Orthographic

Shows true scale in central area, viewed as if mapped from a very great height; distortions increase away from center in areas near edges.

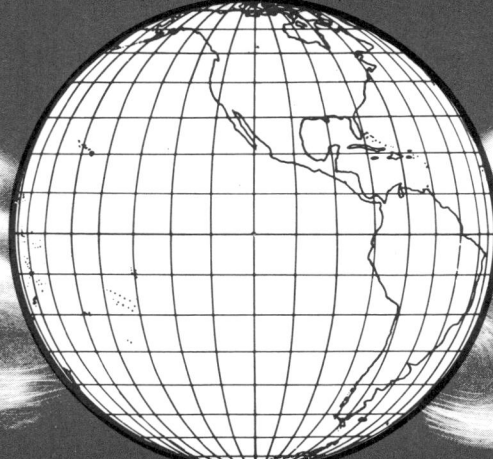

PROJECTIONS

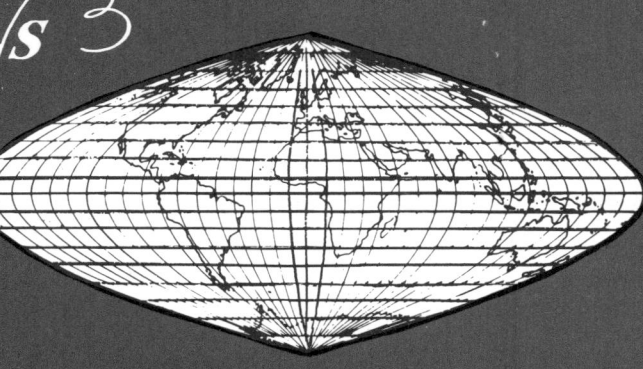

Sinusoidal

An equal-area projection; equator and central meridian are straight lines, parallels correct to scale; other meridians are curved lines.

Polyconic

Based on conic projection with its central meridian a straight line and latitude circles marked on it true to scale.

SEE PAGES XXVI-XXVII FOR FURTHER INFORMATION

Merriam-Webster Pronunciation Key

Symbol	Example	Name	Symbol	Example	Name
ā	āle	long a	N	boN (French bon)	small-capital n
a̋	cha̋otic	half-long a	ng	sing	
â	câre	circumflex a	ō	ōld	long o
ă	ădd	short a	ȯ̇	ȯ̇bey	half-long o
ă	*ă*ccount	italic short a	ô	ôrb	circumflex o
ä	ärm	two-dot a	ŏ	ŏdd	short o
ȧ	ȧsk	one-dot a	ö̆	sö̆ft	short-circumflex o
ȧ	sof*ȧ*	italic one-dot a	*ŏ*	c*ŏ*nnect	italic short o
b	but		oi	oil	
ch	chair		o͞o	fo͞od	long double o
d	day		o͝o	fo͝ot	short double o
du̶̲	verdu̶̲re	ligatured d-u	ou	out	
ē	ēve	long e	p	pen	
ẹ̄	hẹ̄re	hooked long e	r	rat	
ė̄	ė̄vent	half-long e	s	sit	
ĕ	ĕnd	short e	sh	she	
ĕ	sil*ĕ*nt	italic short e	t	to	
ẽ	makẽr	tilde e	th	thin	plain t-h: voiceless
f	fill		t̶h	t̶hen	barred t-h: voiced
g	go		tu̶̲	natu̶̲re	ligatured t-u
h	hat		ū	cūbe	long u
ī	īce	long i	u̇	u̇nite	half-long u
ĭ	ĭll	short i	û	ûrn	circumflex u
ĭ	char*ĭ*ty	italic short i	ŭ	ŭp	short u
j	joke		*ŭ*	circ*ŭ*s	italic short u
k	keep		ü	German grün	umlaut u
ᴋ	=ch in German ich	small-capital k	v	van	
l	late		w	win	
m	man		y	yet	
n	nod		z	zone	
			zh	=z in azure	

For a fuller description of these sounds, see GUIDE TO PRONUNCIATION.
c is used only in the combination **ch**; **q, x** are not used in the respelling for pronunciation.
Foreign sounds for which no special symbols are provided are represented by the nearest English equivalents.
For the apostrophe as in *Eton* (ē′t'n), *Ypres* (ē′pr′), see §§ 66, 66.1, 63.3 in the GUIDE TO PRONUNCIATION.
The principal accent is indicated by a heavy mark (′), and the secondary accent by a lighter mark (′), at the end of the syllable. Foreign words of more than one syllable bearing no accent marks at the ends of syllables have approximately equal accent on all syllables. Syllabic division is indicated by a centered period, or an accent mark, or a hyphen used to join the members of words written or printed with a hyphen.

WEBSTER'S
GEOGRAPHICAL
DICTIONARY

A Merriam-Webster
REG. U.S. PAT. OFF.

A DICTIONARY

OF NAMES OF PLACES

WITH GEOGRAPHICAL AND HISTORICAL
INFORMATION AND PRONUNCIATIONS

Illustrated with Many Maps in the Text

G. & C. MERRIAM CO., PUBLISHERS
SPRINGFIELD, MASS., U.S.A.

REVISED EDITION

Copyright © 1969
BY
G. & C. MERRIAM CO.

Previous Editions
Copyright © 1949, 1955, 1957, 1959, 1960, 1962, 1963, 1964, 1965, 1966, 1967
by G. & C. Merriam Co.

Standard Book Number: 87779-045-0

MADE IN THE U.S.A.
GEORGE BANTA COMPANY, INC., ELECTROTYPERS, PRINTERS, AND BINDERS
THE COLLEGIATE PRESS, MENASHA, WIS., U.S.A.

CONTENTS

CONTENTS

PREFACE

The aim of this MERRIAM-WEBSTER dictionary is to provide in a single handy volume a selection of geographical proper names adequate for the needs of the general user, with full information on the spelling, syllabic division, and pronunciation of the names, and with concise geographical information about the entries and, in many cases, historical information as well.

The names entered (upwards of 40,000) have been selected to include those most likely to meet the needs of the majority of its users. There are, of course, certain items that could not be omitted from a reference work of this kind—the continents and oceans, the countries of the world and their colonies, the principal islands and island groups, the most important natural features of all countries, and the chief cities of the world. But beyond these, within the available space, the editors have included the chief political divisions of important countries both ancient and modern, as well as a generous selection of natural features and of cities, towns, and villages of lesser importance. Many of the last were included because of some fact of historical or other special interest. The rest were entered according to a series of minimum population figures established in advance of the editing. Since the book is intended primarily for English-speaking users and will have its widest distribution in the United States and Canada, names of natural features and places in these two countries, and to a lesser degree in other parts of the English-speaking world, are included on a more generous scale. Thus, at the time of first editing, the minimum population figure for incorporated cities, towns, and villages in the United States and Canada was set at 1500 and the minimum figure for incorporated places in the British Isles, Australia, and New Zealand was set at 5000. In this printing of the book the figures for the United States are taken from the 1960 census and those for Canada and the United Kingdom are from the 1951 censuses. Since these later censuses show a considerable increase in population and in the number of incorporated places above the minimum figures of 1500 and 5000, a number of small places that have now grown beyond the minimum do not appear here. While it is not necessary to list in detail the minimum figures established for all countries or areas, the following list may be of interest: Union of South Africa 3000; Argentina and Brazil 10,000, other republics of South America 5000; countries of western and central Europe 10,000, Union of Soviet Socialist Republics 25,000; China 25,000, India 20,000, Japan 25,000, Philippine Islands 20,000.

Although this book emphasizes current names, which constitute the large majority of its entries, it has not neglected the names of earlier periods of history, from ancient times to the immediate past. The important names of Biblical times, of ancient Greece and Rome, of medieval Europe, and of World War I, for example, are entered and given treatment comparable with that of current names. Thus, both ancient *Mauretania* and modern *Mauritania* are included; *Ionia* appears as an ancient district of Asia Minor, as well as a county and a city in Michigan; the entry of *Lombardy* treats both the medieval kingdom and the modern compartimento.

A feature of the book which the editors hope will be particularly useful is the large number of alternative names and spellings included. Sometimes the alternative is an earlier name, as *Christiania* (former name of *Oslo*) and *Emesa* (ancient name of *Homs*); sometimes it is an alternative form in the same language, as *Derry* (for the county borough *Londonderry*) and *Yezo* (for *Hokkaido*), sometimes an alternative form in another language, as Greek *Imbros* (for Turkish *İmroz*), English *Cracow* (for Polish *Kraków*); sometimes it is a mere variant spelling, as *Lyonais* for *Lyonnais*, *Kadiak* for *Kodiak*.

Maps. All maps in this book were specially prepared for it by the J. W. Clement Company of Buffalo, New York, from copy supplied by the editors. These maps, designed to complement the text matter, are not intended as a substitute for the more detailed maps to be found in a large-scale atlas. Indeed, because of the smaller scale, the number of names and amount of detail on these maps were deliberately restricted, to make them as readable as possible. There are more than 150 black-and-white maps of varying size distributed through the vocabulary, each map being placed at the entry which it complements, or as near to it as possible. Immediately preceding the vocabulary (pages xxviii–xxxi) two double-page maps show the world in different projections: one the long-familiar Mercator projection, the other a polar azimuthal equidistant projection based on the North Pole. Besides the maps themselves there is on pages xxvi–xxvii a very brief discussion of map projections written in such a way that it may be understood by readers relatively unfamiliar with the subject. This article is supplemented by the colored end papers at the front and back of the book, which provide illustrations of several of the common types of projection.

Pronunciation. Despite the growing interest in the pronunciation of place names, it is often difficult to obtain reliable printed information of this kind. Many of the pronunciations in this book, especially of places in the United States and Canada little known outside of their immediate vicinity, were obtained by direct correspondence with residents of those places, such as mayors, postmasters, and school principals. For the pronunciation of most foreign-language names information was supplied by a group of consultants, specialists in various languages, whose names are listed on page vii. The pronunciations are recorded in symbols a large-type key to which will be found on the reverse of the colored end papers at both the front and the back of the book. The *Guide to Pronunciation* on pages x–xvii provides more detailed information of value to all users interested in pronunciation.

Editorial Staff. The planning of this book was carried out under the direction of the Editorial Board of G. & C. Merriam Company consisting, when the initial plans were laid, of the following members: Dr. William Allan Neilson (*chairman*), *Editor in Chief of Merriam-Webster Dictionaries, and formerly President of Smith College;* Mr. Robert C. Munroe, *President of G. & C. Merriam Company;* Dr. John P. Bethel, *General Editor of Merriam-Webster Dictionaries;* Dr. Lucius H. Holt, *Managing Editor of Merriam-Webster Dictionaries.* The Board was ably assisted by Dr. Everett E. Thompson, *Assistant Editor,* of the office staff, to whom special mention is due. For many years Dr. Thompson had been in charge of the Gazetteer work for MERRIAM-WEBSTER dictionaries, so that when this book was projected it was natural that he should have a major share not only in the general planning and in the determining of specific details of selection and presentation of material, but also in the actual writing and reviewing of its entries. Special mention should also be made of the painstaking work of Mr. Edward Artin in preparing the pronunciations, of Miss Ervina Foss and Miss Lucille Brouillet in the complex work of cross-referencing and styling the copy, of Miss Brouillet in adjusting proofs for make-up, of Miss Elsie Mag in assisting with pronunciation, cross-referencing, and styling, and of Miss Sadie Lagoditz in checking innumerable details and performing invaluable clerical assistance. Copy for the maps was prepared by Dr. Thompson, Dr. Holt, and Dr. Bethel, and proofs of the maps themselves were checked by Dr. Thompson, Miss Foss, and Miss Brouillet. Entries and tabular matter were prepared by Dr. Thompson, Dr. Holt, Miss Ruth McIntyre, who prepared much of the historical material for many of the important entries, Mr. Joseph A. Palermo, Mr. Erwin L. Eisold, Miss Mag, Miss Foss, Miss Brouillet, and Mr. Charles Westcott. All matters concerning pronunciation and syllabic

division were under the charge of Mr. Artin, who was assisted by Miss Mag; the *Guide to Pronunciation* (pages x–xvii) was prepared by Mr. Artin. The reading of proofs was done by Dr. Thompson, Miss Brouillet, Miss Foss, Miss Mag, Mr. Hubert Roe, and Miss Rita Goyette.

Consultants. The following persons supplied information on the pronunciation of names in the languages or countries listed in parentheses after their names (the editors, however, being alone responsible for the interpretation of the information supplied and for the pronunciations as they appear in this book):

Mr. William M. Alexander of Aberdeenshire, Scotland (Scotland)
Dr. Rudolph Altrocchi of the University of California (Italian)
Dr. Adriaan Jacob Barnouw of Columbia University (Dutch, Flemish)
Mr. H. A. M. Beckles of Queen's College, British Guiana (British Guiana)
Mr. C. L. Bennet of Dalhousie University, Nova Scotia (New Zealand)
Dr. W. Norwood Brigance of Wabash College (Hawaii)
Dr. Pierre Delattre of the University of Pennsylvania (French)
Dr. Myles Dillon of the Royal Irish Academy (Irish)
Dr. Isidore Dyen of Yale University (Malay)
Dr. M. B. Emeneau of the University of California (Annamese)
Dr. William J. Gedney of Yale University (Siamese)
Dr. Einar Haugen of the University of Wisconsin (Danish, Norwegian)
Mr. Ernest Rudolph Holme of the University of Sydney (Australia)
Dr. Arthur William Hummel of the Library of Congress (Chinese, Japanese, Korean)
Mr. Anthony Joseph Klančar of Portland, Oregon (Bulgarian, Yugoslav)
Dr. Helge Kökeritz of Yale University (Swedish)
Mr. Wolf Leslau of the Asia Institute (Abyssinian, Arabic)
Miss Maria Lantseff Lilienthal of Gladwyne, Pennsylvania (Russian)
Dr. Raven I. McDavid, Jr., of Cornell University (Burmese)
Dr. Isaac Mendelsohn of Columbia University (Hebrew)
Dr. Karl H. Menges of Columbia University (Afghan, Mongolian, Persian, Turkic)
Mr. Ronald E. Mitchell of the University of Wisconsin (Welsh)
Mr. James A. Notopoulos of Trinity College (Modern Greek)
Dr. John B. Olli of the College of the City of New York (Finnish)
Miss Naomi Pekmezian of Washington, D.C. (Armenian)
Dr. Horace I. Poleman of the Library of Congress (India)
Dr. Maxwell Isaac Raphael of Brookline, Massachusetts (Romanian)
Dr. Francis M. Rogers of Harvard University (Portuguese)
Dr. Alfred Senn, Jr., of the University of Pennsylvania (Lithuanian)
Mr. Pedro Vergara of Washington, D.C. (Philippines)
Dr. H. A. Wieschhoff of the University of Pennsylvania (Africa)
Dr. Anna R. Zollinger of Brooklyn College (Romansh)

Acknowledgments. The editors and publishers wish to express their grateful appreciation to these consultants; to all persons who supplied information in response to their letters of inquiry; to technical personnel of the Division of Geodesy of the U.S. Coast and Geodetic Survey who read the manuscript of the article on *Maps and Map Projection;* to the J. W. Clement Company of Buffalo, New York, who prepared the maps, and specifically to Mr. Crawford C. Anderson; to the George Banta Publishing Company of Menasha, Wisconsin, who set the type and prepared the plates and whose staff gave their unfailing co-operation and rendered much valuable assistance, notably in the reading of proof.

John P. Bethel
General Editor.

EXPLANATORY NOTES

In compiling this dictionary, the editors have aimed at clarity of presentation rather than absolute uniformity in arrangement or rigid consistency in typographical and other mechanical details. Consequently, the basic pattern of arrangement that obtains in general throughout the book has been modified to suit the needs of particular instances. The basic pattern of the entries and the principal details of arrangement are described below.

1. General arrangement and kinds of information.

(a) The principal details of each entry (or numbered part of an entry) treating a political division are given usually in the following order: the entry word in heavy-faced type with syllabic division plainly indicated; pronunciation (where not given in a preceding entry); alternative forms and names in heavy-faced type (with syllabic division and pronunciation); descriptive detail and political status; location; area and population; geographical and physical features; economic data; items of general interest, including especially names of colleges and universities and their organization date; and historical information. If the historical information is of sufficient length or relative importance it is placed in a separate paragraph introduced by the label *History*.

Obviously, not all of the details of the basic pattern described above are included at each entry, since in some entries certain details are not applicable or are not of sufficient importance to warrant inclusion.

(b) In entries treating natural features, besides the identifying description and the location, the following kinds of information are included, the amount of such information depending largely on the importance of the entry and the probable value of the information to the user: physical features, such as lengths of rivers, heights of mountains, lengths and areas of islands and of lakes; economic data, such as navigability of rivers, mineral wealth of mountains, agricultural and industrial products of islands; and historical information, as date of discovery, colonization, or acquisition.

(c) Details of information of the states of the United States usually follow a definite basic pattern: the entry word with its syllabic division and pronunciation; descriptive detail; date of admission to the Union; geographical location; rank in area and the area; rank in population and the population; capital; political divisions listed in tabular form; and with an introductory word printed in light italic type: nickname; State flower; motto; chief cities; rivers; mountains; chief industries; and history.

(d) The treatment of long entries of major countries, political divisions, etc., follows more or less closely the general arrangement used for states of the United States (see c, above). Sometimes, however, an entry may contain special information that requires treatment in a separate paragraph with an introductory word (as at **London** a paragraph headed *Treaties, etc.*, or at **Africa** a separate paragraph headed *Political divisions*).

(e) Many political divisions, such as departments, provinces, counties, are entered with only a cross reference to a table at the main entry at which information about the political division can be found. See § 7, below. Others are described briefly at their own entries, following the general arrangement of information (see a, above). Similar treatment is accorded to dams, national parks and monuments, and other kinds of entries.

(f) Except when the population figures are those of an official census which was used for the entire country, most population figures are dated in the text matter. When the date of the official census was old and later estimates were available, as for large divisions and cities, the later figure is included with a date, as well as the figure of the earlier official census.

For the United States the census of 1960 is used; for Great Britain and Canada the censuses of 1951, supplemented by later estimates.

2. Alphabetical arrangement of entries.

(a) For entries in this dictionary, the ordinary rules of alphabetical sequence govern: (1) the single name; (2) this name with a preceding modifier—necessarily represented for alphabetical purposes with the modifier, preceded by a comma, following the name; (3) this name followed by another word or words. Thus:

> George
> George, Cape
> George, Lake
> George Bay
> George Dawson, Mount
> George V Coast
> George Hill

A name containing a numeral, as **George V Coast**, above, is alphabetized as if the numeral were spelled out.

A name spelled as a solid word or a hyphened word precedes the same name when spelled as two words, thus **Georgetown** precedes **George Town**.

(b) Names beginning with the prefix **Mc** or **M'** are all alphabetized as if spelled with the full form of this prefix, **Mac**. In alphabetizing, no distinction is made between these names and other names (such as **Macclesfield**) in which the initial letters **M a c** are not a prefix.

(c) Names of natural features, such as capes, lakes, points, and straits, are generally entered at the significant part of the full name; thus, Cape May is entered at **May, Cape**; Point Barrow is entered at **Barrow, Point;** Lake Michigan is at **Michigan, Lake;** Strait of Malacca is at **Malacca, Strait of;** Paso del Inca is at **Inca, Paso del;** Pointe de Monts is at **Monts, Pointe de.**

(d) As a general rule, the words **Bay, Island, Lake, Mount**, etc., have been included as part of the heavy-faced vocabulary entry. With rare exceptions, the word **River** has been omitted, so that the consultant in looking for the Amazon River should look at **Amazon.**

(e) Names beginning with **Al, El, De, Du, Des, L', La, Le, Les**, etc., are alphabetized at **Al, El, De**, etc., respectively. Except for **The Dalles** and **The Pas**, which are alphabetized at **The**, all names containing "the" are at the main word; thus, **the Everglades** is at **Everglades.**

(f) Two or more names identical in spelling and pronunciation are combined in a single entry. Thus:

> **Bex'ley** (bĕks'lĭ). **1** City, Franklin co., cen. Ohio,
> . . . .
> **2** City, E New South Wales, SE Australia, ...
> **3** Urban district, Kent, SE England, ...

(g) Names of identical spelling that differ in pronunciation or etymology are often entered separately, as the entries at **Acre, Bayonne**, and **Tigre.**

3. Arrangement of parts within entries.

(a) For numbered parts within an entry, the order described below has been followed:

(i) An alphabetical arrangement of countries, except that the United States precedes all other countries. Terri-

tories and dependencies of the United States (Virgin Islands, Puerto Rico, etc.), dominions and colonies of the British Commonwealth and Empire (Australia, Canada, Ceylon, Jamaica, Kenya, etc.), French overseas territories (French Polynesia, New Caledonia, etc.), and other colonial possessions are treated as if independent countries.

When, however, the entry name applies to an independent country (or to a dominion, colony, territory, or the like, that may be regarded as a "country"), this application of the name has generally been made the first item under the entry, followed by the remaining items in the order described above. See the entry at **Denmark.**

(ii) An arrangement of geographical and political categories under the countries, placing natural features in alphabetical order ahead of political entities in descending order (for example, state or province, county, city, town, village).

(b) Names in South Australia and Western Australia are alphabetized at Australia, in Lower Burma and Upper Burma at Burma, Lower Egypt and Upper Egypt at Egypt, etc., in the U.S.S.R., R.S.F.S.R., and other parts of Soviet Russia at Russia. Names in Newfoundland are alphabetized at Newfoundland, not at Canada as are the other provinces, because the union took place too late to permit the necessary rearrangement throughout the book.

4. Composite entries.

The editors have occasionally found it desirable to treat in a single entry names that are related to each other or that form parts of a whole, believing that the consultant will more easily obtain a complete geographical and historical picture. Such names are printed in heavy-faced type. Thus, at **Gaul** are included the early divisions of the ancient country, at **Nile** are described the several sections of the river, at **Taimyr Peninsula** are included the similarly named **Taimyr River, Taimyr Lake, Taimyr Bay,** and **Taimyr Island.**

5. Tables.

To make more usable the information provided, entries of certain classes of names are given in the form of tables, and each name in the table has been made a cross entry at its own alphabetical place in the vocabulary. For example, the counties of the state of Alabama are listed in a *Table* at **Alabama,** and each county name has been cross-entered at its own alphabetical place in the vocabulary; the metropolitan boroughs of London are given in tabular form at **London,** and each name has been cross-entered to the *Table* at **London.** Other examples are the tables of ranges at **Alps** and of dams at **Tennessee Valley Authority,** and the several tables at **Canada** and **United States.**

6. Syllabic division and pronunciation.

(a) *Syllabic division.* Elsewhere than in the respelling for pronunciation (see section b, below), the syllable division shown for a name indicates, for the guidance of printers, proofreaders, writers, and other interested consultants, those points at which the name may be divided at the end of a line of print or writing. A name may be divided wherever (elsewhere than in the respelling for pronunciation) a centered period, a primary or secondary accent, or a hyphen appears in this dictionary. The rules for such division, established for each language by long and widespread practice, are in some respects more or less arbitrary; accordingly the division of a name sometimes differs from that of its respelled pronunciation, which attempts to show how the word is syllabified when spoken.

(b) *Pronunciation.* Pronunciation is indicated by respelling the names in symbols long used in Merriam-Webster dictionaries, a full explanation of which is given on pages x–xvii, and a key to which is provided on the reverse of the decorative end papers. The pronunciation respelling is regularly enclosed within parentheses, but if there is an adjacent pair of parentheses serving some other purpose, the pronunciation is enclosed within square brackets.

Earnest effort has been made to secure accurate information on the pronunciation of all names included. A vast amount of time and effort has been devoted to corresponding with persons living in or near places about the pronunciation of which there was doubt. The pronunciations of foreign-language names are in large measure based on information supplied by consulting specialists (see page vii, above). Where usage has established one, an Anglicized pronunciation has been given in addition to the native pronunciation. Although it is realized that in a large percentage of cases few will be able or will desire to make even a good approximation to the native pronunciation where this alone is given, this pronunciation will usually serve as a useful point of departure from which a satisfactory Anglicized pronunciation can be evolved.

In entries in which no division and pronunciation are shown, the division and pronunciation are those of the nearest preceding entry of identical spelling for which these are shown.

7. Cross references.

Two general types of cross references are found in this dictionary: cross entries in the vocabulary, and cross references in the body of an article. The name to which the consultant is directed is indicated either by the use of special type (light roman capitals and small capitals) or by the placing after the name of the letters q.v. (for Latin *quod vide = which see*), or if reference is to more than one name, qq.v. (for Latin *quae vide = which* [plural] *see*). Thus:

East Peak. = BOUNDARY PEAK.
Tridentine Alps. = *Dolomites:* see *Table* at ALPS.
Jaquemel. Var. of JACMEL.
Düna. German form of DVINA river, N Europe.
Boden See. See Lake CONSTANCE.
Federation of Malaya. See Federation of MALAYA.
Bee. County in Texas. See *Table* at TEXAS.
Apache Lake. See UNITED STATES, *Dams and Reservoirs* (Horse Mesa Dam).
Durobrivae. See ROCHESTER city, England.
Española. One of the Galápagos Is. (*q.v.*).
Krasnoyarsk Territory.... Geographically includes the two national districts of Taimyr and Evenki (*qq.v.*).

Cross references with "see" and "cf." are frequently used in the body of an article. "See" leads to additional information. "Cf." (abbreviation of the Latin word *confer*, meaning "compare") leads to useful, interesting, or related material. See the articles at ASIA MINOR, ATHOS, TAKUTÚ, and TRIPOLI.

Throughout this dictionary, the words UNITED STATES only are used in cross entries and cross references that refer to the entry UNITED STATES OF AMERICA.

8. Abbreviations and symbols.

Abbreviations are used throughout the book, in vocabulary entries, tables, and maps, wherever it is felt that their use permits little or no difficulty of typography or comprehension. Occasionally, as on some maps, where considerations of space necessitated so doing, a few unconventional abbreviations are used. Points of the compass when used as directional points are set in sans-serif type with no following period (thus: SW Maine); when used as part of a name they appear in ordinary type with a following period. A complete list of the abbreviations used is given on pages xviii–xix.

There are only two arbitrary symbols which have been used in the text matter of this book: ✱ meaning *capital* and ⊗ meaning *county seat* or *parish seat.* For symbols used on maps, see the list on page xix.

A GUIDE TO PRONUNCIATION

I. KEY TO THE SYMBOLS USED IN PRONUNCIATION

§ 1. ACCENTS AND HYPHENS. The principal accent is indicated by a heavy mark (′), and the secondary accent by a lighter mark (′), at the end of the syllable. A syllable having no accent is followed by a centered period, except when it is a final syllable, or occurs immediately before a hyphen in a compound word or name. In words of more than one syllable from certain foreign languages (e.g., Japanese, Korean, Siamese), however, in which no accent mark appears at the end of any syllable, there is approximately even accent on all syllables.

FOREIGN SOUNDS for which no special symbols are provided are represented by the nearest English equivalents.

In the following list, the name of each diacritical symbol is given in parentheses immediately after the symbol.

SYMBOLS USED IN RESPELLING FOR PRONUNCIATION

ā (long a*), as in āle, fāte, lā′bor (§ 5).
ȧ (half-long a*), as in chȧ·ot′ic, fȧ·tal′i·ty (§ 6).
â (circumflex a), as in câre, beâr, âir (§ 7).
ă (short a*), as in ădd, lămb, făt (§ 8).
ă̇ (italic short a*), as in ăc·count′, loy′ăl (§ 9).
ä (two-dot a), as in ärm, är·tis′tic, fä′ther (§ 10).
å (one-dot a), as in åsk, ståff, påth (§ 11).
å (italic one-dot a), as in so′fȧ, ȧ·bound′ (§ 12).
b, as in ba′by, be, bit, bob, ab′bey (§ 13).
ch, as in chair, much, ques′tion (-chŭn) (§ 14).
d, as in day, add′ed (§ 15).
du̯ (ligatured d-u), as in ver′du̯re (§ 16).
ē (long e*), as in ēve, mēte, se·rēne′ (§ 17).
ẹ (hooked long e*), as in hẹre, fẹar (§ 18).
ė (half-long e*), as in ė·vent′, crė·ate′ (§ 19).
ĕ (short e*), as in ĕnd, rĕn·di′tion (§ 20).
ĕ̇ (italic short e*), as in si′lĕnt, nov′ĕl (§ 21).
ẽ (tilde e), as in mak′ẽr, pẽr·vert′ (§§ 22, 48).
f, as in fill, buff, phan′tom (făn′-), sap′phire (săf′īr), cough (kôf) (§ 23).
g, as in go, be·gin′, guy (gī) (§ 24).
h, as in hat, hen, hide, hot, hurt, a·head′ (§ 25).
ī (long i*), as in īce, spīre, ī·de′a (§ 26).
ĭ (short i*), as in ĭll, hab′ĭt, bod′y (bŏd′y) (§ 27).
ĭ̇ (italic short i*), as in char′ĭ·ty, pos′sĭ·ble, dĭ·rect′, A′prĭl (§ 28).
j, as in joke, jol′ly, gem (jĕm), edge (ĕj) (§ 29).
k, as in keep, kick (kĭk), cube (kūb), chord (kôrd), pique (pēk) (§ 30).
ᴋ (small capital k), as in German ich (ĭᴋ), ach (äᴋ), Scottish loch (lŏᴋ) (§ 31).
l, as in late, leg, lip, lot, full, hol′ly (§ 32).
m, as in man, men, mine, hum, ham′mer (§ 33).
n, as in no, on, in′ner, sign (sīn) (§ 34).
ɴ (small capital n): without sound of its own, indicates the nasal tone (as in French or Portuguese) of the preceding vowel or diphthong, as in French bon (bôɴ), Portuguese pão (pouɴ) (§ 35).
ng, as in sing, sing′er (sĭng′ẽr), fin′ger (fĭng′gẽr), bank (băngk), can′ker (kăng′kẽr) (§ 36).

ō (long o*), as in ōld, nōte, he′rō (§ 37).
ȯ (half-long o*), as in ȯ·bey′, tȯ·bac′co, a·nat′ȯ·my (§ 38).
ô (circumflex o), as in ôrb, lôrd, ôr·dain′, law (lô), bought (bôt), caught (kôt), all (ôl) (§ 39).
ŏ (short o*), as in ŏdd, nŏt, tŏr′rid, fŏr′est, pŏs·ter′i·ty (§ 40).
ô̆ (short-circumflex o*), as in sô̆ft, dô̆g, clô̆th, lô̆ss, cô̆st (§ 41).
ŏ̇ (italic short o*), as in cŏn·nect′, ŏc·cur′, Bab′y·lŏn (§ 42).
oi, as in oil, nois′y, a·void′, goi′ter (§ 43).
ōō (long double o*), as in fōōd, ōōze, nōōse, rude (rōōd), true (trōō), blue (blōō) (§ 44).
oŏ (short double o*), as in foŏt, woŏl, boŏr, put (poŏt), pull (poŏl), sure (shoŏr) (§ 45).
ou, as in out, now (nou), bough (bou) (§ 46).
p, as in pen, pin, pop, put (§ 47).
r, as in rap, red, hor′rid, far, fur, curd, rhom′boid (rŏm′-), in′ner (§§ 48, 22).
s, as in so, this, haste, cell (sĕl), vice (vīs), scene (sēn), hiss (hĭs) (§ 49).
sh, as in she, ship, shop, ma·chine′ (-shēn′), so′cial (-shăl) (§ 50).
t, as in time, pat, lat′ter, win′ter, thyme (tīm) (§ 51).
t̶h (barred t-h), as in then, though, smooth, breathe (§ 52).
th (plain t-h), as in thin, through, wealth (§ 53).
tu̯ (ligatured t-u), as in na′tu̯re, cul′tu̯re, pic′tu̯re (§ 54).
ū (long u*), as in cūbe, tūne, lūte (§ 55).
u̇ (half-long u*), as in u̇·nite′, em′u̇·late (§ 56).
û (circumflex u), as in ûrn, fûrl, con·cûr′, fern (fûrn), fir (fûr) (§§ 48, 57.1); for German ö, oe, as in schön (shûn), Goe′the (gû′tĕ̇); for French eu, as in jeu (zhû), seul (sûl); etc. (§ 57.2).
ŭ (short u*), as in ŭp, tŭb, ŭn′der, ŭn·do′ (§ 58).
ŭ̇ (italic short u*), as in cir′cŭs, cir′cŭm·stance, de′mon (-mŭn), na′tion (-shŭn) (§ 59).
ü (umlaut u): for French u, as in me·nu′ (mė·nü′); for German ü, as in grün, hübsch; etc. (§ 60).
v, as in van, vent, vote, re·voke′, re·vive′ (§ 61).
w, as in want, win, weed, wood, a·ward′ (-swäd′), choir (kwīr) (§ 62).
y, as in yet, yel′low, be·yond′, on′ion (-yŭn) (§ 63).
z, as in zone, haze, wise (wīz), mu′sic (-zĭk), xy′lo·phone (zī′-) (§ 64).
zh, as in az′ure (ăzh′ẽr), gla′zier (-zhẽr), pleas′ure (plĕzh′ẽr), rouge (rōōzh) (§ 65).
′ as in par′don (pär′d'n), wres′tle (rĕs′'l), indicates that a following consonant is syllabic (§ 66); when not followed by a consonant, it indicates that a preceding consonant is voiceless, as in French nô′tre (nō′tr′), meu′ble (mû′bl′) (§ 66.1), except after y: for its significance in that situation, see § 63.3.

* See § 3.21.

II. PRELIMINARY EXPLANATIONS

§ 2. In the main, English pronunciation is the basis of the following description of sounds. This Dictionary, in common with other works on pronunciation, uses the same symbols for sounds in different languages that are similar but not identical (e.g., ā for the vowel sound in English *gay* and French *gai*, respectively). Although the differences between English sounds and corresponding sounds in foreign languages are often briefly touched on below, no attempt at detailed differentiation has been made, both because of lack of space and because the assigning of the English value to the symbols transcribing foreign names will usually be found adequate in an English context.

§ 3. Explanations (chiefly in the form of definitions) of a number of terms that will be used in the description of sounds may advantageously be made here:

§ 3.1. The **palate** consists of a front, or **hard**, part, and of a back, or **soft**, part. The soft palate is also called the **velum**. The hanging fleshy lobe that constitutes the back part of the soft palate is the **uvula**.

§ 3.2. Phoneticians distinguish the following parts of the **tongue**: the **point**, or **tip**; the **blade**, including the tip and the part just behind it, lying, when at rest, opposite the ridge just behind the upper front teeth (called the *teethridge*); the **front**,—the middle part of the upper surface, which in rest normally lies opposite the hard palate; the **back**,—the part that normally rests opposite the soft palate.

§ 3.3. front, *adj.* Uttered with closure or narrowing of the mouth passage at the front of the mouth, or between the front of the tongue (see § 3.2) and the hard palate.

§ 3.4. back, *adj.* Uttered with closure or narrowing of the mouth passage at the back of the mouth, or between the back of the tongue (see § 3.2) and the soft palate.

§ 3.5. central, *adj.* Uttered with the tongue intermediate in position between front and back. Also called *mixed.*

§ 3.6. advance, *v.* To utter with the tongue farther forward.

§ 3.7. retract, *v.* To utter with the tongue farther back.

§ 3.8. high, *adj.* Of a vowel, uttered with some part of the tongue high up toward the palate (see § 4). Also called *close.*

§ 3.9. low, *adj.* Of a vowel, uttered with a wide opening between the tongue and palate (see § 4). Also called *open.*

§ 3.10. mid, *adj.* Of a vowel, uttered with the tongue intermediate in position between high and low.

§ 3.11. The terms *high* (or *close*) and *low* (or *open*) are also used relatively. Thus o͞o may be described as a lower or more open vowel than o͞o, though absolutely both o͞o and o͞o are high (or close) vowels.

§ 3.12. tense, *adj.* Uttered with the tongue and associated muscles in a relatively tense state.

§ 3.13. lax, *adj.* Uttered with the tongue and associated muscles in a relatively relaxed state.

§ 3.14. round, *v.* To utter with the lips drawn together laterally so as to form a more or less round opening.

§ 3.15. unround, *v.* To utter with the lips spread laterally.

§ 3.16. voiced, *adj.* Uttered with vibration of the vocal cords. Certain consonants are voiced; all vowels are practically always voiced.

§ 3.17. voiceless, *adj.* Uttered without vibration of the vocal cords. Certain consonants are voiceless.

§ 3.18. Every language has pairs of consonants that differ chiefly or only in that one member of each pair is voiced while the other is voiceless. English has the following pairs (each sound symbol is accompanied by a key word):

Voiced		Voiceless	
b	**b**an	p	**p**an
d	**d**ie	t	**t**ie
g	ta**g**	k	ta**ck**
t͟h	ei**th**er	th	e**th**er
v	**v**an	f	**f**an
z	**z**inc	s	**s**ink
zh	confu**s**ion	sh	Confu**ci**an
j	ri**dge**	ch	ri**ch**

§ 3.19. quality, *n.* The identifying character of a vowel sound, determined chiefly by the resonance of the vocal chambers in uttering it.

§ 3.20. quantity *or* **length,** *n.* The relative duration, or time length, of a speech sound. See § 3.21.

§ 3.21. The term **long** for the sounds ā, ē, ī, ō, o͞o, ū, and the term **short** for the sounds ă, ĕ, ĭ, ŏ, o͝o, ŭ, have been established in English by long use; and it has been found convenient to retain them in assigning names to these diacritical symbols (and to certain other derivative symbols) in Division I ("Key to the Symbols Used in Pronunciation") of this Guide. Actually, however, these terms are not strictly accurate phonetically, since the difference between each of these pairs of sounds (e.g., between ā and ă) is primarily one of quality rather than of quantity. Hereafter in this Guide the terms are used in their strict phonetic sense, **long** being applied to a sound of relatively great duration, **short** to a sound of relatively small duration.

§ 3.22. fricative, *adj.* Characterized by frictional rustling of the breath as it is emitted with the mouth passage greatly narrowed, but not closed. Examples: the sounds f, v, s, z.

§ 3.23. trill, *n.* The rapid vibration of one speech organ against another. See § 48.1.

§ 3.24. retroflex, *adj.* Of the tongue, having the tip raised and bent back; of sounds, formed thus. See § 48.

§ 3.25. obscure, *adj.* Uttered without stress;—applied to the unstressed vowel symbolized ȧ, ᵃ, ᵉ, ᶦ, ᵒ, or ᵘ in this Dictionary.

§ 3.26. vanish, *n.* The relatively faint latter part of a diphthong in which the first part has greater stress. Thus, in English, ā often has an ĭ vanish, ō an o͞o vanish.

§ 3.27. open syllable. A syllable ending in a vowel or diphthong. Example: both syllables of *A'da.*

§ 3.28. closed syllable. A syllable ending in a consonant. Example: both syllables of *Ed'ward.*

§ 4. Vowels are often charted or diagramed according to the position assumed by the highest part of the tongue when they are uttered, such position being the chief determinant, or one of the chief determinants, of the quality of each vowel. One common way of charting vowels is shown below. This chart will serve as a rough indication of the relative tongue position of the different vowels.

	FRONT	CENTRAL	BACK
HIGH	ē ĭ		o͞o o͝o
MID	ā ĕ	û, ẽ, ȧ, ŭ	ō
LOW	â ă	ȧ	ô ŏ ä

Note: ī and ū, being diphthongs, are not shown.

III. DESCRIPTION OF SOUNDS

ā

§ 5. As in English āle.

Mid-front tense unrounded. In standard English, usually not a pure, or simple, sound, but diphthongized, with an ĭ vanish (see § 3.26). In another variety, the diphthong begins at or near the mid-front lax vowel ĕ as in *met*. The vanish of the ā sound appears in accented syllables in both England and America when the sound is final or before voiced consonants, as in *day, made*. But in America, before voiceless consonants it is usually not prominent and is sometimes lacking, as in *hate*, and in all positions it is less prominent in America and the North of England than in southern England.

§ 5.1. In foreign languages, ā is usually a pure sound without vanish, and is often higher and tenser than the corresponding pure English sound, or than the first element of the corresponding diphthongal English sound. In some languages it is so high as to suggest ĭ to many English-speaking persons.

å

§ 6. As in English chåotic.

A short sound of ā-like quality, usually without vanish, occurring in unaccented syllables.

â

§ 7. As in English câre.

Low-front unrounded, relatively long, having a tongue position between that for ĕ and for ă. In English, it varies from this position to a higher one, near ĕ, and to a lower one, near ă.

ă

§ 8. As in English ădd.

Low-front unrounded, the mouth being nearly or quite as wide open as for ä in *art*, but the tongue somewhat farther forward and the front (but not the tip) elevated instead of the back.

There is considerable variation in the sound of ă in standard English. In Southern British speech the sound is higher than that generally heard in America. To an American of the North or East the word *back* as pronounced by a Southern English speaker often suggests the word *beck*. In the southern United States, however, the ă resembles in quality that of southern England. In the English of educated Scotsmen and of many Northern Englishmen, the ă is replaced by à (low-central vowel).

ă̇

§ 9. As in English ă̇ccount.

In ordinary English speech, an obscure vowel, like à (see § 12). Occasionally in very deliberate speech pronounced ă.

ä

§ 10. As in English ärm.

Low-back unrounded. Usually somewhat more advanced in southern England than in America. In New England, however, often more advanced than in southern England, in many cases being actually à (low-central vowel).

à

§ 11. As in English àsk.

Low-central unrounded, when used in representing the pronunciation of foreign words. In English words in the respelled pronunciation of which à occurs, the low-central pronunciation is rare in standard English outside of New England, the usual pronunciation being ă (low-front vowel) in America and ä (low-back vowel) in southern England. In English words, accordingly, the symbol à is to be regarded as indicating any of three pronunciations.

à

§ 12. As in English sofà.

Mid-central unrounded. Always obscure.

b

§ 13. As in English baby.

A voiced sound produced by stopping the breath with the lips. Correlative voiceless stop, p; correlative nasal, m.

ch

§ 14. As in English chair.

ch is not a combination of any of the sounds usually borne by *c* and *h* in English, and contains no c or h sound. It is a voiceless sound consisting approximately of t followed by sh (see §§ 51, 50). Voiced correlative, j.

d

§ 15. As in English day.

A voiced sound produced, in English, by stopping the breath by placing the point of the tongue against the teethridge (see § 3.2). In some languages (e.g., French and Italian) the tongue point is placed against the back of the upper front teeth.

Correlative voiceless stop, t; correlative nasal, n.

dū̯

§ 16. As in English verdū̯re.

In words in the respelled pronunciation of which this symbol occurs, the pronunciation dū (= dyo͞o) occurs in most words only in very formal speech. The ligature (‿) indicates that in ordinary speech the dy is usually pronounced j (i.e., d+zh; see § 29). The explanation of this is as follows: The original pronunciation was dy. The sound zh, however, being closer to d than y is, speakers in time began, in accord with a process technically known as assimilation, to take a "path of less resistance" by substituting zh for y.

Also, before consonants the vowel is commonly ê or ŭ, not o͞o.

Correlative sound with voiceless consonant, tū̯.

ē

§ 17. As in English ēve.

High-front tense unrounded. In some languages, higher and tenser than in English.

ẹ̄

§ 18. As in English hẹ̄re.

Used before r in transcribing English words. The inferior modifier indicates that, although the full ē pronunciation does sometimes occur in very formal speech, in ordinary speech a more open sound occurs, this open sound being approximately or exactly a lengthened ĭ.

ė

§ 19. As in English ėvent.

A short sound of ē-like quality occurring in unaccented syllables.

ĕ

§ 20. As in English ĕnd.

Mid-front lax unrounded.

ĕ̇

§ 21. As in English silĕ̇nt.

In ordinary English speech, an obscure vowel, like à. Occasionally in very deliberate speech pronounced ĕ.

ē̇

§ 22. As in English makē̇r.

Used before r in unaccented syllables. In other languages than English, two sounds—an obscure vowel and an r—may be pronounced. For the value of ēr in English words, see § 48.

§ 22.1. ē̇ is used for the obscure vowel in French.

f

§ 23. As in English **f**ill.

A voiceless sound produced by the friction of the breath escaping between the closely juxtaposed upper teeth and lower lip. Voiced correlative, **v**.

g

§ 24. As in English **g**o.

A voiced sound produced by stopping the breath by pressing the back part of the tongue against the soft palate. The tongue is more advanced when the sound occurs with a front vowel (e.g., in *geese* gēs) than when it occurs with a back vowel (e.g., in *goose* gōōs). Correlative voiceless stop, k; correlative nasal, ng.

§ 24.1. In some languages (e.g., Danish, Modern Greek, Portuguese, Spanish, one form of German) the orthographic spelling g may stand for a voiced continuant sound articulated, not by making contact between the back of the tongue and the soft palate, but by merely bringing the back of the tongue close to the soft palate—a sound which is the voiced correlative of κ. This sound is Anglicized as g, and is so represented in this Dictionary.

h

§ 25. As in English **h**at.

An impulse of breath occurring, in English, only at the beginning of a syllable before a vowel or before w (e.g., *white* hwĭt) or y (e.g., *huge* hūj [= hyōōj]). Usually voiceless in English, but sometimes voiced when between vowels.

ī

§ 26. As in English **ī**ce.

A diphthong, not a single sound. Both elements vary somewhat throughout the English-speaking world. In two of the commonest varieties, the diphthong begins with ȧ (low-central vowel) or with ä (low-back vowel) and moves upward toward or to ĭ.

ĭ

§ 27. As in English **ĭ**ll.

High-front lax unrounded.

§ 27.1. The symbol ĭ transcribing Polish *y*, Romanian *â* and *î*, the Russian letter transliterated *y* in this Dictionary, and Turkish *ı*, stands for a high-central unrounded vowel whose nearest counterpart in English is the vowel in *dream* or *rear*.

ĭ

§ 28. As in English char**ĭ**ty.

Transcribes a sound that is an obscure mid-central vowel, like ȧ, with some speakers, ĭ with others.

j

§ 29. As in English **j**oke.

A voiced sound consisting approximately of d followed by zh (see §§ 15, 65). Voiceless correlative, ch.

k

§ 30. As in English **k**eep.

A voiceless sound produced by stopping the breath by pressing the back part of the tongue against the soft palate. The tongue is more advanced when the sound occurs with a front vowel (e.g., in *keel* kēl) than when it occurs with a back vowel (e.g., in *cool* kōōl). Correlative voiced stop, g; correlative nasal, ng.

κ

§ 31. As in German i**ch**, a**ch**, Scottish lo**ch**.

The articulation of this consonant (which occurs in Scottish and in a number of foreign languages—e.g., German and Russian) differs from that of k in that the tongue is merely brought close to the palate, and not actually into contact with it; i.e., the sound is a continuant, and not a stop. As for k and g, in some languages the tongue is more advanced when the sound occurs with a front vowel (e.g., in German *ich* ĭκ) than when it occurs with a back vowel (e.g., in German *ach* äκ).

l

§ 32. As in English **l**ate, fu**ll**.

In the production of this voiced sound in English, the point of the tongue is in contact with the teethridge, as it is for d. However, whereas for d the breath is completely stopped, for l a passage for the breath is left at both sides, or with some speakers at only one side, of the tongue. Thus l is a continuant, d is a stop.

§ 32.1. As in the case of d, in some languages the tongue point is placed against the back of the upper front teeth rather than against the teethridge.

§ 32.2. While the tongue point is in contact with the teethridge, that part of the tongue behind the point is free to assume a variety of positions. These various positions may roughly be reduced to two: when the front of the tongue is raised toward the hard palate, the l is said to be "clear"; when the back of the tongue is raised toward the soft palate, the l is said to be "dark." In general, in English a clear l is pronounced at the beginning of a syllable; a dark l is pronounced (a) at the end of a syllable, (b) before a consonant, and (c) when the l is syllabic (see § 32.4). The difference between a clear l and a dark l never distinguishes words in English, and the same symbol, l, is accordingly used for both varieties.

§ 32.3. Some languages (e.g., French) have a clear l in all positions. In some languages that have both a clear and a dark l, the incidence of the two is not the same as in English: thus in Polish (which has a separate character, *ł*, for dark l) a dark l may occur at the beginning of a syllable and a clear l at the end of a syllable; and the difference between a clear l and a dark l sometimes distinguishes two words otherwise spelled and pronounced the same (e.g., Polish *lawa*, "lava," *ława*, "bench").

§ 32.4. Syllabic l (see § 66). The sound l often forms a syllable by itself, as in *battle* băt′′l, or with other consonants, as in *handled* hăn′d'ld, no vowel whatever being present in the syllable. In pronunciation respellings in this Dictionary a syllabic consonant is preceded by an apostrophe.

m

§ 33. As in English **m**an.

In the production of this sound, the lips are closed as for b, and prevent the breath from escaping through the mouth; however, the soft palate is lowered and the breath escapes through the nose, producing a nasal resonance. Correlative voiced stop, b; correlative voiceless stop, p.

§ 33.1. Syllabic m (see § 66). The sound m sometimes forms a syllable by itself, as in the English suffix *-ism* -ĭz′m, and in one pronunciation of *Clapham* klăp′′m (klăp′′ăm being another pronunciation), no vowel whatever being present in the syllable. In pronunciation respellings in this Dictionary a syllabic consonant is preceded by an apostrophe.

n

§ 34. As in English **n**o.

In the production of this sound, the point of the tongue is placed against the teethridge (in some languages, as French and Italian, against the back of the upper front teeth), as for d, and the breath is unable to escape through the mouth; however, the soft palate is lowered and the breath escapes through the nose, producing a nasal resonance. Correlative voiced stop, d; correlative voiceless stop, t.

§ 34.1. Syllabic n (see § 66). The sound n often forms a syllable by itself, as in *redden* rĕd′′n, or with other consonants, as in *reddened* rĕd′′nd, no vowel whatever being present in the syllable. In pronunciation respellings in this Dictionary a syllabic consonant is preceded by an apostrophe.

N

§ 35. As in French boN**.**

No sound whatever is to be attached to this symbol, which merely indicates that in the utterance of a preceding vowel or diphthong the soft palate is lowered, so that the breath escapes through the nose as well as the mouth, giving the vowel or diphthong a nasal resonance. No trace of any nasal consonant should follow the nasalized vowel unless a nasal consonant is shown in the transcription (see § 35.1). Thus the French word *en* äN consists of only one sound, the vowel ä pronounced with the soft palate lowered.

§ 35.1. In French, a nasal consonant is pronounced after a nasal vowel only in liaison; e.g., *bon accord* bôN′-nȧ′kôr′. In Portuguese and Polish, however, when a nasal vowel is followed by a stop, the nasal consonant corresponding in articulation to the stop is usually inserted between the vowel and the stop (m before b, p; n before d, t; ng before g, k). Examples: Polish *bąbel* bôNm′bĕl, Portuguese *campo* kȧNm′po͞o (contrast French *bambou* bäN′bo͞o′); Polish *pędem* pĕNn′dĕm, Portuguese *conto* kōNn′to͞o (contrast French *contour* kôN′to͞or′); Polish *tęgi* tĕNng′gĕ, Portuguese *banco* bȧNng′ko͞o (contrast French *banquette* bäN′kĕt′).

ng

§ 36. As in English sing**.**

In the production of this sound, which is not a combination of the sounds n and g, contains no n or g sound, and is a single sound, the back part of the tongue is pressed against the soft palate, as for g, and the breath is unable to escape through the mouth; however, the soft palate is lowered and the breath escapes through the nose, producing a nasal resonance. Correlative voiced stop, g; correlative voiceless stop, k.

ō

§ 37. As in English ōld**.**

When accented, ō is usually a diphthong in standard English. In America and in many parts of England, the diphthong begins with the mid-back tense vowel, a pure ō sound, and glides to a vowel resembling o͞o. In the speech of southern England, however, though several varieties of ō exist, the prevailing tendency is to begin the ō sound with the tongue farther forward toward the central position. In the extreme form of this—which is very common in London, Oxford, and Cambridge—the diphthong is approximately û͞o, beginning with the û of *hurt* (the unretroflexed mid-central vowel used by those who "drop" their r's; see § 48).

In America the diphthongal character is less marked. Before voiceless consonants, as in *note*, *oak*, and before r, as in *ore*, the ō is often nearly or quite pure, without vanish. In any case, the beginning of the American sound is a back vowel, not advanced, though sometimes slightly lowered toward ô. The one symbol ō is used in this book to indicate all standard varieties.

§ 37.1. In English words in which ō is shown immediately before r in this Dictionary, the vowel is usually ô in southern England, and sometimes in America.

§ 37.2. In foreign languages, ō is usually a pure vowel without vanish, often higher, tenser, and more lip-rounded than the corresponding pure English sound, or than the first element of the corresponding diphthongal English sound.

ȯ

§ 38. As in English ȯbey**.**

A short sound of ō-like quality, usually without vanish, occurring in unaccented syllables. Where ȯ is shown in English words, the sound is frequently the obscure mid-central vowel (like ȧ), as in the third syllable of *anatomy* ȧ-năt′ȯ-mĭ.

§ 38.1. In words belonging to certain foreign languages (as Hungarian, Italian, and Yugoslav), ȯ is also used in

accented syllables for a sound resembling a pure ō, but much shorter.

ô

§ 39. As in English ôrb**.**

Low-back (but higher than ä, which is also low-back), tense, higher and more lip-rounded in southern England than in America; may be long, as in *law* lô, or relatively short, as in *auspicious* ôs·pĭsh′ŭs.

ŏ

§ 40. As in English ŏdd**.**

In southern England and to some extent in New England, New York City, and the southern United States, this vowel is low-back (lying between ä and ô, which are also low-back), lax, and slightly rounded. In general in the United States, the sound so transcribed is an entirely unrounded vowel identical in quality with ä and of varying length. Where ŏ is shown before r, however (as in *moral* mŏr′ăl), the pronunciation in the United States may be ä or ŏ (with Southern British value) or ô.

§ 40.1. In foreign words, ŏ has a value similar to that which it has in southern England.

ŏ̂

§ 41. As in English sŏ̂ft**.**

This will be recognized as a combination of the symbols ô and ŏ. It is used in transcribing a class of words which in both America and England are pronounced with either ô or ŏ (or an intermediate sound). When these words are pronounced with ŏ in America, the ŏ usually has, not its usual American value ä, but a value similar to that which it has in southern England.

ǒ

§ 42. As in English cǒnnect**.**

In ordinary English speech, an obscure vowel, like ȧ (see § 12). Occasionally in deliberate speech pronounced ŏ.

oi

§ 43. As in English oil**.**

A diphthong consisting of ô+ĭ.

o͞o

§ 44. As in English fo͞od**.**

High-back tense rounded. A single vowel, not two.

§ 44.1. o͞o is also used, in transcribing Swedish and Norwegian *u*, for a high-central rounded long vowel.

o͝o

§ 45. As in English fo͝ot**.**

High-back lax rounded. A single vowel, not two.

§ 45.1. o͝o is also used, in transcribing Norwegian *u*, for a high-central rounded short vowel.

ou

§ 46. As in English out**.**

A diphthong the first element of which varies throughout the English-speaking world. In what is perhaps the commonest variety, the diphthong begins with ȧ and moves upward to or toward o͞o. In two other common varieties the first element is ä and ă, respectively.

p

§ 47. As in English pen**.**

A voiceless sound produced by stopping the breath with the lips. Correlative voiced stop, b; correlative nasal, m.

r

§ 48. As in English ûrn**, r**ap**, fa**r**.**

With American speakers who do not "drop" their r's, the sound of ur in *urn* is a single vowel sound (not two sounds, as the spelling and transcription might suggest)

articulated by raising the point and blade of the tongue toward the hard palate—in technical language, by "retro-flexing" the tongue. ẽr (also a single vowel) is articulated like ûr, but is shorter and laxer, occurring only in completely unaccented syllables.

English consonant r (an r preceding a vowel in the same syllable) is similar in its articulation to the vowel ûr in *urn*, but differs in that (1) the tongue height is greater than is usually the case with the vowel ûr (in some cases so great as to produce audible friction), and in that (2) consonant r holds its position more briefly than does the vowel ûr, the tongue moving immediately toward the position of the vowel that follows. This movement or "glide" is an important characteristic of the consonant, and consonant r bears to the vowel ûr much the same relation that w does to ōō (§ 62) and y does to ē (§ 63).

With Americans who do not "drop" their r's, an *r* following a vowel in the same syllable (except ûr, ẽr: see above) is a vowel of ûr-like quality forming a diphthong with the preceding vowel. In all varieties of American speech, an *r* following an accented vowel and immediately preceding another vowel (e.g., in *carry*) is likewise usually an ûr-like vowel forming a diphthong with the preceding vowel. In Southern British speech, however, such an *r* is usually consonantal.

In eastern New England, New York City, the southern United States, and southern England, r is by most speakers treated differently than in the northern and western part of the United States. With these speakers: (1) The single vowel ûr, ẽr is usually replaced by an unretroflexed single vowel of mid-central articulation (in unaccented syllables—i.e., when the transcription is ẽr—this vowel is the same as *à*). (2) An r shown after any other vowel symbol than û or ẽ in the same syllable in transcriptions in this Dictionary is not pronounced by these speakers, unless a vowel immediately follows without pause in the next syllable (if this next syllable is in a separate word, some of these speakers do not pronounce an r even then). Either the r is dropped entirely (as in *farm*) or a non-syllable-forming mid-central vowel (= *à*) is used for it (as in *fair, feared*). It will be seen from these statements that to speak of these persons as "dropping" their r's is only partially accurate.

§ 48.1. In foreign languages, in which r is usually more vigorously articulated than in English, two common varieties are the tongue-point trill and the uvular r (see § 3.1). In the tongue-point trill the tongue is in light contact at the sides with the upper molars, and the point and blade are raised toward the front palate and rapidly vibrated up and down against the back part of the teethridge (see § 3.2) by the outgoing voiced breath. In uvular r, the voiced breath passes between the raised back of the tongue and the uvula, causing vibration of the latter (uvular trill) or merely producing a strong fricative sound (uvular scrape). Both the tongue-point trilled r and the uvular r occur in French and in German. Italian and Russian have only the tongue-point trill. Danish r is usually uvular. In Spanish, *rr* is pronounced as a tongue-point trill (transcribed rr in Spanish words in this Dictionary), whereas a single *r* has the same place of articulation but usually consists of only a single flip of the tongue point against the teethridge (transcribed r in Spanish words in this Dictionary). In certain positions (e.g., when initial in a word) Spanish *r* may be pronounced rr.

s

§ 49. As in English **s**o.
A voiceless sound produced with the tip and blade of the tongue pressed close to the teethridge, and the point drawn into itself so as to form a very narrow, tubelike channel between the tip and the teethridge. A thread of voiceless breath forced through this channel strikes the points of the teeth (esp. the lower) and produces the characteristic hissing sound. Voiced correlative, z.

sh

§ 50. As in English **sh**e.
sh is not a combination of the sounds s and h, contains no s or h sound, and is a single voiceless sound, pronounced with the tip and blade of the tongue approaching the hard palate a little farther back than for s. The aperture is wider laterally, so that the current of air passing over the tongue is more spread out like a waterfall than for s, in which it is like a jet. The main body of the tongue is also higher toward the roof of the mouth. The broader stream of air rushes against the teeth much as for s, the mouth requiring to be nearly closed. The position of the tongue is on the whole similar to that for y (cf. § 54). Voiced correlative, zh.

When s and h are in separate syllables in the transcription, each has its own sound, as in *sheepshead* shĕps'hĕd'.

t

§ 51. As in English **t**ime.
A voiceless sound produced, in English, by stopping the breath by placing the point of the tongue against the teethridge (see § 3.2). In some languages (e.g., French and Italian) the tongue point is placed against the back of the upper front teeth.

In American English, in certain positions (e.g., in *better, fatal*) the sound is voiced and is articulated very much like the Spanish single-tap r described in § 48.1. Between an n and an unaccented vowel (e.g., in *winter*) the sound may be completely dropped—a pronunciation considered by many to be substandard.

Correlative voiced stop, d; correlative nasal, n.

th

§ 52. As in English **th**en.
th is not a combination of the sounds t and h, contains no t or h sound, and is a single voiced sound. The point of the tongue lightly touches the backs or the points of the upper teeth, in some cases protruding a trifle between upper and lower teeth, while breath buzzes through with a fricative sound. Voiceless correlative, th.

th

§ 53. As in English **th**in.
Voiceless correlative of th (see § 52).

tū̆

§ 54. As in English na**tu**re.
In words in the respelled pronunciation of which this symbol occurs, the pronunciation tū (= tyōō) occurs in most words only in very formal speech. The ligature (‿) indicates that in ordinary speech the ty is usually pronounced ch (i.e., t+sh: see § 14). The explanation of this is as follows: The original pronunciation was ty. The sound sh, however, being closer to t than y is, speakers in time began, in accord with a process technically known as assimilation, to take a "path of less resistance" by substituting sh for y.

Also, before consonants the vowel is commonly ē or *ŭ*, not ōō.

Correlative sound with voiced consonant, dū̆.

ū

§ 55. As in English c**ū**be.
This symbol represents a combination of two sounds. The first element is y or ĭ, the second element ōō (in words transcribed ūr in this Dictionary, the second element is usually ŏō; i.e., ūr is yŏŏr or ĭŏŏr). In words in which ū is shown after certain consonants (notably l, s, z) in this Dictionary, the first element (y or ĭ) is omitted by many or most speakers; e.g., *Lucy*, transcribed lū'sĭ, is often pronounced lōō'sĭ.

 û

§ 56. As in English **û**nite.

The sound ū (see § 55) with briefer second element (often lowered to o͞o, even when not preceding r), occurring in unaccented syllables.

û

§ 57. As in English **û**rn.

In transcriptions of English words, used only before r in syllables having some degree of accent. For its value in these words, see § 48.

§ 57.1. In some foreign languages (e.g., Czech and Yugoslav) in which r may serve as the vowel in an accented syllable, this r (transcribed ûr in this Dictionary) is not the ûr vowel described in § 48, but the tongue-point trill (see § 48.1). Examples: Czech *Brno* bûr′nô, Yugoslav *Vrbas* vûr′bäs.

§ 57.2. In names belonging to some foreign languages, û transcribes, not a mid-central vowel, but either of two mid-front rounded vowels, one close (approximately English ā pronounced with rounded lips), the other open (approximately English ĕ pronounced with rounded lips). Examples: German *Böhmen* bû′mĕn (close), French *Villeneuve* vēl′nûv′ (open). With speakers of English who "drop" their r's, both of these non-English vowels, the close and the open, are commonly Anglicized as the mid-central unretroflexed vowel that these speakers use in a word like *fur* (see § 48); hence the use of the symbol û, and the use of one symbol for two different sounds. With speakers of English who do not "drop" their r's, either of these vowels plus a following r is frequently Anglicized as the mid-central retroflexed vowel that these speakers use in a word like *fur* (see § 48). Thus such speakers would give this sound to ör in German *Görlitz*. When no r follows the vowel, however, such speakers are usually unable to use as their Anglicized pronunciation the mid-central unretroflexed vowel, which is usually as foreign to their speech as the mid-front rounded vowels. In such a case, the Anglicizations used are frequently ā for the mid-front close rounded vowel, ĕ for the mid-front open rounded vowel; i.e., the tongue position is approximately the same as for the non-English vowels, but the lip rounding is omitted: see the first sentence in this paragraph. These pronunciations are also often used even when an r follows the vowel. Examples: German *Döbeln* dā′bĕln, *Göttingen* gĕt′ing·ĕn, *Görlitz* gĕr′lĭts. Cf. § 60.

ŭ

§ 58. As in English **ŭ**p.

In America, usually a mid-central unrounded vowel, the highest part of the tongue being a little lower and farther back than for the *à* in *sofa* or ẽr in *better*. In Southern British, it is pronounced with the tongue slightly farther back.

ŭ

§ 59. As in English circ**ŭ**s.

Mid-central unrounded. Always obscure.

ü

§ 60. As in French men**u** (mē·nü′), German grün.

This symbol transcribes either of two high-front rounded vowels that have no counterpart in English, one close (approximately English ē pronounced with rounded lips), the other open (approximately English ĭ pronounced with rounded lips). These vowels are sometimes Anglicized by omitting the lip rounding; i.e., the close vowel is pronounced as ē, the open as ĭ (cf. § 57.2). Examples: *Tübingen* German tü′bĭng·ĕn, sometimes Anglicized tē′bĭng·ĕn; *Müller* German mül′ēr, sometimes Anglicized mĭl′ēr. Other Anglicizations are yo͞o (= ū) for the close vowel, yo͝o for the open. (Observe that in the yo͞o, yo͝o pronunciations there occur in succession two elements that occur simultaneously in the non-English vowels:

high-front tongue position, supplied by the y; lip rounding, supplied by the o͞o or o͝o. There is of course the additional element of high-back tongue position, supplied by the o͞o or o͝o). Examples: *Debussy* French dē·bü′sē′, Anglicized dē·bū′sĭ; *Müller* German mül′ēr, Anglicized myo͞ol′ēr (as well as mĭl′ēr; see above). Still other Anglicizations (as o͞o, o͝o, ŭ, and—where r follows the vowel—ûr) occur.

v

§ 61. As in English **v**an.

A voiced sound produced by the friction of the breath escaping between the closely juxtaposed upper teeth and lower lip. Voiceless correlative, f.

w

§ 62. As in English **w**ant.

For this sound, the lips are rounded and the back of the tongue raised as for o͞o or o͝o. However, the tongue has this position more briefly than for o͞o or o͝o, moving immediately toward the position of the following vowel.

Although this movement or "glide" is in most cases the distinguishing characteristic of the consonant, in some cases the tongue may be so high as to produce audible friction at the beginning of the sound. This friction is essential to the w sound when it precedes o͞o (as in *woo*), since there could not be any such thing as a movement from o͞o position to o͞o position. Cf. §§ 48, 63.

w and y are commonly called semivowels.

y

§ 63. As in English **y**et.

For this sound, the lips are unrounded and the front of the tongue (the part behind the blade and tip; see § 3.2) is raised toward the hard palate (whence y is called a palatal sound), as for ē or ĭ. However, the tongue has this position more briefly than for ē or ĭ, moving immediately toward the position of the following vowel.

Although this movement or "glide" is in most cases the distinguishing characteristic of the consonant, in some cases the tongue may be so high as to produce audible friction at the beginning of the sound. This friction is essential to the y sound when it precedes ē (as in *ye*), since there could not be any such thing as a movement from ē position to ē position. Cf. §§ 48, 62.

y and w are commonly called semivowels.

§ 63.1. In transcriptions of words from a number of foreign languages, a y following a tongue consonant denotes that the consonant is "palatal" or "palatalized." These two terms are not synonymous. A palatal consonant is one formed with the front of the tongue (the part behind the blade and tip; see § 3.2) near or touching the hard palate, and the tip of the tongue behind the lower front teeth. (The sound y has this articulation [see § 63]; hence the use of y after a consonant to denote that the consonant is palatal.) Common palatal consonants occurring in pronunciations in this Dictionary are ly (the sound of the bold-faced letters in Italian fi**gl**io and Spanish [Castilian pronunciation] o**ll**a), ny (the sound of the bold-faced letters in French a**gn**eau, Italian ba**gn**o, Spanish ca**ñ**ón), dy (the sound of the bold-faced letters in Hungarian **Gy**ula), and ty (the sound of the bold-faced letters in Hungarian ku**ty**a). Whereas in articulating English l, n, d, t the *tip* of the tongue is in contact with the *teethridge* (see § 3.2), in articulating the palatals ly, ny, dy, ty the *front* of the tongue (posterior to the tip; see § 3.2) is in contact with the *hard palate* (posterior to the teethridge), and the *tip* of the tongue is behind the lower front teeth. These palatal sounds can be acquired by placing the tip of the tongue behind the lower front teeth and trying to say l, n, d, t, respectively.

When a consonant (e.g., l, n, d, t) is palatalized, on the other hand, the tip of the tongue is in contact with the teethridge (or, in some languages, with the back of the

upper front teeth), as it is for ordinary l, n, d, t. However, the front of the tongue, posterior to the tip, instead of being somewhat low in the mouth as for ordinary l, n, d, t, is brought to or near the hard palate, thus approximating the position that it has in the articulation of a full palatal sound.

§ 63.2. Palatalization is especially important in Russian. In that language there are a group of five hard, or nonpalatalizing, vowels, and a corresponding group of five soft, or palatalizing, vowels. The palatalizing effect of this group of soft vowels takes, in general, either of two forms: (1) When a soft vowel is immediately preceded by a tongue consonant (except *ch, sh, shch, zh,* which are palatal already), the consonant is palatalized, and a y sound is usually present between the consonant and the vowel. g, k, and к merely have the most forward position possible for these consonants: cf. §§ 24, 30, 31. (2) When a soft vowel is initial in a word, or is immediately preceded by another vowel or by a consonant other than a tongue consonant, the palatalization takes the form of a y sound before the vowel. (Certain exceptions to these two statements are noted below.) Whichever of these two forms the palatalization takes, it is indicated in this Dictionary by the symbol y immediately preceding the vowel; e.g., *Esenin* yĭ·syā′nyĭn.

The usual transliteration of the Russian vowels in this Dictionary, and their usual pronunciation in accented syllables, are as follows:

HARD	SOFT
a (á)	ya (yá)
e (ĕ, ā)	e (yĕ, yā)
y (see § 27.1)	i (yē, ē)
o (ô)	ĕ (yô)
u (o͞o)	yu (yo͞o)

NOTES. It will be observed that the transliteration distinguishes between each pair of hard and soft vowels except hard e and soft e. However, inasmuch as hard e occurs in only two or three genuinely Russian words, one will nearly always be correct in assuming that an e in a Russian name is a soft e.

Observe that the hard vowel y has a value different from that borne by y in the soft vowels ya, yu, where y has its usual English consonantal value. The letters transliterated ya, yu are single letters in Russian, the two-letter transliterations being used to distinguish these soft vowels orthographically from the corresponding hard ones.

i, unlike the other soft vowels, does not have a preceding y sound when it is initial, being pronounced simply ē (ĭ in unaccented syllables). i is also not palatalized when, as it often does, it forms a diphthong with a preceding vowel.

Observe that, whereas in each of the other four pairs the quality of the hard vowel is the same as that of the second (vocalic) element of the soft vowel, in the pair y, i

this quality is different. After sh and zh (but not after ch and *shch:* see § 14) i is pronounced like y.

A consonant may also be palatalized in Russian when not followed by a soft vowel (e.g., when final in a word or when medial and followed by another consonant). Such palatalization is indicated orthographically in Russian by a special letter, not usually transliterated in English and not transliterated in this Dictionary.

§ 63.3. When the symbol y is final in a word or syllable (e.g., in transcriptions of French and other foreign languages), it is followed by an apostrophe, as a precaution against its being mispronounced by English-speaking persons, who, on the analogy of English words having y in such position, might otherwise interpret the symbol as having the value ĭ. Example: *Bastogne* bȧs′tôn′y'.

z

§ 64. As in English **z**one.

A voiced sound produced with the tip and blade of the tongue pressed close to the upper teethridge, and the point drawn into itself so as to form a very narrow, tube-like channel between the tip and the teethridge. A thread of voiced breath forced through this channel strikes the points of the teeth (esp. the lower) and produces the characteristic buzzing sound. Voiceless correlative, s.

zh

§ 65. As in English a**z**ure (ăzh′ẽr; à′zhẽr).

zh is not a combination of the sounds z and h, contains no z or h sound, and is a single voiced sound, pronounced with the tip and blade of the tongue approaching the hard palate a little farther back than for z. The aperture is wider laterally, so that the current of air passing over the tongue is more spread out like a waterfall than for z, in which it is like a jet. The main body of the tongue is also higher toward the roof of the mouth. The broader stream of air rushes against the teeth much as for z, the mouth requiring to be nearly closed. The position of the tongue is on the whole similar to that for y (cf. § 16). Voiceless correlative, sh.

When z and h are in separate syllables in the transcription, each has its own sound, as in *hogshead* hŏgz′hĕd.

,

§ 66. Certain consonants are capable of serving as the vowel in a syllable, and when they so function are called syllabic consonants. In English the chief such consonants are l, n, and (to a much lesser degree) m, which may be syllabic in unaccented syllables after certain consonants. No vowel is present in the syllable. The sign of a syllabic consonant in this Dictionary is an apostrophe immediately preceding the consonant, thus: *battle* băt′'l, *harden* här′d'n, *hardened* här′d'nd, *Clapham* klăp′'m.

§ 66.1. In foreign words (chiefly French), an apostrophe following l or r indicates the unvoicing of these normally voiced sounds, as in French *peuple* pû′pl', *poudre* po͞o′dr'. In such cases, the l' and r' do not form an additional syllable: *peuple* and *poudre* are monosyllables.

ABBREVIATIONS AND SYMBOLS
USED IN THE TEXT, TABLES, AND
MAPS IN THIS BOOK

ABBREVIATIONS

A.	Austria
ab.	about
abbr.	abbreviated, abbreviation
Acad.	Academy
A.C.T.	Australian Capital Territory
A.D.	Anno Domini (Lat., in the year of our Lord)
Ala.	Alabama
Alb.	Albania
alt.	altitude
Alta.	Alberta
Amer.	America, American
anc.	ancient
Angl.	Anglicized
approx.	approximate, approximately
Apr.	April
A.R.	Autonomous Region or Republic
Arab.	Arabic
Arch.	Archipelago
Argen.	Argentine
Ariz.	Arizona
Ark.	Arkansas
AS.	Anglo-Saxon
Assoc.	Association
A.S.S.R.	Autonomous Soviet Socialist Republic
Aug.	August
Aust.	Austria
Austral.	Australasia, Australian
Auton.	Autonomous
A.V.	Authorized Version
B.	Bulgaria
B.C.	Before Christ, British Columbia
Bel.	Belgium
Belg.	Belgian
bet.	between
Bib.	Biblical
bor.	borough
bpl.	birthplace
Br.	British
Braz.	Brazilian
Brit.	British
Bulg.	Bulgarian
B.W.I.	British West Indies
c.	circa (with dates only)
C.	Cabo, Cape, Centigrade
Cal., Calif.	California
Cam.	Cameroun
Can.	Canada, Canadian
cen.	center, central
cent(s).	century, centuries
cf.	confer (Lat., compare)
Chin.	Chinese
Chron.	Chronicles
co.	county
coed.	coeducational
C. of G. H.	Cape of Good Hope
col.	colony

Col.	Colombia, Colonel, Colorado, Colossians
Coll.	College
Colo.	Colorado
comm.	commune
Conn.	Connecticut
cons.	construction
Cor.	Corinthians
cos.	counties
cu.	cubic
CZ.	Czechoslovakia
C.Z.	Canal Zone
Czecho.	Czechoslovakia
d.	died
Dan.	Daniel, Danish
D.C.	District of Columbia
Dec.	December
Del.	Delaware
Den.	Denmark
dept(s).	department(s)
Deut.	Deuteronomy
dist(s).	district(s)
div.	division
Dom. Rep.	Dominican Republic
Dr.	Doctor
Du.	Dutch
E.	East
Eccles.	Ecclesiastes
educ.	educational
e.g.	exempli gratia (Lat., for example)
Eng.	England, English
Eph., Ephes.	Ephesians
Equa.	Equatorial
esp.	especially
est.	estimate, estimated
Est.	Estonia, Estonian
estab.	established
Esth.	Esther
et al.	et alii (Lat., and others)
etc.	et cetera (Lat., and so forth)
excl.	excludes, excluding, exclusive
Exod.	Exodus
Ez., Ezr.	Ezra
Ezek.	Ezekiel
f.	founded
Fahr.	Fahrenheit
Feb.	February
Fed.	Federation
ff.	following
Fin.	Finland
Finn.	Finnish
Fla.	Florida
Flem.	Flemish
form.	former, formerly
fr.	from
Fr.	French
F.S.	Free State
ft.	foot, feet
Ft.	Fort
Ga.	Georgia
Gal.	Galatians
Gen.	General, Genesis

Geo.	George
Ger.	German, Germany
Glos.	Gloucestershire
govt(s).	government(s)
Gr.	Greece, Greek
Gr. Brit., Gr. Britain, Gt. Br.	Great Britain
H.	Hungary
Hab.	Habakkuk
Hag.	Haggai
Heb., Hebr.	Hebrew(s)
Hind.	Hindustani
Hon.	Honduras
Hos.	Hosea
Hun.	Hungary
Hung.	Hungarian
I.	Indian, Isla, Island, Isle
Î.	Île (Fr., Island, Isle)
Icel.	Icelandic
i.e.	id est (Lat., that is)
Ill.	Illinois
in.	inch(es)
incl.	included, includes, including
incorp.	incorporated
Ind.	Indian, Indiana
Inst.	Institution
Ir.	Irish
Ire.	Ireland
Is.	Islands, Islas, Isles
Isa.	Isaiah
Ital.	Italian, Italy
Jan.	January
Jap.	Japan, Japanese
Jas.	James
Jer.	Jeremiah
Josh.	Joshua
Jr.	Junior
Judg.	Judges
Kans.	Kansas
Ky.	Kentucky
L.	Lago, Lagoa, Lake, Latin, Little
La.	Louisiana
Lam.	Lamentations
lat.	latitude
Lat.	Latin, Latvia
Lev.	Leviticus
Lith.	Lithuania, Lithuanian
long.	longitude
m.	mile(s)
M.	Monument
Mal.	Malachi
Man.	Manitoba
Mar.	March
Mass.	Massachusetts
Matt.	Matthew
max.	maximum
Md.	Maryland
Me.	Maine
Medit.	Mediterranean
Mex.	Mexican, Mexico
Mic.	Micah
Mich.	Michigan

Mil. .... Military	*P.O.* .... Post Office	*subdist(s).* .. subdistrict(s)
Minn. ..... Minnesota	*Pol.* .... Poland, Polish	*subprov(s).* .. subprovince(s)
Miss. ...... Mississippi	*polit.* ...... politically	*Sw.* .... Switzerland
Mo. .... Missouri	*pop.* .... population	*S.W.* ...... Southwest
mod. ...... modern	*Port.* ...... Portugal, Portuguese	*S.-W.* ...... South-West
Mon. ...... Monument	*pp.* .... pages	*Swed.* ...... Swedish
Mongol. ... Mongolian	*P.R.* .... Puerto Rico	*Switz.* ...... Switzerland
Mont. ..... Montana	*pron.* ...... pronounced, pronuncia-	*Tan.* .... Tanganyika
MS(S). .... Manuscript(s)	tion	*Tasm.* ..... Tasmania
Mt(s). ..... Mount(s), Mountain(s)	*pron'd.* ..... pronounced	*Tenn.* ...... Tennessee
N. .... National, Netherlands,	*prov(s).* .... province(s)	*Ter., Terr.* .. Territory
North	*Prov.* ...... Proverbs	*Tex.* .... Texas
Nah. ...... Nahum	*Ps., Psa.* .. Psalms	*T.H.* .... Territory of Hawaii
Nat. .... National	*Pt.* .... Point, Punta	*Thess.* ..... Thessalonians
Naut. ...... Nautical	*pub.* .... published	*Tim.* .... Timothy
naut. m. .... nautical mile(s)	*qq.v.* .... quae vide (Lat., which	*trib(s).* ..... tributary, tributaries
N.B. ...... New Brunswick	[plural] see)	*Turk.* ...... Turkish
N.C., N.Car. North Carolina	*Que.* .... Québec	*U.* .... University
N.Dak. .... North Dakota	*q.v.* .... quod vide (Lat., which	*U.K.* ...... United Kingdom
N.E. ...... Northeast	see)	*Ukrain.* .... Ukrainian
Nebr. ...... Nebraska	*R.* .... Reservation, Río, Rio,	*unincorp.* ... unincorporated
Neh. .... Nehemiah	River	*Univ.* ...... University
Neth. ...... Netherlands	*Ra.* .... Range	*U. of S. Afr.* Union of South Africa
Neth. Indies Netherlands Indies	*reincorp.* ... reincorporated	*U.S.* .... United States
Nev. .... Nevada	*Res.* .... Reservation, Reservoir	*U.S.A.* ..... United States of Amer-
Newf. ...... Newfoundland	*Rev.* .... Revelation	ica
N.H. ...... New Hampshire	*R.I.* .... Rhode Island	*U.S.S.R.* ... Union Soviet Socialist
N.I. .... Northern Ireland	*riv(s).* ...... river(s)	Republics
Nic. .... Nicaragua	*Ro.* .... Romania	*usu.* .... usual, usually
N. Island .. North Island	*Rom.* ...... Romania, Romanian,	*Va.* .... Virginia
N.J. .... New Jersey	Romans	*var(s).* ..... variant(s)
N.Mex. .... New Mexico	*Rom. Cath.* . Roman Catholic	*Ven.* .... Venezuela
Nor. .... Northern	*R.R.* .... Railroad	*V.I.* .... Virgin Islands
Norw. ..... Norway, Norwegian	*R.S.F.S.R.* . Russian Soviet Feder-	*Vol.* .... Volcano
Nov. .... November	ated Socialist Repub-	*Vt.* .... Vermont
nr. .... near	lic	*W.* .... West
N.S. .... Nova Scotia	*Russ.* ...... Russian	*Wash.* ..... Washington
N.S.W. .... New South Wales	*Ry(s).* ..... Railway(s)	*W. Australia* Western Australia
N.T. ...... New Testament, North-	*S.* .... South	*Wis.* .... Wisconsin
ern Territory	*S. Afr. D., S.*	*W.Va.* ..... West Virginia
Num., Numb. Numbers	*Afr. Du.* . South African Dutch	*Wyo.* ...... Wyoming
N.W. ...... Northwest	*Sam.* ...... Samuel	*yd(s).* ...... yard(s)
N.W.T. .... Northwest Territories	*Sask.* ...... Saskatchewan	*Yorks.* ...... Yorkshire
N.Y. ...... New York	*S. Australia* South Australia	*Yug.* .... Yugoslavia
N.Z. ...... New Zealand	*S.C., S.Car.* South Carolina	*Yugo.* ...... Yugoslav, Yugoslavian
Ob. .... Obadiah	*Scot.* ...... Scotch, Scotland, Scot-	*Zech.* ...... Zechariah
Obs. .... Obsolete	tish	*Zeph.* ...... Zephaniah
occas. ...... occasional, occasionally	*Sd.* .... Sound	
Oct. .... October	*S.Dak.* ..... South Dakota	
Okla. ...... Oklahoma	*S.E.* .... Southeast	
Ont. .... Ontario	*Sem.* .... Seminary	**SYMBOLS USED IN TEXT MATTER**
opp. .... opposite	*sep.* .... separate, separated	
Ore., Oreg. .. Oregon	*Sept.* ...... September	✳ .... capital
org. .... organized	*Serb.* ...... Serbian	⊗ .... county seat, parish seat
orig. .... original, originally	*S. Island* ... South Island	
O.T. ...... Old Testament	*Sol.* .... Solomon	**SYMBOLS USED ON MAPS**
p. .... page	*Som., Somal.* Somaliland	
P. .... Punta	*Sou., South.* Southern	○ .... location point
Pa. .... Pennsylvania	*Sov.* .... Soviet	◉ .... county seat, capitals of
Pal. .... Palestine	*Span.* ...... Spanish	divisions and, some-
par. .... parish	*sq.* .... square	times, capitals of
Para. ...... Paraguay	*sq. m.* ...... square miles	countries
P.E.I. ..... Prince Edward Island	*Sr.* .... Senior	⊛ .... capitals of countries
penin. ..... peninsula	*S.S.R.* ..... Soviet Socialist Repub-	△ .... peak, mountain
Penn.,	lic	)(........ mountain pass
Penna. ... Pennsylvania	*St.* .... Saint, Sint	∴ .... ruins
Pers. ...... Persian	*Sta.* .... Station	∷ .... national monument
Pet. .... Peter	*Ste.* .... Sainte	✕ .... battlefield
Phil. ...... Philippians	*Str.* .... Strait	⚹ .... lighthouse
Phil. Is. ... Philippine Islands	*sub.* .... suburb	∪∪∪∪ ... reef
		▗▄▖ ... canal
		⌐⌐⌐ ... wall (of China)

GEOGRAPHICAL TERMS

For the convenience of the users of this book we present in the following lists a selection of geographical terms and their equivalents in various foreign languages, including for most terms the chief languages of western Europe. Both the terms and the languages are selected on the basis of their usefulness to the average consultant. Besides names of physical features and of political divisions the lists contain a number of words (such as *old* and *new*, *eastern* and *western* and *central, upper* and *lower*) that are often used in compound proper names.

Each list is arranged in alphabetical sequence, for quickest reference. The first gives foreign terms with their equivalents in English; the second, English terms with their foreign-language equivalents. Names of languages are indicated by abbreviations, which, if not self-evident, may be identified in the list on pages xviii–xix.

LIST I

ab	Pers.	water
-abad	Hind.	city, town
abajo	Span.	lower
acqua	Ital.	water
ada, adasi	Turk.	island
agua	Port., Span.	water
ain	Arab.	spring, well
akrōtērion	Gr.	cape
alt	Ger.	old
altipiano	Ital.	plateau
altiplano	Span.	plateau
alto	Ital., Port., Span.	high, upper
archipel	Du., Fr.	archipelago
archipiélago	Span.	archipelago
arkhipelag	Russ.	archipelago
austral	Span.	southern
ayer	Malay	water
baai	Du.	bay
bab	Arab.	strait, gate
bahia	Port.	bay
bahía	Span.	bay
bahr	Arab.	sea, river
bai	Ger.	bay
baie	Fr.	gulf, bay
baixo	Port.	low, lower
bajo	Span.	low, lower
bana	Jap.	cape
banco	Span.	shoal
band	Pers.	mountain range
bandar	Pers.	port, harbor
baru	Malay	new
bas, basse	Fr.	low
basso	Ital.	low
batu	Malay	rock
bel	Turk.	pass
belyi	Russ.	white
ben	Gaelic	mountain
bereg	Russ.	shore, coast
berg	Du., Ger.	mountain
besar	Malay	great, big
bir	Arab.	spring, well
birket	Arab.	lake
boca	Span.	mouth, estuary
bogaz, boğaz, boghaz	Turk.	strait
bois	Fr.	forest, wood
bolshoi	Russ.	big, great
bucht	Ger.	bay, bight
bugt	Dan.	bay, bight
bukhta	Russ.	bay, bight
bukit	Malay	hill
burnu	Turk.	cape
burun	Turk.	cape
cabo	Port., Span.	cape

campo	Port., Span.	plain
canal	Fr., Span.	channel, canal
canale	Ital.	channel, canal
cap	Fr.	cape
capo	Ital.	cape
cascada	Span.	waterfall
cascata d'acqua	Ital.	waterfall
cataracta	Port.	waterfall
central	Fr., Span.	middle, central
centrale	Ital.	middle, central
cerro	Span.	hill
chaîne	Fr.	mountain range
champ	Fr.	plain, field
chico	Span.	little, small
chiisai	Jap.	little, small
chott	Arab. (Fr. transliteration)	(salt) lake
chute d'eau	Fr.	waterfall
cidade	Port.	city, town
cima	Ital.	peak
cime	Fr.	peak
cité	Fr.	city, town
città	Ital.	city, town
ciudad	Span.	city, town
col	Fr.	pass
colline	Fr.	hill
cordillera	Span.	mountain range
costa	Span.	coast
côte	Fr.	coast
cumbre	Span.	peak
dağ, dagh	Turk.	mountain
dağları	Turk.	mountain range
dal	Du.	valley
darya	Pers.	river
dasht	Pers.	plain, desert
deniz	Turk.	sea, lake
derbent	Pers.	pass
dere	Turk.	valley
désert	Fr.	desert
deserto	Ital.	desert
desht	Pers.	plain, desert
desierto	Span.	desert
détroit	Fr.	strait
djebel	Arab. (Fr. transliteration)	mountain
dlinnyi	Russ.	long
dolina	Slavic	valley
eau	Fr.	water
eiland	Du.	island
erg	Arab.	desert
est	Fr., Ital.	east
este	Port., Span.	east
estrecho	Span.	strait
estreito	Port.	strait

estuaire	Fr.	estuary
estuario	Span.	estuary
étang	Fr.	lake, lagoon
falaise	Fr.	cliff
feld	Ger.	field, plain
fels	Ger.	cliff
fiume	Ital.	river
fleuve	Fr.	river
fluss	Ger.	river
fokani	Arab.	upper
fonn	Norw.	glacier
forêt	Fr.	forest
foz	Port.	estuary
garh	Hind.	hill
gawa	Jap.	river
gebel	Arab.	mountain
gebergte	Du.	mountain range
gebirge	Ger.	mountain range
gegend	Ger.	region
ghat	Hind.	pass
gherb	Arab.	west
gletscher	Dan., Ger.	glacier
gobi	Mongol.	desert
goenoeng	Malay	mount, mountain
göl	Turk.	lake
golf	Dan., Du., Ger.	gulf
golfe	Fr.	gulf
golfo	Ital., Port., Span.	gulf
gölü	Turk.	lake
gora	Russ.	mountain
gorod	Russ.	city
gory	Russ.	mountain range
grand	Fr.	big
grande	Span.	big
groot	Du.	big
gross	Ger.	big
grosso	Ital., Port.	big
guba	Russ.	gulf, bay
gunong	Malay	mountain
gunto	Jap.	archipelago
gunung	Malay	mountain
hafen	Ger.	port
haff	Ger.	lagoon
hai	Chin.	sea
halbinsel	Ger.	peninsula
hammada	Arab.	desert
hamun	Pers.	lake
hanto	Jap.	peninsula
hara	Jap.	plain, field
haut	Fr.	high
higashi	Jap.	east
ho	Chin.	river
hoch	Ger.	high
hochebene	Ger.	plateau
hoek	Du.	cape
hoku	Jap.	north
hoog	Du.	high
hor	Arab.	lake
hsiao	Chin.	little, small
hu	Chin.	lake
île	Fr.	island
ilha	Port.	island
inférieur	Fr.	lower
inferiore	Ital.	lower
insel	Ger.	island
ırmak	Turk.	river
isla	Span.	island
isola	Ital.	island
itadaki	Jap.	peak
jabal	Arab.	mountain
järvi	Finn.	lake
jebel	Arab.	mountain
jezira, jeziret	Arab.	island
jima	Jap.	island
jökull	Icel.	glacier
kaap	Du.	cape
kai	Jap.	sea
kaikyo	Jap.	channel, strait
kaku	Jap.	point
kali	Malay	river
kam	Korean	cape
kap	Dan., Norw., Swed.	cape
kapu	Turk.	pass
kawa	Jap.	river
kebir	Arab.	big
kechil	Malay	small
khrebet	Russ.	mountain range
kiang	Chin.	river
kiao	Chin.	cape, point
kidul	Malay	south
kita	Jap.	north
klein	Du., Ger.	small
ko	Siamese	island
ko	Jap.	lake
koh	Pers.	mountain
koh	Siamese	island
kol	Mongol.	lake
kolpos, kólpos	Gr.	gulf
kong	Chin.	river
kop	S. Afr. Du.	hill
körfez, körfezi	Turk.	gulf, bay
kosui	Jap.	lake
kuh	Pers.	mountain
kul	Mongol.	lake
kulon	Malay	west
kum	Turk.	desert
kyst	Dan.	coast
laag	Du.	low
lac	Fr.	lake
lago	Ital., Port., Span.	lake
lagoa	Port.	lagoon
laguna	Span.	lagoon
land	Ger.	country
lang	Du., Ger.	long
largo	Span.	long
laut	Malay	sea
lembah	Malay	valley
les	Russ.	forest
levante	Ital.	east
litoral	Port.	coast
llano	Span.	plain
long	Fr.	long
longo	Port.	long
lungo	Ital.	long
ma	Arab.	water
maha	Hind.	big, great
maidan	Hind.	plain, field
mali	Russ.	small
mar	Port., Span.	sea
mare	Ital.	sea
massif	Fr.	mountain group
medio	Span.	middle
meer	Du.	lake
meer	Ger.	sea
meio	Port.	middle
mer	Fr.	sea
meridional	Span.	southern
méridional	Fr.	southern
middelst, midden	Du.	middle
midi	Fr.	south
minami	Jap.	south
misaki	Jap.	cape
mittel	Ger.	middle
mizu	Jap.	water
mont	Fr.	mountain
montagna	Ital.	mountain
montagnes	Fr.	mountain range
monte	Ital., Port., Span.	mountain
monti	Ital.	mountain range

more	Russ.	sea
mori	Jap.	mount
moyen	Fr.	middle
mündung	Ger.	river mouth, estuary
mys	Russ.	cape
nada	Jap.	gulf, sea
nagai	Jap.	long
nahr	Arab.	river
naka	Jap.	middle
nan	Chin.	south
negri	Malay	country
neu	Ger.	new
nieder	Ger.	lower
niedrig	Ger.	low
nieuw	Du.	new
nishi	Jap.	west
nizhni	Russ.	lower
noord	Du.	north, northern
nor	Mongol.	lake
nord	Fr.	north
nord-	Ger.	north
nördlich	Ger.	northern
norte	Ital., Port., Span.	north
nos	Russ.	cape
nouveau, nouvelle	Fr.	new
novo	Port.	new
novyi	Russ.	new
nuevo	Span.	new
nuovo	Ital.	new
o	Jap.	big
ö (ø)	Dan., Norw.	island
ö	Swed.	island
ober	Ger.	upper
oblast	Russ.	region
occidental	Fr., Span.	western
occidentale	Ital.	western
occidente	Ital.	west
oceaan	Du.	ocean
océan	Fr.	ocean
oceano	Ital., Port.	ocean
océano	Span.	ocean
oedjoeng	Malay	cape
oeste	Port., Span.	west
oost	Du.	east
oostersch	Du.	eastern
opper	Du.	upper
oriental	Fr., Span.	eastern
orientale	Ital.	eastern
oriente	Span.	east
orta	Turk.	middle
ost-	Ger.	east
östlich	Ger.	east, eastern
ostrov	Russ.	island
oud	Du.	old
ouest	Fr.	west
over	Du.	upper
ozean	Ger.	ocean
ozero	Russ.	lake
padang	Malay	plain
paese	Ital.	country
país	Port., Span.	country
paiz	Port.	country
panchang	Malay	long
paso	Span.	pass
pass	Ger.	pass
passo	Ital., Port.	pass
pays	Fr.	country
peh, pei	Chin.	north
península	Span.	peninsula
penisola	Ital.	peninsula
pequeno	Port.	small
pequeño	Span.	small
pereval	Russ.	pass
petit	Fr.	small
pic	Fr.	peak
picco	Ital.	peak
piccolo	Ital.	small
pico	Port., Span.	peak
piz	Romansh	peak
plaine	Fr.	plain, field
planalto	Port.	plateau
plateau	Fr.	plateau
ploskogorie	Russ.	plateau
poelau	Malay	island
pointe	Fr.	point
poluostrov	Russ.	peninsula
ponta	Port.	point
port	Fr.	port
porto	Ital., Port.	port
poulo	Malay	island
presqu'île	Fr.	peninsula
prezhni	Russ.	old (former)
prokhod	Russ.	pass
proliv	Russ.	strait
puerto	Span.	port
pulau, pulo	Malay	island
punta	Ital., Span.	point
pustnya	Russ.	desert
qum	Turk.	desert
ras	Arab.	cape
ravnina	Russ.	plain, field
região	Port.	region
région	Fr.	region
región	Span.	region
regione	Ital.	region
reka	Russ.	river
retto	Jap.	island (chain)
rio	Port.	river
río	Span.	river
rivier	Du.	river
rivière	Fr.	river
rud	Pers.	river
sabaku	Jap.	desert
sahra (*pl.* sahara)	Arab.	desert
saki	Jap.	cape
san	Jap.	hill, mountain
saut	Fr.	waterfall
schiereiland	Du.	peninsula
see	Ger.	sea, lake
seghir	Arab.	little, small
selat	Malay	channel
selva	Span.	wood, forest
septentrional	Fr., Port., Span.	northern
serra	Port.	mountain range
seto	Jap.	strait
settentrionale	Ital.	northern
shan	Chin.	hill, mountain, mountain range
shang	Chin.	upper
shat, shatt	Arab.	river, (salt) lake
shemal	Arab.	north
sherk	Arab.	east
shima	Jap.	island
shimo	Jap.	lower
shoto	Jap.	archipelago
shott	Arab.	(salt) lake
shui	Chin.	water
si	Chin.	west
sierra	Span.	mountain range
sopka	Russ.	mountain (extinct volcano)
spitze	Ger.	peak
sredni	Russ.	middle
stad	Du.	city, town
stadt	Ger.	city, town
-stan	Pers.	country
step	Russ.	plain
straat	Du.	strait
strasse	Ger.	strait

stretto	Ital.	strait
strom	Ger.	river
su	Turk.	water, river
sud	Fr., Ital., Span.	south
süd-	Ger.	south
südlich	Ger.	southern
suid	S. Afr. Du.	south
suido	Jap.	strait
sul	Port.	south
supérieur	Fr.	upper
superior	Port., Span.	upper
superiore	Ital.	upper
sur	Span.	south
suyu	Turk.	water, river
sziget	Hung.	island
tafelland	Du.	plateau
takai	Jap.	high
tal	Ger.	valley
tandjoeng	Malay	cape, point
tani	Jap.	valley
tanjong	Malay	cape, point
tao	Chin.	island
taung	Burmese	hill
tel, tell	Arab.	hill
temin	Arab.	south
tepe	Turk.	hill
t'ien	Chin.	plain, field
tinggi	Malay	high
to	Jap.	island
toge	Jap.	pass
tua	Malay	old
tung	Chin.	east
ue-no	Jap.	upper
ulu	Turk.	big, great
umi	Jap.	sea
unter	Ger.	lower
ura	Jap.	bay
utan	Malay	forest, woods

utara	Malay	north
val	Ital.	valley
valle	Ital., Port., Span.	valley
vallée	Fr.	valley
vecchio	Ital.	old
veld	S. Afr. Du.	plain (grassland)
velho	Port.	old
veliki	Russ.	great, big
verkhni	Russ.	upper
vershina	Russ.	peak
viejo	Span.	old
vieux, vieille	Fr.	old
vik	Swed.	bay
ville	Fr.	city, town
voda	Russ.	water
vostochni	Russ.	eastern
vostok	Russ.	east
wadi	Arab.	valley (dry water-course)
wald	Ger.	forest, woods
wan	Chin., Jap.	gulf, bay
wasser	Ger.	water
wasserfall	Ger.	waterfall
water	Du.	water
waterval	Du.	waterfall
west	Du., Ger.	west
westlich	Ger.	western
wetan	Malay	east
wüste	Ger.	desert
yama	Jap.	mountain
yug	Russ.	south, southern
zaki	Jap.	cape, point
zaliv	Russ.	gulf
zapad	Russ.	west
zapadni	Russ.	western
zee	Du.	sea
zemlya	Russ.	country, land
zuid	Du.	south

LIST II

archipelago:
Du., Fr.	archipel
Jap.	gunto, shoto
Russ.	arkhipelag
Span.	archipiélago

bay:
Chin.	wan
Dan.	bugt
Du.	baai
Fr.	baie
Ger.	bucht, bai
Jap.	ura, wan
Port.	bahia
Russ.	guba, bukhta
Span.	bahía
Swed.	vik
Turk.	körfez, körfezi

big: see GREAT

bight:
Dan.	bugt
Ger.	bucht
Russ.	bukhta

cape:
Arab.	ras
Chin.	kiao
Dan., Norw., Swed.	kap
Du.	hoek, kaap
Fr.	cap
Gr.	akrōtērion
Ital.	capo
Jap.	bana, saki, misaki, zaki
Korean	kam
Malay	tandjoeng, tanjong, oedjoeng
Port.	cabo
Russ.	mys, nos
Span.	cabo
Turk.	burnu, burun

channel: (see also STRAIT)
Fr., Span.	canal
Ital.	canale
Jap.	kaikyo
Malay	selat

city, town:
Du.	stad
Fr.	ville, cité
Ger.	stadt
Hind.	-abad
Ital.	città
Port.	cidade
Russ.	gorod
Span.	ciudad

cliff:
Fr.	falaise
Ger.	fels

coast:
Dan.	kyst
Fr.	côte
Russ.	bereg
Span.	costa

country, region, land:
Fr.	pays; région; terre
Ger.	land; gegend
Ital.	paese; regione; terra
Malay	negri
Pers.	-stan (as in Hindustan)
Port.	país, paiz; região; terra
Russ.	zemlya; oblast
Span.	país; región; tierra

desert:
Arab.	sahra (*pl.* sahara), hammada, erg
Fr.	désert
Ger.	wüste
Ital.	deserto
Jap.	sabaku
Mongol.	gobi
Pers.	dasht, desht
Russ.	pustnya
Span.	desierto
Turk.	kum, qum

east:
Arab.	sherk
Chin.	tung
Du.	oost
Fr.	est
Ger.	ost-; östlich
Ital.	est, levante
Jap.	higashi

Malay	wetan
Port.	este
Russ.	vostok
Span.	este, oriente

eastern:

Du.	oostersch
Fr., Span.	oriental
Ger.	östlich
Ital.	orientale
Russ.	vostochni

estuary, river mouth:

Fr.	estuaire
Ger.	mündung
Port.	foz
Span.	boca, estuario

field: see PLAIN

forest, wood:

Fr.	forêt, bois
Ger.	wald
Malay	utan
Russ.	les
Span.	selva

glacier:

Dan., Ger.	gletscher
Icel.	jökull
Norw.	fonn

great, big:

Arab.	kebir
Du.	groot
Fr.	grand
Ger.	gross
Hind.	maha
Ital., Port.	grosso
Jap.	o
Malay	besar
Russ.	bolshoi; veliki
Span.	grande
Turk.	ulu

gulf:

Chin.	wan
Dan., Du., Ger.	golf
Fr.	golfe, baie
Gr.	kolpos, kólpos
Ital., Port., Span.	golfo
Jap.	nada, wan
Russ.	guba, zaliv
Turk.	körfez, körfezi

high:

Du.	hoog
Fr.	haut
Ger.	hoch
Ital., Port., Span.	alto
Jap.	takai
Malay	tinggi

hill:

Arab.	tel, tell
Burmese	taung
Chin.	shan
Fr.	colline
Hind.	garh
Jap.	san
Malay	bukit
S. Afr. Du.	kop
Span.	cerro
Turk.	tepe

island:

Arab.	jezira, jeziret
Chin.	tao
Dan., Norw.	ö (ø)
Du.	eiland
Fr.	île
Ger.	insel

Hung.	sziget
Ital.	isola
Jap.	jima, shima, to; retto (chain)
Malay	pulo, poulo, poelau, pulau
Port.	ilha
Russ.	ostrov
Siamese	ko, koh
Span.	isla
Swed.	ö
Turk.	ada, adasi

lagoon:

Fr.	étang
Ger.	haff
Port.	lagoa
Span.	laguna

lake:

Arab.	birket, hor; (salt lake) shat, shatt, shott, or, Fr. transliteration, chott
Chin.	hu
Du	meer
Finn.	järvi
Fr.	lac, étang
Ger.	see
Ital., Port., Span.	lago
Jap.	ko, kosui
Mongol.	kol, kul; nor
Pers.	hamun
Russ.	ozero
Turk.	deniz, göl, gölü

land: see COUNTRY

little, small:

Arab.	seghir
Chin.	hsiao
Du., Ger.	klein
Fr.	petit
Ital.	piccolo
Jap.	chiisai
Malay	kechil
Port.	pequeno
Russ.	mali
Span.	pequeño, chico

long:

Du., Ger.	lang
Fr.	long
Ital.	lungo
Jap.	nagai
Malay	panchang
Port.	longo
Russ.	dlinnyi
Span.	largo

low:

Du.	laag
Fr.	bas, basse
Ger.	niedrig
Ital.	basso
Port.	baixo
Span.	bajo

lower:

Fr.	inférieur
Ger.	nieder, unter
Ital.	inferiore
Jap.	shimo
Port.	baixo
Russ.	nizhni
Span.	bajo, abajo

middle:

Du.	middelst, midden
Fr.	central, moyen
Ger.	mittel

Ital.	centrale
Jap.	naka
Port.	meio
Russ.	sredni
Span.	medio, central
Turk.	orta

mount, mountain:

Arab.	jebel, gebel, jabal, or, Fr. transliteration, djebel
Chin.	shan
Du., Ger.	berg
Fr.	mont, massif (group)
Gaelic	ben
Ital.	montagna, monte
Jap.	mori, san, yama
Malay	goenoeng, gunong, gunung
Pers.	kuh, koh
Port., Span.	monte
Russ.	gora; sopka (extinct volcano)
Turk.	dağ, dagh

mountain range:

Chin.	shan
Du.	gebergte
Fr.	montagnes, chaîne
Ger.	gebirge
Ital.	monti
Pers.	band
Port.	serra
Russ.	khrebet, gory
Span.	cordillera, sierra
Turk.	dağları

new:

Du.	nieuw
Fr.	nouveau, nouvelle
Ger.	neu
Ital.	nuovo
Malay	baru
Port.	novo
Russ.	novyi
Span.	nuevo

north:

Arab.	shemal
Chin.	peh, pei
Du.	noord
Fr.	nord
Ger.	nord-
Ital., Port., Span.	norte
Jap.	hoku, kita
Malay	utara

northern:

Du.	noord
Fr., Port., Span.	septentrional
Ger.	nördlich
Ital.	settentrionale

ocean:

Du.	oceaan
Fr.	océan
Ger.	ozean
Ital., Port.	oceano
Span.	océano

old:

Du.	oud
Fr.	vieux, vieille
Ger.	alt
Ital.	vecchio
Malay	tua
Port.	velho
Russ.	prezhni (former)
Span.	viejo

pass:

Fr.	col
Ger.	pass
Hind.	ghat
Ital., Port.	passo
Jap.	toge
Pers.	derbent
Russ.	prokhod, pereval
Span.	paso
Turk.	kapu, bel

peak:

Fr.	pic, cime
Ger.	spitze
Ital.	picco, cima
Jap.	itadaki
Port.	pico
Romansh	piz
Russ.	vershina
Span.	pico, cumbre

peninsula:

Du.	schiereiland
Fr.	presqu'île
Ger.	halbinsel
Ital.	penisola
Jap.	hanto
Russ.	poluostrov
Span.	península

plain, field:

Chin.	t'ien
Fr.	plaine, champ
Ger.	feld
Hind.	maidan
Jap.	hara
Malay	padang
Pers.	dasht, desht
Port.	campo
Russ.	step, ravnina
S. Afr. Du.	veld (grassland)
Span.	llano, campo

plateau:

Du.	tafelland
Fr.	plateau
Ger.	hochebene
Ital.	altipiano
Port.	planalto
Russ.	ploskogorie
Span.	altiplano

point: (see also CAPE)

Chin.	kiao
Fr.	pointe
Ital., Span.	punta
Jap.	kaku, zaki
Malay	tandjoeing, tanjong
Port.	ponta

port:

Fr.	port
Ger.	hafen
Ital., Port.	porto
Pers.	bandar
Span.	puerto

region: see COUNTRY

river:

Arab.	bahr, shat, shatt, nahr
Chin.	kiang, ho, kong
Du.	rivier
Fr.	fleuve, rivière
Ger.	fluss, strom
Ital.	fiume
Jap.	kawa, gawa
Malay	kali
Pers.	darya, rud
Port.	rio
Russ.	reka
Span.	río
Turk.	irmak, su, suyu

river mouth: see ESTUARY

sea:

Arab.	bahr
Chin.	hai
Du.	zee
Fr.	mer
Ger.	meer, see
Ital.	mare
Jap.	kai, nada, umi
Malay	laut
Port., Span.	mar
Russ.	more
Turk.	deniz

small: see LITTLE

south:

Arab.	temin
Chin.	nan
Du.	zuid
Fr.	sud, midi
Ger.	süd-
Ital.	sud
Jap.	minami
Malay	kidul
Port.	sul
Russ.	yug
S. Afr. Du.	suid
Span.	sud, sur

southern:

Fr.	méridional
Ger.	südlich
Russ.	yug
Span.	meridional, austral

strait:

Arab.	bab
Du.	straat
Fr.	détroit
Ger.	strasse
Ital.	stretto
Jap.	kaikyo, seto, suido
Port.	estreito
Russ.	proliv
Span.	estrecho
Turk.	bogaz, boğaz, boghaz

town: see CITY

upper:

Arab.	fokani
Chin.	shang
Du.	opper, over
Fr.	supérieur
Ger.	ober
Ital.	alto, superiore
Jap.	ue-no
Port., Span.	alto, superior
Russ.	verkhni

valley:

Arab.	wadi (dry water-course)
Du.	dal
Fr.	vallée
Ger.	tal
Ital.	val, valle
Jap.	tani
Malay	lembah
Port., Span.	valle
Slavic	dolina
Turk.	dere

water:

Arab.	ma
Chin.	shui
Du.	water
Fr.	eau
Ger.	wasser
Ital.	acqua
Jap.	mizu
Malay	ayer
Pers.	ab
Port., Span.	agua
Russ.	voda
Turk.	su, suyu

waterfall:

Du.	waterval
Fr.	chute d'eau, saut
Ger.	wasserfall
Ital.	cascata d'acqua
Port.	cataracta
Span.	cascada

west:

Arab.	gherb
Chin.	si
Du., Ger.	west
Fr.	ouest
Ital.	occidente
Jap.	nishi
Malay	kulon
Port., Span.	oeste
Russ.	zapad

western:

Du.	westersch
Fr., Span.	occidental
Ger.	westlich
Ital.	occidentale
Russ.	zapadni

wood: see FOREST

MAPS AND MAP PROJECTION

One of the most difficult problems in map making is projection—the representation of the round surface of the earth on a flat surface such as a page or chart. Although before the Christian era it was known that the earth was round and certain methods of map projection were formulated and carried into execution, most maps remained comparatively crude by modern standards until the age of discovery in the 15th and 16th centuries began to supply the considerable gaps that had up to then existed in man's knowledge of the world as a whole. This widening knowledge in turn stimulated cartographers to devise improved methods of projection.

Although maps of small areas may be true enough to scale throughout so that the distortion is for practical purposes of no consequence, maps of large areas—for example, a continent or a hemisphere—involve distortion of some degree, and this distortion varies throughout the area mapped. The extent that this distortion can reach is vividly brought out by one projection (Mercator) of the world, wherein the poles, which are actually mere points without any dimension, have the same dimension as the equator.

There is no one method of projection that is best for all purposes. All involve distortion of some sort, and what projection is best for a given case is determined by weighing the advantages against the disadvantages of each method in the light of the use to which the map is to be put and the size, configuration, and orientation of the area to be mapped. Not all projections would produce a desirable route map for long-distance airplanes. A country long from north to south and narrow from east to west (e.g., Chile) is not represented to best advantage by the projection that serves best for a country broad from east to west in relation to its depth from north to south (e.g., the United States or the Union of Soviet Socialist Republics).

Reference data employed by projectionists are the parallels of latitude, the meridians of longitude, the poles, and the equator.

The following brief description of some of the more commonly used projections is provided as a complement to the pictures of various projections on the end papers of this book. For those who would like a much fuller treatment, clarified by more detailed illustrations, Special Publication No. 68, *Elements of Map Projection*, published by the U.S. Coast and Geodetic Survey, and the monograph *The Round Earth on Flat Paper*, published (1947) by the National Geographic Society, Washington, D.C., may be suggested.

Hollow rubber balls painted as globes and generously lined with meridians and parallels of latitude can be used to advantage in explaining projections, and an imagined globe of this sort is used in a few of the explanations that follow.

Orthographic. This projection, conceived by Hipparchus about 125 B.C., presents the earth as it would appear to an observer a great distance above it. A sharp picture made by a camera held at a considerable distance from a globe would approximate such a projection. The center is satisfactorily true to scale, but the scale contracts as the distance from the center is increased. Hence this projection is not commonly used for extensive areas.

Azimuthal Equidistant ("azimuthal" means that true direction from the center of the map is preserved). A modern projection that serves well for continents or other large areas. Any point on the globe can be used as a center. (If one of the poles is used, the projection is called *polar azimuthal equidistant*. See map on pages xxx–xxxi.) Like the orthographic, this projection is constructed around a central point, and the scale changes with the distance from this point. However, in the azimuthal equidistant, the scale along radii from this center is constant while the scale expands along circles (parallels of latitude) having this point as center, in proportion to the increasing size of the circles (in a polar projection of the whole world, the antipole is grotesquely exaggerated, appearing as the outermost circle); whereas in the orthographic the scale along such circles is constant, while the scale along the radii contracts in proportion to the distance from the center.

A hemispheric polar azimuthal equidistant projection can be roughly demonstrated by slicing a hollow rubber globe at the equator, cutting along the meridians of one of the halves almost up to the pole, pasting the sections on a flat surface (taking care that all the angles between sections are equal), and painting in the gaps between sections to make the broken land masses continuous.

Lambert's Azimuthal Equal-Area (devised by the German cartographer Johann Heinrich Lambert [1728–1777]). In this projection—which is best used for large areas, such as continents—the quadrilaterals formed by intersecting parallels and meridians are kept equal in area by decreasing the scale in the radial direction from the center inversely as it increases along the parallel circles about the center, with the result that at the edge of the map the quadrilaterals are considerably distorted in shape. (Among the projections that are not equal-area are *conformal* projections. In these the distortion of shape that is necessary to keep the quadrilaterals equal in area is not practiced, with the result that, although there is variation in the area of the quadrilaterals, elementary areas anywhere on the map have their correct shape.)

Mercator. One of the best-known conformal projections, developed by the Flemish geographer Gerhardus Mercator (1512–1594) and first used in his chart of 1569. Such a projection of the earth as a whole is printed as a rectangle on which parallels and meridians appear as straight lines intersecting at right angles. All parallels of latitude have the same length as the central one, the equator (whereas actually they get progressively smaller toward the poles), and all meridians are parallel throughout their entire length (whereas actually they converge to a point at each pole). The presentation of areas not too distant from the equator is satisfactory, but there is great distortion, in scale, of the polar regions. (See map on pages xxviii–xxix.)

The construction of a Mercator projection of the world can be roughly demonstrated in this manner: Cut along one meridian of a hollow rubber globe all the way from north to south pole; cut along all the other meridians from the north pole almost to the equator, and then along all the meridians from the south pole almost to the equator. Flatten out the sectioned globe on a flat surface so that the equator lies directly over a straight line on the surface and the pointed section ends are separated from each other by a space equal to that between two adjacent meridians at the equator. Then paint in the gaps between sections to make the broken land masses continuous.

Mollweide (devised by the German mathematician and astronomer Karl Mollweide [1774–1825]). An equal-area projection of the world as an ellipse whose longer axis is twice the length of its shorter axis. The distortion in shape of the equatorial belt and particularly of the outer regions is the chief defect of this projection.

Sinusoidal. An equal-area projection somewhat similar to the elliptical Mollweide projection, but cone-shaped at the poles rather than flattened, the meridians being sine curves.

Conic and *Polyconic.* The conic projection, which originated with Ptolemy, is well suited to areas of wide spread from east to west lying between the equator and one of the poles, such as the United States or the Mediterranean area. In this projection use is made of the concept of a "standard parallel"—a circle of latitude at all points of which a hollow cone dropped down over a globe is tangent to the globe. With a paper cone and a hollow rubber globe, both with this circle of tangency marked on them, we may roughly demonstrate a conic projection in this manner: The standard parallel should pass about midway through the area being projected. Cut this area out of the rubber globe. Cut along each of the meridians from the north almost up to the standard parallel, and then do the same thing from the south. Unfasten the pasted-together or pinned-together cone so that it will lie flat. Then superimpose the sectioned area from the rubber globe on the cone (taking care that the standard parallel on the globe is lined up with the standard parallel on the cone), paste the globe sections to the cone, and paint in the gaps between the sections so as to make the broken land masses continuous.

The *polyconic* projection, which is well suited to areas long from north to south and narrow from east to west, is accomplished by imagining a number of coaxial cones of varying height, each tangent to the sphere at a different parallel. It was devised in the United States by the first superintendent of the Coast and Geodetic Survey, in whose maps it has been used for more than a century. The central meridian is a straight line, the other meridians are curved; the parallels of latitude are arcs of circles, not concentric, and are true to scale.

Other projections often used but not described above are the *gnomonic, stereographic, parabolic, Albers conical, Lambert conformal conic,* and *Bonne.* A *transverse* projection is one in which the orientation of its axis is not normal; e.g., the axis of a transverse Mercator projection may be a meridian or any oblique great circle instead of the equator, which is its normal axis construction. A *transverse Mercator projection* has been used to chart routes between distant points (e.g., international air routes). A *transverse polyconic projection* was used by the National Geographic Society for its large map (1944) of the Union of Soviet Socialist Republics.

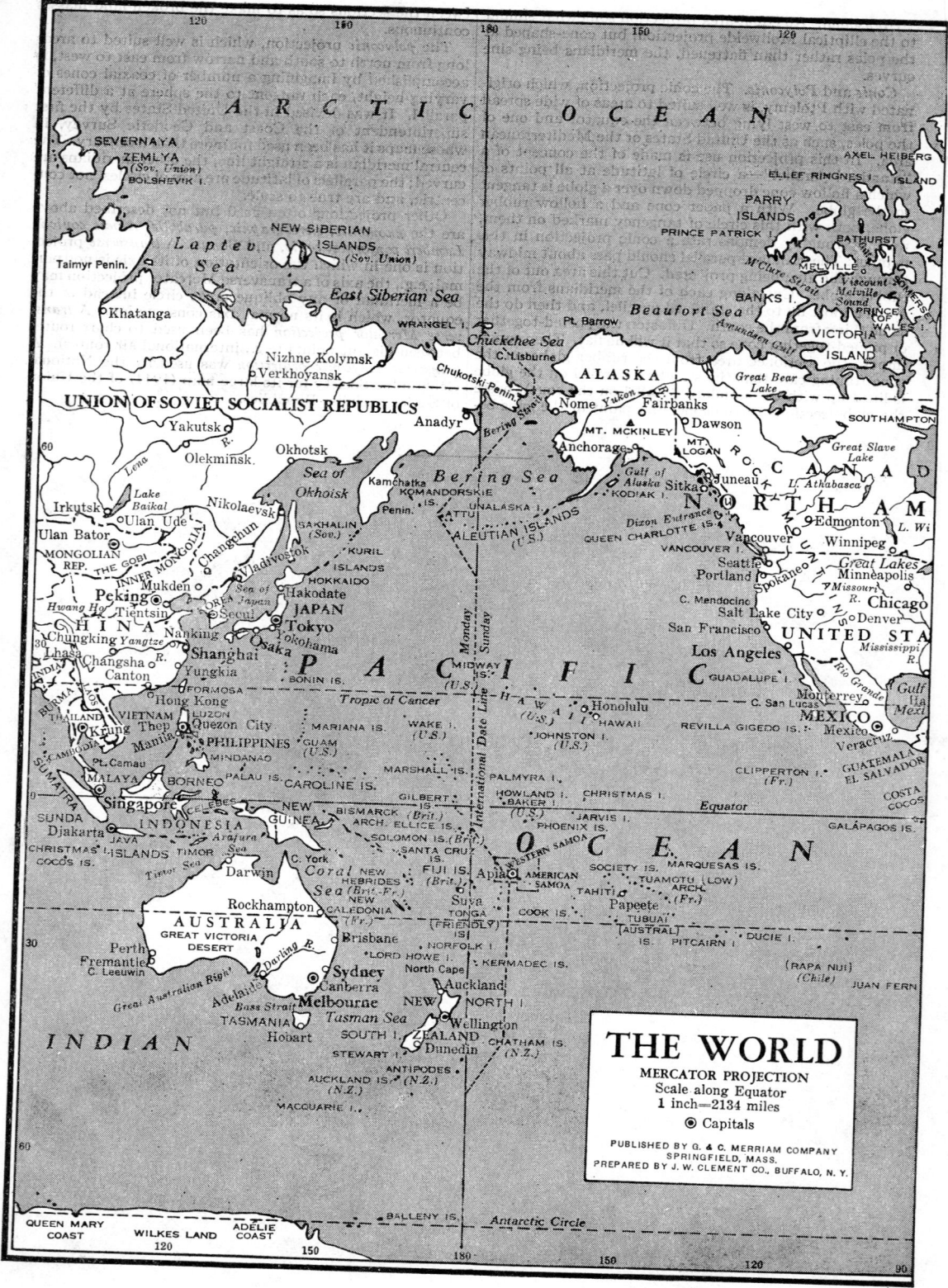

THE WORLD

MERCATOR PROJECTION
Scale along Equator
1 inch=2134 miles

◎ Capitals

PUBLISHED BY G. & C. MERRIAM COMPANY
SPRINGFIELD, MASS.
PREPARED BY J. W. CLEMENT CO., BUFFALO, N. Y.

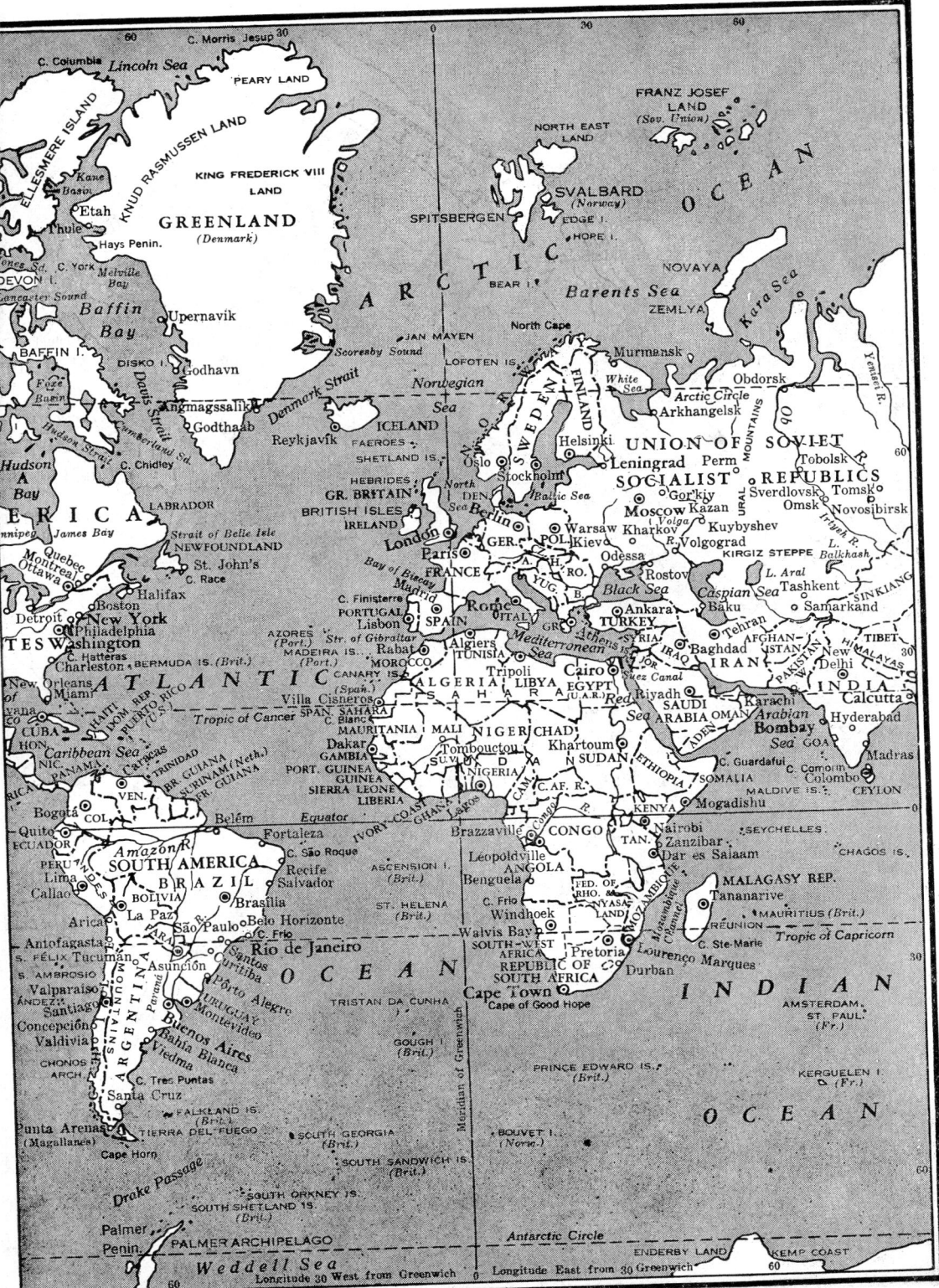

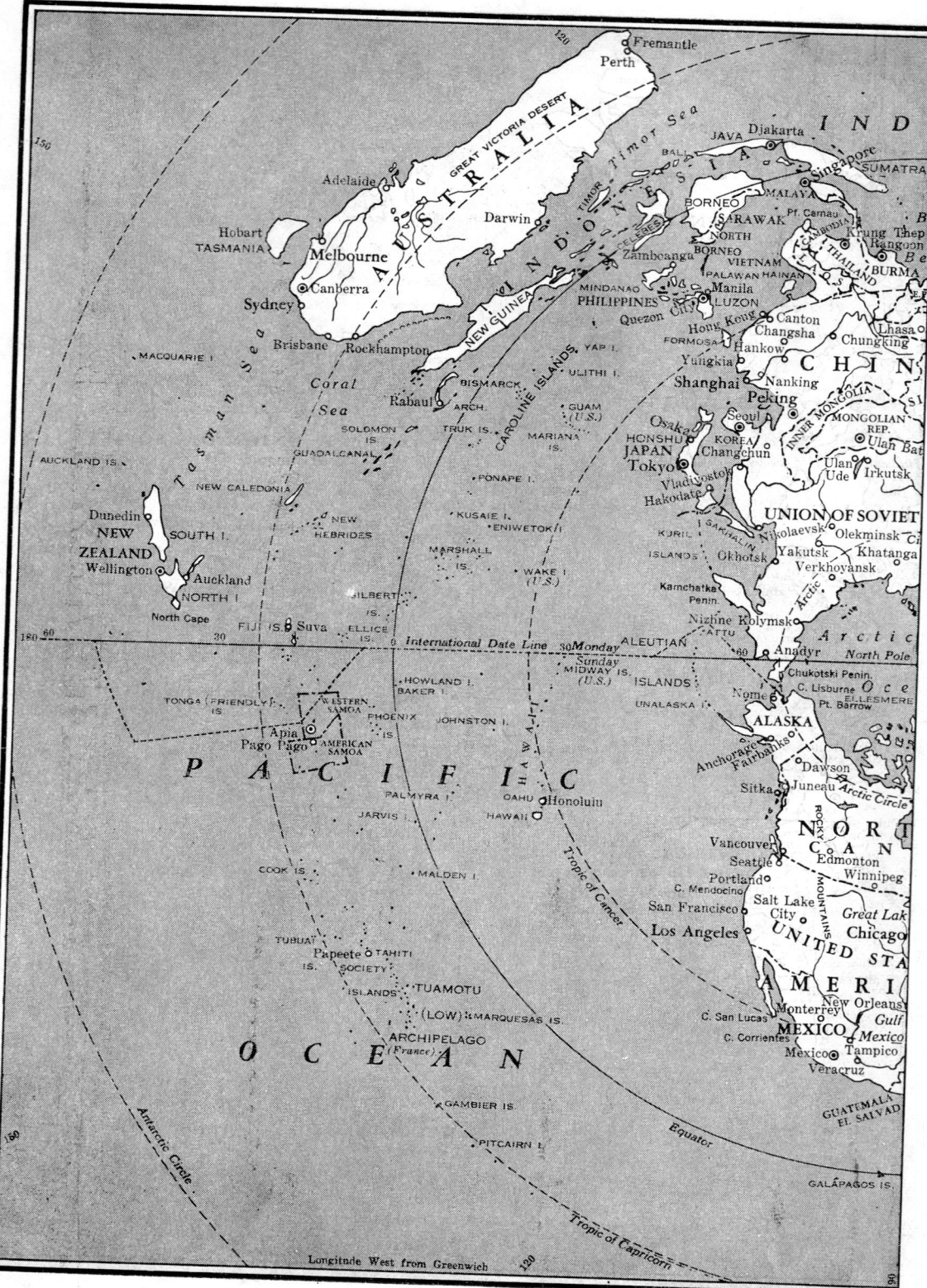

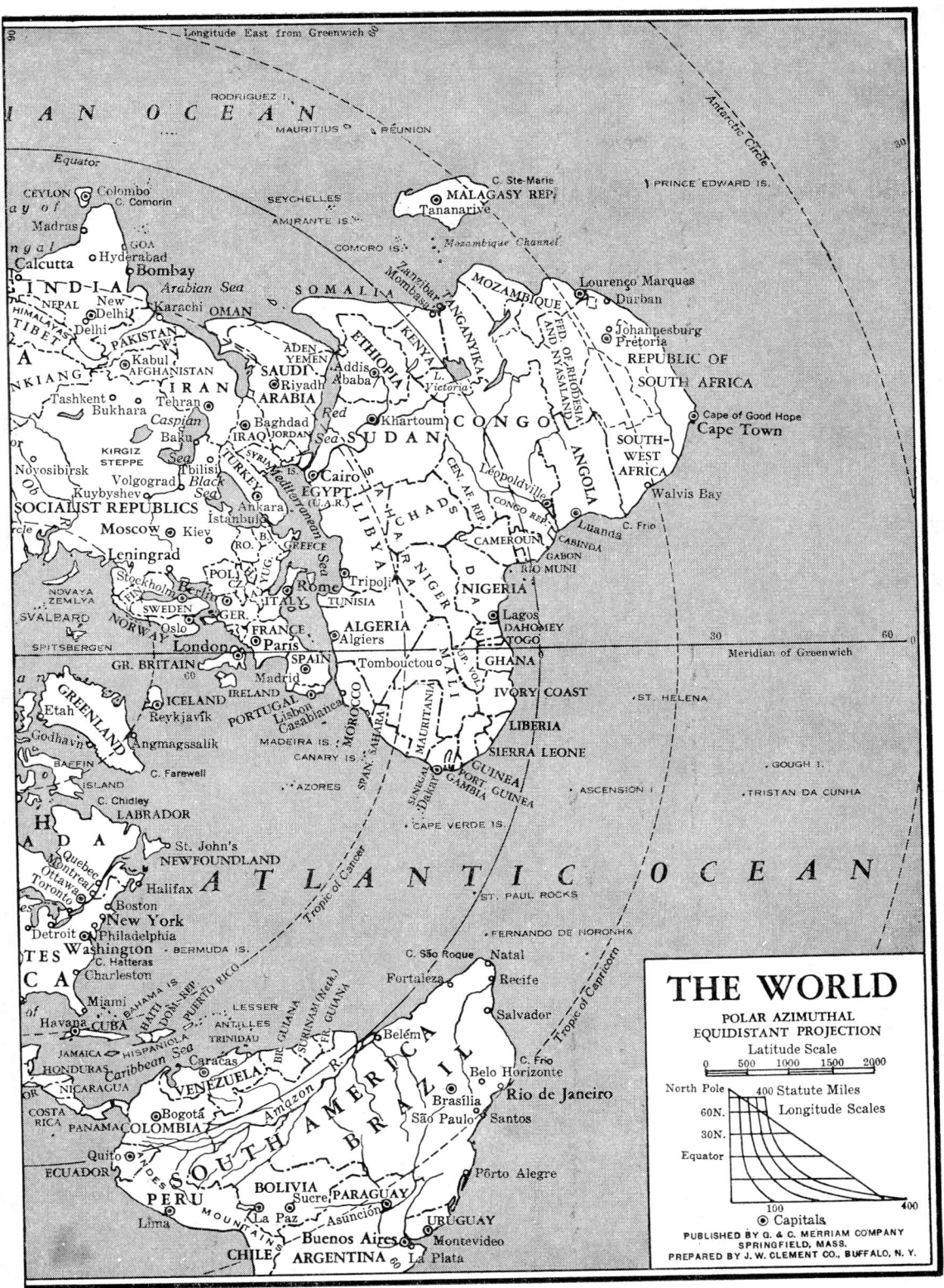

THE WORLD

POLAR AZIMUTHAL
EQUIDISTANT PROJECTION

Latitude Scale

0   500   1000   1500   2000

North Pole   400 Statute Miles
60N.   Longitude Scales
30N.
Equator

⊙ Capitals

PUBLISHED BY G. & C. MERRIAM COMPANY
SPRINGFIELD, MASS.
PREPARED BY J. W. CLEMENT CO., BUFFALO, N. Y.

A

DICTIONARY OF NAMES

OF PLACES

WITH GEOGRAPHICAL AND HISTORICAL INFORMATION, AND PRONUNCIATIONS

Aa (ä). **1** Small river, Nord dept., N France; flows into North Sea near Gravelines.
2 Two rivers of Latvia: (1) = LIELUPE. (2) = GAUYA. Severe fighting bet. Germans and Russians Jan. and Feb. 1917.
3 River, N cen. Switzerland; rises in Lucerne canton, flows N into Aargau canton, expanding into Lakes Baldegg and Hallwil, and continues into Aare river.
4 *or* **Sar′ner–Aa′** (zär′nĕr·ä′). River, cen. Switzerland, in Unterwalden canton; flows N through Lakes Lungern and Sarnen into Lake of Lucerne.

Aa′ben·raa′ (ō′bĕn·rô′). **1** Former county, SE South Jutland, Denmark, now part of Aabenraa-Sönderborg county. See *Table* at DENMARK.
2 *Ger.* **A′pen·ra′de** (ä′pĕn·rä′dĕ). Town at head of fiord opening on Little Belt, 15 m. S of Haderslev, Denmark; pop. (1945) 12,189; formerly German, first known in 13th cent.; received civic rights 1335; passed to Denmark by plebiscite 1920.

Aabenraa–Sön′der·borg (-sŭn′ĕr·bôrg). County of Denmark. See *Table* at DENMARK.

Aa′chen (ä′kĕn). **1** Former government district, W Germany, in Rhine Province, Prussia; 1208 sq. m.
2 *Fr.* **Aix-la-Cha·pelle′** (āks′lä-shȧ·pĕl′; *Fr.* ĕks′lȧ-shȧ′pĕl′, ĕs′-); *anc.* **Aq′uae Gra′ni** (ăk′wē grā′nī; ä′kwē) *or* **Aq′uis·gra′num** (ăk′wĭs·grā′nŭm; ä′kwĭs-). Manufacturing city, its ✳, now in North Rhine-Westphalia state on Belgian border 40 m. WSW of Cologne; pop. (1939) 165,710; railroad junction; trade center; tourist resort; famous mineral springs and baths; fine town hall built 1353 on ruins of Charlemagne's palace; cathedral founded by Charlemagne c. 800; manufactures textiles.
History: Site of Roman baths 1st cent. A.D.; second capital of empire of Charlemagne, who was probably born there; favorite residence of Charlemagne after 768; center of Carolingian culture and site of Charlemagne's great palace (practically destroyed by Northmen 881 but restored 983); given rights of an imperial city 1166 and 1215; coronation city of Holy Roman Empire 813–1531; treaties of Aix-la-Chapelle drawn up here to provide for peace terminating War of Devolution 1668 and War of Austrian Succession 1748; given to France by Peace of Lunéville 1801; returned to Prussia 1815; scene of Conference of Holy Alliance (also called Congress of Aix-la-Chapelle) 1818; Prussian military base in Franco-Prussian War 1870–71; air base in World War I 1914–18. In World War II surrounded by Allied armies Oct. 1944; its surrender demanded Oct. 10; heavily bombarded and nearly destroyed; captured Oct. 20.

Aaland. Variant of ÅLAND.

Aal′borg (ôl′bôrg). **1** County of Denmark. See *Table* at DENMARK.
2 *anc.* **Al·bur′gum** (ăl·bûr′gŭm). Commercial seaport, its ⊗, NE Jutland; pop. (1945) 60,880; has naval school. Seat of trade from 11th cent.; received municipal privileges 1342; in World War II its airfield used in German attack on Norway.

Aa′len (ä′lĕn). Industrial city, Baden-Württemberg, Germany, 44 m. E of Stuttgart; pop. 12,171; iron goods, woolens, linens, and leather goods. Free imperial city 1360–1802; became part of Württemberg 1803.

Aalesund. See ÅLESUND.

Aals′meer (äls′mār). Commune, North Holland prov., Netherlands, 8 m. SW of Amsterdam; pop. 8567; horticultural center.

Aalst (älst) *or* **A′lost′** (ȧ·lôst′). Commune, East Flanders prov., Belgium, 14 m. NW of Brussels, on canalized Dender, tributary of the Schelde; pop. (1938 est.) 41,131; railroad junction; weaving and brewing. Walled city, a former capital of the counts of Flanders; held by France 1667–1706; captured by German vanguard Sept. 1914.

Aal′ten (äl′tĕ[n]). Commune, Gelderland prov., E Netherlands, 29 m. E of Arnhem near German border; pop. 11,195.

Aar′au (ä′rou). Commune, ✳ of Aargau canton, N Switzerland, on Aare river 23 m. W of Zurich; pop. (1941) 12,900; old castle; manufactures cannon, cotton goods, scientific instruments. Founded in 13th century; taken from Hapsburgs by Bern 1415; became capital of Helvetic Republic 1798 (see SWITZERLAND), capital of Aargau canton 1803.

Aa′re (ä′rĕ) *or* **Aar** (är); *anc.* **O·brin′ga** (ô·brĭng′gȧ). River 175 m. long, cen. and N Switzerland; flows NW from Bernese Alps, traversing Hasli Tal (valley) and passing through the Gorge of the Aare (**Aa′re·schlucht′** [ä′rĕ·shlŏŏkt′]) then through Lakes of Brienz and Thun, past Bern, thence NE past Solothurn and Aarau to Rhine; navigable to Thun; connected by canal with Lake of Bienne.

Aar′gau′ (är′gou′); *Fr.* **Ar′go·vie′** (àr·gô′vē′). Swiss canton, in Alps and Jura Mts.; watered by Aare and Reuss rivers. Anciently part of Helvetia; conquered by Franks in 5th cent.; under Hapsburgs 1173–1415; taken by Cantonal League and divided bet. Bern and Lucerne; in part to Helvetic Republic 1798; member of Swiss Confederation 1803; constitution fixed by Congress of Vienna 1815, replaced 1831. See *Table* at SWITZERLAND.

Aar'hus' (ôr'hōōs'). **1** County of Denmark. See *Table* at DENMARK.
2 Seaport city, its ⊗, E Jutland, on Aarhus Bay; pop. (1945) 107,393. One of oldest towns in Denmark; has cathedral begun 1201; important shipping and commercial center with excellent harbor.

Aath. See ATH.

A·ba' (ä·bä'). Town, Calabar prov., Eastern Region, Nigeria, ab. 75 m. W of Calabar on railroad N of Port Harcourt; pop. 58,000.

Ab'a·co (ăb'á·kō). Two of the Bahama Islands, **Great Abaco** (80 m. long) and **Little Abaco**, in Atlantic Ocean E of S Florida; 776 sq. m.; pop. (1943), with adjacent cays, 3461.

A'ba·dan' (ä'bä·dän'; *Angl.* ăb'á·dăn'). **1** Island 40 m. long by 2 to 12 m. wide, W Iran, in Shatt-al-Arab delta; has Shatt-al-Arab on W and Karun and a tributary on E. Probably settled before time of Herodotus; long disputed bet. Persia and Turkey, but definitely assigned to Persia by treaty 1847.
2 Town on Abadan I. on the Shatt-al-Arab, Khuzistan prov., SW Iran, ab. 12 m. SE of Khorramshahr, pop. ab. 40,000; has large oil refineries; terminus of pipe line from Masjid-i-Sulaiman, oil wells at Maidan-i-Naftun; export trade, esp. in oil.

A'ba·deh' (ä'bä·dě'h'). Town, Fars prov., Iran, 110 m. N of Shiraz; noted for its fruit gardens.

A'bae (ā'bē). Ancient town, E Phocis, cen. Greece, on Boeotian border 10 m. SE of Elateia; famous for oracle of Apollo; pillaged by Persians, partially restored through Emperor Hadrian.

Abai. Variant of *Abbai:* see NILE.

A·bai'ang (ä·bī'äng). Island (atoll), NW Gilbert Is., W Pacific Ocean, just N of the equator; 16 m. long by 5 m. wide; pop. (1936) 2424. First residence of American missionaries 1857, under Hiram Bingham.

A·ba·kan' (ŭ·bŭ·kán'). **1** River ab. 210 m. long, Khakass Autonomous Region, Soviet Russia, Asia; rises at W end of Sayan Mts. and flows NE to Yenisei river.
2 Town, ✳ of Khakass Autonomous Region, on left bank of the Yenisei at confluence of the Abakan nearly opp. Minusinsk; pop. 37,281.

A·ba'los Point (ä·vä'lōs). Cape, W coast of Cuba, N of Guadiana Bay.

Abana or **Abanah.** See BARADA.

A'ban·cay' (ä'väng·kī'). Town, ✳ of Apurímac dept., Peru, 130 m. W of Cuzco in valley of Andes; alt. 7200 ft.; pop. (1940 est.) 5789; mining center and important in beet-sugar industry.

A'ba·no Ter'me (ä'bä·nô těr'mä). Commune, Padova prov., Venezia Euganea, Italy, 5 m. S of Padova; pop. 6739; resort; hot springs and mud baths.

Ab'a·rim Mountains (ăb'á·rĭm). Ancient name (*Num.* xxxiii. 47, 48) of low mountain range or bluffs overlooking Dead Sea from NE, now in Jordan; highest point Mt. Nebo (see Mount PISGAH) 2644 ft.

A·ba·shi·ri (ä·bä·shě·rě). Town, Hokkaido prefecture, NE coast of Hokkaido I., Japan; pop. 39,218; railroad terminus on **Abashiri Bay.**

A'ba·so'lo (ä'vä·sō'lô). Town, Guanajuato state, cen. Mexico; pop. 5115.

A'ba·új–Tor'na (ô'bŏ·ōō·y'·tôr'nô). Former county of Hungary.

A·ba'ya, Lake (ä·bä'yä). Lake, SW cen. Ethiopia, E Africa.

Ab·bai' (äb·bī'). See NILE.

Abbasa, El. See EL ABBASA.

Ab'ba·zi'a (ăb'bä·tsě'ä); *Croatian* **O'pa·ti·ja** (ô'pä·tě·yä). Village in Croatia, Yugoslavia, at head of Veliki Kvarner ab. 5 m. W of Rieka; formerly in Italy; pop. (1936) 3666; watering place, known as the "Nice of the Adriatic," noted for its mild climate and beautiful location.

Ab'be·ville (ăb'ê·vĭl; *Sou. also* -v'l). **1** County in South Carolina. See *Table* at SOUTH CAROLINA.

2 City, ⊗ of Henry co., SE Alabama; pop. 2524; agricultural experiment station.
3 City, ⊗ of Wilcox co., S cen. Georgia, on Ocmulgee river; pop. 872.
4 Town, ⊗ of Vermilion parish, S Louisiana, in rice-growing section 20 m. SSW of Lafayette; pop. 10,414, rice mills, cotton gins, sugar factory.
5 City, ⊗ of Abbeville co., W South Carolina, 13 m. W of Greenwood; pop. 5436; settled by Huguenots in 18th cent.; scene of last Confederate cabinet meeting of Jefferson Davis 1865. In agricultural and dairy-farming section; textile mills, bottling works.

Ab'be·ville' (ăb'vēl'); *anc.* **Ab·ba'tis Vil'la** (ă·bä'tĭs vĭl'á). Commune, Somme dept., N France, on Somme river 25 m. NW of Amiens; pop. 19,345; trades in woolens and carpets; has fine late-Gothic church of St. Wulfran begun 1488.
History: Dependent upon St-Riquier abbey 9th cent. A.D.; capital of Ponthieu (*q.v.*); received charter as a commune 1184; under English rule from 1272 to 1369. Allied base in World War I; seized by German armored division May 21, 1940; retaken by Allies Sept. 1944 in advance on W Germany.

Ab·bia'te·gras'so (äb·byä'tä·gräs'sô). Commune, Milano prov., Lombardy, N Italy, 13 m. WSW of Milan; pop. 16,259; market and industrial town.

Ab'bots·ford (ăb'ŭts·fêrd). Estate, Roxburgh co., SE Scotland, on Tweed river 2½ m. W of Melrose; residence 1824–32 of Sir Walter Scott.

Ab'bott·a·bad' (ăb'ŭt·à·băd'; -á·băd'). Town, NW West Pakistan, 63 m. N of Rawalpindi; pop. 10,163; alt. 4120 ft.; hill resort; important military cantonment and sanatorium.

Abd al Ku'ri (ăb'dăl·kōō'rē). Rock and coral reef in Arabian Sea off Cape Guardafui, Africa, and W of the island of Socotra; ab. 1 m. long and bet. 300 and 600 yds. wide.

Ab·de'ra (ăb·dē'rá). City of ancient Thrace on Aegean Sea E of the mouth of the Nestos, nearly opp. Thasos; now in ruins. First settled 7th cent. B.C.; colonized second time by inhabitants of Teos in Ionia c. 544 B.C.; birthplace of several famous Greeks, esp. Democritus and Protagoras. Its inhabitants gained reputation for stupidity, whence the term *Abderite* became one of reproach.

Abdera. See ADRA.

A'bé'ché' (ä'bā'shä'); *also* **A·beshr'** (ä·běsh'ěr). Chief town of Wadai, Chad, N cen. Africa, 400 m. NE of Fort-Lamy, on caravan route bet. Bengasi in Cyrenaica and Darfur prov. of Sudan.

Abela. See ÁVILA.

Abellinum. See AVELLINO commune.

A'bel–Me·ho'lah (ā'běl·mĕ·hō'lá). Ancient town, E Israel, in Jordan valley ab. 10 m. S of Bethshean, Palestine; birthplace of Elisha (*1 Kings* xix. 16).

A'be·ma'ma (ä'bä·mä'mä) or **A'pa·ma'ma** (ä'pä-). Island (atoll), cen. Gilbert Is., nearly on the equator, W Pacific Ocean; 12 m. long by 5 m. wide; pop. (1936) 841; good anchorage. Seized by Japanese 1942; recaptured by American Marines Nov. 21, 1943.

A'bens·berg (ä'běns·běrκ). City, Lower Bavaria govt. dist., Bavaria, Germany, 18 m. SW of Regensburg; pop. 2256; medicinal springs; scene of Austrian defeat by Napoleon April 20, 1809.

A'be·o'ku·ta (ä'bá·ô'kōō·tä). **1** Province of Nigeria. See *Table* at NIGERIA.
2 Town, its ✳, on railroad ab. 60 m. N of Lagos; pop. 45,763; began as refuge from slave hunters; chief town of the Egbas, who made treaty with the British 1893; trade greatly increased with coming of railroad 1899.

Ab'er·av'on (ăb'ĕr·ăv'ŭn; -ā'vŭn; *Welsh* ä'běr·á·vŏn). Former municipal borough, S Wales, now part of Port Talbot.

Aberbrothock. See ARBROATH.

Ab'er·carn' (ăb'ĕr·kärn'); *formerly* **New'bridge** (nū'-

brĭj). Urban district, Monmouthshire, W England, in coal-mining section 26 m. WNW of Bristol; pop. 18,757; iron and tinplate works.

Ab'er·corn (ăb'ẽr·kôrn). Town, ✳ of Tanganyika prov., NE Northern Rhodesia, 15 m. SE of S end of Lake Tanganyika and near Tanganyika Terr. border; alt. 5700 ft. Trading center, beautifully situated; scene of surrender of last of German African forces Nov. 14, 1918.

Ab'er·crom'bie, Mount (ăb'ẽr·krŏm'bĭ; -krŭm'bĭ). Peak 7200 ft., Stevens co., NE Washington.

Ab'er·dare' (ăb'ẽr·dâr'). Mining town (urban dist.), Glamorganshire, S Wales, ab. 4 m. SW of Merthyr Tydfil; pop. 40,916; produces fine steam coal.

Aberdare Mountains. Range, W Kenya, SE Africa; average height 10,000 ft.

Ab'er·deen (ăb'ẽr·dēn). **1** Residential town, Harford co., NE Maryland, 29 m. ENE of Baltimore; pop. 9679. Nearby is **Aberdeen Proving Ground,** a testing ground for U.S. army ordnance, shells, bombs, mines, and other military matériel; a Federal reservation comprising a flat tract of 35,000 acres along W side of upper Chesapeake Bay S of the town.
2 City, ⊗ of Monroe co., NE Mississippi, 24 m. N of Columbus; pop. 6450; shipping point for cotton.
3 City, ⊗ of Brown co., NE South Dakota, ab. 90 m. W of Lake Traverse; pop. 23,073; settled 1880; railroad and wholesale distributing center in agricultural district; flour mills, grain elevators, stockyards and packing plants; manufactures iron and steel machinery, dairy products, etc. Northern State Teachers College (1902).
4 City and port of entry, Grays Harbor co., W Washington, at E end of Grays Harbor 46 m. W of Olympia; pop. 18,741; adjacent to Hoquiam (q.v.), its twin city; lumber center; dairying, fishing, canning industries. Founded 1867, incorp. 1890.
5 Lake 515 sq. m., N cen. Keewatin Dist., Northwest Territories, Canada; expansion of Dubawnt river W of Chesterfield Inlet.

Ab'er·deen' (ăb'ẽr·dēn' [so accented locally]; ăb'ẽr·dēn). **1** or **Ab'er·deen'shire** (ăb'ẽr·dēn'shĭr; -shẽr). County, NE Scotland; area 1971 sq. m.; pop. (1951) 308,055; rivers Dee, Don, Ythan; Grampian Hills in SW section; fisheries (salmon, herring, whitefish), agriculture, cattle raising, quarrying.
2 anc. **De·va'na** (dĕ·vā'nà). Burgh and commercial and industrial center, its ⊗, on the North Sea; pop. (1951) 182,714; part in Kincardine co.; has good harbor at mouth of Dee; exports granite, fish, and cattle.
History: Royal burgh and seat of a bishopric from 12th cent.; a Scottish royal residence 12th–14th cents.; supported Robert Bruce in wars for Scottish independence, captured and for a time made headquarters of Edward I; burned by Edward III 1336; King's College founded 1494, Marischal College 1593 (later Univ. of Aberdeen 1860); welcomed Charles II 1650; occupied by Gen. Monck and Cromwellians 1651; garrisoned by English until 1659.

Ab'er·fel'dy (ăb'ẽr·fĕl'dĭ). Burgh, W Perth co., Scotland, on Tay river 33 m. NW of Perth; pop. 1523; supposed scene of Burns's *Birks of Aberfeldy;* Black Watch regiment raised here 1725.

Ab'er·foyle' (ăb'ẽr·foil'). Parish (pop. 1133) and village, SW Perth co., Scotland, ab. 6 m. SE of Loch Katrine; immortalized by Scott's *Rob Roy;* summer resort for residents of Glasgow.

Ab'er·ga·ven'ny (ăb'ẽr·gà·vĕn'ĭ); anc. **Go·ban'ni·um** (gồ·băn'ĭ·ŭm). Municipal borough, Monmouthshire, W England, on the Usk river 30 m. NW of Bristol; pop. 8844; mining town.

Ab'er·sych'an (ăb'ẽr·sĭk'ăn). Former urban dist., Monmouthshire, W England, since 1935 in Pontypool urban dist.; pop. (1931) 25,748.

A'bert, Lake (ā'bẽrt). Lake ab. 20 m. long and 5 m.

wide, cen. Lake co., S Oregon; has no outlet and is sometimes dry.

Ab'er·til·ler'y (ăb'ẽr·tĭ·lâr'ĭ). Mining town (urban dist.), Monmouthshire, W England, ab. 30 m. NW of Bristol in coal and iron industrial region; pop. 27,617.

Ab'er·yst'wyth (ăb'ẽr·ĭst'wĭth; *Welsh* à'bĕr·ûst'-). Municipal borough, seaport town and watering place, ⊗ of Cardiganshire, W Wales, on Cardigan Bay; pop. 9323; seat of Welsh National Library and of University College of Wales. Castle said to have been built 1109; town built around fortress of Edward I 1277.

Abeshr. See ABÉCHÉ.

a–Bhuird, Ben–. See BEN-A-BHUIRD.

A·bi'a·thar Peak (à·bī'à·thẽr). Mountain 10,800 ft., Yellowstone National Park, NW Wyoming.

Ab–i–Diz (ăb'ĕ·dēz'). River, W Iran, tributary of Karun river (q.v.).

Ab'i·djan' (ăb'ĭ·jän'; *Fr.* à'bē'jän'). Town on lagoon, ✳ of Ivory Coast Republic, W Africa, in SE part; pop. 27,621; terminus of railroad N to Bobo-Dioulasso.

Abila. See Jebel MUSA.

Ab'i·lene (ăb'ĭ·lēn). **1** City, ⊗ of Dickinson co., E cen. Kansas, on Smoky Hill river 25 m. E of Salina; pop. 6746; Eisenhower Memorial Museum; center of flour milling and grain and cattle shipments; former frontier town, railhead 1867–71 for cattle-raising section to SW
2 City, ⊗ of Taylor co., NW cen. Texas, 145 m. WSW of Fort Worth; pop. 90,368; manufactures dairy, food, and cottonseed products, refined oil, etc. Hardin-Simmons Univ. (1891; coed.); Abilene Christian Coll. (1906; coed.); McMurry Coll. (1923; coed.).

Ab'i·le'ne (ăb'ĭ·lē'nē). Region in Syria, E of Anti-Liban Mts.; c. 29 A.D. comprised Tetrarchy of Lysanias (*Luke* iii. 1).

Abindonia. See ABINGDON.

Ab'ing·don (ăb'ĭng·dŭn). **1** City, Knox co., W Illinois, in agricultural section 10 m. S of Galesburg; pop. 3469.
2 Town, ⊗ of Washington co., SW Virginia, in farming and dairying section in Blue Ridge Mts. 15 m. NE of Bristol; pop. 4758; settled c. 1770; site of Black's Fort 1776; manufactures lumber, flour, condensed milk, chemicals; ships tobacco; mountain resort.
3 anc. **Ab'in·do'ni·a** (ăb'ĭn·dō'nĭ·à; -dōn'yà). Municipal borough, Berkshire, S England, on the Thames 6 m. S of Oxford; pop. 10,176; market town; has many interesting antiquities; site of a Benedictine abbey founded 7th cent. A.D.; most prosperous in 13th and 14th cents., declined after 1538.

Abingdon Island. See PINTA ISLAND.

Ab'in·ger (ăb'ĭn·jẽr). Village, Surrey, England, 3 m. WSW of Dorking in 51°12'N, 0°24'W; pop. 1549; government meteorological station for magnetic observations removed from Greenwich 1923.

Ab'ing·ton (ăb'ĭng·tŭn). **1** Town, Plymouth co., SE Massachusetts, 4 m. ENE of Brockton; pop. 10,607; manufactures shoes, textiles, and textile machinery.
2 Urban township, Montgomery co., SE Pennsylvania, N of Philadelphia; pop. 55,831.

Ab'–i–Pandj' (ăb'ĕ·pànj'); *also* **Panj** (pànj) *or* **Pyandzh** (pyänch). River, upper tributary of the Amu Darya in the Pamirs; flows W through Wakhan and N to join the Murghab as boundary stream bet. Afghanistan and Tadzhik S.S.R.

Ab'i·shim' (ăb'ĕ·shĕm'). Mountain 8392 ft., Azerbaijan prov., NW Iran, SW of Lake Urmia.

Ab'i·tib'i (ăb'ĭ·tĭb'ĭ). County of Quebec, Canada. See *Table* at QUEBEC.

Abitibi Lake. Lake on E boundary of Ontario prov., Canada; 356 sq. m.; nearly all in Ontario; source of Abitibi River.

Abitibi River ab. 230 m. long, E Ontario, flowing N to Moose river near James Bay.

Ab·kha'zi·a or **Ab·kha'si·a** (ăb·kä'zhĭ·à; -zhá; *Russ.* ŭp·kä'zyĭ·yà), *officially* **Ab·kha'zian Autonomous Soviet Socialist Republic** (ăb·kä'zhăn). Autonomous republic, NW Georgia, U.S.S.R., on Black Sea

coast at W end of Caucasus Mts.; 3358 sq. m.; pop. (1941 est.) 293,147; ✳ Sukhumi. Has extensive forests and undeveloped mineral resources; chief occupation agriculture; has subtropical products. Abkhazians are a Caucasian race related to the Circassians; chief nationalities Abkhazian 28%, Georgian 33.5%, Armenian 13%. Became Christian under Justinian in 6th cent.; settled in part in 19th cent. after 1829 by Russians and became definitely Russian 1864; created an autonomous republic in Georgia 1919.

A'blain'–Saint'–Na'zaire' (à'blăn'săn'nå'zâr'). Commune, Pas-de-Calais dept., N France, near Vimy Ridge 7 m. N of Arras; pop. (1931) 1098; completely destroyed in second battle of Artois May 21, 1915.

Abo. See TURKU.

Ab'o·mey' (ăb'ô·mā'; à·bō'mĭ; Fr. à'bô'mā'). Town, S Dahomey, West Africa, 60 m. N of Ouidah; pop. ab. 15,000; former slave center, now has trade in ivory, palm oil, and gold; capital of former native kingdom of Dahomey (q.v.); fired and abandoned to French 1892; rebuilt by French and connected with coast by rail 1905.

A'bony (ŏ'bŏn·y'). Commune, cen. Hungary, 10 m. E of Cegléd; pop. 18,342.

Abord à Plouffe, L'. See L'ABORD À PLOUFFE.

Aboukir. See ABUKIR.

Ab·qa'ik (ăb·kä'ĭk). See DHAHRAN.

A'bra (ä'brä). **1** River ab. 100 m. long, NW Luzon, Phil. Is., third in size on the island; rises in S cen. part of Mountain Prov. in Cordillera Central, flows N then W to South China Sea.
2 Inland mountainous province, NW Luzon; 1471 sq. m.; pop. 87,780; chief town and ✳ Bangued. Bounded on N by Ilocos Norte, on E and S by Mountain Prov., and on W by Ilocos Sur. Traversed by middle course of Abra river and its many tributaries N and E; greatly broken by mountain ranges and groups of the Cordillera Central, and by hills; highest point Mt. Manmanoc 6634 ft. on E border. Has heavy rainfall; valleys productive, principal crops being tobacco, rice, and corn; fine timber forests; mineral wealth largely undeveloped. Inhabited chiefly by Ilokanos and Tinggianes.
History: Little settlement attempted by Spanish; suffered serious uprising latter half of 18th cent.; province created 1846; came under American control 1899; civil government established Aug. 19, 1901.

A'bra·ham, Mount (ä'brà·hăm). **1** Mountain 4049 ft., E Franklin co., Maine.
2 Peak 4052 ft., Addison co., W Vermont.

Abraham Lin'coln National Historical Park (lĭng'kŭn). See UNITED STATES, *National Historical Parks.*

Ab'ram (ăb'răm). Urban district, Lancashire, NW England, on Bridgewater Canal 15 m. W of Manchester; pop. 6286.

A·bran'tes (à·vrănn'tĕsh); *anc.* **Au·ran'tes** (ô·răn'tēz). Commune, Santarém district, W cen. Portugal, on Tagus river 32 m. ENE of Santarém; pop. 7215; founded c. 300 B.C.; captured Nov. 24, 1807 by Napoleon's general Junot, who assumed title of duc d'Abrantès.

A·bre'us (à·vrā'ōōs). Municipality (pop. 5968) and town, Las Villas prov., W cen. Cuba, 12 m. NW of Cienfuegos.

'A'bri (ä'brē). Town, Northern Prov., N Sudan, on Nile 100 m. SSW of Wadi Halfa.

A·bro'lhos (à·vrō'lyōōs). Group of pointed rocky islands off Caravelas, S Baía state, Brazil, bet. 17° and 18°S lat.

Abrotonum. See SABRATA.

Abruzzi Apennines; *Ital.* **Appennino Abruzzese.** See APENNINES.

A·bruz'zi e Mo'li·se (à·brōōt'tsĕ â mô'lĕ·zȧ). Compartimento di cen. Italy (for provincial divisions, area, and pop., see *Table* at ITALY); lies bet. Adriatic Sea and Apennines (which attain their greatest height here) and Tronto and Sangro rivers; chiefly forest and pasture land; basin of drained Lake Fucino fertile; watered by

Pescara river; agriculture (olive, vine, grain), sericulture, livestock raising.
History: District formed part of duchy of Spoleto in Lombard times and of Apulia under Normans; in 1240 made a single province by Frederick II, who founded Aquila; province of Angevin kingdom of Naples, to which it was of strategic importance; incorporated in kingdom of Italy as part of Naples 1866.

Ab·sa'ro·ka Mountains (ăb·sär'ô·kà). Range of Rocky Mts. from S Montana across NE corner of Yellowstone Park into NW Wyoming, ab. 175 m. long; highest Franks Peak 13,140 ft.; others Dead Indian 12,253 ft. and Needle Mt. 12,130 ft.

Ab·se'con (ăb·sē'kŭn). City, Atlantic co., SE New Jersey, 6 m. NW of Atlantic City; pop. 4320.

Absecon Inlet. Narrow strait leading from Atlantic Ocean through barrier reefs in Atlantic co., SE New Jersey; its S shore is the N end of **Absecon Beach,** the island (10 m. long) on which Atlantic City is situated.

A'bu (ä'bōō) or **Mount Abu.** District formerly under Brit. administration in Sirohi state, SW Rajputana Agency, NW India; 6 sq. m.; pop. (1941) 4680; on **Mount Abu** 5650 ft. highest point in Aravalli Range (q.v.), famous for its Jain temples, among the most beautiful structures in India. The town (coextensive with the district) was administrative capital of Rajputana Agency; now in S Rajasthan state.

Abuam. See TAFILELT.

A'bu 'A·rish' (ä'bōō ä·rēsh'). Inland town, Asir, SW Arabia, S of As Sabya; pop. ab. 8000.

A·bu'cay (ä·bōō'kĭ). Municipality near E coast of Bataan prov., Luzon, Phil. Is., 3 m. N of Balanga; pop. 10,216. In Japanese attack on Philippines 1941–42 it was anchor point of E end of first line of American defense; scene of Japanese drive Jan. 10–17, 1942 and of strong American counterattack Jan. 25.

A'bu Dha'bi (ä'bōō thä'bē; dä'-; zä'-). Sheikdom and seaport town (pop. ab. 6000) on S coast of Persian Gulf, Trucial Oman, SE Arabia.

A'bu Do·khân', Ge'bel (jä'băl [gä'băl] ä'bōō dô·kän'). Mountain 5492 ft., E Egypt, near coast at N end of Red Sea; porphyry quarries, source of the red building stone much used by the Romans.

A'bu Ha'med (ä'bōō hä'mĕd). Town on right bank of the Nile, N Sudan, 19°34'N; captured by British 1897.

A'bu Ke·mal' (ä'bōō kĕ·mäl'). Town, E Syria, on Euphrates river at the border of Iraq.

Ab·u·kir' or **Ab'ou·kir'** (ä'bōō·kĭr'; à·bōō'kĕr'). **1** Bay, bet. Rosetta mouth of Nile and Alexandria, Egypt.
2 Village (*Arab.* **A'bu Qîr** [ä'bōō kēr']) 13 m. NNE of Alexandria on Abukir Bay; approximate site of ancient Canopus (q.v.). In the bay was fought the "Battle of the Nile" Aug. 1–2, 1798, in which Nelson completely defeated French fleet under Brueys; near the village Napoleon defeated Turks 1799 and Sir Ralph Abercromby landed and defeated French 1801.

A'bu Klea' (ä'bōō klä'). Caravan station and wells, W of the Nile, N Sudan, 63 m. SW of Ed Damer; scene of battle Jan. 17, 1885 in which large force of Mahdists was repulsed by British.

A·bu·ku·ma (ä·bōō·kōō·mä). River 141 m. long, N Honshu I., Japan; flows NNE into Pacific Ocean S of Sendai.

Abu Kurkas. See ABU QURQÂS.

Abulliont. See APULYONT.

A·bu'na (ä·vōō'nä). River, N Bolivia; flows NE forming a section of Brazil-Bolivia boundary and empties into Madeira river at N point of Bolivia.

Abu Qîr. See ABUKIR village.

A'bu Qur·qâs' or **A'bu Kur·kas'** (ä'bōō kōōr·käs'). Town on Nile river, Minya prov., Upper Egypt; pop. ab. 15,000.

Abury. See AVEBURY.

Abus. See HUMBER.

A'bu Sim'bel (ä'bōō sĭm'bĕl) or **Ip'sam·bul'** (ĭp'săm-

bōōl′). Locality on left bank of Nile, Egypt, ab. 22°25′N lat., 40 m. N of Wadi Halfa; site of two rock temples of Ramses II (c. 1250 B.C.), discovered 1812, opened 1817; larger temple has four colossi of the king more than 65 ft. high.

A·bu·ya Mye·da (ä·bōō·yä myä·dä). Peak 13,123 ft., cen. Ethiopia, NE of Addis Ababa.

A·bu′yog (ä·bōō′yôg). Municipality on E coast of Leyte, Phil. Is., 34 m. S of Tacloban; pop. 39,111.

A·by′dos (á·bī′dŏs). **1** Ancient town, Asia Minor, on the Hellespont; scene of crossing of Xerxes' army when he invaded Greece 480 B.C.; resisted Philip V of Macedon 200 B.C.; scene of story of Hero and Leander; toll station until late Byzantine times.
2 Ancient town, Egypt, on left bank of Nile ab. 100 m. below Thebes; one of oldest cities of Egypt, mentioned in early inscriptions; site of temples built from Ist to XXVth dynasty; especially prosperous in XIXth dynasty when temples dedicated to Osiris were built by Seti I and Ramses II; has many tombs of rulers. Near modern Araba el Madfuna.

Abyla. 1 See Jebel MUSA, Morocco.
2 See ÁVILA, Spain.

Ab′ys·sin′i·a (ăb′ĭ·sĭn′ĭ·á; -sĭn′yá); *official name in English* **E′thi·o′pi·a** (ē′thĭ·ō′pĭ·á). Kingdom, E Africa, otherwise known as Ethiopia. For description and history, see ETHIOPIA.

A·ca′di·a (á·kā′dĭ·á). **1** Parish in Louisiana. See *Table* at LOUISIANA.
2 *Fr.* **A′ca′die′** (á′ká′dē′). Original name, of Micmac origin, of Nova Scotia (*q.v.*), first used 1603 in commission to Sieur de Monts, who made first settlement 1604; in early 17th cent. region extended to include all territory bet. St. Lawrence river and gulf and Atlantic Ocean, with indefinite W boundary, but included New Brunswick and E Maine. Settled 1632–1713 by French, who formed peaceful farming community in the Grand Pré district; fought over by England and France in colonial wars of 18th cent.; its inhabitants (ab. 10,000 Acadians) deported by English 1755 and scattered from Maine to Louisiana (see ACADIAN COAST).

Acadia National Park. See UNITED STATES, *National Parks.*

A·ca′di·an Coast (á·kā′dĭ·ăn). District, S Louisiana, W of lower Mississippi river and WNW of New Orleans, settled 1760 and later by exiled Acadians from Nova Scotia; now chiefly in St. James parish.

A′ca·ha·í′ (ä′kä·ä·ē′). Town, Paraguarí dept., S Paraguay; pop. ab. 12,300.

A′ca·jut′la (ä′kä·hōōt′la). Seaport town, Sonsonate dept., SW El Salvador; port formerly an open roadstead; breakwaters and new port facilities constructed 1956–61; oil refineries, cement and chemical fertilizer factories.

A·cám′ba·ro (ä·käm′bä·rô). Town, Guanajuato state, cen. Mexico, 90 m. NW of Mexico City; pop. 17,643; railroad junction.

A·can′thus (á·kăn′thŭs). Ancient town on E coast at base of Acte penin., Chalcidice, N Greece, ab. 4 m. W of site of Xerxes' canal cut across the isthmus of Acte 480 B.C.

A′ca·po·ne′ta (ä′kä·pô·nā′tä). Town, Nayarit state, W Mexico, on **Acaponeta River**; pop. 7111.

A′ca·pul′co, *in full* **A′ca·pul′co de Juá′rez** (ä′kä-pōōl′kô thä hwä′räs). Seaport town, Guerrero state, Mexico, ab. 288 m. S of Mexico City, with fine harbor on Pacific Ocean; pop. 9993; resort and shipping point for cotton, coffee, sugar, and hides. For 250 years (1565–1815) chief port for Spanish trade with Philippines (the "Manila galleons," making yearly voyages across the Pacific to and from Manila) and for transshipment across Mexico; declined after Mexico became independent.

Acarahy, *or* **Acaraí, Serra.** See SERRA ACARAHY.

Ac′ar·na′ni·a (ăk′ēr·nā′nĭ·á; ăk′är-; -năn′yá). **1** Moun-

tainous country of ancient Greece in W part, W of Aetolia and on Ionian Sea, separated from Aetolia by the Achelous river; chief town Stratus. Loosely organized into Acarnanian League; dominated by Sparta 391 B.C. and by Thebes 371 B.C.; allied with Philip of Macedon against Rome; required to give up federal capital and submit to Rome 167 A.D.
2 Division of modern department of Aetolia and Acarnania: see *Table* at GREECE.

A′ca·te·nan′go (ä′kä·tä·näng′gô). Volcano 12,980 ft., Guatemala, ab. 31 m. SW of the city of Guatemala.

A′ca·tlán′ de O·so′rio (ä′kä·tlän′ dâ ô·sō′ryô). Town, Puebla state, SE cen. Mexico, 58 m. S of Puebla; pop. 5591.

A′ca·yu·cán′ (ä′kä·yōō·kän′). Town, SE Veracruz state, E Mexico, 37 m. SE of Tuxtla; pop. 5143.

Accad. See AKKAD.

Accho. See ACRE, Palestine.

Ac′co·mac′ (ăk′ô·măk′). **1** *officially* **Ac′co·mack′.** County in Virginia. See *Table* at VIRGINIA.
2 Town, its ⊗, on N part of Delmarva Penin.; pop. 414; twice a refuge of Gov. Berkeley during Bacon's rebellion 1675–76.

Ac·cra′ *or* **Ak·kra′** (á·krä′; ăk′rá). Seaport city, ✻ of Ghana, W Africa. Has anchorage with breakwater and wharves, cable and wireless connections; terminus of railroad to Kumasi; schools and hospitals.
History: Site of trading forts, James and Crèvecœur, founded by English and Dutch 17th century, and of Danish Fort Christiansborg; Fort Crèvecœur ceded to British 1850, Fort Christiansborg ceded 1871; became capital of Gold Coast Colony 1876. Largest town near "nowhere," i.e. 0° lat. and 0° long. See Cape THREE POINTS.

Ac′cring·ton (ăk′rĭng·tŭn). Municipal borough, Lancashire, NW England, ab. 19 m. N of Manchester; pop. 40,671; coal mines; textile mills; manufactures dyestuffs and textile machinery.

Acelum. See ASOLO.

A·cer′ra (ä·chĕr′rä). Commune, Napoli prov., Campania, S Italy, 9 m. NE of Naples; pop. 21,937; site of ancient city, **A·cer′rae** (á·sĕr′ē), which received Latin rights 332 B.C.; destroyed by Hannibal 216 B.C.; restored 210 B.C.; Roman headquarters in Social War 90 B.C.

Acesines. See CHENAB.

A·chae′a (á·kē′á) *or* **A·cha′ia** (á·kā′yá; á·kī′á). Ancient country, N part of the Peloponnesus, Greece, bordering on Gulfs of Corinth and Patras on N and bounded by Elis, Arcadia, and Sicyonia on SW, S, and SE respectively; chief towns Patrae, Helice, and Aigion.
History: Region presumably settled by the Achaeans, an early Greek people; first given loose political unity by the formation of the Achaean League of twelve Achaean cities, which allied with Athens against Sparta 362 B.C.; aided Greek efforts to stop invasions by Philip and Alexander the Great of Macedon 4th cent. B.C.; renewed 280 B.C. the Achaean League, which supported the wars against Macedon until the Roman defeat of Philip V 197 B.C. and was dissolved by Rome 146 B.C. for assisting Macedon. As a Roman imperial province 146 B.C.–c. 4th cent. A.D. included all of Greece S of Thessaly; a province of the Eastern Roman (Byzantine) Empire until made a Latin principality 1204; overrun by Turks 1460.

Achaea and E′lis (ē′lĭs). Department of Greece. See *Table* at GREECE.

Achaea Phthi·o′tis (thĭ·ō′tĭs). District, S part of ancient Thessaly, Greece, N of Mt. Othrys, extending E to the Pagasaean Gulf.

A′chard′ Point (á′shär′). Cape, W San Cristobal I., SE Solomon Is., W Pacific Ocean.

A·char′nae (á·kär′nē). Village (deme) ab. 6 m. N of Athens, Attica, Greece; charcoal burners of the village gave their name to a play of Aristophanes, *The Acharnians*, performed 425 B.C.

Acheen. See ACHIN.

Ach'e·lo'us (ăk'ê·lō'ŭs); *Mod. Gr.* **A'khe·lō'os** (ä'kä·lō'ôs); *also* **As'pro·pot'a·mos** (ăs'prŏ·pŏt'à·môs; *Mod. Gr.* äs'prŏ·pŏ'tä·môs). River ab. 100 m. long, W Greece; rises in Pindus Mts., NW Thessaly, and flows S to Ionian Sea; forms part of boundary bet. Acarnania and Aetolia.

Acherusia, Palus. See FUSARO.

A·chi' Ba·ba' (ä·chî' bä·bä'); *Turk.* **Al·çı' Te·pe'** (äl·chî' tă·pă'). Height dominating tip of Gallipoli Penin., Turkey in Europe; main position of Turkish defense in Gallipoli fighting of 1915.

Ach'ill (ăk'ĭl). Island ab. 15 m. long off W coast of Ireland, W of Clew Bay, co. Mayo; at W end is cape, **Achill Head.**

A·chin' *or* **A·cheen'** (à·chēn'; ä-); *also* **A·tchin'** (-chēn'). Native sultanate, N Sumatra; now (see ATJEH) a region of Indonesia. Visited by member of da Cunha's fleet 1506; destination of first ventures of Dutch and English East India companies 1599 and 1602; at height of power 1607–36 controlled entire western tip of Sumatra and subject continental states; unsuccessfully attacked Portuguese at Malacca 1615; declined after 17th cent.; treaty with British 1819 to exclude other Europeans lapsed after British ceded Sumatran claims to Dutch; despite continual efforts since 1873 to subdue region, only coastal areas were under effective Dutch control.

A·chinsk' (ŭ·chēnsk'). Town, SW Krasnoyarsk Territory, Soviet Russia, Asia, on Chulym river and on Trans-Siberian R.R. 90 m. W of Krasnoyarsk; has branch railroad connections with Kuznetsk Basin to the S.

Achkel, Lake; *or* **Ga·ra'et–Ach'kel** (gŭ·rä'ĕt·äsh'kĕl). Lake 9 m. long by ab. 4 m. wide, N Tunisia, just SW of Bizerte; control of it gained by American forces May 6, 1943.

Achmetha. See HAMADAN.

A·chray', Loch (lŏk ă·krā'). Small and beautiful lake 1¼ m. long, Perth co., Scotland; connects with Loch Katrine.

Acht'kar'spe·len (äKt'kär'spĕ·lĕn). Commune, Friesland prov., N Netherlands; pop. 14,983.

A'ci·re·a'le (ä'chĕ·rä·ä'lĕ). Seaport, Catania prov., E Sicily, on E coast 10 m. N of Catania; pop. 36,871; resort with sulfur baths; earthquake 1693.

Ack'er·man (ăk'ĕr·măn). Town, ⊗ of Choctaw co., cen. Mississippi, 44 m. WSW of Columbus; pop. 1382; sawmills.

Ack'er Peak (ăk'ĕr). Mountain 10,918 ft. in Sierra Nevada, E Tuolumne co., cen. California.

Ack'ia Battleground National Monument (ăk'yà). See UNITED STATES, *National Monuments.*

Ack'ley (ăk'lĭ). Town, Franklin and Hardin cos., N cen. Iowa, 38 m. W of Waterloo; pop. 1731.

Ack'lins Island (ăk'lĭnz). One of the Bahama Islands, West Indies, in Atlantic Ocean, adjoining Crooked Island and W of Mayaguana; 120 sq. m.; pop. (1943) 1744.

Ac'o·ma (ăk'ō·mà). Pueblo of Acoma Indians on reservation 60 m. W of Albuquerque, Valencia co., New Mexico; (est.) pop. 1000; situated on rock mesa (**Acoma Rock**) 357 ft. high with steep sides and difficult trail. Discovered by Coronado's men 1540; captured by Juan de Oñate 1599; joined in Pueblo revolts against Spanish 1680, 1696; subdued 1692, 1699

Ac'o·mi'ta (ăk'ō·mē'tà). Village, Valencia co., W New Mexico, ab. 53 m. W of Albuquerque; (est.) pop. 500; agricultural community inhabited by Indians chiefly from nearby Acoma pueblo.

Ac'on·ca'gua (ăk'ŭn·kä'gwà; -kăg'wà; *Span.* ä'kông·kä'gwä). **1** Mountain 22,835 ft., W Argentina, near Chilean border at Uspallata Pass; highest peak of Andes and of Western Hemisphere; first climbed 1897. **2** River, cen. Chile; rises on slopes of Aconcagua Mt.; flows W into Pacific Ocean 12 m. N of Valparaíso. **3** Province of Chile. See *Table* at CHILE.

A'con·qui'ja (ä'kông·kē'hä). Peak ab. 16,400 ft. in the Andes, Tucumán prov., N Argentina.

Açores. See AZORES.

Ac'qua·vi'va del'le Fon'ti (äk'kwä·vē'vä dĕl'lä fôn'tē). Commune, Bari prov., Apulia, SE Italy, 15 m. S of Bari; pop. 12,809.

Ac'qui (ăk'kwē); *anc.* **Aq'uae** *or* **Aquae Sta'ti·el'lae** (ăk'wē stä'shĭ·ĕl'ē; ä'kwē). Commune, Alessandria prov., Piedmont, NW Italy, 17 m. SSW of Alessandria; pop. 18,336; sulfurous waters and mud baths, known in Roman times.

Acrae. See PALAZZOLO ACREIDE.

Acragas. See AGRIGENTO.

A'cre (ä'kēr; ā'kēr; ä'krē; ăk'ēr; ăk'rē). **1** Subdistrict, Galilee district, N Palestine; 312 sq. m.; pop. 45,142, (1938 est.) 54,111.
2 *Fr.* **Saint'–Jean'–d'A'cre** (săN'zhäN'dà'kr'). **Ac'cho** (ăk'ō) of O.T., **Ptol'e·ma'ïs** (tŏl'ē·mā'ĭs) of N.T. Seaport city, its *, on promontory N of Mt. Carmel, Palestine, and on **Bay of Acre** (bet. Acre and Haifa, ab. 8 m. across); pop. (1944 est.) 10,695. As a city of Phoenicia, known as Ptolemaïs; captured by Arabs 638 A.D.; a Syrian town under the Seljuk Turks when attacked by Crusaders 12th cent.; as Saint-Jean-d'Acre, included in the Kingdom of Jerusalem set up by Crusaders 1104–87, 1191–1291; conquered by Saladin 1187, reconquered by Philip Augustus 1191; residence of Knights of St. John 13th cent.; became Moslem again at fall of Jerusalem 1291; captured by Turks 1517; declined until 18th cent.; besieged by Napoleon 1799; as part of Syria captured by Mehemet Ali 1832; taken by British 1840 and restored to Ottoman Empire; again taken by British Sept. 23, 1918; part of modern Palestine (*q.v.*).

A'cre (ä'krĕ; *Span.* ä'krä); *formerly* **A'qui·ry'** (ä'kē·rē'). **1** River ab. 330 m. long, W cen. South America, chief tributary of Purús; forms part of boundary bet. Acre Territory, Brazil, and N Bolivia; flows NE to join Purús river in SW Amazonas state, Brazil. **2** Territory, W Brazil; 57,153 sq. m.; pop. (1940 est.) 81,326; * Rio Branco; SW of Amazonas state, borders on E Peru and N Bolivia. Formerly territory of Bolivia; its tropical forests a great rubber supply; encroachment of Brazilian traders led to trouble with Bolivia; revolt 1899 and independence declared; annexed by Brazil by treaty, with payment of about $10,000,000 to Bolivia.

A'cri (ä'krē). Commune, Cosenza prov., Calabria, S Italy, 15 m. NE of Cosenza; pop. 16,213.

Ac'ro·ce·rau'ni·a (ăk'rŏ·sē·rô'nĭ·à; -rôn'yà). Promontory, NW Epirus, ancient Greece, opp. SE point of Italy. To S along coast and inland heights sometimes called **Ac'ro·ce·rau'ni·an Mts.** (-rô'nĭ·ăn; -rôn'yăn), more correctly Ceraunian Mts. (*q.v.*). Promontory now known as Cape Linguetta (*q.v.*) in SW Albania.

Ac'ro·co·rin'thus (ăk'rŏ·kŏ·rĭn'thŭs). Acropolis of Corinth, Greece, a high rock 1887 ft. on which was anciently a citadel, also a temple of Aphrodite; at its foot the Pirene spring; in Middle Ages site of Byzantine fortifications.

A·cro'ï·num (à·krō'ĭ·nŭm) *or* **A·kro'i·non** (à·krō'ĭ·nŏn). Ancient town, S Phrygia, Asia Minor, near the modern Afyon Karahisar; battle 739 A.D. in which Leo III defeated the Moslems.

Ac'te (ăk'tĕ; -tē); *Mod. Gr.* **Ak'tē** (äk'tē). Most easterly of the three peninsulas of Chalcidice, Macedonia, NE Greece, ab. 35 m. long; extends SE into Aegean Sea bet. Strymonic Gulf on the N and Singitic Gulf on the S; at its tip is Mount Athos (see ATHOS). Its narrow isthmus, where it joins the mainland near Acanthus, was cut by a canal by orders of the Persian king Xerxes 480 B.C.

Ac'ti·um (ăk'shĭ·ŭm; -tĭ·ŭm). Promontory and ancient town, NW Acarnania, Greece, on S side of entrance to Ambracian Gulf; scene of naval battle 434 B.C. preliminary to Peloponnesian War and of famous naval victory

of Octavius over Antony and Cleopatra 31 B.C. by which he became emperor of Rome.

Ac′ton (ăk′tŭn). **1** Town, Middlesex co., NE Massachusetts, 13 m. SSE of Lowell; pop. 7238.

2 Village, Halton co., SE Ontario, Canada, 35 m. W of Toronto; pop. 2880.

3 Municipal borough, Middlesex, SE England; pop. 67,424; part of Greater London; known as a center of Puritanism during the Commonwealth.

Acton Vale (văl). Town, Bagot co., S Quebec, Canada, 36 m. NW of Sherbrooke; pop. 3367; railroad junction.

Ac·to′pan (äk·tō′pän). Subdivision of the plateau of Anáhuac (*q.v.*), cen. Mexico; mean elevation 6450 ft.

Ac·tu′ra (äk·tōō′rä). Commune, on railroad ab. 14 m. N of Rio de Janeiro, Brazil.

Açúcar, Pão de. See PÃO DE AÇÚCAR.

Acunum Acusio. See MONTÉLIMAR.

A·cush′net (á·kŏŏsh′nĕt; -nĭt). Town, Bristol co., SE Massachusetts, on inlet of Buzzards Bay 3 m. N of New Bedford; pop. 5755; settled c. 1659; devastated during King Philip's War; scene of battle Sept. 1776 bet. Minutemen and British troops.

A′da (ā′dä). **1** County in Idaho. See *Table* at IDAHO.

2 City, ⊗ of Norman co., NW Minnesota, 32 m. NNE of Moorhead; pop. 2064; dairy products, potatoes.

3 Village, Hardin co., NW cen. Ohio, 15 m. E of Lima; pop. 3918; manufactures; farming; Ohio Northern Univ. (1871).

4 City, ⊗ of Pontotoc co., S cen. Oklahoma, 40 m. SSE of Shawnee; pop. 14,347; settled 1889, incorp. 1910; manufactures flour, cement, brick, tile, etc.; oil fields, livestock ranches nearby; agriculture (cotton, corn, hay, etc.); East Central State College (1909).

5 Mountain 4536 ft., E side of Baranof I., Alaska.

Adabazar. See ADAPAZARI.

A′dai Khokh′ (ä′dī KÔK′). Mountain group and peak 15,240 ft., cen. Caucasus Mts., Soviet Russia, Europe; 42°47′N lat., 43°48′E long.; on boundary bet. North Ossetia and South Ossetia just N of Mamison Pass.

A·dair′ (á·dâr′). **1** Name of counties in four states of the U.S. See *Tables* at IOWA, KENTUCKY, MISSOURI, OKLAHOMA.

2 Bay at NE end of Gulf of California, extending into NW Sonora state, Mexico.

A′dak (ā′dăk). Island, central Andreanof Is., Aleutian Is., SW Alaska; treeless and barren but has several good harbors. In World War II, after Japanese seizure of W Aleutians, occupied 1942 by Americans and developed as air base for attack on Kiska 250 m. W.

A′da·lar′ (ä′dä·lär′). District, comprising group of small islands, E Sea of Marmara, İstanbul vilayet, Turkey in Asia; pop. 16,807.

Adalia. See ANTALYA.

A′dam (ä′dăm). Inland town, E Oman, SE Arabia, W of Sur; pop. ab. 4500.

Ad′am, Mount (ăd′ăm). Peak 2290 ft., highest point in Falkland Is., on N West Falkland.

Ad′a·man′a (ăd′á·măn′á). Village, Apache co., Arizona, 18 m. E of Holbrook; gateway to Petrified Forest National Monument.

Ad′a·ma′wa (ăd′á·mä′wä). Region in W Africa, ab. 50,000 sq. m. bet. Bight of Biafra and Lake Chad; largely a plateau (1500 to 2000 ft.) with highest point about 6000 ft.; crossed by Benue river and tributaries; inhabited by Fulah and Hausa tribes. First explored by Germans, then by French. From about 1900 divided by Germany, France, and England. German portion (former Kamerun) divided 1919 into English and French mandates: French portion a part of French Equatorial Africa; English portion a province of Nigeria (see *Table* at NIGERIA).

A′da·mel′lo, Mon′te (môn′tä ä′dä·měl′lô). Mountain group 11,657 ft., Rhaetian Alps, N Italy, 27 m. WNW of Trento and N of Lake Garda.

Ad′ams (ăd′ămz). **1** Name of counties in twelve states

of the U.S. See *Tables* at COLORADO, IDAHO, ILLINOIS, INDIANA, IOWA, MISSISSIPPI, NEBRASKA, NORTH DAKOTA, OHIO, PENNSYLVANIA, WASHINGTON, WISCONSIN.

2 Town, N Berkshire co., W Massachusetts, 14 m. NNE of Pittsfield; pop. 12,391; lime kilns, textile and paper mills. Settled 1762, incorp. as town 1778.

3 Village, Jefferson co., N New York, 13 m. SSW of Watertown; pop. 1914; agriculture, dairying.

Adams, Mount. **1** Peak 5798 ft., second highest of White Mts., Coos co., New Hampshire, in Presidential Range N of Mt. Washington.

2 Peak 3584 ft., Essex co., NE New York.

3 Peak 12,307 ft. of Cascade Range, SW Yakima co., Washington, S of Mt. Rainier.

Adams, Point. Cape at mouth of Columbia river, NW Oregon.

Adam's Bridge. Chain of shoals ab. 30 m. long bet. Ceylon and SE coast of India (Madras); traditionally, the remains of a causeway built by Rama, hero of the *Ramayana*, to allow the passage of his army from India to Ceylon in order to rescue his wife Sita.

Ad′am's Peak (ăd′ămz); *Singhalese* **Sa′ma·na·la** (sŭ′mä·nä·lä). Mountain 7365 ft., S cen. Ceylon; sacred as place of pilgrimage for Hindus, Buddhists, and Mohammedans;—named, according to the Mohammedan legend, after a large hollow (5 ft. long), resembling a footprint, in rock on its summit, said to have been made by Adam, standing there on one foot for 1000 years as an act of penance for his expulsion from Paradise.

Ad′ams·town′ (ăd′ămz·toun′). **1** Town, E New South Wales, SE Australia, suburb of Newcastle; pop. 4888.

2 Village on Pitcairn Island (*q.v.*).

Adana. See ADEN.

A·da·na′ (ä·dä·nä′) *or* **Sey·han′** (sā·hän′). City, ✳ of Seyhan vilayet, S Turkey in Asia, on left bank of Seyhan river ab. 30 m. from its mouth; pop. (1940) 89,990; fourth city in size in Turkey; railroad and flourishing commercial center. Roman military station; after decline, restored by Harun-al-Rashid c. 782 A.D.; held by Egyptians 1832–40; scene of Armenian massacres of 1909; occupied by French army 1919–21; scene of conference Jan. 30–31, 1943 bet. Prime Minister Churchill for Allies and Turkish officials.

A·da·pa·za·rı′ (ä·dä·pä·zä·rï′), *formerly* **A·da·ba·zar′** (ä·dä·bä·zär′). Chief town, Kocaeli vilayet, NW Turkey in Asia; pop. 24,702; on Sakarya river and on old military road ab. 75 m. E of İstanbul; has rail connections with Üsküdar and important silk and linen industries.

A·dare′ (á·dâr′). Cape, NE Victoria Land, Antarctica, in Ross Dependency, ab. 71°S.

Ad′da (äd′dä). River ab. 80 m. long, Lombardy, N Italy; flows S through Lake Como into Po river 7 m. W of Cremona.

Ad′da·gal′la (äd′á·găl′á; *Ethiopian* äd′dá·gäl′lä). Town, E Ethiopia, E Africa, N of Diredawa; station on Addis Ababa-Djibouti railroad near French Somaliland border.

Addar, Ras. See Cape BON.

Ad′ding·ton (ăd′ĭng·tŭn). See *Lennox and Addington* in *Table* at ONTARIO.

Ad′dis Ab′a·ba (ăd′ĭs äb′á·bá; *Ethiopian* äd·dēs ä·bá·bä); *Ital.* **Ad′dis A·be·ba′** (ăd′dēs ä·bá·bä′). Town, ✳ of Shoa and of Ethiopia, in cen. part; 485 m. by rail to Djibouti, Fr. Somaliland; altitude over 8000 ft.; pop. ab. 150,000. Scene of peace treaty by which Italy recognized the independence of Ethiopia 1896; capital of Ethiopia since 1896; occupied by Italians May 5, 1936 signaling end of Ethiopian resistance to invasion; restored by British April 1941.

Ad′di·son (ăd′ĭ·s'n). **1** County in Vermont. See *Table* at VERMONT.

2 Village, Steuben co., S New York, in agricultural region 24 m. W of Elmira; pop. 2185.

Ad Diwaniya. See DIWANIYAH.

Ad′dys·ton (ăd′ĭs·tŭn). Village, Hamilton co., SW Ohio, on Ohio river 11 m. W of Cincinnati; pop. 1376.

A'del' (ā'dĕl'). City, ⊗ of Cook co., S Georgia; pop. 4321.

A·del' (à·dĕl'). Town, ⊗ of Dallas co., S cen. Iowa, 24 m. W of Des Moines; pop. 2060.

Ad'e·laide (ăd'l·ād). **1** City, * of South Australia, in SE part on Torrens river and 7 m. by rail from its port, Port Adelaide, on Gulf of St. Vincent and ab. 500 m. NW of Melbourne; pop. with suburbs (1966) 726,930. Has wide streets, handsome buildings, and extensive park lands; seat of Univ. of Adelaide (1874), of theological schools, of leading school of mines and industry in Australia, and of two cathedrals; has large export trade. Founded 1837; first municipality in Australia to be incorporated (1840).
2 Town, E Cape Prov., Republic of So. Africa, ab. 95 m. NNE of Port Elizabeth; pop. 3726; trading and wool center.

Adelaide Island. Island ab. 68 m. long and 20 m. wide W of Palmer Peninsula off Graham Coast, Antarctica, Falkland Is. Dependencies.

Adelaide Peninsula. Peninsula, NW Keewatin dist., Northwest Territories, Canada, 68°10′N, 97°30′W, opp. King William Island.

A'dé'lie' Coast or **Land** (ā'dā'lē'; *Angl.* à·dā'lǐ). Part of Antarctica, bet. 66° and 67°S, 136°20′ and 142°20′E; estimated area ab. 150,000 sq. m.; noted for its high winds. First sighted by Capt. d'Urville of French navy 1840; explored by Mawson in his expeditions of 1911–14, 1929–31; placed under French sovereignty by decree Apr. 1, 1938. See WILKES LAND.

Adelsberg. See POSTUMIA.

A'den (ā'd'n; ā'd'n; ăd''n); *anc.* **Ad'a·na** (ăd''n·à). **1** Settlement on coast of SW Arabia; 75 sq. m., including Perim I. 80 sq. m.; pop. (1955) 138,441; became crown colony 1937; now part of South Yemen.
2 Seaport fortress, former * of colony and of Aden Protectorate, on Gulf of Aden ab. 110 m. E of Bab el Mandeb strait; a township comprising a number of settlements (largest settlement, Crater, pop. 55,000).
History: Trading port in Roman times; chief port on medieval Arab trade route between the Red Sea and the Persian Gulf and India; unsuccessfully attacked by Portuguese under Albuquerque 1513; captured by Turks 1538; ruled by Sultan of San'a from 17th century; held by British and governed as part of India 1839–1937; increased greatly in importance as coaling station and transshipment point after opening of Suez Canal 1869; during World War I, political relations managed from Egypt; administered by Colonial Office from 1921; separated from India and made crown colony 1937; a fortified naval base during World War II; joined Federation of South Arabia 1963; since 1967 part of South Yemen.

Aden, Gulf of. Arm of Indian Ocean ab. 550 m. long, bet. S coast of Arabia and Somali Republic, Africa, connecting on W through Bab el Mandeb with the Red Sea. Strategic location on Suez route to India controlled by British after their acquisition of Aden 1839, Perim 1857, and Socotra 1876 (*qq.v.*).

A·de'na (à·dē'nà). Village, Jefferson co., E Ohio, 15 m. SW of Steubenville; pop. 1317.

Aden Protectorate. Hinterland of Aden seaport and strip 750 m. along S coast of Arabia, extending to border of Oman (ab. 53°30′E long.) and including Hadhramaut; formerly ab. 9000 sq. m., increased to 42,000 sq. m., now ab. 112,000 sq. m.; * Aden. Formed from areas adjacent to port of Aden controlled by Arab chiefs in treaty with British government; W portion formed Federation of South Arabia (*q.v.*) 1959.

Adernò. See ADRANO.

Ad'i·a·be'ne (ăd'ǐ·à·bē'nē). Region of ancient Assyria in N part, E of the Tigris and bet. the Great Zab and the Little Zab; later much extended.

A'di·ge (ä'dĕ·jä); *Lat.* **Ath'e·sis** (ăth'ē·sĭs); *Ger.* **Etsch** (ĕch). River ab. 220 m. long, NE Italy; rises in Rhaetian Alps, flows SE and S past Merano, Trento, and Verona

to Adriatic Sea bet. Venice and mouths of Po; navigable for 170 m. Changed its course 587 A.D.; scene of many battles, the best known of which occurred 1799, when General Schérer defeated the Austrians, and in the Austrian-Italian campaign of 1916.

Adigey, Adighe. Vars. of *Adygei*, in ADYGEI AUTONOMOUS REGION.

A'di·grat' (ä'dĕ·grät'). Town, N Ethiopia, E of Aduwa and near border of Eritrea.

A'dil·a·bad' (ŭ'dĭl·à·bäd'; *Angl.* à·dĭl'à·băd). Town, N Andhra Pradesh, cen. India, 160 m. N of Hyderabad.

Ad'i·ron'dack Mountains (ăd'ǐ·rŏn'dăk). Mountain group, NE New York, chiefly in Clinton, Essex, Hamilton, and Franklin cos.; highest Mt. Marcy 5344 ft.; others MacIntyre 5112 ft., Skylight 4920 ft., and Haystack 4918 ft.; includes many lakes, as Saranac, Placid, Tupper, Long, and Raquette; source of Hudson and Ausable rivers; remarkable for fine scenery; has many resorts, esp. for winter sports. In center of mountain region is the **Adirondack Forest Preserve,** area ab. 2,200,000 acres, set aside by state with camp sites for public recreation and to conserve forests and water supply.

Adis Ababa, Adis Abeba. Vars. of ADDIS ABABA.

A'di·ya·man' (ä'dǐ·yä·män'). Chief town, Malatya vilayet, E Turkey in Asia, at foot of mountains N of Euphrates river; pop. 10,305.

Adjar. See ADZHAR.

Ad·jun'tas (äth·hōōn'täs). Municipality (pop. 19,658) and town (pop. 5318), W cen. Puerto Rico; summer resort.

Ad'mi·ral·ty Bay (ăd'mǐ·rǎl·tǐ). See SOUTH SHETLANDS.

Admiralty Inlet. 1 Branch of Puget Sound, NW Washington, bet. Whidbey I. and mainland (Island and Jefferson cos.).
2 Fiord 180 m. long, NW Baffin I., Franklin District, Northwest Territories, Canada, opening into Lancaster Sound; cuts off Brodeur Peninsula to the W.

Admiralty Island. Island ab. 90 m. long by 20 m. wide, N Alexander Archipelago, SE Alaska, bet. mainland on E and Chichagof and Baranof Islands on W.

Admiralty Islands, often **Ad'mi·ral·ties** (-tǐz). Island group, W Pacific Ocean, N of the island of New Guinea and ab. 260 m. W of New Hanover I.; comprises Manus, the only large island, Rambutyo, and ab. 16 small islands. Part of Bismarck Archipelago, constituting with Northwestern Is. the Manus district of the Territory of New Guinea; 800 sq. m.; pop. (1939) 13,712; * Lorengau; chief products coconuts and pearl shell. First seen by Schouten and Le Maire 1615; became part of German protectorate 1884; occupied by Australian forces 1914; mandated to Australia 1920. Seized by Japanese 1942; invaded by Allied forces 1944; Los Negros Is. just E of Manus seized with the airfield (Momote) Feb. 29; Manus and entire group taken over by Mar. 18.

Admiralty Range. Mountains on coast, N part of Victoria Land, Antarctica.

Admiralty Sound. Deep inlet, SW coast of Tierra del Fuego, Chile.

Adoenara. Var. of *Adunara*: see ADONARA.

A'do·na'ra (ä'dō·nä'rä) or **A'du·na'ra** (ä'dōō-). Island bet. E end of Flores and Lomblen Islands, Lesser Sunda Is., Indonesia; ab. 23 m. long by 11 m. wide; 224 sq. m.; pop. 51,544; main settlement Sagu on N coast.

A·do'ni (à·dō'nǐ). Town, W Andhra Pradesh, S Indian Union, 265 m. NW of Madras; pop. 35,635; large trade in locally grown cotton.

A'dour' (à'dōōr'); *anc.* **At'u·rus** (ăt'ū·rŭs; à·tūr'ŭs). River ab. 200 m. long, SW France; flows NW and W from Pyrenees to Bay of Biscay near Biarritz.

Adowa. See ADUWA.

A'dra (ä'thrä); *anc.* **Ab·de'ra** (ăb·dēr'à). Seaport, Almería prov., SE Spain, 30 m. W of Almería; pop.

12,450. Ancient town, Abdera, in Baetica, S Hispania, at foot of hill below present town; a maritime city founded by Carthaginians, taken by Romans.

Adramyttium. See EDREMİT.

A·dra′no (ä-drä′nȯ) *or* **A′der·nò′** (ä′där-nô′); *anc.* **Ha·dra′num** (há·drā′nŭm). Commune, Catania prov., E Sicily, at foot of Mt. Etna and 24 m. NW of Catania; pop. 24,515; founded c. 400 B.C. by Dionysius the Elder; parts of ancient walls still standing; has Norman castle built in 1157. In World War II taken by Allied forces Aug. 1943.

Adranos. See ATRANOS.

A·drar′ (ä-drär′). Name of several mountainous regions in Sahara desert region of NW Africa: (1) Region, W Mauritania, bordering on SE Río de Oro; chief town Ouadane. (2) *in full* **A′drar′ des I′fo′ras′** (*Fr.* à′drär′ dä-zē′fȯ′rà′). Region, cen. Sahara, NE of Tombouctou.

Adria. See ADRIATIC SEA.

A′dri·a (ä′drė·ä); *anc.* **Ha′dri·a** (hä′drĭ·à) *or* **A′tri·a** (ä′trĭ·à). Commune, Rovigo prov., Venezia Euganea, NE Italy, 15 m. E of Rovigo; orig. on Adriatic Sea but now 13 m. inland; pop. 32,762. Ancient Etruscan settlement which gave its name to Adriatic Sea; in Roman times, a port and naval station.

A′dri·an (ā′drĭ·ăn). City, ⊗ of Lenawee co., SE Michigan, on Raisin river 59 m. SW of Detroit; pop. 20,347; center of agricultural and truck-garden region; has large manufacturing interests. Settled 1825, incorp. as city 1853; seat of Adrian College (1845; coed.); Siena Heights College (1919; women).

Adrianople; *anc.* **Adrianopolis** *or* **Hadrianopolis.** See EDİRNE, its modern Turkish name.

A′dri·a Pi·ce′na (ä′drĭ·à pĭ-sē′nà). Variant of *Hadria Picena*: see ATRI.

A′dri·at′ic Sea (ā′drĭ-ăt′ĭk; ăd′rĭ-) *or* **Gulf of Venice;** *Ital.* **Ma′re A′dri·a′ti·co** (mä′rā ä′drē·ä′tē·kȯ); *anc.* **A′dri·a** (ā′drĭ·à) *or* **Ma′re A′dri·at′i·cum** (mä′rē ä′drĭ-ăt′ĭ·kŭm; ăd′rĭ-). Arm of Mediterranean Sea, E of Italy, 500 m. long. Istria, Yugoslavia, and Albania are on its E shore.

Adua. See ADUWA.

A′du·la (ä′dōō·lä). Mountain group, Lepontine Alps, SE Switzerland; highest peak Rheinwaldhorn 11,145 ft.

A·dul′lam (á·dŭl′ăm). Village in hill country of S Canaan, ab. 12 m. SW of Jerusalem; a cave in its vicinity was from early times a place of refuge (*1 Sam.* xxii. 1, 2).

A′du·wa (ä′dŭ·wä), *also* **A′do·wa** (ä′dōō·wä); *Ital.* **A′du·a** (ä′dōō·ä). Town, formerly ✳ of Tigre prov., N Ethiopia, ab. 80 m. S of Asmara; scene of disastrous defeat of Italians March 1, 1896 by Emperor Menelik II, because of which Ethiopia secured recognition of her independence; captured by Italians soon after invasion of Ethiopia Oct. 1935; included in Eritrea 1935–41; retaken by British 1941.

Ad′vent Bay (ăd′vĕnt). Bay in Ice Fjord, West Spitsbergen, Svalbard, Norway; settlements at Longyear City and Advent City.

Advent City. Mining settlement on Advent Bay, West Spitsbergen.

Ad′wick le Street (ăd′ĭk lĕ strēt′). Urban district, West Riding, Yorkshire, England, 20 m. NE of Sheffield; pop. 18,808.

A·dy·gei′ Autonomous Region *or* **A·di·gey′ Autonomous Region** (ŭ·dĭ·gā′ĭ). Autonomous region, S Soviet Russia, Europe; 1505 sq. m.; pop. 241,773, (1941 est.) 254,055; ✳ Maikop; NE of Black Sea, entirely surrounded by Krasnodar Terr.; a subdivision of the R.S.F.S.R.; Kuban river marks N border; land partly river basin, partly hilly; occupations chiefly agricultural, but recent discovery of oil has brought new industry. Predominant ethnic strain Japhetic (Caucasian); chief nationalities Adygei (called Cherkess by the Russians) 47.8%, Russian 25.6%, Ukrainians 23.3%; the Adygei are a tribe of Circassians (see CIRCASSIA).

Formerly part of Kuban prov., inhabited by a Circassian people who had been Christianized in 6th cent. and converted to Mohammedanism 17th cent.; created an autonomous area 1922 and a region 1936. In World War II occupied by Germans in Caucasus drive Aug. 9, 1942, but recaptured by Russians Jan. 31, 1943.

A·dzhar′ *or* **A·djar′** (á·jär′; ä′jär; *Russ.* ŭt·zhàr′); *also* **A·dzhar′i·a** (á·jär′ĭ·à) *or* **A·dzhar′i·stan′** (á·jär′ĭ·stän′; *Russ.* ŭt·zhŭ·ryĭ·stàn′). *Officially* **Adzhar Autonomous Soviet Socialist Republic.** Autonomous republic, SW Georgia, U.S.S.R., on Black Sea coast; 1080 sq. m.; pop. (1941 est.) 169,946; ✳ Batum; on S borders on Çoruh vilayet, NE Turkey; mountainous with dense forests; has heavy rainfall; watered in SW by lower course of Çoruh (Chorokh) river; plain along Black Sea has subtropical vegetation; chief products maize, cotton, rice, tobacco, and fruits. Adzharians are a Caucasian race; chief nationalities Adzharian 53.7%, Georgian 14.5%, Armenian 8%, Russian ab. 8%. Controlled 17th and 18th cents. by Turks who introduced Islamic influences; greater part of region annexed by Russia middle of 19th cent. and Batum acquired 1877–78; after Revolution of 1917 held by Turks for a time but restored to Russia Oct. 1921.

Aea. See KUTAISI.

Aeaea. See Monte CIRCEO.

Ædua. See AUTUN.

Aegadian Isles, Aegates. See EGADI ISLANDS.

Ae·ga′le·os, Mount (ē·gă′lė·ȯs). Mountain 1535 ft., W Attica, Greece, just W of Athens overlooking the Bay of Eleusis and the island of Salamis; on it sat Xerxes watching the defeat of his fleet by the Greeks in the battle of Salamis 480 B.C.

Ae·ge′an Islands (ē·jē′ăn). **1** Islands of the Aegean Sea including the Cyclades, Sporades, Dodecanese, etc.

History: Cyclades and southern islands probably part of Aegean civilization 2d millennium B.C. (see AEGEAN SEA); colonized by Aeolian, Dorian, and Ionian Greeks from mainland c. 1000–700 B.C.; during Greek wars with Persia, islands in Thracian Sea helped Persia, but eastern islands were under influence of revolting Ionian cities; allied with or dependent upon Athens, the leader of the Delian League (see ATHENS), 5th cent. B.C.; except for Cyclades, chiefly controlled by Macedonian empire until they were conquered by Rome 2d cent. B.C.; ruled by Byzantine Empire 5th–13th cents.; ravaged and seized by Roger II of Sicily during Second Crusade 1147; Naxos became center of duchy of Naxos which was established 1207 by Venice from her acquisitions in the Fourth Crusade; in 13th cent. politically controlled by leading Venetian families and commercially dominated by Venetian traders; Imbros (İmroz), Samothrace (Samothrákē), Lesbos (Mytilēnē) recovered by Eastern Empire 1261; western islands remained under Venetian Duchy of the Archipelago; Chios (Khíos) held by Genoese 1261–1329; Rhodes (Rodi) belonged to Knights of St. John of Jerusalem (Hospitalers) 1310–1522; in a series of Venetian wars with Ottoman Turks during 15th and 16th cents., gradually conquered by Turks; part of Ottoman Empire from death of Suleiman I 1566 until joined Greek revolt 1821; most of islands became part of independent Greece by Treaty of Adrianople 1829.

2 *Gr.* **Nē′soi Ai·gai′ou** (nyē′sē á·yà′ōō). Geographical division of modern Greece, comprising departments of Lesbos, Chios, and Samos (see *Table* at GREECE); 1486 sq. m.; pop. (1938 est.) 337,986; chief towns Mytilene, Chios, and Vathy. Administrative division formed 1931.

3 *Ital.* **I′so·le E·ge′e** (ē′zȯ·lä â·jâ′ā). The Italian Aegean Is. (Dodecanese, Rhodes, and Castelrosso) 1923–47.

Aegean Sea. Arm of Mediterranean Sea bet. Asia Minor and Greece, 400 m. long by 200 m. wide. See AEGEAN ISLANDS. It was the center of earliest European civilization, formerly called Mycenean or Minoan but in broader aspects now termed Aegean (c. 3000–1100 B.C.).

Ae′ge·ri, Lake of (ä′gĕ·rē). Small lake, Zug canton, Switzerland, E of Lake of Zug.

Ægidia. See CAPODISTRIA.

Ae·gi′na (ē·jī′nà); *Mod. Gr.* **Ai′gi·na** (ä′yē·nä). **1** Island 9 m. long in the Saronic Gulf, off SE coast of Greece; attached to Attica and Boeotia dept., Greece.
2 Commune, Attica and Boeotia dept., Greece, on W coast of Aegina I.; pop. 6530; sponge fishing.
History: Greek state of maritime importance even in pre-Dorian times; first state in European Greece to coin money in the standard which came to prevail in ancient times; a leading commercial state at the beginning of 5th cent. B.C., but gradually eclipsed by Athens; ravaged Attica in behalf of Thebes; gave submission to Persia 491 B.C.; scene of battle in the so-called First Peloponnesian War in which Aeginetans, allies of Sparta, were defeated by Athens 459 B.C. and forced to join the Delian League; lost its greatness after Athens expelled its people 431 B.C.; destroyed by the Romans 210 B.C. Center of the rebel Greek government after its defeat by the Turks at Mesolóngion 1826.

Aegina *or* **Aigina, Gulf of.** See SARONIC GULF.

Ae′gi·on (ē′jĭ·ŏn), **Ae′gi·um** (-ŭm). Variants of AIGION.

Ae′gos·pot′a·mi (ē′gŏs·pŏt′à·mī) *or* **Ae′gos·pot′a·mos** (-mŏs). Small river and town, ancient Thrace, in the Chersonese. Mouth of river on the Dardanelles scene of Spartan victory under Lysander over Athenian fleet 405 B.C., the last battle of the Peloponnesian War.

Aegusa. See LINOSA.

Aegyptus. See EGYPT.

Aelana. See 'AQABA.

Aelia Capitolina. See JERUSALEM.

Ael′tre (äl′trĕ). Commune, East Flanders prov., Belgium, 12 m. SE of Brugge; pop. 7341.

Æmilia. See EMILIA.

Æmilianum. See MILLAU.

Aenaria. See ISCHIA.

Aenos. See ENEZ.

Aenus. See INN.

Aeoliae Insulae. See LIPARI ISLANDS.

Ae′o·lis (ē′ō·lĭs) *or* **Ae·o′li·a** (ē·ō′lĭ·à; ē·ōl′yà). Ancient country, NW Asia Minor; included island of Lesbos; settled by Aeolian Greeks, a Thessalian people, who founded a number of cities along the coast before 1000 B.C. Religious center at Gryneion, near Cyme. Later formed a district of Mysia and Lydia, overcome by Croesus.

Aequum Tuticum. See ARIANO IRPINO.

Ær′ö′ (â′rû′). Island in the Baltic, Svendborg co., Denmark, S of Fyn I.; ab. 15 m. long; 34 sq. m.; pop. (1925) 11,641.

Aer′schot (är′sкôt). Commune, Brabant prov., cen. Belgium, 23 m. NE of Brussels; pop. 9153; scene of severe fighting Aug.–Sept. 1914.

Æsernia. See ISERNIA.

Æsis. See IESI.

Aethalia. See ELBA.

Ae′thi·o′pi·a (ē′thĭ·ō′pĭ·à). Ancient name for the region of NE Africa, including modern Egypt, Sudan, Ethiopia, and as far S as the knowledge of the ancients extended.

Aetna. See ETNA.

Ae·to′li·a (ē·tō′lĭ·à; ē·tōl′yà). Ancient district, cen. Greece, N of Gulf of Patras and Locris, and E of Acarnania, now part of Aetolia and Acarnania dept. from which it is separated by the Achelous river; a mountainous region.
History: In early times home of a backward group of tribes; first given unity by the formation of the Aetolian League 290 B.C., a military confederation which at its height included most of central Greece and separated Sparta from the Achaean League (see ACHAEA); driven out of area of Peloponnesus by Achaeans and Philip V of Macedon 3d cent. B.C.; helped Rome defeat Mace-

donians at Cynoscephalae 197 B.C.; punished by Rome for aiding Antiochus III of Syria 189 B.C.; incorporated into the Roman province of Achaea 146 B.C.; became part of Eastern (Greek) Empire 1204 A.D.; under Scanderbeg (see ALBANIA), Venetians, and Turks in the course of 15th cent.

Aetolia and Ac′ar·na′ni·a (ăk′ēr·nā′nĭ·à; ăk′är-; -nän′yà). Department of Greece. See *Table* at GREECE.

Af′fo·ri (äf′fô·rē). Town, N suburb of Milan, Milano prov., Lombardy, Italy; pop. (1931) 26,354.

Af·ghan′i·stan (äf·găn′ĭ·stăn). Country, a constitutional monarchy, W Asia; ab. 250,000 sq. m.; pop. ab. 12,000,000; ✻ Kabul; bounded on E by India, on S by Baluchistan, on W by Iran, and on N by U.S.S.R. Has Helmand river in center and SW, flowing into Lake Helmand, Hari Rud in NW, Amu Darya on NE boundary, and Kabul in E, flowing to Indus; very mountainous in cen. and N sections, Hindu Kush ranges 15,000 to 24,000 ft.; many fertile plains and valleys; desert regions in S; Khyber Pass on E border to India; chief cities Kabul, Herat, Kandahar, Mazar-i-Sharif, Ghazni; chiefly an agricultural region; exports timber, skins, carpets, wool, fruits.
History: In early times formed part of Persian and Alexander's empires; little known until Turkoman dynasty set up at Ghazni (*q.v.*) in 10th century; conquered by Mongol emperor Tamerlane c. 1400; part, including Kabul, added to the Mogul Empire of India by its founder, Baber (1483–1530); Kandahar became independent 1706; with western India, seized by Persian Nadir Shah 1737; consolidated as a separate unit by Ahmad Shah Durrani, at whose death (1773) the Afghan empire included eastern Persia, Afghanistan, Baluchistan, Kashmir, and the Punjab; under successive rulers soon lost Punjab and other territory; in 1809 entered first agreement with the British against the Persians and Russians; attacked by British in First Afghan War 1839–42, thereafter throughout 19th century much disturbed; subject of the jealousy and misunderstanding between British and Russians which resulted in the Second Afghan War 1878–79; maintained a degree of independence under Abd-er-Rahman Khan (1880–1901) who confirmed the cession of the Khyber Pass (*q.v.*) to the British; settled boundaries with India 1893, with Russia 1895. Neutral in World War I; recognized as independent by the British in the Treaty of Rawalpindi 1919; entered treaties with Soviet Russia, Turkey and Persia 1921; under the modernizing influence of Amanullah Khan (1919–29), adopted constitution 1923; at the overthrow of Amanullah, established new line of rulers under Nadir Shah (1929–33) whose son joined Turkey, Iraq, and Iran in forming an Oriental Entente 1937. Neutral in World War II; trade pact signed with Soviet Russia July 24, 1940; first Afghan minister to U.S. sent to Washington 1943.

Af′ghan Turkistan (äf′găn). Region, part of Turkistan (*q.v.*), NE Afghanistan, about coextensive with the district around Mazar-i-Sharif. Some include also the district of Badakhshan to the E. Long under Uzbek influence and claimed by Russia; settled in favor of Afghanistan by Anglo-Russian Agreement 1859.

Af·go′i (äf·gô′ē). Town, SE Somalia, E Africa, just NW of Mogadishu on railroad from Mogadishu to Villagio Duca degli Abruzzi.

Afiun Karahissar. See AFYON KARAHISAR.

A·fog′nak (à·fŏg′năk). Island 47 m. long by 22 m. wide on W side of Gulf of Alaska, N of Kodiak I. and separated from mainland by Shelikof Strait; pop. of village on island 197.

à Foux, Cap. See Cap à FOUX.

A′fra·go′la (ä′frä·gô′lä). Commune, Napoli prov., Campania, S Italy, 6 m. NNE of Naples; pop. 29,281.

Af′ri·ca (äf′rĭ·kà). Second largest continent on the globe, 4970 m. long, 4700 m. broad, ab. 11,530,000 sq. m.; pop. (1964 est.) 304,000,000; coast line 16,100 m.; in

both N and S hemispheres with greater part N of the equator.

Boundaries: On N, Mediterranean Sea; most northerly point Cape Blanc, 37°14′N; on NW separated from Europe by Strait of Gibraltar; joined on NE to Asia at Sinai Peninsula. On E, Red Sea and Indian Ocean (chief subdivisions Gulf of Aden and Mozambique Channel); chief island Madagascar, and several small groups; most easterly point Cape Hafun, 51°25′E. On S, Indian and Atlantic Oceans (with arbitrary separation line at 20th meridian E long.); most southerly point Cape Agulhas, 34°50′S. On W, Atlantic Ocean (subdivision Gulf of Guinea); chief islands St. Helena and Ascension in South Atlantic and Cape Verde, Canary, and Madeira Is. groups in North Atlantic; most westerly point Cape Vert, 17°30′W. *Mountains:* Atlas Mts. in NW (highest 13,661 ft.); high plateau region of Ethiopia in NE, Mts. Kenya and Kilimanjaro (its peak Mt. Kibo, highest in Africa 19,317 ft.) and Ruwenzori in E, and the Drakensberg in E part of Republic of So. Africa. Other notable physical features are the great desert of the Sahara in the N, partly desert region of the Sudan, the smaller Libyan and Nubian Deserts of Egypt bordering the Nile valley, and the Kalahari Desert in the S; nearly all the S third of the continent is plateau region. *Rivers:* Nile in NE, Niger and Senegal in W, Congo in cen. part, and Zambezi, Orange, and Limpopo in S. *Lakes:* Victoria, Tanganyika, Albert, and Rudolf in E, sources of the Nile or Congo, and Nyasa in SE with outlet to the Zambezi; in cen. Sudan is Chad, with area much reduced in dry season.

Political divisions: Algeria, Botswana, Burundi (formerly, with Rwanda, the Belgian trust territory of Ruanda-Urundi), Cameroon, Central African Republic (formerly Ubangi-Shari), Chad, Republic of Congo (✳ Brazzaville; formerly Middle Congo), Republic of the Congo (✳ Kinshasa; formerly Belgian Congo), Dahomey, Ethiopia, Gabon, Gambia, Ghana, Guinea, Ivory Coast, Kenya, Lesotho, Liberia, Libya, Malagasy Republic, Malawi (formerly Nyasaland), Mali (formerly Sudanese Republic and, earlier, French Sudan), Mauritania, Morocco, Niger, Nigeria, Rwanda, Senegal, Sierra Leone, Somalia, Republic of South Africa, Republic of the Sudan (formerly Anglo-Egyptian Sudan), Tanzania (formerly Tanganyika and Zanzibar), Togo, Tunisia, Uganda, United Arab Republic, Upper Volta, Zambia (formerly Northern Rhodesia)—all independent countries; also Southern Rhodesia (a British colony); Swaziland (a British dependency); French Somaliland (a French overseas territory); Angola, Cape Verde Islands, Mozambique, Portuguese Guinea, Principe and São Tomé islands (Portuguese overseas territories); Ifni, Spanish Sahara, Río Muni, Fernando Poo (Spanish provinces). For description and history of these countries, see individual entries.

Africa, Roman. Proconsular Roman province (*Lat.* **Af′ri·ca Pro′con·su·la′ris** [ăf′rĭ·ká prō′kŏn·sū·lâr′ĭs]) formed after 146 B.C. from territory around Carthage, extended to include Numidia and N part of modern Libya. Later (bet. 30 B.C. and A.D. 180) Egypt, Cyrenaica, Marmarica, and Mauretania became parts of Roman Empire; lost to Vandals in 5th cent. except for Egypt which was part of Byzantine Empire, later 641 conquered by Mohammedans.

A·fri′ki·ya (ä·frē′kĭ·yá; -yä). Arabic name for TUNISIA.

A·frine′ (ä·frēn′). River ab. 90 m. long in Hatay vilayet and NW Syria; rises in Gaziantep vilayet, S Turkey in Asia, flows S and SW through swamp region to join the Orontes at Antakya (Antioch).

A′frique′, Cape (ä′frēk′). Cape, E Tunisia, N Africa.

Af′ton (ăf′tŭn). 1 River, SE Ayrshire, Scotland, flowing N to the Nith; 9 m. long.
2 Town, Lincoln co., SW Wyoming; pop. 1337.

A·fu′la (ä·fōō′lá). Town, N Israel, 6 m. S of Nazareth; pop. 10,000; railway junction; built 1925.

A·fyon′ Ka′ra·hi·sar′ (ä·fyōn′ kä′rä·hĭ·sär′), *formerly* **A·fiun′ Ka′ra·his·sar′** (ä·fyōōn′). 1 Vilayet, W cen. Turkey in Asia; 4887 sq. m.; pop. 299,248.
2 City, its ✳, on railroad 128 m. NW of Konya; pop. 24,159; center of opium trade. Captured by Greeks March 1921, and retaken by Turks August 1921 during Greco-Turkish war.

Agade. See AKKAD city.

A′ga′dès′ (ä′gà′dĕs′). City, ✳ of Air region, Niger, West Africa; on caravan route from Libya S to Nigeria; said to have been founded by Berbers as center for their trade with Songhai empire.

A′ga·dir′ (ä′gà·dîr′; ăg′à-). Seaport, SW Morocco, S of Mogador and ab. 120 m. SW of Marrakesh; pop. (1958) ab. 45,000; founded in early 16th cent. by Portuguese; later became important port of Morocco. Visited by German gunboat *Panther* 1911 to protect German interests in Morocco (incident which brought on second Moroccan crisis: see MOROCCO); opened to commerce as a projected port Jan. 1, 1930. In World War II Allied forces landed here Nov. 1942; destroyed by earthquakes Feb. 29–Mar. 1, 1960.

A′ga·le′ga Islands (ä′gà·lā′gà; ăg′à-; -lĕg′á). Group of small British islands in Indian Ocean ENE of Madagascar; dependency of Mauritius.

Ag′a·men′ti·cus (ăg′à·měn′tĭ·kŭs; *locally* ăd′à·măt′ĭ·kŭs), **Mount.** Elevation 673 ft., S York co., SW Maine, ab. 4 m. from coast, 43°13′N lat.; a sailors' landmark.

A·ga′na (ä·gä′nyä). Town on W coast of island of Guam, on **Agana Bay** ab. 8 m. NE of Apra Harbor, Mariana Islands, W Pacific Ocean; ✳ of Guam; pop. 1642.

A′gar (ä′gär). Short river, dry at certain seasons, N Tripolitania, NW Libya, N Africa; flows N into Gulf of Sidra.

A′gar (ŭ′gẽr). Town NW Madhya Pradesh, 40 m. NNE of Ujjain; pop. 30,000.

A′gar·ta·la (ŭ′gẽr·tà·lä′). Town, ✳ of Tripura territory, NE Indian Union, 60 m. E of Dacca; pop. 9580.

Ag′as·siz, Mount (ăg′à·sē). Peak 12,433 ft., NW Duchesne co., NE cen. Utah.

Agassiz Needle. Peak 13,882 ft. in Sierra Nevada, E Fresno co., S cen. California.

Agassiz Peak. See SAN FRANCISCO PEAKS.

Agatha. See AGDE.

Ag′at·tu′ (ăg′à·tōō′). Island, Near Is. group at W end of Aleutian Is., SW Alaska, SE of Attu; highest point 3089 ft.; temporarily occupied by Japanese from ab. June to October 1942.

Ag′a·wam (ăg′à·wŏm; -wôm). 1 Indian village on site of Ipswich, Essex co., Massachusetts; sold to white settlers 1638. Cultural center in 17th cent.; residence of Anne Bradstreet and of Nathaniel Ward, author of *The Simple Cobbler of Aggawam in America* (1645).
2 Town, Hampden co., Massachusetts 4 m. SW of Springfield; pop. 15,718; settled 1636, incorp. 1885.

Ag·dam′ (äg·däm′). Town, SW Azerbaidzhan, U.S.S.R., 20 m. NE of Stepanakert.

Agde (ägd); *anc.* **Ag′a·tha** (ăg′à·thá). Commune, Hérault dept., S France, 30 m. SW of Montpellier; pop. 8503. Settled 6th cent. B.C. by Phocaeans; held by Visigoths; episcopal see 400–1790; 12th-cent. medieval fortress cathedral (St. Étienne).

A′ge·da′bia (ä′jà·dä′byä). Road junction, N Libya, N Africa, near E coast of Gulf of Sidra; battle Jan. 1942 bet. British and Germans in first retreat of Rommel's *Afrika Corps.*

A′gen′ (à′zhăɴ′); *anc.* **A·gin′num** (à·jĭn′ŭm). City, ✳ of Lot-et-Garonne dept., SW France, on Garonne river 74 m. SE of Bordeaux; pop. 27,152; manufactures textiles. Capital of Agenais (*q.v.*); a bishopric since 4th cent. A.D.; at end of Albigensian Crusade, location of an inquisition tribunal; joined Catholic League against Huguenots 1589.

A'ge·nais' (ázh'ně') *or* **A'ge·nois'** (ázh'nwȧ'). Historical region, SW France; part of ancient Guienne; * Agen.

History: Home of Nitiobriges in ancient Gaul; in 4th cent. A.D. *Civitas Agennensium* which formed diocese of Agen (*q.v.*); part of Aquitaine (*q.v.*); acquired by dukes of Aquitaine as a hereditary countship 1038; passed to England 1152; given by Richard I as part of dowry of his sister Joan who married Raymond VI of Toulouse 1196; lapsed to French crown 1271; restored to England 1279; changed hands frequently in Hundred Years' War, but French after 1453; reunited to French crown 1615.

A'gen·cy Division (ā'jěn·sĭ). Former district, N Madras prov., E India, comprising the hill regions of Ganjam, Vizagapatam, and East Godavari districts; 19,869 sq. m.; pop. 1,763,765.

Agency Lake. Inlet at N end of Upper Klamath Lake, Klamath co., S Oregon.

Agendicum. See SENS.

Agenois. See AGENAIS.

Agg'te·lek (ŏg'tě·lěk). Village, N Hungary, 28 m. NNW of Miskolc; pop. 648; site of great limestone grotto with stalactites, underground stream, and many passages, of archaeological interest.

Agheila, El. See EL AGHEILA.

Aghri Dagh. Var. of *Aǧrī Daǧï:* see ARARAT.

Aghrim. See AUGHRIM.

Agiguan. See AGUIJAN.

Ag'in·court (ăj'ĭn·kōrt); *Fr.* **A'zin'court'** (à'zăN'kōōr'). Village, Pas-de-Calais dept., N France, 33 m. WNW of Arras; scene of victory of Henry V of England over a larger force of French, demonstrating effectiveness of warfare by archers against heavily armed feudal array Oct. 25, 1415.

Aginnum. See AGEN.

A·ginsk' Bur·yat'–Mon'gol National District (ŭ·gĭnsk' bōōr·yàt'mǒng'gŏl). National district, SE Siberia, in SW part of Chita Region, Soviet Russia, Asia, an area SE of Chita; 10,730 sq. m.; pop. (1941 est.) 32,000; * Aginskoe. Formed 1937; inhabited by a branch of the Buryat-Mongols.

A·gin'sko·e (ŭ·gēn'skŭ·yě). Town, * of Aginsk Buryat-Mongol National District, Soviet Russia, Asia, on a tributary of the Shilka river ab. 70 m. SE of Chita.

Agion Oros. = *Hagion Oros:* see *Mount Athos* at ATHOS.

A·gi'ra (ä·jē'rä); *anc.* **A·gyr'i·um** (à·jĭr'ĭ·ŭm). Commune, Enna prov., cen. Sicily, 15 m. ENE of Enna; pop. 15,350; ancient Siculian city colonized with Greeks by Timoleon 339 B.C. In World War II taken by Americans and Canadians July 29, 1943.

Aglar. See AQUILEIA.

A'gna·del'lo (ä'nyä·děl'lô). Village, Cremona prov., N Italy, N of Lodi; scene of defeat of Venetians by the French (as member of League of Cambrai) May 14, 1509.

Ag'no (äg'nô). River 128 m. long, NW Luzon, Phil. Is.; rises in Benguet subprov. and flows S and SW through Pangasinan prov., then N to Lingayen Gulf near Lingayen; course is through flood plain of rich soil; has many tributaries and extensive delta; one of the important rivers of Luzon. In World War II much fighting on its banks 1942 and when Americans landed January 1945.

A·gno'ne (ä·nyô'nå). Commune, Campobasso prov., Abruzzi e Molise, cen. Italy, 22 m. NW of Campobasso; pop. 9579.

A'goeng, Goe'noeng (gōō'nŏōng ä'gōōng); *or* **Ba'li Peak** (bä'lē). Volcanic mountain (Malay *gunung*) 10,308 ft., NE Bali, Indonesia.

A'goo' (ä'gô·ô'). Municipality, S La Union prov., Luzon, Phil. Is., on main highway and railroad near coast 21 m. S of San Fernando; pop. 13,938; one of oldest towns in the Malay Archipelago. Scene of fight-ing in Japanese invasion Dec. 1941 and on return of American forces Jan. 1945.

A·gor·dat (à·gōr·dàt; *Angl.* à·gôr'dăt, äg'ěr·dăt'). Town, NW Eritrea, NE Africa, ab. 75 m. W of Asmara; terminal of railroad from Massaua and of highway W to Kassala in Sudan. Taken by British Feb. 2, 1941.

Agosta. See AUGUSTA, Italy.

Agostini, Cordillera de. See ANDES.

A'gout' (à'gōō'). River ab. 110 m. long, S tributary of Tarn, Hérault and Tarn depts., S France.

A'gra (ä'grȧ; ä'grä). **1** Former presidency, a division of Bengal Presidency 1833–35, NE India; became 1835 a province with the name of North-West Provinces, which with Oudh was placed under one administrator 1877 and name changed 1902 to United Provinces of Agra and Oudh (*q.v.*).
2 A former province of India; now the W portion of Uttar Pradesh; 82,176 sq. m.; pop. (1941) 40,906,147.
3 Former Division, Agra prov., W cen. Uttar Pradesh; 8646 sq. m.; pop. (1941) 5,326,768.
4 District of Agra div.; 1861 sq. m.; pop. (1941) 1,289,774.
5 City, * of division and district, on right bank of Jumna river 110 m. SE of Delhi; pop. 375,665.

History: Captured by Baber, founder of Mogul Empire, 1526; present city created by Mohammedan conquerors of northern India; stone fort begun by Akbar 1564; Mogul capital until 1658; visited by John Miedenhall, first representative of English East India Co. to reach capital 1603; site of magnificent examples of Indo-Saracenic architecture, including Taj Mahal, built c. 1631–45 as tomb of Shah Jahan's empress, the Fort (within which is the imperial palace of Akbar, the Pearl Mosque or Moti Masjid of Shah Jahan, and the Hall of Private Audience or Diwan-i-Khas) and the Tomb of Itmad-ud-Daulah; captured 1784 by Sindhia, a Maratha dynasty; taken 1803 by British under Lake in Second Maratha War; capital of North-West Provinces 1835–62; besieged by sepoys 1857; after removal of capital to Allahabad, became headquarters of district and division of Agra.

Agra and Oudh, United Provinces of. See UNITED PROVINCES OF AGRA AND OUDH.

Agram. See ZAGREB.

A'gra·mon'te (ä'grä·môn'tå). Municipality and town, Matanzas prov., W cen. Cuba, SE of Matanzas; pop. (munic.) 10,804.

A'gri (ä'grē). Small river, Lucania, S Italy; flows E into the head of Gulf of Taranto.

Aǧ·rï' (ä·rĭ'). Vilayet, E Turkey in Asia; 5142 sq. m.; pop. 103,244; * Bayazıt.

Aǧrï Daǧï. See ARARAT.

Ag'ri Dec'u·ma'tes (äg'rī děk'ů·mā'tēz). Roman district, E and N of the upper Rhine and N of the Danube (approximately Baden and W Württemberg of modern Germany) taken from Germans as they retired eastward; later given to Gauls and to Roman veterans as tithe lands (Lat. *agri decumates*); incorporated in the Empire 2d cent. A.D.

A'gri·gen'to (ä'grē·jěn'tô); *formerly* **Gir·gen'ti** (jěr·jěn'tě). **1** Province of Italy. See *Table* at ITALY.
2 *anc.* **Ag'ri·gen'tum** (äg'rī·jěn'tŭm) *or* **Ac'ra·gas** (ăk'rȧ·gȧs); *Gr.* **Ak'ra·gas**. Commune, its *, SW Sicily, Italy, near SW coast 57 m. SSE of Palermo; pop. 32,951; archaeological ruins; exports sulfur. Founded by colonists from Gela c. 580 B.C.; destroyed by Carthage 406 B.C.; rebuilt by Timoleon, a leader of Syracuse; scene of defeat of Carthaginian general Hanno by Romans 262 B.C. In World War II taken by Americans July 22, 1943.

A'gri·han' (ä'grē·hän') *or* **A'gri·gan'** (-gän'). Volcanic island ab. 6 m. long by 2 m. wide, N end of Mariana Is., W Pacific Ocean, 18°46'N lat. and 145°40'E long.; highest point 3166 ft. American and Hawaiian colony formed here 1810, but destroyed by Spanish. Taken by U.S. forces Aug. 1945.

A·gri′ni·on (ä·grē′nyôn); *formerly also* **Vra·kho′ri** (vrä·kô′rĕ). Town, Aetolia and Acarnania dept., W Central Greece and Euboea, Greece; pop. 14,562; in tobacco-growing region.

A′gua (ä′gwä). Volcano 12,139 ft., SW of Guatemala city, Guatemala.

A′gua Ca′li·en′te (ä′[g]wä käl′ĭ·ĕn′tĕ). Former village, Lower California state, NW Mexico, now a district of Tijuana; races.

A′gua·ca′te (ä′gwä·kä′tä). Municipality and town, La Habana prov., W Cuba, 36 m. E of Havana; pop. (munic.) 11,118.

A′gua Cla′ra (ä′gwä klä′rä). River in Panama E of the Panama Canal; flows SW into E Gatun Lake.

A·gua′da (ä·gwä′thä). Municipality and town, NW Puerto Rico, near S shore of Aguadilla Bay; pop. (munic.) 23,234; founded 1511 and claims to be oldest settlement on island; raises sugar cane.

Aguada de Pa′sa·je′ros (thä pä′sä·hā′rôs). Municipality, SW Las Villas prov., Cuba, 30 m. NW of Cienfuegos; pop. 25,248.

A·gua′das (ä·gwä′thäs). Town, Caldas dept., W cen. Colombia, 50 m. S of Medellín; pop. 7631; Panama hats manufactured, gold and silver mined.

A′gua de Dios (ä′gwä thä thyôs′). Town, Cundinamarca dept., cen. Colombia; pop. 7213.

A′gua·dil′la (ä′gwä·thē′yä). Municipality and seaport, NW Puerto Rico; pop. (munic.) 47,864 and (town) 15,943; has extensive trade in sugar, tobacco, coffee, cotton, and fruit; site of park and memorial. Founded 1775; probably visited by Columbus 1493.

Aguadilla Bay. Bay on W coast of Aguadilla municipality, NW Puerto Rico.

A′gua·dul′ce (ä′gwä·thōol′sä). Pacific coast port, SW cen. Panama, at head of Gulf of Parita; pop. 2829.

A′gua Fri′a (ä′[g]wä frē′ä). River in Arizona; rises in cen. Yavapai co., flows S to empty into Gila river in cen. Maricopa co. W of Phoenix. See LAKE PLEASANT DAM.

A·guán′ (ä·gwän′). River, N Honduras; flows E and NE into Caribbean Sea.

A′gua Pre′ta, Lake (ä′gwá prā′tá). Lake, N Maranhão state, NE Brazil.

A′gua Pri·e′ta (ä′gwä prĕ·ā′tä). Town, Sonora state, NW Mexico; pop. 4106; plan of Agua Prieta 1920 was formal statement of aims of revolutionists seeking to depose Carranza.

A′gua·ri′co (ä′gwä·rē′kô). River ab. 240 m. long, N Ecuador; flows ESE into Napo river.

A′guas Bue′nas (ä′gwäz vwā′näs). Municipality and town, E cen. Puerto Rico; pop. (munic.) 17,034.

A′guas·ca·lien′tes (ä′gwäs·kä·lyän′tás). **1** State, cen. Mexico. See *Table* at MEXICO.
2 City, its ✱, by rail 364 m. NW of Mexico City; pop. 82,234; alt. ab. 6200 ft.; fine climate with mineral springs; built above intricate system of tunnels, prob. work of unknown early race; founded 1575; made capital 1835.

Aguera, La. See LA AGUERA.

A′gui·jan′ (ä′gē·hän′) *or* **A′gi·guan′** (ä′gē·gwän′). Small island, S Mariana Islands, W Pacific Ocean, off S end of Tinian I.

A′gui·lar′ (ä′gē·lär′) *or* **Aguilar de la Fron·te′ra** (thä lä frôn·tā′rä). Commune, Córdoba prov., S Spain, by rail 35 m. S of Córdoba; pop. 16,091; olive groves and vineyards; in Middle Ages on border of Moorish lands.

A′gui·las (ä′gē·läs). Seaport, Murcia prov., SE Spain, 40 m. SW of Cartagena; pop. 15,166.

A·guir′re (ä·gēr′rä). Barrio, Salinas municipality, S Puerto Rico; pop. 8645.

A·gu′ja, Cape (ä·gōō′hä); *Span.* **Ca′bo de la Aguja** (kä′vô thä lä). Cape extending into Caribbean Sea on N coast of Colombia, E of Barranquilla.

Aguja, Point; *Span.* **Pun′ta de Aguja** (pōōn′tä thä). Cape on NW coast of Peru, extending W into the Pacific Ocean.

A·gu·je·re·a′da, Point (ä′gōō·hä′rá·ä′thä). Cape on NW extremity of Puerto Rico.

A′gu·ji′ta (ä′gōō·hē′tä). Town, Coahuila state, NE Mexico; pop. 5069.

A·gul′has, Cape (á·gŭl′ás; *Port.* á·gōō′lyásh). Most S point of Africa, 100 m. ESE of Cape of Good Hope, at 34°50′S lat., 20°E long. (the meridian that serves as dividing line bet. Atlantic and Indian Oceans); lighthouse.

Agulhas Current. See MOZAMBIQUE CURRENT.

A′gung, Gu′nong (gōō′nŏng ä′goong). = Goenoeng AGOENG.

A′gus (ä′gōōs). River ab. 16 m. long, outlet of Lake Lanao, Lanao prov., Mindanao, Phil. Is.; flows N from lake to Iligan Bay.

A·gu′san (ä·gōō′sän). **1** River ab. 150 m. long, Davao and Agusan provs., E Mindanao, Phil. Is.; rises in highlands of SE Davao and flows N through Agusan prov. to Butuan Bay, forming fertile valley 40 to 50 m. wide; navigable in lower course.
2 Province, NE Mindanao, Phil. Is.; 4120 sq. m.; pop. 99,023; ✱ Butuan; bounded on N by Butuan Bay, on NE and E by Surigao prov., on S by Davao prov., and on W by Bukidnon prov.; largely coextensive with wide fertile valley of Agusan river; in NE includes ab. two thirds of Lake Mainit. Mountainous along E and W boundaries, esp. Diuata Mts., highest Mt. Hilonghilong 6027 ft.; in S is large marsh and lake region in middle course of Agusan river. Because of fine climate and rich soil agriculture is chief industry, although fishing along shores of Butuan Bay is important. Chief crops hemp (abacá), tobacco, corn, and fruits; also profitable gold mines. Inhabitants are mainly of the non-Christian tribe of Manobos. Has only three towns of any size Butuan, Cabadbaran, and Buenavista, but many small barrios. In Spanish times a part of Surigao prov.; established as separate province by Americans Sept. 1914; missionaries active on lower Agusan in 17th and 18th cents.; later often suffered from raids of Moros.

A′gu·ta′ya (ä′gōō·tä′yä). Small island in Cuyo group, Palawan prov., cen. Phil. Is., N of Cuyo I.; 6 sq. m.;

Agylla. See CAERE.

Agyrium. See AGIRA.

A·hag′gar (á·hăg′ẽr; ä′hă·gär′), *or* **Hog′gar** (hŏg′ẽr; hŏ·gär′), **Mountains.** High plateau region in cen. Sahara, S part of Oasis Sahariennes Terr., S Algeria; highest peaks 8000–10,000 ft.

A′hi·pa′ra Bay (ä′hē·pä′rä). Bay on extreme NW coast of N extension of North Island, New Zealand.

Ah′len (ä′lĕn). Manufacturing town, W Germany, in West Rhine-Westphalia state 19 m. SE of Münster; pop. 22,357; manufactures zinc and tin ware, machines, shoes, etc.

Ah′mad·a·bad′ (ä′mád·á·bäd′; -á·băd′; *native pron.* ä′mád·á·bäd′) *or* **Ah′med·a·bad′.** **1** Former district in Northern Division of former Bombay prov., W Indian Union; 3879 sq. m.; pop. (1941) 1,372,171.
2 City, its ✱ and ✱ of Gujarat state (formed 1960); on left bank of Sabarmati river 290 m. N of Bombay; pop. (1951) 788,333. One of most beautiful cities of India, has many fine buildings, including Jama Masjid (Great Mosque) and Tomb of Ahmad Shah, Hathi Singh Jain temple (built 1848); important rail junction.
History: Founded in 1411 by Ahmad I of Gujarat on site of previous Hindu cities; built 1411–42; at height in 15th cent. as capital of Gujarat kingdom; declined 1512–72 with Gujarat dynasty; revived under Mogul emperors 1572–1709; reverted to British with other holdings of Peshwa 1818; became modern manufacturing and trading center, esp. noted for cotton textiles; associated with Indian nationalist cause as scene of an anti-British rebellion 1918 and of beginning of Gandhi's efforts 1930 and his arrest 1933.

Ah′mad·na′gar (-nŭg′ẽr) *or* **Ah′med·na′gar.** **1** Dis-

trict, Central division, Bombay prov., W Indian Union; 6646 sq. m.; pop. (1941) 1,142,229.

2 City, its ✱, 64 m. NE of Poona; pop. (1941) 54,193. Founded 1494 as one of the five Mohammedan kingdoms of the Deccan (*q.v.*); conquered by Shah Jahan 1636 when it became part of Mogul Empire; exchanged several times between British and Marathas in wars of 18th cent.; seized by Gen. Wellesley 1803; ceded to British by Treaty of Poona 1817; has fort and cantonment.

A·hos′kie (*à*·hŏs′kĭ). Town, Hertford co., NE North Carolina, 44 m. W of Elizabeth City; pop. 4583; manufactures lumber, baskets; produces tobacco, peanuts, cotton.

A′hua·cha·pán′ (ä′wä·chä·pän′). **1** Department, SW El Salvador; 804 sq. m.; pop. (1942 est.) 103,198.

2 Town, its ✱, near Guatemala border; alt. 2470 ft.; pop. (1942 est.) 13,505; has trade in coffee, tobacco, cereals, sugar.

A′hua·lul′co de Mer·ca′do (ä′wä·lōōl′kŏ thä mĕr·kä′thŏ). Town, Jalisco state, W cen. Mexico, 38 m. W of Guadalajara; pop. 6433.

A′hu·ri′ri (ä′hōō·rē′rē; *colloq.* ou·rẹr′ẹ). River, S cen. South Island, New Zealand; one of the headstreams of the Waitaki.

Ah′ve·nan·maa′ (äk′vĕ·nän·mä′), *or* **Å′land′ Islands** (ō′länd′). Archipelago in S Gulf of Bothnia bet. Sweden and Finland, constituting a dept. of Finland; area including water 581 sq. m.; pop. (1937 est.) 28,248; ✱ Maarianhamina; of ab. 300 total islands and rocky islets, 80 inhabited; chief island **Ahvenanmaa** *or* **Åland.** Colonized early (12th cent.) by Swedes; Swedish fleet defeated and islands seized by Peter the Great 1714; restored by Russia to Sweden 1721; ceded with Finland by Sweden to Russia 1809; subject of international disputes and treaties in 19th cent.; part of independent Finland 1917; neutralized and demilitarized by treaty 1921–22.

Ah·waz′ (ä·wäz′; *native* à·hwäz′). Town, Khuzistan prov., SW Iran, on the Karun river ab. 70 m. NNE of Khorramshahr; pop. ab. 30,000; junction point on old highways; connected by rail with Persian Gulf port of Bandar Shahpur; has oil pipelines; important commercially, esp. in oil business. Under the Arabs in 12th and 13th cents. was a trade center for sugar, rice, and silk; modern town laid out on extensive ruined area of ancient Persian city. Its suburb Bandar Nasiri on the Karun is an official port of entry.

A′i (ā′ĭ; ī). Town in mountains of E Canaan, ancient Palestine, SE of Bethel; destroyed by Joshua (*Josh.* vii–viii).

Ai′bo·ni′to (ī′vō·nē′tō). Municipality (pop. 18,360) and town (pop. 5477), SE cen. Puerto Rico, 30 m. NW of Guayama.

Ai·chi (ī·chē). Prefecture of Japan. See *Table* at JAPAN.

Aidin. See AYDIN.

A′i·e′a (ä′ẹ·ä′ä). Town, Ewa dist., Honolulu co., S Oahu, Hawaii, on E shore of Pearl Harbor; pop. 11,826.

Aigina. See AEGINA.

Ai′gi·on (ä′yôn) *or* **Ae′gi·um** (ē′jĭ·ŭm). Seaport town, Achaea and Elis dept., NW Peloponnesus, Greece, on Gulf of Corinth; pop. 11,011; currant export trade.

Aigues′–Mortes′ (ĕg′môrt′); *anc.* **Aq′uae Mor′tu·ae** (ăk′wē môr′tụ̄·ē; ā′kwē). Commune, Gard dept., S France, in Rhone estuary 25 m. SSW of Nîmes; pop. 3411. Founded by St. Louis who connected it by canal with Gulf of Lions and used it as embarkation point for Sixth Crusade 1248 and Seventh Crusade 1270; fortified 1272 by Philip the Bold; of little importance today except for Tour de Constance and fine medieval military ramparts.

Aiguille d′Argentière. See Aiguille d′ARGENTIÈRE.

Aiguille de Chambeyron. See Aiguille de CHAMBEYRON.

Ai′guille′ Verte (ä′gü̈ē′y′ vĕrt′). Peak 13,520 ft. in the

Pennine Alps, S Switzerland, NE of Mont Blanc.

Ai·gun′ (ī·gōōn′); *Chin.* **Hei′lung′kiang′–cheng′** (hā′lōōng′jĭ·äng′chŭng′). Treaty port, NE Heilungkiang prov., N Manchuria, on the Amur river 20 m. below and S of Blagoveshchensk, Russia; pop. (1931 est.) 38,112. By treaty signed here 1858 China ceded left bank of Amur and right bank below the Ussuri to Russia; destruction by fire 1900 followed by decline in trade.

Aijal. See LUSHAI HILLS.

Ai′ja·lon (ā′jà·lŏn; ĭ′-) *or* **Aj′a·lon** (ăj′à·lŏn). Town in valley of Aijalon, anc. Palestine, 13 m. NW of Jerusalem. On frontier of kingdoms of Ephraim and Judah; valley scene of Biblical episode in which Joshua commanded the sun and moon to stand still (*Josh.* x. 12); assigned to tribe of Dan.

Ai·ka·wa (ī·kä·wä). See SADO.

Ai′ken (ā′kĕn). **1** County in South Carolina. See *Table* at SOUTH CAROLINA.

2 City, its ⊗, W South Carolina, 52 m. SW of Columbia; pop. 11,243; winter health and pleasure resort; textile and lumber mills, kaolin mining and refining; granite quarries. Scene of battle bet. Federal and Confederate troops Feb. 1865.

Ai′lette′ (ā′lĕt′). Small river ab. 40 m. long, Aisne dept., N France, tributary of Oise from SE near Laon; in World War I severe fighting along its banks Oct. 1917 and Sept. 1918.

Ail′sa Craig (āl′sà krāg; krăg). Rocky island 1097 ft. high at mouth of Firth of Clyde 10 m. off coast of SW Scotland; lighthouse.

Aimorés, Serra dos. See SERRA DOS AIMORÉS.

Ain (ăN). **1** River 118 m. long, E France; rises in Jura Mts. and flows S into Rhone river.

2 Department of France. See *Table* at FRANCE.

Aïn′–Beï′da (in[än]′ bā′dà; -dă). Commune, Constantine dept., NE Algeria, ab. 72 m. by highway SE of Constantine; pop. 13,968.

Ain Ja·lut′ (in[än] jà·lōōt′); *Arab.* **‘Ayn Jā·lūt′.** Locality near Nazareth in Palestine; here in 1260 Mongol army of Hulagu destroyed by the Mamelukes of Egypt, and Syria recovered.

‘Ain Jidi. See EN-GEDI.

Ai·no·ta·ke (ī·nŏ·tä·kĕ). See SHIRANE.

Aïn′–Se·fra′ (in[än]′ sŏ·frä′). **1** Territory of Algeria. See *Table* at ALGERIA.

2 Commune, its ✱, in Atlas Mts. 200 m. S of Oran; pop. 15,976.

Ains′worth (ānz′wûrth; -wĕrth). City, ⊗ of Brown co., N Nebraska, 65 m. W of O′Neill; pop. 1982; trade center for agricultural section.

Aintab. See GAZIANTEP.

A′ïn′–Té′mou′chent′ (à′ēn′tä′mōō′shäN′). Commune, Oran dept., NW Algeria, ab. 45 m. SW of Oran; pop. 17,478.

Ain′tree (ān′trē). Locality 5 m. N of Liverpool, Lancashire, England; racecourse where Grand National steeplechase is run every March.

A′ir (à′ēr′); *also* **As′ben** (àz′bĕn′), *better* **Az′bine** (àz′bēn′). Mountainous region of the Sahara, former native kingdom, N cen. Niger Republic, West Africa; ab. 30,000 sq. m.; ✱ Agadès; highest peaks ab. 5000 ft.; valleys and plains fertile with good pasturage; main products dates, millet, and senna. Inhabited by Tuaregs; a native kingdom, called Asben, until conquered by Berbers; recognized as in French sphere from 1890. See AGADÈS.

Air, Point of (âr). Point at mouth of Dee river, Flintshire, NE Wales.

Air′a Force (âr′à fōrs) *or* **Air′ey Force** (âr′ĭ). Waterfall (Scot. *force*) 80 ft. high in small stream flowing into Ullswater Lake, Cumberland, NW England, in the Lake District.

Air′drie (âr′drĭ). Burgh, Lanark co., S cen. Scotland, 11 m. E of Glasgow; pop. 30,308; deposits of coal and

iron nearby; cotton mills, brass founding, and engineering works.

Aire (âr). **1** River 70 m. long, W Yorkshire, England; flows SE and E through Leeds and industrial region to Ouse river; navigable to Leeds. **Aire′dale′** (-dāl′), valley of the Aire, original home of the Airedale terrier. **2** River ab. 80 m. long, Meuse and Ardennes depts., NE France; flows NW through the Argonne to Aisne river near Vouziers; severe fighting on its banks in World War I. **3** anc. **Vi′cus Ju′li·i** (vī′kŭs jōō′lĬ·ī); later **A·tu′ra** (a·tūr′a). Commune, Landes dept., SW France, on left bank of Adour ab. 20 m. SE of Mont-de-Marsan; pop. 3864; residence of the kings of the Visigoths; bishopric in 5th cent., later an episcopal town.

Ai·ro′lo (ī·rō′lō). Commune, Ticino canton, SE cen. Switzerland, at S end of St. Gotthard Tunnel in valley of Ticino river; pop. (1930) 1714.

Air′y, Mount (âr′Ĭ). Peak 6787 ft., SW cen. Lander co., cen. Nevada.

Aisén. See AYSÉN.

Ai′shi·hik (ā′shĬ·hĬk). Lake 107 sq. m., SW Yukon, Canada; outlet through Alsek river to the Pacific.

Aisne (ān; Fr. ân); anc. **Ax′o·na** (ăk′sŏ·na). **1** River ab. 175 m. long, N France; rises in Meuse dept., flows NW and W from Argonne Forest to Oise near Compiègne. Four major battles in valley in World War I: (1) Defeat of Germans Sept. 15–18, 1914 in their retreat from the Marne; (2) French seizure Apr.–July 1917 of heights (Chemin des Dames) N of Aisne; (3) German capture of heights May–June 1918; (4) final defeat of Germans by French and Americans Sept.–Oct. 1918. In World War II crossed Aug. 1944 by American troops in pursuit of Germans. **2** Department of France. See Table at FRANCE.

Ai′ta·pe′ (ī′tä·pā′; ī·tä′pá). **1** Administrative district, NW North-East New Guinea; 11,400 sq. m.; pop. (1930) 61,849. **2** Seaport town, its ✳, ab. 95 m. E of Dutch border; government station. American forces landed here and at Hollandia April 22, 1944; airfields taken; large Japanese force cut off.

Ait′kin (āt′kĬn). **1** County in Minnesota. See Table at MINNESOTA. **2** Village, its ⊗, E cen. Minnesota, on Mississippi river 26 m. ENE of Brainerd; pop. 1829; shipping center for dairy products, turkeys, and small fruits.

Ai·to·li′a (Mod. Gr. â′tô·lyē′ä). Var. of AETOLIA.

Ai·tō·li′a kai A′kar·na·ni′a (â′tô·lyē′ä kâ ä′kär·nä·nyē′ä). Modern Greek form of Aetolia and Acarnania, department of Greece: see Table at GREECE.

Ai′tu·ta′ki (ī′tōō·tä′kē). Island, NW Cook Islands, S Pacific Ocean, NW of Rarotonga; 18°55′S lat.; 7 sq. m.; pop. (1936) 1719; chief village Arutanga; has wide surrounding reef and large lagoon (5 m. across); second to Rarotonga in importance; annexed to New Zealand 1901.

A′iud (ä′yŏŏd); Hung. **Nagy′e′nyed** (nŏd′y·ĕ′nyĕd); Ger. **Strass′burg** (shträs′bŏŏrκ). Town, S Transylvania, Romania, on Mureş river 10 m. N of Alba Iulia; pop. ab. 9000.

Ai·va·li′ (ī·vä·lĭ′). Var. of AYVALIK.

Aix (āks; Fr. ĕks) or **Aix′–en–Pro′vence′** (ĕk′–säN–prô′väNs′); anc. **Aq′uae Sex′ti·ae** (ăk′wē sĕks′tĬ·ē; ä′kwē). City, Bouches-du-Rhône dept., SE France, 20 m. N of Marseilles; pop. 42,615. Founded as military colony by Romans 123 B.C.; scene of defeat 102 B.C. of the Teutones by Marius; chief city of E Narbonensis (4th cent.); occupied by Visigoths 477, by Saracens 731; in Middle Ages as capital of Provence reached high cultural levels; became part of France 1487; seat of parlement of Provence 1501–1789; has cathedral, baths, place; seat of faculties of law and letters of Univ. of Aix-Marseille.

Aix–la–Chapelle. See AACHEN city.

Aix′–les–Bains′ (ĕks′lä·băN′; ĕs′-); anc. **Aq′uae Gra′ti·a′nae** (ăk′wē grä′shĬ·ā′nē; ā′kwē). Commune, Savoie dept., E France, on SE shore of Lake Bourget 9 m. N of Chambéry; pop. 12,889; watering place; its alum or sulfur baths famous in Roman times.

Aiz′pu·te (īz′pōō·tĕ). Administrative district, SW cen. Kurzeme prov., W Latvia; 637 sq. m.

A·jac′cio (à·yät′chŏ). Seaport commune, ✳ of Corse dept. (=island of Corsica), France, on N side of Gulf of Ajaccio on W coast of Corsica; pop. 37,146; episcopal see; coral and sardine fisheries. Became French 1768 (see CORSICA); birthplace of Napoleon; departmental capital 1810; Allied naval base in World War I.

A·jai′garh (à·jī′gär; native -gŭr·h′). Former Indian state, Bundelkhand, Central India group, India, SW of Allahabad; 788 sq. m.; pop. (1941) 96,596.

Ajalon. See AIJALON.

A·jan′ta (à jŭn′tà). Village in hills of cen. Maharashtra, S cen. India, NNE of Aurangabad; in ravine nearby are ab. 30 remarkable caves, the earliest dating from 200 B.C. to A.D. 200 and the latest from 7th cent. A.D., comprising halls and dormitories with walls covered with fresco paintings; caves discovered 1817, excavated by Buddhists.

Ajanta Range. Range of hills, cen. India, extending across N cen. Maharashtra; watershed for tributaries of Tapti and Godavari rivers.

Ajaria, Ajaristan. = ADZHAR.

A′jax Mountain (ā′jăks). Peak 10,900 ft. in Bitterroot Range on Montana-Idaho state boundary.

Aj·dir′ (ăj·dēr′). Town, on N coast of Morocco, near Alhucemas 50 m. W of Melilla; former Riffian capital.

Ajdir, Cape; Arab. **Ras Ajdir** (räs). Cape extending into the Mediterranean Sea on border between Tunisia and Libya.

A·ji·ka·wa (ä·jē·kä·wä). See YODO river.

Aj·mer′ (ŭj·mēr′; -mär′) or **Aj·mere′** (-mēr′). **1** Subdivision of former Ajmer-Merwara prov., NW Indian Union. **2** City, ✳ of Ajmer-Merwara prov., now in Rajasthan, 84 m. SW of Jaipur, situated at base of rocky hill Taragarh (3000 ft.); pop. (1941) 147,258. Conducts large trade in salt; manufactures oils and cotton cloths, and is famous for its dyeing of the latter.
  History: Founded c. 145 A.D.; stronghold of Chauhan Rajputs until 12th cent.; conquered 1193 by the Mohammedan dynasty at Delhi (q.v.); feudal state dependent upon Delhi until 1365; ruled by Udaipur (q.v.) until captured by Mogul emperor Akbar 1556; in 1770 given to Marathas under whom it was scene of violent upheavals until ceded to British 1818 by Maratha ruler of Gwalior after the Pindari War; has notable ruins, esp. dargah (tomb) of famous Mohammedan saint.

Aj·mer′–Mer·wa′ra (-mĕr·wä′rà). Former province of Rajputana, NW Indian Union, on E slopes of Aravalli Range; 2400 sq. m.; pop. (1941) 583,693; ✳ Ajmer.

Aj·na·da′in (ăj′nà·dā′ĭn); better **Jan′na·ba·ta′in** (jăn′à·bà·tā′ĭn). Village, S Palestine, just SW of Jerusalem; scene of victory 634 A.D. by Arabs over Theodorus, brother of Byzantine emperor Heraclius, which opened way for Moslem conquest of Syria.

A′jo (ä′hō). Town, Pima co., S Arizona; pop. 7049; mining.

A·jodh′ya (à·yōd′hyä); also **A·yodh′ya.** Former town, United Provs., N India, on right bank of Gogra river 6 m. E of Fyzabad; now part of that city (now in Uttar Pradesh). In ancient times one of the greatest of Indian cities; capital of kingdom of Kosala, as described in Ramayana; a revived Brahmanism under King Vikramaditya restored it c. 57 B.C. and ab. 400 A.D. it became capital of Chandragupta II; birthplace of founder of Jainism and center of pilgrimages. From it modern Oudh derives its name.

A·jus′co (ä·hōōs′kô). Volcanic mountain 13,612 ft.,

Federal District, Mexico, S of Mexico City and just N of Cuernavaca.

A'juy (ä'hwē). Municipality, NE Iloilo prov., Panay, Phil. Is., on Guimaras Strait NE of Iloilo; pop. 15,469.

Akaba, Akabah. See 'AQABA.

A·ka·gi (ä·kä·gē); *Jap.* **A·ka·gi·san** (-sän). Group of peaks 6210 ft. surrounding a volcanic crater (**Lake Akagi**), Gumma prefecture, cen. Honshu, Japan.

A·kai·shi (ä·kī·shē). Peak 10,145 ft., N part of Shizuoka prefecture, cen. Honshu, Japan.

A'ka·ko'a Point (ä'kä-kō'ä). Cape on N coast of Hawaii I., Hawaii.

A'kal·kot (ŭ'kŭl-kōt). **1** Former Indian state, Deccan and Kolhapur States, SE Bombay prov., W Indian Union; 473 sq. m.; pop. (1941) 103,903.
2 Town, its ✳, now in SE Maharashtra, 25 m. SE of Sholapur; pop. 10,857.

Akamagaseki. See SHIMONOSEKI.

A'ka–ma'ru (ä'kä·mä'rōō). Small island of Gambier Islands, S Pacific Ocean.

Akarai. Var. of *Acarahy:* see SERRA ACARAHY.

A'ka·rit', Wa'di (wä'dē ä'kä-rēt'). Gully in S cen. Tunisia, N of Gabès.

Ak'ar·na'ni·a (ăk'ēr·nä'nĭ·ȧ; ăk'är-; -nän'yȧ; *Mod. Gr.* ä'kär-nä·nyē'ä). Var. of ACARNANIA.

A'ka·ro'a (ä'kȧ·rō'ȧ). Borough, Canterbury provincial dist., E South Island, New Zealand, 30 m. SSE of Christchurch on **Akaroa Harbor**, an inlet in Banks Peninsula. Claimed by British 1840 a few days before arrival of French; some of French immigrants remained and descendants still live here.

A·ka·shi (ä·kä·shē). City, Hyogo pref., W Honshu, Japan, on coast 12 m. W of Kobe; pop. 65,642; separated from N end of Awaji I. by **Akashi Strait**, E end of Inland Sea; resort with fine scenery; its meridian 135°E is standard time meridian for Japan; important industrial city, with big Kawasaki plant.

A·kas'sa (ä·käs'ȧ). Village, SW Owerri prov., Eastern Region, Nigeria, at mouth of Niger. See BRASS.

Ak·çay (äk·chī'). Peak 9940 ft., SW Turkey in Asia, near Mediterranean coast W of Gulf of Antalya.

Ak'dağ' *or* **Ak Dağ** (äk'dä'). Name of several mountains in Turkey in Asia, esp.: (1) Range in cen. part W of SIVAS, highest point 8860 ft. (2) Peak 10,125 ft., SW of Antalya near coast. (3) Peak 9350 ft., in Taurus Mts. E of Cilician Gates. (4) Peak 8186 ft., SSW of Afyon Karahisar.

Ak·dar', Je'bel (jä'băl ăk·där'). Mountain range, Oman, SE Arabia; highest peak Jebel Sham, 9900 ft.

A'kers·hus' (ä'kērs·hōōs'). County of Norway. See *Table* at NORWAY.

Ak Göl (äk gûl). Salt lake (*göl*), S cen. Turkey in Asia, N of Taurus Mts.

A'kha·i'a kai Ē'lis (ä'kä·ē'ȧ kä ē'lyĕs). Modern Greek form of *Achaea and Elis*, department of Greece: see *Table* at GREECE.

A·khal'tsi·khe (ä·käl'tsĕ·kĕ). Town, S Georgia, U.S.S.R., near left bank of upper Kura river 65 m. E of Batum; pop. ab. 15,000; near Turkish border on old caravan route; trades in silk and, especially, in silver filigree work. Capital of Turkish Armenia 1579–1828; chief town of a pashalik of Ottoman Empire and center of slave trade; district ceded to Russia by Treaty of Adrianople 1829.

Akheloös. See ACHELOUS.

A'khi·nou' (ä'kĕ·nōō'), **Lake;** *anc.* **Ker'ki·ni'tis** (kûr'kĭ·nī'tĭs). Lake in course of lower Strymon river, E cen. Macedonia, Greece; town of Serrai is near its N end.

Ak'hi·sar' (äk'hĭ·sär'); *anc.* **Thy'a·ti'ra** (thī'ȧ·tī'rȧ). Town, N Manisa vilayet, W Turkey in Asia, 52 m. NE of İzmir; pop. 21,279. Ancient Greek city of Thyatira in Lydia was colonized and named 280 B.C. by Seleucus Nicator; its inhabitants famous for skill in dyeing purple; one of the Seven Churches of Asia Minor (*Rev.* i. 4, ii. 18–24).

Akh·mîm' *or* **Ekh·mîm'** (ŭк·mēm'); *anc.* **Chem'mis** (kĕm'ĭs); *later* **Pa·nop'o·lis** (pȧ·nŏp'ō·lĭs). Town on right bank of Nile river, Girga prov., Upper Egypt, above Asyût, ab. 26°40'N lat.; pop. ab. 25,000. Chemmis an important city of the Thebais; famous for its manufacture of linen and its limestone quarries; religious center, with temple of Pan (Egyptian Min).

Akhtiar. See SEVASTOPOL.

Akh·to'pol (äk·tŏ'pŏl). Seaport town, SE Bulgaria, on the Black Sea 35 m. SE of Burgas; pop. ab. 1000.

Akh·tyr'ka (ŭk·tĭr'kȧ). Town, Sumy Region, N Ukraine, U.S.S.R., ab. 65 m. WNW of Kharkov; pop. ab. 30,000; has beautiful cathedral, built 1753; center of annual religious pilgrimage.

A·ki (ä·kē). Old province, SW Honshu, Japan; now part of Hiroshima prefecture.

Ak'i·mis'ki Island (äk'ĭ·mĭs'kĭ). Island 60 m. long in James Bay opp. mouth of Attawapiskat river, S Hudson Bay, Keewatin Dist., Northwest Territories, Canada.

A·ki·ta (ä·kē·tä). **1** Prefecture of Japan. See *Table* at JAPAN.
2 City, its ✳, NW Honshu, on right bank of Omono river near its mouth; pop. 126,074; manufactures silk fabrics and gold and silver wares; large trade in lumber.

Ak'kad *or* **Ac'cad** (ăk'ăd; äk'äd). **1** The northern division of ancient Babylonia. From about 4th millennium B.C., inhabited by a leading Semitic people called the Akkadians; after a period of Sumerian rule (see SUMER) under Sargon I and Naram-Sin, developed empire which included Sumer, Elam, the upper Tigris, and northern Syria to the Mediterranean c. 2600–2420 B.C.; adopted Sumerian culture and developed great art (relief of Naram-Sin); lost supremacy after invasion by Gutians c. 2420 B.C.; united with Sumer under latter's leadership; invaded by Amorites (see BABYLON).
2 *anc.* **A·ga'de** (ä·gä'dĕ; ȧ·gä'dĕ). Ancient city, its ✳, in cen. Mesopotamia, placed by some near Sippar, Sargon's capital.

Akkerman. See BELGOROD-DNESTROVSKI.

Akkra. See ACCRA.

A·kla'vik (ȧ·klä'vĭk; ăk·läv'ĭk). Trading post on left bank of Mackenzie river near its mouth, NW Mackenzie District, Northwest Territories, Canada.

Ak Mechet. 1 See SIMFEROPOL.
2 = KZYL ORDA.

Ak'mo·linsk' (äk'mŏ·lĭnsk'; *Russ.* ŭk·mŭ·lyēnsk'). Town, ✳ of Akmolinsk Region, N cen. Kazakh S.S.R., Soviet Russia, Asia, on N bank of Ishim river near its source; pop. 12,770; in center of a steppe region having copper, coal, and gold mines; on caravan route from Tashkent to the S and an important junction point of railroads W to Magnitogorsk, N to Petropavlovsk, E to Pavlodar, and S to Balkhash.

Akmolinsk Region. Subdivision of Kazakh S.S.R., Soviet Russia, Asia, in N cen. part; bounded on N by Kokchetan Region, on E by Pavlodar Region, on S by Karaganda Region, and on W by Kustanai Region, all in the Kazakh Republic; ✳ Akmolinsk. Traversed by Ishim river and by two trunk railroads; Lake Tengiz in S.

A·ko'bo (ȧ·kō'bō). River, E cen. Africa, on border bet. Ethiopia and SE Sudan; flows NW into Pibor river.

Akobo Post. Town, Upper Nile prov., SE Sudan, at confluence of Akobo and Pibor rivers on border of Ethiopia.

A·ko'la (ȧ·kō'lȧ). **1** Former district, W Berar, SW Central Provinces, Indian Union; 4093 sq. m.; pop. (1941) 907,742.
2 City, its ✳, now in Maharashtra, 140 m. WSW of Nagpur; pop. (1941) 62,564; center of cotton trade.

Ak'pa·tok Island (ăk'pȧ·tŏk). Island at mouth of Ungava Bay, SE Franklin District, E Northwest Territories, Canada.

Akragas. See AGRIGENTO commune.

Akritas. See Cape GALLO.

Akroinon. See ACROÏNUM.

Ak'ron (ăk'rŭn). **1** Town, ⊗ of Washington co., NE Colorado; pop. 1890.

2 Village, Erie co., W New York, ab. 22 m. ENE of Buffalo; pop. 2841.

3 Manufacturing and industrial city, ⊗ of Summit co., NE Ohio, 35 m. SE of Cleveland on Little Cuyahoga river; on old Indian Portage Trail bet. Cuyahoga and Tuscarawas rivers; pop. 290,351. Settled ab. 1825, incorporated as village 1836, made county seat 1842, granted charter as city 1865; first rubber factory estab. 1869 by Dr. B. F. Goodrich; after 1910 began phenomenal growth due to demand for tires and other rubber goods; has varied manufactures, including aircraft; seat of former Buchtel College (founded 1870) taken over by city as Univ. of Akron (1913).

A'kro·te'ri Peninsula (ä'krô·tē'rē). Peninsula ab. 10 m. long, on N coast of Crete near W end; Canea is at its base on the W and Suda Bay enclosed by it on SE.

A'kro·ti'ri Bay (ä'krô·tē'rē). Inlet of Mediterranean Sea on S coast of Cyprus; Limassol is on it.

Ak·sa·ray' (äk·sä·rī'). **1** Former vilayet, cen. Turkey in Asia, now parts of Ankara and Niğde vilayets.

2 Town, N Niğde vilayet, NE of Konya; pop. 8344; highway junction point SE of Tuz Lake.

Ak·şe·hir' (äk·shě·hēr'), *formerly* **Ak·shehr'** (äk·shě'-h'r); *anc.* **Phil'o·me'li·on** (fĭl'ô·mē'lĭ·ŏn). Town, Konya vilayet SW cen. Turkey in Asia, on railroad 70 m. NW of Konya; pop. 10,370; on ancient highway in fertile plain S of Akşehir Gölü; known to Cicero and important as frontier town under Byzantine emperors; became a Seljuk town ab. 1400.

Akşehir Gö·lü' (gû·lü'). Lake (*gölü*), W cen. Turkey in Asia, E of Afyon Karahisar.

Ak'su (äk'sōō). **1** = *Aqsu*: see MURGHAB river, Tadzhik S.S.R.

2 River ab. 80 m. long, SW Turkey in Asia; flows S into Gulf of Antalya.

3 Town and oasis, China. See AQSU.

Ak·sum *or* **Ax·um** (äk·sōōm). Decayed town, Tigre prov., N Ethiopia; ab. 12 m. WSW of Aduwa; pop. ab. 5000. Capital of ancient Ethiopian kingdom known as the Axumite Empire which was ruled by Himyaritic emigrants from Arabia, 1st and 2d cents. A.D.; religious center which contained, according to tradition, the Ark of the Covenant brought from Jerusalem by descendant of Solomon and Queen of Sheba.

Ak'sur, el (ăl ōōk'sōōr). = LUXOR.

Aktē. See ACTE.

Ak·tyu'binsk (ŭk·tyōō'bÿĭnsk). Town, ✱ of Aktyubinsk Region, W cen. Kazakh S.S.R., Soviet Russia, Asia; pop. 20,861; chief town on the Chkalov-Tashkent R.R., ab. 125 m. SE of Chkalov; also on oil pipeline running N from Caspian Sea to Orsk.

Aktyubinsk Region. Subdivision of Kazakh S.S.R., Soviet Russia, Asia, in W cen. part; bounded on N by Chkalov Region of R.S.F.S.R., on E by Kustanai Region, on S by Kzyl-Orda Region and Kara-Kalpak A.S.S.R., on SW by Gurev Region, and on W by West Kazakhstan Region; ✱ Aktyubinsk. Steppe region traversed by Emba and Irgiz rivers, by the Chkalov-Tashkent R.R. and by oil pipelines; Lake Chelkar Tengiz in SE.

A'kun (ä'kōōn). Island, Aleutian Is., Alaska, just NE of Akutan I. and separated on NE by Unimak Pass from Unimak I.

A·ku're (ä·kōō'rȧ). Town, ✱ of Ondo province, Western Region, Nigeria, ab. 130 m. NE of Lagos.

A'kur·ey'ri (ä'kür·ā'rĭ). Town, N Iceland, on Eyja Fjord; pop. (1942) 5644; incorporated 1786. Second town in size and importance in Iceland.

A·ku'tan (ä·kōō'tän). One of the Fox Islands, Aleutian Is., Alaska; an active volcano 4244 ft. high; separated on SW from Unalaska I. by **Akutan Pass.**

Ak·yab' (äk·yăb'; ăk'yăb). **1** District, Arakan div., Lower Burma; 5176 sq. m.; pop. 637,580.

2 Town, ✱ of dist. and of Arakan div.; chief seaport on Bay of Bengal, at mouth of Kaladan river 340 m. SE of

Calcutta; pop. 38,094; chief export rice; has excellent harbor and several airfields. Seized by Japanese May 1942; unsuccessfully attacked by Allied Nations Dec. 1942–May 1943, but captured Jan. 1945.

Al'a·bam'a (ăl'ȧ·băm'ȧ). **1** Navigable river 315 m. long, Alabama; formed by confluence of Tallapoosa and Coosa rivers, flows SW from cen. Alabama to join the Tombigbee and form the Mobile and Tensaw rivers flowing into Mobile Bay at Mobile.

2 A southern state of U.S.A., 22d state admitted to Union (1819); bounded on N by Tennessee, on E by Georgia, on S by Florida and the Gulf of Mexico, on W by Mississippi; 29th state in area, 51,609 sq. m. (land area 51,078 sq. m.); 19th state in population, 3,266,740; ✱ Montgomery. See *Table of States* at UNITED STATES. Divided into the following 67 counties (for pronunciation of their names, see their individual entries):

NAME	LOCATION	AREA[1]	POP.[1]	CO. SEAT
Autauga	cen.	599	18,739	Prattville
Baldwin	SW; coastal	1,613	49,088	Bay Minette
Barbour	SE	899	24,700	Clayton and Eufaula
Bibb	cen.	625	14,357	Centreville
Blount	N cen.	640	25,449	Oneonta
Bullock	SE	615	13,462	Union Springs
Butler	S	773	24,560	Greenville
Calhoun	NE	610	95,878	Anniston
Chambers	E	598	37,828	Lafayette
Cherokee	NE	600	16,303	Centre
Chilton	cen.	699	25,693	Clanton
Choctaw	W	918	17,870	Butler
Clarke	SW	1,241	25,738	Grove Hill
Clay	E	603	12,400	Ashland
Cleburne	NE	574	10,911	Heflin
Coffee	SE	677	30,583	Elba and Enterprise
Colbert	NW	616	46,506	Tuscumbia
Conecuh	S	850	17,762	Evergreen
Coosa	E cen.	648	10,726	Rockford
Covington	S	1,034	35,631	Andalusia
Crenshaw	S	611	14,909	Luverne
Cullman	N	743	45,572	Cullman
Dale	SE	560	31,066	Ozark
Dallas	SW cen.	976	56,667	Selma
De Kalb	NE	778	41,417	Fort Payne
Elmore	E cen.	628	30,524	Wetumpka
Escambia	S	962	33,511	Brewton
Etowah	NE	555	96,980	Gadsden
Fayette	NW	627	16,148	Fayette
Franklin	NW	644	21,988	Russellville
Geneva	SE	578	22,310	Geneva
Greene	W	645	13,600	Eutaw
Hale	W	663	19,537	Greensboro
Henry	SE	565	15,286	Abbeville
Houston	SE corner	578	50,718	Dothan
Jackson	NE corner	1,124	36,681	Scottsboro
Jefferson	cen.	1,118	634,864	Birmingham
Lamar	NW	605	14,271	Vernon
Lauderdale[2]	NW corner	688	61,622	Florence
Lawrence	N	686	24,501	Moulton
Lee	E	612	49,754	Opelika
Limestone	N	545	36,513	Athens
Lowndes	S cen.	716	15,417	Hayneville
Macon	E	616	26,717	Tuskegee
Madison	N	803	117,348	Huntsville
Marengo	W	978	27,098	Linden
Marion	NW	743	21,837	Hamilton
Marshall	NE	571	48,018	Guntersville
Mobile[3]	SW corner; coastal	1,248	314,301	Mobile
Monroe	SW	1,035	22,372	Monroeville
Montgomery	SE cen.	790	169,210	Montgomery
Morgan	N	574	60,454	Decatur
Perry	W cen.	734	17,358	Marion
Pickens	W	887	21,882	Carrollton
Pike	SE	673	25,987	Troy
Randolph	E	581	19,477	Wedowee
Russell	E	639	46,351	Seale and Phenix City
Saint Clair	NE cen.	641	25,388	Pell City
Shelby	cen.	800	32,132	Columbiana
Sumter	W	914	20,041	Livingston
Talladega	E cen.	750	65,495	Talladega
Tallapoosa	E	711	35,007	Dadeville
Tuscaloosa	W cen.	1,340	109,047	Tuscaloosa
Walker	NW cen.	809	54,211	Jasper
Washington	SW	1,069	15,372	Chatom
Wilcox	SW cen.	900	18,739	Camden
Winston	NW	633	14,858	Double Springs

[1] Area = land area in sq. m. Pop. from 1960 Census.
[2] Bounded by Tennessee river, including Wilson Dam and Muscle Shoals (*qq.v.*).
[3] Includes Dauphin Island.

ALABAMA

Statute Miles

10	20	30	40

✪ State Capital

PUBLISHED BY G. & C. MERRIAM COMPANY
SPRINGFIELD, MASS.
PREPARED BY J. W. CLEMENT CO., BUFFALO, N.Y.

Nickname: The Cotton State. *State flower:* The golden-rod. *Motto:* We Dare Defend Our Rights. *Chief cities:* Birmingham, Mobile, Montgomery, Huntsville, Tuscaloosa. *Rivers:* Mobile, formed by Alabama and Tombigbee; Alabama (see 1, above); Tombigbee, formed by junction of E and W forks in NE Mississippi; Tennessee, flowing W across N counties (for great dams, Muscle Shoals, Norris, etc., see TENNESSEE river and TENNESSEE VALLEY AUTHORITY); Chattahoochee forming SE boundary with Georgia; Conecuh and Pea, in S and SE part. Mobile and Tensaw (part of its estuary) flow into Mobile Bay, arm of Gulf of Mexico. Martin lake in E is expansion of Tallapoosa river. *Mountains:* S end of Appalachian Mts. (chief ranges Raccoon and Lookout) in NE corner extending as far as Birmingham. Highest point Cheaha Mt. 2407 ft. (a state park) on border bet. Clay and Talladega cos. *Chief industries:* Agriculture (cotton, peanuts, corn, potatoes, fruits, etc.) and mining (great iron and coal deposits in mountains around Birmingham).

History: Explored by Spaniards, notably by De Soto 1539–40; first permanent settlement established 1711 by French at site of Mobile on Mobile Bay; became English 1763; southern part included in West Florida, retroceded to Spain 1783 and claimed by U.S. as part of Louisiana Purchase 1803; rest of Alabama became part of United States 1783, with dividing line under dispute until 1795 when Spain ceded claim north of 31°; included in territory of Mississippi (*q.v.*) 1798; created a territory 1817; 1st constitutional convention July 1819; admitted to Union Dec. 14, 1819; 2d constitutional convention Jan. 7–Mar. 20, 1861 passed ordinance of secession Jan. 11, 1861; government of the Confederate States of America organized at Montgomery Feb. 4, 1861; 3d constitutional convention Sept. 12–30, 1865 declared secession null and void, and abolished slavery; 4th constitutional convention Nov. 5–Dec. 6, 1867; readmitted to Union 1868; present constitution, formulated by 6th constitutional convention, adopted 1901 (see BIRMINGHAM).

Alabama City. Former city, Etowah co., NE Alabama; pop. (1930) 8455; since 1932, part of Gadsden.

A·la·bat' (ä'lä·bät'). Long narrow island ab. 15 m. long, at S end of Lamon Bay off N coast of Tayabas prov., Luzon, Phil. Is.; 74 sq. m.; pop. 11,723.

A·lach'u·a (á·lŏch'ṳ·wä). **1** County in Florida. See *Table* at FLORIDA.
2 City, Alachua co., N Florida; pop. 1974.

A'la·cra'nes (ä'lä·krä'nås). Municipality and town, Matanzas prov., W cen. Cuba, 18 m. S of Matanzas; pop. (town) 5504.

A'la·dağ' (ä'lä·dä') *or* **Ala Dağ.** Name of several mountains in Turkey in Asia, esp.: (1) Mountain chain, SE Asia Minor, N of Adana; highest point 9350 ft.; E end of Taurus Mts. (2) Mountain group 11,515 ft., E Turkish Armenia, N of Lake Van. (3) Mountain group 10,270 ft., NE Turkish Armenia, S of Kars.

A'la·go'as (á'lá·gō'ás). State of Brazil. See *Table* at BRAZIL.

A'la·goí'nhas (á'lá·gwē'nyás). City, Baía state, E Brazil, 70 m. N of Salvador; pop. (1940 est.) 13,461.

A'la·gón' (ä'lä·gōn'). River ab. 120 m. long, W Spain; flows SW into Tagus river 2 m. NE of Alcántara.

A'la·göz' (ä'lä·gûz'); *Russ.* **A·la·gez'** (ŭ·lŭ·gyôs'). Volcanic mountain 13,435 ft., NW Armenian S.S.R., Transcaucasia, U.S.S.R.

A·lai' (ä·lī'). **1** Mountain range running E and W in SW Kirgiz S.S.R., Soviet Russia, Asia; average height 16,000 ft.; highest peak 19,554 ft. Cf. TRANS ALAI.
2 Valley of Kizil Su (a N tributary of the Amu Darya) S of Alai Mts.

Alais. See ALÈS.

A'la·jue'la (ä'lä·hwā'lä). **1** Province, cen. Costa Rica; 3652 sq. m.; pop. (1943 est.) 148,771; healthful plateau region; produces sugar, coffee, hides, cattle.

2 Town, its ✻, 14 m. W of San José; pop. (1943 est.) 9999; center of sugar industry.

A·la Kul' (*Russ.* ŭ·lŭ·kōōl'y'; *Turki* ä'lä·kûl'). Lake, E Kazakh S.S.R., Soviet Russia, Asia, E of Lake Balkhash and near Dzungarian border; has no outlet.

A·la'la·kei'ki (ä·lä'lä·kā'kĕ). Channel 6 m. wide, bet. SW Maui and Kahoolawe, Hawaii.

Alalia. See ALERIA.

Al'a·ma·gan' (ăl'á·má·găn'; ä'lä·mä·gän'). One of the Mariana Islands (*q.v.*), W Pacific Ocean, 165 m. N of Saipan, 17°36′N; included in Japanese mandate 1919; taken by U.S. Aug. 1945.

Al'a·mance (ăl'á·măns). **1** Small stream (**Alamance Creek,** a headstream of Cape Fear river), N cen. North Carolina; on its banks ab. 20 m. W of Hillsboro colonial forces of British governor, William Tryon, decisively defeated Regulators May 16, 1771.
2 County in North Carolina. See *Table* at NORTH CAROLINA.

Al'a·man'ni·a (ăl'á·măn'ĭ·á; -măn'yá). Region, W Europe, on both sides of Upper Rhine (modern E France and SW Germany); home of the Alamanni; in time of Clovis, a Frankish province; later (c. 1000) a duchy.

Al'a·me'da (ăl'á·mē'dá; -mā'dá). **1** County in California. See *Table* at CALIFORNIA.
2 City, Alameda co., W California, on island near E shore of San Francisco Bay, 6 m. E of San Francisco, separated from Oakland by estuary; pop. 61,316; incorp. 1885. Port of entry; naval air base and commercial airports, starting point for first China Clipper flight Nov. 22, 1935; shipping center; manufactures pumps, borax, aircraft parts, diesel engines, pottery; shipbuilding yards; fish canneries; beach resorts.
3 (*pron.* ăl'á·mē'dá) City, Bannock co., SE Idaho, 5 m. NW of Pocatello; pop. 10,660.

Al'a·me'da–Oak'land Tunnel (ăl'á·mē'dá·ōk'lănd; -mā'dá-). Vehicular tunnel 4500 ft. long under an inlet of San Francisco Bay, connecting Alameda with Oakland, California.

Alamein, El. See EL ALAMEIN.

A'la·mi'nos (ä'lä·mē'nôs). Municipality, NW Pangasinan prov., Luzon, Phil. Is., near W shore of Lingayen Gulf; pop. 19,960.

Al'a·mo (ăl'á·mō). **1** Town, ⊗ of Wheeler co., SE cen. Georgia; pop. 822.
2 Town, ⊗ of Crockett co., W Tennessee; pop. 1665.
3 City, Hidalgo co., S Texas, in agricultural section 10 m. E of McAllen; pop. 4121.

Alamo, the. Fort in San Antonio, Texas. Spanish Franciscan mission built c. 1722; converted to a fort 1793; in the Texan war of independence from Mexico, besieged by the Mexicans under Santa Anna Feb. 23–Mar. 6, 1836; defended to the last man of the Texan garrison of 187; became a symbol of Texan fortitude as used in Houston's cry "Remember the Alamo!" at the battle of San Jacinto 46 days later.

Al'a·mo·gor'do (ăl'á·mó·gôr'dō). City, ⊗ of Otero co., S New Mexico, W of Sacramento Mts. 60 m. NE of Las Cruces; pop. 21,723; alt. 4350; to the SW are White Sands Proving Ground (ab. 45 m.), White Sands National Monument (ab. 20 m.), and (ab. 8 m.) **Hol'lo·man Air Force Base** [hŏl'ŏ·măn] (formerly **Alamogordo Air Base**); ab. 55 m. to the NW at N end of the desert which extends between the Rio Grande and the San Andres Mts. is site of the first man-made atomic explosion July 16, 1945.

Alamogordo Dam. Dam, completed 1938, across Pecos river, N De Baca co., New Mexico; height 148 ft.; impounds water, **Alamogordo Reservoir,** for irrigation.

Al'a·mo Heights (ăl'á·mō). City, Bexar co., S cen. Texas, 5 m. NE of San Antonio; pop. 7552; suburb of San Antonio.

Alamos, Los. See LOS ALAMOS.

Al'a·mo'sa (ăl'á·mō'sá; -mōō'sá). **1** County in Colorado. See *Table* at COLORADO.
2 City, its ⊗, S Colorado, on Rio Grande 84 m. WNW of Trinidad; pop. 6205; founded 1878; industrial, shipping, and retail center for San Luis Park; flour mill, meat-packing plant, stockyards. Adams State College (1921).

A·la·mut', Rock of (á·lá·mōōt'). Height, W end of Elburz Mts., N Iran, ab. 70 m. NW of Tehran; stronghold of the Assassins, a secret order of the Ismailians, in medieval ages.

Å'land', Å'land' Islands (ō'länd'). See AHVENANMAA.

Åland Sea. Body of water bet. Ahvenanmaa archipelago at the entrance to the Gulf of Bothnia and the mainland of Sweden.

A'lang·a'lang (ä'läng·ä'läng). Municipality, N Leyte prov., Phil. Is., 11 m. S by W of Tacloban; pop. 21,084.

A'la·o'tra (ä'lä·ō'trá). Lake, NE cen. Madagascar.

A'la·ouites', Territory of the (á·lá'wēt'). = LATAKIA, former republic.

A'la·pi'i Point (ä'lä·pē'ê). Cape on W coast of Kauai I., Hawaii.

A·lar'cos (ä·lär'kōs). Hill and former village, Ciudad Real prov., S cen. Spain, 7 m. W of Ciudad Real; scene of battle 1195 in which the Almohades under al-Mansur defeated Alfonso VIII of Castile.

A'la·şe·hir' (ä'lä·shĕ·hēr'), *formerly* **A'la·shehr'** (-shĕ'h'r); *anc.* **Phil'a·del'phi·a** (fĭl'á·dĕl'fĭ·á; -fyá). City, Manisa vilayet, W Turkey in Asia, on Alaşehir river (tributary of Gediz) and on railroad 75 m. E of İzmir; pop. 8209. Site of ancient city of Philadelphia founded c. 150 B.C. by Attalus II (Philadelphus) of Pergamum; one of the Seven Churches of Asia Minor (*Rev.* i–iii); after a long period of resistance, the last city of Asia Minor to fall to the Turks 1390; said to have been conquered by Tamerlane 1402; largely destroyed by the Greeks 1922.

A'la' Shan' (ä'lä' shän'). **1** Mountain range, SE Ningsia prov., W Inner Mongolia, N China, W of the Hwang Ho; highest ab. 12,000 ft.
2 Desert region of Inner Mongolia, cen. and S Ningsia prov., W of Ala Shan mountain range.

A·las'ka (á·lăs'ká). *Earlier name (to 1867)* **Russian America.** A state of U.S.A., 49th state admitted to Union (1959); the NW part of North America, bounded on N by Arctic Ocean, on E by Yukon and Brit. Columbia, on SW by Pacific Ocean, and on W by Bering Sea and Arctic Ocean; 1st state in area, 586,400 sq. m. (land area 571,065 sq. m.); 50th state in population, 226,167; ✷ Juneau. See *Table of States* at UNITED STATES. *Nickname:* The Last Frontier. *State flower:* The forget-me-not.

Chief cities: Anchorage, Fairbanks, Juneau, Ketchikan, Sitka. *Capes and Islands:* Most northerly point is Point Barrow 71°20'N; Cape Prince of Wales, W point of Seward Penin., separated by Bering Strait (56 m. wide) from Asia; Alaska Penin. and Aleutian Is. in SW extend 1200 m. toward Asia enclosing Bering Sea on S (furthest point W Attu I. 172°30'E); many other islands off coast: St. Lawrence, Nunivak, and Pribilof in Bering Sea, Kodiak and Afognak E of Alaska Penin., and islands of Alexander Archipelago off narrow strip of mainland in SE bordering Brit. Columbia. *Rivers:* Yukon (lower course) crosses from E to W (tributaries: Porcupine, Tanana, Koyukuk), Noatak in N, Kuskokwim in SW, Susitna and Copper in S. *Mts.:* Wrangell Mts. in SE extending to Yukon border, Chugach Mts. along S coast, Alaska Range in S cen. part, Brooks Range in N, and Aleutian Range on Alaska Penin. Highest point Mt. McKinley 20,300 ft. Has one national park, Mount McKinley in Alaska Range, and 3 national monuments, Glacier Bay, Katmai, Sitka. *Chief industries:* Salmon fishing and canning; mining (gold, platinum, silver); furs and seal skins; reindeer (herds of 300,000); has 800 m. of railroads. See ALASKA HIGHWAY.

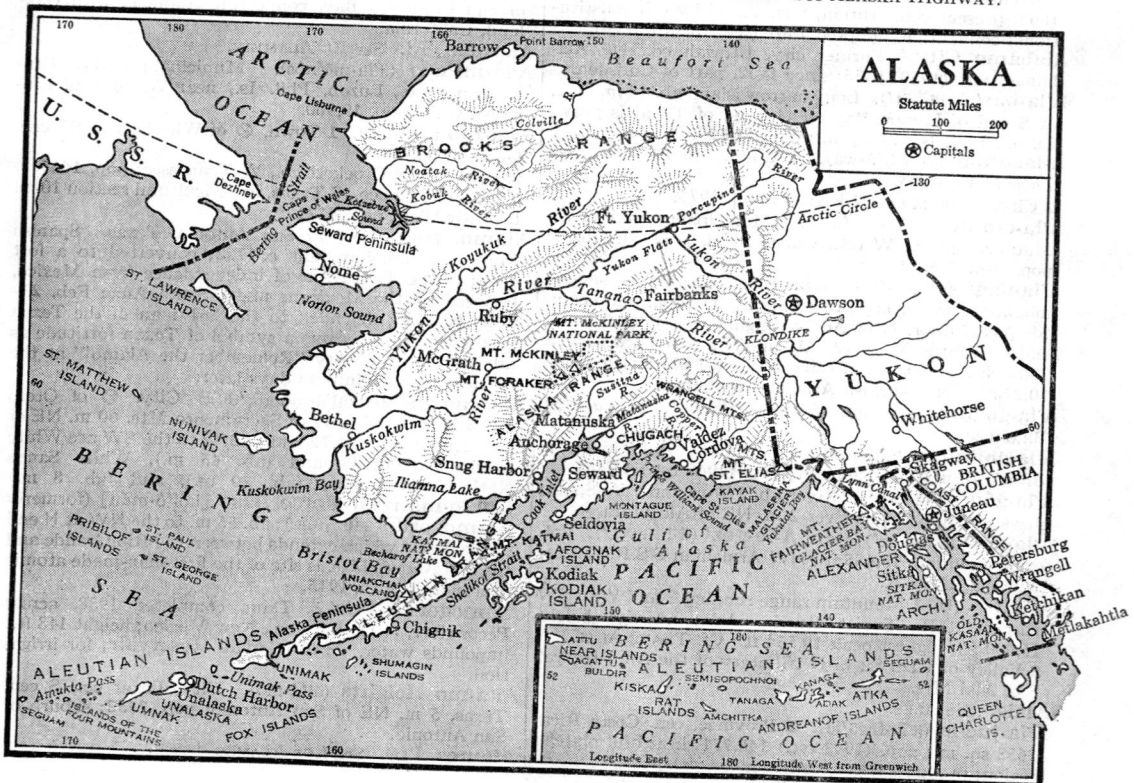

History: Discovered by Russian voyages, esp. of Vitus Bering 1741; first permanent settlement 1783 on Kodiak I.; visited by British explorers Cook, Vancouver, and Mackenzie and by Hudson Bay traders 1778–1847; under trade monopoly of Russian-American Fur Co. 1799–1861, first managed by Aleksandr Baranov; ownership claimed by Russia; region south to 54°40′ ceded by Russia to U.S. for $7,200,000 by treaty of 1867 negotiated by Secretary of State Seward (hence early nickname of Alaska, "Seward's Folly"); organized 1884, received final U.S. territorial status 1912, granted statehood 1959; gold discoveries, including Klondike 1896; disputed boundary with British Columbia arbitrated in favor of U.S. 1903; restriction of seal fisheries by treaties with Great Britain, Russia, and Japan 1911; Univ. of Alaska estab. 1922 at College, near Fairbanks. In World War II Aleutian islands of Attu and Kiska occupied by Japanese June 1942–Aug. 1943.

Alaska, Gulf of. Gulf, S Alaska, bet. Alaska Penin. and Alexander Archipelago.

Alaska Highway. Military and commercial road built as **Al′can′ Highway** [ăl′kăn′] (*A*laska and *Can*ada) by U.S. Army engineers Mar.–Nov. 1942; later, improved and partly relocated; 1523 m. long from Dawson Creek, E Brit. Columbia, NW across N Brit. Columbia, passing through Fort St. John, Fort Nelson, and Lower Post, then through Teslin, Whitehorse, and Kluane in SW Yukon, and Tanacross, Big Delta (where it meets the Richardson Highway, *q.v.*), and Richardson in E Alaska, to Fairbanks. Highest point 4212 ft. bet. Fort Nelson and Watson Lake.

Alaska Peninsula. Long narrow extension ab. 475 m. long, SW Alaska, from Iliamna Lake to Unimak I., geographically a unit with Aleutian Is.

Alaska Range. Mountain range, S Alaska, extending in semicircle from Alaska Penin. to Yukon boundary; highest Mt. McKinley. See Mount MCKINLEY and UNITED STATES, *National Parks* (Mount McKinley National Park).

A·las′ Strait (à·läs′). Channel 10 to 15 m. wide bet. Lombok and Sumbawa Is., Lesser Sunda Is., Indonesia, connecting W Flores Sea with Indian Ocean.

A′la Tau′ (ä′lä tou′). **1** Several ranges 10,000 to 18,000 ft. of the Tien Shan mountain system, E Kazakh and Kirgiz Repubs., Central Asia, around and NE of Issyk Kul. **2** See DZUNGARIAN ALA TAU.

A·la′tri (ä·lä′trē; *anc.* **A·le′tri·um** (á·lē′trĭ·ŭm; à·lĕt′rĭ·ŭm). Commune, Frosinone prov., Latium, cen. Italy, 6 m. N of Frosinone; pop. 18,616; remains of pre-Roman wall of cyclopean masonry.

A·la·tyr′ (ŭ·lŭ·tĭr′y′). Town, SW Chuvash Republic, Soviet Russia, Europe, on left bank of the Sura river 120 m. SW of Kazan; pop. 22,374; important for trade in grain and timber; connected by rail with Kazan.

A′lau·sí′ (ä′lou·sē′). Town, Chimborazo prov., cen. Ecuador, in mountains S of Riobamba; pop. 12,238.

A′la·va (ä′lä·vä). Province of Spain. See *Table* at SPAIN.

Al′a·va, Cape (ăl′à·và). Cape, Clallam co., NW Washington, just S of Cape Flattery, 124°44′W long., 48°10′N lat.; most westerly point of United States mainland excluding Alaska.

A·la·wi′ya or **A·la·wiy′ya** (à·lä·wē′yà; -yä). = LATAKIA.

Al ′A·zi·zi′ya (ăl ä·zē·zē′yà; -yä). Town on Tigris river ab. 50 m. below Baghdad, Iraq.

Al′ba (äl′bä); *anc.* **Al′ba Pom·pe′ia** (ăl′bà pŏm·pē′(y)à). Commune, Cuneo prov., Piedmont, NW Italy, on Tanaro river 33 m. NE of Cuneo; pop. 17,308.

Al′ba·ce′te (äl′vä·thä′tà; -sä′tà). **1** Province of Spain. See *Table* at SPAIN. **2** Commune, its ✳, SE Spain, 138 m. SE of Madrid; pop. (1941 est.) 65,142; manufactures cutlery.

Al′ba Iu′lia (äl′bä yōō′lyä; *Angl.* äl′bà yōōl′yà); *Lat.* **A·pu′lum** (à·pū′lŭm); *Hung.* **Gyu′la·fe′hér·vár** (dyōō′lŏ·fĕ′hār·vär′); *Ger.* **Karls′burg** (kärls′bŏŏrκ). Town on Mureş river, Transylvania, Romania; pop.

12,457. Site of Roman colony; bishopric since 11th cent.; contains tomb of Hungarian national hero, János Hunyadi; 16th-cent. residence of princes of Transylvania (*q.v.*); while under Austria, upper citadel built 1716–35 by Emperor Charles VI; as traditional center of Romanian nationalism, scene of proclamation of union of Transylvania with Romania 1918 and of coronation of King Ferdinand I and Queen Marie 1922.

Al′ba Lon′ga (ăl′bà lŏng′gà). Ancient city, the oldest in Latium, 12 m. SE of Rome, Italy, extending in long line in Alban Hills to E shore of Albanus Lacus. Traditionally founded by Ascanius, son of Aeneas; legendary birthplace of Romulus and Remus, the founders of Rome; razed by Tullus Hostilius 665 B.C.

Albana. See DERBENT.

Al′ban Hills (ôl′băn; äl′-); *Ital.* **Mon′ti Al·ba′ni** (mŏn′tē äl·bä′nē); *anc.* **Al·ba′nus Mons** (ăl·bā′nŭs mŏnz). Mountain group near Albano Laziale, Italy, SE of Rome; a part of the Lower Apennines.

Al·ba′ni·a (ăl·bā′nĭ·à; -bän′yà). **1** Ancient country of E Caucasus region on W side of Caspian Sea, extending N from Cyrus and Araxes rivers and corresponding

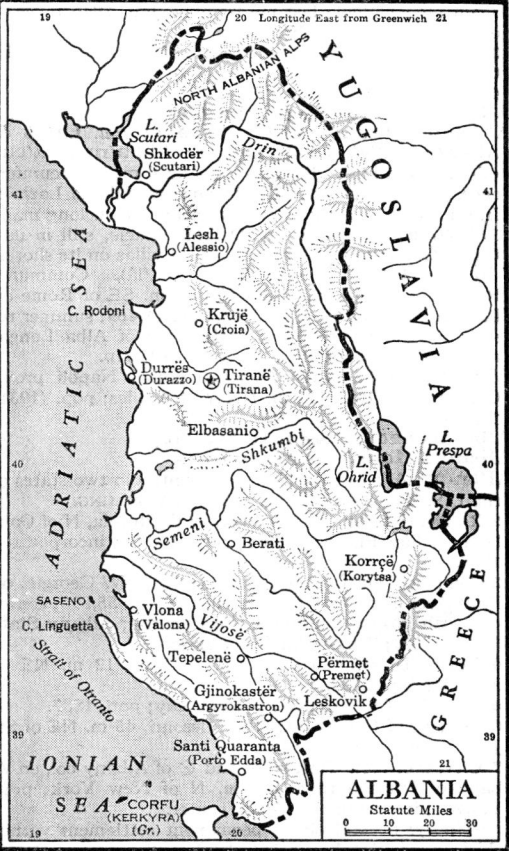

largely to NE Azerbaidzhan and S modern Dagestan. Inhabited by fierce Scythian tribe who fought under Mithridates VI against Pompey.

2 *Albanian* **Shqip·ni′** (shkyĭp·nē′) or **Shqip·ri′** (-rē′). Independent state, W Balkan Penin., bet. Yugoslavia and Greece, on E coast of Adriatic; 10,631 sq. m.; pop. 1,003,068 (1939 est.) 1,063,000; ✳ Tiranë. Very mountainous country; North Albanian Alps in N (highest 6500 to 8700 ft.). *Rivers:* Drin in N, Shkumbi and Semeni in center, Vijosë in S; SE part of Lake Scutari

on N border, outlet Bojana river; parts of Lakes Ohrid and Prespa in SE. *Chief towns:* Tiranë, Shkodër (Scutari), Durrës (Durazzo). Korrçë, and Vlona (Valona).

History: Home of ancient Mediterranean people, divided into Ghegs in the north, Tosks in south; later became Mohammedans converted from Christianity; as a race little affected by Greco-Roman or Slavonic penetration; held by Goths 4th and 5th centuries, Eastern Empire 6th century, and Serbs 7th–14th centuries; despite resistance 1443–68 of national hero, George Castriota (Scanderbeg), overcome by Turks; part of Ottoman Empire until 1912; independence proclaimed as a principality 1912; invaded for brief time 1913 by Serbs; independence again proclaimed 1917 and confirmed 1920 by treaty with Italy and admission into League of Nations; boundary dispute with Yugoslavia settled by League 1921; republic 1925–28; guaranteed territorial integrity and defensive alliance by Italy 1927; monarchy 1928 with Ahmed Bey Zogu as King (Zog I); attacked and overrun April 1939 by Italian troops and placed under rule of king of Italy; invaded in south 1941 by Greek army, which was later driven out by German conquest of Greece. German forces finally driven out Nov. 1944 and again independent; became republic Jan. 1946 by vote of constituent assembly.

3 Ancient name of Highland region of Scotland, N of the Clyde.

4 See AUBAGNE.

Albaniae Pylae. See CASPIAN GATES.

Al·ba·no (äl-bä′nô; *Angl.* ăl-), **Lake**; *Ital.* **La′go di Al·ba′no** (lä′gô dĕ äl-bä′nô); *anc.* **Al·ba′nus La′cus** (äl-bā′nŭs lā′kŭs). Picturesque lake 6 m. in circumference, in crater of extinct volcano near Albano Laziale, Italy; its outlet a rock-hewn tunnel ab. 1 m. long made 398–397 B.C., on advice of Delphic Oracle, still in use. Castel Gandolfo and many beautiful villas on its shores.

Al·ba′no La·zia′le (äl-bä′nô lä-tsyä′lâ). Commune, Roma prov., Latium, cen. Italy, 14 m. SE of Rome on Lake Albano and Appian Way; pop. 11,469; summer resort; Roman ruins. Near early town of Alba Longa, established by Septimius Severus c. 195 A.D.

Al·ba·no′va (äl′bä·nô′vä). Commune, Napoli prov., Campania, S Italy, 11 m. NNW of Naples; pop. (1931) 16,108.

Albanus Lacus. See Lake ALBANO.

Albanus Mons. See ALBAN HILLS.

Al·ba·ny (ôl′bá·nǐ). **1** Name of counties in two states of the U.S. See *Tables* at NEW YORK, WYOMING.

2 Residential city, Alameda co., W California, N of Oakland on San Francisco Bay; pop. 14,804; incorporated 1908.

3 Commercial city, ⊗ of Dougherty co., SW Georgia, on Flint river 65 m. N of Florida border; pop. 55,890; center of pecan groves; radium springs nearby; Albany State Coll. (1903); Turner Air Force Base.

4 Town, Delaware co., E cen. Indiana, 12 m. NE of Muncie; pop. 2132.

5 City, ⊗ of Clinton co., S Kentucky; pop. 1887.

6 City, ⊗ of Gentry co., NW Missouri, 45 m. NE of St. Joseph; pop. 1662.

7 City, ✱ of New York state and ⊗ of Albany co., on W bank of Hudson river 145 m. N of New York; pop. 129,726; important industrial center.

History: Second oldest permanent settlement within thirteen colonies, begun 1614 by establishment of Dutch trading post; actual colonization 1624 when Fort Orange was founded by Dutch West India Company; village, granted independence from the patroon, became Beverwyck 1652; after surrender of Fort Orange to English 1664, Beverwyck became Albany; received charter 1686; long a center for fur trade and contact with Indians; scene of the Albany Congress of the seven English colonies and the Iroquois 1754 when Albany Plan of Union was drafted; seriously menaced by British attack during Revolutionary War, especially in 1777; became capital

of state of New York 1797; expanded as a commercial center after opening of Erie Canal 1825 and of Albany-Schenectady R.R. 1831. Has several notable buildings: state capitol (1871), state education building, and Schuyler mansion (1761); seat of State University College of Education (1844) and several departments of Union Univ.; College of St. Rose (1920; women).

8 City, ⊗ of Linn co., W Oregon, on Willamette river 10 m. NE of Corvallis; pop. 12,926; estab. 1848; manufactures furniture, leather goods, lumber, meat products, foundry products.

9 City, ⊗ of Shackelford co., N cen. Texas, 30 m. NE of Abilene; pop. 2174; ships livestock; oil wells.

10 Seaport municipality, SW Western Australia, on King George Sound ab. 260 m. SE of Perth; pop. 4076; a military settlement 1825. Possesses good harbor; popular vacation and health resort.

11 River 610 m. long, N cen. Ontario, Canada; rises in chain of lakes (largest St. Joseph) in W Ontario and flows E and NE into W James Bay at Fort Albany; chief tributaries the Kenogami and Ogoki rivers.

Alba Pompeia. See ALBA.

Al′ba·tross Point (ăl′bá·trŏs). Cape on NW cen. coast of North Island, New Zealand, at S entrance to Kawhia Harbor.

Al·bay′ (äl-bī′). **1** Province, SE Luzon, Phil. Is.; 1548 sq. m. including subprovince of Catanduanes I. (552 sq. m.); pop. 432,465; ✱ Legaspi. Bounded on N by Camarines Sur, on N and NE by Lagonoy Gulf, on E by Albay Gulf, on S by Sorsogon prov., and on W by Burias Pass. Includes the islands of Batan, Cagraray, Rapu Rapu, and San Miguel. Very mountainous, includes among other peaks the perfect volcanic cone of Mt. Mayon; watered by many small streams; very fertile, esp. well adapted to hemp (abacá), its main crop; other products coconuts, sugar, rice, fruits; also some shipbuilding and mining. Inhabitants are mainly Bikols. Chief towns Legaspi, Tabaco, Daraga, Ligao, and Guinobatan, and Virac on Catanduanes.

History: A populous region before coming of Spaniards but infrequently visited by them before 18th century; became prosperous after 1750 but suffered from great eruption of Mayon 1814; territory decreased 1846 by loss of islands of Masbate and Ticao and by cession of towns to Camarines Sur; civil government established by Americans Apr. 1901. Invaded by Japanese Dec. 1941.

2 Municipality on Albay Gulf, now part of Legaspi (*q.v.*).

Albay Gulf. Inlet of Pacific Ocean in SE Luzon, Phil. Is., on E coast of Albay prov., ab. 30 m. long by 8–12 m. wide; its N shore formed by islands of Cagraray, Batan, and Rapu Rapu. Port of Legaspi is at its head.

Al·ba·zin′ (äl-bä-zēn′). River in extreme N Manchuria; flows NE into Amur river.

Al′be·marle (ăl′bĕ·märl). **1** County in Virginia. See *Table* at VIRGINIA.

2 Town, ⊗ of Stanly co., S cen. North Carolina, 26 m. SE of Salisbury; pop. 12,261; manufactures textiles, cottonseed oil, lumber, bricks.

Albemarle Island. See ISABELA ISLAND.

Albemarle Sound. Inlet of Atlantic Ocean, ab. 60 m. long, in NE North Carolina, forming parts of Currituck, Camden, Pasquotank, Perquimans, and Chowan cos. on the N, Bertie co. on W, and Washington, Tyrrell, and Dare cos. on S; receives the Chowan river in the NW.

Al·ben′ga (äl-bĕn′gä); *anc.* **Al′bum In·gau′num** (ăl′bŭm ĭng·gô′nŭm) *or* **Al′bin·gau′num** (ăl′bĭng·gô′nŭm). Seaport, Savona prov., Liguria, NW Italy, on Ligurian Sea 22 m. SW of Savona; pop. 10,698; Gothic cathedral and well-preserved Roman bridge.

Al·ber′che (äl-vĕr′chä). River ab. 150 m. long, cen. Spain; flows into Tagus river near Talavera.

Al′bères′, Monts (môn′-zàl′bâr′). Easternmost section of the Pyrenees, bet. SW France and NE Spain; highest peak Pic Noulos 4128 ft.

Al·ber′ga (äl-bûr′gá). River ab. 350 m. long, N South

Australia; flows E from Musgrave Range and in rainy season joins with Finke river.

Al·ber'ni (ăl·bûr'nĭ). City, E cen. Vancouver I., Brit. Columbia, Canada, on Alberni Canal near Port Alberni and 95 m. NW of Victoria; pop. 3323. Both towns practically destroyed by fire Aug. 1947.

Alberni Canal. Narrow fiord, S cen. Vancouver I., SW Brit. Columbia, Canada; an inlet of the Pacific ab. 30 m. long opening into Barkley Sound. Port Alberni is at its head.

Al'bert (ăl'bĕrt). County in New Brunswick, Canada. See *Table* at NEW BRUNSWICK.

Al'bert' (ăl'bâr'); *formerly* **An'cre** (äɴ'kr'). Commune, Somme dept., N France, ab. 17 m. NE of Amiens; pop. 6389; on edge of Battle of the Somme 1916, almost completely destroyed in battles of 1918.

Al'bert, Lake; *or* **Al'bert Nyan'za** (ăl'bĕrt nyăn'zȧ; nĭ·ăn'-; nĭ·än'-). Lake (*nyanza*) bet. Uganda and Congo, cen. Africa, ab. 135 m. NW of Lake Victoria, 100 m. long by 20 m. wide; elevation 2200 ft. It receives at SW end the Semliki, outlet of Lake Edward; at NE corner just below Murchison Falls it receives Victoria Nile from Lake Victoria. Its outlet at N end is Albert Nile section of Nile. Discovered by Sir Samuel Baker 1864; circumnavigated by Gessi Pasha 1876 and by Emin Pasha 1884; included in protectorate of Uganda (*q.v.*), but northwest shores leased to Congo Free State 1894 (see BELGIAN CONGO).

Al·ber'ta (ăl·bûr'tȧ). 1 Province, W Canada, most westerly Prairie Province; land area 248,800 sq. m.; pop. 939,501; ✱ Edmonton; has no counties but is subdivided into 17 census divisions. Bounded on N by Mackenzie dist., on E by Saskatchewan, on S by U.S.A. (Montana), and on W by Brit. Columbia. An extensive plateau with higher portion in S; main range of the Canadian Rockies along its SW border; many peaks 8000 to 11,000 ft.; its eastern slopes have been in large part set aside as national recreation areas, remarkable for their scenery (see *Jasper, Banff,* and *Waterton Lakes National Parks* in *Table* at CANADA); in N is the S half of Wood Buffalo National Park; contains also two other smaller national parks and about 14 provincial parks or reserves. Prairie lands well watered, in N by Athabaska and Peace river systems, in center by the North Saskatchewan, and in S by the South Saskatchewan. In NE corner is Lake Claire and W end of Lake Athabaska; in cen. part is Lesser Slave Lake. Mainly devoted to wheat raising; other products cattle, wool, timber, fish; large coal production (35% of Canada's total). Chief cities Edmonton, Calgary, Lethbridge, Medicine Hat.
History: Part of territory ruled by Hudson's Bay Co. until 1870; as part of Northwest Territories, under the Dominion of Canada 1870–82; S part set up as a district, bet. Rocky Mts. and 112°W and S of 55°N, 105,300 sq. m., with capital at Calgary; developed by an increasing number of "homesteaders" after completion of Canadian Pacific R.R. 1886; dominated by ranching until ab. 1900; became famed for its wheat and mineral production; received provincial status 1905.
2 Mountain 13,500 ft., Rocky Mt. range, SW Alberta, at S end of Jasper National Park.

Al'bert Canal (ăl'bĕrt). Canal, NE Belgium, from Liége to Antwerp, 80 m. long, 140 ft. wide; crossed by Germans May 11, 1940; retaken by British Sept. 7, 1944.

Al'bert Ed'ward (ăl'bĕrt ĕd'wẽrd). Peak 13,100 ft. in the Owen Stanley Range, SE Territory of Papua, N of Port Moresby.

Albert Edward Nyanza. See Lake EDWARD.

Albert Lea (lē). City, ⊗ of Freeborn co., S Minnesota, 20 m. W of Austin; pop. 17,108; railroad junction; gasstove factories, meat-packing plant; dairy products.

Albert Mark'ham, Mount (mär'kăm). Peak 10,460 ft. in Victoria Land, Antarctica, 81°S, 158°E; N of Mt. Markham.

Albert Mountains. Mountain range, NW Papua, on North-East New Guinea border; has several peaks over 10,000 ft., highest ab. 13,600; connects with Owen Stanley Mts. on SE.

Albert National Park. Extensive park region 1506 sq. m., E Congo, cen. Africa, bet. Lakes Kivu and Edward; a game preserve and gorilla sanctuary, first set aside 1925 and enlarged 1929. Region explored by American naturalist Carl E. Akeley.

Albert Nile. See NILE.

Albert Nyanza. See Lake ALBERT.

Al'bert·ville (ăl'bĕrt·vĭl; *Sou. also* -v'l). City, Marshall co., NE Alabama, 20 m. NW of Gadsden; pop. 8250; cotton and cottonseed-oil mills.

Al'bert'ville' (*Fr.* ȧl'bâr'vēl'). Port, Katanga prov., W shore of Lake Tanganyika, Congo, Africa; pop. 5710; head of railroad running 170 m. to Congo river at Kabalo; connected by lake steamer with Kigoma on E shore.

Al'bi' (ȧl'bē'); *anc.* **Al·bi'ga** (ăl·bī'gȧ). Commune, ✱ of Tarn dept., S France, on Tarn river 42 m. NE of Toulouse; pop. 30,293; 13th-cent. Gothic cathedral; archbishops' palace. Capital of Romano-Gallic Albigenses and of medieval viscounty of Albigeois, which later became part of Toulouse; not, as is commonly asserted, the center of the Albigensian movement which took on its name.

Al'bi·a (ăl'bĭ·ȧ). City, ⊗ of Monroe co., S Iowa, 22 m. W of Ottumwa; pop. 4582; railroad junction point; coal mining.

Albiga. See ALBI.

Al'bi'geois' (ăl'bē'zhwȧ'). Former region, S France, around Albi, viscounty of Languedoc, now entirely in Tarn dept.; joined to France 1247.

Al·bi'na (ăl·bē'nȧ; *Du.* ȧl·bē'nä). Seaport town, NE Surinam, on W bank of Maroni river opp. Saint Laurent, French Guiana, 80 m. E of Paramaribo; pop. ab. 650; lumber and gold.

Al·bi'na, Point (ăl·bē'nȧ); *Port.* **Pon'ta Al·bi'na** (pōɴn'tȧ äl·bē'nä). Cape on SW coast of Angola, W Africa.

Albingaunum. See ALBENGA.

Al·bi'no (ăl·bē'nō). Commune, Bergamo prov., Lombardy, N Italy, 8 m. NE of Bergamo; pop. (1931) 11,664.

Al'bi·on (ăl'bĭ·ŭn). 1 Village, Cassia co., S Idaho, SE of Burley; pop. 415. Southern Idaho College of Education (1893).
2 City, ⊗ of Edwards co., SE Illinois; pop. 2025.
3 Town, ⊗ of Noble co., NE Indiana; pop. 1325.
4 Industrial city, Calhoun co., S Michigan, 23 m. ESE of Battle Creek; pop. 12,749; manufactures iron products. Albion College (founded as seminary 1835; organized as college 1861; coed.; Methodist).
5 City, ⊗ of Boone co., E cen. Nebraska, 40 m. WSW of Norfolk; pop. 1982.
6 Village, ⊗ of Orleans co., W New York, ab. 10 m. S of Lake Ontario and 32 m. W of Rochester; pop. 5182; shipping center for agricultural, fruit, and vegetable-growing area.
7 Borough, Erie co., NW corner of Pennsylvania, 22 m. SW of Erie; pop. 1630.
8 Oldest name of Great Britain; retained as poetical name of England.

Albis. See ELBE.

Al'blas·ser·dam' (ăl'bläs·ĕr·däm'). Commune, South Holland prov., Netherlands, 9 m. SE of Rotterdam; pop. 6189.

Albona. See LABIN.

Al'bo·rán' (ăl'vȯ·rän'). Island in W Mediterranean Sea, N of Melilla and 45 m. off coast of Spain; belongs to Almería prov., Spain.

Al'box' (ăl·vōк'). Commune, Almería prov., SE Spain, ab. 41 m. NE of Almería; pop. 9939.

Al'brook Field (ôl'brŏŏk). Airfield in Canal Zone, near Ancon and the Pacific terminus of the Panama Canal.

Albuera, La. See LA ALBUERA.

Al'bu·fe'ra (äl'vōō-fā'rä). Lagoon 11 m. long and 4 m. wide, E coast of Spain, 7 m. S of Valencia.

Al'bu·la (äl'bōō-lä). Mountain pass 7595 ft. high, over Rhaetian Alps, Graubünden canton, SE Switzerland; extends from valley of **Albula River** (upper tributary of Rhine) to Upper Engadine Valley; railroad passes through **Albula Tunnel** (3⅔ m. long, alt. 5981 ft.) just S of the pass.

Album Ingaunum. See ALBENGA.

Al'bu·quer'que (ăl'bŭ-kûr'kĕ; ăl'bŭ-kûr'kĕ; -bŭ-). City and health resort, ⊗ of Bernalillo co., cen. New Mexico, on the Rio Grande 55 m. SW of Santa Fe; largest city in the state; pop. 201,189. Divided into old town section (with central Plaza) and modern business section. Old town founded 1706; military post during Spanish and Mexican regimes; outpost of U.S. Military Dept. after Mexican War 1846-70; alternately occupied by Union and Confederate forces during Civil War; new town platted 1880, incorp. as city 1890. Commercial center in agricultural, timber, and mineral region; wool growing; canning, packing, oil refining; Indian and Mexican handicrafts. Univ. of New Mexico (1889); U.S. Indian Training School; Kirtland Air Force Base.

Albuquerque Cays. Group of small islands in Caribbean Sea off SE coast of Nicaragua.

Alburgum. See AALBORG.

Al'bur·quer'que (äl'vōōr-kĕr'kä). Commune, Badajoz prov., SW Spain, N of Badajoz near border; pop. 10,015.

Al'bur·y (äl'bĕr-ĭ). Commercial town, S New South Wales, SE Australia, on Murray river at head of navigation and on main railroad line bet. Melbourne and Sydney 170 m. NE of Melbourne; pop. 10,542; became municipality 1859; widely known for its wines.

Al·cá'cer do Sal (äl-kä'sĕr thŏŏ säl'). Village in Estremadura, Portugal, ab. 25 m. SE of Setúbal; battle 1217 in which King Alfonso II of Portugal defeated the Moors.

Al·ca'ço·vas (äl-kä'sŏŏ-väsh). Town, Évora dist., Alto Alentejo prov., S cen. Portugal, ab. 19 m. SW of Évora; treaty signed here bet. Spain and Portugal Mar. 6, 1480 in which possession of regions in West Africa, Guinea, and Atlantic islands was settled.

Al'ca·lá' de Gua·dai'ra (äl'kä-lä' thä gwä·thī'rä). Commune, Sevilla prov., SW Spain, 10 m. SE of Seville on left bank of Guadaira river; pop. 20,477; flour mills; Moorish remains, esp. the castle (surrendered to Ferdinand III of Castile 1244).

Alcalá de He·na'res (ā-nä'räs); *anc.* **Com·plu'tum** (kŏm·plōō'tŭm). Commune, Madrid prov., cen. Spain, ab. 20 m. ENE of Madrid; pop. 18,419. After reconquest frequently royal residence of Castilian kings; birthplace of Catherine of Aragon, Cervantes, and de Solis; university, second only to Salamanca, founded by Cardinal Jiménez 1508 (moved to Madrid 1846); noted for production (1513-17) of Complutensian Polyglot Bible, so called from ancient name of city.

Alcalá la Re·al' (lä rrĕ-äl'). Commune, Jaén prov., S Spain, ab. 25 m. NW of Granada; pop. 26,058; scene of French victory of Count Sebastiani over Spanish 1810.

Al'ca·mo (äl'kä-mô). Commune, Trapani prov., NW Sicily, 25 m. E by S of Trapani; pop. 38,396; agricultural trade; near site of ancient Segesta; founded by Saracens 828 A.D.; site moved by Frederick II 1233.

Alcan Highway. See ALASKA HIGHWAY.

Al·cân'ta·ra (äl-kän'tá·rá; *Port.* äl-kănn'tá·rá). 1 Seaport, Maranhão state, NE Brazil, on bay opp. São Luiz; pop. 11,179.
2 Village, Rio de Janeiro state, E Brazil, NE of Niteroi.

Al·cán'ta·ra (äl-kän'tá·rá; *Span.* äl-kän'tä·rä). Commune, Cáceres prov., W Spain, on Tagus river near Portuguese border; pop. (1930) 4014. Prob. not the Roman town of **Nor'ba Cae'sa·re'a** (nôr'bá sē'zá·rē'á; sĕs'á-; sĕz'á-). Named from the Roman bridge built here by Hadrian 105 A.D. (total length 670 ft.; its two main arches 110 ft. wide and 210 ft. above normal level of river), one of finest Roman monuments in existence;

home of knightly order (organized 1156, as the Knights of St. Julian, to drive the Moors from Spanish territory) which changed its name to Order of Alcántara when the town was given it 1217 by Alfonso IX.

Alcaraz, Sierra de. See SIERRA DE ALCARAZ.

Al'ca·traz' (äl'ká-trăz'). Rocky island, San Francisco Bay, California, ab. 4 m. NW of the city opp. the Golden Gate; U.S. fortification and penitentiary, estab. 1858 for military prisoners and 1933 for dangerous criminals; closed 1963.

Al'cau·de'te (äl'kou-thä'tä). Commune, Jaén prov., S Spain, bet. Córdoba and Granada; pop. 18,442.

Al·cá'zar de San Juan (äl-kä'thär thä säng hwän'). Commune, Ciudad Real prov., S cen. Spain, 80 m. SE of Madrid; pop. 26,141; center of wine trade. Sometimes identified with Roman **Al'ce** (äl'sĕ) captured by Tiberius Sempronius Gracchus 180 B.C.; district associated with Cervantes and Don Quixote.

Al·ca'zar-qui·vir' (äl-kä'thär-kĕ-vēr') *or* **Al·cá'zar** (äl-kä'thär); *Arab.* **El Qsar el Kbir** (äl k'sŏr' äl kä-bēr'). City, N Morocco, NW Africa, near SW border of former Spanish Morocco, 60 m. S of Tangier; pop. (1936) 30,762; battle Aug. 4, 1578 in which King Sebastian of Portugal was defeated and slain by the Moors.

Al·ci'ra (äl-thē'rä; -sē'rä); *anc.* **Su'cro** (sū'krō). Commune, Valencia prov., E Spain, 23 m. S of Valencia on Júcar river; pop. 24,518; produces oranges and rice.

Alçi Tepe. See ACHI BABA.

Al·co'a (äl-kō'á). City, Blount co., E Tennessee, 15 m. S of Knoxville; pop. 6395; manufactures aluminum.

Al·co·ba'ça (äl'kōō-vä'sá). Village, Leiria dist., W cen. Portugal, 18 m. SSW of Leiria; pop. 2661; famous Cistercian abbey founded 1148 by Alfonso I; tombs of Portuguese kings and Inés de Castro.

Al·co·le'a (äl'kō-lä'á). Village, just E of Córdoba on the Guadalquivir river, Spain; scene of defeat Sept. 28, 1868 of Spanish royal forces by Marshal Serrano during revolution which deposed Isabella II from throne.

Al·co'na (äl-kō'ná). County in Michigan. See *Table* at MICHIGAN.

Al·co'ra (äl-kō'rä). Commune, Castellón de la Plana prov., E Spain, ab. 10 m. WNW of Castellón de la Plana; pop. 4422; noted in 18th cent. for its manufacture of Alcora porcelain, a rich faïence.

Al'corn (ôl'kôrn). 1 County in Mississippi. See *Table* at MISSISSIPPI.
2 Village, SW Claiborne co., Mississippi, 10 m. SW of Port Gibson; Alcorn Agricultural and Mechanical College (1871; coed.).

Al·co'va Dam (äl-kō'vá). Dam completed 1938 across North Platte river below Pathfinder Dam, S cen. Natrona co., cen. Wyoming; height 265 ft.; impounds water, **Alcova Reservoir,** for irrigation.

Al·coy' (äl-koi'). Manufacturing commune, Alicante prov., SE Spain, 22 m. N of Alicante; pop. (1941 est.) 45,857; paper manufacturing.

Al·cu'dia, Bay of (äl-kōō'thyä). Bay on N coast of island of Majorca.

Al·dab'ra (äl-däb'rá). 1 Island group in Indian Ocean N of Madagascar, part of British Indian Ocean Territory; includes Aldabra and Assumption; both flora and fauna are exceptional. Visited by Portuguese 1511; French dependency in 17th cent.; became British 1810.
2 Chief island in group, 20 m. long; 40 sq. m.; an oval atoll enclosing a lagoon.

Al'dan (ôl'dăn). Borough, Delaware co., SE Pennsylvania, 7 m. W of Philadelphia; pop. 4324.

Al·dan' (ŭl-dán'). 1 River 1500 m. long, SE Yakutsk A.S.S.R., Soviet Russia, Asia; rises in Aldan Mts. and flows into Lena river below Yakutsk, forming its chief tributary; navigable for 800 m.
2 Town, SE Yakutsk Repub., in Aldan valley S of the river and on S-to-N highway from the Trans-Siberian R.R. to Yakutsk; pop. ab. 30,000; gold mining.

Al·dan′ Mountains (ŭl·dȧn′). NW spur of Stanovoi Mts., S Yakutsk Repub., Soviet Russia, Asia, forming watershed bet. upper Aldan and Olekma rivers.

Al′de·burgh (ôl[d]′bŭ·rŭ; ôl[d]′brŭ). Municipal borough, Suffolk East, England, on North Sea; pop. 2684; watering place. Received first charter 1529; sent two members to Parliament from 1572 until 1832, long after it had declined to a mere fishing village.

Alder, Ben or **Mount.** See BEN ALDER.

Al′der·ney (ôl′dẽr·nǐ); Fr. **Au′ri′gny′** (ō′rē′nyē′); anc. **Ri·du′na** (rǐ·dū′nȧ). Northernmost of Channel Is., in Guernsey bailiwick; 4½ m. long; 3 sq. m.; pop. 1521; * St. Anne; separated from Cape La Hague, France, by dangerous 8 m.-wide tidal channel, **Race of Alderney.** Agriculture and cattle raising.

Al′der·shot (ôl′dẽr·shŏt). Municipal borough, Hampshire, S England, 32 m. SW of London; pop. 36,184; its permanent military camp (estab. 1855) became 1904–14 center for English military training. Cf. BISLEY.

Al′der·son (ôl′dẽr·s′n). Town, Greenbrier and Monroe cos., SE West Virginia, on Greenbrier river 15 m. E of Hinton; pop. 1225. Federal Industrial Institution for Women (estab. 1926).

Al′drich Deep (ôl′drĭch). One of the deepest parts of the Pacific Ocean, 30,930 ft., in S Pacific E of Kermadec Is., 30°27′S, 176°39′W.

A·le′do (ȧ·lē′dō). City, ⊗ of Mercer co., NW Illinois, 25 m. SSW of Rock Island; pop. 3080.

A·le·gre′te (ȧ′lȧ·grā′tĕ). Municipality (pop. 39,420) and town (pop., 1940 est., 16,475), Rio Grande do Sul state, S Brazil, 260 m. W of Pôrto Alegre.

Aleih. See ALEY.

A·le·ksan′dra Land (ŭ·lyĭ·ksȧn′drȧ). See FRANZ JOSEF LAND.

Aleksandropol. See LENINAKAN.

A·le·ksan′drovsk (ŭ·lyĭ·ksȧn′drŭfsk). **1** or **Aleksandrovsk Sa·kha·lin′ski** (sŭ·ků·lyēn′skǐ). Seaport on W coast of Sakhalin I. on Tatar Strait, Khabarovsk Territory, Soviet Russia, Asia; pop. ab. 18,000; chief town of N part of island; trading center for coal and petroleum.
2 or **Aleksandrovsk Grushevski.** See SHAKHTY, Soviet Russia, Europe.
3 See POLYARNY, Soviet Russia, Europe.
4 See ZAPOROZHE, Ukraine.

A′lek·san·drów Łódz′ki (ä′lĕk·sän′drŏof lōŏts′kĕ). Commune, Łódź dept., Poland, NW suburb of Łódź; pop. (1938–39 est.) 13,246; textile center.

Aleksandr Range. See KIRGIZ RANGE.

A′lek·si·nac (ä′lĕk·sĕ·näts). Town on Morava river, E Yugoslavia, 18 m. NNW of Niš; battle 1876 in which Serbs and Russians were defeated by Turks.

Alemtejo. Older form of ALENTEJO.

A′len′çon′ (ȧ′län′sôn′; Angl. ȧ·lĕn′sŏn, -s′n). Manufacturing city, * of Orne dept., NW France, on Sarthe river 28 m. N of Le Mans; pop. 17,731.
History: Town, center of medieval territory of Alençon, successively a lordship, county, and duchy, the title to which usually belonged to member of royal house 13th–16th cents.; after 1525 seat of court of Margaret of Navarre, sister of Francis I; center for manufacture of point d'Alençon, a lace introduced by Colbert as part of effort to develop French industry (in second half of 17th cent.). In World War II reached by American forces Aug. 1944.

A·len·te′jo (ȧ·länn·tā′zhoō; -tä′zhoō), older **A·lem·te′jo** (ȧ·länn-). Old province, SE Portugal; bounded on S by Algarve prov., W by Atlantic Ocean and Estremadura prov., N by old province of Beira, E by Spain (Cáceres, Badajoz, and Huelva provs.); * Évora; 9189 sq. m.; now forms modern provinces of Alto Alentejo and Baixo Alentejo; drained by Tagus, Sado, and Guadiana rivers. Region occupied by old province now produces rice, fruit, olives; sometimes called "Granary of Portu-

gal"; manufactures olive and other oils, woolens, leather; some mining.

A′le·nu′i·ha′ha (ä′lä·noō′ē·hä′hä). Channel 26 m. wide, Hawaiian Is., bet. Hawaii and Maui.

A′lep′ (ȧ′lĕp′) or **A·lep′po** (ȧ·lĕp′ō); Arab. **Ha′leb** or **Ha′lab** (hä′läb). **1** Former Turkish vilayet, now largely in N Syria.
2 anc. **Be·roe′a** (bĕ·rē′ȧ). City, NW Syria, near Turkish border 60 m. ESE of İskenderon; pop. (1935) 177,313.
History: Ancient city, capital of a kingdom, first taken by Hittites as early as 2000 B.C.; scene of conflict between Hittites and Egyptians, especially in 15th century B.C.; an independent Hittite principality until conquered by Assyrian king 853 B.C.; enlarged by Seleucus Nicator (306–280 B.C.) and named Beroea; see SYRIA for events of significance up to Moslem conquest; taken by Mohammedan Arabs 638 A.D.; temporarily recovered by Greeks under Nicephorus Phocas 969; held by Seljuks 1090–1117; unsuccessfully besieged by Crusaders 1118, 1124; sacked by Mongols 1260 and by Tamerlane 1401; after capture by Ottoman Turks 1517, experienced revival of trade with east; a flourishing trade center in 16th century, gradually declined because of use of sea route to India and later opening of Suez Canal (1869); largely destroyed by earthquakes 1822, 1830; taken by Ibrahim Pasha 1832; in 1918 captured by British and Arabs under Allenby as part of World War I campaign against Turkey; organized as state of French mandate of Syria 1920; united with Damascus to form state of Syria 1925.

A·le′ri·a (ȧ·lẽr′ǐ·ȧ; Ital. ä·lā′ryä) or **A·la′li·a** (ȧ·lä′lǐ·ȧ; ȧ·läl′yä). One of the chief cities of ancient Corsica, near E coast; modern commune is **A′lé′ria** (ȧ′lā′ryä′), pop. (1931) 791.

A·lert′ Bay (ȧ·lûrt′). Village and port on island off NE coast of Vancouver I., Brit. Columbia, Canada, at S end of Charlotte Strait; steamer stop on route from Vancouver to northern ports.

A′lès′ (ȧ′lĕs′), formerly **A′lais′** (ȧ′lĕs′). City, Gard dept., S France, 30 m. NW of Nîmes; pop. 41,385; large trade in raw silk produced in surrounding region.

A·le′si·a (ȧ·lē′zhǐ·ȧ; -zhȧ). Town, NE Celtic Gaul, on a hill, near source of Sequana; site of successful siege of Vercingetorix by which Caesar put down Gallic revolt 52 B.C.

A′les·san′dri·a (ä′läs·sän′drĕ·ä; Angl. ȧl′ĕ·săn′drǐ·ȧ).
1 Province of Italy. See Table at ITALY.
2 Commune, its *, Piedmont, NW Italy, on the Tanaro river 48 m. ESE of Turin; pop. 79,327; railroad and commercial center. Founded 1168; became member of the Lombard League; besieged unsuccessfully by Frederick Barbarossa 1174; seized by Francesco Sforza 1522; attacked by French 1657; captured by Prince Eugene 1707; ceded to Savoy 1713; citadel built 1728; occupied by French 1800–14.

Alessio. See LESH.

Å′le·sund′ or **Aa′le·sund′** (ô′lĕ·soŏn′). Seaport city, Møre og Romsdal co., W Norway, on an island bet. Bergen and Trondheim; pop. 18,350; incorporated 1848; trading center, esp. for Norwegian W coast cod and herring fisheries; headquarters for Arctic sealing fleet.

Aletrium. See ALATRI.

A′letsch·horn′ (ä′lĕch·hôrn′). Mountain 13,721 ft., Bernese Alps, Valais canton, Switzerland, SSE of the Jungfrau.

A·leu′tian Islands (ȧ·lū′shăn; ȧ·loō′-), commonly **A·leu′tians** (-shănz); formerly **Cath′er·ine Archipelago** (kăth′ẽr·ĭn; kăth′rĭn). Chain of volcanic islands extending 1700 m. W from Alaska Penin. 163°W to 172°30′E (but E of Date Line) and separating Bering Sea from North Pacific Ocean; coextensive with Aleutian Islands district of Alaska; pop. 6011. Chief islands and groups from E to W are Fox Is. (including Unimak and Unalaska), Islands of the Four Mountains, Andreanof Is., Rat Is., and Near Is. (including Attu, only 500 m. E of Kamchatka); chief town Dutch Harbor on Unalaska;

several volcanoes still active (highest Shishaldin, on Unimak, 9978 ft.); even climate but much fog and rain; fertile soil; industries fishing, raising fur-bearing animals, and some agriculture. See *Map* at ALASKA.

History: Eastern part discovered by Chirikov and several of western group by Bering 1741 (see ALASKA); exploited by Siberian fur traders; served as approach for Russian expansion to mainland of Alaska; purchased with Alaska by U.S. from Russia 1867; basis of U.S. claim in controversy over seal fisheries that Bering Sea (*q.v.*) was a *mare clausum*; W islands (Attu and Kiska) occupied by Japanese June 1942; Attu retaken by U.S. forces May 1943; Kiska abandoned by Japanese Aug. 1943; U.S. airfields established on Adak and Amchitka.

Aleutian Range. Mountain range along E coast of N Alaska Penin.; includes Mt. Katmai and Katmai National Monument.

Aleutian Trough *or* **Trench.** Deep, 25,190 ft., in North Pacific Ocean at W end of Aleutian Is.

Al'ex·an'der (ăl'ĕg·zăn'dēr; ăl'ĭg-; *Brit. also* -zän'-). Name of counties in two states of the U.S. See *Tables* at ILLINOIS, NORTH CAROLINA.

Alexander, Cape. Cape, NW Choiseul I., W cen. Solomon Islands, W Pacific Ocean, at E end of Bougainville Strait.

Alexander Archipelago. Group of ab. 1100 islands, SE Alaska, made up of tops of submerged mountains, with irregular coast lines and deep channels between them; from N to S chief islands are Chichagof, Admiralty, Baranof, Kupreanof, Prince of Wales, and Revillagigedo; chief towns Sitka and Ketchikan.

Alexander Bay. Bay on extreme NW coast of Cape of Good Hope province, Union of South Africa, at the mouth of Orange river.

Alexander City. City, Tallapoosa co., E Alabama, 5 m. N of Martin Lake; pop. 13,140; formerly Youngville; incorporated 1873; textile mills.

Alexander I Island. Island ab. 235 m. long in Antarctica, W of base of Palmer Penin., Falkland Islands Dependencies, ab. 71°S lat. and 71°W long.; formerly considered part of Antarctic Continent; discovered and named by Bellingshausen on expedition 1819–21.

Alexander Range. = *Aleksandr Range:* see KIRGIZ RANGE.

Al'ex·an'dra (ăl'ĕg·zăn'drà; ăl'ĭg-; *Brit. also* -zän'-). Island, W part of Franz Josef Land, Arctic Regions, 80°30'N, 45°E; belongs to U.S.S.R.

Alexandra, Mount. See Mount RUWENZORI.

Al'ex·an·dret'ta (ăl'ĕg·zăn·drĕt'à; ăl'ĭg-; *Brit. also* -zän-); *Turk.* İs'ken·de·ron' (ĕs'kĕn·dĕ·rōon'). **1** Formerly, a sanjak (administrative district) of Turkey; after World War I (1920) a semiautonomous region of NW Syria extending ab. 100 m. along Gulf of Alexandretta and E Mediterranean, ab. 5000 sq. m., pop. 273,350; chief towns Alexandretta (İskenderon) and Antioch. Set up as a state with limited autonomy 1925 and as the Republic of Hatay 1938; incorporated in Turkish republic by agreement bet. France and Turkey June 23, 1939. Contains Alma Dagh, mountain range, with Musa Dagh at its S end, Orontes and Afrine rivers, and the port of Süveydiye (*anc.* Seleucia), N of mouth of Orontes.

2 *Fr.* A'lex'an'drette' (à'lĕk'sän'drĕt'). Seaport city. See İSKENDERON.

Alexandretta, Gulf of. See Gulf of İSKENDERON.

Al'ex·an'dri·a (ăl'ĕg·zăn'drĭ·à; ăl'ĭg-; *Brit. also* -zän'-). **1** City, Madison co., cen. Indiana, in agricultural section 17 m. WNW of Muncie; pop. 5582; manufactures mineral wool and limestone products.

2 City, ⊗ of Campbell co., N Kentucky; pop. 1318.

3 City, ⊗ of Rapides parish, cen. Louisiana, 100 m. NW of Baton Rouge; pop. 40,279; railroad center and distributing point for section producing cotton, sugar, rice, corn, and timber; manufactures cottonseed oil and building material; rice mills, sawmills.

4 City, ⊗ of Douglas co., W cen. Minnesota, 60 m. WNW of Saint Cloud; pop. 6713; resort center in lake region.

5 City, ⊗ of Hanson co., SE South Dakota; pop. 614.

6 Independent city, Arlington co., N Virginia, on Potomac river 7 m. S of Washington, D.C.; 8 sq. m.; pop. 91,023. Founded 1749 and became busy port (wheat, flour, tobacco) and stage stop; ⊗ of Fairfax co. 1752; incorp. as town 1779; became part of District of Columbia 1791, but was returned to Va. as free city 1846; ⊗ of Alexandria (now Arlington) co. 1847–98; became city 1852; occupied by Federal forces during Civil War; seat of Unionist Alexandria government 1863–65. Railroad center and shipping point; naval torpedo station; residential center and tourist resort; manufactures chemicals, lumber and wood work, brick, pottery, foundry products, etc. Home of George Washington. Protestant Episcopal Theological Seminary (1825) in environs.

7 Municipality, E New South Wales, SE Australia, S suburb of Sydney; pop. 9018.

8 Town, Glengarry co., SE Ontario, Canada, 22 m. N of Cornwall; pop. 2204; has several factories; center of dairying country.

9 *Arab.* **al-Is·kan·da·rî'yah** (ăl·ĭs·kăn·dă·rē'yà; -yä). Governorate (29 sq. m.), coextensive with city, and seaport city, Lower Egypt, on narrow strip of land bet. the Mediterranean and Lake Mareotis and just W of Abukir Bay and Rosetta mouth of Nile; pop. (1937) 685,736. See *Table* at EGYPT. Ancient island (Pharos), on which was famous lighthouse, now a peninsula connected with mainland by sandy isthmus filled in around ancient mole; fine modern harbor is W of peninsula and formed partly by a breakwater. Has railroad connections with Cairo and delta towns; great commercial city of Egypt handling 80% of foreign trade; population very cosmopolitan.

History: Founded by Alexander the Great after his capture of Egypt 332 B.C.; a trading center, also became a center of Hellenistic culture, famed as meeting ground of Greek, Arab, and Jewish ideas; site of greatest library of ancient times which was founded by Ptolemy I (323–285 B.C.) and was alleged to have contained 700,000 rolls of papyri; library lost in a conflagration which occurred when Caesar captured city 48 B.C.; captured by Arabs 640 A.D. and by Turks 1517; occupied by French 1798–1801 during Napoleon's Egyptian campaign (see ABUKIR); after a long period of decline in its significance because of rise of Cairo and neglect to dredge the silted harbor, revived commercially when Mehemet Ali joined it by a canal to the Nile early 19th century; bombarded and occupied by British 1882, after a series of nationalist riots against foreign domination of Egypt; temporarily taken over by British troops because of riots 1921. British naval base in World War II; saved from capture by Rommel by battle of El Alamein Oct.–Nov. 1942.

10 Commune, S Walachia, Romania, on lower Vedea river 30 m. W of Giurgiu; pop. 19,387.

Alexandria Arachosiorum. See KANDAHAR.

Alexandria Bay. Village, Jefferson co., N New York, on St. Lawrence river 25 m. N of Watertown; pop. 1583; summer resort and tourist center for Thousand Islands region.

Alexandria Troas See TROAS.

Al'ex·an·dri'na, Lake (ăl'ĕg·zăn·drē'nà; ăl'ĭg-; *Brit. also* -zän-). Lake, SE South Australia, at mouth of Murray river; actually a lagoon with shallow outlet, a fact that hinders navigation of the Murray; its S arm is the Coorong (*q.v.*).

Alexandropol, Alexandrovsk. Variants of ALEKSANDROPOL, ALEKSANDROVSK.

A'le·xan·drou'po·lis (ä'lâ·ksän·drōo'pô·lyĕs); *formerly Turk.* De'de A·gach' (dĕ'dä ä·äch'). Seaport city, ✳ of Evros dept., Western Thrace, Greece, on Aegean 10 m. NW of mouth of Maritsa river; pop. 12,009; episcopal see; has developed some importance as a trading town. Annexed by Bulgaria 1915–18; by

treaty after World War I returned to Greece. Occupied by Bulgaria 1941.

A·lex′is·ha′fen (ä·lĕk′sĭs·hä′fĕn). Coastal village and mission station on Astrolabe Bay 12 m. N of Madang, North-East New Guinea. Taken by Allies Apr. 26, 1944.

A′ley′ (à′lā′) *or* **A·leih′** (ă·lī′h′; ă·lā′h′). Town, Lebanon, in mountains ab. 10 m. SE of Beirut; summer resort.

Al·fal′fa (ăl·făl′fà). County in Oklahoma. See *Table* at OKLAHOMA.

Al Fal·lu′ja (ăl făl·lōō′jà; -jă). Town, cen. Iraq, on left bank of Euphrates 35 m. W of Baghdad and E of Lake Habbaniya.

Al′föld (ŏl′föld). Great central plain of Hungary, traversed by Danube and Tisza rivers. The **Little Alföld** is a plain in NW Hungary and S Czechoslovakia, near Bratislava.

Al·fon′si·ne (äl·fôn′sĕ·nå). Commune, Ravenna prov., Emilia, N Italy, 10 m. NW of Ravenna; pop. 11,889.

Al′fort′ville′ (àl′fôr′vēl′). Commune, Seine dept., N France, on Seine and Marne rivers 4 m. SE of Paris; pop. 30,078; separated from Maisons-Alfort 1885.

Al′fred (ăl′frĕd; -frĭd). **1** Town, ⊗ of York co., SW Maine; pop. 1201.
2 Village, Allegany co., SW New York, ab. 9 m. SW of Hornell; pop. 2807. Alfred University (coed.; estab. as Select School 1836) includes the State College of Ceramics and the State School of Agriculture (1908).

Alfred, Mount. Peak 8450 ft., Coast Mountains, SW Brit. Columbia, Canada, N of Vancouver.

Al′fre·ton (ôl′frĕ·tŭn; -t′n). Urban district, Derbyshire, N cen. England, 14 m. NNE of Derby; pop. 23,388; coal mines, iron foundries, hosiery, pottery; foundation traditionally ascribed to King Alfred.

Alfsborg. Var. of ÄLVSBORG.

Al Furât. See EUPHRATES.

al-Fustât. See CAIRO city.

Al′gar·ro′bo, Point (äl′gär·rô′vô). Cape on W coast of Puerto Rico.

Algarrobo Bay. Inlet of Pacific Ocean on W cen. coast of Chile below Valparaíso.

Al·gar′ve (äl·gàr′vĕ). **1** Old province, S Portugal; bounded on N by Alemtejo prov., on S and W by Atlantic Ocean; separated in E from Spanish prov. of Huelva by estuary of Guadiana river; ✻ Faro; forms modern district of Faro; Serra do Monchique (highest point 2960 ft.) in N; exports fruits, fish (tunny, sardines, anchovies), salt. Medieval Moorish kingdom (capital Silves) conquered 1251 by Alfonso III and title King of Algarve added to Portuguese crown 1253; later reduced to a province.
2 Province of Portugal. See *Table* at PORTUGAL.

Al′gäu *or* **All′gäu** (äl′goi). District, SW Bavaria, in govt. dist. of Swabia, known esp. for dairy products. In its widest sense, the territory extending N to the Danube, S to the Inn, and W to the Lech.

Algäu, *or* **Allgäu, Alps;** *Ger.* **Al′gäu′er,** *or* **All′-gäu′er, Al′pen** (äl′goi′ẽr äl′pĕn). Mountains bet. Bavaria and Tirol, including such peaks as Hohes Licht (8649 ft.), Mädelegabel (8689 ft.), Hochvogel (8492 ft.); they extend E from Lake of Constance forming W section of Bavarian Alps, and contain sources of the Lech and Iller rivers. See ALPS.

Al′ge·ci′ras (ăl′jĕ·sẽr′às; *Span.* äl′hå·thē′räs). Seaport, Cádiz prov., SW Spain, 6 m. W of Gibraltar; pop. 25,671; exports leather, cork, stone, spirits.
History: Held by Moors 711–1344; after famous siege conquered by Alfonso XI of Castile; Moorish city destroyed and site reoccupied by Spanish 1704 who erected the modern town 1760; station for Spanish fleet during siege of Gibraltar 1780–82; scene of conference of the Powers called to settle first Moroccan crisis 1906; gave name to Act of Algeciras which, in substance, gave France and Spain control of Morocco (*q.v.*).

Algeciras, Bay of. Bay in S extremity of Spain, bet. Algeciras and Gibraltar.

Al′ge·me·sí′ (äl′hå·må·sē′). Commune, Valencia prov., E Spain, ab. 6 m. N of Alcira; pop. 17,373.

Al′ger (ăl′jẽr). County in Michigan. See *Table* at MICHIGAN.

Al′ger′ (àl′zhä′). **1** Department of Algeria, between Constantine and Oran depts. Has mountain ranges along coast and high plateau in interior. Chief towns Algiers, Tizi-Ouzou, Blida. See *Table* at ALGERIA.
2 City, its ✻. See ALGIERS.

Al·ge′ri·a (ăl·jēr′ĭ·à); *Fr.* **Al′gé′rie′** (àl′zhä′rē′). Country in NW Africa; a republic, formerly a government-general of the French Republic, comprising (since 1957) thirteen departments of Northern Algeria and two Saharan departments, formerly Southern Territories (*Fr.* Territoires du Sud); 919,590 sq. m.; pop. 10,265,000; ✻ Algiers. Before 1957 divided by the French into the following departments and territories (for pronunciation of their names, see their individual entries):

NAME	LOCA-TION IN ALGERIA	AREA IN SQ. M.	POPULA-TION 1936	CAPITAL
NORTHERN ALGERIA (DEPARTMENTS)				
Alger	N	21,115	2,240,911	Algiers
Constantine	NE	33,806	2,727,766	Constantine
Oran	NW	25,998	1,623,356	Oran
SOUTHERN TERRITORIES				
Aïn-Sefra	NW	250,958	193,347	Aïn-Sefra
Ghardaïa	N cen.	55,473	166,366	Ghardaïa
Oasis Sahariennes	S	411,669	39,575	
Touggourt	NE	52,058	243,363	Touggourt

Bounded on N by Mediterranean Sea, on E by Tunisia and Libya, on S and SW by Mali and Niger, on W by Mauritania and Río de Oro, and on NW by Morocco; the Southern Territories occupy a large section of N Sahara Desert, nearly 10 times the N part in area, and include the Ahaggar tableland and part of the Adrar des Iforas. The N and settled part is crossed by E Atlas Mts.; coast line has few inlets and rivers are small. In E is lowland around Chott Melrir and Touggourt. Chief products wheat, barley, fruit, and vegetables. Inhabitants are chiefly Berbers with Arab admixtures. Chief cities Algiers, Oran, Constantine, Bône, and Philippeville.
History: Territory known to Romans as Numidia; conquered by Vandals 430–31 A.D., by Eastern Roman Empire 531–34, and by Arabs in 7th century; nominally under rule of Ottoman Empire until 1705; repudiated Turkish rule and controlled by tribal organizations under dey of Algiers until occupied by French 1830; hinterland not subjugated until 1847 after a series of intermittent wars by French against Abd-el-Kader; placed under military rule by Napoleon III; in 1863 given a land law which helped break up tribal organization; after 1879 under civil rule as a part of France; scene of an uprising during French difficulties with Tunis 1881; under a reorganized government after 1898. In World War II under Vichy control until Nov. 1942; occupied by Allied forces Nov. 8–12, 1942; granted independence following referendum of July 1, 1962.

Al·ghe′ro (äl·gâ′rô). Seaport, Sassari prov., NW Sardinia, 17 m. SSW of Sassari; pop. 15,998; exports fruit, wine, oil, coral, preserves; founded by Doria family (Genoese) ab. 1102; settled by Catalonians 14th cent.; under house of Aragon 1354–1720 and subsequently under house of Savoy.

Al·giers′ (ăl·jẽrz′); *Fr.* **Al′ger′** (àl′zhä′); *Arab.* **Al-je-za′ir** (äl′jă·zä′ĭr). **1** Former Barbary state, N Africa, now Algeria.
2 *anc.* **I·co′si·um** (ĭ·kō′sĭ·ŭm; -zĭ·ŭm). Seaport city, ✻ of Algeria and of Alger dept., on W side of **Bay of Algiers**; pop. (1936) 252,321. Has excellent harbor and extensive trade; a modern city built on hills; has government buildings, museum, cathedral, university, national library, and several populous suburbs.
History: Founded in the 10th century on site of a Roman town; held by Spain 1509–17; invaded disas-

trously by Charles V 1541; center of one of the piratical Barbary States which exacted tribute from European shipping; included in U.S. wars against the Barbary States 1801–05, 1815; encouraged by the absence of U.S. naval vessels to attack American shipping in the Mediterranean, finally forced to cease exaction of tribute after defeated by Decatur's punitive expedition 1815; bombarded by British 1816 in effort to force the dey to end Christian slavery; dey deposed by French 1830; became an important trading center as capital of the French colony of Algeria (*q.v.*). Allies landed Nov. 8, 1942.

Al·go′a Bay (ăl·gō′à). Bay on SE coast of Cape Prov., Union of South Africa, ab. 420 m. E of Cape Town; discovered by Portuguese 15th cent.; midway point in voyage to Goa (*q.v.*); town of Port Elizabeth (*q.v.*) founded by British on its shores 1820.

Al·go′ma (ăl·gō′mà). **1** City, Kewaunee co., E Wisconsin, on Lake Michigan 28 m. NE of Green Bay (city); pop. 3855; manufactures dairy products, plywood, veneer, etc.

2 District, Ontario, Canada. See *Table* at ONTARIO.

Al·go′na (ăl·gō′nà). City, ⊗ of Kossuth co., N Iowa, 38 m. N of Fort Dodge; pop. 5702.

Al′go·nac (ăl′gŏ·năk). Village, St. Clair co., SE Michigan, on St. Clair river 24 m. S of Port Huron; pop. 3190; boatbuilding center.

Al·gon′quin Park (ăl·gŏn′kwĭn; -gŏng′-). Canadian provincial park in SE Ontario S of Ottawa river; 2741 sq. m.; game preserve; noted for its fishing waters and beautiful scenery; contains more than 1200 lakes; fine camping facilities. Covers watershed bet. Ottawa river and streams to Georgian Bay.

Algonquin Peak. Mountain 5112 ft. in Adirondack Mountains, Essex co., NE New York.

Al′grange′ (ăl′gränzh′); *Ger.* **Al′gring·en** (ăl′grĭng·ĕn). Commune, Moselle dept., NE France, 19 m. NNW of Metz; pop. (1931) 10,175; iron mines.

Al Hadhr. See HATRA.

Al Hajara. See Al HAJARA.

Al′ha·jue′la (ä′lä·hwä′lä). Village, cen. Panama, on N bank of Chagres river at Madden Dam; outside Canal Zone proper but under U.S. control.

Al·ham′bra (ăl·hăm′brà). **1** Residential city, Los Angeles co., SW California, 5 m. ENE of Los Angeles; pop. 54,807; incorporated 1903.

2 Hill in Granada, Spain; site of remains of Moorish palace and fortifications.

Al′hau·rín′ el Gran′de (ä′lou·rēn′ ĕl grän′dà). Commune, Málaga prov., S Spain, 20 m. SW of Málaga and 5 m. E of Coín by rail; pop. 10,681; marble quarries, oil.

al–Ḥírah. See HIRA.

Al′hu·ce′mas (ä′lōō·thā′mäs; -sā′mäs). Bay and island, Er Rif region, coast of N Morocco ab. 50 m. W of Melilla; bombarded 1923 by Moors in Moroccan revolt against Spanish rule.

A·lia′ga (ä·lyä′gä). Municipality, W Nueva Ecija prov., Luzon, Phil. Is; pop. 15,149.

A′li·bag′ (ä′lĭ·bäg′). See KOLABA.

A′li·can′te (ä·lĭ·kän′tà; *Angl.* ăl′ĭ·kăn′tĕ). **1** Province of Spain. See *Table* at SPAIN.

2 Seaport city, its ✱, SE Spain, 77 m. S of Valencia; pop. (1941 est.) 97,636; episcopal see; produces wines (esp. Alicant red wine), castor oil, cigars, cotton, linen, and woolen goods; agricultural exports. Said to be ancient Roman city of **Lu·cen′tum** (lū·sĕn′tŭm) and, previous to that, a Greek colony; captured by Moors 713; recaptured 1265 by James I of Aragon; besieged by French 1709 and by federalists of Cartagena 1873.

Al′ice (ăl′ĭs). City, ⊗ of Jim Wells co., S Texas, 40 m. W of Corpus Christi; pop. 20,861; railroad division point; produces oil, cotton, farm crops, livestock.

Alice, Mount. Peak 13,310 ft. in Front Range of Rocky Mts. on boundary bet. Boulder and Grand cos., N cen. Colorado.

Alice Springs; *formerly* **Stu′art** (stū′ērt). Town on highway line from Adelaide (994 m.) to Darwin (1105 m.), Australia, in cen. S portion of Northern Territory and virtually the central point of the continent; in Macdonnell Ranges with altitude of 1926 ft.; pop. 4668; center of pastoral and mining region; popular winter resort. Site discovered 1860 by J. McDouall Stuart; capital (1927–31, under the name Stuart) of former Central Australia terr.

Al′ice·ville (ăl′ĭs·vĭl; *Sou. also* -v′l). Town, Pickens co., W Alabama, 35 m. WSW of Tuscaloosa; pop. 3194.

A′li·garh′ (ŭ′lē·gŭr′h′; *Angl.* ăl′ĭ·gär). **1** District, Agra div., Uttar Pradesh, N Indian Union; 1940 sq. m.; pop. (1941) 1,372,641.

2 or **Ko′il–A′li·garh′** (kō′ĭl-). City, its ✱, 43 m. N of Agra; pop. (1941) 112,655; a joint municipality consisting of fortress of Aligarh and the native city of **Ko′il** (kō′ĭl) or **Kol** (kōl); trade and industrial center. Became key Maratha fort under Sindhia 1759; stormed by British Aug. 28, 1803, during Second Maratha War (1803–05); center for western education for Mohammedans (Anglo-Oriental college, opened 1875, transformed 1920 into Aligarh Muslim Univ.).

A′li Khel (ä′lē käl′). Village in Safed Koh, E Afghanistan, on borders of India at W end of Peiwar Pass 50 m. SE of Kabul; scene of fighting 1879 when occupied by Lord Roberts.

Ali Masjid. See KHYBER PASS.

Al′ine, Loch (lŏk äl′ín). Inlet of Atlantic Ocean on coast of W cen. Scotland, in Argyll co.; 3½ m. long.

A′ling Kang′ri (ä′lĭng käng′rĕ) or **A′ling Gang′ri** (gäng′rĕ). Mountain range, W Tibet, Outer China, and mountain peak near its W end (24,000 ft. high) SE of Kashmir.

A′lings·ås′ (ä′lĭngs·ōs′). Town, Älvsborg co., SW Sweden, on lake 25 m. NE of Göteborg; pop. 10,795.

A·li·po′, Cape (ä·lē·pō′); *Turk.* **A·li·po′ Bur·nu′** (ä·lē·pō′ bōōr·nōō′). Cape on SW coast of Turkey in Asia, opp. N end of island of Rhodes.

A′li·pore′ (ä′lĭ·pōr′). See TWENTY-FOUR PARGANAS.

A′li·quip′pa (ăl′ĭ·kwĭp′à). Borough, Beaver co., W Pennsylvania, on Ohio river 19 m. WNW of Pittsburgh; pop. 26,369; steelworks.

A′li·raj′pur (ä′lĭ·räj′pōōr). **1** Former Indian state in SW Central India Agency, cen. India; 849 sq. m.; pop. (1941) 112,754; on July 7, 1947 joined a confederation of Indian states.

2 Town, its ✱, in SW Madhya Pradesh 100 m. WSW of Indore; pop. 5149.

Al′i·sal′ (ăl′ĭ·săl′). Urban community (unincorporated), Monterey co., California, E of Salinas; pop. 16,473.

A·li·şar′ Hü·yük′ (ä·lē·shär′ hü·yük′). Ruins of ancient town on Konak river (tributary of Delice river), cen. Turkey in Asia, ab. 35 m. SE of Yozgat; archaeological site of Hittite town.

al–Iskandaríyah. See ALEXANDRIA.

Al It′ti·had′ (ăl·ĭt′ĭ·hăd′; -häd′). Town, SW Arabian peninsula, W of Aden; ✱ of Federation of South Arabia.

A·li·tus′ or **A·ly·tus′** (ä·lē·tōōs′); *Russ. formerly also* **O·li′ta** (ŭ·lyē′tà). **1** District of Lithuania. See *Table* at LITHUANIA.

2 Town, its ✱, S Lithuania, on Neman river.

A′li·wal′ (ŭ′lĭ·wäl′). Village, W Punjab state, NW India, on S bank of Sutlej ab. 90 m. ESE of Lahore; scene of victory of British over the Sikhs Jan. 28, 1846.

A′li·wal′ North (ä′lĕ·wäl′). Town, NE Cape Prov., Union of South Africa, on Orange river 235 m. NNE of Port Elizabeth; pop. 7645; founded 1849; important health resort with sulfur springs.

Al Jazira or **Al-Jazirah.** See Al JAZIRA.

Al–jezair. See ALGIERS.

Al·ju·bar·ro′ta (ăl·zhōō·vär·rō′tà). Village, Leiria dist., W cen. Portugal, in Lis valley 16 m. SSW of Leiria. Scene of most important battle in Portuguese history in which invading Castilian forces under John I

were defeated 1385 by John I of Portugal; battle established Portuguese independence. See BATALHA.

Al Kadhimain. See KADHIMAIN.

Al·ke·ma'de (äl'kĕ·má'dĕ). Commune, South Holland prov., Netherlands, a suburb of Leiden; pop. 6040.

Alk'maar (älk'mär; *Dutch* älk'már). Commune, North Holland prov., W Netherlands, on North Holland canal 20 m. NNW of Amsterdam, intersected by canals; pop. (1939) 32,815; specially noted for its cheese market; exports also butter and grain; buildings include the town hall, church (Groote Kerk, built 1470–98), and a weigh-house (1582). First Dutch city successfully to resist Spanish 1573; Duke of York forced to capitulate by French under Brune 1799 and permitted to evacuate Russian-English forces.

Al Ku'fa (äl kōō'fá; -fä). Town on W bank of the Euphrates, S cen. Iraq, near An Najaf and ab. 90 m. S of Baghdad. Founded 638 A.D. by Caliph Omar I at the same time as Basra, became one of the two Islamic centers of the early Ommiad caliphs; in 7th and 8th centuries A.D. prosperous capital of perhaps 200,000 population, a Moslem literary, theological, and political center. Overwhelmed by Karmathians 890. Developed the Kufic angular script of Arabic used almost exclusively for the Koran and on monuments and coins.

Al Ku·wait' (äl kōō·wĭt'; -wät') *or* **Ku·wait'.** Seaport town, ✱ of Kuwait principality, at head of Persian Gulf ab. 80 m. due S of Basra; pop. ab. 25,000; has fine harbor and considerable trade. See PERSIAN GULF RESIDENCY.

Al'la·da' (á·lä·dá'). Town, Dahomey, West Africa, about 25 m. N of Ouidah; in 17th and 18th centuries chief town of an extensive kingdom of same name.

Al'la·gash (ăl'á·găsh). River, N Maine, in Piscataquis and Aroostook cos.; flows N into St. John river; outlet of many lakes incl. **Allagash Lake** in N Piscataquis co.

Al'lah·a·bad' (ăl'á·há·bäd'). **1** Division, Uttar Pradesh, N Indian Union; 10,102 sq. m.; pop. (1941) 6,014,813.

2 District of Allahabad division; 2798 sq. m.; pop. (1941) 1,812,981.

3 City, SE Uttar Pradesh, on the Ganges at its junction with the Jumna 72 m. W of Benares; pop. (1941) 260,630; important rail center; trades extensively in locally grown cotton and sugar cane and in European articles. Has historic Jama Masjid (Great Mosque), fine modern buildings, and Univ. of Allahabad.

History: Ancient city, a Holy City of India, long sacred to Hindu pilgrims; under Mohammedan rule 1194–1801; a residence of Mogul emperor, Akbar, who built fort there 1575; taken by British under Clive 1765; restored to ruler of Oudh 1771 in political bargains arranged by Hastings; finally ceded to British 1801; scene of a serious outbreak in Sepoy Mutiny 1857; site of Pillar of Asoka (erected 240 B.C.).

Al·laire' (á·lâr'). Deserted iron-industry village, Monmouth co., E cen. New Jersey, ab. 8 m. SW of Asbury Park; now Camp Burton, gift of Arthur Brisbane to Boy Scouts of America.

Al'la·lin'horn (á'lä·lēn'hôrn). Mountain 13,235 ft., Pennine Alps, Valais canton, Switzerland, ab. 8 m. NNE of Monte Rosa and ab. 8 m. ENE of Zermatt.

Al'la·ma·kee' (ăl'á·má·kē'). County in Iowa. See *Table* at IOWA.

All–American Canal. See IMPERIAL VALLEY.

Al'lan Mountain (ăl'ăn). Peak 9137 ft. in Bitterroot Range, NE Lemhi co., E cen. Idaho.

Al·lan'myo (á·län'myō). Town, Thayetmyo dist., Burma, on Irrawaddy river opp. Thayetmyo; pop. 12,511.

Al'la·too'na (ăl'á·tōō'ná). Hamlet and creek, SE Bartow co., Georgia; battle (**Allatoona Pass**) at creek 12 m. NW of Marietta Oct. 5, 1864 in Sherman's march on Atlanta.

Al'le (äl'ĕ). Tributary of Pregel river, 137 m. long, NE Poland and S Kaliningradsk Region, U.S.S.R.; flows N and E past Pravdinsk (where it becomes navigable) to

Wehlau (where it empties into the Pregel); upper course in Poland known as the Lyna.

Al'lée' Blanche' (á'lá' bländsh'). Pass (alt. 11,690 ft.) and valley in the Savoy Alps, N Italy, 4 m. S of Mont Blanc.

Al'le·gan (ăl'ĕ·găn). **1** County in Michigan. See *Table* at MICHIGAN.

2 City, its ⊗, SW Michigan, in agricultural, dairy, and fruit-growing section 22 m. NNW of Kalamazoo; pop. 4822; manufactures drugs.

Al'le·ga·ny (ăl'ĕ·gā'nĭ; ăl'ĕ·gā'nĭ). **1** Name of counties in two states of the U.S. See *Tables* at MARYLAND, NEW YORK.

2 Village, Cattaraugus co., SW New York, on Allegheny river 4 m. W of Olean; pop. 2064; in agricultural region. St. Bonaventure College and Seminary (founded 1859, chartered 1875) in nearby **St. Bon'a·ven'ture** (sănt bŏn'á·věn'tŭr; bŏn'á·věn'-). Nearby is **Allegany State Park,** 65,000 acres.

Al'le·gha'ny (ăl'ĕ·gā'nĭ; ăl'ĕ·gā'nĭ). Name of counties in two states of the U.S. See *Tables* at NORTH CAROLINA, VIRGINIA.

Alleghany Mountains. Var. of ALLEGHENY MOUNTAINS.

Al'le·ghe'ny (ăl'ĕ·gā'nĭ; ăl'ĕ·gā'nĭ). **1** River 325 m. long, W Pennsylvania, navigable for ab. 200 m.; rises in Potter co., Pa., loops NW into SW New York state, turns S across Pa. border in Warren co., flows S through W Pa., and unites with Monongahela river to form Ohio river at Pittsburgh; chief tributaries the Clarion, French Creek, and the Kiskiminetas.

2 County in Pennsylvania. See *Table* at PENNSYLVANIA.

3 Former city, Allegheny co., SW Pennsylvania, now part of Pittsburgh.

Allegheny Heights. Elevation 3187 ft., Garrett co., NW corner of Maryland.

Allegheny Mountain. Peak 4017 ft., Pendleton co., E West Virginia.

Allegheny Mountains, *also* **Al'le·ghe'nies** (ăl'ĕ·gā'nĭz; ăl'ĕ·gā'nĭz). Ranges of Appalachian system in Pennsylvania, Maryland, Virginia, and West Virginia, W of and generally parallel with the Blue Ridge; varying in height from 2000 to over 4800 ft.; E slope sometimes called **Allegheny Front** and the entire upland area from Cumberland Plateau on S to Mohawk valley in N.Y. is known as the **Allegheny Plateau.**

Al'len (ăl'ĕn; -ĭn). Name of a parish in Louisiana and of counties in four states of the U.S. See *Tables* at LOUISIANA, INDIANA, KANSAS, KENTUCKY, OHIO.

Allen, Bog of. Series of peat bogs, cen. Eire, from ab. 17 m. W of Dublin almost to the Shannon, over 375 sq. m., in Kildare, Offaly, Laoighis, and Westmeath; source of the Brosna, Boyne, and Barrow rivers; cut by Grand and Royal canals.

Allen, Lough (lŏk). Lake (*lough*) ab. 14 sq. m., co. Leitrim, Eire, 8½ m. N of Carrick; the Shannon river flows through it.

Allen, Mount. 1 Peak 9355 ft. in Glacier National Park, NW Montana.

2 Peak 4345 ft. in Adirondack Mts., Essex co., NE New York.

Al'len·dale (ăl'ĕn·dāl; ăl'ĭn-). **1** County in South Carolina. See *Table* at SOUTH CAROLINA.

2 Borough, Bergen co., NE corner of New Jersey, 8 m. N of Paterson; pop. 4092.

3 Town, ⊗ of Allendale co., SW South Carolina, 43 m. SW of Orangeburg; pop. 3114; settled in mid-18th cent.; farming (cotton, melons), fishing, hunting.

Al·len'de (ä-yān'dá). **1** Town, Coahuila state, NE Mexico, 33 m. SW of Piedras Negras; pop. 5613; railroad junction.

2 = SAN MIGUEL DE ALLENDE town in Guanajuato state, Mexico.

Al'len Park (ăl'ĕn; -ĭn). City, Wayne co., SE Michigan, 10 m. WSW of Detroit; pop. 37,052.

Al′len·stein (äl′ĕn·shtīn; *Angl.* ăl′ĕn·stĭn). **1** Former government district, S cen. East Prussia prov., Prussia, Germany; 4458 sq. m. See OLSZTYN.
2 City. See OLSZTYN.

Allenstein-Ma·ri′en·wer′der (-mä·rē′ĕn·vĕr′dĕr). Region made up of several districts of the former Prussian provinces of East Prussia and West Prussia, named from two of the more important: Allenstein in SW East Prussia and Marienwerder (see KWIDZYŃ) in E West Prussia. By a plebiscite taken July 11, 1920, under Treaty of Versailles both sections voted to remain in Germany, but a zone along the E bank of the Vistula around Marienwerder was assigned to Poland.

Al′lens·town (äl′ĕnz·toun; äl′ĭnz-). Town, Merrimack co., S cen. New Hampshire, E of Concord; pop. 1789.

Al′len·town (äl′ĕn·toun; äl′ĭn-). Commercial and industrial city, ⊗ of Lehigh co., E Pennsylvania, on Lehigh river 48 m. N of Philadelphia; pop. 108,347; first platted 1762; sheltered Liberty Bell during Revolution; incorp. as borough 1811 and made ⊗; incorp. as city 1867. Manufactures silk and cotton clothing, cement, mining machinery, steel and metal goods, shoes, cigars, trucks, etc.; limestone quarries. Muhlenberg College (1848; men); Cedar Crest College (1867; women).

Al·lep′pey (ȧ·lĕp′ĭ), *also* **Al·lep′pi.** Town, cen. Kerala state, S India, on Malabar Coast 130 m. S of Calicut; pop. (1941) 56,333. Commercial and industrial community with good harbor; exports copra, coir, pepper, ginger, cardamoms, coconuts.

Al′ler (äl′ĕr). River ab. 100 m. long, W Prussia, Germany; rises near Magdeburg, flows NW into Weser river SE of Bremen; navigable below Celle.

Al·ler′ (ä·lyĕr′). Commune, Oviedo prov., NW Spain, 20 m. SE of Oviedo; pop. 23,600; agricultural produce; coal, iron, and lead mines; coke.

Allgäu, Variant of ALGÄU.

Al′li·a (äl′ĭ·ȧ). Small river of ancient Italy ab. 11 m. N of Rome, flowing into the Tiber on the left bank; identified by some with modern Fosso della Bettina, by others with Fosso di Marcigliana. According to Livy, scene of battle in which Romans were defeated by Gauls under Brennus 390 B.C. and the way opened for sack of Rome.

Al·li′ance (ȧ·lī′ăns). **1** City, ⊗ of Box Butte co., NW Nebraska, 45 m. ENE of Scottsbluff; pop. 7845; trade center for agricultural section; ships seed potatoes.
2 Industrial city, Stark co., NE Ohio, on Mahoning river 16 m. ENE of Canton; pop. 28,362; settled by Quakers 1805; incorp. as village 1854, as city 1889; station on Underground Railroad; manufacturing and distribution center, esp. for cranes, mill machinery, castings, car wheels, etc.; bituminous coal mines and clay deposits nearby. Mount Union College (1846; coed.).

Al′lier′ (ȧ′lyā′); *anc.* **E·la′ver** (ē·lā′vĕr). **1** Navigable river ab. 250 m. long, S cen. France; flows NNW into Loire river ab. 4 m. W of Nevers.
2 Department of France. See *Table* at FRANCE.

Al′li·ga′tor Lake (äl′ĭ·gā′tĕr). Lake in Alligator Swamp, NW Hyde co., E North Carolina.

Alligator Point. Point on E coast of Orleans parish, SE Louisiana, extending into Lake Borgne.

Alligator Swamp. Great swamp, E North Carolina, extending bet. Albemarle Sound and Pamlico Sound and surrounding **Alligator River,** inlet of Albemarle Sound.

Al′li·son (äl′ĭ·s'n). Town, ⊗ of Butler co., NE cen. Iowa; pop. 952.

Al′lis·ton (äl′ĭs·tŭn). Town, Simcoe co., SE Ontario, Canada, 20 m. SSW of Barrie; pop. 1987.

Al′lo·a (äl′ō·ȧ). Seaport burgh, Clackmannan co., Scotland, 25 m. NE of Glasgow near mouth of Forth river; pop. 13,436; seat of the Earls of Mar and the Erskines; manufactures hosiery, yarn, whisky, ale; exports coal.

Al′lo·way (äl′ō·wā). Hamlet, S Ayr co., Scotland, 2¼ m. S of Ayr near mouth of the Doon; birthplace of Robert Burns and scene of his *Tam O'Shanter.*

All Saints Bay; *Port.* **Ba·í′a de To′dos os San′tos**

(bä·ē′ȧ thĕ tō′thoo-zoō sănn′toōs). Bay ab. 100 m. in circumference on E coast of Baía state, E Brazil; at its E entrance is the city of Salvador (Bahia).

Allsch′wil (älsh′vĭl). Commune, Basel-Land demicanton, Basel canton, NW Switzerland, W suburb of Basel; pop. (1930) 7157; manufactures brick and pottery.

Al′lu·mette′ (äl′ú·mĕt′). Island, 70 sq. m., in Ottawa river, SW Quebec prov., Canada, opp. Pembroke, Ont.; the expansion of Ottawa river SW of island sometimes known as **Allumette Lake.**

Al′ma (äl′mȧ). **1** City, ⊗ of Bacon co., SE Georgia; pop. 3515.
2 City, ⊗ of Wabaunsee co., E Kansas, 35 m. W of Topeka; pop. 838.
3 City, Gratiot co., cen. Michigan, 17 m. S of Mt. Pleasant; pop. 8978; beet sugar and petroleum refineries. Alma College (1886; coed.; Presbyterian).
4 City, ⊗ of Harlan co., S Nebraska; pop. 1342.
5 City, ⊗ of Buffalo co., W Wisconsin; pop. 1008.
6 Island, East Lake St. John co., S Quebec, Canada, bet. the outlets of Lake St. John; St. Joseph d'Alma is opp. its E end and Isle Maligne power station is to NE. See SAGUENAY river.

Al′ma (äl′mȧ; *Russ.* äl′y'·mȧ). Small river, SW Crimea, S Soviet Russia, Europe; enters Black Sea 17 m. N of Sevastopol. Scene of defeat of Russians under Prince Menshikov by English and French Sept. 20, 1854, one of earliest battles of Crimean War.

Al′ma-A·ta′ (äl′mä-ä·tä′); *formerly* **Ver′nyi** (vyĕr′nĭ). City, ✶ (since 1928) of Kazakh S.S.R. and ✶ of Alma-Ata Region, Soviet Russia, Asia, in SE part N of Issyk Kul; pop. (1939) 230,528; founded by Russians as a fort 1855; developed as trading center, esp. after building of Turkistan-Siberian R.R.

Alma-Ata Region. Subdivision of Kazakh S.S.R., Soviet Russia, Asia, in SE part; bounded on N by Lake Balkhash, on NE by Taldy-Kurgan Region, on SE by Sinkiang (China), on S by Kirgiz S.S.R., and on W by Dzhambul Region; ✶ Alma-Ata; largely desert, traversed by the Ili river, except in S along N slope of Ala Tau Mts.

Al′ma Daǧ (äl′mä dä′); *anc.* **A·ma′nus** (ȧ·mā′nŭs). Mountains, S Turkey in Asia, branch of Taurus Mts.; S end is in Hatay vilayet.

Al′ma·dén′ (äl′mä·thän′); *anc.* **Sis′a·pon** (sĭs′ȧ·pŏn). Commune, Ciudad Real prov., S cen. Spain, WSW of Ciudad Real bet. two mountains of the Sierra Morena; pop. 12,998; site of world-famous quicksilver mines which produce one third of the world's annual supply of mercury (ab. 1200–1300 tons), hence the name **Almadén del A·zo′gue** (dĕl ä·thō′gä) [Span. *azogue*, "mercury"]; also produces lead and sulfur. Quicksilver mines known to Romans and Moors, leased to Fuggers of Augsburg in 16th cent., worked by the Rothschilds of London in 19th cent.

Al′ma·di′es, Cape (?äl′mȧ·dē′ĕs). The extreme tip of the peninsula forming Cape Vert (*q.v.*), Senegal, W Africa, near Dakar; the westernmost point of Africa.

Almanor, Lake See BIG MEADOWS DAM.

Al·man′sa (äl·män′sä), *older* **Al·man′za** (äl·män′sä). Commune, Albacete prov., SE Spain, 43 m. ESE of Albacete; pop. 16,025; manufactures linen and cotton fabrics, brandy, leather, and soap. Scene of decisive victory 1707 by French under Duke of Berwick over English, Spanish, and Portuguese under Earl of Galway (War of the Spanish Succession).

Al′man·zor′, Pla′za de (plä′thä thä äl′män·thôr′; -sôr′). Highest peak 8692 ft. in Sierra de Gredos, W cen. Spain.

Al′man·zo′ra (äl′män·thō′rä; -sō′rä). River ab. 50 m. long, SE Spain; flows E through cen. Almería prov. into Mediterranean Sea.

Al′ma·ville (äl′mȧ·vĭl). Village, Champlain co., S Quebec, Canada, on St. Maurice river 16 m. NW of Three Rivers; pop. 2282.

Al·mei'da (ăl·mā'dá; *Port.* äl·mā'ě·thá). Fortified commune, Guarda district, NE Portugal, 25 m. NE of Guarda on Spanish frontier; pop. ab. 1600; sulfur waters; formerly one of chief strongholds against Spain; captured 1762 by Spain, but shortly afterward reverted to Portuguese; in Peninsular War captured by French 1810, recaptured by British and Portuguese 1811.

Al'me·lo (ăl'mě·lō). Industrial commune, Overijssel prov., E Netherlands, 22 m. ENE of Deventer at junction of Almelo and Overijssel canals; pop. (1939) 36,247; manufactures cotton and linen fabrics; seat of the Barons van Rechteren 1350 ff. and Counts Limpurg 1711 ff.

Al'me·nar' (äl'má·när'). Commune, Lérida prov., NE Spain, ab. 11 m. NNE of Lérida; scene of defeat of Spanish ruler Philip V by Austrians 1710 during War of Spanish Succession.

Al'me·na'ra (äl'má·nä'rä). Commune, S Castellón de la Plana prov., Spain, 20 m. NNE of Valencia; scene of defeat of Moors 1238 by James I.

Al'men·dra·le'jo (äl'měn·drä·lě'hō). Commune, Badajoz prov., SW Spain, 27 m. ESE of Badajoz; pop. 21,276; farm produce, brandy; annual sheep fair.

Al'me·rí'a (äl'má·rē'ä). **1** Province of Spain. See *Table* at SPAIN.
2 *anc.* **Un'ci** (ŭn'sī) *and* **Por'tus Mag'nus** (pōr'tŭs măg'nŭs). Seaport, its ✱, SE Spain, 60 m. SE of Granada at head of Gulf of Almería; pop. 80,180; episcopal see; exports fruits, esp. white grapes. One of chief Roman harbors after 19 A.D.; after fall of Ommiads as rulers of Spain, became head of small independent Moorish state, then a petty kingdom dependent on Granada; a leading seaport for Moors from which they preyed on Christian commerce; captured by Alfonso VII of Castile 1147, but retaken and held by Moors until 1489.

Almería, Gulf of. Inlet of Mediterranean Sea in S Almería prov., Spain; one of leading harbors of Spain.

Almesbury. Former variant of AMESBURY, England.

Al·mi'na, Point (äl·mē'nä). Point of land extending into the Mediterranean Sea at extremity of peninsula on which Ceuta is situated, NE Morocco, NW Africa; at SE entrance to Strait of Gibraltar.

Al'mi·ran'te (äl'mě·rän'tā). Port on NW side of Chiriquí Lagoon, NW Panama; a headquarters of the United Fruit Company.

Almissa. See OMIŠ.

Al'mo·dó'var (äl'mō·thō'vär). Short stream, SW Spain, in Cádiz prov.; flows W.

Almodóvar del Cam'po (thěl käm'pō). Commune, Ciudad Real prov., S cen. Spain, 22 m. SW of Ciudad Real and 3 m. N of Puertollano coal fields; pop. 14,633; old Moorish fortress.

Al'mond (ä'mŭnd). River 24 m. long, Lanark, West Lothian and Midlothian cos., SE Scotland; flows E and NE to Firth of Forth.

Al'monte (ăl'mŏnt). Industrial town, Lanark co., SE Ontario, Canada, on Mississippi river 32 m. WSW of Ottawa; pop. 2672.

Al·mo'ra (äl·mō'rá). **1** District, Kumaun div., Uttar Pradesh, N Indian Union, in W Himalayas; 5502 sq. mi.; pop. (1941) 687,286.
2 Town and hill station (alt. 5500 ft.), its ✱, 160 m. NE of Delhi; pop. 9688.

Almost–a–Dog Mountain. Peak 8911 ft. in Glacier National Park, S of Upper St. Mary Lake, NW Montana.

Al'mu·ñé'car (äl'mōō·nyä'kär); *anc.* **Sex'i** (sěk'sī). Mediterranean seaport, Granada prov., S Spain, ab. 32 m. S of Granada; pop. 11,110; landing place 756 of Abd-er-Rahman I, founder of the emirate of Córdoba.

Aln *or* **Alne** (ăln). Small river, N Northumberland, N England, flowing E into North Sea at Alnmouth.

Aln'mouth (äl'mouth'; ăln'mouth'). Seaport, Northumberland, England, at mouth of Aln river 3 m. SE of Alnwick; watering place.

Aln'wick (ăn'ĭk). Urban district, Northumberland, N England, on Aln river 37 m. N of Newcastle-on-Tyne; pop. 7366; breweries, grain mills, tobacco factories, and formerly, tanneries; feudal fortress (Alnwick Castle, seat of Dukes of Northumberland) stands at N entrance of town; besieged by Scots 1093, 1135, 1174, 1328, 1448.

A·lo'fi (ä·lō'fē). **1** One of the Futuna Islands (*q.v.*).
2 Chief village of Niue I., Cook Is., on W coast.

A·lo'nē·sos (ä·lô'nyĕ·sôs). Island of the Northern Sporades, NW Aegean Sea, NE of Skopelos; pop. 1005; belongs to Euboea dept., Greece.

A'lor (ä'lôr); *formerly* **Om·bai'** (ôm·bī'). Island, E end of Lesser Sunda Is., Indonesia, 20 m. N of Timor and WSW of Wetar; 906 sq. m.; ab. 60 m. long by 15 m. at E end widening to 26 m. at W end; pop. 51,423; chief town Kalabahi; very mountainous, highest point 5791 ft. at E end; has fine harbor (Kalabahi Bay) at W end. With Pantar forms the **Alor Islands** group (1126 sq. m.; pop. 90,616).

A'lo·ra (ä'lō·rä). Commune, Málaga prov., S Spain, 18 m. WNW of Málaga; pop. 13,968; grain, dates, and fruit, esp. oranges; mineral springs.

A'lor Ga'jah (ä'lôr gä'jä). **1** District, cen. Malacca settlement, Federation of Malaya, N of Malacca municipality; pop. 55,031.
2 Village, its ✱; pop. 1499.

Alor Star (stär). Town, ✱ of Kedah state, near coast in NW part, NW Federation of Malaya, 50 m. N of Penang; pop. 18,568, (1937 est.) 25,000; well laid-out town with modern buildings on highway and railroad N to Thailand; has large airport, 355 m. to Singapore and 800 m. to Rangoon.

Alor Strait. Channel ab. 10 m. wide bet. Lomblen and Pantar Islands in the Lesser Sundas, Indonesia, connecting Flores Sea with Savu Sea.

A·lor'ton (á·lôr't'n). Village, St. Clair co., SW Illinois; pop. 3282.

Alost. See AALST.

A'lo·te·nan'go (ä'lō·tä·näng'gō). Town, Sacatepéquez dept., S cen. Guatemala; pop. 5372.

A'loxe'–Cor'ton' (ä'lôks'kôr'tôn'). Parish, Côte-d'Or dept., E France, just N of Beaune; produces a fine red Burgundy wine (*corton*).

Al'pen (äl'pĕn). German form of *Alps*, as in Berner Alpen: see *Table* at ALPS.

Al·pe'na (ăl·pē'ná). **1** County in Michigan. See *Table* at MICHIGAN.
2 City, its ⊗, NE Michigan, on Thunder Bay, Lake Huron, at mouth of Thunder Bay river 50 m. N of mouth of Saginaw Bay; pop. 14,682; lumber and flour mills, tanneries, fisheries, and extensive lake commerce.

Al'pes (äl'pēz). Latin form of *Alps*. See *Table* at ALPS.

Alpes (álp). French form of *Alps:* (1) See *Table* at ALPS for individual ranges. (2) See *Table* at FRANCE for the following departments of France: **Alpes'–Ma'ri'times'** (álp'má'rē'tēm'), **Basses'–Alpes'** (bäs'-zálp'), **Hautes'–Alpes'** (ōt'-zálp').

Alpesa. See ELVAS.

Al'pha (ăl'fá). Borough, Warren co., NW New Jersey, 3 m. SSE of Phillipsburg; pop. 2406.

Al'phen (äl'fě[n]). Commune, South Holland prov., Netherlands, ab. 19 m. NE of Rotterdam; pop. 17,668.

Al·phe'us (ăl·fē'ŭs); *mod.* **Al·phei·os'** (äl·fyôs'), *also* **Rou·phi·a'** (rōō·fyä'). River ab. 75 m. long, W Peloponnesus, S Greece; rises in Arcadia, flows NW through S Elis into Ionian Sea near Pyrgos; Olympia is on its N bank.

Alp'hu'bel (älp'hōō'bĕl). Mountain 13,803 ft. and pass in the Alps, Valais canton, SW cen. Switzerland, ab. 6 m. NE of Zermatt.

Al'pi (äl'pē). Italian form of *Alps*. See *Table* at ALPS.

Alpi Apuane. = *Apuan Alps:* see APENNINES.

Al'pine (ăl'pīn). **1** County in California. See *Table* at CALIFORNIA.

2 Town, ⊗ of Brewster co., W Texas, 130 m. SE of El Paso; pop. 4740; in mountainous region, raising sheep, goats, cattle; granite quarries and mineral deposits nearby. Sul Ross State Coll. (1920; coed.).

Alportel, São Brás de. See SÃO BRÁS DE ALPORTEL.

Alps (ălps); *anc.* **Al'pes** (ăl'pēz). Mountain system of S cen. Europe extending in crescent shape ab. 660 m. from Mediterranean coast bet. France and Italy into Switzerland and along N boundary of Italy, through SW Austria and into NW and W Yugoslavia; area occupied estimated at ab. 80,000 sq. m.; highest point Mont Blanc (*q.v.*) 15,781 ft.; geologically of many rock types and varied folds and thrusts; remarkable for magnificent scenery with many glaciers, beautiful valleys (Chamonix, Interlaken, Engadine, Lauterbrunnen, Grindelwald, Zermatt) and lakes (Geneva, Thun, Lucerne, Brienz, Zug, Zurich, Constance, Maggiore, Como, Garda, Iseo); source of great rivers or their tributaries (Danube, Rhine, Rhone, Po). See also NORTH ALBANIAN ALPS, AUSTRALIAN ALPS.

The principal ranges (all of which have offshoot ranges and subsidiary groups) are shown in the *Table* on page 33. Famous passes and tunnels are:

Arl'berg (ärl'bĕrK). Pass, SW Austria, alt. 5900 ft., connecting Vorarlberg and the Tirol; railroad tunnel beneath pass 6¼ m. long, on road from Bludenz to Landeck, opened 1884, electrified 1923.

Bren'ner (brĕn'ĕr); *Ital.* **Bren'ne·ro** (brĕn'nă·rō). Pass bet. Innsbruck, Tirol-Vorarlberg prov., Austria, and Bressanone, Venezia Tridentina, Italy, 59 m. (24 m. further to Bolzano); highest point at Brenner, alt. 4494 ft., the lowest of any of the important Alpine passes; much frequented from earliest times; crossed by Teutonic invaders of Italy; carriage road built 1772 and railroad 1864–67 (22 tunnels and 60 large bridges).

Great Saint Ber·nard' (sănt bĕr·närd'); *Fr.* **Grand'– Saint'–Ber'nard'** (grän'săN'bĕr'när'). Pass bet. Valais, SW cen. Switzerland and Aosta prov., Piedmont, N Italy, 50 m. by road from Martigny to Aosta, alt. 8111 ft.; known to Celts and Romans in early times (*Lat.* Mons Jo'vis [mŏnz jō'vĭs]); much frequented by pilgrims and clerics on visits to Rome and later often crossed by medieval emperors and armies; used May 14–20, 1800 by Napoleon for his 40,000 troops for campaign in N Italy; named after the hospice at the summit of the pass, founded in 11th cent. by Saint Bernard of Menthon (923–1008); hospice is a stone building dating from 16th cent. kept by Augustinian monks who, with their famous St. Bernard dogs, give aid to travelers.

Little Saint Ber·nard' (sănt bĕr·närd'); *Fr.* **Pe·tit'– Saint'–Ber'nard'** (pē·tē'săN'bĕr'när'). Pass from Bourg-Saint-Maurice, Savoie dept., France, over Savoy Alps 27 m. to La Thuile, Aosta prov., Piedmont, Italy, alt. 7177 ft.; known in Roman times, has hospice founded in 11th cent. now administered by Order of St. Maurice and St. Lazarus dependent on the house at Aosta.

Mont Ce·nis' (môNs'nē'); *Ital.* **Mon'te Ce·ni'sio** (mŏn'tă chă·nē'zyō). Pass (*col*) bet. Modane, Savoie dept., France, and Susa, Torino prov., Piedmont, Italy, alt. 6831 ft., ab. 46 m. over the Mont Cenis massif in Graian Alps; known since 4th cent. A.D.; crossed by many armies; has been surmised but not proved that it was the pass used by Hannibal; carriage road constructed 1803–13 by order of Napoleon; hospice (at 6332 ft.). **Mont Cenis Tunnel** is 16 m. SW of pass and pierces Massif du Fréjus, 8½ m. from Modane to near Bardonnecchia, Italy; highest point 4246 ft.; constructed 1857–70, opened 1871, first of the great tunnels through the Alps.

Saint Gott'hard (sănt gŏt'ĕrd; *Ger.* [zängkt] gôt'härt) *or* **Got'hard** (sănt gŏt'ĕrd; gŏt'ĕrd); *Fr.* **Saint'– Go'thard'** (săN'gô'tär'). Pass bet. Altdorf in Uri canton and Bellinzona in Ticino canton, Switzerland; actual pass ab. 19 m. over Saint Gotthard group of Lepontine Alps, Göschenen to Airolo, alt. 6935 ft.; road

over pass open since early 13th cent.; named after the hospice in the pass, dedicated to St. Gotthard or Godehardus, bishop of Hildesheim (d. 1038); hospice first built in 14th cent. but has often been destroyed by avalanches; carriage road built 1820–30 but not much used since completion 1882 of **Saint Gotthard Tunnel,** 9½ m., highest point 3788 ft., constructed 1872–80.

Sim'plon (sĭm'plŏn; *Fr.* săN'plôN'; *Ger.* zĭm'plôn); *Ital.* **Sem·pio'ne** (sâm·pyō'nă). Pass bet. Brig, Valais canton, SW cen. Switzerland, and Iselle, NE Piedmont, Italy, 29 m. (40 m. to Domodossola below), alt. 6590 ft., over Alps; marks dividing line bet. Pennine and Lepontine Alps; named from village of Sim'peln (zĭm'pĕln) or Simplon in the pass; hospice at summit founded 1802 by Napoleon (not completed until 1825); carriage road built by Napoleon 1800–07; pass less used since completion of **Simplon Tunnel,** 12½ m., longest in the world, from Brig to Iselle under Monte Leone at W end of Lepontine Alps, alt. at highest point 2313 ft., constructed 1898–1905.

Splü'gen (shplü'gĕn); *Ital.* **Splu'ga** (sploo'gä). Pass bet. Splügen, Graubünden canton, E Switzerland, and Chiavenna, Lombardy, Italy, near head of Lake Como, 25 m. over Rhaetian Alps, alt. 6946 ft.; road built by Austrian government 1818–23.

See also **Mont Blanc Tunnel** at Mont BLANC.

Al'pu·jar'ras, Las (läs ăl'pōō·här'räs). Mountainous region, Granada and Almería provs., S Spain, S of the Sierra Nevada and parallel to it, bet. Motril and Almería; extremely fertile valleys; populated by colonists, esp. from Estremadura, and descendants of Moors who took refuge there after fall of Granada; scene of Moorish uprisings 1500–70.

al-Qâhirah. See CAIRO city.

Al·quí'zar (äl·kē'sär). Municipality and town, La Habana prov., Cuba, 33 m. SW of Havana; pop. (town) 6360.

Al Qur'na (ăl kŏŏr'nå; -nä). Town, SE Iraq, on right bank of the lower Tigris river where it joins the Euphrates to form the Shatt-al-Arab, ab. 45 m. NNW of Basra; captured by British 1914 in World War I.

Als (äls); *Ger.* **Al'sen** (äl'zĕn). Island off E coast of South Jutland, Aabenraa-Sönderborg co., Denmark; 124 sq. m.; pop. (1925) 28,623; in the Little Belt, separated from mainland by Sound of Alsen (**Al'sen·sund'** [äl'zĕn·zōōnt']); fertile, producing esp. apples and grain; lake and sea commercial fishing. Under Danish government to 1864, Prussian 1864–1919, Danish (by plebiscite) from 1919.

Al'sace (ăl'săs; ăl'sās; ăl·sās'; *Fr.* äl'zàs'); *anc.* **Al·sa'ti·a** (ăl·sā'shǐ·å; -shá); *Ger.* **El'sass** (ĕl'zäs). Old German and later French province bet. Rhine river and Vosges Mts., in modern depts. of Bas-Rhin and Haut-Rhin, NE France.

History: Ruled by Rome (see STRASBOURG); gradually penetrated by Germanic peoples; created a Frankish duchy; part of Middle Kingdom (see LORRAINE) assigned to Lothair I by Treaty of Verdun 843 A.D.; belonged to Holy Roman Empire 870–1648; united to duchy of Swabia 925; broken up into feudal principalities controlled chiefly by Bishop of Strasbourg and Hapsburg family in 14th century; Upper Alsace given to Burgundy 1469, but soon broke free; a center of the Peasants' Revolt of 1525; occupied by French in Thirty Years' War; annexed to France by means of Louis XIV's "Chambers of Reunion" 1680; consolidated into provinces of Bas-Rhin and Haut-Rhin after 1789 and under Napoleon; ceded to Germany by Treaty of Frankfurt 1871. For recent history, see ALSACE-LORRAINE.

Al'sace-Lor·raine' (ăl'săs-lŏ·rān'; ăl'sās-; -lō-); *Ger.* **El'sass-Lo'thring·en** (ĕl'zäs-lō'trĭng·ĕn). Frontier region bet. France, Germany, Belgium, and Switzerland; except for Rhine on E has had indefinite boundaries.

History: Formed from French province of Alsace,

English	NAME Classical[1]	Native	LOCATION	HIGHEST POINT
		WESTERN		
Maritime Alps (măr′ĭ·tĭm; -tĭm; -tēm)	Alpes Maritimae (ăl′pēz mȧ·rīt′-ĭ·mē)	*Fr.* Alpes Maritimes (ȧlp′ mȧ′rē′tēm′); *Ital.* Alpi Marittime (äl′pĕ mä-rēt′tĕ·mä)	In S bet. France and Italy	Punta Argentera 10,814 ft.
Ligurian Alps (lĭ·gūr′ĭ·ăn)		*Ital.* Alpi Liguri (äl′pĕ lē′gōō·rĕ)	E extension of Maritime Alps along coast of NW Italy	Saccarello 7,216 ft.
Cottian Alps (kŏt′ĭ·ăn)	Alpes Cottiae (äl′-pēz kŏt′ĭ·ē)	*Fr.* Alpes Cottiennes (ȧlp′ kô′tyĕn′); *Ital.* Alpi Co-zie (äl′pĕ kô′tsyȧ)	N of Maritime Alps bet. Basses-Alpes and Hautes-Alpes depts., France, and Torino prov., Italy	Mount Viso 12,605 ft.
Graian Alps (grā′-yăn; grī′ăn)	Alpes Graiae (äl′pēz grā′yē; grī′ē)	*Fr.* Alpes Graies (ȧlp′ grĕ′); *Ital.* Alpi Graie (äl′pĕ grä′yȧ)	Savoie dept., France, and NW Piedmont, Italy	Gran Paradiso 13,324 ft.
Dauphiné Alps (dō′fē′nā′)		*Fr.* Alpes du Dauphiné (ȧlp′ dü dō′fē′nā′)	In old prov. of Dauphiné (*q.v.*), France, W of Cottian Alps	Barre des Écrins 13,462 ft.
Savoy Alps (sȧ·voi′)		*Fr.* Alpes de Savoie (ȧlp′ dē sȧ′vwȧ′)	In Haute-Savoie dept., France	Mont Blanc 15,781 ft.
		CENTRAL: *Southern*		
Pennine Alps (pĕn′ĭn)	Alpes Penninae (äl′pēz pĕ·nī′nē)	*Fr.* Alpes Pennines (ȧlp′ pĕ′nēn′); *Ital.* Alpi Pennine (äl′pĕ pån·nē′nȧ)	In Valais canton, SW cen. Switz., and N Piedmont, Italy, NE of Graian Alps	Monte Rosa 15,217 ft.
Lepontine Alps (lė·pŏn′tĭn)		*Fr.* Alpes Lépontiennes (ȧlp′ lā′pŏn′tyĕn′); *Ital.* Alpi Lepontine (äl′pĕ lȧ·pŏn·tē′nȧ)	On boundary bet. Switzerland and Italy and in Ticino and Graubünden cantons, Switz.	Monte Leone 11,684 ft.
Rhaetian Alps (rē′shăn)	Alpes Raeticae (äl′pēz rē′tĭ·sē)	*Fr.* Alpes Rhétiques (ȧlp′ rā′tēk′); *Ital.* Alpi Reti (äl′pĕ rȧ′tĕ); *Ger.* Rätische Alpen (râ′tĭ·shĕ äl′pĕn)	E Graubünden canton, Switz.	Piz Bernina 13,295 ft.
		CENTRAL: *Northern*		
Bernese Alps (bûr′nēz′; -nēs′)		*Fr.* Alpes Bernoises (ȧlp′ bĕr′nwȧz′); *Ger.* Berner Oberland *or* Alpen (bĕr′-nēr ō′bĕr·länt, äl′pĕn)	S cen. Switz.—Bern, Valais, and Uri cantons	Finsteraarhorn 14,026 ft.
		EASTERN		
Noric Alps (nŏr′ĭk)	Alpes Noricae (äl′pēz nŏr′ĭ·sē)	*Ger.* Norische Alpen (nō′-rĭ·shĕ äl′pĕn)	Austria, bet. valleys of Mur and Drava	Eisenhut 8,006 ft.
Hohe Tauern (hō′ĕ tou′ĕrn)		*Ger.* Hohe Tauern (hō′ĕ tou′ĕrn)	Bet. Carinthia and Tirol, W Austria	Gross Glockner 12,461 ft.
Carnic Alps (kär′nĭk)	Alpes Carnicae (äl′pēz kär′-nĭ·sē)	*Ger.* Karnische Alpen (kär′nĭ·shĕ äl′pĕn); *Ital.* Alpi Carniche (äl′pĕ kär′nĕ·kȧ)	Bet. S Austria and NE Italy and in Carniola	Kellerwand 9,217 ft.
Dolomites [dŏl′ō·mīts] (Tridentine Alps [trī·dĕn′-tĭn; trĭ-; -tĭn])	Alpes Venetae (äl′pēz vĕn′ĕ·tē)	*Ital.* Dolomiti (dō·lō·mē′-tē)	In Venezia Tridentina and Venezia Euganea, NE Italy, bet. valleys of Adige and Piave	Marmolada 10,965 ft.
Julian Alps (jōōl′yăn)	Alpes Juliae (äl′-pēz jōō′lĭ·ē)	*Ital.* Alpi Giulie (äl′pĕ jōō′lyȧ); *Ger.* Julische Alpen (yōō′lĭ·shĕ äl′pĕn)	In Slovenia, NW Yugoslavia	Triglav 9,394 ft.
Karawanken (kä′rä·väng′kĕn)	Caravanca Mons (kär′ȧ·väng′kȧ mŏnz)	*Ital.* Caravanche (kä′rä-väng′kȧ)	S of the valley of the Drava bet. S Austria and NW Yugoslavia	Hochstuhl 7,334 ft.
Dinaric Alps (dĭ·năr′ĭk)	Alpes Dinaricae (äl′pēz dĭ·năr′-ĭ·sē)	*Ital.* Alpi Dinariche (äl′pĕ dĕ·nä′rĕ·kȧ); *Yugoslav* Dinara Planina (dē′-nä·rä plä′nĕ·nä)	Parallel to W coast of Yugoslavia, S to Albania	Voljnac 7,800 ft.

[1] Latin names given of those ranges known by name to the ancients.

French department of Moselle, and some subdivisions (*arrondissements*) of the former dept. of Meurthe which were ceded to Germany by Treaty of Frankfurt 1871; administered in three divisions, Upper Alsace (*Ger.* O′ber·el′sass [ō′bĕr·ĕl′zäs]), Lower Alsace (Un′ter·el′-sass [ŏŏn′tĕr-]), and Lorraine (Lothringen), under the German Empire 1871–1918; subject to unsuccessful attempts to Germanize 1880–1910; restored to France by Treaty of Versailles 1919. In World War II held by Germany 1940–44; retaken by French and American armies and again restored to France.

Alsatia. See ALSACE.

Al′sek (ăl′sĕk). River 260 m. long, SW Yukon and SE Alaska: rises in Aishihik Lake and flows S through E end of St. Elias Range and Alaska to the Pacific.

Alsen, Alsensund. See ALS.

Alt. See OLT.

Al′ta (al′tà). Winter sports area, Salt Lake co., N Utah, in Wasatch Range SE of Salt Lake City.

Al′ta (äl′tä). River ab. 50 m. long, N Norway; flows N in Finnmark co. into **Alta Fjord** inlet of Arctic Ocean 70°N, hiding place of German fleet in World War II.

Al′ta Ca′li·for′nia (äl′tä kä′lĕ·fôr′nyà). Upper California—the Spanish name for the present state of California, used to differentiate it from Baja California (see LOWER CALIFORNIA).

Al′ta·de′na (ăl′tà·dē′nà). Urban community (unincorporated), Los Angeles co., California, NE of Pasadena; pop. 18,942.

Al′ta·gra′cia (äl′tä·grä′syä). Town, Zulia state, NW Venezuela, on NE shore of Lake Maracaibo and opp. Maracaibo; pop. ab. 7000.

Al′ta Gra′cia (äl′tä grä′syä). Mountain resort, W Córdoba prov., N cen. Argentina, ab. 30 m. SSW of Córdoba; pop. (est.) 12,368.

Al′tai (äl′tī; äl·tī′; *Russ.* ŭl·tī′). Mountain system bet. W Mongolia and NE Sinkiang prov., W China, and bet. Kazakh S.S.R. and Oirot Autonomous Region, Soviet Russia, Asia; highest Belukha 15,157 ft.; source of Irtysh and Ob rivers.

Altai Territory. Territory, SW Soviet Russia, Asia; 71,885 sq. m.; pop. 2,358,653; ✻ Barnaul; formerly included at its E end the Oirot Autonomous Region (*q.v.*); bounded on N by Novosibirsk Region, on E by Kemerovo Region, and on S and SW by Kazakh S.S.R. Traversed by the upper Ob, flowing generally N into Novosibirsk Region. Agricultural region; valuable mineral deposits.

Al′ta·ma·ha′ (ô(l)′tà·mà·hô′). River 137 m. long, SE Georgia, formed by junction of Ocmulgee and Oconee rivers at SE tip of Wheeler co.; flows SE to Atlantic ab. 12 m. N of Brunswick.

Altamaha Sound. Inlet of Atlantic Ocean on SE coast of McIntosh co., SE Georgia, receiving the Altamaha river on the W.

Al′ta·mi′ra (äl′tä·mē′rä). Caverns (*cuevas*) in Santander prov., N Spain, ab. 13 m. WSW of Santander; discovered 1879; prehistoric drawings and paintings of animals, assigned to Upper Magdalenian Age.

Al′ta·mi·ra′no (äl′tä·mē·rä′nŏ). Town, Argentina, 54 m. S of Buenos Aires; pop. ab. 18,000.

Al′ta·mont (ăl′tà·mŏnt). **1** City, Effingham co. SE cen. Illinois; pop. 1656.
2 Urban community (unincorporated), Klamath co., S Oregon, E of Klamath Falls; pop. 10,811.
3 Town, ⊗ of Grundy co., S cen. Tennessee; pop. 552.

Al′ta·mu′ra (äl′tä·mōō′rä); *anc.* **Lu·pa′ti·a** (lû·pā′-shǐ·à; -shà). Commune, Bari prov., Apulia, SE Italy, at foot of the Apennines 28 m. SW of Bari; pop. 31,431; oil, wine, wool; walled city rebuilt 1232 by Emperor Frederick II.

Altan Bulak. See KIACHTA.

Altan–Nor. See ELTON.

Al′ta Peak (ăl′tà). Mountain 11,211 ft. in Sierra Nevada, NE Tulare co., S cen. California.

Al·tar′ (äl·tär′) *or* **Ca′pac–Ur′cu** (kä′päk·ōōr′kōō).

Mountain 17,725 ft. in the Andes, cen. Ecuador, E of Riobamba.

Al′ta Ve′ra·paz′ (äl′tä vā′rä·päs′). Department, cen. Guatemala; 4472 sq. m.; pop. 282,562; ✻ Cobán.

Al′ta·vis′ta (ăl′tà·vĭs′tà). Industrial town, Campbell co., S cen. Virginia, on Roanoke river 23 m. S of Lynchburg; pop. 3299; rayon, cedar chests, etc.

Alt Breisach. See BREISACH.

Alt′dorf (ält′dôrf) *or* **Al′torf** (äl′tôrf). Commune, ✻ of Uri canton, cen. Switzerland, near SE tip of Lake Lucerne 20 m. SE of Lucerne; pop. (1930) 4240; connected with William Tell legend, having a colossal statue of Tell by Kissling on the supposed site of the apple-shooting episode, and a theater for the annual production of Schiller's *William Tell;* site of oldest Capuchin monastery (1581) in Switzerland.

Al′te·na (äl′tĕ·nä). Manufacturing city, W Germany, in North Rhine-Westphalia state 47 m. S of Münster; pop. 16,167; site of ancestral castle of Counts von der Marck; manufactures metalware and wire.

Al′ten·burg (äl′tĕn·bŏŏrk). **1** Manufacturing city, Thuringia, E Germany, in valley of the Pleisse 49 m. E of Weimar; pop. 42,570; trades in grain, cattle, horses; foundries, machinery works; manufactures brushes, gloves, hats, paper, chemicals; lignite mining.
    History: One of oldest German cities east of Saale river (mentioned as early as 976); seat of a burgrave from 12th century; given to Wettin family as fief of Holy Roman Empire 1329; burned by Hussites 1430; held by Ernestine branch of family 1485–1547 and from 1554; scene 1568–69 of conference between Lutherans and Philippists, two groups of German Protestants; from 1603–72 and 1826–1918 capital of independent duchy of Saxe-Altenburg.
2 Town in Hungary. See MAGYARÓVÁR.

Al′ten Fjord (äl′tĕn). Var. of *Alta Fjord:* see ALTA.

Al′ten·kir′chen im Wes′ter·wald′ (äl′tĕn·kĭr′kĕn ĭm vĕs′tĕr·vält′). Town, W Germany, in Rhineland-Palatinate state, 22 m. N of Koblenz; pop. 3011; scene of two battles bet. Austrians and French during War of the First Coalition 1796.

Alt′hei′de (ält′hī′dĕ). Village, S Wrocław dept., SW Poland, 6 m. WSW of Kłodzko; pop. (1925) 2536; formerly in Upper Silesia, Prussia, Germany; has uranium deposits.

Altin Tagh. See ASTIN TAGH.

Alt′kirch (ält′kĭrк). Commune, Haut-Rhin dept., NE France, 29 m. SSW of Colmar; pop. 3455; scene of several battles 1914.

Alt′mühl (ält′mül). River ab. 120 m. long, S Germany; flows E in Bavaria to join the Danube river at Kelheim.

Al′to, Pi′co (pē′kōō äl′tōō). Volcanic peak 7460 ft. on Pico I. in the Azores; highest point in the Azores.

Al′to A′di·ge (äl′tō ä′dĕ·jä). Former district, N Venezia Tridentina, Italy, now Bolzano prov.; mainly German or Ladin speaking.

Al′to A·len·te′jo (äl′tōō ă·länn·tā′zhōō; -tä′zhōō). Province of Portugal. See ALENTEJO and *Table* at PORTUGAL.

Alt′–O′fen (ält′ō′fĕn); *Hung.* **Ó′bu·da** (ō′bŏō·dŏ). District of N Budapest, Hungary.

Al′tofts (ôl′tŏfts). Former urban district, West Riding, Yorkshire, England, on Calder river; pop. (1931) 4981.

Al′ton (ôl′t'n). **1** City, Madison co., SW Illinois, on Mississippi river 22 m. N of East St. Louis; pop. 43,047; industrial center and shipping point; oil refineries, limestone quarries, flour mills, manufacturing plants. Shurtleff College (1827; coed.).
2 City, ⊗ of Oregon co., S Missouri; pop. 677.
3 Urban district, Hampshire, England, on the Wey river ab. 24 m. NE of Southampton; pop. 8636; markets and fairs for hops, corn, and cattle; brewing; iron foundries and paper manufacture.

Al′to·na (äl′tŏ·nä). Before 1937, a city in Schleswig-Holstein prov., Prussia, Germany, on right bank of Elbe river adjoining on the E the Hamburg suburb of St.

Pauli; pop. 185,653; largest and richest city in Schleswig-Holstein; connected with Hamburg by elevated railroad; iron foundries, cotton and woolen mills, breweries, distilleries, glassworks, soap factories, cigar factories, leatherware factories; fishing.

History: Fishing village when passed to Denmark 1640; granted customs privileges with intention of making it rival Hamburg (*q.v.*), its neighbor; burned by Swedes 1713; despite Napoleonic Wars, prospered until 1853 when it lost privileges; occupied 1864 in name of North German Confederation; became Prussian 1866; with Hamburg joined Zollverein 1888; became part of Hamburg 1937.

Al·too′na (ăl·tōō′nȧ). Industrial city, Blair co., S cen. Pennsylvania, near source of Juniata river in bituminous coal region 90 m. E of Pittsburgh; pop. 69,407. Settled 1849, incorp. as city 1868. Extensive manufacturing and repair shops of Pennsylvania R.R.; textile factories; 5 m. W is scenic Horseshoe Curve of railroad.

Al′to Pa′ra·ná′ (*Span.* äl′tŏ pä′rä·nä′; *Port.* äl′tōō pȧ′rȧ·nä′). **1** River. See PARANÁ.
2 Department of Paraguay. See *Table* at PARAGUAY.

Altorf. See ALTDORF.

Al′tos (äl′tŏs). Town, Cordillera dept., cen. Paraguay; pop. ab. 13,800.

Al′to Son′go (äl′tŏ sông′gŏ). Municipality and town, Oriente prov., Cuba, NE of Santiago; pop. (town) 8140.

Alt′ran′städt (ält′rän′shtĕt). Village, in former Prussian province of Saxony, E Germany, 15 m. W of Leipzig. Gave name to two treaties: (1) treaty of 1706, during Great Northern War, by which Augustus II, King of Poland and Elector of Saxony, was forced by Charles XII of Sweden to renounce claim to Polish crown in favor of Stanislas I Leszczyński; (2) treaty of 1707, in which Austrian emperor Joseph I guaranteed to Charles XII religious toleration and freedom for Protestants in Silesia.

Al′trinc·ham (ôl′trĭng·ăm). Urban district, Cheshire, NW England, 9 m. SSW of Manchester; pop. 39,787; typesetting machinery; noted for its market gardens; its annual fair dates from Edward I (1290).

Altsohl. See ZVOLEN.

Alt′stät′ten (ält′shtĕt′ĕn). Commune, St. Gallen canton, NE Switzerland, in fertile Rhine valley 8 m. S of Lake Constance; pop. (1930) 8393; peat; textiles, esp. muslin.

Alt′stet′ten (ält′shtĕt′ĕn). Commune, Zurich canton, NE cen. Switzerland, W suburb of Zurich; pop. 9068.

Al·tu′ras (ăl·tōō′ăs). City, ⊗ of Modoc co., NE corner of California, on Pit river 138 m. NE of Chico; pop. 2819; first settled 1874; called Dorris Bridge until 1874; trade center for livestock, potato, and alfalfa region.

Al′tus (äl′tŭs). City, ⊗ of Jackson co., SW Oklahoma, 58 m. W of Lawton; pop. 21,225; founded 1891; cotton, livestock, grain market.

Altyn Tagh. See ASTIN TAGH.

Al·u′la (ăl·ōō′lȧ). Small port on Gulf of Aden, NE Somalia, W of Cape Guardafui.

Al′um Rock (äl′ŭm). Urban community (unincorporated), Santa Clara co., California, NE of San Jose; pop. 18,942.

Alung Gangri. Var. of ALING KANGRL

A·lush′ta (ȧ·lōōsh′tȧ). Town on SE coast of Crimea, Russia in Europe, ab. 18 m. NE of Yalta.

Aluta. See OLT.

Al′va (äl′vȧ). City, ⊗ of Woods co., NW Oklahoma, 53 m. WNW of Enid; pop. 6258; business center in stockraising, wheat, and dairy-farming region. Northwestern State College (1897; coed.).

Al′va·ra′do (äl′vä·rä′thŏ). **1** Seaside resort, Argentina. See GENERAL ALVARADO.
2 Town, Veracruz state, E Mexico, on coast 33 m. SE of Veracruz; pop. 5776.

Alvarado, Pa′so de (pä′sŏ thä). Andean mountain pass on Argentina-Chile border, bet. W Mendoza prov.,

Argentina, and E Santiago prov., Chile; alt. 12,484 ft.

Al′va·ro O′bre·gón′ (äl′vä·rŏ ŏ′vrä·gôn′); *formerly* **Fron·te′ra** (frŏn·tä′rä). Town, Tabasco state, SE Mexico, on Grijalva river near its mouth; pop. 7439.

Al′vin (äl′vĭn). City, Brazoria co., SE Texas, in agricultural section 25 m. S of Houston; pop. 5643; oil wells.

Älvs′borg′ (ĕlvs′bôr′y′). Province of Sweden. See *Table* at SWEDEN.

Al·wand′, Mount (ăl·vȧnd′); *Pers.* **Kuh–i–Alwand** (kōō′hĕ-); *anc.* **O·ron′tes** (ō·rŏn′tēz). Mountain 10,695 ft., W Iran, just SW of Hamadan.

Al′war, *also* **Al′wur** (ŭl′wĕr). **1** Former Indian state, E Rajasthan, NW India; 3158 sq. m.; pop. (1941) 823,055; a hilly, agricultural region. Founded by Rajput chieftain Pratap Singh in latter part of 18th cent.; joined British against Marathas 1803.
2 City, its ✻, ab. 80 m. SW of Delhi; pop. (1941) 54,143; surrounded by wall and moat; has fine palaces and temples.

Alytus. Var. of ALITUS.

Al′zette′ (äl′zĕt′). River, cen. Luxembourg; flows N into Sauer river.

A′ma·cu′ro (ä′mä·kōō′rŏ), *also* **A′ma·ku′ra** (-kōō′rä). Small river, NE Venezuela, flowing NE then NW to Orinoco delta; along its middle course forms short section of Venezuela-British Guiana boundary (as drawn 1835 by Schomburgk but not accepted by Venezuela until confirmation of British claims by arbitration 1899).

Am′a·de′us, Lake (ăm′ȧ·dē′ŭs). Large lake, cen. Australia, in SW corner of Northern Territory, S of Macdonnell Ranges; has no outlet; discovered 1872 by Ernest Giles, Australian explorer.

A·ma·di′ya (ȧ·mä′dĭ·yȧ; -yä). Town, S Kurdistan, ab. 55 m. NNE of Mosul, N Iraq.

A·madj′uak (ȧ·mäj′wăk). Trading post on S coast of Baffin I. and on Hudson Strait, Franklin Dist., Northwest Territories, Canada.

Amadjuak Lake. Lake in S Baffin Island, E Franklin District, Northwest Territories, Canada, ab. 50 m. N of Amadjuak post.

Am′a·dor (ăm′ȧ·dôr; -dōr). County in California. See *Table* at CALIFORNIA.

Amador, Fort. United States fort in the Canal Zone at the Pacific terminus of the Panama Canal.

A·ma·ga·sa·ki (ä·mä·gä·sä·kĕ). City, Hyogo pref., W Honshu, Japan, on NE shore of Osaka Bay; pop. 279,264; a suburb of Osaka and an important chemical and iron-and-steel center in the Osaka-Kobe industrial area. Frequently bombed by American planes 1945.

A′ma·ger (ä′mȧ·gĕr). Island forming a part of Denmark, lying in Öresund off the NE cen. coast of the island of Sjælland and separated from Sjælland by the harbor of Copenhagen; 25 sq. m.; pop. (1925) 110,404; includes a section of the city of Copenhagen. Inhabitants are largely descendants of 16th-cent. Dutch colonists.

A·mak′nak (ȧ·măk′năk). Small island ab. 4 m. long in Unalaska Bay, Unalaska I., E Aleutian Is.; Dutch Harbor, U.S. Naval Station, on it; highest point 1640 ft.

A·ma·ku·sa (ä·mä·kōō·sä). Island group off W coast of Kyushu, Japan, E of Amakusa Sea and S of Nagasaki, in Kumamoto prefecture; 342 sq. m.; pop. (1945) 216,185; ✻ Hondo; comprises two large islands and ab. 65 small islands.

A·mal′fi (ä·mäl′fē). Town, Salerno prov., Campania, Italy, on north coast of Gulf of Salerno ab. 22 m. SE of Naples; pop. 7598; built on mountain slope; archiepiscopal see; cathedral of Sant'Andrea (11th cent.) with bronze doors cast at Constantinople before 1066.

History: Originally a Byzantine settlement, became important commercial port in 9th century equal to Venice and Genoa; by 839 succeeded in freeing itself from Naples and Benevento; as a leading naval power, helped Pope Leo IV against Saracens 848; one of first Italian cities to become independent republic (under rule of doges) near beginning of 11th century; captured by

Normans under Roger II of Sicily 1131; sacked by Pisans 1135, 1137; declined gradually until inundation of 1373 destroyed much of town and harbor. Notable particularly for the *Tabulae Amalphitanae*, its maritime code, recognized on the Mediterranean till 1750.

A·ma·li·as' (ä'mä-lyäs'). City, Achaea and Elis dept., NW Peloponnesus, Greece; near W coast; pop. 12,365; in fertile region producing wine grapes and currants.

A·mal'ner (ŭ-mŭl'när). Town, East Khandesh dist., Gujerat state., W Indian Union, on tributary of Tapti river 145 m. E of Surat; pop. 23,491.

Amambahy, Serra de. See SERRA DE AMAMBAHY.

A'mam·bay' (ä'mäm-bi'). Department of Paraguay. See *Table* at PARAGUAY.

Amambay, Cordillera de. See SERRA DE AMAMBAHY.

A·ma·mi (ä-mä-mē); *also, officially,* **O·shi·ma** (ō-shē'mä). Island group (**Amami Gun·to** [goōn·tō̄]), N Ryukyu Is., Japan, NE of Okinawa; 498 sq. m.; pop. ab. 185,000; comprises Amami O Shima, or Oshima (largest), Tokuno Shima, Okierabu, Kikai Shima, and others; chief town Naze; naval base and airfields.

A·man·a (á·măn'á). Village, Iowa co., Iowa, 18 m. SW of Cedar Rapids; pop. ab. 200; oldest of seven villages in Iowa co. founded by a religious communal society under Christian Metz, originating in a German Pietist sect, which became established near Buffalo, N.Y. 1842–54 and migrated to Iowa in 1855. Communities incorporated as Amana Society 1859.

A·man'a (á'má'ná'). Peak 1950 ft., S French Guiana, in the Tumuc-Humac range.

Amanus. See ALMA DAĞ.

A'ma·pá' (à'má·pá'). **1** Territory of Brazil. See *Table* at BRAZIL.

2 See MONTENEGRO, Brazil.

A'ma·pa'la (ä'mä·pä'lä). Seaport on Tigre Island, Gulf of Fonseca, Honduras; only good anchorage on Pacific coast of Honduras; pop. (1940) 2058; ab. 114 m. from Tegucigalpa by boat and highway, 70 m. direct.

'A·ma·ra (ä·mä'rŏ). **1** Province (*liwa*), SE Iraq; pop. (1935 est.) 264,508.

2 Town, 'Amara prov., on E bank of Tigris river 100 m. NW of Basra; pop. ab. 28,000; taken by Gen. Townshend as part of Mesopotamian campaign (part of British advance to Baghdad) June 1915. Cf. KUT-AL-IMARA.

A'ma·ran'te (à'má·răn'tě). Town, Piauí state, Brazil, on Parnaíba river ab. 550 m. SW of Fortaleza; trade center for sugar, cotton, cereals, hides, etc.

A'ma·ra'pu·ra' (ŭ'má·rä'poō·rä'). Town on E bank of Irrawaddy river, Mandalay dist., Burma; pop. 8254; a S suburb of Mandalay. Founded 1783 as new capital of kingdom of Burma; destroyed by fire 1810; declined after removal of native court to Ava 1823; capital again 1837–60, when it was abandoned for Mandalay; suffered from earthquake 1839.

A'ma·ra'va·ti (ŭ'má·rä'vá·tē). Ruined city, cen. Andhra Pradesh, E Indian Union, on S bank of Kistna river ab. 60 m. from its mouth; ancient capital of Vengi, Buddhist kingdom of the Andhras; has tope with elaborate carvings of life of Buddha.

Am'ar·go'sa (ăm'är·gō'sá). River, S Nevada and E California; flows into Death Valley, E California.

Amargosa Range. Mountains in SE California, E of Death Valley; highest point 6397 ft.

Am'a·ril'lo (ăm'á·rĭl'ō; -rĭl'ŭ). City, Potter and Randall cos., NW Texas, ⊗ of Potter co., 65 m. E of New Mexico border; pop. 137,969; commercial and industrial center of Texas panhandle; supply center for oil and helium gas (U.S. helium plant); zinc smelters, foundries, grain elevators, oil refineries, meat-packing plants, etc.

'Amarna, Tell el. See TELL EL 'AMARNA.

A·ma'ro (ä·mä'rŏ). Peak 9170 ft. in Abruzzi e Molise dept., SE cen. Italy, in the Apennines.

A·ma·sya' (ä·mä·syä'). **1** Vilayet, N Turkey in Asia; 2142 sq. m.; pop. 128,113.

2 *anc.* **Am'a·si'a** (ăm'á·sī'á). Commercial city, its ✳,

on W banks of Yeşil Irmak 50 m. SSW of Samsun; pop. 12,418.

History: Ancient town capital of kingdom of Pontus (*q.v.*); site of rock-cut tombs of Pontine kings; base of Mithridates' operations against Romans 89, 72, 67 B.C.; made free city by Pompey 65 B.C.; one of chief cities of Greek empire of Trebizond (see TRABZON) and of the Seljuks; withstood siege by Tamerlane; an early residence of Ottoman (Turkish) sultans; birthplace of the geographer Strabo.

Am'a·tig'nak (ăm'á·tĭg'năk). Small island, most southwesterly of the Andreanof Is., Aleutian Is., Alaska.

A'ma·ti'que, Gulf of (ä'mä·tē'kä). Arm of Gulf of Honduras, NE Guatemala and SE Brit. Honduras.

A'ma·ti·tlán' (ä'mä·tē·tlän'). **1** Lake ab. 8 m. long and 3 m. broad in mountains in SE Guatemala; a tourist resort noted for beautiful scenery.

2 Town on the lake 23 m. by rail SW of Guatemala city; pop. 9705; coffee and sugar plantations.

Amatongaland. = TONGALAND.

A'may' (á'mā'). Commune, Liège prov., Belgium, on the Meuse ab. 12½ m. SW of Liège; pop. 6490; quarries, tile and ceramics works, dried fruits.

Am'a·zon (ăm'á·zŏn; -zŭn); *Port.* **Ri'o A'ma·zo'nas** (rē'ōō à'má·zō'nás); *Span.* **Rí'o de las A'ma·zo'nas** (rē'ŏ thä läs ä'mä·sō'näs). *Orig. named* **O'rel·la'na** (ō'rä·yä'nä) *after the explorer.* Called "King of Waters." Largest river in the world (although exceeded in length by the Nile river), flows N in the Peruvian Andes, then E through N Brazil to Atlantic Ocean; its basin ab. 2,320,000 sq. m. (including Tocantins, ab. 2,722,000 sq. m.) extends through 25° of latitude from source of Rio Branco near Mt. Roraima (5°N) to source of a headstream of the Madeira in S Bolivia (ab. 20°S); formed in Peru by union of its two headstreams, the Marañón and Ucayali, just above Iquitos; length of Amazon including Marañón, which rises ab. 100 m. from Pacific Ocean and is usually considered the Amazon proper, 3300 m.; length including Ucayali and its headstream, the Apurímac, 3900 m.; in Brazil called Solimões from Peruvian border to mouth of Negro.

Chief tributaries: On N receives the Napo from N Ecuador and Peru and the Içá (Putumayo), Japurá, Negro, Jamundá, Trombetas, Parú, and Jarí in Brazil; on S the Huallaga in N Peru, Javarí forming part of boundary bet. Peru and Brazil, Jutaí, Juruá, Purús, Madeira, Tapajoz, Xingú, and Tocantins (strictly not a tributary). At its mouth has two branches around island of Marajó (*q.v.*); N branch (at the equator) has Caviana and many smaller islands in it; S and E branch, known as Pará, receives Tocantins; has tidal phenomenon, known as bore, reaching far upstream and at times 16 ft. in height; volume of river so great that its waters can be detected 200 m. out in ocean; navigable for ocean steamers 2300 m. up to Iquitos; its most important port Manaus, at mouth of Negro, 1000 miles from mouth; its high water floods occur in June causing width to vary from 5 to 400 m.; has extremely low gradient, alt. 35 ft. at 2000 m. from the sea. In S Venezuela confluence of Negro and Casiquiare unites Amazon and Orinoco systems.

History: Discovered by Spanish adventurer Vicente Yáñez Pinzón 1500; first descended (from Andes) by Orellana 1541 and ascended by Pedro Teixeira 1637–39; except for occasional ascents in search of slaves, little explored until mid-19th century; opened to world commerce after Emperor Pedro II (of Brazil) authorized steam navigation 1850, and a company, formed 1852, began to operate vessels 1853; valley of Amazon and its tributaries center of crude-rubber industry which reached height in 1910–11 but declined by 1915 after shift of market to East Indies rubber; explored by scientific expeditions, of Roosevelt and Rondon 1913–14, Rice 1910–24, American Geographical Society, and others; perpetual free navigation of Amazon guaranteed by treaty

bet. Colombia and Brazil (ratified by Colombia 1929).

A'ma·zo'nas (à'má·zō'nàs). State of Brazil. See *Table* at BRAZIL.

A'ma·zo'nas (à'mä·sō'nàs). **1** Intendancy of Colombia. See *Table* at COLOMBIA.
2 Department of Peru. See *Table* at PERU.
3 Territory of Venezuela. See *Table* at VENEZUELA.

Am'a·zo'ni·a (ăm'á·zō'nĭ·à; -zōn'yà). The regions about the Amazon river in South America, including the greater part of Brazil and parts of bordering countries, esp. Colombia, Ecuador, Peru, and Bolivia; so called because Orellana and early Spanish explorers thought they saw female warriors on its banks.

Ambacia. See AMBOISE.

Am·ba'la (ŭm·bä'lä). **1** Division, Punjab state, Indian Union; 14,750 sq. m.; pop. (1941) 4,695,462.
2 District of Ambala division; 1851 sq. m.; pop. (1941) 847,745.
3 City, * of division and of dist., 120 m. N of Delhi; pop. (1941) 62,419; market for Simla.

Am'ba·ra'wa (ăm'bä·rä'wä). Town, Central Java prov., Indonesia, S of Semarang; pop. 19,480; scene of fighting by British troops against Indonesian extremists Aug.-Dec. 1945.

Am·bar·chik' (ŭm·bŭr·chēk'). Town on E side of mouth of Kolyma river, NE Yakutsk Repub., Soviet Russia, Asia; air base and port; gold mines nearby.

Am·ba'to (ăm·bä'tŏ). Manufacturing and commercial city, * of Tunguragua prov., cen. Ecuador, ab. 70 m. S of Quito and near N base of Mt. Chimborazo; pop. (1944 est.) 21,692; alt. 8435 ft.; has fine climate, known as "garden city" of Ecuador; raises much fruit; manufactures boots, shoes, and textiles.

Am'ber (ŭm'bĕr). Ruined city, ancient * of Jaipur state, now in E Rajasthan, NW India, 5 m. N of Jaipur, picturesquely situated at mouth of a mountain gorge by beautiful lake; made famous by Rajput structures including the old palace (begun 1600) and the Diwan-i-'Am, richly decorated with sculpture; seized by Rajputs 1037; supplanted by Jaipur 1728.

Am'ber (ăm'bĕr), **Cape**; *Fr.* **Cap d'Am'bre** (kȧp' däN'br'). N point of Madagascar I., ab. 12°S lat.

Am'berg (äm'bĕrK). City, Upper Palatinate government district, Bavaria, W Germany, 35 m. E of Nürnberg; pop. 26,330; formerly capital of Upper Palatinate; manufactures include enamels, earthenware, iron products, woolen cloth, furniture; iron and coal mined in the vicinity. Scene of defeat of French Aug. 24, 1796 by Archduke Charles (of Austria) during War of the First Coalition (1792–97).

Am'ber·gris Cay (ăm'bĕr·grēs; -grĭs). Island in Caribbean Sea off NE British Honduras; encloses S part of Chetumal Bay.

Ambergris Cays. Group of islets or keys in Caicos Is., West Indies.

Ambianum. See AMIENS.

Am'bler (ăm'blĕr). Borough, Montgomery co., SE Pennsylvania, N of Philadelphia; pop. 6765; estab. 1728; asbestos, chemicals, hosiery, sheet-metal products.

Am'ble·side' (ăm'b'l·sīd'). Former urban district, NW England, in Westmorland; now in Lakes urban district.

Am'blève' (äN'blâv'). River ab. 53 m. long, E Belgium; flows NW into Ourthe river a few miles S of Liège; Stavelot is on it. Its banks reached in German offensive Dec. 1944.

Am·bo'di·fo·to'tra (äm·bō'dè·fō·tō'trä). Town, Sainte-Marie I., off NE coast of Madagascar.

Am·boi'na (ăm·boi'nà); *Malay* **Am'bon** (äm'bōn). **1** Southern division of Maluku prov., Indonesia; area 75,801 sq. m.; pop. 400,642; chief island Amboina; chief town Amboina, its *. Comprises islands and island groups around the Banda Sea, esp. Amboina, Ceram, Buru, Aru Is., Kai Is., Tanimbar Is., Babar Is., Wetar, and many small islands, and also the S and

SE portion of mainland of Neth. New Guinea (region of Digoel river).
2 Important island of the Moluccas, Indonesia, Malay Archipelago, off SW coast of Ceram I.; 31 m. long by 10 m. wide; 314 sq. m.; pop. 66,821; formed by two long strips of land connected by narrow isthmus; has high peaks that are active volcanoes (highest Salhutu 4020 ft.); soil fertile; main products tropical fruits and spices, esp. cloves in earlier times.
3 Seaport, chief town and * of Amboina, on fine harbor (**Amboina Bay**); pop. 17,334; naval base and airport; by air 1150 m. ENE of Surabaja and 425 m. SE of Manado; by boat 1292 m. from Manila and 580 m. from Darwin.

History (town and island): Discovered by Portuguese 1510 and settled 1521; source of Portuguese clove monopoly until Portuguese were ousted by Dutch East India Co. 1605; settlement made on the island by English traders 1615; scene of incident known as "massacre of Amboina" 1623 when Dutch killed English on pretext of latter's treachery (until 1654, a bitter issue of Anglo-Dutch relations); entire island claimed by Dutch when they took over suzerainty of Moluccas (1683); captured by British 1796, 1810, but finally restored to Dutch 1814; a separate residency until united with Ternate to form Government of the Moluccas 1927; in 1930 census a division of Moluccas residency. Seized by Japanese Feb. 1942.

Am'boise' (äN'bwàz'); *Lat.* **Am·ba'ci·a** (ăm·bā'shĭ·à; -shà). Commune, Indre-et-Loire dept., NW cen. France, on left bank of Loire river 15 m. E of Tours by rail; pop. 4284; trades in leather (shoe manufacturing) and cloth, esp. woolens; steel and iron founding and manufacture of farm implements; notable particularly for its castle.

History: Lordship under counts of Anjou in 11th century, united to royal domain by Charles VII 1431; castle, rebuilt and beautified by Charles VIII and successors, became a residence of French kings and later a state prison, Abd-el-Kader having been confined there 1848–52; castle's chapel of St. Hubert said to be burial place of Leonardo da Vinci; gave name to conspiracy of Amboise 1560, an unsuccessful plot of Huguenots to remove Francis II from influence of Guise family, and to edict of Amboise 1563, a pacification, concluded by Catherine de Médicis with Huguenots, which guaranteed liberty of worship to Protestant nobility and gentry; castle, confiscated in French Revolution, finally restored to house of Orléans 1872.

Amboland. See OVAMBOLAND.

Am'bos Ca·ma·ri'nes (äm'bōs kä'mä·rē'nàs). Old province, Phil. Is., now divided into the provs. Camarines Norte and Camarines Sur. See CAMARINES NORTE.

Am·bo·si'tra (äm·bō·sē'trä). Inland town, S cen. Madagascar, S of Antsirabe; road junction.

Am'boy (ăm'boi). City, Lee co., N Illinois, 35 m. NW of Ottawa; pop. 2067.

Am·boy'na (ăm·boi'nà). Var. of AMBOINA.

Ambracia. See ARTA city.

Am·bra'cian Gulf (ăm·brā'shăn); *also* **Gulf of Ar'ta** (är'tà; *Mod. Gr.* -tä). Inlet of Ionian Sea, S Epirus, on W coast of Greece; 25 m. long and from 4 to 10 m. wide; on its shores are ruins of several cities important in ancient Greece; battle of Actium (*q.v.*) fought near its entrance 31 B.C.

Ambre, Cap d'. See Cape AMBER.

Am'bridge (ăm'brĭj). Borough, Beaver co., W Pennsylvania, on Ohio river 17 m. WNW of Pittsburgh; pop. 13,865; built on site of German communistic settlement called Economy (estab. 1825); manufactures steel, wrought iron, copper wire, etc.

Am'brim (ăm'brĭm) *or* **Am'brym'** (*Fr.* äN'brăN'). Fertile island 24 m. long by 16 m. wide, NE part of the New Hebrides, SW Pacific Ocean, E of Malekula I.; pop. (native; 1938 est.) 4000. Has active volcano **Mt. Minnei** that had disastrous eruption 1913.

Am·briz′ (ăm·brēz′). Seaport, NW Angola, Africa, 75 m. N of Luanda; pop. 2500.

Am′brose Channel (ăm′brōz). Channel across Sandy Hook bar, entrance to New York harbor SSE of the Narrows, 7½ m. long, 40 ft. deep, and from 1850 to 2000 ft. wide; dredged 1899–1913. **Ambrose Channel Lightship,** marking its entrance is ab. 9 m. E of Sandy Hook.

Ambt–Hardenberg. See HARDENBERG.

Am·bun′ti (ăm·bōōn′tē). Town, ✳ of Sepik administrative district, W North-East New Guinea, on N bank of Sepik river ab. 125 m. from its mouth.

Am·bur′ (ŭm·bōōr′). Town, Madras state, S Indian Union, ab. 107 m. WSW of Madras on Palar river; pop. 24,217; commands pass into the Carnatic; scene of battle 1749.

Am′bu·ra′yan (ăm′bōō·rä′yän). **1** River ab. 60 m. long, SW Mountain Prov., Luzon, Phil. Is.; rises in Benguet subprov., flows W then NW through S Ilocos Sur to South China Sea near Tagudin.
2 Region, NW Luzon; former Spanish military district (*comandancia*), later a subprovince of Mountain Prov.; joined 1920 with Lepanto to form Lepanto-Amburayan subprovince; later divided bet. Ilocos Sur, La Union, and Mountain Prov.

Am·chit′ka (ăm·chĭt′kà). Island ab. 15 m. long by 5 m. wide in the Aleutian Is., at E end of Rat Is. group 69 m. SE of Kiska; occupied 1942 by U.S. task force and air base set up for operations against Japanese on Kiska and Attu Jan.–May 1943.

A·me′ca (ä·mā′kä). **1** River ab. 140 m. long, W cen. Mexico; flows W into Banderas Bay.
2 Town, Jalisco state, W cen. Mexico, on Ameca river 45 m. W of Guadalajara; pop. 13,003.

A·me′ca·me′ca (ä·mā′kä·mä′kä), *in full* **Amecameca de Juá′rez** (thä hwä′räs). Town, México state, cen. Mexico, 36 m. SE of Mexico City; pop. 7573; alt. 7600 ft. Important center of pre-Spanish civilization; has shrine Sacro Monte, hill built over a cave where one of earliest Christian missionaries in Mexico lived, which is visited by thousands of Indians during Holy Week. Starting point for ascents of Popocatepetl and Iztaccihuatl.

A′me·land (ä′mĕ·länt). Island ab. 13 m. long and 2 m. wide of the Netherlands in the West Frisian Is., 4 m. off N coast of Friesland prov. in North Sea; administratively a part of Friesland prov.; has four villages.

A·me′lia (à·mēl′yà; -mē′lĭ·à). County in Virginia. See *Table* at VIRGINIA.

A·me′lia (ä·mā′lyä); *anc.* **A·me′ri·a** (à·mēr′ĭ·à). Commune, Terni prov., Umbria, cen. Italy, 12 m. W of Terni; pop. 11,055; episcopal see since 340; well preserved remains of ancient polygonal city walls.

A·me′lia Courthouse (à·mēl′yà; -mē′lĭ·à). Village, ⊗ of Amelia co., SE cen. Virginia; pop. (est.) 600.

Amelia Island. Island in Atlantic Ocean off coast of Nassau co., NE Florida, ab. 15 m. long by 4 m. wide. Part of Spanish, later of American, Florida; resort of smugglers during U.S. embargo on trade with Europe 1807; scene of incident known as "Amelia Island Affair" in which U.S. sent naval expedition to remove forces of Luis Aury, a South American adventurer, who had set up a government on the island and invited Florida to throw off Spanish rule 1817; captured by U.S. Federal forces from Confederates during American Civil War 1862.

A·me′ni·a (à·mē′nĭ·à; -mēn′yà). Village in Amenia town (pop. 7546), Dutchess co., SE New York, ab. 20 m. NE of Poughkeepsie; agriculture, dairying.

Ameria. See AMELIA.

A·mer′i·ca (à·mĕr′ĭ·kà); *Span.* **A·mé′ri·ca** (ä·mā′rĕ·kä); *Port.* **A·mé′ri·ca** (à·mā′rĕ·kà). A name derived from *Americus* Vespucius, Latinized form of name of Amerigo Vespucci (1451–1512), Italian navigator, and first used in a popular account of his travels in the New

World published 1507 by the German geographer Martin Waldseemüller. Originally (as applied by Waldseemüller), the lands discovered by Columbus, *i.e.* South America and the West Indies; later (as used 1538 by Mercator), the New World, *i.e.* the lands of the Western Hemisphere. In current use: either continent of the Western Hemisphere (North America or South America); often, specifically, the United States of America (*q.v.*); also, although in this application the plural form **the Americas** is the usual one, all the lands of the Western Hemisphere including North America, South America, and the West Indies.

History: Earliest European discovery of any part of the Americas was of NE coast of North America by the Norse (Leif Ericsson 1000, Thorfinn Karlsefni 1004–06); general European knowledge of the Americas dates from the voyages of Columbus, whose first landfall was at San Salvador (island in the Bahamas) Oct. 12, 1492, and who later (voyages of 1495, 1498, 1502) touched coasts of Central and South America; in Europe until 16th and 17th centuries known as *the Indies, West Indies,* or *New World;* separation of North America from Asia established by voyage of Magellan 1519–21. For more detailed information, see NORTH AMERICA, SOUTH AMERICA, CENTRAL AMERICA, WEST INDIES.

America Islands. Name sometimes applied to a group of islands in N part of the Line Is. (*q.v.*), 5°50′N to 2°N, including Palmyra, Washington, Fanning, and Christmas Islands (*qq.v.*).

American Fall *or* **Falls.** See NIAGARA FALLS.

American Falls. City, ⊗ of Power co., SE Idaho; pop. 2123; shipping point for wheat.

American Falls Dam *and* **Reservoir.** See UNITED STATES, *Dams and Reservoirs.*

American Fork. City, Utah co., N cen. Utah, on Utah Lake 14 m. NNW of Provo; pop. 6373; produces and ships poultry and eggs.

American River. River ab. 30 m. long, N cen. California; formed by three forks, flows SW into Sacramento river at Sacramento.

American, *or* **Eastern, Samoa.** Group of islands of Samoa (*q.v.*), SW cen. Pacific Ocean, E of long. 171°W and ab. 14°S lat.; 76 sq. m.; pop. 20,051; ✳ Pago Pago; includes islands of Tutuila, Manua Is. (Tau, Olosega, Ofu), Aunuu, Rose, and Swains. See Territory of WESTERN SAMOA.

History: Ruled by native chiefs until ab. 1860; object of American interest since expedition of Commodore Wilkes 1839; visited by Commander Richard W. Meade, U.S.N., 1872; Pago Pago and trading and extraterritorial rights granted to U.S. 1878; under joint administration of U.S., Germany, and England 1889–99 and by treaty of 1899 granted to U.S.; Swains I. annexed 1925. Administered by U.S. Department of the Navy before 1951 and by U.S. Department of the Interior since then. Constitution, setting up a local legislature, adopted April 1960.

American Virgin Islands. = VIRGIN ISLANDS OF THE UNITED STATES.

A·mer′i·cus (à·mĕr′ĭ·kŭs). Industrial city, ⊗ of Sumter co., SW cen. Georgia; pop. 13,472; shirt factories, lumber mills, canneries; bauxite and kaolin deposits nearby.

A′me·rong′en (ä′mĕ·rông′ĕ[n]). Commune, Utrecht prov., cen. Netherlands, near the Lower Rhine 23 m. SE of Utrecht; pop. 2820; its castle of Count Bentinck was first refuge of Kaiser William II of Germany 1918.

A′mers·foort′ (ä′mĕrs·fōrt′). Commune, Utrecht prov., cen. Netherlands, 12 m. NE of Utrecht; pop. (1939) 48,944; railroad junction; industries include tobacco culture, chemical manufacturing, production of damask, cotton, and woolen goods; has 13th-cent. church, Jansenist college, and 312-ft. Gothic tower built 1441.

Ames (āmz). City, Story co., cen. Iowa, 28 m. N of Des Moines; pop. 27,003. Iowa State Univ. of Science and Technology (1858; coed.); State Forest Nursery.

Ames′bur′y (āmz′bĕr′ĭ; -bĕr·ĭ; -brĭ). **1** Town, Essex co., NE Massachusetts, on Merrimack river 24 m. NE of Lowell; pop. 10,787; manufactures hats.
2 Town, Wiltshire, England, 8 m. N of Salisbury on Avon river; market and fair (grant dating from 1317); known particularly for Stonehenge (1½ m. W), principal surviving megalithic structure in British Isles (cf. AVEBURY); notable in 17th cent. for production of pipe clay and pipes. Scene of a witenagemot 932; site of nunnery built ab. 980.
Amestratus. See MISTRETTA.
Am·ga′ (ŭm·gä′). River 800 m. long, SE Yakutsk Republic, Soviet Russia, Asia; rises in Aldan Mts. and flows NE to Aldan river ab. 175 m. E of Yakutsk.
Am′gun (äm′gŏ͞on). River ab. 400 m. long in Khabarovsk Territory, Soviet Russia, Asia; rises in mountains NW of Khabarovsk and flows NE to the Amur near its mouth above Nikolaevsk.
Am·har′a (äm·här′ȧ; -här′ȧ; -här′ȧ). Province, NW Ethiopia (Abyssinia); ✳ Gondar; former kingdom; a government (province) 1936–41 of Italian East Africa; 76,235 sq. m.; pop. (1939 est.) 2,000,000; gave name (*Amharic*) to official and court language of Ethiopia.
Am′herst (äm′ẽrst; -ûrst). **1** County in Virginia. See *Table* at VIRGINIA.
2 Town, Hampshire co., W Massachusetts, 19 m. N of Springfield; pop. 13,718; Amherst College (1821; men); Univ. of Massachusetts (1863; coed.).
3 Town, Hillsboro co., S New Hampshire, 11 m. SW of Manchester; pop. 2051; settled 1733.
4 Village, Lorain co., N Ohio, 27 m. WSW of Cleveland; pop. 6750; sandstone quarries.
5 Town, ⊗ of Amherst co., cen. Virginia; pop. 1200.
6 District, Tenasserim division, Lower Burma; 7410 sq. m.; pop. 516,233; ✳ Moulmein.
7 Seaport in district, on **Amherst Peninsula**, 30 m. S of Moulmein; pop. ab. 3000; has good harbor. Founded 1826.
8 Town, ⊗ of Cumberland co., N Nova Scotia, Canada, 5 m. E of NE end of Chignecto Bay; pop. 9870. A thriving Acadian village, then known as Les Planches, prior to English occupation; refounded as English town 1760 and named after Jeffrey, Lord Amherst. The inland gateway to Nova Scotia; noted as geographical center of Maritime Provinces; ruins of Forts Lawrence and Beauséjour nearby.
Am′herst·burg (äm′ẽrst·bûrg). Town, Essex co., SE Ontario, Canada, on Detroit river in fertile agricultural section 14 m. S of Windsor; pop. 3638. Founded 1796 on site of old French settlement, visited by La Salle 1679; contains remains of Fort Malden, built 1797–99 and used as a frontier post in War of 1812.
Amherst Island. 1 Island at NE end of Lake Ontario, Ontario, Canada, SW of Kingston.
2 Chief island of the Magdalen Is. in the Gulf of St. Lawrence, Quebec prov., E Canada.
Amherst Mountain. Peak 13,100 ft., La Plata co., SW Colorado.
Amida. See DIYARBEKİR.
Am′i·don (äm′ĭ·dŏn). Village, ⊗ of Slope co., SW North Dakota; pop. 84.
A′miens′ (à′myăn′; *Angl.* ăm′ĭ·ĕnz; *anc.* **Sam′a·ro·bri′va** (săm′ȧ·rō·brī′vȧ, *later* **Am′bi·a′num** (äm′bĭ·ä′nŭm). Manufacturing city, ✳ of Somme dept., N France, on Somme river 72 m. N of Paris; pop. 93,773; site of world-famous cathedral of Notre Dame, largest church in France and one of leading representatives of Gothic architecture in Europe; from 16th cent. one of largest centers of French textile industry, producing chiefly linen, woolens, cotton, velvet, silk, and hemp; noted also for agricultural markets.
History: Capital (as Samarobriva) of the Ambiani; became Roman stronghold; chief city of medieval county **A′mié′nois′** (à′myä′nwà′), which became crown land 1185; passed to Burgundy by Peace of Arras 1435, but

returned to France at death of Duke Charles the Bold 1477; captured by Spanish 1597 and recovered by Henry IV; capital of Picardy to 1790; scene of signing 1802 of Peace of Amiens bet. France and Britain; captured by Prussians 1870; held by Germans for a short time in 1914; gave name to World War I battle (August 1918) which was part of successful Allied counteroffensive against Germany. In World War II taken by Germans May 1940; retaken by British Aug. 31, 1944. Birthplace of Peter the Hermit.
Amindivi Islands. See LACCADIVE ISLANDS.
Am′i·rante Islands (ăm′ĭ·rănt) *or* **Am′i·rantes** (ăm′ĭ·rănts). British island group in Indian Ocean E of Tanganyika and SW of Seychelles Is., ab. 5°30′S lat. and 53°10′E long.; administratively a dependency of Seychelles.
Amisia. See EMS.
Amisus. See SAMSUN.
A·mite′ (ȧ·mēt′). County in Mississippi. See *Table* at MISSISSIPPI.
Amite City. Town, ⊗ of Tangipahoa parish, SE Louisiana, in agricultural section 45 m. ENE of Baton Rouge; pop. 3316; cotton, corn, dairy products.
Am′i·ter′num (ăm′ĭ·tûr′nŭm). Ancient town ab. 58 m. NE of Rome, Italy, 5 m. N of modern Aquila in valley of Aterno river; birthplace of Sallust; ruins of imperial Roman structures; Christian catacombs in vicinity.
Am′i·ty·ville′ (ăm′ĭ·tĭ·vil′). Village, Suffolk co., SE New York, on dividing line bet. Nassau and Suffolk cos., on Great South Bay on Long Island 32 m. E of New York; pop. 8318; residential suburb and seaside summer resort.
Am′li·a (äm′lĭ·ȧ). Island at E end of Andreanof Is., Aleutian Is., SW Alaska.
Am·man′ (äm·män′); *Bib.* **Rab′bah,** *or* **Rab′bath, Am′mon** (răb′ȧ [răb′ăth] äm′ŏn); *anc.* **Phil′a·del′- phi·a** (fĭl′ȧ·dĕl′fĭ·ȧ; -fyȧ). Town, NW Jordan, NW Arabia, 25 m. NE of the Dead Sea on the Damascus-Ma'an railroad; ✳ of Jordan; pop. (1959 est.) 245,000; important junction point on trade routes; has airdrome of British Royal Air Force. Chief city of the Ammonites; besieged and captured by Joab and David (*2 Sam.* xi–xii); improved by Ptolemy II Philadelphus (285–246 B.C.) and named Philadelphia after him; was most southerly of ten cities of the Decapolis; attained greatest prosperity under Eastern Roman Empire.
Am′man·ford (äm′ăn·fẽrd; *Welsh* ä′män·fôrd). Urban district, Carmarthenshire, S Wales, 17 m. ESE of Carmarthen; pop. 6578; coal mining.
Am′me·berg (ôm′mĕ·bär′y). Town, Örebro prov., Sweden, at N end of Lake Vättern; noted zinc mines.
Am′men·dorf (äm′ĕn·dôrf). Commune, in former Prussian province of Saxony, E Germany, 3 m. SSE of Halle; pop. 12,180; center for lignite industries; manufactures paper, cardboard, and chemicals, esp. dyes.
Am′mer (äm′ẽr); *Ger.* **Am′mer·see′** (äm′ẽr·zā′). Lake, Bavaria, S Germany, 21 m. WSW of Munich; 10 m. long; 18 sq. m.; in glacial region characterized by irregular moraine.
Am′mer (äm′ẽr) *or* **Am′per** (äm′pẽr). River, Bavaria, S Germany; rises in Tirol and flows through Ammer Lake into Isar river 2 m. N of Moosburg; Dachau is on its left bank and Oberammergau is near its source.
Am·min (äm·mĕn). Island in the Yellow Sea off W coast of Korea, South Chusei province.
Ammoedara. See HAÏDRA.
Ammonium. See SIWA.
Am′mo·noo′suc (ăm′ȯ·nŏ͞o′sŭk). River ab. 100 m. long, Coos and Grafton cos., New Hampshire; flows W and SW from White Mts. to Connecticut river.
Am′ne′ Ma′chin′ Shan (äm′nĕ′ mä′jĭn′ shän′). Range of the Kunlun Mts. in E cen. Tsinghai, W cen. China, from 18,000 to 25,000 ft. high; source of the Hwang Ho. Its highest peak **Amne Machin** (99°45′E, 34°25′N) is estimated at 25,000 ft.

Amnok. See YALU.

A'mo·chu' (ä'mŏ·chōō'). River, W Bhutan and NE India; flows through Chumbi valley in S Tibet, then SE across SW corner of Bhutan to the Brahmaputra river.

Amol. See AMUL.

A·mor'gos (à·môr'gŏs); *Mod. Gr.* **A'mor·gòs'** (ä'môr-gôs'). Island of the Cyclades, S Aegean Sea, 18 m. SE of Naxos; 52 sq. m.; pop. ab. 3000; belongs to Cyclades dept., Greece. Birthplace of Simonides, Greek poet of 7th cent. B.C.

A'mo·ry (ä'mŏ·rĭ). City, Monroe co., NE Mississippi, 22 m. SSE of Tupelo; pop. 6474; shipping point for cotton, grain, dairy products, timber.

A'mos (ä'mŭs). Town, ⊗ of Abitibi co., SW Quebec, Canada, on Harricana river 50 m. NE of Rouyn; pop. 4265; large sawmills.

Am'os·keag' (ăm'ŭs·kĕg'). Village at **Amoskeag Falls** in Merrimack river, Hillsboro co., S New Hampshire, now part of Manchester; cotton mills.

A'mour' Mountains (à'mōōr'). Range of the Atlas Mts., SE Oran dept., Algeria; highest point ab. 5800 ft.

A·moy' (ä·moi'; à-) *or* **Sze'ming'** (sŏō'mĭng'). Treaty port, Fukien prov., SE China, on Amoy I. and smaller Kulangsu I., ½ m. distant; pop. (1936 est.) 220,000; international settlement (opened 1903), 1½ sq. m., is on Kulangsu; by boat 636 m. S of Shanghai, 293 m. NE of Hong Kong; by air ab. 320 m. ENE of Canton and 130 m. W of Formosa I. In 18th cent. monopolized Chinese junk trade to Straits and Java; first port through which English and Dutch traded with China (former in 1670); occupied by British 1841; opened as treaty port by Treaty of Nanking at close of first British war against China 1842; occupied by Taiping rebels 1853–55; gradually declined as center of tea export; captured by Japanese in 1938 campaign against China and held till end of World War II.

Am·pa'to (äm·pä'tŏ). Peak 20,670 ft., Arequipa dept., S Peru.

Am'pe·nan (äm'pä·nän). Chief seaport, Lombok I., Indonesia, on W coast 250 m. ESE of Surabaja; the port of Mataram.

Amper. See AMMER.

Am·phip'o·lis (äm·fĭp'ŏ·lĭs). Ancient city, E Macedonia, on Strymon river ab. 3 m. above its mouth; colonized by Athens 437 B.C.; in 424 captured by Spartans during Peloponnesian War; became independent after Peace of Nicias 421; occupation by Philip of Macedon caused war with Athens 337 B.C.; headquarters of Roman governor of Macedonia.

Am·phis'sa (äm·fĭs'à; *Mod. Gr.* äm'fĭ·sä) *or* **Sa·lo'na** (sà·lō'nà; *Mod. Gr.* sä·lô'nä). Town, Phthiotis and Phocis dept., Greece, at foot of W slope of Mt. Parnassus; pop. 5294; chief town of ancient Western Locris (see LOCRIS); its rebuilding of Crisa (*q.v.*) was cause of the Fourth Sacred War (339–338 B.C.).

Am·pin (äm·pĕn) *or* **An·ping** (än·pĕng). Seaport, SW coast of Formosa I.; formerly the port of Tainan, but now silted up.

Am'qui' (äN'kē'). Village (unincorporated), ⊗ of Matapédia co. (part of Matane co.), on Gaspé Penin., SE Quebec, Canada, on Matapédia river 25 m. S of Matane; an agricultural community; pop. 2599.

Am·ran' (äm·rän'). Town, N cen. Yemen, SW Arabia, N of San'a.

Am·rao'ti (ŭm·rou'tē). 1 Former district of Berar, SW Central Provinces and Berar, cen. India; 4715 sq. m.; pop. (1941) 988,524.
2 Town NE Maharashtra state, cen. India, on branch of Purna river 86 m. W of Nagpur; pop. (1941) 61,971; important cotton center. Has a fine stupa dating from 2d cent. A.D., whose rich relief decorations are preserved in British Museum (London) and in Madras.

Am·re'li (äm·rā'lĭ). 1 District, SW Gujarat, in S Kathiawar penin., W India; 1077 sq. m.; pop. 173,948.
2 Town, its ✳, 135 m. SW of Baroda; pop. 20,186.

'Am·rit' (ăm·rēt'); *anc.* **Mar'a·thus** (măr'à·thŭs). Town on coast, SW Latakia, Syria, 45 m. S of Latakia and opp. Arwad I. (*anc.* Aradus).

Am·rit'sar (ŭm·rĭt'sēr). 1 District, formerly in Lahore division, Punjab, now in Punjab state, India; 1572 sq. m.; pop. (1941) 1,413,876.
2 Manufacturing city, its ✳, in NW Punjab, India, 32 m. E of Lahore, Pakistan; pop. 325,747; trade center, with large business in skins, hides, and piece goods. Founded by Ram Das 1574 on site granted by Akbar; site of Golden Temple, center of worship of Sikhs; part of Sikh confederacy under Ranjit Singh (d. 1839); as part of Punjab (*q.v.*), annexed by British 1846; scene of incident known as Amritsar affair April 13, 1919 when British, under Gen. Reginald E. H. Dyer, fired on and killed about 400 and wounded many others in a riot caused by Rowlatt Acts (antisedition laws).

Am·ro'ha (äm·rō'hà). Town, Uttar Pradesh, Indian Union, 78 m. E of Delhi; pop. (1941) 55,957; site of tomb of Mohammedan saint, Sheik Saddu, the object of pilgrimages.

Am'rum (äm'rōōm). Island, North Frisian Is., SW of Föhr; 8 sq. m.; belongs to Germany.

Am'ster·dam (ăm'stēr·dăm). 1 Manufacturing city, Montgomery co., E New York, on New York State Barge Canal and Mohawk river 28 m. NW of Albany; pop. 28,772; industrial and shipping center in agricultural district; manufactures carpets and rugs, brooms, sweaters, linseed oil, gloves, silk and rayon textiles, etc. Settled 1783, named Veedersburg; renamed Amsterdam 1804; incorporated as city 1885.
2 (*Du. pron.* äm'stēr·däm') Commercial and manufacturing city, North Holland prov., W Netherlands; ✳ of Netherlands; pop. (1939) 800,594; on former Zuider Zee and connected with North Sea by ship canal (see NORTH SEA CANAL); on N borders Ij (or Y) river; built on piles with canals dividing it into islands, connected by more than 350 bridges.

History: Originally a fishing hamlet, developed by Giesebrecht II and III of Amstel, who built a castle nearby and dammed up the sea (early 13th cent.); received charter as town 1300; joined Hanseatic League 1369; grew steadily in 14th and 15th cents. as evidenced by extent of its walls erected in 1482; received an influx of wealthy merchants from Brabant, and a stream of Portuguese Jews, esp. after decline of Antwerp 1585; with vastly increased population and wealth, became source of the growing Dutch commercial and naval power in 17th cent.; center of Dutch East India and West India Companies (founded in 1602 and 1621) and of Bank of Amsterdam (1609); became leading financial and trade metropolis of Europe, esp. after closure of the Schelde by Treaty of Westphalia (1648) had sealed the fate of its rival Antwerp; opened its dikes against Louis XIV 1672; attracted French Huguenots after revocation 1685 of the Edict of Nantes; after a partial commercial decline in 18th cent. increased its prosperity when connected with North Sea by a canal 1875; capital of the Batavian Republic erected by Napoleon, later of the kingdom of Holland; became part of French Empire 1810; as part of Holland, entered kingdom of the Netherlands 1815; up to the German occupation of the Netherlands in World War II (1940), had been the financial and banking capital of Europe and the chief port for the rich trade with Netherlands Indies; long a center of diamond-cutting industry; contains museums and Rembrandt House which have paintings and works of art of the Dutch masters. When threatened with destruction by German air force, surrendered May 16, 1940.
3 *or* **New Amsterdam.** Volcanic island S Indian Ocean, 38°S, 77°E, near St. Paul I.; 18 sq. m.; belongs to France; formerly a dependency of Madagascar.

Amsterdam Ship Canal. See NORTH SEA CANAL.

A·muay' (ä·mwī'). Port on W coast of Paraguaná Penin., NW Venezuela; petroleum exports.

A·mu′ Dar·ya′ (ä·mōō′ där·yä′; *Angl.* ä′mōō där′yȧ); *anc.* **Ox′us** (ŏk′sŭs); *Arab.* **Jay·hun′** (jī·hōōn′). River, cen. and W Asia, from Pamir plateau to Lake Aral, 1400 to 1500 m.; rises in lakes and mountains of high Pamirs in two headstreams: Murghab or Aq-su (rises in Lake Victoria, alt. 13,400 ft.) and Ab-i-Pandj; flows NW down Hindu Kush slope, forming boundary bet. Tadzhik S.S.R. and NE Afghanistan, then generally W and NW through E Turkmen S.S.R. and W of Uzbek S.S.R. into marshes on S shore of Lake Aral in Kara-Kalpak A.S.S.R., where it forms delta 90 m. long; area of basin ab. 115,800 sq. m.; chief tributaries on N are Vaksh, Kafirnigan, and Surkhab, on S Kunduz; in middle course a source of wide irrigation systems; navigable below Chardzhou (Leninsk) ab. 935 m.; in lower course flows through great expanse of sandy desert. In mid-19th cent., part of course came to be recognized as boundary bet. Afghanistan and Russia. For its history as site of campaigns by Alexander the Great, see SOGDIANA and BACTRIA.

A·muk′ta (ä·mōōk′tä). Volcanic island in Aleutian Is., W of the Islands of the Four Mountains; separated by **Amukta Pass** from Seguam I. on W.

A·mul′ (ô·mōōl′) or **A·mol′** (ô·mōl′). City, Mazanderan prov., N Iran, 23 m. W of Babul; pop. ab. 10,000.

A′mund Ring′nes′ Island (ä′mŏon rĭng′nãs′). One of the Sverdrup Is. (*q.v.*), SW of Axel Heiberg I.

A′mund·sen Gulf (ä′mŏon·sĕn). Body of water bet. the NW coast of Mackenzie District, Northwest Territories, Canada, the S coast of Banks I., and the W coast of Victoria I.

Amundsen Sea. Arm of South Pacific Ocean off Marie Byrd Land, Antarctica, bet. Thurston Penin. on E and Cape Dart on W; ab. 72°S and bet. 123°W and 98°W; explored 1928–29.

A·mur′ (ŭ·mŏor′; *Angl.* ä·mŏor′); *Chin.* **Hei′lung′-kiang′** (hā′lŏong′jĭ·äng′). River, NE Asia, formed by junction of Shilka and Argun rivers (*qq.v.*) at ab. 53°20′N, 121°28′E; length with Argun and Kerulen ab. 2800 m., from junction ab. 1780 m.; forms boundary bet. N Manchuria and two subdivisions of R.S.F.S.R. (Chita Region and Khabarovsk Territory), Soviet Russia, Asia; flows E, SE, and NE to N end of Tatar Strait bet. mainland and Sakhalin I.; below Khabarovsk wholly in Russian territory; est. area of basin 770,000 sq. m.; below junction receives N tributaries Zeya and Bureya, and on S Kumara, Sungari, and Ussuri; chief cities on it: Blagoveshchensk, Khabarovsk, Komsomolsk, and Nikolaevsk (near mouth); navigable for ab. 2000 m. up to Sretensk on the Shilka.

History: Region of Amur valley in contact with Russia from 17th cent.; Russia compelled (by China) to withdraw from valley in Treaty of Nerchinsk (*q.v.*) 1689; settled by Russians from 1847; by Treaty of Aigun (*q.v.*) 1858, left bank of Amur yielded by China to Russia, and Ussuri region by Treaty of Peking 1860; occupied by Russians and developed economically, esp. after building of Trans-Siberian R.R.; Blagoveshchensk (*q.v.*) became chief cultural and commercial center; after Japanese occupation of Manchuria, scene of Soviet-Japanese clashes 1937. See also JEWISH AUTONOMOUS REGION.

Amur Bay. Northwest arm of Peter the Great Bay, Soviet Russia, Asia, ab. 42 m. long; Vladivostok is on inlet of its E shore.

A·my′clae (ȧ·mī′klē). Ancient town, Laconia, SE Peloponnesus, S Greece, ab. 3 m. S of Sparta; chief city of Laconia under the Achaeans and before rise of Dorian Sparta; ultimately conquered by Sparta.

An. Pass in W Burma. See AN PASS.

'A′na (ä′nȧ; -nä). Town, W bank of Euphrates, W Iraq, ab. 75 m. NW of Hit; pop. ab. 15,000. An old town, dating from before 1000 B.C.; in medieval period controlled transport on the river and was starting point for caravan routes across the desert to Syrian cities.

A·na′a (ä·nä′ä), or **Chain** (chān), **Island.** Atoll 19 m. long and 6 m. wide in the Tuamotu Archipelago, French Oceania, S Pacific Ocean; 17°S lat., 146°W long.; has 11 islets around a lagoon; called Chain I. by Captain Cook, who visited it 1769.

An′a·cap′a Islands (ăn′ȧ·kăp′ȧ). Small group of islands in cen. Santa Barbara group, Pacific Ocean; part of Ventura co., SW California; part of group included in Channel Islands National Monument (see UNITED STATES, *National Monuments*).

Anacapa Pass. Strait bet. Anacapa Is. and Santa Cruz I., off NW Los Angeles co., SW California.

An′a·con′da (ăn′ȧ·kŏn′dȧ). City, ⊗ of Deer Lodge co., SW Montana, 23 m. WNW of Butte; pop. 12,054. City started with erection 1884, by Anaconda Copper Mining Co. of Butte, of a copper-smelting plant, later expanded to contain largest nonferrous production plant in world.

Anaconda Mountain. Peak 8300 ft. in Glacier National Park, NW Montana.

An′a·cor′tes (ăn′ȧ·kôr′tĕs). City, Skagit co., NW Washington, on island in Puget Sound 19 m. S of Bellingham; pop. 8414; incorporated 1889; port of call for several steamship companies; fishing and lumbering center.

An′a·cos′ti·a (ăn′ȧ·kŏs′tĭ·ȧ). 1 River ab. 24 m. long in the District of Columbia, flowing into Potomac river immediately S of the city of Washington.
2 Southeastern suburb of Washington, D.C. on left bank of Anacostia river; site of U.S. Naval Air Station.

An′a·dar′ko (ăn′ȧ·där′kō). City, ⊗ of Caddo co., W cen. Oklahoma, on Washita river 18 m. W of Chickasha; pop. 6299; founded 1901; trading center for agricultural region (alfalfa, cotton, corn, etc.); stock raising, cotton ginning, cottonseed-oil milling, dairying, meat packing.

Anadolu. See ANATOLIA.

A·na·dyr′ or **A·na·dir′** (ŭ·nŭ·dĭr′). 1 River 450 m. long, Chukot National District, Soviet Russia, Asia; rises in mountains S of Anadyr Range and flows S and E to Gulf of Anadyr.
2 *formerly* **No′vo Ma·ri′insk** (nô′vŭ mŭ·rye͞′ĭnsk). Town on right bank at mouth of the river, ✳ of Chukot National District; extensive coal mines nearby.

Anadyr, or **Anadir, Gulf of.** Inlet of N Bering Sea S of Chukotski Penin., Chukot National District, Soviet Russia, Asia.

Anadyr, or **Anadir, Range;** *Russ.* **A·na·dyr′ski Khre·bet′** (ŭ·nŭ·dĭr′skĭ ĸryĭ·byĕt′). Mountain range, NW Chukot National District, Soviet Russia, Asia, an extension of the Kolyma Range; runs NW and SE across Arctic Circle to Chukotski Penin.

A·na·far′·ta′ Heights (ä·nä′fär·tä′). Group of hills, W Gallipoli Penin., Turkey in Europe, ab. 4 m. E of Suvla Bay; highest 882 ft.; scene of British attacks 1915 during battle of Suvla Bay (*q.v.*), a part of operations in Gallipoli campaign.

A·na′gni (ä·nä′nyĕ); *anc.* **A·nag′ni·a** (ȧ·năg′nĭ·ȧ). Commune, Frosinone prov., Latium, cen. Italy, on 1500-ft. hill 12 m. NW of Frosinone; pop. 12,396; episcopal see since 487; sulfur mines and springs; 11th-cent. cathedral. Principal town of the Hernici; conquered by Rome 306 B.C.; besieged by Saracens 877 A.D.; scene of the imprisonment and humiliation of Pope Boniface VIII by the emissaries of Philip IV of France.

An′a·heim (ăn′ȧ·hīm). City, Orange co., SW California, 16 m. E of Long Beach; pop. 104,184; in citrus-fruit region; fruit canning, meat packing; manufactures furniture, chemicals, paints; site of Disneyland amusement park. Founded 1857 on communal basis by 50 German families; incorporated 1878.

A·na′ho Bay (ä·nä′hō). Bay, N coast of Nuku Hiva I., Marquesas Is., S Pacific Ocean; chief harbor on the island.

An′a·huac (ăn′ȧ·hwăk). City ⊗ of Chambers co., Texas, 35 m. NE of Galveston on NE shore of Galveston Bay; pop. 1985; formerly a Mexican military post, attacked 1832 by American settlers in Texas in effort to

release William B. Travis and others, thus furnishing issue preliminary to Texan War of Independence.

A·ná′huac (ä-nä′wäk). Great central plateau in Mexico bet. the Sierra Madre Occidental and the Sierra Madre Oriental; includes valley in which the city of Mexico is located; elevation 5000 to 9000 ft. in states of Puebla and Mexico, sloping to 3700 ft. at El Paso on U.S. border; center of pre-Columbian Aztec civilization.

A·nai′za (ä-nī′zȧ; -nä′-; -zȧ). Town, Qasim prov., N cen. Nejd, cen. Saudi Arabia; pop. ab. 15,000; in large oasis.

A·na·ka′pal·le (ŭ-nȧ-kä′pȧl·lä). Town, Vizagapatam dist., NE Andhra Pradesh, 18 m. W of Vizagapatam; pop. 23,376.

Analostan Island. See THEODORE ROOSEVELT ISLAND.

Anam. See ANNAM.

A′na Ma·rí′a, Gulf of (ä′nä mä-rē′ä). Gulf in SW coast of Camagüey prov., E cen. Cuba.

A·nam′bas Islands (ä-näm′bäs). Group of islands of Indonesia, 200 m. NE of Singapore in the South China Sea bet. SE Malay Penin. and W Borneo; 260 sq. m.; pop. 12,371; administratively a part of Riouw province, Sumatra. Chief islands Djemadja and Siantan.

An′a·mo′sa (ăn′ȧ-mō′sȧ). City, ⊗ of Jones co., E Iowa, 23 m. ENE of Cedar Rapids; pop. 4616.

A·na·mur′, Cape (ä-nä-mōōr′); *Turk.* **Anamur Bu·run′** (bōō-rōōn′). Cape on S coast of Turkey in Asia, projecting into Mediterranean Sea opp. Cape Kormakiti on N coast of island of Cyprus.

A·nan′ev or **A·nan′iev** (ŭ-nàn′yĕf). Town, N cen. Odessa Region, SW Ukraine, U.S.S.R., 22 m. SE of Balta; pop. ab. 6100; center for grain trading.

A·nan′ta·pur′ (ȧ-nŭn′tȧ-pōōr′). **1** Former district of Madras prov., S India; 6734 sq. m.; pop. (1941) 1,171,419; chief products food grains, oil seeds, and cotton; in 18th cent. a stronghold of Marathas.
2 Town, its ✳, now in S Andhra Pradesh, about 60 m. SE of Bellary; pop. 15,099.

A·na′pa (ŭ-nȧ′pŭ). Seaport town, W Krasnodar Territory, Soviet Russia, Europe, 20 m. NW of Novorossisk; pop. 13,248. Turkish fortress founded to maintain Turkish relations with Caucasus region 1781; twice captured and restored by Russia, finally remained Russian by terms of Treaty of Adrianople 1829.

An′a·phe (ăn′ȧ-fē); *Mod. Gr.* **A·ná′phē** (ä-nä′fē). Island 7 m. long by 2 m. wide, SE Cyclades, S Aegean Sea, E of Santorin; has no harbor.

A·ná′po·lis (ȧ-nȧ′pōō-lĕs). City, Goiaz state, cen. Brazil, at end of railroad N from São Paulo; pop. (1940 est.) 8204.

Anapurna. See ANNAPURNA.

Anas. See GUADIANA.

A·ñas′co (ä-nyäs′kō). Municipality (pop. 17,200) and town, W Puerto Rico, 6 m. N of Mayagüez.

Añasco Bay. Bay in SW coast of Aguadilla municipality, NW Puerto Rico, at mouth of Grande Añasco river.

Anasquam. See ANNISQUAM.

An′as·ta′si·a Island (ăn′ăs·tä′shĭ·ȧ; -shȧ; -zhĭ·ȧ; -zhȧ). Island ab. 3 m. wide and 14 m. long off coast of St. Johns co., NE Florida, S of St. Augustine, bet. Matanzas river (*q.v.*) and the Atlantic.

A′na·ta·han′ (ä′nä-tä·hän′). Small island, cen. Mariana Is., 80 m. N of Saipan, 16°22′N; highest point 2585 ft.; taken by U.S. Army 1945.

An′a·to′lia (ăn′ȧ·tōl′yȧ; -tō′lĭ·ȧ); *Turk.* **A·na·do·lu′** (ä-nä-dô·lōō′). The part of Turkey in Asia equivalent to the peninsula of Asia Minor (*q.v.*) up to indefinite line on E from Gulf of İskenderon to Black Sea, comprising ab. three fifths of the vilayets of the Turkish republic.

A′na·yac′si (ä′nä-yäk′sē). Peak 18,380 ft., Oruro dept., W Bolivia.

An′cash (äng′käsh), *formerly* **An′cachs** (äng′käsh). Department of Peru. See *Table* at PERU.

An′chor·age (äng′kēr·ĭj). **1** District, S cen. Alaska; pop. 82,833.
2 Seaport city in district at head of Cook Inlet near base

of Kenai Penin.; connected by railroad with Fairbanks 470 m. to N and with Seward 114 m. to S; pop. 44,237. Founded 1914 as construction camp for railroad; now important army post and airport; headquarters of Alaska Defense Command during World War II.

An′co·hu′ma (äng′kō-ōō′mä). The higher peak 21,490 ft. of Mt. Sorata, Bolivia. Cf. ILLAMPU.

An′con (äng′kŏn); *Span.* **An·cón′** (äng·kôn′). Town, Balboa dist., Canal Zone, NW suburb of Panama; pop. 1946; site of American Gorgas Hospital.

An·cón′ (äng·kôn′). **1** Town, S coast of Santa Elena Penin., Ecuador; oil fields.
2 Town and bathing resort 22 m. N of Lima, Lima dept., cen. Peru; pop. (1931) 1505; as a port, superseded by Callao; has Inca remains.
History: Scene of treaty which terminated War of Pacific (1879–83) bet. Chile and Peru Oct. 1883 (see Treaty of VALPARAÍSO for peace bet. Bolivia and Chile) and by which Peru ceded Tarapacá and Chile was to remain in occupation of Tacna and Arica (*qq.v.*) for 10 years until plebiscite should determine final ownership. Failure to carry out plebiscite provision caused Tacna-Arica dispute.

An·co′na (äng-kō′nȧ; *Ital.* äng·kō′nä). **1** Province of Italy. See *Table* at ITALY.
2 Seaport, its ✳, Marches, cen. Italy, on Adriatic coast 117 m. E by S of Florence; pop. 89,198; small, but excellent, harbor; railroad junction; ancient mole designed by Trajan topped by triumphal arch by Apollodorus (erected 115 A.D.); modern mole by Pope Clement II has lighthouse and triumphal arch by Vanvitelli; large import trade; sugar refining, shipbuilding; manufactures silk, paper, sailcloth.
History: Founded by Greek refugees from Syracuse c. 390 B.C.; purple factory founded by Greek merchants; occupied as naval station by Romans during Illyrian war 178 B.C.; taken by Caesar after his crossing Rubicon 49 B.C.; after improvement of harbor by Emperor Trajan who departed from it on second expedition to Moesia and Dacia 105 A.D., became important seaport and naval station; attacked by Goths, Lombards, Saracens; one of the Pentapolis (*q.v.*) under exarchate of Ravenna; chief town of **Mark of Ancona** (in extent about equivalent to modern Marches compartimento), attached to Holy Roman Empire 1138–1254; later a municipal republic under papal protection until taken by Federigo Gonzaga for Clement VII 1532; scene of death of Pope Pius II on eve of a crusade against Turks 1464; taken by French 1797, by Russians 1799; restored to Pope 1814; occupied by French 1832–39, by Austrians 1849–59; captured by Italian troops soon after Castelfidardo (*q.v.*) victory over papal forces 1860; scene of riots leading to strike 1914; bombed by Austrian fleet 1915. In World War II captured by Polish forces July 19, 1944.

An′cre (än′kr′). **1** River 25 m. long, Somme dept., France; from NE flows into Somme river near Corbie ab. 9 m. E of Amiens; scene of several battles 1916–18, esp. of successful Allied advance against Germans Nov. 1916, in which tanks were first used.
2 See ALBERT commune in France.

An·cud′ (äng-kōōth′). Seaport, ✳ of Chiloé prov., S cen. Chile, on N Chiloé I. ab. 608 m. S of Santiago; pop. 13,981; settled 1768; surrendered to Chile by Spaniards 1826; trading center.

Ancud, Gulf of. Inlet of Pacific Ocean on S cen. coast of Chile, E of N Chiloé I.

Ancyra. See ANKARA.

An′da·col′lo (än′dä-kō′yō). Town, Coquimbo prov., cen. Chile, just S of Coquimbo; pop. 6784.

Ån′dals·nes′ (ôn′däls·näs′). Village and railhead port, Romsdal co., W Norway, at head of Romsdalsfjord, in mountain resort region ab. 55 m. E of Ålesund; pop. ab. 500. Occupied by Allied forces Apr. 14–20, 1940; evacuated in May.

An′da·lu′sia (ăn′dȧ·lōō′zhȧ; -shȧ). **1** City, ⊗ of Coving-

ton co., S Alabama, 65 m. W of Dothan; pop. 10,263.

2 *Span.* **An′da·lu·cí′a** (än′dä·lōō·thē′ä; -sē′ä). Region, S Spain; 33,811 sq. m.; comprises the modern provinces of Almería, Granada, Jaén, Málaga, Cádiz, Córdoba, Huelva, and Sevilla; traversed by mountain ranges, among them the Sierra Morena (forming the N boundary) and the Sierra Nevada, and including the Mulhacén (11,420 ft.) and Picacho de Veleta (11,378 ft.) peaks; watered by the Guadalquivir and its principal affluents, the Guadalimar, Guadiato, and Genil rivers; wide range of difference in climate, vegetation, and people; divided into **Upper Andalusia,** valley of upper Guadalquivir, and **Lower Andalusia,** valley of lower Guadalquivir; celebrated for its fertility (often called the "granary" of Spain) and for its picturesque beauty; mountainous regions abound in mineral wealth, esp. copper, lead, mercuric sulfide (cinnabar), coal, silver; agricultural products include wheat, corn, barley, grapes, olives, oranges, lemons, sugar.

History: As kingdom of Tartessus (the Biblical Tarshish, *q.v.*), served as outlet for Spanish minerals and tin from the north in latter half of 2d millennium B.C.; colony of Gadir (see CÁDIZ) established by Phoenicians c. 1100 B.C.; settled by Carthaginians who destroyed the Tartessian kingdom 480 B.C.; under Romans its W part comprised most of province of Baetica; invaded by Vandals and Visigoths 5th cent. A.D.; subjugated by Moors 711–1492; under Moslem Ommiad dynasty of Spain (756–1031), resident at Córdoba (*q.v.*), became intellectual and political center of the peninsula; Lower Andalusia reconquered by Christians 1212; Upper Andalusia, the ancient Moorish kingdom of Granada, reconquered by Ferdinand and Isabella 1492; declined with subjugation of Moors; restored to some importance through discovery of New World and consequent commercial rise of Seville and Cádiz; remained an old Spanish province until divided 1833 into eight modern provinces.

An′da·man and Nic′o·bar Islands (än′då·măn [*or* -măn], nĭk′ŏ·bär), *also known as* **An′da·mans and Nic′o·bars** (-mănz [-mänz], -bärz). Province, Indian Union, comprising two groups of islands in the Bay of Bengal; 3143 sq. m.; pop. (1941) 33,768; ✳ Port Blair; ab. 400 m. directly W of coast of Lower Burma (Tenasserim). United for administration under chief commissioner responsible to governor-general of India 1872, original penal settlement being discontinued. See also ANDAMAN ISLANDS and NICOBAR ISLANDS.

Andaman Islands, *also* **Andamans.** North group of islands in E part of Bay of Bengal; 2508 sq. m.; pop. (1941) 21,316; part of province of Andaman and Nicobar Islands, Indian Union. Chief islands North Andaman, Middle Andaman, and South Andaman, close together in a group (known as Great Andaman) and separated from Little Andaman on the S by Duncan Passage; separated from SW Burma by Preparis Channels and from the Nicobars by Ten Degree Channel. See *Map* at BURMA. Aborigines (Andamanese) have Negrito characteristics.

History: First settled by British 1789; settlement transferred to Port Cornwallis 1792 but abandoned 1796; Port Blair established as Indian penal settlement by Government of India 1858; scene of murder of Viceroy Mayo 1872; joined to Nicobar group to form administrative division of Andaman and Nicobar Islands (*q.v.*); seized by Japanese 1942 but recovered 1945.

Andaman Sea. That part of the Bay of Bengal E of the Andaman and Nicobar Is.; bounded on N and E by coast of Burma, on E and SE by Malay Penin., and on S by Strait of Malacca and Sumatra; ab. 750 m. from N to S.

An′da·va′ka, Cape (än′dä·vä′kä). Cape extending into Indian Ocean on SE coast of island of Madagascar, S of Fort-Dauphin.

Andelys, Les. See LES ANDELYS.

Andematunnum. See LANGRES.

An′denne′ (än′děn′). Industrial commune, Namur prov., Belgium, on right bank of Meuse river 10 m. E of Namur by rail and ab. 22 m. SW of Liége; in region abounding in lead, iron, zinc, and coal mines, marble quarries, and, esp., clay pits; manufactures tobacco pipes, refractory earthenware, brick, porcelain, paper. Grew up around abbey founded by Saint Bregga; taken and burned by inhabitants of Liége ab. 1159; partially burned by Germans Aug. 1914.

An′der·lecht (än′děr·lĕкt). Industrial commune, suburb WSW of Brussels, Brabant prov., Belgium, on Senne river; pop. (1938 est.) 88,048; spinning, weaving, esp. of calicoes and prints; dyeing works; 15th-cent. Gothic church.

An′der′lues′ (än′děr′lü′). Commune, Hainaut prov., Belgium, 60 m. S of Brussels; pop. 11,841; coal mines, metallurgical works, breweries.

An′der·matt (än′děr·mät); *also* **Ur′se·ren** (ŏŏr′zě·rĕn; ŏŏr′zĕrn); *Ital.* **Or·se′ra** (ŏr·sâ′rä). Commune, Uri canton, cen. Switzerland, 17 m. S of Altdorf; pop. (1930) 1088; on route over St. Gotthard Pass; tourist resort, particularly for winter sports.

An′der·nach (än′děr·näк); *anc.* **An′tun·na′cum** (ăn′tŭ·nā′kŭm). City, W Germany, in Rhineland-Palatinate state, on the left bank of the Rhine 10 m. NW of Koblenz; pop. 10,771; manufactures millstones (large export trade) and refractory-clay products; has 12th-cent. watchtower, 13th-cent. late-Romanesque parish church. Founded as a castle by Drusus Senior 12 B.C.; scene of defeat 876 of Charles the Bald by Louis III, son of Louis the German; member of Hanseatic League 1253; burned by the French 1688; to France 1795; ceded to Prussia 1815. In World War II taken by Allies March 1945.

An′der·son (än′děr·s'n). **1** Name of counties in five states of the U.S. See *Tables* at KANSAS, KENTUCKY, SOUTH CAROLINA, TENNESSEE, TEXAS.

2 City, ⊗ of Madison co., cen. Indiana, 17 m. WSW of Muncie; pop. 49,061; founded 1823, incorp. as town 1838, as city 1865; manufactures automobiles and automobile accessories. Prehistoric Indian mounds. Anderson College and Theological Seminary (1917; coed.).

3 Industrial city, ⊗ of Anderson co., NW South Carolina, 28 m. SSW of Greenville; pop. 41,316; commercial and shipping center for agricultural region (cotton, corn, wheat, etc.); manufactures cotton textiles, yarn and twine, lumber, flour, cottonseed products, etc.; site of branch of Confederate treasury 1864–65.

4 Town, ⊗ of Grimes co., E cen. Texas; pop. 2725.

5 River ab. 360 m. long, NW Mackenzie District, Northwest Territories, Canada; rises in lakes N of Great Bear Lake and flows N and into Beaufort Sea.

Anderson Ranch Dam. See UNITED STATES, *Dams and Reservoirs.*

An′der·son·ville (än′děr·s'n·vĭl). Village, Sumter co., Georgia, ab. 55 m. SW of Macon; pop. 263; large national cemetery; site of large Confederate military prison 1864–65, where conditions were so bad that many Union soldiers died.

An′des (än′děz). See VIRGILIO.

An′des (än′děz); *Span.* **Los An′des** (lôs än′dâs) *or, less correctly,* **Cor′dil·le′ra de los An′des** (kôr′thě·yä′rä [*Argen.* -thě·zhä′-] thä lôs än′dâs). Great mountain system of South America extending entire length along W coast from Tierra del Fuego to Panama, 4500 m.; has many volcanoes; source of Cauca, Magdalena, Orinoco, Amazon (Marañón and Ucayali), Pilcomayo, and all large rivers of Argentina except Paraná; in places, esp. N Argentina, Bolivia, Peru, and Colombia, spreads out over high plateaus in several parallel ranges (cordilleras); highest summit Aconcagua 23,081 ft.

Divisions: (1) Range in Tierra del Fuego runs E and W along S shore (highest ab. 7600 ft.). (2) Range from S point of Chile runs due N bet. Chile and Patagonia (**Cordillera de A′gos·ti′ni** [ä′gôs·tē′nē]) with many lakes and peaks bet. 6000 and 12,000 ft. (3) Range from

ab. 42°S lat. N to Bolivia, bet. Chile and Argentina, contains highest peaks of system (many bet. 17,000 and 23,000 ft.); entirely in Chile: Llullaillaco 22,057 ft., Pular 20,340 ft., Copiapó (Cerro del Azufre) 19,947 ft., Pili 19,849 ft.; entirely in Argentina: Aconcagua, Mercedario 22,210 ft., Bonete 21,030 ft., Nevada 21,000 ft.; on boundary line bet. Chile and Argentina: Ojos del Salado 22,572 ft., Tupungato 22,300 ft., Incahuasi 21,720 ft., Tres Cruces 20,853 ft.; many beautiful lakes (resorts) at S end on both sides bet. 39° and 42°S (Nahuel Huapí, Llanquihue, Ranco, Todos los Santos, etc.); passes (*pasos*) at intervals, esp. Uspallata or La Cumbre bet. Mendoza, Argentina, and Santiago, Chile (with the scenic Puente del Inca and the Transandine R.R., tunnel nearly 2 m. long at highest point 13,082 ft.); in N (ab. 23° to 28°S) is Puna de Atacama, desolate plateau region with average height of 11,000 to 13,000 ft., flanked on W in Chile by **Cordillera Do·mey′ko** (thô-mě′ē-kô). (4) Central part in Bolivia covers nearly ⅔ of country in elevated plateau (*altiplano*) 10,000 to 12,000 ft. and encloses Lakes Poopó and Titicaca (part in Peru); main range is **Cordillera Re·al′** (rrě-äl′) with highest peaks Ancohuma 21,490 ft., Illimani 21,184 ft., Illampu 21,276 ft. (5) From Bolivian Andes direction turns NW extending full length of Peru in many ranges covering territory from 200 to 300 m. wide; includes **Cordillera O′rien·tal′** [ō′ryän·täl′] (in SE Peru), **Cordillera Oc′ci·den·tal′** (ôk′sě·thän·täl′) (along the coast), **Cordillera de Ca′ra·ba′ya** [thä kä′rä·vä′yä] (extension of Cordillera Real in SE Peru), **Cordillera Huay′- huash** [wī′wäsh] (cen. Peru, N of Lima, watershed bet. Marañón and Pacific streams); highest peaks: Coropuna 21,720 ft., Huascarán 22,180 ft., Solimana 20,735 ft., Salcantay 20,550 ft. (6) In Ecuador, system (**Cordillera Real**) narrows and runs nearly due N; highest peaks: Chimborazo 20,702 ft., Cotopaxi 19,498 ft., Cayambe 19,160 ft., Antisana 18,885 ft. (7) In Colombia, system spreads out into 3 great ranges: **Cordillera Occidental** near coast; **Cordillera Cen·tral′** [sän träl′] bet. valleys of Cauca and Magdalena rivers; **Cordillera Oriental** in interior (extending as **Cordillera Mé′ri·da** [mä′rě·thä] into W Venezuela); highest peaks: Tolima 18,438 ft., Huila 18,700 ft., Puracé 16,110 ft.; connecting range in E Panama and NW Colombia, Serranía del Darién.

An′des (än′dās). Town, Antioquia dept., NW Colombia; pop. 5991.

An′des, Lake (ăn′děz). Lake, Charles Mix co., S South Dakota.

An′des, Los (lôs än′dās). See LOS ANDES.

An′de·vo·ran′te (än′dā·vô·rän′tä). Coastal town, E cen. Madagascar, E of Tananarive.

An′dhra Pra·desh′ (än′drá prá·dāsh′). State, S India, N of Madras, bordering on Bay of Bengal; formed 1953 from part of Madras state; enlarged 1956 by addition of part of abolished Hyderabad state; ✳ Hyderabad; area 105,963 sq. m.; pop. 31,260,600.

An′di·zhan′ (än′dǐ·zhän′; *Russ.* ŭn·dyǐ·zhän′) *or* **An′- di·jan′** (än′dǐ·jän′; *Uzbek* än′dě·jän′). City, E Uzbek S.S.R., Soviet Russia Asia, 155 m. ESE of Tashkent on upper Syr Darya; pop. 83,691; cotton-trading center.

And·khui′ (änd·ᴋōō′ē). Town, N Afghanistan, Asia, ab. 100 m. W of Balkh near Turkmen S.S.R. border; pop. ab. 15,000; chief town of former khanate.

An·dor′ra (ăn·dôr′á; -dôr′á; *Span.* än·dôr′rä); *Fr.* **An·dorre′** (äṅ·dôr′). **1** Republican state on S slope of E Pyrenees, bet. Ariège dept., France, and Lérida prov., Spain; 191 sq. m.; pop. 5231. Consists of gorges, narrow valleys, and many high peaks; altitude bet. 6500 and 10,170 ft.; contains six villages and has good highway connections with both France and Spain; has excellent pasture land (cattle and sheep raising); produces some tobacco and fruits. Language spoken is Catalan. Of Carolingian origin; placed under joint suzerainty of French counts of Foix and Spanish bishops of Urgel

1278; French rights passed to ruler, Henry IV, 1589, and ultimately to president of France; granted by Napoleon constitution as a republic 1806.
2 Town, its ✳; pop. ab. 1000.

An′do·ver (än′dú·vēr; -dō′vēr). **1** Town, Essex co., NE Massachusetts, 9 m. E of Lowell; pop. 15,878; site of Phillips Academy (preparatory school for boys, estab. 1778, oldest incorporated school in U.S.; cf. EXETER, N.H.), Abbot Academy (preparatory school for girls, founded 1829, oldest incorporated school for girls in New England), Andover Theological Seminary (1808; affiliated with Harvard University since 1908).
2 Municipal borough, Hampshire, S England, on the Anton 22 m. N of Southampton; pop. 14,661.

And′öy (än′û′ü). Northernmost island of the Vesterålen in the Norwegian Sea off NW coast of Norway; 150 sq. m.; pop. 5118; hilly and marshy; has coal beds; chief industries fishing and trade in eider duck feathers and eggs.

An′dre·a′nof Islands (än′drā·ä′nŭf; -nôf; än′drě·än′ŭf; -än′ôf). One of main groups of Aleutian Is., Alaska, extending from 172°W (Seguam I.) to 179°E (Amchitka I. in Rat Is.); chief islands Atka, Tanaga, Adak, Kanaga. In World War II occupied by American army forces and several military bases developed, esp. on Adak I.

An·dre′as, Cape (än·drā′äs; -thrä′-). Cape at end of long narrow peninsula of NE Cyprus, ab. 34°40′E long., 66 m. from coast of Latakia.

An′dré′ba′ (än′drä′bá′). Town on Lake Alaotra, NE cen. Madagascar; N terminus of branch railroad from Moramanga.

An′drew (än′drōō). County in Missouri. See *Table* at MISSOURI.

Andrew Jack′son, Mount (jăk′s'n). Mountain 13,750 ft. at S end of Palmer Penin., ab. 71°31′S, 63°34′W.

Andrew John′son National Monument (jŏn′s'n). See UNITED STATES, *National Monuments.*

An′drews (än′drōōz). **1** County in Texas. See *Table* at TEXAS.
2 Town, Cherokee co., W tip of North Carolina, 78 m. WSW of Asheville; pop. 1404; tannery, lumber mills.
3 Town, Georgetown and Williamsburg cos., E South Carolina, 17 m. W of Georgetown; pop. 2995.
4 City ⊗ of Andrews co., NW Texas; pop. 11,135.

An′dri·a (än′drě·ä). Commune, Bari prov., Apulia, SE Italy, 31 m. WNW of Bari; pop. 56,152; old Gothic cathedral; trades in olives, grain, majolica, and almonds. Founded by Peter, first Norman count of Andria, 1046; favorite residence of Emperor Frederick II who built Castel del Monte (9 m. S).

An′dros (än′drŏs). Chief island of a western group of the Bahamas; largest island of the Bahamas, 1600 sq. m.; with cays constitutes an electoral district; pop. (1943) 6718.

An′dros (än′drŏs; *Mod. Gr.* än′drôs, -thrôs). **1** Island ab. 25 m. long by 10 m. wide, N Cyclades, S Aegean Sea; separated from SE Euboea by narrow strait; pop. 19,000; belongs to Cyclades dept., Greece. Populated chiefly by Ionian Greeks; in mid-7th cent. B.C. sent colonies to Chalcidice; revolted from Athens 411 B.C.; important as naval post, conquered by Macedonian, Ptolemaic, and Pergamene rulers; annexed to Rome as part of Pergamum 133 B.C.
2 Town, its ✳, on E coast; pop. ab. 3000.

An′dros·cog′gin (än′drŭs·kŏg′ǐn). **1** River ab. 157 m. long, NE New Hampshire and SW Maine; rises in Umbagog Lake on Maine-New Hampshire boundary, flows S in New Hampshire, turns E across Maine border and SE into Kennebec river near Bath, S Maine.
2 County in Maine. See *Table* at MAINE.

An·dru′so·vo (ŭn·drōō′sǔ·vǔ). Village a few miles S of Smolensk, W Soviet Russia, Europe. Scene of treaty Jan. 20, 1667 terminating war bet. Poland and Russia (1654–67) and by which Smolensk and E Ukraine, including Kiev, were ceded to Russia.

An·dú′jar (än·dōō′här); *anc.* **Il′li·tur′gis** (ĭl′ĭ·tûr′jĭs). Commune, Jaén prov., S Spain, on right bank of Guadalquivir 24 m. NWN of Jaén: pop. 24,765; known esp. for its mineral springs and for the production of pottery.

A′né′cho′ (ä′nā′kō′). Town, S Togo, West Africa, near border of Dahomey; connected by railroad (27 m. long) with Lomé.

A′ne·cón′ Gran′de (ä′nä·kông′ grän′dä). Peak 6594 ft., SW Río Negro territory, S cen. Argentina.

An′e·ga′da (än′ē·gä′dá; *Span.* ä′nä·gä′thä). Northernmost of Virgin Is., British West Indies, ab. 10 m. long.

A′ne·ga′da Bay (ä′nä·gä′thä). Inlet of Atlantic Ocean on SE coast of Buenos Aires prov., E Argentina, S of Bahía Blanca.

An′e·ga′da Passage (än′ē·gä′dá; *Span.* ä′nä·gä′thä). Channel ab. 40 m. wide E of Anegada I. and Virgin Gorda I. in the Virgin Is., British West Indies.

A·nei′tyum (ä·nĭ′tyŏōm). Most southerly island of the New Hebrides Is., SW Pacific Ocean, 38 m. SSE of Tana; central peak 2788 ft.; has fertile coastal lands and fine harbor on S coast.

Aneiza. = ANAIZA.

A·ne′to, Pi′co de (pē′kō thä ä·nā′tō); *Fr.* **Pic de Né′thou′** (pēk′ dē nā′tōō′). Peak 11,169 ft., highest in the Pyrenees, in the Maladetta range, NE Spain, in Lérida prov. just S of French border.

Anfa. See CASABLANCA.

An′ga (ŭn′gá). Ancient name of E Bihar, NE India; under the rule of Magadha c. 6th to 8th cent.

An′ga·da′nan (äng′gä·thä′nän). Municipality, SW Isabela prov., Luzon, Phil. Is., on left bank of Cagayan river 28 m. S of Ilagan; pop. 16,047.

An·ga′mos, Point (äng·gä′mōs). Cape extending into Pacific Ocean from W cen. Antofagasta prov., N Chile, S of Bay of Mejillones del Sur.

An′gan·gue′o (äng′gäng·gä′ō). Town, Michoacán state, SW Mexico, 78 m. W of Mexico City; pop. 8196.

An·ga·ra′ (ŭn·gŭ·rä′). 1 Navigable river 1100 m. long, Soviet Russia, Asia; flows from SW corner of Lake Baikal N past Irkutsk and then W to Yenisei river, Irkutsk Region; called Upper (Verkhnyaya) Tunguska in its lower course in Krasnoyarsk Territory; chief tributaries Oka and Ilim.

2 *properly* **Verkh′ne** (vyěrᴋ′nyĕ), or **Upper, Angara.** River ab. 200 m. long, N Buryat-Mongol A.S.S.R.; flows SW into N end of Lake Baikal.

An·gat′ (äng·gät′). River ab. 70 m. long, Bulacan prov., Luzon, Phil. Is.; rises in mountains on Tayabas border and flows S and W to the Pampanga river at Calumpit.

Ang·aur′ (äng·our′). Small island at S end of Palau Is. group, W Pacific Ocean, 7 m. SSW of Peleliu; phosphate deposits; chief village Saipan, on W coast. Taken by American forces Sept. 17–Oct. 13, 1944.

An′ge·di′va (än′zhĕ·thē′vá), *formerly* **An′ji·div** (ŭn′jĕ·dēv′). Portuguese island off W coast of India, S of Goa; near Karwar in Mysore state.

Án′gel de la Guar′da (äng′hĕl dä lä gwär′thä). Island ab. 43 m. long off NE cen. Lower California, in upper Gulf of California.

An′ge·les (äng′hä·lâs). Municipality, NW cen. Pampanga prov., Luzon, Phil. Is., on Manila-Dagupan R.R. 10 m. NW of San Fernando; pop. 26,027.

An′ge·les, Los (lôs äng′hä·lâs). See LOS ÁNGELES.

An′ge·les, Mount (än′jĕ·lĕs). Peak 6039 ft., Clallam co., NW Washington.

An′gel Falls (än′jĕl). Waterfall, SE Venezuela, on side of large (ab. 20 m. long) flat-topped mountain E of Caroní river; over 3200 ft. high.

An′ge·li′na (än′jĕ·lē′ná). 1 River 150 m. long, E Texas; flows from Smith co. SSE to Neches river on E boundary of Tyler co.

2 County in Texas. See *Table* at TEXAS.

An′gel Island (än′jĕl). Island in San Francisco Bay, California, 2 m. E of Sausalito; ab. 1 sq. m.; belongs to Marin co.

Ang′eln (äng′ĕln). District, NE Schleswig-Holstein, Germany; area 320 sq. m.; bounded on the N by the Flensburger Föhrde, on E by Kiel Bay, and on S by Schlei Inlet; ground moraine; fertile farm lands; cattle and pig raising; chief town Kappeln (pop. 2653). Traditionally home of Angles, a people who are supposed to have migrated in 5th cent. A.D. to east, central, and north parts of England (see EAST ANGLIA).

Ang′er·app (äng′ĕ·räp). River ab. 90 m. long in former East Prussia prov., Prussia, Germany, now in N Poland and E Kaliningradsk Region, U.S.S.R.; flows N from Masurian Lakes into Pregel river at Chernyakhovsk (Insterburg).

Angerburg. See WĘGORZEWO.

Ång′er·man (ông′ĕr·mán). River 279 m. long, cen. Sweden; rises on W boundary of Sweden, flows SE and S into Gulf of Bothnia just N of Härnösand; navigable for ab. 31 m.; course marked by cataracts and waterfalls; noted for beauty of landscape.

Ång′er·man·land (-länd). Region, formerly a province of E Sweden, on Gulf of Bothnia, ab. coextensive with modern Västernorrland and Västerbotten provs.

Ang′er·mün′de (äng′ĕr·mün′dĕ). City, in former Prussian prov. of Brandenburg, E Germany, 37 m. SSW of Stettin (Szczecin); pop. 10,813; 13th-cent. Gothic church. Scene of defeat of Pomeranians by Elector Frederick I of Brandenburg 1420.

An′gers′ (än′zhā′; *Angl.* än′jērz); *anc.* **Ju′li·om′a·gus** (jōō′lĭ·ŏm′á·gŭs). City, ✱ of Maine-et-Loire dept., W France, on Maine river 48 m. ENE of Nantes; pop. 87,988; episcopal see from 3d cent.; 13th-cent. Gothic cathedral of Saint Maurice; university (closed by French Revolution; reorganized 1875); important slate quarries—whence its sobriquet "Black Angers" or the "Black City"; industrial production of liqueurs, cables, rope, shoes, umbrellas, thread, machines, wire, sparkling wines. Ancient capital of the Andecavi tribe; invaded by Northmen in 9th cent. and by English in 12th and 15th cents.; became seat of counts of Anjou in 9th cent. and later the capital of the duchy (see ANJOU); taken by Huguenots 1585; scene of defeat of Vendean royalists 1793.

An·ghia′ri (äng·gyä′rē). Village, E Tuscany, Italy, NE of Arezzo; pop. 1919; victory of Florentines over Milanese 1440.

Ang′kor (äng′kôr), *orig.* **Angkor Thom** (tôm). Ruined ancient city, old capital of the Khmers, in Cambodia, Indochina, NW of Tonle Sap ab. 4 m. from Siemréap. Founded 1st cent. A.D. by Khmers from NE Burma who transplanted Indian civilization and flourished for several centuries; Angkor Thom built c. 850–900 A.D., a city of 5 sq. m. having moat and walls, and within palaces, temples, and a great tower (Bayon), richly carved, esp. with four faces of Siva. About 1 m. S is **Angkor Wat** or **Vat** (wät), rectangular temple of three stories, with towers, porticoes, galleries, stairways, etc., the entire structure covered with exquisite bas-reliefs. After Siamese conquest of the Khmers in 14th cent. city and temples in ruins and buried in jungle; discovered by French botanist 1860 and later cleared and partially restored by government. See CAMBODIA.

An′glem, Mount (äng′glĕm). Peak 3198 ft., N Stewart I., New Zealand.

An′gle·sey or **An′gle·sea** (äng′g'l·sĭ). 1 *anc.* **Mo′na** (mō′ná). Island, NW Wales, separated from mainland by Menai Strait; 276 sq. m.; most of land given over to cattle and sheep pastures; produces wheat, barley, oats; mineral deposits include lead, silver, copper (esp. at Parys Mt.), asbestos, coal. Welsh spoken by inhabitants; notable druidic ruins, esp. dolmens; subdued by Suetonius Paulinus 61 A.D. who demolished sacred groves of the druids; ruled by princes of North Wales 9th–13th cents.; conquered by Edward I 1282.

2 County in Wales, including Anglesey I. and Holyhead I. See *Table* at WALES.

An′glet′ (äṅ′glĕ′). Commune, Basses-Pyrénées dept., SW France, W suburb of Bayonne; pop. (1931) 11,467.

An′gle·ton (ăng′g'l·tŭn). City, ⊗ of Brazoria co., SE Texas, 36 m. W of Galveston; pop. 7312; oil wells.

An′gleur′ (äṅ′glûr′). Industrial commune, Liège prov., Belgium, 2½ m. SE of Liège near Meuse and Ourthe rivers; pop. 10,985; coal mines and foundries.

Anglia. See ENGLAND.

An′glo-E·gyp′tian Su·dan′ (ăng′glȯ·ė·jĭp′shăn sōō-dän′); *now* **Sudan.** Country bet. Egypt and Uganda, NE Africa, formerly a British and Egyptian condominium; 950,950 sq. m.; pop. (1955 est.) 8,961,000; ✳ Khartoum; ab. 1650 m. from N to S; bounded on N by Egypt, on E by Red Sea, Eritrea, and Ethiopia, on S by Kenya, Uganda, and the Congo, and on W by Central African Republic, Chad, and Libya; crossed by Nile (*q.v.*) which enters from Uganda near Nimule and passes into Egypt just below Wadi Halfa and 2d Cataract; chiefly desert but has hilly regions along Red Sea in NE and in Darfur prov. in W. Has 9 provinces: Northern, Blue Nile, Darfur, Kassala, Khartoum, Kordofan, Bar al Ghazal, Equatoria, and Upper Nile. Chief towns Omdurman (old Dervish capital), Khartoum, Wad Medani, Kassala, and Atbara, and two ports on Red Sea, Port Sudan and Suakin. Chief export cotton; other exports gum arabic (chief source of world supply), salt, grains, and timber. See *Map* at EGYPT.

History: Conquered by Egypt under Hussein, son of Mehemet Ali, 1820–22; under nominal Egyptian authority until 1882; ravaged by slave trade which Sir Samuel Baker and General Charles Gordon (1874–80) sought to suppress; after fanatical Sudanese revolt under the Mahdi 1883 in which the evacuating Egyptian forces were defeated and General Gordon killed (at Khartoum 1885), territory abandoned to rule of the dervishes until Kitchener's campaign 1896–98 defeated them and rescued upper Nile from threat of French advance from west; jointly administered after 1899 by Egypt and Great Britain; after assassination of governor-general in Cairo in 1924 saw withdrawal of Egyptian forces, who were excluded from the country until treaty of 1936 which re-affirmed condominium agreement; saw implementation of first constitution 1953 after Anglo-Egyptian agreement (Feb. 1953) providing for immediate self-government and self-determination in three years; held first parliamentary elections Nov. 1953; became independent republic Jan. 1, 1956.

Ang·mags′sa·lik (äm·mäs′sä·lĭk). Danish settlement and trading post, E coast of Greenland, just below Arctic Circle; pop. 696; its radio station (estab. 1925) broadcasts weather reports. U.S. air base in World War II.

An·gol′ (äng·gȯl′). Town, ✳ of Malleco prov., S cen. Chile, in agricultural and fruit-growing district 325 m. S of Santiago; pop. 12,398.

An·go′la (äng·gō′lȧ). **1** City, ⊗ of Steuben co., NE Indiana, 40 m. N of Fort Wayne; pop. 4746. Tri-State College (1884).

2 Village and resort, Erie co., W New York, near Lake Erie 20 m. S of Buffalo; pop. 2499.

3 (*Port. pron.* ăNng·gô′lȧ) *or* **Portuguese West Africa.** Portuguese colony, SW Africa; 481,226 sq. m.; pop. (1940) 3,738,010; ✳ Luanda; bounded on the N by Rep. of Congo, E by Rep. of Congo and Northern Rhodesia, S by South-West Africa, and W by the Atlantic Ocean; includes also exclave of Cabinda (*q.v.*), N of the Congo river. *Chief rivers:* Congo, which for nearly 100 m. forms part of N boundary; many S tributaries of Kasai, notably the Kwango, which have their source in NE; Cuanza (or Kwanza) in cen. part, flowing NW to Atlantic; Cunene (or Kunene) in S, in part forming boundary with South-West Africa; Cubango (Okovanggo) and Cuito in SE, flowing into the Okovanggo Basin; Kwando (or Cuando), an upper tributary of the Zambezi, in SE. Interior nearly all highland, esp. in Benguela prov. (Bie Plateau); coast low and unhealthy. *Chief towns:* Nova Lisboa (formerly Huambo), Luanda, Benguela, Mossâmedes, Lobito. *Chief products:* Coffee, maize, sugar, palm oil, and palm kernels, wax; has valuable diamond deposits.

History: São Paulo de Loanda (now Luanda) settled by Portuguese 1575; Portuguese rule established over coastal area bet. 1575 and 1648, extended south to Mossâmedes 1840; given Cabinda exclave by agreement with Belgian Congo 1886; frontiers determined by Portuguese treaties with France 1886, Germany 1886, Great Britain 1890, 1891; native uprisings 1902, 1907; given autonomy 1914; settled boundary with South-West Africa 1926; reorganized and divided into 5 provinces 1934.

An·go′ni·land′ (ăng·gō′nĭ·lănd′). Plateau region, SW Nyasaland, bet. Zambezi river and Lake Nyasa; average height 4000 ft.

Angora. See ANKARA.

Angostura. See CIUDAD BOLÍVAR.

An′gou′lême′ (äṅ′gōō′lâm′); *anc.* **Ic′u·lis′ma** (ĭk′ṹ-lĭz′mȧ). City, ✳ of Charente dept., W France, on Charente river 64 m. NNE of Bordeaux; pop. 38,915; episcopal see from 379; Byzantine Romanesque cathedral of St. Pierre (11th and 12th cents.); a center of paper industry; other manufactures include carpets, firearms and gunpowder, liquors, machinery; active trade, esp. in wines.

History: Taken from Visigoths by Clovis, King of Franks, 507 A.D. in which year he built its first cathedral; from 9th cent. center of countship, held by Lusignan family from 1220; ceded to England by Peace of Bretigny 1360 but restored to France by Charles V 1373; passed to house of Orléans 1394; center of duchy (1515–1844) created by Francis I; united to crown 1714; capital of pre-Revolutionary province of Angoumois (*q.v.*).

An′gou′mois′ (äṅ′gōō′mwȧ′). Historical region of W cen. France, bounded on N by Poitou, E by Limousin, SE by Guienne, SW by Gironde estuary, NW by Aunis; ✳ Angoulême; watered by Charente river. Medieval county ceded to England by Peace of Bretigny 1360 and restored 1373 to France by Charles V; appanage of royal crown to 1515; raised to rank of duchy by Francis I 1515.

An′gra do He·ro·ís′mo (äNng′grȧ thōō ė·rōō·ezh′mōō). **1** District of Portugal. See *Table* at PORTUGAL.

2 Seaport, its ✳, in Azores at head of deep bay on S coast of Terceira I.; pop. 10,642; episcopal see; harbor protected by promontory; exports wine, fruit (esp. pineapples), grain, flax. Founded 1534; until 1832 capital of Azores; refuge for Portuguese regency 1830–33.

Angra Pequena. See LÜDERITZ.

An′gri (äng′grė). Commune, Salerno prov., Campania, S Italy, 11 m. WNW of Salerno; pop. 19,468; manufactures textiles, esp. silk and cotton goods. Ancient Mons Lactarius (S of Angri) scene of defeat of Ostrogoths 553 by Narses.

Ang Thong *or* **Ang·thong** (äng·t′hông). **1** Province, S Thailand; 414 sq. m.; pop. 126,776.

2 Town, its ✳, on the Chao Phraya river N of Ayudhya.

An·guil′la (ăng·gwĭl′ȧ). British island, St. Kitts-Nevis territory, Leeward Is., West Indies, ab. 60 m. NW of St. Kitts; 34 sq. m.; pop. (1942 est.) 5175; chief products sea-island cotton, also cattle, phosphate of lime, and salt. See LEEWARD ISLANDS.

Anguilla Cays (kēz; kāz). Group of cays or islets bet. Santaren Channel and Nicholas Channel, N of Cuba; belong to the Bahamas.

An·guille′, Cape (äng·gwĭl′). Cape, SW Newfoundland, S of entrance to St. George Bay.

An·gul′ (ŭng·gōōl′). **1** District of Orissa state, E Indian Union; 1681 sq. m.; pop. 222,736.

2 Town, its ✳, 60 m. WNW of Cuttack.

An′gus (äng′gŭs); *formerly* **For′far** (fôr′fĕr) *or* **For′-far·shire** (-shĭr; -shēr). County, E Scotland; 874 sq. m.; pop. (1951) 274,870; ⊗ Forfar; bounded on the N by

Aberdeen and Kincardine cos., on E by North Sea, on S by Firth of Tay, and on W by Perth co.; irregular, hilly land; cut by North Esk, South Esk, and Isla rivers; agriculture (wheat, potatoes, oats); sheep and cattle raising; salmon fishing; jute and linen manufactures. Chief towns Dundee, Forfar, Montrose, Arbroath.

An′gwin (ăng′(g)wĭn). Town, Napa co., California, ab. 20 m. NNW of Napa; pop. 3593; Pacific Union College (1882; coed.).

An′halt (än′hält). Former German state, cen. Germany; 893 sq. m.; pop. (1939) 436,213; ✳ Dessau; included part of Harz Mts.; watered by Elbe, Mulde, and Saale rivers; produces wheat, corn, flax, potatoes, hops, vegetables; lignite deposits; saltworks.

History: Named from castle of Anhalt built c. 1100; began separate territorial status when inherited as part of Saxony by Duke Henry I of Anhalt (1214–44); in League of German Princes (estab. 1785); subdivided and reunited continuously until reconstituted as duchy of Anhalt by Leopold IV 1863; joined North German Confederation 1866; became part of German Empire 1871; proclaimed republic 1918, receiving its constitution July 18, 1919; lost federal status, becoming a mere administrative unit (Ger. *Land*) of the German Reich 1934.

An′hil·wa′ra (ŭn′hĭl·wä′rà). See PATAN.

An′holt (än′hŏlt). Island, Randers co., Denmark, in middle of Kattegat ab. 45 m. E of Jutland; 8 sq. m.; pop. (1925) 286; lighthouse.

Anhsi. See ANSI.

An′hwei′ *or* **An′hui′** (än′hwā′). Province, E China; 51,888 sq. m.; pop. (1936 est.) 23,265,368; ✳ Hwaining; bounded on N by Kiangsu, on E by Kiangsu and Chekiang, on S by Kiangsi, and on W by Hupeh and Honan; crossed by lower course of Yangtze (ab. ⅓ of province S of river) and in N by Hwai and new course of Hwang Ho; contains Chao Hu (lake) and part of Hungtze Hu; lowland in N and in valley of Yangtze, mountainous in S; chief cities Hwaining, Wuhu, Sihsien, Hofei; chief crops wheat, millet, beans, tea, and rice. Under Ming dynasty (14th–17th cents.), part of province of Kiang-nau (Kiangsu the other part); made separate province in 17th cent. under Manchu (Ch'ing) dynasty.

An′i·ak′chak Volcano (än′ĭ·äk′chăk). Crater 6 m. in diameter, Alaska Penin., SW Alaska, 56°55′N lat.; largest known explosion crater.

A′niche′ (à′nēsh′). Commune, Nord dept., N France, 8 m. ESE of Douai; pop. 8611; noted coal beds.

Anicium. See LE PUY.

A·nie′ne (à·nyâ′nâ); *anc.* **An′io** (än′yō). River 73 m. long, cen. Italy, flowing into the Tiber river just above Rome.

A·ni·wa Bay (ä·nē·wä); *Jap.* **Aniwa Wan** (wän). Bay at S end of Sakhalin I., E Asia.

An·jen′go (ŭn·jĕng′gō). Village, SW India, on coast of Kerala ab. 20 m. NW of Trivandrum; one of the earliest (1684) English settlements in India.

Anjidiv. See ANGEDIVA.

An′jou′ (än′zhōō′; *Angl.* ăn′jōō). Historical region of NW France; bounded on N by Maine, E by Touraine, SE by Saumurois, S by Poitou, and W by Brittany; ✳ Angers; watered by Loire river.

History: County erected as a fief by the Capetian kings; under Fulk III Nerra (987–1040) and his successors, Angevin house acquired Touraine 1044 and Maine 1110; became English 1154 at accession of Henry II (who had inherited it 1151 from his father, Duke Geoffrey of Anjou); returned to French crown when taken from King John 1204; inherited in 1246 by Prince Charles, who became king of Naples and Sicily; raised to a duchy 1297, returned to royal domain through accession of Philip VI 1328; from 1350 to 1480 under third house of Anjou, founded by Louis I (Count of Provence 1339–84 and Duke of Anjou 1360–84), second son of John II (1350–64); became duchy 1360; annexed to French crown by Louis XI 1480.

An′jou·an′ (än′zhwän′) *or* **Jo·han′na** (jô·hăn′à). One of Comoro Is. 80 m. SE of Great Comoro; 89 sq. m.

Anju. See ANSHU.

An′ka·ra (äng′kà·rà; *Turk.* äng′kä·rä′). 1 Vilayet, W cen. Turkey in Asia; 11,164 sq. m.; pop. 534,025; ✳ Ankara. 2 *formerly* **An·go′ra** (ăng·gōr′à; ăng′gō·rà); *anc.* **Ancy′ra** (ăn·sī′rà). Commercial city, ✳ of Turkish republic and of Ankara vilayet, ab. 220 m. ESE of İstanbul; pop. (1940) 155,544; built on a hill 500 ft. above a plain and on **Ankara River** (ab. 115 m. long), a tributary of Sakarya river.

History: Important commercial center (Ancyra) from early times; capital of Celtic kingdom of Galatia (*q.v.*) in 3d cent. B.C., of Roman province of Galatia after 25 B.C.; conquered in succession by Persians, Arabs, Seljuk Turks, Latin Crusaders, and finally 1360 by Ottoman Turks; nearby occurred victory of Mongol conqueror, Tamerlane, over Sultan Bajazet I 1402; part of Ottoman Empire after recovery by Turks 1431; center in which Turkish Nationalists set up provisional government 1920 which in 1923 proclaimed the republic of Turkey (*q.v.*); made capital of Turkey 1923; name officially changed from Angora to Ankara 1930; scene of treaty by which Turkey and Greece recognized territorial status quo and agreed to naval equality in Mediterranean 1930.

An′ka·ra′tra (äng′kä·rä′trä). Mountain group, highest 8675 ft., cen. Madagascar.

Anking. = HWAINING.

An′klam (äng′kläm). City, E Germany, in former Pomerania prov., Prussia, on right bank of Peene river 44 m. NW of Stettin (Szczecin); pop. 14,789; foundries, machinery works, mills (esp. wool and linen), soap factories, sugar manufacturing. Settled in 11th cent.; joined Hanseatic League 1244; sacked during Thirty Years' War and Seven Years' War; acquired by Prussia 1720.

An·ko′ber (äng·kō′bĕr; *native* än′kō′bĕr). Town in Shoa, cen. Ethiopia, on E slope of mountains 85 m. NE of Addis Ababa; pop. ab. 3000.

An·ko′bra (äng·kō′brà). River ab. 125 m. long, W Ghana, West Africa; navigable for 50 miles; enters Gulf of Guinea just W of Axim.

An·ko′le (äng·kō′lä). Plateau region in SW Uganda, bet. Lake Victoria and Lake Edward; formerly a native kingdom; now included in Western Province, British protectorate of Uganda, E Africa; home of the Bahima.

An′lo (än′lō). Commune, Drenthe prov., NE Netherlands, 13 m. SSE of Groningen; pop. 5198.

Ann, Cape (ăn). 1 Eastern peninsula of Essex co., Massachusetts, N of Massachusetts Bay. 2 Cape on coast of Enderby Land, Antarctica, extending into Indian Ocean at 51°17′E.

An′na (ăn′à). City, Union co., SW Illinois, 28 m. SW of Marion; pop. 4280; fruit-shipping center; state hospital for insane.

An′na·berg; *now* **An′na·berg–Buch′holz** (än′ä·bĕrk-bōōK′hōlts). City, Karl-Marx-Stadt dist., East Germany, near Bohemian border in the Erz Gebirge 18 m. S of Karl-Marx-Stadt (Chemnitz); pop. 18,204; center of German lace, braid, and ribbon industry founded by Barbara Uttmann 1550; gained first importance through the mining of silver, tin, bismuth, and cobalt; marble quarries.

An Na·fud′ (ăn′ nä·fōōd′); *also* **Ne·fud′** (nĕ·fōōd′). A desert of red sand in N Saudi Arabia, a northward extension of the great desert of cen. Arabia.

An′nai (än′ī). Village, S cen. British Guiana, on the Rupununi river; center of cattle-raising region.

An Na′jaf (än nä′jäf). Town, S cen. Iraq, on lake W of the Euphrates 35 m. S of Hilla; pop. ab. 25,000; starting point of pilgrimage route to Mecca; contains Ali's shrine.

An·nam′ *or* **A·nam′** (ă·năm′; ä′năm). Region, former French protectorate, cen. Vietnam, situated on E coast of Indochina, with coast line of about 850 m. bordering on South China Sea; 56,974 sq. m.; pop. 5,656,000; ✳ Hue. Bounded on N by Tonkin, on W by Laos, and on

SW by Cambodia and Cochin China; has mountain range extending entire length with peaks 5000 to 7890 ft.; many fine harbors, esp. Camranh Bay; railroad runs along entire coast from Thanhhoa to Saigon. Raises usual tropical products, esp. rice; also exports sugar, cotton and silk tissues, tea, paper, etc. Chief towns Hué, Binh Dinh, and the ports of Tourane, Vinh, and Quangtri.

History: Conquered c. 214 B.C. by Chinese; became independent 1428; came under French influence in late 18th cent., but ruled by emperor of Annam at beginning of 19th cent.; French control extended by various treaties until established as protectorate 1884–86. After World War II became part of Vietnam. See FRENCH INDOCHINA.

An'nan (ăn'ăn). **1** Small river ab. 50 m. long, S Scotland; flows S in Dumfries co. into Solway Firth.

2 Burgh, Dumfries co., S Scotland, on Annan river 2 m. from its mouth; pop. 4631; cotton and rope spinning, sandstone quarrying, shipbuilding, bacon curing.

An'nan·dale (ăn'ăn·dāl). Municipality, E New South Wales, SE Australia, SW suburb of Sydney; pop. 12,205.

An'nan·dale-on-Hud'son (hŭd's'n). Village, Dutchess co., New York, on E bank of Hudson river 21 m. N of Poughkeepsie; Bard College (1860; coed.).

An'na Pau·low'na (ăn'å pô·lō'nå). Commune, North Holland prov., Netherlands, 33 m. N of Amsterdam; pop. 5501.

An·nap'o·lis (ă·năp'ō·lĭs; ă·năp'lĭs). **1** Seaport, ✱ of Maryland and ⊗ of Anne Arundel co., on S bank of Severn river near its mouth at Chesapeake Bay, 22 m. SSE of Baltimore; pop. 23,385. Site of United States Naval Academy (founded 1845 by George Bancroft) and of St. John's College (1696; coed.).

History: Settled as town of Providence by Puritans from Virginia 1649, later known as Anne Arundel Town; became capital of Maryland and renamed Annapolis in honor of Princess (later Queen) Anne 1694; received city charter 1708; scene of meeting of Continental Congress Nov. 26, 1783–June 3, 1784; seat of the Annapolis Convention 1786 in which delegates from five states met but took no action (precursor of Constitutional Convention of 1787).

2 County, Nova Scotia, Canada. See *Table* at NOVA SCOTIA.

Annapolis Basin. Inlet of Bay of Fundy on W coast of Annapolis co., W Nova Scotia, Canada; receives **Annapolis River** (75 m. long) from NE.

Annapolis Roy'al (roi'ăl). Town, ⊗ of Annapolis co., W Nova Scotia, Canada, on S shore of Annapolis Basin 70 m. N of Yarmouth; pop. 784; beautifully situated in noted apple-growing region. One of the oldest settlements in North America N of the Gulf of Mexico; founded as **Port Roy'al** (pōrt roi'ăl; *Fr.* pôr' rwa'yàl') 1605 by Sieur de Monts and Champlain; several times captured by English in 17th cent. and restored to France; became seat of French government in Acadia 1684; finally seized 1710 and became permanently British 1713 by Treaty of Utrecht; name changed in honor of Queen Anne; until 1750 was capital of Nova Scotia.

An'na·pur'na or **A'na·pur'na** (ăn'å·pŏŏr'nå; ŭn'-). Mountain range, Nepal, in the Himalayas; highest peak 26,492 ft.; first climbed 1950 by French expedition.

Ann Ar'bor (ăn' är'bēr). City, ⊗ of Washtenaw co., SE Michigan, in agricultural section 36 m. W of Detroit; pop. 67,340; settled 1824. University of Michigan (founded 1817 in Detroit, reorganized as college in Ann Arbor 1841; coed. since 1870).

An Na'si·ri'ya (ăn nä'sĭ·rĭ'yà; -yä). Town, Basra prov., SE Iraq, on left bank of Euphrates river ab. 100 m. NW of Basra. In World War I taken by British July 25, 1915.

Anne A·run'del (ăn' å·rŭn'd'l). County in Maryland. See *Table* at MARYLAND.

Anne Arundel Town. Early name of ANNAPOLIS, Maryland.

An'ne·cy' (ăn'sē'); *Lat.* **An'ne·ci'a·cum** (ăn'ē·sĭ'-**

å·kŭm). City, ✱ of Haute-Savoie dept., E France, at NW end of Lake Annecy 63 m. ENE of Lyons; pop. 23,293; manufactures linens, cotton yarn, silk, paper; tanneries; noted bell foundry in vicinity (**An'ne·cy'-le-Vieux'** [-lĕ-vyû'], *anc.* **An'ne·ci'a·cum Ve'tus** [vē'tŭs], 1½ m. N). Ancient castle, cathedral, and church of St. Francis. Ruled by counts of the Genevois; under counts of Savoy 1401–1860.

Annecy, Lake. Lake in the Alps, Haute-Savoie dept., E France, 22 m. S of Geneva, 9 m. long, 2 m. wide; connected with Fier river by Thiou canal which runs through Annecy; surrounded by steep, scenic mountains.

An'nen (ăn'ĕn). Formerly, commune, Arnsberg govt. dist., Westphalia prov., Prussia, Germany, 6 m. SW of Dortmund near Witten; coal mining; cast-steel works, glass factories, chemicals, tileworks.

Annesley Bay. See Gulf of ZULA.

An·nette' (ă·nĕt'; ă-). Small island S of Revillagigedo I., SE Alaska; Metlakatla is on it; inhabitants, chiefly Indians and Eskimos, engaged in salmon fishing.

Ann'field Plain (ăn'fēld plān'). Former urban district, Durham, N England, 11 m. SSW of Newcastle; pop. (1931) 15,931; collieries.

An'nis·quam (ăn'ĭs·kwŏm), *earlier* **An'as·quam.** Village and summer resort, N suburb and part of Gloucester, Essex co., NE Massachusetts, on Annisquam Harbor.

Annisquam Harbor. Inlet of Atlantic Ocean on N shore of Cape Ann, E Essex co., NE Massachusetts.

An'nis·ton (ăn'ĭs·tŭn). Manufacturing city, ⊗ of Calhoun co., NE Alabama, 28 m. SE of Gadsden; pop. 33,657; founded as private industrial village; incorporated as city 1879; opened to public 1883; rich iron mines; manufactures iron products, textiles, chemicals.

An'no·bón' (ä'nô·vôn'). Small mountainous island 4 m. long in Gulf of Guinea 120 m. SW of São Tomé; 7 sq. m.; pop. 1204; administered as part of Spanish Guinea; acquired in 1778 but not occupied until 1885.

An'nœul'lin' (ä'nû'lăn'). Commune, Nord dept., N France, 9 m. SSW of Lille; pop. (1931) 6190; coal, brickworks, tanneries.

An'no·nay' (ä'nô·nā'); *anc.* **An'no·ni'a·cum** (ăn'ô·nĭ'å·kŭm). Commune, Ardèche dept., SE France, on Cance river 36 m. N of Privas; pop. 15,669; manufactures paper, kid gloves, woolen hosiery; tanneries, dyeworks, silk mills; 14th-cent. Gothic church; birthplace of Montgolfier brothers.

An·not'to Bay (ă·nŏt'ō). Town on NE coast of Jamaica I., West Indies Federation, 22 m. N of Kingston.

Ann'ville (ăn'vĭl). Locality in Annville township (pop. 4264), Lebanon co., SE cen. Pennsylvania, ab. 4 m. W of Lebanon; platted 1762; dairying; limestone quarries; manufactures hosiery, shoes, etc.; Lebanon Valley College (1866).

A·no'ka (å·nō'kå). **1** County in Minnesota. See *Table* at MINNESOTA.

2 City, its ⊗, E Minnesota, on Mississippi river 17 m. NNW of Minneapolis; pop. 10,562; trade center in agricultural section.

An Pass (än; ăn). Mountain pass in cen. part of Arakan Yoma, W Burma, alt. ab. 5000 ft.; leads from Akyab and coast towns to Magwe and Minbu on the Irrawaddy.

Anping. See AMPIN.

Ans (äNS). Commune, Liège prov., E Belgium, NW suburb of Liège, at source of the Légie tributary of the Meuse; pop. 12,668; coal mines, brickworks, railroad equipment, mine cables.

An'sa·ri'ya, Dje'bel (jä'băl ăn'sä·rē'yå; -yä). Mountain range, NE Latakia, Republic of Syria, running N and S ab. 70 m. along W bank of the Orontes river; highest point ab. 5100 ft.; N extension of Lebanon Mts.

Ans'bach (äns'bäk) *or in English often* **Ans'pach** (ănz'păk). **1** *older* **O'nolz·bach** (ō'nôlts·bäk). City, ✱ of Middle Franconia govt. dist., Bavaria, Germany, 25 m. SW of Nürnberg; pop. 21,923; manufactures cardboard,

paper, combs, motors, textiles. Built around Benedictine monastery founded in 8th cent. by Saint Gumbertus; capital of Ansbach principality.

2 Principality, ruled by Franconian branch of Hohenzollern family of Brandenburg until its transference to Prussia 1791–92; with Bayreuth (forming margraviate of Ansbach-Bayreuth), ceded to Bavaria by Prussia 1806, confirmed by Congress of Vienna 1815.

An·se′ba (ăn-sā′bä). River, Eritrea, NE Africa; rises in cen. Eritrea E of the Barca, flows N and joins the Barca S of the Republic of Sudan border.

An·ser′ma (ăn-sĕr′mä). Town, Caldas dept., W cen. Colombia, 50 m. WSW of Manizales; pop. 5458.

An′shan′ (än′shän′). Town, Liaoning prov., S Manchuria, on railroad 55 m. SSW of Mukden; pop. (1940 est.) 213,865; its steelworks established 1918 by South Manchurian Railway (Japanese), became largest heavy-industry plant in Manchukuo; bombed by U.S. aircraft July and Sept. 1944.

An′shan (ăn′shăn) or **An′zan** (-zăn). Region of ancient Persia NE of Babylonia; a small kingdom, probably in southern Elam (q.v.), closely connected with or inclusive of Susa; seat of authority of early Achaemenian kings, predecessors of Cyrus who founded Persian Empire 6th cent. B.C.

An·shu (än·shoo) or **An·ju** (än·joo). Walled town, South Heian prov., NW Korea, ab. 38 m. N of Heijo; pop. 17,284; commercial market, esp. for extensive coal mines; near rich agricultural plain.

An′shun′ (än′shoon′). City, Kweichow prov., S China, 60 m. SW of Kweiyang; pop. ab. 50,000.

An′si′ (än′sē′) or **An′hsi** (än′shē′). Town, NW Kansu prov., N cen. China, ab. 530 m. NW of Lanchow; station on great highway W to Urumchi and the U.S.S.R.; starting point for northern route to Kashgar, W Sinkiang, via Qomul, Turfan, and Aqsu, and for southern route via Cherchen and Khotan.

An′son (ăn′s'n). **1** County in North Carolina. See *Table* at NORTH CAROLINA.

2 Residential town, Somerset co., W Maine, on Kennebec river 20 m. NW of Waterville; pop. 2252.

3 City, ⊗ of Jones co., NW cen. Texas, 25 m. NNW of Abilene; pop. 2890; cotton-shipping center.

Anson Bay. Inlet of Timor Sea on NW coast of Northern Territory, Australia; receives Daly river.

An·son′go (ăn-sông′gō). Town on left bank of Niger, SE Mali, 50 m. SE of Gao; above this point Niger navigable for 1000 miles.

An·so′ni·a (ăn-sō′nĭ·à; -sōn′yà). Manufacturing city, New Haven co., S Connecticut, on Naugatuck river 8 m. WNW of New Haven; pop. 19,819; settled 1651 as part of Derby, independently organized 1845, became borough 1864, city 1893; manufactures copper, brass, iron castings, machinery, electrical equipment, textiles, roofing, paper boxes. The town (incorp. 1889) is coextensive with the city.

Anspach. See ANSBACH.

An′ta·kya′ (än′tä·kyä′) or **An′ta·ki′yah** (än′tä·kē′yà; -yä). *Anc.* **An′ti·och** (ăn′tĭ·ŏk); *Lat.* **An′ti·o·chi′a** (ăn′tĭ·ō·kī′à); *Greek* **An′ti·o·che′a** (-kē′à). City, Hatay vilayet, S Turkey in Asia, S of Iskenderon; pop. 28,000; on left bank of Orontes river in a fertile plain 20 m. from its mouth. On natural trade route; produces tobacco, maize, and cotton, also olives, carpets, silk goods.

History: Antioch founded by Seleucus Nicator 300 B.C.; became commercial rival of Alexandria; capital of Syria (q.v.) until 64 B.C. when Pompey conquered the province; a mission center for early Christianity; ancient city destroyed by earthquake 526 A.D.; conquered by Arabs 638; captured by Byzantine Empire under Nicephorus Phocas 969; taken by the Seljuk Turks 1085, regained by the Crusaders 1097–98, and as a principality given to Bohemund; subject of dispute bet. Normans and Byzantine emperor whose suzerainty Bohemund agreed to recognize 1099; Latin Christian principality destroyed

by Baybars, Mameluke sultan of Egypt and Syria, 1268. For later history, see SYRIA.

An′tal·ya′ (än′täl·yä′). **1** Vilayet, SW Turkey in Asia; 7519 sq. m.; pop. 242,609.

2 *formerly* **A′da·li·a′** (ä′dä·lē·yä′); *anc.* **At′ta·lei′a** (ăt′à·lī′à); *Bib.* **At′ta·li′a** (ăt′à·lī′à). Seaport town, its ✳, on Gulf of Antalya; pop. 21,659. Ancient city founded c. 150 B.C. on seacoast of Pamphylia by Attalus II Philadelphus, King of Pergamum; from this port Paul sailed with Barnabas to Antioch on his first missionary journey (*Acts* xiv. 25).

Antalya, or **Adalia, Gulf of;** *Turk.* **Antalya Kör′fe·zi′** (kûr′fĕ·zē′). Wide inlet of Mediterranean Sea in SW coast of Turkey in Asia, ab. 110 m. across.

Antananarivo. See TANANARIVE.

Ant·arc′ti·ca (ănt·ärk′tĭ·kà) or **Ant·arc′tic Continent** (-tĭk). The body of land around the South Pole, largely within the Antarctic Circle, ab. 6,000,000 sq. m.; a plateau 6000 to 10,000 ft.. still in the ice age, covered by great icecap; has mountain peaks 10,000 to 15,000 ft. high, some of which are volcanic; isolated by oceans and therefore home of permanent west winds; greater part still unexplored and coast lines not all actually known. By some geographers divided into **West Antarctica** (from Greenwich meridian W to 180th) and **East Antarctica** (E to 180th), by others into four quadrants (Ross, Weddell, Enderby, and Victoria); more commonly subdivided into various lands, coasts, and dependencies, chiefly British, Australian, New Zealand, and Norwegian; esp., Queen Maud Land (Norw.) from 16°30′W to 49°30′E; Enderby Land, Coats Land, and Wilkes Land (Australian, except Adélie Coast, which is French) from ab. 102°E to ab. 142°20′E; Victoria Land (on W side of Ross Sea and Ross Shelf Ice) and Ross Dependency (Brit.) from 160°E to 150°W; Marie Byrd Land and Ellsworth Highland (claimed by U.S.) from 150°W to 80°W; Falkland Islands Dependencies (Brit.) from 80°W to 20°W. See *Map* on page 50.

History: A southern continent mentioned by ancient writers, including Ptolemy, and shown on the maps of medieval cartographers as *terra australis*; its supposed boundaries pushed further southward by voyages of Vasco da Gama, Magellan, Drake, and Tasman (15th–17th cents.); significant exploration of region begun with voyages of Capt. James Cook who proved 1768 that New Zealand was not part of the southern continent, and who first crossed Antarctic Circle in circumnavigation of continent 1772–75; region visited by British and American whalers 1778–1839; first land within Antarctic Circle sighted by Bellingshausen 1819–21; Weddell Sea, Graham Coast, Enderby Land, Adélie Coast discovered during period 1823–40; Ross Sea and Ross Shelf Ice discovered 1841 by Capt. Ross, who established 1842 record of 78°0′S, not surpassed until 1902; discovery of region and scientific study of mainland carried on by successive German. Norwegian, Belgian, and British expeditions, especially after 6th International Geographical Congress of 1895; first landing on continent made by member of Norwegian expedition 1895; Ross Barrier to 82°17′S crossed by Scott 1902–04; southern end of Ross Barrier passed by Shackleton's expedition 1908, and South Magnetic Pole reached by other members of his group 1909; South Pole discovered by Capt. Roald Amundsen Dec. 17, 1911; continuity of coast from George V Coast to Enderby Land demonstrated by land explorations of Sir Douglas Mawson's expeditions 1911–14, 1929–31; explored and mapped from air by Sir Hubert Wilkins 1928–29 and by Commander Richard Byrd 1928–30, 1933–35; part of Pacific coast explored by Byrd's third expedition 1939–40 and fourth 1946–47; Ronne (U.S.) expedition 1946–48 showed Antarctica to be a single continent; Fuchs (Brit.) expedition 1957–58 made first land crossing of the continent.

Antarctic Archipelago. See PALMER ARCHIPELAGO.
Antarctic Peninsula. See PALMER PENINSULA.

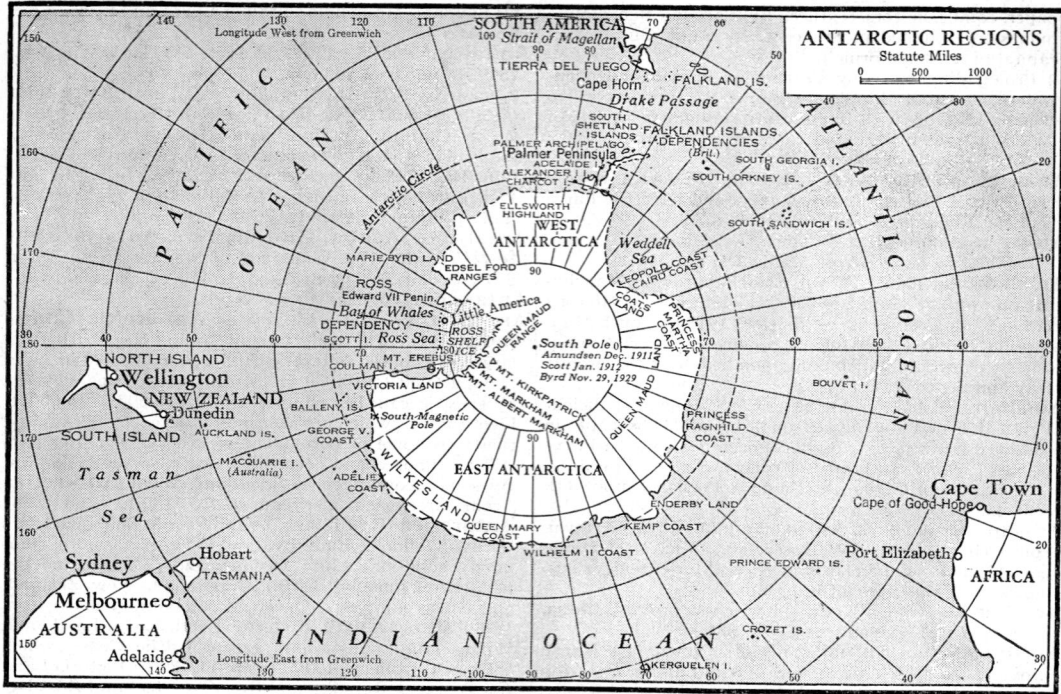

Antarctic Regions. Antarctica (*q.v.*) and the S waters of the Atlantic, Pacific, and Indian Oceans (sometimes inappropriately termed **Antarctic Ocean**); greatest depth recorded in these S waters is the Byrd Deep, 28,152 ft. in ab. lat. 70°S near 180th meridian on N edge of Ross Sea; subpolar conditions extend to lat. 55°S and reach 45°S in area S of Africa. Cf. POLAR REGIONS, ARCTIC REGIONS.

An'te·lope (ăn't'l·ōp). **1** County in Nebraska. See *Table* at NEBRASKA.
2 Island 15½ m. long, SE Great Salt Lake, Utah; forms part of Davis co.

Antelope Peak. 1 Mountain 10,200 ft. in Sierra Nevada on boundary bet. Mono and Alpine cos. E cen. California.
2 Mountain 10,207 ft., SW Eureka co., cen. Nevada.

Antelope Range. Range in NE Nevada, in White Pine and Elko cos.

An·ten'na, Piz'zo (pĕt'tsŏ än·tän'nä). Highest peak 6780 ft. in Madonie Mts., Sicily.

An'te·que'ra (än'tä·kā'rä). **1** Municipality, SW Bohol prov., Phil. Is., 12 m. NNE of Tagbilaran; pop. 15,974.
2 *anc.* **An'ti·quar'i·a** (ăn'tĭ·kwâr'ĭ·à). Commune, Málaga prov., S Spain, 22 m. NNW of Málaga; pop. 37,231; manufactures sugar, textiles; trades in oil, grain; captured from Moors 1410. Caves in vicinity.

An·ter'o, Mount (ăn·tĕr'ō). Peak 14,245 ft. in Sawatch Range, W Chaffee co., cen. Colorado. Cf. ANTERO PEAK.

Antero Peak. Mountain 13,245 ft. in Sawatch Range, Saguache co., S cen. Colorado. Cf. Mount ANTERO.

An'tho·ny (ăn'thô·nĭ). **1** City, ⊗ of Harper co., S Kansas, 62 m. S of Hutchinson; pop. 2744.
2 Village in Coventry town, Kent co., cen. Rhode Island, ab. 7 m. SW of Cranston; settled c. 1805; manufactures cotton cloth.

Anthony Peak. Mountain 10,200 ft. in Sierra Nevada, SE Alpine co., E cen. California.

An'tho·nys Nose (ăn'thô·nĭz). **1** Bold promontory 900 ft., E side of Hudson river, New York, in Putnam co. near Peekskill.

2 Peak 1048 ft., Washington co., E New York.

Anti–Atlas. See ATLAS MOUNTAINS.

An'tibes' (äN'tēb'); *anc.* **An·tip'o·lis** (ăn·tĭp'ō·lĭs). Seaport, Alpes-Maritimes dept., SE France, on Mediterranean 11 m. SW of Nice; pop. 25,014; winter resort; trades in dried fruit, olives, oil, salt fish, anchovies, tobacco, perfumery, wine. Founded c. 340 B.C. by the Phocaeans; became Roman municipium, Roman remains still being extant; episcopal see 400–1244; sacked by Saracens in 9th cent.; heavily fortified, withstanding sieges 1746, 1815. The **Cap' d'An'tibes'** (kȧp' däN'-tēb'), 3 m. SSW, is also a noted winter resort.

An'ti·cos'ti Island (ăn'tĭ·kŏs'tĭ). Large island 130 m. long by ab. 30 m. wide in St. Lawrence estuary and Gulf of St. Lawrence, Quebec prov., E Canada; has well-developed fisheries and extensive forests; chief village Port Menier. Discovered 1534 by Cartier; purchased 1895 by Henri Menier, French chocolate manufacturer.

An·tie'tam Creek (ăn·tē'tăm). Creek in N Maryland, rising in Franklin co., S Pennsylvania, and flowing S through Washington co., Md., to empty into Potomac river 7 m. N of Harpers Ferry. Near its confluence with Potomac is village of **Antietam**, 3 m. N of which, at Sharpsburg, was fought 1862 the battle of Antietam. See SHARPSBURG; UNITED STATES, *National Historical Parks.*

An'ti·fer', Cape (äN'tē'fâr'); *Fr.* **Cap d'An'ti·fer'** (kȧp däN'tē'fâr'). Cape, Normandy, N coast of France, 15 m. NNE of Le Havre; marks W terminus of chalk cliffs of French coast stretching WSW from the Somme and also the NE point of the Bay of the Seine.

An'ti·go (ăn'tĭ·gō). City, ⊗ of Langlade co., NE Wisconsin, 25 m. NE of Wausau; pop. 9691; founded after the Civil War; commercial and shipping center; manufactures lumber, cheese, canned goods, shoes, flour, etc.

An'ti·go·nish' (ăn'tĭ·gŏ·nĭsh'). **1** County, Nova Scotia, Canada. See *Table* at NOVA SCOTIA.
2 Town, its ⊗, N Nova Scotia, on George Bay 35 m. E of New Glasgow; pop. 3196; formerly called Dorchester; first British settlement made 1784 by disbanded officers

and men of Nova Scotian regiment. Site of St. Francis Xavier Univ. (1853; coed.).

An·ti′gua (ăn·tē′gà). Island 12 m. long of E West Indies, 260 m. E of Puerto Rico; 108 sq. m.; in E cen. part of Leeward Is. group, 40 m. E of Nevis; together with Barbuda and Redonda Is. constitutes a territory of Leeward Is., Brit. W. Indies, with total area 171 sq. m. and pop. (1942 est.) 40,122; ✳ St. Johns. Mountainous, partly volcanic and partly of coral formation; many natural harbors, esp. St. Johns on NW, 2 m. long by ¾ m. wide; produces and refines sugar; also raises cotton, fruit, and vegetables.

History: Discovered by Columbus 1493; settled by English from St. Kitts 1632; occupied by French troops in 1666; returned to England by Treaty of Breda 1667; became an associated state of British Commonwealth 1967. Two areas (Parham Harbour on N coast, 430 acres, and shore-line strip on Judge's Bay, 1⅖ sq. m.) leased to U.S. for seaplane base Mar. 27, 1941.

An·ti′gua (än·tē′gwä) *or* **Antigua Gua′te·ma′la** (gwä′tà·mä′lä). City, ✳ of Sacatepéquez dept., S cen. Guatemala, and former ✳ of Guatemala; pop. 12,601; twice wrecked by earthquakes; coffee plantations.

An′ti·ký′thē·ra (än′dē·kyē′thē·rä; *Angl.* ăn′tĭ·kĭ·thēr′à). Small island midway in passage from Sea of Candia to Mediterranean, SE of Cerigo and NW of the NW point of Crete (Cape Busa); part of Argolis and Corinth dept., Greece.

An′ti-Leb′a·non (ăn′tĭ·lĕb′à·nŏn) *or* **An′ti′-Li′ban′** (än′tē′lē′bän′); *anc.* **An′ti·lib′a·nus** (ăn′tĭ·lĭb′à·nŭs); *Arab.* **Je′bel esh Shar′qi** (jă′bĕl ăsh shŭr′kē). Mountain range, SW Levant States, running N and S bet. Lebanon and Syria; highest point Mt. Hermon 9232 ft.

An·til′i·a (ăn′tĭl′ĭ·à; -tĭl′yà) *or* **An·til′la** (ăn·tĭl′à). An ancient mythical land located by Europeans in the unknown West; known in legend as the "Island of the Seven Cities" and the "region away from the sunrise." After 1492 the name, as *Antilles*, came to be identified with certain islands discovered by Columbus.

An·til′la (än·tē′yä). Coastal municipality (pop. 19,899) and town, Oriente prov., E Cuba; chief export sugar.

An·til′les, Greater *and* **Lesser** (ăn·tĭl′ēz; -ēz; *Fr.* äN′tē′y′). Two groups of islands in the West Indies, bounding the Caribbean Sea on the N and E. See WEST INDIES.

An′ti·och (ăn′tĭ·ŏk). **1** City, Contra Costa co., W California, on S bank of San Joaquin river near mouth of the Sacramento; pop. 17,305; settled 1849, incorp. 1890; shipping point for fertile agricultural region producing asparagus, celery, lettuce, almonds, grapes, apricots, wheat; asparagus cannery, fruit-packing plants, lumber mills, steelworks.

2 Village, Lake co., NE Illinois, on Wisconsin border 15 m. WNW of Waukegan; pop. 2268; lake resort.

3 Ancient city in Pisidia, Asia Minor; at certain periods within boundaries of Phrygia; its ruins lie near Yalvaç in N İsparta vilayet, Turkey in Asia, 80 m. WNW of Konya. See St. Paul (*Acts* xiii. 14–52).

4 *Lat.* **An′ti·o·chi′a** (ăn′tĭ·ō·kī′à); *Greek* **An′ti·o·che′a** (-kē′à). Ancient city on the Orontes; now Antakya in Turkey.

History: Founded by Seleucus Nicator 300 B.C.; became commercial rival of Alexandria; capital of Syria (*q.v.*) until 64 B.C. when Pompey conquered the province; a mission center for early Christianity; ancient city destroyed by earthquake 526 A.D.; conquered by Arabs 638; captured by Byzantine Empire under Nicephorus Phocas 969; taken by the Seljuk Turks 1085, regained by the Crusaders 1097–98, and as a principality given to Bohemund; subject of dispute bet. Normans and Byzantine emperor whose suzerainty Bohemund agreed to recognize 1099; Latin Christian principality destroyed by Baybars, Mameluke sultan of Egypt and Syria, 1268. For later history, see SYRIA.

An′ti·o′qui·a (ăn′tĭ·ō′kĭ·à; *Span.* än·tyō′kyä). Department of Colombia. See *Table* at COLOMBIA.

An·tip′a·ros (ăn·tĭp′à·rŏs; ăn′tĭ·pâr′ŏs, -pā′rŏs; *Mod. Gr.* än·dē′pä·rôs). One of the Cyclades Is., S Aegean Sea, SW of Paros I.; 17 sq. m.; pop. ab. 1000; belongs to Cyclades dept., Greece.

Antipatria. See BERATI town.

An′ti·pax′os (ăn′tĭ·păk′sŏs). Small island, S of Paxos, in the Ionian Sea off NW coast of Greece.

An·tip′o·des (ăn·tĭp′ō·dēz). **1** Australia and New Zealand—a colloquial use originating in England but now found also in North America.

2 Group of rocky islands 458 m. SE of Dunedin, New Zealand, 49°S, 180°E or W; 24 sq. m.; belongs to New Zealand. Almost the exact antipodes of London, England.

Antipolis. See ANTIBES.

An′ti·po′lo (än′tē·pō′lŏ). Municipality, S Rizal prov., Luzon, Phil. Is., 12 m. E of Manila; pop. 6135; mecca for pilgrims who come to view miracle-working image of Our Lady of Peace brought from Mexico and placed in the church 1626. Severe fighting in region during latter part of World War II; captured Mar. 10, 1945 by Americans.

Antipyrgos. See TOBRUK.

Antiquaria. See ANTEQUERA.

An·ti′que (än·tē′kā). Province, W Panay, Phil. Is.; 1034 sq. m.; pop. 199,414; ✳ San Jose de Buenavista; has long narrow coast bordering on NE Sulu Sea facing Cuyo Is.; on N bounded by Capiz prov. and on E by Capiz and Iloilo provs.; comprises the plain, valleys, and W mountain slopes of range separating it from the rest of Panay; highest peak, on Capiz border, Mount Nangtud 6724 ft. Has no good harbors; fishing important but agriculture main industry with sugar cane and copra chief export crops. Inhabitants are Visayans. Chief towns San Jose de Buenavista, Sibalom, Dao, Patnoñgon, and Pandan.

History: Probably first settled by peoples from Borneo; Spanish influence not felt until ab. 1600; for a long time troubled by Moro incursions; created a military province 1790 and a province 1798, reorganized 1860, and granted civil government by Americans April 1901.

An′ti·sa′na (än′tē·sä′nä). Volcano 18,885 ft. in the Andes Mts., N cen. Ecuador, just SE of Quito.

An′ti–Tau′rus Mountains (ăn′tĭ·tô′rŭs). Range in E Turkey in Asia, NE of Taurus Mts. of which it is an extension toward the mountains of Armenia.

Antium. See ANZIO.

Antivari. See BAR.

Ant′lers (ănt′lērz). Town, ⊗ of Pushmataha co., SE Oklahoma, 17 m. N of Hugo; pop. 2085; lumbering, agriculture.

An′to·fa·gas′ta (än′tō·fä·gäs′tä). **1** Province of Chile. See *Table* at CHILE.

2 Seaport city, its ✳, N Chile, 680 m. N of Santiago; pop. 49,106; exports nitrate and other minerals; terminus of the international railroad to Oruro and La Paz, Bolivia; has airport and wireless station. Town founded on Bolivian territory 1870; became important as outlet for Chilean nitrate mines; occupied by Chile 1879 and ceded to her by Treaty of Valparaíso 1884 which followed War of the Pacific with Bolivia; became capital of Chilean province of Antofagasta.

An′to·fal′la (än′tō·fä′yä). Volcanic peak 21,129 ft., W Los Andes territory, NW Argentina, near Chile border.

An′ton′gil′ Bay (äN′tôN′zhēl′). Inlet of Indian Ocean on NE coast of island of Madagascar, 50 m. long and 25 m. wide; settled temporarily by French 1642.

An′to·ny′ (äN′tô·nē′). Commune, Seine dept., N France, 5 m. S of Paris; pop. 19,780.

An′trim (ăn′trim). **1** County in Michigan. See *Table* at MICHIGAN.

2 Town, Hillsboro co., S New Hampshire, on Contoocook river 22 m. W of Manchester; pop. 1121; first settled 1741, incorp. 1777.

3 County, NE Northern Ireland; 1098 sq. m.; pop.

231,099 (including Belfast county borough, *q.v.*, 1127 sq. m., pop. 674,769); ⊗ Belfast; bounded on N by Atlantic, NE and E by North Channel, SE by Belfast Lough, S by Lagan river (dividing it from co. Down), SW by Lough Neagh, and on W and NW by Bann river (dividing it from co. Londonderry); coastal area widely covered by basalt, the perpendicular basalt column known as Giant's Causeway being notable; greater part of interior is arable; produces oats, potatoes, flax; peat and rock-salt deposits; linen manufacturing, shipbuilding, fishing, esp. for salmon. Other towns Ballymena, Lisburn, Larne.

4 Town, S co. Antrim, near NE shore of Lough Neagh; pop. 1627; linen manufacturing; has a round tower 92 ft. high, the finest in Ulster.

Ant'si·ra'be (ănt'sĕ·rä'bă); *Fr.* **Ant'si·ra·bé'** (äN'sē'rä'bā'). Commune, cen. Madagascar, in Ankaratra Mts.; pop. (1936) 18,215; thermal springs.

Antsirane. See DIÉGO-SUAREZ.

An·tu'co (än·tōō'kŏ). Volcanic peak 9060 ft. in the Andes Mts., Bío-Bío prov., S cen. Chile, near border of Argentina.

An'tung' (än'dŏong'). **1** Former province (1932–45), S Manchukuo; 16,202 sq. m.; * Antung.

2 Province (created Sept. 1945), S Manchuria; 22,468 sq. m.; pop. (est.) 3,214,000; * Antung.

3 Treaty port, * of Antung prov., S Manchuria, at mouth of Yalu river; pop. (1940 est.) 315,242. Chinese treaty port opened to foreign trade 1906; natural trade outlet (timber, silk, soybeans) for SE Manchuria and NW Korea; important frontier station on railroad from Korea, through which foreign trade became monopolized by Japan; headquarters of Gen. Kuroki during campaign on the Yalu in Russo-Japanese War 1904–05.

Antunnacum. See ANDERNACH.

Ant'werp (änt'wûrp). **1** Agricultural and manufacturing province, N Belgium, immediately S of Netherlands; 1104 sq. m.; pop. (1941 est.) 1,247,675; consists of extensive, sandy, but fertile, plain with tracts of heath and morass in N and NE; watered by Schelde river and its tributaries, the Rupel, Nèthe, and Dyle.

2 *Fr.* **An'vers'** (äN'vâr'); *Flem.* **Ant'wer'pen** (änt'-vĕr'pĕ[n]). Commercial and manufacturing city, its *, on right bank of Schelde river 23 m. N of Brussels; pop. (1938 est.) 273,317; one of busiest and finest modern harbors in Europe; great grain-importing center; large volume of export trade; industries include manufacture of textiles, brewing, distilling, sugar refining, diamond cutting, manufacture of cigars and tobaccos; improved and modernized, its ancient walls having been extended (now ab. 8 m.) and converted into boulevards; vestiges of ancient city remain in the 14th-cent. cathedral of Notre Dame (largest Gothic structure in the Low Countries, containing three celebrated paintings by Rubens), the church of St. Jacques, the hôtel de ville, the Bourse, the Vieille Boucherie, and the Steen (part of ancient castle); fortified by 8 outlying forts, and later, by a second row of 15 forts.

History: By 11th cent., center of margraviate later attached to duchy of Brabant (*q.v.*); received municipal rights 1291; member of Hanseatic League 1315; gradually superseded Bruges as center for cloth trade with England in 15th cent.; part of Burgundian inheritance of Emperor Charles V (see BELGIUM); as distribution center for Spanish and Portuguese colonial trade, became commercial and financial capital of Europe in 16th cent.; attacked in "Spanish Fury" 1576; captured by duke of Parma 1585; declined because of these destructive invasions, eviction of Protestants, and finally, provision in Treaty of Westphalia (1648) closing Schelde to navigation (see AMSTERDAM); center of famous schools of painting (Massys in 16th cent., Van Dyck and Rubens in 17th cent.); began to revive after Napoleon's improvement of harbor c. 1803; part of kingdom of the Netherlands 1815–30; capture by French 1832 and cession to

Belgian nationalists meant success of Belgian revolt from Netherlands; with expanded harbor and dock facilities and aided by free navigation of Schelde 1863, became one of world's leading ports; a fortified city, besieged Sept.–Oct. 1914 by Germans who held it until 1918. In World War II taken by Germans May 18, 1940; recaptured by British Sept. 4, 1944; port almost undamaged but, because of German resistance on Walcheren I. and along Schelde river, proved difficult and costly to open to meet Allied supply problems; port not finally free until Nov. 3.

Antwerp Island. See ANVERS ISLAND.

An Uaimh. See NAVAN.

A·nu'da (ä·nōō'dä), *or* **Cher'ry** (chĕr'ĭ), **Island.** One of the Santa Cruz Is., SW Pacific Ocean, in E part of group on 170°E long.

A·nu·ra'dha·pu'ra (ŭ·nōō·rä'dä·pōō'rä). Town, * of North Central Province, Ceylon, 106 m. NNE of Colombo; pop. 8975. Ancient capital of Singhalese kings of Ceylon; traditionally founded in 5th cent. B.C.; sacred to Buddhists as site of conversion to Buddhism of Ceylonese ruler by Mahinda, son of Asoka, who visited the island ab. 251–246 B.C.; contains sacred Bo Tree, oldest existing historical tree, grown from a slip of the original sacred tree at Buddh Gaya (*q.v.*); abandoned as capital of Singhalese line 11th cent. A.D. in order to escape Tamil invasions; discovered in ruins and reopened by British in 19th cent.

An'vers' (äN'vâr'). See ANTWERP.

Anvers Island; *formerly* **Ant'werp Island** (änt'wûrp). Largest island of the Palmer Archipelago, off W coast of Palmer Penin., Antarctica, 64°30′S, 63°30′W. Visited and named 1898 by a Belgian expedition.

Anxur. See TERRACINA.

An'yang' (än'yäng'). Town, NE Honan prov., E cen. China, on the Peiping-Hankow R.R. 90 m. N of Kaifeng; archaeological site and an ancient capital of Shang or Yin dynasty.

An'ye' Machin (än'yĕ'). Var. of AMNE MACHIN.

A·nyui' (ŭ·nyōō'ĭ). River ab. 420 m. long, N Khabarovsk Territory, Soviet Russia, Asia; rises in Anadyr Range and flows in two branches W to lower Kolyma river.

An'zac Cove (än'zăk). Small bay, an inlet of the Aegean Sea, on Gallipoli Peninsula S of Suvla Bay and 14 m. from its S tip, Turkey in Europe. Anzacs (Australian and New Zealand troops) landed here April 25, 1915, and engaged in actions up to June 30 to retain hold; battle of Sari Bair followed Aug. 6–10, 1915; all troops withdrawn Jan. 1916.

Anzan. See ANSHAN.

An·zhe'ro Sud·zhensk' (ŭn·zhĕ'rŭ sōōd·zhĕnsk'). Town, E cen. Novosibirsk Region, Soviet Russia, Asia, in the Kuzbas 50 m. E of Tomsk on Trans-Siberian R.R.; pop. 71,079.

An'zin' (äN'zăN'). Commune, Nord dept., N France, on Schelde river 26 m. SE of Lille; pop. 14,804; center of richest coal-mining area in France. Destroyed in large part by Germans 1914–18.

An'zio (än'tsyŏ; *Angl.* ăn'zĭ·ō), *formerly* **Por'to d'An'zio** (pôr'tŏ dän'tsyŏ); *anc.* **An'ti·um** (än'shĭ·ŭm). Mediterranean seaport, Roma prov., Italy, 33 m. SSE of Rome; fishing industry; bathing resort, with **Net·tu'no** [năt·tōō'nŏ] (1½ m. E), the favorite of the Romans. In ancient times, a pirate stronghold under the Volscians; lost independence after rising with Latium against Rome 341 B.C.; colonized by Nero who also improved harbor; sacked by Saracens in 9th and 10th cents.; modern town dates from restoration of harbor 1698 by Innocent XII; site of discovery of ancient artifacts, among them the statue often called *Maiden of Anzio;* birthplace of Nero and probably of Caligula. In World War II site of amphibious landing Jan. 22, 1944 of U.S. and British troops, with purpose of disrupting rear communications of Ger-

mans at Cassino; after much severe fighting Allied drive on Rome begun May 25, 1944.

An′zo·á′te·gui (än′sȯ·ä′tȧ·gė). State of Venezuela. See *Table* at VENEZUELA.

Aoba. See OBA.

A·o′la (ä·ō′lä). Chief village and government station, 35 m. E of Henderson Field on N coast of Guadalcanal, E of the cen. part of the island, SE Solomon Is., W Pacific Ocean; at mouth of **Aola River,** a short stream flowing N.

A·o·mo·ri (ä·ȯ·mô·rė). **1** Prefecture of Japan. See *Table* at JAPAN.

2 Seaport city, its ✱, on Mutsu Bay; pop. 93,414; has most important harbor and trading center of N Honshu; ferry service to Hakodate and steamer connections with Vladivostok and Karafuto (Sakhalin I.).

A·o′ni·a (ä·ō′nǐ·ȧ; -ōn′yȧ). A district of Boeotia, E cen. Greece, containing the mountains Helicon and Cithaeron, and hence sacred to the Muses.

A′o·ra′ï, Mount (ä′ō·rä′ė). Peak 6775 ft. in center of Tahiti I., Society Is., French Polynesia, near Mt. Orohena.

A′o·rang′i (ä′ō·räng′ė) *or* **Mount Cook** (kŏok). Peak 12,349 ft. in Southern Alps range, W cen. South I., New Zealand, on boundary bet. Westland and Canterbury provincial dists.

A·or′nos (ä·ôr′nȯs). **1** A great rock in NW India, successfully stormed by Alexander the Great 326 B.C.; long unidentified but now supposed to be in Swat, W of the Indus and NE of Peshawar, Pakistan.

2 See TASHKURGHAN, Afghan Turkistan.

A·o′sta (ä·ôs′tä). **1** Province of Italy. See *Table* at ITALY.

2 *anc.* **Au·gus′ta Prae·to′ri·a** (ô·gŭs′tȧ prē·tōr′ǐ·ȧ). Commune, its ✱, Piedmont, NW Italy, 48 m. NNW of Turin; pop. (1936) 23,641; at junction of Great and Little St. Bernard Passes; cathedral said to have been founded by St. Eusebius; Roman remains, including triumphal arch of Augustus, city walls, ruins of amphitheater; trades in wine, cheese, and leather. Erected c. 24 B.C. as Roman military post by Augustus to celebrate Terentius Varro Murena's victory over the Salassi (25 B.C.).

A′pa (ä′pä). River 125 m. long forming part of E boundary of Paraguay; flows W into Paraguay river.

A·pach′e (ȧ·päch′ė). County in Arizona. See *Table* at ARIZONA.

Apache Lake. See UNITED STATES, *Dams and Reservoirs* (Horse Mesa Dam).

Apache Mountains. Mountain group S of Guadalupe Mts., W Texas, bet. Pecos river and the Rio Grande; highest 5657 ft.

Apaiang. Var. of ABAIANG.

Ap′a·lach′ee Bay (ăp′ȧ·lăch′ė). Inlet of Gulf of Mexico on S coast of Wakulla and Jefferson cos., N Florida, receiving the Aucilla river on the NE.

Ap′a·lach′i·a Dam (ăp′ȧ·lăch′ǐ·ȧ). See *Table* at TENNESSEE VALLEY AUTHORITY.

Ap′a·lach′i·co′la (ăp′ȧ·lăch′ǐ·kō′lä). **1** Navigable river 90 m. long, NW Florida; formed by confluence of Chattahoochee and Flint rivers in SW corner of Georgia, flows S into Apalachicola Bay (Gulf of Mexico). Former boundary bet. East and West Florida (see FLORIDA history). E terminus of Gulf Intracoastal Waterway (*q.v.*) is near its mouth.

2 Seaport city, ⊗ of Franklin co., NW Florida, on Apalachicola Bay at mouth of Apalachicola river; pop. 3099; founded c. 1821 as West Point, incorp. 1827, renamed 1831; port of entry; noted esp. for its oyster beds; game-fishing center, esp. for tarpon.

Apalachicola Bay. Inlet of Gulf of Mexico on S coast of Franklin co., NW Florida, receiving the Apalachicola river on the N.

A·pa′lit (ä·pä′lėt). Municipality, SE Pampanga prov., Luzon, Phil. Is., on right bank of Pampanga river ab. 7

m. SE of San Fernando; pop. 14,330; near the Manila-Dagupan R.R. at SW corner of Candaba swamp.

A·pam′ (ä·päm′). Town, S Ghana, just E of Saltpond; pop. 8589.

A·pam′ (ä·pän′). Town, SE Hidalgo state, E Mexico, N of Tlaxcala; pop. 3959; in center of finest maguey region of Mexico and noted for its pulque.

Apamama. See ABEMAMA.

Ap′a·me′a (ăp′ȧ·mē′ȧ). Name of several ancient cities, esp.: **(1)** City, NW Mesopotomia, on left bank of Euphrates river W of Edessa. **(2) Apamea ad O·ron′tem** (ăd ȯ·rŏn′tĕm), city of W Syria on Orontes river, built by Seleucus Nicator; destroyed by Khosrau II of Persia 7th cent. A.D.; rebuilt, but completely ruined by earthquake 1152. **(3) Apamea Ci·bo′tus** (sǐ·bō′tŭs), city on the Maeander near its source and adjoining Celaenae, S Phrygia, built by Antiochus Soter 3d cent. B.C.; conquered 133 B.C. by Rome which kept control only after Mithridatic Wars (1st cent. B.C.); declined with rise of Constantinople as trade center; taken by Turks 1070.

A′pa·pa (ä′pä·pä). Town, SW Nigeria, across channel W of Lagos; has modern docks, with good anchorage for large vessels.

A′pa·po′ris (ä′pä·pō′rēs). River ab. 500 m. long, S Colombia; flows SE to Brazilian border and empties into Japurá river on Colombia-Brazil boundary of which it forms a small section.

A·par′ri (ä·pär′rė). Municipality on N coast of Cagayan prov., Luzon, Phil. Is., on E side of Cagayan river near its mouth, 55 m. N of Tuguegarao; pop. 26,409; has best harbor on N coast of Luzon with active coast and river trade; site of meteorological station and airfield. First visited by Spaniards 1572; seized by Japanese Dec. 10, 1941; bombed by U.S. aircraft Oct. 15, 1944; retaken by Americans June 21, 1945.

A′pa·ta′ki (ä′pä·tä′kė). Atoll, Tuamotu Archipelago, S Pacific Ocean, ab. 65 m. NW of Fakarava atoll; French administrative headquarters; has lagoon 18 m. long by 15 m. wide with good pearl fishing.

A′pa·tin (ä′pä·tēn). Town, N Yugoslavia, on left bank of Danube 10 m. SW of Sombor; pop. (1921) 13,435.

A·pa′ya·o (ä·pä′yä·ō). Subprovince, N Mountain Province, Luzon, Phil. Is., bet. Cagayan valley and ridge of N Cordillera Central; 1490 sq. m.; pop. 15,614; ✱ Kabugao. Bounded on N by narrow coastal strip of Cagayan prov., on E by Cagayan prov., on S by Kalinga subprov., on SW by Abra prov., and on W by Ilocos Norte; comprises E slopes of the main Cordillera Central, watered by the Abulug and tributaries of the Cagayan; has large forested area. Inhabitants are chiefly Apayaos. In Spanish times a comandancia; made part of Cagayan prov. 1901 by American government and created a subprovince 1907.

A′pel·doorn (ä′pĕl·dōrn). Commune, Gelderland prov., Netherlands, ab. 17 m. N of Arnhem; pop. (1939) 72,666; railroad junction; connected by canals with Zwolle and Zutphen; garden city; noted paper mills; nearby is the Loo (Du. *Het Loo*), summer residence of royal family, originally a hunting lodge of the dukes of Gelder.

Ap′en·nines (ăp′ĕ·nīnz; *Ital.* **Ap′pen·ni′no** (äp′pān·nē′nȯ); *Lat.* **Ap′en·ni′nus Mons** (ăp′ĕ·nī′nŭs mŏnz). Mountain range, cen. Italy, arbitrarily divided from the Ligurian Alps in the NW, extending the full length of the peninsula in a bow-shaped range from near Savona in the NW to Reggio di Calabria in the S; ab. 800 m. long, 25 to 85 m. wide; highest peak Monte Corno 9585 ft. Source of most of the rivers of Italy—many short streams on steep slopes of E side and of longer rivers (Arno, Tiber, Volturno, Garigliano) on W. Crossed by many passes, ab. 13 of main importance. Climate severe in higher areas; vegetation includes (to 1500 ft.) olives, garden plants, and winter pasturage, (to 3000 ft.) chestnut and oak trees and agricultural products, (to 6000 ft.)

NAME English / Italian	LOCATION AND DESCRIPTION	HIGHEST POINT

NORTHERN

Li·gu′ri·an Apennines (lĭ·gūr′ĭ·ăn) — Appennino Li′gu·re (lē′gōō·rå)	From upper Bormida river near Savona SE to La Cisa Pass above La Spezia; along coast of Ligurian Sea; many hydraulic plants	Monte Bue (or Maggiorasca) 5,914 ft.; on N border of Liguria
Tus′can Apennines (tŭs′kăn) — Appennino Tos·ca′no (tôs·kä′nô) or Tosco-E·mi·lia′no (tôs′kô·å·mě·lyä′nô)	From La Cisa Pass SE to sources of the Tiber, 43°50′N; detached range to SW, the Ap′u·an Alps [ăp′û·ăn] (Ital. Al′pi A·pua′ne [äl′pě ä·pwä′nå]), W of the valley of the Serchio and containing marble quarries of Carrara	Monte Cimone 7,095 ft.; in S Emilia, SW of Bologna
Um′bri·an Apennines (ŭm′brĭ·ăn) — Appennino Um′bro (ōōm′brô)	From sources of the Tiber SSE to Scheggia Pass above Gubbio and near Cagli	Monte Nerone 5,005 ft.; in NW Marches

CENTRAL

| Ro′man Apennines (rō′măn) — Appennino Um′bro-Mar′chi·gia′no (ōōm′brô·mär′kě·jä′nô) | From near Cagli SSE to Tronto river, 42°50′N; comprise many parallel ranges with low passes | Monte Vettore 8,128 ft.; in Sibillini Mts. on SW border of Marches |
| A·bruz′zi Apennines (ä·brōōt′tsě) — Appennino A′bruz·ze′se (ä′brōōt·tsä′så) | From the Tronto river SSE to the Sangro; consist of 3 parallel chains and include mountain knot of Gran Sasso d′Italia | Monte Corno 9,585 ft.; NNE of Aquila in Abruzzi e Molise |

SOUTHERN

Ne′a·pol′i·tan Apennines (nē′å·pŏl′ĭ·tăn) — Appennino Na′po·le·ta′no (nä′pô·lå·tä′nô)	From the Sangro and Volturno valleys S to the Ofanto river; include the Ma·te′sian Mts. [må·tē′zhăn] (Ital. Ma·te′se [mä·tā′så])	Monte Miletto 6,725 ft.; on N border of Campania
Lu·ca′ni·an Apennines (lû·kä′nĭ·ăn; -kän′yăn) — Appennino Lu·ca′no (lōō·kä′nô)	From the Ofanto river S to the Crati; mark roughly S limit of limestone Apennines	Monte Pollino 7,450 ft.; on border bet. Calabria and Lucania
Ca·la′bri·an Apennines (kå·lä′brĭ·ăn) — Appennino Ca′la·bre′se (kä′lä·brä′så)	From the Crati river to S tip of toe of peninsula; include granite plateau of Si·la′gi·an Mts. [sĭ·lä′jĭ·ăn] (Ital. La Si′la [lä sē′lä])	Aspromonte 6,420 ft.; S Calabria, E of Reggio di Calabria

NOTABLE PASSES AND TUNNELS

NAME	PRONUNCIATION	DESCRIPTION AND LOCATION
Boc·chet′ta	bôk·kåt′tä	Pass, Liguria, NW Ligurian Apennines, N of Genoa, 2,532 ft.; through it passes highway from Genoa to Alessandria; old Roman road, Genua (Genoa) to Dertona (Tortona)
Ci′sa or La Cisa	lä chē′zä	Pass, marking division bet. Ligurian and Tuscan Apennines, N Tuscany near source of Magra river, 3,414 ft.; railroad from La Spezia to Parma passes under it through tunnel
Fu′ta or La Futa	lä fōō′tä	Pass, S Emilia, in Tuscan Apennines, 2,962 ft.; in valley of the Reno; highway and railroad, Florence to Bologna
Gio′vi	jô′vě	Pass and railroad tunnel (5 m. 250 ft. long, alt. 1,080 ft.), NW Ligurian Apennines, N of Genoa; railroad, Genoa to Turin and Milan
Pe·sca′ra	på·skä′rä	Pass through Abruzzi Apennines along Pescara river, S of Gran Sasso d′Italia; railroad, Pescara to Rome, passes through several tunnels; old Roman road (Valerian Way)
Scheg′gia	skåd′jä	Pass, N Umbria, marking division bet. Northern and Central Apennines, 1,886 ft.; lies bet. Gubbio and Cagli

beech and coniferous trees, and (above 6000 ft.) shrubs, Alpine plants, and summer pasturage; resemble Alps in geological structure. Famous for hill towns Pistoia, Florence, Arezzo, Aquila, Benevento, etc. See LOWER APENNINES.

For the principal ranges and notable passes and tunnels, see *Table* on page 54.

A′pen·ra′de (ä′pĕn·rä′dĕ). German name of former county of Aabenraa: see *Aabenraa-Sönderborg*, in *Table* at DENMARK.

A′pe·ú′ (ä′pä·ōō′). Island in Atlantic Ocean off NE coast of Pará state, Brazil.

Aph′ro·dis′i·as (ăf′rŏ·dĭz′ĭ·ăs). Ancient town, NE Caria, Asia Minor, S of the Maeander and ab. 50 m. ESE of modern Aydın; now in ruins; important as Byzantine town; home of Alexander of Aphrodisias, Greek philosopher, c. 200 A.D.

Aphrodisium. See BÔNE.

A′pi (ŭ′pĕ). Peak 23,899 ft. in the Himalayas, NW corner of Nepal, near source of Kali river.

A′pi (ä′pĕ). See EPI, New Hebrides.

A·pi′a (ä·pē′ä). Seaport on N coast of island of Upolu, Samoa, SW cen. Pacific Ocean; ✳ of the Territory of Western Samoa; pop. ab. 2000; has good harbor, but coral reefs on its borders make it somewhat unsafe; connects by steamship lines with Australia, New Zealand, and the United States; has powerful wireless station. Scene 1899 of naval disaster (see SAMOA for details).

Apiskigamish Lake. See BIENVILLE LAKE.

A·pi′wan (ä·pē′wän). Peak 7600 ft. in NW tip of Santa Cruz territory, S Argentina, on Chile border.

A′pi·za′co (ä′pĕ·sä′kŏ). Town, Tlaxcala state, cen. Mexico, NNE of Tlaxcala; pop. 6768.

Ap′ler·beck (äp′lĕr·bĕk). Commune, North Rhine-Westphalia state, West Germany, 4 m. ESE of Dortmund; pop. 10,938; coal mining.

A′po, Mount (ä′pŏ). Highest mountain in the Philippines, 9689 ft., SE Mindanao, on boundary bet. E Cotabato and W Davao provs. ab. 24 m. WSW of City of Davao; an active volcano with three peaks on its summit; its slopes and immediate vicinity have been established as **Mount Apo National Park,** partly in Cotabato prov.

A·pol′da (ä·pôl′dä). City, Thuringia, East Germany, ENE of Weimar; pop. 25,703; knitted and woven goods (esp. hosiery), metal founding; commerce in grain, leather, cattle.

A′po·li′ma (ä′pŏ·lē′mä). Small island in Territory of Western Samoa, SW cen. Pacific Ocean, in middle of **Apolima Strait** (10 m. wide) bet. E Savaii and W Upolu Is.

A·pol′lo (ä·pŏl′ō). Borough, Armstrong co., W Pennsylvania, 25 m. ENE of Pittsburgh; pop. 2694; manufactures steel, etc.; coal mines, gas wells, limestone quarries.

Ap′ol·lo′nia (ăp′ŭ·lōn′yà; -lō′nĭ·à). **1** Name of numerous ancient towns, esp.: (1) Town on N coast of Cyrenaica, E of Cyrene and its port; belonged to the Pentapolis. (2) Town, Illyria, near coast of Adriatic S of Dyrrhachium; a Greek colony important commercially and culturally; Octavius studied here. (3) Town, E Macedonia, 30 m. SW of Amphipolis; visited by St. Paul (*Acts* xvii. 1). (4) Town, NE Thrace, on Pontus Euxinus coast; *mod.* **So·zo′pol** (sŏ·zô′pŏl), village on Black Sea SSE of Burgas, Bulgaria.

2 Lake, Turkey in Asia. See APULYONT.

A·pop′ka (à·pŏp′kà). City, Orange co., cen. Florida penin., 10 m. NNW of Orlando; pop. 3578; settled 1856 on site of Seminole Indian village; incorp. 1929; trading center and shipping point, ships esp. Boston ferns.

Apopka, Lake. Lake on W boundary of Orange co., cen. Florida penin.

A·pos′tle Islands (à·pŏs′'l). Group of islands in SW Lake Superior, off NW coast of Wisconsin; known also as the **Twelve Apostles,** but there are ab. 20 islands;

they belong chiefly to Ashland co., Wisconsin, esp. islands of Madeline (with only settlement, La Pointe), Outer, Stockton, Oak, Michigan, and Long; Sand Island and two smaller islands belong to Bayfield co.

Apostolic See. See VATICAN CITY.

Ap′pa·lach′i·a (ăp′à·lăch′ĭ·à). Mining town, Wise co., SW Virginia, 40 m. WNW of Bristol; pop. 2456.

Ap′pa·lach′i·a (ăp′à·lăch′ĭ·à; -lä′chĭ·à) or **Appalachian America.** Region of SE United States including the various ranges of the Appalachian Mts., with no definite boundaries but generally comprising SW Pennsylvania and the mountainous parts of Virginia, West Virginia, Kentucky, Tennessee, North Carolina, South Carolina, Georgia, and Alabama; historically (c. 1690 to 1756) included also early settlements beyond the colonies of the Atlantic seaboard.

Ap′pa·lach′i·an Mountains (ăp′à·lăch′ĭ·ăn; -lä′chĭ·ăn; -lăch′ăn; -lä′chăn) or **Ap′pa·lach′i·ans** (-ănz). Mountain system of E North America, extending from the Canadian province of Quebec SW to N Alabama; it includes the White Mts. in New Hampshire, the Green Mts. in Vermont, the Catskills in New York, the Alleghenies in Pennsylvania, the Blue Ridge in Virginia and North Carolina, and the Cumberland Mts. in Tennessee; highest peak Mount Mitchell 6684 ft. in Yancey co., North Carolina.

Appalachian Trail. Footpath extending from Mt. Katahdin in Maine to Mt. Oglethorpe, N Georgia; traverses mountains of the Appalachian range; highest point on the trail Clingmans Dome 6642 ft. in Great Smoky Mts.

Ap′pa·noose (ăp′à·nōōs). County in Iowa. See *Table* at IOWA.

Ap′pe·kun′ny Mountain (ăp′ĕ·kŭn′nĭ). Peak 9053 ft. in Glacier National Park, NW Montana.

Appennino. See APENNINES.

Ap′pen·zell (äp′ĕn·tsĕl; *Angl.* ăp′ĕn·zĕl). **1** Swiss canton; subdivided into demicantons: **Appenzell Inner Rhodes** (rōdz; *Fr.* rôd), Ger. **Ap′pen·zell In′ner Rho′den** (ĭn′ĕr rō′dĕn), almost wholly Catholic, and **Appenzell Outer Rhodes,** Ger. **Ap′pen·zell Aus′ser Rho′den** (ous′ĕr rō′dĕn), almost wholly Protestant. Agricultural and manufacturing canton, notable for scenic beauty; highest point the Säntis 8216 ft. Originally part of dominions of princely abbots of St. Gallen; formed alliance with Swabian imperial cities and adopted own constitution 1377; under protection of Swiss Confederation 1411, becoming a member 1513; divided 1597 into demicantons; assumed present status 1803; known for its institution of the Landsgemeinde. See *Table* at SWITZERLAND.

2 Commune, ✳ of Appenzell Inner Rhodes demicanton, NE Switzerland, 7 m. S of St. Gallen; pop. (1930) 4893; ancient chapel of abbots of St. Gallen, who made summer home here; Capuchin convent and monastery; mountain resort; sheep raising; embroidery; trade in textiles; 2 m. to the SE is **Weiss′bad′** (vīs′bät′), a summer resort, site of one of oldest whey cure establishments in Switzerland.

Ap′pi·an Way (ăp′ĭ·ăn); *Lat.* **Vi′a Ap′pi·a** (vī′à ăp′ĭ·à). First paved Roman road; extended 132 m. straight SE from Rome past Lake Albanus to Tarracina, thence along the coast and inland to Capua; built 312 B.C. by Appius Claudius Caecus, censor; later extended through Beneventum to Brundisium, total of 366 m.; near Rome lined with tombs and monuments.

Ap′pi·sto′ki Peak (ăp′ĭ·stō′kĭ). Mountain 8135 ft. in Glacier National Park, NW Montana, near Two Medicine Lake.

Ap′ple·by (ăp′'l·bĭ). Municipal borough, Westmorland, NW England, on the Eden 26 m. SE of Carlisle; pop. 1704; trade center in agricultural section; baronial castle (rebuilt in 17th cent.).

Ap′ple·gate Peak (ăp′'l·gāt). Mountain 8135 ft., W Klamath co., SW Oregon, on S rim of Crater Lake.

Ap′ple·ton (ăp′'l·tŭn; -t'n). **1** Village, Swift co., W

Minnesota, on Minnesota river 23 m. NW of Monte-video; pop. 2172.

2 Commercial and industrial city, ⊗ of Outagamie co., E Wisconsin, on Fox river 17 m. N of Oshkosh; pop. 48,411; settled c. 1833. Dairying, farming, stock raising; manufactures paper and paper products, flour, knit goods, machinery, etc.; railroad center and river steamer port. Lawrence Coll. (1847; coed.).

Ap'pling (ăp'lĭng). **1** County in Georgia. See *Table* at GEORGIA.

2 Town, ⊗ of Columbia co., E Georgia; pop. 2216.

Ap'po·mat'tox (ăp'ô-măt'ŭks). **1** River ab. 150 m. long, SE cen. Virginia; rises in Appomattox co., flows E into James river at Hopewell; navigable to Petersburg.
2 County in Virginia. See *Table* at VIRGINIA.
3 Town, its ⊗, cen. Virginia, 18 m. E of Lynchburg; pop. 1184; at old Appomattox Courthouse (county town) on April 9, 1865 Confederates under Gen. Robert E. Lee surrendered to Federal army under Gen. Ulysses S. Grant; site now a national monument: see UNITED STATES, *National Monuments* (Appomattox Court House).

Ap'po·naug (ăp'ô-nôg). Village, Kent co., cen. Rhode Island, W of Warwick; shopping center of Warwick; textile bleaching and printing.

A'pra Harbor (ä'prä), *also* **Port Apra**; *formerly* (*Span.*) **San Luis d'A'pra** (sän lōō-ēs' dä'prä). Harbor on W coast of island of Guam, W Pacific Ocean; best anchorage in the island, protected on S by Orote Penin. and on N by Cabras I. and reefs; Piti, the port of entry, is on its NE shore. Scene of Allied landing in invasion of Guam July 20, 1944.

A'pre·mont' (ȧ'prē-môn'; *Angl.* ăp'rē·mŏnt). **1** Village, Ardennes dept., NE France, on Aire river ab. 20 m. NW of Verdun; pop. 272; scene of advance of U.S. division Sept.–Oct. 1918 in battle of the Argonne.
2 Village, Meuse dept., NE France, ab. 4 m. SE of St-Mihiel; pop. (1931) 218; landmark of American front 1918.

A·pri'lia (ȧ·prē'lyȧ). Town, Littoria prov., SW Latium, W Italy, near Anzio and ab. 22 m. S of Rome; founded on reclaimed land of Pontine Marshes 1937. Occupied by American patrols Jan. 25, 1944.

Ap·she·ron' (ŭp·shĕ·rôn'). Peninsula projecting into the Caspian Sea, E Azerbaidzhan Republic, U.S.S.R.; 400 sq. m.; extensive oil fields; Baku is on SW coast.

Apt (ăpt); *anc.* **Ap'ta Ju'lia** (ăp'tȧ jōōl'yȧ; jōō'lĭ·ȧ). Commune, Vaucluse dept., SE France, 29 m. E of Avignon; pop. 5113; ocher and sulfur mines; meteorological station; episcopal see 3d–18th cents.; 8th-cent. church (former cathedral); Roman remains. Capital city of Vulgientes; beautified by Julius Caesar (who added to its name the epithet *Julia*); became French 1481.

Apuan Alps. See APENNINES.

A·pua'nia (ȧ·pwä'nyȧ). **1** Province of Italy. See *Table* at ITALY.
2 Commune, its ✳, Tuscany, cen. Italy, near Gulf of Genoa 60 m. WNW of Florence; pop. 106,378; formed from former communes of Massa (pop. 41,800) and Carrara (pop. 58,511); quarries nearby produce famous Carrara marble; 15th-cent. cathedral, 16th-cent. baroque ducal palace, 13th-cent. castle, academy of sculpture (founded by Napoleon), museum of antiquities.

A·pu'lia (ȧ·pūl'yȧ; -pū'lĭ·ȧ); *Ital.* **Pu'glia** (pōō'lyȧ), *pl.* **Le Pu'glie** (lā pōō'lyȧ). Compartimento of SE Italy (for provincial divisions, area, and pop., see *Table* at ITALY); lies bet. Adriatic on N and Apennines and Gulf of Taranto on S; forms "spur" and "heel" of Italian "boot"; vast coastal plain; watered by Ofanto river; agriculture (wine, olives, grain, fruits, nuts, tobacco), livestock raising, production of salt and niter from coastal lakes.
History: Home of ancient Apulians, a people allied to Rome in second Samnite War (322–304 B.C.), but unfriendly during Punic Wars; scene of fighting during Punic Wars (see CANNAE); came under rule of republican

Rome by end of 3d cent. B.C.; united with Calabria (under this name) to form administrative unit (Regio II) of Roman Empire; conquered by Lombards 668 A.D.; recovered by Byzantine Empire; became county after conquest by Normans 1042; raised to duchy 1059 by Pope Nicholas II who gave it to Robert Guiscard; united with kingdom of the Two Sicilies 1130; invaded by papal forces 1228–29 in struggle bet. Frederick II and Pope Gregory IX. For later history, see kingdom of NAPLES.

Apulum. See ALBA IULIA.

A'pul·yont' (ä'pōōl-yŏnt'), *also* **A'bul·liont'** (ä'bōōl-yŏnt'); *Lat.* **Ap'ol·lo'nia** (ăp'ŭ-lōn'yȧ; -lō'nĭ·ȧ). Lake 18 m. long, 12 m. wide, NW Turkey in Asia, W of Bursa and S of Sea of Marmara; traversed by Atranos river (*Lat.* Rhyndacus).

A·pu're (ä-pōō'rä). **1** River ab. 420 m. long, W Venezuela; rises on E slopes of N Andes, flows E into Orinoco river; navigable for over 300 m.
2 State of Venezuela. See *Table* at VENEZUELA.

A'pu·rí'mac (ä'pōō-rē'mäk). **1** River 500 to 600 m. long in S and cen. Peru; rises in Lake Villafro in Andes Mts. in Arequipa dept., less than 100 m. from the Pacific, flows N to unite with Urubamba river and form Ucayali river, an upper tributary of the Amazon; its lower course for short stretches called the Perené and Tambo.
2 Department of Peru. See *Table* at PERU.

'A'qa·ba *or* **A'ka·ba** (ŭ'kŏ·bȧ; -bǎ) *or* **Qal''at el 'A'qa·ba** (kŏl'ǎt ǎl ŭ'kŏ·bȧ; -bǎ); *anc.* **E'lath** (ē'lǎth); *later* **Ae·la'na** (ē·lā'nȧ). Seaport town, SW Jordan, at head of the Gulf of 'Aqaba and on highway S from Ma'an; at S end of great valley of the Wadi el 'Araba. As ancient Elath was on the caravan route from Egypt to Arabia and just E of Ezion-geber; a chief city of the Edomites. Called Aelana by the Romans and made a strong military post. In medieval times an important port of Palestine; later held by Egypt, then by Turkey; part of Hejaz 1917–25 and in 1925 taken over by Jordan.

'A'qa·ba, Gulf of; *anc.* **Si'nus Ael'a·nit'i·cus** (sī'nŭs ēl'ȧ·nĭt'ĭ·kŭs; ē'lȧ-). Northeast extension of the Red Sea ab. 100 m. long, bet. NW Saudi Arabia and the Sinai Penin., Egypt.

Aqqaqir, El. See EL AQQAQIR.

Aq'su' *or* **Ak'su'** (äk'sōō'). **1** *Chin.* **Wen'suh'** (wŭn'sōō'). Town and oasis, W Sinkiang, W China, at foot of Tien Shan range ab. 250 m. NE of Kashgar and on main caravan highway from China to Kashgar; pop. ab. 40,000; important trade center; Mongol capital in 14th cent.
2 See MURGHAB river, Tadzhik S.S.R.

Aqsur, El (äl ōōk'sōōr). = LUXOR.

Aquae. See ACQUI.

Aquae Augustae. See DAX.

Aquae Calidae. See BATH.

Aquae Flaviae. See CHAVES.

Aquae Grani. See AACHEN city.

Aquae Gratianae. See AIX-LES-BAINS.

Aquae Mortuae. See AIGUESMORTES.

Aquae Panoniae. See BADEN commune, Austria.

Aquae Sextiae. See AIX.

Aquae Solis. See BATH.

Aquae Statiellae. See ACQUI.

Aquae Tarbellicae. See DAX.

A'qui·da·ban', *Span.* **A'qui·da·bán'** (ä'kē·thä·vän'). River ab. 150 m. long, N cen. Paraguay; flows W to Paraguay river. Scene of battle ending war (1865–70) of Paraguay with Argentina, Brazil, and Uruguay, in which Paraguayan forces were completely crushed and Francisco Solano López was killed 1870.

A·quid'neck Island (ȧ·kwĭd'nĕk). Rhode Island (the island), in Narragansett Bay, R.I.

Aq'ui·la (ăk'wĭ·lȧ; *Ital.* ä'kwĕ·lä), *in full* **A'qui·la de'gli A·bruz'zi** (ä'kwĕ·lä dä'lyē ä·brōōt'tsē). **1** Province of Italy. See *Table* at ITALY.
2 Commune, its ✳, Abruzzi e Molise, cen. Italy, in valley of the Aterno 54 m. NE of Rome; pop. 54,722; summer

resort; 2362 ft. above sea level; manufactures linen, leather, paper, wool; trades in saffron and lace.

History: Founded 1240 by Frederick II as outpost against papal forces, destroyed 1259 by Manfred, but rebuilt by Charles I of Anjou; scene of attack by Joanna II of Naples, Pope Martin V, and duke of Milan against Fortebraccio, the condottiere for Aragon, 1424; almost independent republic until subjugation by Spaniards 1521 and union with kingdom of the Two Sicilies 1529.

A'qui·le'ia *or* **A'qui·le'ja** (ä'kwĕ·lâ'yä); *anc.* **Aq'ui·le'ia** (ăk'wĭ·lē'[y]ȧ); *medieval* **A·glar'** (ä·glär'). Town, Friuli prov., Venezia Euganea, Italy, formerly in Austria, 6 m. inland at head of Adriatic and 22 m. WNW of Trieste; pop. 2350; ancient cathedral.

History: Founded by Romans as strongly fortified outpost against Illyrian peoples 181 B.C.; became most flourishing commercial city of northern Italy; ravaged by Attila and Huns 452 A.D., whereupon inhabitants fled to lagoons (see VENICE); seat of patriarch who refused allegiance to Roman see (6th cent.); belonged to Carolingian march of the Friuli in 9th cent., and to march of Verona and Aquileia (fief of Holy Roman Empire); came under authority of Venice in 15th cent.

A·qui'les Ser·dán' (ä·kē'lās sĕr·t̸hän'); *formerly* **San'ta Eu·la'lia** (sän'tä ȧ·ōō·lä'lyä). Town, Chihuahua state, N Mexico, just SE of Chihuahua; pop. 7368.

A·quin'cum (ȧ·kwĭng'kŭm). Ancient town, Pannonia, on the Danube; the modern Buda (see BUDAPEST).

Aquiry. See ACRE.

Aquisgranum. See AACHEN city.

Aq'ui·taine (ăk'wĭ·tān; ăk'wĭ·tān'; *Fr.* à'kē'tĕn'). Historical region of SW France; originally roughly equivalent in extent to Roman Aquitania at time of its conquest by Clovis, later shrinking in size; ✳ Toulouse.

History: For earlier history, see AQUITANIA. After Frankish conquest 507 A.D., became semiautonomous duchy until subjugated by Pepin the Short 768; made subkingdom by Charlemagne and given to his son Louis 781; reunited to French crown 877; after Carolingian decline, became powerful feudal duchy which by 11th cent. controlled most of France south of Loire; passed to Capetian line when Eleanor of Aquitaine married Louis VII 1137, and later to English Plantagenets on Eleanor's second marriage to Henry II 1152; from about 10th cent. called Guienne, a corruption of Aquitaine. For later history, see GUIENNE and GASCONY.

Aq'ui·ta'nia (ăk'wĭ·tān'yȧ; -tā'nĭ·ȧ). A Roman division of SW Gaul; under Caesar consisted of country bet. Pyrenees Mts. and Garonne river peopled by an Iberic race or races, the Aquitani, whom he conquered 56 B.C.; under Augustus made one of 5 divisions of Gaul with capital at Bourges and expanded to include all of Gaul S and W of the Loire (Liger) and Allier (Elaver) rivers; in 3d cent. A.D. subdivided into: **Aquitania Pri'ma** (prī'mȧ), E part of district bet. Loire and Garonne rivers, with capital at Bourges; **Aquitania Secun'da** (sē·kŭn'dȧ), W part of district, with capital at Bordeaux; became the Guienne of medieval France; **Aquitania Ter'ti·a** (tûr'shĭ·ȧ; -shȧ) *or* **No'vem·pop'u·la'na** (nō'vĕm·pŏp'ū·lā'nȧ), the original Aquitania bet. the Pyrenees and the Garonne, with capital at Éauze. Conquered by Visigoths c. 419; became part of Frankish kingdom on defeat of Visigoth king, Alaric II, by Clovis, king of the Franks, in battle near Poitiers 507. For later history, see AQUITAINE and GUIENNE.

Aquitanicus Sinus. See Bay of BISCAY.

Arab, Shatt-al-. See SHATT-AL-ARAB.

'A'ra·ba, Wa'di el (wä'dē äl ŭ'rŏ·bȧ; -bä); *Bib.* **Ar'a·bah** (är'ȧ bȧ). Great valley extending S from the Dead Sea to the Gulf of 'Aqaba, on the border bet. SE Palestine and SW Transjordan.

A·ra'ba el Mad·fu'na (ŭ·rä'bȧ [-bä] äl mäd·fōō'nȧ [-nä]). Village, Girga prov., cen. Upper Egypt; pop. ab. 11,000; site of ancient Abydos (*q.v.*).

A·ra·bat' (ŭ·rŭ·bát') *or* **Tongue of Arabat;** *Russ.*

A·ra·bat'ska·ya Strel'ka (ŭ·rŭ·bát'skŭ·yŭ stryĕl'kŭ). Narrow sandy peninsula ab. 70 m. long on W side of Sea of Azov; part of NE Crimea, Soviet Russia, Europe.

A·ra'bi·a (ȧ·rā'bĭ·ȧ; ȧ·räb'vȧ); *Turk.* **A'ra·bi·stan'** (ä'rä·bē·stän'). Great peninsula of SW Asia extending N and S bet. 12° and 32°N lat. and 35° and 60°E long., ab. 1400 m. long by 1250 m. wide; ab. 1,000,000 sq. m.; est. pop. 10,000,000; chiefly a desert country. In early times divided into: **Arabia Pe·trae'a** (pē·trē'ȧ), *Eng.* Rocky Arabia, the NW part including Sinai Peninsula (not part of modern Arabia), the only part ever conquered, which became a Roman province; **Arabia De·ser'ta** (dē·zûr'tȧ), *Eng.* Desert Arabia, the N part bet. Syria and Mesopotamia; **Arabia Fe'lix** (fē'lĭks), *Eng.* Fertile Arabia (on the assumption that the interior was as fertile as the coastal strip), the main part of the peninsula, but by some geographers restricted to Yemen.

Bounded on N by Transjordan and Iraq, on E by Persian Gulf and Gulf of Oman, on SE by Arabian Sea, on S by Gulf of Aden, on W by Red Sea; fertile in some coastal regions, but arid plateau in its central part; no rivers, but many short wadis; only a few islands along its coast; includes Saudi Arabia, Yemen, Oman, Trucial Oman, and the Aden Protectorate (*qq.v.*).

History: Seat of little-known southern Minaean and Sabaean kingdoms in 1st millennium B.C.; invaded or crossed by Assyrians, Hebrews, and at different times by Romans; part held by Persians 575 A.D.; before Mohammed, occupied by Semitic tribes; consolidation begun by Mohammed and extended after his death 632; center of orthodox caliphate 632–661; under Ommiad caliphate, ruled from Damascus 661–750; lapsed into tribal warfare following Mohammedan disintegration in 8th cent.; dominated by Karmathians in 10th cent.; in general dominated by Mamelukes and after 1517 by the Ottoman Turks but subdivisions of al-Hasa, Oman, Yemen, and Nejd were practically independent; influenced by rise of Wahabi movement centered in Nejd which organized resistance against the Turks (18th–19th cents.); reconquered for Turks by Egyptian Mehemet Ali 1811–20; Wahabi empire re-established 1843–65; internally divided bet. tribes and sects (see HEJAZ and NEJD); in revolt against Turks 1916; resistance directed by Col. Lawrence 1917; gradual consolidation by 1932 of Saudi Arabia under ibn-Saud; independence of Yemen, Oman, Kuwait (*qq.v.*) and other small divisions recognized; maintained a neutrality sympathetic to Great Britain 1939–45.

A·ra'bi·an Desert (ȧ·rā'bĭ·ăn; ȧ·räb'yăn). Desert area, E Egypt, E of Nile and bordering Gulf of Suez and N Red Sea, from ab. 22°N to the Mediterranean.

Arabian Sea. The section of the Indian Ocean lying bet. India on the E and Arabia on the W.

Arabistan. 1 See ARABIA.

2 See KHUZISTAN.

Arabkir. Var. of ARAPKIR.

Arabos, Los. See LOS ARABOS.

Ar'abs Gulf (är'ăbz). Inlet of Mediterranean Sea on N Egyptian coast just W of Alexandria.

Ar'a·by (är'ȧ·bĭ). Archaic or poetic for ARABIA.

A'ra·ca·jú' (ä'rä·kä·zhōō'). City, ✳ of Sergipe state, E Brazil, on the right bank at the mouth of the Cotinguiba river; pop. (1940 est.) 50,670.

A'ra·ca·tí' (ä'rä·kä·tē'). Seaport, Ceará state, NE Brazil, at mouth of Jaguaribe river; pop. (1940 est.) 6803.

A'ra·ça·tu'ba (ä'rä·sä·tōō'vä). City, São Paulo state, SE Brazil; pop. (1940 est.) 17,013.

Ar'a·cho'si·a (ăr'ȧ·kō'zhĭ·ȧ; -zhȧ). Ancient province, E part of Persian Empire and of the empire of Alexander; about equivalent to S part of modern Afghanistan.

Arachthus. See ARAKHTHOS.

A·rad' (ȧ·räd'; *Hung.* ŏ'rŏd). City, W Romania, on Mureș river, pop. (1930 est.) 75,725; industrial and commercial center in agricultural area. A Turkish fort in 17th cent.; belonged to Hungary after 1699 and figured

prominently in Hungarian struggle for independence 1848–49; passed to Romania 1919 after World War I.

A·ra'da (ä·rä'dä). Town, Wadai division of Chad Republic, N cen. Africa, N of Abéché.

A'ra·duey' (ä'rä·thwĕ'ĕ; -thwä'). River ab. 100 m. long, NW cen. Spain; tributary of Duero river.

Aradus. See ARWAD.

A·ra·fat' (ŭ·rŏ·făt'). Granite hill 15 m. SE of Mecca, Arabia; object of pilgrimages.

A'ra·fu'ra Sea (ä'rä·fōō'rä). Sea bet. N Australia and Indonesia, 800 m. long by ab. 350 m. wide; W New Guinea touches it on NE and several groups of islands (Tanimbar, Kai, and Aru) lie along its N border.

Ar'a·gon (ăr'á·gŏn); *Span.* **A'ra·gón'** (ä'rä·gôn').
1 River ab. 80 m. long, N Spain; rises in the Pyrenees and flows SW into Ebro river in Navarra prov.
2 Region and ancient kingdom, NE Spain; 18,294 sq. m.; bounded on N by the Pyrenees, E by Catalonia, SE by Valencia, SW by New Castile, W by Old Castile, and NW by Navarre; comprises the modern provinces of Huesca, Zaragoza, and Teruel; mountainous in N and S portions; produces wheat, corn, olives, wine, etc.; manufactures linens and woolens; copper, lead, sulfur, and salt mines; principal city Saragossa.
History: After overthrow of Carthaginian power in Spain, became part of Roman province of Hispania Tarraconensis; conquered by Visigoths in 5th cent. A.D. and by Moors in 8th cent.; became Carolingian county, emerging from Navarrese rule as independent kingdom 1035; annexed Navarre 1076, Saragossa 1118; united with county of Barcelona 1137 and with Catalonia 1137 and 1164; lost Provence 1196; conquered Balearic Is. 1229–35, Valencia 1238; ruler of Aragon obtained kingdom of the Two Sicilies (1282–85) which he later surrendered for Sardinia and Corsica; held duchy of Athens 1311–88; conquered Naples 1435; united with Castile 1479. See SPAIN.

A'ra·go'na (ä'rä·gō'nä). Commune, Agrigento prov., SW Sicily, 7 m. N of Agrigento; pop. 14,839; sulfur mines; near mud volcano **Mac'ca·lu'ba** (mäk'kä·lōō'bä), 135 ft. high, 860 ft. above sea level.

A·ra'gua (ä·rä'gwä). **1** State of Venezuela. See *Table* at VENEZUELA.
2 *or* Aragua de Bar'ce·lo'na (thä vär'sá·lō'nä). Town. Anzoátegui state, N Venezuela, 62 m. SSW of Barcelona.

A'ra·guai'a *or* **A'ra·guay'a** (ä'rä·gwī'á). River ab. 1100 m. long, cen. Brazil; rises in S cen. Mato Grosso state and flows N into Tocantins river.

A'ra·gua·rí' (ä'rá·gwá·rē'). **1** River ab. 240 m. long, NE Brazil; flows into Atlantic N of Amazon river.
2 City, W Minas Gerais state, E Brazil, 290 m. WNW of Belo Horizonte; pop. (1940 est.) 16,086.

Arahal, El. See EL ARAHAL.

Araish, El. See LARACHE.

A·rai·to (ä·rī·tô). Small island off NW coast of Paramushiro I. at N end of Kuril Is.; its peak 7674 ft. highest point in the Kuril chain.

Ara Jovis. See ARANJUEZ.

A'ra·ka'ka (ä'rá·kä'kä). Town, W British Guiana, on Barima river 140 m. NW of Georgetown; gold fields.

A·ra·kan' (ä·rä·kän'). Division of Lower Burma (see BURMA) along the coast of NE Bay of Bengal; 16,001 sq. m.; pop. 1,008,535; ✲ Akyab; contains Mayu, Kaladan, and Lemro rivers; E border formed by the Arakan Yoma range. Conquered by Burmese 1784; ceded to British 1826 by Treaty of Yandabu (*q.v.*); scene of much fighting bet. Japanese and Allied forces 1942–45.

Arakan Hill Tracts. District of Arakan division, Lower Burma; 1901 sq. m.; pop. 21,418; ✲ Paletwa.

A·ra·kan' Yo'ma (ä·rä·kän' yō'mä). Mountain range in W cen. Burma, extending from Manipur state in Assam, NE India, S to Cape Negrais; highest point Mt. Victoria 10,016 ft.; includes the Naga Hills, Chin Hills, and Lushai Hills and forms barrier between Burma and India.

A'rakh·thos (ä'räk·thôs) *or* **Ar'ta** (är'tå; *Mod. Gr.* -tä); *anc.* **A·rach'thus** (á·räk'thŭs). River ab. 80 m. long in W Greece; chief river of Epirus; flows S to Ambracian Gulf; navigable to Arta.

A·raks' (ŭ·räks'); *Turk.* **A·ras'** (ä·räs'); *anc.* **A·rax'es** (á·räk'sēz). River 635 m. long rising in mountains of Turkish Armenia, S of Erzurum, and flowing E to join the Kura in E Azerbaidzhan, U.S.S.R., ab. 60 m. from its mouth, and also since 1897 flowing by its own mouth into the Caspian Sea; for about half its course, 43°45'E to 48°E, forms the boundary bet. Transcaucasia (Armenian S.S.R. and Azerbaidzhan) on the N and Turkey and NW Iran on the S; has a very rapid current; chief tributaries Zanga from the N and Qara Su from the S.

Ar'al, Lake; *or* **Ar'al Sea** (är'ăl; *Russ.* ŭ·räl'); *Russ.* **A·ral'sko·e Mo're** (ŭ·räl'y'·skŭ·yĕ mô'ryĕ). Inland sea, with ab. 10 per cent salinity, bet. Kazakh S.S.R. and Uzbek S.S.R., SW Soviet Russia, Asia; 26,166 sq. m.; second to Caspian Sea in size in Asia, and fourth largest inland body of water in the world; depth ab. 225 ft.; except on S its shores are steppe or desert and uninhabited; on NE receives the Syr Darya and on S the Amu Darya; its level varies greatly over a period of years.

Ar'am (âr'ăm; ā'răm). Ancient country in SW Asia extending from the Lebanon Mts. to beyond the Euphrates river; the Hebrew name of ancient Syria; named from a northern Semitic people, the Aramaeans, who emerged from Syrian Desert to invade Syria and Upper Mesopotamia (c. 14th cent. B.C.–1100 B.C.) and who (esp. in 10th cent. B.C.) built up numerous highly civilized city-kingdoms, best known of which was Damascus (*q.v.*); gave its name to Aramaic language. See SYRIA.

Ar'an (är'ăn). Island, co. Donegal, Eire, in Atlantic Ocean off NW coast of Ireland; 7 sq. m.; pop. 1480.

A·ran'das (ä·rän'däs). Town, Jalisco state, W cen. Mexico, 70 m. E of Guadalajara; pop. 7254.

Ar'an Islands (är'ăn); *Irish* **Ara na Naomh** (literally, "Aran of the Saints"). Group of small islands, co. Galway, W Eire, off W coast of Ireland at entrance to Galway Bay; 18 sq. m.; pop. 2109; comprises Inishmore or Aranmore (the largest), Inishmaan, Inishere, and (off W of Inishmore) an islet, Eeragh, with lighthouse; chief town Kilronan, on Inishmore; pre-Christian remains.

A'ran·juez' (ä'räng·hwäth'); *anc.* **A'ra Jo'vis** (âr'á jō'vĭs). Commune, Madrid prov., cen. Spain, 26 m. SSE of Madrid; pop. 23,646; planned and built by Ferdinand VI; known chiefly as site of royal summer palace built by Philip II, rebuilt and expanded by Ferdinand VII and Charles III; treaties bet. France and Spain 1745, 1779 1805; abdication of Charles IV 1808.

A'ran Mawdd'wy *or* **Aran Mowdd'wy** (ä'răn mouth'wĭ). Peak 2970 ft. in Merionethshire, W Wales, ab. 30 m. NE of Aberystwyth; highest in Cambrian Mts.

Ar'an·more' (ăr'ăn·mōr'). See ARAN ISLANDS.

A·ran'sas (á·răn'săs). County in Texas. See *Table* at TEXAS.

Aransas Bay. Inlet of Gulf of Mexico NE of Corpus Christi Bay, S Texas, bet. mainland and St. Joseph I.

Aransas Pass. 1 Chief entrance to Aransas Bay.
2 City, Aransas and San Patricio cos., S Texas, on Aransas Bay; pop. 6956; fishing; oil shipping. **Port Aransas** (pop. 551) is a fishing resort on nearby Mustang I.

A·rap'a·ho (á·răp'á·hō). Town, ⊗ of Custer co., W Oklahoma; pop. 351.

A·rap'a·hoe (á·răp'á·hō). County in Colorado. See *Table* at COLORADO.

Arapahoe Peak. Mountain 13,506 ft. in Front Range of Rocky Mts., Grand and Boulder cos., N cen. Colorado.

A'ra·pi'les (ä'rä·pē'lās). Village, Salamanca prov., W Spain, 4 m. SE of Salamanca; pop. (1930) 654; site of battle of Salamanca 1812 in which allied troops under Wellington defeated French under Marmont.

A·rap·kir', *formerly* **A·rab·kir'** (ä·räp·kîr'). Town, E Turkey in Asia, 35 m. N of Malatya; pop. 6810.

Arar. See SAÔNE.

A·ra′ra (ä·rä′rä). Village on N coast of Netherlands New Guinea, nearly opp. Wakde Is. and ab. 125 m. W of Hollandia; scene of landing of Allied troops May 17, 1944.

A′ra·ra·qua′ra (ȧ′rȧ·rȧ·kwä′rȧ). City, cen. São Paulo state, SE Brazil, 150 m. NE of São Paulo; pop. (1940 est.) 28,267.

Ar′a·rat (ăr′ȧ·răt). 1 Ancient kingdom. See URARTU.
2 Mining town and rail junction, W cen. Victoria, Australia, 115 m. WNW of Melbourne; pop. 4913.
3 *Armenian* **Ma·sis′** (mä·sēs′); *Turk.* **Ağ′rı′ Da·ği′** (ä·rï′ dä·ï′); *Pers.* **Koh′–i–nuh′** (kō′ĕ·nōō′). Isolated mountain in E extremity of Turkey, in Ağrı vilayet near Iranian border; has two peaks, Great Ararat (16,873 ft.) and Little Ararat; legendary landing place of Noah's Ark (*Gen.* viii. 4); first climbed in modern times 1829.

Aras. See ARAKS.

A·rau′ca (ä·rou′kä). 1 Commissary of Colombia. See *Table* at COLOMBIA.
2 Town, its ✳, E Colombia, on Arauca river.
3 River ab. 430 m. long, W Venezuela; flows E forming a part of Venezuela-Colombia boundary; empties into Orinoco.

Ar′au·ca′nia (ăr′ô·kän′yȧ; -kä′nĭ·ȧ; *Span.* ä′rou·kä′-nyä). Former region of cen. Chile, S of Bío-Bío river, now included in Concepción, Bío-Bío, and Cautín provinces; home of the Araucanian Indians.

A·rau′co (ä·rou′kŏ). 1 Province of Chile. See *Table* at CHILE.
2 Commune on coast of Arauco prov., S cen. Chile, 35 m. S of Concepción; pop. 15,127.

Arauco, Gulf of. Inlet of Pacific Ocean in coast of S cen. Chile, S of Concepción.

Arausio. See ORANGE city, France.

A·ra′val·li Range *or* **Hills** (ȧ·rä′vȧl·lĭ). Mountain range, NW India, in cen. and S Rajasthan, ab. 300 m. long; average height 1000 to 3000 ft., highest Mt. Abu 5650 ft.; generally bare and thinly inhabited.

A·ra′we (ä·rä′wȧ). Village and peninsula (ending in Cape Merkus) on S coast at W end of New Britain I.; first point of Allied invasion of island Dec. 20, 1943.

A′ra·xá′ (ȧ′rȧ·shä′). Town, Minas Gerais state, E Brazil, 65 m. E of Uberaba; pop. (1940 est.) 10,216.

Araxes. See ARAKS.

Araxos, Araxus. See PAPAS.

A·ra′yat (ä·rä′yät; ȧ·rī′ät). 1 Isolated extinct volcano 3867 ft., NE Pampanga prov., Luzon, Phil. Is.
2 Municipality, NE Pampanga prov., Luzon, at S foot of Mt. Arayat 11 m. N of San Fernando; pop. 22,510.

Arba, L′. See L′ARBA.

Arbe. See RAB.

Arbela, Arbil. See ERBIL.

Ar′ber (är′bĕr). Highest peak 4780 ft. in Bohemian Forest, Lower Bavaria, Germany, E of Regensburg.

Ar·bo′ga (är·bōō′gȧ). Town, Västmanland prov., E Sweden, 8 m. N of Lake Hjälmaren on Arboga river 9 m. W of its mouth in Lake Mälaren; pop. 6487; mineral springs; iron foundries; site of first diet in Sweden 1435 and of diet of 1561 at which Arboga Articles were adopted enabling Eric XIV to curb power of nobility.

Ar′bon′ (är′bôN′); *anc.* **Ar′bor Fe′lix** (är′bĕr fē′lĭks). Industrial commune, Thurgau canton, NE Switzerland, on SW coast of Lake Constance 16 m. SE of Konstanz; pop. (1930) 8615; neolithic pile dwellings.

Arborea. See MUSSOLINIA.

Ar·broath′ (är·brōth′) *or* **Ab′er·bro·thock′** (ăb′ĕr-brŭ·thŏk′). Seaport and manufacturing burgh, Angus co., E Scotland, 45 m. SSW of Aberdeen; pop. 19,503; site of meeting of Robert Bruce with Scottish nobles to resist claims of Edward II 1320.

Ar′buck′le Mountains (är′bŭk′'l). Low mountain region, S cen. Oklahoma.

Ar′ca′chon′ (är′kȧ′shôN′). Commune, Gironde dept., SW France, on S coast of the **Bas′sin′ d′Ar′ca·chon′** [bȧ′săN′ dȧr′-] (inlet of Bay of Biscay), 32 m. WSW of Bordeaux; pop. 13,102; resort; oyster culture, fishing.

Ar·cade′ (är·kād′). Village, Wyoming co., W New York, 33 m. SE of Buffalo; pop. 1930; in dairying region.

Ar·ca′di·a (är·kā′dĭ·ȧ). 1 Residential city, Los Angeles co., SW California, 13 m. ENE of Los Angeles; pop.41,005.
2 City, ⊗ of De Soto co., SW cen. Florida penin., 43 m. ESE of Sarasota; pop. 5889; cattle; winter resort.
3 Town, ⊗ of Bienville parish, NW Louisiana, 52 m. E of Shreveport; pop. 2547; cotton; lumber; salt deposits.
4 City, Trempealeau co., W Wisconsin; pop. 2084.
5 Ancient pastoral country in cen. Peloponnesus, Greece; mountainous, highest ab. 8000 ft.; chief cities Tegea, Mantinea, Orchomenus, and Megalopolis. Home of Arcadians, an ancient Greek people who never attained full political unity; Tegea fought against Sparta c. 800 B.C. but c. 560 B.C. became its subject ally; Arcadian cities later allied with Argos, but were forced to return to Sparta 469 B.C.; formed leagues against Sparta 420 B.C. and 370 B.C.; Megalopolis founded 370 B.C. as federal capital. Suffered in medieval period under Frankish barons, recovered under Turkish rule, again devastated during War of Independence 1821–29.
6 (*Mod. Gr.* är′kä·thē′ä) Department of Greece, nearly coextensive with ancient country. See *Table* at GREECE.

Ar′ca·dy (är′kȧ·dĭ). Archaic and poetic for ARCADIA.

Arcae Remorum. See CHARLEVILLE.

Ar·ca′ta (är·kā′tȧ). City, Humboldt co., NW California, on N end of Humboldt Bay 8 m. NE of Eureka; pop. 5235; Humboldt State College (teachers college; 1913).

Arc Dome (ärk). Peak 11,775 ft., Nye co., cen. Nevada.

Ar·ce′tri (är·chā′trē). Village, Firenze prov., Tuscany, cen. Italy, near Florence; home of Galileo 1634–42.

Ar·ce′via (är·chā′vyä). Commune, Ancona prov., Marches, cen. Italy, 30 m. WSW of Ancona; pop. 12,478.

Archangel See ARKHANGELSK.

Archangel, Gulf of. See DVINA GULF.

Arch′bald (ärch′bôld). Borough, Lackawanna co., NE Pennsylvania; pop. 5471; anthracite coal mines.

Ar′cher (är′chĕr). County in Texas. See *Table* at TEXAS.

Archer City. City, ⊗ of Archer co., N Texas, 25 m. S of Wichita Falls; pop. 1974.

Arch′es National Monument (är′chĕz; -chĭz). See UNITED STATES, *National Monuments*.

Ar′chi·pel′a·go (är′kĭ·pĕl′ȧ·gō). The Aegean Sea—a name originating with Italians in 13th cent.

Archipelago, *Turk.* **Je′za·ir′i–Bahr′i–Se·fid′** (jĕ′-zä·ēr′ĕ bär′ē sĕ·fēd′). Former Turkish vilayet in Asia Minor, composed of islands off W coast; 2660 sq. m.; now mostly Greek.

Archipiélago de Colón. See Archipiélago de COLÓN and GALÁPAGOS ISLANDS.

Archipiélago de los Chonos. See CHONOS ARCHIPELAGO.

Ar′chu·le′ta (är′chŭ·lē′tȧ). County in Colorado. See *Table* at COLORADO.

Arcila. See ARZILA.

Ar′cis′–sur–Aube′ (är′sēs′sür·ōb′). Commune, Aube dept., NE France, 17 m. N of Troyes; pop. 2779; silk and cotton spinning; battle Mar. 20–26, 1814 in which allied forces under Schwarzenberg defeated Napoleon.

Ar′co (är′kŏ). Village, ⊗ of Butte co., Idaho; pop. 1562.

Ar′co (är′kŏ). Commune, S Trento prov., Venezia Tridentina, NE Italy, 4 m. N of Lake Garda; pop. 9215.

Arcobriga. See ARCOS DE LA FRONTERA.

Ar·co′la (är·kō′lȧ). City, Douglas co., E cen. Illinois, 37 m. ESE of Decatur; pop. 2273.

Ar′co·le (är′kŏ·lä). Village, Verona prov., N Italy, 15 m. SE of Verona; pop. 4480; critical battle in Napoleon's early career in which he defeated the Austrians 1796.

Ar′cos de la Fron·te′ra (är′kŏz thä lä frōn·tā′rä); *Lat.* **Ar′co·bri′ga** (är′kŏ·brī′gȧ). Commune, Cádiz prov., SW Spain, 31 m. NE of Cádiz; pop. 18,146; Gothic church; ancient fortifications; ruled by Moors under name of **Me·di′na–Ar′kosh** (mä·dē′nä·ŭr′kōōsh; -dē′nä-); captured by Alfonso el Sabio in 13th cent.

Ar′cot (ŭr′kŏt; *Angl.* är·kŏt′). Town, **E** Madras prov., S Indian Union, on Palar river 65 m. W of Madras; pop. 14,000; capital from 1712 of the Nawabs of the Carnatic (*q.v.*); seized by Robert Clive 1751 during struggle of English against French domination of Carnatic; retaken by French 1760; passed to British with Carnatic 1801.

Arc′tic Archipelago (ärk′tĭk); *also* **Canadian Arctic Islands.** Large group of islands in Arctic Ocean, N of North America, nearly coextensive with Franklin District, Northwest Territories, Canada; includes the large islands of Baffin, Ellesmere, Victoria, Banks, Prince of Wales, Devon, Somerset, and the Parry and Sverdrup groups, and many smaller islands; area ab. 550,000 sq. m.

Arctic Current. The Labrador Current (*q.v.*).

Arctic Ocean. The ocean N of the Arctic Circle; 5,541,000 sq. m.; greatest depth 17,850 ft., in Chuckchee Sea N of Bering Strait, 77°45′N, 175°W; various sections are known by specific names, as Barents Sea, Beaufort Sea, Chuckchee Sea, East Siberian Sea, Greenland Sea, Kara Sea, Laptev Sea, Lincoln Sea, Norwegian Sea.

Arctic Red. River 230 m. long, NW Northwest Territories, Canada; flows NW to the Mackenzie at **Arctic Red River,** post on the Mackenzie SE of Aklavik.

Arctic Regions. The Arctic Ocean and lands in it and adjacent to it about to lat. 70°N; including Point Barrow in Alaska, most of Franklin District in Canada, two thirds of Greenland, Svalbard, Franz Josef Land, Novaya Zemlya, N Siberia. Cf. POLAR REGIONS.

Areas within Arctic Circle first explored 9th–12th cents. A.D. by Norse, who discovered White Sea, Iceland, Greenland, NE North America, and probably Spitsbergen; exploration advanced 16th and 17th cents. by English and Dutch as by-product of search for Northeast or Northwest Passage (*qq.v.*) to China; S part of Baffin I. discovered and Hudson Strait entered by Frobisher 1576–78; Davis Strait explored by John Davis 1585–87; W coast of Novaya Zemlya, Yamal Peninsula, and Spitsbergen discovered by Barents and Nay 1594–97; Hudson Strait and E coast of Hudson Bay navigated by

Hudson 1610–11; knowledge of N Canadian coast advanced by servants of Hudson's Bay Co. and of Siberian coast by Russian merchant expeditions and government expeditions (from 18th cent.); area near Spitsbergen and Greenland frequented by whaling expeditions; in 19th cent. its exploration became scientific rather than commercial; as result of loss of Sir John Franklin, who had proved route of Northwest Passage 1845–47, more than 7000 miles explored by 40 relief expeditions 1848–59; Franz Josef Land discovered by Austrians 1871–74, carefully explored by Russian scientists, annexed by Russia 1928; Northeast Passage first made by Nordenskjöld 1878–79 and Northwest Passage by Amundsen 1903–06; drift across Polar Basin accomplished by Nansen 1893–96; North Pole reached by Peary 1909; Canadian Arctic explored by extensive sledge expeditions (MacMillan, Stefansson, Rasmussen); first explored from air by Byrd and Bennett 1926; traversed from Spitsbergen to Alaska in flight of Amundsen, Nobile, and Ellsworth 1926; northern coasts of Asia and Europe systematically charted by official expeditions of the U.S.S.R.

Ar′cueil′ (är′kü′y′); *Lat.* **Ar′cu·li** (är′kŭ·lī). Commune, Seine dept., N France, 4 m. S of Paris; pop. 16,590; holiday resort; stone quarries; noted for its aqueducts, the first (Arcus Julianus, now in ruins) built by Julian in 4th cent., the second by Marie de Médicis 1613–24, the third, superimposed on the second, 1868–72.

Ard, Loch (lŏĸ ärd′). Small lake in Perth co., cen. Scotland, 2 m. W of Aberfoyle; a source of Forth river.

Ar′da (är′dä). River ab. 110 m. long, S Bulgaria and Turkey in Europe; rises on S slopes of Rhodope Mts. and flows E joining Maritsa opp. Edirne in NW Turkey.

Ar′da·han′ (är′dä·hän′); *Russ.* **Ar·da·gan′** (ŭr·dŭ·gän′). Fortified town, Kars vilayet, NE Turkey in Asia, 45 m. N of Kars; pop. 2863; stormed by Russians 1877 in Russo-Turkish War; ceded to Russia 1878 but with Kars returned to Turkey 1921.

Ar′de·a (är′dē·å). Ancient town, Latium, Italy, near coast SE of Lavinium; chief town of the Rutuli; con-

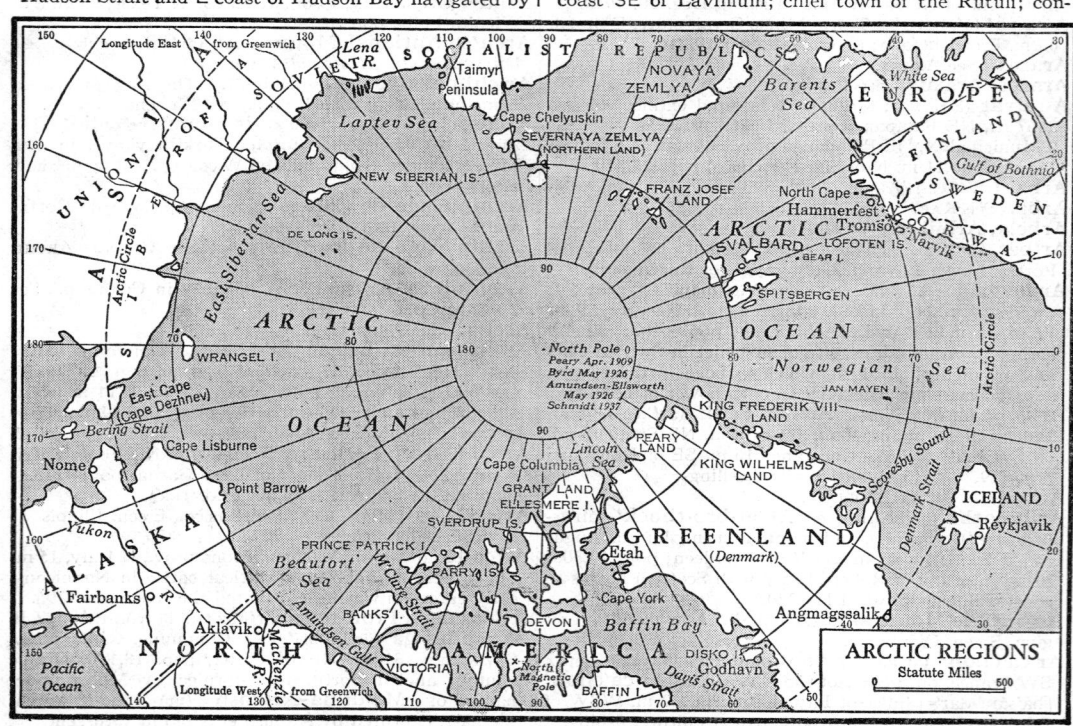

ARCTIC REGIONS
Statute Miles

quered and colonized by the Romans 442 B.C. In area N of the modern village in caves (**Ar′de·a·tine Caves** [är′dĕ·á·tīn]) 336 Italians were massacred by Germans Mar. 24, 1944 as a reprisal measure.

Ar′de·bil′ or **Ar′da·bil′** (är′dá·bēl′). City, E Azerbaijan prov., NW Iran, on the Qara Su 30 m. W of the Caspian Sea; pop. ab. 63,000; important center in the transit trade bet. Iran and Russia; formerly a favorite residence of the Persian court. Home and shrine of Persian saint, Safi-al-Din (1252–1334).

Ar′dèche′ (är′dĕsh′). **1** River 69 m. long, Ardèche dept., SE France; rises in Cévennes Mts., empties into Rhone. **2** Department of France. See *Table* at FRANCE.

Ar′de·lan′ (är′dĕ·län′). Former province, NW Iran; 9364 sq. m.; * Sinneh.

Ar′den, Forest of (är′d′n). Wooded region, N Warwickshire, cen. England, W of Stratford on Avon, 17 m. by 12 m.; originally part of a tract supposed to have covered much of cen. and E England; probably the original of Shakespeare's Forest of Arden in *As You Like It.*

Ar′dennes′ (är′dĕn′; *Angl.* är·dĕn′). **1** *often* **Forest of Ardennes**; *anc.* **Ar′du·en′na Sil′va** (är′dṳ·ĕn′á sĭl′vá). Wooded plateau region, average height less than 1600 ft., E of Meuse river covering most of Belgian province of Luxembourg and part of grand duchy of Luxembourg, and occupying the Meuse valley in French department of Ardennes; coal and iron mines in NW. In World War I scene of frontier battles Aug. 1914 and in Nov. 1918 of the severing of German communications around Sedan. In World War II scene of German offensive May 1940 in which Maginot Line near Sedan was penetrated and Allied forces to N cut off; scene of advance by U.S. troops Sept. 1944 and Dec.–Jan. 1945 of bitter fighting ("Battle of the Bulge") esp. around St-Vith and Bastogne. **2** Department of France. See *Table* at FRANCE.

Ar′di·stan′ (är′dĭ·stän′). Town, cen. Iran, on highway bet. Kashan and Yezd; pop. ab. 10,000.

Ar·djoe′no or **Ar·dju′no** (är·jōō′nō). Volcano 10,955 ft., East Java prov., Indonesia, N of Malang.

Ard′more (ärd′mōr). **1** City, ⊗ of Carter co., S Oklahoma; pop. 20,184; asphalt, zinc, coal mines; oil. **2** Unincorporated community, Montgomery co.. SE Pennsylvania, NW of Philadelphia.

Ardmore Point. Cape on N coast of Mull I. in Inner Hebrides off W coast of Scotland; lighthouse.

Ard′na·mur′chan Point (ärd′ná·mûr′кăn). Cape on NW coast of Argyll co., W Scotland, N of Mull I. and S of Eigg I.; extreme W point of mainland of Great Britain; lighthouse, built 1849, fixed light, visible 18 m.

Ar′dost′ (är′dôst′). Peak 11,444 ft. in the Bulgar Dağları, Taurus Mts., in S cen. Turkey in Asia.

Ar′dres (är′dr′). Commune, Pas-de-Calais dept., N France, 9 m. SE of Calais; pop. 1254; headquarters of Francis I during "Field of the Cloth of Gold" meeting with Henry VIII June 1520. Cf. GUÎNES.

Ard·ros′san (ärd·rŏs′′n). Seaport burgh, Ayr co., SW Scotland, on Firth of Clyde; pop. 8799; shore resort.

Ards′ley (ärdz′lĭ). **1** Residential village, Westchester co., SE New York, 21 m. N of New York; pop. 3991. **2** Urban district, West Riding, Yorkshire, N England, comprising two parishes, **East Ardsley** and **West Ardsley**, 3½ and 4 m. NW of Wakefield; pop. 9216; collieries, iron mines, smelting, woolen manufacturing.

Arduenna Silva. See ARDENNES.

A′re·ci′bo (ä′rá·sē′vô). Municipality (pop. 69,879) and seaport town (pop. 28,828), N Puerto Rico.

A′re·guá′ (ä′rá·gwä′). Town, Central dept., S cen. Paraguay, 10 m. E of Asunción; pop. ab. 6800.

Arelas, Arelate. See ARLES city.

Aremorica. See ARMORICA.

A·re′na, Point (á·rē′ná). Point on SW coast of Mendocino co., W California, 38°57′N.

Ar′e·nac (är′ĕ·năk). County in Michigan. See *Table* at MICHIGAN.

A′re·na′les (ä′rá·nä′läs). Peak 11,285 ft., Aysén prov., S Chile, E of Gulf of Peñas.

A′ren·dal′ (ä′rĕn·däl′). Seaport on the Skagerrak, ⊗ of Aust-Agder co., S Norway; pop. 10,351.

Arensburg. See KURESSARE.

Ar′e·op′a·gus (är′ĕ·ŏp′á·gŭs). Literally, Hill of Ares (Mars' Hill); rocky height 377 ft. in Athens W of the Acropolis; ancient meeting place of court. Scene of St. Paul's address to the Athenians recorded in *Acts* xvii.

A′re·qui′pa (ä′rá·kē′pä). **1** Department of Peru. See *Table* at PERU. **2** City, its *, ab. 475 m. SE of Lima, at foot of El Misti; pop. (1940 est.) 79,185; alt. 7550 ft.; an intellectual, religious, and industrial center and chief distributing point for S Peru; founded by Pizarro on site of Inca town 1540; nearly destroyed by earthquake 1868; university (founded 1821), colleges.

Arequipa, El Vol·cán′ de (ĕl vôl·kän′ dä). = EL MISTI.

Ar′e·thu′sa (är′ĕ·thū′zá; -sá). Fountain on Ortygia I., Syracuse harbor, Sicily; displayed on ancient Syracusan coins; named for Arethusa, a wood nymph of Elis in Greece, who, according to the story of classical mythology, being pursued by the river-god Alpheus, was changed by Artemis into a stream which ran under the sea until its waters rose again in this fountain.

A·rez′zo (ä·rät′tsô). **1** Province of Italy. See *Table* at ITALY. **2** *anc.* **Ar·re′ti·um** (ă·rē′shĭ·ŭm). Commune, its *, Tuscany, cen. Italy, on the Arno 39 m. SE of Florence; pop. 60,284; railroad junction; 13th-cent. Gothic cathedral; in district producing grain, wine, olives, fruits; manufactures silk fabrics, leather goods, textiles. In ancient times, noted esp. for pottery (Arretine ware) and copperwork; city-state from 1098; in struggles of Guelphs and Ghibellines, defeated by Florence at Campaldino 1289; ruled by Florence from 16th cent. until unification of Italy 1860; in World War II taken by British July 16, 1944. Birthplace of Petrarch and Vasari.

Ar′fak (är′fäk). Mountain range in NW West New Guinea; highest point Kwoka 9842 ft.

Ar′ga (är′gä). River ab. 60 m. long, N Spain; rises in the Pyrenees, flows in Aragón river.

Argaeus. See ERCİYAS DAĞI.

Ar·ga′o (är·gä′ô). Municipality on E coast of Cebu I., Phil. Is., on Bohol Strait 36 m. SSW of City of Cebu; pop. 37,331; seized by Japanese 1942; retaken 1945.

Ar′gaon (är′goun) or **Ar′gaum** (är′goum). Village, N Maharashtra state, cen. India, 137 m. W of Nagpur; formerly in W Berar; scene of decisive defeat Nov. 29, 1803 of Marathas by British under Gen. Wellesley.

Ar′gens′ (är′zhäns′). River 72 m. long, Var dept., SE France; flows E to Mediterranean near Fréjus.

Ar·gen′ta (är·jĕn′tá). See NORTH LITTLE ROCK.

Ar·gen′ta (är·jĕn′tä). Commune, Ferrara prov., Emilia, N Italy, 19 m. SE of Ferrara; pop. 28,032.

Ar′gen′tan′ (är′zhäɴ·täɴ′; *Angl.* är′jĕn·tăn). Commune, Orne dept., France, on right bank of Orne river 23 m. NNW of Alençon; pop. 6035; two 15th-cent. churches and 15th-cent. castle; lace, linens, leather goods, stained glass. In World War II the S anchor of Allied line in Normandy campaign, opp. Falaise; W of these two towns six German divisions trapped in Falaise pocket Aug. 18–23, 1944 met disastrous defeat, marking beginning of withdrawal to the Seine.

Ar′gen·ta′rio (är′jän·tä′ryô); *anc.* **Ar′gen·tar′i·us** (är′jĕn·târ′ĭ·ŭs). Mountain 2081 ft., W Italy, off coast at Orbetello 36 m. NW of Civitavecchia; on a promontory, connected with mainland by two tongues of land.

Ar′gen·te′ra, Pun′ta (pōōn′tä är′jän·tâ′rä). Peak 10,814 ft., highest in Maritime Alps, Cuneo prov., SW Piedmont, NW Italy, 32 m. NNE of Nice, France.

Ar′gen′teuil′ (är′zhäɴ′tû′y′). **1** County of Quebec prov., Canada. See *Table* at QUEBEC.

2 Commune, Seine-et-Oise dept., N France, on Seine river 5 m. NNW of Paris; pop. 59,314; residential area; vineyards; metallurgical and chemical industries. Built around nunnery founded 656 by Charlemagne which became famous in 12th cent. through its abbess, Héloïse.

Ar·gen'ti·a (är·jĕn'shĭ·à; -shà). **1** Peninsula, SE Newfoundland, extending into Placentia Bay; leased 1940 for U.S. Army and Navy base and used as aerial base and military training ground.

2 Village, SE Newfoundland, on Placentia Bay (*q.v.*) 22 m. W of St. John's.

Ar'gen·tie'ra (*Ital.* är'jån·tyä'rä). = CIMOLUS.

Ar'gen'tière', Ai'guille' d' (ā'gü·ē'y' dàr'zhän'tyâr'). Peak 12,800 ft. in the Mont Blanc massif Pennine Alps, E France, ab. 8 m. ENE of Chamonix.

Ar'gen·ti'na (är'jĕn·tē'nà; *Span.* är'hän·tē'nä) or **Ar'gen·tine Republic** (är'jĕn·tēn; -tīn). Federal republic, S cen. and S South America, E of Andes Mts.; bounded on N by Bolivia and Paraguay, on E by Brazil, Uruguay, and the Atlantic Ocean, on S and W by Chile; 1,072,745 sq. m.; pop. (1943 est.) 13,906,694; ✷ Buenos Aires; divided into a Federal District (Buenos Aires), 14 provinces, and 9 territories (for pronunciation of their names, see their individual entries):

NAME	LOCATION	AREA[1]	POP.[1]	CAPITAL
Federal District[2]	E	74	2,457,494[3]	
PROVINCES				
Buenos Aires[4]	E	118,752	3,633,256	La Plata
Catamarca	NW	27,773	162,115	Catamarca
Córdoba	N cen.	65,195	1,358,523	Córdoba
Corrientes	NE	34,500	553,013	Corrientes
Entre Ríos	E	29,427	795,867	Paraná
Jujuy	NW	16,859	124,996	Jujuy
La Rioja	NW	35,649	116,688	La Rioja
Mendoza	W	58,239	552,545	Mendoza
Salta	N	50,029	233,465	Salta
San Juan	W	33,257	237,929	San Juan
San Luis	cen.	29,632	210,940	San Luis
Santa Fe	E cen.	51,354	1,613,586	Santa Fe
Santiago del Estero	N	52,222	536,498	Santiago del Estero
Tucumán	N	8,697	590,338	Tucumán
TERRITORIES				
Chaco	N	38,468	345,900	Resistencia
Chubut[5]	S	86,751	89,400	Rawson
Formosa	N	27,825	72,200	Formosa
La Pampa	S cen.	55,382	154,000	Santa Rosa
Los Andes[6]	NW	24,186	7,300	San Antonio de los Cobres
Misiones	NE	11,506	196,600	Posadas
Neuquén	W	36,324	78,500	Neuquén
Río Negro[5]	cen.	78,383	139,600	Viedma
Santa Cruz[5]	S	94,187	19,400	Gallegos
Tierra del Fuego[7]	S	8,074	2,200	Ushuaia

[1] Area in sq. m. Pop. of Federal District and of provinces is 1943 est.; pop. of territories is 1942 est.
[2] Comprises capital city of Buenos Aires.
[3] Includes suburban pop. of Flores and Belgrano.
[4] Does not include the city of Buenos Aires.
[5] In region known as Patagonia.
[6] Former territory, since 1943 divided among provinces of Jujuy, Salta, and Catamarca.
[7] Comprises E half of Tierra del Fuego I. and adjacent islands to E including Staten I.

Chief cities: Buenos Aires, Rosario, Córdoba, Tucumán, Santa Fe, Mendoza, Paraná, Corrientes, and Santiago del Estero; in Buenos Aires there are many large suburbs of the capital including: Avellaneda, La Plata, Lomas de Zamora, and Quilmes. *Chief rivers:* Río de la Plata (estuary of the Paraná and Uruguay); Bermejo, tributary of the Paraguay, and Salado, tributary of the Paraná, which as the Alto Paraná forms the NE boundary; Salado (in cen. part), Colorado, Negro, Chubut. There are many lakes, esp. on slopes of S Andes; among them famous resorts, as Nahuel Huapí. *Chief mountains:* Aconcagua, highest peak of Western Hemisphere, Mercedario, Llullaillaco (volcano), Incahuasi, Tupungato (volcano), and Maipú (volcano), all in W part, near or on the Chilean boundary line, all except Maipú above 21,000 ft. Near Aconcagua is Uspallata

Pass (see ANDES). *Principal industry:* Meat refrigeration; exports are chiefly livestock products but they include also wheat, maize, oats, and linseed.

History: Río de la Plata discovered by Solís 1516; explored by Sebastian Cabot 1526–30; permanent colonization undertaken by Pedro de Mendoza at Buenos Aires (*q.v.*) 1536; Asunción, Santa Fe, Buenos Aires settled by 1580; attached to viceroyalty of Peru 1620; included with regions of modern Uruguay, Paraguay, and Bolivia in viceroyalty of La Plata or Buenos Aires 1776; Buenos Aires attacked by British 1806–07; with setting up of United Provinces of the Plate River 1816, accomplished its independence from Spain; recognized as independent by U.S. 1823, Great Britain 1825; with its recognition of an independent Uruguay, settled strife with Brazil 1828; torn by warfare bet. Federalists and Unitarians; after dictatorship of Rosas (1835–52), set up federal constitution 1853; allied with Brazil and Uruguay in war against Paraguay 1865–70; finally resolved struggle bet. Buenos Aires and provinces 1880; represented at first Pan-American Congress 1890; settled boundaries with Brazil by arbitration 1895, with Chile 1899, 1902; participated in ABC mediation of U.S. dispute with Mexico 1914; neutral in World War I; among first to join League of Nations 1920; withdrew 1921 at failure of its proposals for compulsory arbitration; returned to League 1933; participant in all Pan-American conferences; neutral in World War II; government overthrown by army 1943; army leader, Juan Perón, elected president 1946.

Ar'gen·ti'no, Lake (är'hän·tē'nŏ). Lake ab. 570 sq. m. in W Santa Cruz territory, S Argentina.

Argentoratum. See STRASBOURG.

Ar'geş (är'jĕsh). River ab. 125 m. long in S Romania; joined by the Dâmboviţa SE of Bucharest, flows S into Danube river at Olteniţa; battle Dec. 1–5, 1916 in which Austro-German army defeated the Romanians.

Arghana Maden. = ERGANÍ MADENÍ.

Ar'gi·nu'sae (är'jĭ·nū'sē). Group of small islands off SE coast of island of Lesbos in E Aegean Sea; naval battle in Peloponnesian War 406 B.C., last victory of Athens over Sparta in the war.

Argirocastro. See GJINOKASTËR.

Ar'go (är'gō). **1** Town on the Nile opp. N end of Argo I. **2** Island 25 m. long and 5 m. wide in Nile river, N of Dongola, Northern Province, Anglo-Egyptian Sudan.

Ar'go·lis (är'gō·lĭs; *Mod. Gr.* är'gô·lyēs'). A district of E Peloponnesus, ancient Greece, forming a peninsula; under Mycenaean influence until invaded by Dorians; dominated, although never completely united, by Argos.

Argolis, Gulf of; *also* **Gulf of Nau'pli·a** (nô'pli·à). Inlet of Aegean Sea on E coast of Peloponnesus, S Greece, SE of Argos; Nauplia is at its N end.

Argolis and Cor'inth (kŏr'ĭnth); *Gr.* **Ar'go·lis' kai Ko'rin·thi'a** (är'gô·lyēs' kâ kô'rĕn·thē'ä). Department of Greece. See *Table* at GREECE.

Ar'gonne' (àr'gôn'; *Angl.* är'gŏn, är·gŏn'), *often* **Argonne Forest.** Wooded plateau, NE France, in Meuse, Ardennes, and Marne depts. near Belgian border S of Ardennes, ab. 25 m. long and 10 m. wide, lying bet. the Meuse and the Aisne, with Verdun at its S end; alt. ab. 1150 ft. Scene of campaign of Dumouriez against Prussians before battle of Valmy 1792; also scene of Allied offensive in World War I Sept.–Nov. 1918, often known as the Meuse-Argonne offensive, in which an American army under Pershing advanced from a line S and E of Argonne Forest to Sedan and Stenay by time of Armistice; in World War II overrun by German armies June 1940; crossed by Americans Aug. 30–31, 1944.

Ar'gos (är'gŏs; *Mod. Gr.* är'gôs). City, Argolis and Corinth dept., NE Peloponnesus, Greece, 7 m. NNW of Nauplia; pop. 10,504; railroad junction.

History: As a city-state under King Pheidon c. 680 B.C., claimed hegemony over Peloponnesus; a weak state in continual conflict with Sparta after latter's rise; entered alliances with Spartan enemies, esp. the Quadruple

ARGENTINA, CHILE, PARAGUAY, URUGUAY

Statute Miles

0   100   200   300

⊕ Capitals of Countries

PUBLISHED BY G. & C. MERRIAM COMPANY
SPRINGFIELD, MASS.

PREPARED BY J. W. CLEMENT CO., BUFFALO, N. Y.

Alliance (Corinth, Mantinea, Elis, and Argos) against Sparta 421 B.C. and the alliance with Corinth, Athens, and Thebes in Corinthian War 395–387 B.C.; joined Achaean League 229 B.C.; headquarters of Achaean power under Rome; remained under Byzantine Empire until captured by Franks 1210; held in fief to Athens 1246–61; part of Byzantine Empire 1261–1460 and of Ottoman Empire 1460–1830; seat of national assembly in movement for Greek independence 1822; destroyed by Ibrahim Pasha 1825.

Ar′go·stó′li·on (är′gô·stô′lyôn), *sometimes* **Ar′go·sto′li** (är′gô·stô′lyĕ). Seaport city, ✻ of Cephalonia dept., Ionian Is., Greece, on SW coast of Cephalonia I.; pop. 8293; fine harbor; episcopal see.

Argovie. See AARGAU.

Ar·guel′lo, Point (är·gwĕl′ō). Cape, SW Santa Barbara co., SW California; site of missile-launching center.

Ar·guin′ (är·gwēn′). Island in **Arguin Bay,** N coast of Mauritania, West Africa, ab. 50 m. below Cape Blanc; discovered by Portuguese 15th cent.

Ar′gun′ (är′gōōn′). Navigable river ab. 450 m. long, NE Asia; rises in Hulun Nor, flows NE, forming boundary bet. Manchuria and U.S.S.R., and unites with Shilka river on extreme N boundary to form Amur river.

Ar·gyll′ (är·gĭl′) *or* **Ar·gyll′shire** (-shĭr; -shĕr). County, W Scotland; 3110 sq. m.; pop. (1940 est.) 62,000; ⊗ Lochgilphead; other towns Campbeltown, Dunoon, Oban; mountainous region, a popular tourist resort; coast indented by many lochs and includes many islands (Mull, Islay, Jura, Coll, Tiree, etc.) and the Kintyre Penin.; agriculture, sheep and cattle grazing, fisheries, quarrying (granite, slate).

Argyrokastron. See GJINOKASTËR.

Ar′i·a (är′ĭ·a; à·rī′à). **1** An eastern province of ancient Persian Empire, now in NW Afghanistan and E Iran. **2** City. Ancient name of Herat (*q.v.*).

A·ri·a·ke Bay (ä·rē·ä·kĕ) *Jap.* **Ariake Wan** (wän). Inlet of Pacific Ocean on SE coast of Kyushu I., Japan.

Ar′i·a′na (är′ĭ·ā′nà; -ăn′à). An extensive region of ancient Persian Empire including the eastern provinces of Aria, Arachosia, Carmania, Drangiana, Gedrosia and Parthia; named from Aria.

A·ria′no Ir·pi′no (ä·ryä′nô êr·pē′nô), *formerly* **Ariano di Pu′glia** (dē pōō′lyä). Commune, Avellino prov., Campania, S Italy, 23 m. NE of Avellino; pop. 24,357; built on rocky height in Apennines; subject to earthquakes; episcopal see; many old churches; manufactures earthenware. Occupies supposed site of ancient Samnite town **Ae′quum Tu′ti·cum** (ē′kwŭm tū′tĭ·kŭm).

Ariano nel Po·le′si·ne (nĕl pô·lā′zĕ·nà). Commune, Rovigo prov., Venezia Euganea, NE Italy; pop. 11,875.

Aria Palus. See HAMUN-I-MASHKEL.

A·ri′ca (ä·rē′kä). Seaport city, extreme N Chile, in Tarapacá prov., ab. 1015 m. N of Valparaíso; pop. 14,064; northernmost port of the republic; terminus of railroad from La Paz, Bolivia (277 m.); Peruvian seaport in colonial times; occupied by Chile 1880 after boundary disputes resulting in War of the Pacific 1879–84; by Treaty of Ancón (*q.v.*) 1883, which followed Chilean victory, awarded (with Tacna) to Chile for 10 years with provision for plebiscite; claimed by Peru and Chile in Tacna-Arica dispute which long embittered Chilean-Peruvian relations and came to head 1921–29; access to sea through Arica claimed by Bolivia through League of Nations 1920; by settlement of 1929 awarded to Chile but guaranteed as free port for Peru and outlet for Bolivia via Arica-La Paz R.R. (see TACNA); with its vicinity made a department of Tarapacá prov. 1930.

Ar′i·chat (är′ĭ·shăt). Unincorporated village, ⊗ of Richmond co., on Madame I. off S coast of Cape Breton I., Nova Scotia, Canada; pop. 823; first settled 1713.

A′ri·chu′na (ä′rē·chōō′nä). River 240 m. long, W Venezuela; flows E and joins Arauca river in Apure state.

A·ri′ci·a (à·rĭsh′ĭ·à), *modern* **A·ric′cia** (ä·rēt′chä). Town, Latium, cen. Italy, at foot of Alban Hills on the

Appian Way 16 m. SE of Rome; pop. 5596; summer resort. One of the oldest towns of Italy; subdued by Romans 338 B.C.; famous for its temple and grove of Diana.

A·riège′ (à′ryâzh′) *or* **La Riège** (lá ryâzh′). **1** River ab. 90 m. long, S France; rises in E Pyrenees Mts. forming border bet. Pyrénées-Orientales dept. and Andorra; flows NNW through wide alluvial valley into Garonne river 5 m. S of Toulouse; navigable for ab. 26 m. **2** Department of France. See *Table* at FRANCE.

Ar′i·el Dam (âr′ĭ·ĕl). See UNITED STATES, *Dams.*

A′ri·en′zo San Fe·li′ce (ä′rē·ĕn′tsô säm′ fà·lē′chä). Commune, Napoli prov., Campania, S Italy, 18 m. NE of Naples near the Caudine Forks; pop. 13,682.

Arilica. See PESCHIERA DEL GARDA.

A·ri′ma (à·rē′mà). Borough, N cen. Trinidad, West Indies Fed., 16 m. E of Port of Spain; pop. 5089; center of cacao industry.

Ar′i·ma·the′a (ăr′ĭ·mà·thē′à); *also* **Ar′i·ma·thae′a.** Greek form of Ramah; town, probably in Samaria but not definitely identified, whence came the councillor Joseph who placed the body of Jesus in his own tomb (*Matt.* xxvii. 57 ff.).

Ariminum. See RIMINI.

A·ri′nos (à·rē′nōōs). River ab. 400 m. long, W cen. Brazil; rises in cen. Mato Grosso state, flows N into Juruena river.

A′rio de Ro·sa′les (ä′ryô thä rô·sä′läs). Town, Michoacán state, SW Mexico, 20 m. SE of Uruapan; pop. 5924.

A′ri·pua·nã′ (ä′rē·pwá·nän′). River ab. 600 m. long. W cen. Brazil; rises in N Mato Grosso state, flows N to the Madeira river; in SE Amazonas state it is joined by the Rio Roosevelt; by some the lower course is named the Roosevelt. See Rio ROOSEVELT.

'Arîsh, El. See EL 'ARÎSH.

Ar′is·taz′a·bal′ Island (är′ĭs·tăz′á·bäl′). Island 27 m. long in Pacific Ocean, E side of Hecate Strait, off W British Columbia, Canada, W of Princess Royal Island.

A·ri·ta (ä·rē·tä). Town, Saga prefecture, NW Kyushu I., Japan, 9 m. E of Sasebo; pop. 5730; porcelain.

A′ri·ta′o (ä′rē·tä′ô). Town, Nueva Vizcaya prov., cen. Luzon, Phil. Is., 15 m. SW of Bayombong; taken in American advance toward Cagayan valley June 6, 1945.

Arius. See HARI RUD.

Ar′i·zo′na (är′ĭ·zō′nà). A southwestern state of U.S.A., 48th state admitted to Union (1912); bounded on N by Utah, on E by New Mexico, on S by Mexico, and on W by California and Nevada with the Colorado river separating it from California and in part from Nevada; 6th state in area, 113,909 sq. m. (land area, 113,580 sq. m.); 35th state in population, 1,302,161; ✻ Phoenix. See *Table of States* at UNITED STATES. Divided into the following 14 counties (for pronunciation of their names, see their individual entries):

NAME	LOCATION	AREA[1]	POP.[1]	CO. SEAT
Apache[2]	NE corner	11,174	30,438	St. Johns
Cochise	SE corner	6,256	55,039	Bisbee
Coconino[3]	N	18,573	41,857	Flagstaff
Gila[4]	E cen.	4,750	25,745	Globe
Graham[5]	SE	4,610	14,045	Safford
Greenlee	SE	1,874	11,509	Clifton
Maricopa	SW cen.	9,231	663,510	Phoenix
Mohave[6]	NW corner	13,260	7,736	Kingman
Navajo	NE	9,911	37,994	Holbrook
Pima	S	9,241	265,660	Tucson
Pinal	S	5,378	62,673	Florence
Santa Cruz	S	1,246	10,808	Nogales
Yavapai	cen.	8,091	28,912	Prescott
Yuma	SW corner	9,985	46,235	Yuma

[1] Area = land area in sq. m. Pop. from 1960 Census.
[2] Its NE point the only point in U.S. common to 4 states (Ariz., N.Mex., Colo., and Utah).
[3] Painted Desert in E; many high plateaus and peaks, highest Humphreys Peak 12,611 ft.
[4] Bounded on S by Gila river, including Coolidge Dam and San Carlos Reservoir; Roosevelt Dam and Lake on cen. W border.
[5] Bounded on NW by San Carlos river, including San Carlos Reservoir.
[6] Hoover Dam (Boulder Dam) and Lake Mead on part of NW boundary.

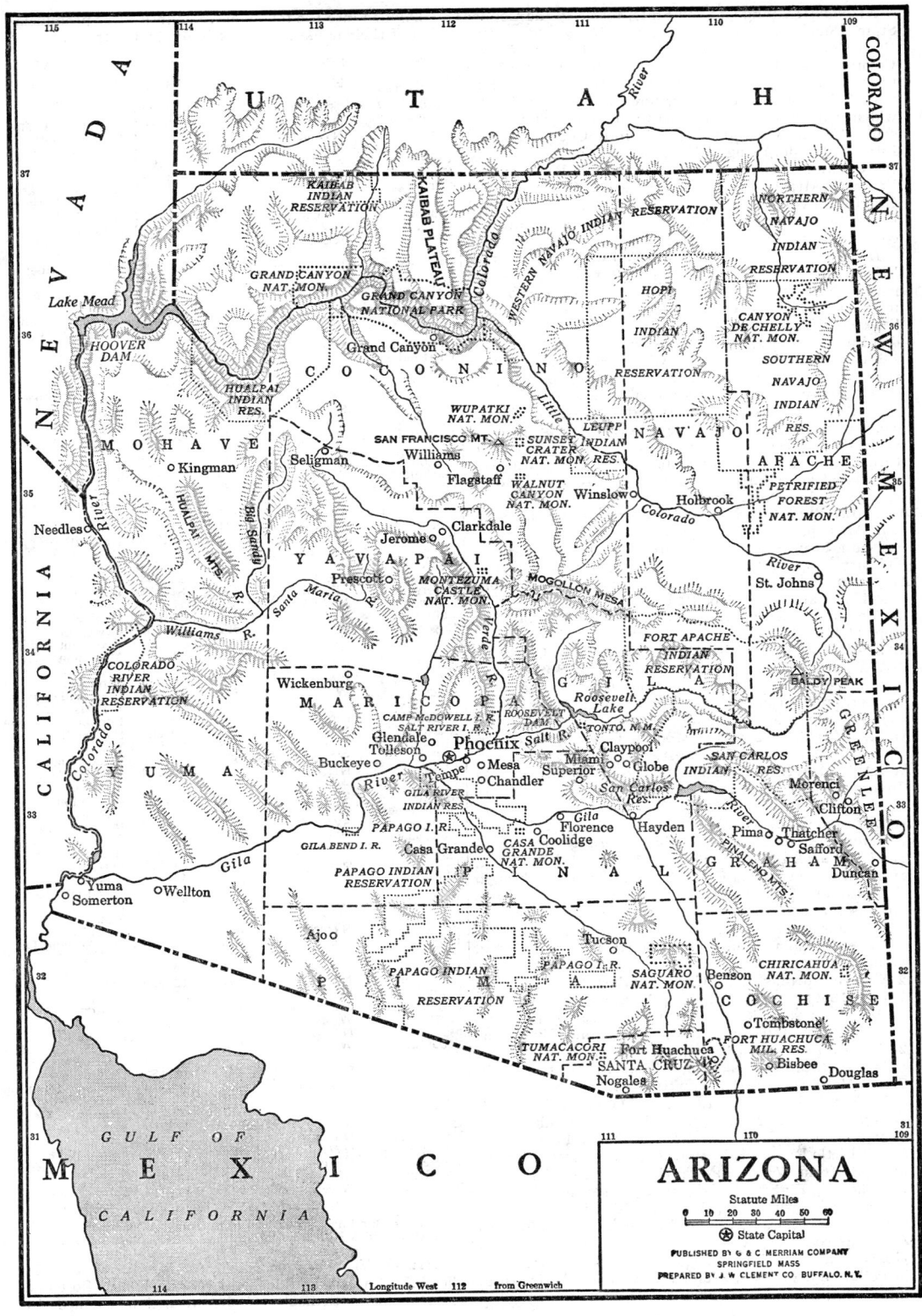

ARIZONA

Statute Miles

0 10 20 30 40 50 60

State Capital

PUBLISHED BY G & C MERRIAM COMPANY
SPRINGFIELD MASS
PREPARED BY J. W. CLEMENT CO. BUFFALO, N. Y.

Nickname: Grand Canyon State, formerly the Copper State. *State flower:* Saguaro cactus. *Motto:* Ditat Deus (God Enriches). *Chief cities:* Phoenix, Tucson. *Rivers:* Colorado on W border, widened at north by Hoover Dam to form Lake Mead; Verde in cen. part flowing SE into Salt; Salt, rising in E region, flowing W into Gila and widened by Roosevelt Dam to form Roosevelt Lake in cen. Arizona; Gila, flowing SW into Colorado river; Little Colorado, rising in E region and flowing NW into the Colorado. *Highest point:* Humphreys Peak, or San Francisco Mt., 12,611 ft. in Coconino co. *Scenic features:* Grand Canyon of the Colorado river in N; Petrified Forest in E. *Chief industries:* Agriculture; stock raising; copper mining.

History: Spanish exploration began with expedition of Franciscan friar Marcos de Niza 1539; ruled by Spain as part of New Spain 1598–1845; inauguration of Spanish missions to Hopis 1638; region acquired by United States by Treaty of Guadalupe Hidalgo 1848 and Gadsden Purchase 1853; organized as separate territory 1863; subjugation of Apaches 1877; with New Mexico refused statehood 1906; submitted a constitution for congressional approval 1911; congressional resolution accepting this constitution vetoed by President Taft chiefly because of provision allowing recall of judges by popular vote; after objectionable matter withdrawn from constitution, admitted to Union Feb. 14, 1912; by state constitutional amendment restored the provision allowing recall of judges Nov. 1912.

Arizona, Plateau of. Tableland extending across N cen. Arizona, marked by many high mountains, including San Francisco Peaks, Slate Mt., Kendrick Peak, O'Leary Peak, Elden Mt., Woody Mt. (*qq.v.*).

Ar·jo′na (är-hō′nä). **1** Town, Bolívar dept., N Colombia, just E of Cartagena; pop. 10,416.
2 Commune, Jaén prov., S Spain, 19 m. WNW of Jaén; pop. 11,112.

Ar′ka·del′phi·a (är′kȧ-dĕl′fĭ·ȧ). City, ⊗ of Clark co., SW Arkansas, on Ouachita river 28 m. S of Hot Springs; pop. 8069; founded 1839; in cotton-growing area; flour, lumber, and cotton mills; Ouachita College (1886); Henderson State Teachers College (1929).

Ar′ka·di′a (är′kä-thē′ä). Modern Greek form of *Arcadia*, department of Greece: see *Table* at GREECE.

Ar·kaig′, Loch (lŏk är-kāg′). Lake 12 m. long, W Inverness co., NW Scotland, 10 m. N of Fort William; 6 sq. m.; trout fishing.

Ar′kan·sas (*in Arkansas*, är′kȧn-sô; *elsewhere* är′kȧn-sô, *occasionally* är-kăn′zȧs, *except in Kansas, where* är-kăn′zȧs *is frequent, esp. for the river*). **1** River 1450 m. long, rising in Lake co., cen. Colorado, and flowing E through S Kansas and SE across NE corner of Oklahoma; bisects Arkansas and empties into Mississippi river in Desha co., SE Arkansas; navigable 650 m.; its largest tributaries are the Canadian and Cimarron rivers. See ROYAL GORGE.

2 A south central state of U.S.A., 25th state admitted to Union (1836); bounded on N by Missouri, on E by Mississippi river separating it from Tennessee and Mississippi, on S by Louisiana. on W by Texas and Oklahoma; 27th state in area, 53,104 sq. m. (land area, 52,725 sq. m.); 32d in population, 1,786,272; ✻ Little Rock. See *Table of States* at UNITED STATES.

Nickname: Wonder State, Land of Opportunity. *State flower:* Apple blossom. *Motto:* Regnat Populus (The People Rule). *Chief cities:* Little Rock, Fort Smith, North Little Rock, Pine Bluff. *Rivers:* Arkansas, bisecting state from W to E and flowing into the Mississippi; Red, flowing E and S in extreme SW area, forming part of boundary with Texas; Ouachita rising in W area and flowing E and then S; White, flowing from N to SE into Arkansas river near confluence with Mississippi. *High points:* Magazine Mt. in Logan co. 2800 ft., Rich Mt. in Polk and Scott cos., 2750 ft. *Industries:* Agriculture; lumbering; mining (coal, manganese, bauxite).

Divided into the following 75 counties (for pronunciation of their names, see their individual entries):

NAME	LOCATION	AREA[1]	POP.[1]	CO. SEAT
Arkansas	E	1,035	23,355	De Witt and Stuttgart
Ashley	SE	933	24,220	Hamburg
Baxter	N	571	9,943	Mountain Home
Benton	NW corner	886	36,272	Bentonville
Boone	N	602	16,116	Harrison
Bradley	S	649	14,029	Warren
Calhoun	S	628	5,991	Hampton
Carroll	NW	634	11,284	Berryville and Eureka Springs
Chicot	SE corner	647	18,990	Lake Village
Clark	SW	878	20,950	Arkadelphia
Clay	NE corner	650	21,258	Corning and Piggott
Cleburne	N cen.	595	9,059	Heber Springs
Cleveland	S	601	6,944	Rison
Columbia	SW	768	26,400	Magnolia
Conway	cen.	560	15,430	Morrilton
Craighead	NE	717	47,303	Jonesboro and Lake City
Crawford	NW	598	21,318	Van Buren
Crittenden	E	623	47,564	Marion
Cross	E	626	19,551	Wynne
Dallas	S cen.	672	10,522	Fordyce
Desha	SE	776	20,770	Arkansas City
Drew	SE	836	15,213	Monticello
Faulkner	cen.	656	24,303	Conway
Franklin	NW	615	10,213	Charleston and Ozark
Fulton	N	611	6,657	Salem
Garland	W cen.	721	46,697	Hot Springs[2]
Grant	S cen.	631	8,294	Sheridan
Greene	NE	579	25,198	Paragould
Hempstead	SW	735	19,661	Hope
Hot Spring	SW cen	621	21,893	Malvern
Howard	SW	600	10,878	Nashville
Independence	NE cen.	755	20,048	Batesville
Izard	N	574	6,766	Melbourne
Jackson	NE	637	22,843	Newport
Jefferson	SE cen.	890	81,373	Pine Bluff
Johnson	NW	676	12,421	Clarksville
Lafayette	SW	537	11,030	Lewisville
Lawrence	NE	592	17,267	Powhatan and Walnut Ridge
Lee	E	620	21,001	Marianna
Lincoln	SE	565	14,447	Star City
Little River	SW	544	9,211	Ashdown
Logan	W	727	15,957	Booneville and Paris
Lonoke	cen.	800	24,551	Lonoke
Madison	NW	832	9,068	Huntsville
Marion	N	628	6,041	Yellville
Miller	SW corner	627	31,686	Texarkana
Mississippi	NE	921	70,174	Blytheville and Osceola
Monroe	E	617	17,327	Clarendon
Montgomery	W	801	5,370	Mount Ida
Nevada	SW	616	10,700	Prescott
Newton	NW	822	5,963	Jasper
Ouachita	S	738	31,641	Camden
Perry	cen.	556	4,927	Perryville
Phillips	E	704	43,997	Helena
Pike	SW	615	7,864	Murfreesboro
Poinsett	NE	762	30,834	Harrisburg
Polk	W	860	11,981	Mena
Pope	NW cen	816	21,177	Russellville
Prairie	E cen.	674	10,515	Des Arc and De Valls Bluff
Pulaski	cen.	781	242,980	Little Rock
Randolph	NE	637	12,520	Pocahontas
Saint Francis	E	636	33,303	Forrest City
Saline	cen.	726	28,956	Benton
Scott	W	898	7,297	Waldron
Searcy	N	664	8,124	Marshall
Sebastian	W	529	66,685	Fort Smith and Greenwood
Sevier	SW	585	10,156	De Queen
Sharp	N	596	6,319	Evening Shade and Hardy
Stone	N	610	6,294	Mountain View
Union	S	1,052	49,518	El Dorado
Van Buren	N cen.	714	7,228	Clinton
Washington	NW	963	55,797	Fayetteville
White	NE cen.	1,042	32,745	Searcy
Woodruff	NE cen.	592	13,954	Augusta
Yell	W cen.	942	11,940	Danville and Dardanelle

[1] Area = land area in sq. m. Pop. from 1960 Census.
[2] City includes Hot Springs National Park, created 1921.

History: Visited by de Soto 1541, Marquette and Jolliet 1673, La Salle and de Tonti 1682; Arkansas Post first permanent settlement (1686); in region claimed by

ARKANSAS

Statute Miles

⊛ State Capital

PUBLISHED BY G. & C. MERRIAM COMPANY
SPRINGFIELD, MASS.
PREPARED BY J. W. CLEMENT CO. BUFFALO, N. Y.

France and yielded to Spain 1762; retroceded to France 1800; included in Louisiana Purchase 1803; parts of Louisiana and Missouri territories before becoming Arkansas Territory 1819; adopted first constitution 1836 and admitted to Union June 15 of same year; seceded 1861; capture of Arkansas Post from Confederates 1863; readmitted into Union 1868.

3 (*pron.* är′kăn·sô) County in Arkansas. See *Table* at ARKANSAS.

Arkansas City. 1 (*pron.* är′kăn-sô) Town, ⊗ of Desha co., SE Arkansas, on Mississippi river; pop. 783.

2 (*pron.* är·kăn′zăs) City, Cowley co., S Kansas, at confluence of Arkansas and Walnut rivers 47 m. S of Wichita; pop. 14,262; oil; flour mills, packing plants.

Ar·kan·sas Post (är′kăn·sô). Village and oldest white settlement (1686) in Arkansas and in lower Mississippi valley, on N bank of Arkansas river just above its junction with the Mississippi; established by Henry de Tonti, one of La Salle's expedition; colonized by John Law 1719; became part of Louisiana Territory 1763; capital of Arkansas Territory 1819–21; captured by Federals Jan. 12, 1863; declined after Civil War. Nearby is **Arkansas Post National Memorial**, 62 acres, created 1960.

Ar·khan′gelsk (ŭr·kän′gĕly'sk); *Eng.* **Arch′an′gel** (ärk′ān′jĕl). **1** Former province, N Russia in Europe.

2 City, ✳ of Arkhangelsk Region, Soviet Russia, on right bank of Northern Dvina near its mouth ab. 460 m. NE of Leningrad; pop. 281,091. At head of Dvina Gulf with very large harbor, closed by ice sometimes as much as 190 days in a year, but recently this handicap much reduced by icebreakers; has much river and canal traffic and is terminus of rail lines to Moscow and Leningrad; exports much timber, also some tar, skins, and flax. Has a monastery dedicated to the Archangel Michael, from which it received its name.

History: Vicinity settled by Northmen 10th cent. A.D.; harbor discovered by English trading expedition under Richard Chancellor who had been sent to discover Northeast Passage 1553; town began with establishment there of first factory (trading station) of Muscovy Co.; opened to trade of other European nations by Boris Godunov (1598–1605); flourished as sole Russian seaport until building of St. Petersburg (see LENINGRAD) 1703; a scene of Allied (British, French, and American) support of north Russian government which resisted Bolshevist government of Russia 1918–19; of great importance in World War II, receiving convoys of lend-lease goods from England and United States 1941–45.

Arkhangelsk Region. Region, N Soviet Russia, Europe, bordering on Barents Sea; 252,367 sq. m.; pop. 1,199,178; ✳ Arkhangelsk. Includes also two large island groups in the Arctic, Novaya Zemlya and Franz Josef Land. Its W coast extends along the White Sea and is broken by Dvina and Onega Bays. Chief rivers Northern Dvina, Onega, and lower course of Mezen. Climate is severe and coastal waters are frozen from late October for an average of 140 days. Chief towns Arkhangelsk, Onega, Molotovsk, Mezen, Kotlas.

Ark′low (ärk′lō). Market town and seaport, co. Wicklow, SE Eire, on E coast at mouth of Avoca river 37 m. S by SE of Dublin; pop. (urban district) 5193; oyster and herring fisheries; manufactures explosives; ancient castle of the Ormondes captured and demolished by Cromwell 1649; Irish insurgents defeated by British 1798.

Ar·ko′na (är·kō′nȧ). Promontory on N coast of Rügen I., Baltic Sea, 148 ft. above sea level; lighthouse (erected 1826); remains of foundation of ancient temple, destroyed 1168 by Danes and Pomeranians, found 1921.

Arl′berg (ärl′bûrg; *Ger.* -bĕrk). Alpine valley, pass, and tunnel in the Tirol, W Austria. In the valley the "Arlberg technique" in skiing was perfected. See ALPS.

Arles (ärl; *Angl.* ärlz, ärl). **1** Medieval kingdom, also called kingdom of Burgundy (*q.v.*), formed from union by Rudolf II in 933 of kingdoms of Cisjurane Burgundy and Transjurane Burgundy; attached to Holy Roman Empire under Emperor Conrad II 1033–34; kingdom had only nominal unity in 11th and 12th cents., although title King of Arles was assumed by German emperors, notably by Frederick Barbarossa 1178; gradually split up, Provence passing to house of Anjou 1246 and to French Crown 1481, and Dauphiné 1349, Franche-Comté 1678, and Savoy 1860 being annexed to France.

2 *anc.* **Ar′e·las** (ăr′ĕ·lăs) *or* **Ar′e·la′te** (ăr′ĕ·lā′tĕ). City, Bouches-du-Rhône dept., SE France, on left bank of Rhone 45 m. NW of Marseilles; pop. 29,165; connected with Mediterranean by canal; ancient Romanesque cathedral; ancient remains, including refurbished Roman amphitheater (Les Arènes), Roman burial place, and ruins of palace of Constantine.

History: Began to prosper as trading center after consul Marius had built canal connecting it with sea 103 B.C., and some of Caesar's legions had settled there; as outlet for commerce of Gaul, surpassed Massilia (see MARSEILLES) and became, next to Rome, most wealthy city of early Roman Empire; episcopal see from 1st cent. A.D.; residence of Emperor Constantine; seat of Council of Arles which decided Donatist controversy 314 A.D. and of several later ones 353, 452, 475; in 5th and 6th cents. captured by Visigoths, besieged by Franks, and taken by Ostrogoths; sacked by Saracens in 8th cent.; capital of kingdom of Arles 933–1246; besieged by Emperor Charles V 1526; archiepiscopal see suppressed by 1790.

Ar′leux′ (är′lû′). Commune, Nord dept., N France, 15 m. E of Arras; pop. (1931) 1724; battle Sept.–Oct. 1918 in advance of Canadians upon Cambrai.

Ar′leux′-en-Go·helle′ (är′lû′än·gwä′y'). Commune, Pas-de-Calais dept., N France, 7 m. NE of Arras; pop. (1931) 487; seized by Canadians Apr. 1917 in one of the battles around Arras.

Ar′ling·ton (är′lĭng·tŭn). **1** County in Virginia. See *Table* at VIRGINIA. Suburb of Washington, D.C., across Potomac river; officially, a county governed as a unit, without districts or other subdivisions and classified as urban with no incorporated place. Site of Arlington National Cemetery (on former estate of Robert E. Lee), containing memorial amphitheater (dedicated 1920) and Tomb of the Unknown Soldier; Pentagon Building, headquarters of U.S. Dept. of Defense; Fort Myer nearby. Alexandria located in county but independent of it.

2 Locality, Riverside co., SE California, SW part of city of Riverside; La Sierra College (1922; coed.).

3 Town, Middlesex co., NE Massachusetts, 6 m. NW of Boston; pop. 49,953; residential suburb of Boston.

4 Manufacturing and residential town, Hudson co., NE New Jersey, on Passaic river ab. 3 m. NNE of Newark; unincorporated, part of Kearny town.

5 Residential community (unincorporated), Dutchess co., New York, E of Poughkeepsie; pop. 8317.

6 City, Kingsbury co., E South Dakota; pop. 996.

7 City, Tarrant co., N Texas, 13 m. E of Fort Worth; pop. 44,775.

Arlington Heights. 1 Village, Cook co., NE Illinois, 25 m. NW of Chicago; pop. 27,878; racecourse.

2 Village, Hamilton co., SW Ohio; pop. 1355; N suburb of Cincinnati.

Ar′lon′ (är′lôN′); *anc.* **Or′o·lau′num** (ŏr′ô·lô′nŭm). Commune, ✳ of Luxembourg prov., SE Belgium, near border of grand duchy of Luxembourg; pop. 11,387; museum of Roman antiquities; wool factories, iron and pottery works, cattle and grain markets. Fortified 1671; occupied by French 1684–97; victories of Jourdan over Imperial forces 1793, 1794; Belgian since 1831. In World War II on edge of German advance Dec. 1944–Jan. 1945.

Ar′ma (är′mȧ). City, Crawford co., SE Kansas, 10 m. N of Pittsburg; pop. 1296.

Ar′ma·ged′don (är′mȧ·gĕd″'n). Greek form of Hebrew name of place, probably Megiddo (*q.v.*), where, according to *Revelation* xvi. 16, a great battle is to be fought.

Ar·magh′ (är·mä′). **1** County, S Northern Ireland; touches S shore of Lough Neagh; 489 sq. m.; pop.

114,226; ⊗ Armagh; other towns Portadown, Lurgan; agriculture (oats, apples, potatoes), livestock raising, quarrying (granite), important linen manufacture.
2 Urban district, its ⊗, 33 m. SW of Belfast; pop. 9279; religious center; seat of Roman Catholic and Protestant archbishops. According to tradition, founded by St. Patrick; seat of famous medieval school of theology; metropolis of Ireland and a leading intellectual center of the western world from 5th to 9th cents.

Ar·ma·gnac′ (är′mȧ·nyȧk′). Small territory in the old province of Gascony, SW France, now included in department of Gers; capitals successively Auch and Lectoure. Known particularly for viticulture, producing famous Armagnac brandy.
  History: Region near Auch (*q.v.*) part of Roman province of Aquitania; part of Gascon county of Fézensac (erected in 9th cent. until it became separate countship of Armagnac c. 960); under Count Gerald III annexed Fézensac 1140; in 15th cent. countship extended from the Garonne to the Adour; first annexed to French Crown 1497, but returned finally by descent through Navarre family 1607; countship granted 1645 by Louis XIV to Henry of Lorraine, Count of Harcourt, by whose family it was held until 1789.

Ar·ma·vir′ (ŭr·mŭ·vyēr′; *Angl.* är′mȧ·vēr′). City, Krasnodar Territory, S Soviet Russia, Europe, 100 m. E of Krasnodar, on Rostov-Baku railroad and NE of Maikop oil fields; pop. 83,677; founded 1848; center of fertile agricultural region. Reached by Germans in Caucasus advance Aug. 1942 and held until Dec. 1942.

Ar·me′ni·a (är·mē′nĭ·ȧ; -mēn′yȧ). **1** *Bib.* **Min′ni** (mĭn′ī). Ancient country in W Asia, now divided bet. the Soviet Union, Turkey, and Iran. It centered in the mountainous region (highest point Mt. Ararat) SE of Black Sea and SW of Caspian Sea; included sources of Euphrates and Araks rivers and lakes Van and Sevan.
  History: Equivalent to ancient kingdom of Van c. 1270–850 B.C. bet. Caucasus and Lake Van; residence of Vannic peoples, skilled in industrial arts and metallurgy; repeatedly attacked by Assyrians who called it Urartu (*q.v.*); conquered by Medes 612 B.C.; occupied by Armenian peoples and under kings of Media 612–549 B.C.; administered as a Persian satrapy 549–331 B.C.; under Alexander and successors 331–317 B.C.; following independence and division into two, reunited with Artaxata as capital by Tigranes (95–55 B.C.), most powerful ruler of Asia; after defeat by Lucullus 69 B.C., became subject to Rome; first to adopt Christianity as national religion 303 A.D.; persecution of Christians 4th–5th cents.; separated from Greek rite 491; changed hands frequently in wars bet. Neo-Persian and Roman Empires 3d–7th cents.; under caliphates, scene of strife bet. Arabs, Seljuks, Byzantines, and Mongols; ruled by Ottoman Turks from 1514; eastern part ceded to Persia 1639; its northern boundary contiguous with Russia 1802 after latter's occupation of Georgia; two districts ceded to Russia 1828, 1829; rise of Armenian nationalism among its scattered peoples 19th cent.; subject of "Armenian question" which plagued European powers after Ottoman Empire failed to carry out reforms first promised in Treaty of Berlin 1878; part ceded to Russia by Turkey by Treaty of San Stefano 1878; scene of a series of massacres which began 1893–94 and continued spasmodically throughout World War I; suffering aggravated as scene of Russo-Turkish hostility during war; after Turkish defeat, Russian part set up as Soviet republic 1921 (see ARMENIAN SOVIET SOCIALIST REPUBLIC); rest remained under Turkey (see Turkish ARMENIA).
  2 = ARMENIAN SOVIET SOCIALIST REPUBLIC.
  3 (*pron.* är·mä′nyä) City, Caldas dept., W cen. Colombia, W of Ibagué; pop. 29,673; in rich coffee district.
  4 (*pron.* är·mä′nyä) Town, Sonsonate dept., SW El Salvador, 25 m. W of San Salvador; pop. (1942 est.) 6568.
Armenia, Greater. Name sometimes given, esp. in medieval times, to region of Armenia.

Armenia, Lesser. See CILICIA.
Armenia, Turkish. The NE part of Turkey in Asia, comprising the whole or parts of 9 vilayets; ab. 57,000 sq. m.; pop. ab. 2,000,000; chief towns Kars, Erzurum, Erzincan. For history, see ARMENIA.
Armenia Mi′nor (mī′nēr). In Roman times, an E district of province of Pontus, bordering W Armenia.
Armenian Soviet Socialist Republic; *Armenian* **Ha′yas·dan′** (hä′yäs·tän′; -dän′). A constituent republic of the U.S.S.R., in S Transcaucasia; 11,580 sq. m.; pop. 1,281,599, (1941 est.) 1,346,709; ✳ Yerevan. One of the three republics of the former Transcaucasian Federation. Bounded on N by Georgia, on E by Azerbaidzhan, on S by Iran and Nakhichevan, and on W by Turkey. Mountainous, with many peaks above 10,000 ft.; highest Alagöz 13,435 ft. Contains Lake Sevan with its outlet the Zanga river, a tributary of the Araks which forms boundary with Turkish Armenia on SW. In Araks valley chief products raised are cotton, mulberry, fruits, rice, and tobacco; cattle raising and lumbering also important. Chief nationalities Armenian 84.7%, Turkic 8.2%. Set up as Soviet republic Apr. 2, 1921; joined Georgia and Azerbaidzhan Mar. 12, 1922 to form the Transcaucasian Federation which on Dec. 30, 1922 became part of the U.S.S.R.; on abolition of the Federation Dec. 5, 1936, became a constituent republic of U.S.S.R.
Ar′men′tières′ (àr′män′tyâr′; *Angl.* är′měn·tyâr′ *or, in a World War I song,* är′měn·tērz′). Commune, Nord dept., N France, 8 m. WNW of Lille; pop. 24,049; industrial center, producing table linen, cotton goods, hemp, lace. Near British front line in World War I; taken and destroyed by Germans April 10, 1918; retaken by British Oct. 1–2, 1918; rebuilt after the war.
Ar·me′ro (är·mā′rŏ). Town, Tolima dept., W cen. Colombia; pop. 6401.
Ar′mi·dale (är′mĭ·dāl). Town, NE New South Wales, SE Australia, 240 m. N of Sydney; pop. 6794.
Ar·mor′i·ca (är·mŏr′ĭ·kȧ), *older* **Ar′e·mor′i·ca** (är′ē·mŏr′ĭ·kȧ). Ancient name for region in NW France comprising the coast of Gaul bet. Seine and Loire rivers. Inhabited by Cymric Celts; with Caesar's subjugation of Veneti 56 B.C., came under Roman rule; organized as Roman province of Lugdunensis; extreme NW part invaded in 5th cent. A.D. by Britons (Celtic peoples from Britain) and thereafter called Brittany (*q.v.*); E part became Normandy.
Ar′mour (är′mēr). City, ⊗ of Douglas co., S South Dakota; pop. 875.
Arm′strong (ärm′strŏng). **1** Name of counties in two states of the U.S. See *Tables* at PENNSYLVANIA, TEXAS. **2** Former county in South Dakota; annexed to Dewey co. 1954.
Ar′na·u′ti, Cape (är′nä·ōō′tē). Western point of Cyprus, 32°15′E long.
Ar·nett′ (är·nět′). Town, ⊗ of Ellis co., NW Oklahoma; pop. 547.
Arn′hem (ärn′hěm). Commune, ✳ of Gelderland prov., E Netherlands, on right bank of Rhine near confluence with IJssel 33 m. ESE of Utrecht; pop. (1939) 90,495; surrounded by residential suburbs; home of the dukes of Gelderland 13th–16th cents.; formerly, member of the Hanseatic League; manufactures mathematical instruments and instruments for use in the physical sciences, also carriages, mirrors, paper; has town hall, Groote Kerk, museum of antiquities. Conquered 1473 by Charles the Bold; came under States-General 1585; taken by French 1672 and 1795 and by Prussians 1813. In World War II captured by Germans 1940; scene of heroic fight Sept. 17–25, 1944 by British 1st Airborne Division encircled by Germans in unsuccessful attempt to secure Rhine bridges, only about one quarter escaping; finally captured Apr. 13, 1945.
Arn′hem, Cape (är′něm). Point, NE Arnhemland, Australia, on NW coast of Gulf of Carpentaria.

Arn'hem·land' (är'nĕm·länd') *or* **Arnhem Land.**
Region on N coast of Northern Territory, Australia; discovered 1623 by expedition of Jan Carstensz.

Ar'no (är'nō). **1** *anc.* **Ar'nus** (är'nŭs). River ab. 140 m.
long in Tuscany, cen. Italy; rises in Monte Falterona,
flows W from the Apennines through Florence into
Ligurian Sea 7 m. below (W of) Pisa; navigable up to
Florence; near Arezzo connected with Tiber by its
canalized tributary, the Chiana; subject to sudden rises
and disastrous floods. In World War II reached by Allied armies in advance N from Rome June–Aug. 1944.
2 Island near S end of Ratak Chain, Marshall Is., N of
Mili; an atoll with 14 islets. Occupied by Allies Feb. 12,
1944.

Ar'nold (är'n'ld). **1** City, Westmoreland co., SW Pennsylvania, on Allegheny river 16 m. NE of Pittsburgh;
pop. 9437; manufactures window glass.
2 Urban district, Nottinghamshire, N cen. England, 5½
m. NE of Nottingham; pop. 21,474; lace, stocking, and
textile manufactures.

Ar'non (är'nŏn); *mod.* (*Arab.*) **Wa'di Mo'jib** *or* **Wa'di
el Mo'jib** (wă'dĭ [ăl] mō'jĭb; mou'-). River in W
Jordan, flowing W into Dead Sea; in ancient times
boundary (*Num.* xxi. 14) bet. Moab on S and country of
Amorites on N; later, boundary bet. Moab and Palestine.

Arn'öy' (är'nŭ'ü). Island in Arctic Ocean off N coast of
Norway, ab. 50 m. NE of Tromsö; pop. 905.

Arn'pri'or (ärn'prī'ēr). Town, Renfrew co., SE Ontario,
Canada, at confluence of Madawaska and Ottawa rivers
37 m. W of Ottawa; pop. 4381; industrial town.

Arns'berg (ärns'bĕrк). **1** Former government district,
Germany, in Westphalia prov., Prussia; 2967 sq. m.
2 City, its *, on Ruhr river 42 m. SSE of Münster; pop.
11,791; ancient capital of Westphalia; paper, resin products, beer and liquors. Founded 1077; received municipal charter 1237; joined Hanseatic League; became
Prussian 1815.

Arn'stadt (ärn'shtät). City, Thuringia, E Germany,
S of Erfurt; pop. 22,024; ancient capital of principality of Schwarzburg-Sondershausen; manufacturing and
agricultural center. First mentioned 704 A.D.; received
municipal rights 1266; bought by counts of Schwarzburg
1306 whose seat it was till 1716.

Arnswalde. See CHOSZCZNO.

Arnus. See ARNO.

Är'ö'. = ÆRÖ.

A'ro (ä'rō). River ab. 100 m. long, cen. Venezuela; flows
N into the Orinoco.

A'roe, *or* **A'ru, Islands** (ä'rōō); *also* **Ar'roe Islands.**
Group of one large and ab. 90 small islands off SW coast
of island of New Guinea, Amboina division, Malaku
prov., Indonesia; 3305 sq. m.; pop. 18,176. Chief
island Tanahbesar ab. 122 m. long by 58 m. wide, divided into six sections by narrow channels; chief town
Dobo on small island on W coast of Tanahbesar I. Islands are flat with swamps and dense forests; chief industry pearl fishing. Japanese air base in World War II.

A'rol·sen (ä'rôl·zĕn). Town, formerly * of Waldeck
principality, Germany, 21 m. WNW of Kassel; pop.
2811; contains a castle, art gallery, and valuable library.

Aromata. See Cape GUARDAFUI.

A·roos'took (å·rōōs'tŏŏk; å·rōōs'-; *locally also* -tĭk).
1 River 140 m. long, N Maine; rises in NE Piscataquis
co., flows NE across New Brunswick border and into St.
John river. This region was scene of "Aroostook War"
Feb.–May 1839, a clash bet. authority of Maine and
New Brunswick over territory near the river, a preliminary to determining the boundary of Maine in Webster-Ashburton Treaty 1842.
2 County in Maine. See *Table* at MAINE.

A'ro·roy' (ä'rō·roi'). Municipality, port on N coast of
Masbate I., Masbate prov., Phil. Is.; pop. 31,289.

Arpachiya. = TELL ARPACHIYA.

Ar·pi'no (är·pē'nō); *anc.* **Ar·pi'num** (är·pī'nŭm).
Commune, Frosinone prov., Latium, cen. Italy, 13 m. E

of Frosinone; pop. 10,564; textile, parchment, and paper
manufacturing; marble quarries. Ancient town of the
Volsci and, later, of the Samnites; conquered by Romans
305 B.C.; given Roman civic privileges 188 B.C. Birthplace of Marius, Cicero, and Marcus Vipsanius Agrippa.

Ar·quà' Pe·trar'ca (är·kwä' pã·trär'kä). Village ab. 15
m. SW of Padua, Venezia, NE Italy, on SE slope of
Euganean Hills; pop. 2487; Petrarch died here 1374.

Arques (ärk), *in full* **Arques'-la-Ba'taille'** (ärk'lä-bä'tä'y'). Village and castle, Seine-Inférieure dept.,
France, just S of Dieppe, Normandy; pop. 2500; scene
of battle Sept. 21, 1589 in which Henry IV defeated
forces of the Holy League under duc de Mayenne.

Arragon. Obsolete variant of ARAGON.

Ar'rah (är'rå). Town, * of Shahabad dist., W Bihar
state, NE Indian Union, 35 m. W of Patna; pop. (1941)
53,122; scene of courageous defense against overwhelming odds by small body of British troops during Sepoy
Mutiny 1857.

Ar'ran (är'ăn). Island, Bute co., in Firth of Clyde, off
SW coast of Scotland; 165 sq. m.; pop. 4506; harbors at
Brodick and Lamlash; prehistoric and Danish relics;
hide-out for Robert Bruce (King's Caves); seat of the
dukes of Hamilton (Brodick Castle).

Ar'ras (är'ăs; *Fr.* à'räs'); *anc.* **Nem'e·to·cen'na** (nĕm'-ĕ·tô·sĕn'å). City, * of Pas-de-Calais dept., N France,
25 m. SSW of Lille; pop. 31,448; episcopal see from 390;
famous cathedral, abbey of St. Vaast, and city hall
ruined by shells in World War I; manufacturing and
trading center; principal grain market in N France.

History: Principal town of the Atrebates (see ARTOIS);
destroyed by Attila 451 A.D. and by Northmen 800;
ruled by county of Flanders; noted as medieval center
for manufacture of tapestries; scene of two treaties:
(1) bet. Burgundians and Armagnacs 1435, and (2) terminating war bet. Maximilian I of Austria and Louis XI
of France 1482; ceded to France by latter treaty and its
name changed (temporarily) by Louis XI to **Fran'-chise'** (frän'shēz'); ceded to Maximilian of Austria 1493
and held by Spanish branch of Hapsburgs to 1640; gave
name to league of Catholic provinces of Netherlands
which were loyal to Spain 1579; taken by Louis XIII of
France 1640, and, as part of Artois, ceded to France
1659; scene of fierce battles 1914–18, during which city
almost completely razed by shellfire; largely rebuilt.
Captured by British Aug. 31, 1944.

Ar're·ci'fe *or* **Puer'to Ar're·ci'fe** (pwĕr'tô är'rĕ·thē'fä;
-sē'fä). Seaport, Las Palmas prov. (E Canary Is.),
Spain, on SE coast of Lanzarote I. 129 m. NE of Las
Palmas; pop. 7733.

Arretium. See AREZZO commune.

Arriaca. See GUADALAJARA, Spain.

Ar Rimal. See RUB' AL KHALI.

Arroe Islands. See AROE ISLANDS.

Ar'ro'manches' (à·rô'mänsh'). Coast village, Calvados
dept., N France, 5 m. NNE of Bayeux; pop. 288; site of
one of two portable harbor installations used by
Allies June 1944 in invasion of Normandy.

Ar'row, Lough (lŏк är'ō). Picturesque lake 4 m. long
by 2½ m. wide, SE co. Sligo, Ireland; its outlet flows ab.
12 m. NW into Owenboy river S of Sligo.

Arrow Lake. A widening of Columbia river in SE British
Columbia, Canada; 93 m. long; 163 sq. m.; often divided
into **Upper Arrow Lake** (to the N) 36 m. long, and
Lower Arrow Lake (to the S) 51 m. long.

Arrow Peak. Mountain 13,810 ft. in San Juan Mts., San
Juan co., SW Colorado.

Ar'row·rock' Dam *and* **Reservoir** (är'ô·rŏk'). See
UNITED STATES, *Dams and Reservoirs.*

Ar·ro'yo (är'rō'yō). Municipality (pop. 13,315) and
town (pop. 3741) on the coast, SE Puerto Rico.

Ar·ro'yos y Es·te'ros (är·rô'yòs ê äs·tā'rōs). Town,
Cordillera dept., cen. Paraguay; pop. ab. 13,450.

Arsanias. See MURAT SUYU.

Arsenaria. See ARZEU.

Ar·sie'ro (är·syȧ'rȯ). Commune, Vicenza prov., Venezia Euganea, NE Italy, 20 m. NNW of Vicenza; pop. 4258; marble quarries; burned by Austrians 1916.

Ar·sin'o·ë (är·sĭn'ō·ē). **1** Ancient town, one of the Pentapolis of Cyrenaica, on the coast NE of Berenice (*mod.* Bengasi).

2 *older* **Croc'o·di·lop'o·lis** (krŏk'ō·dĭ·lŏp'ō·lĭs). City of ancient Egypt, on Lake Moeris near the site of modern El Faiyûm; said to have been founded ab. 2300 B.C.; chief seat of early Egyptian worship of the crocodile; received its later name from sister and wife of Ptolemy II Philadelphus.

3 *later* **Cle'o·pat'ra** (klē'ō·păt'rȧ; -pā'trȧ; -pä'trȧ). City near head of Gulf of Suez.

Ar'ta (är'tȧ; *Mod. Gr.* -tä). **1** See ARAKHTHOS river.

2 Department of Greece. See *Table* at GREECE.

3 *anc.* **Am·bra'ci·a** (ăm·brā'shĭ·ȧ; -shä). City, its ✱, S Epirus, NW Greece, on Arakhthos river N of Ambracian Gulf; pop. 7468; episcopal see. Ambracia founded by Corinthians 7th cent. B.C.; became capital of Pyrrhus, king of Epirus, 295 B.C.; after its decline, new town of Arta founded on its site and became important fortification in Byzantine times; seat of despot of Epirus in 13th and 14th cents.; taken 1449 by Turks, by Ali Pasha 1798, by Reshid Pasha 1822; to Greece 1881.

Arta, Gulf of. See AMBRACIAN GULF.

'Ar·ta·wi'ya (ŭr·tä·wĭ'yȧ; -yȧ). Town, N Arabia, in NE Nejd on highway from Buraida to Al Kuwait; pop. ab. 10,000; founded since 1912 as first Ikhwan colony in Wahabi revival.

Ar·tax'a·ta (är·tăk'sȧ·tȧ). Ruined city, ancient ✱ of Armenia, on left bank of Araks river near village of Kamarlyu 17 m. S of Yerevan, Armenian S.S.R.; destroyed 58 A.D. by Roman general Corbulo.

Ar·tei'jo (är·tĕ'ē·hȯ). Commune, La Coruña prov., Spain, 6 m. SW of La Coruña; pop. 9905.

Artemidorus. See TRIESTE.

Ar·te·mi'sa (är'tȧ·mē'sä). Municipality and town, E Pinar del Río prov., W Cuba; pop. (town) 13,084.

Ar·te·mi'si·um (är'tĕ·mĭzh'ĭ·ŭm; -mĭz'-; -mĭsh'ĭ-); *Gr.* **Ar·te·mí'si·on** (-ŏn). Promontory forming NE point of Greek island of Euboea, Aegean Sea; scene of naval victory of the Greeks over the Persians 480 B.C.

Ar'te·mon' (är'tȧ·mŏn'; *Angl.* är'tĕ·mŏn). See SIPHNOS.

Ar·te'movsk (ŭr·tyĕ'mȯfsk). **1** Town, S Krasnoyarsk Territory, Soviet Russia, Asia; terminus of branch railroad 85 m. NE of Minusinsk; in rich mining region.

2 *formerly* **Bakh'mut** (bȧk'mo͞ot). City, N Stalino Region, E Ukraine, U.S.S.R., 45 m. N of Stalino in the Donets Basin; pop. 55,165; industrial town and railroad junction; extensive salt mines; coal and quicksilver.

Ar·te'sia (är·tē'zhȧ). **1** City, Los Angeles co., California, NE of Long Beach; pop. 9993.

2 City, Eddy co., SE New Mexico, W of Pecos river 38 m. S of Roswell; pop. 12,000; refines oil.

Ar·te'sian Basin (är·tē'zhȧn). Region of E cen. Australia, chiefly in S Queensland, where great quantities of water exist deep below the ground; crossed by the Barcoo and upper tributaries of the Darling.

Artesium. See ARTOIS.

Ar'tha·bas'ka (är'thȧ·băs'kȧ). **1** County, Quebec, Canada. See *Table* at QUEBEC.

2 Town, its ⊗, S Quebec, 38 m. SE of Three Rivers; pop. 2321.

Ar'thing·ton (är'thĭng·tŭn). Town, W Liberia W Africa, 30 m. NNE of Monrovia.

Ar'thur (är'thẽr). **1** County in Nebraska. See *Table* at NEBRASKA.

2 Village, its ⊗, W Nebraska; pop. 165.

3 River ab. 60 m. long, NW Tasmania, Australia; rises in NW part of central highland and flows WNW to Indian Ocean S of Cape Grim.

Arthur Kill (kĭl). Channel, NE New Jersey, bet. New Jersey and Staten I., New York; connects Newark Bay with Raritan Bay.

Arthur Peak. 1 Mountain 10,426 ft. on E boundary of Yellowstone National Park, NW Wyoming.

2 Peak 8800 ft. in N South I., New Zealand.

Ar'thur's Pass (är'thẽrz). Mountain pass through Otira Gorge in Southern Alps, cen. South I., New Zealand.

Arthur's Seat. Hill 823 ft. in Edinburgh, Scotland, overlooking SE section of city; from it King Arthur is said to have watched the defeat of the Picts by his army.

Ar'ti·bo'nite' (är'tē'bȯ'nēt'). River, Haiti, flowing W into Gulf of Gonaïves.

Ar·ti'gas (är·tē'gäs). **1** Department of Uruguay. See *Table* at URUGUAY.

2 *or* **San Eu·ge'nio** (sän ä·o͞o·hā'nyȯ); *also* **San Eugenio del Cua·reim'** (thĕl kwä·rĕ'ĕn). Town, its ✱, NW Uruguay, near Brazil border on W bank of Cuareim river ab. 304 m. N of Montevideo; pop. ab. 16,500.

3 Town, Cerro Largo dept., E Uruguay; pop. 16,500.

Ar'tois' (är'twä'); *Lat.* **Ar·te'si·um** (är·tē'zhĭ·ŭm; -zhŭm; -zĭ·ŭm); *Flemish* **A'trecht** (ä'trĕxt). Historical region of N France; bounded on N by the Strait of Dover, E by Flanders, S and W by Picardy; ✱ Arras.

History: Western part of county of Flanders, given as dowry to Isabella of Hainaut on her marriage to Philip Augustus 1180; inherited by Louis VIII who made it part of royal domain 1222; returned to count of Flanders 1382; passed to dukes of Burgundy who held it 1384–1477; with marriage 1477 of Mary of Burgundy to Hapsburg Maximilian I, passed to Austria, ultimately to Philip IV of Spain 1640; France received final sovereignty over it by Treaties of the Pyrenees 1659 and of Nijmegen 1678; scene of three battles of World War I, Sept. 27–Oct. 10, 1914, May 9–June 18, 1915, and Sept. 25–Oct. 15, 1915.

Art·vin' (ärt·vēn'). Town, Çoruh vilayet, NE Turkey in Asia, SE of Batum; pop. 3460.

A·ru'ba (ä·ro͞o'bä). Dutch island off coast of NW Venezuela; 19 m. long by ab. 5 m. wide; 69 sq. m.; pop. (1942) 33,853; chief town Oranjestad. Administratively part of Curaçao colony ab. 55 m. W of Curaçao; barren; no oil deposits, but has huge refineries where oil from Venezuela is processed. In World War II the refineries were shelled by German submarines Feb. and Apr. 1942 and some damage done. See CURAÇAO.

A·ru'cas (ä·ro͞o'käs). Commune, Las Palmas prov. (E Canary Is.), Spain, on Grand Canary I. 6 m. W of Las Palmas; pop. 21,804; sugar cane.

Aru Islands. See AROE ISLANDS.

Ar'un (är'ŭn). River ab. 40 m. long, Sussex, S England, flowing S into the English Channel at Littlehampton.

Ar'un·del (är'ŭn·d'l; *locally, in Sussex,* ärn'd'l). **1** Municipal borough, West Sussex, England, on Arun river 5 m. from its mouth; pop. 2680; formerly a flourishing seaport connected 1813 by canal with London; now small market town, exporting corn, bark, and timber; site of Arundel Castle, seat of dukes of Norfolk.

2 Small island of the New Georgia Is., cen. Solomon Is., off NW tip of New Georgia and at SW end of Kula Gulf. Occupied by U.S. forces Aug. 1943.

A·run'ta Desert (ȧ·rŭn'tȧ). Large desert area ab. 400 m. N to S in SE Northern Territory, Australia.

A·ru'sha (ȧ·ro͞o'shȧ). Town, ✱ of Northern Province, N Tanganyika, E Africa, 45 m. SW of Mt. Kilimanjaro; pop. ab. 2000.

A'ru·tang'a (ä'ro͞o·täng'ä). Chief village of Aitutaki, Cook Is., S Pacific Ocean; on W coast.

A'ru·wi'mi (ä'ro͞o·wē'mē). River ab. 800 m. long, cen. Africa; rises in NE Congo near Lake Albert, flows SW and W across N Congo into Congo river; called the Ituri in its upper course.

Árva. See ORAVA.

Ar·vad'a (är·văd'ȧ; -vä'dȧ). Town, Jefferson co., Colorado, W of Denver; pop. 19,242.

Ar·vi'da (är·vī'dȧ; *Fr.* är'vē'dä'). City, Chicoutimi co., S Quebec, Canada, 5 m. W of Chicoutimi on the Saguenay; pop. 11,078; important aluminum plant.

Ar′vi′ka (är′vē′kà). Town, Värmland co., W Sweden, ab. 30 m. NW of Lake Vänern; pop. 14,477.

Ar·wad′ (ŭr·wäd′); *Fr.* **Île Rou·ad′** (ēl′ rwäd′); *Bib.* **Ar′vad** (är′văd); *anc.* **Ar′a·dus** (är′á·dŭs). Island ab. 2 m. off the coast of S Latakia, Syria, near Tartus; seaport of ancient Phoenicia (*Ezek.* xxvii. 8) and a flourishing city during Phoenician ascendancy (see TRIPOLI, Lebanon). In World War I first point on Syrian coast occupied by French; made postal station 1916; at end of war became part of French mandate of Latakia.

Ar·za·mas′ (ŭr·zŭ·más′). Town, S Gorki Region, Soviet Russia, Europe, ab. 60 m. S of Gorki; pop. 18,538; a junction point on railroad bet. Moscow and Kazan.

Ar·za′no (är·dzä′nô). Commune, Napoli prov., Campania, S Italy, 3 m. N of Naples; pop. 10,819.

Ar·zeu′ *or* **Ar·zew′** (ŭr·zä′ōō); *anc.* **Ar′se·nar′i·a** (är′-sĕ·när′ĭ·à). Seaport, Oran dept., NW Algeria, N Africa, 22 m. NE of Oran near Cape Ferrat; pop. 7289. One of the landing places of American army Nov. 8, 1942.

Ar′zi·gna′no (är′dzē·nyä′nô). Commune, Vicenza prov., Venezia Euganea, NE Italy, 10 m. W of Vicenza; pop. 13,382.

Ar·zi′la *or* **Ar·ci′la** (är·thē′lä; är·sē′-). Seaport on Atlantic Ocean, NE Morocco, ab. 60 m. S of Tangier; pop. (1936) 6158.
6158.

Aš (äsh); *Ger.* **Asch** (äsh). Town, W Bohemia province, W Czechoslovakia; pop. 22,943; textile mills. One of the first towns occupied by Germans in their seizure of Sudetenland Oct. 1938.

A′sa·han′ (ä′sä·hän′). River ab. 75 m. long, N Sumatra, Indonesia; outlet of Lake Toba flowing ENE into cen. Strait of Malacca.

A·sa·hi Da·ke (ä·sä·hĕ dä·kĕ); *formerly* **I·shi·ka·ri Dake** (ē·shē·kä·rĕ). Mountain 7513 ft., cen. Hokkaido I., Japan.

A·sa·hi·ka·wa (ä·sä·hĕ·kä·wä) *or* **A·sa·hi·ga·wa** (-gä·wä). City, cen. Hokkaido I., Japan, in Hokkaido prefecture; pop. 89,629; in rice-growing area.

A·sa·ma (ä·sä·mä) *or* **A·sa·ma·ya·ma** (ä·sä·mä·yä·mä). Active volcano 8340 ft. on W border of Gumma prefecture, cen. Honshu, Japan, 85 m. NW of Tokyo; one of the largest active volcanoes in Japan; had disastrous explosion 1783.

A′san·sol′ (ä′sän·sōl′). City, Burdwan division, West Bengal, NE Indian Union, 120 m. NW of Calcutta; pop. (1941) 55,797; coal-mining center and rail junction.

Asben. See AIR.

As·bes′tos (ăz·bĕs′tŏs; ăs-). Town, Richmond co., S Quebec, Canada, 26 m. N of Sherbrooke; pop. 8190; site of asbestos mines.

As′bur′y Park (ăz′bĕr′ĭ; -bēr·ĭ). City and summer resort, Monmouth co., E cen. New Jersey, on Atlantic Ocean 24 m. SSE of Perth Amboy; pop. 17,366; orig. developed as summering place chiefly for temperance advocates 1870; became city 1897; oceanside auditorium, convention hall, pier, and boardwalk; summer theater center.

Ascalon. See ASHKELON.

Ascania. See ĪZNĪK LAKE.

As·cen′sion (ä·sĕn′shŭn). **1** Parish in Louisiana. See *Table* at LOUISIANA.
2 British island in S Atlantic Ocean, 9 m. long by 6 m. wide, 7°55′S lat. and 14°25′W long., 750 m. NW of St. Helena; 34 sq. m.; pop. (1940) 169; for 100 years a naval station and garrison of the British Admiralty; since 1922 administratively a part of British colony of St. Helena; only settlement Georgetown. Of volcanic origin, its extinct crater (Green Mt.) 2817 ft.; has little vegetation and scant rainfall but is remarkably healthful; has great numbers of sea turtle, rabbits, wild goats, and sooty tern. Discovered by Portuguese navigator João da Nova on Ascension Day 1501; visited by Dampier 1701. In World War II airfield built by American engineers Apr. 28–July 10, 1942, used as refueling base in transatlantic flights to S Europe, North Africa, and Near East.
3 See PONAPE, Caroline Is.

Asch. See AŠ.

A·schaf′fen·burg (ä·shäf′ĕn·bŏŏrK). City, Lower Franconia govt. dist., Bavaria, Germany, on right bank of Main river 21 m. ESE of Frankfurt am Main; pop. 34,056; manufactures colored paper, clothing, beer and liquors, electrical apparatus, leather, chemicals. Castle built on site of Roman castrum; scene of imperial diet 1447 which produced the Aschaffenburg Concordat; taken several times in Thirty Years' War; part of grand duchy of Frankfurt 1806; ceded with Lower Franconia to Bavaria 1814; taken by U.S. forces Apr. 1945.

A′schers·le′ben (äsh′ĕrs·lā′bĕn). City, E Germany, in the former Prussian province of Saxony, 26 m. SSW of Magdeburg; pop. 28,627; walled city, entered by five gates; potash, coal, and salt mining, manufacture of beet sugar, woolens, paper, chemicals, machinery; nearby is the Wilhelmsbad spa. Founded probably in 11th cent. by Count Esico, ancestor of house of Anhalt; under episcopal see of Halberstadt 1315 and of Brandenburg 1648; to Prussia 1813.

A′sco·li Pi·ce′no (äs′kô·lē pē·chä′nô). **1** Province of Italy. See *Table* at ITALY.
2 *Lat.* **As′cu·lum Pi·ce′num** (äs′kŭ·lŭm pī·sē′nŭm). Commune, its ✻, Marches, cen. Italy, 87 m. NE of Rome; pop. 38,111; episcopal see; Roman and medieval remains, including bridges still in use; manufactures woolens, glass, majolica ware, silks, leather, hats, wax, etc.; in rich agricultural area. One of most ancient cities of Italy; capital of ancient Picenum; taken 268 B.C. by Rome; all Roman citizens within its walls massacred 90 B.C. during Social War; recaptured by Rome 89 B.C.; occupied by Caesar, after crossing the Rubicon 49 B.C.; taken by Totila 545 A.D.; ruled by bishops from 8th cent., became free republic in 12th cent., and joined papal possessions in 15th cent.

Ascoli Sa·tria′no (sä·tryä′nô); *anc.* **Aus′cu·lum Ap′u·lum** (ôs′kŭ·lŭm ăp′û·lŭm) *or* **As′cu·lum** (äs′-kŭ·lŭm). Commune, Foggia prov., Apulia, SE Italy, on E slope of Apennines 18 m. S of Foggia; pop. 8421; episcopal see; site of Roman defeat by Pyrrhus, king of Epirus, 279 B.C. when Pyrrhus lost a large part of his army.

As′cot (äs′kŭt). Village, Berkshire, England, 6 m. SSW of New Windsor, 29 m. SW of London by rail; fashionable two-mile race track (at **Ascot Heath**) established 1711 by Queen Anne.

Asculum. See ASCOLI SATRIANO, ASCOLI PICENO.

As·cut′ney, Mount (ăs·kŭt′nĭ). Peak 3320 ft., SE Windsor co., E Vermont.

A·se′nov·grad′ (ä·sĕ′nŭf·gräd′); *before 1934* **Sta′ni·ma′ka** (stä′nĭ·mä′kä). Town, S Bulgaria, 10 m. SE of Plovdiv; pop. (1934) 17,773.

A·shan′ti (á·shän′tĭ; äsh′ăn·tē′). Region, cen. Ghana; 24,379 sq. m.; pop. 578,078; ✻ Kumasi. Bounded on N by the Northern Region, on E by Volta Region, on S by Western and Eastern Regions, and on W by Ivory Coast. Largely a forest region with plains in NE.
History: Originally a Negro kingdom with capital at Kumasi (*q.v.*); expanded towards Gold Coast and came into conflict with British from early 19th cent.; waged four wars with British, 1824–27, 1873–74, 1893–94, 1895–96; claimed as British protectorate 1894; after capture of Kumasi by Sir Francis Scott 1896 again declared protectorate; rose against British 1900 and besieged Kumasi but repressed; annexed to British Gold Coast Colony 1901; administration reorganized 1934; became a region of the new nation Ghana 1957.

Ash′bourne (äsh′bôrn; -bûrn). Urban district, Derbyshire, England, on a branch of the Dove 11 m. NW of Derby; pop. 5440; cotton and lace manufacturing; iron and copper foundries; site of a defeat of Charles I by Parliamentary party 1644.

Ash′burn (äsh′bĕrn). City, ⊗ of Turner co., S Georgia, 30 m. ENE of Albany; pop. 3291.

Ash'burn·ham (ăsh'bĕrn·hăm). Town, Worcester co., cen. Massachusetts, 7 m. WNW of Fitchburg; pop. 2758; manufactures chairs.

Ash'bur'ton (ăsh'bûr't'n; -bēr·t'n). **1** River ab. 500 m. long, NW Western Australia; flows NW to Indian Ocean near Exmouth Gulf.
2 Urban district, Devonshire, England, 19 m. NE of Plymouth; pop. 2704; market town; manufactures serge, paints; stannaries, breweries, corn mills; lumber; slate, copper, and tin deposits; 15th-cent. church.
3 River ab. 60 m. long, E cen. South I., New Zealand; flows SE into Canterbury Bight.
4 Borough, Canterbury provincial dist., E South I., New Zealand, on Ashburton river near its mouth 50 m. SW of Christchurch; pop. (1941 est.) 7130; in fertile wheat and grain section.

Ash'by de la Zouch (ăsh'bĭ dĕ lä zōōsh'; dĕl'à zōōsh'). Urban district, Leicestershire, England, 15 m. NW of Leicester; pop. 6406; castle, known through Scott's *Ivanhoe* and as prison for Mary, Queen of Scots (1569, 1586), lies S of town; fine late-Perpendicular church; known formerly for manufacture of stockings, woolens, hats, and firebrick, and for its horse markets.

Ash'dod (ăsh'dŏd); *anc. Gr.* **A·zo'tos** (à·zō'tŏs); *Lat.* **A·zo'tus** (à·zō'tŭs). City of ancient Philistia, Palestine, on the coast ab. 18 m. S of Joppa; one of five Philistine city-kingdoms and a center of worship of Dagon (*1 Sam.* v). Besieged for 29 years by Psamtik I of Egypt. The modern village of **Is·dud'** or **Es·dud'** (ĭs·dōōd'), SW Palestine, is on railroad and highway about equally distant from Joppa and Gaza; pop. 3140.

Ash'down (ăsh'doun). City, ⊗ of Little River co., SW Arkansas, 18 m. NNW of Texarkana; pop. 2725.

Ashe (ăsh). County in North Carolina. See *Table* at NORTH CAROLINA.

Ashe'bor'o (ăsh'bûr'ō). Industrial town, ⊗ of Randolph co., cen. North Carolina, 25 m. S of Greensboro; pop. 9449; hosiery, chemicals, lumber, furniture.

Ashe'er·ton (ăsh'ēr·t'n; -tŭn). City, Dimmit co., S Texas, 51 m. S of Uvalde; pop. 1890.

Ashe'ville (ăsh'vĭl). City, ⊗ of Buncombe co., W North Carolina, near E entrance to Great Smoky Mountains National Park; pop. 60,192; health and tourist resort, altitude 2216 ft.; manufactures rayon, blankets, lumber products, hosiery, furniture; dairy, poultry, tobacco, and fruit farms; feldspar, copper, and mica mines. Founded 1794; incorp. 1797; chartered as city 1835.

Ash'field (ăsh'fēld). City, E New South Wales, SE Australia, SW suburb of Sydney; pop. 39,357.

Ash'ford (ăsh'fērd). Urban district, Kent, SE England, on Stour river 20 m. W of Dover; pop. 24,777; rai'road junction; manufactures linen, damask, and agricultural implements; iron foundries; marble quarries; breweries.

A·shi·ka·ga (ä·shē·kä·gä). Commercial city, cen. Honshu, Japan, in Tochigi prefecture 50 m. N of Tokyo; pop. (1950) 52,810; center of weaving industry, probably established several centuries ago; cultural city with celebrated school. As the ancestral home of Ashikaga shoguns, gave its name to a Japanese dynasty (1338–1568).

Ash'ing·ton (ăsh'ĭng·tŭn). Urban district, Northumberland, N England, 13 m. N of Newcastle; pop. 28,723; collieries.

A·shi·o (ä·shē·ō). Commercial city, cen. Honshu, Japan, in Tochigi prefecture near Nikko and ab. 65 m. N of Tokyo; pop. 20,997; copper mines.

A·shi·zu·ri, Cape (ä·shē·zōō·rē); *formerly* **Cape Sa·da** (sä·dä). Cape, W extremity of Shikoku I., Japan, at N end of Bungo Strait, 33°21′N.

Ash'ke·lon (ăsh'kĕ·lŏn) or **As'ca·lon** (ăs'kà·lŏn). Seaport village on coast of Palestine, now ruins near El Majdal, a seat of Philistine worship of Atargatis.
History: Captured by Egyptians under Ramses II 1285 B.C.; one of five city-kingdoms of Philistines who occupied it c. 1200–900 B.C.; conquered by successive ancient empires (see PALESTINE) but never by Israelites

and Jews; conquered by Arabs 636 A.D.; scene of victory of Crusaders under Godfrey of Bouillon and Tancred over sultan of Egypt 1099; captured by Baldwin III 1153; retaken by Saladin 1187 and demolished 1191; finally destroyed by Sultan Baybars I 1270.

Ashkh'a·bad (*Angl.* ăsh'kà·băd; *Pers.* åsh'ĸä·bäd'; *Russ.* ŭs·ĸŭ·båt'); *formerly* **Pol·to·ratsk'** (pŭl·tŭ·råtsk'). City, ✱ of Turkmen S.S.R., in S part on Iran border, Soviet Russia, Asia; pop. 126,580; situated in fertile oasis, well built; established 1883.

Ash'land (ăsh'lănd). **1** Name of counties in two states of the U.S. See *Tables* at OHIO and WISCONSIN.
2 Town, ⊗ of Clay co., E Alabama; pop. 1610.
3 City, ⊗ of Clark co., S Kansas; pop. 1312.
4 Industrial city, Boyd co., NE Kentucky, on Ohio river; pop. 31,283; coal, iron, petroleum, and clay deposits nearby; steel and iron mills, sawmills, brickyards.
5 Town, Aroostook co., N Maine, on Aroostook river 20 m. W of Presque Isle; pop. 1980; shipping center for potatoes and lumber.
6 Town, Middlesex co., NE Massachusetts, 20 m. E of Worcester; pop. 7779.
7 Village, ⊗ of Benton co., N Mississippi; pop. 309.
8 City, Saunders co., E Nebraska; pop. 1989.
9 City, ⊗ of Ashland co., N cen. Ohio, in agricultural section 13 m. NE of Mansfield; pop. 17,419; platted 1815, became city 1844, ⊗ 1846; manufactures pumps, hay tools, rubber goods, automobile parts, medicines. Ashland College (1878; coed.).
10 City, Jackson co., SW Oregon, in farming area 8 m. SSE of Medford; pop. 9119; gold mines, marble and granite quarries nearby; mineral springs (lithia water). Southern Oregon College of Education (1926).
11 Borough, Schuylkill and Columbia cos., E cen. Pennsylvania, 11 m. NE of Pottsville; pop. 5237; platted 1847; coal mining, farming; manufactures mine pumps, knit goods.
12 Town, Hanover co., E cen. Virginia, 16 m. N of Richmond; pop. 2773; began as health resort 1848. Randolph-Macon Coll. (1830; men; moved from Boydton 1868).
13 City and port of entry, ⊗ of Ashland co., N Wisconsin, on Lake Superior 58 m. E of Superior; pop. 10,132; shipping port for iron ore, lumber, black granite, farm products; harbor; airport. Northland Coll. (1892; coed.).

Ashland City. Town, ⊗ of Cheatham co., NW cen. Tennessee; pop. 1400.

Ash'ley (ăsh'lĭ). **1** River ab. 40 m. long, SE South Carolina; rises in Berkeley co. and flows SE into Charleston harbor where it joins the Cooper river.
2 County in Arkansas. See *Table* at ARKANSAS.
3 City, ⊗ of McIntosh co., S North Dakota; pop. 1419.
4 Borough, Luzerne co., E Pennsylvania, 3 m. SW of Wilkes-Barre; pop. 4258; settled 1810; coal mines.

Ash·mûn' (ăsh·mōōn'). Town, Minûfîya prov., Lower Egypt, on railroad in Nile delta 25 m. NW of Cairo.

Ashmûnein, El. See EL ASHMÛNEIN.

A·sho'kan Dam (à·shō'kăn; ăsh'ō·kăn) or **Ol'ive Bridge Dam** (ŏl'ĭv). Dam completed 1912 across Esopus Creek, N Ulster co., SE New York; height 252 ft.; forms **Ashokan Reservoir**, 12 m. long, ab. 13 sq. m., estimated capacity 130 billion gallons, which supplies water for New York City.

Ash'ta·bu'la (ăsh'tà·bū'là). **1** County in Ohio. See *Table* at OHIO.
2 City, Ashtabula co., NE Ohio, on Lake Erie 50 m. ENE of Cleveland; pop. 24,559; settled c. 1801, incorp. 1831, chartered as city 1892; key terminus on Underground Railroad; industrial, commercial, and shipping center; farm implements, foundry castings, hydraulic presses, etc.; tanneries, metalworks, shipyards.

Ash'ta·roth (ăsh'tà·rŏth). Ancient city of Bashan, in the Decapolis region, SW Syria, ab. 32°50′N lat. and 36°E long.; a seat of worship of Astarte. Now ruins at a village 21 m. E of Sea of Galilee.

Ash'ton, *officially* **Ash'ton un'der Lyne** (ăsh'tŭn ŭn'dĕr lin'). Municipal borough, Lancashire, NW England, on Tame river 6 m. E of Manchester; pop. (1951) 46,490; coal mines, textile mills, hat factories.

Ashton in Ma'ker·field (ĭn mā'kĕr·fēld). Urban district, Lancashire, England, 15 m. W of Manchester; pop. 19,053; extensive collieries; manufactures iron goods, cotton goods, pottery.

Ash'ua·nip'i (ăsh'wȧ·nĭp'ĭ). Lake 319 sq. m., SW Labrador, Newfoundland; source of the Hamilton river (*q.v.*), called **Ashuanipi River** in its upper course.

Ashuapmuchuan. See CHAMOUCHOUANE.

Ash·ue'lot (ăsh·wĭl'ŭt; ăsh'ū̇·wĭl'ŭt). River 75 m. long, SW New Hampshire; rises in SE Sullivan co., flows SW into Connecticut river near Massachusetts border; provides power at Keene and other towns in its course.

A'shur (ä'shŏŏr; ăsh'ẽr). **1** See ASSYRIA.
2 Ancient Sumerian settlement; now the village of Sharqat (*q.v.*) on Tigris river S of Mosul.

'Asi, Nahr el. See ORONTES.

A'sia (ā'zhȧ; ā'shȧ). **1** Largest continent on the globe; ab. 16,500,000 sq. m. (not including the Phil. Is. and Indonesia); pop. ab. 1,164,000,000.

Boundaries: On N, Arctic Ocean (chief subdivisions Kara Sea, Laptev Sea, and East Siberian Sea); most northerly point Cape Chelyuskin 77°35′N; chief islands Severnaya Zemlya, New Siberian Is., and Wrangel I. On E, Pacific Ocean (chief subdivisions Bering Sea, Sea of Okhotsk, Sea of Japan, Yellow Sea, East China Sea, and South China Sea; marked by peninsulas of Kamchatka and Korea and by Malay Peninsula; most easterly point East Cape 170°W; chief islands Sakhalin, Japan (4 large islands), Formosa. On S, Indian Ocean (chief subdivisions Bay of Bengal, Arabian Sea, Persian Gulf, and Gulf of Aden); most southerly point Singapore 1°14′N; chief island Ceylon. On W, Red Sea. Isthmus of Suez, Mediterranean Sea, Aegean Sea, and Black Sea, Caucasus Mts., NW Caspian Sea, steppe lands of W Kazakh S.S.R. (E of Volga river) and Ural Mts., the latter having long been conventional boundary bet. Europe and Asia but under the U.S.S.R. the Asiatic portion of R.S.F.S.R. has a region (Molotov Region) W of the range; most westerly point Cape Baba, NW Turkey, 26°10′E; chief island Cyprus. *Mountains, etc.:* The Himalayas in S containing highest peak in the world Mt. Everest 29,002 ft., with branches of Hindu Kush to W, Pamir and Tien Shan to NW, and on the N the great plateau of Tibet (average height above 10,000 ft.) with Kunlun Mts. on N side; Altai Mts. in W Mongolia, Great Khingan Mts. in Manchuria, and Verkhoyansk, Stanovoi, Cherskogo, and Kolyma ranges in E Siberia; many high volcanic peaks in Kamchatka and Japan; in SW the Elburz Mts. of N Iran (highest 18,600 ft.) and the ranges of W and NW Iran. Other notable physical features are Gobi Desert of Mongolia, Takla Makan Desert of Sinkiang, the Deccan plateau of S India, the Plateau of Iran, the great deserts of Syria and Arabia, and the Kirgiz Steppe of SW Soviet Russia. *Rivers:* Ob, Yenisei, Lena in the N, Amur in NE, Hwang Ho, Yangtze, and Si in the E (the three great rivers of China), Mekong, Salween, and Irrawaddy in SE, Brahmaputra, Ganges, and Indus in S (in Tibet and India), Euphrates and Tigris in SW (in Turkey and Iraq), and Ural in W. *Lakes:* Caspian Sea (inland sea) and Lake Aral in SW, Baikal in N, Balkhash in W cen. part, the smaller lakes of Tungting Hu and Poyang Hu in China, and many other comparatively large lakes in Turkey, Iran, Tibet, China, and Mongolia.

Political divisions: Afghanistan, Bhutan, Brunei, Burma, Cambodia, Ceylon, China, Cyprus, India, Indonesia, Iran, Iraq, Israel, Japan, Jordan, Korea, Kuwait, Laos, Lebanon, Malaysia, Maldive Islands, Mongolia, Muscat and Oman, Nepal, Pakistan, Persian Gulf States, Philippines, Saudi Arabia, South Yemen, Syria, Thailand, Tibet, Turkey (part), Union of Soviet Socialist Republics (part), United Arab Republic (part), Vietnam, and Yemen.

2 A Roman province, W part of Asia Minor; ✳ Pergamum, and later Ephesus; formed 133 B.C. out of the kingdom of Pergamum and included Mysia, Lydia, Caria, Phrygia, and smaller districts; reorganized by Sulla 84 B.C.; made a senatorial province 27 B.C.; broken up by Diocletian and under Byzantine Empire known for a time as Asiana.

A'sia·go (ä'zyä·gô). Commune, Vicenza prov., Venezia Euganea, NE Italy, on plateau at foot of the Dolomites 24 m. N of Vicenza; pop. 6318; chief town of the Altipiano dei Sette Comuni (see SETTE COMUNI); makes straw hats. Scene of famous battle with Austrians 1916.

Asia Islands. Group of three small islands, Neth. Indies, ab. 130 m. NW of the Vogelkop Penin., NW New Guinea; usually uninhabited, but occasionally visited by natives from the S to catch turtles. In World War II a Japanese observation post; captured by U.S. forces Nov. 20, 1944.

Asia Mi'nor (mī'nẽr) *or* **An'a·to'li·a** (ăn'ȧ·tō'lĭ·ȧ; -tōl'yȧ). The peninsula forming W extremity of Asia, bet. Black Sea on N and Mediterranean Sea on S and bordering on Aegean Sea on W; forms the greater part of Turkey.

History: Original location of kingdom of Hittites c. 1900–1200 B.C.; western part center of Phrygian kingdom 1000–750 B.C.; west coast settled by Greeks (Aeolians, Dorians, and Ionians) c. 1000 B.C.; western part under kingdom of Lydia (*q.v.*) 670–546 B.C.; conquered by Persian ruler Cyrus 546 B.C.; despite temporary alliance of coastal (Greek) cities with Athens, remained under Persian rule until 4th cent. B.C.; conquered by Alexander of Macedon 333 B.C. who was followed by Antigonus, founder of a separate kingdom which included most of Asia Minor; under Alexander's successors (Diadochi), divided into small kingdoms (see PERGAMUM, CAPPADOCIA, BITHYNIA, and PONTUS) 3d–1st cents. B.C.; coast and southern part contested by Seleucids and Ptolemies; gradually conquered by Rome, west coast in 2d cent. B.C., and rest by 1st cent. A.D.; Christianized after 33 A.D.; after division of Roman Empire (395), ruled by Eastern Roman (Byzantine) Empire; raided occasionally by Arabs after 7th cent.; in 11th cent. conquered by Seljuk Turks who set up Sultanate of Rum (*q.v.*); reconquered in 12th cent. with help of Crusaders who set up Latin Empire and empires of Nicaea and Trebizond (*qq.v.*); overrun by Mongols in 13th cent.; gradually overcome in 14th and 15th cents. by Ottoman Turks, Karaman (*q.v.*) being last state to succumb. For later history, see OTTOMAN EMPIRE and TURKEY.

A·sid' Gulf (ä·sēd'). Arm of Visayan Sea on S coast of Masbate I., Phil. Is.

Asinalunga. See SINALUNGA.

A'si·na'ra (ä'sē·nä'rä). Small Italian island in Mediterranean Sea off NW extremity of the island of Sardinia.

Asinara, Gulf of. Inlet of Mediterranean Sea on N coast of the island of Sardinia, E of Asinara I.

As'i·ne (ăs'ĭ·nē; *Mod. Gr.* ä·sē'nyē). Ancient town on E coast of the Gulf of Argolis, E Peloponnesus, S Greece; an archaeological site near Nauplia.

A·sing'an (ä·sēng'än). Municipality, W cen. Luzon, Phil. Is., 28 m. E of Lingayen; pop. 19,571.

A·sir' (ä·sēr'). Principate, SW coast of Arabia; 13,857 sq. m.; pop. ab. 750,000; ✳ As Sabya; bounded on N by Hejaz, on E by Nejd, on S by Yemen, and on W by the Red Sea. A maritime plain ab. 230 m. along the coast with mountain range (average height 6000 to 7000 ft.) and plateau inland; has good soil for coffee raising and produces dates, cereals, and gum arabic. Inhabitants are mountaineers of Wahabi beliefs. Under Turkish rule control only nominal; became politically active in early part of 20th cent.; acknowledged ibn-Saud 1926; made a division of Saudi Arabia 1933.

Asisium. See ASSISI.

Ask′ja (äsk′yä). Volcanic peak 3376 ft., E cen. Iceland, 65°N lat. and 17°W long.; largest crater in Iceland.

As·ma′ra (ăz·mär′ä; *native* äs·mà·rä). Town, ✳ of Eritrea, NE Africa, ab. 40 m. SW of Massaua; pop. 120,000 (before World War II, 85,000, including 50,000 Italians); altitude 7765 ft.; connected by rail with Massaua and with Cheren in the interior. An old Abyssinian town; in 19th cent. under Egypt; occupied by Italy 1889; capital of a province of Italian East Africa 1936–41; taken by British March 1941.

As′nelles′ (ä′něl′). Village on Normandy coast, France. See CALVADOS REEF.

Ås′nen (ôs′něn). Lake 20 m. long and 15 m. broad, 58 sq. m., Kronoberg prov., S Sweden, 56 m. W of Kalmar.

As′nières′ (ä′nyâr′). Commune, Seine dept., N France, on left bank of Seine river 3 m. NW of Paris; pop. 71,831; boating center notable for its summer regattas; manufactures perfumery, dyes.

A·so (ä·sō) *or* **A·so·san** (ä·sō·sän). Volcanic mountain, cen. Kyushu I., Japan, ab. 25 m. E of Kumamoto; highest of its five peaks 5225 ft.; has huge crater, reputed to be the largest in the world, from 10 to 15 m. in diameter with walls ab. 2000 ft. high.

A′so·la (ä′zō·lä). Commune, Mantova prov., Lombardy, N Italy, on Chiese river 18 m. WNW of Mantua; pop. 10,809.

A′so·lo (ä′zō·lō); *anc.* **Ac′e·lum** (ăs′ě·lŭm). Commune, Treviso prov., Venezia Euganea, NE Italy, 18 m. NW of Treviso; pop. 10,042; made episcopal see in 6th cent.; remains of Roman baths, theater, and aqueduct; residence of Caterina Cornaro 1489–1510.

A′sor (ä′sôr). See ULITHI.

A·so′tin (à·sō′t′n). **1** County in Washington. See *Table* at WASHINGTON.
2 Town, its ⊗, SE Washington; pop. 745.

Aspadana. See ISFAHAN.

As′pen (ăs′pěn). City, ⊗ of Pitkin co., W cen. Colorado, 30 m. W of Leadville; pop. 1101; silver, lead, and zinc ore mills; winter sports center.

Aspen Butte. Mountain 8209 ft., SW Klamath co., S Oregon.

As′per·mont (ăs′pěr·mŏnt). Town, ⊗ of Stonewall co., NW Texas; pop. 1286.

A′spern (äs′pěrn). Former village 5 m. ENE of Vienna, Austria, in the Marchfeld; here and at the nearby village of Essling, May 21–22, 1809, the French under Napoleon were defeated by the Austrians under Archduke Charles Louis; since 1905 part of Vienna.

As′phal·ti′tes, La′cus (lä′kŭs ăs′făl·tī′tēz). The Dead Sea—so called by Josephus.

As′pin·wall (ăs′pǐn·wôl). **1** Borough, Allegheny co., SW Pennsylvania, on Allegheny river 7 m. ENE of Pittsburgh; pop. 3727; residential suburb of Pittsburgh.
2 Former name of city of COLÓN, Panama.

As·pir′ing, Mount (ăs·pīr′ĭng). Peak 9957 ft., SW South I., New Zealand, W of Lake Wanaka.

A′spro·mon′te (äs′prō·mŏn′tä). Mountain ridge of S Apennines, Reggio Calabria, Italy, E of Strait of Messina and Reggio; over 30 m. long; 6420 ft. high at Montalto peak; sharp, heavily wooded slopes. Scene of skirmish Aug. 29, 1862 in which Garibaldi, in his attempt against wishes of Victor Emmanuel II to secure Rome (papal territory) for kingdom of Italy, was wounded and captured by the latter's troops under Pallavicino.

Aspropotamos. See ACHELOUS.

As′pull (ăs′pŭl). Urban district, Lancashire, NW England, 2 m. NE of Wigan; pop. 6522; collieries, iron and steel works, cotton mill.

As′sab (ăs′ăb). Seaport and bay, SE Eritrea, NE Africa, 60 m. N of Bab el Mandeb Strait; acquired as a coaling station 1869; taken over by Italian government 1882; became nucleus of colony of Eritrea.

As·sam′ (ă·săm′; ă·säm′; ăs′ăm). State, NE Indian Union, mostly in Brahmaputra river valley, 49,473 sq. m., pop. (1941) 7,088,131; ✳ Shillong; geographically includes Indian states (Manipur and Khasi States), 12,408 sq. m., pop. (1941) 725,655; total 61,881 sq. m., pop. (1941) 7,813,786. E Himalayas lie along N border; Brahmaputra (here called Dihang) enters through gorges at NE corner; in W cen. part S of Brahmaputra valley are Garo Hills and Khasi Hills; on E and SE various hill ranges (Patkai and Naga on N, Lushai on S) form boundary with Burma; highest point Mt. Japvo 9824 ft. Cherrapunji in Khasi Hills has record for world's heaviest rainfall (annual average 424 inches). Chief industry cultivation and manufacture of tea. Chief towns Shillong, Gauhati, and Imphal (in Manipur). Sadiya in NE is starting point for roads through Sikang to W China. On June 12, 1897 suffered one of severest earthquakes ever known.

History: Strong independent kingdom first founded by Ahoms, invaders from Burma and Chinese frontier, 13th cent.; fought with Mohammedan governor of Bengal 17th cent., but never came under his rule; became dependency of Burmese 1822 and thus a partial cause of First Burmese War (1824–26); ceded to British by Treaty of Yandabu (*q.v.*) 1826; under chief commissioner 1874–1905; part of province of Eastern Bengal and Assam 1905–12 (see BENGAL), separate province 1912. In World War II a British-American base in Burma campaign against the Japanese 1943–45; from Ledo in NE construction of Ledo Road (later Stilwell Road) begun. In division of India in August 1947 lost most of Sylhet district, which was assigned to East Bengal, Pakistan; in 1950 was constituted a state, not including Manipur, area 54,084 sq. m., pop. (1951) 9,043,707.

As′sa·teague Island (ăs′à·tēg). Island, Worcester co., SE Maryland, and Accomac co., N part of E peninsula, Virginia, separating Chincoteague Bay throughout its length from Atlantic Ocean.

As′sa·wa′man Island (ăs′à·wŏm′ăn). Island, E Virginia, on the coast off Accomac county; 4¼ m. long; at the N end is **Assawaman Inlet.**

As′sa·ye (ŭs′sà·yā). Village, cen. Maharashtra state, cen. India, 45 m. NE of Aurangabad; scene of battle Sept. 23, 1803 in which Gen. Wellesley completely defeated Sindhia and Nagpur branches of Marathas.

Assche (äsh; *Flemish* äs′KĚ); *also* **Assche-lez-Bru′-xelles′** (äsh′lä·brü′sěl′; *locally* -brük′sěl′). Commune, Brabant prov., cen. Belgium, 7 m. NW of Brussels; pop. 10,160; hops, flax, wheat; tanneries, breweries.

As′sen (äs′ěn). Commune, ✳ of Drenthe prov., Netherlands, 16 m. S of Groningen; pop. (1939) 20,311; connected by canal with Groningen and Meppel and the Wadden Zee; built around old nunnery now serving as group of public buildings; in vicinity are peat bogs, gardens, the "Giants' Caves" mentioned by Tacitus, and prehistoric stone monuments resembling those at Stonehenge; museum of antiquities.

Asshur. See ASSYRIA.

As·sin′i·boi′a (à·sĭn′ĭ·boi′à; ă·sĭn′ĭ·boi′à). **1** Early region of W Canada, c. 1811–70, with indefinite boundaries; controlled by Hudson's Bay Co. with headquarters at Fort Garry; included Red River Settlement.
2 Former district, formed 1882 out of Northwest Territories, Canada, W of Manitoba and S of Saskatchewan District; 89,000 sq. m.; ✳ Regina. Greater part of it united Sept. 1, 1905 with Saskatchewan District and E part of Athabaska District to form Saskatchewan prov.

As·sin′i·boine (ă·sĭn′ĭ·boin). River 450 m. long, S Canada; rises in SE Saskatchewan, flows S and E across S Manitoba into the Red river at Winnipeg; navigable for ab. 300 m.; has two tributaries, the Qu' Appelle, its main headstream, and the Souris on the S. Discovered by the La Vérendryes 1736; its valley was route to the plains by settlers from the Red River.

Assiniboine, Mount. Mountain 11,870 ft. in Rocky Mts., Canada, on border bet. SE British Columbia and SW Alberta prov., ab. 25 m. SW of Banff in Banff National Park.

As'si'nie' (à'sē'nē'). Trading station, Ivory Coast, West Africa, on SE coast E of Abidjan; pop. ab. 1000.

Assiout, Assiut. See ASYÛT.

Assir, Ras. See Cape GUARDAFUI.

As·si'si (à·sē'zē; *Ital.* äs·sē'zē); *anc.* **A·si'si·um** (à·sĭzh'-ĭ·ŭm). Commune, Perugia prov. Umbria, cen. Italy, on S slope of Monte Subasio 12 m. E by SE of Perugia; pop. 22,514; episcopal see; famous as place of birth and death of St. Francis of Assisi (1182–1226); Gothic Franciscan monastery and Upper and Lower Church of St. Francis, containing paintings by old masters, esp. Giotto.

As·siz' (à·sēs'). City, São Paulo state, SE Brazil, ab. 240 m. WNW of São Paulo; pop. (1940 est.) 9132.

Assomption, L'. See L'ASSOMPTION.

As'sos (ăs'ŏs); *Lat.* **As'sus** (ăs'ŭs). Ancient city of S Troas, in Aeolis, on coast of Gulf of Adramyttium (Edremit) W of Mt. Ida and opp. N shore of Lesbos; founded c. 1000 B.C. and long an important city and port. Aristotle taught here 348–345 B.C. Its ruins now an archaeological site and part of village of **Beh'ram·köy'** (bĕ'räm·kû'ĕ), Çanakkale, NW Turkey.

Assouan, Assuan. See ASWÂN.

As'suad, Cape (ăs'wäd). Cape extending into Indian Ocean on cen. part of E coast of Somalia.

As·su'car. Obsolete spelling of Portuguese *Açúcar:* see PÃO DE AÇÚCAR.

As·sump'tion (ă·sŭmp'shŭn). **1** Parish in Louisiana. See *Table* at LOUISIANA.

2 City, Christian co., cen. Illinois; pop. 1439.

3 See ALDABRA.

Assur. See ASSYRIA.

As'synt, Loch (lŏĸ ăs'ĭnt). Lake ab. 7 m. long, Sutherland co., N Scotland, draining W into Enard Bay.

As·syr'i·a (ă·sĭr'ĭ·à); *anc.* **As'sur** (ä'sŏŏr; ăs'ẽr), **A'shur** (ä'shŏŏr; äsh'ẽr), or **As'shur** (ä'shŏŏr; äsh'ẽr). One of the great ancient empires of the world, holding dominion in W Asia; early ✻ Calah, later ✻ Nineveh; extended along E bank of middle Tigris and over foothills to the E. Probably originated c. 2700 B.C. in Sumerian settlement of Ashur but later became part of Akkadian empire and from c. 1950 to 1850 B.C. was under Babylonian rule; frequently overrun and much influenced by Hittites and Hurrians; after 1800 B.C. hard pressed by Egyptians. Slowly gained control of trade routes under Tiglath-pileser I (c. 1115–1102 B.C.) but was especially powerful in 884 to 782 B.C. when it reached Mediterranean in its conquests under Ashurnasirpal II and Shalmaneser III and in 745 to 626 B.C. when it conquered Israel 734, Damascus 732, and Babylon and Samaria 722, and conducted successful campaigns against Egypt; its greatest rulers then were Tiglath-pileser III, Sargon II, Sennacherib, Esarhaddon, and Ashurbanipal. Lost power rapidly 626–612 B.C. when Nineveh was destroyed by kings of Media and Babylonia (Chaldea). Made a Roman province for a brief time under Trajan 116 A.D.; invaded 627 A.D. by Roman emperor Heraclius; with other Persian provinces became part of the caliphate by 656. For later history of the region, see MESOPOTAMIA.

Astaboras. See ATBARA.

Asta Colonia. See ASTI.

Astacus. See İZMİT.

Asta Pompeia. See ASTI.

As'ta·ra' (äs'tä·rä'; *Russ.* ŭs·tŭ·rá'). Seaport, SE Azerbaidzhan, U.S.S.R., on W coast of Caspian Sea, on border of Iran 20 m. S of Lenkoran.

As'ter·a·bad' (äs'tä·ä·băd'; *Angl.* ăs'tĕr·à·băd', ăs'trà·băd') or **Gur·gan'** (gŏŏr·gän'); *also* **As'tar·a·bad'.** **1** *anc.* **Hyr·ca'ni·a** (hûr·kä'nĭ·à; -kän'yà). Province, N Iran; 5737 sq. m.; mountain district on SE coast of Caspian Sea; ancient Hyrcania, NE of Media and NW of Parthia, often used as a residence of Parthian kings.

2 City, its ✻, ab. 23 m. inland from Caspian Sea; pop. ab. 28,000; formerly important commercially.

A'sti (äs'tē). **1** Province of Italy. See *Table* at ITALY.

2 *anc.* **As'ta** (äs'tà), *or* **Has'ta** (hăs'tà), **Pom·pe'ia** (pŏm·pē'[y]à) *or* **Asta**, *or* **Hasta**, **Co·lo'ni·a** (kŏ·lō'nĭ·à; -lōn'yà). Commune, its ✻, Piedmont, NW Italy, on left bank of Tanaro river 20 m. W of Alessandria; pop. 48,898; has Gothic cathedral built 1348, 8th-cent. and 11th-cent. baptisteries; famous for the sparkling wine Asti spumante; silk mills; known anciently for manufacture of pottery. *History:* Powerful medieval republic; burned by Frederick Barbarossa 1155; captured by the Visconti of Milan 1348; ceded to France 1387 as part of a dowry of daughter of Gian Galeazzo Visconti; given to dukes of Savoy 1529.

Astigi. See ÉCIJA.

As'tin Tagh (äs'tĭn tä'); *formerly* **Al'tin**, *or* **Al'tyn, Tagh** (äl'tĭn). Mountain range (*tagh*), N Tibet and S Sinkiang prov., W China, Central Asia, branch of the Kunlun; highest peak ab. 17,000 ft.

As'ton (ăs'tŭn). Residential township, Delaware co., Pennsylvania, SW of Philadelphia; pop. 10,595.

As'ton Man'or (ăs'tŭn măn'ẽr). Former municipal borough, Warwickshire, England; since 1911 industrial district in NE Birmingham.

As·tor'ga (äs·tôr'gä); *anc.* **As·tu'ri·ca Au·gus'ta** (äs·tūr'ĭ·kà ô·gŭs'tà). Commune, León prov., NW Spain, 28 m. WSW of León; pop. 14,523; episcopal see; manufactures textiles, chocolates; medieval fortifications; Gothic 15th-cent. cathedral. Ancient Roman capital of Asturias and military center; site of church council 446; a famous center of Spanish resistance against Moors in 8th cent.; captured by French 1810 and retaken by Spaniards 1812 (Peninsular War).

As·to'ri·a (äs·tōr'ĭ·à). **1** Former village, Queens co., SE New York, on Long Island, on East river, now residential and industrial section of Long Island City (*q.v.*) in borough of Queens, New York City.

2 City and port of entry, ⊗ of Clatsop co., NW Oregon, on S bank and near mouth of Columbia river; pop. 11,239; near site of Fort Clatsop, estab. by Lewis and Clark expedition 1805. Founded as trading post by John Jacob Astor 1811; taken by British 1813; restored to U.S. 1818. Fisheries, salmon canneries, sawmills, dairies.

As'tra·bad' (ăs'trä·băd'; *Angl.* ăs'trà·băd'). Var. of ASTERABAD.

As'tra·khan (ăs'trà·kăn; -kăn; *Russ.* ăs'trà·ĸän·y'). City, ✻ of Astrakhan Region, Soviet Russia, Europe, on left bank of the Volga at head of its delta ab. 235 m. SE of Stalingrad; pop. 253,655; altitude 50 ft. below sea level and its port, only fair because of silting up of Volga mouths, frozen for about one third of the year; exports fish, caviar, wine, grain. Has fortress, or *kreml* (built ab. 1550 on a hill), and a university (founded 1919).

History: Capital of a Tatar khanate on lower Volga, which became independent of former Kipchak (Golden Horde) empire (1237–1486) [see MONGOLIA and RUSSIA]; conquered 1554–56 by Ivan IV who thus gained control for Russia of entire course of Volga, an important route for eastward expansion; town burned by Turks 1569; center of Peter the Great's campaign against Persia; given special trade privileges by Catherine II; has suffered much from flood, fire, famine, and a cholera epidemic 1830. Reached by Germans 1942.

Astrakhan Region. Region, SE Soviet Russia, Europe, W and SW of the lower Volga with narrow strip along its E bank; newly formed (Oct. 1945) during World War II, chiefly from the Kalmyk A.S.S.R. (*q.v.*) and from part of Stalingrad Region; ✻ Astrakhan.

As'tri·da (äs'trē·dá; *Fr.* äs'trē'dá'). Town, cen. Ruanda-Urundi trust territory, 60 m. NNE of Usumbura.

As'tro·labe, Cape (ăs'trŏ·lāb). Cape, NW point of Malaita I., SE Solomon Is., W Pacific Ocean.

Astrolabe Bay. Inlet of Bismarck Sea on NE cen. coast of North-East New Guinea, at W end of Vitiaz Strait; contains good harbors (Madang and Bogadjim).

A'stro·pa·lia' (ä'strô·pä·lyä'). Var. of ASTYPALAIA.

As'tu·ra (*Lat.* ăs'tụ̄·rá; *Ital.* äs·tōō'rä). Village, Roma prov., Latium, Italy 36 m. SSE of Rome and near Anzio; formerly an islet, now a peninsula; site of a favorite villa of Cicero from which he embarked on the flight that ended with his murder at Formiae 43 B.C.; site of medieval castle of the Frangipani where Conradin, the last Hohenstaufen, unsuccessfully sought refuge after battle of Tagliacozzo 1268.

As·tu'ri·as (ăs·t[y]ōōr'ĭ·ăs; *Span.* äs·tōō'ryäs). **1** Municipality on W coast of Cebu I., Phil. Is., on Tañon Strait 22 m. NW of City of Cebu; pop. 25,468.
2 Region and ancient kingdom, NW Spain; 4206 sq. m.; bounded N by Bay of Biscay, E by Old Castile, S by León and the Cantabrian Mts., and W by Galicia; now forms modern province of Oviedo; picturesque mountain woodlands, steep chasms, fertile valleys; rich pasturage, producing an excellent breed of horses and cattle; deposits of copper, lead, iron, and other minerals; excellent fisheries; produces barley, wheat, corn, olives.
History: Conquered by Romans under Augustus 25 B.C.; refuge for Goths from Saracen onslaught in 8th cent.; kingdom created by Pelayo (718–737), successor to Visigoth ruler, which he successfully defended against Moors; became part of kingdom of León on accession of Alfonso III 866, and later of kingdom of León and Castile; made principality 1388, held until 1931 by heir apparent to the Spanish throne with title Prince of the Asturias; from 1838 officially the province of Oviedo.
3 City, NW Spain. See OVIEDO.

Asturica Augusta. See ASTORGA.

A'sty·pa'lai·a (ä'stĕ·pä'lâ·ä) *or* **As'ty·pa·lae'a** (ăs'tĭ·pȧ·lē'ȧ); *Ital.* **Stam'pa·li'a** (stäm'pä·lē'ä). One of the Dodecanese Is. (*q.v.*), WSW of Kos; 44 sq. m.; pop. 2000.

A'sun·cion' (ä'sōōn·syŏn'; -thyŏn'). Small island, N end of Mariana Is., W Pacific Ocean, 19°40'N lat. Taken by U.S. forces Aug. 1945.

A'sun·ción' (ä'sōōn·syŏn') *or* **Nues'tra Se·ño'ra de la Asunción** (nwäs'trä sä·nyō'rä thä lä). Commercial city, ✻ of Paraguay and of Central dept., in S cen. part of the country on E bank of Paraguay river at the confluence of the Pilcomayo. 650 m. N of Buenos Aires; pop. of urban dist. (1945 est.) 102,537. Chief port of the republic; has sugar refineries, distilleries, tanneries; manufactures shoes, furniture, cigarettes, matches; public buildings include the government palace, national library, national college, and the house of congress.
History: Founded 1538 by expedition under Irala sent inland from coast by Mendoza; first permanent settlement in La Plata region; capital of region until Buenos Aires refounded 1580 and developed; seat of revolutionary junta which threw off rule of Buenos Aires 1811 (see PARAGUAY); occupied 1868 by forces of Brazil, Argentina, and Uruguay in war for Greater Paraguay.

Asunción, La. See LA ASUNCIÓN.

A'sun·ción' Mi'ta (ä'sōōn·syŏn' mē'tä). Town, Jutiapa dept., SE Guatemala; pop. 5343.

As·wân' *or* **As·wan'**, *also* **As·souan'** *or* **As·suan'** (äs·wän'; ăs·wŏn'). **1** Province, SE Upper Egypt. See *Table* at EGYPT.
2 *anc.* **Sy·e'ne** (sĭ·ē'nĕ). City, its ✻, on right bank of the Nile; pop. (1962) 48,000; opp. Elephantine I. and just below the 1st Cataract; popular winter health resort, with modern hotels; has ruins of temple built by Ptolemy Euergetes; on opp. bank tombs of early Egyptian dynasties (VI to XII). Ancient Syene an important town in 1st millennium B.C. Ab. 3½ m. to the S of the city at the beginning of the 1st Cataract is the great Aswân dam, 6400 ft. long, built 1898–1902 to replace 19th-cent. barrage; above it is the High Aswân dam, begun 1960, which will form Lake Nasser, 300 m. long, impounding water for irrigation.

As·yût' *or* **As·yut'**, *also* **As·siout'** *or* **As·siut'** (äs·yōōt'). **1** Province, N Upper Egypt. See *Table* at EGYPT.

2 *anc.* **Ly·cop'o·lis** (lī·kŏp'ō̇·lĭs). City, its ✻ on left bank of the Nile; pop. (1937) 60,338; a well-built city, noted for its pottery and ornamental wood and ivory work; near Nile barrage (completed 1902; 2691 ft. long) and at head of canal to El Faiyûm.

A'ta·ba'po (ä'tä·vä'pŏ). River 140 m. long, S Venezuela; flows N to Orinoco river and forms section of boundary bet. Colombia and Venezuela.

A'ta·ca'ma (ä'tä·kä'mä). Province of Chile. See *Table* at CHILE.
History: While under Bolivian administration. its valuable nitrate deposits were developed by Chilean capital; subject of disagreement bet. Chile and Bolivia which led to War of Pacific (1879–84); control transferred to victorious Chile by Treaty of Valparaíso 1884 (see also ANTOFAGASTA); awarded permanently to Chile 1905.

A'ta·ca'ma, Pu'na de (pōō'nä thä ä'tä·kä'mä). Highland region in Los Andes territory, NW Argentina, with average altitude of 7000 to 13,500 ft. and peaks on its border above 21,000 ft.

Atacama Desert. Arid area extending N from Copiapó in N cen. Chile, covering most of Antofagasta prov. and N part of Atacama prov.; completely barren, with borax lakes and saline deposits and large nitrate deposits; for years a chief source of the world's nitrates.

A'ta·fu' (ä'tä·fōō') *or* **Duke of York.** Island (atoll) in Tokelau group (*q.v.*), cen. Pacific Ocean, bet. Phoenix Is. and Samoa, consisting of a reef ab. 3 m. square with 62 islets. Discovered 1765.

A'tak·pa'mé (ä'täk·pä'mā). Town, Togo, West Africa, 103 m. N of Lomé on Lomé-Blibba railroad.

At'a·lan'te (ăt'ȧ·lăn'tĕ); *Mod. Gr.* **A'ta·lán'tē** (ä'tä·län'dĕ). Channel extending bet. the island of Euboea, Aegean Sea, and Greece, N of Evripos Strait.

A·ta·mi (ä·tä·mē). City on Sagami Sea, on E coast of Izu Penin., Shizuoka prefecture, SE Honshu, Japan, ab. 14 m. S of Odawara; pop. 34,509; watering place.

A'tar (ä'tär). Town, Adrar, NW Mauritania, West Africa; terminus of railroad to St-Louis in Senegal.

A·tas'ca·der'o (ȧ·tăs'kȧ·dĕr'ō̇). Urban community (unincorp.), San Luis Obispo co., California; pop. 5963.

At'a·sco'sa (ăt'ȧ·skō'sȧ). County in Texas. See *Table* at TEXAS.

Atavyrion. See ATTAIRO.

Atax. See AUDE.

At'ba·ra (ăt'bä·rä); *anc.* **As·tab'o·ras** (ăs·tăb'ō̇·rȧs). **1** River ab. 500 m. long, NE Africa; its headstream, the Takkaze, rises in N Ethiopia; flows NW through E Sudan into the Nile at Atbara; last tributary of the Nile.
2 Town, Northern Province, NE Sudan, at the junction of Atbara and Nile rivers just N of Ed Damer; pop. 36,298; victory of Anglo-Egyptian army over Mahdi's forces April 8, 1898.

A·tchaf'a·lay'a ([ȧ·]chăf'ȧ·lī'ȧ). River ab. 225 m. long, S Louisiana; rises in Avoyelles parish, cen. Louisiana, flows S into Atchafalaya Bay; an additional outlet for Red and Mississippi rivers during periods of high water.

Atchafalaya Bay. Inlet of Gulf of Mexico on S boundary bet. St. Mary and Terrebonne parishes, SE Louisiana, receiving (through Grand Lake) the Atchafalaya river on the N.

Atchin. See ACHIN.

Atch'i·son (ăch'ĭ·s'n). **1** Name of counties in two states of the U.S. See *Tables* at KANSAS and MISSOURI.
2 City, ⊗ of Atchison co., NE Kansas, on Missouri river 20 m. N of Leavenworth; pop. 12,529; incorp. 1855; stopping place of westbound caravans in the Gold Rush and later; E terminus of Atchison, Topeka, and Santa Fe R.R. (incorp. 1859; first section completed 1872); railroad and industrial center; flour mills, foundries, industrial alcohol plants. St. Benedict's College (1858; men; Roman Catholic); Mount St. Scholastica College (1863; women; Roman Catholic).

At'co (ăt'kō). Village, Camden co., SW New Jersey, ab. 14 m. SE of Collingswood; pop. (est.) 2200.

A·tel′la di Na′po·li (ä·těl′lä dĕ nä′pō·lė). Commune, Napoli prov., Campania, S Italy, 7 m. N of Naples; pop. (1931) 11,128; includes ruins of ancient Oscan town of **A·tel′la** (á·těl′á), captured by Romans 211 B.C., and famed as the cradle of the early Roman farces *Atellanae Fabulae.*

A·ter′no (ä·těr′nō); *anc.* **A·ter′nus** (á·tûr′nŭs). River ab. 80 m. long, SE cen. Italy; flows out of the Apennines SE and then NE into Adriatic Sea at Pescara; in its lower course known as the **Pe·sca′ra** (pås·kä′rä).

Aternum. See PESCARA seaport.

A·tes′sa (ä·těs′sä). Commune, Chieti prov., Abruzzi e Molise, cen. Italy, 24 m. SE of Chieti; pop. 10,546; cattle and fruit market.

Ateste. See ESTE.

Ath *or* **Aath** (ät). Commune, Hainaut prov., SW Belgium, on left bank of Dender river 55 m. SW of Brussels; pop. 10,606; medieval tower sole remains of ancient town; railroad junction; linen, wool, calico, lace, and glove factories, ironworks, dye works, nail and cutlery factories; population largely Walloon.

Ath′a·bas′ca (ăth′á·bǎs′ká), *also* **Ath′a·bas′ka.**
1 River 765 m. long, S tributary of the Mackenzie, in Alberta prov., W cen. Canada; rises in Rocky Mts. in Jasper National Park, flows NE and N into Lake Athabaska; chief tributaries Pembina, Lesser Slave, and La Biche. Important because of oil sands along its course, believed one of largest oil reservoirs in world.
2 Former district, cen. Canada, formed 1882 out of Northwest Territories bet. 60°N and 55°N, approximately the N part of present Alberta prov.; extended 1885 to include N part of present Saskatchewan prov. Both parts absorbed 1905 by the modern provinces.

Athabasca, Lake. Lake 2842 sq. m., ab. 230 m. long, W cen. Canada, extending across N section of the Alberta-Saskatchewan boundary; on SW receives Athabaska river and on NW discharges into Slave river; connected at its E end by Fond du Lac river with Lake Cree. Chipewyan and Fond du Lac are Hudson's Bay Co. posts on its N shore.

Ath′a·ma′ni·a (ăth′á·mā′nǐ·á; -mān′yá). A district of ancient Epirus, NW Greece, W of Pindus Mts.

Ath′el·ney (ăth′ĕl·nǐ). Locality in Somersetshire, SW England, ab. 8 m. ENE of Taunton; in King Alfred's time an isle in W cen. Wessex, surrounded by marshes; Alfred's refuge from the Danes 878–879. Site of monastery founded by Alfred.

Ath′ens (ăth′ĕnz; -ĭnz; *in Athens, N.Y.,* *also* ā′thĕnz, -thĭnz). **1** County in Ohio. See *Table* at OHIO.
2 City, ⊗ of Limestone co., N Alabama, 12 m. N of Decatur; pop. 9330; agricultural center; hosiery and lumber mills; Athens College (1842; coed.). Occupied by Union troops 1862; site of Campbell's surrender to Confederate general Forrest 1864.
3 City, ⊗ of Clarke co., NE Georgia, 60 m. ENE of Atlanta; pop. 31,355; founded 1785, incorp. 1801; cotton, cottonseed products, lumber. University of Georgia (chartered 1785; estab. 1801), oldest state university.
4 Village, Greene co., SE New York, on Hudson river near Catskill Mts. 26 m. S of Albany; pop. 1754; settled 1686; in fruit and poultry-farming area.
5 Commercial city, ⊗ of Athens co., SE Ohio, 32 m. W of Marietta; pop. 16,470; settled c. 1797, became ⊗ 1805; varied manufactures; coal mines nearby. Ohio Univ. (1804; coed.).
6 Borough, Bradford co., N Pennsylvania, on Susquehanna river 3 m. S of New York border; pop. 4515; settled 1778; foundry products, machine tools, silk.
7 City, ⊗ of McMinn co., SE Tennessee, 27 m. NNE of Cleveland; pop. 12,103; founded 1823, incorp. 1868; manufactures hosiery, woolens, stoves, tables, plows, etc.
8 City, ⊗ of Henderson co., NE Texas, 30 m. WSW of Tyler; pop. 7086; settled 1848; manufactures brick, pottery, cottonseed oil; produces fruit, poultry, vegetables, etc.; clay and lignite deposits and oil wells nearby.

9 Town, Mercer co., S West Virginia, ab. 6 m. NE of Princeton; pop. 1086. Concord Coll. (1872; coed.), teachers college.

10 *anc.* **A·the′nae** (á·thē′nē); *Gr.* **A·the′nai** (ä·thē′-nä). Commercial and manufacturing city, ✳ of Attica and Boeotia dept., E Central Greece and Euboea, and ✳ of Greece, near the Saronic Gulf; pop. ab. 1,850,000; on Attic plain enclosed on three sides by hills; formerly connected with its harbor Piraeus by the Long Walls; contains the Acropolis, the Areopagus (on which hill Paul preached) and the excavated ancient market place Agora; among the principal ancient structures on the Acropolis were the Odeum, Parthenon, Erechtheum, Propylaea, and Dionysiac theater; modern structures include the university, national library, national museum, polytechnic institute, American School of Classical Studies, and numerous schools of archaeology; cultural center of Greek kingdom.

History: Ancient Greek city-state which by the beginning of the 7th cent. B.C. included the territory known as Attica; abolished hereditary kingship 683 B.C.; under Solon's law code of 594 B.C., freed from the Draconian code (published 621 B.C.); ruled by tyrants, the most famous of whom was Pisistratus (560–527 B.C.); largely a democracy after the reforms of Cleisthenes 508 B.C.; under Themistocles, first chosen archon in 493–492 B.C., began building strong fleet in anticipation of Persian invasion; defeated Persia at battle of Marathon (*q.v.*) 490 B.C.; destroyed by Xerxes 480 B.C. in campaign in which Persians were finally defeated by the Peloponnesian League; began fortification of city and Piraeus 479 B.C.; headed the Delian League which was founded in 478 B.C., with headquarters on the island of Delos, as a confederacy against Persia but became the instrument of Athenian empire after subjugation of Naxos 471 B.C. and of Thasos 463 B.C.; at height of its commercial prosperity, leadership in architecture and culture, and political democracy under Pericles 460–431 B.C.; after a long period of opposition to Sparta, withdrew from Peloponnesian League and entered so-called First Peloponnesian War 460–445 B.C.; transferred treasury of Delian League from Delos 454 B.C.; at height of empire (c. 450 B.C.) allied to Thessaly, Achaea, Argos, Samos, Chios, and Lesbos, and had as dependents Euboea, Andros, Naxos, and the remaining Cyclades, most of the extreme western coast of Asia Minor, the entrances to the Propontis and to the Euxine, the coast and islands of the Thracian Sea, and Chalcidice; built Parthenon 447–432 B.C.; lost supremacy in Greece after being defeated in the renewed (Second) Peloponnesian War 431–404 B.C.; sentenced Socrates to death 399 B.C.; allied against Sparta in Corinthian War 395–387 B.C. and again in 377 B.C.; opposed by her former allies in the Social War 357–355 B.C.; anti-Macedonian under Demosthenes, defeated by Philip of Macedon 338 B.C.; under Macedonian hegemony after 322 B.C.

Established friendly relations with Rome 228 B.C. and was aided by Rome against Macedonians, who were finally defeated at Cynoscephalae 197 B.C.; with Roman destruction of the Achaean League 146 B.C., as part of Greece, became subject to Rome; part of Roman province of Achaea (*q.v.*); visited by St. Paul c. 54 A.D.; taken by the Goths 267 A.D.; surrendered to Alaric and the Goths 395; became a duchy after the Latin conquest of Greece 1204; conquered by the Ottoman Empire 1456; Parthenon destroyed during siege by Venetians 1687–88; became the capital of modern Greece 1835. In World War II taken by Germans Apr. 27, 1941; retaken by Greek and British forces Oct. 14, 1944.

Ath′er·ton (ăth′ẽr·t'n; -tŭn). **1** Residential town, San Mateo co., W California, suburb of Redwood City, 22 m. SE of San Francisco; pop. 7717; incorp. 1923.
2 (*pron. also* ăth′ẽr-) Urban district, Lancashire, NW England, 13 m. WNW of Manchester; pop. 20,591; cotton factories, collieries, ironworks.

Atherton Plateau *or* **Tableland.** Plateau region ab. 15,000 sq. m. on NE coast of Queensland, NE Australia, at N end of Eastern Highlands; highest point Mt. Bartle Frere 5287 ft.

Athesis. See ADIGE.

Ath′garh (ŭt′gär; *native* -gŭr·h'). Former Indian state in Eastern States, geographically in SE Orissa, E India, on N bank of Mahanadi river; 163 sq. m.; pop. (1941) 55,498; chief town Athgarh 15 m. NW of Cuttack.

A′thi (ä′tē). River ab. 200 m. long, Kenya, East Africa; rises near Nairobi and flows SE through **Athi Plain**, noted for its numerous wild game, to the Sabaki river. See SABAKI.

A′this′–Mons′ (ȧ′tēs′môNs'). Commune, Seine-et-Oise dept., N France, on Seine river 8 m. SSE of Paris; pop. 7969; naval and aeronautical construction.

'Ath·lit' (äth·lēt'; ät·lēt'). Ancient town and modern archaeological site, on coast of Palestine ab. 8 m. SSW of Haifa; noted for discovery of remarkable fossil specimens. Last place in Holy Land held by Crusaders 1291.

Ath·lone' (äth·lōn'). Urban district, W co. Westmeath, on the Shannon, N cen. Eire; pop. 7257; agricultural center; manufactures woolen and linen goods; salmon fisheries; successfully stormed 1691 by Gen. Godert de Ginkel, after withstanding siege by William of Orange.

Ath·mal′lik (ŭt·mŭl′ĭk). Former Indian state in Eastern States, geographically in S cen. Orissa, E India, on N bank of Mahanadi river; 723 sq. m.; pop. (1941) 72,765.

Ath′ol (äth′ŏl). Industrial town, Worcester co., cen. Massachusetts, 21 m. W of Fitchburg; pop. 11,637; tools, toys, leather goods, wood products.

Ath′oll *or* **Ath′ole** (äth′ŭl). Mountainous district 250 sq. m., N Perth co., cen. Scotland, at S base of Grampian Mts.; includes Tay river and Loch Rannoch; land generally uncultivable; extensive hunting tracts.

Ath′os (äth′ŏs; ā′thŏs; *Mod. Gr.* ä′thôs). Mountain 6670 ft. occupying E end of Acte Penin., Chalcidice, NE Greece; inhabited since 9th cent. A.D. by monastic communities of Greek Rule of St. Basil; the "Holy Mountain" of the Greek Church; as Mount Athos, declared an autonomous republic 1927 (see MOUNT ATHOS).

A·thy' (ȧ·thī'). Urban district, SW co. Kildare, E Eire, 37 m. SW of Dublin; pop. 3753; agricultural center; has two ancient castles; as site of a ford of the Barrow river, strategically important in historic time and scene of many battles.

A′ti·mo′nan (ä′tē·mō′nän). Municipality, S Tayabas prov., Luzon, Phil. Is., on SW shore of Lamon Bay 21 m. E of Lucena; pop. 18,512; harbor. Taken by Japanese Dec. 23, 1941; retaken by Americans Apr. 10, 1945.

A′ti·qui·za′ya (ä′tē·kē·sä′yä). Town, Ahuachapán dept., SW El Salvador, ab. 11 m. W of Santa Ana; pop. (1942 est.) 5901.

A′ti·tlán' (ä′tē·tlän'). **1** Lake 24 m. long by 10 m. wide, SW Guatemala, at 4700 ft. altitude; occupies a crater 1000 ft. deep.
2 Volcano 11,562 ft., S of the lake.
3 Town, Guatemala. See SANTIAGO ATITLÁN.

A′ti·u' (ä′tē·ōō'). Island in cen. part of Cook Is. group, S Pacific Ocean, 116 m. NE of Rarotonga; 20°S lat. and 158°W long.; 26 sq. m.; pop. (1936) 1086.

A′tjeh (ä′chĕ), *officially* **Atjeh and Dependencies;** *commonly* **A·chin** (ȧ·chēn'; ä-). Region, N end of Sumatra, Indonesia; 21,381 sq. m.; pop. 1,003,062; ✳ Kutaradja; comprises an area on both the E and W coasts and also the island of Simeulue and Banjak Is.; very mountainous, with several peaks above 9000 ft.; has railroad along N and NE coasts; chief commercial towns Kutaradja and Sabang on We I. off N tip of Sumatra. For history, see ACHIN.

At′ka (ät′kȧ). Island, largest of the Andreanof group, Aleutian Is., SW Alaska; chief settlement Atka village, pop. 89. In N is Korovin volcano 4852 ft. Inhabited by the Atka, one of the two dialectic divisions of the Aleut. U.S. Army base in World War II.

At′kin·son (ăt′kĭn·s'n). County in Georgia. See *Table* at GEORGIA.

At·lan′ta (ăt·lăn′tȧ). **1** Commercial and industrial city, ✳ of Georgia and ⊗ of Fulton co., located in De Kalb and Fulton cos., NW cen. Ga., 55 m. E of Alabama border; pop. 487,455; largest city in the state; railroad and communication center. Region around Atlanta ceded to Georgia by Creek Indians 1821; selected 1836 by railroad as end of line and named Terminus; incorp. 1843 as town of Marthasville, name changed to Atlanta 1845, reincorporated as city 1847; made county seat of newly created Fulton co. 1853; became market center for its area; Confederate supply depot in Civil War; burned by Sherman Nov. 15, 1864; scene of constitutional convention 1867–68; temporary capital of Georgia 1868, permanent capital from 1887. Educational institutions include the Georgia Institute of Technology (1885; men) and the institutions of the Atlanta University Center, including Atlanta University (1865; coed.), Clark College (1870; coed.), Interdenominational Theological Center (1958), Morehouse College (1867; men), Morris Brown College (1881; coed.), and Spelman College (1881; women). In nearby suburbs are Oglethorpe University (1913; coed.) and Emory University (1836; coed.).
2 Village, ⊗ of Montmorency co., NE Michigan; pop. ab. 400.
3 City, Cass co., NE Texas, on Arkansas border 20 m. S of Texarkana; pop. 4076; lumbering; oil wells.

At·lan′tic (ăt·lăn′tĭk). **1** County in New Jersey. See *Table* at NEW JERSEY.
2 City, ⊗ of Cass co., SW Iowa, 47 m. ENE of Council Bluffs; pop. 6890; manufactures stoves; packing plants.
3 Seaside resort, Accomac co., N part of E peninsula, Virginia, ab. 8 m. SW of Chincoteague.

Atlantic City. City, Atlantic co., SE New Jersey, on Atlantic Ocean ab. 60 m. SE of Philadelphia; pop. 59,544; noted seaside resort; built 1852 on Absecon I. (or Absecon Beach); incorporated as city 1854; railroad terminus; seaplane base; 4-mile-long boardwalk of steel and concrete (built 1896); amusement and recreation piers.

Atlantic Highlands. Borough and summer resort, Monmouth co., E cen. New Jersey, on S shore of Sandy Hook 14 m. ESE of Perth Amboy; pop. 4119.

Atlantic In′tra·coast′al Waterway (ĭn′trȧ·kōs′tăl; -t'l). A system of inland waterways including rivers, bays, and canals along the Atlantic coast of U.S.A. from Cape Cod to Florida Bay; includes the Cape Cod Canal, the Chesapeake and Delaware Canal, the Dismal Swamp Canal, and the Cross-Florida Waterway (*qq.v.*); main points on the system are Trenton, N.J., Norfolk, Va., Beaufort, N.C., Jacksonville, Fla., and Miami, Fla.

At·lán′ti·co (ät·län′tē·kô). Department of Colombia. See *Table* at COLOMBIA.

At·lan′tic Ocean (ăt·lăn′tĭk); *anc.* **O·ce′a·nus At·lan′ti·cus** (ô·sē′ȧ·nŭs ät·län′tĭ·kŭs). Body of water separating North and South America from Europe and Africa; ab. 31,500,000 sq. m. (with its branches 41,000,000 sq. m.); greatest depth Milwaukee Depth 30,246 ft. (discovered 1939), in North Atlantic off NE coast of Dominican Republic. Often divided into **North Atlantic Ocean** and **South Atlantic Ocean** (deepest 26,575 ft., lat. 55°5′S, long. 26°45′W, near South Sandwich Is.). Merges with Arctic Ocean N of 60°N; S of South America connects with Pacific Ocean by Drake Passage; S of Africa arbitrarily separated from Indian Ocean by meridian 20°E. See SARGASSO SEA.

Atlantic Peak. Mountain 12,734 ft., SW Fremont co., cen. Wyoming.

At·lán′ti·da (ät·län′tē·thä). Department, N Honduras; 1914 sq. m.; pop. (1945 est.) 50,413; ✳ La Ceiba.

At′las (ät′läs). Locality, Northumberland co., E cen. Pennsylvania, ab. 1 m. NW of Mount Carmel; pop. 1574.

Atlas Mountains. Mountain system ab. 1500 m. long in NW and N Africa, extending from Cape Noun on SW Morocco coast to Cape Bon on NE Tunisia coast; highest

peak Toubkal in W Morocco 13,661 ft., although Tizi-u-Tanjurt, also in Morocco, has been claimed to be 14,764 ft. In ancient times the name Atlas Mountains was restricted to the Grand Atlas range on the S border of Mauretania. Comprises several ranges: **Grand**, or **High, Atlas** in W and S Morocco containing highest peaks; **An'ti-At'las** (ăn'tĭ-ăt'lăs), to the S and parallel with it, highest point ab. 6750 ft.; **Middle Atlas** (*Fr.* Moy'en' A'tlas'** [mwȧ'yăn'-nȧ'tläs']) in N cen. Morocco, highest ab. 11,000 ft.; **Maritime,** or **Little, Atlas,** coastal ranges, generally lower (averaging 5000 ft.) from Ceuta eastward in Morocco and Algeria to Cape Bon in Tunisia; and **Saharan Atlas** (*Fr.* A'tlas' Sa'ha'rien'** [ȧ'tläs' sȧ'[h]ȧ'ryăn']) in E Morocco and bet. N Algeria and N part of Southern Territories including the Aurès range in E Algeria, highest Djebel Chélia 7609 ft. Not explored extensively until 19th cent.

At'lin Lake (ăt'lĭn). Long, narrow lake 343 sq. m., NW British Columbia and SW Yukon, Canada; connects with Tagish Lake to the W and its outlet the Lewes river. Town of **Atlin** is on its E shore.

A·tlix'co (ȧ-tlēs'kô). Town, Puebla state, SE cen. Mexico, 58 m. SE of Mexico City; pop. 17,034.

At'more (ăt'mōr). City, Escambia co., Alabama, 35 m. NE of Mobile Bay; pop. 8173.

A·to'ka (ȧ-tō'kȧ). **1** County in Oklahoma. See *Table* at OKLAHOMA.

2 City, its ⊗, S Oklahoma, 43 m. SE of Ada; pop. 2877; manufactures flour, lumber, etc.; founded 1867.

A'to·to·nil'co el Al'to (ä'tô-tô-nēl'kô ĕl äl'tô). Town, Jalisco state, W cen. Mexico, 57 m. E of Guadalajara; pop. 9184.

A'to·yac', Rí'o (rē'ô ä'tô-yäk'). River ab. 150 m. long, headstream of the Balsas, cen. Mexico; rises in Tlaxcala and flows S and SW into Guerrero; unnavigable.

A·traf'-i-Bal'da (ȧ-träf'ĕ-bŭl'dȧ). Former district, S cen. Hyderabad state, S cen. India; 2651 sq. m.; pop. 499,661; ✳ Hyderabad.

Atrak. See ATREK.

A'tra·nos' (ä'trȧ-nôs'), also **A'dra·nos'** (ä'drä-nôs'); *anc.* **Rhyn'da·cus** (rĭn'dȧ-kŭs). River ab. 150 m. long, NW Turkey in Asia; flows NW from beyond Kütahya and through Lake Apulyont to the Susıgırlık near the Sea of Marmara.

A·tra'to (ä-trä'tô). River ab. 350 m. long in NW Colombia; flows N into Gulf of Darien. See TRUANDO.

Atrecht. See ARTOIS.

A·trek' (ä-trĕk') or **A·trak'** (ä-träk'). River ab. 300 m. long in NE Iran; flows W forming section of boundary bet. Iran and the Turkmen S.S.R. and empties into SE Caspian Sea in U.S.S.R.

A'tri (ä'trē); *anc.* **Ha'tri·a** (*or* **Ha'dri·a**) **Pi·ce'na** (hä'trĭ-ȧ [hä'drĭ-ȧ] pĭ-sē'nȧ). Commune, Teramo prov., Abruzzi e Molise, cen. Italy, near Adriatic coast 14 m. ESE of Teramo; pop. 12,735; Romanesque-Gothic cathedral; remains of ancient town; manufactures silk, soap, licorice. Became Roman colony 290 B.C.

Atria. See ADRIA.

Atria Picena. Variant of *Hatria Picena:* see ATRI.

Atropatene. See AZERBAIJAN.

A·tsu·gi (ä-tsoō-gĕ; *Angl.* ä-tsoō'gĕ). Town, Kanagawa prefecture, SE Honshu, Japan, 15 m. W of Yokohama; pop. 10,989; airport.

A·tsu·ta (ä-tsoō-tä). Town, Aichi prefecture, S Japan, at head of Ise Bay; pop. 25,000; now port of Nagoya, in S part of city; has famous Shinto shrine.

Atsuta Bay. See ISE BAY.

At·tai'ro (ät-tä'ĕ-rô); *Mod. Gr.* **A'ta·vy'ri·on** (ä'tä-vē'ryôn). Mountain 3986 ft., highest on Rhodes I.

At'ta·la (ăt''l-ȧ). County in Mississippi. See *Table* at MISSISSIPPI.

Attaleia, Attalia. See ANTALYA.

At·tal'la (ă-tăl'ȧ). Industrial city, Etowah co., NE Alabama, 5 m. W of Gadsden; pop. 8257.

At·ta·wa·pis'kat (ăt'ȧ-wȧ-pĭs'kăt). River 465 m. long,

NE Ontario, Canada; rises in chain of lakes in NW Ontario, flows E and NE into James Bay. In long. 88°W flows through **Attawapiskat Lake.**

At'ter (ăt'ēr; *Angl.* ăt'ēr), **Lake;** or **Lake Kam'mer** (käm'ēr; kăm'ēr); *Ger.* **At'ter·see'** (ät'ēr-zā') or **Kam'mer·see'** (käm'ēr-zā'). Lake 12 m. long and 2 m. wide in Upper Austria prov., Austria, 40 m. SW of Linz; its shores form a summer-resort region.

At'ti·ca (ăt'ĭ-kȧ). **1** City, Fountain co., W Indiana, on Wabash river 22 m. WSW of Lafayette; pop. 4341; commercial center; sandstone quarries nearby.

2 Village, Wyoming co., W New York, 31 m. E of Buffalo; pop. 2758; in dairying region.

3 Ancient division and state of E Greece, forming the territory of Athens; bounded on N by Boeotia, on E by Aegean Sea, on S by Saronic Gulf, and on W by Megaris; included the island of Salamis; chief towns were Athens, Piraeus, and Eleusis.

History: In legend divided into **12** independent Pelasgian states; a center of Mycenaean culture 2d millennium B.C.; invaded by Ionian Greeks by c. 1300 B.C.; territory without political unity until gradually unified under Athens by 700 B.C. (traditionally accomplished by King Theseus). For later history, see ATHENS.

Attica and Boe·o'tia (bē·ō'shȧ; -shĭ-ȧ); *Mod. Gr.* **At'ti·kē' kai Boi·ō·ti'a** (ä'tē-kyē' kâ vyô·tē'ä). Department of Greece. See *Table* at GREECE.

Attinianum. See DIGNANO D'ISTRIA.

At'tle·bor'o (ăt''l-bûr'ô). City, Bristol co., SE Massachusetts; pop. 27,118; jewelry; textile mills.

At·tock' (ȧ-tŏk'). **1** District, Rawalpindi division, former Punjab; now in NW West Punjab, Pakistan; 4148 sq. m.; pop. (1941) 675,875; ✳ Campbellpur.

2 Town in district, on Indus river near mouth of Kabul river 42 m. E of Peshawar; pop. 1826; has fortress built by Akbar 1581; important military post.

At'tu (ä'tōō). Rocky island in Near Island group and most westerly of the Aleutian Islands, SW Alaska, 52°55'N lat., 172°30'E long.; highest point more than 3000 ft.; formerly a prosperous Atka Aleut settlement. Occupied by Japanese June 1942; retaken by U.S. forces May–June 1943.

A'tu·a·na (ä'tōō-ä'nä) or **A'tu·o'na** (-ô'nä). Village on S coast of Hiva Oa I., ✳ of Marquesas Is.

A·tuel' (ä-twĕl'). River ab. 300 m. long in W Argentina; rises in the Andes, flows E and SSE in Mendoza prov. to unite with the Salado in N La Pampa prov.

A'tun·ta'qui (ä'tōōn-tä'kĕ). Town, Imbabura prov., N Ecuador; pop. (1944 est.) 8701.

Atura. See AIRE commune, France.

Aturus. See ADOUR.

At'wa'ter (ăt'wô'tēr; -wŏt'ēr). City, Merced co., California, NW of Merced; pop. 7318.

At'wood (ăt'wŏŏd). City, ⊗ of Rawlins co., NW Kansas; pop. 1906.

At'wood Cay (ăt'wŏŏd) or **Sa·ma'na** (sȧ·mä'nȧ). Small island in cen. Bahama Is., 23°9'N, 73°54'W; formerly sometimes identified with Columbus's San Salvador.

A'ty·rá' (ä'tē-rä'). Town, Cordillera dept., cen. Paraguay; pop. ab. 8300.

A'u·a'u Channel (ä'ōō-ä'ōō). Strait 7 m. wide bet. NW Maui I. and Lanai I., Hawaii. See LAHAINA.

Au'bagne' (ō'bàn'y'); *anc.* **Al·ba'ni·a** (ăl-bä'nĭ-ȧ; -bän'yȧ). Commune, Bouches-du-Rhône dept., SE France, 8 m. E of Marseilles; pop. 13,949.

Aube (ōb). **1** River ab. 125 m. long in N cen. France; rises in Haute-Marne dept., flows N and W into Seine river 23 m. NNW of Troyes.

2 Department of France. See *Table* at FRANCE.

Au'be·nas' (ōb'nä'). Commune, Ardèche dept., SE France, on Ardèche river at foot of Cévennes Mts.; pop. 4177; in fertile region near several extinct volcanoes.

Au'bers' (ō'bâr'). Commune, Nord dept., N France, **9** m. W of Lille; pop. (1931) 871; battle March 1915.

Au′ber′vil′liers′ (ō′bĕr′vē′lyā′); *formerly* **No′tre Dame′ des Ver′tus′** (nô′trē dȧm′ [nôt′ dȧm′] dā vĕr′tü′). Commune, Seine dept., N France, NNE suburb of Paris 2 m. from right bank of Seine river; pop. 55,871; manufactures chemical products, perfumes, glass, rubber, cardboard; resort for pilgrims; battle 1814.

Au′bin′ (ō′băɴ′). Commune, Aveyron dept., S France, on Enne river 19 m. NW of Rodez; pop. 5382; coal and iron mines, stone quarries, sulfur and alum mines.

Au′burn (ô′bĕrn). **1** City, Lee co., E Alabama, 8 m. W of Opelika; pop. 16,261; Auburn Univ. (1872; coed.; formerly Alabama Polytechnic Institute).
2 City, ⊗ of Placer co., E California, 36 m. NE of Sacramento; pop. 5586; founded as gold-mining camp 1848, incorp. as city 1888.
3 City, Sangamon co. cen. Illinois, 17 m. S of Springfield; pop. 2209.
4 City, ⊗ of De Kalb co., NE Indiana, 22 m. NNE of Fort Wayne; pop. 6350; commercial center in agricultural section; manufactures automotive parts.
5 City, ⊗ of Androscoggin co., SW Maine, on Androscoggin river opp. Lewiston 30 m. N of Portland; pop. 24,449; shoe manufactories.
6 Town, Worcester co., cen. Massachusetts, 5 m. SSW of Worcester; pop. 14,047; residential suburb of Worcester.
7 City, ⊗ of Nemaha co., SE Nebraska, in fruit-growing section 55 m. SE of Lincoln; pop. 3229.
8 Manufacturing city, ⊗ of Cayuga co., cen. New York, on outlet of Lake Owasco 25 m. WSW of Syracuse; pop. 35,249; founded 1793, became ⊗ 1805, chartered as city 1848. Seat of Auburn Theological Seminary (1819) until its merger in 1939 with Union Theological Seminary in New York City. State prison (built 1816).
9 City, King co., W cen. Washington, 11 m. ENE of Tacoma; pop. 11,933; manufactures pottery, cabinets.
10 City, E New South Wales, SE Australia, W suburb of Sydney; pop. 20,112.

Au′burn·dale (ô′bĕrn-dāl). Residential city, Polk co., cen. Florida penin., 10 m. E of Lakeland; pop. 5595.

Au′bus′son′ (ō′bü′sôɴ′). Commune, Creuse dept., cen. France, on Creuse river 20 m. SE of Guéret; pop. 5860; long celebrated for its carpets and tapestries, the famous Savonnerie carpets and the Beauvais and Gobelin tapestries still being made on hand looms.

Au′by′ (ō′bē′). Commune, Nord dept., N France, 3 m. NNW of Douai; pop. (1931) 7506; coal mines; leading zinc works of France; chemical products.

Auch (ōsh; ōsh); *anc.* **El′im·ber′rum** (ĕl′im·bĕr′ŭm); *later* **Au·gus′ta Aus·co′rum** (ô·gŭs′tȧ ôs·kōr′ŭm). City, ✳ of Gers dept., SW France, on Gers river 42 m. W of Toulouse; pop. 13,313; late-Gothic cathedral (begun 1489) famous for its stained-glass windows and hand-worked choir stalls; museum and library; trades in woolen and cotton goods, Armagnac brandy, wine. Chief town of the Ausci, a Celtiberian tribe; ravaged by Saracens 732; medieval capital of Armagnac; became capital of the generality of Gascony in 17th cent.

Au′chel′ (ō′shĕl′). Commune, Pas-de-Calais dept., N France, 20 m. NW of Arras; pop. (1931) 13,623; coal.

Au′chin·leck′ (ô′kĭn-lĕk′; ô′kĭn-). Parish, Ayr co., SW Scotland; pop. 6808; family home of James Boswell.

Auchterhouse Hill. See SIDLAW HILLS.

Au·cil′la (ô·sĭl′ȧ; ô-) *or* **O·cil′la** (ô-). River ab. 70 m. long, N Florida; flows S from S Georgia into Apalachee Bay.

Auck′land (ôk′lănd). **1** Provincial district of New Zealand. See *Table* at NEW ZEALAND.
2 Seaport city, its ✳, on Waitemata and Manukau Harbors; pop. 149,660, with suburbs 547,900; founded 1840 as capital of New Zealand, but replaced by Wellington 1865; has excellent harbor; trade and distribution center for extensive and prosperous dairy region; residential city with attractive suburbs. Seat of Auckland University College, a unit of New Zealand University.

Auckland Islands. Uninhabited group of islands 200 m. S of New Zealand, 50°32′S, 166°13′E; 234 sq. m.; discovered 1806; mountainous; several good harbors.

Aude (ōd). **1** *anc.* **A′tax** (ā′tăks). River 130 m. long in S France; rises on the slopes of the Pyrenees, flows N and E into Mediterranean Sea near Narbonne.
2 Department of France. See *Table* at FRANCE.

Au′de·narde′ (ōd′nȧrd′); *Flem.* **Ou′de·naar′de** (ou′dĕ-nȧr′dĕ). Commune, East Flanders prov., NW cen. Belgium, on Schelde river 31 m. W of Brussels; pop. 6330; railroad junction; notable for its churches and late-Gothic hôtel de ville; linen, lace, cotton, tobacco; scene of defeat July 11, 1708 of French under duke of Vendôme by Prince Eugene and Marlborough during War of the Spanish Succession; captured by French and American troops Nov. 1, 1918.

Au′den·shaw (ô′d′n·shô). Urban district, Lancashire, NW England, 5 m. E of Manchester; pop. 12,656; cotton mills, manufacture of machines.

Au′der·ghem (ou′dĕr·ᴋĕm). Commune, Brabant prov., cen. Belgium, SE suburb of Brussels (1½ m.); pop. 14,090.

Audh. Var. of OUDH.

Aud′ley (ôd′lĭ). Former urban district, Staffordshire, England, 6 m. NW of Stoke on Trent; pop. (1931) 13,621.

Au·drain′ (ô-drān′; ô′drān′). County in Missouri. See *Table* at MISSOURI.

Au′du·bon (ô′dŭ·bŏn; -bŭn). **1** County in Iowa. See *Table* at IOWA.
2 City, its ⊗, W Iowa, 59 m. NE of Council Bluffs; pop. 2928; in agricultural section; canneries.
3 Borough, Camden co., SW New Jersey, 4 m. SSE of Camden; pop. 10,440; suburb of Camden.

Audubon, Mount. Peak 13,223 ft. in Front Range of the Rocky Mts., Boulder co., N cen. Colorado.

Au′e (ou′ĕ). Industrial city, Karl-Marx-Stadt dist., E Germany, in the Erz Gebirge 13 m. SE of Zwickau; pop. 21,296; iron foundries, machine shops, cotton mills, hardware and tool factories; industrial schools.

Au′er·bach (ou′ĕr·bäᴋ). Industrial city, Karl-Marx-Stadt dist., E Germany, 55 m. S of Leipzig; pop. 19,408; embroidery, carpets, textiles.

Au′er·stedt *or* **Au′er·städt** (ou′ĕr-shtĕt). Village, E Germany, in former Prussian province of Saxony, 14 m. NE of Weimar; scene of defeat of Prussians under duke of Brunswick by French under Davout Oct. 14, 1806, simultaneously with Napoleon's victory over main Prussian army at Jena.

Aufidus. See OFANTO.

Au·ghra′bies Falls (ô·krä′bēs; -grä′-). Falls 450 ft. high in the Orange river, NW Cape Province, Republic of So. Africa, ab. 35 m. E of the South-West Africa border; discovered 1824.

Augh′rim *or* **Agh′rim** (ŏᴋ′rĭm; ŏg′-). Parish and town, co. Galway, Eire, 30 m. E of Galway; pop. 112; scene of decisive victory of William III over James II July 12, 1691, which, together with battle of the Boyne (July 1, 1690), is commemorated in Northern Ireland on Orangemen's Day (July 12).

Au·gi′la (ou·jē′lȧ; ô-; -lä). Oasis and town in S Cyrenaica, Libya, N Africa, 220 m. S by E of Bengasi.

Au·glaize′ (ô·glāz′). **1** River ab. 100 m. long in W Ohio; rises in Auglaize co. and flows W and N to the Maumee river at Defiance.
2 County in Ohio. See *Table* at OHIO.

Au Gres, Point (ō grā′). Point on SE coast of Arenac co., E Michigan, at N entrance to Saginaw Bay.

Augs′burg (ouks′bôorᴋ); *anc.* **Au·gus′ta Vin·del′i·co′rum** (ô·gŭs′tȧ vĭn·dĕl′ĭ·kōr′ŭm). Commercial city, ✳ of Swabia govt. dist., Bavaria, Germany, on the Lech river 30 m. WNW of Munich; pop. (1939) 185,704; consists of ancient inner town and suburbs; buildings include the cathedral, the Rathaus with its notable Golden Hall, and the episcopal palace; center of S German textile industry; machine shops; manufactures acetylene gas, chemicals, leather, paper, jewelry.

History: Roman colony founded by Augustus 14 B.C.; received municipal rights from Hadrian; scene of defeat of Hungarians by Otto I 955 A.D.; recognized as free imperial city 1276; because of location and undertakings of Fugger and Welser families, became center for trade bet. northern and southern Europe in 15th and 16th cents.; scene of diet to which Melanchthon presented Confession of Augsburg 1530, and of drafting of Religious Peace of Augsburg 1555; League of Augsburg against France 1686; lost municipal freedom and became part of Bavaria 1806. In World War II frequently bombed 1940–45; taken by Allied armies April 28, 1945.

Au·gus'ta (ô·gŭs'tà). **1** County in Virginia. See *Table* at VIRGINIA.

2 City, ⊗ of Woodruff co., NE cen. Arkansas, on White river 56 m. SW of Jonesboro; pop. 2272; settled 1848; sawmill, cotton gins. Cf. COTTON PLANT and McCRORY.

3 City, ⊗ of Richmond co., E Georgia, on Savannah river 105 m. ENE of Macon; pop. 70,626; cotton trading; cotton and cottonseed products; kaolin deposits; lumber; settled in 1735 by James Oglethorpe; captured by British 1778, but retaken by Americans under "Lighthorse Harry" Lee 1781; capital of Georgia 1786–96, incorporated as city 1798. Medical Coll. of Georgia (1828; coed.), Paine College (1882; coed.).

4 City, Butler co., S Kansas, 20 m. E of Wichita; pop. 6434; oil refinery and distributing point.

5 City, Bracken co., NE Kentucky, on Ohio river 17 m. NW of Maysville; pop. 1458; shipping point for tobacco.

6 City, ✳ of Maine and ⊗ of Kennebec co., SW Maine, on Kennebec river 25 m. NE of Lewiston; pop. 21,680; at head of navigation on Kennebec river; trading post in 17th cent.; site of Fort Western 1754, incorporated as town 1797, as city 1849; made capital of Maine 1831; lumber and paper mills, shoe factories, textile mills.

7 City, Eau Claire co., W Wisconsin, 20 m. ESE of Eau Claire; pop. 1338.

Au·gu'sta (ou·gōōs'tä) *or* **A·go'sta** (ä·gôs'tä). Commune, Siracusa prov., SE Sicily, 12 m. N of Syracuse; pop. 19,690; on small island, formerly the peninsula of Xiphonia, connected by bridge with Sicilian mainland; fortified naval harbor; saltworks; exports oil, wine, cheese, fruits, honey, sardines. Founded by Frederick II 1232; near site of ancient Megara Hyblaea (*q.v.*); sacked 1286; burned by Turks 1551; almost completely destroyed by earthquake 1693. In World War II taken by British July 1943.

Au·gus'ta, Cape (ou·gōōs'tä). Cape extending into Caribbean Sea on N coast of Colombia at Barranquilla.

Augusta Auscorum. See AUCH.

Augusta Bay. = EMPRESS AUGUSTA BAY.

Augusta Emerita. See MÉRIDA.

Augusta Praetoria. See AOSTA.

Augusta Suessionum. See SOISSONS.

Augusta Taurinorum. See TURIN.

Augusta Treverorum. See TRIER city.

Augusta Vangionum. See WORMS.

Augusta Vindelicorum. See AUGSBURG.

Au'gus·tine (ô'gŭs·tēn). Island ab. 7 m. in diameter, SW part of Cook Inlet, Alaska; highest point 3970 ft.; volcano, eruption 1883.

Augustobona Tricassium. See TROYES.

Augustodunum. See AUTUN.

Augustodurum. See BAYEUX.

Augustonemetum. See CLERMONT-FERRAND.

Augustoritum Lemovicensium. See LIMOGES.

Augustów. See AVGUSTOV.

'Auja, El. See EL 'AUJA.

Au·ké'na (ou·kā'nä). Small island of Gambier Is., S Pacific Ocean.

Au'ki (ou'kē). Chief village, on W coast, of Malaita I., N of cen. part, Solomon Is., W Pacific Ocean.

Auld·earn' (ôld·ûrn'). Village, Nairn co., NE Scotland, E of Nairn; pop. 1065; scene of victory of Montrose over the Covenanters under Sir John Urry May 9, 1645.

Aulie Ata. See DZHAMBUL.

Au'lis (ô'lĭs). Harbor in Boeotia on Evripos Strait, E cen. Greece; according to tradition, starting place of Greek fleet sailing against Troy at beginning of the Trojan War, and scene of the sacrifice of Iphigenia.

Aul·la'gas (ou·yä'gäs), **Lake.** = Lake POOPÓ.

Aul'nay'–sous–Bois' (ō'nā'soo·bwä'). Commune, Seine-et-Oise dept., N France, 6 m. NE of Paris; pop. 31,763.

Aulon. See VLONA.

Au'male' (ō'mál'). **1** Commune, NE cen. Alger dept., N Algeria, NW Africa, ab. 60 m. SE of Algiers; pop. 6781.

2 Commune, Seine-Inférieure dept., N France, 40 m. NE of Rouen; pop. 2402; has fine old church of 16th and 17th cents. Its surrounding territory granted to Odo, half brother of William the Conqueror; ruling family important in French nobility as counts (from 11th cent.) and dukes (after 1547); duchy passed 1618 to ducal house of Nemours (Savoy), thence to Louis XIV by purchase 1675, and finally to House of Orléans 1769.

Aundh (ound). **1** Former Indian state. Deccan and Kolhapur States, S Bombay, Indian Union; joined United Deccan State Aug. 26, 1947; area now in Maharashtra.

2 Town, its ✳, 27 m. SE of Satara; pop. 3741.

Au'nis' (ō'nēs'). Historical region of W cen. France; bounded on N by Poitou, E by Angoumois, S by Gironde estuary, and W by Bay of Biscay; ✳ La Rochelle. Early became a feudal dependency of Poitou.

Aun'je·titz (oun'yĕ·tĭts); *Czech* **U'ně·ti'ce** (ŏŏ'nyĕ·tyĭ'tsĕ). Village just NNW of Prague, Czechoslovakia; site of remains of early bronze culture (c. 2000–1000 B.C.).

Au'nus (ou'nŏŏs). Isthmus, NW Soviet Russia, Europe, extending bet. Lakes Ladoga and Onega; overrun by Russians June 21, 1944.

Au'rang·a·bad' (ou'rŭng·gä·bäd'), *also* **Au'rung·a·bad'.** **1.** District, N Maharashtra, S cen. India; formerly in Hyderabad state and (1956–60) in Bombay state.

2 City, its ✳, ab. 190 m. ENE of Bombay; pop. 29,288; silk, silver, and gold handicrafts. Founded 1610 by Malik Ambar; Aurangzeb's capital in 17th-cent. campaign against southern Indian Mohammedan states; here he erected to his wife a beautiful mausoleum sometimes compared with the Taj Mahal; later the ✳ of independent Nizams before it was removed to Hyderabad.

Au·ra·ni'tis (ô'rá·nī'tĭs). In the time of Herod the Great (37–4 B.C.) that part of Hauran forming NE section of his kingdom, E of the Sea of Galilee.

Aurantes. See ABRANTES.

Au·rar'i·a (ô·râr'ĭ·à). First settlement in Colorado, established 1858; soon united (1860) with two other villages to become Denver.

Au'ray' (ô'rā'). Commune, Morbihan dept., NW France, on Auray river 11 m. W of Vannes; pop. 6474; famed church of Sainte Anne d'Auray (3 m. NW) pilgrimage resort.

Aurelia Aquensis. See BADEN-BADEN.

Aurelianum. See ORLÉANS.

Au·re'li·an Way (ô·rē'lĭ·ăn; ô·rēl'yăn); *Lat.* **Vi'a Au·re'li·a** (vī'à ô·rē'lĭ·à; ô·rēl'yà). Roman highway, called the "Great Coast Road," running NW along the coast of Etruria, at first to Pisae (Pisa), but later extended to Genua (Genoa) in Liguria; near Luna (W of Apuania) it was joined by the Cassian Way.

Au'rès' Mountains (ō'rás'). Mountain massif in the Saharan Atlas, S cen. Constantine dept., NE Algeria; highest peak Djebel Chélia 7609 ft.

Au'rich (ou'rĭk). Town, NW Germany, in Lower Saxony state 12 m. NE of Emden; pop. 9600.

Au'ri'gnac' (ō'rē'nyák'). Commune, Haute-Garonne dept., S France, 37 m. SW of Toulouse; pop. 716; tanneries; caves with significant paleolithic remains, the appropriate subdivision of the Stone Age now being called the Aurignacian period.

Aurigny. See ALDERNEY.

Au′ril′lac′ (ô′rē′yàk′). City, ✻ of Cantal dept., S cen. France, 105 m. NNE of Toulouse; pop. 19,041; manufactures wooden shoes, umbrellas, paper, copper utensils, jewelry; trade in cattle, horses, cheese; 11th-cent. castle. Developed around 9th-cent. abbey of St. Géraud; famous seat of medieval learning.

Au·ro′ra (ô·rôr′à; ŭ·rōr′à). **1** County in South Dakota. See *Table* at SOUTH DAKOTA.
2 Suburban residential city, Adams and Arapahoe cos., NE cen. Colorado, 5 m. E of Denver; pop. 48,548.
3 Industrial city, Kane co., NE Illinois, 37 m. W of Chicago; pop. 63,715; railroad workshops; iron castings, typewriter supplies, etc.; first city to use electricity for street lighting (1881). Aurora College (1893; coed.).
4 City, Dearborn co., SE Indiana, on Ohio river 54 m. SE of Shelbyville; pop. 4119; manufactures furniture, paper boxes, coffins.
5 Village, St. Louis co., NE Minnesota, 13 m. E of Virginia; pop. 2799; trade center for iron-mining section.
6 City, Lawrence co., SW Missouri, 30 m. SW of Springfield; pop. 4683; trade center in dairy and poultry-raising section; zinc and lead deposits nearby.
7 City, ⊗ of Hamilton co., SE cen. Nebraska, 18 m. E of Grand Island; pop. 2576; flour mills, dairies.
8 Village, Cayuga co., cen. New York, on E shore of Cayuga Lake ab. 12 m. SSW of Auburn; pop. 834; settled 1789. Wells College (1868; women).
9 Town, Erie co., New York; pop. 12,888; includes East Aurora village (*q.v.*).
10 Town, York co., SE Ontario, Canada, 25 m. N of Toronto; pop. 3358.
11 Island of the New Hebrides. See MAEWO.

Aur′sund′en (our′sōōn′ĕn). Lake in cen. Norway, N of Femund Lake; drains into headwaters of Glomma river.

Ausa. See VICH.

Au·sa′ble (ô·sā′b'l). River, NE New York; formed by confluence of branches on N boundary of Essex co., flows E into Lake Champlain; in its lower course in Clinton co. flows through a deep scenic gorge, **Ausable Chasm**, ab. 2 m. long; tourist resort.

Au Sa′ble (ô sā′b'l). River 80 m. long, N cen. Michigan; from Crawford co. E into Lake Huron in NE Iosco co.

Au Sable Forks. Village, Essex and Clinton cos., NE New York, at fork of branches of Ausable river SW of Plattsburg; pop. 2026; pulp, paper manufactures.

Au Sable Point. 1 Point on NE coast of Alger co., N Michigan penin., extending into Lake Superior.
2 Point on E coast of Iosco co., NE Michigan, extending into Lake Huron.

Ausangate Knot. See NUDO AUSANGATE.

Auschwitz. See OŚWIĘCIM.

Ausculum Apulum. See ASCOLI SATRIANO.

Aussig. See ÚSTÍ.

Aust′-Ag′der (oust′äg′dĕr). County of Norway. See *Table* at NORWAY.

Aus′ten (ôs′tĕn; -tĭn), **Mount.** Hill and landmark ab. 4 m. S of Henderson Field, cen. Guadalcanal, Solomon Is.; held by Japanese during early part of campaign for the island; taken by U.S. marines Dec. 1942.

Aus′ter·litz (ôs′tĕr·lĭts; *Ger.* ous′-); *Czech* **Slav′kov** (släf′kôf). Commune, Moravia, Czechoslovakia, 12 m. ESE of Brno; pop. 4230; has fine palace and church. Scene of battle Dec. 2, 1805 in which French under Napoleon defeated combined forces of Russians and Austrians led by Kutuzov, thus terminating Third Coalition against France.

Aus′tin (ôs′tĭn). **1** County in Texas. See *Table* at TEXAS.
2 City, ⊗ of Mower co., S Minnesota, 34 m. SW of Rochester; pop. 27,908; food products.
3 Village, ⊗ of Lander co., cen. Nevada, 145 m. ENE of Carson City; pop. 389; founded 1862, became ⊗ 1863; important mining and trading center and post station during early gold-rush period in Nevada.

4 City, ✻ of Texas and ⊗ of Travis co., cen. Texas, on Colorado river 75 m. NE of San Antonio; pop. 186,505. Site first settled as Waterloo 1838; chosen as capital of Republic of Texas 1839, incorp., and renamed Austin; government returned to Houston 1842–45 because of marauding Mexicans and Indians; capital of state of Texas from 1845. Political, commercial, and educational center; distributing point for trading and agricultural area; manufactures furniture, brick, building stone, food products (chili, tamale canneries), cottonseed products, leather goods; packing plants; limestone quarries. Univ. of Texas (1883; coed.); Austin Presbyterian Theological Seminary; Huston-Tillotson College (1877; coed.); St. Edward's Univ. (1881; men; Roman Catholic).

Austin, Lake. Lake in W Salt Lake Region, W Western Australia.

Aus′tral·a′sia (ôs′trăl·ā′zhà; -shà). The portion of Oceania bet. the equator and lat. 47°S; ab. 3,300,000 sq. m.; also, by extension, all of Oceania, but in general, and especially in Australia and New Zealand, the term is not commonly used because of confusion with *Australia*.

Aus·tral′ia (ôs·trāl′yà; -trā′lĭ·à). Island continent, bounded on N by Timor and Arafura Seas, on NE by Coral Sea, on E by South Pacific Ocean, and on S and W by Indian Ocean; 2,948,366 sq. m.; pop. (1933, excluding ab. 51,000 aboriginals) 6,402,240, (1965 est.) 11,359,510. Separated from New Guinea on N by Torres Strait and from Tasmania on S by Bass Strait. West and cen. parts largely desert; many salt lakes, esp. in S (lowest Lake Torrens) and W; low Artesian Basin in E cen. part. Mountain range (Great Dividing Range, or Eastern Highlands) parallel with E coast from N Queensland around to cen. Victoria, highest point Mt. Kosciusko (*q.v.*); also fine plateau uplands in E New South Wales. Coast indented with extensive Gulf of Carpentaria in NE (Cape York Peninsula on E) and Great Australian Bight and Spencer Gulf in S; coast line rugged with few good harbors, but some excellent: Port Jackson (harbor of Sydney), Newcastle (mouth of Hunter river), Brisbane (Moreton Bay), Darwin (Port Darwin), Fremantle (estuary of Swan river), Port Adelaide, Port Pirie, and Port Lincoln in South Australia, and Melbourne (on Port Phillip Bay). Many islands and reefs along coast, esp. Great Barrier Reef on NE, Thursday I. and others in Torres Strait, Melville I. N of Darwin, Kangaroo I. off South Australia, and Fraser I. off SE Queensland. Chief rivers Murray-Darling system; others Fitzroy, Burdekin, Flinders, Swan, Barcoo. See *Map*, page 84.

History: First sighted by Spanish in 16th cent.; missed by Torres, who sailed by Torres Strait (*q.v.*) 1606; not reached by Europeans until landing of Dutch ship *Duyfken* on E coast of Gulf of Carpentaria 1606; in first half of 17th cent. N and W coasts explored by Dutch, who named it New Holland (see also TASMANIA and NEW ZEALAND, both discovered by Dutch mariner Tasman 1642); W coast navigated by Dampier 1688; E part claimed for Britain 1770 by Capt. Cook, who discovered Botany Bay (*q.v.*) and named the land New South Wales; first English settlement 1788, by convicts at Port Jackson (see SYDNEY); circumnavigated by Matthew Flinders 1801–03, who thus proved continental unity of New South Wales and New Holland; came to be called Australia in 19th cent.; granted right of free immigration by British government 1816; entire continent claimed by Britain 1829; given self-government by passage of Australian Colonies Government Act 1850; developed rapidly after gold rush of 1851; adopted, from 1855 in separate colonies, exclusion of Chinese immigrants, thus beginning policy of "White Australia"; crossed from E to W by J. McDouall Stuart 1862; self-dependent for defense after departure of British imperial forces 1870; opened transcontinental telegraph lines 1872; completed railroad from Sydney to Melbourne 1883; carried out federalization 1885–1901 (see Commonwealth of AUSTRALIA).

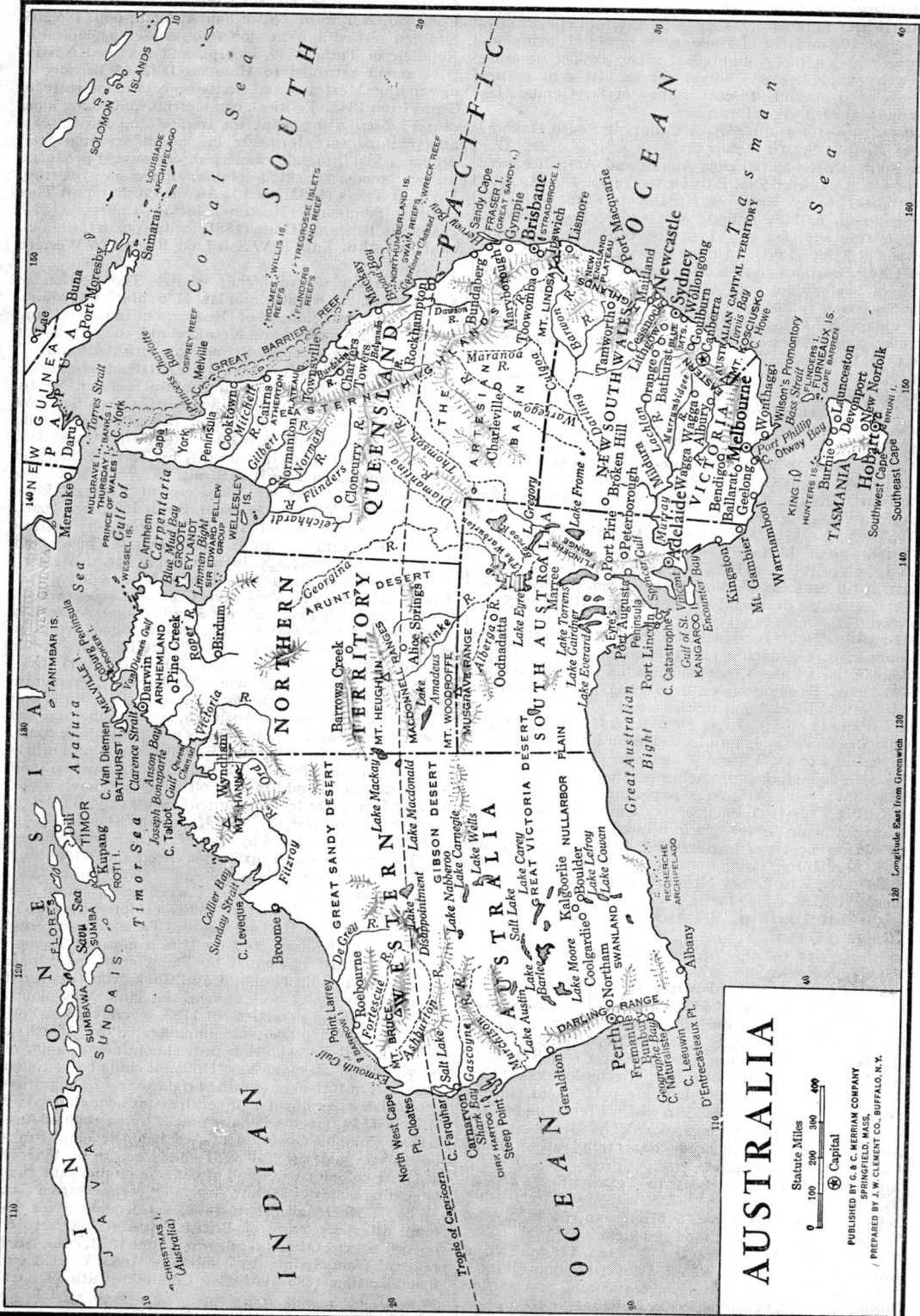

AUSTRALIA

Statute Miles

⊛ Capital

100 200 300 400

PUBLISHED BY G. & C. MERRIAM COMPANY
SPRINGFIELD, MASS.
PREPARED BY J. W. CLEMENT CO., BUFFALO, N.Y.

Australia, Commonwealth of. British self-governing dominion, comprising the six states of New South Wales, Victoria, Queensland South Australia, Western Australia, and Tasmania, and Northern Territory, and Australian Capital Territory (see *Table*, below); 2,974,581 sq. m.; pop. (1933, excluding aboriginals) 6,629,839, (1963 est.) 10,916,249; ✳ Canberra; with Territory of Papua, 3,065,209 sq. m., pop. ab. 10,927,000. Has Federal Parliament with Senate and House of Representatives and a governor-general, who represents the king and who is assisted by an Executive Council of 19 responsible ministers of state.

NAME	LOCA-TION	AREA[1]	POP.[2]	CAPITAL
STATES				
New South Wales	SE	309,432	4,048,598	Sydney
Queensland	NE	670,500	1,566,218	Brisbane
South Australia	S cen.	380,070	1,008,994	Adelaide
Tasmania[3]	S	26,304	361,320	Hobart
Victoria	SE	87,884	3,055,731	Melbourne
Western Australia	W	975,920	772,511	Perth
TERRITORIES				
Australian Capital Territory[4]	SE	939	73,453	
Northern Territory	N	523,620	29,424	Darwin
Territory of Papua	N	90,540	10,697[5]	Port Moresby

[1] Area in sq. m.
[2] Est. of 1963; exclusive of aborigines, of whom there are estimated to be 47,600 of full blood in all Australia.
[3] Including Macquarie I.
[4] Administered from Canberra, the ✳ of the Australian Commonwealth.
[5] White population only (est. of 1962); native pop. ab. 528,856.

Chief cities: Sydney, Melbourne, Brisbane, Adelaide, Perth, Fremantle, Hobart, Canberra, Newcastle, and Geelong. *Chief exports:* Wool, dairy products, wheat, hides and skins, flour, lead, fruits, meats, sugar, ores and concentrates, pig lead, and coal. *Chief mineral products:* Gold, coal, silver, and lead.

History: For years before 1901, see AUSTRALIA. Constitution drafted at National Convocation at Sydney 1891; approved by act of British Parliament 1900 and set in operation 1901; adopted federal tariff and woman suffrage 1902; passed Federal Old Age and Pension Act 1909; administered federal Territory of Papua (*q.v.*) after 1906 and of Northern Territory after 1910; adopted compulsory military service 1909–10, abandoned it 1929; maintained Royal Australian Navy after 1911; participated in World War I and represented at Peace Conference 1919; received mandate of certain German possessions in Pacific (see Territory of NEW GUINEA); occupied new capital Canberra (*q.v.*), 1927; received authority over one third of Antarctica 1933; joined Great Britain in World War II 1939; Darwin and its N coast threatened by Japanese 1941–42 but battle of Coral Sea and campaigns in the Solomon Is. and New Guinea prevented invasion.

Australia Fe′lix (fē′lĭks). A fertile district of cen. Victoria, SE Australia.

Aus·tra′lian Alps (ôs·trāl′yăn; -trā′lĭ·ăn). Mountain range, E Victoria and SE New South Wales, SE Australia, forming the S end of the Great Dividing Range and the watershed bet. the headstreams of the Murrumbidgee river and the short streams flowing S to the Pacific Ocean; average height 2500 to 5000 ft.; highest Mt. Kosciusko 7328 ft.; other peaks, all in Victoria, are Mt. Bogong 6508 ft. Mt. Feathertop 6306 ft., Mt. Hotham 6100 ft., and Mt. Cobberas 6026 ft.

Australian Capital Territory, *formerly known as* **Federal Capital Territory.** Territory of Australia, consisting of enclaves (1) in SE New South Wales, 911 sq. m. including Canberra and (2) area, 28 sq. m., at Jervis Bay on the coast (ceded 1917); total area 939 sq. m., pop. (1933) 8947 (1963 est.) 73,453. Ceded by New South Wales to Commonwealth in 1911; building operations for new government buildings begun 1923 and Parliament opened at Canberra by duke of York 1927.

Austral Islands. See TUBUAÏ ISLANDS.

Aus·tra′sia (ôs·trā′zhà; -shà) *or* **Os·tra′sia** (ŏs-). The eastern dominions of the Merovingian Franks, extending from the Meuse river to the Bohemian Forest.

History: Emerged as eastern part of kingdom of Franks after division of lands which followed death of Clovis (511 A.D.); ruled by Merovingian kings alternately as separate kingdom and as kingdom in conjunction with rule of Neustria (*q.v.*), 6th cent.; original seat of authority of mayors of palace of house of Pepin who founded Carolingian line of Frankish kings in 8th cent.; although recognized as territorial division in partitions of land which were customary at ruler's death, ceased to exist in Frankish empire as it was consolidated by Charlemagne (768–814).

Aus′tri·a (ôs′trĭ·à); *Ger.* **Ö′ster·reich′** (û′stĕr·rīk′). Former empire and later republic, cen. Europe; 32,373 sq. m.; pop. (1951) 6,918,959; ✳ Vienna. Bounded on N by Czechoslovakia (Bohemia and Moravia on N, Slovakia on NE), on E by Hungary, on S by Yugoslavia and Italy, and on W by Switzerland and Bavaria. A mountainous country, N of the Alps, containing many of its spurs and branches; bordered on S by Karawanken, Carnic, and Ötztaler Alps and on S Bavarian border by Bavarian Alps; highest point Gross Glockner in the Hohe Tauern 12,461 ft. Chief passes to Italy are the Brenner and Plöcken, and to Yugoslavia the Loibl. Chief river is the Danube (*Ger.* Donau) crossing in N from Bavaria to Hungary with many tributaries, esp. the Inn, Traun, and Enns; in the S are the Mur and Drau (Drava); Neusiedler Lake on E border is largest lake; in W and S are many other lakes, many of them health and resort centers. Its economy is divided: agriculture prevails in river valleys; industry n N and E, esp. iron and steel, aluminum, chemicals, fertilizers; forestry and tourist trade important. About 97% of people are German-speaking. Chief cities Vienna, Graz, Linz, Salzburg, Innsbruck, and Wiener Neustadt. Republic is divided into 8 provinces (for pronunciation of their names, see their individual entries):

NAME	LOCA-TION	AREA[1]	POPU-LATION[1]	CAPITAL
Burgenland	E	1,529	275,911	Eisenstadt
Carinthia (Kärnten)	S	3,681	474,180	Klagenfurt
Lower Austria[2]	NE	7,092	1,249,610	Krems
Salzburg	W	2,762	324,117	Salzburg
Styria (Steiermark)	SE	6,326	1,106,581	Graz
Tirol[4]	SW	4,884	426,499	Innsbruck
Upper Austria[3]	NW	4,625	1,107,562	Linz
Vienna	NE	469	1,760,784	Vienna
Vorarlberg[4]	W	1,005	193,715	Bregenz

[1] Area in sq. m. Pop. from 1951 Census.
[2] Under German domination (1938–45) called Lower Danube, *Ger.* Niederdonau.
[3] Under German domination (1938–45) called Upper Danube, *Ger.* Oberdonau.
[4] Under German domination (1938–45) Tirol and Vorarlberg were united as Tirol-Vorarlberg province; ✳ Innsbruck.

History: Territory inhabited by Celtic tribes, conquered by Rome 14 B.C.; included Roman settlement of Vindobona (see VIENNA); invaded by Marcomanni and Quadi 2d cent. A.D., by Huns 5th cent.; settled 590 by Slovenes who later formed kingdom of the Avars; erected by Charlemagne into a border state, East Mark (*Ger.* Österreich); became part of Holy Roman Empire under Saxon line; after defeat of Magyars 955, re-established as East Mark by Otto the Great; as an independent duchy 1156, granted to Henry of Austria in return for Bavaria; claimed by Ottokar II, ruler of the Slavic kingdom of Bohemia (1253–78); after defeat of Ottokar by Rudolf of Hapsburg 1278, remained Hapsburg until 1918; failed in effort to enforce control over Swiss cantons; as archduchy, center of imperial authority which also ruled adjacent duchies of Styria, Carinthia, Carniola and count of Tirol; one of ten circles of empire 1512 organized under first great emperor, Maximilian I (1493–1519); with other central European lands of Hapsburgs,

passed to Spanish Charles I (Emperor Charles V 1519–56); continued to be separate from holdings of Spanish Hapsburgs after it was inherited by Ferdinand I 1556; eastern European bulwark against the Turks who besieged Vienna 1529; lost Alsace and more than nominal authority over Holy Roman Empire 1648; saved from Turks by Poles under John Sobieski 1683; by Peace of Karlowitz 1699, received Slavonia, Transylvania, and most of Hungary; awarded Spanish Netherlands (see BELGIUM), Sardinia, and Naples 1713; entered series of wars against Frederick the Great of Prussia (q.v.); lost Silesia 1748; received Galicia in First Partition of Poland 1772; lost Spanish Netherlands 1797, Venice and Tirol 1805 after defeat by Napoleon; became the Austrian Empire at the formal dissolution of the Holy Roman Empire 1806; leading member of the Germanic Confederation formed 1815; in the settlement imposed by the Congress of Vienna 1815, received Lombardy and Venetia, Illyrian provinces, Salzburg and the Tirol, and Galicia; under Metternich, led in maintaining the principle of "legitimacy" against the European nationalistic and liberal revolts up to 1848; with Russian aid put down Hungarian revolt 1848; ruled by Emperor Francis Joseph 1848–1916; in war with Italy and France, lost Lombardy 1859; after defeat by Prussia in 1866, forced to withdraw from German affairs; with Hungary formed "dual monarchy" of Austria-Hungary 1867. (For history of AUSTRIA-HUNGARY, see that entry.) After the collapse of Austria-Hungary, Austria lost its status as a monarchy and was refused permission to unite with Germany; by the Treaty of St-Germain 1919, ceded Bohemia, Moravia, Galicia, Hungary, Bosnia and the Dalmatian coast, Trieste and the Trentino; as a republic 1919–33, suffered severe economic and social disorder; yielded dictatorial powers to Chancellor Dollfuss 1933; occupied by Nazi Germany and incorporated into the German Reich 1938–45 as an administrative unit (*Land*) under official name **Ost′mark** (ôst′märk). During World War II its industrial cities severely bombed by Allies 1944–45; invaded by Russian armies from E in March 1945 and by Allies from W in April and May; reestablished as a republic 1945; occupied by four powers U.S., U.S.S.R., Britain, France 1945–1955.

Aus′tri·a–Hun′ga·ry (ôs′trĭ·à·hŭng′gá·rĭ). Former monarchy, cen. Europe; included Austria, Hungary, and Czechoslovakia, Bucovina and Transylvania in Romania, NW half of Yugoslavia, Galicia in Poland, Venezia Giulia and Venezia Tridentina in Italy; 261,027 sq. m.

History: A "dual monarchy" formed in 1867, restoring partial Hungarian autonomy and creating the Austro-Hungarian Empire from the Austrian Empire and the kingdom of Hungary; after the Treaty of Berlin 1878, administered Turkish provinces of Bosnia and Herzegovina which it annexed in 1908; a member of the Triple Alliance with Germany and Italy 1882–1914; up to 1914 maintained a precarious balance bet. its various minorities; after the assassination (June 28, 1914) of Archduke Francis Ferdinand, issued an ultimatum to Serbia which precipitated the outbreak of World War I 1914; collapsed as the result of defeat in the war and of revolutions by the Czechs, Yugoslavs, and Hungarians 1918. For earlier, before 1867, and later, after 1918, history of AUSTRIA and HUNGARY, see those entries.

Aus′tro·ne′sia (ôs′trô·nē′zhà; -zhĭ·à; -shà; -shĭ·à). In general, the islands of the South Pacific Ocean; more accurately, the vast island area extending from Madagascar in the W, through the Malay Penin. and Archipelago, to Hawaii and Easter I. in the E—a name applied by ethnologists to the region where the peoples speak related agglutinative languages (Austronesian languages). Linguistically the region has three subdivisions: Indonesia, Polynesia, and Melanesia, each inhabited by an Austronesian subfamily.

Aust′våg·öy (oust′vôg·û′ü). Island in the Lofoten group off NW coast of Norway; 203 sq. m.; pop. 6701.

Au·tau′ga (ô·tô′gà). County in Alabama. See *Table* at ALABAMA.

Autesiodorum. See AUXERRE.

Au′teuil′ (ō′tû′y′). District in W part of Paris, France, at SE entrance to Bois de Boulogne (q.v.); famous racecourse for steeplechasing; notable in French literary history through Boileau, Molière, and Mme Helvétius, who held a salon here (known as the Société d'Auteuil).

Au·ti′son Ra′ju (ou·tē′sôn rä′hōō). Peak ab. 20,300 ft. in Cordillera Occidental, Peru.

Au·tlán′ *or* **Autlán de Na·var′ro** (ou·tlän′ dä nä·vär′rô). Town, SW Jalisco state, W cen. Mexico, 80 m. SW of Guadalajara; pop. 10,915.

Autricum. See CHARTRES.

Au′tun′ (ō′tûN′); *anc.* **Æd′u·a** (ĕd′ū·à; ē′dū·à); *later* **Au·gus′to·du′num** (ô·gŭs′tô·dū′nŭm). Commune, Saône-et-Loire dept., E cen. France, 51 m. NNW of Mâcon; pop. 14,863; 11th-cent. Gothic cathedral; 12th-cent. castle; Roman remains; manufactures cloth, carpets, machinery, leather, paper, furniture. Residence of Roman prefects of Gaul; economic and educational center under Romans; ruined by barbaric invasions 406–895; under dukes of Burgundy; burned by British 1379.

Au′vergne′ (ō′vĕrn′y′). Historical region of S cen. France; bounded on N by Bourbonnais, NE by Lyonnais, SE by Languedoc, SW by Guienne, W by Limousin, and NW by Marche; ✳ Clermont (now Clermont-Ferrand); mountains of volcanic origin; medicinal springs.

History: Inhabited by Arverni, Gallic people led by Vercingetorix and defeated by Caesar; yielded to Visigoths 475 A.D.; conquered by Clovis 507; part of Aquitaine; became countship 8th cent.; divided into four lordships, one of which, Terre d'Auvergne, became duchy 1360 (capital Riom), passed to Bourbons 1416, to France 1527.

Auvergne Mountains. Mountain range in cen. France; highest peak Puy de Sancy 6185 ft.

Aux Barques, Pointe (point′ ō bärk′). Point, S Michigan penin., extending into Lake Michigan.

Au′xerre′ (ō′sâr′); *anc.* **Au·te′si·o·do′rum** (ô·tē′sĭ·ô·dōr′ŭm). Commercial city, ✳ of Yonne dept., NE cen. France, on Yonne river 96 m. SE of Paris; pop. 24,282; 13th-cent. cathedral; old abbey; manufactures textiles, wine, leather, earthenware. Flourished in pre-Roman and Roman days; taken by Clovis; part of kingdom of Burgundy; captured by English 1359; united to France by Louis XI; bombarded by Germans 1870.

Au′xonne′ (ō′sôn′). Commune, Côte-d'Or dept., E France, on left bank of Saône river 18 m. ESE of Dijon; pop. 2920; manufactures cloth, plaster of Paris. Chartered 1229; under dukes of Burgundy from 13th cent.; surrendered to Austrians 1815.

Aux Sources, Mont (môN′-tō′sōōrs′). Peak 10,761 ft. in Drakensberg Mts., N Basutoland, on the Natal border; highest mountain in Union of South Africa.

A′va (ā′và). City, ⊗ of Douglas co., S Missouri; pop. 1581.

A′va (ä′và). Ruined city on Irrawaddy river, Sagaing dist., Upper Burma, 6 m. SW of Mandalay; founded in 14th cent.; for 400 years capital of Burma; replaced by Amarapura in 1783; again capital 1823–37.

Av′a·lanche Peak (ăv′à·lánch). Mountain 10,580 ft. on E boundary of Yellowstone National Park, NW Wyoming.

A′val′lon′ (à′và·lôN′). Commune, Yonne dept., NE cen. France, on Cousin river 27 m. SE of Auxerre; pop. 4854; on hill of red granite; 12th-cent. church. Celtic in origin; sacked by Saracens 731, by Normans 843; viscounty in medieval duchy of Burgundy; joined to French crown 1477; pillaged by forces of the League 1593.

Av′a·lon (ăv′à·lŏn). 1 Resort city, Los Angeles co., SW California, at E end of Santa Catalina I. 50 m. S of Los Angeles; pop. 1536; incorp. 1913; recreation center; Indian museum.

2 Residential borough, Allegheny co., SW Pennsylvania, on Ohio river 6 m. NW of Pittsburgh; pop. 6859.

3 Large peninsula of SE Newfoundland, bet. Trinity and Placentia Bays.

Avalon Dam *and* **Lake.** See CARLSBAD, New Mexico.

A·van′ti (*à·vŭn′tē*). Early kingdom of N India 6th–4th cents. B.C., about coextensive with Malwa; * Ujjain.

Avarau. See PALMERSTON.

A′va·ré′ (*à′và·rä′*). City, São Paulo state, SE Brazil, 120 m. W of Campinas; pop. (1940 est.) 10,533.

Avaricum. See BOURGES.

A·var′is (*à·vâr′ĭs*). City of ancient Egypt in E part of Nile delta, the Hyksos capital; completely destroyed, but has been identified with Tanis or Pelusium.

A′va·ru′a (*ä′vä·rōō′ä*). Village on N coast of the island of Rarotonga, Cook Is., S Pacific Ocean; * of Cook Is.

Ave′bur·y (*āv′bẽr·ĭ; ā′bẽr·ĭ*) *or* **A′bur·y** (*ā′bẽr·ĭ*). Village, Wiltshire, England, 29 m. E of Bristol; pop. 525; vast megalithic remains of uncertain date and origin.

A·vei′ro (*à·vā′ĕ·rōō; à·vă′ĕ·rōō*). **1** Salt lagoon on NW coast of Portugal, S of Oporto.

2 District of Portugal. See *Table* at PORTUGAL.

3 Seaport, its *, NW Portugal, on Aveiro lagoon 135 m. N by E of Lisbon, connected by canal with Atlantic Ocean; pop. 12,735; episcopal see; produces sea salt; fisheries (esp. sardines); kaolin and mercury mines. Said to be Roman **Tal′a·bri′ga** (*tăl′à·brĭ′gà*); well known through João Afonso's exploitation of Newfoundland dried codfish trade in 16th cent.

A′vel·la·ne′da (*ä′và·yä·nā′thä; Argentine pron.* *ä′vä·zhä-*). City, Buenos Aires prov., E Argentina, a suburb of Buenos Aires (city); pop. (est.) 399,021.

A′vel·li′no (*ä′văl·lē′nŏ*). **1** Province of Italy. See *Table* at ITALY.

2 *anc.* **Ab′el·li′num** (*ăb′ĕ·lĭ′nŭm*). Commune, its *, Campania, S Italy, 29 m. E by N of Naples; pop. 29,091; earthquake 1930; ruins of ancient town nearby; convent of Monte Vergine (founded 1119) famous pilgrim resort.

A′venches′ (*à′vänsh′*); *anc.* **A·ven′ti·cum** (*à·vĕn′tĭ·kŭm*). Commune, Vaud canton, W Switzerland, near Lake of Morat 8 m. NW of Fribourg; pop. (1930) 1604; one of oldest cities of Switzerland; capital of ancient Helvetia; made Roman colony by Vespasian and Titus, its population then being 60,000; destroyed by Alamanni 264 A.D.; refounded 1076 by Burkhardt, Bishop of Lausanne. Roman antiquities, including ruins of city walls.

Avenio. See AVIGNON.

Av′en·tine (*ăv′ĕn·tīn; -tĭn*). One of the seven hills of Rome. See SEVEN HILLS.

A′ve·reest′ (*à′vĕ·rāst′*). Commune, Overijssel prov., E Netherlands, 13 m. NE of Zwolle; pop. 9582.

A·ver′nus, Lake (*à·vûr′nŭs*); *Ital.* **La′go d′A·ver′no** (*lä′gŏ dä·vĕr′nŏ*); *anc.* **La′cus A·ver′nus** (*lā′kŭs à·vûr′nŭs*). Lake ab. 2 m. in circumference, Napoli prov., Campania, Italy, in crater of extinct volcano 8 m. W of Naples. Because of its dismal aspect and mephitic vapors, considered by the ancients (Homer, Vergil) as entrance to underworld; grove of Hecate, grotto of the Cumaean Sibyl, and home of the Cimmerii placed nearby in ancient legend; transformed by Agrippa into naval base (**Por′tus Iu′li·us** [*pōr′tŭs yōō′lĭ·ŭs*]), and connected with Lacus Lucrinus.

A·ver′sa (*ä·vĕr′sä*). Commercial commune, Napoli prov., Campania, S Italy, 8 m. N by W of Naples; pop. 36,960; famous for its sparkling white wine (Asprino). Built near site of ancient Atella by Normans 1029, being the first settlement in Italy granted them.

A′ver·y (*ā′vẽr·ĭ*). County in North Carolina. See *Table* at NORTH CAROLINA.

A′ves (*ä′väs*), *or* **Bird, Islands.** Group of small Venezuelan islands in Caribbean Sea E of Bonaire.

A′vesnes′ (*à′vân′*). City, Nord dept., N France, 25 m. SE of Valenciennes; pop. 4576. Built around 11th-cent. castle; held by Spain 1559–1659; captured by Prussians 1815; occupied by Germans in World War I.

A′vey′ron′ (*à′vā·rôN′*). **1** River ab. 150 m., S France; flows W into Tarn river 7 m. NW of Montauban.

2 Department of France. See *Table* at FRANCE.

A′vez·za′no (*ä′vĕd·dzä′nŏ*). Commune, Aquila prov., Abruzzi e Molise, cen. Italy, 22 m. S of Aquila; pop. 16,866; episcopal see; 15th-cent. castle; suffered from earthquake 1915.

Av·gu′stov (*ŭv·gōōs′tŭf*); *Pol.* **Au·gu′stów** (*ou·gōōs′-tōōf*). Town, N Białystok dept., NE Poland, 50 m. N of Białystok; pop. (1938–39 est.) 14,900; brewery; trade in fish. Founded 1650 by Sigismund II Augustus of Poland. Battle in World War I in which Russians defeated Germans Sept. 29–Oct. 4, 1914; during World War II held by Germans; taken by Russians Oct. 24, 1944; for a short time 1945–46 in W White Russia.

A′vi·glia′no (*ä′vē·lyä′nŏ*). Commune, Potenza prov., Lucania, S Italy, 7 m. NNW of Potenza; pop. 13,006; marble quarries and mineral springs.

A′vi′gnon′ (*à′vē′nyôN′*); *anc.* **A·ve′ni·o** (*à·vē′nĭ·ō*). Commercial and manufacturing city, * of Vaucluse dept., SE France, near confluence of Rhone and Durance rivers 50 m. NNW of Marseilles; pop. 59,172; ancient cathedral; papal palace; varied manufactures.

History: Founded as Phocaean colony; conquered by Romans. Goths, Burgundians, Ostrogoths, finally Franks; part of kingdom of Arles (*q.v.*); republic 1135–46; part of Venaissin (see COMTAT VENAISSIN); sold by Joanna I of Naples to Pope Clement VI 1348; seat of papacy 1309–77 and of Avignonese popes during Western Schism 1378–1417; united to France 1791.

A′vi·la (*ä′vē·lä*). **1** Province of Spain. See *Table* at SPAIN.

2 *anc.* **Ab′y·la** *or* **Ab′e·la** (*ăb′ĭ·là*). City, its *, cen. Spain, 53 m. WNW of Madrid; pop. 20,261; founded as walled city in late 11th cent.; cathedral; site of university (1455–1807) founded by Ferdinand and Isabella.

A′vi·lés′ (*ä′vē·lās′*). Seaport, Oviedo prov., NW Spain, 14 m. NNW of Oviedo on a winding inlet of the Bay of Biscay; pop. 18,037; iron, copper, and coal mines.

A′vion′ (*à′vyôN′*). Commune, Pas-de-Calais dept., N France, 9 m. NNE of Arras; pop. (1931) 16,465; severe fighting Apr.–June 1917; taken by Canadians.

A·viz′ (*à·vēsh′*). Commune, Portalegre dist., E cen. Portugal, 30 m. SW of Portalegre; gives name to Portuguese and Brazilian Order of Aviz (founded 1147).

Avlona. See VLONA.

A·vo′ca (*à·vō′kà*). **1** Town, Pottawattamie co., SW Iowa, 34 m. ENE of Council Bluffs; pop. 1540.

2 Borough, Luzerne co., E Pennsylvania, 7 m. SW of Scranton; pop. 3562; coal mining; silk mills.

3 *or* **O·vo′ca** (*ō-*). Valley and river in co. Wicklow, E Eire; celebrated in one of Moore's songs.

A′vo′court′ (*à′vō′kōōr′*). Commune, Meuse dept., NE France, 11 m. NW of Verdun; pop. (1931) 242; battles 1916–18, the forest **Bois d′A′vo′court′** (*bwä dä′vō′-kōōr′*) being taken by Germans Mar. 1916 and retaken by American forces Sept. 1918.

A′vo·la (*ä′vō·lä*). Seaport, Siracusa prov., SE Sicily, 14 m. SW of Syracuse; pop. 21,883; almonds and sugar cane; sugar refineries.

A′von. **1** (*ā′vŏn*) Town, W cen. Hartford co., N Connecticut; pop. 5273; incorp. 1830.

2 (*ā′vŏn*) Town, Norfolk co., E Massachusetts, 4 m. N of Brockton; pop. 4301; residential suburb of Brockton.

3 (*ăv′ŭn*) Village, Livingston co., W New York, on Genesee river 18 m. S of Rochester; pop. 2772.

4 (*ā′vŏn*) Village, Lorain co., N Ohio, 17 m. W of Cleveland; pop. 754.

5 (*ā′vŭn*) Upper course of the Swan river (*q.v.*), Western Australia.

6 (*ā′vŭn; ăv′ŭn*) River 65 m. long, S England; rises near Devizes in Wiltshire, flows S into English Channel.

7 (*ā′vŭn*) River 62 m. long, SW England; rises in Gloucestershire, flows S and W through the city of Bristol into Bristol Channel at Avonmouth.

8 (ā'vŭn; ăv'ŭn) River 96 m. long, cen. England; rises in Northamptonshire, flows WSW into the Severn at Tewkesbury; the "Shakespeare" Avon.

9 (ā'vŭn; ăv'ŭn) River 18 m. long, cen. Scotland; flows E into Firth of Forth.

Avon, Ben *or* **Mount.** See BEN AVON.

Av'on-by-the-Sea' (ăv'ŭn-). Borough, Monmouth co., E. cen. New Jersey; pop. 1707; seaside resort.

Av'on·dale (ăv'ŭn-dāl). City, Maricopa co., Arizona, W of Phoenix; pop. 6151.

A'von Lake (ā'vŏn). Village, Lorain co., N Ohio, on Lake Erie 18 m. W of Cleveland; pop. 9403.

A'von·mouth' (ā'vŭn-mouth'). Suburb of Bristol, Gloucestershire, SW cen. England, at mouth of the Avon; deep-sea docks of port of Bristol.

A'von Park (ā'vŏn). City, Highlands co., cen. Florida penin., 43 m. SE of Lakeland; pop. 6073.

A·voy'elles (à-voi'ĕlz; *Fr.* à'vwá'yĕl'). Parish in Louisiana. See *Table* at LOUISIANA.

A'vranches' (à'vräNsh'). Commune, Manche dept., NW France, on inlet 32 m. E of St-Malo; pop. 7130; resort. Taken by Americans July 25–31, 1944; scene of decisive Allied breakthrough.

A'vre (à'vr'). River 36 m. long, Somme dept., N France, flowing into Somme river near Amiens; battles March–May 1918.

Av·şa' (äv-shä'). Island, SW Sea of Marmara, W of Kapudağ Penin., Çanakkale vilayet, Turkey in Asia.

A'waj (ä'wăj). See PHARPAR.

A·wa·ji (ä-wä-jē). Island of Japan, E of Harima Sea, S of Honshu and NE of Shikoku I.; area 243 sq. m.; pop. 186,000; part of Hyogo prefecture; chief town Sumoto.

Awash. See HAWASH.

A·wa·ta (ä-wä-tä). Town, E suburb of Kyoto, Japan; famous for its pottery and Kinkozan ware.

Awe, Loch (lŏk ô'). Lake, Argyll co., cen. Scotland; 23 m. long; 16 sq. m.; extends NNE to base of Ben Cruachan; empties by means of **Awe River** into Loch Etive; has several wooded islands on which are numerous old castles; traveled by steamers.

A·wem'ba (ä-wĕm'bä). Province, NE Northern Rhodesia, S cen. Africa; 37,585 sq. m.; pop. 148,346; ✳ Kasama.

A'woe, Goe'noeng *or* **Gu'nung A'wu** (gōō'nŏŏng ä'wōō). Volcanic peak 6102 ft. on Sangihe I., Sangihe Is. (*q.v.*), Malay Archipelago; eruptions 1856, 1892.

Ax. See DAX.

Ax'ar Fjord (äk'sär). Inlet of the Arctic Ocean on N coast of Iceland, E of Eyja Fjord.

Ax'el (äk'sĕl). Commune, Zeeland prov., SW Netherlands, 20 m. SE of Middelburg; pop. 6060.

Ax'el Hei'berg (äk's'l hī'bûrg). One of the Sverdrup Is. (*q.v.*), W of Ellesmere I.; 13,200 sq. m.

Ax'im (?äk'sĭm). Coast town, SW Ghana, W Africa, at mouth of Ankobra river W of Takoradi; pop. 2189.

Axius. See VARDAR.

Ax'min'ster (ăks'mĭn'stēr). Town, Devonshire, England, on Axe river 23 m. ENE of Exeter; pop. 2673; formerly (1755–1835) famous for its carpets.

Axona. See AISNE.

Axum. See AKSUM.

Ay (ī; *Fr.* à'ē'). Commune, Marne dept., NE France, on Marne river 12 m. S of Reims; pop. 4634; produces Ay wine.

A'ya·cu'cho (ä'yä-kōō'chô). **1** Town, Buenos Aires prov., E Argentina, S of Buenos Aires; district pop. 20,643.

2 Department of Peru. See *Table* at PERU.

3 Town, ✳ of Ayacucho dept., 200 m. SE of Lima; pop. (1940 est.) 18,275; noted for its cathedral and churches. Founded 1539 by Pizarro and known as Guamanga or Huamanga until 1825; decisive battle on small plain of Ayacucho, near the village of La Quinua, Dec. 9, 1824, in which the Spanish viceroy La Serna was defeated by Gen. Sucre, won independence for Peru.

A·ya·guz' (*Russ.* ŭ·yŭ·gōōs'; *Kazakh* ä·yä·gûz'). **1** River ab. 240 m. long, E Kazakh S.S.R., Soviet Russia, Asia; flows generally SW into NE end of Lake Balkhash.

2 *formerly* **Ser·gi·o'pol** (syēr·gyĭ·ô'pŭl·y'). Town, E Kazakh S.S.R., Soviet Russia, Asia, on Ayaguz river 185 m. S of Semipalatinsk; on Turkistan-Siberian R.R.

A'ya·mon'te (ä'yä-môn'tâ). Seaport, Huelva prov., SW Spain, on left bank of Guadiana river near its mouth, 23 m. W of Huelva; pop. 12,136; shipbuilding, fisheries.

A·yan' (ŭ·yàn'). Seaport town on W shore of Sea of Okhotsk, E Khabarovsk Territory, Soviet Russia, Asia.

A'ya So·luk' (ä'yä sô·lōōk'). Village, S İzmir vilayet, W Turkey in Asia, near site of ancient Ephesus (*q.v.*).

A'ya·vi'ri (ä'yä-vē'rê). Town, Puno dept., SE Peru, 55 m. NW of Lake Titicaca; pop. (1940 est.) 6586.

Ay'den (ā'd'n). Town, Pitt co., E North Carolina, 35 m. E of Goldsboro; pop. 3108.

Ay·din' *or* **Ai·din'** (ī·dīn'). **1** Vilayet, SW Turkey in Asia; 2926 sq. m.; pop. 261,078.

2 *anc.* **Tral'les** (trăl'ēz). Town, its ✳, on Menderes river 55 m. SE of İzmir; pop. 15,152; railroad and trading town, producing city of olives, figs, grapes, and cotton. In ancient times Tralles was a flourishing city of Lydia.

Ayer (âr). Town. Middlesex co.. NE Massachusetts, 10 m. E of Fitchburg; pop. 14,927; Fort Devens nearby.

Ayer's Cliff (ârz). Village, ⊗ of Stanstead co., S Quebec, Canada, 18 m. S of Sherbrooke; pop. 697.

Ayles'bur'y (ālz'bĕr'ĭ; *Brit.* -bēr·ĭ, -brĭ). Municipal borough, ⊗ of Buckinghamshire, SE cen. England, 32 m. NW of London; pop. 21,054; in Thames valley **(Vale of Aylesbury)**; noted lace industry.

Ayl'mer (āl'mēr). **1** Town, Elgin co., SE Ontario, Canada, 11 m. E of St. Thomas; pop. 3483.

2 Resort town, Hull co., SW Quebec, Canada, on Ottawa river 7 m. W of Hull; pop. 4375.

Aylmer, Lake. Lake 612 sq. m. in E cen. Mackenzie District, Northwest Territories, Canada.

Ayodhya. See AJODHYA.

Ay'ot Saint Law'rence (ā'ŭt sànt lô'rĕns; lôr'ĕns). Village, cen. Hertfordshire, England, W of Welwyn Garden City; home of George Bernard Shaw.

Ayr (âr). **1** *or* **Ayr'shire** (âr'shĭr; -shēr). County, SW Scotland; area 1132 sq. m.; pop. (1951) 321,184; chief towns Ayr, Kilmarnock, Prestwick, Irvine, Girvan, Troon; rivers Ayr and Doon; agriculture, grazing, dairying, fisheries, coal and iron mining, manufacturing (textile goods, machinery, explosives).

2 Seaport burgh, its ⊗; pop. (1951) 43,011; manufactures chemicals, shoes, carpets, lace; sawmills, shipbuilding and engineering works. Alloway, a suburb of Ayr, was the birthplace of Robert Burns.

Ayre, Point of (âr). North extremity of the Isle of Man, Irish Sea; lighthouse.

Ay·sén' *or* **Ai·sén'** (ī·sān'). **1** Province of Chile. See *Table* at CHILE.

2 Commune, its ✳, S Chile, ab. 830 m. S of Santiago; pop. 13,751.

A·yu·dhy·a *or* **A·yu·thi·a** *or* **A·yut·tha·ya** (ä·yŏŏt·t'hä·yä). **1** Province on the Chao Phraya river N of Bangkok, S Thailand; 976 sq. m.; pop. 326,218.

2 City, 40 m. N of Bangkok, on an island in the lower Chao Phraya; pop. ab. 50,000; former ✳ of Siam; like Venice intersected by many canals and many of its inhabitants live on boats; chief town of one of the richest agricultural sections of the country. Founded 1350 and was Siamese capital until 1767 when it was destroyed by the Burmese; also badly damaged by Burmese 1555; site of battle bet. Dutch and English in 17th cent.

A·yu'tla (ä·yŏŏ'tlä), *in full* **Ayutla de los Li'bres** (thä lôz lē'vräs). Town, Guerrero state, S Mexico, 45 m. E of Acapulco; pop. 2519. Plan of Ayutla (1854), demanding Santa Anna's removal, framing of new constitution, and establishment of representative government, was program of revolution led by Juan Álvarez 1855.

Ay·va·lık' (ī·vä·lĭk'); *anc.* **Her'a·cle'a** (hĕr'à·klē'à).

Coastal town, Balıkesir vilayet, NW Turkey in Asia, on strait opp. Lesbos I.; pop. 12,965.

A'zam·garh' (ä'zĭm-gär'; *native* -gŭr'h'). **1** District, Gorakhpur division, Uttar Pradesh, N India; 2217 sq. m.; pop. (1941) 1,822,893.

2 Town, its *, ab. 50 m. NNE of Benares; pop. 18,046.

A'za·na'que (ä'sä-nä'kå). Peak 16,840 ft., W Bolivia, on SE shore of Lake Poopó.

Azbine. See AIR.

Az'ca·po·tzal'co (äs'kä-pō-tsäl'kō). City, Federal District, cen. Mexico, NW of Mexico City; pop. 31,466.

A'zem·mour or **A'zi·mur** or **A'ze·mur** (ä'zĭ·mōōr). Seaport, NW Morocco, NW Africa, just NE of Mazagan; pop. 14,037.

A'zer·bai·dzhan' or **A'zer·bai·jan'** (ä'zĕr-bĭ-jän'; äz'ēr-), *officially* **Azerbaidzhan Soviet Socialist Republic.** A constituent republic of the Union of Soviet Socialist Republics, E Transcaucasia; 33,200 sq. m.; pop. 3,209,727, (1941 est.) 3,372,794; * Baku. One of the three republics of the former Transcaucasian Federation. Bounded on N by Georgia and Dagestan, on E by the Caspian Sea, on S by Iran, and on W by the Armenian S.S.R. It includes the Nakhichevan Autonomous Soviet Socialist Republic and the Nagorno-Karabakh Autonomous Region. Central part is a plain through which flows the Kura river and its tributaries, esp. the Araks whose upper course forms part of boundary bet. the U.S.S.R. and Iran; N of the plain is E end of Caucasus Mts. and to the S are the E peaks of the mountains of Armenia. Predominant ethnic strain Turko-Tatar. Rich in minerals; oil wells of Baku and vicinity furnish 75% of Russia's output. Other products cotton, wheat, tobacco, wines. Chief towns Baku, Kirovabad, Lenkoran, Nukha.

History: In ancient times home of Scythian tribes and part of Roman Empire; in medieval times overrun by Turks in 11th cent.; after fall of Tamerlane site of several Tatar khanates, esp. Shirvan; again under Persians in 17th cent.; larger part conquered by Russia 1806, 1813; scene of fighting in World War I; with part of Azerbaijan prov. of Persia set up as a republic May 28, 1918; invaded by Turkish Nationalists and Soviet troops 1919–20; established a Soviet government 1920; as member of Transcaucasian Federation (*q.v.*) joined U.S.S.R. Dec. 30, 1922; became constituent republic 1936.

A'zer·bai·jan'. **1** *anc.* **At'ro·pa·te'ne** or **Me'di·a At'ro·pa·te'ne** (mē'dĭ·à ăt'rô·pȧ·tē'nē). Province, NW Iran; 41,150 sq. m.; * Tabriz; separated from Azerbaidzhan S.S.R. by Araks river; mountainous country that includes Lake Urmia, and one of the most fertile regions of Iran; scene of revolt against Iranian government 1945–46. Ancient Media Atropatene (see MEDIA) nearly coincided with the modern province; it was the N part of Media and for some time after the death of Alexander was an independent kingdom.

2 See AZERBAIDZHAN.

Azil, Le Mas d'. See LE MAS D'AZIL.

Azimur. See AZEMMOUR.

Azincourt. Var. of AGINCOURT.

'Aziziya, Al. See AL 'AZIZIYA.

Azof. See AZOV.

A·zo'gues (ä·sō'gås). City, * of Cañar prov., W cen. Ecuador, 80 m. ESE of Guayaquil; pop. (1944 est.) 15,068; manufactures straw hats.

A·zores' (à·zōrz'; ā'zōrz); *Port.* **A·ço'res** (à·sō'rĕsh). Group of nine islands and several islets belonging to Portugal in the N Atlantic Ocean, bet. lat. 36°50' and 39°44'N and long. 25° and 31°16'W; ab. 800 m. off the coast of Portugal; 888 sq. m.; pop. (1940) 484,278; chief town Ponta Delgada; other towns Horta and Angra do Heroísmo. Comprises districts of Angra do Heroísmo, Horta, and Ponta Delgada (see *Table* at PORTUGAL); divided into three groups, the NW group containing

Flores and Corvo, the central group containing Terceira, São Jorge, Pico, Fayal, and Graciosa, and the E group containing São Miguel and Santa Maria. Highest point Pico Alto 7460 ft. Exports fruits, grain, and wines.

History: Date of discovery uncertain, but existence known in Europe in 14th cent.; visited by Portuguese navigator Diogo de Seville 1427–31; known for a time as Flemish Islands owing to Flemish settlement which followed gift of Fayal to Isabella of Burgundy 1466; assigned to Portugal by treaty of Alcaçovas 1480; subject to Spain 1580–1640; famous sea fight off Flores 1591 bet. *Revenge* under Sir Richard Grenville and Spanish fleet; contested by rival claimants of Portuguese crown 1830–31. In World War II naval and air bases granted Great Britain Oct. 16, 1943.

Azotos, Azotus. See ASHDOD.

A·zov' or **A·zof'** (ŭ·zôf'; *also, Angl.,* äz'ôf, ā'zôf, ā'zŏv). Town, SW Rostov Region, Soviet Russia, Europe, near mouth of Don river on S shore of E end of Gulf of Taganrog; pop. 19,266. It is near site of ancient Tanais, a Greek colony. Has some fishing and trade but importance reduced by growth of Rostov and Taganrog. Captured by Vladimir I in 10th cent. and by Genoese in 13th cent., who fortified it and made it a trading port for Oriental goods; sacked by Tamerlane 1395; held alternately by Russians and Turks until 1739 when it was secured to Russia under Empress Anna.

Azov or **Azof, Sea of;** *Russ.* **A·zov'sko·e Mo're** (ŭ·zôf'skŭ·yě mô'ryě); *anc.* **Pa'lus Mae·o'tis** (pā'lŭs mē·ō'tĭs). Sea, NE of the Crimea and bet. the Ukraine on the N and Rostov Region and Krasnodar Territory on the E, S Soviet Russia, Europe; ab. 200 m. long; 14,520 sq. m.; connected with Black Sea on S by Kerch Strait; shallow; sandy shores (see ARABAT); its NE arm, the Gulf of Taganrog, receives the Don river.

Az·pei'tia (äth·pā'tyä; äs-). Commune, Guipúzcoa prov., N Spain, 17 m. SW of San Sebastián; pop. 8024; mineral springs; site nearby (on road to W) of the Santa Casa, said to be birthplace of St. Ignatius of Loyola.

Az'tec (äz'tĕk). City, ⊗ of San Juan co., NW corner of New Mexico; pop. 4137; fruit-growing center.

Aztec Mountain. Peak 13,200 ft. in La Plata co., SW Colorado.

Aztec Ruins National Monument. See UNITED STATES, *National Monuments.*

A'zua (ä'swä). **1** Province, S Dominican Republic. See *Table* at DOMINICAN REPUBLIC.

2 or **Azua de Com'pos·te'la** (thä kôm'pôs·tā'lä). Town, its *, on S coast; pop. (1944 est.) 6561.

A·zua'ga (ä·thwä'gä; -swä'-). Commune, Badajoz prov., SW Spain, 55 m. NW of Córdoba; pop. 16,453.

A·zuay' (ä·swä'ĕ; ä·swī'). Province of Ecuador. See *Table* at ECUADOR.

Azúcar, Pan de. See PAN DE AZÚCAR.

A·zue'ro Peninsula (ä·swä'rô). Peninsula on S Panama coast, W of Gulf of Panama.

A·zu'fre (ä·sōō'frå). Volcanic peak 18,635 ft., SE corner of Antofagasta prov., N Chile, near Argentina border.

Azufre, Cerro del. See COPIAPÓ.

Azufre, Pa'so del (pä'sô thĕl). Andean mountain pass bet. San Juan prov., Argentina, and Coquimbo prov., Chile.

A·zul' (ä·sōōl'). **1** Peak 16,600 ft. in S Los Andes territory, NW Argentina.

2 City, Buenos Aires prov., E Argentina, ab. 170 m. by rail SW of Buenos Aires; pop. (est.) 30,000.

A·zu·ma (ä·zōō·mä). Volcano, one of a group of peaks on S boundary of Yamagata prefecture, W of Fukushima, N Honshu, Japan; peaks range from 5400 ft. to 6641 ft.; eruption 1900.

A·zu·sa (à·zōō'sà). City, Los Angeles co., SW California, 18 m. ENE of Los Angeles; pop. 20,497; settled 1887; shipping center for citrus fruits.

B

Ba. See MBA.

Ba'al·bek (bä′ăl·bĕk; bäl′bĕk; *Arab.* bä′äl·bĕk) *or* **Ba''al·bek** (bä′ăl·bĕk); *anc.* **He'li·op'o·lis** (hē′lĭ·ŏp′ō·lĭs). Village, E Lebanon republic, 35 m. N of Damascus and on railroad and highway from Beirut to Homs; pop. ab. 3000; in ancient times a city of great size and importance, built on the lower W slope of the Anti-Liban Mts.; its identification with the worship of Baal as a Semitic sun-god gave rise to its Greek name Heliopolis, "City of the Sun"; made a Roman colony by Julius Caesar. Its ruins cover a great area; most of the buildings erected under the Romans, esp. during reign of Antoninus Pius (138–161).

Baanfu. See PAAN.

Baarn (bärn). Commune, Utrecht prov., cen. Netherlands, 11 m. NE of Utrecht; pop. 12,141; summer resort.

Ba·ba', Cape (bä·bä′); *Turk.* **Ba'ba Bur·nu'** (bä′bä bōōr·nōō′); *anc.* **Lec'tum** (lĕk′tŭm). Cape on W coast of Turkey, 39°28′N lat., 26°10′E long., N of entrance to Gulf of Edremit; most westerly point of Asia.

Ba·ba', Koh–i– (kō′hē·bä·bä′). Mountain range, E cen. Afghanistan; a SW extension of the Hindu Kush, separated from it by Bamian Pass; highest peak Shah Fuladi 16,872 ft.

Ba·ba·ho'yo (bä′vä·ō′yō) *or* **Bo·de'gas** (bō·thä′gäs). Town, * of Los Ríos prov., W cen. Ecuador, 40 m. NE of Guayaquil; pop. (1944 est.) 13,429; on Bodegas river.

Bab al–Zakak. See Strait of GIBRALTAR.

Ba'bar Islands. Island group of the Netherlands Indies, on S side of Banda Sea ENE of Timor I. and W of Tanimbar Is., E Malay Archipelago; 314 sq. m.; pop. 11,712; attached to Amboina division of Moluccas residency; comprises **Babar Island** (the only large island, 220 sq. m.) and five small islands; densely forested.

Ba'bel (bä′bĕl; -b′l). Biblical city in the plain of Shinar (*Gen.* x. 10; xi. 1–9); the same Akkadian word as that for *Babylon.*

Ba'bel·do·ab (bä′bĕl·dō′äp). Var. of BABELTHUAP.

Bab el Man'deb (băb′ ĕl măn′dĕb). Strait 20 m. wide, bet. SW Arabia and the African coast, uniting Red Sea and Gulf of Aden (Indian Ocean).

Babelsberg. See NOWAWES.

Ba'bel·thu'ap (bä′bĕl·tōō′äp) *or* **Pa·lau'** (pä·lou′). Largest island of Palau group in W Pacific Ocean, ab. 27 m. long and bet. 1 and 8 m. wide; ab. 120 sq. m.; mountainous, well-wooded, and fertile. Included in Japanese mandate 1919; with seizure of Peleliu and Angaur by American forces 1944, its control by air secured.

Ba'bia Gó'ra (bä′byä gōō′rä); *Czech* **Ba'bia Ho'ra** (bä′byä hô′rä). Peak 5659 ft., highest of the Beskids, W Carpathian Mts., in West Beskids on border bet. Slovakia and Kraków dept., Poland.

Ba·bine' Lake (bă·bēn′; băb′ēn). Long narrow lake 306 sq. m. in cen. Brit. Columbia, Canada; drains N through **Babine River** (ab. 55 m. long) into Skeena river.

Babine Mountains. Range of the Coast Mts. in W cen. British Columbia, Canada; highest ab. 8000 ft.

Ba'bo·qui·va'ri Mountains (bä′bō·kē·vä′rē). Small range in S Pima co., S Arizona; highest point 7740 ft.

Ba'bor' Mountains (bä′bôr′). Range of Little Atlas Mts., NW Constantine dept., Algeria; highest ab. 6560 ft.

Ba·bul' (bä·bōōl′); *formerly* **Bar'fu·rush'** (bär′fōō·rōōsh′). City, N Iran, 15 m. S of the Caspian Sea, in Mazanderan prov.; pop. ab. 30,000; has considerable trade through its port Meshed-i-Sar.

Ba'bu·na (bä′bōō·nä). Mountain range, pass, and small river in S Yugoslavia, N of Bitolj.

Ba'bush·kin (bä′bŏŏsh·kĭn); *formerly* **Lo'si·no·o·strovsk'** (lŭ′syĭ·nŭ·ŭ·strôfsk′). City, Moscow Region, Soviet Russia, Europe, NW of Moscow; pop. 70,480.

Ba'bu·yan' (bä′bŏŏ·yän′). Island in Babuyan group, N of Luzon, Phil. Is.; 28 sq. m.

Babuyan Channel. Passage bet. Babuyan Is. and N Luzon, Phil. Is.; ab. 135 m. long and 25 m. wide.

Babuyan Cla'ro (klä′rō). An active volcano 3569 ft. on Babuyan I.

Babuyan Islands *or* **Ba'bu·ya'nes** (bä′bōō·yä′nås). Island group, N Phil. Is., N of Luzon; belongs to Cagayan prov.; contains 24 islands; ab. 225 sq. m.; pop. 3292; of volcanic origin; chief islands Babuyan, Camiguin, Calayan, Fuga, and Dalupiri.

Bab'y·lon (băb′ĭ·lŏn). **1** Village and summer resort, Suffolk co., SE New York, on Great South Bay on Long I., 37 m. E of New York City; pop. 11,062.
2 Ancient city, now in ruins, on Euphrates river ab. 55 m. S of Baghdad, near modern Hilla; * of Babylonia.
History: Ancient town probably in existence from 4th millennium B.C.; one of a number of small city-kingdoms of Babylonia, it was seized by Semitic Amorites before 2200 B.C.; under Amoritic line of kings (c. 2050–1750 B.C.) of which Hammurabi was greatest, became capital of Old Empire of Babylonia and chief commercial city of Euphrates-Tigris valley; ruled by Kassites and Assyrians (see BABYLONIA); destroyed by Sennacherib 689 B.C. but rebuilt; capital of Neo-Babylonian Empire (see CHALDEA) 625–538 B.C.; attained greatest glory under Nebuchadnezzar II 605–562 B.C.; captured by Cyrus the Great 539 B.C. and in 331 B.C. by Alexander of Macedon who died there 323 B.C.; gradual commercial decline accelerated by removal of capital to Seleucia (*q.v.*) by Seleucis Nicator (312–280 B.C.).

Bab'y·lo'ni·a (băb′ĭ·lō′nĭ·à; -lŏn′yà). Ancient country in the lower Euphrates valley, SW Asia, coinciding chiefly with Baghdad prov., S Iraq. See 'IRAQ 'ARABI.
History: For earliest historic period, see SUMER and AKKAD. City-kingdom of Babylon attained hegemony under Ist Dynasty (Amoritic) 2050–1750 B.C.; led by Hammurabi (c. 1955–1913 B.C.), sixth and greatest ruler of Ist Dynasty, conquered all of Mesopotamia and spread its administration (Code of Hammurabi) and civilization over entire area; raided by Hittites; conquered and ruled by Kassites, a non-Semitic people, 1750–1180 B.C.; invaded by Arameans in 11th and 10th cents. B.C.; devastated by wars with Assyria (*q.v.*) which ruled Babylon 729–626 B.C.; ruled 625–538 B.C. by Chaldea (*q.v.*); under Chaldean (Neo-Babylonian) Empire controlled Mesopotamia and Syria, captured Jerusalem 597, 586 B.C.; empire broke up at fall of Babylon 539 B.C.; ruled by Persia 538–331 B.C. when Alexander captured Babylon, by Seleucidae 312–171 B.C., by Parthians 171 B.C.–226 A.D., and by Sassanidae 226–641 A.D. (see PERSIA).

Ba'ca (bä′kà). County in Colorado. See *Table* at COLORADO.

Ba'ca·cay' (bä′kä·kī′). Municipality on E coast of Albay prov., Luzon, Phil. Is., on Tabaco Bay, ab. 10 m. N of Legaspi; pop. 23,863; hemp growing.

Ba·că'u (bä·kŭ′ŏŏ). Industrial city, E Romania, in W Moldavia region on Bistriţa river; pop. 31,264.

Bachan, Bachian. See BATJAN.

Ba'cha·rach (bäk′ä·räk). Village on the Rhine, Germany, 8 m. NW of Bingen; pop. (1933) 1853; wines.

Bachi Channel. Var. of BASHI CHANNEL.

Bač'ka *or* **Bach'ka** (bäch′kä). Former subprovince in N Yugoslavia; now represented approximately by W part of Voivodina autonomous province.

Back Al'le·gha'ny Mountains (ăl′ē·gā′nĭ). Ridge running N and S in Pocahontas co., E cen. West Virginia.

Back'bone' Mountain (băk′bōn′). Mountain 3360 ft. in Garrett co., W extremity of Maryland; highest point in the state; extends SW into N West Virginia.

Backergunge. See BAKARGANJ.

Back River; *formerly* **Great Fish River.** River 605 m. long in N Canada; rises in lakes in E cen. Mackenzie

District, Northwest Territories, flows NE through Lakes Pelly, Garry, and Macdougall, across NW Keewatin District into Chantrey Inlet.

Back'stairs' Passage (băk'stârz'). Channel ab. 7 m. wide bet. E end of Kangaroo I. and mainland of South Australia; forms SE entrance to Gulf of St. Vincent.

Bac'ninh' (bäk'nĭn'y'). Town, E Tonkin, N Vietnam, on railroad 16 m. NE of Hanoi; pop. ab. 10,000.

Ba·co', Mount (bä·kō'). Mountain 8163 ft., cen. Mindoro I., Phil. Is.

Ba'co·li (bä'kô·lê). Commune, Napoli prov., Campania, S Italy, on W shore of Bay of Pozzuoli 9 m. WSW of Naples; pop. 10,438; Roman ruins.

Ba·co'lod (bä·kō'lôd). Chartered city, ✱ of Negros Occidental, Negros, Phil. Is., in NW on Guimaras Strait opp. Guimaras I.; 62 sq. m.; pop. 57,474.

Ba'co·lor' (bä'kô·lôr'). Municipality, former ✱ of Pampanga prov., Luzon, Phil. Is., on a tributary of the Pampanga 3 m. SW of San Fernando; pop. 19,129.

Ba'con (bā'kŭn). County in Georgia. See GEORGIA, *Table.*

Ba·con' (bä·kôn'). Municipality, NE Sorsogon prov., Luzon, Phil. Is., on SE shore of Albay Gulf 6 m. across narrow neck of land from Sorsogon; pop. 18,351.

Ba·cong' (bä·kông'). Municipality, SE Negros Oriental, Negros, Phil. Is., on coast 4 m. S of Dumaguete, opp. Siquijor I.; pop. 10,644; founded 1801.

Ba'co·or' (bä'kô·ôr'). Municipality, NE Cavite prov., Luzon, Phil. Is., on shore of Bacoor Bay SE of City of Cavite and ab. 9 m. SW of Manila; pop. 16,130.

Bacoor Bay. Large inlet of SE Manila Bay, Phil. Is., on Cavite shore S of Cavite Penin.; inner anchorage of Cavite naval base.

Bács'al'más (bäch'ôl'mäsh). Commune, S Hungary, 43 m. SW of Szeged; pop. 12,629.

Bactra. See BALKH ancient city.

Bac'tri·a (băk'trĭ·à), *also* **Bac'tri·a'na** (băk'trĭ·ā'nà; -ăn'à). Ancient country of SW Asia, ab. 250 m. long by 120 m. wide, bet. Hindu Kush Mts. and Oxus river, partly desert; ✱ Bactra; home of nomadic people, the Bactrians; made part of Persian Empire by Cyrus the Great (550–529 B.C.); conquered by Alexander the Great 328 B.C.; from 302 B.C. ruled as province of Seleucid empire; under its Greek satrap, Diodotus, revolted and became independent kingdom c. 250 B.C.; expanded to include part of Afghanistan and of Punjab; after 135 B.C., kingdom destroyed by invasion of Sacae, mixed Scythian, Tatar, and Chinese tribes. In Christian Era region became known as Balkh (*q.v.*).

Ba'cup (bā'kŭp). Municipal borough, Lancashire, NW England, on the Irwell 21 m. N of Manchester; pop. 18,374; coal mines, iron foundries, brass foundries.

Bad (băd). River ab. 110 m. long, SW cen. South Dakota; rises in E Pennington co., flows E into Missouri river opp. Pierre.

Ba'da·csony (bŏ'dŏ·chŏn'y'). Plateau region, Hungary, NW of Lake Balaton; produces white wines.

Ba'da·joz' (bä'thä·hôth'; -hôs'). **1** Province of Spain. See *Table* at SPAIN.

2 *anc.* **Pax Au·gus'ta** (păks ô·gŭs'tà). City, its ✱, SW Spain, on left bank of Guadiana river 52 m. SW of Cáceres near Portuguese border; pop. (1941 est.) 57,004; 13th-cent. cathedral; industrial and border trade center. Center of 11th-cent. Moorish kingdom; captured c. 1227 by Alfonso IX of León; besieged by Portuguese 1660 and by Allies 1705 (War of the Spanish Succession); besieged and taken by French during Peninsular War, retaken by Wellington 1812.

Ba'dakh·shan' (bá'dák·shän'). **1** Former frontier province NE Afghanistan; a mountainous region bet. the upper Amu Darya on the N and the Hindu Kush range on the S, with the Kunduz river as its W boundary; ✱ Faizabad. In ancient times a part of the Greek Bactria; includes district of Wakhan and now forms more important part of administrative province of Kataghan-Badakhshan.

2 See GORNO-BADAKHSHAN, Tadzhik S.S.R.

Ba'da·lo'na (bä'thä·lō'nä); *anc.* **Bae'tu·lo** (bē'tû̇·lō). Industrial commune and seaport, Barcelona prov., NE Spain, 5 m. N of Barcelona; pop. 48,284.

Ba·da'ri (bä·dä'rĭ). Village, Upper Egypt, ab. 19 m. SE of Asyût; in region where excavations by Sir Flinders Petrie revealed evidences of a predynastic neolithic culture, dated before 4000 B.C.

Bad Axe (băd' ăks'). City, ⊗ of Huron co., E Michigan, 15 m. S of mouth of Saginaw Bay; pop. 2998.

Bad·deck' (bă·děk'). Village (unincorporated), ⊗ of Victoria co., NE Nova Scotia, Canada, on N arm of Bras d'Or Lake 30 m. W of Sydney; pop. (1941) 551; scene of first airplane flight in British Empire Feb. 23, 1909.

Bad Dürkheim, Bad Ems. See DÜRKHEIM; EMS.

Ba'den (bā'd'n). Residential borough, Beaver co., W Pennsylvania, 19 m. NW of Pittsburgh; pop. 6109.

Ba'den (bä'děn). **1** *or* **Baden bei Wien** (bī vēn'); *anc.* **Aq'uae Pa·no'ni·ae** (ăk'wē på·nō'nĭ·ē; ā'kwē). Commune, Lower Austria prov., Austria 14 m. SSW of Vienna; pop. (1939) 24,086; famous for warm mineral springs frequented since Roman times.

2 Former German state, SW Germany; 5817 sq. m.; pop. 2,312,462, (1939) 2,518,103; ✱ Karlsruhe; other important cities included Konstanz, Freiburg, Baden-Baden, Mannheim; contained famous Black Forest; bounded W and S by Rhine river; cobalt, iron, tin, and silver-bearing lead mines. Divided into the following 4 districts [Landes komissärbezirke] (for pronunciation of their names, see their individual entries):

NAME	LOCATION WITHIN BADEN	AREA IN SQ. M.	POPULA-TION (1925 CENSUS)	CAPITAL
Freiburg	SW	1,952	599,998	Freiburg im Breisgau
Karlsruhe	N cen.	1,016	667,653	Karlsruhe
Konstanz[1]	SE	1,486	337,508	Konstanz
Mannheim	N	1,363	707,303	Mannheim

[1] Sometimes Anglicized as Constance.

History: Became political unit when Frederick, son of Margrave of Verona, took title of Margrave of Baden 1112; split up and reunited many times before final reunion of all territories under Charles Frederick 1771; member of League of German Princes 1785; became new electorate 1803; supported Napoleon against Austria in War of Third Coalition and received rest of Hapsburg territory in western Germany and rank of grand duchy 1805 (Treaty of Pressburg: see BRATISLAVA); member of Confederation of Rhine until joining Allies against Napoleon 1813; member of Germanic Confederation 1815; received constitution 1818; joined Zollverein 1835; became a leader of German liberal movement and center of action in revolution 1848–49; member of Frankfurt Parliament; supported Austria against Prussia 1866; forced to pay indemnity and become military ally of Prussia; joined North German Confederation 1870 and German Empire 1871; proclaimed republic 1918; became administrative division of the Reich 1933–34; southern part became 1949 a state of Federal Republic of Germany, northern part incorporated in Württemberg-Baden state; both states merged 1951 to form Baden-Württemberg state.

3 City, Baden-Württemberg, Germany. See BADEN-BADEN.

4 Commune, Aargau canton, N cen. Switzerland, 13 m. ENE of Aarau; pop. (1941) 10,388; old castle; sulfur springs and baths, known since Roman times.

Ba'den–Ba'den (bä'děn·bä'děn) *or* **Baden**; *anc.* **Au·re'li·a A·quen'sis** (ô·rē'lĭ·à [-rēl'yà] à·kwěn'sĭs). City, Karlsruhe dist., Baden-Württemberg, Germany, 18 m. SSW of Karlsruhe; pop. 25,692; tourist resort; its thermal baths frequented by ancient Romans.

Ba'den·wei'ler (bä'děn·vī'lẽr). Village, Baden, SW Germany, 28 m. NE of Basel, Switzerland; pop. (1933) 1207; mineral springs; Roman baths.

Ba·den-Würt′tem·berg (bä′děn·vür′těm·běrκ; *Angl.* -wûr′těm·bûrg). State of Federal Republic of Germany, W Germany; formed 1945; 13,800 sq. m., pop. 7,301,900; ✳ Stuttgart.

Bad Freienwalde. See FREIENWALDE.

Badgastein. See GASTEIN.

Badg′er Pass (băj′ĕr). Mountain pass, alt. 7300 ft., cen. California, in Yosemite National Park; skiing.

Bad Godesberg, Bad Harzburg, Bad Homburg. See GODESBERG; HARZBURG; HOMBURG.

Ba·di·an′ (bä·dyän′). Municipality on W coast of Cebu I., Phil. Is., at S end of Tañon Strait; pop. 17,817.

Ba·di′a Po·le′si·ne (bä·dē′ä pô·lā′zĕ·nä). Commune, Rovigo prov., Venezia Euganea, NE Italy; pop. 12,797.

Ba′din (bā′dĭn; -d′n). Town, Stanly co., S cen. North Carolina, ab. 5 m. NE of Albemarle; pop. 1905.

Badin Lake. See YADKIN DAM.

Bad Ischl, Bad Kissingen, Bad Kreuznach. See ISCHL; KISSINGEN; KREUZNACH.

Bad′ Lands′; *orig. Fr.* **Mau′vaises′ Terres′** (mô′vâz′ târ′) or **Terres′ Mau′vaises′** (târ′ mô′vâz′). Barren region with eroded surface in SW South Dakota E of the Black Hills and in NW Nebraska; contains extensive fossil deposits; marked by steep hills, deep gullies, fantastic formations, etc. From this name comes the generic term *badlands* applied also to similar areas in other western states and in South America and Asia.

Bad′lands′ National Monument (băd′lăndz′). See UNITED STATES, *National Monuments.*

Bad Lands Reserve. Canadian provincial park, S Alberta, N of Drumheller near Red Deer river; 1800 acres; contains fossilized remains of prehistoric animals.

Bad Nauheim. See NAUHEIM.

Badnur. See BETUL.

Bad Reichenhall. See REICHENHALL.

Ba·dri·nath′ (bŭ·drē·nät′). Peak 23,210 ft. in the Himalayas, N Garhwal, Uttar Pradesh, N Indian Union; village, temple, and shrine on its slope at 10,291 ft.

Bad River. See BAD.

Bad–Sulza. See SULZA.

Ba·dul′la (bå·dŭl′å). Town, ✳ of Uva prov., SE Ceylon, 85 m. E of Colombo; pop. 9849.

Ba′dung, or **Ba′doeng, Strait** (bä′dŏŏng). Channel ab. 9 m. wide bet. SE Bali and the island of Nusa Besar, Indonesia; connects with Lombok Strait (*q.v.*).

Bad′wa′ter (băd′wô′tĕr; -wŏt′ĕr). Small salt pool 280 ft. below sea level, Death Valley, California; lowest point in North America.

Bad Wildungen. See WILDUNGEN.

Ba·e′na (bä·ā′nä). Commune, Córdoba prov., S Spain, 32 m. SE of Córdoba; pop. 24,830; Roman ruins.

Baeterrae. See BÉZIERS.

Bae′ti·ca (bē′tĭ·kå). A province of the Roman Empire in S Spain, roughly equivalent to W Andalusia.

Baetis. See GUADALQUIVIR.

Baetulo. See BADALONA.

Ba·e′za (bä·ā′thä; -sä). Commune, Jaén prov., S Spain, 19 m. NE of Jaén; pop. 18,136; as medieval Moorish city, sacked by Ferdinand III of Castile 1239.

Ba′fa, Lake (bä′fä); *Turk.* **Ba′fa Gö·lü′** (bä′fä gû·lü′). Large lake in W Turkey in Asia at the mouth of the Menderes river; site of ancient Priene is on its W shore and of Miletus just to S of it.

Baf′fin Bay (băf′ĭn). 1 Large inlet of Atlantic Ocean bet. W Greenland and E Baffin I.; connected with Atlantic Ocean by Davis Strait. Discovered and partly explored by William Baffin 1616.
2 Inlet of Laguna Madre, S Texas.

Baffin Island, *formerly known as* **Baffin Land.** Largest island of Canadian Arctic Archipelago, E Franklin District, Northwest Territories, W of Baffin Bay and Davis Strait; 183,810 sq. m., 5th largest island in the world; pop. 2000, chiefly Eskimos; separated from Quebec prov. on the S by Hudson Strait; in NW is Admiralty Inlet, in S part two lakes, Amadjuak and Nettilling, and

on SE coast two large inlets, Cumberland Sound and Frobisher Bay. Its S part first visited by Frobisher 1576–78; its N part explored by Baffin 1616.

Ba′fing′ (*Fr.* bà′fēn′y′ or -fäng′). The upper course of the Senegal river in Guinea and Mali ab. 350 m. long; rises in the Fouta Djallon highlands and flows NE and N to join the Bakoy at Bafoulabé.

Ba′fou′la′bé′ or **Ba′fu′la′bé′** (*Fr.* bà′fōō′là′bā′). Trading town on Senegal river at confluence of its headstreams, Bafing and Bakoy, 10°48′W, W Mali.

Ba·fra′ (bä·frä′). Town, Samsun vilayet, N Turkey in Asia, on Kızıl Irmak near its mouth; pop. 10,258.

Ba·gac′ (bä·gäk′). Municipality on W coast of Bataan prov., Luzon, Phil. Is., ab. halfway bet. Subic Bay and Mariveles; pop. 2958; fierce fighting nearby Feb. 1942.

Ba′ga·mo′yo (bä′gä·mō′yō). Seaport town, E Tanganyika, E Africa, SW of Zanzibar.

Ba·ga′na (bä·gä′nä). Volcano 6500 ft., Crown Prince Range, S cen. Bougainville I., Bismarck Archipelago.

Ba′gan Si′a·pi·a′pi (bä′gän sē′ä·pē·ä′pē). Town, Sumatra, on Strait of Malacca; pop. 15,321.

Bagaria. See BAGHERIA.

Bagdad. See BAGHDAD.

Ba·gé′ (bà·zhā′). City, S Rio Grande do Sul state, S Brazil, on Uruguayan frontier; pop. 35,300.

Baghailah. Var. of BUGHAILA.

Bagh′dad or **Bag′dad** (băg′dăd; *Arab.* bŭg·dăd′).
1 Province (*liwa*), S and cen. Iraq; pop. (1935 est.) 499,410.
2 City, its ✳ and ✳ of Iraq, on both sides of the Tigris; pop. (1935 est.) 287,000, (1938 est.) 400,000; a very old city, but now modernized; airport; rail connections with Turkey via Mosul and with Basra and Kirkuk.
History: Settlement on site of Baghdad from ancient times; sacked by Moslem Arabs 634 A.D.; rose to importance after its choice 762 A.D. by al-Mansur as capital of Abbasside caliphate; as center of Islam, especially under Caliph al-Mamun (813–833), second only to Constantinople as trade and cultural center (estimated pop. of ab. 2,000,000); though power of Baghdad caliphate declined from about middle of 9th cent., city remained commercially important and continued to rule area corresponding roughly to modern Iraq; almost destroyed when Hulagu, grandson of Genghis Khan (see MONGOLIA), overthrew Abbasside caliphate 1258 and began rule of Il-khans of Persia (1260–1335); conquered by Tamerlane 1401; though captured by Suleiman the Magnificent 1534, did not become part of Ottoman Empire until 1638; objective of British Mesopotamian campaign 1915–17, it was finally captured Mar. 11, 1917; became capital of kingdom of Iraq (*q.v.*) 1921.

Baghdadi, Khan. See KHAN BAGHDADI.

Ba′ghel·khand (bŭg′gĕl·kŭnd). Former agency, E division of Central India Agency, India; 14,706 sq. m.; pop. 1,839,256; ✳ Rewa; a group of Indian states comprising Rewa and 11 minor states.

Ba′ghe·ri′a (bä′gå·rē′ä) or **Ba′ga·ri′a** (bä′gä·rē′ä). Commune, Palermo prov., NW cen. Sicily, near Bay of Palermo 8 m. S by E of Palermo; pop. 25,820.

Bagirmi. See BAGUIRMI.

Ba′gir·pa·şa′ Dağ (bä′ĭr·pä·shä′ dä). Peak 10,768 ft., E Turkey in Asia, SW of Erzurum.

Ba′gi·stan′ (bä′gĭ·stän′). A Moslem region in E India, equivalent to the E part of Pakistan, comprising the N and E two thirds of Bengal and a section of W Assam having a Moslem majority—an occasional term. See EAST BENGAL, PAKISTAN.

Bag′ley (băg′lĭ). Village ⊗ of Clearwater co., NW Minnesota; pop. 1385.

Ba′gna·ca·val′lo (bä′nyä·kä·väl′lō). Commune, Ravenna prov., Emilia, N Italy, 12 m. W by S of Ravenna; pop. 16,596; birthplace of the painter Il Bagnacavallo.

Ba·gna′ra Ca′la·bra (bä·nyä′rä kä′lä·brä). Commune, Reggio di Calabria prov., Calabria, S Italy, 11 m. NNE of Reggio di Calabria; pop. 12,574.

Bag′nell Dam (băg′n′l). See UNITED STATES, *Dams*.

Ba′gnères′–de–Bi′gorre′ (bä′nyär′dĕ-bē′gôr′). Commune, Hautes-Pyrénées dept., SW France, 13 m. SSE of Tarbes; pop. (1931) 9211; health resort, known since Roman times; produces barège, a gauzelike fabric containing wool, first made at Barèges ab. 25 m. SSW.

Ba′gneux′ (bä′nyû′). Commune, Seine dept., N France, S suburb of Paris; pop. 12,492; battle, episode in siege of Paris, Oct. 13, 1870.

Ba′gni di Luc′ca (bä′nyē dĕ lōōk′kä). Commune, Lucca prov., Tuscany, cen. Italy, 13 m. NNE of Lucca; pop. 12,064; thermal mineral springs.

Bagni San Giu·lia′no (sän′ jōō·lyä′nô). Commune, Pisa prov., Tuscany, cen. Italy, 6 m. NNE of Pisa; pop. (1931) 21,894; warm radioactive mineral springs.

Ba′gno a Ri′po·li (bä′nyô ä rē′pô·lē). Commune, Firenze prov., Tuscany, cen. Italy, 4 m. SE of Florence; pop. (1931) 16,857; remains of ancient Roman bath.

Bagno di Ro·ma′gna (dē rô·mä′nyä). Commune, Forlì prov., Emilia, N Italy, 26 m. S by W of Forlì; pop. 10,735; summer resort; thermal springs.

Ba′gno·let′ (bä′nyô′lĕ′). Commune, Seine dept., N France, E suburb of Paris; pop. 28,052.

Ba′go (bä′gô). Municipality, W Negros Occidental, Negros, Phil. Is., on Guimaras Strait ab. 12 m. SSW of City of Bacolod; pop. 53,874.

Bag′ot (băg′ŭt). County, Quebec, Canada. See *Table* at QUEBEC.

Bag′ot·ville (băg′ŭt·vĭl). Town, Chicoutimi co., S Quebec, Canada, on S bank of Saguenay river 10 m. ESE of Chicoutimi; pop. 4136.

Ba′grach Kol (bä′räch kŭl′). Salt lake in cen. Sinkiang prov., W China; drains into Tarim river.

Bagradas. See MEDJERDA.

Ba·gra′ti·o′novsk (bȧ·grȧsh′ĭ·ŏn′ŭfsk; *Russ.* bȧ·grȧ-tyĭ·ô′nŭfsk); *formerly* **Preus′sisch Ey′lau** (proi′sĭsh ī′lou). Town, Kaliningrad Region, Soviet Russia, Europe, 23 m. S of Kaliningrad; formerly in East Prussia prov., Prussia, Germany; pop. (1925) 3584. See EYLAU commune, East Prussia.

Ba′guio, City of (bä′gyô). Chartered city, resort, and summer ✳ of the Philippine Is., geographically an approximately square area of 22 sq. m. in W cen. Benguet subprov. of Mountain Province, NW Luzon, ab. 130 m. N of Manila (160 m. by road); pop. 24,117; healthful location in mountains of Benguet, 4500 to 5500 ft. Visited by Spaniards 1829 but until 20th cent. of less importance than La Trinidad (*q.v.*) to the N; incorporated as City of Baguio 1909; occupied by Japanese Dec. 1941; retaken by Americans Apr. 29, 1945.

Ba·guir′mi *or* **Ba·gir′mi** (bȧ·gĭr′mĭ; *Fr.* bȧ′gēr′mē′). Region, SW Republic of Chad, N cen. Africa, SE of Lake Chad; ✳ before 1898 Massénya; level area ab. 1000 ft. above sea level, traversed by tributaries of the Chari river which forms its W and SW boundary; Fort-Lamy is in NW corner. Explored by Dixon Denham 1826, Heinrich Barth 1852, and Gustav Nachtigal 1872; came under French protection 1897; used as base for operations against Germans in N Cameroons 1914.

Ba·ha′ma Banks (bȧ·hä′mȧ; *in U.S.,* also -hā′-). Two areas of shoal water in the Bahama Is.: **Little Bahama Bank**, N of Grand Bahama I. and bet. it and Abaco on E; **Great Bahama Bank**, covering a large curved area some 330 m. long with Andros on its E rim, separated from Cuba on S by Old Bahama Channel and from Florida on W and NW by Straits of Florida.

Bahama Islands *or* **Ba·ha′mas** (-mȧz). British colony comprising a chain of islands, cays, and reefs lying SE of Florida and N of Cuba; 4404 sq. m.; pop. (1943) 68,846; ✳ Nassau (on island of New Providence); chief islands (from N to S) Grand Bahama, Abaco, Eleuthera, New Providence, Andros, Cat I., San Salvador (or Watlings I.), Exuma, Long I., Crooked I., Acklins I., Mayaguana, Inagua; chain of islands terminates in Turks and Caicos Is. (*q.v.*). Chief occupations agriculture and marine fisheries; exports have included at different periods lumber, dyewood, bark, citrus fruit, tomatoes, sisal, shells, turtle shell, sponges, canned fish, salt; tourist resort.

History: Islands inhabited by Lucayan Indians at time of discovery by Columbus Oct. 12, 1492 (see SAN

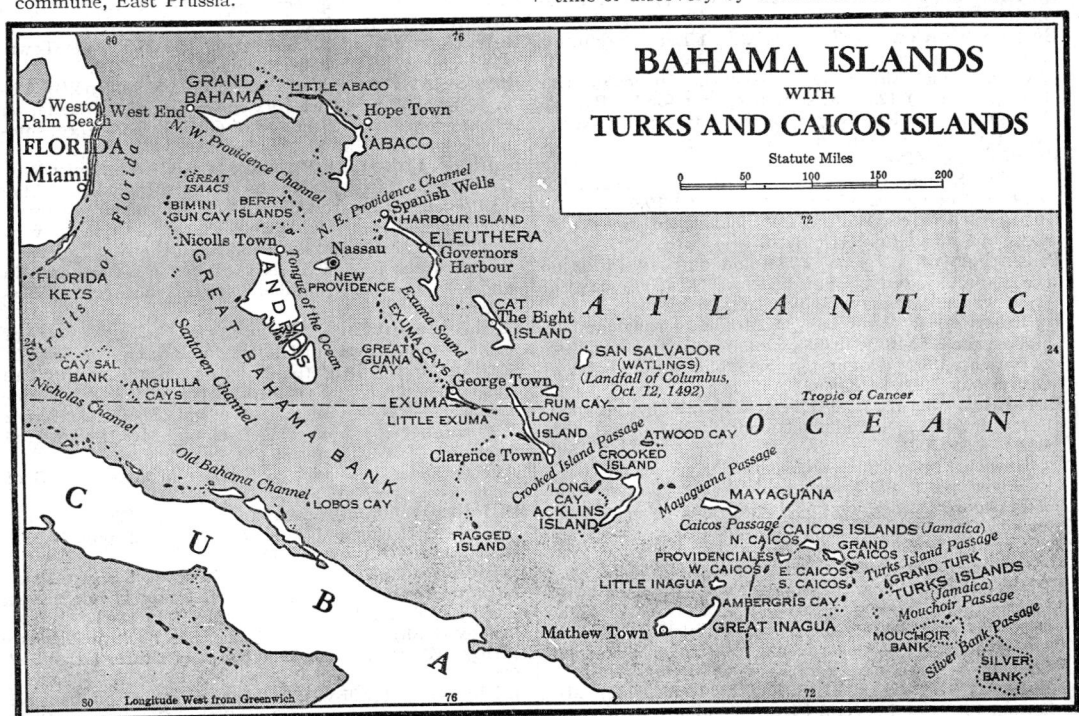

BAHAMA ISLANDS
WITH
TURKS AND CAICOS ISLANDS
Statute Miles

SALVADOR island, Bahamas Is.); assigned to Spain by papal grant but visited only by slave raiders and buccaneers; granted by British crown 1627 to Sir Robert Heath, to whom islands surrendered 1629; suffered from Spanish attacks (as in 1641, 1684, 1719–20) and from use as pirates' base; settlement of islands by company of Eleutherian Adventurers (incorp. 1647) authorized by Parliament 1649; settlements made on Eleuthera and New Providence; islands granted to lords proprietors of Carolina 1670 but civil and military government assumed by crown 1717; piracy in islands ended by Capt. Woodes Rogers, first royal governor, 1718; first meeting of general assembly in Nassau 1729; Nassau seized and disarmed by American force 1776; islands capitulated to Spain 1782 but restored to Great Britain by Treaty of Versailles 1783; influx of American loyalists as settlers 1783–84; proprietary rights of lords proprietors surrendered to crown 1787; Turks Is. under administration of colony 1804–48; abolished slavery 1833; base for blockade running to Southern States 1861–65; site on Mayaguana leased to U.S. for naval base 1940; British air base maintained on New Providence during World War II.

Ba·ha·ri′ya or **Ba·ha·ri′eh** (bä·rē′yȧ; -yä). Oasis in the Libyan Desert, Egypt, in Western Desert prov., ab. 28°N lat. and 29°E long.

Ba·ha′wal·pur′ (bȧ·hä′wȧl·pŏŏr′) or **Bha′wal·pur′** (bä′wȧl·pŏŏr′). **1** Former Indian state, SW Punjab, NW India; 17,494 sq. m.; pop. (1941) 1,341,209; chief Mohammedan state of the Punjab, its ruler a Nawab; region stretches more than 300 m. along the Sutlej, Panjnad, and Indus rivers with practically all of its territory in the Thar Desert. Its rulers became independent of Afghans near end of 18th cent.; made treaty with British 1838; joined Pakistan 1947.
2 Town, its ✱, near Sutlej river ab. 225 m. SW of Lahore; pop. 20,943.

Ba·hi′a (bȧ·ē′ȧ). **1** See BAÍA.
2 See SALVADOR.

Ba·hi′a, Is′las de la (ēz′läz thä lä vä·ē′ä). = BAY ISLANDS.

Ba·hi′a Blan′ca (bä·ē′ä vläng′kä). **1** Large bay in SE Buenos Aires prov., E Argentina.
2 City, Buenos Aires prov., E Argentina, at head of this bay; pop. (est.) 121,055; shipping point for La Pampa, Neuquén, and Río Negro territories; exports cattle, wheat, wool, etc. Dates from fort and trading post 1828.

Ba·hi′a de Ca·rá′quez (bä·ē′ä thä kä·rä′kås) or **Bahía.** Seaport town, Manabí prov., W Ecuador, 115 m. NNW of Guayaquil; pop. (1944 est.) 10,499.

Bahía Gran′de (grän′dȧ). Widemouthed bay on SE coast of Santa Cruz territory, S Argentina.

Bahía Ne′gra (nā′grä). Town and outpost station on the Paraguay river, Olimpo dept., N Paraguay, at point where Paraguay, Bolivia, and Brazil meet.

Ba′ho·ru′co (bä′ō·rōō′kō). **1** Mountain range and its highest peak 5346 ft. in SW Dominican Republic.
2 Province, SW Dominican Republic. See *Table* at DOMINICAN REPUBLIC.

Bah·raich′ (bȧ·rīk′). **1** District, Fyzabad division, E Uttar Pradesh, N Indian Union; 2654 sq. m.; pop. (1941) 1,240,569.
2 Town, its ✱, on affluent of Gogra river 65 m. NE of Lucknow; pop. 33,783; local trade center; contains tomb of Masaud, a champion of Islam, a place of pilgrimage for both Hindus and Mohammedans.

Bah·ram′a·bad′ (bȧ·räm′ä·bäd′). Town, SE cen. Iran, on highway 60 m. W of Kerman; pop. ab. 12,000.

Bah·rein′ Islands (bä·rīn′; -rän′; bä-), also **Bah·rain′ Islands**; *anc.* **Ty′los** (tī′lŏs) or **Ty′ros** (tī′rŏs). Archipelago in W Persian Gulf, 20 m. off al-Hasa coast of Arabia and NW of Qatar Penin.; 213 sq. m.; pop. ab. 120,000; ✱ Manama; comprises low-lying islands of Bahrein (the largest, 27 m. long by 10 m. wide), Muharraq, Sitra, and several islets; headquarters of pearl-

fishing industry of Persian Gulf; extensive oil fields; shipbuilding; makes sail cloth and mats.
History: Occupied by Portuguese 1507–1602, by Arab subjects of Persia to 1783; ruled since 1782 by a member of a Kuwait (*q.v.*) family; nominally an independent sultanate but closely dependent upon British government; Persian ownership denied by British 1928; oil discovered 1932. See PERSIAN GULF RESIDENCY.

Bahr el Abyad. The White Nile. See NILE.

Bahr el A′rab (bä′h′r ăl ŭ′rŏb). River, S Sudan, NE Africa; flows E to join with the Jur and form the Bahr el Ghazal.

Bahr el Azraq. The Blue Nile. See NILE.

Bahr el Gha·zal′ (bä′h′r ăl gŏ·zäl′). **1** River ab. 500 m. long, SW Sudan; formed by confluence of Bahr el Arab and Jur rivers in NW Upper Nile prov.; flows E to unite at Lake No with the Bahr el Jebel and form the White Nile (see NILE).
2 Province, SW Sudan; area 82,530; pop. 991,022; ✱ Wau.

Bahr el Je′bel (ăl jä′băl; gä′băl). Section of the Nile in S Sudan. See BAHR EL GHAZAL.

Bahr en Nil. See NILE.

Bahret el Hule. See Waters of MEROM.

Bahret Lut. See DEAD SEA.

Bahr·gan′, Cape (bä′h′r·gän′). Cape on W coast of Iran, projecting into NE corner of the Persian Gulf.

Bahr Setit. See Bahr SETIT.

Bahr Yusef. See Bahr YUSEF.

Ba′ia (bä′yä); *anc.* **Ba′iae** (bä′yē). Village, Napoli prov., Campania, Italy, ab. 11 m. W of Naples; pop. (1931) 2291; warm sulfur springs; ancient city was popular Roman resort, noted for luxury and immorality.

Ba·i′a (bȧ·ē′ȧ), *formerly spelled* **Ba·hi′a** (bȧ·ē′ȧ). State of Brazil. See *Table* at BRAZIL.

Ba′ia–Ma′re (bä′yä·mä′rĕ); *Hung.* **Nagy′bá′nya** (nŏd′y′·bä′nyŏ). Town, NW Romania, in N Transylvania region on upper Someş river; pop. (1939 est.) 13,882; gold, silver, and copper mines in the vicinity.

Baibazar. Var. of *Beibazar;* see BEYPAZARI.

Baiburt. See BAYBURT.

Baie Co′meau (bā′ kō′mō; *Fr.* bā′ kô′mō′). Town, Saguenay co., SE Quebec, Canada; pop. 3972.

Baie Saint Paul (bā′ sånt pôl′; *Fr.* bā′ săn′ pôl′). Village, ⊗ of West Charlevoix co., S Quebec, Canada, on St. Lawrence river 57 m. NE of Quebec; pop. 3716; summer resort; hunting and fishing.

Bai·kal′, Lake (bī·kȧl′). Lake in S Siberia, Soviet Russia, E Asia, chiefly within the Buryat-Mongol Republic; 13,197 sq. m.; greatest depth 4982 ft.; the largest freshwater basin in Eurasia. Two thirds of its W shore, with the Baikal range, and its S end, with the Angara outlet, lie in Irkutsk Region; it receives on the E the Barguzin and Selenga rivers. Island of Olkhon is in its center. Discovered 1643.

Baikal Mountains. Mountain range along W shore of Lake Baikal, mostly in Irkutsk Region; highest 6890 ft.

Bai·lan′ or **Bei·lan′** (bā·län′); *anc.* **Syr′i·ae Por′tae** (sīr′i·ē pōr′tē) *Eng.* **Syr′i·an Gates** (sĭr′i·ăn). **1** Mountain pass, Hatay vilayet, S Turkey, S of İskenderon; cuts through the Alma Dağ (Amanus Mts.); connected ancient Cilicia with Syria.
2 Town, Hatay vilayet, S Turkey in Asia, just S of İskenderon; pop. ab. 5000.

Bail′don (bāl′dŭn). Urban district, West Riding, Yorkshire, N England, 7 m. N of Bradford; pop. 10,132.

Baile Atha Cliath. See DUBLIN.

Bai·lén′ (bī·lān′). Commune, Jaén prov., S Spain, 20 m. N of Jaén; pop. 10,045; galena and zinc blende mined nearby. Spaniards defeated French July 1808.

Bai′ley (bā′lĭ). County in Texas. See *Table* at TEXAS.

Bailey, Mount. Peak 8360 ft., W of Crater Lake, SW Oregon.

Bai′ley·ville (bā′lĭ·vĭl). Town, Washington co., SE Maine, on St. Croix river 8 m. SW of Calais; pop. 1863.

Bail′leul′ (bä′yûl′). Manufacturing city, Nord dept., N France, near Belgian frontier 15 m. NW of Lille; pop. 10,928; made free commune by counts of Flanders; became French 1678; devastated in World War I.

Bain′bridge (bān′brĭj). **1** Large island in Puget Sound 10 miles directly W of Seattle, Washington, in Kitsap co. **2** City, ⊗ of Decatur co., SW Georgia, on Flint river 13 m. N of Florida border; pop. 12,714.

Bain·siz′za (bīn-sēt′tsä). Plateau N of Gorizia, Venezia Giulia, NE Italy; since 1947 in NW Yugoslavia.

Baird (bârd). City, ⊗ of Callahan co., N cen. Texas, 20 m. E of Abilene; pop. 1633; railroad division point; ships cotton, fruit, berries, etc.; oil wells.

Baird Mountains. Mountain range, W end of Brooks Range, NW Alaska, S of Noatak river.

Baireuth. Var. of BAYREUTH.

Bairns′dale (bârnz′dāl). Town, Victoria, SE Australia, on coast E of Melbourne; pop. ab. 4000; gold fields.

Bai·ro′ko (bī-rō′kō). Village on **Bairoko Harbour** (an inlet of Kula Gulf), NW coast of New Georgia I., cen. Solomon Is.; Japanese supply base bombed by Americans July and Aug. 1943; captured Aug. 25.

Ba′is (bä′ēs). Municipality, E Negros Oriental, Negros, Phil. Is., on Tañon Strait; pop. 22,471.

Baisan. See BEISAN.

Bai·ta′ra·ni (bī·tŭ′rá·nē). River ab. 400 m. long, E India; rises in SE Madhya Pradesh and flows through Orissa into the Bay of Bengal.

Bait Jala. See BEIT JALA.

Bai′xo A·len·te′jo (bī′shoo ȧ·läɴɴ·tä′zhoo). Province of Portugal. See ALENTEJO and *Table* at PORTUGAL.

Ba′ja (bŏ′yŏ). Autonomous city, S Hungary, ab. 60 m. W of Szeged on Danube river; 77 sq. m.; pop. (1939) 31,879; captured by Russian forces Oct. 21, 1944.

Baja California. See LOWER CALIFORNIA.

Ba′ja Ve′ra·paz′ (bä′hä vä′rä·päs′). Department, cen. Guatemala; 1206 sq. m.; pop. 96,182; ✻ Salamá.

Bakan. See SHIMONOSEKI.

Ba′kar·ganj′ *or* **Back′er·gunge′** (bä′kȧr·gŭnj′). District, Dacca division, former Bengal prov., India; since 1947 in East Bengal, Pakistan; 3783 sq. m.; pop. (1941) 3,549,010; ✻ Barisal.

Ba′ker (bā′kẽr). **1** Name of counties in three states of the U.S. See *Tables* at FLORIDA, GEORGIA, OREGON. **2** City, ⊗ of Fallon co., E Montana; pop. 2365. **3** City, ⊗ of Baker co., E Oregon, on fork of Powder river ab. 40 m. SSE of La Grande; pop. 9986; settled in 1863; became ⊗ 1868, incorp. 1874; mineral springs; deposits of volcanic stone, gold, silver, lead, etc., nearby.

Baker, Mount. 1 Peak 12,406 ft., NE Grand co., N Colorado. **2** Peak 10,750 ft. in Cascade Range, cen. Whatcom co., NW Washington.

Baker Butte. Butte in cen. Arizona, at S border of the Mogollon Mesa; 8182 ft. high.

Baker Island. Small island (atoll) in cen. Pacific Ocean near the equator at long. 176°31′W; less than 1 sq. m. Visited for guano 1850 to 1890; claimed by U.S. and Great Britain; occupied by colonists (Hawaiians) for U.S. 1935 and formally proclaimed U.S. territory 1936. Abandoned by U.S. forces early in 1942; reoccupied without opposition Aug. 1944. Cf. HOWLAND ISLAND.

Baker Lake. Lake 1029 sq. m., the expansion of upper (W) Chesterfield Inlet, cen. Keewatin District, Northwest Territories, Canada; receives outlet of Aberdeen Lake at NW and Kazan river in S.

Ba′kers·field (bā′kẽrz·fēld). Commercial city, ⊗ of Kern co., S California, on Kern river at S end of San Joaquin valley 104 m. NNW of Los Angeles; pop. 56,848; center of highly productive petroleum area; oil refining.

Ba′kers·ville (bā′kẽrz·vĭl). Town, ✻ of Mitchell co., W North Carolina; pop. 393; mica mines.

Bakh′chi·sa·rai′ (bäk′chē·sä·rī′). Town, S Crimea, Soviet Russia, Europe, on railroad 15 m. SSW of Simferopol; pop. 10,800; noted for its manufacture of leather

goods, sheepskin cloaks, and articles of copper. From 15th cent. to 1783 capital of Tatar khanate.

Bakhmut. See ARTEMOVSK.

Bakhoy. Var. of BAKOY.

Bakh′ti·a·ri′ (bȧk′tē·yä·rē′). Mountainous region in W Iran; chief town Chigha Khur; highest peaks above 12,000 ft.; home of the nomadic tribe of the Bakhtiari.

Bakhtigan. See NIRIZ.

Ba′kır·köy′ (bä′kĭr·kû′ĕ). Suburban district, Istanbul vilayet, Turkey in Europe; 112 sq. m.; pop. 28,343; its chief town Bakırköy, is SW of İstanbul near coast of Sea of Marmara.

Ba′kony Forest (bŏ′kŏn·y′); *Ger.* **Ba′ko·nyer·wald′** (bä′kŏ·nyẽr·vält′). Mountain range in Hungary bet. the Rába (Raab) river and Lake Balaton; average altitude 2000 ft.

Ba·koy′ *or* **Ba·khoy′** (bä·koi′). River ab. 300 m. long, W Mali, West Africa, a headstream uniting with the Bafing to form the Senegal; chief tributary the Baoulé.

Ba·ku′ (bä·kōō′; *Russ.* bü-). City, ✻ of Azerbaidzhan Republic, U.S.S.R., a port on SW shore of the Apsheron Penin. on the W coast of the Caspian Sea; pop. 809,347; 5th city in size in the U.S.S.R.; center of Russia's most extensive oil region and also of one of the largest oil fields in the world; has oil pipeline to Batum; from it tankers transport oil N to Makhachkala and Astrakhan; petroleum refineries, many mills and factories.

History: Old part of city dates back to 9th cent.; has architectural remains of Arabs and 11th-cent. Persian shahs; Persian town 1509 to 1723; seized by Russians 1723 but restored 1735; finally incorporated in Russia 1806; suffered from disastrous fires and riots 1901, 1904–05, and during the civil war of 1917–21; made capital of Bolshevist government 1917; occupied by British troops July 1918–Aug. 1919; became capital of new republic of Azerbaidzhan 1920.

Ba·kwan′ga (bȧ·kwäng′ȧ). Town, S Congo, in S Kasai prov. E of Luluabourg; pop. 18,900; center of diamond field.

Ba·la′bac (bä·lä′bäk). Island, SW Phil. Is., SW of Palawan I.; 125 sq. m.; pop. 1755; belongs to Palawan prov.; Balabac town on E coast has fine harbor.

Balabac Strait. Passage 34 m. wide bet. S end of Balabac I., Phil. Is., and islands off N coast of Brit. North Borneo; connects Sulu Sea with South China Sea.

Ba′la·ba·la′gan Islands (bä′lä·bä·lä′gän) *or* **Little Pa′ter·nos′ters** (pā′tẽr·nŏs′tẽrz; pãt′ẽr-). Group of about 30 low coral islets in W cen. Makassar Strait, bet. Borneo and Celebes, Indonesia.

Ba′la·ghat (bä′lä·gät). **1** Former district, Chhattisgarh division, cen. Central Provinces, Indian Union; 3614 sq. m.; pop. (1941) 634,350. **2** Town, its ✻, now in Madhya Pradesh, on Wainganga river NE of Nagpur; pop. 9605.

Ba′lah Lakes (bä′lä·h′). Contiguous lakes, N Egypt, on W side of Suez Canal at its N end; contain several islands; connected with Lake Manzala.

Ba′la·kha·ni′ (bä′lä·kä·nē′) *or* **Ba′la·kha·na′** (-nȧ′). Town, Azerbaidzhan Republic, U.S.S.R., just NNE of Baku on the Apsheron Penin.; oil.

Ba·lakh′na (bŭ·läk′nȧ). Town, Gorki Region, Soviet Russia, Europe, ab. 25 m. NW of Gorki; pop. ab. 5000.

Bal′a·kla′va (băl′ȧ·klä′vȧ; -klȧv′ȧ; *Russ.* bȧ·lŭ·klä′vȧ), *also* **Bal′a·cla′va.** Seaport village, SW coast of the Crimea, Soviet Russia, Europe, 8 m. SE of Sevastopol; pop. 1300; scene Oct. 25, 1854 of indecisive battle of Crimean War memorable for charge of Light Brigade.

Bal′a Lake (băl′ȧ). Lake ab. 4 m. long, E Merionethshire, Wales; source of Dee river; largest natural lake in Wales but smaller than the artificial Lake Vyrnwy (*q.v.*).

Ba′lam·ban′ (bä′läm·bän′). Municipality on W coast of Cebu I., Phil. Is., on Tañon Strait; pop. 31,385.

Ba·lan′ga (bä·läng′gä). Municipality, ✻ of Bataan prov., Luzon, Phil. Is., near E coast in central part; pop. 11,684; taken by Japanese Feb. 1942.

Ba'lan·gi'ga (bä'läng·hē'gä). Municipality, S coast of Samar, Phil. Is., on Leyte Gulf; pop. 19,858.

Ba'lan·guin'gui (bä'läng·gēng'gē). **1** Former name of Samales group of islands, Sulu Archipelago, Phil. Is.

2 Most important island of the group, ab. 18 m. E of E tip of Jolo I.; 1 sq. m.

Ba·la·shov' (bȧ·lŭ·shôf'). Town, SW Saratov Region, Soviet Russia, Europe, on left bank of Khoper river 110 m. W of Saratov; pop. 26,846.

Ba'la·si·nor' (bä'lȧ·sǐ·nôr'). **1** Former Indian state, Gujarat States, W Indian Union; 195 sq. m.; pop. (1941) 61,151.

2 Town, its *, now in Gujerat state, 45 m. E of Ahmadabad; pop. 9710.

Ba'la·sore (bŭ'lȧ·sōr). **1** District, E Orissa state, E Indian Union, on coast of Bay of Bengal; 2194 sq. m.; pop. (1941) 1,029,430.

2 Town, its *, near coast SW of Calcutta; pop. 22,851.

Ba'las·sa·gyar'mat (bŏ'lŏsh·shŏ·dyŏr'mŏt). City, N Hungary, 42 m. N of Budapest; pop. 10,804.

Bal'a·ton (bǎl'ȧ·tŏn; *Hung.* bŏ'lŏ·tŏn); *Ger.* **Plat'ten·see'** (plät'ĕn·zā'). Lake 266 sq. m. in W Hungary, 55 m. SW of Budapest; largest lake in central Europe; has many resorts on its shores but no large towns.

Ba'la·ton·fü'red (bŏ'lŏ·tŏn·fü'rĕd) or **Fü'red** (fü'rĕd). Village, W Hungary, on N shore of Lake Balaton.

Ba'la·yan' (bä'lä·yän'). Municipality on SW coast of Batangas prov., Luzon, Phil. Is., on NW shore of Balayan Bay 26 m. NW of Batangas; pop. 15,224.

Balayan Bay. Large inlet of South China Sea in SW Batangas prov., Phil. Is., from 14 to 16 m. wide; Cape Santiago is its SW point and Maricaban I. lies to SE.

Bal'bi (bäl'bē). Active volcano 10,171 ft. in Emperor Range, NW Bougainville I., Solomon Is., W Pacific Ocean; highest point on the island.

Bal·bo'a (bǎl·bō'ȧ; *Span.* bäl·vō'ä). **1** District occupying SE part of Canal Zone; pop. 30,623.

2 Town, Balboa dist., adjacent to Panama at Pacific entrance to Panama Canal; pop. 3139; its port is La Boca.

Balboa Heights. Suburb of Balboa, location of U.S. administrative center for the Canal Zone; pop. 118.

Bal·brig'gan (bǎl·brǐg'ȧn). Seaport and manufacturing town, NE coast of co. Dublin, E Eire, 19 m. NNE of Dublin; pop. 2434; linen, cotton, calico, and stocking manufacturing.

Balch Springs (bôlch). Town, Dallas co., Texas, E suburb of Dallas; pop. 6821.

Bal'cic (bäl'chēk) or **Bal'tchik** (-chēk). Town, Dobruja, NE Bulgaria, on Black Sea W of Cape Caliacra.

Bal·clu'tha (bǎl·klōō'thȧ). Borough near mouth of Clutha river, SE South I., New Zealand; pop. 1570.

Bal'degg (bäl'dĕk). Lake 3½ m. long and 1 m. wide, N cen. Switzerland, in N Lucerne canton, formed by expansion of Aa river.

Bald'face' Mountain (bôld'fās'). Peak 3903 ft. in the Adirondack Mts., Essex co., NE New York.

Bald Hills. Range in Pennington co., SW South Dakota; alt. 5000 ft.

Bald Mountain. **1** Peak 13,974 ft., Summit co., cen. Colorado.

2 Peak 13,694 ft., Summit and Park cos., cen. Colorado.

3 Peak 10,315 ft., cen. Custer co., cen. Idaho.

4 Peak 9389 ft., NW Elmore co., SW cen. Idaho.

5 Peak 8330 ft., Grant co., E cen. Oregon.

6 Peak 7000 ft., Lawrence co., W South Dakota.

7 Peak 11,947 ft., S Summit co., NE Utah.

8 Peak 10,029 ft., Big Horn co., N Wyoming.

9 Peak 10,760 ft. in Wind River Range, W cen. Wyoming.

Bald Mountains. Range of the Appalachian Mts. along the Tennessee-North Carolina boundary, NE of the Great Smoky Mts.; highest ab. 5560 ft.

Bald'win (bôld'wǐn). **1** Name of counties in two states of the U.S. See *Tables* at ALABAMA and GEORGIA.

2 Village, ⊗ of Lake co., W Michigan; pop. 835.

3 Community, Nassau co., SE New York, on S shore of Long I. 23 m. E of Brooklyn; pop. 30,204; fisheries.

4 Borough, Allegheny co., Pennsylvania, on Monongahela river S of Pittsburgh; pop. 24,489.

Baldwin City. City, Douglas co., E Kansas; pop. 1877. Baker University (1858; coed.; Methodist).

Baldwin Park. City, Los Angeles co., California, SE of Monrovia; pop. 33,951.

Baldwin Peninsula. See KOTZEBUE.

Bald'wins·ville (bôld'wǐnz·vǐl). Village, Onondaga co., cen. New York, on N.Y. State Barge Canal 14 m. NW of Syracuse; pop. 5985; natural-gas deposits nearby.

Bald'y, Mount (bôl'dǐ). Peak 12,000 ft., E Beaver co., SW Utah.

Baldy Peak. **1** Mountain 11,496 ft., S Apache co., E Arizona. Also known as **Thom'as Peak** (tŏm'ǎs).

2 Mountain 12,623 ft., Santa Fe co., New Mexico.

3 Mountain, W Texas. See Mount LIVERMORE.

Bâle. See BASEL.

Bal'e·ar'ic Islands (bǎl'ē·ǎr'ǐk); *Span.* **Is'las Ba'le·a'res** (ēz'läz vä'lā·ä'räs). Island group in W Mediterranean Sea near E coast of Spain; 1935 sq. m.; pop. (1941 est.) 410,060; forms Spanish province of **Baleares** (see *Table* at SPAIN); comprises the islands of Majorca, Minorca, Iviza, Formentera, Cabrera (*qq.v.*), and 11 smaller islands; popular resort, noted esp. for its picturesque scenery and mild climate; produces fruits, wine, grain, cattle; rich mineral deposits; fishing, esp. for sardines and anchovies.

History: Became part of Carthaginian empire 5th cent. B.C.; conquered by Rome c. 123 B.C.; overrun by Vandals 465 A.D.; reconquered for Byzantine Empire by Belisarius 534; raided by Arabs in 9th cent. but not permanently conquered until early 10th cent. by Ommiad line at Córdoba (*q.v.*); kingdom of Mallorca taken by James I of Aragon 1229–35 and made a separate kingdom for his son, united to kingdom of Aragon by Pedro IV 1344; Minorca held by British 1709–82 (except for 1756–63); became Spanish province.

Balearis Major. See MAJORCA.

Ba'lem·bang'an (bä'lĕm·bäng'än). Island, N Brit. North Borneo, just S of main channel of Balabac Strait; British settlement here 1762–75.

Ba·ler' Bay (bä·lĕr'). Inlet of Pacific Ocean on E coast of Luzon, Tayabas prov., Phil. Is., 15°50'N. Near its head on short stream is municipality of **Baler** (pop. 11,887), which has one of best harbors on Pacific coast of Luzon; former capital of Principe dist.; occupied by U.S. troops Apr. 14, 1900; in World War II occupied by Japanese; seized by Americans Feb. 12, 1945.

Balesh. See ELVAS.

Baleswar. See GANGES DELTA.

Ba·le'te Pass (bä·lā'tå). Pass in Caraballo Mts., SW Nueva Vizcaya prov., Luzon, Phil. Is., on main highway bet. cen. Luzon and Cagayan valley in the N.

Bâle-Ville (bäl'vēl'). = *Basel Stadt*, Swiss demicanton: see *Table* at SWITZERLAND.

Bal·frin' (bäl·frēn'). Peak 12,474 ft. in the Pennine Alps, Valais canton, SW cen. Switzerland.

Bal·frush' (bȧl·frōōsh'), **Bal'fu·rush'** (bȧl'fōō·rōōsh'). = BABUL.

Bal·gow'lah (bǎl·gou'lȧ). Village, part of Manly and NE suburb of Sydney, New South Wales, Australia.

Ba'li (bä'lē). Island of Indonesia, off E end of Java and bet. Bali Sea and Indian Ocean, westernmost of the Lesser Sunda Is.; ab. 93 m. long by 50 m. wide; 2146 sq. m.; pop. 1,101,393; chief town Singaradja; separated from Java by Bali Strait and from Lombok I. on the E by Lombok Strait; formerly, with Lombok, a residency of Neth. Indies. Famous for its climate and tropical scenery; mountainous, with highest peaks in E (Gunung Agung 10,308 ft.) and N cen. part; at S end has low hook-shaped peninsula; has no good harbors (Buleleng in the N is the best); its rivers are mostly unnavigable and generally run S from the N plateau;

has luxuriant vegetation and grows a great variety of tropical products; principal crop rice.

History: Colonized direct from India in early times, its civilization is Hindu; many fine old temples; little contact with Dutch before 19th cent., when Balinese princes recognized Dutch supremacy but retained local autonomy; native piracy overcome by Dutch expedition 1846; bet. 1882 and 1908 came definitely under Dutch government; naval battle Feb. 19, 1942 off SE coast in Badung Strait, won by Allied Nations, did not prevent occupation of island by Japanese, who made landing Feb. 20; surrendered to Allies Sept. 1945.

Bali and Lom·bok' (lŏm·bŏk'). Former residency, Lesser Sunda Is., Neth. Indies, comprising the islands of Bali and Lombok; 3972 sq. m.; pop. 1,802,683; ✻ Singaradja; had three divisions: Singaradja and South Bali on Bali, and the island of Lombok.

Ba'lian·ga'o (bä'lyäng·gä'ŏ). Municipality, N tip of coast of Misamis Occidental prov., Mindanao, Phil. Is.; pop. 15,810.

Ba'li·ke·sir' (bä'lĭ·kĕ·sēr'). **1** Vilayet, NW Turkey in Asia, 5526 sq. m.; pop. 460,877.

2 City, its ✻, on tributary of the Simav 50 m. S of Sea of Marmara; pop. 26,699; near silver mines; trades in opium and cereals.

Ba·likh' (bä·lēk'). River ab. 120 m. long rising in S Turkey in Asia N of Urfa and flowing S to the Euphrates in N Syria near Rakka.

Ba'lik·pa'pan (bä'lĭk·pä'pän). Seaport town, SE Borneo, Indonesia; pop. 29,843; on **Balikpapan Bay** 225 m. NE of Bandjermasin; has become one of the great oil centers of Borneo. Naval engagement off the bay Jan. 24, 1942 bet. U.S. destroyers and Japanese warships followed a few days later by Japanese occupation of the burned-out port; retaken by Australians July 3, 1945.

Ba'li·li'han (bä'lĕ·lē'hän). Municipality, SW Bohol prov., Phil. Is., 10 m. NE of Tagbiliran; pop. 18,991.

Ba'lin·ga·sag' (bä'lĕng·gä·säg'). Municipality, E Misamis Oriental prov., Mindanao, Phil. Is., on E shore of Macajalar Bay 20 m. NNE of Cagayan; pop. 20,948.

Ba'lin·tang' Channel (bä'lĕn·täng'). Strait 50 m. wide bet. Batan Is. on the N and Babuyan Is. on the S, N Phil. Is.; connects Philippine Sea and South China Sea.

Ba'li Peak (bä'lē). See Goenoeng AGOENG.

Bali Sea. Body of water bet. Kangean Is. on the N and Bali on the S, Indonesia; forms SW part of Flores Sea; Madura Strait opens into it from the W.

Bali Strait. Channel bet. E end of Java and W end of Bali, Indonesia, connecting Bali Sea with the Indian Ocean; only 1 m. wide at narrowest point just N of Banjuwangi, Java.

Ba·li'uag (bä·lē'wäg). Municipality, W Bulacan prov., Luzon, Phil. Is., on right bank of Angat river 10 m. NE of Malolos; pop. 22,972; has large rice market and is noted for its production of bamboo hats. Taken by American forces May 2, 1899 during Philippine rebellion; lost to Japanese Dec. 1941; retaken Jan. 1945.

Bal'kan Mountains (bôl'kăn); *Bulg.* **Sta'ra Pla'ni·na'** (stä'rä plä'nĭ·nä'); *anc.* **Hae'mus** (hē'mŭs). Range of mountains extending E and W across cen. Bulgaria from Yugoslav border to the Black Sea; highest point ab. 7800 ft.; crossed by Shipka Pass, N of Kazanlik.

Balkan Peninsula. Peninsula in SE Europe bet. the Adriatic and Ionian Seas on the W, the Mediterranean Sea on the S, and the Aegean and Black Seas on the E.

Balkan States. Countries occupying the Balkan Peninsula: Yugoslavia, Romania, Bulgaria, Albania, Greece, and Turkey in Europe.

History: For earlier history, see GREECE and MACEDONIA. Incorporated as Roman provinces 168 B.C.–107 A.D. (see EPIRUS, ACHAEA, MACEDONIA, DALMATIA, MOESIA, PANNONIA, THRACE, DACIA, and ILLYRIA); settled by Slavic invaders, Serbs, Croats, Slovenes, and Slavonized Bulgars, who were pushed into Balkan region in 6th cent.; gradually organized into kingdoms (see

BULGARIA, CROATIA, SERBIA, and BOSNIA); except for Montenegro, conquered by Ottoman Turks 14th and 15th cents.; aroused by nationalism and encouraged by decline of Turkish authority, began series of revolts against Turkish rule 1804 (see SERBIA); independence of region, alternately supported and opposed by the Great Powers, was part of issue of European politics known as "Eastern Question"; by 1912, Greece (1829), Serbia, Montenegro, and Romania (all in 1878), and Bulgaria (1908) were recognized as independent states, Croatia, Dalmatia, Bosnia, and Herzegovina belonged to Austria-Hungary, and Macedonia remained in Turkish hands; in First Balkan War 1912–13, Bulgaria, Serbia, Montenegro, and Greece took Macedonia from Turkey, and the independence of Albania (*q.v.*) was proclaimed; in Second Balkan War 1913, former allies and Romania united against Bulgaria; in World War I which was precipitated by Austrian demands on Serbia, only Bulgaria joined Central Powers; Romania, Yugoslavia, Greece, and Turkey signed Balkan Pact 1934, Bulgaria not joining because of desire for revision of boundaries she received by peace treaties of World War I; in World War II, Albania became Italian 1939, Bulgaria joined Axis, Greece was conquered by Germany, and Yugoslavia and Romania were occupied by Axis forces 1941. Yugoslavia 1945, Albania and Bulgaria 1946 proclaimed republics; peace treaties with Bulgaria and Romania signed by United Nations Feb. 10, 1947.

Balkaria. See KABARDINO-BALKARIAN REPUBLIC.

Balkh (bälk). **1** Country of SW Asia, W of Badakhshan and S of the Oxus, in extent corresponding closely to ancient Bactria (*q.v.*); in medieval times on trade route bet. India and Europe; now a district of N Afghanistan (Afghan Turkistan); chief city Mazar-i-Sharif.

2 *anc.* **Bac'tra** (băk'trȧ). Ancient city, ✻ of Bactria and of Balkh; once a center of Zoroastrianism; twice destroyed, first by Genghis Khan and later by Tamerlane; after great epidemic of cholera in 19th cent. reduced to village (Wazirabad) near Mazar-i-Sharif.

3 New town, just N of village of Wazirabad (site of anc. Balkh); pop. ab. 10,000.

Bal·khash'; *Turki* **Bal·qash'** (bäl·käsh'). Town on N shore of Lake Balkhash, E Kazakh S.S.R., Soviet Central Asia; terminus of railroad from Akmolinsk.

Balkhash, Lake; *Turki* **Balqash.** Fresh-water lake in SE Kazakh S.S.R., Soviet Central Asia; alt. 1000 m. E of Lake Aral; 440 m. long and 32 to 51 m. wide; 7200 sq. m.; alt. 900 ft.; has the shape of a broad crescent; its chief feeder is the Ili entering at SE in a wide delta.

Ball, Mount (bôl). Peak 10,865 ft. in SW Canada, on border bet. Alberta and British Columbia.

Bal'la·rat (băl'ȧ·răt). City, S cen. Victoria, SE Australia, 70 m. WNW of Melbourne; pop. 35,681, with suburbs 37,409. Founded 1851; center of one of world's richest gold-mining districts; seat of a school of mines; fine climate; summer resort of residents of Melbourne.

Bal'lard (băl'ẽrd). County in Kentucky. See *Table* at KENTUCKY.

Bal·la·ri (băl·lä'rĭ). Var. of BELLARY.

Bal'la·ter (băl'ȧ·tẽr). Village, Aberdeen co., NE Scotland, on the Dee E of Balmoral; pop. 1301; medicinal springs (see PANNANICH WELLS) nearby.

Bal'le·ny Islands (băl'ĕ·nĭ). Group of volcanic islands in Ross Dependency, Antarctica, ab. 66°S and 163°E.

Bal'li·a (bŏl'ĭ·ȧ). **1** Former district, E Benares division, United Provinces, N Indian Union; 1183 sq. m.; pop. (1941) 1,053,880.

2 Town, its ✻, now in Uttar Pradesh, near N bank of Ganges; pop. 18,143.

Bal'li·na (băl'ĭ·nȧ). Urban district, N co. Mayo, NW Eire, on Moy river; pop. 5728; trade center; salmon fisheries and fish curing; linen weaving.

Bal'li·na·muck' (băl'ĭ·nȧ·mŭk'). Village, N co. Longford, N cen. Eire; scene of surrender 1798 of Irish insurrectionary forces.

Bal′li·na·sloe′ (băl′ĭ·nȧ·slō′). Urban district, E co. Galway, W Eire; pop. 5834; noted annual cattle fair.

Bal′lin·ger (băl′ĭn·jĕr). City, ⊗ of Runnels co., W cen. Texas, 32 m. NE of San Angelo; pop. 5043; manufactures flour, cottonseed oil; ships fruit, cattle, grain.

Bal′lin·skel′ligs Bay (băl′ĭn·skĕl′ĭgz). Inlet of Atlantic on SW coast of Ireland, N of Kenmare river.

Ball′s Bluff (bôlz). Locality in Loudoun co., NE Virginia, on the Potomac 33 m. NW of Washington; battle Oct. 21, 1861 in which Federal force was severely defeated, a conflict of no military importance but one which aroused much criticism in the North.

Ball′ston Spa (bôl′stŭn spä′; spô′). Village, ⊗ of Saratoga co., E New York, ab. 6 m. SW of Saratoga Springs; pop. 4991; mineral springs; founded c. 1787; fashionable watering place before Civil War.

Ball′win (bôl′wĭn). City, St. Louis co., Missouri, W of St. Louis; pop. 5710.

Bal′ly (bä′lĭ). Town, Burdwan division, formerly in Bengal prov.; since 1947 in West Bengal, Indian Union; on Hooghly river across from Calcutta; pop. (1941) 50,397.

Bal′ly·me′na (băl′ĭ·mē′nȧ). Municipal borough, co. Antrim, NE Northern Ireland; pop. 14,165; iron mining; manufactures linen goods and embroidery.

Bal′ly·na·hinch′ (băl′ĭ·nȧ·hĭnch′). Town, co. Down, SE Northern Ireland, 13 m. SW of Belfast; pop. 1919; battle 1798 in which United Irishmen were defeated by the yeomanry.

Bal·main′ (băl·mān′). City, E New South Wales, SE Australia, industrial suburb W of Sydney on Parramatta river; pop. 28,268; chemical works, shipyards.

Bal′maz·új′vá′ros (bŏl′mŏz·ōō′y′·vä′rōsh). Commune, E cen. Hungary, W of Debrecen; pop. 15,699.

Bal·mor′al (băl·mŏr′ăl). Castle in SW Aberdeen co., Scotland, on the Dee river E of Braemar and W of Ballater; Scottish residence of British sovereigns; purchased 1852 by Prince Albert who bequeathed it to Queen Victoria.

Balqash. See BALKHASH.

Bal·quhid′der (băl·hwĭd′ĕr). Village and parish, S Perth co., Scotland, ab. 28 m. NW of Stirling; pop. (parish) 671; district won by Macgregor clan 1558; in the churchyard is grave of Rob Roy who died here 1734.

Bal′sam Lake (bôl′săm). Village, ⊗ of Polk co., NW Wisconsin; pop. 541.

Balsar. See BULSAR.

Bal′sas, Rí′o de las (rē′ō thä läz väl′säs); *known also as the* **Mex·ca′la** (mâs·kä′lä). River 426 m. long, cen. Mexico; rises in Tlaxcala state, flows S and then W through Guerrero into Petachalco Bay; its lower course forms boundary bet. Michoacán and Guerrero.

Bal′ta (băl′tȧ; *Angl.* bôl′tȧ). Town, NW Odessa Region, S Ukraine, U.S.S.R., on a tributary of the Bug river ab. 112 m. NNW of Odessa; pop. 21,374; center of an agricultural region raising especially grain and cattle; has annual fairs. A Turkish town, formerly in Podolia; became Russian by treaty 1792; capital of Moldavian A.S.S.R. 1928–30; in World War II held by Germans 1941–44; retaken by Russians in summer of 1944.

Baltchik. See BALCIC.

Bǎl′ţi *or* **Bal′tzi** (bûlts; bûl′tsĕ). **1** Former department, N cen. Bessarabia, Romania; 2030 sq. m.; pop. 386,476. **2** Town, its *. See BELTSY.

Bal′tic Port (bôl′tĭk). See PALDISKI.

Baltic Provinces. The former Russian governments of Estonia, Livonia, and Kurland (*qq.v.*), which in 1918 were formed into the independent republics of Estonia and Latvia. See BALTIC STATES.

Baltic Sea; *Ger.* **Ost′see′** (ôst′zā′); *Russ.* **Bal·tiy′sko·e Mo′re** (bŭl·tyē′sku·yĕ mô′ryĕ); *anc.* **Ma′re Sue′vi·cum** (mā′rē swē′vĭ·kŭm). Sea in N Europe, an arm of the Atlantic Ocean connecting with the North Sea through the Skaggerak, Kattegat, and Öresund, and extending roughly NE to SW bet. 54° and 66°N lat. and

9°30′ and 30°E long.; ab. 157,000 sq. m.; 1056 m. long; greatest depth ab. 1200 ft.; enclosed by Denmark, Sweden, Finland, U.S.S.R. (Estonia, Latvia, Lithuania), Poland, and Germany. Has two large arms: Gulf of Bothnia, its N extension bet. Sweden and Finland, and Gulf of Finland bet. Finland and Estonia.

Baltic States. The former republics of Estonia, Latvia, and Lithuania (*qq.v.*) on the E shore of the Baltic Sea, which were established as independent states in 1917 out of the Baltic Provinces (*q.v.*) of Russia and the government of Kovno and part of Wilno (later Lithuania); aided by German and Allied forces in forcing out Bolshevist invasion 1919; incorporated in the U.S.S.R. Aug. 3, 1940; overrun by German forces 1941; recovered by Russians in summer and fall of 1944. By some the name was applied to include Finland and Poland as well.

Bal·tiisk′ (bŭl·tyēsk′); *Ger.* **Pil′lau** (pĭl′ou). Town, on sandspit at entrance of the Frisches Haff, Kaliningradsk Region, Soviet Russia, Europe, formerly in East Prussia, Germany; pop. (1933) 7092; harbor; shipbuilding, fishing. Site of landing of Gustavus Adolphus 1626. Assigned to U.S.S.R. at Potsdam Conference 1945.

Bal·tîm′ (băl·têm′). Town, Gharbîya prov., Lower Egypt, near coast in Nile delta midway bet. Rosetta and Damietta mouths and at E end of Lake Burullus.

Bal′ti·more (bôl′tĭ·mōr). **1** County in Maryland. See *Table* at MARYLAND.

2 City, Maryland, on Patapsco river at upper end of Chesapeake Bay ab. 40 m. NE of Washington; pop. 939,024; largest city in the state and 6th largest city in the U.S.; geographically in S Baltimore co. but administratively independent (see *Table* at MARYLAND); port of entry; commercial and industrial center, and important seaport. Johns Hopkins University (1876; part coed.); Goucher College (1885; women; Methodist); Loyola College (1852; men; Rom. Cath.); College of Notre Dame of Maryland (1895; women); Univ. of Baltimore (1925; coed.); Univ. of Maryland (professional schools and hospital; see COLLEGE PARK); St. Mary's Seminary and Univ. (1791; men; Rom. Cath.); Morgan State College (1867; coed.); Peabody Conservatory of Music (1868; coed.).

History: Purchased by Maryland legislature 1729 and made a shipbuilding and export center; during American Revolution, meeting place for American Congress during the British occupation of Philadelphia; incorporated as city 1797; bombing of its Fort McHenry by British Sept. 12–13, 1814 inspired Francis Scott Key to write the *Star-Spangled Banner;* in 1827 organized Baltimore and Ohio R.R. to retain share in trans-Allegheny trade which the Erie Canal threatened to draw entirely to New York; during Civil War, sympathy with the South occasioned riots when Union troops marched through Apr. 19, 1861; suffered from a destructive fire Feb. 7, 1904.

Baltiski. See PALDISKI.

Bal′ti·stan′ (bŭl′tĭ·stän′) *or* **Lit′tle Ti·bet′** (tĭ·bĕt′). Part of Ladakh frontier district, N cen. Kashmir state, N India, bet. 34° and 36°N lat. and 75° and 77°E long.; contains some of highest peaks of W Himalayas; inhabited by Baltis, a non-Mongol Mohammedan people.

Baltiyskoe More. See BALTIC SEA.

Baltzi. Var. of BĂLŢI.

Ba·lu·chi·stan′ (bȧ·lōō′chĭ·stän′; -stän′). Region of W Asia, bounded on N by Afghanistan, on E by India, on S by the Arabian Sea, and on W by Iran; 134,638 sq. m.; pop. (1941) 857,835; divided into: (1) Moslem territory, formerly a province (**British Baluchistan**) of NW Brit. India, S of Afghanistan; since 1947 a part of Pakistan; 9084 sq. m.; * Quetta. (2) Agency territories (leased from Kalat); 37,864 sq. m., and tribal areas 7280 sq. m.; pop. in 1941 of (1) and (2), 501,631; * Quetta. (3) **Baluchistan States:** Kalat, in cen. part, 59,068 sq. m., pop. (1941) 253,305, * Kalat (recognized as independent 1947, joined Pakistan 1948); Kharan in NW 14,210 sq. m., pop. 33,832; and Las Bela, in SE, 7132

sq. m., pop. (1941) 69,067; total area of states 80,410 sq. m., pop. (1941) 356,204. Main territory divided into districts: Quetta-Pishin, Sibi, Zhob, Loralai, and Chagai, and the Bolan subdivision. Country is very mountainous, esp. in NE; Sulaiman Range on NE border, Kirthar Range on SE; ranges of 5000 ft. in cen. part; Hamun-i-Mashkel marsh and desert in NW; much of land is barren with irregular and scant water supply, but with some fertile valleys. *Rivers:* Mashkel, Dasht, Hingol, Hab. *Chief towns:* Quetta (reached by Bolan Pass), Kalat, Bela, Chaman, and Fort Sandeman; also ports of Ormara and Pasni, Gwadar in SW formerly belonged to Oman. Country inhabited chiefly by Baluch, Brahuis, and Afghans.

History: In ancient times, part of Gedrosia; traversed by Alexander the Great 325 B.C.; part of Bactrian kingdom (see BALKH); ruled from 7th–10th cents. A.D. by Arabs who overthrew Persia; except for period when part of Mogul Empire 1595–1638, returned to moderate form of Persian rule; under Nasir Khan of Kalat (1739–95), most of its princes, included several districts of Sind; by treaty of 1876 made virtually a British dependency; districts, assigned at close of Afghan War (1878–79), enlarged; made British province of India 1887; boundaries with Afghanistan and Persia settled 1885 and 1896; became part of Pakistan Aug. 15, 1947.

Baluchistan, Persian. See PERSIAN BALUCHISTAN.

Ba·lut′ (bä·lōōt′). Island, larger and westernmost of the Sarangani Is., SW Davao prov., Mindanao, Phil. Is.; 22 sq. m.; pop. 1377; has semiactive volcano 3110 ft.

Bal·zar′ (bäl·sär′). Town, Guayas prov., W Ecuador, 55 m. N of Guayaquil; pop. (1944 est.) 9306.

Bam (bàm). Town, Kerman prov., SE Iran, on caravan route SE of Kerman; pop. ab. 8500; its trade more important in Middle Ages than in modern times; has famous citadel held by Afghans 1719–1801.

Ba·ma′ko′ (bȧ·mȧ·kō′). Town, ✻ of Mali and of former French Sudan territory, West Africa, on Niger river ab. 90 m. NE of the Guinea border; pop. (1957) 68,600; terminus of railroad from Dakar in Senegal.

Bam′ba·ta′na (bäm′bä·tä′nä). Chief settlement, on cen. part of W coast, of Choiseul I., W cen. Solomon Is., W Pacific Ocean.

Bam′berg (băm′bûrg). **1** County in South Carolina. See *Table* at SOUTH CAROLINA.

2 Town, its ⊗, SW South Carolina, 18 m. SW of Orangeburg; pop. 3081; in pine timber and farming country; textiles.

Bam′berg (bäm′bĕrк; *Angl.* băm′bûrg). Manufacturing city, Upper Franconia govt. dist., Bavaria, Germany, on Regnitz river near its confluence with the Main 30 m. W of Bayreuth; pop. 50,152; 12th-cent. cathedral (Romanesque-Gothic transition); seminary, observatory; manufactures textiles, brewery products.

Bam′burgh (băm′bŭ·rŭ; băm′brŭ), *earlier* **Bam′borough.** Civil parish, E Northumberland co., N England, on coast 17 m. SE of Berwick upon Tweed; pop. 1258; as Bamborough was capital of ancient Bernicia and for a time capital of Northumbria.

Ba′mi·an′ (bȧ′mĕ·yän′). **1** Valley and pass in W Hindu Kush Mts., NE Afghanistan, ab. 60 m. NNW of Kabul; alt. 12,500 ft.

2 Ancient city in Bamian valley, N of the Koh-i-Baba; ruins of great towers and numerous cave dwellings in the walls of the valley, also two colossal images of Buddhist figures, described 630 A.D. by Chinese traveler Hsüan Tsang. Its early history obscure, but it flourished in 12th cent. under Ghuri dynasty; besieged and destroyed 1222 by Genghis Khan.

Bam–i–Dunya. See PAMIR.

Bam·pur′ (bäm·pōōr′). Town, Kerman prov., SE Iran, in a fertile valley; pop. ab. 10,000; inhabitants are chiefly Baluchis; chief town of former Persian Baluchistan.

Bam′ra (bäm′rȧ). Former Indian state, W cen. Orissa, E India; 1974 sq. m.; ✻ Deogarh.

Ba′mu (bä′mōō). Island in Stanley Pool (*q.v.*), in Congo river, W Africa.

Banaba. See OCEAN ISLAND.

Ba·na′hao, Mount (bä·nä′hou). Extinct volcano 7141 ft., SW Tayabas prov., Luzon, Phil. Is., on Laguna border NW of Lucena; last serious eruption 1730.

Ba′nam′ (*Fr.* bȧ′nȧm′). Town, Cambodia, Indochina, on left bank of the Mekong 30 m. SE of Pnompenh; pop. ab. 28,000.

Ba·nan′a (bȧ·năn′ȧ). River, actually a wide part of the lagoon bet. Canaveral Penin. and Merritt I., Brevard co., E Florida.

Ba·na′na (bä·nä′nä). Seaport town, W Léopoldville prov., W Congo, on N side of the mouth of Congo river; pop. ab. 500.

Ba·nan′a Islands (bȧ·năn′ȧ; -nä′nȧ). Group of small islands in Atlantic Ocean off S point of Sierra Leone Penin., Sierra Leone, W Africa, once a station for English slave traders.

Ba·na·nal′ (bȧ·nȧ·näl′). Island over 200 m. long in Araguaia river, NW Goiaz state, Brazil.

Ba·na′na Point (bä·nä′nä). Cape on N side of estuary of Congo river, Africa.

Banaras. See BENARES.

Ba′nas (bŭ′näs). River 300 m. long, S Rajasthan, N cen. India; rises at S end of Aravalli Range in Udaipur, flows NE to the Chambal.

Ba′nas, Cape (bȧ′năs; *Arab.* **Ras Banas** (räs). Cape (*ras*) on E coast of Egypt, projecting into Red Sea N of Foul Bay; lat. 24°N.

Ba·nat′ (*Romanian* bä·nät′; *Yugoslav* bä′nät). **1** Agricultural region (also known as the Voivodina, *q.v.*) formerly in S Hungary E of Tisza river, S of the Mureş, N of the Danube, and W of the Transylvanian Alps; divided bet. Romania and Yugoslavia, except a small strip near Szeged. In Middle Ages, 9th–14th cents., settled chiefly by Magyars and Serbs; fell into neglect under rule of Turks 1552–1718; reclaimed by Maria Theresa (after 1740), incorporated in Hungary 1779, made an Austrian crownland 1849, and reverted to Hungary 1860. After World War I divided bet. Yugoslavia and Romania 1919; in World War II its W part (in Yugoslavia) seized by Hungary 1944–45.

2 Region, W Romania; 7224 sq. m.; formerly part of the Banat region of Hungary, later a province of Romania.

3 Former subprovince in N Yugoslavia kingdom; ✻ Veliki Bečkerek (Petrovgrad); later (1929–45) a part of Dunavska co.; now (since 1945) forms the autonomous province Voivodina in the republic of Yugoslavia.

Ba·na′te (bä·nä′tĕ). Municipality on E coast of Iloilo prov., Panay, Phil. Is., 28 m. NE of City of Iloilo on Guimaras Strait; pop. 16,210.

Ba·na′ue (bä·nä′wȧ). Town (municipal district), NW Ifugao subprov., Mountain Province, Luzon, Phil. Is., ab. 10 m. N of Kiangan; pop. 17,127; in World War II taken by Americans July 1945.

Ban′bridge′ (băn′brĭj′). Urban district, co. Down, SE Northern Ireland, on the Bann river; pop. 6098.

Ban′bur·y (băn′bĕr·ĭ; băm′-). Municipal borough, Oxfordshire, cen. England, on the Cherwell 38 m. SE of Birmingham; pop. 18,917; trade center in agricultural region; famous for its Banbury tarts.

Ban′da (băn′dä; *Angl.* băn′dȧ). **1** Former district, Jhansi division, SW United Provinces, N Indian Union; 2913 sq. m.; pop. (1941) 722,568.

2 Town, its ✻, now in Uttar Pradesh, on Ken river 95 m. W of Allahabad; pop. 22,415.

Banda, La. See LA BANDA.

Ban·dai′ (băn·dī) *or* **Ban·tai** (băn·tī). Volcano 5968 ft. in Fukushima prefecture, N cen. Honshu, Japan, NE of Wakamatsu and N of Lake Inawashiro; had four peaks, one of which was blown off in a destructive eruption July 1888.

Ban′da Islands (băn′dȧ). Island group of the S cen. Moluccas, Indonesia, Malay Archipelago, ab. 60 m.

S of E Ceram; 16 sq. m.; pop. 13,036; ✱ Bandanaira; formerly in Amboina division of Moluccas residency. Comprises three large islands Great Banda, Bandanaira, and Gunung Api, and seven small islands, all of volcanic origin. For centuries important in the spice trade; soil remarkably adapted to growing nutmegs, which are indigenous; also produces other spices, coconuts, fruits; trade controlled by Chinese and Arabs. Discovered and annexed by Portuguese 1512; conquered by Dutch 1621; settlement and interference of English led to Amboina massacre 1623; held by British 1796–1800 and during Napoleonic Wars.

Ban·da′ma (bän·dä′mä). River ab. 370 m. long in cen. Ivory Coast, West Africa; flows S into Atlantic.

Ban′da·mir′ (bän′dà·mēr′). River ab. 175 m. long in SW cen. Iran; flows SE into Lake Niriz.

Ban′da·nai′ra (bän′dä·nī′rä) or **Ban′da Nei′ra** (bän′-dä nī′rä). **1** Small island, most important of the Banda Is., Indonesia.
2 Town on the island, ✱ and port of the Banda Is.; pop. (1930) 4130, (later est.) 6000; its fine harbor is formed by close juxtaposition of Great Banda and Gunung Api (qq.v.); from 16th to 19th cents., an important trade center for spices.

Ban′da O′ri·en·tal′ (bän′dä ō′ryän·täl′). Former name of URUGUAY.

Bandar. See MASULIPATAM.

Ban·dar′ Ab·bas′ (bän·dàr′ äb·bäs′) or **Ben·der′ab-bas′**; Pers. **Ban·dar′ 'Ab·bas′**; formerly **Gom-broon′** (gŏm·brōōn′). Seaport, ✱ of Laristan prov., S Iran, on the Strait of Ormuz; pop. ab. 10,000; founded by Shah Abbas I; has long been one of the chief ports of Iran, English and Dutch factories having been established for trade in 17th cent.; exports carpets, cotton and wool, fruits, and gum.

Ban′dar Ma′ha·ra′ni (bän′där mä′hä·rä′nĕ); also **Mu·ar′** (mōō·wär′). Seaport on the Strait of Malacca, at the mouth of Muar river, NW Johore state, Federation of Malaya; pop. 20,338; chief port of the state.

Ban·dar′ Na′si·ri′ (bän·dàr′ nä′sĕ·rē′). See AHWAZ.

Ban′dar Peng·ga′ram (bän′där pĕng·gä′räm). Seaport on the Strait of Malacca, W Johore state, Federation of Malaya, SE of Bandar Maharani; pop. 13,329.

Ban·dar′ Shah (bän·dàr′ shä′h′). Port, N Iran, at SE corner of Caspian Sea E of Babul; connected by highway and railroad across the Elburz Mts. with Tehran; N terminus of Trans-Iranian R.R. from Bandar Shahpur.

Ban·dar′ Shah·pur′ (bän·dàr′ shä·h′·pōōr′). Town, SW Iran, 55 m. ENE of Abadan; S terminus of Trans-Iranian R.R. and oil port at head of Persian Gulf.

Ban′da Sea (bän′dä). Body of water in E Malay Archipelago, SE of Celebes I., S of Buru I. and Ceram I., W of Kai Is. and Aru Is., NW of the Tanimbar group, and NE of Timor I.; ab. 625 m. long by 275 m. wide.

Ban·dei′ra, Pi′co da (pē′kōō thà vănn·dā′ĕ·rà). Mountain, E Brazil, on border between Espírito Santo and Minas Gerais; highest in Brazil, 9462 ft.

Ban·de·lier′ National Monument (băn′dĕ·lĕr′). See UNITED STATES, National Monuments.

Ban·de′ra (băn·dĕr′à). **1** County in Texas. See Table at TEXAS.
2 Town, its ⊗, SW cen. Texas; pop. (1950) 1036; resort.

Ban·de′ras Bay (băn·dā′räs). Inlet of the Pacific Ocean on W cen. coast of Mexico, chiefly in NW Jalisco state.

Ban′dır·ma′ (bän′dĭr·mä′), formerly **Pan′der·ma** (pän′thär·mä). Town on S shore of Sea of Marmara, Balıkesir vilayet, NW Turkey in Asia; pop. 13,274.

Ban′djer·ma′sin or **Ban′jer·ma′sin** (bän′jĕr·mä′sĭn). Town on Martapura river near its junction with the Barito, SE Borneo, Indonesia; formerly ✱ of South and East Borneo residency; pop. 65,698; about 24 m. from the sea and a port of call for large vessels; trade center for Barito river basin, handling esp. jungle products, coal, and iron; large airport. In early times under Hindu influences; became Mohammedan ab. 1500 under Java-

nese; settled by Dutch 1711; held by English 1811–17; bombed by Japanese and seized by them Feb. 13, 1942; retaken by Allies Aug. 1945.

Ban′doeng or **Ban′dung** (bän′dŏong). City, ✱ of West Java prov., Indonesia, on railroad 75 m. SE of Batavia; pop. 931,477; third largest city in Indonesia; founded in 1810; elevation 2346 ft., surrounded by volcanoes and high mountains; healthful, modern city that has grown remarkably since 1910; has headquarters of several government departments, with schools, hospitals, factories (airplanes, ammunition, instruments, quinine), workshops, etc., and has become a resort; nearby is a radio station, one of the most powerful in the world. In World War II was main defense position of Dutch government and Allied headquarters but was captured by Japanese Mar. 7, 1942; site of Japanese prison camp.

Ban′don (băn′dŭn). Town on Bandon river, S co. Cork, SW Eire; pop. 2839; agricultural center, brewing, distilling; a noted stronghold of Protestantism in the 17th cent.

Ban′dra (bän′drà). Town, Maharashtra, W Indian Union, at S end of Salsette I. on W coast 7 m. N of Bombay; pop. (1941) 71,789; resort town for Parsis and Europeans of Bombay; population includes many native-born Christians who date their religious affiliations back to 16th-cent. and 17th-cent. Portuguese missionaries.

Bandung. See BANDOENG.

Ba′nes (bä′näs). Municipality and seaport, N Oriente prov., E Cuba; pop. (town) 16,000.

Banff (bămf). **1** Resort town near Lake Louise (q.v.) in Banff National Park, SW Alberta, Canada; pop. 2185.
2 or **Banff′shire** (bămf′shĭr; -shēr). County, NE Scotland; area 630 sq. m.; pop. (1951) 50,135; ⊗ Banff; other large town Buckie; rivers Spey and Deveron; quarrying (granite, limestone, slate); salmon and herring fisheries, cattle raising, whisky distilling.
3 Burgh, ⊗ of Banff co.; pop. 3359; fishing, shipping.

Banff National Park. See CANADA, National Parks.

Ban′ga·lore′ (băng′gà·lōr′). **1** District, SE Mysore state, S Indian Union; 2922 sq. m.; pop. 908,056.
2 City, its ✱ and ✱ of Mysore state, 190 m. W of Madras, 500 m. SE of Bombay; pop. (1941) 248,334; had a large British civil and military station, 14 sq. m., pop. (1941) 158,426; total pop. of city 406,760; an important rail and trade center; seat of an institute of science and an agricultural experimentation station; because of its altitude (3113 ft.), healthy and popular residential community. Founded in 16th cent.; later a possession of the Marathas; became a fief of Haidar Ali 1759; taken 1791 by British under Lord Cornwallis; except for civil and military station restored to raja of Mysore 1881.

Ban′ga·na·pal′le (bŭn′gà·nà·pŭl′lä). **1** Former Indian state, Madras States, S India, 210 m. NW of Madras; 259 sq. m.; pop. (1941) 44,592; once under Hyderabad, control ceded to Madras government 1800.
2 Town, its ✱; pop. 5760.

Ban′gas′sou′ (Fr. bän′gà′sōō′). Town, S Central African Republic, N cen. Africa, on N bank of Bomu river.

Bang′gai′ Archipelago (băng′gī′). Group of islands off E coast of Celebes I., Indonesia, Malay Archipelago; includes the large island of Peleng, **Banggai Island**, and about 25 small islands; 1221 sq. m.; pop. 49,836.

Bang′gi (băng′gĕ). Island, N Brit. North Borneo, S of the main channel of Balabac Strait.

Ban′gi′ (bän′gē′). Var. of BANGUI, Africa.

Bang′il (băng′ĭl). Town, East Java prov., Indonesia, near SW coast of Madura Strait; pop. 20,236; on railroad ab. 20 m. S of Surabaja.

Bang′ka (băng′kà). **1** or **Ban′ka** (băng′kà). An island of Indonesia, at NW corner of the Java Sea off SE coast of Sumatra and separated from Sumatra by the narrow **Bangka Strait** (ab. 10 m. wide); 138 m. long by 62 m. wide; 4609 sq. m.; pop. 205,363; chief

town Pangkalpinang; formed greater part of former Bangka residency. One of best tin-producing areas in the world; surface hilly; good roads but no railroads; large pepper plantations destroyed by Japanese; chief port Muntok at N end of Bangka Strait. Formerly belonged to ruler of Palembang; ceded to British 1810; became Dutch by exchange in 1814 for Cochin in India; seized by Japanese in 1942.

2 *officially* **Bangka and Dependencies.** Former residency, SE Sumatra, Neth. Indies; 6475 sq. m.; pop. 278,792; ＊ Pangkalpinang; comprised the islands of Bangka (see 1, above) and Billiton (*q.v.*).

Bang′ka·lan′ (bäng′kä·län′). Town, W coast of Madura I., East Java prov., Indonesia, ab. 16 m. N of Surabaja; pop. 12,359.

Bang′kok (băng′kŏk; bäng·kŏk′); *Siamese* **Krung Thep** (krŏŏng t′häp). Commercial city, ＊ of Thailand (since 1782; see also PHETCHABUN; SARA BURI), on the Chao Phraya ab. 20 m. above its mouth, S Thailand; coextensive with province of Phra Nakhon, 331 sq. m.; pop. 681,214; good river port; old city built on pontoons or piles with many canals; modern city has paved streets and well-built houses. Inhabitants mainly Siamese and Chinese. Only an agricultural village and a fort before 1769 when it became a stronghold against the Burmese; became the capital 1782. Seized by Japanese Dec. 8, 1941; frequently bombed by Allied planes 1944–45.

Ban′gor (băng′gôr; -gẽr). **1** Commercial and industrial city, ⊗ of Penobscot co., E cen. Maine, at head of navigation on Penobscot river 60 m. NE of Augusta; pop. 38,912; lumbering, pulp and paper mills. Bangor Theological Seminary (1816; Congregational); Dow Air Force Base.

2 Borough, Northampton co., E Pennsylvania, 23 m. NE of Allentown; pop. 5766; founded 1773; slate quarries.
3 Municipal borough, co. Down, SE Northern Ireland, on S side of entrance to Belfast Lough 12 m. ENE of Belfast; pop. 20,615; seaside resort; textile mills.
4 Municipal borough and city, Caernarvonshire, NW Wales; pop. 12,822; slate quarries nearby; University College of North Wales (1884).

Bang Phra. See TRAT.

Bang Pla Soi (bäng plä soi); *also* **Chon Bu·ri** (chŭn bŏŏ·rē). **1** Province, Thailand. See CHON BURI.
2 Town, ＊ of Chon Buri prov., Thailand, on N coast of Gulf of Siam 45 m. SE of Bangkok.

Ban·gued′ (bäng·gäd′). Municipality, ＊ of Abra prov., NW Luzon, Phil. Is., on Abra river; pop. 15,287.

Ban′gui′ (*Fr.* bän′gē′). Town, ＊ of Central African Republic (formerly Ubangi-Shari territory), cen. Equatorial Africa, in S part of republic on Ubangi river, 4°28′N; pop. 40,000.

Ban′gui (bäng′gē). Municipality, N Ilocos Norte, Luzon, Phil. Is., on Bangui Bay 25 m. NNE of Laoag; pop. 13,325; N terminus of W coast highway of Luzon.

Bangui Bay. Wide inlet of South China Sea on N coast of Ilocos Norte prov., Luzon, Phil. Is., extending from Dialao Point on NE to Negra Point on SW, ab. 10 m.

Bang′we·u′lu (băng′wĕ·ŏŏ′lŏŏ), *or* **Bang′we·o′lo** (-ŏ′lō), **Lake.** Lake in N Northern Rhodesia, S cen. Africa, SSE of Lake Mweru and SSW of Lake Tanganyika; ab. 50 m. long; area has been estimated at 1670 to 1900 sq. m. but is now gradually drying up; its outlet is the Luapula, a headstream of the Congo. First visited by Livingstone 1868; circumnavigated 1896.

Ba·ní′ (bä·nē′). City, Trujillo prov., S Dominican Republic, SW of Ciudad Trujillo; pop. (1944 est.) 11,731.

Ba′ni·yas′ *or* **Ba′ni·as′** (bä′ni·yäs′). **1** Town on coast of Syria 25 m. S of Latakia; pop. ab. 2000.
2 Village, SW Syria. See CAESAREA PHILIPPI.

Ban′jak (bän′yäk), *or* **Ban′yak, Islands.** Island group, Atjeh govt., Indonesia, in the Indian Ocean off NW coast of Sumatra; 123 sq. m.; pop. 1731; comprises about 65 islands, most of them very small, **Great Banjak,** the largest, being ab. 22 m. by 7 m.

Ba′nja Lu′ka (bä′nyä lōō′kä). Town, NW cen. Yugoslavia, in Bosnia and Herzegovina on Vrbas river; formerly ⊗ of Vrbaska co., Bosnia; pop. (1931) 22,165; commercial and industrial center; thermal springs. Probably dates back to a Roman fort; especially important 16th–18th cents. when it was several times a battlefield bet. Austrians and Turks (1527, 1688, and 1737).

Banjermasin. See BANDJERMASIN.

Ban′joe·mas′ (bän′yōō·mäs′) *or* **Ban′ju·mas′.** **1** Former residency, SW Middle Java prov., Neth. Indies; 2472 sq. m., pop. 2,474,447. First came under Dutch 1705.
2 Town, its ＊, on main highway ab. 25 m. NE of Tjilatjap; pop. 6686.

Ban′joe·wang′i (bän′yōō·wäng′ē) *or* **Ban′ju·wang′i.** Seaport on Bali Strait, East Java prov., Indonesia; pop. 25,185; port for Bali I. and railroad terminus of line from Surabaja.

Banka. See BANGKA.

Bankipore. See PATNA.

Banks (băngks). County in Georgia. See *Table* at GEORGIA.

Banks, Cape. Point on coast of New South Wales, SE Australia, on N shore of entrance to Botany Bay.

Banks Island. 1 Small island in Torres Strait, N of Cape York, Queensland, NE Australia.
2 Island 50 m. long off W cen. British Columbia, Canada, on E side of Hecate Strait.
3 Island 26,400 sq. m., ab. 250 m. long, W Franklin District, Northwest Territories, Canada, NW of Victoria I.; separated from mainland of Mackenzie District by Amundsen Gulf.

Banks Islands. Group of five small islands and a number of islets, SW Pacific Ocean, N of New Hebrides; administered as part of the New Hebrides; chief islands Vanua Lava and Santa Maria; volcanic and fertile, with luxuriant vegetation. Discovered ab. 1595.

Banks Peninsula. Peninsula ab. 35 m. long and 25 m. wide projecting from E cen. coast of South I., New Zealand; Christchurch is at its base on N side, Akaroa Harbor at its SE extremity.

Banks Strait. Passage ab. 13 m. wide separating the Furneaux Group of islands from NE coast of Tasmania.

Banks′town (băngks′toun). City, E New South Wales, SW Australia, SW suburb of Sydney; pop. 25,393.

Ban′ku·ra (bäng′kŏŏ·rä). **1** District, Burdwan division, West Bengal, NE Indian Union; 2646 sq. m.; pop. (1941) 1,289,640.
2 Town, its ＊, on tributary of Hooghly river 100 m. NW of Calcutta; pop. 31,703; produces shellac, silk, tussah.

Ban Mak Khaeng. See UDON THANI.

Ban′me·thu′ot (?bän′mĕ·tōō′ŏt). Town, S Annam, Vietnam, in mountains ab. 110 m. SW of Binh Dinh.

Bann (băn). Name of two rivers in Northern Ireland: the **Upper Bann** 25 m. long, rising in co. Down and flowing NW into Lough Neagh; the **Lower Bann** 33 m. long, flowing N out of Lough Neagh into the Atlantic.

Ban′ner (băn′ẽr). County in Nebraska. See *Table* at NEBRASKA.

Banner Peak. Mountain 12,957 ft. in Sierra Nevada, in NE Madera co., cen. California.

Ban′ning (băn′ing). City, Riverside co., SE California, 25 m. ESE of San Bernardino; pop. 10,250; founded 1883.

Ban′nock (băn′ŭk). County in Idaho. See *Table* at IDAHO.

Ban′nock·burn′ (băn′ŭk·bûrn′; băn′ŭk·bûrn′). Town, Stirling co., cen. Scotland, 2½ m. SSE of Stirling; pop. 4481; battle June 23, 1314 in which Robert Bruce routed the English under Edward II and took Stirling Castle.

Ban′nock Peak (băn′ŭk). **1** Mountain 8321 ft., W of Bannock Range, cen. Power co., SE Idaho.
2 Mountain 10,400 ft. in Yellowstone National Park, NW Wyoming.

Bannock Range. Mountains on W border of Bannock co., SE Idaho.

Ban'nu (bŭn'nōō). **1** Former district, S cen. North-West Frontier Province, NW Pakistan; 1695 sq. m.; pop. (1941) 295,930.

2 or **Ed·war'des·a·bad'** (ĕd·wär'dĕs·à·bäd'). Town, its ✳, on Kurram river 100 m. SSW of Peshawar; pop. 24,768, with cantonment and civil lines pop. 30,539; important military station on border of Waziristan.

Ba·ño'las (bä·nyō'läs). Town, Gerona prov., NE Spain, 10 m. N of Gerona; mineral springs; skull found here 1887 has been classified as Neanderthal type.

Baños, Los. See LOS BAÑOS.

Bans'da (bäns'dà). **1** Former Indian state with Rajput ruler, Gujarat States (formerly in Surat Agency), SE of Surat, N Bombay, W Indian Union; 212 sq. m.; pop. (1941) 54,735.

2 Town, its ✳, now in SE Gujerat state; pop. 4339.

Ban'ská Bys'tri·ca (bàn'skä bĭs'trĭ·tsà); *Hung.* **Besz'-ter·cze·bá'nya** (bĕs'tĕr·tsĕ·bä'nyŏ); *Ger.* **Neu'sohl** (noi'zōl). Commune, cen. Slovakia, Czechoslovakia, on Hron river 100 m. NE of Bratislava; pop. 11,321.

Ban'ská Šti'av·ni'ca (bàn'skä shtĭ'àv·nyĭ'tsà); *Hung.* **Sel'mecz·bá'nya** (shĕl'mĕts·bä'nyŏ); *Ger.* **Schem'-nitz** (shĕm'nĭts). Commune, S cen. Slovakia, Czechoslovakia, SW of Zvolen; pop. (1930) 13,260; an old trading town, noted especially for its gold and silver products.

Ban'stead (băn'stĕd; -stĭd). Civil parish, Epsom rural dist., Surrey, S England; pop. 33,526; Epsom racecourse borders on Banstead Downs.

Bans·wa'ra (bäns·wä'rà). **1** Former Indian state, S Rajputana, NW Indian Union; 1606 sq. m.; pop. (1941) 258,760; for several cents. a Rajput state ruled by a maharaja; joined Union of Rajasthan June 26, 1947.

2 Town, its ✳; pop. 10,444.

Bantai. See BANDAI.

Ban'tam (băn'tăm; *native* bän·täm'). **1** Former residency, West Java prov., Neth. Indies; 3067 sq. m.; pop. 1,028,628; ✳ Serang; comprised W end of Java bet. Java Sea and Indian Ocean, with W coast on Sunda Strait; region mountainous in S, contains Mt. Karang in midst of N plain; well developed agriculturally. In early 16th cent. became powerful Mohammedan sultanate which extended its control over parts of Sumatra and Borneo; invaded by Dutch, Portuguese, and English; recognized Dutch sovereigns 1684, annexed by Dutch 1809; scene of several revolts in 19th cent.; suffered severely from volcanic eruption of Krakatau (*q.v.*) 1883.

2 Town on Bantam Bay, N coast of West Java prov., Indonesia. Capital of Mohammedan sultanate; Portuguese trading station after 1545; site of first Dutch settlement 1596 and of British factory 1603, bet. which great rivalry developed until expulsion of British 1683; under British control 1811–14.

Bantam Bay. Inlet of Java Sea on NW coast of Java, Indonesia, just E of Sunda Strait.

Ban'tam Lake (băn'tăm). Lake 2 sq. m., cen. Litchfield co., NW Connecticut; its outlet is **Bantam River**, a tributary of the Shepaug.

Ban'ta·yan' (bän'tä·yän'). **1** Island, cen. Phil. Is., 9 m. W of N tip of Cebu I. and 20 m. NE of Negros; 45 sq. m.; pop. 35,288; belongs to Cebu prov.

2 Municipality on SW coast of Bantayan I.; pop. 18,805.

Ban·ton' (bän·tôn'). Small island, Romblon prov., Phil. Is., NNW of Romblon I. and N of Simara I.; 11 sq. m.; pop. 4972; S of Marinduque.

Ban'try (băn'trĭ). Town at head of Bantry Bay, SW co. Cork, SW Eire; pop. 2643; fishing center.

Bantry Bay. Bay ab. 25 m. long, SW co. Cork, SW Eire; site of unsuccessful French attempts at landing 1689 and 1796 to help Irish insurrections.

Banyak Islands. See BANJAK ISLANDS.

Ban'yu·mas' (bän'yōō·mäs'). = BANJOEMAS.

Ban'yu·wang'i (bän'yōō·wäng'ē). = BANJOEWANGI.

Ban'zare Coast (băn'zâr). Section of coast of Wilkes Land, Antarctica, extending along Indian Ocean from ab. 121°E long. to 127°E.

Ba'o (bä'ô). Short stream in NW Leyte I., Phil. Is., flowing S into Ormoc Bay; scene of severe fighting bet. Americans and Japanese Nov.–Dec. 1944.

Ba'ou'lé' or **Ba'u'le'** (bà'ōō'lā'). River, W Sudan, West Africa; chief tributary of the Bakoy.

Ba'paume' (bà'pōm'). Commune, Pas-de-Calais dept., N France; pop. 2782; scene of victory of French general Faidherbe over the Prussians Jan. 2–3, 1871; scene of severe fighting in 1916 and 1917 and of successful assault by British forces on the Hindenburg Line Aug. 21–Sept. 1, 1918, the town being completely destroyed.

Ba·'qu'ba (bà·kōō'bà; -kōō'bä). Town, E Iraq, on Diyala river in fertile agricultural region and on railroad 32 m. NE of Baghdad.

Bar (bàr). Town, W Vinnitsa Region, W cen. Ukraine, U.S.S.R., 40 m. W of Vinnitsa; pop. ab. 13,000; important town of Podolia, in 16th cent. a Lithuanian possession, later Polish but held for a short time in 17th cent. (to 1683) by the Turks; headquarters of the Confederation of Bar, formed here 1768 as a Polish patriotic and anti-Russian association, suppressed 1772–76; became Russian 1793 in First Partition of Poland.

Bar (bär) or **An·ti'va·ri** (än·tē'vä·rē). Town, SW Montenegro, S Yugoslavia, near Adriatic Sea; pop. 5544.

Ba'ra Ban'ki (bä'rà bŭn'kē). Former district, Fyzabad division, E cen. United Provinces, N Indian Union; 1722 sq. m.; pop. (1941), 1,162,508; ✳ Nawabganj.

Ba·ra·ba' Steppe (bà·rŭ·bà' stĕp'). Swamp and steppe region, SW Siberia, bet. Ob and Irtysh rivers.

Bar'a·boo (băr'à·bōō). **1** River ab. 90 m. long, S cen. Wisconsin; flows from Juneau co. SE into Wisconsin river below Portage, Columbia co.

2 City, ⊗ of Sauk co., S cen. Wisconsin, 15 m. WSW of Portage; pop. 6672; farm trade center.

Ba'ra·cal'do (bä'rä·käl'dô). Commune, Vizcaya prov., N Spain; pop. 36,165; iron and steel works.

Ba'ra·co'a (bä'rä·kō'ä). Municipality and seaport town on N coast of E Oriente prov., E Cuba; pop. (town) 10,395; has large coconut and banana export trade. Oldest town in Cuba, settled 1512 by Diego Velásquez.

Ba'ra·da (bŭ'rŏ·dà; -dä); *Biblical* **Ab'a·na** or **Ab'a·nah** (ăb'à·nà) [*2 Kings* v. 12]; *classical* **Chry·sor'-rho·as** (krĭ·sŏr'ŏ·ăs). One of the chief rivers of Damascus, W Syria, flowing SE ab. 45 m. from Anti-Liban Mts. past Damascus to swamps at edge of desert.

Bar'a·ga (băr'à·gà). County in Michigan. See *Table* at MICHIGAN.

Ba'ra·gan Steppe (bä'rä·gän stĕp'). Level open tract on the lower Danube river, E Walachia, Romania.

Ba'ra·ho'na (bä'rä·ō'nä). **1** Province, SW Dominican Republic. See *Table* at DOMINICAN REPUBLIC.

2 City, its ✳; pop. (1944 est.) 13,751; sugar, coffee.

Ba·rail' Range (bà·rīl'). Mountain range, NE India, along boundary bet. Assam and Manipur; the S continuation of the Naga Hills; highest Mt. Japvo 9826 ft.

Ba·ra'jas (bä·rä'häs), *officially* **Barajas de Ma·drid'** (bä·rä'häz thä mä·thrē[th]'). Village, Madrid prov., cen. Spain, ab. 10 m. NW of Madrid; pop. 1800; airport.

Ba·rak' (bà·räk'). Upper course of the Surma river in Manipur, NE India. See SURMA.

Baraka. See BARCA river, Africa.

Ba'ram (bä'räm). River ab. 250 m. long, N Sarawak, Borneo; flows NW into South China Sea at Baram Point.

Ba'ram Point (bä'räm); *Malay* **Tan'jong Ba'ram** (tän'jông bä'räm). Cape on N coast of Sarawak, Borneo; projects into South China Sea, ab. 4°30'N.

Ba'ra·mu'la or **Ba'ra·mul'la** (bä'rà·mŏŏl'à). **1** See KASHMIR NORTH.

2 Town, ✳ of Kashmir North dist., Kashmir, N India, ab. 30 m. WNW of Srinagar; pop. (1931) 6886.

Ba·ra'na·gar (bà·rä'nà·gēr). Town, Twenty-four Parganas dist., West Bengal, Indian Union, N suburb of Calcutta on Hooghly river; pop. (1941) 54,451.

Ba·ra·no'a (bä'rä·nō'ä). Town, Atlántico dept., N Colombia, near Barranquilla; pop. 6899.

Bar'a·nof (bär'á·nŏf; *Russ.* bŭ·rà'nŭf). Island ab. 100 m. long, W Alexander Archipelago, SE Alaska, S of Chichagof I.; Sitka is on its W coast.

Ba·ra'no·vi·chi (bŭ·rä'nŭ·vyĭ·chĭ; bŭ·rŭ·nô'vyĭ·chĭ); *Pol.* **Ba'ra·no·wi'cze** (bä'rä·nô·vě'chě). City, ✻ of Baranovichi Region, W cen. White Russia, U.S.S.R., 85 m. SW of Minsk (formerly in Nowogródek dept., Poland); pop. (1938–39 est.) 30,119; important railroad junction; was Polish frontier station to Russia. Scene of violent fighting bet. Germans and Russians June and July 1916; in World War II seized by Germans July 1941 and held until retaken by Russians July 8, 1944.

Baranovichi Region. Region, W cen. White Russia, U.S.S.R.; ✻ Baranovichi.

Ba'ra·nya (bä'rä·nyä). Former subprovince in N Yugoslavia bet. the Drava and Danube rivers.

Ba'raque' Mi'chel' (bá'rák' mē'shěl'). Peak 2200 ft. in Hohe Venn Mts., near Spa, E Belgium; highest point in Belgium.

Bar'a·tar'i·a Bay (băr'á·târ'ĭ·á). **1** Inlet of Gulf of Mexico on boundary bet. Jefferson and Plaquemines parishes, SE Louisiana.
2 Bayou and village, SE Louisiana, W of the mouth of the Mississippi; region connected with legends and activities (1810–15) of Jean and Pierre Lafitte, who led a band of privateers and smugglers.

Ba·raun'dha (bá·roun'dá). Former Indian state, W Baghelkhand, once in E Central India Agency, India, SSW of Rewa; 228 sq. m.; pop. (1941) 17,306.

Bar'ba (bär'vä). Volcano 8700 ft. cen. Costa Rica, N of San José.

Bar'ba·ce'na (bàr'bá·sā'ná). City, S Minas Gerais state, E Brazil, 125 m. N of Rio de Janeiro; pop. (1940 est.) 19,466; center of agricultural district; altitude 3500 ft.; healthful climate; large sanatorium.

Bar'ba·co'as (bär'vä·kō'äs). Municipality and river port, Nariño dept., SW Colombia, 45 m. E of Tumaco; pop. ab. 9000.

Bar·ba'dos (bär·bä'dōz). Island in the Lesser Antilles, West Indies, E of cen. Windward Is.; former British colony, since 1966 an independent dominion of British Commonwealth; 166 sq. m.; pop. (1965 est.) 246,452; ✻ Bridgetown. Chiefly of coral formation with no good harbors and only small streams; generally level but with hills in cen. part, highest point 1105 ft.; has healthful climate; chief industry sugar; exports molasses and rum.
History: Probably discovered by Portuguese in 16th cent.; claimed for England in 1605 when it was visited by Leigh's Guiana expedition; first settled under auspices of Courteen 1626; included in grant to earl of Carlisle 1627 whose settlers overcame those of Courteen 1629; leased by Lord Willoughby, a Royalist, who governed until forced to yield to Commonwealth 1652; taken over by Crown 1663; became prosperous as sugar producer, esp. in 17th and 18th cents.; suffered from wars of England with France, Spain, and later with U.S.; abolished slavery 1834; seat of government for Windward Is. 1833 to 1885, when made separate administration.

Bar'ba·ry (bär'bá·rĭ). Coastal region in N Africa, extending from Egypt to the Atlantic Ocean.
History: For early history, see MAURETANIA, NUMIDIA, and CIRENAICA. Overrun by Vandals under Genseric 5th cent. A.D.; conquered by Belisarius for Byzantine Empire 533–534; gradually overcome by Islam 7th cent.; broken up into independent Moslem states known as **Barbary States** (see MOROCCO, ALGIERS, TUNIS, TRIPOLI); European penetration begun by occupation of Ceuta by Portuguese 1415; Oran, Bougie, and Tripoli conquered by Spanish 1509–11; dominion of corsair Barbarossa reduced by victory 1535 of expedition of Charles V under Andrea Doria, but Algiers held out against Charles until 1541; Tripoli (*q.v.*) lost to Turks 1551; carried on piracy against European commerce and collected tribute from leading European states; after U.S. war with Tripoli 1801–05, U.S. expedition to Algiers 1815, and bombardment of Algiers by British 1816, ceased exaction of tribute and Christian slavery. For later history, see under separate states.

Bar'bas, Cape (bär'väs). Cape on SW coast of Río de Oro, Spanish Sahara, NW Africa.

Bar·bas'tro (bär·väs'trô). Town and commune, Huesca prov., Spain; pop. (commune, 1930) 6601; old city, known in Roman times; 16th-cent. cathedral.

Bar·ba'te, Río (rrē'ô vär·vä'tä). Short stream in Cadiz prov., SW Spain, flowing SW to the Atlantic Ocean just E of Cape Trafalgar; on its banks in 711 A.D. is supposed to have been fought the battle in which Roderick, last king of the Visigoths, was defeated and probably slain by the Moslems under Tariq.

Bar'ber (bär'bẽr). County in Kansas. See *Table* at KANSAS.

Bar'be·ri'no di Mu·gel'lo (bär'bá·rē'nô dê mōō·jěl'lô). Commune, Firenze prov., Tuscany, cen. Italy, 16 m. N of Florence; pop. 11,791.

Bar'bers Point (bär'bẽrz); *also* **Ka·la'e·lo'a Point** (kä·lä'â·lō'á). Cape on SW corner of Oahu I., Hawaii, W of Pearl Harbor.

Bar'ber·ton (bär'bẽr·t'n; -tŭn). **1** Manufacturing city, Summit co., NE Ohio, 7 m. SSW of Akron; pop. 33,805; produces rubber goods, matches, machinery, aluminum, asbestos; founded 1893.
2 Town, E Transvaal, Union of South Africa, 180 m. S of Pretoria; pop. 3844; center of De Kaap gold fields; asbestos, magnesite, talc, and nickel in vicinity.

Bar'bi·zon (bär'bĭ·zŏn; *Fr.* bår'bē'zôN'). Village, Seine-et-Marne dept., N France, S of Melun, near forest of Fontainebleau; pop. (1931) 651; center of Barbizon School of French painters.

Bar'bour (bär'bẽr). Name of counties in two states of the U.S. See *Tables* at ALABAMA and WEST VIRGINIA.

Bar'bours·ville (bär'bẽrz·vĭl). Village, Cabell co., W West Virginia, 9 m. E of Huntington; pop. 2331; scene of Federal victory in Civil War July 13, 1861.

Bar'bour·ville (bär'bẽr·vĭl). City, ⊗ of Knox co., SE Kentucky, 22 m. NNW of Middlesborough; pop. 3211. Union College (1879; coed.; Methodist).

Bar·bu'da (bär·bōō'dá). Flat, coral island in E West Indies, a part of Antigua territory of the Leeward Islands, 25 m. N of Antigua; 62 sq. m.; pop. ab. 1000; principal crop sea-island cotton.

Bar'ca (bär'ká). **1** River in NE Africa, chiefly in Eritrea; rises in cen. Eritrea, flows N, receives the Anseba from E; crosses into Sudan where it is called **Ba'ra·ka** (bŭ'rŏ·ká; -kä); empties into Red Sea.
2 Region, NW Cyrenaica, NE Libya, N Africa, esp. the height of land (**Barca Plateau,** highest point ab. 2340 ft.) surrounding the ancient town of Barca; part of the Pashalik of Tripoli under the Ottoman Turks.
3 *Ital.* **Bar'ce** (bär'chä); *Arab.* **El Merg** (ăl mŭrg'). Town, N Cyrenaica, Libya, Africa, ab. 60 m. NE of Bengasi; pop. ab. 3000; in region of fighting 1941–42. Ancient **Barca** in Cyrenaica was founded ab. 550 B.C.; became center for Greek refugees, but was a Libyan, not a Greek, town; plundered by Persians 512 B.C.; declined under the Ptolemies; again important under Moslems.

Bar'cel·lo'na (bär'chäl·lō'nä), *in full* **Barcellona Poz'zo di Got'to** (pŏt'tsô dê gôt'tô). Commune, Messina prov., NE Sicily on Longano river 18 m. W by S of Messina; pop. 27,134; summer resort; sulfur baths.

Bar'ce·lo'na (bär'sě·lō'ná; *Span.* bär'thä·lō'nä, bär'sâ-). **1** Province of Spain. See *Table* at SPAIN.
2 *anc.* **Bar'ci·no** (bär'sĭ·nō), *later* **Bar'ci·no'na** (bär'sĭ·nō'ná). City, its ✻, NE Spain, on the Mediterranean 315 m. ENE of Madrid; pop. (1941 est.) 1,087,099; largest city, chief manufacturing center, and principal seaport in Spain; 13th-cent. Spanish Gothic cathedral; ancient ruins; old Roman wall fortifications destroyed 1868, now replaced by modern boulevards; university (founded 1430).
History: Traditionally, city founded 3d cent. B.C. by

Hamilcar Barca of Carthage; ruled by Romans, Visigoths; taken by Moors 713 A.D.; retaken by Franks for Charlemagne 801 and made capital of Spanish March (see CATALONIA); Frankish county of Barcelona became almost independent in 9th cent.; after Catalonia united with Aragon 1137, city became flourishing commercial center, an originator of deposit banking, and the rival of Italian ports; captured in 1652 as center of resistance in great Catalonian rebellion; abandoned by Allies 1714; in 19th cent. became center of radical social movements and of movement for Catalonian separatism; seized in military coup of Primo de Rivera 1923; loyalist capital 1937–39; its capture in 1939 brought collapse of Catalonian resistance.

Bar'ce·lo'na (bär'sĕ·lō'nȧ; *Span.* bär'sȧ·lō'nä). Town, ✻ of Anzoátegui state, N Venezuela, 150 m. E of Caracas; pop. (1941 est.) 12,910; in low and unhealthful but fertile region with considerable trade. Founded 1637.

Bar'ce·lo·ne'ta (bär'sä·lō·nā'tä). Municipality (pop. 19,334) and town (pop. 762), N Puerto Rico, on the Manatí river and on railroad 28 m. W of San Juan.

Barcino, Barcinona. See BARCELONA.

Bar·coo' (bär·kōō'); *or* **Coo'per's Creek** (kōō'pẽrz; kō͝op'ẽrz). River ab. 600 m. long, Australia; flows from SW Queensland to Lake Eyre in South Australia; discovered 1845.

Bar·daï' (bär·dī'). Town, extreme N Chad Republic, N Africa, in Tibesti Mts.; chief town of the Tibesti region.

Bar'de·jov (bär'dyĕ·yôf); *Hung.* **Bárt'fa** (bärt'fŏ); *Ger.* **Bart'feld** (bärt'fĕlt). Town, E Slovakia, Czechoslovakia, in S foothills of Carpathian Mts. 20 m. N of Presov; pop. 7606; hot springs.

Bar·de'ra (bär·dâ'rä). Town, S Somalia, E Africa, on the Juba river ab. 250 m. W of Mogadishu; pop. 1500; head of steamship service on the Juba.

Bar'dia (bär'dyä; bär·dē'ä); *also* **Por'to Bardia** (pôr'tō). Town on coastal road, extreme NE Cyrenaica, Libya, N Africa, near Egyptian border; pop. 2370. Has good harbor, airfield, supply and radio station. Several times captured in World War II: starting point of Italian attack Sept. 1940; taken by British Dec. 1940–Jan. 1941; lost to Rommel's forces Apr. 1941; taken and lost again by British 1941–42; finally recaptured Nov. 13, 1942.

Bar·do'li (bär·dō'lĕ). Town, SE Gujarat state, India, just E of Surat.

Bard'sey (bärd'zĭ). Island, Caernarvonshire, Wales, in the Irish Sea off the W Welsh coast N of entrance to Cardigan Bay; fishing, farming; ruins of 13th-cent. abbey on foundation thought to date from 516; anciently a place of religious pilgrimage.

Bards'town (bärdz'toun). City, ⊗ of Nelson co., cen. Kentucky, 36 m. SSE of Louisville; pop. 4798.

Barduli. See BARLETTA.

Bardwan. See BURDWAN.

Bard'well (bärd'wĕl; -wĕl). City, ⊗ of Carlisle co., SW Kentucky; pop. 1067.

Ba'règes' (bȧ'râzh'). Village, Hautes-Pyrénées dept., SW France, in the Pyrenees Mts. 23 m. S of Tarbes; health resort. See BAGNÈRES-DE-BIGORRE.

Ba·reil'ly *or* **Ba·re'li** (bȧ·rā'lĭ). **1** = ROHILKHAND division of United Provinces.
2 Former district, Rohilkhand division, N cen. United Provinces, N India, 1591 sq. m.; pop. (1941) 1,176,197.
3 City, its ✻, now in NW cen. Uttar Pradesh, on Ramganga river 130 m. E of Delhi; pop. (1941) 192,688; site of a military cantonment and government college; important railroad junction. Founded 1537.

Bar'ents Island (bär'ĕnts; *Du.* bä'rĕnts). Island, E Spitsbergen archipelago, Arctic Ocean, N of Edge I.; 37 m. long; 554 sq. m.

Barents Sea. Part of Arctic Ocean N of Norway and Soviet Russia, Europe, and bet. Spitsbergen and Novaya Zemlya.

Bar'fleur' (bȧr'flûr'). Town, Manche dept., NW France, on NE point of Cotentin Penin. 2 m. S of **Point Bar-**
fleur, which marks the NW point of the Bay of the Seine; pop. (1931) 1069; resort; fishing; in Middle Ages an important port.

Barfurush. See BABUL.

Bar'ga (bär'gä). **1** Commune, Lucca prov., Tuscany, cen. Italy, 17 m. N of Lucca; pop. 11,708.
2 Mongol region, NW Manchuria, W of the Great Khingan Mts.

Barge Canal. = NEW YORK STATE BARGE CANAL.

Bar·gu·zin' (bĕr·go͝o·zyēn'). **1** Mountain range, parallel with the Barguzin river and bet. it and Lake Baikal, W Buryat-Mongol Republic, Soviet Russia, Asia; highest point 8862 ft.
2 River ab. 225 m. long, W Buryat-Mongol Republic, flowing SW to Lake Baikal.
3 Town on right bank near mouth of the river; pop. 2217.

Bar Har'bor (bär' här'bẽr). Town, Hancock co., SE Maine, on Mt. Desert I. on Frenchman Bay; pop. 2444; first permanent English settlement 1763; summer resort; greatly damaged by fire 1947.

Ba'ri (bä'rĕ), *in full* **Bari del'le Pu'glie** (dâl'lä pōō'lyä). **1** Province of Italy. See *Table* at ITALY.
2 *anc.* **Bar'i·um** (bâr'ĭ·ŭm). Commercial seaport, its ✻, Apulia, SE Italy, on Adriatic Sea 139 m. E by N of Naples; pop. 196,747; trades in wine, oil, grain, almonds; manufactures cotton and linen goods, soap, glass, hats, liquors, organs, pianos; 11th-cent. cathedral and church; pilgrim resort; university. Leading commercial center of Apulia since 2d cent. B.C.; successively dominated by Goths, Greeks, Saracens, Byzantines, Normans, Germans, and Venetians; became part of kingdom of Naples 1588. In World War II taken by British Sept. 1943; Allied ships in harbor bombed by Germans Dec. 2, 1943.

Ba'ri·a (bä'rĭ·yȧ) *or* **Ba'ri·ya.** Former Indian state, E Gujarat States, W Indian Union, once in Rewa Kantha Agency; 810 sq. m.; pop. (1941) 189,062; ✻ Devgad Baria.

Ba'ria (bä'ryä). River in S Venezuela; rises in mountains on border, Serra Curupirá, in extreme S tip of Venezuela, flows N into Casiquiare river.

Ba'ri Do·ab' (bä'rĭ dō·äb'). Plain region bet. Sutlej and Ravi rivers, NW India; chiefly in Lahore and Multan divisions, West Punjab, Pakistan, but upper (NE) part, traversed by Upper Bari Doab Canal, now in Amritsar dist., Punjab state, India.

Ba·ri'li (bä·rē'lĕ). Municipality near W coast of Cebu I., Phil. Is., 30 m. SW of City of Cebu; pop. 29,247.

Ba·ri·lo'che *or* **San Car'los de Ba·ri·lo'che** (säng kär'lŏs thä bä'rĕ·lō'chä). Town, SW Río Negro territory, S cen. Argentina, on S shore of Lake Nahuel Huapí; pop. ab. 3500; resort.

Ba·ri'ma (bä·rē'mä). River in NW British Guiana; flows SE, then curves to the NW, crosses the Venezuelan border and empties into Atlantic Ocean at the S Orinoco delta; navigable for ab. 40 m.

Ba·ri'nas (bä·rē'näs). **1** *formerly* **Za·mo'ra** (sä·mō'rä). State of Venezuela. See *Table* at VENEZUELA.
2 Town, its ✻, W cen. Venezuela, 260 m. SW of Caracas; pop. (1941 est.) 2485.

Ba·rin'go, Lake (bä·rĭng'gō). Lake ab. 180 sq. m., Kenya, E Africa, NE of Lake Victoria.

Ba'ri·pa'da (bä'rĭ·pä'dä). Town, former ✻ of Mayurbhanj state, Eastern States, NE Indian Union, 115 m. SW of Calcutta; now in Orissa state; pop. ab. 6000.

Ba'ri·sal' (bŭ'rĭ·säl'). Town, ✻ of Bakarganj dist., Dacca division, East Bengal, Pakistan, near Tetulia mouth of Ganges river 130 m. E of Calcutta; pop. (1941) 61,316; river port with active trade; noted for natural phenomenon known as "Barisal guns," noises like distant thunder or cannon fire, supposed to be of seismic origin.

Ba'ri·san' Mountains (bä'rĕ·sän'). Mountain system ab. 1000 m. long extending the length of the island of Sumatra, Indonesia, chiefly along the W coast, containing many volcanic peaks from 6000 to more than

12,400 ft.; highest Mt. Kerintji 12,467 ft.; for the most part made up of two parallel chains with a series of mountain lakes in the high valley bet. them, largest of which is Toba (*q.v.*).

Ba·ri'to (bä-rē'tō). River ab. 550 m. long, SE Borneo, Indonesia; rises in E ranges of Muller Mts., flows S into Java Sea; its lower course flows through wide marshy region in which cross branches connect with other streams; one of the largest rivers of Borneo, navigable for steamers of moderate size for about 250 m.

Barium. See BARI.

Bariya. See BARIA.

Bar'king Town (bär'kǐng) *or*, *popularly*, **Bar'king.** Urban district, Essex, SE England, E suburb of London near the Thames river; pop. (1951) 78,197; part of Greater London; site of ruins of ancient nunnery (c. 670 A.D.).

Bark'ley Sound (bärk'lǐ). Inlet of Pacific Ocean, in SW Vancouver I., SW British Columbia, Canada.

Bark'ly Tableland (bärk'lǐ). Plateau region, alt. ab. 1000 ft., Australia, mostly in E Northern Territory, but its SE end in Queensland; cattle raising.

Barkly West. Town, Griqualand West, Cape Province, Union of South Africa, on N bank of Vaal river; pop. 1817; formerly most important town in Griqualand.

Bar'kol' (bär'kûl'), *also* **Bar'kul'** (-kûl'); *Chin.* **Chen'si'** (jŭn'shē'). Town and oasis, E Dzungaria, NE Sinkiang, W China; pop. ab. 4000; in mountain region on SE shore of lake (**Bar Kol**), off main highway ab. 60 m. NW of Qomul.

Bâr·lad' (bûr·läd'), *formerly* **Bêr·lad'.** City, E Romania, 60 m. NNW of Galaṭi; pop. 26,189.

Bar'–le–Duc' (bär'lĕ-dük'), *unofficially* **Bar'–sur–Or'nain'** (-sür-ôr'năn'). Commune, ✳ of Meuse dept., NE France, 128 m. E of Paris; pop. 16,697; 14th-cent. church; old Roman gate; varied manufactures.

Bar'lee, Lake (bär'lē). Large salt lake, S Salt Lake Region, W Western Australia.

Bar·let'ta (bär-lĕt'ä); *anc.* **Bar'du·li** (bär'dụ̄·lǐ). Seaport, Bari prov., Apulia, SE Italy, on Adriatic coast near mouth of Ofanto river 34 m. WNW of Bari; pop. 57,386; 12th-cent. Romanesque cathedral and 13th-cent. Gothic church; college founded by Ferdinand IV.

Bar'lin' (bär'lăn'). Commune, Pas-de-Calais dept., N France, NW of Arras; pop. (1931) 10,410; coal mines.

Bar'men (bär'mĕn). Former city (pop. 187,099), west Germany; since 1929 part of Wuppertal (*q.v.*).

Bar'mouth (bär'mŭth). Town, Merionethshire, N Wales, on coast of Cardigan Bay; pop. 2466; resort.

Bar'nard, Mount (bär'nẽrd). Peak 14,003 ft. in Sierra Nevada, near Mt. Whitney, SE cen. California.

Barnard Castle. Urban district, Durham, N England, on Tees river 17 m. W of Darlington; pop. 4433; 13th-cent. castle figures in Sir Walter Scott's poem *Rokeby*.

Bar·na·ul' (bĕr·nŭ·ōōl'). Town, ✳ of Altai Territory, Soviet Russia, Asia, on the Ob river 110 m. S of Novosibirsk; pop. 148,129; located on navigable river and on Turkistan-Siberian railroad; in rich mining region; large manufactures; meteorological observatory (founded 1841), mining school, museums. Founded 1730.

Bar'ne·gat (bär'nē·găt; -găt). Town, Ocean co., E New Jersey, ab. 14 m. S of Toms River; pop. (1940) 1133.

Barnegat Bay. Inlet of Atlantic Ocean, ab. 30 m. long, extending N to S in Ocean co., New Jersey.

Barnegat Inlet. Strait bet. Long Beach I. and Island Beach leading from Atlantic Ocean into Barnegat Bay.

Barnegat Light; *before 1948* **Barnegat City.** Borough, New Jersey, at N tip of Long Beach I. on Barnegat Inlet; pop. 287; site of lighthouse built 1855, abandoned 1930.

Barnes (bärnz). **1** County in North Dakota. See *Table* at NORTH DAKOTA.
2 Urban community (unincorporated), Douglas co., Oregon, N of Roseburg; pop. 5076.
3 Municipal borough, Surrey, S England, SW suburb of London, on the Thames; pop. 40,558.

Barnes'bor'o (bärnz'bûr'ō). Borough, Cambria co., SW cen. Pennsylvania, 24 m. WNW of Altoona; pop. 3035; soft-coal mines; manufactures clothing.

Barnes'ville (bärnz'vĭl). **1** City, ⊗ of Lamar co., W cen. Georgia, 35 m. WNW of Macon; pop. 4919; cotton mills; pecan-processing plant.
2 Village, Belmont co., E Ohio, 38 m. SW of Steubenville; pop. 4425; manufactures evaporated milk, mine cars and parts, glass, paper, nursery and lumber products; coal and natural gas deposits nearby.

Bar'net (bär'nĕt; -nĭt). Urban district, Hertfordshire, SE England, 12 m. N of London; pop. 25,017; residential section and part of Greater London; scene of decisive Yorkist victory Apr. 14, 1471 in the Wars of the Roses, in which the earl of Warwick was killed.

Bar'ne·veld (bär'nĕ·vĕlt). Commune, Gelderland prov., E Netherlands, 10 m. E of Amersfoort; pop. 13,747.

Bar·nolds'wick (bär·nōldz'wĭk; bär'lĭk). Urban district, West Riding, Yorkshire, N England, 9 m. N of Burnley; pop. 10,282; cotton-spinning works.

Barns'dall (bärnz'dôl). City, Osage co., N Oklahoma, 16 m. SW of Bartlesville; pop. 1663; called Bigheart until 1921; oil and gas wells; agriculture.

Barns'ley (bärnz'lĭ). County borough, West Riding, Yorkshire, N England, on the Dearne 30 m. ENE of Manchester; pop. (1951) 75,625; has textile mills; iron and steel manufacturing; coal deposits nearby.

Barn'sta·ble (bärn'stà·b'l). **1** County in Massachusetts. See *Table* at MASSACHUSETTS.
2 Town, its ⊗, SE Massachusetts, on S shore of Cape Cod Bay; pop. 13,465; cranberries; summer resort.

Barn'sta·ple (bärn'stà·p'l; *locally* -b'l). Municipal borough, Devonshire, SW England, on the Taw estuary 50 m. N of Plymouth; pop. 16,302; lace and glove factories, iron foundries, potteries; one of the oldest of royal boroughs; site of Cluniac priory of 11th cent.

Barnstaple Bay. Bay on NW coast of Devonshire, SW England; receives the Taw river from the E.

Barn'well (bärn'wĕl; -wĕl). **1** County in South Carolina. See *Table* at SOUTH CAROLINA.
2 City, its ⊗, SW South Carolina, 36 m. SW of Orangeburg; pop. 4568.

Ba'ro (bä'rō). River ab. 220 m. long in W Ethiopia; unites with Pibor river on border of SE Sudan to form Sobat river.

Ba·ro'da (bà·rō'dà; *native* bà·rō·dà). **1** Former Indian state, W Indian Union; 8176 sq. m.; pop. (1941) 2,855,010; had four divisions, three in Gujarat (Kadi, Baroda, and Navsari) and one in peninsula of Kathiawar (Amreli, with Okhamandal). Once a part of Mogul Empire; in 18th cent. its princes belonged to Maratha Confederacy; c. 1721 secured part of Gujarat; in 19th cent. subject to British administrative control until gaekwar (ruler) given full powers 1881; became part of Bombay state 1948 and of Gujerat state 1960.
2 Division of former Baroda state, E of Surat; 1922 sq. m.; pop. 711,481.
3 City, former ✳ of Baroda state, now in SE Gujerat state, 244 m. N of Bombay; pop. (1941) 152,326; in fertile district producing cotton, rice, tobacco; famous for its jewelry and silver-interwoven cloth.

Baroda and Gu'ja·rat' States Agency (gōō'jà·rät'). A political agency of W India 1937–47 consisting of the state of Baroda and a number of smaller states formerly in the Rewa Kantha, Kaira, Surat, Nasik, and Thana agencies.

Ba·ro'ghil Pass (bà·rō'gĭl). Pass, alt. 12,457 ft., over the Hindu Kush bet. Chitral, N West Pakistan prov., and the Wakhan valley.

Ba'rop (bä'rōp). Former commune, Arnsberg govt. dist., Westphalia, Prussia, Germany, SSW of Dortmund; pop. 11,331; mining; manufactures machinery.

Ba·ro·tac' Nue'vo (bä'rō·täk' nwä'vō). Municipality, SE Iloilo prov., Panay, Phil. Is., near left bank of lower Jalaur river 16 m. NNE of City of Iloilo; pop. 20,572.

Ba·rot'se (bà·rŏt'sĕ). Province, W Northern Rhodesia, S cen. Africa; 60,890 sq. m.; pop. 332,958; ✻ Mongu, native ✻ Lealui; crossed by Zambezi river; practically coextensive with **Ba·rot'se·land'** (-lănd'), region inhabited by the Barotse, a powerful Negro people. See NORTHERN RHODESIA.

Bar'qui·si·me'to (bär'kĕ·sĕ·mā'tô). City, ✻ of Lara state, NW Venezuela, 170 m. WSW of Caracas; pop. (1941 est.) 53,865; at N end of Cordillera Mérida at alt. of ab. 2000 ft.; export center for coffee, sugar, cacao, and rum. Founded 1552.

Bar'ra (bär'à; *locally* bà'rä). Chief island of S group in the Outer Hebrides, off NW coast of Scotland; ab. 8 m. long and bet. 2 and 3 m. wide; chief village Castlebay, with ruins of Kisamul Castle, seat of the ancient Clan Macneil; with ab. 20 smaller islands (including Vatersay, Sandray, Mingulay, Berneray) constitutes parish of **Barra** or **Barra Islands** (pop. 2250); administratively a part of Inverness co.; cockle and herring fisheries; many Norse and Celtic remains.

Barra, Sound of. Channel bet. South Uist I. and Barra I. in the Outer Hebrides, off NW coast of Scotland.

Bar'rack·pore' (bŭr'ăk·pōr'), *also* **Bar'rack·pur'** (-pŏŏr'). Town, West Bengal state, India, 15 m. N of Calcutta on left bank of Hooghly river; pop. 40,778; station for troops since 1772; scene of mutiny 1824 which was suppressed; scene of disbandment of first Sepoy regiment to mutiny Mar. 1857.

Bar'ra do Pi·ra·í' (bär'rà thŏŏ pê·rà·ē'). City, Rio de Janeiro state, SE Brazil; pop. (1940 est.) 15,313; railroad junction point ab. 45 m. NW of Rio de Janeiro.

Bar'ra·fran'ca (bär'rä·fräng'kä). Commune, Enna prov., cen. Sicily, 14 m. SSW of Enna; pop. 13,111; sulfur mines.

Bar'ra Head (bär'à; bà'rä). Cape on Berneray I., the S point of Barra Is., Outer Hebrides, off W coast of Scotland; lighthouse.

Barram. Var. of BARAM.

Bar'ra Man'sa (bär'rà măn'sà). City, Rio de Janeiro state, SE Brazil, NW of Rio de Janeiro; pop. (1940 est.) 8957.

Bar·ran'ca·ber·me'ja or **Bar·ran'ca Ber·me'ja** (bär·räng'kä·vĕr·mĕ'hä). River port, NW cen. Colombia, in Santander dept. on the Magdalena river ab. 50 m. W of Bucaramanga; pop. 9307; petroleum.

Bar·ran'cas (bär·räng'käs). River in SW cen. Argentina; rises near Chilean border, flows SE to unite with Río Grande and form Colorado river.

Bar·ran'co (bär·räng'kô). Town, S suburb of Lima, Peru, on the coast; pop. (1931) 13,984.

Bar'ran·que'ras (bär'räng·kä'räs). River port, Chaco territory, N Argentina, on Paraná river near Corrientes and Resistencia; ships hardwoods and cotton.

Bar·ran·quil'la (bär'räng·kē'yä; *Angl.* băr'ăn·kē'[y]à). City and port, ✻ of Atlántico dept., N Colombia, on Magdalena river 10 m. from its mouth; pop. 150,395; river channel deepened for ocean-going vessels 1935.

Bar·ran·qui'tas (bär'räng·kē'täs). Municipality (pop. 18,978) and town (pop. 4684), cen. Puerto Rico.

Bar're (bär'ĕ). **1** Town, Worcester co., cen. Massachusetts, 19 m. WNW of Worcester; pop. 3479; woolen mills, foundries, dairies.
2 City, Washington co., N cen. Vermont, 7 m. SSE of Montpelier; pop. 10,387; settled c. 1788; organized as town 1793, as city 1894; extensive granite quarries and works; manufactures machines and tools.

Barre des É'crins' (bär' dā·zā'krăn'). Highest peak 13,462 ft. in the Dauphiné Alps and in the Pelvoux group of that range, SE France. See *Table* at ALPS.

Bar'ren (băr'ĕn). **1** River ab. 120 m. long, S Kentucky, flowing NW out of Monroe co. into Green river.
2 County in Kentucky. See *Table* at KENTUCKY.

Barren Grounds. Low level treeless plains of N Canada, chiefly in Mackenzie District E of the Mackenzie basin and in Keewatin District NW of Hudson Bay;

marked by many lakes, swamps, thin soil; sparsely inhabited by Eskimos and trappers.

Bar·re'to (bà·rā'tŏŏ). Village, N suburb of Niterói, Rio de Janeiro state, SE Brazil.

Bar·re'tos (bär·rā'tŏŏs). City, N São Paulo state, SE Brazil, 240 m. NW of São Paulo; pop. (1940 est.) 17,272.

Bar'rett Dam (băr'ĕt; -ĭt). Dam completed 1922 across Cottonwood Creek, S San Diego co., SW California; height 213 ft.; impounds water for water supply.

Barr'head' (bär'hĕd'). Manufacturing burgh, Renfrew co., SW Scotland, on Levern river; pop. 12,971; cotton mills, engineering works, iron and brass founding.

Bar'rie (băr'ĭ). Town, ⊗ of Simcoe co., SE Ontario, Canada, on W extremity of Lake Simcoe; pop. 12,514; summer resort; railroad shops, tanneries, grist mills.

Bar'ri·er (băr'ĭ-ēr), **Cape.** Cape on S end of Great Barrier I., off NE North I., New Zealand.

Barrier, or **Stan'ley** (stăn'lĭ), **Range.** Mountain range, W New South Wales, SE Australia; highest ab. 2000 ft.; rich in lead, silver, and zinc ores. See BROKEN HILL.

Bar'ri·ga'da, Mount (băr'ĭ·gä'dà). Elevation 674 ft. in E cen. Guam, Mariana Is., 5 m. E of Agana; in reconquest of Guam by Americans taken Aug. 3, 1944.

Bar'ring·ton (băr'ĭng·tŭn). **1** Village, Cook and Lake cos., NE Illinois, 33 m. NW of Chicago; pop. 5434.
2 Borough, Camden co., SW New Jersey, 6 m. SSE of Camden; pop. 7943.
3 Town, Bristol co., E Rhode Island, E of Narragansett Bay and 8 m. ESE of Providence; pop. 13,826; incorp. by Massachusetts 1717, became part of Rhode Island 1746-47, incorp. by Rhode Island 1770. Residential and resort center; shipbuilding, fishing industries.

Bar'ro Col'o·ra'do (băr'ō kŏl'ô·rä'dō; -răd'ō; *Span.* bär'rô kō'lô·rä'thô). Island 6 sq. m. in Gatun Lake, Canal Zone; biological station; wild-life preserve.

Bar'ron (băr'ŭn). **1** County in Wisconsin. See *Table* at WISCONSIN.
2 City, its ⊗, NW Wisconsin, 8 m. SW of Rice Lake (city); pop. 2338; creamery products, lumber.

Bar·ro'sa (bär·rô'sä). Village, Cádiz prov., Spain, SE of Cádiz; British victory over French nearby 1811.

Bar'row (băr'ō). **1** County in Georgia. See *Table* at GEORGIA.
2 Village in Alaska. See Point BARROW.
3 Island off NW coast of Western Australia, NE of North West Cape.
4 or **Barrow in Fur'ness** (fûr'nĕs; -nĭs). County borough, Lancashire, NW England, on Furness Penin. opp. Isle of Walney 52 m. N of Liverpool; pop. (1951) 67,473; has steelworks, smelters, shipbuilding yards; hematite deposits nearby.
5 River 112 m. long, SE Ireland; flows S from SE co. Offaly to Waterford Harbour.

Barrow, Point. Most northerly point of Alaska, 71°20'N, 156°W, on Arctic Ocean ab. 550 m. NE of Nome and an equal distance NW of Fairbanks; has small Eskimo settlement (Nuvuk). Town, **Barrow,** ab. 12 m. S, is government station with post office and radio and weather bureau stations, pop. 1314; has been important in explorations and aviation. Barrow Arctic Science Station opened by U.S. Navy 1947.

Barrow Creek. Post and telegraph station in desert region of cen. Northern Territory, Australia.

Bar'row·ford (băr'ô·fērd). Urban district, Lancashire, NW England, on Leeds and Liverpool Canal 27 m. N of Manchester; pop. 4765.

Barrow Strait. Channel from 40 to 65 m. wide bet. Bathurst and Cornwallis Is. on the N and Prince of Wales and Somerset Is. on the S, N Franklin District, Northwest Territories, Canada.

Bar'ry (băr'ĭ). **1** Name of counties in two states of the U.S. See *Tables* at MICHIGAN and MISSOURI.
2 City, Pike co., W Illinois, ESE of Quincy; pop. 1422.
3 Municipal borough and seaport, Glamorganshire, SE Wales, pop. 40,979; shipping point for coal; resort.

Bar'sac' (bär'såk'). Commune, Gironde dept., SW France, near the Garonne; pop. (1931) 2514; produces fine sauterne wine (see SAUTERNES).

Bar'si (bär'sĭ). Town, S Maharashtra state, W Indian Union, 200 m. ESE of Bombay; pop. 27,610; active trade center, esp. in cotton and oil seeds.

Bar'stow (bär'stō). City, San Bernardino co., California; pop. 11,644; early mining and frontier town.

Bar'-sur-Aube' (bär'sür-ōb'). Commune, Aube dept., NE France; pop. (1931) 4264; evidences of Roman occupation found nearby; destroyed by Huns 5th cent.; rebuilt, gained commercial importance; now market center for agricultural region producing wine, grain. Scene of battle Feb. 27, 1814 in which Allies defeated the French.

Bar-sur-Ornain. See BAR-LE-DUC.

Bartenstein. See BARTOSZYCE.

Bártfa, Bartfeld. See BARDEJOV.

Bar·thol'o·mew (bär·thŏl'ô·mū). County in Indiana. See *Table* at INDIANA.

Bartholomew Bayou. River 275 m. long, SE Arkansas and NE Louisiana; navigable 150 m.; rises in Jefferson co., SE cen. Arkansas, winds SE and S across Louisiana border into the Ouachita river in NE Louisiana.

Bar·ti'ca (bär·tē'kȧ). Town, N British Guiana, in Essequibo co., at confluence of Essequibo, Mazaruni, and Cuyuni rivers 45 m. SW of Georgetown; pop. (1931) 1585; point of departure for gold and diamond fields.

Bar'tle Frere (bär't'l frēr). Mountain 5287 ft. in Atherton Plateau, S of Cairns, NE Queensland, N Australia.

Bar'tles·ville (bär'tlz·vĭl). City, ⊗ of Washington co., NE Oklahoma, 41 m. N of Tulsa; pop. 27,893; founded 1877; oil and gas wells; manufactures oil-field equipment.

Bart'lett (bärt'lĕt; -lĭt). **1** Village, ⊗ of Wheeler co., NE cen. Nebraska; pop. 125.
2 Town, Carroll co., E New Hampshire, on Saco river 11 m. NW of Conway; pop. 1013; resort in White Mts.
3 City, Bell and Williamson cos., cen. Texas, 20 m. S of Temple; pop. 1540; farm trade center.

Bartlett Dam. Dam completed 1939 across Verde river in Salt River Indian Reservation, E Maricopa co., S cen. Arizona; height 287 ft.; impounds water for irrigation.

Bartlett Deep. Area of NW Caribbean Sea bet. Cayman Is. and Jamaica where ocean floor exceeds 3000 fathoms in depth; its deepest point thus far recorded is 22,788 ft., in ab. 19°15'N, 79°35'W.

Bart'lett's Fer'ry Dam' (bärt'lĕts; -lĭts). Dam completed 1926 across Chattahoochee river on Georgia-Alabama border ab. 18 m. N of Columbus, Ga.; height 145 ft.; impounds water for power, forming **Bart'lett's Fer'ry Lake'**.

Bar'ton (bär't'n). **1** Name of counties in two states of the U.S. See *Tables* at KANSAS and MISSOURI.
2 Village, Orleans co., N Vermont; pop. 1169.

Bar'ton up·on' Hum'ber (bär't'n, hŭm'bẽr). Urban district, Parts of Lindsey, Lincolnshire, E England, 8 m. SW of Hull; pop. 2218; important port in 14th cent.

Bar'ton·ville (bär't'n·vĭl). Village, Peoria co., NW cen. Illinois, 7 m. SW of Peoria; pop. 7253.

Bar'to·szy'ce (bär'tô·shī'tsĕ); *Ger.* **Bar'ten·stein** (bär'tĕn·shtīn). Town, N Olsztyn dept., N Poland, N of Olsztyn; pop. (1946) 12,576.

Bar'tow (bär'tō). **1** County in Georgia. See *Table* at GEORGIA.
2 City, ⊗ of Polk co., cen. Florida penin., 15 m. SSE of Lakeland; pop. 12,849; settled 1851; phosphate mining, citrus canning, cigar making.

Bar·wa'ni (bŭr·wä'nĭ). **1** Former Indian state, SW Central India, Indian Union, in Satpura Range S of Narbada river; now in SW Madhya Pradesh; 1189 sq. m.; pop. (1941) 176,666.
2 Town, its ⁕; pop. 8949.

Bar'won (bär'wŭn). Upper course of Darling river in NE New South Wales, SE Australia; rises in SE Queensland and flows SW ab. 400 m.; forms part of boundary bet. Queensland and New South Wales.

Barygaza. See BROACH.

Basarabia. See BESSARABIA.

Bas'co (bäs'kŏ), *in full* **San'to Do·min'go de Bas'co** (sän'tŏ thô·mēng'gŏ thä väs'kŏ). Town, ⁕ of Batanes prov., N Phil. Is., on W shore of Batan I. ab. 150 m. N of Aparri; pop. 2782.

Bas·cu·ñán', Cape (bäs'kōō·nyän'). Cape on SW coast of Atacama prov., N cen. Chile.

Ba'sel (bä'zĕl), *older* **Basle** (bäl); *Fr.* **Bâle** (bäl). **1** Swiss canton; subdivided into demicantons: **Ba'sel-Land'** (bä'zĕl-länt'), *also* **Baselland** *or* **Basel (Land)**, and **Ba'sel-Stadt'** (-shtät'), *also* **Baselstadt** *or* **Basel (Stadt)**. See *Table* at SWITZERLAND.
2 City, ⁕ of Basel-Stadt demicanton and of Basel canton, NW Switzerland, on both sides of Rhine river 43 m. N of Bern; pop. (1941) 162,105; 11th-cent. cathedral; university (founded 1460); manufactures silk goods, ribbons, cotton prints, linen, leather, gloves. Scene of famous church council which lasted through 45 sessions from 1431 until 1443; became member of Swiss Confederation 1501; Confession of Basel adopted by Protestants 1534; peace treaties signed here Apr. 5, July 22, and Aug. 28, 1795, bet. Prussia, Spain, and France.

Ba'sey' (bä·sĕ'ē; -sä'). Municipality, S Samar, Phil. Is., on N shore of San Pedro Bay; pop. 28,296.

Ba'shahr (bŭ'shēr); *also* **Bus'sa·hir** (bŏŏs'sȧ·hēr). Former Indian state, one of the Punjab Hill States, NW India, on SW slope of the Himalayas; 3439 sq. m.; pop. 100,192; geographically in East Punjab, Indian Union.

Ba'shan (bä'shăn; -shăn). Fertile region in ancient Palestine, E and NE of the Sea of Galilee.

Ba'shi Channel (bä'shē), *formerly* **Ba'chi Channel** (bä'chē). Strait ab. 92 m. wide bet. Batan Is. of the Philippines and S end of Formosa; traversed at approximately 21°25'N by the boundary line as determined by Treaty of Paris Dec. 10, 1898.

Bashi Islands. Earlier name of Batan Islands.

Bash'kir Republic (bäsh'kir; băsh·kir'; *Russ.* bŭsh-kēr'), *officially* **Bashkir Autonomous Soviet Socialist Republic**; *also* **Bash·kir'i·a** (bäsh·kir'ĭ·ȧ). Autonomous republic, E Soviet Russia, Europe; 54,233 sq. m.; pop. (1941 est.) 3,304,476; ⁕ Ufa; a subdivision of the R.S.F.S.R.; bounded on N by Molotov and Sverdlovsk regions and on E by Chelyabinsk Region, all three in Soviet Russia, Asia; on S and SW by Chkalov Region, and on W by Tatar Republic. A plateau and mountainous (Southern Urals) area, watered by the Belaya and its tributary the Ufa; has Ural river on its E border; has extensive forests and valuable mineral deposits in the mountains; main occupations agriculture, esp. grain crops, grazing, and raising of horses. Predominant ethnic strain is Turko-Tatar. Chief towns Ufa, Sterlitamak, Beloretsk. Bashkirs came under Russian control 1556, but have rebelled several times since.

Ba'si·du' (bä'sĕ·dōō'). Town, Laristan prov., S Iran, on W end of Qishm I.

Ba·si'gon (bä·sē'gôn). River ab. 35 m. long, cen. Camarines Norte prov., Luzon, Phil. Is.

Ba·si'lan (bä·sē'län). **1** Island group, SW of Mindanao, Phil. Is.; ab. 530 sq. m.; comprises Basilan I. and about 50 small islands.
2 Island in Basilan group, separated from Zamboanga by Basilan Strait; 495 sq. m.; pop. 57,561; chief town Isabela; forms part of City of Zamboanga. Mountainous, with highest point 3320 ft.; has fine forests of valuable woods; inhabitants mainly Moros whose chief occupation is fishing. Occupied by Americans Mar. 18, 1945.

Basilan Strait. Passage ab. 10 m. wide bet. Basilan I. and SW Mindanao, S Phil. Is.; connects Moro Gulf with the Sulu Sea.

Basilicata. See LUCANIA.

Bas'i·lisk Harbour (băs'ĭ·lĭsk; băz'-). Large inlet in Utupua I., Santa Cruz Is., SW Pacific Ocean.

Ba'sin (bā's'n). Town, ⊗ of Big Horn co., N Wyoming; pop. 1319.

Ba'sing·stoke (bā'zĭng·stōk). Municipal borough, Hampshire, S England, 46 m. WSW of London; pop. 16,979; an old town with many antiquities; at **Ba'sing** (bā'zĭng) parish to the E occurred Ethelred's victory over the Danes 871.

Ba'sir·hat' (bŭ'sĭr·hät'). Town, West Bengal, India, on Kalindi river 30 m. E of Calcutta; pop. 21,287.

Ba'sit', Cape (bá'sēt'); *Arab.* **Ras el Ba·sit'** (räs' ăl bă·sēt'). Cape, N coast of Latakia, Syria, ab. 35°40'N.

Bas'ka·tong (băs'kȧ·tŏng). Lake, Gatineau co., SW Quebec, Canada; outlet S through Gatineau river.

Basle. See BASEL.

Bas·man', *or* **Baz·man'**, **Kuh'-i–** (kōō'hĕ·bȧz·män'). Peak of an extinct volcano 11,447 ft. in SE Iran.

Ba·so'ko (bȧ·sō'kō). Town, Oriental prov., NE Congo, at junction of Aruwimi and Congo rivers.

Basque Provinces (băsk); *Span.* **Pro·vin'cias Vas'·con·ga'das** (prŏ·vēn'thyȧz [-syȧz] väs'kông·gä'thäs). Region, N Spain; 2739 sq. m.; bounded N by Bay of Biscay, E by Navarre, S and W by Old Castile; comprises modern provinces of Vizcaya, Álava, and Guipúzcoa; has Pyrenees on E and E end of Cantabrian Mts. on W; forests, orchards, vineyards; center of iron-mining district; copper mining, marble quarrying; fisheries.
History: Inhabited by Basques, a people of obscure racial and linguistic origin who retained virtual autonomy until 19th cent.; little affected by Moorish conquest of Spain; Álava and Vizcaya successively dependent upon kingdoms of Asturias, Navarre, and Castile; took part in Carlist War 1834–76, but allowed by Alfonso XII to keep only certain amount of administrative autonomy; given autonomy soon after outbreak of Civil War 1936 but conquered by Insurgents 1936–37.

Bas'ra (băs'rä; *Angl.* bŭs'rȧ). **1** Province (*liwa*), S Iraq; pop. (1935 est.) 286,512.
2 *formerly* **Bus'ra** *or* **Bus'rah** (bŭs'rȧ). Port, its *, at head of the Shatt-al-Arab ab. 75 m. from the Persian Gulf, SE Iraq; pop. (1938 est.) 180,000. Third most important town in Iraq; connected by rail with Baghdad. Founded by Caliph Omar I 638; famous under the Abbassides; known in *Arabian Nights* as **Bas'so·rah** (băs'ō·rȧ); taken by Turks 1668 but declined as a trade center until World War I; in World War II occupied by British 1941, became important for transshipment of supplies to Turkey and U.S.S.R.

Bas'–Rhin' (bä'răn'). Department of France. See *Table* at FRANCE.

Bas'sac (bäs'säk). Town on right bank of Mekong river, N Cambodia; pop. ab. 4000; in region ceded by Japanese to Siam 1941–45.

Bassae. See PHIGALIA.

Bassam. See GRAND BASSAM.

Bas·sa'no (bäs·sä'nō), *in full* **Bassano del Grap'pa** (dál gräp'pä). Commune, Vicenza prov., Venezia Euganea, NE Italy, on left bank of Brenta river 19 m. NE of Vicenza; pop. 21,750; has 12th-cent. Romanesque church and 13th-cent. castle; manufactures majolica ware, leather, straw hats, wax. First mentioned 998; joined Venetian republic 1402; scene of defeat of Austrians by Napoleon Sept. 8, 1796; made duchy by Napoleon and conferred upon Maret 1809.

Bassas da India. See Bassas da INDIA.

Bassée, La. See LA BASSÉE.

Bas·sein' (bȧ·sān'; *Burmese* -thän'). **1** River ab. 160 m. long in Bassein dist., Lower Burma; a navigable outlet of the Irrawaddy in W part of its delta.
2 District, Irrawaddy division, Lower Burma; 4145 sq. m.; pop. 571,043.
3 City, its * and * of Irrawaddy division, in the Irrawaddy delta 90 m. W of Rangoon; pop. 45,662; center of rice-growing region. Badly damaged by Japanese 1942; reoccupied by British May 25, 1945.

Bas·sein' (bȧ·sān'). Seaport, NW Maharashtra state, W Indian Union, 25 m. N of Bombay; pop. (1930) 12,689. Captured by Portuguese 1536 and was a large,

flourishing port until taken by Marathas in 1739; since decayed.

Bas'sen·thwaite (băs'ʼn·thwāt). Lake 4 m. long in the Lake District, NW England, in Cumberland co. E of Cockermouth; an expansion of Derwent river.

Basses'–Alpes' (bäs'-zȧlp'). Department of France. See *Table* at FRANCE.

Basses'–Py'ré'nées' (bäs'pē'rä'nā'). Department of France. See *Table* at FRANCE.

Basse'terre' (bäs'târ'). Seaport on St. Kitts I., Leeward Is., West Indies Fed., * of St. Kitts I. and of St. Kitts-Nevis territory, Leeward Islands; pop. (1938 est.) 8000.

Basse'–Terre' (bäs'târ'). **1** Island 35 m. long in the French West Indies; the W part of the island of Guadeloupe, or Guadeloupe proper.
2 Seaport on SW coast of Basse-Terre I., * of the French dept. of Guadeloupe; pop. (1936) 13,638; founded 1643.

Bas'sett (băs'ĕt; -ĭt). Village, ⊗ of Rock co., N Nebraska; pop. 1023.

Bas'setts (băs'ĕts; -ĭts). Urban community (unincorp.). Henry co., Virginia, NW of Martinsville; pop. 3148.

Bass Island (băs), **North, Middle,** *and* **South.** Three islands in W Lake Erie, N of E Ottawa co., N Ohio; Put in Bay, scene of Perry's naval victory 1813, is on South Bass Island.

Bassorah. See BASRA city.

Bass Rock (băs). Large isolated greenstone rock, S of entrance to Firth of Forth, SE Scotland; lighthouse; site of ruins of 17th-cent. castle, seized by Jacobites 1691 and held 3 years before surrendering to William of Orange.

Bass Strait. Strait separating Australia from Tasmania, 80 to 150 m. wide, 185 m. long; discovered 1798 by George Bass, British surgeon and navigator.

Bas'tar (bŭs'tĕr). Former Indian state, Eastern States, geographically in SE Central Provinces, Indian Union; 13,701 sq. m.; pop. (1941) 633,888; * Jagdalpur.

Bas'ti (bŭs'tĭ). **1** Former district, Gorakhpur division, NE United Provinces, N Indian Union; 2822 sq. m.; pop. (1941) 2,185,641.
2 Town, its *, now in SE Uttar Pradesh, 115 m. NNE of Allahabad; pop. 22,526.

Bas'ti (băs'tĭ). See BAZA, Spain.

Ba·sti'a (bäs·tē'ȧ; *Fr.* bȧs'tyá'). Seaport city, Corse dept., France, on NE coast of island of Corsica 65 m. NE of Ajaccio; pop. 52,208; principal commercial and industrial city of Corsica; citadel; cathedral. Taken by British 1745; became French 1768; made capital of Corsica 1791 (later superseded by Ajaccio).

Bas'togne' (bás'tôn'y'). Town, E Luxembourg prov., SE Belgium; pop. 4005; an upland town of the Ardennes 43 m. S of Liége; important railroad and highway junction point. In World War II in the German offensive (Battle of the Bulge) of December 1944, an American division surrounded here Dec. 22–27; held after severe fighting until German forces driven back Jan. 1945.

Bas'trop (băs'trŭp). **1** County in Texas. See *Table* at TEXAS.
2 City, ⊗ of Morehouse parish, N Louisiana, 24 m. NNE of Monroe; pop. 15,193; paper mills; natural gas.
3 City, ⊗ of Bastrop co., S cen. Texas, on Colorado river 28 m. ESE of Austin; pop. 3001; lignite mines nearby.

Ba·su'to·land' (bȧ·sōō'tô·lănd'). Former British protectorate surrounded by South Africa; since 1966 the independent constitutional monarchy of **Le·so'tho** (lĕ·sō'tō); 11,716 sq.m.; pop. 975,000; * Maseru. Bounded on W and N by Orange Free State, on E by Natal and Griqualand East, and on S by Cape Province; mountainous, greater part 5000 to 6500 ft. above sea level; has Drakensberg Mts. along E border; watered by upper Orange river and tributaries and Caledon on W border; chief crops wheat, maize, and sorghum. Before 1800 mostly uninhabited; in early 19th cent. many quarrels with Boers; first received British protection 1843; annexed 1868 and made part of Cape Colony 1871; brought under direct control of British government 1884.

Ba'ta (bä'tä). Seaport and chief town, Río Muni, Spanish Guinea, W Africa; pop. ab. 3000.

Ba·taan' (bá·tän'; bá·tän'; *Span.* bä·tä'än). Province, W Luzon, Phil. Is., forming a peninsula 30 m. long by 15 m. wide on W side of Manila Bay; 517 sq. m.; pop. 85,538; ✳ Balanga. Traversed by S end of Zambales Mts. terminating in Mt. Mariveles, highest point 4700 ft. in province; has many short streams and few indentations on its coast; Mariveles Bay at its S end is best harbor; its NW coast forms E shore of the large safe anchorage of Subic Bay; western half is covered with forests and jungle; eastern coastal plain is most populous; chief towns Balanga, Orion, Dinalupihan, Mariveles.
History: Bet. 1600 and 1650 the scene of several conflicts with the Dutch; in early times a part of Pampanga; created separate province by Spanish governor general 1754; civil government established March 1901. In World War II scene of final struggle of American and Filipino forces under Gen. Douglas MacArthur against Japanese conquest of Phil. Is. Northern end occupied about Jan. 10, 1942, after fall of Manila, by American forces, who after withdrawal southward toward Mariveles, surrendered Apr. 9, 1942; remnant of force retired to Corregidor (*q.v.*) which also gave up May 6. Retaken by Americans Feb. 15–21, 1945.

Ba·ta·ba·nó' (bä'tä·vä·nö'). Municipality and town, S La Habana prov., W Cuba; pop. (town) 5447; sponge and turtle fisheries.

Batabanó, Gulf of. Widemouthed gulf S of La Habana and Pinar del Río provs., W Cuba, and N of Isle of Pines.

Ba'tac (bä'täk). Municipality, SW Ilocos Norte prov., Luzon, Phil. Is., 10 m. S of Laoag; pop. 22,207.

Ba·taisk' (bŭ·tīsk'). City, SW Rostov Region, Soviet Russia, Europe, 12 m. S of Rostov; pop. 22,852; important railroad junction point with main line running SE to Caucasus; handles much grain and cattle. Key point in struggle for Rostov 1918 in civil war; seized by German armies July 1942; recaptured Feb. 1943.

Ba'tak·land' (bä'täk·länd'); *Du.* **Ba'tak·lan'den** (bá·täk·län'den). Region around Lake Toba, N Sumatra, Indonesia, formerly in Tapanoeli residency and Sumatra East Coast government; original home of the Battaks, an important Indonesian people, formerly cannibals, now numbering more than 1,000,000; country not controlled by Dutch until after middle of the 19th cent.

Ba·ta'la (bá·tä'lá). Town, NW Punjab state, NW Indian Union, ab. 55 m. ENE of Lahore; pop. 33,204.

Ba·ta'lha (bá·tä'lyá). Commune, Leiria dist., W cen. Portugal, 6 m. S of Leiria; pop. 4371; famous for its Dominican monastery, now a national monument containing tomb of John I of Portugal and other kings, built by John I of Portugal to commemorate his victory 1385 over John I of Castile at Aljubarrota nearby.

Batalpashinsk. See CHERKESSK.

Ba·tam' (bä·täm'). Island in the Riouw Archipelago, Indonesia, opp. Singapore; 163 sq. m.; pop. 13,258; its N shore borders on Singapore Strait.

Ba·tan' (bä·tän'). **1** Island, E Albay prov., Luzon, Phil. Is., in center of chain of three islands N of Albay Gulf and forming part of S shore of Lagonoy Gulf; ab. 13 m. long by 5 m. wide; 35 sq. m.; has valuable coal mines. **2** Chief island of Batan Is. group, N Phil. Is.; 27 sq. m.; pop. 6043. See BATANES.

Bat'a·nae'a (băt'á·nē'á). Roman name of S Bashan, ancient Palestine, forming the SW part of the region ruled over by Philip the Tetrarch (4 B.C.–34 A.D.).

Ba·ta'nes (bä·tä'näs). Province, comprising the **Ba-tan' Islands** (bä·tän'), N of Luzon, N Phil. Is.; 76 sq. m.; pop. 9512; ✳ Basco, on Batan I.; separated from Formosa by Bashi Channel and from the Babuyan Is. to the S by Balintang Channel; comprises Itbayat, Batan, and Sabtang Is. and 11 islets; mountainous, with an extinct volcano on Batan I. Long inhabited; first conquered by Spanish 1791; made a province 1909.

Ba'tang' (bä'täng'). See PAAN, China.

Ba'tang (bä'täng). Town, Central Java prov., Indonesia, just E of Pekalongan; pop. 28,655.

Ba·tan'gas (bá·täng'gás; *Span.* bä·täng'gäs). **1** Province, S Luzon, Phil. Is.; 1191 sq. m.; pop. 442,034; ✳ Batangas; numerous mountains, esp. in W and NE; many small streams; in cen. part is large Lake Taal with Taal volcano forming an island in its center; three large bays Balayan, Batangas, and Tayabas; main products sugar, lumber, coconut oil, and some manufactured cloths. Chief towns Batangas, Lipa, Rosario, Tanauan, Lemery.
History: Populous region in pre-Spanish times; explored by Spaniards 1570 and created a province 1581, much larger than at present; in 17th cent. suffered from Moro attacks and in 18th cent. from severe eruptions of Taal volcano; active in revolution against Spanish; civil government established May 1901. **2** Municipality, its ✳, in S part of province on NE coast of Batangas Bay 58 m. S of Manila; pop. 49,164; Japanese landed here Dec. 24, 1941.

Batangas Bay. Inlet in S coast of Batangas prov., Luzon, Phil. Is., ab. 9 m. across at mouth; island of Maricaban on SW; Batangas and Bauan at its head.

Ba'tang Lu'par (bä'täng loo'pär). River 120 m. long, SW Sarawak, Borneo; flows W into the South China Sea.

Batan Island, Batan Islands. See BATAN, BATANES.

Ba·tan'ta (bä·tän'tä). Island ab. 40 m. long off N coast of Salawati (*q.v.*) I., Neth. New Guinea.

Ba·ta'vi·a (bá·tä'vĭ·á; -tāv'yá). **1** Industrial city, Kane co., NE Illinois, 35 m. W of Chicago; pop. 7496; manufactures farm implements, engines, and foundry products; stone quarries. **2** Manufacturing city, ⊗ of Genesee co., W New York, 33 m. WSW of Rochester; pop. 18,210; settled 1801, incorporated 1914; manufactures shoes, flavoring extracts, farm machinery. **3** Village, ⊗ of Clermont co., SW Ohio, 17 m. E of Cincinnati; pop. 1729; tobacco, corn, wheat.

Ba·ta'vi·a (bá·tä'vĭ·á; -tāv'yá; *Du.* bá·tä'vĕ·á). **1** Former residency, NW West Java prov., Neth. Indies; 3098 sq. m.; pop. 2,637,035; ✳ Batavia. Included lowlands along NW coast of Java on Java Sea and Batavia Bay and the Thousand Is. group is SW Java Sea; region has many short streams; extensive rubber and coconut plantations and market gardens; thickly settled. **2** *now* **Dja·kar'ta** *or* **Ja·kar'ta** (já·kär'tá). Seaport city on N coast of West Java prov., ✳ of West Java prov., and ✳ of Indonesia; pop. 1,492,100. Located on Batavia Bay at mouth of Tjiliwong river; has three divisions: (1) old city on both sides of the river on swampy ground; marked by canals, and houses and streets in style of Holland; (2) modern town, Weltevreden, farther inland, well laid out with wide streets, parks, European shops, clubs, etc.; (3) Tandjungpriok, 6 m. to the E, constituting the port. The largest city and principal port of Indonesia; central station for railroads to Serang on W and to E end of island; airport; radio station. Founded 1619 on site of Jacatra (*q.v.*) by Jan P. Coen; became headquarters of Dutch East India Company; gradually extended control over neighboring sultanates and principalities; suffered severe earthquake 1699; in 18th cent. notorious for its unhealthful condition but destruction of walls of old city and establishment of Weltevreden (c. 1810) prevented abandonment; defended by Allies 1942 but captured by Japanese Mar. 5. **3** Coastal town, N Surinam, near mouth of the Coppename river 48 m. W of Paramaribo.

Batavia Bay; *now* **Djakarta Bay.** Inlet of Java Sea on NW coast of Java, Indonesia; site of the old city of Batavia and of Tandjungpriok.

Ba·ta'vi·an Republic (bá·tä'vĭ·ăn; -tāv'yăn). The name given to Holland by the French after its conquest in 1795; lasted until 1806 when kingdom of Holland was set up with Louis, brother of Napoleon, as its ruler.

Bates (bāts). County in Missouri. See *Table* at MIS-SOURI.

Bates'burg (bāts'bûrg). Town, W cen. South Carolina, 32 m. W of Columbia; pop. 3806.

Bates'ville (bāts'vĭl; *Sou. also* -v'l). **1** City, ⊗ of Independence co., NE cen. Arkansas; pop. 6207; first settled 1812; marble and manganese in vicinity. Arkansas College (1872; incorp. 1836 as Batesville Academy; coed.). **2** City, Ripley co., SE Indiana, 31 m. ESE of Shelbyville; pop. 3349; furniture manufacturing. **3** Town, a ⊗ of Panola co., NW Mississippi, 35 m. ENE of Clarksdale; pop. 3284; in agricultural section.

Bath (bàth). **1** Name of counties in two states of the U.S. See *Tables* at KENTUCKY and VIRGINIA. **2** City, ⊗ of Sagadahoc co., S Maine, on Atlantic Ocean inlet 28 m. NE of Portland; pop. 10,717; incorporated 1781; port of entry and trading center; shipbuilding. **3** Village, ⊗ of Steuben co., S New York, 19 m. E of Hornell; pop. 6166; settled 1793; in agricultural region. **4** Borough, Northampton co., E Pennsylvania, 10 m. NNE of Allentown; pop. 1736. **5** See BERKELEY SPRINGS, West Virginia. **6** *anc.* **Aq'uae Cal'i·dae** (ăk'wē kăl'ĭ·dē; ā'kwē) *or* **Aquae So'lis** (sō'lĭs). City and county borough, Somersetshire, SW England, on the Avon 12 m. ESE of Bristol; pop. (1951) 79,275. Has Roman remains; was a royal borough in 10th cent.; granted charter 1189. Health resort, with thermal springs, esp. popular in 18th cent.

Ba·the·lé'mont', *in full* **Ba·the·lé'mont'–lès–Bau'ze·mont'** (bȧt'lä'môn'lĕ·bōz'môn'). Village, Meurthe-et-Moselle dept., NE France, 6 m. N of Lunéville; pop. 109; here on Nov. 3, 1917 fell the first three American soldiers killed in World War I.

Bath'gate (bàth'gāt; -gĭt). Manufacturing burgh, West Lothian co., SE Scotland; pop. 11,290; coal mines, stone quarries; whisky distilling; steelworks.

Bath'urst (bàth'ûrst; -ẽrst). **1** City, E New South Wales, SE Australia, on Macquarie river in Blue Mts. 100 m. WNW of Sydney; pop. 10,415; founded 1819; center of wheat-growing district; fruit, tobacco, cereals; gold, copper and silver mines; stone quarries. **2** Town and summer resort, ⊗ of Gloucester co., NE New Brunswick, Canada, on Nipisiguit Bay at mouth of Nipisiguit river; pop. 4453; important salmon center and shipping port for lumber. **3** Seaport on the Island of St. Mary in the Gambia river, Gambia crown colony, W Africa; ✳ of the colony and of Gambia protectorate; pop. (1931) 14,370; chief trade in tropical products, hides, ivory, gold. During World War II developed as important airport. **4** Village, SE Cape Province, Union of South Africa, 90 m. ENE of Port Elizabeth; pop. 832; first home and administrative center of British settlers of 1820.

Bathurst, Cape. Cape, NW Mackenzie District, Northwest Territories, Canada, extending into Beaufort Sea, 127°30′W.

Bathurst Inlet. Large inlet of Coronation Gulf, NE Mackenzie District, Northwest Territories, Canada.

Bathurst Island. **1** Island, NW of Northern Territory, Australia, W of Melville I.; 30 m. long; 786 sq. m.; separated from mainland by Clarence Strait. **2** Island, N Canada, one of the Parry Is., NW Franklin District, Northwest Territories.

Ba'tis'can' (bȧ'tēs'kän'). River ab. 50 m. long, S Quebec, Canada; rises in W Quebec co., flows S into St. Lawrence river near Batiscan in Champlain co.

Ba't jan (bä'chän), *also* **Ba'chan** *or* **Ba'chian** (-chän). Largest island of a group in Moluccas, Indonesia, Malay Archipelago, just SW of Halmahera; lat. 30′S and long. 127°30′E; 50 m. long by ab. 23 m. wide; 914 sq. m.; pop. ab. 10,000; irregular in shape, mountainous and volcanic; highest point 6926 ft.; remarkable for its fauna and flora. Formerly a sultanate; seized by Dutch 1609 and put under control of Sultan of Ternate. The group (2268 sq. m., pop. 17,934), includes the smaller islands of

Kasiroeta and Mandioli to the W and the large group of Obi Is. (*q.v.*) to the S.

Bat'ley (băt'lĭ). Municipal borough, West Riding, Yorkshire, N England, 6 m. SSW of Leeds; pop. 40,192; manufactures shoddy and machinery.

Bat'na (băt'nä; -nȧ). Commune, cen. Constantine dept., NE Algeria; pop. 6143; station on railroad to Biskra.

Ba·to' (bä·tô'). Municipality, SE Catanduanes I., Phil. Is., near coast E of Virac; pop. 17,230.

Bato, Lake. Small lake on S boundary of Camarines Sur prov., Luzon, Phil. Is., partly in NW Albay prov.; total area 15 sq. m.; receives many streams of Albay that rise near the foot of Mt. Mayon; outlet is the Bicol river.

Ba'toe (bä'tōō) *or* **Ba'tu.** Island group, Indonesia, in the Indian Ocean off W cen. coast of Sumatra; 463 sq. m.; pop. 12,619; crossed by the equator; contains about 48 islands with only three of any size, Tanahmasa, Tanahbala, and Pini.

Ba'toe·da'ka *or* **Ba'tu·da'ka** (bä'tōō·dä'kä). See SCHILDPAD ISLANDS.

Ba·to'ka (bȧ·tō'kȧ). Province, S Northern Rhodesia, S cen. Africa; 32,460 sq. m.; pop. 155,463; ✳ Livingstone; bordered on S by Zambezi river.

Bat'on Rouge (băt'′n rōōzh′). **1** For parishes in Louisiana, see *East Baton Rouge* and *West Baton Rouge* in *Table* at LOUISIANA. **2** City, ✳ of Louisiana and ⊗ of East Baton Rouge parish, SE cen. Louisiana, on Mississippi river 78 m. WNW of New Orleans; pop. 152,419; 3d largest city in the state, located on bluffs on E side of the river; petroleum refineries, chemical manufacturing; trading center for agricultural section. Louisiana State University and Agricultural and Mechanical College (1859; coed.).

History: Transferred from France to Great Britain by Treaty of Paris 1763, and made a part of West Florida; conquered by Spain during American Revolution; ceded by Spain to France 1800; claimed again by Spain at time of Louisiana Purchase 1803; established independence by rebellion 1810, and declared itself county by the name of Feliciana; after admission of Louisiana to the Union 1812, incorporated as a town 1817; state capital 1849–61 and 1882 to date; held by Union forces for greater part of Civil War.

Ba·trun' (bȧ·trōōn'); *Fr.* **Ba'troun'** (bȧ'trōōn'). Town, on coast in N Lebanon Republic; pop. 5000.

Bat'tam·bang (băt'ăm·bäng). Town, W Cambodia, W of Tonle Sap, Indochina; pop. ab. 25,000, in 1936 ab. 16,000; in a fertile plain in large rice-growing area. Ceded to Siam by Cambodia 1809 and by Siam to French Indochina 1907; under Japanese pressure yielded by the French Vichy government to Siam Mar. 1941; returned to Cambodia 1946.

Bat'ten·berg (băt'′n·bûrg; *Ger.* bät'ĕn·bĕrк). Village, W Germany, in former Hesse-Nassau, 15 m. NNW of Marburg; seat of family of counts whose title died out c. 1314 and was revived 1851 for a royal branch, English members of which renounced the title 1917 and assumed the surname Mountbatten.

Battersea. Metropolitan borough of London. See *Table* at LONDON.

Bat'ti·ca·lo'a (bŭt'ĭ·kȧ·lō'ȧ). Seaport town, ✳ of Eastern Province, Ceylon, on Bay of Bengal; pop. 11.585. Located on a lagoon noted for its "singing fish," a natural phenomenon, still unexplained, consisting of musical notes rising from the water. Taken from Portuguese 1639 by Dutch, who erected a fort 1682.

Bat'ti·pa'glia (bät'tē·pä'lyä). Commune, Salerno prov., S Campania, S Italy, 12 m. ESE of Salerno; pop. 8168; road junction, taken by Allies Sept. 12, 1943.

Bat'tle (băt'′l). **1** River ab. 340 m. long, cen. Alberta and Saskatchewan provs., Canada; flows E from cen. Alberta into the North Saskatchewan at Battleford. **2** Former urban district, East Sussex, England, 6 m. NW of Hastings; pop. (1931) 3491; named from the Battle of Hastings that took place 1066 on a hill SE of the town.

Site of Battle Abbey, founded by William the Conqueror and consecrated 1094, now mostly in ruins. The "Roll of Battle Abbey," a list of Norman surnames, probably compiled in 14th cent.

Bat′tle Creek′. Industrial city, Calhoun co., S Michigan, 22 m. E of Kalamazoo; pop. 44,169; manufactures breakfast foods, also printing presses, gas stoves, farm machinery; site of Battle Creek Sanitarium.

Bat′tle·ford (băt′'l·fôrd). Town, W Saskatchewan, Canada, at junction of Battle and North Saskatchewan rivers opposite North Battleford; pop. 1319; flour mills and mineral-water works. Founded 1875; capital of Northwest Territories 1876–82, and of Saskatchewan dist. 1882–1905; invested by Indians during second Riel rebellion 1885.

Battle Harbour. Village on small island off SE Labrador coast, N of N end of Strait of Belle Isle, on sheltered roadstead; site of a Grenfell Mission Hospital, estab. 1893, which was destroyed by fire 1923.

Bat′tle·ment Mountain (băt′'l·mĕnt). Peak 11,900 ft. in W Park co., NW Wyoming.

Battle Mountain. 1 Peak 4431 ft. in Fall River co., SW corner of South Dakota.

2 Village, Lander co., cen. Nevada, ab. 80 m. N of Austin; pop. (est.) 1050; mines and smelters.

Bat′to·nya (bŏt′tŏ·nyō). Commune, SE Hungary, 42 m. E of Szeged on Romanian border; pop. 14,539.

Batu. See BATOE.

Ba′tu A′nam (bä′tōō ä′näm). Village on railroad, N Johore, Federation of Malaya, near Gemas; severe fighting bet. Australians and Japanese Jan. 1942.

Ba′tu Ga′jah (bä′tōō gä′jä). Town, cen. Perak state, Federation of Malaya, on railroad just S of Ipoh; pop. 6759; residential district, and headquarters of Kinta Valley tin-producing area.

Ba·tu′lao, Mount (bä·tōō′lou). Mountain 2894 ft., NW Batangas prov., Luzon, Phil. Is., W of Lake Taal.

Ba·tum′ (bä·tōōm′) *or* **Ba′tu·mi** (bä′tōō·mĭ). City and seaport, ✲ of Adzhar A.S.S.R., SW Georgia, U.S.S.R., on Black Sea near Turkish border; pop. 70,807. Has finest port at E end of Black Sea, but with heavy rainfall and considerable malaria is not very healthy; connected by rail and oil pipe line with Tiflis and Baku; exports petroleum, naphtha, raw silk, maize, and hardwood. Long a possession of Persia and Turkey; acquired by Russia 1878; occupied by British 1918; one of the Black Sea bases of Russian fleet.

Ba′uan (bä′wän). Municipality on N coast of Batangas Bay, Batangas prov., Luzon, Phil. Is., 4 m. NW of Batangas; pop. 37,043; piña cloth embroidery.

Ba′uang (bä′wäng). Municipality, S cen. La Union prov., Luzon, Phil. Is., at a river mouth near the coast 6 m. S of San Fernando; pop. 16,304.

Bau′chi (bou′chĕ). **1** Province of Nigeria. See *Table* at NIGERIA.

2 Commercial town, its ✲, 150 m. SE of Kano; pop. ab. 11,000.

Bau·dette′ (bô·dĕt′). Village, ⊗ of Lake of the Woods co., N Minnesota, on Rainy river; pop. 1597.

Baudh (boud) *or* **Bod** (bōd). **1** Former Indian state, S Orissa, Indian Union; 1156 sq. mi.; pop. (1941) 146,175.

2 *or* **Baudh Raj** (räj). Town, its ✲, on S bank of Mahanadi river 100 m. WNW of Cuttack.

Baudissin. See BAUTZEN city.

Bauld, Cape (bôld). Cape at NE tip of Newfoundland, at N entrance to the Strait of Belle Isle.

Baule. See BAOULÉ.

Baule, La. See ESCOUBLAC.

Bau′res (bou′räs). River in NE Bolivia; flows NW into Guaporé river on Brazilian border; with headstream Blanco ab. 360 m. long.

Bau·rú′ (bou·rōō′). City, S cen. São Paulo state, SE Brazil, 175 m. NW of São Paulo; pop. (1940 est.) 33,418.

Bau′ta (bou′tä). Municipality and town, La Habana prov., W Cuba, 14 m. SW of Havana; pop. (town) 8304.

Baut′zen (bou′tsĕn). **1** Circle of Saxony, Germany. See *Table* at SAXONY.

2 *older* **Bu′dis·sin** (bōō′dĭ·shĭn) *or* **Bau′dis·sin** (bou′-). Manufacturing city, its ✲, on Spree river 32 m. ENE of Dresden; pop. 40,335; textiles, leather, paper, machinery, iron goods, etc.; scene of defeat of Prussian and Russian armies by Napoleon May 20–21, 1813.

Baux, Les. See LES BAUX.

Bau′ya (bou′yà). Native town, W Sierra Leone, W Africa; junction for two inland railroads extending E and NE; to W connected by rail with Freetown.

Bauzanum. See BOLZANO commune.

Ba·var′i·a (bȧ·vâr′ĭ·ȧ); *Ger.* **Bay′ern** (bī′ẽrn). State of Federal Republic of Germany, S Germany; 27,232 sq. m.; pop. (1957) 9,192,800; ✲ Munich; other important cities include Nürnberg, Würzburg, Augsburg, Regensburg; mountains include the Bavarian Alps, the Fichtel Gebirge, and the Bohemian Forest (Böhmer Wald); watered by Danube and Main rivers; produces grain, vegetables, fruit, wine; slate, marble, graphite, and gypsum mining; manufactures iron goods, scientific instruments, dyes, etc. Divided into the following government districts (Regierungsbezirke):

ENGLISH NAME	GERMAN NAME	LOCATION IN BAVARIA	AREA IN SQ. M.	POPULATION (1925 CENSUS)	CAPITAL
Lower Bavaria[1]	Niederbayern	SE	4,148	755,769	Landshut
Lower Franconia	Unterfranken	NW	3,260	762,744	Würzburg
Middle Franconia	Mittelfranken	W	2,935	998,386	Ansbach
Palatinate, The	Pfalz	—[2]	2,125	931,755	Speyer
Swabia	Schwaben	SW	3,805	859,397	Augsburg
Upper Bavaria	Oberbayern	S	6,441	1,684,766	Munich
Upper Franconia	Oberfranken	NE	2,898	757,515	Bayreuth
Upper Palatinate[1]	Oberpfalz	E	3,729	629,262	Regensburg

[1] *Lower Bavaria* and *Upper Palatinate* combined into one govt. dist. c. 1932; German name Niederbayern und Oberpfalz; ✲ Regensburg.

[2] Exclave; bounded W by Saarland, NW by Prussia, NE by Hesse, E by Baden, S by France.

History: Territory conquered by Romans 1st cent. B.C. (see NORICUM and RAETIA); invaded by Germanic peoples (Marcomanni) who became tributary to Franks in 6th cent. A.D.; conquered by Charlemagne and incorporated in his empire 788; assigned to East Frankish kingdom in divisions of Frankish empire 817, 843; one of great stem duchies of Holy Roman Empire; Bavarian East Mark became separate duchy of Austria (*q.v.*) 1156; taken from Saxony (*q.v.*) and given to house of Wittelsbach by Frederick Barbarossa 1180; divided into Upper and Lower Bavaria 13th cent.; under Louis IV of Upper Bavaria, who was crowned emperor 1328, added temporarily Brandenburg, Tirol, and Netherlandish counties; became electorate 1623; under Maximilian I leader of Catholic League in Thirty Years' War; received Upper Palatinate 1648; allied with France 1701–04, during War of Spanish Succession; after War of Bavarian Succession 1778–79, united with Palatinate; its boundaries and make-up changed several times during Napoleonic era; granted constitution 1818; in 1833 merged its customs union with that of Prussia, laying basis of later Zollverein; joined Austria in war on Prussia 1866; joined North German Confederation 1870 and German Empire 1871; deposed King Louis III and proclaimed republic 1918; Munich the scene of "Beer Hall Putsch" 1923 when Ludendorff and Adolf Hitler attempted, unsuccessfully, to overthrow Bavarian government; after rise of Hitler 1933, placed under federal governor; in 1934 became mere administrative unit; overrun and conquered by American armies Mar.–May 1945; in American zone in postwar temporary division of Germany.

Ba·var'i·an Alps (bȧ·vâr'ǐ·ăn). Range of the Alps bet. S Bavaria, Germany, and Tirol, Austria, extending E and W from Lake Constance to Salzburg; highest point the Zugspitze 9719 ft. The Algäuer Alps form its W end.

Ba'vio (bä'vyồ). Town, Buenos Aires prov., E Argentina, ab. 50 m. SE of Buenos Aires.

Bawd'win (bôd'wǐn). Town, N Shan State, E cen. Burma, in mountains 30 m. WNW of Lashio; has wolframite deposits that have been an important source of tungsten; also has valuable silver, lead, and zinc deposits and ruby mines.

Ba'we·an (bä'vä·än). Island of Indonesia, in the Java Sea 100 m. N of Surabaja; area 77 sq. m.; pop. 29,862. Invaded by Japanese Feb. 25, 1942; just NE of the center of the naval battle of Java Sea Feb. 26–28, 1942; surrendered to Allies Sept. 1945.

Baw'lake (bô'lāk). Native state, cen. Karenni dist., E Burma; 568 sq. m.; pop. 13,802.

Baxar. See BUXAR.

Bax'ley (băks'lǐ). City, ⊗ of Appling co., SE Georgia, 38 m. N of Waycross; pop. 4268; tobacco, pecans.

Bax'ter (băks'tẽr). County in Arkansas. See *Table* at ARKANSAS.

Baxter, Mount. Peak 13,118 ft. in Sierra Nevada, on the boundary between Fresno and Inyo cos., SE cen. California.

Baxter Springs. City, Cherokee co., SE corner of Kansas; pop. 4498; zinc and lead mines nearby.

Bay (bā). **1** Name of counties in two states of the U.S. See *Tables* at FLORIDA and MICHIGAN.

2 or **Bay Village.** City, Cuyahoga co., N Ohio, on Lake Erie 12 m. W of Cleveland; pop. 14,489.

Bay, La·gu'na (lä·gōō'nä thä vä'ė̇; vī'). Large crescent-shaped lake, cen. Luzon, Phil. Is., SE of Manila; ab. 32 m. long; 344 sq. m.; largest lake of the Philippines; its outlet is the Pasig at the NW.

Bayadiya, El. See EL BAYADIYA.

Ba'yam·bang' (bä'yäm·bäng'). Municipality, S Pangasinan prov., Luzon, Phil. Is., 21 m. SE of Lingayen on N bank of Agno river; pop. 25,578.

Ba·ya'mo (bä·yä'mồ). Municipality and town, Oriente prov., E Cuba; pop. (town) 16,161; on **Bayamo River** (tributary of the Cauto) 27 m. E of Manzanillo; founded 1514. A center of revolutionary movement against Spain 1868–98; here Cuban soldier Calixto García Íniguez received 1898 the "Message to Garcia."

Ba·ya·món' (bä'yä·mồn'). **1** River in E cen. Puerto Rico; flows N into Atlantic Ocean.

2 Municipality (pop. 72,221) and town (pop. 15,109), NE cen. Puerto Rico; according to tradition, the first municipality in Puerto Rico to be settled; produces fruit, tobacco, sugar, coffee.

Bayan Tumen. See KERULEN town.

Bay'ard (bā'ẽrd). City, Morrill co., W Nebraska, on North Platte river 20 m. ESE of Scottsbluff; pop. 1519; beet-sugar refinery.

Ba·ya·zit' or **Ba·ya·zid'** (bä·yä·zǐt'). Town, ✳ of Ağrı vilayet, E Turkey in Asia, just S of Mt. Ararat; pop. 1734; site of fortress on ancient trade route.

Bay·bay' (bī·bī'). Municipality on W coast of Leyte I., Phil. Is., on Camotes Sea 42 m. SSW of Tacloban; pop. 42,526; important hemp port.

Bay'bor'o (bā'bûr'ồ). Town, ⊗ of Pamlico co., E North Carolina, near Pamlico Sound; pop. 545.

Bay Bulls (bā' bŏolz'). Seaside resort, SE Newfoundland, on Atlantic Ocean 20 m. S of St. John's.

Bay·burt' or **Bai·burt'** (bī·bŏort'). Town, Gümüşane vilayet, NE Turkey in Asia, on Çoruh river 60 m. WNW of Erzurum; pop. 10,211.

Bay City. 1 City, ⊗ of Bay co., E Michigan, at head of Saginaw Bay 13 m. N of Saginaw; pop. 53,604; formerly, lumbering center; now, fishing, beet-sugar, and coal-mining center.

2 City, ⊗ of Matagorda co., SE Texas, 70 m. WSW of Galveston; pop. 11,656; sulfur mines and oil wells.

Bay de Verde (bā' dě vûrd'). Seaport, SE Newfoundland, at mouth of Conception Bay; pop. 867.

Bayern. See BAVARIA.

Ba·yeux' (bȧ·yōō'; *Fr.* bȧ'yû'); *anc.* **Au·gus'to·du'-rum** (ô·gŭs'tồ·dūr'ŭm). Town, Calvados dept., Normandy, NW France, ab. 15 m. WNW of Caen and ab. 5 m. inland from the English Channel; pop. 7351. An old town, with bishopric after 4th cent.; taken by Norsemen 890; several times besieged and captured in wars bet. 12th and 16th cents. Has fine 13th-cent. Gothic church and a museum containing the famous Bayeux tapestry (probably of 11th cent.), representing in 72 panels incidents in the life of William the Conqueror.

Bay'field (bā'fēld). County in Wisconsin. See *Table* at WISCONSIN.

Bayındır. See CAŸSTER.

Bay Islands (bā). Group of islands in Caribbean Sea off N Honduras coast, including Roatán, largest of the group, and Guanaja; a department of Honduras (*q.v.*).

Bay'lor (bā'lẽr). County in Texas. See *Table* at TEXAS.

Bay Mi·nette' (bā' mǐ·nět'). City, ⊗ of Baldwin co., SW Alabama, 22 m. NE of Mobile; pop. 5197.

Bay of Islands. 1 Inlet of Bering Sea, W coast of Adak I., Andreanof Is., Aleutian Is.

2 Inlet of Gulf of St. Lawrence, W coast of Newfoundland; receives the Humber river.

3 Inlet of South Pacific Ocean, NE coast of North I., New Zealand.

Bay of Pigs. See COCHINOS BAY.

Bay of Whales. See Bay of WHALES.

Ba'yom·bong' (bä'yồm·bồng'). Municipality, ✳ of Nueva Vizcaya prov., Luzon, Phil. Is., on Magat river; pop. 12,146. Captured by Americans June 7, 1945.

Bay·onne' (bā·ōn'; bā·yōn'). City, Hudson co., NE New Jersey, on peninsula that separates Upper New York Bay from Newark Bay 5 m. SW of Jersey City; pop. 74,215; connected with Staten I. by Bayonne Bridge (steel arch, with channel span of 1675 ft.) over Kill van Kull; important petroleum refining and exporting center; manufactures chemicals, paint, wire, boilers, radiators, electric motors and generators; extensive docks; motorboat and yacht-building yards; U.S. naval supply depot. Site visited by Henry Hudson 1609; original grant 1646; incorp. as city of Bayonne 1869.

Ba'yonne' (bȧ·yồn'; *Angl.* bā·[y]ōn', -[y]ŏn', bĭ-); *anc.* **La·pur'dum** (lȧ·pûr'dŭm). Commercial and manufacturing city, Basses-Pyrénées dept., SW France, at confluence of the Nive with the Adour near Bay of Biscay 55 m. WNW of Pau; pop. 31,350; 13th-cent. cathedral; citadel; arsenal; mint; shipbuilding works; manufactures famous Bayonne hams, woolens, chocolate, soap, brandy, leather, linens, glass.

History: Taken by English 1199; held by French since 1451; meeting place of Catherine de Médicis and duke of Alva 1565 where Massacre of St. Bartholomew is said to have been planned; famous in 16th and 17th cents. for manufacture of cutlery and armaments, the bayonet having been invented here (whence its name); meeting of Napoleon, Charles IV of Spain, and Prince of the Asturias 1808 which led to abdication of Spanish monarchs in favor of Napoleon.

Bay'port (bā'pōrt). Village, Washington co., E Minnesota, on St. Croix river 15 m. ENE of St. Paul; pop. 3205; state prison.

Bay·reuth' (bī·roit'; *in English, also* bī'roit). Industrial city, ✳ of Upper Franconia govt. dist., Bavaria, Germany, 41 m. NE of Nürnberg; pop. 35,306; 16th-cent. and 18th-cent. palaces; the Festspielhaus (designed by composer Richard Wagner), where the Wagner festivals have been held at irregular intervals since its opening 1876. Founded 1194 under Bishop Otto II of Bamberg; under burgrave of Nürnberg 1248–1398, margraves of Brandenburg-Kulmbach 1603–1769; to Prussia 1791, Napoleon 1806, Bavaria 1810. In World War II taken by Allies Apr. 1945.

Bay Rob′erts (rŏb′ẽrts). Town on W shore of Conception Bay Newfoundland, S of Harbour Grace and 27 m. W of St. John's; pop. 1222; port of entry.

Bayrut. See BEIRUT.

Bay St. Lou′is (bā′ sănt lōō′ĭs). City, ⊗ of Hancock co., S Mississippi, on Gulf of Mexico 15 m. W of Gulfport; pop. 5073; seashore resort.

Bay′ Shore′. Town and resort, Suffolk co., SE New York, on S shore of Long I. and Great South Bay ab. 40 m. E of Brooklyn; pop. (1950) 9665.

Bay′ Springs′. Town, a ⊗ of Jasper co., SE cen. Mississippi; pop. 1544.

Bay′town′ (bā′toun′). City, Harris co., SE Texas, on Galveston Bay ab. 22 m. ESE of Houston; pop. 28,159; oil wells; large toluene factory.

Bay′ville (bā′vĭl). Village on N shore of Long I., Nassau co., SE New York; pop. 3962.

Ba′za (bä′thä; -sä); *anc.* **Bas′ti** (băs′tĭ). Commune, Granada prov., S Spain, 53 m. NE of Granada; pop. 20,772; besieged by Isabella of Castile 1489; scene of French victory over Spaniards 1810.

Ba′zan′court′ (bä′zäɴ′kōōr′). Town, Marne dept., France, NE of Reims; pop. 1272; scene of battle Oct. 7, 1918 when Germans were forced to evacuate it.

Ba·zar·dyu′ze (bä′zär-dü′zĕ). Peak 14,728 ft. in E Caucasus Mts., bet. Dagestan and Azerbaidzhan.

Ba·zar′gic (bä-zär′jĕk); *Bulg.* **Do′brich** (dô′brĭch), *after 1949* **Tol·bu′khin** (tôl·bōō′kĭn). City, NE Bulgaria, in Dobruja region; pop. 29,938; in Romania 1913–40.

Bazman, Kuh–i–. See Kuh-i-BASMAN.

Beach (bēch). City, ⊗ of Golden Valley co., W North Dakota; pop. 1460.

Beach Haven Inlet. Narrow strait leading from Atlantic Ocean into S extremity of Barnegat Bay off SE tip of Ocean co., New Jersey.

Beach′wood (bēch′wŏŏd). Village, Cuyahoga co., Ohio, E of Cleveland; pop. 6089.

Beach′y Head (bēch′ĭ). Headland 575 ft. high on S coast of East Sussex, S England, projecting into English Channel; lighthouse. Scene June 30, 1690 of naval victory of French over British and Dutch.

Bea′con (bē′kŭn; -k'n). City, Dutchess co., SE New York, at foot of Mt. Beacon on Hudson river opp. Newburgh; pop. 13,922.

Beacon Falls. Town, W cen. New Haven co., S Connecticut; pop. 2886; settled 1678, incorp. 1871.

Bea′cons·field (bē′kŭnz-fēld; *in England, usu.* bĕk′ŭnz-). **1** Town, N Tasmania, Australia, on Tamar river 25 m. NW of Launceston; pop. 827; center of gold field. **2** Town, Buckinghamshire, S cen. England, 22 m. NW of London; pop. 7909; noted for its associations with Edmund Burke, Benjamin Disraeli, and G. K. Chesterton. **3** Town, Griqualand West, N Cape Province, Union of South Africa, SE suburb of Kimberley; pop. ab. 20,000; united with Kimberley 1912.

Bea′dle (bē′d'l). County in South Dakota. See *Table* at SOUTH DAKOTA.

Bea′gle Channel (bē′g'l). Channel bet. S Tierra del Fuego I. and S group of Chilean islands in Tierra del Fuego archipelago, off S tip of South America.

Bear (bâr). River ab. 350 m. long, SE Idaho and N Utah; rises in Uinta Mts., N Utah, flows N crossing Wyoming border twice, turns NW into SE Idaho, bends S and empties into Great Salt Lake, N Utah.

Bear Butte (bâr′ būt′). Peak 4422 ft. in Meade co., W South Dakota.

Beards′town (bẽrdz′toun). City, Cass co., W cen. Illinois, on Illinois river 45 m. WNW of Springfield; pop. 6294; railroad workshops, flour mills.

Bearhaven. See BEREHAVEN.

Bear Island (bâr). **1** = *Bere Island:* see BEREHAVEN. **2** Island in Barents Sea 240 m. N of Norway; 69 sq. m.; with Spitsbergen group forms Svalbard, Norway.

Bear Islands; *Russ.* **Med·ve′zhi Os·tro·va′** (myĕd-vyä′zhĭ ŭs·trŭ·vä′). Group of small islands opp. mouth of Kolyma river, East Siberian Sea, off NE coast of Yakutsk, Soviet Russia, Asia.

Bear Lake. 1 Lake ab. 20 m. long and 7 m. wide on E Idaho-Utah border; depth 175 ft.; outlet is tributary of Bear river. **2** County in Idaho. See *Table* at IDAHO.

Bear Mountain. 1 Peak 12,955 ft. in San Juan co., SW Colorado. **2** Mountain 2355 ft. in town of Salisbury, extreme NW Connecticut. **3** Mountain 1314 ft. on Hudson river in Bear Mountain Park (1000 acres, a section of Palisades Interstate Park), New York; Bear Mountain Bridge, opened 1924, crosses Hudson here. **4** Mountain in NE Dauphin co., SE cen. Pennsylvania, on the edge of the Bear Valley coal basin. **5** Peak 7172 ft. in Pennington co., SW South Dakota.

Bé′arn′ (bā′är′; -ärn′); *Lat.* **Ben′e·har′num** (bĕn′ĕ-här′nŭm). Historical region of SW France; bounded anciently on W, N, and E by Gascony and on S by Pyrenees; ✳ Pau. Part of Aquitania under Romans; devastated by Vandals, Visigoths, and later by Saracens; hereditary viscountship in 11th cent.; countship of Béarn held by Henry IV and retained when he became king of France 1589; united with French crown 1620; province of France 1620–1789.

Bear River. See BEAR.

Bear′wal′low Mountain (bâr′wŏl′ō). Peak 6487 ft. in Yancey co., W North Carolina.

Be′as *or* **Bi′as** (bē′äs); *anc.* **Hyph′a·sis** (hĭf′à·sĭs). River ab. 300 m. long, one of the "Five Rivers" of the Punjab, N India; rises in the Himalayas E of Dharmsala, Punjab state, flows W and SW to the Sutlej river in W Punjab state SW of city of Kapurthala.

Be′as de Se·gu′ra (bā′äz thä sā·gōō′rä). Commune, Jaén prov., S Spain, 55 m. NE of Jaén; pop. 14,953; in region producing wine, oil, fruits, flax.

Be·a′ta, Cape (bä·ä′tä). Cape extending into Caribbean Sea from S cen. coast of Hispaniola.

Be·a′ta Island (bä·ä′tä). Small island in the Caribbean Sea off S cen. coast of Hispaniola.

Be·a′ten·berg (bä·ä′tĕn·bĕrк) *or* **Sankt Beatenberg** (zängkt). Village, Bern canton, Switzerland, NW of Interlaken; pop. 1088; resort.

Be·at′rice (bē·ăt′rĭs). City, ⊗ of Gage co., SE Nebraska, 35 m. S of Lincoln; pop. 12,132; in grain and livestock-raising section; manufactures windmills, irrigation equipment, farm machinery, gasoline engines, dairy products.

Beat′tie Peak (bē′tĭ). Mountain 13,200 ft. in San Juan and San Miguel cos., SW Colorado.

Beat′ton (bĕt′'n). River ab. 145 m. long in E British Columbia, Canada; flows E and S into Peace river.

Beat′ty·ville (bā′tĭ·vĭl). City, ⊗ of Lee co., E Kentucky; pop. 1048.

Beau Bas′sin′ (bō′ bȧ′săɴ′). See ROSE HILL.

Beau′caire′ (bō′kâr′); *anc.* **U·ger′num** (û·jûr′nŭm), *later* **Bel′li Quad′rum** (bĕl′ĭ kwŏd′rŭm). Commercial commune, Gard dept., S France, on right bank of Rhone river (opp. Tarascon) 15 m. E of Nîmes; pop. 10,059; 14th-cent. churches. Formerly famous for great annual fair (founded 1217 by Raymond VI, Count of Toulouse).

Beauce (bōs). **1** County, Quebec, Canada. See *Table* at QUEBEC. **2** Ancient district of N cen. France, now part of departments of Loir-et-Cher and Eure-et-Loir; ✳ Chartres.

Beauce′ville East (bōs′vĭl ēst′); *Fr.* **Beauce′ville′–Est′** (bōs′vēl′ ĕst′). Town, ⊗ of Beauce co., S Quebec, Canada, on Chaudière river SSE of Quebec; pop. 1573.

Beau′court′–sur–l'An′cre (bō′kōōr′sür·läɴ′kr′). Village, Somme dept., NE France, 5 m. N of Albert; fighting Aug. 1918.

Beau′fort. 1 (bō′fẽrt). County in North Carolina. See *Table* at NORTH CAROLINA.

2 (bū′fẽrt) County in South Carolina. See *Table* at
SOUTH CAROLINA.
3 (bō′fẽrt) Town and seaside resort, ⊗ of Carteret co.,
SE North Carolina, on inlet of Atlantic Ocean 35 m. SE
of New Bern; pop. 2922; estab. 1722; port of entry at
terminus of an inland waterway; canning plants, commercial fisheries; lumbering, farming.
4 (bū′fẽrt) City, ⊗ of Beaufort co., S South Carolina, on
Port Royal 52 m. SW of Charleston; pop. 6298; con-
quered by British in the Revolution; fell into hands of
Federal fleet 1861; tourist center; truck farms, canneries,
shrimp and oyster industries; phosphate mines.
5 (bō′fẽrt) Town, SW British North Borneo, NE of
Brunei Bay and on railroad 45 m. SSW of Jesselton.
Beau′fort Sea (bō′fẽrt). That part of the Arctic Ocean
NE of Alaska, NW of Canada, and W of Banks I. in the
Arctic Archipelago.
Beau′fort West (bō′fẽrt). Town, S cen. Cape Province,
Republic of So. Africa, 260 m. ENE of Cape Town; pop.
7967; in Great Karroo region; sheep raising.
Beau′har′nois′ (bō′är′nwå′). **1** County, Quebec, Can-
ada. See *Table* at QUEBEC.
2 Manufacturing town, its ⊗, on St. Lawrence river 20
m. SW of Montreal; pop. 5694.
Beau′lieu (bū′lĭ). Parish, New Forest rural dist.,
Southampton, S England; ruins of Beaulieu Abbey,
wealthy Cistercian house founded by King John 1204.
Beau′ly (bū′lĭ). Small river in N cen. Scotland, flowing
NE into Moray Firth W of Inverness.
Beau·mar′is (bō·mŏr′ĭs; -mắr′ĭs; *locally also* bŭ·mŏr′ĭs).
Municipal borough, Anglesey, NW Wales, on **Beaumaris Bay**; pop. 2128; 13th-cent. castle.
Beau′mont (bō′mŏnt). **1** City, Riverside co., SE Cali-
fornia, 21 m. SE of San Bernardino; pop. 4288; fruit.
2 Industrial city and port of entry, ⊗ of Jefferson co.,
SE Texas, on Neches river 7 m. E of Houston; pop.
119,175; connected with Gulf of Mexico by Sabine-
Neches Canal. Settled 1835, ⊗ 1838, incorp. 1881. Oil-
refining center and oil port, with oil and natural gas pipelines; lumbering, rice and cotton growing; manufactures
oil-well machinery, paper; shipyards.
Beau′mont′-Ha′mel′ (bō′mỗN′å′mĕl′). Village,
Somme dept., NE France, near the Ancre ab. 5 m. N of
Albert; fighting July–Nov. 1916; taken by British Nov.
13, 1916, a phase of the battle of the Somme.
Beaune (bōn); *Lat.* **Bel′na** (bĕl′nå). Commercial and
manufacturing city, Côte-d′Or dept., E France, 23 m.
SSW of Dijon; pop. 12,161; 12th-cent. church; large
hospital (founded 1443); 15th-cent. ramparts; school of
viticulture; trades in Burgundy wines.
Beau′port (bō′pôr′). Market town. Quebec co., S
Quebec, Canada, NE suburb of Quebec on St. Lawrence
river; pop. 5390. Granted to Robert Gifford 1634, be-
came first seigneury established in New France; served as
Montcalm′s headquarters 1759.
Beau′re·gard (bō′rĕ·gärd). Parish in Louisiana. See
Table at LOUISIANA.
Beau′sé′jour′ (bō′sā′zhōōr′; bō′zĕ·zhōōr′). Town, SE
Manitoba, Canada, 30 m. ENE of Winnipeg; pop. 1376.
Beau′so·leil′ (bō′sō′lâ′y′). Commune, Alpes-Maritimes
dept., SE France, near Ligurian Sea 8 m. ENE of Nice;
pop. (1931) 13,051; winter resort.
Beau′vais′ (bō′vā′; *Fr.* -vĕ′); *anc.* **Bel·lov′a·cum**
(bĕ·lŏv′å·kŭm) *and* **Cae′sar·om′a·gus** (sē′zẽr·ŏm′å-
gŭs). Manufacturing commune, ✱ of Oise dept., N
France, 42 m. NNW of Paris; pop. 18,869; 13th-cent.
cathedral (unfinished); 10th-cent. and 12th-cent.
churches; 12th-cent. palace; ancient Roman ramparts;
manufactures tapestries and carpets (for which it has
long been famed), woolens, lace, buttons, brushes.
Became commune 1096; made heroic resistance to large
army of Burgundians under Charles the Bold 1472.
Beaux, Les. See LES BAUX.
Bea′ver (bē′vẽr). **1** River, W Pennsylvania; formed by
confluence of Shenango and Mahoning rivers in Law-

rence co., flows S into Ohio river at Rochester, cen.
Beaver co.
2 Name of counties in three states of the U.S. See *Tables*
at OKLAHOMA, PENNSYLVANIA, UTAH.
3 Town, ⊗ of Beaver co., NW Oklahoma; pop. 2087;
capital of the "Territory of Cimarron" 1887–90.
4 Residential borough. ⊗ of Beaver co., W Pennsylvania, on Ohio river 26 m. NW of Pittsburgh; pop. 6160.
5 City, ⊗ of Beaver co., SW Utah, 42 m. SE of S end of
Sevier Lake; pop. 1548.
6 River 305 m. long, tributary of Churchill river in
Saskatchewan and Alberta provs., Canada.
Beaver City. City, ⊗ of Furnas co., S Nebraska; pop.
818.
Beaver Creek. River 200 m. long, NW Kansas and SW
Nebraska; rises in Kit Carson co., E Colorado, flows NE
across NW corner of Kansas into Nebraska and joins
Sappa river 10 m. before emptying into Republican
river in Harlan co., S Nebraska.
Beaver Dam. City, Dodge co., SE cen. Wisconsin, 29
m. SSW of Fond du Lac; pop. 13,118; manufactures
stoves and foundry products, shoes, soap.
Beaver Dam Creek. See MECHANICSVILLE.
Beaver Dam Mountains. Range in extreme SW
Utah.
Beaver Dams. See MERRITTON.
Beaver Falls. Industrial city, Beaver co., W Pennsylva-
nia, on Beaver river 18 m. S of New Castle; pop. 16,240;
settled 1806; manufactures cold-drawn steel, chinaware,
metal, paper, and cork products; coal mines, clay pits,
oil and gas wells. Geneva College (1848; coed.).
Bea′ver·head′ (bē′vẽr·hĕd′). County in Montana. See
Table at MONTANA.
Beaverhead Mountains. Mountain range, part of
Bitterroot Range, in Continental Divide, forming part
of the boundary bet. SW Montana and E Idaho.
Bea′ver·hill′ Lake (bē′vẽr·hĭl′). Lake in cen. Alberta,
Canada, ab. 35 m. E of Edmonton.
Beaver Island. **1** Island in N Lake Michigan, W of
Emmet co., N Michigan; a part of Charlevoix co.
2 One of the Falkland Is. (*q.v.*).
Beaver Meadows. Borough, Carbon co., E Pennsylva-
nia, 21 m. S of Wilkes-Barre; pop. 1392; coal mining.
Beaver River. See BEAVER.
Bea′ver·ton (bē′vẽr·t′n; -tŭn). City, Washington co.,
Oregon, W of Portland; pop. 5937.
Be·a′war (bå·ä′wär). Town, cen. Rajasthan, on affluent
of Luni river 115 m. SW of Jaipur; pop. 28,342.
Be′be·dou′ro (bā′vĕ·thō′rōō). City, N São Paulo state,
SE Brazil, 215 m. NNW of São Paulo; pop. (1940 est.)
11,876; railroad junction point.
Beb′ing·ton and Brom′bor·ough (bĕb′ĭng·tŭn,
brŏm′bŭ·rŭ [-brŭ]). Urban district, Cheshire, NW
England, on the Mersey opp. Liverpool; pop. 47,742.
Bec. Abbey. See LE BEC-HELLOUIN.
Bé′can′cour′ (bā′kän′kōōr′). Village, ⊗ of Nicolet co.,
S Quebec, Canada, on St. Lawrence river; pop. 312.
Bec′cles (bĕk′′lz). Municipal borough, East Suffolk, E
England, 100 m. NE of London; pop. 6869.
Be′ce·lae′re (bā′så·lâ′rĕ). Small commune, West Flan-
ders prov., NW Belgium; pop. 2588; a stronghold in the
German front line in World War I.
Bech′a·rof Lake (bĕch′å·rŏf). Lake ab. 30 m. long, N
Alaska Penin., SW of Katmai National Monument.
Bec-Hellouin, Le. See LE BEC-HELLOUIN.
Bech′u·a′na·land′ (bĕch′ōō·ä′nå·länd′; bĕ·chwä′nå-).
1 = BECHUANALAND PROTECTORATE.
2 = BRITISH BECHUANALAND.
Bechuanaland Protectorate. Former British protec-
torate, S cen. Africa; since 1966 the independent republic
of **Bo·tswa′na** (bŏt·swä′nå); ab. 222,000 sq. m.; pop.
(1964) 543,105; ✱ Gaberones. Bounded on NW by
Caprivi Concession and Zambezi river, on NE by Southern Rhodesia, on SE by Transvaal, on S by Cape
Province, and on W by South-West Africa. The Oko-

vanggo Basin and salt lakes in the N and the Kalahari Desert in W and S fill most of the protectorate; the Molopo and Limpopo rivers border it on the S. Inhabitants are mainly Bechuanas, Bamangwatos and other Bantu tribes. Chief towns, along E border, Serowe, Palapye, Francistown, Mochudi. See *Map* at UNION OF SOUTH AFRICA. Formerly governed by a resident commissioner, under the high commissioner for Basutoland, Bechuanaland Protectorate, and Swaziland.

History: Occupied by British at instigation of Cecil Rhodes 1884; organized as British protectorate 1885, divided into British Bechuanaland and Bechuanaland Protectorate which was N of Molopo river; included in grant to British South Africa Co. 1889 but never administered by it; when British Bechuanaland (*q.v.*) was attached to Cape of Good Hope 1895, N part remained a protectorate.

Beck'en·ham (bĕk′′n·ăm; bĕk′năm). Urban district, Kent, SE England, S suburb of London; pop. (1951) 74,834; part of Greater London.

Beck'er (bĕk′ẽr). County in Minnesota. See *Table* at MINNESOTA.

Beck'ham (bĕk′ăm). County in Oklahoma. See *Table* at OKLAHOMA.

Beck'ley (bĕk′lĭ). City, ⊗ of Raleigh co., S West Virginia, 35 m. N of Bluefield; pop. 18,642; coal mining.

Beck'um (bĕk′ōōm). Manufacturing city, W Germany, in former Westphalia prov., Prussia, 23 m. SE of Münster; pop. 10,660.

Beda, El. See DOHA.

Bedd·gel'ert (bāth·gĕl′ẽrt; bĕth-). Village, Caernarvon, NW Wales, S of Snowdon Mt.; pop. 1213; resort, noted for its beautiful location; scene of legend of Prince Llewellyn and his hound.

Bed'ding·ton and Wal'ling·ton (bĕd′ĭng·tŭn, wŏl′ĭng·tŭn). Urban district, Surrey, S England, S suburb of London; pop. 32,751; part of Greater London.

Bed'ford (bĕd′fẽrd). **1** Name of counties in three states of the U.S. See *Tables* at PENNSYLVANIA, TENNESSEE, VIRGINIA.

2 City, ⊗ of Lawrence co., S Indiana, 20 m. S of Bloomington; pop. 13,024; limestone quarries.

3 City, ⊗ of Taylor co., SW Iowa, 73 m. SE of Council Bluffs; pop. 1807.

4 City, ⊗ of Trimble co., N. Kentucky; pop. 717.

5 Town, Middlesex co., NE Massachusetts, 10 m. S of Lowell; pop. 10,969.

6 Agricultural town, Hillsboro co., S New Hampshire, 3 m. SW of Manchester; pop. 3636.

7 City, Cuyahoga co., N Ohio, 11 m. SE of Cleveland; pop. 15,223; residential suburb of Cleveland.

8 Borough, ⊗ of Bedford co., S Pennsylvania, on branch of Juniata river 30 m. S of Altoona; pop. 3696; mineral springs nearby in **Bedford Springs**, a summer resort. Settled as **Rays'town** (rāz′toun) c. 1750; Fort Bedford, an important frontier station in last half of 18th cent., built 1751; town laid out 1766.

9 Town, ⊗ of Bedford co., SW cen. Virginia, 22 m. WSW of Lynchburg; pop. 5921.

10 Town, ⊗ of Missisquoi co., S Quebec, Canada, 40 m. SE of Montreal; pop. 2073.

11 County in England. See BEDFORDSHIRE.

12 Municipal borough, ⊗ of Bedfordshire, SE cen. England, on the Ouse 48 m. NNW of London; pop. 53,065; manufactures agricultural implements. Dates back to 6th cent.; scene of John Bunyan's imprisonment 1660–72 and 1675 (when he is supposed to have written *Pilgrim's Progress*, published 1678).

Bedford Heights Village, Cuyahoga co., Ohio, S of Cleveland; pop. 5275.

Bed'ford·shire (bĕd′fẽrd·shĭr; -shẽr) *or* **Bed'ford** (bĕd′fẽrd) *or* **Beds** (bĕdz). County, SE cen. England; area 473 sq. m.; pop. (1951) 311,844; ⊗ Bedford; other towns Luton, Dunstable; watered by the Ouse; agriculture, manufacture of farm implements and lace.

Bed'ling·ton (bĕd′lĭng·tŭn). Parish, Northumberland, N England; pop. 7148; famous for its terriers; a part of **Bed'ling·ton·shire** (-shĭr; -shẽr), urban district on the Blyth near its mouth in North Sea 11 m. N of Newcastle, pop. (1951) 28,836.

Bed'loe's Island (bĕd′lōz); *since 1956 officially* **Lib'er·ty Island** (lĭb′ẽr·tĭ); *formerly also* **Bed'loe Island** (bĕd′lō). Small island in Upper New York Bay; purchased by City of New York 1758 and c. 1800 ceded to U.S. government; location of Bartholdi's statue Liberty Enlightening the World.

Bed'min'ster (bĕd′mĭn′stẽr). Locality in Bedminster township (pop. 2740), Bucks co., SE Pennsylvania, ab. 20 m. SE of Allentown.

Be'dra·shen' (bă′dẽr·shĭn′; -shăn′). Village on left bank of the Nile, Lower Egypt, S of Cairo; site of ruins of ancient Memphis.

Beds. = BEDFORDSHIRE.

Bed'was and Ma'chen (bĕd′wås, măk′ăn). Urban district, Monmouthshire, W England, 27 m. WNW of Bristol; pop. 8712.

Bed·well'ty (băd·wĕl′tĭ). Urban district, Monmouthshire, W England, 31 m. WNW of Bristol; pop. 28,826.

Bed'worth (bĕd′wûrth; -wẽrth). Urban district, Warwickshire, cen. England; pop. 24,866.

Bę'dzin (bĕn′jēn); *Russ.* **Ben'din** (byăn′dyĭn); *Ger.* **Bend'zin** (bĕn′tsēn). Commune, Śląsk dept., S Poland, 78 m. SW of Kielce; pop. (1938–39 est.) 50,721; coal and iron deposits; steelworks; sugar raising.

Bee (bē). County in Texas. See *Table* at TEXAS.

Beech Grove (bēch grōv). City, Marion co., cen. Indiana, 7 m. SE of Indianapolis; pop. 10,973.

Bee'croft Head (bē′krŏft). Peninsula and point of land, SE New South Wales, Australia, enclosing Jervis Bay on the N. See Cape SAINT GEORGE, Australia.

Bee'mer·ang, Mount (bē′mẽr·ăng). Mountain 4100 ft. high of Blue Mts., E New South Wales, Australia.

Bee'ren·berg (bâr′ẽn·bûrg). Extinct volcano 8347 ft. on Jan Mayen I., Arctic Ocean; highest point on island.

Beeroth. See BIRE.

Be'er·she'ba (bē′ẽr·shē′bá; bẽr·shē′bá; bē·ûr′shē·bá). **1** Subdistrict, Gaza district, S Palestine; 4855 sq. m.; pop. 51,082, (1938 est.) 51,505.

2 *Arab.* **Bir es Sa'ba** (bĭr′ ăs să′bă). Frontier town in Beersheba subdist., S Palestine, on ancient caravan route ab. 45 m. SW of Jerusalem; pop. 2959. Marked the extreme S limit of Palestine (*Judges* xx. 1): see DAN. Scene of victory of British over Turks Oct. 31, 1917.

Bees'ton and Sta'ple·ford (bēs′tŭn, bē′s'n; stā′p'l-fẽrd). Urban district, Nottinghamshire, N cen. England, 4 m. SW of Nottingham; pop. 49,849.

Bee'ville (bē′vĭl). City, ⊗ of Bee co., S Texas, 48 m. NNW of Corpus Christi; pop. 13,811; oil wells.

Be'gi·che·va (byă′gĭ·chĕ·vá). Island, NW Yakutsk Republic, Soviet Russia, Asia, N of Nordvik Bay, at mouth of Khatanga river.

Bè'gles (bě′gl′). Commune, Gironde dept., SW France, on Garonne river 4 m. SSE of Bordeaux; pop. 20,989.

Beg'na (bĕng′nä). River in S Norway; flows S into Tyrifjord Lake, whence it issues as the Drammenselv.

Bé'hague', Pointe (pwănt′ bā′ág′). Cape extending into Atlantic Ocean from E coast of French Guiana.

Behar. See BIHAR.

Beharieh. Var. of BAHARÎYA.

Beh·be·han' (bĕ·h′·bĕ·hän′). Town, Fars prov., SW Iran, E of Bandar Shahpur; pop. 15,000 to 20,000; once a flourishing city, now considerably decayed; near ruins of an ancient Persian city.

Be·hei'ra (bōō·hī′rŏ; -hā′-). Province, N Lower Egypt. See *Table* at EGYPT.

Behisni. See BESNI.

Be'his·tun' (bā′hĭs·tōōn′; *Pers.* bá′-) *or* **Bi'si·tun'** *or* **Bi'su·tun'** (bē′sŭ·tōōn′). Ruined town in W Iran, 22 m. E of Kermanshah, Luristan prov. On limestone cliff above present village is monument of Darius the Great

consisting of sculptures in relief and trilingual (cuneiform) inscriptions, the "Rosetta Stone of Asia"; decipherment by Henry Rawlinson in 1846 furnished key to our knowledge of Assyrian and Babylonian records.

Behnesa. See OXYRHYNCHUS.

Behramköy. See ASSOS.

Behring. Var. of BERING.

Beibazar. See BEYPAZARI.

Bei'da (bā'dá). Town, NE Libya, in Cyrenaica NE of Bengasi; palace of King of Libya.

Bei'jer·land (bī'yĕr·länt) or **Hoek'sche Waard** (hōōk'sĕ várt'). Island 6 m. S of Rotterdam, attached to South Holland prov., Netherlands.

Bei Kem (bĕ'ĕ kĕm'). See YENISEI.

Beilan. See BAILAN.

Bei'ra (bā'ĕ·rá). 1 Old province, N cen. Portugal; ✻ Coimbra; now forms modern provinces of Beira Alta, Beira Baixa, and part of Beira Litoral; soil rocky, except on coast; watered by Douro, Tagus, Mondego, and numerous other rivers; traversed by Serra da Estrela. Region occupied by old province now produces grain, oil, wine, chestnuts; coal, iron, salt, marble mines. 2 Seaport on SE coast of Mozambique, SE Africa, 120 m. SW of mouth of the Zambezi; ✻ of Manica and Sofala prov.; pop. (1935 est.) 24,502. Chief port for Southern Rhodesia, Nyasaland, and cen. Mozambique; exports maize, rubber, cotton, sugar.

Bei'ra Al'ta (bā'·rá äl'tá). Province of Portugal. See BEIRA and *Table* at PORTUGAL.

Beira Bai'xa (bī'shá). Province of Portugal. See BEIRA and *Table* at PORTUGAL.

Beira Li·to·ral' (lĕ·tōō·räl'). Province of Portugal. See BEIRA; ESTREMADURA (old province); *Table* at PORTUGAL.

Bei·rut' or **Bay·rut'** (bā·rōōt'); *Fr.* **Bey'routh'** (bā'·rōōt'); *anc.* **Be·ry'tus** (bĕ·rī'tŭs). City, ✻ of Republic of Lebanon, built on a promontory with Lebanon Mts. behind it; pop. 211,006 (1960 est. 500,000); has extensive trade; connected by highway with Damascus and Baghdad. Seat of American university.

History: Ancient Phoenician settlement mentioned in Tell el-Amarna tablets; ruled by Romans until Arab capture of Syria (*q.v.*) 635 A.D.; captured for kingdom of Jerusalem (*q.v.*) by Baldwin I 1110; object of struggle bet. Crusaders and Saracens until latter finally captured it 1291; although came to be ruled by Druses, technically belonged to Ottoman Empire; in 1840 bombarded and captured by British and French who intervened in Syria to quell revolt of Mehemet Ali against sultan (see EGYPT); captured by French in campaign against Turkey 1918; capital of Lebanon since 1920.

Bei·san' (bā·sän') or **Bai·san'** (bī-). 1 Subdistrict, Galilee dist., N Palestine; 139 sq. m.; pop. 15,123, (1938 est.) 18,338.
2 *Bib.* **Beth'she'an** or **Beth'–She'an** (bĕth'shē'ăn; -shē·än'); *anc.* **Scy·thop'o·lis** (sĭ·thŏp'ō·lĭs). Town, its ✻, in the Valley of Jezreel W of the Jordan ab. 18 m. SE of Nazareth; pop. 3830. Site of settlement of Early Bronze Age (c. 3000–2000 B.C.) and rich in archaeological material of the pre-Israelite period; important in Hittite and early Egyptian history. As Bethshean taken by Joshua; later known as Scythopolis. One of the ten cities of Decapolis.

Beit'bridge (bīt'brij). Town, S Southern Rhodesia, on the Limpopo opp. Messina in Transvaal.

Beit Ja'la (bāt jă'lá; -lä) or **Bait Ja'la** (bīt-); *Bib.* **Gal'lim** (găl'ĭm). Town, Bethlehem subdist., Jerusalem dist., Palestine, NW of Bethlehem.

Beit Jibrin. See ELEUTHEROPOLIS.

Be'ja (bā'zhá). 1 District of Portugal. See *Table* at PORTUGAL.
2 *anc.* **Pax Ju'li·a** (păks jōō'lĭ·á; jōōl'yá). Commune, its ✻ and ✻ of Baixo Alentejo prov., S Portugal, 85 m. SE of Lisbon; pop. 12,985; manufactures oil, pottery, textiles, leather; Roman ruins, including an aqueduct.

Bé'ja' (bā'zhá'); *anc.* **Vac'ca** (văk'á). Town, N Tunisia, N Africa, 65 m. W of the city of Tunis; pop. ab. 11,000. Fighting on highway running N to Bizerte in final stage of Tunisia campaign Apr. 1943 in World War II.

Bejapur. See BIJAPUR.

Bejraburana. See PHETCHABUN.

Bejraburi. See PHET BURI.

Be'ju·cal' (bĕ'hōō·käl'). Municipality and town, La Habana prov., W Cuba; pop. (town) 8319.

Be·káa' (bĭ·kä'). 1 Former sanjak in E Lebanon.
2 See EL BIKA.

Be·ka'si (bĕ·kä'sĭ). Village, W Java, E of Djakarta; destroyed Dec. 1945 by British in retaliation against Indonesians.

Bek–Budi. See KARSHI.

Bé'kés (bā'kāsh). Commune, SE Hungary; pop. 30,593; trade center in agricultural region.

Bé'kés·csa'ba (bā'kāsh·chŏ'bŏ). City, SE Hungary, S of Békés; pop. (1939) 49,973; commercial and industrial center; manufactures esp. linen goods.

Be'la (bā'lá). Town, W Pakistan, in Baluchistan, 110 m. NW of Karachi; pop. 8043.

Be'la Crk'va (bĕ'lä tsûrk'vä); *Hung.* **Fe'hér·tem'plom** (fĕ'här·tĕm'plŏm); *Ger.* **Weiss'kir'chen** (vīs'·kĭr'kĕn). Town, Voivodina, E Yugoslavia, 45 m. E of Belgrade near border of Romania; pop. (1931) 9662.

Bel Air (bĕl âr'). Town, ⊗ of Harford co., NE Maryland, 23 m. NE of Baltimore; pop. 4300.

Be·la'jan (bá·lä'yän). River ab. 150 m. long in E Borneo, Indonesia; a N tributary of the Mahakam.

Be'lal·cá'zar (bā'läl·kä'thär; -sär). Commune, Córdoba prov., S Spain, 51 m. NNW of Córdoba; pop. 9471; wheat, barley, wine, oil, fruit, garden truck; argentiferous lead mining.

Be'la–Sla'ti·na (byä'lä slä'tĕ·nä). Town, Vrattsa dept., NW cen. Bulgaria; pop. (1926) 7247.

Be·la'wan (blä'wän) or **Be·la'wan–De'li** (-dä'lĕ). Town and seaport at mouth of Deli river, Sumatra, Indonesia; port of Medan.

Be·la·ya (byĕ'lá·yá). Navigable river ab. 700 m. long in Bashkir Republic, E Soviet Russia, Europe; rises in Southern Urals S of Zlatoust and flows S, W, and NW to the Kama river S of Sarapul.

Be·la·ya Tser'kov (byĕ'lá·yá tsyĕr'kúf·y'). Town, W Kiev Region, N Ukraine, U.S.S.R., on a tributary of the Dnieper 50 m. S of Kiev; pop. ab. 42,000; commercial and agricultural center on the central Ukraine railroad. Held by Germans in World War II from 1941 until late in 1943.

Belbeis. See BILBEIS.

Bel'cher Islands (bĕl'chĕr). Island group in SE Hudson Bay, Keewatin District, Northwest Territories, Canada.

Bel'cher·town (bĕl'chĕr·toun). Town, Hampshire co., W Massachusetts, 15 m. NE of Springfield; pop. 5186;

Bel·chi'te (bĕl·chē'tá). Commune, Zaragoza prov., NE Spain, 22 m. SSE of Saragossa; pop. (1930) 3812; in Peninsular War scene of victory of French forces under Suchet over Spanish forces under Blake June 1809.

Bel'ding (bĕl'dĭng). City, Ionia co., S cen. Michigan, 25 m. ENE of Grand Rapids; pop. 4887; silk mills.

Be·lém' (bĕ·lĕN'; *Port.* -lãĕN'); *sometimes called* **Pa·rá'** (pá·rá'). Seaport city, ✻ of Pará state, N Brazil, at 1°28'S; pop. (1940 est.) 166,662; on Pará river 90 m. from the sea; distributing center for Amazon valley; exports rubber, Brazil nuts, cocoa, timber.

Be·len' (bĕ·lĕn'). Village, Valencia co., W New Mexico, on the Rio Grande 30 m. S of Albuquerque; pop. 4495; railroad division point; alfalfa, cereals, fruit, wool.

Be·lén' (bá·län'). Town, Concepción dept., N cen. Paraguay, 125 m. N of Asunción; pop. ab. 7000.

Bel'ep Islands (bĕl'ĕp). Group of small islands bet. parallel coral reefs 28 m. NW of NW tip of New Caledonia, SW Pacific Ocean.

Be·le'ri·um (bĕ·lĕr'ĭ·ŭm). Ancient name of CORNWALL county, SW England.

Bel′fast (bĕl′fȧst). **1** Seaport city, ⊗ of Waldo co., S Maine, on Penobscot Bay 30 m. SSW of Bangor; pop. 6140, settled 1769; tourist center.
2 (*locally also* bĕl·fȧst′) County borough and seaport, ✳ of Northern Ireland and ⊗ of co. Antrim, E Northern Ireland; pop. 443,670; one of the chief shipbuilding centers of the world; also center of the linen industry in Ireland; Queen's University (1909).
History: Site of Norman castle in possession of earls of Ulster, granted to Sir Arthur Chichester 1604 who settled colonists (see ULSTER); town incorporated by James I of England (1603–25); settled by Scots from 17th cent., it became center of Irish Protestantism.
3 Town, SE cen. Transvaal, Union of South Africa, 125 m. E of Pretoria; pop. 2135; summer resort.
Bel′fast Lough (bĕl′fȧst [bĕl·fȧst′] lŏκ). Inlet of the North Channel on E coast of Northern Ireland; the city of Belfast lies at its head.
Bel·fo′dio (bȧl·fô′dyô). Town, W Ethiopia, near border of Sudan.
Bel′fort′ (bĕl′fôr′; bā′fôr′). Fortified commune, ✳ of Territoire de Belfort, E France, 88 m. ENE of Dijon; pop. 45,625; commands pass (Belfort Gap, *q.v.*) bet. Vosges and Jura Mts.; manufactures iron wire, sheet iron, clocks, hats, leather. Ceded to France by Austria 1648; fortified by Vauban; unsuccessfully besieged by Allies 1814; besieged by Germans 1870–71; the only·part of Alsace left to France after cession of 1871.
Belfort, Ter′ri′toire′ de (tĕ′rē′twȧr′ dē). Department of France. See *Table* at FRANCE.
Bel′fort Gap (bĕl′fôr găp′); *Fr.* **Trou′ée′ de Bel′fort′** (trōō′ā′ dē bĕl′fôr′; bā′fôr′). Pass bet. Vosges and Jura Mts., E France, through which passes historic route from Saône valley to the Rhine; highest point 1158 ft. In World War II seized by Germans June 17, 1940; occupied by American and French forces Aug.–Sept. 1944.
Bel·fort′ Ro′xo (bĕl·fôr′ rō′shōō). Village, Rio de Janeiro state, SE Brazil, ab. 10 m. NW of Rio de Janeiro.
Belgard. See BIAŁOGARD.
Bel·gaum′ (bĕl·goum′). **1** Former district, Southern Division, Bombay, W Indian Union; 4527 sq. m.
2 Town, its ✳, 240 m. SSE of Bombay, now in Mysore state; pop. (1941) 58,319; trade center noted for its hand-loom weaving.
Bel′gian Con′go (bĕl′jăn [-jĭ·ăn] kŏng′gō); *Fr.* **Con′go′ belge** (kôn′gō′ bĕlzh′); *Flem.* **Bel′gisch Con′go** (bĕl′gĭs kông′gō). *Earlier* **Congo Free State.** Former Belgian colony, S cen. Africa; became (as **Republic of the Congo**) independent 1960; 895,348 sq. m.; pop. (1957) 13,290,700; ✳ Kinshasa; formerly included trust territory of Belgian East Africa (Ruanda-Urundi). Bounded on NW and N by Equatorial Africa, on NE by Sudan and Uganda, on E by Tanganyika Territory and Lake Tanganyika, on SE and S by Northern Rhodesia, and on SW by Angola; its W extremity forms narrow corridor along lower Congo with less than 25 m. of coast line on the Atlantic. A tropical country, crossed by the equator in N cen. part; occupies greater part of Congo river basin. *Chief tributaries of Congo* (upper course known as the Lualaba): Ubangi (on NW and N border), Aruwimi, Lindi, Lomami, Lukuga (outlet of Lake Tanganyika), Lulonga, Ruki, and Kasai. *Lakes:* Tanganyika and Mweru on E and SE borders, Kivu in E, Edward and Albert on NE border, Léopold II in W and Stanley Pool. Mostly low plateau, with marshes along Congo in NW. *Mountains:* Ranges in SE with several peaks ab. 6000 ft., higher ranges along W shore of Lake Tanganyika, and high mountains on E (highest point of Virunga group 14,786 ft., of Ruwenzori 16,791 ft.). Divided since 1966 into 12 provinces. *Chief towns:* Kinshasa, Lubumbashi, Coquilhatville, Kisangani, Boma, Luluabourg. *Chief products:* Rubber, palm oil, cotton, forest products; minerals, esp. copper, diamonds, gold, silver, uranium.
History: Territory developed by International Asso-

ciation of the Congo (1878) which was controlled by Leopold II of Belgium; Congo Free State, with Leopold as sovereign, established and recognized by Berlin Conference 1885; boundaries determined by Berlin Conference, treaties with Great Britain (1894 and 1914), and with France, Germany, and Portugal (see FRENCH EQUATORIAL AFRICA and ANGOLA); after international criticism of treatment of natives, annexed to Belgium 1908; divided into four provinces 1914; by negotiations with Great Britain and League (1919–23), granted mandate of Ruanda-Urundi (*q.v.*) which had been taken from Germany 1916; capital changed from Boma to Léopoldville 1923; exchanged small piece of territory in southwest with Portugal 1927; granted independence June 30, 1960.
Belgian East Africa. = RUANDA-URUNDI.
Bel′gi·ca (bĕl′jĭ·kȧ). Ancient country, NE Gallia; one of the five administrative areas into which Augustus and Tiberius divided Gaul; corresponds in part with modern Belgium.
Bel′gium (bĕl′jŭm; -jĭ·ŭm); *Fr.* **Bel′gique′** (bĕl′zhēk′); *Flem.* **Bel′gi·ë** (bĕl′gē·ĕ). Constitutional monarchy, NW Europe; bounded on NW (ab. 65 m. of coast line) by the North Sea, on N by Netherlands, on E by Germany, on SE by the duchy of Luxembourg, and on S and W by France; 11,774 sq. m.; pop. 9,026,778; ✳ Brussels; divided into the following 9 provinces (for pronunciation of their names, see their individual entries):

NAME	LOCATION	AREA[1]	POP.[1]	CAPITAL
Antwerp	N	1,104	1,247,675	Antwerp
Brabant	cen.	1,267	1,755,942	Brussels
East Flanders	NW cen.	1,147	1,200,121	Gent
Hainaut	SW	1,436	1,214,101	Mons
Liège	E	1,525	870,447	Liège
Limburg	NE	929	427,740	Hasselt
Luxembourg	SE	1,705	217,721	Arlon
Namur	S	1,413	352,173	Namur
West Flanders	NW	1,248	971,472	Brugge

[1] Area is in sq. m. Pop. is 1941 est.

Chief rivers: Schelde and its tributaries (Lys, Dender, Senne, Rupel) in W cen. part and the Meuse in E and SE (also as boundary in NE along Maastricht prov. of Netherlands); chief tributaries of the Meuse: Sambre, Ourthe, Amblève; extensive canal system connects many of the streams. Mostly plain with wooded hill region (Ardennes) in S; chief port on North Sea is Oostende, but Antwerp near mouth of Schelde has much greater trade. *Chief cities:* Brussels, Antwerp, Gent, Liège, Mechelen, but many other towns, now declined in importance, were great cities in medieval times: Bruges (now Brugge), Louvain (Leuven), Courtrai (Kortrijk), Ypres (Ieper), Tournai. An important industrial and commercial country, but industrialization has been at expense of agriculture; before World War II iron and steel production was high; other lines of importance were textiles, diamond cutting, glassware; has two coal regions.
History: Inhabited in ancient times by Belgae, a people of Celtic stock, who were conquered by Caesar 57 B.C.; Belgica, a Roman province, erected by Augustus; invaded by Germanic peoples, including the Franks who incorporated territory in their kingdom; part of Carolingian kingdom of Lotharingia (see LORRAINE); except for duchy of Flanders which became dependency of France, attached to medieval empire as duchy of Lower Lorraine; broke up into semi-independent territories, such as Brabant, Limburg, Luxembourg (*qq.v.*); by 1484, territories of Netherlands, of which future Belgium was a part, gradually united into Burgundian state which passed to Hapsburgs 1477; the center of European commerce in 16th cent. (see ANTWERP); allotted to Spanish Hapsburgs 1555; basis of modern Belgium laid in southern Catholic provinces, reclaimed from revolt against Spain and split from northern Protestant provinces after

BELGIUM AND LUXEMBOURG

Statute Miles

0   10   20   30

Longitude East from Greenwich

Union of Utrecht 1579 (see NETHERLANDS); Artois, Lille, Maubeuge, and Cambrai lost to France in 17th cent.; Spanish Netherlands became Austrian 1713; overrun by French 1792 (see JEMAPPES) and incorporated in France 1801; reunited to Holland as independent kingdom of the Netherlands 1815; after revolt begun in 1830, recognized (by treaties of 1831 and 1839) as independent kingdom of Belgium, its neutrality guaranteed by the Great Powers; received half of duchies of Limburg and Luxembourg; under Leopold II, Congo Free State in personal union with Belgium 1885 and annexed in 1908 (see BELGIAN CONGO); invasion by Germany 1914 the occasion of British entrance into World War I; in peace treaty 1919, awarded Moresnet, Eupen-et-Malmédy, and mandate of Ruanda-Urundi (qq.v.); by treaty with England and France 1926, abrogated former status of neutrality; in World War II invaded May 1940 and occupied by Germans; cen. and E part overrun by Allied armies Sept. 1944; Battle of the Bulge in E Dec. 1944–Jan. 1945; formed customs union with Netherlands and Luxembourg 1947.

Bel'go·rod (byĕl'gŭ·rŭt), *also* **Byel'go·rod.** City, S Kursk Region, Soviet Russia, Europe, on upper Donets river and on railroad 50 m. N of Kharkov; pop. ab. 26,000; built on a hill of chalk; trades in chalk, lumber, soap, leather. Of ecclesiastical importance in 17th cent. and later a fortified point in conflicts with the Tatars. Held by Germans in World War II 1941–42; scene of bitter fighting Feb.–Mar. 1943; retaken by Russians Aug. 5, 1943.

Bel'go·rod–Dnes·trov'ski (-d'nyĕs·trôf'skĭ); *formerly* **Ak·ker·man'** (ŭk·kĕr·mán'); *Romanian* **Ce·ta'tea Al'bă** (chĕ·tä'tyä äl'bä); *anc.* **Ty'ras** (tĭ'răs). City, Izmail Region, SW Ukraine, U.S.S.R., on right bank of Dniester estuary 28 m. SE of Odessa; pop. 33,495; has shallow harbor but considerable trade in salt, fish, wool, tallow, and especially in wine; a well-built city with

beautiful gardens and old fortifications. On site of old Milesian colony of Tyras (founded 7th cent. B.C.); held by Macedonians and Romans; in medieval times under control of Tatars and Genoese, and in 1484 captured by Turks; seized several times by Russians who finally acquired it by treaty 1826; became a Romanian town 1918, a port of Bessarabia; ceded to the Soviet Union June 1940 but seized by Germans 1941; retaken by Russians 1944 and name changed 1946 from Akkerman.

Bel'grade (bĕl'grād; bĕl'grād'); *Serbian* **Be'o·grad** (bĕ'ô·gräd). **1** Former county, E Yugoslavia kingdom; 93 sq. m.; pop. 291,738; ⊗ Belgrade; incorporated 1945 in federated republic of Serbia in republic of Yugoslavia. **2** *anc.* **Sin'gi·du'num** (sĭn'jĭ·dū'nŭm). Industrial city, ✳ of Yugoslavia and of the federated republic of Serbia (since 1945), on right bank of Danube river where the Sava joins it; pop. (1931) 266,849; capital of former kingdom of Serbia and ⊗ (1929–45) of former Belgrade co.; an important transportation and communications center.

History: Roman fortification, Singidunum; destroyed by Avars 6th cent. A.D.; held by Avars to 9th cent., Bulgars in 10th, Byzantines from 11th to 13th, and by Serbs in 14th cent.; saved from siege by Turks when Hunyadi defeated them nearby 1456 (see HUNGARY); captured by Suleiman the Magnificent (see OTTOMAN EMPIRE) 1521; ceded to Austria 1718 by Treaty of Passarowitz and recovered by Turks in Peace of Belgrade 1739; in 19th cent. capital of independent principality of Serbia (q.v.); bombardment by Turks 1862 the cause of forced withdrawal of Turkish garrisons 1867; in World War I captured and lost by Austrians 1914, held by Central Powers 1915–18; scene of proclamation of Kingdom of Serbs, Croats, and Slovenes of which it became capital (see YUGOSLAVIA). In World War II devastated and captured by Germans Apr. 13, 1941; retaken by Ukrainians and Yugoslavs Oct. 20, 1944.

Bel·gra′no (bĕl·grä′nṓ). **1** Peak 7526 ft. in NW Santa Cruz territory, S Argentina, NE of **Lake Belgrano.** **2** District of Buenos Aires (city), E Argentina.

Bel·gra′vi·a (bĕl·grä′vĭ·à; -grāv′yà). A fashionable residence district in the west end of London, centering at Belgrave Square.

Bel·ha′ven (bĕl·hā′vĕn). Town, Beaufort co., E North Carolina, on Pamlico Sound 38 m. NE of New Bern; pop. 2386; lumbering, fisheries.

Be′ling·ton (bē′lĭng·tŭn). City, Barbour co., N West Virginia, 8 m. NNW of Elkins; pop. 1528; coal mining.

Belitung or **Belitoeng.** See BILLITON.

Be·lize′ (bĕ·lēz′); *Span.* **Be·li′ce** (bä·lē′sä). **1** River ab. 150 m. long, British Honduras; rises in NE Guatemala and flows E into the Gulf of Honduras at Belize. **2** = BRITISH HONDURAS. **3** District, E British Honduras; 1623 sq. m.; pop. (1943 est.) 24,577. **4** Seaport, ✱ of district and of British Honduras; at mouth of Belize river; pop. (1943) ab. 18,000; trading center for colony, esp. in mahogany and logwood.

Beljak. See VILLACH.

Bel′knap (bĕl′năp). County in New Hampshire. See *Table* at NEW HAMPSHIRE.

Belknap Peak. Mountain 12,131 ft. on boundary bet. Piute and Beaver cos., SW cen. Utah.

Bell (bĕl). **1** Name of counties in two states of the U.S. See *Tables* at KENTUCKY and TEXAS. **2** Residential city, Los Angeles co., SW California, 5 m. S of Los Angeles; pop. 19,450; incorporated 1927.

Bel′la Coo′la River (bĕl′à kōō′là). Short stream in SW British Columbia, Canada; flows W into Burke Channel.

Bel·laire′ (bĕ·lâr′; bĕ-). **1** Village, ⊗ of Antrim co., NW Michigan; pop. 689. **2** City, Belmont co., E Ohio, on Ohio river 26 m. S of Steubenville; pop. 11,502; coal, clay, limestone deposits; manufactures glass, enamelware, stoves, caskets. **3** City, Harris co., Texas, entirely within city of Houston; pop. 19,872.

Bel·la′ry (bĕ·lä′rĭ). Town, SW Andhra Pradesh, S cen. India, 270 m. NW of Madras; pop. (1941) 56,148.

Belle Alliance, La. See LA BELLE ALLIANCE.

Bel′leau′ (bĕ′lō′). Village, Aisne dept., N France, 9 m. NW of Château-Thierry; pop. (1931) 193; American military cemetery (dedicated 1923).

Bel′leau′ Wood (bĕl′ō′; *Fr.* bĕ′lō′); *Fr.* **Bois de Bel′-leau′** (bwäd′ bĕ′lō′). Wood S of Belleau village, France; scene of battle June 6–25, 1918, in which five German divisions were defeated by 4th U.S. Marine Brigade, stopping German advance on Paris, but with heavy loss to the marines.

Belle′chasse′ (bĕl′shàs′). County, Quebec, Canada. See *Table* at QUEBEC.

Bel·leek′ (bĕ·lēk′). Parish and village, co. Fermanagh, Northern Ireland, on the Erne river; famous for its china.

Belle·fon′taine (bĕl·foun′t'n; -fŏn′-). City, ⊗ of Logan co., W Ohio, 30 m. N of Springfield; pop. 11,424; former site of Shawnee Indian village; settled 1806; in agricultural region; varied manufactures.

Bellefontaine Neighbors. City, St. Louis co., Missouri, N of St. Louis; pop. 13,650.

Belle′fonte (bĕl′fŏnt). **1** Town, New Castle co., N Delaware, on Delaware river NE of Wilmington; pop. 1536; **2** Industrial borough, ⊗ of Centre co., cen. Pennsylvania, 25 m. NNW of Lewistown; pop. 6088.

Belle Fourche (bĕl′ fōōsh′). **1** River ab. 350 m. long, NE Wyoming and W South Dakota; rises in NE Wyoming, flows NE and E into Cheyenne river in E Meade co., S.Dak. In S Butte co., S.Dak., flows through **Belle Fourche Reservoir,** used for irrigation and formed by **Belle Fourche Dam** (completed 1911, height 112 ft.) across Owl Creek, a N tributary. **2** City, ⊗ of Butte co., W South Dakota, on Belle Fourche river 25 m. N of Lead; pop. 4087; manufactures beet sugar, flour, bricks, creamery products.

Belle Glade (bĕl′ glād′). City, Palm Beach co., SE Florida, on SE shore of Lake Okeechobee; pop. 11,273; built 1925, laid waste by hurricane 1928, rebuilt.

Belle′-Île′-en-Mer′ (bĕ′lēl′äɴ·mâr′). Island in N Bay of Biscay, off S coast of Morbihan dept. (to which it belongs), NW France; 35 sq. m.; pop. (1931) 6063.

Belle Isle (bĕl′ īl′). Island ab. 15 sq. m. in Atlantic Ocean at entrance to Strait of Belle Isle; administratively part of Newfoundland; lighthouse.

Belle Isle, Strait of. Channel bet. N tip of Newfoundland and SE Labrador, 10 to 15 m. wide, connecting Gulf of St. Lawrence with Atlantic Ocean.

Belle Meade (bĕl′ mēd′). City, Davidson co., N cen. Tennessee; pop. 3082.

Bellenz. See BELLINZONA.

Belle Plaine (bĕl′ plān′). City, Benton co., E cen. Iowa, 34 m. W of Cedar Rapids; pop. 2923; pottery works.

Belle·rive′ (bĕl·rēv′). Residential suburb of Hobart, Tasmania, directly opp. on left bank of the Derwent.

Belle Ver′non (bĕl vûr′nŭn). Borough, Fayette co., SW Pennsylvania, on Monongahela river 24 m. SSE of Pittsburgh; pop. 1784; settled 1791; coal, glass, steel.

Belle′ville (bĕl′vĭl). **1** Industrial city, ⊗ of St. Clair co., SW Illinois, 14 m. SE of East St. Louis; pop. 37,264; in coal-mining region; manufactures boilers, nails, agricultural implements, stoves; Scott Field (*q.v.*) nearby. **2** City, ⊗ of Republic co., N Kansas, 17 m. N of Concordia; pop. 2940; in agricultural section. **3** Town, Essex co., NE New Jersey, on Passaic river 4 m. N of Newark; pop. 35,005; an old Dutch settlement of 17th cent., originally known as Second River section of Newark; became separate community 1839; manufactures brass and copper, wire cloth, rubber tires, chemicals, brick, etc. **4** Industrial city, ⊗ of Hastings co., SE Ontario, Canada, on Bay of Quinte 47 m. W of Kingston; pop. 19,519; founded 1790; good harbor; trades in lumber and is in fine dairying section; produces much cement. Seat of Albert College (founded 1857), an affiliate of Univ. of Toronto, and of Ontario School for the Deaf.

Belle′vue′ (bĕl′vū′). **1** Town, Jackson co., E Iowa, on Mississippi river 20 m. SSE of Dubuque; pop. 2181; pottery works. **2** City, Campbell co., N Kentucky, on Ohio river just above Newport; pop. 9336; a suburb of Covington, Ky., and Cincinnati, Ohio. **3** City, Sarpy co., E Nebraska, on Missouri river 8 mi. S of Omaha; pop. 8831; oldest town in Nebraska; on site of fur-trading post; missionary station 1833. **4** City, Huron and Sandusky cos., N Ohio, 14 m. SSW of Sandusky; pop. 8286; settled 1815; limestone quarries; farm implements, automobile accessories. **5** Borough, Allegheny co., SW Pennsylvania, on Ohio river; pop. 11,412; residential suburb of Pittsburgh. **6** City, King co., Washington, E of Seattle; pop. 12,809.

Bell′flow′er (bĕl′flou′ẽr). City, Los Angeles co., California, N of Long Beach; pop. 45,909.

Bell Gardens. Urban community (unincorporated), Los Angeles co., California, NW of Downey; pop. 26,467.

Bel′li′court′ (bĕ′lē′kōōr′). Commune, Aisne dept., N France, 8 m. N of Saint-Quentin; pop. 716; in World War I part of Hindenburg Line, taken by Americans Sept. 29, 1918. American military cemetery.

Bel′ling·ham (bĕl′ĭng·hăm). **1** Town, Norfolk co., E Massachusetts, 19 m. SE of Worcester; pop. 6774; birthplace of William T. Adams ("Oliver Optic"). **2** Commercial and industrial city, ⊗ of Whatcom co., NW Washington, on **Bellingham Bay** ab. 18 m. S of Canadian border; pop. 34,688. Settled 1852 as Whatcom and became ⊗ 1854; incorp. with adjoining town of Fairhaven 1890 and named Fairhaven; merged with New Whatcom and renamed Bellingham 1903. Port of call for steamers; coal mining; lumbering; salmon fisheries, fruit and salmon canneries. Western Washington State College (1893; coed.).

Bel'lings·hau'sen Sea (běl'ĭngz·hou'z'n). Inlet of South Pacific Ocean on coast of Antarctica; extends along coast from Alexander I Island to Thurston Penin., ab. long. 75° to 98°W and bet. 70° and 72°S.

Bel·lin·zo'na (bâl·lēn·tsō'nä; *Angl.* běl'ĭn·zō'nà); *Ger.* **Bel'lenz** (běl'ĕnts). Commune, ✳ of Ticino canton, SE cen. Switzerland, near Ticino river 92 m. SE of Bern; pop. (1941) 10,948; railroad junction. Fortified in Roman times; to city of Como 1231, to Milan 1396, to Swiss Confederation 1503.

Belli Quadrum. See BEAUCAIRE.

Bell Island (běl). **1** Island in Atlantic Ocean, off NE coast of Newfoundland, 50°45'N.
2 Island in Conception Bay, Newfoundland, W of city of St. John's; pop. (1942 est.) 6300; rich in iron deposits.

Bell'mawr' (běl'mär'). Borough, Camden co., New Jersey, SW of Camden; pop. 11,853.

Bell'mead' (běl'mēd'). City, McLennan co., Texas, NE suburb of Waco; pop. 5127.

Bell'more (běl'mōr). Urban community (unincorp.), Nassau co., SE New York, on Long I.; pop. 12,784.

Bel'lo (bā'yŏ). Town, Antioquia dept., NW Colombia; pop. 8180.

Bello Horizonte. See BELO HORIZONTE.

Bel·lo'na (bě·lō'nà). Small island ab. 110 m. S of Guadalcanal and ab. 20 m. WNW of Rennell I. in SE Solomon Is., W Pacific Ocean.

Bellovacum. See BEAUVAIS.

Bel'lows Falls (běl'ōz). Industrial village, in Rockingham town, Windham co., SE corner of Vermont, on Connecticut river 21 m. N of Brattleboro; pop. 3831; settled 1753; manufactures paper, farm machinery.

Bell Rock. See INCHCAPE ROCK.

Bell Sound (běl). Large inlet on SW coast of West Spitsbergen I., Svalbard.

Bel·lu'no (bâl·lōō'nô). **1** Province of Italy. See *Table* at ITALY.
2 Commune, its ✳, Venezia Euganea, NE Italy, on Piave river 50 m. NW of Venice; pop. 25,547; cathedral; manufacturing and trade center. Became Roman 180 B.C.; in middle ages became Lombard duchy and later a Frankish countship; part of Venetian Republic 1420–1797; occupied by Austro-German forces 1917.

Bell'ville (běl'vĭl). **1** City, ⊗ of Austin co., SE cen. Texas; pop. 2218.
2 Town, SW Cape Province, Union of South Africa, 12 m. ENE of Cape Town; pop. 3027.

Bell Vil'le (bězh vē'zhä). Town, Córdoba prov., N cen. Argentina, 120 m. W of Rosario; pop. (est.) 24,038.

Bell'wood (běl'wŏŏd). **1** Residential village, Cook co., NE Illinois, 13 m. W of Chicago; pop. 20,729.
2 Borough, Blair co., S cen. Pennsylvania, 8 m. NNE of Altoona; pop. 2330; coal mines; farming.

Bel'ly (běl'ĭ). River ab. 75 m. long, SW Alberta, Canada; rises in Glacier National Park, Montana, and flows NNE to Oldman river E of Macleod.

Bel'mar (běl'mär). Borough, Monmouth co., E cen. New Jersey; pop. 5190; seashore resort; fishing.

Bél'mez (běl'māth; -mäs). Commune, Córdoba prov., S Spain, 35 m. NW of Córdoba; pop. 10,440.

Bel'mond (běl'mŏnd). City, Wright co., N cen. Iowa, 28 m. SW of Mason City; pop. 2506; beet-sugar plant.

Bel'mont (běl'mŏnt). **1** County in Ohio. See *Table* at OHIO.
2 City, San Mateo co., W California, 10 m. SSE of San Francisco; pop. 15,996.
3 Town, Middlesex co., NE Massachusetts, 7 m. WNW of Boston; pop. 28,715; residential suburb of Boston.
4 Village Mississippi co., SE Missouri, 15 m. S of Cairo, Illinois; scene of battle Nov. 7, 1861 in which Gen. Grant's attacking force was driven back by Confederate forces under Gen. Leonidas Polk.
5 Village, ⊗ of Allegany co., SW New York; pop. 1146.
6 City, Gaston co., SW North Carolina, 7 m. E of Gastonia; pop. 5007; manufactures yarn, hosiery, dyes.

Belna. See BEAUNE.

Be·loeil' (bě·lû'y'). Town, Verchères co., S Quebec, Canada, on Richelieu river NE of Montreal; pop. 2992.

Beloe More. See WHITE SEA.

Be'lo·e O'ze·ro (byě'lŭ·yě ô'zyĭ·rŭ) *or* **Byel·o'ze·ro** (byĭ·lô'zyĭ·rŭ). Lake (*ozero*) 433 sq. m. in W Vologda Region, Soviet Russia, Europe; outlet to Rybinsk Reservoir by Sheksna river; along its W and S shores is a part of the Mariinsk Canal System (*q.v.*).

Be'lo Ho·ri·zon'te (bâ'lô·rě·zōNn'tě), *formerly* **Bel'lo Ho·ri·zon'te.** City, ✳ of Minas Gerais state, in S cen. part, E Brazil, 376 m. N of Rio de Janeiro; pop. (1940 est.) 179,770; alt. ab. 3000 ft.; excellent climate; region important for cotton and cattle and diamond cutting.

Be·loit' (bě·loit'). **1** City, ⊗ of Mitchell co., N cen. Kansas, on Solomon river 51 m. NW of Salina; pop. 3837; trading center in agricultural section.
2 Industrial city, Rock co., S Wisconsin, on Rock river on Illinois border; pop. 32,846. Beloit Coll. (1846; coed.). Indian mounds nearby.

Be'lo·morsk' (běl'ô·môrsk'; *Russ.* byĭ·lŭ·môrsk'); *formerly* **So·ro'ka** (sŭ·rô'kà). Seaport town on W coast of Onega Bay, SW White Sea, E Karelia, U.S.S.R., on railroad S of Kem; exports lumber.

Be'lo·retsk' (běl'ô·rětsk'; *Russ.* byĭ·lŭ·ryětsk'). Town, E Bashkir Republic, Soviet Russia, Europe, on Belaya river in Southern Ural Mts.; pop. ab. 20,000.

Belorussia. Var. of BYELORUSSIA.

Belostok. See BIAŁYSTOK.

Belovar. Variant of BJELOVAR.

Bel·pas'so (bâl·päs'sô). Commune, Catania prov., E Sicily, on S slope of Mt. Etna; pop. 10,281; rebuilt just N of older town destroyed by lava in 1669.

Bel'per (běl'pēr). Urban district, Derbyshire, N cen. England, on the Derwent 8 m. N of Derby; pop. 15,716.

Bel'pre (běl'prě). Village, Washington co., SE Ohio, on Ohio river 10 m. SSW of Marietta; pop. 5418; Blennerhassett I. nearby.

Bel'sen, *in full* **Ber'gen-Bel'sen** (běr'gěn·běl'zěn). Locality in NW Germany, in Lower Saxony ab. 12 m. NNW of Celle; site of Nazi concentration camp taken by Allies Apr. 14, 1945.

Belt, Great *and* **Little.** See GREAT BELT, LITTLE BELT.

Bel·ter'ra (bâl·těr'rà). Town, Pará state, NE Brazil, on right bank of Tapajoz river near its confluence with the Amazon; ab. 26 m. S of Santarém; one of the Ford rubber plantations. Cf. FORDLANDIA.

Bel'ton (běl't'n). See WEST GLACIER.
2 Town, Anderson co., NW South Carolina, 9 m. E of Anderson; pop. 5106; cotton mills.
3 City, ⊗ of Bell co., cen. Texas, W of Temple; pop. 8163; Mary Hardin-Baylor College (1845; women).

Bel·tram'i (běl·trăm'ĭ). County in Minnesota. See *Table* at MINNESOTA.

Belts'ville (bělts'vĭl). Village, Prince Georges co., Maryland, ab. 12 m. NE of Washington; principal experiment station, U.S. Department of Agriculture.

Bel'tsy (byěl'tsĭ); *Romanian* **Băl'ți** (bûlts; bûl'tsě). Town, N cen. Moldavian Republic, U.S.S.R., on a W tributary of the Dniester 70 m. NW of Kishinev; pop. 30,667; formerly in Romania.

Beluchistan. Variant of BALUCHISTAN.

Be·lu'kha (byĭ·lōō'kà), *also* **Bye·lu'kha.** Highest peak 15,157 ft. in the Altai mountain system, on border bet. Kazakh S.S.R. and Oirot Autonomous Region, Soviet Russia, Asia.

Bel'vi·dere (běl'vĭ·dēr). **1** City, ⊗ of Boone co., N Illinois, 15 m. E of Rockford; pop. 11,223.
2 Town, ⊗ of Warren co., NW New Jersey, on Delaware river 11 m. NNE of Phillipsburg; pop. 2636.

Bel·yan'do (běl·yăn'dō). River ab. 250 m. long, E Queensland, NE Australia; flows N along E slope of Eastern Highlands to join Burdekin river.

Bel·zo'ni (běl·zō'nĭ). City, ⊗ of Humphreys co., W Mississippi, 28 m. SW of Greenwood; pop. 4142.

Be·midj′i (bĕ·mĭj′ĭ). City, ⊗ of Beltrami co., N Minnesota, 28 m. S of Lower Red Lake; pop. 9958, summer resort; manufactures lumber, cement, bricks, woolen goods. Bermidji State College (1913; coed.).

Bemis Heights. See SARATOGA.

Be′na Be′na (bā′nà bā′nà). Village, E cen. part of North-East New Guinea, ab. 90 m. NW of Lae; held by Japanese in World War II.

Ben–a–Bhuird (bĕn′à·bōōrd′). Mountain 3924 ft. on N border of W Aberdeen co., NE Scotland.

Benacus, Lacus. See Lake GARDA.

Ben′a·dir′ (bĕn′à·dīr′). Coast region, S Somalia, E Africa; its chief town is Mogadishu.

Ben Al′der (bĕn ôl′dĕr). Mountain 3757 ft., N cen. Scotland, on W side of Loch Ericht, SE Inverness co.

Be·na′res (bĭ·nä′rĕs; -rĕz) or **Ba·na′ras** (bà·nä′ràs) or **Va·ra′na·si** (vä·rä′nà·sĭ). **1** Division, SE United Provinces of Agra and Oudh, N Indian Union; 9460 sq. m.; pop. (1941) 5,545,257.

2 earliest name **Ka′si** (kä′sē). City, its ✳, now in SE Uttar Pradesh, on Ganges river 400 m. WNW of Calcutta; pop. (1941) 255,744. One of India's most ancient and picturesque cities; maintains numerous marts and bazaars; manufactures include silk brocades, gold filigree work, lacquered toys, beaten-brass vessels, gold and silver thread, and jewelry. Holy City of the Hindus and the object of constant pilgrimages; also sacred to Jains, Sikhs, and Buddhists, and it is said that Buddha preached his first sermon here in the Deer Park. Has 1500 temples and large mosques; among its most famous structures are the Bisheshwar or Golden Temple, the Mosque of Aurangzeb, and the Durga Kund, a Maratha temple. Seat of a Hindu university, the first private sectarian university established by law in India.

3 Former Indian state, SE United Provinces, N Indian Union, in two parts along the Ganges near Benares; 866 sq. m.; pop. (1941) 451,428; ✳ Ramnagar.

Be′nas, Ras (räs bä′näs). Var. of Cape BANAS.

Ben′a·vi′des (bĕn′à·vē′dĕs). City, Duval co., S Texas, 60 m. W of Corpus Christi; pop. 2459, oil and gas wells; sulfur mines; clay pits.

Ben Av′on (bĕn ăv′ŭn). Borough, Allegheny co., SW Pennsylvania, on Ohio river 7 m. NW of Pittsburgh; pop. 2553; suburb of Pittsburgh.

Ben A′von (bĕn än′). Mountain 3843 ft., NE cen. Scotland, in SW Aberdeen co. on boundary of Banff co.

Benbaun. See Twelve Pins of BUNNABEOLA.

Ben·bec′u·la (bĕn·bĕk′û·là). Island ab. 8 m. long of the Outer Hebrides, bet. the islands of North Uist and South Uist, off NW coast of Scotland; in Inverness co.

Ben′bon·yath′e (?bĕn′bŏn·yäth′ĕ), **Mount.** Peak 3470 ft. in Flinders Range, E South Australia.

Ben Cleuch. See OCHIL HILLS.

Ben·coe′len (bĕn·kōō′lĕn; bĕng-). Var. of BENKOELEN.

Ben Cru′a·chan (krōō′à·hän). Mountain 3689 ft. in N Argyll co., W Scotland, SE of Loch Etive.

Bend (bĕnd). Industrial city, ⊗ of Deschutes co., cen. Oregon, on Deschutes river 95 m. E of Eugene; pop. 11,936; center of recreational region.

Ben Da′vis Point (bĕn dā′vĭs). Point on SW coast of Cumberland co., SW New Jersey, in Delaware Bay.

Ben Dearg or **Ben Derg** (bĕn jĕr′ĕk). Mountain 3547 ft. in Ross and Cromarty co., N Scotland, SE of Loch Broom.

Benderabbas. See BANDAR ABBAS.

Ben·de′ry (byĕn·dyĕ′rĭ) or **Ben·der′** (Turk. bĕn·dĕr′); Romanian **Ti·ghi′na** (tĕ·gē′nä). Town, Moldavian S.S.R., U.S.S.R., near right bank of the Dniester in its lower course 30 m. SE of Kishinev; pop. 31,698; on rail line bet. Kishinev and Odessa; has some industrial plants and a trade in timber, fruits, and tobacco. Genoese trading town in 12th cent.; controlled by many different peoples down to 18th cent.; site of fortress erected 1558 by Suleiman the Magnificent; headquarters of Charles XII for his campaign in Russia 1709 and place

where he was held prisoner 1712–14; became part of Bessarabia, Romania, 1918; ceded to Russia 1940; held by Axis powers 1941–44.

Ben′di·go (bĕn′dĭ·gō); formerly **Sand′hurst** (sănd′hûrst). City, cen. Victoria, SE Australia, 80 m. NNW of Melbourne; pop. 25,342; founded 1851; important mining and market center. One of earliest places where alluvial gold was discovered (1851).

Bendin or **Bendzin.** See BĘDZIN.

Ben Dou′ran (bĕn dōōr′ăn) or **Ben Do′ran** (dōr′ăn). Mountain 3523 ft. in Grampian Mts., NE Argyll co., W Scotland.

Be′ne·dikt·beu′ern (bā′nà·dĭkt·boi′ĕrn). Village, S Upper Bavaria, SW Germany, on railroad 30 m. S of Munich in N foothills of Alps; pop. (1925) 1470; noted Benedictine monastery founded 733 where was discovered 13th-cent. MS., the Carmina Burana, a collection of goliardic songs, now in Munich.

Be′ne·fac′tor′ (bā′nà·fàk·tôr′). Province of Dominican Republic. See Table at DOMINICAN REPUBLIC.

Beneharnum. See BÉARN.

Ben′e·lux (bĕn′ĕ·lŭks). The countries of Belgium, Netherlands, and Luxembourg—from their initial letters—so-called since formation of customs union 1947.

Be·ne·ven′to (bā·nà·věn′tō; Angl. bĕn′ĕ·věn′tō). **1** Province of Italy. See Table at ITALY.

2 anc. **Mal′e·ven′tum** (măl′ĕ·věn′tŭm), changed euphemistically by Romans to **Ben′e·ven′tum** (bĕn′ĕ·věn′tŭm). Commune, its ✳, Campania, S Italy, at confluence of Calore and Sabbato rivers 34 m. NE of Naples; pop. 37,865; antiquities include a 9th-cent. Lombard-Saracenic cathedral and the Porta Aurea (Ital., golden gate), a triumphal arch of Trajan, erected 114 A.D.; manufactures gold and silver plate, leather, parchment.

History: Ancient town of the Samnites; became Roman colony 268 B.C.; became seat of Lombard duchy of Benevento 571 A.D.; fell to Saracens and later to Normans; under papal control through most of its modern history; made principality by Napoleon 1806 and conferred upon Talleyrand; under papal control 1815 until its unification with the kingdom of Italy 1860.

Ben′e·wah (bĕn′ĕ·wä). County in Idaho. See Table at IDAHO.

Ben′field·side (bĕn′fēld·sīd). Former urban district, Durham, N England, on the Derwent 13 m. SW of Newcastle; since 1937 part of Consett.

Ben′fleet (bĕn′flēt). Urban district, Essex, SE England, on inlet of Thames estuary 29 m. E of London; pop. 19,881.

Ben·gal′ (bĕn·gôl′; bĕng·gôl′; attributively usu. Ben′gal), earlier **Bengal Presidency.** Former province, NE Brit. India, 77,442 sq. m., pop. (1941) 60,306,525; ✳ Calcutta; included geographically Indian states of Tripura and Cooch Behar, 5370 sq. m., pop. (1941) 1,153,852; total area 82,812 sq. m., pop. (1941) 61,460,377. Bounded on N by Sikkim and Bhutan, on E by Assam and Burma, on S by Bay of Bengal, and on W by Bihar and part of Eastern States. Most of S part known as Sundarbans, occupied by delta of Ganges and Brahmaputra (see GANGES DELTA); S ranges of Himalayas in N and hills in Chittagong and Tripura in SE. Staple crop rice, with some tobacco, hemp, tea; jute the most important manufacture. Chief cities Calcutta, Howrah, Dacca, Chittagong, Kharagpur, Darjeeling.

History: Ancient Hindu region introduced to Buddhism by Asoka 3d cent. B.C.; northeast part of older Bengal (see MAGADHA and BIHAR) nucleus of Maurya and Gupta empires; conquered by an Afghan ruler, Mohammed of Ghor (see GHOR), c. 1199; eastern Bengal made province under Tughlak dynasty 1324; Bengal under independent dynasty 1338–1539; in 1576 taken from Afghans by Moguls; first visited by factors of English East India Co. 1633; Calcutta (q.v.) founded by English 1690 and Bengal made a presidency 1699; soon after Clive's victory at Plassey (q.v.) 1757 came to be

under the Company's financial and military control; seat of authority of governor-general 1774–1834; Eastern Bengal and Assam separated from Bengal province 1905, but restored in 1912 when the whole was constituted as new presidency; made autonomous province 1937 (see BRITISH INDIA); divided Aug. 15, 1947 into East Bengal, now part of Pakistan, and West Bengal, part of Indian Union (see these terms for former divisions and districts of Bengal assigned to each).

Bengal, Bay of. Part of Indian Ocean bet. E India and W coasts of Burma and the Malay Penin.

Ben·ga′si (bĕn·gä′zē) or **Ben·ga′zi**, also **Ben·gha′zi.**
1 Former province of N (Italian) Libya, N Africa; 58,684 sq. m.; pop. (1936) 96,193; ✷ Bengasi.
2 anc. **Ber′e·ni′ce** (bĕr′ĕ·nī′sĕ). Coastal city, ✷ of Cyrenaica and of Bengasi prov., Libya, on NE shore of Gulf of Sidra 350 m. W of Egypt; pop. (1938 est.) 64,641. Under Italian administration developed as seaport and naval and air base; center of colonization of Italian North Africa, esp. after 1938. In World War II Italian supply base; captured by British Feb. 7, 1941, by Germans Apr. 4, 1941; again taken by British Dec. 25, 1941; given up Jan. 28, 1942, retaken Nov. 20, 1942.

Bengawan. See SOLO river.

Beng·ka′lis (bĕng·kä′lĭs). **1** Island, E Sumatra, Indonesia, at S end of Strait of Malacca.
2 Town and fishing port on W side of island ab. 120 m. W of Singapore; pop. 3291.

Bengkoelen, Bengkulu. See BENKOELEN.

Ben′go (bĕng′gō), **Bay of.** Inlet of Atlantic Ocean on NW coast of Angola, W Africa; Luanda is on it.

Ben′gore Head (bĕn′gōr; bĕng′-). Cape, E of Giant's Causeway, co. Antrim, NE Ireland.

Ben·guel′a (bĕn·gĕl′à; bĕng′-), also **Ben·guel′la.**
1 Province, W Angola, SW Africa, along the coast.
2 Seaport town, W Angola; pop. (1934) ab. 6000; railroad terminus; exports beeswax, maize, cattle, hides. Fort built here 1587; town founded 1617.

Benguela, or **Benguella, Current.** A cold ocean current moving northward along the W coast of southern Africa.

Ben′gué′rir′ (băn′gā′rēr′). Town, W cen. Morocco, NW Africa, ab. 45 m. NNE of Marrakesh on railroad and highway to Casablanca.

Ben·guet′ (bĕng·gĕt′). Subprovince, S Mountain Province, N Luzon, Phil. Is., in mountainous region of S Cordillera Central and Caraballo Mts.; 987 sq. m.; pop. 115,339; ✷ La Trinidad; agriculture; gold mining. Formed by Spanish as a military district (comandancia) 1846; made subprovince 1908. Baguio, its most important town, administered separately.

Ben′ha (bĕn′hà). City, ✷ of Qalyubîya prov., Lower Egypt; pop. (1937) 28,922; on railroad E of the Damietta branch of the Nile ab. 28 m. N of Cairo.

Ben Hill (bĕn hĭl′). County in Georgia. See Table at GEORGIA.

Be′ni (bā′nĕ). **1** River over 1000 m. long in N and cen. Bolivia; rises in E cordillera of Andes in Cochabamba dept., flows N to unite with Mamoré river and form Madeira river; near its mouth receives large tributary from the W, the Madre de Dios.
2 better **El Beni** (ĕl). Department of Bolivia. See Table at BOLIVIA.

Be′ni-Ab·bès′ (bă′nē·äb·bĕs′). Town, W Southern Territories, Algeria, near Morocco border ab. 390 m. SSW of Oran; outpost station.

Be·ni′cia (bĕ·nē′shà). City, Solano co., cen. California, on N shore of Carquinez Strait 18 m. NNE of Oakland; pop. 6070; fishing, canning, manufacture of dredging machinery; U.S. Army Arsenal. Founded 1848; capital of California 1853–54; chartered as city 1861.

Be′ni Ha′san (bā′nē hä′sän). Village on Nile river, Egypt, 75 m. N of Asyût; site of rock tombs (XIIth dynasty, c. 2000 B.C.).

Be·nin′ (bĕ·nĭn′; -nēn′; bĕ-). **1** Formerly part of Upper

Guinea, bet. the Volta river and Rio del Rey, including all of Slave Coast and the Niger delta region.
2 Name formerly given by French to their possessions on the Guinea coast including Dahomey.
3 River more than 100 m. long, S Nigeria, flowing into Bight of Benin; connects with W part of Niger delta.
4 Province of Nigeria: see Table at NIGERIA. Former native kingdom, one of the most highly organized of the Negro states of West Africa before the coming of the Portuguese 1485; exerted great influence in 17th cent., then known to Europeans as **Great Benin;** control taken over by British 1897–99.

Benin, Bight of. Widemouthed bay in N section of the Gulf of Guinea, W Africa.

Benin City. Town, Nigeria, ✷ of Benin prov., in W delta of the Niger ab. 150 m. E of Lagos; pop. ab. 15,000; a flourishing place in 17th and 18th cents.

Be′ni–Saf′ (bă′nē·säf′). Seaport and commune NW Oran dept., NW Algeria, ab. 50 m. SW of Oran; pop. (commune) 11,819; exports iron ore.

Be′ni Su·ef′ (bă′nē·sŏŏ·wāf′). **1** Province, N Upper Egypt. See Table at EGYPT.
2 City, its ✷, on W bank of Nile 22 m. SE of El Faiyûm; pop. (1937) 45,492; trade center; cotton manufacture.

Ben′ja·min (bĕn′jà·mĭn). City, ⊗ of Knox co., N Texas; pop. 338.

Ben′kel·man (bĕng′kĕl·măn). Village, ⊗ of Dundy co., S Nebraska; pop. 1400.

Ben·koe′len or **Ben·ku′len** (bĕn·kŏŏ′lĕn; bĕng-) or **Beng·koe′len** (bĕng-) or **Beng·ku′lu** (bĕng·kŏŏ′lŏŏ).
1 Former residency of Neth. Indies, on the SW coast of Sumatra; 10,132 sq. m.; pop. 323,123; ✷ Benkoelen; comprised the elevated region of the S Barisan Mts. and a narrow coastal strip.
2 Town, its ✷, a port in 3°48′S, ab. 350 m. NW of Djakarta; pop. 13,418. Settlement established by British 1684 and fort built a few years later; in early years a center of pepper and spice trade; ceded to Dutch 1824 in exchange for Malacca.

Ben Laoigh (bĕn lŭ′ĭ). = BEN LUI.

Ben Law′ers (bĕn lô′ĕrz). Mountain 3984 ft., NW of Loch Tay, Perth co., cen. Scotland.

Benld (bĕ·nĕl[d]′; bĕn′ĕl[d]′). City, Macoupin co., SW cen. Illinois, 26 m. NE of Alton; pop. 1848.

Ben Led′i (bĕn lĕd′ĭ). Mountain 2875 ft. in SW Perth co., cen. Scotland, NE of Loch Katrine.

Ben Lo′mond (bĕn lō′mŭnd). **1** Mountain 10,900 ft., Utah, just N of Ogden.
2 Mountain ab. 5000 ft. in NE New South Wales, SE Australia; highest in New England range.
3 Mountain 5160 ft., NE Tasmania, bet. the North and South Esk rivers; highest point in Tasmania.
4 Mountain 3192 ft. on E side of Loch Lomond, Stirling co., S cen. Scotland; dominating peak of the region.

Ben Lu′i (bĕn lŏŏ′ĭ). Mountain 3708 ft. on border bet. Perth and Argyll cos., cen. Scotland, N of Ben Lomond.

Ben Mac·dhu′i (bĕn′ măk·dŏŏ′ĭ), also **Ben Muich-dhu′i.** Mountain 4296 ft. in NE cen. Scotland, bet. Aberdeen and Banff cos.; one of the Cairngorm group.

Ben More (bĕn mōr′; mồr′). **1** Mountain 3169 ft. in cen. part of the island of Mull off W coast of Scotland.
2 Mountain 3843 ft. in SW Perth co., cen. Scotland.
3 Mountain 3273 ft. in Sutherland co., N Scotland.

Ben′net Island (bĕn′ĕt; -ĭt). Westernmost island of De Long group in Arctic Ocean, NE of New Siberian Is., 150°E; belongs to Yakutsk A.S.S.R.

Ben′nett (bĕn′ĕt; -ĭt). County in South Dakota. See Table at SOUTH DAKOTA.

Bennett, Lake. Lake, the W arm of Tagish Lake, on border bet. British Columbia and Yukon Territory, Canada, N by E of Chilkoot Pass; station on its shores was active town during the Klondike rush.

Ben′netts·ville (bĕn′ĕts·vĭl; -ĭts-). City, ⊗ of Marlboro co., NE South Carolina, 30 m. N of Florence; pop. 6963; manufactures yarn, tire fabrics, lumber, etc.

Ben Ne′vis (bĕn nĕ′vĭs; nĕv′ĭs). Peak 4406 ft. in Grampian Mts., W cen. Scotland, in Inverness co. E of N end of Loch Linnhe; highest peak in Great Britain.

Ben′ning·ton (bĕn′ĭng·tŭn). **1** County in Vermont. See *Table* at VERMONT.

2 Village in Bennington town (pop. 13,002), a ⊗ of Bennington co., SW corner of Vermont, 31 m. W of Brattleboro; pop. 8023; manufactures textiles, knit goods, paper, knitting machinery; Bennington Coll. (founded 1925, opened 1932; women). Chartered by New Hampshire 1749, settled 1761; claimed by both New York and New Hampshire before Vermont became state; during the Revolution an important supply base for Continental Army; battle of Bennington fought nearby Aug. 16, 1777 in which Americans under Gen. Stark defeated Col. Baum, in command of a raiding force from Gen. Burgoyne's army. See HOOSIC FALLS, N.Y.

Be·no′ni (bĕ·nō′nĭ). Town, S Transvaal, NE Republic of So. Africa, in the Witwatersrand 20 m. E of Johannesburg; pop. 77,760; mining center with some of the richest gold mines in the world; important industrial town.

Bénoué. See BENUE.

Ben′rath (bĕn′rät) *or* **Benrath am Rhein** (äm rīn′). Former commune, Rhine Province, Prussia, Germany, on Rhine river; since 1929 part of city of Düsseldorf.

Bens′berg (bĕns′bĕrK). Mining commune, W Germany, in former Rhine Province, Prussia, 10 m. ENE of Cologne; pop. 12,632; ironworks.

Ben′sen·ville (bĕn′s'n·vĭl). Village, Du Page co., NE Illinois, 18 m. WNW of Chicago; pop. 9141.

Bens′heim (bĕns′hīm). City, Starkenburg prov., Hesse, Germany, 16 m. S of Darmstadt; pop. 10,067.

Ben′son (bĕn′s'n). **1** County in North Dakota. See *Table* at NORTH DAKOTA.

2 Town, Cochise co., SE corner of Arizona, 42 m. ESE of Tucson; pop. 2494.

3 City, ⊗ of Swift co., W Minnesota, 26 m. N of Montevideo; pop. 3678; agriculture and dairying.

4 Town, Johnston co., E North Carolina, 28 m. S of Raleigh; pop. 2355.

Benson *or* **Ben′sing·ton** (bĕn′sĭng·tŭn). Parish and village, SE Oxfordshire, cen. England, on the Thames; scene of battle 777 A.D. in which Offa of Mercia defeated Cynewulf of Wessex.

Ben Sta′rav (bĕn stä′räv). Mountain 3541 ft., N Argyll co., W Scotland, E of Loch Etive.

Bent (bĕnt). County in Colorado. See *Table* at COLORADO.

Ben′tinck Island (bĕn′tĭngk; -tĭk). Island, cen. Mergui Archipelago (q.v.).

Bent′ley·ville (bĕnt′lĭ·vĭl). Borough, Washington co., SW Pennsylvania, 23 m. S of Pittsburgh; pop. 3160; coal.

Bent′ley with Ark′sey (bĕnt′lĭ, ärk′sĭ). Urban district, West Riding, Yorkshire, N England; pop. 19,826.

Ben′ton (bĕn′t'n). **1** Name of counties in nine states of the U.S. See *Tables* at ARKANSAS, INDIANA, IOWA, MINNESOTA, MISSISSIPPI, MISSOURI, OREGON, TENNESSEE, WASHINGTON.

2 City ⊗ of Saline co., cen. Arkansas, 20 m. SW of Little Rock; pop. 10,399; founded 1836; furniture.

3 City, ⊗ of Franklin co., S Illinois, 25 m. S of Mount Vernon; pop. 7023; coal mining, farming.

4 City, ⊗ of Marshall co., W Kentucky, 22 m. SE of Paducah; pop. 3074; tobacco, corn, strawberries.

5 Village, ⊗ of Bossier parish, NW Louisiana; pop. 1336.

6 Town, ⊗ of Scott co., SE Missouri; pop. 554.

7 Town, ⊗ of Polk co., SE Tennessee; pop. 638.

Benton Harbor. City, Berrien co., SW corner of Michigan, on Lake Michigan 48 m. WSW of Kalamazoo; pop. 19,136; manufactures foundry products, automobile accessories, ships; seat of the communistic religious colony known as the House of David (organized 1903).

Benton Heights. Urban community (unincorporated), Berrien co., Michigan, NE of Benton Harbor; pop. 6112.

Ben′ton·ville (bĕn′t'n·vĭl; *Sou. also* -v'l). **1** City, ⊗ of

Benton co., NW corner of Arkansas, 22 m. N of Fayetteville; pop. 3649; founded 1837.

2 Village, Johnston co., cen. North Carolina, 37 m. SE of Raleigh; indecisive battle Mar. 19, 1865 bet. Confederates under Johnston and left wing of Sherman's army.

Be′nue (bā′nwā) *or* **Bin′ue** (bĭn′wā) *or* **Bé′noué′** (bā′nwā′). **1** River ab. 870 m. long in W Africa, chief tributary of Niger river from E; rises in N Cameroun, flows W across E cen. Nigeria.

2 Province of Nigeria. See *Table* at NIGERIA.

Ben Ve·nue′ (bĕn′ vĕ·nōō′; -nū′). Mountain 2393 ft. in SW Perth co., cen. Scotland, just S of Loch Katrine.

Ben Vor′lich (bĕn vôr′lĭK). Mountain 3224 ft., S Perth co., cen. Scotland, S of Loch Earn.

Ben′wood (bĕn′wŏŏd). City, Marshall co., N West Virginia, on Ohio river 3 m. S of Wheeling; pop. 2850; coal mining, steel industries.

Ben Wyv′is (bĕn wĭv′ĭs; wē′vĭs). Mountain 3429 ft. in E Ross and Cromarty co., N Scotland.

Ben′-y-Gloe′ (bĕn′ĭ-glō′). Mountain 3671 ft. in NE Perth co., cen. Scotland.

Ben′zie (bĕn′zĭ). County in Michigan. See *Table* at MICHIGAN.

Be′o (bā′ō). See TALAUD ISLANDS.

Beograd. See BELGRADE.

Bep′pu (bĕp′ōō; *Jap.* bĕp·pŏŏ). City, on **Beppu Bay** (an arm of W end of Inland Sea), NE Kyushu I., Japan, in Oita prefecture; pop. 93,033; hot springs.

Be′quia (bĕk′wā). An island of the Grenadines, E West Indies, S of St. Vincent; pop. 1870; administratively a part of St. Vincent.

Be·rar′ (bā·rär′). Division of former Central Provinces and Berar, cen. India, in SW part N of Hyderabad; 17,809 sq. m.; pop. (1941) 3,604,866; ✳ Amraoti; divided into six districts; crossed by Ajanta Range; bordered on E by Wardha river and on S by the Penganga. Founded 1484, one of the five Mohammedan kingdoms of the Deccan (q.v.); lasted until 1572 when it became part of Mogul Empire; overrun by Marathas near end of 17th cent.; with help of Wellesley, territory west of Wardha river acquired by ruler of Hyderabad; taken over by British government as Assigned Districts of Hyderabad 1853; transferred to administration of Central Provinces 1903. In Madhya Pradesh 1947–56; in Bombay state 1956–60; in Maharashtra since 1960.

Be·rat′i (bĕ·rät′ĭ) *or* **Be·rat′** (bĕ·rät′). **1** Prefecture, S cen. Albania; 1518 sq. m.; pop. 142,616.

2 *anc.* **An′ti·pat′ri·a** (ăn′tĭ·păt′rĭ·à; -pā′trĭ·à). Town, Berati prefecture, ab. 30 m. NE of Vlona; pop. 10,403.

Berau. See VOGELKOP.

Beraun. 1 River. See BEROUNKA.

2 Town. See BEROUN.

Ber′ber (bûr′bĕr). **1** Former province, NE Anglo-Egyptian Sudan, now in Northern Province, Sudan.

2 Town, SE Northern Province, Sudan, on E bank of the Nile river ab. 30 m. N of Ed Damer; pop. (1938 est.) 10,000; in earlier days starting point for caravans going across the Nubian Desert to Suakin; taken by the Mahdists 1884, not recovered until 1897.

Ber′be·ra (bûr′bĕr·à). Seaport, Somalia, in former British Somaliland, E Africa, on S shore of Gulf of Aden; pop. varies bet. 15,000 in the hot season and 30,000 in the cool season.

Ber′bé′ra·ti′ (*Fr.* bĕr′bā′rá·tē′). Town, N Congo Republic (formerly Middle Congo); highway junction.

Ber·bice′ (bûr·bēs′). **1** River ab. 300 m. long in E British Guiana; flows N into Atlantic Ocean near New Amsterdam; navigable for 125 m.

2 County, E British Guiana; 16,920 sq. m.; pop. (1931) 75,919; ⊗ New Amsterdam.

Ber′chem (bĕr′Kĕm). Commune, Antwerp prov., N Belgium; pop. (1938 est.) 45,576; S suburb of Antwerp.

Berch′tes·ga′den (bĕrK′tĕs·gä′dĕn). Town, SE Bavaria, Germany, in E Bavarian Alps ab. 10 m. S of Salzburg; pop. 3772; resort (alt. 1889 ft.); site of villa

built as hide-out for Hitler to which he often retired during World War II; scene of important conferences. Bombed by Allies Mar. 1945 and occupied May 7.

Berck (bĕrk). Commune, Pas-de-Calais dept., N France, on English Channel NW of Arras; pop. 16,700; resort.

Ber·di'chev (byĕr·dyĕ'chĕf). City, S Zhitomir Region, W cen. Ukraine, U.S.S.R., 22 m. S of Zhitomir; pop. 66,306; railroad junction; center of district that trades in farm products, iron and wooden wares, and fish. Assigned to Lithuania 1546 by treaty; later Polish; captured by Russia 1768. Held by Germans 1941–44.

Berdyansk, Berdiansk. See OSIPENKO.

Be·re'a (bĕ·rē'ȧ). **1** City, Madison co., E cen. Kentucky, 28 m. E of Danville; pop. 4302. Berea College (1855; coed.).

2 City, Cuyahoga Co., N Ohio, 12 m. SW of Cleveland; pop. 16,592, greenhouses for scientific growing of vegetables. Baldwin-Wallace College (1845; coed.).

3 Variant of BEROEA.

Bere·ha'ven or **Bear'ha'ven** (bâr'hȧ'vĕn; also **Cas'·tle·town·bere'** (kȧs''l·toun·bâr'), officially **Cas'tle-town Bear'ha'ven.** Small town, co. Cork, SW Eire, on N coast of Bantry Bay; pop. 728; has fine harbor partly enclosed by **Bere Island** (bâr); formerly used as a British naval base.

Be're·ho'vo (bĕ'rĕ·hô'vô); Hung. **Be'reg·szász** (bĕ'rĕg·säs), Russ. **Be·re·go'vo** (byĭ·ryĕ·gô'vŭ). Town, formerly in Carpathian Ruthenia prov., E Czechoslovakia, ab. 15 m. S of Mukachevo; pop. (1930) 19,026; a Hungarian town included 1918 in Czechoslovakia; returned to Hungary 1939–45; now in U.S.S.R.

Ber'e·ni'ce (bĕr'ĕ·nī'sĕ). **1** Ruined city, SE Egypt, on a bay of the Red Sea; ancient seaport sheltered on N by point of land (mod. Cape Banas); founded by Ptolemy II 3d cent. B.C.

2 See BENGASI city; CIRENAICA.

Beres'ford (bĕrz'fĕrd). City, Lincoln and Union cos., SE South Dakota, 35 m. S of Sioux Falls; pop. 1794; dairy, stock, grain, poultry farms.

Be·res·tecz'ko (bĕ'rĕs·tĕch'kô). Village, NW Ukraine, U.S.S.R., ab. 30 m. S of Lutsk; disastrous defeat July 1, 1651 of Cossack hetman Bogdan Chmielnicki by Poles.

Be'ret·tyó (bĕ'rĕ·tyō). River ab. 150 m. long, E Hungary and W Romania; rises in W Transylvania, flows W and SW to the Körös.

Be·ret·tyó·új'fa·lu (bĕ'rĕ·tyō·ōō'y'·fŏ·lŏŏ). Commune, E Hungary, S of Debrecen; pop. ab. 9000.

Be·re'zi·na (byĕ·ryä'zyĭ·nȧ). River 350 m. long in White Russia, U.S.S.R.; flows SE into Dnieper river W of Gomel; connects by canal with Dvina river. Battle fought at the crossing of the river near Borisov Nov. 26–28, 1812 by Napoleon's army in the retreat from Moscow, when three Russian armies inflicted enormous losses on it. In World War II scene of fierce fighting July 3–8, 1944 during German advance on Smolensk.

Be·rez'ni·ki (byĭ·ryôz'nyĭ·kĭ). City, cen. Molotov Region, Soviet Russia, Europe (politically, in Asia; see SIBERIA), at foot of W slope of Ural Mts. on left bank of Kama river; pop. 63,575; industrial city.

Be·re'zo·vo (byĕ·ryô'zŭ·vŭ), formerly **Be·re'zov** (-zŭf). Town, NW Khanty-Mansi National District, Soviet Russia, Asia, on left bank of lower Ob where Sosva joins it; pop. 4706; established as Cossack trading post 1593; place of exile.

Berg (bĕrκ). Former duchy on the Rhine E of Cologne, Germany; ab. 1120 sq. m.; bounded on N by duchy of Cleve and on W by Jülich; made countship 1108, became duchy 1380, associated with Jülich 1423, with Cleve 1511; became part of Prussia 1815. See DÜSSELDORF.

Ber'ga·ma (bĕr'gä·mä'). Town, İzmir vilayet, W Turkey in Asia, 58 m. N of İzmir; pop. 14,839. See PERGAMUM.

Ber'ga·mo (bĕr'gä·mô). **1** Province of Italy. See Table at ITALY.

2 anc. **Ber'go·mum** (bûr'gŏ·mŭm). Commune, its *,

Lombardy, N Italy, in foothills of Alps 30 m. NE of Milan; pop. 86,043; 12th-cent. Romanesque cathedral, ancient walls; industrial and commercial center. Settled by Gauls; became Roman municipium under Caesar; destroyed by Attila; became Lombard duchy; fell to Milan 1264; ruled by the Visconti of Lombardy 1296–1428, by Venetian Republic 1428–1797; conquered by Napoleon 1796; under Austrian rule 1814–59.

Ber'ge·dorf (bĕr'gĕ·dôrf). Section of Hamburg, Germany, on branch of Elbe river; observatory. Made a city 1275; belonged to Lübeck and Hamburg 1420–1868; became part of Hamburg 1938.

Ber'gen (bûr'gĕn). County in New Jersey. See Table at NEW JERSEY.

Ber'gen (bĕr'κĕ[n]). See MONS.

Ber'gen (bĕr'gĕn) or **Bergen auf Rü'gen** (ouf rü'gĕn). Chief town of island of Rügen, Germany; pop. 4598.

Ber'gen (bär'gĕn; Angl. bûr'-). Seaport city, SW Norway, constituting a county (see Table at NORWAY), and itself ⊗ of Hordaland co.; pop. 98,303, (1938 est.) 106,500; 2d largest city in Norway; exports fish and imports coal, grain, iron, and foodstuffs; manufactures cordage, paper, pottery, and alcohol. Founded 1070; N outpost of Hanseatic League in 15th and 16th cents.; cathedral dating from 13th cent. Occupied by Germans Apr. 9, 1940 and held until end of World War II.

Ber'gen·field (bûr'gĕn·fēld). Borough, Bergen co., NE corner of New Jersey, 9 m. E of Paterson; pop. 27,203; manufactures clothing, pianos, machinery.

Ber'gen op Zoom (bĕr'κĕn ôp zōm'). Commune, North Brabant prov., S Netherlands, at mouth of small stream (Zoom) on Schelde estuary; pop. (1939) 25,343; formerly strongly fortified; fisheries, potash refineries, iron foundries; manufactures ceramics; shipping center.

Bergen–Belsen. See BELSEN.

Ber'ge·rac' (bĕr'zhē·råk'). Commune, Dordogne dept., SW cen. France, on Dordogne river 25 m. SSW of Périgueux; pop. 18,902; fine 19th-cent. Gothic church; varied manufactures. Captured by English 1345 and fortified; taken by French 1450.

Ber'gisch Glad'bach (bĕr'gĭsh glät'bäκ). Industrial city, W Germany, in former Rhine Province, Prussia, 9 m. NE of Cologne; pop. 18,192; summer resort.

Bergomum. See BERGAMO.

Bergues (bĕrg). Town, Nord dept., N France, ab. 5 m. S of Dunkerque; pop. 3756; built as a frontier fortress and often besieged in Flemish wars.

Ber·ha'la Strait (bĕr·hä'lä). Channel bet. the island of Singkep, Lingga Archipelago, and the E cen. coast of Sumatra, Indonesia.

Ber'ham·pore (bĕr'ȧm·pōr). Town, cen. West Bengal, NE Indian Union, on left bank of Bhagirathi river 110 m. N of Calcutta; pop. 27,403; founded as military station 1767; scene of first overt act of Sepoy Mutiny 1857. Includes remnant of **Cos'simba'zar** (kä'sĭn·bä'zär), a city formerly important.

Ber'ham·pur (bĕr'ȧm·pŏŏr). Town, cen. Orissa state, E Indian Union, 100 m. SW of Cuttack and ab. 9 m. from the sea; pop. 37,750; exports sugar. Kallikota College.

Be'ring (bēr'ĭng; bĕr'-; bâr'-; Dan. bā'rĕng), or **Be'rin·ga** (byä'ryĭn·gȧ). Island. See KOMANDORSKIE ISLANDS.

Bering Sea. Part of North Pacific Ocean; 878,000 sq. m.; greatest depth 13,422 ft.; enclosed on E by mainland of Alaska, on SE and S by Aleutian Is., on SW by Kamchatka Penin., and on NW by E Siberia; connects by Bering Strait with Arctic Ocean; contains St. Lawrence I., Nunivak I., Pribilof Is. (all American) and Komandorskie Is. (Russian); latter two groups famous as fur-seal breeding grounds; receives Yukon river; crossed diagonally by International Date Line. Explorations of its waters and of Bering Strait 1728 and 1741 by Danish navigator Vitus Bering in employ of Russia formed chief basis for Russian claims to Alaska. Bering Sea Controversy bet. Great Britain and U.S. 1886–93 settled by

court of arbitration at Paris 1893 in favor of Great Britain, denying U.S. the right to prohibit pelagic hunting of fur seals in Bering Sea.

Bering Strait. Strait ab. 56 m. wide connecting Arctic Ocean and Bering Sea (*q.v.*), and separating Asia (U.S.S.R.) from North America (Alaska); Diomede Is. (*q.v.*) in middle. Traversed by Vitus Bering 1728.

Ber′ja (bĕr′hä). Commune, Almería prov., SE Spain, 20 m. W of Almería; pop. 12,476; viticulture; lead mining; metal and textile industries.

Berke′ley (bûrk′lĭ). **1** Name of counties in two states of the U.S. See *Tables* at SOUTH CAROLINA and WEST VIRGINIA.

2 Residential and industrial city, Alameda co., W California, on San Francisco Bay N of Oakland; pop. 111,268; manufactures food products, soaps, engines, serums, vaccines, inks, foundry products. Univ. of California (1855); Armstrong Coll. (1918; coed.). Founded 1853, incorporated as city 1909; most of N section of city destroyed by fire 1923 and since rebuilt.

3 City, St. Louis co., E Missouri, NW suburb of St. Louis; pop. 18,676; incorporated as a city 1937.

4 (*pron. also* bärk′lĭ) Plantation on left bank of the James river, Charles City co., E Virginia, at **Har′rison's Landing** (här′ĭ·s'nz); birthplace of Benjamin Harrison, signer of the Declaration of Independence, and of William Henry Harrison, 9th president of the U.S.; plundered by Benedict Arnold 1781; base for Union army after Malvern Hill.

Berkeley Springs; *legal name* **Bath** (båth). Town and health resort, ⊗ of Morgan co., NE West Virginia, near Potomac river 18 m. NW of Martinsburg; pop. 1138; mineral springs; chartered 1776.

Berkhampstead. = GREAT BERKHAMPSTEAD.

Berk′ley (bûrk′lĭ). Residential city, Oakland co., SE Michigan, 12 m. SSE of Pontiac; pop. 23,275; in the Detroit suburban area.

Ber·ko′vi·tsa *or* **Ber·ko′vi·ca** (bĕr·kô′vė·tsä). Town, Vrattsa dept., NW cen. Bulgaria; pop. (1926) 5961.

Berks. 1 (bûrks) County in Pennsylvania. See *Table* at PENNSYLVANIA.

2 (bärks; bûrks) = BERKSHIRE, England.

Berk′shire (bûrk′shĭr; -shēr). County in Massachusetts. See *Table* at MASSACHUSETTS.

Berk′shire (bärk′shĭr; -shēr; *rarely, in England,* bûrk′-) *or* **Berks** (bärks; bûrks). County, S England; 725 sq. m.; pop. (1951) 402,939; ⊗ Reading; largely in the Thames river basin; agriculture and livestock raising (Berkshire hogs).

Berkshire Hills (bûrk′-), *commonly* **Berk′shires** (-shĭrz; -shērz). Range in Berkshire co., W Massachusetts; highest peak Mount Greylock 3505 ft.

Bêrlad. See BÂRLAD.

Ber·len′gas (bĕr·lāng′gàsh). Group of small islands off W coast of Portugal, lat. 39°25′N; lighthouse.

Ber′lin (bûr′lĭn). **1** Industrial town, S Hartford co., cen. Connecticut, 11 m. SSW of Hartford; pop. 11,250.

2 City, Coos co., N New Hampshire, in White Mts., at confluence of Dead and Androscoggin rivers 17 m. S of Umbagog Lake; pop. 17,821; manufactures paper, woodfiber string, wood pulp, artificial leather; U.S. government fish hatchery nearby; winter sports.

3 Borough, Camden co., SW New Jersey, 15 m. SE of Camden; pop. 3578.

4 Borough, Somerset co., S Pennsylvania, 28 m. S of Johnstown; pop. 1600; farm and dairy products.

5 Manufacturing city, Green Lake and Waushara **cos.**, cen. Wisconsin, 20 m. W of Oshkosh; pop. 4838.

6 (bûr·lĭn′; bĕr·) = KITCHENER, Canada.

7 Town, SE Cape Province, S Union of South Africa, 20 m. WNW of East London; pop. 1429; resort.

Ber·lin′ (bûr·lĭn′; bĕr·lĭn′; *often* bûr′lĭn *before an accented syllable, as in* "*Ber′lin, Germany*"; *Ger. pron.* bĕr·lēn′). **1** Former province of Prussia. See *Table* at PRUSSIA.

2 Commercial, industrial, and administrative city, in former Prussia, Germany, on the Spree river 163 m. SE of Hamburg; pop. (1939) 4,332,242, (1950) 3,336,475; before 1945, coextensive with Berlin prov. and Greater Berlin, ✳ of Prussia and of Germany. Before World War II (1939), 4th largest city in the world; one of leading financial and industrial cities of world; famous structures and institutions included the Marienkirche, the Imperial Palace, former Royal Palace (later a museum), the Opera House, Royal Guard House, the Schlossbrücke (bridge), Prussian State Library, Old Royal Library (later part of university), the Rathaus or Town Hall, the Schauspielhaus (theater), the Brandenburg Gate, the Tiergarten and other fine parks, the university (founded 1810 by Frederick William III), most of these buildings being destroyed during World War II.

History: Kölln and Berlin, both Wendish villages, founded in early 13th cent.; member of Hanseatic League 14th cent.; united under name of Berlin, it became residence of Hohenzollerns and capital of Brandenburg (*q.v.*); from 1701 capital of kingdom of Prussia (*q.v.*); grew to be industrial and commercial center, especially under Frederick II (1740–86); entered by Austrians 1757 and by Russians 1760; occupied by French under Napoleon, who issued here the Berlin decree 1806; capital of German Empire 1871–1918, of Republic 1919–32, of Third Reich 1933–45; scene of Congress of Berlin 1878 and of Berlin Conference 1885; much of city destroyed by Allied bombing 1941 and 1943–45; occupied by Russians Apr.–May 1945; divided June 1945 into four occupation zones (American, British, French, and Russian); on setting up of independent governments in east and west Germany 1949, West Berlin became part of the West German Federal Republic (made a state 1950 but not yet formally incorporated), and East Berlin was made ✳ of the East German Democratic Republic.

Ber′lin (bûr′lĭn), **Mount.** Peak 9081 ft. in N Nye co., cen. Nevada.

Ber·lin′–Britz′ (bĕr·lēn′brĭts′), **Ber·lin′–Frie′de·nau** (-frē′dĕ·nou), **Ber·lin′–Tem′pel·hof** (-tĕm′pĕl·hôf), etc. Former suburbs, now parts of Berlin, Germany.

Ber·me′jo (bĕr·mĕ′hô). **1** River ab. 1000 m. long in N Argentina; rises on the Bolivian frontier and flows SE into Paraguay river on the Paraguay-Argentina boundary; its middle course known as the Teuco.

2 Town, Tarija dept., S Bolivia, on Argentine border.

Ber·me′o (bĕr·mā′ô). Commune, Vizcaya prov., N Spain, on Bay of Biscay 15 m. NE of Bilbao; pop. 11,739.

Bermondsey. Metropolitan borough of London. See *Table* at LONDON.

Ber·mu′da (bĕr·mū′dà), *also* **Bermuda Islands** *or* **Ber·mu′das** (-dàz); *formerly* **Som′ers Islands** (sŭm′-ẽrz). British colony comprising a group of about 360 islands (of which only some 20 are inhabited) about 640 m. ESE of Cape Hatteras in W North Atlantic Ocean ab. 32°14′ to 32°25′ N lat. and 64°38′ to 64°52′W long.; 19 sq. m.; pop. (1939) 30,814; principal island **Bermuda Island**, *also called* **Great Bermuda** *or* **Long Island;** ✳ Hamilton, on Bermuda I.

History: Visited by Spanish 1515 and named for Juan de Bermúdez; English called them Somers Islands after Sir George Somers who was forced to land there while on his way to Virginia 1609; first colonized by English (sent by members of Virginia Co.) on St. George's I. 1612; settled and governed under the Somers Island Co. 1615–84; taken over by Crown 1684; capital removed from St. George to Hamilton 1815; sites for military and naval bases leased to U.S. 1940.

Bermuda Hundred. Village, a settlement of Jamestown colony 1613, on peninsula, Chesterfield co., SE cen. Virginia, bet. James and Appomattox rivers; a Federal base in Grant's campaign against Richmond 1864.

Bern (bûrn; *Ger.* bĕrn) *or* **Berne** (bûrn; *Fr.* bĕrn). **1** Swiss canton. See *Table* at SWITZERLAND.

2 City, ✳ of Bern canton and of Switzerland, on Aare river 59 m. SW of Zurich; pop. (1941) 130,331; has three

fine bridges over Aare river; 15th-cent. Gothic cathedral, 15th-cent. Gothic town hall, hall of Swiss Federal Council, university (founded in 16th cent.; reorganized 1834), libraries; headquarters of Universal (or International) Postal Union (founded 1874); manufactures textiles, machinery, scientific instruments, chocolate.

History: Founded as military post by Duke Berchtold V of Zäringen 1191; became free imperial city 1218; achieved final independence 1339; entered Swiss Confederation 1353 (see SWITZERLAND); accepted Reformation 1528; became powerful in 18th cent. when it ruled Vaud, Fribourg, Aargau, and the region of the Bernese Alps; after French occupation 1798, made member of Helvetic Republic; made capital of Switzerland 1848.

Ber·nal′ Hill (bŭr·näl′). Peak 7020 ft. in SW San Miguel co., NE cen. New Mexico.

Ber′na·lil′lo (bŭr′nà·lē′yō). 1 County in New Mexico. See *Table* at NEW MEXICO.

2 Town, ⊗ of Sandoval co., NW cen. New Mexico, on the Rio Grande 12 m. N of Albuquerque; pop. 2574. Approximate site of Coronado's headquarters 1540–42; settled 1698.

Ber′nam (bĕr′näm). River ab. 120 m. long on boundary bet. S Perak state and N Selangor, Federation of Malaya; flows W into the Strait of Malacca; navigable for steam launches for over 100 m.

Ber′nards·ville (bŭr′nĕrdz·vĭl). Borough, Somerset co., N cen. New Jersey, 8 m. SW of Morristown; pop. 5515.

Ber′nay′ (bĕr′nā′). Commune, Eure dept., France, 25 m. WNW of Évreux; pop. 7700; has important textile manufactures; annual horse fair; grew up around Benedictine Abbey (founded 1013).

Bern′burg (bĕrn′bŏŏrK). Manufacturing city, East Germany, on Saale river 22 m. W of Dessau; pop. 34,305. Fortified town in 10th cent.; capital of duchy of Anhalt-Bernburg. Site of bomber manufacturing plants, object of British and American air raids 1944–45.

Bern·cas′tel Cues (bĕrn′käs′tĕl kōōs′; bĕrn′käs′tĕl, kōō′ĕs), *formerly* **Bern·kas′tel.** Commune, W Germany, in former Rhine Province, Prussia, on the Mosel 21 m. NE of Trier; pop. 4507; white wine (Bernkasteler).

Berne. 1 (bûrn) City, Adams co., E Indiana, 32 m. S of Fort Wayne; pop. 2644; founded 1852 by Mennonite immigrants from Bern, Switzerland; official publishing house for the Mennonite General Conference.

2 (bûrn; *Fr.* bĕrn) See BERN, Switzerland.

Ber′ne·ray (bûr′nĕ·rā). See BARRA.

Ber′nese′ Alps (bûr′nēz′; -nēs′), **Bernese O′ber·land** (ō′bĕr·lănd′); *Ger.* **Ber′ner Al′pen, Berner O′ber·land′** (bĕr′nĕr äl′pĕn, ō′bĕr·länt′). See OBERLAND and *Table* at ALPS.

Ber·ni′ci·a (bûr·nĭsh′ĭ·à). Anglian kingdom of 6th cent. A.D., located bet. Tyne and Forth, with capital at Bamborough; united with Deira (*q.v.*) to form kingdom of Northumbria (*q.v.*).

Ber′ni·er (bûr′nĭ·ĕr). Island off W coast of Western Australia, at entrance to Shark Bay.

Ber·ni′na (bûr·nē′nä; *Angl.* bĕr·nē′nà). Southern extension of the Rhaetian Alps, on border bet. Italy and Switzerland; its highest peak and the highest in the Rhaetian Alps is **Piz Bernina** (pēts bĕr·nē′nä) 13,295 ft. on the Italian border but in Switzerland. **Bernina Pass** 7645 ft. is E of the peak.

Bernkastel. See BERNCASTEL CUES.

Be·roe′a (bē·rē′à). See (1) VEROIA, Greece; (2) BIRE, Palestine; (3) ALEP, Syria.

Be′roun (bĕ′rô·ōōn); *Ger.* **Be′raun** (bā′roun). Town, cen. Bohemia prov., W Czechoslovakia, ab. 17 m. WSW of Prague; pop. (1930) 13,143.

Be′roun·ka (bĕ′rô·ōōng·kà); *Ger.* **Be′raun** (bā′roun). River ab. 85 m. long in W Czechoslovakia; formed by union of several streams near Plzeň, flows E into Vltava river.

Ber′ra (bĕr′rä). Commune, Ferrara prov., Emilia, N Italy; pop. (1931) 10,875.

Berre, É′tang′ de (ä′tänd′ bĕr′). Lagoon 13 m. long and 3 to 8 m. wide, S Bouches-du-Rhône dept., S France, E of the Rhone; has narrow outlet to Gulf of Lions.

Ber′ri·en (bĕr′ĭ·ĕn). Name of counties in two states of the U.S. See *Tables* at GEORGIA and MICHIGAN.

Berrien Springs. Village, Berrien co., SW Michigan, 47 m. WSW of Kalamazoo; pop. 1953. Emmanuel Missionary College (1874; Seventh-Day Adventist).

Ber′ry′ *or* **Ber′ri′** (bĕ′rē′; *Angl.* bĕr′ĭ). Historical region of cen. France; bounded anciently on N by Orléanais, E by Nivernais, SE by Bourbonnais, SW by Marche, W by Touraine; ✳ Bourges. Originally inhabited by the Bituriges Cubi who opposed Vercingetorix; under Romans was part of Aquitania Prima; countship in Carolingian period; fell to Crown in 11th cent.; made duchy 1360; returned to French Crown 1601; province to 1789.

Ber′ry′–au–Bac′ (bĕ′rē′ō·bȧk′). Village, Aisne dept., N France, 11 m. NW of Reims; crossing of Aisne river here frequently of importance in World War I, esp. in Chemin des Dames battles 1917–18.

Ber′ry Islands (bĕr′ĭ). Group of small islands in the Bahamas, N of Andros I.; 14 sq. m.; pop. (1943) 403.

Ber′ry·ville (bĕr′ĭ·vĭl; *Sou. also* -v′l). 1 City, a ⊗ of Carroll co., NW Arkansas; pop. 1999.

2 Town, ⊗ of Clarke co., N Virginia; pop. 1645.

Ber′si·mis′ (bĕr′sē·mē′). River ab. 240 m. long, tributary of the St. Lawrence river in Quebec prov., Canada, flowing SSE; enters the St. Lawrence NE of Tadoussac.

Ber′thier′ (bĕr′tyä′). 1 County, Quebec, Canada. See *Table* at QUEBEC.

2 Town, its ⊗, on St. Lawrence river 37 m. WSW of Three Rivers; pop. 3325.

Ber′thoud Pass (bûr′thŭd). Mountain pass 11,315 ft., Clear Creek and Grand cos., N Colorado, in Front Range of the Rocky Mts.; ski runs; highway.

Ber·tie′ (bûr·tē′). County in North Carolina. See *Table* at NORTH CAROLINA.

Ber′tin·court′ (bĕr′tăn′kōōr′). Village, Pas-de-Calais dept., N France, ab. 6 m. E of Bapaume; pop. 866; fighting Mar. 1917 and Mar. 1918 in World War I.

Be′ru (bā′rōō). Island (atoll) 11 m. long at S end of Gilbert Is. S of the equator, W Pacific Ocean; pop. (1936) 2468; headquarters and school of missionaries.

Ber′wick (bûr′wĭk). 1 Town, St. Mary parish, S Louisiana, 53 m. S of Baton Rouge; pop. 3880; fishing center; oyster and shrimp works; shell deposits.

2 Town, York co., SW Maine, on New Hampshire border 25 m. SW of Biddeford; pop. 1557.

3 Industrial borough, Columbia co., E cen. Pennsylvania, on Susquehanna river 23 m. WSW of Wilkes-Barre; pop. 13,353; founded 1786; manufactures steel cars, silk, garments, foundry and machine-shop products.

Ber′wick (bĕr′ĭk) *or* **Ber′wick·shire** (-shǐr; -shēr). County, SE Scotland; area 457 sq. m.; pop. (1951) 25,060; ⊗ Duns; agriculture, livestock grazing, fisheries.

Ber′wick up·on′ Tweed (bĕr′ĭk, twēd′). Municipal borough, Northumberland, N England, on North Sea at mouth of the Tweed near Scottish border; pop. 12,550; herring and salmon fisheries; iron manufacturing.

Ber′wyn (bûr′wĭn). 1 Residential city, Cook co., NE Illinois, 10 m. W of Chicago; pop. 54,224.

2 Locality, Chester co., SE Pennsylvania, ab. 9 m. NE of West Chester.

Berwyn Mountains. Range in N Wales, along the border bet. Merionethshire and Montgomeryshire; highest point Moel Sych 2718 ft.

Berytus. See BEIRUT.

Be·san′çon′ (bē·zän′sôN′); *anc.* **Ve·son′ti·o** (vē·zŏn′shĭ·ō; -shō). Commercial and manufacturing city, ✳ of Doubs dept. (and, earlier, ✳ of Franche-Comté), E France, 47 m. E of Dijon; pop. 65,022; citadel by Vauban; university (founded 1485); Roman ruins, including triumphal arch of Marcus Aurelius, aqueduct, and amphitheater; extensive watch and clock industry. Captured by Julius Caesar 58 B.C.

Besi. See SANANA island.

Be·si·ka′ Bay (bĕ′sĕ·kä′). Roadstead bet. Asia Minor and the N end of Bozcaada (Tenedos) I.

Be·şik·taş′ (bĕ′shĕk·täsh′). District and suburb of İstanbul, Turkey in Europe, on the Bosporus NE of Beyoğlu; pop. 55,007.

Bes′kids, East and **West** (bĕs′kĭdz; bĕs·kēdz′). Mountain ranges, W Carpathians, on NE boundary of Czechoslovakia; highest peak Babia Góra, in West Beskids, 5659 ft.

Bes·ni′ (bĕs·nē′), formerly **Be′his·ni′** (bĕ′hĭs·nē′). Town, Gaziantep vilayet, S Turkey, in mountains 53 m. ENE of Maraş; pop. 8266.

Be·soe′ki (bȧ·sōō′kĕ) or **Be·su′ki** Former residency, East Java prov., Neth. Indies; 3913 sq. m.; pop. 2,083,309; ✻ Bondowoso; included E end of Java bet. Madura Strait on the N, Indian Ocean on the S.

Be·son′ti·um (bē·zŏn′shĭ·ŭm; -shŭm). Variant of Vesontio: see BESANÇON.

Bes′sa·ra′bi·a (bĕs′ȧ·rä′bĭ·ȧ; -räb′yȧ). 1 Region of SE Europe, bet. Dniester and Prut rivers extending from Black Sea N to Poland. In Roman times a part of the colony of Dacia; later a borderland overrun by barbarian migrations; named after Bassarab dynasty of Walachia, 14th cent. A.D.; became part of principality of Moldavia (q.v.) 1367; fought over by Turks and Russians 1711–1812; ceded by Turkey to Russia 1812; part yielded 1856 to Moldavia after Crimean War but most of it recovered by Russia 1878 by Treaty of Berlin; formed a government under Russia 1812–1917 (17,147 sq. m., pop. [c. 1910] 2,440,000; ✻ Kishinev). 2 Romanian **Ba′sa·ra′bia** (bä′sä·rä′byä). Former province, E Romania; 17,147 sq. m.; pop. 2,863,409; ✻ Chişinău (Kishinev). Proclaimed independence from Russia as Moldavian (Bessarabian) Republic 1917; joined Romania Apr. 9, 1918 and recognized as Romanian by Treaty of Versailles 1919 but still claimed by Soviet Union. Seized by Soviet Union June 27, 1940; with Bucovina incorp. Aug. 1940 as Moldavian Federal Soviet Republic (see MOLDAVIAN REPUBLIC), a part of the U.S.S.R., SW of the Ukraine. Retaken by Germans and Romanians June 1941; recovered by Russia 1944.

Bes′se·mer (bĕs′ĕ·mēr). 1 Manufacturing city, Jefferson co., Alabama, SW of Birmingham; pop. 33,054. 2 City, ⊗ of Gogebic co., NW upper Michigan penin., 5 m. E of Ironwood; pop. 3304; in iron-mining section. 3 Borough, Lawrence co., W Pennsylvania, 9 m. W of New Castle; pop. 1491.

Bessemer City. Town, Gaston co., SW North Carolina, 7 m. W of Gastonia; pop. 4017; cotton, tobacco.

Besuki. See BESOEKI.

Besztercze. See BISTRIȚA.

Beszterczebánya. See BANSKÁ BYSTRICA.

Beth′a·nie or **Beth′a·ny** (bĕth′ȧ·nĭ). Town, S South-West Africa, 130 m. E of Lüderitz; pop. ab. 1800.

Beth′a·ny (bĕth′ȧ·nĭ). 1 City, ⊗ of Harrison co., N Missouri, 43 m. NW of Chillicothe; pop. 2771. 2 City, Oklahoma co., cen. Oklahoma, 7 m. W of Oklahoma City; pop. 12,342; Bethany Nazarene College (1899; coed.; removed from Oklahoma City 1909). 3 Town, Brooke co., N West Virginia, ab. 12 m. NE of Wheeling; pop. 992. Bethany Coll. (1840; coed.). 4 Village, Palestine, on Mount of Olives ab. 2 m. E of Jerusalem on the Jericho road.

Beth′el (bĕth′′l). 1 Village, W Alaska, near mouth of Kuskokwim river; pop. 1258; U.S. airport. 2 Manufacturing town, N cen. Fairfield co., SW Connecticut; pop. 8200; hats. 3 Town, Oxford co. W Maine, 36 m. WNW of Lewiston; pop. 2408; in the Rangeley Lakes region; resort. 4 Village, Clermont co., SW Ohio; pop. 2019. 5 Borough, Allegheny co., Pennsylvania, S of Pittsburgh; pop. 23,650. 6 Town, Windsor co., E Vermont, ab. 16 m. NNW of Woodstock; pop. 1356.

Beth′el (bĕth′′l; bĕth′ĕl; bĕth′ĕl′). Ruined town, Palestine, ab. 11 m. N of Jerusalem; in early history of Israel considered a holy place (Gen. xii. 8; xxviii. 19).

Be·thes′da (bĕ·thĕz′dȧ). Residential district (pop. 56,527), Montgomery co., cen. Maryland; residential section for Washington, D.C.

Beth′–ho′ron (bĕth′hōr′ŏn; -hŏr′ŏn). Town in mountain pass, N Judaea, Palestine, ab. 11 m. NW of Jerusalem; in Old Testament times a strategical place where there were often conflicts (Josh. x. 11; 1 Kings ix. 17).

Bé′thin′court′ (bā′tăn′kōōr′). Village, Meuse dept., NE France, 6 m. NW of Verdun; held by Germans in siege of Verdun 1916–17.

Beth′le·hem (bĕth′lĕ·ĕm; -hĕm). 1 Town, Grafton co., W New Hampshire, ab. 5 m. SE of Littleton; pop. 898; settled 1787; summer resort; headquarters of American Hay Fever Assoc. 2 City, Lehigh and Northampton cos., E Pennsylvania, on Lehigh river 5 m. E of Allentown; pop. 75,408; manufactures steel, munitions, hosiery, iron products, silk, cigars, furnaces. Lehigh Univ. (1865); Moravian College (1742; coed.). Founded by Moravians 1741; housed hospital for Continental soldiers during Revolution; incorp. as borough 1845; became city 1917. Music center (home of annual Bach festival); chief center of Moravian sect in U.S. 3 Subdistrict, Jerusalem dist., cen. Palestine; 258 sq. m.; pop. 23,725, (1938 est.) 25,834. 4 Town, ✻ of Bethlehem subdist., Palestine, 5½ m. SW of Jerusalem; pop. (1944 est.) 8889. An ancient town of Judaea, the early home of David. Regarded by Christendom as the site of the Nativity. 5 Town, NE Orange Free State, E cen. Union of South Africa, 150 m. ENE of Bloemfontein; pop. 10,377; railroad center; large railroad shops and industrial plants; in fertile agricultural region; mountain scenery.

Bethnal Green. Metropolitan borough of London. See Table at LONDON.

Beth′page′ (bĕth′pāj′). Urban community (unincorporated), Nassau co., New York, in cen. Long I. S of Hicksville; pop. (incl. Old Bethpage) 20,515.

Beth·sa′i·da of Gal′i·lee (bĕth·sā′ĭ·dȧ, găl′ĭ·lē) or of **Gau′lo·ni′tis** (gô′lô·nī′tĭs), also **Bethsaida Ju′li·as** (jōō′lĭ·ăs; jōōl′yăs). Ruined town on NE side of the Sea of Galilee on E side of the river Jordan near where it enters the sea; was probably partly in Galilee.

Bethshean, Beth–shean. See BEISAN.

Beth′–she′mesh (bĕth′shē′mĕsh). Town, cen. Judaea, Palestine, ab. 24 m. W of Jerusalem; archaeological site; occupied by Hyksos ab. 1600 B.C. and later by Egyptians and Assyrians; often mentioned in the Bible.

Be·thu′lie (bĕ·tōō′lĕ). Town, S Orange Free State, E cen. Republic of So. Africa, near N bank of Orange river 100 m. S of Bloemfontein; pop. 3267.

Bé′thune′ (bā′tün′). Commune, Pas-de-Calais dept., N France, 17 m. NNW of Arras; pop. 20,073; coal mines. During World War I held by British and several times attacked, esp. Apr. 1918.

Be′ti·o (bā′tsĭ·ō; bāt′shĭ·ō; bā′shĭ·ō). Islet and village, S end of Tarawa (q.v.) atoll, Gilbert Is., W Pacific Ocean.

Bet′si·bo′ka (bĕt′sĭ·bō′kȧ). River, cen. Madagascar; flowing N into Bombetoka Bay.

Bet′ten·dorf (bĕt′′n·dôrf). Industrial city, Scott co., E Iowa, on Mississippi 5 m. E of Davenport; pop. 11,534.

Bet′ti·ah (bāt′tĭ·ȧ). Town, NW Bihar prov., NE Indian Union, 100 m. NNW of Patna; pop. 27,941.

Bet′tws y Coed (bĕt′ŭs ĭ koid′; bā′tōōs). Parish and urban district, Caernarvonshire, NW Wales; pop. 776; on the Conway river ab. 16 m. S of Llandudno in beautiful glen and river scenery; tourist and artist center.

Be′tul (bā′tōōl); formerly **Bad′nur** (bäd′nōōr). Town, NE Maharashtra, 95 m. NW of Nagpur; pop. 9614.

Bet′wa (bāt′wä). River 360 m. long, cen. India; rises in W Madhya Pradesh, flows NE and E into Jumna river near Hamirpur; feeds large irrigation system.

Beu′el (boi′ĕl); *formerly* **Vi′lich** (fē′lĭк). Manufacturing commune, W Germany, in the former Rhine Province, Prussia, on Rhine river opp. Bonn; pop. 17,543.

Beu′lah (bū′lȧ). Village, ⊗ of Benzie co., NW Michigan; pop. 436.

Beu′ron (boi′rôn). Village and monastery, Sigmaringen government dist., SW Germany, on the N bank of the Danube ab. 8 m. NE of Tuttlingen; pop. (1925) 600. Monastery founded 1077 by Augustinians, secularized 1802, taken over by Benedictines 1863; library.

Beuthen. See Bytom.

Be′ve·land (bā′vĕ·länt). Two islands, **North Beveland** (35 sq. m.; pop. 7536) and **South Beveland** (144 sq. m.; pop. 50,733), of the Netherlands, in Zeeland prov. in the estuary of the Schelde river, separated by narrow channel. In World War II South Beveland occupied by Allies Oct. 10–30, 1944.

Be′ve·ren (bā′vĕ·rĕ[n]). Commune, East Flanders prov., NW cen. Belgium, 6 m. W of Antwerp; pop. 12,312.

Bev′er·ley (bĕv′ēr·lĭ). Municipal borough, ⊗ of East Riding, Yorkshire, N England, 7 m. NNW of Hull; pop. 15,499; incorp. 1129; has two fine churches.

Bev′er·ly (bĕv′ēr·lĭ). **1** City, Essex co., NE corner of Massachusetts, 16 m. NE of Boston; pop. 36,108.
2 City, Burlington co., S cen. New Jersey, on Delaware river 13 m. NE of Camden; pop. 3400.

Beverly Hills. 1 Residential city, Los Angeles co., SW California, W suburb of Los Angeles; pop. 30,817.
2 Village, Oakland co., SE Michigan, S of Pontiac; pop. 8633.

Be′ver·wijk′ (bā′vēr·vīk′). Commune, North Holland prov., W Netherlands; pop. (1939) 21,272.

Bew·cas′tle (bū·kàs′'l). Village, Cumberland, NW England, 10 m. NE of Brampton; has remarkable cross of 7th (or 10th) cent., with runic inscriptions.

Bex (bĕ). Commune, Vaud canton, W Switzerland, near the Rhone SE of E end of Lake of Geneva; pop. 4433; salt mines, brine baths.

Bexar (bâr). County in Texas. See *Table* at Texas.

Bex′hill′ (bĕks′hĭl′). Municipal borough, East Sussex, S England, on English Channel; pop. 25,668.

Bex′ley (bĕks′lĭ). **1** City, Franklin co., cen. Ohio, 3 m. E of, adjacent to, and almost surrounded by, Columbus; pop. 14,319. Capital Univ. (1850; coed.).
2 City, E New South Wales, SE Australia, suburb (9 m. S) of Sydney; pop. 20,539.
3 Urban district, Kent, SE England, on the Cray 14 m. SE of London; pop. 88,781; part of Greater London.

Be·ya·zit′ (bĕ·yä·zĭt′). = Bayazit.

Bey Dağ′la·ri′ (bĕ′ĕ dä′lä·rĭ′). Mountain range in SW Turkey in Asia, W of the Gulf of Antalya; highest point Akdağ 10,125 ft.

Bey·koz′ (bĕ·ĕ·kôz′). Town, Kocaeli vilayet, NW Turkey in Asia, on E shore of the Bosporus N of Üsküdar.

Bey′o·ğlu′ (bĕ′ĕ·ō·lōō′); *formerly* **Pe′ra** (pâ′rä). City, a division of İstanbul, Turkey in Europe; pop. 234,750; the section N of the Golden Horn and the chief residential quarter of European communities.

Bey′pa·za·rɪ′ (bĕ′ĕ·pä·zä·rĭ′), *formerly* **Bei′ba·zar′** (bĕ′ĕ·bä·zär′). Town, Ankara vilayet, W cen. Turkey in Asia, 60 m. W of Ankara; pop. 5728; noted for its fine fruit; important under the Byzantine emperors.

Beyrouth. See Beirut.

Bey′şe·hir′ (bĕ′ĕ·shĕ·hĕr′). Town on SE shore of Lake Beyşehir, Konya vilayet, Turkey; pop. 2805.

Beyşehir Lake; *Turk.* **Beyşehir Gö·lü′** (gȯ·lū′). Lake 35 m. long, SW cen. Turkey, W of Konya.

Be·zhi·tsa (bĕzh′ĭ·tsȧ; *Russ.* byä′zhĭ·tsȧ); *during World War II until Jan. 1944 known as* **Or′dzho·ni·kid′ze·grad** (ȯr′jȯn·ĭ·kĭd′zĕ·grȧd; *Russ.* ūr·jŭ·nyĭ·kĕd′zĕ·grȧt′). Town, W cen. Orel Region, Soviet Russia, Europe, on the Desna just N of Bryansk; pop. 82,331; important locomotive-construction center.

Bé′ziers′ (bā′zyä′); *anc.* **Bae·ter′rae** (bē·tĕr′ē). Commercial and manufacturing city, Hérault dept., S France,

38 m. SW of Montpellier; pop. 73,305; surrounded by old walls; 12th-cent. Gothic cathedral; regional trade center; extensive brandy distilleries. Ancient Gallic fortress; captured by Romans 120 B.C.; massacre 1209 of 20,000 inhabitants for having harbored (1200) the Albigenses; episcopal see to 1790.

Be·zons′ (bĕ·zôn′). Commune, Seine-et-Oise dept., N France, NW suburb of Paris; pop. 13,964.

Bez·wa′da (bāz·wä′dȧ); *now* **Vi′ja·ya·va′da** (vĭj′-ȧ·yȧ·vŭd′ȧ). Town, NE Madhya Pradesh, SE India, on Kistna river at the head of its delta 155 m. ESE of Hyderabad; pop. 161,200. Headquarters of Kistna irrigation canal system; active trade center and rail junction. Village of **Un′da·val′le** (ȯȯn′dȧ·vŭl′lä) nearby has interesting rock temples and ruins.

Bha′dar (bŭ′dēr). River ab. 120 m. long, Kathiawar Penin., W India, flowing WSW into Arabian Sea.

Bhad′gaon (bŭd′goun). Town, adjoining Katmandu on the E, E cen. Nepal; pop. 93,176.

Bhad·res′war (bŭd rās′wēr). Town, West Bengal, India, on Hooghly river 20 m. N of Calcutta; pop. 22,992.

Bha′gal·pur′ (bä′gȧl·pȯȯr′). **1** Division, NE Bihar state, NE India; 18,701 sq. m.; pop. 9,598,025.
2 City, its ✱, on right bank of Ganges river 205 m. NNW of Calcutta; pop. (1941) 93,254; rail and trade center.

Bha·gi′ra·thi (bä·gē′rȧ·tĭ). **1** The Ganges river at its source, near Gangotri, N Indian Union.
2 Upper course of the Hooghly (*q.v.*), West Bengal, NE Indian Union; one of the Ganges distributaries. See also Ganges Delta.

Bha′kra Dam (bŭk′rȧ). Dam in gorge of Sutlej river near village of Bhakra, Punjab state, N India, NW of Bilaspur; 680 ft. high. With **Nan′gal Dam** (nŭng′gȧl), forms part of Bhakra-Nangal irrigation and hydroelectric project, completed 1954.

Bha·mo′ (bä·mō′). **1** District, Sagaing division, Upper Burma, now in Kachin State; 4146 sq. m.; pop. 121,193.
2 Town, its ✱, on E bank of upper Irrawaddy river 100 m. S of Myitkyina and 65 m. NW of Namhkam; pop. 7827. About 40 m. from China border and has active trade with towns in Yunnan prov.; head of navigation of the Irrawaddy, with steamer connections with Rangoon. Important station on Stilwell Road (earlier Ledo Road) connecting Myitkyina with Burma Road; lost to Japanese Apr. 1942 and scene of much fighting before its recovery Oct.–Dec. 1944.

Bhan·da′ra (bŭn·dä′rä). Town NE Maharashtra, cen. India, on branch of Wainganga river 33 m. E of Nagpur; pop. 16,738.

Bha′rat (bŭ′rŭt). India; —its ancient name and the name now used officially in India.

Bha′rat·pur′ (bŭ′rŭt·pȯȯr′) *or* **Bhurt′pore** (bûrt′-pōr). **1** Former Indian state, Eastern Rajputana States, NW India; 1978 sq. m.; pop. (1941) 575,625.
2 City, its ✱, now in Rajasthan state, 34 m. W of Agra; pop. 30,173; known for beauty and workmanship of its chowries, made from sandalwood, ivory, and silver. Strongly fortified; unsuccessfully besieged 1805 by British under Lord Lake; besieged by Lord Combermere 1825–26 and captured.

Bharoch. Var. of Broach.

Bha·tin′da (bŭ·tĭn′dȧ). Town, Punjab state, India, 100 m. SSE of Lahore; pop. 22,771; rail center.

Bhat·pa′ra (bät·pä′rȧ). City, West Bengal, India, on Hooghly river 22 m. N of Calcutta; pop. 134,916.

Bhav·na′gar *or* **Bhau·na′gar** (bou·nŭg′ēr). **1** Former Indian state, belonging to the Western India States, E Kathiawar, on W shore of Gulf of Cambay, W Indian Union; 2961 sq. m.; pop. (1941) 618,429; now in Gujerat state. Region first settled by Gohel Rajputs about 1260; came into close relations with Bombay government in 18th cent. and its lands consolidated by British in 1807.
2 Town and seaport, its ✱, on W coast of Gulf of Cambay 200 m. N of Bombay; pop. 75,594, (1941) 102,851; founded 1723; chief seaport of Kathiawar Penin.

Bhawalpur. See BAHAWALPUR.

Bhawanipatna. See KALAHANDI.

Bhe'ra (bā'rà). Town, N West Punjab, Pakistan, on Jhelum river 105 m. NW of Lahore; ancient Indian mounds nearby.

Bhi'ma (bē'mä). River ab. 400 m. long, S India; rises in Maharashtra state in Western Ghats E of Bombay, flows SE in S Maharashtra, N Mysore, and cen. Andhra Pradesh to Kistna river near Raichur.

Bhir (bēr) or **Bir** (bēr). Town, cen. Maharashtra, cen. India, 65 m. SSE of Aurangabad; pop. ab. 18,000.

Bhi·wa'ni (bǐ·wä'nē). Town, S Punjab state, India, 70 m. W of Delhi; pop. 35,866.

Bho·pal' (bō·päl'). **1** Former state, S Central India States, India, incorporated 1956 in Madhya Pradesh; 6921 sq. m.; pop. (1941) 785,322. Chief state of former Bhopal Agency and next to Hyderabad the most important Moslem state in all India. Surface broken by Vindhya Mts.; Narbada river formed its S border. Founded 1723 by Dost Mohammed Khan, an Afghan chieftain who had served under Aurangzeb; made treaty arrangements with British government 1817; ruled by female line (Begums of Bhopal) 1844-1926.
2 City, its ✻, since 1956 ✻ of Madhya Pradesh; about 182 m. NW of Nagpur; pop. (1941) 75,228.

Bhopal Agency. Formerly, a group of nine Indian states (including Bhopal), a subdivision of Central India Agency; 9073 sq. m.; pop. 1,051,976; ✻ Bhopal.

Bhor (bōr). **1** Former Indian state, one of Deccan and Kolhapur States in Western Ghats, W Indian Union; 910 sq. m.; pop. (1941) 155,961.
2 Town, its ✻, 25 m. S of Poona; now in S cen. Maharashtra; pop. 5185.

Bhot (bōt), **Bho'ti·ya** (bō'tǐ·yä), **Bho'ti·yal** (bō'-tǐ·yäl). Old names for TIBET.

Bhotan. See BHUTAN.

Bhubaneswar. See BHUVANESHWAR.

Bhuj (bōōj). Town, ✻ of former Cutch state, Western India States, W Indian Union, 190 m. W of Ahmadabad; pop. 21,859; known for silverwork.

Bhuket. See PHUKET.

Bhurtpore. See BHARATPUR.

Bhu·sa'val or **Bhu·sa'wal** (bōō·sä'vàl). Town, N Maharashtra, W India, on Tapti river; pop. 27,989.

Bhu·tan' (bōō·tän'; bōō·tǎn'), also **Bho·tan'** (bō·tän'). Semi-independent country in E Himalayas on NE border of India; bounded on N and E by Tibet, on S by Assam, and on W by Sikkim and Tibet; ab. 18,000 sq. m.; pop. 700,000; ✻ Thimbu (Tashi Chho Dzong); summer ✻ Paro. Crossed for most part by short high mountain ridges (peaks up to 24,000 ft.) running N to S and separated by deep valleys (12,000 to 18,000 ft.). Inhabitants (Bhutanese) are a branch of Tibetan Mongolians (chiefly Buddhists). Relations with British began about 1772; outrages against British subjects 1863 led to invasion 1865 when by treaty portions were annexed to India; since 1907 under rule of hereditary maharaja; government of India has voice in external relations.

Bhu'va·nesh'war or **Bhu'ba·nes'war** (bōō'và-nāsh'wēr). Town, ✻ of Orissa, E Indian Union, 30 m. N of Puri; has 500 (originally several thousand) remarkable temples in Orissan style of architecture, erected bet. 8th and 12th cents. A.D.; the Great Temple one of the finest Hindu shrines in India.

Biache–Saint–Vaast (byash'säN·vàst'). Commune, Pas-de-Calais dept., N France, near Douai; pop. 2427; severe fighting in July 1916 and Aug. 1918.

Biac'na·ba'to or **Biak'–na·ba'to** (byäk'nä·bä'tō). Village in mountains of NE Bulacan prov., Luzon, Phil. Is., 28 m. NE of Malolos; noted for its caves. Area NE of village now forms Biak-na-bato National Park. Scene Dec. 14, 1897 of signing of Pact of Biacnabato bet. Aguinaldo, head of provisional government, and Spanish governor-general in attempt to terminate the revolution.

Bi·a'fra, Bight of (bē·ä'frà). Widemouthed bay in E section of the Gulf of Guinea, W Africa.

Bi·ak' (bē·yäk'); also **Wi·ak'** (wē·yäk'). Island, largest of the Schouten Is., off N coast of Neth. New Guinea; 45 m. long by 23 m. wide; 948 sq. m.; pop. ab. 20,000. Northwest part hilly; several populous towns on coast including Bosnek; three airfields. Seized by Japanese 1942; retaken after fierce fighting May 27-June 20 1944 by Allied forces.

Bia'la (byä'lä). **1** River 71 m. long in E Kraków dept., Poland, a branch of the Dunajec river; battles May 1915 in German offensive under Mackensen.
2 River 21 m. long in W Kraków dept., Poland, tributary of the upper Vistula.
3 or **Biała Kra·kow'ska** (krä·kôf'skä). Commune, Kraków dept., Poland, on Biała river 43 m. WSW of Kraków; pop. (1938-39 est.) 30,337; agricultural trading center, esp. in cattle; manufactures textiles.
4 or **Biała Pod·la'ska** (pôd·lä'skä). Commune, Lublin dept. Poland, 60 m. NNE of Lublin; pop. (1938-39 est.) 22,000.

Bia·lo'gard (byä·lô'gärt); Ger. **Bel'gard** (bĕl'gärt). City, NE Szczecin dept., NW Poland, 72 m. NE of Stettin; formerly in Pomerania, Germany; pop. (1946) 14,801; industrial and transportation center; assigned to Poland by the Potsdam Conference 1945.

Bia'ly Ka'mień (byä'lǐ kä'myĕn·y'); Ger. **Weiss-stein** (vīs'shtīn). Town, W Wrocław dept., SW Poland, NW suburb of Wałbrzych; pop. (1946) 17,348; coal mining. Assigned to Poland by Potsdam Conference 1945.

Bia·ly'stok (byä·lǐ'stôk); Russ. **Be·lo·stok'** or **Bie-lo·stok'** (byi·lŭ·stôk'). **1** Former department, NE Poland; 10,038 sq. m.; pop. 1,643,485; ✻ Białystok; added to White Russia 1944-45 as Belostok; with Suwałki ceded back to Poland by U.S.S.R. Aug. 1945 and made new department (ab. 11,000 sq. m., pop. 600,000).
2 Industrial city, its ✻, 105 m. NE of Warsaw; pop. 105,346; textile center; important railroad junction. Founded in 14th cent.; annexed to Prussia 1795-1807, then Russian until taken by Germans Aug. 1915; restored to Poland 1919. In World War II overrun by Germans July 1941; retaken by Russians July 1944.

Bian'ca·vil'la (byäng'kä·vēl'lä); older **I·nes'sa** (ē·nĕs'-sä). Commune, Catania prov., E Sicily, at foot of Mt. Etna; pop. 16,644. Founded 1480 as Albanian colony.

Bianco, Monte. See Mont BLANC.

Biar, El. See EL BIAR.

Bi·a'ro (bē·ä'rō). See SANGIHE ISLANDS.

Biar'ritz' (byä'rēts'). Commune, Basses-Pyrénées dept., SW France, on Gulf of Gascogne 5 m. WSW of Bayonne; pop. 20,691; fashionable summer and winter resort; mineral baths; sea bathing.

Bi'as (bē'äs). See BEAS.

Bi'as Bay (bī'ǎs). Inlet of South China Sea on coast of Kwangtung prov., SE China, E of Kowloon.

Bi'bane' Mountains (Fr. bē'bàn'). Range of the Little Atlas Mts., E Alger and W Constantine depts., Algeria.

Bibb (bĭb). Name of counties in two states of the U.S. See Tables at ALABAMA and GEORGIA.

Bibb City. Town, Muscogee co., W Georgia, 5 m. N of Columbus; pop. 1213.

Bib·bie'na (bēb·byâ'nä). Commune, Arezzo prov., Tuscany, cen. Italy, on Arno river; pop. 10,214.

Bi'be·rach (bē'bĕ·räk). Industrial city, Baden-Württemberg state. Germany, 56 m. SE of Stuttgart; pop. 10,065; famous bell foundries; leather, toys, machinery. Scene of defeat of Austrians by French 1796 and 1800.

Bi·bi' Ei·bat' (bē·bē' ā·bät'). Locality, Apsheron Penin., Azerbaidzhan, U.S.S.R., 5 m. W of Baku; has one of oldest and richest oil fields in Europe.

Bi·brac'te (bǐ·brǎk'tē). Ancient town, E Gaul, near modern Autun; capital of the Aedui; battlefield 58 B.C. where Julius Caesar defeated the Helvetii.

Bi'brax (bī'brǎks). Ancient town of the Remi, Belgica, NE Gaul, near the Aisne on or near site of Laon.

Bices'ter (bǐs'tēr). Town (urban district), Oxfordshire, England, 12 m. NNE of Oxford; pop. 4171.

Bi'cê'tre (bē'sâ'tr'). South suburb of Paris, France; famous lunatic asylum founded by Richelieu.

Biche, La. See LA BICHE.

Biche, Lac la (lȧk' lȧ bǐsh'). Lake, E cen. Alberta prov., Canada; drains W into Athabaska river.

Bichitra. See PHICHIT.

Bick'nell (bǐk'n'l). City, Knox co., SW Indiana, 13 m. ENE of Vincennes; pop. 3878; coal mines.

Bicocca, La. See LA BICOCCA.

Bi'col or **Bi'kol** (bē'kōl). River ab. 75 m. long, W cen. Camarines Sur prov., Luzon, Phil. Is.; flows NW from Lake Bato to San Miguel Bay; fertile valley.

Bicol Peninsula. SE extension of Luzon, Phil. Is., inhabited principally by the Bikol; comprises Camarines Norte, Camarines Sur, Albay, and Sorsogon provs.

Bi'da (bī'dȯ). See DOHA.

Bi'da (bē'dä). City, Niger prov., Northern Region, Nigeria, near left bank of the Niger; pop. 25,358 (chiefly Hausas); famous for its brass and copper work. Founded 1859; came under British 1901.

Bi'dar (bē'dēr). 1 Former district, W cen. Hyderabad state, S cen. India; 4825 sq. m.; pop. 873,615. One of the five Mohammedan kingdoms of the Deccan 1492–c. 1609. 2 Town, NE Mysore, 70 m. NW of Hyderabad; pop. 12,434; dynastic capital of Bidar kingdom in 16th cent.

Bi'das·so'a (bē'ᵗhä·sō'ä). Short stream ab. 33 m. long at N frontier of Spain; rises in Spain and flows W and N to Bay of Biscay at Fuenterrabia; for ab. 7 m. its lower course forms boundary bet. France and Spain.

Bid'de·ford (bǐd'ē·fērd). Industrial city, York co., SW Maine, across the Saco river from Saco; pop. 19,255; settled 1630; textile mills, textile machinery factories.

Bid'dulph (bǐd'ŭlf). Urban district, Staffordshire, W cen. England, 8 m. N of Stoke on Trent; pop. 10,898.

Bid'e·ford (bǐd'ē·fērd). Municipal borough, Devonshire, SW England, near mouth of Torridge river 45 m. N of Plymouth; pop. 10,100; manufacturing.

Bi'don' (Fr. bē'dôn'). Town SE Aïn-Sefra territory, SW Algeria, on trans-Saharan caravan route.

Bie'brich (bē'brĭk). Former city (pop. 21,250), Wiesbaden govt. dist., Hesse-Nassau prov., Prussia, Germany; now part of city of Wiesbaden (q.v.).

Bie'brza (byě'bzhä); *Russ.* **Bobr** (bō'bēr). River ab. 130 m. long, N Poland, flowing into Narew river.

Biel (bēl); *Fr.* **Bienne** (byěn). Commune, N Bern canton, Switzerland, near Lake of Biel 17 m. NNW of Bern; pop. (1941) 41,219; railroad junction; manufactures clocks, machinery, earthenware, paper. Founded in early 13th cent. by bishops of Basel; to France 1798; to Bern canton 1815.

Biel, *Fr.* **Bienne, Lake of.** Lake, W Switzerland, in Bern canton 3 m. NE of Lake of Neuchâtel; 10 m. long and bet. 1 and 3 m. wide; 16 sq. m.; contains St. Pierre I., Rousseau's residence 1765.

Bie·la'wa (byě·lä'vä); *Ger.* **Lang'en·bie'lau** (läng'-ěn·bē'lou). Town, S Wrocław dept., SW Poland, 37 m. SSW of Wrocław; pop. (1946) 20,116; textiles.

Bie'le·feld (bē'lě·fělt). Manufacturing city, W Germany, in the former Westphalia prov., Prussia, 38 m. E of Münster; pop. (1939) 128,714; manufactures include linens, silks, shirts, machinery, bicycles, automobiles; 11th-cent. castle (now museum) nearby.

Biel'la (byěl'lä). Manufacturing commune, Vercelli prov., Piedmont, NW Italy, 25 m. NW of Vercelli; pop. 28,289; railroad terminus; in rich agricultural area.

Bielostok. See BIAŁYSTOK.

Biel'sko (byěl'skô); *Ger.* **Bie'litz** (bē'lǐts). Commune, Śląsk dept., S Poland, at NW foot of Carpathians 29 m. S of Katowice; pop. (1938–39 est.) 32,000.

Bien'ho'a (byěn'hō'ä). Town, Cochin China, S Vietnam, 20 m. N of Saigon; pop. ab. 20,000; industrial town, formerly capital of Cambodia; Buddha statues.

Bienne. See BIEL.

Bi·en'ville (bē·ěn'vǐl; *Sou.* also -v'l; *Fr.* byäɴ'vēl'). Parish in Louisiana. See *Table* at LOUISIANA.

Bi·en'ville (bē·ěn'vǐl; *Can. Fr.* byäɴ'vēl'), or **A·pis'ki·ga·mish'** (ȧ·pǐs'kǐ·gȧ·mǐsh'), **Lake.** Lake 392 sq. m., N cen. Quebec prov., Canada, with outlet through Great Whale river into Hudson Bay.

Bie Plateau (bē). Highland region ab. 5000 ft. alt. cen. Angola, SW Africa.

Bier'stadt, Mount (bēr'stǎt). Peak 14,046 ft., Clear Creek co., N cen. Colorado.

Big An'ne·mes'sex River (ǎn'ē·měs'ěks; -ĭks). Inlet of Tangier Sound, Somerset co., SE Maryland.

Big Bay Point (bā). Point on N coast of Marquette co., N Michigan penin., extending into Lake Superior.

Big Bear Lake (bâr). Reservoir in San Bernardino Valley, SW San Bernardino co., SW California, formed by damming small natural lake; center of resort area.

Big Bend National Park (běnd). See UNITED STATES, *National Parks.*

Big Beth'el (běth''l). Locality, Warwick co., Virginia, ab. 10 m. NW of Fort Monroe; battle June 10, 1861.

Big Black. River 330 m. long, W cen. Mississippi; rises in Webster co., N cen. Miss., flows SW into the Mississippi river in NW Claiborne co., SW Miss.

Big Black Mountain. Peak 4150 ft. in Harlan co., SE Kentucky; highest point in the state.

Big Black Mountains. Range of the Cumberland Mts. along S section of Virginia-Kentucky boundary.

Big Blue. River 300 m. long, flowing from Hamilton co., SE cen. Nebraska, SE into Kansas river at Manhattan, Riley co., NE Kansas.

Big Bone Lick. Locality, Boone co., N Kentucky, just E of Ohio river; deposit of mammoth fossils; probably discovered 1729; visited by Daniel Boone 1770.

Big Cy'press Swamp (sī'prěs; -prĭs). Swamp region 2400 sq. m.; W part of the Everglades, S Florida.

Big Delta. Village and post station, E Alaska, on Tanana river and on Alaska Highway at its junction with Richardson Highway, 65 m. SE of Fairbanks; pop. (1950) 155.

Big Diomede. See DIOMEDE ISLANDS.

Bi'gej (bē'gěj). Islet, SE Kwajalein atoll, W Marshall Is., just N of Kwajalein I.; taken by Allies Feb. 6, 1944.

Big Elk Peak (ělk). Mountain 9478 ft. in E Bonneville co., SE Idaho.

Big Flats (flǎts). Town, Chemung co., S New York, ab. 9 m. NW of Elmira near Chemung river; pop. 3665.

Big Fork (fôrk). River ab. 120 m. long, N Minnesota; rises in NW Itasca co., flows N into Rainy river on United States-Canada boundary.

Big'gar (bǐg'ēr). Market town, SW cen. Saskatchewan, Canada, 58 m. W of Saskatoon; pop. 2214.

Big'gles·wade (bǐg'lz·wād). Urban district, Bedfordshire, SE cen. England, 42 m. N of London; pop. 7280.

Bigheart. See BARNSDALL.

Big Hole Battlefield National Monument (hōl). See UNITED STATES, *National Monuments.*

Big'horn' (bǐg'hôrn'). River 336 m. long, formed by confluence of Popo Agie and Wind rivers in Fremont co., W cen. Wyoming, and flowing N into Yellowstone river in SW Treasure co., SE cen. Montana.

Big Horn (bǐg' hôrn'). Name of counties in two states of the U.S. See *Tables* at MONTANA and WYOMING.

Bighorn Mountain. Peak 4713 ft. in Banner co., W Nebraska.

Big Horn Mountains. Range in N Wyoming, extending N and S from Montana border to Natrona co.; highest point Cloud Peak 13,165 ft.

Big Jay Peak. See JAY PEAK.

Big Lake. 1 Lake in N Mississippi co., NE Arkansas, reaching to Missouri boundary; outlet Pemiscot Bayou. 2 Lake in E Maine, in cen. Washington co. 3 Town, ⊗ of Reagan co., W Texas; pop. 2668.

Big Mead'ows Dam (měd'ōz). Dam completed 1927 across North Fork of Feather river, NW Plumas co., NE

California; height 130 ft.; impounds water, **Lake Al'ma·nor** (ăl'má·nôr), for water power.

Big Mud'dy (mŭd'ĭ). River ab. 100 m. long, SW Illinois; rises in S cen. Illinois, flows SW into Mississippi in W Jackson co., SW Illinois.

Big Nemaha. See NEMAHA.

Bigorra. See TARBES.

Bi'gorre' (bē'gôr'). Medieval countship in W Pyrenees, SW France, in valley of the Adour; ✴ Tarbes; attached to Béarn 1425.

Big Pine Key (pīn). One of the Florida Keys.

Big Rap'ids (răp'ĭdz). City, ⊗ of Mecosta co., cen. Michigan, 35 m. WNW of Mt. Pleasant; pop. 8686; in section producing natural gas; manufactures furniture; Ferris Institute (1884; coed.).

Big Sa'ble Point (sā'b'l). Point on W coast of Mason co., W Michigan, extending into Lake Michigan.

Big Sand'y (săn'dĭ). **1** River ab. 80 m. long, W Arizona; joins Santa Maria river on SE boundary of Mohave co. to form Williams river.
2 Navigable river 22 m. long, E Kentucky; formed by confluence of Levisa Fork and Tug Fork (*qq.v.*) in E Lawrence co., E Kentucky, flows N forming N section of Kentucky-West Virginia boundary, and empties into Ohio river near Catlettsburg, NE Kentucky.

Big Sandy Creek. River 200 m. long, E Colorado; rises in N El Paso co., flows SE into Arkansas river.

Big San'ta A·ni'ta Dam (săn'tá á·nē'tá). Dam completed 1927 across Big Santa Anita creek, California; height 235 ft.; impounds water for flood control.

Big Sioux (sōō). River ab. 300 m. long, South Dakota and Iowa; rises in W Grant co., NE South Dakota, flows S and SE to form South Dakota-Iowa boundary, and empties into Missouri river at extreme SE corner of South Dakota on W boundary of Sioux City.

Big Slide Mountain (slīd). Peak 4255 ft. in the Adirondack Mountains, Essex co., NE New York.

Big Southern Butte. Peak 7659 ft. in S Butte co., SE cen. Idaho.

Big Spring (sprĭng). City, ⊗ of Howard co., NW Texas, 78 m. NW of San Angelo; pop. 31,230; oil; cotton.

Big Stone (stōn). County in Minnesota. See *Table* at MINNESOTA.

Big Stone Gap. Town, Wise co., SW Virginia, in Cumberland Mts. 40 m. WNW of Bristol; pop. 4688.

Big Stone Lake. Narrow lake ab. 35 m. long, bet. NE corner of South Dakota and W Minnesota.

Big Sur (sûr). Village, Monterey co., California, near coast SE of Point Sur on Big Sur river (ab. 10 m. long).
2 Resort region, Monterey co., California, extending from vicinity of Point Sur S ab. 80 m. along coast W of Santa Lucia Range.

Big Tim'ber (tĭm'bẽr). City, ⊗ of Sweet Grass co., S cen. Montana, on Yellowstone river; pop. 1660; wool.

Big Tu·jun'ga No. 1 (tōō·jŭng'gá). Dam completed 1932 across Big Tujunga creek, Los Angeles co., California; height 250 ft.; impounds water for flood control.

Big Tupper Lake. See TUPPER LAKES.

Big Wood. River 95 m. long, S Idaho; rises on S slopes of Sawtooth Mts., flows S, then W to Snake river.

Bi'hać (bē'hách) or **Bi'hach** (-hách). Town, Croatia, Yugoslavia, on Una river; pop. (1931) 8374.

Bi·har' (bē·här') or **Be·har'** (bē-). **1** State, NE India; 67,164 sq. m.; pop. 38,779,562; ✴ Patna, summer ✴ Ranchi. Bounded on N by Nepal, on E by West Bengal, on S and SW by Orissa and Madhya Pradesh, and on W by Uttar Pradesh. Plateau region in S (Chota Nagpur) and Ganges valley in N; rich agricultural lands with rice as staple crop; coal and iron mining in S. Chief towns Patna, Gaya, Bhagalpur, and Jamshedpur. Prominent in political and religious history of India; its limits nearly the same as ancient kingdom of Magadha with records dating back to c. 600 B.C. Under Bimbisara, Gautama began his preaching at Buddh Gaya (*q.v.*). Succeeded by Maurya empire, followed 320 A.D.

by Gupta empire, with Pataliputra (Patna) as capital. Native dynasty overcome in 12th cent. by Mohammedans and about 1497 annexed to Delhi; came into possession of East India Company 1765 and made a part of Bengal; set up as part of province of Bihar and Orissa 1912 but made a separate province 1936.
2 Division, Bihar state; 42,633 sq. m.; pop. (1941) 28,823,802.
3 Town, cen. Bihar, 40 m. SE of Patna; pop. (1941) 54,551; produces muslins and gold and silver brocades; has many mosques and graves holy to Moslems and is a place of pilgrimage. Capital of Magadha until seat of government moved to Patna in 16th cent.

Bihar and O·ris'sa (ô·rĭs'á). Former province 1912–36 of Brit. India; 83,054 sq. m.; pop. 37,677,576; ✴ Patna; geographically included Indian States, 28,648 sq. m.

Bi·hor' (bē·hôr'), *Hung.* **Bi'har** (bĭ'hôr), **Mountains.** Mountains, W cen. Transylvania, Romania, NW of the Transylvanian Alps; highest point ab. 6065 ft.

Biisk. See BISK.

Bi·ja·gos', I'lhas dos (ē'lyázh thōōzh vĕ·zhá·gôsh'); *Eng.* **Bis·sa'gos Islands** (bĭ·sä'gŭs). Group of low, unhealthful islands Portuguese Guinea, W Africa, off coast SW of Bissau; largest are Orango, Formosa, Caravela; on easternmost island, Bolama, is town and port of Bolama.

Bijanagar. See VIJAYANAGAR.

Bi·ja·pur' (bĭ·jä'pŏŏr), *also* **Be·ja'pur** (bĭ-). Town, SE Bombay prov., W Indian Union, 240 m. SE of Bombay; pop. 39,747. Adopted 1489 by Yusuf Adil Shah as capital of independent kingdom; one of the five Mohammedan kingdoms of the Deccan (*q.v.*). Has numerous pre-Mohammedan ruins and large mosques, palaces, and buildings in Islamic style; also an impressive citadel and fort. Kingdom conquered by Aurangzeb 1686, ceded to Marathas 1760, and taken over by British 1818.

Bi·ja'war (bĭ·jä'wẽr). Former Indian state, Bundelkhand, Central India States, Indian Union; 980 sq. m.; pop. (1941) 120,990; ✴ Bijawar; pop. (1931) 5748.

Bi·je'lji·na (bē·yĕ'lyĕ·nä). Town, NW Bosnia and Herzegovina, cen. Yugoslavia; pop. (1931) 12,367.

Bij'nor (bĭj'nôr), *also* **Bij'naur** (-nour). Town, NW Uttar Pradesh, N India, 3 m. from left bank of Ganges river 80 m. NE of Delhi; pop. 23,520.

Bi·ka', El (ăl bĭ·kä'); *also* **Be·káa'** (bĭ·kä') or **Buk'a'a** (bōōk'ä); *Arab.* **El Be·qa'** (ăl bā·kä'); *anc.* **Coe'le-Syr'i·a** or **Coe'le·syr'i·a** (sē'lĕ·sĭr'ĭ·á). Valley in SW Levant States in Lebanon and Syria, 100 m. long and 10 m. wide, bet. the Lebanon and Anti-Liban mountain ranges; traversed by the upper Orontes (flowing N) and the Litani (flowing S) rivers. By the ancients Coele-Syria was also used, during the wars bet. the Seleucids and Egypt, of a wider area comprising much of S Syria.

Bi'ka·ner' (bē'kŭ·när'; *Angl.* bĭk'á·nẽr'). **1** Former Indian state, N Rajputana, NW India; 23,181 sq. m.; pop. 1,292,938. Desolate tract, part of Thar Desert without a single stream; N part watered by irrigation canals from Punjab. Principal industry raising camels, horses, and sheep; people skillful in handicrafts. Founded ab. 1465 by Rajput chief; adhered loyally to Mogul Empire; waged wars with Jodhpur through 18th cent.; received British political agent 1883.
2 City, its ✴, ab. 245 m. W of Delhi; pop. (1941) 127,226; founded 1485 by Bika, a Rajput chief of Marwar; renowned for its carpets and blankets; surrounded by stone wall and overlooked by citadel; its temples and palaces constructed of bright-red sandstone.

Bi·ki'ni (bĭ·kē'nĭ; *native* bĭk'ĭ·nĭ). Atoll with ab. 20 islets, NW end of Ratak Chain, Marshall Is., Micronesia, 11°35'N lat., 165°25'E long.; lagoon 21½ m. long by 11 m. wide; ab. 190 m. E of Eniwetok and 170 m. NW of Kwajalein. Largest islets Bikini, Enyu, and Namu; entrance to lagoon is through Enyu Channel on the SE, 9 m. wide. Population of 167 removed to Rongerik before American tests of atomic bomb July 1 and 25, 1946.

Bikol. See BICOL.

Bi·la·a′ Point (bē′lä·ä′). Most northerly point of Mindanao, Phil. Is., at NE corner, Surigao prov.

Bilâd-es–Sudan. See SUDAN.

Bilá Hora. See WHITE MOUNTAIN, Czechoslovakia.

Bi·las′pur (bĭ·läs′pŏŏr). Town, NE Madhya Pradesh, cen. India, on tributary of Mahanadi river 210 m. ENE of Nagpur; pop. 31,374.

Bilaspur or **Kah·lur′** (kä·lŏŏr′). **1** Former state, one of Punjab States, East Punjab, NW Indian Union; merged 1954 in Himachal Pradesh and now forming an administrative district; 453 sq. m.; pop. (1941) 110,336. **2** Town, its ✳, on Sutlej river NW of Simla; pop. 2387.

Bi·lauk′taung Range (bē·louk′toun). Mountain range 2000 to ab. 5000 ft. along boundary bet. SE Lower Burma and SW Thailand.

Bil·ba′o (bĭl·bä′ō; *Span.* bēl·vä′ō). Commercial and manufacturing city, ✳ of Vizcaya prov., N Spain, 7 m. from the Bay of Biscay; pop. (1941 est.) 195,890; manufactures iron, steel, glass, paper, pottery, tobacco; exports linen, wine, and, esp., iron ore; shipbuilding. Founded 1300; besieged by Carlists 1833–35, 1872–76.

Bil·beis′ or **Bel·beis′** (bĭl·bās′). Town, Sharqîya prov., Lower Egypt, 30 m. NE of Cairo; pop. ab. 16,000.

Bilbilis. See CALATAYUD.

Bildt, de. See DE BILDT.

Bi′le·cik′ (bē′lĕ·jēk′). **1** Vilayet, NW Turkey in Asia; 1826 sq. m.; pop. 124,314. **2** Town, its ✳, 37 m. NW of Eskişehir; pop. 3992.

Bí′li·na (bē′lĭ·nà); *Ger.* **Bi·lin′** (bĕ·lēn′; bē′lēn). City, NW Bohemia prov., W Czechoslovakia; pop. (1939) 10,698; watering place, with mineral springs.

Bi·li′ran (bē·lē′rän). Island N of Leyte, cen. Phil. Is.; 192 sq. m.; pop. 48,934; chief town Caibiran.

Bilkas. See BILQÂS.

Bille′ri·ca (bĭl′rĭ·kà). Town, Middlesex co., NE Massachusetts, 6 m. S of Lowell; pop. 17,867.

Bil′linge and Win′stan·ley (bĭl′inj, wĭn′stăn·lĭ). Urban district, Lancashire, NW England, 12½ m. NE of Liverpool; pop. 6157.

Bil′ling·ham (bĭl′ing·ăm). Urban district, Durham, N England, 29 m. SSE of Newcastle; pop. 23,944.

Bil′lings (bĭl′ingz). **1** County in North Dakota. See *Table* at NORTH DAKOTA. **2** City, ⊗ of Yellowstone co., S cen. Montana, on Yellowstone river; pop. 52,851; trading and shipping point for livestock, poultry, and wool; beet-sugar factories. Eastern Montana College of Education (1927); Rocky Mountain College (1883).

Bil·li′ton (bĭ·lē′tŏn) or **Be·li′tung** (bà·lē′tŏŏng); *Du.* **Be·li′toeng** (-tŏŏng). Island, Indonesia, in the Java Sea off the SE coast of the island of Sumatra; 55 m. long by 43 m. wide; 1866 sq. m.; pop. 73,429; chief town Tandjungpandan; tin mines.

Bill Wil′liams Mountain (bĭl′ wĭl′yǎmz). Peak 9264 ft. in SW Coconino co., N cen. Arizona.

Bil′ly′–Mon′ti·gny′ (bē′yē′môn′tē′nyē′). Commune, Pas-de-Calais dept., N France, 11 m. NE of Arras; pop. (1931) 10,492; coal mines.

Bil′ma (bĭl′mà). Oasis in Niger Republic, West Africa, in central E Sahara ab. 800 m. S of Tripoli.

Bi·lox′i (bĭ·lŭk′sĭ; -lŏk′sĭ). City, Harrison co., SE Mississippi, on Gulf of Mexico 13 m. E of Gulfport; pop. 44,053; first permanent white settlement in the Mississippi valley (1699); now a shore and fishing resort; commercial oyster and shrimp fisheries; Keesler Air Force Base with U.S. Air Force Technical School.

Bil·qâs′ or **Bil·kas′** (bĭl·käs′). Town, Gharbîya prov., Lower Egypt, in Nile delta 30 m. SW of Damietta.

Bil′ston (bĭl′stǔn). Urban district, Staffordshire, W cen. England, 10 m. WNW of Birmingham; pop. 33,464; coal and iron mining; potteries.

Bi′ma Bay (bē′mà). Inlet of Flores Sea on NE coast of Sumbawa I., Lesser Sunda Is., Indonesia; one of best harbors in Indonesia; town of Raba on it.

Bim′i·ni (bĭm′ĭ·nĭ) or **Bim′i·nis** (-nĭz). Two small islands of the Bahamas E of S Florida and separated from Florida by the Straits of Florida; 9 sq. m.; pop. (1943) 718. Named for mythical island of Bimini, supposed site of "fountain of youth" the quest for which led to discovery of Florida 1513 by Ponce de Leon.

Bi′nal·ba′gan (bē′näl·bä′gän). Municipality, W coast of Negros Occidental prov., Negros, Phil. Is., on Panay Gulf 33 m. S of City of Bacolod; pop. 18,112.

Bi′na·lo′nan (bē′nä·lō′nän). Municipality, E Pangasinan prov., Luzon, Phil. Is., 23 m. E of Lingayen; pop. 19,376; important road center.

Bi·ñan′ (bē·nyän′). Municipality, W Laguna prov., Luzon, Phil. Is., near SW coast of Laguna de Bay; pop. 16,238; important terminus for roads to Cavite.

Bi′nang·o′nan (bē′näng·ō′nän). Municipality, S Rizal prov., Luzon, Phil. Is., on W shore of peninsula on Laguna de Bay 10 m. SE of Pasig; pop. 16,588; large quarries of building stone nearby.

Binche (bănsh). Commune, Hainaut prov., SW Belgium, on Haine river 10 m. E of Mons; pop. 11,422; lace.

Bindhachal. See MIRZAPUR.

Bindloe Island. See MARCHENA ISLAND.

Bin′dra·ban (bĭn′drä·bàn). Var. of BRINDABAN.

Bin·du′ra (bĭn·dŏŏr′à). City, Southern Rhodesia, in Mashonaland prov. NE of Salisbury; pop. (est.) 25,000.

Bing′en (bĭng′ĕn). City, Rheinhessen dist., Hesse, Germany, at confluence of Rhine and Nahe rivers 17 m. W of Mainz; pop. 10,186; 15th-cent. Gothic church; Klopp castle nearby; famous Drususbrücke (bridge; built by Drusus 13 B.C.) over the Nahe river; ancient Mäuseturm (Mouse Tower; according to legend, Archbishop Hatto devoured by mice here c. 970); Rhenish Technical College; manufactures leather, liquors, tobacco. Inhabited by ancient Belgae; scene of defeat of Gauls by Romans 70 A.D.; Emperor Henry IV imprisoned in nearby castle 1105; burned by French 1689; under French rule 1797–1814; to Hesse 1815.

Bin′ger·ville′ (băn′zhä′vēl′). Seaport town, Ivory Coast, West Africa; former territorial ✳; pop. ab. 1000; on lagoon bet. Abidjan and Grand Bassam.

Bing′ham (bĭng′ăm). County in Idaho. See *Table* at IDAHO.

Bingham Canyon. Town, Salt Lake co., N Utah, 20 m. SSW of Salt Lake City; pop. 1516; copper, silver, gold, lead mines.

Bing′ham·ton (bĭng′ăm·tǔn). Manufacturing and industrial city, ⊗ of Broome co., S New York, at confluence of Chenango and Susquehanna rivers 65 m. S of Syracuse; pop. 75,941; with Johnson City and Endicott one of so-called Triple Cities; first permanent settlement 1787; incorporated as village 1834, city 1867; site of first farm bureau in U.S. (1911).

Bingian, Slieve. See SLIEVE BINGIAN.

Bing′ley (bĭng′lĭ). Urban district, West Riding, Yorkshire, N England, on the Aire 13 m. WNW of Leeds; pop. 21,566; woolen mills, paper mills.

Bin·göl′ (bĕng·gŭl′). Vilayet, E Turkey in Asia, formed from parts of Muş and Elâziz vilayets; pop. (1940) 70,184; ✳ Bingöl (pop. 300).

Bin·göl′ Da·ği′ (bĕng·gŭl′ dä·ĭ′). Mountain range (*daği*), Armenia, E Turkey in Asia, NW of Lake Van; highest point 11,975 ft.

Bin·go Sea (bĕn·gō) or **Sea of Bingo.** Expansion of the Inland Sea, Japan, in its central part, N of Shikoku I.

Binh Dinh (bĭn′y′ dĭn′y′). Town near coast, SE Annam, S Vietnam; pop. 75,000; its port is Quinhon.

Bin′ma·ley′ (bēn′mä·lā′). Municipality, cen. Pangasinan prov., Luzon, Phil. Is., in Agno delta 3 m. E of Lingayen on S shore of Lingayen Gulf; pop. 20 455.

Bin′tan (bĭn′tän) or **Bin′tang** (-täng). Island, largest of the Riouw Archipelago, Indonesia, off S tip of the Malay Peninsula; 415 sq. m.; pop. ab. 20,000; bauxite mines.

Bin·tu′lu (bĭn·tŏŏ′lŏŏ). Coastal town, W Sarawak, NW Borneo, 175 m. SW of Brunei.

Binue. See BENUE.

Bí'o–Bí'o (bē'ô·vē'ô). **1** River 238 m. long in S cen. Chile; flows from the Andes Mts. into the Pacific Ocean at the city of Concepción. **2** Province of Chile. See *Table* at CHILE.

Bipontium. See ZWEIBRÜCKEN.

Bir (bẽr). See BHIR.

Bir, Cape (bẽr); *Arab.* **Ras Bir** (räs bēr). Cape projecting from E coast of French Somaliland into the Gulf of Aden at entrance to Bab el Mandeb.

Bir·ca'o (bẽr·kä'ô) or **Bur Ga'vo** (bōōr gä'vô); *formerly* **Port Durn'ford** (dûrn'fẽrd). Seaport, S Somalia, E Africa; in Jubaland, formerly part of Kenya.

Bird Islands. See AVES ISLANDS.

Birds'bor'o (bûrdz'bûr'ô). Industrial borough, Berks co., SE Pennsylvania, on Schuylkill river 9 m. SSE of Reading; pop. 3025; founded 1740; steel castings.

Bir'dum (bûr'dŭm). Town, N cen. Northern Territory, Australia, on railroad ab. 300 m. SE of Darwin.

Bi're or **Bi'reh** (bē'rē); *Biblical* **Be·e'roth** (bē·ē'rŏth; bẽr'ōth); *anc.* **Be·roe'a** (bē·rē'à). Town, Palestine, 9 m. N of Jerusalem on a rocky hilltop; battle 161 B.C.

Bi're·cik' (bē'rĕ·jēk') or **Bi'ri·jik'** (bē'rĕ·jēk'). Town on left bank of the Euphrates river, Urfa vilayet, SE Turkey in Asia, 45 m. WSW of Urfa; pop. 9669.

Bir el–Go'bi (bẽr' ăl·gō'bī). Village and pass in the hills 37 m. S of Tobruk, NE Cyrenaica, Libya, N Africa; severe fighting 1941–42.

Bir en Na·trun' (bẽr' ăn nă·trōōn'). Town, SW Northern Province, N Sudan, in Libyan Desert 250 m. WSW of Dongola.

Bir es Saba. See BEERSHEBA.

Bir Ha·cheim' (bēr' hōō·kī'yĭm; -kä'-). Village, NE Cyrenaica, Libya, N Africa, 40 m. SSW of Tobruk; in World War II scene of much fighting 1942, esp. when taken by Germans under Rommel June 1942.

Bir·han' (bĭr·hän'). Peak 13,628 ft. in cen. Ethiopia, NNW of Addis Ababa.

Birijik. See BIRECIK.

Bir·jand' (bēr·jänd'). Town, SE Khurasan prov., NE Iran; pop. ab. 25,000; on a plateau (alt. 4440 ft.) and on the highway from Meshed to Zahidan.

Bir'ken·feld (bĭr'kĕn·fĕlt). **1** District of Oldenburg. See *Table* at OLDENBURG. **2** Town, its ✳, 25 m. ESE of Trier; pop. 2579.

Bir'ken·head (bûr'kĕn·hĕd). **1** (*locally also* bûr'kĕn·hĕd'). County borough, Cheshire, NW England, on the Mersey estuary opposite Liverpool; pop. 147,803, (1951) 142,392; shipbuilding and shipping center; has flour mills; steel manufacturing. Connected with Liverpool by tunnel under the Mersey 2⅓ m. long. First iron vessel in England built here 1829; new docks opened 1847; Confederate privateer *Alabama* launched 1862. **2** Borough, Auckland provincial dist., North I., New Zealand, suburb of Auckland on N shore of Waitemata Harbor; pop. 3355.

Bir'ket Qâ·rûn' (bĭr'kĕt kä·rōōn'). Shallow lake ab. 30 m. long and 5 m. wide in Faiyûm prov., N Egypt; occupies part of basin of ancient Lake Moeris (*q.v.*).

Bir'ming·ham (bûr'mĭng·hăm; *Brit. and occas. U.S.*, -mĭng·ăm). **1** Industrial city, ⊗ of Jefferson co., N cen. Alabama; pop. 340,887; incorp. 1871; consolidated with a dozen surrounding towns 1910; area rich in coal, hematite, and many other minerals; manufactures iron and steel products, electrical equipment, carbide, cotton and cottonseed products, cigars, machinery, soap, tanks. Howard College (1842; coed.); Birmingham-Southern College (1856; coed.); Miles College (1907; coed.). **2** Residential city, Oakland county, SE Michigan, 8 m. SSE of Pontiac; pop. 25,525. **3** City and county borough, Warwickshire, Staffordshire, and Worcestershire, W cen. England, 98 m. NW of London; pop. 1,002,603, (1951) 1,112,340; is a great railroad focus and metal-manufacturing center; also manufactures rubber products, hardware, jewelry, munitions of

war; coal and iron fields nearby. Grammar school founded 1552 by King Edward VI; Queen's College (1828) became part of Birmingham Univ. (founded 1898). Before 13th cent. a market town; swept by plague 1665; enfranchised by Reform Act 1832; bombed by German planes 1940–41.

Bir'nie (bûr'nĭ). Island 1 sq. m. in center of Phoenix Islands group, S of Canton I., cen. Pacific Ocean.

Bi'ro·bi·dzhan' or **Bi'ro–Bi·djan'** (bĭr'ô·bĭ·jän'; -jän'; *Russ.* byĭ·rŭ·byĭ·jän'). **1** See JEWISH AUTONOMOUS REGION. **2** Town, ✳ of Jewish Autonomous Region, Soviet Russia, Asia, on Trans-Siberian R.R. ab. 110 m. W of Khabarovsk; pop. ab. 38,000.

Birr (bûr) or **Par'sons·town** (pär's'nz·toun). Urban district, W co. Offaly, cen. Eire; pop. 3297; brewing, distilling; castle, noted as astronomical observatory.

Birsen. See BIRZHAI.

Bir'stall (bûr'stôl). Former urban district, West Riding, Yorkshire, N England; since 1937 part of Batley.

Bir'zhai (bĭr'zhī); *Russ.* **Bir·zhai'** (byĭr·zhī'); *Ger.* **Bir'sen** (bĭr'zĕn). Town, ✳ of Birzhai-Pasvalys dist., N Lithuania; pop. (1938 est.) 8211. Alliance bet. Peter the Great of Russia and Augustus II of Poland formed here 1701 against Sweden.

Bir'zhai–Pas'va·lys' (bĭr'zhī·pås'và·lēs'). District of Lithuania. See *Table* at LITHUANIA.

Bisanthe. See TEKIRDAĞ.

Bisayas. See VISAYAN ISLANDS.

Bis'bee (bĭz'bē). City, ⊗ of Cochise co., SE corner of Arizona, 58 m. E of Nogales; pop. 9914; incorp. 1900; center of one of richest copper-producing regions in America; also mines gold, silver, lead.

Bis·ca'ri (bēs·kä'rē). Village, Ragusa prov., SE Sicily, 15 m. E of Gela; pop. (1931) 4130. In World War II its airfield captured by U.S. Army July 14, 1943.

Bis'cay (bĭs'kā; -kĭ) or **Bis·ca'ya** (bēs·kä'yä). Province of Spain. See *Vizcaya*, in *Table* at SPAIN.

Bis'cay, Bay of (bĭs'kā; -kĭ); *anc.* **Ma're Can·tab'-ri·cum** (mā'rē kăn·tăb'rĭ·kŭm) or **Aq'ui·tan'i·cus Si'nus** (ăk'wĭ·tăn'ĭ·kŭs sī'nŭs), *also* **Si'nus Can·tab'-ri·cus** (kăn·tăb'rĭ·kŭs) or **Can'ta·ber O·ce'a·nus** (kăn'tà·bẽr ō·sē'à·nŭs). Great inlet of the Atlantic Ocean on W coast of France and N coast of Spain, from Ushant I. on the N to Cape Ortegal, Spain, on the S; receives the Loire, Garonne, and Adour rivers on the E.

Bis'cayne Bay (bĭs'kān; bĭs·kān'). Inlet of Atlantic Ocean on E coast of Dade co., SE Florida; the city of Miami is on its NW shore and the island of **Biscayne Key** is on the NE.

Bi·sce'glie (bē·shā'lyå). Seaport, Bari prov., Apulia, SE Italy, on Adriatic 21 m. WNW of Bari; pop. 33,552.

Bisch'heim' (*Fr.* bē'shĕm'; *Ger.* bĭsh'hīm). Commune, Bas-Rhin dept., NE France, NW suburb of Strasbourg; pop. (1931) 10,955.

Bisch'off, Mount (bĭsh'ôf). Mountain near Waratah (*q.v.*), Tasmania, Australia; tin ore.

Bish'en·pur' (bĭsh'ĕn·pōōr'). Town on lake, S cen. Manipur state, NE Indian Union, ab. 20 m. SSW of Imphal; severe fighting near here Apr. 1944 in which Japanese advance was stopped.

Bish'nu·pur' (bĭsh'nōō·pōōr'). Town, Bankura dist., West Bengal, NE Indian Union, 75 m. NW of Calcutta; pop. 19,398; in ancient times an important city.

Bish'op (bĭsh'ŭp). City, Inyo co., E California, in Owens river valley 35 m. W of Nevada border; pop. 2875; stock raising and tungsten mining.

Bishop and Clerks (klärks). Group of small rocky islands in St. George's Channel, off Pembrokeshire, SW coast of Wales; 5 m. W of St. David's Head.

Bishop Auck'land (ôk'lănd). Urban district, Durham, N England, at confluence of Wear and Gaunless rivers 23 m. S of Newcastle; pop. 36,350.

Bish'op's Falls (bĭsh'ŭps fôlz'). **1** Waterfall in Exploits river, cen. Newfoundland, ab. 14 m. from its mouth.

2 Lumber town on Exploits river near the falls; pop. (1942 est.) 2300; pulp and paper mills.

Bishop's Stort′ford (stôr′ferd; stôrt′ferd). Urban district, Hertfordshire, SE England, on the Stort 28 m. NNE of London; pop. 12,772.

Bishop's Wearmouth. See SUNDERLAND, England.

Bish′op·ville (bĭsh′ŭp·vĭl). Town, ⊗ of Lee co., NE cen. South Carolina, 22 m. NNE of Sumter; pop. 3586.

Bisitun. See BEHISTUN.

Bisk (byĕsk) *or* **Biisk** (byē′ĭsk). Town, E Altai Territory, Soviet Russia, Asia, on the Biya river near its junction with the Katun 80 m. SE of Barnaul; pop. 80,190.

Bis′kra (bĭs′krŏ). **1** Commune, S Constantine dept., NE Algeria, at an oasis ab. 120 m. S of the city of Constantine; pop. 18,944; winter resort. In fort here French garrison massacred by Arabs May 12, 1844.

2 Adjacent unorganized commune in Touggourt territory; pop. 16,578.

Bis′ku·pitz (bĭs′kŏŏ·pĭts). Former commune, Oppeln govt. dist., Silesia, Germany; 1927–45 a section (pop. 17,272) of city of Hindenburg (see ZABRZE).

Bis′ley (bĭz′lĭ). Village, Surrey, S England, ab. 29 m. SW of London and ab. 7 m. NE of Aldershot; scene since 1890 (cf. WIMBLEDON) of annual meet of National Rifle Association.

Bis′marck (bĭz′märk). City, ✻ of North Dakota and ⊗ of Burleigh co., S cen. North Dakota, on Missouri river; pop. 27,670. First settled 1871–72; became territorial capital 1883. Railroad division point and terminal; base of upper Missouri river navigation; trading center in heart of spring-wheat region; manufactures flour, farm machinery, feeds; packing plants.

Bis′marck Archipelago (bĭz′märk). Island group in W Pacific Ocean N of E end of island of New Guinea, including islands of New Britain, New Ireland, New Hanover, Admiralty Is., and about 200 other islands and islets; 22,920 sq. m.; pop. ab. 202,000; part of the Territory of New Guinea; seat of government Lae on New Guinea (before 1941 Rabaul, *q.v.*, on New Britain). Islands are of volcanic origin with active volcanoes, esp. on New Britain; main part of archipelago is circular in form enclosing extensive Bismarck Sea and lies bet. 1° and 6°20′S lat. and 145° and 154°E long.; natives mainly Melanesians, with many different languages; chief products copra, cocoa, and shellfish. See *Map* at NEW GUINEA.

History: First visited in early part of 17th cent.; coasts of New Britain explored by Dampier 1700 and after 1767 other islands by Carteret and others. Proclaimed German protectorate 1884. Occupied by Australians 1914 and included in mandate (Territory of New Guinea) to Australia 1920. Seized by Japanese Jan. 1942; Rabaul, Gasmata, Kavieng frequently bombed by Allied forces 1943–44; parts of New Britain and the Admiralty Is. seized 1944 but Japanese forces in many places bypassed in advance of Allies to Philippine Is.

Bismarckburg. See KASANGA.

Bis′marck·hüt′te (bĭs′märk·hüt′ĕ). Former commune, Polish Silesia; since 1934 a part of Chorzów.

Bis′marck Range (bĭz′märk). Mountain range, E New Guinea I., in North-East New Guinea; highest peak ab. 15,400 ft.

Bis′marck Sea (bĭz′märk). Part of the W Pacific Ocean enclosed by the islands of the Bismarck Archipelago, ab. 500 m. across from E to W. In battle of Bismarck Sea Mar. 2–3, 1943 Allied planes completely destroyed Japanese fleet of 10 warships, 12 transports, 63 planes.

Bisnulok. See PHITSANULOK.

Bi′son (bī′s′n; -z′n). Town, ⊗ of Perkins co., NW South Dakota; pop. 457.

Bi·son′ti·um (bī·zŏn′shĭ·ŭm; -shŭm). Variant of *Vesontio:* see BESANÇON.

Bissagos Islands. See Ilhas dos BIJAGOS.

Bis·sau′ (bĭ·sou′) *or* **Bis·são′** (bē·souN′). Chief port and ✻ of Portuguese Guinea, W Africa; pop. 18,309.

Bis′ti·neau, Lake (bĭs′tĭ·nō). Lake ab. 30 m. long and 2 m. wide on boundary bet. Bienville and Bossier parishes, NW Louisiana; navigable for steamboats; connected by outlet stream S with Red river.

Bis′tri·ţa (bēs′trĕ·tsä) *or* **Bis′tri·tsa.** River 185 m. long in NE Romania; rises in SE Carpathian Mts., flows SE into Siret river near Bacău in Moldavia.

Bistriţa *or* **Bistritsa;** *Hung.* **Besz′ter·cze** (bĕs′tĕr·tsĕ). **1** River ab. 60 m. long, an upper tributary of the Someş in N Transylvania.

2 City, N Transylvania region, N cen. Romania, on Bistriţa river ab. 40 m. N of Târgu-Mureş; pop. 13,251; founded by German colonists in 12th cent.

Bisutun. See BEHISTUN.

Bitche (bēch); *Ger.* **Bitsch** (bĭch). Commune, Moselle dept., NE France, near Saar border 60 m. NW of Strasbourg; pop. 5552. Citadel on rocky hill dominating the town defended in several wars; in World War II a strong point of German defense, taken by U.S. troops Jan. 1945.

Bi·thyn′i·a (bĭ·thĭn′ĭ·à). Ancient country in NW Asia Minor, bordering on the Propontis and Euxine and adjoining Paphlagonia on the E and Galatia, Phrygia, and Mysia on the S. Mountainous and well-forested; on the W indented by two inlets and crossed by the Sangarius (*mod.* Sakarya) river. Settled by a Thracian tribe. Its first king, Nicomedes I, founded Nicomedia (*mod.* İzmit) as capital 264 B.C.; prosperous until overcome by Mithridates of Pontus; became Roman province 74 B.C. with varying boundaries; known as **Bithynia et (and) Pon′tus** (ĕt pŏn′tŭs) 98–117 A.D.; under Byzantine Empire divided into two parts.

Bithynium. See CLAUDIOPOLIS.

Bit·lis′ (bĕt·lēs′). **1** Vilayet, E Turkey in Asia, formed from part of Muş vilayet; pop. (1940) 68,825.

2 Commercial and manufacturing town, its ✻, ab. 16 m. SW of Lake Van; pop. 10,122; at altitude 4700 ft., with good climate.

Bi′tolj (bē′tôl·y′) *or* **Mon′as·tir′** (mŏn′ăs·tîr′; *Turk.* mô·nä·stēr′). City, Macedonia federated republic, Yugoslavia; pop. (1931) 33,024; industrial and commercial center; founded by Slavs 1014 near ancient **Her′a·cle′a Lyn·ces′tis** (hĕr′à·klē′à lĭn·sĕs′tĭs). On plain at altitude of 2019 ft., strategically situated; passed to Turks 1382 and strengthened by them about 1820; taken from Turks in Second Balkan War and assigned to Serbia by Treaty of Bucharest 1913. In World War I taken 1915 by Bulgaria but retaken by Allies; again captured 1941 by Bulgarians in World War II.

Bi·ton′to (bē·tôn′tô); *anc.* **Bu·tun′tum** (bû·tŭn′tŭm). Commune, Bari prov., Apulia, SE Italy, 8 m. W of Bari; pop. 30,622; 12th-cent. Romanesque cathedral.

Bitsch. See BITCHE.

Bit′ter·feld (bĭt′ẽr·fĕlt). Industrial city, E Germany, in former Prussian province of Saxony, 45 m. SE of Magdeburg; pop. 19,384; lignite works; manufactures chemicals, clayware and stoneware, machinery, etc., and in recent years large synthetic-oil works. Founded 1153; conquered by landgrave Dietrich von Meissen 1476; under Saxon rule; passed to Prussia 1815.

Bit′ter·fon·tein′ (bĭt′ẽr·fŏn·tān′). Town, W Cape Prov., Union of South Africa, 180 m. N of Cape Town.

Bit′ter Lakes (bĭt′ẽr). Two lakes, **Great Bitter Lake** and **Little Bitter Lake,** Isthmus of Suez, Egypt, just N of Suez; connected and traversed by the Suez Canal (23 m. across). Originally in ancient bed of Red Sea; in modern times marshy depressions until filled by the cutting of the canal.

Bit′ter·root′ *or* **Bitter Root** (bĭt′ẽr·rōōt′; -rŏŏt′). River, W Montana; rises in S Ravalli co., flows N and joins Clark Fork near Missoula in cen. Missoula co.

Bitterroot, *or* **Bitter Root, Range** *or* **Mountains.** A range of the Rocky Mts. ab. 400 m. long extending along the Idaho-Montana boundary; highest peak Garfield Mt. 10,961 ft.; pierced by **Bitterroot Tunnel,** a railroad tunnel nearly 2 m. long.

Biv′ouac Peak (bĭv′wăk; bĭv′o͝o·ăk). Mountain 11,045 ft. in N Grand Teton National Park, NW Wyoming.

Bi·wa (bē·wä) *or* **O·mi** (ō·mē). Lake in W cen. Honshu, Japan, NE of Kyoto; 40 m. long and 12 m. wide; altitude 285 ft.; remarkable for its scenic beauty and famous in Japanese legends; its outlet is the Yodo.

Bix′schoo′te (bĭk′sκō′tĕ). Village, West Flanders prov., NW Belgium, 5 m. N of Ieper (Ypres); pop. 758; scene of first German gas attack Apr. 22, 1915 in World War I.

Bi′ya (bē′yȧ; *Russ.* byĕ′yȧ). River ab. 350 m. long, N Oirot Autonomous Region, Soviet Russia, Asia; flows NW, joins the Katun to form the Ob.

Bi·ya′la (bĭ·yă′lȧ; -lȧ). Town, Gharbîya prov., Lower Egypt, ab. 14 m. NW of El Mansûra; pop. ab. 16,000.

Bi′zerte′ (bē′zĕrt′; *Angl.* bĭ·zûrt′ *and, popularly,* bĭ·zûr′tĕ) *or* **Bi·zer′ta** (bĭ·zûr′tȧ; *Span.* bĕ·thĕr′tä, -sĕr′-); *anc.* **Hip′po Za·ry′tus** (hĭp′ō zȧ·rī′tŭs). Fortified seaport, N Tunisia, N Africa; northernmost town in Africa; pop. (1936) 28,468; threefold harbor: outer harbor on Mediterranean with breakwater and two jetties, inner harbor (Bay of Sebra) connected with outer by canal, and Lake Bizerte (*q.v.*) with well-developed naval port and arsenal (Sidi Abdallah); military post, Ferryville, on S shore of lake. In early times a Roman colony; taken by Arabs 7th cent.; subject for many years to Tunis and Constantine and scene of frequent revolts. Harbor fell into neglect but after French seizure in 1881, remade and opened 1895. In World War II captured by Allies May 7–9, 1943.

Bizerte *or* **Bizerta, Lake.** Deep-water lagoon 50 sq. m. forming a landlocked harbor for Bizerte (*q.v.*).

Bi·zo′ni·a (bĭ·zō′nĭ·ȧ). The western part of Germany comprising the two zones of occupation controlled by U.S. and Great Britain, assigned 1945 at end of World War II; united Aug. 1947 and set up Jan. 8, 1948 as new nonpolitical economic administration; occupation statute revoked 1955. See GERMANY.

Bi′zot′ (bē′zō′). Commune, Constantine dept., NE Algeria, just N of Constantine; pop. 10,845.

Bje′lo·var (byĕ′lô·vär). Town, Croatia, N Yugoslavia, 43 m. E of Zagreb; pop. (1931) 10,279.

Björk′ö′ (byûrk′û′). Swedish name of Koivisto, fortress and outer port of Viipuri, Finland (now Vyborg in U.S.S.R.); scene of signing of treaty July 24, 1905 bet. William II of Germany and Nicholas II, tsar of Russia, in an unsuccessful attempt to form a coalition against Great Britain. See KOIVISTO.

Björneborg. See PORI.

Blaa′vand (blô′vȧn), **Cape;** *Dan.* **Blaa′vands Huk** (blô′vȧns ho͝ok′). Cape on W cen. coast of Jutland Penin., Denmark.

Black (blăk). 1 River ab. 70 m. long, E cen. Louisiana; formed by confluence of Ouachita and Tensas rivers; flows S into Red river forming section of boundary bet. Catahoula and Concordia parishes, E cen. Louisiana. 2 River 280 m. long, SE Missouri and NE Arkansas; navigable 100 m.; rises in NE Reynolds co., SE Missouri, flows S into White river on boundary of Jackson and Independence cos., NE cen. Arkansas. 3 River 125 m. long, N cen. New York; rises in Herkimer co., flows W and NW into Lake Ontario near Watertown, Jefferson co.; navigable for 40 m. 4 River, SE North Carolina; flows S from Sampson co. into Cape Fear river ab. 10 m. above Wilmington. 5 River, E South Carolina; rises in Sumter co., flows SE into Winyah Bay in E Georgetown co. 6 River, N Vermont; rises in S Orleans co., flows N into Lake Memphremagog. 7 River, SE Vermont; flows S and SE in Windsor co. into Connecticut river. 8 River ab. 200 m. long, W cen. Wisconsin; rises in Taylor co., flows SW into Mississippi river at La Crosse.

Black Belt. A strip of rolling prairie land extending across cen. Alabama and Mississippi, with black clayey soil, good for growing cotton.

Black Broth′ers (brŭth′ẽrz). Mountain 6620 ft. in Yancey co., W North Carolina.

Black′burn (blăk′bẽrn). County borough, Lancashire, NW England, 21 m. NNW of Manchester; pop. 122,697, (1951) 111,217; has textile mills, one of the greatest cotton-weaving centers in the world; coal fields nearby.

Blackburn, Mount. Mountain 16,140 ft., Wrangell Mts., SE Alaska, 120 m. NE of mouth of Copper river.

Black Butte. Isolated peak 3468 ft. in Slope co., SW North Dakota; highest point in the state.

Black Canyon. 1 Canyon of the Colorado river bet. Arizona and Nevada; ab. 15 m. long; site of Boulder Canyon project ab. 25 m. SE of Las Vegas, Nevada. See UNITED STATES, *Dams and Reservoirs* (Hoover Dam). 2 Canyon of the Gunnison river in NE Montrose co., W Colorado, where the river cuts through granite, gneiss, and black schist; ab. 50 m. long, averages 1300 ft. wide, walls 3000 ft. at highest point; most picturesque part is now the **Black Canyon of the Gunnison National Monument:** see UNITED STATES, *National Monuments.*

Black Country. The Midland districts of S Staffordshire and N Warwickshire, England—so called because of the grime from the coal and iron mines and industries.

Black Di′a·mond (dī′ȧ·mŭnd). Town, King co., W cen. Washington, ab. 22 m. E of Tacoma; pop. (1940) 1026; coal mines.

Black Dome. Peak 3990 ft. in the Catskill Mts., Greene co., SE New York.

Black Down. See MENDIP HILLS.

Black′foot′ (blăk′fo͝ot′). 1 River ab. 100 m. long, SE Idaho; flows out of **Blackfoot River Reservoir,** Caribou co., NW and W into Snake river in cen. Bingham co. 2 City, ⊗ of Bingham co., SE Idaho, 23 m. N of Pocatello; pop. 7378; sugar beets; sugar refinery.

Blackfoot Mountain. Peak 9597 ft. in cen. Glacier National Park, NW Montana, SW of St. Mary Lakes; has glacier on N slope.

Black′ford (blăk′fẽrd). County in Indiana. See *Table* at INDIANA.

Black Forest; *Ger.* **Schwarz′wald′** (shvärts′vält′). Mountainous region in SW Germany, in the states of Württemberg and Baden, along E bank of upper Rhine from the Neckar to the Swiss border; highest peak Feldberg 4695 ft.; higher parts thickly forested; has many lakes and mineral springs, contains sources of Neckar and Danube rivers; favorite tourist resort.

Black Hawk (blăk′ hôk′). County in Iowa. See *Table* at IOWA.

Black′head′ (blăk′hĕd′). 1 Peak 12,500 ft., San Juan Mts., E Archuleta co., S Colorado. 2 Cape on NE coast of Ireland, on N side of entrance to Belfast Lough; lighthouse.

Black Head (blăk′ hĕd′). 1 Peak 3937 ft. in the Catskill Mts., Greene co., SE New York. 2 Cape on W coast of Ireland, on S side of entrance to Galway Bay.

Black′heath′ (blăk′hēth′). Common and pleasure resort, 267 acres, SE London, England, mainly in Lewisham metropolitan borough S of the Thames; headquarters of Kentish rebels 1381 under Wat Tyler and again 1450 under Jack Cade; later notorious for its highwaymen. Here golf first introduced into England 1608.

Black Hills. Group of mountains in W South Dakota and NE Wyoming; total area ab. 6000 sq. m.; contains gold, lead, and other mineral deposits; highest mountain 7242 ft. Harney Peak, South Dakota; drained chiefly by the Belle Fourche and South fork of Cheyenne river.

Blackhope Scar. See MOORFOOT HILLS.

Black Lake. 1 Lake ab. 13 m. long in N Natchitoches parish, NW cen. Louisiana; outlet is to Red river; part of a large fish and game preserve. 2 Lake ab. 20 m. long in W St. Lawrence co., N New York; outlet from N end into Oswegatchie river. 3 Town, Megantic co., S Quebec, Canada, 5 m. SSW of Thetford Mines; pop. 2800; asbestos mines.

Black Me′sa (mä′så). Elevation 4978 ft., extreme NW Oklahoma, in Cimarron co.; highest point in the state.

Black′more, Mount (blăk′mŏr). Peak 10,196 ft. in cen. Gallatin co., S Montana.

Black Mountain. 1 Peak 3600 ft. in Dawson and Gilmer cos., N Georgia.
2 Peak 9020 ft. in N Grant co., SW New Mexico.
3 Town, Buncombe co., W North Carolina, 13 m. E of Asheville; pop. 1313; summer tourist center.

Black Mountains. 1 Ridge in W Mohave co., NW cen. Arizona, along E bank of Colorado river.
2 Range of Blue Ridge Mts. in W North Carolina, chiefly in Yancey and Buncombe cos.; highest peak Mount Mitchell 6684 ft.
3 Range in Brecknockshire, SE Wales, E of the Usk river; highest peak 2660 ft.

Black Pine Peak. Mountain 9386 ft. in SE Cassia co., S Idaho.

Black′pool′ (blăk′pōōl′). County borough. Lancashire, NW England, on Irish Sea 30 m. N of Liverpool; pop. 101,553, (1951) 147,131; seaside pleasure resort.

Black River. 1 Name of several rivers in U.S.: see BLACK, above.
2 Town on SW coast of Jamaica, West Indies Fed.

Black River Falls. City, ⊗ of Jackson co., W cen. Wisconsin, on falls of Black river 25 m. N of Sparta; pop. 3195; lumber and grist mills; dairying; poultry.

Black′rock′ (blăk′rŏk′). Residential urban district, co. Dublin, E Eire; pop. 11,982; a SE suburb of Dublin on the coast near Dun Laoghaire.

Black Rock Desert. Alkaline sink in NW Nevada; ab. 70 m. long and 20 m. wide; 1000 sq. m.; **Black Rock Range** (highest point 8618 ft.) extends along its W side, in Humboldt co.

Blacks′burg (blăks′bûrg). **1** Town, Cherokee co., N South Carolina, 27 m. ENE of Spartanburg; pop. 2174.
2 Town, Montgomery co., W Virginia, 28 m. W of Roanoke; pop. 7070; Virginia Polytechnic Institute (1872).

Black Sea; *also* **Eux′ine** (ūk′sĭn; *Brit. usually* -sīn) **Sea;** *Russ.* **Cher′no·e Mo′re** (chôr′nŭ·yě mô′ryě); *anc.* **Pon′tus** *or* **Pon′tus Eux·i′nus** (pŏn′tŭs ūk·sĭ′nŭs). Sea bet. Europe and Asia; 168 500 sq. m.; greatest depth ab. 7200 ft.; connected with Aegean Sea through the Bosporus, Sea of Marmara, and Dardanelles, and with the Sea of Azov, its N arm, by Kerch Strait; receives many rivers, esp.: Danube, Dniester, Bug, Dnieper, Kuban (of Europe); Kızıl Irmak and Sakarya (of Turkey in Asia); the Sea of Azov receives the Don.

Black′shear′ (blăk′shẽr′). City, ⊗ of Pierce co., SE Georgia, 10 m. NE of Waycross; pop. 2182.

Black′sod′ Bay (blăk′sŏd′) Inlet of Atlantic Ocean on W coast of Ireland, S of Erris Head. enclosed on the W by Mullet Penin.

Black′stock′ Knob (blăk′stŏk′). Peak 6386 ft. in Buncombe co., W North Carolina.

Black′stone (blăk′stōn). **1** River 40 m. long, S cen. Massachusetts and NE Rhode Island; rises in S cen. Worcester co., Mass., flows SE across NE corner of Rhode Island, becomes the Sekonk at Pawtucket.
2 Town, Worcester co., cen. Massachusetts, 20 m. SE of Worcester; pop. 5130; textiles.
3 Town, Nottoway co., S cen. Virginia, 36 m. WSW of Petersburg; pop. 3659; tobacco market.

Black Stream. See JAPAN CURRENT.

Black′town′ (blăk′toun′). Town, E New South Wales, SE Australia, on railroad ab. 10 m. NW of Sydney.

Black Volta. See Black VOLTA.

Black War′ri·or (wŏr′ĭ-ẽr; wôr′yẽr). Navigable river 178 m. long, cen. Alabama; formed by confluence of Locust and Mulberry forks in Jefferson co. flows SW, through coal fields, into Tombigbee river near Demopolis; furnishes water power above Tuscaloosa.

Black′wa′ter (blăk′wô′tẽr; -wŏt′ẽr). **1** River ab. 85 m. long, cen. Missouri; rises in W Johnson co., flows E into Missouri river in N Cooper co.

2 River, SE Virginia; rises in Prince George co., joins Nottoway river on North Carolina boundary to form the Chowan.
3 River ab. 130 m. long, S cen. British Columbia, Canada; flows E into Fraser river.
4 River 100 m. long, S Eire; rises 16 m. NE of Killarney, flows E across co. Cork, then S to Youghal Bay.
5 River ab. 40 m. long, co. Meath, E Eire; flows SE from co. Cavan into the Boyne river at Navan.
6 River 40 m. long, W Essex co., SE England; rises near Saffron Walden and flows SE into the North Sea.
7 River, SW cen. Northern Ireland; rises in co. Tyrone and flows along boundary bet. cos. Tyrone and Armagh into SW Lough Neagh.

Blackwater Falls. Falls 63 ft. high in Blackwater river (tributary of Cheat river) above **Blackwater Canyon** (gorge ab. 10 m. long with rugged walls 1000 ft. high) in **Blackwater Falls State Park,** Tucker co., NE West Virginia, at N end of Monongahela National Forest.

Black′well (blăk′wĕl; -wĕl). City, Kay co., N Oklahoma; pop. 9588; oil refining, zinc smelting, meat packing.

Black′wells Island (blăk′wĕlz; -wĕlz). See WELFARE ISLAND.

Bla′den (blā′d′n). County in North Carolina. See *Table* at NORTH CAROLINA.

Bla′dens·burg (blā′d′nz·bûrg). Town, Prince Georges co., S cen. Maryland, 7 m. ENE of Washington; pop. 3103; site of battle Aug. 24, 1814 in which American defeat by British resulted in the burning of most of the public buildings of Washington Aug. 24–25, 1814.

Blaen·av′on (blīn·ăv′ŭn). Urban district, Monmouthshire, W England, 31 m. NW of Bristol; pop. 9777.

Bla·go·dat′, Mount (blŭ·gŭ·dăt′). See NIZHNI TAGIL.

Bla′go·vesh′chensk (blăg′ŏ·vĕsh′chĕnsk; *Russ.* blŭ-gŭ·vyăsh′chĕnsk). Commercial city on Amur river, near Khabarovsk Territory, Soviet Russia, Asia, near junction with Zeya river; pop. 58,761; trading center, at head of navigation. Founded 1856 by Nikolai Muraviëv; scene of Russo-Japanese naval incident 1937; base for Russian advances into Manchuria Aug. 1945.

Blaina. See NANTYGLO AND BLAINA.

Blaine. **1** Name of counties in four states of the U.S. See *Tables* at IDAHO, MONTANA, NEBRASKA, OKLAHOMA.
2 Village, Anoka co., Minnesota, NW of Minneapolis; pop. 7570.
3 City and port of entry, Whatcom co., NW Washington, near Canadian boundary 20 m. NNW of Bellingham; pop. 1735; in farming section; tourist center.

Blair (blâr). **1** County in Pennsylvania. See *Table* at PENNSYLVANIA.
2 City, ⊗ of Washington co., E Nebraska, on Missouri river 22 m. N of Omaha; pop. 4931; trade center in agricultural section. Dana College (1884; coed.).

Blair′more (blâr′mŏr). Coal-mining town, S Alberta, Canada, near Brit. Columbia border 72 m. W of Lethbridge; pop. 1933.

Blairs′town (blârz′toun). Township, Warren co., NW New Jersey, 12 m. WSW of Newton; pop. 1797; farming.

Blairs′ville (blârz′vĭl). **1** Town, ⊗ of Union co., N Georgia; pop. 437.
2 Borough, Indiana co., W cen. Pennsylvania, on Conemaugh river 21 m. W of Johnstown; pop. 4930.

Bla′kang Ma′ti (blä′käng mä′tē). Fortified island ab. 2 m. long in Singapore Strait just SSW of Singapore, Malaya; part of the defense of Singapore harbor.

Blake Deep (blāk). One of the deepest parts 28,300 ft. of Atlantic Ocean, N of Puerto Rico.

Blake′ly (blāk′lĭ). **1** City, ⊗ of Early co., SW Georgia, 47 m. WSW of Albany; pop. 3580; founded 1821.
2 Borough, Lackawanna co., NE Pennsylvania, 7 m. NE of Scranton; pop. 6374; suburb of Scranton; coal mining.

Blake Point (blāk). Point at NE extremity of Isle Royale, NW Lake Superior.

Blam·bang′an Peninsula (blām·bäng′än). Narrow strip of land forming southeasternmost point of Java, Indonesia, bet. S end of Bali Strait and Indian Ocean.

Blanc, Cape (blän; *Angl.* blängk, blăngk). Cape on N tip of Tunisia; northernmost point of Africa, 37°14′N.

Blanc (blän; *Angl.* blängk, blăngk), *or* **Blan′co** (bläng′-kô), **Cape.** Cape on NW coast of Africa; a narrow peninsula extending S into Atlantic Ocean; bisected by the boundary bet. Río de Oro zone of Spanish Sahara and Mauritania, West Africa.

Blanc, Mont (môn′ blän′; *Angl.* mŏnt′ blängk′, blăngk′); *Ital.* **Mon′te Bian′co** (môn′tä byäng′kô). Highest mountain 15,781 ft. of the Alps, Savoy Alps, Haute-Savoie dept., SE France, on Italian border. Beneath it is **Mont Blanc Tunnel** (7½ m.) connecting Chamonix, France, with Courmayeur, Italy; longest vehicular tunnel in the world.

Blan′ca, La·gu′na (lä·gōō′nä vläng′kä). Large freshwater lake in extreme S Chile, E of Skyring Water.

Blan′ca Peak (bläng′ka). Mountain 14,390 ft. in Castilla, Huerfano, and Alamosa cos., S Colorado; highest peak in the Sangre de Cristo Mts.

Blanche Bay (blänch). Inlet of Pacific Ocean on NE coast of New Britain I., Bismarck Archipelago; its inner part, Simpson Harbour, is site of Rabaul.

Blanche Harbour. Protected body of water in Treasury Is., S of Bougainville I., Solomon Is., bet. Mono and Stirling Is.: affords good anchorage.

Blan′ches·ter (blăn′chĕs′tēr; -chĭs·tēr). Industrial village, Clinton co., SW Ohio, 29 m. ENE of Cincinnati; pop. 2944; manufactures pumps, textiles. Settled 1832.

Blanc–Mesnil, Le. See LE BLANC-MESNIL.

Blanc′-Nez′ (bläN′nā′). Literally "White Nose"; white chalk cliff forming a cape on Strait of Dover, N France, 5 m. W of Calais; its companion cape is Gris-Nez (*q.v.*).

Blan′co (bläng′kô). County in Texas. See *Table* at TEXAS.

Blan′co (bläng′kô). **1** River ab. 230 m. long in E Bolivia; flows NW into Baures river.
2 River ab. 45 m. long in N Honduras; flows out of Lake Yojoa (*q.v.*) into the Ulúa river.

Blan′co, Cape (bläng′kô). Cape on NW coast of Curry co., SW corner of Oregon; westernmost point of Oregon, 124°32′W.

Blan′co, Cape (bläng′kô). **1** See Cape BLANC, Africa.
2 Cape at S extremity of Nicoya Penin., on W coast of Costa Rica, at the entrance to the Gulf of Nicoya.
3 Cape at extreme NW tip of Peru.

Blan′co, Pi′co (pē′kô vläng′kô). Mountain 11,693 ft. in SE Costa Rica, in the Cordillera de Talamanca.

Blanc Sa′blon′ (bläN′ sá′blôN′). Village, E Quebec, Canada, on **Blanc Sablon Bay,** inlet at S end of Strait of Belle Isle on boundary bet. Labrador and Quebec.

Bland (blănd). **1** County in Virginia. See *Table* at VIRGINIA.
2 Village, its ⊗, western Virginia.

Blan′ken·ber′ghe (bläng′kĕn·bĕr′kĕ). Commune, West Flanders prov., NW Belgium; pop. 7277; resort.

Blan′ken·burg *or* **Blankenburg am Harz** (bläng′-kĕn·bŏŏrk äm härts′). City, Magdeburg dist., East Germany, in Harz Mts. 36 m. SE of Brunswick; pop. 12,062; tourist resort; manufactures tile, wooden goods.

Blan′ke·ne′se (bläng′kĕ·nā′zĕ). Former commune, Schleswig govt. dist., Schleswig-Holstein prov., Prussia, Germany, on Elbe river 9 m. W of Hamburg; in 1929 made part of Hamburg.

Blan·quil′la (bläng·kē′yä). Venezuelan island in Caribbean Sea 74 m. NNE of La Tortuga I.

Blan·tyre′ (blăn·tīr′). Town Shire Highlands, S Malawi, SE Africa; combined with Limbe into municipality 1959; total pop. 62,600; chief commercial center of Malawi.

Blar′ney (blär′nĭ). Town, cen. co. Cork, SW Eire, 4 m. NW of Cork; pop. 723; in its 15th-cent. Blarney Castle is the "Blarney stone," which is said to make anyone who kisses it proficient in blarney (i.e., smooth wheedling talk or flattery).

Blas′dell (blāz′dĕl). Village, Erie co., W New York, on Lake Erie 7 m. S of Buffalo; pop. 3909.

Blas′ket Islands (blás′kĕt; -kĭt). Group of small islands off SW coast of Ireland, N of entrance to Dingle Bay; in co. Kerry; largest is Great Blasket.

Bla′vet′ (blá′vĕ′). River ab. 90 m. long, Brittany, NW France; rises in Côtes-du-Nord dept.. flows SSW to the Bay of Biscay; its estuary forms the harbor of Lorient.

Blaw′nox (blô′nŏks). Industrial borough, Allegheny co., SW Pennsylvania, on Allegheny river 9 m. ENE of Pittsburgh; pop. 2085; steel and iron manufactures.

Blay′don (blā′d′n). Urban district, Durham, N England, on the Tyne 5 m. W of Newcastle; pop. 30,791; iron and steel manufactures, brick kilns; coal.

Bleck′ley (blĕk′lĭ). County in Georgia. See *Table* at GEORGIA.

Bled (blĕd). Resort village in mountains of NW Yugoslavia ab. 30 m. NW of Ljubljana.

Bled′soe (blĕd′sō). County in Tennessee. See *Table* at TENNESSEE.

Ble′king·e (blā′kĭng·ĕ). Province of Sweden. See *Table* at SWEDEN.

Blencathara. See SADDLEBACK.

Blen′heim. 1 (blĕn′ĭm; -ĕm; *Fr.* blĕ′nĕm′); *Eng. and French form of German* **Blind′heim** (blĭnt′hīm). Village on Danube, W Bavaria, Germany, 23 m. NNW of Augsburg; scene of victory Aug. 13, 1704 of English under Marlborough and Prince Eugene over French and Bavarians under Marshals Tallard and Marsin in War of Spanish Succession; called also battle of Höchstädt (*q.v.*).
2 (blĕn′ĭm; -ĕm) Town, Kent co., SE Ontario, Canada, 10 m. SE of Chatham; pop. 2459.
3 (blĕn′ĭm; -ĕm) Borough, ✳ of Marlborough provincial dist., NE South I., New Zealand; pop. (1941 est.) 5200; harbor for smaller vessels.

Blen′heim Park (blĕn′ĭm; -ĕm). Civil parish, orig. seat **(Blenheim Palace)** of duke of Marlborough, near Woodstock, Oxfordshire, cen. England; granted to duke by government in Queen Anne's reign.

Blen′ner·has′sett Island (blĕn′ēr·hăs′ĕt; -ĭt). Island in Ohio river 2 m. below Parkersburg, West Virginia, famous as meeting place 1805 of Aaron Burr and Harman Blennerhassett who had purchased part of island 1798.

Blesae. See BLOIS.

Bletch′ley (blĕch′lĭ). Urban district, Buckinghamshire, SE cen. England, 43 m. NW of London; pop. 10,916.

Blgariya. See BULGARIA.

Blib′ba (blĭb′á; *Fr.* blĕ′bá′). Town, Togo, W Africa, on railroad ab. 143 m. N of Lomé.

Bli′da (blē′dá; -dä). City, N Alger dept., N Algeria, just SW of the city of Algiers; pop. (1960) 93,000; beautifully situated on edge of a plain at base of Maritime Atlas Mts.; active trade in oranges and flour. Dates from 16th cent.; important under the Turks; airfield taken by Americans Nov. 8, 1942.

Blindheim. See BLENHEIM.

Blind River (blīnd). Town, Algoma dist., S Ontario, Canada, port on North Channel at mouth of Mississagi river 70 m. E of Sault Ste. Marie; pop. 2512; railroad town in mining district; lumber; paper mills.

Bliss′field (blĭs′fēld). Village, Lenawee co., S Michigan, 32 m. S of Ann Arbor; pop. 2653.

Bli′tar (blē′tär). Town, East Java prov., Indonesia, SE of Kediri; pop. 27,846.

Block Island (blŏk). **1** Island 7 m. long by 3½ m. wide in Atlantic Ocean at E entrance to Long Island Sound, ab. 9 m. SW of Point Judith, Rhode Island; part of Washington co., Rhode Island; coextensive with town of New Shoreham; summer resort and deep-sea fishing center; has two good harbors and two lighthouses. First settlement 1661; admitted to the colony 1664.
2 Village in town of New Shoreham, Washington co., SE Rhode Island; resort.

Block Island Sound. Body of water bet. Washington co., S Rhode Island and Block I., connecting Atlantic Ocean on E with Long Island Sound on W.

Bloe'men·daal' (blōō'měn·dàl'). Commune, North Holland prov., W Netherlands, just N of Haarlem; pop. 14,086.

Bloem'fon·tein' (blōōm'fôn·tān'). City, * of Orange Free State, in cen. part, Union of South Africa, 295 m. W of Durban on a tributary of Modder river; pop. 145,273. Founded 1852; made municipality 1880; occupied by British 1900 without opposition. Trading center for cattle and sheep; seat of University College of the Orange Free State (formerly Grey University); possesses Lamont Telescope, largest in southern hemisphere; site of University of Michigan's southern observatory and of Boyden Station of Harvard Observatory.

Bloem'hof (blōōm'hôf). Town, SW Transvaal, NE Republic of South Africa, on Vaal river 95 m. NNE of Kimberley; pop. 2375; diamond mining; cattle.

Blois (blwà); *anc.* **Ble'sae** (blē'sē). Manufacturing city, Loir-et-Cher dept., N cen. France, on right bank of Loire river 35 m. SW of Orléans; pop. 26,025; 17th-cent. cathedral; ancient Roman aqueduct. Famous castle rich in historical associations: residence of counts of Blois; became a favorite residence of French kings.

Blom'i·don, Cape (blŏm'ĭ·dŭn). Cape and promontory (670 ft. high) on W coast of Nova Scotia, Canada, S of entrance to Minas Basin.

Blön'du·ós' (blûn'dü·ōs'). Village, NW Iceland, on E side of Húna Bay; pop. (1925) 273.

Bło'nie (błō'nyě). Village, Warszawa dept., Poland, ab. 17 m. W of Warsaw; in World War I in Russian W defense line, taken by Germans July 20, 1915.

Bloods'worth Island (blŭdz'wûrth; -wẽrth). Island in Chesapeake Bay, S Dorchester co., Maryland.

Bloody Nose Ridge. Name given by U.S. marines to Umurbrogol Mt. on Peleliu I., S Palau Is., W Pacific Ocean; scene of severe fighting Sept. 19–26, 1944 which resulted in isolation of Japanese.

Bloo'mer (blōō'mẽr). City, Chippewa co., W Wisconsin, 13 m. NNW of Chippewa Falls; pop. 2834.

Bloom'field (blōōm'fēld). **1** Residential and agricultural town, cen. Hartford co., N Connecticut, NNW of Hartford; pop. 13,613; incorp. 1835; tobacco raising.
2 Town, ⊗ of Greene co., SW Indiana, 24 m. WSW of Bloomington; pop. 2224; grain, livestock, lumber.
3 City, ⊗ of Davis co., SE Iowa, 18 m. S of Ottumwa; pop. 2771; distributing point in sheep-raising section.
4 City, ⊗ of Stoddard co., SE Missouri; pop. 1330.
5 Town, Essex co., NE New Jersey, 4 m. NNW of Newark; pop. 51,867; orig. part of Newark, made separate township 1812; manufactures electric appliances, cosmetics, porcelain enamel, woolens.

Bloom'ing·dale (blōōm'ĭng·dàl). Borough, Passaic co., N New Jersey, 9 m. WNW of Paterson; pop. 5293.

Bloom'ing Grove (blōōm'ĭng). See CORSICA, Ohio.

Bloom'ing·ton (blōōm'ĭng·tŭn). **1** City, ⊗ of McLean co., cen. Illinois, 35 m. ESE of Peoria; pop. 36,271; in coal-mining, farming, and dairy section; ironworks. Illinois Wesleyan University (1850; coed.).
2 City, ⊗ of Monroe co., S cen. Indiana, 45 m. SW of Indianapolis; pop. 31,357; settled 1815; limestone quarries. Indiana University (1820; coed. from 1867).
3 Village, Hennepin co., SE cen. Minnesota, SW of Minneapolis; pop. 50,498.

Blooms'burg (blōōmz'bûrg). Industrial town, ⊗ of Columbia co., E cen. Pennsylvania, 26 m. NNW of Pottsville; pop. 10,655; Bloomsburg State Coll. (1839; coed.).

Blooms'bur·y (blōōmz'bĕr·ĭ; -brĭ). A central district of London; British Museum, Univ. of London; once fashionable but now largely a lodginghouse area.

Blo'ra (blō'rä). Town, central Java prov., Indonesia, E of Semarang; pop. 18,451; in hilly region where much teak is produced.

Blore Heath (blōr). Area near Market Drayton, Shropshire, W England; site of Yorkist victory 1459.

Bloss'burg (blôs'bûrg). Borough, Tioga co., N Pennsylvania, on Tioga river 30 m. N of Williamsport; pop. 1956; iron foundries; coal mines.

Blount (blŭnt). Name of counties in two states of the U.S. See *Tables* at ALABAMA and TENNESSEE.

Blounts'town (blŭnts'toun). City, ⊗ of Calhoun co., NW Florida, on Apalachicola river 47 m. W of Tallahassee; pop. 2375; lumber and naval-stores center.

Blount'ville (blŭnt'vĭl; *Sou.* also -v'l). Unincorporated community, Sullivan co., NE Tennessee; pop. 9158.

Blu'cher Point (blōō'chẽr). Point of land on NE coast of Huon Penin., SE North-East New Guinea.

Blu'denz (blōō'děnts). Commune, in the Vorarlberg prov., SW Austria, on the Ill river 25 m. S of Bregenz; pop. ab. 7000; tourist resort; fine castle.

Blue (blōō). **1** River ab. 40 m. long, S Indiana; rises in Washington co., flows S into Ohio river.
2 Upper course of East Fork of the White river (*q.v.*), Indiana, to cen. Bartholomew co.

Blue Ash (ăsh). Village, Hamilton co., SW Ohio, NE of Cincinnati; pop. 8341.

Blue Earth. 1 County in Minnesota. See *Table* at MINNESOTA.
2 City, ⊗ of Faribault co., S Minnesota, 18 m. E of Fairmont; pop. 4200; in agricultural section.

Blue'field' (blōō'fēld'). **1** Town, Tazewell co., SW Virginia, on border adjoining Bluefield, West Virginia, 32 m. WNW of Pulaski; pop. 4235.
2 City, Mercer co., S West Virginia, in Blue Ridge Mts. contiguous with Bluefield, Virginia; pop. 19,256; near coal field, also iron, limestone, and silica mines; lumber mills. Bluefield State College (1895; coed.).

Blue'fields' (blōō'fēldz'). **1** River in Nicaragua. See ESCONDIDO.
2 Town, * of Zelaya dept., Nicaragua, on SE coast at mouth of the Escondido river; pop. (1943 est.) 10,292; export center for bananas, coconuts, and cabinet woods.

Blue'grass', the (blōō'grâs'). Region in central Kentucky where Kentucky bluegrass (*Poa pratensis*) abounds; noted for breeding of fine horses.

Blue Grot'to (grŏt'ō). Cavern ab. 175 ft. long and 50 ft. high on N shore of island of Capri, in Bay of Naples, Italy; renowned for the dazzling blue light inside.

Blue'hill' Bay (blōō'hĭl'). Inlet of Atlantic Ocean on S coast of Hancock co., Maine, W of Mt. Desert I.

Blue Island. City, Cook co., NE Illinois, 15 m. S of Chicago; pop. 19,618; industrial suburb of Chicago.

Blue Knob. Peak 3136 ft. in Bedford co., S Pennsylvania, N of Bedford.

Blue Licks (lĭks). Locality, including mineral springs (**Blue Licks Springs**), Nicholas co., NE Kentucky, on right bank of Licking river ab. 40 m. NE of Lexington; scene of battle Aug. 19, 1782 in which Kentucky pioneers were defeated by a force of Indians and Canadians; site now **Blue Licks Battlefield State Park.**

Blue Mountain. 1 See RICH MOUNTAIN, Arkansas.
2 Peak 3187 ft. in Franklin co., W Maine.
3 Peak 6007 ft. in N Clallam co., NW Washington.
4 Town, Tippah co., N Mississippi; pop. 471; Blue Mountain College (1873; women).

Blue Mountains. 1 Mountain range, NE Oregon and SE Washington; highest peak Rock Creek Butte 9097 ft. (*q.v.*).
2 Range in NE Pennsylvania, part of Kittatinny Mountain (*q.v.*).
3 Range in E Jamaica, West Indies; highest **Blue Mountain Peak** 7388 ft., on whose slopes is raised Blue Mountain coffee.
4 or **Blue Plateau.** Part of Great Dividing Range, E New South Wales, SE Australia; highest ab. 4460 ft.

Blue Mud Bay. Inlet of W Gulf of Carpentaria on Arnhemland coast, N Northern Territory, Australia.

Blue Nile (nīl). River, Sudan, NE Africa. See NILE.
2 or **Ge·zi'ra** (jě·zēr'à; *Arab.* jä·zē'rȯ). Province, E

Sudan; 54,880 sq. m.; pop. 2,069,646; ✳ Wad Medani.

Blue Point. Locality, Suffolk co., Long Island, New York, on Great South Bay; SW of Patchogue; noted for its oyster beds.

Blue Ridge. 1 *also* **Blue Ridge Mountains.** The eastern and southeastern range of the Appalachian Mts., extending from a point near Harpers Ferry, West Virginia, SW across western Virginia and W North Carolina into N Georgia; by some considered to include the N extension into Maryland, Pennsylvania, and New York; its highest peaks are in the Black Mountains (*q.v.*) of North Carolina; average elevation 2000 to 4000 ft.
2 City, ⊗ of Fannin co., N Georgia; pop. 1406.

Blue Ridge Dam. See *Table* at TENNESSEE VALLEY AUTHORITY.

Blue River. Name of two rivers in Indiana: see BLUE, above.

Blue Sulphur Springs. Mineral springs and village, Greenbrier co., SE West Virginia.

Bluff (blŭf); *formerly* **Camp′bell·town** (kăm′bĕl·toun). Borough on peninsula (**the Bluff**), S South I., New Zealand, at entrance to **Bluff Harbour**, an inlet of Foveaux Strait; port of Invercargill; pop. 1625.

Bluff, Mount. Peak 3350 ft. in the Blue Ridge, western Virginia.

Bluff′ton (blŭf′tŭn). **1** City, ⊗ of Wells co., NE Indiana, 23 m. S of Fort Wayne; pop. 6238; manufactures farm implements and lumber products.
2 Village, Allen co., NW Ohio, 15 m. NE of Lima; pop. 2591; distribution point for crushed stone and limestone of vicinity. Bluffton College (1900; Mennonite; coed.).

Blu·me·nau′ (blōō·mĕ·nou′). Town on the Itajaí river, Santa Catarina state, S Brazil; pop. 22,627; founded 1851 by German immigrants.

Blu′men·thal (blōō′mĕn·täl). Former commune, Stade govt. dist., Hannover prov., Prussia, Germany, on Weser river 15 m. E of Oldenburg; now part of Bremen.

Blüm′lis·alp′ (blüm′lēs·älp′). Range in the Bernese Alps, S cen. Switzerland; highest peak **Blüm′lis·alp′-horn′** (-älp′hôrn′) 12,038 ft.

Blunts Reef (blŭnts). Reef just off Cape Mendocino, California; has lightship.

Blyth (blīth; blī; blīth). Municipal borough, Northumberland, N England, on North Sea at mouth of the **Blyth River** (20 m. long) 12 m. NNE of Newcastle; pop. 34,742; fisheries, shipbuilding yards; exports coal.

Blythe (blīth). City, Riverside co., SE California, near the Colorado river; pop. 6023; settled 1910; cotton.

Blythe′ville (blīth′vǐl; *Sou.* also -v′l). City, ⊗ of Mississippi co., NE Arkansas, 5 m. S of Missouri border; pop. 20,797; trade center for agricultural region.

Bo (bō) *or* **Song′–Bo′** (sông′bō′); *in China called* **Pa′pien′** (bä′byĕn′). River nearly 500 m. long, SE Asia; rises in cen. Yunnan, China, and flows SE in parallel course to the Coi, with which it unites near Sontay, in N Vietnam.

Bo′ac (bō′äk). Municipality, ✳ of Marinduque prov., Marinduque I., Phil. Is., on river 2 m. from W coast; pop. 20,977; an old Spanish-built town.

Bo·a′co (bō·ä′kō). **1** Department, SW cen. Nicaragua; 2085 sq. m.; pop. (1943 est.) 42,382.
2 Town, its ✳; pop. (1943 est.) 3299.

Boa Esperança, Cabo de. See Cape of GOOD HOPE.

Bo·a′no (bō·ä′nō). Small island 18 m. long by 12 m. wide off W end of Ceram I., Indonesia.

Boars Head (bōrz). Peak 2100 ft. in Schuylkill co., E cen. Pennsylvania.

Bo′a Vis′ta (bō′à·vēsh′tà). Easternmost of Cape Verde Is.; 234 sq. m.; pop. ab. 3000; chief town Sal.

Bo′a Vis′ta (bō′à vēsh′tà). **1** *formerly* **Boa Vista do To·can·tins′** (thōō tōō·kănn·tēns′). Town, N Goiaz state, cen. Brazil, on left bank of Tocantins river.
2 *or* **Boa Vista do Ri′o Bran′co** (thōō rē′ōō vrănng′-kōō). Town, ✳ of Rio Branco territory, W Brazil, on right bank of upper Rio Branco.

Bo′az (bō′ăz). City, Marshall and Etowah cos., NE Alabama, 17 m. NW of Gadsden; pop. 4654.

Bob′bi·li (bŏb′ĭ·lĭ). Town, NE Anhdra Pradesh, E India, 70 m. N of Vizagapatam; pop. 20,544; when attacked by French and natives 1756, held out until every man was dead or mortally wounded.

Bo′bi′gny′ (bō′bē′nyē′). Commune, Seine dept., N France, NE suburb of Paris; pop. 17,676.

Bo′bo-Diou·las′so (bō′bō·dyōō·läs′ō). Town, W Upper Volta, West Africa; pop. 18,589; terminus of railroads from Abidjan and Ouagadougou.

Bo·bon′ (bô·bôn′). Municipality, NW coast of Samar, Phil. Is., 55 m. N of Catbalogan; pop. 15,449.

Bobr (bô′bĕr); *Ger.* **Bo′ber** (bō′bĕr). **1** River ab. 155 m. long, chiefly in W Wrocław dept., SW Poland; rises in Sudeten Mts. and flows N to the Odra (Oder) SE of Frankfurt; formerly in Silesia, Germany.
2 See BIEBRZA.

Bo′brek Karb (bō′brĕk kärp′). Industrial commune, E Śląsk dept., SW Poland; pop. (1946) 22,095; WSW suburb of Bytom; formerly in Silesia, Germany; coal mines; manufactures steel, coke, ammonia. Assigned to Poland by Potsdam Conference 1945.

Bobrik. See STALINOGORSK.

Bo·bruisk′ (bŭ·brōō′ĭsk). City, ✳ of Bobruisk Region, White Russia, U.S.S.R., 90 m. SE of Minsk; pop. 84,107; on Berezina river; center for trade in grain and lumber. Fortified by Alexander I; withstood attack of French army 1812; nearly destroyed by great fire 1902; seized by Germans July 1, 1941, recovered June 1944.

Bobruisk Region. Region, cen. White Russia, ✳ Bobruisk.

Boca, La. See LA BOCA.

Bo′ca Chi′ca (bō′kà chē′kà). Island in Florida Keys adjacent to Key West; U.S. Naval Air Station.

Bo′ca Chi′ca (bō′kä chē′kä), **Bo′ca Gran′de** (grän′-dä). See CORREGIDOR.

Bo·cai·u′va *or* **Bo·cay·u′va** (bōō·kī·ōō′và). Town, Minas Gerais state, E Brazil, on railroad ab. 190 m. N of Belo Horizonte; pop. ab. 4000; visited by scientists to observe eclipse of the sun May 20, 1947.

Bo′ca Ra·ton′ (bō′kà rà·tōn′). City, Palm Beach co., SE Florida, on the coast 17 m. N of Fort Lauderdale; pop. 6961; radar training center of U.S. Air Force.

Bo′cas del To′ro (bō′käz thĕl tō′rō). **1** Province, W Panama; 3508 sq. m.; pop. 25,496.
2 Atlantic coast port, its ✳, on an island off NW coast of Panama; pop. 2101; exports bananas, coffee, cacao.

Boc′ca Ti′gris (bŏk′à tē′grĭs). Literally "Tiger's Mouth"; narrow channel bet. the upper and lower Pearl rivers, bet. Canton and Hong Kong. See PEARL river.

Bocchetta Pass. See APENNINES.

Bochkarevo. See KUIBYSHEVKA.

Boch′nia (bôK′nyä). Mining commune, Kraków dept., Poland, 31 m. ESE of Kraków; pop. (1938–39 est.) 14,780; salt mines; gypsum quarries; trades in agricultural products. Taken 1702 by Charles XII.

Bo′cholt (bōK′ôlt). Manufacturing city, W Germany, in North Rhine-Westphalia, near Dutch border; pop. 30,268; cotton and iron goods.

Bo′chum (bō′Kōōm). Industrial city, W Germany, in North Rhine-Westphalia, in Ruhr valley 37 m. SSW of Münster; pop. (1950) 289,804; schools of mining and metallurgy; iron, steel, and coal; in World War II bombed by British.

Böck′ing·en (bŭk′ĭng·ĕn). City, Baden-Württemberg, Germany, 25 m. N of Stuttgart; pop. 11,593.

Bod. See BAUDH.

Bo·dai·bo′ (bŭ·dī·bô′). Town, NE Irkutsk Region, Soviet Russia, Asia, on right bank of Vitim river NE of Lake Baikal; center of rich gold district.

Bo·de′gas (bō·thā′gäs). **1** River in W cen. Ecuador; its estuary known as the Guayas river (*q.v.*); navigable for ab. 200 m.
2 Town, Ecuador. See BABAHOYO.

Bo·de′le (bô·dä′lå); *Fr.* **Bo′dé′lé′** (bô′dä′lā′). Low area, N Chad, N cen. Africa, NE of Lake Chad and S of Tibesti Mts.; tobacco, cotton, forage grasses.

Bo′den (bōō′děn). Town, Norrbotten co., N Sweden, on Lule river 22 m. NNW of Luleå; pop. 10,058.

Bodenbach. See PODMOKLY.

Boden See. See Lake CONSTANCE.

Bo′derg, Lough (lŏк bō′děrg; -dûrg). Lake in N cen. Ireland, S of Lough Allen; one of the chain of lakes traversed by the Shannon river.

Bod′ie Island (bō′dĭ). Long narrow island, NE North Carolina, separating Albemarle and Roanoke Sounds from the Atlantic Ocean; lighthouse at its S end.

Bo′di·na·yak′ka·nur′ (bō′dĭ·nä·yŭk′kȧ·nōōr′). Town, S Madras prov., S Indian Union, 55 m. W of Madura; pop. 27,036.

Bodincomagus. See CASALE MONFERRATO.

Bo′djo·ne·go′ro (bō′jȯ·nȧ·gō′rō) or **Bo′jo·ne·go′ro.**
1 Former residency, NW East Java prov., Neth. Indies; 2634 sq. m.; pop. 1,984,408; ✴ Bodjonegoro.
2 Town, its ✴, on Solo river 60 m. W of Surabaja; pop. 19,784; central market for teak.

Bod′kin Point (bŏd′kĭn). Point, Anne Arundel co., cen. Maryland, on S side of mouth of Patapsco river.

Bod′min (bŏd′mĭn). Municipal borough Cornwall, SW England, 26 m. WNW of Plymouth; pop. 6058.

Bodnjan. See DIGNANO D'ISTRIA.

Bod′ö′ (bō′dû′). Seaport, ⊗ of Nordland co., N Norway, ab. 100 m. SW of Narvik; pop. 5142; trade center; shipping point for copper ore and marble; tourist resort, with the midnight sun from June 1 to July 12.

Bodotria. See Firth of FORTH.

Bod′rog (bŏd′rŏg). Small river in NE Hungary; flows SW into Tisza river near Tokaj.

Bo·drum′ (bō·drōōm′); *anc.* **Hal′i·car·nas′sus** (hăl′i·kär·năs′ŭs). Seaport on S side of **Bodrum Peninsula** on Aegean Sea, Mụḡla vilayet, SW Turkey in Asia; pop. 4531; opp. Kos I. See HALICARNASSUS.

Bodza. See BUZĂU.

Boe′la (bōō′lå). See CERAM.

Boe′le (bō′lě). Formerly, commune, Arnsberg govt. dist., Westphalia prov., Prussia, Germany, 8 m. S of Dortmund; now part of Hagen.

Boe′le·leng (bōō′lě·lěng) or **Bu′le·leng.** Seaport town, N coast of Bali I., Lesser Sunda Is., Indonesia; port of Singaradja; harbor unsafe during west monsoon.

Bo·è′o (bô·â′ô), or **Li·li·be′o** (lē·lē·bâ′ô), **Cape.** Westernmost point of Sicily.

Boe·o′tia (bē·ō′shȧ; -shĭ·ȧ). 1 District and ancient republic in E cen. Greece; bounded on N by Locris Opuntia, on E by the Atalante channel and the Evripos, on S by Attica, Megaris, and Gulf of Corinth, on W and NW by Phocis; chief cities Orchomenus and Thebes (qq.v.).

History: Inhabited by Boeotians, an Aeolian people from Thessaly; politically significant after formation of Boeotian League under headship of Thebes c. 600–550 B.C.; a Medized state during Greek war with Persia; hostile to Athens which succeeded in breaking up Boeotian League and forcing members, except Thebes, to join Delian League 457 B.C.; revolted against Athens and restored League 447 B.C.; in Peloponnesian War, defeated Athenians at Delium 424 B.C.; after battle of Leuctra (q.v.) 371 B.C., led by Thebes, dominated Greece; declined after Philip of Macedon's victory at Chaeronea 338 B.C. and the destruction of Thebes by Alexander the Great 336 B.C.

2 *Mod. Gr.* **Voi·o·ti′a** (vyô·tē′ä). Division of modern department of Attica and Boeotia: see *Table* at GREECE.

Boer′ne (bûr′ně). City, ⊗ of Kendall co., S cen. Texas; pop. 2169; tourist and health resort.

Boe′roe (bōō′rōō) or **Bu′ru.** Island of the W Moluccas, Indonesia, Malay Archipelago, W of Ceram, 3°30′S, 126°40′E; area 3400 sq. m.; pop. 19,625; chief villages Namlea and Kajeli, on E coast; 90 m. long by 50 m. wide; generally elevated, esp. in the NW (highest point

Mt. Tomahu 7969 ft.); hardwood forests. Long subject to the Sultan of Ternate; taken over by the Dutch 1683.

Boe′toeng or **Bu′tung** (bōō′tŏŏng); or **Bu′ton** (bōō′tôn). Island ab. 100 m. long by 10 to 30 m. wide, off SE coast of Celebes I., Indonesia; ab. 2000 sq. m.; pop. ab. 100,000; separated from Muna I. on the W by **Boetoeng Strait** (ab. 65 m. long); chief town Baubau (pop. 2500) on SW coast.

Boeuf River or **Bayou** (bŭf; bōŏf). River ab. 200 m. long, NE Louisiana; rises just N of Arkansas border, flows SW into Ouachita river in N Catahoula parish.

Bo·ga′djim (bô·gä′jĭm). Village and port at head of Astrolabe Bay, ab. 12 m. S of Madang, North-East New Guinea. Taken by Americans Apr. 1944.

Bo′ga·lu′sa (bō′gȧ·lōō′sȧ). Industrial city, Washington parish, E Louisiana, 60 m. NNE of New Orleans; pop. 21,423; paper and lumber mills; tung oil.

Bo′gaz·ka·le′ (bō′äz·kä·lě′). Var. of BOGAZKÖY.

Bo′gaz·köy′ or **Bo′ghaz·keui′** (bō′äz·kû′ē) or **Hat′tu·shash′** (kät′tŏŏ·shäsh′); *Gr.* **Pte′ri·a** (tẹr′ĭ·ȧ). Village containing ancient Hittite ruins, in mountains of N cen. Turkey in Asia, 16 m. NW of Yozgat and ab. 90 m. E of Ankara; remarkable remains of probable capital of powerful Hattic dynasty (c. 16th–12th cents. B.C.).

Bog′do U′la (bôg′dō ōō′lȧ) or **Bog′do-o′la** (-ō′lȧ). Mountain range, E Tien Shan, bet. Urumchi and Barkol, cen. Sinkiang, W China; highest peak ab. 18,000 ft., average height 14,000 ft.

Bo′gen·fels (bō′gěn·fělz; *S. Afr. D.* bōō′ěn·fěls). Town, SW South-West Africa, on coast 50 m. S of Lüderitz; has remarkable natural rock archway.

Bog′nor Re′gis (bŏg′nēr rē′jĭs). Urban district, West Sussex, S England, on the coast ab. 17 m. E of Portsmouth; pop. 25,624; seaside resort.

Bo·go′ (bō·gô′). Municipality on E coast of Cebu I., Phil. Is., on inlet of Visayan Sea 54 m. N of City of Cebu; pop. 27,517; fine harbor.

Bo·go·du′khov (bŭ·gŭ·dōō′кŭf). Town, E Ukraine, U.S.S.R., ab. 30 m. WNW of Kharkov; pop. 16,013.

Eo′gong, Mount (bō′gŏng). Mountain 6509 ft., SE Victoria, SE Australia, in Darg Plateau at S end of Great Dividing Range; highest point in Victoria.

Bogor. See BUITENZORG.

Bogorodsk. See NOGINSK.

Bo′go·slof (bō′gȯ·slôf). Small island in Bering Sea ab. 60 m. W of N Unalaska I., Alaska, built up by submarine volcano; uninhabited; first reported by Russian navigators ab. 1796 when it appeared as a single peak. Violent eruptions 1823, 1883, 1900, and 1907 have changed its aspect; now has several peaks joined by a land strip.

Bo·go′ta (bō·gō′tȧ). Borough, Bergen co., NE corner of New Jersey, 8 m. ESE of Paterson; pop. 7965.

Bo′go·tá′ (bō′gȯ·tä′; *in English, also* bō′gȯ·tô′); *orig.* **San′ta Fe** (sän′tä fā′), *or later* **Santa Fe de Bo′go·tá′** (thä vō′gȯ·tä′). City, W cen. Colombia, its ✴ and ✴ of Cundinamarca dept., on plateau (alt. 8563 ft.) of eastern Andes; pop. 325,658; called "Athens of South America"; has fine cathedral (rebuilt 1814), National University (founded 1572), observatory. Originally center of Chibcha culture; Spanish settlement founded 1538 by Gonzalo Jiménez de Quesada, conquistador; capital of viceroyalty of New Granada; audiencia established 1549; scene of revolt 1810–11 against Spanish rule; recovered by Spaniards 1816–19; freed by victory of Bolívar at Boyacá 1819; capital of Greater Colombia and later (1831) of New Granada (Colombia); Pan American Conference Mar.–Apr. 1948.

Bog′ra (bŏg′rȧ). Town, Rajshahi division, N East Bengal, Pakistan; pop. 14,819.

Bogue (bōg). = BOCCA TIGRIS.

Bogue Sound (bōg). Sound bet. S mainland of Carteret co., SE North Carolina, and barrier reefs off the coast; connects at W end with Atlantic Ocean through the **Bogue Inlet.**

Boguszów. See GOTTESBERG.

Bo·he′mi·a (bô·hē′mǐ·à); *Czech* **Če′chy** (chĕк′ĭ); *Ger.* **Böh′men** (bû′mĕn). Province, W Czechoslovakia; area (1935) 20,101 sq. m.; pop. (1930) 7,109,376; ✻ Prague (*Czech* Praha); agriculture, mining, manufacture of textiles, metal and wood products, glass, and pottery. Encircled by mountains: Erz Gebirge on NW, Sudeten on NE, Bohemian-Moravian Highlands on SE, and the Bohemian Forest on SW; highest point 5266 ft. in the Riesen Gebirge, a range of the Sudeten. Chief rivers the Elbe (here called the Labe) and its tributaries the Vltava (Moldau) and Ohře (Eger); chief towns Prague, Plzeň, České Budêjovice, Pardubice.

History: Settled in 5th cent. A.D. by west Slavic people, Czechs; tributary to Charlemagne's empire (see FRANCE); part of kingdom of Moravia (*q.v.*) founded 870; converted to Latin Christianity by German missionaries 9th cent.; after dissolution of Moravia 906, became duchy which in 10th cent. was forced to accept German suzerainty; under rule of Přemysl family, expanded to include Moravia, parts of Silesia, Slovakia, and Kraków (forced to yield Polish conquests by Emperor Henry III 1041); in 12th cent. raised to rank of electorate and hereditary kingdom within Holy Roman Empire; at height of power under Ottokar II (1253–78) who conquered Styria from Hungary and Austrian territories but was defeated by Emperor Rudolf (of Hapsburg) 1278; last ruler of Přemysl line (d. 1306) also king of Poland; during reign of Charles I 1347–78 (also Emperor Charles IV) of Luxembourg line (1308–1437) reached "golden age," controlling Upper and Lower Lusatia, Moravia, Silesia, and Brandenburg; alienated by anti-Huss Council of Constance (see KONSTANZ), plunged into Hussite wars 1420–36; from election of Ferdinand as king (see AUSTRIA) 1526, remained under Hapsburg rule to 1918; deposition of ruler (Defenestration of Prague) 1618 inaugurated Thirty Years' War (see GERMANY); Protestantism exterminated and independence lost at battle of White Mountain 1620; by 18th cent. completely incorporated in Austrian Empire; battleground in wars of Frederick II and in 1866 (see PRUSSIA); with Moravia and Slovakia, declared independence 1918 (see CZECHOSLOVAKIA); invaded by Germans and made part of German Protectorate of Bohemia and Moravia Mar. 1939; part of restored Czechoslovakia 1945.

Bohemia and Mo·ra′vi·a (mô·rä′vǐ·à). German protectorate comprising the two western divisions of Czechoslovakia, set up Mar. 1939, dissolved 1945.

Bo·he′mi·an Forest (bô·hē′mǐ·ăn); *Ger.* **Böh′mer Wald** (bû′mēr vält′); *Czech* **Čes′ký Les** (chĕs′kē lĕs′). Mountain range along the boundary bet. Bavaria, S Germany, and Bohemia, W Czechoslovakia; highest peak Arber, in Bavaria, 4780 ft.

Bo·he′mi·an–Mo·ra′vi·an Highlands (bô·hē′mǐ·ăn-mô·rä′vǐ·ăn). Mountain range forming boundary bet. SE Bohemia and W Moravia, Czechoslovakia; highest point ab. 2700 ft.; runs NE and SW.

Böhmisch–Brod. See ČESKÝ-BROD.

Böhmisch-Leipa. See ČESKÁ LÍPA.

Bo·hol′ (bô·hôl′). Island, S cen. Phil. Is., N of Mindanao, one of the Visayan Is.; 1492 sq. m.; also, with smaller adjacent islands, forms a province, 1575 sq. m., pop. 491,608, ✻ Tagbilaran. Has fairly regular coast line with many islands, largest Panglao on SW and Lapinin on W side of Canigao Channel; few good anchorages; highest peaks ab. 2600 ft.; short rivers; produces rice, sugar, coconuts, hemp, tobacco; weaving an important industry; chief towns, mostly on the coast, Tagbilaran, Loon, Talibon. Visited by Legaspi 1565; in early days under jurisdiction of Cebu; suffered from rebellion 1622 and again 1744; made separate province by the Spanish 1854; civil government created Apr. 20, 1901; came under Japanese control 1942; invaded and recovered Apr. 1945 by U.S. forces.

Bohol Strait. Passage from 12 to 25 m. wide bet. SE Cebu and W Bohol, Phil. Is.; connects Camotes Sea on the N with Mindanao Sea on the S.

Bo·hot′le (bô·hôt′lå). Town, N Somalia, E Africa, SE of Berbera on Ethiopia border.

Boinu. See KALADAN.

Boi′ro (boi′rô). Coastal commune, La Coruña prov., NW Spain, 54 m. SSW of La Coruña; pop. 11,668; cattle raising; fishing; sardine canneries.

Bois. See BOIS DE BOULOGNE.

Bois Blanc Island (bŏb′ lō′). 1 Island in NW Lake Huron, a part of Mackinac co., Michigan. 2 Long, narrow island in Detroit river, SE Michigan, opp. Amherstburg, Ontario prov., Canada.

Bois Brule. See BRULE.

Bois′–Co′lombes′ (bwä′kô′lônb′). Manufacturing commune, Seine dept., N France, NW suburb of Paris; pop. (1931) 25,892.

Bois d'Avocourt. See AVOCOURT.

Bois de Belleau. See BELLEAU WOOD.

Bois de Bou·logne′ (bwä′ dē boo-lōn′; -loin′; *Fr.* boo′lôn′y′); *familiarly* **Bois** (bwä). Large park 2155 acres, formerly a forest, just W of Paris, France, in a loop of the Seine adjoining Neuilly on the N and Boulogne on the W; acquired by the city of Paris 1852 and transformed into a recreational area; contains the famous race tracks of Longchamp in SW part and Auteuil (steeplechases) in SE.

Bois de la Brigade Marine. See BELLEAU WOOD.

Bois de Sioux (boi′ sōō′). River, W Minnesota; flows N out of Lake Traverse, forms S section of North Dakota-Minnesota boundary, unites with Otter Tail river to form Red River of the North.

Bois′–du–Roi′ (bwä′dü-rwä′). Highest peak 2959 ft. in Morvan Mts., E cen. France.

Boi′se (boi′sǐ; -zǐ). 1 River ab. 60 m. long below Arrowrock Dam, SW cen. Idaho, formed by forks uniting in NW Elmore co.; flows W through Boise (city) and Canyon co. into Snake river. 2 County in Idaho. See ⊗ *Table* at IDAHO. 3 City, ✻ of Idaho and ⊗ of Ada co., SW Idaho; largest city in the state; pop. 34,481; founded 1863 on the site of an army camp; incorporated as city 1864; capital of Idaho Territory 1864, and of the state from 1890; creameries, packing houses, stone quarries.

Boise City (bois). Town, ⊗ of Cimarron co., NW Oklahoma, 60 m. W of Guymon; pop. 1978.

Bois–le–Duc. See 's HERTOGENBOSCH.

Boj′a·dor, Cape (bŏj′à·dôr; *Port.* boō·zhá·thôr′). Cape extending into Atlantic Ocean on W cen. coast of Spanish Sahara, NW Africa, S of Canary Is. at 26°15′N.

Bo′ja·na or **Bo′ya·na** (bô′yä·nä). Small river in NW Albania, the N mouth of the Drin river; flows out of Lake Scutari SW into Adriatic Sea along boundary line bet. Albania and Yugoslavia.

Bo·je·a·dor′, Cape (bô·hâ·à·thôr′). Point on NW coast of Ilocos Norte prov., Luzon, Phil. Is.; lighthouse.

Bo′jo·la′li (bō′yō·lä′lĕ). Town, W Surakarta, cen. Java, Indonesia, at foot of Mt. Merapi; pop. 10,261.

Bojonegoro. See BODJONEGORO.

Bo′ké′ (bô′kā′). Town on Nunez river, W Guinea, W Africa, 110 m. NW of Conakry.

Bokhara. See BUKHARA.

Bokn Fjord (bôk′ĕn), *also* **Bukn Fjord** (boŏk′ĕn). Inlet of the North Sea on SW coast of Norway, N of Stavanger; ab. 35 m. long; 10 to 15 m. wide.

Bokonka, Bo Kunka. Variants of MINYA KONKA.

Bo·ko′ro (bô·kō′rō). Town, SW cen. Chad Republic, N cen. Africa, 120 m. E of Fort-Lamy.

Boks′burg (bŏks′bûrg). Town, S Transvaal, NE Union of South Africa, 15 m. E of Johannesburg; pop. 50,126; important gold-mining center.

Bo·la′ma (bô·lä′må) or **Bu·la′ma** (boō-). 1 Island of the Ilhas dos Bijagos (see Ilhas dos BIJAGOS). 2 Town on Bolama I., former ✻ of Portuguese Guinea, W Africa; pop. ab. 4000.

Bo·lan′gir (bō·län′gĭr). See PATNA.

Bo·lan′ Pass (bō·län′). Mountain pass ab. 60 m. long, elevation at crest 5900 ft., bet. Sibi and Quetta in N Baluchistan; very narrow and with precipitous sides.

Bo·la′rum (bō·lä′rŭm). See SECUNDERABAD.

Bol′bē, Lake (bŏl′bē; *Mod. Gr.* vôl′vē). Lake in N part of Chalcidice, Macedonia, Greece.

Bol′bec′ (bŏl′bĕk′). Industrial commune, Seine-Inférieure dept., N France, WNW of Rouen; pop. 10,209.

Bolbitine, Bolbitinic Mouth. See ROSETTA.

Bolbok. See SAN JUAN.

Bo·le·chów (bô·lĕ′kōōf). Town, W Ukraine, U.S.S.R., 37 m. WNW of Stanislav (formerly in Stanisławów dept., Poland); pop. (1938–39 est.) 11,744; health resort.

Bolerium. See LANDS END.

Boleslav Mladá. = MLADÁ BOLESLAV.

Bolesławice. See BUNZELWITZ.

Bo·le·sła′wiec (bô·lĕ·slä′vyĕts); *Ger.* **Bunz′lau** (bŏonts′lou). Town, W Wrocław dept., SW Poland, on Bobr river W of Legnica; pop. (1946) 21,946; formerly in Silesia, Germany; famous for its pottery. In section assigned to Poland by Potsdam Conference 1945.

Bol·grad′ (bŭl·grät′). Town, Izmail region, SW Ukraine, U.S.S.R., ab. 25 m. N of Izmail; pop. 12,821.

Bo′li·na′o (bō′lĕ·nä′ô). **1** Cape, 16°20′N, NW point of the peninsula of W Pangasinan prov., Luzon, Phil. Is., on South China Sea coast W of Lingayen Gulf.

2 Municipality, NW Pangasinan, just E of the cape and opp. Santiago I.; pop. 14,914.

Bol′i·var (bŏl′ĭ·vẽr). **1** County in Mississippi. See *Table* at MISSISSIPPI.

2 City, ⊗ of Polk co., SW Missouri; pop. 3219.

3 Town, ⊗ of Hardeman co., SW Tennessee; pop. 3338.

Bo·lí′var (bō·lē′vär). **1** Department of Colombia. See *Table* at COLOMBIA.

2 Province of Ecuador. See *Table* at ECUADOR.

3 State of Venezuela. See *Table* at VENEZUELA.

4 Town, Buenos Aires prov., E Argentina, ab. 170 m. SW of Buenos Aires; pop. ab. 10,000; trading center.

5 Municipality, Cauca dept., SW Colombia, 47 m. NNE of Pasto; pop. 18,720; mining town at alt. 6435 ft.

Bo·lí′var, Cer′ro (sĕr′rô bō·lē′vär); *formerly called* **La Pa·ri′da** (lä pä·rē′thä). Hill, E Bolivia, in Bolívar state S of Ciudad Bolívar; ab. 6 m. long, 2000 ft. high; iron mining.

Bo·lí′var, Pi′co (pē′kŏ bō·lē′vär). Mountain, W Venezuela, in Mérida state; highest in the Cordillera Mérida and in Venezuela, 16,411 ft.

Bol′i·var Peninsula *or* **Point** (bŏl′ĭ·vẽr). Peninsula ab. 23 m. long at E entrance to Galveston Bay, Texas.

Bo·liv′i·a (bô·lĭv′ĭ·à; *Span.* bô·lē′vyä). Republic, W cen. South America; bounded on N and E by Brazil, on SE by Paraguay, on S by Argentina, and on W by Peru and Chile; has no coastline, outlets to sea being in Chile and Peru; 513,086 sq. m.; pop. (1945 est.) 3,722,700; administrative ✳ La Paz, constitutional ✳ Sucre; divided into the following nine departments (for pronunciations, see their individual entries):

NAME	LOCA-TION	AREA[1]	POP.[1]	CAPITAL
Chuquisaca	S	33,148	370,300	Sucre
Cochabamba	cen.	20,584	619,100	Cochabamba
El Beni	N	94,160	69,200	Trinidad
La Paz	W	43,065	1,173,300	La Paz
Oruro	W	20,381	199,800	Oruro
Pando[2]	NW	32,414	18,300	Cobija
Potosí	SW	45,855	754,600	Potosí
Santa Cruz	E	142,105	387,500	Santa Cruz
Tarija	S	81,374[3]	130,600	Tarija

[1] Area in sq. m. Pop. is 1945 est.
[2] Formerly Colonial Territories.
[3] Includes 46,561 sq. m. in the Chaco region.

In eastern part has low, hot, fertile land, watered by many rivers; in central part on E slope of mountains high

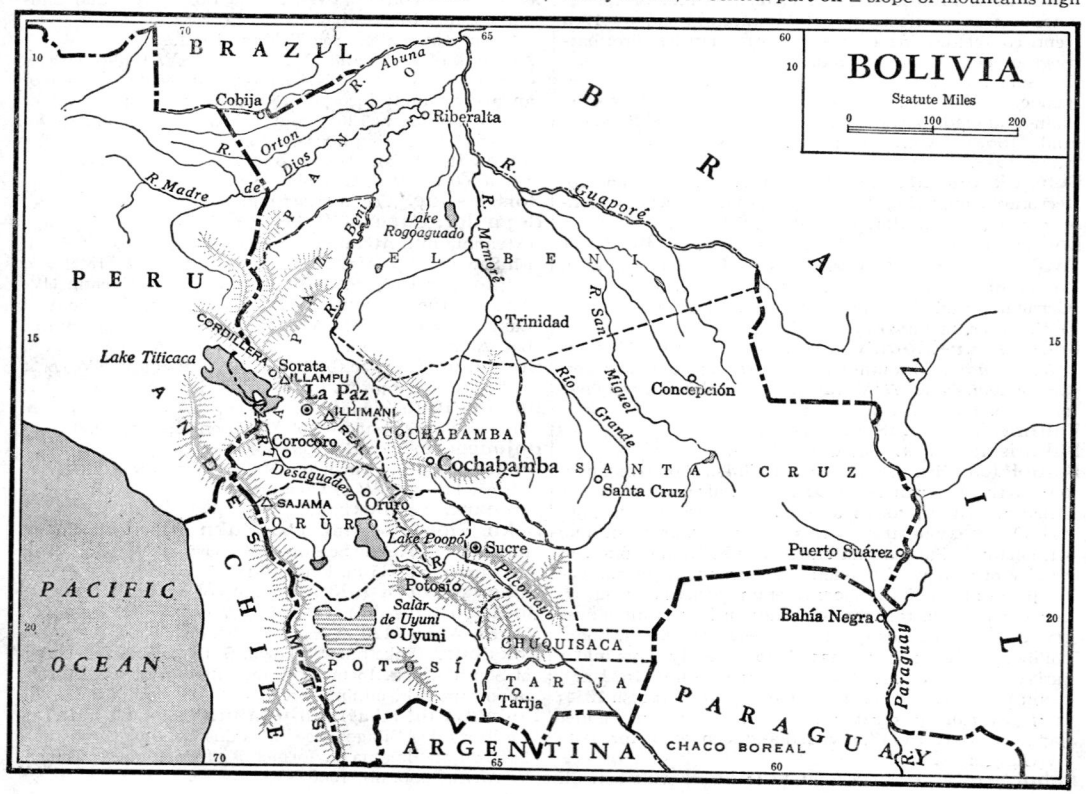

BOLIVIA

Statute Miles

0   100   200

plateau region; in W part the central ranges of the Andes, esp. the Cordillera Real E of Lake Titicaca, highest peaks Sorata (Ancohuma and Illampu) 21,490 ft., Sajama 21,390 ft., Illimani 21,184 ft.; many volcanic peaks; in SW in Oruro and Potosí depts. are elevated nitrate deserts, esp. Salar de Uyuni. Chief rivers are large headstreams of the Madeira: Guaporé (along Brazilian border) and its tributaries Baures and Itonama; Mamoré, with many tributaries draining E slopes of the Andes; Beni and its tributary the Madre de Dios; Abuna (forming in N part of boundary with Brazil); upper Pilcomayo in the S. Includes part of Lake Titicaca (*q.v.*) which receives waters of Lake Poopó in SW cen. part through the Desaguadero river. Chief cities La Paz, Sucre, Cochabamba, Oruro, Potosí, Santa Cruz. Economic resources mainly mineral (tin, silver, copper, lead, and zinc); also exports much rubber and forest products.

History: Home of the Aymaras, Indians with a high pre-Inca culture, who were conquered by Incas in 14th cent.; conquered 1538 by Hernando Pizarro, half brother of conqueror of Peru (*q.v.*); organized as dependency of Charcas or Upper Peru; joined to Viceroyalty of Buenos Aires 1776; although struggles against royalists continuous from 1809, achieved independence from Spain only in 1825 when Sucre invaded Charcas, and called congress to proclaim republic of Bolivia; long troubled by internal strife and series of unsuccessful wars; lost seacoast in War of the Pacific against Chile (*q.v.*) 1879–84; after dispute with Brazil, ceded Acre (*q.v.*) 1903; finally made peace 1904 with Chile which retained Arica (*q.v.*); renewed dispute 1920–29; lost most of Chaco (*q.v.*) by treaty 1938 which settled war with Paraguay (1932–35).

Bol·khov' (bŭl·Kôf'). Town, Orel Region, Russia in Europe, 40 m. N of Orel; pop. 17,532; center for hemp and livestock; in midst of fighting area 1941–43.

Bol'li·gen (bŏl'ĭ·gĕn). Town, Bern canton, Switzerland, E suburb of Bern; pop. (1930) 7839.

Bol'lin (bŏl'ĭn). River 20 m. long, Cheshire, NW England; tributary of the Mersey.

Bol'lin·ger (bŏl'ĭn·jẽr; bŏol'ĭng·ẽr, bō'lĭng-). County in Missouri. See *Table* at MISSOURI.

Bol'ling·ton (bŏl'ĭng·tŭn). Urban district, Cheshire, NW England, 25 m. E of Liverpool; pop. 5313.

Bo·lo'gna (bō·lō'nyä; *Angl.* bô·lōn'yȧ, -lō'nȧ). **1** Province of Italy. See *Table* at ITALY.

2 *anc.* **Fel'si·na** (fĕl'sĭ·nȧ); *later* **Bo·no'ni·a** (bō·nō'nĭ·ȧ). Commune, its ✻, Emilia, N Italy, at foot of Apennines 51 m. N by E of Florence; pop. 269,687; railroad center; manufactures macaroni, sausage, liquors, leather, linen, silk goods, velvet, glass, machinery; Gothic 14th-cent. church of San Petronio.

History: Site of Etruscan town Felsina; made Roman military colony 189 B.C.; belonged to Byzantine exarchate of Ravenna (*q.v.*); after short period of Lombard rule became free commune, receiving charter in 12th cent.; seat of oldest European university, founded 1088; joined Lombard League against Frederick Barbarossa 1167; helped break power of Frederick II; in course of 15th cent. ruled temporarily by Bentivoglio and Visconti families; incorporated in States of the Church (*q.v.*) by Pope Julius II 1506; scene of crowning of Emperor Charles V 1530; after French occupation 1796, made capital of Cispadane Republic (*q.v.*); restored to States of the Church 1815; occupied by Austria after revolts 1831, 1848; voted annexation to kingdom of Italy 1860. In World War II after surrender of Italy Sept. 1943, controlled by Germans; attacked by Allied armies Sept. 1944, taken Apr. 21, 1945.

Bo·lon'da (bō·lŏn'dȧ). Settlement on S coast of Guadalcanal I., SE Solomon Is., W Pacific Ocean.

Bo·lon·drón' (bō·lôn·drōn'). Municipality (pop. 11,823) and town (pop. 3710), Matanzas prov., W cen. Cuba.

Bolos. See VOLOS.

Bo·lot'no·e (bŭ·lôt'nŭ·yĕ). Town, E Novosibirsk Re-

gion, Soviet Russia, Asia, 75 m. NE of Novosibirsk.

Bol·se'na (bŏl·sâ'nä); *anc.* **Vol·sin'i·i** (vŏl·sĭn'ĭ·ī). Commune, Viterbo prov., N Latium, Italy, on Lake Bolsena; pop. (1931) 3825; 11th-cent. church.

Bolsena, Lake. Lake 10 m. long and 8 m. wide in N Latium, cen. Italy, 20 m. NNW of Viterbo; discharges through Marta river SW into N Tyrrhenian Sea.

Bolshaya. See Mount MCKINLEY.

Bol'she·vik (bŏl'shĕ·vĭk; bōl'-; *Russ.* bŭl·y'·shĭ·vyĕk'). Island, SE Severnaya Zemlya, in Arctic Ocean off Taimyr Penin., Soviet Russia, Asia.

Bol·shoi' (bŏl·shoi'; bōl-; *Russ.* bŭl·y'·shoi'). Largest island of the Lyakhov Is. (*q.v.*).

Bolshoi Kavkaz. See CAUCASUS MOUNTAINS.

Bolsón de Mapimí. See Bolsón de MAPIMÍ.

Bol'so'ver (bŏl'zō'vẽr). Urban district, Derbyshire, N cen. England, 13 m. SSE of Sheffield; pop. 10,815.

Bols'ward (bôls'värt). Commune, Friesland prov., Netherlands, 15 m. SW of Leeuwarden; pop. 6866.

Bolt Head (bōlt). Headland on S coast of Devonshire, SW England, W of Start Point.

Bol'ton (bōl't'n), *in full* **Bolton-le-Moors** (-lē-mŏorz'). County borough, Lancashire, NW England, on the Croal 10 m. NW of Manchester; pop. 177,250, (1951) 167,162; has textile mills, ironworks, paper mills, chemical manufacturing; coal deposits nearby; one of the oldest centers of the woolen trade, where Richard Arkwright invented the spinning frame (1769) and S. Crompton the spinning mule (1779).

Bol'ton Brown, Mount (bōl't'n broun'). Peak 13,527 ft. in Sierra Nevada, E Fresno co., S cen. California.

Bolton upon Dearne (dûrn). Former urban district, West Riding, Yorkshire, N England; pop. (1931) 14,245.

Bo·lu' (bō·lōō'). **1** Vilayet, NW Turkey in Asia; 4300 sq. m.; pop. 248,027.

2 Town, its ✻; pop. 6978; terminus of railroad branch from Adapazarı 64 m. to the W.

Bo'lus Head (bō'lŭs). Cape on SW coast of Ireland, on W side of entrance to Ballinskelligs Bay.

Bol·za·ne'to (bŏl·tsä·nā'tô). Commune, Genova prov., Liguria, Italy; pop. 12,565; a N suburb of Genoa.

Bol·za'no (bŏl·tsä'nô). **1** Province of Italy. See *Table* at ITALY.

2 *Ger.* **Bo'zen** (bō'tsĕn); *anc.* **Bau·za'num** (bô·zā'nŭm). Commune, its ✻, Venezia Tridentina, NE Italy, in S Tirol at confluence of the Isarco river with the Adige 87 m. NNW of Venice; pop. 45,505; trade center for region producing wine and fruits; 14th-cen. Gothic cathedral; Franciscan monastery. Ancient Roman town; fell to Lombards 680 A.D., to Franks 740; seat of Bavarian border countships; fell to episcopate of Trent 1027; under Hapsburgs from 1363 sharing the history of the Tirol; conquered by Italy 1918.

Bo'ma (bō'mȧ). Town, W Léopoldville prov. W Congo, ab. 60 m. from the mouth of the Congo river on N bank; pop. 20,531; until 1923 ✻ of Belgian Congo. Founded as a slave market in 16th cent.

Bo'mar·sund (bō'mȧr·sŭnd'). **1** Strait in the Ahvenanmaa Is. in the Gulf of Bothnia.

2 Russian fort on Ahvenanmaa captured Aug. 16, 1854 by British and French (Crimean War).

Bom'ba (bŏm'bȧ; *Ital.* bôm'bä). Town, NE Cyrenaica, Libya, N Africa, bet. Derna and Tobruk on the **Gulf of Bomba.**

Bom·ba'la (bŏm·bä'lȧ). Town, SE New South Wales, SE Australia, 110 m. S of Canberra and ab. 38 m. W of Eden harbor; pop. 931; one of many sites considered 1903–04 for Commonwealth capital; at one time actually selected by Federal Senate.

Bom·bay' (bŏm·bā'; *before an accented syllable, as in* Bombay Island, *often* bŏm'bā'). **1** Former state, W India; area (1956) 190,919 sq. m.; pop. 48,000,000; ✻ Bombay; a presidency (until 1937) and province (1947) of British India, a province of Indian Union 1947–56; reorganized 1956 as state incorporating Kutch and Saurashtra and

the Marathi-speaking parts of Hyderabad and Madhya Pradesh, small areas being transferred at that time to Mysore and Rajasthan states; divided 1960 into two states: Gujerat and Maharashtra (*qq.v.*). Extended along W coast from West Pakistan boundary on the NW to Mysore on the S, with Western Ghats along most of its length (highest 4500 ft.) and in N the lower courses of the Narbada and Tapti rivers flowing into Gulf of Cambay; sources of several large rivers (Godavari, Bhima, Kistna) of central India within its boundaries. Some sections devoted to agriculture; chief industry cotton manufacturing. Chief cities Bombay, Poona, Ahmadabad, Nagpur, Sholapur, Baroda.

History: Under various Hindu and Moslem dynasties during early Christian era down to c. 1500, but not an important center; Goa (*q.v.*) taken 1510 by Portuguese and Bombay town 1534; first English settlement at Surat 1612; territory much increased by districts from Gujarat 1805–18, from Kathiawar 1807–20, and from sections along E slope of Ghats 1819–27; received Aden 1839 and Sind 1843. Sind made separate province 1936 and Aden a crown colony 1937; constituted an autonomous province 1937; became part of Indian Union Aug. 15, 1947; divided May 1, 1960 into a Gujarati-speaking state (Gujerat, ✳ Ahmadabad) and a Marathi-speaking state (Maharashtra, ✳ Bombay).

2 City, its ✳ and (since 1960) ✳ of Gujerat state, on Bombay I.; pop. (1951) 2,994,444; magnificent harbor, ocean gateway to western India; exports raw cotton, grain, and seeds and imports piece goods, metals, and machinery; a center of textile and cotton industry; seat of Univ. of Bombay.

History: Town acquired by Portuguese 1534; ceded to English as part of dowry of wife of Charles II 1661; granted to East India Co. 1668; developed by the Company's governor of Surat (*q.v.*) who made it headquarters 1672; in 1708 became center of British authority in India; first Indian railroad constructed 1853 bet. it and Thana; after opening of Suez Canal 1869 and construction of other railroads, became largest distributing center in India.

Bombay Island. Island 10 m. off W cen. coast of India; 24 sq. m.; coextensive with the municipality of Bombay; encloses **Bombay Harbor** on the E; connected by bridges and causeways with Salsette I. to the N.

Bombay States. A former group of 151 Indian states, most of them small, which were in political relations with the Bombay Government; later divided between Baroda and the Gujarat States Agency, Kolhapur and Deccan States, and Western India States Agency.

Bom·be·to′ka Bay (bŏm′bĕ·tō′kä). Inlet of Mozambique Channel on NW coast of the island of Madagascar.

Bombon, Lake. See Lake TAAL.

Bomfim. See BONFIM.

Bom Je·sús′ (bōn′ zhä·zōōs′). Small island in Guanabara Bay, N of the city of Rio de Janeiro, Brazil.

Böm′lo (bûm′lö). Island 21 m. long, SW Norway, in Hordaland co. S of Bergen; 70 sq. m.

Bommes (bôm). Village, Gironde dept. SW France; pop. 519; produces wine (see SAUTERNES).

Bom′o·seen Lake (bŏm′ō·zēn). Lake ab. 8 m. by 1½ m. in NW Rutland co., W Vermont; summer resort.

Bo′mu (bō′mōō) *or* **Mbo′mu** (′m·bō′mōō). River ab. 500 m. long, cen. Africa; flows W forming boundary bet. N Republic of the Congo and S Central African Republic and unites with Uele river to form Ubangi river.

Bomvanaland. See TEMBULAND.

Bon, Cape (kāp bŏn′; *Fr.* bôn′); *or* **Ras Ad·dar′** (räs äd·där′). Peninsula ab. 50 m. long extending NE from extreme NE Tunisia, N Africa. Occupied by German troops in retreat from Egypt and Libya May 1943; surrendered to Allied army May 11–12.

Bona. See BÔNE.

Bo′na (bō′nä), **Mount.** Mountain 16,420 ft. at E end of Wrangell Mts. near Yukon border, SE Alaska.

Bonacca. See GUANAJA.

Bon′a·gai (bŏn′à·gī). Village on N coast of Woodlark I., off SE New Guinea; its port is Kulamadau.

Bo′nai (bō′nī). Former princely state, NE Indian Union, ab. 110 m. NW of Cuttack; 1280 sq. m.; ✳ **Bo′naigarh′** (bō′nī·gär′; *native* -gŭr′h′), pop. 1852.

Bon′aire′ (bō·nâr′); *Span.* **Buen Ai′re** (bwän i′rä). Island, Neth. West Indies, off coast of Venezuela 30 m. E of Curaçao; 95 sq. m.; pop. (1942) 5796; chief town Kralendijk; part of Curaçao overseas territory.

Bo·nan′za Peak (bō·năn′zà). Mountain 9500 ft. in N Chelan co., cen. Washington.

Bo′na·parte (bō′nà·pärt). Former name of RÉUNION.

Bon′a·ven′ture (bŏn′à·vĕn′tūr; *Fr.* bô′nà′vän′tür′). **1** River ab. 60 m. long on Gaspé Peninsula, SE Quebec, Canada; flows S into Chaleur Bay.

2 County, Quebec, Canada. See *Table* at QUEBEC.

Bon′a·vis′ta (bŏn′à·vĭs′tà). Seaport, E Newfoundland, on E side of Bonavista Bay near Cape Bonavista; pop. 3718; one of island's oldest fishing stations.

Bonavista Bay. Inlet of Atlantic Ocean in E Newfoundland ab. 40 m. wide bet. Cape Freels on NW and **Cape Bonavista** on SE; contains numerous small islands.

Bond (bŏnd). County in Illinois. See *Table* at ILLINOIS.

Bon·de′no (bōn·dā′nō). Commune, Ferrara prov., Emilia, N Italy, 12 m. NW of Ferrara; pop. 27,192.

Bon′di (bŏn′dī). Town on coast, part of Waverley municipality, city of Sydney, New South Wales, Australia; famous beach (**Bondi Beach**).

Bon·doc′ (bôn·dŏk′). Peninsula ab. 37 m. long, SE end of Tayabas prov., Luzon, Phil. Is.; its S extremity is **Bondoc Point**, on N side of Sibuyan Sea.

Bon′dou′kou′ (*Fr.* bôn′dōō′kōō′). Interior native town, E Ivory Coast, West Africa; pop. ab. 3000.

Bon′do·wo′so (bôn′dō·wō′sō). Town, East Java prov., Indonesia, 90 m. SE of Surabaja; pop. 18,751; in valley W of Idjen Mts.

Bon′dy′ (bôn′dē′). Commune, Seine dept., N France, ENE suburb of Paris; pop. 20,539; chemical products; near forest (**Forest of Bondy**) formerly notorious as haunt of brigands.

Bône (bōn); *known as* **Bo′na** (bō′nä) *down to French occupation*. Seaport and commune, N Constantine dept., NE Algeria, 70 m. NE of Constantine; pop. (1936) 83,275; inner harbor of 25 acres and spacious outer harbor; large trade in phosphates, iron and zinc, and barley, wool, cork, etc.; considerable manufacturing. Largely a modern French city, built on coastal plain at mouth of Seybouse river and at foot of range of hills. Identified with **Aph′ro·dis′i·um** (ăf′rō·dĭz′ĭ·ŭm; -dĭzh′ĭ·ŭm), the port of ancient **Hippo** *or* **Hip′po Re′gi·us** (hĭp′ō rē′jĭ·ŭs), whose ruins are 1 m. to the S, a rich city of Roman Africa to c. 300 A.D. and the bishopric and home 396–430 of St. Augustine. Hippo and its port severely damaged by Vandals 431 and Arabs 646 and Bona built on latter site by Arabs in 7th cent. Held in medieval times by Italians, Spaniards, Genoese, Algerines; occupied by French 1832; entered by Allies Nov. 12, 1942.

Bo′ne *or* **Bo′ni** (bō′nĕ), **Gulf of.** Large inlet of Flores Sea extending deep into S coast of Celebes I.

Bo′ness. See BORROWSTOUNNESS.

Bo·ne′te (bō·nā′tā). Peak 21,030 ft. in N La Rioja prov., NW Argentina.

Bon·fim′ (bōN·fēN′), *formerly* **Bom·fim′** (bōN-). **1** Town, Baía state, E Brazil, on railroad 200 m. NE of Salvador; pop. 7269.

2 Town, Goiaz state, E cen. Brazil, ab. 50 m. E of Goiaz.

Bon′ga (bŏng′gà). Chief town, Kafa prov., SW Ethiopia, E Africa.

Bong·a′bon (bông·ä′bŏn). Municipality, E cen. Nueva Ecija prov., Luzon, Phil. Is. 16 m. NE of Cabanatuan; pop. 11,885; an early capital of the province.

Bon′ham (bŏn′ăm). City ⊗ of Fannin co., NE Texas, 23 m. E of Sherman; pop. 7049; manufactures gasoline pumps, cotton goods, dairy products.

Bon Homme (bŏn'ŭm). County in South Dakota. See *Table* at SOUTH DAKOTA.

Boni, Gulf of. See Gulf of BONE.

Bo·ni·fa'cio (bô-nē-fä'chō). Commune, S point of Corsica, on Strait of Bonifacio; pop. 3628; on narrow peninsula with steep cliffs on three sides. A historic town, said to have been settled 828; became Genoese 1187, later practically an independent republic.

Bonifacio, Strait of. Strait bet. islands of Corsica and Sardinia in Mediterranean Sea; 7 m. at narrowest part.

Bon'i·fay (bŏn'ĭ·fā). Town, ⊗ of Holmes co., NW Florida, 96 m. ENE of Pensacola; pop. 2222.

Bo'nin (bō'nĭn), *or* O·ga·sa·wa·ra (ō·gä·sä·wä·rä), **Islands**; *Jap.* **Ogasawara Gun·to** (gōōn·tō). Group of twenty-seven volcanic islands in the W Pacific Ocean, 600 m. S of Tokyo bet. lat. 26°30' and 27°44'N and long. 141° and 143°E; 40 sq. m.; pop. before World War II ab. 5000; belongs to Tokyo prefecture. Largest island Chichi Jima in center; other important islands Haha Jima, Muko Jima, and Yome Jima. First known to Japanese c. 1600; first colonized 1830 by small group of Europeans and Hawaiians; occupied by Japanese 1862, annexed 1876. In World War II attacked by U.S. task force Sept. 1944; frequently bombed by U.S. planes 1944–45. Administered by U.S. since 1945.

Bo'ni·ra'u (bō'nē·rä'ōō). Mountain 7546 ft., N Vogelkop Penin., NW Neth. New Guinea, near coast.

Bonn (bŏn). Manufacturing city and educational center, W Germany, in North Rhine-Westphalia state on the left bank of Rhine river 16 m. SSE of Cologne; pop. (1965) 140,789; fine 13th-cent. Romanesque cathedral, 18th-cent. town hall; famous university; manufactures chemicals, porcelain, machinery, musical instruments, jute, cement. Birthplace of Beethoven. Bombed by Allies 1944–45, captured Mar. 7–8, 1945; meeting place of constituent assembly which drafted constitution, approved May 8, 1949, for West German republic (comprising American, British, and French occupation zones); chosen as capital of the new republic (often called **Bonn Republic**) May 1949.

Bonne Bay (bŏn). Inlet of the Gulf of St. Lawrence, W Newfoundland.

Bon'ner (bŏn'ẽr). County in Idaho. See *Table* at IDAHO.

Bon'ners Ferry (bŏn'ẽrz). Village, ⊗ of Boundary co., N Idaho, 75 m. NNE of Coeur d'Alene; pop. 1921.

Bon'ner Springs (bŏn'ẽr). City, Wyandotte co., NE Kansas, 15 m. W of Kansas City; pop. 3171.

Bonne Terre (bŏn târ'). City, St. Francois co., E Missouri, 52 m. SSW of St. Louis; pop. 3219; lead mining.

Bon'ne·ville (bŏn'ĕ·vĭl). **1** County in Idaho. See *Table* at IDAHO.
2 Town, Multnomah co., NW Oregon, at Bonneville Dam. ab. 32 m. NE of Portland; pop. ab. 150.

Bonneville, Mount. Peak 12,530 ft. in E Sublette co., W Wyoming.

Bonneville Dam. See UNITED STATES, *Dams.*

Bonneville Salt Flats *or* **Bonneville Flats.** A stretch of barren salt flat land ab. 100 sq. m., Tooele co., NW Utah, E of Wendover; part of bed of the Pleistocene Lake Bonneville; several world automobile speed records established here since 1935.

Bon'ny (bŏn'ĭ). Seaport village at mouth of **Bonny River** (one of the mouths of the Niger, *q.v.*), SE Owerri prov., Eastern Region, Nigeria; formerly important, now its trade taken over by Port Harcourt.

Bononia. See (1) VIDIN, Bulgaria (2) BOULOGNE, France (3) BOLOGNA commune in Italy.

Bon Se·cour' Bay (bŏn sē·kōōr'). Inlet of Gulf of Mexico on SW coast of Baldwin co., SW Alabama.

Bon·thain' (bŏn·tīn'). Port at S end of SW peninsula of Celebes I., Indonesia; pop. 6711.

Bonthain, Mount. = LOMPOBATANG.

Bon'the (bŏn'tĭ). **1** District, Sierra Leone, W Africa; 1350 sq. m.; pop. 97,822; includes Sherbro I., Turner's Penin., and two small areas on the mainland.

2 Seaport town, its ✻, on E coast of Sherbro I.; pop. 4404; an important trading town.

Bon·toc' (bôn·tôk'; *Angl.* bŏn·tŏk'). **1** Subprovince, cen. Mountain Province, Luzon, Phil. Is., E of cen. Cordillera Central; 906 sq. m.; pop. 72,871; ✻ Bontoc.
2 Municipal district, its ✻ and ✻ of Mountain Province, on upper Chico river, in W part of province; pop. 611.

Bo'ny' (bô'nē'). Village. Aisne dept., NE France. 10 m. NNW of St-Quentin; battle Sept. 29 1918; American military cemetery.

Boom (bōm). Commune, Antwerp prov., N Belgium, on the Rupel 8 m. S of Antwerp; pop. 19,373.

Boo'mer (bōō'mẽr). Residential town, Fayette co., S cen. West Virginia, SE of Charleston; pop. (with Harewood) 1657.

Boom'plaats (bōōm'pläts). Locality, S Orange Free State, Republic of So. Africa, near Jagersfontein, SW of Bloemfontein; scene Aug. 29, 1848 of defeat of Boers under Pretorius by Sir Harry Smith.

Boone (bōōn). **1** Name of counties in eight states of the U.S. See *Tables* at ARKANSAS, ILLINOIS, INDIANA, IOWA, KENTUCKY, MISSOURI, NEBRASKA, WEST VIRGINIA.
2 City, ⊗ of Boone co., cen. Iowa, 35 m. NNW of Des Moines; pop. 12,468; railroad, coal-mining. and industrial center; Indian antiquities discovered nearby.
3 Town, ⊗ of Watauga co., NW North Carolina, 22 m. NNW of Lenoir; pop. 3686. Appalachian State Teachers College (1903; coed.).

Boones'bor'o, *earlier* **Boones'bor'ough** (bōōnz'-bûr'ō). Former village, Madison co., E cen. Kentucky, on Kentucky river; site of a fort founded by Daniel Boone 1775.

Boone's Trail (bōōnz). = WILDERNESS ROAD.

Boone'ville (bōōn'vĭl). **1** City, a ⊗ of Logan co., W Arkansas, 34 m. SE of Fort Smith; pop. 2690; sawmills and cotton gins; tuberculosis sanatorium.
2 City, ⊗ of Owsley co., E Kentucky; pop. 143.
3 Town, ⊗ of Prentiss co., NE Mississippi; pop. 3480.

Boons'bor'o (bōōnz'bûr'ō). Town Washington co., N Maryland; pop. 1211; ab. 10 m. S of Hagerstown near a gap in South Mountain (*q.v.*); scene of Federal victory Sept. 14, 1862.

Boon'ton (bōōn't'n; -tŭn). Town, Morris co., N New Jersey, 8 m. NNE of Morristown; pop. 7981; settled 1762, incorp. 1867; in farming and industrial area; important ironmaking center during middle of 19th cent.

Boon'ville (bōōn'vĭl). **1** City, ⊗ of Warrick co., SW Indiana, 17 m. ENE of Evansville; pop. 4801.
2 City, ⊗ of Cooper co., cen. Missouri, on Missouri river 25 m. W of Columbia; pop. 7090; scene June 17, 1861 of first land battle of Civil War in Missouri, in which Union troops under Gen. Nathaniel Lyon defeated Confederate force under Col. John S. Marmaduke.
3 Village, Oneida co., cen. New York, 20 m. N of Rome; pop. 2403; in dairy-farming section.

Booth'bay' Harbor (bōōth'bā'). Seaport town, Lincoln co., S Maine, on Atlantic Ocean 34 m. ENE of Portland; pop. 2252; fishing center and summer resort.

Boo'thi·a, Gulf of (bōō'thĭ·á). Gulf bet. Boothia Penin. and Melville Penin. and S of NW Baffin I., Northwest Territories, Canada.

Boothia Peninsula, *formerly* **Boothia Fe'lix Peninsula** (fē'lĭks). Peninsula, almost an island, in S Franklin District, Northwest Territories, Canada; separated from Baffin I. on the E by Gulf of Boothia and from Prince of Wales I. on the NW by Franklin Strait. The North Magnetic Pole was formerly located on its W shore (see MAGNETIC POLE). Its N tip is northernmost point of mainland of North America, at ab. 72°N.

Boo'tle (bōō't'l). County borough, Lancashire, NW England, on the Mersey, suburb of Liverpool; pop. 74,302; shipping center; metal manufacturing, flour milling; lumberyards.

Bo·po'lu (bô·pō'lōō). Native settlement, NW Liberia, W Africa, ab. 70 m. N of Monrovia.

Bo′que·rón′ (bō′kä·rŏn′). **1** Department of Paraguay. See *Table* at PARAGUAY.

2 Port, a barrio of Cabo Rojo municipality, SW Puerto Rico, on **Boquerón Bay**.

Bo′ra Bo′ra *or* **Bo′ra·bo′ra** (bōr′ä·bōr′ä). One of the Leeward Is. group of the Society Is., French Polynesia, 9 m. W by N of Tahaa; pop. 1330.

Bo′rah Peak (bōr′ä). Mountain 12,655 ft. in Lost River Range, Custer co., cen. Idaho; highest point in the state.

Bo′ran (bōr′ăn). Region, S Ethiopia, bordering on Kenya.

Bo·rås′ (bōō·rōs′). Town, Älvsborg prov., SW Sweden, 35 m. E of Göteborg; pop. 51,453; textile mills; founded 1632 by Gustavus Adolphus.

Bo·raz·jan′ (bô·räz·jän′; -jōōn′). Town, SW Iran, just NE of Bushire; pop. ab. 6000.

Borbetomagus. See WORMS.

Bor·bon′ (bôr·bôn′). Municipality on NE coast of Cebu I., Phil. Is., 38 m. N of City of Cebu; pop. 16,680.

Borbonensis Ager. See BOURBONNAIS.

Bor′deaux′ (bôr′dō′); *anc.* **Bur·dig′a·la** (bûr·dĭg′a·lä). Commercial seaport and industrial city, ✱ of Gironde dept., SW France, 13 m. above confluence of Garonne and Dordogne rivers 310 m. SSW of Paris; pop. 258,348; archiepiscopal see; famous for its fine red and white wines; important structures include a 17-arch stone bridge (1821), city gate (Porte de Bourgogne), 8th-cent. Gothic church, 10th-cent. Romanesque church. 11th-cent. Gothic cathedral; university (1441); exports wine, brandy, drugs, dyes, etc.; shipbuilding; manufactures sugar, textiles, pottery, soap, rope, liquors.

History: Under Roman rule was capital of Aquitania Secunda; taken by Goths and Normans; passed to French king Louis VII; held by England 1154–1451; suffered during Revolution as a Girondist center; joined with Bourbon forces 1814; seat of government of National Defense 1870; an American military base 1918; French government temporarily removed here 1918; occupied by Germans 1940–45; relieved Apr. 1945.

Bor′den (bôr′d′n). County in Texas. See *Table* at TEXAS.

Borden Island. Island, N Parry Is., Franklin District, Northwest Territories, Canada.

Bor′den·town (bôr′d′n·toun). City, Burlington co., S cen. New Jersey, on Delaware river 6 m. SSE of Trenton; pop. 4974; settled 1682 by English Quakers; partly destroyed by British 1778; incorporated as city 1867.

Bor′di·ghe′ra (bôr′dē·gâ′rä). Commune, Imperia prov., Liguria, NW Italy, ESE of Ventimiglia; seaport; winter resort; pop. 8621.

Bordj′–bou–Ar′ré′ridj′ (bôrj′bōō′ä′rä′rēj′). Commune, Constantine dept., NE Algeria, ab. 100 m. W of Constantine; pop. 13,089.

Bordj′–Mé′na′iel′ (bôrj′mä′nä′yĕl′). Commune, Alger dept., N Algeria, ab. 35 m. E of Algiers; pop. 26,607.

Bord′ö′ (bôr′dû′). An island of the Faeroes (*q.v.*).

Borgå. See PORVOO.

Bor′gar·nes′ (bôr′gär·nâs′). Village, SW coast of Iceland, just N of Reykjavík; pop. 337.

Bor′gen Bay (bôr′gĕn). Inlet of Bismarck Sea on N coast of New Britain I., Bismarck Archipelago, at W end just E of Cape Gloucester; strategic Hill 660 on the bay captured by marines Jan. 14, 1944 after a ten-day battle.

Bor′ger (bôr′gēr). City, Hutchinson co., NW Texas, in the panhandle; pop. 20,911; gas and petroleum.

Bor′ger·hout (bôr′ĸĕr·hout). Commune, Antwerp prov., N Belgium, an E suburb of Antwerp; pop. (1938 est.) 54,626.

Borg′holm (bôrg′hŏm; *Swed.* bôr′y′·ĥŏlm). Seaport, Kalmar prov., SE Sweden, on W coast of Öland I.; pop. 2025; chief town of island; seaside resort.

Borgne, Lake (bôrn; *Fr.* bôrn′y′). Inlet of Mississippi Sound in Orleans and St. Bernard parishes, SE Louisiana; connects Lake Pontchartrain with Gulf of Mexico.

Bor′go Grap′pa (bôr′gō gräp′pä). Village, Latium, W Italy, near Cisterna and ab. 10 m. S of Velletri, where the

Anzio and southern armies of U.S. joined May 25, 1944 in advance on Rome.

Bor′go·ma·ne′ro (bôr′gô·mä·nâ′rô). Commune, Novara prov., NW Italy, 19 m. NNW of Novara; pop. 13,434.

Borgo San Donnino. See FIDENZA.

Bor′go San Lo·ren′zo (bôr′gō sän′ lô·rĕn′tsô). Commune, Firenze prov., Tuscany, cen. Italy, 14 m. NNE of Florence; pop. 16,805; sulfur springs; summer resort.

Bor′go·se′sia (bôr′gô·sâ′zyä). Commune, Vercelli prov., Piedmont, NW Italy, on Sesia river 27 m. NNW of Vercelli; pop. 13,716; textiles.

Bor′go Val di Ta′ro (bôr′gō väl′ dē tä′rô). Commune, Parma prov., Emilia, N Italy, in Taro valley 36 m. SW of Parma; pop. 15,209; lignite deposits nearby.

Bor′gu (bôr′gōō); *Fr.* **Bor′gou′** (bôr′gōō′). District in N Dahomey and W Ilorin prov., W Northern Region, Nigeria, W Africa, bounded on NE and E by the Niger; inhabited by several pagan Negro tribes; an area contested by France and Great Britain 1894–98; divided by convention of June 1898; chief town Nikki.

Bo′ri′nage′ (bô′rē′nàzh′). Coal-mining district surrounding Mons, Hainaut prov., Belgium.

Bo′rin·quén′ (bō′rĕng·kān′). Early native name of PUERTO RICO.

Borinquén, Point. Cape at NW end of Puerto Rico, at E side of entrance to Mona Passage.

Bo·ri′slav (bŭ·rȳē′slàf); *Pol.* **Bo·ry′sław** (bô·rī′släf). City, W Ukraine, U.S.S.R., at N foot of Carpathians 44 m. SW of Lvov (formerly in Lwów prov., Poland); pop. (1938–39 est.) 45,037; oil field; natural-gas deposits.

Bo·ri′so·glebsk′ (bô·rīs′ô·glĕpsk′; *Russ.* bŭ·ryĭ·sŭ·glyĕpsk′). City, E Voronezh Region, Soviet Russia, Europe, at junction of Vorona and Khoper rivers; pop. 52,055; established 1646 as a fort against the Crimean Tatars; center of grain-producing area; annual fairs.

Bo·ri′sov (bŭ·rȳē′sŭf). Town, N cen. White Russia, U.S.S.R., on left bank of Berezina river 50 m. NE of Minsk; pop. 25,844; tanneries, sawmills. Held by Germans July 1941 to July 1944. See BEREZINA.

Bo·ri′sov·ka (bŭ·rȳē′sŭf·kà). **1** Town, S Kazakh S.S.R., Soviet Central Asia, on railroad 145 m. NW of Tashkent. **2** Town, SW Kursk Region, Soviet Russia, Europe, on left bank of Vorskla river near its source 52 m. N of Kharkov; pop. 33,424. Held by Germans 1941–43.

Bor′ja (bôr′hä). Town, Guairá dept., S Paraguay, S of Villarrica; pop. ab. 10,300.

Borkhaya. See BUOR KHAYA.

Bor′ku (bôr′kōō). A region in E Sahara, N Chad Republic, N cen. Africa.

Bor′kum (bôr′kŏom). German island ab. 6 m. long and 2 m. wide in North Sea at mouth of Ems river 26 m. NW of Emden, the westernmost of the East Frisian Islands; a favorite summer resort.

Bor′mi·da (bôr′mĕ·dä). River ab. 100 m. long mostly in Piedmont, NW Italy; rises at E end of Maritime Alps, flows NE to the Tanaro below Alessandria.

Bor′na (bôr′nä). Mining and manufacturing city, Leipzig dist., E Germany, 15 m. SSE of Leipzig; pop. 10,978.

Bor′ne·o (bôr′nĕ·ō). Island in the Malay Archipelago, E of Sumatra, N of Java, and W of Celebes; lat. 7°3′N to 4°10′S and long. 108°50′ to 119°20′E; third largest island in the world; 289,993 sq. m.; pop. 2,966,536. Northern part (sometimes called collectively **British Borneo**) includes British colonies of North Borneo and Sarawak, and protectorate of Brunei; S section (*Indonesian* **Ka′li·man′tan** [kä′lē·män′tän]), formerly a division (**Dutch Borneo**) of the Neth. Indies, now belongs to Indonesia; area 208,286 sq. m., pop. 3,676,000. Touches South China Sea on W and NW, Sulu Sea on NE, Celebes Sea and Makassar Strait on E, and Java Sea on S. Crossed by the equator in S cen. part; has indented coast line with numerous good harbors. Mountainous throughout N and cen. parts; chief ranges Muller, Schwaner, and Kapuas; highest point Mt. Kinabulu 13,455 ft. in N Brit. North Borneo. Most important rivers are the

Barito, Kapuas, Mahakam, and Rajang. Raises rice, maize, tobacco, millet, and vegetables; exports forest products; mineral wealth very great: gold, copper, coal, iron, and oil.

History: Invaded c. 6th cent. A.D. by people from S India; S part influenced in turn by Sumatra and Java (*qq.v.*); sultanate of Brunei (*q.v.*) on N coast probably founded from Malaya and gave its name in corrupted form to entire island; visited by Portuguese, Dutch, and English traders 16th and 17th cents.; Sarawak, Brunei, and North Borneo (*qq.v.*) dependencies of British since 19th cent. (see also LABUAN); rest claimed by Dutch who subdued coast, esp. in wars 1850–54, 1859–62. In World War II seized by Japanese Dec. 1941–Feb. 1942; frequently bombed by U.S. planes 1944–45; invasion begun at Tarakan by Australian troops May 1, 1945 and operations continued until surrender of Japan Aug. 14, 1945. Dutch Borneo reorganized 1947 as a federation of autonomous provinces to be included in the projected United States of Indonesia; reorganized again as part of Republic of Indonesia 1950.

Borneo, South and East. Former residency occupying S and E parts of Dutch Borneo, Neth. Indies, on island of Borneo; 151,582 sq. m.; pop. 1,366,214; ✻ Bandjermasin; now divided into South Kalimantan and East Kalimantan provs. of Indonesia. Region is mountainous in N and W, esp. along border of West Borneo; highest point above 7300 ft. Many rivers, including the Barito, Mahakam, Kajan, and Kahajan. Noted for its great wealth in oil (Tarakan and Balikpapan). Has a few good harbors and several coastal islands (see LAOET).

Borneo, West. Former residency occupying W section of Dutch Borneo, Neth. Indies, on island of Borneo; 56,650 sq. m.; pop. 802,447; ✻ Pontianak. Mountain ranges on Sarawak border and in NE; highest point 5768 ft.; chief river the Kapuas; chief town Pontianak in the delta of the Kapuas river on the equator. See BORNEO island.

Born·holm (bôrn'hōlm). Island, constituting a county of Denmark, in Baltic Sea 25 m. S of Sweden; 228 sq. m.; pop. 45,930; ⊗ Rönne. See *Table* at DENMARK. Generally hilly; has become a popular tourist resort. In early times the home of pirates; seized by the Hanseatic League 1510; down to 1660 held for varying periods by Denmark, Lübeck, Sweden; Danish since 1660.

Born·höved' (bôrn·hûft'). Village, SE Schleswig-Holstein, NW Germany, 10 m. E of Neumünster; pop. (1925) 970; battle here July 22, 1227 in which Danes under Waldemar II were defeated by Germans, decisively ending Danish dominion over Baltic region.

Bor Nor (bûr' nōr') or **Buir Nor** (bōō'y'r). Lake in NW Manchuria, on the border of Mongolia S of Hulun Nor; outlet is Khalka river.

Bor'nu (bôr'nōō). Province of Nigeria; includes part (5149 sq. m., pop. 194,000) of Cameroons trust territory. See *Table* at NIGERIA. A vast plain surrounding and sloping toward Lake Chad; inhabited chiefly by Kanuri Negroes. With territory now in S Niger, Fr. W. Africa, constituted a Mohammedan native kingdom from ab. 11th cent.; together with Kanem formed an empire from ab. 13th cent., at height of its power 1571–1603; came in conflict with Fulahs ab. 1808; after 1835 visited by Europeans and by 1900 French, Germans, and British each had spheres of influence; in 1902 became part of protectorate of Nigeria under British.

Borny. See COLOMBEY.

Bo'ro·boe·doer' (bōr'ō·bōō·dōōr') or **Bo'ro·bu·dur'.** Ruins of a great Buddhist temple, Central Java prov., Indonesia, ab. 10 m. S of Magelang and 18 m. NW of Jogjakarta; about 1000 years old, built of volcanic lava over a hill, with eight galleries of some 1500 exquisite bas-relief carvings and 430 life-size images of Buddha. Has been completely restored and is now under government care.

Bo·ro·di·no' (bŭ·rŭ·dyĭ·nô'). Village, W Moscow Re-

gion, Soviet Russia, Europe, 70 m. WSW of Moscow on the Moscow-Smolensk highway (now on railroad). Scene of great battle of Napoleonic Wars Sept. 7, 1812 in which Napoleon defeated Gen. Kutuzov with heavy losses on both sides. In World War II scene of severe fighting Oct. 15–16, 1941.

Bo·ron'ga Islands (bŭ·rŏn'gä). Group of small islands in Bay of Bengal off W coast of cen. Burma, S of Akyab.

Bo·rong'an (bō·rông'än). Municipality. SE Samar, Phil. Is., on coast 36 m. E of Catbalogan; pop. 21,340; has extensive coconut plantations.

Bo·ro'vi·chi (bŭ·rô'vyĭ·chĭ). Town, SE Novgorod Region, Soviet Russia, Europe, on Msta river 160 m. SE of Leningrad; pop. 28,402.

Bor'ro·me'an Islands (bŏr'ō·mē'ăn); *Ital.* **I'so·le Bor'ro·me'e** (ē'zō·lā bŏr'rō·mâ'ā). Four small islands in Lake Maggiore, NW Italy; noted for their scenery.

Bor'row·dale' (bŏr'ō·dāl'). Valley in Cumberland, NW England, near Keswick; famed for its beauty; through it flows the Derwent.

Bor'row·stoun·ness' (bō·nĕs'; bŏr'ō·stō·nĕs'); *original, and still official, name for* **Bo'·ness'** (bō·nĕs'). Seaport burgh, West Lothian co., SE Scotland, on Firth of Forth; pop. 9949; coal mining, iron founding.

Bor·sip'pa (bôr·sĭp'ȧ). Ancient Akkadian city near Babylon; its ruins are just S of Hilla.

Bor'stal (bôr'st'l). Village near Rochester, Kent, SE England; site of Borstal reformatory (founded 1902) which pioneered the segregation of young offenders from mature criminals, and other reforms (Borstal system).

Boryslaw. See BORISLAV.

Borysthenes. See DNIEPER.

Bor'zya (bôr'zyȧ). Town, S Chita Region, Soviet Russia, Asia, on Russian-Manchurian R.R. ab. 170 m. SE of Chita.

Bo'san·ska Gra'diš·ka (bō'sän·skä grä'dĕsh·kä). Town, NW cen. Yugoslavia, on Sava river N of Banja Luka; pop. (1931) 6526.

Bos'ca·wen (bŏs'kwĭn; bŏs'koin; bŏs'kô'ĭn). Town, Merrimack co., S cen. New Hampshire, on Merrimack river 9 m. N of Concord; pop. 2181.

Bos·caw'en (bŏs·kô'ĭn; -kô'ĭn). See TAFAHI.

Bos'co·bel (bŏs'kō·bĕl). **1** City, Grant co., SW corner of Wisconsin, on Wisconsin river; pop. 2608; farm trade center; founding place of the Gideons, society of commercial travelers (1899).

2 Locality, Shropshire, W England, E of Shrewsbury; site of Royal Oak in which Prince Charles (later Charles II) hid in his flight after battle of Worcester 1651.

Bos'co·re·a'le (bôs'kō·rā·ä'lā) *and* **Bo'sco·tre·ca'se** (-trä·kä'zä). Adjoining towns in commune of Torre Annunziata, Napoli prov., Campania, Italy, at foot of S slope of Vesuvius near Pompeii; important discoveries of antiquities have been made at Boscoreale.

Bos'ham (bŏz'ăm). Village, South Downs, West Sussex, England, on coast 4 m. W of Chichester; resort and fishing village. A historical site said to have been residence of King Canute and Roman Emperor Vespasian.

Bos'hof (bŏs'hŏf). Town, health resort, W Orange Free State, E cen. Union of South Africa, 30 m. ENE of Kimberley; pop. 2268; a center of wool industry.

Bo'silj·grad (bō'sĕl·y'·gräd). Town, SE Yugoslavia, NE of Skoplje; pop. 3000; with surrounding district, 320 sq. m., ceded to Yugoslavia by Bulgaria 1920.

Bos'koop (bôs'kōp). Commune, South Holland prov., Netherlands, 2 m. NW of Gouda; pop. 7704; famous for its nurseries of roses, azaleas, and other flowering shrubs.

Bos'kop (bŏs'kŏp). Locality in the Transvaal, Union of South Africa; site of discovery of fossilized skull 1913.

Bos'na (bŏz'nä; *Yugo.* bôs'nä). **1** River 150 m. long in W cen. Yugoslavia; flows N into Sava river 24 m. E of Brod.

2 See BOSNIA.

Bos'nek (bŏz'nĕk; bôs'-). Village on SE coast of Biak I., Schouten Is., Neth. New Guinea; with Mokmer airfield a few miles W taken by Allies May–June 1944.

Bos′ni·a (bŏz′nĭ·á); *Yugo.* **Bos′na** (bôs′nä). Region, cen. Yugoslavia; separated from Slavonia on N by the Sava river, from Serbia on E by the Drina river, borders Montenegro on S, Herzegovina on SW, and Dalmatia and Croatia on W; Dinaric Alps along W border; chief town Sarajevo.

History: Ruled by Croatian kings c. 958 A.D.; subject to Hungary 1000–1200; organized c. 1200 under a ban who later took province of Herzegovina; after period of Serbian rule, became strong lordship with territory reaching seacoast (Stephen Kotromanić, ban, 1322–53); independent kingdom with its ruler, Stephen Tvrtko, taking title "King of Bosnia and Serbia" 1376; took part in battle of Kosovo (*q.v.*) 1389; kingdom disintegrated from 1391, the S part becoming independent duchy Herzegovina (*q.v.*); stronghold of Bogomile heresy; conquered by Turks 1463, made Turkish province; scene of insurrections against Turkish rule 1821–51; after rising 1875 which encouraged revolt in Bulgaria (*q.v.*), placed under control of Austria-Hungary 1878 and made part of province of **Bosnia and Her′ze·go·vi′na** (hûr′tsĕ·gō·vē′nä), which was formally annexed to Austria-Hungary 1908 and became a province of Yugoslavia 1918 (ab. 23,000 sq. m., ✶ Sarajevo); at reorganization of Yugoslavia 1929 comprised counties of Vrbaska, Drinska, part of Primorje; reunited with Herzegovina 1945 as a federated republic of Yugoslavia (19,904 sq. m.; pop. [1931] 1,185,040).

Bos′o·ra (bŏs′ō·rá). Var. of BOSRA.

Bos′po·rus (bŏs′pō·rŭs); *Turk.* **Ka′ra·de·niz′ Bo′-ga·zɪ′** (kä′rä·dĕng·ēz′ bō′ä·zɪ′); *anc.* **Bos′po·rus Thra′ci·us** (thrā′shĭ·ŭs). *Also, commonly but incorrectly,* **Bos′pho·rus** (bŏs′fō·rŭs). Narrow strait bet. Turkey in Europe and Turkey in Asia connecting the Sea of Marmara with the Black Sea; ab. 20 m. long and from ab. ½ to 2¾ m. wide. See *Map* at TURKEY. Noted for its fine scenery on both banks and on European side lined with many residential suburban villages of İstanbul. From ancient times, important as thoroughfare of commerce bet. Black Sea and Aegean and Mediterranean; of great importance in medieval trade of Constantinople; controlled by Turks since 1452, when they completed fortification of its shores. See also DARDA-NELLES and, for later history, the STRAITS.

Bosporus, Cim·me′ri·an (sĭ·mẽr′ĭ·ăn); *anc.* **Bosporus Cim·me′ri·us** (sĭ·mẽr′ĭ·ŭs). **1** Kerch Strait (*q.v.*). **2** Ancient kingdom. See CIMMERIAN BOSPORUS.

Bos′que (bŏs′kā; -kĕ). County in Texas. See *Table* at TEXAS.

Bos′ra (bŏz′rá) *or* **Bus′ra** (bōŏs′rŏ); *also* **Boz′rah** (bŏz′rá). Ruins of town in the Hauran, now a village in SW Syria on SW border of Jebel ed Druz; not the Bozrah of Edom (*Gen.* xxxvi. 33) or of Moab (*Jer.* xlviii. 24), neither of which, however, has been definitely identified. In the time of the Maccabees a caravan junction point; known to Romans as **Bos′tra** (bŏs′trá) and became capital of Roman province of Arabia.

Bos′sier (bō′zhẽr). Parish in Louisiana. See *Table* at LOUISIANA.

Bossier City. Industrial town, Bossier parish, NW Louisiana, E suburb of Shreveport; pop. 32,776.

Bos′ton (bôs′tŭn). **1** Seaport city, ✶ of Massachusetts, and ⊗ of Suffolk co., E Massachusetts, on Massachusetts Bay at mouths of Charles and Mystic rivers; pop. 697,197; largest city in the state and 13th largest city in U.S. Industrial, commercial, and financial center; important fish market, and greatest wool market in U.S.; varied manufactures. Home of the Unitarian movement in U.S.; headquarters of antislavery agitation in period preceding Civil War; birthplace of the Christian Science movement. Famous buildings include: Christ Church (Old North Church 1723), from the steeple of which the signal was given to Paul Revere to inform him of the route taken by the British in their march on Concord; Old South Meetinghouse (1729); Faneuil Hall (1742,

known as the "Cradle of Liberty"); the old State House (1748); U.S. Custom House; Boston Public Library; Boston Museum of Fine Arts. Boston University (1869; coed.; Methodist); New England Conservatory of Music (1867); Northeastern University (1898); Simmons College (1899; women); Emmanuel College (1919; women; Catholic); Suffolk University (1906; coed.); Emerson Coll. (1880; coed.); Calvin Coolidge Coll. (1934; coed.).

History: Settled by Gov. John Winthrop 1630 (see CHARLESTOWN); made capital of Massachusetts Bay Colony 1632; began first continuously published colonial newspaper 1704; leader in opposition to British trade restrictions and other policies leading to the outbreak of the American Revolution; scene of the Boston Massacre Mar. 5, 1770, and the so-called Boston Tea Party Dec. 16, 1773; trade shut off by Boston Port Bill 1774; battle of Bunker Hill June 17, 1775; British withdrew from city Mar. 17, 1776; opposed to Jefferson's embargo policy and War of 1812; incorporated as a city 1822. **2** Village (est. pop. 300) and town (pop. 5106) including it, Erie co., W New York, ab. 20 m. SSE of Buffalo. **3** Village, ⊗ of Bowie co., NE Texas.

Boston; *formerly* **St. Bot′olph's Town** (sȧnt bŏt′ŏlfs). Municipal borough, ⊗ of The Parts of Holland, Lincolnshire, E England, on the Witham near its mouth 49 m. E of Nottingham; pop. 24,453; shipping, fisheries; trade center in agricultural section.

Boston Bay. Western section of Massachusetts Bay, E Massachusetts; the city of Boston is situated at its W end on **Boston Harbor.**

Boston Corner. Town, Columbia co., New York; former SW corner of Massachusetts ceded to New York 1853; 1½ sq. m.

Boston Mountains. Ridge 1000 to 2000 ft. in Ozark Plateau in NW Arkansas.

Bostra. See BOSRA.

Bos′well (bŏz′wĕl; -wĕl). Borough, Somerset co., S Pennsylvania, 13 m. SSW of Johnstown; pop. 1508.

Bos′worth Field (bŏz′wûrth; -wẽrth). Area in rural district of Market Bosworth, Leicestershire, cen. England; site of final battle 1485 in Wars of the Roses in which Richard III was defeated and killed.

Bo·ta·fo′go Bay (bōō·tà·fō′gōō). Inlet of Guanabara Bay in S section of Rio de Janeiro, Brazil, enclosed on SE by Pão de Açúcar (Sugarloaf Mt.).

Bot′a·ny (bŏt′à·nĭ). Town, E New South Wales, Australia, suburb of Sydney on Botany Bay; pop. 8287.

Botany Bay. Inlet of South Pacific Ocean, on S border of city of Sydney, New South Wales, SE Australia, 9 m. S of Port Jackson; ab. 6 m. at greatest width. Scene of first landing on Australian soil by Capt. Cook Apr. 1770; selected 1787 as site for penal settlement; landing made Jan. 1788; settlement transferred later to Port Jackson

Botany Point. Cape on W end of St. Thomas I., Virgin Is., West Indies.

Bot′e·tourt (bŏt′ĕ·tŏt). County in Virginia. See *Table* at VIRGINIA.

Both′ni·a (bŏth′nĭ·á). Former name of the region about the Gulf of Bothnia.

Bothnia, Gulf of. Northern arm of the Baltic Sea, extending bet. Sweden on the W and Finland on the E.

Both′well (bŏth′wĕl; -wĕl; bŏth′-). Parish and town, Lanark co., Scotland, ab. 7 m. SE of Glasgow; ruins of Bothwell Castle of 13th cent.; at **Bothwell Bridge** over the Clyde the Royalists under Monmouth and Claverhouse defeated the Covenanters June 22, 1679.

Botocan. See PAGSANJAN.

Bo·to·şa′ni *or* **Bo·to·sha′ni** (bŏ·tŏ·shän′; -shä′nĕ). Commercial town, NE Romania, in Moldavia region; pop. 32,107; trade center for agricultural area.

Botswana. See BECHUANALAND PROTECTORATE.

Bot′ti·neau′ (bŏt″ĭ·nō′). **1** County in North Dakota. See *Table* at NORTH DAKOTA.
2 City, its ⊗, N North Dakota, 59 m. NE of Minot; pop. 2613; in summer resort region.

Bot′tom, the (bŏt′ŭm). See SABA.

Bot′trop (bŏt′rŏp). Coal-mining city, W Germany, in North Rhine-Westphalia state, Prussia, 5 m. NNW of Essen; pop. 77,315; coke furnaces.

Bo·tu·ca·tú′ (bō·tŏŏ·ká·tŏŏ′). City, São Paulo state, SE Brazil, 115 m. NW of São Paulo; pop. 19,753.

Bot′wood (bŏt′wŏŏd). Town, E Newtoundland, 160 m. WNW of St. John's; pop. (1942 est.) 1200; has large seaplane base and 30 m. to the E is large airport, western terminus for transatlantic planes. See GANDER.

Bot′zen (bŏ′tsĕn). Variant of *Bozen*: see BOLZANO.

Bötzow. See ORANIENBURG.

Boua′ké′ (bwà′kā′) *or* **Bwa′ke** (bwä′kā). Commercial town, S cen. Ivory Coast, West Africa, on railroad 180 m. NNW of Abidjan; pop. 70,000.

Bou–Am. See TAFILELT.

bou–Aou·kaz′, Dje′bel (jä′bal bŏŏ′ou·kăz′). Hill 2000 ft. high in NW cen. Tunisia, N Africa; severe fighting in British attack on Tunis Apr. 27–30, 1943.

Bou A′ra·da (bŏŏ ŭ′rŏ·dă). Town, N Tunisia, ab. 45 m. SW of Tunis; fighting 1943.

Bou′cau′ *or* **Le Bou′cau′** (lĕ bŏŏ′kō′). Commune, Basses-Pyrénées dept., France, 3 m. N of Bayonne; pop. 5738; an industrial suburb.

Bouches′–du–Rhône′ (bŏŏsh′dü·rōn′). Department of France. See *Table* at FRANCE.

Bou′fa′rik′ (*Fr.* bŏŏ′fà′rēk′). Commune, N Alger dept., N Algeria, ab. 21 m. SSW of Algiers; pop. 14,752.

Bou′gain·ville (bŏŏ′gắn·vĭl; bō′-; *Fr.* bŏŏ′găN′vēl′). Largest of the Solomon Islands, W Pacific Ocean; ab. 125 m. long by ab. 40 m. wide; 3500 sq. m.; pop. (1930) 46,300; chief town and administrative headquarters Kieta, a part of Kieta district, Territory of New Guinea. Traversed lengthwise by a mountain range called Emperor Range in N and Crown Prince Range in S, highest peak Mount Balbi 10,171 ft. in N section; much of the interior unexplored. Has rich, volcanic soil and many coconut plantations; other products are coffee and cocoa. On N is Buka I. separated from it by narrow Buka Passage, and on the S are Shortland Is. Good harbors are at Kieta (Rawa Harbour), Buka Passage, and Buin (Tonolai Harbour) at S end; on W coast is anchorage in Empress Augusta Bay. Discovered by Louis de Bougainville 1768; came under control of a German trading company 1882 and was a German possession 1899–1914; taken by Australians in World War I and included 1920 in mandated New Guinea. Occupied Jan. 1942 by Japa-nese who developed harbors and made airfields; bombed by Allied air forces 1943 and landings made by U.S. Marines Nov. 1, 1943 on coast of Empress Augusta Bay, but most of island and Japanese forces by-passed 1944 until campaign by Australians in 1945.

Bougainville Strait. Channel ab. 30 m. wide bet. S Bougainville and NW Choiseul Is., W cen. Solomon Is., through which passes boundary line bet. the Solomon Is. of the Australian trust territory and the British Solomon Is.

Bou′ga·roun′, Cape (bŏŏ′gá·rŏŏn′). Cape on N coast of Constantine dept., NE Algeria.

Bou′gie′ (bŏŏ′zhē′); *anc.* **Sal′dae** (săl′dē). Seaport and commune on W shore of **Gulf of Bougie,** NW Constantine dept., NE Algeria, ab. 115 m. E of Algiers; pop. of commune (1936) 30,659; has good harbor, is beautifully situated, and has considerable trade in oils, wool, hides, and minerals; in 5th cent a fortified city of Genseric the Vandal; in 11th cent. capital of powerful Berber dynasty; later under the Hafsids, Barbary pirates, and Spaniards; taken by French 1833. Occupied by British troops Nov. 11, 1942.

Bouil′lon′ (bŏŏ′yôN′). Town in the Ardennes, Luxembourg prov., Belgium, on the Semois ab. 7 m. NNE of Sedan; pop. 2869; made capital of small duchy 1088 of crusader Godfrey of Bouillon; later attached successively to Liège, Sedan, France, Netherlands, Belgium.

Bou·ï′ra′ (bŏŏ′ē′rá′). Commune, Alger dept., N Algeria; pop. 11,007.

Boukhara. Variant of BUKHARA.

Boul′der (bōl′dēr). **1** County in Colorado. See *Table* at COLORADO.
2 City, its ⊗, N cen. Colorado, 25 m. NW of Denver; pop. 37,718; incorp. 1871 and 1878; summer and health resort; in mining region producing gold, silver, and esp. coal; region also produces fruits, vegetables, poultry, livestock. University of Colorado (1876; coed.).
3 Town, ⊗ of Jefferson co., SW cen. Montana; pop. 1394.
4 Town, S Western Australia, in gold-mining district 335 m. ENE of Perth; pop. 5809.

Boulder Canyon. Former canyon of the Colorado river ab. 20 m. above Black Canyon (site of Hoover Dam) bet. Arizona and Nevada; now covered by Lake Mead.

Boulder City. Model city, Clark co.. SE corner of Nevada; pop. 4059; built by U.S. government in 1932 as construction headquarters during work on Hoover Dam and as permanent administrative headquarters for Reclamation and National Park Service forces in area.

Boulder Dam. See UNITED STATES, *Dams.*

Boulder Peak. Mountain 10,966 ft. in S Custer co., cen. Idaho.

Bou·lin′da, Mount (bŏŏ·lĭn′dá). Peak 4078 ft. in cen. part of island of New Caledonia, SW Pacific Ocean.

Bou·logne′ (bŏŏ·lōn′; -loin′; *Fr.* bŏŏ·lôN′y′) *or* **Bou′-logne′–sur–Mer′** (bŏŏ′lôN′y′·sür·mâr′); *anc.* **Ges′o·ri′a·cum** *or* **Ges′so·ri′a·cum** (jĕs′ô·rĭ′á·kŭm), *later* **Bo·no′ni·a** (bô·nō′nĭ·á). Seaport city, Pas-de-Calais dept., N France, on English Channel 61 m. NW of Arras; pop. 52,371; fishing center; 13th-cent. castle; Italian Renaissance cathedral; Roman remains; large English population. Inhabitants massacred by Northmen 882 A.D.; taken by Henry VIII of England 1544; sold back to France 1550; demolished by Emperor Charles V 1553; place where Napoleon gathered large army 1808 in preparation for attack on England. In World War II taken by Germans May 21, 1940; stormed by Canadians Sept. 18, 1944 after four days of hard fighting.

Bou′logne′–Bil′lan′court′ (bŏŏ′lôN′y′·bē′yäN′kŏŏr′), *formerly* **Bou′logne′–sur–Seine′** (-sür·sân′). Industrial commune, Seine dept., N France, SW suburb of Paris on Seine river; pop. 97,379; near Bois de Boulogne; manufactures automobiles, airplanes, chemical products.

Bound′a·ry (boun′dá·rĭ). County in Idaho. See *Table* at IDAHO.

Boundary Bay. Inlet of Strait of Georgia in extreme SW British Columbia on U.S.-Canada border bet. Point Roberts and Blaine, Washington.

Boundary Peak. Mountain 13,145 ft. in W Esmeralda co., SW Nevada, on Nevada-California boundary; highest point in Nevada.

Bound Brook (bound′ brŏŏk′). Borough, Somerset co., N cen. New Jersey, on Raritan river 7 m. NW of New Brunswick; pop. 10,263; settled c. 1660; scene of attack by British force under Cornwallis 1777; manufactures paints, chemicals, clothing, asbestos products.

Boun′ti·ful (boun′tĭ·f'l). City, Davis co., N Utah, 8 m. N of Salt Lake City; pop. 17,039; truck gardens; fruit (esp. cherry) orchards.

Boun′ty Islands (boun′tĭ). Group of 13 islets 415 m. ESE of Dunedin, New Zealand, in lat. 47°43′S and long. 179°E; 1 sq. m.; uninhabited; under New Zealand administration; discovered 1788 by Capt. William Bligh in H.M.S. *Bounty.*

Bou·quet′ Canyon Dam (bōō·kā′; bō·kā′). Dam completed 1934 across **Bouquet Creek,** California; height 225 ft.; impounds water for water power.

Bou·rail′ (bōō·rī′). Town, New Caledonia I., SW Pacific Ocean, on coastal highway 80 m. NW of Nouméa.

Bour′bon (bûr′bŭn). Name of counties in two states of the U.S. See *Tables* at KANSAS and KENTUCKY.

Bour′bon (bōōr′bŭn; *Fr.* bōōr′bôn′). See RÉUNION.

Bour′bon·nais′ (bōōr′bŭ·nā′; *Fr.* bōōr′bô′nĕ′); *Lat.* **Bor·bo·nen′sis A′ger** (bôr′bō·nĕn′sĭs ā′jẽr). Historical region of cen. France; bounded anciently on NE by Nivernais, E by Burgundy, SE by Lyonnais, S by Auvergne, SW by Marche, and NW by Berry; ✳ (from late 15th cent.) Moulins.

History: Part of Celtic Gaul under Caesar, then of Aquitania under Augustus; began separate existence in 10th cent. A.D. under Aimar, founder of first house of Bourbon (became extinct 1218); ruled by second house of Bourbon until 1272; given in dowry to Robert of Clermont (6th son of Louis IX) who founded the third and most famous house of Bourbon; became part of royal domain 1527 and subsequently a province of France.

Bourbon–Vendée. See LA ROCHE-SUR-YON.

Bou·rem′ *or* **Bu·rem′** (bōō·rĕm′). Town, Mali, West Africa, on Niger river E of Tombouctou; terminus of trade route to Algeria.

Bou·resches′ (bōō′rĕsh′). Village, Aisne dept., NE France, 7 m. WNW of Château-Thierry; taken by Americans June 1918 in battle of Belleau Wood.

Bourg (bōōr; *Fr.* bōōr), *also* **Bourg′–en–Bresse′** (bōōr′–kän′brĕs′). Commune, ✳ of Ain dept., E France, 45 m. W of Geneva, Switzerland; pop. 24,746; 16th-cent. Gothic church; museum of antiquities; manufactures hosiery, linen, cotton goods. See BRESSE.

Bourges (bōōrzh; *Fr.* bōōrzh); *anc.* **A·var′i·cum** (á·văr′ĭ·kŭm). Commune, ✳ of Cher dept., cen. France, 126 m. S of Paris; pop. 49,263; fine 13th-cent. Gothic cathedral; archiepiscopal palace; military center: arsenal, cannon foundry, government powder works; manufactures cloth, iron goods, leather. Taken by Caesar 52 B.C.; under Augustus became capital of Roman province of Aquitania; at division of Aquitania in 3d cent. was made capital of Aquitania Prima; site of numerous medieval councils; university founded 1463 but abolished during Revolution.

Bour·get′ (bōōr·zhā′; *Fr.* bōōr′zhĕ′). Lake 11 m. long in E France, in Savoie dept.

Bourget, Le. See LE BOURGET.

Bourg–la–Reine (bōōr′lȧ·rān′; *Fr.* bōōr′lȧ·rân′). Commune, Seine dept., N France; pop. 8946; suburb of Paris.

Bourg′–Ma′dame′ (bōōr′mȧ′dăm′; *Fr.* bōōr′mȧ′dȧm′). Village, Pyrénées-Orientales dept., S France; pop. 468; international bridge over a tributary of the Segre to Puigcerdá marks the Franco-Spanish frontier.

Bourgogne. See BURGUNDY.

Bour′goin′ (bōōr′gwăn′). Commune, Isère dept., SE France; pop. (1931) 8020; industrial town 34 m. NW of Grenoble.

Bourg′–Saint–Mau′rice′ (bōōr′săn′mô′rēs′). Commune, Savoie dept., E France; pop. 2610; in a valley in Graian Alps at alt. 2668 ft.; railroad terminal and French (W) terminus of Little Saint Bernard Pass; tourist center.

Bourke (bûrk). Town, N New South Wales, SE Australia, on Darling river 410 m. NW of Sydney; pop. 1778; first settled as a fort 1835.

Bour′la′maque′ (bōōr′lȧ′măk′). Town, Abitibi co., SW Quebec, Canada; pop. 2460.

Bour′lon′ (bōōr′lôn′). Village (pop. 1273) and forested area (**Bourlon Wood**), Pas-de-Calais dept., N France, 5 m. W of Cambrai; fighting Nov. 20–30, 1917.

Bourne (bōrn). Town, Barnstable co., SE Massachusetts, on Cape Cod Canal 14 m. W of Barnstable; pop. 14,011; summer resort trade.

Bourne′mouth (bōrn′mŭth; bōōrn′-). County borough, Hampshire, S England, on English Channel at mouth of the Bourne 28 m. WSW of city of Southampton; pop. 116,797, (1951) 144,726; resort.

Bourn′ville (bōrn′vĭl; bōōrn′-). Model industrial town, a S suburb of Birmingham, England; pop. ab. 8000; founded by George Cadbury 1879.

Bouscat, Le. See LE BOUSCAT.

Bous′sa (bōō′sȧ). = BUSA.

Bous′su′ (bōō′sü′). Commune, Hainaut prov., SW Belgium, just W of Mons; pop. 13,159; industrial town.

Bou′vet Island (bōō′vā). Norwegian island in S Atlantic Ocean 1600 m. SSW of Cape of Good Hope, ab. lat. 54°S and long. 5°E.

Bou′vines′ (bōō′vēn′). Village, Nord dept., NE France, 10 m. SE of Lille; battlefield July 27, 1214 where French under Philip Augustus completely defeated Emperor Otto IV, King John of England, and their allies.

Bow (bō). River 315 m. long, SW Alberta, Canada; rises in Banff National Park on the E slopes of the Rocky Mts., flows SE through the park just E of Lake Louise then E past Calgary to unite with the Oldman and form the South Saskatchewan river.

Bow *or* **Strat′ford le Bow** (străt′fẽrd lē bō′). Parish, Poplar borough, E London, England; pop. 37,003.

Bow′bells′ (bō′bĕlz′). City, ⊗ of Burke co., NW North Dakota; pop. 687.

Bow′doin Lake (bō′d'n). Lake ab. 5 m. long in N cen. Phillips co., N Montana, 12 m. ENE of Malta; Federal migratory bird refuge.

Bow′en (bō′ĕn). Seaport, E Queensland, NE Australia, 290 m. NW of Rockhampton; pop. 2618.

Bow Fell (bō fĕl). Mountain 2960 ft., SE Cumberland, NW England, in the Lake District.

Bow′ie (bōō′ĭ). **1** County in Texas. See *Table* at TEXAS. **2** Town, Prince Georges co., Maryland, NE of Washington; pop. 1489; Bowie State Coll. (1925; coed.). **3** City, Montague co., N Texas, 42 m. S of Wichita Falls; pop. 4566; oil, gas, coal, clay deposits nearby.

Bow Island. See HAO.

Bowl′ing (bōl′ĭng). Village, Dunbarton co., W cen. Scotland, on Clyde river ab. 3 m. SE of Dumbarton; shipbuilding.

Bowl′ing Green′ (bōl′ĭng). **1** City, ⊗ of Warren co., S Kentucky, 64 m. SE of Owensboro; pop. 28,338; trade center in agricultural section; limestone quarries. Western Kentucky State College (1906; coed.). **2** City, ⊗ of Pike co., E Missouri; pop. 2650. **3** City, ⊗ of Wood co., NW Ohio, 18 m. S of Toledo; pop. 13,574; agriculture, meat packing, oil wells; manufacturing. Bowling Green State Univ. (1910; coed.). **4** Town, ⊗ of Caroline co., E Virginia; pop. 528.

Bow′man (bō′mȧn). **1** County in North Dakota. See *Table* at NORTH DAKOTA. **2** City, its ⊗, SW corner of North Dakota; pop. 1730.

Bow′man·ville (bō′mȧn·vĭl). Industrial town, Durham co., SE Ontario, Canada, on Lake Ontario 42 m. ENE of Toronto; pop. 5430; flour mills, canning factory.

Bow River. River in Canada: see Bow, above.

Box Butte (bŏks′ būt′). County in Nebraska. See *Table* at NEBRASKA.

Box El′der (bŏks′ ĕl′dēr). County in Utah. See *Table* at UTAH.

Box Hill. 1 Town, S Victoria, SE Australia, NE suburb of Melbourne; pop. 15,334.
2 See DORKING.

Box′tel (bôks′tĕl). Commune, North Brabant prov. S Netherlands, ab. 12 m. E of Tilburg; pop. 10,944.

Bo′ya·cá′ (bō′yä·kä′). **1** Department of Colombia. See *Table* at COLOMBIA.
2 Town, Boyacá dept., cen. Colombia; pop. 7660; battle in which Spanish were defeated by small army under Bolívar Aug. 7, 1819. See BOGOTÁ.

Boyana. See BOJANA.

Boyd (boid). Name of counties in two states of the U.S. See *Tables* at KENTUCKY and NEBRASKA.

Boyd′ton (boid′tŭn). Town, ⊗ of Mecklenburg co., S Virginia; pop. 449.

Boy′er (boi′ēr). River 123 m. long, W Iowa; rises in Buena Vista co., NW Iowa, flows SW into Missouri river in W Pottawattamie co., SW Iowa.

Boy′er·town (boi′ēr·toun). Borough, Berks co., SE Pennsylvania, 16 m. E of Reading; pop. 4067.

Boyle (boil). **1** County in Kentucky. See *Table* at KENTUCKY.
2 Town, N co. Roscommon, N cen. Eire; pop. 2093; ruins of Cistercian abbey dating from 12th cent.

Boyne (boin). River 70 m. long in E Ireland; rises in the Bog of Allen, co. Kildare, flows NNE into the Irish Sea just below Drogheda; important battle fought on its banks 3 m. W of Drogheda July 1, 1690 in which the forces under King William III of England defeated the Jacobites under King James II. See AUGHRIM.

Boyne City. City, Charlevoix co., NW Michigan, 40 m. SW of Cheboygan; pop. 2797; fishing and summer resort.

Boyn′ton Beach (boin′t′n; -tŭn). City, Palm Beach co., SE Florida, S of West Palm Beach; pop. 10,467.

Boz, Cape (bōz); *Turk.* **Boz′bu·run′** (bōz′bŏŏ·rŏŏn′). Cape on NW coast of Turkey in Asia, projecting W into the Sea of Marmara.

Boz′ca·a·da′ (bōz′jä·ä·dä′); *anc.* **Ten′e·dos** (tĕn′ē·dŏs). Turkish island in NE Aegean Sea off W coast of Turkey in Asia, S of the island of İmroz and ab. 12 m. S of the Dardanelles; in the Trojan legend the station of the Greek fleet; used as base by Xerxes in the Persian War and later an ally of Athens. See GREECE.

Boz Dağ (bōz′ dä′); *anc.* **Tmo′lus** (t′mō′lŭs; mō′-). Mountain range ab. 6200 ft. high in W Turkey 20 m. E of İzmir; divides valleys of Gediz and Caÿster.

Boze′man (bōz′măn). City, ⊗ of Gallatin co., S Montana, 80 m. ESE of Butte; pop. 13,361. Montana State College (1893; coed.; oldest unit of Univ. of Montana).

Bozeman Pass. Mountain pass near Bozeman, S Montana, alt. ab. 4700 ft., on the **Bozeman Trail** which extended from Julesburg, Colorado, on the South Platte river to Virginia City, mining town in SW Montana; traced by John M. Bozeman 1863–65; its use by gold seekers opposed by Indians and abandoned after 1868; after 1877 became important cattle route.

Bozen. See BOLZANO commune.

Boz′rah (bōz′rȧ). **1** See BOSRA, Syria.
2 *mod.* **El Bu·sei′ra** (ăl bŏŏ·sī′rŏ; -sā′rŏ). Town of Jordan, formerly in Arabia and ancient capital of Edom (*Gen.* xxxvi. 33) SSE of Dead Sea and near Petra; noted for its sheep.

Bra (brä). Commune Cuneo prov., Piedmont, NW Italy, 25 m. NE of Cuneo; pop. 21,914.

Bra·bant′ (brȧ·bănt′; *now infrequent*, brä′bänt; *Fr.* brȧ′bän′; *Du.* brä·bänt′). **1** Old duchy of the Netherlands, covering territory of what is now S Netherlands and central and N Belgium.
History: Region settled by Franks in 5th cent. A.D.; in 9th cent. included in kingdom of Lotharingia and after 959 in duchy of Lower Lorraine (see LORRAINE); in late 12th cent. became independent duchy; finally passed to house of Burgundy 1430; inherited by Hapsburgs 1477; from 15th cent. a center of culture and commerce (see ANTWERP and BRUSSELS); northern section took part in revolt from Spain and by treaty of 1609 was awarded to United Provinces (see NETHERLANDS); southern (and larger) section remained part of Spanish, later Austrian Netherlands; united under French rule 1794–1814 and in kingdom of Netherlands 1815–30; provinces of Antwerp and southern Brabant joined revolt of Belgium (*q.v.*) 1830.
2 Province, cen. Belgium; 1267 sq. m.; pop. (1941 est.) 1,755,942; ✳ Brussels; densely populated region; rivers Senne, Dyle, Demer. Formerly, part of the old duchy of Brabant; overrun by the Germans in 1914 and 1940 and occupied by them through World Wars I and II.

Brabant Island. Island, second in size in Palmer Archipelago, Antarctica; 33 m. long.

Brač (bräch) *or* **Brach** (bräch); *Ital.* **Braz′za** (brät′-tsä). Yugoslav island in the Adriatic Sea off the Dalmatian coast; 152 sq. m.; pop. (1931) 17,317.

Bracara Augusta. See BRAGA.

Brac·cia′no, Lake (brät-chä′nō); *anc.* **Sab′a·ti′nus** (săb′ȧ·tī′nŭs). Lake 22 sq. m. in W cen. Italy 17 m. NW of Rome; drains SW into the Tyrrhenian Sea.

Brace′bridge (brās′brĭj). Town, ⊗ of Muskoka dist., SE Ontario, Canada, 5 m. S of S end of Lake Muskoka; pop. 2684; mills, factories; summer resort.

Brack′en (brăk′ĕn). County in Kentucky. See *Table* at KENTUCKY.

Brack′en·ridge (brăk′ĕn·rĭj). Borough, Allegheny co., SW Pennsylvania, on Allegheny river 18 m. NE of Pittsburgh; pop. 5697; coke, stainless steel.

Brack′ett·ville (brăk′ĕt·vĭl). City, ⊗ of Kinney co., SW Texas, 28 m. E of Del Rio; pop. 1662; cattle, sheep.

Brack′we′de (brăk′vā′dĕ). Commune, W Germany, in North Rhine-Westphalia state, 36 m. E of Münster and just S of Bielefeld; pop. 11,943; manufactures metal goods, glass, leather; cattle market.

Bra·da′no (brä·dä′nō). River ab. 60 m. long in S Italy; flows SE into the head of the Gulf of Taranto.

Brad′dock (brăd′ŭk). Industrial borough, Allegheny co., SW Pennsylvania, on Monongahela river 8 m. E of Pittsburgh; pop. 12,337; scene of Braddock's defeat July 9, 1755 by French and Indians; manufactures steel and iron foundry products, machinery.

Bra′den·ton (brā′d′n·tŭn). City, ⊗ of Manatee co., W Florida penin., at S end of Tampa Bay 11 m. N of Sarasota; pop. 19,380; winter resort; travertine quarries.

Brad′ford (brăd′fērd). **1** Name of counties in two states of the U.S. See *Tables* at FLORIDA and PENNSYLVANIA.
2 Village, Darke and Miami cos., W Ohio, 28 m. NNW of Dayton; pop. 2148.
3 Industrial city, McKean co., N Pennsylvania, 18 m. W of Allegheny river as it crosses New York border; pop. 15,061; oil and gas wells; coal deposits.
4 Village in Westerly town, Washington co., S Rhode Island, ab. 4 m. SE of Hopkinton; pop. (1950) 1024.
5 County borough, West Riding, Yorkshire, N England, near the Aire 10 m. W of Leeds; pop. 298,041, (1951) 292,394; center of worsted industry; coal and iron.

Bradford on A′von (ā′vŭn; ăv′ŭn). Urban district, Wiltshire, S England, 6 m. ESE of Bath; pop. 5627; ancient Saxon church.

Brad′ley (brăd′lĭ). **1** Name of counties in two states of the U.S. See *Tables* at ARKANSAS and TENNESSEE.
2 Village, Kankakee co., NE Illinois, 3 m. N of Kankakee; pop. 8082.

Bradley, Mount. Peak 13,280 ft. in Sierra Nevada, NE Tulare co., S cen. California.

Bradley Beach. Borough, Monmouth co., E cen. New Jersey, on Atlantic Ocean 2 m. S of Asbury Park; pop. 4204; seaside resort; fisheries.

Bra′dy (brā′dĭ). City, ⊗ of McCulloch co., cen. Texas,

46 m. SSW of Brownwood; pop. 5338; shipping point for poultry, esp. turkeys; trades in cotton, wool, mohair.

Brae·mar' (brā·mär'). **1** District in SW Aberdeen co., NE Scotland comprising the upper valley of the Dee river ab. 24 m. long; tourist resort.
2 Village, SW Aberdeen co., NE Scotland, 7 m. W of Balmoral Castle; site of a castle, seat of the earl of Mar; standard of revolt raised here 1715 by 6th earl.

Brae·ri'ach (brā·rē'ăk). Peak 4248 ft., N cen. Scotland, on border bet. Inverness and Aberdeen cos.

Bra'ga (brä'gȧ). **1** District of Portugal. See *Table* at PORTUGAL.
2 *anc.* **Brac'a·ra Au·gus'ta** (brăk'ȧ·rȧ ô·gŭs'tȧ). Commune, its * and * of Minho prov., NW Portugal, 197 m. N by E of Lisbon; pop. (1940) 29,875; capital of old province of Entre-Douro-e-Minho and ancient capital of Lusitania; said to have been founded by Carthaginians; Roman ruins; 12th-cent. cathedral; archiepiscopal see and primacy of Portugal; manufactures textiles, cutlery, firearms, gold and silver articles.

Bra·ga'do (brä·gä'thŏ). Town, Buenos Aires prov., E Argentina; pop. (est.) 16,329.

Bra·gan'ça (brä·găN'sȧ). **1** Town, NE Pará state, N Brazil, ab. 120 m. E of Belém; railroad terminus.
2 City, São Paulo state, SE Brazil, 40 m. N of São Paulo; pop. (1940 est.) 12,942.

Bra·gan'ça (brä·găN'sȧ) *or* **Bra·gan'za** (brä·găn'zȧ). **1** District of Portugal. See *Table* at PORTUGAL.
2 Commune, its *, NE Portugal, near Spanish border 88 m. ENE of Braga; pop. 6089; former capital of old province of Trás-os-Montes; episcopal see; famous feudal castle of dukes of Braganza; manufactures textiles, olive oil; trades in cattle and grain.

Brah'man·ba'ri·a (brä'mȧn·bär'ĭ·ȧ). Town, Dacca division, SE East Pakistan, 200 m. ENE of Calcutta; pop. 26,662.

Brah'ma·ni (brä'mȧ·nē). River ab. 280 m. long in Orissa, E India; rises in S Bihar and flows S to join the Mahanadi delta N of Cuttack.

Brah'ma·pu'tra (brä'mȧ·pōō'trȧ); *anc.* **Dy'ar·da·nes** (dī'är·dā'nēz) *or* **Oe·da'nes** (ē·dā'nēz). River 1800 m. long in Tibet (where its upper course is called **Tsang'·po'** [tsäng'pô']) and NE India; rises in SW Tibet in the Kailas Range (Himalayas) near 82°E; as the Tsangpo or **Ma'tsang'** (mä'tsäng') flows E 700 m. across S part of Tibet; on its S bank is Shigatse. Below Tsela Dzong at about 95°E turns abruptly S and breaks through E Himalayas in great gorges (known in this section as the **Dihang**) and turns again SSW near Sadiya in NE Assam to flow W through Assam valley and S in East Bengal, Pakistan, where it becomes the Jamuna and merges with the Ganges in the Ganges-Brahmaputra Delta (*q.v.*). Navigable for 800 m. to Dibrugarh; drains an area of 361,000 sq. m. Its upper course long unknown, esp. its identity with the Tsangpo, first established by exploration 1884–86; the Dihang explored 1913.

Braich'-y-Pwll' (brīk'ĭ·pōōl'). Cape, Lleyn Penin., NW coast of Wales.

Bră·i'la (brȧ·ē'lä). City, E Romania, on Danube river 12 m. S of Galaţi; pop. (1939 est.) 68,561; ships grain; important in wars of Turks, Walachians, and Russians.

Braine'-l'Al'leud (brân'lä'lü'). Commune, Brabant prov., cen. Belgium, 11 m. S of Brussels; pop. 10,873; manufactures glass.

Braine'-le-Comte' (brân'lē·kôNt'). Commune, Hainaut prov., Belgium; pop. 10,072.

Brai'nerd (brā'nẽrd). City, ⊗ of Crow Wing co., cen. Minnesota, on Mississippi river 53 m. N of St. Cloud; pop. 12,898; dairy products; near lake resort region.

Brain'tree (brān'trē; -trḗ). **1** Town, Norfolk co., E Massachusetts, 10 m. S of Boston; pop. 31,069; residential and industrial suburb of Boston.
2 (*locally also* brän'trē) Urban district, Essex, SE England, on the Blackwater 39 m. NE of London; pop. 17,480; textile mills, ironworks.

Brak'pan (brăk'păn). Town, S Transvaal, NE Republic of South Africa, in the Witwatersrand, 23 m. E of Johannesburg; pop. 54,811; formerly part of Benoni, became separate municipality 1919; rich gold mines.

Brambanan. See PRAMBANAN.

Bram'bau'er (brăm'bou'ēr). Formerly, a commune, Arnsberg govt. dist., Westphalia prov., Prussia, Germany, N of Dortmund; pop. 13,351; coal mining.

Bram'ham Moor (brăm'ăm). Locality, Yorkshire, N England, ENE of Leeds; battle Feb. 1408 in which Sir Henry Percy was defeated and killed.

Bramp'ton (brăm[p]'tŭn). **1** Industrial town, ⊗ of Peel co., SE Ontario, Canada, 20 m. W of Toronto; pop. 8389; boots and shoes, woolens, flour.
2 Market town in Brampton parish (pop. 7932), Cumberland, NW England, 11 m. NE of Carlisle.

Branch (brănch). County in Michigan. See *Table* at MICHIGAN.

Bran'co, Ri'o (rē'ōō vrăNng'kŏō); *or* **Pa·ri'ma** (pȧ·rē'mä). River ab. 350 m. long, N Brazil; formed by confluence of the Uraricoera and Takutú; flows S into the Rio Negro.

Bran'den·burg (brăn'dĕn·bûrg). City, ⊗ of Meade co., NW cen. Kentucky; pop. 1542.

Bran'den·burg (brăn'dĕn·bûrg; *Ger.* brän'dĕn·bōōrk). **1** Historical region and province of Prussia, NE cen. Germany (see *Table* at PRUSSIA); surrounds the city of Berlin. Has numerous lakes and fir forests; produces vegetables, tobacco; manufactures woolens, cotton goods, machinery; mining.
History: Earliest Germanic inhabitants replaced by Slavic Wends who were unsubdued by Charlemagne; overcome in 12th cent. by Albert the Bear, margrave of Brandenburg, who established order, planted German colonists, and laid basis for expansion of territory secured by co-operation of his successors with Teutonic Knights (see PRUSSIA); recognized as one of seven imperial electorates 1356; declined and lost territory under rule of Wittelsbach and Luxembourg houses 1323–1411; given by emperor to Frederick of Nürnberg who became margrave 1415 and elector 1417; helped Teutonic Knights in war against Poland (see PRUSSIA) 15th cent.; extended boundaries and crushed nobility; accepted Reformation c. 1540; acquired Cleves and Ravensberg 1614 by marriage of Elector John Sigismund, who became duke of Prussia 1618; added East Friesland under Great Elector, Frederick William (1640–88), whose successful participation in wars against Sweden made Brandenburg-Prussia a leading power; its elector became king of Prussia 1701.
2 *or* **Brandenburg an der Ha'vel** (än dĕr hä'fĕl). Industrial city, E Germany, in Brandenburg, on Havel river 37 m. WSW of Berlin; pop. 59,297; 12th-cent. Romanesque cathedral, 14th-cent. town hall; varied manufactures. Episcopal see 948–1598; seat of Prussian National Assembly 1848; former residence of reigning family of Prussia.

Bran'der, Pass of (brăn'dēr). Mountain pass ab. 7 m. long in N Argyll co., W Scotland, through which the waters of Loch Awe pass to Loch Etive.

Bran'don (brăn'dŭn). **1** Town, ⊗ of Rankin co., S cen. Mississippi; pop. 2139.
2 City, SW Manitoba, Canada, on S bank of Assiniboine river; pop. 20,598; railroad divisional point; grain elevators, oil refineries, creameries, various manufactories. Seat of Brandon College (affiliate of University of Manitoba), industrial school for Indians, and a Dominion experimental farm. Founded 1879; named after Brandon House, a Hudson's Bay post 17 m. E, established 1794.
3 Mountain 3127 ft. in co. Kerry, near the sea W of Brandon Bay, SW Ireland.

Brandon and By'shot'tles (bī'shŏt''lz). Urban district, Durham, N England, on the Deerness 17 m. S of Newcastle; pop. 19,751.

Brandon Bay. Inlet of Atlantic Ocean on SW coast of Ireland, W of Tralee Bay.

Bran'dy·wine' (brăn'dĭ·wīn'). A creek in Pennsylvania and Delaware uniting with Christiana creek (now Christina river) at Wilmington, Delaware; battlefield on the creek in Pennsylvania 10 m. NW of Wilmington where on Sept. 11, 1777 the British under Gen. Howe defeated the Americans under Gen. Washington and entered Philadelphia Sept. 27. See CHADDS FORD.

Bran'ford (brăn'fẽrd). Borough, New Haven co., S Connecticut, on Long Island Sound 6 m. ESE of New Haven; pop. 2371; settled 1644, incorp. 1893; varied manufactures; fishing, esp. for oysters; in town of Branford (pop. 16,610) incorporated 1930.

Bra·nie'wo (brä·nyĕ'vô); *Ger.* **Brauns'berg** (brouns'-bĕrk). City, NW Olsztyn dept., N Poland, NE of Elbląg; pop. (1946) 21,143; formerly in Königsberg govt. dist., East Prussia, Germany; cigars, leather, and beer.

Brans'field Strait (brăns'fēld). Channel bet. South Shetlands on N and Palmer Penin. on S, Antarctica, ab. 60 m. wide and extending NE and SW for ab. 200 m.

Brant (brănt). County, Ontario, Canada. See *Table* at ONTARIO.

Bran'tas (brăn'tȧs) or **Ke·di'ri** (kĕ·dẽr'ė). River 195 m. long in E cen. Java, Indonesia; flows W, N, and NE into Madura Strait, one branch (Kali Mas) at Surabaja and the other 25 m. S at the town of Bangil.

Brant'ford (brănt'fẽrd). Industrial city, ⊗ of Brant co., SE Ontario, Canada, on Grand river 22 m. WSW of Hamilton; pop. 36,727; founded 1830; manufacturing center; headquarters for the united Iroquois tribes of Six Nations; early home of Alexander Graham Bell.

Brant'ley (brănt'lĭ). County in Georgia. See *Table* at GEORGIA.

Bras d' Or' (brä·dôr'; *Fr.* brá·-). Salt lake ab. 50 m. long in cen. Cape Breton I., Nova Scotia, Canada; 230 sq. m. Its N extension is **Little Bras d'Or**, 130 sq. m.

Brasil. See BRAZIL.

Bra·sí'lia (brȧ·zēl'yȧ). City, ✻ of Brazil, in cen. Brazil, in Federal District, E Goiaz state, on the Paraná, a headstream of the Tocantins; construction begun 1956; capital moved from Rio de Janeiro 1960; pop. (1959) 65,000.

Bra·şov' or **Bra·shov'** (brä·shŏv'); *Hung.* **Bras'só** (brŏsh'shō); *Ger.* **Kron'stadt** (krōn'shtät). City, cen. Romania, in the foothills of Transylvanian Alps; pop. (1939 est.) 61,827; manufactures textiles, chemicals, leather, and metal products; Gothic church built 1385–1425. Founded by Saxon settlers in 13th cent.; a leader in Reformation in Transylvania in 16th cent.; *in 1950 renamed* **Sta'lin** (stä'lĭn; -lēn; stăl'ĭn; -ēn).

Brass (brȧs). Town at mouth of **Brass River** (100 m. long, a channel of the Niger delta), S Owerri prov., Eastern Region, Nigeria; formerly a flourishing trading settlement, visited by Portuguese and British; traded in slaves; territory taken after massacre of Christians at Akassa 1895.

Bras·schaet' (brä·sKät'). Commune, Antwerp prov., N Belgium; pop. 11,779.

Brass'town' Bald (brȧs'toun' bôld') or **Mount E·no'-tah** (ê·nō'tȧ). Mountain 4784 ft. on boundary of Towns and Union cos., N Georgia; highest point in the state.

Bra'ti·sla'va (brȧ·tyĭ·slä'vȧ; *Angl.* brăt'ĭ·slä'vȧ); *Ger.* **Press'burg** (prĕs'bŏŏrk); *Hung.* **Po'zsony** (pŏ'zhŏn·y'). City, ✻ of province of Slovakia, E cen. Czechoslovakia, on left bank of Danube ab. 30 m. E of Vienna; pop. (1930) 123,852; large Gothic cathedral (begun 1090, rebuilt 1845–67) where kings of Hungary were formerly crowned; extensive industries; shipping center, with chief trade in corn. As Pressburg an old town dating back to 9th cent.; capital of Hungary 1541–1784 and seat of Diet until 1848; scene of signing of Treaty of Pressburg Dec. 26, 1805 bet. France and Austria, by which Austria lost much territory and recognized Napoleon as king of Italy. On formation of Czechoslovakia became capital of province of Slovakia 1918–39; capital of German protected state of Slovakia 1939–45.

Brats'berg (bräts'bắr). Former name of Telemark co., Norway: see *Table* at NORWAY.

Brat'tle·bor'o (brăt''l·bûr'ô). Town, Windham co., SE corner of Vermont, on Connecticut river 8 m. N of Massachusetts border; pop. 11,734; settled by garrison of Fort Dummer 1724, chartered 1753, incorp. as village 1832. Manufactures pipe organs, cotton goods, wooden products, granite memorials, etc.; resort.

Braunsberg. See BRANIEWO.

Braunschweig. See BRUNSWICK, Germany.

Braun'ston (brôn's'n; brän'-). Village, Northamptonshire, cen. England, 3 m. NW of Daventry; pop. 481; terminus of the Grand Junction Canal which here goes through a tunnel 1½ m. long.

Bra'va (brá'vȧ). Southernmost island of the Cape Verde Islands; 23 sq. m.; pop. 9013.

Bra'va (brä'vä). Coast town, SE Somalia, 90 m. SW of Mogadishu; pop. ab. 4000.

Bra'va Point (brä'vä). Cape on S coast of Uruguay near Montevideo extending into the Río de la Plata (56 m. wide here) opp. Piedras Point in Argentina.

Bravo, or Bravo del Norte, Río. See RIO GRANDE.

Braw'ley (brô'lĭ). Commercial city, Imperial co., SE corner of California, in Imperial Valley S of Salton Sea; pop. 12,703; 115 ft. below sea level.

Brax'ton (brăks'tŭn). County in West Virginia. See *Table* at WEST VIRGINIA.

Bray (brā). **1** Urban district and port, NE co. Wicklow, E Eire; pop. 10,111; on wide bay, just N of Bray Head. **2** Civil parish, Berkshire, S England; pop. 4141; residence of a vicar who is said to have been twice a Roman Catholic and twice a Protestant in four successive English reigns bet. 1520 and 1560. **3** Small region in N France in Somme, Seine-Inférieure, and Seine-et-Oise depts.; chief town Neufchâtel. **4** or **Bray'–sur–Somme'** (brā'sür·sôm'). Village, Somme dept., N France, on the Somme SE of Albert; pop. ab. 1000; battle in Allied retreat Mar. 25–26. 1918.

Bray Head (brā). **1** Cape at SW end of Valentia I., co. Kerry, SW coast of Ireland, S of entrance to Dingle Bay. **2** Point on E coast of Ireland, just S of Dublin.

Bra·zeau' (brȧ·zō'). River ab. 125 m. long, SW Alberta, Canada; a tributary of the upper North Saskatchewan.

Brazeau, Mount. Peak 11,386 ft. in Jasper National Park, SW Alberta, Canada, near source of Brazeau river.

Bra·zil' (brȧ·zĭl'), *officially* **United States of Brazil**, *Port.* **Es·ta'dos U·ni'dos do Bra·sil'** (ảsh-tä'thōōz ōō·nē'thōōz thōō brȧ·zĭl'); *Span.* **Bra·sil'** (brä·sēl'). Federal republic, E cen. South America; 3,286,169 sq. m.; pop. (1960) 70,967,185; ✻ (since 1960) Brasília; former ✻ Rio de Janeiro. Bounded on NW by Colombia, on N by Venezuela, British Guiana, Surinam, French Guiana, on E by the Atlantic Ocean, on S by Uruguay, and on W by Argentina, Paraguay, Bolivia, and Peru.

Mountain ranges (averaging less than 4000 ft.) and plateau region are chiefly in E and S parts; highest point is the Pico da Bandeira, 9462 ft. high, located in the eastern part on the border between the states of Minas Gerais and Espírito Santo; in northern part on Guiana and Venezuela borders are Tumuc-Humac, Acarahy, Pacaraima, Parima, and other ranges (*serras*). Its entire N and central part is lowland region, occupied by the Amazon (*q.v.*) and its many great tributaries; other rivers: in plateau region in E the São Francisco, Parnaíba, and Jequitinhonha; in the SW the Paraguay, Alto Paraná, and Uruguay (each in part a boundary stream); in the Iguassú, tributary of the Alto Paraná, are the famous Iguassú Falls. Has few lakes of any size; largest is Lagoa dos Patos, in Rio Grande do Sul. Except for the large islands of Marajó and Caviana at the mouth of the Amazon and Maracá to the N there are no large islands along the 5000 miles of the Atlantic coast line; 225 m. ENE of Cape São Roque, in 32°30'W, is the important small island of Fernando de Noronha, now a

BRAZIL

Statute Miles

0   100   200   300   400

⊕ Capitals of Countries
⊙ Capitals of States

PUBLISHED BY G. & C. MERRIAM COMPANY
SPRINGFIELD, MASS.
PREPARED BY J. W. CLEMENT CO., BUFFALO, N.Y.

territory. Has good harbors at Belém, Salvador, Rio de Janeiro, Santos, and Pôrto Alegre. Its immense forests (*selvas*) of the Amazon region are source of many forest products (rubber, balata, Brazil nuts. vegetable oils); the savannas or grasslands (*campos*) are source of cattle and agricultural products; its plateau region in E and S is of great importance for its coffee, cacao, tobacco, cotton, and yerba maté, and its varied minerals and precious stones. Chief cities Rio de Janeiro, São Paulo, Recife, Salvador, Pôrto Alegre, Belém, and Belo Horizonte.

Divided (until 1960) into the following 20 states, 6 territories, and Federal District (for pronunciation of their names, see their individual entries):

NAME	LOCATION	AREA[1]	POP.[1]	CAPITAL
Federal District[2]	SE	451	1,781,567	
STATES				
Alagoas	E	11,031	957,628	Maceió
Amazonas	W	595,474	427,264	Manaus
Baía	E	215,329	3,938,909	Salvador
Ceará	NE	57,371	2,101,325	Fortaleza
Espírito Santo	E	16,543	758,535	Vitória
Goiaz	cen.	244,330	832,869	Goiânia
Maranhão	NE	133,674	1,242,721	São Luiz
Mato Grosso	SW	485,405	423,089	Cuiabá
Minas Gerais	E	226,179	6,798,647	Belo Horizonte
Pará	N	470,752	935,679	Belém
Paraíba	E	21,591	1,432,618	João Pessoa
Paraná	S	82,741	2,012,863	Curitiba
Pernambuco	E	38,315	2,693,551	Recife
Piauí	NE	94,819	826,320	Teresina
Rio de Janeiro	SE	16,372	1,862,900	Niterói
Rio Grande do Norte	NE	20,236	774,464	Natal
Rio Grande do Sul	S	110,150[3]	3,350,120	Pôrto Alegre
Santa Catarina	S	31,118	1,140,511	Florianópolis
São Paulo	SE	95,459	7,239,711	São Paulo
Sergipe	E	8,321	545,962	Aracajú
TERRITORIES				
Acre	W	57,153	81,326	Rio Branco
Amapá	N	55,489	21,191	Montenegro
Fernando de Noronha[4]		7	1,065	
Guaporé	W	96,986	25,015	Velho
Rio Branco	NW	97,438	12,130	Boa Vista
Serra dos Aimorés[5]	E	3,435	67,103	

[1] Area in sq. m. Pop. is 1940 est.
[2] Since 1960, called Guanabara state; coextensive with the city of Rio de Janeiro; new Federal District (officially since 1960) is in Goiaz state: see BRASÍLIA.
[3] Including area 5062 sq. m.
[4] Island off E coast.
[5] Disputed area bet. Minas Gerais and Espírito Santo.

History: Northern coast discovered by Vicente Pinzón, a Spaniard, 1500; although allotted to Portugal by Treaty of Tordesillas 1494, not formally claimed by discovery until Cabral accidentally touched there 1500; title confirmed to John III of Portugal by Congress of Badajoz 1524; first settled at São Vicente under system of hereditary captaincies 1532; settled for short periods by French at Rio de Janeiro 1555–60 and at Maranhão (São Luiz) 1612, by Dutch at Pernambuco 1630–54; neglected during period of Spanish rule of Portugal 1580–1640; fought war which resulted in expulsion of Dutch 1641–54; made viceroyalty with capital at Bahia 1640–1762 and at Rio de Janeiro from 1763; interior opened by Paulistas (people of São Paulo) and others who developed production of mineral wealth, gold and diamonds, and planting of sugar and coffee, especially in 18th cent.; expanded Portuguese boundaries recognized in treaties of Madrid 1750 and San Ildefonso 1777; in 1808 became refuge and seat of government of John VI, prince regent, when Napoleon invaded Portugal; opened to foreign commerce 1808; United Kingdom of Portugal, Brazil, and Algarve proclaimed and ruled from Brazil 1815–21; forced grant of constitution by John VI who returned to Portugal 1821; in 1822 proclaimed independence (see SÃO PAULO city) under Pedro who became

Emperor Pedro I (1822–31); fought war with Argentina over Banda Oriental 1825–28 (see URUGUAY); prosperous and internally peaceful during reign of Emperor Pedro II (succeeded 1831, ruled 1841–89); helped overthrow dictatorship of Rosas 1852 (see ARGENTINA); allied with Argentina and Uruguay in war against Paraguay 1865–70; deposed Pedro II 1889 and adopted constitution for federal republic United States of Brazil 1891; settled peaceably numerous boundary disputes 1895–1909; declared war on Germany 1917; entered League of Nations 1920 but withdrew 1928; under President Getulio Vargas set up constitutions 1934 and 1937, second of which established dictatorial powers; joined Allies in World War II Aug. 1942. Brasília made capital 1960.

Bra·zil' (brå·zĭl'). City, ⊗ of Clay co., W Indiana, 15 m. ENE of Terre Haute; pop. 8853; clay products.

Brazil, Plateau of. Highland region in SE Brazil, chiefly in Minas Gerais and São Paulo states.

Brazil Current. A warm ocean current flowing S along the coast of Brazil.

Bra·zo'ri·a (brå·zōr'ĭ·å). County in Texas. See *Table* at TEXAS.

Braz'os (brăz'ŭs). **1** River, cen. Texas; 870 m. long, navigable 40 m. (300 m. in high water); formed by confluence of Salt Fork and Double Mountain Fork in Stonewall co., N Texas, flows SE into Gulf of Mexico in S Brazoria co.
2 County in Texas. See *Table* at TEXAS.

Brazos Peak. Mountain 11,274 ft. in NE Rio Arriba co., N New Mexico.

Brazza. See BRAČ.

Braz'za·ville (brăz'å·vĭl; *Fr.* brả·zả'vēl'). River port on NW shore of Stanley Pool in the Congo river, ✳ of Congo Republic (formerly Middle Congo) and of former French Equatorial Africa and Middle Congo; pop. (1955) ab. 81,000. By air line distance 250 m. from mouth of the Congo; connected with Atlantic seaboard by railroad completed 1934; center for river trade for 1000 m. up the Congo. Founded 1880 by Pierre Brazza, French explorer; used as base for later claims of France to vast territory to NE.

Bre'a (brē'å). City, Orange co., SW California, 22 m. NE of Long Beach; pop. 8487.

Bread·al'bane (brĕd·ôl'bån). District in W Perth co., cen. Scotland; traversed by the Grampians.

Breath'itt (brĕth'ĭt). County in Kentucky. See *Table* at KENTUCKY.

Breaux Bridge (brō). Town, St. Martin parish, S Louisiana, 8 m. ENE of Lafayette; pop. 3303.

Bre'bes (brā'bĕs). Town, cen. Java, Indonesia, W of Tegal; pop. 13,707.

Bré'cey' (brā'sā'). Commune, Manche dept., NW France, E of Avranches; pop. (1931) 2159.

Brèche'–de–Ro'land' (brĕsh'dē–rô'län'). Defile, alt. 9200 ft., in Hautes-Pyrénées dept., SW France, in the Pyrenees on the Franco-Spanish boundary 35 m. S of Tarbes; in medieval legend said to have been hewn by the knight Roland with one blow of his sword Durendal.

Bre'chin (brē'chĭn; -kĭn). Burgh, Angus co., E Scotland; pop. 7264; paper mills, distilleries; linen weaving.

Bre·chou' (brē·shōō'). One of the Channel Islands, just W of Sark; 74 acres.

Breck'en·ridge (brĕk'ĕn·rĭj). **1** Town, ⊗ of Summit co., cen. Colorado; pop. 393.
2 City, ⊗ of Wilkin co., W Minnesota; pop. 4335.
3 City, ⊗ of Stephens co., N cen. Texas, 50 m. ENE of Abilene; pop. 6273; ships grain, cattle; oil and gas wells.

Breckenridge Hills. Village, St. Louis co., Missouri, NW of St. Louis; pop. 6299.

Breck'in·ridge (brĕk'ĭn·rĭj). County in Kentucky. See *Table* at KENTUCKY.

Breck'nock (brĕk'nŏk) *or* **Brec'on** (brĕk'ŭn). **1** Municipal borough, ⊗ of Brecknockshire, SE Wales; pop. 6466; manufactures textiles (woolens, flannels).
2 See BRECKNOCKSHIRE.

Brecknock, or **Brecon, Beacons.** Two sandstone peaks, Brecknockshire, Wales, S of Usk valley; highest massif in S Wales; highest point Pen y Fan 2907 ft.

Brecknock Peninsula. Peninsula extending westward from SW Tierra del Fuego I.

Breck'nock·shire (brĕk'nŏk·shǐr; -shẽr) or **Brec'on-shire** (brĕk'ŭn·shǐr; -shẽr), also **Brecknock** or **Brecon.** County, SE Wales; area 733 sq. m.; pop. (1951) 56,484; ⊗ Brecknock; mountainous region; rivers Usk and Wye; agriculture, livestock raising, coal and iron mining, quarrying (limestone), textile manufacturing.

Brecks'ville (brĕks'vĭl). Village, Cuyahoga co., N Ohio, 12 m. S of Cleveland; pop. 5435.

Břec'lav (brzhĕts'lȧf); Ger. **Lun'den·burg** (lōōn'dĕn-bōōrk). Town, S Moravia prov., cen. Czechoslovakia; pop. (1930) 13,694; a border town 45 m. NNE of Vienna.

Brec'on (brĕk'ŭn). See BRECKNOCK; BRECKNOCKSHIRE.

Bre·da' (brā·dä'). Commune, North Brabant prov., S Netherlands, on the Merk river 14 m. W of Tilburg; pop. (1939) 51,804; manufactures carpets, cloth, and cigars; has fine Gothic church. An old town, strongly fortified in early times; Compromise of Breda signed 1566 by the Dutch and Spanish; seized by duke of Parma 1581 but retaken 1590 by Maurice of Nassau; after siege of a year surrendered 1625 to Spaniards; retaken by Dutch 1637; Declaration of Breda (amnesty proclamation) issued Apr. 1660 by Charles II of England; Peace Treaties of Breda concluded 1667 bet. Britain, France, and Netherlands; important in wars of French Revolution 1793–95. In World War II fell to Germans May 1940, retaken by British Oct. 29, 1944.

Bre·das'dorp (brĕ·däs'dȯrp). Town, SW Cape Province, S Union of South Africa, 105 m. ESE of Cape Town; pop. 3112; produces wool, tobacco, and grain.

Bred'bur·y and Rom'i·ley (brĕd'bẽr·ĭ [-brĭ], rŏm'-ĭ·lĭ). Urban district, Cheshire, NW England, 6 m. SE of Manchester; pop. 17,810.

Bree'de (brā'dĕ). River 165 m. long in SW Cape Prov., Union of South Africa; flows SE into Indian Ocean.

Breed's Hill. See BUNKER HILL.

Breese (brēz). City, Clinton co., SW cen. Illinois, 33 m. E of East St. Louis; pop. 2461.

Bre'ga (brā'gä). Town, N Libya, bet. Agedabia and El Agheila near SE coast of Gulf of Sidra.

Bre'genz (brā'gĕnts); anc. **Bri·gan'ti·um** (brĭ-găn'shĭ·ŭm). City, ✳ of Vorarlberg prov., Austria, at E end of Lake Constance 78 m. WNW of Innsbruck; pop. (1939) 18,504; lake harbor and tourist resort; has a museum of Roman and Celtic antiquities; manufactures silk goods, shoes, clocks, cottons; coal mines. Ancient Celtic settlement; important station under Romans; in Middle Ages under counts of Bregenz, later under counts of Montfort; passed to Hapsburgs 1523; stormed by Swedes 1647; under Bavarian rule 1805–14.

Brei'di Fjord (brā'thĭ). Bay on W coast of Iceland.

Brei'sach or Alt **Brei'sach** (ält brī'zäk); anc. **Mons Bri·si'a·cus** (mŏnz brĭ·sī'ȧ·kŭs). Town, Baden-Württemberg, W Germany, on right bank of Rhine W of Freiburg; pop. 2507; an old fortified town of the Sequani on left bank of Rhine, captured by Ariovistus c. 61 B.C.; one of chief fortresses of the German Empire during Middle Ages; resisted Protestants during Thirty Years' War but capitulated after siege by French 1638 and ceded to France 1648 by Treaty of Westphalia; to Austria 1697; to Baden by Treaty of Pressburg 1805.

Brei'ten·feld (brī'tĕn·fĕlt). Village in Saxony, E Germany, 6 m. NNW of Leipzig; scene of two battles of the Thirty Years' War: (1) Sept. 17, 1631 in which Swedes and Saxons under Gustavus Adolphus completely defeated the Imperialist forces under Count von Tilly; (2) Nov. 2 1642 in which the Swedish army under Torstenson defeated the Imperialists under Archduke Leopold William and Prince Piccolomini.

Breit'horn' (brīt'hȯrn'). Peak 13,685 ft. on the Swiss-Italian border S of Zermatt, Valais canton, Switzerland.

Bre'men (brē'mĕn). **1** Industrial city, Haralson co., W Georgia, 40 m. W of Atlanta; pop. 3132; cotton mills. **2** Town, Marshall co., N Indiana; pop. 3062.

Bre'men (brā'mĕn; Angl. also brĕm'ĕn). **1** Archbishopric and duchy, covering territory bet. lower Weser and lower Elbe rivers, NW of former duchy of Brunswick-Lüneburg; ab. 2000 sq. m.; made archbishopric in 13th cent.; created a duchy 1648 under supremacy of Sweden; became part of electorate of Hannover 1715. **2** Former German state, NW Germany; 99 sq. m.; pop. (1939) 400,086; ✳ Bremen; comprised district around city of Bremen; lost sovereignty at accession of National Socialist regime 1933. **3** State of Federal Republic of Germany; includes cities of Bremen and Bremerhaven (see WESERMÜNDE); 156 sq. m.; pop. (1957 est.) 664,000. **4** Commercial city, ✳ of Bremen state (not a part of earlier duchy), Germany, on Weser river 59 m. SW of Hamburg; pop. (1939) 342,113; important port of entry; together with its port Wesermünde (q.v.), principal seat of German import and export trade; varied manufactures; 11th-cent. Romanesque cathedral.
History: Became episcopal see 788, seat of an archbishopric 847; one of the important Hanse Towns; became free city under elector of Brunswick; part of French empire 1810–13. In World War II submarine and naval base; largely destroyed by Allied bombing 1943–45; taken by British Apr. 27, 1945.

Bre'mer (brē'mẽr). County in Iowa. See *Table* at IOWA.

Brem'er·ha·ven (brĕm'ẽr·hä'vĕn; Ger. brä'mẽr·hä'fĕn). **1** Former city (pop. 23,896) and port of Bremen at the mouth of the Weser 35 m. N of Bremen, forming an exclave of Bremen state, Germany; part of Wesermünde 1932–47; shipbuilding and trading center, often bombed by Allied air forces in World War II. **2** See WESERMÜNDE.

Bre'mers·dorp (brē'mẽrz·dȯrp). Town, cen. Swaziland, SE Africa; before 1902 capital of Swaziland.

Brem'er·ton (brĕm'ẽr·t'n; -tŭn). City, Kitsap co., W Washington, on Puget Sound 15 m. W of Seattle; pop. 28,922; site of Puget Sound Navy Yard (1891).

Bren'ham (brĕn'ȧm). City, ⊗ of Washington co., SE cen. Texas, 35 m. S of Bryan; pop. 7740.

Bren'ner (brĕn'ẽr); Ital. **Bren'ne·ro** (brĕn'nâ·rô). Village and customs station at Italian end of Brenner Pass; scene of conferences bet. Hitler and Mussolini 1940–41; surrendered to Allies May 5, 1945.

Brenner Pass; Ital. **Pas'so Bren'ne·ro** (päs'sô brĕn'nâ·rô). Alpine pass. See ALPS.

Bren'ta (brĕn'tä); anc. **Me·do'a·cus Ma'jor** (mĕ·dō'-ȧ·kŭs mā'jẽr; mä'jôr). River ab. 100 m. long in Venezia Tridentina, NE Italy; flows SE through Venezia into the lagoons of Venice.

Brent'ford and Chis'wick (brĕnt'fẽrd, chĭz'ĭk). Urban district, Middlesex, SE England, on the Thames 10 m. W of London; pop. 62,618, (1951) 59,354; is a part of Greater London. Brentford was scene of defeat of the Danes 1016 by Edmund Ironside, and of the defeat of the Parliamentarians Nov. 12, 1642 by Prince Rupert.

Bren'ton, or **Bren'ton's, Point** (brĕn't'n[z]; -tŭn[z]). Southernmost point of the island of Rhode Island, Newport co., SE Rhode Island, S of Newport.

Brent'wood (brĕnt'wŏŏd). **1** Town, Prince Georges co., S cen. Maryland, 5 m. NE of Washington; pop. 3693. **2** City, St. Louis co., E Missouri, 8 m. W of St. Louis; pop. 12,250; residential suburb of St. Louis. **3** Urban community (unincorporated), Suffolk co., SE New York, in Islip town, cen. Long I.; pop. 15,387. **4** Residential borough, Allegheny co., SW Pennsylvania, 5 m. S of Pittsburgh; pop. 13,706. **5** Urban district, Essex, SE England, 20 m. ENE of London; pop. 29,898; seat of a grammar school dating from the middle 16th cent.

Bre'scia (brā'shä). **1** Province of Italy. See *Table* at ITALY.

2 *anc.* **Brix′i·a** (brĭk′sĭ·à). Walled commune, its ✻, Lombardy N Italy, at foot of Alps 54 m. E by N of Milan; pop. 123,332; manufacturing center, producing esp. firearms, paper, leather, iron products, silk, linen, oil; trades in raw silk; 9th-cent. and 17th-cent. cathedrals; the Broletto palace (12th cent.), and the Palazzo della Loggia; many fine Roman remains. Ancient Celtic town; became seat of Roman colony c. 15 B.C. and later a Roman municipium; devastated by Goths 412 A.D. and later by Attila; rebuilt 452; fell to Lombardy; free city 936–1426; held by Venice 1426 ff., France 1796 ff., Austria 1815 ff., Sardinia 1859–60; became part of kingdom of Italy 1860; entered by Allies Apr. 28–29, 1945.

Bres′kens (brĕs′kĕns). Town, Zeeland prov., SW Netherlands, on S shore of Schelde estuary opp. Flushing; pop. 3003; unsuccessfully attacked by Allies Oct. 8–9, 1944.

Bres′lau (brĕs′lou; *in English, also* brĕz′-). **1** Former government district, cen. Silesia prov., Prussia, Germany; 5019 sq. m.
2 City, its ✻. See WROCŁAW.

Bres·sa·no′ne (brås·så·nō′nå); *Ger.* **Bri′xen** (brĭk′sĕn). Commune, Bolzano prov., Venezia Tridentina, NE Italy, at S end of Brenner Pass in S Tirol on Isarco river, 20 m. NE of Bolzano; pop. 9503; cathedral; health resort; ceded to Italy 1919 by Austria.

Bresse (brĕs). District ab. 60 m. long and 20 m. wide, E France; fertile region specializing in poultry and cattle. Ancient countship comprised the plain around Bourg and the Revermont; under house of Savoy from 1272 with Bourg its capital; ceded to Henry IV 1601.

Bres′soux′ (brĕ′sōō′). Commune, Liège prov., E Belgium, NE suburb of Liège; pop. 15,067.

Bres′suire′ (brĕ′sü·ēr′). Commune, Deux-Sèvres dept., W France, 38 m. N of Niort; pop. 5324; a historical town damaged and pillaged in several wars 1214, 1598, 1794.

Brest (brĕst). **1** Fortified seaport commune, Finistère dept., NW France, on Atlantic Ocean 32 m. NW of Quimper; pop. 79,342; chief naval station of France, planned by Richelieu and fortified by Vauban in 17th cent.; manufactures chemicals, shoes, linens; trades in wine, coal, timber, flour, fruit, vegetables; naval schools; fine botanical gardens. Unsuccessfully attacked by English and Dutch 1694; blockaded by English, and French fleet defeated 1794; important debarkation point for American troops and supplies in World War I. In World War II occupied by Germans June 1940; used as submarine base and frequently bombed by Allies; reached by U.S. forces Aug. 26–28, 1944 and captured Sept. 19, 1944.
2 *or* **Brest Li·tovsk′** (brĕst′ lĭ·tôfsk′; *Russ.* bryĕst′ lyĭ·tôfsk′); *Pol.* **Brześć nad Bu′giem** (bzhĕsts′y′ nåd bōō′gyĕm). City on right bank of Bug river, ✻ of Brest Region, SW White Russia, U.S.S.R., 112 m. E of Warsaw; formerly ✻ of Polesie dept., Poland; pop. (1938–39 est.) 55,374; important railroad junction; trade center. Taken by Germans 1915; scene of signing of treaty (Brest Litovsk) bet. Germany and Russia Mar. 3, 1918; in World War II taken by Germans Sept. 28, 1939 but after division of Poland by Germany and Russia remained in Russian part 1939–41; taken by Germans June 24, 1941; retaken by Russians July 18, 1944.

Brest Region. Region, SW White Russia, U.S.S.R.; ✻ Brest; nearly coextensive with former Polesie dept. of Poland.

Bretagne. See BRITTANY.

Bre′ti·gny′ (brā′tē·nyē′); *Fr.* **Bré′ti·gny′.** Village of Normandy just SE of Chartres, Eure-et-Loir dept., N cen. France; treaty May 8, 1360 bet. England and France, closing the first part of the Hundred Years' War.

Bret′on, Cape (brĭt′'n; brĕt′'n). **1** Cape, most easterly point of Cape Breton I., NE Nova Scotia, Canada.
2 See CAPE BRETON.

Bret′on Sound (brĕt′'n; *Fr.* brē·tôN′). Inlet of Gulf of Mexico off NE coast of Plaquemines parish, SE Louisiana.

Brett, Cape (brĕt). Cape on NE coast of N extension of North I., New Zealand, E of Bay of Islands.

Bret′ton Woods (brĕt′'n). Fashionable hotel center and resort, Coos co., N New Hampshire, ab. 18 m. SSE of Littleton; site of United Nations Monetary and Financial Conference July 1–22, 1944 at which an International Monetary Fund was established.

Bre·vard′ (brĕ·värd′). **1** County in Florida. See *Table* at FLORIDA.
2 Town and summer resort, ⊗ of Transylvania co., SW North Carolina, 26 m. SSW of Asheville; pop. 4857; produces lumber, tanning extract, cotton goods.

Bré′vent′ (brā·väN′). Peak 8285 ft. in the Alps, Haute-Savoie dept., E France, near Mont Blanc N of Chamonix.

Břev′nov (brzhĕv′nôf); *Ger.* **Brew′now** (brĕv′nō). Commune, W suburb of Prague, Bohemia, Czechoslovakia; pop. 12,750.

Brew′er (brōō′ēr). Commercial and industrial city, Penobscot co., E cen. Maine, on Penobscot river opp. Bangor; pop. 9009; wood pulp, paper, brick.

Brewer, Mount. Peak 13,886 ft. on boundary bet. Fresno and Tulare cos., S cen. California, in Sierra Nevada.

Brew′ster (brōō′stēr). **1** County in Texas. See *Table* at TEXAS.
2 Town, Barnstable co., SE Massachusetts, on Cape Cod Bay; pop. 1236.
3 Village, ⊗ of Blaine co., cen. Nebraska; pop. 44.
4 Residential village, Putnam co., SE New York, 23 m. ESE of Newburgh; pop. 1714; in lake resort area.
5 Village, Stark co., NE Ohio, 12 m. WSW of Canton; pop. 2025.

Brewster, Cape. Point on E coast of Greenland, in 70°N lat.

Brewster, Mount. Peak 3018 ft. in Panama, E of Panama Canal.

Brew′ton (brōō′t'n). City, ⊗ of Escambia co., S Alabama, 60 m. ENE of Mobile bay; pop. 6309.

Brey′ten (brā′t'n). Town, E Transvaal, Union of South Africa, 120 m. E of Johannesburg; railroad junction point in stock-raising district.

Bri·an′çon′ (brē′äN·sôN′); *anc.* **Bri·gan′ti·o** (brĭ·găn′-shĭ·ō). Town, Hautes-Alpes dept., SE France, 48 m. SE of Grenoble; pop. 6822; frontier town and tourist resort at N end of Cottian Alps; connects with Italy by the Col de Genèvre (alt. 6102 ft.). Said to have been founded by the Greeks; in Roman times important station on road from N Italy to SE Gaul.

Briansk. See BRYANSK.

Bri·an′za (brē·än′tsä). Hilly but fertile district S of Lake Como, Lombardy, N Italy.

Bri′ar·cliff′ Man′or (brī′ēr·klĭf′ măn′ēr). Residential village, Westchester co., SE New York, E of Hudson river 31 m. N of New York; pop. 5105; permanent camps of Girl Scouts and Camp Fire Girls.

Brices Cross Roads Battlefield Site (brīs′ĕz; -ĭz). See UNITED STATES, *National Historical Parks.*

Bri′dal·veil (brī′d'l·vāl′). Waterfall 620 ft. in Yosemite National Park, E cen. California.

Bridge′burg (brĭj′bûrg). Former town, Welland co., SE Ontario, Canada; joined with Fort Erie village 1932 to form Fort Erie town.

Bridge′hamp′ton (brĭj′hăm[p]′tŭn). Village, Suffolk co., SE New York, on Long I. near Atlantic Ocean, ab. 19 m. E of Riverhead; pop. (est.) 900; settled 1660.

Bridg′end′ (brĭj′ĕnd′). Urban district, Glamorganshire, SE Wales; pop. 13,646; trade center in agricultural section; brickworks, stone quarries, tanning and brewing.

Bridge′port (brĭj′pōrt). **1** City, Jackson co., NE corner of Alabama, on Tennessee river 3 m. S of Tennessee border; pop. 2906; textiles, lumber.
2 Village, ⊗ of Mono co., E California; pop. (est.) 300
3 Industrial city, ⊗ of Fairfield co., SW corner of Connecticut, on Long Island Sound at mouth of Pequonnock river, 17 m. SW of New Haven; pop. 156,748; manufac-

tures electrical goods, machinery and machine tools, munitions, metal goods and hardware, airplanes, marine engines, sewing machines, textiles, clothing, pharmaceuticals, radios; Bridgeport Univ.; State Trade School. First settled 1639 as Pequonnock, later called New Fairfield, Stratfield, and Fairfield Village; incorporated as city 1836; industrial development accelerated after Civil War; first high school established 1876; town (incorp. 1821) and city consolidated and made coextensive 1889. **4** City, Lawrence co., SE Illinois, 17 m. E of Olney; pop. 2260; in agricultural and oil-producing section. **5** City, ⊗ of Morrill co., W Nebraska, on North Platte river 32 m. ESE of Scottsbluff; pop. 1645. **6** Village, Belmont co., E Ohio, on Ohio river opp. Wheeling, West Virginia, 22 m. S of Steubenville; pop. 3824; glass, sheet metal, tin; boat building. **7** Borough, Montgomery co., SE Pennsylvania, on Schuylkill river 14 m. NW of Philadelphia; pop. 5306; iron and coke works, woolen mills; quarries. **8** City, Wise co., N Texas, 40 m. NNW of Fort Worth; pop. 3218; incorp. 1913; in agricultural section. **9** Town, Harrison co., N West Virginia, 5 m. E of Clarksburg; pop. 4199; shipping point for cattle.

Bridgeport Dam. Dam completed 1931 across W fork of Trinity river, Wise co., NE of Fort Worth, N Texas; height 110 ft.; impounds water, **Lake Bridgeport,** for flood control and water supply.

Bridg'er's Pass (brĭj'ẽrz). Mountain pass, cen. Wyoming, S of South Pass; discovered by James Bridger and later used by pony express and Union Pacific R.R.

Bridges Creek. See WAKEFIELD.

Bridge'ton (brĭj'tŭn). **1** Town, St. Louis co., Missouri, NW of St. Louis; pop. 12,250. **2** City, ⊗ of Cumberland co., SW New Jersey, 10 m. N of mouth of Delaware river; pop. 20,966; founded by Quakers c. 1686; made port of entry 1790; incorp. 1865; packing and shipping center esp. for tomatoes; peas; beans, and small fruits; glassworks.

Bridge'town (brĭj'toun). **1** Town, ⊗ of Annapolis co., W Nova Scotia, Canada, on Annapolis river; pop. 1038. **2** Commercial port, SW Barbados I., West Indies Fed., ✳ of Barbados; pop. (1938 est.) 15,000; main exports sugar, molasses, and rum.

Bridge View. Village, Cook co., NE Illinois, SW of Chicago; pop. 7334.

Bridge'ville (brĭj'vĭl). Industrial borough, Allegheny co., SW Pennsylvania, 9 m. SW of Pittsburgh; pop. 7112; coal mines; manufactures steel and iron.

Bridge'wa'ter (brĭj'wô'tẽr; -wŏt'ẽr). **1** Industrial town, Plymouth co., SE Massachusetts, 7 m. S of Brockton; pop. 10,276. Massachusetts State Coll. (1840). **2** Residential borough (P.O. **West Bridgewater**), Beaver co., W Pennsylvania, on Ohio river 25 m. NW of Pittsburgh; pop. 1292. **3** Town, Rockingham co., N Virginia, SW of Harrisonburg; pop. 1815; Bridgewater Coll. (1880; coed.). **4** Town, Lunenburg co., S Nova Scotia, Canada, on Lahave river, 52 m. WSW of Halifax; pop. 4010; founded ab. 1812; first school in Canada established 1632 in this vicinity by six Capuchin monks, later moved to Port Royal (Annapolis Royal); lumbering.

Bridg'north' (brĭj'nôrth'). Municipal borough, Shropshire, W England, on the Severn 23 m. W of Birmingham; pop. 6244.

Bridg'ton (brĭj'tŭn). Town, Cumberland co., SW Maine, 25 m. W of Lewiston; pop. 2707; in resort area.

Bridg'wa'ter (brĭj'wô'tẽr; -wŏt'ẽr). Municipal borough, Somersetshire, SW England, on the Parret 10 m. from Bristol Channel and 28 m. SSW of Bristol; pop. 22,221; seaport; Bath brick and cement works.

Brid'ling·ton (brĭd'lĭng·tŭn; *locally* bûr'lĭng·tŭn, bŏl'ĭ-tŭn). Municipal borough, East Riding, Yorkshire, N England, on North Sea 25 m. NNE of Hull; pop. 24,767; excellent harbor; summer resort.

Brid'port (brĭd'pōrt). Municipal borough, Dorsetshire,

S England, on English Channel 63 m. WSW of Southampton; pop. 6273; manufactures ropes, nets, sailcloth.

Brie (brē). Agricultural district and medieval county, NE France, E of Paris, now in departments of Aisne, Marne, and Seine-et-Marne; chief town was Meaux; noted for its vineyards and pastures, and esp. for its cheese (Brie cheese).

Brieg. See BRZEG.

Briel'le (brē'lĕ), *also* **Briel** (brēl) *or* **Bril** (brĭl); *in English, esp. formerly,* **The Brill** (brĭl). Commune, South Holland prov., W Netherlands, on N coast of Voorne I. on the Nieuwe Maas, 14 m. W of Rotterdam; pop. 3546; has good harbor, its inhabitants have long been pilots and fishermen. First place seized by Dutch (the Gueux led by William de la Marck in 1572) in reconquest of Netherlands from the Spanish, and held against attack by land and sea.

Bri'enne' (brē'ĕn'). **1** Small former county in the Champagne, NE France, 23 m. NNE of Troyes; held from 10th cent. to end of 18th cent. by Brienne family; its most famous member was the Crusader, John of Brienne (1148–1237), King of Jerusalem (1210–25). **2** *or* **Bri'enne'-le-Châ'teau'** (-lĕ·shä'tō'). Town, Aube dept., ✳ of former county; pop. 2218; site of military school at which Napoleon studied 1779–84; partly destroyed in battle Jan. 29, 1814 in which Napoleon gained a slight victory over Blücher.

Bri·enz' (brē·ĕnts'). Commune, Bern canton, Switzerland, at NE end of Lake of Brienz; pop. 2474; noted for its fine scenery and for its wood-carving industry.

Brienz, Lake of. Lake 8¾ m. long in SE Bern canton, Switzerland; traversed by the Aare river.

Bri'er·field (brī'ẽr·fēld). Urban district, Lancashire, NW England, 23 m. N of Manchester; pop. 7005.

Bri'er·ley Hill (brī'ẽr·lĭ). Urban district, Staffordshire, W cen. England, 10 m. W of Birmingham; pop. 48,943.

Bri'eulles'-sur-Meuse' (brē'ûl'sür·mûz'). Village, Meuse dept., NE France, 18 m. NW of Verdun; pop. 579; has monument marking crossing of Meuse Nov. 1, 1918 by American forces in last phase of World War I.

Bri'ey' (brē'ē'; brē'ā'). Commune, Meurthe-et-Moselle dept., NE France, 12 m. NW of Metz; pop. 2804; center of **Briey Basin,** a district containing extensive iron fields and smelting furnaces.

Brig (brēk); *Fr.* **Brigue** (brēg); *Ital.* **Bri'ga** (brē'gä). Commune, Valais canton, SW cen. Switzerland, on Rhone river 31 m. ENE of Sion; pop. (1930) 2961; tourist resort; station at Swiss end of Simplon Tunnel.

Brig'an·tine Beach (brĭg'ăn·tēn). Narrow sandy island off N Atlantic coast, SE New Jersey.

Brigantinus Lacus. See Lake CONSTANCE.

Brigantio. See BRIANÇON.

Brigantium. See BREGENZ.

Bri'ga-Ten'da (brē'gä·tĕn'dä). Area in NW Italy in Cuneo prov., Piedmont, and Imperia prov., Liguria, in Maritime Alps near the S end of the French-Italian border, ab. 32 m. NE of Nice; comprises two small towns, **Briga Ma·rit'ti·ma** [mä·rēt'tĕ·mä] (pop. of commune 1147) and **Tenda** (pop. of commune 1864), on a small stream (Roja) in mountain area containing important hydroelectric developments. Demanded by France 1946 as reparation from Italy and ceded by treaty 1947.

Brig'ham City (brĭg'ăm). City, ⊗ of Box Elder co., NW corner of Utah, 20 m. N of Ogden; pop. 11,728; woolen goods, beet sugar, canning industries; peaches.

Brig'house' (brĭg'hous'). Municipal borough, West Riding, Yorkshire, N England, 20 m. SW of Leeds; pop. 30,587.

Brigh'ton (brī't'n). **1** City, ⊗ of Adams co., NE cen. Colorado, 18 m. NE of Denver; pop. 7055; founded 1889, incorp. as city 1922; sugar-beet center. **2** Town, SE South Australia, suburb 10 m. SW of Adelaide on Gulf of St. Vincent; pop. 4888. **3** Municipality, SE Tasmania, Australia, 12 m. N of Hobart; pop. 1917; in agricultural and orchard region.

4 Town, S Victoria, SE Australia, on E side of Port Phillip Bay, suburb 8 m. S of Melbourne; pop. 29,706; port of call and watering place.

5 Village, Northumberland co., SE Ontario, Canada, near N shore of Lake Ontario 20 m. WSW of Belleville; pop. 1967; resort for fishermen and vacationists.

6 County borough, East Sussex, S England, on English Channel 50 m. S of London; pop. 147,427, (1939 est.) 156,440; seaside resort, with chalybeate springs; has no harbor. Mentioned in Domesday Book; for several hundred years merely a fishing village.

Bright'wa·ters (brīt'wô'tẽrz; -wŏt'ẽrz). Village, Suffolk co., SE New York, on Great South Bay on Long Island, 39 m. E of New York; pop. 3193.

Brigue. See BRIG.

Brig'us (brĭg'ŭs). Seaport, SE Newfoundland, on S shore of Conception Bay 25 m. W of St. John's; pop. 2010; fishing center.

Bri·hue'ga (brḗ-wā'gä). Commune, Guadalajara prov., cen. Spain, 17 m. NE of Guadalajara; pop. (1930) 2543; scene of English defeat by Philip V Dec. 9, (1710).

Bril, The Brill. See BRIELLE.

Bril'liant (brĭl'yănt). Village, Jefferson co., E Ohio, on Ohio river 7 m. S of Steubenville; pop. 2174.

Brin'da'ban (brĭn'dä'bản). Town, Uttar Pradesh, N Indian Union, on Jumna river ab. 80 m. S of Delhi; pop. 14,632; Hindu holy city.

Brin'di·si (brĭn'dĭ·zĭ; *Ital.* brēn'dē·zē). **1** Province of Italy. See *Table* at ITALY.

2 *anc.* **Brun·du'si·um** (brŭn-dū'zhĭ·ŭm; -zĭ·ŭm) *or* **Brun·di'si·um** (-dĭzh'ĭ·ŭm; -dĭz'ĭ·ŭm). Fortified seaport, its ✳, Apulia, SE Italy, on Strait of Otranto in Adriatic, 139 m. E by S of Naples; pop. 41,699; naval base during World War I; trades in wine, figs, olive oil; two 11th-cent. churches; 12th-cent. cathedral; 13th-cent. castle. Original settlement captured by Romans 267 B.C.; became Roman naval station; death place of Vergil 19 B.C.; taken by Saracens 836 and Normans 1071; later lost most of its importance until 1870.

Brink'ley (brĭngk'lĭ). City, Monroe co., E Arkansas, 64 m. E of Little Rock; pop. 4636; cotton and lumber.

Bri·o'ni (brḗ-ō'nḗ). Island group in the Adriatic Sea near Pulj, Istria; now in Yugoslavia; noted marble quarries.

Bri'on' Island (brḗ'ôN'). Small island in the Gulf of St. Lawrence, E Canada, N of Magdalen Is.

Bri'oude' (brḗ-ood'); *anc.* **Bri'vas** (brī'văs). Town, Haute-Loire dept., S cen. France, 36 m. S of Clermont-Ferrand; pop. 5039; trade center of a fertile plain; captured by Goths 532; later taken by Burgundians, Saracens (732), and Normans; Romanesque church.

Briovera. See SAINT-LÔ.

Bris'bane (brĭz'bản [*locally*]; -bān). **1** River 100 m. long, SE Queensland, Australia; flows E to Moreton Bay.

2 Seaport city, ✳ of Queensland, Australia, on N bank of Brisbane river near its mouth, 14 m. E of Moreton Bay; pop. with suburbs 299,782; founded 1824 as a penal colony; made capital of newly created colony of Queensland 1859; has active port, maintains a dry dock. Seat of Queensland University.

Bris'coe (brĭs'kō). County in Texas. See *Table* at TEXAS.

Bri·si·ghel'la (brḗ-zē·gĕl'lä). Commune, Ravenna prov., Emilia, N Italy, SW of Ravenna; pop. 15,652.

Bris'tol (brĭs't'l). **1** Name of counties in two states of the U.S. See *Tables* at MASSACHUSETTS and RHODE ISLAND.

2 Industrial city, SW Hartford co., N Connecticut, 15 m. WSW of Hartford; pop. 45,499; settled 1727, incorp. 1911; famous in its early history as clockmaking center; manufactures bells, coaster brakes, ball bearings, springs, clocks; brass and iron foundries. The town (incorp. 1785) is coextensive with the city.

3 City, ⊗ of Liberty co., NW Florida; pop. 614.

4 Town, Grafton co., W New Hampshire, 14 m. WNW of Laconia; pop. 1470; summer resort.

5 Industrial borough, Bucks co., SE Pennsylvania, on Delaware river 19 m. ENE of Philadelphia in Bristol township (pop. 59,298); pop. 12,364; settled 1697; early port of call for river traffic; manufactures carpets, machinery, worsted and woolen goods.

6 Town and port of entry, ⊗ of Bristol co., E Rhode Island, on Narragansett Bay 13 m. ESE of Providence; pop. 14,570; settled 1669; figured in King Philip's War; incorp. by Plymouth Colony 1681; annexed to R.I. 1746; bombarded by British ships 1775; burned and pillaged by British 1778. Once important for whale fishing and shipbuilding; now center for yachting; yacht works; fish and shellfish industries; manufactures woolen, cotton, and rubber goods, shoes, wire.

7 City, Sullivan co., NE Tennessee, 22 m. NNE of Johnson City on Tennessee-Virginia line, contiguous with Bristol, Virginia, the two cities having a common main thoroughfare through which the state line runs; pop. 17,582; in mineral and timber region; ships livestock; manufactures rayon, pulp and paper, leather goods, mine cars, furniture. King College (1867; coed.).

8 Town, Addison co., W Vermont, 10 m. NNE of Middlebury; pop. 2159; settled 1786; German summer school courses of Middlebury Coll.

9 City, SW Virginia, contiguous with Bristol, Tennessee; in Washington co. but politically independent; pop. 17,144; iron, lumber, textiles, paper, leather, pharmaceuticals; livestock market.

10 City and county borough, Gloucestershire, SW cen. England, at confluence of Avon and Frome rivers 119 m. by rail W of London; pop. 397,012, (1951) 442,281; important shipping center; imports grain, fruit, sugar, tobacco, oils, hides, cattle; exports chemicals, tin, salt, machinery, chocolate, glass, pottery, leather goods, soap. Bristol University (chartered 1909), cathedral (1142), library (1613), art gallery, museum, and Clifton Suspension Bridge over the Avon. From early times a place of commerce; received first charter 1172; active in medieval trade; point of departure 1497 of John Cabot; in Civil War taken 1643 by Royalists under Prince Rupert and in 1645 captured by Parliamentarians; scene of Reform riots 1831; in World War II repeatedly bombed by German air force 1940 and 1941.

Bristol Bay. Arm of Bering Sea in its SE part, on W side of N end of Alaska Penin., SW Alaska; one of richest salmon-fishing areas in the world.

Bristol Channel. Arm of Atlantic Ocean extending bet. S Wales and SW England; ab. 85 m. long and bet. 5 and 43 m. wide.

Bris'tow (brĭs'tō). City, Creek co., E cen. Oklahoma, 20 m. WSW of Sapulpa; pop. 4795; supply and shipping center for oil and gas fields; manufactures cottonseed oil, fuel and lubricating oils, machinery.

Brit'ain (brĭt''n). Anglicized form of Latin **Bri·tan'ni·a** (brĭ·tăn'ĭ·à; -tăn'yà), applied historically to the island of Great Britain especially during its pre-Roman and Roman periods and in the early Anglo-Saxon period until the merging of the Heptarchy into the England of King Alfred. See GREAT BRITAIN.

2 Short for GREAT BRITAIN.

Bri·tan'ni·a (brĭ·tăn'ĭ·à; -tăn'yà). **1** See BRITAIN.

2 Now, poetically, Great Britain and the Dominions.

Britannia Minor. See BRITTANY.

British America. 1 *specif.* **British North America.** British possessions N of United States, that is, Canada. **2** Sometimes, all British possessions in, or adjacent to, North and South America.

British Baluchistan. See BALUCHISTAN.

British Bechuanaland. Former colony lying bet. Orange and Molopo rivers bordering Griqualand West on SE; organized as part of British protectorate 1885 (see BECHUANALAND PROTECTORATE); attached to Cape of Good Hope 1895 and with it became 1910 part of the

Republic of South Africa; chief towns Mafeking, Vryburg (*q.v.*), Taungs, and Kuruman.

British Borneo. See BORNEO.

British Central Africa Protectorate. Early name of *Malawi*. See NYASALAND.

British Columbia. Province, Canada, on Pacific coast; land area 359,279 sq. m.; pop. 817,861; ✳ Victoria; has no counties, subdivided into 10 divisions; bounded on N by Yukon Territory and Mackenzie District, E by Alberta prov., S by U.S.A. (Washington, Idaho, and Montana), and W by Pacific Ocean and Alaska. Has four national parks and a large area (ab. 14,000 sq. m.) set aside in 50 provincial parks. Most mountainous province of Canada; in N crossed by Rocky Mts. which on SE form boundary with Alberta; has several subsidiary ranges, nearly parallel: Cariboo Mts., Selkirk Mts., Monashee Mts., Purcell Range, etc.; farther W along the coast are the Coast Mts., a continuation of the Cascade Range of U.S. Its chief river is the Fraser which with tributaries waters most of central and S parts; in SE are Columbia and headstreams, and in NE the Liard and Peace rivers and tributaries, each a part of the Mackenzie river system; along the coast are many shorter streams (as Stikine, Skeena, Nass) with lower courses generally long narrow fiords. Lakes, mostly of the finger type, are numerous in all parts. Off its Pacific shores are many islands, notably Vancouver and the Queen Charlotte group; many good harbors. Large ocean trade; forest products, minerals (gold, lead, zinc, copper, and coal), agricultural products, fish. Chief cities Vancouver, Victoria, New Westminster.

History: Its shores visited by Sir Francis Drake 1578–79, by Juan de Fuca 1592, and by Capt. Cook 1778; careful survey of coast made by Capt. George Vancouver 1792–94 and overland explorations made by several (Mackenzie, Lewis and Clark, Thompson, and Fraser) bet. 1793 and 1811; for a time (1849–58) known as New Caledonia and formed part of Hudson's Bay Company's concession; part claimed by U.S. (see OREGON); gold discovered in Fraser river basin 1856. Established as British crown colony 1858; united with Vancouver I. 1866, with N boundary extended to 60°N; joined Dominion 1871. Canadian Pacific Railway completed to Vancouver 1885.

British Commonwealth of Nations. 1 The United Kingdom of Great Britain and Northern Ireland (see GREAT BRITAIN), as the governing power of the British Empire (*q.v.*), together with the self-governing dominions and republics: Canada (granted dominion status 1867), Australia (1901), New Zealand (1907), South Africa (1910; withdrew 1961), and Eire (1921; withdrew 1948), India and Pakistan (1947), Ceylon (1948), Ghana (1957), Malaysia (1957), Nigeria (1960), Cyprus and Sierra Leone (1961), Jamaica, Trinidad and Tobago, and Uganda (1962), Kenya (1963), Tanzania, Malawi, Malta, and Zambia (1964), Gambia and Singapore (1965), Guyana, Botswana, Lesotho, and Barbados (1966), Mauritius (1968)—as originally determined by two imperial conferences (the Imperial War Conference of 1918 where autonomy for the dominions was first proposed, and the Imperial Conference of 1926, which declared that Great Britain and the dominions were "autonomous communities within the British Empire, equal in status, in no way subordinate one to another . . . though united by a common allegiance to the Crown") and established by Statute of Westminster 1931.

2 *or* **Commonwealth of Nations.** The United Kingdom and the British dominions and republics together with all the British dependencies.

British East Africa. 1 Former name of Kenya (*q.v.*). **2** British countries in E Africa, including Kenya, Uganda, Zanzibar, and Tanganyika; 679,961 sq. m.

British Empire. The British Commonwealth of Nations (*q.v.*) and the aggregation of separate geographical and political units under the more or less direct control

of the British Parliament, including the colonies, protectorates, and dependencies, and such trust territories (former mandates) and condominiums as are not restricted in their government by the terms of trusteeship or by joint agreements with other authorities; ab. 11,758,590 sq. m.; pop. ab. 156,662,000 (excluding the British Commonwealth, ab. 3,657,163 sq. m.; pop. [various estimates 1939–44] 115,234,000); ✳ London.

☞ All figures given above are exclusive of India.

History: (1) *Territorial development:* Territorial acquisition began in early 17th cent. with group of settlements in North America and Caribbean and East Indian trading posts founded by private individuals and trading companies; captured Gibraltar 1704; by 18th cent., held 13 Atlantic seaboard colonies (see UNITED STATES) and began to add territory in India (see INDIA, 1); as result of French defeat (completed by 1763) secured Acadia, Canada, eastern Mississippi valley, and supremacy in India; began to build power in Malaya 1786 (see PENANG); acquired Cape of Good Hope, Ceylon, and Malta as result of Napoleonic Wars; secured Aden 1839, Hong Kong 1841, and controlled Suez Canal from 1875; in 19th cent. European partition of Africa, acquired Nigeria, Egypt, and territories later comprising British East Africa and Union of South Africa; after World War I, secured mandates to German East Africa, Cameroons, part of Togo, German South-West Africa, Mesopotamia, Palestine, and part of German Pacific islands. (2) *Political development:* Prior to 1783, Crown and Parliament claimed full authority over colonial legislatures; after 1783 evolved system of self-government for advanced colonies; gave dominion status to Canada 1867, then to Australia 1901, New Zealand 1907, Union of South Africa 1910, and Irish Free State 1921; by Statute of Westminster 1931 gave legal expression to the British Commonwealth of Nations (*q.v.*); granted republic status to India 1947 and dominion status to Pakistan 1947 (republic 1956), Ceylon 1948, Malaya 1957, Ghana 1957 (republic 1960), Cyprus and Nigeria 1960; Burma granted complete independence 1948.

British Gui·a′na (gē-ä′nȧ; -än′ȧ) *or since 1966* **Guy·an′a** (gī-än′ȧ; -ä′nȧ). Country, N South America, on the Atlantic; former British crown colony; since 1966 an independent dominion of British Commonwealth; 83,000 sq. m.; pop. (1964 est.) 638,030; ✳ Georgetown; divided into the three counties of Berbice, Demerara, and Essequibo; has low-lying, marshy coastal region (coast line ab. 270 m.) with inland plains sloping up to mountain ranges on W and S; highest range Pacaraima Mts., the NE extension of the Serra Pacaraima along the Venezuela-Brazil boundary, culminating in Roraima 8620 ft. near the junction of the Venezuela-Brazil-Brit. Guiana boundaries; in S is Serra Acarahy, highest peak ab. 2500 ft., densely wooded, and the W extension of the Tumuc-Humac range along the Brazilian border. Has many rivers, all flowing to the Atlantic; among them the Essequibo, in cen. part with main tributaries: Cuyuni, Mazaruni, and Potaro (containing the Kaieteur Falls); the Courantyne on Surinam boundary in E; and the commercially important, but shorter streams, Demerara and Berbice, in the NE. Chief exports sugar, molasses, rum, forest products; also produces rice, gold, and diamonds. Chief cities Georgetown, New Amsterdam; also trading villages of Springlands and Bartica, and Suddie (U.S. base in World War II).

History: For history of region, see GUIANA; colony of Essequibo founded by Dutch probably c. 1620; Berbice founded 1624 under auspices of Dutch West India Co. and Demerara 1645, an offshoot of Berbice; in 18th cent., settled by non-Dutch, including many English; first captured by British and Georgetown (*q.v.*) founded 1781; after final recapture from Dutch 1803, ceded to British 1814; Essequibo, Berbice, and Demerara united as crown colony of British Guiana 1831; its boundary with Venezuela, long subject of controversy, became serious

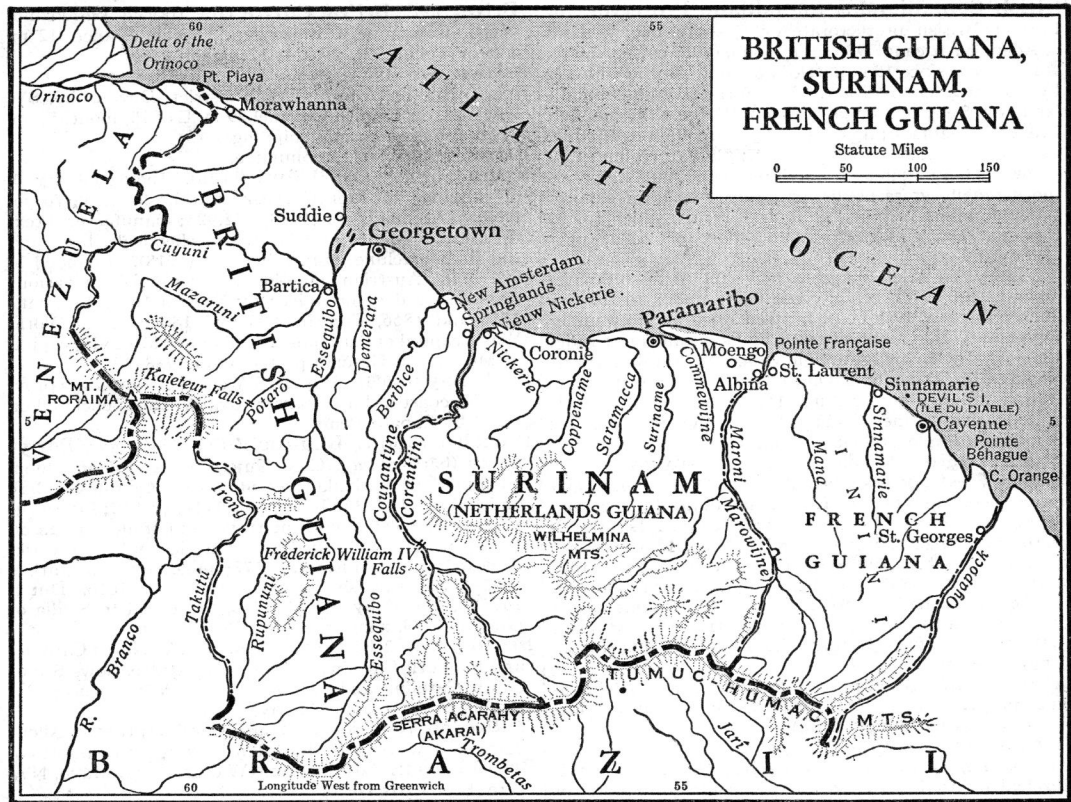

BRITISH GUIANA,
SURINAM,
FRENCH GUIANA

Statute Miles
0   50   100   150

issue, involving U.S. (Olney Doctrine) in 1895; in arbitration award 1899, most of British claims upheld; boundary with Brazil arbitrated 1904; sites (on Demerara river and near Suddie) for military and naval bases leased to U.S. 1940.

British Honduras. British crown colony, Central America; 8688 sq. m.; pop. (1943 est.) 62,512; ✳ Belize; administratively divided into 5 districts: Belize, Cayo, Northern, Stann Creek, and Toledo; bounded on NW and N by Mexico, on E by the Caribbean Sea, on SE by Honduras Bay, and on S and W by Guatemala. Generally low and marshy along the coast, rising inland, hilly in S with highest point ab. 3681 ft.; separated from Quintana Roo, Mexico, on the N by the Hondo river and from Guatemala on the S by the Sarstoon; traversed in central part by the Belize river which rises in NE Guatemala and flows E to the Caribbean at Belize; off coast are many islets, reefs, and cays; in NE is Ambergris Cay, and opp. Belize are Turneffe Is. Chief towns Belize and Corozal; economic resources coconuts, bananas, citrus fruits, and forest products.

History: Probably settled in 1638 by English logwood cutters from Jamaica; maintained existence despite Spanish opposition which was finally defeated 1798; made British superintendency of Belize 1786 to which Great Britain sought to add Bay Islands 1841; intended expansion by British (see also MOSQUITO COAST) part of background of Clayton-Bulwer Treaty bet. England and the U.S. 1850; southern boundary with Guatemala fixed by treaty 1859; declared a colony subordinate to Jamaica 1862; independent of Jamaica since 1884.

British India. That part of India formerly under direct British administration: that is, the Indian Empire (see INDIA, 2) exclusive of the Indian States; 865,446 sq. m.; pop. (1941) 295,808,722; ✳ New Delhi.

British Indian Ocean Territory. British colony, Indian Ocean, formed 1965 from Chagos Islands (formerly part of Mauritius) and Aldabra, Farquhar, and Desroches Islands (formerly part of Seychelles); administered by governor of Seychelles.

British Isles, the. Island group in W Europe, comprising Great Britain, Ireland, and adjacent islands.

British Kaffraria. See KAFFRARIA.

British Malaya. 1 Former British possessions in the Malay Penin. and the Malay Archipelago, SE Asia, including the Straits Settlements and Malay States in S part of Malay Penin. and Brunei in NW Borneo; 53,345 sq. m.; ✳ Singapore. See Federation of MALAYA, STRAITS SETTLEMENTS, BRUNEI.

History: British settlements began with acquisition of Penang 1786; Malacca captured from Dutch 1795 and Singapore founded 1819. For further history, see PENANG, STRAITS SETTLEMENTS, MALACCA, MALAY STATES, and the individual states. In World War II entire area seized by Japanese Dec. 8–9, 1941–Feb. 15, 1942; not recovered until end of war Aug. 1945. A constitutional Union of Malaya set up Apr. 1, 1946 consisting of 9 Malay States, with Malacca and Penang; reorganized Feb. 1948 as the Federation of Malaya.

2 Malay lands of SE Asia still in British Empire after 1946 (Singapore colony, North Borneo, Sarawak).

British New Guinea. See Territory of PAPUA.

British North America. See BRITISH AMERICA and The Dominion of CANADA.

British North Borneo. See NORTH BORNEO.

British Solomon Islands. British protectorate comprising the Solomon Islands (except Bougainville, Buka and adjacent small islands) and the Santa Cruz Islands; 12,780 sq. m.; pop. (1931) 100,000; ✳ Honiara. See SOLOMON ISLANDS.

British Somaliland *or* **Somaliland Protectorate.**
Former British protectorate on S shore of the Gulf
of Aden, E Africa; 67,936 sq. m.; pop. (1938 est.) 350,000;
✳ Hargeisa; since 1960 part of Somalia. Bordered on N
by Gulf of Aden, on E and SE by former Italian Somaliland, on S by Ethiopia, and on W by Ethiopia and
French Somaliland; its coast ranges are 4000 to 5000 ft.
with highest point in NE 7900 ft.; plateau region in W
known as Guban; inland, inhabited by nomadic tribes, is
thorn jungle, grass plains, or semidesert; chief exports
skins, hides, livestock, gum and resins; chief towns
Berbera, Hargeisa, Burao, and port of Zeila, near
Djibouti.

History: In Middle Ages a powerful Arab sultanate;
broken up in 17th cent.; coast came under British influence in early 19th cent. but remained actually under
Egypt until 1884; administered by Government of India
1884–98, by British Foreign Office 1898–1905; transferred to British Colonial Office Apr. 1, 1905; occupied by
Italian military forces Aug. 16, 1940–Mar. 16, 1941;
united with former Italian Somaliland to form (as
Somalia) an independent republic 1960.

British Virgin Islands. See VIRGIN ISLANDS.

British West Indies. Islands of the West Indies (*q.v.*)
forming colonies of Great Britain, including Jamaica and
its dependencies, the Bahama Is., Leeward Is., Windward Is., Barbados, Trinidad and Tobago; 12,507 sq. m.;
pop. (1942) ab. 2,400,000. For history, see separate
entries. All of the British West Indies except the British
Virgin Is. (in the Leeward Is.) and the Bahamas united
1958 to form the West Indies Federation. See *Maps* at
BAHAMA ISLANDS, JAMAICA, LESSER ANTILLES, and
VIRGIN ISLANDS.

Bri′to (brē′tô). Small port on Pacific coast, SW Nicaragua; proposed as outlet with locks for W end of Nicaragua Canal (see NICARAGUA).

Brit′on Ferry (brĭt′′n). Seaport, Glamorganshire, S
Wales, at mouth of the Neath river; pop. 9383; metallurgical industries; port of Neath, center of export for
coal-mining region.

Britt (brĭt). Town, Hancock co., N Iowa, 30 m. W of
Mason City; pop. 2042.

Brit′ta·ny (brĭt′′n·ĭ); *Fr.* **Bre·tagne′** (brẽ·tȧn′y′); *Lat.*
Bri·tan′ni·a Mi′nor (brĭ·tăn′ĭ·ȧ [-tăn′yȧ] mĭ′nẽr
[mĭ′nôr]). Historical peninsular region of NW France;
bounded anciently on N by English Channel, NE by
Normandy, E by Maine and Anjou, SE by Poitou, S and
W by Atlantic Ocean; exactly equivalent to modern departments of Ille-et-Vilaine, Loire-Inférieure, Côtes-
du-Nord, Morbihan, Finistère; ✳ Rennes; numerous
short rivers; traditionally divided by Bretons into the
Armor (coastal regions) and the *Argoat* (hinterland).

History: For early history of region, see ARMORICA;
region occupied by Bretons, Celtic people, whom the
Anglo-Saxon invasion of Britain drove through SW
England to NW corner of France 5th–6th cents. A.D.;
subdued by Clovis, King of Franks, but never effectively
part of Merovingian or Carolingian kingdoms; at end of
10th cent., Geoffrey I, former count of Rennes, took title
of duke of Brittany, unrecognized by France until 1213;
acquired as fief of England 1169 through betrothal of its
heiress to Geoffrey, son of Henry II; at death of Duke
Arthur 1203, claimed as vassal state of France; territory
expanded to include mouth of Loire; until 15th cent.
practically a separate state; came to French crown
through marriages of Duchess Anne to Charles VIII 1491
and to Louis XII 1499 and of heiress, Claudia, to
Francis I 1514; incorporated in France 1532; up to
French Revolution, a French province; involved in Wars
of the Vendée (see POITOU).

Brit′ton (brĭt′′n). City, ⊗ of Marshall co., NE South
Dakota, 45 m. ENE of Aberdeen; pop. 1442.

Briva Isarae. See PONTOISE.

Brivas. See BRIOUDE.

Brive′–la–Gail′larde′ (brēv′lȧ·gȧ′yȧrd′),   *formerly*

Brive; *anc.* **Bri′va Cur·re′ti·a** (brī′vȧ kŭ·rē′shĭ·ȧ;
-shȧ). Commune, Corrèze dept., S cen. France, 12 m.
SW of Tulle; pop. 29,074; 12th-cent. church.

Brixen. See BRESSANONE.

Brix′ham (brĭk′săm). Urban district, Devonshire, SW
England, on English Channel 29 m. E of Plymouth; pop.
8761; fisheries, coastal shipping.

Brixia. See BRESCIA commune.

Br′no (bûr′nô); *Ger.* **Brünn** (brün). Industrial city, ✳
of province of Moravia, cen. Czechoslovakia, 70 m.
NNE of Vienna; pop. (1930) 264,925; manufactures textiles, esp. woolens, also hardware, chemicals, beer, and
the Bren machine gun; university (1918). Founded in
9th cent.; Austrian imperial free city 1278; in various
wars besieged or occupied: by Swedes 1645, Prussians
1742 and 1866, French 1805 and 1809; before World
War I capital of Austrian crownland of Moravia; capital
of Moravia in German protectorate 1938–45.

Bro′a Bay (brō′ä). Bay on SW coast of Matanzas prov.
and SE coast of La Habana prov., W Cuba; enclosed on
the S by Zapata Penin.

Broach (brōch) *or* **Bha·roch′** (bȧ·rōch′); *anc.* **Bar′y-
ga′za** (băr′ĭ·gä′zȧ). City, Gujerat state, Indian Union,
on N bank of Narbada river 30 m. from Gulf of Cambay
and 190 m. N of Bombay; pop. (1941) 55,810; for centuries one of most important travel and trade centers on
India's west coast, famed for its fabrics and ivory work.
Annexed to Mogul Empire 1572; under rule of Marathas
1685–1772; English factory established 1616, Dutch
1626; captured by British 1772, but ceded to Sindia of
Gwalior 1783, again taken by British 1803.

Broad (brôd). **1** River ab. 220 m. long, W North Carolina
and N South Carolina; rises in Blue Ridge, flows S into
South Carolina and unites with Saluda river near Columbia to form Congaree river.

2 River ab. 70 m. long, S South Carolina; rises in Allendale co., flows SE into the Atlantic Ocean in Beaufort co.

Broad Haven. Sea inlet on NW coast of co. Mayo, NW
Eire, E of Erris Head.

Broads, the (brôdz). Low-lying district in Norfolk
(**Norfolk Broads**) and Suffolk (**Suffolk Broads**),
E England, characterized by lakelike expansions of the
rivers, esp. along the lower courses of the **Yare** (yâr),
Bure (būr), and **Wave′ney** (wāv′nĭ), and by shallow
lagoons connected with the rivers by channels.

Broad Sound. Inlet of Pacific Ocean on E coast of
Queensland, Australia, S of Mackay.

Broad′stairs′ and Saint Pe′ter's (brôd′stârz′, sånt
pē′tẽrz). Urban district, Kent, SE England, on North
Sea 67 m. E of London; pop. 15,082; includes **Broadstairs,** a watering place near Ramsgate.

Broad′top′ Mountain (brôd′tŏp′). Coal field 80 sq. m.
in Bedford and Huntingdon cos., S Pennsylvania.

Broa′dus (brō′dŭs). Town, ⊗ of Powder River co., SE
Montana; pop. 628.

Broad′view′ (brôd′vū′). Village, Cook co., Illinois, W
of Chicago; pop. 8588.

Broadview Heights. Village, Cuyahoga co., NE Ohio,
S of Cleveland; pop. 6209.

Broad′wa′ter (brôd′wô′tẽr; -wŏt′ẽr). County in Montana. See *Table* at MONTANA.

Brock′en (brŏk′ĕn; *Ger.* brôk′-). Highest peak 3747 ft.
in the Harz Mts., Germany, in former prov. of Saxony,
Prussia 32 m. S of Brunswick; celebrated in legends, esp.
in connection with the Faust legend.

Brock′port (brŏk′pōrt). Village, Monroe co., W New
York, 18 m. W of Rochester; pop. 5256; dairy and truck
farms; nurseries; canneries. New York State College of
Education (1841).

Brock′ton (brŏk′tŭn). Industrial city, Plymouth co.,
SE Massachusetts, 19 m. S of Boston; pop. 72,813; shoe
manufacturing. Land deeded by Indians 1649, settled
1700; until 1821 a part of Bridgewater, name Brockton
adopted 1874; incorp. 1881.

Brock′ville (brŏk′vĭl). Industrial town, Leeds co., SE

Ontario, Canada, on St. Lawrence 48 m. ENE of Kingston; pop. 12,301; ⊗ of Leeds and Grenville cos.

Brock′way (brŏk′wā). Borough, Jefferson co., W cen. Pennsylvania, 9 m. N of Du Bois; pop. 2563.

Brod (brŏd). Town, N cen. Yugoslavia, on Sava river 120 m. WNW of Belgrade; pop. 13,778.

Bro′deur′ Peninsula (brŏ′dûr′). Northwest section of Baffin I., Northwest Territories, Canada.

Brod′head′ (brŏd′hĕd′; brŏd′-). City, Green co., S Wisconsin, 13 m. E of Monroe; pop. 2444.

Bro′dy (brŏ′dĭ). Commercial city, W Ukraine, U.S.S.R., 40 m. NNW of Ternopol (formerly in Tarnopol dept., Poland); pop. (1938–39 est.) 16,400. Founded 1584; made city 1684; free city 1779–1879; occupied by Russians in World War I; battle 1916; held by Germans 1941–44.

Bro′ken Ar′row (brō′kĕn ăr′ō). City, Tulsa co., NE Oklahoma, 14 m. SE of Tulsa; pop. 5928; coal, oil.

Broken Bow (bō′). **1** City, ⊗ of Custer co., cen. Nebraska, 65 m. ENE of North Platte; pop. 3482.
2 Town, McCurtain co., SE corner of Oklahoma, 47 m. E of Hugo; pop. 2087; lumber; farming.

Broken Hill. **1** officially **Broken Hill and Willyam′a** (wĭl·yăm′ȧ; -yä′mȧ). Mining city, W New South Wales, SE Australia, in Barrier Range 260 m. NE of Adelaide (335 m. by rail); pop. 26,921; founded 1884; in subarid region at elevation of 1000 ft.; center of district noted for production of lead, zinc, and silver.
2 Town, ✳ of Luangwa prov., cen. Northern Rhodesia, S cen. Africa, on railroad ab. 70 m. N of Lusaka; pop. 8859; mining (lead, zinc, vanadium); nearby was discovered 1921 the Broken Hill skull, a prehistoric human skull (Rhodesian man), proto-Australoid in type.

Bro′lo (brŏ′lŏ). Town, Messina prov., NE Sicily, on N coast; pop. ab. 2000; heavy fighting Aug. 13, 1943.

Bromberg. See BYDGOSZCZ.

Brome (brōm). County, Quebec, Canada. See Table at QUEBEC.

Brom′ley (brŭm′lĭ; brŏm′-). Municipal borough, Kent, SE England, 9 m. SE of London; pop. 45,374.

Bro′mo (brŏ′mō). Volcano 7839 ft. in Malang residency, East Java prov., Indonesia, one of the Tengger Mountains (q.v.); famous for its frequent activity.

Bromp′ton (brŏm[p]′tŭn; brŭm[p]′-). A W cen. district of London, England, S of Hyde Park.

Bromp′ton·ville (brŏm[p]′tŭn·vil). Town, Richmond co., S Quebec, Canada, N of Sherbrooke; pop. 2025.

Bröm′se·bro′ (brŭm′sĕ·brōō′). Town, Kalmar prov., SE Sweden, on coast NE of Karlskrona; treaty of peace signed here 1645 bet. Sweden and Denmark.

Broms′grove (brŏmz′grōv). Urban district, Worcestershire, W cen. England; pop. 27,924.

Bron (brôN). Commune, Rhône dept., E cen. France, ESE suburb of Lyons; pop. (1941) 12,423; airfield.

Bron′son. 1 (brŏn′s′n). Town, ⊗ of Levy co., NW Florida penin.; pop. 707.
2 (brŭn′s′n). City, Branch co., S Michigan, 30 m. S of Battle Creek; pop. 2267.

Bron′te (brŏn′tä). Commune, Catania prov., E Sicily, at W foot of Mt. Etna; pop. 17,918.

Bronx (brŏngks). **1** River, New York City; rises Westchester co., flows S into East River, nearly bisecting Bronx borough.
2 County in New York. See Table at NEW YORK state.
3 or **the Bronx.** Residential and industrial borough, forming N part of New York City; ⊗ of Bronx co. and coextensive with the county; 41 sq. m.; pop. 1,424,815; only borough of New York City on the mainland, comprising the section NE of Harlem river, with adjacent islands (City, Hunter's, Hart's, Riker's); traversed by Bronx river. Settled 1641; made separate county 1913; park system includes notably Pelham Bay (containing Orchard Beach), Van Cortlandt Park, and Bronx Park (containing N.Y. Zoological Park and Botanical Garden and museum); well-known educational institutions include Fordham Univ. (1841; Roman Catholic), part of

N.Y. Univ., Hunter College (1870). Governed as part of New York City; has a borough president, with local and county functions conducted independently of central municipal government. See also NEW YORK city.

Bronx′ville (brŏngks′vĭl). Residential village, Westchester co., SE New York, 17 m. NNE of New York; pop. 6744; Sarah Lawrence College (1926; women).

Brooke (brŏŏk). County in West Virginia. See Table at WEST VIRGINIA.

Brooke's Point (brŏŏks). Port and municipal district, SE coast of Palawan, Phil. Is., on Sulu Sea; pop. 21,839.

Brook Farm. See WEST ROXBURY.

Brook′field (brŏŏk′fēld). **1** Village, Cook co., NE Illinois, 10 m. W of Chicago; pop. 20,429; site of Chicago Zoological Park (Brookfield Zoo).
2 Town, Worcester co., cen. Massachusetts, 15 m. W of Worcester; pop. 1751.
3 City, Linn co., N Missouri, 27 m. E of Chillicothe; pop. 5694; in agricultural section; coal deposits nearby.
4 City, Waukesha co., SE Wisconsin; pop. 19,812.

Brook·ha′ven (brŏŏk·hā′vĕn). **1** City, ⊗ of Lincoln co., SW Mississippi, 23 m. N of McComb; pop. 9885.
2 Town, Suffolk co., Long I., New York, E of Patchogue; pop. 109,900 ab. 7 m. to the NE is Upton, site of Brookhaven National Laboratory for Nuclear Research.
3 Borough, Delaware co., SE Pennsylvania, SE of Philadelphia; pop. 5280.

Brook′ings (brŏŏk′ĭngz). **1** County in South Dakota. See Table at SOUTH DAKOTA.
2 City, its ⊗, E South Dakota, 53 m. N of Sioux Falls; pop. 10,558; became city 1883. South Dakota State College of Agriculture and Mechanic Arts (1881; coed.).

Brookland. See WEST COLUMBIA.

Brook′lands (brŏŏk′lăndz). Village, S Manitoba, Canada, a suburb of Winnipeg; pop. 2915.

Brook′lawn (brŏŏk′lôn). Borough, Camden co., SW New Jersey, 4 m. S of Camden; pop. 2504.

Brook′line (brŏŏk′lĭn). Town, Norfolk co., E Massachusetts, 4 m. WSW of Boston; pop. 54,004; birthplace of John F. Kennedy, 35th president of the U.S.

Brook′lyn (brŏŏk′lĭn). **1** Residential town, cen. Windham co., NE corner of Connecticut; pop. 3312.
2 Village, St. Clair co., SW Illinois; pop. 1922.
3 Residential borough, forming part of New York City, ⊗ of Kings co. (see Table at NEW YORK state) and coextensive with the county, in SW extremity of Long Island; 71 sq. m.; pop. 2,627,319 (largest in one of five boroughs of New York City); separated from Manhattan by East river; includes districts of Flatbush, Red Hook, Greenpoint, Bushwick, New Utrecht, Williamsburg, Brownsville, Bay Ridge, Shore Road, Ridgewood, and Brooklyn Heights; brewing; shipbuilding; food processing; manufactures shoes, paint, varnish, machinery, foundry and machine-shop products, building equipment, gyroscopes and other steamship and airplane equipment; large grain-shipping facilities. Educational institutions include Brooklyn College (1930; municipal), Packer Collegiate Inst. (1845), Polytechnic Institute of Brooklyn (1854; men), Pratt Institute (1887), Long Island Univ. (1926), St. Francis College (1858, chartered 1884; men), St. Joseph's College for Women (1916). Brooklyn Museum, Prospect Park, Marine Park, Botanical Garden; Coney Island; Greenwood Cemetery; Floyd Bennett Field; U.S. (Brooklyn) Navy Yard (1801). Governed as part of New York City; has a borough president, with local and county functions conducted independently of central municipal government. See also NEW YORK city.

History: Settlements made along Gowanus and Jamaica Bays at Wallabout Bay (later incorp. as Williamsburg) by Dutch and Walloons 1636 and 1637; settlement established 1645 near present site of borough hall and named *Breuckelen;* New Utrecht settled ab. 1650, Flatbush (at first called Midwout) ab. 1651; scene of battle of Long Island Aug. 27, 1776 in which British under Sir William Howe defeated Americans under Israel

Putnam; incorporated as city 1834; annexed Williamsburg and Bushwick 1855, included all of Kings co. by 1896; borough of New York City 1898.

4 City, Cuyahoga co., NE Ohio, SW of Cleveland; pop. 10,733.

Brooklyn Center. Village, Hennepin co., SE cen. Minnesota, 8 m. NNW of Minneapolis; pop. 24,356.

Brooklyn Park. Village, Hennepin co., Minnesota, NW of Minneapolis; pop. 10,197.

Brook Park. Village, Cuyahoga co., NE Ohio, SW of Cleveland; pop. 12,856.

Brooks (brŏŏks). Name of counties in two states of the U.S. See *Tables* at GEORGIA and TEXAS.

Brooks Islands. Former name of MIDWAY.

Brooks Range. Mountain range averaging 5000 to 10,000 ft., across N Alaska from Kotzebue Sound to Canadian border, forming watershed bet. Yukon basin on S and Arctic coast on N; includes smaller groups or ridges of De Long, Baird, and Endicott Mts.

Brooks'ville (brŏŏks'vĭl). **1** City, ⊗ of Hernando co., W Florida penin., 42 m. N of Tampa; pop. 3301.

2 City, ⊗ of Bracken co., NE Kentucky; pop. 601.

Brook'ville (brŏŏk'vĭl). **1** Town, ⊗ of Franklin co., E Indiana, 28 m. SSW of Richmond; pop. 2596.

2 Village, Montgomery co., SW Ohio, 12 m. WNW of Dayton; pop. 3184; structural steel, bridges.

3 Industrial borough, ⊗ of Jefferson co., W cen. Pennsylvania, 18 m. W of Du Bois; pop. 4620.

Brook'wood (brŏŏk'wŏŏd). Village, Surrey, England, 4 m. SW of Woking and 28 m. SW of London; American military cemetery.

Broom, Loch (lŏk brŏŏm'; brŏŏm'). Sea inlet on NW coast of Scotland, in Ross and Cromarty co.; **Little Loch Broom** is a parallel inlet just to the S.

Broome (brŏŏm; brŏŏm). **1** County in New York. See *Table* at NEW YORK state.

2 Seaport town, NW Western Australia, on Roebuck Bay; pop. ab. 1000; bombed by Japanese Mar. 1942.

Broughton Bay. See EAST CHOSEN BAY.

Brough'ty Ferry (brŏ'tĭ). Suburb of Dundee, Angus co., E Scotland, on Firth of Tay ab. 3½ m. E of main part of the city; castle dating from 1498.

Brow'ard (brou'ĕrd). County in Florida. See *Table* at FLORIDA.

Brown (broun). Counties in nine states of the U.S. See *Tables* at ILLINOIS, INDIANA, KANSAS, MINNESOTA, NEBRASKA, OHIO, SOUTH DAKOTA, TEXAS, WISCONSIN.

Brown, Mount. Peak 8541 ft. in Glacier National Park, NW Montana.

Brown, Point. Point on SW coast of Grays Harbor co., W Washington, at N entrance to Grays Harbor.

Brown Clee Hill. See CLEE HILLS.

Brown Deer. Village, Milwaukee co., SE Wisconsin, N of Milwaukee; pop. 11,280.

Brown'field (broun'fēld). City, ⊗ of Terry co., NW Texas, 38 m. SSW of Lubbock; pop. 10,286.

Brown'hills' (broun'hĭlz'). Urban district, Staffordshire, England, 13 m. N of Birmingham; pop. 21,482.

Brown'ing (broun'ĭng). Town, Glacier co., NW Montana; pop. 2011; tourist resort; headquarters of the Blackfeet Indian Reservation.

Browns'burg (brounz'bûrg). Village, Argenteuil co., SW Quebec, Canada, WNW of Montreal; pop. 3238.

Browns'town (brounz'toun). **1** Town, ⊗ of Jackson co., S Indiana, 32 m. SE of Bloomington; pop. 2140.

2 Borough, Cambria co., SW cen. Pennsylvania, near Johnstown; pop. 1379.

Browns'ville (brounz'vĭl). **1** Urban community (unincorporated), Escambia co., Florida, W of Pensacola; pop. 38,417.

2 City, ⊗ of Edmonson co., cen. Kentucky; pop. 473.

3 Industrial borough, Fayette co., SW Pennsylvania, on Monongahela river 13 m. NW of Uniontown; pop. 6055.

4 City, ⊗ of Haywood co., W Tennessee, 27 m. W of Jackson; pop. 5424; fruit, cotton, sawmills.

5 City and port of entry, ⊗ of Cameron co., S Texas, on Rio Grande opp. Matamoros, Mexico, 25 m. from Gulf of Mexico; pop. 48,040. Began as trading post; Fort Brown (orig. Fort Taylor) established 1846; town founded 1848; scene of Mexican disorders 1859; served as one of principal ports of Confederacy during Civil War. Ships citrus fruits, vegetables, canned goods, oil; resort.

Brown'ville (broun'vĭl). Town, Piscataquis co., N cen. Maine, 37 m. NNW of Bangor; pop. 1641.

Brown Wil'ly (wĭl'ĭ). Mountain 1375 ft., highest point in Cornwall, SW England, 4½ m. SE of Camelford.

Brown'wood (broun'wŏŏd). Industrial city, ⊗ of Brown co., cen. Texas, 64 m. SSE of Abilene; pop. 16,974; ships cotton, grain, pecans, wool, mohair, poultry, dairy products. Daniel Baker Coll. (1889; coed.); Howard Payne Coll. (1889; coed.).

Bru·ay'–en–Ar'tois' (brü-ā'äN-når'twä'). Commune, Pas-de-Calais dept., N France, 17 m. NW of Arras; pop. (1931) 31,831; coal mines.

Bruce (brŏŏs). County, Ontario, Canada. See *Table* at ONTARIO.

Bruce, Mount. Mountain 4024 ft. in plateau region S of Fortescue river, highest point in Western Australia.

Bruce Coast. Northeast section of Coats Land, Antarctica; along coast of South Atlantic E of Weddell Sea, ab. 16°30'W to 23°W.

Bruce Peninsula. Peninsula of SE Ontario, Canada; extends N bet. Lake Huron and Georgian Bay.

Bruch'sal (brŏŏĸ'zäl). City, Baden-Württemberg state, W Germany, on a tributary of the Rhine 11 m. NE of Karlsruhe; pop. 16,469; railroad junction; fine 18th-cent. baroque castle; manufactures soap, paper, railroad signals. Founded before 937 A.D.; residence of princebishops of Speyer from 12th cent.; to Baden 1802.

Bruck, *or* **Bruck an der Mur** (brŏŏk' än dẽr mŏŏr'). Commune, Styria prov., Austria, at confluence of Mürz and Mur rivers 25 m. NNW of Graz; pop. 12,198; old Gothic church; manufactures iron goods, paper, cable.

Brug'ge (brüg'ĕ) *or* **Bruges** (brŏŏzh; brŏŏ'jĭz; *Fr.* brüzh). Commune, * of West Flanders prov., NW Belgium, ab. 55 m. NW of Brussels; pop. (1938 est.) 51,884; an important commercial city on canals connecting with Zeebrugge and Oostende on the North Sea; manufactures laces, linens, cotton and woolen goods; has many fine old buildings; known as "City of Bridges."

History: Flemish town dating at least from 9th cent. A.D. when count of Flanders built castle; a member of Hanseatic League in 13th cent.; Bruges developed into chief Hanseatic market; drove out French rulers ("Matins of Bruges") 1302; as center of English wool trade and Flemish cloth industry, became commercial and financial hub of northern Europe; residence of dukes of Burgundy who founded there Order of Golden Fleece 1429; art and cultural center in 15th cent. (Jan van Eyck, Hans Memling, etc.); sanding up of the Zwyn (small stream connecting it with North Sea), falling off of cloth industry, civil strife, and rise of rival Antwerp (*q.v.*) caused its decline from late 15th cent.

Brugh na Boinne (brŏŏ' nà boin'). Locality, co. Meath, NE Eire, on N bank of Boyne river, WSW of Drogheda; site of ancient royal cemetery, includes three great mounds, including Newgrange (*q.v.*).

Brühl (brül). City, W Germany, in North Rhine-Westphalia near Rhine river 8 m. S of Cologne; pop. 11,228.

Bru'ja Point (brŏŏ'hä). Cape at S extremity of Canal Zone, W of the Pacific terminus of the Panama Canal.

Bruk'ka·ros, Mount (brŭk'à·rōs). Mountain ab. 5200 ft. in S cen. South-West Africa; an extinct volcano.

Brule (brŏŏl; brŏŏ'là, -lĭ). County in South Dakota. See *Table* at SOUTH DAKOTA.

Brule *or* **Bois Brule** (boi' brŏŏl'). **1** River ab. 40 m. long, Douglas co., NW corner of Wisconsin; flows N near E boundary of Douglas co., into Lake Superior.

2 River, NE Wisconsin; rises in N Forest co., flows E and forms section of Wisconsin-Michigan boundary until it

joins the Michigamme river to form the Menominee river on N boundary of Florence co.

Bru′nan·burh (broo′năn·bûrg; *Anglo-Saxon* broo′nän-boŏrk). Battlefield of uncertain location in S Scotland or N England; site of victory of Athelstan over a league of Welsh, Scots, and Danes 937 A.D.

Brun′didge (brŭn′dĭj). Town, Pike co., SE Alabama, 60 m. SSE of Montgomery; pop. 2523.

Brundusium *or* **Brundisium.** See BRINDISI seaport.

Bru·nei′ (broo·nī′; broo·nä′). **1** River in Borneo. See LIMBANG.

2 Sultanate in NE part of Borneo, a British protectorate; 2226 sq. m.; pop. 30,135, (1938 est.) 38,000; divided geographically into two parts, each entirely surrounded by Sarawak and each having coast line on South China Sea and Brunei Bay; the two sections separated by Limbang river valley. Exports rubber, cutch, sago. In pre-Spanish times a powerful and populous state; visited by Magellan's ships 1521; captured by Spaniards 1580 but not held; declined in influence and became a resort for pirates; its sultan in 1841 handed over Sarawak to Raja James Brooke and in 1846 entered into treaty with Great Britain, ceding Labuan; placed under British protection 1888; in 1906 definitely yielded all administration to a British Resident; occupied by Japanese Dec. 1941, retaken by Australians June 1945. **3** Seaport, its ✳, on Brunei Bay; pop. 10,453.

Brunei Bay. Inlet of South China Sea on the NW coast of Borneo; its shores touched by North Borneo, Brunei, and Sarawak; in its N part is Labuan I.; landing place of Australian and Dutch forces June 10, 1945.

Bru′ni *or* **Bru′ny** (broo′nī; *Fr.* brü′nē′). Island 149 sq. m., and ab. 32 m. long, off SE coast of Tasmania, SW of Storm Bay; its S point is Tasman Head.

Brü′nig (brü′nĭk). Mountain pass 3396 ft. in Bernese Oberland, Switzerland, E of Brienz; connects valley of the Aare with Lake of Lucerne.

Brun′ke·berg (broong′kĕ·bärk). Village, Telemark co., S Norway, ab. 42 m. NW of Skien; pop. ab. 1000; battle Oct. 10, 1471 in which Danes were defeated.

Brünn. See BRNO.

Bruns′büt·tel·koog′ (broons′büt′ĕl·kōk′). Town, Schleswig-Holstein, Germany, on Elbe river at S entrance to Kiel Canal; pop. 5244.

Bruns′sum (brŭn′sŭm). Commune, Limburg prov., SE Netherlands, 11 m. NE of Maastricht; pop. 16,036.

Bruns′wick (brŭnz′wĭk). **1** Name of counties in two states of the U.S. See *Tables* at NORTH CAROLINA and VIRGINIA.

2 Seaport city, ⊗ of Glynn co., SE Georgia, on Atlantic Ocean; pop. 21,703; shrimp fishing; shipbuilding.

3 Village, Cumberland co., SW Maine, 23 m. NE of Portland; pop. 15,797; trade center for resort regions; textile mills, paper factories. Bowdoin College (1794; men).

4 Town, Frederick co., N Maryland, on Potomac river 15 m. WSW of Frederick; pop. 3555.

5 City, Chariton co., N cen. Missouri, on Missouri river 33 m. SE of Chillicothe; pop. 1493.

6 Village, Medina co., Ohio, NW of Akron; pop. 6453.

7 City, S Victoria, SE Australia, N suburb of Melbourne; pop. 54,348.

Bruns′wick (brŭnz′wĭk); *Ger.* **Braun′schweig** (broun′shvīk). **1** Former German state, cen. Germany; 1417 sq. m.; pop. (1939) 599,208; ✳ Brunswick.

2 *older German* **Bruns′wich** (broons′vĭk). Manufacturing and commercial city, cen. Germany, on Oker river ab. 125 m. W of Berlin; pop. (1964 est.) 238,537; ✳ of free state of Brunswick until its incorporation into Lower Saxony state; has 12th-cent. cathedral, numerous fine churches of 12th cent. and later, a 13th to 14th-cent. Gothic Rathaus, and the Collegium Carolinum (1745).

History (state and city): Reputedly founded by Bruno c. 861; made city 1031; important member of Hanseatic League in 13th cent.; joined Schmalkaldic League during

Reformation; in 1671 passed to dukes of **Brunswick-Wol′fen·büt′tel** (vôl′fĕn·büt′ĕl) who made it their residence 1753; duchy of Brunswick annexed to kingdom of Westphalia 1807–13; member of German Confederation; duchy proclaimed republic Nov. 8, 1918; in World War II important industrial center, esp. in manufacture of fighter airplanes; frequently bombed by Allied air forces 1943–45; taken by Americans Apr. 13, 1945.

Brunswick-Lü′ne·burg (-lü′nĕ·boŏrk). Duchy, cen. Germany, an early possession of the Welf family, created 1235 by Frederick II for Otto the Child, who held town of Brunswick and surrounding territory; holdings gradually expanded until its subdivision resulted in several branches of Brunswick house; as younger branch of house of Brunswick, its rulers given electorate of Hannover 1692 (establishing English royal house of Hanover 1714–1901); made part of kingdom of Westphalia 1807–13, but restored as independent state in 1815; joined customs union (Zollverein) 1844, North German Confederation 1866, and became state of German Empire 1871; last ruler, Ernest Augustus, abdicated 1918 and duchy declared a republic 1918; lost sovereign rights to Third Reich by law of 1934.

Brunswick Peninsula. Peninsula extending S from S tip of mainland of South America (Chile), bet. Strait of Magellan on S and E and Otway Water on NW. Cape Froward, its S tip, is most southerly point of mainland of South America, 53°53′43″S.

Brunswick-Wolfenbüttel. See BRUNSWICK.

Bruny. See BRUNI.

Brusa, Brussa. See BURSA.

Brush (brŭsh). Town, Morgan co., NE Colorado, 10 m. E of Fort Morgan; pop. 3621.

Brus′sels (brŭs′′lz); *Fr.* **Bru·xelles′** (brü′sĕl′; *locally* brük′sĕl′); *Flemish* **Brus′sel** (brüs′ĕl). City, cen. Belgium, ✳ of Belgium and of Brabant prov., on Senne river; pop. (1938 est.) 191,678, with suburbs 912,774; has town hall, palaces, cathedral (founded 1010), museums, churches, monuments; manufactures carpets, tapestries, lace; printing, publishing; foundries, breweries.

History: Village grew up about chapel on island in Senne; among holdings of Louvain (Leuven) and later of dukes of Brabant (*q.v.*) who made it their residence; slower than Flemish towns to develop cloth industry, it had become, by 14th cent., chief town of Brabant; in 1530 made capital of Netherlands under Hapsburgs; took part in revolt against rulers 1576; won back for Hapsburgs by Alexander of Parma 1585; bombarded by Villeroi during wars of Louis XIV of France; under kingdom of the Netherlands 1815–30; center of Belgian revolution 1830 and capital of Belgium since 1830; scene of several international conferences: 1874 (on usages of war), 1876 (on exploration of central Africa), 1890 (to extirpate African slave trade).

Brü′ster Ort (brüs′tĕr ôrt′). Cape on coast of East Prussia, on NE side of the Gulf of Danzig; now in Poland.

Bruttium. See CALABRIA.

Brüx. See MOST.

Bruxelles. See BRUSSELS.

Bry′an (brī′ăn). **1** Name of counties in two states of the U.S. See *Tables* at GEORGIA and OKLAHOMA.

2 City, ⊗ of Williams co., NW corner of Ohio, 52 m. W of Toledo; pop. 7361; manufactures aviation equipment, pharmaceutical supplies; artesian wells.

3 City, ⊗ of Brazos co., E cen. Texas, 72 m. SSE of Waco; pop. 27,542; cotton gins and compresses.

Bryansk (bryänsk; *Angl.* brī·ănsk′), *also* **Briansk** (bryänsk; brī·änsk′). City, formerly in W cen. Orel Region, Soviet Russia, Europe, on Desna river at head of navigation, W of Orel and 215 m. SW of Moscow; since 1946 ✳ of Bryansk Region; pop. 87,473; important railroad junction point; trades in timber, forest products, and cattle; sawmills, flour mills, distilleries, and nearby in a N suburb (Maltsevsk) large ironworks, locomotive plant, and glass and rope factories; has long been a cul-

tural center. Founded 1146; independent principality to 1356; later subject to Lithuania but became Russian in 17th cent.; in World War II held by Germans Oct. 13, 1941 to Sept. 1943.

Bryansk Region. Region, SW Soviet Russia, Europe, created 1946 from Orel Region; ✳ Bryansk.

Bryce, Mount (brīs). Peak 11,507 ft. in E British Columbia, Canada, near Alberta border.

Bryce Canyon National Park. See UNITED STATES, *National Parks.*

Bryn Ath′yn (brĭn′ ăth′ĭn). Residential borough, Montgomery co., SE Pennsylvania, ab. 16 m. NE of Philadelphia; pop. 1057; seat of Bryn Athyn Cathedral, center of Swedenborgianism in the U.S.

Bryn′mawr′ (brĭn′mour′; -môr′). Urban district, Brecknockshire, SE Wales; pop. 6524; market town; coal mining and steel manufacture.

Bryn Mawr (brĭn′ mär′). Unincorporated residential community, Montgomery co., SE Pennsylvania, ab. 7 m. S of Norristown; pop. (est.) 9500. Bryn Mawr College (1880; women).

Bry′son City (brī′s′n). City, ⊗ of Swain co., W North Carolina, on edge of Great Smoky Mountains National Park 53 m. W of Asheville; pop. 1084; resort.

Brzeg (bzhĕk); *Ger.* **Brieg** (brēk); *anc.* **Civ′i·tas Al′tae Ri′pae** (sĭv′ĭ·tăs ăl′tē rī′pē). City, E Wrocław dept., SW Poland, on Odra (Oder) river 27 m. SE of Wrocław; pop. (1946) 31,419; formerly in Silesia, Germany; 14th-cent. Gothic churches, town hall; cattle fair; manufactures tobacco, cigars, textiles. Received city rights 1250; captured by Prussia in First Silesian War 1741; fortifications destroyed by French 1806; taken by Russians Feb. 7, 1945; assigned to Poland by Potsdam Conference 1945.

Brześć nad Bugiem. See BREST, White Russia.

Brze·ża′ny (bzhĕ·zhä′nĭ). Town, W Ukraine, U.S.S.R. (formerly in Tarnopol dept., Poland), 30 m. WSW of Ternopol; pop. 11,721. Scene of German breakthrough Aug. 28, 1915, retaken by Russians July 1, 1916.

Brze·zi′ny (bzhĕ·zē′nĭ). Industrial commune, Łódź dept., Poland, 11 m. E of Łódź; pop. (1938–39 est.) 13,009; textiles; scene of World War I battle bet. Germans and Russians Nov. 1914.

Bua. See ČIOVO.

Buad (bwäd). Island off W coast of Samar, Phil. Is., across entrance to Maqueda and Villareal Bays; 14 sq. m.; pop. 6704. Town of Zumarraga is on its W coast.

Bu·bas′tis (bū·băs′tĭs). Ancient city, Lower Egypt, in Nile delta; ruins (excavated 1886–87) near modern city of Zagazig, called **Tell Bas′ta** (tĕl′ băs′tá; *Arab.* tăl băs′tă); chief seat of worship of the goddess Bast, usually represented as lion-headed or cat-headed; chosen 945 B.C. by Sheshonk I as capital of XXIId (Bubastite) dynasty; destroyed by Persians c. 350 B.C.

Bu′be·neč (boo′bĕ·nĕch). City, N suburb of Prague, Bohemia, Czechoslovakia; pop. ab. 30,000.

Bu′bi·yan′ (boo′bē·yän′). Island at head of Persian Gulf off N coast of Kuwait and W of mouth of Shatt-al-Arab; administratively a part of Kuwait.

Bu·ca·ra·man′ga (boo′kä·rä·mäng′gä). City, ✳ of Santander dept., N cen. Colombia; pop. 41,714; in the Cordillera Oriental of the Andes at alt. of 3030 ft.; center of region producing coffee, cacao, tobacco, and cotton.

Bu·cas′ Gran′de (boo·käs′ grän′dá). Island off NE Mindanao, Phil. Is., a part of Surigao prov.; 50 sq. m.; pop. 2556; highest point 3012 ft.

Buc′ca·neer′ Archipelago (bŭk′á·nēr′). Group of islands off N coast of Western Australia at entrance to King Sound.

Buch′an (bŭk′ăn; *Scot.* bŭk′-). Region N of the Ythan river, NE Aberdeen co., Scotland; includes Buchan Ness and the Bullers of Buchan (*qq.v.*).

Bu·chan′an (bū·kăn′ăn; bū-). **1** Name of counties in three states of the U.S. See *Tables* at IOWA, MISSOURI, VIRGINIA.

2 City, ⊗ of Haralson co., W Georgia; pop. 753.

3 City, Berrien co., SW corner of Michigan, 53 m. SW of Kalamazoo; pop. 5341.

4 Village, Westchester co., SE New York, on Hudson river 37 m. N of New York; pop. 2019.

5 See GRAND BASSA, Liberia.

Buchanan Dam; *formerly* **Ham′il·ton Dam** (hăm′ĭl·tŭn; -t′n). Dam completed 1937 across Colorado river, Burnet and Llano cos., cen. Texas; height 158 ft.; impounds water for power.

Buch′an Ness (bŭk′ăn nĕs′; *Scot.* bŭk′ăn). Headland on NE coast of Scotland, S of Peterhead; lighthouse; easternmost point of Scotland.

Bu′cha·rest (boo′ká·rĕst; bū′-); *Romanian* **Bu′cu·reş′ti** (boo′koo·rĕsht′; -rĕsh′tĕ). City, SE Romania, on Dâmboviţa river; ✳ of Romania; pop. (1939 est.) 648,162; industrial and commercial center; manufactures machinery, textiles, chemicals, leather, metal goods; university (founded 1864); fine public gardens.

History: Residence of rulers of Walachia (*q.v.*) from 14th cent.; became capital of Romania (*q.v.*) 1861; scene of negotiation of several important treaties: (1) Peace of Bucharest 1812 bet. Russia and Turkey; (2) peace bet. Serbia and Bulgaria 1886 (see EASTERN RUMELIA); (3) Treaty of Bucharest 1913, stripping Bulgaria (*q.v.*) of her conquests. Occupied by Germans 1916–18; after abdication of King Carol Sept. 6, 1940, scene of rioting and assassinations; under Nazi control 1940–44; occupied by Russians Aug. 31, 1944.

Bu′chen·wald′ (boo′kĕn·vält′). Village, Thuringia, E Germany, near Weimar; site of concentration camp, taken Apr. 13, 1945 by American forces. One of the worst of German camps for prisoners.

Buchhorn. See FRIEDRICHSHAFEN.

Bück′e·burg (bük′ĕ·boork). Town, ✳ of Schaumburg-Lippe, former state of NW Germany, 30 m. WSW of Hannover; pop. 5632.

Buck′eye (bŭk′ī′). Town, Maricopa co., SW cen. Arizona, near Gila river 30 m. W of Phoenix; pop. 2286.

Buck·han′non (bŭ·kăn′ŭn). **1** River ab. 45 m. long, NE cen. West Virginia; rises in SW Randolph co., flows N into Tygart river in Barbour co.

2 City, ⊗ of Upshur co., NE cen. West Virginia, on Buckhannon river 14 m. E of Weston; pop. 6386; farming and grazing center; coal mines, gas wells; manufactures leather, lumber, etc. West Virginia Wesleyan Coll. (1890; coed.).

Buck·ha′ven and Meth′il (bŭk·hā′vĕn, mĕth′ĭl). Burgh comprising two ports, Fife co., E Scotland, 7 to 8 m. NE of Kirkcaldy; pop. 20,154.

Buck′hurst Hill (bŭk′hûrst). Former urban district, Essex, SE England, near the Roding 10 m. NNE of London; pop. (1931) 5486; part of Greater London.

Buck′ie (bŭk′ĭ). Seaport burgh, Banff co., NE Scotland, ab. 13 m. E of Elgin; pop. 7705; herring fisheries.

Buck′ing·ham (bŭk′ing·hăm; *Brit.* -ing·ăm). **1** County in Virginia. See *Table* at VIRGINIA.

2 Town, its ⊗, cen. Virginia; pop. 218.

3 Industrial town, Papineau co., SW Quebec, Canada, on Lièvre river 17 m. NE of Ottawa; pop. 6129; pulp and paper mills; phosphate, graphite, and mica mines.

4 County in England. See BUCKINGHAMSHIRE.

5 Municipal borough, Buckinghamshire, SE cen. England, 20 m. NE of Oxford; pop. 3944. Seat (Stowe, with famous gardens) of former dukes of Buckingham.

Buck′ing·ham·shire (bŭk′ing·ăm·shĭr; -shēr) *or* **Buck′ing·ham** (bŭk′ing·ăm) *or* **Bucks** (bŭks). County, SE cen. England; area 749 sq. m.; pop. (1951) 386,164; ⊗ Aylesbury; rivers Thames, Ouse, Thame; agriculture, dairying, livestock raising.

Buck′land (bŭk′lănd). Town, Franklin co., NW Massachusetts, 9 m. W of Greenfield; pop. 1664.

Buck′ley (bŭk′lĭ). Manufacturing urban district, Flintshire, NE Wales; pop. 7699.

Buckley, Mount. Peak 6599 ft. in W North Carolina.

Buck Mountain (bŭk). **1** Peak 4630 ft. in Grayson co., SW Virginia. **2** Peak 11,923 ft. in S cen. Grand Teton National Park, NW Wyoming.

Buck′ner Bay (bŭk′nēr); *Jap.* **Na·ka·gu·su·ku Wan** (nä·kä·gōō·sōō·kōō wän). Inlet of the Pacific Ocean in SE coast of Okinawa I., Ryukyu Is., Japan; U.S. fleet anchorage in Okinawa campaign Apr.–June 1945.

Bucks (bŭks). **1** County in Pennsylvania. See *Table* at PENNSYLVANIA. **2** See BUCKINGHAMSHIRE.

Buck′skin, Mount (bŭk′skĭn). Peak 13,800 ft. in Lake and Park cos., cen. Colorado.

Bucks′port (bŭks′pōrt). Town, Hancock co., SE Maine, on Penobscot river 17 m. S of Bangor; pop. 3466.

Bu′co·vi′na *or* **Bu′ko·vi′na** (bōō′kŏ·vē′nä; *Angl.* -nå). Region, E cen. Europe, 4031 sq. m.; formerly an Austrian crownland; as province (1918–40) of N Romania, 4031 sq. m., pop. ab. 850,000, ✳ Cernăuţi (*Ger.* Czernowitz). Occupies foothills of E Carpathian Mts., thickly wooded and source of Dniester, Prut, and Siret rivers flowing to Black Sea.

History: Inhabited by Ruthenian tribes; part of principality of Moldavia (*q.v.*); occupied by Austria 1774 and formally ceded by Turkey 1777; ruled by Austria as part of Galicia until 1849 when Bucovina was made separate crownland; became independent at collapse of Austria-Hungary 1918 and joined Romania 1918–40; seized by Soviet Union June 27, 1940 and incorporated with Bessarabia Aug. 1940 in Moldavian Republic; held by German and Romanian forces 1941–45; N half became part of Ukrainian S.S.R. 1945 (chief town Chernovtsy) and S half, including towns Rădăuţi and Siret, remained in Romania.

Buc′quoy′ (bü′kwå′). Village, Pas-de-Calais dept., France, 10 m. S of Arras; pop. ab. 1000; scene of fierce fighting July 1918.

Bucureşti. See BUCHAREST.

Bu·cy′rus (bu̇·sī′rŭs). Industrial city, ⊗ of Crawford co., N cen. Ohio, on Sandusky river 17 m. NNE of Marion; pop. 12,276; settled 1818, became ⊗ 1830; manufactures highway construction machinery, plows, cranes, hoists, steel castings, copper kettles, clay products.

Bu′czacz (bōō′chäch). Town, W Ukraine, U.S.S.R., on Strypa river 34 m. SSW of Ternopol (formerly in Tarnopol dept., Poland); pop. 11,120; manufactures artistic tapestries; agriculture, horse breeding, distilling. Treaty bet. Poland and Turkey signed here 1672; key point in fighting in World War I Dec. 1915–Jan. 1916 and again in Brusilov's offensive June 1916.

Bu′da·fok (bōō′då·fôk). City, S suburb of Budapest, cen. Hungary, on Danube river; pop. 15,014.

Bu′da·pest′ (bōō′då·pĕst′; bū′-; *Hung.* bŏō′dŏ·pĕsht′). Autonomous city, ✳ of Hungary, in cen. part, 135 m. SE of Vienna; 181 sq. m.; pop. (1939) 1,115,877; united since 1872 former towns of **Bu′da** (*Hung.* bōō′dŏ) on right bank of Danube and **Pest** (*Hung.* pĕsht) on left bank; political, financial, industrial, and commercial center of Hungary. Pest is more the commercial and industrial center and contains most of the modern cultural activities: theaters, museums, parks, the Royal Hungarian Univ., and government buildings; in Buda are more historical buildings.

History: Buda site of Roman camp (*anc.* **A·quin′cum** [å·kwĭng′kŭm]) set up in 2d cent. A.D.; Buda and Pest both towns inhabited by Germans in 13th cent.; Buda fortified by Matthias Corvinus in 15th cent. and became capital of Hungary; captured and held by Turks 1541–1686; Buda (Pest almost destroyed earlier) retaken from Turks by Charles of Lorraine 1686; became free imperial city; in 1848–49 both towns disturbed by nationalistic revolt, Pest (which in 18th cent. had outstripped Buda) becoming capital of Kossuth's revolutionary government (see HUNGARY); capital of Hungary under Dual Monarchy 1867 (see AUSTRIA-HUNGARY);

united as Budapest 1872; center of revolt for independence of Hungary 1918; occupied by Romanians in war against government of Béla Kun 1919. In World War II an aircraft and supply center for German forces; bombed 1944–45 by U.S. Air Force and Buda badly damaged; taken by Russians Feb. 13, 1945 after long bitter fighting.

Bu·daun′ (bōō·doun′). Town, NW cen. Uttar Pradesh, N India, 123 m. ESE of Delhi; pop. 52,077; founded ab. 905 A.D.; has ruins of old fort and a splendid mosque converted in 13th cent. from an ancient Hindu temple by Altamsh, King of Delhi; became British 1801.

Budd Coast (bŭd′). Mountainous section of Antarctica coast, 67°S, S of Perth, Australia bet., 110°30′E and 114°E.; part of Wilkes Land and part of Australian claim.

Buddh Ga·ya′ (bŏŏd′ gå·yä′). Village, cen. Bihar state, NE Indian Union, 7 m. S of Gaya. One of the holiest sites of Buddhism; here Gautama Buddha is said to have experienced his Enlightenment under the sacred Bo Tree. A temple and other structures built on the site have been destroyed and a rebuilt temple devoted to Vishnu now marks the place.

Bud′don Ness (bŭd′′n nĕs′). Headland on E cen. coast of Scotland, at N entrance to Firth of Tay; lighthouse.

Bude (būd). Village, N Cornwall, England, SW of Bideford on **Bude Bay**; summer resort.

Budějovice, České. See ČESKÉ BUDĚJOVICE.

Budge′–Budge′ (bŭj′bŭj′). Town, West Bengal, NE India, on Hooghly river WSW of Calcutta; pop. 24,183.

Budissin. See BAUTZEN city.

Bu′dri·o (bōō′drĕ·ŏ). Commune, Bologna prov., Emilia, N Italy, 10 m. E by N of Bologna; pop. 16,870.

Bu·drum′ (bōō·drōōm′). = BODRUM.

Budweis. See ČESKÉ BUDĚJOVICE.

Bu′e (bōō′å) *or* **Mag′gio·ra′sca** (mäd′jŏ·räs′kä) **Mon′te** (mŏn′tå). Highest mountain in the Ligurian Apennines. See APENNINES.

Bu·e′a *or* **Bu·ë′a** (bōō·ā′å). Town, W Cameroun, near the coast at foot of Cameroon Mt., connected by highway with its port Victoria; formerly ✳ of British Cameroons trust territory and before 1919 ✳ of German Cameroons (Kamerun).

Bued (bwād). River ab. 35 m. long, NW Luzon, Phil. Is.; rises on the plateau of Baguio and flows SW through Benguet and Pangasinan to Lingayen Gulf near Mangaldan.

Buen Aire. See BONAIRE.

Bue′na Park (bwā′nå). City, Orange co., California, W of Anaheim; pop. 46,401.

Bue′na·ven·tu′ra (bwā′nä·vän·tōō′rä; *Angl.* bwĕn′å·vĕn·tŏŏr′å). Important Pacific port, Valle dept., W Colombia, 210 m. W of Bogotá on Chocó Bay; pop. 14,515; has steamer connections with Panama and is terminus of railroads in W Colombia; exports coffee, gold, and platinum.

Bue′na Vis′ta (bū′nå vĭs′tå). **1** County in Iowa. See *Table* at IOWA. **2** City, ⊗ of Marion co., W Georgia; pop. 1574. **3** City, W cen. Virginia, in Rockbridge co. but politically independent, 25 m. NW of Lynchburg; 3 sq. m.; pop. 6300; manufactures paper, silk, brick, flour; tannery.

Bue′na Vis′ta (bwā′nä vēs′tä). **1** Mountain 10,820 ft., S Costa Rica. **2** Battlefield near Saltillo, Coahuila state, NE Mexico; defeat of Santa Anna by U.S. forces under Zachary Taylor Feb. 1847 ended northern campaign in Mexican War. **3** See VATILAU, Solomon Is.

Bue′na Vis′ta Lake *or* **Reservoir** (bū′nå vĭs′tå). Reservoir, SW of Bakersfield, in Kern co., S California, into which the lower course of the Kern river flows.

Bue′na Vis′ta Peak (bū′nå vĭs′tå). Mountain 9692 ft. in Sierra Nevada, E Mariposa co., cen. California; in S part of Yosemite National Park.

Bue′nos Ai′res (bwā′nŭs âr′ĕz; bō′nŭs; ĭ′rĕz; *Span.* bwä′nôs ĭ′räs). **1** Province of Argentina. See *Table* at ARGENTINA.

2 See LA PLATA viceroyalty.

3 City, ✳ of Argentina and itself constituting the Federal District or Capital, on estuary of the Río de la Plata, E Argentina, ab. 130 m. from the sea; pop. (1943 est.) 2,457,494, including suburban pop. of Flores and Belgrano. Largest city in the world S of the equator and third largest in Western Hemisphere; on level plain, connected by many railroads with all parts of Argentina; laid out regularly with wide streets and many plazas; fine Capitol and government buildings, cathedral, opera house, art gallery, museums, and many churches; university (1821). Shallow port but highly developed; exports meat, grain, hides, wool, dairy products.

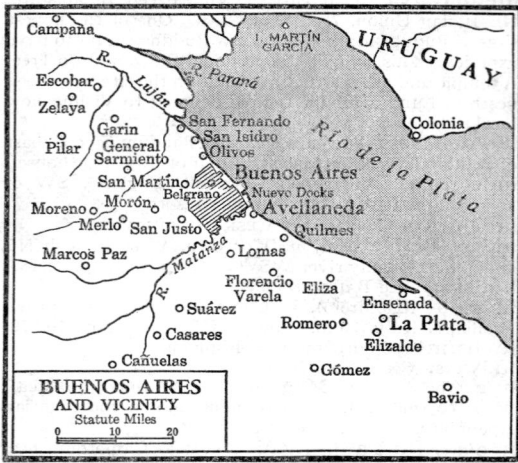

BUENOS AIRES
AND VICINITY
Statute Miles
0   10   20

History: First colonized by Pedro de Mendoza 1536 as Santa María del Buen Aire; not permanently settled until 1580; capital of subordinate division of viceroyalty of Peru, it became in 1776 the seat of viceroyalty of La Plata (*q.v.*) or Buenos Aires; blockaded by British in dispute over intervention in Uruguay 1845; drew up constitution separate from provinces in 1854 and began intermittent conflict with them over control of government of Argentina; erection into federal district, as capital of Argentina but separate from province of Buenos Aires, settled war with provinces 1880; seat of Pan-American Congresses 1910, 1936.

Buenos Aires, Lake. Lake 75 m. long in SE Chile, on the Chile-Argentina boundary.

Buenos Aires, Point. Cape on NW point of Váldez Penin., enclosing Gulf of San José, NE coast of Chubut territory, S Argentina.

Buer (boor; *Ger.* boor). Former city, Münster govt. dist., Westphalia prov., Prussia, Germany; pop. (1925) 99,058; became part of Gelsenkirchen (*q.v.*) in 1928.

Bu·et′, Mont (môn′ bü·ĕ′). Peak 10,200 ft. in the Pennine Alps, E Haute-Savoie dept., E France.

Buey (bwĕ′ĕ; bwä). Cape on N coast of Tabasco state, SE Mexico, extending into the Bay of Campeche.

Bufarik. Var. of BOUFARIK.

Buf′fa·lo (bŭf′á·lō). **1** River ab. 100 m. long, W Tennessee; rises in N Lawrence co., flows W, then N into Duck river in cen. Humphreys co.

2 Name of counties in three states of the U.S. See *Tables* at NEBRASKA, SOUTH DAKOTA, WISCONSIN.

3 Village, ⊗ of Wright co., S cen. Minnesota, 31 m. WNW of Minneapolis; pop. 2322.

4 City, ⊗ of Dallas co., SW cen. Missouri; pop. 1477.

5 Residential, commercial, and industrial city and port, ⊗ of Erie co., W New York, at NE point of Lake Erie

and on Niagara river ab. 16 m. SE of Niagara Falls; pop. 532,759; W terminus of N.Y. State Barge Canal and E terminus of Great Lakes; connected with Fort Erie, Canada, by Peace Bridge (opened 1927) across Niagara river; point of departure for Niagara Falls; in agricultural and industrial area; railroad and distributing cen-

BUFFALO, NIAGARA FALLS
AND VICINITY
Statute Miles
0   5   10

ter; grain and coal elevators; railroad shops, meat-packing plants, lumber, livestock, and iron-ore industry; manufactures metal and machine-shop products, automobile parts, food products, chemicals, etc. Albright Art Gallery, Grosvenor Library. Canisius Coll. (1870; part coed.), New York State Coll. of Education (1867; coed.), D'Youville Coll. (1908; women), Univ. of Buffalo (1846; coed.). Settled by Indians 1780; site platted by Joseph Ellicott 1799; sold in lots 1803; incorporated 1810; military post in War of 1812; burned by British and Indians 1813; rebuilt 1814–15; incorporated as village 1816; became W terminus of Erie Canal (opened 1825); became city 1832; important station on Underground Railroad. Scene of Pan-American Exposition 1901 where President McKinley was assassinated.

6 Town, ⊗ of Harper co., NW Oklahoma; pop. 1618.

7 Town, Union co., NW South Carolina, ab. 3 m. W of Union; pop. 1209.

8 Town, ⊗ of Harding co., South Dakota, on Grand river 36 m. SE of NW corner of state; pop. 652.

9 City, ⊗ of Johnson co., N Wyoming, 33 m. S of Sheridan; pop. 2907; in livestock-raising section.

10 River ab. 50 m. long, SE Cape Province, Union of South Africa; flows SE past Kingwilliamstown to the Indian Ocean at East London.

Buffalo Bay. Inlet of Lake of the Woods in SE Manitoba, Canada; extends W from the American part of the lake.

Buf′fa·lo Bill Reservoir (bŭf′á·lō bĭl′). Reservoir at Shoshone Dam, Wyoming. See UNITED STATES, *Dams and Reservoirs.*

Buffalo Fork. River ab. 120 m. long, N Arkansas; rises in SW Newton co., N Arkansas, flows E and NE into White river on SE boundary of Marion co., N cen. Arkansas.

Buffalo National Park. See CANADA, *National Parks.*

Buffalo Peaks. Mountain 13,541 ft. in Chaffee and Park cos., cen. Colorado.

Bu′ford (bū′fẽrd). City, Gwinnett co., N Georgia, 35 m. NE of Atlanta; pop. 4168; trading center; tannery.

Bug (bŏŏg; *Pol.* bŏŏk). River over 450 m. long, cen. Poland; rises in W Ukraine U.S.S.R., flows N to Brest, turns W and NW into Poland to the Vistula river 18 m. NW of Warsaw; navigable below Brest. In World War I several battles fought along its course in 1915. About 200 m. of its central course formed part of the Curzon Line, laid down by the Supreme Council after World War I Dec. 1919 as Poland's eastern frontier; this same section included in the Russo-German boundary of 1939 and retained after World War II in the boundary bet. U.S.S.R. and Poland.

Bug (bŏŏg; *Russ.* bŏŏk); *anc.* **Hyp′a·nis** (hĭp′á·nĭs); *also known as* **Southern Bug**. River ab. 500 m. long, SW Ukraine, U.S.S.R.; rises in Kamenets Podolsk Region near former Polish border and flows SE to the Dnieper estuary; has many rapids and is not navigable above Voznesensk; largest tributary is the Ingul, which joins it at Nikolaev. In World War II crossed by Germans July 1941 and by Russians Mar. 15, 1944.

Bu′ga (bŏŏ′gä). City, Vallee dept., W Colombia; pop. 19,595; trading center for sugar, coffee, and cacao.

Bu·gan′da (bŭ·găn′dá; bŏŏ·gän′dä). Native kingdom, a province of SE Uganda, E Africa; ✳ Kampala; includes islands in N part of Lake Victoria.

Bu·ghai′la (bŏŏ·gī′lá; -lä). Town, Iraq, on the Tigris 25 m. W of Kut-el-Amara.

Bu·gul·ma′ (bŏŏ·gŏŏl·má′). Town, SE Tatar Republic, Soviet Russia, Europe, on Ulyanovsk-Ufa R.R. 160 m. SE of Kazan; pop. 8100.

Bu·gu·ru·slan′ (bŏŏ·gŏŏ·rŏŏ·slän′). Town, NW Chkalov Region, Soviet Russia, Europe, on railroad 95 m. NE of Kuibyshev; pop. ab. 19,000; on N bank of the Kinel river.

Bu′hi (bŏŏ′hē). Municipality, SE Camarines Sur prov., Luzon, Phil. Is., on S shore of **Lake Buhi** (10 m. long by 4 m. wide); pop. 22,391.

Buhl (būl). **1** City, Twin Falls co., S Idaho, 17 m. W of Twin Falls; pop. 3059; agricultural and dairy products. **2** Village, St. Louis co., NE Minnesota, 8 m. ENE of Hibbing; pop. 1526; iron mining.

Builth Wells (bĭlth′ wĕlz′). Town, N Brecknockshire, S cen. Wales, on the Wye 14 m. N of Brecknock; pop. 1708; spa, market town; notable in Welsh history, dating back to 11th cent.

Bu·in′ (bŏŏ·ēn′). Settlement at S end of Bougainville I., NW Solomon Islands, W Pacific Ocean; on Tonolai Harbour on Bougainville Strait N of Shortland Is. Held by Japanese as base and bypassed by Americans in conquest of the Solomon Is. 1942–43.

Bui·naksk′ (bŏŏ·ĭ·näksk′); *formerly* **Te′mir–Khan–Shu·ra′** (tĕ′mĭr·ĸän·shŏŏ·rä′). Town, N cen. Dagestan, SE Soviet Russia, Europe, on branch railroad 25 m. WSW of Makhachkala; pop. 15,897; has large fruit-preserving works.

Buir Nor. See BOR NOR.

Buitengewesten. See OUTER PROVINCES.

Bui′ten·zorg (boi′tĕn·zôrĸ). **1** Former residency, W cen. West Java prov., Neth. Indies; 4484 sq. m.; pop. 2,212,997; ✳ Buitenzorg; included former West Preanger residency. In N of this area are mountains of central range of Java (see SALAK and GEDE); produces tea and coꞌfee, rice, sugar, and rubber. **2** *now* **Bo′gor** (bŏ′gôr). City, 36 m. S of Djakarta; pop. 65,431; summer ✳; palace, formerly residence of the governor general; at elevation of ab. 870 ft.; magnificent mountain scenery; notable botanical garden (founded 1817) with more than 10,000 kinds of plants. Town founded 1745.

Bu′ja·lan′ce (bŏŏ′hä·län′thä; -sä). Commune, Córdoba prov., S Spain, 23 m. E of Córdoba; pop. 15,728; manufactures textiles, tile, chinaware, flour; ruins of 10th-cent. Moorish castle.

Buj·nurd′ (bŏŏj·nŏŏrd′). Town in mountains of N Khurasan prov., NE Iran; pop. ab. 8000.

Bujumbura. See USUMBURA.

Bu′ka (bŏŏ′ká). One of the Solomon Islands just N of Bougainville I. (*q.v.*) and separated from it by **Buka Passage**, containing excellent anchorage; 190 sq. m.; pop. (1930) 7560; with Bougainville and adjacent small islands forms Kieta district of the Territory of New Guinea. Mostly level with mangrove swamps and some forest and grassland regions. Best anchorage is Queen Carola Harbour. Held by Japanese in World War II but by-passed by U.S. forces Feb. 1944.

Buka′a. See El BIKA.

Bu·ka′ma (bŏŏ·kä′má). Town, S cen. Katanga, SE Republic of the Congo; trading town on navigable Lualaba river.

Bukavu. See COSTERMANSVILLE.

Bu·kha′ra *or* **Bo·kha′ra** (bŏŏ·kär′á, bŏ-; -kär′á; *Persian* bŏŏ·kä·rä′; *Russ.* bŏŏ·ká′rá, bŏŏ·kŭ·rá′). **1** Former emirate occupying region around city of Bukhara, W Asia; later, a state in Russian Central Asia. In early times region known as Sogdiana and Transoxiana (*qq.v.*). Ruled effectively by Moslem Arabs from c. 710 A.D.; built up into powerful Islamic kingdom by Samanids (874–999); as capital of Samanid realm, which included territory from Baghdad to borders of India and from Bukhara to Persian Gulf, became intellectual center of Islam and wealthy mart for trade of central Asia; destroyed by Genghis Khan 1219; under various dynasties, the prize of Mongols, Turks, Uzbeks (see TURKISTAN), and others; in 19th cent., its emir controlled khanates of Kokand and Khiva; conquered 1866–68 and made a Russian protectorate; proclaimed a Soviet republic 1920; since 1924 has formed part of Uzbek S.S.R. (*q.v.*). **2** City, W Uzbek S.S.R., E of the Amu Darya and ab. 140 m. W of Samarkand; pop. 50,382; chief city of emirate and of Russian state; has many mosques and minarets and was once second only to Mecca as a holy place of Islam; long a training center for Moslem priests.

Bu·kid′non (bŏŏ·kĭd′nŏn; bŏŏ·kēd′nŏn). Province, N Mindanao, Phil. Is.; 3104 sq. m.; pop. 57,561; ✳ Malaybalay. Mountainous and plateau region with no coast line; highest point Mt. Katanglad, in W cen. part, 7804 ft.; in N many short streams flowing N and NW to Gingoog and Macajalar Bays; largest stream is the Pulangi in E and S forming the upper course of the Rio Grande de Mindanao. Has fertile soil esp. suitable for grazing; chief crops corn, coffee, hemp (abacá), rice, and camotes. Inhabitants are mainly Bukidnons, with some Manobos and Moros. Malaybalay and Talakag are the only municipalities of any size. Region never adequately explored until recent years; since ab. 1850 a part of Misamis and in 1901 erected as a subprovince; from 1907 to 1914 a subprovince of Agusan.

Bukittinggi. See FORT DE KOCK.

Bukn Fjord. See BOKN FJORD.

Bu·ko′ba (bŏŏ·kō′bá). **1** Former province in N Tanganyika, E Africa, now part of Lake prov. **2** Town on W shore of Lake Victoria, Lake province, NW Tanganyika, E Africa; coffee plantations.

Bukovina. See BUCOVINA.

Bul, Kuh–i– (kŏŏ′hē·bŏŏl′). Mountain 13,009 ft. in SW cen. Iran, 175 m. NE of Bushire.

Bu′la·can′ (bŏŏ′lä·kän′). **1** Province, cen. Luzon, Phil. Is.; 1021 sq. m.; pop. 332,807; ✳ Malolos. Western part is in central Luzon plain; hills and mountains in the E, highest Mt. Oryod in SE 3838 ft. Watered by the Angat, a large tributary of the Pampanga; delta of the latter covers a large area of swampy land in SW along shore of Manila Bay. Principal crops corn, rice, sugar, fruit. Chief towns Malolos, Hagonoy, San Miguel.

History: Had large towns before coming of the Spanish; one of earliest provinces created by them 1578; was center of opposition to British 1762–63; increased in population and trade during following century; scene of several notable events of Revolution of 1897 (see

BIACNABATO and MALOLOS); civil government established by Americans Feb. 1901. In World War II taken by Japanese Jan. 1942 but recovered Jan.–Feb. 1945.
2 Municipality, SW Bulacan prov., 7 m. SE of Malolos; pop. 11,931; former capital of the province.

Bulama. See BOLAMA.

Bu′lan (bōō′län). Municipality, SW Sorsogon prov., Luzon, Phil. Is., port on Ticao Pass 22 m. SSW of Sorsogon; pop. 29,414; largest town in province.

Bu′land·shahr′ (bōō·lŭnd·shär′; native bōō·lŭnd·shŭ′-h′r). Town, W Uttar Pradesh, N India, on Kali Nadi river 45 m. ESE of Delhi; pop. 24,898; taken over by British in 1803.

Bu·laq′ or **Bu·lak′** (bōō·läk′). Port of Cairo, Egypt, located on the Nile; now part of Cairo; pop. ab. 112,000; originally site of museum (now in Cairo) founded 1863 by the French Egyptologist Mariette.

Bu′la·wa′yo or **Bu′lu·wa′yo** (bōō′lŭ·wä′yō). Town, SW Southern Rhodesia, S Africa, 380 m. N of Pretoria; chief town of Matabeleland; pop. (1962 est.) 210,900, including suburbs; founded 1893; important railroad center and trade headquarters for vast grazing area; gold and coal found in region.

Bul·dir′ (?bōōl·dîr′). Rocky islet in W Aleutian Is., in channel bet. Kiska on E and Near Is. on W.

Buldur. See BURDUR.

Buleleng. See BOELELENG.

Bul′gar Dağ′la·ri′ (bōōl′gär dä′lä·rï′). Range in the Taurus Mts., S Turkey in Asia; highest peak Ardost 11,444 ft. Cf. CILICIAN GATES.

Bul·gar′i·a (bŭl·gâr′ï·à; bōōl-); Bulgarian **Bl·ga′ri·ya** (bŭl·gä′rĕ·yä). Republic, SE Europe, bounded on N by Romania, on E by Black Sea, on SE by Turkey, on S by Greece, and on W by Yugoslavia; 42,858 sq. m.; pop. (1959) 7,798,000, (1963 est.) 8,100,000; ✳ Sofia. Crossed in cen. part by Balkan Mts. (locally, the Stara Planina) 3500 to 7800 ft.; in SW and S by Rhodope range; highest point Mt. Musala 9595 ft.; surface varied in plateau,

plain, and river valley regions. *Chief rivers:* Maritsa, flowing E into Turkey, and its tributary the Tundzha; Struma and Mesta in SW flowing S into Greece; Danube, forming most of N boundary with Romania. *Chief products:* Cereals, cotton, sugar, tobacco, considerable livestock; also silk and attar of roses. *Chief towns:* Sofia, Plovdiv, Varna, Ruse, Burgas, Pleven.

History: For earlier history of Bulgarian territory, see MOESIA and THRACE. Invaded by Bulgars, a Ural-Altaic people who in 6th cent. A.D. lived bet. Don and Caucasus and in 7th cent. settled in Bessarabia, crossed Danube, became Slavicized, and founded first organized Slavic power in Balkans; soon after baptism of King Boris 865, joined Greek Church; powerful under Tsar Simeon (893–927) who introduced Byzantine culture; invaded by Russians and Byzantines 967–972; western part erected by Samuel (976–1014) into new state but lost independence 1014; part of Byzantine Empire 1018–1185; under Asen family, built second Bulgarian Empire 1185–1366; part of Ottoman Empire from Turkish conquest (1369–72) to 20th cent.; revived nationalism in 19th cent.; premature rising in 1876 caused "massacres" by Turks which made Bulgarian problem a European concern; at close of Russo-Turkish War (1877–78), autonomous Bulgarian principality (including most of Macedonia) erected by Treaty of San Stefano; divided by Congress of Berlin which returned Macedonia to Turkey and set up autonomous Eastern Rumelia 1878; annexed Eastern Rumelia 1885 thereby invoking war with Serbia; under Prince Ferdinand, reconciled with Russia 1896; declared complete independence from Turkey 1908; took a leading part in First Balkan War and, because of increased territory, caused Second Balkan War (see BALKAN STATES); forced to cede Dobruja to Romania and most of Macedonia to Serbia, Greece, and Turkey 1913; entered World War I on side of Central Powers 1915; by Treaty of Neuilly (see NEUILLY-SUR-SEINE) lost position on Aegean seaboard

BULGARIA
Statute Miles
0 10 20 30 40 50 60

1919; by pact with Yugoslavia 1937, began to co-operate with Balkan powers; recovered southern Dobruja from Romania 1940; signed Axis pact 1941; taken over by Germany; invaded by Russia Sept. 8, 1944; proclaimed Bulgarian People's Republic Sept. 15, 1946.

Bul'har (bo͞ ol'här). Seaport town, N Somalia, E Africa, on Gulf of Aden 40 m. W of Berbera; pop. ab. 7000.

Bulk'ley (bŭlk'lĭ). River ab. 130 m. long, W cen. British Columbia, Canada, E of Bulkley Mts.; flows N into Skeena river.

Bulkley Mountains. Range of the Coast Mts., W cen. British Columbia, Canada, W of Babine Mts.

Bul'lard's Bar Dam (bo͞ ol'ĕrdz bär'). Dam completed 1924 across N fork of Yuba river, N Yuba co., N cen. California; height 199 ft.; impounds water, **Bullard's Bar Reservoir,** for water power.

Bul'le·court' (bül'ko͞ or'). Village, Pas-de-Calais dept., N France, 9 m. SE of Arras; pop. 281; battles 1917–18, esp. six weeks of severe fighting May–June 1917.

Bul'ler (bo͞ ol'ĕr). River 105 m. long, N South Island, New Zealand; flows W to Tasman Sea.

Buller, Mount. Mountain 5911 ft. at W end of Great Dividing Range, E Victoria, Australia.

Bul'lers of Buch'an (bo͞ ol'ĕrz; bŭk'ăn, *Scot.* bŭĸ'-). Basin ab. 200 ft. deep and 50 ft. wide in rocky coast of Buchan region, NE Aberdeen co., Scotland, 6 m. S of Peterhead.

Bull Hill (bo͞ ol). Peak 13,773 ft. in Lake co., cen. Colorado.

Bul'litt (bo͞ ol'ĭt). County in Kentucky. See *Table* at KENTUCKY.

Bul'loch (bo͞ ol'ŭk). County in Georgia. See *Table* at GEORGIA.

Bul'lock (bo͞ ol'ŭk). County in Alabama. See *Table* at ALABAMA.

Bull Point (bo͞ ol). Cape on extreme NW point of Devonshire, SW England, S of entrance to Bristol Channel; lighthouse.

Bull Run (bo͞ ol' rŭn'). Stream, NE Virginia; runs SE and forms boundary bet. Fairfax and Prince William cos., E of Manassas, and empties into Potomac river; scene of Civil War battles (1) July 21, 1861 in which Federal leader Gen. Irvin McDowell was defeated by Confederate generals J. E. Johnston and P. G. T. Beauregard, and (2) Aug. 29–30, 1862 in which Gen. Lee defeated Federal forces under Gen. John Pope. Both battles called Manassas by Confederates; a phase of second battle also known as battle of Groveton.

Bulls Bay (bo͞ olz). Inlet of Atlantic Ocean on NE coast of Charleston co., SE South Carolina; enclosed on SW by **Bulls Island.**

Bu·lo'lo (bo͞ o-lō'lō). 1 River, an upper tributary of the Markham river, forming **Bulolo Valley,** part of the Morobe gold fields of SE North-East New Guinea, high in the mountains W of Huon Gulf.
2 Mining town on the Bulolo river.

Bul·sar' *or* **Bal·sar'** (bŭl·sär'). Seaport town, S Gujerat state, W India, 115 m. N Bombay; pop. 19,481; in early days of East India Company an important trading center.

Bul·sha'ia. Var. of *Bolshaya:* see Mount McKINLEY.

Bu·lu'an (bo͞ o-lo͞ o'än). Town (municipal district), E cen. Cotabato prov., Mindanao, Phil. Is., near **Lake Buluan** (24 sq. m.); pop. 15,724.

Bu'lun (bo͞ o'lo͞ on). Village on W bank of Lena river near its mouth, N Yakutsk Republic, Soviet Russia, Asia, in coal-bearing region.

Bu·lu'san (bo͞ o-lo͞ o'sän). Volcano 5118 ft., 5 m. inland, S cen. Sorsogon prov., Luzon, Phil. Is. Visible 60 m. at sea and a landmark for ships in San Bernardino Strait; last eruption 1852.

Buluwayo. See BULAWAYO.

Bum'ba (bo͞ om'bä). Town, Equator prov., Congo, on Congo river at its N point; airport.

Bu'na (bo͞ o'nä). Village on Holnicote Bay, N coast of E Papua, New Guinea I.; formerly port for shipment of gold from inland gold fields; after Japanese landings here and at Gona July 1942, used as base for attacks on Port Moresby; captured by Allied forces Jan. 18–20, 1943.

Bun'bur·y (bŭn'bĕr·ĭ). Port, SW Western Australia, on Geographe Bay about 110 m. S of Perth; pop. 5139; outlet for timber and farming region.

Bun'combe (bŭng'kŭm). County in North Carolina. See *Table* at NORTH CAROLINA.

Bun·cra'na (bŭn·krä'nä). Urban district, NE co. Donegal, N Eire, on E shore of Lough Swilly; pop. 2295.

Bun'da·berg (bŭn'dä·bûrg). Seaport town, E Queensland, Australia, on Burnett river 10 m. from Pacific Ocean and 200 m. N of Brisbane; pop. 11,466.

Bun'del·khand (bo͞ on'dĕl·kŭnd). Formerly, one of the chief agency divisions, in E part of Central India Agency, India; 10,081 sq. m.; pop. 1,289,015; ✳ Nowgong (in Chhatarpur state). Consisted of 9 states (most important Orchha) and 13 estates. An uneven country of hills and plains; became subject c. 1500 to Delhi and to Marathas; rights transferred to the British by treaty 1817.

Bunder Abbas. Var. of BANDAR ABBAS.

Bun'di (bo͞ on'dĭ). 1 Former Indian state in Eastern Rajputana States, NW India, in SE part of Rajputana; 2205 sq. m.; pop. (1941) 249,374; founded about 1342, it came under British protection by treaty in 1818. On June 26, 1947 became a part of Rajasthan.
2 Town, its ✳, 95 m. SE of Ajmer; pop. 17,991.

Bu Ngem (bo͞ on' gĕm'). Village at road junction, NW Libya, N Africa, 90 m. SW of Sirte.

Bun·go Strait *or* **Channel** (bo͞ on·gô); *formerly* **Haya·su·i Strait** (hä·yä·so͞ o·ē). Channel 20 to 25 m. wide NE of Kyushu, Japan, separating it from Shikoku.

Bun'ker Hill (bŭng'kĕr). Height in Charlestown, Boston, Mass.; battle June 17, 1775 on adjacent **Breed's Hill** (brēdz), where Bunker Hill monument now stands.

Bun'kie (bŭng'kĭ). Town, Avoyelles parish, cen. Louisiana, 28 m. SSE of Alexandria; pop. 5188; cottonseed-oil mills.

Bun'na·be'o·la (bŭn'ä·bē'ô·lä), **Twelve Pins,** *or* **Bens** (bĕnz), **of.** Mountain group in Connemara, W co. Galway, W Ireland; highest peak **Ben·baun'** (bĕn·bôn') 2395 ft.

Bun·nell' (bŭ·nĕl'). City, ⊗ of Flagler co., NE Florida; pop. 1860.

Bun'ting (bŭn'tĭng). Island in Andaman Sea off NW coast of Kedah state, W side of Malay Penin.

Bunyoro. See NORTHERN PROVINCE.

Bun'zel·witz (bo͞ on'zĕl·vĭts); *Pol.* **Bo'le·sła·wi'ce** (bô'lĕ·slä·vē'tsĕ). Village, formerly in Silesia, Prussia, Germany, now in Wrocław dept., SW Poland, 7 m. N of Świdnica; battle 1761 bet. forces of Frederick the Great and combined Austrian and Russian forces.

Bunzlau. See BOLESŁAWIEC.

Bu'or Kha'ya (bo͞ o'ôr kä'yä) *or* **Bor·kha'ya** (bôr·kä'yä). Cape, N Yakutsk A.S.S.R., Soviet Russia, Asia, extending into Laptev Sea at 133°20′E, just E of the Lena delta, and marking NE point of **Buor Khaya Gulf.**

Buq'buq (bo͞ ok'bo͞ ok). Coastal village, NW Egypt, E of Salûm and W of Sidi Barrâni; fighting in World War II North African campaigns, esp. Dec. 1940.

Bu·rai'da (bo͞ o·rī'dä; -rä'-; -dä). Town, Qasim prov., N cen. Nejd, Arabia; pop. ab. 20,000; has extensive palm groves; important commercially.

Bu·ra'no (bo͞ o·rä'nô). Island and village in the Lagoon of Venice, NE Italy, ab. 5 m. NE of Venice; part of Venice commune.

Bu·ra'o (bo͞ o·rä'ð). Town, N Somalia, E Africa, on caravan route ab. 80 m. SSE of Berbera; pop. ab. 10,000.

Bu·ra'uen (bo͞ o·rä'wän). Municipality, cen. Leyte I., Phil. Is., W of Dulag and 21 m. SW of Tacloban; pop. 33,505; at foot of central mountain range and near sulfur deposits. Captured by Americans Oct. 25, 1944 after severe fighting; airfield.

Bur'bank (bûr'băngk). City, Los Angeles co., SW California, 10 m. NW of Los Angeles; pop. 90,155; airport terminal; airplane factories.

Bur'de·kin (bûr'dĕ·kĭn). River 425 m. long, E Queensland, Australia; flows SE from Eastern Highlands and after junction with Belyando flows N and E to Pacific Ocean.

Burdigala. See BORDEAUX.

Bur·dur' (bŏŏr·dŏŏr') or **Bul·dur'** (bŏŏl·dŏŏr'). **1** Vilayet, SW Turkey in Asia; 2553 sq. m.; pop. 111,400. **2** Town, its ✳, 2 m. SE of Lake Burdur, in hills (alt. 3150 ft.) and on railroad to Antalya; pop. 13,424.

Burdur, Lake; *Turk.* **Burdur Gö·lü'** (gû·lü'). Lake in SW Turkey in Asia, SW of Eğridir Lake.

Bur·dwan' or **Bar·dwan'** (bûr·dwän'). **1** Division, formerly in SW Bengal, since Aug. 1947 the larger part of West Bengal, NE Indian Union; 14,135 sq. m.; pop. (1941) 10,287,369.

2 Town, Burdwan division, on Damodar river 70 m. NNW of Calcutta; pop. (1941) 62,910; has numerous temples and fine palace; headquarters of the Maharajadhiraj Bahadur of Burdwan, head of an important Bengal house.

Bure. See the BROADS.

Bu'reau (bûr'ō). County in Illinois. See *Table* at ILLINOIS.

Burem. See BOUREM.

Bu·re'ya (bŭ·rā'à; *Russ.* bŏŏ·ryĕ'yà). River 480 m. long, a N tributary of the Amur in S Khabarovsk Territory, Soviet Russia, Asia; flows SW to the Amur below Blagoveshchensk.

Burg (bŏŏrK). **1** *also* **Burg bei Mag'de·burg** (bī mäk'dĕ·bŏŏrK) or **Burg an der Ih'le** (än dĕr ē'lĕ). City, E Germany, formerly in Saxony province, Prussia, on Ihle Canal near Elbe river 12 m. NE of Magdeburg; pop. 24,406; leather goods, iron, machinery, furniture. **2** Chief town on Fehmarn I. See FEHMARN.

Bur·gas' (bŏŏr·gäs'). **1** Department, SE Bulgaria; 5258 sq. m.; pop. (1934) 554,947.

2 Seaport, its ✳, on the Gulf of Burgas; pop. (1934) 36,230; terminal of railroad to Sofia; exports grain, iron ore, wine, and butter.

Burgas, Gulf of. Inlet of the Black Sea on the central part of the coast of Bulgaria.

Bur'gaw (bûr'gô). Town, ⊗ of Pender co., SE North Carolina; pop. 1750.

Burg'dorf (bŏŏrK'dôrf). Commune, Bern canton, Switzerland, on Emme river ab. 11 m. NE of Bern; pop. (1941) 10,197; has a castle dating from 11th cent.; Pestalozzi principal of a school here 1799–1804.

Bur'gen·land (bŏŏr'gĕn·länt). Province, E Austria, on Hungarian border in foothills of the Alps and on edge of the Hungarian plain; area 1529 sq. m.; pop. 275,911; ✳ Eisenstadt; includes northern two thirds of Neusiedler Lake; before 1919 part of Hungary; by Treaties of Saint-Germain and Grand Trianon entire region was to be transferred to Austria but on Hungary's objection, a plebiscite was held Dec. 1921 and all but Sopron transferred Feb. 1922; as part of German Ostmark, absorbed by Styria. Occupied by Russians Apr. 1945 in World War II.

Bur'gess Hill (bûr'jĕs; -jĭs). Urban district, East Sussex, S England; pop. 8524.

Bur'getts·town (bûr'gĕts·toun). Borough, Washington co., SW Pennsylvania, 24 m. W of Pittsburgh; pop. 2383; zinc, coal, molybdenum industries.

Bur'ghers·dorp (bûr'gĕrz·dôrp). Town, NE Cape Province, S Union of South Africa, 70 m. NNW of Queenstown; pop. 4855; health resort.

Bürg'len (bür'glĕn). Village, Uri canton, Switzerland, near SE tip of Lake Lucerne SE of Altdorf; legendary birthplace of William Tell.

Bur'gos (bŏŏr'gŏs). **1** Province of Spain. See *Table* at SPAIN.

2 City, its ✳, N cen. Spain, 132 m. N of Madrid; pop.

(1941 est.) 60,328; manufactures woolens, paper, chocolates; noted for its old buildings, among them castle of counts of Castile and esp. the cathedral (1221), one of most noted examples of Gothic architecture in Europe; home and burial place of the Cid. Founded 884; made capital of Old Castile; to 1560 a royal residence and capital of kingdom of León and Castile.

Bur'gun·dy (bûr'gŭn·dĭ); *Fr.* **Bour'gogne'** (bŏŏr'gôn'y'). Region of varying limits in E Gaul and pre-Revolutionary France. Name was originally applied to a kingdom in Rhone valley and W Switzerland (see GENEVA) founded by a Germanic people, the Burgundians, who fled from Germany in early 5th cent. It was conquered by the Merovingians c. 500 and incorporated into the Frankish empire; in division of Carolingian empire by the Treaty of Verdun 843, included in Middle Kingdom (see LORRAINE) of Lothair I; region later divided into the kingdoms of Cisjurane (Lower) Burgundy or Provence, founded 879, and Transjurane (Upper) Burgundy, founded 888, which united 933 to form the kingdom of Burgundy or Arles (*q.v.*). After absorption of Arles by Holy Roman Empire 1033, the name was retained in the Free County of Burgundy or Franche-Comté (*q.v.*) and especially in the duchy of Burgundy which was formed in 9th cent. from lands in NW part of original kingdom S of 48th parallel chiefly bet. Saône and Loire rivers. On death of Philippe de Rouvre 1361, the duchy escheated to French Crown; given as appanage by King John II to his 4th son, Philip the Bold; passed in direct succession to John the Fearless, Philip the Good, and Charles the Bold, before whose death in 1477, the Burgundian house had controlled Nivernais, Franche-Comté, Lorraine (*qq.v.*), and Low Countries; seized from Charles's daughter, Duchess Mary of Burgundy, by King Louis XI and annexed to French Crown; a province until the Revolution.

Bur·han'pur (bŏŏr·hän'pŏŏr). Town, N Maharashtra state, cen. India, on the Tapti river S of Khandwa and 185 m. W of Nagpur; pop. (1941) 53,987; known for its brocades, gold and silver embroideries, flowered silks, and gold wire; a walled city of the Moguls, founded 1400, and for several centuries capital of independent Mohammedan princes; later the capital of the Deccan under the Mogul of Delhi; captured 1803 by British but not retained; ceded to British in 1861.

Bu'rias (bŏŏ'ryäs). Island 43 m. long just SE of Luzon, Phil. Is.; 164 sq. m.; pop. 4469; forms part of Masbate prov. Long narrow mountainous island, N of Masbate and separated from Luzon on NE by Burias Pass; on NE border of Sibuyan Sea.

Burias Pass. Channel ab. 12 m. wide bet. E Burias I. and the mainland of SE Luzon, Phil. Is.

Buriat, or **Buriat–Mongolian, A.S.S.R.** See BURYAT-MONGOL AUTONOMOUS SOVIET SOCIALIST REPUBLIC.

Bu·ri'ca, Point (bŏŏ·rē'kä). Cape on S extremity of Costa Rica, on boundary with Panama, extending S into Pacific Ocean.

Bu'rin (bûr'ĭn). Fishing town, S Newfoundland, on W shore of Placentia Bay at its mouth; pop. 796; has landlocked harbor; extensive fisheries.

Bu·ri·ram (bŏŏ·rē·räm); *also* **Pu·ri·ram·ya** (bŏŏ·rē·räm—*sic.*). **1** Province, SE Thailand; 3703 sq. m.; pop. 241,410.

2 Town, its ✳, 65 m. E of Nakhon Ratchasima.

Burkatów. See BURKERSDORF.

Burk'bur·nett' (bûrk'bĕr·nĕt'; *earlier* bûrk·bûr'nĕt, -nĭt). City, Wichita co., N Texas, near Red river 15 m. N of Wichita Falls; pop. 7621; livestock, oil wells.

Burke (bûrk). **1** Name of counties in three states of the U.S. See *Tables* at GEORGIA, NORTH CAROLINA, NORTH DAKOTA.

2 City, ⊗ of Gregory co., S South Dakota; pop. 811.

Burke Channel. Inlet of Pacific Ocean, ab. 45 m. long, W British Columbia, Canada; ab. 52°N.

Burke Mountain. Peak 3500 ft. on boundary bet. Caledonia and Essex cos., NE Vermont.

Bur′kers·dorf (bŏŏr′kĕrs-dôrf); *Pol.* **Bur·ka′tów** (bŏŏr·kä′tŏŏf). Village, S Wrocław dept., SW Poland; formerly in Silesia, Germany; battle July 21, 1762 in which Frederick the Great defeated the Austrians under Daun.

Burkes′ville (bûrks′vĭl; *Sou. also* -v′l). City, ⊗ of Cumberland co., S Kentucky; pop. 1688.

Bur′kett, Mount (bûr′kĕt; -kĭt). Mountain 9600 ft. near Alaska-Brit. Columbia boundary, SE Alaska. 30 m. N of Wrangell.

Bur′leigh (bûr′lĭ). County in North Dakota. See *Table* at NORTH DAKOTA.

Bur′le·son (bûr′lĕ·s′n). County in Texas. See *Table* at TEXAS.

Bur′ley (bûr′lĭ). City, ⊗ of Cassia co. S Idaho, on Snake river 38 m. E of Twin Falls; pop. 7508; beet-sugar factory; flour mill; shipping point for wheat, potatoes, and livestock.

Bur′lin·game (bûr′lĭn·gām; -lĭng·gām). Residential city, San Mateo co., W California, on W shore of San Francisco Bay 10 m. S of San Francisco; pop. 24,036.

Bur′ling·ton (bûr′lĭng·tŭn). **1** County in New Jersey. See *Table* at NEW JERSEY.

2 Town, ⊗ of Kit Carson co., E Colorado; pop. 2090.

3 Town, W Hartford co., N Connecticut; pop. 2790; settled 1780, incorp. 1806; trout hatchery; Nepaug State Forest nearby.

4 City, ⊗ of Des Moines co., SE Iowa, on Mississippi river; pop. 32,430; settled 1829 on the site of an Indian village; incorporated as town 1837; temporary seat of government of Iowa Territory 1838; now a railroad and industrial center; manufactures iron and iron products, soap, furniture, buttons.

5 City, ⊗ of Coffey co., E Kansas, 28 m. SE of Emporia; pop. 2113; oil field nearby.

6 Town, ⊗ of Boone co., N Kentucky; pop. (est.) 350.

7 Town, Middlesex co., NE Massachusetts, 11 m. SSE of Lowell; pop. 12,852; in agricultural section.

8 City, Burlington co., S cen. New Jersey, on Delaware river 11 m. SSW of Trenton; pop. 12,687; shipping point for farm and dairy products and fruit; manufactures iron pipe, artificial hair, artificial limbs, silk, clothing, architectu·al millwork. Settled by Quakers 1677; became capital of West Jersey and port of entry 1681; alternated with Perth Amboy (*q.v.*) as provincial capital after union of East and West Jersey in 1702; invaded by Hessians 1776; bombarded by British 1778.

9 City, Alamance co., N cen. North Carolina, 20 m. E of Greensboro; pop. 33,199; industrial center in agricultural region; manufactures textiles, furniture, etc.

10 City and port of entry, ⊗ of Chittenden co., NW Vermont, on Lake Champlain 34 m. WNW of Montpelier; pop. 35,531; largest city in the state. Chartered by Province of New Hampshire 1763; settled 1773; organized 1797; figured as military center and base for naval activity on Lake Champlain in War of 1812; incorp. 1865. Industrial center and shipping point; manufactures textiles, marble, lumber, and wooden products, brush fibers, corn foods, Venetian blinds, etc.; summer and winter resort; grave of Ethan Allen. University of Vermont (1791; coed.); Trinity Coll. (1925; women; Roman Cath.).

11 City, Skagit co., NW Washington, 20 m. S of Bellingham; pop. 2968.

12 City, Racine co., SE Wisconsin, 24 m. W of Racine; pop. 5856; settled 1833; dairying center; manufactures food products, beer, brassware, etc.; limestone quarry.

13 Town, Halton co., S Ontario, Canada, on Lake Ontario 7 m. NE of Hamilton; pop. 6017.

Bur′ma (bûr′má). Republic, SE Asia, formerly a British dependency; bounded on N by Tibet, on E by Chinese province of Yunnan, Indochina, and Thailand, on SW by Andaman Sea, and on W by the Bay of Bengal, states of East Bengal and Assam, and territory of Manipur; extends from ab. lat. 10° to 28°15′N and long. 92° to 101°E, constituting NW section of Indochinese peninsula; total area 261,610 sq. m., pop. 14,667,146; divided in 1931 Census bet. regularly administered area (divisions and districts) 171,157 sq. m., pop. 13,102,048, specially administered areas (Federated Shan States and Karenni) 62,335 sq. m., pop. 1,565,098, and certain unenumerated areas (including Wa States and Naga Hills region on NW border) 28,118 sq. m., (no pop. figures); ✻ Rangoon. See *Map*, p. 175. Estimated total pop. (1939) 16,119,000. Often divided into **Lower Burma** (the coastal region—Arakan, Irrawaddy, Pegu, and Tenasserim divisions) and **Upper Burma** (the N or inland part—Magwe, Mandalay, and Sagaing divisions).

POLITICAL DIV.	LOCA-TION IN BURMA	AREA SQ. M.	1931 POP.	CAPITAL
LOWER BURMA				
Arakan	W	16,001	1,008,535	Akyab
Irrawaddy	SW	13,460	2,334,774	Bassein
Pegu	S cen.	13,799	2,549,637	Rangoon
Tenasserim	S	37,614	1,872,668	Moulmein
UPPER BURMA				
Magwe	W cen.	27,693	1,722,044	Magwe
Mandalay	N cen.	12,504	1,696,332	Mandalay
Sagaing	N	50,086	1,918,058	Sagaing
EASTERN STATES				
Karenni	E	4,519	58,761	Loikaw
Northern Shan States[1]	E cen.	21,400	636,107	Taunggyi[1]
Southern Shan States[1]	E cen.	36,416	870,230	Taunggyi[1]
Unenumerated Area		28,118		

[1] Comprises the Federated Shan States (✻ Taunggyi) which include also the Wa States and for administrative purposes Karenni district.

Mountainous along India border, in N part, and in Shan States; other important ranges are the Arakan Yoma, Pegu Yoma, and Dawna and Bilauktaung Ranges. Basin of the Irrawaddy, with its tributaries Chindwin, Shweli, Myitnge, occupies most of country; Salween and Sittang are the main streams of E part. Long coast line and numerous islands provide several good harbors. An agricultural country; main product rice, others sesamum, peanuts, cotton, maize; mineral output important, esp. petroleum, lead, tungsten, silver, and zinc, and rubies and sapphires. Inhabitants chiefly Burman groups; others are Shan, Karen, Kachin, Mon, Wa, and Chinese peoples. Chief cities Rangoon in the S, Mandalay in the N, Moulmein, Bassein, Akyab.

History: Inhabited by people of Mongolian stock and probably of Tibetan origin; in 3d cent. A.D. settled on coast and at river mouths by Hindus who converted Burma to Buddhism; first united in 11th cent. under a dynasty at Pagan which was overthrown by Mongols in 13th cent.; Toungoo, Pegu, and Ava the larger of the petty states which now sprang up; united under Toungoo dynasty assisted by Portuguese who first traded there 1519; short-lived Dutch and English factories were founded in 17th cent.; modern Burmese state founded in 18th cent. by Alompra and his successors who conquered Arakan, Tenasserim coast, Manipur, Assam, and eventually came into conflict with the English East India Co.; fought three wars with British: First (1824–26), Second (1852–53), and Third (1886); as result of First Burmese War by Treaty of Yandabu (*q.v.*) British acquired Assam, Arakan, Tenasserim, and Pegu; after Second Burmese War Rangoon (*q.v.*) retained by British and Lower Burma formed 1862; as result of Third Burmese War Upper Burma formed 1886, including Mandalay (*q.v.*), a kingdom founded by native dynasty in 19th cent.; as province of British India, under lieutenant governor until 1923 when raised to governor's province; separated

from India and made crown colony in 1937. In World War II overcome by Japanese 1942 (Rangoon occupied Mar. 8); government located at Simla; reconquest carried on 1943–45; Ledo Road constructed and Akyab, Myitkyina, and N part retaken by Feb. 1945; Mandalay captured in March. Granted independence by pact signed with Great Britain Oct. 17, 1947, effective Jan. 4, 1948.

Burma Road. Motor highway from Lashio (at railhead from Mandalay), E Burma, NE to Kunming in Yunnan, 717 m. by road (320 m. by airline); crosses Burma-China border near Namhkam, Burma, and Wanting (lowest point on road 3200 ft.), China; then proceeds generally E across Salween and Mekong river valleys through Paoshan and Tali to Kunming; alt. in Salween-Mekong region 6000 to 8500 ft. Extension (often considered a part of the Burma Road) E from Kunming to Kweiyang in Kweichow, then N through Tsunyi to Chungking, ab. 700 m. by road. Total length, Chungking to Rangoon (in Burma by rail from Lashio through Hsipaw, Maymyo, and Mandalay), ab. 2100 m. In early part of World War II a vital transportation connecting link (opened Dec. 1938) for supplies to Chinese government; closed for three months July 18–Oct. 18, 1940; lower part in Burma and Yunnan seized by Japanese Mar. 1942. Reopened Jan. 1945 by completion of Stilwell Road, earlier Ledo Road (*qq.v.*), connecting with India through Namhkam, Bhamo, and Myitkyina in Burma. Part in India and Burma abandoned by the military 1946.

Bur′net (bûr′nĕt; -nĭt). County in Texas. See *Table* at TEXAS.
2 Town and resort, its ⊗, cen. Texas, 43 m. NNW of Austin; pop. 2214; in agricultural section.
Bur·nett′ (bûr·nĕt′; bẽr-). **1** County in Wisconsin. See *Table* at WISCONSIN.
2 River, SE Queensland, NE Australia; flows NE past Bundaberg and into Hervey Bay.
Burn′ham (bûr′năm). Borough, Mifflin co., cen. Pennsylvania, 2 m. N of Lewistown; pop. 2755; iron and steel works.
Burnham on Sea. Urban district, Somersetshire, SW England, on Bristol Channel 24 m. SW of Bristol; pop. 5120.
Bur′nie (bûr′nĭ). Town on N coast of Tasmania, Australia, 75 m. WNW of Launceston; pop. 3390.
Burn′ley (bûrn′lĭ). County borough, Lancashire, NW England, at confluence of Burn and Calder rivers 22 m. N of Manchester; pop. 98,258, (1951) 84,950; has textile mills, iron foundries; coal mines nearby.
Burns (bûrnz). City, ⊗ of Harney co., SE Oregon, 20 m. N of Malheur Lake; pop. 3523; capital of old cattle empire, modern livestock center of Oregon including Paiute Indian village within the city boundaries; lumber mills.
Burns′ville (bûrnz′vĭl; *Sou.* also -v′l). Town, ⊗ of Yancey co., W North Carolina; pop. 1388.
Burnt′is′land (bûrnt′ī′lănd; *Scot.* also brŭnt′-). Seaport burgh, Fife co., E Scotland, on the Firth of Forth opposite Edinburgh; pop. 5668; watering place; fisheries; shipbuilding.
Burnt Mountain (bûrnt). Peak 10,602 ft. in Sierra Nevada, E Fresno co., S cen. California.
Bur′ra (bûr′à) or **Koo·rin′ga** (kōō·rĭng′gà). Town, South Australia, ab. 80 m. NE of Adelaide; pop. 1725; nearby copper mines, of rich yield 1847–77, now closed; region devoted to sheep and wheat.
Bur·rard′ Inlet (bŭ·rärd′). Inlet 9 m. long of the Strait of Georgia, extending E into British Columbia, Canada; the city of Vancouver is on S side at its mouth and Port Moody at its head. One of the best natural harbors on the Pacific coast of North America.
Bur·ria′na (bŏŏr·ryä′nä). Commune, Castellón de la Plana prov., E Spain, 8 m. S of Castellón de la Plana; pop. 18,473; trades in wine, oil, and fruit, esp. oranges.
Bur′rill·ville (bûr′ĭl·vĭl). Town, Providence co., N Rhode Island, 22 m. NW of Providence; pop. 9119; ad-

ministrative center Harrisville; was part of Providence until 1731, part of Glocester 1731–1806; now includes ten small villages; manufactures textiles, woolen goods.
Bur′row Head (bûr′ō). Cape on S coast of Scotland, bet. Luce Bay and Wigtown Bay.
Burr′wood (bûr′wŏŏd). U.S. Engineers′ station at mouth of W course of Mississippi river in the delta.
Bur′ry Inlet (bûr′ĭ). E arm of Carmarthen Bay, SW Wales, bet. Carmarthenshire and Glamorganshire.
Burry Port. Urban district and seaport, Carmarthenshire, S Wales; pop. 5927.
Bur·sa′ (bŏŏr·sä′), *formerly* **Bru·sa′** or **Brus·sa′** (brŏŏ·sä′). **1** Vilayet, NW Turkey in Asia; 5236 sq. m.; pop. 443,867.
2 *anc.* **Pru′sa** (prōō′sà). City, its ✳, ab. 13 m. from SE shore of Sea of Marmara; pop. (1940) 77,348; connected by rail with its port Mudanya; noted for its carpets and silk stuffs. As ancient Prusa founded at foot of (Mysian) Mt. Olympus as seat of Bithynian kings; flourished under Roman and Byzantine emperors and became capital of the Ottomans 1327–61; plundered by the Tatars 1402.
Bur′sa (bûr′sà). See BYRSA.
Burs′lem (bûrz′lĕm). Former municipal borough, Staffordshire, W cen. England; became part of Stoke on Trent 1910; known for manufacture of pottery since 17th cent.; home of Josiah Wedgwood; Wedgwood Inst. (1863). See the POTTERIES.
Burt (bûrt). County in Nebraska. See *Table* at NEBRASKA.
Burt Lake. Lake in W Cheboygan co., N Michigan; resort area in state park.
Bur′ton (bûr′t′n). Unincorporated town, ⊗ of Sunbury co., S cen. New Brunswick, Canada, on right bank of St. John river 18 m. E of Fredericton; pop. 1336.
Burton, Lake. Reservoir in Tallulah river, Rabun co., NE Georgia; outlet into Chattooga river.
Burton on Trent or **Burton upon Trent** (trĕnt). County borough, Staffordshire, W cen. England, 26 m. NNE of Birmingham; pop. 49,169; breweries.
Burt′scheid (bŏŏrt′shīt). Suburb of Aachen, W Germany; formerly a town, part of Aachen since 1897; thermal springs.
Buru. See BOEROE.
Bu·ru·jird′ (bŏŏ′rŏŏ·jĭrd′). City, W Iran, 60 m. WSW of Iraq; pop. ab. 22,000; chief town of Luristan prov.
Bu·rul′lus (bŭ·rŭl′ŭs), **Lake.** Coastal lake in Nile delta just E of Rosetta mouth, N Egypt; Baltîm is at its E end.
Burundi. See URUNDI.
Bur′wash (bûr′ish; bẽr′ish). Civil parish, E Sussex, SE England; pop. 2078.
Bur′wash Land′ing (bûr′wŏsh). Station on W shore of Kluane Lake, SW Yukon, Canada, on Alaska Highway.
Bur′well (bûr′wĕl; -wĕl). City, ⊗ of Garfield co., cen. Nebraska; pop 1425.
Burwell, Mount. Peak 11,738 ft. in S Park co., NW Wyoming.
Bur′wood (bûr′wŏŏd). City, E New South Wales, SE Australia, W suburb of Sydney; pop. 19,371.
Bur′y (bĕr′ĭ). County borough, Lancashire, NW England, 10 m. NNW of Manchester; pop. 56,182, (1951) 58,829; textile mills.
Bur·yat′ or **Bur·iat′**, *formerly* **Bur·yat′–Mon′gol** (bŏŏr·yät′mŏng′gŏl) or **Bur·yat′–Mon·go′lian** (bŏŏr·yät′mŏng·gōl′yăn; -gō′lĭ·ăn;-mŏn-), **Autonomous Soviet Socialist Republic.** Autonomous republic of the R.S.F.S.R. in S Siberia, Asia, E of Lake Baikal; 127,020 sq. m.; pop. 542,170; ✳ Ulan-Ude. Bounded on N and W by Irkutsk Region, on E and SE by Chita Region, on S by Outer Mongolia; touches Tuva Autonomous Region on SW. Includes practically all of Lake Baikal, Barguzin river, the lower courses of the Selenga and Khilok rivers, and the upper course of the Vitim. Main area consists of plateau and mountain ranges, the Yablonoi along E border, the Barguzin and Baikal ranges

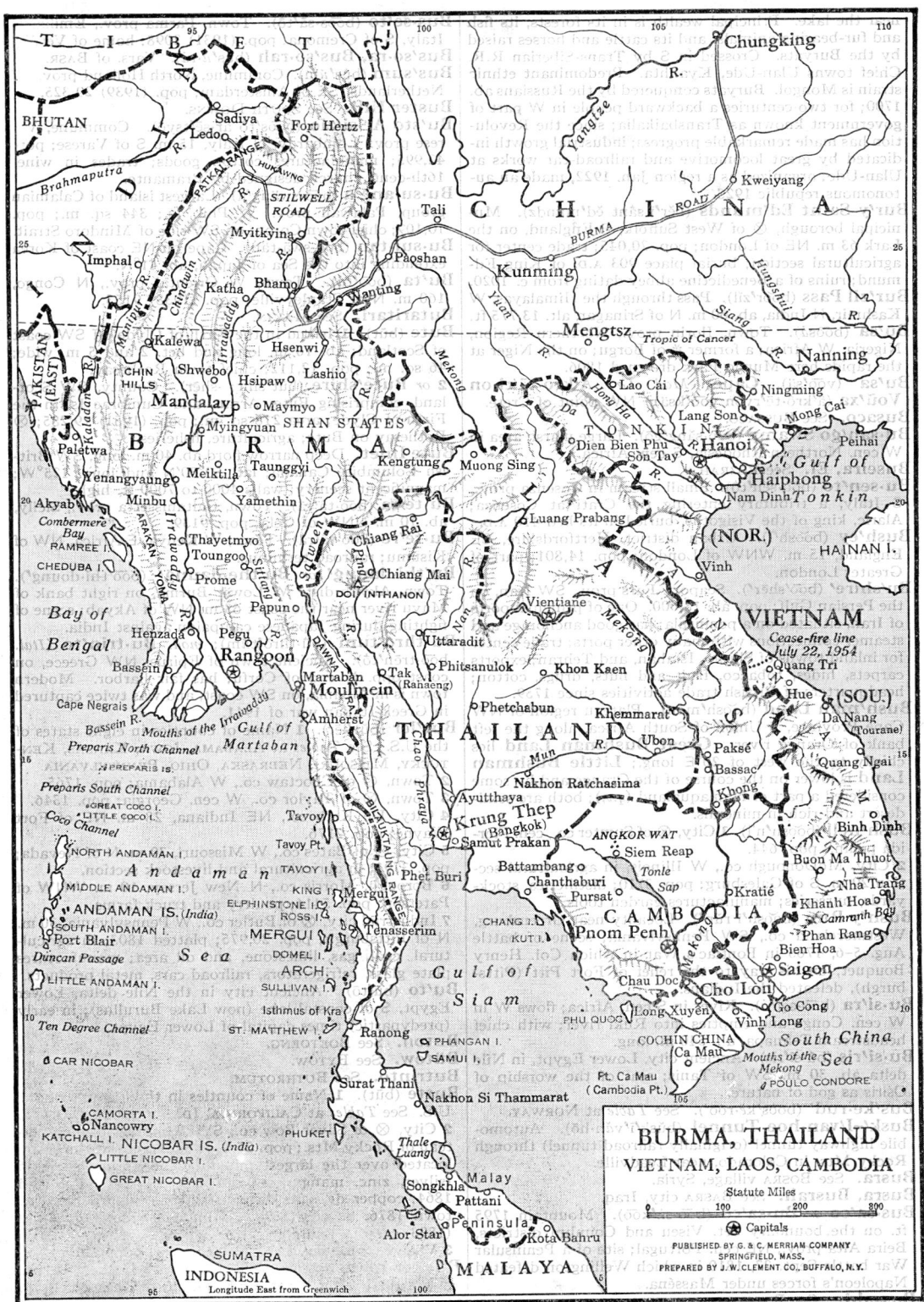

BURMA, THAILAND
VIETNAM, LAOS, CAMBODIA

Statute Miles

0   100   200   300

⊕ Capitals

PUBLISHED BY G. & C. MERRIAM COMPANY
SPRINGFIELD, MASS.
PREPARED BY J. W. CLEMENT CO., BUFFALO, N.Y.

near the lake. Principal wealth is in its forests, its fish and fur-bearing animals, and its cattle and horses raised by the Buryats. Crossed in S by Trans-Siberian R.R. Chief towns Ulan-Ude, Kyakhta. Predominant ethnic strain is Mongol. Buryats conquered by the Russians ab. 1700; for two centuries a backward people in W part of government known as Transbaikalia; since the Revolution has made remarkable progress; industrial growth indicated by great locomotive and railroad-car works at Ulan-Ude; organized as a region Jan. 1922, made an autonomous republic 1923.

Bur'y Saint Ed'munds (bĕr'ĭ sănt ĕd'mŭndz). Municipal borough, ⊗ of West Suffolk, E England, on the Lark 63 m. NE of London; pop. 20,045; trade center for agricultural section; burial place 903 A.D. of King Edmund; ruins of a Benedictine abbey dating from c. 1020.

Bur'zil Pass (bŏŏr'zĭl). Pass through the Himalayas, W Kashmir, N India, ab. 60 m. N of Srinagar, alt. 13,775 ft.

Bu'sa (bōōsá). Town, Ilorin prov., Northern Region, Nigeria, W Africa; a former ✳ of Borgu; on the Niger at the rapids here Mungo Park drowned 1806.

Bu'sa (vōō'sä), **Cape**; Mod. Gr. **A'kro·tē'ri·on Voū'xa** (ä'krô·tē'ryôn vōō'ksä). NW point of Crete.

Busaco. See BUSSACO.

Bu·san'go Swamp (bōō·săng'gō). Large marsh area in W cen. Northern Rhodesia, S cen. Africa.

Buseira, El. See BOZRAH.

Bu·sen'to (bōō·sĕn'tô). Small stream in Cosenza prov., S Italy, a tributary entering the Crati at Cosenza; Alaric, king of the Visigoths, buried in its bed 410 A.D.

Bush'ey (bŏŏsh'ĭ). Urban district, Hertfordshire, SE England, 15 m. WNW of London; pop. 14,801; part of Greater London.

Bu'shire' (bōō'shēr'). Seaport, Fars prov., SW Iran, on the Persian Gulf; pop. ab. 18,000. One of principal ports of Iran, situated on a peninsula; has good anchorage and steamer connections with many other ports; trade center for inland towns of Shiraz, Isfahan, and Tehran; exports carpets, hides, tobacco, fruit and nuts, drugs, cotton; headquarters of British trade activities since 1759.

Bush'man Land (bŏŏsh'măn). Plateau region of NW Cape Province, S Union of South Africa, along the left bank of Orange river. **Great Bushman Land** lies chiefly to the west of 20°E long.; **Little Bushman Land** is lower on the course of the Orange and by some considered a part of Namaqualand (q.v.); both are semidesert and rich in minerals.

Bush'nell (bŏŏsh'n'l). 1 City, ⊗ of Sumter co., cen. Florida penin.; pop. 644.
2 City, McDonough co., W Illinois, in agricultural section 29 m. S of Galesburg; pop. 3710; distilleries, stockyards, nurseries; manufactures garden tools.

Bush'y Run (bŏŏsh'ĭ rŭn'). Locality near Greensburg, Westmoreland co., SW Pennsylvania; scene of battle Aug. 5–6, 1763 in Pontiac's War in which Col. Henry Bouquet, on his way to the relief of Fort Pitt (Pittsburgh), defeated the Indians.

Bu·si'ra (bōō·sēr'á). River in S cen. Africa; flows W in W cen. Congo and empties into Ruki river; with chief headstream Tshuapa, ab. 540 m. long.

Bu·si'ris (bū·sī'rĭs). Ancient city, Lower Egypt, in Nile delta ab. 30 m. SW of Tanis; seat of the worship of Osiris as god of nature.

Bus'ke·rud' (bŏŏs'kĕ·rōō'). See Table at NORWAY.

Busk'–I'van·hoe Tunnel (bŭsk'ĭ'văn·hō'). Automobile highway tunnel (originally railroad tunnel) through Rocky Mts. in Colorado, near Leadville.

Busra. See BOSRA village, Syria.

Busra, Busrah. See BASRA city, Iraq.

Bus·sa'co or **Bu·sa'co** (bōō·sà'kōō). Mountain 1795 ft. on the boundary bet. Viseu and Coimbra districts, Beira Alta prov., NE cen. Portugal; site of a Peninsular War battle Sept. 27, 1810 in which Wellington defeated Napoleon's forces under Masséna.

Bussahir. See BASHAHR.

Bus·se'to (bōōs·sā'tô). Town, Parma prov., Emilia, N Italy, S of Cremona; pop. (1931) 2098; home of Verdi.

Bus'so·ra, Bus'so·rah (bŭs'ŭ·rá). Vars. of BASRA.

Bus'sum (bûs'ŭm). Commune, North Holland prov., W Netherlands, SE of Amsterdam; pop. (1939) 29,325.

Buster Hill. See SOUTH DOWNS.

Bu'sto Ar·si'zio (bōōs'tô är·sē'tsyô). Commune, Varese prov., Lombardy, N Italy, 15 m. S of Varese; pop. 42,995; manufactures cotton goods; trades in wine; 16th-cent. church designed by Bramante.

Bu·su·ang'a (bōō·swäng'ä). Largest island of Calamian group, Palawan prov., W Phil. Is.; 344 sq. m.; pop. 10,109; chief town Coron; on SW side of Mindoro Strait.

Bu·sui·tan (bōō·swā·tän). Cape on NE coast of Korea extending into the Sea of Japan, ab. 41°N.

Bu'ta (bōō'tá). Town, W Oriental prov., N Congo, 160 m. N of Stanleyville; pop. (1938) 9153.

Butaritari. See MAKIN.

Bute (būt). 1 Island in the Firth of Clyde off SW coast of Scotland; ab. 16 m. long and bet. 2 and 5 m. wide; 46 sq. m.; pop. 12,112; chief town Rothesay.
2 or **Bute'shire** (būt'shĭr; -shēr). County, SW Scotland, comprising Bute, Arran, and Cumbrae Is. in the Firth of Clyde; area 218 sq. m.; pop. (1951) 19,285; ⊗ Rothesay on Bute; agriculture, fisheries.

Bute Inlet. Deep narrow fiord ab. 40 m. long, SW British Columbia, Canada; lat. 50°30′N and long. 125°W; magnificent scenery; walls 4000 to 7000 ft. high.

Bu·te'ra (bōō·tā'rä). Town, Caltanissetta prov., Sicily, ab. 10 m. NNW of Gela; pop. 7639.

Bu·te're (bōō·tā'rá). Town, W Kenya, E Africa, NW of Kisumu; railroad terminus.

Bu'thi·daung' or **Bu'the·daung'** (bōō'thĭ·doung'). Town, Akyab dist., W Lower Burma, on right bank of Mayu river near the coast 63 m. NW of Akyab; scene of fighting during Japanese campaign against India.

Bu·thro'tum (bū·thrō'tŭm); mod. **Bu·trin'to** (Ital. bōō·trēn'tô). Ancient town of Epirus, NW Greece, on coast opp. N end of Corfu; has fair harbor. Modern town is in Albania, on SW coast, and was twice captured in Greek-Italian war of 1941.

But'ler (bŭt'lẽr). 1 Name of counties in eight states of the U.S. See Tables at ALABAMA, IOWA, KANSAS, KENTUCKY, MISSOURI, NEBRASKA, OHIO, PENNSYLVANIA.
2 Town, ⊗ of Choctaw co., W Alabama; pop. 1765.
3 Town, ⊗ of Taylor co., W cen. Georgia; pop. 1346.
4 City, De Kalb co., NE Indiana, 28 m. NE of Fort Wayne; pop. 2176.
5 City, ⊗ of Bates co., W Missouri, 30 m. N of Nevada; pop. 3791; in agricultural and livestock section.
6 Borough, Morris co., N New Jersey, 10 m. WNW of Paterson; pop. 5414; poultry and truck farms.
7 Industrial city, ⊗ of Butler co., W Pennsylvania, 30 m. N of Pittsburgh; pop. 20,975; platted 1803; in agricultural, coal, gas, limestone, and oil area; manufactures plate glass, refrigerators, railroad cars, metal products.

Bu'to (bū'tô). Ancient city in the Nile delta, Lower Egypt, S of coastal lake (now Lake Burullus); in early (predynastic) times capital of Lower Egypt.

Buton. See BOETOENG.

Bütow. See BYTÓW.

Butrinto. See BUTHROTUM.

Butte (būt). 1 Name of counties in three states of the U.S. See Tables at CALIFORNIA, IDAHO, SOUTH DAKOTA.
2 City, ⊗ of Silver Bow co., SW Montana in high plateau of Rocky Mts.; pop. 27,877; 3d largest city in state; located over the largest mineral deposits in the world (silver, zinc, manganese, and esp. copper). Founded 1864; copper deposits discovered 1880; incorporated as town 1876, as city 1879. Montana School of Mines (1893; coed.).
3 Village, ⊗ of Boyd co., N Nebraska; pop. 526.

But'ter·mere (bŭt'ẽr·mẽr). Lake in the Lake District, NW England, in Cumberland 7 m. SW of Keswick; 1¼ m. long; maximum depth 94 ft.

But'ter·milk' Channel (bŭt'ẽr·mĭlk'). Channel ab. 2½ m. long in Upper New York Bay, bet. Governors I. and Brooklyn, New York.

But'ter·worth (bŭt'ẽr·wûrth; -wẽrth). **1** Chief town of Province Wellesley, Penang settlement, Federation of Malaya, on coast opp. George Town; pop. 13,540.
2 Town, ✻ of the Transkei, E Cape Province, S Union of South Africa, 50 m. NNE of East London; pop. 1280.

Butt of Lewis. See Butt of LEWIS.

Butts (bŭts). County in Georgia. See *Table* at GEORGIA.

Bu·tu'an (bōō·tōō'än). Municipality, ✻ of Agusan prov. NE Mindanao. Phil. Is., in N part on left bank of Agusan river ab. 5 m. from its mouth; pop. 18,295.

Butuan Bay. Large inlet of SE Mindanao Sea in N Agusan prov., NE Mindanao, Phil. Is.; ab. 24 m. wide from Diuata Point to E shore; receives Agusan river.

Butung. See BOETOENG.

Butuntum. See BITONTO.

Bu·tur·li'nov·ka (bōō·tōōr·lyē'nŭf·kȧ). Town, E cen. Voronezh Region, Soviet Russia, Europe, 60 m. SE of Voronezh; pop. 25,342; in cattle-raising region.

Bux'ar or **Bax'ar** (bŭk'sẽr). Town, W Bihar state NE Indian Union, on Ganges 77 m. W of Patna; pop. 13,449; victory Oct. 23, 1764 of British under Major Hector Munro over forces of Siraj-ud-daula and Mir Kasim, which established British control over Bengal.

Bux'ton (bŭks'tŭn). **1** Town, York co., SW Maine, 15 m. W of Portland; pop. 2339.
2 Coastal town, N British Guiana, in Demerara co., 11 m. by rail E of Georgetown.
3 Municipal borough, Derbyshire, N cen. England, 20 m. SE of Manchester; pop. 19,556; resort, mineral springs.

Buynaksk. Var. of BUINAKSK.

Bü'yük A·da' (bü'yük ä·dä'). Island in E Sea of Marmara, W Turkey, SE of entrance to the Bosporus; largest of the Princes Is.

Bü'yük·de·re' (bü'yük·dĕ·rĕ'). Town on the Bosporus, Turkey in Europe, ab. 11 m. NE of İstanbul; residential suburb in valley from which İstanbul gets water.

Bu·za'chi (bōō·zä'chē). Large peninsula projecting into NE Caspian Sea, N of Mangyshlak Penin., Kazakh S.S.R., Soviet Central Asia.

Bu·zan'cy' (bü'zän'sē'). **1** Village, Aisne dept., NE France, ab. 3 m. S of Soissons; taken by British and French July 28–30, 1918.
2 Village, Ardennes dept., NE France, 12 m. E of Vouziers; pop. 666; taken by Americans Nov. 2, 1918.

Bu·zău' (bōō·zŭ'ōō); *Hung.* **Bod'za** (bŏd'zŏ). **1** River ab. 150 m. long in cen. Romania; rises in Transylvania and flows SE through **Buzău Pass** in Transylvanian Alps and NE into Siret river near Galaţi.
2 City, Muntenia, SE Romania, on Buzău river 62 m. NE of Bucharest; pop. 36,115; trade center in rich oilfield region, esp. for salt, oil, and lumber.

Bu·zu·luk' (bōō·zōō·lōōk'). City, W Chkalov Region, Soviet Russia, Europe, on left bank of Samara river and on railroad 90 m. ESE of Kuibyshev; pop. 30,400; trading town at the edge of the steppe region; deals esp. in grain and cattle; large Tatar population.

Buz'zards Bay (bŭz'ẽrdz). **1** Inlet of Atlantic Ocean, 30 m. long and 5 to 10 m. wide, in SE Massachusetts; the W end of Cape Cod Canal is at its NE extremity.
2 Town, Barnstable co., SE Massachusetts, on Cape Cod Canal near entrance of inlet; pop. 2170.

Bwa·ga·oi'a (bwä'gä·oi'ä). See LOUISIADE ARCHIPELAGO.

Bwake. See BOUAKÉ.

Bwa'na M'kub'wa or **Bwa'na·mkub'wa** (bwä'näm·kōōb'wä). Town, N Luangwa prov., cen. Northern Rhodesia, S cen. Africa; pop. 1901; copper mines.

By'am Mar'tin (bī'ăm mär't'n; mär'tĭn). Island in channel bet. Melville and Bathurst Is., Parry Is., Franklin District, Northwest Territories, Canada.

Byblos. See JUBAYL.

Byd'goszcz (bĭd'gôshch); *Ger.* **Brom'berg** (brôm'-**berk**). Commercial and industrial city, ✻ of Pomorze dept., Poland, 67 m. NE of Poznań; pop. (1938–39 est.) 141,000. Originally a commercial city of the Teutonic Knights; enlarged and developed by Frederick the Great in 18th cent.; under Prussian rule 1772–1919. In World War II held by Germans 1939–45.

Byel–. Literally "white" in Russian. For names beginning *Byel-*, see BEL-, as *Belgorod, Belomorsk, Belukha.*

Byelorussian Soviet Socialist Republic; *shortened form* **Byelorussia.** See WHITE RUSSIA.

Byes'ville (bīz'vĭl). Village, Guernsey co., E Ohio, 24 m. E of Zanesville; pop. 2447; coal mining.

By'lot Island (bī'lŏt). Island 5100 sq. m. N of Baffin Island and W of Baffin Bay, E Franklin District, Northwest Territories, Canada.

Byrd Deep (bûrd). Ocean depth 28,152 ft. on N edge of Ross Sea at ab. 70°S and near the 180th meridian.

Byrds'town (bûrdz'toun). Town, ⊗ of Pickett co., N Tennessee; pop. 613.

Byron. See NUKUNAU.

By'ron, Cape (bī'rŭn). Cape, New South Wales, Australia, extreme E point of continent, in 153°38′E long.

Byr'sa or **Bur'sa** (bûr'sȧ). The citadel of Carthage.

By'tom (bī'tôm); *Ger.* **Beu'then** (boi'tĕn). Industrial city, cen. Śląsk dept., SW Poland, just NW of Chorzów and 100 m. SE of Wrocław; pop. (1946) 100,842; formerly in Silesia, Germany; iron, zinc, and lead works; coal mines. Became part of Prussia 1742. Taken by Russians Jan. 1945; in section assigned to Poland by Potsdam Conference 1945.

By'tów (bī'tōōf); *Ger.* **Bü'tow** (bü'tō). Town, SW Gdańsk dept., N Poland, ab. 100 m. E of Koszalin; pop. (1946) 9713; railroad junction and market town; Polish town in 15th cent., came under Brandenburg 1657. Assigned to Poland by Potsdam Conference 1945.

Bytown. See OTTAWA, Canada.

By·za'ci·um (bǐ·zā'shǐ·ŭm). The S part of the Roman province of Africa; corresponds to S half of Tunisia.

By·zan'tine Empire (bǐ·zǎn'tǐn; -tǐn; bǐ-; bǐz'ǎn·tǐn; -tǐn). Empire of SE and S Europe and W Asia, 4th–15th cents., with boundaries varying greatly; in earliest period generally termed **Eastern Roman Empire**, 395–474, with capital at Constantinople (earlier Byzantium); first Byzantine emperor, so called, Zeno the Isaurian (474–491). Reached its greatest extent under Justinian (527–565), who reconquered most of Western Empire, erected Church of Saint Sophia, and issued basic codification of Roman law (*Corpus Juris Civilis*); divided into themes for administration; withstood attacks of Persians, Arabs, and Bulgars 7th–10th cents.; ab. 1000 A.D. comprised S Balkans, Greece, Asia Minor, and parts of S Italy. Long controversy over iconoclasm within Eastern Church prepared for break with Roman Church; attained great wealth and cultural supremacy of Mediterranean world because of its control of commerce bet. east and west and its preservation of classical heritage; lost holdings in Italy and, as result of Manzikert (see MALAZKERT), yielded Asia Minor to Seljuks; declined under Comnenian dynasty and forced to give commercial control to Venice (*q.v.*) which profited most from Crusades; Constantinople sacked by Fourth Crusade 1204 and Empire split up into (1) Latin Empire (*q.v.*), Greek empires of (2) Trebizond and (3) Nicaea, and (4) miscellaneous Venetian, Latin, and Greek holdings (see ACHAEA, ATHENS, EPIRUS, SALONIKA); partly restored by capture of Constantinople by Michael VIII 1261; in 14th cent. gradually lost territory to Turks until there remained only Constantinople, Morea, and Salonika; capture of Constantinople in 1453 marked formal end of Byzantine Empire (see OTTOMAN EMPIRE).

By·zan'ti·um (bǐ·zǎn'shǐ·ŭm; bǐ-; -shŭm; -tǐ·ŭm). Ancient city, site of modern İstanbul (*q.v.*).

Bzu'ra (bzōō'rä). River ab. 90 m. long in cen. Poland, flowing into Vistula river from the S; its source is just N of Łódź.

C

Ca·a·cu·pé' (kä'ä·koō·pā'). Town, ✳ of Cordillera dept., cen. Paraguay; pop. ab. 11,300.

Ca·a·gua·zú' (kä'ä·gwä·soō'). Department of Paraguay. See *Table* at PARAGUAY.

Ca·a·ma·ño Sound (kä'ä·mä'nyō). Inlet of Hecate Strait W of Princess Royal I. and N of Aristazabal I., off W coast of British Columbia, Canada.

Ca·a·pu·cú' (kä'ä·poō·koō'). Town, Paraguarí dept., S Paraguay, ab. 70 m. SSE of Asunción.

Ca·a·za·pá' (kä'ä·sä·pä'). **1** Department of Paraguay. See *Table* at PARAGUAY.
2 City, its ✳, SE Paraguay; pop. ab. 19,950.

Ca·bad'ba·ran (kä·bäd'bä·rän). Municipality, N Agusan prov., Mindanao, Phil. Is., on E shore of Butuan Bay ab. 12 m. N of Butuan; pop. 20,254.

Ca'bai·guán' (kä'vī·gwän'). Municipality and town, Las Villas prov., W cen. Cuba, 37 m. SE of Santa Clara; pop. (town) 15,656.

Ca·bal'lo or **Pu·lo' Ca·bal'lo** (poō·lō' kä·vä'yō). Rocky islet in Corregidor group, ab. 1 m. SE of Corregidor I., in entrance to Manila Bay, Phil. Is.; alt. 420 ft.; lighthouse; site of Fort Hughes. Surrendered to Japanese May 1942; recaptured by U.S. Mar. 1945.

Ca·bal'lo Dam (kä·bä'yō). Secondary dam completed 1938 across Rio Grande river below Elephant Butte Dam, Sierra co., New Mexico; height 96 ft.; impounds water for irrigation.

Ca·ba'ñas (kä·vä'nyäs). **1** Seaport municipality on NE coast of Pinar del Río prov., W Cuba; pop. 21,623.
2 Department, N cen. El Salvador; 316 sq. m.; pop. (1942 est.) 81,632; ✳ Sensuntepeque.

Ca'ba·na·tuan' (kä'bä·nä·twän'). Municipality, ✳ of Nueva Ecija prov., Luzon, Phil. Is., in S cen. part on left bank of Pampanga river; pop. 46,626; a highway junction point and trade center. Site of large Japanese prison camp (near Cabu village) for American and Filipino soldiers captured at Bataan and Corregidor, which was taken by U.S. forces Jan. 30, 1945.

Ca'ba·no' (kä'bä·nō'). Village, Témiscouata co., S Quebec, Canada, on Lake Témiscouata; pop. 2594.

Ca·bar'rus (kä·bär'ŭs). County in North Carolina. See *Table* at NORTH CAROLINA.

Ca'bar·ru'yan Island (kä'bär·roō'yän). Island on NW shore of Lingayen Gulf, Pangasinan prov., Luzon, Phil. Is.; 30 sq. m.; pop. 8989; forested; chief town Anda.

Ca'ba·tu'an (kä'bä·toō'än). Municipality, W cen. Iloilo prov., Panay, Phil. Is., NW of Iloilo; pop. 21,054.

Ca'be·de'lo (kä'vä·thä'loō). Seaport, Paraíba state, E Brazil; pop. (1940 est.) 5897; port for João Pessoa.

Cab'ell (kăb'ĕl). County in West Virginia. See *Table* at WEST VIRGINIA.

Cabellio. See CAVAILLON.

Ca'bes (kä'bĕs). Var. of GABÈS.

Ca'bes Point (kä'väs). Cape on E coast of St. Thomas I., Virgin Is., West Indies, N of Pillsbury Sound.

Ca·be'za del Buey (kä·vä'thä [-sä] thĕl vwĕ'ĕ; vwä'). Commune, Badajoz prov., SW Spain, 90 m. E of Badajoz; pop. 11,762; cattle; lead, galena, and iron mines.

Cabeza del Mo'ro (mō'rō). Highest peak 5110 ft. in the Guadalupe Mts., Cáceres prov., W Spain.

Cabillonum. See CHALON-SUR-SAÔNE.

Ca·bi'mas (kä·vē'mäs). Town, N Zulia state, NW Venezuela, on NE coast of Lake Maracaibo; pop. 11,193.

Ca·bin'da (kä·bin'dä; *Port.* kä·vēNN'dä). **1** Portuguese territory N of Congo river; ab. 3000 sq. m.; exclave attached to Congo dist., Angola, 1886, by agreement with Belgian Congo.
2 Seaport, N of the mouth of the Congo river, W Africa; ✳ of Congo dist., Angola; pop. ab. 12,000.

Cab'i·net Mountains (kăb'ĭ·nĕt; -nĭt). A range of the Rocky Mts. in NW Montana and N Idaho; highest point ab. 9000 ft.

Cabira. See SIVAS.

Cabo de Hornos. See Cape HORN.

Ca'bo Del·ga'do (kä'voō thȧl·gä'thoō). **1** Former district, NE Mozambique, SE Africa; ✳ Porto Amelia; with Niassa dist., 73,000 sq. m., pop. ab. 464,000; now part of Niassa prov.
2 See Cape DELGADO.

Ca'bo Gra'cias a Dios (kä'vŏ grä'syäs ä thyŏs'). Comarca, extreme NE Nicaragua; pop. (1940) 20,218; ✳ Cabo Gracias a Dios (pop. 268). Politically included in Zelaya dept.

Cabo Juby. See CABO YUBI.

Ca'bo Ro'jo (kä'vŏ rō'hō). Municipality (pop. 24,858) and town (pop. 3086), SW Puerto Rico, 7 m. S of Mayagüez.

Cab'ot Head (kăb'ŭt hĕd'). Cape, SE Ontario prov., Canada; NE point of Bruce Penin. on Georgian Bay.

Cabot Strait. Channel ab. 60 m. wide bet. SW Newfoundland and N Cape Breton I., connecting the Gulf of St. Lawrence with the Atlantic Ocean.

Ca'bourg' (kȧ'boōr'). Village, Calvados dept., NW France; pop. 1846; adjoins Dives-sur-Mer on the W; one of the finest beaches among the Channel resorts.

Cabo Verde, Ilhas do. See CAPE VERDE ISLANDS.

Ca'bo Yu'bi (kä'vŏ yoō'vē) or **Cabo Ju'by** (hoō'-); *also* **Vil'la Bens** (bē'lyä vĕns). Town, SW Morocco, in former Spanish enclave on Cape Yubi; former seat of administration of Spanish Sahara and Ifni; pop. 1981.

Ca'bra (kä'vrä); *anc.* **I·gab'rum** (ĭ·găb'rŭm). Commune, Córdoba prov., S Spain, 37 m. SE of Córdoba; pop. 20,779; manufactures linen, bricks; captured from Moors by Ferdinand III 1240; recaptured 1311.

Cab'ra·mat'ta and Can'ley Vale (kăb'rȧ·măt'ȧ, kăn'lĭ). Town (joint municipality), E New South Wales, SE Australia, a W suburb of Sydney; pop. 6108.

Cab'ras Island (kăb'räs; *Span.* kä'vräs). Narrow island ab. 2 m. long and ¼ m. wide off W coast of Guam; forms part of N shelter of Apra Harbor.

Ca·bre'ra (kä·vrā'rä); *anc.* **Ca·prar'i·a** (kȧ·prär'ĭ·ȧ). Small island of the Balearic Is., Baleares prov., Spain, 9 m. S of Majorca; a part of Palma commune.

Ca'bri·el' (kä'vrē·ĕl'). River ab. 130 m. long in E Spain; flows S through Cuenca prov. and into Júcar river.

Ca·bril'lo National Monument (kȧ·brē'[y]ō; -brĭl'ō). See UNITED STATES, *National Monuments.*

Ca'bu (kä'boō). Village, cen. Nueva Ecija prov., Luzon, Phil. Is., barrio, ab. 7 m. ENE of Cabanatuan. Site 1942–45 of Cabanatuan prison camp (see CABANATUAN).

Ca·bu'gao (kä·boō'gou). Municipality, N Ilocos Sur, Luzon, Phil. Is., on coast 17 m. N of Vigan; pop. 13,867.

Cabul. Var. of KABUL.

Ca'ca·hua·mil'pa Caverns (kä'kä·wä·mēl'pä). Large natural caverns in NE Guerrero state near Cuernavaca, cen. Mexico.

Ča'čak (chä'chäk) or **Cha'chak.** Town, Serbia, Yugoslavia, ab. 62 m. S of Belgrade; pop. 9116.

Ca·ca'pon (kȧ·kä'pŭn). River ab. 130 m. long, NE West Virginia; rises in S Hardy co., flows N into Potomac river.

Cac'cia, Cape (kät'chä). Cape on NW coast of the island of Sardinia.

Cá'ce·res (kä'thā·râs; kä'sâ-). **1** Province of Spain. See *Table* at SPAIN.
2 Commune, its ✳, W Spain, on Cáceres river 152 m. SW of Madrid; pop. 39,392; manufactures linen, woolens, hats, leather, soap; remains of Roman fortifications; held by Moors 1142–1229.

Ca'chan' (kȧ·shäN'). Commune, Seine dept., N France, S suburb of Paris on Bièvre river; pop. (1931) 12,790.

Cache (kăsh). **1** River ab. 230 m. long, NE Arkansas; rises in NE Arkansas and flows S into the White river in Monroe co., E cen. Arkansas.
2 County in Utah. See *Table* at UTAH.

Cache la Pou'dre (kăsh' lẽ pōō'drẽ). River ab. 125 m. long, N Colorado; flows from a point near Milner Pass N and E to the South Platte near Greeley.

Ca·chí', Ne·va'do de (nä·vä'thõ thä kä·chē'). Peak 21,325 ft. in Salta prov., N Argentina.

Ca'cho·ei'ra (kȧ'shōō·ā'ē·rȧ). **1** City, Baía state, E Brazil, near W coast of All Saints Bay ab. 45 m. W of Salvador; pop. (1940 est.) 10,431.
2 City, cen. Rio Grande do Sul state, S Brazil, on Jacuí river 110 m. W of Pôrto Alegre; pop. (1940 est.) 17,498.

Ca'cho·ei'ro de I·ta·pe·mi·rim' (kȧ'shōō·ā'ē·rōō thē ē·tȧ·pā·mē·rēn'). City, Espírito Santo state, E Brazil, 65 m. SW of Victoria; pop. (1940 est.) 19,208.

Ca·cou'na (kȧ·kōō'nȧ; *Fr.* kȧ'kōō'nȧ'). Village and summer resort, Quebec prov., Canada; pop. ab. 1000; on S shore of St. Lawrence NE of Rivière du Loup.

Cad'do (kăd'ō). A parish in Louisiana and a county in Oklahoma. See *Tables* at LOUISIANA and OKLAHOMA.

Caddo Lake. Lake ab. 20 m. long on N Texas-Louisiana boundary; connected with Soda Lake and Red river; navigable for steamboats.

Ca'der Fron·wen' (kä'dĕr vrôn·wĕn'). Peak 2568 ft. in the Berwyn Mts., N Wales.

Cader Id'ris (ĭd'rĭs). Peak 2927 ft. in Merionethshire, W Wales, S of Dolgelley.

Cad'il·lac (kăd'l·ăk). City, ⊗ of Wexford co., NW Michigan, 36 m. SSE of Traverse City; pop. 10,112; manufactures automobile tires, wood and metal products.

Ca'diz. **1** (kā'dĭz) City, ⊗ of Trigg co., SW Kentucky; pop. 1980.
2 (kăd'ĭz) Village, ⊗ of Harrison co., E Ohio, 20 m. WSW of Steubenville; pop. 3259; sheep raising; coal.
3 (kä'thĕs) Municipality, N Negros Occidental, Negros, Phil. Is., on Visayan Sea NE of Bacolod; pop. 41,905.

Cá'diz (*Span.* kä'thĕth, -thĕs); *Angl.* **Ca·diz'** (kȧ·dĭz'; kä'dĭz; kăd'ĭz). **1** Province of Spain. See *Table* at SPAIN.
2 *anc.* **Ga'dir** (gä'dĭr), *later* **Ga'des** (gä'dēz). Seaport city, its ✱, SW Spain, on Bay of Cádiz 58 m. NW of Gibraltar and 62 m. SSW of Seville; pop. (1941 est.) 89,623; center of Spanish-American trade; principal Spanish naval station; 13th-cent. and 18th-cent. cathedrals (with paintings by Murillo), bull ring, lighthouse.
History. Founded as Phoenician trading colony c. 1100 B.C.; outlet for Spanish mineral wealth, tin and amber from N; ruled by Carthaginians, Romans, Visigoths; held by Moors from 711 A.D. until captured 1262 by Alfonso of Castile; one of two centers for Spanish trade with American colonies (see SEVILLE) 16th–18th cents.; scene of raid of earl of Essex 1596; became seat of Casa de Contratación (clearing house for American trade) 1718; besieged by French 1810–12; seat of national assembly (Span. *Cortes*) which promulgated liberal constitution of 1812; witnessed beginning of revolution which deposed Queen Isabella 1868.

Cádiz, Bay of. Inlet of the Gulf of Cádiz on SW coast of Spain, affording excellent harbor for the city of Cádiz.

Cádiz, Gulf of. Widemouthed inlet of Atlantic Ocean on SW coast of Spain.

Ca·do're (kä·dō'rā), *or* **Ca·dor'ic, Alps** (kȧ·dôr'ĭk). A name of the Dolomites bet. Venezia Euganea and Venezia Tridentina, NE Italy.

Cadurcum. See CAHORS.

Cae'li·an (sē'lĭ·ăn; sēl'yăn); *Lat.* **Cae'li·us Mons** (sē'lĭ·ŭs mŏnz). One of the seven hills of Rome. See SEVEN HILLS.

Caen (kän). Commercial and manufacturing city, ✱ of Calvados dept., Normandy, NW France, on Orne river ab. 9 m. from coast of English Channel and 126. m WNW of Paris; pop. 61,334; trade center for agricultural and dairying region; notable structures include L'Abbaye-aux-Dames (founded 1066 by Matilda, wife of William the Conqueror), L'Abbaye-aux-Hommes (founded by William the Conqueror 11th cent.), church of Saint Pierre; university (founded 1431 by Henry VI of England); industries include shipbuilding, dyeworks, foundries, and the manufacture of Angora-rabbit gloves, linens, woolens, cotton goods, leather. Under English rule 1346, 1417–50; suffered in religious wars; captured by Protestants 1562. In World War II one of the main objects of Allied invasion; attacked by British on D day, June 6, 1944; became part of German defense line; again attacked June 25 and taken by British and Canadians July 9; much of the city destroyed.

Caene, Caenepolis. See QENA.

Cae're (sē'rē) *or* **A·gyl'la** (ȧ·jĭl'ȧ); *mod.* **Cer·ve'te·ri** (chĕr·vā'tā·rē). City, ancient stronghold of Etruria, near coast ab. 22 m. WNW of Rome; Etruscan tombs; according to legend, the refuge 390 B.C. of the Vestal Virgins when the Gauls took Rome.

Caer Gybi. See HOLYHEAD urban district.

Caer·le'on (kär·lē'ŏn); *anc.* **Is'ca Sil'u·rum** (ĭs'kȧ sĭl'û·rŭm). Urban district, Monmouthshire, W England, on Usk river; pop. 4711. Thought to be the "Carlion" (where Arthur was crowned and held his court) of Malory's *Morte d'Arthur*.

Caer Luel. See CARLISLE, England.

Caer·nar'von (kär·när'vŭn). **1** = CAERNARVONSHIRE.
2 Municipal borough and seaport, ⊗ of Caernarvonshire, NW Wales; pop. 9255; shipping point for slate; famous 13th-cent. castle, birthplace of Edward II.

Caernarvon Bay. Bay bet. Caernarvonshire and Anglesey, NW Wales; Menai Strait connects it with Beaumaris Bay.

Caer·nar'von·shire (kär·när'vŭn·shĭr; -shēr) *or* **Caernarvon.** County, NW Wales; 569 sq. m.; pop. (1951) 124,074; ⊗ Caernarvon; mountainous area; rivers Conway, Ogwen, Glaslyn; quarrying (esp. slate), mining (lead, zinc, manganese), agriculture, livestock raising.

Caer·phil'ly (kär·fĭl'ĭ). Urban district, Glamorganshire, SE Wales; pop. 35,194; trade center in coal-mining section; known esp. for its cheese; has 13th-cent. castle.

Caesaraugusta. See SARAGOSSA.

Cae'sa·re'a (sē'zȧ·rē'ȧ; sĕs'ȧ-; sĕz'ȧ-). **1** See CHERCHEL, Algeria.
2 *mod.* **Qi·sar'ya** (kē·sär'yȧ; -yă). Ancient seaport on coast of Samaria and Roman capital of Palestine, 55 m. NW of Jerusalem; pop. 706. Founded by Herod the Great; made Roman capital after Vespasian's reign; site of an early Christian church and frequently mentioned in the New Testament; council held here 195 A.D.

Caesarea Mazaca. See KAYSERI.

Caesarea Phi·lip'pi (fĭ·lĭp'ī; fĭl'ĭ·pī). Ancient city at foot of Mt. Hermon near the source of the Jordan, NW Decapolis, Palestine. Has temple which was built by Herod the Great and enlarged by Philip the Tetrarch; important in Roman times. Now modern village of **Ba'ni·yas'** (bä'nĭ·yăs') in SW Syria.

Caesarodunum. See TOURS.

Caesaromagus. See BEAUVAIS.

Cae'sar's Head (sē'zẽrz). Range 3225 ft. of the Blue Ridge, in N Greenville co., NW South Carolina; the S face is a 1500-ft. precipice.

Caesena. See CESENA.

Caetité. See CAITETÉ.

Ca·gar'ras Islands (kȧ·gȧr'räs). Islands in Atlantic Ocean off S Rio de Janeiro state, SE Brazil.

Ca'ga·yan' (kä'gä·yän'). **1** *or* **Ri'o Gran'de de Ca·gayan** (rē'õ grän'dä thä). River 220 m. long, NE Luzon, Phil. Is.; flows N to Babuyan Channel; largest river in Luzon; chief tributary the Chico; valley 50 m. wide bet. the Cordillera Central on the W and the Sierra Madre on the E; navigable for much of its course. Near its mouth is the port of Aparri.
2 River ab. 50 m. long, Mindanao, Phil. Is.; flows N from Bukidnon to Macajalar Bay.
3 Province, NE Luzon, Phil. Is.; 3470 sq. m.; pop.

292,270; ✳ Tuguegarao; occupies lower basin of Cagayan river, including part of its tributary the Chico with Sierra Madre range averaging ab. 3500 ft. E of valley along Pacific Ocean; includes Babuyan Is. (*q.v.*) to the N; northernmost tip is Cape Engaño; valley region fertile, esp. suitable for tobacco. Chief towns Tuguegarao, Aparri, Gattaran, and Solana.

History: Visited and explored by Spaniards 1572–81; recognized as a political division by 1583; scene of several uprisings in 17th cent.; suffered from injustices of the tobacco monopoly c. 1782–1830; civil government established Sept. 1901. In World War II Aparri occupied by Japanese Dec. 10, 1941; Cagayan valley reconquered by American forces May–June 1945.

4 *also* **Cagayan de Mi·sa′mis** (dä mē·sä′mēs). Municipality, ✳ of Misamis Oriental prov., Mindanao, Phil. Is., in E part near S shore of Macajalar Bay ab. 3 m. from mouth of Cagayan river; pop. 48,084.

Cagayan Islands, *or* **Ca′ga·ya′nes** (kä′gä·yä′näs) Group of seven small islands in N part of Sulu Sea, Phil. Is., 70 m. W of SW Negros in 9°30′N; ab. 5 sq. m.; pop. 3029; only settlement **Ca′ga·yan·cil′lo** (kä′gä·yän-sē′yô); belong to Palawan prov.

Cagayan Su′lu (sōō′lōō). Small island in SW Sulu Sea, SW Phil. Is., lat. 7°N, ab. 70 m. off the NE coast of North Borneo; 26 sq. m.; surrounded by 13 islets; remarkable for its scenery, fertility, fauna and flora; suffered much in 19th cent. from Moro pirates. With Sibutu I. (*q.v.*) inadvertently omitted from Philippine lands sold by Spain to U.S. by treaty of Dec. 10, 1898; acquired for sum of $100,000 by special agreement of Nov. 7, 1900, proclaimed Mar. 23, 1901.

Ca′gli (kä′lyē). Commune, Pesaro e Urbino prov., Marches, cen. Italy, 29 m. SSW of Pesaro; pop. 12,658.

Ca′glia·ri (kä′lyä·rē). **1** Province of Italy. See *Table* at ITALY.

2 *anc.* **Car′a·lis** (kăr′a·lĭs). Fortified seaport, its ✳, and ✳ of Sardinia, at head of Gulf of Cagliari on S coast of Sardinia 252 m. SW of Rome; pop. 106,649; 14th-cent. cathedral; ancient Roman remains; university (founded 1596; modernized 1765). Founded by Phoenicians; held successively by Romans, Saracens, Pisans, Spain, Austria, and (as kingdom of Sardinia) by Savoy.

Cagliari, Gulf of. Inlet of Mediterranean Sea on S coast of the island of Sardinia.

Cagnes–sur–Mer (kán′y′·sür·mâr′). Commune, Alpes-Maritimes dept., SE France; pop. 7866; resort on the Riviera just W of Nice.

Ca′gra·ray′ (kä′grä·rī′). Island, E Albay prov., Luzon, Phil. Is., ab. 11 m. NE of Legaspi; 28 sq. m.; pop. 8122; lies bet. Lagonoy Gulf and Albay Gulf.

Ca′gua (kä′gwä). Town, Aragua state, N Venezuela; pop. (1941 est.) 5029.

Cagua, Mount. Mountain 3927 ft. of volcanic origin near N end of Sierra Madre range, NE Cagayan prov., Luzon, Phil. Is.

Ca′guas (kä′gwäs). Municipality (pop. 65,098) and town (pop. 32,015), E cen. Puerto Rico; in fertile agricultural region.

Ca·ha′ba (kȧ·hô′bȧ; -hä′bȧ), *sometimes* **Ca·haw′ba** (-hô′-). River ab. 200 m. long, cen. Alabama; rises in St. Clair co., flows S through coal fields into Alabama river in Dallas co. ab. 10 m. SW of Selma.

Ca·ho′ki·a (kȧ·hō′kĭ·ȧ). Village, St. Clair co., SW Illinois, just S of East St. Louis; pop. 15,829; founded 1699 by the French, one of first permanent white settlements in Illinois. The **Cahokia Mounds,** a group of prehistoric Indian mounds including one which is the largest prehistoric earthwork in the U.S., are not in this village but are located ab. 4 m. NE of East St. Louis.

Ca′hors′ (kȧ·ôr′); *anc.* **Ca·dur′cum** (kȧ·dûr′kŭm) *and* **Di′vo·na** (dī′vô·nȧ; dĭv′ô-). City, ✳ of Lot dept., S cen. France, on Lot river 59 m. N of Toulouse; pop. 13,269; episcopal see (from 4th cent.); 12th-cent. cathedral; 14th-cent. fortified bridge; episcopal palace (now pre-

fecture); coal in vicinity. Important center of finance in Middle Ages; university (consolidated with Toulouse university 1751) founded 1322 by Pope John XXII, a native; under English rule 1360–1428.

Ca·hul′ (kä·hōōl′). **1** Former department, SW Bessarabia, Romania; 1730 sq. m.; pop. 194,631.

2 Town, its ✳. See KAGUL.

Cai′ba·rién′ (kī′vä·ryän′). Municipality and town, Las Villas prov., W cen. Cuba; pop. (town) 19,815; port on N coast 30 m. E of Santa Clara.

Cai′cos Islands (kä′kŭs). See TURKS AND CAICOS ISLANDS.

Caicos Passage. Channel ab. 45 m. wide in the Bahama Is., West Indies, NW of Caicos Is.

Caieta. See GAETA.

Cail′lou Lake (kä′lōō; kȧ·lōō′; *Fr.* kȧ′yōō′). Lake 5 m. long in S Terrebonne parish, SE Louisiana; **Grand Caillou Bayou** runs through the lake.

Cai·ma·ne′ra (kī′mä·nä′rä). Seaport barrio on W side of Guantánamo Bay, SE Oriente prov., E Cuba.

Cainargea–Mică. See KUCHUK KAINARJI.

Caird Coast (kârd). Ice-covered section of Antarctica, 75°S lat. and 23° to 29°W long., on SE coast of Weddell Sea NE of Leopold Coast; part of Coats Land and included in Falkland Islands Dependencies (*q.v.*).

Cairn Eige (kärn ě′ě) *or* **Carn Eige** (kärn ě′ě). Peak 3877 ft., NW Scotland, in S Ross and Cromarty co.

Cairn′gorm′ Mountains (kârn′gôrm′). Range of The Grampians in NE cen. Scotland; highest peak Ben Macdhui, 4296 ft. high; includes **Cairngorm** 4084 ft., in W Banff co.; chief source of a smoky-brown variety of quartz (cairngorm).

Cairn Hill (kârn). Peak 2545 ft. in the Cheviot Hills along the border bet. England and Scotland.

Cairns (kârnz). Seaport, NE Queensland, Australia, on Trinity Bay within Great Barrier Reef 865 m. NW of Brisbane (1040 m. by rail); pop. 12,004; on narrow lowland strip E of Atherton Plateau; outlet and supply center for silver-lead, tin, and copper mines and for agricultural and dairy country; principal crop sugar.

Cairn Toul (kârn′ tōōl′; toul′). Peak 4241 ft., N cen. Scotland, in the Cairngorm group, SW Aberdeen co.

Cai′ro (kâr′ō; kä′rō). **1** Industrial and commercial city, ⊗ of Grady co., SW Georgia, 50 m. S of Albany; pop. 7427; sugar cane sirup, pecans.

2 City, ⊗ of Alexander co., SW Illinois, at confluence of Ohio and Mississippi rivers; pop. 9348; sawmills, flour mills, foundries and machine shops; port of entry; settled c. 1846; incorp. 1857; depot for Federal military supplies during Civil War. The "Eden" of Charles Dickens's novel *Martin Chuzzlewit.*

Cai′ro (kī′rō). **1** Governorate, N Egypt. See **2**, below, and *Table* at EGYPT.

2 *Arab.* **al–Qâ′hi·rah** (ăl·kä′hĭ·rŏ). City in N Egypt; ✳ of Egypt and of United Arab Republic, on right bank of Nile ab. 9 m. above division into two main branches of the delta; pop. (1937) 1,312,096; constitutes the governorate of Cairo. Largest city in Africa; its Arab quarter ancient but much of city modern; has 250 mosques (many in ruins), esp. Sultan Hasan Mosque, Mohammed Ali Mosque, and El Azhar (a university); one of main educational centers of Islam; center of many industries.

History: Near site of Roman city Babylon which was captured by Arabs 641 A.D.; Old Cairo (**al–Fus·tât′** [ăl·fŏŏs·tät′] by Arabs), built as military camp 642; new part (**al–Qâ′hi·rah** [ăl kä′hĭ·rŏ]) built by Fatimid dynasty (see EGYPT) 968 and made their capital 973, known as "City of Victory"; citadel erected in late 12th cent. by Saladin, ruler of Egypt and Syria at time of Third Crusade; while capital of Mameluke sultans (from 13th cent.), reached greatest prosperity as trade and cultural center; taken by Ottoman Turks 1517; held by French 1798–1801; capital of semi-independent pashalik (province) ruled by Mehemet Ali, and of independent kingdom of Egypt (*q.v.*). British and U.S. base in North

Africa campaign 1942. Site of conference Nov. 22–26, 1943 of President Roosevelt, Prime Minister Churchill, and Generalissimo Chiang Kai-shek.

Cai'ro, Mount (kī'rō). Mountain 5474 ft. dominating Monte Cassino, Italy, on NNW.

Cai'ro·çu', Point (kī'rōō·sōō'). Cape on S coast of Rio de Janeiro state, SE Brazil, S of Ilha Grande Bay.

Cai'te·te' or **Cae'ti·té'** (kī'tě·tâ'). Municipality and town, S Baía state, Brazil; pop. (municipality) 29,754.

Caith'ness (kāth'něs; kāth·něs'). County, N Scotland; area 686 sq. m.; pop. (1951) 22,705; ⊗ Wick; agriculture, fisheries.

Cai·va'no (kī·vä'nō). Commune, Napoli prov., Campania, S Italy, 8 m. NNE of Naples; pop. 16,356; trade center for agricultural area; medieval fortified town.

Ca'ja·bam'ba (kä'hä·väm'bä). Town, Chimborazo prov., cen. Ecuador, 9 m. W of Riobamba; pop. (1944 est.) 15,043.

Ca'ja·mar'ca (kä'hä·mär'kä). **1** Department of Peru. See *Table* at PERU.

2 Town, its ⊗, on E slope of the Andes ab. 370 m. NW of Lima; pop. (1940 est.) 15,553; alt. 9000 ft.; in mining and grain-growing region; hot sulfur springs (known as Baths of the Incas) nearby. Atahualpa, last of the Inca sovereigns, executed here by Pizarro 1533.

Ca·jon' Pass (kà·hōn'). Pass bet. San Gabriel Mts. on W and San Bernardino Mts. on E, S California, N of San Bernardino and ENE of Los Angeles; southeastern gateway for overland travel to the coast since 1831.

Cal'a·bar (kăl'à·bär). **1** Province of Nigeria. See *Table* at NIGERIA.

2 Town, its ⊗, and port on left bank of **Calabar River** (flows into Cross estuary); pop. 16,653; trades in palm oil and palm kernels; an Efik center.

Ca'la·ba·zar' de Sa'gua (kä'lä·vä·sär' thä sä'gwä). Municipality and town, Las Villas prov., W cen. Cuba, 15 m. N of Santa Clara; pop. (town) 8131.

Ca'la·bo'zo (kä'lä·vō'sō). Town, Guárico state, N cen. Venezuela, 110 m. S of Caracas; pop. 7123; cattle and agricultural center in the llanos.

Ca·la'bri·a (kà·lä'brĭ·à). **1** Region of ancient Italy, a peninsula forming the "heel" of Italian "boot"; now the S part of Apulia prov.

2 *Ital.* **Ca·la'bri·a** (kä·lä'brě·ä), *pl.* **Le Ca·la'bri·e** (lā kä·lä'brě·â); *anc.* **Brut'ti·um** (brŭt'ĭ·ŭm). Compartimento of S Italy (for provincial divisions, area, and pop., see *Table* at ITALY); occupies entire "toe" of Italian "boot"; consists of marshy coastal flatlands, well-watered and fertile valleys, and a central ridge of granite mountains; heavily forested; subject to severe earthquakes (disastrous ones having occurred 1783–87, 1905, 1908); agriculture, stock raising, and quarrying.

History: Ancient Bruttium, founded as Greek colony, taken by Romans 268 B.C.; retaken in 9th cent. A.D. by Byzantine Empire; conquered by Normans under Robert Guiscard who became duke of Apulia and Calabria 1059; united to Norman kingdom of Naples and Sicily 11th cent., and with kingdom of Italy 1860.

Calabrian Apennines; *Ital.* **Appennino Calabrese.** See APENNINES.

Calae. See CHELLES.

Ca'la·fat' (kä'lä·fät'). Town, Oltenia, S Romania, on the Danube opp. the Bulgarian city of Vidin; pop. 7705; founded in 14th cent. by colonists from Genoa who developed the ship-repairing industry and whose workmen (*calfats*) gave the town its name; later became grain-trading center; battleground during Russo-Turkish conflicts in 19th cent.

Calagurris. See CALAHORRA.

Ca'lah (kā'là); *mod.* **Nim·rud'** (nĭm·rōōd'). Biblical name (*Gen.* x. 11, 12) of **Ka'lakh** (kä'läk), an ancient capital of Assyria, on E bank of Tigris river ab. 20 m. SSE of Mosul. Built probably in 13th cent. B.C.; under Ashurnasirpal II (884–859 B.C.) replaced Nineveh as capital and remained royal residence for 150 years.

Ca·la·hor'ra (kä·lä·ôr'rä); *anc.* **Cal'a·gur'ris** (kăl'à·gŭr'ĭs). Commune, Logroño prov., N Spain, on right bank of Ebro 26 m. SE of Logroño; pop. 12,004; trades in wine and cattle. Ancient town, Calagurris, taken by Pompey after four years' siege 76–73 B.C.

Cal'ais (kăl'ĭs). City, Washington co., E Maine, on St. Croix river; pop. 4223; port of entry, connected with St. Stephen, N.B., by International Bridge.

Ca'lais' (kà·lě'; *Angl.* kăl'ā, kā·lā', kăl'ĭs). Seaport and manufacturing city, Pas-de-Calais dept., N France, on Strait of Dover 64 m. NW of Arras; pop. 67,568; fortified place; 18th-cent. and modern town halls; Hôtel de Guise (founded by Edward III of England), Hôtel Dessin; barracks; technical schools; manufactures silk and cotton tulle, linen, lace, hosiery, nets, fishing vessels. Town of old county of Artois taken 1347 by Edward III of England; after 1450 only remaining English possession in France; recaptured 1558 by duke of Guise; held by Spanish 1596–98; objective, together with Dunkerque, of famous German "drive to the sea" in World War I. In World War II taken by Germans May 22, 1940; launching base for robot bombs June 15–Sept. 1, 1944; surrounded by Canadian Army Sept. 6, 1944 and taken Sept. 30.

Ca'la·mar' (kä·lä·mär'; *Angl.* kăl'à·mär'). Town, N Bolívar dept., N Colombia, on lower Magdalena river E of Cartagena; pop. 6934; railroad terminus.

Ca·lam'ba (kä·läm'bä; kä'läm·bä'). Municipality on S shore of Laguna de Bay, W Laguna prov., Luzon, Phil. Is.; pop. 32,363; birthplace of José Rizal.

Ca'la·mian' Islands (kä'lä·myän'), or **Ca'la·mia'nes** (kä'lä·myä'nås). Island group, SW Phil. Is., bet. Mindoro and Palawan Is.; 677 sq. m.; pop. 17,437; comprises 3 large islands Busuanga, Culion, and Coron, and ab. 95 small ones; part of Palawan prov. Mountainous and well forested; chief town Coron.

Calamine, La. See MORESNET.

Ca·lam'i·ty, Mount (kà·läm'ĭ·tĭ). Peak 3641 ft. in the Adirondack Mts., Essex co., NE New York.

Cal'a·mus (kăl'à·mŭs). River ab. 70 m. long, N cen. Nebraska; rises in Brown co., flows SE into North Loup river in Garfield co., cen. Nebraska.

Ca·la'ñas (kä·lä'nyäs). Commune, Huelva prov., SW Spain, 32 m. N of Huelva; pop. 11,285; pyrite mines.

Ca·lan'che (kä·läng'kä). Region on W cen. coast of Corsica remarkable for its red granite formations.

Ca·la·pan' (kä·lä·pän'). Municipality, ⊗ of Mindoro prov., Phil. Is., on NE coast of Mindoro I. at E end of Verde Island Passage; pop. 17,158.

Ca·la'pe (kä·lä'på). Municipality on W coast of Bohol, Phil. Is., on Bohol Strait N of Tagbilaran; pop. 21,319.

Că·lă·ra'şi (kà·là·räsh'; -rä'shě). Town, SE Romania, in Muntenia region, on the Danube ab. 63 m. ESE of Bucharest; pop. 17,890; commercial center; fisheries.

Ca'lar·cá' (kä'lär·kä'). Town, Caldas dept., W cen. Colombia; pop. 7453.

Ca'la·si·a'o (kä'lä·sě·ä'ō). Municipality, cen. Pangasinan prov., Luzon, Phil. Is., on a branch of the Agno 7 m. E of Lingayen; pop. 19,325; noted for its hat industry.

Ca'la·ta·fi'mi (kä·lä'tä·fē'mě). Commune, Trapani prov., NW Sicily, 21 m. ESE of Trapani; pop. 11,484; site of Garibaldi's defeat May 15, 1860 of Neapolitans.

Ca'la·ta·gan' (kä'lä·tä·gän'). Municipality on SW coast of Batangas prov., Luzon, Phil. Is.; pop. 7710.

Ca'la·ta·yud' (kä'lä·tä·yōōth'). Commune, Zaragoza prov., NE Spain, 45 m. SW of Saragossa; pop. 18,419; trade center; sulfur baths; ruins of Moorish forts. Founded in 8th cent.; conquered 1120 by Alfonso I of Aragon. Birthplace of the Latin epigrammatist Martial 2 m. E at ancient **Bil'bi·lis** (bĭl'bĭ·lĭs).

Ca'la·tra'va (kä'lä·trä'vä). **1** Municipality, NE coast of Negros Occidental prov., Negros, Phil. Is., on Tañon Strait 36 m. E of City of Bacolod; pop. 38,695.

2 Ancient fortress, cen. Spain, just ENE of Ciudad Real near Guadiana river; defended against Moors by two Cistercians who presented it to Sancho III of Castile

1158 and instituted Order of Calatrava; captured by Moors 1197, retaken 1212; taken over by Order of Alcántara 1218 when Order of Calatrava built new convent ab. 8 m. S (New Calatrava); only a tower now on site.

Calauria. See POROS.

Cal′a·ver′as (kăl′à·vĕr′ás). **1** River ab. 70 m. long, cen. California; flows SW into San Joaquin river. **2** County in California. See *Table* at CALIFORNIA.

Ca′la·vi′te, Cape (kä′lä·vē′tå). Northwest point of Mindoro I., Phil. Is., 13°27′N, 120°18′E; just to the E is **Mount Calavite** 4990 ft.

Ca′la·yan′ (kä′lä·yän′). Island in Babuyan group, N of Luzon, Phil. Is.; 73 sq. m.; pop. 1911.

Cal·ba′yog (käl·bä′yôg). Municipality, W Samar, Phil. Is., on Samar Sea 29 m. NW of Catbalogan; pop. 25,786.

Cal′be (käl′bĕ); *also* **Kal′be** (käl′bĕ) *or* **Calbe an der Saa′le** (än dĕr zä′lĕ). Manufacturing city, E Germany, in former Prussian province of Saxony, on Saale river 16 m. S of Magdeburg; pop. 11,583.

Cal′ca·sieu (käl′kà·shōō). **1** River ab. 200 m. long, SW Louisiana; rises in N Vernon parish, flows in wide curve E, SE, and SW, through **Calcasieu Lake** (ab. 15 m. long, in Cameron parish, surrounded by marshes which cover almost entire parish), and into Gulf of Mexico through **Calcasieu Pass** (ab. 5 m. long). **2** Parish in Louisiana. See *Table* at LOUISIANA.

Cal·ce′ta (käl·sā′tä). Town, Manabí prov., W Ecuador, 100 m. N of Guayaquil; pop. (1944 est.) 13,366.

Calchi. See KHALKĒ.

Cal·cut′ta (käl·kŭt′à). City, S West Bengal, NE Indian Union, on Hooghly river ab. 90 m. from its mouth; 34 sq. m.; pop. (1941) 2,108,891, with suburbs and Howrah 2,488,183; * of former Bengal province and Presidency Division and, until 1912, seat of government of India. Has one of world's most active ports; exports jute and jute manufactures, tea, rubber, hides and leather, and flaxseed. Seat of Univ. of Calcutta and educational center of India. Has fine maidan or park (2 sq. m.) which contains Fort William, a Jain temple, botanical garden, and government buildings.

History: English factory established by Job Charnock on site 1690; Fort William erected 1696; seat of Bengal presidency 1707; captured by Siraj-ud-daula, nawab of Bengal, who imprisoned English (Black Hole of Calcutta) 1756; retaken by Clive 1757; capital of British India until 1912 (see DELHI).

Cal′das (käl′däs). Department of Colombia. See *Table* at COLOMBIA.

Cal·dei′ra (käl·dā′ĕ·rá). Mountain peak ab. 3350 ft. on Fayal I. in the Azores.

Cal′der (kôl′dĕr). **1** Small river in Lancashire, NW England, flowing into the Ribble river. **2** River in N cen. England, in SW Yorkshire; flows NE into the Aire river at Castleford below Leeds.

Cal·de′ra (käl·dā′rä). Seaport and commune, Atacama prov., N cen. Chile, ab. 440 m. N of Santiago; pop. (commune) 2078; chief port of province and the port of Copiapó (54 m. by rail); exports nitrate and copper.

Cal′der·wood′ Dam (kôl′dĕr·wood′). See *Table* at TENNESSEE VALLEY AUTHORITY.

Cal·die′ro (käl·dyā′rô). Commune, Verona prov., SW Venezia Euganea, NE Italy, E of Verona; pop. 2202; scene of battles of Napoleonic Wars in which Masséna defeated the Austrians under Archduke Charles Louis Oct. 30, 1805 but was defeated Nov. 12, 1805.

Cald′well (kôld′wĕl; -wĕl; kŏld′-; *in South, also* kà·wĕl′). **1** Name of a parish in Louisiana and of counties in four states of the U.S. See *Tables* at LOUISIANA, KENTUCKY, MISSOURI, NORTH CAROLINA, TEXAS. **2** City, ⊗ of Canyon co., SW Idaho, 25 m. W of Boise; pop. 12,230; College of Idaho (1891; coed.). **3** City, Sumner co., S Kansas, 33 m. W of Arkansas City; pop. 1788; in grazing and wheat section. **4** Borough, Essex co., NE New Jersey, 9 m. NNW of Newark; pop. 6942; birthplace of Grover Cleveland.

5 Village, ⊗ of Noble co., SE Ohio, 21 m. N of Marietta; pop. 1999; coal mines, oil wells, salt mines. **6** City, ⊗ of Burleson co., E cen. Texas, 20 m. SW of Bryan; pop. 2204; manufactures cottonseed oil, ice.

Cal′dy, *or* **Cal′dey, Island** (käl′dĭ). Island at W entrance to Carmarthen Bay, S Wales; lighthouse; site of 5th-cent. monastery at which St. David was a scholar; ancient stone inscribed in ogam and Latin.

Cal′e·don (käl′ĕ·dŏn). **1** River ab. 230 m. long in SE Africa; rises in the Drakensberg mountain range near the NW boundary of Natal, E Union of South Africa, flows WSW forming the boundary bet. Orange Free State and Basutoland, and empties into Orange river. **2** Town, SW Cape Province, S Union of South Africa, 70 m. E of Cape Town; pop. 3221; thermal springs.

Cal′e·do′nia (käl′ĕ·dōn′yá; -dō′nĭ·á). **1** County in Vermont. See *Table* at VERMONT. **2** Village, ⊗ of Houston co., SE corner of Minnesota, 30 m. S of Winona; pop. 2563; agricultural trade center. **3** Ancient name for N Britain; Scotland.

Cal′e·do′nian Canal (käl′ĕ·dōn′yăn; -dō′nĭ·ăn). Ship canal extending diagonally across cen. Scotland from Loch Linnhe on the SW to Moray Firth on the NE; built by uniting Lochs Ness, Oich, Lochy, and Eil with a navigable channel; begun 1805, opened 1822, completed 1847; 60½ m. long, including 22 m. of channel construction and 38¼ m. in the lochs; 110 ft. wide at water surface; has 29 locks with an average lift of 8 ft.

Ca·le′ra (kä·lā′rä). Town, Vaiparaíso prov., cen. Chile, ab. 40 m. NE of Valparaíso; pop. 8426; railroad junction.

Ca·lex′i·co (kà·lĕk′sĭ·kō). City, Imperial co., SE corner of California, on Mexican border adjacent to Mexicali, Mexico; pop. 7992; fruit and cotton.

Calf of Man. See Calf of MAN.

Cal′ga·ry (käl′gà·rĭ). City, S Alberta, Canada, on Bow river; pop. 129,060; trading center of an extensive stock-raising and wheat region; base of supplies for surrounding mining districts; has large grist and flour mills, grain elevators, brick and cement works, lumber mills, oil refineries, and packing houses. Seat of Provincial Institute of Technology and Art (1916; coed.) and of a provincial normal school. Begun as a fort of the Northwest Mounted Police 1875 and as a town 1884; became capital of Alberta district.

Cal·houn′ (käl·hōōn′; *esp. attributively,* käl′hōōn). **1** Name of counties in eleven states of the U.S. See *Tables* at ALABAMA, ARKANSAS, FLORIDA, GEORGIA, ILLINOIS, IOWA, MICHIGAN, MISSISSIPPI, SOUTH CAROLINA, TEXAS, WEST VIRGINIA. **2** City, ⊗ of Gordon co., NW Georgia, 22 m. NNE of Rome; pop. 3587; incorp. 1852; largely destroyed by Sherman 1864 but rebuilt; cotton mills. **3** City, ⊗ of McLean co., W Kentucky; pop. 817.

Calhoun Falls. Town, Abbeville co., W South Carolina, 27 m. WSW of Greenwood; pop. 2525.

Ca′li (kä′lĕ). City, * of Valle dept., W Colombia; pop. 88,366; at the confluence of Cali river with the Cauca at alt. 3000 ft.; connected by rail with port of Buenaventura 105 m. to W; center of valley trade, esp. livestock, lumber, and mineral products. Founded 1536.

Ca·lia′cra *or* **Ka·lia′kra, Cape** (kä·lyá′krä). Cape, NE Bulgaria, on the Black Sea in the Dobruja.

Cal′i·cut (käl′ĭ·kŭt; -kŭt; *now also* **Ko′zhi·kode′** (kō′zhĭ·kōd′). City, cen. Kerala, S India, on the Malabar Coast ab. 350 m. WSW of Madras; pop. (1951) 158,724; exports coconuts, coffee, tea, spices; gave its name to the cloth *calico*. Visited by Vasco da Gama 1498; unsuccessfully attacked by Albuquerque 1510; site of Portuguese fortified factory 1513–25 (abandoned); visited by British 1615; site of trading posts of British (estab. 1664), French (estab. 1698), Danish (1752–84); occupied by British troops 1790; transferred by treaty to British 1792. Seat of two colleges.

Cal′i·en′te (käl′ĭ·ĕn′tĕ). City, Lincoln co., E Nevada, ab. 23 m. S of Pioche; pop. 792; railroad division point.

Cal′i·for′nia (kăl′ĭ·fôrn′yà; -fôr′nĭ·à). **1** A western state of U.S.A., 31st state admitted to Union (1850); bounded on N by Oregon, on E by Nevada and Arizona, on S by Mexican territory of Lower California, and on W by the Pacific Ocean; 3d state in area, 158,693 sq. m. (land area 156,740 sq. m.); 2d state in population, 15,717,204; ✻ Sacramento. See *Map* pp. 184, 185; also *Table of States* at UNITED STATES. Divided into the following 58 counties (for pronunciations, see their individual entries):

NAME	LOCATION	AREA[1]	POP.[1]	CO. SEAT
Alameda	W	733	905,670	Oakland
Alpine	E	723	397	Markleeville
Amador	cen.	594	9,990	Jackson
Butte	N	1,663	82,030	Oroville
Calaveras	cen.	1,028	10,289	San Andreas
Colusa	N cen.	1,153	12,075	Colusa
Contra Costa	W	734	409,030	Martinez
Del Norte	NW corner; coastal	1,003	17,771	Crescent City
El Dorado	E	1,725	29,390	Placerville
Fresno[2]	S cen.	5,985	365,945	Fresno
Glenn	N	1,317	17,245	Willows
Humboldt	NW; coastal	3,573	104,892	Eureka
Imperial[3]	SE corner	4,284	72,105	El Centro
Inyo[4]	E	10,091	11,684	Independence
Kern	S	8,170	291,984	Bakersfield
Kings	SW cen.	1,395	49,954	Hanford
Lake	W	1,256	13,786	Lakeport
Lassen[5]	NE	4,548	13,597	Susanville
Los Angeles[6]	SW; coastal	4,071	6,038,771	Los Angeles
Madera[7]	cen.	2,148	40,468	Madera
Marin	W; coastal	521	146,820	San Rafael
Mariposa[8]	cen.	1,455	5,064	Mariposa
Mendocino	W; coastal	3,510	51,059	Ukiah
Merced	cen.	1,983	90,446	Merced
Modoc	NE corner	4,094	8,308	Alturas
Mono	E	3,028	2,213	Bridgeport
Monterey	W; coastal	3,324	198,351	Salinas
Napa	W cen.	790	65,890	Napa
Nevada	E	979	20,911	Nevada City
Orange	SW; coastal	782	703,925	Santa Ana
Placer	E	1,431	56,998	Auburn
Plumas	NE	2,570	11,620	Quincy
Riverside	SE	7,179	306,191	Riverside
Sacramento	N cen.	985	502,778	Sacramento
San Benito	W	1,396	15,396	Hollister
San Bernardino	SE	20,131	503,591	San Bernardino
San Diego	SW corner; coastal	4,258	1,033,011	San Diego
San Francisco[10]	W; coastal	45	742,855	San Francisco
San Joaquin	cen.	1,410	249,989	Stockton
San Luis Obispo	SW; coastal	3,326	81,044	San Luis Obispo
San Mateo	W; coastal	454	444,387	Redwood City
Santa Barbara[11]	SW; coastal	2,745	168,962	Santa Barbara
Santa Clara	W	1,305	642,315	San Jose
Santa Cruz	W; coastal	439	84,219	Santa Cruz
Shasta[12]	N	3,800	59,468	Redding
Sierra	NE	958	2,247	Downieville
Siskiyou	N	6,313	32,855	Yreka
Solano	cen.	827	134,597	Fairfield
Sonoma	W; coastal	1,579	147,375	Santa Rosa
Stanislaus	cen.	1,506	157,294	Modesto
Sutter	N cen.	607	33,380	Yuba City
Tehama	N	2,976	25,305	Red Bluff
Trinity	NW	3,191	9,706	Weaverville
Tulare[13]	S cen.	4,845	168,403	Visalia
Tuolumne[14]	cen.	2,275	14,404	Sonora
Ventura[15]	SW; coastal	1,857	199,138	Ventura
Yolo	N cen.	1,034	65,727	Woodland
Yuba	N	638	33,859	Marysville

[1] Area = land area in sq. m. Pop. from 1960 Census.
[2] SE part occupied by Kings Canyon National Park.
[3] Contains Imperial Valley and (in NW) most of Salton Sea, both below sea level.
[4] Death Valley in E and S.
[5] Part of Lassen Volcanic National Park in SW.
[6] Includes Santa Catalina and San Clemente Is., separated from mainland by San Pedro Channel.
[7] Part of Yosemite National Park in NE.
[8] E portion occupied by part of Yosemite National Park.
[9] Largest county in U.S.
[10] Coextensive with city of San Francisco.
[11] Includes northernmost group of Santa Barbara Is. (San Miguel, Santa Rosa, and Santa Cruz), separated from mainland by Santa Barbara Channel.
[12] SE corner contains part of Lassen Volcanic National Park, including Lassen Peak.
[13] NE portion contains Sequoia National Park.
[14] SE portion occupied by part of Yosemite National Park.
[15] Includes small islands of central part of chain of Santa Barbara Islands.

Nickname: Golden State, also El Dorado. *State flower:* Golden poppy. *Motto:* Eureka (I Have Found It). *Chief cities:* Los Angeles, San Francisco, San Diego, Oakland, Long Beach, San Jose. *Rivers:* Colorado, forming border in extreme SE with Arizona; Sacramento, flowing from near Mt. Shasta into San Francisco Bay; Pit, a tributary of the Sacramento; San Joaquin, flowing NW from Sierra Nevada area to join the Sacramento. *Chief lakes:* Tahoe in E on Nevada border, Owens in SE, and Salton Sea in Imperial Valley in extreme S. *Mts.:* Coast Ranges, in two parts, broken by San Francisco Bay and extending along most of the coast; a higher range, Sierra Nevada, extends along E border and contains Mt. Whitney, highest peak in state (and in continental U.S.) 14,495 ft., and at N end Mt. Shasta 14,162 ft.; in this range are Yosemite Valley and Sequoia National Parks, Lassen Peak (only volcano in U.S. proper) and Lassen Volcanic National Park; at its S end is Death Valley, a National Monument and lowest spot in U.S., and Mojave and Colorado Deserts. Along the coast in central part are San Francisco and San Pablo Bays discharging through Golden Gate into the Pacific Ocean, Monterey Bay, and in the S the Gulf of Santa Catalina and Santa Barbara Is. *Chief industries:* Agriculture (esp. fruitgrowing), petroleum, mining (gold, silver, copper, lead, quicksilver).

History: Coast explored by voyage of Cabrillo and Ferrelo who established Spanish claim to region 1542–43; coast reached by Sir Francis Drake 1579; first Franciscan mission established at San Diego 1769; remained under Spanish control, and later under Mexican control until conquered by U.S. forces during Mexican War (1846–47); ceded to U.S. by Treaty of Guadalupe Hidalgo 1848; settlement by Americans begun in 1841, greatly accelerated after discovery of gold at Coloma (Sutter's Mill) in 1848 which brought influx of miners and adventurers (the "forty-niners"); admitted to Union Sept. 9, 1850 as a free state under Compromise Act; present constitution drawn up by constitutional convention Sept. 28, 1878–Mar. 3, 1879, ratified by people, and in force Jan. 1, 1880; large sections of San Francisco destroyed by fire following an earthquake 1906. **2** City, ⊗ of Moniteau co., cen. Missouri, 22 m. W of Jefferson City; pop. 2788; trading center. **3** Borough, Washington co., SW Pennsylvania, on Monongahela river 15 m. NW of Uniontown; pop. 5978; coal mining. California State College (1852).

California, Gulf of; *formerly known as the* **Ver·mil′ion Sea** (vẽr·mil′yŭn). Arm of the Pacific Ocean extending in NW direction bet. the Mexican district of Lower California on the W and the Mexican states of Sonora and Sinaloa on the E.

California, Lower. See LOWER CALIFORNIA.

California Current. An ocean current flowing S off W coast of North America.

Ca·li′ma (kä·lē′mä). River ab. 50 m. long in W Colombia; flows into the San Juan N of Buenaventura.

Cal′i·mere, Point (kăl′ĭ·mẽr). Cape, E Madras prov., SE coast of India, N of Palk Strait.

Calimno, Calino. See KALYMNOS.

Ca′li·nog′ (kä′lē·nôg′). Municipality, N Iloilo prov., Panay, Phil. Is., N of Iloilo; pop. 22,175.

Cal′i·pa′tri·a (kăl′ĭ·pà·trĭ′à). City, Imperial co., SE corner of California, 26 m. N of El Centro; pop. 2548.

Cal′i·sto′ga (kăl′ĭ·stō′gà). City, Napa co., W cen. California, 12 m. NE of Santa Rosa; pop. 1514; settled 1859; trade center esp. for wine grapes; hot springs and geysers.

Calivo. See KALIBO.

Cal′la·han (kăl′à·hăn). County in Texas. See *Table* at TEXAS.

Cal′lan·der (kăl′ăn·dẽr). Village, Parry Sound dist., SE Ontario, Canada, on railroad at E end of Lake Nipissing ab. 7 m. SSE of North Bay.

Cal·la′o (kä·yä′ō). **1** Constitutional province of Peru with departmental status. See *Table* at PERU.

CALIFORNIA AND NEVADA

Statute Miles

0 20 40 60 80

★ State Capital

PUBLISHED BY G. & C. MERRIAM COMPANY
SPRINGFIELD, MASS.
PREPARED BY J. W. CLEMENT CO. DEPEW N.Y.

2 City, its ✱, chief seaport of Peru on Callao Bay 8 m. W of Lima; pop. (1940 est.) 84,438; modern well-equipped maritime terminal. Founded 1537, incorp. as a town 1671; destroyed by tidal wave and earthquake 1746; bombarded by Spanish 1866, and again 1880 by Chilean forces who took possession during War of the Pacific 1879–84.

Cal′la·way (kăl′á·wā). County in Missouri. See *Table* at MISSOURI.

Calle, La. See LA CALLE.

Calleva Atrebatum. See SILCHESTER.

Cal·lic′u·la (kă·lĭk′ů·lá). Mountain, N of Capua and ab. 4 m. NE of Teanum Sidicinum (*mod.* Teano), Campania, Italy; here Hannibal on his way back to Apulia 217 B.C. outwitted Fabius Maximus Cunctator.

Cal′li·ni′cum (kăl′ĭ·nĭ′kŭm). Ancient town on left bank of the Euphrates, N Syria, S of Edessa; on E frontier of Roman Empire in 6th and 7th cents. A.D.; Belisarius defeated here 531 by the Persian king Kavadh I.

Callipolis. See GELIBOLU.

Callithea. See KALLITHEA.

Cal′lo·way (kăl′ő·wā). County in Kentucky. See *Table* at KENTUCKY.

Calmar. Var. of KALMAR.

Cal′no (kăl′nō) *or* **Cal′neh** (kăl′nĕ). Biblical city of N Syria (*Isa.* x. 9).

Ca′lonne′-Ri′cou·art′ (kà·lôn′rē′kwàr′). Commune, Pas-de-Calais dept., N France; pop. (1931) 11,497.

Ca′lo·o′can (kä′lô·ô′kän). Municipality, NW Rizal prov., Luzon, Phil. Is., just N of Manila; pop. 38,820.

Ca·loo′sa·hatch′ee (kà·lōō′sà·hăch′ē). River, S Florida; rises in Glades co., S cen. Florida penin., flows W into Gulf of Mexico below Fort Myers; connected by canal with Lake Hicpochee, constitutes W portion of the Cross-Florida Waterway (*q.v.*).

Ca·lo′re (kä·lō′rā); *anc.* **Ca′lor** (kā′lôr). River, E headstream of the Volturno, S Italy.

Calpe. See PILLARS OF HERCULES; Rock of GIBRALTAR.

Cal′ta·gi·ro′ne (kăl′tä·jĕ·rō′nå). Commune, Catania prov., E Sicily, 37 m. SW of Catania; pop. 39,349.

Cal′ta·nis·set′ta (kăl′tä·nĭ·sĕt′å; *Ital.* käl′tä-nĕs-sät′-tä). **1** Province of Italy. See *Table* at ITALY.

2 Commune, its ✱, cen. Sicily, Italy, 59 m. SE of Palermo; pop. 50,467; sulfur; mineral springs; cathedral; Norman monastery (built 1153 by Roger II).

Ca′luire′-et-Cuire′ (kà′lü·ēr′å·kü·ēr′). Commune, Rhône dept., E cen. France, N suburb of Lyons on left bank of Saône river; pop. (1931) 16,126; coal mines.

Cal′u·met (kăl′ů·mĕt; -mĭt). **1** County in Wisconsin. See *Table* at WISCONSIN.

2 Village, Houghton co., NW Michigan penin., 70 m. NW of Marquette; pop. 1139; copper mines.

3 Industrial area, NW Indiana and NE Illinois, SE of and adjacent to Chicago, Illinois; includes chiefly the cities of East Chicago, Gary, Hammond, and Whiting, Indiana, and Calumet City and Lansing, Illinois.

Calumet City. Industrial city, Cook co., NE Illinois, 20 m. S of Chicago on Indiana border; pop. 25,000; glue and chemical factories; meat-packing plants; steelworks.

Calumet Harbor. Harbor district, SE Chicago, Illinois, on Lake Michigan at mouth of Calumet river (8 m. long) draining Lake Calumet in S Chicago.

Calumet Park. Village, Cook co., NE Illinois, S suburb of Chicago; pop. 8448.

Ca′lum·pit′ (kä′lŏŏm·pēt′). Municipality, SW Bulacan prov., Luzon, Phil. Is., NW of Malolos; pop. 17,047.

Cal′va′dos′ (kăl′vá·dôs′; -dōs′). Department of France. See *Table* at FRANCE.

Calvados Reef; *Fr.* **Ro′chers′ du Calvados** (rô′shä′dü). Long reef of rocks off village of Asnelles on Normandy coast, Calvados dept., France, W of the mouth of the Orne; was bet. the central and eastern beachheads on which Allies landed June 6, 1944.

Cal′va·ry (kăl′vá·rĭ); *Heb.* **Gol′go·tha** (gŏl′gŏ·thà). The place, outside of the ancient city of Jerusalem, where Christ was crucified (*Luke* xxiii. 33); the traditional site is within the walls of modern Jerusalem and is occupied by the Church of the Holy Sepulcher, actual site is uncertain.

Cal′ven (käl′vĕn). Narrow gorge, Venezia Tridentina, NE Italy, near the border of Graubünden canton, Switzerland; scene of defeat May 22, 1499 of Maximilian I by the Swiss of the Grisons (Graubünden) who thereby gained their independence.

Cal′vert (kăl′vērt). **1** County in Maryland. See *Table* at MARYLAND.

2 City, Robertson co., E cen. Texas; pop. 2073.

Cal′vi (käl′yē). Seaport, NW Corsica; pop. 2517; founded 13th cent.; repulsed forces of Henry II of France 1553; conquered by Nelson 1794 after 7 weeks' siege in which he lost an eye; erroneously claimed to be birthplace of Columbus.

Cal·vin′i·a (kăl·vĭn′ĭ·à). Town, W Cape Province, Union of South Africa, 180 m. NNE of Cape Town; pop. 2671; center of sheep and wheat section.

Calycadnus. See GÖKSU.

Cal′y·don (kăl′ĭ·dŏn). Ancient city, S Aetolia, cen. Greece, near coast of Gulf of Patras; scene in Greek legend of the Calydonian boar hunt.

Calydon, Gulf of. See Gulf of PATRAS.

Calymna, Calymnos. See KALYMNOS.

Cam (kăm). River ab. 40 m. long in Cambridgeshire, E cen. England; flows into the Ouse 3½ m. S of Ely; the city of Cambridge, on its banks, derives its name from the river.

Ca′ma·güey′ (kä′mä·gwĕ′ē; -gwā′). **1** Province of Cuba. See *Table* at CUBA.

2 Municipality and city, its ✱, in cen. part, E cen. Cuba; pop. (city) 78,458; distributing center for cattle-raising and agricultural district. Founded 1528; in early part of 19th cent. was capital of Spanish West Indies. Its port is Nuevitas.

Camagüey Archipelago. Group of islands off N coast of Camagüey prov., E cen. Cuba; principal islands are cayos Romano, Sabinal, Coco, and Guajaba.

Ca′ma·io′re (kä′mä·yō′rā). Commune, Lucca prov., Tuscany, cen. Italy, 12 m. NW of Lucca; pop. 22,291.

Ca′ma·jua·ní′ (kä′mä·hwä·nē′). Town, Las Villas prov., W cen. Cuba, E of Santa Clara; pop. 12,087.

Ca·ma′lig (kä·mä′lĕg). Municipality, E Albay prov., Luzon, Phil. Is., at S base of Mt. Mayon and on railroad ab. 6 m. W of Legaspi; pop. 22,230.

Ca·ma′no Island (kä·mä′nō). Island ab. 14 m. long in upper Puget Sound, off W coast of Snohomish co., NW Washington, a part of Island co., Washington.

Ca′ma·rat′, Cape (kà′mä′rä′). Cape, Var dept., SE France, NE of the Hyères Is.

Ca′ma·ret′ (kà′mä′rĕ′), *in full* **Camaret-sur-Mer** (-sür-mâr′). Village, Finistère dept., NW France, at tip of a peninsula just S of Brest; pop. 3528.

Camargue, La. See LA CAMARGUE.

Ca′ma·ri·ñal′, Cape (kä′mä·rē·nyäl′). Cape on SW coast of Spain, S of Cape Trafalgar.

Ca′ma·ri′nes (kä′mä·rē′nås). See CAMARINES NORTE.

Camarines Nor′te (nôr′tå). Province, SE Luzon, Phil. Is., on Pacific coast; 829 sq. m.; pop. 98,324; ✱ Daet. Mountains are volcanic and a continuation of ranges in Tayabas and Camarines Sur; highest peak Labo 3094 ft. on S border; soil very fertile, produces esp. rice, corn, hemp, and tobacco; much mineral wealth. Chief towns Daet, Jose Pañganiban, Paracale.

History: Was united with Camarines Sur for more than two centuries as one political unit under Spanish rule, known at first as Camarines 1573–1829 and later 1854–57, 1893–1919, as Ambos Camarines; in other years a separate province; region explored by Juan de Salcedo 1571; Franciscan mission established early in 17th cent.; civil government set up Apr. 1901.

Camarines Sur (sōōr′). Province, comprising cen. part of long peninsula of SE Luzon, Phil. Is., with coasts on

both the Pacific Ocean and inland waters of the Archipelago; 2060 sq. m.; pop. 385,695; ✳ Naga. Mountain ranges extend along W coast and through Caramoan Penin.; volcanic peaks of Isarog and Iriga in cen. and S parts; the Bicol flows generally NW from Lake Bato to San Miguel Bay; on extreme E separated by narrow channel from Catanduanes I. (part of Albay). Chief exports hemp, copra, forest products, and fish. Chief towns Naga, Iriga, Nabua, Libmanan, and Caramoan.

History: See CAMARINES NORTE. From early times a well-settled region; suffered from revolt ab. 1650; civil government established Apr. 1901; finally set up as separate province 1919.

Camarões. See CAMEROONS.

Ca'ma·rón', Cape (kä'mä·rôn'). Cape on N coast of Honduras, projecting into the Caribbean Sea.

Cam'as (kăm'ăs). **1** County in Idaho. See *Table* at IDAHO.
2 Industrial city, Clark co., SW Washington, on Columbia river 12 m. E of Vancouver; pop. 5666; in farming section; paper and pulp industry; fruit packing.

Ca·mau' (kȧ·mou'; *Fr.* kȧ'mō'). Town, S Cochin China, Vietnam, near Point Camau.

Camau, Point, *formerly* **Cam·bo'di·a Point** (kăm-bō'dĭ·ȧ). The S end of Cochin China, Vietnam; extends W into South China Sea and marks the SE corner of Gulf of Siam.

Cam'ba·luc (kăm'bȧ·lŭk) *or* **Cam'ba·lu** (kăm'bȧ·lōō). Marco Polo's name for Khanbalik (*q.v.*), the Mongol capital of China.

Cam·bay' (kăm·bā'). **1** Former Indian state, Gujarat, Indian Union, at head of Gulf of Cambay; 392 sq. m.; pop. (1941) 96,592. Founded ab. 1730.
2 Town, its ✳, at N end of Gulf of Cambay and at mouth of Mahi river 240 m. N of Bombay; pop. 31,877. Mentioned by Marco Polo in 1293 as one of India's two most important seaports; silting up of harbor in recent times has diverted former trade; has interesting Jain ruins and remains of encircling wall. Captured by British 1780, restored to Marathas 1783, and ceded to British by treaty 1803.

Cambay, Gulf of. Inlet of Arabian Sea on W coast of India, SE of Kathiawar Penin.; gradually being filled with silt; receives Narbada, Tapti, and Mahi rivers.

Camberiacum. See CHAMBÉRY.

Cam'ber·well (kăm'bēr·wĕl; -wĕl). **1** City, S Victoria, SE Australia, E suburb of Melbourne; pop. 50,059.
2 Metropolitan borough of London. See *Table* at LONDON.

Cam·bo'di·a (kăm·bō'dĭ·ȧ); *also, formerly,* **Cam·bo'ja** (kăm·bō'jȧ); *Fr.* **Cam'bodge'** (kän'bōj'). Country, Indochina; a kingdom, formerly a French protectorate; area 69,866 sq. m.; pop. (1953 est.) 3,860,000; ✳ Pnompenh. In S part of Indochina, bordering on Thailand on N and W, on Gulf of Siam on SW, and on Vietnam on SE. Generally level with mountain range (Phanom Dong Rak) along N border and peaks along the coast 2300 to 5700 ft. Most of the kingdom lies in basin of lower Mekong with the large lake, Tonle Sap, in its W part. Has large jungle areas; agriculture and fishing are two main industries; much rice is produced; other exports cotton, tobacco, maize, rubber, and pepper. Cambodians are descendants of the Khmers. Chief towns Pnompenh, Battambang, Kratié.

History: In early times under Hindu influence; Khmer kingdom flourished around city of Kambodja founded c. 435 A.D.; at its height 9th–12th cents. when it ruled entire Mekong valley and tributary Shan States and built Angkor Thom as capital (see ANGKOR); from 13th cent. attacked by Annamese, Thais, and Siamese city-states; became province alternately of Annam or Siam; Battambang ceded to Siam 1809; became reluctant vassal of Siam 1844; a French protectorate 1863, recognized by Siam 1867; had border controversy with Siam, settled in favor of Cambodia 1907; lost Battambang and sur-

rounding area to Siam again 1941–46; became fully independent 1954.

Cambodia Point. See Point CAMAU.

Cam'borne–Red'ruth (kăm'bôrn·rĕd'rŏŏth; -bĕrn-; -rĕd·rŏŏth'). Urban district, Cornwall, SW England, 53 m. WSW of Plymouth; pop. 35,829; coal mines.

Cam'brai' (kän'brā'; *Angl.* kăm·brā'), *older* **Cam'-bray'** (-brā'); *Flem.* **Kam'bryk** (käm'brĭk); *anc.* **Cam'e·ra'cum** (kăm'ēr·ā'kŭm). Industrial city, Nord dept., N France, on Schelde river 34 m. S by E of Lille; pop. 29,655; archiepiscopal see; manufactures linen goods (esp. cambric and cambresine—both named for the city), cotton, lace, thread, leather goods, sugar, soap.

History: A Frankish capital 445 A.D.; made commune 1076; league against Venice formed here 1508; Peace of Cambrai signed 1529; to France 1678. Occupied by Germans 1914–18; important battles of World War I fought in villages to SW: (1) a surprise British attack with tanks on German lines and German counterattack Nov. 20–Dec. 7, 1917; in closing phase of war of attrition, a partial British success; (2) complete victory of British and Canadians Sept. 27–Oct. 5, 1918.

Cam'bri·a (kăm'brĭ·ȧ). **1** County in Pennsylvania. See *Table* at PENNSYLVANIA.
2 Latin name of Wales, used by modern poets.

Cam'bri·an Mountains (kăm'brĭ·ăn). Range extending N to S through cen. Wales; highest peak Aran Mawddwy 2970 ft.

Cam'bridge (kām'brĭj). **1** Village, ⊗ of Henry co., NW Illinois; pop. 1665; in agricultural section.
2 City, ⊗ of Dorchester co., SE Maryland, on E shore of Chesapeake Bay 38 m. SE of Annapolis; pop. 12,239; packing houses for fish, oysters, and crabs; lumber, flour, and textile mills; shipbuilding yards.
3 City, a ⊗ of Middlesex co., NE Massachusetts, 3 m. W of Boston; pop. 107,716; educational center; also manufacturing and commercial center, 2d city in Massachusetts in value of goods manufactured; machinery, inks, glass, rubber goods, wire cables, boilers, valves, paper boxes. Founded 1630 as one of the Massachusetts Bay settlements and known as New Towne until 1636; Harvard College (first institution of learning in U.S.) founded 1636 and first printing press in U.S. set up 1640 by Stephen Day; under an elm, standing until 1923, Gen. Washington took command of American Army July 3, 1775; at Craigie House (built 1759), his headquarters 1775–76, Cambridge flag first used Jan. 2, 1776; in 19th cent. home of many American literary leaders; incorporated as city 1846; has many presses, schools, seminaries; Harvard University; Radcliffe College (1879; women), affiliated with Harvard Univ.; Massachusetts Institute of Technology (founded in Boston 1861; removed to Cambridge 1915); Episcopal Theological School (1867).
4 Village, ⊗ of Isanti co., E Minnesota, 41 m. N of Minneapolis; pop. 2728.
5 City, Furnas co., S Nebraska, on Republican river; pop. 1090; fossilized bones of saber-toothed tiger discovered 1947.
6 Village, Washington co., E New York, 26 m. NNE of Troy; pop. 1748; agriculture, stockbreeding.
7 City, ⊗ of Guernsey co., E Ohio, 21 m. ENE of Zanesville; pop. 14,562; settled 1806; coal, iron, pottery clay, oil, and natural-gas deposits nearby; mining; manufacturing; produces pottery, glassware.
8 County in England. See CAMBRIDGESHIRE.
9 *Lat.* **Can'ta·brig'i·a** (kăn'tȧ·brĭj'ĭ·ȧ). Municipal borough, ⊗ of Cambridgeshire, E England, on the Cam 48 m. NNE of London; pop. 66,789, (1951) 81,463. Has many churches, esp. the Holy Sepulchre (round church, c. 1130) and Saint Benedict. Dates from early times, its site probably occupied by Romans. Chiefly important because of Cambridge University (dating from the 12th cent., probably c. 1110), one of the two great English universities.

Cambridge City. Town, Wayne co., E Indiana, 15 m. W of Richmond; pop. 2569.

Cam'bridge·shire (kăm'brĭj·shĭr; -shēr) or **Cambridge.** 1 Formerly, and still as a postal and geographical name, a county in E England comprising the modern administrative counties of Cambridge (see 2, below) and the Isle of Ely (q.v.).
2 Administrative county in E England; 492 sq. m.; pop. (1951) 166,863; ⊗ Cambridge; the rivers Ouse, Cam, Lark, Nene; chief industry agriculture.

Cambridge Springs. Borough and resort, Crawford co., NW Pennsylvania; pop. 2031; manufactures evaporated milk, etc.; mineral spring.

Cam·bu'ni·an Mountains (kăm·bū'nĭ·ăn; -būn'yăn). Mountain range on N border of Thessaly, NE Greece, and separating it from SW Macedonia; terminates in Mt. Olympus on the E.

Cam'den (kăm'dĕn). 1 Name of counties in four states of the U.S. See *Tables* at GEORGIA, MISSOURI, NEW JERSEY, NORTH CAROLINA.
2 Town, ⊗ of Wilcox co., SW cen. Alabama; pop. 1121.
3 City, ⊗ of Ouachita co., S Arkansas, on Ouachita river 29 m. N of El Dorado; pop. 15,823; made ⊗ 1843, incorp. 1844; oil and natural gas in vicinity.
4 Town, Knox co., S Maine, on W shore of Penobscot Bay 37 m. E of Augusta; pop. 3988; resort.
5 City and port of entry, ⊗ of Camden co., SW New Jersey, on Delaware river across from Philadelphia, with which it is connected by bridge; pop. 117,159; settled c. 1681; originally part of Newton township; incorporated as city 1828; railroad terminus 1834; made ⊗ of Camden co. 1844; grew rapidly in industrial expansion following Civil War; industrial, marketing, and transportation center of S New Jersey; manufactures radios, phonographs, canned soups, soap, steel pens, chemicals; shipyards; home of Walt Whitman 1873–92.
6 Village, Oneida co., cen. New York, 16 m. WNW of Rome; pop. 2694; in agricultural section.
7 Village, ⊗ of Camden co., NE North Carolina, 4 m. E of Elizabeth City; pop. (est.) 300.
8 City, ⊗ of Kershaw co., N cen. South Carolina, near Wateree river 31 m. ENE of Columbia; pop. 6842. First settled 1733–34 near scene of American defeat (under Gen. Gates) and mortal wounding of Gen. De Kalb in battle of Camden Aug. 16, 1780, and of Rawdon-Hastings' victory over Americans under Gen. Nathanael Greene at Hobkirk's Hill Apr. 25, 1781; became Confederate storehouse, hospital, and haven of refuge until burned by Sherman in 1865. Winter resort and sports center; markets naval stores, agricultural products; manufactures textiles, cottonseed oil, lumber, veneers.
9 Town, ⊗ of Benton co., W Tennessee; pop. 2774.

Cam'den·ton (kăm'dĕn·tŭn). Town, ⊗ of Camden co., S cen. Missouri; pop. 1405.

Camden Town. District, St. Pancras borough, London, England.

Cam'el (kăm'ĕl; -'l). Small river in Cornwall, SW England; flows NW into Atlantic Ocean E of Trevose Head.

Cam'el·ford (kăm'ĕl·fĕrd; kăm'l-). Rural district, Cornwall, SW England, on the Camel river; pop. 7577.

Cam'e·lot (kăm'ĕ·lŏt). In the Arthurian legends, the place where King Arthur had his palace and court and where the Round Table was; has been variously located in Somersetshire, at or near Winchester, and in Wales.

Cam'els Hump (kăm'ĕlz; -'lz). Peak 4083 ft. of the Green Mts., Vermont, 20 m. SE of Burlington.

Cam'em·bert' (kăm'ĕm·bâr'; *Fr.* ká'mäṅ'bâr'). Village, Orne dept., NW France, E of Falaise; pop. 258; Camembert cheese first made here ab. 1761, chief center for the cheese now in nearby Vimoutiers (q.v.).

Cameracum. See CAMBRAI.

Ca'me·ri'no (kä'mä·rē'nô); *anc.* **Cam'e·ri'num** (kăm'ĕ·rī'nŭm). Commune, Macerata prov., Marches, cen. Italy, 23 m. SW of Macerata; pop. 12,012; university (founded 1727); manufactures silks.

Ca'me·ri'no Men·do'za (kä'mä·rē'nô mĕn·dô'sä); *formerly* **San'ta Ro'sa Ne·cox'tla** (sän'tä rrô'sä nä·kôs'tlä). Town, Veracruz state, E Mexico; pop. 10,962.

Cam'er·on (kăm'ĕr·ŭn). 1 Name of a parish in Louisiana and of counties in two states of the U.S. See *Tables* at LOUISIANA, PENNSYLVANIA, and TEXAS.
2 Town, ⊗ of Cameron parish, SW corner of Louisiana; pop. (est.) 1500.
3 City, Clinton and De Kalb cos., NW Missouri, 47 m. NNE of Kansas City; pop. 3674; in agricultural section.
4 City, ⊗ of Milam co., cen. Texas, 27 m. SE of Temple; pop. 5640; agricultural center (cotton, cattle, bees, etc.).
5 City, Marshall co., N West Virginia, 12 m. SE of Moundsville; pop. 1652; in farming section.

Cameron, Mount. Peak 14,238 ft. in Park co., cen. Colorado.

Cameron Bay. Mining town on E shore of Great Bear Lake, Northwest Territories, Canada, just S of Arctic Circle; center of a radium-producing region.

Cameron Pass. Mountain pass 10,285 ft., Larimer and Jackson cos., N Colorado, in Medicine Bow Range.

Cam'er·oon' (kăm'ĕr·ōōn'). 1 or **Fa'ko** (fä'kō). Massif 13,353 ft. in N Cameroun, W Africa, near coast.
2 River ab. 140 m. long in W Cameroun, W Africa; flows into Gulf of Guinea.
3 see CAMEROUN.

Cam'er·oons' (kăm'ĕr·ōōnz'; *Port.* **Ca·ma·rões'** (kä·mä·rōēṅsh'); *Ger.* **Ka'me·run'** (kä'mĕ·rōōn'); *Fr.* **Ca'me·roun'** (kàm'rōōn'). 1 Former German protectorate in West Africa; 1920–46 NW portion (34,081 sq. m., pop. ab. 797,000) a British mandate attached to Nigeria, remainder a French mandate (see CAMEROUN); became a trust territory under United Nations 1946.
History: Factory established by 1868; proclaimed German protectorate 1884; boundaries with Nigeria and French Congo determined 1893, 1894; captured by British and French during World War I; divided bet. mandates to France and Great Britain.
2 Province of Nigeria; part of the former British trust territory. Formerly included two separate areas: Southern Cameroons, which in 1961 by plebiscite joined the Republic of Cameroun, and Northern Cameroons, which then voted to remain part of Nigeria.

Ca'me·roun' (kàm'rōōn') or **Cam'er·oon'** (kăm'ĕr·ōōn'). Republic, W Africa, on the Gulf of Guinea; ab. 183,000 sq. m.; pop. ab. 4,000,000; ✲ Yaoundé. Bounded on N, E, and S by Equatorial Africa, on SW by Río Muni and Bight of Biafra, and on W by Nigeria. Plateau country inland, marshes along coast and lower courses of rivers; chief rivers Cameroon and Sanaga; products are tropical: ground nuts, palm oil, cotton, coffee, ivory, and hides. Chief towns Yaoundé, Edéa, and the ports Douala and Kribi. Formerly part of German-held Cameroons (q.v.); French mandate 1919–46; administered as part of French Equatorial Africa. Established as trust territory under Charter of the United Nations 1946; became independent Jan. 1, 1960; annexed former British trusteeship territory of Southern Cameroons Oct. 1, 1961.

Ca'mi·guin' (kä'mĕ·gēn'). 1 Island in Babuyan group, N of Luzon, Phil. Is.; 63 sq. m.; pop. 585; mountainous; has **Camiguin** volcano. ab. 2750 ft., in N part.
2 Island in Mindanao Sea ab. 6 m. off N coast of Mindanao, Phil. Is.; 96 sq. m.; pop. 40,805; part of Misamis Oriental prov.; mountainous; highest peak 5620 ft.; produces much sugar, tobacco, rice, cacao; volcanic in formation; eruptions in 1871 and 1948; chief towns Mambajao, Catarman, and Sagay.

Ca'mi·ling' (kä'mĕ·lēng'). Municipality, NW Tarlac prov., Luzon, Phil. Is., on a tributary of the Agno 19 m. NW of Tarlac; pop. 25,824; important market town.

Ca·mil'la (ká·mĭl'á). City, ⊗ of Mitchell co., SW Georgia, 25 m. S of Albany; pop. 4753.

Ca·mil'lus (ká·mĭl'ŭs). Village, Onondaga co., cen. New York, 9 m. W of Syracuse; pop. 1416; farming,

dairying; claims title of "birthplace of the Republican party" (1852).

Ca·mi'ri (kä·mē'rē). Town, Santa Cruz dept., S Bolivia, ab. 250 m. SE of Sucre; oil refineries.

Ca·mi'rus (ká·mī'rŭs). Ancient town on W coast of island of Rhodes; chief town of the island before Rhodes was founded. See PENTAPOLIS.

Cam'lan (kăm'lăn). Locality, SW England, where King Arthur is said to have died in battle 537; site unidentified but possibly near Camelford in Cornwall.

Ca'mo·cim' (ká'mōō·sēN'). City and port, Ceará state, NE Brazil, ab. 170 m. WNW of Fortaleza; pop. 8299.

Ca'mo·ghe' (kä'mō·gä'). Peak 7303 ft. in Ticino canton, SE cen. Switzerland.

Ca·mo'ni·ca (kä·mō'nē·kä). Valley 50 m. long in the Alps, in Brescia prov., N Italy.

Ca·mor'ta (ká·môr'tá). Island, cen. Nicobar Is., Indian Union; 58 sq. m.; pop. 548; just N of Nancowry I.

Ca·mo'tes Islands (kä·mō'tås). Group of three islands, Poro, Pacijan, and Ponson, N of Camotes Sea near W coast of Leyte and ab. 20 m. E of the N end of Cebu I.; Visayan Is., E cen. Phil. Is.; 86 sq. m.; pop. 43,345; largest town San Francisco on Pacijan I. Belong to Cebu prov.; mountainous and productive; formerly part of Leyte prov.

Camotes Sea. Body of water in Visayan Is., E cen. Phil. Is., E of N end of Cebu I., N of Bohol, W of Leyte, and S of Camotes Is. Scene of several naval and air battles during Leyte campaign 1944.

Camp (kămp). County in Texas. See *Table* at TEXAS.

Camp (kämp). See CAMPERDOWN, Netherlands.

Cam·pa'gna (käm·pä'nyä). 1 = CAMPAGNA DI ROMA. 2 Commune, Salerno prov., Campania, S Italy, 18 m. E by S of Salerno; pop. 10,818; cathedral.

Campagna di Ro'ma (dē rō'mä; *Eng. often* **Roman Campagna.** Region surrounding Rome, Italy; ab. 800 sq. m.; almost coextensive with Rome commune; in recent years largely reclaimed and repopulated.

Cam'pal·di·no (käm'päl·dē'nō). Village, Tuscany, Italy, on the upper Arno ESE of Florence; scene of battle June 11, 1289 in which the Ghibelline supporters of Arezzo were severely defeated by the Guelphs of Florence.

Cam·pa'na (käm·pä'nä). 1 Town, Buenos Aires prov., E Argentina, on the Paraná river 45 m. NW of Buenos Aires; pop. (1943) 23,000; commercial center with meat-freezing, oil-refining, and grain-storage industries. 2 Island ab. 55 m. long and 10 m. wide in Pacific Ocean off SW coast of Chile, NW of Wellington I.

Cam'pa·na'rio (käm'pä·nä'ryō). Peak 13,190 ft. on Argentina-Chile boundary, bet. SW Mendoza prov., W Argentina, and E Talca prov., cen. Chile.

Cam'pa·nel'la, Point (käm'pä·nĕl'lä). Cape at S end of the Bay of Naples, Italy, opp. island of Capri.

Cam·pa'nia (käm·pän'yá; -pä'nĭ·á). 1 See CHAMPAGNE, France. 2 (*Ital.* käm·pä'nyä) Compartimento of S Italy (for provincial divisions, area, and pop., see *Table* at ITALY); lies on Tyrrhenian Sea bet. Latium and Lucania; exceedingly fertile and generally mountainous region; produces principally wine, olives, citrus fruits, and grain; fine Mediterranean climate; noted in ancient times as a favorite resort of distinguished Romans; noted for its natural beauty and famous old towns (Cumae, Stabiae, Pompeii, Capua, Salernum, Neapolis, etc.). Occupied successively by Oscans, Greeks, Etruscans, Samnites, and from 350 B.C. by Romans.

Camp'bell (kăm'bĕl; -ĕl). 1 Name of counties in five states of the U.S. See *Tables* at KENTUCKY, SOUTH DAKOTA, TENNESSEE, VIRGINIA, WYOMING. 2 Former county in Georgia; part annexed to Fulton co. 1926, the rest 1932. 3 City, Santa Clara co., W California, SW of San Jose; pop. 11,863. 4 City, Dunklin co., SE Missouri; pop. 1964.

5 Industrial city, Mahoning co., NE Ohio, 4 m. SE of Youngstown; pop. 13,406; iron and steel works.

Campbell, Cape. Cape on NE coast of South I., New Zealand, at W side of S Cook Strait.

Camp'bell·ford (kăm'bĕl·fĕrd; kăm'ĕl-). Town, Northumberland co., SE Ontario, Canada, on Trent river 28 m. E of Peterborough; pop. 3235; produces lumber, pulp, flour, woolens, and shoes.

Campbell Hill. Eminence 1550 ft. near Bellefontaine, Logan co., W Ohio; highest point in the state.

Campbell Island. Island in S Pacific Ocean, lat. 52°33'S and long. 169°9'E; 44 sq. m.; discovered 1810; has good harbors; annexed to New Zealand.

Campbell Mountain. Peak 8207 ft. in Glacier National Park, NW Montana.

Camp'bell·pur' (kăm'bĕl·pŏŏr'). Town, N West Pakistan, SE of Peshawar; pop. 11,694.

Camp'bell's Bay (kăm'bĕlz; kăm'ĕlz). Village, ⊗ of Pontiac co., SW Quebec, Canada, on Ottawa river opp. Calumet I. 50 m. NW of Ottawa; pop. 975.

Camp'bells·ville (kăm'bĕlz·vĭl; kăm'ĕlz-). City, ⊗ of Taylor co., cen. Kentucky, SW of Danville; pop. 6966; tobacco growing.

Camp'bell·ton (kăm'bĕl·tŭn; kăm'ĕl-). Town, Restigouche co., N New Brunswick, Canada, on Restigouche river 15 m. from its mouth; pop. 7754; founded 1776; at head of deep-water navigation; exports fish and lumber; resort; almost completely destroyed by fire 1910.

Camp'bell·town (kăm'bĕl·toun; kăm'ĕl-). 1 Municipality and town, E Tasmania, Australia, 40 m. SSE of Launceston; pop. (municipality) 1670. 2 Former name of BLUFF, New Zealand.

Camp'bel·town (kăm'bĕl·toun). Seaport burgh, Argyll co., W Scotland, on the E side of S end of Kintyre Penin.; pop. 7169; fisheries, distilleries.

Camp Bor'den (bôr'd'n). Station of Royal Canadian Air Force, Simcoe co., Ontario, Canada, near Lake Simcoe 12 m. WSW of Barrie.

Cam·pe'che (käm·pē'chĕ; *Span.* käm·pā'chä). 1 State, SE Mexico. See *Table* at MEXICO. 2 City, its ✻, on W coast of Yucatán penin.; pop. 23,277; exports logwood and mahogany, chicle, sisal, hides. Founded 1540.

Campeche, Bank of; *Span.* **Ban'co Cam·pe'che** (bäng'kō käm·pā'chä). Shoal N of Yucatán penin., state of Yucatán, SE Mexico.

Campeche, Bay of. SW section of the Gulf of Mexico, forming a wide shallow bay extending into SE Mexico.

Cam·pe·chue'la (käm'pä·chwä'lä). Town, Oriente prov., E Cuba, on coast of Gulf of Guacanayabo 15 m. SW of Manzanillo; pop. 6013.

Cam'per·down (kăm'pēr·doun); *Mod. Dutch* **Camp** (kämp). Village, North Holland prov., W Netherlands, on North Sea coast 8 m. NW of Alkmaar; nearby occurred naval battle Oct. 11, 1797 in which British under Duncan defeated Dutch under De Winter.

Camp Hill (kămp). Residential borough, Cumberland co., S Pennsylvania, 5 m. WSW of Harrisburg; pop. 8559; suburb of Harrisburg.

Cam'pi Bi·sen'zio (käm'pē bē·zĕn'tsyō). Commune, Firenze prov., Tuscany, cen. Italy, 7 m. WNW of Florence; pop. 15,537.

Campi Flegrei. See PHLEGRAEAN FIELDS.

Cam·pi'glia Ma·rit'ti·ma (käm·pē'lyä mä·rēt'tē·mä). Commune, Livorno prov., Tuscany, cen. Italy, 35 m. S by E of Leghorn; pop. 11,591; airport.

Câm'pi·na (kĭm'pē·nä). Commune, Muntenia, S Romania, NW of Ploești; pop. 11,983; oil wells.

Cam·pi'na Gran'de (kănm·pē'ná gränn'dĕ). City, E Paraíba state, E Brazil, 100 m. NW of Recife; pop. (1940 est.) 34,023; terminus of railroad from João Pessoa.

Cam·pi'nas (kănm·pē'nás). City, E São Paulo state, SE Brazil, 68 m. NNW of São Paulo; pop. (1940 est.) 78,914; center of coffee-producing district; also in an area that raises cotton, cereals, and sugar.

Cam'pli (kăm'plē). Commune, Teramo prov., Abruzzi e Molise, cen. Italy, 4 m. N by E of Teramo; pop. 11,109.

Cam'po or **Kam'po** (käm'pō). **1** River, S Cameroun, W Africa; forms part of boundary with Río Muni.
2 Seaport town, Cameroun, W Africa, at mouth of the Campo river just N of the Río Muni boundary.

Cam'po·bas'so (käm'pō·bäs'sō). **1** Province of Italy. See *Table* at ITALY.
2 Commune, its ✱, Abruzzi e Molise, cen. Italy, in Apennines ab. 95 m. NE of Naples; pop. 29,573; 15th-cent. feudal castle; cathedral. In World War II marked the point in the Volturno campaign Oct. 1943 where the British and American forces joined.

Cam'po·bel'lo (käm'pō·bĕl'ō). Island ab. 10 m. long by 2 to 3 m. wide, Charlotte co., SW New Brunswick, Canada; pop. 1176; just E of Eastport, Maine, separated from U.S. by Lubec Channel. Owned by Adm. William Owen and descendants 1767–1880; bought by New York syndicate and converted into summer resort; Roosevelt Memorial Bridge to Lubec, Maine, completed 1962.

Cam'po·bel'lo di Li·ca'ta (käm'pō·bĕl'lō dē lē·kä'tä). Commune, Agrigento prov., SW Sicily, 20 m. ESE of Agrigento; pop. 11,732.

Campobello di Ma·za'ra (mä·tsä'rä). Commune, Trapani prov., NW Sicily, SSE of Trapani; pop. 10,285.

Cam'po de Crip·ta'na (käm'pō thä krĕp·tä'nä). Commune, Ciudad Real prov., S cen. Spain, 52 m. NE of Ciudad Real; pop. 15,427; agricultural products.

Cam'po de la Cruz (käm'pō thä lä krōōs'). Town, Atlántico dept., N Colombia; pop. 5458.

Cam'po·for'mi·do (käm'pō·fôr'mǐ·dō; *Ital.* käm'pō·fôr'mě·dō; *formerly* **Cam'po·for'mi·o** (käm'pō·fôr'mǐ·ō; käm'pō·fôr'myō). Village, Friuli prov., E Venezia Euganea, NE Italy, SW of Udine; pop. 1130; treaty Oct. 17, 1797 bet. France and Austria ending first phase of Napoleonic Wars.

Cam'po Gran'de (kăNm'pōō grăNn'dě). City, Mato Grosso state, SW Brazil; pop. (1940 est.) 23,460; on railroad in center of S part of the state.

Cam'pos (kăNm'pōōs). City, Rio de Janeiro state, SE Brazil, 35 m. from mouth of the Paraíba river; pop. (1940 est.) 52,677; sugar, coffee, and tobacco center.

Camp'ton (kăm[p]'tŭn). **1** City, ⊗ of Wolfe co., E Kentucky; pop. 484.
2 Town, cen. New Hampshire, in Grafton co., 25 m. NNW of Laconia; pop. 1058; settled 1765; resort.

Câm'pu·lung (kǐm'pōō·lōōng'). **1** or **Kim'po·lung'** (kǐm'pō-). City, cen. Romania, in Muntenia region, 80 m. NW of Bucharest; pop. 13,454; in S foothills of Transylvanian Alps; summer resort. Founded by German colonists in 12th cent.
2 Town, N Romania, in former Bucovina region, on Moldava river 50 m. WSW of Botoşani; pop. 10,124.

Camp Up'ton (ŭp'tŭn). Army camp on Long I., Suffolk co., New York, ab. 10 m. WSW of Riverhead; estab. in World War I, rebuilt 1940 for use in World War II; site since 1947 of Brookhaven National Laboratory for Nuclear Research.

Cam'ranh' Bay (käm'rän'y'; *Angl.* kăm'răn'). Inlet of South China Sea on SE coast of Annam, Federation of Indochina, ab. 12°N, bet. Phanrang and Nhatrang Former French naval base with large protected anchorage; used by Japanese 1940–45; Japanese vessels bombed by Allied planes Jan. 11, 1945.

Cam'rose (kăm'rōz). Town, S cen. Alberta, Canada, 44 m. SSE of Edmonton; pop. 4131; seat of a Lutheran college and a provincial normal school.

Camulodunum. See COLCHESTER.

Ca·muy' (kä·mwē'). Municipality (pop. 19,739) and town (pop. 2341) NW Puerto Rico, W of Arecibo.

Ca'na (kā'nä), *often* **Cana of Gal'i·lee** (găl'ǐ·lē). Village, Galilee dist., N Palestine, ab. 4 m. NE of Nazareth, where Christ performed his first miracle.

Ca'naan (kā'năn). **1** Village, N Litchfield co., NW corner of Connecticut; pop. 1146; incorp. 1739.

2 Town, Grafton co., W New Hampshire, on Indian river 11 m. E of Lebanon; pop. 1507; resort.
3 The old and native name of that part of Palestine bet. the Jordan and the Mediterranean, but sometimes vaguely used as the equivalent of all of Palestine; had settlements in Early Bronze Age (3200–2100 B.C.), probably Amorites and Hittites; later, its inhabitants, a pre-Israelite race (Canaanites), overcome by Jews c. 1200 B.C. returning from Egypt (the Promised Land (Land of Promise) of the Israelites (*Exod.* iii. 8).

Canaan Mountain. Peak 3702 ft. in Preston co., N West Virginia.

Ca'ña·ca'o Bay (kä'nyä·kä'ō). Inlet of Manila Bay at end of Cavite Penin., Cavite prov., Luzon, Phil. Is.; fine anchorage; the N harbor of Cavite naval base.

Can'a·da (kăn'à·dà); *often, esp. before 1867, called* **British North America.** Country in northern North America; a federal state constituting a self-governing unit (dominion) of the British Commonwealth of Nations; land area 3,610,097 sq. m.; pop. 14,009,429; ✱ Ottawa; comprises the following 10 provinces and 2 territories (for pronunciations, see their individual entries):

NAME	LOCA-TION	AREA[1]	POP.[1]	CAPITAL
Alberta	W	248,800	939,501	Edmonton
British Columbia	SW	359,279	1,165,210	Victoria
Manitoba	cen.	219,723	776,541	Winnipeg
New Brunswick	SE	27,473	515,697	Fredericton
Newfoundland[2]	SE	147,994	361,416	St. John's
Northwest Terrs.	N	1,253,438	16,004	Yellowknife
Nova Scotia	SE	20,743	642,584	Halifax
Ontario	S and cen.	363,282	4,597,542	Toronto
Prince Edward I.	SE	2,184	98,429	Charlotte-town
Quebec	E	523,860	4,055,681	Quebec
Saskatchewan	W	237,975	831,728	Regina
Yukon Terr.	NW	205,346	9,096	Whitehorse

[1] Area = land area in sq. m. Pop. from 1951 Census.
[2] Including Labrador (see LABRADOR, 2).

Bounded on N by Arctic Ocean, on E by the Atlantic (including Davis Strait and Baffin Bay), on S by U.S. and on W by Alaska and the Pacific; includes many islands in N, most northerly point (83°) of which is Cape Columbia on Ellesmere I.; has large inlet of Hudson Bay in NE. *Rivers:* St. Lawrence (draining Great Lakes and in part forming boundary with U.S.), Columbia (upper course, flows into Washington state, U.S.), Mackenzie (with great tributaries Liard, Slave, Peace, Athabaska, etc.), Yukon (upper course, flows into Alaska), Nelson (with upper tributaries of North and South Saskatchewan), Red River of the North (lower course), Dubawnt, Fraser, Severn, Albany, Ottawa, and Saguenay. *Lakes:* Parts of Lakes Ontario, Erie, Huron, Superior, and Lake of the Woods; Great Bear, Great Slave, Athabaska, Winnipeg, Winnipegosis, and many smaller ones such as Nipigon, Mistassini, and Louise (Banff National Park). *Mountains:* Rocky Mts. in W with many high peaks extending from Alaska to U.S. border (including Selkirk, Cariboo, and other ranges), Coast Mts. along Brit. Columbia coast, Laurentian Hills in Quebec; highest point Mt. Logan 19,850 ft. in Yukon Terr., second in height in North America; other peaks: Lucania (Yukon) 17,150 ft.; St. Elias and Fairweather (on W boundary); Mts. Waddington 13,260 ft. in Brit. Columbia, Robson 12,972 ft., Assiniboine 11,870 ft., and Edith Cavell 11,033 ft., in the Rocky Mts. *Largest cities:* Montreal, Toronto, Vancouver, Winnipeg, Hamilton, Ottawa, Quebec, Windsor, Edmonton, Calgary, London, and Halifax. *Economic resources:* Field crops, esp. wheat, oats, barley, and rye; farm animals and dairy products; lumber and wood pulp; furs; fisheries; minerals, esp. gold, nickel (leads in world production), copper, silver, zinc, cobalt. See *Maps* at MARITIME PROVINCES and NEWFOUNDLAND.

History: Early (c. 1000 A.D.) discovered by Norsemen;

Atlantic coast frequented by European fishermen from 15th cent. (see NEWFOUNDLAND); mainland discovered by explorers in search of Northwest Passage to Asia (see HUDSON BAY and ARCTIC REGIONS); Gulf of St. Lawrence and river to sites of Quebec and Montreal discovered by Cartier 1534–41 under whom French attempted their first colony; Quebec (city) founded 1608 by Champlain, who explored St. Lawrence, discovered Lake Champlain, and penetrated interior to Georgian Bay 1603–15; Hudson Bay entered by Henry Hudson 1610; under influence of French missionaries after 1615; part of New France granted to Company of the Hundred Associates 1627 (returned to French crown 1664); Montreal founded by Maisonneuve 1642; expeditions of Nicolet, Marquette and Jolliet, and La Salle; object of Anglo-French rivalry from 17th cent.; Acadia (see NOVA SCOTIA), Newfoundland, and Hudson Bay region relinquished to England 1713; rest of country ceded by Treaty of Paris 1763; region of Ottawa and St. Lawrence rivers organized 1774 as Quebec prov. (q.v.). Boundaries with U.S. settled 1783 (see NORTHWEST TERRITORY), 1846 (see OREGON COUNTRY), and 1903 (see ALASKA). Dominion of Canada established 1867 by union of New Brunswick and Nova Scotia with Quebec, whose two parts (formerly known as Upper and Lower Canada) became present Ontario and Quebec provs.; purchased 1869 the western regions explored by Hudson's Bay Co. (chartered 1670 by Charles II) and North West Co. (consolidated with Hudson's Bay Co. 1821); put down Riel's Rebellion 1869; admitted as provinces Manitoba 1870, British Columbia 1871, Prince Edward Island 1873, Alberta and Saskatchewan 1905, Newfoundland 1949; see NORTHWEST TERRITORIES, YUKON; entered World War I 1914, World War II 1939.

NATIONAL HISTORIC PARKS

NAME	ESTAB-LISHED	AREA (IN ACRES)	LOCATION	HISTORICAL SIGNIFICANCE
Fort Anne	1917	31	Annapolis Royal, W Nova Scotia	Site of early Acadian settlement at Port Royal; first fort built c. 1635; named 1710 in honor of Queen Anne of England; several times rebuilt and added to by English
Fort Battleford	1951	36.7	South of North Battleford, Saskatchewan	North West Mounted Police post built 1876
Fort Beauséjour	1926	59	Near Sackville, SE New Brunswick	Fort built by French 1751–55; captured by English 1755; its defenses strengthened in Amer. Revolution, War of 1812.
Fort Chambly	1941	2.5	Chambly Canton on Richelieu river, 20 m. E of Montreal	Fort built by French 1665; burned by Indians 1702; rebuilt of stone 1709–11; captured by U.S. forces 1775; contains museum
Fort Lennox	1941	210	On Île-aux-Noix in Richelieu river, 12 m. S of St. Johns	Advance post against Indians in 18th cent.; present fortifications built by English 1812–27
Fort Malden	1941	3	Amherstburg, Ontario	Built by English 1797–99 on Detroit river; important frontier defense post in War of 1812
Fort Prince of Wales	1941	50	Churchill, NE Manitoba, on Hudson Bay	Built by English 1733–71 to control Hudson Bay; now in ruins
Fortress of Louisbourg	1941	339.5	Near Louisburg, E Cape Breton I., Nova Scotia	Built by French 1720–40 as strategic military and naval base; captured by New England volunteers 1745; restored to France but captured by British 1758 in Seven Years' War; now group of picturesque ruins
Fort Wellington	1941	8.5	Prescott, Ontario, on St. Lawrence	Defense post built 1812–13; strengthened during rebellion of 1837–38; blockhouse within earthworks and palisade
Halifax Citadel	1956	37	Halifax, Nova Scotia	Defense post constructed 1828–42
Lower Fort Garry	1951	13	20 m. N of Winnipeg, Manitoba	Hudson's Bay Company fort built between 1831 and 1839
Port Royal	1941	17	Lower Granville village, 8 m. SW of Annapolis Royal, Nova Scotia	Replica on Annapolis Basin of "Habitation" built 1605 by Champlain and De Monts; site of first permanent settlement in Canada
Signal Hill	1958	243.4	St. John's, Nfld.	Location of fortifications and site of battles in 1700's
Woodside	1954	11	Kitchener, Ontario	Boyhood home of W. L. Mackenzie King

NATIONAL PARKS

NAME	ESTAB-LISHED	AREA (IN SQ. M.)	LOCATION	FEATURES
Banff	1885	2,585	SW Alberta	Mountains, glaciers; game sanctuary; summer and winter sports center; resorts of Banff and Lake Louise
Cape Breton Highlands	1936	390	N Cape Breton Island, N.S.	Rugged highland and coastal scenery
Elk Island	1913	51	E cen. Alberta ab. 30 m. E of Edmonton	Fenced enclosure containing buffalo, moose, deer, wapiti; recreational and camping resort
Georgian Bay Islands	1929	5.37	Thirty islands in Georgian Bay	Limestone caves and formations; resort
Glacier	1886	521	SE British Columbia	Peaks, glaciers, valleys in heart of Selkirk Mts.
Jasper	1907	4,200	W Alberta	Mountains, lakes; big-game sanctuary; resorts
Kootenay	1920	587	SE British Columbia	Mountains, canyons, hot mineral springs
Mount Revelstoke	1914	100	SE British Columbia	Plateau region on Mt. Revelstoke, W slope of Selkirk Mts.
Point Pelee	1918	6	Ontario, on Lake Erie	Most southerly mainland point in Canada; resort
Prince Albert	1927	1,869	Central Saskatchewan	Forested region with many lakes and waterways; resort
Prince Edward Island	1937	7	Strip 25 m. long on N coast of Prince Edward Island	Bathing beaches and recreational area
Riding Mountain	1929	1,148	SW Manitoba	Highland forested area, with many lakes; game preserve
St. Lawrence Islands	1914	185.6 (acres)	Mainland area and 13 islands of the Thousand Islands	Recreational areas
Waterton Lakes	1895	220	S Alberta; Canadian part of Waterton-Glacier International Peace Park (q.v.)	Mountain recreational area
Wood Buffalo (includes former Buffalo National Park, established 1908, 197.5 sq. m., in Alberta)	1922	17,300	N Alberta and S Northwest Territories, W of Slave river and bet. Athabaska and Great Slave Lakes	Immense forested and plains region; large herd of buffalo and other game
Yoho	1886	507	SE British Columbia	Peaks, waterfalls, lakes, valleys, on W slopes of Rocky Mts.

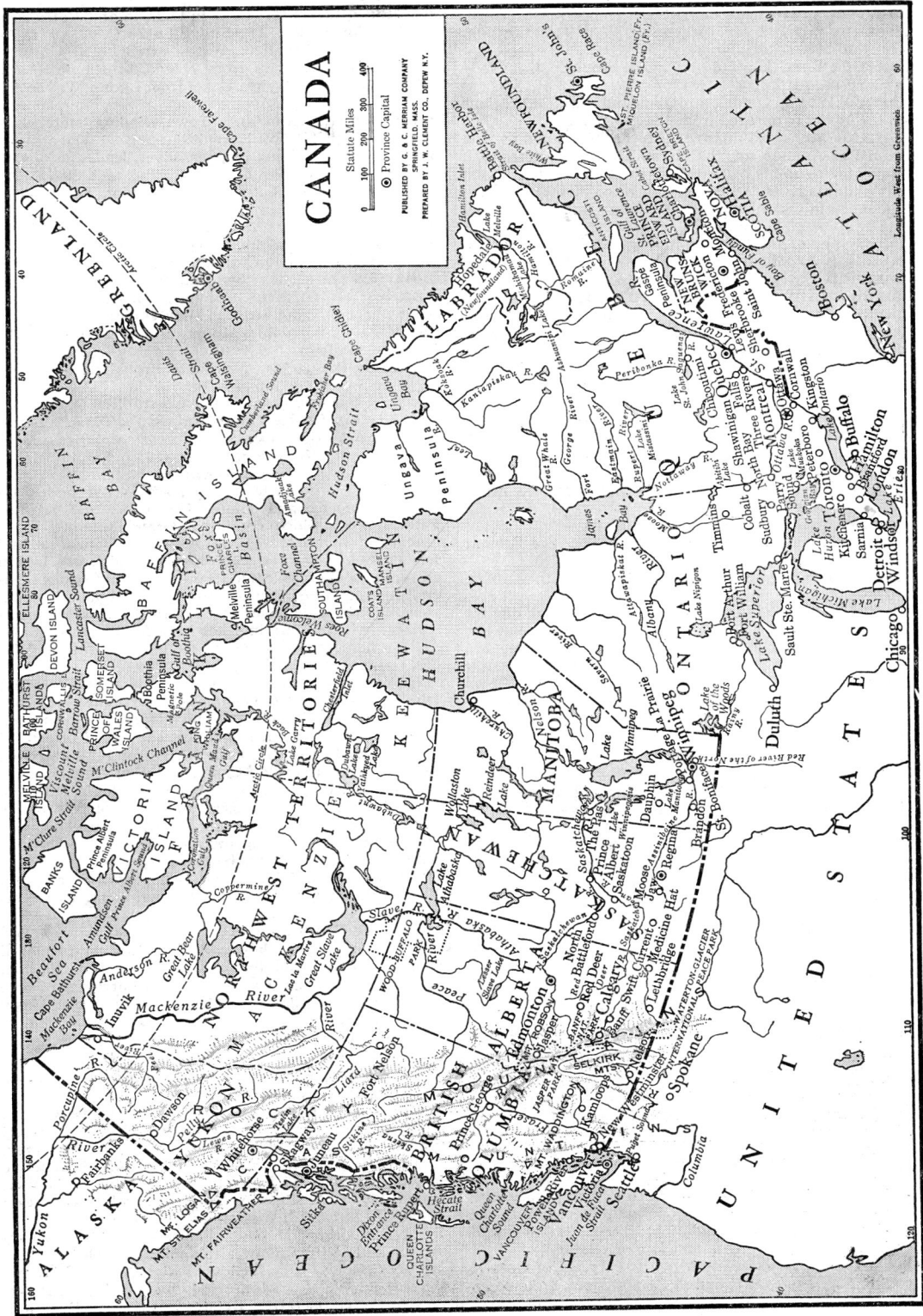

Ca·ña'da de Gó'mez (kä·nyä'thä thä gō'mäs). Town, Santa Fe prov., E cen. Argentina, W of Rosario; pop. (est.) 16,808.

Can'a·da East (kăn'á·dá). Quebec province, Canada—a name used from 1841 to 1867.

Canada West. Ontario province and unsettled regions to the W—a name used from 1841 to 1867.

Ca·na'di·an (ká·nā'dĭ·ǎn). **1** River 906 m. long, flowing from Las Animas co., S Colorado, S and E across NE New Mexico and NW Texas and through cen. Oklahoma to Arkansas river in SE Muskogee co., E Oklahoma. **2** County in Oklahoma. See *Table* at OKLAHOMA. **3** Town, ⊗ of Hemphill co., NW Texas, 38 m. NE of Pampa; pop. 2239; in cattle-raising and farming section.

Canadian Arctic Islands. See ARCTIC ARCHIPELAGO.

Canadian Fall or **Falls.** See NIAGARA FALLS.

Canadian Shield. See LAURENTIAN HIGHLANDS.

Can'a·jo·har'ie (kăn'á·jō·hăr'ĭ). Village, Montgomery co., E New York, on Mohawk river 21 m. W of Amsterdam; pop. 2681; settled c.1730; figured in Revolution as meeting place (Fort Rensselaer); food-packing plants.

Ça'nak·ka·le' (chä'näk·kä·lě'). **1** Vilayet, NW Turkey, extending on both sides of the Dardanelles (European section 560 sq. m., pop. 34,402; Asiatic section 2930 sq. m., pop. 188,823); total area 3490 sq. m.; pop. 223,225. **2** *formerly* **Cha·nak'** (chä·näk'). Commercial town and fort, its ✻, on the Asiatic shore of the Dardanelles; pop. 15,187; unsuccessfully bombarded Mar. 1915 by Allied fleet in World War I.

Çanakkale Boğazı. See DARDANELLES.

Ca·nal' (ká·năl'). Governorate, NE Egypt. See *Table* at EGYPT.

Ca·nal' Zone (ká·năl' zōn'). Strip of territory 10 m. wide in Panama, under perpetual lease to United States for Panama Canal; includes Gatun Lake and district above Alhajuela for a reservoir (Madden Dam), but not cities of Panama and Colón; 648 sq. m. (including 276 sq. m. of water); pop. 52,822; administrative center Balboa Heights. Chief cities Cristobal, Ancon, Balboa.

History: Acquisition of zone by U.S. provided for in Hay-Herrán Treaty with Colombia (not ratified by Colombia); rights over it granted to U.S. by treaty with Panama 1903; governed and operated according to act of Congress of 1912; boundaries determined 1914; sovereignty disputed by U.S. and Panama 1926.

Can'an·dai'gua (kăn'ǎn·dā'gwá). City, ⊗ of Ontario co., W New York, at N end of Canandaigua Lake 26 m. SE of Rochester; pop. 9370; in agricultural and grape-growing region; resort; varied manufactures.

Canandaigua Lake. Lake in Ontario and Yates cos., W New York; one of the Finger Lakes (*q.v.*); ab. 15 m. long and 2 m. wide at its greatest extent. The **Canandaigua Outlet** flows from N end of the lake into Seneca river N of Cayuga Lake; from Lyons, Wayne co., also called the Clyde river.

Ca'na·ne'a (kä'nä·nā'ä). Town, Sonora state, NW Mexico, 135 m. NNE of Hermosillo; pop. 11,006; altitude 5150 ft.; cattle; mining (copper, silver, lead, zinc).

Cana of Galilee. See CANA.

Ca·ñar' (kä·nyär'). **1** Province of Ecuador. See *Table* at ECUADOR. **2** Town, Cañar prov., W cen. Ecuador, in the Andes 70 m. ESE of Guayaquil; pop. (1944 est.) 11,925.

Canarias, Islas. See CANARY ISLANDS.

Ca·nar'ies (ká·nâr'ĭz). See CANARY ISLANDS.

Canaries Mountain. Mountain mass 3145 ft. on Saint Lucia I., Windward Is., West Indies.

Ca·na'rio (ká·nä'ryōō). Mountain peak 5449 ft. on the island of Madeira.

Ca·nar'sie (ká·när'sĭ). Section of Brooklyn, New York City, in S part on Jamaica Bay.

Ca·nar'y Islands (ká·nâr'ĭ) or **Ca·nar'ies** (ká·nâr'ĭz); *Span.* **Is'las Ca·na'rias** (ēz'läs kä·nä'ryäs). Island group in Atlantic Ocean off NW coast of Africa 823 m. SW of Spain; 2807 sq. m.; pop. (1930) 557,489, (1941 est.) 696,982; forms two provinces of Spain: (1) Santa Cruz de Tenerife prov. which comprises Tenerife, La Palma, Gomera, and Hierro (*qq.v.*) Is., and (2) Las Palmas prov. which comprises Grand Canary, Fuerteventura, Lanzarote (*qq.v.*), Alegranza, Graciosa, and Isla de Lobos Is., the last three of which are barren and uninhabited; volcanic in origin; mountainous, generally rugged in contour; has some fertile valleys; mild, pleasant climate; subject to severe droughts and tornadoes; irrigated farming; has both Mediterranean and African flora; produces grain, fruits, esp. oranges, lemons, figs, and peaches, vegetables, wines.

History: Known in ancient times as the "Fortunate Isles"; rediscovered and claimed by Portuguese 1341 but awarded to Castile by papal bull 1344; taken possession of by Castile 1402; their conquest the object of expedition sent by Prince Henry the Navigator 1425 who tried to secure them to cut off Castilian trade to West Africa; later acquired by Aragon; thought to be W limit of world (see HIERRO); on usual route of Spanish vessels in trade with New World; supplied wine in exchange for fish brought by New England traders 17th to early 19th cents.; divided 1927 into the two provinces.

Can'a·sto'ta (kăn'á·stō'tá). Village, Madison co., cen. New York, on N.Y. State Barge Canal 22 m. E of Syracuse; pop. 4896; settled c. 1806.

Canati. See FELANITX.

Ca·nav'er·al, Cape (ká·năv'ẽr·ǎl). Cape on E coast of Canaveral Penin. E of Merritt I., in Brevard co., Florida, at lat 28°28' N, long. 80°32' W; site of Patrick Air Force base and test missile test center; in 1963 renamed **Cape Ken'ne·dy.**

Canaveral Peninsula. Narrow strip of land ab. 100 m. long off E coast of Florida, extending S from SE Volusia co.; encloses Indian River; near central part is separated from Merritt I. by Banana river.

Can'ber·ra (kăn'běr·á). City in Australian Capital Territory, SE New South Wales, on Molonglo river, branch of Murrumbidgee river, 204 m. SW of Sydney, ✻ of Commonwealth of Australia; pop. 70,775; in active farming section (principally wheat and livestock); chosen 1908 to be site of Australian capital; construction of city begun 1913; first meeting of Commonwealth's Parliament held 1927. Seat of Australian National University and of Commonwealth's military college.

Can'by (kăn'bĭ). City, Yellow Medicine co., SW Minnesota, 31 m. WSW of Montevideo; pop. 2146; headquarters for a co-operative livestock, wool-shipping, and creamery association.

Can'cale' (kăn'kȧl'). Town, Ille-et-Vilaine dept., NW France, on coast E of Saint-Malo; pop. 3291; oysters.

Can·da'ba (kän-dä'vä). Municipality, E Pampanga prov., Luzon, Phil. Is., on left bank of Pampanga river 10 m. ENE of San Fernando; pop. 19,956; on W margin of large lagoon and swamp area E of the Pampanga, known as **Candaba Swamp** (*Span.* **Pi·nag' de Candaba** [pĕ·näg' thä̃]).

Can·de·la'ria (kän'dä̇-lä'ryä). **1** Municipality, Pinar del Río prov., W Cuba; pop. 14,018; includes town on railroad 45 m. SW of Havana.
2 River in S Campeche state, Mexico; flows W and N into Laguna de Términos.

Can'di·a (kăn'dǐ·ȧ). **1** Island. See CRETE.
2 *or* **He·rak'li·on** (hē·răk'lǐ·ǒn; hĕr'ȧ·klǐ'ŏn); *Mod. Gr.* **Hē·rá'klei·on** (ē·rä'klē·ôn); *anc.* **Her'a·cle'um** (hĕr'ȧ·klē'ŭm). Seaport city, ✻ of Hērákleion dept., E cen. Crete, on N shore of island; pop. 33,404; episcopal see. Founded by Saracens near site of ancient Knossos; occupied by Venetians (whence its Italian name Candia) 13th–17th cents.; captured by Turks 1669; in modern times largest city in Crete; before 1841 capital of the island; devastated in German invasion May 1941.

Candia, Sea of; *Gr.* **Krē'ti·kòn' Pé'la·gos** (krē'tē·kôn' pä'lä·gôs). Part of the E Mediterranean Sea N of Crete and S of the Cyclades Is.

Can'dler (kănd'lēr). County in Georgia. See *Table* at GEORGIA.

Can'dle·wood', Lake (kăn'd'l·wŏŏd'). Lake 15 m. long in W Connecticut, near New York border bet. Litchfield and Fairfield cos.; drains N into Housatonic river.

Can'do (kăn'dōō). City, ⊗ of Towner co., N North Dakota; pop. 1566.

Can·don' (kän-dôn'). Municipality, S Ilocos Sur prov., Luzon, Phil. Is., near coast and on main highway 25 m. S of Vigan; pop. 20,528; coastwise trade.

Ca·ne'a (kȧ·nē'ȧ; *Ital.* kä-nâ'ä); *Gr.* **Kha·nia'** (кä-nyä'). **1** Department of Greece. See *Table* at GREECE.
2 *anc.* **Cy·do'ni·a** (sĭ-dō'nĭ·ȧ; -dōn'yȧ). Commercial seaport city, its ✻ and ✻ of Crete since 1841, on N coast of island at base of Akroteri Penin. on Bay of Canea; pop. 26,604; Orthodox and Catholic bishoprics. Prospered under Venetian rule; taken by Turks 1646; suffered heavily during German invasion May 1941.

Canea, Bay of. Inlet of Sea of Candia on N coast of Crete at its W end; enclosed on E by Akroteri Penin.

Ca·ne·lo'nes (kä'nä·lō'näs). **1** Department of Uruguay. See *Table* at URUGUAY.
2 *or* **Gua'da·lu'pe** (gwä'thä·lōō'pä). Town, its ✻, S Uruguay, 27 m. N of Montevideo; flour mills.

Ca·ñe'te (kä·nyä'tä). **1** River ab. 100 m. long in W cen. Peru; flows SW into Pacific Ocean 80 m. S of Lima.
2 Town at mouth of the Cañete, Peru; pop. ab. 5000.

Ca'ney (kā'nǐ). City, Montgomery co., SE Kansas, 20 m. SW of Independence; pop. 2682.

Ca·ney' (kä-nā'; *Span.* -nĕ'ĕ). See EL CANEY.

Ca·ney', Point (kä-nā'; *Span.* -nĕ'ĕ). Cape on SE coast of Las Villas prov., W cen. Cuba.

Ca'ney Fork (kā'nǐ). River, cen. Tennessee; formed by confluence of branches in SE White co., flows W and NW into Cumberland river near Carthage, Smith co.; traverses Great Falls Lake (bet. White, Van Buren, and Warren cos.), formed by Great Falls Dam, one of the dams of the Tennessee Valley Authority (*q.v.*).

Can'gas (käng'gäs). Commune, Pontevedra prov., NW Spain, on Bay of Vigo 14 m. SW of Pontevedra; pop. 15,836; cloth manufactures, sardine canning; cattle.

Can'gas de Nar·ce'a (-gäs thä när·thä'ä), *also called* **Cangas de Ti·ne'o** (tĕ·nä'ō). Commune, Oviedo prov., NW Spain, 37 m. WSW of Oviedo; pop. 21,296; coal mining, farming, stock raising.

Cangas de O·nís' (thä ō·nēs'). Commune, Oviedo prov., NW Spain, 35 m. E of Oviedo; pop. 9936; agriculture, stock raising, copper and coal mining; tanneries. Ancient seat of Asturian kings. See COVADONGA.

Can'go Caves (käng'gō). Stalactite caves in the Zwartberg Mts., S Cape Province, Union of South Africa, N of Oudtshoorn.

Ca'ni·cat·tì' (kä'nē·kät·tē'). Commune, Agrigento prov., SW Sicily, 16 m. E by N of Agrigento; pop. 29,680; sulfur mines. Taken by Americans July 1943.

Ca'ni·ga'o Channel (kä'nē·gȧ'ō). Passage 18 to 28 m. wide bet. SW Leyte and E Bohol, S cen. Phil. Is.; connects NE Mindanao Sea with Camotes Sea.

Ca'ni'gou' (kȧ'nē·gōō'). Peak 9135 ft., S Pyrénées-Orientales dept., S France, in the E Pyrenees ab. 20 m. SW of Perpignan.

Ca·nil'las (kä-nē'lyäs; -nē'yäs). Commune, Madrid prov., cen. Spain, NE suburb of Madrid; pop. 20,924.

Ca·ni'no (kä-nē'nō). Village, Roma prov., W Latium, cen. Italy, WNW of Viterbo; pop. 3626; in 1814 made a principality for Lucien Bonaparte.

Can'is·te'o (kăn'ĭs·tē'ō). **1** River ab. 60 m. long, SW New York; rises in Allegany co., flows SE into Tioga river ab. 5 m. SW of Corning in SE Steuben co.
2 Residential village, Steuben co., S New York, on Canisteo river 6 m. SSE of Hornell; pop. 2731. Former Indian village; settled by whites 1788.

Çan'kı·rı' (chäng'kǐ·rǐ') *or* **Chan'ki·ri'**. **1** Vilayet, N cen. Turkey in Asia; 3345 sq. m.; pop. 177,587.
2 *anc.* **Gan'gra** (găng'grȧ); *later* **Ger·man'i·cop'o·lis** (jĕr·măn'ĭ·kŏp'ō·lís). Town, its ✻, on tributary of Kızıl Irmak ab. 60 m. NE of Ankara; pop. 9762; scene of Synod of Gangra c. 340 A.D.

Can'la·on', Mount (kăn'lä·ôn'); *or* **Ma'la·spi'na** (mä'lä·spē'nä). Active volcano 8087 ft., N cen. Negros I., cen. Phil. Is.; in eruption 1866 and 1893.

Can'na (kăn'ȧ). Island 4½ m. long of the Inner Hebrides, off W coast of Scotland; part of Inverness co.

Can'nae (kăn'ē). Battlefield near modern Barletta, Bari prov., Apulia, SE Italy, where, in 216 B.C. during Second Punic War, Hannibal inflicted on Roman army the severest defeat ever sustained by Rome.

Can'na·nore (kăn'ȧ·nōr) *or* **Ka'na·nur'** (kŭ'nȧ·nōōr'). Town, N Kerala, SW India, on the Malabar Coast 50 m. NNW of Kozhikode; pop. 34,236; has some export trade. Visited by Vasco da Gama 1498; Portuguese settlement made 1501, fort built 1505; present fort built by Dutch 1656; captured by British 1790.

Can'nel·ton (kăn'ĕl·tŭn). City, ⊗ of Perry co., S Indiana, on Ohio river 43 m. E of Evansville; pop. 1829.

Cannes (kăn; *Fr.* kȧn). Seaport and commune, Alpes-Maritimes dept., SE France, on Mediterranean 18 m. SW of Nice; pop. (commune) 49,032; resort; manufactures perfumes, soap; exports fruit, oils, anchovies. Twice destroyed by Moors; Napoleon landed nearby on his escape from Elba Mar. 1815; in World War II marked E limit of landing of Americans Aug. 15, 1944.

Cannet, Le. See LE CANNET.

Can'nock (kăn'ŭk). Urban district, Staffordshire, W cen. England, 16 m. NNW of Birmingham; pop. 40,927; coal mining.

Can'non (kăn'ŭn). **1** River ab. 95 m. long, SE Minnesota; rises S Le Sueur co., flows NE to the Mississippi.
2 County in Tennessee. See *Table* at TENNESSEE.

Can'non·ball' (kăn'ŭn·bôl'). River ab. 140 m. long, SW North Dakota; rises in Slope co., flows E into Missouri river on NW boundary of Sioux co.

Cannon Falls. City, Goodhue co., SE Minnesota, 24 m. NE of Faribault; pop. 2055; farm products.

Cannon Mountain. 1 Peak 8460 ft. in Glacier National Park, NW Montana.
2 *or* **Pro'file Mountain** (prō'fīl). Peak 4077 ft. in N Grafton co., W New Hampshire, in White Mts. on W side of Franconia Notch; on a SE shoulder is a natural formation (the Profile, or Old Man of the Mountain) which resembles a human face seen in profile; on NE is a formation resembling a cannon; aerial tramway.

Can'nou·an' (kăn'ŏŏ·än'). Small island, N Grenadines, Windward Is., West Indies.

Cann'statt *or* **Kann'statt** (kän'shtät). Northern suburb of Stuttgart, Baden-Württemberg, W Germany; formerly an independent town, became part of Stuttgart 1905; mineral springs; site of discovery 1700 of human skull (the Cannstatt skull) thought to be representative of a neolithic race.

Ca·no'as (kȧ·nō'ȧs). City, Rio Grande do Sul state, S Brazil, a N suburb of Pôrto Alegre; pop. 12,066.

Can'on City (kăn'yŭn). City, ⊗ of Fremont co., S cen. Colorado, on Arkansas river 35 m. SW of Colorado Springs; pop. 8973; settled 1859; resort in rich mining district; marble, limestone quarries; state penitentiary.

Can'ons·burg (kăn'ŭnz·bûrg). Borough, Washington co., SW Pennsylvania, 18 m. SSW of Pittsburgh; pop. 11,877; platted 1787; active center of Whisky Insurrection 1794; coal-mining center; gas and oil wells.

Ca·no'pus (kȧ·nō'pŭs). Ancient city on the coast of Lower Egypt, 15 m. E of Alexandria at Abukir; in early times of much importance because of its great temple of Serapis; the most westerly branch of the Nile delta then had its mouth here (**Ca·no'pic Mouth** [kȧ·nō'pĭk]).

Ca·no'sa di Pu'glia (kä·nō'sä dē pōō'lyä); *anc.* **Ca·nu'si·um** (kȧ·nū'zhĭ·ŭm; -zĭ·ŭm). Commune, Bari prov., Apulia, SE Italy, 43 m. W by N of Bari; pop. 28,377; Romanesque cathedral built 1101; ruined castle; ancient Roman remains.

Canossa. See Ciano d'Enza.

Canóvanas. See Loíza.

Can'so (kăn'sō). Fishing town, Guysborough co., E Nova Scotia, Canada, on Atlantic Ocean at mouth of Chedabucto Bay near Cape Canso; pop. 1313; reputed to have been inhabited by European fishermen and fur traders shortly after Columbus' discovery of America; became English post 1718; recaptured by French 1744 but left unoccupied; held by British 1745–49; had repeated Indian trouble; ravaged and largely destroyed by privateers 1812. American terminus of several Atlantic cables and port of call for Gloucester fishing fleet.

Canso, Cape. Cape at NE end of Nova Scotia mainland, Canada, at S entrance to Chedabucto Bay.

Canso, Strait, *or* **Gut, of.** Deep, narrow channel bet. NE Nova Scotia mainland and S Cape Breton I., Canada; ab. 14½ m. long and 1 m. wide.

Cantaber Oceanus. See Bay of Biscay.

Can·ta'bri·an Mountains (kăn·tā'brĭ·ăn); *Span.* **Cor·dil·le'ra Can·tá'bri·ca** (kôr'thē·[l]yä'rä kän·tä'vrē·kä). Range in N and NW Spain; highest peak Torre de Cerredo 8787 ft.

Cantabrigia. See Cambridge, England.

Can'tal' (käN'tȧl'). Department of France. See *Table* at France.

Can'ter·bur'y (kăn'tēr·bĕr'ĭ; *esp. Brit.,* -bĕr·ĭ, -brĭ).
1 City, E New South Wales, SE Australia, SW suburb of Sydney; pop. 79,058.
2 *anc.* **Du'ro·ver'num** (dūr'ō·vûr'nŭm); *ecclesiastical Lat.* **Can'tu·ar'i·a** (kăn'tū·âr'ĭ·ȧ); *AS.* **Cant'wa'ra·burh'** (kȧnt'wȧ·rȧ·bōōrk'). City and county borough, Kent, SE England, on the Stour 53 m. ESE of London; pop. 27,778; ecclesiastical metropolis of England since the founding 602 of a monastery by Saint Augustine. Church, later the cathedral, destroyed by fire 1067, E part rebuilt, destroyed again by fire 1174, rebuilt 1175–80; improved by changes and additions 1379–1503; scene of murder of Thomas à Becket 1170 and after his canonization 1172 made a place of pilgrimage (shrine, built after 1175, destroyed by Henry VIII 1538); damaged by German bombing May 31, 1942.
3 Provincial district of New Zealand. See *Table* at New Zealand.

Canterbury Bight (bīt). Wide inlet of Pacific Ocean, E cen. coast of South I., New Zealand, S of Banks Penin.

Can'tho' (kŭn'tō'). Town, cen. Cochin China, S Vietnam, on right bank of the Mekong in its delta 90 m. SW of Saigon; pop. 27,000; has considerable trade in rice and fish; a port of call for river and coastal steamers.

Can'ti'gny' (käN'tē'nyē'). Village, Somme dept., N France, ab. 18 m. S of Amiens; pop. (1931) 106; battle May 28, 1918, first offensive by U.S. forces in World War I.

Can·ti'les Cay (kăn·tē'lȧs). Island in N Caribbean Sea, E of Isle of Pines and S of W Cuba.

Can'ton (kăn't'n; -tŭn). **1** Manufacturing town, W Hartford co., N Connecticut; pop. 4783; incorp. 1806; watered by Farmington river; includes Collinsville (*q.v.*).
2 City, ⊗ of Cherokee co., NW Georgia, 33 m. NNW of Atlanta; pop. 2411.
3 City, Fulton co., W cen. Illinois, 25 m. WSW of Peoria; pop. 13,588; settled 1825; incorp. 1854; manufactures farm implements, lumber and clay products.
4 Industrial town, Norfolk co., E Massachusetts, 14 m. SSW of Boston; pop. 12,771; manufactures rubber goods, textiles, electrical equipment; site of Paul Revere's brass and bell foundry.
5 City, ⊗ of Madison co., cen. Mississippi, 25 m. NNE of Jackson; pop. 9707; cotton.
6 City, Lewis co., NE Missouri, on Mississippi river 33 m. N of Hannibal; pop. 2562; lumber mills, canneries, poultry farms. Culver-Stockton College (1853; coed.), oldest coeducational college west of the Mississippi.
7 Village, ⊗ of St. Lawrence co., N New York, 18 m. ESE of Ogdensburg; pop. 5046; in dairy farming region. St. Lawrence University (1856; coed.).
8 Town, Haywood co., W North Carolina, 15 m. W of Asheville; pop. 5068; pulp, paper, tannic extract.
9 Industrial city, ⊗ of Stark co., NE Ohio, 20 m. SSE of Akron; pop. 113,631; settled c. 1805; became ⊗ 1809; incorporated as village 1822, as city 1854. Manufactures steel, vacuum cleaners, roller bearings, safes and vaults, motors, brick and tile, rubber goods. Home of Pres. McKinley, who is buried here in National McKinley Memorial (erected 1907).
10 Borough, Bradford co., N Pennsylvania, 30 m. NNE of Williamsport; pop. 2102; commercial center.
11 City, ⊗ of Lincoln co., SE South Dakota, on Big Sioux river 20 m. S of Sioux Falls; pop. 2511; shipping point for corn and poultry; road machinery.
12 Town, ⊗ of Van Zandt co., NE Texas; pop. 1114.

Can·ton' (kăn·tŏn'; kăn'tŏn). **1** *officially* **Kwang'chow'** (kwäng'jō'). Commercial city and treaty port, ✳ of Kwangtung prov., SE China, on Pearl river in Si delta ab. 80 m. from the sea; pop. (1936 est.) 1,122,600; chief port and city of S China; city proper (Old City) enclosed by walls with twelve gates; has very large floating population (approximately 200,000) on river boats; noted esp. for its great volume of trade, both imports and exports; in business transactions with foreigners has developed a trade jargon ("pidgin English").

History: In early history of China an outpost of minor importance; incorporated in empire 3d cent. B.C.; made capital of Kwangtung under the Mings; first seaport of China opened to foreigners; regularly visited for centuries by Arab, Hindu, and Parsi traders, in 16th cent. by Portuguese; in 1684 granted right to English East India Company to establish factory; later opened to French and Dutch and (except for Macao) remained the only Chinese trading port down to 1842; its resistance to English opium trade led to war with Great Britain 1841–42; became one of the first treaty ports by Treaty of Nanking 1842. Scene of incident 1856 that led to second war with Great Britain; occupied by British and French 1856–61; granted 1859 new concession area (Shameen) to foreigners; its commercial prosperity affected by growth of Hong Kong; in 19th cent. seat of nationalist ideas and Kuomintang (see Kwangtung); occupied by Japanese Oct. 21, 1938; base for later Japanese offensives, esp. in 1944.
2 River, China. See Pearl river.

Can'ton (kăn't'n; -tŭn), *formerly* **Mar'y** (mâr'ĭ), **Island.** One of the more important of the Phoenix Is. (*q.v.*), cen. Pacific Ocean, 2°48′ S lat., 171°43′W, an atoll

8 m. long by 4 m. wide, enclosing large lagoon; has stunted vegetation, with coconut groves at S end; affords excellent base for seaplanes and airplanes. Visited by expedition to observe total eclipse of sun June 8, 1937; since 1939 has become important aviation station under Anglo-American condominium on S route from Honolulu to New Caledonia.

Can·tù' (kän·too'). Commune, Como prov., Lombardy, N Italy, 5 m. SSE of Como; pop. 18,517; sericulture.

Cantuaria, Cantwaraburh. See CANTERBURY.

Cantyre. See KINTYRE.

Ca·ñue'las (kä·nywä'läs). Town, Buenos Aires prov., E Argentina, ab. 37 m. SW of Buenos Aires; pop. ab. 6000.

Canusium. See CANOSA DI PUGLIA.

Can'yon (kǎn'yŭn). **1** County in Idaho. See *Table* at IDAHO.

2 City, ⊗ of Randall co., NW Texas, in the Panhandle 18 m. S of Amarillo; pop. 5864; farming, stock raising. West Texas State Coll. (1909; coed.).

Canyon City. Town, ⊗ of Grant co., E cen. Oregon; pop. 654.

Canyon de Chel'ly National Monument (dě shā'). See UNITED STATES, *National Monuments.*

Can'yon Di·ab'lo (kǎn'yŭn dĭ·äb'lō). Gorge, SE Coconino co., N Arizona, in **Canyon Diablo River,** a tributary of the Little Colorado river; ab. 225 ft. deep and 500 ft. wide; Crater Mound is nearby.

Canyon Lake. See MORMON FLAT DAM.

Cao'bang (kou'bäng). Town, Tonkin, N Vietnam, near China border ab. 115 m. N of Hanoi.

Ca·or'le (kä·ôr'lā). Commune, Venezia prov., Venezia Euganea, NE Italy, on Gulf of Venice at mouth of Livenza river; pop. 10,077; cathedral; watering place.

Cap, Le. See CAP HAITIEN.

Capac–Urcu. See ALTAR.

Ca·pan'no·ri (kä·pän'nō·rē). Commune, Lucca prov., Tuscany, cen. Italy, 4 m. E of Lucca; pop. 41,033; consists of group of 38 villages.

Ca·par'ra (kä·pär'rä). Settlement on Puerto Rico near San Juan, founded 1509 by Ponce de León, abandoned 1511.

Ca'pas (kä'päs). Town, S Tarlac prov., Luzon, Phil. Is.; pop. 13,178; airfield just N of Clark Field.

Cap'–Chat' (kåp'shä'). Village, West Gaspé co., Gaspé Penin., SE Quebec, Canada, on St. Lawrence river 46 m. ENE of Matane; pop. 1642; summer resort.

Cap de la Ma'de·leine (kåp' dē là mà'dlěn'). City, Champlain co., S Quebec, Canada, on N bank of St. Lawrence river 4 m. ENE of Three Rivers; pop. 18,667.

Cape, the (kāp). Colloquial form of reference to various capes and peninsulas, including: Cape HORN, Cape of GOOD HOPE, CAPE COD.

Cape Bar'ren Island (bǎr'ěn). Island in the Furneaux Group, NE of Tasmania, Australia.

Cape Bret'on (brĭt'n; brět'n). **1** See Cape BRETON.
2 County, Nova Scotia, Canada. See *Table* at NOVA SCOTIA.

Cape Breton Highlands National Park. See CANADA, *National Parks.*

Cape Breton Island. Island, E part of Nova Scotia prov., E Canada; 3975 sq. m.; pop. 150,157; comprises four counties: Cape Breton, Inverness, Richmond, and Victoria; separated from mainland by narrow Strait of Canso; in central part are Bras d'Or salt lakes; has many summer resorts and one national park; its extensive Sydney coal fields are of great economic value. Formally assigned to France 1632 and retained by Treaty of Utrecht 1713; ceded to England 1763; independent of Nova Scotia 1784–1820 (❋ Sydney).

Cape Charles (chärlz). **1** See Cape CHARLES.
2 Town, Northampton co., S Virginia penin., on Chesapeake Bay 33 m. NNE of Norfolk; pop. 2041; sea-food industries.

Cape Coast, *formerly* **Cape Coast Castle.** Seaport town, SW Ghana, W Africa, 75 m. WSW of Accra; pop.

(1937 est.) 19,412; first settlement by Portuguese 1610; site of castle (hence the early name) built by Swedes 1652; seized by English 1664 and held against various attacks; capital of colony to 1876.

Cape Cod (kŏd), *often* **the Cape. 1** Sandy peninsula, SE Massachusetts, nearly coextensive with Barnstable co.; 1 to 20 m. wide, ab. 65 m. long, extends E from the mainland and forms a wide curve toward the N enclosing Cape Cod Bay; has open ocean (Atlantic) on the E,

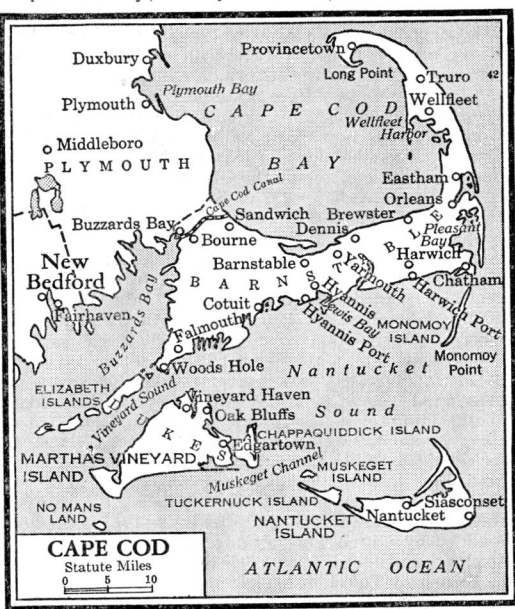

CAPE COD
Statute Miles
0   5   10

Nantucket Sound on the S (separating it from Martha's Vineyard and Nantucket I.), Buzzards Bay on the SW; its base on the W is crossed by the Cape Cod Canal (8 m. long); extending from its SE corner is Monomoy Point, a long narrow sand spit, and extending from its SW corner are the Elizabeth Is. Its N tip, N of Provincetown, discovered by Gosnold 1602; Pilgrims from *Mayflower* landed near Provincetown Nov. 1620.
2 The N tip of the peninsula.

Cape Cod Bay. South end of Massachusetts Bay off E coast of Massachusetts; formed within the northward sweep of Cape Cod; see CAPE COD CANAL.

Cape Cod Canal. Ship canal crossing Cape Cod at its base, in Barnstable co., Massachusetts; connects Buzzards Bay with Cape Cod Bay; 8 m. long, 500 ft. wide, 32 ft. deep; completed 1914, owned by U.S. government.

Cape Colony. See CAPE OF GOOD HOPE prov.

Cape E·liz'a·beth (ê·lĭz'à·běth). Town, Cumberland co., SW Maine, on Atlantic Ocean 7 m. S of Portland; pop. 5505; summer resort.

Cape Fear (fēr). River ab. 202 m. long, cen. and SE North Carolina; navigable to Fayetteville; formed by confluence of Deep and Haw rivers in Chatham co., flows SE into Atlantic Ocean in E Brunswick co.

Cape Gi·rar'deau (jĭ·rä[r]'dō; -dŭ). **1** County in Missouri. See *Table* at MISSOURI.
2 City, Cape Girardeau co., SE Missouri, on Mississippi river 30 m. NNW of its confluence with Ohio river; pop. 24,947; shoe factories, cement plants, sawmills. Southeast Missouri State College (1873; coed.).

Cape Hat'ter·as National Seashore Park (hǎt'ēr·ǎs). See *Table, Note 5,* at NORTH CAROLINA.

Cape Horn Mountain (hôrn). Peak 9500 ft. in Salmon River Mts., W Custer co., cen. Idaho.

Cape May (mā). **1** Cape, S New Jersey. See Cape MAY.
2 County in New Jersey. See *Table* at NEW JERSEY.

3 City, Cape May co., S New Jersey, ab. 40 m. SW of Atlantic City on Atlantic Ocean; pop. 4477; early settlement (from ab. 1664) known as Cape Island; one of oldest Atlantic coast resorts.

Cape May Court House. Village, ⊗ of Cape May co., S New Jersey, 28 m. SW of Atlantic City; pop. 1749.

Cape of Good Hope. 1 Cape, S Union of South Africa. See Cape of GOOD HOPE.

2 *often called* **Cape′ Prov′ince,** *formerly (before 1910)* **Cape′ Col′o·ny.** Province, S Republic of So. Africa; 277,169 sq. m.; pop. (1936) 3,529,900, including 791,574 Europeans; ✻ Cape Town; much of its N boundary formed by Orange river, its principal stream, which separates it from Orange Free State on NE and from South-West Africa on NW (Griqualand West and British Bechuanaland, now parts of the province, are N of Orange river; bounded in extreme NE by Basutoland and Natal; rivers include the Olifants and Great Berg in SW and streams flowing S or SE to South Atlantic and Indian Oceans, as the Breede, Gouritz, Great Fish, Great Kei, and Umzimvubu; has inner plateau bordered by an escarpment roughly parallel with the coast; many short ranges 6000 to 8500 ft. in height; S of the escarpment in central part is the Great Karroo, a dry tableland 2000 to 3000 ft. above sea level; its most southerly point—also most southerly point of continent of Africa—is Cape Agulhas 34°50′S (Cape of Good Hope 92 m. WNW, in 34°21′S). Divided into several regions (generally not considered to be political subdivisions): Griqualand West, Transkeian Territories, Bushman Land (*qq.v.*). *Chief products:* Grains, kaffir corn, tobacco, livestock, fruits, hides, wool. *Chief cities:* Cape Town, Port Elizabeth, East London, Kimberley, Uitenhage, Paarl.

History: Cape of Good Hope discovered 1488 by Bartholomeu Dias while en route to India 1487–88; colony founded by Dutch who began settlement at Table Bay 1652; occupied by British 1795–1803 and 1806–14; ceded to British by Dutch 1814; Natal united with Cape Colony for administrative purposes 1844–56; annexed British Kaffraria 1865 and British Bechuanaland 1895; administered Basutoland 1871–84; received responsible government 1872; joined Union of South Africa 1910.

Ca·per′na·um (ka·pûr′na·ŭm; -ni·ŭm). Ruined city of ancient Palestine, on the NW shore of the Sea of Galilee; home of Jesus during most of the period of his ministry.

Cape Sa′ble Island (sā′b'l). Small island off the SW tip of Nova Scotia, Canada; Cape Sable is its S point.

Ca′pes′terre′ (ka′pĕs′târ′). Commune, SE Marie-Galante I., Guadeloupe, Fr. West Indies; pop. ab. 7000.

Capesterre–le–Ma′ri′got′ (-lĕ·ma·rē′gō′). Commune, SE Basse-Terre, Guadeloupe, Fr. West Indies; pop. ab. 10,000.

Cape Town *or* **Cape′town′** (kāp′toun′); *S. Af. Du.* **Kaap′stad** (käp′stät). Seaport city, ✻ of Cape of Good Hope prov. and seat of legislature of Republic of South Africa, in SW part on Table Bay; pop. 344,223; well laid out; resort; has commodious harbor well sheltered by artificial breakwater; chief port of South Africa; has Africa's second largest grain elevator; exports gold and diamonds, fruits, wines, skins, wool, mohair, maize, and flowers; has Royal Observatory, source of time signals throughout South Africa. First settlement at Table Bay founded 1652 by Dutch navigator, Jan van Riebeeck, for the Dutch East India Company; served as a stopover for ships plying the Europe-to-India route; under Dutch rule until 1795, when it was captured by a British force; returned to the Dutch by the Treaty of Amiens 1803, retaken by the British 1806. Formerly site of South African College (founded 1829; became University of Cape Town 1918), now at Rondebosch (*q.v.*).

Cape Verde Islands (vûrd); *Port.* **I′lhas do Ca′bo Ver′de** (ē′lyȧzh tнōō kä′vōō vär′dĕ). Group of volcanic islands in the Atlantic Ocean ab. 320 m. W of Cape Vert, bet. 14°47′ and 17°13′N lat.; 1557 sq. m.; pop. (1936) 162,055, (1940 est.) 181,286; ✻ Praia on São Tiago; constitutes a Portuguese colony; main islands: São Tiago, Santo Antão, São Vicente, São Nicoláo, Sal, Boa Vista, Fogo, Maio, Brava, Santa Luzia. Generally mountainous, highest peak 9348 ft. on Fogo; produces some sugar, tobacco, oranges and other fruits, coffee, castor oil; chief towns are Praia the capital and Porto Grande on São Vicente, an important coaling station. Discovered 1456 by Ca Da Mosto, Venetian navigator in service of Prince Henry of Portugal; ruled privately 1456–95; became part of royal domain 1495.

Cape York Peninsula (yôrk). Peninsula ab. 450 m. long forming NE part of Queensland, Australia; terminates in Cape York on Torres Strait.

Cap Hai′tien (kàp hā′shĕn); *Fr.* **Cap′-Ha′i′tien′** (kà′pà′ē′syän′; -tyän′); *locally* **Le Cap** (lĕ kàp′). Seaport, N Haiti, pop. (1936 est.) 12,000; earthquake 1842.

Ca·pha′reus (ka·fâr′ūs); *Mod. Gr.* **Ka′phē·revs′** (kä′-fĕ·râfs′). *Also* **Do′ro** (dô′rō). Cape, SE coast of Euboea I.; extends into Aegean Sea as rocky and dangerous promontory; in legend, scene of wreck of Greek fleet returning from Troy.

Ca′pia·tá′ (kä′pyä·tä′). City, Central dept., S cen. Paraguay; pop. ab. 15,520.

Ca′pi·ba·ri′be (kä′pĕ·vä·rē′vĕ). River 140 m. long, Pernambuco state, NE Brazil; flows E into Atlantic Ocean at Recife.

Ca·pil′la del Mon′te (kä·pē′yä [*Argentine* -pē′zhä] тнĕl môn′tā). Mountain resort, W Córdoba prov., N cen. Argentina; altitude ab. 3000 ft.

Capital Federal. See FEDERAL DISTRICT, Argentina.

Capitan, El. See EL CAPITAN.

Cap′i·tan′ Peak (kăp′i·tăn′). Mountain 10,023 ft., cen. Lincoln co., cen. New Mexico.

Cap′i·tol Heights (kăp′i·t'l). Town, Prince Georges co., S cen. Maryland, 6 m. E of Washington; pop. 3138.

Cap′i·to·line (kăp′i·tô·līn; ka·pīt′'l·īn). One of the seven hills of Rome; once had 2 peaks, the Arx and the **Cap′i·to′li·um** (kăp′i·tō′li·ŭm). See SEVEN HILLS.

Cap′i·tol Peak (kăp′i·t'l). Mountain 14,100 ft. in Pitkin co., W cen. Colorado.

Capitol Reef National Monument. See UNITED STATES, *National Monuments.*

Ca′piz (kä′pēs). **1** Province, N Panay, Phil. Is.; 1703 sq. m.; pop. 405,285; ✻ Capiz; borders Sibuyan Sea on the N with Jintotolo Channel on NE; good harbors at Capiz and in Pilar Bay; mountainous in W and SW; fertile plain in the E in the Panay valley. Produces sugar and rice, timber and forest products. Chief towns Capiz, Pontevedra, Ibajay, Pilar, and Libacao.

History: Town of Panay second Spanish settlement in the Philippines, built 1569; native settlements increased in 17th cent.; region organized 1716 as a politico-military province; seized by Revolutionists 1898; civil government established Apr. 1901.

2 Municipality, its ✻, on good harbor at mouth of Panay river; pop. 29,021; connected by rail with Iloilo; port of call for steamers; has large rice trade.

Ca′po·di′stri·a (kä′pō·dēs′trē·ä); *Angl.* kăp′ō·dĭs′trĭ·à); *Slovenian* **Ko′per** (kô′pĕr); *Serbo-Croatian* **Ko′par** (kô′pär); *anc.* **Æ·gid′i·a** (ē·jĭd′i·à); *later* **Jus′tin·op′-o·lis** (jŭs′tĭn·ŏp′ô·lĭs). Seaport, Istria penin., Yugoslavia, in Slovenia on Gulf of Trieste just SSW of Trieste; pop. 11,995; cathedral; old fort. Before achieving independence 1478, belonged alternately to Venice and Genoa from 10th cent.; became capital of Istria; fell to Austria 1797–1805, 1814–1918, and to Italy 1918–47.

Ca′po·ret′to (kä′pō·rât′tō; *Angl.* kăp′ô·rĕt′ō); *Ger.* **Kar′freit** (kär′frīt); *Yugo.* **Ko′ba·rid** (kô′bä·rēd). Village, formerly in Gorizia prov., NW Venezia Giulia, NE Italy, on the Isonzo 21 m. NE of Udine; since treaty of 1947 in Slovenia, NW Yugoslavia; pop. 6273; in World War I campaign from Oct. 24 to Dec. 26, 1917, scene of a major defeat of Italian forces under Gen. Cadorna who were driven back to the Piave by Austro-German forces under Gen. Otto von Below.

Cap'pa·do'ci·a (kăp'*à*·dō'shǐ·*à*; -shà). Mountainous district of E Asia Minor (cen. modern Turkey) of varying boundaries; watered by the Halys river; a satrapy of the Persian Empire, it became a semi-independent kingdom under Ariarathes I, a contemporary of Alexander of Macedon; established as a separate dynasty c. 255 B.C.; aided Rome in her wars in Asia Minor; Roman province 17 A.D.; Caesarea Mazaca was its chief city.

Ca·pra'ia (kä·prä'yä). Island ab. 3½ m. long and 1½ m. wide in Mediterranean Sea NNW of Elba and E of N tip of Corsica; belongs to Genova prov., Italy; penal colony.

Ca·pra'ra, Point (kä·prä'rä). Northern point of Asinara I. off NW coast of Sardinia.

Capraria. See CABRERA.

Ca'pra·ro'la (kä'prä·rō'lä). Commune, Viterbo prov., N Latium, cen. Italy, 9 m. SE of Viterbo; pop. 5525; castle built 1547–59 for Alessandro Farnese.

Ca'pre·ol (kä'prē·ŏl; kăp'rē-). Town, Sudbury dist., SE Ontario, Canada, 15 m. N of Sudbury; pop. 2002.

Ca·pre'ra (kä·prā'rä). Island in Tyrrhenian Sea off NE coast of Sardinia; 6 sq. m.; a part of Sassari prov., Sardinia, Italy; Garibaldi's home 1856–82.

Ca·pre'se or **Caprese Mi·chel·an'ge·lo** (kä·prā'sā mē·kāl·än'jā·lō). Commune, Arezzo prov., E Tuscany, Italy; pop. (1931) 3195; birthplace of Michelangelo.

Ca'pri (kä'prē); *anc.* **Cap're·ae** (kăp'rē·ē). Island in the Bay of Naples, Italy, in Napoli prov.; ab. 5 sq. m.; pop. (1931) ab. 7000; cliffs on E side rise 900 ft.; highest point 1920 ft. is on W side; on N shore is the Blue Grotto (*q.v.*); fertile soil. During Napoleonic Wars captured by British 1806, French 1808; returned to Ferdinand I of the Two Sicilies 1815.

Cap'ri·corn Channel (kăp'rǐ·kôrn). Passage in Pacific Ocean off E coast of Queensland, Australia; entrance to waters inside Great Barrier Reef at its S end.

Ca·pri'vi Concession (kä·prē'vē); *Ger.* **Ca·pri'vi·zip'-fel** (kä·prē'vē·tsǐp'fĕl). Strip of land, NE South-West Africa; 40 m. wide, runs E ab. 300 m. bet. Angola and Northern Rhodesia on N and Bechuanaland Protectorate on S; ab. 7000 sq. m.; known also as "Caprivi's Finger"; obtained 1890 by the German chancellor Count Georg Leo von Caprivi in negotiations with the British.

Capsa. See GAFSA.

Cap San'té' (kăp' sän'tā'). Village (unincorporated), ⊗ of Portneuf co., S Quebec, Canada, on N bank of St. Lawrence river 28 m. WSW of Quebec; pop. 1129; an old parish dating back to 17th cent.; noted as a resort.

Cap'u·a (kăp'ū·à; *Ital.* kä'pwä). Commune, Napoli prov., Campania, S Italy, on Volturno river 19 m. N of Naples; pop. 14,183; 9th-cent. cathedral (modernized); agriculture. Founded 856 A.D. on site of ancient **Cas'i·li'num** (kăs'ĭ·lī'nŭm) 2½ m. SE of the original ancient city of **Cap'u·a** [kăp'ū·à] (devastated by Genseric 456 A.D., completely destroyed 840 by the Saracens); captured 1501 by Caesar Borgia; as fortified city, one of defenses of kingdom of Naples; fell to kingdom of Italy 1860; scene of heavy fighting Oct. 1943 in World War II.

Ca·pu'lin Mountain National Monument (kä·pū'lǐn). See UNITED STATES, *National Monuments.*

Ca·puz'zo (kä·pōōt'tsō), **Fort.** Village and fort, NE Cyrenaica, Libya, on Egyptian border S of Bardia; base for Italian operations Sept. 1940; captured by British Dec. 16, 1940, figured in later campaigns 1941–42.

Ca'que·tá' (kä'kā·tä'). **1** Name given in Colombia to the upper course of the Japurá river. See JAPURÁ.
2 Commissary of Colombia. See *Table* at COLOMBIA.

Car, Slieve. See SLIEVE CAR.

Ca'ra·bal'lo Mountains (kä'rä·vä'yō, *also known as the* **Ca'ra·bal'los** (-vä'yōs). **1** The mountain group in cen. and S Nueva Vizcaya prov., cen. Luzon, Phil. Is. with general elevation of 2000 to 5000 ft.; joined from the N by the Cordillera Central and on the E by the Sierra Madre; the range extending to the S into Tayabas prov. is sometimes called the **Caraballo Sur** (sōōr').
2 The Cordillera Central, Phil. Is.;—formerly so called.

Ca'ra·ban·chel' Al'to (kä'rä·vän·chĕl' äl'tō). Commune, Madrid prov., cen. Spain, SW suburb of Madrid; pop. 10,682.

Carabanchel Ba'jo (vä'hō). Commune, Madrid prov., cen. Spain, SW suburb of Madrid; pop. 26,970.

Ca'ra·ba'o (kä'rä·vä'ō). Islet off W shore of Cavite prov. on S side of entrance to Manila Bay, Phil. Is.; has American fortification, Fort Frank. See CORREGIDOR.

Carabaya, Cordillera de. See CORDILLERA DE CARABAYA.

Ca'ra·bo'bo (kä'rä·vō'vō). **1** State of Venezuela. See *Table* at VENEZUELA.
2 Village in Carabobo state, ab. 20 m. SW of Valencia; battle June 24, 1821 in which Sucre defeated royalists thereby winning independence for Venezuela.

Ca'ra·cal' (kä'rä·käl'). City, Oltenia region, S Romania, 30 m. ESE of Craiova; pop. (1939 est.) 16,000.

Ca·rac'as (kà·räk'às; *Span.* kä·rä'käs). City, ✱ of Venezuela and of the Federal District, N Venezuela; pop. (1950) 495,064, metropolitan area (1957 est.) 1,162,780; beautiful city, well laid out, at alt. of ab. 3000 ft.; connected with its seaport La Guaira, 8 m. directly N, by a railroad ab. 23 m. long. University, cathedral (1614).

History: Founded 1567 by Diego de Losada; attacked by Drake 1595; capital of captaincy-general of Caracas erected 1731; birthplace of Simón Bolívar 1783; under Bolívar's leadership, first colony to revolt from Spain 1810; visited by earthquake which helped those loyal to Spain to recover city 1812; re-entered by Bolívar 1813 and occupied by him again June 29, 1821 (after Carabobo); became capital of independent Venezuela.

Ca'ra·co'les (kä'rä·kō'lās). Town, Antofagasta prov., Chile; pop. ab. 5000; silver mines.

Ca'ra·gua·tay' (kä'rä·gwä·tä'ē; -tī'). Town, E cen. Cordillera dept., cen. Paraguay, 50 m. E of Asunción; pop. ab. 18,900.

Caralis. See CAGLIARI seaport.

Caraman, Caramania. Vars. of KARAMAN, KARAMANIA.

Ca'ra·mo'an (kä'rä·mō'än). Municipality at E end of Caramoan Penin., NE Camarines Sur prov., Luzon, Phil. Is., near shore of Lagonoy Gulf; pop. 22,750.

Caramoan Peninsula. Peninsula ab. 53 m. long by 13 m. wide extending into Pacific Ocean and forming NE part of Camarines Sur prov., SE Luzon, Phil. Is.; on W is San Miguel Bay and on SE Lagonoy Gulf.

Ca'ran·go'la (kä'räNng·gō'lä). City, SE Minas Gerais state, E Brazil, 133 m. SE of Belo Horizonte; pop. 8892.

Ca'ra·pa·che'ta (kä'rä·pä·chā'tä). Peak 16,400 ft., cen. Cochabamba dept., cen. Bolivia.

Ca'ra·pe·guá' (kä'rä·pā·gwä'). Town, Paraguarí dept., S cen. Paraguay, ab. 40 m. SE of Asunción; pop. ab. 20,300; founded 1725.

Car'a·quet (kär'à·kĕt). Village, NE New Brunswick, Canada, on S shore of Chaleur Bay; in 19th cent. an important cod-fishing village, with 22 m. of beach.

Ca'ra·tas'ca Lagoon (kä'rä·täs'kä). Large lagoon on E coast of Honduras, an inlet of the Caribbean Sea.

Ca'ra·va'ca (kä'rä·vä'kä). Commune, Murcia prov., SE Spain, 38 m. WNW of Murcia; pop. 20,645; manufactures paper, textiles, leather, brandy, chocolate, oil.

Ca'ra·vag'gio (kä'rä·väd'jō). Commune, Bergamo prov., Lombardy, N Italy, 13 m. S of Bergamo; pop. 10,691; formerly defended by walls, castle, and moat; birthplace of Michelangelo da Caravaggio.

Car'a·van'ca Mons (kär'à·väng'kä mŏnz); *Ital.* **Ca'ra·van'che** (kä'rä·väng'kā). = *Karawanken:* See *Table* at ALPS.

Ca'ra·ve'las (kà'rà·vâ'lás). Seaport town, S Baía state, Brazil; pop. ab. 8000.

Ca'ra·zo' (kä'rä·sō'). Department, SW Nicaragua; 367 sq. m.; pop. (1943 est.) 63,123; ✱ Jinotepe.

Car·bal'lo (kär·vä'[l]yō). Commune, La Coruña prov., NW Spain, 19 m. SW of La Coruña; pop. 18,159; thermal mineral springs and baths.

Car′ber′ry Hill (kär′bĕr′ĭ; -bēr·ĭ). Hill ab. 500 ft., East Lothian, Scotland, E of Edinburgh; Mary, Queen of Scots, surrendered to barons here June 15, 1567.

Carbilo. See SAINT-NAZAIRE.

Car′bon (kär′bŭn). Counties in four states of U.S. See *Tables* at MONTANA, PENNSYLVANIA, UTAH, WYOMING.

Car′bo·na′ra, Cape (kär′bō·nä′rä). Cape on SE extremity of Sardinia, E of the Gulf of Cagliari.

Car′bon·ate Mountain (kär′bŭn·āt). Peak 13,900 ft. in Chaffee co., cen. Colorado.

Car′bon·dale (kär′bŭn·dāl). **1** City, Jackson co., SW Illinois, 17 m. W of Marion; pop. 14,670; Southern Illinois University (opened 1874; coed.).

2 City, Lackawanna co., NE Pennsylvania, 14 m. NE of Scranton; pop. 13,595; mining and railroad center.

Car′bo·near′ (kär′bō·nēr′). Seaport, SE Newfoundland, on W shore of Conception Bay 27 m. WNW of St. John's; pop. (1951) 3351; has important fish trade.

Car′bon Hill (kär′bŭn). Mining city, Walker co., NW cen. Alabama, 50 m. NW of Birmingham; pop. 1944.

Car·bo′nia (kär·bō′nyä). Recently built town, SW Sardinia, near coast; pop. ab. 12,000; near coal mines.

Car′ca·gen′te (kär′kä·hän′tā). Commune, Valencia prov., E Spain, on Júcar river 29 m. SSW of Valencia; pop. 17,846; textiles; Roman and Moorish ruins.

Car′car (kär′kär). Municipality on E coast of Cebu I., Phil. Is., 22 m. SW of City of Cebu; pop. 36,308.

Car′ca·ra·ñá′ (kär′kä·rä·nyä′). River in cen. Argentina; formed by Saladillo and Tercero rivers, flows E into Paraná river above Rosario.

Car′cas′sonne′ (kár′kä·sôn′); *anc.* **Car′ca·so** (kär′kä·sō). Manufacturing city, ✱ of Aude dept., S France, on Aude river 54 m. SE of Toulouse; pop. 33,441; fine twelve-arch bridge; partly surrounded by walls attributed in part to Visigoths; castle; 13th-cent. Gothic cathedral; manufactures woolen cloth (for which it is chiefly noted), paper, linen, leather, iron goods, soap, pottery. Taken by Visigoths 725 A.D.; viscountship 11th–13th cents.; taken by Simon de Montfort 1209; joined to French crown 1247; pillaged and destroyed by Black Prince 1355; Huguenots massacred here 1566.

Car′che·mish (kär′kĕ·mĭsh; kär·kē′-). Ruined city on the W bank of the Euphrates river at Syrian border, N Turkey, 35 m. SE of Gaziantep; ancient city of Mitanni kingdom in 2d millennium B.C.; later a chief city of the Hittites; captured by Egyptians under Thutmose III in 15th cent. B.C., came under Assyria after 717 B.C.; scene of great battle 605 B.C. in which Nebuchadnezzar II of Babylon defeated Necho II and destroyed Egyptian power in Asia (*2 Chron.* xxxv. 20; *Jer.* xlvi. 2).

Car′chi (kär′chē). Province of Ecuador. See *Table* at ECUADOR.

Car′cross (kär′krŏs). Village and station, on N shore of Lake Bennett, S Yukon, Canada; on railroad; terminus of a short branch of the Alaska Highway.

Car′da·mon Hills (kär′dà·mŭn). Range, S India, on E border of Kerala state; averages 2000 to 4000 ft.

Cár′de·nas (kär′thā·näs). **1** Seaport city on **Cárdenas Bay**, N Matanzas prov., W cen. Cuba, 23 m. E of Matanzas; pop. 37,144; exports sugar and sisal fiber.

2 Town, San Luis Potosí state, cen. Mexico, on railroad 85 m. E of San Luis Potosí; pop. 8478.

Car′diff (kär′dĭf). **1** Town, Onondaga co., New York, S of Syracuse; the "Cardiff giant" reported found nearby 1869 was a rude figure of a man 10½ ft. high, carved out of gypsum obtained at Fort Dodge, Iowa, exhibited for a time as a "petrified man."

2 County borough and seaport city, ⊗ of Glamorganshire and ✱ of Wales, SE Wales; pop. (1951) 243,627; ships coal; shipbuilding, steel manufacturing, paper mills, chemical works; Cardiff Castle, dating from 1090, now residence of the marquess of Bute; University College of South Wales and Monmouthshire.

Car′di·gan (kär′dĭ·găn). **1** Mountain 3121 ft., S Grafton co., W New Hampshire.

2 = CARDIGANSHIRE.

3 Municipal borough, Cardiganshire, W Wales; pop. 3497; site of ancient Celtic castle, rebuilt by Normans and demolished by Cromwell's Parliamentarians.

Cardigan Bay. Widemouthed inlet of St. George's Channel on W coast of Wales.

Car′di·gan·shire (kär′dĭ·găn·shĭr; -shēr) *or* **Cardigan.** County, W Wales; area 692 sq. m.; pop. (1951) 53,267; ⊗ Aberystwyth; livestock raising, lead mining.

Car′di·nal (kär′dĭ·năl; -n'l). Village, Grenville co., SE Ontario, Canada, 46 m. S of Ottawa; pop. 1782.

Cardinal Mountain. Peak 13,388 ft., E Fresno co., S cen. California, in Sierra Nevada.

Car·do′na (kär·thō′nä). Commune, Barcelona prov., Spain, 45 m. NW of Barcelona; pop. (1930) 4820; nearby is a hill 260 ft. formed of rock salt.

Car·dross′ (kär·drŏs′). Parish and village, Dunbarton co., Scotland, on the Firth of Clyde ab. 4 m. NW of Dumbarton; pop. 13,604; nearby is the castle where Robert Bruce died 1329.

Card′ston (kärd′stŭn). Town, S Alberta, Canada, on St. Mary river 40 m. SSW of Lethbridge; pop. 2487.

Ca·rei′ (kä·rě′ě), *also* **Ca·reü′ Ma′re** (kä·rě′o͝o mä′rě); *Hung.* **Nagy′ká′roly** (nŏd′y'·kä′rôl·y′). Commune, NW Transylvania, Romania, SW of Satu-Mare; pop. 16,085; formerly belonged to Hungary; once seat of Károlyi family; Piarist monastery.

Ca′ren′tan′ (kä′rän′tän′). Town, Manche dept., NW France, at base of Cotentin Penin. 23 m. W of Bayeux; pop. (1931) 3641; has small port; strong fortress in Middle Ages; suffered much during religious wars of 16th cent.; during World War II captured by U.S. troops after severe battle June 8–12, 1944.

Car′ew (kär′o͝o; kär′ĭ). Village, Pembrokeshire, SW Wales, on Milford Haven 5 m. E of Pembroke; ½ m. N are ruins of a castle of ab. 13th cent.; 14-ft. Celtic cross near the castle entrance.

Car′ey (kâr′ĭ). Village, Wyandot co., NW cen. Ohio, 14 m. ESE of Findlay; pop. 3722; ships onions, celery, etc.

Carey, Lake. Lake, Salt Lake Region, S cen. Western Australia.

Car′fin (kär′fĭn). Mining village, N Lanark co., S Scotland; shrine dedicated to Our Lady of Lourdes.

Car′i·a (kâr′ĭ·à). Ancient division of SW Asia Minor bordering on the S and SW on the Aegean Sea, on the N on Lydia, and on the E on Phrygia and Lycia; coast line marked by several long peninsulas (esp. Bodrum) and gulfs and numerous Aegean Is. (now parts of the Dodecanese); covered with fairly high mountains; traversed in the N by the Maeander. In early times settled by Doric and Ionic colonies; absorbed by Lydia but for a time under independent king, Mausolus, c. 377–353 B.C.; taken from Persia 334 B.C. by Alexander; came under Syria and Pergamum and in 125 B.C. incorporated in the Roman province of Asia. Chief cities Halicarnassus (the capital), Miletus, Cnidus, Magnesia, and Tralles.

Ca·ria′co, Gulf of (kä·ryä′kō). Inlet of Caribbean Sea on NE coast of Venezuela, S of Araya Penin.

Ca′ria·man′ga (kä′ryä·mäng′gä). Town, Loja prov., SW Ecuador; pop. (1944 est.) 15,598.

Ca′ri·ba′na, Point (kä′rě·vä′nä). Cape on NW coast of Colombia, at E side of Gulf of Darien.

Car′ib·be′an Sea (kär′ĭ·bē′ăn; kă·rĭb′ē·ăn). Arm of the Atlantic Ocean bounded by the West Indies on the N and E, N South America on the S, and Central America on the W; connects with Gulf of Mexico on the NW through Yucatán Channel; ab. 750,000 sq. m.; greatest depth 22,788 ft. in Bartlett Deep (*q.v.*).

Caribbees. See WEST INDIES.

Car′i·boo Mountains (kär′ĭ·bо͞o). Range of the Rocky Mts. ab. 200 m. long, E cen. British Columbia, Canada, in the great bend of the Fraser river; separated from main range of Rocky Mts. by upper Fraser river; highest point ab. 11,750 ft.; district in W foothills scene of famous gold rush of 1860.

Cariboo Road. Highway, British Columbia, W Canada; follows Fraser river, turns NW at N end of Cariboo Mts. and ends at Hazelton (*q.v.*); modern highway is ab. 500 m. long; original road (begun 1862, opened 1865) was ab. 400 m. long and passable for stagecoaches.

Car′i·bou (kăr′ĭ·bōō). **1** County in Idaho. See *Table* at IDAHO.

2 Town, Aroostook co., N Maine, on Aroostook river 13 m. N of Presque Isle; pop. 12,464; potato-shipping center.

Caribou Highway. = CARIBOO ROAD.

Caribou Mountain. Peak 9805 ft. in SE Bonneville co., SE Idaho.

Caribou Mountains. Range, N Alberta prov., Canada, N of Peace river; average height ab. 2000 ft.; N part in Wood Buffalo National Park.

Ca′ri·brod (tsä′rĕ·brôd); *Bulg.* **Tsa′ri·brod**; *in 1950 renamed* **Di·mi′trov·grad′** (dĕ·mē′trôv·gräd′). Town, E Yugoslavia, ab. 50 m. SE of Niš on Nišava river; pop. ab. 4000; in Bulgaria before 1919.

Ca′ri·ga·ra (kä′rē·gä′rä). Municipality on Carigara Bay, N Leyte I., Phil. Is., 22 m. W of Tacloban; pop. 23,236; taken by Americans Nov. 2, 1944.

Carigara Bay. Southern part of Samar Sea at N end of Leyte I., Phil. Is.; enclosed on NW by Biliran I.

Ca′ri·huai·ra′zo (kä′rē·wī·rä′sō). Peak 16,515 ft., cen. Ecuador, NNE of Riobamba, in the Andes Mts.

Ca·ri′ni (kä·rē′nē). Commune, Palermo prov., NW cen. Sicily, 10 m. W of Palermo; pop. 14,762; 14th-cent. Gothic castle; scene of defeat of Sicilian revolutionists by Bourbon forces 1860.

Ca·ri′no·la (kä·rē′nô·lä). Commune, Napoli prov., Campania, Italy, 29 m. NNW of Naples; pop. 11,536.

Ca·rin′thi·a (ka·rĭn′thĭ·a). Province of Austria. See *Table* at AUSTRIA. Forms basin watered by the Drau (Drava) with several beautiful lakes (Wörther See, Millstätter See, etc.), center of a summer resort area; bordered on S by Karawanken and Carnic Alps and separated from Salzburg prov. on NW by the Hohe Tauern.

History: Inhabited originally by Celtic stock; part of Roman province of Noricum; invaded by Germans, then by Slovenes in period of migrations; in 8th cent. A.D. belonged to Carolingian empire (part of Bavaria); made a separate duchy 976 which, for a time, included Verona and Styria and finally came to Hapsburgs in 1335; parts of Carinthia belonged to Illyrian Provinces (*q.v.*) 1809–13; became Austrian crownland 1849; after 1918 southern part taken by Yugoslavia; in 1920, possession of S part by Yugoslavia confirmed by a plebiscite, but Klagenfurt region retained by Austria.

Car′is·brooke (kăr′ĭz·brŏŏk; kär′ĭs-). Village and parish, Isle of Wight, S England; pop. (parish) 5232; castle in which Charles I was imprisoned 1647–48.

Car′len·ti·ni (kär′lĕn·tē′nē). Commune, Siracusa prov., SE Sicily, 22 m. NW of Syracuse; pop. (1931) 11,548.

Carle′ton (kärl′tŭn; -t′n). **1** County, New Brunswick, Canada. See *Table* at NEW BRUNSWICK.

2 County, Ontario, Canada. See *Table* at ONTARIO.

Carleton Place. Industrial town, Lanark co., SE Ontario, Canada, on Mississippi river at foot of Mississippi Lake, 28 m. SW of Ottawa; pop. 4725; resort.

Câr′li·ba·ba (kĭr′lĕ·bä′bä). Village, NE Transylvania, Romania, W of Câmpulung; pop. ab. 1000; on **Cârlibaba Pass** in Carpathian Mts.

Car′ling·ford Lough (kär′lĭng·fĕrd lŏk). Inlet of Irish Sea on E coast of Ireland, on boundary bet. SE Northern Ireland and NE Eire.

Car′lin·ville (kär′lĭn·vĭl). City, ⊗ of Macoupin co., SW cen. Illinois, 38 m. SSW of Springfield; pop. 5440; Blackburn Coll. (coed.; 1835).

Car·lisle′ (kär·līl′; kär′līl). **1** County in Kentucky. See *Table* at KENTUCKY.

2 City, ⊗ of Nicholas co., NE Kentucky; pop. 1601.

3 Borough, ⊗ of Cumberland co., S Pennsylvania, 19 m. W of Harrisburg; pop. 16,623; settled 1751; scene of treaty bet. Ohio Indians and Benjamin Franklin 1753;

headquarters of Washington during Whisky Insurrection 1794; station on Underground Railroad before Civil War; attacked by Confederates July 1, 1863. Manufactures silks, clothing, shoes, railroad frogs and switches, carpets and rugs. Site of Carlisle Indian School 1879–1918, now occupied by Carlisle Barracks and U.S. Army Medical Field Service; Dickinson College (1783; coed.). Home and grave of Molly Pitcher.

4 *anc.* **Lu′gu·val′li·um** (lū′gŭ·văl′ĭ·ŭm) *or* **Lu′guval′lum** (-văl′ŭm), *later* **Caer Lu′el** (kär lōō′ĕl). City and county borough, ⊗ of Cumberland, NW England, on Eden river 8 m. from Solway Firth and 108 m. N of Liverpool; pop. 57,304, (1951) 67,894; railroad center; cathedral (begun in 12th cent.); textile mills, ironworks. Important Roman station; refounded by William Rufus; as a border fortress often attacked by Scots; place of imprisonment of Mary, Queen of Scots, May–July 1568.

Car′lo·for′te (kär′lô·fôr′tā). See SAN PIETRO.

Car′los Ro′jas (kär′lôs rrō′häs). Municipality, Matanzas prov., W cen. Cuba, ESE of Matanzas; pop. 8925.

Carlota, La. See LA CARLOTA.

Car′low (kär′lō). **1** County, SE Eire, in Leinster prov.; 346 sq. m.; pop. 34,452; agriculture, dairy farming.

2 Urban district, its ⊗, SE Eire; pop. 7649; ruins of great Norman castle; burned by Rory Oge O′More late 16th cent.; taken by Cromwell′s forces 1650.

Carlowitz. Var. of KARLOWITZ.

Carls′bad (kärlz′băd). **1** City, San Diego co., SW California, NW of San Diego; pop. 9253.

2 City, ⊗ of Eddy co., SE New Mexico, on Pecos river 70 m. S of Roswell; pop. 25,541; settled 1888; important potash mines; to the SW are Carlsbad Caverns (*q.v.*), and to the N is the Carlsbad Reclamation Project (developed by U.S. government 1906 ff.) consisting of **Avalon Dam** and **McMillan Dam** across the Pecos river, with the lakes thus formed and miles of canals and ditches.

Carlsbad. See KARLOVY VARY.

Carls′bad Caverns (kärlz′băd). Series of limestone caves near Carlsbad, SE New Mexico; Big Room over ½ m. long, 400 ft. wide at its widest part, and 348 ft. high; now included in **Carlsbad Caverns National Park** (see UNITED STATES, *National Parks*).

Carlsruhe. See KARLSRUHE city.

Carl′stadt (kärl′stăt). Borough, Bergen co., NE corner of New Jersey, 8 m. SE of Paterson; pop. 6042; bought co-operatively from original American owners by German exiles and liberals seeking political freedom; brass, onyx, and marble works; varied manufactures.

Carl′ton (kärl′tŭn; -t′n). **1** County in Minnesota. See *Table* at MINNESOTA.

2 Village, its ⊗, E Minnesota; pop. 862.

3 Urban district, Nottinghamshire, N cen. England, 4 m. NE of Nottingham; pop. 34,248.

Car·lyle′ (kär·līl′; kär′līl). City, ⊗ of Clinton co., SW cen. Illinois, 40 m. E of East St. Louis; pop. 2903; flour and grain trading center; flour mills, paper factories.

Car′ma·gno′la (kär′mä·nyô′lä). Commune, Torino prov., Piedmont, NW Italy, on Po river 17 m. S of Turin; pop. 12,737; ruins of ancient castle; manufactures textiles; gave its name to the *carmagnole*, costume worn in S France by Piedmontese workmen and adopted, after 1792, by the French Revolutionists, whose revolutionary song was *La Carmagnole*.

Car′man (kär′măn). Market town, S Manitoba, Canada, 48 m. SW of Winnipeg; pop. 1867; railroad junction.

Carmana, Carmania. See KERMAN.

Car·mar′then (kär·mär′then; *esp. Brit.*, kẽr-). **1** See CARMARTHENSHIRE.

2 Municipal borough and commercial seaport, ⊗ of Carmarthenshire, S Wales; pop. 12,121; ruins of Norman castle on site of ancient Roman station; residence of Sir Richard Steele at time of his death 1729.

Carmarthen Bay. Inlet of Bristol Channel on S coast of Wales; Caldy I. is at its W entrance.

Car·mar′then·shire (-shĭr; -shĕr) *or* **Carmarthen**. County, S Wales; area 919 sq. m.; pop. (1951) 171,742; ⊗ Carmarthen; hilly area; chief river the Towy; agriculture, coal and iron mining, quarrying, textiles.

Car′maux′ (kär′mō′). Commune, Tarn dept., S France, 48 m. NE of Toulouse; pop. 10,448; coal mining.

Car′mel (kär′mĕl). Residential village and resort in Carmel town (pop. 9113), ⊗ of Putnam co., SE New York, 20 m. ESE of Newburgh; pop. (1950) 1526.

Car·mel′ (kär·mĕl′) *or* **Carmel–by–the–Sea**. City, Monterey co., W California, on Pacific Ocean S of Monterey Bay; pop. 4580; founded c. 1904 by several artists as rustic refuge; art and recreation center.

Car′mel, Mount (kär′mĕl). Mountain ab. 1800 ft. in NW Palestine near Mediterranean coast; extends southeasterly ab. 15 m. along S bank of the Qishon river; early became sacred to both Yahweh and Baal (cf. *1 Kings* xviii. 19 ff.); after 6th cent. A.D. a favored site for monasteries, esp. that of the Order of Carmelites founded 1156 A.D.

Car·me′lo (kär·mā′lō). Town at mouth of the Uruguay river, Colonia dept., SW Uruguay, 140 m. NW of Montevideo; pop. ab. 12,000; historic ruins in vicinity.

Car′men (kär′mĕn; *Span.* -mān). **1** Town, Bolívar dept., N Colombia; pop. 8228.
2 Island enclosing Laguna de Términos, SE Bay of Campeche, Campeche state, SE Mexico; on its W end is town of **Carmen** *or* **Ciu·dad′ del Car′men** (syōō·thä′thĕl kär′mān), pop. 7687, which has a good port.
3 Small island off SE coast of Lower California, NW Mexico, in the Gulf of California; salt deposits.

Car′men del Pa′ra·ná′ (kär′mān dĕl pä′rä·nä′). Town, Itapúa dept., SE Paraguay, on Paraná river W of Encarnación; pop. ab. 14,400.

Car′mi (kär′mī). City, ⊗ of White co., SE Illinois, 45 m. ESE of Mt. Vernon; pop. 6152.

Car′mi′chael (kär′mī′kĕl; -k′l; kär·mī′-). Urban community (unincorporated), Sacramento co., N cen. California, NE of Sacramento; pop. 20,455.

Car′mi·gna′no (kär′mĕ·nyä′nō). Commune, Firenze prov., Tuscany, cen. Italy; pop. (1931) 12,577.

Car·mo′na (kär·mō′nä); *anc.* **Car′mo** (kär′mō). Industrial and commercial commune, Sevilla prov., SW Spain, 18 m. ENE of Seville; pop. 24,876; ancient Roman necropolis, city gates, Moorish wall and alcazar; captured from Moors 1247 by Ferdinand III.

Car′nac (kär′năk; *Fr.* kár′nák′). Commune, Morbihan dept., NW France, on Quiberon Bay ab. 17 m. SE of Lorient; pop. (1931) 2960; region noted for many stone monuments including dolmens and long rows of menhirs; mounds; remains of a Gallo-Roman town.

Car·na′ro (kär·nä′rō). Former province of Italy including the islands of the Gulf of Quarnero (Cherso, Lussino, Unie)—name used by D'Annunzio. Now by treaty of 1947 part of Croatia, NW Yugoslavia.

Car·nar′von (kär·när′vŭn; kĕr-). **1** Town, W Western Australia, on Shark Bay; pop. 1453.
2 Town, cen. Cape Province, S Union of South Africa, 290 m. NE of Cape Town; pop. 2583; sheep.
3 Var. of CAERNARVON.

Carnarvonshire. Var. of CAERNARVONSHIRE.

Car·nat′ic (kär·năt′ĭk) *or* **Kar·na′tik** (kĕr·nä′tĭk). A region and old division bet. Eastern Ghats and Coromandel Coast, S India, S of 16°N; now a part of Madras state and Andhra Pradesh, India; orig. the country of the Kanarese, an irregular area in S cen. India including Mysore and parts of Andhra Pradesh. Historically of great importance; divided for centuries bet. Pandya and Chola kingdoms; from 1310 to 1710 under Moslems and the Delhi kings; for a time independent, with capital at Arcot; during 18th cent. the scene of Anglo-French rivalry, British gaining ascendancy after seizure of Arcot 1751 and defeat of Haidar Ali in Second Mysore War (1780–84); annexed by British 1801.

Car′nedd Da′fydd (kär′nĕth dà′vĭth). Mountain 3426

ft. in E Caernarvonshire, NW Wales, NE of Snowdon.

Carnedd Llew·el′yn (lōō·ĕl′ĭn; *Welsh* lĕ′ōō·ĕ′lĭn). Mountain 3484 ft. in E Caernarvonshire, NW Wales.

Car′ne·gie (kär·nĕg′ĭ; kär·nēg′ĭ; -nā′gĭ). **1** Town, Caddo co., W cen. Oklahoma, on Washita river 37 m. NNW of Lawton; pop. 1500; cotton gin, elevators; farming.
2 Borough, Allegheny co., SW Pennsylvania, 6 m. WSW of Pittsburgh; pop. 11,887; coal, steel, iron, petroleum.

Carnegie, Lake. Lake on W edge of Gibson Desert, cen. Western Australia.

Carn Eige, Carn Toul (kärn). Vars. of CAIRN EIGE, CAIRN TOUL.

Car·ne′ro, Point (kär·nā′rō). Point on S coast of Spain extending into the Strait of Gibraltar at W entrance to the Bay of Algeciras.

Carnes′ville (kärnz′vĭl; *Sou. also* -v′l). City, ⊗ of Franklin co., NE Georgia; pop. 481.

Car′neys Point (kär′nĭz). Town, Salem co., SW New Jersey, on Delaware river; pop. (est.) 3500.

Car′nia (kär′nyä). Region S of the Carnic Alps in Venezia, N Italy.

Car′nic Alps (kär′nĭk). See *Table* at ALPS.

Car Nic′o·bar *or* **Kar Nicobar** (kär′ nĭk′ō·bär). Most northerly island of Nicobar group, Andaman and Nicobar Is., Indian Union; 49 sq. m.; pop. 7492.

Car·nio′la (kärn·yō′lä; kär′nĭ·ō′lä; *Ital.* kär·nyō′lä); *Ger.* **Krain** (krīn). **1** Region of S Europe NE of head of Adriatic Sea; mountainous country, having E end of Carnic Alps in NW and traversed on W by the Julian Alps; chief town Ljubljana (Laibach).
History: Belonged to Roman province of Pannonia; received influx of Slovenes c. 590 A.D.; with Carinthia, ruled by Carolingian mark of Bavaria; twice founded as independent mark; in 13th cent. a part of the Holy Roman Empire (**March of Carniola**) in SE bordering on kingdom of Hungary; came under the Hapsburgs 1335 who took title of duke of Carinthia; ceded to Napoleon by Austria 1809–13 (see ILLYRIAN PROVINCES), remained duchy of Austria until 1849.
2 Former Austrian crownland 1849–1919 bounded on N by Carinthia, on NE by Styria, on E, SE, and S by Croatia, and on W by Italy (Istria and Gorizia); divided after World War I bet. Italy (782 sq. m.) and Yugoslavia (3060 sq. m.); by 1947 treaty entirely in Yugoslavia.

Carn Mairg. See MONADHLIATH MOUNTAINS.

Car·nous′tie (kär·nōōs′tĭ). Seaport burgh, SE Angus co., E Scotland, on North Sea ab. 11 m. ENE of Dundee; pop. 5195; resort with fine beach and golf course.

Carn′sore Point (kärn′sōr). Cape on SE extremity of Ireland, projecting into St. George's Channel.

Car·nun′tum (kär·nŭn′tŭm). Ancient town, N Pannonia, on S bank of the Danube; ruins near Hainburg, Austria; originally Celtic, became important Roman post from the time of Augustus; used as base 172–175 A.D. by Marcus Aurelius in his campaign against the Marcomanni; destroyed by Germans 4th cent.

Car′o (kär′ō). Village, ⊗ of Tuscola co., E Michigan, 28 m. E of Saginaw; pop. 3534; beet-sugar refinery.

Ca′ro·la Ha′fen (kä′rō·lä hä′fĕn). = QUEEN CAROLA HARBOUR.

Car′ol City (kär′ŭl). Urban community (unincorporated), Dade co., SE Florida, NW of Miami Beach; pop. 21,749.

Car′o·leen′ (kăr′ō·lēn′). Town, Rutherford co., SW North Carolina; pop. 1168.

Car′o·li′na (kăr′ō·lī′nà). Early American colony; as granted by Charles II to eight Lords Proprietors 1663 included land from ocean to ocean bet. 31st and 36th parallels; in 1665 boundaries extended to include area around Albemarle Sound where settlers from Virginia had located since ab. 1650. Fundamental Constitutions by John Locke adopted by proprietors in 1669 and later abandoned; first permanent settlement by English 1670 (in South Carolina); Spanish ceded claim to territory 1670; because of neglect of proprietors to defend colony in

Tuscarora War (1711–12) and Yamassee War (1715–16) and other reasons, charter abrogated and separate royal governments established in North and South Carolina (*qq.v.*) 1729—hence, the Carolinas.

Ca′ro·li′na (kä′rô·lē′nä). Municipality (pop. 40,923) and town (pop. 3075), NE Puerto Rico, 11 m. ESE of San Juan.

Ca′ro·li′na, La (lä kä′rô·lē′nä). See LA CAROLINA.

Car′o·line (kăr′ô·lĭn). Name of counties in two states of the U.S. See *Tables* at MARYLAND and VIRGINIA.

Caroline Island. Small atoll of the Line Is. in cen. Pacific Ocean 10°S of the equator, ab. 400 m. E of Tongareva I.; 6 m. long by 1 m. wide with shallow lagoon.

Caroline Islands *or* **Car′o·lines** (-līnz). Extensive archipelago in W Pacific Ocean, E of S Philippine Is.; lat. ab. 5° to 10°N and long. 135° to 163°E; includes 550 to 680 islands, according to what is termed an island; has many coral islets and reefs; 333 sq. m., including lagoons 550 sq. m.; pop. (1935) 48,048; most important islands Yap, Ponape, Truk, and Kusaie. The Palau Is. are by some considered a part of the Carolines (**Western Carolines**) and Koror I. in the Palaus was Japanese headquarters for all islands of the mandate. Some islands are fertile and populous; the larger are volcanic, the smaller are atolls, generally uninhabited; natives are Micronesians; on some islands are massive ruins, still unexplained, indicating presence of numerous and capable people centuries ago (cf. EASTER ISLAND). Annexed by Spain 1686; rarely visited down to latter part of 19th cent.; German seizure of Yap 1885 aroused protest (dispute settled 1887 by decision of Pope Leo XIII); islands purchased by Germany 1899; seized by Japan 1914 and granted as mandate to Japan 1919; after 1935 prohibited territory to all foreigners; fortified by Japan; Ulithi and southern islands (Peleliu and Angaur) of the Palau group occupied by Americans Sept.– Oct. 1944; became part of Trust Territory of the Pacific Islands, assigned to U.S. 1947.

Carolopolis. See CHARLEVILLE.

Ca′ro·ní′ (kä′rô·nē′). River 550 m. long in E Venezuela; rises in Serra Pacaraima in SE Venezuela; flows N into Orinoco river near its mouth.

Caronium. See LA CORUÑA.

Ca·ro′ra (kä·rō′rä). Town, Lara state, NW Venezuela, ab. 53 m. W of Barquisimeto; pop. (1941 est.) 8806.

Ca′rouge′ (kà′rōōzh′). Commune, Geneva canton, SW Switzerland; pop. (1930) 8035; suburb of Geneva.

Car·pa′thi·an Mountains (kär·pā′thĭ·ăn) *or* **Car·pa′thi·ans** (-ănz); *anc.* **Car′pa·tes** (kär′pà·tēz). Mountain system 800 m. long, maximum breadth ab. 240 m., extending along boundary bet. Czechoslovakia and Poland; highest peak Gerlsdorfer Spitze 8737 ft.; subdivided into East and West Beskids (see BESKIDS) and the Tatra Mts. (or High Tatra) in cen. part; extensions to SW are Little Carpathian Mts. and White Carpathian Mts. (*qq.v.*); Transylvanian Alps are sometimes called the South Carpathians. Source of Vistula, Dniester, and Tisza rivers; many battles fought on or near its slopes, esp. in World Wars I and II; among best-known passes are Jablonica Pass and Lupków Pass.

Carpathian Ru·the′ni·a (rōō·thē′nĭ·à; -thēn′yà); *Czech* **Pod′kar·pat′ská Rus** (pôt′kär·pàt′skä rōōs′). Former province, E Czechoslovakia, S of the Carpathian Mts.; 4871 sq. m.; pop. (1938) 798,310, including ab. 500,000 Ukrainians; ✸ Uzhorod (Uzhgorod); agriculture and livestock raising; region comprised several counties of NE Hungary which in 1918 were incorporated in Czechoslovakia. As **Car·pa′tho–U·kraine′** (kär-pā′thô·û·krān′; -ū′krān; - û·krīn′; -ū′krīn) *or* **Ruthenia** became again part of Hungary 1939–45 with consent of Germany; after World War II ceded by Czechoslovakia to the U.S.S.R. Sept. 29, 1945 and made a part of the Ukraine; called **Za′kar·pat′ska·ya** (zà′kŭr·pàt′skà·yà) by the Russians.

Carpathus, Carpathos. See KARPATHOS.

Carpenisi. See KARPENISION.

Car′pen·tar′i·a, Gulf of (kär′pĕn·târ′ĭ·à). Large gulf, NE Australia, inlet of Arafura Sea ab. 480 m. N to S and 420 m. E to W, bordered on W by Arnhemland and Northern Territory, Australia, and on E by Cape York Penin. of Queensland; for the most part shallow (average 30 to 40 fathoms).

Carpenter Dam. See Lake HAMILTON, Arkansas.

Car′pen·ters·ville (kär′pĕn·tẽrz·vĭl). Village, Kane co., NE Illinois, N of Elgin; pop. 17,424.

Car′pen′tras (kàr′păṅ′trás′); *anc.* **Car·pen′to·rac′te** (kär·pĕn′tô·răk′tĕ). Manufacturing city, Vaucluse dept., SE France, 12 m. NE of Avignon; pop. 13,732; Gothic cathedral; Roman remains, including triumphal arch, aqueduct. A former episcopal see; scene of council 527; residence of Pope Clement V 1313; former capital of papal countship of Venaissin.

Car′pi (kär′pē). Commune, Modena prov., Emilia, N Italy, 10 m. N of Modena; pop. 34,189; episcopal see; 16th-cent. castle; city walls and citadel; sericulture.

Car′pin·te·ri′a (kär′pĭn·tĕ·rē′à). Urban community (unincorporated), Santa Barbara co., SW California, SE of Santa Barbara; pop. 4998.

Car·qui′nez Strait (kär·kē′nĕs). Strait 8 m. long joining San Pablo and Suisun Bays, California.

Car′ra·belle′ (kăr′à·bĕl′). City, Franklin co., NW Florida, on Gulf of Mexico E of Apalachicola river; E terminal of the Gulf Intracoastal Waterway; pop. 1146; resort.

Carrae. Var. of *Carrhae*: see HARAN.

Car·ran·tu′al (kär′ăn·tōō′ăl). Highest peak 3414 ft. in Ireland, in Macgillicuddy's Reeks, co. Kerry.

Car·ra′ra (kà·rär′à; *Ital.* kär·rä′rä). Former commune, Italy; now part of commune of Apuania (*q.v.*).

Car·re′ño (kär·rĕ′nyô). Commune, Oviedo prov., NW Spain, on Bay of Biscay 16 m. N of Oviedo; pop. 10,009.

Car·re′ta, Point (kär·rĕ′tä). Cape, S Uruguay, extending into the Río de la Plata near Montevideo.

Carrhae. See HARAN.

Car′ri·a·cou′ (kär′ĭ·à·kōō′). Largest island of the Grenadines (*q.v.*); 13 sq. m.; pop. (1939 est.) 9358; chief town Hillsborough; administered as part of Grenada.

Car′rick·fer′gus (kăr′ĭk·fûr′gŭs). Municipal borough, co. Antrim, NE Northern Ireland, on N shore of Belfast Lough 9½ m. NE of Belfast; pop. 8650; seaport; historic settlement of Scottish protestants.

Car′rick·ma·cross′ (kăr′ĭk·mà·krŏs′). Town, co. Monaghan, NE Eire, 68 m. NNW of Dublin; pop. 2045; manufactures lace.

Car′rick on Shan′non (kăr′ĭk, shăn′ŭn). Town, ⊗ of co. Leitrim, N Eire, 28 m. SE of Sligo; pop. 1660.

Carrick on Suir (shōōr). Urban district, SE co. Tipperary, S Eire, 18 m. WNW of Waterford; pop. 4761; slate quarrying; 14th-cent. castle; at nearby Carrickbeg are ruins of a 14th-cent. abbey.

Car′ri·er Mills (kăr′ĭ·ẽr), *also* **Car′ri·ers Mills** (kăr′-ĭ·ẽrz). Village, Saline co., SE Illinois, 17 m. E of Marion; pop. 2006.

Car′ri·gain, Mount (kăr′ĭ·gĭn). Mountain 4647 ft., Grafton co., New Hampshire, in White Mts.

Car′ring·ton (kăr′ĭng·tŭn). City, ⊗ of Foster co., E cen. North Dakota, NNW of Jamestown; pop. 2438.

Carr Inlet (kär). Inlet, S end of Puget Sound, W of Tacoma, Washington.

Car′ri·zal′ (kär′rē·säl′). Village, Chihuahua state, Mexico, ab. 85 m. S of Ciudad Juárez; scene of skirmish June 21, 1916 in which Mexican government troops defeated Pershing's forces who were in pursuit of Villa.

Car′ri·zo Springs (kär′rē·zō). City ⊗ of Dimmit co., S Texas, 47 m. S of Uvalde; pop. 5699.

Car′ri·zo′zo (kär′ĭ·zō′zō). Town, ⊗ of Lincoln co., cen. New Mexico, 75 m. W of Roswell; pop. 1546.

Car′roll (kăr′ŭl). **1** Name of counties in thirteen states of the U.S. See *Tables* at ARKANSAS, GEORGIA, ILLINOIS, INDIANA, IOWA, KENTUCKY, MARYLAND, MISSISSIPPI, MISSOURI, NEW HAMPSHIRE, OHIO, TENNESSEE, VIR-

GINIA. For parishes of Louisiana, see *East Carroll* and *West Carroll* in *Table* at LOUISIANA.

2 City, ⊗ of Carroll co., W cen. Iowa, 47 m. SW of Fort Dodge; pop. 7682; trade and manufacturing center.

Car′roll·ton (kăr′ŭl·tŭn). **1** Town, ⊗ of Pickens co., W Alabama; pop. 894.

2 City, ⊗ of Carroll co., W Georgia, 40 m. WSW of Atlanta; pop. 10,973; incorp. 1856; textile mills.

3 City, ⊗ of Greene co., W Illinois, 33 m. NNW of Alton; pop. 2558; settled 1818, incorp. as city 1853.

4 City, ⊗ of Carroll co., N Kentucky, on Ohio river 37 m. N of Frankfort; pop. 3218.

5 Town, a ⊗ of Carroll co., cen. Mississippi; pop. 343.

6 City, ⊗ of Carroll co., NW cen. Missouri, 30 m. S of Chillicothe; pop. 4554; in agricultural section.

7 Village, ⊗ of Carroll co., E Ohio, 21 m. SE of Canton; pop. 2786; manufactures; coal mines nearby.

Car′ron (kăr′ŭn). **1** River in S cen. Scotland, in Stirling co.; flows E into the Firth of Forth 3 m. NE of Falkirk.

2 Village, Stirling co., Scotland, on Carron river ab. 2 m. NW of Falkirk; noted for ironworks, established 1760.

Car′rot (kăr′ŭt). River ab. 220 m. long, cen. Saskatchewan, Canada; flows ENE across Manitoba border into Saskatchewan river.

Car′rum (kăr′ŭm). Town, Victoria, SE Australia, on E shore of Port Phillip Bay; pop. ab. 7000.

Car·shal′ton (kẽr-shôl′t'n; kär-; *locally also* kās-hô[l]′-, kä·shô′-). Urban district, Surrey, S England, 12 m. S of London; pop. 28,763, (1951) 62,804.

Car′so (kär′sō); *Yugo.* **Kras** (kräs); *Ger.* **Karst** (kärst). Mountain plateau N of Trieste and E of the Isonzo river, formerly in Venezia Giulia e Zara, NE Italy; battles in World War I: (1) May 1916, and (2) May 1917 in which the Italians were victors over the Austrians (but lost their gains Oct. 1917). Since treaty of 1947 greater part in NW Yugoslavia.

Car′son (kär′s'n). **1** River ab. 170 m. long, rising in Alpine co., E California, and flowing N and E into Carson Lake, SW Churchill co., W Nevada.

2 County in Texas. See *Table* at TEXAS.

3 Urban community (unincorporated), Los Angeles co., California, SE of Los Angeles; pop. 38,059.

4 Village, ⊗ of Grant co., S North Dakota; pop. 501.

Carson City. City, ✳ of Nevada and ⊗ of Ormsby co., W Nevada, near Lake Tahoe and Carson river 23 m. S of Reno; pop. 5163; settled 1858 and named for Kit Carson; became ✳ 1861; in silver-mining, agricultural, and lumbering region; site of branch of U.S. mint 1870–93.

Carson Lake. Lake ab. 12 m. long in SW Churchill co., W Nevada; receives Carson river from S; no outlet.

Carson Pass. Mountain pass 8634 ft., Alpine co., E California, in main range of the Sierra Nevada Mts.; discovered during winter 1843–44 by Capt. John Frémont and Kit Carson; used by the forty-niners.

Carson Peak. Mountain 13,600 ft. in Hinsdale co., SW Colorado.

Carson Sink. Shallow marshy lake in N Churchill co., W Nevada. Cf. CARSON LAKE.

Car′stensz, Mount (kär′stěnz); *Du.* **Car′stensz Top′pen** (kär′stěns tôp′ěn). Peaks (Du. *toppen*) in W cen. Neth. New Guinea, in the Nassau Range; highest 16,404 ft., highest mountain in New Guinea.

Car·ta·ge·na (kär·tá·jē′ná; -gä′ná; *Span.* kär′tä·hä′nä). **1** Seaport on NW coast of Colombia, ✳ of Bolívar dept., 60 m. SW of Barranquilla; pop. 73,190; has fine harbor with narrow entrance; considerable trade in cattle, hides, tobacco, cabinet woods. Founded 1533, became one of the most important cities of Spanish America; in 17th cent. second only to Mexico City in western hemisphere; strongly fortified in Spanish times; often attacked by the French and English (Drake in 1585 and Vernon in 1741); Spanish until 1815 when it was taken by Bolívar but soon lost, retaken 1821.

2 *anc.* **Car·tha′go No′va** (kär·thā′gō [-tä′gō] nō′vá). Seaport city, Murcia prov., SE Spain, on Mediterranean

28 m. ESE of Murcia; pop. (1941 est.) 113,622; naval arsenal; lead, iron, zinc, copper mines; medieval Gothic cathedral; ancient castle.

History: Founded by Carthaginians under Hasdrubal c. 225 B.C.; captured by Scipio Africanus 210 B.C. and made a Roman colony; sacked by Vandals 425 A.D.; taken by Byzantines 534 and Visigoths 624; held by Moors from 711 until freed by James I of Aragon 1276; sacked by Sir Francis Drake 1585; occupied by duke of Berwick 1707; site of communistic revolt 1873–74.

Car·ta′go (kär·tä′gō). **1** Town, Valle dept., W Colombia, 125 m. W of Bogotá; pop. 14,750.

2 Province, cen. Costa Rica; 1121 sq. m.; pop. (1943 est.) 106,242; sugar, coffee, bananas, dairy products.

3 City, its ✳, Costa Rica, at foot of Mt. Irazú 14 m. SE of San José; alt. 4930; pop. (1943 est.) 9667; former capital of Costa Rica; founded 1553; destroyed by earthquakes 1841 and 1910; center of rich agricultural district.

Car·te′ia (kär·tē′yá). Ancient town and port on S coast of Spain (Hispania), at head of bay bordered on E by Mt. Calpe (*mod.* Gibraltar); founded by Phoenicians; colonized 170 B.C. by Roman soldiers.

Car′ter (kär′tẽr). Name of counties in five states of the U.S. See *Tables* at KENTUCKY, MISSOURI, MONTANA, OKLAHOMA, TENNESSEE.

Carter, Mount. Peak 9834 ft. in Glacier National Park, NW Montana.

Carter Dome (dōm). Peak 4860 ft. in SE Coos co., N New Hampshire, E of **Carter Notch.**

Car′ter·et′ (kär′tẽr-ĕt′; kär′tẽr·ĕt). **1** County in North Carolina. See *Table* at NORTH CAROLINA.

2 Borough, Middlesex co., cen. New Jersey, 6 m. NNE of Perth Amboy near Staten I.; pop. 20,502; metal and oil refining; manufactures steel, tobacco, chemicals.

Car′te·ret′ (kär′tē·rĕ′). Village, W coast of Manche dept., NW France, 20 m. SW of Cherbourg; pop. (1931) 714; small port. When reached by Allied forces June 18, 1944, N part of Cotentin Penin. (*q.v.*) was cut off; important point in battle of Normandy.

Car′ters·ville (kär′tẽrz·vil; *Sou. also* -v'l). City, ⊗ of Bartow co., NW Georgia, 35 m. NW of Atlanta; pop. 8668; in coal-mining region.

Car′ter·ville (kär′tẽr·vil). **1** City, Williamson co., S Illinois, 10 m. W of Marion; pop. 2643; coal mining.

2 City, Jasper co., SW Missouri, 7 m. NNE of Joplin; pop. 1443; lead and zinc deposits nearby.

Car′thage (kär′thij). **1** City, ⊗ of Hancock co., W Illinois, 38 m. NNE of Quincy; pop. 3325; place where Joseph Smith was imprisoned and killed 1844. Carthage College (1870; coed.; Lutheran).

2 Town, ⊗ of Leake co., cen. Mississippi, 48 m. NE of Jackson; pop. 2442.

3 City, ⊗ of Jasper co., SW Missouri, 14 m. NE of Joplin; pop. 11,264; livestock; lead and zinc deposits.

4 Village, Jefferson co., N New York, 16 m. E of Watertown; pop. 4216; manufactures paper, cheese boxes, processed dairy products; foundries; machine shops.

5 Town, ⊗ of Moore co., cen. North Carolina; pop. 1190.

6 Town, ⊗ of Smith co., N cen. Tennessee, on Cumberland river 21 m. E of Lebanon; pop. 2021.

7 City, ⊗ of Panola co., E Texas, 28 m. S of Marshall; pop. 5262; in agricultural section.

8 *anc.* **Car·tha′go** (kär·thā′gō; -tä′gō). Ancient city and state, N Africa, on coast NE of modern Tunis; built on tip of a peninsula, originally around a citadel known as the Byrsa; comprised inner and outer harbor, extensive walls, old and new city (suburb of Megara).

History: Founded by colonists from Phoenician kingdom of Tyre 814 B.C.; from 6th cent. B.C. began conquests in western Africa, Sicily, and Sardinia; after defeat at Himera (*q.v.*) 480 B.C., developed sea power and, under descendants of Hamilcar, came to dominate western Mediterranean; fought Sicily 4th cent. B.C.; engaged in series of bitter wars with Rome, known as Punic Wars: In First Punic War 264–241 B.C. conquered Spain to

Ebro but Rome acquired Sicily; in Second (led by Hannibal) 218–201 B.C. fought battles of Cannae and Zama (*qq.v.*); at end of Third 149–146 B.C. city utterly destroyed by the younger Scipio; site of colony founded by Caesar 44 B.C.; captured by Vandals 439 A.D.; won for Byzantine Empire by Belisarius 533–34; lost to Arabs 698.

Carthago Nova. See CARTAGENA.

Cart'wright (kärt'rīt). Coast village and fine harbor on inlet of SE Labrador, SE of Hamilton Inlet.

Ca'rua·rú' (kä′rwä·rōō′). City, E Pernambuco state, E Brazil, ab. 70 m. W of Recife; pop. (1940 est.) 24,634.

Ca·rú'pa·no (kä·rōō′pä·nô). Seaport, N Sucre state, N Venezuela, on Paria Penin. 100 m. ENE of Barcelona; pop. (1941 est.) 16,220; oil fields nearby.

Ca·ruth'ers·ville (kȧ·rŭth′ẽrz·vĭl). City, ⊗ of Pemiscot co., SE corner of Missouri, on Mississippi river 60 m. SW of its conjunction with Ohio river; pop. 8643.

Car'ver (kär′vẽr). County in Minnesota. See *Table* at MINNESOTA.

Car'vin' (kȧr′văn′). Commune, Pas-de-Calais dept., N France, 18 m. NNE of Arras; pop. 18,696; coal mines.

Car·vo·ei'ro, Cape (kẽr·vwā′ē·rōō). Cape on W coast of Portugal, opp. the Berlengas.

Ca·rys'tus (kȧ·rĭs′tŭs). Ancient town at S end of island of Euboea, Greece; noted for marble and asbestos.

Cas'a·blan'ca (kăs′ȧ·blăng′kȧ; *Span.* kä′sä·vläng′kä); *Arab.* **Dar el Bei·da'** or **Dar–al–Bai·da'** (där′ ăl bī·dä′; bä·dä′). Seaport city, W coast of Morocco, NW Africa, at 33°38′N lat.; pop. (1936) 257,430, (1960 est.) 700,000; largest city in Morocco; large harbor, recently extensively improved. Founded by Portuguese on site of ancient city of Anfa, destroyed in 1465; occupied 1757 by Moroccan sultan and in 1907 by French as result of murder of some French workers. In World War II surrendered to Allies Nov. 11, 1942; scene of conference bet. Prime Minister Churchill and President Roosevelt Jan. 14–26, 1943, at which the "unconditional surrender" of Axis countries was determined upon.

Cas'a Gran'de (kăs′ȧ grän′dĕ). City, Pinal co., S Arizona, 43 m. SSE of Phoenix; pop. 8311; to NE is **Casa Grande National Monument:** see UNITED STATES, *National Monuments.*

Ca·sa'le Mon'fer·ra'to (kä·sä′lā mŏn′fär·rä′tô). Commune, Alessandria prov., Piedmont, NW Italy, on Po river 18 m. NNW of Alessandria; pop. 37,098; 12th-cent. cathedral; citadel (founded 1590 by Duke Vicenzo) one of strongest in Italy. Founded 730 on site of ancient **Bo'din·com'a·gus** (bō′dĭng·kŏm′ȧ·gŭs); fell to marquises of Montferrat 1246, becoming capital of the duchy of Montferrat; later fell to Mantua 1559, Savoy, France 1681, Piedmont 1703, Italy 1860.

Ca·sal'mag·gio're (kä·säl′mäd·jō′rȧ). Commune, Cremona prov., Lombardy, N Italy, on Po river 23 m. ESE of Cremona; pop. 15,345; cathedral; manufactures majolica, glassware, leather, chemicals; Venetians defeated by Francesco Sforza in battle 1448.

Ca·sa'mance' (kȧ·zȧ′mäns′). **1** River, Senegal, West Africa, S of Gambia; has wide estuary 100 m. long.
2 Region bet. Gambia and Portuguese Guinea, W Africa, a part of Senegal; ✳ Ziguinchor.

Ca·sa·ra'no (kä·sä·rä′nô). Commune, Lecce prov., Apulia, SE Italy, 22 m. S of Lecce; pop. 11,225.

Ca·sa'res (kä·sä′rȧs). Town, Buenos Aires prov., E Argentina, on railroad ab. 30 m. WSW of Buenos Aires.

Ca'sas Gran'des (kä′säz grän′dȧs). Town, NW Chihuahua state, N Mexico, on Casas Grandes river; pop. ab. 2000; nearby to the S are ruins of ancient city, perhaps built by Aztecs 1000 years ago.

Cascadas, Las. See LAS CASCADAS.

Cas·cade' (kăs·kād′; *attributively, also* kăs′kād′).
1 County in Montana. See *Table* at MONTANA.
2 Village, ⊗ of Valley co., W cen. Idaho; pop. 923.

Cascade Point. Cape on S cen. part of W coast of South I., New Zealand; lat. 44°S.

Cascade Range. Mountain range, N continuation of Sierra Nevada Mts., extending N from Lassen Peak, NE California, across Oregon and Washington; highest peak Mt. Rainier 14,408 ft., in Washington; its continuation N in British Columbia is known as the Coast Mts.

Cascade Tunnel. Railroad tunnel 7.79 m. long, Chelan and King cos., cen. Washington, ab. 100 m. E of Seattle, through Cascade Range.

Cascate delle Marmore. See VELINO.

Ca'sci·na (kä′shĕ·nä). Commune, Pisa prov., Tuscany, cen. Italy, on Arno river 8 m. ESE of Pisa; pop. 27,941; Florentine victory over Pisans 1364.

Cas'co Bay (kăs′kō). Inlet of Atlantic Ocean on SE coast of Cumberland co., SW Maine, containing many islands including Orrs I. and Chebeague I.; the city of Portland is situated on its W shore.

Casco Peak. Mountain 13,884 ft. in Lake co., cen. Colorado.

Case Inlet (kās). Inlet at S end of Puget Sound, bet. Mason and Pierce cos., Washington.

Ca'sel·li'na e Tor'ri (kä′sȧl·lē′nä ā tôr′rȧ). Commune, SW suburb of Florence, cen. Italy; pop. ab. 20,000.

Ca·ser'ta (kä·zĕr′tä). Commune, Napoli prov., Campania, S Italy, 16 m. NNE of Naples; pop. 49,462; 12th-cent. cathedral; palace (begun 1752; designed by Vanvitelli) built by Charles III of Spain; often called the "Versailles of Naples." Headquarters of Garibaldian campaigns 1860. Field Marshal Alexander's headquarters during latter part of Italian campaign in World War II; here "Act of Surrender" of German Army Group in Italy and Yugoslavia signed Apr. 29, 1945.

Ca'sey. **1** (kā′sĭ) County in Kentucky. See *Table* at KENTUCKY.
2 (kā′zĭ; -sĭ) City, Clark co., E Illinois, 67 m. SE of Decatur; pop. 2890.

Cash'el (kăsh′ĕl). Urban district (pop. 2831), S cen. co. Tipperary, S Eire, at the base of **Rock of Cashel** 306 ft. high, on which are the ruins of a cathedral, a chapel, and a round tower. Irish chieftains of Munster here submitted to Henry II of England 1171.

Cashmere. See KASHMIR.

Ca'si·gu'ran (kä′sĕ·gōō′rän). Port, cen. Sorsogon prov., SE Luzon, Phil. Is., on Sorsogon Bay; pop. 12,412.

Casiguran Sound. Long narrow inlet of Pacific Ocean on E coast of Luzon, Tayabas prov., Phil. Is., with Cape San Ildefonso marking its SE point of entrance.

Ca·sil'da (kä·sēl′dä). Town, Santa Fe prov., E cen. Argentina, 210 m. NW of Buenos Aires and 34 m. W of Rosario; pop. (est.) 16,200.

Casilinum. See CAPUA.

Ca·si'no (kȧ·sē′nō). Town, NE New South Wales, SE Australia, 110 m. S of Brisbane; pop. 5293.

Casinum. See CASSINO.

Ca'si·quia're (kä′sȧ·kyä′rȧ). River ab. 125 m. long, S Venezuela; connects the upper course (Guainía) of Rio Negro with the Orinoco river; a unique stream, not having a reversible current but flowing in a channel over marshy land of slight relief; strictly an arm of the Orinoco.

Cas'ket Mountain (kăs′kĕt; -kĭt). Peak 6180 ft. in Jeff Davis co., W Texas.

Cás'lav (chäs′läf); *Ger.* **Tschas'lau** (chäs′lou). City, province of Bohemia, W Czechoslovakia, 45 m. ESE of Prague; pop. (1930) 10,637.

Caso. See KASOS.

Ca·so'ria (kä·sô′ryä). Commune, Napoli prov., Campania, S Italy, 3 m. N by E of Naples; pop. 20,241.

Cas'per (kăs′pẽr). City, ⊗ of Natrona co., cen. Wyoming, on North Platte river; pop. 38,930; petroleum deposits nearby; oil refineries.

Cas'pi·an (kăs′pĭ·ăn). City, Iron co., SW Michigan penin., 32 m. WNW of Iron Mountain; pop. 1493.

Caspian Gates; *anc.* **Cas'pi·ae Py'lae** (kăs′pĭ·ē pī′lē) or **Al·ba'ni·ae Pylae** (ăl·bā′nĭ·ē). Narrow pass on W shore of Caspian Sea near Derbent (*q.v.*) at 42°N; trade route for centuries.

Caspian Sea; *anc.* **Cas′pi·um Ma′re** (kăs′pĭ·ŭm mä′rē) *or* **Hyr·ca′num Mare** (hûr·kā′nŭm). Inland salt lake bet. Europe and Asia, 760 m. long and 270 m. wide; 169,381 sq. m.; the largest inland body of water in the world; about 85 ft. below sea level. Receives the Volga, Ural, and Emba rivers at the N, and the Terek and Kura (with Araks) on the W. Has no outlet; loses more by evaporation than it receives from the streams. Except for S shore, which belongs to Iran, its borders are entirely within the U.S.S.R. Chief ports Baku in U.S.S.R. and Resht and Bandar Shah in Iran. Important as commercial route during Middle Ages when it formed a part of Mongol-Baltic trade route for goods from Asia.

Cass (kăs). **1** River, E Michigan; total length ab. 100 m.; formed by union of headstreams in Tuscola co., flows W into the Saginaw river, Saginaw co., cen. Michigan.
2 Name of counties in nine states of the U.S. See *Tables* at ILLINOIS, INDIANA, IOWA, MICHIGAN, MINNESOTA, MISSOURI, NEBRASKA, NORTH DAKOTA, TEXAS.
Cassai. See KASAI.
Cassandreia. See POTIDAEA.
Cas·sa′no al·l′Io′nio (käs·sä′nô äl·lyô′nyô). Commune, Cosenza prov., Calabria, S Italy, 33 m. N of Cosenza; pop. 11,428; episcopal see; castle.
Cassano d′Ad′da (däd′dä). Commune, Milano prov., Lombardy, N Italy, on the Adda 16 m. E of Milan; pop. (1931) 5604; scene of defeat of Ghibellines by Guelphs 1259, victory of duke of Vendôme over Eugene of Savoy Aug. 16, 1705 in War of Spanish Succession, and in Napoleonic Wars the victory of Suvorov over French forces of Moreau Apr. 27, 1799.
Cassel. See KASSEL city.
Cas′sel·ton (kăs′l·tŭn). City, Cass co., E North Dakota, 21 m. W of Fargo; pop. 1394; railroad center.
Cas′sia (kăsh′á). County in Idaho. See *Table* at IDAHO.
Cas′sian Way (kăsh′ăn); *Lat.* **Vi′a Cas′si·a** (vī′á kăsh′ĭ·á). Ancient Roman road from Rome to Florence; its line, through Bolsena, Chiusi, and Arezzo, is followed closely by modern Rome-Florence highway; extension ran NW to the Aurelian Way near Luna.
Cas·si′no (kȧ·sē′nô; *Ital.* käs·sē′nô); *before 1871* **San Ger·ma′no** (sän′ jär·mä′nô); *anc.* **Ca·si′num** (kȧ·sī′nŭm). Commune, Frosinone prov., Latium, cen. Italy, near Rapido river 28 m. ESE of Frosinone; pop. 20,064; ancient ruins; Benedictine monastery of Monte Cassino (*q.v.*) nearby; peace signed here by Emperor Frederick II and Pope Gregory IX 1230; defeat of Murat by Austrians Mar. 16, 1815. In World War II a key position in the German Gustav Line, barring entrance to Allies into valley of Liri river and road to Rome; battle for it began Feb. 1, 1944, but through Feb. and Mar. infantry, artillery, and air assaults were unsuccessful; second battle begun May 11 and town captured May 17; monastery completely destroyed.
Cassiquiare. Var. of CASIQUIARE.
Cas′si·ter′i·des (kăs′ĭ·tĕr′ĭ·dēz). Ancient name of tin-producing (Gr. *kassiteros* tin) islands of W Europe; originally applied to Scilly Isles off Britain, but location unknown.
Cass Lake (kăs). **1** Lake on NW boundary of Cass co., N cen. Minnesota, extending into Beltrami co.
2 Village, Cass co., N cen. Minnesota, on Cass Lake 15 m. ESE of Bemidji; pop. 1586; nurseries.
Cas·sop′o·lis (kȧ·sŏp′ô·lĭs). Village, ⊗ of Cass co., SW Michigan; pop. 2027.
Cass′ville (kăs′vĭl). City, ⊗ of Barry co., SW Missouri; pop. 1451.
Castalian Spring. See PARNASSUS.
Ca·stel′buo′no (käs·tĕl′bwô′nô). Commune, Palermo prov., NW cen. Sicily, ESE of Palermo; pop. 11,155.
Ca·stel′fi·dar′do (käs·tĕl′fē·där′dô). Commune, Ancona prov., Marches, cen. Italy, S of Ancona; pop. (1931) 7460; scene of battle Sept. 18, 1860 in which Italians (Piedmontese) decisively defeated papal forces.

Ca·stel′fio·ren·ti′no (käs·tĕl′fyô·rän·tē′nô). Commune, Firenze prov., Tuscany, cen. Italy, 19 m. SW of Florence; pop. 13,056.
Ca·stel′fran′co del·l′E·mi′lia (käs·tĕl′fräng′kô däl·lä·mē′lyä). Commune, Modena prov., Emilia, N Italy, 7 m. SE of Modena; pop. 19,360.
Castelfranco Ve′ne·to (vä′nä·tô). Commune, Treviso prov., Venezia Euganea, NE Italy, 15 m. W of Treviso; pop. 17,349; birthplace of Il Giorgione.
Ca·stel′ Gan·dol′fo (käs·tĕl′ gän·dôl′fô). Commune, Roma prov., Latium, cen. Italy, on W shore of Lake Albano 13 m. SE of Rome; pop. 2740; includes a group of papal estates; papal palace begun by Urban VIII; summer residence of the popes. See VATICAN CITY.
Ca·stel′lam·ma′re, Gulf of (käs·tĕl′läm·mä′rä). Inlet of Tyrrhenian Sea on NW coast of the island of Sicily.
Castellammare del Gol′fo (däl gôl′fô). Seaport, Trapani prov., NW Sicily, on Gulf of Castellammare E of Trapani; pop. 18,032; tuna fisheries; watering place.
Castellammare di Sta′bia (dē stä′byä); *anc.* **Sta′-bi·ae** (stä′bĭ·ē). Fortified seaport, Napoli prov., Campania, S Italy, on Bay of Naples 16 m. SE of Naples; pop. 46,469; episcopal see; ruins of 13-cent. castle of Frederick II; royal arsenal; dockyards; summer resort. Built on site of, and from ruins of, ancient Stabiae, destroyed by the eruption of Vesuvius 79 A.D. in which Pliny the Elder perished; English and Neapolitans defeated by French under Macdonald 1799.
Ca·stel·la′na (käs′täl·lä′nä). Commune, Bari prov., Apulia, SE Italy, 16 m. SE of Bari; pop. (1931) 11,994.
Cas·tel·la′na, La (lä käs′tä·yä′nä). See LA CASTELLANA.
Ca·stel·la·ne′ta (käs·tĕl′lä·nä′tä). Commune, Ionio prov., Apulia, SE Italy, 19 m. NW of Taranto; pop. 10,424; 12th-cent. cathedral; trade center.
Cas·tel·lón′ de la Pla′na (käs′tä·[l]yôn′ dä lä plä′nä). **1** Province of Spain. See *Table* at SPAIN.
2 Manufacturing city and Mediterranean seaport, its ✳, E Spain, 40 m. NNE of Valencia; pop. 46,876; manufactures paper, porcelain, sailcloth, woolen and hempen fabrics; captured from Moors by James I of Aragon 1233.
Castellorizo. See KASTELORRIZON.
Ca·stel′mas′sa (käs·tĕl′mäs′sä). Commune, Rovigo prov., Venezia Euganea, NE Italy; pop. 10,475.
Cas′tel′nau′da′ry′ (käs′tĕl′nô′dȧ′rē′). Commune, Aude dept., S France, ab. 22 m. WNW of Carcassonne; pop. 8054; important in ancient Languedoc and in the wars against the Albigenses in 13th cent.; battle Sept. 1, 1632 in which Louis XIII defeated duke of Montmorency and Gaston d′Orléans.
Castelnuovo. See ERCEGNOVI.
Ca·stel′nuo′vo Be·rar·den′ga (käs·tĕl′nwô′vô bâ·rär·dĕng′gä). Commune, Siena prov., Tuscany, cen. Italy, 8 m. E by N of Siena; pop. (1931) 10,559.
Cas·te′lo Bran′co (käsh·tā′lōō vrăng′kōō). **1** District of Portugal. See *Table* at PORTUGAL.
2 Commune, its ✳, and ✳ of Beira Baixa prov., E cen. Portugal, 114 m. NE of Lisbon; pop. 9820; cathedral.
Castelrosso. See KASTELORRIZON.
Ca·stel′ San Gio·van′ni (käs·tĕl′ sän′ jô·vän′nē). Commune, Piacenza prov., Emilia, N Italy, 15 m. W of Piacenza; pop. 10,191; French defeated here by Austrians and Russians 1799.
Castel San Pie′tro del·l′E·mi′lia (säm pyä′trô däl·lä·mē′lyä). Commune, Bologna prov., Emilia, N Italy, 15 m. SE of Bologna; pop. 15,263; mineral baths.
Ca·stel′ter′mi·ni (käs·tĕl′tĕr′mê·nê). Commune, Agrigento prov., SW Sicily, near Agrigento; pop. 12,256.
Castelvetere. See CAULONIA.
Ca·stel′ve·tra′no (käs·tĕl′vâ·trä′nô). Commune, Trapani prov., NW Sicily, 29 m. SSE of Trapani; pop. 26,129; ruins of ancient Selinus (*q.v.*) nearby.
Ca′sti·glio′ne del La′go (käs·tē·lyō′nä däl lä′gô). Commune, Perugia prov., Umbria, cen. Italy, on Lake Trasimeno 18 m. W by N of Perugia; pop. 16,828; castle.

Castiglione del′le Sti·vie′re (dä̀l′lä̀ stĕ·vyâ′rä̀). Commune, Mantova prov., Lombardy, N Italy, 22 m. NW of Mantua; pop. 8353; Austrians under Wurmser defeated by French under Napoleon Aug. 5, 1796.

Ca′sti·glion′ Fio·ren·ti′no (käs′tĕ·lyōn′ fyô-rän-tē′nô). Commune, Arezzo prov., Tuscany, cen. Italy, 10 m. S by E of Arezzo; pop. 14,830.

Cas·tile′ (kăs·tēl′); *Span.* **Cas·til′la** (käs·tē′[l]yä). Region and ancient kingdom, cen. and N cen. Spain; 53,500 sq. m.; comprises the modern provinces of Ávila, Burgos, Ciudad Real, Cuenca, Guadalajara, Logroño, Madrid, Palencia, Santander, Segovia, Soria, Toledo, and Valladolid; divided into two historical regions: in the N, Old Castile (*q.v.*), and in the S, New Castile (*q.v.*); extensive plains, forming tablelands hemmed in on all sides by mountains; some fertile regions, esp. in the S, but in general arid; watered chiefly by the Duero, Guadiana, Tagus, and Júcar rivers.

History: Originally an extension of kingdom of León (*q.v.*); in 10th cent. A.D. countship of Castile made hereditary and practically autonomous by Count González of Burgos; united with Navarre 1026 which began conquest of León; León united with Castile by Ferdinand I 1037; expanded by series of conquests of Moorish kingdoms: Toledo (New Castile) 1085, Córdoba 1236, Seville 1248, and Murcia 1266; took Canary Is. 1402 and Gibraltar 1462; union with Aragon (*q.v.*) 1479 (after marriage of Isabella of Castile to Ferdinand of Aragon 1469) completed with accession of their grandson, Charles I of Spain, 1516. See SPAIN.

Castilla la Nueva. See NEW CASTILE.

Castilla la Vieja. See OLD CASTILE.

Cas·til′lo de San Mar′cos National Monument (kăs·tē′yō dĕ sän mär′kŭs). See UNITED STATES, *National Monuments.*

Cas′til′lon′ (käs′tē′yôN′) *or* **Cas′til′lon′-et-Ca′pi′-tour′lan′** (käs′tē′yôN′-nä·kà′pē′tōōr′län′). Commune, Gironde dept., SW France, on the Dordogne river 26 m. E of Bordeaux; pop. 3099; scene of English defeat July 17, 1453 in last battle of Hundred Years' War.

Cas·tine′ (kăs·tēn′; *attributively, also* kăs′tēn). Town, Hancock co., SE Maine, on E side of Penobscot Bay 35 m. S of Bangor; pop. 824; fishing and resort center.

Cas·tle·bar′ (kàs′′l·bär′). Urban district, ⊗ of co. Mayo, NW Eire; pop. 5158; site of Norman castle, home of the de Burghs; nearby is site of runaway victory ("Castlebar Races") of French auxiliaries and Irish insurrectionists over militia and yeomanry 1798.

Cas′tle Dale′ (kàs′′l). City, ⊗ of Emery co., E cen. Utah; pop. 617.

Cas′tle·ford (kàs′′l·fẽrd). Urban district, West Riding, Yorkshire, N England, 11 m. ESE of Leeds; pop. 43,116; glass, earthenware, chemicals.

Cas′tle Gate′ (kàs′′l). Town, Carbon co., Utah, near Price river; pop. 321; huge sandstone formations at the entrance to Price river canyon.

Castle Harbour. Gulf off NE end of Bermuda I. in the Bermuda Is., formed by St. George's I. and St. David I. on N and small islands on E.

Castle Hill. Elevation (Hill 193) near the Benedictine monastery, Cassino, Italy; after bitter fighting captured by Indian troops Mar. 15–20, 1944.

Castle Island. One of the Bahama Is., at SE entrance to Crooked Island Passage; lighthouse (estab. 1868).

Cas′tle·maine′ (kàs′′l·mān′). Town, cen. Victoria, SE Australia, 65 m. NW of Melbourne; pop. 5221; its gold mines among the first to be opened in Australia.

Cas′tle Mountain (kàs′′l). See Mount EISENHOWER.

Castle Peak. 1 Mountain 10,668 ft. in Sierra Nevada Mts., E Fresno co., S cen. California.
2 Mountain 14,259 ft., Gunnison and Pitkin cos., W cen. Colorado.
3 Mountain 11,820 ft., SW Custer co., cen. Idaho.

Castle Point. Peak 6300 ft., W Klamath co., S Oregon, SW of Crater Lake.

Castle Rock. Town, ⊗ of Douglas co., cen. Colorado; pop. 1152.

Castle Shan′non (shăn′ŭn). Borough, Allegheny co., SW Pennsylvania, 6 m. S of Pittsburgh; pop. 11,836.

Cas′tle·ton (kàs′′l·t′n; -tŭn). Town and summer resort, Rutland co., W Vermont, ab. 10 m. W of Rutland; pop. 1902; mobilization center of Ethan Allen and Green Mountain boys before attack on Ticonderoga 1775. Castleton Teachers College (1787; coed.).

Castleton on Hud′son (hŭd′s′n) *or* **Castleton-on-Hudson.** Village, Rensselaer co., E New York, on Hudson river 9 m. S of Albany; pop. 1752; high-level bridge, railroad cutoff, with channel span of 1008 ft.

Cas′tle·town (kàs′′l·toun). Town, former ✳ of Isle of Man, on S coast of the island; pop. 1713.

Castletown Bearhaven, Castletownbere. See BEREHAVEN.

Ca′stor (*Ger.* käs′tôr; *Eng.* käs′tēr). Peak 13,879 ft. in the Pennine Alps on Swiss-Italian border, the E peak of the **Zwil′ling·e** [tsvil′ing·ĕ] (Twins), just W of Monte Rosa. The W peak is **Pol′lux** (*Ger.* pôl′ōōks; *Eng.* pôl′ŭks) 13,432 ft.

Cas′tor Peak (kàs′tēr). Mountain 10,800 ft. in Yellowstone National Park, NW Wyoming.

Castra Regina. See REGENSBURG.

Cas′tres (kàs′tr′); *anc.* **Cas′tra Al′bi·en′si·um** (kăs′-trà ăl′bĭ·ĕn′sĭ·ŭm). Commercial and manufacturing city, Tarn dept., S France, on Agout river 24 m. S of Albi; pop. 29,133; fine town hall (former episcopal palace) with gardens on plan of Tuileries; 17th-cent. church. Founded on site of Roman camp around Benedictine monastery 647; to Crown 1225; episcopal see 1317–1789; made countship 1356; conquered by Louis XIII 1629.

Cas′tries′ *or* **Port Cas′tries′** (kàs′trē′; kȧs′trēs). Seaport on NW coast of Saint Lucia I., Windward Is., British West Indies; ✳ of British colony of Saint Lucia; pop. ab. 8000; coaling station.

Cas′tro (kàs′trō). County in Texas. See *Table* at TEXAS.

Cas′tro (käs′trô). Small port on E shore of Chiloé I., Chiloé prov., S cen. Chile; pop. 5518.

Ca′stro (käs′trô), **Ca′stron** (käs′trôn). Variants of KÁSTRON.

Cas′tro Al′ves (kȧsh′trōō äl′vĕs). City Baía state, E Brazil, on railroad ab. 68 m. W of Salvador; pop. 7349.

Cas′tro del Rí′o (käs′trô ᵺĕl rē′ô). Commercial and manufacturing commune, Córdoba prov., S Spain, 22 m. SE of Córdoba; pop. 17,298.

Castrogiovanni. See ENNA commune.

Ca′strop–Rau′xel (käs′trôp-rouk′sĕl), *also* **Ka′strop–Rau′xel.** Industrial city, W Germany, in North Rhine-Westphalia state, 32 m. SSW of Münster; pop. 53,218; coal mining; manufactures cement, chemicals, tile.

Ca′stro·re·a′le (käs′trô-rä·ä′lä). Commune, Messina prov., NE Sicily; pop. 12,240; warm sulfur springs.

Cas′tro–Ur·dia′les (käs′trô-ōōr·ᵺyä′läs). Seaport, Santander prov., N Spain, on Bay of Biscay 30 m. ESE of Santander; pop. 11,963; iron mining; ancient Roman colony; destroyed by French 1813; later rebuilt.

Cas′tro Valley (käs′trō). Urban community (unincorporated), Alameda co., W California, N of Hayward; pop. 37,120.

Ca′stro·vil′la·ri (käs′trô-vēl′lä-rê). Commune, Cosenza prov., Calabria, S Italy, 35 m. N of Cosenza; pop. 11,943.

Castrum. See EL QASR.

Castua. See KASTAV.

Cas′tu·lo (käs′tū·lô). Ancient Iberian town of Hispania Tarraconensis (in modern S Spain) on the Baetis (Guadalquivir) river; important Roman town near silver and lead mines. Scipio Africanus defeated Carthaginians here 208 B.C. Site of modern **Caz·lo′na** (käz-lō′nä; käth-), Jaén prov., 2 m. N of Linares.

Ca′sus (kā′sŭs). = KASOS.

Cas′well (kăz′wĕl; -wĕl). County in North Carolina. See *Table* at NORTH CAROLINA.

Catabathmus Magna. See SALÛM.

Ca'ta·ca'os (kä'tä·kä'ŏs). Town, Piura dept., NW Peru, SW of Piura; center of Peruvian Panama-hat industry.

Catacium. See CATANZARO.

Ca'ta·co'cha (kä'tä·kō'chä). Town, Loja prov., SW Ecuador; pop. (1944 est.) 14,240.

Ca'ta·gua'zes (kä'tá·gwá'zĕs). City, SE Minas Gerais state, E Brazil, 120 m. NNE of Rio de Janeiro; pop. (1940 est.) 9206.

Cat'a·hou'la (kăt'á·hōō'lá). Parish in Louisiana. See *Table* at LOUISIANA.

Catahoula Lake. Lake in S La Salle parish, Louisiana.

Ca'ta·ing'an (kä'tä·ēng'än). Municipality, SE coast of Masbate I., Phil. Is., on Samar Sea; pop. 38,709.

Catalaunian Plains. See CHÂLONS-SUR-MARNE.

Ça'tal·ca' (chä'täl·jä'); *Angl.* **Cha'tal·ja'.** Town, İstanbul vilayet, Turkey in Europe, ab. 20 m. W of İstanbul; pop. 4571; center of heavily fortified line across peninsula from Black Sea to Sea of Marmara, where Turks made final stand Nov. 1912 in First Balkan War; temporary W boundary of Turkey in Europe 1912–13.

Catalina. = SANTA CATALINA island, Santa Barbara Is.

Cat'a·lo'nia (kăt'á·lōn'yá; -lō'ni·á); *Span.* **Ca'ta·lu'ña** (kä'tä·lōō'nyä); *Catalan* **Ca'ta·lu'nya** (kä·tá·lōō'nyá). Historical region, in northeast corner of Spain; 12,431 sq. m.; pop. ab. 2,790,000; bounded N by France and the Pyrenees, E and S by the Mediterranean, SW by Valencia, W by Aragon; comprises the modern provinces of Barcelona, Gerona, Lérida, and Tarragona; traversed by spur of Pyrenees; watered principally by the Ebro; generally rugged land, but containing fertile valleys and coast lands; rich in minerals and agricultural products; people retain own language (Catalan) and strong sense of regional unity.

History: Originally settled by numerous independent tribes, and subsequently by Phoenicians and Greeks; invaded by Carthaginians under Hamilcar Barca and Hannibal; conquered by Romans under whom it became a wealthy province with its capital at Tarragona; invaded by Visigoths early 5th cent. A.D.; S portion taken by Arabs 711 but reconquered by Charlemagne who set up Spanish March 795 with its capital later (801) at Barcelona; became independent Frankish county of Barcelona (or Catalonia) 9th cent.; united with Aragon (*q.v.*) 1164; by 13th cent. had extensive territory N of Pyrenees (including Cerdagne, Roussillon, part of Provence); Barcelona became a European trade center and point of departure for Aragonese expansion in Mediterranean (see MAJORCA; SICILY); engaged in long struggle to maintain political and cultural autonomy against frequent attempts at centralization and unification by Castile; revolted 1640–59 as result of policy of Olivares; Cerdagne and Roussillon lost to France 1659; during War of the Spanish Succession (1701–14) sided with Archduke Charles of Austria; entered most recent movement for autonomy 1917–19; autonomous 1932–34; again autonomous after joining Loyalists in Spanish Civil War 1936; lost autonomy 1939 after fall of Barcelona (Loyalist capital from 1937) and forbidden use of Catalan by Franco government.

Cat'a·mar'ca (kăt'á·mär'ká; *Span.* kä'tä·mär'kä). **1** Province of Argentina. See *Table* at ARGENTINA.

2 Town, its ✳, NW Argentina, 115 m. S by W of Tucumán; pop. (est.) 22,000; at altitude of 1600 ft. in foothills of E Andes; agricultural and mining center.

Catana. See CATANIA.

Ca'tan·dua'nes (kä'tän·dwä'nás). Island off SE Luzon, E Phil. Is.; 552 sq. m.; pop. 63,530; ✳ Virac; forms a subprovince of Albay. With Luzon coast forms Lagonoy Gulf; covered with hills and low mountain ranges, highest peak ab. 3000 ft.; soil fertile producing rice, corn, cotton, hemp, and coconuts. Included in Albay prov. by government enactment July 16, 1901.

Ca'tan·du'va (kä'tăNN·dōō'vá). City, São Paulo state, SE Brazil, 230 m. NW of São Paulo; pop. 17,073.

Ca·ta'nia (ká·tän'yá; *Ital.* kä·tä'nyä). **1** Province of Italy. See *Table* at ITALY.

2 *anc.* **Cat'a·na** (kăt'á·ná). Manufacturing and commercial commune, its ✳, E Sicily, at foot of Mt. Etna on Gulf of Catania; pop. 244,972; episcopal see; ancient Roman ruins; Norman cathedral (founded 1091); university (founded 1444); chemicals, sulfur, cement, textiles, leather.

History: Founded by Greeks 729 B.C.; Athenian base of operations against Syracuse 432 B.C.; taken by Romans 263 B.C. (First Punic War); taken by Saracens A.D. 902 and by Normans c. 1090; devastated by earthquakes, esp. in 1169 and 1693, and by volcanic eruptions, esp. in 1669; off nearby coast scene of naval victory of French under Duquesne over the Spanish and Dutch fleet under de Ruyter 1676. In World War II a German defense point; under attack by British from July 12, 1943; outflanked and abandoned Aug. 5.

Catania, Gulf of. Inlet of Mediterranean Sea on E coast of the island of Sicily.

Ca·ta'ño (kä·tä'nyõ). Municipality (pop. 25,208) and town (pop. 8276), San Juan dist., NE Puerto Rico; town is on S shore of San Juan harbor S of San Juan.

Ca'tan·za'ro (kä'tän·dzä'rõ). **1** Province of Italy. See *Table* at ITALY.

2 *anc.* **Ca·ta'ci·um** (ká·tä'shi·ŭm). City, its ✳, Calabria, S Italy, near Gulf of Squillace 183 m. SE of Naples; pop. 45,400; cathedral; academy of sciences; summer resort; devastated by earthquake 1783 and 1908.

Cat'a·o'nia (kăt'á·ōn'yá; -ō'ni·á). Ancient region of Asia Minor bet. Cappadocia and Cilicia, including NE part of Taurus Mts.

Ca'ta·ra'ma (kä'tä·rä'mä). Town, Los Ríos prov., W cen. Ecuador; pop. (1944 est.) 6705.

Ca'tar·man' (kä'tär·män'). Municipality, N coast of Samar, Phil. Is., 55 m. NNE of Catbalogan; pop. 21,007.

Cat'a·sau'qua (kăt'á·sô'kwá). Borough, Lehigh co., E Pennsylvania, on Lehigh river 4 m. N of Allentown; pop. 5062; manufactures textiles, cement, flour.

Ca·tas'tro·phe, Cape (ká·tăs'trõ·fē). Cape at W entrance to Spencer Gulf, S South Australia.

Ca'ta·tum'bo (kä'tä·tōōm'bõ). River in N South America; rises in N Colombia, flows NE across Venezuelan border and into Lake Maracaibo.

Ca·taw'ba (ká·tô'bá). **1** River ab. 250 m. long, from Blue Ridge Mts., W North Carolina, S into South Carolina, where it is known as the Wateree (*q.v.*).

2 County in North Carolina. See *Table* at NORTH CAROLINA.

Cat'a·wis'sa (kăt'á·wĭs'á). Borough, Columbia co., E cen. Pennsylvania, NNW of Pottsville; pop. 1824.

Cat'ba·lo'gan (kăt'bä·lõ'gän). Municipality, ✳ of Samar prov., Phil. Is., on W coast of Samar I. in central part; pop. 26,654; has fair harbor on Samar Sea.

Cateau, Le. See LE CATEAU.

Catelet, Le. See LE CATELET.

Ca'te·ma'co (kä'tä·mä'kõ). Town, Veracruz state, E Mexico, just E of Tuxtla; pop. 5374.

Ca'ter·ham and War'ling·ham (kä'tẽr·ăm, wôr'ling·ăm). Urban district, Surrey, S England, S of London; pop. 31,290; a part of Warlingham lies within Greater London.

Ca·thay' (kă·thā'). An old name for China, esp. during Middle Ages; introduced by Marco Polo. It comes from the Persian *Khitai*, after the Khitans, a Tatar race occupying the Sungari basin in the 10th cent. A.D. Used in cen. Asia and in countries to the W, but never by the Chinese themselves. The modern Russian form is *Kitai*.

Cat'head' Point (kăt'hĕd'). Point at N extremity of Leelanau co., NW Michigan, on Lake Michigan.

Ca·the'dral Mountain (ká·thē'drál). Peak 6850 ft. in Brewster co., W Texas.

Cathedral Peak. **1** Mountain 10,933 ft., NE Mariposa co., California, in Sierra Nevada Mts. in Yosemite National Park.

2 Mountain 14,100 ft., Pitkin co., W cen. Colorado.

3 Mountain 10,600 ft. in Yellowstone National Park, NW Wyoming.

Cathedral Rocks. Mountain 6551 ft., Mariposa co., California; rises 2592 ft. above Yosemite valley.

Catherine, Mount. See Gebel KATHERINA.

Catherine Archipelago. See ALEUTIAN ISLANDS.

Cath′kin Peak (kăth′kĭn) *or* **Cham′pagne′ Cas′tle** (shăm′pān′). Peak 10,357 ft. in Drakensberg Mountains, Union of South Africa.

Cath·lam′et (kăth-lăm′ĕt; -ĭt). Town, ⊗ of Wahkiakum co., SW Washington; pop. 615.

Cat Island (kăt). **1** Island in Gulf of Mexico, off S coast of Harrison co., S Mississippi.

2 One of the Bahama Is., in Atlantic Ocean SE of Eleuthera I. and WNW of San Salvador; 160 sq. m.; pop. (1943) 3780; formerly identified with the San Salvador of Columbus (see SAN SALVADOR island).

Cat′letts·burg (kăt′lĕts-bûrg; -lĭts-). City, ⊗ of Boyd co., NE Kentucky, 5 m. S of Ashland; pop. 3874.

Ca·to′che, Cape (kä-tō′chå). NE extremity of Yucatán penin., SE Mexico, projecting into Yucatán Channel.

Ca′tons·ville (kā′tŏnz-vĭl). Urban community (unincorporated), Baltimore co., Maryland, SW of Baltimore; pop. 37,372.

Ca·too′sa (kå-tōō′så). County in Georgia. See *Table* at GEORGIA.

Ca·tron′ (kå-trŏn′). County in New Mexico. See *Table* at NEW MEXICO.

Cats′kill (kăts′kĭl). Village, ⊗ of Greene co., SE New York, on W side of Hudson river 30 m. S of Albany; pop. 5825; summer resort, gateway to Catskill Mts.; settled by Dutch c. 1680; incorp. 1806.

Catskill Mountains. Group of the Appalachian system, SE New York, along W bank of the Hudson chiefly in Greene, Ulster, and Delaware cos.; highest peak Slide Mt. 4204 ft.; heavily wooded; many resorts.

Cat′tail′ Peak (kăt′tāl′). Mountain 6609 ft. in Yancey co., W North Carolina, near Mt. Mitchell.

Cat′ta·rau′gus (kăt′å-rô′gŭs). County in New York. See *Table* at NEW YORK.

Cattaraugus Creek. River ab. 70 m. long, W New York; forms boundary bet. Erie and Cattaraugus cos. and flows W into Lake Erie.

Cattaro. See KOTOR.

Cattegat. = KATTEGAT.

Cau′a·bu·rí′ (kou′å-vōō-rē′). River ab. 100 m. long in NW Brazil; from S tip of Venezuela S into Rio Negro.

Ca·ua′yan (kä-wä′yän). Municipality, SW Negros Occidental, Negros, Phil. Is., on Panay Gulf; pop. 25,645.

Cau′ca (kou′kä). **1** River ab. 600 m. long, W Colombia; rises in Andes Mts., flows N into Magdalena river.

2 Department of Colombia. See *Table* at COLOMBIA.

Cau·ca′sia (kô-kā′zhå; -shå) *or* **Cau′ca·sus** (kô′kå-sŭs). Region bet. the Black and Caspian Seas; ab. 154,250 sq. m.; pop. ab. 14,410,000; extends SE and NW ab. 750 m. from Apsheron Penin. to mouth of Kuban river on Black Sea; contains the Caucasus Mts. (*q.v.*) which divide it into **Cis′cau·ca′sia** (sĭs′-), N of the range, and **Trans′cau·ca′sia** (trăns′-), on the S.

History: Inhabited from ancient times by peoples of Caucasian race to which successive invaders added numerous other elements; known to ancient Greeks (see COLCHIS); penetrated, during Middle Ages, by Greek Christianity; East Caucasus later converted to Islam; under nominal Persian and Turkish suzerainty until gradually forced into connection with Russia whose acquisition of Astrakhan (*q.v.*) had brought her to the Caspian; conquered by Russia, to the Kuban and Terek 1774, Derbent 1796 and Baku 1806, Georgia 1801, Shirvan and Karabakh 1813, Persian Armenia 1828, Akhaltsikhe 1829; mountain tribes of Caucasus became Russian subjects after arrest of their leader Shamyl 1859; Circassians surrendered 1864; Kars, Ardahan, and Batum ceded by Turkey to Russia 1878. For later his-

tory of southern part, see TRANSCAUCASIAN FEDERATION. In World War II its oil fields goal of German advance July–Nov. 1942; Ordzhonikidze farthest point reached Nov. 10–19; German armies driven out by Jan. 1943.

Caucasus Indicus. See HINDU KUSH.

Cau′ca·sus Mountains (kô′kå-sŭs); *Russ.* **Bol·shoi′ Kav·kaz′** (bŭl·y′·shoi′ kŭf·kåz′). Range ab. 700 m. long bet. the Black and Caspian Seas, S Soviet Russia; formerly often considered the boundary bet. Europe and Asia; separates Ciscaucasia from Transcaucasia of volcanic origin; has many peaks above 15,000 ft., highest Mt. Elborus 18,481 ft., highest peak in Europe; crossed by high passes, the two best known being Daryal and Mamison (*qq.v.*).

Cauda. See GAVDOS.

Cau′dé′ran′ (kō′dā′rän′). Commune, Gironde dept., SW France, suburb of Bordeaux; pop. (1931) 20,384.

Cau′dine Forks (kô′dĭn). Mountain passes on the road bet. Capua and Beneventum, Campania, S Italy, near Caudium; defeat of Romans by the Samnites 321 B.C.

Cau′di·um (kô′dĭ-ŭm). Ancient town, Samnium, S Italy, E of Beneventum.

Cau′dry′ (kō′drē′). Commune, Nord dept., N France, 40 m. SSE of Lille; pop. 13,031; textiles.

Cau·é′ (kou-â′). Mountain, S cen. Minas Gerais state, SE Brazil, ab. 50 m. NE of Belo Horizonte; iron-ore deposits; the town of Itabira is on its S slope.

Caugh′ley (käf′lĭ). Village, E Shropshire, England; site of pottery factories (abandoned ab. 1815) where willow pattern was first made ab. 1780.

Caugh′na·wa′ga (kôg′nå-wô′gå). Indian village, S Quebec, Canada, on the St. Lawrence S of Montreal.

Ca′uit Point (kä′wēt). Point of land, E Surigao prov., Mindanao, Phil. Is., SE of entrance to Lanuza Bay.

Caul′field (kôl′fēld). City, S Victoria, SE Australia, SE suburb of Melbourne; pop. 65,298.

Cau·lo′nia (kou-lō′nyä); *formerly* **Ca·stel′ve′te·re** (käs-tĕl′vâ′tâ-râ). Commune, Reggio di Calabria prov., Calabria, S Italy; pop. (1931) 12,607.

Cau·que′nes (kou-kā′nås). Town, ✳ of Maule prov., S cen. Chile, ab. 198 m. S of Santiago; pop. 12,987; in region severely damaged by earthquake Jan. 24, 1939.

Cau′ra (kou′rä). River ab. 450 m. long, cen. Venezuela; rises in the Serra Pacaraima, flows N into the Orinoco.

Cau′sap′scal′ (kō′zăp′skăl′). Village, Matane co., Gaspé Penin., SE Quebec, Canada, on Matapédia river 37 m. SSE of Matane; pop. 2609; resort for fishermen.

Causses (kōs). District, S cen. France, on S border of the Massif Central; a limestone region, noted for gorges and subterranean rivers.

Cau′te·rets′ (kō′tṛĕ′). Commune, SW Hautes-Pyrénées dept., SW France; pop. 1577; hot sulfur springs.

Cau·tín′ (kou-tēn′). Province of Chile. See *Table* at CHILE.

Cau′to (kou′tô). River ab. 150 m. long, E Cuba; rises in cen. Oriente prov., flows W into Guacanayabo Bay; navigable for ab. 70 m.

Cau′ve·ry (kô′vĕr-ĭ) *or* **Ka′ve·ri** (kä′vĕr-ĭ). River 475 m. long, cen. Madras state, S India; rises in N Kerala state, flows E and SE, and enters Bay of Bengal in a wide delta. On the border of Mysore it forms island of Sivasamudram on either side of which are the **Cauvery Falls**, descending ab. 320 ft. and supplying water power. Navigable in short sections for small vessels only; source of extensive irrigation system; noted for its scenery; entire course, but esp. the sections at Seringapatam and Trichinopoly, regarded as sacred.

Ca′va de′ Tir·re′ni (kä′vä dâ tĕr·râ′nĕ). Commune, Salerno prov., Campania, S Italy, 3 m. WNW of Salerno; pop. 35,051; cathedral; summer resort; manufactures textiles; famous Benedictine monastery (founded 1025 by Saint Alferius over a cave he occupied) nearby.

Ca′val′lon (kä′vä′yôN′); *anc.* **Ca·bel′li·o** (kå·bĕl′ĭ-ō). Commune, Vaucluse dept., SE France, on Durance river 13 m. SE of Avignon; pop. 12,522; 12th-cent. cathedral.

Cav′a·lier′ (kăv′à·lẽr′; attributively, also kăv′à·lẽr′).
1 County, North Dakota. See Table at NORTH DAKOTA.
2 City, ⊗ of Pembina co., NE corner of North Dakota;
pop. 1423.
Ca·val′la (kà·văl′à). = KAVALLA, department and sea-
port of Greece.
Ca·val′ly or **Ka·val′li** (kà·văl′ĭ). River ab. 300 m. long,
W Africa, bet. Ivory Coast and Liberia.
Cav′an (kăv′ăn). **1** County, N Eire, in Ulster prov.; 730
sq. m.; pop. 76,670; chief industry agriculture.
2 Urban district, its ⊗: pop. 3393; burned 1690 by
Enniskillen partisans of William of Orange after their
defeat of Jacobite forces.
Ca′va·ra′ya (kä′vä·rä′yä). Peak 19,193 ft. in N Chile,
W of Lake Poopó.
Ca·var′ze·re (kä·vär′dzä·rå). Commune, Venezia prov.,
Venezia Euganea, NE Italy, on Adige river 25 m. SSW
of Venice; pop. 25,199.
Cave of the Winds. See NIAGARA FALLS.
Ca·via′na (kà·vyä′nà). Island in N branch of the mouth
of the Amazon river, NE Brazil; belongs to Pará state.
Ca·vi′te (kä·vē′tå). **1** Province, SW Luzon, Phil. Is.;
498 sq. m.; pop. 238,581; ✳ City of Cavite. On S side of
Manila Bay; western end of NW shore is on South Channel (see CORREGIDOR). A plain except for the low mountain range in S on Batangas border; its many streams
flow N or NW to Manila Bay. Fertile volcanic soil produces rice, sugar, coffee, copra. Chief towns Cavite,
Imus, General Trias.
History: Not populous in early Spanish times, but increased in importance with establishment of navy yard
at Cavite; attacked by Dutch 1647; became stronghold
of religious orders; in 19th cent. the center of revolutionary activity against Spanish government, esp. 1872 and
1896; civil government established June 11, 1901.
2 officially **City of Cavite.** Chartered city, its ✳, in NE
part, on narrow point of land (**Cavite Peninsula**) 8 m.
across Manila Bay SW of Manila; pop. 38,254. A walled
town with old forts and arsenals; its harbor part of Bacoor Bay (bet. the peninsula and the mainland); in early
times made a naval base by the Spanish government.
Scene of defeat of Spanish fleet by Admiral Dewey May
1, 1898, known as the battle of Manila Bay (q.v.). Chief
naval base and coaling station of U.S. fleet in Asiatic
waters 1898–1941. Created a chartered city May 26,
1940. Partly destroyed by Japanese air attacks Dec.
8–10, 1941; captured by Japanese Jan. 2, 1942; retaken
by Americans Feb. 13, 1945.
Caw′dor (kô′dēr). Parish, Nairn co., N Scotland, 5 m.
SW of Nairn; pop. 823; famous castle where the murder
of King Duncan in Shakespeare's *Macbeth* takes place.
Cawn′pore (kôn′pōr) or **Cawn′pur** (-pŏŏr). City,
Allahabad division, S cen. Uttar Pradesh, N Indian
Union, on right bank of Ganges river 245 m. SE of Delhi;
pop. (1941) 487,324; important rail junction; most important industrial center of the state; leather, cotton,
wool, and sugar industries. Garrisoned by British troops
in 1778. Known for the massacre by Nana Sahib of British soldiers and European families during Sepoy Mutiny
July 15, 1857.
Ca′xa·mar′ca (kä′hä·mär′kä). Older spelling of CAJA-
MARCA.
Ca′xam·bú′ (kà′shäNm·bōō′). Town, S Minas Geraïs
state, E Brazil, 130 m. NW of Rio de Janeiro; pop. (1940
est.) 6005; mineral springs.
Ca·xi′as (kà·shē′às). **1** City, NE Maranhão state NE
Brazil, 182 m. SE of São Luiz; pop. (1940 est.) 7254.
2 City, Rio de Janeiro state, SE Brazil; pop. (1940 est.)
24,050.
3 City, Rio Grande do Sul state, S Brazil, 60 m. N of
Pôrto Alegre; pop. (1940 est.) 17,409.
Cay (kē; the first is the West Indian pron.). For **Cay
Lobos,** etc., see LOBOS, etc.
Ca·yam′be (kä·yäm′bå). **1** Peak 19,160 ft. in the Andes
Mountains, N Ecuador.

2 Town, Pichincha prov., N cen. Ecuador, 33 m. NE of
Quito; pop. (1944 est.) 11,855.
Cay′ce (kā′sê). City, Lexington co., W cen. South
Carolina, SW of Columbia; pop. 8517.
Cay·enne′ (ki-ĕn′; kä-ĕn′; attributively, also ki′ĕn,
kä′ĕn). City, ✳ of French Guiana; pop. 11,704; on NW
coast of **Cayenne Island,** ab. 30 m. in circumference,
formed by the **Cayenne River,** a small stream that
divides into two channels before emptying into the At-
lantic. Founded by French 1604; held twice by Dutch in
17th cent.; received little attention until 19th cent. when
French Guiana (q.v.) made a penal colony.
Cayes or **Aux Cayes** (ō kä′y′; ō kā′y′). Seaport on S
Tiburon Penin., SW Haiti; pop. (1936 est.) 11,875.
Ca·yey′ (kä·yē′ē; -yä′). Municipality (pop. 38,061) and
town (pop. 8276), SE Puerto Rico, 9 m. NNW of
Guayama in section producing tobacco, sugar, coffee.
Cay·man′ Islands (kä·măn′; kā′măn). Island group
in NW Caribbean Sea ab. 200 m. NW of Jamaica of
which it was formerly a dependency; 104 sq. m.; pop.
8803; a Brit. colony. Group comprises three islands:
Grand Cayman, the largest, ab. 22 m. long, pop.
(1943) 5311, with Georgetown, ✳ of the group, on its W
end; NE of Grand Cayman **Little Cayman,** 10 m. long,
pop. (1943) 63, and **Cayman Brac** (brăk), 12 m. long,
pop. (1943) 1296. Discovered by Columbus 1503 but
never occupied by Spaniards; colonized from ab. 1734 by
English from Jamaica.
Ca′yo (kä′yô). For **Cayo Coco, Cayo Largo,** etc.,
see COCO CAY, LARGO CAY, etc.
Ca′yo (kä′yô). **1** District, W British Honduras; 1830 sq.
m.; pop. (1943 est.) 8296; ✳ El Cayo.
2 See EL CAYO.
Cay Sal Bank (kē′ săl′). Bank in W Bahamas, bet.
Straits of Florida and N cen. Cuba; separated from
Great Bahama Bank on E by Santaren Channel; Cay
Sal lighthouse (established 1839) in NW corner.
Ca·ÿs′ter (kà·ĭs′tēr); mod. **Ba′yin·dir′** (bä′yĭn·dĭr′).
River ab. 85 m. long, SW Asia Minor, N of the Maean-
der; flows W to Aegean Sea near Ephesus; celebrated in
Homer.
Cay·u′ga (kà·ōō′gà; kà·yōō′gà; kĭ·ōō′gà; kū′gà).
1 County in New York. See Table at NEW YORK.
2 Village, ⊗ of Haldimande co., SE Ontario, Canada, 22
m. S of Hamilton; pop. 719.
Cayuga Lake. Lake in W cen. New York, chiefly in
Cayuga and Seneca cos.; one of the Finger Lakes (q.v.);
ab. 40 m. long and 2 m. average width; deepest point
ab. 435 ft.; connected at N end with Seneca Lake by
the **Cayuga and Sene·a Canal** (sĕn′ē·kà), part of
N.Y. State Barge Canal system.
Ca·zal′la de la Sier′ra (kä·thä′lyä [kä·sä′yä] thä lä
syēr′rä). Commune, Sevilla prov., SW Spain, on S slope
of the Sierra Morena 40 m. NNE of Seville; pop. 10,058;
iron and lead mining.
Caz′e·no′vi·a (kăz′′n·ō′vĭ·à). Village and resort, Madi-
son co., cen. New York, 18 m. ESE of Syracuse, pop.
2584; traditional birthplace of Hiawatha.
Cazlona. See CASTULO.
Ca·zor′la (kä·thôr′lä; -sôr′-). Commune, Jaén prov., S
Spain, 42 m. ENE of Jaén; pop. 13,031; reached peak of
importance under Moors.
Cazza. See SUŠAC.
Ceanannus. See KELLS.
Ce·a·rá′ (sâ·à·rä′). **1** State of Brazil. See Table at
BRAZIL.
2 City, its ✳. See FORTALEZA.
Ce′ba·co or **Cé′ba·co** (sā′vä·kô). Island at the entrance
to the Gulf of Montijo, S of SW Panama.
Cebenna. See CÉVENNES.
Ce′bo·ru′co (sā′vô·rōō′kô). Active volcano 7100 ft. in
Nayarit state, W Mexico, SE of city of Tepic.
Ce·bu′ (sâ·bōō′); Visayan **Sug·bu·** (sōōg·bōō′). **1** Is-
land, one of the Visayan Is., 1707 sq. m., E cen. Phil.
Is., constituting with adjacent islands a province, 1880

sq. m., pop. 1,068,078, ✳ City of Cebu; 139 m. long by ab. 20 m. wide, with mountain chain extending its entire length (highest 3324 ft.), crossed by only six passes. Touches Visayan Sea on N and Camotes Sea on E, separated from Bohol on SE by Bohol Strait, and from Negros on W by Tañon Strait. Its more important adjacent islands are Bantayan W of N end and Camotes group and Mactan on the E. Produces sugar, corn, coconuts, rice, tobacco, gold, and coal. Its inhabitants are Visayans. Chief towns Cebu. Argao, Carcar.

History: Before coming of Spaniards one of the more populous and prosperous islands; discovered Apr. 7, 1521 by Magellan (see MACTAN); occupied by Legaspi 1565; often raided by Moro pirates 16th and 17th cents.; opened to foreign trade 1863; evacuated by Spanish 1898; civil government created by U.S. 1901. Occupied by Japanese Apr. 1942; retaken by U.S. forces Mar. 1945.
2 *officially* **City of Cebu.** Chartered city, ✳ of Cebu prov., in cen. part of E coast of Cebu I.; 128 sq. m.; pop. 146,817. Oldest Spanish town in the Philippines; has excellent harbor, sheltered on E by Mactan I.; contains Santo Niño Church in front of which is the cross Magellan set up at the first Mass on the island; cathedral, old Spanish stone fort. Occupied by Legaspi 1565 and until 1571 capital of Spanish possessions in the Philippines. Seized by Japanese Apr. 18, 1942, practically destroyed May 22; recaptured by U.S. forces Mar. 27, 1945.

Cec·ca'no (chäk·kä'nö). Commune, Frosinone prov., Latium, cen. Italy, on Sacco river 5 m. S of Frosinone; pop. 15,139. Taken by American forces May 1944.

Čechy. See BOHEMIA.

Ce'cil (sē's'l). **1** County in Maryland. See *Table* at MARYLAND.
2 Locality in Cecil township (pop. 8563), Washington co., SW Pennsylvania, SW of Pittsburgh; pop. (1950) 1550.

Ce'ci·na (chä'chē·nä). Coastal commune, Livorno prov., Tuscany, cen. Italy, near mouth of **Cecina River,** 20 m. S by E of Leghorn; pop. 10,527.

Ce'dar (sē'dēr). **1** River 329 m. long flowing from SE Minnesota SE to Iowa river in Louisa co., SE Iowa.
2 River, E cen. Nebraska; rises in Garfield co., flows SE into Loup river in Nance co.
3 Name of counties in three states of the U.S. See *Tables* at IOWA, MISSOURI, NEBRASKA.

Cedar Bergen. See CEDAR MOUNTAINS.

Cedar Breaks National Monument (bräks). See UNITED STATES, *National Monuments.*

Ce'dar·burg (sē'dēr·bûrg). City, Ozaukee co., E Wisconsin, 17 m. N of Milwaukee; pop. 5191.

Cedar City. Town, Iron co., SW Utah; pop. 7543; settled 1851; iron ore deposits; Zion National Park to the S, Cedar Breaks National Monument to the E.

Cedar Creek. 1 River ab. 125 m. long, SW North Dakota; flows E into Cannonball river.
2 Small stream in Shenandoah co., N Virginia, flowing into the north fork of the Shenandoah river; battle Oct. 19, 1864 in which Union forces under Gen. Sheridan defeated the Confederates under Gen. Early.

Cedar Creek Dam *and* **Reservoir.** Dam and reservoir in Cedar Creek (branch of Salmon Falls Creek), SW Twin Falls co., SW Idaho. Cf. SALMON FALLS DAM.

Cedar Creek Peak. Mountain 7586 ft. in E Cassia co., S Idaho.

Cedar Falls. City, Black Hawk co., NE cen. Iowa, 6 m. W of Waterloo; pop. 21,195; manufactures rotary pumps, elevator equipment, concrete mixers, brooms. State College of Iowa (1876; coed.).

Cedar Grove. Town, Essex co., NE New Jersey, 6 m. SSW of Paterson; pop. 14,603.

Ce'dar·hurst' (sē'dēr·hûrst'). Residential village, Nassau co., SE New York, on Long Island 17 m. ESE of New York; pop. 6954.

Cedar Keys. Small group of islands in Gulf of Mexico, off SW coast of Levy co., NW Florida penin.

Cedar Lake. 1 Urban community (unincorporated), Lake co., NW corner of Indiana, SW of Valparaiso; pop. 5766.
2 Lake 285 sq. m., NW of Lake Winnipeg, W Manitoba, Canada; Saskatchewan river flows through it to Lake Winnipeg.

Cedar Mountain. Locality in Culpeper co., Virginia, 10 m. S of Culpeper; battle Aug. 9, 1862 in which Union forces under Gen. Banks were defeated by Gen. Ewell's Confederate troops.

Cedar Mountains; *Dutch* **Ce'der Ber'gen** (sä'der bĕr'gĕ). Range in W Cape Province, Union of South Africa; highest peak 6339 ft.

Cedar Point. 1 Point, SE Mobile co., Alabama, at W entrance to Mobile Bay.
2 Point, E St. Marys co., S Maryland, on S side of mouth of Patuxent river.
3 Tip of long narrow peninsula on Lake Erie at entrance to Sandusky Bay, Erie co., Ohio; resort.

Cedar Rapids. City, ⊗ of Linn co., E Iowa, 105 m. ENE of Des Moines; pop. 92,035; settled 1838, incorp. 1856; railroad center; manufactures prepared cereals, starch, dairy and creamery equipment; packing houses. Coe College (1851; coed.; Presbyterian).

Cedar River. See CEDAR, above.

Ce'dar·town' (sē'dēr·toun'). Industrial city, ⊗ of Polk co., NW Georgia, 17 m. S of Rome; pop. 9340.

Ce'dar·ville (sē'dēr·vil). **1** Town, Cumberland co., SW New Jersey, ab. 7 m. S of Bridgeton; pop. 1095.
2 Village, Greene co., SW cen. Ohio, NE of Xenia; pop. 1702; Cedarville College (1894; coed.).

Ceder Bergen. See CEDAR MOUNTAINS.

Ce'dros (sē'drŏs; *Span.* sä'thrŏs). Island 30 m. long in the Pacific Ocean, off the coast of Lower California.

Ce·fa·lù' (chä·fä·lōō'); *anc.* **Ceph'a·loe'di·um** (sĕf'a·lē'dĭ·ŭm). Seaport, Palermo prov., NW cen. Sicily, on Tyrrhenian Sea 37 m. E by S of Palermo; pop. 10,730; cathedral; marble quarrying. Ancient city an ally of Carthage 396 B.C.; conquered by Dionysius the Elder and later by Agathocles; taken by Moors 858 A.D.

Ceg'léd (tsĕg'lād). City, cen. Hungary, 42 m. SE of Budapest; pop. 39,203.

Ce'glie Mes·sa'pi·co (châ'lyä mâs·sä'pē·kô). Commune, Brindisi prov., Apulia, SE Italy, 22 m. W of Brindisi; pop. 20,764; castle.

Ce'he·gín' (thä'ĕ·hēn'; sä'ĕ-). Industrial and commercial commune, Murcia prov., SE Spain, 34 m. WNW of Murcia; pop. 17,316.

Cei'ba (sē'ĕ·vä; sā'vä). Municipality (pop. 9075) and town (pop. 1644), E Puerto Rico, SE of San Juan.

Ceiba, La. Seaport in Honduras. See LA CEIBA.

Celaenae. See DINAR.

Ce·la'no (chä·lä'nö). Commune, Aquila prov., Abruzzi e Molise, cen. Italy, on N shore of the former Lake Fucino 22 m. SSE of Aquila; pop. 11,653; castle.

Celano, Lake. See FUCINO.

Ce·la'ya (sä·lä'yä). City, Guanajuato state, cen. Mexico, 45 m. SE of Guanajuato; pop. 22,766; altitude 5750 ft.; railroad junction.

Cel'e·bes (sĕl'ĕ·bēz; sĕ·lē'bēz; *Du.* sĕ·lä'bĕs) *Indonesian* **Su'la·we'si** (sōō'lä·wä'sĕ). **1** Island, Indonesia, in Malay Archipelago E of Borneo, S of the Philippine Is.; lat. 1°45'N to 5°37'S, and long. 118°49' to 125°5'E; 69,255 sq. m.; including adjacent dependent islands, 72,967 sq. m., pop. 4,231,906. Formerly a division of the Outer Provinces of Neth. Indies made up of the government of Celebes and the residency of Manado (for physical features, see CELEBES, 2, below, and MANADO).

History: Probably first visited by Portuguese 1512 while developing spice trade of the Moluccas; first foreign settlement on island was by Dutch 1607 at Makassar; Manado established 1657; scene in 17th cent. of various wars bet. Dutch and native sultans; ruler of Makassar overcome 1667; wars with Buginese pirates (of S Celebes) 17th and 18th cents.; direct Dutch rule

over both N and S parts gradually established, but sultanate in SE not completely conquered until 1905. Overrun by Japanese Jan.–Feb. 1942; Manado, Kendari, and Makassar occupied; often bombed by Americans 1944–45; surrendered to Australians Sept. 1945.
2 A government (now called **South Sulawesi**) occupying S section of the island of Celebes; 38,776 sq. m.; pop. 3,093,251; ✳ Makassar; includes the two long peninsulas to the SW and SE and various adjacent islands: Butung, Muna, Tukangbesi Is., Salajar, Kabaena, etc. Mountainous, with several peaks in cen. part above 9500 ft. and one peak Rantemario 11,286 ft. in N cen. part of SW peninsula. Produces rice, copra, maize, sugar, and tobacco and many forest products (rattans, copal, dammar, etc.). For history see sense 1, above.

Celebes Sea. Part of the Pacific Ocean, ab. 420 m. from N to S and 520 m. E to W at widest parts; enclosed on N by Sulu Archipelago and Mindanao of the Phil. Is., on E by Sangihe Is., on S by Celebes, and on W by Borneo; connected with Java Sea by Makassar Strait on SW.

Celestial Empire. See CHINA.

Ce′li·ca (sā′lē·kä). Town, Loja prov., SW Ecuador, ab. 58 m. S of Machala; pop. (1944 est.) 10,904.

Ce·li′na (sē·lī′nà). **1** City and summer resort, ⊗ of Mercer co., W Ohio, on W end of Lake St. Marys; pop. 7659; manufactures furniture; canneries.
2 Town, ⊗ of Clay co., N Tennessee; pop. 1228.

Ce′lje (tsě′lyĕ); *Ger.* **Cil′li** (tsĭl′ē). Town, Slovenia, NW Yugoslavia, NE of Ljubljana; pop. 7602; thermal springs.

Cel′le (tsěl′ē). Industrial city, in Lower Saxony state, W Germany, on Aller river 22 m. NE of Hannover; pop. 25,545; 13th-cent. ducal palace; 16th-cent. town hall; 19th-cent. courthouse; manufactures include paper, printer's ink, dyes, leather, machinery, soap, cigars.

Celles (sĕl). Village, Namur prov., SE Belgium, ab. 8 m. E of Dinant; pop. 729; farthest point W reached Dec. 24–25, 1944 by German counteroffensive (Battle of the Bulge); retaken by Allies Dec. 26.

Ce′lo, Mount (sē′lō). Peak 6351 ft. in Yancey co., W North Carolina.

Celt′i·be′ri·a (sĕl′tĭ·bēr′ĭ·à). Mountainous district of ancient Spain, in NE bet. the Ebro and Tagus rivers.

Cemenelum. See CIMIEZ.

Cemetery Ridge. Low ridge extending in N and S direction S of Gettysburg, Adams co., Pennsylvania; at its N end just to the E and ab. ¼ m. S of the town are **Cemetery Hill** and **Culp's Hill** (kŭlps) where much of the fighting of the first two days of the battle of Gettysburg July 1–2, 1863 took place, partly a Confederate success; meanwhile the ridge as far S as Round Top (*q.v.*) was occupied by the center of the Federal defense and received on July 3 the Confederate assault led by Gen. Pickett, who was repulsed with loss of three fourths of his division.

Cen·chre′ae (sĕng·krē′ē; sĕng′krē·ē). Ancient town, NE coast of Peloponnesus, S Greece, on Saronic Gulf SE of Corinth; visited by Paul on second missionary journey (*Acts* xviii. 18).

Ce·nis′, Mont (môns′nē′); *Ital.* **Mon′te Ce·ni′sio** (mŏn′tä chä·nē′zyō). Alpine pass and tunnel. See ALPS.

Cen′ter (sĕn′tēr). **1** Town, Saguache co., S Colorado, 25 m. NW of Alamosa; pop. 1600.
2 Village, ⊗ of Knox co., NE Nebraska; pop. 147.
3 Village, ⊗ of Oliver co., North Dakota; pop. 476.
4 City, ⊗ of Shelby co., E Texas, 45 m. N of Lufkin; pop. 4510; lumber, brooms, mattresses; cotton gins.

Center. See also CENTRE.

Center City. Village, ⊗ of Chisago co., E Minnesota; pop. 293.

Cen′ter·dale (sĕn′tēr·dāl′). Village, Providence co., N Rhode Island, ab. 3 m. NW of Providence; pop. (est.) 2000; shopping and administrative center of North Providence.

Center Line *or* **Cen′ter·line′.** Residential city, Macomb co., SE Michigan, 11 m. N of Detroit; pop. 10,164.

Cen′ter·ville (sĕn′tēr·vĭl). **1** City, ⊗ of Bibb co., cen. Alabama; pop. 1981.
2 Village, N New Castle co., Delaware, NW of Wilmington; elevation ab. 440 ft.; highest point in state.
3 City, ⊗ of Appanoose co., S Iowa, 30 m. SW of Ottumwa; pop. 6629; coal mining.
4 Village, ⊗ of St. Joseph co., S Michigan; pop. 971.
5 Village, ⊗ of Reynolds co., SE Missouri; pop. 163.
6 Borough, Washington co., SW Pennsylvania, on Monongahela river 17 m. WNW of Uniontown; pop. 5088.
7 City, Turner co., SE South Dakota, 35 m. SSW of Sioux Falls; pop. 887; farm trade center.
8 Town, ⊗ of Hickman co., Tennessee; pop. 1678.
9 City, ⊗ of Leon co., E cen. Texas; pop. 836.
10 *or* **Cen′tre·ville** (sĕn′tēr·vĭl). Village, Fairfax co., Virginia, near field of first battle of Bull Run.

Centerville. See also CENTREVILLE.

Cen′to (chĕn′tō). Commune, Ferrara prov., Emilia, N Italy, 18 m. WSW of Ferrara; pop. 22,371.

Centorbi. See CENTURIPE.

Cen·tral′ (sän·träl′). Department of Paraguay. See *Table* at PARAGUAY.

Central Africa. The British dependencies Northern Rhodesia, Southern Rhodesia, and Nyasaland lying in the interior of S Africa; became political federation 1953; dissolved 1963.

Central African Republic. See UBANGI-SHARI.

Cen′tral America (sĕn′trăl). The S portion of North America from S boundary of Mexico to NW Colombia, South America; 228,578 sq. m.; pop. ab. 8,750,000; includes the 6 republics of Guatemala, Honduras, El Salvador, Nicaragua, Costa Rica, and Panama, and the colony of British Honduras (*qq.v.*); bordered on SW by Pacific Ocean and on NE by Caribbean Sea. By some geographers regarded as beginning at Isthmus of Tehuantepec and thus including also Quintana Roo territory and 4 states of Mexico: Yucatán, Campeche, Tabasco, and Chiapas. Its many mountains a connecting link between western North American system and the Andes; numerous volcanoes, many of them active; highest point Tajumulco volcano, W Guatemala, 13,816 ft. See MIDDLE AMERICA.

History: Atlantic coast from Honduras to Gulf of Darien skirted by Columbus 1502; first settlement 1510 on Gulf of Darien; explored by agents of Pedrarias from Panama; coast of Nicaragua explored and Lake Nicaragua discovered by Gil González de Ávila 1522; Granada and León founded by Córdoba 1523; Gulf of Honduras explored 1524 by Olid and Las Casas sent by Cortes from Mexico; Guatemala and El Salvador conquered by Alvarado 1524; organized (except for Chiapas and Panama) into Spanish captaincy general of Guatemala; independent in 1821; joined Mexico under Iturbide for brief period during 1822–23; loosely united as United Provinces of Central America 1823–39; separated into independent republics 1838–39; from 1848 control of Isthmian transit an issue bet. U.S. and Great Britain (see NICARAGUA and PANAMA); organized briefly as Greater Republic of Central America 1895–98; treaties of amity drawn up by Washington conference of Central American states 1923.

Central Asia, Soviet. Region of W Asia; before 19th cent., part ruled by Moslem khanates of Bukhara, Khiva, and Kokand, and rest inhabited by uncontrolled and warlike nomad Turkmen tribes who were subdued by Russians under Alexander II 1865 when Russian province of Turkistan was constituted, khanates being subdued later (Bukhara 1868, Khiva 1873, and Kokand 1875); Turkmen tribes broken by battle of Geok Tepe 1881; after Russian Revolution, reorganized as Uzbek, Turkmen, Tadzhik, Kazakh, and Kirgiz Soviet Socialist Republics (in U.S.S.R.); total area 1,508,445 sq. m.; pop. (1939) 16,626,760, (1941 est.) 17,471,466.

Central Australia. A territory of Australia 1927–31, 20th to 26th parallels of S lat., in cen. part of continent;

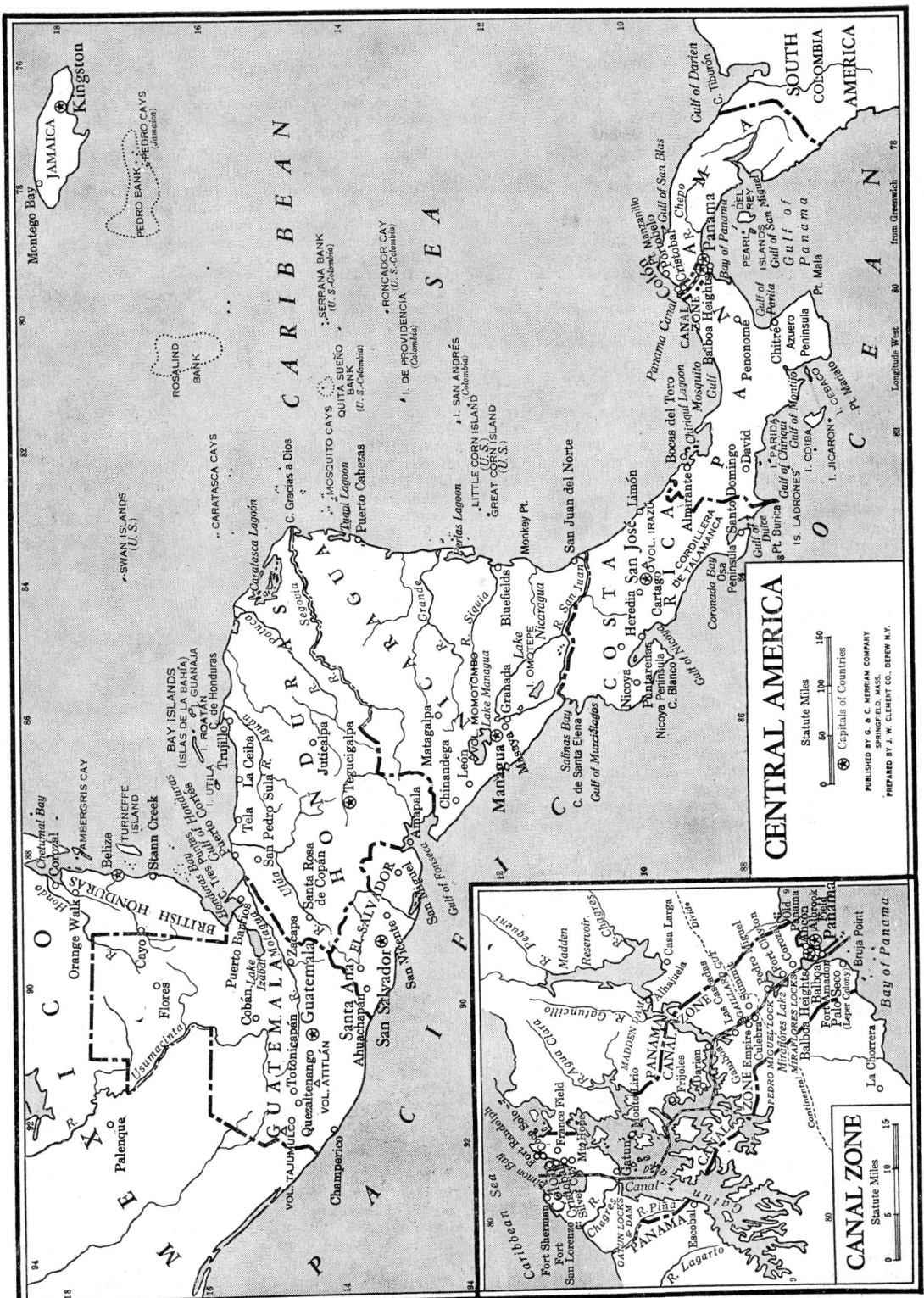

CENTRAL AMERICA

Statute Miles

⊛ Capitals of Countries

PUBLISHED BY G. & C. MERRIAM COMPANY
SPRINGFIELD, MASS.
PREPARED BY J. W. CLEMENT CO. DEPEW N.Y.

CANAL ZONE

Statute Miles

* Stuart (now known as Alice Springs, *q.v.*); formerly S part of Northern Territory; in 1931 restored.

Central Black Earth Area; *also* **Cher·no·zem′ Area** (chĭr·nŭ·zyôm′). Former subdivision (estab. 1928) of Soviet Russia, Europe in SW part; 74 112 sq. m.; * Voronezh; divided into several regions 1936.

Central City. 1 Town, ⊗ of Gilpin co., N cen. Colorado; pop. 250; center of gold-mining region.
2 Village, Marion co., S cen. Illinois, suburb of Centralia; pop. 1422; nurseries.
3 City, Muhlenberg co., W Kentucky, 32 m. S of Owensboro; pop. 3694; railroad center.
4 City, ⊗ of Merrick co., E cen. Nebraska, on Platte river 23 m. ENE of Grand Island; pop. 2406; railroad junction. Nebraska Central College (1899; coed.).
5 Borough, Somerset co., S Pennsylvania, 18 m. SSE of Johnstown; pop. 1604.

Central Division. Former division, cen. Bombay prov., W India; 37,296 sq. m.; pop. (1941) 8,197,393.

Central Europe. Indefinite and occasional term applied to the countries of the central part of Europe, approximately those bet. the Baltic Sea on N and Alps on S and bet. Russia on E and North Sea and France on W. Apparently first used in political sense (**Mit′tel·eu·ro′pa** [mĭt′ĕl·oi·rō′pä], that is, **Middle Europe**) by Georg Friedrich List c. 1840 to denote Germany, Austro-Hungary, Switzerland, and the Low Countries; in recent use extended to include also Poland and Romania, but usually not the Baltic and Balkan States; by some in period following World War I made equivalent to the Little Entente (Czechoslovakia, Romania, and Yugoslavia).

Central Falls. Industrial city, Providence co., N Rhode Island, on Blackstone river just N of Pawtucket; pop. 19,858; textiles, glass (electric-light bulbs).

Central Greece and Eu·boe′a (û·bē′à). Geographical division of Greece; includes island of Euboea, the Northern Sporades, and cen. part of Greek mainland; 9651 sq. m.; pop. (1938 est.) 1,799,169; comprises departments of Aetolia and Acarnania, Attica and Boeotia, Euboea, and Phthiotis and Phocis (see *Table* at GREECE).

Cen·tra′lia (sĕn·trāl′yà; -trā′lĭ·à). **1** City, Clinton and Marion cos., SW cen. Illinois, 58 m. E of East St. Louis; pop. 13,904; founded 1853, incorp. 1859; coal, iron, oil.
2 City, Boone co., cen. Missouri, 22 m. NNE of Columbia; pop. 3200; coal deposits nearby.
3 Borough, Columbia co., E cen. Pennsylvania, 12 m. NNW of Pottsville; pop. 1435; iron and coal mining.
4 City, Lewis co., SW Washington, 23 m. S of Olympia; pop. 8586; one community with its sister city, Chehalis.

Central India Agency *or* **Central India.** Formerly, a group of Indian states under supervision of a British political agent, bet. 21° and 26°N and 74° and 83°E; 52,047 sq. m.; pop. (1941) 7,506,427; * Indore; comprised 89 states, most important: Indore, Bhopal, and Rewa; bulk of population Hindu. Since Aug. 15, 1947 all have affiliated with the Indian Union.

Central Java. See MIDDLE JAVA.

Central Karroo. See KARROO.

Central Province. 1 Province, S cen. Ceylon; 2290 sq. m.; pop. 953,388; * Kandy; mountainous terrain with highest peak on the island Pidurutalagala 8294 ft.; source of the Mahaweli; tea culture.
2 Province, S cen. Kenya colony, E Africa; * Nairobi.
3 Province, cen. Tanganyika, E Africa; 37,497 sq. m.; pop. 582,442.

Central Provinces and Be·rar′ (bà·rär′). Former province, cen. Indian Union, * Nagpur; consisted of **Central Provinces**, 80,766 sq. m., and **Berar**, 17,809 sq. m.; reorganized 1950 and renamed **Ma′dhya Pra·desh′** (mŭ′dyà prà·dāsh′), * Bhopal, 24,600 sq. m., pop. (1951) 3,577,431. Indian states formerly a part of this province assigned 1937–47 to Central India Agency and Eastern States Agency. Lies partly in Vindhya Mts. and Satpura Range, and in valleys of Narbada,

Tapti, and N tributaries of Godavari rivers; has several distinct plateau regions. Principal crops cotton, rice, wheat. Peopled chiefly by Hindus, but also by members of aboriginal and old Dravidian races, esp. Gonds.

History: Territory in Central Provinces conquered by Marathas in 18th cent. and ruled from Nagpur (*q.v.*); taken for British by Dalhousie under doctrine of lapse 1853; Berar (*q.v.*) transferred to Central Provinces 1903; constituted an autonomous province 1937. *Chief cities:* Indore, Jubbulpore, Bhopal, Raipur.

Central Range; *Russ.* **Sre·din′ny Khre·bet′** (sryi-dyē′nĭ κryĭ·byĕt′). Mountain range extending the length of Kamchatka Penin., Khabarovsk Territory, Soviet Russia, Asia; average height 3000 ft.; highest Ichinskaya Sopka 11,834 ft.

Central Valley. Valley of Sacramento and San Joaquin rivers (*qq.v.*) in California, bet. Sierra Nevada and Coast Ranges; over 400 m. long, 20–50 m. wide.

Cen′tre (sĕn′tĕr). **1** County in Pennsylvania. See *Table* at PENNSYLVANIA.
2 Town, ⊗ of Cherokee co., NE Alabama; pop. 2392.

Centre. See CENTER.

Cen′tre·ville (sĕn′tĕr·vĭl). **1** City, St. Clair co., SW Illinois, SE of St. Louis, Missouri; pop. 12,769.
2 Town, ⊗ of Queen Annes co., E Maryland; pop. 1863.

Centreville. See also CENTERVILLE.

Centum Cellae. See CIVITAVECCHIA.

Cen·tu′ri·pe (chän·tōō′rĕ·pà); *earlier* **Cen·tor′bi** (chän·tôr′bĕ); *anc.* **Cen·tu′ri·pa** (sĕn·tūr′ĭ·pà). Commune, Enna prov., cen. Sicily, 28 m. E by N of Enna; pop. 10,802; sulfur; marble; soda; destroyed by Frederick II 1233; rebuilt 1548.

Ceos. See KEOS.

Cephaloedium. See CEFALÙ.

Ceph′a·lo′ni·a (sĕf′à·lō′nĭ·à; -lōn′yà); *Gr.* **Ke′phal·lē·ni′a** (kyâ′fä·lyĕ·nyē′ä); *anc.* **Ceph′al·le′ni·a** (sĕf′à·lĕ′nĭ·à; -lēn′yà). One of Ionian Is. in Ionian Sea off W coast of Greece; 277 sq. m.; pop. 57,578; with Ithaca forms Cephalonia dept. (see *Table* at GREECE). Chief town Argostolion on inlet on SW coast. Mountainous, highest point ab. 5300 ft. Seized by Romans 189 B.C.; British 1809–64, Greek since 1864.

Ce·phi′sus (sĕ·fī′sŭs) *or* **Ce·phis′sus** (sĕ·fĭs′ŭs). **1** River in Attica and Boeotia dept. in cen. Greece, flowing from Mt. Pentelikon S into the Saronic Gulf, passing to W of Athens.
2 River ab. 60 m. long, cen. Greece; rises in Phthiotis and Phocis dept., near Mt. Oeta, flows E through W Attica and Boeotia dept. to site of former Lake Copais (*q.v.*).

Ce·pra′no (chā·prä′nō). Commune, Frosinone prov., SE Latium, cen. Italy; pop. 7570; nearby are the ruins of ancient Fregellae (*q.v.*).

Ce′ram (sī′räm). Large island, cen. Moluccas, Indonesia; 6621 sq. m.; pop. ab. 83,000. Chief settlements Bula and Piru. Has many mountains (highest 10,023 ft.), small islands in Manipa Strait off W end and the Gorong group to SE, dense tropical forests. Came under nominal Dutch control about 1650.

Ceram Sea. Section of W Pacific Ocean ab. 250 m. long by 80 m. wide in cen. Moluccas, Indonesia; bet. Buru and Ceram Is. to S, Sula Is. to W, Obi island group to N, and Misoöl I. to E.

Cerasus. See GÍRESUN.

Ce·rau′ni·an Mountains (sĕ·rô′nĭ·ăn; -rôn′yăn). Mountain range along coast of NW Epirus, NW Greece; highest peak ab. 6300 ft. See ACROCERAUNIA.

Cercina. See KERKENNAH ISLANDS.

Cer′dagne′ (sĕr′dàn′y); *Span.* **Cer·da′ña** (thĕr·thä′nyä; sĕr-). Old division of Europe in the E Pyrenees, partly in France and partly in Spain.

Ce·re′a (chā·rā′à). Commune, Verona prov., Venezia Euganea, NE Italy, 19 m. SSE of Verona; pop. 10,343.

Ce′res (sĭr′ēz; sē′rēz). Town, SW Cape Province, S Union of South Africa, 63 m. ENE of Cape Town; pop. 3571; health resort with dry and bracing climate.

Ceresio, Lago; Ceresius, Lacus. See Lake LUGANO.

Ce·re·so'le Al'ba (chä·rā·zō'lä äl'bä). Commune, Cuneo prov., Piedmont, NW Italy; pop. 2145; battle Apr. 14. 1544 in which French were defeated by imperial forces of Charles V.

Ce·ri·gno'la (chä·rē·nyō'lä). Commune, Foggia prov., Apulia, SE Italy, 22 m. SE of Foggia; pop. 39,540; manufactures linen; college; defeat of French by Spanish 1503.

Ce'ri·go (chā'rē·gō); *Gr.* **Ký'thē·ra** (kyē'thē·rä); *Lat.* **Cy·the'ra** (sĭ·thēr'à). Southernmost of the Ionian Is. in the Mediterranean Sea off SE coast of Peloponnesus ab. 8 m. S of Cape Malea; 110 sq. m.; pop. 9092; ✳ Kýthēra; in department of Argolis and Corinth, Greece. Rocky, but with fertile districts. In antiquity had temple of Aphrodite (Cytherea) who according to one legend emerged here from the sea. See PAPHOS.

Cer'na (chĕr'nä). = CRNA.

Cernăuţi. See CHERNOVTSY.

Cer'na–Vo'dă *or* **Cer'na·vo'da** (chĕr'nä·vô'dà). Commercial port, Dobruja, SE Romania, on the Danube WNW of Constanţa; pop. 6461; occupied Oct. 25, 1916 by Bulgarian-German forces.

Cer·ral'vo (sĕr·räl'vô). Small island off the SE coast of Lower California, at the mouth of the Gulf of California.

Cer·re'do, Tor're de (tôr'rĕ thä ther·rĕ'thô [sĕr-]); *or* **Cerredo, Pe'ña de** (pā'nyä). Highest peak 8787 ft. in the Cantabrian Mts., W Santander prov., N Spain.

Cer·ri'tos (sĕr·rē'tôs). Town, San Luis Potosí state, cen. Mexico, 48 m. NE of San Luis Potosí; pop. 6980.

Cer'ro de las Me'sas (sĕr'rô thä läz mā'säs). Village, Veracruz state, E Mexico, SE of Veracruz; archaeological site, jades found here 1941.

Cer'ro del A·zu'fre (sĕr'rô thĕl ä·sōō'frä). See COPIAPÓ.

Cer'ro de Pas'co (sĕr'rô thä päs'kô). **1** Mountain 15,100 ft. in Junín dept., cen. Peru; copper mines.

2 Mining town, ✳ of Pasco dept., cen. Peru, ab. 112 m. NE of Lima; formerly ✳ of Junín dept.; pop. (1940 est.) 19,187; altitude 14,208 ft.; in one of the most famous copper, silver, and gold-mining districts.

Cer'ro de Pun'ta (sĕr'rô thä pōōn'tä). Peak 4398 ft. in cen. Puerto Rico, in E Cordillera Central; highest mountain in Puerto Rico.

Cer'ro Gor'do (sĕr'ô gôr'dō). **1** County in Iowa. See *Table* at IOWA.

2 (*Span.* sĕr'rô gôr'thô) Mountain pass bet. Veracruz and Jalapa, E Mexico; battle Apr. 18, 1847 in which Americans under Gen. Scott defeated Mexicans.

Cer'ro Lar'go (sĕr'rô lär'gô). Department of Uruguay. See *Table* at URUGUAY.

Cer'ro Pal·pa'na (sĕr'rô päl·pä'nä). Peak 19,833 ft. in N Chile, near Bolivian border.

Cer·tal'do (chär·täl'dô). Commune, Firenze prov., Tuscany, cen. Italy, 18 m. SW of Florence; pop. 12,094; castle; home of Boccaccio.

Cer·van'tes (sĕr·vän'tâs). Municipality, E Ilocos Sur prov., Luzon, Phil. Is., on left bank of Abra river; pop. 7155.

Cerveteri. See CAERE.

Cer'via (chĕr'vyä). Commune, Ravenna prov., Emilia, N Italy, on Adriatic 14 m. SSE of Ravenna; pop. 12,319; cathedral; saltworks; sea bathing.

Cervin, Mont. See MATTERHORN.

Ce·sa'no Ma·der'no (chä·zä'nô mä·dĕr'nô). Commune, Milano prov., Lombardy, N Italy, 9 m. N of Milan; pop. (1931) 11,448.

Ce·se'na (chä·zā'nä); *anc.* **Cae·se'na** (sĕ·zē'nà). Commune, Forlì prov., Emilia, N Italy, 12 m. SE of Forlì; pop. 61,314; episcopal see (one of the oldest in Italy); citadel; library (founded 1452); produces sulfur, sugar, wine, hemp, silk, vegetables. Withstood attack by Albornoz 1357; pillaged 1377; under the Malatestas 1385–1465; taken by Cesare Borgia during his campaign 1499–1501 in Romagna and became part of the papal domain; captured by British forces Oct. 1944.

Ce·se·na'ti·co (chä·zä·nä'tē·kô). Commune, Forlì prov., Emilia, N Italy, on Adriatic 18 m. E of Forlì; pop. 11,646; fisheries; sea bathing.

Cēsis. See TSESIS.

Čes'ká Lí'pa (chĕs'kä lē'pà); *Ger.* **Böh'misch–Lei'pa** (bû'mĭsh·lī'pä). Town, N Bohemia prov., W Czechoslovakia, 40 m. N of Prague; pop. (1930) 14,230; manufacturing center.

Čes'ké Bu'dě·jo'vi·ce (chĕs'kä bōō'dyĕ·yô'vĭ·tsĕ); *Ger.* **Bud'weis** (bŏŏt'vīs). City, S Bohemia prov. W Czechoslovakia, on Vltava river 75 m. S of Prague; pop. (1930) 43,788; varied manufactures; breweries; cathedral.

Čes'ko·slo'ven·ská Re'pu·bli'ka (chĕs'kô·slô'vĕn·skä rĕ'pŏŏ·blī'kà) *or* **Čes'ko·slo'ven·sko** (-skô). = CZECHOSLOVAKIA.

Čes'ký–Brod (chĕs'kē·brôt'); *Ger.* **Böh'misch–Brod** (bû'mĭsh·brôt'). Town, cen. Bohemia, Czechoslovakia, 19 m. E of Prague; pop. (1921) 4460; battle May 30, 1434 in which Hussite leader, Andrew Procop, was killed.

Český Les. See BOHEMIAN FOREST.

Český Těšín. Var. of TĚŠÍN ČESKÝ.

Cess (sĕs). River in Liberia.

Cess'nock (sĕs'nŏk). Town, E New South Wales, SE Australia, 25 m. W of Newcastle; pop. 14,387.

Ce·ta'tea Al'bă (chĕ·tä'tyä äl'bà). **1** Former department, S Bessarabia, Romania; 2932 sq. m.; pop. 340,459. **2** City, its ✳, now in Izmail Region, SW Ukraine, U.S.S.R. See BELGOROD-DNESTROVSKI.

Ce'ti·nje (tsĕ'tĕ·nyĕ). Town, Montenegro (✳ of Montenegro until after World War II), Yugoslavia; in mountainous region 19 m. SE of Kotor; pop. 6366. Founded in latter part of 15th cent. by Montenegrin king, Ivan the Black; several times sacked and burned by Turkish invaders; contains tombs of Montenegrin rulers; 1929–45 capital of Zetska co.

Cette. See SÈTE.

Ceu'ta (thä'ŏō·tä; sä'ŏō·tä). Seaport and Spanish presidio, N Morocco, at E end of Strait of Gibraltar opp. Gibraltar; pop. 56,909; belongs to Spanish province of Cádiz. Long a flourishing trading town under the Arabs; taken by Portuguese 1415; became Spanish 1580. See PILLARS OF HERCULES.

Cé'vennes' (sā'vĕn'); *anc.* **Ce·ben'na** (sĕ·bĕn'à). **1** Mountain range in S France extending NE and SW, W of the Rhone, from N Ardèche dept. to SW Hérault dept.; highest peak Mt. Mézenc 5753 ft. **2** Old district, France, NE part of Languedoc, comprising the region of the Cévennes Mts.; ✳ Mende. Inhabitants known as Cevenoles; refuge of Protestants in time of crusade against the Albigenses 13th cent.; also scene 1702 of uprising of Camisards in religious wars following the Edict of Nantes (1685).

Cey·han' (jä·hän'). **1** *formerly* **Ji·hun'** (jĭ·hōōn'); *anc.* **Pyr'a·mus** (pĭr'à·mŭs). River ab. 230 m. long in E Asia Minor, flowing from the Anti-Taurus Mts. S and SSW through Cilicia into Gulf of İskenderon. **2** Town, Seyhan vilayet, S Turkey in Asia, on Ceyhan river and on railroad 25 m. E of Adana; pop. 9978.

Cey·lon' (sĕ·lŏn'); *anc.* **Ser'en·dib** (sĕr'ĕn·dĭb; *Arab.* sŭ·rŏn·dēb'); *Lat. and Gr.* **Ta·prob'a·ne** (tà·prŏb'à·nē). Called "Pearl of the Orient." Dominion in the British Commonwealth of Nations; island, ab. 270 m. long and up to ab. 140 m. wide; 25,332 sq. m.; pop. 8,103,648, (1957 est.) 9,172,042; divided into 9 provinces; ✳ Colombo. In Indian Ocean, S of India, with which it is connected by Adam's Bridge, a chain of shoals which divides Palk Strait on N from Gulf of Mannar on S; highest point Pidurutalagala 8294 ft. Rich in tropical vegetation; chief products tea, rubber, coconuts, pearls. Chief cities Colombo, Kandy, Galle, Jaffna, Trincomalee. Original inhabitants were Veddas and Sinhalese; became center of Buddhist civilization 3d cent. B.C. with capital at Anuradhapura (now ruins); first settled by Portuguese 1505, Dutch 1658, English 1796; made crown

colony 1833; in World War II bombed by Japanese airplanes Apr. 4 and 9, 1942; granted dominion status Feb. 4, 1948.

Cha'blais' (shä'blē'). Ancient region of Savoy; ✻ Thonon; now part of Haute-Savoie dept., E France, S of Lake Geneva; gained by counts of Savoy 11th cent.; became Calvinist 1535; won back 1594–98 to Catholicism by Saint Francis of Sales; part of France 1860.

Cha'blis' (shä'blē'; *Angl.* shăb'lē). Commune, Yonne dept., NE cen. France, ab. 11 m. E of Auxerre; pop. 1935; region produces white Burgundy wines.

Cha'ca·bu'co (chä'kä·vōō'kō). **1** Town, Buenos Aires prov., E Argentina, ab. 120 m. E of Buenos Aires; pop. ab. 15,000; in center of important agricultural district.
2 Village just N of Santiago, cen. Chile; scene of battle Feb. 12, 1817 in which San Martín with O'Higgins defeated the Spanish royalists.

Cha·ca'o Channel (chä·kä'ō). Strait bet. N Chiloé I. and the mainland of S cen. Chile, connecting the·Gulf of Ancud with the Pacific Ocean.

Chachak. See ČAČAK.

Cha·cha'ni (chä·chä'nē). Peak ab. 20,000 ft. in Arequipa dept., S Peru; meteorological station.

Cha'cha·po'yas (chä'chä·pō'yäs). Town, ✻ of Amazonas dept., N Peru, ab. 160 m. NE of Trujillo; pop. (1940 est.) 5494; altitude 7600 ft.; industrial center.

Cha'choeng'sao' or **Cha'xerng'sao'** (chä'chŭng'-sou'). **1** Province, S Thailand; 2182 sq. m.; pop. 201,175.
2 Town, its ✻, on railroad 40 m. E of Bangkok.

Cha'co (chä'kō); *Span.* **Cha'co** (chä'kō) or **El Chaco** (ĕl) or **Gran Chaco** (grän). **1** Region, S cen. South America; ab. 248,000 sq. m.; thinly populated, swampy, drained by Paraguay river and its chief W tributaries the Pilcomayo and Bermejo; principal divisions: (1) **Chaco Bo're·al'** (vō'rä·äl'). Main part of region, in fork of the Paraguay and Pilcomayo; its ownership a matter of dispute bet. Bolivia and Paraguay for 86 years, and a cause of war bet. them 1932–35; by peace treaty (signed at Buenos Aires July 21, 1938, effective Aug. 29) larger central and E part (95,313 sq. m.) to Paraguay, smaller W part (ab. 46,561 sq. m.) to Bolivia. Paraguayan region divided administratively into 3 departments; Bolivian region attached to Tarija dept. (2) **Chaco Cen·tral'** (sän·träl'). Part of the Chaco in N Argentina bet. the Pilcomayo and Bermejo rivers; ab. 40,000 sq. m.; comprises Formosa territory (27,825 sq. m.) and N part of Salta prov. (ab. 12,000 sq. m.). (3) **Chaco Aus·tral'** (ous·träl'). S part of Chaco in N Argentina S of Bermejo river; ab. 66,000 sq. m.; coextensive with NE part of Santiago del Estero prov., cen. part of Salta prov., and territory of Chaco (see 2, below).
2 Territory in Argentina. See *Table* at ARGENTINA.

Cha'co Canyon National Monument (chä'kō). See UNITED STATES, *National Monuments*.

Chad (chăd), *officially* **Tchad** (*Fr.* chåd). Republic, N cen. Africa; area 495,600 sq. m.; pop. 2,580,000; ✻ Fort-Lamy. Comprises much desert area; mountains of Tibesti (highest over 11,000 ft.) and Ennedi in N, Bodele depression in NW, and Lake Chad and marshy region on W border; S part well forested; chief river the Chari; raises much livestock; exports ivory and palm oil. Contains former native kingdoms of Kanem, Wadai, and Baguirmi. Chief towns Fort-Lamy, Abéché, Bokoro. Formerly a French military territory, part of Ubangi-Shari-Chad; in 1920 made a separate colony; became a republic in French Community Nov. 28, 1958.

Chad, Lake. Lake in NW cen. Africa, at junction of boundaries of former Fr. West Africa and Fr. Equatorial Africa, and NE Nigeria; fed by Chari river from S and by numerous other streams; has no outlet but remains fresh; its shrinking area varies greatly, often being only half its maximum of ab. 10,000 sq. m.; ab. 3 ft. deep in NW, 15 ft. in S where it is navigable. First explored by Denham, Oudney, and Clapperton 1823. See FRENCH EQUATORIAL AFRICA.

Chad'bourn (chăd'bẽrn). Town, Columbus co., S North Carolina, 52 m. W of Wilmington; pop. 2325.

Chad'der·ton (chăd'ẽr·t'n; -tŭn). Urban district, Lancashire, NW England, suburb of Oldham, on the Irk 8 m. NE of Manchester; pop. 31,114; cotton mills.

Chadds Ford (chădz' fôrd'). Village, Delaware co., Pennsylvania, on Brandywine creek; originally Chad's Ford, a crossing of the Brandywine, where the main action of the battle of Sept. 11, 1777 was fought.

Cha'di·le'o (chä'thē·lā'ō). Name given to lower course of Río Salado, La Pampa territory, S cen. Argentina.

Chad'ron (shăd'rŭn). City, ⊗ of Dawes co., NW Nebraska, 50 m. N of Alliance; pop. 5079; livestock raising. Nebraska State Coll. (1911; coed.).

Chad'wicks (chăd'wĭks). Village, Oneida co., cen. New York, ab. 9 m. SW of Utica.

Chaer'o·ne'a (kĕr'ō·nē'ȧ; kẽr'ō-) or **Chaer'o·nei'a** (-nī'ȧ). Ancient city, now in ruins, of W Boeotia, E cen. Greece, SE of Mt. Parnassus and near Orchomenus; scene of victory of Philip of Macedon 338 B.C. over a confederation of Greek states, and of the defeat of Mithridates VI by Sulla 86 B.C.

Cha'fa·ri'nas (chä'fä·rē'näs), or **Zaf'a·rin** (zăf'ȧ·rĭn), **Islands.** Island group in the Mediterranean Sea off N end of Morocco, near Melilla; pop. ab. 320.

Chaf'fee. 1 (chă'fē). County in Colorado. See *Table* at COLORADO.
2 (chăf'ē'). City, Scott co., SE Missouri, 12 m. SW of Cape Girardeau; pop. 2862; trade center in agricultural section.

Cha'gai (chä'gī). District, NW Baluchistan, Pakistan; 19,429 sq. m.; pop. (1941) 29,250; mountainous and desert region; annexed in 1896.

Chagai Hills. Range, highest 8061 ft., extending E and W along Afghan boundary of Chagai dist., Pakistan.

Cha'gos Islands (chä'gōs). Group of British islands in Indian Ocean S of Maldive Is.; part of British Indian Ocean Territory; 76 sq. m.; pop. ab. 1000; chief island Diego Garcia.

Chag'res (chăg'rĕs; *Span.* chä'grās). River in Panama and the Canal Zone; rises in cen. Panama E of the Canal Zone, flows SW into Gatun Lake, and drains NW out of Gatun Lake into the Caribbean Sea.

Cha·grin' Falls (shȧ·grĭn'; *locally also* shŏŏg'rĭn, shăg'-rĭn). Residential village, Cuyahoga co., N Ohio, 15 m. ESE of Cleveland; pop. 3458.

Cha'gua·ra'mas (chä'gwä·rä'mäs). Tract of land, NW Trinidad, West Indies Federation, on **Chaguaramas Bay,** inlet of the Gulf of Paria, WNW of Port of Spain; site of U.S. naval base, leased 1940.

Cha'har' (chä'här'). Former province, E Inner Mongolia, N China; ✻ Wanchuan (Kalgan); bounded NW and N by Outer Mongolia, on E by Jehol and Manchuria, on S by Hopeh and Shansi provs. of China, and on SW and W by Suiyuan. Taken from Japanese 1935; after end of World War II came under control of Chinese Communists. Partitioned 1952 among other provinces.

Chah·bar' or **Char·bar'** (chä·bär'). Seaport, Makran, SE Iran, on coast of Gulf of Oman at S end of E Iranian highway from Meshed.

Chai·ba'sa (chī·bä'sä). See SINGHBHUM.

Chai·nat or **Jai·nat** (chī·nät). **1** Province, SW cen. Thailand; 1084 sq. m.; pop. 152,236.
2 Town, its ✻, 35 m. S of Nakhon Sawan.

Chain Island. See ANAA ISLAND.

Chai·ya·phum or **Ja·ya·bum** (chī·yä·p'hoom). **1** Province, N Thailand; 2930 sq. m.; pop. 237,465.
2 Village, its ✻, 90 m. SE of Chiang Rai.

Cha'ke Cha'ke (chä'kĕ chä'kĕ). Town, ✻ of Pemba I., Zanzibar colony, E Africa.

Cha·kra'ta (chȧ·krä'tȧ). Town and hill station, N Uttar Pradesh, N India; pop. 1374 (in hot weather pop. c. 6000); at 7000 ft. overlooking Jumna valley.

Chalantun. See YALU.

Cha'la·te·nan'go (chä'lä·tā·näng'gō). **1** Department,

NW El Salvador; 1292 sq. m.; pop. (1942 est.) 112,939.

2 Town, its ✱; pop. (1939 est.) 10,017.

Chal'ce·don (kăl'sĕ·dŏn; -dŭn; kăl·sē'd'n), *better* **Chal'-che·don** (kăl'kĕ·dŏn; -dŭn; kăl·kē'd'n). See KADIKÖY.

Chal'chi·co·mu'la (chäl'chē·kŏ·moo'lä). Village, Puebla state, SE cen. Mexico, at foot of Mt. Citlaltepetl.

Chal·chua'pa (chäl·chwä'pä). City, Santa Ana dept., W El Salvador, near Santa Ana; pop. (1942 est.) 9626.

Chal·ci'di·ce (kăl·sĭd'ĭ·sē); *Gr.* **Khal'ki·di·kē'** (käl'-kyĕ·thĕ·kyē'). **1** Peninsula of E Macedonia, NE Greece, projecting SE into N Aegean Sea bet. Strymonic Gulf on E and Gulf of Salonika on W; terminates in three long peninsulas: (from E to W) Acte, Sithonia, and Pallene (*qq.v.*). In N part at its base are Lakes Bolbē and Lankada and the city of Salonika. See ATHOS.

2 Department of Greece. See *Table* at GREECE.

Chal'cis (kăl'sĭs) *or* **Chal'kis** (käl'kĭs); *also called* **Ev'ri·pos** (ăv'rē·pŏs) *or* **Neg'ro·pont** (nĕg'rŏ·pŏnt); *Gr.* **Khal·kis'** (käl·kyēs'). City, ✱ of Euboea dept., Greece, on Euboea I. on Evripos strait; pop. 17,297; important as early as 7th cent. B.C.; founded many cities in Macedonia, Italy, Sicily; invasion point for campaigns against Greece. Aristotle died here. See ERETRIA.

Chal'co (chäl'kŏ). Lake in cen. Mexico, ab. 25 m. SE of Mexico City; alt. 7480 ft.

Chal·de'a (kăl·dē'à), *also* **Chal·dae'a** (-dē'à). Ancient region on the Euphrates river and the Persian Gulf, Asia; originally the S part of Babylonia. Frequently, and esp. in Biblical use (*Gen.* xi. 28; *Dan.* ix. 1), equivalent to Babylonia (*q.v.*) after it was occupied by the Chaldeans, a Semitic people from the S who had attacked it since 11th cent. B.C. and finally secured throne under Nabopolassar 625 B.C.; with Medes, brought about fall of Assyrian Empire 612 B.C.; while ruled by Nebuchadnezzar II, subdued Judaea, and captured Jerusalem 597 and 586 B.C.; Chaldean (or Neo-Babylonian) Empire fell when Persians captured Babylon 539 B.C.

Chal'di·ran' (chäl'dĭ·rän') *or* **Chal·dran'** (chäl·drän'). Town in Armenia, S of Kars; battle Aug. 23, 1514 in which Selim I, Ottoman sultan, defeated Persians.

Cha·leur' Bay (shà·loor'; -lûr'); *Fr.* **Baie de Cha·leur'** (bäd' shà'lûr'). Inlet ab. 85 m. long of W Gulf of St. Lawrence, SE Canada, extending bet. N New Brunswick and the Gaspé Penin. in SE Quebec prov.; receives the Restigouche river; famous as a fishing ground, esp. for salmon. Discovered 1535 by Cartier.

Chalkar Tengis. Var. of CHELKAR TENGIZ.

Chalkis. See CHALCIS.

Chalk River (chôk). Village near Ottawa river, 20 m. NW of Pembroke, SE Ontario, Canada; atomic pile set up by Canadian government here during World War II.

Chal'lis (chăl'ĭs). Village, ⊗ of Custer co., cen. Idaho; pop. 732.

Chal·mette' National Historical Park (shăl·mĕt'). See UNITED STATES, *National Historical Parks.*

Châ'lons'–sur–Marne' (shä'lôN'sür·màrn'). Commune, ✱ of Marne dept., NE France, on Marne river 99 m. E of Paris; pop. 35,530; cathedral, restored under Louis XIV; 12th-cent. Romanesque church; manufactures woolens, cotton goods, leather. Chief town of the ancient Catalauni; fortified by Romans; early center of Christianity 250; on plains to the S (Catalaunian Plains) Attila defeated by Aëtius 451 A.D.; united to France 1360; captured by Germans 1870.

Cha'lon'–sur–Saône' (shä'lôN'sür·sōn'); *anc.* **Cab'il·lo'num** (kăb'ĭ·lŏ'nŭm). Manufacturing city, Saône-et-Loire dept., E cen. France, on Saône river 35 m. N of Mâcon; pop. 33,201; 17th-cent. Gothic cathedral; 14th-cent. church; 15th-cent. episcopal palace.

Chaltel. See FITZ ROY.

Chama. See RIO CHAMA.

Cha'ma·lha'ri (chä'mä·hlä'rē). Var. of CHOMO LHARI.

Cha'man (chŭ'mŭn). Town, W Baluchistan, Pakistan, 60 m. NW of Quetta on Afghanistan border; railroad terminus; on highway over **Chaman Pass.**

Cha'mar·tín' de la Ro'sa (chä'mär·tēn' dä lä rrô'sä). Commune, Madrid prov., cen. Spain, NNE suburb of Madrid; pop. 64,485.

Cham'ba (chŭm'bà). **1** Former Indian state, N Punjab, NW India; area 3127 sq. m.; pop. (1941) 168,908; in mountainous country, enclosed on N and W by Kashmir. Founded in 6th cent. A.D.; nominally subject to Mogul Empire; came under British influence 1846.

2 Town, its ✱, on gorge of upper Ravi river; pop. 6219.

Cham'bal (chŭm'bŭl). Unnavigable river 650 m. long, cen. India; rises in W Vindhya Mts. near Indore and flows NE, E, and SE into the Jumna W of Cawnpore.

Cham'ber·lain (chām'bēr·lĭn). City, ⊗ of Brule co., S South Dakota, on Missouri river 10 m. N of its confluence with White river; pop. 2598; stock raising.

Chamberlain Lake. Lake in N Piscataquis co., N cen. Maine.

Cham'bers (chām'bērz). **1** Island in Green Bay, NE Wisconsin, in Door co.

2 Name of counties in two states of the U.S. See *Tables* at ALABAMA and TEXAS.

Cham'bers·burg (chām'bērz·bûrg). Industrial borough, ⊗ of Franklin co., S Pennsylvania, 50 m. WSW of Harrisburg; pop. 17,670; settled 1730; burned by Confederates 1864. Limestone, freestone, marble quarries. Wilson College (1869; women).

Cham'bé·ry' (shäN'bā'rē'); *Lat.* **Cam'be·ri'a·cum** (kăm'bĕ·rĭ'à·kŭm). Commercial and manufacturing city, ✱ of Savoie dept., E France, 54 m. E of Lyons; pop. 28,073; cathedral.

Cham'bey'ron', Ai'guille' de (ä'gü·ē'y' dĕ shäN'bā'-rôN'). Mountain 11,155 ft. in the Cottian Alps, Basses-Alpes dept., SE France.

Cham·be'zi (chăm·bē'zĭ; chäm·bä'zĕ). A headstream of the Congo river, Africa; rises in N Zambia, flows SW, forms multiple channel in swamp S of Lake Bangweulu from which it emerges as the Luapula.

Cham'blee (chăm'blē). City, De Kalb co., NW cen. Georgia, N of Atlanta; pop. 6635.

Cham'bly (shăm'blĭ; *Fr.* shäN'blē'). **1** County, Quebec, Canada. See *Table* at QUEBEC.

2 *or* **Cham'bly' Bas'sin'** (shäN'blē' bà'săN'). Village, Chambly co., S Quebec, Canada, on Richelieu river 14 m. ESE of Montreal; pop. 2160; served as a main base of operations for Carleton and Burgoyne 1776–77.

Chambly Canal. Canal, part of Richelieu river system, from Chambly to St. Johns, Quebec, Canada; 11.78 m. long, with 9 locks.

Chambly Canton. Village, Chambly co., S Quebec, Canada, on Richelieu river 15 m. E of Montreal; pop. 1636. Site of fort built in 1665: see CANADA, *National Historic Parks* (Fort Chambly).

Cham'bolle'–Mu'si'gny' (shäN'bôl'mü'zē'nyē'). Commune, Côte-d'Or dept., E France, near Dijon; pop. (1931) 445; celebrated wines (red Burgundy) from vineyard of Musigny.

Chambon–Feugerolles, Le. See LE CHAMBON-FEUGEROLLES.

Cham'bord' (shäN'bôr'). **1** Village, Lake St. John co., S Quebec, Canada, on Lake St. John; pop. 1070.

2 Village, Loir-et-Cher dept., N cen. France, ab. 10 m. NE of Blois; pop. 325; château built by Francis I.

Cham'do (chäm'dō) *or* **Chang'tu'** (chäng'doo'). Town, Sikang prov., S China, on left bank of the Mekong 130 m. NW of Paan; pop. ab. 2000; crossroads town on several important trade routes.

Cha'me·le·cón' (chä'mā·lā·kôn'). River in NW Honduras; flows NE into the Gulf of Honduras.

Cha'me Point (chä'mā). Cape on S coast of Panama, at W side of entrance to the Bay of Panama.

Cha'mi·zal' (chä'mē·säl'; *Angl.* shăm'ĭ·zăl'). Tract of 437 acres N of the Rio Grande adjoining El Paso, Texas; originally in Mexico, later in U.S. because of change of course of Rio Grande; after long controversy ceded to Mexico by U.S. in 1963.

Cha′mo, Lake (chä′mō). Lake in SW Ethiopia, S of Lake Abaya and NE of Lake Rudolf.

Cha′mo′nix′ (shä′mô′nē′) *or* **Cha′mou′ni′** (shä′mōō′-nē′). Noted valley ab. 14 m. long and bet. 1 and 2⅓ m. wide in Haute-Savoie dept., E France, near NW entrance to new Mont Blanc tunnel; winter sports; mountain climbing; best starting point for ascent of Mont Blanc to the SE, at the town of **Cha′mo′nix′-Mont–Blanc** (-môn′blän′).

Cha′mou′chou·ane′ (shä′mōō′shwän′) *or* **Ash·uap′-mu·chuan′** (ăsh·wäp′mōō·chwän′). River 165 m. long, S Quebec, Canada, flowing SE into Lake St. John.

Cham′pa (chăm′pä). Ancient coastal kingdom of Indochina, occupying region closely corresponding to S Annam; flourished 3d cent. A.D. to end of 15th cent. Its inhabitants were Chams, related to the Cambodians.

Cham·pagne′ (shăm·pān′; *Fr.* shän′pän′y′); *Lat.* **Cam·pa′nia** (kăm·pān′yà; -pā′nĭ-à). Region of NE France, bounded on N by Low Countries; ✳ Troyes; watered by Marne, Aube, Aisne, Meuse, Yonne rivers; famous for its wines. An important medieval French county, held by houses of Vermandois, Blois, and Navarre; by marriage 1284 of heiress, Jeanne de Navarre, to Prince Philip (later Philip IV) of France, came to French crown; province before 1789; scene of battles of World War I 1915, 1917, 1918, esp. in hilly region ENE of Reims.

Cham·pagne′ Cas′tle (shăm′pān′). See CATHKIN PEAK.

Cham·paign′ (shăm·pān′). **1** Name of counties in two states of the U.S. See *Tables* at ILLINOIS and OHIO. **2** City, Champaign co., E cen. Illinois, 45 m. ENE of Decatur; pop. 49,583; settled ab. 1855, incorp. as city 1860; adjoins Urbana; commercial and industrial center in agricultural section.

Cham′pa·quí′ (chäm′pä·kē′). Peak 9350 ft. in W Córdoba prov., N cen. Argentina; highest of the Sierras de Córdoba.

Champ′au′bert′ (shän′pō′bâr′). Village, Marne dept., NE France, ab. 17 m. SSE of Épernay; scene of battle Feb. 10, 1814 in which Napoleon defeated the Allies.

Cham′pe·ri′co (chäm′pā·rē′kô). Seaport, Retalhuleu dept., SW Guatemala; pop. ab. 2000; port for Retalhuleu and Quezaltenango; chief export coffee.

Cham′pi′gny′–sur–Marne′ (shän′pē′nyē′sür·mârn′). Commune, Seine dept., N France, SSE suburb of Paris on Marne river; pop. (1931) 27,450; battles Nov. 30 and Dec. 2, 1870 in which the French attempted unsuccessful sorties from Paris.

Cham′pi·on′s Hill (chăm′pĭ·ŭnz). Hill, Hinds co., SW cen. Mississippi, 20 m. E of Vicksburg; battle May 16, 1863 in which Union forces under Gen. Grant drove Confederates back toward Vicksburg.

Cham·plain′ (shăm·plān′, shăm′plān′; *Fr.* shän′plän′). County, Quebec, Canada. See *Table* at QUEBEC.

Cham·plain′, Lake (shăm·plān′). Lake on N part of boundary bet. Vermont and New York, extending ab. 6 m. into Canada; ab. 125 m. long, ¼ to 14 m. wide; ab. 600 sq. m.; greatest depth ab. 600 ft. Discovered 1609 by French explorer Samuel de Champlain; scene of American naval victory over British Sept. 11, 1814.

Cham′plain′ Ca·nal′ (shăm′plān′). Canal connecting Lake Champlain at Whitehall, New York with the Erie Canal at Waterford, New York; 60 m. long, with 11 locks; part of the N.Y. State Barge Canal system.

Cham·po′eg (chăm·pō′ĕg). Settlement in Willamette valley, Oregon, S of Portland, where "Champoeg meeting" was held May 2, 1843 which organized a provisional government, the only government in the Pacific Northwest until Oregon Territory organized Mar. 1848; site commemorated by Champoeg Memorial State Park.

Chanak. See ÇANAKKALE.

Chanaq. Var. of *Chanak:* see ÇANAKKALE.

Cha·nar′ (chà·när′). = CHUNAR.

Cha′ña·ral′ (chä′nyä·räl′). Port, Atacama prov., N cen. Chile; pop. 3955; exports nitrates and copper.

Chança. See CHANZA.

Chan′ce·lade′ (shäns′làd′). Commune, Dordogne dept., SW cen. France; pop. (1931) 1095; skeleton unearthed near here in 1888 considered to be representative of a late paleolithic race (Chancelade).

Chan′cel·lors·ville (chăn′sĕ·lērz·vĭl), *now* **Chan′cel·lor** (chăn′sĕ·lēr). Locality in Spotsylvania co., Virginia, just W of Fredericksburg; scene of battle May 2–3, 1863 which resulted in defeat of Union forces under Hooker by Confederates under Lee and Jackson and death of Jackson May 10.

Chan′da (chăn′dà). Town E Maharashtra, cen. India, on affluent of Wardha river 85 m. S of Nagpur; pop. 28,138; old capital of ancient Gond dynasty.

Chan′da·lar′ (shăn′dà·lär′). River ab. 200 m. long, NE Alaska; flows SE from Endicott Mts. to upper Yukon.

Chan·dau′si (chŭn·dou′sĕ). Town, W Uttar Pradesh, N India, on affluent of Ganges river 95 m. E of Delhi; pop. 26,768; rail and trade center.

Chan′de·leur′ Islands (shăn′dĕ·lûr′; *Fr.* shän′dlûr′). Chain of small islands off E coast of SE Louisiana, in St. Bernard parish, lying bet. **Chandeleur Sound** and the Gulf of Mexico.

Chan′der·na·gor′ (chŭn′dēr·nà·gôr′) *or* **Chan′dar·na′gar** (chŭn′dēr·nŭg′ēr). Settlement and adjoining territory, SE India, on the Hooghly river 21 m. N of Calcutta; ab. 4 sq. m.; pop. (1941) 38,284. At first a trading post (factory) founded by Colbert's French East India Co. and granted to French by Emperor Aurangzeb 1688; in 18th cent. a thriving center for maritime trade; captured by English 1757, restored to French 1763; recaptured 1794, and restored permanently 1816; under jurisdiction of governor at Pondichéry (*q.v.*). Voted 1949 to join India; became part of Republic of India 1950.

Chan′di·garh′ (chŭn′dē·gär′). City, N India; a federally administered territory, joint ✳ of Punjabi Suba and Hariana; pop. 150,000.

Chan′dler (chănd′lēr). **1** City, Maricopa co., SW cen. Arizona, 17 m. SE of Phoenix; pop. 9531; winter resort. **2** City, ⊗ of Lincoln co., cen. Oklahoma, 26 m. N of Shawnee; pop. 2524; pecans; honey. **3** Village, East Gaspé co., SE Quebec, Canada, on SE Gaspé Penin. 23 m. SW of Percé; pop. 2326.

Chang′an′ *or* **Ch′ang′-an′** (chäng′än′). Early name of Sian (*q.v.*); also one one of its modern official names.

Chan′ga·na′che·ri (chŭng′gà·nä′chēr·ĭ). Town, cen. Kerala, SE of Alleppey; S India; pop. 24,201.

Chang′bha·kar′ (chäng′bà·kär′). Former princely state, NE Central Provinces, India; 899 sq. m.; pop. (1941) 21,266; now part of Madhya Pradesh.

Chang–chêng. See GREAT WALL.

Chang′chih′ (chäng′chĭr′) *or* **Lu·an′** (lōō·än′). Town, S Shansi prov., E China, ab. 100 m. NW of Kaifeng; communications center and Chinese military base in Chinese-Japanese War 1937–45.

Chang′chow′ (chäng′jō′). **1** See LUNGKI. **2** See WUTSIN.

Chang′chuen′ (chäng′chün′); *Eng.* **Saint John Island** (sânt jŏn′). Island, Kwangtung prov., S coast of China, SW of Macao.

Chang′chun′ (chäng′chŏŏn′); *Jap. official name* **Hsin′king′** (shǐn′jǐng′). City, ✳ of Kirin prov., S cen. Manchuria, on railroad 165 m. NNE of Mukden; pop. (1940 est.) 544,202; on edge of fertile Sungari river plain; rail junction point; trades esp. in soybeans. Small village until end of 18th cent. when small farmers were brought into district from Shantung; gained in importance after 1900; made capital of new Japanese state of Manchukuo 1932; became special municipality 1933. In World War II captured by Russian paratroopers Aug. 22, 1945; scene of conflicts in Chinese civil war 1946–47.

Changkiakow. See WANCHUAN.

Chang′ku′feng′ (jäng′gou′fŭng′). Hill on left bank of Tumen river near its mouth in disputed area on frontier of U.S.S.R., Korea, and Manchuria; controls Russian

Poseta Bay to the NE; claimed by Japan 1938; scene of fighting bet. Russians and Japanese July–Aug. 1938.

Chang Kwan Sai Ling (jäng kwäng tsī lǐng). Mountain range extending NE and SW in cen. Kirin prov., E Manchuria, E of Harbin; highest ab. 4400 ft.

Chang Pai Shan (chäng bī shän). Mountain range, SE Manchuria, along N Korea border, highest point 9003 ft.; source of rivers Sungari, Yalu, and Tumen. Many Manchu legends connected with it.

Chang′sha′ (chäng′shä′). City and treaty port, ✳ of Hunan prov., SE cen. China, on right bank of the Siang ab. 45 m. S of Tungting Hu (lake); pop. (1936 est.) 311,600. Formerly enclosed by wall with 12 gates, first wall built according to tradition ab. 202 B.C.; once famed as a literary center; noted for its silk, linen, and brassware industries. First opened to foreign missionaries 1901; made a treaty port 1904; successfully withstood a siege of 90 days by Taiping rebels 1852. In World War II captured by Japanese Sept. 1941 but soon given up; in three other battles 1941–42 Japanese severely defeated; finally taken by Japanese June 21, 1944 and held until end of war. Has university 700 years old; also American "Yale in China."

Chang Tang (jäng′ däng′). Northern region of Tibet (q.v.); a desert plateau at average altitude of 17,000 ft.; has many lakes, including Nam Tso.

Chang′teh′ (chäng′dǔ′). City, N Hunan prov., SE cen. China, on left bank of Yuan river near its mouth; pop. ab. 300,000. A treaty port with certain restrictions; center of China's "Rice Bowl." Has high mountains to the W. In World War II severely damaged in four unsuccessful attacks 1939–43 by Japanese in their campaigns against Changsha; finally fell 1944.

Chang′ting′ (chäng′tǐng′) or **Ting′chow′** (tǐng′jō′). City, SW Fukien prov., China, on upper Han river near Kiangsi border 18 m. N of Swatow.

Chang′tse′ (chäng′tsě′). North peak 24,730 ft. of Mt. Everest group, Himalayas, S Tibet, on Nepal border.

Changtu. See CHAMDO.

Chang′yang′ (chäng′yäng′). Town, S Hupeh, E cen. China, on tributary of the Yangtze 12 m. S of Ichang.

Cha·nia′ (kä·nyä′). = CANEA.

Chan′kiang′ (chän′kǐ·äng′). New name of Kwangchowan, after its restoration 1946 to China by France.

Chankiri. See ÇANKIRI.

Chan′nel (chän′′l). Town, SW Newfoundland, on coast E of Port-aux-Basques; pop. 2634.

Channel Islands. **1** British group of islands in the English Channel 10 to 30 m. off W coast of Manche dept., France; 75 sq. m.; pop. (1931) 93,205; comprise Jersey, Guernsey, Alderney, and Sark, and several islets. Originated noted breeds of cattle, esp. Jersey and Guernsey breeds. Fertile islands, exporting fruit, vegetables, and flowers, chiefly to England. Inhabitants are part of Norman descent, part English. *History:* Cromlechs, menhirs, etc., indicate occupation by prehistoric race; became part of Normandy 933; united to British crown at time of Norman Conquest 1066 and union made permanent 1154; British claims recognized by Philip II of France in Treaty of Bretigny 1360; domestically independent, not controlled by Imperial Parliament; an asylum for political refugees. Occupied by Germans June 30, 1940–May 9, 1945.
2 The Santa Barbara Islands, California.

Channel Islands National Monument. See UNITED STATES, *National Monuments.*

Chan′ning (chän′ǐng). Town, ⊗ of Hartley co., NW Texas; pop. 351.

Chantabun. See CHANTHABURI.

Chan·ta′da (chän·tä′thä). Commune, Lugo prov., NW Spain, 32 m. SSW of Lugo; pop. 15,127; stock raising; manufactures leather, soap, bricks and tile, linens.

Chan·tha·bu·ri (chän·t′hä·bōō·rē); *also* **Chan·ta·bun** (chän·t′hä·bōōn) or **Chan·ta·bu·ri.** **1** Province, S Thailand; 2326 sq. m.; pop. 101,084.

2 Commercial town, its ✳, near NE coast of Gulf of Siam 140 m. SE of Bangkok; pop. ab. 7000; has good port.

Chan′til′ly (shän′tĭl′ĭ). Village, Fairfax co., Virginia, 20 m. W of Washington; battle Sept. 1, 1862 in which Jackson attempted unsuccessfully to prevent withdrawal of Pope's Federals after 2d battle of Bull Run; Dulles International Airport.

Chan′til′ly′ (shän′tē′yē′). Commune, Oise dept., N France; pop. 5959; château and park; horse racing; formerly manufactured the delicate Chantilly lace.

Chan′trey Inlet (chän′trĭ). Inlet on N coast of Keewatin District, Northwest Territories, Canada.

Cha·nute′ (shà·nōōt′). City, Neosho co., SE Kansas, 44 m. WSW of Fort Scott; pop. 10,849; market city near oil, gas, and clay deposits; oil refineries; cement works.

Chanute Field. U.S. Air Force base in Rantoul, Illinois, location of an Air Force Technical School.

Cha′ny, Lake (chä′nǐ). Lake ab. 1300 sq. m., SW Novosibirsk Region, Soviet Russia, Asia, E of Omsk; gradually drying up.

Chan′za (chän′thä; -sä); *Port.* **Chan′ça** (shän′sà). River in SW Spain; flows SSW, forming a section of the Spanish-Portuguese boundary, and empties into Guadiana river ab. 20 m. from its mouth.

Chao′an′ (chou′än′) or **Chao′chow′** (chou′jō′). City, E Kwangtung prov., SE China, on Han river ab. 20 m. above Swatow; pop. ab. 300,000. Made treaty port 1858 but river too shallow for large vessels; large river trade by junk. Scene of banishment of the great poet, philosopher, and opponent of Buddhism, Han Yü (768–824 A.D.), under the T′ang dynasty.

Chao Hu (chou′ hōō′). Lake (*hu*), cen. Anhwei, E China, W of Wuhu; outlet on SE to the Yangtze.

Cha·o′ni·a (kà·ō′nǐ·à; -ōn′yà). District of ancient Epirus, NW Greece, extending along the coast N of the Kalamas river; its Pelasgian inhabitants were among the earliest peoples to enter Greece.

Chao Phra·ya (chou p′hrä·yä); *often in English sources,* **Me Nam** *or* **Me·nam** (mä·näm] (Thai, "river"). River, Thailand, 750 m. long, flowing S from highlands on N border to head of Gulf of Siam near Bangkok; strictly, name applies only to lower course, 160 m., from junction of Nan and Ping rivers in 15°42′N; lower course has many branches, the W branch being the Tha Chin (q.v.). See NAN, PING, WANG, YOM.

Chao′tung′ (jou′tōong′). City, NE Yunnan, S China, near the Yangtze ab. 175 m. NNE of Kunming; pop. ab. 30,000; commercial, stock-farming, and mining center.

Cha·pa′evsk (chŭ·pä′yěfsk). Town, S Kuibyshev Region, Soviet Russia, Europe, on Kuibyshev-Syzran R.R. 30 m. W of Kuibyshev; pop. 57,995.

Cha·pa′la, Lake (chä·pä′lä) Lake 50 m. long by 12 m. wide in Jalisco state, Mexico; traversed by the Santiago river (q.v.).

Cha′pa·ré′ (chä′pä·rä′). River ab. 180 m. long in cen. Bolivia; flows N into the upper Mamoré river.

Cha′par·ral′ (chä′pär·räl′; *Angl.* chăp′ă·răl′). Town, Tolima dept., W cen. Colombia, on the Magdalena 80 m. SW of Bogotá; pop. 5506.

Chapei. See SHANGHAI.

Chap′el Hill (chăp′ěl; -′l). Town, Orange co., N North Carolina, 11 m. WSW of Durham; pop. 12,573; Univ. of North Carolina (chartered 1789, opened 1795; coed.).

Chap′man, Mount (chăp′măn). Peak 6425 ft. in Great Smoky Mts., Sevier co., E Tennessee.

Chapman Peak. Mountain 9375 ft. in Glacier National Park near N boundary, NW Montana.

Chap′pa·quid′dick Island (chăp′à·kwĭd′ĭk). Island in Nantucket Sound off SE coast of Martha's Vineyard, Massachusetts.

Chap′pell (chăp′ěl; -′l). Village, ⊗ of Deuel co., W Nebraska; pop. 1280.

Cha′pra (chŭ′prä). Commercial town, W Bihar, NE India, on Ganges river just below junction with the Gogra; pop. (1941) 55,142.

Cha·pul'te·pec' (chä-pŏŏl'tå-pĕk'). Mexican fortress on isolated rocky hill 3 m. SW of Mexico City, captured by American assault Sept. 12–13, 1847 during the Mexican War; scene of meeting of Inter-American Conference Feb. 21–Mar. 8, 1945 that drafted Act of Chapultepec (approved Mar. 6, 1945) pledging for duration of World War II use of combined force in preserving American boundaries (act extended and implemented by conference at Petrópolis, Brazil, Aug. 15–Sept. 2, 1947).

Cha·ram'bi·rá' Point (chä-räm'bĕ-rä'). Cape on Pacific coast of Colombia, 4°N lat.

Cha'ran–Ka·no'a (?chä'rän-kå-nō'å). Village on SW coast of Saipan, Mariana Is.; beachheads 2 m. S and 2 m. N secured by U.S. Marines June 15, 1944; base for advance N to Garapan and S to Aslito airfield.

Charbar. See CHAHBAR.

Char'cas (chär'käs). **1** Town, San Luis Potosí state, cen. Mexico, 62 m. N of San Luis Potosí; pop. 6081.

2 or **Las Char'cas** (läs chär'käs). Early name for the Spanish audiencia of Upper Peru (q.v.).

Char'co A·zul' Bay (chär'kŏ ä·sŏŏl'). Inlet of Gulf of Chiriquí on the N, in extreme SW Panama.

Char'cot' Is'land (shär'kō'). Island in Palmer Archipelago, Antarctica; 75°W long. and 70°S lat.

Chard (chärd). Town, Somersetshire, SW England, N of Lyme Regis; pop. 5218; market center; manufactures lace, textiles; 15th-cent. church; two Roman villas.

Char'don (shär'd'n). Village, ⊗ of Geauga co., NE Ohio, 24 m. ENE of Cleveland; pop. 3154; maple-syrup and maple-sugar center.

Char·dzhou' (chär·jō'ŏŏ); also **Char·jui'** (chär·jŏŏ'ē); in 1926–27 called **Len'insk** (lĕn'ĭnsk; Russ. lyä'nyĭnsk). Town, E Turkmen S.S.R., Soviet Central Asia, on left bank of Amu Darya ab. 60 m. SW of Bukhara; pop. 54,739; important center in cotton trade; airport.

Cha'rente' (shà'ränt'). **1** Navigable river 225 m. long, W France; rises in Haute-Vienne dept., flows W into the Bay of Biscay opp. Oléron I.

2 Department of France. See Table at FRANCE.

Cha'rente'–Ma'ri'time' (-må'rē'tēm'); formerly **Cha'-rente'–In'fé'rieure'** (-ăN'fā'ryûr'). Department of France. See Table at FRANCE.

Cha'ren'ton'–le–Pont' (shà'räN'tôNl'pôN'). Commune, Seine dept., N France, SE suburb of Paris, at confluence of Marne and Seine rivers; pop. 20,946; manufactures boats, pianos, porcelain, rubber goods; stone bridge across Marne river formerly important in defenses of Paris. Includes **Con'flans'** or **Con'flans'–l'Ar'che·vêque'** [kôN'fläN'lär'shĕ·vâk'] (pop. 10,283) where treaty bet. Louis XI and the League of Public Weal was signed 1465.

Char·gog'ga·gogg'man·chau'ga·gogg'chau·bun'-a·gun'ga·maugg (chär·gŏg'å·gŏg'män·chô'gå·gŏg'-chô·bŭn'å·gŭng'gå·môg), **Lake.** The long (Indian) name of Lake Chaubunagungamaugg (q.v.).

Cha'ri (shà'rē') or **Sha'ri** (shä'rē). River ab. 1400 m. long; flows from Central African Republic NW into Lake Chad, Chad Republic; its wide delta borders in part on Brit. Cameroons; many tributaries in N Central African Republic. Fort-Lamy is at head of delta.

Char'ing Cross (chăr'ĭng). District in London, England, S of Trafalgar Square, on site of old village of Cherringe; formerly site of an Eleanor Cross, destroyed 1647, now has a modern memorial cross, erected 1865.

Char'i·ton (shär'ĭ·t'n). **1** River 280 m. long, S Iowa and N cen. Missouri; rises in Clarke co., S Iowa, flows E, then S across Missouri border and into the Missouri river.

2 County in Missouri. See Table at MISSOURI.

3 City, ⊗ of Lucas co., S Iowa, 42 m. SSE of Des Moines; pop. 5042; foundry, machine shops, dairy.

Charjui. = CHARDZHOU.

Char·kha'ri (chĕr·kä'rē). Former Indian state, in Bundelkhand, NE Central India Agency, India, ab. 100 m. W of Allahabad; 785 sq. m.; pop. (1941) 123,594; geographically in SW Uttar Pradesh.

Char'khliq' (chĭ·ä'kŭ·lĭk'). Town, S cen. Sinkiang, W China, on highway S of the Takla Makan Desert 155 m. E of Cherchen.

Charle'mont (chärl'mŏnt). Village, co. Armagh, S Northern Ireland, on the Blackwater 6 m. N of Armagh; pop. 1220; terminus of Ulster Canal.

Char'le·roi (shär'lē·roi). Borough, Washington co., SW Pennsylvania, on Monongahela river 22 m. S of Pittsburgh; pop. 8148; coal mining, glass, steel industries.

Char'le·roi' or **Char'le·roy'** (shär'lē·rwä'). Commune, Hainaut prov., SW Belgium; pop. (1938 est.) 27,274; industrial center in a coal and iron mining section; captured by Germans after fierce fighting Aug. 23, 1914.

Charles (chärlz). **1** River 47 m. long, E Massachusetts; flows into Boston Bay; its estuary separates Boston from Cambridge; navigable for 7 m.

2 County in Maryland. See Table at MARYLAND.

Charles, Cape. Cape at S tip of Northampton co., Virginia, N of entrance to Chesapeake Bay.

Charles'bourg' (shàrl'bŏŏr'). Residential village, Quebec co., S Quebec, Canada, 3 m. N of Quebec; pop. 5734.

Charles City (chärlz). **1** County in Virginia. See Table at VIRGINIA.

2 City, ⊗ of Floyd co., N Iowa, 30 m. ESE of Mason City; pop. 9964; nurseries, tractor manufactory.

3 Village, ⊗ of Charles City co., E Virginia; birthplaces of William Henry Harrison and John Tyler, 9th and 10th presidents of the U.S., nearby.

Charles Island. See SANTA MARÍA island.

Charles Mix (mĭks). County in South Dakota. See Table at SOUTH DAKOTA.

Charles Mound. Elevation 1241 ft. in Jo Daviess co., NW Illinois; highest point in the state.

Charles River. River in Massachusetts: see CHARLES.

Charles'ton (chärl'stŭn; chärlz'tŭn). **1** County in South Carolina. See Table at SOUTH CAROLINA.

2 Town, a ⊗ of Franklin co., NW Arkansas; pop. 1036.

3 City, ⊗ of Coles co., E cen. Illinois, 50 m. ESE of Decatur; pop. 10,505; flour, shoes, dairy products. Eastern Illinois University (1895; coed.).

4 City, a ⊗ of Tallahatchie co., NW Mississippi, 31 m. ESE of Clarksdale; pop. 2528.

5 City, ⊗ of Mississippi co., SE Missouri, 28 m. SSE of Cape Girardeau; pop. 5911; cotton; shoe factories.

6 Seaport city, ⊗ of Charleston co., SE South Carolina, on Atlantic Ocean; pop. 65,925; 2d largest city in state; formerly protected by Forts Sumter and Moultrie; ships coal, phosphates, petroleum products, cotton, cotton goods, tobacco, rice, lumber. College of Charleston (1770); The Citadel (1842; men). Charleston Navy Yard is just above the city.

History: Founded 1670 on Albemarle Point on W bank of Ashley river by an English colony under William Sayle; removed across Ashley river to present location 1680; became center of wealth and culture in the South; first American fire insurance company established here 1736; successfully opposed attacks by British fleet 1776 and 1779, but was captured May 12, 1780 by Sir Henry Clinton, and held by British until Dec. 14, 1782; became center of movement for nullification 1832 and of other movements to resist federal authority; site of the convention which proclaimed secession of South Carolina from the Union Dec. 1860; scene of outbreak of hostilities in the Civil War 1861 (see FORT SUMTER); evacuated by Confederate forces Feb. 17, 1865 after two years of siege; seriously damaged by earthquake Aug. 31, 1886.

7 Industrial city, ✳ of West Virginia and ⊗ of Kanawha co., W cen. West Virginia, at confluence of Elk and Kanawha rivers; pop. 85,796; distributing point for region producing coal, oil and gas, salt, hardwood timber; manufactures chemicals, glass, foundry products, furniture and veneers. Morris Harvey Coll. (1888; removed from Barboursville 1935). Settled around Fort Lee shortly after the Revolution; incorporated as town 1794, as city 1870; ✳ of W.Va. 1870–75, and from 1885.

Charleston Peak. Mountain 10,874 ft. in W Clark co., SE Nevada.

Charles'town (chärlz'toun). **1** City, Clark co., S Indiana, NE of Jeffersonville; pop. 5726.
2 Former city, Middlesex co., Massachusetts, since 1874 part of Boston; on Boston Harbor bet. mouths of Charles and Mystic rivers; U.S. Navy Yard; state prison (until 1956). Founded ab. 1628, oldest part of Boston; almost destroyed June 17, 1775 in battle of Bunker Hill (*q.v.*); chartered as city 1847.
2 Town, Sullivan co., SW New Hampshire, on Connecticut river 10 m. S of Claremont; pop. 2576; military base for Colonial troops during last years of French and Indian War; rendezvous for Gen. Stark and New Hampshire troops en route to battle of Bennington.
3 Town and summer resort, Washington co., S Rhode Island, on inlet of Block Island Sound SW of Newport; pop. 1966; taken from Westerly and incorp. 1738. Site of Indian burial ground and of Coronation Rock, where until 1770 Indians crowned their chieftains.
4 Chief town on Nevis I., Territory of Leeward Is., West Indies Federation; pop. (1938 est.) 1200.
Charles Town. City, ⊗ of Jefferson co., NE West Virginia, 14 m. S of Martinsburg; pop. 3329; scene of trial and execution of John Brown 1859.
Char'le·ville (chär'lĕ-vĭl; *nonlocally, also* chärl'vĭl). Town, S Queensland, Australia, on Warrego river 423 m. WNW of Brisbane; pop. 3204.
Char'le·ville (shär'lē-vēl'); *medieval* **Ar'cae Re·mo'rum** (är'sē rē·mōr'ŭm) *and* **Car'o·lop'o·lis** (kăr'ō-lŏp'ō·lĭs). Commune, Ardennes dept., NE France, on Meuse river opp. Mézières; pop. 22,557; hardware, etc.
Char'le·voix (*in Mich.:* shär'lĕ·voi; *in Can.: Eng.* shär'lĕ·vwä, *Fr.* shär'lĕ·vwä'). **1** County in Michigan. See *Table* at MICHIGAN.
2 City, its ⊗, NW Michigan, on Lake Michigan 41 m. NNE of Traverse City; pop. 2751; resort, fishing.
3 County, S Quebec, Canada; divided into **East Charlevoix** (*Fr.* **Char'le·voix'–Est'** [shär'lĕ·vwä'ĕst']), 719 sq. m., pop. 14,511, ⊗ La Malbaie, *and* **West Charlevoix** (*Fr.* **Char'le·voix'–Ouest'** [-wĕst']), 1496 sq. m., pop. 13,748, ⊗ Baie Saint Paul.
Char'lotte (shär'lŏt; *the city in Mich. is* shär'lŏt', shĕr-). **1** Name of counties in two states of the U.S. See *Tables* at FLORIDA and VIRGINIA.
2 City, ⊗ of Eaton co., S Michigan, SW of Lansing; pop. 7657; furniture, automobile accessories.
3 Commercial and industrial city, ⊗ of Mecklenburg co., S North Carolina, in Piedmont Region 15 m. N of South Carolina border; pop. 201,564; largest city in the state; important distribution point for cotton, tobacco, and peanut-growing region; center for mill engineering and of hydroelectric development; manufactures esp. cotton yarn and cotton goods. Johnson C. Smith Univ. (1867; coed.); Queens College (1857; women). Settled c. 1748, incorporated 1768, made ⊗ 1774; occupied by British under Cornwallis 1780; headquarters of Gen. Gates 1780; center of gold rush at end of 18th cent.; branch of United States mint estab. c. 1836 (closed 1913); last meeting place of Confederate Cabinet 1865.
4 Town, ⊗ of Dickson co., NW cen. Tennessee; pop. 551.
5 County, New Brunswick, Canada. See *Table* at NEW BRUNSWICK.
Char'lotte A·ma'lie (shär'lŏt ȧ·mäl'yĕ); *formerly* (*1921–37*) **St. Thom'as** (sȧnt tŏm'ȧs). Seaport, ✳ of St. Thomas I. and of the Virgin Islands of the United States, West Indies; pop. 9801; at head of St. Thomas Harbor on S shore of St. Thomas I.
Char'lotte Courthouse (shär'lŏt). Town, ⊗ of Charlotte co., S Virginia; pop. 555.
Char'lotte Harbor (shär'lŏt). Inlet of Gulf of Mexico on W coast of SW Florida, in Charlotte and Lee cos.; receives Peace river in NE; Pine I. extends S of it.
Char·lot'ten·burg (shär·lŏt'′n·bûrg; *Ger.* shär·lŏt'′ĕn-bōŏrk). Residential section of Berlin, Germany; before

1920 an independent city; site of 17th-cent. palace (damaged in World War II) of Queen Sophia Charlotte, wife of Frederick I of Prussia. Now in western sector.
Char·lot'ten·burg (shär·lŏt'′n·bûrg; *Du.* shär·lŏt'′ĕn-bûrk). Coastal town, NE Surinam, on Cottica river.
Char'lottes·ville (shär'lŏts·vĭl). City, ⊗ of Albemarle co., cen. Virginia, but politically independent, 70 m. WNW of Richmond; 6 sq. m.; pop. 29,427. Settled c. 1737; chartered as city 1888. Manufactures woolen cloth for military uniforms and other textiles; publishes law books. Univ. of Virginia (1819; part coed.). Monticello (home of Jefferson; now national memorial) and Ash Lawn (home of James Monroe) nearby.
Char'lotte·town (shär'lŏt·toun). City, ✳ of Prince Edward I., Canada, and ⊗ of Queens co., in cen. part of island, on Hillsborough Bay; pop. 15,887. Founded by French ab. 1720; became ✳ 1765; chief export center of the island; good harbor; manufactures woolen goods, foundry products, and lumber; important fisheries. Prince of Wales College and Normal School (1860); St. Dunstan's Coll. (1831; Rom. Cath.).
Charlotte Town. See GOUYAVE.
Charl'ton (chärl't'n; -tŭn). **1** County in Georgia. See *Table* at GEORGIA.
2 Town, Worcester co., cen. Massachusetts, 12 m. SW of Worcester; pop. 3685; agricultural trade center.
Char'ny' (shär'nē'). Village, Levis co., S Quebec, Canada, on Chaudière river 8 m. SSW of Quebec; pop. 3300.
Charran. See HARAN.
Char'ters Tow'ers (chär'tĕrz tou'ĕrz). Town, E Queensland, Australia, near Burdekin river 75 m. SW of Townsville; pop. 6982; in gold-mining region.
Char'tres (shär'tr'; *Angl.* shär'tr'); *anc.* **Au'tri·cum** (ô'trĭ·kŭm) *and* **Civ'i·tas Car·nu'tum** (sĭv'ĭ·tăs kär-nū'tŭm). Commercial city, ✳ of Eure-et-Loir dept., N cen. France, on Eure river 48 m. SW of Paris; pop. 27,077; famous 13th-cent. Gothic cathedral, noted particularly for its two spires; enclosed by ramparts; manufactures woolens, leather, hosiery; important grain and cattle market. Was capital of ancient Beauce; second crusade preached here by St. Bernard 1145; taken by English 1417; recovered 1432; Henry IV crowned in cathedral here 1594; occupied by Germans 1870.
Char'treuse', La Grande (là gränd' shär'trûz'). Chief house, until 1903, of Carthusian order, near the village of **Saint–Pierre–de–Chartreuse** (săn'pyâr'dĕ-), Isère dept., SE France, ab. 12½ m. N of Grenoble; religious settlement founded by St. Bruno of Cologne 1084; present buildings date from 1676; monks expelled 1903 as result of Associations Law (1901) dissolving monastic associations; noted for liqueur.
Cha·ryb'dis (kȧ·rĭb'dĭs). Whirlpool near Messina, Sicily, now called Galofalo (*q.v.*). See SCILLA.
Chas·co·mús' (chäs'kō·mōos'). Town, Buenos Aires prov., E Argentina, 50 m. S of La Plata; pop. 8400.
Chase (chās). Name of counties in two states of the U.S. See *Tables* at KANSAS and NEBRASKA.
Chase City. Town, Mecklenburg co., S Virginia, 28 m. ENE of South Boston; pop. 3207; tobacco market.
Chas'ka (chăs'kȧ). City, ⊗ of Carver co., SE cen. Minnesota, on Minnesota river 20 m. SW of Minneapolis; pop. 2501; beet-sugar refinery.
Chatalja. See ÇATALCA.
Cha'teau·bri·ant' (shä·tō'brē'äN'). Commune, Loire-Inférieure dept., NW France, 40 m. NNE of Nantes; pop. 8271; castle.
Châ'teau·dun' (shä'tō·dûN'). Commune, Eure-et-Loir dept., N cen. France, 28 m. SSW of Chartres; pop. 7057; dates from Gallo-Roman period; château.
Cha'teau·gay, *in Canada* **Châ'teau·guay** (shăt'ȧ·gē; -gā; *Fr.* shä'tō'gā'). River ab. 60 m. long, New York and Canada, rises in N N.Y. in Chateaugay Lakes on border bet. Clinton and Franklin cos. and flows N through Châteauguay co. in S Quebec to the St. Lawrence ab. 14 m. above Montreal. On its banks in Canada about 15

m. from its mouth a battle was fought Oct. 26, 1813 in which the American forces under Gen. Wade Hampton were repulsed.

Chateaugay Lakes. Two lakes in NE New York, **Upper Chateaugay** in W Clinton co. and **Lower Chateaugay** in E Franklin co.; outlet, Chateaugay river flowing out of N end of Lower Chateaugay; resort.

Châ′teau·guay (shăt′ȧ·gē; -gä; *Fr.* shä′tō′gä′). **1** See CHATEAUGAY.

2 County, Quebec, Canada. See *Table* at QUEBEC.

3 Town, Châteauguay co., S Quebec, Canada, on St. Lawrence river 14 m. SW of Montreal; pop. 2240; near mouth of Châteauguay river and opp. the Ottawa.

Châ′teau·neuf′–de–Ran′don′ (shä′tō′nûf′dĕ·räN′-dôN′). Village, Lozère dept., S France, NE of Mende; besieged 1380 by Du Guesclin who died here.

Châ′teau′ Ri′cher′ (shä′tō′ rē′shä′). Town (unincorporated), a ⊗ of Montmorency co., S Quebec, Canada, on N bank of St. Lawrence river 25 m. NE of Quebec; pop. 2348; dairying and market gardening.

Châ′teau′roux′ (shä′tō′rōō′); *during Revolution called* **In′dre·ville′** (ăN′drĕ·vēl′). Manufacturing and commercial commune, ✻ of Indre dept., cen. France, on Indre river 80 m. S of Orléans; pop. 28,578; 10th-cent. castle.

Châ′teau′–Thier′ry′ (shä′tō′tyĕ′rē′). Commune, Aisne dept., N France, on right bank of Marne river 37 m. SSW of Laon; pop. 7246; manufactures scientific and musical instruments, woolen yarn, etc.; trades in wine; stone quarried nearby; Thierry castle said to have been built by Charles Martel 730; birthplace of La Fontaine. Battles 1814; occupied by Germans 1870; initial successes against Germans won by American troops in nearby Belleau Wood June 6, 1918, and town retaken July 21; American Military Cemetery. See MARNE.

Châtelard, Le. See LE CHÂTELARD.

Châ′te·let′ (shä′tlĕ′). Industrial commune, Hainaut prov., SW Belgium, on Sambre river; pop. 15,110.

Châ′te·li′neau′ (shä′tlē′nō′). Commune, Hainaut prov., SW Belgium, opp. Châtelet; pop. 18,350.

Châ′tel′le·rault′ (shä′tĕl′rō′); *in Eng. usage* **Châ′tel′-he·rault′** (shä′tĕl′rō′). Commune, Vienne dept., W cen. France, on Vienne river 21 m. NNE of Poitiers; pop. 19,369; manufactures small arms, cutlery. Built around 11-cent. castle; capital of a 16th-cent. duchy.

Chat′field (chăt′fēld). City, Fillmore and Olmsted cos., SE Minnesota, 18 m. SE of Rochester; pop. 1841.

Chat′ham (chăt′ăm; *Chatham, Mass., is often* -(h)ăm). **1** Name of counties in two states of the U.S. See *Tables* at GEORGIA and NORTH CAROLINA.

2 Town, Barnstable co., SE Massachusetts, on Atlantic Ocean 18 m. E of Barnstable; pop. 3273; resort.

3 Residential borough, Morris co., N New Jersey, on Passaic river 6 m. SE of Morristown; pop. 9517.

4 Village, Columbia co., SE New York 22 m. SSE of Albany; pop. 2426; railroad center.

5 Town, ⊗ of Pittsylvania co., S Virginia; pop. 1822.

6 Seaport town, Northumberland co., E New Brunswick, Canada, on estuary of Miramichi river; pop. 5223; fine harbor; lumber trade; shipyards, foundries, pulp mills; center for fishing and hunting. Founded 1800.

7 City, ⊗ of Kent co., SE Ontario, Canada, on Thames river 16 m. E of Lake St. Clair; pop. 21,218; agricultural center, esp. for fruit and livestock; canneries, machine shops, mills, and an automobile factory. Settled 1835.

8 Municipal borough, Kent, SE England, on the Medway 30 m. ESE of London; pop. 46,940; one of the chief naval and military stations of Great Britain. First used for naval purposes by Henry VIII; Royal Dockyard founded ab. 1700 and greatly developed since 1867.

Chatham Island. 1 See SAN CRISTÓBAL island, Ecuador.

2 See CHATHAM ISLANDS.

Chatham Islands. Island group in S Pacific Ocean 536 m. E of New Zealand; 44°S lat. and 176° W long.; 372 sq. m.; pop. (1936) 702; constitute a county of South

I., New Zealand; comprise two islands: Chatham (347 sq. m.) and Pitt (25 sq. m.). Discovered 1790.

Chatham Strait. Narrow passage bet. Admiralty and Kuiu Is. on E and Baranof and Chichagof Is. on W, SE Alaska.

Châ′til′lon′ (shä′tē′yôN′). Commune, Seine dept., N France, S suburb of Paris; pop. 10,895; Fort de Châtillon site since 1949 of France's first atomic pile.

Châtillon–sur–Seine (-sür·sân′). Commune, Côte-d'Or dept., E France, 43 m. NW of Dijon; pop. 4727; ruined 13th-cent. castle of dukes of Burgundy; unsuccessful conference Feb. 5–Mar. 19, 1814 bet. Napoleon and the Allies. In World War II junction point Sept. 12, 1944 of two American armies.

Chat′om (chăt′ŭm). Town, ⊗ of Washington co., SW Alabama; pop. 993.

Châ′tou′ (shä′tōō′). Commune, Seine-et-Oise dept., N France, NNW suburb of Paris on Seine river; pop. (1931) 12,023; summer resort; 13th-cent. church.

Chats′wood (chăts′wŏod). Urban center, N suburb of Sydney, New South Wales, Australia.

Chats′worth (chăts′wûrth; -wērth). **1** City, ⊗ of Murray co., N Georgia; pop. 1184.

2 Seat of the dukes of Devonshire, Derbyshire, N cen. England, ab. 20 m. N of Derby; one of the most splendid residences in England.

Chat′ta·hoo′chee (chăt′ȧ·hōō′chē). **1** Navigable river 410 m. long, rising in Towns co., NE Georgia, and flowing SW to Alabama border at West Point, W cen. Georgia, then S forming a section of Alabama-Georgia boundary and a section of Georgia-Florida boundary; unites with the Flint river to form the Apalachicola river (*q.v.*).

2 County in Georgia. See *Table* at GEORGIA.

3 Town, Gadsden co., NW Florida, NW of Tallahassee; pop. 9699.

Chat′ta·noo′ga (chăt′ȧ·nōō′gȧ). Industrial city and port of entry, ⊗ of Hamilton co., SE Tennessee, on Tennessee river just N of Georgia border; pop. 130,009; in scenic region, with Missionary Ridge to the E and Lookout Mt. to the SW; manufactures iron and steel products, farm implements, textiles and hosiery, furniture; railroad center; main headquarters of TVA since 1935; iron and coal mines. Univ. of Chattanooga (1886; coed.). Chickamauga and Chattanooga National Military Park nearby (see UNITED STATES, *National Historical Parks*). First permanent white settlement c. 1835; became salt-trading center; chartered 1839, as city 1851; developed river trade (cotton, etc.) and became transportation center; served as Union base during Civil War 1863 ff.; scene of engagements including battle of Chickamauga 1863 and battle of Chattanooga Nov. 23–25, 1863 (battle of Lookout Mt., called "Battle above the Clouds," and battle of Missionary Ridge).

Chat′ter·is (chăt′ēr·ĭs). Urban district, Isle of Ely, E England, 67 m. N of London; pop. 5528.

Chat·too′ga (chȧ·tōō′gȧ). **1** See TUGALOO river.

2 County in Georgia. See *Table* at GEORGIA.

Cha·tu′ge Dam (chȧ·tōō′gĕ). See *Table* at TENNESSEE VALLEY AUTHORITY.

Chau·bun′a·gun′ga·maugg, Lake (chô·bŭn′ȧ·gŭng′-gȧ·môg); *or* **Lake Web′ster** (wĕb′stēr). Lake in S Worcester co., cen. Massachusetts, near Webster.

Chau′dière′ (shō′dyâr′). River ab. 120 m. long, S Quebec, Canada; rises in Lake Megantic and flows N to the St. Lawrence just above Quebec.

Chaudière Falls. Falls in Ottawa river at Ottawa city, Ontario, Canada; river narrows to 200 ft., descends 50 ft.; site of extensive water-power development.

Chau′doc′ (chŭ′ŏŏ·dŏk′). Town, W Cochin China, Vietnam, on Mekong river on Cambodia border; pop. ab. 4500; export port for Cambodia.

Chauk (chouk). Town, Magwe dist., Lower Burma, on Irrawaddy ab. 60 m. N of Magwe; pop. 12,830.

Chau′kan Pass (chou′kän). Pass over mountains NE of Patkai Range, alt. 7979 ft., on NW boundary of

Burma N of the Ledo Road and S of Fort Hertz; on highway from Myitkyina N to Sadiya in Assam.

Chaulnes (shōn). Commune, Somme dept., N France, 11 m. SW of Péronne; pop. 1626; scene of much fighting in World War I, 1914–17 and 1918.

Chau′mont′ (shō′môN′); *formerly* **Chau′mont′-en-Bas′si′gny′** (-äN·bȧ′sē′nyē′). Commune, * of Haute-Marne dept., NE France, at confluence of Marne and Suize rivers 140 m. ESE of Paris; pop. 18,069; 13th-cent. Gothic church; fine town hall; manufactures gloves, hosiery, leather, cutlery, textiles. Treaty 1814 bet. Great Britain, Russia, Austria, and Prussia renewing and strengthening alliance against Napoleon; headquarters of American Expeditionary Force under Pershing in World War I. In World War II taken by Germans June 15, 1940; retaken by American armies Sept. 1944.

Cha·un′ Bay (chŭ·ōōn′). Inlet of the Arctic Ocean, NW Chukot National District, NE Soviet Russia, Asia, 69°N lat. and 170°E long.

Chau′ny′ (shō′nē′). Commune, Aisne dept., N France, on Oise river S of St-Quentin; pop. 8951; destroyed in World War I.

Chau·tau′qua (shȧ·tô′kwȧ). **1** Name of counties in two states of the U S. See *Tables* at KANSAS and NEW YORK. **2** Town, Chautauqua co., SW corner of New York, on Chautauqua Lake; pop. 4376. Chautauqua system of popular education inaugurated 1874.

Chautauqua Lake. Lake ab. 18 m. long and from 1 to 2½ m. wide, Chautauqua co., SW corner of New York; outlet from SE end flows into Allegheny river.

Chaux-de-Fonds, La. See LA CHAUX-DE-FONDS.

Chav′es (chăv′ĕs). County in New Mexico. See *Table* at NEW MEXICO.

Cha′ves (shȧ′vĕsh); *anc.* **Aq′uae Fla′vi·ae** (ăk′wē flā′vĭ·ē; ā′kwē). Commune, Vila Real dist., N Portugal, near Spanish border 22 m. NNE of Vila Real; pop. 6482; thermal salt baths and springs; cathedral; tomb of Alfonso I, Duke of Braganza; manufactures linens and silks; Convention of Chaves Sept. 18, 1837 signed here.

Cha′ville′ (shȧ′vēl′). Commune, Seine-et-Oise dept., N France, SW suburb of Paris; pop. (1931) 10,948.

Cha·vin′da (chä·vēn′dä). Town, Michoacán state, SW Mexico; pop. 5131.

Chaxerngsao. See CHACHOENGSAO.

Cha·zy′ (shä·zē′). Village, Clinton co., NE New York, near Lake Champlain ab. 13 m. N of Plattsburg; pop. 3386; limestone formations of geological interest.

Chazy Lake. Lake ab. 4 m. long, Clinton co., NE corner of New York; source of Great Chazy river.

Chea′dle and Gat′ley (chē′d′l, găt′lĭ). Urban district, Cheshire, NW England, S of Manchester; pop. 31,508.

Chea′ha′ (chē′hô′). Mountain 2407 ft. in Clay and Talladega cos., E Alabama; highest point in state.

Cheat (chēt). River ab. 150 m. long, N West Virginia; formed by confluence of forks in S Tucker co., flows N across Pennsylvania border and into Monongahela river in SW Fayette co., SW Pa.; E of Morgantown are lake, dam, and gorge; hydroelectric power development.

Cheat′ham (chēt′ăm). County in Tennessee. See *Table* at TENNESSEE.

Cheat Mountain (chēt). Mountain 3478 ft. in Randolph co., NE cen. West Virginia.

Cheb (кĕp); *Ger.* **E′ger** (ā′gĕr). City, W Bohemia prov., W Czechoslovakia, in the valley of the Ohře ab. 50 m. NW of Plzeň; pop. (1930) 31,546; industrial community; scene of assassination of Wallenstein 1634.

Che·beague′ (shĕ·bēg′). Island in Casco Bay, Cumberland co., off coast of SW Maine.

Che·bo·ksa′ry (chĭ·bŭ·ksȧ′rĭ). Town, * of Chuvash Republic, Soviet Russia, Europe, on the Volga 80 m. W of Kazan; pop. 12,008; commercial and cultural center of the republic; local industries; important fair.

Che·boy′gan (shĕ·boi′găn). **1** River ab. 40 m. long, N Michigan; flows N into Lake Huron at Cheboygan.

2 County in Michigan. See *Table* at MICHIGAN.

3 City, its ⊗, N Michigan, on Lake Huron at mouth of the Cheboygan river; pop. 5859; summer resort and fishing center; formerly a lumbering center.

Chech, Erg. See EL ERG.

Che·chen′o-In·gush′ Republic (chĕ·chĕn′ŏ·ĭn·gōōsh′), *officially* **Checheno-Ingush Autonomous Soviet Socialist Republic.** Autonomous republic on N slopes of Caucasus Mts., SE Soviet Russia, Europe; 6060 sq. m.; pop. (1941 est.) 732,838; * Grozny; a subdivision of the R.S.F.S.R.; formed Nov. 1920 by combining the Chechen and Ingush autonomous areas, then in the North Caucasus region; dissolved 1943–44 for collaboration with Germans during World War II; reconstituted 1957; chief nationalities Chechen, a warlike people, 58%, and Ingush, a related Caucasian people, 13% (see INGUSH), both of Mohammedan religion.

Che·co′tah (chĕ·kō′tȧ). City, McIntosh co., E Oklahoma, 22 m. SSW of Muskogee; pop. 2614; coal, clay.

Ched′a·buc′to Bay (shĕd′ȧ·bŭk′tō). Inlet of Atlantic Ocean in NE tip of the mainland of Nova Scotia, Canada, SE of Strait of Canso.

Ched′dar (chĕd′ĕr). Village, Somersetshire, SW England, 22 m. SW of Bristol; pop. 2154; cliffs and stalactite caverns; known also for its cheese (Cheddar cheese) originally made here.

Che·du′ba (chĕ·dōō′bȧ; chĕd′ōō·bȧ). Island, Arakan, W Burma, in Bay of Bengal S of Ramree I.; 220 sq. m.; pop. ab. 30,000; held by Japanese May 1942–Jan. 1945.

Cheek′to·wa′ga (chēk′tŏ·wä′gȧ). Urban community (unincorporated), Erie co., W New York, E of Buffalo; pop. 65,128.

Chees′man Dam (chēz′măn). Dam completed 1904 across South Platte river, SW Douglas co., cen. Colorado; height 232 ft.; forms Cheesman Lake.

Che′fang′ (chĕ′fäng′). Town, SW Yunnan prov., S China, on the Burma Road near Wanting; alt. ab. 3200 ft.; held by Japanese May 1942–Nov. 26, 1944.

Che·foo′ (jŭ′fōō′) *or* **Yen′tai′** (yĕn′tī′). Commercial city and treaty port on N coast of E end of Shantung Penin., NE China, 112 m. NE of Tsingtao; pop. (1931 est.) 131,659; at E end of Pohai Strait; exports silk, lace, hairnets; school of China Inland Mission for children of missionaries. Made open port 1863; Chefoo Convention, signed 1876, forced China to open additional ports and to improve status of foreigners in China.

Che·ha′lis (chĕ·hā′lĭs). **1** River ab. 125 m. long, W Washington; rises in Lewis co., flows NW into Grays Harbor at Aberdeen.

2 City, ⊗ of Lewis co., SW Washington, 5 m. S of its sister city Centralia (*q.v.*); pop. 5199; dairy, poultry, fruit farms; lumber, brick, milk-condensing plants.

Chehalis, Point. Point on SW coast of Grays Harbor co., W Washington, at S entrance to Grays Harbor.

Cheik–Sa′ïd′ (shāk′sȧ′ĕd′); *Arab.* **Sheikh Sa′id** (shĭk [shāk] sȧ·ēd′). Small French territory, SW tip of Arabia, on Bab el Mandeb Strait opp. Perim I.; ab. 1 sq. m.; pop. ab. 1000; first acquired 1868 by French commercial company; ceded to French government 1886.

Cheju. See SAISHU.

Che′kiang′ (jŭ′ji·äng′). Coast province, E China, 39,780 sq. m.; pop. (1936 est.) 21,230,749; * Hangchow; bounded on N by Kiangsu prov., on E by East China Sea, on S by Fukien prov., and on W by Kiangsi and Anhwei provs. The smallest province of China Proper but one of the most densely populated. N part lies just S of the delta of the Yangtze; cen. part drained by the Fuchun, flowing into Hangchow Bay; the S part drained by the Wu; many hills and low mountain ranges. The Chu Shan Archipelago is off NE coast. Chief products wheat, beans, rice, cotton, tea, and silk. Chief cities Hangchow, Ninghsien, Yungkia, and Shaohing. A cultural center of early China; during 12th and 13th cents. A.D. its chief city, Hangchow, was capital of China under Sung dynasty; after Mongol conquest 1280 became center of Mangi (the empire of S China).

Che·lan′ (shĕ·lăn′). **1** County in Washington. See *Table* at WASHINGTON.

2 Town, Chelan co., cen. Washington, at S end of Lake Chelan; pop. 2402; summer resort.

Chelan, Lake. Lake ab. 55 m. long and from 1 to 2 m. wide in Chelan co., cen. Washington; outlet from S end flows into Columbia river.

Chelan Range. Range in cen. Washington, extending along the W shore of Lake Chelan, in Chelan co.

Che·le·ken′ (chĭ·lyĭ·kĕn′). Island, SE Caspian Sea, off W coast of Turkmen Republic, Soviet Central Asia.

Ché′lia′, Dje′bel′ (jā′bĕl′ shā′lyá′); *Arab.* **Je′bel She·li′a** (jä′bāl shä·lī′yá; -yä). Highest peak 7609 ft. in Aurès Mts., NE Algeria.

Cheliabinsk. Var. of CHELYABINSK.

Ché′liff′ (shā′lēf′); *also* **She·liff** (shĕ·lēf′). River ab. 430 m. long in Algeria, NW Africa; rises in Atlas Mts., flows N and W into Mediterranean Sea E of Oran.

Cheliuskin. Var. of CHELYUSKIN.

Chel·kar′ Teng·iz′ (chĕl·kär′ tĕng·ēz′). Lake, cen. Kazakh S.S.R., Soviet Central Asia, ab. 110 m. NE of Lake Aral.

Chel′la′ (*Fr.* shĕ′lá′). Town, Morocco, S of Rabat; necropolis.

Chelles (shĕl); *anc.* **Ca′lae** (kā′lē). Commune, Seine-et-Marne dept., N France, near N bank of the Marne 7 m. E of Paris; pop. 14,658; prehistoric remains found nearby, whence the name "Chellean epoch"; site of famous convent 650–1790.

Chel′ly Canyon (shā′). = *Canyon de Chelly National Monument:* see UNITED STATES, *National Monuments.*

Chelm (kĕlm); *Russian* **Kholm** (kôlm). Commune, Lublin dept., Poland, 42 m. ESE of Lublin; pop. (1938–39 est.) 29,100; just W of the Bug; fine cathedral; trade center for fertile agricultural region. Battle Aug. 1–3, 1915 resulting in German victory.

Chelm′no (kĕlm′nô); *Ger.* **Culm** *or* **Kulm** (kŏŏlm). Commercial and industrial commune, Pomorze dept., Poland, on Vistula river 24 m. NNW of Toruń; pop. (1938–39 est.) 13,525; manufactures iron goods, beer. Founded 1231 by Teutonic Knights, made city 1233; member of the Hanse; belonged to Prussia 1773–1807, 1815–1919.

Chelms′ford (chĕms′fērd; chĕmz′-; *nonlocally, also* chĕlmz′-). **1** Town, Middlesex co., NE Massachusetts, 4 m. SSW of Lowell; pop. 15,130; textiles.

2 Municipal borough, ⊗ of Essex. SE England, on the Chelmer 30 m. NE of London; pop. 37,888.

Chelm′ża (kĕlm′zhä); *Ger.* **Culm′see′** *or* **Kulm′see′** (kŏŏlm′zā′). Commune, Pomorze dept., Poland, 12 m. N of Toruń; pop (1938–39 est.) 13,462; 13th-cent. cathedral; manufactures beet sugar.

Chel′sea (chĕl′sĭ). **1** Town, Kennebec co., SW Maine, 6 m. SE of Augusta; pop. 1893.

2 Industrial city, Suffolk co., E Massachusetts, 3 m. NNE of Boston; pop. 33,749; rubber and rubber goods, boots and shoes, paper stock; Mass. Soldiers' Home and U.S. Naval Hospital. Settled 1624, set off from Boston 1739; suffered great fire Apr. 12, 1908.

3 Village, Washtenaw co., SE Michigan, 15 m. W of Ann Arbor; pop. 3355.

4 City, Rogers co., NE Oklahoma; pop. 1541.

5 Village in Chelsea town (township), ⊗ of Orange co., E Vermont, 14 m. S of Barre; pop. (town) 957.

6 Metropolitan borough of London. See *Table* at LONDON.

Chel′ten·ham. 1 (chĕl′t'n·hăm). Township, Montgomery co., SE Pennsylvania, NNE of Philadelphia; pop. 35,990.

2 (chĕlt′năm; chĕl′t'n·ăm). Municipal borough, Gloucestershire, SW cen. England, on the river Chelt 42 m. S of Birmingham; pop. (1951) 62,823; popular watering place, with mineral springs.

Che·lya′binsk (chĭ·lyä′byĭnsk), *also* **Che·lia′binsk.** City, ✷ of Chelyabinsk Region, in cen. part, Soviet Russia, Asia, 125 m. S of Sverdlovsk; pop. 273,127; industrial center; makes tractors, tanks, agricultural implements, leather goods; on the Trans-Siberian R.R. Founded 1658. Headquarters of Czechoslovak legion in fighting after Revolution of 1917.

Chelyabinsk Region. Region, W Soviet Russia, Asia, E of southern Urals; 63,111 sq. m.; pop. 2,802,949; ✷ Chelyabinsk. Has much fertile and forested land; chief crops wheat, rye, millet, oats; large coal deposits. In former Ural Area and since discovery after World War I of great deposits of iron (see MAGNITOGORSK) has formed the S part of the Ural Industrial Area (*q.v.*). Chief cities Chelyabinsk, Magnitogorsk, Zlatoust, Troitsk. Organized as a subdivision of Soviet Russia in Asia 1936; in World War II greatly reduced by organization of Kurgan Region from its E part.

Che·lyus′kin, Cape (chĭ·lyoōs′kĭn); *also* **Cape Che·lius′kin.** Cape on Taimyr Penin., NW Soviet Russia, Asia; northernmost point of Asia, 77°35′N, 105°E.

Che·min′ des Dames (shĕ·măn′ dā dám′). Highway ab. 4 m. N of and parallel with the Aisne river, N France, with its E end near Craonne; literally, "Ladies Road," so called because constructed for the journeys of the daughters of Louis XV. Scene of much severe fighting in World War I, esp. as phases of several important battles, Sept. 1914, Apr., May, and Oct. 1917, and May 1918. In World War II taken by Germans June 1940.

Chemmis. See AKHMÎM.

Chem′nitz (kĕm′nĭts). **1** Circle of Saxony, Germany. See *Table* at SAXONY.

2 *after 1953* **Karl-Marx-Stadt** (kärl′märks′shtät′). City, its ✷, on Chemnitz river at foot of Erz Gebirge 43 m. SE of Leipzig; pop. (1939) 334,563; manufactures include textiles (for which it is chiefly noted), carpets, chemicals, automobiles, electrical equipment and machinery. Made free imperial city 1125; sometimes called the "Saxon Manchester." In World War II bombed by Allies; taken by American forces Apr. 1945.

Chemulpo. See JINSEN.

Che·mung′ (shĕ·mŭng′). **1** River, S New York; formed by confluence of Cohocton and Tioga rivers in Steuben co., flows SE across Pennsylvania border and into Susquehanna river. See ELMIRA.

2 County in New York. See *Table* at NEW YORK.

Che·nab′ (chĕ·näb′); *anc.* **A·ces′i·nes** (á·sĕs′ĭ·nēz). River ab. 590 m. long, N India, one of the "Five Rivers" of the Punjab; rises in N East Punjab in the Himalayas, flows NW, then W and SW through Kashmir and W cen. West Punjab, Pakistan, to unite with the Sutlej to form the Panjnad; joined by the Jhelum in West Punjab; source of extensive canal and irrigation system.

Che·nan′go (shĕ·năng′gō). **1** River ab. 100 m. long, S cen. New York; rises near Madison-Oneida co. boundary, flows S into Susquehanna river at Binghamton.

2 County in New York. See *Table* at NEW YORK.

Chê′née′ (shĕ′nā′). Commune. Liège prov., Belgium, SE suburb of Liège; pop. 9981.

Che′ney (chē′nĭ). City, Spokane co., E Washington, 14 m. SSW of Spokane; pop. 3173. Eastern Washington State College (1890; coed.).

Cheney Cobble. Peak 3673 ft. in the Adirondack Mts., Essex co., NE New York.

Chengchiatun. See LIAOYUAN.

Cheng′chow′ (jŭng′jō′) *or* **Cheng′hsien′** (-shyĕn′). City, ✷ of Honan prov., on right bank of Hwang Ho, E cen. China, 40 m. W of Kaifeng; important railroad junction of the north-south line (Peiping to Hankow) and the west-east line (Sian to Tunghai). Considerable fighting in 1944 for adjacent sections of the railroad.

Cheng′teh′ (chŭng′dŭ′) *or* **Je·hol′** (jĕ·hōl′). City, ✷ of Jehol prov., NE China, in S part of province on Lwan river ab. 110 m. NE of Peiping; pop. 46,951; historically famous as the summer residence of the Manchu emperors of China. The imperial estates, begun 1703 by Emperor K'ang-hsi, covered a great park; here Emperor Ch'ien

Lung received in 1793 the historic British trade mission under Lord Macartney.

Cheng'tu' (chŭng'dōō'). City, ✳ of Szechwan prov., S cen. China, in NW corner of Red Basin; pop. 440,988; located on remarkable irrigation system of the Min and other streams devised more than 2000 years ago, the center of an exceptionally fertile region. One of the oldest cities of China; in early times for certain periods an imperial capital; walls and broad streets; tombs and other remains of early eras; West China Union University. In World War II American air base for B-29 bombers 1944-45.

Chensi. See BARKOL.

Chenstokhov. See CZĘSTOCHOWA.

Chen'yuan' (jŭn'yü·än'). Town, E Kweichow, S China, 110 m. E of Kweiyang; gold and copper mines.

Che·o'ah Dam (chē·ō'ȧ). See *Table* at TENNESSEE VALLEY AUTHORITY.

Che·pach'et (chē·păch'ĕt; -ĭt). Village, Providence co., N Rhode Island, ab. 15 m. NNW of Central Falls; pop. (est.) 800; governmental center of Glocester; dairy farms.

Che'po (chä'pō). River in E cen. Panama; flows W and SW into the Bay of Panama E of the city of Panama.

Chep'ping, *or* **Chip'ping, Wyc'ombe** (chĭp'ĭng wĭk'ŭm); *now* **High Wycombe.** Municipal borough, Buckinghamshire, SE cen. England, on the Wye 29 m. WNW of London; pop. 39,352; paper mills, furniture factories.

Chep'stow (chĕp'stō). Urban district, Monmouthshire, W England, on Wye river; pop. 5285; high tides.

Cheq'uers (chĕk'ẽrz). The official country seat of the prime minister of England, a historic Tudor mansion 35 m. NW of London, presented to the government by Lord and Lady Lee of Fareham 1917.

Cher (shâr). **1** River ab. 220 m. long, cen. France; rises in Creuse dept., flows NW into Loire river.

2 Department of France. See *Table* at FRANCE.

Che·ra'sco (kä·räs'kô). Commune, Cuneo prov., Piedmont, Italy, on Tanaro river ab. 22 m. NE of Cuneo; pop. 8937; treaty Apr. 26, 1631 bet. France and Spain; armistice Apr. 28, 1796 bet. France and Italy that ended Italian support of Austria.

Cher'aw (chē'rô). Town, Chesterfield co., NE South Carolina, on Pee Dee river 14 m. WNW of Bennettsville; pop. 5171. Settled c. 1752; site of Confederate supply depot until captured by Sherman 1865. Manufactures cotton textiles, lumber, brick, foundry products.

Cher'bourg (shâr'bŏŏrg; -bŏŏr; *Fr.* shĕr'bŏŏr'). Manufacturing seaport and naval arsenal, Manche dept., NW France, on N coast of Cotentin Penin. on English Channel; pop. 39,105; strongly fortified; naval station; consists of old or civil town and Port Militaire, the new or military town; transatlantic port of embarkation and debarkation; shipbuilding. Occupies site of ancient Roman station; under English rule to 1200; pillaged by English 1295; sustained sieges 1378, 1418, 1450; taken by English 1758 and held for ransom. In World War II held from June 1940 by Germans; attacked from S by Allies June 21-22, 1944, taken June 27; harbor practically destroyed by Germans.

Cher'chel' *or* **Sher'shel'** (shĕr'shĕl'); *anc.* **Cae'sa·re'a** (sē'zȧ·rē'ȧ; sĕs'ȧ-; sĕz'ȧ-). Seaport, N Alger dept., N Algeria; pop. 12,650.

Cher'chen' (jü·ûr'chŭng'). **1** River ab. 420 m. long, W China; flows from N slopes of cen. Kunlun Mts. N and NE along SE border of Takla Makan Desert to Lop Nor.

2 Town and oasis, S Sinkiang, W China, on Cherchen river; pop. ab. 4000; on caravan and motor highway.

Cher'e·miss' (chĕr'ē·mĭs'; *Russ.* chĭ·ryĭ·myĕs'). = MARI.

Che·rem'kho·vo (chĭ·ryĕm'ќȧ·vṳ; chĭ·ryĕm·ќô'vṳ). Town, S Irkutsk Region, Soviet Russia, Europe, on Trans-Siberian R.R. 80 m. NW of Irkutsk; pop. 65,907; largest coal fields in Russian Far East nearby.

Che'ren (*Ital.* kâ'rän) *or* **Ke'ren** (kā'rĕn). Town, E cen. Eritrea, NE Africa; pop. 7500; connected by rail with Asmara. Captured by British Mar. 28, 1941.

Che·re·po·vets' (chĭ·ryĭ·pŭ·vyĕts'; *Angl.* chĕr'ĕ·pṳ·vĕts'). City, SW Vologda Region, Soviet Russia, Europe, 70 m. W of Vologda, near junction of Suda and Sheksna rivers just before they enter Rybinsk Reservoir (*q.v.*); pop. 24,900; distilleries; manufactures agricultural implements and boots and shoes; center for hunting, fishing, and lumbering. Originally a settlement (in Novgorod principality) which grew up near a monastery founded before 15th cent.; became a town 1780.

Cher'gui, Chott ech; Shatt el Sher'gui (shŏt' ăsh shŭr'gē). Marshy saline lake, NW Algeria.

Cher'i·bon' (chĕr'ĭ·bŏn'). **1** Former residency, NE West Java prov., Neth. Indies, on coast of Java Sea; 2097 sq. m.; pop. 2,069,690; ✳ Cheribon; fertile coastal plain, with one high mountain Tjareme in the SE; chief products sugar and rice. A center of Mohammedanism in Java since 1526 but the sultanate became subject to the Dutch in 17th cent.

2 *or* **Tji're·bon'** (chē'rĕ·bôn'). City, Indonesia, a seaport on Java Sea near volcano Tjareme and on railroad ab. 130 m. E of Djakarta; pop. 54,079; a place of Mohammedan pilgrimage.

Cher'i·ton (chĕr'ĭ·t'n; -tŭn). Former urban district, Kent, SE England, near coast W of Dover; pop. 8089.

Cher·kas'sy *or* **Cher·ka'si** (chĕr·kàs'sĭ). City, SE Kiev Region, cen. Ukraine, U.S.S.R., on the Dnieper 100 m. SE of Kiev; pop. 51,693; center of region raising sugar beets and tobacco; refineries; timber mills. In 15th cent. an important Cossack town, esp. for trading; under Polish rule until Chmielnicki's revolt 1648; became Russian 1795; held by Germans 1941-43.

Cher·kess' Autonomous Region (chĕr·kĕs'; *Russ.* chĭr-). Autonomous region, SE Soviet Russia, Europe, in valley of upper Kuban river; 1273 sq. m.; pop. (1941 est.) 97,233; ✳ Cherkessk; a subdivision of the R.S.F.S.R. Bounded on N, E, and S by Stavropol Territory, and on W by Krasnodar Territory; mountainous. United with the Karachaev Autonomous Region 1922 to form an autonomous unit; made a national district 1926 and raised to rank of autonomous region 1928.

Cher·kessk' (chĕr·kĕsk'; *Russ.* chĭr-); *formerly* **Ba·tal·pa·shinsk'** (bŭ·tăl·pŭ·shĭnsk') *and* **Su·li'mov** (sŏŏ·lē'môf; *Russ.* sŏŏ·lyē'mŭf). Town, ✳ of Cherkess Autonomous Region, Soviet Russia, Europe, on Kuban river 160 m. SE of Krasnodar; railroad terminus; sawmills, oil presses, factories. For a time before World War II known as **Ye'zho·vo–Cherkessk** (yā'zhṳ·vṳ-), but name restored to Cherkessk in 1938.

Cherna. See CRNA.

Cher'na·ya (chôr'nȧ·yȧ). Small river in the Crimea, S Soviet Russia, Europe, E of Sevastopol; flows W into the Black Sea; scene of victory of Allies over Russians Aug. 16, 1855 during Crimean War.

Cherniakovsk. = CHERNYAKHOVSK.

Cher·ni'gov (chĕr·nyē'gŭf). **1** Medieval principality, cen. Russia, extending NE from Kiev to borders of Ryazan; ✳ Chernigov; at height of power in 11th and 12th cents.

2 Region, N Ukraine, U.S.S.R.; most of W boundary formed by the Dnieper; touches White Russia on NW and Bryansk Region of R.S.F.S.R. on N.

3 City, its ✳, on right bank of Desna river 77 m. NNE of Kiev; pop. 67,356; manufactures footwear and flour. A very old town, mentioned as early as 907; in 11th cent. capital of Chernigov principality, at which time its cathedral (still preserved) was built; partly destroyed by Mongols 1240; annexed by Lithuania in 14th cent. but lost to Poland; occupied by Russia 1686; captured by Germans Sept. 13, 1941; retaken late in 1943.

Chernoe More. See BLACK SEA.

Cher·nov'tsy (chĕr·nôf'tsĭ); *Romanian* **Cer'nă·u'ţi** (chĕr'nȧ·ōōts'; -ōō'tsĕ); *Ger.* **Czer'no·witz** (chĕr'nŏ·vĭts'). **1** Region, W Ukraine, U.S.S.R., formerly a de-

partment of Bucovina in N Romania; to U.S.S.R. 1940. **2** Industrial and commercial city, its ✳ and former ✳ of Bucovina, on right bank of Prut river; pop. (1939 est.) 109,698; cultural center; university, opened by Germans 1875. Grew from small village after Austrian occupation in 1775; battlefield 1915–17 in World War I; became Romanian 1918; ceded to U.S.S.R. 1940.

Chernozem Area. See CENTRAL BLACK EARTH AREA.

Cher·nya′khovsk (chĭr-nyá′kŭfsk); *Ger.* **In′ster·burg** (ĭn′stēr-bŏŏrĸ). City, formerly in East Prussia prov., Prussia, Germany, on Angerapp river; now in Kaliningradsk Region, W Soviet Russia, Europe; 53 m. E of Kaliningrad (Königsberg); pop. 39,311; railroad junction; 14th-cent. castle; manufactures include tile, chemicals, stoves, sugar, vinegar. Founded c. 1336; became city 1583; taken by Russians Jan. 1945; assigned to U.S.S.R. by Potsdam Conference 1945.

Cher′o·kee′ (chĕr′ô·kē′; chĕr′ô·kē′). **1** Name of counties in eight states of the U.S. See *Tables* at ALABAMA, GEORGIA, IOWA, KANSAS, NORTH CAROLINA, OKLAHOMA, SOUTH CAROLINA, TEXAS.
2 City, ⊗ of Cherokee co., NW Iowa, 48 m. ENE of Sioux City; pop. 7724; makes farm implements.
3 City, ⊗ of Alfalfa co., N Oklahoma, 38 m. NW of Enid; pop. 2410; feed crops, livestock; milling.

Cherokee Dam. See *Table* at TENNESSEE VALLEY AUTHORITY.

Cherokee Outlet *or* **Cherokee Strip.** Strip of land ab. 12,000 sq. m. along S border of Kansas; guaranteed to Cherokee Indians by treaties of 1828 and 1833; held by Cherokee Nation until 1891 when it was purchased by United States for ab. $8,596,000; opened to settlers Sept. 16, 1893; became part of Territory of Oklahoma.

Cher′ra·pun′ji, *earlier* **Cher′ra Poon′jee** (chĕr′á·pŏŏn′jĭ; *native* chŭ·rä·pōōn′jē). Village and former British military station, cen. Assam, NE Indian Union; alt. ab. 4590 ft.; has record for world's heaviest rainfall (annual average 424 inches).

Cher′ry (chĕr′ĭ). Co. in Nebr. See *Table* at NEBRASKA.

Cherry Hill. See DELAWARE.

Cherry Island. See ANUDA.

Cher′ry·vale (chĕr′ĭ·vāl′). City, Montgomery co., SE Kansas, 10 m. ENE of Independence; pop. 2783.

Cherry Valley. Village, Otsego co., New York, 50 m. W of Albany; pop. 668; medicinal springs; Cherry Valley Massacre by Butler's Rangers and Indians Nov. 11, 1778.

Cher′ry·ville (chĕr′ĭ·vĭl). Town, Gaston co., SW North Carolina, 10m. ENE of Shelby; pop. 3607; manufactures cotton, machinery.

Cher·sko′go Range (chĕr·skô′vŭ—*sic*), *also* **Cher′ski Range** (chĕr′ski). Mountain range, NE Yakutsk Republic, Soviet Russia, Asia, N of the Sea of Okhotsk; runs NW and SE; highest point 10,217 ft.

Cherso. See CRES.

Cher′so·nese, The (kûr′sŏ·nēz; -nēs); *anc.* **Cher′so·ne′sus** (-nē′sŭs). Literally, "peninsula"; in ancient geography applied to several peninsulas in Europe and Asia with designating adjectives: (1) **Chersonesus Au′re·a** (ô′rĕ·á). The Golden Chersonese. See MALAY PENINSULA. (2) **Chersonesus Cim′bri·ca** (sĭm′brĭ·kà). See JUTLAND. (3) **Chersonesus Her′a·cle·ot′i·ca** (hĕr′á·klē·ŏt′ĭ·kà). See KHERSON. (4) **Chersonesus Tau′ri·ca** (tô′rĭ·kà). See CRIMEA. (5) **Chersonesus Thrac′i·ca** (thrăs′ĭ·kà). See GALLIPOLI PENINSULA.

Chert′sey (chûrt′sĭ). Urban district, Surrey, S England, on S bank of the Thames; pop. 31,029; market gardens.

Cher′well (chär′wĕl; -wŏl). River ab. 30 m. long, cen. England; rises in Northamptonshire, flows S through Oxfordshire into the Thames (Isis) at Oxford.

Ches′a·ning (chĕs′á·nĭng). Village, Saginaw co., cen. Michigan, 20 m. SW of Saginaw; pop. 2770.

Ches′a·peake (chĕs′á·pēk). City, SE Virginia, S of Norfolk, formed 1963 by merger of former city of South Norfolk and former county of Norfolk; pop. 73,647.

Ches′a·peake and Del′a·ware Canal (chĕs′á·pēk; dĕl′á·wâr, -wēr). Canal ab. 14 m. long, 90 ft. wide, and 12 ft. deep at medium low water, from Delaware City, Delaware, to Chesapeake City, Maryland, connecting Chesapeake and Delaware Bays.

Chesapeake Bay. Inlet of Atlantic Ocean, 200 m. long and from 4 to 40 m. wide, its lower section in Virginia and its upper section in Maryland; receives the Susquehanna river in the N, the Patuxent and Potomac on the W, the Chester, Choptank, and Nanticoke on the E, and the Rappahannock, York, and James rivers on the SW.

Chesapeake City. Town, Cecil co., NE Maryland; pop. 1104; terminus of Chesapeake and Delaware Canal.

Chesh′am (chĕsh′ám; *locally usu.* chĕsh′ăm). Urban district, Buckinghamshire, SE cen. England, 25 m. WNW of London; pop. 11,428.

Chesh′ire (chĕsh′ēr; *less often,* -ĭr). **1** County in New Hampshire. See *Table* at NEW HAMPSHIRE.
2 Residential town, N cen. New Haven co., S Connecticut, 5 m. WNW of Wallingford; pop. 13,383; incorp. 1780; agriculture; formerly copper and barytes mining center.
3 Town, Berkshire co., W Massachusetts, 9 m. NNE of Pittsfield; pop. 2472; dairy products, esp. cheese.

Cheshire *or* **Ches′ter** (chĕs′tēr). County, NW England; area 1502 sq. m.; pop. (1951) 1,258,050; ⊗ Chester; other towns Birkenhead, Stockport, Wallasey, Crewe, Macclesfield; rivers Dee, Weaver, and Mersey; farming, dairying (Cheshire cheese), coal and salt mining, shipbuilding, chemical and textile manufacturing.

Chesh′ska·ya Bay (chĕsh′skà·yà). Inlet of the Arctic Ocean (Barents Sea), Arkhangelsk Region, N coast of Soviet Russia, Europe, E of Kanin Penin.

Ches′hunt (chĕs′n't). Urban district, Hertfordshire, SE England, 15 m. N of London; pop. 23,016; part of Greater London.

Ches′ley (chĕs′lĭ). Town, Bruce co., SE Ontario, Canada, 22 m. S of Owen Sound; pop. 1672.

Ches′ter (chĕs′tēr). **1** River ab. 40 m. long, E Maryland; flows W along boundary of Kent and Queen Annes cos. into Chesapeake Bay.
2 Name of counties in three states of the U.S. See *Tables* at PENNSYLVANIA, SOUTH CAROLINA, TENNESSEE.
3 Town, S cen. Middlesex co., S Connecticut, on Connecticut river; pop. 2520; settled as part of Saybrook c. 1690, incorp. 1836; manufactures bits, augers, needles.
4 City, ⊗ of Randolph co., SW Illinois, on Mississippi river 58 m. SSE of East St. Louis; pop. 4460; shipping center for iron, lead, sand, and coal.
5 Town, Hampden co., SW Massachusetts, 17 m. SE of Pittsfield; pop. 1155.
6 Town, ⊗ of Liberty co., N Montana; pop. 1158.
7 City and port of entry, Delaware co., SE Pennsylvania, on Delaware river 14 m. WSW of Philadelphia; pop. 63,658; shipbuilding yards, steel mills, automobile assembly plants, oil refineries, munitions and locomotive works. Crozer Theological Seminary (1867); Pennsylvania Military Coll. (1821; incorp. 1862). Settled by Swedes 1644 (second oldest settlement in Pa.); under Dutch control 1655, English control 1664; became borough 1701, ⊗ 1789–1851, city c. 1866.
8 City, ⊗ of Chester co., N South Carolina, 18 m. SSW of Rock Hill; pop. 6906; manufactures cotton textiles, yarn, flour; granite works.
9 Residential city, Hancock co., N tip of West Virginia panhandle, on Ohio river; pop. 3787; potteries.
10 County in England. See CHESHIRE.
11 *anc.* **De′va** (dē′và) *or* **De·va′na Cas′tra** (dĕ·vā′nà kăs′trà). City and county borough, ⊗ of Cheshire, NW England, on the Dee 15 m. S of Liverpool; pop. 48,229; manufactures leather goods and paint; cheese market; active port and railroad center. Noted for its well-preserved walls, famous "Rows" of houses, and cathedral. For several centuries after 60 A.D. Roman "camp on the Dee"; after Romans left held in turn by British, Saxons, and Danes; rebuilt 908; last place in England to surrender (1070) to William the Conqueror; during 13th

to 16th cents. scene of presentation of mystery plays of the Chester Cycle.

Ches·ter·field (chĕs′tēr·fēld). **1** Name of counties in two states of the U.S. See *Tables* at SOUTH CAROLINA and VIRGINIA.

2 Town, ⊗ of Chesterfield co., NE South Carolina; pop. 1532.

3 Village, ⊗ of Chesterfield co., Virginia; pop. (est.) 135.

4 Municipal borough, Derbyshire, N cen. England, 11 m. S of Sheffield; pop. (1951) 68,540; coal and iron mines, steelworks, textile mills, potteries.

Chesterfield Inlet. 1 Inlet of Hudson Bay ab. 250 m. long and 25 m. wide, E Keewatin District, Northwest Territories, N Canada; inland expands into Baker Lake (*q.v.*).

2 Station on NW coast of Hudson Bay on S side of mouth of Chesterfield Inlet.

Chesterfield Islands. Group of eleven coral islets in cen. Coral Sea bet. N New Caledonia I. and E coast of Queensland, Australia; total area ab. 4 sq. m. Owned by France; uninhabited; guano deposits.

Ches′ter le Street (chĕs′tēr lĕ strēt′). Urban district, Durham, N England, 10 m. S of Newcastle; pop. 18,539; coal and iron mines nearby.

Ches′ter·ton (chĕs′tēr·t′n; -tŭn). Town, Porter co., NW Indiana, 5 m. S of Lake Michigan; pop. 4335.

Ches′ter·town (chĕs′tēr·toun). Town, ⊗ of Kent co., NE Maryland, 32 m. ESE of Baltimore; pop. 3602; seat of Washington College (1782; coed.), of whose first board of governors George Washington was a member.

Chestnut, Mount (chĕs′nŭt; chĕst′-; -nŭt). Peak 4600 ft. in Rabun co., NE Georgia.

Chestnut Hill. 1 Suburb of Boston, Massachusetts; seat of Boston College (1863; Roman Catholic; men).

2 Residential district, NW Philadelphia (city), Pennsylvania; Chestnut Hill College (1871; women).

Chestnut Ridge. Ridge ab. 130 m. long extending from Preston co., West Virginia, NE to cen. Indiana co., W cen. Pennsylvania; highest point 2293 ft.

Che·sun′cook Lake (chē·sŭn′kŏŏk). Lake ab. 20 m. long in cen. Piscataquis co., N cen. Maine; traversed by West Branch of the Penobscot river.

Che·to′pa (shĕ·tō′pȧ). City, Labette co., SE Kansas, 34 m. SW of Pittsburg; pop. 1538.

Che′tu·mal′ (chä′tŏŏ·mäl′). Town, ✴ of Quintana Roo territory, E Yucatán penin., Mexico.

Chetumal Bay. Inlet ab. 70 m. long of NW Caribbean Sea in SE coast of Quintana Roo territory, Mexico, and NE coast of British Honduras.

Chev′er·ly (shĕv′ēr·lĭ). Town, Prince Georges co., S cen. Maryland, E of Washington, D.C.; pop. 5223.

Chev′i·ot (shĭv′ĭ·ŭt; shĕv′-). City, Hamilton co., SW corner of Ohio, 8 m. NW of Cincinnati; pop. 10,701.

Chev′i·ot Hills (chĕv′ĭ·ŭt; chē′vĭ-; chĭv′ĭ-; -[v]yŭt). Range of hills extending NE to SW along the English-Scottish border; highest peak Cheviot 2676 ft.

Che·we′lah (chē·wē′lȧ). Industrial City, Stevens co., NE Washington, 46 m. NNW of Spokane; pop. 1525; magnesite mines; manufactures building materials.

Chey·enne′ (shī·ĕn′; -ăn′). **1** River 290 m. long, W cen. South Dakota; formed by confluence of South Fork and Beaver Creek in Fall River co., flows N and NE into Missouri river on S boundary of Armstrong co.

2 Name of counties in three states of the U.S. See *Tables* at COLORADO, KANSAS, NEBRASKA.

3 Town, ⊗ of Roger Mills co., W Oklahoma; pop. 930; Custer's Battlefield (Nov. 27, 1868) nearby.

4 City, ✴ of Wyoming and ⊗ of Laramie co., SE Wyoming, 10 m. N of Colorado border; pop. 43,505; railroad center; ships cattle and sheep; packing houses, oil refineries, creameries; founded 1867, incorp. and made state capital 1869. See FORT FRANCIS E. WARREN.

Cheyenne Wells. Town, ⊗ of Cheyenne co., E Colorado; pop. 1020.

Chey′ney (chā′nĭ). Village, Delaware co., SE Pennsyl-

vania, W of Media; pop. (1950) 288; Cheyney State College (1837; coed.).

Chha′tar·pur′ (chŭ′tēr·pŏŏr′; *native* ch′hŭ′-). Former Indian state, NE Central India, Indian Union; 1170 sq. m.; pop. (1941) 184,720; ✴ Chhatarpur.

Chhat′tis·garh′ (chŭt′ĭs·gär′; *native* ch′hŭt′tēs·gŭr′h′). **1** Former division, E Central Provinces, Indian Union; 27,742 sq. m.; pop. (1941) 5,592,621; ✴ Raipur.

2 Former agency, forming a group of 16 Indian states, N, W, and S of Chhattisgarh division, geographically in E Central Provinces, India; 37,688 sq. m.; pop. (1941) 4,050,000; chief states Bastar, Surguja, Kalahandi, Patna.

Chhin·dwa′ra (chĭn·dwä′rȧ; *native* ch′hĭn-). Town, S Madhya Pradesh, 64 m. NNW of Nagpur; pop. ab. 17,000.

Chhota Udepur. See CHOTA UDAIPUR.

Chiahsing. See KASHING.

Chiambone, Ras. See DICKS HEAD.

Chiamdo. Var. of CHAMDO.

Chiamis. See TJIAMIS.

Chiamussu. See KIAMUSZE.

Chia′na (kyä′nä). River ab. 25 m. long, cen. Italy, flowing N from near Chiusi to the Arno at Arezzo; its valley (**Val′le di Chiana** [väl′lä dē]), formerly marshy and malarial, has been drained and canalized.

Chiang-ling. See KIANGLING.

Chiang Mai (chē·äng′ mī′) or **Chieng′mai′** (chē·ĕng′mī′). **1** Province, NW Thailand; 8839 sq. m.; pop. 544,001.

2 City, its ✴, on upper course of Ping river ab. 80 m. E of Burma border; pop. ab. 100,000; important trade center esp. in teak; railroad terminus. Formerly capital of united Lao kingdom, later subject to Burma.

Chiang Rai (chē·äng′ rī′) or **Chieng′rai′** (chē·ĕng′rī′). **1** Province, N Siam; 5853 sq. m.; pop. 443,476.

2 Town, its ✴, on tributary of the Mekong 90 m. NE of Chiang Mai; trading town on junction of highways N to Shan States and NW Indochina and S to Lampang.

Chianjur. See TJIANDJOER.

Chian·ning. See NANKING.

Chi·an′ti Mountains (kĭ·än′tĭ; *Ital.* **Mon′ti Chian′ti** (mŏn′tē kyän′tē). Mountain range of the Apennines in Tuscany, cen. Italy. The region is noted for its wines, esp. a dry red variety.

Chiapa, *in full* **Chia′pa de Cor′zo** (chyä′pä thä kôr′sō). Town, Chiapas state, SE Mexico; pop. 5450.

Chia′pas (chyä′päs). State, SE Mexico. See *Table* at MEXICO.

Chia·ra·mon′te Gul′fi (kyä′rä·mŏn′tä gŏŏl′fē). Commune, Ragusa prov., SE Sicily; pop. 12,324.

Chia′ri (kyä′rē); *anc.* **Clar′i·um** (klär′ĭ·ŭm). Commune, Brescia prov., Lombardy, N Italy, 16 m. W of Brescia; pop. 13,880; manufactures textiles; old fortifications; scene of defeat of French and Spanish army by Prince Eugene Sept. 1, 1701.

Chias′so (kyäs′sō). Commune, Ticino canton, Switzerland, on Italian frontier W of SW end of Lake Como; pop. ab. 6000; customs station on St. Gotthard railroad.

Chi·a′tu·ra (chē·ä′tŏŏ·rä) or **Chi·a′tu·ri** (-rē). Town, cen. Georgian S.S.R., in S foothills of Caucasus Mts. ab. 85 m. NW of Tiflis; rich manganese mines.

Chia′va·ri (kyä′vä·rē). Commune, Genova prov., Liguria, NW Italy, on Gulf of Rapallo 22 m. ESE of Genoa; pop. 17,520; manufactures silk, lace; fisheries.

Chia·ven′na (kyä·vĕn′nä). Town, Sondrio prov., N Lombardy, Italy, at N end of Lake Como; pop. 3713; S terminal of Splügen Pass.

Chiazza. See PIAZZA ARMERINA.

Chi′ba (chē′bȧ; *Jap.* chē·bä). **1** Prefecture of Japan. See *Table* at JAPAN.

2 City, its ✴, on E shore of Tokyo Bay; pop. 57,446; capital of a powerful daimio family 12th–16th cents.; reduced to a poor fishing village at end of 16th cent., but now prosperous commercial town.

Chi·ca′go (shǐ·kä′gō; -kŏg′ō; -kô′gō). **1** Small river in Chicago, Illinois, consisting of North Branch and South Branch; South Branch connected with the Des Plaines river at Lockport by the **Chicago Drainage Canal,** since 1930 called the **Sanitary and Ship Canal** (see ILLINOIS WATERWAY).
2 City, ⊗ of Cook co., NE Illinois, on Lake Michigan; pop. 3,550,404; important port, and 2d largest city in United States; central United States market and distributing point; world's greatest grain and livestock market; meat-packing plants, grain elevators, railroad shops, etc.; manufactures electrical equipment, farm implements and machinery, railroad cars, iron and steel

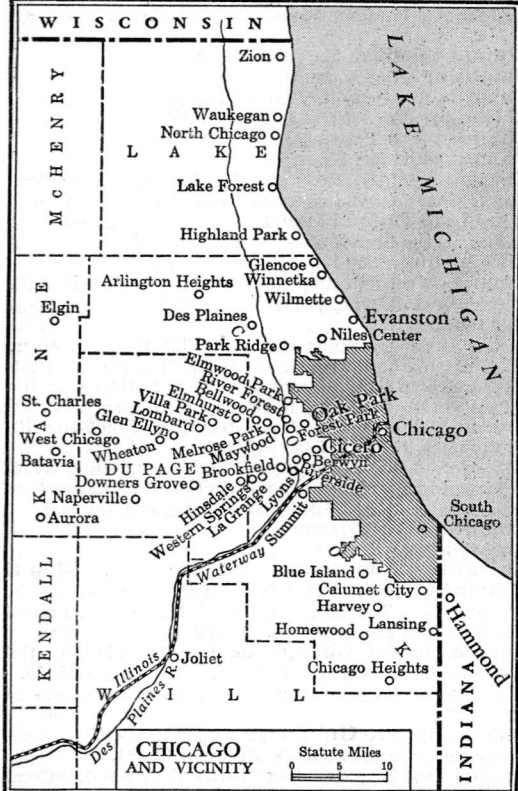

W I S C O N S I N

Zion

Waukegan
North Chicago

L A K E

Lake Forest

Highland Park

Glencoe
Arlington Heights Winnetka
Wilmette

Elgin
Des Plaines

Park Ridge
Niles Center
Evanston

Elmwood Park
River Forest
Bellwood
St. Charles Elmhurst
Villa Park
Glen Ellyn Lombard
West Chicago Wheaton Maywood
Batavia DU PAGE Brookfield
Downers Grove Riverside
Naperville
Aurora

Hinsdale Springs
La Grange
Western Lyons
Waterway Summit

Blue Island
Calumet City
Harvey
Homewood Lansing

Joliet

Chicago Heights

W Illinois
Des Plaines R.
I L L

Oak Park
Forest Park
Cicero
Chicago
Berwyn

South Chicago

CHICAGO
AND VICINITY
Statute Miles
0   5   10

L A K E   M I C H I G A N

O Hammond
I N D I A N A

McHENRY   LAKE   COOK   KENDALL

products, etc.; its important buildings include the Public Library, John Crerar Library (scientific works), Shedd Aquarium, Planetarium, Chicago Natural History Museum, Chicago Art Institute, Hull House; its educational institutions include University of Chicago (1891; coed.), Illinois Institute of Technology (1940; coed.) combining Armour College of Engineering (1892) and Lewis Institute of Arts and Sciences (1894), Loyola University (1869; coed.), De Paul University (1898; coed.), St. Francis Xavier College for Women (1912), Northwestern University (branch; 1926), Chicago Teachers College (1869; Central Y.M.C.A. College (1919; coed.), Mundelein College (1929; women), Roosevelt College (1945; coed.).
History: In 17th cent. name associated with portage (bet. Des Plaines and Chicago rivers) which connected St. Lawrence-Great Lakes system with Mississippi; strategic position on route for travel to Mississippi important to French, British, and Americans; tract, 6 miles square, at river mouth, acquired by U.S. from Indians 1795; Fort Dearborn built 1803, abandoned during War of 1812; gradually settled and received city charter

1837; expanded rapidly after completion of Illinois and Michigan Canal 1848, connecting Chicago and Mississippi rivers, and its connection with railroads from east 1853; more than half destroyed by great fire of 1871; scene of Haymarket riot 1886, Pullman strike 1894.
Chicago Heights. Industrial city, Cook co., NE Illinois, 27 m. S of Chicago; pop. 34,331.
Chicago Ridge. Village, Cook co., NE Illinois, SW of Chicago; pop. 5748.
Chi·ca′pa (*Port.* shē·kä′pả). River 310 m. long in the Congo basin, S Africa; rises in E cen. Angola, flows N into Kasai river.
Chich′a·gof (chǐch′ả·gôf; *Russ.* chǐ·chä′gŭf). Island, NW Alexander Archipelago, SE Alaska, N of Baranof I.
Chichagof Harbor. Inlet on NE coast of Attu I. at W end of Aleutians Is.; Japanese force wiped out here May–June 1943.
Chi·chén′ It·zá′ (chě·chän′ ět·sä′). Village in Yucatán state, Mexico, ab. 20 m. W of Valladolid; once one of the principal centers of the Mayas; extensive ruins, but some of the temples, pyramids, towers, etc., of brick, marble, or stone, rich with sculptures, are still well preserved.
Chich′es·ter (chǐch′ǐs·tēr). Municipal borough, ⊗ of West Sussex, S England, 16 m. ENE of Portsmouth; pop. 19,110; early Norman cathedral (begun c. 1090).
Chi·chi Ji·ma (chē·chē jē·mä). **1** Group of islands in the Bonin Is. (*q.v.*).
2 Largest island in the group and in the Bonin Is.
Chick′a·hom′i·ny (chǐk′ả·hŏm′ǐ·nǐ). River ab. 90 m. long, E Virginia; rises 16 m. NW of Richmond, flows SE into James river.
Chick′a·mau′ga (chǐk′ả·mô′gả). City, Walker co., NW Georgia, 18 m. WNW of Dalton; pop. 1824; near **Chickamauga Creek** (tributary of the Tennessee river) where a battle was fought Sept. 19–20, 1863 in which Confederates under Bragg defeated Federals under Rosecrans; part of the campaign for Chattanooga.
Chickamauga and Chat′ta·noo′ga National Military Park (chăt′ả·noō′gả). See UNITED STATES, *National Historical Parks.*
Chickamauga Dam. See *Table* at TENNESSEE VALLEY AUTHORITY.
Chick′a·saw (chǐk′ả·sô). **1** Name of counties in two states of the U.S. See *Tables* at IOWA and MISSISSIPPI.
2 City, Mobile co., SW Alabama, NW of Prichard; pop 10,002.
Chickasaw Bayou. An arm of the Mississippi river, W Mississippi, just N of Vicksburg and near the lower Yazoo; attack Dec. 29, 1862 by Union forces on heights **(Chickasaw Bluffs)** along its bank unsuccessful in attempt to capture Vicksburg.
Chick′a·sa′whay (chǐk′ả·sô′wā) or **Chick′a·sa′wha** (-wả). River 200 m. long, SE Mississippi; rises in E cen. Mississippi, flows S to unite with Leaf river in N George co. and form Pascagoula river.
Chick′a·sha (chǐk′ả·shả). City, ⊗ of Grady co., cen. Oklahoma, on Washita river 40 m. SW of Oklahoma City; pop. 14,866; manufactures cottonseed oil, flour, machinery; dairy products, cattle raising; oil and gas wells. Oklahoma College for Women (1908).
Chi·cla′na de la Fron·te′ra (chē·klä′nä thả lä frôntā′rä). Commune, Cádiz prov., SW Spain, 12 m. SE of Cádiz; pop. 17,047; thermal sulfur baths.
Chi·cla′yo (chē·klä′yō). Coastal city, ✲ of Lambayeque dept., NW Peru; pop. (1940 est.) 32,646; in rice and sugar district; its ports are Eten and Pimentel.
Chi′co (chē′kō). **1** City, Butte co., N California, 80 m. N of Sacramento; pop. 14,757; food processing and packing; manufactures beet sugar, lumber, cement. Settled 1847, incorporated as city 1923. Chico State College (1887).
2 Either of two rivers in S Argentina, one flowing NE out of Lake Musters in S Chubut territory and emptying into Chubut river, the other in Santa Cruz territory flowing SE into Atlantic Ocean at Santa Cruz.
3 River ab. 130 m. long, a W tributary of the Cagayan,

in NE Luzon, Phil. Is.; rises in the mountains of SW Bontoc subprov. and flows NNE to the Cagayan.

4 *or* **Pam·pan′ga Chico** (päm·päng′gä). River ab. 60 m. long, a W tributary of the Pampanga river, cen. Luzon, Phil. Is.; flows S.

Chic′o·pee (chĭk′ŭ·pē; -pē). **1** River, SW cen. Massachusetts; formed by junction of Quaboag and Swift rivers in N Hampden co., flows W into Connecticut river. **2** Industrial city, Hampden co., SW Massachusetts, on Connecticut river 3 m. N of Springfield; pop. 61,553; includes **Chicopee Falls, Chicopee Center, Wil′·li·man′sett** (wĭl′ĭ·măn′sĕt; -sĭt), **Fair′view** (fâr′vū′), and **Al′den·ville** (ôl′dĕn·vĭl); manufactures rubber and rubber goods, sporting goods. College of Our Lady of the Elms (1928; women). Westover Field, U.S. Air Force base, is nearby.

Chi′cot (shē′kō). County in Arkansas. See *Table* at ARKANSAS.

Chi′cot, Point (shē′kō; *Fr.* shē·kō′). Point on E coast of St. Bernard parish, SE Louisiana, on Breton Sound.

Chi·cou′ti·mi (shĭ·kōō′tĭ·mĭ; *Fr.* shē′kōō·tē′mē′). **1** River ab. 100 m. long, S Quebec, Canada; rises in Laurentides Provincial Park, flows N to Lake Kenogami and then E to the Saguenay at Chicoutimi; in its lower course drops nearly 500 ft.; noted for its scenery. **2** County, Quebec, Canada. See *Table* at QUEBEC. **3** River port, its ⊗, on Saguenay river at head of navigation at mouth of Chicoutimi river; pop. 23,216; lumber, pulp, paper; center of great water-power developments; seat of a Roman Catholic see. Founded 1650.

Chi·dam′ba·ram (chĭ·dŭm′bà·ràm). Town, N cen. Madras state, S India, 125 m. SSW of Madras; pop. 25,084; has numerous pagodas and temples, the principal temple sacred to Siva, much visited by pilgrims.

Chid′ley, Cape (chĭd′lĭ). Cape at N tip of Labrador, on Killinek I. on S side of entrance to Hudson Strait.

Chief Mountain (chēf). Peak 9056 ft. in Glacier National Park, NW Montana.

Chief's Head (chēfs). Peak 13,579 ft. in Boulder co., N cen. Colorado.

Chiem, Lake (kēm); *Ger.* **Chiem′see′** (kēm′zä′). Largest lake in Bavaria, S Germany, ab. 40 m. ESE of Munich; 32 sq. m.; 1600 ft. above sea level. Has three islands; outlet is the Alz by which course of 30 m. to the Inn.

Chiengmai. See CHIANG MAI.

Chiengrai. See CHIANG RAI.

Chie′ri (kyä′rē). Commune, Torino prov., Piedmont, NW Italy, 8 m. SE of Turin; pop. 13,736; walled city; large Gothic church; manufactures textiles.

Chie′ti (kyâ′tē). **1** Province of Italy. See *Table* at ITALY. **2** *anc.* **Te·a′te** (tē·ä′tē). Commune, its ✻, Abruzzi e Molise, cen. Italy, near right bank of Pescara river 93 m. ENE of Rome; pop. 30,266; archiepiscopal see; manufactures textiles; fine Gothic church. Ruled successively by Greeks, Romans, Lombards, Franks, and Normans; under Normans was capital of the Abruzzi; taken by French 1802; Theatine Order named for ancient city.

Chi′fu′. Var. of CHEFOO.

Chi·gha′ Khur (chē·gä′ kŏŏr′). Chief town of the Bakhtiari in mountains of W Iran.

Chig′na·hua·pán′ (chēg′nä·wä·pän′). Town, NW Puebla state, SE cen. Mexico; pop. 4156.

Chig·nec′to (shĭg·nĕk′tō). Isthmus joining Nova Scotia, Canada, to the mainland, comprising Cumberland co. and part of Colchester co.; in its narrowest part, at Amherst, ab. 12 m. wide; on N borders on Northumberland Strait and on S on Chignecto Bay and Minas Basin.

Chignecto Bay. N extremity of Bay of Fundy, Canada, ab. 50 m. long, lying bet. SE New Brunswick and NW Nova Scotia mainland; extremely high tides.

Chig′nik (chĭg′nĭk). **1** Bay, inlet on SE coast of Alaska Penin., S Alaska. **2** Village, on S shore of bay; pop. (1950) 253.

Chih′feng (chĭr′fŭng′). Town and treaty port, cen. Jehol prov., NE China; pop. 39,712.

Chih′kiang′ (jĭr′jĭ·äng′); *formerly* **Yuan′chow′** (yü-än′jō′). City, W Hunan prov., SE cen. China, on railroad 210 m. WSW of Changsha near border of Kweichow prov. In World War II important American air base unsuccessfully attacked by Japanese Apr.–May 1945.

Chih′li (chē′lē′; *Chin.* jĭr′lē′). Former province in NE China Proper; 115,830 sq. m.; ✻ Peking; divided 1928 largely into Hopeh (in China Proper), Jehol (in Manchuria), and Chahar (in Inner Mongolia) provs.

Chihli, Gulf of. See Po HAI.

Chi·hua′hua (chē·wä′wä). **1** State, N Mexico. See *Table* at MEXICO. **2** City, its ✻; pop. 56,808; altitude 4600 ft.; center of rich silver-mining district.

Chi·jol′ Canal (chē·hôl′). Canal 6 ft. deep and 25 ft. wide connecting Tampico (Pánuco river) with Tuxpan in E Veracruz state, Mexico.

Chi·ku·ho (chē·kōō·hô). Town, Fukuoka prefecture, N Kyushu, Japan; largest coal mines in Japan.

Chikuraj. See TJIKOERAJ.

Chilachap. See TJILATJAP.

Chilapa, *in full* **Chi·la′pa de Al′va·rez** (chē·lä′pä thä äl′vä·räs). Town, Guerrero, S Mexico; pop. 6094.

Chil·co′tin (chĭl·kō′t′n). River 145 m. long, S cen. British Columbia, Canada; flows SE into Fraser river.

Chil′dress (chĭl′drĕs; -drĭs). **1** County in Texas. See *Table* at TEXAS. **2** City, its ⊗, NW Texas, 80 m. E of Plainview; pop. 6399; railroad division point.

Chil′e (chĭl′ē; *Span.* chē′lā). Republic, SW South America; long, narrow country bet. Andes Mts. and the Pacific Ocean, ab. 2600 m. from ab. 17°30′S to Cape Horn in 56°S and nowhere above 221 m. wide; 286,396 sq. m.; pop. (1964 est.) 8,515,023; ✻ Santiago; bounded on N by Peru, on E by Bolivia and Argentina, on S by Drake Passage, and on W by the Pacific Ocean. Divided into the following 25 provinces (for pronunciation of their names, see their individual entries):

NAME	LOCA-TION	AREA[1]	POP.[1]	CAPITAL
Aconcagua	cen.	3,940	121,206	San Felipe
Antofagasta	N	47,515	154,087	Antofagasta
Arauco	S cen.	2,222	68,870	Lebu
Atacama	N cen.	30,843	90,105	Copiapó
Aysén	S	34,357	16,700	Aysén
Bío-Bío	S cen.	4,343	118,578	Los Ángeles
Cautín	S cen.	6,707	348,756	Temuco
Chiloé	S cen.	9,052	91,355	Ancud
Colchagua	cen.	3,423	133,491	San Fernando
Concepción	S cen.	2,201	335,281	Concepción
Coquimbo	cen.	15,401	250,953	La Serena
Curicó	cen.	2,215	90,490	Curicó
Linares	S cen.	3,791	133,705	Linares
Llanquihue	S cen.	7,107	113,087	Puerto Montt
Magallanes[2]	S	52,285	51,171	Punta Arenas
Malleco	S cen.	5,512	145,299	Angol
Maule	S cen.	2,172	65,418	Cauquenes
Ñuble	S cen.	5,487	226,904	Chillán
O'Higgins	cen.	2,746	201,599	Rancagua
Osorno	S cen.	3,867	80,299	Osorno
Santiago	cen.	6,559	1,463,441	Santiago
Talca	cen.	3,722	149,920	Talca
Tarapacá	N	21,346	99,724	Iquique
Valdivia	S cen.	7,723	210,256	Valdivia
Valparaíso	cen.	1,860	476,737	Valparaíso

[1] Area in sq. m. Pop. is 1943 est.
[2] Includes Strait of Magellan and all Chilean islands of the Tierra del Fuego archipelago (*q.v.*).

Has low coastal ranges; N part is high plateau (desert of Atacama). In N includes several peaks above 19,000 ft. (Mts. Copiapó, Palpana, Llullaillaco), but most of highest Andean peaks are on the boundaries with Bolivia and Argentina. Has no rivers of any size; largest Bío-Bío, Maipo, Itata, Maule, Copiapó; many lakes in S cen. part in resort region (Llanquihue, Ranco); S of 42° coast marked by many inlets, islands, and archipelagoes; owns W half of Tierra del Fuego and island on which is Cape Horn; also possesses small islets of Juan Fernández, Easter I., and others far out in the Pacific. Agriculture, forestry, and fishing important but most important ex-

ARGENTINA, CHILE,
PARAGUAY, URUGUAY

Statute Miles

0   100   200   300

⊛ Capitals of Countries

PUBLISHED BY G. & C. MERRIAM COMPANY
SPRINGFIELD, MASS.
PREPARED BY J. W. CLEMENT CO., BUFFALO, N.Y.

ports copper, nitrates, iodine, iron, gold, sulfur. Chief cities Santiago, Valparaíso, Concepción, Temuco, Viña del Mar; important ports Iquique, Antofagasta, Coquimbo, and Puerto Montt.

History: In 15th cent. northern part conquered by Incas; first invaded by Spanish under Almagro 1535; settlement begun at Santiago by Pedro de Valdivia 1541; governed under viceroyalty of Peru, becoming a separate captaincy general 1778; revolted against Spain 1810, but not finally independent until Feb. 12, 1818, after battle of Chacabuco (1817); independence assured by victory of San Martín at Maipo Apr. 5, 1818; governed by O'Higgins to 1823; under presidency of Prieto (1831–41), received centralized constitution 1833 and orderly conservative government; fought confederation of Peru and Bolivia (see YUNGAY) 1836–39; took part in war with Spain 1866; in War of the Pacific against Peru and Bolivia 1879–84, won the rich nitrate fields on coast of Bolivia (see ANTOFAGASTA and IQUIQUE) and occupied Tacna and Arica (*qq.v.*) which, until 1929, were subject of dispute with Peru; boundary disputes with Argentina 1899 and 1902 settled by arbitration; one of A.B.C. powers; neutral in World War I; erected new constitution 1925; member of League of Nations 1919–38; neutral in World War II.

Chiledug. See TJILEDOEG.

Chil′i (chĭl′ĭ). English var. of CHILE.

Chilia. See KILIYA river.

Chilia–Nouă. See KILIYA town.

Chi′li·an·wa′la *or* **Chil′li·an·wa′la** (chĭl′ĭ·ăn·wä′lä). Village, N West Punjab, Pakistan, 5 m. E of the Jhelum; pop. ab. 5000; battle Jan. 13, 1849 in Sikh Wars in which English under Sir Hugh Gough defeated Sikhs.

Chiliwong. See TJILIWONG.

Chil′ka Lake (chĭl′kä). Shallow inland gulf on the NE coast of Indian Union, in E Orissa state, lat. 19°40′N.

Chil′kat (chĭl′kăt). River 55 m. long flowing SE to **Chilkat Inlet** at head of Lynn Canal (*q.v.*), SE Alaska.

Chil′ko Lake (chĭl′kō). Lake 171 sq. m., S cen. British Columbia, Canada; outlet is the **Chilko River** flowing N into Chilcotin river.

Chil′koot Inlet (chĭl′kōot). E arm of Lynn Canal (*q.v.*), SE Alaska.

Chilkoot Pass. Pass in coast range, N Rocky Mts.; extends 29 m. from former village of Dyea at head of Taiya Inlet, Lynn Canal, SE Alaska, to Lake Bennett in Yukon Territory, Canada; highest point 3502 ft.; used 1896–98 by gold seekers until opening of White Pass farther E.

Chil·la′lo (chēl·lä′lô). Peak 11,991 ft. in cen. Ethiopia.

Chil·lán′ (chē·yän′). Commercial city, ✳ of Ñuble prov., S cen. Chile, 56 m. NE of Concepción; pop. 42,817; birthplace of the liberator Bernardo O'Higgins; orig. town, known as **Chillán Vie′jo** (vyĕ′hô), now a subdivision of the city (pop. 4310), founded 1594; destroyed by earthquake 1835 and rebuilt on present site 1836; again suffered severe earthquake destruction 1939. About 45 m. SE are the hot sulfur springs of Chillán, discovered 1795.

Chillán, Ne·va′do de (nä·vä′thô thä). Volcano 10,367 ft., S cen. Chile, SE of Chillán; active 1861, 1864.

Chil′li·coth′e (chĭl′ĭ·kŏth′ē). **1** City, Peoria co., NW cen. Illinois, on Illinois river N of Peoria; pop. 3054.

2 City, ⊗ of Livingston co., N Missouri, 75 m. NE of Kansas City; pop. 9236; in dairy-farming and livestock-raising section; coal and limestone deposits nearby.

3 Industrial city, ⊗ of Ross co., S Ohio, on Scioto river 44 m. S of Columbus; pop. 24,957; in agricultural and coal-mining region; printing and publishing; manufactures paper, shoes, furniture. Camp Sherman is N of city. Settled 1796; became capital of Northwest Territory 1800, capital of new state of Ohio 1803–10, 1812–16.

Chil′li·wack (chĭl′ĭ·wăk). City, S Brit. Columbia, Canada, on left bank of Fraser river 55 m. E of Vancouver; pop. 5663; creameries, fruit canneries, sawmills.

Chil′lon′ (shē′yôN′; *Angl.* shĭl·lŏn′, shĭl′ŭn). Castle in Vaud, W Switzerland, at E end of Lake Geneva; place of imprisonment 1530–36 of François de Bonnivard, hero of Lord Byron's poem *The Prisoner of Chillon.*

Chi′lo·é′ (chē′lō·ā′). **1** Island 4700 sq. m. in Pacific Ocean off SW coast of Chile, forming with several smaller islands a province of Chile; coal deposits.

2 Province of Chile. See *Table* at CHILE.

Chilpancingo, *in full* **Chil′pan·cin′go de los Bra′·vos** (chēl′pän·sēng′gô thä lôz vrä′vôs). Town, S Mexico, ✳ of Guerrero state; pop. 8834.

Chil′tern Hills (chĭl′tẽrn) *or* **Chil′terns** (-tẽrnz). Range of chalk hills 55 m. long in Oxfordshire and Buckinghamshire, S cen. England; highest point Coombe Hill, ab. 850 ft.

Chiltern Hundreds. Three hundreds (early divisions of a county)—Stoke, Burnham, and Desborough—in the Chiltern Hills, Buckinghamshire, England, the stewardship of which has long been a nominal office under the Chancellor of the Exchequer.

Chil′ton (chĭl′t′n; -tŭn). **1** County in Alabama. See *Table* at ALABAMA.

2 City, ⊗ of Calumet co., E Wisconsin, 18 m. E of Oshkosh; pop. 2578; manufactures cheese, aluminum, flour.

Chi′lung′ (chē′lōong′). = KEELUNG: see KIRUN.

Chil′wa, Lake (chĭl′wä). Lake ab. 40 m. long, SE Nyasaland and NW Mozambique, SE of Lake Nyasa.

Chilwell. See NEWTON AND CHILWELL.

Chimahi. See TJIMAHI.

Chi·mal′te·nan′go (chē·mäl′tä·näng′gô). **1** Department, S cen. Guatemala; 764 sq. m.; pop. 177,123.

2 Town, its ✳; pop. 7898.

Chi′may′ (shē′mā′). Commune, Hainaut prov., SW Belgium, 30 m. SW of Dinant; pop. 3368; castle, marble quarries; manufactures faïence.

Chim·bai′ (chĭm·bī′). Town, former ✳ of Kara-Kalpak Republic, Uzbek S.S.R., Soviet Central Asia; pop. 5400; in the delta of the Amu Darya, S of Lake Aral.

Chim·bo·ra′zo (chĭm′bô·rä′zō; -rä′-; shĭm′-; *Am. Span.* chēm′bô·rä′sô). **1** Peak 20,702 ft. in W cen. Ecuador; highest point in the Cordillera Real.

2 Province of Ecuador. See *Table* at ECUADOR.

Chim·bo′te (chēm·bô′tä). Seaport town, Ancash dept., W Peru, at mouth of Santa river; pop. ab. 1000; on Pan American Highway.

Chim·kent′ (chĭm·kĕnt′). Town, ✳ of South Kazakhstan Region, S Kazakh S.S.R., Soviet Central Asia, on Turkistan-Siberian R.R. 75 m. N of Tashkent; pop. 74,185; a trading and industrial center; health resort.

Chim′ney Point (chĭm′nĭ). Village and promontory, Addison co., Vermont, on S part of Lake Champlain; E terminal of Champlain bridge.

Chimney Rock. Peak 4242 ft. in Morrill co., W Nebraska.

Chim′ney·top′, Mount (chĭm′nĭ·tŏp′). Peak 4229 ft. in Union co., N Georgia.

Chi′na (chī′nà); *Chinese* **Chung–Hua Min–Kuo** (chōong′hwä′ mĭn′kwô′), "Republic of China"; *formerly* (until Jan. 1912) **Chinese Empire.** Known also as **Flowery Kingdom, Middle Kingdom,** and **Celestial Empire.** A republic of E and cen. Asia; total area 3,691,500 sq. m.; pop. (1964 est.) 700,000,000; ✳ Peking (Peiping). Comprises: (1) **China** *or* **China Proper,** now officially divided into 36 provinces; 2,903,455 sq. m.; pop. (1936 est.) 422,707,868; made up as follows: (a) the original China Proper ("18 Provinces") of the Empire and Republic: Anhwei, Chekiang, Fukien, Honan, Hopei, Hunan, Hupei, Kansu, Kiangsi, Kiangsu, Kwangsi, Kwangtung, Kweichow, Shansi, Shantung, Shensi, Szechwan, and Yunnan, 1,458,847 sq. m., pop. (1936 est.) 411,040,814. To these in recent years have been added: (b) **Inner Mongolia,** comprising 3 provinces of Chahar, Ningsia, and Suiyuan, 326,285 sq. m., pop. (1936 est.) 5,142,793; and (c) three regions, formerly considered as outer dependencies, now the provinces of

Sinkiang, Sikang, and Tsinghai, 1,118,323 sq. m., pop. (1936 est.) 6,524,261. (2) **Outer China,** comprising Tibet (only nominally a province), Manchuria, Jehol, and Formosa; 965,591 sq. m.; pop. (1936 est.) 38,365,580. For the period 1907–32 the 3 original provinces (Liaoning, Kirin, and Heilungkiang) of Manchuria were incorporated in China Proper; in 1932 they were, together with Jehol in 1933, set up by Japan as an independent kingdom, Manchukuo. In 1945, 3 original provinces of Manchuria (redivided into 9 provinces) and Jehol restored to China. The island of Formosa returned to China (Sept. 1945); former province of Outer Mongolia declared its independence (Oct. 1945). See *Map*, pages 230–231.

Rivers: Its three great rivers—the Hwang Ho in the N, Yangtze in the cen. part, and the Si in the S—great commercial highways; the Amur forming N boundary of Manchuria, and its tributary the Sungari; the Salween and Mekong of SE Asia, rising in the Tibetan plateau and mountains of Tsinghai; and the Tsangpo (Brahmaputra) flowing across S Tibet and SW Sikang. *Chief lakes:* Tungting Hu and Poyang Hu in SE cen. part, Tai Hu and Hungtze Hu in E, Tsing Hai (or Koko Nor) in Tsinghai, and many large lakes without outlet in Sinkiang and Tibet. *Mountains:* The Himalayas along the S and SW border of Tibet, itself a great plateau of more than 10,000 ft. elevation; the Kunlun Mts. stretching E and W along the N edge of Tibet, with many subsidiary ranges, esp. the Astin Tagh and the Nan Shan; the Tien Shan in W Sinkiang; the Great Khingan Mts. in Manchuria; and in China Proper, esp. in S and W, many shorter and lower ranges; highest known peak Minya Konka 24,900 ft. in E Sikang; Amne Machin (estimated at 25,000 ft.) in Tsinghai may be higher. *Other notable physical features:* the Gobi and Takla Makan Deserts, Tarim basin and Turfan depression, Yangtze Gorges, Hainan I., Liaotung, Shantung, and Luichow Penins., Gulf of Po Hai and Hangchow Bay. Many good harbors on its long coast.

An agricultural land but in recent years has developed cotton, wool, and silk manufacturing; produces cereals, soybeans, rice, cotton, hemp, and flax; animal industry is important; in minerals, esp. coal and iron, its resources are enormous but little developed; tin, antimony, and tungsten mined. Chief cities Shanghai, Chungking, Canton, Peiping, Nanking, Hankow, Tientsin, Changsha, Mukden. See HONG KONG; MACAO; MANCHUKUO; MANCHURIA.

History: Civilization probably spread from Hwang Ho (Yellow River) valley where it existed c. 3000 B.C.; Chou dynasty (1122–255 B.C.) the first vouched for by valid historical evidence; from mouth of Yangtze river to Great Wall under Chou control but from 8th to 3d cents. B.C. divided into warring feudal states; Taoism and Confucianism founded in 6th cent. B.C.; under Ch'in (Ts'in) dynasty (255–206 B.C.) expanded south of Yangtze and built Great Wall against invasion from north; members of Han dynasty (202 B.C.–220 A.D.) reconquered Annam and Canton, took northern Korea and, through mastery of central Asian tribes, gained first direct overland contact with west (Rome); Buddhism (see INDIA) introduced by 1st cent. A.D.; split up bet. 220 and 280 into three kingdoms Shu (Han), Wu, and Wei; Nestorian Christianity and Mohammedanism introduced 618–907, and "Golden Age" of Chinese literature began under T'angs whose authority extended to Cambodia and to Persia and the Caspian; ruled by Sung dynasty (960–1127), and, after invasion of Kin Tatars in north, by Southern Sungs (1127–1280); in 13th cent. became seat of Mongol empire which included all of China (not Indochina), and stretched across Asia into Europe as far as Lithuania and Novgorod; Kublai Khan, first of Yüan (Mongol) dynasty (1260–1368), visited by Marco Polo 1275–92; southern China drove out Mongols and founded Ming dynasty (1368–1644); reached in 1521 by

Portuguese whose traders and missionaries were at first admitted to interior but were later strictly limited (see MACAO); under Manchus (1644–1912) Chinese Empire included Manchuria, Mongolia, Tibet, and Turkistan, and claimed as tributaries Korea, Annam, Siam, Burma, and Nepal; in first treaty with European power (see NERCHINSK) 1689, defined northern boundary with Russia; from 1717 Macao and Canton alone open to European trade until, at close of First Opium War 1842, China forced to cede Hong Kong and open five treaty ports; eastern Siberia, as far as Vladivostok (*q.v.*) ceded to Russia 1858–60; lost Korea, Formosa, and Pescadores (Treaty of Shimonoseki) 1895 to Japan; lease of Kiaochow to Germany in 1898 began European scramble for concessions; northern China scene of Boxer risings 1900; overthrew Manchus and erected Chinese Republic 1912; forced to yield to Twenty-one Demands of Japan 1915; entered World War I 1917; subject of Nine-Power Treaty after Washington Conference 1922; after civil war 1920–26 nationalist government formed at Nanking by Chiang Kai-shek 1928, 1931; Manchuria (*q.v.*) occupied by Japan 1931–32; engaged in war with Japan 1937–45; one of the four Great Powers in world-wide conflict of Allied Nations against Axis countries 1939–45; civil war 1945–50, during which Communist regime took over mainland China.

China Grove. Manufacturing town, Rowan co., cen. North Carolina, 10 m. SW of Salisbury; pop. 1500.

Chi'na·me'ca (chē'nä·mā'kä). Town, San Miguel dept., E El Salvador; pop. (1942 est.) 6502.

Chinan. See TSINAN.

Chi'nan·de'ga (chē'nän·dā'gä). **1** Department, NW Nicaragua; 1776 sq. m.; pop. (1943 est.) 83,741. **2** Town, its ✳; pop. (1943 est.) 15,525; sugar mill.

China Proper. See CHINA.

China Sea. Part of Pacific Ocean reaching from Japan to S end of Malay Penin.; divided by Formosa into **East China Sea** or **Eastern Sea** (enclosed by E China, S Korea, Kyushu and Ryukyu Is., and Formosa) and **South China Sea,** often called simply **China Sea** (enclosed by SE China, Indochina, Malay Penin., Borneo, Philippine Is., and Formosa).

Chi·na'ti Peak (chē·nä'tē). Mountain 7730 ft. in Presidio co., W Texas.

Chin'cha (chēn'chä). River ab. 60 m. long, cen. Peru; flows W into Pacific Ocean 115 m. SSE of Lima.

Chincha Al'ta (äl'tä). Town, Ica dept., SW Peru, near mouth of Chincha river; pop. (1940 est.) 12,768.

Chincha Islands. Group of small islands in Pacific Ocean off coast of W cen. Peru, Ica dept.; guano.

Chinchaycocha. See Lake JUNÍN.

Chin'chou' (jĭn'jō'), *formerly* **Kin'chow'** (jĭn'jō'). Town, Kwantung Leased Territory, S Manchuria, on NW coast of Liaotung Penin. and on railroad; pop. 13,000; a customs substation of Dairen.

Chinchow. See CHINHSIEN.

Chin'co·teague (shĭng'kŏ·tēg; chĭng'kŏ-). Town, NE Accomac co., E Virginia, on Chincoteague I., bet. S end of Assateague I. and the mainland; pop. 2131; fisheries.

Chincoteague Bay. Long narrow bay bet. Assateague I. and the mainland (Maryland and Virginia).

Chin'de (chĭn'dĕ). Seaport town on only navigable mouth of the Zambezi, SE cen. Mozambique; pop. (1935 est.) 3894; formerly chief port for Nyasaland and Northern Rhodesia; partly superseded by Beira.

Chin'di·o (chĭn'dĭ·ō). Town, Manica and Sofala prov., S Mozambique, SE Africa, on Zambezi river; S terminus of Nyasaland railroad.

Chin'dwin' (chĭn'dwĭn'). River ab. 550 m. long in W Upper Burma; chief tributary of the Irrawaddy. Rises in Kumon Range in N Burma, flows NW through Hukawng Valley, then S along India border and SE to the Irrawaddy at Myingyan; generally navigable below its confluence with the Uyu, its chief tributary. Scene of much fighting 1942–44.

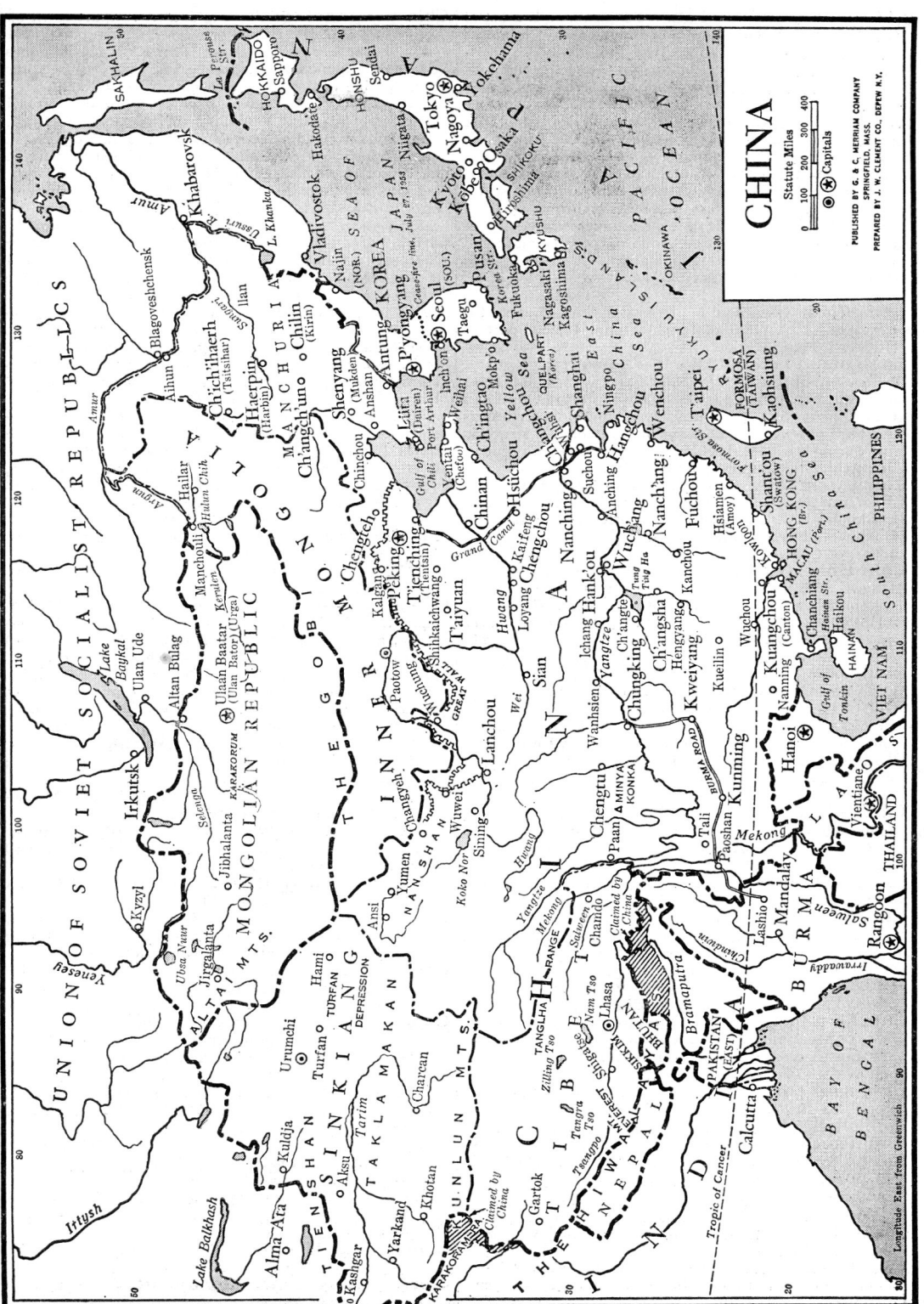

CHINA

Statute Miles

0   100   200   300   400

◉ Capitals

PUBLISHED BY G. & C. MERRIAM COMPANY
SPRINGFIELD, MASS.
PREPARED BY J. W. CLEMENT CO., DEPEW, N.Y.

Chi·nen Peninsula (chĕ·nĕn). Peninsula on E coast of Okinawa, at S end of island S of Buckner Bay; Japanese on it cut off by U.S. marines June 5–6, 1945.

Chinese Turkistan *or* **Kash·gar′i·a** (kăsh·gâr′ĭ·à). The part of Turkistan (*q.v.*) under Chinese control, now comprising the W and cen. parts of the modern province of Sinkiang, W China; chief town was Kashgar. Since earliest times occupied successively by the Hiung-Nu, Yuechi, Chinese, Ephthalites, Uigurs, Mohammedans, and Mongols. Khotan was long the most important city. In 14th and 15th cents. visited by many Moslem scholars, but tolerance then established overthrown by cruel Chinese conquest in 18th cent.; under leadership of Uzbeks rebelled against China 1866; reconquered 1877–78 and made part of Sinkiang.

Chinese Wall. See GREAT WALL.

Ching. See KING.

Ching′ford (chĭng′fĕrd). Urban district, Essex, SE England, 12 m. NNE of London; pop. 48,330; part of Greater London.

Chinghai. **1** Lake in China. See TSING HAI.
2 Province of China. See TSINGHAI.

Chin′gle·put (chĭng′g'l·pŏŏt). Town, Madras, S Indian Union, 14 m. SW of Madras; pop. 14,358; important as a capital of Vijayanagar kings in 16th cent.; a strategic fort during wars bet. French and English in 18th cent.

Chingtehchen. Var. of KINGTEHCHEN.

Ching′yuan′ (chĭng′yü·än′). Var. of TSINGYUAN.

Chin′hai′ (chĭn′hī′). **1** City and port, NE Chekiang prov., E China, ab. 12 m. ENE of Ninghsien on SE shore of Hangchow Bay; pop. ab. 35,000.
2 Var. of *Chinghai:* see TSINGHAI.

Chin Hills (chĭn). **1** Range of hills along W border of Magwe division, Upper Burma, part of Arakan Yoma system; highest 7998 ft.; inhabited by Chin tribes.
2 Hill district, W Magwe division, Upper Burma; 10,377 sq. m.; pop. 171,237; ✳ Falam; scene of much fighting in Japanese campaign against Manipur 1942–44.

Chin′hsien′ (jĭn′shyĕn′); *formerly* **Chin′chow′** (jĭn′jō′). Town, SW Liaoning prov., Manchuria, at head of Gulf of Po Hai on W side; pop. (1940 est.) 142,606; commercial center, esp. for cattle trade, on Tientsin-Mukden railroad. Fighting here 1945 in Chinese civil war.

Chin′i·ot (chĭn′ĭ·ŭt). Town, cen. West Punjab, Pakistan, on E bank of Chenab river 80 m. W of Lahore; pop. 25,841.

Chin′ju′ (jĭn′jōō′) *or* **Shin′shu′** (shĭn′shōō′). Town, South Keisho prov., S Korea, 55 m W of Fusan; pop. 30,269; center of cotton district.

Chin′kai′ (chĭn′kī′). Seaport town, South Keisho prov., S Korea, on inlet of Chosen Strait 22 m. W of Fusan; former Japanese naval base.

Chin′kiang′ (*Angl.* chĭn′kyăng′; *Chin.* jĭn′jĭ·äng′). City and treaty port, ✳ of Kiangsu prov., E China, on S bank of Yangtze 43 m. below Nanking at the junction of the Grand Canal with the river; pop. (1931 est.) 199,776. About 2000 years old; important in time of Marco Polo and under Ming and Manchu dynasties.

Chin Ling Shan, *formerly* **Tsin′ling′ Shan** (chĭn′lĭng′ shän′). Mountain range in N China, running E–W from SE Kansu across cen. Shensi into W Honan; watershed bet. Wei and Han rivers; highest peak ab. 11,000 ft.

Chin·nam·po (chĕn·năm·pŏ). City, South Heian prov., Korea, on the W coast 25 m. SW of Heijo; pop. (1938 est.) 61,457; treaty port; opened to foreign trade 1897.

Chinnereth, Sea of. See Sea of GALILEE.

Chi′no (chē′nō). City, San Bernardino co., SE California, 30 m. E of Los Angeles; pop. 10,305; founded 1887; trade center for citrus fruits and sugar beets.

Chi′non′ (shē′nôn′). Commune, Indre-et-Loire dept., NW cen. France, on the Vienne river; pop. 4169; birthplace of Rabelais.

Chi·nook′ (shĭ·nŏŏk′). Town, ⊗ of Blaine co., N Montana, 22 m. E of Havre; pop. 2326; beet-sugar refinery.

Chinsura. See HOOGHLY.

Chin′wang′tao′ (chĭn′hwäng′dou′). Seaport town on Gulf of Po Hai, NE Hopeh prov., NE China; pop. (1931 est.) 20,020; first created as outlet for Kaiping coal mines 100 m. distant; opened as treaty port 1901; ice-free, has considerable winter trade of Tientsin and Newchwang.

Chiog′gia (kyôd′jä); *anc.* **Fos′sa Clau′di·a** (fŏs′à klô′dĭ·à). Seaport, Venezia prov., Venezia Euganea, NE Italy, on island in Venetian lagoon 15 m. S of Venice; pop. 42,569; built on piles and connected with mainland by 800-ft. stone bridge; 17th-cent. cathedral; chief fishing port of Italy; coastal trade; manufactures textiles, lace, bricks, ships; supremacy of Venice over Genoa decided here in naval battle Dec. 23, 1379.

Chi′os (kī′ŏs); *Mod. Gr.* **Khí′os** (κε̄′ôs); *Turk.* **Sa·kis′-A·da·si′** (sä·kĭz′ä·dä·sī′); *Ital.* **Sci′o** (shē′ô). **1** Island in the Aegean Sea off W coast of Turkey in Asia, by some included among the Southern Sporades (see SPORADES); 30 m. long by 8 to 15 m. wide; 355 sq. m.; pop. (1938 est.) 82,914; administratively a department of Greece (see *Table* at GREECE). Hilly, fertile; produces much fruit, esp. figs. Noted in antiquity for its claims as Homer's birthplace and for its school of epic poets, the Homeridae; also for its sculptors. Colonized by Ionians and became powerful state; became subject to Persia 494 B.C.; joined Delian League 478 B.C.; revolted several times but prospered under Romans and Byzantines; later passed successively to Turks, Venetians, Genoese, Ottomans, and finally 1912 to Greece. British and Greek troops landed here Oct. 6, 1944. Birthplace of Theopompus of Chios. See AEGEAN ISLANDS.
2 *or* **Ka′stron** (kä′strôn). City on E coast of Chios I., ✳ of Chios dept.; pop. 22,122.

Chip′ley (chĭp′lĭ). Town, ⊗ of Washington co., NW Florida, 105 m. ENE of Pensacola; pop. 3159.

Chi·po′la (chĭ·pō′là). River ab. 130 m. long, SE Alabama and W Florida; flows S from Henry co., SE Alabama, and empties into the Apalachicola river ab. 10 m. from its mouth; navigable for a short distance.

Chip′pa·wa (chĭp′à·wä; -wô). Village, Welland co., SE Ontario, Canada, on Niagara river 2 m. above Niagara Falls; pop. 1762; founded by Loyalists in 1783. American force defeated the British here on July 5, 1814.

Chip′pen·ham (chĭp′ĕn·ăm). Municipal borough, Wiltshire, S England, on the Avon 20 m. E of Bristol; pop. 11,850.

Chip′pe·wa (chĭp′ĕ·wä; -wô). **1** River, W cen. Minnesota; flows S into Minnesota river.
2 River 183 m. long, W cen. Wisconsin; rises in Sawyer co., flows S and SW into Mississippi river; navigable 50 m. to Eau Claire, Wisconsin.
3 Name of counties in three states of the U.S. See *Tables* at MICHIGAN, MINNESOTA, WISCONSIN.

Chippewa Falls. Industrial city, ⊗ of Chippewa co., W Wisconsin, on Chippewa river 10 m. NNE of Eau Claire; pop. 11,708; railroad and highway focus.

Chippewa Lake. Lake in Sawyer co., NW Wisconsin; a source of Chippewa river.

Chipping Wycombe. See CHEPPING WYCOMBE.

Chip′ut·net′i·cook Lakes (shĭp′ŏŏt·nĕt′ĭ·kŏŏk). Chain of lakes forming upper course of St. Croix river, on boundary bet. W New Brunswick, Canada, and E Maine; largest is Grand Lake (*q.v.*).

Chi·qui·mu′la (chē′kē·mōō′lä). **1** Department, SE Guatemala; 917 sq. m.; pop. 144,011; coffee, sugar, rice.
2 City, its ✳; pop. 10,868.

Chi·qui·mu·lil′la (chē′kē·mōō·lē′yä). Town, Santa Rosa dept., S Guatemala; pop. 5637.

Chi·quin′qui·rá′ (chē·kēng′kē·rä′). Town, Boyacá dept., cen. Colombia, 65 m. N of Bogotá; altitude 8365 ft.; pop. 6998; emerald mines nearby; pilgrimages.

Chire. See SHIRE.

Chir′i·ca′hua Mountains (chĭr′ĭ·kä′wà). Small range in E Cochise co., SE Arizona.

Chiricahua National Monument. See UNITED STATES, *National Monuments.*

Chi·ri·quí' (chē'rē·kē'). **1** Volcanic peak 11,070 ft., W Panama, near the border of Costa Rica.
2 Province, W Panama; 3693 sq. m.; pop. 111,294; * David.

Chiriquí, Gulf of. Inlet of the Pacific Ocean in extreme SW Panama.

Chiriquí Lagoon. Inlet of the Caribbean Sea on the NW coast of Panama, W of Mosquito Gulf.

Chi·ro'mo (chǐ·rō'mō). Commercial town on Shire river, S Nyasaland, SE Africa.

Chirpan. See CIRPAN.

Chir'ri·pó' Gran'de (chēr'rē·pō' grän'då). Mountain 12,589 ft. in SE cen. Costa Rica, in the Cordillera de Talamanca; highest point in Costa Rica.

Chi·sa'go (shǐ·sā'gō). County in Minnesota. See *Table* at MINNESOTA.

Chishima Retto, Chishima Strait. See KURIL ISLANDS, KURIL STRAIT.

Chis'holm (chǐz'ŭm). City, St. Louis co., NE Minnesota, 4 m. ENE of Hibbing; pop. 7144; iron mining.

Chisholm Trail. A cattle trail leading N from near San Antonio, Texas, to Abilene, Kansas; used esp. immediately after the Civil War when large herds of cattle were driven to markets in the N.

Chi·si·ma'io (kē·zē·mä'yō) *or* **Kis·ma'yu** (kĭs·mä'yōō). Seaport, S Somalia, E Africa; pop. ab. 10,000; occupied by British Feb. 14, 1941.

Chi'şi·nău' (kē'shē·nû'ōō). City, * of Bessarabia and later of Moldavian Republic. See KISHINEV.

Chis'le·hurst and Sid'cup (chĭz''l·hûrst, sĭd'kŭp). Urban district, Kent, SE England, 10 m. SE of London; pop. 83,837; part of Greater London.

Chi'sos Mountains (chē'sōs). Range in Big Bend National Park, S Brewster co., W Texas; highest 7835 ft.

Chi·sto'pol (chǐ·stô'pŭl·y'). Town, cen. Tatar Republic, Soviet Russia, Europe, on left bank of Kama river 65 m. SE of Kazan; pop. 15,798; a trade center esp. in lumber, grain, and textiles; has Tatar advanced schools.

Chiswick. See BRENTFORD AND CHISWICK.

Chi·ta' (chĭ·tà'). City, * of Chita Region, in SW part, Soviet Russia, Asia, on Chita river near its confluence with the Ingoda; pop. 102,555; on Trans-Siberian R.R. 260 m. E of Ulan-Ude; center of a rich mineral region (coal, iron, gold, wolfram, bismuth, and molybdenum); rapid industrial development in recent years.

Chi·ta, Ne·va'do de (nå·vä'thô thå chē'tä). Peak 18,022 ft. in the Cordillera Oriental, N cen. Colombia, near Chinavita.

Chit'al·droog *or* **Chit'al·drug** (chĭt''l·drŏog). Town, N Mysore state, S Indian Union, 137 m. N of Mysore; pop. 10,732.

Chi·tam'bo (chĭ·tăm'bō). Village, NE Zambia, S cen. Africa, S of the marshes on S shore of Lake Bangweulu; David Livingstone died 1873 at Old Chitambo, a small village NNW of Chitambo.

Chi·ta' Region (chĭ·tà'). Region, SE Soviet Russia, Asia; 180,455 sq. m.; pop. 1,159,478; * Chita. Its chief streams are the Amur on its SE border, the Shilka and Argun (headstreams of the Amur), and the Olekma and Zeya. Region is a plateau area, with the Yablonoi Mts. on the W and extensions of mountain ranges of Khabarovsk Territory in the E. Produces grains and vegetables, but esp. timber, furs, and minerals; raises cattle. Crossed by the Trans-Siberian R.R. in the S and by the new transcontinental BAM near its N and E borders. Chief cities Chita, Nerchinsk, Sretensk. Forms part of one of the earliest settled regions of E Siberia, then known as Transbaikalia; after the Revolution 1917 a part of the Far Eastern Region (*q.v.*); designated as a new subdivision of Soviet Russia in Asia 1936.

Chit'i·na (chĭt''n·ô). Village, N of Chugach Mts. on Copper river 75 m. NNE of Cordova, SE Alaska; pop. (1950) 92.

Chi·tral' (chĭ·träl'). **1** River ab. 300 m. long in NW India and NE Afghanistan; flows S through Chitral state and into Afghanistan, where it is called the Kunar, and empties into Kabul river near Jalalabad.
2 Former Indian state, N North-West Frontier Province, Pakistan; ab. 4500 sq. m.; pop. ab. 35,000; on Afghan border on S slope of Hindu Kush Mts.; ruled by independent Moslem dynasty for 300 years; occupied by British when succession disputed 1895; on Aug. 15, 1947 became part of Pakistan.
3 Town, its *, on Chitral river at over 5000 ft. Small British force withstood siege Mar.–Apr. 1895.

Chi·tré' (chē·trā'). Town, * of former Herrera prov., S Panama; pop. 4790.

Chit'ta·gong (chĭt'à·gŏng). **1** Division, formerly part of Bengal, NE Brit. India, now wholly within East Bengal, Pakistan; 11,765 sq. m.; pop. (1941) 8,477,890.
2 Town, its *, on Karnaphuli river 12 m. from its mouth and 225 m. E of Calcutta; pop. (1941) 92,301. Trade center; exports Assam tea, Burmese mineral oil, jute, cotton, rice, and hides. In one of the regions of heaviest annual rainfall in the world. Known to early Portuguese mariners; conquered by nawab of Bengal 1666; ceded to British East India Company 1760.

Chittagong Hill Tracts. District of Chittagong division, since Aug. 15, 1947 in East Bengal, Pakistan; 5007 sq. m.; pop. (1941) 247,053; * Rangamati. Hilly region along Burmese border, inhabited by descendants of Arakanese and aboriginal tribes.

Chit'ten·den (chĭt''n·děn). County in Vermont. See *Table* at VERMONT.

Chittenden Reservoir. Reservoir at upper end of East Creek tributary of Otter Creek, W cen. Vermont.

Chit'ten·don, Mount (chĭt''n·dŭn). Peak 10,000 ft. in Yellowstone National Park, NW Wyoming.

Chit·toor' (chĭ·tŏor'). Town, S Andhra Pradesh, SE India, ab. 90 m. W of Madras; pop. 22,018.

Chiu'si (kyōō'sē); *anc.* **Clu'si·um** (klōō'zhĭ·ŭm; -zǐ·ŭm). Commune, Siena prov., SE Tuscany, cen. Italy, ab. 40 m. SE of Siena; pop. 8043; one of the 12 cities of ancient Etruria, flourished 7th–6th cents. B.C.; became subject to Rome 295 B.C.; declined in Middle Ages because of proximity to swamps of Chiana river.

Chi·u'ta, Lake (shē·ōō'tà). Lake in NW Mozambique, SE Africa; the Lugenda river issues from its N end.

Chi·vas'so (kē·väs'sō). Commune, Torino prov., Piedmont, NW Italy, on Po river NE of Turin; pop. 11,590; sulfur baths; fortifications destroyed by French 1804.

Chi'vil·coy (chē'vēl·koi'). City, Buenos Aires prov., E Argentina, 90 m. W of Buenos Aires; pop. ab. 37,000.

Chi·xoy' (chē·hoi'). See USUMACINTA.

Chka'lov (ch'kà'lŭf) *or* **O'ren·burg** (ôr'ĕn·bŏorg; *Russ.* ŭ·ryĕn·bŏork'). City, * of Chkalov Region, Soviet Russia, Europe, on Ural river; on railroad from Kuibyshev to Tashkent; pop. 172,925; long a trading center. First established as a fort 1735; a point of severe fighting after Revolution of 1917; suffered greatly from famine of 1920–21; capital of Kirgiz Autonomous Republic 1920–24; name changed 1938 in honor of V. P. Chkalov, Russian aviator, leader of first transpolar flight June 1937 from Moscow to Vancouver, Washington; again renamed Orenburg 1957.

Chkalov Region *or* **Orenburg Region.** Region, E Soviet Russia, Europe; 47,787 sq. m.; pop. 1,677,013; * Orenburg; hilly in N and E; traversed by Ural river and tributaries and by the Samara in the W; has some mineral wealth; produces leather goods and shawls.

Choaspes. See KARKHEH.

Cho'be (chō'bè). Swamp and lower course of Kwando river in Caprivi Concession, South-West Africa.

Chocim. See KHOTIN.

Cho·có' (chô·kō'). **1** Large bay, W coast of Colombia; Buenaventura is on it.
2 Intendancy of Colombia. See *Table* at COLOMBIA.

Cho·cor'u·a, Mount (shŭ·kŏr'ōō·à). Peak 3475 ft. in W cen. Carroll co., E New Hampshire, in Sandwich Range of the White Mts.

Choc'taw (chŏk'tô). Counties in three states of the U.S. See *Tables* at ALABAMA, MISSISSIPPI, OKLAHOMA.

Choc'taw·hatch'ee (chŏk'tô-hăch'ê). River ab. 180 m. long, NW Florida; rises in S Alabama; flows S, forming boundary bet. Walton and Washington cos., into **Choctawhatchee Bay,** inlet of Gulf of Mexico.

Choi'seul' (shwä'zûl'). One of the Solomon Is., W Pacific Ocean, ab. 32 m. E of SE Bougainville I. and midway bet. Bougainville and Santa Isabel Is.; 85 m. long and bet. 4 and 20 m. wide; ab. 1500 sq. m.; was under German control 1886–99; became part of British Solomon Is. protectorate; chief settlement Bambatana on W coast; highest point 2470 ft.; nearly surrounded by barrier reef; densely forested.

Choi'sy'–le–Roi' (shwä'zē'lĕ-rwä'). Commune, Seine dept., N France, SSE suburb of Paris on left bank of Seine river; pop. 28,476; Rouget de Lisle buried here.

Choj·ni'ce (Koi·nē'tsĕ); *Ger.* **Ko'nitz** (kō'nĭts). Commune, Pomorze dept., Poland, 65 m. NW of Toruń; pop. (1938–39 est.) 16,975. Scene of last great victory of Teutonic Knights over Poles 1454; recovered from Prussia after World War I.

Choj'nów (Koi'nōof); *Ger.* **Hay'nau** (hī'nou). Manufacturing city, cen. Wrocław dept., SW Poland, 11 m. N of Legnica; pop. (1946) 11,114; formerly in Silesia, Germany; assigned to Poland 1945. Battle bet. French and Prussians May 26, 1813.

Cho·kai (chō-kī). Volcano 7423 ft., N Yamagata prefecture, N Honshu, Japan, near coast; last eruption 1861.

Cho'la (chō'lä). Early kingdom in Carnatic, SE India; known from 4th cent. B.C. but especially powerful under Chola dynasty of Tamil kings (888–1267 A.D.); extended from Pudukkottai N to Nellore, with capitals at Kumbakonam and Tanjore.

Cho'let' (shô'lĕ'). Commune, Maine-et-Loire dept., W France, on Maine river 32 m. SSW of Angers; pop. 23,385; manufactures textiles, paper; 15th-cent. bridge; completely destroyed in Wars of the Vendée 1793–94.

Cho'lon' *or* **Cho Lon** (chō'lôn'). City, S Vietnam, in E Cochin China; SW suburb of Saigon; pop. 481,000; has many canals and houses built on piles; varied industries. Founded by Chinese immigrants ab. 1780.

Cho·lu'la (chō-lōō'lä), *in full* **Cholula de Ri'va·da'bia** (thä rē'vä-thä'vyä). Town, 8 m. W of Puebla, Puebla state, SE cen. Mexico; pop. 8424; site of the truncated Pyramid of Quetzalcoatl (base covers 42 acres), used by the Aztecs for their human sacrifices. Cf. TEOTIHUACÁN.

Cho'lu·te'ca (chō'lōō-tā'kä). **1** River ab. 150 m. long, S Honduras; flows E, S, and SW to Gulf of Fonseca.
2 Department, S Honduras; 1966 sq. m.; pop. (1945 est.) 96,559.
3 Town, its ✻; pop. (1940) 5057; cattle center.

Cho'mo Lha'ri (chō'mô hlä'rê) *or* **Chu'ma·lha'ri** (chōō'mä-). Mountain peak 23,930 ft. in the Himalayas bet. Tibet and NW Bhutan.

Chomo–lungma. See Mount EVEREST.

Cho'mŭ·tov (Kô'mōō-tôf); *Ger.* **Ko'mo·tau** (kō'mô-tou). Manufacturing city, NW Bohemia, W Czechoslovakia, 52 m. NW of Prague; pop. (1930) 33,279.

Chon Bu·ri (chŭn bōō-rē); *also* **Bang Pla Soi** (bäng plä soi). **1** Province, S Thailand; 1727 sq. m.; pop. 149,918.
2 Town, its ✻. See BANG PLA SOI.

Cho'ne (chō'nä). **1** River ab. 60 m. long in W Ecuador; flows from Andes Mts. W into Pacific Ocean.
2 City, Manabí prov., W Ecuador, 110 m. WSW of Quito; pop. (1944 est.) 21,834; cacao, coffee, and sugar.

Chongjin. See SEISHIN.

Chonju. See ZENSHU.

Cho'nos Archipelago (chō'nôs); *Span.* **Ar'chi·pié'la·go de los Chonos** (är'chĕ-pyä'lä-gŏ thä lôs). Group of islands in S Pacific Ocean off SW coast of Chile, N of Madre de Dios Archipelago.

Chon·ta'les (chôn-tä'lâs). Department, S cen. Nicaragua; 4170 sq. m.; pop. (1943 est.) 65,376; ✻ Juigalpa.

Cho'pi·col'qui (chō'pĕ-kôl'kĕ). Peak ab. 22,000 ft. in the Cordillera Occidental, Peru.

Chop'tank' (chŏp'tănk'). River ab. 100 m. long, E Maryland; rises in W cen. Delaware, flows SW across Maryland border to Chesapeake Bay in SE Talbot co.

Cho·ras'mi·a (kô-răz'mĭ-á). Province of ancient Persia on the Oxus, W Asia, extending W to the Caspian Sea; in 12th cent. ab. equivalent to empire of Khwarizm (*q.v.*) which became the khanate of Khiva (*q.v.*). The Chorasmians, who were Aryans, formed a contingent under Xerxes.

Chor'ley (chôr'lĭ). Municipal borough, Lancashire, NW England, 19 m. WNW of Manchester; pop. 32,636; cotton weaving and calico printing.

Chorlu. See ÇORLU.

Chorokh. See ÇORUH.

Cho·rol'que (chô-rôl'kä). Peak 18,380 ft. in Potosí dept., SW Bolivia.

Chorrera, La. See LA CHORRERA.

Chor·ril'los (chôr-rē'yôs). Residential town, ab. 9 m. S of Lima, Peru; pop. (1931) 7293; resort; scene of Chilean victory over Peruvians Jan. 13, 1881.

Chorum. See ÇORUM.

Cho'rzów (kô'zhōof). Manufacturing and mining city, Śląsk dept., SW Poland, 5 m. NNW of Katowice; pop. (1938–39 est.) 109,500; formed 1934 from former communes of Chorzów, Królewska Huta, and Hajduki Nowe. Iron and coal mines; one of largest nitrate plants in world; blast furnaces; manufactures include iron goods, glass, cement, brick and tile, brandy.

Cho·sen (chō-sĕn). See KOREA.

Chosen Archipelago; *also* **Ko·re'an Archipelago** (kô-rē'ăn). Group of small islands in Chosen Strait, off S coast of Korea.

Chosen Strait. Channel ab. 35 m. wide bet. S Korea and Tsushima connecting Sea of Japan with Yellow Sea and East China Sea; NW part of Korea Strait (*q.v.*).

Cho·shi (chō-shê). Seaport town on SE coast of Honshu, Japan, in Chiba prefecture, at mouth of Tone river 60 m. E of Tokyo; pop. 73,512; chief industry fishing.

Cho·shu (chō-shōō). Strictly, a Japanese clan, uniting in latter part of 19th cent. with three others in opposition to foreigners and in rebellion against the emperor; often applied to the old province of Nagato, their feudal territory, in SW extremity of Honshu I.; now part of Yamaguchi prefecture.

Cho·si'ca (chô-sē'kä). Town, 25 m. by rail E of Lima, Peru; altitude 2800 ft.; winter resort.

Choszcz'no (Kôshch'nô); *formerly* **Arns'wal'de** (ärns'-väl'dĕ). Town, S Szczecin dept., NW Poland, 40 m. SE of Stettin; pop. (1946) 12,725; before 1945 in Prussia, Germany; coal mines, iron foundries; spinning and weaving.

Cho'ta Nag'pur (chō'tá näg'pŏŏr). Former division, SW Bihar prov., NE India; 27,112 sq. m.; pop. (1941) 7,516,349; a plateau region, covered with forests and inhabited chiefly by aboriginal races.

Chota Nagpur States. A group of nine former Indian states, earlier in Eastern States Agency in Chota Nagpur, NE India.

Cho'ta U·dai'pur (chō'tá ōō-dī'pŏŏr; ōō'dī-pŏŏr'), *also* **Chho'ta U·de'pur** (ch'hō'tä ōō-dâ'pŏŏr). **1** Former Indian state, Gujarat States, W India; 894 sq. m.; pop. (1941) 162,177; founded ab. 1484 and ruled by a Rajput family.
2 Town, its ✻, ab. 50 m. E of Baroda; pop. 6434.

Cho'teau (shō'tō). City, ⊗ of Teton co., NW cen. Montana; pop. 1966.

Chotin. See KHOTIN.

Chott (shŏt). French form of Arabic *shatt* (saline lake). For names beginning **Chott** see the second element, as **Chott Djerid,** see DJERID, **Chott ech Chergui,** see CHERGUI.

Cho'tu·sitz' (Kô'tōō-zĭts'); *Czech* **Cho'tu·si·ce** (Kô'tōō-sĭ'tsĕ). Village, Bohemia, W Czechoslovakia, near

Čáslav; scene of victory of Frederick the Great over Austrians May 17, 1742 as result of which Prussia acquired most of Silesia from Maria Theresa.

Chou'kou'tien' (jō'kō'tyĕn'), *also* **Chow Kow Tien** (jō' kō' tyĕn'). Village, Hopeh prov., NE China, 37 m. SW of Peiping; site of discovery 1929 of skull, jaws, and teeth of extinct Peking man (*Sinanthropus pekinensis*).

Chou'teau (shō'tō). County in Montana. See *Table* at MONTANA.

Cho·wan' (chŏ·wŏn'). **1** River ab. 50 m. long, NE North Carolina; formed by confluence of Blackwater and Nottoway rivers, flows SE into Albemarle Sound.
2 County in North Carolina. See *Table* at NORTH CAROLINA.

Chow·chil'la (chou·chĭl'à). City, Madera co., cen. California, 35 m. NW of Fresno; pop. 4525.

Chow Kow Tien. See CHOUKOUTIEN.

Chow'tsun' (jō'tsŭn'). Town and treaty port, cen. Shantung, NE China, on railroad 58 m. E of Tsinan; pop. 46,200; largest silk manufacturing town in Shantung.

Christ'church (krīs[t]'chûrch). **1** Municipal borough, Hampshire, S England, at confluence of Avon and Stour rivers near English Channel 23 m. WSW of city of Southampton; pop. 9190.
2 City, ✱ of Canterbury provincial dist., near E coast of South I., New Zealand, on small Avon river 8 m. NW of its port, Lyttelton; pop. 88,500, with suburbs 126,040, (1941 est.) 135,500; center of New Zealand's most productive wheat and grain region. Seat of Canterbury University Coll. 1873 (a unit of Univ. of New Zealand) and Christ's Coll. Founded 1850 by English Anglicans.

Chris'tian (krĭs'chǎn). Counties in three states of the U.S. See *Tables* at ILLINOIS, KENTUCKY, MISSOURI.

Chris'ti·an'a (krĭs'tĭ·ăn'à). See CHRISTINA river.

Chris'ti·a'na (krĭs'tĭ·ä'nà). Town, SW Transvaal, NE Republic of So. Africa, on Vaal river 65 m. NNE of Kimberley; pop. 3432; diamonds.

Christiania. Former name of OSLO.

Christiansand. See KRISTIANSAND.

Chris'tians·burg (krĭs'chǎnz·bûrg). Town, ⊗ of Montgomery co., western Virginia, 27 m. WSW of Roanoke; pop. 3653; founded 1792; stockyards.

Chris'tians·haab' (krĕs'tyáns·hôp'). Danish settlement on Disko Bay, W coast of Greenland; pop. 599.

Chris'tian Sound (krĭs'chǎn). Inlet of Pacific Ocean at S end of Chatham Strait, S of Baranof I., SE Alaska.

Chris'tian·sted' (krĭs'chǎn·stĕd'; *Dan.* krĕs'tyǎn-stĕth'). Town on NE coast of St. Croix I., Virgin Is. of the United States, West Indies; former ✱ of the Danish West Indies; pop. 4495.

Christiansund. See KRISTIANSUND.

Chris·ti'na (krĭs·tē'nà), *formerly* **Chris'ti·an'a** (krĭs'tĭ·ăn'à). A river in N Delaware uniting with Brandywine creek and flowing into Delaware river at Wilmington.

Christ'mas Island (krĭs'mǎs). **1** British island in Indian Ocean ab. 225 m. S of W end of Java, at 10°30'S lat. and 105°34'E long.; 11 m. long by 4½ m. wide; 60 sq. m.; pop. 1059, (1940 est.) 1440; deposits of phosphate of lime. Known to navigators since ab. 1650; formally annexed by British June 1888, placed under Straits Settlements 1889, and incorporated with Singapore settlement 1900; to Australia 1958. Seized by Japanese Apr. 10, 1942.
2 One of the Line Islands (*q.v.*) in cen. Pacific Ocean S of Hawaii and 160 m. SE of Fanning I., ab. 1°57'N lat. and 157°27'W long.; largest atoll in the Pacific, 234 sq. m. of which 94 sq. m. is land; pop. 42. Discovered by Capt. Cook 1777; annexed by Great Britain 1888; included in colony of Gilbert and Ellice Is. 1919; British control disputed by United States 1936–38 but island remained British; important as air base. Cf. AMERICA ISLANDS.

Chris'to·pher (krĭs'tŏ·fēr). City, Franklin co., S Illinois, 28 m. SSW of Mount Vernon; pop. 2854; coal.

Chru'dim (krōō'dyĭm). Industrial town, E Bohemia, W Czechoslovakia, 35 m. N of Brno; pop. (1930) 13,292.

Chrysopolis. See ÜSKÜDAR.

Chry·sor'rho·as (krĭ·sŏr'ō·ǎs). See BARADA.

Chrza'nów (KSHä'nōof). Commune, W Kraków dept., S Poland, 27 m. WNW of Kraków; pop. (1938–39 est.) 20,540; agriculture; lead and coal mining.

Chu (chōō). River ab. 600 m. long, SE Kazakh S.S.R., Soviet Central Asia, flowing from the Tien Shan W to small lake in desert.

Chuanchow. See TSINKIANG.

Chuapa. See TSHUAPA.

Chu·but' (chōō·vōōt'). **1** River in S Argentina; rises in Andes Mts., flows E across Chubut territory, and empties into Atlantic Ocean near Rawson.
2 Territory of Argentina. See *Table* at ARGENTINA.

Chuchow. See LISHUI.

Chuck'chee Sea (chŏŏk'chē; *Russ.* **Chu·kot'sko·e Mo're** (chōō·kôt'skŭ·yĕ mô'ryĕ). Sea, part of Arctic Ocean N of Bering Strait bet. Asia and North America.

Chu'do·vo (chōō'dŭ·vŭ). Village, N Novgorod Region, Soviet Russia, Europe, on Volkhov river; on railroad 65 m. SE of Leningrad. Held by Germans 1941–43.

Chud'sko·e O'ze·ro (chōōt'skŭ·yĕ ô'zyĭ·rŭ). Russian name of Lake Peipus (*q.v.*), Europe, and its official name since 1940.

Chüfou. See KUFOW.

Chu'gach Mountains (chōō'gǎch). Mountain range along coast of S Alaska, extending from head of Cook Inlet ab. 280 m. eastward to W end of St. Elias Range.

Chu'gu'chak' (chōō'gōō'chǎk'). **1** District, N Sinkiang, W China; formerly a part of W Outer Mongolia.
2 Town, its ✱. See TAHCHENG.

Chu'hsien' (chü'shyĕn'). City, W Chekiang prov., E China, on railroad 120 m. SW of Hangchow. In World War II American air base; severe fighting 1942.

Chuk'chi (chŏŏk'chē). Var. of *Chuckchee* in CHUCKCHEE SEA and *Chukotski* in CHUKOTSKI PENINSULA.

Chu–kiang. See PEARL river.

Chu·kot' National District (chōō·kôt'). District, Soviet Russia, Asia, comprising Chukotski Penin. and territory occupied by Anadyr river system and Anadyr Range E of Yakutsk A.S.S.R. and N of Koryak National District; 254,991 sq. m.; pop. (1941 est.) 14,983; ✱ Anadyr; inhabited by the Chukchi of Palaeo-Asiatic origin; chief occupations reindeer breeding, hunting, and fishing. Formed 1930 and formerly a part of Khabarovsk Territory; of increasing importance in air communication bet. America and the Far East.

Chu·kot'ska·ya Kult·ba'za (chōō·kôt'skǎ·yà kŏŏl-y't·bá'zá). Town in Chukot National District, Soviet Russia, Asia, on Bering Strait S of East Cape.

Chu·kot'ski (chōō·kôt'skĭ), *or* **Chu·kot'** (chōō·kôt'), **Peninsula.** Peninsula, E Chukot National District, NE Soviet Russia, Asia, bet. Bering Sea on the S and Chuckchee Sea on the N; its E point is East Cape (*q.v.*).

Chukotskoe More. Russian form of CHUCKCHEE SEA.

Chu'la Vis'ta (chōō'là vĭs'tà). City, San Diego co., SW California, S of San Diego; pop. 42,034.

Chu'lu·ca'nas (chōō'lōō·kä'näs). Town, Piura dept., NW Peru, 32 m. NE of Piura; pop. (1940 est.) 12,622.

Chu·lym' (chōō·lĭm') *or* **Chu·lim'** (-lĭm'). Navigable river ab. 700 m. long, S Siberia, Soviet Russia, Asia; rises in mountains of SW Krasnoyarsk Territory and flows N and W into Ob river below Tomsk.

Chumalhari. See CHOMO LHARI.

Chum'bi (chŏŏm'bē). Fertile valley, alt. 9500 ft., in the Himalayas in S Tibet, bet. Sikkim and Bhutan; crossed by the usual trade route bet. India and Tibet.

Chumbul. Var. of CHAMBAL.

Chum·phon *or* **Jum·porn** (chŏŏm·p'hôn). **1** Province, SW Thailand; 2202 sq. m.; pop. 101,535.
2 Town, its ✱; port on Malay Penin. on W shore of Gulf of Siam 245 m. S of Bangkok, on railroad.

Chuna. See UDA.

Chu·nar' (chŭ·när'). Fortified and ancient town on S bank of Ganges 20 m. SSW of Benares, SE Uttar Pra-

desh, N Indian Union; pop. 8050; captured by Akbar 1575; came under control of British 1763; treaty signed here 1781 bet. Warren Hastings and nawab of Oudh.

Chung'hsien' (jŏŏng'shyĕn'), *formerly* **Chung'chow'** (-jō'). City, E cen. Szechwan prov., S cen. China, on Yangtze ab. 100 m. below Chungking; pop. 50,000.

Chung–Hua Min–Kuo. See CHINA.

Chung'king' (chŏŏng'king'; *Chin.* -chǐng'); *officially* **Pa'hsien'** (bä'shyĕn'). City, S Szechwan prov., S China, on N bank of Yangtze at its junction with Kialing; 1937–46 ✱ of China; pop. (1931 est.) 635,000, (1946 est.) 1,002,787; surrounded by wall 5 miles in circuit; has high mountain directly back of it. Natural gateway of trade for products of Szechwan; has important banks and industries. Declared open port 1891; scene of serious native rebellion 1896–98; made headquarters of Chinese Nationalist armies 1938 and political capital of China (from Nov. 1937) by Kuomintang; became site of many transported industrial plants, schools and colleges, and government offices, and new residence of many Chinese. Bombed severely by Japanese after 1938; American air base 1944–45.

Chung'shan'kong' (jŏŏng'shän'kông'). Town, Kwangtung prov., SE China, on W side of estuary of Canton river N of Macao and opp. Hong Kong; developed by Chinese as a port to rival Hong Kong.

Chung Tiao Shan (jŏŏng'tyou'shän'). Mountain range along border bet. Honan and Shansi provs., NE cen. China; in bend of the Hwang Ho.

Chupriya. See ČUPRIJA.

Chu'qui·ca·ma'ta (chōō'kĕ·kä·mä'tä). Subdivision (pop. 19,202) of Calama commune, N Chile; largest known single copper-mining property in the world.

Chu'qui·sa'ca (chōō'kĕ·sä'kä). **1** Department of Bolivia. See *Table* at BOLIVIA.
2 Former name of SUCRE.

Chur (kōōr); *Romansh* **Cue'ra** (kwâ'rä); *Ital.* **Co'i·ra** (kô'ê·rä); *Fr.* **Coire** (kwàr); *anc.* **Cu'ri·a Rhae·to'rum** (kūr'ĭ·à rê·tōr'ŭm). Commune, ✱ of Graubünden canton, E Switzerland, 43 m. E of Altdorf; pop. (1941) 17,060; ancient cathedral (oldest part dating from 4th cent.); important tourist resort. Mentioned as city and episcopal see in 5th cent. A.D.; imperial city in 15th cent.; became capital of Graubünden canton 1820.

Church (chûrch). Urban district, Lancashire, NW England, on Leeds and Liverpool Canal 20 m. N of Manchester; pop. 5199.

Church'ill (chûrch'[h]ĭl). **1** County in Nevada. See *Table* at NEVADA.
2 River 1000 m. long, cen. Canada; rises in Lake la Loche in NW Saskatchewan, flows E across Saskatchewan and N Manitoba provs. and turns NE into Hudson Bay at Churchill; many rapids; passes through many large lakes, esp. Churchill and Snake in Saskatchewan and Granville and Southern Indian in Manitoba; chief tributaries the Reindeer and Beaver.
3 River, E Canada: see HAMILTON.
4 Seaport, NE Manitoba, Canada, on Hudson Bay at mouth of Churchill river; pop. ab. 400; terminus of branch railroad from The Pas; best harbor on W coast of Hudson Bay; construction of port for direct shipment of wheat to Europe finished 1931. Settled as Fort Churchill 1688 by Hudson's Bay Company.

Churchill, Cape. Headland on W shore of Hudson Bay, E of Churchill, NE Manitoba, Canada.

Churchill Downs (dounz). Race track, Louisville, Kentucky; scene of annual Kentucky Derby, foremost American horse-racing event, held since 1875.

Churchill Falls. See GRAND FALLS.

Church Mountain (chûrch). Peak 6245 ft. in W cen. Whatcom co., NW Washington.

Church Point. Town, Acadia parish, S Louisiana, 18 m. NW of Lafayette; pop. 3606.

Chu'ru (chōō'rōō). Town, Rajasthan, NW India, 110 m. NNW of Jaipur; pop. 21,965.

Chu'ru·bus'co (chōō'rōō·vōōs'kō). Locality near Mexico City, Mexico; battle Aug. 20, 1847 in which Gen. Winfield Scott defeated Mexican forces of Santa Anna.

Chusei Hoku, Chusei Nan. See NORTH CHUSEI; SOUTH CHUSEI.

Chu Shan (chōō' shän'; *Chin.* jō' shän') *or* **Chu'san'** (chōō'sän'; *Chin.* jō'shän'). **1** Archipelago of ab. 100 islands in East China Sea off NE coast of Chekiang prov. at entrance to Hangchow Bay, E China; pop. ab. 400,000; ✱ Tinghai, on Chu Shan I.; for several centuries a base for trade with foreign governments, esp. Japan and Great Britain. See PUTO SHAN.
2 Island 20 m. long by 10 m. wide, largest of the Chu Shan archipelago, East China Sea, ab. 50 m. E of Ninghsien; on its S shore is Tinghai.

Chu·shu (chōō·shōō). Inland town, North Chusei prov., S cen. Korea, 65 m. SE of Seoul; pop. 25,906.

Chu·so·va'ya (chōō·sŭ·vä'yà). River ab. 430 m. long in Sverdlovsk and Molotov Regions, Soviet Russia, Asia; rises near Sverdlovsk and flows NW to Kama river.

Chust. See KHUST.

Chu'ti·a Nagpur (chōō'tĭ·à). Var. of CHOTA NAGPUR.

Chu'vash (chōō'văsh; *Russ.* chŏŏ·väsh') **Republic,** *officially* **Chuvash Autonomous Soviet Socialist Republic;** *also* **Chu·vash'i·a** (chōō·väsh'ĭ·à). Autonomous republic, E cen. Soviet Russia, Europe, S of the Volga; 6909 sq. m.; pop. 1,132,360, (1941 est.) 1,110,592; ✱ Cheboksary; a subdivision of the R.S.F.S.R. In level country of Volga basin, crossed by lower Sura river, which also forms part of W boundary; has extensive forests; chief occupation lumbering; peasant industries in woodworking. Predominant ethnic strain Turko-Tatar; Chuvashes, originally a Bulgarian people allied to the Mordvinians and nominally Christian, have been affected by Tatar elements. Chief towns Cheboksary and Alatyr. Under the tsars an undeveloped region; suffered much during civil war 1918–20 and in the famine that followed; created an autonomous area June 1920 and an autonomous republic Apr. 1925.

Chu·zen·ji (chōō·zĕn·jê). Lake in Tochigi prefecture, cen. Honshu, Japan, 7 m. W of Nikko; 15 m. in circumference; alt. 4375 ft.; resort; noted for its mountain scenery; shrines.

Cia'les (syä'läs). Municipality (pop. 18,106) and town (pop. 3275), cen. Puerto Rico, 17 m. SE of Arecibo.

Ciam·pi'no (chäm·pē'nô). Village, cen. Italy, in Latium 10 m. SE of Rome; international airport.

Cia'no d'En'za (chä'nô dĕn'tsä). Commune, Reggio nell'Emilia prov., Emilia, N Italy, 12 m. SW of Reggio nell'Emilia; pop. (1931) 5279; includes village of **Ca·nos'sa** [kà·nôs'à; *Ital.* kä·nôs'sä] (pop. 224) containing ruins of castle in which Emperor Henry IV submitted 1077 to Pope Gregory VII and did public penance, this humiliation of Henry giving rise to the phrase (reputedly first used by Bismarck 1871) "going to Canossa," meaning "humble submission."

Ci·ba'o (sê·vä'ô). Fertile valley, cen. Dominican Republic, running E and W parallel with and N of the Cordillera Central; chief towns Santiago de los Caballeros and La Vega.

Cí'bo·la (sē'bô·là). Vague historical region in present N New Mexico including seven pueblos (the "Seven Cities of Cíbola") believed by earliest Spanish explorers of the region to contain vast treasures.

Ci'bo·lo (sē'bô·lô). River ab. 150 m. long, Texas; rises on Edwards Plateau, flows SE and enters San Antonio river in cen. Karnes co.

Cib'y·ra (sĭb'ĭ·rà). Important ancient city of Greater Phrygia, on the border of Caria; became part of Roman Empire 83 B.C.

Cic'er·o (sĭs'ĕr·ō). Industrial town, Cook co., NE Illinois, W suburb of Chicago; pop. 69,130; electrical equipment and malleable iron castings, pumps, engines.

Ci'dra (sē'thrä). Municipality (pop. 21,891) and town (pop. 3191), E cen. Puerto Rico.

Cie·cha'nów (chĕ·ĸä'nōōf). Commune, Warszawa dept., Poland, 49 m. NNW of Warsaw; pop. (1938–39 est.) 15,200; agricultural industries.

Cie'go de Á'vi·la (syä'gŏ thä ä'vĕ·lä). Municipality and town, W Camagüey prov., E cen. Cuba; pop. (town) 29,130; railroad junction in sugar-producing region.

Cié'na·ga (syä'nä·gä). Coastal town, N Magdalena dept., N Colombia, 40 m. E of Barranquilla; pop. 22,783; exports cotton, tobacco, bananas, cocoa.

Cien·fue'gos (syän·fwä'gôs). Municipality (1938 est. pop. 92,258) and town (pop. 49,452) on **Cienfuegos bay**, SW Las Villas prov., W cen. Cuba; branch of Arnold Arboretum of Harvard University nearby; exports sugar. First visited by Columbus on first voyage; surveyed by Ocampo 1508; settled 1819.

Cie'szyn (chĕ'shǐn); *Ger.* **Te'schen** (tĕsh'ĕn); *Czech* **Tě'šín** (tyĕ'shēn). Industrial city, Śląsk dept., SW Poland, 40 m. SSW of Katowice; pop. (1938–39 est.) 28,000; divided 1920 bet. Poland (**Cieszyn**, on E bank of Olsa river) and Czechoslovakia (Těšín Český, on W bank of Olsa); reunited under Polish rule 1938 but W town returned to Czechoslovakia at end of World War II. Railroad junction; varied manufactures. First mentioned 1155; seat of duchy 1290–1653; treaty ending War of the Bavarian Succession signed 1779; in World War I Austrian headquarters till 1917. See TESCHEN.

Cie'za (thyä'thä; syä'sä). Manufacturing commune, Murcia prov., SE Spain, on Segura river 25 m. NNW of Murcia; pop. 23,499; manufactures linen and hempen fabrics, flour, brown paper, lumber; remains of Roman fort, Arab ruins, medieval church.

Ci·fuen'tes (sē·fwän'tās). Municipality, Las Villas prov., W cen. Cuba; pop. 8472; railroad junction point 10 m. S of Sagua la Grande.

Ci·lan' (sē·län'). Early Portuguese form of CEYLON.

Ci·li'ci·a (sǐ·lǐsh'ǐ·à; -lǐsh'à). Ancient country and region in SE Asia Minor, extending along Mediterranean coast S of Taurus Mts. from the Amanus Mts. to Pamphylia; conquered by Cyrus and made satrapy of Persian Empire; subdued by Alexander the Great who entered it through Cilician Gates; conquered by Pompey and made a Roman province, which at first included Pamphylia and Isauria, 62 B.C.; invaded by Arabs 710–711 A.D.; theme of Byzantine Empire; an independent Armenian principality (also called Little Armenia) founded 1080, which usually joined Crusaders against Greeks; became kingdom 1198; conquered by Turks 15th cent.; a scene of Armenian massacres 1909. As a modern region in Turkey, called also **Lesser Armenia**, it includes İçel and the S parts of Seyhan and Maraş vilayets; pop. ab. 540,000, including many Armenians.

Ci·li'cian Gates (sǐ·lǐsh'ăn); *anc.* **Ci·li'ci·ae Py'lae** (sǐ·lǐsh'ǐ·ē pī'lē); *Turk.* **Gü·lek' Bo·gaz'** (gü·lĕk' bō·äz'). Pass through Bulgar Dağları, a range in the Taurus Mts., S Turkey in Asia, 38 m. NW of Adana; has been used for centuries by armies and traders.

Cilli. See CELJE.

Cim'ar·ron (sĭm'à·rŏn; -rŏn). **1** River 600 m. long, rising in Colfax co., NE New Mexico, and flowing across SW Kansas and cen. Oklahoma into Arkansas river in SE Pawnee co., N Oklahoma.

2 County in Oklahoma. See *Table* at OKLAHOMA.

3 City, ⊗ of Gray co., SW Kansas; pop. 1115.

Cim'bri·an, *or* **Cim'bric**, **Cher'so·nese** (sĭm'brǐ·ăn [sĭm'brǐk] kûr'sô·nēz; -nēs); *also* **Cimbrian Peninsula.** Jutland. See CHERSONESE.

Ci'miez (sē'myâz'); *anc.* **Cem'e·ne'lum** (sĕm'ĕ·nē'lăm). Fashionable and hotel section of Nice, France; ancient town a Gallo-Roman provincial capital, destroyed during Lombard invasions; a few ruins.

Ci'mi·ni, Mon'ti (mŏn'tē chē'mē·nē); *Eng.* **Ci·min'i·an Hills** (sǐ·mǐn'ǐ·ăn). Small mountain range, Latium, cen. Italy, just SE of Viterbo; highest point **Mon'te Ci'mi·no** (mŏn'tā chē'mē·nō) 3454 ft.

Ci·mi·te'ro (chē·mē·tâ'rō). See VENICE.

Cim·me'ri·an Bos'po·rus (sǐ·mẽr'ǐ·ăn bŏs'pô·rŭs). **1** See Cimmerian BOSPORUS.

2 An ancient kingdom on and around the Cimmerian Bosporus (mod. Kerch Strait); first settlement was by Milesians (5th cent. B.C.) at town of Panticapaeum, later capital of the kingdom; gradually included all of the Crimea; came under Mithridates of Pontus c. 100 B.C.; conquered by Rome 66 B.C.

Ci·mo'lus (sǐ·mō'lŭs); *Mod. Gr.* **Kí'mo·los** (kyē'mô·lôs). Island 16 sq. m., SW Cyclades, S Aegean Sea, just NE of Melos; in Cyclades dept., Greece; has produced much cimolite, an aluminum silicate in the form of a fine white earth, used by fullers.

Ci·mo'ne, Mon'te (mŏn'tä chē·mō'nå). Peak 7095 ft. in the Tuscan Apennines, Modena prov., N Italy.

Ci·na·ru'co (sē'nä·rōō'kô). River ab. 280 m. long in NE Colombia and W Venezuela; flows E to the Orinoco; joined on S by the **Ci'na·ru·qui'to** (sē'nä·rōō·kē'tô), ab. 250 m. long, its main tributary.

Cin'ca (thēng'kä; sēng'-). River ab. 70 m. long in NE Spain; rises in the Pyrenees on the French frontier, flows S into Segre river above its junction with the Ebro.

Cin'cin·na'ti (sĭn'sǐ·năt'ǐ; -năt'à). Commercial and manufacturing city, ⊗ of Hamilton co., SW corner of Ohio, on Ohio river; pop. 502,550; railroad center and distributing port (esp. coal, iron, lumber, salt); slaughtering and packing (esp. pork), brewing, printing; varied manufactures. Cincinnati Conservatory of Music (1867); Univ. of Cincinnati (1870; coed.); Xavier Univ. (1831; part coed.); Hebrew Union College (1875). Laid out 1788 (Fort Washington built 1789); became ⊗ 1790; incorp. as town 1802, as city 1819; developed esp. with opening of Miami and Erie Canal 1827; became grape culture center and wine market following influx of Germans 1840. Known as "Queen City" or "Queen of the West." Birthplace of William Howard Taft.

Cin'go·li (chēng'gô·lē). Commune, Macerata prov., Marches, cen. Italy, NW of Macerata; pop. 15,496.

Ci·ni·sel'lo Bal'sa·mo (chē·nē·zĕl'lô bäl'sä·mô). Commune, N Italy, 4 m. N of Milan; pop. (1931) 10,086.

Cin'ko·ta (tsǐng'kŏ·tŏ). Commune, Hungary, E suburb of Budapest; pop. ab. 13,000.

Cin'na·min'son (sǐn'à·mǐn's'n). Township, Burlington co., S cen. New Jersey, near Riverton; pop. 8302; known as initial port of entry of Japanese beetle in 1916.

Cinque Ports (sĭngk). A number of seaport towns on the coast of Kent and Sussex in England, originally five —Dover, Sandwich, Romney, Hastings, and Hythe—to which were later added Winchelsea, Rye, and other minor places; enfranchised by Edward the Confessor; in return for special sea service in defense of the coast, granted many special privileges, as of civil and criminal jurisdiction, most of which have been annulled.

Cin'ta·la'pa (sēn'tä·lä'pä). Town, Chiapas state, SE Mexico, 40 m. W of Tuxtla; pop. 5043.

Cin'to, Mont (mônt chēn'tô). Mountain 8881 ft., NW Corsica.

Cintra. See SINTRA.

Ciotat, La. See LA CIOTAT.

Či'o·vo (chē'ô·vô); *Ital.* **Bu'a** (bōō'ä). Yugoslav island in the Adriatic Sea off the Dalmatian coast opp. Trogir; pop. ab. 2000.

Ci·pan'go (sǐ·päng'gō), *also* **Ci·pan'gu** (-gōō). In medieval legend a marvelous island, or islands, east of Asia, described by Marco Polo by the name Zipangu. It was sought by Columbus and is generally identified with the modern Japan. See NIPPON.

Circars. See NORTHERN CIRCARS.

Cir·cas'si·a (sẽr·kăsh'ǐ·à; -kăsh'à). Region in S Soviet Russia, Europe, N of the W end of the Caucasus Mts. and on the NE coast of the Black Sea; has no political significance. Inhabited from ab. 13th cent. by races subject to Georgia, who became independent in first half of 15th cent. They occupied the basins of tributaries of the Terek and Kuban rivers, a warlike people noted for

their beautiful women; their two leading branches are today the Adygei and Cherkess, now forming two autonomous regions of the R.S.F.S.R. (see ADYGEI AUTONOMOUS REGION and CHERKESS AUTONOMOUS REGION). Taken over by Russians by 1829; after long war of resistance to Russia 1830–59, large numbers deported 1864 to Turkey. After Revolution 1917 autonomous areas established for remaining members of race.

Cir·ce'o, Mon'te (mŏn'tä chĕr·chä'ō); *anc.* **Circae'um Prom'on·to'ri·um** (sûr·sē'ŭm prŏm'ŭn·tōr'ĭ·ŭm). Mountain and promontory 1775 ft. on N side of the Gulf of Gaeta, W Italy, W of Terracina; in very early times an island called **Ae·ae'a** (ē·ē'ȧ), legendary home of Circe.

Cir'cle (sûr'k'l). **1** Village, E Alaska, on upper Yukon river ab. 85 m. above Ft. Yukon; pop. (1950) 83; mining village settled ab. 1890, deserted during Klondike rush. **2** Town, ⊗ of McCone co., E Montana; pop. 1117.

Cir'cle·ville (sûr'k'l·vĭl). City, ⊗ of Pickaway co., S cen. Ohio, on Scioto river 25 m. S of Columbus; pop. 11,059; settled 1806 on site once occupied by mound builders; incorp. as village 1814, as city 1853; agricultural center (corn, broomcorn, wheat, etc.).

Cir'cu·lar Head (sûr'kû·lẽr). **1** A bold promontory 478 ft. high at tip of a peninsula on N coast of Tasmania, Australia, ab. 40 m. NE of Burnie; a steep mass of greenstone; at its foot on mainland side is the town of Stanley.
2 Earlier name of STANLEY.

Ci·re·na'i·ca (chē·rä·nä'ē·kä); *now usu.* **Cyr'e·na'i·ca** (sĭr'ē·nā'ĭ·kȧ; sī'rĕ-). Region, later a province, E Libya, including Oases of Kufra; ab. 330,170 sq. m.; pop. 291,328; ✳ Bengasi. Ancient Cyrenaica settled by Greeks who founded Cyrene (Cirene) c. 630 B.C.; under Greek dynasty established by Battus of Thera, kingdom of Cyrene or Cyrenaica took form, and other cities were founded; after death of Alexander the Great, ruled by Ptolemies who called it *Pentapolis* because it included 5 cities (Cyrene, Arsinoë, Berenice, Ptolemaïs, Apollonia); bequeathed to Romans 96 B.C. and in 67 B.C. made Roman province which included Crete; overrun by Arabs in 7th cent. A.D.; nominally under Ottoman Empire after conquest of Egypt (*q.v.*); part of Tripoli (*q.v.*) which was annexed to Italy 1911 (see LIBYA). Scene of many battles in World War II 1940–42: see BARDIA, DERNA, TOBRUK, BENGASI, BIR HACHEIM.

Ci'ren·ces'ter (sĭ'rĕn·sĕs'tẽr; sĭs'ĭ[s]·tẽr; *older* sĭz'ĭ·tẽr); *anc.* **Co·rin'i·um** (kô·rĭn'ĭ·ŭm). Urban district, Gloucestershire, SW cen. England, 14 m. SE of Gloucester; pop. 11,188; remains of an abbey dating from 1117.

Ci·re'ne (chē·rä'nā); *now usu.* **Cy·re'ne** (sī·rē'nė). Town, N Cyrenaica, NE Libya, N Africa, 110 m. ENE of Bengasi. Greek city (Cyrene) founded by King Battus from island of Thera c. 630 B.C.; became prosperous trading and cultural center; capital of kingdom of Cyrenaica; a city of the Pentapolis; suffered complete decline and abandoned by 4th cent. A.D.

Ci'res, Point (thē'rås; sē'-). Cape on coast of N Morocco, on Strait of Gibraltar nearly opp. Tarifa.

Ci'rey', *in full* **Cirey-sur-Blaise** (sē'rā'sür·blâz'). Village, Haute-Marne dept., NE France, NW of Chaumont; on Blaise river, tributary of Marne; château of Mme du Châtelet; residence of Voltaire 1734–49.

Ci·riè' (chē·ryĕ'). Commune, Torino prov., Piedmont, NW Italy, 12 m. NNW of Turin; pop. 10,210.

Čir·pan' (chĭr·pän') *or* **Chir·pan'**. Town, Stara Zagora dept., S cen. Bulgaria, E of Plovdiv; pop. (1926) 11,137.

Cirque de Gavarnie. See GAVARNIE.

Cirque Mountain (sûrk). Highest point 5500 ft. in Torngat Mts., Labrador, at S end of the range.

Cirta. See CONSTANTINE.

Cis·al'pine Gaul (sĭs·ăl'pīn [-pĭn] gôl). See GAUL.

Cisalpine Republic. Republic in N Italy created by Napoleon 1797 by combining the Cispadane and Transpadane Republics; ✳ Milan; embraced lands around

Milan N of the Po and around Ferrara and Bologna S of Po; incorporated into kingdom of Italy 1805.

Cisa, *or* **La Cisa, Pass.** See APENNINES.

Cis'cau·ca'sia (sĭs'kô·kä'zhȧ; -shȧ). Region N of the Caucasus Mts. in the R.S.F.S.R., Soviet Union; 82,600 sq. m.; pop. ab. 5,969,000 (see CAUCASIA); comprises Grozny Region, S half of Krasnodar Territory, and the Dagestan, Kabardino-Balkarian, and North Ossetian Autonomous Soviet Socialist Republics.

Cis'co (sĭs'kō). City, Eastland co., N cen. Texas, 40 m. E of Abilene; pop. 4499; gas and oil wells.

Cis'lei·tha'nia (sĭs'lī·thăn'yȧ; -thä'nĭ·ȧ). Formerly, that part of Austria-Hungary W of Leitha river.

Cis·ne'ros (sēz·nā'rōs). Town, Antioquia dept., NW Colombia, 40 m. NE of Medellín; pop. 5423.

Cis'pa·dane' Gaul (sĭs'pȧ·dān' gôl; sĭs·pā'dän). See GAUL.

Cispadane Republic. Republic in N Italy created by Napoleon 1796 from lands S of Po around Modena, Reggio, Ferrara, and Bologna; ✳ Bologna; incorporated 1797 into Cisalpine Republic (*q.v.*).

Cisplatine Province. See URUGUAY.

Cistercium. See CÎTEAUX.

Ci·ster'na di Lit·to'ria (chēs·tẽr'nä dē lēt·tō'ryä), *formerly* **Cisterna di Ro'ma** (rō'mä). Commune, Littoria prov., Latium, cen. Italy, just N of Pontine Marshes 10 m. N by W of Littoria; pop. 12,471; castle. In World War II taken May 25, 1944 by U.S. forces.

Ci·ster·ni'no (chēs·tär·nē'nō). Commune, Brindisi prov., Apulia, SE Italy, 28 m. WNW of Brindisi; pop. (1931) 10,573.

Cit'a·del, Mount (sĭt'ȧ·dĕl; -d'l). Peak 9024 ft. in Glacier National Park, NW Montana.

Ci'teaux' (sē'tō'); *Lat.* **Cis·ter'ci·um** (sĭs·tûr'shĭ·ŭm; -shŭm). Village in the commune **Saint'–Ni'co'las'–lès–Cîteaux** (săn'nē'kô'lä'lĕ-), Côte-d'Or dept., E France, ab. 16 m. SSE of Dijon; pop. 360; abbey of Cistercian Order, founded 1098 by Robert of Molesmes.

Ci·thae'ron (sĭ·thē'rŏn) *or* **Ki'thai·rōn'** (kyē'thä·rôn'); *also* **El'a·te'a** (ĕl'ȧ·tē'ȧ). Mountain 4629 ft., cen. Attica and Boeotia dept., Greece; on NW border of ancient Attica; sacred to Dionysus and the Muses.

Citharista. See LA CIOTAT.

Ci'ti·um (sĭsh'ĭ·ŭm). Ancient city on SE coast of Cyprus, center of Phoenician influence in the island; part of its site is now port of Larnaca. Founded before Phoenician era; under control of Assyria in 7th cent. B.C. In the Bible known as **Kit'tim** [kĭt'ĭm] (*Gen.* x. 4; *Isa.* xxiii. 1). During period of Greek revolts was loyal to Persia. Birthplace of Zeno, Greek Stoic philosopher.

Ci'tlal·te'petl (sē'tläl·tā'pĕt'l) *or* **O'ri·za'ba** (ōr'ĭ·zä'bä; *Span.* ō'rē·sä'vä). Volcanic peak 18,700 ft. in cen. Veracruz state, Mexico; highest point in Mexico.

Cit'ro·nelle' (sĭt'rō·nĕl'). Town, Mobile co., SW Alabama, 30 m. NW of Mobile; pop. 1918; surrender of last Confederate army E of Mississippi river May 4, 1865.

Cit'rus (sĭt'rŭs). County in Florida. See *Table* at FLORIDA.

Cit·ta·del'la (chēt·tä·dĕl'lä). Manufacturing commune, Padova prov., Venezia Euganea, NE Italy, 16 m. N by W of Padua; pop. 12,966; manufactures paper, textiles; founded 1220; ancient city walls and tower.

Cit·tà' del·la Pie've (chēt·tä' däl'lä pyä'vä). Commune, Perugia prov., Umbria, cen. Italy, WSW of Perugia; pop. 9374; cathedral. Birthplace of Il Perugino.

Città del Vaticano. See VATICAN CITY.

Cit·tà' di Ca·stel'lo (chēt·tä' dē käs·tĕl'lō). Commune, Perugia prov., Umbria, cen. Italy, on Tiber river 27 m. NNW of Perugia; pop. 32,658; Renaissance cathedral; mineral springs; ironworks.

Cit·ta·no'va (chēt·tä·nō'vä). Commune, Reggio di Calabria prov., Calabria, S Italy; pop. 14,043.

Cittavecchia. See STARI GRAD.

Cit·tà' Vec'chia (chēt·tä' vĕk'kyä) *or* **No·ta'bi·le** (nō·tä'bē·lä). Fortified city, cen. Malta I., 6 m. W of

Valletta; pop. ab. 9000; capital of the island until 1570; cathedral, catacombs.

Cit′y Island (sĭt′ĭ). Island in Long Island Sound off E coast of the Bronx, New York City.

City Point. Formerly a village, now part of Hopewell, Prince George co., Virginia, on James river; base of operations in Civil War.

Ciu·dad′ Bo·lí′var (syōō·thäth′ vô·lē′vär). River port, ✳ of Bolívar state, NE Venezuela, on the narrows (Span. *angosturas*) of the Orinoco river, whence its former popular name **An′gos·tu′ra** (äng′gôs·tōō′rä; *Angl.* äng′gôs-tōōr′ȧ); pop. (1941 est.) 19,764.

Ciudad Ca·mar′go (kä·mär′gô). Town, SE Chihuahua state, N Mexico, 85 m. SE of Chihuahua; pop. 7705.

Ciudad de las Ca′sas (thä läs kä′säs). = *San Cristóbal de las Casas:* see SAN CRISTÓBAL city, Mexico.

Ciudad del Carmen. See CARMEN.

Ciudad de Valles. See VALLES.

Ciu·dad′ de Vic·to′ria (syōō·thä′ thä vĕk·tō′ryä). = DURANGO city, Mexico.

Ciu·da·de′la (thyōō′thä·thä′lä; syōō′-). Manufacturing seaport, Baleares prov., Spain, on W coast of Minorca I. 70 m. NE of Palma; pop. 10,716.

Ciu·dad′ Gar·cí′a (syōō·thäth′ gär·sē′ä). Town, Zacatecas state, cen. Mexico, W of Zacatecas; pop. 8755.

Ciudad Gon·zá′lez (gôn·sä′läs). Town, Guanajuato state, cen. Mexico, 33 m. N of Guanajuato; pop. 6562.

Ciudad Guayana. See SANTO TOMÉ DE GUAYANA.

Ciudad Guz·mán′ (gōōz·män′). City, Jalisco state, W cen. Mexico, 35 m. S of Lake Chapala; pop. 22,170.

Ciudad Hi·dal′go (ē·thäl′gô). Town, Michoacán state, SW Mexico; pop. 7594.

Ciudad Ixtepec, *formerly* **San Je·ró′ni·mo Ix′te·pec′** (säng′ hä·rō′nĕ·mô ēs′tä·pĕk′). Town, Oaxaca state, SE Mexico, just N of Oaxaca; pop. 7069.

Ciudad Juá′rez (hwä′rås). City, Chihuahua state, N Mexico, opp. El Paso, Texas; pop. (1959 est.) 280,323; alt. 3117 ft.; connected with El Paso by bridge over the Rio Grande; founded in latter part of 17th cent.; important as early transportation center and as headquarters of Benito Juárez while in exile.

Ciudad Lerdo. See LERDO.

Ciu·dad′ Ma·de′ro (syōō·thäth′ mä·thā′rô); *also* **Vil′la Ce·ci′lia** (bē′yä sä·sē′lyä). City, Tamaulipas state, E Mexico, S suburb of Tampico; pop. 28,075.

Ciudad Men·do′za (mån·dō′sä). Town, Veracruz state, E Mexico, just SW of Orizaba; pop. 10,970.

Ciudad Nan′te (nän′tâ). Town, Tamaulipas state, E Mexico; pop. 8690.

Ciudad O′bre·gón′ (ō′vrä·gôn′). Town, Sonora state, NW Mexico, 65 m. SE of Guaymas; pop. 12,497.

Ciudad Porfirio Díaz. See PIEDRAS NEGRAS.

Ciu·dad′ Re·al′ (thyōō·thäth′ [syōō-] rrĕ·äl′). **1** Province of Spain. See *Table* at SPAIN.
2 Commune, its ✳, S cen. Spain, near Guadiana river 99 m. S of Madrid; pop. 32,931; makes woolen and linen goods, brandies; Gothic cathedral; founded by Alfonso el Sabio; Spaniards defeated by French nearby 1809.

Ciudad Ro·dri′go (rrô·thrē′gô). Manufacturing commune, Salamanca prov., W Spain, 53 m. WSW of Salamanca; pop. 12,082; cathedral (begun 1190); taken by English 1706 but recovered 1707; in Peninsular War twice captured: by the French under Ney July 10, 1810 and by the British under Wellington Jan. 19, 1812.

Ciu·dad′ Ser·dán′ (syōō·thäth′ sĕr·thän′). Town, Puebla state, SE cen. Mexico, on railroad from Veracruz to Puebla 48 m. E of Puebla; pop. 7891.

Ciudad Tru·jil′lo (trōō·hē′yô); *now* **San′to Do·min′go** (sän′tô thô·mēng′gô; *Angl.* săn′tô dô·mĭng′gô). City, S Dominican Republic, in the District of Santo Domingo; ✳ of the Dominican Republic; pop. (1958 est.) 316,292; founded (as Santo Domingo) 1946 by Bartholomew Columbus, brother of Christopher Columbus; first permanent settlement by Europeans in the New World; razed by cyclone 1930; rebuilt under President

Trujillo, for whom it was renamed 1936; former name (Santo Domingo) restored 1961 at fall of Trujillo regime; cathedral contains supposed remains of Christopher Columbus.

Ciudad Vic·to′ria (vĕk·tō′ryä). Town, E cen. Mexico; ✳ of Tamaulipas state; pop. 19,513; in center of sugar-growing region 150 m. SE of Monterrey. Founded 1750.

Ciudad Vie′ja (vyĕ′hä). Town, Sacatepéquez dept., S cen. Guatemala; pop. 6011.

Ci·vi·da′le del Fri·u′li (chē·vē·dä′lä dål frē·ōō′lē; frē′ōō·lē); *anc.* **Fo′rum Ju′li·i** (fōr′ŭm jōō′lĭ·ī). Commune, Friuli prov., Venezia Euganea, NE Italy, 9 m. E by N of Udine; pop. 10,424; 15th-cent. cathedral.

Ci′vi·ta Ca′stel·la′na (chē′vē·tä käs′tĕl·lä′nä); *anc.* **Fa·le′ri·i** (fȧ·lēr′ĭ·ī). Commune, Viterbo, N Latium, cen. Italy, N of Rome; pop. 7745; 13th-cent. cathedral of Santa Maria; ancient Falerii one of 12 cities of Etruria; built on plateau surrounded except on W side by gorges 200 ft. deep; conquered by Romans 241 B.C.

Civita Lavinia. See LANUVIUM.

Civitas Altae Ripae. See BRZEG.

Civitas Carnutum. See CHARTRES.

Civitas Eburovicum. See ÉVREUX.

Ci·vi·ta·vec′chia (chē·vē·tä·vĕk′kyä); *anc.* **Cen′tum Cel′lae** (sĕn′tŭm sĕl′ē) *and* **Tra·ja′ni Por′tus** (trȧ·jā′nī pōr′tŭs; pôr′-). Fortified seaport, Roma prov., Latium, cen. Italy, on Tyrrhenian Sea 39 m. WNW of Rome; pop. 31,858; episcopal see; chief port of Rome (cf. OSTIA); citadel (designed by Michelangelo; erected by Pope Urban VIII); arsenal (designed by Bernini and Bramante), aqueduct; Etruscan and ancient Roman antiquities; sea bathing; manufactures calcium carbide, cement, ships. Occupied by French 1849–70.

Ci·vi·tel′la del Tron′to (chē·vē·tĕl′lä dål trôn′tô). Commune, Teramo prov., Abruzzi e Molise, cen. Italy, 8 m. N of Teramo; pop. 10,609.

Ciz·re′ (jēz·rĕ′); *formerly* **Je·zi′ret ibn O′mar** (jĕ·zē′-rĕt ĭb′n ō′mär). Town, SE Mardin vilayet, SE Turkey in Asia, on the Tigris on Syrian border; pop. 5283.

Clack′a·mas (klăk′ȧ·măs). **1** River ab. 80 m. long, NW Oregon; flows NW into Willamette river.
2 County in Oregon. See *Table* at OREGON.

Clack·man′nan (klăk·măn′ăn). **1** *or* **Clack·man′-nan·shire** (-shĭr; -shēr). County, cen. Scotland; 55 sq. m.; pop. (1951) 37,528; agriculture, coal mining.
2 Parish and town, its ⊗, ab. 7 m. E of Stirling; pop. 2585; associated with Robert Bruce and Robert Burns.

Clac′ton (klăk′tŭn). Urban district, Essex, SE England, on North Sea 59 m. ENE of London; pop. 24,065; watering place.

Clai′borne (klā′bērn). Name of a parish in Louisiana and of counties in two states of the U.S. See *Tables* at LOUISIANA, MISSISSIPPI, TENNESSEE.

Claire, Lake (klâr). Lake 404 sq. m., NE Alberta, Canada, W of Lake Athabaska.

Claire′mont (klâr′mŏnt). Town, ⊗ of Kent co., NW Texas; pop. (1950) 175.

Clair′ton (klâr′t′n). Industrial city, Allegheny co., SW Pennsylvania, on Monongahela river 12 m. SSE of Pittsburgh; pop. 18,389; settled 1770; manufactures coke and its by-products, also steel, chemicals; coal mines.

Clair′vaux′ (klĕr′vō′). Hamlet, Aube dept., NE France, 40 m. ESE of Troyes; contains Cistercian abbey, since 1808 a prison, founded 1115 by St. Bernard of Clairvaux.

Clal′lam (klăl′ăm). County in Washington. See *Table* at WASHINGTON.

Cla′mart′ (klȧ′mär′). Commune, Seine dept., N France, suburb of Paris near Forest of Meudon; pop. 32,427.

Cla′me·cy′ (klȧm′sē′). Commune, Nièvre dept., cen. France, 36 m. NNE of Nevers on the Canal of Nivernais; pop. (1931) 5434; seat of bishops of Bethlehem after Saladin's capture of Jerusalem 1188 and until 1789.

Clan′ton (klăn′t′n; -tŭn). City ⊗ of Chilton co., cen. Alabama, 41 m. NW of Montgomery; pop. 5683.

Clap′ham (klăp′ăm; -′m), **North** *and* **South.** Wards

of Wandsworth metropolitan borough, London, England (see *Table* at LONDON).

Clare (klâr). **1** County, Michigan. See MICHIGAN, *Table*. **2** City, Clare co., cen. Michigan, 15 m. N of Mt. Pleasant; pop. 2442; near petroleum and natural-gas field. **3** Market town and parish, SW Suffolk, England, on Stour river; castle mounds. **4** County, W Eire, in Munster prov.; 1231 sq. m.; pop. 89,879; ⊗ Ennis; agriculture, livestock raising, lead mining, quarrying (marble, slate), fishing. **5** Island off W coast of Ireland at entrance to Clew Bay and S of Achill I.; administratively in co. Mayo. **6** River, co. Galway, Eire; flows S through center of county then W and into Lough Corrib near its S end.

Clare′mont (klâr′mŏnt). **1** City, Los Angeles co., SW California, 28 m. E of Los Angeles; pop. 12,633; seat of Pomona College (1887; coed.), Claremont University College (1925; coed.), Scripps College (1926; women), Claremont Men's College (1946), and Harvey Mudd College (1955; coed.). **2** City, Sullivan co., SW New Hampshire, 30 m. N of Keene; pop. 13,563; machinery, textiles, footwear. **3** Town, W Western Australia, W suburb of Perth on Melville Water, the estuary of Swan river; pop. 5949. **4** Town, SW Cape Province, S Republic of So. Africa, ab. 7 m. SSE of Cape Town; pop. ab. 6000.

Clare′more (klâr′mōr). City and health resort, ⊗ of Rogers co., NE Oklahoma, 25 m. ENE of Tulsa; pop. 6639; mineral springs; gas, oil, coal deposits; agriculture. Oklahoma Military Acad. (1920). Birthplace of Will Rogers nearby bet. Claremore and Oologah (to NW).

Clar′ence (klăr′ĕns). **1** River 240 m. long, NE New South Wales, SE Australia; flows SE to Pacific Ocean. **2** River 125 m. long, NE South I., New Zealand; flows NE, E, and SE to Pacific S of Waipapa Point.

Clarence Island. 1 Chilean island in Tierra del Fuego Archipelago (*q.v.*), SW of Brunswick Penin. **2** Small island in Scotia Sea, in NE part of South Shetlands, Falkland Is. Dependencies; ab. 54°W long.

Clarence Peak. Peak ab. 9348 ft. on Fernando Poo I.

Clarence Strait. 1 Narrow passage ab. 135 m. long, SE Alaska, bet. Prince of Wales I. on W and Wrangell and Revillagigedo Is. and mainland on E. **2** Channel ab. 90 m. long bet. Bathurst and Melville Is. on N and mainland of Northern Territory, Australia, on S; connects Van Diemen Gulf with Timor Sea. **3** Strait in E Persian Gulf, extending bet. Qishm I. and the mainland of Iran.

Clar′en·don (klăr′ĕn·dŭn). **1** County in South Carolina. See *Table* at SOUTH CAROLINA. **2** City, ⊗ of Monroe co., E Arkansas; pop. 2293. **3** City, ⊗ of Donley co., NW Texas, in the Panhandle 52 m. ESE of Amarillo; pop. 2172; cattle, cotton. **4** Parish, England. See CLARENDON PARK.

Clarendon Hills. Village, Du Page co., NE Illinois, SW of Chicago; pop. 5885.

Clarendon Park *or* **Clarendon.** Parish, S Wiltshire, England, 2 m. SE of Salisbury; scene 1164 of council of bishops and barons who issued the *Constitutions of Clarendon* defining and limiting the rights of the clergy.

Cla′rens′ (klả·räɴ[s]′). Village, one of the Montreux group, Vaud canton, Switzerland, at E end of Lake Geneva; chief scene of Rousseau's *Nouvelle Héloïse*.

Cla·ri′den·stock (klả·rē′dĕn·shtôk). Peak 10,730 ft. in the Alps, Uri canton, cen. Switzerland.

Cla·rin′da (klả·rĭn′dả). City, ⊗ of Page co., SW Iowa; pop. 4903.

Clar′i·on (klăr′ĭ·ŭn). **1** River, NW cen. Pennsylvania; rises in McKean co., flows SW into Allegheny river. **2** County in Pennsylvania. See *Table* at PENNSYLVANIA. **3** City, ⊗ of Wright co., N cen. Iowa; pop. 3232. **4** Borough, ⊗ of Clarion co., W Pennsylvania, on Clarion river; pop. 4958. Clarion State College (1866; coed.).

Clarium. See CHIARI.

Clark (klärk). **1** Name of counties in twelve states of the U.S. See *Tables* at ARKANSAS, IDAHO, ILLINOIS, INDIANA, KANSAS, KENTUCKY, MISSOURI, NEVADA, OHIO, SOUTH DAKOTA, WASHINGTON, WISCONSIN. **2** Township, Union co., NE New Jersey, SW of Elizabeth; pop. 12,195. **3** City, ⊗ of Clark co., NE South Dakota; pop. 1484.

Clark, Mount. 1 Peak 11,506 ft. in Sierra Nevada, E Mariposa co., cen. California. **2** Highest peak 4733 ft. in Franklin Mts., Mackenzie District, Northwest Territories, Canada. **3** Peak 7085 ft. in N South I., New Zealand.

Clark′dale (klärk′dāl). Town (unincorporated), Yavapai co., cen. Arizona; pop. 1095; copper smelting.

Clarke (klärk). Name of counties in five states of the U.S. See *Tables* at ALABAMA, GEORGIA, IOWA, MISSISSIPPI, VIRGINIA.

Clarkes′ville (klärks′vĭl). City, ⊗ of Habersham co., NE Georgia; pop. 1352.

Clark Field (klärk). United States air base in the Philippine Islands, NW Pampanga prov., Luzon, near Fort Stotsenburg and ab. 48 m. NW of Manila; bombed by Japanese and airplanes destroyed Dec. 8, 1941; captured Jan. 1942; retaken by Americans Jan. 25, 1945.

Clark Fork. River ab. 300 m. long, rising near Butte, Silver Bow co., SW Montana, and flowing NW across Idaho border to Pend Oreille Lake in N Idaho.

Clarks′burg (klärks′bûrg). Industrial city, ⊗ of Harrison co., N West Virginia, on West Fork, headstream of the Monongahela river; pop. 28,112; settled 1764. Coal mines, oil and gas, limestone and clay deposits; glass.

Clarks′dale (klärks′dāl). City, ⊗ of Coahoma co., NW Mississippi, 53 m. NNW of Greenwood; pop. 21,105; trade and shipping center for cotton-growing section.

Clarks Fork (klärks). River ab. 120 m. long, NW Wyoming and S Montana; rises in Absaroka Mts. in S Montana, flows E through NW Wyoming, then N into Yellowstone river in S cen. Montana.

Clarks Summit (klärks). Borough, Lackawanna co., NE Pennsylvania, 7 m. N of Scranton; pop. 3693.

Clarks′ton (klärks′tŭn). City, Asotin co., SE Washington, on Snake river opp. Lewiston, Idaho; pop. 6209.

Clarks′ville (klärks′vĭl). **1** City, ⊗ of Johnson co., NW Arkansas, near Arkansas river 56 m. E of Fort Smith; pop. 3919; settled 1837. College of the Ozarks (1891). **2** Town, Clark co., S Indiana; pop. 8088. **3** City, ⊗ of Montgomery co., N Tennessee, on peninsula at confluence of Cumberland and Red rivers 40 m. WNW of Nashville; pop. 22,021; settled 1784; tobacco. **4** City, ⊗ of Red River co., NE Texas, 29 m. E of Paris; pop. 3851; cotton, livestock, lumber, grain.

Clat′sop (klăt′sŭp). County in Oregon. See *Table* at OREGON.

Clauda. See GAVDOS.

Claude (klôd). City, ⊗ of Armstrong co., NW Texas, in the Panhandle; pop. 895.

Clau·di·op′o·lis (klô′dĭ·ŏp′ō·lĭs); *earlier* **Bi·thyn′-i·um** (bĭ·thĭn′ĭ·ŭm). Ancient city in Bithynia, Asia Minor, near modern Bolu; destroyed by earthquake.

Claus′thal–Zel′ler·feld (klous′täl-tsĕl′ĕr·fĕlt), *also* **Klaus′thal–Zel′ler·feld** (klous′-). Mining city, W Germany, in the former Prussian province of Hannover, in NW Harz Mts. 32 m. SSW of Brunswick; pop. 12,418; iron, lead, copper, silver, zinc; government mint; 17th-cent. church (largest wooden church in Germany).

Claw′son (klô′s′n). City, Oakland co., SE Michigan, 11 m. SE of Pontiac; pop. 14,795.

Clax′ton (klăks′tŭn). City, ⊗ of Evans co., SE cen. Georgia, 48 m. W of Savannah; pop. 2672.

Clay (klā). **1** Name of counties in eighteen states of the U.S. See *Tables* at ALABAMA, ARKANSAS, FLORIDA, GEORGIA, ILLINOIS, INDIANA, IOWA, KANSAS, KENTUCKY, MINNESOTA, MISSISSIPPI, MISSOURI, NEBRASKA, NORTH CAROLINA, SOUTH DAKOTA, TENNESSEE, TEXAS, WEST VIRGINIA. **2** Town, ⊗ of Clay co., cen. West Virginia; pop. 486.

Clay, Mount. Peak 5532 ft. of the White Mts. in S Coos co., N New Hampshire, just N of Mt. Washington.

Clay Center. 1 City, ⊗ of Clay co., NE cen. Kansas, NW of Manhattan; pop. 4613; grain elevators, flour mills.

2 City, ⊗ of Clay co., S Nebraska; pop. 792.

Clay Cross (klā krôs). Urban district, Derbyshire, N cen. England, 15 m. S of Sheffield; pop. 8552.

Clay'pool (klā'pōōl). Town (unincorporated), Gila co., E cen. Arizona, NW of Globe; pop. 2505; copper region.

Clay'ton (klā't'n). 1 Name of counties in two states of the U.S. See *Tables* at GEORGIA and IOWA.

2 Town, a ⊗ of Barbour co., SE Alabama; pop. 1313.

3 City, ⊗ of Rabun co., NE corner of Georgia; pop. 1507.

4 City, ⊗ of St. Louis co., E Missouri, 8 m. W of St. Louis; pop. 15,245; residential suburb of St. Louis.

5 Borough, Gloucester co., SW New Jersey, 21 m. S of Camden; pop. 4711; in farming section.

6 Town, ⊗ of Union co., NE corner of New Mexico, on high plateau near Texas and Oklahoma borders; pop. 3314.

7 Village, Jefferson co., N New York, on St. Lawrence river in Thousand Is. region, 20 m. NNW of Watertown; pop. 1996; summer resort, fishing center; port of entry.

8 Town, Johnston co., E North Carolina, 13 m. SE of Raleigh; pop. 3302; manufactures lumber, cotton.

Clay'ton le Moors (klā't'n lĕ mōōrz'; mōrz'). Urban district, Lancashire, NW England, 21 m. N of Manchester; pop. 6823; coal mining.

Cla·zom'e·nae (klà·zŏm'ĕ·nē). Ancient city in Asia Minor, 20 m. W of İzmir, on the Gulf of İzmir; one of the 12 Ionian Cities, celebrated for its temples. Birthplace of the philosopher Anaxagoras.

Clear, Cape (klēr). Headland, S Clear I., off SW Eire.

Clear Creek. 1 River ab. 80 m. long, cen. Colorado; rises SW Clear Creek co., flows E into South Platte river.

2 County in Colorado. See *Table* at COLORADO.

Clear'field (klēr'fēld). 1 County in Pennsylvania. See *Table* at PENNSYLVANIA.

2 Borough, its ⊗, W cen. Pennsylvania 20 m. ESE of Du Bois; pop. 9270; settled 1805; industrial center.

3 City, Davis co., N Utah, S of Ogden; pop. 8833.

Clear Fork (klēr). River ab. 200 m. long, N cen. Texas; flows E across Jones co., follows winding course through Shackelford, Throckmorton, and Stephens cos., unites with Salt Fork in S Young co. to form the Brazos river.

Clear Island. Island 3 m. long and ab. 1 m. wide off S coast of co. Cork, Eire; its S point is Cape Clear; 4 m. to the SW is Fastnet lighthouse.

Clear Lake. 1 Lake 25 m. long and 2 to 10 m. wide, Lake co., W California.

2 Reservoir in California. See CLEAR LAKE RESERVOIR.

3 City on Clear Lake, Cerro Gordo co., N Iowa, 14 m. W of Mason City; pop. 6158.

4 City, ⊗ of Deuel co., E South Dakota; pop. 1137.

Clear Lake Reservoir or **Clear Lake.** Large reservoir in NW Modoc co., NE California, ab. 10 m. below Oregon border; its outlet, an upper tributary (Lost River) of the Klamath, flows into Oregon.

Clear'wa'ter (klēr'wô'tēr; -wŏt'ēr). 1 River, NW Idaho; formed by forks uniting in N Idaho co., flows N and W into Snake river at Lewiston, NW Nez Perce co.

2 Name of counties in two states of the U.S. See *Tables* at IDAHO and MINNESOTA.

3 City, ⊗ of Pinellas co., W Florida penin., on Gulf of Mexico 18 m. NW of St. Petersburg; pop. 34,653; incorp. 1891; citrus fruit, flowers, fish; connected by two-mile causeway with **Clearwater Island**, a beach resort.

4 Lake 478 sq. m., Quebec prov., Canada; outlet on W connects it with Richmond Gulf (*q.v.*).

5 River 100 m. long, SW Alberta, Canada; flows from N Banff National Park to North Saskatchewan river.

6 River ab. 130 m. long, cen. Canada; rises in lakes in NW Saskatchewan and flows W to the Athabasca in NE Alberta; midway in its course is accessible from Lake la Loche (source of Churchill river) by La Loche Portage.

Clearwater Mountains. Mountain group in Idaho co., N cen. Idaho, highest ab. 8000 ft.

Clea'tor Moor (klē'tēr). Former urban district, Cumberland, NW England, on the Eden 36 m. SW of Carlisle; pop. (1931) 6581; coal mining.

Cle'burne (klē'bērn). 1 Name of counties in two states in the U.S. See *Tables* at ALABAMA and ARKANSAS.

2 City, ⊗ of Johnson co., N cen. Texas, 27 m. S of Fort Worth; pop. 15,381; shipping and trading center for agricultural area (esp. cotton, livestock, dairy products).

Clee Hills (klē). Range of hills 14 m. long in S Shropshire, W England; highest peaks **Brown Clee Hill** (broun) 1792 ft. and **Tit'ter·stone Clee Hill** (tĭt'ĕr·stōn') 1750 ft.

Cle El'um (klē ĕl'ŭm). City, Kittitas co., cen. Washington, at junction of Cle Elum and Yakima rivers 35 m. WSW of Wenatchee; pop. 1816; coal mining.

Cle Elum Lake. Lake 8 m. NE of Cle Elum, NW Kittitas co., cen. Washington; source of **Cle Elum River,** which flows into Yakima river at Cle Elum; **Cle Elum Dam** (135 ft.; completed 1933) at S end of lake aids in water conservation for irrigation.

Clee'thorpes (klē'thôrps). Urban district, Parts of Lindsey, Lincolnshire, E England, at mouth of the Humber 18 m. SE of Hull; pop. 29,558; seaside resort.

Cleeve Cloud (klēv' kloud'). Highest point 1031 ft. in the Cotswold Hills, in NE Gloucestershire, SW cen. England, 3¼ m. NE of Cheltenham.

Clem'en·ton (klĕm'ĕn·tŭn). Borough, Camden co., SW New Jersey, SSE of Camden; pop. 3766; charcoal pits.

Clem'son (klĕm's'n); *formerly* **Clemson College.** Town, Pickens co., NW South Carolina, SE of Walhalla; pop. 1587; Clemson Agricultural Coll. (1889).

Cleofás. = MARÍA CLEOFÁS.

Cleopatra. See ARSINOË.

Cler'ken·well (klär'kĕn·wĕl; -wĕl). District, metropolitan borough of Finsbury, N London, England (see *Table* at LONDON); gatehouse of ancient priory, founded 1100, of the Knights of St. John of Jerusalem.

Cler'mont (klĕr'mŏnt). 1 County in Ohio. See *Table* at OHIO.

2 City, Lake co., cen. Florida penin., 24 m. W of Orlando; near Lake Apopka; pop. 3313.

Cler'mont (klĕr'môⁿ'). 1 Commune, Oise dept., N France, 41 m. N of Paris; pop. (1931) 5870; once seat of countship, united to crown by St. Louis who gave it 1269 to his son Robert de France, first of the House of Bourbon; pillaged 1359 and 1415 by English.

2 See CLERMONT-FERRAND.

Cler'mont'-Fer'rand' (klĕr'môⁿ'fĕ'räⁿ'). Commercial and manufacturing city, ✳ of Puy-de-Dôme dept., S cen. France, 88 m. E of Limoges; pop. 101,128; manufactures rubber goods, chemicals, linen, machinery; 13th-cent. Gothic cathedral; 6th-cent. church; observatory.

History: Clermont, *anc.* Au·gus'to·nem'e·tum (ô·gŭs'tŏ·nĕm'ĕ·tŭm), founded by Romans; capital of the Arverni; made episcopal see 250; scene of several councils, esp. the council 1095 giving rise to the Crusades; became capital of duchy of Auvergne 1556; officially united 1731 with **Mont'fer'rand'** (môⁿ'fĕ'räⁿ'), nearby town founded 11th cent. by lords of Auvergne.

Cler'mont'-l'Hé'rault' (-lā'rō'). Commune, Hérault dept., S France; pop. (1931) 5657; dates from Roman times; occupied by Saracens; scene of much conflict during 16th-cent. religious wars in Languedoc.

Clermont-Tonnerre. See RÉAO.

Clé'ry'-sur-Somme' (klā'rē'sür·sôm'). Commune, Somme dept., N France, on the Somme near Péronne; pop. (1931) 567; destroyed by Germans in World War I.

Cleuch, Ben. See OCHIL HILLS.

Cle've or **Kle've** (klā'vĕ); *Eng.* **Cleves** (klēvz); *Fr.* **Clèves** (klâv). Manufacturing and resort city, in the former Rhine Province of Prussia, W Germany, near the Rhine river 66 m. WSW of Münster; pop. 20,241; old ducal castle (Schwanenburg). Seat of old duchy of

same name whose Duke John, a leader of German Protestantism, was father of Anne of Cleves (1515-57) fourth wife of Henry VIII; passed to Elector of Brandenburg by treaty 1614 and later to Prussia; to France 1805; reverted to Prussia 1814; after World War I occupied by Belgians to 1925; in World War II N anchor of German Westwall, taken by Canadians Feb. 12, 1945.

Cleve′don (klĕv′dŭn). Urban district, Somersetshire, SW England, on Bristol Channel 11 m. W of Bristol; pop. 9467; seaside resort.

Cleve′land (klēv′lănd). **1** Name of counties in three states of the U.S. See *Tables* at ARKANSAS, NORTH CAROLINA, OKLAHOMA.
2 City, ⊗ of White co., NE Georgia; pop. 657.
3 City, a ⊗ of Bolivar co., NW Mississippi, 30 m. NNE of Greenville; pop. 10,172; in cotton-growing section. Delta State Teachers College (1924; coed.).
4 Commercial and industrial city and port of entry, ⊗ of Cuyahoga co., N Ohio, at mouth of Cuyahoga river on Lake Erie (see *Map* at OHIO); pop. 876,050; largest city in the state, and 8th largest city in the U.S.; distributing center and market for iron ore and coal, grain and lumber; manufactures iron and steel, foundry and machine-shop products, freight-handling equipment, motor vehicles and parts, batteries, gas and electric fixtures, stoves, paints; slaughtering and meat-packing plants; printing and publishing. Western Reserve Univ. (1826); Case Institute of Technology (1880; men); Fenn College (1923; coed.). Surveyed by Moses Cleaveland for Conn. Land Co. 1796; incorp. as village 1814, as city 1836; expanded following opening of first section of Ohio and Erie Canal 1827; annexed rival Ohio City 1854.
5 City, Pawnee co., N Oklahoma, on Arkansas river 30 m. WNW of Tulsa; pop. 2519; oil center.
6 Industrial city, ⊗ of Bradley co., SE Tennessee, 26 m. ENE of Chattanooga; pop. 16,196; settled 1820; manganese and silica mines.
7 City, Liberty co., E Texas, 42 m. NNE of Houston; pop. 5838; manufactures lumber; oil wells.
8 District ab. 420 sq. m., North Riding, Yorkshire, England; bounded on N by Tees estuary and North Sea, on S by **Cleveland Hills** (highest ab. 1400 ft.); yields iron, manufactured chiefly at Middlesbrough on W border; Cleveland bay horses first bred in this region.

Cleveland, Mount. Peak 10,438 ft., highest point in Glacier National Park, NW Montana.

Cleveland Heights. City, Cuyahoga co., N Ohio, 7 m. E of Cleveland; pop. 61,813; residential suburb.

Cleves (klēvz). Village, Hamilton co., SW corner of Ohio, on Ohio river 13 m. W of Cincinnati; pop. 2076.

Cleves, Clèves. See CLEVE.

Clew Bay (klōō). Inlet of Atlantic Ocean in co. Mayo, NW Eire; ab. 8 m. wide, extends inland 15 m.

Cli′chy′ (klē′shē′) or **Clichy–la–Ga′renne′** (-là-gà′rĕn′); *anc.* **Clip·pi′a·cum** (klĭ-pī′à-kŭm). Manufacturing commune, Seine dept., N France, NW suburb of Paris; pop. 56,475; manufactures rubber, chemical goods, starch; a residence of the court in 7th cent.

Clif′den (klĭf′dĕn). Town and seaport, W co. Galway, W Eire; pop. 1019; lobster fishing.

Cliff′side′ (klĭf′sīd′). Village, Rutherford co., SW North Carolina, ab. 10 m. SE of Forest City; pop. 1275.

Cliffside Park. Borough, Bergen co., NE corner of New Jersey, on Hudson river 8 m. NNE of Jersey City and opp. New York City; pop. 17,642; residential suburb.

Clif′ton (klĭf′tŭn). **1** Town, ⊗ of Greenlee co., SE Arizona, on San Francisco river 110 m. NE of Tucson near New Mexico border; pop. 4191; settled 1872.
2 City, Passaic co., N New Jersey, NNW of Passaic; pop. 82,084; formerly part of Passaic, made separate city 1917; manufactures steel, textiles, chemicals.
3 Township, Ashe co., NW North Carolina, ab. 30 m. NW of North Wilkesboro; pop. 1619.
4 Town, Spartanburg co., NW South Carolina, ab. 7 m. NE of Spartanburg; pop. 1249; cotton mills.

5 City, Bosque co., cen. Texas, NW of Waco; pop. 2335.
6 See NIAGARA FALLS city, Canada.
7 Residential suburb of Bristol, Gloucestershire, England, on the Avon where it forms a gorge 245 ft. deep which is crossed by a suspension bridge, 702-ft. span, built 1832-64 by I. K. Brunel; hot springs.

Clifton Forge (fōrj; fôrj). City, western Virginia, in Alleghany co. but politically independent, 10 m. E of Covington; 1 sq. m.; pop. 5268; railroad and iron center.

Clifton Heights. Manufacturing borough, Delaware co., SE Pennsylvania, 7 m. W of Philadelphia; pop. 8005.

Clifton Springs. Village, Ontario co., W New York, 29 m. ESE of Rochester; pop. 1953; sulfur springs.

Cli′max (klī′măks). Village, Lake co., cen. Colorado, NE of Leadville on Fremont Pass; pop. 1609; site of Harvard Observatory high-altitude station for solar research; world's largest molybdenum mine.

Clinch (klĭnch). **1** River ab. 200 m. long, E Tennessee; rises in Tazewell co., SW Virginia, flows SW across Tennessee border and joins the Tennessee river in Roane co.; passes through Norris Lake, earlier named **Clinch′-Pow′ell Reservoir** (klĭnch′pou′ĕl), formed by Norris Dam near junction of Powell and Clinch rivers, one of the dams of the Tennessee Valley Authority (*q.v.*).
2 County in Georgia. See *Table* at GEORGIA.

Clinch′co (klĭnch′kō). Town, Dickenson co., SW Virginia, ab. 17 m. NE of Grundy; pop. (1950) 1390.

Clinch Mountain (klĭnch). Ridge 4724 ft. extending from SW Virginia SW across border into NE Tennessee, bet. the Clinch and Holston rivers.

Cling′mans Dome (klĭng′mănz). Mountain in the Great Smoky Mts., on Tennessee-North Carolina boundary; highest peak 6642 ft., highest point in Tennessee.

Clin′ton (klĭn′t'n; -tŭn). **1** Name of counties in nine states of the U.S. See *Tables* at ILLINOIS, INDIANA, IOWA, KENTUCKY, MICHIGAN, MISSOURI, NEW YORK, OHIO, PENNSYLVANIA.
2 City, ⊗ of Van Buren co., N cen. Arkansas; pop. 744.
3 Town, SW Middlesex co., S Connecticut, on Long Island Sound and on Hammonasset river; pop. 4166.
4 City, ⊗ of De Witt co., cen. Illinois, 22 m. N of Decatur; pop. 7355; in agricultural section; railroad center.
5 City, Vermillion co., W Indiana, 12 m. N of Terre Haute; pop. 5843; agriculture; coal mining.
6 City, ⊗ of Clinton co., E Iowa, on Mississippi river 30 m. NE of Davenport; pop. 33,589; trade and industrial center; ironworks, machine shops.
7 City, ⊗ of Hickman co., SW Kentucky, 24 m. WSW of Mayfield; pop. 1647; in agricultural section.
8 Town, ⊗ of East Feliciana parish, E Louisiana; pop. 1568.
9 Industrial town, Worcester co., cen. Massachusetts, 12 m. NNE of Worcester; pop. 12,848; textiles.
10 Town, Hinds co., SW cen. Mississippi; pop. 3438; Mississippi Coll. (1826; men; Baptist).
11 City, ⊗ of Henry co., W Missouri, 40 m. SW of Sedalia; pop. 6925; dairies, chick hatcheries.
12 Village, Oneida co., cen. New York, 9 m. WSW of Utica; pop. 1855; Hamilton College (1812; men).
13 Town, ⊗ of Sampson co., SE North Carolina; pop. 7461; lumbering, berry growing (esp. huckleberries).
14 City, Custer co., W Oklahoma, on Washita river 86 m. W of Oklahoma City; pop. 9617; founded 1903; shipping center for cattle and wheat country; grain elevator, cotton gins, bottling works.
15 City, Laurens co., NW South Carolina, 27 m. NE of Greenwood; pop. 7937; manufactures cotton cloth, hosiery, lumber. Presbyterian College (1880; coed.)
16 Town, ⊗ of Anderson co., E Tennessee, 15 m. NW of Knoxville; pop. 4943; site of Clinton Engineer Works covering 59,000 acres, built 1943 as a part of Manhattan District (*q.v.*) to produce plutonium and operated by University of Chicago. See OAK RIDGE.
17 Town, Huron co., SE Ontario, Canada, 12 m. SE of Goderich; pop. 2547; piano factory; flour mills.

Clinton, Mount. Peak 4275 ft. of the White Mts., in S Coos co., N New Hampshire, SW of Mt. Washington.

Clinton–Col′den Lake (kŏl′děn). Lake 674 sq. m. in E cen. Mackenzie District, Northwest Territories, Canada, NE of Great Slave Lake.

Clin·ton·ville (klĭn′t′n-vĭl; -tŭn-). City, Waupaca co., E cen. Wisconsin, 30 m. NNW of Appleton; pop. 4778; manufactures autotrucks, conveyors, dairy products.

Clint′wood (klĭnt′wŏŏd). Town, ⊗ of Dickenson co., SW Virginia; pop. 1400.

Cli′o (klī′ō). City, Genesee co., SE cen. Michigan, 12 m. N of Flint; pop. 2212.

Clip′per·ton (klĭp′ẽr·t′n; -tŭn). Uninhabited island ab. 2 sq. m., E Pacific Ocean, 670 m. SW of Mexico, 10°N lat. and 109°W long.; a low atoll bet. 2 and 3 m. in diameter, enclosing a rock 82 ft. high. Discovered and used as a base by John Clipperton, English pirate, in early 18th cent.; claimed by France 1858; forcibly occupied by Mexico 1897; awarded to France 1930 by King of Italy as arbitrator, turned over 1932.

Clippiacum. See CLICHY.

Clith′er·oe (klĭth′ẽr·ō). Municipal borough, Lancashire, NW England, on the Ribble 28 m. N of Manchester; pop. 12,057; ancient castle; textiles.

Cli·tum′nus (klī·tŭm′nŭs); *mod.* **Cli·tun′no** (klē·tōōn′nô). River, Umbria, cen. Italy; rises W of Spoleto in a beautiful spring (described by Pliny the Younger: *Epistles*, viii. 8) and flows N into the Topino.

Cloates, Point (klōts). Cape on Indian Ocean, W Western Australia, S of North West Cape.

Clon′a·kil′ty (klŏn′à·kĭl′tĭ). Urban district, S coast of co. Cork, SW Eire, at head of **Clonakilty Bay,** an inlet of Atlantic Ocean; pop. 2747; fisheries, breweries; trade in farm produce. Birthplace of Michael Collins.

Clon′ard (klŏn′ērd). Village, co. Meath, E Eire, on the Boyne 30 m. WNW of Dublin; ruins of famous college, founded c. 520 by St. Finnian, at which St. Columba was a pupil.

Clon·cur′ry (klŏn·kûr′ĭ). Small town in rich mining district, W Queensland, Australia.

Clon′fert (klŏn′fẽrt). Village, SE co. Galway, W Eire; has ruined cathedral founded by St. Brendan, who established monastery here ab. 553.

Clon′mac·noise′ (klŏn′măk·noiz′). Parish, NW co. Offaly, cen. Eire, on Shannon river ab. 9 m. S of Athlone; early center of Christianity, site of an abbey founded 541; laid waste by English 1552.

Clon·mel′ (klŏn·mĕl′; klŏn′mĕl). Municipal borough, ⊗ of co. Tipperary, S Eire; pop. 10,491.

Clon·tarf′ (klŏn·tärf′; klŏn′tärf). Residential suburb of Dublin, Eire, on N shore of Dublin Bay; watering place; scene Apr. 23, 1014 of defeat of Danes by Brian Boru, who was killed here.

Clo·quet′ (klō·kā′). **1** River, NE Minnesota; rises in Lake co., flows SW into St. Louis river in S St. Louis co. **2** City, Carlton co., E Minnesota, 17 m. WSW of Duluth; pop. 9013; manufactures paper and wood products.

Clos′ter (klŏs′tẽr). Borough, Bergen co., NE corner of New Jersey, 11 m. ENE of Paterson; pop. 7767.

Closter–Zeven. = *Kloster-Zeven:* see ZEVEN.

Cloud (kloud). County in Kansas. See *Table* at KANSAS.

Cloud′cap′ (kloud′kăp′). Mountain 8070 ft. in W Klamath co., near E shore of Crater Lake, SW Oregon.

Cloud Peak. Mountain 13,165 ft., highest point in Big Horn Mts., on boundary bet. Big Horn and Johnson cos., N Wyoming.

Clouds Rest (kloudz). Mountain 9930 ft., Mariposa co., cen. California; rises 5964 ft. above Yosemite Valley, in Yosemite National Park.

Cloud′veil′ Dome (kloud′vāl′). Peak 12,026 ft. in cen. Grand Teton National Park, NW Wyoming.

Cloud′y Bay (kloud′ĭ). Inlet of Cook Strait on NE coast of South I., New Zealand; Blenheim is on its S shore.

Clo·vel′ly (klō·vĕl′ĭ). Village, Devonshire, SW England, on SW shore of Barnstaple Bay ab. 11 m. WSW of Bide-

ford; pop. 528; on a cliff, its main street is like a staircase and is too steep for wheeled vehicles; resort.

Clo′ver (klō′vẽr). Town, York co., N South Carolina, 17 m. NW of Rock Hill; pop. 3500; cotton; lumber.

Clo′vis (klō′vĭs). **1** City, Fresno co., S cen. California, 10 m. NE of Fresno; pop. 5546. **2** City, ⊗ of Curry co., E New Mexico, near Texas boundary; pop. 23,713; four-way railroad division point; trade center for wheat and cattle region.

Cloyne (kloin). Village, co. Cork, SW Eire, 15 m. ESE of Cork; pop. (1926) 712; ancient bishopric of which Berkeley was bishop 1734–53; 14th-cent. cathedral.

Cluj (klōozh); *Ger.* **Klau′sen·burg** (klou′zĕn-bŏŏrҡ; *Hung.* **Ko′lozs·vár** (kō′lôzh-vär′). City, NW cen. Romania, in Transylvania in hills on right bank of the Little Someş; pop. (1939 est.) 100,272; begun 12th cent. as German settlement on site of older town; industrial and commercial center; seat of an Orthodox bishop, and of bishops of the Reformed and Uniat churches; university; national theater.

Clunia. See FELDKIRCH.

Clu′ny (klōō′nĭ; *Fr.* klü′nē′). Commune, Saône-et-Loire dept., E cen. France; pop. (1931) 4099; remains of Benedictine abbey of Cluny, founded c. 910 by William I, Duke of Aquitaine; Cluny lace, formerly made in Auvergne, named from its use by monks of the abbey.

Clusium. See CHIUSI.

Clu′tha (klōō′thȧ). River 210 m. long in SE South I., New Zealand; flows SE into the Pacific Ocean; headstreams rise in Lakes Wanaka and Wakatipu.

Clw′yd (klōō′ĭd). River in N Wales; flows N into Irish Sea at Rhyl; vale of Clwyd noted for scenery.

Clyde (klīd). **1** River, W New York, from Lyons in Wayne co. to Seneca river; part of Canandaigua Outlet. **2** Town, former ⊗ of Bryan co., SE Georgia; pop. (1950) 119. **3** Village, Wayne co., W New York, on N.Y. State Barge Canal 18 m. NW of Auburn; pop. 2693; makes shoe counters, steam engines, farm implements, glass. **4** Village, Sandusky co., N Ohio, 17 m. SW of Sandusky; pop. 4826; settled c. 1820; farming; canneries. **5** River, S Scotland; 106 m. long from the source of its true headstream the Daer Water; rises in S Lanarkshire; flows N, near Lanark descends by four waterfalls a distance of 320 ft. in less than four miles; flows NW, near Hamilton, past Glasgow (head of navigation for ocean-going vessels), and Renfrew; at Dumbarton expands into the **Firth of Clyde,** an estuary extending 64 m. to the island of Ailsa Craig where it is ab. 37 m. wide. **Clydes′-dale** (klīds′dāl′), the valley of the upper Clyde, ab. 50 m. long, has coal and iron; noted also for agriculture and for a breed of heavy draft horses (*Clydesdale*).

Clyde′bank′ (klīd′băngk′). Burgh, Dunbarton co., W cen. Scotland, on the Clyde; pop. (1951) 44,625; has shipbuilding yards, engineering works.

Cly′mer (klī′mẽr). Borough, Indiana co., W cen. Pennsylvania, 25 m. N of Johnstown; pop. 2251.

Clyth Ness (klĭth′ nĕs′). Headland projecting into North Sea on NE coast of Scotland, E cen. Caithness co., S of Wick; lighthouse.

Cni′dus (nī′dŭs). Ruins of ancient town at Cape Krio, end of long promontory of Caria, SW Asia Minor; a Dorian city noted for its wealth, temples, statues, and fine buildings; belonged to the Pentapolis of Asia Minor. Nearby was fought naval battle 394 B.C. in which Athenian leader Conon defeated Spartans under Pisander.

Cnossus. See KNOSSOS.

Co′a·chel′la Valley (kō′ȧ·chĕl′ȧ). Valley in SE California bet. Salton Sea and the San Bernardino Mts.

Coa·ho′ma (kō·hō′mȧ). County in Mississippi. See *Table* at MISSISSIPPI.

Co·a·hui′la (kō′ȧ·wē′lä). State, NE Mexico. See *Table* at MEXICO.

Coal (kōl). County in Oklahoma. See *Table* at OKLAHOMA.

Coal City. City, Grundy co., NE Illinois, 20 m. SSW of Joliet; pop. 2852; in coal-mining section.

Coal′dale (kōl′dāl). Borough, Schuylkill co., E cen. Pennsylvania, 20 m. ENE of Pottsville; pop. 3949; coal.

Coal′gate (kōl′gāt). City, ⊗ of Coal co., S Oklahoma, 33 m. SE of Ada; pop. 1689; oil and gas wells in vicinity.

Coal Grove. Village, Lawrence co., S Ohio, on Ohio river 3 m. SE of Ironton; pop. 2961.

Coal·in′ga (kō·lĭng′gá). City, Fresno co., S cen. California, 50 m. SW of Fresno; pop. 5965; oil fields.

Coal′ville (kōl′vĭl). **1** City, ⊗ of Summit co., NE Utah; pop. 907.
2 Urban district, Leicestershire, cen. England, 14 m. WNW of Leicester; pop. 25,739; coal mining.

Co·a′mo (kō·ä′mō). Municipality (pop. 26,082) and town (pop. 12,146), S cen. Puerto Rico, ENE of Ponce.

Coast′ers Harbor Island (kōs′tērz). See NEWPORT, R.I.

Coastland. See KÜSTENLAND.

Coast Province (kōst). Province, SE Kenya colony and protectorate, E Africa; ✳ Mombasa.

Coast Ranges. Mountains along the Pacific coast of North America from the southern part of California, where they meet the Sierra Nevada Mts. (see SAN BERNARDINO MOUNTAINS), through Oregon and Washington, into British Columbia and Alaska (Vancouver I., Queen Charlotte Is., Alexander Archipelago, St. Elias and Chugach ranges, Kenai Peninsula, and Kodiak I.); in California peaks are from 3800 ft. to 8826 ft. (Mt. Pinos); in Oregon from 2500 ft. to 7000 ft.; in Washington to 7954 ft. (highest point in the Olympic Mts.). The **Coast Mountains** of British Columbia, including Mt. Waddington 13,260 ft., are not a continuation of the U.S. Coast Ranges but of the Cascade Range (q.v.).

Coat′bridge (kōt′brĭj). Manufacturing burgh, Lanark co., S cen. Scotland, 9 m. E of Glasgow; pop. (1951) 47,538; coal and iron mining; iron founding; manufactures steam boilers, firebrick, railroad rolling stock.

Co·a′te·pec′ (kō·ä′tā·pĕk′). Town, Veracruz state, E Mexico, just S of Jalapa; pop. 11,459.

Co·a·te·pe′que (kō·ä′tā·pā′kā). Town, Quezaltenango dept., SW Guatemala; pop. 6425; in coffee-growing area.

Coates′ville (kōts′vĭl). City, Chester co., SE Pennsylvania, 28 m. E of Lancaster; pop. 12,971; manufactures steel, brass and iron products, textiles.

Co·at′i·cook (kō·ăt′ĭ·kook). Industrial town, Stanstead co., S Quebec, Canada, 20 m. S of Sherbrooke; pop. 6341; wood products, woolens, bricks, milk products.

Coats Island (kōts). Island in N Hudson Bay, Keewatin District, Northwest Territories, Canada.

Coats Land. Largely ice-covered section of Antarctica on SE coast of Weddell Sea from 18°W to 40°W; includes Caird Coast and Leopold Coast. The greater part is included in Falkland Islands Dependencies (q.v.).

Co·at′za·co·al′cos (kō·ät′sä·kō·äl′kōs). **1** River in the Isthmus of Tehuantepec, Mexico; rises in the Sierra Madre, flows NE into the Bay of Campeche.
2 formerly **Puer′to Mé′xi·co** (pwĕr′tō mĕ′hē·kō). Town, Veracruz state, E Mexico; pop. 13,740; located on Coatzacoalcos river 1 m. from its mouth; port of entry.

Co·bá′ (kō·vä′). Ancient Maya city, NE Yucatán penin., Mexico; ruins now in Quintana Roo Territory.

Co′balt (kō′bôlt). Mining town, Timiskaming dist., SE Ontario, Canada, 70 m. N of North Bay and just W of Lake Timiskaming; pop. 2230; extensive deposits containing silver and cobalt, discovered 1903; large floating population; mining for silver has much declined but in World War II mining for cobalt resumed.

Co·bán′ (kō·vän′). City, ✳ of Alta Verapaz dept., cen. Guatemala; pop. 8001; in rich coffee-growing area.

Co′bar (kō′bär). Town, cen. New South Wales, SE Australia, 360 m. WNW of Sydney; pop. 1163; formerly had rich copper and gold mines.

Cobb (kŏb). County in Georgia. See *Table* at GEORGIA.

Cob′ble Mountain Dam (kŏb′'l). Dam completed 1932 across Little river, W Hampden co., W Massachu-

setts; height 263 ft.; impounds water, **Cobble Mountain Reservoir,** for water supply and power.

Cob′e·quid Bay (kŏb′ĕ·kwĭd). Eastern arm of Minas Basin, cen. Nova Scotia, Canada; Truro at its head.

Cobh (kōv); *formerly* **Queens′town** (kwēnz′toun). Urban district and seaport on Great I. in Cork Harbour, SE co. Cork, SW Eire; pop. 5713; port of call for ocean liners. Adjacent Haulbowline I. was formerly an important British naval base.

Co·bi′ja (kō·vē′hä). **1** City, ✳ of Pando dept., NW Bolivia, on Acre river; pop. (1943 est.) 5000; rubber.
2 Former name of GATICO, Chile.

Coblenz. See KOBLENZ.

Co′bles·kill′ (kō′b'l·skĭl′; -b'lz·kĭl′). Village, Schoharie co., E New York, SW of Amsterdam; pop. 3471; battle May 30, 1778 bet. patriots and Indians led by Tories.

Co′bourg (kō′bûrg). Manufacturing town, Northumberland co., SE Ontario, Canada, on Lake Ontario 70 m. ENE of Toronto; pop. 7470; ⊗ of Northumberland and Durham cos.; fine harbor; summer resort.

Co′bourg, or **Co′burg, Peninsula** (kō′bûrg). Peninsula 50 m. long and 20 m. broad, N Australia; on N side of Van Diemen Gulf.

Co′bre or **El Co′bre** (ĕl kō′vrä). Municipality, Oriente prov., E Cuba, 8 m. W of Santiago de Cuba; pop. 36,435; copper mines, worked since 1547.

Co′burg (kō′bûrg). **1** City, S Victoria, SE Australia, N suburb of Melbourne; pop. 38,122.
2 (Ger. kō′boork) Manufacturing and commercial city, Upper Franconia govt. dist., Bavaria, Germany, 36 m. NW of Bayreuth; pop. 24,701; 13th-cent. church; 16th-cent. castle (Ehrenberg). First mentioned 1056; passed to Ernestine line of dukes of Saxony 1485; seat of dukes of Coburg; residence of dukes of Saxe-Coburg-Gotha; capital of Saxe-Coburg 1735; to Bavaria 1920.

Coc′a·na′da (kŏk′á·nä′dá) or **Ka′ki·na′da** (kä′kĭ-). City, NE Andhra Pradesh, E India, on Bay of Bengal at N side of Godavari delta, 300 m. NNE of Madras; pop. 99,952; harbor facilities maintained with difficulty because of alluvial soil; chief exports rice, cotton, oil seeds.

Co′cha·bam′ba (kō′chä·väm′bä). **1** Department of Bolivia. See *Table* at BOLIVIA.
2 City, its ✳, W cen. Bolivia, ab. 80 m. NE of Oruro; 8448 ft. above the sea; pop. (1943 est.) 60,000; second largest city of the republic, originally known as Oropeza; founded 1574; chief distributing point for eastern Bolivia; cathedral, university.

Co·che′co (kō·chē′kō). River ab. 33 m. long, SE New Hampshire; flows S to Salmon Falls river.

Co′chin (kō′chĭn; kŏch′ĭn). **1** Region, former state, SW Indian Union, on Malabar Coast; merged 1949 with Travancore forming state of **Travancore and Cochin** which became in 1956 part of new state of Kerala; area 1493 sq. m.; ✳ Ernakulam; has fine forested regions and is center of trade in coconut products. Its history is practically that of the town Cochin (see below).
2 Town, N Kerala state, SW Indian Union; situated on a long strip of land on Malabar Coast 125 m. W of Madura; pop. 22,818; maintains harbor facilities with difficulty, esp. from May to August; exports mainly coconut products, tea, and nuts. Portuguese factory founded by Vasco da Gama 1502; fort built by Albuquerque 1503, first European fort in India; British settled 1635 but forced out by Dutch 1663, under whom town became important trade center; came under sovereignty of Haidar Ali 1776 but was surrendered by his son Tipu Sahib to the British 1791; occupied by British 1795 and fortifications destroyed; formally ceded by Dutch 1814. Burial place of Albuquerque.

Co′chin Chi′na (kō′chĭn chĭ′ná; kŏch′ĭn); *Fr.* **Co′chin′chine′** (kô′shăn′shēn′). Former autonomous republic in the Federation of Indochina, S Vietnam, S of Annam and Cambodia with coast on South China Sea and Gulf of Siam; 29,974 sq. m.; pop. 4,616,000; ✳ Saigon; with exception of few hills (c. 3000 ft.) in N part,

flat alluvial plain of Mekong delta and several short streams; river channels and irrigation canals form one of greatest rice-producing areas in Asia; fishing an important industry. Inhabitants are mainly Annamese, with some Cambodians, Chams, Chinese. Chief towns Saigon, Cholon, Longxuyên, Cantho.

History: Vassal of Chinese Empire; later part of Khmer kingdom of Cambodia (*q.v.*) and of empire of Annam; in French war with Annam, Saigon was occupied 1859; by Treaty of Saigon 1862, its three eastern provinces were ceded to French who occupied its western provinces in 1867 and made it a colony; united administratively with French protectorates of Annam, Tonkin, and Cambodia to form French Indochina (*q.v.*) 1887; made an autonomous republic within the French Union 1946; incorporated in Vietnam 1949.

Co·chi′nos Bay (kô-chē′nôs) *or* **Bay of Pigs.** Bay on SW coast of Las Villas prov., W cen. Cuba; scene of attempted invasion of Cuba by anti-Castro force April 17, 1961.

Co·chi′nos Point (kô-chē′nôs). Point at S end of Bataan Penin., Luzon, Phil. Is., near Mariveles; actually formed by group of islets, Los Cochinos.

Co·chise′ (kô-chēs′). County in Arizona. See *Table* at ARIZONA.

Coch′ran (kŏk′răn). **1** County in Texas. See *Table* at TEXAS.

2 City, ⊗ of Bleckley co., cen. Georgia; pop. 4714.

Coch′rane (kŏk′răn). **1** District, Ontario, Canada. See *Table* at ONTARIO.

2 Town, its ⊗, E Ontario, Canada, 48 m. NNE of Timmins; pop. 3401; railroad divisional point.

Cock′burn Channel (kō′bērn). Passage off S Chile extending S and W from Strait of Magellan to the Pacific bet. Clarence I. on W and SW Tierra del Fuego.

Cockburn Island. Island in N Lake Huron, off W tip of Manitoulin I., administratively a part of Manitoulin dist., S Ontario prov., Canada.

Cocke (kŏk). County in Tennessee. See *Table* at TENNESSEE.

Cock′er (kŏk′ēr). Small river in Cumberland, NW England; flows out of Lake Buttermere N into the Derwent at **Cock′er·mouth** (kŏk′ēr·mouth; -mŭth), urban district, Cumberland, pop. 5234; birthplace of William Wordsworth.

Cocks′comb′ Mountains (kŏks′kōm′). Range in S British Honduras; highest point Victoria Peak 3681 ft.

Co·clé′ (kō-klā′). Province, cen. Panama; 1470 sq. m.; pop. 55,737; * Penonomé.

Coco. See SEGOVIA.

Co′coa (kō′kō). City, Brevard co., E Florida, on Indian river 42 m. SE of Orlando; pop. 12,294; incorporated 1895; citrus-shipping center; fishing resort.

Co′co Cay (kō′kō); *Span.* **Ca′yo Co′co** (kä′yô kō′kô). Island off NW coast of Camagüey prov., E cen. Cuba.

Co′co Channel (kō′kō). Strait off N point of North Andaman I., Andaman Is., Bay of Bengal.

Co′co·ni′no (kō′kô-nē′nō). County in Arizona. See *Table* at ARIZONA.

Coconino Plateau. Tableland in cen. Coconino co., N cen. Arizona, S of Grand Canyon National Park.

Co′co·nut′ Grove (kō′kô-nŭt′; - nŭt). South suburban section of Miami, Florida.

Co′cos Island (kō′kôs). Uninhabited island 18 sq. m., Pacific Ocean, SW of Costa Rica, 5°35′N, 87°2′W.

Co′cos (kō′kôs; *Angl.* -kŭs), *or* **Kee′ling** (kē′lĭng), **Islands.** Group of ab. 20 small coral islands in the Indian Ocean, ab. 580 m. SW of Java; lat. 12°5′S and long. 96°53′E; 1 sq. m.; pop. 1142; British possession attached to Singapore colony until 1955 when it was transferred to Australia; chief product coconuts. Acquired by Great Britain 1857, placed under Ceylon governor 1878, under Straits Settlements 1886; incorporated with Singapore settlement 1903; scene of sinking of German cruiser *Emden* by Australian cruiser *Sydney* Nov. 9, 1914.

Co′co So′lo (kō′kō sō′lō). Village on inlet just E of Colón, N end of Canal Zone, N of France Field; pop. 1133; U.S. Naval Reservation and Fleet Air Base.

Co·cu′la (kô-kōō′lä). Town, Jalisco state, W cen. Mexico, 32 m. SW of Guadalajara, pop. 7706.

Cocuy, Sierra Nevada de. See SIERRA NEVADA DE COCUY.

Cod, Cape. See CAPE COD.

Co·de′ra, Cape (kô-thä′rä). Cape extending into Caribbean Sea on N cen. coast of Venezuela, E of Caracas.

Co·di·go′ro (kô-dē·gô′rô). Commune, Ferrara prov., Emilia, N Italy, 25 m. E of Ferrara; pop. 17,028.

Cod′ing·ton (kŏd′ĭng·tŭn). County in South Dakota. See *Table* at SOUTH DAKOTA.

Co·do′gno (kô-dō′nyô). Commune, Milano prov., Lombardy, N Italy, 34 m. SE of Milan; pop. 11,424; scene of defeat of Austrians by French 1796.

Cod′ring·ton (kŏd′rĭng·tŭn). Village on Barbuda I., British colony of Leeward Is., West Indies.

Co·dro′i·po (kô-drô′ē·pô). Commune, Friuli prov., Venezia Euganea, NE Italy, SW of Udine; pop. 13,771.

Co′dy (kō′dĭ). City, ⊗ of Park co., NW Wyoming, on Shoshone river E of Buffalo Bill Reservoir; pop. 4838; tourist resort at E entrance to Yellowstone Park.

Cody Peak. Mountain 10,246 ft. on E boundary of Yellowstone National Park, NW Wyoming.

Coele–Syria, Coelesyria. See EL BIKA.

Coes′feld (kōs′fĕlt), *also* **Koes′feld** (kōs′-). City, W Germany, in North Rhine-Westphalia state 21 m. W of Münster; pop. 10,857; 13th-cent. town hall; manufactures textiles, iron goods, paper, chairs, soap. Became city 1197; under bishop of Münster 1246; member of Hanseatic League; to Prussia 1815.

Coet′qui′dan′ (kwĕt′kē′däN′). Military camp, Morbihan dept., NW France; site of St. Cyr after 1945.

Coeur d′A·lene′ (kôr′d′l·ān′). **1** River ab. 100 m. long, N Idaho; flows W from Shoshone co. into Coeur d′Alene Lake.

2 City, ⊗ of Kootenai co., N Idaho, 32 m. E of Spokane, Washington; pop. 14,291; on site of military post established 1879; discovery of silver and lead deposits 1882; mining, lumbering, farming.

Coeur d′Alene Lake. Lake in Kootenai co., N Idaho; ab. 30 m. long; ab. 60 sq. m.; center of large resort area.

Cof′fee (kôf′ĭ). Name of counties in three states of the U.S. See *Tables* at ALABAMA, GEORGIA, TENNESSEE.

Cof′fee·ville (kôf′ĭ·vĭl). Town, a ⊗ of Yalobusha co., N Mississippi; pop. 813.

Cof′fey (kôf′ĭ). County in Kansas. See *Table* at KANSAS.

Cof′fey·ville (kôf′ĭ·vĭl). City, Montgomery co., SE Kansas, 15 m. S of Independence; pop. 17,382; former frontier town and cattle-shipping point; near oil and gas fields; manufactures structural steel, chemicals.

Cof′fin Island (kôf′ĭn). See MAGDALEN ISLANDS.

Co′fre de Pe·ro′te (kō′frä thä pä·rō′tä); *Indian name* Nau′cham·pa·te′petl (nou′chäm·pä·tä′pĕt·′l). Mountain 13,552 ft. in Veracruz state, Mexico.

Co·ghi′nas (kô-gē′näs). River ab. 60 m. long in N Sardinia; flows N into Gulf of Asinara.

Coglians, Monte. See KELLERWAND.

Co′gnac (kō′nyăk; kôn′yăk; *Fr.* kô′nyäk′); *anc.* **Compni′a·cum** (kŏmp·nĭ′ă·kŭm). Commune, Charente dept., W France, on Charente river 24 m. W of Angoulême; pop. 16,305; famous for its distilleries producing cognac (named for it). Belonged to Richard Cœur de Lion; made commune 1352; Protestant stronghold in latter part of 16th cent.; a center for ceramic manufactures in 18th cent.

Co·has′set (kô-hăs′ĕt; -ĭt). Town, Norfolk co., E Massachusetts, on Atlantic Ocean 15 m. SE of Boston; pop. 5840; summer resort.

Cohasset Rocks. See MINOTS LEDGE.

Co·hoc′ton *or* **Con·hoc′ton** (kô-hŏk′tŭn). River ab. 60 m. long, S New York; flows SE and unites with Tioga river near Corning to form Chemung river.

Co·hoes' (kō·hōz'). City, Albany co., E New York, at confluence of Mohawk and Hudson rivers near E terminus of N.Y. State Barge Canal, 10 m. N of Albany; pop. 20,129; manufacturing center, with power from 70-foot falls of Mohawk river. First settled by Dutch 1665; chartered as city 1870; headquarters of Gen. Gates in Revolutionary War.

Coi (koi) *or* **Song'koi** (sŏng'koi'); *also, literally*, **Red** (*Fr.* **Rouge** [rōōzh]) **River.** River (*song*) ab. 500 m. long of SE Asia; rises in cen. Yunnan, S China, flows SE across Tonkin in N Indochina, past Hanoi, and into Gulf of Tonkin; has wide fertile delta E of Hanoi; known as the Yuan in China; chief tributaries the Gam from the N and the Bo, or Noire, from the S.

Coi'ba (koi'vä). Island 20 m. long in Pacific Ocean off SW coast of Panama.

Coile. See COYLE.

Coim'ba·tore' (koim'bȧ·tōr'). City, W Madras, S Indian Union, on Noyil river 280 m. SW of Madras; pop. (1941) 130,348; on S slope of Nilgiri Hills; has cotton mills, tanneries, coffee and sugar factories; agricultural college; 3 m. to the E is the Pagoda of **Pe·rur'** (pā·rōōr'), of archaeological interest.

Co·im'bra (kō·ĭm'brȧ; *Port.* kwēNM'brȧ). 1 District of Portugal. See *Table* at PORTUGAL.

2 *anc.* **Co·nim'bri·a** (kō·nĭm'brĭ·ȧ) *or* **Co·nim'bri·ga** (kō·nĭm'brĭ·gȧ). City, its ✳, W cen. Portugal, on Mondego river 108 m. NNE of Lisbon; pop. (1940) 35,437; ✳ of Beira Litoral prov.; former ✳ of Portugal (1139–c. 1260); manufactures earthenware, combs; 12th-cent. cathedral; University of Coimbra (founded 1290 at Lisbon; transferred to Coimbra 1537). Powerful city under Romans; conquered by Visigoths and later by Moors; reconquered 1064 by Ferdinand I the Great and the Cid; Inés de Castro murdered here 1355.

Co·ín' (kō·ēn'). Commune, Málaga prov., S Spain, 19 m. W of Málaga; pop. 17,348; manufactures soap, paper, textiles, oil, wine, esparto mats; marble quarries nearby.

Coira, Coire. See CHUR.

Co·je'des (kō·hā'thås). State of Venezuela. See *Table* at VENEZUELA.

Co·ju'te·pe'que (kō·hōō'tå·pā'kå). City, ✳ of Cuscatlán dept., cen. El Salvador, 16 m. E of San Salvador; pop. (1942 est.) 14,912; produces rice, coffee, sugar, indigo.

Coke (kōk). County in Texas. See *Table* at TEXAS.

Co·lac' (kō·lăk'). Town, S Victoria, SE Australia, 40 m. WSW of Geelong; pop. 5600.

Col'bert (kŏl'bērt). County in Alabama. See *Table* at ALABAMA.

Col'by (kŏl'bĭ). City, ✳ of Thomas co., NW Kansas, 38 m. E of Goodland; pop. 4210; in agricultural section.

Colby Mountain. Peak 9615 ft. in Sierra Nevada, in E Tuolumne co., cen. California.

Col·cha'gua (kŏl·chä'gwä). Province of Chile. See *Table* at CHILE.

Col'ches'ter (kŏl'chĕs'tēr; -chĭs·tēr). 1 Town, NW New London co., SE Connecticut; pop. 4648; settled 1699; includes borough of Colchester (pop. 2260).

2 County, Nova Scotia, Canada. See *Table* at NOVA SCOTIA.

3 *anc.* **Cam'u·lo·du'num** (kăm'ū·lô·dū'nŭm). Municipal borough, Essex, SE England, on the Colne 53 m. NE of London; pop. (1931) 48,701; (1951) 57,436; oyster fisheries, agriculture; site of ancient Roman settlement, the first Roman colony in Britain, founded by Claudius 43 A.D.; burned by Boadicea's warriors.

Col'chis (kŏl'kĭs). Ancient country on the Black Sea S of Caucasus Mts. corresponding to W part of the Soviet republic of Georgia; watered by the Phasis (*mod.* Rion); ✳ Aea; in Greek legend the home of Medea and magic, where in a sacred grove was the Golden Fleece sought by the Argonauts; in 1st cent. B.C. Colchians were overcome by Mithridates VI, King of Pontus.

Col'den Mountain (kōl'dĕn). Peak 4713 ft. in the Adirondack Mts., in Essex co., NE New York.

Cold Harbor (kōld). Locality, Hanover co., E cen. Virginia, N of the Chickahominy river ab. 10 m. ENE of Richmond; site of two battles of the Civil War: (1) in 1862, better known as Gaines' Mill (*q.v.*); (2) June 1 and 3, 1864, in which Gen. Lee forced Federals to retire with heavy losses.

Cold'spring' (kōld'sprĭng'). Village, ✳ of San Jacinto co., E Texas; pop. (est.) 500.

Cold Spring. Village, Putnam co., SE New York, on Hudson river 20 m. S of Poughkeepsie; pop. 2083; in farming country; made Parrott guns used in Civil War.

Cold'stream' (kōld'strēm'). Burgh, Berwick co., SE Scotland; on English border; pop. 1294; the Coldstream Guards originally organized here by Gen. Monck 1659–60; once a popular runaway-marriage resort.

Cold'wa'ter (kōld'wô'tēr; -wŏt'ēr). 1 River ab. 150 m. long, NW Mississippi; rises in NE Marshall co., flows SW and S, into Tallahatchie river in Quitman co.

2 City, ✳ of Comanche co., S Kansas; pop. 1164.

3 City, ✳ of Branch co., S Michigan, 28 m. S of Battle Creek; pop. 8880; manufactures furnaces, marine engines, shoes, cement, flour.

4 Village, Mercer co., W Ohio, 33 m. SW of Lima; pop. 2766.

Cole (kōl). County in Missouri. See *Table* at MISSOURI.

Cole'brook (kōl'brŏŏk). Town, Coos co., N New Hampshire, on Connecticut river 33 m. NNW of Berlin; pop. 2389; tourist center; potato growing, lumbering.

Cole'man (kōl'măn). 1 County in Texas. See *Table* at TEXAS.

2 City, its ✳, cen. Texas, 28 m. WNW of Brownwood; pop. 6371; manufactures cottonseed oil, bricks.

3 Coal-mining town, S Alberta, Canada, ab. 74 m. W of Lethbridge; pop. 1961.

Co·len'so (kō·lĕn'zō). Village on Tugela river, W Natal, Union of South Africa, 65 m. NW of Pietermaritzburg; pop. 1123; scene of battle Dec. 1899 in Boer War which halted Gen. Butler's advance to relief of Ladysmith 14 m. N; occupied by British Feb. 20, 1900.

Cole·raine' (kōl·rān'; kōl'rān). Municipal borough and shipping port, co. Londonderry, NW Northern Ireland, on Bann river; pop. 10,748; fisheries, distilleries, linen manufacture.

Cole'roon (kōl'rōōn; kō'lĕ·rōōn). The northern and largest branch of the Cauvery river (*q.v.*), India, in its delta; empties into Bay of Bengal S of Cuddalore.

Coles (kōlz). County in Illinois. See *Table* at ILLINOIS.

Coles'berg (kōlz'bŭrg). Town, N Cape Province, S Union of South Africa, 130 m. SW of Bloemfontein; pop. 2905; occupied by Boers during Boer War and scene of repeated clashes 1899–1900.

Col'fax (kōl'făks). 1 Name of counties in two states of the U.S. See *Tables* at NEBRASKA and NEW MEXICO.

2 City, Jasper co., S cen. Iowa, 18 m. E of Des Moines; pop. 2331; near coal fields.

3 Town, ✳ of Grant parish, cen. Louisiana; pop. 1934.

4 City, ✳ of Whitman co., SE Washington, 15 m. NNW of Pullman; pop. 2860; produces wheat and livestock.

Col·hué' (kōl·wā') *or* **Colhué Hua·pí'** (wä·pē'). Lake in S Chubut territory, S Argentina, E of Lake Musters.

Co·li'ma (kō·lē'mä). 1 Volcano 12,792 ft. in Jalisco state, W cen. Mexico.

2 State, SW Mexico. See *Table* at MEXICO.

3 City, its ✳, SW Mexico; pop. 22,601; altitude 1600 ft.; cattle raising and farming.

Coll (kŏl). Island ab. 12 m. long of the Inner Hebrides, W of N Mull I., off W coast of Scotland; administratively a part of Argyll co.

Col'la·dor' (kō'yä·thôr'). Peak 12,835 ft. in Cajamarca dept., N Peru.

Col·la'ti·a (kŏ·lā'shĭ·ȧ). Ancient Sabine town, Latium, Italy, ab. 10 m. NE of Rome; scene, in Roman legend, of the rape of Lucrece, wife of Tarquinius Collatinus; referred to as **Col·la'ti·um** (-ŭm) in Shakespeare's poem *The Rape of Lucrece*.

Col′le di Val d'El′sa (kôl′lä dĕ väl dâl′sä). Industrial commune, Siena prov., Tuscany, cen. Italy, 14 m. NW of Siena; pop. 11,052; 13th-cent. cathedral; ironworks.

Col′lege (kŏl′ĕj; -ĭj). Village, W suburb of Fairbanks, Alaska; seat of Univ. of Alaska (authorized 1915; opened 1922; coed.); pop. 1755.

Col′lege·bor′o (-bûr′ŏ). See STATESBORO, Ga.

Col′lege·dale (-dāl). Village, Hamilton co., SE Tennessee, E of Chattanooga; pop. (1950) 277; Southern Missionary Coll. (1893; coed.).

College Park. 1 City, Clayton and Fulton cos., NW cen. Georgia, 8 m. SSW of Atlanta; pop. 23,469.

2 City, Prince Georges co., Maryland, 8 m. NE of Washington; pop. 18,482; site of Maryland State College of Agriculture (chartered 1856 as Maryland Agricultural Coll.), since 1920 part of University of Maryland.

College Place. See WALLA WALLA, Washington.

College Station. City, Brazos co., E cen. Texas, 4 m. S of Bryan; pop. 11,396; Agricultural and Mechanical College of Texas (1871; men).

Col′lege·ville (kŏl′ĕj-vĭl; -ĭj-). 1 Township, Stearns co., cen. Minnesota, 10 m. W of St. Cloud; pop. 1812; St. John's Univ. (1857; Roman Catholic).

2 Borough, Montgomery co., SE Pennsylvania, ab. 8 m. NW of Norristown; pop. 2254; Ursinus College (1869; coed.).

Col·le′gno (kôl-lā′nyŏ). Commune, Torino prov., Piedmont, NW Italy, NW of Turin; pop. (1931) 11,522.

Col′le Sal·vet′ti (kôl′lä säl-vät′tĕ). Commune, Livorno prov., Tuscany, Italy, NE of Leghorn; pop. (1931) 10,174.

Col′le·ton (kŏl′ĕ-t′n; -tŭn). County in South Carolina. See *Table* at SOUTH CAROLINA.

Col′lie (kŏl′ĭ). Town, SW Western Australia, 110 m. S of Perth; pop. 3785.

Col′lier (kŏl′yẽr). County in Florida. See *Table* at FLORIDA.

Collier Bay. Large inlet of Indian Ocean, N coast of Western Australia.

Colli Euganei. See EUGANEAN HILLS.

Col′lin (kŏl′ĭn). County in Texas. See *Table* at TEXAS.

Col′ling·dale (kŏl′ĭng-dāl). Borough, Delaware co., SE Pennsylvania, 7 m. WSW of Philadelphia; pop. 10,268.

Col′lings·wood (kŏl′ĭngz-wŏŏd). Borough, Camden co., SW New Jersey, 3 m. SE of Camden; pop. 17,370; settled by Quakers 1682, incorp. 1888; residential.

Col′lings·worth (kŏl′ĭngz-wûrth). County in Texas. See *Table* at TEXAS.

Col′ling·wood (kŏl′ĭng-wŏŏd). 1 City, S Victoria, SE Australia, NE suburb of Melbourne; pop. 30,661.

2 Lake town, Simcoe co., SE Ontario, Canada, on Nottawasaga Bay 29 m. WNW of Barrie; pop. 7413; shipbuilding; steelworks, foundries, machine shops; government fish hatchery.

Collingwood Bay. Inlet of Solomon Sea on N coast of E Papua, New Guinea I., ab. 9°S lat.

Col′lins (kŏl′ĭnz). 1 Short stream, cen. Tennessee; rises near W boundary of Sequatchie co., flows N into Caney Fork at Great Falls Lake; forms part of system of Tennessee Valley Authority (*q.v.*).

2 Town, ⊗ of Covington co., S Mississippi; pop. 1537.

Collins, Mount. Peak 6255 ft. in Great Smoky Mts., on boundary bet. Tennessee and North Carolina 2½ m. NE of Clingmans Dome.

Collins Landing. See THOUSAND ISLANDS.

Col′lins·ville (kŏl′ĭnz-vĭl). 1 Subdivision (pop. 1682) of the town of CANTON, Connecticut; manufactures axes and other edged tools.

2 City, Madison co., SW Illinois, 10 m. E of East St. Louis; pop. 14,217; in coal-mining section; has zinc smelter, cannery; manufactures women's clothing.

3 City, Tulsa co., NE Oklahoma, 17 m. NNE of Tulsa; pop. 2526; near oil and gas wells.

Col′lo (kŏl′lŏ). Coastal town and commune, Constantine dept., NE Algeria, N of the city of Constantine; pop. (commune) 4651; lead and mercury mines.

Col′mar (kŏl′mär; *Fr.* kôl′màr′); *Ger.* **Kol′mar** (kŏl′mär; *Ger.* kôl′mär). Manufacturing commune, ✳ of Haut-Rhin dept., NE France, 105 m. E of Chaumont; pop. 49,448; manufactures printed goods, calicoes, silks, cotton goods, leather. Became free imperial city 1226; under Swedes 1632–34; to France 1697, Germany 1871, France 1919; in World War II taken by Germans June 17, 1940 retaken by French Feb. 2, 1945.

Cöln. See COLOGNE.

Colne (kōn; kōln). 1 River 35 m. long, Essex, SE England; flows SE into North Sea.

2 River 35 m. long in Hertfordshire and Buckinghamshire, SE cen. England, flowing into the Thames.

3 Municipal borough, Lancashire, NW England, 27 m. N of Manchester; pop. 20,674; cotton mills, quarries.

Col′nett, Mount (kŏl′nĕt; -nĭt). Peak 4954 ft., NE coast of New Caledonia I., SW Pacific Ocean.

Co·lô′a·ne (kōō-lō′á·nĕ). See MACAO colony.

Co·lo′gna Ve′ne·ta (kȯ-lō′nyä vâ′nâ·tä). Commune, Verona prov., Venezia Euganea, NE Italy; pop. 10,700.

Co·logne′ (kȯ-lōn′); *Ger.* **Köln**, *less often* **Cöln** (kûln); *anc.* **Op′pi·dum U′bi·o′rum** (ŏp′ĭ·dŭm ū′bĭ-ōr′ŭm), *later, because birthplace of Nero's mother, Agrippina,* **Co·lo′ni·a Ag′rip·pi′na** (kȯ-lō′nĭ·á [-lŏn′yä] ăg′rĭ-pī′nȧ). Manufacturing and commercial city, W Germany, in North Rhine-Westphalia state on W bank of Rhine river 20 m. SSE of Düsseldorf; pop. (1939) 768,426; before World War II buildings included an 11th-cent. church, famous 13th-cent. cathedral (completed 19th cent.), 14th-cent. Gothic town hall; university (founded 1388); one of leading industrial cities of Germany; manufactured machinery, electrical goods, chemicals, textiles, foodstuffs, paper, iron goods, vehicles, lumber, rubber goods, and Cologne water; important river port.

History: Roman name, Colonia Agrippina, given in 50 A.D. to colony of veterans and of German Ubii; captured by Franks; became an episcopal see 4th cent. and archiepiscopal see 785; its archbishop increased holdings (acquired duchy of Westphalia 1180) until he became one of most powerful princes of Germany; one of most important centers of Hanseatic League; after battle of Worringen 1288, citizenry established their independence of archbishop; a center of medieval German art and learning; archbishop confirmed as elector of the empire 1356; city's prosperity declined, esp. after Thirty Years' War; occupied by French 1794; territories of archbishop secularized 1803; given to kingdom of Prussia by Congress of Vienna 1815; after World War I occupied by British troops 1918–26. In World War II object of first great air raid of the war May 30, 1942; frequently bombed 1943–45 by British and American air forces, by spring of 1945 practically entirely destroyed except for the cathedral; entered by American troops Mar. 5–6, 1945.

Co·lo′ma (kȯ-lō′mȧ). Village, El Dorado co., California, near Placerville 36 m. NE of Sacramento; pop. (1950) 606; site of Sutter's Mill where gold was discovered Jan. 24, 1848.

Colomb *or* **Co′lomb′–Bé′char′** (kȯ-lôn′bā′shàr′). Commune, Aïn-Sefra territory, NW Algeria; S terminus of railroad leading N through Oran dept.; pop. 23,008.

Co′lombes′ (kȯ-lônb′). Manufacturing commune, Seine dept., N France, NW suburb of Paris; pop. 61,944.

Colombey *or* **Co′lom′bey′–Nouil′ly** (kȯ-lôn′bā′-nōō′yē′). Village, Moselle dept., NE France, ab. 4 m. E of Metz; scene of battle (called also battle of Borny and of Courcelles from towns nearby) Aug. 14, 1870 in which Steinmetz failed to check Bazaine's retreat.

Co·lom′bi·a (kȯ-lŭm′bĭ·ȧ; *Span.* kȯ-lôm′byä). Republic, NW South America; 439,825 sq. m.; pop. (1944 est.) 9,905,448; ✳ Bogotá; bounded on N by the Caribbean Sea, on E by Venezuela and Brazil, on S by Peru and Ecuador, on W by the Pacific Ocean and Panama; divided into the following 14 departments, 6 commissaries,

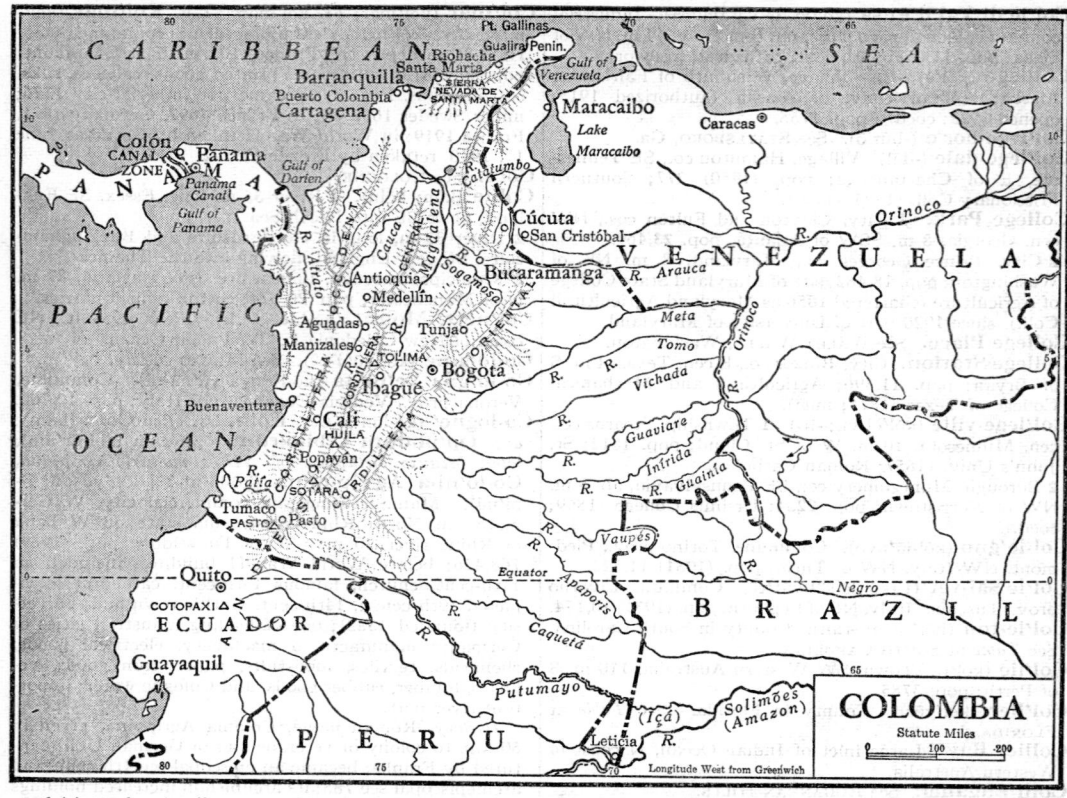

and 4 intendancies (for pronunciation of their names, see their individual entries):

NAME	LOCA-TION	AREA[1]	POP.[1]	CAPITAL
DEPARTMENTS				
Antioquia[2]	NW	25,409	1,331,000	Medellín
Atlántico	N	1,340	327,909	Barranquilla
Bolívar[2]	N	22,996	897,780	Cartagena
Boyacá[2]	cen.	24,934	764,640	Tunja
Caldas	W cen.	5,162	919,480	Manizales
Cauca[2]	SW	11,660	403,300	Popayán
Cundinamarca[2]	cen.	9,108	1,315,400	Bogotá
Huila	S cen.	7,992	227,770	Neiva
Magdalena[2]	N	20,819	397,996	Santa Marta
Nariño	SW	11,548	512,580	Pasto
Norte de Santander	N	8,297	387,630	Cúcuta
Santander[2]	N cen.	12,382	681,290	Bucaramanga
Tolima[2]	W cen.	8,876	639,103	Ibagué
Valle	W	8,085	785,990	Cali
COMMISSARIES				
Arauca	E	9,973	11,490	Arauca
Caquetá	S	39,764	21,650	Florencia
Guajira	NE	4,726	62,190	Uribia
Putumayo	S	10,220	16,240	Mocoa
Vaupés	SE	57,857	8,040	Mitú
Vichada	E	39,764	9,920	Puerto Carreño
INTENDANCIES				
Amazonas	SE	48,008	6,640	Leticia
Chocó	W	17,981	115,150	Quibdó
Meta	cen.	32,903	55,630	Villavicencio
San Andrés y Providencia[3]		21	6,630	San Andrés

[1] Area in sq. m. Pop. of departments is 1944 est.; pop. of commissaries and intendancies, 1942 est.
[2] Originally a separate sovereign state; sovereign rights abolished 1886 although certain prerogatives, as issuing postage stamps, were retained as late as 1904.
[3] Islands in Caribbean Sea E of Nicaragua.

Mountains: Covered in W and cen. parts by N end of great Andes system, here separating into 3 parallel ranges: Cordillera Oriental (E), extending into NW Venezuela; Cordillera Central (cen.); and Cordillera Occidental (W); highest peak Huila 18,700 ft.; other peaks, above 16,000 ft., are Tolima, Chita, Puracé; has many volcanoes. *Rivers:* In cen. part the Magdalena and the Cauca (W tributary of Magdalena), both flowing N bet. main ranges of the Andes; in W the Atrato flowing N to Gulf of Darien and many short rapid streams on the coast flowing W to the Pacific; in E tributaries of the Orinoco (Meta, Vichada, Guaviare), the Vaupés (tributary of the Rio Negro), and in SE the Apaporis and Caquetá; in S the Putumayo forming most of boundary with Peru. *Economic resources:* Coffee, bananas, hides, cacao, oil, forest products, minerals, esp. platinum and gold. *Chief cities:* Bogotá, Medellín, Cali, Manizales, Ibagué, Barranquilla, Cartagena.

History: Coasts visited by Spanish adventurer, Ojeda, 1500; first successfully colonized after Jiménez de Quesada had defeated Chibchas, a nation of highly civilized Indians, on Colombian plateau 1536–38; Santa Fé de Bogotá founded 1538; in 1718 and 1740 made separate viceroyalty of New Granada (*q.v.*) which included modern Colombia, Panama, Ecuador, and Venezuela; after unsuccessful attempt in 1811, achieved independence from Spain under leadership of Bolívar 1819 (see Boyacá); lost Venezuela and Ecuador by secession 1830; reorganized into: Grenadine Confederation 1858, United States of New Granada 1861, United States of Colombia 1863, and republic of Colombia (including Panama) 1886; lost Panama (*q.v.*) by revolt after failure to ratify Hay-Herrán Treaty 1903; neutral in World War I; settled Panama controversy with U.S. 1921; settled border disputes with Ecuador 1919, Venezuela 1922, Brazil 1929; settled Leticia dispute with Peru 1934, after it had threatened war 1932; in World War II broke off relations 1941 with Axis countries but did not declare war. See also GREAT COLOMBIA.

Co·lom'bo (kô·lŭm'bō). Seaport and commercial city, ✳ of Dominion of Ceylon and of Western Province, near mouth of Kelani river on Indian Ocean; pop. 284,155, mostly Singhalese; Ceylon's largest city and port; has artificial harbor; native handicrafts, little industry; University College and Royal College. Occupied 1517 by Portuguese, captured by Dutch 1656, and taken over by English 1796 (see CEYLON). A British defense base in Indian Ocean 1942–45.

Co·lón' (kô·lōn'; *Span.* -lôn'). 1 Town, Entre Ríos prov., E Argentina; pop. 10,180.

2 Municipality and town, Matanzas prov., W cen. Cuba, 27 m. SE of Cárdenas; pop. (town) 11,833.

3 Department, N Honduras; 17,104 sq. m.; pop. (1945 est.) 27,802; ✳ Trujillo.

4 Province, N cen. Panama; area 2810 sq. m.; pop. 78,119.

5 *formerly* **As'pin·wall** (ăs'pĭn·wôl). City, ✳ of Colón prov., N cen. Panama, on Limon Bay at N entrance to Panama Canal; pop. 44,393; N terminus of Panama R.R. (built 1850–55); founded 1850 and named for William H. Aspinwall, one of builders of railroad; before work of Panama Canal Commission was very unhealthful; with its suburb Cristobal (*q.v.*) an important port.

Co·lón', Ar'chi·pié'la·go de (är'chĕ·pyä'lä·gô thä kô·lôn'). Territory, Ecuador, comprising the Galápagos Is.; 3029 sq. m.; pop. (1944 est.) 661; ✳ San Cristóbal.

Co·lo'nia (kô·lō'nyä). 1 Department of Uruguay. See *Table* at URUGUAY.

2 *or* **Colonia del Sa'cra·men'to** (thĕl sä'krä·mān'tô). Seaport and resort, its ✳, SW Uruguay, on La Plata river opp. Buenos Aires; pop. ab. 7700; founded by Portuguese from Brazil 1680; fought over by Spanish and Portuguese; acquired by Spain in treaties of 1777 and 1778; center of rich agricultural and dairying district.

Co·lo'ni·a Ag'rip·pi'na (kô·lō'nĭ·à [-lōn'yà] ăg'rĭ·pī'nà). See COLOGNE.

Co·lo'ni·a Ju'lia Fa·nes'tris (kô·lō'nĭ·à [-lōn'yà] jōōl'yà [jōō'lĭ·à] fà·nĕs'trĭs). See FANO.

Co·lo'ni·al Beach (kô·lō'nĭ·ăl). Town and resort, Westmoreland co., E Virginia, on Potomac river 30 m. E of Fredericksburg; pop. 1769; fisheries.

Colonial Heights. Independent city, SE cen. Virginia, on Appomattox river opp. Petersburg; pop. 9587.

Colonial National Historical Park. See UNITED STATES, *National Historical Parks.*

Colonial Territories; *Span.* **Co·lo'nias** (kô·lō'nyäs). Former name of PANDO dept., Bolivia.

Col'o·nie' (kŏl'ô·nē'). Village, Albany co., New York, NW of Albany; pop. 6992.

Co·lon'na, Cape (kô·lôn'nä); *anc.* **Su'ni·um Prom'on·to'ri·um** (sū'nĭ·ŭm prŏm'ŭn·tōr'ĭ·ŭm). Cape on S extremity of Attica and Boeotia dept., E cen. Greece; summit contains ruins of ancient temple.

Co·lon'ne, Cape (kô·lôn'nä); *anc.* **La·cin'i·um Prom'on·to'ri·um** (là·sĭn'ĭ·ŭm prŏm'ŭn·tōr'ĭ·ŭm). Cape on E coast of Calabria, S Italy, projecting into Ionian Sea S of Gulf of Taranto.

Col'on·say (kŏl'ŭn·zā; -sā). Island of the Inner Hebrides, W Scotland; ab. 16 sq. m.; part of Argyll co.

Co·lo'nus (kô·lō'nŭs). Ancient village, Attica, Greece, ab. 1½ m. N of Athens; birthplace of Sophocles.

Col'o·ny (kŏl'ô·nĭ). Province, Nigeria. See LAGOS, former colony; *Table* at NIGERIA.

Col'o·phon (kŏl'ô·fŏn). Ancient city, one of the 12 Ionian Cities, 15 miles NW of Ephesus, in Lydia, Asia Minor; famous for its troop of cavalry; destroyed by Lysimachus 287 B.C.

Col'o·ra'do (kŏl'ô·rä'dō; -răd'ō). 1 River 1450 m. long, SW United States; rises in NE Grand co., N Colorado; flows SW across Colorado receiving the Gunnison from SE, across SE corner of Utah receiving Green river from N and the San Juan from E, across NW corner of Arizona receiving the Little Colorado from SE; turns S and becomes lower section of Arizona-Nevada boundary and

entire California-Arizona boundary; joined in SW Arizona by Gila river from E; flows through Mexico ab. 90 m., empties into Gulf of California. Passes through two notable canyons, Grand Canyon and Black Canyon (*qq.v.*). See SALTON SINK.

2 River 840 m. long, cen. Texas; rises in Dawson co., flows SE into Matagorda Bay; navigable to Austin.

3 A west central state of U.S.A., 38th state admitted to Union (1876); bounded on N by Wyoming and Nebraska, on E by Nebraska and Kansas, on S by Oklahoma and New Mexico, on W by Utah; 8th state in area, 104,247 sq. m. (land area 103,922 sq. m.); 33d state in population, 1,753,947; ✳ Denver. See *Table of States* at UNITED STATES. Divided into the following 63 counties (for pronunciations, see their individual entries):

NAME	LOCA-TION	AREA[1]	POP.[1]	CO. SEAT
Adams	NE cen.	1,246	120,296	Brighton
Alamosa	S	720	10,000	Alamosa
Arapahoe	NE cen.	820	113,426	Littleton
Archuleta	S	1,364	2,629	Pagosa Springs
Baca	SE corner	2,565	6,310	Springfield
Bent	SE	1,533	7,419	Las Animas
Boulder[2]	N cen.	753	74,254	Boulder
Chaffee	cen.	1,039	8,298	Salida
Cheyenne	E	1,772	2,789	Cheyenne Wells
Clear Creek	N cen.	394	2,793	Georgetown
Conejos	S	1,271	8,428	Conejos
Costilla	S	1,215	4,219	San Luis
Crowley	E	803	3,978	Ordway
Custer	S cen.	737	1,305	Westcliffe
Delta	W	1,157	15,602	Delta
Denver[3]	NE cen.	66	493,887	Denver
Dolores	SW	1,028	2,196	Rico
Douglas	cen.	843	4,816	Castle Rock
Eagle	NW cen.	1,685	4,677	Eagle
Elbert	E cen.	1,864	3,708	Kiowa
El Paso[4]	E cen.	2,158	143,742	Colorado Springs
Fremont	S cen.	1,562	20,196	Canon City
Garfield	W	2,994	12,017	Glenwood Springs
Gilpin	N cen.	149	685	Central City
Grand[2]	N	1,867	3,557	Hot Sulphur Springs
Gunnison	W cen.	3,242	5,477	Gunnison
Hinsdale	SW	1,057	208	Lake City
Huerfano	SW	1,578	7,867	Walsenburg
Jackson	N	1,623	1,758	Walden
Jefferson	cen.	786	127,520	Golden
Kiowa	E	1,792	2,425	Eads
Kit Carson	E	2,171	6,957	Burlington
Lake	cen.	380	7,101	Leadville
La Plata	SW	1,689	19,225	Durango
Larimer[2]	N	2,619	55,343	Fort Collins
Las Animas	SE	4,794	19,983	Trinidad
Lincoln	E	2,593	5,310	Hugo
Logan	NE	1,827	20,302	Sterling
Mesa	W	3,313	50,715	Grand Junction
Mineral	S	921	424	Creede
Moffat	NW corner	4,754	7,061	Craig
Montezuma[5]	SW corner	2,095	14,024	Cortez
Montrose[6]	W	2,239	18,286	Montrose
Morgan	NE	1,282	21,192	Fort Morgan
Otero	SE	1,267	24,128	La Junta
Ouray	SW	540	1,601	Ouray
Park	cen.	2,166	1,822	Fairplay
Phillips	NE	680	4,440	Holyoke
Pitkin	W cen.	974	2,381	Aspen
Prowers	SE	1,626	13,296	Lamar
Pueblo	SE cen.	2,401	118,707	Pueblo
Rio Blanco	NW	3,263	5,150	Meeker
Rio Grande	S	916	11,160	Del Norte
Routt	NW	2,330	5,900	Steamboat Springs
Saguache	S	3,144	4,473	Saguache
San Juan	SW	392	849	Silverton
San Miguel	SW	1,283	2,944	Telluride
Sedgwick	NE corner	544	4,242	Julesburg
Summit	cen.	615	2,073	Breckenridge
Teller	cen.	554	2,495	Cripple Creek
Washington	NE	2,525	6,625	Akron
Weld	N	4,004	72,344	Greeley
Yuma	NE	2,383	8,912	Wray

[1] Area = land area in sq. m. Pop. from 1960 Census.
[2] Rocky Mountain National Park occupies SW corner of Larimer co., NE corner of Grand co., and NW corner of Boulder co.
[3] Coextensive with city of Denver.
[4] Pikes Peak within county, near W boundary.
[5] Its SW point the only point in U.S. common to four states (Colo., Utah, Ariz., and N.Mex.). Mesa Verde National Park in SE cen. part.
[6] Black Canyon of the Gunnison (National Monument) in NE part.

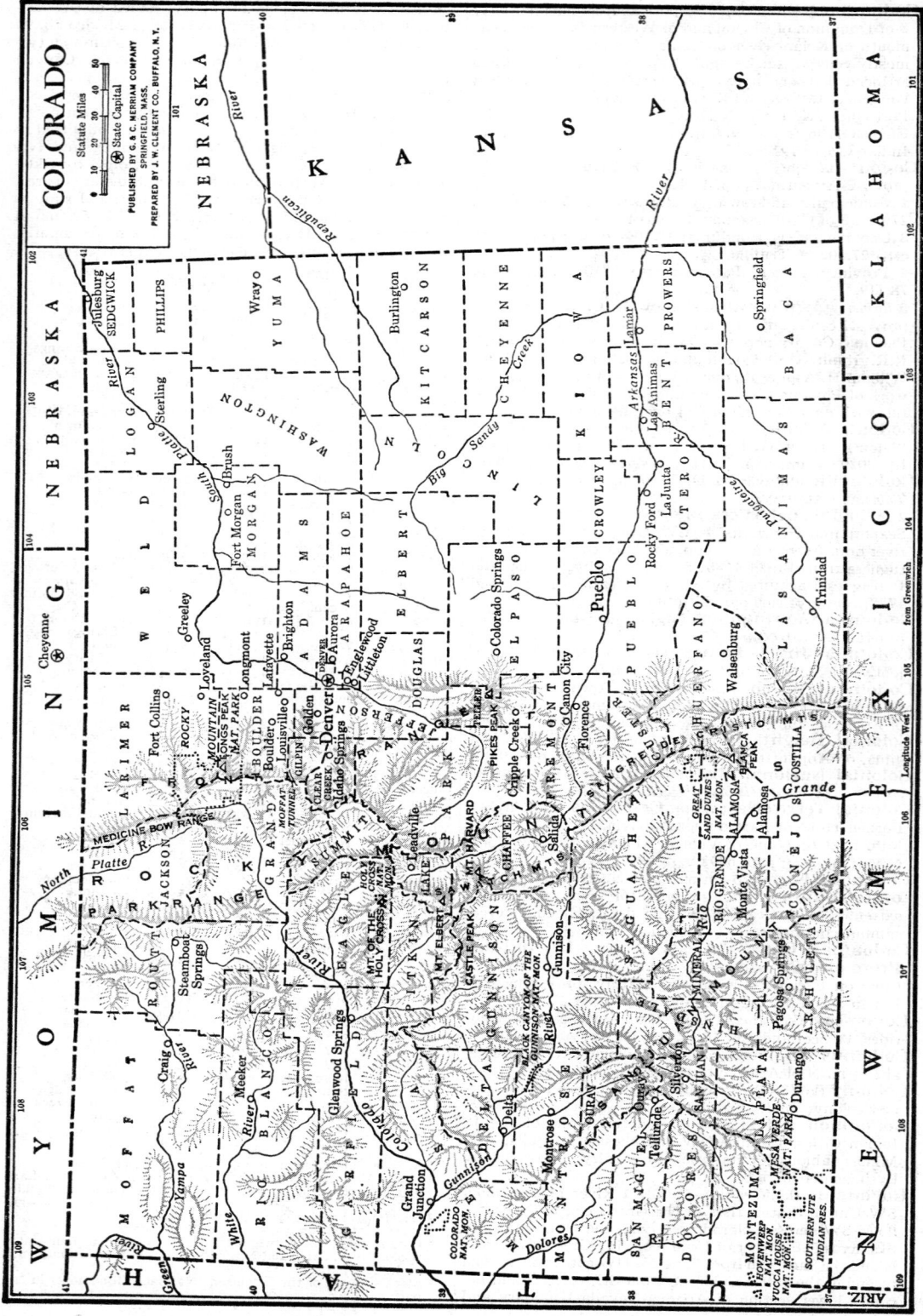

COLORADO

Statute Miles

PUBLISHED BY G. & C. MERRIAM COMPANY
SPRINGFIELD, MASS.
PREPARED BY J. W. CLEMENT CO. BUFFALO, N.Y.

⊛ State Capital

Nickname: Centennial State, also Silver State. *State flower:* Columbine. *Motto:* Nil Sine Numine (Nothing Without the Divine Will). *Chief cities:* Denver, Pueblo, Colorado Springs, Aurora. *Rivers:* Colorado (see 1, above); Arkansas, from cen. region E into Kansas; South Platte, from cen. region NE into Nebraska; Rio Grande, rising in SW, flowing SE into New Mexico. *Highest point:* Mount Elbert 14,431 ft., in Lake co.; has 51 peaks above 14,000 ft. and 1500 above 10,000 ft. *Chief industries:* Mining; stock raising.

History: Explored (chiefly during 18th cent.) and claimed by Spanish; E part included in Louisiana Purchase (*q.v.*) 1803, rest in territory yielded by Mexico 1848; explored by Pike 1806, Long 1820, Frémont 1842–53, and by a host of fur trappers; gold, discovered at Cherry Creek near Pikes Peak in 1858, attracted American settlers; first settlement at Auraria 1858; organized as territory 1861; held first constitutional convention 1864; admitted as state Aug. 1, 1876.
4 County in Texas. See *Table* at TEXAS.
5 *or* **Colorado City.** City, ⊗ of Mitchell co., NW cen. Texas, on Colorado river 25 m. W of Sweetwater; pop. 6457; oil; livestock.
Co·lo·ra·do (kō′lō·rä′thō; *Angl.* kŏl′ō·rä′dō, -răd′ō). River in cen. Argentina; formed by confluence of Río Grande and Barrancas river near Chilean border, flows SE into Atlantic Ocean below Bahía Blanca.
Col′o·ra′do Desert (kŏl′ō·rä′dō; -răd′ō). Arid region ab. 2000 sq. m. in SE California, W of the Colorado river; includes Salton Sink. See IMPERIAL VALLEY.
Colorado National Monument. See UNITED STATES, *National Monuments.*
Co′lo·ra′dos (kō·lō·rä′thōs). Mountain group, highest point 19,846 ft., on border bet. Los Andes territory, NW Argentina, and NE Atacama prov., Chile.
Col′o·ra′do Springs (kŏl′ō·rä′dō; -răd′ō). Residential and resort city, ⊗ of El Paso co., E cen. Colorado, at foot of Pikes Peak; pop. 70,194; founded 1871, incorp. as city 1878; trade center for Cripple Creek gold field. Colorado College (1874, coed.); U.S. Air Force Academy (1954; transferred 1958 from Lowry Air Force Base, Denver, Colorado, to site NNW of city).
Co·los′sae (kō·lŏs′ē). An ancient city in SW Phrygia; a flourishing commercial town in time of Herodotus but declined on founding of Laodicea nearby; seat of an early Christian church to which Saint Paul wrote the *Epistle to the Colossians.*
Co′lo·tlán′ (kō′lō·tlän′). Town, Jalisco state, W cen. Mexico, ab. 70 m. W of Aguascalientes; pop. 5093.
Col′quitt (kŏl′kwĭt). **1** County in Georgia. See *Table* at GEORGIA.
2 City, ⊗ of Miller co., SW Georgia; pop. 1556.
Col′ter Peak (kōl′tēr). Mountain 10,500 ft. in Yellowstone National Park, NW Wyoming.
Col′ton (kōl′t′n; -tŭn). City, San Bernardino co., SE California, 3 m S of San Bernardino; pop. 18,666.
Co·lum′bi·a (kō·lŭm′bĭ·à). **1** River ab. 1270 m. long, SW Canada and NW United States; rises in Columbia Lake, SE British Columbia, flows NW, around N end of Selkirk Mts., turns S; widens into Arrow Lake (*q.v.*); crosses Washington boundary, forms large curve to W, called Big Bend; near Oregon border receives its largest tributary, Snake river, from E; turns W and becomes W part of Washington-Oregon boundary; turns N below Portland and empties into Pacific; its mouth the only deepwater harbor bet. San Francisco and Cape Flattery; navigable 95 m. for seagoing boats; upper course source of hydroelectric power (see UNITED STATES, *Dams and Reservoirs* [Bonneville and Grand Coulee Dams]). Discovered 1792 by Capt. Robert Gray of Boston.
2 Name of counties in eight states of the U.S. See *Tables* at ARKANSAS, FLORIDA, GEORGIA, NEW YORK, OREGON, PENNSYLVANIA, WASHINGTON, WISCONSIN.
3 City, Monroe co., SW Illinois; pop. 3174.
4 City, ⊗ of Adair co., S cen. Kentucky; pop. 2255.

5 Village, ⊗ of Caldwell parish, Louisiana; pop. 1021.
6 City, ⊗ of Marion co., S Mississippi, 32 m. W of Hattiesburg; pop. 7117; agriculture, dairying.
7 City, ⊗ of Boone co., cen. Missouri, 27 m. N of Jefferson City; pop. 36,650; in agricultural section. University of Missouri (1839; coed.).
8 Town, ⊗ of Tyrrell co., E North Carolina; pop. 1099.
9 Industrial borough, Lancaster co., SE Pennsylvania, on Susquehanna river 11 m. W of Lancaster; pop. 12,075; settled by Quakers 1726; proposed as site for national capital 1789; manufactures steel, foundry products, glass, textiles, tobacco.
10 City, ✳ of South Carolina and ⊗ of Richland co., in W cen. part of the state on Congaree river, 12 m. E of Lake Murray; pop. 97,433. Settled c. 1700; founded as capital of the state 1786; incorp. as village 1805, as city 1854; figured as city of refuge in Revolution; shelled, entered, and burned by Sherman 1865. Manufactures cotton goods (esp. duck), cottonseed oil, fertilizer, lumber; granite quarries; timber, cotton. Univ. of South Carolina (1801; coed.); Columbia College (1854; women); Columbia Bible Coll. (1923); Allen Univ. (1870; coed.); **Benedict College (1870; coed.).**
11 City, ⊗ of Maury co., W cen. Tennessee, on Duck river 43 m. SSW of Nashville; pop. 17,624; first settled 1807; mule and livestock market; manufactures.
Columbia, Cape. Northernmost point, 83°, of Canada, on N coast of Ellesmere I., NE Arctic Archipelago.
Columbia, District of. See DISTRICT OF COLUMBIA.
Columbia, Mount. 1 Peak 14,070 ft. in Chaffee co., Colorado.
2 Peak 12,294 ft. bet. SW Alberta prov. and SE British Columbia, Canada, on S border of Jasper National Park.
Columbia City. City, ⊗ of Whitley co., NE Indiana, 18 m. WNW of Fort Wayne; pop. 4803.
Columbia Heights. Residential city, Anoka co., E Minnesota, on Mississippi river 5 m. N of Minneapolis; pop. 17,533.
Columbia Lake. Lake ab. 14 m. long, SE British Columbia, W Canada; source of the Columbia river.
Co·lum′bi·an′a (kō·lŭm′bĭ·ăn′à). **1** County in Ohio. See *Table* at OHIO.
2 Town, ⊗ of Shelby co., cen. Alabama; pop. 2264.
3 Village, Columbiana co., E Ohio, 15 m. S of Youngstown; pop. 4164; foundries, machine shops.
Columbia River Reservoir. See UNITED STATES, *Dams and Reservoirs* (Grand Coulee Dam).
Co′lum·bre′tes (kō′lōōm·brā′tās). Group of small islands in Mediterranean Sea off E Spain, 39°50′N lat.
Co·lum·bus (kō·lŭm′bŭs). **1** County in North Carolina. See *Table* at NORTH CAROLINA.
2 City, ⊗ of Muscogee co., W Georgia, on Chattahoochee river 80 m. WSW of Macon; pop. 116,779; established 1828 as frontier post; cotton gins and cotton mills, ironworks, packing houses; Fort Benning (*q.v.*) 8 m. S.
3 City, ⊗ of Bartholomew co., cen. Indiana, 34 m. E of Bloomington; pop. 20,778; manufactures diesel engines, automobile accessories, leather.
4 City, ⊗ of Cherokee co., SE corner of Kansas, 18 m. SW of Pittsburg; pop. 3395; lead and zinc works; coal.
5 City, NW Hickman co., SW Kentucky, on Mississippi river just below confluence with the Ohio; pop. 357; fortified 1861 by Confederates but evacuated 1862.
6 City, ⊗ of Lowndes co., E Mississippi, 7 m. W of Alabama border; pop. 24,771; temporary capital of Mississippi 1863 when Jackson was occupied by Union troops. Mississippi State College for Women (1884).
7 Town, ⊗ of Stillwater co., S cen. Montana; pop. 1281.
8 City, ⊗ of Platte co., E Nebraska, at confluence of Loup and Platte rivers; pop. 12,476; headquarters of Loup River Public Power District Project.
9 Town, ⊗ of Polk co., SW North Carolina; pop. 725.
10 Commercial and manufacturing city, ✳ of Ohio and ⊗ of Franklin co., cen. Ohio, on the Scioto 97 m. NE of Cincinnati; pop. 471,316; in agricultural country, near

supplies of coal, iron, natural gas, limestone, clay; meat-packing plants, foundries, paper and printing plants; varied manufactures. Ohio State Capitol, Gallery of Fine Arts, Battelle Memorial Institute (1929), Ohio State Penitentiary; Lockbourne Air Force Base. Ohio State Univ. (1870; coed.), Capital Univ. (1850; coed.), Franklin Univ. (1902; Y.M.C.A.; coed.); St. Mary of the Springs (1911; women). First settlement at Franklinton 1797 on W bank of Scioto; site opposite laid out 1812 as new capital and named Columbus; made ⊗ 1824; became city 1834; absorbed Franklinton 1871.

11 Town, ⊗ of Colorado co., SE cen. Texas, on Colorado river 33 m. S of Brenham; pop. 3656; ships rice, cotton.
12 City, Columbia co., S cen. Wisconsin, 25 m. NE of Madison; pop. 3467; settled 1839; agriculture, dairying.

Columbus Grove. Village, Putnam co., NW Ohio, 12 m. N of Lima; pop. 2104.

Co·lu'sa (kǒ·lōō'sá). **1** County in California. See *Table* at CALIFORNIA.
2 City, ⊗ of Colusa co., N cen. California, on Sacramento river 53 m. NW of Sacramento; pop. 3518.

Col'ville (kŏl'vĭl). **1** City, ⊗ of Stevens co., NE Washington, ab. 68 m. N of Spokane; pop. 3806.
2 River ab. 320 m. long, N Alaska, flows E along N slope of Brooks Range, then N to Beaufort Sea.

Colville, Cape. Cape on N coast of North I., New Zealand, on E side of Hauraki Gulf.

Col'vin, Mount (kŏl'vĭn). Peak 4074 ft. in the Adirondack Mts., Essex co., NE New York.

Col'vos Passage (kŏl'vŭs). Strait at S end of Puget Sound, Washington, W of Vashon I.

Col'wyn (kŏl'wĭn). Borough, Delaware co., SE Pennsylvania, 6 m. WSW of Philadelphia; pop. 3074.

Col'wyn Bay (kŏl'wĭn). Urban district, Denbighshire, N Wales; pop. 22,276; popular seaside resort.

Co·mac'chio (kô·mäk'kyô); *anc.* **Co·mac'ti·um** (kô·mäk'shĭ·ŭm; -tĭ·ŭm). Fortified commune, Ferrara prov., Emilia, N Italy, 30 m. ESE of Ferrara; pop. 13,894; built on 13 islands connected by bridges; fisheries.

Com'a·ge'ne (kŏm'á·jē'nê). Var. of COMMAGENE.

Co·mal' (kô·mäl'). County in Texas. See TEXAS, *Table*.

Co·ma·la'pa (kô'mä·lä'pä). Town, Chimaltenango dept., S cen. Guatemala; pop. 10,461.

Co·ma'na (kô·mä'ná). Ancient city of S Cappadocia, Asia Minor, in Taurus Mts. on upper Seyhan river; exact site uncertain; important religious center 1st cent. B.C.

Co·man'che (kô·măn'chê). **1** Counties in three states of the U.S. See *Tables* at KANSAS, OKLAHOMA, TEXAS.
2 City, Stephens co., S Oklahoma; pop. 2082; oil.
3 City, ⊗ of Comanche co., cen. Texas, 24 m. ENE of Brownwood; pop. 3415; gas and oil wells.

Co·ma·ya'gua (kô'mä·yä'gwä). **1** Department, S cen. Honduras; 1919 sq. m.; pop. (1945 est.) 60,452.
2 Town, its ✳, S cen. Honduras, 35 m. W of Tegucigalpa; pop. (1940) 4758; former ✳ of Honduras.

Combaconum. See KUMBAKONAM.

Com'ba·hee (kŭm'bē). River ab. 140 m. long, S South Carolina; formed by confluence of Salkehatchie and Little Salkehatchie rivers; flows SE to Atlantic Ocean.

Combarelles. See Les EYZIES.

Combe Ca'pelle (kônb' kȧ'pĕl'). Rock shelter, near Bergerac, Dordogne dept., SW cen. France; noted for discovery 1909 of a skeleton, the type specimen of the Combe-Capelle race of the Aurignacian period.

Com'ber·mere Bay (kŭm'bēr·mēr). Inlet of Bay of Bengal on W coast of Burma, SE of Akyab.

Combin, Grand. See GRAND COMBIN.

Com'bles (kôn'bl'). Commune, Somme dept., NW France, 6 m. NNW of Péronne; pop. (1931) 905; scene of much fighting during World War I; left in ruins.

Come'ragh Mountains (kŭm'rá). Mountain range in S Ireland, in co. Waterford; highest peak **Knock'a-naf'frin** (nŏk'á·năf'rĭn) 2597 ft.

Co'me·rí'o (kō'mä·rē'ô). Municipality (pop. 18,583) and town (pop. 5232), E cen. Puerto Rico.

Co·mil'la (kô·mĭl'á) *or* **Ku·mil'la** (kōō·mĭl'lä). Town, ✳ of Tippera dist., East Bengal, Pakistan, on affluent of Meghna river 200 m. ENE of Calcutta; pop. 31,365.

Co'mines' (kô'mēn'). Industrial commune, West Flanders prov., NW Belgium; pop. 7524; birthplace of French chronicler Philippe de Comines; on Lys river opp. **Comines**, Nord dept., N France, pop. (1931) 6512.

Co·mi'no (kô·mē'nô). **1** Island 1 sq. m. of the Malta group in the Mediterranean Sea, bet. Malta and Gozo.
2 Cape on E coast of Sardinia, N of Gulf of Orosei.

Co'mi·so (kō'mē·zô). Commune, Ragusa prov., SE Sicily, 7 m. W of Ragusa; pop. 22,163; castle; airport.

Comitán, *in full* **Co·mi·tán' de Do·mín'guez** (kō'-mē·tän' dä thô·mēng'gäs). Town, Chiapas state, SE Mexico, ab. 70 m. ESE of Tuxtla; pop. 8683.

Com'mack (kŏm'ăk). Urban community (unincorporated), Suffolk co., New York, in cen. Long I. ESE of Huntington; pop. 9613.

Com'ma·ge'ne (kŏm'á·jē'nê). District of ancient Syria, bet. Taurus Mts. and Euphrates river SE of Cappadocia; independent under a branch of the Seleucids; came under Romans in Vespasian's reign; ✳ Samosata.

Commander Islands. See KOMANDORSKIE ISLANDS.

Commedagh, Slieve. See SLIEVE COMMEDAGH.

Com'merce (kŏm'ûrs; -ērs). **1** City, Los Angeles co., SW California, NW of Downey; pop. 9555.
2 City, Jackson co., NE Georgia; pop. 3551.
3 City, Ottawa co., NE corner of Oklahoma, 65 m. ENE of Bartlesville; pop. 2378; zinc and lead mines.
4 City, Hunt co., NE Texas, 15 m. ENE of Greenville; pop. 5789. East Texas State Coll. (1889; coed.).

Commerce Town. Town, Adams co., NE cen. Colorado, NE of Denver; pop. 8970.

Com'mer'cy' (kô'mēr'sē'). Commune, Meuse dept., NE France, on Meuse river; pop. (1931) 7303.

Com'me·wij'ne (kŏm'ě·vī'ně). **1** *or* **Com'me·wy'ne** (-vī'ně). River ab. 100 m. long in NE Surinam; flows NNW into the Suriname estuary near Paramaribo.
2 District of Surinam; pop. (1941) 25,963.

Commonwealth of Nations. See BRITISH COMMONWEALTH OF NATIONS.

Communism, Mount. See STALIN PEAK.

Co'mo (kō'mô). **1** Province of Italy. See *Table* at ITALY.
2 *anc.* **Co'mum** (kō'mŭm). Commune, its ✳, Lombardy, N Italy, at SW end of Lake Como 24 m. N of Milan; pop. 53,210; 14th-cent. cathedral; silk, velvet, clothing, metal goods, optical goods. Headquarters of Ghibelline party in 11th and 12th cents.; destroyed 1127 by Milanese and rebuilt 1159 by Frederick I; from 1335 under the Visconti family; center of Garibaldian agitation 1859. Mussolini arrested here Apr. 28, 1945 and shot.

Co'mo, Lake (kō'mô); *anc.* **La'cus Lar'i·us** (lā'kŭs lâr'i·ŭs). Lake in Lombardy, N Italy, expansion of Adda river; 37 m. by ab. 3 m.; 56 sq. m.; surrounded by mountains 3000 to 7000 ft. high; many resorts.

Co'mo·do'ro Ri'va·da'via (kō'mô·thô'rô rē'vä·thä'vyä). Seaport on SE coast, Chubut territory, S Argentina, on Gulf of San Jorge; pop. ab. 22,000; petroleum.

Co'mon·fort' (kō'môm·fôrt'). Town, Guanajuato state, cen. Mexico, 38 m. SE of Guanajuato; pop. 6510.

Com'o·rin, Cape (kŏm'ô·rĭn). Cape on S extremity of India, in Kerala state.

Com'o·ro Islands (kŏm'ô·rō); *Fr.* **Îles Co'mores'** (ēl' kô'môr'). French group of volcanic islands in N Mozambique Channel, bet. NE Mozambique and NW Madagascar; includes islands of Great Comoro, Anjouan, Mayotte, and Mohéli; 790 sq. m.; pop. (1936) 128,608; exports vanilla, sugar, copra, sisal. Mayotte occupied by French 1843, other islands secured by treaty 1886; became 1914 a colony attached administratively to Madagascar; made a territory 1946.

Com'piègne' (kôn'pyěn'y'). Commune, Oise dept., N France, on left bank of Oise river 34 m. E of Beauvais; pop. 18,885; 16th-cent. Gothic town hall; fine château.
History: Taken from duke of Burgundy by Charles VI

1415; scene of capture of Joan of Arc by English 1430; German headquarters 1870–71; armistice ending World War I signed in forest nearby Nov. 11, 1918; armistice bet. France and Germany signed on same spot June 22, 1940; retaken by Allies Aug. 1944.

Complutum. See ALCALÁ DE HENARES.

Compniacum. See COGNAC.

Compostela, Santiago de. See SANTIAGO.

Comp′ton (kŏmp′tŭn). **1** Industrial city, Los Angeles co., SW California, 13 m. S of Los Angeles; pop. 71,812. **2** County in Quebec, Canada. See *Table* at QUEBEC.

Com′stock (kŭm′stŏk). Village, Washington co., E New York, NE of Glens Falls; pop. (1950) 1590.

Com′stock Lode (kŭm′stŏk). See VIRGINIA CITY.

Com′tat′ Ve·nais′sin′ (kôn′tá′ vĕ-nĕ′săn′) or **Comtat** or **Venaissin.** Historical region of SE France; bounded on N by Dauphiné, E and S by Provence, W by Languedoc; ✳ Carpentras; under papal rule 1274–1791.

Comum. See COMO.

Con′a·kry or **Kon′a·kri** (kŏn′á·krĭ). Seaport town, ✳ of Guinea (formerly French Guinea), W Africa, on Tombo I. (*q.v.*); pop. (1951) 49,200.

Co·nan′i·cut Island (kō-năn′ĭ-kŭt). Island in Narragansett Bay W of Rhode Island (island); a part of Newport co., Rhode Island; coextensive with Jamestown.

Con′a·sau′ga (kŏn′á·sô′gá). River, NW Georgia; rises in SE Tennessee, flows S into Georgia, unites with Coosawattee river to form Oostanaula river.

Conca. See CUENCA.

Con′car′neau′ (kôn′kàr′nō′). Commune, Finistère dept., NW France, on Atlantic coast NW of Lorient; pop. (1931) 5815; old part of town walled, on an island, new part on mainland a seaside resort; sardine fishing.

Con′cep·cion′; *Span.* **Con′cep·ción′** (kôn′sĕp·syôn′; *Angl.* kŏn·sĕp′shŭn). Municipality, SE Tarlac prov., Luzon, Phil. Is., 13 m. SSE of Tarlac; pop. 32,702.

Con′cep·ción′ (kôn′sĕp·syôn′; *Angl.* kŏn·sĕp′shŭn). **1** Town, Santa Cruz dept., E Bolivia, near source of Baures river 165 m. NE of Santa Cruz; pop. ab. 2000. **2** Province of Chile. See *Table* at CHILE. **3** Commercial city, ✳ of Concepción prov., S cen. Chile, on the Bío-Bío river 6 m. from its mouth and 260 m. SW of Santiago; pop. 85,813; distributing center for S Chile; its ports are Tomé and Talcahuano. Founded by Pedro de Valdivia ab. 6 m. from its present site 1550; laid waste by Araucanian Indians 1555; refounded 1557; destroyed by earthquakes 1570, 1730, 1751; rebuilt on present location 1755; again ruined by earthquake 1835; severely damaged by earthquake of Jan. 24, 1939. **4** Volcano, occasionally active, 5105 ft., Nicaragua; one of two peaks (see MADERA) on the island of Ometepe in Lake Nicaragua. **5** Department of Paraguay. See *Table* at PARAGUAY. **6** or **Vil′la Concepción** (bē′yä). Town and river port, ✳ of Concepción dept., E Paraguay, on E bank of Paraguay river 125 m. N of Asunción; pop. ab. 16,500. **7** See GRENADA island, British West Indies.

Concepción, La. See LA CONCEPCIÓN.

Concepción Bay. Inlet of Pacific Ocean in coast of S cen. Chile, near city of Concepción.

Concepción de la Vega. See LA VEGA commune.

Concepción del U′ru·guay′ (dĕl ōō′rōō·gwī′). River port, Entre Ríos prov., E Argentina, on the border of Uruguay; pop. 31,498; National Univ. (founded 1778).

Concepción Strait or **Channel.** Strait S of Duke of York I. (Madre de Dios Archipelago), off SW Chile, leading from Pacific Ocean NE into Trinidad Gulf.

Con·cep′tion, Point (kŏn·sĕp′shŭn). Point on SW extremity of Santa Barbara co., SW California.

Conception Bay. Inlet ab. 40 m. long of Atlantic Ocean in SE Newfoundland, W of city of St. John's.

Con′cha (kôn′chä). Peak 15,223 ft. in the Cordillera Mérida, W Venezuela.

Con·cha′gua (kôn·chä′gwä). Volcano ab. 3900 ft. in El Salvador, ab. 70 m. ESE of the city of San Salvador.

Con′chas, Las (läs kôn′chäs). See LAS CONCHAS.

Con′chas Dam (kôn′chäs). Dam completed 1939 across South Canadian river, E San Miguel co., New Mexico; height 235 ft.; impounds water for flood control and irrigation, forming **Conchas Reservoir** (ab. 25 sq. m.).

Con′cho (kôn′chō). **1** River ab. 150 m. long, W cen. Texas; flows E into Colorado river in NE Concho co. **2** County in Texas. See *Table* at TEXAS.

Con′chos (kôn′chōs). River ab. 300 m. long, Chihuahua state, N Mexico; flows N into the Rio Grande.

Con′cord (kŏng′kĕrd). **1** River, NE Massachusetts; formed by junction of Sudbury and Assabet rivers, flows N into the Merrimack river at Lowell. **2** City, Contra Costa co., W California, NNE of Berkeley; pop. 36,208. **3** Residential town, Middlesex co., NE Massachusetts, 12 m. S of Lowell; pop. 12,517; settled 1635; in 1775 had storehouse of munitions and military supplies which the British were marching to seize when they were checked by minutemen in battles at Lexington and Concord April 19, 1775; statue of the *Minute Man of Concord* by D. C. French at the bridge over Concord river where battle was fought; residence of A. Bronson Alcott, Louisa May Alcott, Ralph Waldo Emerson, Margaret Fuller, Nathaniel Hawthorne, Henry David Thoreau. **4** City, ✳ of New Hampshire and ⊗ of Merrimack co., S cen. New Hampshire, on Merrimack river 15 m. N of Manchester; pop. 28,991; transportation center of state; varied manufactures; granite quarries; St. Paul's School (preparatory school; 1856); home of Mary Baker Eddy. Original grant 1659; settled 1727; incorp. by Massachusetts as Rumford 1733, by New Hampshire as "parish of Concord" 1765, town 1784, city 1853; became capital 1808; figured in Indian wars, esp. in massacre of 1746. **5** (kŏng′kĕrd; kông′-) City, ⊗ of Cabarrus co., S cen. North Carolina, 18 m. NE of Charlotte; pop. 17,799; former gold-mining center (gold discovered 1799); manufactures cotton goods, cottonseed oil, lumber, flour. Barber-Scotia Coll. (1867; coed.). **6** (kŏng′kĕrd, -kôrd; kŏn′kôrd) City, E New South Wales, SE Australia, W suburb of Sydney on S bank of lower Parramatta river; pop. 23,220.

Con·cor′di·a (kŏn-kôr′dĭ·á; kŏng-). **1** Parish in Louisiana. See *Table* at LOUISIANA. **2** City, ⊗ of Cloud co., N Kansas, 50 m. N of Salina; pop. 7022; in agricultural section; creamery, brick kilns.

Con·cor′dia (kông-kôr′thyä). City, Entre Ríos prov., E Argentina, on right bank of Uruguay river opp. Salto in Uruguay; pop. (est.) 37,764.

Con·cor′dia sul′la Sec′chia (kông-kôr′dyä sōōl′lä säk′kyä). Commune, Modena prov., Emilia, N Italy, on Secchia river 20 m. N of Modena; pop. 11,143.

Con′da·mine (kŏn′dá·mĭn). River of SE Queensland, Australia; flows W through Darling Downs; joins Maranoa to form Culgoa.

Con′da′mine′, La (là kôn′dá′mēn′). See LA CONDAMINE.

Con·da′te (kŏn-dä′tĕ). Name, meaning "at the confluence of two rivers," given to many towns in ancient Gaul, esp. modern Cosne, Montereau-faut-Yonne, Rennes, and Saint-Claude (*qq.v.*), and retained in its modern French form **Con′dé** (kôn′dā′) in many such names.

Con′dé′–Smen′dou′ (kôn′dā′smän′dōō′). Commune, Constantine dept., NE Algeria; pop. 17,349.

Con′dé′–sur–l′Es′caut′ (kôn′dā′sür·lĕs′kō′). Commune, Nord dept., N France, 7 m. NE of Valenciennes and 2 m. from Belgian border; pop. (1931) 7228; principality from which the Condé branch of house of Bourbon held their title.

Con′dé′–sur–Noi′reau′ (-nwà′rō′). Commune, Calvados dept., NW France, 33 m. SSW of Caen; pop. (1931) 4852; important during Middle Ages; held by English 1417–49; noted for cotton spinning and weaving.

Con′de·ú′ba (kōⁿn′dá·ōō′vá). City, S Bahía state, E Brazil, 270 m. SW of Salvador.

Condivincum. See NANTES.

Con'dom' (kôn'dôN'). Commune, Gers dept., SW France, 20 m. SW of Agen; pop. (1931) 6310; founded 8th cent.; episcopal see 1317–1790; sacked 1569 by Huguenots; trades in armagnac, the brandy made in this region.

Con'don (kŏn'dŭn). City, ⊗ of Gilliam co., N Oregon; pop. 1149.

Con'dore', Pou'lo' (pōō'lō' kôn'dôr'). Island (*poulo*) in the South China Sea, off S coast of Cochin China, S Vietnam; occupied by French 1861–1954.

Co·ne'cuh (kô·nā'kŭ). **1** River ab. 175 m. long, S Alabama; flows into the Escambia river.
2 County in Alabama. See *Table* at ALABAMA.

Co·ne·glia'no (kô·nā·lyä'nō). Manufacturing commune, Treviso prov., Venezia Euganea, NE Italy, 15 m. N of Treviso; pop. 15,434; wine, textiles (esp. silks).

Co·ne'jos (kô·nā'ŭs; -hŭs). **1** County in Colorado. See *Table* at COLORADO.
2 Village, its ⊗, S Colorado; pop. (1950) ab. 200.

Con'e·maugh (kŏn'ĕ·mô). River ab. 45 m. long, SW Pennsylvania; formed by confluence of **Little Conemaugh River** and Stony Creek at Johnstown, in Cambria co., flows W to unite with Loyalhanna Creek and form Kiskiminetas river. See JOHNSTOWN.

Con'es·to'ga (kŏn'ĕs·tō'gà). Township, Lancaster co., Pennsylvania, SSW of Lancaster; pop. 2230; place of manufacture of Conestoga wagon, developed ab. 1750.

Co'ney Island (kō'nĭ). Pleasure resort, Brooklyn borough, New York City; formerly an island 5 m. long, now part of Long Island (since silting up of Coney Island Creek); first pavilion and bathhouse erected 1844.

Conflans, Conflans–l'Archevêque. See CHARENTON-LE-PONT.

Con'flans'–Sainte–Ho'no'rine' (kôn'flän'săN'-tô'nô'-rēn'). Commune, Seine-et-Oise dept., N France, at confluence of Oise and Seine rivers; pop. 10,283.

Confluentes. See KOBLENZ.

Con·fu'so (kôn·fōō'sō). River, S Chaco Boreal, W Paraguay; rises in swamp of the Pilcomayo, flows E, parallel to Pilcomayo for ab. 200 m., into the Paraguay.

Cong (kŏng). Village, co. Galway, Eire, bet. Lough Mask and Lough Corrib; abbey and stone cross; caves; region noted for archaeological remains and for connection with legends of the Firbolg. Cf. MOYTURA.

Con'ga·mond, Lake (kŏng'gà·mŏnd). Series of ponds 3 m. long in S Hampden co., SW Massachusetts, on Mass.-Conn. boundary line.

Con'ga·ree (kŏng'gà·rē). River ab. 60 m. long, cen. South Carolina; formed by confluence of Broad and Saluda rivers near Columbia· forms S boundary of Richland co., unites with Wateree river to form Santee river.

Con'gle·ton (kŏng'g'l·tŭn). Municipal borough, Cheshire, NW England, 22 m. S of Manchester; pop. 15,492.

Con'go (kŏng'gō). **1** *also* **Kon'go.** River bet. 2500 and 3000 m. long, W cen. Africa, one of largest rivers in the world; formed by confluence of Luapula and Lualaba rivers: the Luapula, a continuation of the Chambezi (*q.v.*), after it flows through the swamp S of Lake Bangweulu, flows N through Lake Mweru forming the boundary bet. Northern Rhodesia and Rep. of Congo; the Lualaba rises in SE Rep. of Congo and flows N to join the Luapula at ab. 6°45′S, 26°50′E. From this junction to Stanley Falls (*q.v.*), the Congo is sometimes known as the Lualaba; below Stanley Falls, turns NW and W in a big curve, receiving the Lindi and Aruwimi rivers from the N and the Lomami from the S; begins to turn SW, receives Mongala from N, turns more sharply S and is joined by the Ubangi; from this point to ab. 200 m. from mouth on Atlantic Ocean forms boundary bet. Congo Republic and Republic of Congo; receives the Kasai from the E; at Stanley Pool (*q.v.*) ab. 330 m. from its mouth are located Brazzaville and Léopoldville; navigable for 83 m. from mouth to Matadi and for 1050 m. bet. Stanley Pool and Stanley Falls, and for

585 m. above the falls. Estuary ab. 7 m. wide from Banana Point on N to Sharks Point on S; drainage area ab. 1,600,000 sq. m. Its mouth discovered 1484 by Diogo Cam, Portuguese navigator; lower course ascended by British expedition 1816; headstreams traced by David Livingstone 1867–73; entire river system explored by Henry M. Stanley 1874–84.
2 Indefinite term rather frequently used for territory in central Africa on both sides of the Congo river.
3 District, N Angola, SW Africa, including Cabinda exclave; ✶ Cabinda; site of native (Kongo) kingdom 16th to 18th cents., with capital at São Salvador
4 The Republic of the Congo, formerly Belgian Congo (*q.v.*)
5 The Republic of Congo, formerly Middle Congo (*q.v.*)

Congo Belge. See BELGIAN CONGO.

Congo Free State. See BELGIAN CONGO.

Conhocton. See COHOCTON river.

Coni. See CUNEO commune.

Con'i·cal Hill (kŏn'ĭ·kál). Elevation, S Okinawa, Ryukyu Is., E of Naha; severe fighting May 1945.

Conimbria, Conimbriga. See COIMBRA.

Con'is·brough (kŏn'ĭs·brŭ). Urban district, West Riding, Yorkshire, N England, on the Don near Doncaster; pop. 16,412; has fine Norman castle of 12th cent., home (Coningsburgh) of Athelstane in *Ivanhoe.*

Con'is·ton (kŏn'ĭs·tŭn). **1** Industrial town, Sudbury dist., SE Ontario, Canada; suburb of Sudbury; pop. 2292.
2 Village, N Lancashire, England, at N end of Coniston Water; burial place of John Ruskin.

Coniston Fells. Mountain range in N Lancashire, NW England; highest peak **Coniston Old Man** *or* **Old Man of Coniston** 2635 ft.; on W side of **Coniston Water** *or* **Lake**, ab. 5 m. long, maximum depth 184 ft.

Con·jee've·ram (kŏn·jē've·răm), *a British corruption of* **Kan·chi'pu·ram** (kän·chē'pŏō·rám). Town, NE Madras, S Indian Union, 40 m. WSW of Madras; pop. (1941) 74,635; noted for silk and cotton fabrics and saris; very ancient city with numerous temples and shrines—for Hindus, one of India's seven most sacred cities. Capital of Pallava dynasty in early cents. A.D.; under sovereignty of Delhi 1310 and in realm of the Great Mogul 1646; captured by Clive 1752.

Conn, Lough (lŏk kŏn'). Lake 8 m. long and 4 m. wide in co. Mayo, NW Eire.

Con'nacht (kŏn'ŭkt; -ŭt), *formerly* **Con'naught** (kŏn'ôt; kŭ·nôt'). Province, NW Eire; 6611 sq. m.; pop. 525,468; counties: Galway, Leitrim, Mayo, Roscommon, Sligo.
History: An ancient native kingdom in W Ireland; converted to Christianity by St. Patrick c. 432; from 11th cent. dominated by the O'Connors of Roscommon whose feuds with other kingdoms led to English invasion in 12th cent. (see IRELAND); led by Bourkes, rose against English 16th cent.; divided into counties 1590.

Con'nah's Quay (kŏn'àz kē'). Urban district, Flintshire, NE Wales; pop. 7365.

Con'naught. See CONNACHT.

Connaught Tunnel. Railroad tunnel through Selkirk Mts. at Rogers Pass, British Columbia, Canada; 5 m. long; alt. 3790 ft.; constructed 1913–16.

Con'ne·aut' (kŏn'ĕ·ôt'). City, Ashtabula co., NE corner of Ohio, on Lake Erie; pop. 10,557; ore and coal port.

Con·nect'i·cut (kŏ·nĕt'ĭ·kŭt). **1** River 407 m. long, NE United States; rises in Connecticut Lakes, N New Hampshire, near Canadian border, flows S, its west bank forming New Hampshire-Vermont boundary, crosses W cen. Massachusetts and cen. Connecticut, empties into Long Island Sound near Saybrook; chief tributaries are White river in Vt., Ashuelot in N.H., Deerfield, Millers, Westfield, and Chicopee in Mass., and Farmington in Conn.; navigable to Windsor; provides water power for industries. See *History* of state, below.
2 An eastern state of U.S.A., an original state of the Union, the 5th to ratify the Federal Constitution (Jan.

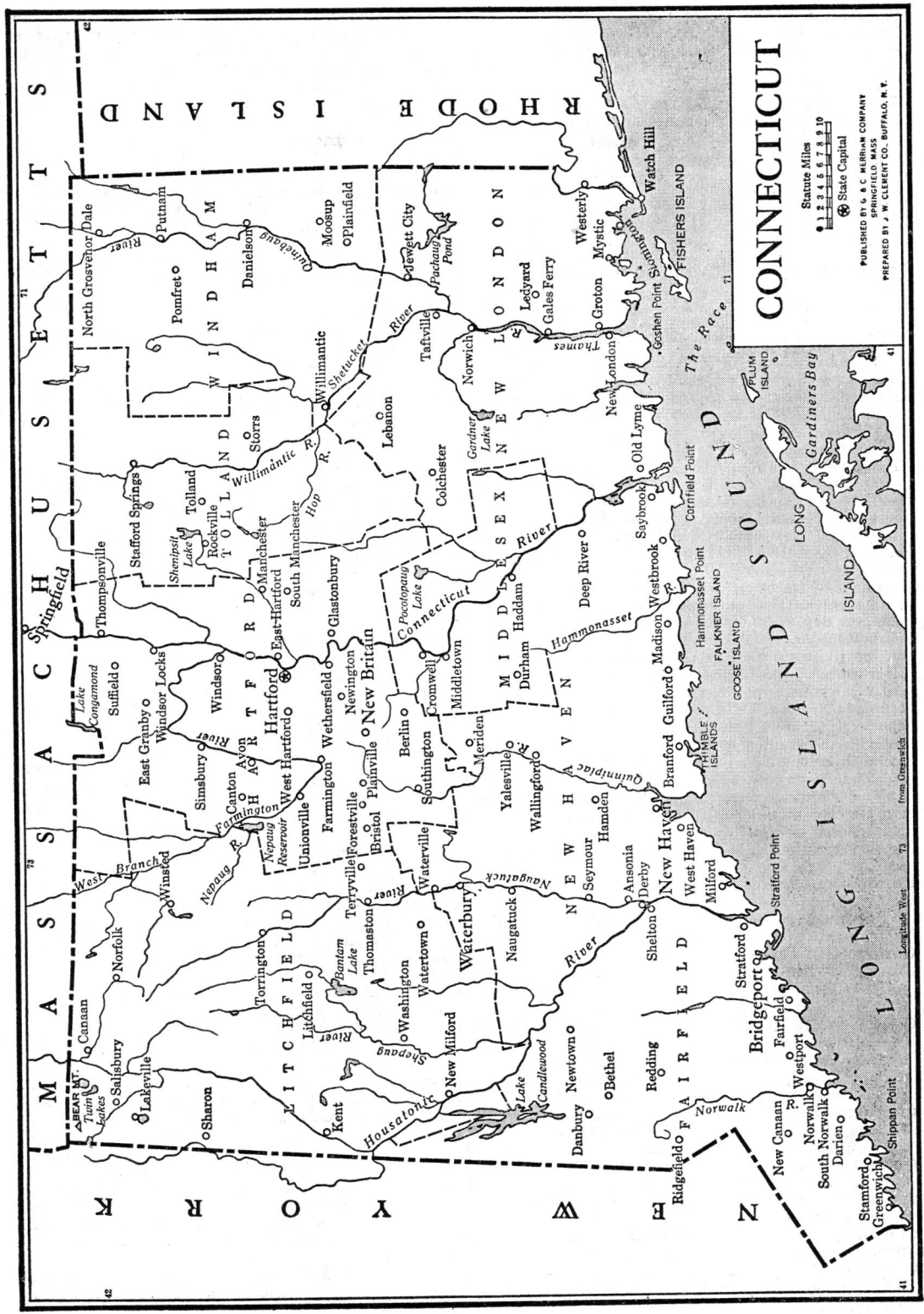

CONNECTICUT

Statute Miles

⊕ State Capital

PUBLISHED BY G & C MERRIAM COMPANY
SPRINGFIELD MASS
PREPARED BY J W CLEMENT CO. BUFFALO. N.Y.

9, 1788); southernmost of the New England states, bounded on N by Massachusetts, on E by Rhode Island, on S by Long Island Sound, and on W by New York; 48th state in area, 5009 sq. m. (land area 4899 sq. m.); 25th state in population, 2,535,234; * Hartford. See *Table of States* at UNITED STATES. Divided into the following 8 counties (for pronunciation of their names, see their individual entries):

NAME	LOCATION	AREA[1]	POP.[1]	CO. SEAT
Fairfield	SW corner; coastal	633	653,589	Bridgeport
Hartford	N	740	689,555	Hartford
Litchfield	NW corner	938	119,856	Litchfield
Middlesex	S; coastal	374	88 865	Middletown
New Haven	S; coastal	610	660,351	New Haven and Waterbury
New London	SE corner; coastal	672	185,745	New London and Norwich
Tolland	N	416	68,737	Tolland
Windham	NE corner	516	68,572	Putnam and Willimantic

[1] Area = land area in sq. m. Pop. from 1960 Census.

Nickname: Nutmeg State, also Land of Steady Habits, Blue Law State, Constitution State. *State flower:* Mountain laurel. *Motto:* Qui Transtulit Sustinet (He Who Transplanted Sustains). *Chief cities:* Hartford, Bridgeport, New Haven, Waterbury, New Britain. *Rivers:* Connecticut (see 1, above); Housatonic in W and Thames in E, flowing S into Long Island Sound. Highest point Mt. Frissell 2380 ft. in Litchfield co. *Chief industries:* Manufacturing (electrical machinery, metal products, textiles, hats), tobacco growing, insurance.

History: Coast explored and Connecticut river discovered by Adrian Block, a Dutch trader, 1614; lower course of river explored by men from Plymouth 1632; fort built by Dutch on present site of Hartford 1633; first permanent settlements made by colonists from Massachusetts Bay who founded the three river towns Hartford, Windsor, and Wethersfield 1635–36; New Haven colony the settlement of third (Puritan) group 1638; river towns adopted Fundamental Orders 1639, the first American constitution based on the consent of the governed; in New England Confederation 1643–84; received charter 1662 which united Connecticut and New Haven colonies and granted strip of land extending to Pacific; included in Dominion of New England, the government of Connecticut was taken over by Andros 1687; relinquished claims to western lands 1786 except for Western Reserve to which it abandoned jurisdiction 1800; participated in Hartford Convention 1814–15; adopted new constitution 1818, in force until 1965, when it was replaced by another.

Connecticut Lakes. Four small lakes in N Coos co., N New Hampshire; the fourth lake, within half a mile of the Canadian border, and the third lake are the ultimate sources of the Connecticut river.

Connecticut Reserve. = WESTERN RESERVE.

Con'nells·ville (kŏn'lz·vĭl). Industrial city, Fayette co., SW Pennsylvania, on Youghiogheny river 12 m. NNE of Uniontown; pop. 12,814; settled 1770; coal.

Con·ne·ma'ra (kŏn'ĕ·mä'rȧ). Barren, mountainous coastal district in W co. Galway, W Eire; bounded on N by Clew Bay, on E by Lough Mask and Lough Corrib, on S by Galway Bay, on W by Atlantic Ocean; Twelve Pins of Bunnabeola in W (highest point 2395 ft.).

Con'ners·ville (kŏn'ērz·vĭl). City, ⊗ of Fayette co., E Indiana, 18 m. SW of Richmond; pop. 17,698; manufactures automobile accessories, furniture, products.

Con·ness', Mount (kŏ·nĕs'). Peak 12,556 ft. in the Sierra Nevada, in E Tuolumne co., cen. California.

Con'rad (kŏn'rȧd). City, ⊗ of Pondera co., NW Montana; pop. 2665.

Con'roe (kŏn'rō). City, ⊗ of Montgomery co., E Texas, 38 m. N of Houston; pop. 9192; oil wells; timber.

Con·se·lhei'ro La·fa·ie'te (kôN'sĕ·lyā'ĕ·rōō lȧ'fȧ·yā'tĕ). City, Minas Gerais state, E Brazil; pop. (1940 est.) 14,488.

Consentia. See COSENZA.

Con'sett (kŏn'sĕt; -sĭt). Urban district, Durham, N England, on the Derwent SW of Newcastle; pop. 39,456.

Con'sho·hock'en (kŏn'shō·hŏk'ĕn). Industrial borough, Montgomery co., SE Pennsylvania, on Schuylkill river 13 m. NW of Philadelphia; pop. 10,259; tires, steel and iron products, textiles, surgical instruments.

Con·so·la·ción' del Nor'te (kŏn'sō·lä·syôn' dĕl nôr'tä). Municipality, Pinar del Río prov., W Cuba, near N coast; pop. 18,371.

Consolación del Sur (sōōr'). Municipality (pop. 43,790) and town (1943 pop. 5495), Pinar del Río prov., W Cuba, 13 m. NE of Pinar del Río.

Con'stance. See KONSTANZ.

Constance, Lake; *Ger.* **Bo'den See** (bō'dĕn zā'); *anc.* **Brig'an·ti'nus La'cus** (brĭg'ăn·tī'nŭs lā'kŭs). Lake on the border bet. SW Germany, W Austria, and NE Switzerland, enclosed by Baden, Württemberg, Bavaria, Vorarlberg and Switzerland; 46 m. long; 207 sq. m.

Constance, Mount. Peak 7777 ft. in Olympic Mts., in E Jefferson co., W Washington.

Con·stan'ţa *or* **Con·stan'tsa** (kôn·stän'tsä); *Turk.* **Küs'ten·ja'** (küs'tĕn·jä'); *anc.* **Con·stan'ti·a'na** (kŏn·stän'shǐ·ä'nȧ; -än'ȧ), **To'mi** (tō'mī), *or* **To'mis** (tō'mǐs). Seaport city, Dobruja, SE Romania, on the Black Sea; pop. (1939 est.) 61,412; chief seaport of Romania, exporting esp. petroleum. Under the Turks from 1413 to 1878; captured by Russians Aug. 29, 1944.

Constantia. 1 See SALAMIS, Cyprus.

2 Commune, Manche dept., France. See COUTANCES.

3 Lake port, Baden, Germany. See KONSTANZ.

Cons'tan·ti·na (kôns'tän·tē'nä). Commune, Sevilla prov., SW Spain, 40 m. NNE of Seville; pop. 14,433; lead mining; founded by the Roman Emperor Constantine; Roman ruins.

Cons'tan'tine' (kôns'tän'tēn'; *Angl.* kŏn'stăn·tēn). 1 Department of Algeria. See *Table* at ALGERIA.

2 *anc.* **Cir'ta** (sûr'tȧ). Fortified city, its *, NE Algeria, 200 m. ESE of Algiers; pop. (1936) 106,830; its port is Philippeville; built by Arabs on rocky height over 800 ft. above river valley; has medieval walls and gates; Roman ruins nearby. Capital of Numidian kings at height of influence under Micipsa 2d cent. B.C.; ruined in wars, restored by Constantine 313 A.D.; taken by French 1837 after long siege; occupied by U.S. troops Nov. 1942.

Con'stan·tine Harbor (kŏn'stăn·tēn). Inlet at E end of Amchitka I. on N coast, Aleutian Is.; airport.

Constantinople. See İSTANBUL.

Constantiola. See OLTENIŢA.

Constantsa. See CONSTANŢA.

Constanz. See KONSTANZ.

Cons'ti·tu·ción' (kôns'tē·tōō·syôn'; *Angl.* kŏn'stǐ·tū'shŭn). 1 Port and summer resort, Maule prov., S cen. Chile, near mouth of the Maule river ab. 163 m. S of Valparaíso; pop. 7053; exports grain and lumber.

2 Port, Argentina. See VILLA CONSTITUCIÓN.

Con'sti·tu'tion Island (kŏn'stǐ·tū'shŭn). Small island in Hudson river opp. West Point, New York.

Con'tal'mai'son' (kôn'tȧl'mā'zôn'). Village, Somme dept., N France, 3 m. ENE of Albert; pop. (1931) 128; taken by British from Germans July 11, 1916, one of the first of the battles of the Somme; completely destroyed.

Continental Divide *or* **Great Divide.** The watershed of the North American continent; the line of highest points of land separating the waters flowing W from those flowing N or E and extending SSE from NW Canada across W United States through Mexico and Central America to South America where it joins the Andes Mts.; in Canada and U.S. generally coincides with various ranges of the Rocky Mts.; in Mexico comprises the great plateau bet. the Sierra Madre ranges (Occidental and Oriental); in Central America lies generally much nearer the Pacific Ocean than the Caribbean Sea. Its central point is the state of Colorado where it comprises many peaks above 13,000 ft.

Con·tooc'ook (kŭn·tŏŏk'ŭk). River ab. 80 m. long, S New Hampshire; rises in Hillsboro co., flows N and NE into the Merrimack above Concord.

Con'tra Cos'ta (kŏn'trȧ kŏs'tȧ). County in California. See *Table* at CALIFORNIA.

Con·tra·ta·ción' (kŏn'trä·tä·syôn'). Town, Santander dept., N cen. Colombia; pop. 5238.

Con·tre'ras (kôn·trä'räs). Town, Federal District, cen. Mexico, 14 m. SSW of Mexico City; pop. 6853; scene of battle Aug. 19–20, 1847 in which the Americans under Gen. Winfield Scott defeated the Mexican forces.

Con'vent (kŏn'vĕnt). Village, ⊗ of St. James parish, SE Louisiana; pop. (est.) 400.

Convent Station. Village, Morris co., New Jersey, SE of Morristown; pop. (est.) 900; College of St. Elizabeth (1899; women).

Con·ver·sa'no (kŏn·vär·sä'nȯ). Commune, Bari prov., Apulia, SE Italy, near Adriatic coast 17 m. ESE of Bari; pop. 15,903; Norman castle, 11th-cent. cathedral.

Con'verse (kŏn'vûrs; -vērs). County in Wyoming. See *Table* at WYOMING.

Con'way (kŏn'wā). **1** County in Arkansas. See *Table* at ARKANSAS.

2 City, ⊗ of Faulkner co., cen. Arkansas, 25 m. NNW of Little Rock; pop. 9791; founded 1871, incorp. 1874. Hendrix College (1884; coed.); Arkansas State Teachers College (1907; coed.)

3 Town, Carroll co., E New Hampshire, 36 m. NNE of Laconia in S region of the White Mts.; pop. 4298; summer and winter resort.

4 Borough, Beaver co., W Pennsylvania, on Ohio river 20 m. NW of Pittsburgh; pop. 1926.

5 Town, ⊗ of Horry co., E South Carolina, on Waccamaw river 35 m. NNE of Georgetown; pop. 8563; river port; manufactures lumber, cotton, tobacco.

6 River 30 m. long, N Wales; flows N, forming boundary bet. Denbighshire and Caernarvonshire, into Beaumaris Bay at Conway.

7 Municipal borough, Caernarvonshire, NW Wales, at mouth of the Conway river; pop. 10,237; castle dating from 13th cent.; remains of ancient Roman fort.

Con'yers (kŏn'yĕrz). City, ⊗ of Rockdale co., N cen. Georgia; pop. 2881.

Coo. See Kos.

Cooch Be·har' (kŏŏch' bĕ·här'). **1** Former Indian state, NE India; 1321 sq. m.; pop. (1941) 640,842; once under the government of Bengal, later one of the states of the Eastern States Agency; since 1947 part of West Bengal state, India; a triangular plain in area where the Tista joins the Brahmaputra; produces rice, jute, and tobacco. Settled by Koches, a tribe akin to Indo-Chinese races; in earlier times a powerful state in Assam; came under British control 1772.

2 Town, its ✳, 265 m. N of Calcutta; pop. 11,837.

Cook (kŏŏk). Name of counties in three states of the U.S. See *Tables* at GEORGIA, ILLINOIS, MINNESOTA.

Cook, Mount. 1 Mountain 13,760 ft., SE Alaska, N of Yakutat Bay, in St. Elias Range SE of Mt. Logan.

2 Mountain in New Zealand. See AORANGI.

Cook and Northern Islands. A name sometimes given to the Cook Is. and Northern Cook (Manihiki) Is., S Pacific Ocean.

Cooke (kŏŏk). County in Texas. See *Table* at TEXAS.

Cooke'ville (kŏŏk'vĭl). Town, ⊗ of Putnam co., N cen. Tennessee, 79 m. N of Chattanooga; pop. 7805; poultry shipping center; Tenn. Polytechnic Institute (1915).

Cook Inlet (kŏŏk). Arm of Pacific Ocean, S Alaska, W of Kenai Penin.; ab. 220 m. long and 60 m. at its widest point; Anchorage is at its head; has largest tidal bore in U.S. with 45-foot range in one arm of its mouth. First explored by Capt. Cook 1778.

Cook Islands. Group of islands in S Pacific Ocean, SW of Society Is. and ab. 975 m. E of Tonga Is.; lat. 16° to 23°S and long. 156° to 160°W; includes Rarotonga, Aitutaki, Atiu, Mangaia, Mauke, Mitiaro, and Hervey Is.; 84 sq. m.; pop. (1936) 10,243; an outlying dependency of New Zealand since 1901; administratively includes the Manihiki or Northern Cook Is. Fertile and healthful group, inhabited by Polynesians of the race that orig. colonized New Zealand in 13th or 14th cent.; some of smaller islands discovered 1773 by Capt. Cook.

Cook'shire (kŏŏk'shĭr; -shēr). Town, ⊗ of Compton co., S Quebec, Canada, 14 m. E of Sherbrooke; pop. 1209.

Cook Strait. Channel bet. North I. and South I., New Zealand; 16 to 90 m. wide; discovered by Capt. Cook 1770.

Cook'town (kŏŏk'toun). Town, NE Queensland, Australia, on Coral Sea within Great Barrier Reef 295 m. N of Townsville; trades with New Guinea; place where Capt. James Cook beached the *Endeavor* for repairs 1770.

Cool·gar'die (kŏŏl·gär'dĭ). Municipality and district, SW Western Australia, 351 m. E of Perth, in goldmining region; pop. (district) 2478.

Coo'lidge (kŏŏ'lĭj). City, Pinal co., S Arizona; pop. 4990.

Coolidge, Mount. Peak 6400 ft. in Custer co., SW South Dakota.

Coolidge Dam *and* **Reservoir.** See UNITED STATES, *Dams and Reservoirs.*

Coolin Hills. See CUILLIN HILLS.

Coomassie. See KUMASI.

Coombe. See The MALDENS AND COOMBE.

Coon Butte. See CRATER MOUND.

Coo·noor' (kŏŏ·nŏŏr'). Town and sanatorium in Nilgiri Hills, Madras, S Indian Union; pop. 14,000.

Coon Rapids (kŏŏn). **1** Town, Carroll co., W cen. Iowa, 60 m. WNW of Des Moines; pop. 1560.

2 Village, Anoka co., E Minnesota; pop. 14,931.

Coo'per (kŏŏ'pẽr; kŏŏp'ẽr). **1** County in Missouri. See *Table* at MISSOURI.

2 City, ⊗ of Delta co., NE Texas, 21 m. SSW of Paris; pop. 2213; in cotton-raising section.

Cooper's Creek. See BARCOO.

Coo'pers·town (kŏŏ'pẽrz·toun; kŏŏp'ẽrz-). **1** Residential village, ⊗ of Otsego co., cen. New York, at S end of Otsego Lake near Susquehanna river, 31 m. SSE of Utica; pop. 2553; site bought 1785 by William Cooper, father of James Fenimore Cooper, who made it the setting of his *Leatherstocking Tales;* scene 1939 of the official celebration of the centenary of the origin of baseball; National Baseball Museum.

2 City, ⊗ of Griggs co., E North Dakota; pop. 1424.

Coorg *or* **Kurg** (kŏŏrg). Formerly a province of S British India, SW of Mysore state; 1593 sq. m.; pop. (1941) 168,726; ✳ Mercara; mountainous region on top of Western Ghats. Inhabited by Kodagu and Yerava. In earlier times a kingdom comprising more territory; occupied by Haidar Ali 1780–82 and later by Tipu Sahib; came under British 1834; administered by chief commissioner of Mysore 1881–1947; now in Mysore state.

Coo'rong, the (kŏŏ'rŏng). Southern arm of Lake Alexandrina, SE South Australia; ab. 100 m. long, extends SE parallel with the coast.

Co·os' (kō·ŏs'; kō'ŏs). County in New Hampshire. See *Table* at NEW HAMPSHIRE.

Coos (kŏŏs). County in Oregon. See *Table* at OREGON.

Coo'sa (kŏŏ'sȧ). **1** Navigable river 286 m. long, Alabama; formed by confluence of Etowah and Oostanaula rivers near Rome, Floyd co., NW Georgia, flows W across border into Alabama and SW to join Tallapoosa river S of Wetumpka, Elmore co., to form Alabama river; has great locks and water-power developments.

2 County in Alabama. See *Table* at ALABAMA.

Coosa Bald. Peak 4287 ft. in Union co., N Georgia.

Coo'sa·wat'tee (kŏŏ'sȧ·wŏt'ė). River, NW Georgia; rises in Gilmer co., flows SW to unite with the Conasauga river and form the Oostanaula river.

Coos Bay (kŏŏs). **1** Inlet on coast of Coos co., SW Oregon, at mouth of the Coos river.

2 *until* 1944 *called* **Marsh'field** (märsh'fēld). City, Coos co., SW Oregon, on inlet of Pacific Ocean; pop. 7084; port of entry; ships lumber; fisheries.

Coo′ta·mun′dra (kōō′tå·mŭn′drå). Town, SE New South Wales, SE Australia, ab. 80 m. NW of Canberra; pop. 4683.

Co′pa·ca·ban′a Beach (kō′på·kå·bån′å); *Port.* **Prai′a de Co·pa·ca·ba′na** (prī′å thĕ kōō·på·kå·vä′nå). Beach on Atlantic Ocean, SE part of city of Rio de Janeiro, Brazil, at W side of entrance to Guanabara Bay; resort.

Co′pa·hué′ (kō′på·wä′). Volcanic peak 9875 ft. in W Neuquén territory, W Argentina, on Chile border.

Co·pa′is (kō·pā′ĭs); *Mod. Gr.* **Ko′pa·ïs′** (kō′pä·ēs′) *or* **To·po′lia** (tô·pô′lyä). Former lake in N Boeotia, Greece; received the Cephisus; formed extensive marsh land, at several periods drained by underground channels to Euboean Sea; in 1886 properly drained and much ground reclaimed for agriculture.

Co·pán′ (kō·pän′). **1** Department, W Honduras; 1430 sq. m.; pop. (1945 est.) 87,631; ✱ Santa Rosa. **2** Ruined city near Santa Rosa (*q.v.*).

Cop′co No. 1 (kŏp′kō). Dam completed 1922 across Klamath river, N Siskiyou co., N California; height 247 ft.; impounds water for water power.

Co′pen·ha′gen (kō′pĕn·hā′gĕn; -hä′gĕn); *Danish* **Kö′ben·havn′** (kû′p'n·houn′). **1** County of Denmark. See *Table* at DENMARK. **2** Industrial and commercial city and seaport on E coast of Sjælland I. and N part of Amager I., Denmark, ✱ of Denmark; 28 sq. m.; pop. (1945) 731,707, with suburbs, **Greater Copenhagen,** (1945) 1,078,892; shipping center; shipbuilding, brewing and distilling, sugar refining; manufactures porcelain, diesel engines; exports esp. dressed meat and dairy products. Copenhagen Univ. (founded 1478); royal palace (Christiansborg), town hall, national (Thorwaldsen) museum, cathedral (rebuilt after 1807); cultural center of northern literature and art. A fishing village fortified by Absalon in 12th cent.; given municipal privileges 1254; frequently attacked and taken by Hanseatic League; made capital of kingdom of Denmark 1443; besieged unsuccessfully by Charles X of Sweden 1658–59; scene of treaty 1660 by which Denmark ceded to Sweden the southern part of Scandinavian penin.; harbor scene of destruction of Danish fleet by British under Nelson 1801; bombarded 1807; occupied by Germans Apr. 1940 to May 5, 1945.

Cö′pe·nick *or* **Kö′pe·nick** (kû′pĕ·nĭk). Former commune, now part of Greater Berlin, Germany; scene of trial of Crown Prince Frederick (Frederick the Great) 1730 after his attempt to escape to England.

Co·per·ti′no (kō·pår·tē′nô). Commune, Lecce prov., Apulia, SE Italy; pop. 12,787; Angevin château.

Co′piague (kō′pāg; -pĕg). Urban community (unincorporated), Suffolk co., SE New York, on Long I. W of Lindenhurst; pop. 14,081.

Co·pi′ah (kō·pī′å). County in Mississippi. See *Table* at MISSISSIPPI.

Co′pia·pó′ (kō′pyä·pō′). **1** River, Atacama prov., N cen. Chile; flows NW and W into the Pacific Ocean. **2** *or* **Cer′ro del A·zu′fre** (sĕr′rô thĕl ä·sōō′frä). Volcano 19,947 ft. in N cen. Chile, E of the town of Copiapó. **3** Town, N cen. Chile, on the Copiapó river ab. 420 m. N of Santiago; ✱ of Atacama prov.; pop. 15,693; important as a silver and copper-mining center; settled ab. 1540; ruined by earthquakes 1819, 1822, and 1851.

Cop′lay (kŏp′lĭ). Borough, Lehigh co., E Pennsylvania, on Lehigh river 5 m. N of Allentown; pop. 3701.

Cop·pa′ro (kŏp·pä′rô). Commune, Ferrara prov., Emilia, N Italy, 13 m. ENE of Ferrara; pop. 23,777; in Po delta, formerly undrained marshland.

Cop′pe·na′me (kŏp′ĕ·nä′mĕ). River ab. 150 m. long in N Surinam; flows N into Atlantic Ocean.

Cop′per (kŏp′ēr). River ab. 300 m. long, S Alaska; flows S around W end of Wrangell Mts. and through Chugach Range to Gulf of Alaska.

Copper Center. Village, SE Alaska, 90 m. N of Cordova; pop. (est.) 145; on Copper river and on Richardson Highway near its junction with Glenn Highway.

Copper Cliff. Mining town, Sudbury dist., SE Ontario, Canada, 5 m. WSW of Sudbury; pop. 3974; mining center with large nickel-copper smelter.

Cop′per·mine′ (kŏp′ēr·mīn′). River 525 m. long, Mackenzie District, Northwest Territories, Canada; rises in lakes of cen. part, flows NW and N to Coronation Gulf.

Coptos. See QIFT.

Co′pul·hué′, Pa′so (pä′sô kō′pōōl·wä′). Andean mountain pass at alt. 6986 ft. on boundary bet. Neuquén territory, W Argentina, and Bío-Bío prov., S cen. Chile.

Co′quet (kō′kĕt). **1** Island in the North Sea off NE coast of Northumberland, N England. **2** River ab. 40 m. long in N Northumberland, N England; rises in the Cheviot Hills, flows E into the North Sea.

Co′quil′hat′ville′ (kō′kē′yå′vēl′). **1** *now called* **Equator Province.** Province, NW Republic of Congo, cen. Africa; 158,003 sq. m.; native pop. (1938) 1,557,972. **2** Town, its ✱, on the Congo river where it is joined by the Ruki, 4′N; pop. (1938) 10,503.

Co·quille′ (kō·kēl′). **1** River, SW Oregon; formed by confluence of branches in Coos co., flows N and W into Pacific Ocean; with longest branch ab. 70 m. long; navigable to Coquille. **2** City, ⊗ of Coos co., SW Oregon, on Coquille river 13 m. S of Marshfield; pop. 4730.

Co·quim′bo (kō·kēm′bô). **1** Province of Chile. See *Table* at CHILE. **2** Port, Coquimbo prov., cen. Chile, 215 m. N of Valparaíso; pop. 18,863; the port for La Serena.

Co′ra·co′ra (kōr′å·kōr′å; *Span.* kō′rä·kō′rä). Mining town, S Ayacucho dept., S Peru; pop. ab. 8000.

Cor′al Bay (kŏr′ål). Bay on E end of St. John I., Virgin Is. of the United States, West Indies.

Coral Ga′bles (gā′b'lz). City, Dade co., SE Florida, on Biscayne Bay 5 mi. SW of Miami; pop. 34,793; incorporated 1925. Univ. of Miami (1925; coed.).

Coral Harbour. Port and station on inlet on S coast of Southampton I., Keewatin District, Northwest Territories, Canada; airport.

Coral Sea. Part of the Pacific Ocean bet. Queensland, Australia, on the W, and the New Hebrides and New Caledonia on the E; bordered on N by Papua and Solomon Is.; N part known as the Solomon Sea (*q.v.*). Scene of U.S. victory over Japanese May 7–8, 1942.

Co·rang′a·mite, Lake (kō·răng′å·mīt). Lake, Victoria, Australia, 50 m. W of Port Philip Bay; 72 sq. m.

Corantijn. See COURANTYNE.

Co′ra·op′o·lis (kōr′ĭ·ŏp′ô·lĭs). Borough, Allegheny co., SW Pennsylvania, on Ohio river 11 m. WNW of Pittsburgh; pop. 9643; settled c. 1760; iron, steel, glass; Greater Pittsburgh U.S. Air Force Base.

Co·rato′ (kō·rä′tô). Commune, Bari prov., Apulia, SE Italy, 25 m. W by N of Bari; pop. 44,661.

Co′ra·zón′ (kō′rä·sôn′). Town, Cotopaxi prov., cen. Ecuador; pop. (1944 est.) 5571.

Cor′beil′ (kôr′bâ′y); *anc.* **Cor·bo′li·um** (kôr·bō′li·ŭm). Commune, Seine-et-Oise dept., N France, at confluence of Seine and Essonne rivers 16 m. SSE of Paris; pop. 11,180; flour mills (noted since 12th cent.). Under Carolingian kings capital of a countship; annexed to France 1108; royal residence; treaty bet. St. Louis and king of Aragon signed here 1258.

Cor′bie′ (kôr′bē′). Commune, Somme dept., N France, 10 m. NE of Amiens; pop. (1931) 4825; ruins of Benedictine abbey, founded 7th cent. by Bathilde, Queen of Clovis II; ruined 1918.

Cor′bin (kôr′bĭn). City, Knox and Whitley cos., SE Kentucky; pop. 7119; coal mining.

Corbolium. See CORBEIL.

Cor′bridge (kôr′brĭj). Market town, Northumberland, N England, on N bank of Tyne river just E of Hexham; pop. 2050; nearby is site of Corstopitum, Roman military post; capital of Northumbria in 8th cent.

Cor′co·ran (kôr′kō·răn). City, Kings co., SW cen. California, 45 m. SE of Fresno; pop. 4976.

Cor′co·va′do (kôr′kŏ·vä′dō)—*Port. and Span.*, literally "hunchbacked." **1** (*Port.* kōōr·kōō·vȧ′thōō) Peak 2310 ft. on S side of city of Rio de Janeiro, SE Brazil; has gigantic concrete figure of Christ the Redeemer on its top; funicular railway.
2 (*Span.* kôr′kŏ·vä′thŏ) Volcanic peak 7550 ft. in the Andes Mts. in S Chile, opp. Chiloé I.
Corcovado Gulf. Inlet of Pacific Ocean lying bet. Chiloé I. and the mainland of SW Chile.
Corcyra. See CORFU.
Corcyra Nigra. See KORČULA.
Cor′dele′ (kôr′dēl′; kôr′dēl′). City, ⊗ of Crisp co., SW cen. Georgia, 35 m. NE of Albany; pop. 10,609; trading center; cotton mills, sawmills, peanuts.
Cor′dell′ (kôr′dĕl′; kôr′dĕl′). City, ⊗ of Washita co., W Oklahoma, 16 m. S of Clinton; pop. (1950) 2920; produces cotton, grain, livestock; gas and oil wells nearby.
Cor′dil·le′ra (kôr′thĕ·yä′rä). Department of Paraguay. See *Table* at PARAGUAY.
Cor′dil·le′ra Can·tá′bri·ca (kôr′thĕ·[l]yä′rä kän·tä′vrĕ·kä). See CANTABRIAN MOUNTAINS.
Cor′dil·le′ra Cen·tral′ (kôr′thĕ·yä′rä sän·träl′).
1 Range of the Andes (*q.v.*) in Colombia.
2 Chief range of the Dominican Republic; includes Pico Duarte, 10,417 ft. high.
3 Range of the Andes extending NW and SE in N cen. Peru, E of the Marañón.
4 The main mountain range of N Luzon, Phil. Is., extending from N edge of its central plain to N coast of the island; highest point Mt. Pulog 9606 ft.; unites with the Caraballo Mts. (*q.v.*) in cen. Luzon.
5 Mountain range in SW cen. Puerto Rico; highest peak Cerro de Punta 4398 ft.
Cordillera de Agostini. See ANDES.
Cordillera de Amambay. See SERRA DE AMAMBAHY.
Cor′dil·le′ra de Ca′ra·ba′ya (kôr′thĕ·yä′rä thä kä′rä·vä′yä). A range of the Andes (*q.v.*) E of Cuzco, SE Peru; highest point Nudo Ausangate 20,013 ft.
Cordillera de Los Andes. See ANDES.
Cor′dil·le′ra de Ta′la·man′ca (kôr′thĕ·yä′rä thä tä′lä·mäng′kä). Range in S Costa Rica, extending SE into W Panama; highest point Chirripó Grande 12,589 ft.
Cordillera de Ve′ne·zue′la (thä vā′nå·swā′lä). Mountain range in N Venezuela; highest point ab. 8530 ft.
Cordillera Domeyko. See ANDES.
Cordillera Huayhuash. See ANDES.
Cor′dil·le′ra Ma·rí′ti·ma (kôr′thĕ·yä′rä mä·rē′tĕ·mä). The Cordillera Occidental in Peru: see ANDES.
Cordillera Mé′ri·da (mā′rĕ·thä), *also* **Sier′ra Ne·va′da de Mérida** (syĕr′rä nå·vä′thä thä). Range of mountains extending NE and SW in W Venezuela, a NE extension of the Andes; highest point Pico Bolívar, 16,411 ft.
Cordillera Oc′ci·den·tal′ (ŏk′sĕ·thän·täl′). See ANDES.
Cordillera O′rien·tal′ (ō′ryän·täl′). **1** Eastern range of the Andes in cen. Bolivia.
2 Eastern range of the Andes in Colombia. See ANDES.
3 Eastern range of the Andes in N Peru.
4 Eastern range of the Andes in SE Peru; highest point Salcantay 20,550 ft.
Cordillera Re·al′ (rrĕ·äl′). **1** Range of the Andes, W Bolivia. See ANDES.
2 Range of the Andes in Ecuador. See ANDES.
Cór′do·ba (kôr′thŏ·vä). **1** Province of Argentina. See *Table* at ARGENTINA.
2 City, its ✱, N cen. Argentina, on the Primero river 387 m. NW of Buenos Aires; pop. (1943 est.) 287,598; third city in size in the republic; founded 1573; industrial and commercial center; university (founded 1613), second oldest university in America (cf. LIMA, Peru).
3 Town, Veracruz state, E Mexico, 55 m. WSW of Veracruz; pop. 17,865; alt. 2700 ft.; chief product coffee.
4 *Eng.* **Cor′do·va** (kôr′dŏ·vȧ). Province of Spain. See *Table* at SPAIN.

5 *Eng.* **Cordova**; *anc.* **Cor′du·ba** (kôr′dų·bȧ). City, ✱ of Córdoba prov., S Spain, on Guadalquivir river 73 m. ENE of Seville; pop. (1941 est.) 144,942; produces gold and silver; manufactures leather and leather goods; Roman and Moorish remains, including an 8th-cent. mosque (now a cathedral) built by Abd-er-Rahman I, an alcazar, and a Moorish bridge over the Guadalquivir.
History: Probably founded by Phoenicians; ruled by Romans, Visigoths, and 711–1236 by the Arabs; in 756 A.D. became independent of Damascus caliphate and under Abd-er-Rahman I and successors, became seat of emirate, later the Western Caliphate of Córdoba; flourishing capital of the most powerful state in Spain (at height in 10th cent.); under Arabic rule became renowned throughout Europe as home of most brilliant intellectual achievements of its time—whence the epithet "Athens of the West"; declined gradually after overthrow of caliphate 1031; captured by Ferdinand III of Castile 1236; pillaged by French 1808 and 1811.
Cor′do·va (kôr′dŏ·vȧ). **1** Town, Walker co., NW cen. Alabama, 28 m. NW of Birmingham; pop. 3184.
2 See CÓRDOBA, Spain.
Cor·do′va (kôr·dō′vȧ). Coast town, SE Alaska, on inlet at SE corner of Prince William Sound; pop. 1128; cans clams and salmon; airport.
Cór′do·va Island (kôr′dŏ·vȧ). Tract of 385 acres on N bank of the Rio Grande forming an enclave of Mexico within the city of El Paso, Texas. Northern 193 acres ceded to U.S. in return for Chamizal (*q.v.*) 1963.
Corduba. See CÓRDOBA, Spain.
Corduene. See GORDYENE.
Core Sound (kōr). Sound bet. mainland of Carteret co., SE North Carolina, and **Core Bank,** one of chain of islands or reefs, having Cape Lookout at S tip.
Cor·fin′i·um (kôr·fĭn′ĭ·ŭm). Ancient town, Samnium, Italy, ab. 7 m. N of Sulmo, on the Valerian Way; capital of short-lived republic of Italia, formed by Allies during Social War (90–88 B.C.).
Cor·fu′ (kôr·fōō′; kôr·fū′); *Mod. Gr.* **Kér′ky·ra** (kyär′kyĕ·rä); *anc.* **Cor·cy′ra** (kôr·sī′rȧ). **1** One of the Ionian Is. in the Ionian Sea off the coast of SW Albania and NW Greece; 40 m. long by 7 to 20 m. wide; 227 sq. m.; pop. 103,214; with Paxos forms a department of Greece (see *Table* at GREECE); fertile, produces olives, olive oil, and fruits. Settled by Corinthians c. 700 B.C.; probably the **Sche′ri·a** (skēr′ĭ·ȧ) of Homer; off its coasts first naval battle of Greek history fought c. 664 B.C.; 435 B.C. sought help of Athens against Corinth, one of the causes of Peloponnesian War; became Roman possession 229 B.C.; Venetian from 1386 to 1797, when it took the name Corfu; under British 1809–64; since 1864 part of Greece. In World War I refuge of Serbs 1916–19 and scene of signing July 20, 1917 of "Pact of Corfu" which established new Serb, Croat, and Slovene state; in World War II fell to Germans Apr. 1941, retaken by Greek and British forces Oct. 6, 1944.
2 Seaport city, ✱ of Corfu dept., Ionian Is., W Greece, on E coast of the island; pop. 32,221; has palace.
Corfu Straits *or* **Channel.** Narrow channel bet. NE Corfu I. and SW coast of Albania.
Co′ria del Rí′o (kō′ryä thĕl rrē′ō). Commune, Sevilla prov., SW Spain, on Guadalquivir river 9 m. SSW of Seville; pop. 11,038.
Corigliano, *in full* **Co·ri·glia′no Ca′la·bro** (kō·rē·lyä′nŏ kä′lä·brŏ). Commune, Cosenza prov., Calabria, S Italy, near W shore of Gulf of Taranto 25 m. NNE of Cosenza; pop. 16,285; olive groves; castle; aqueduct.
Corinium. See CIRENCESTER.
Co·rin′na (kō·rĭn′ȧ). Town, Penobscot co., E cen. Maine, 26 m. WNW of Bangor; pop. 1895.
Cor′inth (kôr′ĭnth; *Corinth, N.Y., is also* kŏ·rĭnth′). **1** City, ⊗ of Alcorn co., NE Mississippi; pop. 11,453; railroad junction; textiles, dairy products; severe fighting Oct. 3–4, 1862, when Union forces under Rosecrans repulsed Confederates under Van Dorn.

2 Village, Saratoga co., E New York, on Hudson river 28 m. NE of Amsterdam; pop. 3193; paper mills.
3 *Gr.* **Kó′rin·thos** (kô′rĕn·thôs). Division (*Lat.* **Co·rin′thi·a** [kō·rĭn′thĭ·á]) of ancient Greece, occupying greater part of Isthmus of Corinth and part of NE Peloponnesus; bounded on N and W by Gulf of Corinth, on NE by Megaris, on E by Saronic Gulf, on S by Argolis, and on W by Sicyonia.
4 Subdivision of modern Argolis and Corinth dept., which see in *Table* at GREECE.
5 City, Argolis and Corinth dept., NE Peloponnesus, Greece, on Gulf of Corinth; pop. 9944; 3 m. NE by E of site of ancient city of Corinth. See ACROCORINTHUS.

History: Ancient Corinth appears to have been founded in 9th cent. B.C. by Dorian invaders of Greece; by position on Isthmus of Corinth became leading commercial city and founded Syracuse, Corcyra (see CORFU) c. 700 B.C. and numerous other colonies, including Potidaea 609 B.C.; member of Peloponnesian League in Peloponnesian War (see SPARTA); in Corinthian War 395–387 B.C., joined Athens, Thebes, and Argos against Sparta; joined Achaean League 243 B.C.; destroyed by Roman general, Mummius, 146 B.C.; refounded by Roman colony sent out by Caesar 44 B.C.; scene of early mission of St. Paul 52–54 A.D.; taken from Byzantine Empire by Latin Crusaders 1205; after a period of Venetian rule, conquered by Ottoman Turks 1458; controlled by Venice 1682–1715, Turks 1715–1822, and Greece from 1822; old city destroyed by earthquake and new city founded 1858. In World War II occupied by Germans Apr. 1941; liberated by British Oct. 10, 1944.

Corinth, *or* **Le·pan′to** (lĕ·păn′tō; *Ital.* lä′pän·tô), **Gulf of;** *anc.* **Si′nus Cor′in·thi′a·cus** (sī′nŭs kŏr′ĭn·thĭ′á·kŭs). Inlet of Mediterranean Sea, cen. Greece, NE of the Peloponnesus, extending E from Lepanto Strait to Isthmus of Corinth (*q.v.*).
Corinth, Isthmus of. Isthmus from 4 to 8 m. wide connecting Peloponnesus with Attica and Boeotia dept., E cen. Greece; crossed by a ship canal (4 m. long; constructed 1881–93) connecting the Gulf of Corinth with the Saronic Gulf.
Co·rin′to (kō·rēn′tō). Seaport, Chinandega dept., NW Nicaragua; pop. (1940) 2500; most important port in Nicaragua; exports coffee, sugar, hides.
Co·ri′o·li (kō·rī′ō·lī). Ancient Volscian town, Latium, Italy; legendary scene of siege 493 B.C. by Romans under Gaius Marcius Coriolanus.
Co·ris′co (kō·rĭs′kō; *Span.* -rēs′kō). Spanish island at the entrance to **Corisco Bay** (14 m. long) in Bight of Biafra, off SW coast of Río Muni, W Africa; 5½ sq. m.; pop. ab. 1000; originally a slave-trading station; later a trading and shipbuilding post.
Corizza. See KORRÇË.
Cork (kôrk). **1** County, SW Eire, in Munster prov.; 2881 sq. m.; pop. 355,957; ⊗ Cork.
2 City or county borough, its ⊗, SW Eire, at mouth of Lee river at head of Cork Harbour 15 m. from the Atlantic Ocean; pop. 80,765; seaport; its ocean steamer port is Cobh (*q.v.*); seat of University College (1845), a constituent college of the Univ. of Ireland (1908). Frequently ravaged by the Danes (9th–11th cents.); taken by Henry II 1172 and by Oliver Cromwell 1649.
Cork Harbour. Harbor on S coast of Ireland; 1 m. wide at the entrance, expands to width of 4 m. inland.
Cor·le·o′ne (kôr·lā·ō′nā). Commune, Palermo prov., NW cen. Sicily; pop. 14,725; cathedral; Saracenic origin.
Çor·lu′ (chôr·lōō′) *or* **Chor·lu′**. Town, Tekirdağ vilayet, Turkey in Europe, NE of Tekirdağ; pop. 11,721.
Cormantyne. = KORMANTINE.
Cor·ne′lia (kôr·nēl′yá; kĕr-; -nē′lĭ·á). City, Habersham co., NE Georgia, 39 m. NNW of Athens; pop. 2936.
Cor·nell′ (kôr·nĕl′). City, Chippewa co., W Wisconsin, 20 m. NNE of Chippewa Falls; pop. 1685.
Cornell, Mount. Peak 3906 ft. in the Catskill Mts., Ulster co., SE New York.

Cor′ner Brook (kôr′nẽr). Town at head of estuary of Humber river, W Newfoundland; pop. (1951) 6831; has fine harbor; paper mill; pulpwood factory.
Corneto. See TARQUINIA.
Cor′niche′ (kôr′nēsh′). Road, actually three more or less parallel highways, ab. 19 m. long along the Riviera, France, from Nice to Menton, cutting across the precipitous cliffs (Fr. *corniche,* "shelf, cornice") of the Maritime Alps: (1) Grande Corniche, the upper road, part of great military road built by Napoleon 1806; for through and heavy traffic; (2) Petite Corniche, the lower road, along the coast; and (3) Moyenne Corniche, the middle road, affording better access to the towns.
Cor·ni·glia′no Li′gu·re (kôr·nē·lyä′nō lē′gōō·rä). Town, Genoa commune, Liguria, Italy; on coast, a W suburb of Genoa; pop. (1931) 22,267.
Cor′ning (kôr′nĭng). **1** City, a ⊗ of Clay co., NE corner of Arkansas; pop. 2192.
2 City, Tehama co., N California, 5 m. W of Sacramento river and 21 m. NW of Chico; pop. 3006; olives; olive oil.
3 City, ⊗ of Adams co., SW Iowa; pop. 2041.
4 Manufacturing city, Steuben co., S New York, on Chemung river 14 m. W of Elmira; pop. 17,085; settled 1789; manufactures many kinds of glassware, radio tubes, lenses (including the 200-in. lens for the telescope of Mount Palomar observatory in Calif. 1934), also electrical and railroad supplies, tools, saws, furnaces.
Cor′nish (kôr′nĭsh). Town, Sullivan co., SW New Hampshire, ab. 8 m. NW of Claremont; pop. 1106; art and literary colony.
Corn Islands (kôrn). Two small islands, **Great Corn Island** and **Little Corn Island,** in Caribbean Sea ab. 40 m. off E coast of Nicaragua; site of U.S. naval station; leased by Nicaragua to U.S. Feb. 18, 1916 as a protection for possible canal across Nicaragua.
Cor′no, Mon′te (mŏn′tä kôr′nō). Peak 9585 ft., Teramo prov., cen. Italy, in the Gran Sasso d'Italia, Abruzzi Apennines; highest peak in the Apennines.
Corn′wall (kôrn′wôl; -wăl; *Brit. usu.* -wăl). **1** Village, Orange co., SE New York, on Hudson river S of Newburgh; pop. 2785; contains villages of **Cornwall** (pop. 2211) and **Cornwall on the Hudson,** summer resort on Hudson river at foot of Storm King Mt.
2 Borough, Lebanon co., SE cen. Pennsylvania, 17 m. N of Lancaster; pop. 1934; iron-ore deposits.
3 Manufacturing town, Stormont co., SE Ontario, Canada, on St. Lawrence river 53 m. SE of Ottawa; pop. 16,899; ⊗ of Stormont, Dundas, and Glengarry cos.; port for river steamers; textile, paper, pulp, flour, and planing mills; at lower end of **Cornwall Canal** (11 m. long, with 6 locks); founded 1776.
4 Maritime county, extreme SW part of England; 1357 sq. m.; pop. (1951) 345,612; ⊗ Truro; forms a peninsula ab. 75 m. long (45 m. wide at base), terminating in Lands End; has rocky coast, much indented. Highest point Brown Willy 1375 ft. *Chief towns:* Bodmin, Falmouth, Penzance, Truro. *Rivers:* Tamar, Camel. *Chief industries:* tin mining (famous as source of tin for Phoenicians in ancient times), copper mining, pilchard fishing. Has uranium deposits. Many remains (cromlechs, dolmens, etc.) of early inhabitants. Given by William the Conqueror to his brother Robert as an earldom; created a duchy 1337 by Edward III for Prince of Wales and still is appanage of male member of highest rank in reigning family, next to sovereign.
Corn·wal′lis Island (kôrn·wŏl′ĭs). One of the Parry Is., cen. Franklin District, Northwest Territories, Canada, bet. Bathurst I. and Devon I., N of Barrow Strait.
Co′ro (kō′rō), *formerly* **San′ta A′na de Coro** (sän′tä ä′nä thä). Town, * of Falcón state, NW Venezuela, SE of Gulf of Coro at base of Paraguaná Penin.; pop. (1941 est.) 18,750; La Vela (La Vela de Coro), its port, 14 m. ENE; founded 1527; for a few years before 1578 capital of Venezuela; site of Miranda's unsuccessful attempt 1805 to free Venezuela from Spain.

Co·ro·co·ro (kō'rô-kō'rô). Town, La Paz dept., W Bolivia, ab. 55 m. SSW of La Paz near Desaguadero river; pop. ab. 4500; copper mining.

Cor'o·man'del Channel (kŏr'ô-măn'd'l). Strait ab. 10 m. wide bet. S end of Great Barrier I. and mainland of North I., New Zealand.

Coromandel Coast. Coast of SE India from Point Calimere N to mouths of Kistna river; has low shore line with no good harbors; beaten by heavy seas throughout the year, especially during northeast monsoon (Oct. to Apr.); chief ports Nellore, Madras, Pondichéry, Cuddalore, Tranquebar, and Negapatam.

Co·ron' (kô-rôn'). **1** Island, Calamian Is., W Phil. Is., off SE coast of Busuanga I.; 27 sq. m.; high, rocky, and thinly inhabited; noted for edible bird's nests.
2 Municipality, chief town of Busuanga I., N Palawan prov., Phil. Is., on SE coast; pop. 11,354.

Co·ro'na (kô-rō'nå). City, Riverside co., SE California, 12 m. SW of San Bernardino; pop. 13,336; settled 1898, incorp. 1906; shipping center for citrus fruits.

Co·ro·na'da Bay (kō'rō-nä'thä). Widemouthed inlet of Pacific Ocean on W coast of Costa Rica.

Cor'o·na'do (kŏr'ô-nä'dō). Residential city, San Diego co., SW California, on bay opp. San Diego; pop. 18,039.

Cor·o·na'tion Gulf (kŏr'ô-nä'shŭn). Gulf, N Mackenzie District, Northwest Territories, Canada, bet. the mainland and S Victoria I., ab. 109°-115°W.

Coronation Island. Largest island of the South Orkney group, South Atlantic Ocean; 60°32'S, 46°52'W.

Cor'o·ne'a (kŏr'ô-nē'å). Town in W part of ancient Boeotia, E cen. Greece, SW of Lake Copais; scene of battles: (1) 447 B.C. Boeotians defeated the Athenians, and (2) 394 B.C. Spartans under Agesilaus in the Corinthian War defeated the coalition led by Thebes.

Co·ro·nel' (kō'rô-nĕl'). Seaport, Concepción prov., S cen. Chile, 17 m. S of Concepción; pop. 14,799; important coal-mining center; scene of a naval battle Nov. 1, 1914 bet. British squadron under Rear Admiral Sir Christopher Cradock and German squadron under Vice-Admiral von Spee in which British were defeated, Cradock himself going down with his flagship the "Good Hope." See *History* at FALKLAND ISLANDS.

Coronel Bo·ga'do (vô·gä'thô). Town, Itapúa dept., SE Paraguay; pop. ab. 11,100.

Coronel O·vie'do (ô·vyä'thô). City, ✶ of Caaguazú dept., E Paraguay; pop. 33,100.

Coronel Suá'rez (swä'räs). Town, Buenos Aires prov., E Argentina, SSW of Buenos Aires; pop. 13,200.

Co·ro'nie (kô-rō'nĕ). Coastal town, NW Surinam, 75 m. W of Paramaribo, in district producing coconuts.

Co·ro·pu'na, Ne·va'do (nä-vä'thô kō'rō-pōō'nä). Peak ab. 21,720 ft. in Andes (Cordillera Occidental) NW of Arequipa, S Peru.

Co·ro·zal' (kō'rō·säl'). **1** Seaport, NE British Honduras, ✶ of Northern dist.; pop. (1943 est.) 8120; produces sugar, rum, corn.
2 Town, Canal Zone, on the Panama Canal ab. 2 m. NNW of Balboa; military reservation.
3 Municipality (pop. 23,570) and town (pop. 3166), N cen. Puerto Rico; town 16 m. SW of San Juan.

Cor'pus Chris'ti (kŏr'pŭs kris'tĭ); *colloquially shortened to* **Corpus**. City and port of entry, ⊗ of Nueces co., S Texas, on SW shore of Corpus Christi Bay at mouth of Nueces river; pop. 167,690; settled 1839, incorp. 1852; figured in Mexican and Civil Wars; railroad and shipping center; seaside and fishing resort; oil and gas fields; oil refineries; fisheries; naval air training station. See GULF INTRACOASTAL WATERWAY.

Corpus Christi Bay. Inlet of Gulf of Mexico in NE Nueces co., S Texas; sheltered from the Gulf by Mustang I., its connection with the Gulf being the strait **Corpus Christi Pass** (S of the island).

Cor·ral' (kôr-räl'). Port and commune, Valdivia prov., S cen. Chile, near mouth of Valdivia river; pop. 8619; scene of Chilean victory 1819 in War of Independence.

Cor·ra·lil'lo (kôr'rä·lē'yô). Municipality, Las Villas prov., W cen. Cuba, 40 m. E of Cárdenas; pop. 9932.

Cor·reg'gio (kôr·räd'jô; *Angl.* kŏ·rĕj'ō, -rĕj'ĭ·ō). Commune, Reggio nell'Emilia prov., Emilia, N Italy, 8 m. NE of Reggio; pop. 19,046; birthplace of Correggio.

Cor·reg'i·dor (kô·rĕg'ĭ·dôr; *Span.* kôr'rĕ·hĕ·thôr'). Island in entrance to Manila Bay, Phil. Is., 3½ m. off S point of Bataan Peninsula, ab. 6 m. SE of Mariveles and 28 m. WSW of Manila; belongs to Cavite prov.; rocky; area about 2 sq. m.; highest point 649 ft.; before World War II had one village, San Jose, pop. 5681; pop. of the island (1948) 36; divides entrance to Manila Bay into two channels: North Channel (Span. Boca Chica), 2 m. wide, and South Channel (Span. Boca Grande), 6½ m. wide; nearby are two small islands La Monja and Caballo I., site of Fort Hughes; associated with it before the war as an American military defense unit were the small islands of El Fraile, site of Fort Drum, and Carabao I., site of Fort Frank. Semaphore station, four lighthouses, and American-built fortification, Fort Mills; extensive tunnels in the rock. First fortified by Spanish 18th cent.; passed successfully by Admiral Dewey's fleet May 1, 1898; made a U.S. military station 1900 and later strengthened by other fortifications (see 1, above); after Japanese invasion of the Philippines Dec. 1941 chosen with Bataan (*q.v.*) by Gen. MacArthur as major defense position; after long resistance, Jan.–Apr. 1942, surrendered May 6, 1942; invaded by Americans Feb. 16, 1945, all Japanese overcome by Feb. 22.

Cor·rèze' (kô'râz'). Department of France. See *Table* at FRANCE.

Cor'rib, Lough (lŏk kŏr'ĭb). Lake in W co. Galway, W Eire, S of Lough Mask; 27 m. long; 71 sq. m.; has outlet, **Corrib River**, on SE flowing into Galway Bay.

Corridor (Polish). See POLISH CORRIDOR.

Cor·rien'tes (kôr-ryän'täs). **1** Province of Argentina. See *Table* at ARGENTINA.
2 Commercial city, its ✶, NE Argentina, on the Paraná river opp. Resistencia and ab. 25 m. below confluence of Paraná and Paraguay rivers; pop. (est.) 59,323.

Corrientes, Cape. 1 Cape extending into Atlantic Ocean from E Argentina, SE Buenos Aires prov.
2 Cape extending into Pacific Ocean from cen. part of W coast of Colombia.
3 Cape on SW coast of Pinar del Río prov., W Cuba.
4 West extremity of state of Jalisco, W cen. Mexico, projecting into the Pacific Ocean, 20°22'N.

Corrientes Bay. Bay in SW coast of Pinar del Río prov., W Cuba, W of Cape Corrientes.

Cor'ry (kŏr'ĭ). City, Erie co., NW corner of Pennsylvania, 28 m. ESE of Erie; pop. 7744; manufactures aircraft parts, metal products, furniture.

Cor'ry·vreck'an *or* **Cor'rie·vrech'an** *or* **Cor'rie-vrek'in** (kŏr'ĭ·vrĕk'ăn). Whirlpool and strait off W coast of Scotland, N of Jura I.

Corse (kôrs). French for CORSICA island, also a department of France: see *Table* at FRANCE.

Corse, Cape; *anc.* **Sa'crum Pro'mon·to'ri·um** (sä'krŭm prôm'ŭn·tôr'ĭ·ŭm). Northern point of Corsica.

Corse'wall' Point (kôrs'wôl'). Cape on N coast of The Rinns, Wigtown co., SW Scotland; lighthouse.

Cor'si·ca (kôr'sĭ·kä). **1** *Fr.* **Corse** (kôrs). French island in the Mediterranean Sea W of N Italy and ab. 100 m. SE of SE coast of France; since 1815 a department (Corse) of France; 3367 sq. m.; pop. 322,854; ✶ Ajaccio; ab. 114 m. long from Cape Corse in the N to the Strait of Bonifacio on the S separating it from Sardinia; mountainous with highest point Mont Cinto 8881 ft.; has numerous short streams; E coast line is unbroken by harbors or bays but W coast is quite irregular with Gulf of Ajaccio its largest inlet. Chief products wine, olive oil, citrus fruits, chestnuts, silk; chief towns Ajaccio, Bastia, Calvi, Corte, Bonifacio. See *Map* at FRANCE.

History: Settled in ancient times by Etruscan, Phoenician, Phocaean, and Carthaginian traders; conquered

by Romans in 3d cent. B.C., by Vandals in 5th cent. A.D., and by Belisarius (for Byzantine Empire) 534; overrun by Goths, Franks, Saracens; came under rule of Pisa which was finally ousted after a bitter struggle with republic of Genoa; most of the time from 1347 to 1768 ruled by Genoa; in revolt 1729–68; sold by Genoa to France 1768; occupied by British 1794–96 and 1814–15. In World War II occupied by Axis forces Nov. 1942–Sept. 1943.

2 *now* **Bloom′ing Grove** (bloom′ĭng). Village, Morrow co., cen. Ohio; birthplace of Warren G. Harding, 29th president of the U.S.

Cor′si·can′a (kôr′sĭ·kăn′à). City, ⊗ of Navarro co., NE cen. Texas, S of Dallas; pop. 20,344; cotton goods and cottonseed products; oil and gas wells; oil refineries.

Cor′son (kôr′s′n). County in South Dakota. See *Table* at SOUTH DAKOTA.

Corson Inlet. Narrow strait leading from Atlantic Ocean through barrier reefs off NE coast of Cape May co., S New Jersey.

Cor·stop′i·tum (kôr·stŏp′ĭ·tŭm). See CORBRIDGE.

Cor′ta·zar′ (kôr′tä·sär′). Town, Guanajuato state, cen. Mexico, just W of Querétaro; pop. 9044.

Cor′te (kôr′tâ). Commune, cen. Corsica; pop. (1936) 4828; partly built on steep, high rock; home 1755–69 of Pasquale di Paoli; marble quarries nearby; wine trade.

Cor′te Ma·der′a (kôr′tĕ mà·dêr′à). Town, Marin co., W coastal California, N of San Francisco; pop. 5962.

Cor·te·nuo′va (kôr·tâ·nwô′vä). Commune, Bergamo prov., Lombardy, Italy, bet. Bergamo and Brescia; pop. (1931) 1412; scene of victory Nov. 27, 1237 of Emperor Frederick II over the Lombards.

Cor·tés′ (kôr·tās′). Department, NW Honduras; 2350 sq. m.; pop. (1945 est.) 99,796; ✻ San Pedro Sula.

Cor′tez (kôr′tĕz; kôr·tĕz′). City, ⊗ of Montezuma co., SW corner of Colorado; pop. 6764; sheep, cattle.

Cor·ti′na (kôr·tē′nà); *in full* **Cor·ti′na d′Am·pez′zo** (kôr·tē′nä däm·pĕt′tsô). Village, N Italy, in Belluno prov. N of Belluno; noted ski resort, in the Dolomites.

Cort′land (kôrt′lănd). **1** County in New York. See *Table* at NEW YORK.

2 City, its ⊗, cen. New York, 30 m. S of Syracuse; pop. 19,181; settled 1792; canneries; manufactures motor trucks, motorboats, airplane equipment. Univ. of New York College of Education (1863; coed.).

Cor·to′na (kôr·tō′nà; *Ital.* kôr·tō′nä). Commune, Arezzo prov., Tuscany, cen. Italy, 14 m. SSE of Arezzo; pop. 31,518; cathedral; remains of cyclopean walls, Roman baths, temple; museum of Etruscan antiquities, tomb of St. Margaret. Ancient Etruscan city; confederated with Rome 310 B.C.; under Casale family 14th cent.; passed to Naples 1409, to Florence 1412.

Corubal. See Rio GRANDE, W Africa.

Ço·ruh′ (chô·rōōK′) *or* **Cho·rokh′** (chô·rôK′). **1** River ab. 200 m. long in NE Turkey in Asia; flows ENE, then N across Russian border into Black Sea S of Batum.

2 Vilayet, NE Turkey in Asia; 3408 sq. m.; pop. 143,267.

3 Seaport, its ✻. See RIZE.

Ço·rum′ (chô·rōōm′) *or* **Cho·rum′.** **1** Vilayet, N cen. Turkey in Asia; 4339 sq. m.; pop. 284,773.

2 Town, its ✻, E of the Kızıl Irmak 116 m. ENE of Ankara; pop. 20,170.

Co·rum·bá′ (kô·rōōnm·bà′). Commercial city on the Paraguay river, Mato Grosso state, SW Brazil, ab. 11 m. from the border of SE Bolivia; pop. (1940 est.) 13,345.

Coruña, La; Corunna. See LA CORUÑA.

Co·run′na (kô·rŭn′à). City, ⊗ of Shiawassee co., S cen. Michigan, 23 m. W of Flint; pop. 2764; furniture.

Cor′u·pe′di·on (kôr′û·pē′dĭ·ŏn; kôr′ōō-) *or* **Cor′u·pe′di·um** (-ŭm). Literally "plain of Corus"; battlefield in ancient Lydia, Asia Minor, ENE of Magnesia, where Seleucus Nicator defeated Lysimachus 281 B.C.

Cor·val′lis (kôr·văl′ĭs). City, ⊗ of Benton co., W Oregon, on Willamette river 30 m. SSW of Salem; pop. 20,669; settled 1845. Oregon State Univ. (1868; coed.).

Cor′vo (kôr′vōō). Island, NW Azores, in the district of Horta; 7 sq. m., smallest island of the group.

Corycian Cave. See PARNASSUS.

Cor′y·don (kôr′ĭ·d′n). **1** Town, ⊗ of Harrison co., S Indiana, 18 m. WSW of New Albany; pop. 2701; capital of Indiana Territory 1813–16 and of the state of Indiana until 1825; captured and held for a short time 1863 by Confederate raiding party under Gen. J. H. Morgan.

2 Town, ⊗ of Wayne co., S Iowa; pop. 1687.

Co′ry·ell′ (kôr′ĭ·ĕl; kôr′ĭ·ĕl′). County in Texas. See *Table* at TEXAS.

Cos. See Kos.

Cos Cob (kŏs′ kŏb′). Subdivision of town of GREENWICH, Connecticut; marine motors.

Coscomatepec, *in full* **Cos·co′ma·te·pec′ de Bra′vo** (kôs·kō′mä·tà·pĕk′ thä vrä′vô). Town, Veracruz state, E Mexico; pop. 5266.

Co·se·güi′na (kō′sà·gwē′nä). Volcano 3830 ft. in Nicaragua, on the Gulf of Fonseca; eruption Jan. 20, 1835.

Cosel. See KOŹLE.

Cose′ley (kōz′lĭ). Urban district, Staffordshire, W cen. England, suburb of Wolverhampton; pop. 34,414.

Co·sen′za (kō·zĕn′tsä). **1** Province of Italy. See *Table* at ITALY.

2 *anc.* **Con·sen′ti·a** (kŏn·sĕn′shĭ·à; -shà). Commune, its ✻, Calabria, S Italy, at confluence of Busento and Crati rivers 150 m. SE of Naples; pop. 40,032; 13th-cent. cathedral containing tombs of Louis III of Anjou and Isabella of Aragon; college; manufactures faïence, iron and steel products. Ancient capital of the Brutii; important in Second Punic War; devastated by earthquakes 1181, 1638, 1783, 1854, 1870, 1908.

Co·shoc′ton (kō·shŏk′tŭn). **1** County in Ohio. See *Table* at OHIO.

2 City, its ⊗, E cen. Ohio, on Muskingum river; pop. 13,106; on site of Indian village destroyed 1781; pottery.

Cos′mo·le′do Islands (kŏz′mô·lā′dô). Group of small islands in the Aldabra Is. (*q.v.*).

Cosne (kōn); *anc.* **Con·da′te** (kŏn·dä′tĕ). Commune, Nièvre dept., cen. France, on the Loire 37 m. NNW of Nevers; pop. (1931) 7289; important military post in Middle Ages, taken by English 1420; 12th-cent. church.

Co·spi′cua (kō·spē′kwä). Urban district, SE Malta, across the harbor from Valletta; pop. ab. 12,000; with adjacent towns of **Sen·gle′a** (sàng·glâ′ä) and **Vit·to·rio′sa** (vĕt·tô·ryô′sä), pop. ab. 27,000; group often called the "Three Cities."

Cossimbazar. See BERHAMPORE.

Cossyra. See PANTELLERIA.

Cos′ta Bra′va (kōs′tä brä′vä). The coast of Catalonia, Spain, NE of Barcelona.

Cos′ta del Sol (kōs′tä thĕl sôl). The southern coast of Spain from Estepona to Motril.

Cos′ta Me′sa (kŏs′tà mā′sà). City, Orange co., SW coastal California, SSW of Santa Ana; pop. 37,550.

Cos′ta Ri′ca (kŏs′tà rē′kà). Republic, C Central America; 19,238 sq. m.; pop. (1943 est.) 706,596; ✻ San José; bounded on N by Nicaragua, on E by Caribbean Sea and Panama, on S and W by the Pacific Ocean. Traversed from NW to SE by the mountains of the Continental Divide, its SE section known as the Cordillera de Talamanca; highest point Chirripó Grande 12,589 ft.; chief volcanoes Irazú, Turrialba, and Barba. Only large river is the San Juan on NE boundary; its main tributaries are San Carlos and Sarapiquí. Its Caribbean coast line has only one good harbor, Puerto Limón; on Pacific coast has large peninsula of Nicoya in NW and smaller peninsula of Osa in S, the Gulfs of Nicoya and Dulce, and the wide Bay of Coronada. Economic resources coffee, bananas, and cacao. Chief cities San José, Cartago, Puerto Limón, Heredia.

History: Discovered by Columbus on last voyage 1502; Gulf of Nicoya object of expedition sent by Pedrarias, governor of Isthmus of Panama; region conquered by Spanish by 1530; province of captaincy general of Guate-

mala; with other countries of Central America (*q.v.*), revolted from Spain 1821; in Iturbide's Mexican empire 1821–23; nominally part of United Provinces of Central America 1823–38; declared itself independent republic 1848; boundary with Panama arbitrated 1900 but continued to be cause of dispute; bloodless revolution 1917 brought trouble with U.S.; entered World War I 1918; joined League of Nations 1920; refused to join Central American Union 1921; in World War II declared war on Axis countries Dec. 8, 1941.

Cos′ter·mans·ville (kŏs′tẽr·mănz·vĭl). **1** *now called* **Ki′vu** (kē′vōō). Province, E Republic of Congo (formerly Belgian Congo), S cen. Africa; 87,409 sq. m.; native pop. (1938) 1,302,432.
2 *or* **Bu·ka·vu** (bōō·kä′vōō). Town, its ✶, in E part at S end of Lake Kivu; pop. 26,792.

Cos·til′la (kŏs·tē′[y]ä). County in Colorado. See *Table* at COLORADO.

Costilla Peak. Mountain 12,634 ft. in Sangre de Cristo Range, NW Colfax co., N New Mexico.

Co·sum′nes (kŏ·sŭm′nĕz). River, N cen. California; rises in El Dorado co., flows SW into Mokelumne river.

Cos′wig *or* **Kos′wig** (kôs′vĭk). Industrial city, East Germany, on Elbe river 11 m. ENE of Dessau; pop. 10,103; river port; pottery, matches, paper, chemicals.

Cosyra. See PANTELLERIA.

Co′ta·ba′to (kō′tä·bä′tō). **1** Province, SW Mindanao, Phil. Is.; 8868 sq. m.; pop. 298,935; ✶ Cotabato; mountainous in S and on E and N borders; Mt. Apo (*q.v.*), in E on Davao boundary the highest mountain 9689 ft. in the Phil. Is.; mountains densely wooded with much fine, hard timber. Central and W part occupied with basin of the Mindanao river and lower course of its tributary, the Pulangi. Chief product rice, but forest products and fish important; has long coast line, near SE end of which is Sarangani Bay. Inhabitants chiefly the Moro people, known as the Magindanao, also several pagan tribes. No municipalities except Cotabato.
History: Became Moslem stronghold, probably toward end of 15th cent.; practically an independent Moro sultanate until ab. 1850; in almost constant conflict with Spaniards 1850–99; became district of Moro Province 1903 and a prov. of dept. of Mindanao and Sulu 1914.
2 Municipality, its ✶, in NW part in the delta of the Mindanao; pop. 10,166; founded as a fort by the Spanish ab. 1862; has good harbor 7 m. from town.
3 River, Mindanao, Phil. Is. See MINDANAO.

Co′ta·ca′chi (kō′tä·kä′chē). Town, Imbabura prov., N Ecuador, 50 m. NNE of Quito; pop. (1944 est.) 7703.

Co·teau′ Landing (kô·tō′). Village, ⊗ of Soulanges co., S Quebec, Canada, on St. Lawrence river; pop. 387.

Cote Blanche Bay (kōt blänsh). Inlet of Gulf of Mexico on SW coast of St. Mary parish, S Louisiana, divided into **East Cote Blanche Bay** and **West Cote Blanche Bay.**

Côte d′A′zur (kōt′ då′zür′). The Mediterranean coast of France, esp. its E end; part of the Riviera (*q.v.*).

Côte des Allemands. See GERMAN COAST.

Côte d′Ivoire. See IVORY COAST.

Côte d′Or (kōt′ dôr′). Range of hills, Côte-d′Or dept., E France, SW of Dijon; noted for rich vineyards.

Côte-d′Or (kōt′dôr′). Department of France. See *Table* at FRANCE.

Côte française des Somalis. See FRENCH SOMALILAND.

Co·ten′tin′ Peninsula (kô′täN′tăN′). Peninsula formed by N end of Manche dept., NW France, bet. Channel Is. and Bay of the Seine. In World War II scene of fighting from beginning of Allied invasion June 6, 1944 to capture of Cherbourg June 27.

Côtes–du–Nord (kōt′dü·nôr′). Department of France. See *Table* at FRANCE.

Cöthen. See KÖTHEN.

Co·tin′ga (kô·tēng′gà). River, 120 m. long, N Brazil; rises near border, flows S into the Takutú.

Co′to (kō′tō). Small stream in SE Costa Rica, flowing into Gulf of Dulce; ownership of region disputed with Panama.

Co′to·nou′ *or* **Ko′to·nu′** (kō′tô·nōō′). Seaport, former ✶ of Dahomey, West Africa; pop. 56,200.

Co′to·pax′i (kō′tô·păk′sĭ; *Span.* kō′tô·pä′hē). **1** Volcano 19,498 ft. in N cen. Ecuador; said to be world's highest active volcano.
2 *formerly* **Le·ón′** (lā·ôn′). Province of Ecuador. See *Table* at ECUADOR.

Cotrone. See CROTONE.

Cots′wold Hills (kŏts′wōld; -wŭld) *or* **Cots′wolds** (-wōldz; -wŭldz). Range of hills in Gloucestershire, SW cen. England; highest point Cleeve Cloud 1031 ft.

Cot′tage Grove (kŏt′ĭj grōv′). City, Lane co., W Oregon, S of Eugene; pop. 3895; lumbering, stock raising.

Cott′bus *or* **Kott′bus** (kŏt′bŭs; *Ger.* kôt′bōōs). City, East Germany, formerly in Brandenburg prov., Prussia, on Spree river 64 m. SE of Berlin; pop. 50,432; railroad center; makes cloth, carpets, metal goods; cattle markets. First mentioned 1156; passed 1445 to elector of Brandenburg, 1807 to Saxony, 1813 to Prussia; in World War II captured by Russians Apr. 24, 1945.

Cot′tes·loe (kŏt′ĕs·lō). Town, W Western Australia, 7 m. SW of Perth on Indian Ocean; pop. 5860.

Cot′ti·an Alps (kŏt′ĭ·ăn). See *Table* at ALPS.

Cot′ti·ca (kŏt′ĭ·kà). Navigable river ab. 80 m. long in N Surinam; flows W into the Commewijne near its mouth; large bauxite deposits along its course.

Cot′ting·ham (kŏt′ĭng·ăm). Former urban district, East Riding, Yorkshire, N England; pop. (1931) 6179.

Cot′tle (kŏt′′l). County in Texas. See *Table* at TEXAS.

Cot′ton (kŏt′′n). County in Oklahoma. See *Table* at OKLAHOMA.

Cotton Plant (plănt′). City, S Woodruff co., NE cen. Arkansas; pop. 1704; battle 1862.

Cot′ton·wood′ (kŏt′′n·wŏŏd′). **1** River ab. 140 m. long, S Minnesota; rises in Lyon co., flows E into Minnesota river below New Ulm in Brown co.
2 County in Minnesota. See *Table* at MINNESOTA.

Cottonwood Creek. Creek in S San Diego co., SW California; contains Barrett Dam and Morena Dam (*qq.v.*).

Cottonwood Falls. City, ⊗ of Chase co., E cen. Kansas; pop. 971.

Cottonwood Mountain. Peak 9321 ft. in S Idaho co., N cen. Idaho.

Co·tu′it (kô·tū′ĭt; -tōō′-). Town, Barnstable co., SE Massachusetts, on Nantucket Sound; pop. (est.) 700; summer resort; noted oyster beds.

Co·tul′la (kô·tŭl′à). City, ⊗ of La Salle co., S Texas, 70 m. N of Laredo; pop. 3960; in farming section.

Cotyora. See ORDU.

Coucy-le-Château, *in full* **Cou′cy′-le-Châ′teau′-Auf′rique′** (kōō′sēl′shä′tō′frēk′). Commune, Aisne dept., N France, 18 m. WSW of Laon; pop. (1931) 1069; ruins of a feudal castle, destroyed by Germans during World War I.

Cou′de·kerque′–Branche′ (kōōd′kĕrk′bränsh′). Commune, Nord dept., N France, SE suburb of Dunkerque; pop. (1931) 11,867; textiles.

Cou′ders·port (kou′dẽrz·pōrt). Borough and mountain resort, ⊗ of Potter co., N Pennsylvania, on Allegheny river 36 m. ESE of Bradford; pop. 2889.

Couil′let′ (kōō′yĕ′). Commune, Hainaut prov., SW Belgium, just SE of Charleroi; pop. 12,831.

Cou′lee Dam (kōō′lĭ dăm). Town, Grant, Douglas, and Okanogan cos., NE cen. Washington, on Columbia river; includes former town of Mason City; pop. 1344.

Coul′man Island (kōl′măn). Island in Ross Dependency off coast of Victoria Land, Antarctica, ab. lat. 73°25′S and long. ab. 170°E.

Coul′miers′ (kōōl′myä′). Commune, Loiret dept., N cen. France, W of Orléans; pop. (1931) 347; scene of battle Nov. 9, 1870 in which Bavarians were defeated by the French under Aurelle de Paladines.

Cou·lom'miers' (kōō'lô'myã'). Commune, N Seine-et-Marne dept., N France; pop. (1931) 6679; 13th–16th cent. church of St. Denis; suffered during World War I.

Couls'don and Pur'ley (kōlz'dŭn, pûr'lĭ). Urban district, Surrey, S England, 11 m. S of London; pop. 37,702, (1951) 63,770; part of Greater London.

Coun'cil (koun'sĭl). **1** Village, ⊗ of Adams co., W Idaho; pop. 827; in apple-growing area.
2 Village, W Alaska, NE of Nome.

Council Bluffs (blŭfs). City, ⊗ of Pottawattamie co., SW Iowa, on Missouri river opp. Omaha, Nebraska; pop. 54,361; site of Mormon settlement 1846–52; outfitting point for emigrants to California during gold rush 1849–50; selected as eastern terminus of Union Pacific R.R. 1863; grain elevators, nurseries, vineyards.

Council Grove (grōv). City, ⊗ of Morris co., E cen. Kansas, 25 m. NW of Emporia; pop. 2664.

Coupe'ville (kōōp'vĭl). Town and resort, ⊗ of Island co., NW Washington, on Whidbey I.; pop. 740.

Cour'an·tyne (kōr'ăn·tīn); **Du.** **Co'ran·tijn'** (kō'răn·tīn'). River ab. 300 m. long in N South America; rises in the Serra Acarahy, flows N to Atlantic Ocean forming boundary bet. British Guiana and Surinam.

Cour'be·voie' (kōōr'bĕ·vwà'). Manufacturing commune, Seine dept., N France, on the Seine, a NW suburb of Paris; pop. 58,638; foundries.

Cour'ce·lette' (kōōr'sĕ·lĕt'). Village, Somme dept., N France, 5 m. NE of Albert; pop. (1931) 194; in World War I captured by Canadians 1916 during battle of the Somme; taken and retaken in 1918.

Cour'celles' (kōōr'sĕl'). **1** Commune, Hainaut prov., SW Belgium, just NNW of Charleroi; pop. 17,717.
2 or **Courcelles-sur-Nied** (-sür-nyä'). Village, Moselle dept., NE France, 7 m. SE of Metz; battle fought nearby at Colombey (q.v.) Aug. 14, 1870.

Courland. See KURLAND.

Cour'ma'yeur' (kōōr'mà'yûr'). Village, Aosta prov., NW Italy, SE of Mont Blanc; pop. 719; resort.

Courneuve, La. See LA COURNEUVE.

Cour'rières' (kōō'ryâr'). Commune, Pas-de-Calais dept., N France, SSW of Lille; pop. (1931) 5306; coal.

Courte'nay (kōrt'nĭ). City, E Vancouver I., Brit. Columbia, Canada, on Strait of Georgia 90 m. WNW of Vancouver; pop. 2553.

Court'house' Rock (kōrt'hous'). Height 4100 ft. in Cheyenne co., W Nebraska; ab. 500 ft. above surrounding country; historic landmark.

Court'land (kōrt'lănd). Town, ⊗ of Southampton co., SE Virginia; pop. 855; nearby was scene of Nat Turner's Insurrection Aug. 1831.

Cour'trai' (kōōr'trä'). See KORTRIJK.

Cour'ville (kōōr'vĭl; **Fr.** kōōr'vĭl'). Town, Quebec co., S Quebec, Canada, on St. Lawrence river 6 m. NE of Quebec; pop. 3138.

Cou·shat'ta (kōō·shăt'à). Town, ⊗ of Red River parish, NW Louisiana; pop. 1663.

Cou·tances' (kōō'täns'); **anc.** **Con·stan'ti·a** (kŏn·stăn'shĭ·à; -shà). Commune, Manche dept., NW France, 17 m. WSW of Saint-Lô; pop. (1931) 6502; ancient Celtic town, in 3d cent. fortified by Constantius Chlorus and named in his honor; often besieged in Middle Ages; in World War II captured by Allies July 28, 1944.

Cou'tras' (kōō'trä'). Commune, Gironde dept., SW France, 56 m. NE of Bordeaux; pop. (1931) 5211; wine-producing region; scene Oct. 20, 1587 of battle in which Henry of Navarre defeated the Catholics.

Co'va·don'ga (kō'vä·thông'gä). Village, Oviedo prov., NW Spain, 5 m. from Cangas de Onís; scene of victory of Pelayo over the Moors 718.

Cove Neck. See OYSTER BAY village, New York.

Cov'en·try (kŏv'ĕn·trĭ). **1** Manufacturing town, S cen. Tolland co., N Connecticut; pop. 6356; incorp. 1712.
2 Town, Kent co., cen. Rhode Island, 15 m. SW of Providence; pop. 15,432; governmental seat Washington village; taken from Warwick and incorporated 1741.

3 City and county borough, Warwickshire, cen. England, near the Avon 18 m. ESE of Birmingham; pop. 167,083, (1951) 258,211; manufactures automobiles and bicycles, motorcycles, airplanes, machinery, motors, watches. Home of Lady Godiva, who, with her husband, founded a Benedictine abbey here c. 1043; meeting place of parliaments under Henry IV and Henry VI; probably center of the presentation of the Coventry Mysteries 15–16th cents. In World War II its devastation Nov. 14–15, 1940 by the German Luftwaffe gave rise to the term *coventrize.*

Co·vi·lhã' (kōō·vĕ·lyăN'). Commune, Castelo Branco dist., E cen. Portugal, N of Castelo Branco; pop. 15,640; manufactures woolen and cotton cloth; dyeworks.

Co'ville, Lake (kō'vĭl); *formerly* **Nak'nek Lake** (năk'nĕk). Lake, SW Alaska, near base of Alaska Penin.; almost entirely within Katmai National Monument.

Co·vi'na (kō·vē'nà). City, Los Angeles co., SW California, 20 m. E of Los Angeles; pop. 20,124.

Cov'ing·ton (kŭv'ĭng·tŭn). **1** Counties in two states of the U.S. See *Tables* at ALABAMA and MISSISSIPPI.
2 City, ⊗ of Newton co., N cen. Georgia, 32 m. ESE of Atlanta; pop. 8167; incorporated 1822; cotton mills.
3 City, ⊗ of Fountain co., W Indiana, on Wabash river 27 m. WNW of Crawfordsville; pop. 2759.
4 City, a ⊗ of Kenton co., N Kentucky, at confluence of Ohio and Licking rivers opp. Cincinnati; pop. 60,376; commercial and industrial center; X-ray equipment, safes and locks; packing houses, distilleries. Villa Madonna Coll. (1921; coed.).
5 City, ⊗ of St. Tammany parish, SE Louisiana, 37 m. N of New Orleans; pop. 6754; fishing and hunting.
6 Village, Miami co., W Ohio; pop. 2473.
7 Town, ⊗ of Tipton co., W Tennessee, 39 m. NE of Memphis; pop. 5298; in cotton-growing territory.
8 City, western Virginia, ⊗ of Alleghany co. but politically independent; pop. 11,062; makes paper, rayon, textiles.

Cow'an, Lake (kou'ăn). Lake, S Western Australia, in E Swanland S of Kalgoorlie.

Cow'ans·ville (kou'ănz·vĭl). Town, Missisquoi co., S Quebec, Canada, 48 m. ESE of Montreal; pop. 4431.

Cow'den·beath' (kou'd'n·bēth'). Burgh, Fife co., E Scotland; pop. 13,153; coal mining; place where much of the drafting of the Solemn League and Covenant was done (c. 1642).

Cow'en, Mount (kou'ĕn). Mountain 11,190 ft., Park co., S Montana.

Cowes (kouz). Urban district, N Isle of Wight, S England, 9 m. WSW of Portsmouth; pop. 17,154; seaport and shipbuilding center; yachting resort.

Co·we'ta (kō·wē'tà; kĭ·ē'tà). County in Georgia. See *Table* at GEORGIA.

Cow'ley (kou'lĭ). County in Kansas. See *Table* at KANSAS.

Cow'litz (kou'lĭts). **1** River ab. 150 m. long, SW Washington; formed by confluence of forks in E Lewis co., flows W, then S into Columbia river in Cowlitz co.
2 County in Washington. See *Table* at WASHINGTON.

Cow'pas'ture (kou'pàs'tûr). River ab. 60 m. long, western Virginia; rises in Highland co., flows SW, unites with Jackson river to form the James.

Cow'pens' (kou'pĕnz'). Town, Spartanburg co., NW South Carolina, in the Piedmont 8 m. ENE of Spartanburg; pop. 2038; formerly cattle-raising center; just N of town is scene of battle Jan. 17, 1781 in which Gen. Daniel Morgan defeated British under Col. Tarleton, commemorated by **Cowpens Battlefield Site** (see UNITED STATES, *National Historical Parks*).

Cow'ra (kou'rà). Mining town, SE cen. New South Wales, SE Australia, 100 m. N of Canberra; pop. 5056.

Cox'comb' Mountain (kŏks'kōm'). Peak 11,000 ft. in cen. Park co., NW Wyoming.

Coxcomb Peak. Mountain 13,660 ft. in Hinsdale and Ouray cos., SW Colorado.

Coxin's Hole. See ROATÁN town.

Cox·sack′ie (kŏŏk·săk′ĭ). Village, Greene co., SE New York, on Hudson river 22 m. S of Albany; pop. 2849.

Coy′le or **Coi′le** (koi′lå). River ab. 180 m. long, Santa Cruz territory, S Argentina; rises near Chilean border, flows E and NE into Atlantic Ocean.

Co′yo·a·cán′ (kō′yō·ä·kän′). City, Federal District, cen. Mexico, suburb of Mexico City; pop. 23,690; contains the old Cortes palace, first seat of the Spanish government, now used as a municipal building.

Coy·o′te Peaks (kī·ō′tĕ). Mountain 10,919 ft. in Sierra Nevada, E Tulare co., S cen. California.

Co·zad′ (kō·zăd′). City, Dawson co., S cen. Nebraska, on Platte river; pop. 3184; shipping point for alfalfa.

Co′zu·mel′ (kō′sōō·mĕl′). Island 24 m. long and 7 m. wide off NE coast of Quintana Roo territory, SE Mexico.

Crab Island. See VIEQUES.

Cracow. See KRAKÓW.

Cra′dle Mountain (krā′d'l). Mountain 5069 ft., NW cen. Tasmania, Australia, on W edge of cen. highlands.

Crad′ock (krăd′ŭk). Town, SE cen. Cape Province, S Union of South Africa, on Great Fish river 123 m. N of Port Elizabeth; pop. 9268; at ab. 3000 ft. surrounded by mountains; cattle, sheep, and Angora goats; health resort, warm sulfur baths.

Craf′ton (krăf′tŭn). Borough, Allegheny co., SW Pennsylvania, 4 m. W of Pittsburgh; pop. 8418; residential.

Craggy Dome, Craggy Gardens, Craggy Pinnacle. See GREAT CRAGGY MOUNTAINS.

Craig (krāg). **1** Name of counties in two states of the United States. See *Tables* at OKLAHOMA and VIRGINIA. **2** Town on W coast of Prince of Wales I., SE Alaska; pop. 273; government telegraph station. **3** City, ⊗ of Moffat co., NW corner of Colorado, on Yampa river; pop. 3984; center of oil-producing region.

Craig′a·vad′ (krāg′å·väd′). Suburb of Belfast, Northern Ireland, on Belfast Lough ab. 8 m. NE of Belfast; scene of meeting July 12, 1913 of 150,000 Ulstermen to protest against the Home Rule Bill.

Crai′gen·put′tock (krā′gĕn·pŭt′ŭk). Farm near Dumfries, S Scotland; home of Thomas Carlyle 1828–34.

Craig′head′ (krāg′hĕd′). County in Arkansas. See *Table* at ARKANSAS.

Craig Head. Cape on N coast of Moray co., NE Scotland; lighthouse.

Cra·io′va (krä·yō′vä). City, S Romania, on the Jiu river 112 m. W of Bucharest; pop. (1939 est.) 55,442; an industrial and commercial center of Walachia; cathedral.

Cra′mer·ton (krā′mēr·t′n; -tŭn). Unincorporated town, Gaston co., SW North Carolina; pop. 3123; textile mills.

Cram′ling·ton (krăm′lĭng·tŭn). Former urban district, Northumberland, N England, 8 m. N of Newcastle; pop. (1931) 8238.

Cran′ber′ry Lake (krăn′bĕr′ĭ; -bĕr·ĭ). Lake 6 m. long in S St. Lawrence co., N New York.

Cran′brook (krăn′brŏŏk). City, SE Brit. Columbia, Canada, in Kootenay Valley 70 m. E of Nelson; pop. 3621; active trade center, esp. in lumber.

Cran′don (krăn′dŭn). City, ⊗ of Forest co., NE Wisconsin, 25 m. E of Rhinelander; pop. 1679; lakeside resort, built around and bet. four lakes.

Crane (krān). **1** County in Texas. See *Table* at TEXAS. **2** City, its ⊗, W Texas; pop. 3796.

Crane Lake. Lake on N boundary of St. Louis co., NE Minnesota; receives Vermilion river on the W.

Cran′ford (krăn′fērd). Township, Union co., NE New Jersey, 5 m. W of Elizabeth; pop. 26,424.

Cran′non (krăn′ŏn) or **Cra′non** (krā′nŏn). Ancient town in cen. Thessaly, NE Greece, ab. 13 m. SW of Larisa; scene of battle 322 B.C. in which Antipater defeated the league of cities of cen. Greece.

Cran′ston (krăn′stŭn). Industrial city, Providence co., N Rhode Island, on Pawtuxet river 5 m. S of and adjoining Providence; pop. 66,766; settled c. 1638; manufactures cotton print goods, mill machinery, metal goods; coal and graphite deposits.

Craonne (krän; krän). Village, Aisne dept., N France, ab. 15 m. SE of Laon; pop. 116; battle Mar. 7, 1814 in which Napoleon repulsed the Allies; in struggle for Chemin des Dames in World War I taken and retaken three times 1917 and 1918.

Cra′ter Lake (krā′tēr). Lake in Cascade Mts., W Klamath co., S Oregon; ab. 6 m. long, 5 m. wide, and 1932 ft. deep; occupies crater of Mt. Mazama, an extinct volcano; remarkable esp. for the intensity of color of the water; region has been set aside as **Crater Lake National Park** (see UNITED STATES, *National Parks*).

Crater Mound or **Me′te·or Crater** (mē′tĕ·ēr); *also known as* **Coon Butte** (kōōn′ būt′). Depression 4000 ft. in diameter, 600 ft. deep, SE Coconino co., Arizona, 20 m. W of Winslow; encircled by a ridge 100–150 ft. high, containing loose pieces of rock and sand; many small fragments of meteoric iron are found in the region; by some believed to be caused by a great meteor, but more probably produced by a volcanic steam explosion.

Crater Peak. Mountain 7425 ft. in W Klamath co., S Oregon, S of Crater Lake.

Cra′ters of the Moon National Monument (krā′tērz). See UNITED STATES, *National Monuments*.

Cra′ti (krä′tĕ); *anc.* **Cra′this** (krā′thĭs). River 58 m. long, Calabria, S Italy; rises S of Cosenza, flows to Gulf of Taranto; ancient Sybaris at its mouth.

Cra′to (krä′tōō). City, S Ceará state, NE Brazil; pop. (1940 est.) 10,142; a railroad terminus.

Cra′ven (krā′vĕn). County in North Carolina. See *Table* at NORTH CAROLINA.

Craw′ford (krô′fērd). **1** Name of counties in eleven states of the U.S. See *Tables* at ARKANSAS, GEORGIA, ILLINOIS, INDIANA, IOWA, KANSAS, MICHIGAN, MISSOURI, OHIO, PENNSYLVANIA, WISCONSIN. **2** City, Dawes co., NW Nebraska, 50 m. NW of Alliance; pop. 1588; trade center in irrigated agricultural section.

Crawford Notch. Defile in White Mts. (*q.v.*) in NW Carroll co., New Hampshire, traversed by Saco river.

Craw′fords·ville (krô′fērdz·vĭl). Commercial city, ⊗ of Montgomery co., W cen. Indiana, 43 m. WNW of Indianapolis; pop. 14,231; Wabash College (1832; men).

Craw′ford·ville (krô′fērd·vĭl). **1** Village, ⊗ of Wakulla co., NW Florida; pop. (est.) 600. **2** City, ⊗ of Taliaferro co., NE cen. Georgia; pop. 786.

Cray′ford (krā′fērd). Urban district, Kent, SE England, ESE of London; pop. 27,951; part of Greater London.

Cra′zy Mountains (krā′zĭ). Mountain group, Meager, Park, and Sweet Grass cos., S Montana; highest point, Crazy Peak 11,178 ft., is in N Sweet Grass co.

Cré′cy′ (krā′sē′), *in full* **Cré′cy′–en–Pon′thieu′** (-än-pôn′tyû′); *Eng.* **Cres′sy** (krĕs′ĭ). Commune, Somme dept., N France, ab. 12 m. N of Abbeville; pop. (1931) 1365; scene Aug. 26, 1346 of first decisive battle of Hundred Years' War, a victory for Edward III of England over Philip VI of Valois; noted for weapons and tactics of the English, who used longbows, small bombards, one of earliest forms of artillery, and dismounted men-at-arms; established England as a military power.

Cred′i·ton (krĕd′ĭ·t′n). Market village, Devonshire, SW England, ab. 8 m. NW of Exeter; episcopal see 909–1049; important wool industries 13th–17th cents.

Cree (krē). Lake 406 sq. m., N Saskatchewan, Canada; discharges through **Cree River** (ab. 90 m. long) to the Fond du Lac river.

Creede (krēd). Town, ⊗ of Mineral co., S Colorado, in gorge of Rio Grande; pop. 350; founded 1890 as mining camp (silver, gold, zinc).

Creek (krēk). County in Oklahoma. See *Table* at OKLAHOMA.

Crefeld. See KREFELD-UERDINGEN AM RHEIN.

Creil (krā′y′). Commune, Oise dept., N France, on Oise river 28 m. N of Paris; pop. 10,899; stone quarries; mills.

Cre′ma (krā′mä). Commune, Cremona prov., Lombardy, N Italy, on Serio river 23 m. NW of Cremona; pop. 25,163; cathedral; produces wine, silk, linen, lace,

hats. Taken 1160 by Frederick Barbarossa; under Milan 1338–1453, Venice 1453–1797, and Austria 1815 until becoming part of the kingdom of Italy.

Cre·mo'na (krě·mō'nȧ; *Ital.* krä·mō'nä). **1** Province of Italy. See *Table* at ITALY.

2 Fortified commune, its ✱, Lombardy, N Italy, on Po river 49 m. ESE of Milan; pop. 64,019; 12th-cent. cathedral; 13th-cent. palace; manufactures machinery, textiles, earthenware; once celebrated for the manufacture of terra cotta and, in 16th–18th cents., for the fine violins manufactured by the Amati and Guarnieri families and by Antonio Stradivari. Colonized by Romans 218 B.C. as fort against Gallic tribes; destroyed 69 A.D. by Vespasian, who helped rebuild it; medieval town incorporated by Milan 1334.

Cren'shaw (krěn'shô). County in Alabama. See *Table* at ALABAMA.

Cré'py *or* **Cres'py'** (krā'pē'). Commune, Aisne dept., N France, ab. 6 m. NW of Laon; pop. (1931) 1272; treaty of Crépy signed Sept. 18, 1544 bet. Francis I of France and Emperor Charles V.

Cré'py'–en–Va'lois' (krā'pē'äⁿ·vȧ'lwȧ'). Commune, Oise dept., N France, ab. 16 m. S of Compiègne; ancient capital of Valois; remains of castle; church of Saint Denis.

Cres (tsrěs); *Ital.* **Cher'so** (kěr'sô). Island in the Veliki Kvarner (Gulf of Quarnero), at the head of the Adriatic Sea; 158 sq. m.; pop. (1931) ab. 9000; belonged to Austria before World War I, to Italy 1919–47, since 1947 part of Croatia, NW Yugoslavia.

Cres'cent, Lake (krěs'ʼnt). Lake, Clallam co., NW Washington, in Olympic Mts.; source of the blueback trout (*Salmo beardsleei*).

Crescent City. City, ⊗ of Del Norte co., NW corner of California, on coast; pop. 2958.

Cres'co (krěs'kō). City, ⊗ of Howard co., N Iowa, 18 m. WNW of Decorah; pop. 3809.

Crespy. See CRÉPY.

Cress'kill (krěs'kĭl). Borough, Bergen co., NE corner of New Jersey, 11 m. E of Paterson; pop. 7290.

Cres'son (krěs'ʼn). Borough and resort, Cambria co., SW cen. Pennsylvania; pop. 2659; magnesia springs.

Cres·so'na (krě·sō'nȧ). Borough, Schuylkill co., E cen. Pennsylvania, 3 m. S of Pottsville; pop. 1854.

Cressy. See CRÉCY.

Crest (krěst). Commune, Drôme dept., SE France; pop. (1931) 5379; the keep of a 12th-cent. castle (destroyed 17th cent.) used as a prison; makes silk, woolens, paper.

Crest Hill. City, Will co., NE Illinois, W of Hammond, Indiana; pop. 5887.

Crest'line' (krěst'lĭn'). Village, Crawford co., N cen. Ohio, 12 m. W of Mansfield; pop. 5521.

Cres'ton (krěs'tŭn). City, ⊗ of Union co., S Iowa, 57 m. SW of Des Moines; pop. 7667; in bluegrass section.

Cres'tone Needle (krěs'tōn). Peak 14,130 ft. in Custer and Saguache cos., S cen. Colorado.

Crestone Peak. Peak 14,291 ft. in Custer and Saguache cos., S cen. Colorado.

Crest'view' (krěst'vū'). Industrial city, ⊗ of Okaloosa co., NW Florida, 47 m. ENE of Pensacola; pop. 7467; blueberry and pecan packing.

Crest'wood' (krěst'wŏŏd). City, St. Louis co., E Missouri; pop. 11,106.

Crêt de la Neige (krěd' lȧ nâzh'). = RECULET.

Crete (krēt). **1** Village, Will co., NE Illinois, 30 m. S of Chicago; pop. 3463.

2 City, Saline co., SE Nebraska, 19 m. SW of Lincoln; pop. 3546. Doane College (1872; coed.; Congregational).

3 *Gr.* **Krē'tē** (krē'tĕ); *anc.* **Cre'ta** (krē'tȧ), *also often* **Can'di·a** (kăn'dĭ·ȧ; *Ital.* kän'dyä). Greek island in E Mediterranean Sea, SSE of Greece; ab. 160 m. long and from 6 to 35 m. wide; 3199 sq. m.; pop. (1938 est.) 441,687; ✱ Canea; politically a division of Greece, comprising the departments of Canea, Hērákleion, Lasithion, and Rethymnon. Has high central range of mountains, highest Ida 8195 ft.; many short streams, watering dis-

tricts that produce various fruits; has several prominent capes (as Busa, Krio, Sidero) and is indented by many bays, esp. Suda, Canea, Messara; chief towns Canea, Candia, Rethymnon. See *Map* at GREECE.

History: Developed an advanced civilization which was based upon copper and bronze (Early Minoan or Aegean) c. 3000–2100 B.C.; c. 2000 B.C. its cities Knossos and Phaistos centers of Cretan dynasties; its culture expanded to islands and to mainland (Middle Minoan) c. 2100–1600 B.C.; ab. 16th cent. B.C., the cultural center of Aegean and eastern Mediterranean (see MYCENAE and TIRYNS); decline hastened by invasion from mainland c. 1400 B.C. and later under pressure of Greeks; 67 B.C. annexed to Rome for having given aid to pirates of Cilicia; part of Byzantine Empire; became headquarters of Saracen pirates in 9th cent. A.D.; reconquered for Byzantines by Nicephorus Phocas 960–961; sold to Venice by Boniface III, Count of Montferrat, a leader of 4th Crusade (1202–04); conquered 1669 by Ottoman Turks who completed Venetian expulsion 1715. In late 19th cent., sought independence and annexation to Greece; by Pact of Halepa 1878 received practical self-government (see HALEPA); after three unsuccessful revolts, obtained assistance of Greece 1896 (cause of Greco-Turkish War 1897); occupied by forces of powers 1898; semi-independent state, preliminary union with Greece 1908, and final annexation 1913. In World War II captured by German airborne forces May 20–30, 1941, first successful use of airborne forces in a major campaign.

Cré'teil' (krā'tâ'y'). Commune, Seine dept., N France, SE suburb of Paris on Marne river; pop. (1931) 11,596; battle during siege of Paris 1870.

Creus, Cape (krā'ōōs). Cape on extreme NE coast of Spain; W limit of Gulf of Lions.

Creuse (krûz). **1** River ab. 150 m. long in cen. France; rises in Creuse dept., flows NW into Vienne river.

2 Department of France. See *Table* at FRANCE.

Creusot, Le. See LE CREUSOT.

Creutz'wald'–la–Croix' (krûts'vȧld'lȧ·krwä'). Commune, Moselle dept., NE France; pop. (1931) 10,329.

Creux (krû). Chief landing place on the island of Sark, Channel Is.

Cre·val·co're (krā·väl·kô'rȧ). Commune, Bologna prov., Emilia, N Italy; pop. (1931) 13,549.

Creve Coeur (krēv' kŏŏr'). **1** Village, Tazewell co., cen. Illinois; pop. 6684.

2 City, St. Louis co., E Missouri, W of St. Louis; pop. 5122.

Cre'vil·len'te (krā'vě·[l]yän'tȧ). Commune, Alicante prov., SE Spain, 20 m. SW of Alicante; pop. 11,403.

Crewe (krōō). **1** Town, Nottoway co., S cen. Virginia, 42 m. W of Petersburg; pop. 2012; hosiery manufactures.

2 Municipal borough, Cheshire, NW England, 30 m. SE of Liverpool; pop. 52,415; important railroad center; manufactures locomotives and railroad cars. A hamlet in 1840; incorporated 1877.

Crick'lade (krĭk'lād). Market town, Wiltshire, England, on the Thames 9 m. NW of Swindon; very old, mentioned in *Anglo-Saxon Chronicle*.

Crieff (krēf). Burgh, Perth co., cen. Scotland; pop. 5473; health resort; before 1770 scene of famous cattle fair.

Cril'lon, Mount (krĭl'ŭn). Peak 12,725 ft., S Alaska, on Fairweather Penin. S of Mt. Fairweather; summit reached for first time July 19, 1934.

Cri·me'a (krī·mē'ȧ; krī-); *Russ.* **Krim** (krĭm); *anc.* **Cher'so·ne'sus Tau'ri·ca** (kûr'sō·nē'sŭs tô'rĭ·kȧ). **1** Peninsula, S Soviet Russia, Europe, extending into the Black Sea and having the Sea of Azov to the NE; joined to mainland (SE Kherson Region, S Ukraine) by isthmus of Perekop which has Karkinit Bay on W and Sivash or Putrid Sea on E; its E extension is the Kerch Penin., separated from Russian mainland (Krasnodar Territory) by Kerch Strait, the entrance to the Sea of Azov; from W end of Kerch Penin. a long narrow spit of sand, the Arabat, extends NW bet. Sea of Azov and the

Sivash; N two thirds is steppe country, with good soil for agriculture; along SE shore extends the Yaila Range reaching a height of 5000 ft.; its rivers are short unnavigable streams. For history, see 2, below.

2 *or* **Crimea Republic;** *officially* **Cri·me′an Autonomous Soviet Socialist Republic** (krī·mē′ǎn; krĭ-). Former autonomous republic, S Soviet Russia, Europe, coextensive with the peninsula; 10,036 sq. m.; pop. 1,126,824, (1941 est.) 1,184,060; ✻ Simferopol; since 1945 a region of the R.S.F.S.R. Predominant ethnic strain is Turko-Tatar; chief nationalities Tatar 25%, Russian 42%. *Chief occupations:* shipbuilding, mining, fishing, manufacturing; by land has rail connection with Melitopol and Kherson. *Chief towns:* Simferopol, Sevastopol, Yalta, and Kerch.

History: Inhabitants in very early times (8th cent. B.C.) were Cimmerians, who were expelled by Scythians 7th cent.; settled on the southern coast 6th cent. B.C. (see KERCH and FEODOSIYA) by Greek traders; in early 5th cent. B.C., seat of Greek kingdom of the Cimmerian Bosporus with which Athens had extensive commercial relations; invaded by Goths, Huns, and by Khazars, who held Crimean part of their kingdom in southern Russia from ab. 7th cent. A.D. to 10th cent.; Greek coastal towns (theme of Cherson) in Byzantine Empire until c. 1000; after Tatar invasion 13th cent. belonged to Khanate of Golden Horde (see RUSSIA); 15th cent. became independent Khanate of Crimea which at first extended beyond the peninsula; southeast coastal strip held by Genoese; Tatar khanate overthrown by Ottoman Turks 1475; recognized as Russian dependency in Treaty of Kuchuk Kainarji 1774; incorporated by Russia 1783. Scene of Crimean War (England, France, Sardinia against Russia) 1854–56; proclaimed independent Crimean Republic 1918; entered Soviet Russia (R.S.F.S.R.) 1921. In World War II overrun by Nazi armies in fall of 1941 (see SEVASTOPOL); isolated by Russians Oct. 1943 and retaken Mar.–May 1944; republic liquidated 1945 for collaboration with Nazis. See YALTA.

Cri·mi′sus (krĭ·mī′sŭs) *or* **Cri·mis′sus** (krĭ·mĭs′ŭs). River, W Sicily; scene of battle in which Timoleon defeated the Carthaginians 341 B.C.

Crim′mit·schau *or* **Krim′mit·schau** (krĭm′ĭt·shou). Manufacturing city in Karl-Marx-Stadt dist., East Germany, 36 m. S of Leipzig; pop. 27,119; textiles.

Crip′ple Creek (krĭp′'l krēk′). City, ⊗ of Teller co., cen. Colorado, SW of Colorado Springs; pop. 614; in one of world's great gold-producing districts.

Cri′sa (krī′sȧ). Ancient city of Phocis, cen. Greece, near Delphi and bet. it and its port on the Gulf of Corinth; destroyed by Amphictyonic Council in First Sacred War c. 590 B.C.; its rebuilding by Amphissa brought on Fourth Sacred War 339 B.C. See DELPHI.

Cri·şa·na–Ma′ra·mu′reş (krĕ·sha′nä·mä′rä·mōō′rĕsh). Former province of Romania, in NW part.

Cris′field (krĭs′fēld). City, Somerset co., SE Maryland, on Chesapeake Bay 32 m. SW of Salisbury; pop. 3540; shipping point for oysters, crabs, and fish.

Crisp (krĭsp). County in Georgia. See *Table* at GEORGIA.

Cris·to′bal (krĭs·tō′bǎl); *Span.* **Cris·tó′bal** (krĕs·tō′väl). **1** District in NW Canal Zone; pop. 11,499.

2 Town in the district, at Atlantic entrance to Panama Canal; a suburb of Colón and Silver City; pop. 817.

Crit′ten·den (krĭt′'n·dĕn). Counties in two states of the U.S. See *Tables* at ARKANSAS and KENTUCKY.

Cr′na (tsûr′nä) *or* **Cher′na** (chĕr′nä). River ab. 120 m. long in S Yugoslavia; flows SE and N into Vardar river.

Crna Gora. See MONTENEGRO.

Croagh Pat′rick (krō păt′rĭk). Mountain 2510 ft. in S co. Mayo, W Ireland; according to tradition, place where Saint Patrick began his missionary work in Ireland.

Cro′a·tan (krō′ȧ·tăn′), *or* **Cro′a·to′an** (krō′ȧ·tō′ǎn), **Island.** Island off coast of North Carolina, bet. Pamlico Sound and the Atlantic Ocean—formerly so called, probably same as Ocracoke I.; thought to be place to

which Raleigh's colony from Roanoke I. moved 1587, since Croatan Indians were friendly, but disappearance of all members of colony by 1591 never has been satisfactorily explained.

Croatan Sound. Strait bet. Roanoke I. and the mainland of Dare co., E North Carolina.

Cro·a′ti·a (krō·ā′shĭ·ȧ; -shȧ); *Serb.* **Hr′vat·ska** (hûr′vät·skä). Region in SE Europe, now (since 1945) a federated republic of Yugoslavia; in its most restricted sense name designates territory S of the Sava and W of the Una, bounded on N by Slovenia, on E by Slavonia, on S by Bosnia and Dalmatia, and on W by Adriatic Sea; boundaries however have varied greatly at different periods: as medieval kingdom extended at times NE to the Drava and S to Montenegro; as separate county 1939 included coastal region as far S as Mostar, and in World War II under German rule included territory around Banja Luka. Chief towns Zagreb, Karlovac, Osijek (in Slavonia).

History: For earlier history of region, see PANNONIA. From 7th cent. A.D., inhabited by Croats, a south Slavic people, whom Charlemagne made tributary to Franks; formed into kingdom under Tomislav 924; joined with Hungary in dynastic union (1102), whence the Croats became westernized and separated from Slavs under Serbian influence; retained autonomy under Hungarian crown; with Slavonia taken by Turks in 16th cent., N part restored by Treaty of Karlowitz 1699; parts of Croatia included in Napoleon's Illyrian Provinces (*q.v.*) 1809–13; helped Austria to put down Hungarian revolution 1848–49 and as a result set up with Slavonia as separate Austrian crownland **Croatia and Sla·vo′ni·a** (slȧ·vō′nĭ·ȧ; -vōn′yȧ), which was reunited to Hungary as part of *Ausgleich* 1867 (see AUSTRIA-HUNGARY) and set up as a Hungarian crownland, became a leader in prewar agitation 1912–14 of South Slavs for independence from Austria-Hungary, and united with other Yugoslav areas to proclaim kingdom of Serbs, Croats, and Slovenes 1918 (see YUGOSLAVIA); at reorganization of Yugoslavia 1929 Croatia and Slavonia became Savska co., which in 1939 was united with Primorje co. to form county of Croatia, which in turn became federated republic of Croatia 1945 (✻ Zagreb).

Crock′er Land (krŏk′ẽr). An Arctic land supposed to have been seen 1906 by Robert E. Peary, in long. 100°W, lat. 83°N, WNW of Grant Land; proven nonexistent by expedition of Donald MacMillan 1914.

Crock′ett (krŏk′ĕt; -ĭt). **1** Name of counties in two states of the U.S. See *Tables* at TENNESSEE and TEXAS.

2 City, ⊗ of Houston co., E Texas, 32 m. S of Palestine; pop. 5356; cottonseed-oil mills, lumber mills; pecans.

Croc′o·dile (krŏk′ō·dīl). **1** See LIMPOPO river.

2 A headstream of the Komati river, Transvaal, Union of South Africa.

Crocodilopolis. See ARSINOË.

Croia. See KRUJË.

Croi·silles′ (krwä′zē′y′). Village, Pas-de-Calais dept., N France, 8 m. SE of Arras; pop. (1931) 853; destroyed during World War I in battles of 1917–18.

Croix (krwä). Industrial commune, Nord dept., N France, NE suburb of Lille; pop. (1931) 20,652; metalworks, dyeworks, breweries.

Cro′ker Island (krō′kẽr). Island in Arafura Sea off N coast of Cobourg Penin., Northern Territory, Australia.

Cro–Magnon. See Les EYZIES.

Crom′ar·ty Firth (krŏm′ẽr·tĭ). Inlet of Moray Firth, Ross and Cromarty co., N Scotland.

Cro′mer (krō′mẽr). Urban district, Norfolk, England, on North Sea coast 24 m. N of Norwich; pop. (1951) 4658; watering place; coast guard and lifeboat station.

Cromp′ton (krŭmp′tŭn). Urban district, Lancashire, NW England, NE of Manchester; pop. 12,558; textiles.

Crom′well (krŏm′wĕl; -wĕl). **1** Town, NW Middlesex co., S Connecticut, on Connecticut river; pop. 6780; incorporated 1851; manufactures hardware.

2 Borough, Otago provincial dist., S South I., New Zealand, on upper Clutha river in lake region; pop. 600.

Cro'nen·berg or **Kro'nen·berg** (krō'nĕn-bûrg; *Ger.* -bĕrk). Manufacturing city, North Rhine-Westphalia state, W Germany, 21 m. NNE of Cologne; pop. 14,051; iron industry; silk weaving.

Cron'stadt (krŏn'stăt). = KRONSHTADT.

Cro·nul'la (krŏ-nŭl'á). Coastal village on Port Hacking, New South Wales, Australia just S of Sydney.

Crook (krook). **1** Name of counties in two states of the U.S. See *Tables* at OREGON and WYOMING.

2 Urban district, Durham, N England, 20 m. SSW of Newcastle; pop. 27,606.

Crook'ed (krook'ĕd; -ĭd). River ab. 150 m. long, cen. Oregon; flows W and NW into Deschutes river.

Crooked Creek. River ab. 100 m. long in W Illinois, flowing into Illinois river.

Crooked Island. One of the Bahama Is., Brit. W. Indies, in cen. part of group S of San Salvador (Watlings I.); 76 sq. m.; pop. (1943) 1078.

Crooked Island Passage. Deep-water channel ab. 40 m. wide in the Bahama Is., Brit. W. Indies, S and SE of Long I. and NW of Crooked I. and Acklins I.

Crooked Lake. See KEUKA LAKE.

Crooks'ton (krooks'tŭn). City, ⊗ of Polk co., NW Minnesota, 32 m. SW of Thief River Falls; pop. 8546; livestock raising; wheat, sugar beets, dairy products.

Crooks'ville (krooks'vĭl). Village, Perry co., SE cen. Ohio, 13 m. S of Zanesville; pop. 2958; manufactures stoneware, chinaware, tile; coal mines, clay deposits.

Crop'red'y (krŏp'rĕd'ĭ). Village, N Oxfordshire, cen. England, ab. 3½ m. N of Banbury; scene of battle (Cropredy Bridge) June 29, 1644 in which the Royalists defeated the Parliamentarians under Sir William Waller.

Cros'by (krŏz'bĭ). **1** County, Texas. See *Table* at TEXAS.

2 Village, Crow Wing co., cen. Minnesota, 16 m. NE of Brainerd; pop. 2629; iron and manganese mining.

3 City, ⊗ of Divide co., NW North Dakota; pop. 1759.

4 or **Great Crosby.** Municipal borough, Lancashire, NW England, on Irish Sea at mouth of the Mersey 6 m. NNW of Liverpool; pop. 58,362.

Crosby, Mount. Peak 12,435 ft. in S Park co., NW Wyoming.

Cros'by·ton (krŏz'bĭ·t'n; -tŭn). City, ⊗ of Crosby co., NW Texas, E of Lubbock; pop. 2088; cattle, grain.

Cross (krŏs). **1** County in Arkansas. See *Table* at ARKANSAS.

2 River ab. 300 m. long, Brit. Cameroons and SE Nigeria; flows W and S to Gulf of Guinea; large estuary.

Cross, Cape. Cape on NW coast of South-West Africa; point farthest S (22°S) reached by Diogo Cam 1484; stone cross erected here by him.

Cross Bay. Bay on NW coast of West Spitsbergen I.

Cross City. Town, ⊗ of Dixie co., N Florida penin., 50 m. W of Gainesville; pop. 1857; lumber center.

Cros'sett (krŏs'ĕt; -ĭt). City, Ashley co., SE Arkansas, 42 m. E of El Dorado; pop. 5370; lumber.

Cross Fell. See PENNINE CHAIN.

Cross'–Flor'i·da Waterway; *officially* **O'kee·cho'bee Waterway** (ō'kĕ-chō'bĕ). Waterways linking the Atlantic coast at Stuart, Florida, with the Gulf of Mexico at the mouth of the Caloosahatchee river by way of St. Lucie Canal, Lake Okeechobee, and Lake Hicpochee.

Cross Keys (kēz). Formerly a post village, S Rockingham co., Virginia, 20 m. NE of Staunton; battle June 8, 1862 in which Confederates under Gen. Ewell defeated Federal troops under General Frémont.

Cross Mountain. Peak 12,140 ft. in Sierra Nevada, in N Tulare co., S cen. California.

Cross River. See CROSS.

Cross Sound. Inlet of Pacific Ocean bet. SE Alaska and N Chichagof I.; joins S end of Glacier Bay.

Cross'ville (krŏs'vĭl; *Sou. also* -v'l). Town, ⊗ of Cumberland co., E cen. Tennessee, 28 m. W of Harriman; pop. 4668; rubber products, appliances, knit goods.

Cro'ton (krō't'n). River ab. 60 m. long in SE New York; flows from Dutchess co. S and SW through Putnam and Westchester cos. into Hudson river; important source of water supply for New York City since 1842, when **Croton Aqueduct** (tunnel 31 m. long when completed) first brought in water from original reservoir near its mouth; now contains a system of dams and reservoirs including Croton Falls and New Croton.

Cro·to'ne (krō·tō'nĕ); *sometimes called* **Co·tro'ne** (kō-trō'nĕ); *anc.* **Cro·to'na** (krō-tō'ná) or **Cro'ton** (krō'-tŏn). Commune, Catanzaro prov., Calabria, S Italy, on Gulf of Taranto; pop. 21,496; cathedral; old castle. Ancient Greek republic, founded by Achaeans c. 700 B.C.; home of Milo and, 540–530 B.C., of Pythagoras; scene of battles before and during Second Punic War; scene of defeat of Otto II by Byzantines and Saracens 982 A.D.

Cro'ton Falls Dam (krō't'n fôlz'). Dam completed 1911 across west branch of Croton river, Putnam co., SE New York; height 167 ft.; forms **Croton Falls Reservoir,** part of Croton system of water supply for New York City.

Cro'ton-on-Hud'son (krō't'n, hŭd's'n). Village, Westchester co., SE New York, on Hudson river near mouth of Croton river, 34 m. N of New York; pop. 6812.

Crow (krō). River ab. 160 m. long, S Minnesota; formed by junction of North Fork and South Fork on boundary bet. Hennepin and Wright cos., flows NE into Mississippi river above Anoka.

Crow'ell (krō'ĕl). City, ⊗ of Foard co., N Texas, 30 m. SW of Vernon; pop. 1703; grain, stock, poultry.

Crow'ley (krou'lĭ). **1** County in Colorado. See *Table* at COLORADO.

2 City, ⊗ of Acadia parish S Louisiana, 24 m. W of Lafayette; pop. 15,617; rice mills, rice experiment station.

Crown Mountain (kroun). **1** Peak 13,600 ft. in Hinsdale and San Juan cos., SW Colorado.

2 Peak 7186 ft. in S Brewster co., W Texas.

3 or **Crown Hill.** Peak 1550 ft. in W cen. St. Thomas I., in the Virgin Is. of the United States, West Indies; highest point in the Virgin Is. Marine air base nearby.

Crown Point. **1** City, ⊗ of Lake co., NW corner of Indiana, 13 m. S of Lake Michigan; pop. 8443.

2 Village in Crown Point town (pop. 1685), Essex co., NE New York, on W shore of S part of Lake Champlain ab. 7 m. S of Ticonderoga; became an English trading post 1714 and strategic point on route from New York to Canada; called Pointe à la Chevelure (Scalp Point) by the French who built Fort St. Frédéric here 1731 as proposed capital of territory; goal of expedition led by Sir Wm. Johnson 1755 ending in battle of Lake George; taken by Gen. Jeffrey Amherst 1759 who began Fort Amherst (renamed Fort Crown Point); captured by Seth Warner and Green Mountain Boys 1775; again held by British 1777 until after defeat at Saratoga; seat of Crown Point Reservation (includes ruins of forts, etc.).

Crown Prince Range. Mountain range in S part of Bougainville I., NW Solomon Is., highest peak 7743 ft.

Crown Prince Ru'dolf Island (roo'dŏlf). Northernmost island of Franz Josef Land, Arctic Ocean.

Crown Princess Mar'tha Land (mär'thá). See PRINCESS MARTHA COAST.

Crow Peak (krō). Mountain 5772 ft. in Lawrence co., W South Dakota.

Crow's Nest (krōz). Mountain 1396 ft. in Orange co., New York, on W bank of Hudson above West Point.

Crows'nest' Pass (krōz'nĕst'). Pass, alt. 5500 ft., through the Rocky Mts., in SE Brit. Columbia, Canada, on Alberta border; lat. 49°35′N; Canadian Pacific R.R.

Crows Nest Peak (krōz). Mountain 6683 ft. in Pennington co., W South Dakota.

Crow Wing (krō' wing'). **1** River, cen. Minnesota; formed by branches in N Wadena co., flows SE and E into the Mississippi on SW boundary of Crow Wing co.

2 County in Minnesota. See *Table* at MINNESOTA.

Croy'don (kroi'd'n). County borough, Surrey, S Eng-

land; pop. 233,032, (1951) 249,592; residential suburb in S part of Greater London; airport; varied manufactures, including aircraft, electrical apparatus.

Cro'zet' Islands (krô'zĕ'). Five uninhabited small French islands in S Indian Ocean, ab. lat. 46°30'S and long. 51°E; discovered 1772 by Marion-Dufresne.

Cruachan, Ben. See BEN CRUACHAN.

Cru'ces (krōō'sås). Municipality and town (pop. 9043), Las Villas prov., W cen. Cuba, WSW of Santa Clara.

Crum El'bow (krŭm ĕl'bō). Double bend in Hudson river ab. 4 m. above Poughkeepsie, New York.

Crum'mock Water (krŭm'ŭk). Lake in Cumberland, NW England; 2½ m. long, maximum depth 144 ft.

Cruz, Cape (krōōs; *Angl.* krōōz). Cape at SW point of Oriente prov., E Cuba, projecting into Caribbean Sea.

Cruz, Point (krōōz). Small coral promontory just W of mouth of Matanikau river, NW coast of Guadalcanal I., SE Solomon Is.; in World War II scene of considerable fighting, esp. in Oct. and Nov. 1942.

Cruz Al'ta (krōōz äl'tȧ). City, Rio Grande do Sul state, S Brazil; pop. (1940 est.) 16,331.

Cruz Bay (krōōz). Town at W end of St. John I., Virgin Is. of the United States, West Indies.

Cruz del E'je (krōōz' thĕl ĕ'hȧ). Town, Córdoba prov., N cen. Argentina; pop. (est.) 19,173.

Cru·zei'ro (krōō·zā'ē·rōō). City, Santa Catarina state, S Brazil, on tributary of Uruguay river 190 m. W of Florianópolis; pop. (1940 est.) 11,863.

Cruz Gran'de (krōōz' grän'då). Seaport, Coquimbo prov., cen. Chile, 32 m. N of Coquimbo; pop. 685; subdivision of **La Hi·gue'ra** (lä ē·gā'rä) commune (pop. 6956); shipping point for iron ore from the nearby mines of El Tofo.

Crys'tal (krĭs't'l). Village, Hennepin co., SE cen. Minnesota, 15 m. W of Minneapolis; pop. 24,283.

Crystal Beach. Village, Welland co., Ontario, on shore of Lake Erie; pop. 1204; bathing, amusement park.

Crystal City. 1 City, Jefferson co., E Missouri, on Mis-

sissippi river 30 m. S of St. Louis; pop. 3678; plate glass. **2** City, ⊗ of Zavala co., S Texas, 35 m. S of Uvalde; pop. 9101; shipping center for winter garden area growing esp. spinach.

Crystal Falls. City, ⊗ of Iron co., SW Michigan penin., 23 m. NNW of Iron Mountain (city); pop. 2203; iron mines of the Menominee Range area.

Crystal Lake. City, McHenry co., N Illinois, 28 m. WSW of Waukegan; pop. 8314; summer resort.

Crystal Springs. City, Copiah co., SW Mississippi, 23 m. SSW of Jackson; pop. 4496; ships tomatoes.

Csallóköz. See GREAT SCHÜTT.

Cse'pel (chĕ'pĕl). **1** Island 30 m. long in Danube river S of Budapest, cen. Hungary. **2** Industrial commune on N tip of the island; incorporated with Budapest 1950.

Cson'grád (chŏn'gräd). City, S Hungary, at the confluence of the Körös and Tisza rivers; pop. 28,234; market center for farm products, cattle, and wine.

Ctes'i·phon (tĕs'ĭ·fŏn; tē'sĭ-). Ancient ruined city in cen. Iraq, on E bank of the Tigris opp. Seleucia and 20 m. SSE of Baghdad; capital of the ancient kingdom of Parthia (*q.v.*) and of later Sassanid empire (see PERSIA); part of the great vaulted hall of this later period still standing. Captured by Arabs 637 A.D.; declined after building of Arab capital at Baghdad (*q.v.*); scene of battle won by Turks over the British Nov. 21, 1915.

Cuando. See KWANDO.

Cuango. See KWANGO.

Cuan'za or **Kwan'za** (kwän'zȧ). River ab. 500 m. long cen. Angola, SW Africa; rises in S cen. Angola, flows NW into Atlantic Ocean near Luanda.

Cuau'tla (kwou'tlä). Town, Morelos state, S cen. Mexico, ab. 18 m. SE of Cuernavaca; pop. 6431; alt. 4350 ft.; sulfur springs; resort.

Cu'ba (kū'bȧ; *Span.* kōō'vä). Island in the Greater Antilles, West Indies, S of Florida and N of W Caribbean Sea; with adjacent islands forms Republic of Cuba,

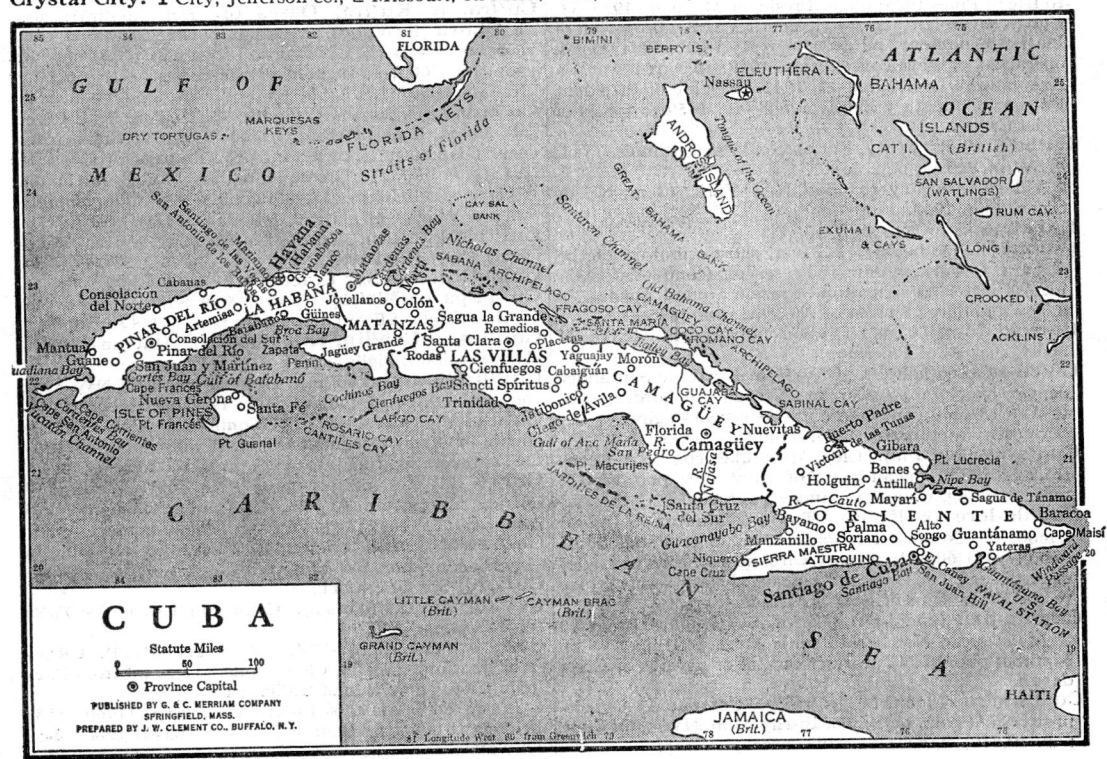

46,736 sq. m.; pop. (1966 est.) 7,800,000; ✻ Havana; divided into the following six provinces (for pronunciation of their names, see their individual entries):

PROVINCES	LOCATION	AREA[1]	POP.[1]	CAPITAL
Camagüey[2]	E cen.	10,172	487,791	Camagüey
La Habana	W	3,174	1,235,939	Havana
Las Villas[3]	W cen.	8,267	938,581	Santa Clara
Matanzas	W cen.	3,260	361,079	Matanzas
Oriente[4]	E	14,132	1,356,489	Santiago de Cuba
Pinar del Río	W	5,212	398,794	Pinar del Río

[1] Area is in sq. m. Pop. is 1943 Census.
[2] Formerly Puerto Príncipe prov.
[3] Formerly Santa Clara prov.
[4] Formerly Santiago de Cuba prov.

Island ab. 760 m. long from Cape Maisí on E to Cape San Antonio on W; varies in width from 25 to 125 m.; has coast line of ab. 2000 m. with many cays and islands (largest Isle of Pines off SW); largely flat or rolling country; highest point in Oriente prov. (Pico Turquino 6560 ft.); rivers mostly short and rapid. Chief trade is with U.S., chief product sugar (second largest producer in the world); other products tobacco, molasses, coffee, cocoa, fruits. Chief cities Havana, Holguín, Camagüey, Santiago de Cuba.

History: Discovered by Columbus on his first voyage 1492; conquered by Spanish under Velásquez 1511, present site of Havana settled 1519; part of viceroyalty of New Spain; Havana captured by British 1762, but restored to Spain 1763; became captaincy general 1777 and entered prosperous period under Las Casas from 1790; revolted unsuccessfully 1868–78; rose again in 1895, as result of which United States entered Spanish-American War 1898; in 1901 adopted constitution including Platt Amendment which made Cuba virtually a protectorate of U.S.; took over government May 20, 1902 from American military authorities; occupied by U.S. marines 1906–09 and on other occasions; entered World War I 1917; joined League of Nations 1920; given full claim to Isle of Pines 1925; under President Machado 1925–33; Cuban sovereignty unrestricted after U.S. abrogation of Platt Amendment and certain treaty rights 1934; began operation of new constitution 1940; declared war on Axis powers Dec. 9 and 11, 1941. Regime of President Fulgencio Batista y Zaldívar fell Jan. 1959 to forces of Fidel Castro.

Cu'ba (kū'bȧ). **1** City, Fulton co., W cen. Illinois, 35 m. WSW of Peoria; pop. 1380.
2 Village, Allegany co., SW New York, 13 m. NE of Olean; pop. 1949.

Cubango. See OKOVANGGO.

Çu·buk' (choo·book'). **1** River, short tributary of the Ankara, N Turkey; dam and reservoir (completed 1935) furnish water for irrigation in region around Ankara.
2 Town on river 8 m. N of Ankara; pop. 1615.

Cuc'cio, Mon'te (mŏn'tā̇ koōt'chō). Height 3448 ft., N Sicily, just W of Palermo.

Cú'cu·ta (koō'koō·tä). City, ✻ of Norte de Santander dept., N Colombia, near the Venezuelan border; pop. (1958) 131,410; on Colombia-Venezuela highway; destroyed by earthquake 1875, rebuilt.

Cud'a·hy (kŭd'ȧ·hī). City, Milwaukee co., SE Wisconsin, on Lake Michigan 7 m. S of Milwaukee; pop. 17,975; meat packing, tanning; foundry products.

Cud'da·lore' (kŭd''l·ôr'). Town, E Madras, S Indian Union, on Coromandel Coast 18 m. S of Pondichéry; pop. (1941) 60,632; seaport with mostly coastal trade; exports sugar, oilseeds and oil cake; health resort. Just to the N are ruins of Fort St. David (*q.v.*).

Cud'da·pah (kŭd'ȧ·pä). Town, SW Andhra Pradesh, S India, near Northern Penner river 140 m. NW of Madras; pop. 22,602; former capital of nawabs of Cuddapah.

Cu'dil·le'ro (koō'thē·[l]yā'rō). Commune, Oviedo prov., NW Spain, on Bay of Biscay 22 m. NW of Oviedo; pop. 10,630; manganese mines nearby.

Cud'worth (kŭd'wûrth; -wērth). Urban district, West Riding, Yorkshire, N England; pop. 8757.

Cuen'ca (kwäng'kä). **1** City, ✻ of Azuay prov., S Ecuador, ab. 68 m. SE of Guayaquil; pop. (1944 est.) 52,519; alt. 8640 ft.; founded by Spanish 1557 on site of native town called Tumibamba; made episcopal see 1786; cathedral, normal institute, and university; called "Athens of Ecuador"; manufactures Panama hats.
2 Province of Spain. See *Table* at SPAIN.
3 *anc.* **Con'ca** (kŏng'kä). Commune, ✻ of Cuenca prov., E cen. Spain, on Júcar river 89 m. ESE of Madrid; pop. 24,702; castle; 13th-cent. Gothic cathedral; built by Moors; captured by Alfonso VIII of Castile 1177; made municipality 1257; under attack by English 1706, by French 1808 and 1810, and by Carlists 1874.

Cuenca, Serranía de. See SERRANÍA DE CUENCA.

Cuera. See CHUR.

Cuer'na·va'ca (kwěr'nä·vä'kä). Town, ✻ of Morelos state, S cen. Mexico; pop. 14,336; alt. 4500 ft.; Cacahuamilpa Caverns, among largest in North America, are nearby; resort.

Cuer'nos of Ne'gros (kwěr'nôs, nā'grōs). Highest peak 6244 ft. in Negros Oriental prov., Negros, Phil. Is., in SE part W of Dumaguete.

Cue'ro (kwâr'ō). City, ⊗ of De Witt co., S Texas, on Guadalupe river 27 m. NNW of Victoria; pop. 7338; center for cotton-growing and turkey-raising area.

Cuers (kü·âr'). Commune, Var dept., SE France, N of Hyères; pop. 3517; **Cuers–Pierre'feu'** (-pyěr'fü') airdrome bet. Cuers and commune of Pierrefeu to the E.

Cuesmes (kwäm'). Commune, Hainaut prov., SW Belgium; pop. 10,250; coal mines.

Cuet'za·lán' (kwět'sä·län'). Town, Puebla state, SE cen. Mexico; pop. 7087.

Cue'vas del Al'man·zo'ra (kwā'väz thĕl äl'män·thō'rä; -sō'rä); *formerly* **Cuevas de Ve'ra** (thä vā'rä). Commune, Almería prov., SE Spain, 42 m. NE of Almería; pop. 9526; silver, lead, and iron mining.

Cu'fra, *or* **Ku'fra, Oases of** (*Ital.* koō'frä); *also* **Ku'fa·ra** (koō'fä·rȧ). Group of five oases in cen. Libyan Desert, S Cyrenaica, Libya; ab. 7000 sq. m.; pop. ab. 7000; stronghold of the Senusi, overcome by Italians 1930–31.

Cu'ia·bá'; *formerly* **Cu'ya·bá'** (koō'yȧ·vȧ'). **1** River ab. 300 m. long, in Mato Grosso state, SW Brazil; rises near Diamantino, flows S into São Lourenço river.
2 City, ✻ of Mato Grosso state, SW Brazil, on Cuiabá river; pop. (1940 est.) 18,940; active river trade; on highway at W edge of plateau; founded in 18th cent.

Cui'cas (kwē'käs). Town, Trujillo state, W cen. Venezuela; pop. (1941 est.) 5068.

Cuicuilco. See SAN CUICUILCO.

Cui·la'pa (kwĕ·lä'pä). Town, ✻ of Santa Rosa dept., S Guatemala; ⊗ of Guatemala; pop. (1938 est.) 2914.

Cuil'lin, *or* **Coo'lin, Hills** (koō'lǐn). Hills on Skye I., NW Scotland; highest peak 3234 ft.

Cuillin Sound (koō'lǐn). Body of water off NW coast of Scotland, bet. Skye and Rum Is., Inner Hebrides.

Cuin'chy' (kü·ăn'shē'). Commune, Pas-de-Calais dept., N France, 8 m. ESE of Béthune; pop. (1931) 1512; severe fighting, esp. 1915, in World War I.

Cui'to (kwē'tō). River more than 400 m. long, SW Africa; rises in cen. Angola, flows through marshland, S and SE into Okovanggo river on Angola border.

Cuit·ze'o, Lake (kwĕt·sā'ō). Lake 31 m. long in Michoacán state, SW Mexico.

Cularo. See GRENOBLE.

Cul'ber·son (kŭl'bēr·s'n). County in Texas. See *Table* at TEXAS.

Cu·le'bra (kŭ·lā'brä; -lĕb'rä; *Span.* koō·lā'vrä). **1** Railroad station, Panama Canal Zone, ab. 10 m. from Panama City, on W side of Gaillard Cut.
2 Island off E coast of Puerto Rico, pop. (1960) 573; belongs to Puerto Rico; site of U.S. naval base. See DEWEY.

Culebra Gulf. See Gulf of MURCIÉLAGOS.

Culebra Mountain. Hill, SE Canal Zone, through which **Culebra Cut** (see GAILLARD CUT) was made.

Culebra Peak. Mountain 14,069 ft. in Costilla and Las Animas cos., S Colorado, in cen. part, called the **Culebra Range**, of the Sangre de Cristo Range.

Cul·go'a (kŭl·gō′à). River ab. 200 m. long, SE Queensland and NE New South Wales, Australia; formed by junction of Maranoa and Condamine rivers, flows SW; with these streams the longest tributary of the Darling.

Cu'lia·cán' (kōō′lyä·kän′), *officially* **Culiacán-Rosa'les** (-rrô·sä′läs). Commercial city, ✳ of Sinaloa state, W Mexico, on **Culiacán River** (ab. 175 m. long) 40 m. from its mouth; pop. 22,025; founded 1599.

Cu·lion' (kōō·lyôn′). 1 Island, S part of Calamian Is., N Palawan prov., Phil. Is.; 150 sq. m.; pop. 7328; has fertile soil and healthful climate; on it is **Culion Reservation**, a leper colony established 1906.
2 Town (leper colony) on NE coast of island; fine port.

Cul·le'ra (kōō·[l]yä′rä). Commune, Valencia prov., E Spain, on Júcar river near its mouth on the Mediterranean 24 m. SSE of Valencia; pop. 15,005; fishing, stock raising; captured from Moors by James I of Aragon.

Cul'li·nan (kŭl′ĭ·năn; -năn). Town, S cen. Transvaal, NE Union of South Africa, 20 m. E of Pretoria; site of the Premier diamond mine (opened 1902, closed 1932) in which was discovered 1905 the Cullinan diamond.

Cull'man (kŭl′măn). 1 County in Alabama. See *Table* at ALABAMA.
2 City, its ⊗, N Alabama, 45 m. N of Birmingham; pop. 10,883; shipping center, esp. for strawberries.

Cul·lod'en Moor (kŭ·lŏd′n; -lô′d′n); *also called* **Drum·mos'sie Moor** (drŭm·môs′ĭ). Moor in Inverness co., NW Scotland; battle Apr. 16, 1746 in which British force under duke of Cumberland defeated Highland Jacobite force under Prince Charles Edward, thus ending last armed outbreak of the Stuart cause; notorious for slaughter of Highland wounded after battle.

Cul'lo·whee (kŭl′ŭ·[h]wē). Town in Cullowhee township (pop. 2500), Jackson co., SW North Carolina, ab. 16 m. SW of Waynesville. Western Carolina College (1889; coed.).

Culm. See CHEŁMNO.

Culmsee. See CHEŁMŻA.

Cul'pep'er (kŭl′pĕp′ẽr). 1 County in Virginia. See *Table* at VIRGINIA.
2 Town, its ⊗, N Virginia, W of Fredericksburg; pop. 2412; muster place in 1775 for Culpeper minutemen.

Culp's Hill. See CEMETERY RIDGE.

Cul'ver (kŭl′vẽr). Town, Marshall co., N Indiana, 33 m. SSW of South Bend; pop. 1558.

Culver City. City, Los Angeles co., SW California, SW of Los Angeles; pop. 32,163; motion-picture studios.

Cu'mae (kū′mē). Ancient town, Campania, Italy, on coast W of Neapolis (Naples); oldest Greek colony in Italy or Sicily, founded before 721 B.C.; defeated the Etruscans 524 B.C.; allied with Hiero of Syracuse in his defeat of Etruscans in naval battle 474 B.C.; came under supremacy of Rome ab. 340 B.C.; destroyed by Neapolitans 1205 A.D. On the site near the shore is the acropolis containing caves said to have been seat of the oracle of the Cumaean Sibyl.

Cu·ma·ná' (kōō′mä·nä′). Seaport city, ✳ of Sucre state, N Venezuela, 185 m. E of Caracas; pop. (1941 est.) 25,811; exports tobacco, cacao, fish, cotton textiles, coffee. Settled 1520 by Las Casas who established a model Indian colony; destroyed by natives 1522; settled again 1523 by Diego Castellón under the name Nueva Toledo; oldest existing European settlement in South America; has often suffered from earthquakes, esp. 1766, when it was almost completely destroyed, and Jan. 1929.

Cum·bal' (kōōm·bäl′). Volcano 16,000 ft. in the Andes, Nariño dept., SW Colombia, on border of Ecuador.

Cum'ber·land (kŭm′bẽr·lănd). 1 Navigable river 687 m. long, S Kentucky and N Tennessee; formed by confluence of forks in Harlan co., SE Kentucky, flows W through S Kentucky, turns S in Monroe co. and makes great loop in N Tennessee, re-enters Kentucky running N into Ohio river in W Livingston co., W Kentucky. The **Cumberland**, or **Great, Falls** (63 ft. high, over 100 ft. wide) are in cen. Whitley co., Ky. See *Table* at TENNESSEE VALLEY AUTHORITY (Great Falls Dam).
2 Name of counties in eight states of the U.S. See *Tables* at ILLINOIS, KENTUCKY, MAINE, NEW JERSEY, NORTH CAROLINA, PENNSYLVANIA, TENNESSEE, VIRGINIA.
3 City, Harlan co., SE Kentucky, 21 m. SSE of Hazard; pop. 4271; mining center.
4 City, ⊗ of Allegany co., NW Maryland, on Potomac river; pop. 33,415; railroad and industrial center; coal mines; iron and steel products, glass, cement, tires.
5 Town, Providence co., N Rhode Island, 4 m. SE of Woonsocket; pop. 18,792; governmental center Valley Falls. Originally part of Massachusetts; annexed to Rhode Island 1746, incorp. 1747. Textiles, ironware.
6 Village, ⊗ of Cumberland co., cen. Virginia; pop. (est.) 250.
7 City, Barron co., NW Wisconsin, 13 m. W of Rice Lake (city); pop. 1860; creameries, canneries.
8 County, Nova Scotia. See *Table* at NOVA SCOTIA.
9 County, NW England; area 1520 sq. m.; pop. (1951) 285,347; ⊗ Carlisle; other towns Whitehaven, Workington, Penrith; lakes include Derwentwater, Ullswater, Thirlmere; rivers include Derwent, Ehen, Esk; coal and iron mining, limestone quarrying, sheep raising.

Cumberland Caverns. Large cave, Warren co., cen. Tennessee, 10 m. SE of McMinnville.

Cumberland Gap. Pass, alt. 1315 ft., through Cumberland Plateau in Claiborne co., NE Tennessee; discovered 1750, became an early emigrant route; used by Daniel Boone in his pioneer trips into Kentucky 1767–71 and when he led settlers to site of Boonesborough 1775 blazing and clearing the Wilderness Road (*q.v.*); first mail route through Gap to Danville, Ky., 1792; strategic point in Civil War.

Cumberland Island. Island in Atlantic Ocean, off mainland of Camden co., SE Georgia.

Cumberland Islands. Group of small islands off E coast of Queensland, Australia, SE of Townsville.

Cumberland Lake. Lake 166 sq. m. in NE Saskatchewan prov., Canada; drains S into Saskatchewan river.

Cumberland Peninsula. Peninsula, E Baffin I., E Franklin District, Northwest Territories, Canada; its easternmost point, Cape Dyer, on Davis Strait.

Cumberland Plateau *or* **Mountains.** Tableland extending NE to SW from S West Virginia to NE Alabama N of Birmingham; extends along border bet. Kentucky and Virginia and in E Tennessee W of the Tennessee river; average height ab. 2000 ft., average width ab. 50 m.; structurally the W section of the Appalachian Mts. and a part of the Allegheny highlands. Rich deposits of bituminous coal in the Tennessee area.

Cumberland Road. First national road in the United States; originally started at Cumberland, Maryland; construction began 1811; extended to Vandalia, Illinois.

Cumberland Sound. 1 Inlet of Atlantic Ocean on Georgia-Florida boundary; receives the St. Marys river.
2 Inlet of Davis Strait, SE Baffin I., Northwest Territories, N Canada, SW of Cumberland Penin.

Cum·braes', the (kŭm·brāz′; kŭm′brāz). Two islands in the Firth of Clyde, forming a civil parish (pop. 2079) of Bute co., SW Scotland: **Great Cumbrae Island**, WSW of Largs; 5 sq. m.; summer resort; **Little Cumbrae Island**, S of Great Cumbrae; 1 sq. m.; lighthouse.

Cum'bre, La (lä kōōm′brä). = *Uspallata Pass:* see ANDES.

Cum'bre Ne'gra (kōōm′brä nā′grä). Peak 6273 ft. in W Chubut territory, S Argentina, on Chile border.

Cum'bres Pass (kŭm′brĕs). Mountain pass 10,003 ft., Conejos co., S Colorado, in San Juan Mts.; used by Indians and early Spanish explorers; highway.

Cum′bri·a (kŭm′brĭ·à). Ancient Celtic kingdom, NW Britain; in Alfred's time formed S half of Strathclyde. Name survives in *Cumberland.*

Cum′bri·an Mountains (kŭm′brĭ·ăn). Range of hills in Cumberland, Westmorland, and Lancashire, NW England; highest peak Scafell Pike 3210 ft., highest mountain in England.

Cu′mières′ (kü′myâr′), *in full* **Cumières-le-Mort-Homme** (-lĕ·môr′-tôm′). Former village, Meuse dept., NE France, ab. 6 m. NW of Verdun just E of Le Mort Homme, on the Meuse; destroyed in fighting around Verdun during World War I.

Cu′mi·ná′ (kōō′mē·ná′). River ab. 150 m. long in N Brazil; flows S and unites with Curuá Panemá to form Curuá river emptying into the Amazon.

Cum′ing (kŭm′ĭng). County in Nebraska. See *Table* at NEBRASKA.

Cum′ming (kŭm′ĭng). Town, ⊗ of Forsyth co., N Georgia; pop. 1561.

Cu·nax′a (ků·năk′sà). Town in ancient Babylonia, E of the Euphrates river ab. 87 m. NW of Babylon; scene of battle 401 B.C. bet. Artaxerxes II of Persia and his brother Cyrus the Younger in which the latter was killed; as a result of the demoralization of Cyrus' army, the Greek mercenary force, originally led by Clearchus, made (401–399 B.C.) their famous Retreat of the Ten Thousand (the *Anabasis*) under Xenophon to Cotyora on the Black Sea.

Cun·di·na·mar′ca (kōōn′dē·nä·mär′kä). Department of Colombia. See *Table* at COLOMBIA.

Cu·ne′ne *or* **Ku·ne′ne** (kōō·nā′nĕ). River 700 m. long, SW Angola, SW Africa; flows S and W to Atlantic Ocean; in its lower course forms a section of the boundary bet. Angola and South-West Africa; in its westward descent to coast are several cataracts, esp. the **Great Cataract** (in 17°25′S, 14°20′E) which falls 330 ft.

Cu′ne·o (kōō′nā·ō). 1 Province of Italy. See *Table* at ITALY.

2 *Fr.* **Co′ni′** (kô′nē′). Commune, its ✱, Piedmont, NW Italy, 69 m. W of Genoa; pop. 35,321; episcopal see.

Cuor·gnè′ (kwôr·nyĕ′). Commune, Aosta prov., Piedmont, NW Italy, 28 m. SE of Aosta; pop. 10,983.

Cu′par (kōō′pēr; -pär). Burgh, ⊗ of Fife co., E Scotland; pop. 5530; site of a 12th-cent. castle of the MacDuffs, earls of Fife.

Cu′pri·ja (tyōō′prē·yä) *or* **Chu′pri·ya** (chōō′-). Town, Serbia, E Yugoslavia, ab. 70 m. SE of Belgrade; pop. 8235; during World War I central ammunition depot of Serbian army; occupied by Germans in World War II.

Cura. See VILLA DE CURA.

Cu·ra·çao′ (kōōr′à·sou′; kür′à·sō′). 1 *since 1949 officially called* **Netherlands Antilles.** Territory of the Netherlands in the West Indies; formerly a colony, now an integral part of the Netherlands kingdom; comprises islands of Curaçao, Bonaire, and Aruba off Venezuela coast, and St. Martin (S section), St. Eustatius, and Saba at N end of Leeward Is.; 403 sq. m.; pop. (1942) 113,956; ✱ Willemstad (on Curaçao). See *Maps* at LESSER ANTILLES and WEST INDIES.

2 Largest island in territory, in the Caribbean Sea 60 m. N of W Venezuela; 36 m. long by 8 m. wide; 210 sq. m.; pop. (1942) 70,022; chief town Willemstad (✱ of the overseas territory); surface generally flat, highest point 1220 ft.; chief products cereals, phosphate, cattle fruits; chief industries oil refining (oil from Venezuela) and manufacture of curaçao liqueur.

History: Discovered by Spaniards 1499, first settled by them 1527; captured by Dutch West India Co. 1634; held by British 1807–15; with Aruba awarded to Netherlands by Treaty of Paris 1815; capital temporarily seized by Venezuelan revolutionaries 1929; in World War II oil refineries on Aruba and Curaçao damaged by shells from German submarines Feb. and Apr. 1942.

Cu·ra·cau·tín′ (kōō′rä·kou·tēn′). Town, Malleco prov., S cen. Chile, 45 m. NE of Temuco; pop. 5740.

Cu·ra·ni·la′hue (kōō·rä′nē·lä′wå). Commune, Arauco prov., S cen. Chile; pop. 13,026; coal mines.

Cu′ra·ray′ (kōō′rä·rä′ē; -rī′). River ab. 190 m. long, rising in E cen. Ecuador and flowing E into Napo river in N Loreto dept., NE Peru.

Cu·re·pipe′ (kür′pēp′). Town and health resort, cen. Mauritius; pop. 19,421.

Cu′res (kū′rēz). Ancient town, Latium, Italy, NE of Rome; famous in legend as original home of Sabines who settled the Quirinal and as birthplace of Numa Pompilius, second king 715–673 B.C. of Rome; site is a hill with two summits and a ditch around the base.

Curia Rhaetorum. See CHUR.

Cu′ri·có′ (kōō′rē·kō′). 1 Province of Chile. See *Table* at CHILE.

2 City, its ✱, cen. Chile, 110 m. S of Santiago; pop. 21,153; founded 1742.

Cu·ri·ti′ba (kōō′rē·tē′vá), *formerly* **Cu′ry·ti′ba** (kōō′-rē-). City, ✱ of Paraná state, S Brazil, ab. 70 m. from the coast; pop. (1940 est.) 101,204.

Cu′ri·ti·ba′nos (kōō′rē·tē·vä′nōos). City, cen. Santa Catarina state, S Brazil; pop. 20,552.

Cur′ragh (kûr′à). Plain in co. Kildare, E Eire, on W bank of the Liffey; site of a racecourse.

Cur·ral′ das Frei′ras (kōōr·räl′ däsh frā′ē·räsh). Vast natural amphitheater in cen. Madeira I.

Cur′rent (kûr′ĕnt). River ab. 250 m. long, flowing from Texas co., S Missouri, E and SE into Black river in Randolph co., NE Arkansas.

Cur′ri·tuck (kûr′ĭ·tŭk). 1 County in North Carolina. See *Table* at NORTH CAROLINA.

2 Village, its ⊗, NE North Carolina; pop. (est.) 250.

Currituck Sound. Sound W of barrier reef in E Currituck co., NE North Carolina, extends N ab. 35 m. from mouth of Albemarle Sound.

Cur′ry (kûr′ĭ). Name of counties in two states of the U.S. See *Tables* at NEW MEXICO and OREGON.

Cur′tea–de–Ar′geş (kōōr′tyä·dĕ·är′jĕsh). Commune, S cen. Romania, on the Argeş SW of Câmpulung; pop. 6831; episcopal see since end of 18th cent.; Byzantine cathedral in monastery grounds to the N.

Cu·ruá′ (kōō·rwä′). River 65 m. long in N Brazil; formed by confluence of Curuá Panemá and Cuminá rivers; flows S into the Amazon.

Curuá Pa′ne·má′ (pá′nĕ·má′). River ab. 170 m. long in N Brazil; flows S and unites with Cuminá river to form Curuá river emptying into the Amazon.

Curupirá, Serra. See SERRA CURUPIRÁ.

Cu′ru·zú′ Cua·tiá′ (kōō′rōō·sōō′ kwä·tyä′). Town, Corrientes prov., NE Argentina, 160 m. SSE of Corrientes; pop. (est.) 15,000.

Cur′wens·ville (kûr′wĕnz·vĭl). Borough, Clearfield co., W cen. Pennsylvania, on West Branch of Susquehanna river 16 m. ESE of Du Bois; pop. 3231; settled 1812; produces fire brick, leather, clay, stone, shirts, hosiery.

Curytiba. See CURITIBA.

Curzola. See KORČULA.

Cur′zon Line (kûr′z'n). A line suggested by Lord Curzon to the Supreme Council in Dec. 1919 as a practical line of demarcation bet. Soviet Russia and the then new state of Poland; began at the S tip of Lithuania just N of Grodno, extended S to the right bank of the Bug river near Brest, then followed the Bug for ab. 200 m., turned W near Sokal and SSW across E Galicia to the N boundary of Czechoslovakia at a point ab. 50 m. S of Przemyśl; primarily an ethnic boundary with areas to W inhabited chiefly by Poles and those to E by Russians. Again used 1920 as basis for armistice bet. Russians and Poles but final E boundary of Poland, fixed by Treaty of Riga 1920, was approximately parallel but 120 to 160 m. farther E. Used in part for German-Russian partition of Poland Sept. 1939 but with W extensions at N and S ends; by Yalta Conference and later action claimed by U.S.S.R. as basis for new boundary bet. U.S.S.R. and Poland.

Cus′ca·tlán′ (kōōs′kä·tlän′). Department, cen. El Salvador; 672 sq. m.; pop. (1942 est.) 106,079; ✳ Cojutepeque.

Cusco. See Cuzco.

Cush or **Kush** (kŭsh). Ancient country in the Nile valley, adjoining Egypt, S of ab. lat. 24°N.

Cush′ing (kōōsh′ĭng). City, Payne co., N cen. Oklahoma, 40 m. W of Sapulpa; pop. 8619; founded 1892; oil and gas wells and refineries; industrial center.

Cushing, Mount. Mountain 8676 ft., N British Columbia, Canada, highest in Stikine Mts.

Cush′man, Lake (kōōsh′măn). Reservoir ab. 10 m. long created by dams (275 and 240 ft. high) completed 1926 across N fork of Skokomish river, Mason co., W Washington; supplies water power for Tacoma.

Cus′set′ (kü′sĕ′). Commune, Allier dept., cen. France, ab. 2 m. E of Vichy; pop. (1931) 8732; mineral springs.

Cus·se′ta (kŭ·sē′tá). Town, ⊗ of Chattahoochee co., W Georgia; pop. 768.

Cus′ter (kŭs′tẽr). **1** Name of counties in six states of the U.S. See *Tables* at COLORADO, IDAHO, MONTANA, NEBRASKA, OKLAHOMA, SOUTH DAKOTA.
2 City and summer resort, ⊗ of Custer co., SW South Dakota, 30 m. SW of Rapid City; pop. 2105; tourist center (near Wind Cave National Park and other scenic spots); gold, silver, lead mines nearby.

Custer, Mount. Peak 8700 ft., NW Montana, in Glacier National Park on Continental Divide.

Custer Battlefield National Monument. See UNITED STATES, *National Monuments.*

Custer Peak. Mountain 6794 ft. in Lawrence co., W South Dakota.

Cu·stoz′za (kōōs·tô′tsä) or **Cu·stoz′za** (-tôt′tsä). Village, Verona prov., Venezia Euganea, NE Italy, 11 m. SW of Verona; pop. (1931) 854; scene of two Italian defeats in wars for unity and independence: (1) July 24, 1848 by Austrians under Count Radetzky; (2) June 24, 1866 by forces of Archduke Albert.

Cüstrin. See KOSTRZYN.

Cut′ Bank′. Town, ⊗ of Glacier co., NW Montana, 95 m. NNW of Great Falls; pop. 4539.

Cutch or **Kutch** (kŭch). Former Indian state in N part of Western Indian States; now in Gujerat state; 8461 sq. m.; pop. (1941) 500,800; ✳ Bhuj; enclosed on W by E mouth of Indus, on SW and S by Arabian Sea and Gulf of Cutch; covered in N and E by the Rann of Cutch; a wild country, with rocky and sandy wastes and scant water supply; population three-quarters Hindu and remainder Mohammedan. Under rule of Mohammedan line of kings from 13th cent. to 19th; established relations with British 1815–22; separated from Bombay prov. 1924.

Cutch, or **Kutch, Gulf of.** Inlet of Arabian Sea S of Cutch and NW of Kathiawar; at its head adjoins the Little Rann of Cutch.

Cutch, or **Kutch, Rann of** (rŭn). Large salt marsh, ab. 9000 sq. m. in NW Gujerat state NW India; the N section is the **Great Rann of Cutch,** and the E section is the **Little Rann of Cutch.**

Cu′thah (kū′thá). Ancient city, Babylonia; devoted to worship of Nergal, ruler of Aralu, the abode of the dead; one of cities from which people were taken by the king of Assyria to colonize Samaria (*2 Kings* xvii. 24).

Cuth′bert (kŭth′bẽrt). City, ⊗ of Randolph co., SW Georgia, 38 m. WNW of Albany; pop. 4300; incorporated 1834; cannery, lumber mills, cotton mills.

Cut′off′ Peak (kŭt′ôf′). Mountain 10,300 ft. in S Montana, in Yellowstone National Park.

Cut′tack (kŭt′ăk). City, formerly ✳ of Orissa, E Indian Union, on Mahanadi river 220 m. SW of Calcutta; pop. 102,505; on Orissa canal system; noted for its excellent silver filigree work; seat of government college and school of engineering. Successively capital of Orissa for Hindu kings, the Great Mogul, and Maratha governors; captured by British in Second Maratha War 1803.

Cutts Peak (kŭts). Mountain 4080 ft. in Washington co., N cen. Vermont.

Cut′ty·hunk′ Island (kŭt′ĭ·hŭngk′). Island, SW Elizabeth Is., Buzzards Bay, SE Massachusetts.

Cux·ha′ven (kōōks·hä′fĕn). Seaport, in West Germany, on North Sea at mouth of Elbe river; pop. 17,648; important fisheries; bathing resort; shipbuilding; frequently bombed by Allied air forces in World War II.

Cuyabá. See CUIABÁ.

Cuy·a·hog′a (kī·á·hŏg′á; kī′á-; ká-; -hô′gá; -hō′gá). **1** River ab. 100 m. long, NE Ohio; rises in Geauga co., flows SW through Portage co. into Summit co., turns abruptly N and flows into Lake Erie at Cleveland; near Akron receives the **Little Cuyahoga** river.
2 County in Ohio. See *Table* at OHIO.

Cuy·a·hog′a Falls (ká·hŏg′á; kí-; -hô′gá; -hō′gá). City, Summit co., NE Ohio, on Cuyahoga river 5 m. N of Akron; pop. 47,922; rubber goods, tires, tools, dies.

Cu′ya·po′ (kōō′yä·pô′). Municipality, NW Nueva Ecija prov., Luzon, Phil. Is.; pop. 24,570.

Cu′yo (kōō′yô). **1** Island group, cen. Phil. Is., N of Sulu Sea and ab. 65 m. E of N end of Palawan I.; ab. 50 sq. m.; pop. 21,358; comprises Cuyo and Agutaya Is., and ab. 45 islets; forms part of Palawan prov.
2 Largest island in group, volcanic in origin; 22 sq. m.; highest point ab. 600 ft.
3 Municipality, coextensive with Cuyo I. and nearby islets; pop. 17,492.

Cuy·u′na Range (kī·ū′ná). Iron-ore belt, cen. Minnesota, in Crow Wing and Aitkin cos., NW of Mille Lacs.

Cu·yu′ni (kōō·yōō′nē). River ab. 300 m. long in N South America; rises in E Venezuela, flows N, then E forming section of Venezuela-British Guiana boundary, continues E across N British Guiana to the Essequibo river near its mouth; just before entering the Essequibo, is joined by the Mazaruni river.

Cuz′co (kōōs′kô), *sometimes written* **Cus′co** (kōōs′-). **1** Peak 17,830 ft. in Potosí dept., SW Bolivia.
2 Department of Peru. See *Table* at PERU.
3 City, its ✳, ab. 350 m. SE of Lima; pop. (1940 est.) 45,158; alt. 11,024 ft.; university, national college, Renaissance cathedral. Sometimes called the "Archaeological Capital of South America," was once capital of vast Inca empire and known as the "City of the Sun"; supposedly founded in 11th cent. by Manco Capac; taken by the Spanish under Pizarro 1533; famous for its ruins of Inca temples, fortresses, walls, and palaces, esp. of the fortress of Sacsahuaman and of the nearby city of Machu Picchu (*qq.v.*) and of the Temple of the Sun.

Cwm·am′man (kōōm·ám′án). Urban district, Carmarthenshire, S Wales; pop. 4593.

Cyc′la·des (sĭk′lá·dēz); *Gr.* **Ky·kla′des** (kyê·klä′thâs). Group of ab. 220 islands in S Aegean Sea, bet. the Peloponnesus and the Dodecanese; 996 sq. m.; pop. 146,987 (1938 est.); administratively a division and a department of Greece (see *Table* at GREECE); ✳ Hermoupolis; chief islands: Andros, Tenos, Naxos, Amorgos, Melos, Paros, Syros, Keos, Kythnos, Seriphos, Ios, and Santorin. So called by the ancients because they formed a circle or cluster (Gr. *kyklos*) around the small island of Delos, then the seat of Delian League (see ATHENS).
History: Under Mycenaean culture 2d millennium B.C.; held successively by Persians, Athenians (after Mycale 479 B.C.), Carians, Ptolemaic Egypt, and Macedonia; ruled by Venetians as duchy of Naxos after 1207; for rest of history, see as part of AEGEAN ISLANDS.

Cy′clone Mountain (sī′klōn). Peak 13,800 ft. in Chaffee co., cen. Colorado.

Cyd′nus (sĭd′nŭs). Historic river in Cilicia, in modern İçel vilayet, Turkey in Asia; flows SE from Taurus Mts. past Tarsus to the Mediterranean.

Cy·do′ni·a (sī·dō′nĭ·á; -dōn′yá). Ancient city on NW coast of Crete, on whose site is modern Canea (q.v.).

Cyl·le′ne (sĭ·lē′nē); *Mod. Gr.* **Kyl·lē′nē** (kĭ·lē′nê; *Gr.* kyê·lyē′nyê) or **Zir′i·a** (zĭr′ĭ·á; *Gr.* zē′ryä). Mountain

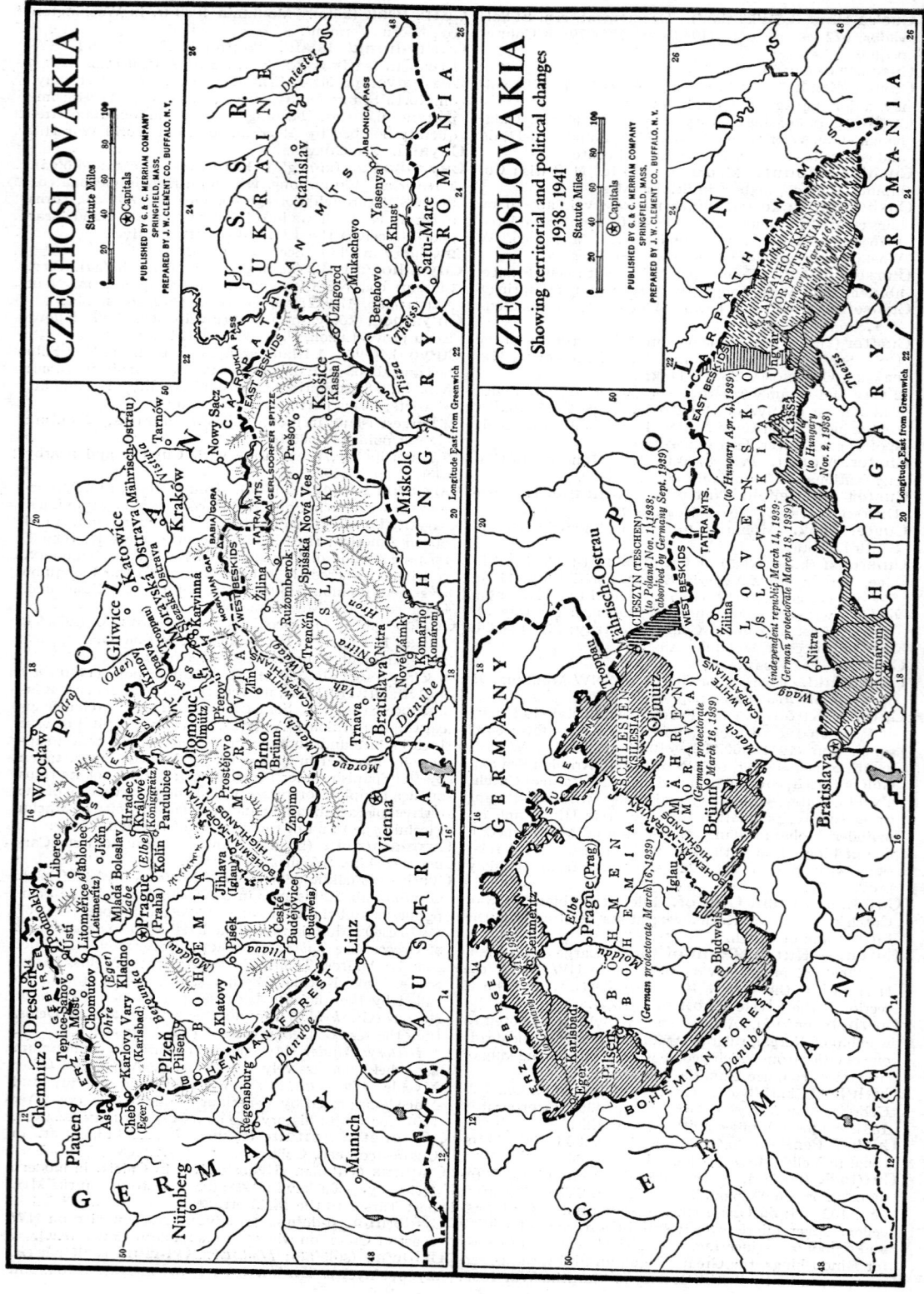

7789 ft., NE Peloponnesus, S Greece; in ancient times was on border bet. Achaea and Arcadia; in Greek legend sacred to Hermes as his birthplace.

Cy'me (sī'mē). City of ancient Aeolis, in Asia Minor, on the W coast N of the mouth of the Hermus.

Cyn'os·ceph'a·lae (sĭn'ŭ·sĕf'á·lē; sī'nŭ-). Two hills in a low range ab. 18 m. SSE of Larissa, SE Thessaly, NE Greece; scene of battles: (1) 364 B.C. in which the Thebans under Pelopidas defeated the tyrant of Pherae; and (2) 197 B.C., the decisive battle of the Second Macedonian War, in which the Roman general T. Quinctius Flamininus defeated King Philip V of Macedon.

Cy'nos·se'ma (sī'nŏ·sē'má; sĭn'ŏ-). Promontory on E side of Chersonesus Thracica (Gallipoli Penin.) off which occurred naval battle 411 B.C. in which Athenians under Alcibiades and Thrasybulus defeated Spartans.

Cyn'o·su'ra (sĭn'ŏ·sōōr'á; sī'nŏ-) or **Kyn'o·su'ra** (kĭn'ŏ·sōōr'á; kī'nŏ-). Promontory, E Salamis I., just SE of Salamis town and opp. Mt. Aegaleos on coast of Attica, Greece, off which occurred battle of Salamis 480 B.C.

Cyn'thi·an'a (sĭn'thĭ·ăn'á). City, ⊗ of Harrison co., N Kentucky, 27 m. NNE of Lexington; pop. 5641.

Cyn'thus (sĭn'thŭs). Mountain, Delos I., Cyclades Is., Aegean Sea; legendary birthplace of Apollo and Artemis.

Cy'press Hills Park (sī'prĕs; -prĭs). Canadian provincial park, S of Maple Creek, SW Saskatchewan prov.

Cy'prus (sī'prŭs). Island, a republic and formerly a British colony, E Mediterranean Sea, 60 m. W of coast of Syria and 40 m. S of coast of Turkey; area 3572 sq. m.; pop. (1956) 528,879; ✳ Nicosia; of irregular shape with a number of wide bays and prominent capes, esp. Cape Andreas which terminates a long narrow peninsula on the NE; in cen. part has a plain, enclosed on N by mountain range which reaches 3357 ft. and on S by range culminating in Mt. Troodos 6403 ft.; no rivers or lakes of any size. Chief occupations agriculture and cattle raising; exports carobs, cattle, wine, raisins, cotton, barley; in early times famous for its copper (the English word derived from Greek name of island, *Kypros*, through the Latin *cuprum*), now produces some chromium ore, asbestos, and gypsum. Chief towns: Nicosia, Limassol, Larnaca, Famagusta, and Kyrenia; has ruins of several famous towns of ancient times, esp. Citium and Paphos.

History: Colonized by Phoenicians and ancient Greeks; ruled by Assyrian, Persian (after 525 B.C.), Ptolemaic, and Roman Empires (see PAPHOS); as part of Byzantine Empire, frequently raided or captured by Saracens 7th–10th cents. A.D.; captured by Richard I of England during Third Crusade 1191; sold to Lusignan dynasty which ruled 1192–1474; Famagusta, leading port, held by Genoese 1376–1464; 1489 acquired by Venetians whom Turks expelled 1571; according to convention with Turkey, administered by Great Britain 1878–1914; annexed by British at outbreak of war with Turkey 1914; made a crown colony 1925; became a republic in the British Commonwealth 1960.

Cyr'e·na'i·ca (sĭr'ē·nā'ĭ·ká; sī'rĕ-). See CIRENAICA.

Cy·re'ne (sī·rē'nē); *Ital.* **Ci·re'ne** (chē·rā'nā). Ancient city in North Africa, founded by Greeks c. 630 B.C.; original capital of Cyrenaica and a city of the Pentapolis; taken by Alexander the Great 331 B.C. and soon after came under the Ptolemies; belonged to Romans after 96 B.C.; has interesting ruins. See CIRENE.

Cyrus. See KURA.

Cythera. See CERIGO.

Cythnos. See KYTHNOS.

Cyz'i·cus (sĭz'ĭ·kŭs). **1** *modern* **Ka'pı·da·ğı'** (kä'-pĭ·dä·ĭ'). Peninsula, triangular in shape, on S coast of the Sea of Marmara, Balıkesir vilayet, NW Turkey in Asia; in ancient times said to have been an island. **2** Ancient city, Mysia, Asia Minor, on isthmus leading to Cyzicus Penin. on Sea of Marmara; founded by Greeks from Miletus 756 B.C.; in naval battle off its shore 410 B.C. Alcibiades destroyed Spartan fleet.

Czar'no·ho'ra (chär'nô·hô'rä). Peak 6750 ft., SW Ukraine, U.S.S.R., on former boundary bet. Poland and Carpathian Ruthenia, Czechoslovakia.

Czech'i·a (chĕk'ĭ·á). Occasional short form of CZECHOSLOVAKIA.

Czech'o·slo·va'ki·a, *also* **Czech'o–Slo·va'ki·a** (chĕk'ŏ·slō·vä'kĭ·á; -văk'ĭ·á); *Czech* **Čes'ko·slo'ven·sko** (chĕs'kŏ·slŏ'vĕn·skô). Republic, cen. Europe; as created 1918 was bounded on N by Germany and Poland, on extreme E by Romania, on S by Hungary and Austria, and on W by Germany; area (1935) 54,244 sq. m., (1945) 49,373 sq. m.; pop. (1930) 14,729,536, (1946) 13,452,980; ✳ Prague; now has U.S.S.R. on extreme E. *Mountains:* Mountainous country, Bohemia shut in on SW by the Bohemian Forest (Böhmer Wald), on the NW by Erz Gebirge, and on NE by the Sudeten Mts. which also extend into N Moravia; Moravia crossed by several ranges NE to SW, esp. the Bohemian-Moravian Highlands on W border; Slovakia separated from Poland on N by Carpathian Mts. (containing highest point in country Gerlachovka 8737 ft.) and on NW by White Carpathian Mts. *Rivers:* Labe (upper Elbe) in Bohemia and its important branches, the Ohře, Berounka, and Vltava; in Moravia the upper courses of the Oder (*Czech* Odra) and March (*Czech* Morava); in Slovakia numerous tributaries of the Danube and Tisza (Váh, Nitra, Hron). *Industries:* Manufacture of sugar, beer, foodstuffs, shoes, glassware; agriculture, lumbering, and mining also extensively developed. *Chief cities:* Prague, Brno, Moravská Ostrava, Bratislava, Plzeň, and Olomouc. For administrative purposes divided since 1945 in 3 provinces, Bohemia, Moravia and Silesia, and Slovakia.

History: See BOHEMIA, MORAVIA, SLOVAKIA, SILESIA, and CARPATHIAN RUTHENIA; republic formed in 1918 by Czechs and Slovaks from territories formerly part of the Austro-Hungarian Empire; Tomáš G. Masaryk first president 1918–35; received Teschen after dispute with Poland 1919–20; ratified constitution and began its operation 1920; entered treaty with Yugoslavia 1920, with Romania 1921 (basis of Little Entente); allied with France 1924; political life disturbed by minority demands for autonomy, including those of Sudeten Germans who were supported by Hitler's Germany; after Munich agreement which settled German-Czech crisis of 1938, Sudetenland annexed to Germany, Teschen to Poland, and a strip of Slovakia and of Ruthenia to Hungary; Slovakia and Ruthenia, given autonomy 1938, declared independence 1939; remainder of Czech state became German protectorate of Bohemia and Moravia (*q.v.*) 1939–45; after World War II lost Carpathian Ruthenia (Carpatho-Ukraine) to the U.S.S.R.; formed close political and economic union with Russia, and by Communist coup Feb. 1948 came under Soviet domination. ◼

Czeg'léd (tsĕg'lād). = CEGLÉD.

Cze'ladź (chĕ'lädz·y'); *Ger.* **Tsche'li·ads** (chä'lĕ·äts). Commune, E Śląsk dept., SW Poland, 4 m. NW of Sosnowiec; pop. (1938–39 est.) 21,035; coal industry.

Czenstochau. See CZĘSTOCHOWA.

Czernowitz. See CHERNOVTSY.

Czę'sto·cho'wa (chĕn'stô·kô'vä); *Russian* **Chen·sto·khov'** (chĭn·stŭ·kôf'); *Ger.* **Czen'sto·chau** (chĕn'stô-kou). Industrial city, Kielce dept., Poland, on Warta river 65 m. WSW of Kielce; pop. (1938–39 est.) 138,000; episcopal see; railroad junction; manufactures include textiles, paper, steel, iron, leather; famous shrine of Virgin in ancient monastery. A historic town, very wealthy in 15th cent.; resisted siege by Swedes 1655 and 1705; taken by Russians 1772, by Prussians 1793; in World War I captured by Germans Nov. 1914, in World War II again captured by Germans Sept. 1939.

Czort'ków (chôrt'kŏŏf). Town, W Ukraine, U.S.S.R., 38 m. S of Ternopol (formerly in Tarnopol dept., Poland); pop. (1938–39 est.) 19,038; chief occupation agriculture; manufactures brandy, tobacco.

D

Da·an'ban'ta·yan' (dä-än'bän'tä-yän'). Municipality on coast at N tip of Cebu I., Phil. Is., 69 m. N of City of Cebu; pop. 24,198.

Daba, El. See EL DABA.

Da·bhoi' (däb·hoi'). Town, SE Gujerat state, W India, 20 m. SE of Baroda; pop. 18,156; has fine architectural remains of Hindu temples, gates, etc.

Da'bob Bay (dä'bŏb). Inlet of Hood Canal, Jefferson co., W Washington.

Dą·bro'wa Gór·ni'cza (dônm·brô'vä gōōr·nē'chä); *Ger.* **Dom'brau** (dôm'brou). Coal-mining commune, Śląsk Dąbrowski dept., S Poland, just E of Katowice; pop. (1938–39 est.) 41,373.

Dac'ca (dăk'à). **1** Division, formerly in E Bengal, NE Brit. India; since Aug. 1947 forms cen. part of East Bengal, Pakistan; 15,498 sq. m.; pop. (1941) 16,683,714. **2** City, its ✳, just W of Meghna river 160 m. ENE of Calcutta; pop. (1941) 213,218; produces fine muslins, gold and silver jewelry, and handsomely carved shells; operates shipyards. Site of French, Dutch, and English trading posts at various times; capital of Mogul province of East Bengal 1608–1704 and of former British province of Eastern Bengal and Assam 1905–12. Seat of Dacca Univ. (estab. 1921).

Da'chau (däκ'ou). Town, Upper Bavaria govt. dist., Bavaria, Germany, 10 m. NNW of Munich on the Ammer river; pop. 7148; site, prior to and during World War II, of large concentration camp, captured by Allies Apr. 29, 1945 (32,000 prisoners liberated).

Dach'stein' (däκ'shtīn'). Highest peak 9829 ft. in the **Dachstein Mountains** in W cen. Austria, ab. 35 m. SE of Salzburg; mountains form part of boundary where the three provinces—Salzburg, Styria, and Upper Austria—meet.

Da'ci·a (dä'shǐ·à; -shá). Ancient country, cen. Europe; ✳ Sarmizegetusa; bounded on N by Carpathians, NE by the Tyras (Dniester), E and S by Danubius (Danube), and W by the Tissus (Tisza); roughly equivalent to modern Romania including Transylvania.

History: Inhabited before Roman conquest by Getae and Dacians, peoples of Thracian stock, who invaded Roman Empire in Domitian's reign; conquered by Trajan, and made Roman province at death of Dacian king, Decebalus, 107 A.D.; fortified and colonized by Rome as its trans-Danube frontier; abandoned to Goths when Aurelian withdrew Roman colonists to a new Dacia carved out of Moesia (*q.v.*) 270; region of older Dacia invaded by Goths, Huns, Avars, Bulgars, Magyars, Pechenegs, and Cumans before founding of principalities, Walachia and Moldavia (*qq.v.*).

Dade (dād). Name of counties in three states of the U.S. See *Tables* at FLORIDA, GEORGIA, MISSOURI.

Dade City. City, ⊗ of Pasco co., W Florida penin., 35 m. NE of Tampa; pop. 4759; center of truck-farming and citrus-growing region; kaolin deposits nearby.

Dade'ville (dād'vĭl; *Sou. also* -v'l). Town, ⊗ of Tallapoosa co., E Alabama; pop. 2940; lumber; asbestos.

Daer Water. See CLYDE river, Scotland.

Da'et (dä'āt). Municipality, ✳ of Camarines Norte, near coast in SE part of province, Luzon, Phil. Is.; pop. 20,066; chief commercial town of province; rice mills.

Da·ga'mi (dä·gä'mĕ). Municipality, N cen. Leyte I., Phil. Is., 16 m. SSW of Tacloban; pop. 22,776; on E slope of mountains. Taken by Americans Oct. 29, 1944.

Dag'en·ham (dăg'năm). Urban district, Essex, SE England, NE suburb of London; pop. 89,362, (1951) 114,588; part of Greater London; automobiles.

Dag'es·tan' *or* **Dagh'es·tan'** (dăg'ĕs·tăn'; *Russ.* dà·gĕ·stän'); *officially* **Dagestan Autonomous Soviet Socialist Republic.** Autonomous republic, SE Soviet Russia, Europe, on W shore of Caspian Sea; 13,124 sq. m.; pop. 930,527, (1941 est.) 977,800; ✳ Makhachkala; a

subdivision of the R.S.F.S.R.; bounded on NW and N by Grozny Region, on E by Caspian Sea, on S by Azerbaidzhan, and on W by Georgian S.S.R. Along its S and SW border stretch the Caucasus Mts.; the S two thirds a mountainous region, the N part and along the Caspian mostly sandy plain and salt marsh; the rivers are comparatively short mountain streams; forests small, little good agricultural land; main occupation raising cattle and sheep; large but undeveloped mineral resources, esp. oil, iron, sulfur, quicksilver. Predominant ethnic strain Japhetic (Caucasian); chief nationalities Lezghian 64½%, Russian 12½%. Chief towns Makhachkala, Derbent.

History: From early times inhabited by warlike tribes; ceded by Persia to Russia 1813; not subjugated until 1859 (see GUNIB); rose again during Russo-Turkish War 1877; formed separate republic 1917; scene of severe fighting until 1921 and of subsequent famine; became autonomous republic 1921 in North Caucasus Region of U.S.S.R.; reorganized 1936 with change of boundaries.

Dag'gett (dăg'ĕt; -ĭt). Co. in Utah. See *Table* at UTAH.

Dagö. See KHIUMA.

Da'go Peak (dä'gō). Mountain 4999 ft. in Shoshone co., NE Idaho.

Da·gu'pan (dä·gōō'pän). Municipality, N Pangasinan prov., Luzon, Phil. Is., on S shore of Lingayen Gulf 6 m. E of Lingayen; pop. 32,602; most important commercial port of the province; manufacturing.

Da'ha·na (dä'há·nà). See RUB' AL KHALI.

Dah'lak Archipelago (dä'lăk; *Arab.* dä'h'·läk); *Ital.* **I'so·le Da'ha·lach'** (ē'zō·lä dä'ä·läk'). Island group, S Red Sea, off Bay of Massaua on coast of Eritrea; pop. ab. 2000; belongs to Eritrea; **Dahlak,** chief island, 23 m. long and 15 m. wide.

Dah·lon'e·ga (dä·lŏn'ĕ·gà). City, ⊗ of Lumpkin co., N Georgia; pop. 2152; settled 1833; gold-mining town; trading center; site of a branch of United States mint 1838–61. North Georgia Coll. (1873; coed.).

Dah'na (dä'h'·nà). See RUB' AL KHALI.

Da·ho'mey (dà·hō'mĭ; *Fr.* dà·ō'mā'). Republic, former French territory, West Africa, extending N from the Gulf of Guinea bet. Republic of Togo and Nigeria; 44,696 sq. m.; pop. 1,351,936, (1945 est.) 1,458,000; ✳ Porto-Novo; from the coast, which is a line of lagoons, inland the land is at first flat and covered with vegetation, then (at ab. 50 m.) extends as a great marsh, opening up N to the Niger in a high plateau (part of Borgu region); chief products palm oil and palm kernels, also cotton, coffee, and maize; inhabited by Fon branch of Ewe-speaking tribes; chief towns Porto-Novo, Cotonou, Ouidah, Abomey.

History: Negro kingdom which, in 17th cent., rose around Abomey; expanded north and to Slave Coast on south; coastal footholds, Cotonou and Porto-Novo, gained by French who finally captured Abomey and deposed ruler in 1892; made a French colony 1894 and part of French West Africa 1895; boundaries with Togo and Lagos determined in treaties with Germany 1897 and Great Britain 1898; made an overseas territory of the French Union 1946; became an autonomous republic of the French Community.

Dahr el Qa·dib' (dä'h'r ăl kŏ·dēb'). Highest peak 10,131 ft. of the Lebanon Mts., N Lebanon.

Dah·shûr' *or* **Da·shur'** (dä·shoor'; *Arab.* dä·h'·shoor'). Site near Memphis, Egypt, of pyramid built by Sesostris III (c. 1887–1849 B.C.).

Dai·do (dī·dō) *or* **Tae·dong** (tä·dŏong). River and inlet, NW Korea; river ab. 200 m. long) flows SSW into the Yellow Sea near Chinnampo.

Dai'gle·ville (dä'g'l·vĭl; *Sou. also* -v'l). Urban community (unincorporated), Terrebonne parish, SE Louisiana, S of Baton Rouge; pop. 5906.

Dai·ho·ku (dī·hŏ·kŏō). = TAIHOKU.

Dai·miel′ (dī·myĕl′). Manufacturing commune, Ciudad Real prov., S cen. Spain, 19 m. ENE of Ciudad Real; pop. 19,759; manufactures linens, woolens, liquors, soap, lace; Gothic and Doric parish churches.

Dai·nan (dī·nän). = TAINAN.

Dain′ger·field (dān′jẽr·fēld). Town, ⊗ of Morris co., NE Texas; pop. 3133.

Dai Nippon. See JAPAN; NIPPON.

Dai′qui·rí′ (dī′kǐ·rē′; *Span.* -kê-). Barrio, El Caney municipality, Oriente prov., E Cuba, on coast 14 m. E of Santiago Bay; American troops landed June 22, 1898.

Dai′ren′ (dī′rĕn′); *Russ.* **Dal′ny** (dàl′y′·nyǐ); *Chin.* **Ta′lien′** or **Ta′lien′wan′** (dä′lĕ·ĕn′wän′). City and treaty port, ✳ of former Japanese leased territory of Kwantung on S coast of Liaotung Penin., 20 m. E of Port Arthur; pop. (1938 est.) 533,696; has one of finest harbors on East Asia coast; sheltered on N, W, and S by hills; connects by rail with Mukden and railroad system of E China. A fine modern city, first laid out as commercial seaport and terminus of Siberian railroad by edict of Russian tsar July 30, 1899; opened to commerce 1901; in Russo-Japanese War occupied by Japanese May 1904; part of Kwantung (*q.v.*) leased to Japan by Treaty of Portsmouth Sept. 1905; again a free port 1906. In World War II bombed by American planes Sept.–Dec. 1944; taken by Russians Aug. 1945; by Chinese-Soviet treaty of Aug. 1945 remained under Chinese sovereignty but a port with preferential rights for Russians.

Dai Sen (dī sĕn) or **O·ya·ma** (ō·yä·mä; *Angl.* ō·yä′mȧ). Peak 5620 ft. in Tottori prefecture, W Honshu, Japan, SE of Matsue; a beautiful cone-shaped peak, the highest of the volcanic peaks of SW Honshu.

Dai·set′ta (dā·zĕt′ȧ). City, Liberty co., E Texas, ab. 32 m. W of Beaumont; pop. 1500; oil wells; sawmills.

Da′ja·bón′ (dä′hä·vôn′). Commune, ✳ of Libertador prov., NW Dominican Republic; pop. (1941) 9267.

Dakahliya. Var. of *Daqahlīya:* see *Table* at EGYPT.

Da·kar′ (dä·kär′; dȧ-). Seaport, ✳ of Senegal and of former French West Africa, on S side of Cape Vert Penin.; pop. (1956 est.) 230,900; with Gorée, Rufisque, and adjacent area formed from 1924 to 1946 an autonomous circumscription, **Dakar and Dependencies** (60 sq. m.); has one of best harbors on Atlantic coast of Africa; of strategic importance as dominating W tip of Africa equidistant (1860 m.) from Brazil and Europe; airport is at Ouakam just NNW.

History: Founded 1857 opp. settlement of Gorée (*q.v.*) which had been French since 17th cent.; railroad built from Dakar to Saint-Louis 1882–85; became naval base and, in 1902, capital of French West Africa (*q.v.*); after defeat of France, attacked unsuccessfully by forces of Free French and British Sept. 23–25, 1940; by decree of May 17, 1946 reunited with Senegal. Became capital of Senegal 1958.

Dakh′la (däk′lä). Oasis in Southern Desert prov., Egypt, lat. 25°30′N and long. 29°E; chief town El Qasr.

Da·ko′ta (dȧ·kō′tȧ). **1** *often called* **James** (jāmz). Name, by act of Territorial legislature, of river in North Dakota and South Dakota; 710 m. long; rises in Wells co., cen. North Dakota, flows S across E cen. South Dakota and empties into Missouri river at Yankton, Yankton co., SE South Dakota.

2 Name of counties in two states of the U.S. See *Tables* at MINNESOTA and NEBRASKA.

Dakota City. 1 Town, ⊗ of Humboldt co., NW cen. Iowa; pop. 706.

2 Village, ⊗ of Dakota co., NE Nebraska; pop. 928.

Dakota Territory. Former territory, U.S.A., named from important group of Siouan tribes; comprised the region on both sides of the middle course of Missouri river and W of the Red River of the North. First visited by La Vérendrye brothers 1742–43; greater part included in Louisiana Purchase 1803; N limit of NE section determined by treaty with Great Britain 1818; parts included in various territories of the U.S. bet. 1805 and 1861; or-

ganized as Dakota Territory (capital Yankton 1861–83, Bismarck 1883–89) Mar. 2, 1861 including much of Wyoming and Montana; reduced to area of present two states 1868; settlement hastened by discovery of gold 1874 in the Black Hills; admitted to the Union Nov. 2, 1889, by division into two states, "the Dakotas"— North Dakota and South Dakota (*qq.v.*).

Đakovica, Đakovo. See DJAKOVICA, DJAKOVO.

Dak′shin (dŭk′shǐn). Island 615 sq. m. in Meghna river, SE East Bengal, Pakistan.

Dal (dŭl). Lake near Srinagar (*q.v.*), Kashmir, India.

Dal (däl). River 250 m. long in S cen. Sweden, formed by two forks, the **Ös′ter Dal** (ûs′tẽr) and **Väs′ter Dal** (vĕs′tẽr); flows SE into Gulf of Bothnia.

Da′la·gue′te (dä′lä·gä′tȧ). Municipality on E coast of Cebu I., Phil. Is., near S end on Bohol Strait 46 m. SSW of City of Cebu; pop. 27,284.

Dalai Nor. See HULUN NOR.

Da·la·man′ (dä·lä·män′). River ab. 100 m. long in SW Turkey in Asia; flows S to the Mediterranean.

Dalarna, Dalarne. See DALECARLIA.

Dalbo. See VÄNERN.

Dal′by (dôl′bǐ). Town, SE Queensland, Australia, in Darling Downs region on Condamine river 115 m. WNW of Brisbane; pop. 2965.

Dale (dāl). **1** County in Alabama. See *Table* at ALABAMA.

2 Borough, Cambria co., SW cen. Pennsylvania, near Johnstown; pop. 2807.

Dal′e·car′li·a (dăl′ē·kär′lǐ·ȧ); *Swed.* **Da′lar·na′** (dä′lär·nä′) or **Da′lar·ne** (-nĕ). Region in W cen. Sweden, about equivalent to the province of Kopparberg (see *Table* at SWEDEN); region of many historical associations; its people noted for their dialect, colorful costumes, and patriotism, esp. in 15th and 16th cents. (revolted against Eric XIII 1434–36, were strong supporters of Gustavus Vasa 1519–23). Rich in forests and iron and copper mines.

Dale′garth Force (dāl′gärth fōrs′). Waterfall in W Cumberland, NW England, in the Lake District.

Dal′elf′, Dal′älv′ (däl′ĕlv′). = DAL river, Sweden.

Dal′ga (däl′gȧ). Town, Asyût prov., Upper Egypt, on left bank of Nile ab. 45 m. below Asyût; pop. ab. 15,000.

Dal′hart (dăl′härt). City, Dallam and Hartley cos., NW corner of Texas, in the Panhandle; ⊗ of Dallam co.; 70 m. NNW of Amarillo; pop. 5160; ships cattle and grain.

Dal·hou′sie (dăl·hou′zǐ). **1** Seaport town, ⊗ of Restigouche co., N New Brunswick, Canada, on Chaleur Bay at mouth of Restigouche river; pop. 4939; founded 1810; extensive lumber, lobster, and salmon trade; resort.

2 (*Ind.* dŭl·hou′zē) Town and hill station, Gurdaspur dist., N East Punjab, NW Indian Union, 140 m. NE of Lahore; pop. 1030; in Himalayas just E of upper Ravi river, geographically in Chamba state; elevation 7700 ft.

Dali. See IDALIUM.

Da·lí′as (dä·lē′äs). Commune, Almería prov., SE Spain, 18 m. WSW of Almería; pop. 11,697; lead mines; mineral baths nearby.

Dal·keith′ (dăl·kēth′; dȧl-). Burgh, Midlothian co., SE Scotland; pop. 8786; trading center for grain; coal mining, brass founding; Dalkeith palace, residence of several British monarchs, has a noted picture gallery.

Dall (dôl). Narrow island ab. 45 m. long, SW of Prince of Wales I., S Alexander Archipelago, SE Alaska.

Dal′lam (dăl′ăm). County in Texas. See *Table* at TEXAS.

Dal′las (dăl′ăs; *Sou.* also -ĭs). **1** Name of counties in five states of the U.S. See *Tables* at ALABAMA, ARKANSAS, IOWA, MISSOURI, TEXAS.

2 City, ⊗ of Paulding co., NW Georgia, 30 m. WNW of Atlanta; pop. 2065; lumber and cotton mills; scene of indecisive battle bet. the armies of Grant and Lee May 25–28, 1864 (battle of New Hope Church).

3 Town, Gaston co., SW North Carolina, 5 m. N of Gastonia; pop. 3270; was ⊗ 1846–1911.

4 City, ⊗ of Polk co., NW Oregon, 15 m. W of Salem; pop. 5072; settled 1845; lumber, leather, prunes.

5 Residential borough, Luzerne co., E Pennsylvania, 9 m. NNW of Wilkes-Barre; pop. 2586. College Misericordia (1923; women).

6 Industrial and commercial city, ⊗ of Dallas co., NE Texas, on Trinity river ab. 33 m. E of Fort Worth; pop. 679,684; site first settled 1841; platted 1846 and became ⊗; incorp. as town 1856, as city 1871. Cotton market, oil capital, and insurance center; manufactures cotton gins and other machinery, cottonseed and petroleum products, cotton textiles, airplanes and parts, furniture; meat packing, motorcar assembling, printing and publishing; Hensley Field, U.S. Air Force base. Southern Methodist Univ. (1910; coed.); Dallas Theological Seminary and Graduate School of Theology (1925); Univ. of Dallas (1956; coed.). Scene of Texas Centennial Exposition (1936), Pan American Exposition (1937).

Dallas, Lake. See GARZA DAM, Texas.

Dallas Peak. Mountain 13,800 ft. in Ouray and San Miguel cos., SW Colorado.

Dal′las·town (dăl′ăs·toun). Borough, York co., S Pennsylvania, 6 m. SE of York; pop. 3615.

Dalles, The. 1 *or* **Dalles City.** See THE DALLES, Oregon.

2 See SAINT CROIX river, Wisconsin and Minnesota.

Dal·ma′ti·a (dăl·mā′shǐ·à; -shà); *Serbo-Croat.* **Dal′-ma·ci·ja** (däl′mä·tsĕ·yä). Former Austrian crownland on the Adriatic coast; ab. 4916 sq. m.; extended from near Albanian border on the S to Zadar on the N and included many islands; name later applied to most of the Yugoslav coast; mountainous (Dinaric Alps), many good harbors.

History: Conquered by Rome 34 B.C.; province of prefecture of Illyricum (*q.v.*) under Diocletian (d. 313 A.D.); in western part of Roman Empire after division of 395; part of Gothic kingdom of Odoacer; reconquered by Eastern Roman Empire under Justinian; invaded and settled by Slavonic peoples in 7th cent.; possession of coastal towns the goal of successive rulers of Croatia, Hungary, and Serbia, with Venetians endeavoring to gain foothold from 10th cent.; coast came under rule of Venice, 1420–1699; province, including interior, finally ceded to Venice by Turkey 1718; with suppression of Venetian Republic, held by Austria 1797–1805, 1813–1918 (part of Illyrian Provinces 1809–13); partly occupied by Italy 1918–19; joined kingdom of Serbs, Croats, and Slovenes 1918 (see YUGOSLAVIA); Zara (Zadar) held by Italy which was forced to give up her other Dalmatian claims in Treaty of Rapallo 1920. In World War II seizure attempted by Germans but for the most part held under control of Yugoslav partisans; since 1945 included in federated republics of Croatia and Montenegro in Yugoslavia.

Dal·men′y (dăl·mĕn′ǐ; dăl-). Village and parish, West Lothian co., Scotland, on Firth of Forth; pop. (parish) 3691; cathedral.

Dal·ness′ (dăl·nĕs′; dăl-). Deer forest, N Argyll co., W Scotland, NE of Loch Etive; 7520 acres.

Dalny. See DAIREN.

Dal′ri·a·da (dăl′rǐ·à′dà; *Angl.* dăl′rǐ·à′dà, -ăd′à). **1** Ancient kingdom, N Ireland; now N part of co. Antrim.

2 Ancient kingdom, Argyll co., W Scotland; founded ab. 500 A.D. by emigrants from the Irish kingdom.

Dal′ton (dôl′t′n). **1** Industrial city, ⊗ of Whitfield co., NW Georgia, 38 m. N of Rome; pop. 17,868; incorp. 1847, ⊗ 1851; headquarters of Gen. Joseph E. Johnston 1863–64; cotton and lumber mills; center of candlewick bedspread industry.

2 Town, Berkshire co. W Massachusetts, 5 m. ENE of Pittsfield; pop. 6436; paper manufacturing.

Dal′ton·ganj′ (dôl′t′n·gŭnj′; dŭl′tŏn·gŭnj′). Town, Chota Nagpur division, W Bihar state, NE Indian Union; pop. 12,040; coal-mining region.

Dal′ton in Fur′ness (dôl′t′n; fûr′nĕs, -nǐs). Urban

district, Lancashire, NW England, near Irish Sea 52 m. N of Liverpool; pop. 10,394.

Da′lu·pi′ri (dä′loo·pē′rē). **1** Island in Babuyan group, N of Luzon, Phil. Is.; 24 sq. m.; pop. 240.

2 Island off NW coast of Samar, Phil. Is., on S side of San Bernardino Strait bet. Capul I. and Samar coast; 11 sq. m.; pop. (San Antonio municipality) 6421.

Da′ly (dā′lǐ). River ab. 300 m. long, N Northern Territory, Australia, flows W to Anson Bay; navigable for 70 m.

Daly City. Residential city, San Mateo co., W California, S suburb of San Francisco; pop. 44,791; absorbed town of Colma 1936.

Daly Waters. Village and post station on upper Roper river, N cen. Northern Territory, Australia; on Defense Highway and terminus of railroad to Darwin.

Dam (dăm). Town on Suriname river, E Surinam; terminus of only railroad in Surinam, 107 m. S from Paramaribo.

Da′man·hûr′ (dä′măn·hoor′); *anc.* **Her·mop′o·lis Par′va** (hĕr·mŏp′ô·lǐs pär′và). City, ✳ of Beheira prov., N Lower Egypt, on railroad E of Alexandria and W of Rosetta branch of the Nile; pop. (1937) 61,962.

Da·mão′ (dȧ·moun′) *or* **Da·man′** (dȧ·män′). **1** District of Portuguese India, including Nagar Aveli region; 148 sq. m.; pop. 57,000.

2 Its chief town, a seaport, W India, on Gulf of Cambay at mouth of Damanganga river 100 m. N of Bombay; pop. ab. 7000; once an active harbor, but now of decreasing importance; carries on fishing, shipbuilding, salt extracting, and cotton weaving; destroyed by Portuguese 1531, and recaptured and annexed 1559.

Da·mar′ (dȧ·mär′). See DHAMAR, Yemen, Arabia.

Da′mar (dä′mär). Group of small islands in S Banda Sea NW of Babar Is., S Moluccas, E Malay Archipelago; part of the Serawatti Is.; pop. ab. 2000. Chief island Damar, ab. 11 m. in diameter, has active volcano.

Da·ma·ra·land′ (dȧ·mär′à·länd′; dăm′à·rȧ-). Region, cen. South-West Africa; a plateau region inhabited chiefly by the Damara, a race including two different peoples: the warlike Herero of Bantu stock (hence **Her·re′ro·land′** [hĕ·rā′rô·länd′] as an alternative name) and the Hill Damara of Hottentot and mixed breeds. Chief occupation cattle raising.

Dam′a·ri·scot′ta River (dăm′à·rǐ·skŏt′à; *locally* dăm′-à·skŏt′ǐ). Narrow inlet of the Atlantic Ocean, 22 m. long, on the coast of Lincoln co., S Maine.

Da·mas′cus (dȧ·măs′kŭs); *French* **Da′mas′** (dȧ′mä′; -mäs′); *Arab.* **Esh Shâm** (ăsh shäm′). City, ✳ of the Republic of Syria, on the Barada river, with Anti-Liban Mts. to the W and desert to the E; pop. (1935) 193,912; believed to be the oldest city in the world having continuous existence; connected by highway and railroad across the mountains with Beirut ab. 53 m. to the NW and by rail with Homs and Hama to the N and with Ma′an in Jordan to the S; for centuries a great trade mart with many shops and bazaars; situated on edge of an oasis near beautiful gardens and groves; has Great Mosque (partly ruined), many small mosques, schools, and missions.

History: Ancient city ruled by Egyptians and Hittites before it became an independent Aramaean kingdom c. 1000 B.C.; prominent in Hebrew history; fell before Assyrians 732 B.C.; later included in kingdoms of Babylonians, Persians, Alexander the Great, Ptolemies, and Seleucids; 661 A.D. became residence of caliph until overthrow of Ommiad line 750; frequently attacked during Crusades; occupied 1918 by British and Arabs as part of campaign in Syria; center of Syrian independence movement until seized by French 1920 and made a state in French mandate of Syria; united with Alep to form state of Syria 1925; forced by bombardment to submit to French after its occupation 1925 by Druses; captured by Free French and British June 1941.

Damavand. See DEMAVEND.

Dâm′bo·vi′ţa (dĭm′bô·vē′tsä). River ab. 150 m. long in S cen. Romania; flows out of the Transylvanian Alps SSE past Bucharest into the Argeş river.

Damer, Ed. See ED DAMER.

Dam·ghan′ (däm·gän′). Town, NW Khurasan prov., NE Iran; pop. ab. 16,500; on main highway from Tehran to Khurasan and terminus of railroad E from Tehran; has large trade in almonds and pistachios; was of greater importance in the Middle Ages; has interesting ruins dating from the 11th cent. See HECATOMPYLOS.

Dam′i·et′ta (däm′ĭ·ĕt′á; däm·yĕt′á); *Arab.* **Dim·yāṭ′** (dŏŏm·yät′). **1** Governorate, N Egypt. See 2, below, and *Table* at EGYPT.

2 Commercial city, N Egypt, port at mouth of the Damietta branch of the Nile, on E bank in the Nile delta 8 m. from the sea; pop. (1937) 40,332; constitutes the governorate of Damietta; conquered by Crusaders 1219; taken by French Crusaders 1249.

3 *anc.* **Phat·nit′ic** (făt·nĭt′ĭk). Eastern mouth of the Nile, W of Port Said; partly silted up and not navigable to large vessels.

Dam′loup′ (däN′lŏŏ′). Village, Meuse dept., NE France, 5 m. NE of Verdun; pop. (1931) 118; severe fighting 1916 during World War I.

Dam·mam′ (däm·mäm′). Oil center, al-Hasa, Saudi Arabia, near coast of Persian Gulf opp. Bahrein I.

Dam′ma′rie′, Cape (dá′má·rē′). Cape at NW point of Tiburon Penin., SW Haiti, on S side of entrance to Gulf of Gonaïves.

Dammarie-les-Lys (-lä·lēs′). Commune, Seine-et-Marne dept., N France, near Melun; pop. (1931) 5074; ruins of 13th-cent. abbey founded by Blanche of Castile.

Da′mo·dar (dä′mō·där). Navigable river ab. 350 m. long in cen. Bihar and West Bengal states, NE Indian Union; flows ESE into Hooghly river just below Nadia; planned to be a great power development.

Da′moh (dŭm′ō). Town, N Madhya Pradesh, **190 m. N** of Nagpur; pop. 20,728; market place **for cattle and** farm produce of district; pillaged by **mutineers in Sepoy** Mutiny 1857.

Dam′pier Archipelago (däm′pēr). Group of ab. 20 small rocky islands off NW coast of Western Australia, lat. 20°40′S.

Dampier Land. Peninsula, N Western Australia, bet. Indian Ocean and King Sound; Cape Leveque at tip.

Dampier Strait. 1 Passage ab. 15 m. wide off W end of New Britain I., Bismarck Archipelago, W Pacific Ocean; separates New Britain from Umboi I.

2 Channel ab. 100 m. long and 35 m. wide bet. Waigeo I. and W end (Vogelkop) of the island of New Guinea.

Damp′re·my′ (däNr′mē′). Commune, Hainaut prov., SW Belgium; pop. 13,373; coal mines.

Dan (dän). **1** River 180 m. long, S Virginia; rises in Patrick co., flows S into North Carolina, then E crossing state border several times before joining Roanoke river in S Virginia.

2 Ancient village at N extremity of Palestine (*Judges* xx. 1) on Lebanon border N of the Waters of Merom; now a mound 4 m. W of Baniyas. See BEERSHEBA.

Da′na, Mount (dä′ná). Peak 13,055 ft. in Sierra Nevada, in E Tuolumne co., cen. California.

Dan′a·kil (dän′á·kĭl), *Ital.* **Dan·ca′lia** (däng·käl′yä). Desert region, E Africa, in NE Ethiopia, SE Eritrea, and N French Somaliland; mostly in Great Rift Valley; inhabited by the Danakil, or Afar, people.

Da Nang. See TOURANE.

Da·na′o (dä·nä′ō). Municipality on E coast of Cebu I., Phil. Is., 17 m. NNE of City of Cebu; pop. 28,387; port for nearby coal mines.

Danastris. See DNIESTER.

Dan′bur′y (dän′bĕr′ĭ; -bēr·ĭ). **1** City, Fairfield co., SW Connecticut, 20 m. NW of Bridgeport; pop. 22,928; manufactures felt hats, hat-making machinery, silk, paper, silver-plated goods, electrical goods, roller and ball bearings, chemicals; Danbury State College (1903). Set-

tled 1684; burned by British 1777 during Revolutionary War; became borough 1822, incorp. as city 1889; point of origin of Danbury's Hatters' Case 1902 (Supreme Court decision 1908 against boycott by labor organizations). Forms part of town of Danbury (pop. 39,382).

2 Town, ⊗ of Stokes co., N North Carolina; pop. 175.

Dancalia. See DANAKIL.

Dan′dridge (dän′drĭj). Town, ⊗ of Jefferson co., E Tennessee; pop. 829.

Dane (dān). County in Wisconsin. See *Table* at WISCONSIN.

Dane′law′ (dān′lô′), *also* **Dane′lagh′** (dän′lô′). The NE part of England where Danish law was in force 9th and 10th cents.; covered East Anglia, Essex, a large part of Mercia, and most of Northumbria. See WEDMORE.

Dan′ger, Point (dän′jēr). Cape on E coast of Australia, most northerly point of New South Wales, at 28°9′S, 153°34′E.

Danger Islands. Island group in W Manihiki Is., cen. Pacific Ocean, N of Cook Is., chief island Pukapuka; pop. (1936) 651; administered by New Zealand with Cook Is.

Dangerous Islands. = TUAMOTU ARCHIPELAGO.

Dangla, Dang·la. 1 Mountain pass. See TANG-LA.

2 Mountain range. See TANGLHA.

Dangra Yum. Var. of TANGRA TSO.

Dangrek Mountains. = DONREK MOUNTAINS.

Dangs, The (dängz). Former group of 14 petty Indian states (once included in the Rewa Kantha Agency), subordinate to Gujarat States Agency, W India; 667 sq. m.; pop. (1941) 40,498; now semi-independent.

Da′ni·a (dä′nĭ·á). City, Broward co., SE Florida, on Atlantic Ocean 20 m. N of Miami; pop. 7065; incorporated 1927; tomato-growing center.

Dan′iels (dän′yĕlz). County in Montana. See *Table* at MONTANA.

Dan′iel·son (dän′yĕl·s′n; dän′′l-). Borough (pop. 4642) in town of KILLINGLY, Connecticut; incorporated 1854; cotton-manufacturing center.

Dan′iels·ville (dän′yĕlz·vĭl). City, ⊗ of Madison co., NE Georgia; pop. 362.

Danish West Indies. See VIRGIN ISLANDS.

Dan·lí′ (dän·lē′). Town, El Paraíso dept., S Honduras, 45 m. E of Tegucigalpa; pop. (1940) 3209; produces coffee, tobacco, sugar; gold mine nearby.

Danmark. See DENMARK.

Dan′ne·mo′ra (dän′ĭ·môr′á; -môr′á). **1** Village, Clinton co., NE corner of New York, 13 m. W of Plattsburg; pop. 4835; iron deposits; manufactures toweling, ticking, yarn; Clinton State Prison (1845).

2 (*Swed.* dän′nĕ·mōō′rá). Commune, Uppsala prov., SE Sweden, 22 m. N of Uppsala; pop. 1062; iron mines.

Dan′ne·virke (dän′ĕ·vûrk). Borough, Hawke's Bay provincial dist., SE North I., New Zealand, 110 m. NE of Wellington; pop. 4470; founded by Scandinavians.

Dan no U·ra *or* **Dan·no·u·ra** (dän·nō·ōō·rä). Locality, E end of Shimonoseki (*q.v.*), Japan; naval battle 1185 in which the Taira clan was totally defeated by the Minamoto.

Dan River. See DAN.

Dan·sa′lan, City of (dän·sä′län). Chartered city, ✻ of Lanao prov., Mindanao, Phil. Is., in E cen. part on N shore of Lake Lanao; 11 sq. m.; pop. 11,319; summer resort; created a city Aug. 19, 1940.

Dans′ville (dänz′vĭl). Village, Livingston co., W New York, 21 m. NW of Hornell; pop. 5460; fruit tree nurseries, canneries; health resort, sanitarium; birthplace of American Red Cross (founded by Clara Barton 1881).

Dan′ta (dän′tá). Former Indian state, Rajputana, NW India, NW of Jaipur; 347 sq. m.; pop. (1941) 31,110.

Dant′zig (dän[t]′sĭg; *Fr.* däNt′sēk′). French form, and occasional variant spelling in English, of DANZIG.

Dan′ube (dän′ūb). **1** *Ger.* **Do′nau** (dō′nou); *Hung.* **Du′na** (dōō′nō); *Romanian* **Du′nă·rea** (dōō′nă·ryä). *Anc.* **Da·nu′bi·us** (dá·nū′bĭ·ŭs) *or* **Is′ter** [ĭs′tēr]

(lower course). River 1725 m. long in cen. Europe, second longest river in Europe (Volga is longest); formed by confluence of Brege and Brigach rivers in the Black Forest, Baden, Germany, 37 m. WNW of Lake Constance; flows E across Württemberg and Bavaria, across N Austria and Hungary; ab. 20 m. N of Budapest turns S and traverses cen. Hungary before entering Yugoslavia where it turns SE; flows E as it forms section of the Romanian-Bulgarian boundary; finally turns N across SE Romania and E into the Black Sea through several mouths (delta ab. 1000 sq. m. in area), the northernmost channel, the Kiliya mouth, now forming boundary bet. Romania and the Ukraine, U.S.S.R. Has many tributaries (approximately 300) draining the various ranges of the Alps and the Carpathians; chief tributaries on the left (N): Altmühl, Naab (Germany), March (Austria and Czechoslovakia), Váh, Nitra, Hron (Czechoslovakia), Tisza (Yugoslavia and Hungary), Olt, Argeş, Siret (Romania), and Prut (Romania and Moldavian S.S.R.); on the right (S): Iller, Lech, Isar, Inn (Germany), Enns, Leitha (Austria), Rába (Hungary), Drava (Hungary and Yugoslavia), Sava, Morava (Yugoslavia), and Isker (Bulgaria). Navigable as far as Ulm by boats of limited draft; in Austria bet. Linz and Vienna passes through defiles with picturesque scenery; just W of Turnu-Severin in Romania passes through the famous defile of the Iron Gate (*q.v.*).

History: Long an important highway for trade bet. central and eastern Europe, its significance increased with development of steam navigation in 19th cent.; free navigation of Danube established in 1856 (Declaration of Paris) and placed under supervision of a European Commission which was renewed several times; closed to ships of war 1878; internationalized 1919 by Treaty of Versailles; regulated by postwar commission operating under Danube Convention of 1921; part of regulation passed to Romania 1938; dominated by Germany who was admitted to membership of commission 1939.

2 = *Donau*, circle of Württemberg: see *Table* at WÜRTTEMBERG.

3 = DUNAVSKA, former county of Yugoslavia.

Da·nu′bi·a (dă·nū′bĭ·à). Occasional name for countries and regions of the Danube basin.

Da·nu′bi·an Principalities (dă·nū′bĭ·ăn). Former name for Moldavia and Walachia (*qq.v.* for earlier history); ruled by Turkish governors although by treaty of Kuchuk Kainarji 1774, Russian intervention permitted; occupied by Russia 1810 and made subject to further Russian control 1812; guaranteed withdrawal of Turkish troops and greater autonomy 1829; occupied by Russia 1829–34, 1849–51, and 1853–56; as United Principalities of Moldavia and Walachia, had separate identical administrations 1858–61; completely united and named Romania 1861; union recognized by Sultan 1862; for later history, see ROMANIA.

Danubius. See DANUBE.

Danum. See DONCASTER.

Dan′vers (dăn′vẽrz). Town, Essex co., NE corner of Massachusetts, 16 m. NNE of Boston; pop. 21,926; manufactures leather and leather goods and chemicals; birthplace of Israel Putnam, Revolutionary commander.

Dan′ville (dăn′vil; *Sou. also* -v′l). **1** City, a ⊗ of Yell co., N cen. Arkansas; pop. 955.

2 City, ⊗ of Vermilion co., E Illinois, 33 m. E of Champaign; pop. 41,856; made ⊗ 1827, incorp. 1869; commercial center of farming, dairy, and coal-mining section; flour and lumber mills, brick and glass manufactories.

3 Town, ⊗ of Hendricks co., cen. Indiana, 20 m. W of Indianapolis; pop. 3287; Canterbury Coll. (1946; coed.).

4 City, ⊗ of Boyle co., cen. Kentucky, 32 m. SSW of Lexington; pop. 9010; founded 1775; seat of government for the area 1785–92; market center for tobacco, hemp, and livestock, esp. horses. Centre College of Kentucky (1819; coed.; Presbyterian).

5 Borough, ⊗ of Montour co., E cen. Pennsylvania, 30

m. SE of Williamsport; pop. 6889; settled 1792; iron ore, coal, limestone deposits; manufactures iron and steel, stoves, textiles.

6 Industrial city, S Virginia, in Pittsylvania co. but politically independent, on Dan river 3 m. N of North Carolina border; 6 sq. m.; pop. 46,577; tobacco market; shipping and trading center; manufactures textiles, brick, flour, paint, proprietary medicines; Confederate Memorial Mansion. Founded 1793; seat of government briefly during last days of Southern Confederacy 1865.

Dan′zig (dăn[t]′sig; dăn′zig; *Ger.* dän′tsĭk); *Pol.* **Gdańsk** (g′dän′y′sk). **1** City, commercial seaport, Gdańsk dept., N Poland, on Gulf of Danzig just W of mouth of the Vistula; pop. (1929) 256,403; situated on delta arm of the Vistula ab. 5 m. from its actual port, Neufahrwasser; has large shipping business with trade in lumber, grain, and coal; also important manufacturing industries and railroad and air-line connections; population before 1939 was mostly German.

History: Mentioned in 10th cent. A.D. as Polish town of Gdańsk; capital of dukes of Pomerania 13th cent.; ruled by Teutonic Order 1309–1454; joined Hanseatic League and became one of leading centers for Hanseatic trade and monopolized Polish foreign trade; in 1466, after revolt of part of western Prussia, became free city under Polish protection; captured by Russia 1734; ceded to Prussia in 3d partition of Poland 1793; by Article 102 of Versailles Treaty, city of Danzig, with adjoining territory, erected as free state under League of Nations 1919–20; within Polish customs union, it served as Polish outlet to sea; in continuous postwar friction with Poland; after 1933, threatened by competition of Gdynia (*q.v.*) and by rise of Nazis in Germany; cession of Danzig to Germany the immediate issue of conflict bet. Poland and Germany which began World War II; incorporated in Germany 1939; named Hanseatic City of Danzig 1940; recovered 1945 by Allies, made part of Poland.

2 *in full* **Free City of Danzig.** Territory on Gulf of Danzig, now part of Gdańsk dept., N Poland; 754 sq. m.; pop. (1929) 407,517; chief city Danzig; other communities in the territory are Sopot, a seaside resort, and the small towns of Nowy Staw (Neuteich) and Nowy Dwór Gdański (Tiegenhof); for history, see 1, above.

Danzig, Gulf, *or* **Bay, of.** Wide inlet of S Baltic Sea, N Poland.

Da′o (dä′ō; dou). **1** Municipality, S Antique prov., Panay, Phil. Is., on coastal highway 16 m. S of San Jose de Buenavista; pop. 21,249.

2 Municipality, E cen. Capiz prov., Panay, Phil. Is., on the Panay river and on railroad 15 m. SSW of Capiz; pop. 13,886; has active trade in forest products.

Daph′nae (dăf′nē); *Bib.* **Tah′pan·hes** (tä′păn·hēz; tá·păn′hēz); *mod.* **Tel De·fen′neh** (tĕl dĕ·fĕn′ĕ). Ancient fortress, NE Egypt, W of Suez Canal near El Qantara; archaeological site.

Daph′nē (dăf′nē; *Mod. Gr.* thäf′nyĕ). Town on coast near tip of Acte Penin., Chalcidice, Greece; in Mount Athos republic; has famous monastery.

Da′piak (dä′pyäk), **Mount.** Mountain 8620 ft., NE Zamboanga prov., Mindanao, Phil. Is., 25 m. SSE of Dipolog; highest peak in province.

Da·pi′tan (dä·pē′tän). Municipality, N Zamboanga prov., Mindanao, Phil. Is., on Dapitan Bay (inlet of S side of passage bet. Sulu Sea and Mindanao Sea); pop. 28,295, important trade center with good harbor; one of the oldest towns in the Philippines; place where Dr. José Rizal spent four years of exile 1893–96.

Dapsang. See GODWIN AUSTEN.

Da·qah·lî′ya (dŭ·kŏ·lē′yá; -yă). Province, Lower Egypt. See *Table* at EGYPT.

Da′ra (där′à). Ancient fortress in N Mesopotamia; captured by Persians 573 A.D. during war of Khosrau I against Justin II, ruler of Byzantine Empire.

Da·rab′ (dä·räb′). Town, Fars prov., SW Iran, 130 m. SE of Shiraz; pop. ab. 12,000; noted for its groves of

oranges and lemons and for the large sculptured bas-relief nearby commemorating the victory 260 A.D. of Shapur I over the Roman emperor Valerian.

Da·ra′ga (dä·rä′gä). Municipality, E Albay prov., Luzon, Phil. Is., on railroad 2 m. W of Legaspi; pop. 29,484.

Da·ram′ (dä·räm′). Largest of coastal islands of Samar, Phil. Is., off W coast in Samar Sea, W of Buad I.; 39 sq. m.; pop. ab. 13,000.

Dar·bhan′ga (dĕr·bŭng′gá; *native* dŭr·b'hŭng′gä). City, Tirhut division, N Bihar state, NE Indian Union, 70 m. NE of Patna; pop. (1941) 69,203; chief distribution and trade point for district's agricultural interests; seat of a medical college, has fine palace of former maharaja.

Dar′by (där′bĭ). Borough, Delaware co., SE Pennsylvania, 5 m. W of Philadelphia; pop. 14,059; settled 1660; manufactures textiles, filters, tanks, tools.

Dar′da·nelle′ (där′d'n·ĕl′). City, a ⊗ of Yell co., W cen. Arkansas, on Arkansas river; pop. 2098.

Dar′da·nelles′ (där′d'n·ĕlz′); *Turkish* **Ça′nak·ka·le′ Bo′ğa·zı′** (chä′näk·kä·lĕ′ bō′ä·zı′); *anc.* **Hel′les·pon′-tus** (hĕl′ĕs·pŏn′tŭs), *Angl.* **Hel′les·pont** (hĕl′ĕs·pŏnt). Narrow strait, 40 m. long, ¾ m. to 4 m. wide, bet. Europe (Gallipoli Penin.) and Turkey in Asia; connects Sea of Marmara with Aegean Sea. See *Map* of *Turkey in Europe*, at TURKEY.

  History: Ancient Hellespont the scene of Xerxes' crossing to Europe in invasion of Greece 480 B.C. (see PERSIA); crossed by Alexander the Great 334 B.C.; part of Eastern Roman (Byzantine) Empire until 14th cent.; crossed 1356 by Ottoman Turks who had settled at Gelibolu (*q.v.*) and fortified by Sultan Mohammed II 1462; with expansion of Russia to Black Sea, increased in strategic importance as only outlet for Russian fleet to Mediterranean; for history of control as an issue of European politics, part of Near Eastern Question, see the STRAITS; scene of Allied campaign during World War I 1915 (for land attack see GALLIPOLI PENINSULA).

Dar′di·stan′ (där′dĭ·stän′). Region, NW Kashmir, N India, and N North-West Frontier Province, Pakistan; inhabited by the Dard, an Indo-Aryan people of the upper Indus valley, an important linguistic group.

Dare (dâr). County in North Carolina. See *Table* at NORTH CAROLINA.

Dar el Beida, Dar-al-Baida. See CASABLANCA.

Dar′ent (där′ĕnt). River 20 m. long, W Kent, SE England; flows NE to the Thames; navigable to Dartford.

Dar es Sa·laam′ *or* **Dar′es·sa·lam′** (där′ ĕs sá·läm′; *Arab.* där′ ăs sä·läm′). **1** District, Eastern Province, Tanganyika, E Africa; pop. 154,000.

  2 Seaport city, E Tanganyika; ⁂ of Tanganyika and, since 1964, of Tanzania; pop. 128,742; founded 1862 by sultan of Zanzibar; taken by Carl Peters for German East Africa Co. 1887; made capital of German East Africa 1891; captured by British 1916.

Dar′field (där′fēld). Urban district, West Riding, Yorkshire, N England; pop. 6238.

Dar′fur′ (där′fŏŏr′). Province, W Sudan, NE Africa; 191,650 sq. m.; pop. 1,328,765; ⁂ El Fasher; an independent kingdom until annexed by Egypt 1874; made part of Anglo-Egyptian Sudan 1898.

Dar′ga·ville (där′gá·vil). Borough, N Auckland provincial dist., North I., New Zealand, on Wairoa river near W coast 80 m. NNW of Auckland; pop. 1980.

Darg Plateau (därg). Highland region, S end of Great Dividing Range, E Victoria, SE Australia; highest Mt. Bogong 6509 ft.

Dar Ha·mid′ (där′ hă·mēd′). Desert region, cen. Kordofan prov., Sudan.

Darial, *or* **Dariel, Pass.** See DARYAL PASS.

Dar′i·en′ (dâr′ĭ·ĕn′; dâr′ĭ·ĕn; *in Georgia*, dâr′ĭ·ĕn, dä′-rĭ·ĕn). **1** Residential town, SW Fairfield co., SW Connecticut, on Long Island Sound; pop. 18,437; incorporated 1820; floral gardening.

  2 City, ⊗ of McIntosh co., SE Georgia; pop. 1569.

3 *Span.* **Da·rién′** (dä·ryān′). Settlement and colony (originally named **San′ta Ma·rí′a la An·ti′gua del Da·rién′** [sän′tä mä·rē′ä lä än·tē′gwä thĕl dä·ryān′]) established by Spaniards on W shore of Gulf of Urabá on N coast (Pearl Coast) of Isthmus of Darien (later Isthmus of Panama, discovered early in 16th cent.); colony founded 1510 by Balboa, Pizarro, and others, by removing unsuccessful settlement (1509) of San Sebastián from E side of gulf; from here Balboa crossed the isthmus 1513 to discover the South Sea (Pacific); center of early Spanish exploration until replaced 1519 by Panama (Panamá); part of province of New Granada; in 1698 site of New Caledonia, founded by Darien company, a Scottish undertaking under William Paterson which sought to cut off Spanish colonies but was not maintained. For later history, see PANAMA.

  4 Former province, E Panama, now included in Panama prov. (*q.v.*).

  5 Village, Canal Zone, on SE shore of Gatun Lake.

Darien, Gulf of. Inlet of the Caribbean Sea extending bet. E Panama and NW Colombia; receives the Atrato river; its inner section is the Gulf of Urabá.

Darien, Isthmus of. See Isthmus of PANAMA.

Da·rién′, Ser′ra·ní′a del (sĕr′rä·nē′ä thĕl dä·ryän′). Range in E Panama, extending in part along the Panama-Colombia boundary; average height ab. 3000 ft.

Dariorigum. See VANNES.

Dar·jee′ling *or* **Dar·ji′ling** (där·jē′lĭng). **1** District, Rajshahi division, formerly in Bengal, NE Brit. India, now in West Bengal, NE Indian Union; 1192 sq. m.; pop. (1941) 376,369.

  2 Town and hill station, India; pop. 19,903, including cantonments of Jalapahar and Lebong; on Sikkim border at elevation of ab. 6000 ft., highest point 7886 ft.; commands one of finest views in the world including Mt. Kanchenjunga, 40 m. directly N, and Mt. Everest (visible on clear days from nearby **Ti′ger Hill** [ti′gĕr] 8515 ft.) 110 m. to the NW. Inhabitants chiefly Nepalese and Bhutanese; British connection began 1816. Hot weather headquarters of Bengal government. See SILIGURI.

Darke (därk). County in Ohio. See *Table* at OHIO.

Dar′kot Pass (där′kŏt; *native* dŭr′kŏt). Mountain pass 15,000 ft. in a range of the E Hindu Kush Mts., from Gilgit, in Kashmir, to Chitral, in North-West Frontier Province, Pakistan.

Dar′las·ton (där′lås·tŭn). Urban district, Staffordshire, W cen. England; pop. 22,024; manufacturing community in coal and iron section.

Dar′ling (där′lĭng). River 1160 m. long, S Queensland and N and W New South Wales, SE Australia; navigable in part and at certain seasons, but its volume is very irregular; has headstreams in Great Dividing Range and Darling Downs; flows SW into Murray river near South Australia border.

Darling Downs (dounz). Pastoral district ab. 25,000 sq. m., SE Queensland, Australia, W of Brisbane; drained by upper tributaries of Darling river.

Darling Range. Mountain range ab. 250 m. long, SW Western Australia, parallel with the coast; highest point not more than 1500 ft.

Dar′ling·ton (där′lĭng·tŭn). **1** County in South Carolina. See *Table* at SOUTH CAROLINA.

  2 Town, its ⊗, NE South Carolina, 10 m. NW of Florence; pop. 6710; settled 1798; trade center for agricultural region; manufactures cotton goods, tobacco, veneers, desks and chairs.

  3 City, ⊗ of Lafayette co., S Wisconsin, 18 m. E of Platteville; pop. 2349.

  4 County borough, Durham, N England, on the Skerne 50 m. NE of Leeds; pop. (1931) 72,086, (1951) 84,861; railroad center; locomotive works, iron foundries, steel plants, woolen mills.

Darm′stadt (därm′shtät; *in English, also* därm′stăt). City, S Hesse state, Germany, 17 m. S of Frankfurt-am-Main; former ⁂ of Hesse; pop. (1957) 128,700; museum;

16th-cent. town hall; manufactures include machinery, iron goods, brewery products, carpets, chemicals, tobacco, scientific instruments. Made city 1330; became capital of Hesse-Darmstadt 1567; burned by French 1688 and 1693; in World War II taken by Americans Mar. 26, 1945.

Dar'rell's, or **Dar'rell, Island** (där'ĕl[z]). Small island in Great Sound, Bermuda, SW of Hamilton; transatlantic air base.

Dart (därt). River, S Devonshire, SW England; flows SE to English Channel at Dartmouth.

Dart, Cape. Cape at foot of Mt. Siple promontory, Marie Byrd Land, Antarctica, 123°W.

Dart'ford (därt'fĕrd). Urban district, Kent, SE England, on the Darent 15 m. ESE of London; pop. 40,544; site of the first paper mill in England; scene of the outbreak of Peasants' Revolt (Wat Tyler's Rebellion) June 1381.

Dart'moor (därt'mŏor; -mōr). Tableland, 215 sq. m., mean elevation 1500 ft., in S Devonshire, SW England; has wild open places, many tors (highest High Willhays 2039 ft.), and morasses; source of all principal Devonshire rivers; its forests, in cen. part, are only small tracts of dwarf oaks; prehistoric remains; prison at Princetown built 1806 for French captives, convict station since 1850.

Dart'mouth (därt'mŭth). **1** Town, Bristol co., SE Massachusetts, 6 m. SW of New Bedford; pop. 14,607; formerly a shipbuilding center; fishing.
2 Coastal town, Halifax co., S Nova Scotia, Canada, on Halifax harbor across from Halifax; pop. 15,037; manufactures soap, cordage, lumber, beer, bolts; founded by the English 1750; destroyed by Indians 1751 and rebuilt. Fort Clarence below the town overlooks narrow eastern passage of Halifax harbor.
3 Municipal borough, Devonshire, SW England, on English Channel at mouth of the Dart 25 m. E of Plymouth; pop. 5842; shipbuilding yards; naval cadet college.

Dar'ton (där't'n). Urban district, West Riding, Yorkshire, N England; pop. 14,400.

Da'ru (där'ōō). Town and port of entry on a small island, lat. 9°10'S and long. 143°10'E, SW Territory of Papua, New Guinea, on N side of Torres Strait.

Dar–ul–A·man' (där'ōōl·ä·män'). Suburb of Kabul, Afghanistan; planned by Amanullah Khan before his downfall 1929 as new modern capital; contains unfinished parliament buildings, a few modern homes, beautiful rose gardens.

Da'ru·var (dä'rōō·vär). Commune, N Yugoslavia, 64 m. ESE of Zagreb; pop. 2706; thermal springs.

Dar'vel Bay (där'v'l). Inlet of Celebes Sea, on SE coast of British North Borneo, opp. W end of Sulu Archipelago of the Philippines.

Dar'wen (där'wĕn; där'ĕn). Municipal borough, Lancashire, NW England, 17 m. NNW of Manchester; pop. 30,827; coal mines, stone quarries; manufactures paper and cotton.

Dar'win (där'wĭn); orig. **Palm'er·ston** (päm'ĕr·st'n); also formerly **Port Darwin.** Seaport, ✳ of Northern Territory, Australia, on Port Darwin (an inlet of Clarence Strait); pop. 1566; one of the best harbors in the Commonwealth; supply and shipping point for northern Australia; terminus of overland telegraph and highway from Adelaide; center of sparsely populated and largely undeveloped region. Founded 1869; headquarters of Allied armies in northern Australia 1941–45; bombed by Japanese 1942.

Darwin, Mount. Peak 13,841 ft. in Sierra Nevada, on boundary bet. Fresno and Inyo cos., SE cen. California.

Dar·yal' (dĕr·yäl'; där·yäl'; Russ. dŭr·yäl'y'), or **Dar'-i·al'** (där'ĭ·ăl'), Pass; also **Dar'i·el' Pass** (där'ĭ·ĕl'). Gorge, ab. 8 m. long, alt. 4122 ft., in the Caucasus Mts., Soviet Russia, Europe, E of Mt. Kazbek; traversed by Terek river; has vertical rock walls 5900 ft. high. Probably the only early passage across the Caucasus; fortified

as early as 150 B.C.; through it was constructed 1811–64 the Georgian Military Road from Tiflis to Vladikavkaz (Dzaudzhikau).

Darya yi Namak. See Darya yi NAMAK.

Dasht (däsht). River ab. 255 m. long, SW Baluchistan; flows SW into Arabian Sea.

Dasht–i–Ka·vir' (däsht'ĕ·kȧ·vēr') or **Great Salt Desert.** Salt desert, a plateau, alt. 2500 ft., in N cen. Iran.

Dasht–i–Lut (-lōōt'). Tableland, largely desert, alt. 1000 ft., in cen. and E cen. Iran.

Dashur. See DAHSHÛR.

Da·sol' Bay (dä·sôl'). Inlet of South China Sea on SW coast of Pangasinan prov., Luzon, Phil. Is.

Das·pal'la (dŭs·pŭl'lä). Former Indian state, SE Eastern States, NE Indian Union, W of Cuttack; area now in Orissa state; 556 sq. m.; pop. (1941) 53,833.

Da'ta (dä'tä). Mountain 7577 ft. in S part of Cordillera Central, N Luzon, Phil. Is.

Date Line. A hypothetical line coinciding approximately with the meridian 180° from Greenwich, fixed by

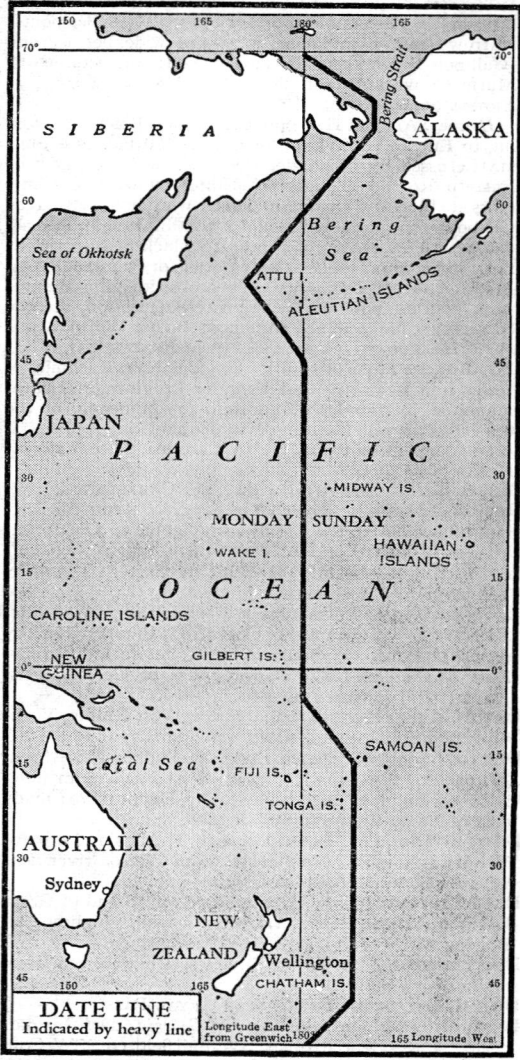

DATE LINE
Indicated by heavy line

international or general agreement as the place where each calendar day first begins. The day for any given

locality commences when it is midnight at that place; hence, any given day, say Monday, first begins at midnight on the date line, and following the midnight line begins continuously farther westward, in New Zealand, Australia, etc. It is thus Monday from the date line westward to the midnight line and Sunday from the date line eastward to the midnight line. Finally, as the midnight line reaches the date line again, it is for the instant Monday over practically the whole world; then Tuesday begins, and so on. Thus for the greater part of the twenty-four hours Hawaii has the same day name as San Francisco, and Manila the same day name (one day later than the day of Hawaii) as Australia. Thus, when it is Monday noon, May 1, at San Francisco, it is 4 o'clock (standard time) or 14 minutes past 4 (local mean time) Tuesday morning, May 2, at Manila. A vessel crossing the date line to the westward sets the date forward by one day, as from Sunday to Monday; if the line is crossed in going eastward, the date is set back. To avoid dividing places in close intercourse, the line is deflected bet. 45°N lat. and 80°N lat., so that all Asia lies to the W of it, all North America, including the Aleutian Is., to the E; and bet. 12°S lat. and 56°S lat. the line is deflected so that Chatham Is. and the Tonga group lie to the W.

Da′ti·a (dŭt′ĭ·ä); *also* **Dut′ti·a** (dŭt′ĭ·ä). **1** Former Indian state, Bundelkhand, N Central India, Indian Union; 846 sq. m.; pop. (1941) 174,072; came under British government by treaty 1802; now part of Madhya Pradesh.

2 Town, its ✳, 45 m. SSE of Gwalior; pop. 18,292; has fine palace of Hindu architecture.

Dat′il Range (dăt′l). Range in W cen. New Mexico, extending across N part of boundary bet. Catron and Socorro cos.

Dat′teln (dät′ĕln). Commune, W Germany, in N North Rhine-Westphalia state in the valley of the Lippe 24 m. SSW of Münster; pop. 20,114; coal mining; manufactures leather, chemicals, wire.

Da·tu′, Cape (dä·tōō′); *Du.* **Tan′djoeng Da·toek′** (tän′jŏong dä·tŏok′). Cape, W Borneo, projecting into South China Sea at ab. 109°30′E, marking the boundary bet. W Sarawak and the SW part of Dutch Borneo.

Datu Bay. Inlet of South China Sea in SW Sarawak, bet. delta of Rajang river and mouth of Sarawak river, N of Kuching; receives the Batang Lupar.

Daugava. **1** River, N Europe. See DVINA.

2 See DAUGAVGRĪVA.

Dau′gav·grī′va (dou′gáv·grē′và); *Russ.* **Dau′ga·va** (dou′gȧ·vȧ), *formerly* **Ust Dvinsk** (ōōst′ dvĭnsk′; *Russ.* ōōst′y′ dvyēnsk′); *Ger.* **Dü′na·mün′de** (dü′nä-mün′dĕ). Harbor and fortress on island at mouth of the Dvina on the Gulf of Riga, cen. Latvia, U.S.S.R., 8 m. N of Riga; serves as Riga's port in winter; held by Germans 1917–18 in World War I and 1941–44 in World War II.

Dau′gav·pils (dou′gáf·pĭls). **1** Administrative district, S Latgale prov., E Latvia, U.S.S.R.; 1849 sq. m.

2 *Russ.* **Dau′gav·pils** (dou′gáf·pyĭls) *or* **Dvinsk** (dvĭnsk; *Russ.* dvyēnsk); *Ger.* **Dü′na·burg** (dü′nä-bōōrk). City, ✳ of Latgale prov., E Latvia, U.S.S.R., on Dvina river; pop. (1935) 45,160; railroad junction 120 m. SE of Riga; trade center for lumber and agricultural products (esp. grain, flax). Founded ab. 1275 by Teutonic Knights; under Polish rule 1559–1772, Russian rule 1772–1915; resisted repeated attacks by Germans 1915–18; occupied 1918 by Bolshevik army, which was expelled Jan. 1920 by Latvian-Estonian-Polish force; held 1941–44 by Germans in World War II.

Da′uin (dä′wĭn). Municipality, SE Negros Oriental, Negros, Phil. Is., on coast 8 m. S of Dumaguete, opp. Siquijor I.; pop. 12,234; founded 1787.

Da′uis (dä′wĕs). Municipality on Panglao I., Bohol, Phil. Is., on narrow strait NE of island, nearly opp. Tagbilaran; pop. 12,154.

Dau′lat·a·bad′ (dou′lȧt·ȧ·bäd′). Town, NW cen.

Maharashtra state, S cen. India, ab. 10 m. NW of Aurangabad; has remarkable fortress on rock ab. 600 ft. high within which are ruins of tower, palace, temple, and other structures. As **De·o′gi·ri** (dĕ·ō′gĭ·rĭ) founded c. 1187; captured 1294 by Ala-ud-din of the Khilji dynasty; made capital of India by Mohammed Tughlak in 1339 who gave it its present name; later, held by various Moslem rulers; after 1707 came into possession of nizam of Hyderabad.

Dau′lat·a·bad′ (dou′lȧt·ô·bôd′). Town, W cen. Iran, ab. 40 m. SSE of Hamadan; pop. ab. 4500.

Dau′le (dou′lā). **1** River ab. 55 m. long in NW Ecuador; flows N into Esmeraldas river.

2 Town, Guayas prov., W Ecuador, on E bank of Daule river 22 m. N of Guayaquil; pop. (1944 est.) 18,089.

Dau′lis (dô′lĭs). Ancient city of Phocis, cen. Greece, 12 m. E of Delphi; scene of legend of Philomela.

Dau′phin (dô′fĭn). **1** County in Pennsylvania. See *Table* at PENNSYLVANIA.

2 River ab. 70 m. long, S cen. Manitoba, Canada, connecting Lake Manitoba with Lake Winnipeg; passes through Lake St. Martin.

3 Town, SW cen. Manitoba, Canada, 10 m. W of S end of Lake Dauphin; pop. 6007; distributing center.

Dauphin, Lake. Lake 200 sq. m. in SW Manitoba, Canada, W of N Lake Manitoba.

Dau′phi·né′ (dō′fē′nā′). Historical region and former province of SE France; bounded anciently on N by Burgundy, E by Savoy (kingdom of Sardinia), S by Provence, SW by Comtat Venaissin, W by Languedoc, NW by Lyonnais; equivalent to modern departments of Drôme, Hautes-Alpes, Isère; ✳ Grenoble; watered by Drôme, Isère, and Durance rivers; mountainous in E.

History: Region occupied by Burgundians, later by Franks; formed part of Lothair's kingdom (see LORRAINE) and of kingdom of Arles (*q.v.*); from 10th to 13th cents. consolidated and expanded by counts of Vienne who were vassals of Holy Roman Empire; acquired by Philip VI of France 1349; became appanage of eldest son of French king who assumed title (*dauphin*) attached to the land.

Dauphiné Alps. See *Table* at ALPS.

Dau′phin Island (dô′fĭn). Island at entrance to Mobile Bay, off SW coast of Alabama; included in Mobile co.; discovered by Iberville 1699.

Da·van′ge·re (dä·vŭn′gĕ·rĕ). Town, E Mysore state, S Indian Union, 155 m. NW of Bangalore; pop. 23,155.

Da′vao (dä′vou). **1** Province, SE Mindanao, Phil. Is.; 7529 sq. m.; pop. 292,600; ✳ City of Davao; second province in area in the Philippines; very mountainous with high peaks in E and Mt. Apo 9689 ft., highest in the Philippines, on W border. Agusan river rises in SE and flows N to Agusan prov.; other short streams flow E to Pacific or S or E to Davao Gulf; at N end of Davao Gulf is large Samal I. and off Tinaca Point in SW are Sarangani Is. Has exceptionally fertile volcanic soil and fine climate; chief product abacá (Manila hemp); produces also copra, cacao, coffee, rice, and forest products; inhabitants mostly pagan tribes, esp. Bagobos, Mandayas; Santa Cruz, Malita, Tagum (municipal district), and Pantukan are important municipalities.

History: Visited by Spaniards in 16th cent. but region under jurisdiction of sultanate of Mindanao until middle of 19th cent.; organized as a Spanish province 1849 and changed to a military district 1860; under Americans became part of Moro Province 1903; granted civil government 1914; from ab. 1902 when Japanese colonies were formed to raise hemp, received increasing numbers of Japanese, until in 1940 there were ab. 20,000 of them; seized by Japanese navy Dec. 20, 1941.

2 *officially* **City of Davao.** Chartered city, its ✳, in W cen. part on NW shore of Davao Gulf opp. Samal I.; pop. 95,546; fourth largest city in the Philippines; trading center for region producing hemp (abacá) of superior quality; several airfields in vicinity. Founded 1849; in

20th cent. developed as part of Japanese colony; seized by Japanese navy Dec. 20, 1941 and made a naval base; bombed by U.S. planes Sept. 1944; retaken by Allied forces May 1945.

Davao Gulf. Large inlet of Pacific Ocean, S Davao prov., Mindanao, Phil. Is., ab. 80 m. long by 45 m. wide; marked on SE side of entrance by Cape San Agustin and on SW by Kalian Point; Samal I. is at its N end.

Dav′en·port (dăv′ĕn-pōrt; dăv′m-). **1** City, ⊗ of Scott co., E Iowa, on Mississippi river across from Rock Island, Ill.; pop. 88,981; railroad, commercial, and industrial center; shipping point for grain; manufactures railroad equipment, cereal products, cement, farm implements. St. Ambrose College (1882; men; Roman Catholic). Founded 1835 on the site of an Indian village; made ⊗ 1838; site of the first railroad bridge across the Mississippi river, completed 1856.
2 Town, ⊗ of Lincoln co., E Washington; pop. 1417.

Dav′en·try (dăv′ĕn-trĭ; *locally also* dān′trĭ). Municipal borough, Northamptonshire, cen. England; pop. 4078; large overseas broadcasting station.

Da·vid′ (dȧ-vēth′). Town, W Panama, ✳ of Chiriquí prov.; pop. 9222; its port, Pedregal, is 5 m. to the S.

Da′vid City (dā′vĭd). City, ⊗ of Butler co., E Nebraska, 39 m. NNW of Lincoln; pop. 2304; trade center.

Da·vid′-Go·ro·dok′ (dŭ·vyēd′gŭ·rŭ·dôk′); *Pol.* **Da′-wid·gró′dek** (dä′vēd·grōō′dĕk). Town, S White Russia, U.S.S.R., on Goryn river 49 m. E of Pinsk (formerly in Polesie dept., Poland); pop. 11,374.

Da′vid Point (dā′vĭd). Cape on S side of W St. Thomas I., Virgin Is., West Indies, W of Fortuna Bay.

Da′vids Island (dā′vĭdz). Island in Long Island Sound, New York, near New Rochelle; Fort Slocum (*q.v.*).

Da′vid·son (dā′vĭd·s'n). **1** Name of counties in two states of the United States. See *Tables* at NORTH CAROLINA and TENNESSEE.
2 Town, Mecklenburg co., S North Carolina, 18 m. N of Charlotte; pop. 2573; Davidson College (1837; men).

Davidson, Mount. Peak 7870 ft., site of Virginia City, Storey co., W Nevada.

Da′vie (dā′vĭ). County in North Carolina. See *Table* at NORTH CAROLINA.

Da′viess (dā′vĭs). Name of counties in three states of the U.S. See *Tables* at INDIANA, KENTUCKY, MISSOURI.

Da′vis (dā′vĭs). **1** Name of counties in two states of the U.S. See *Tables* at IOWA and UTAH.
2 City, Yolo co., N cen. California, 15 m. W of Sacramento; pop. 8910; University of California at Davis (1923); experimental farm.
3 Town, Murray co., S Oklahoma, on Washita river 23 m. N of Ardmore; pop. 2203.

Davis Bridge Dam. Dam completed 1924 across Deerfield river in S Vermont; height 200 ft.; impounds water for power.

Davis Islands. Three man-made islands, Tampa, Florida, at mouth of Hillsborough river; municipal hospital and several recreational centers.

Davis Mountain. See NEGRO MOUNTAIN.

Davis Mountains. Small range in N Jeff Davis co., W Texas; includes Mt. Livermore 8382 ft.

Da′vi·son (dā′vĭ·s'n). County in South Dakota. See *Table* at SOUTH DAKOTA.

Da′vis Peak (dā′vĭs). Mountain 7150 ft., N Cascade Range, NW Washington.

Davis Strait. Strait bet. SW Greenland and E Baffin I., connecting Baffin Bay with the Atlantic Ocean; width at its narrowest point 200 m. Discovered by John Davis during voyage in search of Northwest Passage (*q.v.*) 1585; Greenland side of strait explored by Davis in 1587 when he sailed through it into Baffin Bay.

Da·vos′ (dä·vōs′). Commune, Graubünden canton, E Switzerland, in Davos valley 13 m. ESE of Chur; pop. (1930) 11,164; consists of villages of **Da·vos′–Platz′** (-pläts′) and **Da·vos′–Dorf′** (-dôrf′); famous as a center for winter sports and, owing to its dry and sunny cli-

mate, as a winter and summer health resort, esp. for tuberculars.

Da·wa′ (dȧ·wä′). River ab. 370 m. long, S Ethiopia; flows SE to join the Ganale Dorya and Webbe rivers and form the Juba; also forms part of the boundary bet. Ethiopia and Kenya.

Da·wa′sir (dȧ·wä′sĭr). Watercourse in SW cen. Saudi Arabia; flows NE, then NW; dry at some seasons.

Dawes (dôz). County in Nebraska. See *Table* at NEBRASKA.

Dawidgródek. See DAVID-GORODOK.

Daw′ley (dô′lĭ). Urban district, Shropshire, W England, on Shrewsbury Canal 28 m. WNW of Birmingham; pop. 8369.

Daw′lish (dô′lĭsh). Coast town, Devonshire, SW England, on the English Channel 12 m. S of Exeter; pop. (1951) 7512; seaside resort.

Daw′na Range (dô′nȧ). Mountain range extending NW and SE along boundary bet. E cen. Burma and W Thailand, W of Thaungyin river; highest point 6821 ft.

Daw′ros Head (dô′rŏs). Cape on W coast of co. Donegal, N Eire, N of Donegal Bay.

Daw′son (dô′s'n). **1** Name of counties in four states of the U.S. See *Tables* at GEORGIA, MONTANA, NEBRASKA, TEXAS.
2 City, ⊗ of Terrell co., SW Georgia, 22 m. NW of Albany; pop. 5062; trade center.
3 City, Lac qui Parle co., W Minnesota, 16 m. W of Montevideo; pop. 1766.
4 Coal mining town, Colfax co., N New Mexico, ab. 22 m. NW of Springer.
5 River ab. 380 m. long, E Queensland, Australia, S tributary of Fitzroy river; flows N.
6 City, in Yukon Territory, N Canada, on right bank of the Yukon near where it is joined by the Klondike; pop. 783; ab. 50 m. E of Alaska boundary, elevation 1400 ft.; a receiving and distributing center of the Klondike mining region; has steamer connections both up and down the Yukon; temperature frequently averages 40° below zero for several days. Had its beginnings in 1896 in the Klondike gold rush, when for several years it was much larger than now; capital of the Yukon 1898–1953.
7 Chilean island in Tierra del Fuego archipelago (*q.v.*) off W coast of Tierra del Fuego I.; separated from Brunswick Penin. on W by Strait of Magellan.

Dawson, Mount. Mountain 10,982 ft., SE British Columbia, Canada; in Selkirk Mts., in Glacier National Park.

Dawson Creek. City, NE Brit. Columbia, Canada, 315 m. NW of Edmonton near Alberta border; pop. 10,946; terminus of Northern Alberta R.R. from Edmonton (495 m. by rail) and W of Peace River (278 m. by rail); starting point of the Alaska Highway (*q.v.*); population much increased since beginning of construction of highway.

Dawson Springs. Resort City, Hopkins co., W Kentucky, 53 m. E of Paducah; pop. 3002; mineral springs.

Daw′son·ville (dô′s'n·vĭl; *Sou. also* -v'l). Town, ⊗ of Dawson co., N Georgia; pop. 307.

Dax (däks) *or* **Ax** (äks); *anc.* **Aq′uae Tar·bel′li·cae** (ăk′wē tär·bĕl′ĭ·sē; ā′kwē), *later* **Aquae Au·gus′tae** (ô·gŭs′tē). Commune, Landes dept., SW France, on Adour river 30 m. SW of Mont-de-Marsan; pop. 13,056; hot saline springs; mineral baths; 14th-cent. castle; 18th-cent. cathedral; terminus of French-Spanish tunnel. Ancient Gallic town; made episcopal see early in Christian era; capital of viscountship in Béarn during Middle Ages.

Day (dā). County in South Dakota. See *Table* at SOUTH DAKOTA.

Day′ton (dā′t'n). **1** City, Campbell co., N Kentucky, on Ohio river 3 m. above Newport; pop. 9050.
2 Village, Lyon co., W Nevada, ab. 11 m. NE of Carson City; pop. 489; gold discovered here 1849.
3 Manufacturing city, ⊗ of Montgomery co., SW Ohio, on Miami river 47 m. N of Cincinnati; pop. (with Silver

City) 262,332; aviation and aeronautical research center, site of government-owned Wright-Patterson Air Force Base and Fairfield Air Depot; municipal airport; manufactures cash registers, electric refrigerators, air-conditioning equipment, paper, computing scales, machinery and tools, automotive parts and accessories, rubber products, U.S. stamped envelopes, household appliances. Univ. of Dayton (1850; coed.), Bonebrake Theological Seminary (1871). Settled 1796, became ⊗ 1803, incorp. 1805; suffered from disastrous flood Mar. 1913; first large city to adopt commission-manager form of government (1914). Home of Wilbur and Orville Wright.
4 City, ⊗ of Rhea co., E cen. Tennessee; pop. 3500; scene of Scopes test case evolution trial July 1925; manufactures hosiery, lumber, flour; coal mining. William Jennings Bryan College (1930; coed.).
5 City, ⊗ of Columbia co., SE Washington, 27 m. NE of Walla Walla; pop. 2913; fruit and vegetable canneries and packing plants, sawmills, creamery; ships wheat and apples.
Day·to'na Beach (dā·tō'nȧ). Winter resort city, Volusia co., E Florida, on Atlantic Ocean 92 m. SSE of Jacksonville; pop. 37,395; settled c. 1870; formed 1926 by consolidation of municipalities of Seabreeze, Daytona Beach, and Daytona; noted esp. for its hard, white beach; Daytona International Speedway. Bethune-Cookman College (1872; coed.).
De Aar (dě är'). Town, cen. Cape Province, S Union of South Africa, 240 m. NNW of Port Elizabeth; pop. 5118; important railroad junction of main lines from Cape Town and Port Elizabeth; in grazing region.
Dead Indian Peak. Mountain 12,253 ft., W Park co., NW Wyoming, in the Absaroka Mts., 28 m. WNW of Cody.
Dead'man' Mountain (děd'măn'). Peak 10,365 ft., W Wyoming, in N Lincoln co.
Dead'mans' Bay (děd·mănz'). Inlet of Gulf of Mexico on coast of upper Dixie and lower Taylor cos., NW Florida penin.
Dead Man's Hill. = LE MORT HOMME.
Dead River. See NAHR EL MIFJIR.
Dead Sea; *anc.* **La'cus As'phal·ti'tes** (lā'kŭs ăs'făl·tī'tēz); *Arab.* **Bah'ret Lut** (bă'h'·rĕt lōot'). Salt lake on the boundary between Palestine and Jordan; 46 m. long, 10 m. wide at its greatest breadth; 370 sq. m.; surface 1296 ft. below the level of the Mediterranean Sea, lowest point on earth's surface; receives the Jordan at N end; has had many names and has figured in many events of Biblical history.
Dead'wood' (děd'wŏŏd'). **1** River in Valley and Boise cos., W cen. Idaho; tributary of S fork of Payette river; **Deadwood Dam** (height 165 ft.; completed 1931) and **Deadwood Reservoir** in S Valley co. impound its waters for irrigation purposes.
2 City, ⊗ of Lawrence co., W South Dakota, in Deadwood Gulch in N Black Hills, 4 m. N of Lead; pop. 3045; trade center for surrounding mining camps and cattle ranches; mining, ore smelting and refining, lumbering, livestock raising; tourist center; laid out in 1876 following discovery of gold in Deadwood Gulch (1875).
Deaf Smith (děf smith; dēf). County in Texas. See *Table* at TEXAS.
Deal (dēl). **1** Borough and summer resort, Monmouth co., E cen. New Jersey, on Atlantic Ocean ab. 4 m. S of Long Branch; pop. 1889.
2 Municipal borough, Kent, SE England, on Strait of Dover 8 m. NNE of Dover; pop. 24,276; large safe anchorage; boatbuilding center; reputed landing place of Julius Caesar 55 B.C.
Deal Island. 1 Small island, partly marshland, in Tangier Sound, Chesapeake Bay, NW Somerset co., Maryland.
2 Town, NW part of the island; pop. 810.
Dean, Forest of (dēn). Royal forest 117,560 acres, W Gloucestershire, SW cen. England, bet. the Severn and the Wye; contains iron and coal mines.

Dean Channel. Inlet of Pacific Ocean (Queen Charlotte Sound) ab. 75 m. long, W British Columbia, Canada; receives **Dean River** (ab. 150 m. long) from the E; connects with Burke Channel on S.
De·án' Fu'nes (dā·än' fōō'nâs). Town, Córdoba prov., N cen. Argentina, on railroad 75 m. NNW of Córdoba; pop. (est.) 11,755.
Dear'born (dęr'bôrn; -bērn). **1** County in Indiana. See *Table* at INDIANA.
2 City, Wayne co., SE Michigan, 10 m. W of Detroit; pop. 112,007; site of the Ford automobile-manufacturing plant; incorporated as city 1927.
Dearg, Ben. See BEN DEARG.
Dearne (dûrn). River 25 m. long, West Riding, Yorkshire, N England; tributary of the Don.
Dease (dēs). River ab. 120 m. long, N Brit. Columbia, Canada; flows N from small Dease Lake to the Liard at Lower Post on the Alaska Highway.
Dease Strait. Channel bet. S Victoria I. and N Canada mainland, E of Coronation Gulf.
Death Valley (děth). **1** Valley in Inyo co., E California, bet. Panamint Mts. on W and Amargosa Range on E; Amargosa river flows into it from S; contains small pool, Badwater, lowest point in U.S., 280 ft. below sea level, less than 80 m. from Mt. Whitney (14,495 ft.), highest point in U.S. outside of Alaska); has been set aside as **Death Valley National Monument: see** UNITED STATES, *National Monuments.*
2 Post office, Inyo co., E California, E of Death Valley National Monument.
Deau'ville' (dō'vēl'; *Angl.* dō'vĭl). Commune, Calvados dept., NW France, on the Bay of the Seine ab. 20 m. NE of Caen; pop. (1931) 4827; resort, racecourse; just E of Normandy invasion coast 1944.
De Ba'ca (dě bä'kȧ). County in New Mexico. See *Table* at NEW MEXICO.
De'bar (dě'bär). Fortified town, W Macedonia federated republic, Yugoslavia, near the Drin river and Albanian border; pop. 6913; commercial center; cattle breeding; nearby sulfurous springs. Assigned to Serbia 1913; belonged to Vardarska co. 1929–45.
Debba, Ed. See ED DEBBA.
Deb'dou' (děb'dōō'). Town, NE Morocco, NW Africa, SSW of Oudjda.
de Bildt (dě bĭlt'). Commune, Utrecht prov., cen. Netherlands, a suburb of Utrecht; pop. 11,151.
Dę'blin (děNm'blěn; *Angl.* děm'blĭn); *Russ.* **I·van'go-rod** (ĭ·vän'gŭ·rŭt; *Angl.* ĭ·văn'gŏ·rŏd). Town at junction of Wieprz and Vistula rivers, Lublin prov., E Poland; taken by Germans Aug. 4, 1915.
De'bo, Lake (dā'bō). Lake, cen. Mali, West Africa, ab. 150 m. SW of Tombouctou; traversed from SW to N by the Niger river.
De'bra Mar'kos (dû'brû mär'kōs; *Angl.* děb'rȧ). Town in W Ethiopia, 110 m. NW of Addis Ababa; ✳ of former Gojjam prov.; pop. ab. 5000.
De'bre·cen (dě'brě·tsěn). Autonomous city, E Hungary, 120 m. E of Budapest; 369 sq. m.; pop. (1939) 122,517; commercial center in agricultural and livestock-raising region; scene of Kossuth's proclamation 1849 decreeing deposition of the Hapsburgs; in World War II taken by Russians Sept. 1944; meeting place of provisional Hungarian National Assembly Dec. 21, 1944.
De·cap'o·lis (dě·kăp'ŏ·lĭs). Region in N of ancient Palestine, beginning W of Jordan river at E end of Plain of Esdraelon and stretching to the E and NE of the Sea of Galilee; settled by many Greeks following Alexander's conquests, but got its name (Greek, literally, "ten cities") from the league of 10 (originally) Greek cities formed after Pompey's campaign 64–63 B.C.; generally under Roman control. Damascus was only important city; Scythopolis (Beisan) the only one W of the Jordan.
De·ca'tur (dě·kā'tẽr). **1** Name of counties in five states of the U.S. See *Tables* at GEORGIA, INDIANA, IOWA, KANSAS, TENNESSEE.

2 Industrial city, ⊗ of Morgan co., N Alabama, on Tennessee river 75 m. N of Birmingham; pop. 29,217; chartered as city 1826; devastated by Civil War; consolidated 1927 with city of Albany.

3 City, ⊗ of De Kalb co., NW cen. Georgia, 5 m. E of Atlanta; pop. 22,026; residential suburb of Atlanta; incorporated 1823; Agnes Scott College (1889; women).

4 City, ⊗ of Macon co., cen. Illinois, on Sangamon river 35 m. E of Springfield; pop. 78,004; incorporated as city 1836; in corn-growing and coal-mining section; manufactures starch, corn meal, corn sirup, livestock feed, and metal products; railroad center; in May 1860, Abraham Lincoln here received his first endorsement by a party convention for the presidential nomination. Millikin University (1901; coed.).

5 City, ⊗ of Adams co., E Indiana, 20 m. SSE of Fort Wayne; pop. 8327; in agricultural, dairy, and lumbering section.

6 Village, Van Buren co., SW Michigan, 24 m. WSW of Kalamazoo; pop. 1827.

7 Town, ⊗ of Newton co., E cen. Mississippi; pop. 1340.

8 Town, ⊗ of Meigs co., SE Tennessee; pop. 681.

9 City, ⊗ of Wise co., N Texas, 25 m. W of Denton; pop. 3563; trade center and shipping point for agricultural and dairy region.

Decatur, Lake. Lake 13 m. long by ½ m. wide made by damming Sangamon river E of Decatur, Macon co., cen. Illinois.

Decatur City. Town, Decatur co., S Iowa, 5 m. W of Leon; pop. 6435.

De·ca′tur·ville (dė·kā′tẽr·vǐl; *Sou. also* -v′l). Town, ⊗ of Decatur co., W Tennessee; pop. 571.

De·caze′ville′ (dė·käz′vēl′). Mining and manufacturing commune, Aveyron dept., S France, on Lot river 20 m. NW of Rodez; pop. 12,365; coal mines; foundries, steel mills.

Dec′can (dĕk′ăn; dĕk′ăn; dė·kăn′). The peninsula of India S of the Narbada river; by some restricted to the tableland bet. the Narbada and Kistna, comprising Maharashtra and parts of Madhya Pradesh, Andhra Pradesh, Mysore, and Orissa. See SOUTHERN DECCAN, UNITED DECCAN STATE. Region of predominantly Dravidian population not reached by Aryan invasion (see INDIA); states of Deccan vassals of Maurya rulers c. 3d cent. B.C.; gradually passed under rule of kings of Andhra, a state which expanded from original location on E coast of Deccan to become paramount in cen. and N India 1st cent. B.C.–3d cent. A.D.; invaded by Moslems in 13th cent. and conquered in 14th cent.; ruled by independent Mohammedan Bahmani sultanate which later split up into five Mohammedan kingdoms of Deccan (Ahmadnagar, Berar, Bidar, Bijapur, and Golconda); in 18th cent. became scene of rivalry of British and French and subsequently of British struggle against Marathas.

Deccan and Kol′ha·pur States (kō′là·poŏr). Former agency division, W India, comprising 18 Indian states (6 salute and 12 nonsalute), in S Bombay prov. and W Deccan; 10,870 sq. m.; pop. (1941) 2,785,428; chief state Kolhapur, with former agency headquarters at city of Kolhapur; area of 6 salute states (Bhor, Janjira, Kolhapur, Mudhol, Sangli, and Savantvadi) 6888 sq. m., pop. (1941) 1,969,442. On Aug. 26, 1947, seven of the states (Aundh, Bhor, Kurundwad [Sr.], Miraj [Jr.], Phaltan, Ramdurg, and Sangli) formed a new state, the United Deccan State.

De·cep′tion Island (dė·sĕp′shŭn). See SOUTH SHETLAND ISLANDS.

Dě′čín (dyě′chēn); *Ger.* **Tet′schen** (tā′chěn). City, N Bohemia prov., W Czechoslovakia, on the Labe (Elbe) opp. Podmokly, near border of Saxony; pop. (1930) 13,034; manufactures chemicals, confectionery, cotton goods; 17th-cent. castle.

De·cize′ (dė·sēz′). Commune, S Nièvre dept., cen. France; pop. 3477; S terminus of the Canal du Nivernais.

De·co′rah (dė·kōr′à). City, ⊗ of Winneshiek co., NE Iowa, 62 m. NE of Waterloo; pop. 6435; Luther College (1861; coed.; Lutheran).

Dede Agach. See ALEXANDROÚPOLIS.

Ded′ham (dĕd′ăm). Town, ⊗ of Norfolk co., E Massachusetts, on Charles river 9 m. SW of Boston; pop. 23,869; primarily residential; one of oldest towns in state, settled 1635; first free school in America supported by general tax, built 1649.

Dee (dē). **1** River 90 m. long in NE Scotland; rises on the slopes of the Cairngorm Mts., flows E into North Sea at Aberdeen; noted for its scenery and its salmon fishing.

2 River 50 m. long in S Scotland; flows S in Kirkcudbright co. into Solway Firth.

3 River 70 m. long in N Wales and W England; rises in Bala Lake, N Wales; flows E, NE, and N, forming a section of the English-Welsh boundary; crosses into W England, passes through Chester, and empties into Irish Sea through a broad estuary.

Deel (dēl). River 26 m. long, co. Limerick, SW Ireland, flowing into Shannon river.

Deep (dēp). River ab. 130 m. long, N cen. North Carolina; rises in Guilford co., flows SE and E to unite with Haw river in Chatham co. and form Cape Fear river.

Deep Bay. 1 Bay NW of Kowloon Penin., Hong Kong, SE China; controlled by Great Britain.

2 Inlet on SE cen. coast of Malaita I., SE Solomon Is.

Deep Bot′tom (bŏt′ŭm). Hamlet, Henrico co., E cen. Virginia; scene of fighting during Civil War 1864.

Deep Creek Lake. Artificial lake, Garrett co., NW corner of Maryland; 4000 acres; formed by dam of the Youghiogheny Hydro-Electric Power Co. in **Deep Creek** near its confluence with the Youghiogheny river.

Deep′ha·ven (dēp′hā′věn). Village, Hennepin co., SE cen. Minnesota, W of Minneapolis; pop. 3286.

Deep Hole Harbor. Inlet of Nantucket Sound on S coast of W Barnstable co., SE Massachusetts.

Deep River. 1 River, North Carolina. See DEEP.

2 Town, Connecticut: see SAYBROOK.

3 Village, Middlesex co., Connecticut, in town of Deep River (before 1947 called Saybrook); pop. 2166.

Deer, Old (ōl dẽr). Parish, Aberdeen co., NE Scotland, W of Peterhead; pop. 2990; site of ancient abbey the founding of which is related in the *Book of Deer*, a MS. copy of portions of the Gospels in Latin Vulgate version containing marginal notes in Gaelic; the oldest Scottish document containing Gaelic, it was discovered 1857 at Cambridge University by Henry Bradshaw; no part of the original abbey remains.

Deer Creek. River 80 m. long, cen. Ohio; rises in Madison co., flows SE through Pickaway co., enters Scioto river in N Ross co.

Deer Creek Dam. Dam completed 1941 across Provo river, N cen. Utah; height 235 ft.; impounds water, **Deer Creek Reservoir**, for irrigation.

Deer′field (dẽr′fēld). **1** River ab. 100 m. long, NW Massachusetts; rises in Windham co., SE Vermont, flows S across Mass. border and E into Connecticut river in cen. Franklin co., NW Mass.

2 *now* **Deerfield Beach.** Town, Broward co., SE Florida, on Atlantic Ocean 38 m. N of Miami; pop. 9573; incorporated 1925; agricultural center.

3 Village, Lake co., NE corner of Illinois, 18 m. S of Waukegan; pop. 11,786.

4 Town, Franklin co., NW Massachusetts, 4 m. S of Greenfield; pop. 3338; one of oldest towns in Connecticut valley, founded 1669–72; suffered from two serious Indian attacks, the Bloody Brook massacre 1675, and the raid of 1704 when a band of Indians and French burned the town, killed 49 and carried ab. 100 captive to Canada. Seat of Deerfield Academy (estab. 1797), now a boys' preparatory school.

Deer′ Flat′ Dam′. Earth-embankment dam forming **Lake Low′ell** (lō′ĕl) or **Deer Flat Reservoir**, in Canyon co., SW Idaho; reservoir filled by water diverted through canal from Boise river.

Deer Island. **1** Island on E side of entrance to Penobscot Bay, SE Maine; part of Hancock co.; chief village Deer Isle.

2 Island bet. Boston Bay and Boston Harbor, Massachusetts.

3 Island, Charlotte co., SW New Brunswick, Canada, in S part of Passamaquoddy Bay near coast of Maine; chief village Fairhaven.

Deer Isle. **1** Island 9 m. long adjacent to Deer I., in Penobscot Bay, SE Maine; noted for its pink granite.

2 Town, Hancock co., SE Maine, on Deer I. in Penobscot Bay; pop. 1129; fishing and summer resort.

Deer Lodge. **1** County in Montana. See *Table* at MONTANA.

2 City, ⊗ of Powell co., W Montana, 37 m. WSW of Helena; pop. 4681.

Deer Mountain. **1** Peak 6233 ft. in W North Carolina.

2 Peak 5500 ft. in Pennington co., SW South Dakota.

Deer Park. **1** Unincorporated community, Suffolk co., New York, in cen. Long I. N of Babylon; pop. 16,726.

2 City, Hamilton co., SW corner of Ohio, 9 m. NNE of Cincinnati; pop. 8423.

De·fi'ance (dĕ·fī'ăns). **1** County in Ohio. See *Table* at OHIO.

2 City, its ⊗, NW Ohio, at confluence of Auglaize and Maumee rivers 40 m. NNW of Lima; pop. 14,553; on site of Fort Defiance built by Gen. Anthony Wayne 1794; incorp. as village 1836, as city 1881; manufacturing, agricultural, trading, and shipping center; manufactures machines and machinery, automobile parts and accessories, service station equipment, hardware, steel, dairy products. Defiance College (founded 1850, as college 1885; coed.).

De Fu'ni·ak Springs (dĕ fū'nĭ·ăk). Town, ⊗ of Walton co., NW Florida, 70 m. ENE of Pensacola; pop. 5282; in region producing cotton, rice, sugar cane, grapes, peaches; manufactures turpentine; large fresh-water spring; site of Florida Chautauqua (second in U.S.).

Degh (dāg). River ab. 200 m. long, N India; flows SW out of S Kashmir through E West Punjab, Pakistan, to the Ravi river SW of Lahore.

De'go (dā'gō). Commune, Savona prov., W cen. Liguria, NW Italy; pop. (1931) 3032; scene Apr. 14, 1796 of defeat of Austrians by Napoleon's forces.

De Grey (dĕ grā'). River ab. 300 m. long, NW Western Australia, flows N and NW to Indian Ocean near Point Larrey.

De·hi·bat' (dā·hĭ·băt'). Town, SE Tunisia, on Tripolitania boundary 95 m. S of Médenine.

De'hi·wa'la–Mount La·vin'i·a (dā'hĭ·wä'lá mount' lá·vĭn'ĭ·á). Urban district, W Western Province, Ceylon, on Indian Ocean 8 m. S of Colombo; pop. 34,288; health and pleasure resort located on rock ledge.

Dehli. See DELHI.

Deh'ra Dun (dā'rá dōon'). Town, NW Uttar Pradesh, N India, 140 m. NNE of Delhi; pop. 144,216; headquarters of Government Forest Department and Trigonometrical Survey; also seat of Indian Forest College and its associated Research Institute and India Military College (1934); has large military cantonment for Gurkha troops; fine temple in Mohammedan style erected 1699 by the Sikh guru, Ram Rai.

Deim Zu·beir' (dīm' zōo·bĭr'; dām' zōo·bār'). Town, SW Sudan, in Equatoria prov.

De'i·ra (dā'ē·rá). Anglian kingdom which emerged in second half of 6th cent. A.D. and extended from Tees river to the Humber (eastern part of modern Yorkshire); after long conflict with its northern neighbor, Bernicia, both were united in 7th cent. to form kingdom of Northumbria (q.v.); partitioned by Danes in 9th cent.; before Norman Conquest a separate earldom, occasionally united with Bernicia.

Deir el–Bah'ri (dĭr' [dār'] ăl·bä'h'·rī). Temple site, Egypt, on W bank of Nile near Thebes and opp. Karnak; important archaeological site; tombs opened by Maspero 1881; temple, excavated 1906 and later, built by Queen Hatshepsut; situated at base of a cliff 400 ft. high; contains pictorial representations on its walls of expedition to land of Punt on the Somali coast.

Deir–ez–Zor (dĭr'ăz·zōor'; dār'-; -zōr'), *also* **Deir.** Town, E Syria, on the right bank of Euphrates river; pop. 6659; most important town of a large area, ✳ of former region of Zor; lies at junction of river route from Alep to Baghdad and from Damascus NE to Mosul.

Dej (dĕzh); *Hung.* **Dés** (dāsh). City, Transylvania region, NW Romania, on the Someş river; pop. (1939 est.) 12,595.

Dej'vi·ce (dĕ'i·vĭ·tsĕ); *Ger.* **Dej'witz** (dā'vĭts). Part of Prague, Bohemia, Czechoslovakia; pop. ab. 24,000.

De Kaap (dĕ käp'). Mountain, N Drakensberg Mts., Transvaal, NE Union of South Africa; gold fields in **De Kaap Valley** where town of Barberton was founded during the gold rush of 1884 and later.

De Kalb (dĕ kălb'; *in Ga., also* kăb'). **1** Name of counties in six states of the U.S. See *Tables* at ALABAMA, GEORGIA, ILLINOIS, INDIANA, MISSOURI, TENNESSEE.

2 City, De Kalb co., N Illinois, 28 m. SSE of Rockford; pop. 18,486; incorporated 1877; manufactures farm equipment, wire products, esp. barbed wire; Northern Illinois Univ. (1895; coed.).

3 Town, ⊗ of Kemper co., E Mississippi; pop. 880.

Dekkan. Var. of DECCAN.

De la Beche (dĕl'á·bāsh'). Mountain 10,058 ft., Southern Alps, South I., New Zealand, 9 m. NE of Aorangi.

Del'a·go'a Bay (dĕl'á·gō'á). Inlet 55 m. long of the Indian Ocean on extreme SE coast of Mozambique, SE Africa; the city of Lourenço Marques lies at its head.

History: Discovered by Portuguese 1502; neighboring territory explored 1544 by Lourenço Marques; site of trading settlement of Dutch 1721–30; islands in bay occupied by British 1861; claimed by Portuguese and British until attempt of Transvaal to occupy it 1868 brought dispute to a head; awarded to Portugal by arbitration 1875; after building of Delagoa Bay R.R. connecting Lourenço Marques (q.v.) with Pretoria 1895, as economic outlet for Transvaal, it became subject of British agreements with Germany (1898) and Portugal (1899); by Delagoa Bay R.R. arbitral award 1900, Portugal forced to pay indemnity for seizure of road.

De Lan'cey (dĕ lăn'sĭ). Locality, Jefferson co., W cen. Pennsylvania, ab. 14 m. SW of Du Bois.

De Land (dĕ lănd'). City, ⊗ of Volusia co., E Florida, 22 m WSW of Daytona Beach; pop. 10,775; founded 1876; center of citrus-growing region; winter resort; Ponce de Leon springs nearby; John B. Stetson University (founded 1883, incorp. 1889; coed.).

De·la'no (dĕ·lā'nō). City, Kern co., S California, 30 m. NNW of Bakersfield; pop. 11,913; ships grain and fruit.

Del'a·no, Mount (dĕl'á·nō). Peak 10,200 ft. of Rocky Mts., in Beaverhead co., SW Montana.

Del'a·no Peak (dĕl'á·nō). Mountain 12,162 ft. on boundary bet. Piute and Beaver cos., SW cen. Utah.

De·la'tyn (dĕ·lä't'n; *Pol.* dĕ·lä'tĭn). Town, SW Ukraine, U.S.S.R., at E end of Jablonica Pass on Prut river, 28 m. SSW of Stanislav (formerly in Stanisławów dept., Poland); pop. 8815; salt deposits, mineral baths. Occupied by Russians 1916; reoccupied 1917 by Germany.

Delatyn Pass. See JABLONICA PASS.

Del'a·van (dĕl'á·văn). City and summer resort, Walworth co., S Wisconsin, 19 m. S of Janesville; pop. 4846; manufactures knit goods, electric pumps, cigars.

Del'a·ware (dĕl'á·wâr; -wēr). **1** River 296 m. long, Pennsylvania and Delaware; formed by junction of east and west branches in Delaware co., S New York, flows SE to form Pennsylvania-New York, Pennsylvania-New Jersey, and Delaware-New Jersey boundaries, and empties into Delaware Bay; navigable to Trenton, New Jersey. See WASHINGTON CROSSING.

2 Middle Atlantic state of U.S.A., an original state of the Union, the first state to ratify the Federal Constitution,

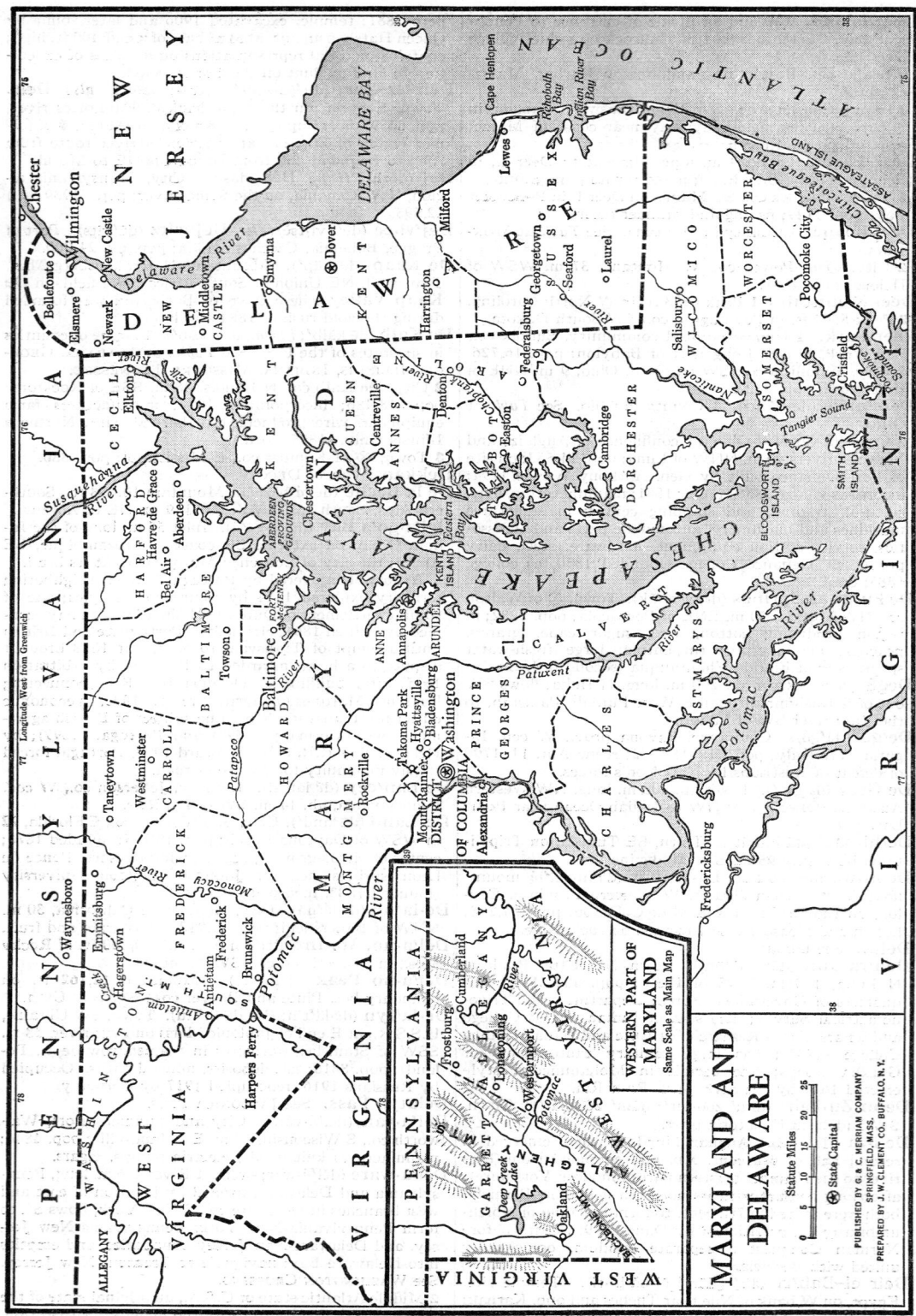

MARYLAND AND DELAWARE

WESTERN PART OF MARYLAND
Same Scale as Main Map

Statute Miles
0 5 10 15 20 25

⊕ State Capital

PUBLISHED BY G. & C. MERRIAM COMPANY
SPRINGFIELD, MASS.
PREPARED BY J. W. CLEMENT CO., BUFFALO, N.Y.

Dec. 7, 1787; bounded on N and NW by Pennsylvania, on E by Delaware river and Delaware Bay and the Atlantic Ocean, and on S and W by Maryland; 49th state in area, 2057 sq. m. (land area 1978 sq. m.); 46th state in population, 446,292; ✳ Dover. See *Table of States* at UNITED STATES. Divided into the following 3 counties (for pronunciations, see their individual entries):

NAME	LOCATION	AREA[1]	POP.[1]	CO. SEAT
Kent	cen.	595	65,651	Dover
New Castle	N	437	307,446	Wilmington
Sussex	S; coastal	946	73,195	Georgetown

[1] Area = land area in sq. m. Pop. from 1960 Census.

Nickname: Diamond State; also Blue Hen State. *State flower:* Peach blossom. *Motto:* Liberty and Independence. *Chief cities:* Wilmington, Newark. *River:* Delaware (see 1, above). *Highest point:* Centerville (440 ft.), in New Castle co. *Chief industries:* Fruitgrowing, chemical manufacture (Du Pont Co., in Wilmington).

History: Earliest settlements made by Dutch 1631, first permanent settlements made by Swedes 1638 (see NEW SWEDEN; WILMINGTON); New Sweden captured by Dutch 1655 and, as part of New Netherland, by English 1664; became part of a grant made to Penn (see PENN-SYLVANIA) 1682; in 1703 lower counties received right to separate legislative assembly, but remained under governor of Pennsylvania until 1776; active in American Revolution; formulated first constitution 1776, adopted present constitution 1897.

3 Name of counties in six states of the U.S. See *Tables* at INDIANA, IOWA, NEW YORK, OHIO, OKLAHOMA, PENN-SYLVANIA.

4 *or since 1961* **Cherry Hill.** Urban township, Camden co., W cen. New Jersey, E of Camden; pop. 31,522.

5 City ⊗ of Delaware co., cen. Ohio, 23 m. N of Columbus; pop. 13,282; founded 1808; manufactures chairs, stoves, machine screws, tiles, rubber goods; mineral springs; Ohio Wesleyan Univ. (1842; coed.). Birthplace of Rutherford B. Hayes, 19th president of U.S.

Delaware Bay. Arm of Atlantic Ocean, bet. SW coast of New Jersey and E coast of Delaware.

Delaware City. Town, New Castle co., N Delaware; pop. 1658; terminus of Chesapeake and Delaware Canal.

Delaware Water Gap. Borough, Monroe co., E Pennsylvania, E of Stroudsburg; pop. 554; summer resort on Delaware river at **Delaware Water Gap,** a gorge ab. 2 m. long through the Kittatinny Mt., having on W Mount Minsi, Pa. (ab. 1500 ft.) and on E Mount Tammany, N.J. (1480 ft.).

Del Car'men Mountains (děl kär'měn). Range 8000 to 10,000 ft. in N Coahuila state, N Mexico, a subsidiary range of the Sierra Madre Oriental. See SANTIAGO MOUNTAINS.

De·lé'mont' (dē-lā'môN'); *Ger.* **Dels'berg** (děls'běrк). Commune, N Bern canton, Switzerland, in the Jura Mts.; pop. (1930) 6393; watchmaking.

De Le·on' (dě lē·ŏn'). City, Comanche co., cen. Texas, 35 m. NNE of Brownwood; pop. 2022; in farming section.

Delft (dělft). Commune, South Holland prov., SW Netherlands; pop. (1939) 54,897; during 17th–18th cents. noted for its pottery manufacture (delftware); scene of the assassination of William the Silent 1584; birthplace of Grotius. Occupied by Germans May 1940.

Delft Island. Island in waters bet. Palk Strait and Palk Bay, off NW coast of Ceylon.

Delf·zijl' (dělf-zĭl'). Commune, Groningen prov., NE Netherlands, on Ems estuary; pop. 9666.

Del·ga'da Point (děl·gä'thä). Cape extending into Atlantic Ocean from S end of Váldez Penin., off E cen. coast of Argentina, S of the Gulf of San Matías.

Del·ga'do, Cape (děl·gä'dō; *Port.* dâl·gá'thoō). Cape extending into Indian Ocean on extreme NE coast of Mozambique, SE Africa.

Del'hi (děl'hī). **1** Village, ⊗ of Delaware co., S New York, 50 m. S of Utica; pop. 2307; dairying, agriculture.

2 Village, Norfolk co., SE Ontario, Canada, 25 m. SSW of Brantford; pop. 2517.

Del'hi (děl'ĭ); *more correctly* **Dil'li** (dĭl'lē) *or* **Deh'li** (dě'h'·lē). **1** Territory, N Indian Union, SE of the Punjab and formerly a part of the Punjab; 574 sq. m.; pop. (1951) 1,744,072; created 1912 for administrative purposes when city of Delhi was made capital of India; includes 65 villages on E bank of Jumna, formerly in Meerut division, United Provinces.

2 *or* **Old Delhi.** City, its ✳; the S and new part (officially **New Delhi**) ✳ of Indian Empire 1912–47, since 1947 ✳ of the Indian Union; on W bank of Jumna river; pop. including suburbs (1941) 521,849; important rail and trade center; produces gold and silver filigree work and embroidery, jewelry, shawls, muslins, pottery, wood and ivory carvings; has splendid examples of Mohammedan and Hindu architecture, among the finest being the Imperial Palace (better known as the "Fort," contains the Diwan-i-Am or Hall of Public Audience, where was formerly placed the famous Peacock Throne, and the Diwan-i-Khas or Hall of Private Audience), the Jama Masjid or Great Mosque (one of largest mosques in the world), the tomb of Humayun, and the Kutb Minar (one of world's most perfect towers). South of the old walled city (Old Delhi, or **Shah'ja·han'a·bad'** [shä'ja·hän'-ä·bäd'], as it is still called locally) is located the modern seat of the Indian government (New Delhi) with symmetrically planned streets, attractive buildings, and an imposing capitol. The present city, seventh on this site (the most ancient known as **In'dra·pras'tha** [in'drá-prŭs'tá]), was reconstructed by Shah Jahan (see below). Seat of the Univ. of Delhi and of several colleges. See FIROZABAD; TUGHLAKABAD.

History: Chosen as capital by founder of Mohammedan Slave dynasty 1206; at height in 13th cent. when Sultanate of Delhi controlled northern India; laid waste by invasion of Tamerlane 1398; conquered by Baber, founder of Mogul dynasty in India, 1526; although Mogul capital mostly at Agra (*q.v.*), city beautified, beginning in 1631 with building under Shah Jahan; pillaged by Nadir Shah 1739; with its surrender to Marathas 1772, Mogul emperor came under Maratha control; taken by British under Lake 1803; a center of Sepoy Mutiny 1857, held by mutineers for several weeks; scene of coronation durbars 1903, 1911; replaced Calcutta as capital of British India 1912 (see NEW DELHI).

De'li (dā'lē). Short but important stream of NE Sumatra, Indonesia, flows NE to Strait of Malacca at Belawan, the port of Medan.

De·li'ce (dě·lē'jě). River ab. 175 m. long in cen. Turkey in Asia; flows NW and N into the Kızıl Irmak.

De·li'cias (då·lē'syäs). Town, Chihuahua state, N Mexico; pop. 6020.

De'litzsch (dā'lĭch). Manufacturing city, E Germany, in former Saxony prov., Prussia, 22 m. SSE of Dessau; pop. 14,892; manufactures cigars, chocolates, shoes, sugar; rolling mills. Made city 1306.

De'li·um (dē'lĭ·ŭm). Ancient seaport in Boeotia, E cen. Greece, on the E coast; battle 424 B.C. in which Boeotians defeated the Athenians.

Del'len·baugh, Mount (děl'ěn·bô). Peak 6750 ft. in N Mohave co., NW Arizona.

Dell Rapids (děl). City and resort, Minnehaha co., SE South Dakota, on Big Sioux river 20 m. N of Sioux Falls; pop. 1863; rock quarries.

Del'lys' (dě·lēs'). Seaport and commune (pop. 18,864), NE Alger dept., N Algeria, 45 m. E of Algiers.

Del·mar'va Peninsula (děl·mär'vá). Peninsula, E United States, bet. Chesapeake and Delaware Bays; includes Eastern Shore (*q.v.*) and all of Delaware;—so called from *Del*aware, *Mar*yland, *Va.* (Virginia).

Del'men·horst (děl'měn·hôrst). Commercial and manufacturing commune, Lower Saxony state, West Germany, 9 m. WSW of Bremen; pop. 24,700; manufactures linoleum, textiles, coaches.

Del Mon'te (dĕl mŏn'tĕ). **1** Seaside resort, Monterey co., W California, on S shore of Monterey Bay.
2 (*Span.* dĕl môn'tä). Town, N Bukidnon prov., N Mindanao, Phil. Is., 15 m. SE of Cagayan; airfield; pineapple plantation.

Del Norte (dĕl nôrt'). **1** County in California. See *Table* at CALIFORNIA.
2 Town, ⊗ of Rio Grande co., S Colorado, on the Rio Grande 30 m. WNW of Alamosa; pop. 1856.

De Long Islands (dĕ lŏng'). Group of three small islands (Bennet, Henrietta, and Zhokova) in Arctic Ocean NE of New Siberian Is.; belong to Yakutsk A.S.S.R.

De Long Mountains. Range, W end of Brooks Range, N of Noatak river, NW Alaska; highest 5000 ft.

Del'o·raine (dĕl'ō-rān'). Town, N Tasmania, Australia, 25 m. W of Launceston; pop. 1552; dairying; farming.

De'los (dē'lŏs); *Gr.* **Dē'los** (*Mod. Gr.* thē'lôs). Smallest island 2 sq. m. of the Cyclades, S Aegean Sea, in the narrow passage bet. Mykonos and Rhenea Is. By ancient Greeks considered the center of the archipelago (whence the name: see CYCLADES), sacred as the legendary birthplace of Apollo and Artemis; guarded treasure of Delian League 478–454 B.C. (see ATHENS); became flourishing commercial center and important slave market, especially after Rome made it a free port 166 B.C.; sacked during Mithridatic Wars; gradually declined and became deserted; excavations by the French since 1877 have uncovered many remains of interest.

Del'phi (dĕl'fī). **1** City, ⊗ of Carroll co., NW cen. Indiana, on Wabash river 30 m. WNW of Kokomo; pop. 2517.
2 *modern* **Del·phoi'** (thȧl·fē'); *in early times* **Py'tho** (pī'thō). Town, Phthiotis and Phocis dept., Greece; pop. 1085; situated nearly equidistant (ab. 6 m.) from N shore of Gulf of Corinth and from Mt. Parnassus. From at least 7th cent. B.C., visited by ancient Greeks as the seat of Delphic oracle and of worship of Apollo Pythius and Dionysus; scene of Pythian games, held every fourth year; c. 590 B.C. Crisa punished by Thessaly and allies for levying tolls upon pilgrims to the oracle (First Sacred War); enriched by gifts from all Greece, it became coveted booty, as when Phocians used its wealth to finance Third Sacred War (355–346 B.C.), and its temples were plundered by Sulla and other Romans.

Del'phos (dĕl'fŏs). City, Allen and Van Wert cos., NW Ohio, 13 m. WNW of Lima; pop. 6961; settled 1834; manufactures motor trucks, trailers, bank furniture.

Del'ray' Beach (dĕl'rā'). City, Palm Beach co., SE Florida, on Atlantic Ocean 18 m. S of West Palm Beach; pop. 12,330; settled 1901, incorp. 1927; tourist resort.

Del Ri'o (dĕl rē'ō). City and port of entry, ⊗ of Val Verde co., SW Texas, on Rio Grande 37 m. SE of its confluence with Pecos river; pop. 18,612; market and distributing center for agricultural area; ships wool, lambs, mohair; grape culture.

Delsberg. See DELÉMONT.

Del'ta (dĕl'tȧ). **1** Name of counties in three states of the U.S. See *Tables* at COLORADO, MICHIGAN, TEXAS.
2 City, ⊗ of Delta co., W Colorado, on Gunnison river 35 m. SE of Grand Junction; pop. 3832; ships fruit.
3 Village, Fulton co., NW Ohio, 24 m. W of Toledo; pop. 2376.

Del'ta A'ma·cu'ro (dĕl'tä ä'mä·kōō'rō). Territory of Venezuela. See *Table* at VENEZUELA.

Del'ville Wood (dĕl'vĭl; *Fr.* dĕl'vĕl'). Forested area near Longueval, Somme dept., N France; taken by Allies as part of the battle of the Somme 1916.

Del'vi·në (dĕl·vē'nĕ); *Ital.* **Del'vi·no** (dĕl'vē·nō). Town, S Albania, just S of Gjinokastër; pop. ab. 7000.

De'mar·ca'tion Point (dē'mär·kā'shŭn). Cape extending N into Beaufort Sea, marking boundary bet. Alaska and Yukon Territory, Canada, 69°45′N, 141°W.

Dem'a·vend (dĕm'ȧ·vĕnd) *or* **Da'ma·vand'** (dä'mä·vänd'). Peak 18,600 ft., N Iran, NE of Tehran; highest in the Elburz Mts.

De'mer (dā'mĕr). River 47 m. long in E cen. Belgium; flows W in Limburg and Brabant provs., empties into Dyle river 6 m. N of Louvain.

Dem'e·rar'a (dĕm'ē·rär'ȧ; -rär'ȧ). **1** River ab. 200 m. long, British Guiana; flows N parallel with and E of the Essequibo river, empties into Atlantic Ocean at Georgetown; navigable for over 100 m.
2 County in British Guiana; 4420 sq. m.; pop. (1931) 185,184; ⊗ Georgetown.

De·me'tri·as (dē·mē'trĭ·ȧs). Ruined city, SE Thessaly, NE Greece, near modern Volos and just SE of Iolcus; founded c. 290 B.C. by Demetrius Poliorcetes and a favorite residence of Macedonian kings.

Dem'ing (dĕm'ĭng). Village and health resort, ⊗ of Luna co., SW New Mexico, W of Las Cruces; pop. 6764.

Demir Hissár, Demir Hisar. See SIDEROKASTRON.

Dem·min' (dĕ·mēn'). Manufacturing city, E Germany, in the former Pomerania prov. of Prussia, on Peene river 73 m. NW of Stettin; pop. 12,787; manufactures barrel staves, sugar, brewery products. One of oldest Slavic settlements in Pomerania; unsuccessfully besieged by Germans 1148; conquered by Henry the Lion 1164; became member of Hanseatic League 1283; to Sweden 1648, Prussia 1720.

Dem·nat' (dĕm·nät'). Town, S cen. Morocco, NW Africa, 60 m. E of Marrakech.

Dem'o·crat, Mount (dĕm'ō·krăt). Peak 14,142 ft. in Park and Lake cos., cen. Colorado.

Demonesi Insulae. See PRINCES ISLANDS.

De·mop'o·lis (dē·mŏp'ō·lĭs). City, Marengo co., W Alabama, on Tombigbee river 48 m. W of Selma; pop. 7377; cotton and allied products.

Dem'o·rest (dĕm'ō·rĕst). Town, Habersham co., NE Georgia, 7 m. from Clarkesville; pop. 1029; Piedmont College (1897; coed.).

De·mot'i·ca (dē·mŏt'ĭ·kȧ; *Ital.* dä·mô'tē·kä). Var. of *Dimotika*. See DIDYMOTEIKHON.

Dem'po (dĕm'pō). Volcanic peak 10,364 ft. in S Sumatra, Indonesia, in the Barisan Mts. E of Benkulen.

De·nain' (dē·năN'). Commune, Nord dept., N France, 26 m. SE of Lille; pop. 26,478; coal mining; metal works. Fortified at early date; scene of battle July 24, 1712 (during War of Spanish Succession) in which Marshal Villars defeated Prince Eugene of Savoy.

Denali. See Mount McKINLEY.

Den'bigh (dĕn'bĭ). **1** Former village, ⊗ of former Warwick co., SE Virginia; now part of city of Newport News.
2 County in Wales. See DENBIGHSHIRE.
3 Municipal borough, Denbighshire, N Wales; pop. 8127; agriculture, stone quarrying; ruined Norman castle besieged for eleven months by Cromwell's Parliamentarians before it capitulated 1645.

Den'bigh·shire (dĕn'bĭ·shĭr; -shēr) *or* **Denbigh.** County, N Wales; area 669 sq. m.; pop. (1951) 170,699; ⊗ Ruthin; hilly area; rivers Dee, Conway, Clwyd; agriculture, stock raising, mining (lead, zinc, iron, copper), quarrying (limestone, slate).

Den'der (dĕn'dĕr). **1** River 250 m. long, E Sudan; rises in Ethiopia, flows NW into Blue Nile N of Sennar.
2 Navigable river 42 m. long in W cen. Belgium; flows N out of Hainaut prov. into the Schelde river at Termonde.

Den'de·ra (dăn'dŭ·rȧ); *anc.* **Ten'ty·ra** (tĕn'tĭ·rȧ). Village, Upper Egypt, on left side of Nile opp. Qena; ancient city dedicated to worship of goddess Hathor; temple was begun 1st cent. B.C. and added to by the Romans, esp. Augustus and Domitian; among temple decorations was a celebrated zodiac now in Bibliothèque Nationale in Paris.

Den'der·mon'de (dĕn'dĕr·môn'dĕ). = TERMONDE.

Den'ham Springs (dĕn'ăm). Town, Livingston parish, SE Louisiana, E of Baton Rouge; pop. 5991.

Den Hel'der (dĕn hĕl'dĕr). Commune, North Holland prov., W Netherlands; pop. (1939) 37,325; fortified port on the Mars Diep, an outlet from Wadden Zee into North Sea; fortified by Napoleon 1811; Dutch naval station.

De′nia (dā′nyä); *anc.* **Di·a′ni·um** (dī·ā′nĭ·ŭm). Seaport commune, Alicante prov., SE Spain, on Mediterranean Sea 45 m. NE of Alicante; pop. 12,323.

De·nil′i·quin (dĕ·nĭl′ĭ·kwĭn). Town, S New South Wales, SE Australia, 250 m. W of Canberra; pop. 3192; in the Riverina, a pastoral and agricultural region.

Den′i·son (dĕn′ĭ·s'n). **1** City, ⊗ of Crawford co., W Iowa, 58 m. NNE of Council Bluffs; pop. 4930; in section producing grain, cattle, hogs, dairy products. **2** City, Grayson co., NE Texas, in valley of Red river 10 m. N of Sherman; pop. 22,748; railroad center; shipping point for agricultural region (esp. cheese, cotton, processed pecans and peanuts); grape culture; birthplace of Dwight D. Eisenhower, 34th president of the U.S.

Denison Dam. See UNITED STATES, *Dams*.

De·niz·li′ (dĕ·nĕz·lē′). **1** Vilayet, SW Turkey in Asia; 4304 sq. m.; pop. 270,327. **2** Town, its ✳, on a tributary of the Menderes ab. 112 m. SE of İzmir, with which it has rail connections; pop. 16,847; beautifully situated with fine gardens; during wars bet. Seljuks and Byzantines in 12th cent. replaced ancient **La·od′i·ce′a** (lā·ŏd′ĭ·sē′à; lā′ŏd-) *or* **Laodicea ad Ly′cum** (ăd lī′kŭm), now in ruins nearby, founded by Antiochus II and several times destroyed by earthquake or conquest, but recovered; one of the Seven Churches of Asia Minor (*Rev.* i–iii).

Den′mark (dĕn′märk). **1** *Danish* **Dan′mark** (dàn′märk). Kingdom, NW Europe, comprising most of Jutland (*Dan.* Jylland) Penin. and a group of islands in Baltic Sea, the most prominent of which are Sjælland, Fyn, Falster, Lolland, Langeland, and Bornholm (90 m. E of Sjælland); bounded on the N by the Skagerrak, on the E by the Kattegat, Öresund and the Baltic Sea, on the S by Germany, and on the W by the North Sea; 16,576 sq. m.; pop. 3,680,605, (1945) 4,045,232; ✳ Copenhagen; outlying possessions are the Faeroes (540 sq. m., pop. [1945] 29,198) and the colony of Greenland (839,800 sq. m., pop. [1945] 18,431); divided into the city of Copenhagen (28 sq. m., pop. 666,269; 1945 census 731,707) and the following 22 counties (for pronunciation of their names, see their individual entries):

COUNTY[1]	LOCATION	AREA[2]	POP.[2]
Aabenraa-Sönderborg[3]	SE Jutland	475	82,338
Aalborg	NE Jutland	1,129	194,423
Aarhus	E Jutland	971	274,320
Bornholm[4]	Bornholm I.	228	45,930
Copenhagen[5]	E Sjælland	453	358,734
Farö[6]	Faeroes	540	25,744
Frederiksborg[7]	N Sjælland	519	119,465
Haderslev	SE Jutland	518	63,294
Hjörring	NE Jutland	1,102	153,261
Holbæk	NW Sjælland	676	121,120
Maribo	Lolland and Falster Is.	693	132,109
Odense	N Fyn I.	699	214,929
Præstö	SE Sjælland	654	118,659
Randers	E Jutland	952	152,810
Ribe	SW Jutland	1,184	148,076
Ringköbing	W Jutland	1,800	158,259
Sorö	SW Sjælland	571	114,554
Svendborg	SE Fyn I.	643	142,345
Thisted	NW Jutland	686	84,054
Tönder[8]	SW Jutland	505	39,100
Vejle	SE Jutland	907	174,929
Viborg	N cen. Jutland	1,180	147,371

[1] Unless otherwise noted, its county seat has the same name.
[2] Area = land area in sq. m. Pop. from 1935 Census.
[3] Comprises the former cos. of Aabenraa (305 sq. m.) and Sönderborg (170 sq. m.). County seat Aabenraa.
[4] County seat Rönne.
[5] County seat Roskilde.
[6] County seat Thorshavn.
[7] County seat Hilleröd.
[8] Ceded by Germany to Denmark after World War I.

Low, flat land with highest point (on E coast of Jutland) not above 550 ft.; has no large rivers and few lakes,

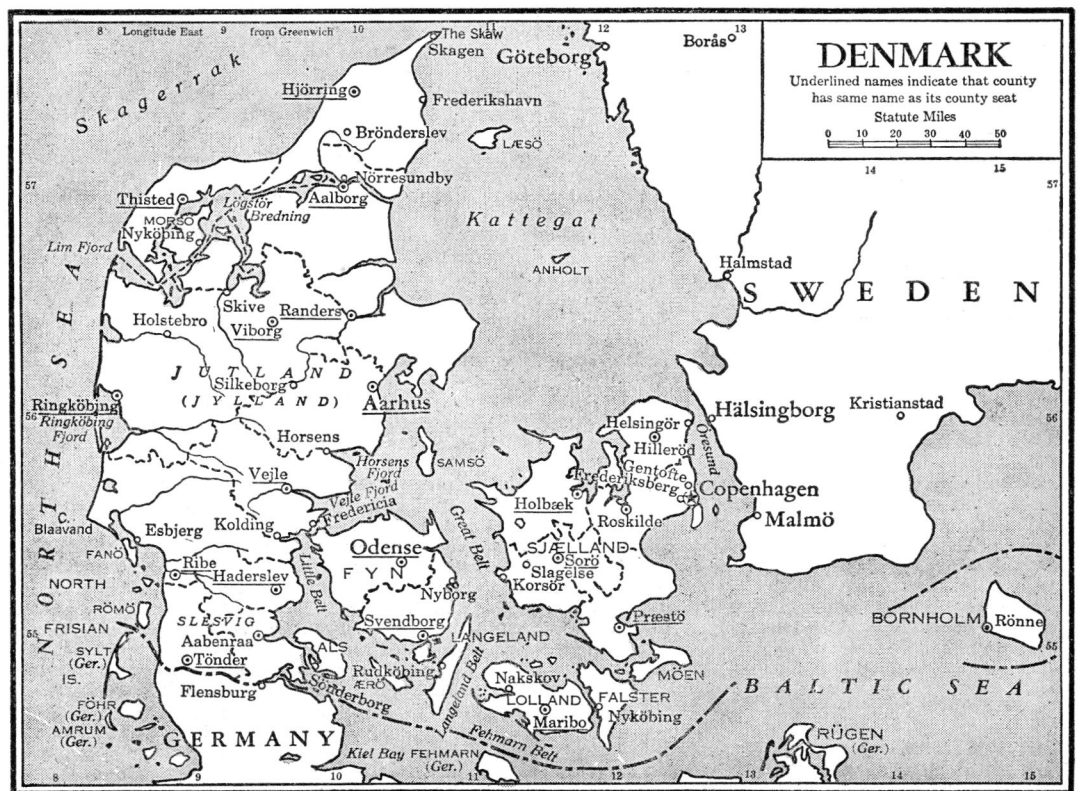

DENMARK
Underlined names indicate that county
has same name as its county seat
Statute Miles
0   10   20   30   40   50

but its shore line, esp. in N and W of Jutland, is indented by many lagoons and fiords; most important is Lim Fjord extending across N Jutland from North Sea to Kattegat. Great Belt is passage bet. Sjælland and Fyn, and Little Belt a narrower channel bet. Fyn and mainland. Agriculture and cattle raising are chief industries; fishing and brewing also important; grains (wheat, rye, oats, and barley) and dairy products (esp. butter) are chief products. Chief cities Copenhagen, Aarhus, Odense, Aalborg, Esbjerg, Randers, Horsens.

History: Settled by Danes, a Scandinavian branch of Teutons, c. 6th cent. A.D.; participated in Viking raids on England, France, and Low Countries 8th–10th cents.; by 1014 the united Danish kingdom occupied Schleswig (*q.v.*), southern Sweden, and England; under Canute the Great 1018–35, converted to Christianity and ruled a short-lived "northern empire" which included Norway; Copenhagen (*q.v.*) made the capital and expansion begun along southern shore of Baltic by dynasty founded by Waldemar the Great (1157–82); by 14th cent., despite opposition of Waldemar IV, came increasingly under German influence, and, especially after Peace of Stralsund 1370, was dominated by Hanseatic League (see HANSE TOWNS); Scandinavia united under Margaret of Denmark 1387 (Union of Kalmar 1397); Danish monarchy of the Oldenburg line 1448–1863; Sweden (*q.v.*) became independent and began to threaten Danish supremacy; accepted Protestant Reformation 1536; lost power and territory in wars with Sweden in 17th cent.; abolished serfdom under Bernstorff; in Leagues of Armed Neutrality 1780 and 1800; after bombardment of Copenhagen 1807, joined Napoleon; forced to cede Norway and Helgoland 1814; duchies of Schleswig and Holstein (*qq.v.*) lost in war with Austria and Prussia 1864; neutral in World War I; sold Danish West Indies (see VIRGIN ISLANDS) to U.S. 1917; recognized Iceland (*q.v.*) as sovereign state in personal union with Denmark 1918; received Northern Schleswig (*Dan.* Nord Slesvig) by plebiscite 1920; in 1933, awarded eastern Greenland (occupied by Norway 1931); taken over by Germany Apr. 1940 and held until May 1945.

2 Town, Bamberg co., SW South Carolina, 21 m. SW of Orangeburg; pop. 3221; railroad center; lumber.

Denmark Strait. Channel 130 m. wide bet. SE Greenland and Iceland; connects Arctic Ocean with the North Atlantic; here in World War II on May 24, 1941 the German battleship *Bismarck* sank the British *Hood*.

Den′ne·witz (dĕn′ĕ·vĭts). Village, Brandenburg, Germany, 42 m. SSW of Berlin; scene of victory Sept. 6, 1813 of Prussians under von Bülow over the forces of Marshal Ney.

Den′nis (dĕn′ĭs). Town, Barnstable co., SE Massachusetts, on Cape Cod 7 m. ENE of Barnstable; pop. 3727; summer and fishing resort; site of the Cape Playhouse and Cape Cinema.

Dennis Ness (nĕs′). Headland on N coast of North Ronaldsay I., Orkney Is., off N Scotland; lighthouse.

Den′ni·son (dĕn′ĭ·s'n). Village, Tuscarawas co., E Ohio, 27 m. S of Canton; pop. 4158; meat packing; manufactures sewer pipe, clay products, batteries, sheet iron. See UHRICHSVILLE.

Den′ny and Dun′i·pace (dĕn′ĭ, dŭn′ĭ·pās). Burgh, Stirling co., cen. Scotland; pop. 6692; manufactures.

De·nou′sa (thâ·nōō′sä). Small island, E Cyclades, S Aegean Sea, 12 m. E of Naxos; in Cyclades dept., Greece.

Den·pa′sar (dĕn·pä′sär); *also* **Den Pasar**. Town, S Bali, Lesser Sunda Is., Indonesia; pop. 16,639. administrative and commercial center; has seaport and airport.

Dent (dĕnt). County in Missouri. See *Table* at MISSOURI.

Dent Blanche (dän′ blänsh′). Peak 14,318 ft. in the Pennine Alps, S Switzerland.

Dent d' Hérens. See Dent d' HÉRENS.

Dent du Mi′di′ (dän′ dü mē′dē′). Mountain 10,690 ft., SW Switzerland, near French border SSW of Bex.

Den′ton (dĕn′t'n; -tŭn). **1** County in Texas. See *Table* at TEXAS.

2 City, Jeff Davis co., SE cen. Georgia, SW of Hazlehurst; pop. 1726.

3 Town, ⊗ of Caroline co., E Maryland, 40 m. E of Annapolis; pop. 1938; canneries; strawberry shipping point.

4 City, ⊗ of Denton co., N Texas, 35 m. NNW of Dallas; pop. 26,844; trade and agricultural center; North Texas State College (1890; coed.); Texas State College for Women (1901).

5 Urban district, Lancashire, NW England, 6 m. ESE of Manchester; pop. 25,612; felt hats.

D'En′tre·cas′teaux′ Channel (dän′trē·kàs′tō′). Strait separating S end of Bruni I. from Tasmania mainland, Australia.

D'Entrecasteaux Islands. Island group in the W Pacific Ocean, off SE coast of New Guinea I.; 1200 sq. m.; pop. ab. 40,000; British-owned, attached to the Territory of Papua; chief settlement Dobu; include Goodenough, Fergusson, and Normanby Is. and many islets, small coral atolls, and reefs; separated from the mainland by Ward Hunt and Goschen Straits; mountainous, with many extinct volcanoes.

D'Entrecasteaux Point. Cape, SW point of Australia, in Western Australia.

Den′ver (dĕn′vēr). **1** County in Colorado. See *Table* at COLORADO.

2 City, its ⊗ and ✳ of Colorado, in NE cen. part of the state on South Platte river; largest city in the state; pop. 493,887; alt. 5280 ft.; railroad, commercial, and industrial center, and resort; headquarters for mining (gold, silver, coal) and beet-sugar industries in the surrounding area; manufactures include mining machinery, rubber products, scientific apparatus, machine shop and packing house products; Lowry Air Force Base with U.S. Air Force Technical School. University of Denver (1864; coed.; Methodist); Iliff School of Theology (1892; coed.; Methodist); Regis College (1877; men; Roman Catholic). Settlement called Auraria (*q.v.*) made 1858 by gold prospectors and miners and united with two other villages to form Denver 1860; incorp. as city 1861; made state capital 1867.

3 Borough, Lancaster co., Pennsylvania, NE of Ephrata; pop. 1875.

Den′ville (dĕn′vĭl). Town, Morris co., N New Jersey, 7 m. N of Morristown; pop. (est.) 8400; rail junction; Indian Lake, summer resort, at SW tip.

De′o·band′ (dē′ō·bŭnd′; dä′-). Town, Meerut division, NE Uttar Pradesh, N Indian Union, 75 m. NNE of Delhi; pop. 22,126; an ancient town, with numerous temples, ghats, etc., a resort of pilgrims; seat of well-known Arabian college.

De·o·do′ro (dĕ·ōō·thō′rōō). Town, W suburb of Rio de Janeiro, Brazil.

De′o·garh (dē′ō·gär; dä′-; *native* -gŭr′h′). **1** Town, ✳ of Bamra state, E Indian Union, on a tributary of the Brahmani river 100 m. NW of Cuttack.

2 See DEOGHAR.

De′o·ghar *or* **De′o·garh** (dē′ō·gär; dä′-; *native* -gŭr′h′). Town, E Bihar state, NE India, 170 m. NW of Calcutta; pop. ab. 14,000; has temple dedicated to Hindu god Siva; visited by many pilgrims; health resort.

Deogiri. See DAULATABAD.

De Pere (dĕ pĕr′). City, Brown co., E Wisconsin, on Fox river 5 m. S of Green Bay (city); pop. 10,045; agricultural and industrial center; manufactures paper, boats, medicines, feeds, brick; site of St. Francis Xavier Mission, first permanent Jesuit church in Wisconsin (estab. 1671); St. Norbert Coll. (1898; men) at West De Pere.

De·pew′ (dĕ·pū′). Village, Erie co., W New York, 9 m. E of Buffalo; pop. 13,580; industrial suburb of Buffalo; manufactures storage batteries, food products, steel castings.

De·pos′it (dĕ·pŏz′ĭt). Village and summer resort,

Broome and Delaware cos., S New York, 25 m. E of Binghamton; pop. 2025.

Deptford. Metropolitan borough of London. See *Table* at LONDON.

De·pue′ (dĕ-pū′). Village, Bureau co., N Illinois, on Illinois river 25 m. W of Ottawa; pop. 1920.

De Queen (dĕ kwēn′). City, ⊗ of Sevier co., SW Arkansas; pop. 2859; incorporated 1897; made ⊗ 1905; shipping point for tomatoes, strawberries, cantaloupes, etc.

De Quin′cy (dĕ kwĭn′sĭ). Town, Calcasieu parish, SW Louisiana, 20 m. NW of Lake Charles; pop. 3928; in section yielding rice, sugar, lumber; petroleum and natural-gas deposits nearby.

Der·'a′ (dŭr-ă′); *Fr.* **Dé′ra·a′** (dā′rä·ä′). Town, SW Syria, on railroad from Damascus to Ma'an near Jordan border; pop. ab. 4000.

De′ra Gha′zi Khan (dā′rȧ gä′zĭ kän′). Town in Multan division, West Punjab, Pakistan, on Indus river 45 m. W of Multan; pop. 23,468; founded at close of 15th cent. by Ghazi Khan, son of a Baluch chieftain.

De′ra Is′mail Khan (ĭs′mĭl kän′). Town, Pakistan, in N West Pakistan, on the right bank of the Indus river 155 m. S of Peshawar; pop. 38,956; founded at close of the 15th cent. by Ismail Khan, a Baluch chieftain; active bazaar; conducts large caravan trade with Afghanistan through the Gumal Pass (*q.v.*).

De·ra·i′yeh *or* **Der·a′yah** (dŭr-ē′yȧ; -yä). Town, cen. Saudi Arabia, just W of Riyadh; formerly capital of the Wahabis; ruined by Ibrahim Pasha 1819.

Der′be (dûr′bĕ; -bē). Ancient town, S Lycaonia, Asia Minor, on border of Cilicia; visited by St. Paul on first and second journeys; exact site not known.

Der·bent′ (dĕr·bĕnt′) *or* **Der·bend′** (-bĕnd′); *anc.* **Al·ba′na** (ăl-bā′nȧ). Town, SE Dagestan, SE Soviet Russia, Europe, on Caspian Sea 70 m. SE of Makhachkala; pop. 27,476; in narrow strip of land with high hills immediately behind, actually forming a pass, **Derbent Gateway;** hills covered with orchards and vineyards; chief industries making of wine, fishing, wool spinning.

History: At S end of pass are remains of wall anciently known as Caspian Gates (Caspiae Pylae), a Persian defense against inroads of nomadic tribes of the N; wall and citadel supposed to have been built (6th cent.) by Khosrau I; seized by Arabs 728; noted as a residence of Harun al-Rashid, who made it a cultural center; captured by Mongols 1220; seized by Peter the Great 1722 but lost to Russians by 1736; again conquered from Persia 1796 and finally annexed 1813; largely destroyed in civil war of 1917–21.

Der′by (dûr′bĭ). 1 Urban community (unincorporated), Adams co., NE cen. Colorado, NE of Denver; pop. 10,124.

2 Manufacturing city, New Haven co., S Connecticut, at confluence of Naugatuck and Housatonic rivers opp. Shelton, 8 m. W of New Haven; pop. 12,132; settled 1642, incorp. 1893; manufactures sponge rubber, metal (brass, copper, bronze) specialties, pins, hardware. The town (incorp.) is coextensive with the city.

3 City, Sedgwick co., S cen. Kansas, ab. 13 m. SE of Wichita; pop. 6458.

4 Town in Vermont. See DERBY LINE.

5 (*Brit.* där′bĭ, *occasionally* dûr′-) County in England. See DERBYSHIRE.

6 (*Brit.* där′bĭ, *occasionally* dûr′-) County borough, ⊗ of Derbyshire, N cen. England, on the Derwent 37 m. NNE of Birmingham; pop. 142,400, (1951) 141,264; railroad and manufacturing center; manufactures automobiles, textiles, paper, silk, pottery (Chelsea-Derby ware); birthplace of Herbert Spencer; home of George Eliot.

Der′by Line (dûr′bĭ lĭn′). Village in Derby town (pop. 2506), Orleans co., N Vermont, on Canadian border ab. 7 m. NE of Newport; pop. 849; forms single community with Canadian villages of Stanstead and Rock Island in Quebec.

Der′by·shire (där′bĭ-shĭr; -shēr; *occasionally* dûr′bĭ-) *or* **Derby.** Mining and manufacturing county, N cen.

England; area 1012 sq. m.; pop. (1951) 826,336; ⊗ Derby; other chief town Chesterfield; rivers include the Derwent and the Trent; sheep raising, dairying, textile manufacture, porcelain and paper making.

Derg, Ben. See BEN DEARG.

Derg, Lough (lŏk dûrg′). 1 Lake in SE co. Donegal, NW Ireland; according to legend, the entrance to Saint Patrick's Purgatory was on a small island in this lake. 2 Lake ab. 24 m. long and bet. 2 and 6 m. wide in Galway, Clare, and Tipperary cos., SW cen. Ireland; traversed N to S by the Shannon river.

De Rid′der (dĕ rĭd′ēr). City, ⊗ of Beauregard parish, SW Louisiana, 42 m. N of Lake Charles; pop. 7188; in section yielding soybeans, corn, rye, oats, and oranges, also turpentine and lumber.

Der′mott (dûr′mŭt). City, Chicot co., SE corner of Arkansas, 12 m. W of Mississippi river; pop. 3665; settled 1832; trading point; lumber mills.

Der′na (dĕr′nȧ). 1 Former province of (Italian) Libya, E of Bengasi prov.; 43,143 sq. m.; pop. (1936) 41,233. 2 Coastal city, its ✳; pop. (1938 est.) 21,547; site of Italian colonies since 1915; exports wool, corn, wax, honey, bananas. Captured by American navy Apr. 1805 in war with Barbary pirates; in World War II changed hands several times 1941–42.

Dern′berg, Cape (dûrn′bûrg; *Ger.* dĕrn′bĕrK). Cape extending into Atlantic Ocean on SW coast of South-West Africa.

Der′ne (dĕr′nĕ). Industrial commune, W Germany, in North Rhine-Westphalia state near Dortmund; pop. 13,009; coal mining; ironworks.

Der′ry (dĕr′ĭ). 1 Manufacturing town, Rockingham co., SE New Hampshire, 10 m. SE of Manchester; pop. 6987; manufactures boots and shoes. 2 Borough, Westmoreland co., SW Pennsylvania, 21 m. W of Johnstown; pop. 3426. 3 County and county borough in Northern Ireland. See LONDONDERRY.

Dertona. See TORTONA.

Dertosa. See TORTOSA.

Der′went (dûr′wĕnt). 1 River ab. 130 m. long, S cen. Tasmania, Australia; rises in Lake St. Clair and flows SE to Storm Bay; has many affluents on its left bank, outlets of the lakes of the central highlands, esp. the Dee, Ouse, Clyde, and Jordan; navigable to Hobart on its right bank on the estuary (4 m. wide). 2 River 33 m. long in Cumberland, NW England; flows N through lakes Derwentwater and Bassenthwaite, turns WSW to Solway Firth at Workington. 3 River ab. 60 m. long in N Derbyshire, N cen. England; flows SE into the Trent on border of Leicestershire. 4 River 30 m. long in Durham and Northumberland, N England; flows NE to the Tyne 3 m. W of Gateshead. 5 River 57 m. long in Yorkshire, N England; flows N into the Ouse.

Der′went·wa′ter (dûr′wĕnt·wô′tēr; -wŏt′ēr). Lake ab. 3 m. long in the Lake District, Cumberland, NW England; has several islands on one of which, Lord's Island, was the residence of the earls of Derwentwater; traversed from S to N by the Derwent river; in S receives also the brook which contains Lodore waterfall; to the NE is the town of Keswick.

Dés. See DEJ.

Des·a·gua·de′ro (dās′ä·gwä·thā′rô). 1 Name given to upper course of Río Salado in W Argentina. 2 River ab. 160 m. long in W Bolivia; flows from Lake Titicaca on the Peruvian border to Lake Poopó.

Des·a′güe, Ca·nal′ del (kä·näl′ dĕl däs·ä′gwä). Canal ab. 30 m. long built bet. 1879 and 1900 to drain the Valley of Mexico, cen. Mexico; removed danger of floods from the city of Mexico.

Des Al′le·mands, Lake (dĕs ăl′măn; *Fr.* dā′-zȧl′mäN′). Lake in S Saint John the Baptist parish, SE Louisiana.

Des Arc (dĕz ärk′). Town, a ⊗ of Prairie co., E cen. Arkansas, on White river; pop. 1482; river port.

Des′ca·be·za′do (dãs′kä·vä·sä′thŏ). Two mountains **Descabezado Gran′de** (grän′dä) 12,562 ft. and **Descabezado Chi′co** (chē′kŏ) 10,660 ft., in E cen. Chile, near Argentine border.

Des′chail′lons′, *in full* **Deschaillons sur St. Lau′rent′** (dä′shä′yŏN′ sür säN′ lô′räN′). Village, Lotbinière co., S Quebec, Canada, on St. Lawrence river 27 m. ENE of Three Rivers; pop. 1185.

Des′chutes′ (dā′shōōt′). **1** River 250 m. long, cen. and N Oregon; rises in SW Deschutes co., flows N into Columbia river forming part of boundary bet. Wasco and Sherman cos.
2 County in Oregon. See *Table* at OREGON.

De′se·a′do (dā′sā·ä′thŏ). River ab. 300 m. long in S Argentina; flows E from Andes Mts. in NW Santa Cruz territory on the Chilean border and empties into Atlantic Ocean at Puerto Deseado.

De′se·che′o Island (dā′sā·chā′ŏ). Small island off NW corner of Puerto Rico.

De′sen·ga′ño, Cape (dā′säng·gä′nyŏ). Cape extending into Atlantic Ocean on E coast of Santa Cruz territory, S Argentina.

De·sen·za′no del Gar′da (dä·zĕn·tsä′nŏ dâl gär′dä). Commune, Brescia prov., Lombardy, N Italy, on S shore of Láke Garda 16 m. ESE of Brescia; pop. 10,360; important harbor.

Des′er·et′ (dĕz′ĕr·ĕt′). The provisional state organized 1849 by a convention of Mormons, comprising the greater part of the southwestern United States S of the 42d parallel and W of the Rocky Mts.; ✳ Salt Lake City; refused recognition by U.S. Congress and Territory of Utah created in its stead 1850.

Des′er·on′to (dĕz′ĕr·ŏn′tō). Town, Hastings co., SE Ontario, Canada, on Bay of Quinte 17 m. E of Belleville; pop. 1522; trades in lumber; summer resort.

De·ser′tas (dĕ·zâr′täsh). Small group of rocky islets in the Madeira Is. (*q.v.*), 30 m. SE of Madeira; lat. 32°31′N and long. 16°30′W.

De·sha′ (dĕ·shä′). County in Arkansas. See *Table* at ARKANSAS.

De·shi·ma (dĕ·shē·mä). Artificial island 600 ft. long and 250 ft. wide at the head of Nagasaki harbor, Kyushu, Japan; the residence of representatives of the Dutch East India Co. 1641–1859; during these two centuries, when Japan was closed to all foreigners, the only point of contact bet. the Japanese and the outside world; usually six or eight Dutch agents in residence to carry on a restricted trade, they were allowed to leave the island only once a year, when they made a journey to Yedo to report to the shogun.

Desh′ler (dĕsh′lēr). Village, Henry co., NW Ohio, 17 m. NW of Findlay; pop. 1824.

Desiderii Fanum. See SAINT-DIZIER.

De′sio (dâ′zyŏ). Commune, Milano prov., Lombardy, N Italy, 11 m. NNW of Milan; pop. 13,499.

Dé′si′rade′ (dā′zē′räd′). Island in French West Indies, a dependency of Guadeloupe; 11 sq. m.; pop. (1938 est.) 1710.

De Smet (dĕ smĕt′). City, ⊗ of Kingsbury co., E South Dakota; pop. 1324.

Des Moines (dĕ moin′). **1** River 327 m. long, Iowa, formed by junction of east and west forks in Humboldt co., NW cen. Iowa, flows SE diagonally across Iowa to empty into the Mississippi at Keokuk, SE extremity of Iowa; including west fork which rises in Murray co., SW Minnesota it is 533 m. long; forms extreme E section of Iowa-Missouri boundary.
2 County in Iowa. See *Table* at IOWA.
3 City, ✳ of Iowa, and ⊗ of Polk co., S cen. Iowa, at confluence of Des Moines and Raccoon rivers; largest city in the state; pop. 208,982; in the Iowa corn belt and coal-mining section; packing houses, clothing manufactories, chemical works, dairies, flour mills; Drake University (1881; coed.; Disciples of Christ). Fort Des Moines built on this site 1843; settlement incorporated as Fort Des

Moines 1851; made capital of Iowa and chartered as city of Des Moines 1857. Army post (cavalry), Fort Des Moines, estab. 1900, adjoins the city on the S; in World War II location of first WAC training center (opened July 20, 1942).

Des′mond (dĕz′mŭnd). Ancient kingdom, S Munster, S Ireland; comprised present cos. Cork and Kerry.

Des·na′ (dĕs·nä′; *Russ.* dyĕs·nä′). River ab. 550 m. long in SW Soviet Russia, Europe, and N Ukraine; rises E of Smolensk and flows generally S to join the Dnieper near Kiev; navigable to Bryansk and is an important channel for the lumber trade; chief tributary the Seim; much fighting on its banks 1943.

De′so·la·ción (dā′sŏ·lä·syôn′); *also Eng.* **Des′o·la′tion** (dĕs′ŏ·lā′shŭn). Uninhabited Chilean island 70 m. long, northernmost of the Tierra del Fuego archipelago.

Desolation Island. 1 See DESOLACIÓN.
2 See KERGUELEN.

Des′o·la′tion Point (dĕs′ŏ·lā′shŭn). Point at N end of Dinagat I., Surigao prov., Mindanao, Phil. Is., on E side of Surigao Strait.

De So′to (dĕ sō′tō; dĕ). **1** Name of a parish in Louisiana and of counties in two states of the U.S. See *Tables* at LOUISIANA, FLORIDA, MISSISSIPPI.
2 City, Jefferson co., E Missouri, 38 m. SSW of St. Louis; pop. 5804; lead and zinc deposits nearby.

De·spair′, Mount (dĕ·spâr′). Peak 8585 ft. in Glacier National Park, NW Montana.

Des Plaines (dĕs plānz′). **1** River 150 m. long, NE Illinois; rises in SE Wisconsin, flows S to unite with the Kankakee river and form the Illinois river. See ILLINOIS WATERWAY.
2 City, Cook co., NE Illinois, 20 m. NW of Chicago; pop. 34,886; manufactures electrical supplies.

Despoto Planina. See RHODOPE.

Des′sau (dĕs′ou). Manufacturing city, Halle dist., E Germany, on Mulde river 71 m. SW of Berlin; pop. (1939) 120,732; 16th-cent. palace, parliament buildings, municipal theater, old and new town halls, 16th-cent. church; manufactures include refined sugar, carpets, paper, textiles, machinery, railroad coaches, distillery products; agricultural trade center; in recent years had airplane factory. Said to have been founded by Albert the Bear 12th cent.; made city 1213; capital of Anhalt-Dessau 1603; scene of victory of Wallenstein over Count Mansfeld Apr. 15–25, 1626 (Thirty Years' War); made capital of Anhalt 1863; in World War II frequently bombed 1942–45; taken by Allies Apr. 21, 1945.

Des′sie *or* **Des′sye** (dā′syā). Town, Wallo region, N cen. Ethiopia, SE of Magdala.

Destêrro. See FLORIANÓPOLIS.

De·struc′tion Island (dĕ·strŭk′shŭn). Island in Pacific Ocean, cen. coast, W Washington.

Det′mold (dĕt′mōld; *Ger.* dĕt′mŏlt). City, North Rhine-Westphalia, Germany, 54 m. E of Münster; formerly ✳ of Lippe; pop. 16,051; summer resort; large statue to Arminius, conqueror of Varus (9 A.D.) nearby; manufactures textiles, biscuits, furniture, tobacco, leather, buttons, beer; near marble and gypsum quarries. Charlemagne defeated Saxons nearby (at ancient Theotmalli) 783 A.D.; founded c. 1300; became city 1350.

De·tour′ (dĕ·tŏŏr′; dē′tŏŏr). Village, SE tip of Chippewa co., E and NE Michigan penin.; pop. 669; at mouth of St. Marys river which enters Lake Huron through **Detour Passage**, a strait bet. the mainland and Drummond I.

Detour, Point. Point at SE extremity of Delta co., S Michigan penin., extending into Lake Michigan.

Détour des Anglais. See ENGLISH TURN.

De·troit′ (dĕ·troit′). **1** River ab. 31 m. long, SE Michigan; connects Lake St. Clair with Lake Erie and forms part of U.S.-Canada boundary; crossed by railroad tunnel (2668 ft. long) and vehicular tunnel (2200 ft. long), connecting Detroit, Mich. with Windsor, Canada.

2 City, ⊗ of Wayne co., SE Michigan, on Detroit river just W of Lake St. Clair; pop. 1,670,144; largest city in the state and 5th largest city in U.S.; automobile-manufacturing center; also manufactures airplanes, military tanks, electric machinery, aluminum products, hardware, chemicals. University of Detroit (1877; coed.; Roman Catholic); Detroit Institute of Technology (1891; men and women); Marygrove College (1910; women; Roman Catholic); Wayne State University (1933; coed.); Mercy College (1941; women).

History: Fort Pontchartrain du Détroit (Ft. Pontchartrain of the Straits) founded by French 1701 as part of chain of posts intended to control Illinois country; from foundation, it was trading and political center for Great Lakes region; surrendered to English during Seven Years' War 1760; besieged by Pontiac 1763–64; chief center of British control of western country during War of Independence; finally turned over to U.S. 1796; almost destroyed by fire 1805; surrendered by Hull to British 1812 but reoccupied by Americans 1813; capital of Michigan Territory 1805–37 and of state 1837–47; incorporated as village 1815, as city 1824; auto manufacturing begun in the city 1899.

Detroit Lakes. City, ⊗ of Becker co., NW cen. Minnesota, 42 m. E of Fargo, North Dakota; pop. 5633; trade center and summer resort in a lake region.

Detskoe Selo. See PUSHKIN.

Det′ti·foss′ (dĕt′tĭ·fôs′). Waterfall 257 ft. high in Jökulsá river, NE Iceland.

Det′ting·en (dĕt′ĭng·ĕn). Village, Lower Franconia, Bavaria, Germany; pop. ab. 1000; scene in War of the Austrian Succession of victory of George II of England, commanding an army of English, Hanoverian, and Hessian troops, over the French June 27, 1743.

Deu′el (dū′ĕl). Name of counties in two states of the U.S. See *Tables* at NEBRASKA and SOUTH DAKOTA.

Deur′ne (dûr′nĕ). **1** Commune, Antwerp prov., N Belgium; pop. (1938 est.) 56,664; E suburb of Antwerp. **2** Commune, North Brabant prov., S Netherlands, just E of Eindhoven; pop. 10,806.

Deutsch–Brod. See NĚMECKÝ BROD.

Deutsches Reich. See GERMANY.

Deutsch–Eylau. See IŁAWA.

Deutsch–Krone. See WAŁCZ.

Deutschland. See GERMANY.

Deutsch–Südwestafrika. See SOUTH-WEST AFRICA.

Deutz (doits). Part of Cologne, Germany, on right bank of Rhine; independent town until 1888; castle, made Benedictine monastery 1002.

Deux–Mon′tagnes′ (dû′môn′tȧn′y′). County, Quebec, Canada. See *Two Mountains* in *Table* at QUEBEC.

Deuxponts. See ZWEIBRÜCKEN.

Deux–Sè′vres (dû′sâ′vr′). Department of France. See *Table* at FRANCE.

De′va (dē′vȧ). See CHESTER.

De′va (dĕ′vä); *Ger.* **Diem′rich** (dēm′rĭк). City, Tran-

sylvania region, W cen. Romania, on the Mureş river 78 m. ESE of Arad; pop. 10,593.

De Valls Bluff (dē vălz′). Town, a ⊗ of Prairie co., E cen. Arkansas, on White river; pop. 654.

Devana. See ABERDEEN.

Devana Castra. See CHESTER.

Dé′va·vá′nya (dā′vȯ·vä′nyȯ). Commune, SE Hungary, 47 m. SW of Debrecen; pop. 15,319.

De·ve·li′ (dĕ·vĕ·lē′). Town, Kayseri vilayet, cen. Turkey in Asia, ab. 33 m. SW of Kayseri; pop. 10,328.

De′ven·ter (dā′vĕn·tēr). Commercial commune, Overijssel prov., E Netherlands, on IJssel river; pop. (1939) 41,096; iron foundries, carpet factories; belonged to Hanseatic League; occupied by Germans 1940.

Dev′er·on (dĕv′ēr·ŭn). Small river in NE Scotland, flowing into North Sea at Banff.

Dev′gad Ba′ri·a (dăv′gȧd bä′rĭ·yȧ). Town, E Gujerat state, formerly ✳ of Baria state, W Indian Union, 52 m. NE of Baroda; pop. 6976.

De·vies′ Mountain (dĕ·vēs′). Peak 2760 ft. in Fayette co., SW Pennsylvania.

Dé′ville′–lès–Rou·en′ (dā′vēl′lĕ′rwän′). Commune, Seine-Inférieure dept., N France, ab. 2 m. W of Rouen of which it is an industrial suburb; pop. (1931) 7403.

Dev′ils (dĕv′′lz). River ab. 125 m. long, SW Texas; rises in N Crockett co., flows S into Rio Grande in S Val Verde co.

Dev′il′s Bit Mountains (dĕv′′lz bĭt′). Range in N co. Tipperary, S cen. Ireland; highest peak 1583 ft.

Devil′s Bridge. Locality, Cardiganshire, W Wales, on Rheidol river; noted for scenery, stone bridges, glen with cataract of 210 ft. drop.

Devil′s Ear Mountain. Peak 3903 ft. in the Adirondack Mts., NE New York.

Devil′s Island; *Fr.* **Île du Dia′ble** (ēl′ dü dyȧ′bl′). One of the Safety Is. (*q.v.*) off the N coast of French Guiana; became a penal colony of the French government in latter part of 19th cent.; here Captain Alfred Dreyfus was a prisoner 1895–99; its gradual abandonment as a penal colony begun 1946.

Dev′ils Lake (dĕv′′lz). **1** Saline lake bet. Ramsey and Benson cos., NE cen. North Dakota. **2** City, ⊗ of Ramsey co., NE North Dakota, on former N shore of Devils Lake; pop. 6299; railroad and trading center in agricultural section.

Dev′ils Post′pile′ National Monument (dĕv′′lz pōst′pīl′). See UNITED STATES, *National Monuments.*

Devils River. See DEVILS.

Devils Tower National Monument. See UNITED STATES, *National Monuments.*

De·vi′zes (dē·vī′zĕz; -zĭz). Municipal borough, Wiltshire, S England, on the Kennet 28 m. ESE of Bristol; pop. 7892; market center; agricultural implements.

Dev′on (dĕv′ŭn). **1** Town, York co., SW New Brunswick, Canada, on St. John river across from Fredericton; pop. (1941) 2337; annexed to Fredericton 1945. **2** County in England. See DEVONSHIRE. **3** River ab. 34 m. long, E Scotland; rises in Ochil Hills, Perth co., flows into Forth river in Clackmannan co. ab. 3 m. NW of Alloa.

Devon Island. Island 21,900 sq. m. in NE Franklin District, Northwest Territories, Canada, N of Baffin I. and at the head of Baffin Bay.

Dev′on·port (dĕv′ŭn·pōrt). **1** Town, on N coast of Tasmania, Australia, at mouth of Mersey river 50 m. WNW of Launceston; pop. 5153; active port; an attractive bathing and recreational resort. **2** Seaport, Devonshire, SW England; on E side of Tamar estuary NW of Plymouth, of which it is a part; royal dockyard, military and naval station. **3** Borough, Auckland provincial dist., North I., New Zealand, suburb of Auckland on N side of Waitemata Harbor; pop. 10,310; important naval station.

Dev′on·shire (dĕv′ŭn·shĭr; -shēr) *or* **Devon.** County, SW England; area 2612 sq. m.; pop. (1951) 798,283; ⊗

Exeter; other towns Plymouth, Torquay, Paignton, Newton Abbot, Barnstaple, Brixham, Dartmouth, Exmouth; rivers Exe and Dart; agriculture, livestock raising (Devon cattle), mining (tin, copper), quarrying, fisheries, manufacturing (textiles, paper, pottery).

De·vrek′ (dĕ·vrĕk′). River ab. 120 m. long in N cen. Turkey in Asia; flows E into the Kızıl Irmak.

De·was′ (dă·wäs′). **1** Two former Indian states, Central India, Indian Union, in former Malwa Agency: Senior Branch, 449 sq. m., pop. (1941) 89,352; Junior Branch, 419 sq. m., pop. (1941) 83,669. Founded in first half of 18th cent. by two brothers, Maratha chieftains.
2 Town, their ✳, 23 m. NE of Indore; pop. 16,810.

De·wets′dorp (dĕ·vĕts′dôrp). Town, SE Orange Free State, E cen. Union of South Africa, 40 m. SE of Bloemfontein; pop. 2428.

Dew′ey (dū′ĭ). **1** Name of counties in two states of the U.S. See *Tables* at OKLAHOMA and SOUTH DAKOTA.
2 City, Washington co., NE Oklahoma, 6 m. NE of Bartlesville; pop. 3994; manufactures cement, gasoline.
3 Town in the municipality of Culebra, Puerto Rico; pop. (1950) 693.

De Witt (dĕ wĭt′). **1** Name of counties in two states of the U.S. See *Tables* at ILLINOIS and TEXAS.
2 City, a ⊗ of Arkansas co., E Arkansas, 40 m. E of Pine Bluff; pop. 3019; rice mills, cotton gins; shipping point for lumber and livestock.
3 City, Clinton co., E Iowa, 18 m. W of Clinton; pop. 3224.

Dews′bur·y (dūz′bĕr·ĭ). County borough, West Riding, Yorkshire, N England, on the Calder 9 m. S of Leeds; pop. 54,302, (1951) 53,476; has ironworks, woolen goods manufactures.

Dex′ter (dĕks′tĕr). **1** Industrial town, Penobscot co., E cen. Maine, 30 m. WNW of Bangor; pop. 2720; textile mills.
2 City, Stoddard co., SE Missouri, 26 m. E of Poplar Bluff; pop. 5519; trade and industrial center; cotton gin, flour mill, shirt factory, poultry packing house.

Dezhnev, or **Dezhneva, Cape.** See EAST CAPE.

Dhah·ran′ (dä·rän′; *Arab.* thă·hrän′; dă-; ză-). Former village, al-Hasa dist., E Saudi Arabia, near W coast of Persian Gulf near Bahrein Is.; adjacent to Dammam in extensive oil regions; has developed into large town; pipeline connection with Abqaiq oil field 40 m. to the SW; airport of U.S. Air Force.

Dha·mar′ (thă·mär′; dă-; ză-) or **Da·mar′** (dă·mär′). Town, S cen. Yemen, SW Arabia, SSE of San'a.

Dha′nush·ko′di (dŭ′nōosh·kō′dĭ). Seaport at E tip of Rameswaram I., Madras, SE Indian Union, bet. Palk Strait and Gulf of Mannar; created 1913.

Dhar (där). **1** Former Indian state, SW Central India, Indian Union; 1798 sq. m.; pop. (1941) 253,210; founded by Rajputs 9th cent. A.D.; conquered by Mohammedans 13th cent.; made a fief of the Marathas 1742; came under British control 1819; now in W Madhya Pradesh.
2 Town, its ✳, 33 m. SW of Indore; pop. 19,607; of great antiquity; famous in medieval India as capital of Rajput dynasty of Malwa; long a center of culture and learning; has fine Pillar Mosque and other structures of interest.

Dha′ram·pur (dŭ′răm·pōor). **1** Former Indian state, SE Gujarat States, W Indian Union; 719 sq. m.; pop. (1941) 123,326.
2 Town, its ✳, 115 m. N of Bombay; pop. 7218.

Dhar′ma (thŭr′mà; -mă; dŭr′-; zŭr′-). Town, cen. Nejd, Saudi Arabia, ab. 45 m. W of Riyadh.

Dharm′jay·garh (därm′jĭ·gär′; *native* d'hŭrm′jĭ·gŭr'h) See UDAIPUR.

Dharm·sa′la (därm·sä′là; *native* d'hŭrm-). Town and cantonment, Jullundur division, Punjab, NW Indian Union; pop. 6359; a hill station and sanatorium, elevation 6000 ft.

Dhar·war′ (där·wär′). Town, NW Mysore state, Indian Union, 290 m. SSE of Bombay and 75 m. E of

Pangim; pop. 41,671; rail center with lively trade; important cotton industry.

Dhau′la·gi′ri, Mount (dou′là·gĭ′rĭ). Peak 26,810 ft. in the Himalayas, W cen. Nepal, N India, 28°45′N, 83°30′E; now in Orissa.

Dhen·ka′nal (dān·kä′näl). **1** Former Indian state, E Eastern States, NE Indian Union; 1428 sq. m.; pop. (1941) 324,212.
2 Town, its ✳, 25 m. NW of Cuttack; pop. 7480.

Dhi·ban′ (thē·băn′; dē-; zē-); *anc.* **Di′bon** (dī′bŏn). Ruins of an ancient city in Palestine, E of the Dead Sea and a few miles N of the Arnon river; place where the Moabite stone was found 1868, a block of black basalt bearing an inscription of 34 lines, dating from the 9th cent. B.C. and written in the Moabite alphabet, an important representative of the Phoenician script. See MOAB.

Dhib·ban′ (thĭb·băn′; dĭb-; zĭb-). Town on right bank of the Euphrates near N shore of Lake Habbaniya, cen. Iraq; headquarters of British Royal Air Force.

Dhol′pur (dōl′pōor). **1** Former Indian state, E Rajputana, NW India; 1173 sq. m.; pop. (1941) 286,901; from 1805 under Jat rulers; under Mogul emperors 1527–1707; now in Rajasthan.
2 Town, its ✳, 34 m. S of Agra; pop. 19,586.

Dhon·bu·ri (t'hŭn·bōo·rē). Province, Thailand; 149 sq. m.; pop. 204,939.

Dho·ra′ji (dō·rä′jĭ). Town, Gondal state, cen. Kathiawar, Western India States, Indian Union, near Bhadar river 250 m. NW of Bombay; pop. 29,302.

Dhor el Khodib. = DAHR EL QADIB.

Dhran′ga·dhra (dräng′gà·drä). **1** Former Indian state, NE Kathiawar, Western India States, Indian Union; 1167 sq. m.; pop. (1941) 94,417; under Rajput rulers of a clan of great antiquity.
2 Town, its ✳, 75 m. W of Ahmadabad; pop. 17,538.

Dhrol (drōl). Former Indian state, N Kathiawar, Western India States, Indian Union, E of Jamnagar; 283 sq. m.; pop. (1941) 33,617; now in Gujerat state.

Dhu′bri (dōo′brĭ). Town, NW Assam, NE Indian Union, on right bank of Brahmaputra river ab. 260 m. NNE of Calcutta; pop. 9435.

Dhu′li·a (dōo′lĭ·à). Town, N Maharashtra, W Indian Union, on Panjhra river 200 m. NE of Bombay; pop. (1941) 53,308; important cotton market.

Di′a (dē′ä). Small island off N coast of Crete, E Mediterranean Sea, ab. 10 m. NNE of Candia.

Diable, Île du. See DEVIL'S ISLAND.

Dia′ble·rets′ (dyà′blē·rĕ′). Peak 10,645 ft. in the Bernese Alps, Valais canton, SW cen. Switzerland.

Di·ab′lo, Canyon (dī·äb′lō). See CANYON DIABLO.

Diablo, Mount. Isolated peak 3849 ft. in Contra Costa co., W California, 18 m. E of Oakland.

Diablo Dam *and* **Reservoir.** See UNITED STATES, *Dams and Reservoirs.*

Dia′blo′tin′, Morne (môrn′ dyà′blō′tăn′). Peak 5314 ft. on the island of Dominica, West Indies.

Diala. See DIYALA.

Di′a·la′o Point (dē′à·lä′ō). Point on N coast of Ilocos Norte prov., Luzon, Phil. Is., W of Mayraira Point; marks NE point of Bangui Bay, ab. 18°38′N.

Di′al Mountain (dī′ăl). Peak 4023 ft. in the Adirondack Mts., Essex co., NE New York.

Dia·man′te (dyä·män′tà). **1** River in Mendoza prov., W Argentina; rises in Andes Mts. near Chile-Argentina border, flows E to the Río Salado.
2 Town, Entre Ríos prov., E Argentina, on left bank of the Paraná 60 m. N of Rosario; pop. (est.) 11,518.

Di′a·man·ti′na (dī′à·măn·tē′nà). River ab. 470 m. long, SW Queensland, Australia; upper tributary of the Warburton river.

Di·a·man·ti′na (dĕ·à·măn·tē′nà). City, cen. Minas Gerais state, E Brazil; pop. (1940 est.) 9907; center of the diamond industry.

Di·a·man·ti′no (dĕ·à·măn·tē′nōo). Town, Mato

Grosso state, SW Brazil, near source of Paraguay river 80 m. NNW of Cuiabá.

Di'a·mant' Punt (dē'à·mänt' pûnt'); *Eng.* **Di'a·mond Point** (dī'à·mŭnd). Cape on NE tip of Sumatra, Indonesia, at NW end of Strait of Malacca.

Di'a·mond, Cape (dī'à·mŭnd). Promontory, alt. 333 ft., E end of city of Quebec, Canada; site of citadel.

Diamond Harbour. Port, West Bengal, NE Indian Union, at the head of the estuary of the Hooghly, 30 m. SSW of Calcutta with which it is connected by rail.

Diamond Head. Cape and landmark 761 ft. high, SE Oahu I., SE of Honolulu, Hawaii.

Diamond Mountains. 1 Range in E cen. Nevada, extending from SW Elko co. S along boundary bet. Eureka and White Pine cos.

2 *Jap.* **Kon·go·san** (kŏn·gō·sän). Group of mountain peaks along cen. part of E coast of Korea, S of Genzan, mostly in Kogen prov., covering area of ab. 75 sq. mi.; highest ab. 5600 ft.; remarkable for geological formation with many beautiful scenic wonders; even more notable as center of Buddhist religion for centuries, with temples, cloisters, colossal Buddha images, etc. In early Korean legend, the land of "twelve thousand peaks"; probably first visited by Buddhist priests in 4th cent. A.D. but after 16th cent. declined under persecution.

Diamond Peak. 1 Mountain 13,105 ft. in Sierra Nevada, in E Fresno co., S cen. California.

2 Mountain 8750 ft. in SE tip of Lane co., W Oregon.

Diamond Point. See DIAMANT PUNT.

Dianium. See DENIA.

Diarbekr. See DIYARBEKIR.

Di'bang' (dē'bäng') or **Di'bong'** (-bŏng'). Tributary of the Brahmaputra river, in NE India and SW Sikang; flows into the Brahmaputra at the great bend in NE Assam.

Di'bër (dē'bēr); *Ital.* **Di'bra** (dē'brä). Prefecture, NE cen. Albania; 921 sq. m.; pop. 86,992; ❋ Peshkopi.

Dibio. See DIJON.

Dibon. See DHIBAN.

Di'bru·garh' (dī'brōō·gär'; *native* -gŭr'h'). Town, NE Assam, NE Indian Union, head of navigation on left bank of Brahmaputra river; pop. 18,734; center of tea-raising region; in World War II an Allied air base.

Dibse. See THAPSACUS.

Di'cio·sân'măr·tin' (dē'chô·sîn'mēr·tēn'). Commune, N Romania, SW of Târgu-Mureş; pop. 6355.

Dick'e·busch (dĭk'ĕ·bŭs). Small commune, West Flanders prov., NW Belgium, 3 m. from Ieper (Ypres); pop. 1126; defended by the British against the German drive Apr. 1918.

Dick'ens (dĭk'ĕnz; -ĭnz). **1** County in Texas. See *Table* at TEXAS.

2 City, its ⊗, NW Texas; pop. 302.

Dick'en·son (dĭk'ĕn·s'n; -ĭn·s'n). County in Virginia. See *Table* at VIRGINIA.

Dick'ey (dĭk'ĭ). County in North Dakota. See *Table* at NORTH DAKOTA.

Dick'in·son (dĭk'ĭn·s'n). **1** Counties in three states of the U.S. See *Tables* at IOWA, KANSAS, MICHIGAN.

2 City, ⊗ of Stark co., SW North Dakota, 100 m. W of Bismarck; pop. 9971; founded c. 1880; became ⊗ 1884; livestock and wheat shipping point; manufactures brick, pottery; lignite coal mines, clay deposits. State Teachers College (1916; coed.).

Dicks Head (dĭks); *Arab.* **Ras Chiam·bo'ne** (räs' kyäm·bō'nå). Promontory extending into Indian Ocean at boundary bet. NE Kenya and SE Somalia.

Dick'son (dĭk's'n). **1** County in Tennessee. See *Table* at TENNESSEE.

2 Town, Dickson co., NW cen. Tennessee, 35 m. WSW of Nashville; pop. 5028; cigars, raincoats, shuttles.

Dickson City. Borough, Lackawanna co., NE Pennsylvania, 5 m. NE of Scranton; pop. 7738; coal-mining center; foundry and machine-shop products, silks.

Dickson Island. Small island off NW coast of Siberia,

Soviet Russia, Asia, at mouth of Yenisei river, ab. 73°30′N lat., 80°30′E long.; has settlement and harbor.

Dic·le' Ne·hri' (dĭj·lĕ' nĕ·hrē'). Turkish name of upper Tigris river.

Dicte. See DIKTĒ.

Did'y·ma (dĭd'ĭ·mà). Ruins of town on W coast of Asia Minor, S of Miletus; in ancient times was in Caria; oracle of Apollo; famous temple.

Didyme. See SALINA island.

Di·dy·mo'tei·khon (thĕ·thĕ·mô'tĕ·ʁon); *Bulgarian* **Di·mo'ti·ka** (dĭ·mô'tĭ·kä). Town, Evros dept., NE Greece, formerly ❋ of the department, on Maritsa (*Gr.* Evros) river S of Edirne; pop. 9500.

Die·cio'cho de Mar'zo (dyä·syō'chô thä mär'sô). Town, Tamaulipas state, E Mexico; pop. 5163.

Diedenhofen. See THIONVILLE.

Die'go Gar·ci'a (dyä'gô gär·thē'ä). Chief island of the Chagos Is. (*q.v.*).

Die'go Ra·mí'rez (dyä'gô rä·mē'râs). Chilean island group, southernmost of the Tierra del Fuego archipelago (*q.v.*), 60 m. SW of Cape Horn.

Dié'go–Sua'rez (dyä'gô–swä'râs) or **An'tsi·ra'ne** (än'tsĕ·rä'nå). Harbor and town near N end of Madagascar; pop. (1936) 12,237; harbor is one of best in world; has served as French naval base.

Die'kirch (dē'kĭrʁ). Commune, grand duchy of Luxembourg; pop. 3858.

Diemrich. See DEVA.

Dien Bien Phu (dyĕn' byĕn' fōō'). Village, SW Tonkin, N Vietnam; French military post in Indochina war; in 1954 besieged 55 days, fell to Vietminh May 7.

Dieng Plateau (dēng). Small plateau area, alt. ab. 6880 ft., on Mt. Prahoe, cen. Java, Indonesia, SW of Semarang; once a crater; on it are ruins of Hindu (Brahmanic) temples, built c. 9th cent. A.D.

Di·eppe' (dē·ĕp'; *Fr.* dyĕp). Seaport, Seine-Maritime dept., N France, on English Channel 34 m. N of Rouen; pop. 25,500; known esp. for manufacture of ivory and bone goods, which dates from 15th cent.; shipbuilding; trades in fish, silk, wine, brandy, fruit, manufactured goods. Important naval base in 17th cent.; suffered from plague 1668, 1670; destroyed by English and Dutch 1694; occupied by Germans 1870–71 in Franco-Prussian War and 1940–44 in World War II; site of commando raid by Canadians and British Aug. 19, 1942; captured by Canadians Aug. 31, 1944.

Diest (dēst). Manufacturing commune, Brabant prov., cen. Belgium; pop. 8384; breweries.

Die'ti·kon (dē'tĕ·kôn). Commune, Zurich canton, Switzerland, NE of Zurich; pop. 6487.

Dif'fer'dange' (dē'fĕr'dänzh'); *Ger.* **Dif'fer·ding'en** (dĭf'ĕr·dĭng'ĕn). Town, SW grand duchy of Luxembourg, 12 m. SW of Luxembourg; pop. (1945) 14,158.

Dig (dēg). Town, NE Rajasthan, NW India; pop. 11,166; has palace ruins and fort, built 1730; scene of battle 1803 in which Gen. Lake defeated Marathas.

Dig'by (dĭg'bĭ). **1** County, Nova Scotia, Canada. See *Table* at NOVA SCOTIA.

2 Resort town, its ⊗, W Nova Scotia, Canada, on Annapolis Basin 57 m. NNE of Yarmouth; pop. 2047; founded 1783 by body of Loyalists from New England; exports "Digby chickens," a variety of small herring.

Digby Gut (gŭt'). Passage in W Nova Scotia, Canada, 2 m. long and ½ m. wide, forming outlet of Annapolis Basin into Bay of Fundy; actually a gap or cleft in elevated ridge along SW coast of Nova Scotia, its steep sides 400 to 600 ft. high; strong tides and winds.

Digh'ton (dī't'n). **1** City, ⊗ of Lane co., W Kansas; pop. 1526.

2 Town, Bristol co., SE Massachusetts, 7 m. N of Fall River; pop. 3769; market gardening. On E bank of Taunton river opp. the town is **Dighton Rock,** a boulder of green stone curiously marked; many theories of its origin have been given but now generally believed to be American Indian; first observed c. 1680.

Di·gna'no d'I'stri·a (dē-nyä'nô dēs'trē-ä); *now, officially,* *Yugoslav* **Bod'njan** (bôd'nyän); *anc.* **At·tin'i·a'num** (ă·tĭn'ĭ·ā'nŭm). Commune on Istria Penin., 8 m. N of Pulj (Pola); pop. 11,265; before World War I belonged to Austria; in Venezia Giulia, Italy, 1918–47; awarded to Yugoslavia by treaty signed Feb. 10, 1947.

Digne (dēn'y'). Commune, ⁜ of Basses-Alpes dept., SE France, 71 m. NE of Marseilles; pop. 4371; 13th-cent. cathedral; mineral springs nearby.

Di'goel (dē'gōōl) *or* **Di'gul**. Navigable river ab. 400 m. long, SE Neth. New Guinea; rises in E end of Snow Mts. and flows S and W to Arafura Sea, N of Frederik Hendrik I.; its basin largely swampy jungle.

Di'goin' (dē'gwän'). Commune, W Saône-et-Loire dept., E cen. France, on the Loire; pop. (1931) 6736; manufactures pottery and porcelain.

Digue, La. See SEYCHELLES.

Di'hang' (dē'häng') *or* **Di'hong'** (dē'hông'). Name applied to the Brahmaputra river (*q.v.*) in its middle course, where it turns and breaks through the Himalayas in Tibet and Assam.

Di'jon' (dē'zhôn'); *anc.* **Dib'i·o** (dĭb'ĭ·ō). Commercial and manufacturing city, ⁜ of Côte-d'Or dept., E France, on Ouche river 168 m. SE of Paris; pop. 96,257; surrounded by eight forts; 13th-cent. church; 14th-cent. town hall (former palace of dukes of Burgundy); university; trade center for Burgundy wine and mustard; manufactures machinery, chemicals, automobiles, shoes, flour. Birthplace of Bossuet. Occupied by Germans 1870.

Dikh Tau. = DYKH TAU.

Diks·mui'de *or* **Dix·mui'de** (dĭks·moi'dĕ); *Fr.* **Dix'-mude'** (dēks'müd'; dēs'-). Commune, W Flanders prov., Belgium, 13 m. N of Ieper (Ypres); pop. 3146; in World War I destroyed during heavy fighting Oct. 22–Nov. 10, 1914 when Germans were prevented from reaching the sea by flooding of the area.

Dik'tē (thĕk'tē); *Eng.* **Dic'te** (dĭk'tē). Mountain peak 7170 ft. in Lasithi Mts., E Crete, SE of Candia; in Greek mythology the place where Zeus was reared.

Dik'wa (dĭk'wä). 1 District, Bornu prov., NE Nigeria; 5149 sq. m.; pop. 194,373; the N part of Brit. Cameroons trust territory, S of Lake Chad.
2 Town, its ⁜, near SW shore of Lake Chad.

Di'lam (dī'lăm). Town, cen. Nejd, Saudi Arabia, ab. 60 m. SE of Riyadh.

Dil'a·ram' (dĭl'ä·räm'). Town, SW cen. Afghanistan, on main highway 150 m. WNW of Kandahar.

Di'le Point (dē'lä). Most westerly point of Ilocos Sur prov., Luzon, Phil. Is., ab. 4 m. W of Vigan.

Dil'i *or* **Dil'li** (dĭl'ē). Town, ⁜ of Portuguese Timor, on N coast, E section of the island of Timor; pop. ab. 3000; good harbor for small craft; held by Japanese from Feb. 1942 to end of World War II.

Dil'len·burg (dĭl'ĕn·bŏŏrk). Town, W Germany, in Hesse state, ab. 25 m. WSW of Marburg; pop. 6011; ruins of castle where William the Silent was born.

Dil'li 1 (dĭl'ē) See DELHI.
2 (dĭl'ē) See DILI.

Dil'ling·en (dĭl'ĭng·ĕn). 1 Town, Schwaben govt. dist., Bavaria, Germany, on the N bank of the Danube 19 m. NE of Ulm; pop. 6091; taken by Allies Apr. 27, 1945 after several days' fighting.
2 Commune, Saarland, Germany, on the Saar 28 m. S of Trier; pop. ab. 10,000.

Dil'lon (dĭl'ŭn). 1 County in South Carolina. See *Table* at SOUTH CAROLINA.
2 City, ⊗ of Beaverhead co., SW Montana, 53 m. S of Butte; pop. 3690; shipping point for wool; Montana State Normal College (1893; coed.).
3 Town, ⊗ of Dillon co., NE South Carolina, 29 m. ENE of Florence; pop. 6173; textiles, flour, lumber.

Dil'lon Bay (dĭl'ŭn). Bay with good anchorage on W coast of Eromanga I., New Hebrides, SW Pacific; site of Martyrs' Memorial Church, in memory of several

missionaries killed on the island by natives 1839–72.

Dil'lon·vale (dĭl'ŭn·vāl). Village, Jefferson co., E Ohio, 13 m. SSW of Steubenville; pop. 1232; coal mining.

Di·lo'lo (dē·lō'lō). Lake in E Angola, SW Africa, near Congo border, lat. 11°30'S and long. 22°20'E.

Dil'worth (dĭl'wûrth; -wĕrth). Village, Clay co., W Minnesota, near Moorhead; pop. 2102.

Di'ma·pur (dē'mä·pŏŏr). Town, Assam Valley division, Assam prov., NE Indian Union; at foot of W slope of Naga Hills and key point on Bengal-Assam R.R.; goal of Japanese advance 1944 but not taken.

Di·ma'sa·lang' (dē·mä'sä·läng'). Municipality, E coast of Masbate I., Phil. Is., 20 m. SE of Masbate; pop. 24,471.

Di·mashq' (dĭ·măshk'). = DAMASCUS.

Dimitrovgrad. See CARIBROD.

Dim'mit (dĭm'ĭt). County in Texas. See *Table* at TEXAS.

Dim'mitt (dĭm'ĭt). Town, ⊗ of Castro co., NW Texas; pop. 2935.

Dimotika. See DIDYMOTEIKHON.

Dimyāṭ. See DAMIETTA.

Di·na'gat (dē·nä'gät). 1 Island, N of extreme NE point of Mindanao, SE Phil. Is., a part of Surigao prov.; 309 sq. m.; pop. ab. 14,600; separated from Mindanao by channel ab. 5 m. wide, from Siargao I. on E by **Dinagat Sound**, and from S Leyte and Panaon Is. on N W by Surigao Strait (*q.v.*); has chain of mountains from N to S with several peaks above 1700 ft. and highest 3300 ft.; chief towns Dinagat and Loreto.
2 Municipality and chief town of Dinagat I., on SW coast; pop 9533.

Di·naj'pur (dĭ·näj'pŏŏr). 1 District, formerly in Rajshahi division, cen. Bengal, NE Brit. India; in 1947 divided bet. East Bengal, Pakistan, and West Bengal, Indian Union; 3953 sq. m.; pop. (1941) 1,926,833.
2 Town, its ⁜, in Pakistan; pop. 19,156.

Di·na·lu·pi·han (dē'nä·lōō·pē'hän). Municipality, N Bataan prov., Luzon, Phil. Is., near Pampanga border and ab. 14 m. NNW of Balanga; pop. 8821; scene of fierce fighting with Japanese Jan. 1942.

Di·nan' (dē·nän'). City, Côtes-du-Nord dept., NW France, on Rance river 35 m. E of Saint-Brieuc; pop. 11,822; remains of 13th-cent. ramparts; 15th-cent. cloister; 12th-cent. churches.

Di·nant' (dē·nän'). Commune, Namur prov., S Belgium, on the Meuse; pop. 7003; in the Ardennes forest region, sacked by the Germans Aug. 15, 1914.

Di·na·pur (dĭ'nä·pŏŏr) *or* **Di'na·pore** (-pōr). Town, NW Bihar state, NE Indian Union, on right bank of Ganges river 12 m. W of Patna; pop. 24,221; iron foundries; produces excellent wood carvings; includes military cantonment; Sepoy troops stationed here joined mutiny in 1857.

Di·nar' (dĭ·när'); *anc.* **Ce·lae'nae** (sĕ·lē'nē). Town, Afyon Karahisar vilayet, W cen. Turkey in Asia, on railroad 50 m. SSW of Afyon Karahisar; pop. 4106; ancient Celaenae a great city of Phrygia at the source of the Maeander; setting of legend of Apollo and Marsyas.

Di·nar', Kuh-i- (kōō'hē·dē·när'). Peak 14,030 ft. in N Fars prov., SW Iran, ab. 100 m. NW of Shiraz.

Di'nard' (dē'när'). Commune, Ille-et-Vilaine dept., NW France, on the Gulf of Saint-Malo at the mouth of the Rance, opp Saint-Malo; pop. 9090; watering place.

Di·nar'ic Alps (dĭ·när'ĭk); *Yugoslav* **Di'na·ra Pla'-ni·na** (dē'nä·rä plä'nē·nä). See *Table* at ALPS.

Din'di·gul (dĭn'dĭ·gŭl). Town, S Madras, S Indian Union, 35 m. N of Madura; pop. (1941) 56,275; trade center, especially for tobacco and cigars; includes overlooking fort formerly of great strategic importance during the wars with the Marathas and in the time of Haidar Ali.

Din'dings (dĭn'dĭngz). Former division of Penang settlement, Straits Settlements, an outlying part on W Malay Penin.; included Pangkor I. and territory on opp. mainland; 182 sq. m.; pop. 19,592; chief town Lumut

(pop. 1898); ceded to Penang by Perak 1874, returned 1935; with Perak joined Federation of Malaya 1946.

Din'dy·mus, Mount (dĭn'dĭ·mŭs). See PESSINUS.

Ding·a'lan Bay (dĕng·ä'län). Inlet of Pacific Ocean on E coast of Luzon, Tayabas prov., Phil. Is., S of Baler Bay; its coast subleased to and exploited by Japanese before World War II.

Din'gle (dǐng'g'l). Seaport, W co. Kerry, SW Eire; on a small harbor on NW shore of **Dingle Bay** (an inlet of Atlantic Ocean extending ab. 30 m. inland); pop. 1800; as a port of Desmond important in 16th cent.

Din·gras' (dĕng·gräs'). Municipality, S cen. Ilocos Norte prov., Luzon, Phil. Is., on a tributary of the Laoag river 8 m. ESE of Laoag; pop. 22,434.

Ding'wall (dǐng'wôl; -wŭl). Burgh, ⊗ of Ross and Cromarty co., N Scotland, near the head of Cromarty Firth; pop. 3367; whisky distilling.

Din'kels·bühl (dǐng'kĕls·bül). Town, W Bavaria, Germany, ab. 45 m. SW of Nürnberg; pop. 5067; free imperial city 1351–1802.

Di'no·saur National Monument (dī'nô·sôr). See UNITED STATES, *National Monuments.*

Dins'la'ken (dǐns'lä'kĕn). Industrial city, W Germany, in North Rhine-Westphalia state near Rhine river 10 m. N of Duisburg; pop. 25,075; coal mining; manufactures steel. wire. nails, tile, lumber.

Di·nu'ba (dī·nū'bà). City, Tulare co., S cen. California, 25 m. SE of Fresno; pop. 6103; in irrigated district.

Din·wid'die (dǐn·wǐd'ǐ; dǐn'wǐd'ǐ). **1** County in Virginia. See *Table* at VIRGINIA.
2 Village. its ⊗, SE Virginia, 15 m. SW of Petersburg; pop (est.) 200; scene of Sheridan's defeat of Pickett near Dinwiddie Courthouse before fall of Petersburg Mar. 31, 1865, a part of the battle of Five Forks.

Di·oc'le·a (dī·ŏk'lê·à). See SALONA.

Di'o·mede Islands (dī'ô·mēd). Two islands **Big Diomede** (Russian) and **Little Diomede** (American) in middle of Bering Strait, ab. 2 m. apart; separated by date line; pop. of Little Diomede 129. Discovered and named by Vitus Bering, Danish explorer in the employ of Russia, on Aug. 16, 1725 (St. Diomedes' Day); Big Diomede has important Soviet weather station.

Dio'ny·si·a'des (thyô'nvĕ·sē·ä'thâs; *Angl.* dī'ô·nǐ·sī'à·dēz). Group of small islands in Mediterranean Sea just W of Cape Sidero, NE point of Crete; belong to Greece.

Dioscurias. See SUKHUMI.

Di'os·györ' (dī'ösh·dyür'). Commune, N Hungary, 7 m. W of Miskolc; pop. 21,222.

Di·os'po·lis (dī·ŏs'pō·lǐs); *also* **Diospolis Mag'na** (mäg'nà). Literally "City of God"; a late name of Thebes in Egypt, esp. as used of the XVIIIth, XIXth, and XXth (Diospolite) dynasties of Egyptian kings of the New Kingdom (c. 1580–1090 B.C.).

Diour'bel' (dvoor'bĕl'). Town, Senegal, West Africa, E of Dakar; pop. (1942) 18,006.

Di·po'log (dê·pô'lôg). Municipality, N Zamboanga prov., Mindanao, Phil. Is., on S coast of passage bet. Sulu Sea and Mindanao Sea; pop. 31,604.

Dir (dǐr). **1** Former independent state, S Malakand, N cen North-West Frontier Province, Pakistan; pop. ab. 100,000; on route bet. Peshawar and Chitral.
2 Its chief town. 85 m. N of Peshawar.

Di·rec'tion. Cape (dī·rĕk'shŭn; dǐ-). Cape, cen. E coast ot Cape York Penin., Queensland, NE Australia.

Di're·da·wa' *or* **Di're Da·wa'** (dē'rä·dà·wä'). City, E Ethiopia, on the Addis Ababa-Djibouti railroad; pop. ab. 30,000; taken by British Mar. 31, 1941.

Di·riam'ba (dê·ryäm'bä). Town, Carazo dept., SW Nicaragua, 20 m. S of Managua; pop. (1943 est.) 8971.

Dirk Har'tog Island (dûrk här'tŏg). Island 239 sq. m. off W coast of Western Australia, crossed by lat. 26°S.

Dirschau. See TCZEW.

Dis'ap·point'ment, Cape (dǐs'à·point'mĕnt). Cape on SW extremity of Pacific co., SW Washington, on N side of entrance to Columbia river.

Disappointment, Lake. Lake, N cen. Western Australia, crossed by Tropic of Capricorn.

Disappointment Islands. Small island group, N Tuamotu Archipelago, S Pacific Ocean.

Dis·cov'er·y Bay (dǐs·kŭv'ẽr·ǐ). Inlet of Indian Ocean, S coast of Australia, at boundary bet. Victoria and South Australia.

Dis·gra'zia, Mon'te del'la (mŏn'tâ dâl'lä dĕz·grä'-tsyä). Peak 12,067 ft. in the Bernina Alps, N Italy, NNW of Sondrio.

Dis'ko (dǐs'kō). Island 3200 sq. m. in Davis Strait, on W coast of Greenland, 70°N lat.; has extensive coal deposits; part of Danish colony; Godhavn is on S shore.

Disko Bay. Bay on the W coast of Greenland, S of Disko I.

Dis'mal Swamp (dǐz'măl). Swamp area ab. 30 m. long and 10 m. wide in SE Virginia and NE North Carolina; traversed by **Dismal Swamp Canal** (22 m. long) connecting Chesapeake Bay with Albemarle Sound.

Dis·na' (dǐs·nä'; *Russ.* dyǐs·nà'); *Pol.* **Dzis'na** (jēs'nä). **1** River ab. 85 m. long in N White Russia; flows E into Dvina river at Disna, formerly on Russian border.
2 Town, N White Russia, U.S.S.R., 128 m. NE of Vilnyus; formerly in Wilno dept., Poland; pop. 4788.

Di'son' (dē'zôn'). Manufacturing commune, Liège prov., E Belgium; pop. 10,599.

District Heights. Town, Prince Georges co., S cen. Maryland, SE of Washington, D.C.; pop. 7524.

District of Co·lum'bi·a (kô·lŭm'bǐ·à). Federal district of U.S.A., coextensive with the city of Washington (*q.v.*); bounded on N, E, and S by Maryland, and on W by Virginia; 69 sq. m. (land area 61 sq. m.); pop. 763,956, estimated wartime pop. 1,250,000. *Official flower:* American Beauty rose. *Motto:* Justitia Omnibus (Justice to All).

History: Territory for seat of Federal government originally 100 square miles; authorized by Congressional act 1790 and granted by Maryland and Virginia 1790–91; site of Washington (*q.v.*), chosen by President Washington, occupied by government 1800; part (see ALEXANDRIA) retroceded to Virginia 1846; slave trade forbidden in District 1850 and slavery abolished with compensation 1862; governed since 1874 by Commission appointed by President (permanent arrangement 1878); by consolidation of Georgetown (*q.v.*) with Washington became coterminous with Washington. Granted national suffrage 1961 by 23d amendment to U.S. Constitution.

Dis·tri'to Fe'de·ral' (dĕs·trē'tô fä'thâ·räl'). Spanish for FEDERAL DISTRICT, Argentina, Mexico, and Venezuela.

Dis·tri'to Fe·de·ral' (dĕsh·trē'too fâ·thĕ'räl'), *formerly* **Dis·tric'to Federal** (dĕsh·trē'too). Portuguese for FEDERAL DISTRICT, Brazil.

Di·sûq' (dǐ·sook'). Town, Gharbîya prov., Lower Egypt, on Rosetta branch of the Nile E of Damanhûr.

Dith'mar'schen (dǐt'mär'shĕn); *Eng.* **Dit'marsh** (dǐt'märsh). Region, SW Schleswig-Holstein, northern Germany, bet. the Elbe and Eider rivers; partly marsh, partly sandy; in Charlemagne's time known as **Nord'al·bin'gi·a** (nôrd'ăl·bǐn'jǐ·à); peasant independent self-government formed in 13th cent., finally overcome in 1559 and divided; annexed to Schleswig-Holstein 1866.

Dit'ters·bach (dǐt'ẽrs·bäĸ). Commune, Śląsk Dolny dept., SW Poland, S suburb of Wałbrzych; pop. 14,916; coal mining; formerly in Prussia, Germany.

Di'u (dē'oo). District of Portuguese India, comprising island and seaport town (pop. 13,844; fortified town, formerly important trade center), S extremity of Kathiawar Penin., W India, 170 m. NW of Bombay; 20 sq. m.; includes also two small towns on the mainland; came into Portuguese possession in 1535.

Di·ua'ta Mountains (dê·wä'tä). Mountain range, NE Mindanao, Phil. Is., running N and S bet. Surigao and Agusan provs.; highest Mt. Hilonghilong 6027 ft.

Diuata Point. Point on NE coast of Mindanao, Phil.

Is., marking boundary bet. Agusan and Misamis Oriental provs. and also W side of entrance to Butuan Bay.

Dives, *in full* **Dives–sur–Mer** (dēv′sür·mâr′). Town, Calvados dept., NW France; pop. 4239; on the Bay of the Seine ab. a mile inland from the harbor from which William the Conqueror set sail on his first attempt to reach England 1066 (cf. SAINT-VALÉRY-SUR-SOMME).

Di′vi, Point (dī′vi). Cape, E coast of India, E of Kistna delta and S of Masulipatam.

Di·vide′ (dǐ·vīd′). County in North Dakota. See *Table* at NORTH DAKOTA.

Divide Mountain. Peak 8647 ft. on E border of Glacier National Park, NW Montana.

Di·vid′ing Ridge (dǐ·vīd′ĭng). Ridge extending along W section of boundary between Virginia and West Virginia.

Di′vion′ (dē′vyôN′). Commune, Pas-de-Calais dept., N France, 17 m. NW of Arras; pop. (1931) 10,156; coal mining.

Di·vi′sion Peak (dǐ·vĭzh′ŭn). Mountain 8585 ft. in W Humboldt co., NW Nevada.

Divisões, Serra das. See SERRA DAS DIVISÕES.

Divodurum *or* **Divodurum Mediomatricum.** See METZ.

Divona. See CAHORS.

Di′wa·ni′yah (dē′wǎ·nē′yȧ; -yǎ); *Arab.* **Ad Di′wa·ni′ya** (ăd dē′-). **1** Province (*liwa*), cen. Iraq; pop. (1935 est.) 416,831.
2 Town, S cen. Iraq, on the Euphrates river 40 m. SE of Hilla; on the Baghdad-Basra railroad.

Dix (dĭks). River, cen. Kentucky; flows N into Kentucky river. See DIX RIVER DAM.

Dix′field (dĭks′fēld). Town, Oxford co., W Maine, 33 m. NNW of Lewiston; pop. 2323; wooden products.

Dix′ie (dĭk′sǐ). **1** The southern states of the U.S.
2 County in Florida. See *Table* at FLORIDA.

Dix Mountain (dĭks). Peak 4842 ft. in the Adirondack Mts., Essex co., NE New York.

Dixmuide, Dixmude. See DIKSMUIDE.

Dix′on (dĭk′s'n). **1** County in Nebraska. See *Table* at NEBRASKA.
2 City, ⊗ of Lee co., N Illinois, 40 m. SSW of Rockford; pop. 19,565; founded 1830; commercial center.
3 City, ⊗ of Webster co., W Kentucky; pop. 541; coal mining.

Dixon Entrance. Strait ab. 40 m. wide bet. N Queen Charlotte Is., Canada, and S Prince of Wales I., SE Alaska, and W Brit. Columbia; connects Hecate Strait with the Pacific Ocean.

Dix River Dam (dĭks). Dam completed 1925 across Dix river in Kentucky; height 270 ft.; water power.

Di·ya′la (dǐ·yä′lä; *Angl.* dǐ·yǎl′ȧ) *or* **Di·a′la** (dǐ·äl′ȧ). **1** River ab. 300 m. long in E Iraq; rises in mountains of W Iran, flows SW across Iraq border into the Tigris river at Baghdad; navigable for 50 m.; traverses a fertile region.
2 Province, E cen. Iraq; pop. (1935 est.) 215,900.

Di·yar′ba·kir′ (dē·yär′bä·kǐr′) *or* **Di·ar′bekr′** (dē·yär′bĕk′ẽr). **1** Vilayet, SE Turkey in Asia; 5742 sq. m.; pop. 213,283.
2 *anc.* **Am′i·da** (ăm′ĭ·dȧ). Commercial city, its ✳, on right bank of the Tigris; pop. (1940) 43,264; trades in wool, mohair, and copper; esp. flourishing in 19th cent. As Amida became Roman colony 230 A.D.; captured after long siege 363 A.D. by Shapur II of Persia; several times taken by Persians and Arabs before finally being taken by the Turks 1515.

Diz·ful′ (dĭz·fōōl′). Town, Khuzistan prov., SW Iran, ab. 130 m. N of Khorramshahr; pop. ab. 15,000; on a tributary of the Karun and on railroad and highway to the N; has fine large stone bridge across the river; its chief local industries are dyeing and manufacture of felts. The ruins of ancient Susa are ab. 15 m. S.

Dj-. For some words beginning thus, see J-.

Djai·lo′lo (jī·lō′lō). See HALMAHERA.

Djailolo Passage. Strait bet. SE Halmahera I. on the

W and the small islands off W Waigeo I. on the E, in the Moluccas, E Malay Archipelago; connects Ceram Sea with the Pacific Ocean; extreme width is ab. 100 m.

Dja·kar′ta (jȧ·kär′tȧ). City, Java, ✳ of Indonesia. See BATAVIA.

Djakarta Bay. See BATAVIA BAY.

Dja′ko·vi′ca *or* **Đa′ko·vi′ca** (dyä′kō·vē′tsä). Town, S Yugoslavia, near Albanian border, now (since 1945) in the Kosovo-Metohija autonomous prov., formerly in Vardarska co.; pop. 13,773.

Dja′ko·vo *or* **Đa′ko·vo** (dyä′kō·vȯ). Town, N Yugoslavia, 22 m. SW of Osijek; pop. 7987; episcopal see, one of whose bishops was Joseph G. Strossmayer, leader of Croatian National Party.

Djam′bi *or* **Jam′bi** (jäm′bē). **1** Former residency, S cen. Sumatra, Neth. Indies, extending nearly across the island from Barisan Mts. to South China Sea; 17,341 sq. m.; pop. 245,272; ✳ Djambi; its low marshy area drained by Hari river; rubber and petroleum.
2 Town, its ✳, a river port on the Hari river ab. 60 m. from its mouth; pop. 22,071; an important oil center and trading town; in 17th and 18th cents. capital of an influential sultanate; later a vassal of Batavia.
3 River. See HARI.

Dja·pa′ra *or* **Ja·pa′ra** (jä·pä′rä). Town, on coast of Central Java prov., Indonesia, 35 m. NNE of Semarang; pop. 8356; seat of important sultanate in 17th cent.

Djapara–Rem′bang *or* **Japara–Rem′bang** (-rĕm′-bäng). Former residency, NE Middle Java prov., Neth. Indies; 2339 sq. m.; pop. 1,885,548; ✳ Kudus; long coast line on Java Sea; bordered Semarang residency on SW and S and Bodjonegoro residency of East Java province on E; lowland around Kudus but volcanic mountains in NW and S; petroleum; sugar; rice.

Djatinegara. See MEESTER CORNELIS.

Dja′ti·wang′i *or* **Ja′ti·wang′i** (jä′tē·wäng′ē). Town, West Java prov., Indonesia, ab. 20 m. W of Cheribon; pop. 11,022.

Dja′wa (jä′wä). Indonesian form of JAVA.

Djebeïl. See JUBAYL.

Djebel. See JEBEL.

Djeb′el Druze (jĕb′ĕl drōōz′; *Fr.* jä′bĕl′ drüz′). = JEBEL ED DRUZ.

Dje·bo′id, Lake (jĕ·bō′ĭd). Large lake SE of Alep, NW Syria; size varies with the season.

Djed′dah (jĕd′ȧ). = JIDDA.

Dje·dei′da (jĕ·dā′dȧ; *Arab.* jōō·dī′dȧ, -dā′-, -dȧ). Railroad junction town on the Medjerda river, N Tunisia, ab. 17 m. W of the city of Tunis; in World War II held by British for a few days in Nov. 1942; German base in Tunisian campaign, taken by Allied armies May 1943.

Djel′fa (jĕl′fȧ). Town, Ghardaïa territory, Algeria, N Africa, S of Algiers; railroad terminal.

Djem, El. See EL DJEM.

Dje·ma′dja (jĕ·mä′jä). Largest island of Anambas Is., Indonesia, in W part of group.

Djem′ber *or* **Jem′ber** (jĕm′bẽr). Town, East Java prov., Indonesia, S of Bondowoso; pop. 20,222.

Djen′né *or* **Jen′né** (jĕ′nā′). Commercial town, S cen. Mali (formerly French Sudan), West Africa, 250 m. SW of Tombouctou; pop. (1940) 4969; founded probably 8th cent. by the Songhai, for a time their capital; flourished 12th–16th cents.; name thought by some to be origin of name, Guinea, now applied to NW coast region; taken by the French 1893.

Djerablous. See JERABLUS.

Djer′ba *or* **Jer′ba** (jĕr′bȧ); *anc.* **Me′ninx** (mē′nĭngks). Island in cen. Mediterranean Sea, off SE coast of Tunisia, at S side of entrance to the Gulf of Gabès; ab. 16 sq. m.; pop. ab. 35,000; a fertile island producing much fruit; exports olive oil and dates; contains remains of ancient Roman civilization.

Dje·rid′, Chott (shŏt′ jĕ·rēd′); *Arab.* **Shatt el Je·rid′** (shŏt′ ăl jŭ·rēd′); *anc.* **Pa′lus Tri·to′nis** (pā′lŭs trī·tō′nĭs). Large saline lake ab. 120 m. long in SW cen.

Tunisia, N Africa; in Greek mythology believed by some to have been the scene of the birth of Athena, whence her name *Athena Tritogeneia.*

Djev'dje·li·ja (dyĕv'dyĕ·lĕ·yä). Town, Macedonia, SE Yugoslavia, on Vardar river at Greek border.

Dji·bou'ti *or* **Ji·bu'ti** (jĭ·bōō'tĭ). City, ✳ of French Somaliland, E Africa, on S shore of Gulf of Tadjoura; pop. (1936) 14,870, (1939 est.) 20,000; terminus of railroad from Addis Ababa, Ethiopia; has large landlocked harbor; founded as port by French 1888; made capital 1892.

Dji·djel'li *or* **Ji·jel'li** (jĭ·jĕl'ĭ); *anc.* **I·gil'gi·li** (ĭ·jĭl'ji·lĭ). Commune, NW Constantine dept., NE Algeria, on coast 50 m. NW of Constantine; pop. 11,871.

Djoc'ja *or* **Djok'ja** (jŏk'yà; jŏk'yà). Common short form of *Djokjakarta:* see JOGJAKARTA.

Djokjakarta. See JOGJAKARTA.

Djom'bang (jŏm'bäng). Town, East Java prov., Indonesia, in wide plain ab. 40 m. SW of Surabaja; pop. 20,380.

Djouf, El. See EL DJOUF.

Djulfa. See DZHULFA.

Djur·dju'ra (jŏŏr·jŏŏr'à). Mountain range of the Little Atlas Mts., NE Alger dept., Algeria; highest point ab. 7570 ft.

Dmi'tri·ev (dĕ·mē'trĭ·ĕf; *Russ.* d'myē'tryĭ·yĕf). Town, NW Kursk Region, Soviet Russia, Europe, on railroad 50 m. NW of Kursk; pop. 51,436.

Dmi'trov (dĕ·mē'trôf; *Russ.* d'myē'trŭf). Town, Moscow Region, W cen. Soviet Russia, Europe, on railroad ab. 40 m. N of Moscow; pop. 6390; dates from 12th cent.; suffered damage from the Tatars; has iron, metal, and cellulose factories; reached by Germans Dec. 1941.

Dnepr. See DNIEPER.

Dne'pro·dzer·zhinsk' (nĕp'rô·dĕr·zhĭnsk'; *Russ.* d'nyĭ·prŭ·dyĕr·zhĭnsk'); *formerly* **Ka'men·sko·e** (kà'myĭn·skŭ·yĕ). City, cen. Dnepropetrovsk Region, E cen. Ukraine, U.S.S.R., on right bank of the Dnieper ab. 20 m. W of Dnepropetrovsk; pop. 147,829.

Dne'pro·pe·trovsk' (nĕp'rô·pĕ·trôfsk'; *Russ.* d'nyĭ·prŭ·pyĕ·trôfsk'). **1** Region, E cen. Ukraine, U.S.S.R.; crossed by the Dnieper river.
2 *formerly* **E·ka'te·ri'no·slav** (ĕ·kät'ĕr·ē'nô·slàv; *Russ.* yĭ·kà·tyĭ·ryē'nŭ·slàf'). City, its ✳, on right bank of the Dnieper at its big bend, 120 m. SW of Kharkov; pop. 500,662; an industrial city and railroad junction, a center of the wheat trade of cen. Ukraine, also handles coal, iron, timber, and manufactured products; situated near head of rapids of lower Dnieper which extend ab. 25 m. S nearly to Zaporozhe (see DNEPROSTROI); has railroad bridge across the Dnieper; cathedral, museum, library, and other cultural buildings. Founded by Potëmkin 1786 and named Ekaterinoslav after Empress Catherine II; occupied by Germans Aug. 23, 1941; retaken Oct. 25, 1943.

Dne'pro·stroi' (nĕp'rô·stroi'; *Russ.* d'nyĭ·prŭ·stroi'). Dam 2500 ft. long and 200 ft. high across the lower Dnieper at foot of main rapids below Dnepropetrovsk and above Zaporozhe, Ukraine, U.S.S.R.; largest hydroelectric plant in the world, built under direction of American engineers 1927-32; dam proper surmounted by piers with 47 crest gates of 40-foot span; locks on left bank provide navigation around rapids. Partly destroyed Aug. 23, 1941 by Russians in "scorched earth" policy to prevent use by Germans; rebuilding begun immediately after recapture of Dnepropetrovsk, completed by end of 1947.

Dnestr. See DNIESTER.

Dnie'per (nē'pēr); *Russ.* **Dne'pr** (d'nyĕ'pr'); *anc.* **Bo·rys'the·nes** (bô·rĭs'thĕ·nēz). River ab. 1400 m. long in W and SW Soviet Russia, Europe; rises in Smolensk Region in S Valdai Hills near the source of the Volga, flows SW, then S through E White Russia, SE and SW through the Ukraine, with a big bend at Dnepropetrovsk, into the Black Sea near Kherson; third

longest river of Europe (after the Volga and the Danube), has drainage basin of ab. 200,000 sq. m.; navigable for most of its course to a point above Smolensk; dammed below Dnepropetrovsk by huge Dneprostroi dam (*q.v.*). Chief tributaries the Berezina, Sozh, Pripyat, Desna, Sula, Psel, and Vorskla rivers. Chief cities on its course Smolensk, Orsha, Mogilev, Kiev, Cherkassy, Kremenchug, Dnepropetrovsk, Zaporozhe, Nikopol, and Kherson. In 1667 became frontier bet. Russia and Poland; large territories on upper Dnieper acquired by Russia in first partition of Poland 1772.

Dnies'ter (nēs'tēr); *Russ.* **Dnes'tr** (d'nyĕs'tr'); *Romanian* **Ni'stru** (nē'strōō); *anc.* **Ty'ras** (tī'ràs) *or* **Da·nas'tris** (dà·năs'trĭs). River 850 m. long, SE Europe; rises in SW Ukraine on N slope of Carpathian Mts. and flows SE in winding course to the Black Sea SW of Odessa; 360 m. of its course were formerly in Poland above Khotin where it crosses the old Russian border; recent improvements at rapids of Yampol have rendered it navigable to Khotin; has considerable traffic and an abundance of fish. Chief tributaries the Seret and Stry; chief towns on its course Khotin, Mogilev Podolski, Bendery, and Belgorod-Dnestrovski. Has long been the E boundary of Bessarabia; since 1940 its entire course in U.S.S.R.

Do·ab' (dō·äb'). Literally, in Hindustani, "two waters"; in India, a tract of land bet. two rivers whose courses are approximately parallel; specifically, the region in Uttar Pradesh bet. the Ganges and the Jumna rivers from the Siwalik Hills to their junction, called also **Great Doab.**

Doane, Mount (dōn). Peak 10,500 ft. in Yellowstone National Park, NW Wyoming.

Doane Mountain. Peak 5500 ft. in Pennington co., SW South Dakota.

Dobbs Ferry (dŏbz). Village, Westchester co., SE New York, on Hudson river 20 m. N of New York; pop. 9260; residential suburb of New York City; seat of Children's Village, home and training school for problem children (estab. in New York 1851; moved here 1901); place where Generals Washington and Rochambeau planned the Yorktown campaign and where Washington met with Clinton and Sir Guy Carleton May 6, 1783.

Dö'beln (dû'bĕln). Industrial city, East Germany, on the Mulde river 36 m. ESE of Leipzig; pop. 22,508; railroad junction; manufactures machinery, metal and wooden goods, chocolates, cigars, sugar; 15th-cent. church; monument to Luther.

Do·be·ran' (dō'bĕ·rän'). Town, Mecklenburg, E Germany, ab. 2 m. from shore of Bay of Mecklenburg 7 m. W of Rostock; pop. 5570; watering place; ruins of 12th-cent. Cistercian Abbey, 14th-cent. Gothic church.

Do'bo (dō'bō). Village and only port of Aru Is., Indonesia, on small island off W coast of Tanahbesar I.

Dobrich. See BAZARGIC.

Dobromierz. See HOHENFRIEDEBERG.

Do'bru·ja *or* **Do'bru·dja** (dô'brōō·jä); *Romanian* **Do'bro·gea** (dô'brô·jä). Region, SE Romania and NE Bulgaria, comprising Black Sea coastal strip S of Danube river; a province of Romania 1913-40, area 8979 sq. m., chief town Constanța; S half to Bulgaria 1940.

Dob'son (dŏb's'n). Town, ⊗ of Surry co., N North Carolina; pop. 684.

Do'bu (dō'bōō). Chief settlement of D'Entrecasteaux Is., E of SE Papua, New Guinea I., on small island bet. Fergusson and Normanby Is.

Do'ce (dō'sĕ). River ab. 360 m. long, E Brazil; rises in S cen. Minas Gerais state, flows E across border of Espírito Santo state and into Atlantic Ocean N of Vitória; in a region of many rich iron-ore deposits.

Doch'art, Loch (lŏk dŏk'ērt). Lake 3 m. long in Perth co., cen. Scotland.

Dodabetta, Mount. See NILGIRI HILLS.

Dod'dridge (dŏd'rĭj). County in West Virginia. See *Table* at WEST VIRGINIA.

Do·dec'a·nese (dō·děk'á·nēs; -nēz) *or* **Do'dec·a·ne'-sus** (dō'děk·à·nē'sŭs; dō·děk'-). Literally, Greek, "twelve islands"; group of islands in SE Aegean Sea, included in the Southern Sporades (see SPORADES); 486 sq. m.; pop. (1936) 76,724; formerly part of Italian Aegean Is. (Isole Egee); includes 12 main islands (Greek and Italian names): Astypalaia (Stampalia), Kalymnos (Calino), Karpathos (Scarpanto), Kasos (Caso), Khalkē (Calchi), Kos (Coo), Leros (Lero), Lipsos (Lisso or Lipso), Nisyros (Nisiro), Patmos (Patmo), Symē (Simi), Telos (Piscopi), and numerous small islands; administrative center Rhodes. Held as part of Ottoman Empire until 1912; seized (with Rhodes) by Italy in war with Turkey over Tripoli 1912; promised by Italians to Greece 1913 but not surrendered; turned over to Greece after Turkey had ceded them to Italy by Treaty of Sèvres 1920; Rhodes, Dodecanese, and Kastelorrizon (*q.v.*) given to Italy in Treaty of Lausanne 1923, restored to Greece by treaty of March 31, 1947. See AEGEAN ISLANDS, RHODES.

Dodge (dŏj). Counties in four states of the U.S. See *Tables* at GEORGIA, MINNESOTA, NEBRASKA, WISCONSIN.

Dodge City. City, ⊗ of Ford co., S Kansas, on Arkansas river 120 m. E of Colo. border; pop. 13,520; formerly frontier town and cattle-shipping point on the old Santa Fe Trail; industrial center in wheat-growing section.

Dodge'ville (dŏj'vĭl). City, ⊗ of Iowa co., SW Wisconsin, 24 m. NE of Platteville; pop. 2911; retail and shipping center for dairy and corn-hog district and pea-growing region; lead and zinc mines nearby.

Dod'man Point (dŏd'măn). Cape on SE coast of Cornwall, SW England.

Do'do·ma (dō'dō·mä). Town, Central Prov., Tanganyika, E Africa; pop. 12,262; railroad and highway center.

Do·do'na (dō·dō'nà). Town and oracle on Mt. Tomarus, Epirus, NW Greece, in E part of Thesprotia; a center of Pelasgic worship; dedicated to Zeus and consulted from very early times; temple destroyed by Aetolians 219 B.C. but oracle survived several centuries.

Doe'tin·chem (dōō'tĕ·Kĕm). Commune, Gelderland prov., E Netherlands, at Arnhem; pop. 14,329.

Dog'ger Bank (dŏg'ẽr). Submerged sand bank in cen. North Sea, ab. 60 m. E of England; fishing; naval battle nearby Jan. 24, 1915 bet. battle cruiser squadrons of Vice-Admiral Beatty and Rear-Admiral Hipper in which the Germans escaped with one cruiser, the *Blücher*, lost.

Dog Island (dŏg). Island off S Franklin co., NW Florida, separated from mainland by St. George Sound.

Do·go (dō·gô). See OKI ARCHIPELAGO.

Do'ha (dō'há; -hà) *or* **Bi'da** (bĭ'dŏ); *formerly* **El Be'da** (ăl bā'dŏ). Town, ✻ of sheikdom of Qatar, Arabia, on the Persian Gulf on the E coast of Qatar Penin.; residence of the sultan.

Do'had (dō'hŭd). Town, E Gujerat state, W India, 105 m. E of Ahmadabad; pop. 22,093.

Doi In·tha·non (dŏi ĭn·t'hä·nŭn). Mountain 8468 ft., NW Thailand, near the upper course of the Ping river 35 m. WSW of Chiang Mai; highest mountain in Thailand.

Doj'ran, *or* **Doi'ran, Lake** (dŏi'rän). Small lake 18 sq. m. on boundary line bet. N Macedonia, Greece, and SE Yugoslavia, E of the Vardar; divided bet. the two countries; scene 1916–17 of conflict bet. Allies (British and French armies) and Central Powers (Germans and Bulgarians). On W shore is the Yugoslav commune **Dojran** (pop. ab. 8000).

Dok'kum (dŏk'ŭm). Town, Friesland prov., N Netherlands, ab. 12 m. NE of Leeuwarden; pop. 4895; scene of death of Saint Boniface 755.

Dol, *in full* **Dol–de–Bre·tagne'** (dŏl'dē·brĕ·tàn'y'). Commune, Ille-et-Vilaine dept., NW France, SE of Saint-Malo; pop. (1931) 4473; menhir ab. 30 ft. high nearby; 13th-cent. cathedral. On frontier bet. Normandy and Brittany, formerly an important fortress; captured by Henry II of England 1164.

Dol'beau' (dŏl'bō'). Town, East Lake St. John co., S Quebec, Canada, on Mistassini river 8 m. N of Lake St. John; pop. 4307.

Dôle (dōl). 1 Commercial and manufacturing commune, Jura dept., E France, on Doubs river 30 m. N of Lons-le-Saunier; pop. 18,117; 16th-cent. church; hospital in Renaissance style; Roman ruins.
2 *or* **La Dôle** (là). Peak ab. 5505 ft. in Vaud canton, W Switzerland, on French border ab. 16 m. N of Geneva.

Dol·gel'ley (dŏl·gĕl'ĭ; -gĕth'lĭ; *Welsh* -gĕ'hlĭ). Urban district, ⊗ of Merionethshire, W Wales; pop. 2246.

Dolge'ville (dŏlj'vĭl). Village, Fulton and Herkimer cos., E New York, 25 m. E of Utica; pop. 3058.

Do·li'na (dō·lē'nä). Town, W Ukraine, U.S.S.R., ab. 30 m. W of Stanislav; pop. 9916; formerly in Stanisławów prov., S Poland.

Dol'lar Law (dŏl'ẽr lô'). Mountain 2680 ft., Peebles co., S Scotland.

Dol'lart (dŏl'ärt). Basin of upper (S) end of the Ems estuary, NW Germany and NE Netherlands, 10 m. long by 7 m. wide; Emden is on its N shore.

Dolnja Tuzla. See TUZLA.

Dol'o·mites (dŏl'ô·mīts); *Ital.* **Do·lo·mi'ti** (dō·lō·mē'tē). See *Table* at ALPS.

Dolon. See TOLUN.

Do·lo'res (dō·lōr'ĕs; -ĕz; *Span.* -lō'räs). 1 River 230 m. long, SW Colorado; rises in NW end of San Juan Mts., flows SW, then N and NW across Utah boundary into Colorado river in E cen. Grand co., E Utah.
2 County in Colorado. See *Table* at COLORADO.
3 Town, Buenos Aires prov., E Argentina, ab. 126 m. SE of Buenos Aires.
4 Port, Soriano dept., SW Uruguay, on San Salvador river ab. 18 m. above its confluence with the Uruguay, ab. 145 m. NW of Montevideo; pop. ab. 11,500; shipping point for grain.

Do·lo'res Hi·dal'go (dō·lō'räs ē·thäl'gô). Town, Guanajuato state, cen. Mexico, on railroad 30 m. NE of Guanajuato; pop. 5915.

Do·lo'res Peak (dō·lōr'ĕs). Mountain 13,502 ft. in Dolores and San Miguel cos., SW Colorado.

Dol'phin, Cape (dŏl'fĭn). Cape extending into South Atlantic Ocean from NW coast of East Falkland I., off SE South America.

Dolphin and Un'ion Strait (ūn'yŭn). Channel bet. SW Victoria I. and N Canada mainland; connects Coronation Gulf with Amundsen Gulf.

Dolphin Depth. Point 27,972 ft. deep in Atlantic Ocean N of Puerto Rico.

Dolphin Head. 1 Promontory extending into Atlantic Ocean on SW cen. coast of South-West Africa.
2 Peak 1813 ft. in W Jamaica, West Indies.

Dol'ton (dŏl't'n). Village, Cook co., NE Illinois, 17 m. S of Chicago; pop. 1874.

Dom (dōm). Highest peak 14,942 ft. in Mischabelhörner, Valais canton, SW cen. Switzerland.

Domb'ås' (dŏm'ôs'; dŏōm'-). Village, Opland co., S cen. Norway, on S edge of Dovrefjell; pop. 321; scene of fighting bet. Allies and Germans Apr. 30–May 2, 1940.

Dom'basle' (dôn'bäl'). Commune, Meurthe-et-Moselle dept., NE France, ab. 10 m. SE of Nancy; pop. (1931) 8082; soda factories.

Dombes (dôNb). Region, S Ain dept., E France, bet. the Ain, Rhone, and Saône rivers; has many low hills and stagnant ponds; unhealthful. Once part of kingdom of Arles, later principality with capital at Trévoux; united to crown 1762. See BRESSE.

Dombrau. See DĄBROWA GÓRNICZA.

Dombrek. See SIMOÏS.

Dôme, Puy de (pü·ēd' dōm'). Peak 4805 ft., Puy-de-Dôme dept., S cen. France, W of Clermont-Ferrand.

Do'mel Island (dō'mĕl). Island, cen. Mergui Archipelago (*q.v.*), Burma.

Dome Peak (dōm). 1 Mountain 8860 ft. in N Washington, on boundary bet. Chelan and Skagit cos.

2 Mountain 6586 ft. in Yakima co., S Washington.

Dome Rock. Height 4560 ft. in Scotts Bluff co., W Nebraska.

Do·mes·nes, Cape (dōōm'ĕs·nâs'). Cape on NW coast of Latvia, U.S.S.R., on S side of entrance to Gulf of Riga.

Domeyko, Cordillera. See ANDES.

Dom'front' (dôN'frôN'). Commune, W Orne dept., NW France, 30 m. E of Avranches; pop. (1931) 3894; dates from 6th cent.; Norman stronghold of Middle Ages, scene of fighting in many wars 14th–16th cents.; in World War II taken by Americans Aug. 13–15, 1944 after having been once taken and lost.

Dom'i·ni'ca (dŏm'ĭ·nē'ka; dŏ·mĭn'ĭ·ka). Island, Windward Is., British West Indies in center of Lesser Antilles bet. Guadeloupe (S Leeward Is.) and Martinique (N Windward Is.); territory, formerly a presidency in Leeward Is. colony; ab. 29 m. from N to S, 16 m. wide; 305 sq. m.; pop. (1942) 53,686; ✱ Roseau; mountainous and volcanic; highest peak Morne Diablotin 5314 ft., highest point in the Lesser Antilles; fertile, with fine forests, but not developed agriculturally.

History: Discovered by Columbus 1493; included in grant to earl of Carlisle but Caribs left in possession until 18th cent.; settled by French from whom English took it 1759; captured by French 1778 but restored to Great Britain 1783; incorporated with Leeward Is. 1833; administration transferred to Windward Is. Jan. 1, 1940.

Do·min'i·can Republic (dŏ·mĭn'ĭ·kăn; *officially* **Re·pú'bli·ca Do·mi'ni·ca'na** (rrĕ·pōō'vlē·kä thŏ·mē'nĕ·kä'nä). Republic occupying E two thirds of Hispaniola I., West Indies; 18,816 sq. m.; pop. (1960)

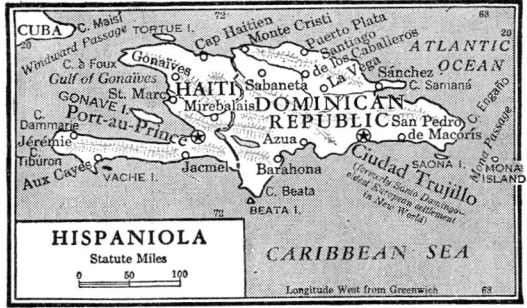

462,192; ✱ Santo Domingo (from 1936 to 1961 called Ciudad Trujillo); divided into the following 17 provinces and the District of Santo Domingo (as of 1949; there have been several reorganizations since that date; for pronunciation of their names, see their individual entries).

NAME	LOCA-TION	AREA[1]	POP.[1]	CAPITAL
Azua	S	1,359	77,215	Azua
Bahoruco	SW	1,347	65,397	Neiba
Barahona	SW	1,341	61,457	Barahona
Benefactor	W cen.	1,344	97,504	San Juan de la Maguana
Duarte	N cen.	1,116	148,718	San Francisco de Macorís
Espaillat	N cen.	254	108,338	Moca
La Vega	cen.	1,782	221,600	La Vega
Libertador	NW	356	36,244	Dajabón
Monseñor de Meriño	E cen.	981	61,655	Monte Plata
Montecristi	NW	1,150	78,791	Montecristi
Puerto Plata	N	822	143,793	Puerto Plata
Samaná	NE	546	30,334	Samaná
San Pedro de Macorís	SE	520	91,988	San Pedro de Macorís
San Rafael	W	788	36,046	Elías Piña
Santiago	N cen.	1,367	259,616	Santiago
Santo Domingo, District of	S	548	136,702	Ciudad Trujillo
Seibo	E	2,715	174,522	Seibo
Trujillo	S	793	139,853	San Cristóbal

[1] Area in sq. m. Pop. from 1944 est. Census.

On E terminates in Cape Engaño on Mona Passage

(separates Hispaniola from Puerto Rico); Capes Isabela and Francés Viejo are prominent points on N coast and Cape Beata on SW; coast line generally regular except for long peninsula of Samaná on N enclosing Bay of Samaná; N part covered by rich Vega Real valley formed by two streams flowing in opposite directions; cen. part traversed by the Cordillera Central; highest point Pico Duarte, 10,417 ft., several peaks above 5000 ft.; mountainous SW part contains Lake Enriquillo. Chief industry agriculture and chief products are sugar, cocoa, tobacco, maize, molasses. Chief towns Santo Domingo, Santiago de los Caballeros, San Pedro de Macorís, and Puerto Plata.

History: For earlier history, see HISPANIOLA. Created 1844 after revolt against Boyer's rule of entire island of Hispaniola; except for brief period (1861–65) of annexation to Spain, has since then been independent, although its customs were controlled by United States 1905–41, and it was under U.S. military occupation 1916–24; new constitution adopted 1924; broke off diplomatic relations with Germany 1917 in World War I; declared war on Axis powers 1941 in World War II.

Do·min'ion (dŏ·mĭn'yŭn). Town, Cape Breton co., E Nova Scotia, Canada, on Atlantic Ocean 7 m. ENE of Sydney; pop. 3143; coal mines.

Dom'joch' (dŏm'yôK'). Mountain pass 14,060 ft. over the Mischabelhörner, S of the Dom, Valais canton, SW cen. Switzerland.

Dom'mel (dŏm'ĕl). River, S Netherlands; rises in Belgium, flows N across the border through cen. North Brabant prov., S Netherlands, into the Maas (Meuse).

Do'mo (dō'mō). Small village, E Ethiopia, near the border of Somalia.

Do·mo·dos'so·la (dō·mô·dôs'sō·lä); *anc.* **Do'mus De'i** (dō'mŭs dē'ĭ). Commune, Novara prov., Piedmont, NW Italy, in river valley 47 m. N of Novara near Italian end of Simplon Tunnel; pop. 10,645; made countship under bishop of Novara by Charlemagne; captured by Swiss 1416; laid waste by Valaisans 1487; to Austria 1714, Savoy 1735.

Dom Pe·dri'to (dōNm' pĕ·thrē'tōō). City, Rio Grande do Sul state, S Brazil, just E of Livramento; pop. (1940 est.) 10,078.

Dom'ré'my'-la-Pu'celle' (dôN'rā'mē'lä·pü'sĕl'). Village, Vosges dept., NE France, on the Meuse; pop. (1931) 279; birthplace of Joan of Arc.

Domus Dei. See DOMODOSSOLA.

Do·mu'yo (dō·mōō'yō). Volcanic peak 15,450 ft. in the Andes Mts., N Neuquén territory, Argentina, near Chilean boundary.

Don (dŏn). **1** River ab. 55 m. long in N cen. England, in Yorkshire; flows NE into the Ouse at Goole.

2 River 62 m. long in Aberdeen co., NE Scotland; flows E into North Sea 1½ m. N of Aberdeen.

3 (*Russ.* dôn); *Tatar* **Du'na** (dōō'nä); *anc.* **Tan'a·is** (tăn'ä·ĭs). River ab. 1200 m. long in SE Soviet Russia, Europe; rises just SE of Tula, flows SE in a big bend to within 48 m. of the Volga, then turns SW to the Sea of Azov (Gulf of Taganrog) at Rostov; its drainage basin of ab. 166,000 sq. m. covers E part of rich black earth region; has abundant fish (salmon and herring) and along its banks are many fishing villages; the only cities of size along its course are Rostov and Voronezh; chief tributaries the Manych, Donets, Chir, Medveditsa, Khoper, Voronezh, and Sosna rivers. Although shallow it is navigable for larger vessels as far as the bend, where a Volga-Don canal is planned. See Territory of the DON COSSACKS.

Do'ña A'na (dōn'yà ăn'à). County in New Mexico. See *Table* at NEW MEXICO.

Don'ald·son·ville (dŏn'l[d]·s'n·vĭl). City, ⊗ of Ascension parish, SE Louisiana, on Mississippi river 28 m. SSE of Baton Rouge; pop. 6082; state capital 1830–31.

Don'al·son·ville (dŏn'l·s'n·vĭl). City, ⊗ of Seminole co., SW Georgia; pop. 2621; peanuts; naval stores.

Donard, Slieve. See SLIEVE DONARD.

Do'nau (dō'nou). **1** See DANUBE.

2 Circle of Württemberg. See *Table* at WÜRTTEMBERG.

Do'nau·wörth' (dō'nou·vûrt'). Town, Swabia, Bavaria, Germany, on the Danube 25 m. N of Augsburg; pop. 4821; an old town with fort and castle; in 13th cent. seat of duke of Upper Bavaria; became imperial city 1348; important in Thirty Years' War; site of two battles: (1) 1704 in which it was captured by duke of Marlborough and Louis of Baden; (2) 1805 in which Austrians were defeated by Marshal Soult.

Do'na·witz (dō'nä·vĭts). Commune, Styria prov., Austria, on the Mur 27 m. NW of Graz; pop. (1939) 17,623; manufactures iron and steel; lignite mining.

Don'bas or **Don'bass** (dŏn'băs; *Russ.* dŭn·bàs') or **Do·nets' Basin** (dŏ·nĕts'; *Russ.* dŭ·nyĕts'). Region ab. 230 m. from W to E and ab. 100 m. wide in plain of Donets river and lower Dnieper, E Ukraine, U.S.S.R., producing 60% of Russia's coal; adjoins the rich iron field of Krivoi Rog; contains many great industrial cities, as Artemovsk, Donetsk, Voroshilovgrad, Makeevka, Gorlovka, Yenakiyevo; in World War II occupied by Germans Oct. 1941 to Jan. 1943.

Don Be·ni'to (dôm bä·nē'tô). Commune, Badajoz prov., SW Spain, 57 m. ENE of Badajoz; pop. 20,931.

Don'cas·ter (dŏng'kăs·tẽr); *anc.* **Da'num** (dā'nŭm). County borough, West Riding, Yorkshire, N England, on the Don river 45 m. E of Manchester; pop. 63,316, (1951) 81,896; coal; railroad cars, farm machines; horse racing center (scene of the annual St. Leger).

Don Cos'sacks, Territory of the (dŏn kŏs'ăks; -ăks). Region in the basin of the lower Don river, SE Soviet Russia, Europe, now nearly coextensive with Rostov Region; once held by Khan of the Crimea (*q.v.*); settled by Cossacks by 16th cent.; lower Don basin, although controlled by Russia in early 17th cent., not formally acquired until Turkey ceded to Russia her claim to Azov 1699; Cossack communities had special political status in return for military service; in 1918, erected Republic of the Don, soon defeated by Bolsheviki; part of North Caucasus Region 1923–36.

Don'do (dŏn'dō). **1** Town, NW Angola, SW Africa, on Cuanza river at head of navigation; pop. ab. 4000.

2 Town, SE cen. Mozambique, SE Africa, ab. 30 m. NNW of Beira; railroad junction.

Don'dra Head (dŏn'drà). Cape on S extremity of the island of Ceylon, 6°N, projecting into the Indian Ocean.

Don'e·gal' (dŏn'ē·gôl'; dŏn'ē·gôl'). **1** County, N Eire, in Ulster prov.; 1865 sq. m.; pop. 142,310; ⊗ Lifford; rivers Foyle, Derg, Finn; agriculture, livestock grazing, fishing, quarrying (granite, sandstone); linen and woolen goods.

2 Town, S co. Donegal, N Eire, at head (25 m. inland) of **Donegal Bay** and at mouth of Eask river; pop. 1315; ancient seat of the O'Donnell clan; ruins of a Franciscan monastery (founded 1474) and of a 17th-cent. castle.

Don'el·son (dŏn'l·s'n). Urban community (unincorp.), Davidson co., N Tennessee, E of Nashville; pop. 17,195.

Do·nets' (dŏ·nĕts'; *Russ.* dŭ·nyĕts'). River ab. 670 m. long in E Ukraine and S Soviet Russia, Europe, rises in E Kursk Region N of Belgorod and flows SE into the Don river ENE of Rostov; chief tributary the Oskol; navigable for ab. three quarters of its course and flows through the Donbas (**Donets Basin**), affording means of transportation of heavy products. See DONBAS.

Dong·ga'la (dŏng·gä'lä). Town and port, Celebes I., Indonesia, on W coast on Makassar Strait 310 m. N of Makassar; pop. 3821.

Don'go·la (dŏng'gô·là; *popularly* dŏng·gō'là, dŏn-). **1** Former province, N Anglo-Egyptian Sudan, NE Africa, now part of Northern Province, Sudan.

2 or **New Dongola**; *also* **El Or'de** (ĕl ôr'dĕ). Town, Northern Province, N Sudan, on Nile river, lat. 19°11'N, ab. 47 m. above the Third Cataract; pop. (1938 est.) 9000; an old town, capital of the Nubian kingdom 6th to 14th cents.

Don'i·phan (dŏn'ĭ·făn). **1** County in Kansas. See *Table* at KANSAS.

2 City, ⊗ of Ripley co., S Missouri, 28 m. WSW of Poplar Bluff; pop. 1421.

Don'jek (dŏn'jĕk). River, SW Yukon Territory, NW Canada; flows into White river at **Donjek**; crossed by Alaska Highway NW of Burwash Landing.

Don'ley (dŏn'lĭ). County in Texas. See *Table* at TEXAS.

Don'na (dŏn'à). City, Hidalgo co., S Texas, 12 m. E of McAllen; pop. 7522; ships citrus fruits, vegetables, canned goods; sugar refining.

Dön'na (dûn'nä), *also* **Dön'naes·ö'** (dûn'nĕs·û'). Island in Norwegian Sea off W coast of Norway, in Nordland co.; pop. 1892.

Don'na·co'na (dŏn'à·kō'nà). Town, Portneuf co., S Quebec, Canada, on St. Lawrence river 27 m. W of Quebec; pop. 3663.

Don'nai' (*Fr.* dô'nā'). River ab. 200 m. long, NE Cochin China, Indochina; rises in Annam, flows W and S to unite with other streams (on one of which is Saigon) and form an extensive delta just N of the Mekong delta.

Don'ner Lake (dŏn'ēr). Small lake, Nevada co., E California, in Sierra Nevada Mts. ab. 13 m. NW of Lake Tahoe; W of the lake are **Donner Peak** 8315 ft. and **Donner Pass** 7135 ft., traversed by highway and site of U.S. Weather Bureau observatory.

Don'ners·berg (dŏn'ērs·bĕrk). Mountain 2254 ft., N Rhineland-Palatinate, Germany, at N end of Vosges Mts.; the surrounding district was a department of France 1801–14 with capital at Kaiserslautern.

Don'ny·brook (dŏn'ĭ·brŏŏk). Suburb of city of Dublin, E Eire; pop. 37,228; scene of an annual fair, founded 1204 by King John and suppressed 1855, notorious for debauchery and fighting.

Do·no'ra (dô·nōr'à). Industrial borough, Washington co., SW Pennsylvania, on Monongahela river 20 m. SSE of Pittsburgh; pop. 11,131; wire, steel, zinc.

Don Pe'dro Dam (dŏn pē'drō; pĕd'rō). Irrigation dam completed 1923 across Tuolumne river (*q.v.*), SW Tuolumne co., cen. California; height 288 ft.

Don'rek (dŏn'rĕk), *or* **Dang'rek** (däng'rĕk), **Mountains.** = PHANOM DONG RAK mountain range, on boundary bet. Cambodia and Siam.

Don·sol' (dŏn·sôl'). Municipality, NW Sorsogon prov., Luzon, Phil. Is., on W coast at N end of Ticao Pass 28 m. W of Sorsogon; pop. 18,050.

Doobaunt. *Var.* of DUBAWNT.

Doo'ly (dōō'lĭ). County in Georgia. See *Table* at GEORGIA.

Doon (dōōn). Small river ab. 25 m. long in Ayrshire, SW Scotland; flows through Loch Doon and empties into Firth of Clyde 3 m. S of Ayr; immortalized by Burns.

Doon, Loch (lŏk dōōn'). Lake ab. 5 m. long in Ayrshire, SW Scotland, 22 m. SSE of Ayr.

Doone Valley (dōōn). Valley, N Devonshire, SW England, just N of Exmoor, Somersetshire; scene of legend of the Doones, a band of outlaws of 17th cent. who figured in Blackmore's novel *Lorna Doone*.

Door (dōr). County in Wisconsin. See *Table* at WISCONSIN.

Door'man (dōr'măn); *Du.* **Door'man Top** (dōr'män tôp'). Peak (Du. *top*), N cen. part of Snow Mts., cen. West New Guinea; 13,287 ft. high.

Doorn (dōrn). Commune, Utrecht prov., cen. Netherlands, ab. 10 m. SE of Utrecht; pop. 4134; residence (from 1920) of Kaiser William II of Germany.

Doornik. See TOURNAI.

Doorn'kop (dōōrn'kôp). Village, Transvaal, NE Republic of So. Africa, 15 m. SW of Johannesburg; scene Jan. 2, 1896 of Jameson's surrender to Cronjé after the raid on Johannesburg.

Door Peninsula (dōr). Peninsula, E Wisconsin, bet. Green Bay and Lake Michigan; includes Door co. and parts of Kewaunee and Brown cos.

Dor, Dora. See TANTURA.

Do′ra Bal′te·a (dō′rä bäl′tå·ä). River ab. 100 m. long in NW Italy; rises at foot of Little Saint Bernard Pass and flows E and SE into Po river ab. 20 m. below Turin.

Dorada, La. See LA DORADA.

Do·ra′do (dō·rä′thō). Municipality (pop. 13,460) and town (pop. 2120), N Puerto Rico; town near coast 10 m. W of San Juan.

Do′rah (dōr′å), or **Du′rah** (dōōr′å), **Pass.** Mountain pass 14,800 ft. in Hindu Kush Mts., from Afghanistan to Chitral in Pakistan.

Doran, Ben. See BEN DOURAN.

Do′ra Ri·pa′ria (dō′rä rē·pä′ryä). River ab. 60 m. long in Piedmont, NW Italy; rises in Cottian Alps, flows E into Po river near Turin.

Dor′cheat (dôr′chēt). Bayou ab. 100 m. long, S United States; rises in S Nevada co., SW Arkansas, flows S into N end of Bistineau Lake, Webster parish, NW Louisiana.

Dor′ches′ter (dôr′chĕs′tĕr; -chĭs·tẽr). **1** Name of counties in two states of the United States. See *Tables* at MARYLAND and SOUTH CAROLINA.

2 Former town, since 1870 a ward of the city of Boston, E Massachusetts; settled 1630; extended nearly to Rhode Island boundary; included **Dorchester Heights** (a hill SE of Boston) the fortification of which resulted in the evacuation of Boston by the British Mar. 17, 1776.

3 County, Quebec, Canada. See *Table* at QUEBEC.

4 Town (unincorporated), ⊗ of Westmorland co., SE New Brunswick, Canada, near mouth of Petitcodiac estuary 6 m. W of Sackville.

5 *anc.* **Dur′no·var′i·a** (dûr′nō·vâr′ĭ·å). Municipal borough, ⊗ of Dorsetshire, S England, on the Frome; pop. 11,623; the Casterbridge of Thomas Hardy's Wessex novels.

Dor′dogne′ (dôr′dôn′y′). **1** *anc.* **Du·ra′ni·us** (dū·rā′nĭ·ŭs). River ab. 300 m. long in SW France; formed by confluence of Dor and Dogne rivers in Puy-de-Dôme dept., S cen. France, flows SW and W to unite with Garonne river 13 m. N of Bordeaux and form the Gironde estuary; navigable for ab. 190 m.

2 Department of France. See *Table* at FRANCE.

Dor′drecht (dôr′drĕkt). **1** or **Dort** (dôrt). Commune, South Holland prov., SW Netherlands, on Maas (Meuse) river ab. 12 m. ESE of Rotterdam; pop. (1939) 62,980; commercial and shipping center; scene of meeting of first congress of Protestant provinces of the Netherlands July 15, 1572; scene of religious congress known as Synod of Dort 1618–19.

2 Town, E Cape Province, S Union of South Africa, 120 m. NNW of East London; pop. 2749; health and pleasure resort; alt. 5389 ft.

Dore, Monts (môn′ dôr′). Mountain group in Auvergne Mts., Puy-de-Dôme dept., S cen. France; highest Puy de Sancy 6185 ft.

Do′ris (dōr′ĭs; dŏr′ĭs). **1** Small country in cen. part of ancient Greece, bet. Mts. Oeta and Parnassus and containing sources of Cephisus river; important in Greek history only as home of the Hellenic people that entered and conquered Greece 12th cent. B.C. Corinth and Sparta were Dorian cities.

2 District or region on coast of Caria, Asia Minor, and adjacent islands, made up of Dorian settlements.

Dor′king (dôr′kĭng). Urban district, Surrey, S England, 22 m. SSW of London; pop. 20,252; market and residential community; home of George Meredith (at Box Hill, a few miles N).

Dor′mont (dôr′mŏnt). Residential borough, Allegheny co., SW Pennsylvania, 4 m. S of Pittsburgh; pop. 13,038.

Dor′nach′ (dōr′näk′; *Ger.* dôr′näĸ). Industrial suburb of Mulhouse, Haut-Rhin dept., NE France.

Dorn′birn (dôrn′bǐrn). Manufacturing commune, Tirol-Vorarlberg prov., Austria, 6 m. S of Bregenz; pop. (1939) 17,664; textiles, machinery.

Dor′noch (dôr′nŏĸ; -nŭĸ). Burgh on Dornoch Firth, ⊗ of Sutherland co., N Scotland; pop. 1921; health resort; scene 1722 of last execution in Scotland for witchcraft.

Dornoch Firth. Inlet of North Sea on NE coast of Scotland bet. Sutherland and Ross and Cromarty cos.

Doro. See CAPHAREUS.

Do′ro·hoi′ (dô′rô·hoi′). Commercial city, Moldavia region, NE Romania, 75 m. NW of Iaşi; pop. 15,375.

Dorozsma. See KISKUNDOROZSMA.

Dorpat. See TARTU.

Dor′set, Cape (dôr′sĕt; -sĭt). Cape, SW Baffin I., S tip of Foxe penin.

Dor′set·shire (dôr′sĕt·shĭr; -shẽr; dôr′sĭt-) or **Dorset.** County, S England; area 973 sq. m.; pop. (1951) 291,157; ⊗ Dorchester; other towns Swanage, Weymouth, Portland, Poole, Sherborne; rivers Stour and Frome; agriculture, dairy farming, sheep grazing, fisheries, quarrying, textile manufacture. See WESSEX.

Dort. See DORDRECHT.

Dort′mund (dôrt′mŏŏnt). Industrial, mining, and commercial city, West Germany, in North Rhine-Westphalia state, on the Ems river in the Ruhr 31 m. S of Münster; pop. (1939) 537,000; connected with North Sea by Dortmund-Ems canal; well-developed harbor; important railroad center; manufactures machinery, steel rails, wire rope, safes, metal plate. Ancient walled city; first mentioned 899 A.D.; in 12th cent. called **Tre·mo′ni·a** (trê-mō′nĭ·å); member of Hanseatic League; to Prussia 1815; occupied by French troops 1923–24; phenomenal growth after World War I; bombed many times by Allies 1943–45; fell to Allied armies Apr. 1945.

Dor′val′ (dôr′vál′). Residential town, Montreal I., S Quebec, Canada, 10 m. WSW of Montreal; pop. 5293.

Dorylaeum. See ESKİŞEHİR.

Dos Ba·hí′as, Cape (dōz′ vä·ē′äs). Cape extending into Atlantic Ocean on E coast of Chubut territory, S Argentina, at N side of entrance to Gulf of San Jorge.

Dos Her·ma′nas (dōs ĕr·mä′näs). Commune, Sevilla prov., SW Spain, 10 m. SSE of Seville; pop. 18,881.

Dospad Dagh. See RHODOPE.

Do′than (dō′thăn). **1** City, ⊗ of Houston co., SE Alabama, 15 m. N of Florida border and 15 m. W of Chattahoochee river; pop. 31,440; settled 1885; trading center for large agricultural region; manufactures hosiery, cotton compresses, fertilizers, peanut oil.

2 Ancient town of Samaria, Palestine, on the highway N of Samaria at a pass leading to the Plain of Esdraelon; here Joseph was sold into slavery (*Gen.* xxxvii. 17).

Dou·ai′ (dōō·ā′; *Fr.* dwä), formerly **Dou·ay′** (dōō·ā′; *Fr.* dwä); *anc.* **Du·a′cum** (dū·ā′kŭm). Commercial and manufacturing city, Nord dept., N France, on Scarpe river 19 m. S of Lille; pop. 42,021; important educational center to 1889; gives its name to the Douay Bible or Version, an English version from the Latin Vulgate for Roman Catholics (New Testament published at Rheims 1582, Old Testament at Douai 1609–10).

Dou·a′la or **Du·a′la** (dōō·ä′lå). Seaport, Cameroun, W equatorial Africa, on Bight of Biafra; pop. ab. 118,857; most important port of country; terminus of railroad inland; taken from Germans Sept. 1914 in World War I.

Dou·ar′ne·nez′ (dwär′nē·nâz′; -nā′). Commune, Finistère dept., NW France, 12 m. NW of Quimper; pop. 11,032; fisheries.

Dou·au′mont′ (dwō′môn′). Fort in Meuse dept., NE France, just N of Verdun; fighting June to Oct. 1916.

Double Mountain Fork. River ab. 200 m. long, rising in E New Mexico, flowing into Salt Fork in Stonewall co., NW Texas.

Double Springs. Town, ⊗ of Winston co., NW Alabama; pop. 811.

Dou′ble·top′ Peak (dŭb′l·tŏp′). Mountain 11,715 ft. in N Sublette co., W Wyoming.

Doubs (dōō). **1** *anc.* **Du′bis** (dū′bĭs). River ab. 270 m. long in E France; rises in Jura Mts., flows NE; becomes French-Swiss border; flows into Switzerland, turns N then, in France, N and finally SW to enter the Saône.

2 Department of France. See *Table* at FRANCE.

Doubt, River of. See Rio ROOSEVELT.

Dougga. See THUGGA.

Dou'gher·ty (dŏ'ĕr·tĭ). County in Georgia. See *Table* at GEORGIA.

Doug'las (dŭg'lăs). **1** Name of counties in twelve states of the U.S. See *Tables* at COLORADO, GEORGIA, ILLINOIS, KANSAS, MINNESOTA, MISSOURI, NEBRASKA, NEVADA, OREGON, SOUTH DAKOTA, WASHINGTON, WISCONSIN. **2** Town on Douglas I., SE Alaska; pop. 1042. **3** City, Cochise co., SE corner of Arizona, on Mexican border; pop. 11,925; stock raising; copper and lead smelters. **4** City, ⊗ of Coffee co., S Georgia, 35 m. WNW of Way-cross; pop. 8736; agricultural trading center. **5** Town, Worcester co., cen. Massachusetts, 14 m. S of Worcester; pop. 2559; woolen manufacturing. **6** Town, ⊗ of Converse co., E Wyoming, on North Platte river 50 m. E of Casper; pop. 2822; livestock; petroleum deposits. **7** Island on Gastineau Channel opp. Juneau, SE Alaska. **8** Town, ✳ of Isle of Man, England, in SE part of island; pop. 20,288; seaside resort.

Douglas, Mount. Peak 11,300 ft. in S Sweet Grass co., S cen. Montana.

Douglas Channel. Inlet of Pacific Ocean ab. 60 m. long, W British Columbia, Canada, joining Gardner Canal at its mouth, N of Princess Royal Island.

Douglas Dam. See *Table* at TENNESSEE VALLEY AUTHORITY.

Doug'las·ville (dŭg'lăs·vĭl; *Sou.* also -v'l). City, ⊗ of Douglas co., W Georgia, 20 m. W of Atlanta; pop. 4462.

Douglas Water. River in S cen. Scotland, flowing NE in Lanark co. to empty into Clyde river.

Dou·ka'to (dōō·kä'tô), *or* **Du·ca'to** (*Ital.* dōō·kä'tô), **Cape;** *anc.* **Leu·ca'tes** (lū·kä'tēz). Promontory and S point of island of Leukas, Ionian Is.; traditional scene of Sappho's leap into the sea.

Doul'lens' (dōō'läN'). Commune, Somme dept., N France, N of Amiens; pop. (1931) 5705; medieval stronghold; scene of inter-Allied conference Mar. 1918.

Dour (dōōr). Commune, Hainaut prov., SW Belgium, 9 m. WSW of Mons; pop. 11,925.

Douran, Ben. See BEN DOURAN.

Dourga Strait. See PRINCESS MARIANNA STRAIT.

Dou'ro (dō'rōō); *Span.* **Due'ro** (dwā'rô); *anc.* **Du'ri·us** (dūr'ĭ·ŭs). River ab. 485 m. long in Spain and Portugal; rises in Soria prov., N cen. Spain; flows W to NE Portugal, then turns S, forming section of Portuguese-Spanish boundary, then W into Atlantic Ocean 2 m. S of Oporto; in Portugal goes through deep gorges, has many rapids, but navigation facilities have been improved.

Dou'ro Li·to·ral' (dō'rōō lē·tōō·räl'). Province of Portugal. See *Table* at PORTUGAL.

Douve (dōōv). River ab. 40 m. long, Normandy, NW France, in Manche dept.; flows S and E into Bay of the Seine NE of Carentan, which is near it on a tributary.

Dou'vres (dōō'vr'). **1** Commune, Calvados dept., NW France, N of Caen; pop. (1931) 1559; held by Germans against Allied advance June 7–11, 1944. **2** See DOVER, England.

Dove (dŭv; dōv). Small river ab. 39 m. long in Derbyshire, cen. England; flows S from near Buxton and empties into the Trent below Burton; favorite stream of Izaak Walton.

Do'ver (dō'vĕr). **1** Commercial city, ✳ of Delaware and ⊗ of Kent co., cen. Del., 40 m. S of Wilmington; pop. 7250; laid out 1717, made state capital 1777; incorp. as town 1829, as city 1929; market and shipping point for fruits and vegetables; canneries, packing plants; manufactures silk hosiery, rubber products, baskets, mattresses, plumbing supplies. **2** City, ⊗ of Stafford co., SE New Hampshire, 11 m. NNW of Portsmouth; pop. 19,131; settled c. 1622; attacked by Indians June 28, 1689; incorporated as city 1855; manufactures textiles, shoes, machinery.

3 Town, Morris co., N New Jersey, 8 m. NNW of Morristown; pop. 13,034; settled 1722; chartered 1875; center of iron-ore area; government munition depot; manufactures explosives, knit goods, silk. **4** Village, Ohio. See WESTLAKE. **5** City, Tuscarawas co., E Ohio; pop. 11,300; coal mines. **6** Town, ⊗ of Stewart co., NW Tennessee; pop. 736; burned by Union forces 1862. **7** *Fr.* **Dou'vres** (dōō'vr'); *anc.* **Du'bris Por'tus** (dū'brĭs pōr'tŭs). Municipal borough, Kent, SE England, on the Strait of Dover 67 m. ESE of London; pop. 35,217; chief of the Cinque Ports; port, naval base, and resort and in normal times the usual gateway to the Continent. In Roman times an important landing place; Dover castle, a stronghold of medieval England, besieged by Dauphin Louis (later Louis VIII of France) and rebellious barons 1216; held by Parliamentarians during Civil War; scene of secret treaty bet. Charles II and Louis XIV 1670; headquarters of Dover patrol which protected shipping during World War I; in World War II under fire from German heavy guns Aug. 10, 1940 to Sept. 30, 1944.

Dover, Strait of; *also* **Straits of Dover;** *Fr.* **Pas de Ca'lais'** (päd' kä'lĕ'); *anc.* **Fre'tum Gal'li·cum** (frē'tŭm găl'ĭ·kŭm). Channel bet. SE England and N France, the easternmost and narrowest section of the English Channel; 20 m. wide at narrowest point.

Do'ver–Fox'croft (dō'vĕr·fŏks'krôft). Town, ⊗ of Piscataquis co., N cen. Maine, 34 m. NW of Bangor; pop. 4173; woolen mills.

Dovey. See DYFI.

Dov're·fjell (dôv'rĕ·fyĕl'). Plateau in cen. Norway; highest point ab. 7565 ft.

Do·wa'giac (dô·wŏj'ăk). City, Cass co., SW Michigan, 35 m. SW of Kalamazoo; pop. 7208; stoves and furnaces.

Down (doun). County, SE Northern Ireland; 952 sq. m.; pop. 241,105; ⊗ Downpatrick; other towns Bangor, Newry, Banbridge; rivers Bann, Newry, Lagan; agriculture, stock raising (esp. race horses and hogs), quarrying (granite), linen weaving.

Dow'ners Grove (dou'nĕrz). Village, Du Page co., NE Illinois, 20 m. W of Chicago; pop. 21,154; manufactures furniture and tools; dairy products.

Dow'ney (dou'nĭ). City, Los Angeles co., SW California, SE of Los Angeles; pop. 82,505; manufactures textiles, asbestos, aircraft, chemicals.

Dow'nie·ville (dou'nĭ·vĭl). Village, ⊗ of Sierra co., NE California, 78 m. NNE of Sacramento; pop. (est.) 400.

Dow'ning·town (dou'nĭng·toun). Industrial borough, Chester co., SE Pennsylvania, on E branch of Brandywine Creek 32 m. W of Philadelphia; pop. 5598; manufactures textiles, brick, metal products.

Down·pat'rick (doun·păt'rĭk). Urban district, ⊗ of co. Down, SE Northern Ireland, at SW end of Strangford Lough; pop. 3878; cathedral; linen weaving; burial place of St. Patrick, St. Columba, and St. Brigid.

Downs, the (dounz). **1** Range of hills in S England. See NORTH DOWNS, SOUTH DOWNS. **2** Roadstead ab. 9 m. long and 6 m. wide in English Channel, along SE coast of Kent bet. North and South Foreland; affords excellent anchorage, protected by a natural breakwater, the Goodwin Sands; scene of battle of Goodwin Sands 1652, English naval victory over Dutch, and of drawn battle bet. English and Dutch 1666.

Doyles'town (doilz'toun). Borough, ⊗ of Bucks co., SE Pennsylvania, 25 m. N of Philadelphia; pop. 5917; settled 1735; manufactures; farming and dairying.

Dra, Wad (wăd' drä'). River, often dry, SW Morocco, NW Africa; empties into Atlantic Ocean at Cape Noun.

Drabescus. See DRAMA.

Dra'chen·fels' (dräk'ĕn·fĕls'). Literally "Dragon's Rock," one of the Siebengebirge, on E bank of Rhine S of Bonn, W Germany; 1053 ft. high; resort; in German legend said to be scene of the slaying of the dragon by Siegfried.

Dra'cut (drā'kŭt). Town, Middlesex co., NE Massachusetts, 2 m. N of Lowell; pop. 13,674.

Dra·go·ne'ra (drä'gô·nä'rä). Small Spanish island 1⅔ sq. m. in Mediterranean Sea off W coast of Majorca.

Drag'on's Mouths (drăg'ŭnz). Strait ab. 10 m. wide bet. Paria Penin., NE Venezuela, and NW coast of Trinidad; so called because of the many small rocky islands in its several channels.

Dra'gui'gnan' (drä'gē'nyäɴ'). Commune, ✳ of Var dept., SE France, 40 m. NE of Toulon; pop. 12,130; tanneries; resort.

Dra'kens·berg Mountains (drä'kĕnz·bûrg) *or* **Quath·lam'ba** (kwät·läm'bá). Mountain range ab. 600 m. long extending from SW to NE in Cape Province and Natal, Union of South Africa; highest peak Mont aux Sources 10,761 ft.

Drake Passage *or* **Strait** (drāk). Strait bet. Cape Horn on N and South Shetland Is., connecting South Atlantic Ocean (Scotia Sea) and South Pacific Ocean.

Drake's Bay (drāks). Inlet of Pacific E of Pt. Reyes, Marin co., W California; U.S. Coast Guard station. Landing of Sir Francis Drake from *Golden Hind* June 15, 1579.

Drakhmani. See ELATEIA.

Dra'ma (drä'má). **1** Department of Greece. See *Table* at GREECE.

2 *anc.* **Dra·bes'cus** (drá·bĕs'kŭs). City, its ✳, Macedonia, N Greece; pop. 29,339; in fertile valley bet. Struma and Nestos rivers; raises tobacco.

Dram'men (dräm'mĕn). Seaport, ⊗ of Buskerud co., S Norway, at mouth of the **Dram'mens·elv** (dräm'mĕns·ĕlv') on a branch of Oslo Fjord; pop. 25,493; sawmills, paper mills, cellulose factories.

Dran'cy' (dräɴ'sē'). Commune, Seine dept., N France, NE suburb of Paris; pop. 42,938; scene of battles bet. French and Prussians Nov. 29 and Dec. 21, 1870.

Dran·gi·a'na (drăn·jĭ·ā'ná; -ăn'á). Ancient region of Asia, a part of Ariana and a province of ancient Persian Empire and of the Grecian empire of Alexander; now included in W Afghanistan and E Iran. See SEISTAN.

Dra'no·va Island (drä'nô·vä). Island, E Romania, in S part of Danube delta.

Dra'va (drä'vä) *or* **Dra've** (drä'vĕ); *Ger.* **Drau** (drou); *anc.* **Dra'vus** (drā'vŭs). River 450 m. long in Austria and Yugoslavia; rises in the Hohe Tauern, W Carinthia, S Austria, flows E into and across N Yugoslavia, then SE forming section of Yugoslav-Hungarian boundary, empties into Danube river 14 m. E of Osijek, Yugoslavia; navigable for small boats for 350 m.

Dra·vos'burg (drá·vōs'bûrg). Borough, Allegheny co., SW Pennsylvania, on Monongahela river 9 m. SE of Pittsburgh; pop. 3458.

Drav'ska (dräv'skä). Former county (1929–45), NW Yugoslavia; 6151 sq. m.; pop. 1,120,549; ⊗ Ljubljana); since 1945 nearly coextensive with Slovenia.

Dre'her Shoals Dam (drā'ĕr). See UNITED STATES, *Dams and Reservoirs.*

Dre·ke'ti (drĕ·kĕ'tĕ) *or* **Ndre·ke'ti** ('n·drĕ·kĕ'tĕ). Chief river of Vanua Levu I., Fiji Is., SW Pacific Ocean.

Dren'the (drĕn'tĕ). Province, NE Netherlands; 1030 sq. m.; pop. (1939) 246,879; ✳ Assen; livestock raising.

Drepanum. See TRAPANI.

Dres'den (drĕz'dĕn). **1** Town, ⊗ of Weakley co., NW Tennessee; pop. 1510.

2 Town, Kent co., SE Ontario, Canada, 13 m. N of Chatham; pop. 2052.

3 (*Ger.* dräs'dĕn) Circle of Saxony. See *Table* at SAXONY.

4 (*Ger.* dräs'dĕn) Industrial city, ✳ of Dresden dist. and former ✳ of Saxony, E Germany, on Elbe river 63 m. ESE of Leipzig; pop. (1939) 625,174; palace; law courts; polytechnic school, military academy, conservatory of music, academy of fine arts, world-famous art galleries, and museums containing collections of porcelain, medieval artifacts, zoological specimens, etc.; varied manufactures (including Dresden china which, however, is

chiefly manufactured at Meissen, *q.v.*); coal mining in vicinity.

History: Original Slavonic settlers subjugated c. 922 A.D.; residence of margraves of Meissen at beginning of 13th cent.; residence of Albertine dukes of Saxony 1485–1918; bombarded by Frederick the Great 1760; occupied by Austrians 1809; scene of famous battle Aug. 26–27, 1813, in which Allies under Schwarzenberg unsuccessfully attempted to wrest it from Napoleonic troops in occupation; occupied by Prussians 1866; in World War II captured by Russians May 8, 1945.

Dreux (drû); *anc.* **Du'ro·cas'ses** (dūr'ô·kăs'ēz), *later* **Dro'cae** (drō'sē). Commune, Eure-et-Loir dept., N cen. France, 20 m. NNW of Chartres; pop. 13,361; tanneries; manufactures hats.

Drew (drōō). **1** County in Arkansas. See *Table* at ARKANSAS.

2 Town, Sunflower co., W Mississippi, 27 m. S of Clarksdale; pop. 2143.

Drew'ry's Bluff (drōōr'ĭz), *formerly* **Dru'ry's Bluff** (drōōr'ĭz). Height on right bank of James river 5 m. S of Richmond, Virginia, near Bermuda Hundred; in campaign for Richmond 1864 Union advance under Gen. Butler stopped here May 12–16 by Gen. Beauregard.

Dri'burg (drē'bŏŏrk). Town, W Germany, in North Rhine-Westphalia state just E of Paderborn; pop. 4160; mineral springs.

Driggs (drĭgz). Village, ⊗ of Teton co., E Idaho; pop. 824.

Drin (drēn) *or* **Dri'ni** (drē'nē); *anc.* **Dri'lo** (drī'lō). River ab. 170 m. long in Yugoslavia and Albania; flows N out of Lake Ohrid into E Albania, turns W in N Albania and empties into Adriatic Sea; its N mouth is the Bojana river.

Dri'na (drē'nä); *anc.* **Dri'nus** (drī'nŭs). River ab. 160 m. long in cen. Yugoslavia, constituting a large section of the boundary bet. Serbia and Bosnia; flows N into Sava river ab. 60 m. W of Belgrade.

Drin'i·u'mor (drĭn'ĭ·ōō'môr). Short stream, E of Aitape, North-East New Guinea; scene of Japanese attack on American line July 11, 1944 and of fighting to July 31.

Drin'ska (drēn'skä). Former county (1929–45), cen. Yugoslavia; 11,417 sq. m.; pop. 1,693,073; ⊗ Sarajevo; since 1945 divided bet. the two federated republics of Serbia and of Bosnia and Herzegovina.

Drö'bak (drû'bäk). Seaport town, Akershus co., SE Norway; pop. 2087; used as a winter port for Oslo; summer resort.

Drobeta. See TURNU-SEVERIN.

Drocae. See DREUX.

Dro'court' (drô'kōōr'). Commune, Pas-de-Calais dept., N France, 9 m. NE of Arras; pop. (1931) 2646; N end of Drocourt-Quéant Line, strong German defense line 1917, extending N from Quéant in the Hindenburg Line; taken by Allies Sept. 1918.

Dro'ghe·da (drô'ĕ·dá). Municipal borough and port, S co. Louth, NE Eire, on Boyne river; pop. 14,494; salmon fisheries, cotton mills, tanneries, soap works. Site of noted synod 1152; besieged 1649 by Cromwell who stormed it and put most of the Royalist garrison to the sword; surrendered to William of Orange immediately after battle of the Boyne.

Dro·go·bych' (drŭ·gŭ·bĭch'); *Pol.* **Dro·ho'bycz** (drô-hô'bĭch). **1** Region, W Ukraine, U.S.S.R., formerly part of Lwów dept., Poland.

2 City, SW Ukraine, U.S.S.R., 39 m. SW of Lvov (formerly in Lwów dept., Poland); pop. (1938–39 est.) 34,527; petroleum; trades in cattle and agricultural goods; scene of battle 1915 bet. Austrians and Russians; taken by Russians Sept. 1939 and by Germans June 1941.

Droit'wich (droit'wĭch). Municipal borough, Worcestershire, W cen. England; pop. 6453; brine springs; health resort.

Drôme (drōm). **1** River ab. 60 m. long in SE France; rises in Hautes-Alpes dept., flows NW and W into Rhone river 12 m. SSW of Valence.

2 Department of France. See *Table* at FRANCE.

Dro·more' (drŏ-mōr'). Urban district, co. Down, SE Northern Ireland, on Lagan river 17 m. SW of Belfast; pop. 2390; linen weaving.

Droyls'den (droilz'dĕn). Urban district, Lancashire, NW England, E suburb of Manchester; pop. 26,365.

Drug (drōōg). Town, SE Madhya Pradesh, E cen. India, 140 m. E of Nagpur; pop. 13,172.

Drum·clog' (drŭm·klŏg'). Moorland in Lanark co., S cen. Scotland, 16 m. SE of Glasgow; scene of defeat of Royalists under John Graham of Claverhouse by the Covenanters June 11, 1679.

Drum'hel'ler (drŭm'hĕl'ẽr). Mining city, S Alberta, Canada, on Red Deer river 62 m. ENE of Calgary; pop. 2601; produces lignite.

Drum'mond (drŭm'ŭnd). County, Quebec, Canada. See *Table* at QUEBEC.

Drummond, Lake. Lake in SE Virginia, in Dismal Swamp near North Carolina border; ab. 7 m. long by 5 m. wide; ab. 20 ft. above sea level.

Drummond Island. Island in N Lake Huron, off SE extremity of mainland of Chippewa co., NE Michigan, a part of Chippewa co.; site of fort built by the British 1815 and held by them until 1822; pop. 501.

Drum'mond·ville (drŭm'ŭnd·vĭl). Industrial city, ⊗ of Drummond co., S Quebec, Canada, on St. Francis river 32 m. S of Three Rivers; pop. 14,341.

Drummossie Moor. See CULLODEN MOOR.

Drum·moyne' (drŭ·moin'). City, E New South Wales, SE Australia, W suburb of Sydney on S bank of Parramatta river; pop. 29,214.

Drum'right (drŭm'rīt). City, Creek co., E cen. Oklahoma, 30 m. W of Sapulpa; pop. 4190; oil refining.

Drury's Bluff. See DREWRY'S BLUFF.

Druze, Jeb'el (jĕb'ĕl drōōz') or **Je'bel ed Druz** (*Arab.* jä'bäl ăd drōōz'). **1** Mountain 5791 ft. cen. Jebel ed Druz dist., Republic of Syria.

2 See JEBEL ED DRUZ.

Drwę'ca (dĕr·vĕnn'tsä). River ab. 75 m. long, Pomorze dept., N Poland; flows SW into the Vistula at Toruń.

Dry'burgh Ab'bey (drī'bŭ·rŭ; -brŭ). Ruin on the Tweed, Berwick co., SE Scotland; Walter Scott's tomb.

Dry'den (drī'd'n). Town, Kenora dist., W Ontario, Canada, 76 m. E of Kenora; pop. 2627; pulp and paper mill; provincial experimental farm.

Dry·gal'ski Island (drĭ·gäl'skĭ). Island off Queen Mary Coast, Antarctica, ab. 66°S lat., 93°E long.; discovered by Rawson 1912 but named after German explorer Erich von Drygalski who first observed it from balloon 1902.

Dry Tor·tu'gas (tôr·tōō'gäz). Small group of islands W of Marquesas Keys, at entrance to Gulf of Mexico, a part of Monroe co., SW Florida; site of Fort Jefferson National Monument (see UNITED STATES, *National Monuments*).

Duacum. See DOUAI.

Duala. See DOUALA.

Duar'te (dwär'tè). City, Los Angeles co., SW California, E of Pasadena; pop. 13,962.

Duar'te (dwär'tä). Province, N cen. Dominican Republic. See *Table* at DOMINICAN REPUBLIC.

Duarte, Pico. See Monte TRUJILLO.

Du·bawnt' (dōō·bônt'; dōō'bônt). River 580 m. long in N cen. Canada; rises in lakes in SE Mackenzie District, Northwest Territories, flows N through **Dubawnt Lake** (1654 sq. m.) and E through Aberdeen Lake into Baker Lake, cen. Keewatin District.

Dub'bo (dŭb'ō). Town, E cen. New South Wales, SE Australia, on Macquarie river 165 m. NW of Sydney; pop. 8344; center of coal and copper mining region.

Dü'ben·dorf (dü'bĕn·dôrf). Commune, Zurich canton, NE cen. Switzerland, NE of Zurich; airport, scene of start of Piccard-Cosyns stratosphere balloon flight Aug. 18, 1932 that attained alt. of 55,577 ft.

Dubis. See DOUBS.

Dub'lin (dŭb'lĭn). **1** City, ⊗ of Laurens co., cen. Georgia, 47 m. ESE of Macon; pop. 13,814; incorp. and made ⊗ 1812; lumber industry.

2 Town, Cheshire co., SW corner of New Hampshire, ab. 12 m. SSE of Keene; pop. 684; summer resort.

3 City, Erath co., N cen. Texas, 43 m. NE of Brownwood; pop. 2443; railroad center; agricultural market.

4 County, E Eire, in Leinster prov.; 356 sq. m.; pop. 586,925; ⊗ Dublin.

5 *Gael.* **Bai'le A'tha Cli'ath** (blä'klē'à); *anc.* **Eb'la·na** (ĕb'là·nà). Seaport and county borough, * of Eire and ⊗ of co. Dublin, E Eire, at mouth of Liffey river on **Dublin Bay**; pop. 468,103; iron founding, shipbuilding, glass manufacture, stout brewing; noted castle, founded c. 1200; Christ Church cathedral (Anglican), started 1053, the only one of Danish foundation in British Isles; St. Patrick's cathedral (Anglican), which had Jonathan Swift as dean 1713–45; seat of Trinity College (called also University of Dublin), founded 1591, and of University College of the National University of Ireland.

History: Stronghold of Norse power in Ireland from 9th cent.; in battle of Clontarf (suburb of Dublin) occurred the Danish defeat at hands of Irish led by Brian Boru 1014; given charter and made center of English Pale by Henry II in expedition of 1171–72; besieged 1646 and surrendered to Parliamentarians 1647; scene of Phoenix Park murders May 6, 1882 and of Easter Rebellion Apr. 24, 1916 (see IRELAND).

Du'blon (dōō'blŏn). Main island of Truk (*q.v.*), in E part.

Dub'no (dōōb'nô). Town, W Ukraine, U.S.S.R., 30 m. SE of Lutsk (formerly in Wołyń dept.); pop. (1938–39 est.) 18,167; tobacco. In World War I scene of battles 1915, 1916, 1918; occupied by Austrians Sept. 1915–June 1916; by Germans Feb. 1918 ff.; in World War II held by Russians until July 1941 when it was taken in German advance.

Du·bois' (dōō·bois'; *also* dōō'bois, *esp. when followed by a word, as* Coun'ty, *accented on 1st syllable*). **1** County in Indiana. See *Table* at INDIANA.

2 Village, ⊗ of Clark co., E Idaho; pop. 447.

Du Bois (*pron. as for preceding entry*). Industrial city, Clearfield co., W cen. Pennsylvania, 46 m. NNW of Altoona; pop. 10,667; in coal-mining and agricultural region.

Du·bov'ka (dōō·bôf'kà). Town, cen. Stalingrad Region, Soviet Russia, Europe, on the Volga 33 m. N of Stalingrad; pop. 10,135; formerly an important Cossack center.

Du·bré'ka (dōō·brā'kà). Town near coast, W Guinea, West Africa, just N of Conakry.

Dubris Portus. See DOVER.

Du'brov·nik (dōō'brŏv·nĕk); *Ital.* **Ra·gu'sa** (rä·gōō'zä). Seaport, S Dalmatia, Yugoslavia, on the coast ab. 40 m. NW of Kotor; pop. 18,767; resort. Founded 7th cent. by Greeks; independent republic until conquered by Napoleon 1808; in Illyrian Provinces 1809–13; center of art and literature in Middle Ages; passed to Austria 1814; 17th-cent. cathedral, 15th-cent. palace.

Du·buque' (dŭ·būk'). **1** County in Iowa. See *Table* at IOWA.

2 City, its ⊗, E Iowa, on Mississippi river; pop. 56,606; important river port, has shipbuilding yard, packing houses, lumber mills. University of Dubuque (1852; coed.; Presbyterian), Clarke College (1843; women; Roman Catholic), Loras College of Dubuque (1839; men; Roman Catholic). First settled permanently 1833 (oldest city in Iowa); incorporated 1841.

Ducato, Cape. See Cape DOUKATO.

Ducatus Romae. See Duchy of ROME.

Duch'cov (dōōκ'tsôf); *Ger.* **Dux** (dōōks). City, NW Bohemia prov., Czechoslovakia, in foothills of Erz Gebirge 48 m. NW of Prague; pop. (1930) 12,877.

Du·chesne' (dōō·shän'). **1** River ab. 120 m. long, NE

Utah; rises in Uinta Mts., flows S and E into Green river.

2 County in Utah. See *Table* at UTAH.

3 City, ⊗ of Duchesne co., NE cen. Utah; pop. 770.

Du'cie Island (dū'sĭ). Uninhabited coral island in S Pacific Ocean; lat. 24°40′ and long. 124°48′W, 325 m. E of Pitcairn I.; annexed by Britain 1902 and attached to Pitcairn I. colony.

Duck (dŭk). River ab. 200 m. long, W cen. Tennessee; rises in Coffee co., flows W and NW into Tennessee river.

Duck Mountain Park. Canadian provincial park, SE Saskatchewan, on Manitoba boundary, 15 m. NE of Kamsack; forests, lake.

Duck'town (dŭk'toun). City, Polk co., SE corner of Tennessee, ab. 30 m. SE of Cleveland; pop. 741; copper smelting.

Dud'don (dŭd′′n). River ab. 20 m. long flowing bet. Lancashire (Furness) and Cumberland, NW England, into the Irish Sea by an estuary 7 m. long.

Du'de·lange' (düd'länzh′); *Ger.* **Dü·de·ling'en** (dü'-dĕ·lĭng′ĕn). Industrial commune, S Luxembourg, Europe, on French border 10 m. S of Luxembourg city; pop. (1945) 12,680.

Du·din'ka (dōō-dĭng'ká; *Russ.* dōō-dyēn′ká). Town, ✳ of Taimyr National District, Soviet Russia, Asia, on Yenisei river near its mouth; port; coal mines.

Dud'ley (dŭd'lĭ). **1** Industrial town, Worcester co., cen. Massachusetts, 16 m. SSW of Worcester; pop. 6510.

2 County borough, Worcestershire, W cen. England, 10 m. WNW of Birmingham; pop. 59,583, (1951) 62,536; coal mines, brick kilns, iron and brass foundries.

Dud'na (dōōd'ná). River, E Maharashtra state, S cen. India; flows SE into Godavari river W of Nander.

Dud'wei'ler (dōōt'vī'lĕr). Industrial town, Saarland, SW Germany, just N of Saarbrücken; pop. 23,647.

Dueim, Ed or **El.** See ED DUEIM.

Due'ñas (dwā'nyäs). Municipality, N cen. Iloilo prov., Panay, Phil. Is., near Jalaur river 25 m. N of City of Iloilo; pop. 16,310.

Duero. See DOURO.

Due West (dū' wĕst'). Town in Due West township, Abbeville co., W South Carolina, ab. 17 m. NW of Greenwood; pop. 1166; Erskine College (1839; coed.).

Duf'fel (dŭf'ĕl). Commune, Antwerp prov., N Belgium, 10 m. SSE of Antwerp; pop. 10,142; foundries, distilleries, paper factory; a coarse woolen cloth (*duffel*) originally made here.

Duf'fer·in (dŭf'ĕr·ĭn). County, Ontario, Canada. See *Table* at ONTARIO.

Duff Islands (dŭf). Small island group in N part of Santa Cruz Is., SW Pacific Ocean; lat. 9°55′S and long. 167°E.

Du·four'spit'ze (dü·fōōr'shpĭt'sĕ). Highest peak 15,217 ft. of Monte Rosa, in the Pennine Alps, on the Swiss-Italian border.

Du'gi O'tok (dōō'gĕ ō'tŏk; *Yugoslav* ō'tŏk); *Ital.* **I'so·la Lun'ga** (ē'zō·lä lōōng'gä). Yugoslav island in the Adriatic Sea off the Dalmatian coast; 27 m. long; 46 sq. m.; pop. ab. 4000.

Dui'da (dwē'thä). Mountain 8103 ft., cen. Amazonas territory, S Venezuela.

Duis'burg, *formerly* **Duis'burg–Ham·born'** (düs'-bōōrK·häm·bôrn'; -häm'born; *Angl.* dōōz'bûrg·häm'-bôrn, dōōs'-). Industrial city and river port, W Germany, in North Rhine-Westphalia on the Rhine river at confluence of the Ruhr 12 m. NNW of Düsseldorf; pop. (1939) 431,256; Europe's largest inland river port (above tidewater); on W border of Ruhr industrial district; manufactures steel, zinc, copper, machinery, chemicals; shipbuilding. Ancient town; became member of Hanseatic League; site of a university 1655–1818; formed 1929 by consolidation of former cities of Duisburg (residence of Gerhardus Mercator 1552 to his death 1594) and Hamborn; in World War II frequently bombed by Allied air forces 1943–45; taken by Allies Mar. 1945.

Dui've·land (doi'vĕ·länt). East part of Schouwen I., Zeeland prov., SW Netherlands; pop. ab. 7000.

Duke of Clarence. Island in Tokelau Is., cen. Pacific Ocean. See NUKUNONO.

Duke of Glouces'ter Islands (glŏs'tĕr; glôs'-). Group of 3 small uninhabited islands in S Pacific Ocean, 470 m. SE of Tahiti and 360 m. NE of Raïvavaé in the Tubuaï Is.; generally considered a part of the Tuamotu Archipelago.

Duke of York Island (yôrk). **1** Island in Madre de Dios Archipelago, in S Pacific Ocean off SW coast of Chile, at entrance to Concepción Strait.

2 Island in Tokelau Is., cen. Pacific Ocean. See ATAFU.

Duke of York Islands. Group of 13 small islands at N end of St. George's Channel bet. NE New Britain I. and SW New Ireland I. in Bismarck Archipelago, W Pacific Ocean.

Dukes (dūks). County in Massachusetts. See *Table* at MASSACHUSETTS.

Duk'in·field (dŭk'ĭn·fēld). Municipal borough, Cheshire, NW England, 6 m. E of Manchester; pop. 18,445; cotton textiles, firebricks.

Du'kla (dōō'klä). Town, SE Poland, in Rzeszów dept. 43 m. SE of Tarnów; pop. 2277; just N of **Dukla Pass** in Carpathian Mts., through which Russian army entered Hungary 1849 and which was used again by Russians 1915 and Jan. 1945.

Du'lag (dōō'läg). Municipality on E coast of Leyte I. on Leyte Gulf, Phil. Is., 19 m. S of Tacloban; pop. 28,693; marked S limit of beachhead in invasion by U.S. forces on Oct. 20, 1944: town and airfield seized.

Du·laim' (dōō·līm'). Province (*liwa*), W Iraq; pop. (1935 est.) 129,836.

Du·la'wan (dōō·lä'wän). Municipality, N cen. Cotabato prov., Mindanao, Phil. Is., on the Mindanao river 21 m. SE of Cotabato; pop. 55,329.

Dul'ce (dōōl'sâ). **1** River ab. 360 m. long in N cen. Argentina; rises in Tucumán prov., flows SE through several channels into the marsh region N of Mar Chiquita in N Córdoba prov.; in upper course called the **Sa'la·dil'lo** (sä'lä·thē'yō; *usu. in Argentina,* -thē'zhô).

2 River in SE Guatemala; flows from Lake Izabal (or Dulce Gulf) into Honduras Bay; link in commercial waterway from Panzós on the Polochic river to the Caribbean Sea.

Dulce, Gulf of. Inlet of Pacific Ocean in S Costa Rica, E of Osa Penin.

Dulce Gulf. See Lake IZABAL.

Dulcigno. See ULCINJ.

Dül'ken (dül'kĕn). Industrial city, W Germany, in West Rhine-Westphalia state 20 m. WNW of Düsseldorf; pop. 11,374; textiles, machinery; in World War II taken by Allies Mar. 1945.

Du·luth' (dŭ·lōōth'). City, ⊗ of St. Louis co., NE Minnesota, at W end of Lake Superior; pop. 106,884; third largest city in the state; commercial and industrial center; excellent harbor. University of Minnesota, Duluth Branch (1905); College of Saint Scholastica (1912; women). Region probably explored by Radisson and Groseilliers 1654–60; site of city visited by Daniel Greysolon, Sieur Duluth, in 1679; first permanent settlement 1852; incorporated 1870.

Dul'wich (dŭl'ĭj, -ĭch). District of Camberwell metropolitan borough, S London, England; residential; Dulwich College, founded and endowed 1619 by English actor Edward Alleyn, contains notable picture gallery of works esp. of Dutch and Flemish masters.

Du'ma·gue'te (dōō'mä·gā'tâ). Municipality, ✳ of Negros Oriental, Negros, Phil. Is., in SE part on coast at S end of Tañon Strait; pop. 22,236; oldest town in the province; Silliman Univ. (1901; Presbyterian; coed.).

Du·ma'lag (dōō·mä'läg). Municipality, S Capiz prov., Panay, Phil. Is., on upper Panay river 21 m. SSW of Capiz; pop. 13,642; noted for its natural bridge and caves.

Du·man′gas (dōō·mäng′gäs). Municipality, SE Iloilo prov., Panay, Phil. Is., near coast E of Jalaur river 13 m. ENE of City of Iloilo; pop. 24,539.

Du′man·jug′ (dōō′män·hōōg′). Municipality on W coast of Cebu I., Phil. Is., on Tañon Strait 37 m. SW of City of Cebu; pop. 20,973.

Du′ma·ran′ (dōō′mä·rän′). Island in Sulu Sea off NE coast of Palawan I., Palawan prov., W Phil. Is.; 120 sq. m.; pop. 2409; chief town Dumaran on E coast; thickly wooded.

Du′mas (dōō′mås). **1** City, Desha co., SE Arkansas, 39 m. SE of Pine Bluff; pop. 3540.
2 City, ⊗ of Moore co., NW Texas, 30 m. WNW of Borger; pop. 8477; agriculture, cattle; oil wells.

Dum·bar′ton (dŭm·bär′t′n; dŭm-). **1** or **Dum·bar′-ton·shire** (-shír; -shēr). = DUNBARTONSHIRE.
2 Burgh, ⊗ of Dunbartonshire, W cen. Scotland, on Leven river near its junction with the Clyde; pop. 23,703; shipbuilding; engineering works; in S part rising abruptly from the bank of the Clyde is the Rock of Dumbarton, a twin-peaked hill, site of Pictish and Norse fortresses and of a Scottish castle, which was prison of William Wallace before his removal to London for trial and execution (1305) and residence from which infant Mary, Queen of Scots, was spirited away to France 1548. Capital of medieval Celtic kingdom of Strathclyde.

Dum′bar′ton Oaks (dŭm′bär′t′n ōks′). Mansion at Georgetown, suburb of Washington, D.C., where representatives of China, U.S.S.R., United Kingdom, and U.S. met Aug. 21 to Oct. 7, 1944 and formulated proposals for a world organization which were the basis of the organization of the United Nations as created at San Francisco Apr. 1945.

Dum′–Dum′ (dŭm′dŭm′). Town, West Bengal, NE India, near Calcutta; pop. (3 municipalities) 28,356, military station (headquarters of Bengal artillery 1783–1853) and ammunition factory where dumdum bullets were first made; treaty bet. Siraj-ud-daula and Clive signed here 1757.

Du·mei′ra (dōō·mēr′á). Small island off coast of Eritrea, NE Africa, in Bab el Mandeb strait.

Dum·fries′ (dŭm·frēs′; dŭm-). **1** or **Dum·fries′shire** (-frēsh′shír; -shēr). County, S Scotland; 1073 sq. m.; pop. (1951) 85,656; ⊗ Dumfries; the rivers Nith, Annan, Esk; agriculture, livestock grazing, quarrying (limestone, sandstone), salmon fisheries.
2 Burgh, its ⊗, S Scotland; pop. 26,320; trade and industrial center; manufactures esp. hosiery and tweeds; residence (1791–96) and burial place of Robert Burns.

Dum′ka (dōōm′kä). See SANTAL PARGANAS.

Du′mont (dū′mŏnt). Borough, Bergen co., NE corner of New Jersey, 9 m. E of Paterson; pop. 18,882.

Dum·yat′ (dōōm·yät′). Var. of *Dimyâṭ*: see DAMIETTA.

Du′na. **1** (dōō′nŏ). Hungarian form of DANUBE river.
2 (dōō′nä). Tatar form of DON river, Soviet Russia, Europe.

Dü′na (dü′nä). German form of DVINA river, N Europe.

Dünaburg. See DAUGAVPILS.

Du′na·föld′vár (dōō′nŏ·fúld′vär). Commune, S Hungary, 50 m. S of Budapest on right bank of the Danube; pop. 12,226.

Du·na·gi′ri (dōō′nä·gī′rĭ). Mountain 23,181 ft. in the Himalayas, Garhwal dist., Uttar Pradesh, N India.

Du·na′jec (dōō·nä′yĕts). River ab. 130 m. long in Kraków prov., S Poland; flows N from Carpathian Mts. into Vistula river; in World War I scene of battles in the two stages of Austro-German offensive under Gen. Mackensen against Russia May 1–14, 1915 and May 24–June 15, 1915; in World War II overrun by German armies by Sept. 14, 1939.

Dünamünde. See DAUGAVGRĪVA.

Dunărea. See DANUBE river.

Du′nav (*Yugoslav* dōō′näv; *Bulg.* dŏŏ′näf). = DANUBE river.

Du′nav·ska (dōō′näv·skä). Former county (1929–45),

NE Yugoslavia; 11,461 sq. m.; pop. 2,310,220; ⊗ Novi Sad; since 1945 divided bet. federated republic of Serbia and autonomous province of Voivodina.

Dun′bar (dŭn′bär). City, Kanawha co., W cen. West Virginia, on Kanawha river W of Charleston; pop. 11,006.

Dun·bar′ (dŭn·bär′; dŭn-). Burgh, East Lothian co., SE Scotland, at mouth of the Firth of Forth E of Edinburgh; pop. 4115; fishing port and summer resort; scene of Cromwell's victory Sept. 3, 1650 over Leslie's Covenanters.

Dun·bar′ton (dŭn·bär′t′n; dŭn-) or **Dun·bar′ton·shire** (-shír; -shēr). County, W cen. Scotland; area 244 sq. m.; pop. (1951) 164,263; ⊗ Dumbarton; its only important river the Clyde; stock raising, dairying, shipbuilding, coal mining, textiles, quarrying, fishing.

Dun′can (dŭng′kăn). **1** Town, Greenlee co., SE Arizona; pop. 862; marketing center.
2 City, ⊗ of Stephens co., S Oklahoma, 27 m. E of Lawton; pop. 20,009; founded 1891 in Indian Territory; oil wells; manufactures cottonseed oil, asphalt, gasoline, oil-well machinery.
3 City, SE Vancouver I., Brit. Columbia, Canada, 28 m. NNW of Victoria; pop. 2784.

Dun·can′non (dŭn·kăn′ŭn). Borough and summer resort, Perry co., S cen. Pennsylvania, on Susquehanna river 13 m. NNW of Harrisburg; pop. 1800.

Dun′can Passage (dŭng′kăn). Channel ab. 32 m. wide separating Rutland and Great Andaman Is. on the N from Little Andaman I. on the S, E Bay of Bengal.

Dun′cans·bay Head (dŭng′kănz·bĭ). Extreme NE point of the mainland of Scotland; 210 ft. high.

Dun′dalk (dŭn′dôk). Urban community (unincorporated), Baltimore co., N Maryland; pop. 82,428.

Dun·dalk′ (dŭn·dô[l]k′). Urban district and seaport, ⊗ of co. Louth, NE Eire, on Dundalk Bay near mouth of Castletown river; pop. 14,684; fisheries; trades in livestock and farm products. Captured 1315 by Edward Bruce who proclaimed himself king here; nearby was scene of Bruce's defeat and death in battle against forces of Edward II 1318.

Dun′dalk′ Bay (dŭn′dô[l]k′ bā′). Inlet of Irish Sea on extreme NE coast of Eire.

Dun·das′ (dŭn·däs′; dŭn′dăs). **1** Town, E New South Wales, SE Australia, W suburb of Sydney; pop. 6017.
2 County, Ontario, Canada. See *Table* at ONTARIO.
3 Manufacturing town, Wentworth co., SE Ontario, Canada, 5 m. W of Hamilton; pop. 6846.

Dun′das Strait (dŭn′däs). Passage ab. 18 m. wide from Van Diemen Gulf to Arafura Sea, separating Cobourg Penin. from Melville I.

Dun·dee′ (dŭn·dē′; dŭn′dē). **1** Village, Monroe co., SE corner of Michigan, 23 m. S of Ann Arbor; pop. 2377.
2 Seaport and manufacturing burgh, Angus co., E Scotland; pop. (1951) 177,333; the fourth largest burgh in Scotland; jute fabrics, linen, canvas, automobiles; shipbuilding. University College, now part of University of St. Andrews. Ravaged many times in Scottish-English wars.
3 Town, W Natal, E Union of South Africa, 120 m. NNW of Durban; pop. 5591; center of rich iron and coal district; battle of Talana Hill, which opened Boer War, fought nearby Oct. 20, 1899.

Dun·drum′ Bay (dŭn·drŭm′; dŭn′drŭm, -drŭm). Inlet of Irish Sea on SE coast of Northern Ireland, in co. Down, S of Strangford Lough.

Dun′dy (dŭn′dĭ). County in Nebraska. See *Table* at NEBRASKA.

Dun·e′din (dŭn·ē′d′n). **1** City, Pinellas co., W Florida penin., on Gulf of Mexico 20 m. NW of St. Petersburg; pop. 8444; settled c. 1855, incorp. 1927; resort.
2 City, ✳ of Otago provincial dist., SE South I., New Zealand, at head of Otago Harbor 190 m. SW of Christchurch; pop. with suburbs (1941 est.) 82,200; founded 1848 by Scottish Presbyterians; port; exports wool and gold, which has been mined in vicinity since its discovery

1861; Otago University (1869), a unit of New Zealand University; base for ships of Byrd's Antarctic explorations (1928–30, 1933–35).

Dun·el′len (dŭn·ĕl′ĕn; -ĭn). Borough, Middlesex co., cen. New Jersey, 7 m. N of New Brunswick; pop. 6840.

Dun·ferm′line (dŭn·fûrm′lĭn; dŭm-). Burgh, Fife co., E Scotland; pop. (1951) 44,710; manufactures linen and metal products, cordage, fire clay; coal mining; Dunfermline Abbey, burial place of Robert Bruce and of many Scottish kings (11th–17th cents.); birthplace of Andrew Carnegie.

Dun·gan′non (dŭn·găn′ŭn). Urban district, co. Tyrone, W cen. Northern Ireland, 8 m. W of Lough Neagh; pop. 5674; in coal-mining section; linen, pottery.

Dun′gar·pur (dŏong′gĕr·pŏor). **1** Former Indian state, S Rajputana, NW India; 1460 sq. m.; pop. (1941) 274,282; ruled by descendants of Mewar chieftains; came under British protection 1818; joined Union of Rajasthan June 26, 1947.
2 Town, its ✳, 90 m. NE of Ahmadabad; pop. 8560.

Dun·gar′van (dŭn·gär′văn). Urban district and seaport, on **Dungarvan Harbour** at mouth of Colligan river, S co. Waterford, S Eire; pop. 5426; remnants of a castle built by King John and of 14th-cent. priory.

Dunge′ness′ (dŭnj′nĕs′). Headland on SE coast of England, projecting into Strait of Dover; lighthouse.

Dunge′ness′ Point (dŭnj′nĕs′ point′). Cape in S Argentina, at N side of entrance to Strait of Magellan.

Dun′geon Gill Force (dŭn′jŭn gĭl′ fōrs′). Waterfall 90 ft. in Westmorland, NW England, near Grasmere in Lake District.

Dunheved. See LAUNCESTON, England.

Dunholme. See DURHAM municipal borough, England.

Dun·keld′ (dŭn·kĕld′). Town, Perth co., cen. Scotland, on Tay river NW of Perth; pop. 833; ruins of early 9th-cent. Culdee abbey and of 12th-cent. cathedral.

Dun′kerque′ (dŭn′kĕrk′); *Eng.* **Dun′kirk** (dŭn′kûrk; dŭn·kûrk′); *earlier French* **Dun′querque′** (dŭn′kĕrk′). Fortified seaport and industrial city, Nord dept., N France, on Strait of Dover 44 m. NW of Lille; pop. 31,017; 16th-cent. church, 15th-cent. chapel.

History: Founded before 9th cent. A.D.; as part of Flanders, ruled by Burgundians, Spanish; besieged by English and French who defeated Spanish in "Battle of the Dunes" June 4, 1658; awarded to England 1659 and sold to France by Charles II 1662; center for piracy 17th cent.; in 1713 (Treaty of Utrecht) and in succeeding treaties, France promised to demolish its fortifications; in World War I object of German drives. In World War II scene of evacuation of 225,000 British and ab. 112,000 French and Belgian soldiers from Flanders after fall of France May 29–June 2, 1940; at end of war surrendered by Germans May 9, 1945.

Dun′kirk (dŭn′kûrk). **1** City, Blackford and Jay cos., E Indiana, 11 m. NE of Muncie; pop. 3117.
2 City and port of entry, Chautauqua co., SW corner of New York, on Lake Erie 35 m. SW of Buffalo; pop. 18,205; in grape-growing region; manufactures locomotives, oil-refining machinery.
3 (dŭn′kûrk; dŭn·kûrk′). See DUNKERQUE.

Dunk Island (dŭngk). Island, 2½ m. off E coast of Queensland, NE Australia, ab. 60 m. S of Cairns; home for 25 years of the Australian naturalist and journalist Edmund James Banfield, author of *The Confessions of a Beachcomber*.

Dunk′lin (dŭngk′lĭn). County in Missouri. See *Table* at MISSOURI.

Dun Laoghai′re (dŭn lā′rĕ) or **Dun·lea′ry** (dŭn·lēr′ĭ); *formerly* **Kings′town** (kĭngz′toun; kĭng′stŭn). City borough, SE co. Dublin, on S shore of Dublin Bay, E Eire; pop. 39,785; seaport noted for export of live cattle; fisheries; noted yachting center.

Dun′lap (dŭn′lăp). **1** Town, Harrison co., W Iowa, 42 m. NNE of Council Bluffs; pop. 1254.
2 City, ⊗ of Sequatchie co., SE Tennessee; pop. 1026.

Dun·man′us Bay (dŭn·măn′ŭs). Inlet of Atlantic Ocean on SW coast of Ireland, S of Bantry Bay.

Dun·more′ (dŭn·mōr′; dŭn′mōr). Manufacturing borough, Lackawanna co., NE Pennsylvania, 3 m. E of Scranton; pop. 18,917; center of anthracite mining region.

Dun′more Head (dŭn′mōr hĕd′). Promontory, co. Kerry, Munster prov., SW Eire, N of Dingle Bay; most W point of mainland of Ireland, 10°30′W.

Dun′mow (dŭn′mō) or **Little Dunmow**. Village, Essex, SE England, 35 m. NE of London; known for the custom (originated 13th cent., revived 1855) of awarding a flitch of bacon to any couple who will swear that they have not quarreled or repented of their marriage within a year and a day of its celebration.

Dunn (dŭn). **1** Name of counties in two states of the U.S. See *Tables* at NORTH DAKOTA and WISCONSIN.
2 Town, Harnett co., cen. North Carolina, 24 m. NE of Fayetteville; pop. 7566.

Dun′net Head (dŭn′ĕt; -ĭt). Cape on NE coast of Scotland; the northernmost point of the Scottish mainland, 58°40′N; lighthouse.

Dunn′ville (dŭn′vĭl). Town, Haldimand co., SE Ontario, Canada, on Grand river 29 m. SSE of Hamilton; pop. 4478.

Dun·oon′ (dŭn·ōon′). Coastal burgh, Argyll co., W Scotland; pop. 9940; watering place; ruins of ancient castle; statue of Burns's "Highland Mary," who was born nearby.

Dunquerque. See DUNKERQUE.

Dun·ra′ven, Mount (dŭn·rā′věn). Mountain 12,548 ft., Larimer co., N cen. Colorado, in Rocky Mountain National Park.

Duns (dŭnz). Burgh, ⊗ of Berwick co., SE Scotland; pop. 2028; castle.

Dun·score′ (dŭn·skōr′). Civil parish, Dumfries co., S Scotland; pop. 962; site of Craigenputtock, farm home of Thomas Carlyle.

Dun′si·nane′ (dŭn′sĭ·nān′; dŭn′sĭ·nān′; dŭn·sĭn′ăn). Hill 1012 ft. in Sidlaw Hills, Perth co., cen. Scotland; scene of defeat of Macbeth by Siward 1054.

Duns′muir (dŭnz′mūr). City, Siskiyou co., N California, near Mt. Shasta. 100 m. ENE of Eureka; pop. 2873; summer resort (hunting and fishing).

Dun′sta·ble (dŭn′stà·b′l). Municipal borough, Bedfordshire, SE cen. England, 32 m. NNW of London; pop. 17,108; ancient Roman walled camp; venue of court at which Cranmer ruled Catherine of Aragon's marriage to Henry VIII invalid (1533).

Dun·veg′an, Loch (lŏk dŭn·věg′ăn). Sea inlet on W coast of Skye I. in the Inner Hebrides, off NW coast of Scotland; enclosed on W by peninsula ending in **Dunvegan Head,** 100 ft. high.

Du Page (dŭ pāj′). County in Illinois. See *Table* at ILLINOIS.

Du′plin (dū′plĭn). County in North Carolina. See *Table* at NORTH CAROLINA.

Dup′ni·ca or **Dup′ni·tsa** (dŏop′nĭ·tsä). Commune, SW Bulgaria, on Struma river 31 m. SSW of Sofia; pop. (1934) 16,017.

Du′po (dū′pō). Village, St. Clair co., SW Illinois, 10 m. S of East St. Louis; pop. 2937.

Du·pont′ (dà·pònt′). Borough, Luzerne co., E Pennsylvania, 9 m. NE of Wilkes-Barre; pop. 3669; coal mining.

Düppel. See DYBBÖL.

Du·pree′ (dŏo·prē′). Town, ⊗ of Ziebach co., NW cen. South Dakota; pop. 548.

Du·quesne′ (dŏo·kān′). City, Allegheny co., SW Pennsylvania, on Monongahela river 10 m. ESE of Pittsburgh; pop. 15,019; manufactures steel and iron.

Du Quoin (dŏo koin′). City, Perry co., SW Illinois, 30 m. SW of Mount Vernon; pop. 6558; flour mills, meatpacking plants, shoe factories.

Du′ra-Eu·ro′pos (dūr′à-û·rō′pŏs). Ancient town of Mesopotamia on right bank of the Euphrates; now vil-

lage of **Sa′la·hi′yeh** (sä′lä·hē′yà; -yă) in SE Syria near Iraqi border; important archaeological site.

Durah Pass. See DORAH PASS.

Durán. See ELOY ALFARO.

Du′rance′ (dü′räns′). River 160 m. long in SE France; rises in Hautes-Alpes dept., flows SW into Rhone river 3 m. SW of Avignon.

Du·rand′ (dū·rănd′). **1** City, Shiawassee co., S cen. Michigan, 17 m. WSW of Flint; pop. 3312; railroad and trade center.
2 City, ⊗ of Pepin co., W Wisconsin, 16 m. S of Menomonie; pop. 2039.

Du·ran′go (dŏŏ·răng′gō). City, ⊗ of La Plata co., SW Colorado, 18 m. N of New Mexico border and 70 m. ENE of SW corner of Colo.; pop. 10,530; settled 1880. Fort Lewis A. & M. College (1910; coed.).

Du·ran′go (dŏŏ·räng′gō). **1** State, NW cen. Mexico. See *Table* at MEXICO.
2 *officially* **Vic·to′ria de Du·ran′go** (bĕk·tō′ryä thä thŏŏ·räng′gō). City, its ✱, NW cen. Mexico; pop. 33,318; alt. ab. 6200 ft.; center of lumbering, mining, and farming district. Founded 1564; important political and religious center in early history of N Mexico.

Duranius. See DORDOGNE.

Du·rant′ (dū·rănt′). **1** Town, Holmes co., W cen. Mississippi, 36 m. SE of Greenwood; pop. 2617; in agricultural section.
2 City, ⊗ of Bryan co., S Oklahoma, 46 m. ESE of Ardmore; pop. 10,467; settled 1870; cotton gins and compresses, cottonseed oil. Southeastern State College (1909; coed.).

Du·raz′no (dŏŏ·räs′nŏ). **1** Department of Uruguay. See *Table* at URUGUAY.
2 *or* **San Pe′dro del Durazno** (säm pā′thrŏ thĕl). Town, its ✱, S cen. Uruguay, near Yi river 105 m. N of Montevideo; pop. ab. 27,000.

Durazzo. See DURRËS.

Dur′ban (dûr′băn; -bӑn; dûr·băn′). Seaport, E Natal, Republic of So. Africa, on landlocked lagoon, inlet of Indian Ocean; pop. with suburbs 681,492; South Africa's largest grain elevator; headquarters of whaling fleet; resort; large Indian and Malayan population; seat of Howard College and of a technical college. Founded 1824, oldest settlement in Natal; township laid out 1835 and named after Sir Benjamin D'Urban, then governor of Cape Colony; British garrison, besieged by Boers 1842, saved by famous 600-mile ride of Dick King to Grahamstown. See NATAL.

Dü′ren (dü′rĕn); *anc.* **Mar′co·du′rum** (mär′kŏ·dū′-rӑm). Industrial city, W Germany, in the former Rhine Province, Prussia, on Rur river 18 m. E of Aachen; pop. 37,176; railroad junction; 13th–16th-cent. pilgrimage church; botanic garden, astronomical observatory. Probably of Roman origin; scene of diets held by Charlemagne 775 and 779; burned by Emperor Charles V 1543; to France 1801, Prussia 1814; in World War II city and vicinity scene of severe fighting Dec. 1944 to Mar. 1945.

Dur′fee Hill (dûr′fê). Elevation 805 ft., Providence co., Rhode Island, NW of Providence.

Dur′ge Nur (dŏŏr′gĕ nŏŏr′). Salt lake, W Outer Mongolia, S of Khara Nur.

Dur′ham (dûr′ăm). **1** County in North Carolina. See *Table* at NORTH CAROLINA.
2 Town, Middlesex co., S Connecticut, 6 m. S of Middletown; pop. 3096; settled 1699.
3 Town, Strafford co., SE New Hampshire, 5 m. SSW of Dover; pop. 5504; settled 1635; scene of Indian massacres, notably 1675, 1694, 1704; Univ. of New Hampshire (founded at Hanover as part of Dartmouth College 1866; removed to Durham 1893; coed.).
4 Industrial city, ⊗ of Durham co., NE cen. North Carolina, 20 m. NW of Raleigh; pop. 78,302; settled c. 1750, incorp. 1867, made ⊗ 1881; important tobacco and cotton market. Duke Univ. (1838; coed.); North Carolina College at Durham (1910; coed.).

5 County, Ontario, Canada. See *Table* at ONTARIO.
6 Town, Grey co., SE Ontario, Canada, 28 m. S of Owen Sound; pop. 1839.

Dur′ham (dûr′ăm; *Brit.* dŭr′-). **1** County, N England; area 1015 sq. m.; pop. (1951) 1,463,416; ⊗ Durham; other towns Sunderland, Gateshead, South Shields, Darlington, West Hartlepool; rivers include Tees and Wear; shipbuilding, coal and iron mining, iron and steel manufacturing, grazing and farming.
2 *Saxon* **Dun′holme** (dŭn′ăm). Municipal borough, its ⊗, N England, on the Wear 15 m. S of Newcastle; pop. 19,283; shipbuilding yards, coal and iron mines, chemical and glass manufactures; cathedral; castle; University of Durham.

Durius. See DOURO.

Dürkheim *or* **Bad Dürk′heim** (bät dürk′hïm). Town, Palatinate govt. dist., Bavaria, S Germany, 15 m. NW of Speyer; pop. 7770; mineral springs.

Dur′lach (dŏŏr′läk). City, Baden-Württemberg, W Germany, 3 m. ENE of Karlsruhe; pop. 18,016; manufactures bicycles, sewing machines, dental instruments, organs. First mentioned 1161; to margraves of Baden 1227; burned by French 1689.

Durle′ston Head (dûrl′stŭn). Headland on S coast of Dorsetshire, S of Bournemouth, S England; lighthouse.

Dur′mi·tor (dŏŏr′mĕ·tŏr). Mountain 8294 ft., cen. Montenegro, Yugoslavia, ESE of Mostar; highest point of inland mountain ranges of Yugoslavia.

Durnovaria. See DORCHESTER municipal borough, England.

Durobrivae. See ROCHESTER city, England.

Durocasses. See DREUX.

Durocortorum. See REIMS.

Durostorum. See SILISTRA.

Durovernum. See CANTERBURY.

Dur′rës (dŏŏr′rĕs); *Ital.* **Du·raz′zo** (dŏŏ·rät′tsŏ). **1** Prefecture, W Albania; 616 sq. m.; pop. 77,890.
2 *anc.* **Ep′i·dam′nus** (ĕp′ĭ·dăm′nŭs), *later* **Dyr·ra′-chi·um** *or* **Dyr·rha′chi·um** (dĭ·rā′kĭ·ŭm). Seaport, its ✱, W Albania, on Adriatic Sea; pop. 8739; outlet for Tiranë and shipping point esp. for grain, olive oil, and tobacco; has large Moslem population; modern Grand Mosque.
History: Ancient Epidamnus a colony founded by Corcyra and Corinth c. 625 B.C.; dispute over it a cause of Peloponnesian War; under Romans (after 229 B.C.) an important port at start of overland route across Greece; by Emperor Augustus made over to his veterans after Actium 31 B.C.; theme of Dyrrachium a division of Byzantine Empire; taken by Robert Guiscard (see SICILY) 1081–82 and by Normans 1185; after its capture by Angevins 1272, changed hands frequently bet. Albanians, Serbians, and Angevins; ruled by Venice 1392–1501, and by Turks 1501–1913; after occupation by Serbs 1913, made part of principality of Albania (*q.v.*). In World War I occupied by Italians 1915 and by Austrians 1916; as Austrian naval base destroyed 1918 by Allied naval force; in World War II during Italian-Greek conflict 1940 repeatedly bombed by Greeks and British.

Dur Shar·ru′kin (dŏŏr shä·rŏŏ′kĭn). See KHORSABAD.

Dürt·men′ Da·ğı′ (dürt·mĕn′ dä·ï′). Peak 5380 ft. in N Turkey in Asia, WNW of Samsun.

d′Ur′ville, Cape (dûr′vil). Cape on N coast of Neth. New Guinea, just E of Geelvink Bay near mouth of the Mamberamo river.

D′Urville Island. Island lying bet. Tasman Bay and Cook Strait off N coast of South I., New Zealand.

Dur′yea (dŏŏr′yä; dŏŏr′ĭ·à). Borough, Luzerne co., E Pennsylvania, 7 m. SW of Scranton; pop. 5626; coal mines; silk manufactures.

Du·sham′be (dŏŏ·shàm′bĕ). Var. of *Dyushambe:* see STALINABAD.

Düs′sel (düs′ĕl). River ab. 20 m. long, in North Rhine-Westphalia state, W Germany; flows SW into the Rhine at Düsseldorf.

Düs'sel·dorf (düs'ĕl·dôrf; *Angl.* dōō's'l·dôrf, dōōs''l-, dĭs''l-). **1** Government district, W Germany; area 2122 sq. m.
2 Industrial city and river port, its ✳ and ✳ of North Rhine-Westphalia, W Germany, on Rhine river 21 m. NNW of Cologne; pop. 675,900; 14th-cent. Gothic church; 18th-cent. Academy of Art; home of famous school of painting; metallurgical, glass, and chemical manufactures. Birthplace of Heinrich Heine. Founded before 11th cent.; residence of dukes of Berg, electors of the Palatinate; 1805 became center of grand duchy of Berg created by Napoleon; taken by Prussians 1815; occupied by Allies 1921–25; in World War II bombed by Allies May 1943 to 1945, partly occupied by Allies Mar. 1945, final surrender Apr. 17, 1945.

Dutch Borneo. See BORNEO.

Dutch East Indies. See NETHERLANDS INDIES.

Dutch'ess (dŭch'ĕs, -ĭs; dŭch·ĕs'). County in New York. See *Table* at NEW YORK.

Dutch Guiana. See SURINAM.

Dutch Harbor. Port, village, and U.S. Naval Station on E Amaknak I. in Unalaska Bay, on N side of E end of Unalaska I., E Aleutian Is., SW Alaska; has harbor 1¾ m. long by ¾ m. wide; the port, ab. 1½ m. N of Unalaska village, is used as port of call for steamers; in early days the capital of the fur-sealing industry; deteriorated until taken over by Navy; attacked by the Japanese June 1942.

Dutch New Guin'ea (gĭn'ĭ). = NETHERLANDS NEW GUINEA.

Dutch Timor. See NETHERLANDS TIMOR.

Dutch West Indies. See NETHERLANDS WEST INDIES.

Duttia. See DATIA.

Dut'ton, Mount (dŭt''n). Peak 10,800 ft. in NW Garfield co., S Utah.

Du'val (dōō'vôl; dū'-). Name of counties in two states of the U.S. See *Tables* at FLORIDA and TEXAS.

Du'ver·gé' (dōō'vĕr·hā'). Commune (1941 pop. 12,974) and town (1944 est. pop. 5521), Barahona prov., SW Dominican Republic.

Dúvida, Rio da. See Rio ROOSEVELT.

Du·wa'mish (dŭ·wä'mĭsh) *or* **Dwa'mish** (dwä'mĭsh). Navigable river, W cen. Washington; formed by confluence of Green and White rivers in SW King co., flows N into Puget Sound at Seattle.

Dux. See DUCHCOV.

Dux'bur'y (dŭks'bĕr'ĭ; -bēr·ĭ). Residential town, Plymouth co., SE Massachusetts, on Plymouth Bay 17 m. ESE of Brockton; pop. 4727; summer resort.

Duzdab. See ZAHIDAN.

Dvi·na' (dvē·nä'; *Russ.* dvyĭ·ná'). **1** River, N Russia in Europe. See NORTHERN DVINA.
2 *Lettish* **Dau'ga·va** (dou'gà·và); *Ger.* **Dü'na** (dü'nä). *Known also as the* **Southern Dvina** *or* **Western Dvina;** *Russ.* **Za'pad·na·ya Dvina** (zà'pàd·nà·yà). River ab. 630 m. long, N Europe; rises in Valdai Hills, NW Soviet Union, near sources of the Volga and the Dnieper, flows SW and W across N White Russia and SE and S Latvia to Gulf of Riga near Riga; drainage basin ab. 33,000 sq. m.; generally navigable to Vitebsk; has many short tributaries; connected by canal systems with the Neva, Volga, and Dnieper rivers.

Dvina Gulf *or* **Bay;** *also* **Gulf of Dvinsk** (dvĭnsk; *Russ.* dvyēnsk); *Russ.* **Dvin'ska·ya Gu·ba'** (dvyēn'skà·yà gōō·bá'). *Formerly* **Gulf of Arch'an'gel** (ärk'ăn'jĕl). Southeast arm of White Sea, Arkhangelsk Region, N Soviet Russia, Europe; receives Northern Dvina river; port of Arkhangelsk at its head.

Dvinsk. See DAUGAVPILS.

Dvůr Krá'lo·vé nad La'bem (dvōōr krä'lô·vâ nàt là'bĕm); *Ger.* **Kö'ni·gin·hof'** (kû'nĕ·gĭn·hōf'). Town, NE Bohemia prov., W Czechoslovakia, 65 m. ENE of Prague on Labe (Elbe) river; pop. (1930) 16,588.

Dwamish. See DUWAMISH.

Dwar'ka (dwär'kä). Seaport, Gujerat state, W India, at W end of Kathiawar Penin.; pop. 7632; temple of Krishna; one of the seven sacred cities of India.

Dwight (dwīt). Village, Livingston co., NE cen. Illinois, 35 m. SW of Joliet; pop. 3086.

Dwin (dvēn) *or* **Tvin** (tĭën). Ancient town in Armenia, SW of Lake Sevan; medieval capital of Armenia.

Dwy'ka (dwī'kà). River ab. 90 m. long in Great Karroo region of Cape Province, Union of South Africa; flows into the Gamka NW of Oudtshoorn; has given its name to a geological division of South Africa.

Dyardanes. See BRAHMAPUTRA.

Dyaul (dyoul; joul). Island ab. 14 m. long, 30 m. off the NW coast of New Ireland, Bismarck Archipelago, W Pacific Ocean.

Dyb'böl (düb'ûl); *Ger.* **Düp'pel** (düp'ĕl). Town, S Jutland, Denmark, on coast 6 m. SW of Sönderborg; pop. ab. 1000; scene of several struggles bet. Danes and Germans 1848 and 1849; held by Denmark 1860 until recaptured by Prussians 1864; held by Germany until returned to Denmark under plebiscite 1920.

Dy'ea (dī'ā'). Former village at head of Taiya Inlet, N end of Lynn Canal, SE Alaska; after discovery of gold (1896–97) in Klondike region, became supply center and starting point for trail over Chilkoot Pass to Dawson and northern mining fields; just NW of Skagway, which superseded it on opening of White Pass.

Dy'er (dī'ēr). County in Tennessee. See *Table* at TENNESSEE.

Dyer, Cape. Easternmost point, 61°20'W, of Cumberland Penin., Baffin I., Canada, on Davis Strait.

Dy'ers·burg (dī'ērz·bûrg). City, ⊗ of Dyer co., NW Tennessee, 45 m. NW of Jackson; pop. 12,499; cotton, wheat; manufactures textiles, cottonseed oil, flour.

Dy'ers·ville (dī'ērz·vĭl). City, Delaware and Dubuque cos., E Iowa, 25 m. W of Dubuque; pop. 2818.

d'Yeu, Île. See Île d'YEU.

Dy'fed (dĭv'ĕd). Ancient region in SW Wales, now Pembrokeshire.

Dy'fi (dĭv'ĭ) *or* **Dov'ey** (dŭv'ĭ). River 30 m. long, W Wales; flows S and SW into Cardigan Bay.

Dyke Ac'land Bay (dīk ăk'lănd). Inlet of Solomon Sea on N coast of SE Papua, New Guinea, SE of Holnicote Bay. See ORO BAY.

Dyke Lake (dīk). Large lake in W Labrador; forms part of course of Hamilton river.

Dykh Tau *or* **Dykh'tau'** (dīk'tou'). Mountain (*tau*) 17,085 ft. in a N spur of the Caucasus Mts., S Kabardino-Balkarian Republic, Soviet Russia, Europe; lat. 43°5'N and long. 43°15'E.

Dy'le (dī'lĕ; *Fr.* dēl). River ab. 50 m. long in Belgium; flows N and W in Brabant and Antwerp provs. and unites with the Nethe river 4 m. NW of Mechelen to form the Rupel river; Belgian and British line of defense May 1940.

Dyrrachium, Dyrrhachium. See DURRËS.

Dy'sart (dī'zērt). Former burgh and seaport, Fife co., Scotland, on the Firth of Forth; since 1930 part of Kirkcaldy; ruins of chapels of St. Dennis and St. Serf; in 15th and 16th cents. manufactured salt.

Dytikē Thrakē. = *Western Thrace:* see THRACE.

Dyushambe. See STALINABAD.

Dza–chu. See MEKONG.

Dzaoudzi. See MAYOTTE.

Dzau·dzhi'kau (dzou·jē'kou); *Russ.* **Or'dzho·ni·kid'ze** (ôr'jŏn·ĭ·kĭd'zĕ; *Russ.* ŭr·ju·nyĭ·kēd'zĕ); *formerly* **Vla'di·kav·kaz'** (vlăd'ĭ·kăf·kăz'; *Russ.* vlà·dyĭ·kŭf·kàs'). Commercial and industrial city, ✳ of North Ossetia, SE Soviet Russia, Europe; pop. 127,172; on plateau, alt. 2345 ft., on both sides of the Terek 70 m. WSW of Grozny; at N end of Georgian Military Road leading S through Daryal Pass to Tiflis. Founded 1784 as a fort, became town 1860; after the Revolution one of chief towns of North Caucasus region and the Mountain Republic; for a time capital of Ingushetia; name changed 1937 to Ordzhonikidze and again 1944 to the Ossetian

name, Dzaudzhikau; marked the farthest advance of German armies into Caucasus Mts. Nov. 10–19, 1942.

Dzer·zhinsk′ (dyĕr·zhĭnsk′). City, W Gorki Region, Soviet Russia, Europe, just W of Gorki on Oka river; pop. 103,415; a new industrial city of rapid growth.

Dzha·lal′ A·bad′ (jà·läl′ ä·bäd′). Town, SW Kirgiz S.S.R., Soviet Central Asia, in upper Syr Darya valley on the Uzbek border, NE of Andizhan; pop. 19,800.

Dzham·bul′ (jàm·bōōl′); *formerly* **Au′li·e A′ta** (ou′-lĕ·yĕ ä′tà). Town, ✻ of Dzhambul Region, SE Kazakh S.S.R., Soviet Central Asia, on Turkistan-Siberian R.R. 130 m. NE of Tashkent; pop. 62,723.

Dzhambul Region. Subdivision of Kazakh S.S.R., Soviet Central Asia, in SE part; ✻ Dzhambul; mostly steppe and desert; traversed by Chu river.

Dzhan·koi′ (jŭn·koi′). Town, N Crimea, Soviet Russia, Europe, 55 m. N of Simferopol; pop. 8300; railroad junction; several industrial plants; center for grain export; held by Germans 1941–44.

Dzhib′kha·lan·tu′ (jĭb′кä·län·tōō′); *Mongol* **U′lias-su·tai′** *or* **U′la·su·tai′** (ōō′lyä·sōō·tī′). Town, W cen. Outer Mongolia, in mountainous district ab. 460 m. W of Urga; pop. ab. 6000; important transport and trading center; square fortress built 1765.

Dzhir′ga·lan·tu′ (jĭr′gä·län·tōō′); *formerly* **Kob′do** (kôb′dō) *or* **Khob′do** (кôb′dō). Town, chief trading center of W Outer Mongolia, SW of Khobdo river at foot of Altai Mts., ab. 260 m. W of Dzhibkhalantu; pop. ab. 6000; market for cattle, sheep, skins, and wool.

Dzhul·fa′ *or* **Djul·fa′** (jōōl·fä′); *formerly* **Jul·fa′**. Town in Nakhichevan A.S.S.R., Azerbaidzhan, U.S.S.R., on Araks river 25 m. SE of Nakhichevan; junction point of Russian railroad lines for Tabriz in Iran; important town in Armenian history; has ruins of churches and monasteries.

Dzier·żo′niów (jĕr·zhô′nyōōf); *Ger.* **Rei′chen·bach** (rī′кĕn·bäк). Town, S cen. Wrocław dept., SW Poland, SE of Świdnica; pop. (1946) 22,000; formerly in Silesia, Germany; manufactures machinery, textiles; grain and cattle market. Founded in 13th cent.; scene of battle of Reichenbach Aug. 16, 1762 in which Frederick the Great defeated the Austrians; scene of diplomatic congress 1790 and of conference bet. Prussia and Russia 1813; assigned to Poland by Potsdam Conference 1945.

Dzisna. See DISNA.

Dzun·gar′i·a ([d]zōōng·gâr′ĭ·à; [d]zŭng-) *or* **Zun-gar′i·a** (zōōng-; zŭng-); *also* **Sun·gar′i·a** (sōōng-; sŭng-). Region, N Sinkiang, W China, N of the Tien Shan; includes the more modern district of Chuguchak; its chief centers in rich valley of the Ili river. From 11th to 14th cents. a Mongol kingdom; devastated by Tamerlane 1389; ruled by a Kalmuck confederation until 1758–59 when it was conquered by Chinese, made part of Sinkiang.

Dzun·gar′i·an A′la Tau (-ăn ä′lä tou′). Mountain range bet. E Kazakh S.S.R. and NW Sinkiang prov., W China; highest peak 16,550 ft.

E

Eads (ēdz). Town, ⊗ of Kiowa co., E Colorado; pop. 929

Ea'gle (ē'g'l). **1** County in Colorado. See *Table* at COLORADO.

2 Settlement, E Alaska, on the Yukon on Canadian border; pop. 92.

3 Town, ⊗ of Eagle co., NW cen. Colorado; pop. 546.

Eagle Grove. City, Wright co., N cen. Iowa, 20 m. NE of Fort Dodge; pop. 4381.

Ea'gle·hawk' (ē'g'l·hôk'). Town, cen. Victoria, Australia, 6 m. NW of Bendigo; pop. 3789; gold mines.

Eagle Lake. **1** Lake in Lassen co., NE California.

2 Lake in N Aroostook co., N Maine; drains into a tributary of Aroostook river.

3 Lake in N Piscataquis co., N cen. Maine.

4 Town, Aroostook co., N Maine, 13 m. S of Fort Kent at W end of Eagle Lake; pop. 1138.

5 City, Colorado co., SE cen. Texas, 40 m. S of Brenham; pop. 3565; rice-milling center.

6 Lake 128 sq. m., SW Ontario, Canada, in Kenora dist., chief outlet through Rainy Lake.

Eagle Mountain. Peak 7510 ft. in Hudspeth co., W Texas.

Eagle Pass. City and port of entry, ⊗ of Maverick co., SW Texas, on the Rio Grande 52 m. SSE of Del Rio; pop. 12,094; site of U.S. Army encampment (Camp Eagle Pass) during war with Mexico; on one of favorite routes to California during gold rush of 1849; resort.

Eagle River. **1** Village, ⊗ of Keweenaw co., N Michigan penin., on Lake Superior; pop. (1950) 194.

2 City, ⊗ of Vilas co., N Wisconsin; pop. 1367.

Eagles Rest (ē'g'lz). Peak 11,257 ft. in N Grand Teton National Park, NW Wyoming.

Ea'gle·ton Village (ē'g'l·t'n; -tŭn). Urban community (unincorporated), Blount co., E Tennessee, S ot Knoxville; pop. 5068.

Ea'ling (ē'lĭng). Municipal borough, Middlesex, SE England, W suburb of London; pop. 117,707, (1951) 187,306; part of Greater London; birthplace of Thomas Huxley.

Ear'by (ẽr'bĭ). Urban district, West Riding, Yorkshire, N England; pop. 5348.

Earle (ûrl). City, Crittenden co., E Arkansas, 27 m. WNW of Memphis, Tenn.; pop. 2391; cotton.

Ear'ling·ton (ûr'lĭng·tŭn). City, Hopkins co., W Kentucky, 28 m. N of Hopkinsville; pop. 2786; coal mining.

Earl's Seat. See LENNOX HILLS.

Earls'ton (ûrl'stŭn); *orig.* **Er'cel·doune** (ûr's'l·dōōn'), *also* **Er'cil·doune** (ûr's'l·dōōn'). Parish and market town, S Berwick co., SE Scotland, near Melrose; pop. 1761; ruin of ancient tower, the "Rhymer's Castle," residence of Thomas Learmont or Thomas of Erceldoune, seer and poet; manufactures tweed and gingham.

Ear'ly (ûr'lĭ). County in Georgia. See *Table* at GEORGIA.

Earn (ûrn). River ab. 40 m. long in Perth co., cen. Scotland; flows out of Loch Earn and into the Tay river.

Earn, Loch (lŏk ûrn'). Lake 6½ m. long in Perth co., cen. Scotland.

Earns'law, Mount (ûrnz'lô). Peak 9250 ft. in Southern Alps, SW cen. South I., New Zealand.

Ear of Di·o·ny'si·us (dī·ō·nĭsh'ĭ·ŭs; -nĭsh'ŭs; -nĭs'ĭ·ŭs). A narrow cavern in one of the ancient quarries of Syracuse, Sicily. tapering to an orifice above, where the tyrant Dionysius the Elder is said to have listened, as one still may, to conversation below.

Ears'don (ẽrz'dŭn; ûrz'-; *locally also* yô'z'n). Former urban district, Northumberland, N England, 7 m. NE of Newcastle; pop. (1931) 13,086.

Eas'ley (ēz'lĭ). City, Pickens co., NW South Carolina, 13 m. W of Greenville; pop. 8283; cotton, flour.

East, the. **1** The countries of Asia and of the Asiatic archipelagoes; the countries E of Europe; the Orient; *the*

East usually connotes the civilized Asiatic countries, either ancient or modern. See FAR EAST, MIDDLE EAST, NEAR EAST.

2 In United States history and geography, formerly the part E of the Allegheny Mts., esp. the New England states; now, often, the region E of the Mississippi river.

East Africa Protectorate. See KENYA.

East Alton. Village, Madison co., SW Illinois, on Mississippi river 5 m. E of Alton; pop. 7630.

East and West Maitland. See East and West MAITLAND.

East and West Mole'sey (mōl'zĭ). Former urban district, Surrey, S England; pop. (1931) 8464; since 1933 in Esher.

East An'gli·a (ăng'glĭ·à). **1** Ancient division, England, including modern Norfolk and Suffolk; probably settled by Angles (see ANGELN), it emerged as one of kingdoms in Anglo-Saxon Heptarchy (*q.v.*); converted to Christianity and subjugated by Mercia 7th cent.; practically absorbed in Mercia by 8th cent.; Danish territory according to the Peace of Wedmore 878; conquered by Wessex 10th cent.; Danish earldom under Canute.

2 Geographical region of modern England; the counties of Norfolk and Suffolk.

East An'gus (ăng'gŭs). Mill town, Compton co., S Quebec, Canada, on St. Francis river; pop 3714.

East Antarctica. See ANTARCTICA.

East Aurora. Village, Erie co., W New York, 15 m. ESE of Buffalo; pop. 6791; settled 1804; seat of former Roycroft colony (handicrafts) and Roycroft Press, estab. by Elbert Hubbard 1895.

East Australian Current. Warm ocean current flowing S off E coast of Australia.

East Bar'net Valley (bär'nĕt; -nĭt). Urban district, Hertfordshire, SE England, 10 m. N of London; pop. 40,414; part of Greater London.

East Baton Rouge. Parish in Louisiana. See *Table* at LOUISIANA.

East Bengal. Region, E Pakistan, formerly a province of Pakistan; merged 1955 with other smaller areas to form **East Pakistan** prov.; comprises part of former Bengal prov., Brit. India, including all of Chittagong and Dacca divisions, the Rangpur, Bogra, Rajshahi, and Pabna dists. of Rajshahi division, parts of Dinajpur, Jalpaiguri, and Malda dists. of Rajshahi division, Khulna dist. and parts of Nadia and Jessore dists. of Presidency division, and most of Sylhet dist. of Assam; total est. area 52,550 sq. m.

East Beskids. See BESKIDS.

East Boston. Section of Boston, Massachusetts, on E side of Charles river estuary; Boston airport.

East'bourne (ēst'bōrn). County borough, East Sussex, S England, on English Channel 57 m. S of London; pop. (1951) 57,801; resort.

East Bridgewater. Town, Plymouth co., SE Massachusetts, 5 m. SE of Brockton; pop. 6139.

East Cape. **1** Most easterly point of the island of New Guinea, 151°E lat., on SE tip of Papua; marks NE corner of Milne Bay.

2 Cape on E coast of North I., New Zealand, easternmost point of North I.

3 *or* **Cape Dezh'nev** (dĕzh'nĕf; *Russ.* dyäsh'nyĕf) *or* **Dezh'ne·va** (dĕzh'nĕ·và; dyäsh'nyĕ·và). Cape at the NE extremity of Asia, projecting into Bering Strait; at E end of Chukotski Penin., Chukot National District, Soviet Russia, 66°N, 170°W.

East Carroll. Parish, Louisiana. See LOUISIANA, *Table*.

East Charlevoix. See CHARLEVOIX.

East'cheap (ēs[t]'chēp). Street, formerly a market and square, in SE part of City of London near N end of London Bridge; site of Boar's Head tavern of Shakespeare's time.

East Chicago. City, Lake co., NW corner of Indiana, on Lake Michigan 18 m. SE of Chicago; pop. 57,669; manufactures steel, chemicals, railroad equipment, tinplate; refines oil.

East China Sea. See CHINA SEA.

East Cho·sen Bay (chō·sĕn); *formerly* **Brough'ton Bay** (brô't'n). Inlet of the Sea of Japan in E coast of Korea, ab. lat. 39°N.

East Cleveland. City, Cuyahoga co., N Ohio, 5 m. ENE of Cleveland; pop. 37,991; residential suburb; manufactures electrical appliances; electrical research laboratories.

East Conemaugh. Borough, Cambria co., SW cen. Pennsylvania, 3 m. NE of Johnstown; pop. 3334.

East Dere'ham (dĕr'ăm). Urban district, Norfolk, E England, 14 m. W of Norwich; pop. 6441; home of Cowper 1796–1800.

East Detroit. Residential city, Macomb co., SE Michigan, 10 m. NE of Detroit; pop. 45,756.

East End. The eastern portion of London, England, comprising the densely populated industrial and shipping districts and including most of the poorest districts.

Eas'ter Island (ēs'tẽr); *Span.* **Pas'cua** (päs'kwä); *native* **Ra'pa Nu'i** (rä'pä nōō'ē). Island in S Pacific Ocean, lat. 27°6'S and long. 109°17'W, ab. 2000 m. W of the Chilean coast; ab. 50 sq. m.; pop. ab. 250; has gigantic statues and other archaeological remains of unknown origin. Discovered on Easter day 1722 by Dutch admiral, Roggeveen; annexed by Chile 1888.

Eastern Bay. Inlet of Chesapeake Bay on SW coast of Queen Annes co., E Maryland.

Eastern Bengal. 1 Former province of India. See ASSAM and BENGAL.
2. = EAST BENGAL, Pakistan.

Eastern Desert. = ARABIAN DESERT.

Eastern Empire. = *Eastern Roman Empire:* see BYZANTINE EMPIRE.

Eastern Erg. = *Grand Erg Oriental:* see EL ERG.

Eastern Euphrates. See MURAT SUYU.

Eastern Ghats. See GHATS.

Eastern Highlands. = GREAT DIVIDING RANGE, Australia.

Eastern Island. See MIDWAY.

Eastern Islands. See LAU ISLANDS.

Eastern Kathiawar. Former agency, subdivision of Western India States Agency, W India; 2845 sq. m.; pop. (1941) 323,019; chief town Wadhwan Civil Station (pop. 13,344).

Eastern Locris. See LOCRIS.

Eastern Manych. See MANYCH.

Eastern Province. 1 Province, Republic of Congo (formerly Belgian Congo). See STANLEYVILLE.
2 Province, E Ceylon, on Bay of Bengal; 3840 sq. m.; pop. 212,421; ✳ Trincomalee.
3 Province, E Tanganyika; 26,713 sq. m.; pop. 541,414; ✳ Dar es Salaam.
4 Province, E Uganda protectorate; ✳ Jinja.

Eastern Provinces; *now* **Eastern Region.** Southeast division of Nigeria. See *Table* at NIGERIA.

Eastern Punjab. = EAST PUNJAB.

Eastern Rajputana States Agency. Eastern part of former Rajputana Agency, NW India, comprising states of Bharatpur, Bundi, Dholpur, Jhalawar, Karauli, and Kotah (*qq.v.*); on June 26, 1947 the states of Bundi, Karauli, and Kotah joined the Union of Rajasthan.

Eastern Range. Mountain range, Kamchatka (*q.v.*), Soviet Russia, Asia; has several high volcanic peaks, including Klyuchevskaya Sopka 15,666 ft., highest in Siberia.

Eastern Region; **Span. Re·gión' O'rien·tal'** (rrĕhyôn' ō'ryän·täl'). The part of Ecuador beyond (E of) the Andes Mts.; boundaries of region have been in dispute bet. Ecuador, Colombia, and Peru since 1860; by settlement of 1942 at Rio de Janeiro Conference now comprises the provinces of Napo-Pastaza and Santiago-Zamora (*qq.v.*).

Eastern Roman Empire. See BYZANTINE EMPIRE.

Eastern Rumelia. Balkan region, now S part of Bulgaria, including Rhodope Mts. and Maritsa river valley; 12,585 sq. m.; chief town Plovdiv (Philippopolis); established as autonomous province of Turkey 1878; annexed to Bulgaria 1885; Bulgarian annexation caused Serbian war against Bulgaria 1885–86 and a crisis in European diplomacy (1885–88) in which Russia failed to achieve separation of region from Bulgaria.

Eastern Samoa. See AMERICAN SAMOA.

Eastern Sea. = *East China Sea:* see CHINA SEA.

Eastern Shore. The part of Maryland E of Chesapeake Bay and the counties of Accomac and Northampton in Virginia; sometimes includes all of Delaware and then considered as equivalent to the Delmarva Penin.

Eastern Siberian Region. See EAST SIBERIA REGION.

Eastern Sierra Madre. = SIERRA MADRE ORIENTAL.

Eastern Silesia. Former duchy in N Austria-Hungary, bet. Prussian Silesia and Moravia; chief town Troppau; in 20th cent. its W two thirds became Czech province of Slezsko (Silesia); its E section was nearly equivalent to Teschen (*q.v.*).

Eastern States. 1 The New England states: Maine, New Hampshire, Vermont, Massachusetts, Rhode Island, and Connecticut—popularly so called; in certain groupings, as in the Federal Land Bank system, New York and New Jersey are included.
2 The states of the U.S. along the Atlantic seaboard E of the Allegheny Mts.—a term occasionally used in the Mississippi valley and in states W of it. See the EAST.
3 Former group of Indian states, NE India; area 66,989 sq. m.; pop. 8,084,332; comprised 42 states, two of which, Cooch Behar and Tripura (*qq.v.*), were on E border of Bengal prov.; others in region bet. Bihar on NE and Central India on SW, at one time part in Central Provinces and part (Orissa Feudatory States; 18,151 sq. m.; pop. [1941] 3,023,731) in Orissa. Under the British government had direct relations with the Crown Representative through Resident at Calcutta, assisted by two political agents at Sambalpur and Raipur; July 15, 1947, 39 of the 42 states formed an administrative union within the Indian Union for more co-ordinated action on matters of common interest.

Eastern Thrace. See THRACE.

Eastern Townships. Towns of S Quebec prov., Canada, E of Montreal and S of the St. Lawrence—popularly so called; chief center Sherbrooke.

Eastern Turkistan. = CHINESE TURKISTAN.

East Falkland. See FALKLAND ISLANDS.

East Fe·li'ci·an'a (fĕ·lĭsh'ĭ·ăn'á). Parish in Louisiana. See *Table* at LOUISIANA.

East Flanders. Province, NW cen. Belgium; 1147 sq. m.; pop. (1941 est.) 1,200,121; ✳ Gent; formerly part of the county of Flanders (*q.v.*); rivers Schelde, Lys; grows wheat and flax; manufactures linen and laces.

East Florida. See *History* at FLORIDA.

East Fremantle. See FREMANTLE, Australia.

East Friesland. = OSTFRIESLAND.

East Frisian Islands. See FRISIAN ISLANDS.

East Gary. Town, Lake co., NW corner of Indiana, 5 m. S of Lake Michigan; pop. 9309.

East Gaspé. See GASPÉ.

East Granby. Town, Hartford co., N Connecticut, 12 m. N of Hartford; pop. 2434; incorporated 1858; nearby is Newgate Prison, used in Revolutionary days and one of early state prisons. See SIMSBURY.

East Grand Forks. City, Polk co., NW Minnesota, on Red river opp. Grand Forks, North Dakota; pop. 6998; beet-sugar refinery.

East Grand Lake. See GRAND LAKE, Maine.

East Grand Rapids. City, Kent co., W Michigan, suburb of Grand Rapids; pop. 10,924; incorporated as a village 1891, as a city 1926.

East Green'ville. Borough, Montgomery co., SE Pennsylvania, 14 m. S of Allentown; pop. 1931.

East Green'wich (grĕn'ĭch). Manufacturing town and summer resort, ⊗ of Kent co., cen. Rhode Island, 12 m. WSW of Providence; pop. 6100; ships shellfish.

East Grin'stead (grĭn'stĕd; -stĭd). Urban district, East Sussex, S England; pop. 10,845; brick and tile.

East Haddam. Town, E Middlesex co., S Connecticut, on Connecticut river; pop. 3637; incorporated 1734; manufactures cotton goods.

East'ham. 1 (ĕs'tăm) Town, Barnstable co., SE Massachusetts, ab. 25 m. from Provincetown; pop. 1200. 2 (ĕst'hăm) Parish, Cheshire, NW England, on the Mersey 6 m. SE of Birkenhead; pop. 2990; terminus of Manchester Ship Canal.

East Ham (ĕst' hăm'). County borough, Essex, SE England, an E suburb of London; pop. 142,394, (1951) 120,873; part of Greater London; docks, shipyards, ironworks, chemical factories.

East'hamp'ton (ĕst'hăm[p]'tŭn; -hăm[p]'tŭn). Town, Hampshire co., W Massachusetts, 12 m. NNW of Springfield; pop. 12,326; manufactures yarns, thread, buttons; Williston Academy, boys' preparatory school.

East Hamp'ton (ĕst' hăm[p]'tŭn). 1 Residential, manufacturing, and agricultural town, NE Middlesex co., S Connecticut; pop. 5403; incorporated as Chatham 1767. 2 Village and summer resort, Suffolk co., SE New York, on Long I., on Atlantic Ocean 20 m. W of Montauk Point; pop. 1772; settled 1648; considered part of Connecticut until 1664; seat of Clinton Academy (1784), first academy of higher education in N.Y.; home of John Howard Payne, author of *Home, Sweet Home.*

East Hartford. Town, E cen. Hartford co., N Connecticut, on E side of Connecticut river opp. Hartford; pop. 43,977; settled c. 1650; manufactures airplanes.

East Haven. Suburban residential town, S New Haven co., Connecticut, on Long Island Sound; pop. 21,388; incorporated 1785; summer resort; includes Lake Saltonstall, site of first iron mill in Connecticut.

East Helena. Town, Lewis and Clark co., W cen. Montana, 5 m. E of Helena; pop. 1490.

East Hills. Village, Nassau co., New York, in SW cen. Long I.; pop. 7184.

East In'dies (ĭn'dĭz; -dēz). 1 *also* **East In'di·a** (ĭn'-dĭ·ȧ). Collective name applied, loosely and vaguely, to India, Indochina, and the Malay Archipelago. 2 In better usage, politically, the Republic of Indonesia, formerly the Netherlands East Indies. See INDIES. By some writers used to include all the islands of the Malay Archipelago; that is, the Republic of Indonesia, parts of the British Empire (E New Guinea, N Borneo), the Philippine Is., and Portuguese Timor.

East Indonesia. Former state of the United States of Indonesia (see NETHERLANDS INDIES); included Celebes, the Moluccas, Bali, Lombok, Flores, Netherlands Timor, and other smaller islands of cen. Malay Archipelago; pop. ab. 8,000,000; ✳ Makassar. Established Dec. 25, 1946, first state to be set up with the approval of the Netherlands in movement to form the United States of Indonesia.

East I'slip (ī'slĭp). Village, Suffolk co., SE New York, on S shore of Long I.; pop. (est.) 7000.

East Jaffrey. See JAFFREY, New Hampshire.

East Java. Province of Indonesia comprising the island of Madura and the E section of the island of Java; 18,498 sq. m.; pop. 15,055,714; ✳ Surabaja; chief towns Surabaja, Malang, Kediri, Madiun, and Probolinggo.

East Jer'sey (jûr'zĭ). Eastern and northern New Jersey constituting a proprietary colony from 1676 to 1702 when it was united with West Jersey to form the royal province of New Jersey (*q.v.*); ✳ (from 1686) Perth Amboy; held by William Penn and associates from 1682.

East Jor'dan (jôr'd'n). City, Charlevoix co., NW Michigan, 35 m. NE of Traverse City; pop. 1919.

East Kalimantan. See BORNEO, SOUTH AND EAST.

East Kazakhstan Region. Subdivision of Kazakh S.S.R., Soviet Central Asia, in E part; bounded on N by Altai Territory, on NE by Oirot Autonomous Region on E and S by Sinkiang, China, and on W by Semipalatinsk Region; ✳ Ust Kamenogorsk.

East Killingly. Subdivision of town of KILLINGLY, Connecticut; absorbent cotton.

East Lake Saint John. See LAKE SAINT JOHN county, S Quebec, Canada.

East'land (ĕst'lănd). 1 County in Texas. See *Table* at TEXAS. 2 City, its ⊗, N cen. Texas, 50 m. E of Abilene; pop. 3292; oil; trade center in farming region.

East Lansdowne. Borough, Delaware co., SE Pennsylvania, near Philadelphia; pop. 3224.

East Lansing. City, Ingham co., S Michigan, 5 m. E of Lansing; pop. 30,198; Michigan State Univ. of Agriculture and Applied Science (1855; coed.).

East'lawn (ĕst'lôn). Urban community (unincorporated), Washtenaw co., SE Michigan; pop. 17,652.

East'leigh' (ĕst'lē'). Municipal borough, Hampshire, S England, 6 m. NNE of city of Southampton; pop. 30,557.

East Liverpool. City, Columbiana co., E Ohio, on Ohio river 18 m. N of Steubenville; pop. 22,306; settled 1798, incorp. 1834; center of ceramic industry.

East Lon'don (lŭn'dŭn); *orig.* **Port Rex** (rĕks). City, SE Cape Province. S Union of South Africa, at mouth of Buffalo river 150 m. ENE of Port Elizabeth; pop. with suburbs 60,563; founded 1847, an early settlement in British Kaffraria; wool center; resort; seat of Selborne College and a technical college.

East Longmeadow. Town, Hampden co., SW Massachusetts, 5 m. SE of Springfield; pop. 10,294.

East Los Angeles. Urban community (unincorporated), Los Angeles co., SW California; pop. 104,270.

East Lothian *or* **Had'ding·ton** (hăd'ĭng·tŭn) *or* **Had'ding·ton·shire** (-shĭr; -shĕr). County, SE Scotland; area 267 sq. m.; pop. (1951) 52,240; ⊗ Haddington; chief river the Tyne; agriculture, fishing; coal.

East Lu·ang'wa (lōō·äng'wä). Province, E Northern Rhodesia; 22,350 sq. m.; pop. 225,076; ✳ Fort Jameson.

East Lyme (līm). Residential town, SW New London co., SE Connecticut, on Long Island Sound; pop. 6782; incorporated 1839; quarries pink granite.

East McKeesport. Residential borough, Allegheny co., SW Pennsylvania, 12 m. E of Pittsburgh; pop. 3470.

East'main (ĕst'mān). River 375 m. long, W Quebec, Canada; flows W into James Bay.

East'man (ĕst'măn). City, ⊗ of Dodge co., S cen. Georgia, 52 m. SE of Macon; pop. 5118.

East Mauch Chunk. See JIM THORPE.

East Massapequa. Urban community (unincorporated), Nassau co., New York, on Long I., SE of Mineola; pop. 14,779.

East Meadow. Urban community (unincorporated), Nassau co., New York, on Long I. E of Hempstead; pop. 46,036.

East Millinocket. Town, Penobscot co., E cen. Maine, 50 m. SW of Houlton; pop. 2392; paper mill.

East Moline. City, Rock Island co., NW Illinois, a suburb of Moline on Mississippi river; pop. 16,732; manufactures farm implements.

East Na'ra (nä'rȧ). River ab. 220 m. long, NW India; flows N in Sind prov. and Khairpur, Pakistan, to the Indus river at Sukkur; its lower course canalized.

East Newark. Manufacturing borough, Hudson co., NE New Jersey, on Passaic river opp. Newark; pop. 1872.

East Northport. Urban community (unincorporated), Suffolk co., New York, on Long I. E of Huntington; pop. 8381.

Eas'ton (ēs'tŭn) 1 Town, Aroostook co., N Maine, 7 m. ESE of Presque Isle; pop. 1389. 2 Town, ⊗ of Talbot co., E Maryland, on E shore of Chesapeake Bay 28 m. ESE of Annapolis; pop. 6337.

3 Manufacturing town, Bristol co., SE Massachusetts, 7 m. SW of Brockton; pop. 9078; shoes, shovels.
4 City, ⊗ of Northampton co., E Pennsylvania, at junction of Lehigh and Delaware rivers 15 m. ENE of Allentown; pop. 31,955; became ⊗ 1752, incorp. as borough 1789, as city 1887; ships coal; manufactures iron and steel, cement, silk, crayons, paints, hosiery, mining and quarrying machinery. Lafayette Coll. (1826; men).

East Orange. City, Essex co., NE New Jersey, residential suburb ab. 4 m. WNW of Newark; pop. 77,259; largest of "The Oranges" (Orange, East Orange, West Orange, South Orange); incorp. as separate township 1863, as city 1899; manufactures motors and generators, hydrants, aeronautic and automotive equipment, pharmaceuticals. Upsala College (1893; coed.).

East Pakistan. That part of Pakistan in the east of the peninsula of India; a province since 1955.

East Palestine. City, Columbiana co., E Ohio, 18 m. S of Youngstown; pop. 5232; estab. 1828; manufactures pottery ware, automobile tires; clay, coal, petroleum.

East Paterson. Borough, Bergen co., NE corner of New Jersey, 2 m. SE of Paterson; pop. 19,344.

East Peak. = BOUNDARY PEAK.

East Peoria. City, Tazewell co., cen. Illinois, across Illinois river from Peoria; pop. 12,310.

East·pha′lia (ēst-fāl′yà; -fā′li·à). East section of the ancient duchy of Saxony, Germany; bordered on the E by the Elbe river and on the S by the Harz Mts.

East Pittsburgh. Industrial borough, Allegheny co., SW Pennsylvania, 10 m. E of Pittsburgh; pop. 4122; electrical equipment.

East Point. 1 City, Fulton co., NW cen. Georgia, 7 m. SSW of Atlanta; pop. 35,633; incorporated 1887.
2 Point at E tip of Prince Edward I., Canada, extending into the Gulf of St. Lawrence.
3 Cape at E end of Vieques I., E of Puerto Rico in the West Indies.
4 Cape at E end of island of St. Croix in the Virgin Is. of the U.S., West Indies.
5 Cape at E end of Anegada I. in the British Virgin Is., West Indies.

East′port (ēst′pōrt). City, Washington co., SE corner of Maine, on island in Passamaquoddy Bay 24 m. SE of Calais; pop. 2537; easternmost city in U.S.; fisheries, sardine canneries.

East Prai′rie (prâr′ĭ). City, Mississippi co., SE Missouri, 38 m. S of Cape Girardeau; pop. 3449.

East Preanger. See PREANGER.

East Providence. City, Providence co., N Rhode Island; pop. 41,955; suburb of Providence; originally part of Seekonk, Mass.; set off and incorporated 1862; oyster shipping, petroleum refining; manufactures chemicals.

East Prussia; *Ger.* **Ost′preus′sen** (ōst′proi′sĕn). Historical region and former province of Prussia, E of Pomerania; see *Table* at PRUSSIA. On SE Baltic shore, inhabited by Old Prussians, conquered by Teutonic Knights 1226 (see PRUSSIA); after (Second) Peace of Thorn 1466, retained by Teutonic Knights as vassal of Poland; included in duchy of Prussia secularized by Albert of Brandenburg 1525; province of kingdom of Prussia; scene of Hindenburg's successful resistance against Russians (see TANNENBERG and MASURIAN LAKES) in World War I; 1919 separated from rest of Germany by Polish Corridor (*q.v.*) and southern part returned to Germany by plebiscite; reunited with territory of the Reich by German conquest of Poland 1939; invaded by Russian armies in fall of 1944 and overrun Jan.–May 1945; by decision of Potsdam Conference 1945, divided bet. U.S.S.R. and Poland, with Königsberg, Insterburg, and all N of a line drawn E to W just S of the Pregel assigned to U.S.S.R. and S two thirds to Poland (see MAZURY).

East Punjab. Eastern part of former Punjab prov., India; since 1947 a province (later **Punjab** state, ✳ Chandigarh) of NW Indian Union; comprising all of Jullundur and Ambala divisions of the former Punjab, the entire Amritsar dist. and parts of Gurdaspur and Lahore dists. of Lahore division; 47,456 sq. m. In 1966 divided into states of Punjabi Suba and Hariana (*qq.v.*).

East Rai′nelle (rā′nĕl). Town, Greenbrier co., SE West Virginia, 23 m. NW of Hinton; pop. 1244.

East Ret′ford (rĕt′fērd). Municipal borough, Nottinghamshire, N cen. England, on the Idle 23 m. E of Sheffield; pop. 16,312.

East Ridge. Town, Hamilton co., SE Tennessee, on Georgia border 5 m. ESE of Chattanooga; pop. 19,570.

East Riding. See YORKSHIRE.

East River. Strait connecting Long Island Sound and Upper New York Bay, New York; separates Manhattan from Brooklyn and Queens on Long I.

East River Mountain. Mountain 3480 ft. bet. Tazewell co., SW Virginia, and Mercer co., S West Virginia.

East Rochester. Manufacturing village, Monroe co., W New York, 7 m. E of Rochester; pop. 8152.

East Rockaway. Residential village and resort, Nassau co., SE New York, on cen. Long Island 20 m. ESE of New York City; pop. 10,721.

East Rutherford. Industrial borough, Bergen co., NE corner of New Jersey, 8 m. NNE of Newark; pop. 7769.

East Saint Louis. Manufacturing city, St. Clair co., SW Illinois, on Mississippi river opp. St. Louis, Mo.; pop. 81,712; railroad center; important livestock market; iron and steel products, glass, aluminum, chemicals.

East Schelde Estuary. Inlet of the North Sea on SW coast of Netherlands, at mouth of Schelde river, N of Walcheren, North Beveland, and South Beveland Is.

East Siberian Sea. Part of Arctic Ocean, N of Yakutsk Republic and Chukot National District, Soviet Russia, Asia; extends from New Siberian Is. to Wrangel I.

East Siberia, *or* **Eastern Siberian, Region.** Formerly one of the three subdivisions of Russia in Asia, consisting of the cen. and E parts of Siberia (see SIBERIA, 2); chief town Irkutsk.

East Side. The E part of Manhattan borough, New York City, esp. below 14th St. (Lower East Side), formerly peopled by the poorer classes. Site of headquarters district of United Nations (42d St. to 48th St.).

East Spencer. Town, Rowan co., cen. North Carolina, 4 m. ENE of Salisbury; pop. 2171.

East Stoke. See East STOKE.

East Stroudsburg. Borough, Monroe co., E Pennsylvania, 32 m. NNE of Allentown; pop. 7674; East Stroudsburg College (1893; coed.).

East Suffolk. See SUFFOLK.

East Sussex. See SUSSEX.

East Syracuse. Village, Onondaga co., cen. New York, 5 m. E of Syracuse; pop. 4708; steel products.

East Ta′was (tô′wàs). City, Iosco co., NE Michigan, at N side of mouth of Saginaw Bay; pop. 2462.

East Thomaston. Village, Upson co., W cen. Georgia, 36 m. W of Macon; pop. 2237.

East Tirol; *Ger.* **Ost′ti·rol** (ōst′tē·rōl′). Eastern part of the Austrian Tirol; before World War II formed an exclave of Tirol prov., SW Austria, and the political district of Lienz; 763 sq. m.; pop. 28,237.

East Turkistan. = CHINESE TURKISTAN.

East Vandergrift. Borough, Westmoreland co., SW Pennsylvania, on Kiskiminetas river; pop. 1388.

East′view′ (ēst′vū′). Town, Carleton co., SE Ontario, Canada, E of Ottawa on Ottawa river; pop. 13,799.

East′ville (ēst′vil; *Sou. also* -v'l). Town, ⊗ of Northampton co., S part of E Virginia penin.; pop. 261.

East Washington. Borough, Washington co., SW Pennsylvania, SW of Pittsburgh; pop. 2483.

East Whittier. Urban community (unincorporated), Los Angeles co., SW California; pop. 19,884.

East Wilmington. Urban community (unincorp.), New Hanover co., SE North Carolina; pop. 5520.

East Windsor. 1 Town, N cen. Hartford co., N Connecticut, on Connecticut river; pop. 7500.

2 Former city, Essex co., SE Ontario, Canada; annexed to Windsor 1935.

East′wood (ēst′wŏŏd). Urban district, Nottinghamshire, N cen. England, 8 m. NW of Nottingham; pop. 9896; in coal-mining section.

Ea′ton (ē′t'n). **1** County in Michigan. See *Table* at MICHIGAN.

2 Village, ⊗ of Preble co., SW Ohio, 22 m. W of Dayton; pop. 5034; founded 1806; raw fur market.

Eaton Rapids. City, Eaton co., S Michigan, 15 m. SSW of Lansing; pop. 4052; woolen mills.

Ea′ton·ton (ē′t'n·tŭn). City, ⊗ of Putnam co., cen. Georgia, 38 m. NNE of Macon; pop. 3612.

Ea′ton·town (ē′t'n·toun). Borough, Monmouth co., E cen. New Jersey, 6 m. NNW of Asbury Park; pop. 10,334.

Eau Claire (ō′ klâr′). **1** River ab. 70 m. long, W cen. Wisconsin; rises in Clark co., flows W into Chippewa river at Eau Claire. See *Table* at WISCONSIN.

2 County in Wisconsin.

3 Commercial and industrial city, ⊗ of Eau Claire co., W Wisconsin, on Chippewa river; pop. 37,987; settled in 1840's; developed as outlet for Chippewa lumber district. Wisconsin State University (1916; coed.).

Eau Gal′lie (ō′ găl′ĭ). City, Brevard co., cen. E Florida, SSE of Orlando; pop. 12,300.

Eaux–Bonnes (ō′bôn′). Town, Basses-Pyrénées dept., SW France, ab. 23 m. S of Pau; pop. 174; thermal mineral waters (50° to 90°) famous since 14th cent.; ab. 5 m. to the SW is the watering place of **Eaux–Chaudes** (ō′shōd′), with warm sulfur springs (52° to 97°).

Eaux Vives (ō′ vēv′). Former commune, Geneva canton, Switzerland; now in E part of city of Geneva.

L′auze′ (à′ōz′). Commune, W Gers dept., SW France, 15 m. NW of Auch; pop. 1520; ancient capital of Aquitania Tertia.

Eba, Mount. See MOUNT EBA.

E′bal, Mount (ē′băl). Mountain 3084 ft. in Samaria, Palestine, N of Nablus.

Eb′bw (ĕb′ŏŏ). River 24 m. long, NW Monmouthshire, W England; flows S into the Usk S of Newport.

Ebbw Vale. Urban district, Monmouthshire, W England, on the Ebbw 35 m. NW of Bristol; pop. 29,205; coal and iron mines; steelworks.

Eben Emael, Fort. See FORT EBEN EMAEL.

Eb′ens·burg (ĕb′ĕnz·bûrg). Borough, ⊗ of Cambria co., SW cen. Pennsylvania, 15 m. NE of Johnstown; pop. 4111.

E′bers·wal′de (ā′bĕrs·väl′dĕ). City, E Germany, in the former Potsdam govt. dist., Brandenburg prov., Prussia, 28 m. NE of Berlin; pop. 29,571; 14th-cent. Gothic church; summer resort for Berliners; prehistoric (1050–850 B.C.) gold artifacts found here 1913.

E′bing·en (ā′bĭng·ĕn). City, Baden-Württemberg state, West Germany, 41 m. S of Stuttgart; pop. 12,128; manufactures knitted goods, velvet, and precision tools.

E′bi Nor (ā′bĕ nōr′). Salt lake (*nor*), W Dzungaria, NW Sinkiang, W China, bet. the Dzungarian Ala Tau Mts. and N ranges of Tien Shan; alt. 2300 ft.

Eblana. See DUBLIN.

E′bo·la (ĕb′ō·là). Headstream of the Mongala river (*q.v.*), N Congo; flows W.

E′bo·li (ā′bō·lē). Commune, Salerno prov., Campania, S Italy, 16 m. ESE of Salerno; pop. 14,727; old castle.

Eb′on (ĕb′ŭn). Atoll at S end of Ralik Chain, Marshall Is., W Pacific Ocean; ab. 4°32′N lat., 300 m. SSE of Kwajalein; 22 islets (largest Ebon).

Ebora. See EVORA.

Eboracum. See YORK, England.

Éboulements, Les. See LES ÉBOULEMENTS.

E′bro (ā′brō; *Span.* ā′vrō); *anc.* **I·be′rus** (ī·bē′rŭs). River ab. 480 m. long in NE Spain; rises in the Cantabrian Mts. in Santander prov., flows ESE into Mediterranean Sea ab. 80 m. SW of Barcelona; has drainage basin of ab. 32,000 sq. m.; chief tributaries the Aragon,

Segre, and Jalón rivers; has long been used for irrigation; navigable to seafaring vessels as far as Tortosa (ab. 22 m. from its mouth) and to small boats as far as Tudela (in Navarra prov.).

Ebudae. See HEBRIDES.

Eb′u·ra′cum (ĕb′ū·rā′kŭm). Var. of *Eboracum:* see YORK, England.

Eburodunum. 1 See EMBRUN commune, France.

2 See YVERDON commune, Switzerland.

Ebusus. See IVIZA.

Ecbatana. See HAMADAN.

Ec′cle·fech′an (ĕk″l·fĕk′ăn; *Scot.* -fĕk′ăn). Village near Dumfries, Dumfries co., S Scotland; birthplace of Thomas Carlyle.

Ec′cles (ĕk′'lz). Municipal borough, Lancashire, W England, on the Irwell 4 m. W of Manchester; pop. 43,927; cotton and silk textiles.

Ec′cle·shall (ĕk″l·shăl; -shôl). Market town, Staffordshire, England, 7 m. NW of Stafford; pop. 3532; walls and moat of castle which was episcopal residence 13th cent. to 1867.

E·cha′gue (â·chä′gwå). Municipality, S Isabela prov., Luzon, Phil. Is. on W bank of Cagayan river 34 m. S of Ilagan; pop. 16,249; taken by Americans June 15, 1945.

Ech′mi·a·dzin′ (ĕch′mē·ä·dzēn′) *or* **Ej′mi·a·dzin′** (ĕj′-). Monastery, Armenian S.S.R., Soviet Union, near Vagarshapat at the foot of Mt. Alagöz, 12 m. W of Yerevan; seat of the Armenian patriarch; founded by Gregory the Illuminator c. 302 A.D.; contains large and valuable library of Armenian literature.

Ech′o, Lake (ĕk′ō). Lake, cen. Tasmania, Australia, ab. 60 m. NW of Hobart; source of Dee river, a tributary of the Derwent.

Echo Canyon. Ravine in Summit co., NE Utah, with walls 800 to 1200 ft. high; railroad passes through it; important in early history of the state.

Echo Dam. Dam completed 1930 across Weber river, Summit co., N Utah, NE of Salt Lake City; height 125 ft.; impounds water for irrigation, forming **Echo Reservoir.**

Echo Lake. Small lake, alt. 1931 ft., N Grafton co., W New Hampshire, in White Mts. near Franconia; shut in by mountains (Cannon Mt. on W).

Ech′ols (ĕk′lz). County in Georgia. See *Table* at GEORGIA.

Echt (ĕkt). Commune, Limburg prov., SE Netherlands, 20 m. NE of Maastricht; pop. 9420.

Ech′ter·nach (ĕk′tĕr·näk). Town, NE Luxembourg, Europe, on the Sauer 18 m. NE of Luxembourg city; pop. 3070; an old town famous for its festival on Whit-Tuesday; place where St. Willibrord is buried. Figured in fighting in Battle of the Bulge 1944–45.

E·chu′ca (ĕ·chōō′kà). Town, N Victoria, SE Australia, on Murray river 112 m. N of Melbourne; pop. 4411; trades in wool, wine, and timber.

É′ci·ja (ā′thē·hä; ĕ′thē·hä); *anc.* **As′ti·gi** (ăs′tĭ·jī). Manufacturing city, Sevilla prov., SW Spain, 48 m. ENE of Seville; pop. 34,895; episcopal see; ancient Roman colony; Roman ruins.

Eck′ern·för′de (ĕk′ĕrn·fûr′dĕ). Seaport, Schleswig-Holstein, northwestern Germany, on Kiel Bay, just NW of Kiel; pop. 7328.

Eckmühl. See EGGMÜHL.

Écluse. See SLUIS.

Ec′no·mus (ĕk′nō·mŭs). Hill near Licata, S Sicily; naval battle in nearby waters 256 B.C. in which Roman fleet defeated the Carthaginians.

E·con′o·my (ē·kŏn′ō·mĭ). Borough, Beaver co., W Pennsylvania, NW of Pittsburgh; pop. 5925. See AMBRIDGE.

E′corse (ē′kôrs). City, Wayne co., SE Michigan, on Detroit river 8 m. SW of Detroit; pop. 17,328; steel manufacturing.

Écrins, Barre des. See BARRE DES ÉCRINS.

Ec′tor (ĕk′tēr). County in Texas. See *Table* at TEXAS.

Ec'ua·dor (ĕk'wȧ·dôr; *Span.* ā'kwä·thôr'). Republic, NW South America; bounded on N by Colombia, on E and S by Peru, and on W by the Pacific Ocean; 104,510 sq. m.; pop. (1944 est.) 3,171,367; ✳ Quito; divided into the following 17 provinces and one territory (for pronunciation of their names, see their individual entries):

NAME	LOCA-TION	AREA[1]	POP.[1]	CAPITAL
Azuay	S	3,011	263,873	Cuenca
Bolívar	W	1,246	110,270	Guaranda
Cañar	W cen.	1,034	125,109	Azogues
Carchi	N	1,383	79,155	Tulcán
Chimborazo	cen.	2,379	276,685	Riobamba
Cotopaxi	cen.	1,781	202,385	Latacunga
El Oro	SW	2,288	83,712	Machala
Esmeraldas	NW	6,134	59,246	Esmeraldas
Guayas	W	8,208	431,903	Guayaquil
Imbabura	N	1,854	148,993	Ibarra
Loja	SW	4,438	212,429	Loja
Los Ríos	W cen.	2,292	134,805	Babahoyo
Manabí	W	7,306	331,153	Portoviejo
Napo-Pastaza	E	[2]	[2]	Tena
Pichincha	N cen.	6,474	321,569	Quito
Santiago-Zamora	E	[2]	[2]	Macas
Tungurahua	cen.	1,237	209,872	Ambato
Colón (territory)[3]		3,029	661	San Cristóbal

[1] Area in sq. m. Pop. is 1944 est.
[2] Napo-Pastaza and Santiago-Zamora constitute the Eastern Region (*Span.* Región Oriental). Combined area is 50,416 sq. m.; combined pop. (1944 est.) is 179,433.
[3] Comprises the Galápagos Is.

Mountains: Central range of the Andes Mts. with highest volcanic peaks Chimborazo 20,702 ft., Cotopaxi 19,498 ft., Cayambe 19,160 ft., Sangay 19,144 ft.; country subject often to volcanic disturbances and earthquakes. *Rivers:* Short streams flowing W to Pacific, in-

cluding the Esmeraldas, with its tributary the Daule in N, and the Guayas flowing to wide Gulf of Guayaquil in SW; streams on E slope of Andes in Eastern Region, tributaries of the Amazon and of its headstream the Marañón, most important being the Napo and its tributary the Curaray, the Tigre, Pastaza, Morona (Makumma in Ecuador), and Santiago (Zamora in Ecuador). *Island possessions:* The Galápagos Is. (*q.v.*) ab. 600 m.

off the coast, constituting Colón territory. *Chief natural resources:* Cacao, coffee, ivory nuts, hats, balsa wood, petroleum, and several minerals, esp. copper and lead. *Chief cities:* Quito (nearly on the equator, alt. ab. 9300 ft.), Guayaquil, Cuenca, Ambato, Riobamba, Loja, Latacunga.

History: Quito, ancient name of Ecuador, conquered by Peru before advent of Spanish; conquered by Spanish 1534; a presidency under viceroyalty of Peru, later of New Granada; after earlier unsuccessful risings, won final independence from Spain at battle of Mt. Pichincha May 24, 1822; part of Great Colombia until 1830 when it seceded to become republic of Ecuador; in league with Chile and Peru in war against Spain 1866; its political history a turbulent one; its boundaries, especially with Peru, a long-standing cause of friction with its neighbors; boundary with Colombia settled 1916 but that with Peru, in spite of treaties of 1860, 1887, and 1890, not settled until July 1945 when the larger part of the region bet. the Marañón and the Putumayo was assigned to Peru.

E·dam' (à·dăm'; *Angl.* ē'dăm, ē'dăm). Commune and seaport, North Holland prov., W Netherlands, on the IJsselmeer; pop. 8295; market for the cheese to which it gives its name (Edam cheese).

Ed'couch (ĕd'kouch). Town, Hidalgo co., S Texas, 20 m. ENE of McAllen; pop. 2814; railroad junction.

Ed Da'mer (ĕd dä'mĕr; *Arab.* ăd dä'mŭr). Town, ✳ of Northern Province, N Sudan, on the Nile.

Ed Deb'ba (ĕd dĕb'à; *Arab.* ăd dăb'bà, -bă). Town, N cen. Sudan, in Northern Province, on the Nile WSW of Merowe.

Ed'dra·chil'lis Bay (ĕd'rà·kĭl'ĭs). Bay on NW coast of Scotland, in Sutherland co.

Ed Du·eim' *or* **El Du·eim'** (ĕd dōō·ām'; *Arab.* ăd dōō·wĭm' -wām'). Town, Blue Nile prov., E Sudan, on White Nile; ✳ of former White Nile prov.; pop. ab. 10,000.

Ed'dy (ĕd'ĭ). Name of counties in two states of the U.S. See *Tables* at NEW MEXICO and NORTH DAKOTA.

Eddy Mountain. Peak 9151 ft. in S cen. Siskiyou co., N California.

Ed'dy·stone (ĕd'ĭ·stŏn). Borough, Delaware co., SE Pennsylvania, on Delaware river 12 m. WSW of Philadelphia; pop. 3006; locomotive works; munitions center during World War I.

Ed'dy·stone Rock (ĕd'ĭ·stŏn; *Brit.* -stŭn). Rocky islet in the English Channel 14 m. SSW of Plymouth; lighthouse.

Ed'dy·ville (ĕd'ĭ·vĭl; *Sou. also* -v'l). City, ⊗ of Lyon co., W Kentucky, on Cumberland river 30 m. E of Paducah; pop. 1858.

E'de (ā'dĕ). Commune, Gelderland prov., E Netherlands, 13 m. NW of Arnhem; pop. (1939) 36,436.

E'de (ā'dà). City, Oyo prov., W Western Region, Nigeria, 45 m. NNE of Ibadan; pop. 52,392; a Yoruba city.

E·dé'a (à·dā'à). Town, E Cameroun, W Africa, on railroad ab. 40 m. SE of Douala.

E'den (ē'd'n). **1** Village, Concho co., W cen. Texas, 38 m. ESE of San Angelo; pop. 1486; railroad terminus; sheep and goats, cotton.
2 Seaport town with large and safe harbor on Twofold Bay, SE New South Wales, SE Australia.
3 River ab. 65 m. long in Westmorland and Cumberland, NW England, flowing N into head of Solway Firth.
4 River 18 m. long in Fife co., E Scotland, flows NE into St. Andrews Bay.

E'den Reservoir (ē'd'n). Reservoir in a tributary of Green river, NW Sweetwater co., SW Wyoming.

E'den·ton (ē'd'n·tŭn). Town, ⊗ of Chowan co., NE North Carolina, on Albemarle Sound near mouth of Chowan river; pop. 4454; formerly horse-racing center; produces peanuts, cotton; shad and herring fisheries. Settled 1658; capital of colony 1722–66; scene of "Eden-

ton tea party" Oct. 25, 1774, a meeting of 51 ladies who signed a pact resolving not to drink tea or wear clothing made in England until the tax on tea should be repealed.

E′der (ā′dĕr). River ab. 84 m. long, chiefly in Hesse, W Germany; flows E to join the Fulda just S of Kassel; in its course is Eder reservoir dam, largest in Germany, which was bombed by R.A.F. May 16, 1943.

E·des′sa (ĕ·dĕs′à; *Mod. Gr.* ä′thä·sä) *or* **Vo′de·na′** (vô′thä·nä′). City, * of Pella dept., W Macedonia, Greece, 48 m. WNW of Salonika; pop. 13,115; textiles, tobacco; anciently a capital of Macedonian kings; scene of assassination of Philip II of Macedon 336 B.C.

Edessa. Ancient city of NW Mesopotamia, now in SE Turkey in Asia. See URFA.

Edfu. See IDFU.

Ed′gar (ĕd′gẽr). County in Illinois. See *Table* at ILLINOIS.

Ed′gard (ĕd′gärd). Village, ⊗ of Saint John the Baptist parish, SE Louisiana; pop. (est.) 750.

Ed′gar·town′ (ĕd′gẽr·toun′). Town, ⊗ of Dukes co., SE Massachusetts, E Martha's Vineyard on **Edgartown Harbor**, an inlet of Nantucket Sound; pop. 1474.

Edge′combe (ĕj′kŭm). County in North Carolina. See *Table* at NORTH CAROLINA.

Edge′cumbe, Mount (ĕj′kŭm). Extinct volcano 3467 ft. at S end of Kruzof I. opp. Sitka, SE Alaska; known also as **Cape Edgecumbe.**

Edge′field (ĕj′fēld). **1** County in South Carolina. See *Table* at SOUTH CAROLINA.
2 Town, its ⊗, W South Carolina, 21 m. NW of Aiken; pop. 2876; agriculture.

Edge Hill *or* **Edge′hill′.** Ridge in S Warwickshire, cen. England, 7 m. NW of Banbury; scene of an indecisive battle Oct. 23, 1642 bet. Royalists under Charles I and forces of Parliament under earl of Essex.

Edge Island. Island 1970 sq. m., SE Spitsbergen archipelago, Arctic Ocean.

Edge′mont (ĕj′mŏnt). City, Fall River co., SW corner of South Dakota, near Black Hills 22 m. WSW of Hot Springs; pop. 1772; sanitarium.

Edg′er·ton (ĕj′ẽr·t'n; -tŭn). City, Rock co., S Wisconsin, 11 m. N of Janesville; pop. 4000; tobacco.

Edge′wa′ter (ĕj′wô′tẽr; -wŏt′ẽr). **1** Town, Jefferson co., cen. Colorado, 5 m. W of Denver; pop. 4314.
2 Borough, Bergen co., NE corner of New Jersey, on Hudson river 7 m. NNE of Jersey City; pop. 4113; manufactures linseed and castor oil, aluminum.

Edge′wood (ĕj′wŏŏd). **1** Village, S Harford co., NE Maryland, 18 m. NE of Baltimore; pop. 1670; site of **Edgewood Arsenal,** with Army Chemical Center and Chemical Corps School.
2 Borough, Allegheny co., SW Pennsylvania, 7 m. E of Pittsburgh; pop. 5124.

Edge′worth (ĕj′wûrth). Borough, Allegheny co., SW Pennsylvania, on Ohio river 13 m. WNW of Pittsburgh; pop. 2030; birthplace of Ethelbert Nevin.

E·di′na (ĕ·dī′nà). **1** Village, Hennepin co., SE cen. Minnesota, 8 m. SW of Minneapolis; pop. 28,501.
2 City, ⊗ of Knox co., NE Missouri, 22 m. E of Kirksville; pop. 1457.

Ed′in·bor′o (ĕd′'n·bûr′ô). Borough, Erie co., NW corner of Pennsylvania, on a lake ab. 18 m. S of Erie; pop. 1703; Edinboro State College (1859; coed.).

Ed′in·burg (ĕd′'n·bûrg). **1** Town, Bartholomew and Johnson cos., cen. Indiana, 30 m. SSE of Indianapolis; pop. 3664; veneer mill, furniture factory.
2 City, ⊗ of Hidalgo co., S Texas, 10 m. NNE of McAllen; pop. 18,706; trade center for agricultural region.

Ed′in·burgh (ĕd′'n·bûr′ô; *Brit.* -bŭ·rŭ, -brŭ). **1** *or* **Ed′in·burgh·shire** (-shĩr). See MIDLOTHIAN.
2 City and burgh, * of Scotland and ⊗ of Midlothian co., SE Scotland, on S shore of Firth of Forth; pop. (1931) 439,010, (1951) 466,770; built on several hills; the Old Town is on a rock, very steep on W end where castle stands and sloping toward the E where Holyrood palace

is located; New Town is W of the castle rock, separated from it by a valley, now site of public gardens; important printing and publishing center; university (1583).

History: Probably originated with castle erected by Edwin of Northumbria who defeated the Picts early in 7th cent. A.D.; royal residence of Malcolm Canmore in 11th cent.; Canongate, later annexed to Edinburgh, rose about the abbey of Holyrood (*q.v.*); granted charter and rights over town of Leith by Robert the Bruce; capital of Scottish kingdom and meeting place of Parliament after 1436; lost political importance after accession of James VI to English throne 1603 and union of Scotland (*q.v.*) with England 1707; proclaimed Charles II king 1649 and captured by Cromwell 1650; New Town built in 18th cent.; became a literary and educational center (Athens of the North).

Ed′ing·ton (ĕd′ĭng·tŭn). Village and parish, Wiltshire, S England; 14th-cent. priory church; scene of Alfred's victory over the Danes 878.

E·dir′ne (ĕ·dĭr′nĕ; *Turkish* ĕ·dĕr′nĕ); *formerly* **A′dri·an·o′ple** (ā′drĭ·ăn·ō′p'l). **1** Vilayet, W Turkey in Europe, a part of E Thrace; 2920 sq. m.; pop. 184,840.
2 *anc.* **A′dri·an·op′o·lis** (ā′drĭ·ăn·ŏp′ō·lĭs) *or* **Ha′dri·an·op′o·lis** (hā′drĭ·ăn·ŏp′ō·lĭs). City, its *, on both banks of the Tundzha river at its confluence with the Maritsa (Meriç) 130 m. NW of İstanbul, NW Turkey in Europe; pop. (1940) 45,168; varied manufactures; exports fruits, cotton, raw silk, attar of roses.

History: Early Thracian town rebuilt and renamed by Roman emperor Hadrian c. 125 A.D.; scene of the important battle in which the Roman emperor Valens fell before the Visigoths who had crossed the Danube 378; scene of defeat of the Bulgarian dynasty of Asen by the Greek emperor Theodore II 1254; conquered by the Avars, Bulgarians, and Crusaders, became Turkish 1361; residence of sultans until 1453; captured by the Russians 1829, 1879; by Treaty of Adrianople 1829 Russia secured control of Danube mouths; taken by Bulgaria 1913, restored to Turks 1922.

Ed′i·son (ĕd′ĭ·s'n). Urban township, Middlesex co., cen. New Jersey, SW of Elizabeth; pop. 44,799.

Ed′is·to (ĕd′ĭs·tō). River ab. 150 m. long, S and SW South Carolina; rises (**South Fork Edisto**) in E Edgefield co., flows SE into Atlantic Ocean.

Edisto Island. 1 Island at mouth of Edisto river, S extremity of Charleston co., SE South Carolina.
2 Village on the island, in Edisto Island township.

E′dith·burg (ē′dĭth·bûrg). Town, SE South Australia, on Gulf of St. Vincent opp. Adelaide; pop. 610; resort.

E′dith Cav′ell, Mount (ē′dĭth kăv′'l). Peak 11,033 ft. in Jasper National Park, SW Alberta, Canada, near British Columbia border.

Ed′mond (ĕd′mŭnd). City, Oklahoma co., cen. Oklahoma, 13 m. N of Oklahoma City; pop. 8577; gas and oil wells. Central State College (1891; coed.).

Ed′monds (ĕd′mŭndz). City, Snohomish co., NW cen. Washington, N of Seattle; pop. 8016.

Ed′mon·son (ĕd′mŭn·s'n). County in Kentucky. See *Table* at KENTUCKY.

Ed′mon·ton (ĕd′mŭn·tŭn). **1** City, ⊗ of Metcalfe co., S Kentucky; pop. 749.
2 City, * of Alberta, Canada, in S cen. part of province on both banks of North Saskatchewan river; pop. 159,631; portion on S bank is former town of **Strath·co′na** (străth·kō′nà), annexed 1911; most important rail and air center in Canadian Northwest; distribution point of rich farm country and coal-mining region, hub of large fur trade; varied manufactures; seat of University of Alberta (1906) and of a Jesuit college, an affiliate of Laval University. Originally established 1795 as a fort and trading post of the Hudson's Bay Co.
3 Municipal borough, Middlesex, SE England, on New river just N of London; pop. 77,658, (1951) 104,244; part of Greater London; residence of Charles Lamb, William Cowper, and John Keats.

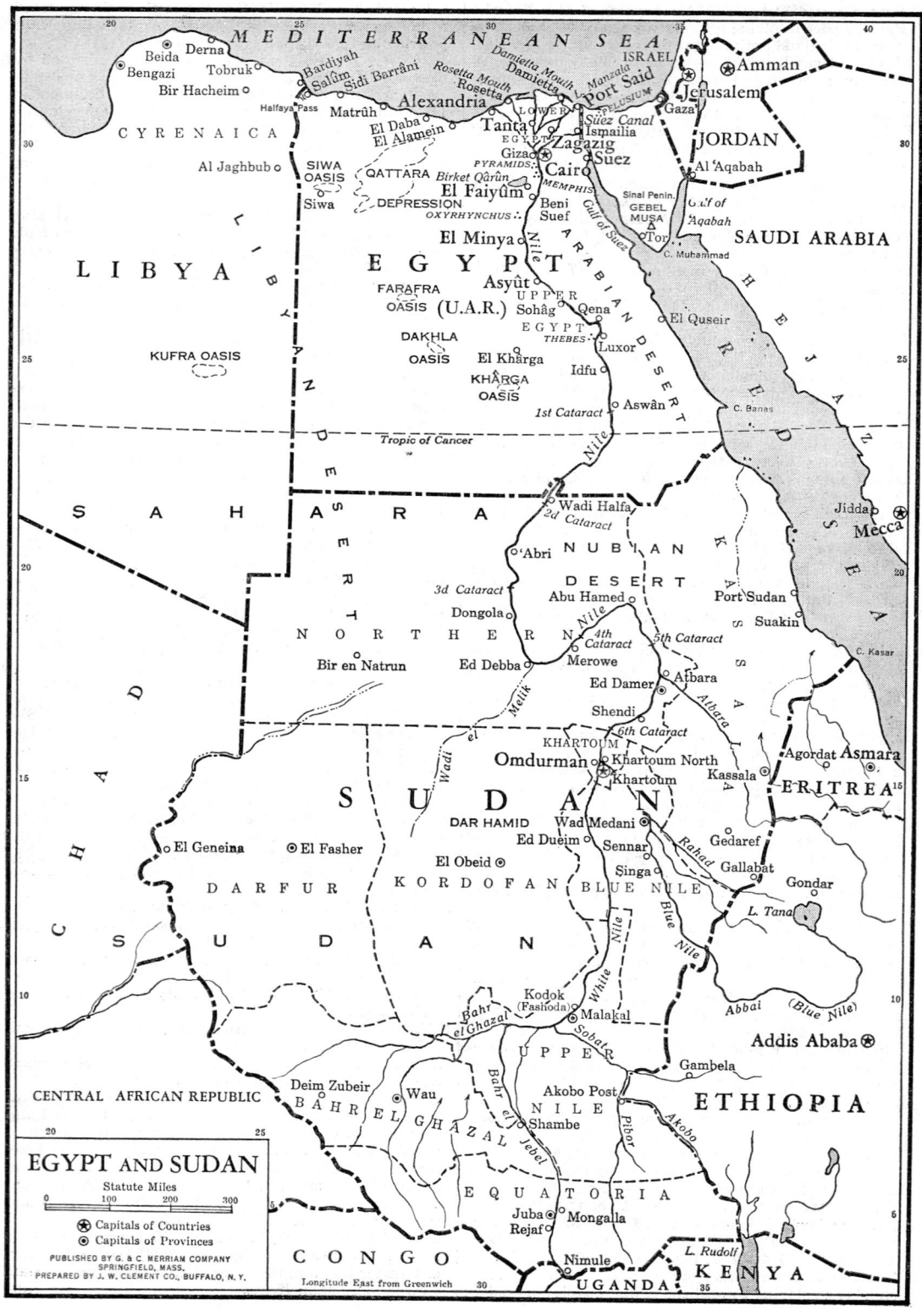

EGYPT AND SUDAN

Statute Miles

0   100   200   300

⊛ Capitals of Countries
⊙ Capitals of Provinces

PUBLISHED BY G. & C. MERRIAM COMPANY
SPRINGFIELD, MASS.
PREPARED BY J. W. CLEMENT CO., BUFFALO, N. Y.

Longitude East from Greenwich

Ed'munds (ĕd'mŭndz). County in South Dakota. See *Table* at SOUTH DAKOTA.

Ed'munds·ton (ĕd'mŭn[d]·stŭn). Town, ⊗ of Madawaska co., NW New Brunswick, Canada, on upper St. John river across from NE Maine; pop. 10,753; lumber.

Ed'na (ĕd'nà). City, ⊗ of Jackson co., SE Texas, 25 m. ENE of Victoria; pop. 5038.

Edo. See TOKYO.

E'dom (ē'dŭm); *also known as* **Se'ir** (sē'ĭr). Ancient country S of Dead Sea, along both sides of the Wadi el 'Araba, with indefinite boundaries; on NE touched Moab, on E Arabia, and on W the Sinai Penin.; mountainous and largely barren; included summits of Hor and Seir; according to Bible (*Gen.* xxxvi) the land given to Esau (or Edom); chief town and capital Sela (Petra); with some shifting of boundaries to include S Judaea, became known in Maccabean and Roman times as Idumaea (*q.v.*).

E'dre·mit' (ĕ'drĕ·mēt'); *anc.* **Ad'ra·myt'ti·um** (ăd'rà·mĭt'ĭ·ŭm). Town, Balıkesir vilayet, NW Turkey in Asia, near Aegean Sea at head of Gulf of Edremit; pop. 12,603.

Edremit, *anc.* **Adramyttium, Gulf of.** Inlet of Aegean Sea on W coast of Turkey in Asia, opp. N coast of island of Lesbos.

Ed'sel Ford Ranges (ĕd's'l fôrd'). Mountain groups and ranges, NW Marie Byrd Land, Antarctica; extend S from shelf ice at long. 140° to 145°W and lat. 76° to 78°S; highest peak ab. 14,000 ft.

Edsin. See ETSIN.

E·du'ni, Mount (ĕ·dōō'nĭ). Peak 7200 ft. in W Mackenzie District, Northwest Territories, Canada, in NE part of Mackenzie Mts.

Ed'ward, Lake (ĕd'wĕrd). Lake in E cen. Africa, on the boundary between NE Congo and SW Uganda, S of Lake Albert with which it is connected by the Semliki river; ab. 830 sq. m.; discovered by Stanley 1889; formerly called **Al'bert Ed'ward Ny·an'za** (ăl'bĕrt ĕd'wĕrd nĭ·ăn'zà; nĭ-).

Edward VIII Bay. Inlet of Indian Ocean on coast of Antarctica, ab. 12 m. wide, bet. Kemp Coast and Enderby Land, at ab. 57°20′E.

Edwardesabad. See BANNU.

Ed'wards (ĕd'wĕrdz). Name of counties in three states of the U.S. See *Tables* at ILLINOIS, KANSAS, TEXAS.

Edward VII Peninsula; *formerly* **King Edward VII Land.** Peninsula, Marie Byrd Land, on E shore of Ross Sea, Antarctica, in lat. 77°45′S, long. 156°W; claimed for Britain by Capt. Scott 1902; included in Ross Dependency (*q.v.*).

Edwards Plateau. Highland region of W Texas, alt. bet. 2000 and 5000 ft.; source of tributaries of the Colorado, Nueces, and Rio Grande rivers and bordered on the W by the Pecos; centers in Schleicher and Sutton cos.

Ed'wards·ville (ĕd'wĕrdz·vĭl). **1** City, ⊗ of Madison co., SW Illinois, 17 m. NE of East St. Louis; pop. 9996; coal mining; radiators and brass products.

2 Borough, Luzerne co., E Pennsylvania, 3 m. WNW of Wilkes-Barre; pop. 5711; coal mining.

Eeck'e·ren (āk'ĕ·rĕ[n]). Commune, Antwerp prov., N Belgium; pop. 13,596; a N suburb of Antwerp.

Eek'loo (āk'lō). Commune, East Flanders prov., NW cen. Belgium, 11 m. NW of Gent; pop. 14,657.

Eel (ēl). River, NW California; rises in N Mendocino co., flows NW into Pacific Ocean.

Ee'ragh (ē'răk). See ARAN ISLANDS.

Eesti. See ESTONIA.

Ees'ti·maa' (ās'tĭ·mä'). = *Eesti:* see ESTONIA.

E·fa'te (ĕ·fä'tà) *or* **Va'té'** (*Fr.* và·tā'). Island, cen. New Hebrides Is., SW Pacific Ocean; 26 m. long by 14 m. wide; 200 sq. m.; pop. (native; 1938 est.) 2483; chief town Vila, which is the administrative center of New Hebrides Is.; good harbors at Vila and Havannah.

Ef'fing·ham (ĕf'ĭng·hăm). **1** Name of counties in two states of the U.S. See *Tables* at GEORGIA and ILLINOIS.

2 City, ⊗ of Effingham co., SE cen. Illinois; pop. 8172.

E·fo'gi (?ĕ·fō'gĭ). Village in Owen Stanley Range, E Papua, New Guinea, 25 m. NE of Port Moresby near Kokoda; severe fighting Sept.–Oct. 1942.

E'ga·di Islands (ĕg'à·dĭ); *Ital.* **I'so·le E'ga·di** (ē'zŏ·lâ ā'gä·dē); *Eng.* **Ae·ga'di·an Isles** (ĕ·gā'dĭ·ăn); *anc.* **Ae·ga'tes** (ĕ·gā'tēz). Group of islands in Mediterranean Sea off W coast of Sicily; 15 sq. m.; pop. 6196; politically constitute Favignana commune in Trapani prov., NW Sicily, Italy; chief islands Marettimo and Favignana. Scene of naval battle in which Romans destroyed the Carthaginian fleet thus terminating the First Punic War 241 B.C.

E'ge·des·min'de (ā'gĕ·thĕs·mēn'ĕ). Danish settlement on S Disko Bay, W Greenland; pop. 1646.

Egee, Isole. See AEGEAN ISLANDS.

E'ger (ā'gĕr). **1** River in Germany and Czechoslovakia. (*q.v.*).

2 City in Czechoslovakia. See CHEB.

E'ger (ĕ'gĕr); *Ger.* **Er'lau** (ĕr'lou). City, N cen. Hungary, 25 m. SW of Miskolc; pop. 30,150; exports wine.

Egerdir. Var. of EĞRIDIR.

E'ger·sund' (ā'gĕr·sōōn'). Seaport town, Rogaland co., SW Norway, 35 m. S of Stavanger; pop. 3401; fisheries.

Eg'gen·berg (ĕg'ĕn·bĕrk). Former commune, Styria prov., Austria, now a WNW section of Graz.

Eg'gerts·ville (ĕg'ĕrts·vĭl). Urban community (unincorp.), Erie co., New York, E of Buffalo; pop. 44,807.

Egg Harbor (ĕg). Early name of Somers Point, New Jersey.

Egg Harbor City. City, Atlantic co., SE New Jersey, 17 m. NW of Atlantic City; pop. 4416; founded by German immigrants 1850; vineyards.

Egg Island. Barren rock off Niihau, NW Hawaii. See LEHUA ISLAND.

Egg Island Point. Point on S coast of Cumberland co., SW New Jersey, extending into Delaware Bay.

Egg'mühl (ĕk'mül) *or* **Eck'mühl.** Village, Bavaria, Germany, S of Regensburg; scene of battle Apr. 22, 1809 in which French, Bavarians, and Württembergers under Napoleon defeated Austrians under Archduke Charles.

Eg'ham (ĕg'ăm). Urban district, Surrey, S England, on the Thames 20 m. WSW of London; pop. 24,515; the field of Runnymede (*q.v.*) lies along the riverside; Royal Holloway College for Women (1886).

Eg'ma Plateau (ĕg'mà). Highland region of cen. Sinai Penin., NE Egypt; highest point Ras el Geneina 5328 ft.

Eg'mont (ĕg'mŏnt); *Maori* **Ta'ra·na'ki** (tä'rä·nä'kĕ). Volcanic peak 8260 ft. in W cen. North I., New Zealand; noted for its symmetry and beauty.

Egmont, Cape. Cape on SW cen. coast of North I., New Zealand, at end of W bulge of North I.

Egmont Cape. **1** Cape, NE Cape Breton I., Nova Scotia, SE Canada.

2 Cape at S end of **Egmont Bay** (inlet of Northumberland Strait). W Prince Edward I., SE Canada.

Egorevsk. See YEGOREVSK.

Eg're·mont (ĕg'rĕ·mŏnt). Parish, formerly urban district, Cumberland, NW England, on the Ehen 38 m. SW of Carlisle; pop. 6213.

Eğ'ri·dir' (ā'rĭ·dĭr'). Town, Isparta vilayet, Turkey in Asia, at S end of Eğridir Lake; pop. 5793.

Eğridir Lake; *Turk.* **Eğridir Gö·lü'** (gù·lü'). Lake (*gölü*) in W Turkey in Asia, NE of Isparta; 30 m. long by 3 to 10 m. wide; no known outlet.

Egripos. See EVRIPOS.

E'gypt (ē'jĭpt); *Arab.* **El Qutr el Mas'ri** (ăl kōōt'răl mĭs'rē); *anc.* **Ae·gyp'tus** (ĕ·jĭp'tŭs). Country, NE Africa with small part in NE (Sinai Penin.) in Asia; coextensive (since 1961) with United Arab Republic; area ab. 386,198 sq. m., of which the cultivated and settled area is only ab. 13,574 sq. m. (1937) 15,920,694; ✳ Cairo; comprises: **Lower Egypt** (the Nile Delta), area 8483 sq. m., pop. 7,138,676; **Upper Egypt** (the Nile

valley S of 30°N lat.); area 4773 sq. m., pop. 6,423,412; governorates (Cairo, Alexandria, Damietta, Suez, Canal), area 139 sq. m., pop. 2,248,996; and frontier provinces and district, area 179 sq. m., pop. 109,610; divided into the following administrative divisions (for pronunciation of their names, see their individual entries):

NAME	LOCATION IN EGYPT	AREA IN SQ. M.	POP. (1937 CENSUS)	CAPITAL
GOVERNORATES¹				
Alexandria	N	29	685,736	
Cairo	N	62	1,312,096	
Canal¹	NE	40	161,146	
Damietta	N	1	40,332	
Suez	NE	7	49,686	
LOWER EGYPT—PROVINCES				
Beheira	N	1,719	1,061,596	Damanhûr
Daqahlîya	N	1,023	1,218,502	El Mansûra
Gharbîya	N	2,818	1,967,894	Tanta
Minûfîya	N	622	1,159,701	Shibin el Kôm
Qalyubîya	N	368	610,157	Benha
Sharqîya	N	1,933	1,120,826	Zagazig
UPPER EGYPT—PROVINCES				
Aswân	SE	363	305,096	Aswân
Asyût	cen.	812	1,205,321	Asyût
Beni Suef	N	423	561,312	Beni Suef
Faiyûm	N	670	602,122	El Faiyûm
Girga	cen.	609	1,118,402	Girga
Giza	N	409	685,331	Giza
Minya	cen.	782	928,259	El Minya
Qena	E cen.	705	1,017,569	Qena
FRONTIER PROVINCES AND DISTRICT				
Red Sea District	E	24	9,914	
Sinai Province	NE	35	18,011	
Southern Desert Province²	S	47	29,109	
Western Desert Province³	W	73	52,576	

¹ Coextensive with cities of the same name, with exception of governorate of Canal which comprises cities of Port Said and Ismailia.
² Includes Dakhla and Khârga oases.
³ Includes Siwa, Baharîya, and Farafra oases.

Mountains: Only mountains are those in Sinai Penin. in NE (bet. Gulf of Suez on W and Gulf of 'Aqaba on E) where Egma Plateau culminates in Ras el Geneina 5328 ft. and Gebel Musa group (Biblical Mt. Sinai) 8652 ft. and in the range (3000 to 7165 ft.) extending along Red Sea coast from Suez to border of Republic of Sudan. *Deserts:* Has 3 large deserts: (1) Arabian, in E bet. the Nile and the mountains along the Red Sea and Gulf of Suez; (2) Western, in W cen. part; (3) E part of Libyan Desert along SW border; best known oases the Khârga (S cen. part), Dakhla (cen.), Farafra (W cen.), and Siwa (NW); bet. Western Desert and Mediterranean coast is the remarkable Qattara Depression. *Rivers:* Only its great river the Nile, which has no tributaries of importance in Egypt. SW of Cairo on W bank of the Nile near El Faiyûm is the Birket Qârûn (what is left of ancient Lake Moeris). *Economic resources:* Cotton, grains (wheat, rice, barley, millet, maize), and vegetables. *Chief cities:* Cairo, Alexandria, Port Said, Tanta, El Mansûra, El Faiyûm.

History: A very ancient kingdom, by about 3000 B.C. Egypt had developed one of the two early civilizations of ancient world; Thinite dynasty, founded by Menes, which united Upper and Lower Egypt c. 3400 B.C., the first of 30 dynasties which ruled ancient Egypt (c. 3400–332 B.C.); pyramids built under IVth dynasty (2900–2750 B.C.) of Old Kingdom which had capital at Memphis; Karnak, near Thebes, monument of XIIth dynasty (2000–1788 B.C.) under which Egypt began expansion as an imperial power, conquering Ethiopia, and later, under Thutmose III 1501–1447 B.C. (XVIIIth dynasty), Palestine and Syria; in decline dominated by priest-kings, Libyan, Ethiopian, Assyrian, and Persian rulers; driven from Asiatic holdings by Nebuchadnezzar (see BABYLON)

605 B.C.; history of ancient dynasties closed with Alexander's conquest 332 B.C.; ancient Egyptians invented calendar (traditional date 4241 B.C.), papyrus and hieroglyphic writing, earliest sea-going ships, created massive architectural monuments, pyramids, temples, sculpture (see ABU SIMBEL, ABYDOS, GIZA, PYRAMIDS, KARNAK, LUXOR, etc.).

Center of Hellenistic culture at Alexandria (*q.v.*) under Ptolemies 323–30 B.C.; part of Roman Empire from 30 B.C. until Arab conquest 640 A.D.; Cairo (*q.v.*) seat of Fatimid caliphate which ruled Egypt 968–1171; ruled by Mamelukes 1250–1517; nominally part of Ottoman Empire 1517–1914; invaded by Napoleon 1798, but French forced to withdraw (see ABUKIR); became virtually independent with accession of pasha, Mehemet Ali, 1805; by revolts against Sultan 1832 and 1839, obtained status of autonomous hereditary principality; under Khedive Ismail Pasha, Suez Canal (*q.v.*) completed 1869; occupied 1882 by British, who shared dual control with France 1879–82; (for problem of Sudan, see ANGLO-EGYPTIAN SUDAN); administered by Evelyn Baring (Lord Cromer) 1883–1907; declared British protectorate 1914. Secured independence 1922, but issues of British military occupation and Sudan only settled by treaty of 1936; 1923 constitution reintroduced 1935. Neutral in World War II; invaded Sept. 1940 by Italians, who were driven out by British Dec. 1940; invaded by Germans Nov. 1941 and again June–July 1942 when they reached El Alamein, but they were driven out after battle of El Alamein Oct. 1942. Became a republic 1953, a year after overthrow of King Farouk by a military coup.

E′hen (ē′ĕn). Small river in Cumberland, NW England; flows out of Ennerdale Water past Egremont and on S to the Irish Sea.

E·hi·me (ĕ·hē·mĕ). Prefecture of Japan. See *Table* at JAPAN.

Eh′ren·breit′stein (ā′rĕn·brīt′shtīn). Town, W Germany, on the right bank of the Rhine river opposite Koblenz; pop. 2926; at foot of a rocky ridge 387 ft. high, which was formerly site of an ancient fortress; ridge became a possession 1018 of Emperor Henry II; fortress often besieged, later strengthened during wars of 18th cent., and finally razed by Treaty of Versailles; taken by American army Mar. 27, 1945.

E·ia′o (ĕ·yä′ō). Small island 6½ m. long, Marquesas Is., ab. 56 m. NW by N of Nuku Hiva I.; formerly a place of exile for French convicts; now uninhabited.

Éi′bar (ĕ′ĕ·vär). City, Guipúzcoa prov., N Spain, 27 m. WSW of San Sebastián; pop. 11,772; manufactures steel products.

Ei′ben·stock (ī′bĕn·shtôk). Town, Saxony, Germany, near Mulde river ab. 16 m. SW of Zwickau; pop. (1933) 9356; tambour embroidery introduced 1775; manufactures curtains, lace, tin and iron; cattle market; has belonged to Saxony since 1534.

Ei′ber′gen (ī′bĕr′ĸĕ[n]). Commune, Gelderland prov., Netherlands, near German border; pop. 9135.

Ei′bhinn (ā′vĭn). Mountain 3611 ft., NW cen. Scotland, in S Inverness co. 6 m. W of Loch Ericht.

Eichs′feld (īĸs′fĕlt). Hilly district in former Saxony prov., Prussia, Germany, just NW of Thuringia; contains source of Leine river.

Eich′stätt (īĸ′shtĕt) *or* **Eich′stadt** (-shtät). Town, Middle Franconia, W Bavaria, Germany, on the Altmühl ab. 67 m. NNW of Munich; pop. 8006; old town and place of pilgrimage containing tomb of St. Willibald (700?–786); has fine Gothic cathedral. Originally a Roman station; made bishopric 745 by Boniface, its bishops becoming princes of the empire; in 19th cent. a princedom granted to Eugène de Beauharnais, subject to Bavaria.

Eick′el (ī′kĕl). Former town in Westphalia prov., Prussia, Germany; since 1927 part of Wanne-Eickel (*q.v.*).

Ei′der (ī′dēr). River ab. 115 m. long in N Germany, forming boundary bet. Schleswig and Holstein; rises E of

Rendsburg and flows W into North Sea S of the Eiderstedt Penin.; importance decreased since completion of the Kiel Canal. In 19th cent. gave its name to a Danish party (the *Eider Danes*) which advocated the incorporation of Schleswig into Denmark.

Ei'der·stedt (ī'dēr-shtĕt). Peninsula extending into Heligoland Bight on W coast of Schleswig-Holstein, Germany.

Eids'vold (ĕ'īts·vôl). Commune, Akershus co., SE Norway, 30 m. NE of Oslo; pop. 11,267; new constitution drawn up here May 17, 1814 providing for a unicameral national assembly and denying the king an absolute veto.

Ei'el·son Field (ī'ĕl·s'n). U.S. airfield, E Alaska, on Tanana river on Alaska Highway, 26 m. SE of Fairbanks; formerly known as **Mile 26.**

Ei'fel (ī'fĕl). Hilly region ab. 40 m. long and 20 m. wide in W Germany, W of the Rhine river, NW of the Moselle river and NE of Luxembourg; highest point 2493 ft. in E part; a barren region, chiefly of geologic interest; shows evidence of volcanic action; limestone moors, many lakes (called crater lakes); overrun by American armies Mar. 1945.

Ei'ger (ī'gēr). Peak 13,040 ft. in the Bernese Alps, W cen. Switzerland, NW of the Finsteraarhorn.

Eigg (ĕg). Small island of the Inner Hebrides, off W coast of Scotland; pop. 138; administratively a part of Inverness co.

Ei'jer·land (ī'yēr·länt). North section of Texel I., Netherlands.

Eil (īl). Coastal town, NE Somalia, E Africa; terminus of road from Mogadishu.

Eilat. See ELATH.

Eil, Loch (lŏκ ēl'). Sea inlet, on border bet. Argyll and Inverness cos., W Scotland, extending 8½ m. W from N end of Loch Linnhe; connects on E with Caledonian Canal system.

Eil'don Hills (ēl'dŭn). Three conical peaks, Roxburgh co., SE Scotland, S of Melrose; highest 1385 ft.; prehistoric and Roman remains; rich in legendary lore.

Ei'len·burg (ī'lĕn·boŏrκ). Manufacturing city, E Germany, in the former Saxony prov. of Prussia on the Mulde river 13 m. NE of Leipzig; pop. 18,172; railroad junction; textiles, machinery, furniture, pianos, sugar; castle dating at least from the 10th cent.; town dates from 981; passed to Prussia 1815.

Ei'len·dorf (ī'lĕn·dôrf). Commune, North Rhine-Westphalia state, West Germany, 4 m. E of Aachen; pop. 11,566; stone quaries; chemicals, refractory products.

Eil Malk (āl' mälk'). Island, S cen. Palau Is., W Pacific Ocean, S of Urukthapel; bet. it and Peleliu I. 10 m. to the SW are many islets and reefs.

Eimeo. One of the Windward Is., Society Is., French Polynesia. See MOORÉA.

Ein'beck (īn'bĕk). Industrial town, S Lower Saxony state, W Germany, S of Hildesheim; pop. 9593; important esp. 15th–17th cents.; manufactures Einbeck (bock) beer. Grew up around monastery founded 1080; seat of princes of Grubenhagen (branch of the ducal house of Brunswick) 14th cent. to 1596; member of Hanseatic League.

Eind'ho·ven (īnt'hō'vĕ[n]). Commercial and industrial commune, North Brabant prov., S Netherlands, 55 m. SE of Rotterdam; pop. (1939) 113,128; produces electrical and radio apparatus; in World War II marked S point of region invaded by Allied airborne troops Sept. 1944.

Ein'sie·deln (īn'zē'dĕln). Commune, Schwyz canton, E cen. Switzerland, 9 m. NNE of Schwyz; pop. (1930) 8053; 18th-cent. Benedictine abbey (founded 9th or 10th cent.) containing a famous image of the Virgin which is the object of annual pilgrimages; Zwingli parish priest here 1516–18; birthplace of Paracelsus.

Ei'pel (ī'pĕl). German name of river in Czechoslovakia and Hungary. See IPEL'.

Ei're (*Ir.* ā'rĕ; *in English, also* ā'rĕ, âr'ĕ, âr'ĕ, ī'rĕ, ī'rĕ) or **Ire'land** (īr'lănd); *from 1922 to 1937* **I'rish Free State** (ī'rĭsh), *Gaelic* **Saor'stat' Eir'eann** *or* **Saor'stát' Éir'eann** (sâr'stôt' âr'ĭn); *since Apr. 18,* 1949 *officially called* **Republic of Ireland.** Republic occupying S, cen., and NW Ireland; 26,602 sq. m.; pop. 2,968,420; ✻ Dublin. See *Map,* p. 327. Divided into the following 4 provinces and 26 counties (for pronunciation of their names, see their individual entries):

COUNTY[1]	LOCATION	AREA[2]	POP.[2]	CO. SEAT
PROVINCE OF CONNACHT				
Galway	W	2,293	168,198	Galway
Leitrim	N	589	50,908	Carrick on Shannon
Mayo	NW	2,084	161,349	Castlebar
Roscommon	N cen.	951	77,566	Roscommon
Sligo	N	694	67,447	Sligo
PROVINCE OF LEINSTER				
Carlow	SE	346	34,452	Carlow
Dublin	E	356	586,925	Dublin
Kildare	E	654	57,892	Naas
Kilkenny	SE	796	68,614	Kilkenny
Laoighis	cen.	664	50,109	Maryborough
Longford	N cen.	403	37,847	Longford
Louth	NE	317	64,339	Dundalk
Meath	E	903	61,405	Trim
Offaly	cen.	771	51,308	Tullamore
Westmeath	N cen.	681	54,706	Mullingar
Wexford	SE	908	94,245	Wexford
Wicklow	E	782	58,569	Wicklow
PROVINCE OF MUNSTER				
Clare	W	1,231	89,879	Ennis
Cork	SW	2,881	355,957	Cork
Kerry	SW	1,815	139,834	Tralee
Limerick	SW	1,037	141,153	Limerick
Tipperary[3]	S	1,643	137,835	Clonmel
Waterford	S	710	77,614	Waterford
PROVINCE OF ULSTER[4]				
Cavan	N	730	76,670	Cavan
Donegal	N	1,865	142,310	Lifford
Monaghan	NE	498	61,289	Monaghan

[1] In Irish idiom, *county* precedes the name, as in *county Cork, county Meath.*
[2] Area in sq. m. Pop. from 1936 Census.
[3] Divided for administrative purposes into Tipperary North Riding (771 sq. m.; pop. 59,551) and Tipperary South Riding (872 sq. m.; pop. 78,284).
[4] See ULSTER former province.

Extends bet. 51°27'N (Mizen Head in co. Cork the southernmost point of the island) and 55°25'N (Malin Head in co. Donegal the northernmost point of Ireland); comprises most of the territory of Ireland, which consists geographically of a central plain with lakes (*loughs*) in N, cen., and W parts, with groups of hills averaging 2000 to 3000 ft. on N, W, and S; chief lakes in Eire: Loughs Mask, Corrib, and Conn in W, Ree and Derg in cen. part, and the beautiful Lakes of Killarney in SW; shares with Northern Ireland the Erne and Foyle rivers (*qq.v.*) and Loughs Foyle and Carlingford (*qq.v.*); chief rivers the Shannon (ab. 240 m. long, longest in the British Isles), in cen. part, Boyne and Liffey in E, Barrow, Nore, and Suir in SE, Blackwater and Lee in S. Contains the island's highest point Carrantual 3414 ft., in Macgillicuddy's Reeks in SW. Coast line irregular, esp. in SW and W where it is indented by Bantry Bay, Kenmare River, Dingle Bay, Galway Bay, Clew Bay, Sligo Bay, Donegal Bay, and the estuary of the Shannon; has many good harbors. Chief cities Dublin, Cork, Limerick, Dun Laoghaire, Waterford, Galway, Dundalk, Drogheda.

History: As Irish Free State, estab. **1922,** a dominion in the British Commonwealth of Nations, Northern Ireland (*q.v.*) having been formed 1920; adopted constitution 1922; settled boundary with Northern Ireland 1925; under De Valera, gradually abandoned ties with British crown, in 1937 declaring Eire (its official new name) a sovereign, independent democratic state; remained associated for certain purposes with British Commonwealth

of Nations; neutral throughout World War II; refused request of Britain and United States Mar. 1944 to expel Axis representatives; by Republic of Ireland Act Dec. 1948 declared itself completely independent with no allegiance to British crown or membership in British Commonwealth of Nations; officially proclaimed the Republic of Ireland Apr. 18 (Easter Monday), 1949. See IRELAND.

Ei′rinn (ā′rĭn; âr′ĭn). = ERIN.

Ei′se‧nach (ī′zĕ‧näк). Manufacturing city, Thuringia, Germany, 31 m. W of Erfurt; pop. 43,385; 16th-cent. town hall. Birthplace of Johann Sebastian Bach; place where Luther attended school 1498–1501. Originated in 12th cent.; capital of Thuringian landgraves; residence 1596 ff. of Ernestine line of princes; capital of duchy of Eisenach 1672–1741; united with Weimar 1741; part of Thuringia 1815.

Ei′sen‧berg (ī′zĕn‧bĕrк). City, Thuringia, Germany, 38 m. E of Erfurt; pop. 11,317; 16th-cent. town hall; manufactures sausages, porcelain, pianos.

Eisenburg. See VASVÁR.

Ei′sen‧erz′ (ī′zĕn‧ĕrts′). Mining commune, N Styria prov., Austria, 16 m. NW of Leoben; pop. 8654; nearby is the Erzberg (q.v.).

Ei′sen‧how′er, Mount (ī′z′n‧hou′ẽr): *formerly* **Cas′tle Mountain** (kås′′l). Mountain 9390 ft. in Canadian Rockies, S Alberta, Canada, W of Calgary; in Banff National Park; renamed 1946.

Ei′sen‧hut (ī′zĕn‧hōot). Mountain 8006 ft., highest in Noric Alps, in SW Styria, Austria, NW of Klagenfurt.

Ei′sen‧stadt (ī′zĕn‧shtät). Town, ✻ of Burgenland, Austria, just W of Neusiedler Lake; pop. 3260; until 1921 in Hungary.

Eisernes Tor. See IRON GATE.

Eisk. See YEISK.

Eis′le′ben (īs′lā′bĕn). Mining city, in the former Saxony prov., Prussia, Germany, in the E spurs of Harz Mts. 22 m. NW of Merseburg; pop. 23,694; 16th-cent. town hall; house in which Martin Luther was born (a museum since 1917) and the house in which he died; copper and silver.

Eitape. Var. of AITAPE.

Ejmiadzin. See ECHMIADZIN.

E′ka‧lak′a (ē′kà‧lăk′à). Town, ⊗ of Carter co., SE corner of Montana; pop. 738.

Ekaterinburg. See SVERDLOVSK.

Ekaterinenstadt. See MARKSSHTADT.

Ekaterinodar. See KRASNODAR.

Ekaterinoslav. See DNEPROPETROVSK.

E′ke (ā′kå). See MAUI.

E′ke‧näs (ě′kě‧näs). Town, Uusimaa dept., S Finland, W of Helsinki, on Gulf of Finland near Hangö; pop. 3225.

Ekhmîm. See AKHMÎM.

Ek′ron (ĕk′rŏn). Ancient city, SW Palestine; one of the 5 chief city-kingdoms of Philistia, on the border of Judah 5 m. SSW of Er Ramle.

El Ab‧ba′sa (ăl ăb‧bă′sà; -să). Town, Sharqîya prov., Lower Egypt, just E of Zagazig; pop. ab. 16,000.

Elabuga. See YELABUGA.

El A‧ghei′la (ĕl à‧gā′là). Town on coastal road, N Libya, near SE end of the Gulf of Sidra; starting point for caravans S; scene of several battles of World War II; reached by British Feb. 1941 during offensive against the Italian army and again in Dec. 1941 during retreat of Germans; site of first blow of Rommel's offensive against British Jan. 23, 1942; again reached by Allies Nov. 13, 1942 and captured Dec. 17.

E′lah (ē′là), **Vale of.** Valley of middle course of northern branch of Nahr Suqreir, S cen. Judaea, S Palestine, ab. 15 m. W of Bethlehem; probable site of the combat bet. David and Goliath (*1 Sam.* xvii. 2, 19).

El Aksur. = LUXOR.

El A′la‧mein′ (ĕl ăl′à‧mān′). Village on coastal road, N Egypt, ab. 65 m. W of Alexandria and N of NE corner of Qattara Depression; farthest German advance July 1, 1942 in campaign to seize Alexandria, Cairo, and the Suez Canal; scene of battle Oct. 19–Nov. 3, 1942 in which Allies defeated Germans. See EL AQQAQIR.

E′lam (ē′lăm); *also known as* **Su′si‧a′na** (sū′zĭ‧ā′nà; -ăn′à). Ancient kingdom at head of Persian Gulf E of Babylonia, dating back possibly to 5th millennium B.C.; from c. 3000 B.C., there was a conflict between Elamites, non-Semitic inhabitants of Elam, and the Sumerians and Akkadians; with its capital at Susa, kingdom of Elam flourished c. 1200–c. 640 B.C. when it was absorbed by Assyria, which destroyed Susa; Susa later became one of capitals of Persian Empire of Cyrus the Great (see PERSIA).

E′lands‧laag′te (ē′länts‧läk′tĕ). Settlement, NW Natal, Union of South Africa; scene of battle Oct. 21, 1899 in which Boers under Joubert were temporarily repulsed by British.

El Aq‧qa′qir (ăl ŭk‧kä′kīr). Village, N Egypt, near El Alamein; scene of tank battle Nov. 2–3, 1942 in which Germans were severely beaten; closing phase of battle of El Alamein.

El Aq′sur (ăl ŏŏk′sŏŏr). = LUXOR.

El A′ra‧hal′ (ĕl ä′rä‧äl′). Commune, Sevilla prov., SW Spain, 23 m. ESE of Seville; pop. 13,517.

El Araish. See LARACHE.

El ′A‧rîsh′ (ĕl ä‧rēsh′); *anc.* **Rhi′no‧co‧lu′ra** (rī′nô‧kô‧lūr′à). Town, Sinai prov., NE Egypt, on Mediterranean Sea near frontier of Palestine; pop. ab. 4000; in World War I important point in advance of British toward Palestine; taken Dec. 20, 1916.

El Ash′mû‧nein′ (ăl ăsh′mŏŏ‧nān′; -nĭn′). Village, Egypt, near W bank of the Nile, 27°46′N; site of **Her‧mop′o‧lis Mag′na** (hûr‧mŏp′ô‧lĭs măg′nà), in ancient times center of the worship of Anubis or Thoth.

Elatea. 1 Mountain. See CITHAERON.
2 Town. See ELATEIA.

E‧la′tei‧a (ā‧lā′tyà) *or* **Drakh‧ma′ni** (тнräk‧mä′nyĕ); *anc.* **El′a‧te′a** (ĕl′à‧tē′à). Town, NE Phthiotis and Phocis dept., Greece, NE of Mt. Parnassus; pop. 1719.

E′lath (ē′lăth). 1 See ′AQABA.
2 *or* **Ei‧lat′** (ā‧lät′). Seaport, S Israel, W of ′Aqaba at head of Gulf of ′Aqaba; built since 1948.

El ′Au′ja (ăl ou′jà; -jă). Village, S Palestine, 45 m. S of Gaza on Egypt boundary.

Elaver. See ALLIER.

E′lâ‧ziz′ (ă′lä‧zēz′). 1 Vilayet, E cen. Turkey in Asia; 5858 sq. m.; pop. 174,603.
2 Town, its ✻, 75 m. NW of Diyarbekir; pop. 23,456.

El′ba (ĕl′bà). 1 City, a ⊗ of Coffee co., SE Alabama; pop. 4321.
2 *anc.* **Il′va** (ĭl′và) *or* **Ae‧tha′lia** (ē‧thăl′yà; -thă′lĭ‧à). Italian island in Mediterranean Sea bet. NE coast of Corsica and mainland of Italy; 86 sq. m.; pop. (1931) ab. 27,000; politically a part of Italian province of Livorno; chief town Portoferraio; has iron-ore deposits which have been worked since ancient times. Residence of Napoleon after his first abdication May 1814 to Feb. 26, 1815 when he left secretly to begin his career of the "Hundred Days"; in World War II taken from Germans by French June 17–19, 1944.

Elba, Cape. See Ras HADARBA.

El Bahnasa. See OXYRHYNCHUS.

El Bahr. See NILE.

El Ban′co (ĕl väng′kô). Town, Magdalena dept., N Colombia, ab. 100 m. SE of Cartagena; pop. 5626.

El′ba‧sa′ni (ĕl′bä‧sä′nĕ) *or* **El′ba‧san′** (-sän′). 1 Prefecture, E cen. Albania; 1141 sq. m.; pop. 111,422.
2 Town, its ✻, E cen. Albania, on Shkumbi river 20 m. SE of Tiranë; pop. 13,796; market center in agricultural region producing esp. tobacco, fruit, and olive oil; E terminus of railroad line from Durrës; Italian base in early part of World War II.

El Ba′ya‧di′ya (ăl bä′yä‧dē′yà; -yä). Town, Qena prov., Upper Egypt, just S of Luxor; pop. ab. 16,000.

El′be (ĕl′bĕ; *sometimes Angl.* ĕlb); *Czech* **La′be** (lä′bĕ); *anc.* **Al′bis** (ăl′bĭs). River ab. 720 m. long in Czechoslo-

IRELAND

Statute Miles

0   25   50   75   100

✹ Capitals

PUBLISHED BY G. & C. MERRIAM COMPANY
SPRINGFIELD, MASS.
PREPARED BY J. W. CLEMENT CO. BUFFALO, N. Y.

ıkia and Germany; rises on S slopes of the Riesen Ge-rge, Czechoslovakia, flows S, W, and NW in Czecho-slovakia, then WNW across cen. Germany into North Sea at Cuxhaven; navigable to beyond Czechoslovakian border; just N of Litoměřice (Leitmeritz) cuts through the Erz Gebirge in a narrow gorge. Chief tributaries Vltava and Ohře (Eger) in Czechoslovakia, and Mulde, Saale, Schwarze Elster, Havel, and Elde in Germany; connected by canals with Oder river and Baltic Sea. Meeting point Apr. 27, 1945 of British and American ar-mies with Russian armies (see TORGAU); part of lower course established 1945 as line of demarcation bet. Brit-ish and Russian zones of administration in Germany.

El Beda. See DOHA.

El Be′ni (ĕl vä′nĕ) or **Be′ni** (bā′-). Department of Bo-livia. See *Table* at BOLIVIA.

El Beqa′. See El BIKA.

El′ber·feld′ (ĕl′bĕr-fĕlt′). Former city (pop. 167,577), Düsseldorf govt. dist., Rhine Province, Prussia, Ger-many; since 1929 part of Wuppertal (q.v.).

El′ber·on (ĕl′bĕr-ŭn). Village, Monmouth co., E cen. New Jersey, next to Long Branch; pop. (est.) 1350; sea-shore resort; President James A. Garfield died here 1881.

El′bert (ĕl′bẽrt). Name of counties in two states of the U.S. See *Tables* at COLORADO and GEORGIA.

Elbert, Mount. Peak 14,431 ft. in Lake co., cen. Colo-rado; highest peak in the state and in the Rocky Mts.

El′ber·ton (ĕl′bẽr-t′n; -tŭn). City, ⊗ of Elbert co., NE Georgia, E of Athens; pop. 7107; quarries granite.

El′beuf′ (ĕl′bûf′). Commune, Seine-Inférieure dept., N France, on Seine river 14 m. SSW of Rouen; pop. 17,506; manufactures clothing; fine Renaissance churches.

El Bi·ar′ (ăl′bĭ-är′). Commune, Alger dept., N Algeria; pop. 11,430.

El′bląg (ĕl′blôNngg); *Ger.* **El′bing** (ĕl′bĭng). Seaport and industrial city, Gdańsk dept., N Poland, 30 m. ESE of Gdańsk; formerly in East Prussia prov., Germany, near the Frisches Haff; pop. 67,878, (1947 est.) 89,952; important shipbuilding and repair yards. Founded 1237; became member of Hanseatic League; taken by Poland 1454; annexed to Prussia 1772; captured by Russians Jan. 26–Feb. 7, 1945, after severe fighting; in section of East Prussia assigned to Poland by Potsdam Conference 1945.

El′bo·rus′ (ĕl′bŏ-rōōz′) or **El·brus′** (ĕl·brōōz′; *Russ.* ĭl·y′·brōōs′). Highest mountain 18,481 ft. (W peak, E peak slightly lower) in the Caucasus Mts. (q.v.) and in Europe; in N Georgian Soviet Socialist Republic, U.S.S.R.; actually in a N subsidiary spur of the main range of the Caucasus.

El′bow Lake (ĕl′bō). Village, ⊗ of Grant co., W Minne-sota, 29 m. W of Alexandria; pop. 1521.

El·burz′ Mountains (ĕl·bōōrz′). Range in N Iran, ex-tending W to E parallel with S shore of Caspian Sea, from which it is separated by a lowland strip not at any point more than 25 m. wide; highest peak Demavend 18,600 ft.; has many peaks above 10,000 ft.

El Buseira. See BOZRAH.

El Ca·jon′ (ĕl kà·hōn′). City, San Diego co., SW coastal California, E of San Diego; pop. 37,618.

El Cam′po (ĕl kăm′pō). City, Wharton co., SE Texas, 25 m. NW of Bay City; pop. 7700; rice; oil and sulfur.

El Ca·ney′ (ĕl kä·nā′; *Span.* -nĕ′ĕ) or **Ca·ney′.** Mu-nicipality, Oriente prov., E Cuba; pop. 19,078; scene of battle July 1, 1898, in the Spanish-American War, in which Gen. Henry Lawton's division defeated the Span-iards; this and victory at San Juan Hill (q.v.) on same day led to American control of Santiago de Cuba and destruction of Cervera's fleet July 3.

El Cap′i·tan′ (ĕl kăp′ĭ·tăn′). **1** Peak 7564 ft. in Sierra Nevada, Yosemite Valley, cen. California; largest ex-posed monolith in the world, rising 3604 ft. above the valley floor.
2 Peak 9936 ft. in Ravalli co., W Montana.
3 Peak 8078 ft. in Guadalupe Mts., NW Culberson co., W Texas.

El Capitan Dam. Dam completed 1935 across San Diego river, California; height 270 ft.; impounds water for water supply.

El Ca′yo (ĕl kä′yŏ) or **Cayo.** Town, ✱ of Cayo dist., W British Honduras; pop. (1943) ab. 7300.

El Cen′tro (ĕl sĕn′trō). City, ⊗ of Imperial co., SE corner of California, in Imperial Valley 86 m. E of San Diego, near Mexican border; pop. 16,811; settled 1905; 52 ft. below sea level; shipping point for melons, dates, lettuce, etc.

El Cer·ri′to (ĕl sĕ·rē′tō). Residential city, Contra Costa co., W California, on San Francisco Bay 6 m. N of Oak-land; pop. 25,437.

El Cerro del Mercado. See IRON MOUNTAIN, Mexico.

El Chaco. See CHACO.

El′che (ĕl′chà); *anc.* **Il′i·ci** (ĭl′ĭ·sī). City, Alicante prov., SE Spain, 13 m. SW of Alicante; pop. 46,666; dates, palm fronds; manufactures leather, and shoes and san-dals of esparto grass; episcopal palace; scene of annual mystery play; ancient Roman colony; held by Moors 8th–13th cents.

El Cobre. See COBRE, Cuba.

El′da (ĕl′dä). Commune, Alicante prov., SE Spain, 18 m. NW of Alicante; pop. 20,050; agricultural produce; manufactures paper and esparto articles; remains of old Gothic castle.

El Da′ba (ăd dä′bà; -bă). Village on coastal road, NW Egypt, E of Matrûh and W of El Alamein; seized by Germans June 1942 in their advance to El Alamein.

El′de (ĕl′dĕ). River ab. 130 m. long in Mecklenburg, N Germany; flows SW through several lakes into Elbe river 62 m. SE of Hamburg.

El′den Mountain (ĕl′dĕn). Peak 9280 ft. in cen. Coco-nino co., N cen. Arizona.

El Djem (ĕl jĕm′). Town, NE Tunisia, 40 m. S of Sousse.

El Djouf (ăl jōōf′) or **El Juf.** Desert region at W end of the Sahara in E Mauritania and W Mali, West Africa.

El′don (ĕl′dŭn). **1** City, Wapello co., SE Iowa, 12 m. SE of Ottumwa on Des Moines river; pop. 1386.
2 City, Miller co., cen. Missouri, 23 m. SW of Jefferson City; pop. 3158; cheese; clothing.

El·do′ra (ĕl·dōr′à). City, ⊗ of Hardin co., N cen. Iowa, 24 m. NNW of Marshalltown; pop. 3225; agricul-ture; dairying.

El′do·ra′do (ĕl′dŏ·rä′dō). **1** Commercial city, Saline co., SE Illinois, 25 m. W of confluence of Ohio and Wabash rivers; pop. 3573;
2 Town, ⊗ of Schleicher co., W cen. Texas, 45 m. S of San Angelo; pop. 1815.

El Do·ra′do (ĕl′ dŏ·rä′dō). County in California. See *Table* at CALIFORNIA.

El Do·ra′do (ĕl′ dŏ·rä′dō). **1** City, ⊗ of Union co., S Arkansas, 80 m. ESE of Texarkana; pop. 25,291; settled 1843, made ⊗ 1844, incorp. 1851; chief city of Arkansas oil industry; oil discovered 1921.
2 City, ⊗ of Butler co., S Kansas, 28 m. ENE of Wichita; pop. 12,523; agriculture, livestock; oil refineries.

El′do·ra′do Range (ĕl′dŏ·rä′dō). Range in extreme S tip of Nevada, running N to S along Colorado river.

El′do·ra′do Springs (ĕl′dŏ·rä′dō). City, Cedar co., W Missouri, 18 m. E of Nevada; mineral springs.

El′do·ret′ (ĕl′dŏ·rĕt′). Town, W cen. Kenya colony, E Africa, on railroad ab. 50 m. NE of Kisumu.

El Dueim. See ED DUEIM.

Elea. See VELIA.

E·lec′tra (ē·lĕk′trà). City, Wichita co., N Texas, 25 m. WNW of Wichita Falls; pop. 4759; oil; manufactures drilling tools, oil-well equipment.

E·lec′tric Peak (ē·lĕk′trĭk). Mountain 11,155 ft. in S Montana, near Wyoming border, in Yellowstone Na-tional Park; highest point in Gallatin Range.

E′le·e′le (ā′lā·ā′lĕ). Village, Koloa dist., S coast of Kauai I., Hawaii, E of Hanapepe; pop. 1184.

El′e·phant (ĕl′ē·fănt). **1** Island ab. 28 m. long and 15 m. wide in Scotia Sea, in NE part of South Shetland Is.,

Falkland Islands Dependencies; ab. 61°05′S, 55°10′W.

2 River ab. 250 m. long in SE cen. South-West Africa; flows SE into Oup river.

El′e·phan′ta (ĕl′ĕ·făn′tä); *Hind.* **Gha′ra·pu′ri** (gä′rä·pōō′rē). Small island in Bombay harbor, W Indian Union, ab. 6 m. E of the city; famous for its Temple Caves, excavations cut out of solid rock probably 1000 to 1200 years ago; contains colossal carved figures of the Trimurti, Siva, Parvati, and other Hindu deities.

El′e·phant Butte Dam *and* **Reservoir** (ĕl′ĕ·fănt). See UNITED STATES, *Dams and Reservoirs.*

El′e·phan·ti′ne (ĕl′ĕ·făn·ti′nē; -tē′nē). Island in Nile river, in Upper Egypt, opp. Aswân just below the First Cataract; ruins of many structures—Egyptian, Roman, Saracen, and Arabic; at its upper end had ancient Nilometer; site of discovery 1903 of the *Elephantine papyri*, dating from end of 5th cent. B.C. and containing varied information about the Jewish people.

El′e·phant Mound (ĕl′ĕ·fănt). Prehistoric earthwork 4 m. S of Wyalusing, NW Grant co., SW Wisconsin, on Mississippi river; once thought to resemble an elephant; first noticed 1872.

Elephant Mountain. Peak 6230 ft. in W Brewster co., W Texas.

Elephant Tusk. See INDIANOLA PEAK.

El Erg. See El ERG.

El Es·co′ri·al (ĕl ĕs·kōr′ĭ·ăl; *Span.* äs′kô·ryäl′). Commune, Madrid prov., cen. Spain, 25 m. NW of Madrid in NW Sierra de Guadarrama; pop. 6357; site of the Escorial, a vast structure erected 1563–84 at the direction of Philip II, comprising a royal palace, a royal mausoleum, a church, a college, and a monastery, and containing many works of art.

Elets. See YELETS.

E·leu′sis (ê·lū′sĭs); *Gr.* **E′lev·sis′** (â′lâf·sēs′). Village with ruins of an ancient city, ab. 14 m. NW of Athens, in Attica and Boeotia dept., Greece, on N shore of Bay of Eleusis opp. Salamis I.; pop. 4436; a place of great antiquity; in early times independent of Athens; seat of the Eleusinian Mysteries, the most famous of the Greek religious mysteries, in honor of Demeter; sacred buildings destroyed 396 A.D. by Alaric.

Eleusis, Bay of. Inlet of Saronic Gulf, Attica and Boeotia dept., Greece, almost completely shut in by Salamis I.

E·leu′ther·a (ê·lū′thēr·à). One of the Bahama Is., in the Atlantic Ocean E of New Providence I.; ab. 80 m. long; 164 sq. m.; pop. (1943) 6430; one of the earliest islands in the Bahamas to be colonized, in mid-17th cent.

E·leu′ther·op′o·lis (ê·lū′thēr·ŏp′ô·lĭs); *mod.* **Beit Ji·brin′** (bāt [bīt] jĭ·brēn′). Ancient city in Palestine, in S Judaea, ab. 40 m. WNW of Hebron; site of Roman ruins; sacked or destroyed several times; rebuilt and renamed by Septimius Severus 200 A.D.; important in time of Crusades.

Eleven Thousand Virgins, Cape of the. See VÍR-GENES.

El Fai·yûm′ *or* **El Fa·yum′** (ăl fā·yōōm′; fī-). Town, ✳ of Faiyûm prov., N Upper Egypt, ab. 70 m. SW of Cairo; pop. (1937) 63,703; important modern town on the Bahr Yusef bet. the Nile and Birket Qârûn; lies in bed of ancient Lake Moeris near site of Arsinoë, in region rich in archaeological objects and papyri.

El Fa′sher (ăl fä′shēr). Town, ✳ of Darfur prov., W Sudan; pop. 26,161; on caravan and motor routes from Khartoum to Abéché and Lake Chad.

Elfeld. See ELTVILLE.

El Fer·rol′ (ĕl fĕr·rôl′); *officially since 1939* **El Ferrol de Cau·dil′lo** (thä kou·thē′yō). City, La Coruña prov., NW Spain, 11 m. NE of La Coruña on a fine natural harbor; pop. (1945 est.) 63,714; important naval station; shipbuilding; chosen as site of naval arsenal by Charles IV 1726; shipbuilding established in mid-18th cent.; surrendered to English 1805; occupied by French Jan.–June 1809.

El Frai′le (ĕl frī′lä; frä′ĕ·lä). Rocky islet on S side of South Channel, part of entrance to Manila Bay, Phil. Is., ab. 2 m. from Cavite shore; had American fortification, Fort Drum. See CORREGIDOR.

Elfsborg. Var. of ÄLVSBORG.

El Fung (ĕl fōōng′). Former province, E Anglo-Egyptian Sudan, now part of Blue Nile prov., Sudan.

El Ga·le′ras (ĕl gä·lā′räs). Volcanic peak ab. 14,000 ft. in Andes Mts., SW Colombia.

El Ga·za′la (ĕl gà·zäl′à). Village, Cyrenaica, NE Libya, on coast W of Tobruk; in World War II an Axis supply port; in early part of 1942 part of British defense line, evacuated in June.

El Ge·nei′na (ăl jōō·nā′nà). Town, W Darfur prov., W Sudan, on border W of El Fasher.

El Gha·na′yim (ăl gŏ·nä′ĭm). Town, Asyût prov., Upper Egypt, on W bank of Nile SE of Asyût; pop. 15,000.

El Gha′raq es Sul·ta′ni (ăl gŏ′rŏk ăs sōōl·tä′nē). Town, Faiyûm prov., Upper Egypt, just SW of El Faiyûm; pop. ab. 18,000.

El′gin (ĕl′jĭn). City, Cook and Kane cos., NE Illinois, 38 m. WNW of Chicago; pop. 49,447; dairy products, esp. butter; watch manufacturing.

El′gin (ĕl′gĭn). **1** City, Bastrop co., S cen. Texas, 23 m. E of Austin; pop. 3511; railroad junction.

2 County, Ontario, Canada. See *Table* at ONTARIO.

3 Burgh, ⊗ of Moray co., NE Scotland; pop. 10,535; distilleries; wool, iron; ruins of noted cathedral.

4 *or* **Elginshire.** County in Scotland. See MORAY.

El Gizeh. See GIZA.

El′gon, Mount (ĕl′gŏn). Volcanic peak 14,176 ft. in E cen. Africa, on the Uganda-Kenya boundary, NE of Lake Victoria.

El Grul′lo (ĕl grōō′yô). Town, Jalisco state, W cen. Mexico; pop. 5433.

El Guet·tar′ (ĕl gĕ·tär′). Village, S cen. Tunisia, ab. 12 m. SE of Gafsa; taken by American troops Mar. 17, 1943.

El Habesha. See ETHIOPIA.

El Hamad. See SYRIAN DESERT.

El Ham′ma (ĕl hăm′à). Town, cen. Tunisia, on E shore of Chott Djerid 16 m. W of Gabès.

El Ham·mâm′ (ăl hăm·măm′). Village on coastal road, N Egypt, bet. El Alamein and Alexandria.

El Hasa. See al-HASA.

Elias, Mount. = Mount SAINT ELIAS of the Saint Elias Range.

E·lí′as Pi′ña (â·lē′äs pē′nyä). Commune, ✳ of San Rafael prov., Dominican Republic.

Elichpur. Var. of ELLICHPUR.

Elimberrum. See AUCH.

Eliocroca. See LORCA.

El′i·ot (ĕl′ĭ·ŭt; ĕl′yŭt). Town, York co., SW Maine, 28 m. SSW of Biddeford; pop. 3133.

E′lis (ē′lĭs; *Mod. Gr.* ē′lyĕs). **1** Ancient country in NW Peloponnesus, Greece; bounded on N by Achaea, on E by Arcadia, on S by Messenia, and on W by Ionian Sea; extent varied in accordance with changes in its political influence; district of Triphylia in S for a time held by Arcadia. Watered by Peneus and Alpheus rivers; mountain range on E border including Mt. Erymanthus (at NE corner); chief town Elis; in S was plain of Olympia (*q.v.*). After First Peloponnesian War involved in most of the wars of Greece, usually but not always as ally of Sparta; control of Olympian games for several centuries gave Eleans considerable prestige.

2 City, ✳ of ancient Elis, in W cen. part on Peneus river; now only ruins.

3 Subdivision of Achaea and Elis dept. of modern Greece. See *Table* at GREECE.

E·lis′a·beth·ville (ê·lĭz′à·bĕth·vĭl). **1** *now called* **Ka·tan′ga** (kà·tăng′gà). Province, SE Republic of Congo (formerly Belgian Congo), S cen. Africa; 186,933 sq. m.; native pop. (1938) 1,023,060.

2 *now called* **Lu·bum·ba′shi** (lōō′bōōm·bä′shĕ). City, SE Katanga, near border of Zambia; pop. (1964) ab.

),000; founded 1910 and named after Belgian queen; s had remarkable growth in recent years.

Elisavetgrad. See KIROVOGRAD.

Elisavetpol. See KIROVABAD.

Elista. See STEPNOI.

E·li′za (å·lē′sä). Town, Buenos Aires prov., E Argentina, ab. 25 m. SE of Buenos Aires.

E·liz′a·beth (ê·lĭz′á·bĕth). 1 Navigable river, Norfolk co., SE Virginia, emptying into Hampton Roads; the cities of Norfolk and Portsmouth are on its banks.
2 City, ⊗ of Union co., NE New Jersey, on Newark Bay 5 m. S of Newark; pop. 107,698; residential suburb of New York City; connected with Staten I. by Goethals Bridge; transships coal and iron; manufactures machinery, chemicals, beds, printing presses, clothing; has oil refineries, foundries, steelworks, shipbuilding yards. Purchased by English from Indians 1664 and settled as Elizabethtown; capital of New Jersey until 1686; meeting place of colonial assembly 1668–82; important point in Washington's maneuvers during Revolution; chartered as borough of Elizabeth 1740 and 1789, as town 1796, as city 1855; original seat of Princeton Univ. (see PRINCETON, N.J.); home of Alexander Hamilton and Aaron Burr.
3 Borough, Allegheny co., SW Pennsylvania, on Monongahela river 14 m. SSE of Pittsburgh; pop. 2597; formerly important boatbuilding center.
4 Town, ⊗ of Wirt co., W West Virginia; pop. 727.

Elizabeth, Cape. 1 Cape on coast of SW Maine, 8 m. S of Portland, in Cumberland co.
2 *Russ.* **Ye·li·za·ve′ty** (yĭ·lyĭ·zŭ·vyĕ′tĭ). North point of Sakhalin I., Khabarovsk Territory, Soviet Russia, Asia, 54°30′N.

Elizabeth City. 1 Former county in Virginia; since 1958, comprises independent city of Hampton.
2 Town, ⊗ of Pasquotank co., NE North Carolina, on N arm of Albemarle Sound; pop. 14,062; excellent harbor; fisheries; manufactures cotton textiles, veneer, furniture; U.S. Coast Guard air base, shipyard, and supply base; Elizabeth City State College (1891; coed.). Became ⊗ 1799; naval victory won near here by Federals 1862.

Elizabeth Island. See HENDERSON ISLAND.

Elizabeth Islands. Group of 16 small islands extending SW from SW point of Cape Cod (Barnstable co.), in SE Massachusetts; in Dukes co., SE Mass., separated from Martha's Vineyard by Vineyard Sound and from mainland of Mass. by Buzzards Bay.

Elizabeth Point. Cape on SW coast of South-West Africa, S of Lüderitz.

E·liz′a·beth′ton (ê·lĭz′á·bĕth′tŭn). City, ⊗ of Carter co., NE Tennessee, on Watauga river 9 m. E of Johnson City; pop. 10,896; manufactures rayon and rayon yarn; manganese deposits.

E·liz′a·beth·town′ (ê·lĭz′á·bĕth·toun′). 1 Village, ⊗ of Hardin co., SE Illinois; pop. 524.
2 City, ⊗ of Hardin co., cen. Kentucky, 40 m. S of Louisville; pop. 9641.
3 Village, ⊗ of Essex co., NE New York, in Adirondack Mts. 32 m. S of Plattsburg; pop. 779.
4 Town, ⊗ of Bladen co., S North Carolina, on Cape Fear river 35 m. SSE of Fayetteville; pop. 1625; peanut products.
5 Borough, Lancaster co., SE Pennsylvania, 18 m. WNW of Lancaster; pop. 6780; founded 1732; Elizabethtown College (1899; coed.).

E′li·zal′de (ā′lē·säl′dä). Town, Buenos Aires prov., E Argentina, ab. 35 m. SE of Buenos Aires.

El Jadida. See MAZAGAN.

El Jezira. See GEZIRA.

Elk (ĕlk). 1 River ab. 40 m. long, flowing S from Chester co., SE Pennsylvania, into N Chesapeake Bay in NE corner of Maryland; has wide estuary ab. 13 m. long.
2 River ab. 150 m. long, flowing SW from Grundy co., S Tennessee, into Tennessee river near upper end of Muscle Shoals, N Alabama.

3 River ab. 180 m. long, cen. West Virginia; rises in Pocahontas co., flows N, NW, and W into Kanawha river at Charleston in Kanawha co.
4 Name of counties in two states of the U.S. See *Tables* at KANSAS and PENNSYLVANIA.

Ełk (ĕlk); *Ger.* **Lyck** (lĭk). Manufacturing city, Białystok dept., NE Poland, ab. 60 m. NW of Białystok; formerly in East Prussia, Germany; pop. 16,900; railroad junction; horse and cattle market; assigned to Poland by Potsdam Conference 1526.

El·ka′der (ĕl·kä′dĕr). Town, ⊗ of Clayton co., NE Iowa, 46 m. NW of Dubuque; pop. 1526.

El Kan′ta·ra (ĕl kăn′tá·rá; *Arab.* äl kŏn′tŭ·rŏ). Oasis N of Biskra, Algeria, at S end of gorge through Atlas Mts., on edge of Sahara Desert.

Elk City (ĕlk). City, Beckham co., W Oklahoma, 27 m. WSW of Clinton; pop. 8196; gin machinery.

El Kef. See LE KEF.

El Ke′rak (äl kŭ′rŏk), *also* **Kerak**; *anc.* **Kir Mo′ab** *or* **Kir of Moab** (kûr mō′ăb). Town, W Jordan, E of S end of Dead Sea; pop. ab. 4000; fortified 1136 by Crusaders, who called it **Le Crac** (lĕ kråk′); taken by Saladin 1188; taken by Turks 13th cent.; suffered considerably in World War I.

Elk Grove Village (ĕlk). Village, Cook co., NE Illinois, NW suburb of Chicago; pop. 6608.

El Khalil. See HEBRON.

El Khâr′ga (ĕl kär′gá; *Arab.* äl kär′gá, -gă). Town in the Khârga oasis, Southern Desert prov., Lower Egypt; pop. ab. 6000.

Elk′hart (ĕlk′härt; ĕl′kärt). 1 County in Indiana. See *Table* at INDIANA.
2 City, Elkhart co., N Indiana, 15 m. E of South Bend; pop. 40,274; manufactures band instruments, proprietary medicines, railroad supplies.

Elk Hills (ĕlk). United States naval oil reservation in Kern co., S California; leased by Secretary of the Interior Albert B. Fall at time of Teapot Dome oil scandals but lease canceled 1924.

Elk′horn′ (ĕlk′hôrn′). 1 River ab. 200 m. long, NE Nebraska; rises in Rock co., flows SE into Platte river.
2 City, ⊗ of Walworth co., S Wisconsin, 24 m. E of Janesville; pop. 3586; musical instruments, shoes.

El′kin (ĕl′kĭn). Industrial town, Surry co., N North Carolina, on Yadkin river; pop. 2868.

El′kins (ĕl′kĭnz). City, ⊗ of Randolph co., NE cen. West Virginia, 37 m. SE of Clarksburg; pop. 8307; railroad shops. Davis and Elkins Coll. (1903; coed.).

Elk Island National Park. See CANADA, *National Parks.*

Elk′land (ĕlk′lănd). Borough, Tioga co., N Pennsylvania, on New York border; pop. 2189; leather.

Elk Mountain (ĕlk). Peak 11,162 ft., one of the highest peaks in Medicine Bow Range, S cen. Wyoming.

El′ko (ĕl′kō). 1 County, Nevada. See NEVADA, *Table.*
2 City, its ⊗, NE corner of Nevada, on Humboldt river 32 m. NNW of Franklin Lake; pop. 6298; formerly site of Univ. of Nevada 1874–85 (see RENO, Nevada).

Elk Point (ĕlk). City, ⊗ of Union co., SE corner of South Dakota; pop. 1378.

Elk River. 1 See ELK.
2 Village, ⊗ of Sherburne co., cen. Minnesota, on Mississippi river NW of Minneapolis; pop. 1763.

Elk′ton (ĕlk′tŭn). 1 City, ⊗ of Todd co., SW Kentucky; pop. 1448.
2 Town, ⊗ of Cecil co., NE Maryland, on Elk river; pop. 5989; American "Gretna Green" until passage of a 48-hour marriage law 1938; paper, flour, fertilizer.

El Ku·nei′tra *or* **El Qu·nei′tra** (ĕl kōō·nā′trá; *Arab.* äl kōō·nā′trŏ, -nĭ′-). Town, SW Syria, ab. 40 m. SW of Damascus on highway to Safad and Haifa.

El′land (ĕl′ănd). Urban district, West Riding, Yorkshire, N England; pop. 19,273; woolens; ironworks.

Ellas. See GREECE.

Ellasar See LARSA.

El'la·ville (ĕl'ȧ·vĭl; *Sou. also* -v'l). City, ⊗ of Schley co., SW cen. Georgia; pop. 905.

El Ledj'a (ĕl lĕj'ȧ; *Arab.* ăl lăj'ȧ, -ă) *or* **Ledja.** Region of lava wilderness, containing many caves, on W frontier of Jebel ed Druz, SW Syria, S of Damascus; formerly haunt of robber bands.

El'lef Ring'nes' Island (ĕl'ĕf rĭng'nās'). One of the Sverdrup Is. (*q.v.*); 4800 sq. m.

El'len, Mount (ĕl'ĕn; -ĭn). **1** Peak 11,485 ft. in NE Garfield co., S Utah.
2 Peak 4135 ft. in Washington co., N cen. Vermont.

El'len·dale (ĕl'ĕn·dāl). City, ⊗ of Dickey co., S North Dakota, 63 m. S of Jamestown; pop. 1800; North Dakota State Normal and Industrial College (1889; coed.).

El'lens·burg (ĕl'ĕnz·bûrg). City, ⊗ of Kittitas co., cen. Washington, on Yakima river 27 m. N of Yakima; pop. 8625; coal mines; Central Washington College of Education (1891; coed.).

El'len's Isle (ĕl'ĕnz). Small island in Loch Katrine, Perth co., cen. Scotland; Ellen's haunt in Sir Walter Scott's *Lady of the Lake.*

El'len·ville (ĕl'ĕn·vĭl). Residential village, Ulster co., SE New York, in Shawangunk Mts. 26 m. W of Poughkeepsie; pop. 5003.

Elles'mere (ĕlz'mēr). Urban district, Shropshire, W England, 10 m. SW of Whitchurch, on **Ellesmere Canal** (not now in use); pop. 2159; dairy farming.

Ellesmere, Lake. Coastal lake 107 sq. m. in E South I., New Zealand, on S side of Banks Penin. at its base.

Ellesmere Island. Island 76,600 sq. m., N Franklin District, Northwest Territories, Canada, W of NW Greenland; its N point, Cape Columbia, is the northernmost point of Canada (in 83°).

Ellesmere Port and Whit'by (hwĭt'bĭ). Urban district, Cheshire, NW England, on the Mersey 10 m. SSE of Liverpool; pop. 32,594.

El'lice (ĕl'ĭs), *or* **La·goon'** (lȧ·gōōn'), **Islands.** Island group consisting of 9 coral atolls, all inhabited, in W Pacific Ocean, N of Fiji Is. and SE of Gilbert Is., extending from 5° to 10°30'S lat. and 176°E long. to 179°58'W long. (all lie W of the date line); 14 sq. m.; pop. (1940) 4613; government headquarters and chief village on Funafuti I.; belongs to British colony of Gilbert and Ellice Islands; chief islands Funafuti, Nukufetau, Nukulaelae, and Nanumea. Group has interesting ethnological history: in early centuries Ellice Islanders and Gilbertese of same race (Melanesian) but in 16th cent. Ellice Is. invaded and occupied by Samoans who established Polynesian race. Nanumea probably discovered 1781 and Funafuti 1819; in 19th cent. visited often by blackbirders who gradually decimated the population; made part of Gilbert and Ellice Islands Colony 1915.

El'lich·pur' *or* **El'ich·pur'** (ĕl'ĭch·pŏŏr'). Town, N Maharashtra state, cen. Indian Union, 110 m. W of Nagpur; pop. 28,592; active trade, chiefly in timber and cotton. Supposedly founded 11th cent.; became seat of Imad Shah dynasty of Berar 1484; hereditary ruler in 1803 received the title of nawab; family died out in 19th cent.

El'li·cott City (ĕl'ĭ·kŭt). Town, ⊗ of Howard co., cen. Maryland; pop. 9575.

El'li·jay' (ĕl'ĭ·jā'). City, ⊗ of Gilmer co., N Georgia; pop. 1320.

El'ling·ton (ĕl'ĭng·tŭn). Agricultural town, NW Tolland co., N Connecticut; pop. 5580; incorporated 1786.

El'lin·wood (ĕl'ĭn·wŏŏd). City, Barton co., cen. Kansas, 43 m. NW of Hutchinson; pop. 2729.

El'li·ott (ĕl'ĭ·ŭt; ĕl'yŭt). County in Kentucky. See *Table* at KENTUCKY.

Elliott Bay. Inlet of Puget Sound, waterfront of the city of Seattle, Washington.

El'lis (ĕl'ĭs). **1** Name of counties in three states of the U.S. See *Tables* at KANSAS, OKLAHOMA, TEXAS.
2 City, Ellis co., cen. Kansas, 60 m. NW of Great Bend; pop. 2218.

Ellis Island. Island, Upper New York Bay, ab. 1 m. SW of S point of Manhattan I.; sold by N.Y. state to national government 1808; became immigrant station 1891 and for many years received great majority of immigrants and nonimmigrant aliens entering the U.S.; ceased as immigration station 1954.

El'lis·land' (ĕl'ĭs·lănd'). Farm, Dumfries co., S Scotland, on the Nith 6 m. NW of Dumfries; home of Robert Burns 1788–91; property of British nation since 1928.

El'lis·ville (ĕl'ĭs·vĭl; *Sou. also* -v'l). City, a ⊗ of Jones co., SE Mississippi, 8 m. SW of Laurel; pop. 4592.

El·lo'ra (ĕ·lōr'ȧ). Village, cen. Maharashtra state, S cen. India, 15 m. NW of Aurangabad; famous for its rock temples, a series of caves carved out of the rocky hillside 1¼ m. long; in 3 sections: Buddhist, Brahmanical, and Jain; finest is Kailas of the Brahmanical group.

El·lore' (ĕ·lōr'). City, NE Andhra Pradesh, E India, 255 m. NNE of Madras at junction of Godavari and Kistna canal systems; pop. (1941) 64,911; large grain trade, important carpet manufactures; its fort was constructed of materials from nearby ruins of Pedda Vegi, supposed remains of Buddhist kingdom of Vengi; former capital of Northern Circars.

Ells'worth (ĕlz'wûrth; -wẽrth). **1** County in Kansas. See *Table* at KANSAS.
2 City, ⊗ of Ellsworth co., cen. Kansas, 36 m. W of Salina; pop. 2361; winter wheat; petroleum, limestone.
3 City, ⊗ of Hancock co., SE Maine, 27 m. SE of Bangor; pop. 4444.
4 Borough, Washington co., SW Pennsylvania, 23 m. S of Pittsburgh; pop. 1456.
5 Village, ⊗ of Pierce co., W Wisconsin; pop. 1701.

Ellsworth, Mount. Peak 8595 ft. in Glacier National Park, NW Montana.

Ellsworth Highland; *formerly* **James W. Ellsworth Land** (jāmz). High plateau of Antarctica extending E from Marie Byrd Land to W coast of Weddell Sea S of Palmer Penin., bet. 60° and 100° E.

Ell'wang'en (ĕl'väng'ĕn). Town, E Baden-Württemberg state, Germany, 46 m. ENE of Stuttgart; pop. 5653; captured by Allies Apr. 25, 1945.

Ell'wood City (ĕl'wŏŏd). Borough, Beaver and Lawrence cos., W Pennsylvania, 11 m. S of New Castle; pop. 12,413; metal products (pipe, tubing); coal mines.

El Maghreb el Aqsa. See MOROCCO.

El Mahalla el Kubra. = MAHALLA EL KUBRA.

El Maj'dal (ăl măj'dăl). **1** Ancient town on Sea of Galilee, N Palestine. See MAGDALA.
2 *anc.* **Mig'dal-Gad'** (mĭg'dăl-găd'). Town on railroad and highway, SW Palestine, 13 m. NNE of Gaza, in Gaza subdist.; pop. 6398; nearby are ruins of Ashkelon.

El'ma·li' (ĕl'mä·lĭ'). Town, W Antalya vilayet, SW Turkey in Asia, on highway in mountains 45 m. W of Antalya; pop. 5056; inhabited by direct descendants of the ancient Lycians.

El Man·su'ra (ĕl măn·sŏŏr'ȧ; *Arab.* ăl mŏn·sŏŏ'rŏ). Commercial and industrial city, ✳ of Daqahliya prov., Lower Egypt; pop. (1937) 69,036; on right bank of Damietta branch of the Nile SW of Lake Manzala; scene of battle Feb. 8, 1250 in which Crusaders (Sixth Crusade) under King Louis IX of France were severely defeated and Louis was captured.

El Man'te (ĕl män'tā). Town, Tamaulipas state, E Mexico; pop. 8690.

El Mar del Sur. Spanish for SOUTH SEA.

El Ma'ta·ri'ya (ăl măt'ȧ·rē'yȧ). **1** Town, Daqahliya prov., Lower Egypt, a NE suburb of Cairo; pop. ab. 20,000; near ruins of Heliopolis.
2 Town on shore of Lake Manzala and W of Port Said, NE Egypt; railroad terminus.

El Me·chi'li *or* **Me·ki'li** (ĕl mĕ·kē'lĭ). Town, NE Cyrenaica, Libya, N Africa, SSW of Derna on road connecting Salûm and Bengasi; set up as a gasoline depot by the British Dec. 1940; taken by Germans in advance on Egypt but retaken Nov. 1942.

El·Me·nar′ (ĕl mĕ·när′). Town, N Morocco, near coast of Strait of Gibraltar ab. 6 m. E of Tangier.

El′men·dorf Field (ĕl′mĕn·dôrf). U.S. airfield just E of Anchorage, at head of Cook Inlet, S cen. Alaska.

El Merg. See BARCA town.

Elm′hurst (ĕlm′hûrst). Residential city, Du Page co., NE Illinois, 17 m. W of Chicago; pop. 36,991; Elmhurst College (1871; coed.; Evangelical and Reformed Church).

El·mi′na (ĕl·mē′nȧ). Seaport town, S Ghana, W Africa; pop. ab. 5000; founded by Portuguese traders 1482.

El Min′ya (ĕl mĭn′yȧ). City, * of Minya prov., Upper Egypt, on left bank of the Nile 90 m. S of El Faiyûm; pop. (1937) 51,026.

El·mi′ra (ĕl·mī′rȧ). **1** Industrial city, ⊗ of Chemung co., S New York, on Chemung river 48 m. W of Binghamton; pop. 46,517; large coal shipments; dairying industry; manufactures office equipment, business machines, fire-fighting apparatus and chemicals, fabricated steel; site of Elmira College (1855), one of first in U.S. to grant degrees to women; Elmira State reformatory for men (1876), pioneer in modern penological methods. Nearby at Newtown (name also of the city 1815–28) was fought Aug. 29, 1779 the battle in which forces of expedition under Gen. John Sullivan and Gen. James Clinton defeated Indians and Tories who had been harassing New York and Pennsylvania frontiers, also sometimes known as battle of Chemung river; settled c. 1788; became ⊗ 1836; chartered as city 1864; home and burial place of Mark Twain. **2** Town, Waterloo co., SE Ontario, Canada, 12 m. N of Kitchener; pop. 2589; in fertile agricultural district.

Elmira Heights. Village, Chemung co., S New York, N suburb of Elmira; pop. 5157.

El Mis′ti (ĕl mēs′tē). Volcano 19,110 ft. in S Peru, NE of Arequipa.

El′mont (ĕl′mŏnt). Urban community (unincorporated), Nassau co., New York, on Long I. SW of Garden City; pop. 31,138.

El Mon′te (ĕl mŏn′tē). City, Los Angeles co., SW California, 12 m. E of Los Angeles; pop. 13,163; lion farm.

El·mo′ra (ĕl·mōr′ȧ). Locality, Cambria co., SW cen. Pennsylvania, ab. 22 m. NNE of Johnstown; pop. (est.) 1141.

El′more (ĕl′mōr). Name of counties in two states of the U.S. See *Tables* at ALABAMA and IDAHO.

El Mor′ro National Monument (ĕl mŏr′ō). See UNITED STATES, *National Monuments*.

Elms′ford (ĕlmz′fērd). Village, Westchester co., SE New York, 26 m. N of New York; pop. 3795; residential suburb.

Elms′horn (ĕlms′hôrn). Manufacturing city, Schleswig govt. dist., Schleswig-Holstein, northwestern Germany, 20 m. NW of Hamburg; pop. 15,392; railroad junction.

Elm′wood (ĕlm′wŏŏd). **1** Subdivision of town of WEST HARTFORD, Connecticut. **2** City, Peoria co., NW cen. Illinois, 20 m. WNW of Peoria; pop. 1882; birthplace of the sculptor Lorado Taft.

Elmwood Park. Residential village, Cook co., NE Illinois, suburb of Chicago; pop. 23,866.

Elmwood Place. Village, Hamilton co., SW corner of Ohio, 7 m. N of Cincinnati; pop. 3813; manufactures steel and foundry products.

Elne (ĕln); *anc.* **Il·lib′e·ris** (ĭ·lĭb′ēr·ĭs). Commune, Pyrénées-Orientales dept., S France, 10 m. SSE of Perpignan; pop. (1931) 4046; early 12th-cent. Romanesque cathedral; scene of murder of Emperor Constans 350.

El O·beid′ (ĕl ō·bād′). Town, * of Kordofan prov., cen. Sudan, 220 m. SW of Khartoum; pop. 52,372; important trade center; battle fought nearby Nov. 1–4, 1883 in which Gen. William Hicks and Egyptian army were defeated by the Mahdi.

E′lo·bey′, Great *and* **Little** (ā′lō·vā′; *Span.* -vĕ′ē). Two islands in Gulf of Guinea, W Africa; combined area ab. 1 sq. m.; attached to Spanish Guinea.

E′lon College (ē′lŏn). Town, Alamance co., N cen. North Carolina, ab. 3 m. NNW of Burlington; pop. 1284; Elon College (1889; coed.).

El Orde. See DONGOLA.

El O′ro (ĕl ō′rō). Province of Ecuador. See *Table* at ECUADOR.

El O′ro de Hi·dal′go (ĕl ō′rō thä ē·thäl′gō). Town, México state, cen. Mexico, 67 m. NW of Mexico City; pop. 8638.

El Oued (ĕl wĕd′); *also* **El Wad** (äl wăd′). Town (pop. ab. 11,000), oasis, and commune (pop. 68,203), cen. Touggourt territory, NE Algeria; on highway 50 m. NE of Touggourt.

E·loy′ Al·fa′ro (ā·loi′ äl·fä′rō); *formerly* **Du·rán′** (dōō-rän′). Railroad center, Guayas prov., W Ecuador, on Guayas river opp. Guayaquil; starting point of Guayaquil-Quito railroad, completed 1908.

El Pa·ra·í′so (ĕl pä′rä·ē′sō). Department, S Honduras; 3310 sq. m.; pop. (1945 est.) 73,597; * Yuscarán.

El Pas′o (ĕl păs′ō). **1** Name of counties in two states of the U.S. See *Tables* at COLORADO and TEXAS. **2** City, Woodford co., N cen. Illinois; pop. 1964. **3** City and port of entry, ⊗ of El Paso co., W tip of Texas, on Rio Grande river opp. Ciudad Juárez, Mexico; pop. 276,687; commercial, jobbing, and manufacturing center in region growing fruit, vegetables, and cotton (irrigation furnished by Elephant Butte Dam); railroad center and gateway to Mexico; ore smelters, copper and oil refineries. Texas Western College (1913; coed.); Fort Bliss (*q.v.*) and Biggs Air Force Base nearby. First settled 1827; alternately occupied by Federal and Confederate troops during Civil War; incorporated 1873.

El Paso del Nor′te (dĕl nôr′tĕ). Gorge of the Rio Grande river near El Paso, Texas.

El Paso de Robles. City, California. See PASO ROBLES.

El′phin·stone Island (ĕl′fĭn·stōn; -stŭn). Island, NW Mergui Archipelago (*q.v.*), Burma.

El Pro·gre′so (ĕl prō·grā′sō). **1** Department, N Guatemala; 742 sq. m.; pop. 65,302. **2** Town, * of El Progreso dept., Guatemala, on a tributary of the Usumacinta river near Mexican border. **3** Town, Yoro prov., NW Honduras, on Ulúa river 25 m. from its mouth; pop. (1940) 5409.

El Puerto. See PUERTO DE SANTA MARÍA.

El Qan′ta·ra (ĕl kăn′tȧ·rȧ; *Arab.* äl kŏn′tŭ·rŏ). Village on E bank of Suez Canal, Sinai prov., NE Egypt, bet. Port Said and Ismailia.

El Qa′ra (äl kä′rŏ). Village on W border of Qattara Depression, NW Egypt.

El Qasr (äl kŏs′r′); *Lat.* **Cas′trum** (kăs′trŭm). Literally "castle, stronghold"; chief town of Dakhla oasis, Southern Desert prov., Egypt; pop. bet. 5000 and 10,000.

El Qa·tra′ni (äl kŏ·trä′nē). Town, W cen. Jordan, on railroad ab. 50 m. S of Amman.

El Qsar el Kbir. See ALCAZARQUIVIR.

El Quds esh Sherif. See JERUSALEM.

El Quneitra. See EL KUNEITRA.

El Qu·seir′ *or* **El Qo·seir′** (äl kōō·sār′; -sīr′); *also, formerly* **Kos·seir′** (kōō-). Seaport, E Egypt, on the Red Sea E of Qena; pop. ab. 3000; on ancient caravan route to the Nile.

El Qusur. See LUXOR.

El Qutr el Masri. See EGYPT.

El Re′no (ĕl rē′nō). Industrial city, ⊗ of Canadian co., cen. Oklahoma, 27 m. W of Oklahoma City; pop. 11,015; Fort Reno (*q.v.*) and U.S. reformatory nearby.

El′roy (ĕl′roi). City, Juneau co., cen. Wisconsin, 30 m. ESE of Sparta; pop. 1505; butter.

El′sah (ĕl′sȧ). Village, Jersey co., W Illinois, on Mississippi river; pop. 218; The Principia College (1910; coed.; Christian Science).

El Sal′to (ĕl säl′tō). **1** Town, S Durango state, NW cen. Mexico, in Sierra Madre Occidental 75 m. NE of Mazatlán; pop. 6070. **2** Town, Jalisco state, W cen. Mexico; pop. 5531.

El Sal·va·dor (ĕl săl'vȧ·dôr; *Span.* ĕl säl'vä·thôr'). Republic, Central America; bounded on NW by Guatemala, on N, NE, and E by Honduras, on S and SW by the Pacific Ocean; area 8268 sq. m.; pop. 2,612,139 (1942 est.) 1,862,980; ✻ San Salvador; divided for administrative purposes into 14 departments; smallest and most densely populated of the Central American republics and the only one without an Atlantic seaboard. Crossed from NW to SE by two mountain ranges with many volcanic peaks, highest Santa Ana 8300 ft., San Miguel 7120 ft., San Salvador, and San Vicente; narrow coastal region is low plain, but most of country is plateau averaging 2000 ft. Only river the Lempa; several lakes in plateau region, largest Ilopango. Main industry agriculture; chief products coffee, sugar, beans, sisal, balsam. Chief cities San Salvador, Santa Ana, San Miguel, Ahuachapán, San Vicente.

History: Discovered by Alvarado 1523; in captaincy general of Guatemala; with rest of Central America (*q.v.*), became independent of Spain 1821, of Mexico 1823; member of United Provinces of Central America 1823–39; a leading advocate of various other projects for union; adopted new constitution 1939; remained neutral in World War I but declared war on Axis powers 1941 in World War II.

Elsass, Elsass–Lothringen. See ALSACE, ALSACE-LORRAINE.

Els'ber·ry (ĕlz'bĕr'ĭ; -bĕr·ĭ). City, Lincoln co., E Missouri, on Mississippi river 30 m. NNW of St. Charles; pop. 1491.

El Se·gun·do (ĕl sĕ·gŭn'dō; -gōōn'-). Oil city, Los Angeles co., SW California, 14 m. SW of Los Angeles; pop. 14,219; founded by Standard Oil Co., incorp. 1917.

El'si·nore (ĕl'sĭ·nōr). 1 City, Riverside co., SE California, on Elsinore Lake 30 m. S of San Bernardino; pop. 2432; mineral springs in vicinity.
2 Seaport, Denmark. See HELSINGÖR.

Els'mere (ĕlz'mēr). 1 Residential town, New Castle co., N Delaware, suburb of Wilmington; pop. 7319.
2 City, Kenton co., N Kentucky, 8 m. SW of Covington; pop. 4607.

El Sollum. See SALŪM.

El'ster (ĕl'stēr). 1 Name of two rivers in Germany: (1) **Schwar'ze Elster** (shvär'tsĕ), literally "Black Elster," in cen. part, ab. 125 m. long; flows N and NW out of Saxony into Elbe river 8 m. E of Wittenberg. (2) **Weis'se Elster** (vī'sĕ), literally "White Elster," ab. 120 m. long; rises in NW Czechoslovakia and flows N past Leipzig to the Saale near Halle.
2 Town, East Germany, in Saxony on the Weisse Elster just W of Leipzig; pop. (1933) 2205; mineral springs, baths.

El'stow (ĕl'stō; -stŭ). Village, Bedfordshire, S England, ab. 1 m. S of Bedford; birthplace of John Bunyan.

Els'tree (ĕls'trē). Parish, S Hertfordshire, England, NW of London; motion-picture industry.

Els'wick (ĕl'sĭk; ĕl'zĭk; ĕlz'wĭk). Ward of Newcastle upon Tyne, Northumberland, N England; site of engineering works and shipyard founded by Sir W. G. Armstrong, now part of Vickers Armstrong, Ltd.

El Teb (ĕl tĕb'). Locality, NE Sudan, near coast of Red Sea S of Port Sudan; scene of two battles Feb. 1884.

El'te·keh (ĕl'tĕ·kĕ). Ancient village in W Palestine, W of Jerusalem and near Ekron; scene of battle 701 (or 700) B.C. in which Sennacherib defeated Egyptians.

El Te·nien'te (ĕl tä·nyān'tä). Mining town, O'Higgins prov., cen. Chile, 45 m. S of Santiago; pop. 11,761; has large copper mines. See SEWELL.

El'tham (ĕl'thăm). Borough, Taranaki provincial dist., SW North I., New Zealand; pop. 2040.

El Tih (ĕl tē'). Plateau, cen. Sinai Penin., NE Egypt, just N of the Egma Plateau; 1800 to 3600 ft.

El To·cu'yo (ĕl tō·kōō'yō). Town, Lara state, NW Venezuela; pop. (1941 est.) 5365; in Cordillera Mérida 40 m. SW of Barquisimeto.

El To'fo (ĕl tō'fō). Mining town, Coquimbo prov., cen. Chile, ab. 250 m. N of Valparaíso; pop. 1717; subdivision of La Higuera commune; iron mines.

El'ton (ĕl't'n; *Russ.* ĕl'y·tŭn) or **El'ton·sko·e** (ĕl'y·tŭn·skŭ·yĕ; *Kalmyk* **Al'tan–Nor** (äl'tän·nōr'). Salt lake in E Stalingrad Region, Soviet Russia, Europe, in steppe E of Volga river; very shallow, much of it dry in the summer; yields large quantities of salt.

El Tro'na·dor' (ĕl trō'nä·thôr'). Volcano 11,350 ft. on Argentina-Chile boundary near Lake Nahuel Huapí; a feature of Gran Parque Nacional in Argentina.

Elt'ville (ĕlt'vĭl) or **El'feld** (ĕl'fĕlt). Town, W Germany, in Hesse state, on the Rhine 5 m. SW of Wiesbaden; pop. (1933) 4362; Gutenberg established his press here 1465.

El Uqsor. See LUXOR.

E·lu'ra (ĕ·lōōr'ȧ). = ELLORA.

El Va'do Dam (ĕl vä'thō). Dam completed 1935 across Chama river, NW cen. Rio Arriba co., NW New Mexico; height 175 ft.; impounds water, **El Vado Reservoir,** for irrigation.

El Val'le (ĕl vä'yä). Town in Federal District, N Venezuela; pop. (1941 est.) 5384.

El'vas (âl'väsh); *Lat.* **Al·pe'sa** (ăl·pē'sȧ); *Arab.* **Ba'lesh** (bä'läsh). Fortified city, Portalegre dist., E cen. Portugal, near Spanish frontier 30 m. SSE of Portalegre; pop. 11,747; manufactures jewelry, firearms, cannon; 15th-cent. cathedral, Moorish aqueduct. Fortified by Moors; taken by Portugal 1226; conquered by French 1808; ceded to Portugal by Convention of Sintra 1808.

El'vend (ĕl'vĕnd). Var. of ALWAND.

El've·rum (ĕl'vĕ·rōōm). Town, Hedmark co., E Norway, SE of Lillehammer; pop. 11,509; temporary meeting place of Norwegian government Apr. 1940.

El Vie'jo (ĕl vyĕ'hō). Town, a NW suburb of Chinandega, NW Nicaragua; pop. (1941 est.) 5321.

El'vins (ĕl'vĭnz). City, St. Francois co., E Missouri, 57 m. SSW of St. Louis; pop. 1818.

El Vol·cán' de A're·qui'pa (ĕl vôl·kän' dä ä'rä·kē'pä). = EL MISTI.

El Wad. See EL OUED.

El'wood (ĕl'wŏŏd). 1 City, Madison co., cen. Indiana, 25 m. WNW of Muncie; pop. 11,793; industrial center in tomato-growing section.
2 Village, ⊗ of Gosper co., S Nebraska; pop. 481.

E'ly (ē'lĭ). 1 City, St. Louis co., NE Minnesota, 40 m. NE of Virginia; pop. 5438; in iron-mining section.
2 City, ⊗ of White Pine co., E Nevada, 63 m. SSE of Ruby Lake; pop. 4018; copper mines; Lehman Caves National Monument nearby.
3 Urban district, Isle of Ely, E England, on the Ouse 18 m. NNE of Cambridge; pop. 9989; beet-sugar refining; its cathedral, begun 1083, one of the most notable in architecture in England; stronghold of Hereward the Wake 1070–71.

Ely, Isle of. Administrative county in E England, formerly and still in postal and geographical use, the N part of Cambridgeshire (*q.v.*); largely drained fenland; 372 sq. m.; (1951) 89,038; ⊗ March; other towns are Ely, Wisbech; chiefly agricultural.

Ely, Mount. Peak 7310 ft. in N cen. Lincoln co., E Nevada.

El'y·ma'is (ĕl'ĭ·mā'ĭs). Greek form of Elam (*q.v.*), sometimes used to designate a district of ancient Elam, in its S part at head of Persian Gulf, inhabited by the Elymeans.

E·lyr'i·a (ĕ·lĭr'ĭ·ȧ). Industrial city, ⊗ of Lorain co., N Ohio, 23 m. WSW of Cleveland; pop. 43,782; settled 1817.

El Yun'que (ĕl yōōng'kä). 1 Anvil-shaped peak on Más a Tierra I. in the Juan Fernández group in the Pacific Ocean, 365 m. W of Valparaíso, Chile.
2 Peak 3496 ft. in the Luquillo Mts., E Puerto Rico.

E'ma (ĕ'mä). River 130 m. long, E Estonia, U.S.S.R.; outlet of Lake Virts flowing E to Lake Peipus.

E·man′u·el (ē·măn′ū·ĕl). County in Georgia. See *Table* at GEORGIA.

Emaus. See EMMAUS.

Em·ba′ (ĕm·bä′). River ab. 350 m. long, W Kazakh S.S.R., Soviet Central Asia, flowing SW into NE corner of Caspian Sea; extensive oil fields on its lower course.

Em′ba·baan′ (ĕm′bä·bän′). Var. of MBABANE.

Em·bar′ca·de′ros, Point (ăm·bär′kä·thä′rôs). Cape on NE coast of Puerto Rico, W of Cape San Juan.

Em′bar·ras or **Em′bar·rass** (ăm′brô). River ab. 150 m. long, E Illinois; rises in Champaign co., flows S and SE into Wabash river.

Em′bos·ca′da (äm′bôs·kä′thä). Town, W Cordillera dept., cen. Paraguay, NE of Asunción; pop. ab. 7080.

Em′brun′ (äN′brûN′); *anc.* **Eb′u·ro·du′num** (ĕb′ū·rô·dū′nŭm). Commune, Hautes-Alpes dept., SE France, on the Durance ab. 100 m. NE of Marseilles; pop. (1931) 2711; archiepiscopal see c. 800–1791; 12th-cent. cathedral.

Em′den (ĕm′dĕn). Seaport and city, Lower Saxony, NW Germany (in the former Hannover prov. of Prussia) at mouth of Ems river on N coast of the Dollart, 46 m. WNW of Oldenburg; pop. 27,770; connected with interior by means of Dortmund-Ems and other canals; protected by dikes; 12th-cent. church; 16th-cent. town hall; shipbuilding. Founded 10th cent.; annexed to Hamburg 1433; made free city 1595; free port 1751; passed to Holland 1806 and to Hannover 1815; to Prussia 1866; in World War II an important naval base with oil tanks and refineries; frequently heavily bombed by Allies 1943–45; taken by Canadian forces Apr. 1945.

Emerald Isle. See IRELAND.

Emerita Augusta. = *Augusta Emerita*: see MÉRIDA.

Em′er·son (ĕm′ēr·s'n). **1** Borough, Bergen co., NE New Jersey, NE of Paterson; pop. 6849.
2 Town, SE Manitoba, Canada, on Red River of the North, at Minnesota border 63 m. S of Winnipeg; pop. 884; frontier customs town.

Em′er·y (ĕm′ēr·ĭ; ĕm′rĭ). County in Utah. See *Table* at UTAH.

Em′er·y·ville (ĕm′ēr·ĭ·vĭl; ĕm′rĭ-). Town, Alameda co., W California, on San Francisco Bay, suburb of Oakland; pop. 2686; packing houses, stockyards, iron foundries.

Emesa. See HOMS.

Em′i·grant Peak (ĕm′ĭ·grănt). **1** Mountain 10,960 ft. in S Park co., S Montana.
2 Mountain 6805 ft. in Esmeralda co., SW Nevada.

E′mi Kous′si (ā′mē kōō′sē). Peak 11,201 ft. in the Sahara, highest point of Tibesti massif, N Chad.

E·mi′lia (â·mē′lyä); *anc.* **Æ·mil′ia** (ê·mĭl′yä; -mĭl′ĭ·â). Compartimento of N Italy; for provincial divisions, area, and pop. see *Table* at ITALY; on Adriatic Sea bet. Tuscany and Lombardy; mountainous in S, fertile plain (**E·mil′ian Plain** [ê·mĭl′yän]) in N; formerly formed duchies of Parma and Modena and the papal Romagna; named for ancient Æmilian Way (built 187 B.C., ran from Rimini to Piacenza, 176 m.).

Em′i·nence (ĕm′ĭ·nĕns). City, ⊗ of Shannon co., S Missouri; pop. 516.

E′min·ö·nü′ (ĕ′mĕn·ū·nū′). District and suburb of İstanbul, Turkey in Europe; pop. 100,933.

E′mi·rau′ (ā′mĭ·rou′). Island in S part of St. Matthias group, Bismarck Archipelago, W Pacific Ocean; occupied by U.S. Marines Mar. 19, 1944.

Em′ma·ha′ven (ĕm′â·hä′vĕ[n]; *Angl.* ĕm′â·hä′vĕn, -hä′vĕn); *now* **Tu′luk·ba′jur** (tōō′lŏŏk·bä′yŏŏr). Port of Padang, W Sumatra, Indonesia, on NW shore of Koninginne Bay 4 m. S of Padang.

Em′ma·stad (ĕm′â·stät; *Angl.* ĕm′â·stăd). Town on island of Curaçao, Netherlands West Indies, near Willemstad; oil refineries.

Em·ma′us (ĕ·mā′ŭs), *formerly* **E′maus** (ē′mous; -môs). Borough, Lehigh co., E Pennsylvania, 5 m. S of Allentown; pop. 10,262; founded by Moravians c. 1740; manufactures pipe, tubing, rubber products, textiles.

Em·ma′us (ĕ·mā′ŭs). **1** Ancient village, Palestine;

probably modern **Qa·lun′ya** (kä·lōōn′yä; -yä), pop. 632, 4 m. NW of Jerusalem.
2 *or* **Emmaus Ni·cop′o·lis** (nĭ·kŏp′ō·lĭs; nĭ-). Ancient town, Judaea, Palestine, 20 m. NNW of Jerusalem near the Roman road to Joppa; probably modern **'Im·was'** (ĭm·wäs′), pop. 1021.

Em′me (ĕm′ĕ). River 45 m. long in W cen. Switzerland; flows NNW in Bern canton, joins the Aare river 1½ m. NE of Solothurn.

Em′men (ĕm′ĕ[n]). Commune, Drenthe prov., NE Netherlands, near German border ab. 28 m. SE of Groningen; pop. (1939) 48,586.

Em′me·rich (ĕm′ĕ·rĭk). City, North Rhine-Westphalia state, W Germany, near the Dutch border on Rhine river 61 m. WSW of Münster; pop. 13,647; river port; 15th-cent. town hall; varied manufactures. First mentioned 697 A.D.; passed to counts of Gelder 1233; made city 1247; passed to Cleves 1402; member of Hanseatic League 1407; with Cleves, passed to Brandenburg 1614; in World War II frequently bombed; in 1945 one of the crossings of the Rhine made here by Allies.

Em′met (ĕm′ĕt; -ĭt). Name of counties in two states of the U.S. See *Tables* at IOWA and MICHIGAN.

Em′mets·burg (ĕm′ĕts·bûrg; ĕm′ĭts-). City, ⊗ of Palo Alto co., N Iowa, 48 m. NW of Fort Dodge; pop. 3887.

Em′mett (ĕm′ĕt; -ĭt). City, ⊗ of Gem co., SW Idaho, 23 m. NW of Boise; pop. 3769; estab. as trading post 1864, incorp. 1900; ships fruit, esp. cherries; lumber.

Em′mits·burg (ĕm′ĭts·bûrg). Town, Frederick co., N Maryland, 20 m. N of Frederick; pop. 1369; Mount St. Mary's College (1808; men; Rom. Cath.); St. Joseph's College (1809; women; Rom. Cath.).

Em′mons (ĕm′ŭnz). County in North Dakota. See *Table* at NORTH DAKOTA.

Emmons Peak. Mountain 13,428 ft. in N Duchesne co., NE cen. Utah.

Emona. See LJUBLJANA.

Em′o·ry (ĕm′ô·rĭ; ĕm′rĭ). **1** Village, ⊗ of Rains co., NE Texas; pop. 559.
2 Town, Washington co., SW Virginia; pop. (1950) 176; Emory and Henry Coll. (1838; coed.).

Emory Peak. Mountain 7835 ft., the highest peak in Chisos Mts., S Brewster co., W Texas.

Em′pe·dra′do (ām′pâ·thrä′thô). Town, Corrientes prov., NE Argentina, on left bank of the Paraná just S of Corrientes.

Em′per·or Range (ĕm′pēr·ēr). Mountains forming N part of range that traverses Bougainville I., Solomon Is.; includes Mt. Balbi 10,171 ft., highest point in entire range; S extension is Crown Prince Range.

Em′pire (ĕm′pīr). Town on the canal in Gaillard Cut, Canal Zone, Panama, NW of Panama City.

Empire, the. = HOLY ROMAN EMPIRE.

Em′po·li (ām′pō·lē). Commune, Firenze prov., Tuscany, cen. Italy, on Arno river 18 m. WSW of Florence; pop. 26,212; manufactures cotton goods, leather, straw goods, faïence, glass, macaroni; 11th-cent. cathedral.

Em·po′ri·a (ĕm·pōr′ĭ·â). **1** City, ⊗ of Lyon co., E Kansas, 52 m. SW of Topeka; pop. 18,190; founded 1857; railroad division point; flour mills, cheese factory; Kansas State Teachers College (1863); College of Emporia (1882; coed.; Presbyterian). Home of William Allen White, editor and proprietor of Emporia *Gazette* from 1895 to his death 1944.
2 Manufacturing town, ⊗ of Greensville co., S Virginia, 38 m. S of Petersburg; pop. 5535; composed of North Emporia and South Emporia.

Em·po′ri·um (ĕm·pōr′ĭ·ŭm). Borough, ⊗ of Cameron co., N cen. Pennsylvania, 38 m. SSE of Bradford; pop. 3397; manufactures radio tubes, leather.

Em′press Au·gus′ta Bay (ĕm′prĕs [-prĭs] ô·gŭs′tâ). Widemouthed inlet of Solomon Sea on W coast of Bougainville I., NW Solomon Is., W Pacific Ocean; scene Nov. 1, 1943 of first landing by U.S. Marines in invasion of Bougainville (*q.v.*).

Ems (ĕms; *Angl.* ĕmz); *anc.* **A·mi'si·a** (*á·*mĭzh'ĭ·*á*). River ab. 200 m. long, NW Germany; rises in E Westphalia and flows NW and N through Westphalia and Hannover to the North Sea; its mouth is a wide estuary bordering on NE Netherlands, the upper part forming the Dollart (*q.v.*) and the lower comprising the navigable main channel which divides, passing to the W (**West Ems**) and E (**East Ems**) of Borkum I. in the East Frisian Is.; connected with the Ruhr region by the Dortmund-Ems canal system.

Ems (ĕms; āms; *Angl.* ĕmz); *called also* **Bad Ems** (bät'ĕms'; āms') Town, West Germany, in Hesse state on the Lahn river 11 m. SE of Koblenz; pop. (1933) 7672; watering place; here on Aug. 25, 1786 the four Roman Catholic archbishops of Cologne, Trier, Mainz, and Salzburg prepared the Punctation of Ems asserting episcopal rights against the Pope; also scene of interview bet. the King of Prussia and the French ambassador July 13, 1870 resulting in the sending by Bismarck of the famous Ems dispatch, a direct cause of the Franco-Prussian War 1870–71.

Ems'det'ten (ĕms'dĕt'ĕn). Commune, W Germany, in North Rhine-Westphalia state on Ems river 16 m. NNW of Münster; pop. 13,297; textiles.

Ems'worth (ĕmz'wûrth; -wêrth). Residential borough, Allegheny co., SW Pennsylvania, on Ohio river 8 m. WNW of Pittsburgh; pop. 3341.

E'nard Bay (*á*'närd). Bay on NW coast of Scotland, S of Point of Stoer and N of Loch Broom.

E'na·re, Lake (ā'n*á*·rĕ). = Lake INARI.

En·can'to, Cape (ång·kän'tŏ); *or* **Encanto Point.** Cape on E coast of Luzon, Phil. Is., at SE point of Baler Bay.

En'car·na·ción' (äng'kär·nä·syōn'). 1 *in full* **Encarnación de Dí'az** (d*á* thē'äs). Town, Jalisco state, W cen. Mexico, just S of Aguascalientes; pop. 5962.

2 Town, ✳ of Itapúa dept., SE Paraguay, on Paraná river opp. Posadas, Argentina, with which it is connected by ferry, 180 m. SE of Asunción; pop. ab. 16,000; founded 1614; railroad terminus; in agricultural and grazing district.

En'con·tra'dos (äng'kôn·trä'thŏs). Town, Zulia state, NW Venezuela, on Catatumbo river 125 m. SW of Maracaibo; center of coffee-growing region near Colombia border.

En·coun'ter Bay (ĕn·koun'tēr). Inlet of Indian Ocean, SE South Australia, at outlet of Murray river.

En'cru·ci·ja'da (äng'krōō·sē·hä'thä). Municipality and town, Las Villas prov., W cen. Cuba, 15 m. N of Santa Clara; pop. (town) 7511.

En'dau (ĕn'dou). River ab. 80 m. long in NE Johore and SE Pahang states, S Malay Penin.; flows NE into South China Sea near SE boundary of Pahang state.

En'de (ĕn'dĕ). Town and port on S coast of Flores I., Lesser Sunda Is., Indonesia; pop. 7226; chief administrative center of E Sunda Is.

En'der·bur'y (ĕn'dēr·bēr'ĭ; -bēr·ĭ). One of the more important of the Phoenix Is., cen. Pacific Ocean, 3°S lat. and 171°W long.; an atoll 3 m. long by ¾ m. wide; 4 sq. m.; formerly worked for guano. As an important airplane base visited and claimed 1937–39 by both Great Britain and U.S.A.; with Canton I. placed 1939 under joint control; has no good anchorage and no seaplane facilities, its lagoon being merely a shallow pool.

En'der·by Land (ĕn'dēr·bĭ). Semicircular projection of Antarctica, extending from Ice Bay in 49°30'E to Edward VIII Bay at ab. 57°20'E and extending S from ab. lat. 66°S; first sighted by John Biscoe 1831–32; claimed by British, whose claims, according to some, extend as far W as 40°E.

Enderby Quadrant. Formerly, the quarter section of the Antarctic Continent (see ANTARCTICA) bet. the Greenwich meridian and 90°E; now chiefly Queen Maud Land, Enderby Land, Mac-Robertson Coast, and Leopold and Astrid Coast.

En'der·lin (ĕn'dēr·lĭn). City, Ransom co., SE North Dakota, 29 m. SE of Valley City; pop. 1596; railroad division point.

En'di·cott (ĕn'dĭ·kŭt). Village, Broome co., S New York, on Susquehanna river, 8 m. W of Binghamton; pop. 18,775; with Binghamton and Johnson City, one of so-called Triple Cities; manufactures shoes, business machines.

Endicott Mountains. Subsidiary mountain range, cen. part of Brooks Range, N Alaska; highest ab. 9000 ft.

En'dor (ĕn'dôr); *mod.* **In·dur'** (ĭn·dōōr'). Ancient village in Palestine, near Mt. Tabor 6 m. SE of Nazareth (*1 Sam.* xxviii. 7).

En'dröd (ĕn'drûd). Commune, SE Hungary, on Körös river 60 m. SW of Debrecen; pop. 15,807.

E·nez' (ĕ·nĕz'); *anc.* **Ae'nos** (ē'nŏs). Town and port, Edirne vilayet, NW Turkey in Europe, on Meriç (Maritsa) river in its delta.

En·fi'da·ville (ĕn·fē'd*á*·vĭl; *Fr.* än'fē'd*á*·vēl'). Town, NE Tunisia, near the coast ab. 30 m. S of Hammamet; in World War II center of fighting Apr. 1943, taken by British Apr. 20.

En'field (ĕn'fēld). 1 Manufacturing town, NE Hartford co., N Connecticut, on E bank of Connecticut river on Mass. border; pop. 31,464; settled 1681 as part of Massachusetts; annexed to Connecticut 1749; tobacco raising; includes Thompsonville (*q.v.*).

2 Manufacturing town, Grafton co., W New Hampshire, 6 m. E of Lebanon; pop. 1867; formerly site of Shaker settlements.

3 Town, Halifax co., NE North Carolina, 18 m. NNE of Rocky Mount; pop. 2978; ⊗ of Edgecombe co. 1745–58.

4 Town, E New South Wales, SE Australia, SW suburb of Sydney; pop. 14,782.

5 Urban district, Middlesex, SE England, on New river 10 m. N of London; pop. 67,874, (1951) 110,458; a part of Greater London; residential section; rifle manufacturing.

En'ga·dine (ĕng'g*á*·dēn; *Fr.* än'g*á*·dēn'); *Ger.* **En'ga·din'** (ĕng'gä·dēn'); *Ital.* **En·ga·di'na** (äng·gä·dē'nä). Swiss portion ab. 60 m. long of valley of the Inn river, in E Graubünden canton, E Switzerland; SW part is called the **Upper Engadine** and NE part the **Lower Engadine**; Saint-Moritz is near SW end.

Engannim. See JENIN.

Engano. See ENGGANO.

En·ga'ño, Cape (äng·gä'nyŏ). 1 Cape at E end of island of Hispaniola, on NW side of Mona Passage.

2 Northeast point of Cagayan prov., Luzon, Phil. Is., formed by N tip of Palaui I., 18°31'N; lighthouse; important naval battle off this cape Oct. 25, 1944 in which American fleet defeated Japanese force.

En·ge'bi (ĕng·gä'bĕ). Islet of Eniwetok (*q.v.*) atoll, Marshall Is.; captured by Americans Feb. 17–19, 1944.

En·ge'di (ĕn·gē'dĭ; -dĭ; -gĕd'ĭ); *mod.* **'Ain Ji'di** (än jī'dē; ĭn). Village and spring on W shore of Dead Sea, SE Judaea, Palestine, 18 m. E of Hebron (*1 Sam.* xxiv. 1).

Eng'el·berg (ĕng'ĕl·bĕrk). Valley in the Alps, in Unterwalden canton, cen. Switzerland.

En'gel·mann Peak (ĕng'gĕl·mǎn). Mountain 13,500 ft. in Clear Creek co., N cen. Colorado.

Eng'els (*Ger.* ĕng'ĕls; *Russ.* ĕn'gĕly's); *formerly* **Po·krcvsk'** (pŭ·krôfsk'). Town, ✳ of former German Volga Republic, SE Soviet Russia, Europe, on the Volga opp. Saratov; pop. 73,279; an agricultural center; renamed 1932 in honor of Friedrich Engels.

Eng·ga'no *or* **En·ga'no** (ĕng·gä'nŏ). Island in the Indian Ocean off SW coast of Sumatra, Indonesia; 18 m. long by 11 m. wide, area (with nearby islets) 171 sq. m.; pop. 469; chief export copra.

En'ghien' (än'gǎN'). See MONTMORENCY, France.

En'ghien'–les–Bains' (-lä·bǎN'). Commune, Seine-et-Oise dept., N France, N suburb of Paris; pop. (1931) 11,324; mineral springs and baths.

ENGLAND AND WALES

Statute Miles

0   25   50   75   100

⊛ Capitals of Countries

PUBLISHED BY G. & C. MERRIAM COMPANY
SPRINGFIELD, MASS.
PREPARED BY J. W. CLEMENT CO., BUFFALO, N.Y.

Eng'land (ĭng'glănd). **1** *Lat.* **An'gli·a** (ăng'glĭ·å). South part of the island of Great Britain, excluding Wales; largest division of the United Kingdom of Great Britain and Northern Ireland; 51,356 sq. m.; pop. (1931) 37,794,003, (1951) 41,572,585; ✻ London; divided into the following counties (for pronunciation of their names, see their individual entries):

NAME[1]	LOCA-TION	AREA[2]	POP.[2]	CO. SEAT
Bedfordshire	SE cen.	473	311,844	Bedford
Berkshire	S	725	402,939	Reading
Buckinghamshire	SE cen.	749	386,164	Aylesbury
Cambridgeshire[3]	E	492	166,863	Cambridge
Cheshire	NW	1,502	1,258,050	Chester
Cornwall	SW	1,357	345,612	Truro
Cumberland	NW	1,520	285,347	Carlisle
Derbyshire	N cen.	1,012	826,336	Derby
Devonshire	SW	2,612	798,283	Exeter
Dorsetshire	S	973	291,157	Dorchester
Durham	N	1,015	1,463,416	Durham
Ely, Isle of[3]	E	372	89,038	March
Essex	SE	1,528	2,043,574	Chelmsford
Gloucestershire	SW cen.	1,257	938,618	Gloucester
Hampshire[4]	S	1,503	1,196,617	Winchester
Herefordshire	W	842	127,092	Hereford
Hertfordshire	SE	632	609,735	Hertford
Huntingdonshire	E cen.	366	69,273	Huntingdon
Kent	SE	1,525	1,563,286	Maidstone
Lancashire	NW	1,875	5,116,013	Preston
Leicestershire	cen.	832	630,893	Leicester
Lincolnshire[5]	E			
The Parts of Holland		420	101,545	Boston
The Parts of Kesteven		724	131,566	Sleaford
The Parts of Lindsey		1,520	473,463	Lincoln
London	SE	117	3,348,336	London
Middlesex[6]	SE	232	2,268,776	
Monmouthshire[7]	W	546	424,647	Newport
Norfolk	E	2,055	546,550	Norwich
Northamptonshire[8]	cen.	914	359,550	Northampton
Northumberland	N	2,019	798,175	Newcastle
Nottinghamshire	N cen.	844	841,083	Nottingham
Oxfordshire	cen.	749	275,765	Oxford
Peterborough, Soke of[8]	E cen.	84	63,784	Peterborough
Rutlandshire	E cen.	152	20,510	Oakham
Shropshire	W	1,347	289,844	Shrewsbury
Somersetshire	SW	1,620	551,188	Taunton
Southampton	= *Hampshire*, above.			
Staffordshire	W cen.	1,153	1,621,013	Stafford
Suffolk[5]	E			
East Suffolk		871	321,849	Ipswich
West Suffolk		611	120,590	Bury St. Edmunds
Surrey	S	722	1,601,555	Kingston on Thames
Sussex[5]	S			
East Sussex		829	618,083	Lewes
West Sussex		628	318,661	Chichester
Warwickshire	cen.	976	1,860,874	Warwick
Westmorland	NW	789	67,383	Kendal
Wight, Isle of	S	147	95,594	Newport
Wiltshire	S	1,345	387,379	Trowbridge
Worcestershire	W cen.	699	522,974	Worcester
Yorkshire[5]	N			
East Riding		1,172	510,800	Beverley
North Riding		2,127	525,496	Northallerton
West Riding		2,780	3,480,066	Wakefield
York, City of[9]		10	105,336	

[1] For county names ending in -*shire*, the -*shire* is often omitted in informal use when there is no ambiguity. In legal use, except of *Gloucester, Hereford, Stafford*, etc., not *Gloucestershire, Herefordshire*, etc., is preferred. The redundant *county of Gloucestershire, Herefordshire* etc., is incorrect.
[2] Area in sq. m. Pop. is 1951 Census and includes county boroughs.
[3] Cambridgeshire, as an official postal and geographical name, includes the Isle of Ely.
[4] *Hampshire*, not *Southampton*, is the popular, and official postal, name. See HAMPSHIRE in *Vocab.*
[5] Preferred, as an official postal and geographical designation, to names of its subdivisions.
[6] Middlesex, now largely in Greater London, has no county seat. Administration offices are in Westminster.
[7] Monmouthshire is often considered a part of Wales.
[8] Northamptonshire, as an official postal and geographical name, includes the Soke of Peterborough.
[9] The City of York is a county of itself, outside any of the three Ridings.

Islands: Isle of Man in Irish Sea off NW coast, Isle of Wight in English Channel off S coast, Lundy I. at entrance to Bristol Channel, and Scilly Is. off Lands End

(the SW tip of England). *Mountains and highland regions:* In N the Pennine Chain, Cumbrian Mts. (including Scafell Pike 3210 ft., highest in country), and Cheviot Hills (along Scottish border); in SW the Cotswold Hills and plateau regions of Exmoor and Dartmoor; in SE the Downs, and in S Salisbury Plain. *Chief rivers:* Thames in S, Ouse in cen. and E, Humber (with Ouse and Trent) in NE, Mersey in W, and Severn in SW. *Chief lakes:* Bassenthwaite, Derwentwater, Ullswater, Windermere, all of great scenic beauty in the Lake District in Cumberland, Westmorland, and Lancashire in NW. *Chief industries:* Production of iron and steel, coal mining, shipbuilding, and all kinds of manufacturing are of importance. *Chief cities:* London, Birmingham, Liverpool, Manchester, Sheffield, Leeds, and Bristol.

For history, see GREAT BRITAIN.

2 City, Lonoke co., cen. Arkansas, 22 m. SE of Little Rock; pop. 2861; cotton.

En'gle·wood (ĕng'g'l·wŏŏd). **1** Suburban residential city, Arapahoe co., NE cen. Colorado, 5 m. S of Denver; pop. 33,398.

2 Residential city, Bergen co., NE corner of New Jersey, W of Hudson river 10 m. E of Paterson; pop. 26,057; incorporated as city 1895; Palisades Interstate Park nearby.

Eng'lish (ĭng'glĭsh). **1** Town, ⊗ of Crawford co., S Indiana, 33 m. W of New Albany; pop. 698.

2 River ab. 100 m. long, largest tributary of the Winnipeg, in SW Ontario, Canada; flows W through chain of large lakes.

English Ba·zar' (bå·zär'). Town, ✻ of Malda dist., West Bengal, NE Indian Union, 170 m. N of Calcutta; pop. 16,907.

English Channel; *often,* **the Channel**; *Fr.* **La Manche** (là mäNsh'), i.e., "the Sleeve"; *anc.* **O·ce'a·nus Bri·tan'ni·cus** (ô·sē'å·nŭs brĭ·tăn'ĭ·kŭs). Strait bet. S England and N France; connects with Atlantic Ocean on the W and with North Sea (through the Strait of Dover) on the NE; varies in width bet. 20 and 100 m.

Eng'lish·man Bay (ĭng'glĭsh·măn). Inlet of Atlantic Ocean on S cen. coast of Washington co., SE Maine.

English Turn (tûrn); *Fr.* **Dé·tour' des An'glais'** (dā'tōōr' dā·zäN'glĕ'). Bend of Mississippi river just below New Orleans, Louisiana, also the village (pop. ab. 100) in the bend; place where an English expedition was turned back Sept. 1699 by Bienville's story that strong French forces were farther up the river.

Enguinegatte. See GUINEGATE.

Engyum. See GANGI.

E'nid (ē'nĭd). City, ⊗ of Garfield co., N Oklahoma, 68 m. NNW of Oklahoma City; pop. 38,859; founded 1893; grain elevators, oil refineries; stockyards; market for horses and mules. Phillips Univ. (1907; coed.).

Enikale Strait. See KERCH STRAIT.

E·ni'peus (ē·nī'pūs; *Mod. Gr.* â'nyĕ·pâfs'). River in Thessaly, Greece, tributary of the Salambria; rises in Othrys Mts.

Enisei, Eniseisk. See YENISEI, YENISEISK.

E·ni'we·tok (ĕ·nē'wĕ·tŏk; *popularly* ĕn'ĭ·wē'tŏk). Atoll at extreme NW end of Ralik Chain, NW Marshall Is., W Pacific Ocean, 11°30′N lat. and 162°15′E long.; circular in shape with 40 islets around lagoon 23 m. in diameter; fine anchorage; main islets Eniwetok in S and Engebi in N; taken by Americans from Japanese Feb. 17–22, 1944 and made into a naval base; in 1947 designated by U.S. Atomic Energy Commission as permanent mid-Pacific proving ground for atomic weapons.

Enk·hui'zen (ĕngk·hoi'zĕ[n]). Commune and seaport, North Holland prov., W Netherlands, on W shore of IJsselmeer 28 m. NE of Amsterdam; pop. 9347; important commercial and fishing center in early 17th cent.

En'na (ĕn'à; *Ital.* ĕn'nä). **1** Province of Italy. See *Table* at ITALY.

2 *before 1927 called* **Ca'stro·gio·van'ni** (käs'trô·jô·vän'nē); *anc.* **En'na** (ĕn'à) *or* **Hen'na** (hĕn'à). Com-

mune, * of Enna prov., cen. Sicily, Italy, 64 m. SE of Palermo; pop. 23,817; summer resort; trades in sulfur and rock salt; cathedral (founded 1307), old feudal fortress, castle built by Frederick II of Aragon. Ancient site of principal temple of Ceres (Demeter) and, in mythology, her birthplace; headquarters of slaves in First Servile War 132 B.C.; nearby Lake of Pergusa site of fabled rape of Proserpine by Pluto; captured by Saracens 9th cent. and by Normans 11th cent.

En Na·hud′ (ăn nă·hōōd′). Commercial town, W Kordofan prov., cen. Sudan, 135 m. WSW of El Obeid; trades in cattle, ostrich feathers, ivory, and cotton goods.

En Na·qu′ra (ăn nä·kōō′rŏ). Village and cape (*Arab.* **Ras en Naqura** [räs]) on SW coast of Lebanon Republic, on N border of Palestine.

En Nasira. See NAZARETH.

En Nebk (ăn năb′ăk), *also* **Neb′ek** (nĕb′ĕk). Town, SW Syria, ab. 42 m. NE of Damascus.

En′ne·di′ (*Fr.* ĕn′dē′). Mountains, NE Chad, N cen. Africa; highest peak 4756 ft.

En′ner·dale Water (ĕn′ēr·dāl). Lake in the Lake District, Cumberland, NW England; 2½ m. long; maximum depth 148 ft.

En Nîl. See NILE.

En′nis (ĕn′ĭs). **1** Industrial city, Ellis co., NE cen. Texas, 20 m. N of Corsicana; pop. 9347; cotton compresses and gins; cottonseed oil.
2 Urban district, ⊗ of co. Clare, W Eire; pop. 5897; limestone quarrying, brewing, whisky distilling; ruins of two noted abbeys nearby.

En′nis·cor′thy (ĕn′ĭs·kôr′thĭ). Urban district, cen. co. Wexford, SE Eire, on river Slaney; pop. 5873; brewing, manufacture of woolens, tanning; agricultural trading center; remains of 13th-cent. castle.

En′nis·kil′len (ĕn′ĭs·kĭl′ĕn) *or* **In′nis·kil′ling** (ĭn′ĭs-kĭl′ĭng). Municipal borough, ⊗ of co. Fermanagh, SW Northern Ireland, on an island in the Erne river just S of Lough Erne; pop. 6318; trading center for agricultural section; manufactures cutlery. Scene of battle 1689 in which forces of William II defeated those of James II; famous regiment of Enniskillen Dragoons formed at the time.

En Nofilia. See NOFILIA.

Enns (ĕns; *Angl.* ĕnz). **1** River ab. 160 m. long, cen. Austria; flows E and N from Styria prov. into Danube river 11 m. SE of Linz; forms section of boundary bet. Upper Austria and Lower Austria.
2 Town, on Enns river near its confluence with the Danube; pop. 4192; one of the oldest towns in Austria, on old trade route across the Danube; in medieval times a prosperous market town; nearby is famous Augustinian monastery of St. Florian, with fine manuscript library.

E·no′la (ĕ·nō′lă). Locality, Cumberland co., S Pennsylvania, near Susquehanna river ab. 5 m. NW of Harrisburg; pop. (est.) 3200.

En′o·ree′ (ĕn′ŏ·rē′). River ab. 80 m. long, NW South Carolina; rises in Blue Ridge Mts. in Greenville co., flows SE into Broad river.

Enotah, Mount. See BRASSTOWN BALD.

En′ri·quil′lo, Lake (ăn′rĕ·kē′yŏ). Salt lake, SW Dominican Republic, E Hispaniola I., West Indies; 150 ft. below sea level.

En′sche·de′ (ĕn′sKĕ·dā′). Industrial commune, Overijssel prov., E Netherlands, near German frontier; pop. (1939) 91,494; manufactures and trades in cotton textiles.

En′se·na′da (ĕn′sĕ·nä′dä; *Span.* än′sā·nä′thä). **1** Town on coast of Río de la Plata, Buenos Aires prov., E Argentina, ab. 35 m. SE of Buenos Aires; forms part of the port of La Plata.
2 Seaport, N Lower California, NW Mexico, on Pacific Ocean; pop. 4616; former capital of Northern District of Lower California.
3 Village in Guánica municipality, on coast of SW Puerto Rico; pop. 3229.

En·teb′be (ĕn·tĕb′ĕ). Town, formerly * of Uganda, E Africa, 19 m. SW of Kampala, on N shore of Lake Victoria; pop. ab. 11,000; on the equator; connected by rail via Nairobi with Mombasa; founded 1893; made capital of British protectorate of Uganda 1894.

En′ter·prise (ĕn′tēr·prīz). **1** City, a ⊗ of Coffee co., SE Alabama, 27 m. W of Dothan; pop. 11,410; peanuts.
2 City, ⊗ of Wallowa co., NE corner of Oregon, 54 m. NE of Baker; pop. 1932; pine timber; ranching, agriculture.

En′tre-Dou′ro-e-Mi′nho (äNN′trĕ·thŏ′rōō·ĕ·mē′nyŏō), *popularly* **Mi′nho** (mē′nyŏō). Old province, NW Portugal; 2749 sq. m.; * Braga; now forms modern provinces of Minho and Douro Litoral.

En′tre Ri′os (äNN′trĕ rē′ōōs). City, Rio de Janeiro state, SE Brazil, 50 m. N of Rio de Janeiro; pop. (1940 est.) 10,600; transportation center.

En′tre Ri′os (än′trä rrē′ôs). Province of Argentina. See *Table* at ARGENTINA.

E·nu′gu (ā·nōō′gŏō). City, Onitsha prov., Eastern Region, Nigeria; pop. 12,959; * of the Eastern Region.

E′num·claw (ē′nŭm·klô). Town, King co., W cen. Washington, 23 m. E of Tacoma; pop. 3269; gateway to recreation areas of Mount Rainier.

En′yu, Enyu Channel (ĕn′yŏō). See BIKINI.

Enzeli. See PAHLEVI.

Eolie, Isole. See LIPARI ISLANDS.

E·o′lus (ĕ·ō′lŭs). Mountain 3185 ft. in NW Bennington co., SW Vermont.

Eolus, Mount. Peak 14,086 ft. in La Plata co., SW Colorado.

Éparges, Les. See LES ÉPARGES.

Ep′au·let Mountain (ĕp′ŏ·lĕt). Peak 13,500 ft. in Clear Creek co., N cen. Colorado.

E′pe (ā′pĕ). Commune, Gelderland prov., E Netherlands, 9 m. N of Apeldoorn; pop. 13,410.

E′pe·cuén, Lake (ā′pā·kwän′). Lake ab. 94 sq. m. in S Buenos Aires prov., E Argentina; resort.

E′pe·hy′ (ĕ′pē′). Village, Somme dept., N France, S of Cambrai; pop. (1931) 1408; destroyed in World War I; taken by the British Sept. 1918.

Epeiros. See EPIRUS.

Eperjes. See PREŠOV.

É′per′nay′ (ā′pĕr′nā′); *anc.* **Spar′na·cum** (spär′nă·kŭm). Commune, Marne dept., NE France, on the Marne 21 m. WNW of Châlons-sur-Marne; pop. 20,406; in region famous for production of champagne wines; manufactures earthenware. Fortified city in Middle Ages; besieged by Henry IV 1592; scene of violent fighting and air raids 1914–18.

Eph′e·sus (ĕf′ē·sŭs). Ruins of ancient Ionian city, W Asia Minor, near coast of Aegean Sea 35 m. SSE of İzmir, in fertile plain near the mouth of the Caÿster river, near modern village of Aya Soluk. Traditionally founded by Carians; one of the 12 Ionian Cities; conquered by Persians; its democracy restored by Alexander the Great 334 B.C.; had famous temple, a center of cult of Diana; finally came to Romans from king of Pergamum (*q.v.*); capital of Roman province of Asia; early seat of Christianity (visited by Saint Paul on second and third missionary journeys, church to which he wrote the *Epistle to the Ephesians*); sacked by Goths 262 A.D.; seat of church council which condemned heresy of Nestorius 431.

E′phra·im (ē′frā·ĭm; ē′frĭ·ŭm). **1** City, Sanpete co., cen. Utah, 43 m. WSW of Price; pop. 1801; settled 1853; center of turkey and sheep-raising area.
2 Mountainous region or range (**Mount Ephraim**) of cen. Palestine, originally the country allotted to the tribe of Ephraim; extended S from near Shechem to neighborhood of Bethel.
3 Sometimes, the Northern Kingdom, or Kingdom of Israel (see ISRAEL).

Eph′ra·ta (ĕf′rȧ·tȧ). Borough, Lancaster co., SE Pennsylvania, 13 m. NE of Lancaster; pop. 7688; stock rais-

ing. Founded c. 1732 as German Seventh-day Baptist monastic community (Society of the Solitary) by Johann Conrad Beissel; Ephrata Cloisters built and printing press established 1745.

E·phra′ta (ĭ-frā′tà). City, ⊗ of Grant co., cen. Washington at S end of the Grand Coulee; pop. 6548.

E′pi (ā′pē) *or* **A′pi** (ä′pē). One of the New Hebrides Is., SW Pacific Ocean, in E part of the group, 25 m. SE of Malekula; 27 m. long by 11 m. wide; pop. (native; 1938 est.) 2500; has mountain peak 2785 ft., fertile soil, and fine plantations (esp. coconut).

Ep:damnus. See DURRËS.

Ep′i·dau′rus (ĕp′ĭ-dô′rŭs). Ancient seaport town in Greece, on E coast of Argolis on Saronic Gulf, 25 m. E of Argos; site of famous temple dedicated to Asclepius, Greek god of medicine and healing; also site of theater and a Greek round structure (*tholos*, rotunda); much visited for centuries; until Roman times town and vicinity were semi-independent.

É′pi·nal′ (ā′pē′nàl′). Commune, ✳ of Vosges dept., NE France, on Moselle river 65 m. E of Chaumont; pop. 27,708; freestone and marble quarried nearby; manufactures cotton goods, hats, and iron and brass goods. Founded 10th cent.; in World War II captured by U.S. forces Sept. 25, 1944.

É′pi·nay′–sur–Seine′ (ā′pē′nā′sür-sân′). Industrial commune, Seine dept., N France, N suburb of Paris on the Seine; pop. (1931) 14,505.

Epiphania. See HAMA.

Epiphanie, L′. See L′EPIPHANIE.

E·pi′rus (ė·pī′rŭs); *Gr.* **E′pei·ros** (ĕ′pē-rôs). **1** An ancient country in NW Greece, bounded on N by Illyria, on E by Macedonia and Thessaly, on S by Aetolia and Acarnania, and on W by Ionian Sea, extending along coast of latter from Acroceraunia promontory on N to the Ambracian Gulf on S; mountainous, traversed by main range of Pindus Mts. and parallel ranges; mountains cut by Inachus, Achelous, and Kalamas rivers; more important of its districts were Athamania, Thesprotia (*q.v.*), Molossis, and Chaonia; chief towns Phoenice, Dodona, Buthrotum.

History: United by King Pyrrhus (d. 272 B.C.); made a republic c. 200 B.C.; after Roman defeat of Macedonians 197 B.C. retained independence; punished by Rome for supporting Perseus 168 B.C.; set up as Roman province 146 B.C.; under Byzantine Empire until Michael Angelus Comnenus erected an independent state 1204; conquered by Turks 1430; Greece received E part 1881, captured Ioannina 1913, and was awarded 1919 the W part as far N as a point on the coast off N Corfu; N part is now in S Albania; formed battleground for Greeks and Italians 1940–41.

2 Geographical division of modern Greece, its W part N of the Peloponnesus; 3611 sq. m.; pop. (1938 est.) 298,930; forms departments of Arta, Ioannina, and Preveza (see *Table* at GREECE).

E·po·me′o, Mon′te (môn′tā ā·pô·mā′ô). Highest point 2588 ft. on island of Ischia (*q.v.*).

Eporedia. See IVREA.

Ep′ping (ĕp′ing). **1** Manufacturing town, Rockingham co., SE New Hampshire, 15 m. W of Portsmouth; pop. 2006; shoes, bricks.

2 Urban district, Essex, SE England, 17 m. NE of London; pop. 6934; on N edge of **Epping Forest**, a former royal forest of large extent, now a pleasure ground.

Ep′som (ĕp′sŭm). Town, Surrey, S England, on the edge of Banstead Downs in Epsom and Ewell municipal borough; pop. (1931) 27,089; the seat of Epsom College; nearby is **Epsom Downs** racecourse, where the Derby and the Oaks are run annually; magnesia springs in the vicinity from which Epsom salts formerly were made.

Epsom and Ew′ell (ū′ĕl). Municipal borough, Surrey, SE England, 13 m. SW of London; pop. 35,500, (1951) 68,049.

Ep′worth (ĕp′wûrth; -wẽrth). Parish in the Parts of Lindsey, Lincolnshire, E England; pop. 1795; birthplace of John Wesley—hence the name Epworth League for the Methodist young people's organization founded 1889 at Cleveland, Ohio.

E·qua′tor (ê-kwā′tẽr). = EQUATOR PROVINCE.

E′qua·to′ri·a (ē′kwà-tōr′ĭ-à; ĕk′wà-). **1** Occasional name used somewhat indefinitely for the equatorial regions of Africa.

2 Province, S Sudan; 131,528 sq. m.; pop. 903,503; ✳ Juba.

Equatorial Africa. = FRENCH EQUATORIAL AFRICA.

Equatorial Countercurrent. The surface current moving E in a few places in the oceans near the equator.

Equatorial Current. The surface current moving W in the oceans near the equator.

Equator Province. Province, Republic of the Congo (formerly Belgian Congo). See COQUILHATVILLE.

E′qui·nox Mountain (ē′kwĭ-nŏks; ĕk′wĭ-). Peak 3816 ft. in Taconic range, in Bennington co., SW Vermont.

Erakleion. Var. of *Hērákleion:* city, see CANDIA; dept., see *Table* at GREECE.

E·ran′dio (â·rän′dyô). Commune, Vizcaya prov., N Spain, N suburb of Bilbao; pop. (1930) 11,268.

E′rath (ē′răth). County in Texas. See *Table* at TEXAS.

Er′bil (ĭr′bĭl) *or* **Ar′bil** (ĭr′bĭl). **1** Province (*liwa*), N Iraq; pop. (1935 est.) 180,671.

2 *anc.* **Ar·be′la** (är-bē′là). City in fertile region of N Iraq, 50 m. E of Mosul and S of the Great Zab; pop. ab. 25,000; a very old city, probably a Sumerian settlement that came to be one of chief places of Assyria; still has important trade; not scene of battle of Arbela, which was really fought at Gaugamela (*q.v.*) 331 B.C.; neighborhood overrun and conquered by Mongols 1236 A.D.

Er′ceg·no′vi (ĕr′tsĕg-nō′vê); *Ital.* **Ca·stel′nuo′vo** (käs·tĕl′nwô′vô). Seaport, S Yugoslavia, on N shore of Gulf of Kotor; pop. 12,096.

Erceldoune, Ercildoune. See EARLSTON.

Er′ci·yas′ Da·ğı′ (ĕr′jê-yäs′ dä-ĭ′); *anc.* **Ar·gae′us** (är-jē′ŭs). Peak 12,848 ft. in cen. Turkey in Asia, S of Kayseri; highest mountain in Asia Minor.

Erdély. See TRANSYLVANIA.

Er′e·bus, Mount (ĕr′ĕ-bŭs). Peak 13,200 ft. on Ross I. in Ross Sea, Antarctica; lat. 77°35′S and long. 167°10′E; an active volcano.

E′rech (ē′rĕk; ĕr′ĕk); *Akkadian* **U′ruk** (ōō′rook). Ancient Sumerian city (c. 2300 B.C.) in S Babylonia, on the Euphrates NW of Ur of the Chaldees; the modern **War·ka′** (wür·kä′); in the Bible a city of Nimrod's kingdom in land of Shinar (*Gen.* x. 10); excavations on the site have been considerable, uncovering walls, a temple, base of a ziggurat, and a valuable library.

E′reğ·li′ (ĕ′rĭ-lē′). **1** Town, Konya vilayet, SW cen. Turkey in Asia, 85 m. ESE of Konya; pop. 9463; textile manufacturing.

2 *anc.* **Her′a·cle′a Pon′ti·ca** (hĕr′à·klē′à pŏn′tĭ·kà). Seaport on Black Sea, Zonguldak vilayet, NW Turkey in Asia, 40 m. ENE of mouth of the Sakarya river; pop. 5879.

E′re·pe·cú′, Lake (ā′rĕ·pĕ·kōō′). Lake, NW Pará state, N Brazil, N of the Amazon; traversed by Trombetas river, a tributary of the Amazon.

E′re·pe·cu·rú′ (ā′rĕ·pĕ·kōō·rōō′). River ab. 250 m. long, N Brazil; formed by confluence of Parú (Oeste) and Marapí rivers, flows S into Trombetas river just before it empties into the Amazon.

E·re′tri·a (ė·rē′trĭ·à; ĕ·rĕt′rĭ·à). City of ancient Greece, on S coast of Euboea I. ab. 15 m. SSE of Chalcis, its rival in the early period. Founded as an Ionian colony; destroyed by Persians 490 B.C. (before battle of Marathon) for earlier assistance to revolting Ionian Greeks; rebuilt but less significant.

E′retz Yis′ra·el′ *or* **E′rets Yis′ra·el′** (ĕ′rĕts yĭs′rä-āl′). Literally, Hebrew, "Land of Israel"; modern Jewish name for Palestine. See ISRAEL.

Erevan. See YEREVAN.

Erft (ĕrft). River ab. 70 m. long, in the Rhineland, western Germany; rises in Eifel region and flows N to the Rhine near Neuss.

Er′furt (ĕr′fŏŏrt; *in English, also* -fĕrt). **1** Government district of former Saxony prov., Prussia, E Germany; 1364 sq. m.
2 Manufacturing city, its ✲, 64 m. WSW of Leipzig; pop. (1939) 166,661; 12th-cent. cathedral; commercial flower growing, large trade in plants and seed; manufactures shoes, metal goods, machinery, clothing. According to tradition, founded 6th cent.; episcopal see founded by Saint Boniface 741; famous university founded 1378 (suppressed 1816); signed protective treaty with Saxony 1483; residence of Luther as Augustinian monk 1505–08; passed to elector of Mainz 17th cent.; scene of Congress of Erfurt (Napoleon, Alexander of Russia, numerous German sovereigns) 1808; taken by Prussia 1813; Prussian rule confirmed by Congress of Vienna 1814; captured by American forces Apr. 12, 1945.

Erg, El (ĕl ĕrg′). Any of certain regions of sand dunes in the Sahara, N Africa, including: **Erg I′gui′di′** (ē′gē′dē′) in W Algeria and N Mauritania; **Erg Chech** (shĕsh′) in SW Algeria and N Republic of Mali; **Grand Erg Oc′ci′den′tal′** (grän′-tĕrg′ŏk′sē′dän′tȧl′) in N cen. Algeria S of Oran dept.; **Grand Erg O′rien′tal′** (ô′ryän′tȧl′) in E Algeria S of Constantine dept.

Er·ga·ni′ ma·de·ni′ (ĕr·ȧ·nē′ mä·dĕ·nē′); *also* **Ar·gha·na′ Ma·den′** (är·ȧ·nä′ mä·dĕn′). Town, Elâziz vilayet, E cen. Turkey in Asia, on upper Tigris 40 m. NW of Diyarbekir; pop. 2751; copper mines.

Er·ge·ne′ (ĕr·gĕ·nĕ′). River ab. 110 m. long, cen. Turkey in Europe; rises near Black Sea coast, flows W into Maritsa (Meriç) river on Greek border.

Er′gi·ri′ (ĕr′gĕ·rē′). = GJINOKASTĚR.

Erh Hai (ĕr′ hī′) *or* **Ta′li Lake** (tä′lē). Lake in W Yunnan prov., S China, just N of Burma Road; 30 m. long by 10 to 15 m. wide; alt. ab. 6600 ft.; has Tali city on W shore; resorts, many white marble pagodas built 1000 years ago by Sung dynasty; outlet to Yangpi river, a tributary of the Mekong.

Er′icht, Loch (lŏκ ĕr′ῐκt). Lake 14 m. long in Perth and Inverness cos., N cen. Scotland.

Er′ick (ĕr′ῐk). City, Beckham co., W Oklahoma, 50 m. NNW of Altus; pop. 1342; cattle ranches, gas wells.

Er′ics·son, Mount (ĕr′ῐk·s′n). Peak 13,625 ft. in Sierra Nevada, in N Tulare co., S cen. California.

Eridanus. See PO.

E′ri·du (ā′rῐ·dŏŏ). Ancient city, the chief seaport of Sumer and Babylonia, close to shore of Persian Gulf; its site now 120 m. from the gulf near the lower Euphrates, S of An Nasiriya and near Ur of the Chaldees; the first royal city of Sumerian tradition; perhaps dates back to 7000 B.C.; seat of the god Ea; excavations begun 1855.

E′rie (ĕr′ῐ). **1** Name of counties in three states of the U.S. See *Tables* at NEW YORK, OHIO, PENNSYLVANIA.
2 City, ⊗ of Neosho co., SE Kansas; pop. 1309.
3 City and port of entry, ⊗ of Erie co., NW corner of Pennsylvania, on Lake Erie; pop. 138,440; large harbor, ships lumber, coal, iron ore, petroleum, grain, fish; coal and natural gas deposits; manufactures boilers and engines, stoves, machinery, electric locomotives, flour and gristmill products; Villa Maria College (1925; women), Mercyhurst College (1926; women). Laid out 1795 on site of old French Fort Presque Isle (1753); incorp. as borough and became ⊗ 1803; headquarters of Commodore Perry (most of whose vessels were built here) in War of 1812; chartered as city 1851.

Erie, Lake. Lake in U.S. and Canada, 4th in size of the 5 Great Lakes (*q.v.*); bounded on W and N by Ontario prov., Canada, on E by New York, on S by Pennsylvania and Ohio, and on SW by Michigan, the U.S.-Canada boundary passing through the lake; ab. 240 m. long; 9940 sq. m.; greatest depth 210 ft.; elevation 572 ft.; at W end connected through Detroit river, Lake St. Clair, and St. Clair river with Lake Huron, and at E end

through Niagara river and Welland Ship Canal with Lake Ontario. Battle of Lake Erie, in which Commodore Perry defeated British naval force, fought in Put in Bay Sept. 10, 1813. See ERIE CANAL; NEW YORK STATE BARGE CANAL.

Erie Canal. Canal, 363 m. long, 40 ft. wide at surface, and 4 ft. deep, from Buffalo, New York, on Lake Erie to Albany, New York, on Hudson river; built 1817–25; enlarged several times and finally (work begun 1909) made a barge canal and became main waterway (340 m. long, 150 ft. wide, and 12 ft. deep) of the New York State Barge Canal (*q.v.*).

Eriha. See JERICHO.

E·ri·mo, Cape (ĕ·rē·mô). Cape on SE coast of Hokkaido I., Japan.

E′rin (ĕr′ῐn). Town, ⊗ of Houston co., NW Tennessee; pop. 1097.

Er′in (ĕr′ῐn; ĕr′ῐn). Ireland—now a poetic name.

Er′ith (ĕr′ῐth; ĕr′ῐth). Urban district, Kent, SE England, on the Thames 14 m. E of London; pop. 46,263; part of Greater London; summer resort and yachting headquarters; gunpowder factory.

Er′i·tre′a (ĕr′ῐ·trē′ȧ; *Ital.* â·rē·trâ′ä). Former Italian colony on Red Sea, NE Africa, extending from Cape Kasar (lat. 18°2′N) to a point just S of Assab on Bab el Mandeb (lat. 12°30′N), ab. 670 m.; 45,754 sq. m.; pop. (1931) 600,573; ✲ Asmara; bounded on NE and E by Red Sea, on SE by French Somaliland, on S by Ethiopia, and on W and NW by the Sudan Republic; includes the many islands of the Dahlak Archipelago and Zuqar I. farther S; has low coastal plain and interior mountain range with peaks 5300 ft. to 9882 ft.; has two streams in the N, the Anseba and Barca, headstreams of the Baraka flowing N to Red Sea in Sudan, and crossing its W part the Gasc, tributary of Atbara. Products are cotton and hides. Chief towns Asmara, Massaua, Assab, Cheren.

History: Part of ancient Ethiopia (*q.v.*); Assab (*q.v.*) taken over by Italian government 1882; organized as a colony Jan. 1890; incorporated as a state or government of Italian East Africa June 1, 1936; increased by additions of Ethiopian districts Tigre, Dancalia, and Aussa; conquered by British forces 1941; became federated with Ethiopia 1952.

Erivan. See YEREVAN.

Er′ji·as′ (ĕr′jĕ·yäs′). = ERCIYAS DAĞI.

Er′lang′en (ĕr′läng′ĕn). City, Middle Franconia govt. dist., Bavaria, Germany, on Regnitz river 12 m. NNW of Nürnberg; pop. 29,597; 18th-cent. baroque town hall; 18th-cent. castle; manufactures cotton goods, electrical instruments; university (Friedrich-Alexander University, founded at Bayreuth 1742, removed here 1743). Received city rights 1398; passed to burgraves of Nürnberg 1460, margraves of Bayreuth 1541, Prussia 1791, Bavaria 1810.

Er′lang′er (ûr′läng′gĕr). Residential city, Kenton co., N Kentucky, 7 m. SW of Covington and 4 m. SE of Greater Cincinnati airport; pop. 7072.

Erlau. See EGER.

Er′me·land (ĕr′mĕ·länt) *or* **Erm′land** (ĕrm′länt). Region, W cen. East Prussia, now in Mazury dept., N Poland, extending SE from Frisches Haff; ab. 1650 sq. m.; became bishopric under Teutonic Knights 1250; attached to Poland by Treaty of Thorn 1466; became part of Prussia 1772.

Er′me·lo (ĕr′mĕ·lō). **1** Commune, Gelderland prov., N Netherlands, 14 m. NE of Amersfoort; pop. 14,718.
2 Town, SE Transvaal, NE Union of South Africa, 120 m. E of Johannesburg near source of Vaal river; pop. 4836.

Er′mine Street (ûr′mῐn). Ancient Roman road from London to York, Britain, passing through Lincoln and Doncaster; from York had an extension past Hadrian's Wall to Scotland; one of four great Roman roads of Britain (see FOSSE WAY, ICKNIELD STREET, WATLING STREET).

Er·na′ku·lam (ĕr·nä′kŏŏ·lăm). Town, cen. Kerala state, S India, on Malabar Coast 120 m. W of Madura; pop. 36,638.

Erne (ûrn). River ab. 60 m. long in N Ireland; rises in co. Cavan, N Eire, flows N across border of Northern Ireland, turns NW and widens into **Upper Lough Erne** (lŏк ûrn′), 13 m. long; continues as a winding river past Enniskillen and expands into **Lough Erne** (18 m. long, 5 m. wide at widest point), then flows W into Donegal Bay; fine waterfall bet. Lough Erne and the bay.

E·rode′ (ê·rōd′). Town, cen. Madras, S Indian Union, on right bank of Cauvery river 75 m. WNW of Trichinopoly; pop. 33,672; trade center.

Er′o·mang′a or **Er′ro·mang′a** (ĕr′ô·mäng′ä; -mäng′-gà). Island 35 m. long by 25 m. wide in S group of New Hebrides Is., SW Pacific Ocean, 62 m. SSE of Efate; has several mountain ranges, highest point 2600 ft., and several bays with good anchorages, esp. Dillon Bay on W coast.

Er Rafa. See Rafa′.

Er Ram′le (ŭr rŏm′là; -lă) or **Ramle. 1** Subdistrict, Lydda dist., cen. Palestine; 358 sq. m.; pop. 70,579, (1938 est.) 102,125.

2 Ancient town, its ✱, 11 m. SE of Jaffa; pop. (1944 est.) 14,930; an important junction town on Roman road from Jerusalem to the coast; key fortress in time of Crusades.

Er Ri·ad′ (ăr rĭ·yäd′). = Riyadh.

Er′ri·boll, Loch (lŏк ĕr′ĭ·bŏl). Inlet of Atlantic Ocean on extreme N coast of Scotland; ab. 10 m. long.

Er Rif or **Er Riff** (ĕr rĭf′). Hilly coastal area in N Morocco, NW Africa, constituting cen. and E parts of former Spanish Morocco extending from a point E of Melilla, or ab. 2°W to ab. 5°30′W; inhabited by Berber tribes (Riffians), who rose in revolt 1921; at first they defeated Spanish forces and, under leadership of Abd-el-Krim from 1923, they held out until overcome by combined Spanish and French forces 1926.

Er′ri·gal′, Mount (ĕr′ĭ·gôl′; ĕr′ĭ·gôl′). Peak 2466 ft. in co. Donegal, N Eire.

Er′ris Head (ĕr′ĭs). Cape on NW coast of co. Mayo, NW Eire, projecting into Atlantic Ocean.

Erromanga. See Eromanga.

Érsekújvár. See Nové Zámky.

Er′skine·ville (ûr′skĭn·vĭl). Town, E New South Wales, SE Australia, S suburb of Sydney; pop. 6644.

Er′win (ûr′wĭn). **1** Town, Harnett co., cen. North Carolina, ab. 4 m. NW of Dunn; pop. 3183; cotton manufactures.

2 Town, ✱ of Unicoi co., NE Tennessee, 12 m. S of Johnson City; pop. 3210; pottery manufactures.

Er′y·man′thus (ĕr′ĭ·măn′thŭs); Gr. **Er′y·man′thos** (-thŏs; Mod. Gr. â·rē′măn·thôs) or **O′lo·nos′** (Mod. Gr. ô′lô·nôs′). Peak 7295 ft. in Achaea and Elis dept., NW Peloponnesus, S Greece; in ancient times was where Arcadia, Achaea, and Elis met; in Greek mythology, scene of killing of the Erymanthian boar by Hercules.

Er′y·thrae (ĕr′ĭ·thrē). Ancient city of Lydia, on coast of the peninsula opp. island of Chios; one of the 12 Ionian Cities; dwelling place of a sibyl, Herophile, regarded usually as identical with the Cumaean sibyl.

Er′y·thrae′an Sea (ĕr′ĭ·thrē′ăn); Lat. **Ma′re Er′y·thrae′um** (mä′rê ĕr′ĭ·thrē′ŭm). In ancient geography, the part of the Indian Ocean now known as the Arabian Sea and the Persian Gulf; also called the Red Sea, the **Mare Ru′brum** (rōō′brŭm).

Er′y·thrai′on, Cape (ĕr′ĭ·thrī′ŏn; Mod. Gr. â′rê·thrä′ôn). The SE point of Crete, extending into the Mediterranean Sea.

Eryx. See Monte San Giuliano.

Erz′berg′ (ĕrts′bĕrк′; ärts′-). Mountain 5032 ft. at Eisenerz, Styria prov., Austria; rich in iron ore; the mines have been worked for over 1000 years.

Erzerum. See Erzurum.

Erz′ge·bir′ge (ĕrts′gĕ·bĭr′gĕ; ärts′-); Eng. **Ore Mountains.** Mountain range bet. Saxony, E cen. Germany,

and the province of Bohemia in Czechoslovakia; highest peak Keilberg 4080 ft.

Er′zin·can′ (ĕr′zĭn·jän′) or **Er′zin·jan′** (-jän′). **1** Vilayet, E cen. Turkey in Asia; 5078 sq. m.; pop. 158,377.

2 Town, its ✱, on N bank of Kara Su 96 m. W of Erzurum, in Turkish Armenia; pop. 17,426; in fertile river plain in midst of orchards and gardens; chief agricultural products wheat, fruit, and cotton; cotton and silk industries; a military station with barracks and hospital; nearby in 4th cent. A.D. was home of Gregory the Illuminator. Came under control of Seljuks 1071 but they were defeated here by Mongols 1243; added to Ottoman Empire by Sultan Mohammed II 1473.

Er′zu·rum′ or **Er′ze·rum′** (ĕr′zŭ·rōōm′; ĕrz·rōōm′; ûr′zŭ-; ûrz-). **1** Vilayet, NE Turkey in Asia; 11,182 sq. m.; pop. 325,758.

2 City, its ✱, on Turkish-Russian railroad near source of the Kara Su; pop. (1940) 36,414; in mountains of W Turkish Armenia, a military station of strategical importance; large caravan traffic, esp. with Trabzon. Of great antiquity, important in Armenian and Arabic history; seized by Seljuks 1201; came under Turks 1517; three times captured by Russians—1828, 1878, 1916; meeting of First Nationalist Congress July 23, 1919.

Es′bjerg (ĕs′byărk). Seaport, Ribe co., SW Jutland Penin., Denmark, on North Sea; pop. (1945) 43,241; exports meats and dairy products; fisheries; cement works; only good harbor on W coast of Jutland.

Es′ca·lan′te (ĕs′kà·län′tê). River ab. 80 m. long, S Utah; flows SE into Colorado river.

Es′ca·lan′te (ās′kä·län′tà). Municipality, NE Negros Occidental, Negros, Phil. Is., on coast at N end of Tañon Strait; pop. 60,152; important local trade center, founded ab. 1860.

Es·cam′bi·a (ĕs·kăm′bĭ·à). **1** Navigable river ab. 75 m. long, flowing S from SW Alabama into Florida, where it forms boundary bet. Escambia and Santa Rosa cos.; empties into Pensacola Bay.

2 Name of counties in two states of the U.S. See *Tables* at Alabama and Florida.

Es′ca·na′ba (ĕs′kà·nä′bà). **1** River ab. 100 m. long, N Michigan penin.; rises in Marquette co., N Michigan penin., flows SE into Little Bay de Noc.

2 City, ⊗ of Delta co., S Michigan penin., on Little Bay de Noc; pop. 15,391; port of entry; ships iron ore; manufactures paper, chemicals, iron.

Es′car·pa′do, Point (ās′kär·pä′thŏ). Cape on SW coast of Panama, at S side of entrance to Gulf of San Miguel.

Es′cau′dain′ (ĕs′kō′dăN′). Commune, Nord dept., N France, 23 m. SSE of Lille; pop. (1931) 11,238; coal.

Escaut. See Schelde.

Esch, officially **Esch–sur–Al′zette** (ĕsh′sür·àl′zĕt′). Industrial commune, S grand duchy of Luxembourg, on French border 10 m. SW of Luxembourg; pop. (1945) 24,374; in coal-mining area.

Esch′we′ge (ĕsh′vä′gĕ). Industrial city, W Germany, in NE Hesse and formerly in Hesse-Nassau prov., Prussia, on Werra river 25 m. ESE of Kassel; pop. 12,723; 14th-cent. castle; 17th-cent. town hall; varied manufactures, including soap, esp. a mottled type known as Eschwege, or Eschweger, soap.

Esch′wei′ler (ĕsh′vī′lĕr). City, W Germany, in SW North Rhine-Westphalia state, 11 m. NE of Aachen; pop. 26,107; manufactures include iron, zinc, and copper goods, tin plate, machinery, boilers; coal, lead, and calamine mining in vicinity. In World War II town and vicinity scene of severe fighting 1944.

Es′co·bal′ (ās′kō·väl′). Town, Colón prov., Panama, on W shore of Gatun Lake on border of Canal Zone.

Es′co·bar′ (ās′kō·vär′). **1** Town, Buenos Aires prov., E Argentina, ab. 25 m. NW of Buenos Aires.

2 Town, Paraguarí dept., S cen. Paraguay, just SE of Asunción; pop. ab. 4800.

Es′co·ce′sa Bay (ās′kō·sā′sä). Bay on NE coast of

Dominican Republic, NW of Cape Samaná, Hispaniola I., West Indies.

Es'con·di'do (ĕs'kŏn·dē'dō). City, San Diego co., SW corner of California, 28 m. N of San Diego; pop. 16,377; founded 1885; extensive vineyards.

Es'con·di'do (äs'kôn·dē'thô) *or* **Blue'fields'** (blōō'-fēldz'). Navigable river ab. 65 m. long in S cen. Nicaragua; formed by the Siquia and other headstreams, flows E into the Caribbean Sea at Bluefields.

Escorial, El. See EL ESCORIAL.

Es'cou'blac' (ĕs'kōō'blàk'). Commune, Loire-Inférieure dept., NW France, near Saint-Nazaire; pop. (1931) 6126; because of shifting sands town was forced to move 2 m. inland 1779; nearby on coast is **La Baule**, one of the finest beach resorts in Brittany.

Es'cu·dil'la Mountain (ĕs'kŭ·dē'à). Peak 10,691 ft. in E Arizona, SE extremity of Apache co.

Escuinapa, *in full* **Es'cui·na'pa de Hi·dal'go** (äs'-kwē·nä'pä thä ē·thäl'gō). Town, Sinaloa state, W Mexico, on railroad ab. 40 m. SE of Mazatlán; pop. 5864.

Es·cuin'tla (äs·kwēn'tlä). **1** Department, S Guatemala; 1693 sq. m.; pop. 176,280.
2 City, its ✳, 30 m. SSW of Guatemala; pop. 6158; medicinal baths; fruit-growing.

Es·cu'mi·nac, Point (ĕs·kū'mǐ·năk). Cape, E Northumberland co., E New Brunswick prov., SE Canada, on S side of entrance to Miramichi Bay.

Es'dra·e'lon (ĕz'drȧ·ē'lŏn; -drä-). Plain in N Palestine, in valley of the Qishon river, E of Mt. Carmel; its E end, traversed by the Jalud river, tributary of the Jordan, is known as the **Valley of Jez're·el** (jĕz'rê·ĕl; jĕz'rēl). See MEGIDDO.

Esdud. See ASHDOD.

E'sher (ē'shēr), *formerly* **Esher and The Dit'tons** (dǐt'nz). Urban district, Surrey, S England, 15 m. SW of London; pop. 51,217; includes The Dittons and, since 1933, East and West Molesey; site of the mansion, Esher Place, occupied 1529 by Cardinal Wolsey.

Eshnunna. See TELL ASMAR.

Esh'o·we (ĕsh'ô·wä). Village, chief town of Zululand, NE Natal, Union of South Africa, 70 m. NNE of Durban; pop. 2223; beautifully located, resort.

Esh Shâm. 1 Arabic for DAMASCUS.
2 Arabic for SYRIA.

Esk (ĕsk). **1** River in NE England, flowing E into North Sea at Whitby.
2 River ab. 40 m. long in S Scotland; rises in NE Dumfries co. and flows S into the head of Solway Firth; its lower course for a few miles lies in Cumberland, England; bet. it and the Sark (a small stream of Dumfries, Scotland) is a small tract of land (8 m. long by 4 m. wide) known for years as the "Debatable Land," a disputed border tract; the Sark established as boundary bet. Scotland and England 1552; Gretna Green is on N bank of Sark.
3 River, Midlothian co., SE Scotland; formed by confluence of **North Esk** and **South Esk** in Dalkeith, flows N to Firth of Forth at Musselburgh.
4 See NORTH ESK and SOUTH ESK.

Esk Hause (ĕsk' hôs'). Mountain pass 2490 ft. in W Cumberland, NW England, in the Lake District.

Es·ki'·Džu'ma·ya' (ĕs·kǐ'jōō'mä·yä'). Town, Shumen dept., NE Bulgaria, 37 m. S of Ruse; pop. (1926) 10,490.

Es'ki·fjör'dur (ĕs'kyǐ·fyûr'thür). Fiord on E coast of Iceland.

Eski Foça. See FOÇA.

Eskije. See XANTHE.

E'skil·stu'na (ā'shǐl·stōō'nä). City, Södermanland prov., SE Sweden, S of Lake Mälaren 45 m. W of Stockholm; pop. 45,245; steelworks, engineering plants; manufactures esp. cutlery and swords.

Es'ki·şe·hir' (ĕs'kĕ·shĕ·hēr') *or* **Es'ki·shehr'** (ĕs'kĕ·shĕ'h'r). **1** Vilayet, W cen. Turkey in Asia; 5147 sq. m.; pop. 183,205.
2 City, its ✳, on tributary of Sakarya river, 128 m. W of

Ankara; pop. (1940) 60,614; healthful location; famous for its deposits of meerschaum; nearby are ruins of ancient Phrygian city of **Dor'y·lae'um** (dŏr'ĭ·lē'ŭm), a city that was mentioned in wars of Lysimachus and Antigonus and acquired importance in Byzantine times; scene of defeat of Seljuk sultan, Kilij Arslan, 1097 by Godfrey of Bouillon; taken by Turks 1176.

Es'la (äz'lä). River ab. 150 m. long in NW Spain; rises in N León prov., flows SSW into Duero river ab. 15 m. below Zamora.

Es'me·ral'da (ĕz'mẽ·räl'dȧ). County in Nevada. See *Table* at NEVADA.

Es'me·ral'das (äz'mä·räl'däs). **1** River ab. 150 m. long in NW Ecuador; flows W from Andes Mts. into Pacific Ocean.
2 Province of Ecuador. See *Table* at ECUADOR.
3 Town, ✳ of Esmeraldas prov., NW Ecuador, 2 m. from mouth of Esmeraldas river 118 m. NW of Quito; pop. (1944 est.) 13,881; gold mines in vicinity.

Esna. See ISNA.

E·so'pus (ê·sō'pŭs). Town (pop. 6597) and village in Ulster co., SE New York, on the Hudson river ab. 8 m. S of Kingston; in apple-growing area.

Esopus Creek. Creek in Ulster co., SE New York; rises in Catskill Mts., flows SE then N into Hudson river ab. 10 m. above Kingston. See ASHOKAN DAM.

Es'pail'lat' (ĕs'pä'yà'). Province, N cen. Dominican Republic. See *Table* at DOMINICAN REPUBLIC.

España. See SPAIN.

Es'pa·ño'la (ĕs'pän·yō'lȧ; *Span.* äs'pä·nyō'lä). **1** *also known as* **Hood Island** (hŏŏd). One of the Galápagos Is. (q.v.).
2 See HISPANIOLA.

Es'pe·rance, Cape (ĕs'pēr·äns). Cape on NW coast of Guadalcanal I., SE Solomon Is., W Pacific Ocean; landing place for Japanese forces 1942–43; naval battle off coast near here Oct. 11–12, 1942; last Japanese foothold on island. See SAVO.

Es'pe·ran'za (äs'pä·rän'sä). **1** Town, Santa Fe prov., E cen. Argentina, just W of Santa Fe; pop. (est.) 16,192.
2 Town, Las Villas prov., W cen. Cuba, on railroad 10 m. W of Santa Clara; pop. 18,081.

Esperanza, La. See LA ESPERANZA.

Es'pi·chel', Cape (ĕsh'pê·shâl'). Promontory on SW coast of Portugal, 21 m. S of Lisbon.

Es'pi·nal' (äs'pê·näl'). Municipality, Tolima dept., W cen. Colombia, on the upper Magdalena 30 m. SE of Ibagué; pop. 5666.

Es·pí'ri·to San'to (ĕsh·pē'rê·tŏŏ sănn'tŏŏ). **1** Island a few hundred yards off mainland of Espírito Santo state, E Brazil; site of the city of Vitória.
2 State of Brazil. See *Table* at BRAZIL.

Es·pí'ri·tu San'to (äs·pē'rê·tŏŏ sän'tŏ) *or* **Ma·ri'na** (mä·rē'nä); *also known as* **San'to** (sän'tŏ). Largest island of the New Hebrides in NW part of group, SW Pacific Ocean; 76 m. long by 45 m. wide, 1875 sq. m.; pop. (native; 1938 est.) 7242; has mountain range along W coast, highest point Mt. Santo 6195 ft.; coast line marked on the N by two peninsulas, largest on NW, with St. Philip and St. James Bay bet. them; agriculturally well developed; principal settlement Luganville, on SE coast. During World War II site of military and naval bases established by Americans, who first landed Mar. 12, 1942.

Es·pí'ri·tu San'to (äs·pē'rê·tŏŏ sän'tŏ). Island 13 m. long off SE coast of Lower California, near mouth of Gulf of California.

Es·pí'ri·tu San'to, Cape (äs·pē'rê·tŏŏ sän'tŏ). Northeast point of Samar I., E Phil. Is., 12°35′N, 125°9′E.

Es·pí'ri·tu San'to, Cape (äs·pē'rê·tŏŏ sän'tŏ). Cape on N coast of Tierra del Fuego I., S of entrance to Strait of Magellan.

Es·pí'ri·tu San'to Bay (äs·pē'rê·tŏŏ sän'tŏ). Inlet of Caribbean Sea on E coast of Yucatán penin., Quintana Roo territory, Mexico, S of Ascension Bay.

Es′qui·line (ĕs′kwĭ·lĭn; -lĭn). One of the seven hills of Rome. See SEVEN HILLS.

Es·qui′malt (ĕs·kwĭ′môlt). Seaport and naval station, SE Vancouver I., Brit. Columbia, Canada, on Juan de Fuca Strait 4 m. W of Victoria of which it is a suburb; pop. (of district municipality) 10,153; spacious harbor; British navy station until 1905 when Canadian government took it over; its drydock (built 1888) transferred to Canada 1910; shipyard, salmon cannery.

Es′qui·pu′las (ās′kē·pōō′läs). Town, Chiquimula dept., SE Guatemala, 73 m. E of Guatemala; pop. 1263; church contains a black image of Christ (the "Black Christ") worshiped by the Indians.

Es′rom (ĕs′rŭm). Lake in NE Sjælland I., Denmark.

Es Salt (ăs sălt′). Town, NW Jordan, W of Amman.

Es′sen (ĕs′'n; ĕs′ĕn), *also* **Essen an der Ruhr** (än dĕr rōōr′; *Ger.* rōōr′). Industrial city, W Germany, in North Rhine-Westphalia state, 18 m. NNE of Düsseldorf, near right bank of the Ruhr river ab. 13 m. from where it enters the Rhine; pop. (1939) 659,871; 10th-cent. cathedral; famous for Krupp works, manufacturing armaments, locomotives, agricultural implements, the most extensive iron and steel works in Europe; includes numerous adjacent communes and towns. Founded 9th cent.; made a city 10th cent.; passed to Prussia 1803; bombed in World War I; heavily bombed by Allies 1943–45, esp. the Krupp works; taken with other cities in fall of the Ruhr Apr.–May 1945.

Es′sen·don (ĕs′'n·dŭn). City, S Victoria, SE Australia, NW suburb of Melbourne; pop. 46,099.

Es′sen·tu′ki (ĕs′'n·tōō′kĭ; *Russ.* yĭ·syĕn·tōō′kĭ). Town, Stavropol Territory, SE Russia in Europe, on N slopes of Caucasus Mts. 10 m. W of Pyatigorsk; pop. 23,000.

Es′se·qui′bo (ĕs′ĕ·kwē′bō). **1** River ab. 600 m. long in British Guiana; largest river of the colony, rises in Serra Uassary on Brazilian border, flows N into Atlantic Ocean; has wide estuary; navigable for some distance; main tributaries all from W: the Cuyuni and Mazaruni near its mouth, Potaro in cen. part, and Rupununi in S cen. part.

2 County, W British Guiana; 68,140 sq. m.; pop. (1931) 49,830; chief town Bartica; in early times about equivalent to the colony (see BRITISH GUIANA).

Es′sex (ĕs′ĕks; -ĭks). **1** Name of counties in five states of the U.S. See *Tables* at MASSACHUSETTS, NEW JERSEY, NEW YORK, VERMONT, VIRGINIA.

2 Agricultural and manufacturing town, SE Middlesex co., S Connecticut, on W bank of Connecticut river near its mouth; pop. 4057; settled 1690, incorp. 1852; as maritime trade center, attacked by British in War of 1812.

3 Urban community (unincorporated), Baltimore co., Maryland, E of Baltimore; pop. 35,205.

4 Town in Vermont. See ESSEX JUNCTION.

5 County, Ontario, Canada. See *Table* at ONTARIO.

6 Town, Essex co., SE Ontario, Canada, 16 m. ESE of Windsor; pop. 2741; bricks, flour; canning factory.

7 County, SE England; area 1528 sq. m.; pop. (1951) 2,043,574; ⊗ Chelmsford; other towns West Ham, East Ham, Walthamstow, Southend on Sea, Harwich, Clacton; rivers Thames, Stour, Colne, Blackwater, Lea, Crouch; agriculture, fisheries, manufacturing (machinery, textiles, chemicals, cement).

History: Region a Roman center before invasion by East Saxons; Anglo-Saxon kingdom of Heptarchy (*q.v.*) with its center at London; received Christianity and submitted to Mercia (*q.v.*) 7th cent. A.D.; its subkings later disappeared; included in territory under the Danelaw 9th cent.; reconquered by Wessex, it became a shire and later a powerful English earldom.

Essex Junction. Industrial village in Essex town (pop. 7090), Chittenden co., NW Vermont, on Winooski river 5 m. E of Burlington; pop. 5340; Fort Ethan Allen nearby.

Es′sex·ville (ĕs′ĭks·vĭl). City, Bay co., E Michigan, on Saginaw Bay 4 m. E of Bay City; pop. 4590.

Es′sing·ton (ĕs′ĭng·tŭn). Locality, Delaware co., SE Pennsylvania, on Delaware river ab. 4 m. NE of Chester; pop. (1950) 1545; settled by Swedes 1643.

Ess′ling (ĕs′lĭng). Village near Vienna, Austria; see ASPERN.

Ess′ling·en (ĕs′lĭng·ĕn). Manufacturing city, Baden-Württemberg state, W Germany, on the Neckar river 6 m. ESE of Stuttgart; pop. 40,562; founded in 8th cent.; free imperial town; became part of Swabian League of cities.

Es′sonne′ (ĕ′sôn′). River ab. 56 m. long, N France; rises in Loiret dept., flows N to the Seine at Corbeil.

Es′sonnes′ (ĕ′sôn′). Commune, Seine-et-Oise dept., N France, 20 m. SSE of Paris; pop. 10,505; paper factories; 12th-cent. church.

Es Sur. See TYRE.

Es Su·wei′da (ĕs sōō·wī′dà; -wä′-; -dä); *Fr.* **Sou·ei·da′** (swä′dä′). Town, ✳ of former Druse territory of Jebel ed Druz, now a part of Republic of Syria, railroad terminus ab. 56 m. S of Damascus; pop. ab. 8000; on site of an ancient Roman settlement.

Estados, Isla de los. See STATEN ISLAND, Argentina.

Estados Unidos de Venezuela. Official name for VENEZUELA.

Estados Unidos Mexicanos. See MEXICO.

Es·tan′cia (ĕs·tăn′chà; -shà). Town, ⊗ of Torrance co., cen. New Mexico; pop. 797.

Es·tân′cia (ĕsh·tän′syà). Town on coast, S Sergipe state, E Brazil; pop. (1940 est.) 10,422.

Est′court (ĕst′kōrt). Town, W Natal, E Union of South Africa, 85 m. NW of Durban; pop. 2676.

E′ste (ĕs′tā; *anc.* **A·tes′te** (à·tĕs′tē). Commune, Padova prov., Venezia Euganea, NE Italy, 17 m. SW of Padua; pop. 14,438; medieval fortress; campanile; manufactures iron products, pottery, cordage, chemicals. Ancient Roman military colony; seat of Este family until their expulsion by Paduans 1275; with Padua fell to Venetians 1405.

Es′te·lí′ (ās′tā·lē′). **1** Department, W Nicaragua; 772 sq. m.; pop. (1943 est.) 53,872.

2 Town, its ✳, 65 m. N of Managua; pop. (1943 est.) 5747.

Es′te·po′na (ās′tā·pō′nä). Seaport commune, Málaga prov., S Spain, on Mediterranean Sea 46 m. SW of Málaga; pop. 11,851.

Es′té·rel′ (ĕs′tā′rĕl′). Mountainous, forested region, S France, on coast of departments of Var and Alpes-Maritimes, bet. Fréjus and Cannes; highest point Mont Vinaigre 2020 ft.

Es′té′rias′, Cape (*Fr.* ĕs′tā′ryàs′). Cape extending into Gulf of Guinea on coast of Gabon, W equatorial Africa, bet. Corisco Bay on the N and Gabon river on the S; Libreville is on its S coast.

Es′tes Park (ĕs′tĕz). **1** A high-level valley of the Front Range, Rocky Mts., N Colorado; now a part of Rocky Mountain National Park (see UNITED STATES, *National Parks*).

2 Village in Larimer co., N Colorado, 28 m. SW of Fort Collins; pop. 1175; alt. 7500 ft.; entrance to Rocky Mountain National Park.

Es′te·van (ĕs′tĕ·văn). Town, SE Saskatchewan, Canada, on Souris river 54 m. SE of Weyburn; pop. 3935; flour mills, lumberyards, coal mines.

Es′ther, Mount (ĕs′tĕr). Peak 4270 ft. in the Adirondack Mts., Essex co., NE New York.

Es′ther·ville (ĕs′tĕr·vĭl). City, ⊗ of Emmet co., N Iowa, 58 m. NE of Cherokee; pop. 7927.

Esthonia. See ESTONIA.

Es′till (ĕs′t'l). County in Kentucky. See *Table* at KENTUCKY.

Es′ton (ĕs′tŭn). Urban district, North Riding, Yorkshire, N England, near Tees estuary and North Sea 33 m. SSE of Newcastle and 4 m. ESE of Middlesbrough; pop. 33,315; near the iron-ore deposits of the Cleveland dist.; manufactures iron and steel.

Es·to′ni·a (ĕs·tō′nĭ·à; -tōn′yà); *less correctly* **Es·tho′-ni·a** (ĕs·tō′nĭ·à; -tōn′yà; -thō′-; -thŏn′-); *Estonian* **Ees′-ti** (ās′tĭ). Republic, N Europe, on Baltic Sea, annexed by U.S.S.R. 1940 and incorporated in Soviet Union as **Es·to′ni·an Soviet Socialist Republic** (-tō′nĭ·ăn; -tōn′yăn); 18,361 sq. m.; pop. (1934) 1,126,413, (1940 est.) 1,120,000; ✱ Tallin; bounded on N by Gulf of Finland, on E by Leningrad and Pskov Regions of R.S.F.S.R., on S by Latvia, and on W by Baltic Sea; constituted 1918 from former Russian government of Estonia (see BALTIC PROVINCES) and N third of Livonia; divided into the following 11 provinces (for pronunciations, see individual entries):

NAME	LOCA-TION	AREA[1]	POP.[1]	CAPITAL
Harju	N	2,194	253,466	Tallin
Järva	N cen.	1,066	59,398	Paide
Lääne	W	1,846	73,891	Haapsalu
Pärnu	SW	2,108	89,984	Pärnu
Petseri	SE	730	65,166	Petseri
Saare	W	1,144	56,048	Kuressare
Tartu	E	2,710	175,140	Tartu
Valga	S	583	39,154	Valga
Vilyandi	S cen.	1,567	74,092	Vilyandi
Viru	NE	2,852	141,705	Rakvere
Võru	SE	1,561	81,184	Võru

[1] Area is in sq. m. Pop. is 1937 est. of towns and provinces; to the total of these figures must be added 26,819, borough population enumerated separately.

Coast is low and there are no heights of land; its SW coast is N shore of Gulf of Riga; includes four islands in Baltic Sea off W coast: Sarema (Saaremaa), Khiuma (Hiiumaa), Muhu, and Vormsi; on E shares ab. one half of Lakes Peipus (*q.v.*) and Pskov with the R.S.F.S.R.; has many other lakes, largest of which is Virts, in S cen. part; many streams, most important being the Pärnu, Kasari, and Narova rivers. Chief occupations agriculture, dairy farming, and livestock raising; exports butter, lumber, flax, meat products, and cellulose. Predominant ethnic strain is Finno-Ugrian; chief nationalities, Estonian 88%, Russian 8%. Chief cities Tallin, Tartu, Narva, Pärnu.

History: Estonians conquered by Danes who founded Reval (see TALLIN) 1219; after ferocious revolt of peasantry 1343–45, taken over by Teutonic Order 1346; under rule of Swedish who captured Reval 1561; ceded to Russia (see BALTIC PROVINCES) 1721; became independent republic Feb. 24, 1918; recognized by U.S.S.R. 1920 (peace signed at Tartu); joined League of Nations 1921; ruled as dictatorship 1934–37; joined nonaggression pact with Germany (see LATVIA) 1939; occupied by Russian army June 1940 and annexed to U.S.S.R. as Estonian S.S.R. Aug. 3, 1940; overrun by German army 1941 and retaken by Russians 1944; incorporation in U.S.S.R. not recognized by United States.

Es·to·ril′ (ĕsh·tōō·rĭl′). Resort town, W Estremadura prov., Portugal, on coast W of Lisbon; pop. (est.) 3000.

Es·tot′i·land (ĕs·tŏt″l-ănd). A mythical land in America, placed by old geographers in region of Newfoundland, Labrador, and Canada E of Hudson Bay; referred to by Milton as "cold Estotiland" (*Paradise Lost* x. 686); earliest mention about 1558.

Estrada, La. See LA ESTRADA.

Estrella, Serra da. See SERRA DA ESTRELLA.

Es′tre·ma·du′ra (ĕs′trĕ·mà·dōōr′à). **1** (*Port.* ĕsh·trĕ-mà·thōō′rà) Old province, W Portugal; ✱ Lisbon; now forms modern provinces of Estremadura, Ribatejo, and part of Beira Litoral; chief river the Tagus.
2 Province of Portugal. See *Table* at PORTUGAL.
3 (*Span.* ās′trä·mä·thōō′rä) *or* **Ex′tre·ma·du′ra** (ās′-trä·mä·thōō′rä; ĕks′-). Region, W cen. Spain; 16,065 sq. m.; bounded on N by León, E by New Castile, S by Andalusia, W by Portugal; comprises modern provinces of Cáceres and Badajoz; tableland; watered by Tagus and Guadiana rivers; raises sheep and swine; large forests in N portion, agricultural land in S; noted for its ilex trees; deposits of silver, coal, copper.

Es·tre·moz′ (ĕsh·trĕ·môsh′). Town, Alto Alentejo prov., Portugal, ab. 25 m. NE of Évora; pop. 9718; ruins of ancient castle; marble quarries; pottery; Portuguese victories over Spanish nearby 1663, 1665.

Estrondo, Serra do. See SERRA DO ESTRONDO.

E·su·to·ru (ĕ·sōō·tō·rōō). Seaport town on NW coast of Karafuto, Sakhalin I., on Gulf of Tatary; pop. (1939 est.) 28,556; formerly Japanese.

Eszék. See OSIJEK.

Esz′ter·gom (ĕs′tĕr·gôm); *Ger.* **Gran** (grän). City, N Hungary, on the Danube 27 m. NW of Budapest; pop. 18,255; cathedral; ancient ecclesiastical center.

Établissements de l'Océanie *or* **Établissements français de l'Océanie.** See FRENCH POLYNESIA.

Établissements français dans l'Inde. See FRENCH INDIA.

E′tah (ē′tà). **1** Eskimo settlement in NW Greenland, on Smith Sound N of Cape York, 78°20′N; known as point of departure for polar exploration expeditions.
2 Town, Agra division, W cen. Uttar Pradesh, N India, 46 m. NE of Agra; pop. (1931) 11,473.

E·ta·ji·ma (ĕ·tä·jĕ·mä). Island on N coast of Inland Sea, SW Honshu, Japan, opp. Kure and S of Hiroshima; Imperial Naval College.

É′tampes′ (ā′tänp′). Commune, Seine-et-Oise dept., N France, 30 m. SSW of Paris; pop. 10,610; dates back to early 7th cent.; scene of a council which recognized Innocent II as legitimate pope 1130.

Étang de Berre, Étang de Thau, etc. See Étang de BERRE, Étang de THAU, etc.

É′ta′ples (ā′tàp′l′). Commune, Pas-de-Calais dept., N France, on Canche estuary S of Boulogne; pop. (1931) 6673; fishing; boatbuilding; treaty 1492 bet. Henry VII of England and Charles VIII of France; important British base in World War I.

E·ta′wah (ĕ·tä′wà). Town, SW Uttar Pradesh, N India, on left bank of Jumna river 67 m. SE of Agra; pop. (1941) 53,114; cotton mills, hornware factories; has a ruined fort and several mosques including the Jama Masjid, adapted from a Hindu temple.

E·taw′ney Lake (ĕ·tô′nĭ). Lake 625 sq. m., N Manitoba, Canada, NE of Southern Indian Lake.

Etchmiadzin. = ECHMIADZIN.

E′ten (ā′tĕn). Seaport ab. 12 m. S of Chiclayo, Lambayeque dept., NW Peru; open roadstead.

E·ter′ni·ty, Cape (ĕ·tûr′nĭ·tĭ). Promontory, Quebec, Canada, on S shore of Saguenay river 39 m. from its mouth; 1400 ft. high; forms E portal of inlet of **Eternity Bay.** See Cape TRINITY.

E′thi·o′pi·a (ē′thĭ·ō′pĭ·à). **1** Ancient country W of Red Sea, NE Africa, bet. ab. lat. 24° and 10°N; included S Egypt, E Republic of the Sudan, Eritrea, and N (modern) Ethiopia; sometimes name referred just to the Nile valley above Syene (Aswân), but in classical writings it (see AETHIOPIA) referred to that part of Africa S from Egypt as far as Zanzibar; dominated by Egypt from XIth dynasty; became independent of Egypt during XXIIId dynasty; the Biblical land of Cush; part of Sabaean kingdom of Aksum ruled by dynasty descended from Menelik, traditionally son of Hebrew King Solomon and Queen of Saba (Sheba); under Jewish influence until converted to Christianity by bishop Frumentius 4th cent. A.D.; became Monophysite Christian 7th cent.; from 675 cut off from rest of Christian world by Moslem conquest of Egypt and Nubia; 1490 resumed contact when visited by Covilhão who was believed to have found kingdom of Prester John; aided by Portuguese in expelling Moslem sultan of the Somali 1541; center of missionary activity of Jesuits until their expulsion 1633; explored 1768–73 by James Bruce who reported decayed empire restricted to region N of Blue Nile. For later history, see sense 2, below.
2 *or* **Ab′ys·sin′i·a** (ăb′ĭ·sĭn′ĭ·à; -sĭn′yà), *from a Portuguese corruption of the Arab.* **El Ha′be·sha** (ăl hă′bă-shá; -shä). Independent country in E Africa; 305,731 sq.

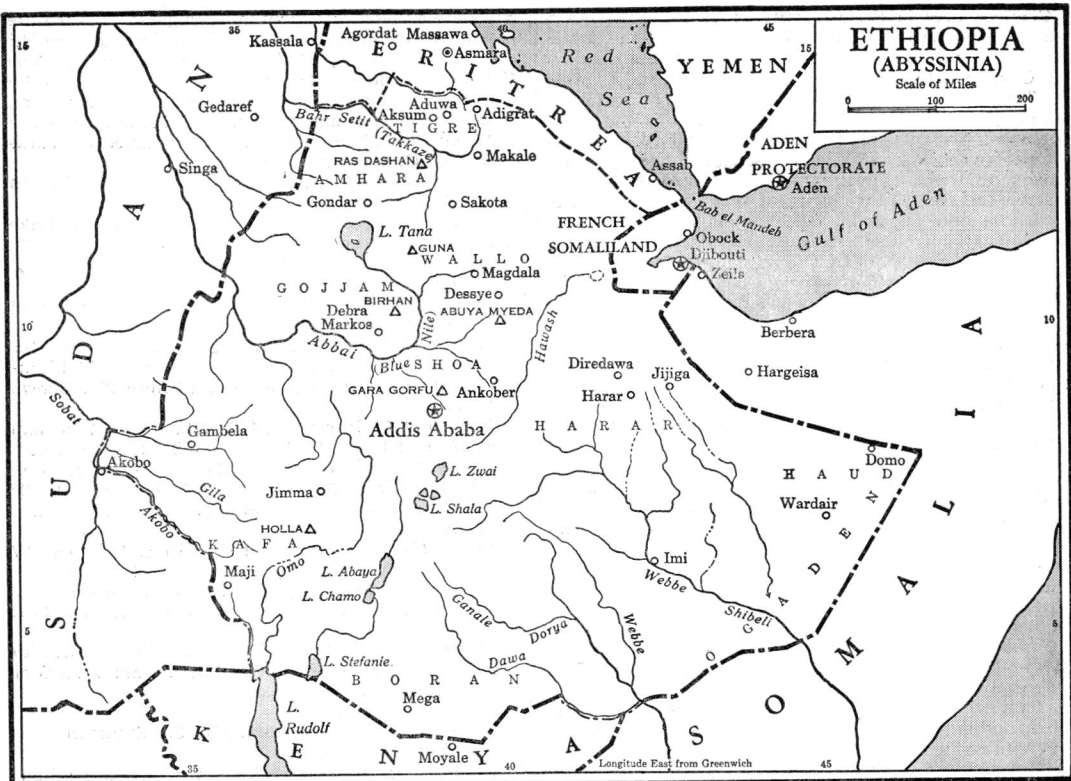

ETHIOPIA
(ABYSSINIA)
Scale of Miles
0   100   200

m.; pop. (1939 est.) 9,450,000; ✳ Addis Ababa; bounded on N by Eritrea, on E by French Somaliland and Somalia, on SE by Somalia, on S by Kenya, and on W by Republic of the Sudan; divided administratively into 12 provinces, some of which (as Asmara, Gojjam, Tigre, Shoa, Kafa) nearly coincide with ancient kingdoms of same name.

(Before Portuguese discoveries, Ethiopia the common name for region, see 1, above, but modern usage establishes no clear-cut distinction bet. Ethiopia and kingdom of Abyssinia; 19th-cent. maps show Abyssinia (Ethiopia) and texts vary, although Abyssinia would appear to refer strictly to the Amharic nucleus of the Ethiopian empire. The independent rulers of 19th and 20th cents. used Ethiopia as did the Italian conqueror.)

Mountains: Mountainous in N, cen., and S parts with many peaks 7000 to 13,000 ft., highest Ras Dashan in N 15,160 ft.; lowlands on E border include Danakil Desert in NE and the Haud in SE extending into coastal Somalia. *Rivers:* Main streams in N and NW the Takkaze (Bahr Setit) and the Abbai (Blue Nile), the outlet of Lake Tana, both tributaries of the Nile; in SW the Omo flowing S to Lake Rudolf on Kenya border; in E the Hawash, rising in cen. part SE of Addis Ababa and losing itself in Danakil Desert; in SE many streams flowing SE forming headstreams of the Juba and Webbe Shibeli rivers in Somaliland. Has no coast line but has outlet to the sea by railroad which connects Addis Ababa with the port of Djibouti in French Somaliland; chief products hides and skins, coffee, grain, bananas, cotton. *Chief cities:* Addis Ababa, Diredawa, Harar, Debra Markos, Gondar.

History: Modern Ethiopia began with Theodore's rule, established by conquest of other chiefs 1855 and terminated by Napier's expedition 1868; cut off from Red Sea by Egypt 1872–79 but saved from Egyptian con-

quest; Assab (*q.v.*) made Italian 1882; claimed as an Italian protectorate (through Treaty of Uccialli 1889); coastal region made separate Italian colony 1890 (see ERITREA); under Menelik, defeated Italians at Aduwa 1896; territorial integrity recognized by Great Britain, France, and Italy 1906; admitted to League of Nations 1923; after failure of League to settle an Italo-Ethiopian clash at Walwal 1934, invaded by Italy 1935; formally annexed to Italy and organized with Eritrea and Italian Somaliland as Italian East Africa (1936–41); regained independence after being liberated by British 1941; became federated with Eritrea 1952.

Et′ive, Loch (lŏk ĕt′iv). Inlet of Atlantic Ocean extending from Firth of Lorne inland E (8½ m.) and NE (10½ m.) in Argyll co., W Scotland.

Et′na (ĕt′nȧ). Manufacturing borough, Allegheny co., SW Pennsylvania, on Allegheny river 5 m. NNE of Pittsburgh; pop. 5519; iron and steel products.

Et′na (ĕt′nȧ; *Ital.* ĕt′nä); *Lat.* **Aet′na** (ĕt′nȧ). Volcano 10,741 ft. in NE Sicily, near the coast; ab. 80 eruptions have been recorded, notably destructive ones 1169, 1693, and 1832.

Et′na (ĕt′nȧ), **Mount.** Peak 13,800 ft. in Chaffee co., cen. Colorado.

E·to′lin Strait (ʔē·tō′lĭn). Passage in Bering Sea separating Nunivak I. from mainland of SW Alaska.

E′ton (ē′t'n). Urban district, Buckinghamshire, SE cen. England, on the Thames opp. Windsor; pop. 3250; Eton College founded by Henry VI 1440.

E·to·ro·fu (ĕ·tō·rō·fŏŏ) or **I′tu·rup** (ē′tŭ·rŭp). Largest of the Kuril Is. (*q.v.*), Soviet Russia, Asia, at S end NE of Hokkaido, Japan; 140 m. long; 2657 sq. m.; chief town Shana.

E·to′sha Pan (ȧ·tō′shȧ). Large salt basin in N Southwest Africa.

Et′o·wah (ĕt′ō·wä). **1** River ab. 150 m. long, NW

Georgia; rises in SE extremity of Tennessee, flows S across Georgia border, then W to unite with the Oostanaula near Rome in Floyd co. and form Coosa river.

2 County in Alabama. See *Table* at ALABAMA.

3 Town, McMinn co., SE Tennessee, 25 m. NE of Cleveland; pop. 3223; railroad division point.

Etowah Mound. Prehistoric earthwork, 3 m. SE of Cartersville, Bartow co., NW Georgia, on Etowah river; a quadrilateral, truncated pyramid, base covers ab. 3 acres, top ab. 170 by 176 ft.; 61 ft. high; copper plates with repoussé figures have been found in it.

É'tre·tat' (ā'trĕ·tä'). Town, Seine-Maritime dept., N France, on coast N of Le Havre; pop. 1687; resort.

E·tru'ri·a (ĕ·trōōr'ĭ·à). Ancient country in cen. Italy, covering region now comprising the compartimento of Tuscany and part of Umbria compartimento; home of Etruscans, a people who probably migrated from Asia Minor c. 900 B.C.; their chief confederation, traditionally of 12 cities, included Veii, Florentia, Volsinii, etc.; traded extensively with Greeks and Phoenicians and built up civilization, noted for its art, at height c. 500 B.C.; at its peak Etruscan power extended into N Italy; gradually declined after defeat of its sea power off Cumae (*q.v.*) and absorption of its cities, one by one, by Rome (by 3d cent. B.C.); kingdom of Etruria erected by Napoleon in 1801 incorporated in French Empire 1808.

Etsch. See ADIGE.

Et·sin' (ĕt·sēn'), *also* **Ed·sin'** (ĕd·zēn'). River ab. 200 m. long in N China; formed by confluence of the Hwei (rises on N side of Nan Shan range in Kansu) with another headstream near Ningsia border; flows N to Gashiun Nor, NW Ningsia.

Et Ta·fi'la (ĕt tŏ·fē'lä; - lä). Town, cen. Jordan, SE of Dead Sea on railroad N of Ma'an.

Et'ten en Leur (ĕt'ĕn ĕn lûr'). Commune, North Brabant prov., Netherlands, just W of Breda; pop. ab. 10,000; residence of van Gogh 1881.

Et'ter·beek (ĕt'ĕr·bāk). Commune, Brabant prov., cen. Belgium, a suburb of Brussels; pop. 45,328.

Et'trick (ĕt'rĭk). **1** Town (unincorporated), Chesterfield co., SE cen. Virginia, on the Appomattox opp. Petersburg; pop. 2998; Virginia State College (1882; coed.).

2 Small river ab. 32 m. long in SE Scotland, flows NE through Selkirk co. into the Tweed.

Ettrick Forest. Former forest and hunting ground in Selkirk co., SE Scotland; now converted into a pastoral region; James Hogg (1770-1835), Scottish poet, a native of this region, was known as "The Ettrick Shepherd."

Etymander. See HELMAND.

Et'za·tlán' (ĕt'sä·tlän'). Town, Jalisco state, W cen. Mexico, 45 m. W of Guadalajara; pop. 5641.

Etzina. See KARAKHOTO.

Eu (û). Commune, Seine-Inférieure dept., N France, 17 m. NE of Dieppe; pop. (1931) 5617; ancient countship, supposedly descended from dukes of Normandy, which passed successively to houses of Brienne, Artois, Cleves, Lorraine-Guise, and Orléans; château begun in 16th cent., largely destroyed by fire 1902; extensive forest to SE.

E'u·a (ā'ōō·ä). Island 33 sq. m. of the Tongatabu group in S Tonga Is., SW Pacific Ocean, 9 m. SE of Tongatabu I.

Eu·boe'a (û·bē'à); *Mod. Gr.* **Ev'voi·a** (â'vyä); *Ital.* **Ne·gro·pon'te** (nä·grô·pŏn'tä); *Eng.* **Neg'ro·pont** (nĕg'rŏ·pŏnt). Largest island of Greece, in the Aegean Sea NE of Attica and Boeotia; 90 m. long by 4 to 30 m. wide; 1586 sq. m.; pop. (1938 est.), including islands of Northern Sporades, 179,523; ✱ Chalcis; with Northern Sporades forms a department of the Central Greece and Euboea geographical division (see *Table* at GREECE). Separated on N from Magnesia and Achaea Phthiotis by narrow strait, on NW from Locris by the Atalante channel, and in cen. part of W coast separated from Boeotia by narrow Evripos strait, on which Chalcis and ruins of

Aulis are situated; its mountains (highest 5725 ft.) are part of the chain in Thessaly and the Cyclades; on NE coast is promontory of Artemisium and on SE Cape Caphareus. Connected with Boeotia by a bridge built by Chalcidians; dominated by Athens in 5th cent. B.C.; from 146 B.C. in Roman province of Macedon; to Venice 1204 but not subdued until 1366; conquered by Turks 1470 See CHALCIS and ERETRIA.

Eu·boe'an Sea (û·bē'ǎn); *anc.* **Ma're Eu·bo'i·cum** (mā'rē û·bō'ĭ·kŭm). = ATALANTE channel.

Eu'clid (ū'klĭd). City, Cuyahoga co., N Ohio, on Lake Erie 9 m. NE of and adjoining Cleveland; pop. 62,998; settled 1798; grape culture; manufactures machinery, airplane parts.

Eu·do'ra (û·dôr'à). City, Chicot co., SE corner of Arkansas, 85 m. E of El Dorado; pop. 3598.

Eu·fau'la (û·fô'lä). **1** City, a ⊗ of Barbour co., SE Alabama, on Chattahoochee river 75 m. SE of Montgomery; pop. 8357; shipping center; before 1843 known as Irwinton.

2 City, ⊗ of McIntosh co., E Oklahoma, on Canadian river 27 m. NNE of McAlester; pop. 2382; agriculture.

Eu·ga'ne·an Hills (û·gā'nê·ǎn; ū'gà·nē'ǎn); *Ital.* **Col'li Eu·ga'ne·i** (kôl'lē â·ōō·gä'nä·ē). Range of hills ab. 2000 ft. high in W Padova prov., Venezia Euganea, NE Italy.

Eu·gene' (û·jēn'). Industrial city, ⊗ of Lane co., W Oregon, on Willamette river 62 m. S of Salem; pop. 50,977; settled 1851, became ⊗ 1853, incorp. as city 1864; gold and silver mines. Univ. of Oregon (1872; coed.).

Eu·ge'nia, *or* **San'ta Eugenia, Point** (săn'tá û·jēn'yà). Cape on W coast of Lower California, S of Sebastián Vizcaíno Bay.

Eugubium. See GUBBIO.

Eu'len Ge·bir'ge (oi'lĕn gĕ·bĭr'gĕ). See SUDETEN.

Eumolpias. See PLOVDIV.

Eu'nice (ū'nĭs). **1** Town, St. Landry parish, S cen. Louisiana, 32 m. NW of Lafayette; pop. 11,326; cotton, rice,

2 City, Lea co., SE corner of New Mexico, ab. 18 m. S of Hobbs; pop. 3531; oil (discovered in nearby Jal 1927); founded 1909, made city 1937.

Euonymus. See PANARIA.

Eupatoria. See YEVPATORIYA.

Eu'pen' (*Fr.* û'pĕn'; *Ger.* oi'pĕn). Commune, E Liège prov., E Belgium, 21 m. E of Liège; pop. 13,157; formerly in Germany; transferred with Malmédy and Moresnet to Belgium by Treaty of Versailles 1919; in World War II taken in Allied advance Sept. 12, 1944; with Malmédy (*q.v.*) forms **Eu'pen'-et-Mal'mé'dy** (û'pĕn'ā·mál'mä'dē'), district, 382 sq. m.

Eu·phra'tes (û·frā'tēz); *Turk.* **Frat** (frät) *or* **Fı·rat'** (fī·rät'); *Arab.* **Al Fu·rât'** (ăl fōō·rät'). River 1700 m. long in SW Asia; formed by confluence of the Murat Suyu (Eastern Euphrates) and the Kara Su (Western Euphrates, the main stream) in E Turkey in Asia; flows S and SE across NE Syria, through W and cen. Iraq to unite with the Tigris and continue, as Shatt-al-Arab, to Persian Gulf; has few important tributaries but in Syria on the N receives the Balikh and the Khabur; in middle course crosses Syrian Desert; in lower course in Iraq is used for irrigation, expands into swamps and side streams; navigable for small vessels below Hit. Has on its banks several modern cities of importance: Erzincan (on the Kara Su), Rakka, Deir-ez-Zor, An Najaf, and Nasiriya, and ruins of many ancient cities. Its valley was extensively irrigated in ancient times and gave growth to civilizations of Babylonia, Assyria, Chaldea (see MESOPOTAMIA).

Eur·a'sia (ūr·ā'zhà; -shà). Name given to Europe and Asia as one continent.

Eure (ûr). **1** River 140 m. long in NW France; rises in Orne dept., flows N into the Seine above Rouen; navigable for ab. 50 m.

2 Department of France. See *Table* at FRANCE.

Eure′–et–Loir′ (ûr′ā·lwàr′). Department of France. See *Table* at FRANCE.

Eu·re′ka (ū·rē′ká). **1** County in Nevada. See *Table* at NEVADA.
2 City, ⊗ of Humboldt co., NW California, on Humboldt Bay 83 m. S of Oregon border; pop. 28,137; port of entry; redwood mills, chief redwood outlet for Pacific coast; settled 1850, incorp. as city and made ⊗ 1856.
3 City, ⊗ of Woodford co., N cen. Illinois, 17 m. E of Peoria; pop. 2538; Eureka College (1848; coed.).
4 City, ⊗ of Greenwood co., SE Kansas, 40 m. S of Emporia; pop. 4055; livestock.
5 Village, ⊗ of Eureka co., cen. Nevada, 42 m. SSW of Ruby Lake; pop. 496.
6 City, McPherson co., N South Dakota, 62 m. WNW of Aberdeen; pop. 1555; wheat market.
7 City, Juab co., W Utah, 30 m. SW of Provo; pop. 771; gold, silver, copper, lead, zinc mines.

Eureka Springs. City, a ⊗ of Carroll co., NW Arkansas, 35 m. NE of Fayetteville; pop. 1437; resort notable for numerous medicinal springs.

Eu·ri′pos (û·rī′pŭs; *Mod. Gr.* âv′rē·pôs). Var. of EVRIPOS.

Eu·ro′pa (û·rō′pá). Small French island, S cen. Mozambique Channel, 22°20′S; dependency of Madagascar.

Eu·ro′pa (*Lat.* û·rō′pá; *Ger.* oi·rō′pä; *Ital.* ä·ōō·rô′pä; *Span.* ä·ōō·rō′pä). Latin, German, Italian, and Spanish form of EUROPE.

Eu·ro′pa Point (û·rō′pá). Southernmost tip of Gibraltar, on Strait of Gibraltar.

Eu′rope (ūr′ŭp). Continent, smallest except Australia; ab. 3,800,000 sq. m.; pop. (1939 est.) 545,620,000. *Boundaries:* on N, Arctic Ocean (chief subdivisions Kara Sea, Barents Sea, White Sea); most northerly point North Cape, Norway, 71°10′20′′N; chief islands Vaigach, Novaya Zemlya, Kolguev (U.S.S.R.), Svalbard (Norway). On E, Asia, with which it is sometimes considered as one continent, Eurasia, the conventional boundary being Ural Mts. and Ural river, but now, in political division of the U.S.S.R. into European and Asiatic portions, Molotov Region, W of the Urals, is considered as part of Asia; on SE Caspian Sea. On S, Iran and Turkey in Asia, Black Sea, and Mediterranean (chief subdivisions Aegean Sea, Ionian Sea, Adriatic Sea, Tyrrhenian Sea, Ligurian Sea); marked by Crimean, Balkan, Italian, and Iberian penins.; most southerly point Point Marroquí, Spain, 36°2′N; chief islands Aegean Is., Crete, Ionian Is. (Greece), Sicily, Sardinia (Italy), Corsica (France), and Balearic Is. (Spain). On W, Atlantic Ocean (chief subdivisions Bay of Biscay, North Sea, Norwegian Sea); indented on NW by Baltic Sea (subdivisions Gulf of Bothnia, Gulf of Finland) which is connected with North Sea by the Kattegat and the Skagerrak; marked by peninsulas of Jutland (Denmark) and Scandinavia; most westerly point of mainland Cape Roca, Portugal, 9°30′W, of British Isles, Dunmore Head, Eire, 10°30′W; chief islands British Isles, with smaller groups: Shetland, Orkney, and Outer Hebrides; Faeroes (Denmark), Lofoten Is. (Norway). Chief islands of Baltic Sea; Ahvenanmaa Is. (Finland), Sarema, Khiuma (Estonia, U.S.S.R.), Gotland, Öland (Sweden), Bornholm, Sjælland, Fyn, Falster, Lolland (Denmark), and Rügen (Germany). European mainland separated from British Isles by English Channel and Strait of Dover; from NE Africa by Strait of Gibraltar; from Turkey in Asia by Dardanelles, Sea of Marmara, and Bosporus.
Mountains, etc.: Numerous high mountain regions; Pyrenees (bet. Spain and France), Alps (Switzerland, France, Italy, Austria), Apennines (Italy), Bohemian Forest, Erz Gebirge, and Sudeten Mts. (Germany and Czechoslovakia), Carpathian Mts. (Czechoslovakia, Poland, and Romania), Kjölen Mts. (Norway and Sweden), Transylvanian Alps (Romania), Rhodope Mts., Balkan Mts. (Bulgaria), Caucasus (including highest point of continent, Mt. Elborus, 18,481 ft.) and Ural Mts.

(U.S.S.R.). Other physical features: high plateau of Spain with several mountain ranges (Cantabrian, Sierra de Guadarrama, Sierra Nevada) and extensive level plain of most of Russia; lowest point is Caspian Sea (ab. 85 ft. below sea level). *Rivers:* Volga, Dnieper, Dniester, Don, Northern Dvina (U.S.S.R.), Vistula (Poland), Oder, Elbe (Germany and Czechoslovakia), Rhine (chiefly Germany), Thames (England), Seine, Loire, Rhone (France), Ebro, Guadalquivir (Spain), Douro, Tagus (Spain and Portugal), Po, Tiber (Italy), Danube (Germany, Austria, Hungary, Yugoslavia, Romania, Bulgaria, U.S.S.R.). *Lakes:* Many small lakes in Switzerland (esp. Geneva, Neuchâtel, Zurich), Constance (Switzerland and Germany), Balaton (Hungary), Como, Garda, Maggiore (Italy), Scutari (Yugoslavia and Albania), Vänern, Vättern, Mälaren (Sweden), hundreds of lakes in Finland, and the large lakes of Ladoga, Onega, and Peipus (U.S.S.R.).
Political divisions: Union of Soviet Socialist Republics (in Europe), Poland, Germany, Czechoslovakia, Hungary, Romania, Bulgaria, Greece, Turkey in Europe, Albania, Yugoslavia, Italy, Switzerland, France, Spain, Portugal, Luxembourg, Belgium, Netherlands, Denmark, Finland, Sweden, Norway, United Kingdom, and Eire.

Europus. See RHAGES.

Eu′ros (ūr′ŏs; *Mod. Gr.* âv′rŏs). = *Evros*, department of Greece: see *Table* at GREECE.

Eu·ro′tas (û·rō′tás; *Mod. Gr.* âv·rô′täs); *mod.* **I′ri** (ē′rē). River ab. 60 m. long in S Peloponnesus, Greece, flowing S into Gulf of Laconia; ancient Sparta on it.

Eu·rym′e·don (û·rĭm′ē·dŏn). Ancient name of a small river in S Asia Minor; scene of battle 466 B.C. in which the Greek leader Cimon defeated the Persians.

Eu·se′bio A·ya′la (ā·ōō·sā′vyô ä·yä′lä). Town, S Cordillera dept., cen. Paraguay, E of Caacupé; pop. ab. 12,000.

Eus′kir′chen (ois′kĭr′kĕn). Manufacturing city, W Germany, in SW North Rhine-Westphalia state, 20 m. SSW of Cologne; pop. 14,603.

Eus′tis (ūs′tĭs). City, Lake co., cen. Florida, on **Lake Eustis** 30 m. NW of Orlando; pop. 6189; incorp. 1925.

Eu′taw (ū′tô). City, ⊗ of Greene co., W Alabama; pop. 2784; agriculture; incorporated 1838.

Eutaw Springs. Locality on **Eutaw Creek,** a tributary of the Santee river, South Carolina, in Berkeley co. ab. 45 m. N of Charleston; scene of battle in Revolutionary War Sept. 8, 1781, last important conflict in South Carolina, its results more favorable to Americans.

Eu·tin′ (oi·tēn′). Commune, Schleswig-Holstein, western Germany, ab. 20 m. N of Lübeck; pop. 7037.

Eut′suk Lake (ōōt′sŭk). Lake in W cen. British Columbia prov., Canada; drains E through Nechako river; largest lake in Tweedsmuir (Provincial) Park.

Euxine Sea; *Lat.* **Pontus Euxinus.** See BLACK SEA.

Euyuk. See HÜYÜK.

E·van′ge·line (ē·văn′jē·lēn). Parish in Louisiana. See *Table* at LOUISIANA.

Ev′ans (ĕv′ănz). County, Georgia. See GEORGIA, *Table.*

Evans, Mount. 1 Peak 14,260 ft. in Clear Creek co., N cen. Colorado; on its crest is Cosmic Ray Laboratory of Univ. of Denver, built 1936; jointly sponsored 1948 with four other universities as the Inter-University High-Altitude Laboratory; automobile highway to summit.
2 Peak 13,590 ft. in Park and Lake cos., cen. Colorado.

Evans City or **Ev′ans·burg** (ĕv′ănz·bûrg). Residential borough, Butler co., W Pennsylvania, 23 m. N of Pittsburgh; pop. 1825.

Ev′ans·dale (ĕv′ănz·dāl). Town, Black Hawk co., NE cen. Iowa, SE of Waterloo; pop. 5738.

Ev′ans·ton (ĕv′ăn·stŭn; –ănz·tŭn). **1** Residential city, Cook co., NE Illinois, 15 m. N of Chicago; pop. 79,283; Northwestern University (1851; coed.); Garrett Biblical Institute (1855); Seabury-Western Theological Seminary (1933; Episcopalian); National College of Education (1886; women).

2 Town, ⊗ of Uinta co., SW corner of Wyoming, on Bear river 5 m. E of Utah border; pop. 4901; dairy farming, agriculture; coal, iron, and petroleum deposits.

Ev·ans·ville (ĕv'ănz·vĭl). **1** City, ⊗ of Vanderburgh co., SW Indiana, on Ohio river 29 m. ENE of confluence with Wabash river; pop. 141,543; 4th largest city in the state; manufactures automobile bodies, foundry products gas engines, gas refrigerators; breweries. Evansville College (1854; coed.).

2 City, Rock co., S Wisconsin, 15 m. WNW of Janesville; pop. 2858; settled 1839; manufactures windmills, auto trailers, dairy products, farm machinery.

Ev'arts (ĕv'ĕrts). City, Harlan co., SE Kentucky, in Cumberland Mts. 35 m. ENE of Middlesborough; pop. 1473.

Ev'e·leth (ĕv'ĕ·lĕth). City, St. Louis co., NE Minnesota, 5 m. S of Virginia; pop. 5721; in iron-mining section.

Eve'ning Shade (ēv'nĭng). Town, a ⊗ of Sharp co., N Arkansas; pop. 232.

E·ven'ki or **E·ven'ky** (ĕ·vĕng'kĭ). National district in E part of Krasnoyarsk Territory, Soviet Russia, Asia; 209,057 sq. m.; pop. 38,804; ✳ Tura; in N cen. Siberia, crossed by the Lower (Nizhnyaya) Tunguska river; formed 1930; inhabited by Evenkis, a race of Mongol origin.

Ev'er·ard, Lake (ĕv'ĕr·ärd). Lake, S South Australia, W of Lake Gairdner.

E've·re (ā'vĕ·rĕ). Commune, Brabant prov., cen. Belgium, NE of Brussels; pop. 9894; agriculture, horticulture (esp. production of witloof); airport.

Ev'er·est, Mount (ĕv'ĕr·ĕst; -ĭst); _Tibetan_ **Cho'mo·lung'ma** (chō'mō·lŏŏng'mä). Highest known mountain in the world 29,028 ft. (by a former measurement 29,002 ft.), in the Himalayas bet. Nepal and Tibet, in 27°59′N, 87°5′E, 110 m. NW of Darjeeling; scene of numerous climbing attempts 1921–52; summit first photographed from airplane Apr. 19, 1933 and first reached May 29, 1953 by members of a British expedition led by Sir John Hunt.

Ev'er·ett (ĕv'ĕr·ĕt; -ĭt). **1** City, Middlesex co., NE Massachusetts, 3 m. N of Boston; pop. 43,544; coal and petroleum storage plants; manufactures paints and varnishes, iron and iron castings.

2 Borough, Bedford co., S Pennsylvania, 28 m. S of Altoona; pop. 2279; coal mines; stone quarries.

3 Industrial city and seaport, ⊗ of Snohomish co., NW cen. Washington, on Puget Sound at mouth of Snohomish river 28 m. N of Seattle; pop. 40,304; lumbering center; fisheries, canneries.

Everglades, the. A vast tract of marshland in Palm Beach, Broward, Dade, Monroe, and Collier cos., S Florida, lying S of Lake Okeechobee; large area has been reclaimed by drainage canals with locks and levees; the S part has been set aside as **Everglades National Park**: see UNITED STATES, _National Parks_.

Ev'er·green' (ĕv'ĕr·grēn'). City, ⊗ of Conecuh co., S Alabama, 80 m. NE of Mobile Bay; pop. 3703; mineral springs; agricultural experiment station.

Evergreen Park. Village, Cook co., NE Illinois, 10 m. SW of Chicago; pop. 24,178.

Ev'ers·ley (ĕv'ĕrz·lĭ). Village, NE Hampshire, S England, NW of Aldershot; residence of Charles Kingsley.

Ev'er·son (ĕv'ĕr·s'n). Borough, Fayette co., SW Pennsylvania, 16 m. NNE of Uniontown; pop. 1304.

Eve'sham (ēv'shăm; ē'shăm; ē'săm). Municipal borough, Worcestershire, W cen. England, on the Avon 27 m. S of Birmingham; pop. 12,066; trade center in section raising fruit and vegetables; scene of battle Aug. 4, 1265 in which Simon de Montfort was defeated and killed.

É'vian' (ā'vyäN') or **É'vian'-les-Bains'** (-lā·băN'). Commune, Haute-Savoie dept., E France, on S shore of Lake Geneva; pop. 4353; fashionable health resort.

É'vo·ra (ā'vōō·rà). **1** District of Portugal. See _Table_ at PORTUGAL.

2 _anc._ **Eb'o·ra** (ĕb'ŏ·rà) or **Lib'er·al'i·tas Ju'li·a**

(lĭb'ĕr·ăl'ĭ·tăs jōō'lĭ·à; jōōl'yà). Commune, its ✳, also ✳ of Alto Alentejo prov., and of old prov. of Alentejo, SE cen. Portugal, 68 m. E by S of Lisbon; pop. (1940) 21,851; manufactures cotton, cloth; iron founding; 13th-cent. Gothic cathedral. Roman temple of Diana, Roman aqueduct, archiepiscopal library. Captured by Sertorius 80 B.C., by Moors 712 A.D., by Portuguese 1166; residence of Portuguese court 15th and 16th cents.

Evpatoria See YEVPATORIYA.

É'vreux' (ā'vrû'); _anc._ **Civ'i·tas E·bu'ro·vi'cum** (sĭv'ĭ·tăs ĕ·būr'ō·vī'kŭm). Commune, ✳ of Eure dept., N France, 55 m. WNW of Paris; pop. 20,116; one of oldest towns in France; ancient Norman church; 11th–18th cent. cathedral; Roman ruins. Taken from Romans by Clovis; pillaged by Normans 892; taken and burned by Henry I of England 1119; captured by Philip Augustus of France 1194, 1199; alternated bet. English and French control in 15th cent.

Ev'ri·pos (ĕv'rē·pôs). **1** or **E'gri·pos** (ā'grē·pôs). Narrow strait bet. cen. part of W Euboea I. and the mainland of Greece, S of Atalante channel; the tide or current flows through it violently.

2 City on Euboea I., Greece. See CHALCIS.

Ev'ros (ĕv'rŏs; _Gr._ âv'rŏs). **1** River. See MARITSA.

2 Department of Greece. See _Table_ at GREECE.

Ev·ry'khou (âv·rē'kōō). Village, W cen. Cyprus; terminus of railroad from Famagusta.

Evstrátios, Hagios. See HAGIOS EVSTRÁTIOS.

Evvoia. See EUBOEA.

E'wa (ĕ'và). **1** District, Honolulu co., S Oahu I., Hawaii; pop. 78,666; sugar plantations.

2 Town in district at W end of Pearl Harbor; pop. 3257.

E·wau'na, Lake (ĕ·wô'nà). Small lake, SW Klamath co., S Oregon, just S of Upper Klamath Lake; source of Klamath river.

Ewe, Loch (lŏκ ū'). Inlet of the Atlantic Ocean on W coast of Ross and Cromarty co., N Scotland; 10 m. long; connected with Loch Maree by a river 3 m. long.

E'we·land (ā'và·lănd'; ā'wà-). Region extending ab. 80 m. along coast of W Africa, bet. mouth of Volta river and Grand Popo at mouth of the Mono; ab. 10,000 sq. m.; pop. ab. 1,000,000; inhabited by the Ewe tribe; part of former Slave Coast.

Ew'ing (ū'ĭng). Township, Mercer co., W cen. New Jersey, NNW of Trenton; pop. 26,628.

Ex·cel'si·or Mountain (ĕk·sĕl'sĭ·ẽr; ĭk-). Peak 12,440 ft. in Sierra Nevada, in Mono co., E California.

Excelsior Mountains. Mountain range in Mineral co., SW Nevada; highest Pilot Peak 9207 ft.

Excelsior Springs. City, Clay co., NW Missouri, 25 m. NE of Kansas City; pop. 2864; mineral springs; resort.

Ex·cheq'uer Dam _and_ **Reservoir** (ĕks·chĕk'ẽr; ĕks'-chĕk·ẽr). See UNITED STATES, _Dams and Reservoirs._

Exe (ĕks). River 55 m. long in SW England; rises in NW Somersetshire, flows S past Tiverton and Exeter into English Channel at Exmouth.

Ex'e·ter (ĕk'sĕ·tẽr). **1** City, Tulare co., S cen. California, 45 m. SE of Fresno; pop. 4264; in agricultural region.

2 Manufacturing town, ⊗ of Rockingham co., SE New Hampshire, 12 m. WSW of Portsmouth; pop. 7243; settled and incorporated 1638; capital of N.H. in Revolutionary days 1775 ff. Phillips Exeter Academy (boys' preparatory school, estab. 1781, opened 1783; cf. ANDOVER, Mass.).

3 Borough, Luzerne co., E Pennsylvania, on Susquehanna river 9 m. W of Scranton; pop. 4747; coal mines; timber.

4 Town, Washington co., S Rhode Island, 13 m. WNW of Newport; pop. 2298; formerly part of North Kingstown.

5 Village, Huron co., SE Ontario, Canada, 27 m. W of Stratford; pop. 2547.

6 _anc._ **Is'ca Dam·no'ni·o'rum** (ĭs'kà dăm·nō'nĭ-ōr'ŭm). City and county borough, ⊗ of Devonshire, SW England, on the Exe 37 m. NE of Plymouth; pop. 66,029, (1951) 75,479; has cathedral; railroad center; agricul-

tural center; shipping (city connected with tidal estuary of the Exe by a ship canal). Probably a trading center and fort existed here even before Roman times; a center of resistance of Britons to Anglo-Saxon invasion; withstood Danish attack 1001, but captured by Sweyn 1003; capitulated to William the Conqueror 1068; Royalist stronghold in Civil War 1642–46; in World War II site of largest U.S. Navy supply depot in England.

Ex'moor (ĕks'mo͞or; -mōr). Tract of moorland in Somersetshire, SW England; 32 sq. m.; highest point 1707 ft.

Ex'mouth (ĕks'mouth). Urban district, Devonshire, SW England, on English Channel at mouth of the Exe, 10 m. SSE of Exeter; pop. 17,232; summer resort, fishing and yachting.

Exmouth Gulf. Inlet of Indian ocean, W Western Australia, bet. 21° and 23°S lat.; North West Cape is its NW point.

Exmouth Peninsula. Peninsula extending S from SW coast of Chile, E of Wellington I.

Ex'ploits (ĕks'ploits). River ab. 150 m. long in Newfoundland; flows NE through Red Indian Lake into Notre Dame Bay.

Ex·plor'ing Islands (ĕks·plōr'ĭng; ĭks-). Island group, N end of Lau group, E Fiji Is., SW Pacific Ocean; ab. 17°10'S lat. and 179°W long.; ab. 10 islands, largest Vanua Mbalavu.

Ex'port (ĕks'pōrt). Borough, Westmoreland co., SW Pennsylvania, 20 m. E of Pittsburgh; pop. 1518; coal mining.

Extremadura. See ESTREMADURA, region of Spain.

Ex·u'ma (ĕk·so͞o'má; ĕg·zo͞o'-; ĭk-; ĭg-). Island group of the Bahama Is., in Atlantic Ocean S of New Providence I.; consists of **Great Exuma, Little Exuma,** and adjacent cays; 100 sq. m.; pop. (1943) 3784.

Exuma Sound. Body of water in Bahama Is., West Indies, S of New Providence and Eleuthera Is. and W of Cat I.

Eye (ī). Peninsula extending into North Minch on NE coast of island of Lewis with Harris Outer Hebrides, off NW coast of Scotland.

Ey'ja Fjord (ā'yä). Inlet of Arctic Ocean on N coast of Iceland E of Skaga Fjord.

Ey'lau (ī'lou). 1 or **Preus'sisch Eylau** (proi'sĭsh). Commune, former East Prussia prov., Germany (see BAGRATIONOVSK); scene of a bloody but indecisive battle Feb. 8, 1807 bet. the allied Russians and Prussians and the French under Napoleon.
2 = *Deutsch-Eylau:* see ILAWA.

Ey'non (ī'nŭn). Locality, Lackawanna co., NE Pennsylvania, ab. 6 m. SW of Carbondale.

Eyn'sham (ĕn'shăm; ān'-) or **En'sham** (ĕn'-). Parish and village Oxfordshire, cen. England, 7½ m. NW of Oxford; few remains of ancient Benedictine abbey of which Ælfric Grammaticus was first abbot (1005).

Ey'rar·bak'ki (ā'rär·bäk'yĭ). Village, SW coast of Iceland, ab. 32 m. SE of Reykjavík.

Eyre, Lake (âr). Shallow salt lake 3700 sq. m., NE South Australia, lat. 27°50' to 29°20'S, from 39 to 60 ft. below sea level.

Eyre Peninsula (âr). Large peninsula, S South Australia, W of Spencer Gulf, lat. 33° to 35°S.

Eysk. Var. of *Eisk:* see YEISK.

Eystrátios, Hagios. See HAGIOS EVSTRÁTIOS.

Ey'zies', Les (lā-zā'zē'); *in full* **Les Eyzies–de–Ta'yac'** (-dĕ·tá'yȧk'). Commune, Dordogne dept., SW cen. France, SE of Périgueux on the Vézère; pop. (1931) 955; region containing many caves, notably **Cro–Ma'-gnon'** (krō'má'nyôN'), where type specimens of the Cro-Magnon race dating from the Aurignacian period were found 1868, and **Com'ba'relles'** (kôN'bȧ'rĕl') and **Font–de–Gaume** (fôND'gōm') discovered 1901, decorated with paleolithic paintings and engravings. See also LE MOUSTIER and LA MADELEINE.

E·zan, Cape (ĕ·zän). Cape on S coast of Hokkaido, Japan, at S of entrance to Uchiura Bay.

E·zei'za (â·sĕ'ê·sä). Airport, Buenos Aires prov., E Argentina, ab. 15 m. from Buenos Aires center; developed 1946–47; one of largest civilian airfields in the world.

E'zi·on·ge'ber (ē'zĭ·ŏn·gē'bĕr). Ancient town, now an archaeological site, the modern village of Tell el Khalifa, near 'Aqaba at head of Gulf of 'Aqaba, SW corner of Jordan; place where Solomon built a navy (*1 Kings* ix. 26); came under control of Edomites in middle of 8th cent. B.C.

Ezo. See HOKKAIDO.

Ez'ra Church (ĕz'rá). Site in SW Atlanta, Georgia, of battle July 28, 1864 in which Confederates tried unsuccessfully to check Sherman's advance.

Ez Zue·ti'na (ĕz zwȧ·tē'ná). Town on coastal road, N Libya, N Africa, on E shore of Gulf of Sidra bet. Bengasi and Agedabia.

F

Fa′bens (fā′bĕnz). Town, El Paso co., W tip of Texas, on the Rio Grande ab. 25 m. SE of El Paso; pop. 3134; stock raising, mining.

Fa′bri·a′no (fä′brē·ä′nô). Commune, Ancona prov., Marches, cen. Italy, 38 m. SW of Ancona; pop. 26,382; manufactures paper; sulfur springs.

Fa′ca·ta′ti·vá′ (fä′kä·tä′tē·vä′). City, Cundinamarca dept., cen. Colombia, 25 m. NW of Bogotá; alt. 8270 ft.; pop. 9779.

Fad·de′ev·ski (fŭ·dyä′yĕf·skĭ). One of New Siberian Is. (*q.v.*).

Faemund. See FEMUND.

Fa·en′za (fä·ĕn′tsä; *Angl.* -ĕn′zȧ); *anc.* **Fa·ven′ti·a** (fȧ·vĕn′shĭ·ȧ; -shȧ). Commune, Ravenna prov., Emilia, N Italy, 19 m. SW of Ravenna; pop. 47,199; connected with Adriatic Sea by canal (opened 1782); early-Renaissance cathedral; iron and salt springs; pottery center; International Museum of Ceramics; Scene of victory of Sulla over followers of Marius 82 B.C. and of Totila over the Byzantines 542 A.D.; became famous in 15th and 16th cents. for its manufacture of Faenza ware and faïence (both named for the town); during World War II in center of fighting Dec. 1944.

Faer′oes (fâr′ōz); *Dan.* **Fær′ö′er·ne** (fâr′û′ĕr·nĕ). Island group in Atlantic Ocean N of British Isles, ab. 190 m. NW of Shetland Is.; of the 22 islands only 17 are inhabited, largest Strömö; constitute a county, **Fær′ö′** (fâr′û′), of Denmark; 540 sq. m.; pop. 25,744, (1945) 29,198; ⊗ Thorshavn; see *Table* at DENMARK. Islands generally hilly and precipitous; highest point ab. 3000 ft.; fishing and sheep raising. Possession of Denmark since 1380; inhabitants, of Norse descent, have control of local affairs and are represented in Danish Parliament; unsuccessfully sought independence 1946.

Faesulae. See FIESOLE.

Fa·e′te, Mon′te (môn′tä fä·ā′tä). Mountain ab. 3000 ft., S of Rome, Italy; taken by American forces June 2, 1944 just before capture of Rome on June 4.

Fă·gă·ras′ (fä·gȧ·räsh′). Town, N cen. Romania, on Olt river NW of Braşov; pop. 22,700.

Fa′ger·sta (fä′gĕr·stà′). Town, Västmanland prov., E cen. Sweden, 37 m. N of Västeräs; pop. 10,022; manufactures pig iron.

Fa′gui′bine′ (fȧ·gē′bēn′), *or* **Fa′gi·bi′ni** (fä′gē·bē′nĕ), **Lake.** Lake ab. 70 m. long, Mali, cen. West Africa, W of Tombouctou and N of Niger river.

Fahlun. See FALUN.

Fa′ïd Pass (fä′yĭd). Mountain pass, N Tunisia, N Africa, E of Sbeitla and on highway to Sfax; scene of American defeat by Germans under Rommel Feb. 14, 1943; retaken in April.

Fai′fo′ (fī′fō′). Coastal town, E Annam, Vietnam, 14 m. S of Tourane; pop. ab. 8000; dates back to the Cham race and to Chinese domination.

Fails′worth (fālz′wûrth). Urban district, Lancashire, NW England, 5 m. NE of Manchester; pop. 18,033.

Fair′banks (fâr′băngks). Town, Alaska, at junction of Tanana and Chena rivers; pop. 13,311; alt. 448 ft.; chief town of cen. Alaska; port of entry; terminus of railroad to Seward and of Alaska Highway; Univ. of Alaska (1922, coed.) at suburban village of College (ab. 2 m. W); gold mining, lumbering. Founded 1902 as result of a gold rush.

Fair′born (fâr′bôrn). City, Greene co., SW Ohio, NE of Dayton; pop. 19,453; formed 1950 by consolidation of former villages of Fairfield and Osborn.

Fair′burn (fâr′bĕrn). City, Fulton co., NW cen. Georgia, 18 m. SW of Atlanta; pop. 2470.

Fair′bur′y (fâr′bĕr′ĭ; -bēr·ĭ). **1** City, Livingston co., NE cen. Illinois, 33 m. NE of Bloomington; pop. 2937.

2 City, ⊗ of Jefferson co., SE Nebraska; pop. 5572; packing plant; manufactures windmills, pumps.

Fair′chance′ (fâr′chȧns′). Borough, Fayette co., SW Pennsylvania, 6 m. S of Uniontown; pop. 2120.

Fair′fax (fâr′făks). **1** County in Virginia. See *Table* at VIRGINIA.

2 Town, Marin co., W California, 15 m. NW of San Francisco; pop. 5813.

3 Town, Osage co., N Oklahoma, 25 m. ESE of Ponca City; pop. 2076; oil wells, refineries.

4 Town, ⊗ of Fairfax co., NE Virginia; pop. 13,585.

Fair′field (fâr′fēld). **1** Name of counties in three states of the U.S. See *Tables* at CONNECTICUT, OHIO, SOUTH CAROLINA.

2 City, Jefferson co., cen. Alabama, 5 m. W of Birmingham; pop. 15,816; founded 1910; planned city, laid out by U.S. Steel Corp. (see also GARY, Indiana); once known as Corey.

3 City, ⊗ of Solano co., cen. California, 40 m. SW of Sacramento; pop. 14,968; Travis Air Force Base.

4 Town, SE Fairfield co., SW Connecticut, on Long Island Sound; pop. 46,183; settled 1639; port of entry; summer resort; gold and silver refining.

5 Village, ⊗ of Camas co., S cen. Idaho; pop. 474.

6 City, ⊗ of Wayne co., SE Illinois, 30 m. E of Mt. Vernon; pop. 6362.

7 City, ⊗ of Jefferson co., SE Iowa, 24 m. E of Ottumwa; pop. 8054; iron products, gloves, glass, brushes; Parsons College (1875; coed.; Presbyterian).

8 Town, Somerset co., W Maine, on Kennebec river 4 m. N of Waterville; pop. 5829; pulp and woolen mills.

9 Town, ⊗ of Freestone co., E cen. Texas; pop. 1781.

10 Town, Franklin co., NW Vermont, 8 m. E of St. Albans; pop. 1225; birthplace of Chester A. Arthur, 21st president of the U.S.

11 Town, E New South Wales, SE Australia, ab. 12 m. W of Sydney center; pop. 8705.

Fair′ha′ven (fâr′hā′vĕn). **1** Town, Bristol co., SE Massachusetts, on Buzzards Bay across harbor from New Bedford; pop. 14,339; former whaling center; boatyards.

2 See BELLINGHAM, Washington.

Fair′ Ha′ven. **1** Borough and resort, Monmouth co., E cen. New Jersey, 16 m. SE of Perth Amboy; pop. 5678.

2 Village, Rutland co., W Vermont, on Poultney river 15 m. W of Rutland; pop. 2378; chartered 1783; slate.

Fair′ Ha′vens (hā′vĕnz). Sheltered harbor on S coast of Crete, E of Bay of Messara; port where Paul's ship touched on his journey to Rome (*Acts* xxvii. 8).

Fair Head. Basaltic headland 630 ft. high projecting into North Channel on extreme NE coast of Ireland.

Fair′hope (fâr′hōp). Town, Baldwin co., SW Alabama, on Mobile Bay SE of Mobile; pop. 4858; resort; settled 1893–94 on basis of single-tax doctrine promulgated by Henry George; School of Organic Education, known for experiments in progressive education.

Fair Lawn. Borough, Bergen co., NE corner of New Jersey, 3 m. ENE of Paterson; pop. 36,421; textiles, cement products.

Fair′mont (fâr′mŏnt). **1** City, ⊗ of Martin co., S Minnesota, 41 m. SSW of Mankato; pop. 9745.

2 Town, Robeson co., S North Carolina, 41 m. SSW of Fayetteville; pop. 2286.

3 Manufacturing city, ⊗ of Marion co., N West Virginia, on Monongahela river 18 m. NNE of Clarksburg; pop. 27,477; center of coal-mining area; Fairmont State Coll. (1867; coed.). Settled 1793, became ⊗ 1842.

Fairmont City. Village, St. Clair co., SW Illinois, 5 m. E of East St. Louis; pop. 2688.

Fair′mount (fâr′mount). Town, Grant co., N cen. Indiana, 9 m. S of Marion; pop. 3080.

Fair Oaks. Locality just E of Richmond, Virginia; battlefield (called also Seven Pines), scene of engagement May 31–June 1, 1862 in which Federal troops under McClellan repulsed Confederates under Johnston

(Johnston wounded; on June 1 Robert E. Lee took command of Confederate forces).

Fair Plain. Urban community (unincorporated), Berrien co., SW Michigan, WSW of Kalamazoo; pop. 7998.

Fair′play (fâr′plā′). Town, ⊗ of Park co., cen. Colorado; pop. 404; alt. 9964 ft.

Fair′port (fâr′pōrt). **1** Industrial village, Monroe co., W New York, 10 m. E of Rochester; pop. 5507.
2 Village (post office **Fairport Harbor**), Lake co., NE Ohio, on Lake Erie 28 m. NE of Cleveland; pop. 4267; fisheries.

Fair′view (fâr′vū′). **1** See CHICOPEE, Massachusetts.
2 Borough, Bergen co., NE corner of New Jersey, 7 m. N of Jersey City; pop. 9399; bleachery, fireworks plant.
3 Urban community (unincorporated), Dutchess co., SE New York, NE of New York City; pop. 8626.
4 City, ⊗ of Major co., NW Oklahoma, 37 m. WSW of Enid; pop. 2213.

Fairview Park. City, Cuyahoga co., N Ohio, SW suburb of Cleveland; pop. 14,624.

Fair′way (fâr′wā). City, Johnson co., E Kansas, SE of Kansas City; pop. 5398.

Fair′weath′er, Cape (fâr′wĕth′ẽr). Cape on SE coast of Alaska, 58°55′N, 138°W, ab. 35 m. S of Mt. Fairweather.

Fairweather, Mount. Peak 15,318 ft. on boundary bet. Alaska and NW British Columbia, Canada, on NW border of Glacier Bay National Monument.

Fa·i′si (fä·ē′sē). Town, E coast of Shortland I., NW Solomon Is., W Pacific Ocean; government station, chief town of Shortland Is.; became naval base under Japanese; center of copra trade.

Fai·yûm′ or **Fa·yûm′** (fä·yōōm′; fī-). Province, N Upper Egypt; ✱ El Faiyûm. See *Table* at EGYPT.

Faiyûm, El. See EL FAIYÛM.

Faiz′a·bad′. 1 (fīz′ä·bäd′; *native* fīz′ä·bäd′) Town, NE Afghanistan; ✱ of Badakhshan and of modern Kataghan-Badakhshan prov.; pop. 62,482.
2 (fīz′ä·bäd′; *native* fâz′ä·bäd′) Var. of FYZABAD, Indian Union.

Fa·jar′do (fä·här′thō). Municipality (pop. 18,321) and town (pop. 12,409), NE Puerto Rico.

Fa′ka·o′fo (fä′kä·ō′fō). Atoll of Tokelau group, cen. Pacific Ocean, N of Samoa; lagoon 7 m. by 4 m.; has chief settlement (**Fakaofo**) of the group.

Fa′ka·ra′va (fä′kä·rä′vä). Atoll, lat. 16°S and long. 146°W, in Tuamotu Archipelago, French Oceania, South Pacific Ocean; 32 m. long by 10 m. wide; chief village Rotoava.

Fak′fak′ (fäk′fäk′). Coastal settlement at W end of Neth. New Guinea, just S of entrance to McCluer Gulf; pop. ab. 1000; one of best ports of Neth. New Guinea.

Fako. See CAMEROON.

Fa·laise′ (fȧ·lāz′; *Fr.* fȧ′lâz′). Commune, S Calvados dept., NW France, 19 m. SE of Caen; pop. (1931) 5616; ruined castle; celebrated since 11th cent. for fair, held annually in Aug., for livestock and wool at Guibray, a suburb. Seat of dukes of Normandy, probably birthplace of William the Conqueror; held by English 1417–50; in World War II Normandy campaign captured by Canadians Aug. 16, 1944 and formed N point of Falaise pocket (see ARGENTAN).

Fa·la′lop (fä·lä′lŭp). See ULITHI.

Fa·lam′ (fä·läm′). Town, ✱ of Chin Hills dist., W Upper Burma, on Manipur river 175 m. NW of Mandalay.

Fal′con (fô[l]′kŭn); *native* **Fo·nu′a·fo′o** (fô·nōō′ä·fō′ō). Small volcanic island in SW Pacific Ocean, ab. 55 m. NW of Tongatabu in Tonga Is., ab. lat. 20°19′S and long. 175°25′W. In latter part of 18th cent. observed by navigators as a reef; appeared as an island 1885 and again in 1896 after a violent eruption; subsided c. 1899 but as a result of eruptions in 1927 became an island ab. 1½ m. long; disappeared again by Mar. 1949.

Fal·cón′ (fäl·kōn′). State of Venezuela. See *Table* at VENEZUELA.

Fal′con·er (fôl′kŭn·ẽr). Manufacturing village, Chautauqua co., SW New York; pop. 3343.

Falcon Heights. Village, Ramsey co., E Minnesota, N suburb of St. Paul; pop. 5927.

Fa′lé·mé′ (fä′lā′mā′). River ab. 200 m. long in Senegal, West Africa; tributary of Senegal river.

Falerii. See CIVITA CASTELLANA.

Fal·fur′ri·as (făl·fŏŏr′ĭ·ȧs). City, ⊗ of Brooks co., S Texas, 58 m. SW of Corpus Christi; pop. 6515.

Fal′ken·stein (fäl′kĕn·shtīn); *also* **Falkenstein in Sach′sen** (ĭn zäk′sĕn). Industrial city, Saxony, East Germany, 36 m. SW of Chemnitz; pop. 15,626.

Fal′kirk (fôl′kûrk). Burgh, Stirling co., cen. Scotland, 20 m. ENE of Glasgow; pop. (1951) 37,528; coal and iron mines, flour mills, chemical factories, and breweries. Scene of two battles: (1) July 22, 1298, in which Edward I of England defeated Scots under Wallace; (2) Jan. 17, 1746, in which Prince Charles Edward and his Highlanders defeated Gen. Hawley.

Falk′land Islands (fôk′lănd; *less often*, fôlk′-); *Span.* **Is′las Mal·vi′nas** (ēz′läs mäl·vē′näs). British crown colony in South Atlantic Ocean, 300 m. E of Strait of Magellan, comprising two principal islands, **East Falkland** (with adjacent small islands 2580 sq. m.) and **West Falkland** (with adjacent small islands 2038 sq. m.); the smaller islands include Weddell I., Pebble I., and Jason Is.; total area 4618 sq. m.; pop. (1939 est.) 2425; ✱ Stanley; main islands of quite irregular shape with wide channel (**Falkland Sound**) bet. them; many fiords and bays; highest point Mt. Adams 2290 ft. on West Falkland; whaling, sheep raising, sealing.
History: Discovered 1592; not occupied until French made short-lived settlement 1764; settlement of English and their expulsion by Spanish 1770 at one time threatened to cause war bet. England and countries party to Family Compact; although claimed by Argentina after she won independence (and still claimed), occupied by British 1833; in nearby waters a British fleet destroyed German Pacific fleet Dec. 8, 1914.

Falkland Islands Dependencies. All land areas bet. 20° and 50°W long. S of 50°S lat. (including South Georgia I., South Orkney Is., South Sandwich Is., and the shores of Weddell Sea; see COATS LAND) and bet. 50° and 80°W long. S of 58°S (including the Palmer Penin. and South Shetlands Is., Palmer Archipelago), administered as dependencies of the Falkland Is. since 1908; area of South Georgia I. 1450 sq. m., permanent pop. (in whaling industry) ab. 750; other sections not inhabited and no estimates of areas available; entire area claimed by Argentina.

Falk′ner Island (fôk′nẽr). Island in Long Island Sound off SE coast of New Haven co., Connecticut.

Falk′nov (fälk′nôf); *Ger.* **Fal′ke·nau** (fäl′kĕ·nou). Town, W Bohemia prov., W Czechoslovakia, on Ohře river 11 m. WSW of Karlovy Vary; pop. (1930) 11,284.

Fal′kö′ping (fäl′chŭ′pĭng). Town, Skaraborg prov., S Sweden, W of Lake Vättern; pop. (1928) 6860; scene of battle Feb. 24, 1389 in which Albert, Duke of Mecklenburg, was defeated and taken prisoner by forces of Margaret of Denmark.

Fall′en Tim′bers (fôl′ĕn tĭm′bẽrz). Locality on Maumee river SW of Toledo, NW Ohio; scene of victory Aug. 20, 1794 of Anthony Wayne over the Indians which led to enforcement of Jay's Treaty (Nov. 1794) and British evacuation of border forts.

Fal′lon (fäl′ŭn). **1** County in Montana. See *Table* at MONTANA.
2 City, ⊗ of Churchill co., W Nevada, near Carson Lake and Carson Sink 53 m. E of Reno; pop. 2734.

Fall River (fôl). **1** County in South Dakota. See *Table* at SOUTH DAKOTA.
2 Seaport and manufacturing city, a ⊗ of Bristol co., SE Massachusetts, on Mt. Hope Bay at mouth of Taunton river 12 m. NW of New Bedford; pop. 99,942; in 19th cent. one of largest centers in U.S. for cotton mills and

textile machinery works. Originally part of Plymouth colony; settled 1656; severe fires 1843 and 1928.

Falls (fôlz). **1** County in Texas. See *Table* at TEXAS.
2 Township, Bucks co., SE Pennsylvania, N of Philadelphia; pop. 29,082.

Falls Church. Independent city, NE Virginia, 10 m. NW of Alexandria; pop. 10,192.

Falls City. City, ⊗ of Richardson co., SE corner of Nebraska, 65 m. ESE of Beatrice; pop. 5598.

Falluja, Al. See AL FALLUJA.

Fal'mouth (făl'mŭth). **1** City, ⊗ of Pendleton co., N Kentucky, 30 m. SSE of Covington; pop. 2568; apiaries.
2 Town, Cumberland co., SW Maine, 6 m. N of Portland; pop. 5976.
3 Residential and resort town, Barnstable co., SE Massachusetts, 16 m. ESE of New Bedford near E shore of Buzzards Bay; pop. 13,037; formerly whaling and boatbuilding center; Otis Air Force Base; includes **Woods Hole** (wŏŏdz), seat of Woods Hole Oceanographic Institution (founded 1930).
4 Seaport town on S coast of island of Antigua, Leeward Is., British West Indies.
5 Coastal town, NW Jamaica I., British West Indies; pop. (1943 est.) 2561.
6 Municipal borough, Cornwall, SW England, on English Channel at mouth of the Fal 44 m. WSW of Plymouth; pop. 17,036; port, fishing center, seaside resort; a U.S. Naval training base 1943–45.

False Bay (fôls). Bay on SW coast of Cape Province, Union of South Africa, E of Cape of Good Hope.

False Cape. See Kaap VALSCH.

False Cape Horn. Cape at SE tip of Hoste I., S of Tierra del Fuego I. and NW of Cape Horn.

False Pass. Village on E coast of Unimak I. opp. tip of Alaska Penin., Aleutian Is.

False Point. Cape on NE coast of India, in Orissa prov., projecting into Bay of Bengal just N of mouth of Mahanadi river.

Fal'so, Cape (fäl'sô). Southwest extremity of Lower California, extending into Pacific Ocean.

Fal'ster (fäl'stēr). Island forming a part of Denmark, lying in Baltic Sea S of the island of Sjælland (with which it is connected by a bridge over 10,000 feet long), SW of Möen, and E of Lolland; 198 sq. m.; pop. (1925) 44,771; together with Lolland forms Maribo co.

Făl'ti·ce'ni (fûl'tê·chěn'; -chě'nê). City, Moldavia region, NE Romania, 68 m. NW of Bacău; pop. 14,347.

Fa'lun' *or* **Fah'lun'** (fä'lŭn'). City, ⁎ of Kopparberg prov., cen. Sweden, 130 m. NW of Stockholm; pop. 15,327; railroad car factories, iron mines and foundries, pyrite mines; former copper-mining center.

Fa'ma·gu'sta (fä'mä·gŏŏs'tà; *Ital.* fä'mä·gŏŏs'tä). **1** District, E island of Cyprus, E Mediterranean Sea; 781 sq. m.; pop. (1931) 71,472.
2 Seaport, its ⁎, on Famagusta Bay on E coast NW of Cape Greco; pop. (1942 est.), with suburb of Varosha, 13,331; 3 m. S of ruins of Salamis (*q.v.*); has fortifications, castle, and large cathedral (now a mosque); connected by rail with Nicosia. Important during Crusades, receiving many refugees after fall of Acre 1291; taken by Genoese 1376 and by Turks 1571 after siege of a year; British internment camp for Jews attempting illegally to enter Palestine 1946–48.

Famagusta Bay. Broad inlet of Mediterranean Sea on E coast of Cyprus.

Famatina. For **Nevado de Famatina** and **Sierra de Famatina**, see SIERRA DE FAMATINA.

Fan'ad Head (făn'ăd). Cape on N coast of Ireland, at W of entrance to Lough Swilly; lighthouse.

Fan'nin (făn'ĭn). Name of counties in two states of the U.S. See *Tables* at GEORGIA and TEXAS.

Fannin, Camp. Station of the Army Ground Forces, Infantry, near Tyler, Smith co., NE Texas.

Fan'ning Island (făn'ĭng). One of the Line Is. (*q.v.*) in cen. Pacific Ocean, S of Hawaii; lat. 4°N and long.

159°W; 15 sq. m.; included 1916 in British colony of Gilbert and Ellice Is.; station on the Pacific cable bet. Canada, Fiji Is., New Zealand, and Australia; pop. (1940) 255; discovered 1798 by American navigator, Capt. Edmund Fanning. Cf. AMERICA ISLANDS.

Fa·no' (fä·nô'); *anc.* **Pha'nos** (fā'nŏs); *Mod. Gr.* **O'tho·nói'** (ô'thô·nyē'). Island of the Ionian Is., 14 m. NW of Corfu.

Fa'no (fä'nô); *anc.* **Fa'num For·tu'nae** (fā'nŭm fôr·tū'nē), *later* **Co·lo'ni·a Ju'lia Fa·nes'tris** (kô·lō'nĭ·à [-lōn'yà] jōōl'yà [jōō'lĭ·à] fà·nĕs'trĭs). Commune, Pesaro e Urbino prov., Marches, cen. Italy, on Adriatic Sea near mouth of Metauro river, 6 m. SE of Pesaro; pop. 31,617; manufactures silk, oil, hemp; fisheries; cathedral; remains of triumphal arch and city walls. Under Papal States 1463–1860; first printing press with movable Arabic type set up here 1513 by Pope Julius II; seat of a university until 1828. See PENTAPOLIS.

Fan'ö' (fän'û'). Island of Denmark, in North Sea off SW coast of Jutland Penin.; in North Frisian Is.; 22 sq. m.; pop. (1925) 2731.

Fan'wood (făn'wŏŏd). Borough, Union co., NE New Jersey, 9 m. W of Elizabeth; pop. 7963.

Fa'o (fä'ô). Port, SE Iraq, near Persian Gulf at mouth of the Shatt-al-Arab, which is 1 m. wide here but obstructed by bar across channel.

Fara. See SHURUPPAK.

Fa'ra·fan·ga'na (fä'rä·fäng·gä'nä). Town, SE coast of Madagascar, S of Manakara.

Fa·raf'ra (fŭ·rŏf'rô). Oasis, Western Desert prov., Egypt, in Libyan Desert, 27°N, 28°E; pop. ab. 1000.

Fa·rah' (fä·rä'h). **1** River ab. 200 m. long, rising in mountains in W cen. Afghanistan and flowing SW into Lake Helmand.
2 A minor province, SW Afghanistan.
3 Town in Farah prov., 140 m. S of Herat; pop. ab. 5000.

Far'al·lon Islands (făr'ă·lŏn). Small group of islands in Pacific Ocean, a part of San Francisco co., W cen. California, ab. 30 m. W of Golden Gate.

Fa·ra·san' Islands (fŭ·rŏ·sän'). Group of islands in SE Red Sea, off SW coast of Asir, Saudi Arabia.

Far'ciennes' (fár'syĕn'). Commune, Hainaut prov., SW Belgium, near Charleroi; pop. 10,570.

Far East. 1 The countries of E Asia bordering on Pacific Ocean: China, Japan, E Siberia, Korea, Indochina, Malay Archipelago (including the Philippine Is., etc.); the Orient.
2 The E strip of Siberia along the coast, in 19th cent. a viceroyalty of Russian empire, later known as Maritime Province. See FAR EASTERN REGION; SIBERIA.

Far Eastern Region *or* **Area.** Former division of Soviet Russia in Asia, including Pacific coast and borders of Manchuria; 900,745 sq. m.; coincides roughly with more recent Khabarovsk and Maritime Territories and Chukot and Koryak National Districts; first known as **Far Eastern Republic,** formed 1920 of four republics of E Siberia with capital at Chita, which was supplanted 1922 by Far Eastern Region, with capital first at Vladivostok and later at Khabarovsk; reorganized 1926 as Far Eastern Area; reorganized again 1938 when it was divided.

Fa·regh' (fà·rĕg'). Short river in W Cyrenaica, NE Libya, N Africa; drains W into marshes S of El Agheila.

Fare'ham (fâr'ăm). Urban district, Hampshire, S England, on NW Portsmouth harbor 6 m. NNW of Portsmouth; pop. 42,470.

Fare'well', Cape (fâr'wĕl'). **1** *Dan.* **Kap Far·vel'** (kàp' fär·vĕl'). Southern point of Greenland, 60°N, 44°W.
2 Northernmost point of South I., New Zealand.

Far'go (fär'gō). City, ⊗ of Cass co., E North Dakota, on Red river at head of navigation; largest city in the state; pop. 46,662; settled 1871, incorp. 1875; distributing point esp. for farm machinery, automobiles, sweet clover; flour mill, creameries, meat-packing plants (in suburbs of

West Fargo and **Southwest Fargo**); manufactures steel, wood, and glass products. North Dakota State Univ. of Agriculture and Applied Science (1890; coed.).

Fargues (fàrg). Village, Gironde dept., SW France; pop. (1931) 622; produces wine (see SAUTERNES).

Far′i·bault (făr′ĭ·bō). **1** County in Minnesota. See *Table* at MINNESOTA.
2 City, ⊗ of Rice co., S Minnesota, 47 m. S of Minneapolis; pop. 16,926; on site of trading post established 1826 by Alexander Faribault.

Fa·rid′kot (fä·rēd′kōt). **1** Former Indian state, East Punjab, NW India, S of the Sutlej; 637 sq. m.; pop. (1941) 199,283; under British influence 1809–1947.
2 Town, its ✳, 65 m. SSE of Lahore; pop. 16,759.

Fa·rid′pur (fä·rēd′pŏor). **1** District, Dacca division, formerly in Bengal, NE Brit. India, now in East Bengal, Pakistan; 2821 sq. m.; pop. (1941) 2,888,803.
2 Town, its ✳, on S bank of an old channel of the Ganges, 35 m. W of Dacca; pop. 15,516.

Fa·ri·lhões′ (fä·rē·lyōĕNsh′). Group of Portuguese islets off W cen. coast of Portugal, just N of the Berlengas Is.

Farm′er City (fär′mẽr). City, De Witt co., cen. Illinois, 34 m. NE of Decatur; pop. 1838.

Farm′ers Branch (fär′mẽrz). City, Dallas co., NE Texas, NNE suburb of Dallas; pop. 13,441.

Farm′ers·ville (fär′mẽrz·vĭl; *Sou. also* -v′l). City, Collin co., NE Texas, W of Greenville; pop. 2021; onions.

Farm′er·ville (fär′mẽr·vĭl; *Sou. also* -v′l). Town, ⊗ of Union parish, N Louisiana; pop. 2727.

Farm′ing·dale (fär′mĭng·dāl). Village, Nassau co., SE New York, on Long I. 30 m. E of New York City; pop. 6128; manufactures airplanes.

Farm′ing·ton (fär′mĭng·tŭn). **1** River, N Connecticut; formed by confluence in NE Litchfield co. of East Branch and West Branch (ab. 30 m. long) both of which rise in Massachusetts; flows into Connecticut river at Windsor.
2 Residential and industrial town, W cen. Hartford co., N Connecticut; pop. 10,813; watered by Farmington river; settled 1640, incorp. 1645. Includes 2 communities: (1) Farmington, former industrial center, now residential suburb; and (2) Unionville (*q.v.*).
3 City, Fulton co., W cen. Illinois; pop. 2831.
4 Town, ⊗ of Franklin co., W Maine, 26 m. WNW of Waterville; pop. 5001; Farmington State Teachers College (1864; coed.).
5 Residential city, Oakland co., SE Michigan, 14 m. SSW of Pontiac; pop. 6881.
6 Village, Dakota co., SE Minnesota, 22 m. S of St. Paul; pop. 2300.
7 City, ⊗ of St. Francois co., E Missouri, 59 m. S of St. Louis; pop. 5618; lead deposits.
8 Town, Strafford co., SE New Hampshire, 6 m. NW of Rochester; pop. 3287; shoe manufacturing.
9 Commercial town, San Juan co., NW corner of New Mexico, on San Juan river near NE corner of Northern Navajo Indian Reservation; pop. 23,786.
10 City, ⊗ of Davis co., N Utah, on Great Salt Lake 15 m. N of Salt Lake City; pop. 1951.

Farm′ville (färm′vĭl; *Sou. also* -v′l). **1** Town, Pitt co., E North Carolina, 21 m. SSE of Wilson; pop. 3997; markets esp. tobacco.
2 Town, ⊗ of Prince Edward co., S cen. Virginia, 45 m. E of Lynchburg; pop. 4293; settled 1754; tobacco warehouses; lumber mills; Longwood College (1884; women).

Farn′bor·ough (färn′bûr′ō; *Brit.* -bŭ·rŭ, -brŭ). **1** Urban district, Hampshire, S England, 31 m. WSW of London; pop. 27,702; Royal Air Force station.
2 Town, Kent, SE England ab. 14 m. S of London; pop. 4373.

Farne Islands (färn). Group of 17 small islands off NE coast of Northumberland, N England; scene of wreck of the *Forfarshire* 1838 and the rescue, from Longstone lighthouse, by Grace Darling.

Farn′ham (fär′năm). **1** Industrial town, Missisquoi co., S Quebec, Canada, on Yamaska river 35 m. ESE of Montreal; pop. 4926; important railroad junction.
2 Urban district, Surrey, S England, on Wey river 38 m. SW of London; pop. 23,911; ruins of Waverley Abbey, founded 1128, earliest Cistercian abbey in England.

Farnham, Mount. See PURCELL RANGE.

Farn′worth (färn′wûrth; -wẽrth). Urban district, Lancashire, NW England, 7 m. NW of Manchester; pop. 28,614; collieries, iron foundries; manufactures paper, cotton, bricks.

Fa′ro (fä′rōō). **1** District of Portugal. See *Table* at PORTUGAL.
2 Seaport commune, its ✳, S Portugal, on Atlantic Ocean 137 m. SSE of Lisbon; pop. (1940) 19,695; ✳ of Algarve prov.; trades in fish, wine, oil, cork, dried and fresh fruits, basketry; antimony and salt deposits; cathedral; earthquakes 1722, 1755.

Fär′ö′ (fôr′û). Island 44 sq. m. in Baltic Sea off NE coast of Gotland I.; a part of Gotland prov., Sweden.

Fa′ro, Cape (fä′rō); *Ital.* **Pun′ta del Faro** (pōōn′tä däl); *anc.* **Pe·lo′rus** (pē·lōr′ŭs). Cape on NE extremity of Sicily.

Far′oe Islands, Far′oes (fär′ō, -ōz). = FAEROES.

Far′quhar, Cape (fär′kwẽr; -kẽr). Point on W coast of Western Australia, near Tropic of Capricorn.

Farquhar Islands. Group of small British islands in Indian Ocean NE of Madagascar; part of British Indian Ocean Territory.

Far′rell (fär′ĕl). City, Mercer co., W Pennsylvania, on Shenango river 17 m. NNW of New Castle; pop. 13,793; steel mills.

Far Rock′a·way (fär′ rŏk′à·wā′). Seashore resort, Queens borough, New York City, on S shore of Long I. SE of Jamaica Bay.

Far·rukh′a·bad (fẽr·rŏŏk′ä·bäd). **1** Former district, Allahabad division, cen. United Provinces, N Indian Union; 1642 sq. m.; pop. (1941) 955,377; on both sides of the Ganges, one of healthiest regions of the Doab.
2 *or* **Farrukhabad–cum–Fa′te·garh** (-kŭm·fŭ′tä·gär′; *native* -gûr′h′). City, its ✳, now in Uttar Pradesh, on right bank of Ganges river 100 m. WNW of Lucknow; pop. (1941) 59,580; government gun-carriage factory in Fategarh. Farrukhabad founded 1714; scene of defeat of Marathas by Lord Lake 1804; in Sepoy Mutiny 1857–58 scene of a massacre of English and of several engagements.

Fars (färs) *or* **Far′si·stan′** (fär′sĕ·stän′); *anc.* **Per′sis** (pûr′sĭs). Province, SW Iran; 68,319 sq. m.; ✳ Shiraz; ancient Persis the original home of Persians and nucleus of later Persian Empire, in extent corresponded closely with modern Fars; chief cities were Persepolis and Pasargadae. See PERSIA.

Fars·hut′ (färs·hōōt′). Town, Qena prov., Upper Egypt, near left bank of the Nile ab. 35 m. W of Qena; pop. ab. 12,000.

Fars′ley (färz′lĭ). Former urban district, West Riding, Yorkshire, N England; pop. (1931) 6158; since 1937 in Pudsey.

Far′tak, Cape (fär′tăk); *Arab.* **Ras Far′tak** (räs fûr′tăk). Cape on coast of Hadhramaut, S Arabia, SW of Qamr Bay projecting into Arabian Sea.

Farther India. See INDOCHINA.

Farther Pomerania. See POMERANIA.

Farvel, Kap. See Cape FAREWELL, Greenland.

Far′well (fär′wĕl; -wĕl). City, ⊗ of Parmer co., NW Texas; pop. 1009.

Far West. The part of the United States W of Mississippi river, or, now more generally, the part W of Great Plains.

Fas. See FÈS.

Fa·sa′no (fä·zä′nô). Commune, Brindisi prov., Apulia, SE Italy, near Adriatic Sea 33 m. NW of Brindisi; pop. 21,923.

Fasher, El. See EL FASHER.

Fashoda. See KODOK.

Fast′net (fàs[t]′nĕt; -nĭt). Rocky islet in Atlantic

Ocean 4 m. SW of Cape Clear, off S Ireland, 51°22′N, 9°35′W; lighthouse.

Fa·stov′ (fŭ·stôf′). Town, W Kiev Region, N cen. Ukraine, U.S.S.R., 35 m. SW of Kiev; pop. ab. 10,000.

Fategarh. See FARRUKHABAD city.

Fa′teh·pur (fŭ′tŭ·pŏŏr). 1 Former district, Allahabad division, S United Provinces, N Indian Union; 1621 sq. m.; pop. (1941) 806,944.

2 Town, now in Uttar Pradesh, 50 m. SE of Cawnpore; pop. 18,947.

3 Town, E Rajasthan, NW India, formerly in NW Jaipur state, Rajputana; pop. 19,505.

Fatehpur Si′kri (sē′krē). Town SW Uttar Pradesh, N Indian Union, 23 m. W of Agra; pop. 6998; ancient city founded 1570 by Akbar, who made it his capital of the Mogul Empire; abandoned after his death 1605; remains include magnificent structures, partly in ruins: palaces, audience halls, tombs, great gate of victory (Boland Darwaza), etc.

Father, the. See ULAWUN.

Fa·tih′ (fä·tē′h′). District and suburb of Istanbul, Turkey in Europe, N cen. part of Stamboul; pop. 172,201.

Fá′ti·ma (fà′tē·mà). Village, cen. Portugal, SE of Leiria; shrine of the Virgin (Our Lady of Fátima).

Fatshan. See NAMHOI.

Fa′tu Hi′va (fä′tōō hē′và), *formerly* **Mag′da·le′na** (mäg′dà·lē′nà). Island 8 m. by 4 m., Marquesas Is., South Pacific Ocean, ab. 36 m. S of E end of Hiva Oa I.; pop. ab. 300.

Faulk (fôk). County in South Dakota. See *Table* at SOUTH DAKOTA.

Faulk′ner (fôk′nēr). County in Arkansas. See *Table* at ARKANSAS.

Faulk′ton (fôk′tŭn). City, ⊗ of Faulk co., N cen. South Dakota; pop. 1051.

Fau′quier′ (fô′kēr′). County in Virginia. See *Table* at VIRGINIA.

Faure′smith (four′smĭth). Town, S Orange Free State, Union of South Africa, just W of Jagersfontein and ab. 75 m. SW of Bloemfontein; pop. 2014; founded 1848, year of battle of Boomplaats (*q.v.*).

Fau′ro (?fou′rō). Island, one of Shortland Is. group S of Bougainville I., NW Solomon Is., W Pacific Ocean; ab. 10 m. long.

Fa·va′ra (fä·vä′rä). Commune, Agrigento prov., SW Sicily, 5 m. E of Agrigento; pop. 21,878; castle; sulfur mines, marble quarries.

Faventia. See FAENZA.

Fav′er·sham (făv′ēr·shăm; *U.S. also* -shăm). Municipal borough, Kent, SE England, on Faversham Creek 45 m. ESE of London; pop. 12,294; oyster fisheries, gunpowder factory; tombs of King Stephen, his queen Matilda, and his son.

Fa′vi·gna′na (fä′vē·nyä′nà). An island and commune of Egadi Is. (*q.v.*).

Fax′a Bay (fäk′sä); *Icel.* **Fax′a·fló′i** (fäk′sä·flō′ĭ). Bay on SW coast of Iceland on SE shore of which Reykjavík is situated.

Fa·yal′ (fà·yäl′). Westernmost island of cen. group of the Azores, W of Pico I.; lat. 38°35′N and long. 28°50′W; 64 sq. m.; pop. ab. 19,000; in district of Horta; presented by Alfonso V to his aunt, Isabella of Burgundy 1466; Horta, its chief town, on SE coast, the sailing port for shipping trade of Azores 18th and 19th cents.

Fay·ette′ (fā·ĕt′; fá′ĕt; fä′ĕt). 1 Name of counties in eleven states of the U.S. See *Tables* at ALABAMA, GEORGIA, ILLINOIS, INDIANA, IOWA, KENTUCKY, OHIO, PENNSYLVANIA, TENNESSEE, TEXAS, WEST VIRGINIA.

2 City, ⊗ of Fayette co., NW Alabama, 35 m. NNW of Tuscaloosa; pop. 4227.

3 Town, Fayette co., NE Iowa, 32 m. S of Decorah; pop. 1597; Upper Iowa University (1857; coed.).

4 Town, ⊗ of Jefferson co., SW Mississippi; pop. 1626; lumbering.

5 City, ⊗ of Howard co., N cen. Missouri, 25 m. NW of

Columbia; pop. 3294; Central College (estab. 1855, opened 1857; coed.; Methodist).

6 Town, Seneca co., W cen. New York; pop. 2825; scene of organization by Joseph Smith Apr. 6, 1830 of Church of Jesus Christ of Latter-day Saints.

Fayette City. Borough, Fayette co., SW Pennsylvania, on Monongahela river 25 m. SSE of Pittsburgh; pop. 1159.

Fay′ette·ville (fā′ĕt·vĭl; *Sou. also* -v′l). 1 City, ⊗ of Washington co., NW Arkansas, 50 m. N of Fort Smith; pop. 20,274; rail and trade center; summer mountain resort; manufactures hardwood products, farm implements; University of Arkansas (1871; coed.); Agricultural Experiment Station. Settled 1828; incorp. as city 1910; battle of Pea Ridge (Mar. 7–8, 1862) fought nearby.

2 City, ⊗ of Fayette co., W Georgia; pop. 1389.

3 Manufacturing village, Onondaga co., cen. New York, 10 m. E of Syracuse; pop. 4311.

4 Manufacturing city, ⊗ of Cumberland co., S cen. North Carolina, on Cape Fear river at head of navigation, 50 m. S of Raleigh; pop. 47,106; formerly important turpentine and lumber center; Fayetteville State Teachers College (1867; coed.). Founded by Scottish colonists 1739; occupied by Cornwallis 1781; state capital 1789–93; occupied by Gen. Sherman 1865.

5 Commercial and manufacturing town, ⊗ of Lincoln co., S Tennessee, 44 m. SW of Columbia; pop. 6804; site of Camp Blount, where Andrew Jackson mobilized his troops 1813 for victory over Creek Indians 1814.

6 Town, ⊗ of Fayette co., S cen. West Virginia; pop. 1848.

Fayum. See FAIYÛM.

Fa·zog′li (fä·zôg′lĭ). District, E Sudan, E Africa, on Ethiopia border S of Sennar; traversed by the Blue Nile; conquered 1821 by Mehemet Ali.

Fear, Cape (fēr). Cape on Smith I., SE coast of Brunswick co., North Carolina, at mouth of Cape Fear river.

Feath′er (fĕth′ēr). River ab. 100 m. long, N cen. California; including its forks 250 m. long; rises in Plumas co. and flows SW into Sacramento river above city of Sacramento. See BIG MEADOWS DAM.

Feath′er·stone (fĕth′ēr·stŭn; -stōn). Urban district, West Riding, Yorkshire, N England, E of Wakefield; pop. 13,925; coal mining.

Feath′er·top′, Mount (fĕth′ēr·tŏp′). Peak 6306 ft., E cen. Victoria, SE Australia, in Darg Plateau region.

Fé′camp′ (fā′kän′); *anc.* **Fis·cam′num** (fĭs·kăm′nŭm). Seaport, Seine-Inférieure dept., N France, on English Channel 40 m. NW of Rouen; pop. 17,708; fisheries; Benedictine liqueurs, still made (now by secular corporation) in same place where formula was discovered in early 16th cent. by monks of Benedictine monastery.

Fe·da′la (fĕ·dä′là; -lă). Town, Morocco, N Africa, on coast 14 m. NE of Casablanca; one of landing places of American troops Nov. 7, 1942.

Federal Capital Territory. See AUSTRALIAN CAPITAL TERRITORY.

Federal District; *Span.* **Dis·tri′to Fe′de·ral′** (dĕs-trē′tō fā′thä·räl′); *Port.* **Dis·tri′to Fe′de·ral′** (dĕsh-trē′tōō fā′thĕ·räl′). 1 *or* **Federal Capital;** *Span.* **Ca′pi·tal′ Fe′de·ral′** (kä′pĕ·täl′ fā′thä·räl′). The city of Buenos Aires, ✳ of Argentina, not included in province of Buenos Aires; 74 sq. m.; pop. (1943 est.), including suburban pop. of Flores and Belgrano, 2,457,494.

2 Former seat of national government, SE Brazil; 451 sq. m.; coextensive with city of Rio de Janeiro.

3 Large area on plateau of SE Goiaz state, cen. Brazil; 2260 sq. m.; site of Brasília, capital (since Apr. 21, 1960) of Brazil.

4 Area containing the capital of Mexico, Mexico City; 573 sq. m.; pop. 1,773,627.

5 Capital area, N Venezuela; 745 sq. m.; pop. (1941 est.) 380,099; ✳ Caracas.

Fed′er·als·burg (fĕd′ēr·ǎlz·bûrg). Town, Caroline co., E Maryland, 25 m. NNW of Salisbury; pop. 2060.

Federated Ma·lay′ States (mȧ·lā′; mā′lā). Formerly a federation, under British protection, of the states of Pahang, Perak, Selangor, and Negri Sembilan in British Malaya, at S extremity of Malay Penin.; 27,540 sq. m.; pop. 1,732,688, (1940–41 est.) 2,212,052; ✳ Kuala Lumpur. Entered treaties providing for their protection by British government (Perak 1874, the other states later); federated 1895; occupied by Japanese 1941–42; since 1946 in Federation of Malaya. See Federation of MALAYA.

Federated Shan States (shän; shăn). Now called **Shan State**. Region comprising the Northern Shan States (q.v.) and Southern Shan States (q.v.), E Burma; 57,816 sq. m.; pop. 1,506,337; ✳ Taunggyi; includes Wa States on E frontier; inhabitants chiefly Shan, of Thai stock, also found in NW Siam and in Yunnan prov., China. Original Shan States flourished 12th to 16th cents.; became part of old Burmese kingdom; not overcome by British until 1887; federated since 1922; Northern States crossed by Burma Road; entire region overrun by Japanese 1942.

Federation of Malaya. See Federation of MALAYA.

Fe′djedj, Chott el (shŏt′ ăl fĕ′jĕj). Marshy saline lake, S cen. Tunisia, N Africa; an E extension of Chott Djerid; ab. 60 m. long.

Fe′fan (fā′fän). Island in E part of Truk (q.v.); highest point 1026 ft.

Fehértemplom. See BELA CRKVA.

Feh′marn (fā′märn). Island in W Baltic Sea, on NW side of entrance to Bay of Mecklenburg; 72 sq. m.; pop. ab. 12,000; fine pastureland; chief town Burg (pop. 3390); attached to Schleswig-Holstein (formerly province, Prussia), Germany.

Fehr′bel·lin′ (fār′bĕ·lēn′). Town, Brandenburg, E Germany, NW of Berlin; pop. (1933) 2122; scene June 18, 1675 of victory of Elector Frederick William of Brandenburg over the Swedes under Karl Gustav Wrangel.

Feil′ding (fēl′dǐng). Borough, Wellington provincial dist., SW North I., New Zealand, 85 m. NNE of Wellington; pop. 4265.

Fei′ra de San·ta′na (fā′ĕ·rȧ thē sănn·tä′nȧ), formerly **Feira**. City, Baía state, E Brazil, just NNW of Salvador; pop. (1940 est.) 14,222.

Fe′jér (fĕ′yār). Former Hungarian county.

Fe′la·nitx′ (fā′lä·nēch′) or **Fe′la·ni′che** (fā′lä·nē′chȧ); anc. **Ca·na′ti** (kȧ·nä′tĭ). Commune, Baleares prov., Spain, SE Majorca I., 27 m. SE of Palma; pop. 11,759; pottery industry dates from 3d cent. B.C.

Feld′berg (fĕlt′bĕrκ). Highest peak 4695 ft. in Black Forest, Baden, SW Germany, SE of Freiburg.

Feld′kirch (fĕlt′kĭrκ); anc. **Clu′ni·a** (kloo′nĭ·ȧ). City, in the Vorarlberg, west Austria, on Liechtenstein frontier on Ill river 20 m. SSW of Bregenz; pop. 4898; castle; railroad junction, on the route over the Arlberg Pass to the E.

Félegyháza. See KISKUNFÉLEGYHÁZA.

Felicitas Julia. See LISBON.

Fe·li′pe Car·ril′lo Puer′to (fȧ·lē′pȧ kär·rē′[l]yỏ pwĕr′tỏ). Town, E cen. Quintana Roo Territory, Yucatan penin., Mexico; formerly Santa Cruz de Bravo.

Fe′lix·stowe (fē′lĭk·stō). Urban district, East Suffolk, E England; pop. 15,080; seaside resort.

Fel′le·tin′ (fĕl′tän′). Commune, S Creuse dept., cen. France, S of Aubusson (q.v.); pop. 2557; celebrated for manufacture of tapestries.

Fellin. See VILYANDI.

Fel′ling (fĕl′ǐng). Urban district, Durham, N England, 4 m. S of Newcastle; pop. 25,286; industrial suburb of Gateshead.

Felsina. See BOLOGNA commune.

Fel′sö·gal·la (fĕl′shu·gŏl′lŏ). Commune, NW Hungary, 28 m. W of Budapest; pop. 17,339.

Fel′sted or **Fel′stead** (fĕl′stĕd; -stĭd). Village, Essex, SE England, in Saffron Walden municipal borough; pop. 1845; school, founded 1564 as grammar school, became

popular with Puritans 17th cent. and a notable public school late 19th cent.

Felt′ham (fĕl′tăm). Urban district, Middlesex, SE England, WSW suburb of London; pop. 44,830; part of Greater London.

Fel′tre (fâl′trā; Angl. fĕl′trā); anc. **Fel′tri·a** (fĕl′trĭ·ȧ). Commune, Belluno prov., Venezia Euganea, NE Italy, 17 m. SW of Belluno; pop. 17,777; cathedral; trades in silk, wine, oil; besieged by Austrians 1917–18.

Fe′mund′ or **Fae′mund′** (fā′moon′). Lake 37 m. long, E Norway, in Hedmark co. 85 m. SE of Trondheim.

Fen or **Fen Ho** (fŭn′ hŭ′). River ab. 300 m. long, cen. Shansi prov., NE China; an E tributary of the Hwang Ho, flows SSE.

Feng′cheng′ (fŭng′chŭng′); Jap. official name **Feng′-hwang′cheng′** (fŭng′hwäng′chŭng′). Town and treaty mart, S Liaoning prov., S Manchuria, on railroad 22 m. NNW of Antung; pop. ab. 25,000; Japanese army base in Russo-Japanese War 1904–05.

Feng′hwa′ (fŭng′hwä′). Town, NE Chekiang prov., E China, ab. 10 m. SSW of Ninghsien (Ningpo); birthplace of Generalissimo Chiang Kai-shek.

Feng′kieh′ (fŭng′jĭ·ĕ′) or **Kwei′chow′** (gwä′jō′). City, E Szechwan, S cen. China, on N bank of Yangtze river at head of Yangtze Gorges (q.v.), 120 m. WNW of Ichang; pop. ab. 25,000; has long been of great strategic importance.

Feng′tai′ (fŭng′tī′). Railroad junction town, N Hopei prov., NE China, ab. 6 m. SW of Peiping; important exchange market of goods from Mongolia for those of north and middle China.

Feng′tien′ (fŭng′tĭ·ĕn′). **1** Province of Manchuria. See LIAONING.

2 Former name of MUKDEN.

3 Former province (1932–45), S Manchukuo; 29,263 sq. m.; pop. (1940 est.) 10,325,530; ✳ Mukden.

Feng′tu′ (fŭng′doo′). City, SE Szechwan prov., S cen. China, on N bank of the Yangtze 85 m. ENE of Chungking; pop. ab. 50,000; nearby (Pingtu-shan) is sacred pilgrimage center of Taoists.

Feng′yi′ (fŭng′yē′). Town, W cen. Yunnan prov., S China on Burma Road near SE shore of Erh Hai (Tali Lake).

Fen Ho. See FEN.

Fe′ni Islands (fā′nĕ). Group of small islands ab. 40 m. off SE coast of New Ireland, Bismarck Archipelago, W Pacific Ocean.

Fen′ni·more (fĕn′ĭ·mōr). City, Grant co., SW corner of Wisconsin, 20 m. NNW of Platteville; pop. 1747.

Fen′no·scan′di·a or **Fen′no–Scan′di·a** (fĕn′ȯ·skăn′dĭ·ȧ). The part of N Europe comprising Finland, Sweden, Norway, and Denmark—specifically used in geology.

Fens, the (fĕnz); also **Fen Country** (fĕn). Low-lying districts, once marshland but long-since drained and cultivated, in E England, esp. in Lincolnshire near shores of the Wash.

Fen′ton (fĕn′t'n; -tŭn). **1** Village, Genesee co., SE cen. Michigan, 15 m. S of Flint; pop. 6142; manufactures cement; summer resort.

2 See the POTTERIES, England.

Fen′tress (fĕn′trĕs; -trĭs). County in Tennessee. See Table at TENNESSEE.

Fen′yang′ (fŭn′yäng′). City, cen. Shansi prov., NE China, near E bank of Fen river 60 m. SW of Yangku.

Fe′o·do′si·ya (fĕ′ȯ·dô′shĭ·ȧ; Russ. fyĭ·ŭ·dô′syĭ·yȧ); Ital. **Kaf′fa** (käf′fä); Tatar **Ke·fe′** (kyĕ·fĕ′); anc. **The′o·do′si·a** (thē′ȯ·dō′shĭ·ȧ; -shȧ). Seaport town, SE Crimea, Soviet Russia, Europe, 55 m. WSW of Kerch; pop. 27,339; fine harbor, rail connections with Kerch and Dzhankoi, important esp. for its oyster fishing and preparation of caviar; health resort. Site of Greek colony founded by Milesians by 6th cent. B.C.; formed part of kingdom of Cimmerian Bosporus (q.v.); as Kaffa was a flourishing Genoese trading colony 13th cent.; captured

by Turks 1475 and ceded to Russians 1774; bombarded by Turks Oct. 1914; held by Germans 1942–Apr. 1944.

Fer, Cape (kāp′ fär′); *Fr.* **Cap de Fer** (kȧp′ dĕ fâr′). Cape on NE coast of Constantine dept., NE Algeria, N Africa.

Fère, La. See LA FÈRE.

Fère–en–Tar′de·nois′ (fâr′äṉ·tȧr′dĕ·nwä′). Town, Aisne dept., N France; pop. 1948; type station for Tardenoisian culture; nearby, at village of **Se·ringes′–et–Nesles′** (sĕ·rănzh′ā·nĕl′), just to the E, is the Oise-Aisne American Military Cemetery, second largest Am. cemetery in Europe; scene of several battles in World War I in 1914 and 1918 (July 21 taken by Allies).

Fe·ren·ti′no (fâ·rän·tē′nō; *Angl.* fĕr′ĕn-); *anc.* **Fer′en·ti′num** (fĕr′ĕn·tī′nŭm). Commune, Frosinone prov., Latium, cen. Italy, 6 m. NW of Frosinone; pop. 15,516; cathedral; ancient city walls; mineral baths.

Fer·ga′na or **Fer·ghá′na** (fĕr·gä′nȧ). **1** Region, W cen. Asia, W of the Tien Shan; overrun by Arabs 719; conquered by Genghis Khan and Tamerlane and ruled in 15th cent. by descendants of Tamerlane; in 1513 conquered by the Uzbegs and became part of Kokand; taken by Russians 1875–76 and made a division of Russian Turkistan; under Soviet government divided bet. Uzbek S.S.R. and Kirgiz S.S.R.
2 Subdivision, E Uzbek S.S.R.
3 *formerly* **Sko′be·lev** (skô′bĕ·lĕf; *Russ.* skô′byĭ·lyĕf). City, E Uzbek S.S.R., Soviet Russia, Asia, in fertile valley of region of the Alai Mts. 40 m. E of Kokand; pop. 14,275; deposits of ferganite (a uranium mineral) in vicinity; built by Russians 10 m. SE of old town of Margelan and earlier known as **New Margelan.**

Fer′gus (fûr′gŭs). **1** County in Montana. See *Table* at MONTANA.
2 Village, Wellington co., SE Ontario, Canada, 13 m. NW of Guelph; pop. 3387; railroad junction.

Fergus Falls. City, ⊗ of Otter Tail co., W cen. Minnesota, 50 m. SE of Moorhead; pop. 13,733; flour mills, co-operative creamery.

Fer′gu·son (fûr′gŭ·s'n). City, St. Louis co., E Missouri, 10 m. NNW of St. Louis; pop. 22,149.

Fer′gus·son (fûr′gŭ·s'n) or **Ka′lu·wa′wa** (kä′lōō-wä′wä). One of the D'Entrecasteaux Is., in W Pacific Ocean, 4 m. E of Goodenough I.; ab. 38 m. long and 16 m. wide; 518 sq. m.; several good harbors; extinct volcanoes, hot springs, and geysers.

Fer′i·an′a (fĕr′i·än′ä; *Arab.* fär·yä′nȧ·h′). Town, W Tunisia, SSW of Kasserine Pass, on highway from Gafsa to Tebessa; taken by Germans Feb. 1943.

Fer·man′agh (fĕr·măn′ȧ). County, SW Northern Ireland; 653 sq. m.; pop. 53,040; ⊗ Enniskillen; chief river the Erne; agriculture, livestock grazing.

Fer′mo (fĕr′mō; *Ital.* fâr′mō); *anc.* **Fir′mum Pi·ce′num** (fûr′mŭm pĭ·sē′nŭm). Commune, Ascoli Piceno prov., Marches, cen. Italy, near Adriatic Sea 23 m. NNE of Ascoli Piceno; pop. 25,203; cathedral and 14th-cent. archiepiscopal palace; trades in grain, wool. Founded by Sabines before foundation of Rome.

Fer·moy′ (fĕr·moi′). Urban district, NE co. Cork, SW Eire, on Blackwater river; pop. 4123; agricultural trading center; angling.

Fer·nan·di′na (fûr′năn·dē′nȧ) or **Fernandina Beach.** City, ⊗ of Nassau co., NE corner of Florida, on Atlantic Ocean 25 m. NE of Jacksonville; pop. 7276.

Fer·nan·di′na (fĕr′nän·dē′nä). **1** An early name of CUBA.
2 *also known as* **Nar′bor·ough Island** (när′bŭ·rȧ; -brŭ). One of the Galápagos Is. (*q.v.*).

Fer·nan′do de No·ro′nha (fĕr·năn′dōō thĕ nōō·rō′nyȧ). Brazilian island in Atlantic Ocean ab. 300 m. off E bulge of Brazil; constitutes a territory; 7 sq. m.; pop. (1940 est.) 1065; used as a penal colony.

Fer·nan′do Po′o (*Span.* fĕr·nän′dō pō′ô) or **Fernan′do Po** (fĕr·năn′dō pō′). Spanish island in Bight of Biafra, S of SE Nigeria, W Africa; ab. 800 sq. m.; pop.

26,405; a part of Spanish Guinea; chief town Santa Isabel, capital of Spanish Guinea; mountainous, highest point ab. 10,000 ft.; has fertile soil, produces cacao, coffee, palm oil, bananas, coconuts. Discovered by Portuguese 1471; became Spanish 1778, abandoned, but finally took possession of again 1844.

Fer·não′ Ve·lo′so Bay (fĕr·nouɴ′ vĕ·lō′zōō). Inlet of Mozambique Channel on NE coast of Mozambique, SE Africa, S of Cape Loguno.

Fern′dale (fûrn′dāl). **1** Residential city, Oakland co., SE Michigan, 9 m. N of Detroit; pop. 31,347.
2 Residential borough, Cambria co., SW cen. Pennsylvania, 3 m. S of Johnstown; pop. 2717.

Ferne Islands (färn). = FARNE ISLANDS.

Fer′ney (fĕr′nā), *in full* **Ferney–Vol′taire′** (-vôl′târ′). Town, Ain dept., E France, on shore of Lake Geneva ab. 4 m. from Geneva; pop. 978; château; grew up around the colony of watchmakers established by Voltaire, who lived here 1758–78.

Fer′nie (fûr′nĭ). City, SE Brit. Columbia, Canada, E of Kootenay river, on W slope of Rocky Mts.; pop. 2551; extensive coal mines; sawmills, machine shops.

Ferns (fûrnz). Village, co. Wexford, E Eire, ab. 8 m. N of Enniscorthy; once capital of kingdom of Leinster; cathedral.

Fe·rolle′, Point (fĕ·rōl′). Cape, NW Newfoundland, on SE of entrance to Strait of Belle Isle.

Fe·roze′pore (fĕ·rōz′pōr) or **Fi·roz′pur** (fĭ·rōz′pŏor). **1** District, Jullundur division, formerly in Punjab, NW Brit. India, now in Punjab state, India; 4085 sq. m.; pop. (1941) 1,423,076.
2 City, its ✳, ab. 4 m. from S bank of Sutlej river 45 m. SSE of Lahore; pop. 64,634; has large cotton and grain trade; site of a military cantonment with India's largest arsenal. British rule first established here 1835.

Fe·roze′shah (fĕ·rōz′shä). Village in Ferozepore dist., Punjab state, NW India, 13 m. E of Ferozepore; scene of battle of First Sikh War, a victory (but with heavy losses) of British under Sir Hugh Gough over Sikhs Dec. 21–22, 1845.

Fer·ra′ra (fĕ·rär′ä; *Ital.* fär·rä′rä). **1** Province of Italy. See *Table* at ITALY.
2 *anc.* **Fo′rum Al·li·e′ni** (fōr′ŭm ăl′ĭ·ē′nī). Commune, its ✳, Emilia, N Italy, near the Po 57 m. SW of Venice; pop. 119,265; seven-mile city wall; cathedral; castle; fortified citadel; art gallery, university (founded 1264; reopened 1815); birthplace of Savonarola; trades in agricultural products; manufactures leather, glass, silk goods. Bestowed by pope upon margrave of Tuscany ab. end of 10th cent. A.D.; in 1208 came to be ruled by d'Este family; seat of Council of Ferrara (1438) which removed to Florence; raised to a duchy 15th cent., became seat of brilliant Renaissance court; brought under direct rule of papacy 1598; ceded to French 1797; restored to papacy 1815; joined kingdom of Sardinia (see SAVOY) 1859; scene of severe fighting Apr. 1945, taken by Allies Apr. 23.

Fer′ri·day (fĕr′ĭ·dā). Town, Concordia parish, E cen. Louisiana, 10 m. NW of Natchez, Miss.; pop. 4563.

Ferro. See HIERRO.

Ferrol, El. See EL FERROL.

Fer′ry (fĕr′ĭ). County in Washington. See *Table* at WASHINGTON.

Fer′ry·land (fĕr′ĭ·lănd). Town, SE Newfoundland, on Atlantic Ocean 38 m. S of St. John's; harbor; site of colony established 1621–29 by Sir George Calvert, Lord Baltimore.

Fer′ry·ville (fĕr′ĭ·vĭl; *Fr.* fĕ′rē′vēl′). Town, N Tunisia, N Africa, on S shore of Lake Bizerte; pop. (1936) 6330; occupied by U.S. troops May 7, 1943.

Ferté, La. See LA FERTÉ.

Ferté–Bernard, La. See LA FERTÉ-BERNARD.

Ferté–Milon, La. See LA FERTÉ-MILON.

Fertile Crescent. A semicircle of fertile land, stretching from Palestine on the Mediterranean around Syrian

Desert N of Arabia to Persian Gulf; scene of struggles and migrations of some of the earliest known peoples (Sumerians, Assyrians, Semitic tribes)—a term used by some historians of the prehistory of southwestern Asia.

Fertö, Lake. See Lake NEUSIEDLER.

Fès (fĕs) *or* **Fez** (fĕz); *Arab.* **Fas** (fäs). Commercial city, N cen. Morocco, ab. 150 m. NE of Casablanca; pop. (1936) 144,424; one of the sacred cities of Islam, founded 793; many mosques; for many years a traditional capital of the sultanate of Morocco.

Fes′sen·den (fĕs′'n·dĕn). City, ⊗ of Wells co., cen. North Dakota; pop. 920.

Festiniog. See FFESTINIOG.

Fes′tu′bert′ (fĕs′tü′bâr′). Village, Pas-de-Calais dept., N France, near Béthune; pop. ab. 1000; destroyed during World War I, in battles 1914, 1915, 1918.

Fes′tus (fĕs′tŭs). Commercial and residential city, Jefferson co., E Missouri, on Mississippi river 29 m. S of St. Louis; pop. 7021.

Fet′lar (fĕt′lär). One of Shetland Is., NE of Scotland.

Feu′er·bach (foi′ĕr·bäĸ). Industrial city, cen. Baden-Württemberg, Germany, NE suburb of Stuttgart; pop. 17,617; sandstone quarries.

Fez. See Fès.

Fezara. See FEZZARA.

Fé′zen′sac′ (fā′zän′säk′). See ARMAGNAC.

Fez·zan′ (fĕ·zän′); *anc.* **Pha·za′ni·a** (fá·zā′nĭ·á). Region of desert and oases in SW Libya, N Africa; area ab. 212,750 sq. m.; pop. 54,438; ✳ Sebha; under Turkish control from 16th cent. to 1912; made part of Tripoli by Italians 1912; invaded by Free French forces Mar. 1942; made a province of Libya 1949.

Fez·za′ra *or* **Fe·za′ra** (fĕ·zär′á; *Arab.* fäz·zä′rŏ). Lake ab. 30 m. long in Algeria, N Africa, SW of Bône.

Ffes·tin′i·og *or* **Fes·tin′i·og** (fĕs·tĭn′ĭ·ŏg). Urban district, Merionethshire, W Wales; pop. 6923; slate quarries.

Fia·na′ran·tso′a (fyá·nä′rán·tsō′á). Commune, SE Madagascar; pop. (1936) 14,740; terminus of railroad from Manakara.

Fich′tel·ge·bir′ge (fĭĸ′tĕl·gĕ·bĭr′gĕ). Mountain range in NE Bavaria, S cen. Germany; highest peak Schneeberg 3447 ft.

Ficks′burg (fĭks′bûrg). Town, E Orange Free State, E cen. Republic of So. Africa, on Caledon river 105 m. ENE of Bloemfontein; pop. 5133; center of wheat region.

Fi·den′za (fē·dĕn′tsä; *Angl.* fĭ·dĕn′zȧ); *before 1927* called **Bor′go San Don·ni′no** (bôr′gŏ sän dŏn·nē′nŏ); *anc.* **Fi·den′ti·a** (fī·dĕn′shĭ·á; -shá; fĭ-), *later* **Fi·den′ti·o′la** (-dĕn′shĭ·ō′lá). Commune, Parma prov., Emilia, N Italy, 14 m. W by N of Parma; pop. 17,352; site of victory of Metellus Pius over Carbo 82 B.C.; St. Domninus said to have been beheaded here 304 A.D.— whence its former name; part of duchy of Parma 1545–1859.

Fiel′dale (fēl′dāl). Town, Henry co., S Virginia, ab. 4 m. W of Martinsville; pop. 1499.

Fier (fyâr). River 41 m. long, Haute-Savoie dept., E France; flows W through Annecy to the Rhone; connected with Lake Annecy by Thiou canal which runs through Annecy; noted for scenery of its gorges.

Fie′scher·horn′, Gross′ (grōs′ fē′shĕr·hôrn′). Peak 13,285 ft., S cen. Switzerland, in Bernese Alps E of the Jungfrau.

Fie′so·le (fyâ′zȯ·lâ); *anc.* **Fae′su·lae** (fē′zṳ·lē). Commune, Firenze prov., Tuscany, cen. Italy, 4 m. NE of Florence; pop. 11,153; health resort; Romanesque cathedral (1028); episcopal palace; ruins of Etruscan city walls, Roman baths and theater; home of Fra Angelico. Ancient Etruscan town; withstood siege by Byzantine general, Belisarius, in 6th cent. A.D.; eclipsed by rise of Florence (*q.v.*), which overcame it in 11th cent.

Fife (fīf) *or* **Fife′shire** (fīf′shīr; -shēr). County, E Scotland, bet. firths of Tay and Forth; 505 sq. m.; pop. (1951) 306,855; ⊗ Cupar; other towns are Dunfermline,

Kirkcaldy, St. Andrews; rivers Eden and Leven; agriculture, quarrying (limestone), coal mining, linen manufacture, fisheries.

Fife Ness (nĕs). Headland on E coast of Fife co., E Scotland.

Fifteen–Mile Falls Dam. Dam completed 1930 across Connecticut river ab. 8 m. S of St. Johnsbury, Vermont; height 175 ft.; impounds water for power, forming a lake 7 m. long.

Figig. See FIGUIG.

Fi·gli′ne Val·dar′no (fē·lyē′nä väl·där′nŏ). Commune, Firenze prov., Tuscany, cen. Italy, on Arno river 17 m. SE of Florence; pop. 12,621.

Fi·gue′ras (fē·gā′räs). Manufacturing and commercial city, Gerona prov., NE Spain, in E Pyrenees Mts. 24 m. N of Gerona; pop. 16,337; citadel built by Ferdinand VI; occupied by French 1794, 1808, 1811, 1823.

Fi·guig′ (fī·gēg′), *also* **Fi·gig′** (fī·gĭg′). Oasis bet. SE Morocco and Algeria; 5 sq. m.; pop. ab. 15,000.

Fi′ji (fē′jĕ; -jē). 1 British crown colony in SW Pacific Ocean, comprising Fiji Is. and island of Rotuma (since 1881); 7083 sq. m.; pop. (1940) 220,787; ✳ Suva on Viti Levu I.

2 *or* **Fiji Islands.** Island group in SW Pacific Ocean, E of the New Hebrides and SW of Samoa, bet. 16° and 19°20′S lat. and 178°W and 177°E long.; crossed by 180th meridian but lies W of date line; group contains over 300 islands, of which 106 are inhabited; 7069 sq. m.; pop. (1964) 456,390 including ab. 190,000 natives, 230,000 Indians (brought in for coolie labor); chief islands Viti Levu, Vanua Levu, Tavenui, Kandavu, Koro, Ngau, and Ovalau; important groups Lau Is. (including Exploring and Lakemba Is.), Yasawa Is., and Lomai Viti; together with Rotuma I. constitutes British crown colony of Fiji. Volcanic in origin, with fertile soil; highest point Mt. Victoria, on Viti Levu, 4341 ft.; chief products for export sugar, copra, and fruit; chief occupations fishing and agriculture; Fijians are dark, frizzly-haired race of Melanesian origin, formerly cannibals, now mostly professed Christians.

History: Discovered by Tasman 1643; visited by Capt. Cook 1774; used by escaped convicts from Australia as early as 1804; explored by Commander Charles Wilkes of U.S. 1840; offered to Great Britain 1858 by native ruler who was pressed by dispute with U.S.; annexed by British 1874.

Filch′ner, Cape (fĭlĸ′nēr). Point on coast of Antarctica extending into Indian Ocean at 91°52′E long. and ab. 66°30′S lat.; forms dividing point bet. Queen Mary Coast and Wilhelm II Coast.

Filchner Shelf Ice. Large area of shelf ice at head of Weddell Sea, Antarctica, at W end of Coats Land, in ab. 77°30′S, 38°W; discovered 1912.

Filipinas, Islas. Spanish for PHILIPPINE ISLANDS.

Fill′more (fĭl′mōr). 1 Name of counties in two states of the U.S. See *Tables* at MINNESOTA and NEBRASKA.

2 City, Ventura co., SW California, 43 m. WNW of Los Angeles; pop. 4808; hunting and fishing resort.

3 City, ⊗ of Millard co., W Utah, 20 m. NW of Richfield; pop. 1602; capital of Utah territorial government 1851–56.

Fi·lot·tra′no (fē·lŏt·trä′nŏ). Commune, Ancona prov., Marches, cen. Italy, 16 m. SSW of Ancona; pop. 10,145.

Fi·na′le Li′gu·re (fē·nä′lā lē′gōō·rä). Commune (group of villages), Savona prov., Liguria, NW Italy, on Ligurian Sea 11 m. SW of Savona; pop. (1931) 9851; health resort.

Finale nel l′E·mi′lia (nȧl′lá·mē′lyä). Commune, Modena prov., Emilia, N Italy, on Panaro river 22 m. NE of Modena; pop. 16,691; manufactures silk.

Fin′cas′tle (fĭn′kàs′'l). Town, ⊗ of Botetourt co., W cen. Virginia; pop. 403.

Finch′ley (fĭnch′lĭ). Urban district, Middlesex, SE England, NW suburb of London; pop. 58,964, (1951) 69,990; part of Greater London; residential area; Finch-

ley Common once a haunt of highwaymen, notably Dick Turpin and Jack Sheppard.

Find'horn (fīnd'hôrn). River ab. 45 m. long in NE Scotland; flows NE in Nairn and W Moray cos. to empty into Moray Firth.

Find'lay (fĭn'lĭ; fĭnd'lĭ). City, ⊗ of Hancock co., NW Ohio, 40 m. S of Toledo; pop. 30,344; incorporated 1890; in heart of petroleum and gas section of state; manufactures petroleum, foundry, and clay products, tires and machinery. Findlay College (1882; coed.).

Fin'gal (fĭng'găl). Town and municipality, NE Tasmania, Australia, 50 m. ESE of Launceston; pop. (municipality) 3655.

Fingal's Cave. See STAFFA.

Fin'ger Lakes (fĭng'gẽr). Group of long narrow lakes in W New York, including notably lakes Seneca, Cayuga, Keuka, Canandaigua, Owasco, and Skaneateles (qq.v.).

Fin·go·land' (fĭng'gō·lănd'). A district of Transkei (q.v.), Cape Province, Union of South Africa, E of Great Kei river; inhabited by Fingus (Amafingu).

Fi'ni (fē'nē) or **Mfi'ni** ('m·fē'nē). River in W Congo, SW cen. Africa, being the section of Lukenie river bet. Lake Leopold II outlet and Kasai river.

Fi'niels', Pic de (pēk' dē fē'nyĕls'). Mountain 5585 ft. in Lozère dept., S France; highest peak in Lozère range of the Cévennes Mts.

Fin'is·tère' (fĭn'ĭs·târ'; Fr. fē'nēs'târ'). Department of France. See Table at FRANCE.

Fin'is·terre', Cape (fĭn'ĭs·târ'; Span. fē'nēs·tĕr'rē); anc. **Ne'ri·um Pro'mon·to'ri·um** (nē'rĭ ŭm prŏm'-ŭn·tōr'ĭ·ŭm). Westernmost point of Spanish mainland, on coast of La Coruña prov., NW Spain, 9°18'W.

Fin'is·terre' Range (fĭn'ĭs·târ' rānj'). Mountain range, E New Guinea, bet. coast and Markham valley, extending NW from W part of Huon Penin. to near Madang; scene of fighting Jan.–Feb. 1944.

Finke (fĭngk). River ab. 400 m. long, Australia; flows SE in S Northern Territory and N South Australia; in some seasons joins Alberga river to flow into Lake Eyre.

Fin'land (fĭn'lănd); Finnish **Suo'mi** (swô'mĭ) or **Suo'men Ta'sa·val'ta** (swô'mĕn tä'sä·väl'tä). Republic, N Europe, bounded on the N by Norway, on the E by Russia (Murmansk and Karelia), on the S by the Gulf of Finland, and on the W by the Gulf of Bothnia and Sweden; 130,165 sq. m. (including 12,190 sq. m. of inland water); pop. (1940) 3,887,217; ✳ Helsinki; divided into the following 10 departments (for pronunciation of their names, see their individual entries):

DEPART-MENT	LOCA-TION	AREA[1]	POP.[1]	CAPITAL
Ahvenanmaa	off W coast	572	27,676	Maarianhamina
Häme	SW	7,118	420,438	Tampere
Kuopio	S	13,806	398,512	Kuopio
Lappi	N	36,308	143,679	
Mikkeli	S	6,750	203,627	Mikkeli
Oulu	N	21,887	327,422	Oulu
Turku-Pori	SW	8,500	536,079	Turku and Pori
Uusimaa	S	4,435	601,710	Helsinki
Vaasa	W	15,062	599,774	Vaasa
Viipuri	SE	3,537	628,300	Kotka

[1] Area excludes inland water area; figures for 1945. Pop. from 1940 Census.

Land of few hills or mountains (highest Haltiatunturi 4344 ft., in NW on Norwegian border) but of many lakes (nearly 1/10 of total area) and streams (esp. Oulu and Kemi in the N). Chief lakes Oulujärvi, Saimaa, Näsijärvi, Keitele, Pielisjärvi (all in S or cen. part), and Inari (in the N). Has long coast line with several excellent ports; chief islands the Ahvenanmaa group (formerly Swedish), and Kimito, Vallgrund, and Karlö, in Gulf of Bothnia. Chief industries agriculture, lumbering, textile manufacturing, and manufacture of wood products. Chief cities Helsinki, Tampere, Turku, Vaasa, and Oulu; lost to Russia 1944 Viipuri (see VYBORG) and Petsamo, its Arctic port (see PECHENGA).

History: Region settled by Finnish people by the beginning of the 8th century A.D.; conquered and con- verted by Swedes in 12th cent.; E part (see KARELIA) ceded to Russia 1721; ceded to Russia by Sweden which had been defeated in War of Third Coalition 1809; organized as autonomous grand duchy in personal union with Tsar; 1899–1917 suffered from policy of Russification which took away constitution and other rights; proclaimed independence 1917; after civil war in which Germans helped drive out Reds 1918–19, ended war with Russia 1920; awarded Åland Is. 1922 after dispute with Sweden; forced to cede Karelian Isthmus and other border districts to Russia as result of defeat in war 1939–40; joined Germany against Russia June 1941; regained lost territory temporarily 1941–44 but again forced to yield to Russia the same territory, with slight changes (retention of Hangö by Finland in exchange for Porkkala Penin. near Helsinki and loss of Petsamo territory).

Finland, Gulf of. Arm of Baltic Sea 260 m. long and from 45 to 85 m. wide, S of Finland and N of Estonia (U.S.S.R.); at E end narrows to Kronstadt Bay; chief islands Hogland, Lavansaari, and Kotlin (Kronstadt); chief cities on it Helsinki and Kotka (Finland), Vyborg, Leningrad, Narva, and Tallin (U.S.S.R.).

Fin'lay (fĭn'lĭ). River 250 m. long in N British Columbia, Canada, from N cen. British Columbia flows S and E to unite with Parsnip river at 56°N and form Peace river; regarded as ultimate headstream of Mackenzie river.

Fin'ley (fĭn'lĭ). City, ⊗ of Steele co., E North Dakota; pop. 808

Fin'mark'en (fĭn'mär'kĕn). ☞ *Finnmark:* see Table at NORWAY.

Finn (fĭn). **1** River ab. 24 m. long in co. Donegal, N Eire; flows E out of Lough Finn (lŏk fĭn') across co. Donegal to unite with Mourne river on Northern Ireland border and form Foyle river.
2 River, N Ireland; flows from SE co. Fermanagh, Northern Ireland, into cos. Monaghan and Cavan in Eire and into Upper Lough Erne, Northern Ireland.

Fin'ney (fĭn'ĭ). County in Kansas. See Table at KANSAS.

Finn'mark' (fĭn'märk'). See Table at NORWAY.

Finsbury. Metropolitan borough of London. See Table at LONDON.

Finsch'ha'fen (fĭnsh'hä'fĕn; Angl. fĭnch'hä'fĕn). Settlement on SE coast of North-East New Guinea, at extremity of Huon Penin. 65 m. ENE of Lae; early headquarters of German trading company; occupied by Japanese Mar. 8, 1942, retaken by Australians Oct. 2, 1943.

Fin'ster·aar'horn (fĭn'stĕr·är'hôrn). Peak 14,026 ft., highest of the Bernese Alps, S Switzerland.

Fin'ster·wal'de (fĭn'stĕr·väl'dĕ). Manufacturing city, Brandenburg, eastern Germany, 61 m. SSE of Berlin and 30 m. WSW of Cottbus; pop. 13,389; manufactures include textiles, machinery, furniture; 16th-cent. Gothic church. Taken 1130 by German counts; to Bohemia 1373, Electorate of Saxony 1635, Prussia 1815; taken by Russians May 1945.

Fiord'land', or Sounds, National Park (fyôrd'lănd', soundz'). National park, SW corner of South I., New Zealand; extends 200 m. along the coast, here indented with many sounds that resemble Norwegian fiords.

Fio·ren·zuo'la d'Ar'da (fyô·rän·tswô'lä där'dä). Commune, Piacenza prov., Emilia, N Italy, 13 m. SE of Piacenza; pop. 10,261.

Firat. See EUPHRATES.

Fir·daus' (fĭr·dous'); formerly **Tun** (tōōn). Town, NE cen. Iran, in Khurasan prov.; pop. ab. 7500.

Fire Island or **Fire Island Beach** (fīr). Long narrow sandy spit of land, ab. 30 m. long by ¼ to ½ m. wide, off S cen. Long I., New York, bet. Great South Bay and Atlantic Ocean; lighthouse and signal station for reporting transatlantic liners approaching New York; summer resort.

Fi·ren'ze (fē·rĕn'tsâ). **1** Province of Italy. See Table at ITALY.

2 Commune, its ✳. See FLORENCE, Italy.

FINLAND

Statute Miles

50   100

⊕ ⊛ Capitals

PUBLISHED BY G. & C. MERRIAM COMPANY
SPRINGFIELD, MASS.
PREPARED BY I W CLEMENT CO BUFFALO N.Y

Fi·ren·zuo'la (fĕ·răn·tswô'lä). Commune, Firenze prov., Tuscany, cen. Italy, on N slope of Apennines 24 m. NNE of Florence; pop. 12,259; summer resort.

Fir'mi'ny' (fēr'mē'nē'). Commune, Loire dept., SE cen. France, 6 m. WSW of St-Étienne; pop. 20,257; coal; manufactures railroad, artillery, and marine supplies.

Firmum Picenum. See FERMO.

Fi·roz'a·bad (fĭ·rōz'ȧ·băd; -ä·bäd). **1** One of the earlier cities on site of modern Delhi (*q.v.*), Indian Union, founded 1354 by Firuz Shah III, king of Delhi; abandoned after Tamerlane's invasion 1398–99.

2 Town, W Uttar Pradesh, N India, on railroad N of Jumna river 22 m. E of Agra; pop. 23,154.

Firozpur. See FEROZEPORE.

Fi·roz'shah (fĭ·rōz'shä). = FEROZESHAH.

Firth of Clyde, Firth of Forth. See CLYDE, FORTH.

Fiscamnum. See FÉCAMP.

Fischern. See RYBÁŘE.

Fish'er (fĭsh'ẽr). County in Texas. See *Table* at TEXAS.

Fish'er·mans Island (fĭsh'ẽr·mănz). Island at N side of entrance to Chesapeake Bay, S extremity of Northampton co., Virginia.

Fish'er's Hill (fĭsh'ẽrz). Village, Shenandoah co., N Virginia, 8 m. NNE of Woodstock; scene Sept. 22, 1864 of Sheridan's defeat of Confederates under Gen. Early.

Fish'ers Island (fĭsh'ẽrz). Island nearly 8 m. long and ab. 1 m. wide off NE end of Long I. and off S coast of Connecticut, from which it is separated by **Fishers Island Sound;** a part of New York state; resort.

Fisher Strait. Channel ab. 50 m. wide bet. S Southampton I. and Coats I. in E Keewatin District, Northwest Territories, Canada.

Fish'guard (fĭsh'gärd). Urban district and commercial seaport, Pembrokeshire, SW Wales; pop. 4840; an attempted French invasion defeated by local militia 1797.

Fish'kill' Landing (fĭsh'kĭl'). Former village, Dutchess co., SE New York; part of Beacon since 1913.

Fismes (fēm). Town, Marne dept., NE France, on the Vesle; pop. 2869; nearly destroyed in fighting of World War I, esp. on Aug. 4, 1918 when Americans finally captured it from Germans.

Fitch'burg (fĭch'bûrg). City, a ⊗ of Worcester co., cen. Massachusetts, 22 m. N of Worcester; pop. 43,021; transportation and industrial center; manufactures foundry and machine-shop products, saws, and textiles; Massachusetts State College (1894; coed.). Settled 1740; city chartered 1872.

Fitz·ger'ald (fĭts·jẽr'ăld). City, ⊗ of Ben Hill co., S cen. Georgia, 50 m. E of Albany; pop. 8781; founded 1895 by veterans of Union army, incorp. 1896.

Fitz'roy (fĭts'roi; fĭts·roi'). **1** River 180 m. long, E cen. Queensland, Australia, flows E to Pacific Ocean at Rockhampton.

2 River ab. 300 m. long, N Western Australia; flows W and NW into King Sound.

3 Manufacturing city, S Victoria, SE Australia, N suburb of Melbourne; pop. 30,919.

Fitz Roy (fĭts' roi; fĭts roi') *or* **Chal·tel'** (chäl·tĕl'). Peak 10,958 ft. on Argentina-Chile boundary, near Lake Viedma.

Fiu'me (fyoo'mâ). **1** Former name of *Carnaro* prov., Italy: see *Table* at ITALY.

2 City and seaport. See RIEKA.

Fiu·mi·ci'no (fyoo'mē·chē'nō). **1** See RUBICON.

2 Town, Latium, cen. Italy, on Tyrrhenian Sea 15 m. SW of Rome and 3 m. WNW of Ostia; pop. 1121; Leonardo da Vinci International Airport (opened 1961).

Five Forks. Locality, Dinwiddie co., SE Virginia, just SW of Petersburg; scene Mar. 31–Apr. 1, 1865 of victory of Federals under Sheridan over Confederates under Pickett. See DINWIDDIE.

Five Northern Provinces. Five northern provinces of China, including Shantung, Hopeh, and Shansi of China Proper (see CHINA) and Chahar and Suiyuan of Inner Mongolia; contain immense deposits of coking coal and iron ore; control of region primary aim of Japanese in Chino-Japanese War 1937–45.

Five Towns, the. See the POTTERIES.

Fi·viz·za'no (fĕ·vēd·dzä'nō). Commune, Apuania prov., Tuscany, cen. Italy, 15 m. N of Apuania; pop. 17,818; mineral springs; marble quarries; earthquake 1920.

Flag Island (flăg). Small island, Gulf of Mexico, off coast of NW Florida; on S edge of Apalachicola Bay.

Flag'ler (flăg'lẽr). County in Florida. See *Table* at FLORIDA.

Flag'staff' (flăg'stȧf'). City, ⊗ of Coconino co., N Arizona, 63 m. NE of Prescott; pop. 18,214; in Coconino Plateau S of San Francisco Peaks at 6907 ft. above sea level; health resort; lumber mills; Northern Arizona University (1899; coed.); Lowell Observatory (1894). Settled 1876, became ⊗ 1891, incorp. as city 1928.

Flam'beau (flăm'bō). River ab. 150 m. long, N Wisconsin; flows out of Lac du Flambeau SW into Chippewa river.

Flam'bor'ough Head (flăm'bûr'ō; *Brit.* -bŭ·rŭ, -brŭ). Promontory on E coast of Yorkshire, N England, 18 m. SE of Scarborough; lighthouse, 214 ft. above water; chalk cliffs with many caverns; in 54°7′N, 0°5′W.

Fla·men'co (flä·mĕng'kō). Small fortified island, Bay of Panama, just off SE end of Panama Canal.

Flam'ing Cliffs (flăm'ĭng). A highland in S Outer Mongolia, where fossils and dinosaur eggs were discovered by Roy Chapman Andrews expedition 1925. See SHABARAKH USU.

Fla·min'i·an Way (flȧ·mĭn'ĭ·ăn; -mĭn'yăn); *Lat.* **Vi'a Fla·min'i·a** (vī'ȧ flȧ·mĭn'ĭ·ȧ; -mĭn'yȧ). Ancient road, Italy; ran due N from Rome, over 200 m., to Rimini; constructed 220 B.C. by Gaius Flaminius.

Flan'ders (flăn'dẽrz; *Brit. usu.* flän'-); *Fr.* **Flan'dre** (fläɴ'dr'); *Flemish* **Vlaan'de·ren** (vlän'dĕ·rĕ[n]). Medieval county extending along coast of Low Countries; ✳ Lille; now constitutes Belgian provinces of East Flanders and West Flanders (*qq.v.*) and part of the French department of Nord; given by Charles the Bald to Baldwin I 862 A.D.; by 14th cent. Flemish towns (Brugge, Ieper, etc.), becoming industrial (cloth and metals) and commercial centers of northern Europe, were in conflict with French-dominated rulers; rose against counts 1302, 1337, and 1382 under leadership of van Arteveldes; passed to Burgundy by marriage; as part of Spanish Netherlands, some territory secured for France by Louis XIV; ceded to France temporarily 1797; region scene of fighting during both World Wars. Cf. ARTOIS.

Flan'dreau (flăn'drōō). City, ⊗ of Moody co., E South Dakota, 35 m. N of Sioux Falls; pop. 2129.

Flan'nan Islands (flăn'ăn); *also called* **Seven Hunters.** Group of seven small uninhabited islands in Atlantic Ocean W of Lewis I. in the Outer Hebrides, W of Scotland.

Flat (flăt). Village, SW cen. Alaska, in mountainous region E of the Yukon ab. 175 m. NE of Bethel; pop. (1950) 146; airport.

Flat'bush' (flăt'bŏŏsh'). See BROOKLYN.

Flat'head' (flăt'hĕd'). **1** River, 245 m. long, W Montana; rises in SE British Columbia, flows S across U.S.-Canada boundary to **Flathead Lake** (ab. 30 m. long, 12 to 14 m. wide), thence S and W into Clark Fork.

2 County in Montana. See *Table* at MONTANA.

Flat River. City, St. Francois co., E Missouri, 55 m. SSW of St. Louis; pop. 4515; lead mines.

Flat'ter·y, Cape (flăt'ẽr·ĭ). Cape on NW extremity of Clallam co., N Washington, on S side of entrance to Juan de Fuca Strait.

Flat Top. See Peaks of OTTER.

Flèche, La. See LA FLÈCHE.

Fleet'wood (flēt'wŏŏd). **1** Borough, Berks co., SE Pennsylvania, 10 m. NE of Reading; pop. 2647.

2 Urban district, Lancashire, NW England, on More-

cambe Bay at mouth of the Wyre 20 m. N of Blackpool; pop. 27,525; trading port; seaside resort.

Flegrei, Campi. See PHLEGRAEAN FIELDS.

Fleisch'manns (flīsh'mănz). Village and summer resort, Delaware co., S New York, in Catskill Mts. ab. 32 m. NW of Kingston; pop. 450.

Flek'ke·fjord (flĕk'kĕ·fyōr'). Town, on extreme SW coast of Norway, in Vest-Agder co.; pop. 2252.

Flé'malle' (flā'mȧl'). Two communes, Liège prov., Belgium, SW of Liège: **Flémalle–Grande** (-gränd'), on the Meuse, pop. 5840, crystal-glass factories; **Flémalle–Haute** (-ōt'), pop. 6074; nearby is Flémalle fort, one of circle of forts around Liège.

Flem'ing (flĕm'ĭng). County in Kentucky. See *Table* at KENTUCKY.

Flem'ings·burg (flĕm'ĭngz·bûrg). City, ⊗ of Fleming co., NE Kentucky; pop. 2067.

Flem'ing·ton (flĕm'ĭng·tŭn). Borough, ⊗ of Hunterdon co., NW cen. New Jersey, 21 m. N of Trenton; pop. 3232; settled c. 1750; poultry and eggs; scene of trial of Bruno R. Hauptmann Jan. 1935 for Lindbergh murder.

Flens'burg (flĕns'bŏŏrk; *Angl.* flĕnz'bûrg). Seaport and manufacturing city, Schleswig govt. dist., Schleswig-Holstein, Germany, at head of a 30-mile-long inlet **(Flens'burg'er Föhr'de** [flĕns'bŏŏr'gēr fûr'dĕ]) of Baltic Sea near Danish border 20 m. N of Schleswig; pop. 63,139; shipbuilding; iron foundries, rolling mills, woodworking plants; 13th-cent. late-Gothic church; 12th-cent. Romanesque church. Became city 1284; conquered by Imperial forces 1627 and by Swedish forces 1643; by plebiscite Mar. 1920 voted to remain in Germany; in World War II a naval base, frequently bombed.

Flers (flâr). Industrial commune, Orne dept., NW France, 38 m. NW of Alençon; pop. 12,900; textiles.

Fletsch'horn' (flĕch'hôrn') or **Ross'bo'den·horn'** (rôs'bō'dĕn·hôrn'). Peak 13,127 ft. in Pennine Alps, S Switzerland, S of Simplon Pass.

Fleu'rus' (flü'rüs'). Commune, Hainaut prov., SW Belgium; pop. 6736; scene of battle June 26, 1794 in which French under Marshal Jourdan defeated Austrians under prince of Saxe-Coburg.

Fleu'ry', *in full* **Fleury-de·vant'–Dou·au'mont'** (flü'rēd'väN'dwō'môN'). Commune, Meuse dept., NE France; pop. (1914) 450, (1931) 77; 2 m. NE of Verdun; one of defenses of Verdun in World War I; severe fighting 1916.

Flevo Lacus. See ZUIDER ZEE.

Flin'ders (flĭn'dērz). **1** Largest island of the Furneaux Group off NE Tasmania, Australia, 20 m. wide by 40 m. long; place where aboriginal Tasmanians were forced to take refuge 1831.
2 River 500 m. long, N Queensland, Australia, flows NW to Gulf of Carpentaria.

Flinders Range. Mountain range, E South Australia, E of Lake Torrens; highest peak St. Mary Peak 3900 ft.

Flinders Reefs. Group of reefs outside Great Barrier Reef, Queensland, Australia, 17°45'S.

Flin Flon (flĭn' flŏn'). Mining town, NW Manitoba, Canada, on Saskatchewan border 70 m. N of The Pas; pop. (district) 9899; railroad terminus; discovery of uranium 1948 caused large increase in population.

Flinsch Peak (flĭnch). Mountain 9225 ft. on Continental Divide in Glacier National Park, NW Montana.

Flint (flĭnt). **1** River 265 m. long, W Georgia; formed by junction of Mud and Camp creeks in Fayette co., flows S to unite with the Chattahoochee in SW extremity of Georgia and form the Apalachicola river.
2 River, SE Michigan; flows NW to unite with Shiawassee river to form Saginaw river.
3 City, ⊗ of Genesee co., SE cen. Michigan, 58 m. NNW of Detroit; pop. 196,940; manufactures automobiles, airplane engines, paints and varnishes, automobile accessories. Settled 1820, chartered as city 1855; automobile industry first established 1904.
4 Small British island at S end of Line Is. in cen. Pacific

Ocean S of Hawaii, 11°26'S lat., and ab. 450 m. NNW of Tahiti; large coconut plantation.
5 County of Wales. See FLINTSHIRE.
6 Municipal borough and seaport, Flintshire, NE Wales; pop. 14,257; coal and lead deposits; manufactures alkali and chemicals; scene of Richard II's submission to Bolingbroke 1399.

Flint'shire (flĭnt'shĭr; -shēr) or **Flint.** County, NE Wales; area 256 sq. m.; pop. (1951) 145,108; ⊗ Mold; other towns Flint, Rhyl; rivers Dee, Clwyd; agriculture, livestock raising, dairying, mining (coal, iron, lead, copper), manufacturing (chemicals, artificial silk, pottery).

Flod'den (flŏd''n). Hill in N Northumberland, N England, 12 m. E of Kelso near Scottish border; site of battle (also known as **Flodden Field**) Sept. 9, 1513 in which English under Earl of Surrey defeated with great slaughter Scots under James IV, who was killed.

Flo'ra (flōr'ȧ). City, Clay co., SE cen. Illinois, 33 m. NE of Mt. Vernon; pop. 5331; manufactures shoes, furniture; dairy products; redtop grass seed.

Flor·al'a (flŏr·ăl'ȧ; flŭ·răl'ȧ). City, Covington co., S Alabama, on Florida border; pop. 3011; sawmills.

Flo'ral Park (flōr'ăl). Residential village, Nassau co., SE New York, on Long I. 15 m. E of New York City; pop. 17,499; flower culture.

Flor'ence (flŏr'ĕns). **1** Name of counties in two states of the U.S. See *Tables* at SOUTH CAROLINA and WISCONSIN.
2 Industrial city, ⊗ of Lauderdale co., NW corner of Alabama, on Tennessee river by Wilson Dam; pop. 31,649; founded 1818, incorp. 1826, chartered as city 1889; manufactures textiles, iron products; foodpacking plants, lumber mills. Muscle Shoals airport; Alabama State College (1873; coed.).
3 Town, ⊗ of Pinal co., S Arizona, on Gila river 50 m. SE of Phoenix; pop. 2143; founded 1866.
4 City, Fremont co., S cen. Colorado, on Arkansas river 35 m. SSW of Colorado Springs; pop. 2821; founded as coal-mining center 1860, incorp. as city 1887; in oil-producing district.
5 City, Boone co., N Kentucky, SW of Cincinnati, Ohio; pop. 5837.
6 Manufacturing village, Burlington co., S cen. New Jersey, on Delaware river 7 m. SSW of Trenton; pop. (with Roebling) 4215.
7 Manufacturing city, ⊗ of Florence co., E South Carolina, 40 m. ENE of Sumter; pop. 24,722; transportation and trade center; manufactures furniture, plows. In Civil War shipping center and point of embarkation for troops, hospital town, and prison.
8 Town, ⊗ of Florence co., NE Wisconsin; pop. 1251.
9 *Ital.* **Fi·ren'ze** (fē·rĕn'tsä); *anc.* **Flo·ren'ti·a** (flō·rĕn'shǐ·ȧ; -shä). Manufacturing commune, ✲ of Firenze prov., Tuscany, cen. Italy, at head of navigation on Arno river at foot of Apennines, 146 m. NNW of Rome; pop. 322,535; archiepiscopal see; university; seat of Accademia della Crusca. Notable structures include 13th-cent. Duomo or Cathedral of Santa Maria del Fiore, churches of Santa Croce (13th cent.), Santa Maria Novella (13th cent.), the 14th-cent. Ponte Vecchio, the Campanile, the Bargello or Palazza del Podestà (national museum), the Strozzi palace, the Pitti palace, the Loggia dei Lanzi, the Uffizi gallery, the Laurentian library, the Medici-Riccardi palace, the Accademia delle Belle Arti, the Magliabechiana library, and the Palazzo Vecchio.

History: Founded at foot of hill on top of which stood Etruscan town of Faesulae (see FIESOLE); in Roman times located on Cassian Way; escaped capture by Goths 5th cent. A.D.; in medieval margraviate of Tuscany (*q.v.*); by end of 12th cent. a flourishing trade and industrial center; came to be governed chiefly by members of wealthy guilds; torn by bitter civil strife which reflected Guelph-Ghibelline struggle in Italy; republic gradually secured control of extensive surrounding terri-

tory, including Pistoia 1306, Arezzo, Volterra, Pisa 1406, and Leghorn; after 1434 ruled by the Medici (Cosimo 1434–64, Lorenzo the Magnificent 1469–92), members of powerful banking family, who fostered development of Italian Renaissance in which Florence was a leader; republic under Savonarola 1494–98; final expulsion of Medici occurred 1527 but they were restored as dukes of Florence 1531 and as grand dukes of Tuscany 1569; probably greatest cultural and artistic center of western Europe (14th–16th cents.); its language diffused throughout Italy, subsequently becoming standard language of the country; capital of Italy 1864–70. In World War II abandoned July 29, 1944 by Germans, who destroyed all but one of the Arno bridges; entered by British Aug. 4–10, 1944.

Florence Lake *and* **Florence Lake Dam.** See SAN JOAQUIN river, California.

Flo·ren'cia (flō-rān'syä). Town, * of Caquetá commissary, S Colombia, 120 m. ENE of Pasto.

Flo·ren'cio Va·re'la (flō-rän'syō vä·rā'lä). Town, Buenos Aires prov., E Argentina, ab. 15 m. SE of Buenos Aires.

Florentia. See FLORENCE, Italy.

Flo'res (flōr'ĕs; -ēz; flôr'-; *Braz.* flō'rēs; *Port.* flō'rĕsh; *Span.* flō'rås). **1** Island, NW Azores (*q.v.*), in district of Horta; 57 sq. m.; pop. ab. 7000; discovered by Portuguese 1452.
2 City, Pernambuco state, E Brazil, on a tributary of the São Francisco ab. 200 m. W of Recife; pop. 13,015.
3 Town, * of Petén dept., N Guatemala, on an island in a lake; pop. (1938 est.) 1993; produces chicle and timber; stronghold of Itza Indians who preserved it from Spaniards until 1697.
4 Island of the Lesser Sunda Is., Indonesia; largest island in the chain extending from Java to Timor, lies E of Sumbawa and bet. Flores Sea and Savu Sea; ab. 224 m. long and 37 m. wide near W end; 5509 sq. m.; pop. 600,000; chief towns Ende and Larantuka. Volcanic in origin; several isolated peaks above 5000 ft., highest 7874 ft. in W cen. part; coast line has few inlets; no large rivers; exports chiefly copra, grows maize and rice. In early times subject to the princes of Celebes; came partly under Dutch influence c. 1667, although the E end, around Larantuka, was claimed and held by Portugal until 1851; entire island came under Dutch control 1907; occupied by Japanese Mar. 1942.
5 Division of former Timor residency, Lesser Sunda Is., Neth. Indies, comprising large island of Flores and smaller adjacent islands of Komodo, Rintja, Solor, Adonara, Lomblen, and Alor Is. group; 7751 sq. m.; pop. 717,300.
6 Department of Uruguay. See *Table* at URUGUAY.

Flores, Laguna de. See PETÉN lake.

Flores, Las. See LAS FLORES.

Flo'res Sea (flōr'ĕs; -ēz; flôr'-). Body of water ab. 175 m. wide bet. E end of Java Sea and W end of Banda Sea, bet. S Celebes and Lesser Sunda Is. in Indonesia; in SW merges with Bali Sea.

Flo'res·ville (flōr'ĕs·vĭl). City, ⊗ of Wilson co., S cen. Texas, 30 m. SSE of San Antonio; pop. 2126.

Flor'ham Park (flôr'ăm). Borough, Morris co., N New Jersey, 4 m. E of Morristown; pop. 7222.

Flo'ri·a·na (flōr'ĭ·ä'ná; -än'á). Suburb of Valletta, on island of Malta; pop. ab. 7000.

Flo'ri·a·nó'po·lis (flōr'ĭ·á·nŏp'ō·lĭs; *Port.* flō'ryá·nō'-pōō·lĕsh; *formerly* **Des·têr'ro** (dĕsh·tär'rōō). City, * of Santa Catarina state, S Brazil, on Santa Catarina I.; pop. (1940 est.) 25,253; excellent harbor; considerable coastwise trade.

Flor'i·da (flôr'ĭ·dá). **1** Southeast state of U.S.A., 27th state admitted to Union (1845); bounded on N by Alabama and Georgia, on E by Atlantic Ocean, on S by Straits of Florida and the Gulf of Mexico, on W by Gulf of Mexico and Alabama; 22d state in area, 58,560 sq. m. (land area 54,262 sq. m.); 10th state in population,

4,951,560; * Tallahassee. See *Table of States* at UNITED STATES. Divided into the following 67 counties (for pronunciation of their names see their individual entries):

NAME	LOCATION	AREA[1]	POP.[1]	CO. SEAT
Alachua	N penin.	892	74,074	Gainesville
Baker	NE	585	7,363	Macclenny
Bay	NW coast	753	67,131	Panama City
Bradford	NE	293	12,446	Starke
Brevard[2]	cen. E coast	1,032	111,435	Titusville
Broward[3]	SE coast	1,218	333,946	Fort Lauderdale
Calhoun[4]	NW	557	7,422	Blountstown
Charlotte	SW coast	705	12,594	Punta Gorda
Citrus	W penin. coast	570	9,268	Inverness
Clay	NE	598	19,535	Green Cove Springs
Collier[3]	SW coast	2,032	15,753	Naples
Columbia	N	786	20,077	Lake City
Dade[3,5]	SE corner; coastal	2,054	935,047	Miami
De Soto	SW cen. penin.	648	11,683	Arcadia
Dixie	NW penin. coast	688	4,479	Cross City
Duval	NE coast	777	455,411	Jacksonville
Escambia	NW corner; coastal	657	173,829	Pensacola
Flagler	NE coast	483	4,566	Bunnell
Franklin[5]	NW coast	544	6,576	Apalachicola
Gadsden[6]	N	508	41,989	Quincy
Gilchrist	NW penin.	339	2,868	Trenton
Glades	S cen. penin.	745	2,950	Moore Haven
Gulf[4]	NW coast	557	9,937	Wewahitchka
Hamilton	N	514	7,705	Jasper
Hardee	cen. penin.	630	12,370	Wauchula
Hendry	S	1,187	8,119	La Belle
Hernando	W penin. coast	488	11,205	Brooksville
Highlands	cen. penin.	1,041	21,338	Sebring
Hillsborough	cen. W penin. coast	1,040	397,788	Tampa
Holmes	NW	483	10,844	Bonifay
Indian River[2]	cen. E coast	511	25,309	Vero Beach
Jackson[4]	NW	942	36,208	Marianna
Jefferson	N coast	598	9,543	Monticello
Lafayette	NW penin.	543	2,889	Mayo
Lake	cen. penin.	996	57,383	Tavares
Lee	SW coast	786	54,539	Fort Myers
Leon	N	685	74,225	Tallahassee
Levy	NW penin. coast	1,103	10,364	Bronson
Liberty[6]	NW	838	3,138	Bristol
Madison	N	702	14,154	Madison
Manatee	cen. W penin. coast	701	69,168	Bradenton
Marion	N cen. penin.	1,617	51,616	Ocala
Martin	SE coast	559	16,932	Stuart
Monroe[3,5]	SW corner; coastal	994	47,921	Key West
Nassau[7]	NE corner; coastal	650	17,189	Fernandina
Okaloosa	NW coast	944	61,175	Crestview
Okeechobee	SE cen. penin.	780	6,424	Okeechobee
Orange	cen. penin.	916	263,540	Orlando
Osceola	cen. penin.	1,325	19,029	Kissimmee
Palm Beach[3]	SE coast	1,978	228,106	West Palm Beach
Pasco	cen. W penin. coast	751	36,785	Dade City
Pinellas	cen. W penin. coast	264	374,665	Clearwater
Polk	cen. penin.	1,861	195,139	Bartow
Putnam	NE penin.	803	32,212	Palatka
Saint Johns	NE coast	609	30,034	St. Augustine
Saint Lucie[2]	cen. E coast	588	39,294	Fort Pierce
Santa Rosa	NW coast	1,024	29,547	Milton
Sarasota	cen. W penin. coast	586	76,895	Sarasota
Seminole	cen. penin.	321	54,947	Sanford
Sumter	cen. penin.	561	11,869	Bushnell
Suwannee	N	677	14,961	Live Oak
Taylor	N coast	1,032	13,168	Perry
Union	NE	240	6,043	Lake Butler
Volusia	E coast	1,115	125,319	De Land
Wakulla	NW coast	614	5,257	Crawfordville
Walton	NW coast	1,046	15,576	De Funiak Springs
Washington	NW	597	11,249	Chipley

[1] Area = land area in sq. m. Pop. from 1960 Census.
[2] Indian River (inlet) along full extent of shore line.
[3] These counties include the Everglades region.
[4] On E bounded by Apalachicola river, former boundary of old colonies of East and West Florida.
[5] Includes part of Florida Keys (island chain).
[6] On W bounded by Apalachicola river.
[7] Includes Amelia I., S end of Sea Is. chain.

Nickname: Sunshine State, also Peninsular State. *State flower:* Orange blossom. *Motto:* In God We Trust. *Chief cities:* Miami, Tampa, Jacksonville, St. Petersburg,

FLORIDA

Statute Miles

0 10 20 30 40 50

⊛ State Capital

PUBLISHED BY G. & C. MERRIAM COMPANY
SPRINGFIELD, MASS.
PREPARED BY J. W. CLEMENT CO., BUFFALO, N. Y.

WESTERN PART OF
FLORIDA
Same Scale as Main Map

Orlando. *Rivers:* St. Johns, rising in E cen. part and flowing N into Atlantic Ocean; Caloosahatchee, outlet of Lake Okeechobee in the S flowing W; Indian River (actually a tidal inlet) in the E extending 165 m. along the coast; Kissimmee, chief headstream of the lake of same name; Withlacoochee, in the W; Suwannee and Apalachicola in the N, and the boundary rivers Perdido in the NW and St. Marys in the NE. *Highest point:* Iron Mountain 325 ft., in Polk co. *Chief industries:* Fruit-growing (oranges, grapefruit, pineapples), fishing.

History: Spanish Florida, which included southeastern part of present U.S., discovered by Ponce de León 1513; St. Augustine (*q.v.*) settled 1565; ceded to England 1763; divided into two provinces (known as the **Flor′i·das** [flŏr′ĭ·dáz]), East and West Florida; retroceded to Spain 1783; West Florida claimed by U.S. as part of Louisiana Purchase 1803 and occupied 1813; border crossed by Jackson in raid on Seminoles 1818; purchase for $5,000,000 by U.S. completed in Adams-Onís Treaty 1819; organized as territory 1822; admitted to Union as state Mar. 3, 1845; passed ordinance of secession Jan. 10, 1861; annulled ordinance of secession Oct. 28, 1865 and abolished slavery; readmitted to Union 1868; adopted present constitution 1885; in land boom 1925.
2 Village, Monroe co., NE Missouri, on Salt river 28 m. SW of Hannibal; birthplace of Mark Twain.

Flo·ri′da (flô·rē′thä). **1** Municipality, Camagüey prov., Cuba, 23 m. NW of Camagüey; pop. (1931) 28,283.
2 Department of Uruguay. See *Table* at URUGUAY.
3 Town, * of Florida dept., S cen. Uruguay, 60 m. N of Montevideo; pop. ab. 16,000; grain-trading center.

Flor′i·da, Cape (flŏr′ĭ·dà). Point, SE end of Biscayne Key, Biscayne Bay, off SE coast of Florida; lighthouse.

Flor′i·da, Straits of (flŏr′ĭ·dà); *also* **Florida Strait.** Channel ab. 110 m. wide bet. Florida Keys (S end of Florida) and N coast of Cuba, connecting Atlantic Ocean and Gulf of Mexico.

Flor′i·da Bay (flŏr′ĭ·dà). Body of water bet. S tip of Florida mainland and Florida Keys.

Flo·ri′da·blan′ca (flô·rē′thä·vläng′kä). Municipality, W Pampanga prov., Luzon, Phil. Is.; pop. 17,521.

Flor′i·da Island (flŏr′ĭ·dà; flô·rē′dà) *or* **N′·Ge′la** (′ng·gä′lä). Island in SE Solomon Is. in SW Pacific Ocean, N of cen. Guadalcanal and W of Malaita I.; 22 m. long and ab. 6 m. wide; belongs to British Solomon Islands protectorate; off its W shore is Olevuga I. and close to its S shore are the three islands of Tulagi (*q.v.*), Gavutu, and Tanambogo; off SE coast stretching across to Guadalcanal are shoals and reefs, interrupted in center by Sealark Channel. Occupied by Japanese May 4, 1942, taken by Americans Aug. 7 (see also SAVO Island).

Flor′i·da Keys (flŏr′ĭ·dà). A chain of islands extending in a curve to the SW off S tip of Florida, on N side of Straits of Florida; partly in Dade co. but chiefly in Monroe co., Florida; more important islands Key Largo, Upper Matecumbe Key, Lower Matecumbe Key, Long Key, Key Vaca, Big Pine Key, Sugarloaf Key, and Key West at SW extremity of the group; devastated by hurricane 1935; traversed by Overseas Highway, completed 1938, which crosses Card Sound from the mainland to Key Largo and extends to Key West over many miles of causeways and bridges. See KEY WEST.

Flo·ri′dia (flô·rē′dyä). Commune, Siracusa prov., SE Sicily, 8 m. W by N of Syracuse; pop. 14,473.

Flo·ri′na (flô′rĭ·nä). **1** Department of Greece. See *Table* at GREECE.
2 *also transliterated* **Phló′ri·na**; *Serb.* **Le·rin′** (lĕ·rēn′). City, its *, W Macedonia, N Greece, near Yugoslav border; pop. 10,585; seized by Germans Apr. 1941.

Flor′is·sant (flŏr′ĭ·sănt). City, St. Louis co., E Missouri, NW of St. Louis; pop. 38,166.

Flor′ö′ (flô′rû′). Coastal town, ⊗ of Sogn og Fjordane co., W Norway, on a peninsula N of Sunn Fjord; pop. 1405.

Flowery Kingdom. See CHINA.

Floyd (floid). **1** River ab. 80 m. long, NW Iowa; rises in O′Brien co., flows SW into Missouri river at Sioux City.
2 Name of counties in six states of the U.S. See *Tables* at GEORGIA, INDIANA, IOWA, KENTUCKY, TEXAS, VIRGINIA.
3 Town, ⊗ of Floyd co., SW Virginia; pop. 487.

Floyd·a′da (floi·dā′dà). Town, ⊗ of Floyd co., NW Texas, 28 m. SE of Plainview; pop. 3769.

Fluchthorn. See SILVRETTA.

Flume Mountain (floom.). Peak 4327 ft. in Franconia Mts., Grafton co., New Hampshire, E of Franconia Notch; on W side is the **Flume**, a canyon, 12 ft. wide at narrowest point, ab. 70 ft. deep.

Flu′men·do′sa (floo′mĕn·dō′sä). River ab. 80 m. long in SE Sardinia; flows into Tyrrhenian Sea.

Flu′mi·ni Man′nu (floo′mē·nē män′noo). River ab. 50 m. long, S Sardinia; enters Gulf of Cagliari at Cagliari.

Flush′ing (flŭsh′ing). **1** Village, Genesee co., SE cen. Michigan, 10 m. WNW of Flint; pop. 3761.
2 Former village, Queens co., SE New York, on Long I.; since 1898 part of borough of Queens, New York City; mostly residential; one of oldest nursery centers in U.S.; seat of Queens College (1937; coed.); N.Y. World's Fair of 1939–40 held in **Flushing Meadow**, now site of Flushing Meadow Park; temporary headquarters of United Nations (1946–49). See also QUEENS borough, New York City.
3 Commune and seaport, Netherlands. See VLISSINGEN.

Flushing Bay. Inlet of East river, N shore of Long I., New York.

Flu·van′na (floo·văn′à). County in Virginia. See *Table* at VIRGINIA.

Fly (flī). River ab. 650 m. long in W Papua, SE New Guinea I.; largest river in New Guinea, navigable for more than 500 m.; flows S and SE into Gulf of Papua in wide estuary; part of its middle course forms boundary with Neth. New Guinea.

Fo′a (fō′à; *native* fō′ä). Island in Haabai group, Tonga Is., SW cen. Pacific Ocean.

Foard (fōrd). County in Texas. See *Table* at TEXAS.

Fo·ça′ (fô·chä′) *or* **Fo·cha′.** Two seaports on Gulf of İzmir, İzmir vilayet, W Turkey in Asia: (1) **Ye·ni′** (yĕ·nē′) (New Foça), founded 1421 by Genoese; pop. 2619. (2) **Es·ki′** (ĕs·kē′) **Foça** (Old Foça), *anc.* **Pho·cae′a** (fô·sē′à), ab. 5 m. S of Yeni Foça; most northerly of the 12 Ionian Cities on W coast of Asia Minor; a flourishing maritime state c. 800–600 B.C.; established Massilia colony (Marseilles) 600 B.C.; conquered by Persians 540 B.C.

Foc·şa′ni (fôk·shän′; -shä′nè). City, E cen. Romania, in S Moldavia region; pop. 32,799; scene of battles: (1) Aug. 1, 1789 in which a combined Austrian-Russian army defeated the Turks; (2) Jan. 8, 1917 when it was taken by Austro-German forces; truce signed here Dec. 6, 1917.

Fog′gia (fôd′jä). **1** Province of Italy. See *Table* at ITALY.
2 Commune, its *, Apulia, SE Italy, 162 m. ESE of Rome; pop. 62,340; center of great Apulian plain or "tavoliere"; ruins of castle of Frederick II who held parliament here 1240; extensive airfields, captured by British Army Sept. 27, 1943.

Fo′go (fō′gōō). One of Cape Verde Is., in S part of group; ab. 190 sq. m.; pop. ab. 8000; contains volcano 9348 ft., highest point in islands; eruption 1847.

Fo′go (fō′gō). Seaport town (1942 est. pop. 1200), E Newfoundland, on N shore of **Fogo Island**, E of entrance to Notre Dame Bay.

Föhr (fûr). Island off W coast of Schleswig-Holstein, northwestern Germany, one of North Frisian Is.; 32 sq. m.; pop. ab. 7000; chief town Wyk (pop. 2782).

Foix (fwà). Commune, * of Ariège dept., S France, at foot of the Pyrenees 47 m. S of Toulouse; pop. 4445; steelworks, tanneries.

Foix, Countship of. Historical region of S cen. France; bordered anciently on N and E by Languedoc, SE by Roussillon, S by the Pyrenees, W by Gascony;

capitals Foix and Pamiers; watered by Ariège river; made countship 1012; joined to French crown at ascension of Henry IV to throne of France.

Fol'croft (fŏl'krôft). Borough, Delaware co., SE Pennsylvania, 7 m. WSW of Philadelphia; pop. 7013.

Fo'ley (fō'lĭ). Village, ⊗ of Benton co., cen. Minnesota, 15 m. ENE of St. Cloud; pop. 1112.

Fo·li'gno (fô·lē'nyô); *anc.* **Ful·gin'i·um** (fŭl·jĭn'ĭ·ŭm). Manufacturing commune, Perugia prov., Umbria, cen. Italy, 18 m. SE of Perugia; pop. 39,483; cathedral; two Renaissance palaces. Founded 8th cent.; devastated by Perugians 1281; ruled by the Guelph Trinci family 1305–1439; part of Papal States 1439–1860, of Italy from 1860.

Folke'stone (fōk'stŭn). Municipal borough, Kent, SE England, on Strait of Dover 6 m. WSW of Dover; pop. 45,200; seaport, summer resort; fisheries; dates back to Roman and Saxon times.

Folk'ston (fōk'stŭn). City, ⊗ of Charlton co., SE Georgia; pop. 1810.

Fol'lans·bee (fŏl'ănz·bē). City, Brooke co., N West Virginia, on Ohio river 19 m. N of Wheeling; pop. 4052; steel products.

Fol'som (fōl'sŭm). **1** City, Sacramento co., California, NE of Sacramento; pop. 3925; state penitentiary.
2 Village, Union co., NE New Mexico, E of Raton; pop. 142; nearby in 1925 were found artifacts, esp. chipped stone projectile points (*Folsom points*), considered as representative of culture of a Stone Age people supposed to have lived in North America at end of last glacial period (late Pleistocene).

Fomboni. See Mohéli.

Fo·men'to (fô·mān'tô). Municipality and town, Las Villas prov., W cen. Cuba; pop. (town) 17,381.

Fon'da (fŏn'dà). Manufacturing village, ⊗ of Montgomery co., E New York, on Mohawk river 12 m. W of Amsterdam; pop. 1004; railroad center; settled by Dutch c. 1775; burned by Loyalist troops 1780; became ⊗ 1836.

Fond du Lac (fŏn'dŭ lăk'; dŭ). **1** County in Wisconsin. See *Table* at Wisconsin.
2 Manufacturing city and resort, ⊗ of Fond du Lac co., E Wisconsin, at S end of Lake Winnebago; pop. 32,719; settled 1836.
3 River ab. 100 m. long in N Saskatchewan, Canada; flows W to Lake Athabaska.

Fon'di (fŏn'dē; *Angl.* fŏn'dĭ); *anc.* **Fun'di** (fŭn'dī). Commune, Littoria prov., Latium, cen. Italy, 29 m. E by S of Littoria; pop. 15,456; on ancient Appian Way; ruins of castle of Colonna family; Gothic cathedral.

Fon'douk (fŏn'dōok; *Arab.* fōon'-). Town, N cen. Tunisia, 20 m. WSW of Kairouan; near mountain pass whose capture by Allies Apr. 12, 1943 resulted in capture of Kairouan.

Fon'sa·gra'da (fôn'sä·grä'thä). Commune, Lugo prov., NW Spain, 27 m. ENE of Lugo; pop. 14,832.

Fon·se'ca, Gulf of (fôn·sā'kä); *or* **Fonseca Bay.** Large inlet of Pacific Ocean with El Salvador on N, Honduras on E, and Nicaragua on S.

Fon'taine·bleau (fŏn't'n·blō; -tĭn-; *Fr.* fôɴ'tĕn'blō'). Commune, Seine-et-Marne dept., N France, near left bank of the Seine 35 m. SSE of Paris; pop. 17,724; in forest of Fontainebleau; barracks, military college, communal college, school of designing and engineering; famous for its château (SE of town), former residence of French kings, now summer residence of presidents of the Republic; place where revocation of Edict of Nantes was signed 1685 and where Pius VII was held prisoner by Napoleon 1812–14.

Fon·tan'a (fŏn·tăn'à). City, San Bernardino co., S California, W of San Bernardino; pop. 14,659.

Fon·tan'a Dam (fŏn·tăn'à). See *Table* at Tennessee Valley Authority.

Fontarabia. See Fuenterrabia.

Font-de-Gaume. See Les Eyzies.

Fon'te·nay'-le-Comte (fôɴt'nā'lĕ·kôɴt'). Town, SE Vendée dept., W France, 25 m. NE of La Rochelle; pop.

7435; dates from time of the Gauls; belonged to English 1360–72; scene of much fighting during 16th cent. and in 1793; capital of department of Vendée 1790–1806.

Fontenay–sous–Bois (-soo-bwä'). Commune, Seine dept., N France, SE suburb of Paris; pop. 31,546.

Fon'te·noy' (fôɴt'nwá'). **1** Commune, Hainaut prov., SW Belgium, 5 m. ESE of Tournai; pop. 854; scene of battle May 11, 1745 in which Marshal Saxe with help of Irish Brigade defeated a combined force of British, Hanoverians, Austrians, and Dutch under duke of Cumberland.
2 *formerly* **Fon'ta'net'** (fôɴ'tà'nĕ'). Town, Yonne dept., NE cen. France, S of Sens; pop. 113; scene of defeat of Emperor Lothair by his brothers Charles the Bald and Louis the German 841.

Fon'te·vrault'–l'Ab'baye' (fôɴ'tĕ·vrō'lä'bā'). Town, Maine-et-Loire dept., W France, ESE of Saumur; pop. 1121; abbey, founded 1100, where early Plantagenet kings were buried, since 1804 a prison.

Fonuafoō. Native name for Falcon island.

Foochow. See Minhow.

Foots'cray (fōots'krā). Manufacturing city, S Victoria, SE Australia, W suburb of Melbourne; pop. 46,270; bluestone quarries; dry docks.

For'a·ker, Mount (fôr'à·kēr; -ĭ·kēr). Mountain 17,000 ft. in Alaska Range in Mount McKinley National Park, S cen. Alaska, SW of Mt. McKinley.

For'bach (fôr'bák'; *Ger.* fôr'bäK). Commune, Moselle dept., NE France, 32 m. E of Metz; pop. 12,167; glass and pottery; coal mines; scene of battle Aug. 6, 1870 in which General Frossard was defeated by the Prussians.

Forbes (fôrbz). Town, E cen. New South Wales, SE Australia, 185 m. WNW of Sydney; pop. 5356; flour mills, sawmills, breweries.

Forbes, Mount. Peak 11,902 ft. in Banff National Park, SW Alberta, Canada.

Forbidden City. 1 Lhasa, ✳ of Tibet, Outer China—so called because of hostility of the lamas to foreign visitors other than pilgrims.
2 In Peiping, China, the walled enclosure (ab. ⅓ of a sq. m.) containing the Imperial Palace, with its pleasure grounds, reception halls, pavilions, and offices of state— so called because it was formerly closed to the public.

For·ca'dos (fôr·sä'dŭs; *Port.* fōor·sà'thōosh). **1** The main navigable channel of Niger river, S Nigeria.
2 Town, Warri prov., Western Region, Nigeria, on coast 160 m. SE of Lagos; main port of entry at mouth of Niger river.

Ford (fōrd). Name of counties in two states of the U.S. See *Tables* at Illinois and Kansas.

Ford City. Borough, Armstrong co., W Pennsylvania, on Allegheny river 34 m. NE of Pittsburgh; pop. 5440; manufactures plate glass.

Ford'ham (fôr'dăm). Former village now included in Bronx borough, New York City; Fordham University (1841; men; Roman Catholic).

Ford Island. Island in Pearl Harbor, S Oahu, Hawaiian Is., N Pacific Ocean; naval base.

Ford·lan'di·a (fōrd·lăn'dĭ·à). Town, Pará state, NE Brazil, on right bank of Tapajoz river ab. 110 m. S of Santarém; one of the Ford rubber plantations. See also Belterra.

For'dyce (fôr'dīs). City, ⊗ of Dallas co., S cen. Arkansas, 30 m. NE of Camden; pop. 3890.

Fo·rel', Mount (fô·rĕl'). Mountain 11,100 ft., E Greenland, near coast N of Angmagssalik.

Fore'land, North *and* **South** (fōr'lănd). Two headlands in Kent, SE England: North Foreland, 2½ m. SE of Margate, has one lighthouse; South Foreland, 3 m. NE of Dover, has two lighthouses.

Foreland Sound. See Prince Charles Foreland.

Fore River, *in full* **Wey'mouth Fore River** (wā'mŭth fōr). Inlet of Boston Bay on coast of Norfolk co., E Massachusetts; large Fore River shipyards on it at Quincy.

For′est (fôr′ĕst; -ĭst). **1** Name of counties in two states of the U.S. See *Tables* at PENNSYLVANIA and WISCONSIN.
2 City, ⊗ of Scott co., cen. Mississippi, 41 m. E of Jackson; pop. 3917.
3 Town, Lambton co., SE Ontario, Canada, 23 m. ENE of Sarnia; pop. 1790; near S end of Lake Huron.
Fo′rest′ (fô′rĕ′). Commune, Belgium. See VORST.
For′est Can′tons, the Four (fôr′ĕst [-ĭst] kăn′t′nz [-tŭnz; -tŏnz]); *Ger.* **Die Vier Wald′stät′ter** (dē fēr vält′shtĕt′ēr). Uri, Schwyz, Unterwalden, and Lucerne cantons, Switzerland, surrounding Lake of Lucerne (Lake of the Four Forest Cantons); Uri, Schwyz and Unterwalden, first to unite against Hapsburgs 1291, were nucleus of Swiss confederation. See SWITZERLAND.
Forest City. 1 City, ⊗ of Winnebago co., N Iowa, 25 m. WNW of Mason City; pop. 2930.
2 Town, Rutherford co., SW North Carolina, 20 m. W of Shelby; pop. 6556; textiles, lumber, bricks.
3 Borough, Susquehanna co., NE Pennsylvania, 20 m. NNE of Scranton; pop. 2651; coal mining; textiles.
Forest Grove. City, Washington co., NW Oregon, 22 m. W of Portland; pop. 5628; Pacific Univ. (1849; coed.).
Forest Hill. Village, York co., SE Ontario, Canada, in Greater Toronto area; pop. 15,305.
Forest Hills. 1 Residential community in Queens borough, New York City, on Long I.; scene of national lawn tennis (grass-court) tournaments.
2 Borough, Allegheny co., SW Pennsylvania, 8 m. E of Pittsburgh; pop. 8796.
Forest Park. 1 Town, Clayton co., NW cen. Georgia, SSE suburb of Atlanta; pop. 14,201.
2 Residential village, Cook co., NE Illinois, W suburb of Chicago; pop. 14,452.
For′est·ville (fôr′ĕst·vĭl; -ĭst-). Subdivision of town of BRISTOL, Connecticut.
Fo′rez′ (fô′râz′). Ancient region, cen. France, a plain bet. the upper Loire and the Allier, W of Lyons; bordered on W by **Forez Mountains;** medieval countship dependent on Burgundy; united with France 1531.
For′far (fôr′fēr). **1** or **For′far·shire** (-shĭr; -shēr). County of Scotland. See ANGUS.
2 Burgh, ⊗ of Angus co., E Scotland; pop. 9981; jute, linen goods; site of castle, scene of several Scottish parliaments (11th–14th cents.).
Fork′ed Deer (fôr′kĕd; -kĭd). River ab. 15 m. long, W Tennessee; formed by confluence of long north and south forks in S Dyer co.; flows W into Mississippi river. Cf. OBION river.
For·lì′ (fôr-lē′). **1** Province of Italy. See *Table* at ITALY.
2 *anc.* **Fo′rum Liv′i·i** (fôr′ŭm lĭv′ĭ-ī). Commune, its ✳, Emilia, N Italy, 165 m. N by W of Rome; pop. 65,683; episcopal see; old citadel; 14th-cent. Palazzo Communale; manufactures. Allied with Ravenna 12th cent.; taken by Martin IV 1282; became part of Papal States 1504; to Italy 1860.
For′man (fôr′măn). City, ⊗ of Sargent co., SE North Dakota; pop. 530.
Form′by (fôrm′bĭ). Urban district, Lancashire, NW England, on Irish Sea 10 m. N of Liverpool; pop. 10,429.
For′men·te′ra (fôr′măn-tā′rä); *anc.* **Oph′i·u′sa** (ŏf′ĭ-ū′sà). Fourth largest island of the Balearic group, Baleares prov., Spain, in W Mediterranean Sea S of Iviza I. and 82 m. SW of Majorca; 40 sq. m.; pop. (1930) 2929; fisheries, salt making. See BALEARIC ISLANDS.
For′men·tor′, Cape (fôr′măn-tôr′). Cape on N extremity of island of Majorca, W Mediterranean Sea.
For′mia (fôr′myä); *formerly* **Mo′la di Ga·e′ta** (mō′lä dē gä-â′tä); *anc.* **For′mi·ae** (fôr′mĭ-ē). Commune, Littoria prov., Latium, cen. Italy, on Gulf of Gaeta 41 m. ESE of Littoria; pop. 16,905; summer resort; active seaport. Ancient town of the Volsci; on Appian Way; received limited citizenship rights from Rome 322 B.C. and full rights 188 B.C.; site of a summer villa of Cicero, who was murdered nearby (see ASTURA); in World War II taken by Americans May 18, 1944.

For·mi′ga (fōōr·mē′gà). City, Minas Gerais state, E Brazil, 100 m. WSW of Belo Horizonte; pop. 9216.
For·mi′gi·ne (fôr·mē′jĕ·nà). Commune, Modena prov., Emilia, N Italy, 7 m. SW of Modena; pop. 10,985.
For′mi′gny′ (fôr′mē′nyē′). Village, Calvados dept., NW France, ab. 27 m. WNW of Caen; scene of battle Apr. 15, 1450 in which French defeated English in next-to-last battle of Hundred Years' War (see CASTILLON).
For·mo′sa (fôr·mō′sà) or **Tai·wan** (tī·wän). Island in China Sea, off Fukien prov., SE China, formerly in S part of Japanese Empire; in lat. 21°53′ to 25°18′N and long. 120° to 122°E; ab. 225 m. long; 13,857 sq. m. (including Pescadores, *q.v.*); pop. (1935) 5,315,642, (1962) 11,375,085; ✳ Taipei; has lofty mountain range extending through E cen. part, highest peaks Niitaka 13,599 ft. and Tsugitaka 12,894 ft.; no long rivers; its S point, Garan Bi, on Bashi Channel, which separates it from Batan Is. of the Philippines. Inhabitants chiefly Chinese, some Japanese, and two small groups of aborigines; produces sugar, rice, tea, fruit, forest products; mines gold and coal. Chief cities Taipei and its two ports, Kirun and Tansui, Tainan, Kagi, Takao, Taichu, and Shinchiku. See *Map* at JAPAN.
History: Probably known to Chinese from earliest times but not settled by them until quite late; explored by Portuguese and Spanish 16th cent.; named Formosa by the Portuguese because of its beautiful scenery (Port. *formosa* pretty); site of fort built 1624 by Dutch who were driven out by Manchus 1662; not open to Europeans again until two ports opened 1858 by Treaties of Tientsin; ceded to Japan 1895; in World War II made a strong military base by the Japanese; frequently bombed 1944–45 by U.S. planes; after defeat of Japan returned to China; seat of Chinese Nationalist government since 1949.
For·mo′sa (fôr·mō′sà; *Span.* -sä). **1** Territory of Argentina. See *Table* at ARGENTINA.
2 Town, its ✳, N Argentina, on a tributary of the Paraguay river; pop. (est.) 18,500.
For·mo′sa Bay (fôr·mō′sà). Inlet of Indian Ocean on SE coast of Kenya, E Africa; receives Tana river.
Formosa, *or* **Taiwan, Strait.** Channel ab. 115 m. wide bet. Fukien prov., SE China, and Formosa I.; connects East China Sea with South China Sea.
For·mo′so, Cape (fôr·mō′sō). Cape on coast of Nigeria, W Africa, near Nun mouth of Niger river.
Forn′felt (fôrn′fĕlt). City, Scott co., SE Missouri, 8 m. S of Cape Girardeau; pop. (1950) 1539.
For′res (fôr′ĭs; -ĭz). Burgh, Moray co., NE Scotland, 11 m. SW of Elgin; pop. 4462; site of castle at which Macbeth is said to have killed Duncan; nearby is the heath where, in the Shakespeare play, Macbeth met the three witches.
For′rest (fôr′ĕst; -ĭst). County in Mississippi. See *Table* at MISSISSIPPI.
Forrest City. Commercial city, ⊗ of St. Francis co., E Arkansas; pop. 10,554; manufactures textiles, brooms.
Forst (fôrst), *also* **Forst in der Lau′sitz** (ĭn dēr lou′zĭts). Industrial city, eastern Germany, in Brandenburg on Neisse river 14 m. E of Cottbus and 75 m. SE of Berlin; pop. 35,962; important textile center; produces Forst, one of finest white wines of the Palatinate.
For·syth′ (fôr-sīth′; fēr-sīth′; fôr′sĭth). **1** Name of counties in two states of the U.S. See *Tables* at GEORGIA and NORTH CAROLINA.
2 City, ⊗ of Monroe co., cen. Georgia, 22 m. NW of Macon; pop. 3697; Bessie Tift College (1847; women).
3 City, ⊗ of Taney co., S Missouri; pop. 489.
4 City, ⊗ of Rosebud co., SE Montana; pop. 2032.
Fort Al′ba·ny (ôl′bà·nĭ). Trading post, Cochrane dist., E Ontario, Canada, on James Bay at mouth of Albany river; established ab. 1670 by Hudson's Bay Co.
Fort Aleksandrovsk. See FORT SHEVCHENKO.
For′ta·le′za (fôr′tà·lā′zà); *sometimes called* **Ce′a·rá′** (sā′à·rà′). City and port, ✳ of Ceará state, NE Brazil,

ab. 270 m. NW of Natal; pop. (1940 est.) 142,453; open roadstead, new port works at Point Mucuripe 5 m. E; exports sugar, coffee, cotton, hides; founded early in 17th cent.; made capital 1810.

Fort An'cient (ăn'shĕnt). Prehistoric Indian fortification, Warren co., SW Ohio; overlooks Little Miami river; earth wall over 3½ m. long, 6-10 ft. high, encloses ab. 100 acres in two divisions, the Old Fort and the New Fort.

Fort Anne National Historic Park (ăn). See CANADA, *National Historic Parks.*

Fort Ar'cham·bault (är'shăm·bō; *Fr.* ȧr'shäⁿ'bō'). Station on Chari river, N Central African Republic (formerly Ubangi-Shari, French Equatorial Africa); pop. 1745; airport.

Fort At'kin·son (ăt'kĭn·s'n). City, Jefferson co., SE Wisconsin; pop. 7908; farm and dairy equipment.

Fort Bay'ard (fôrt bā'ērd; bī'ĕrd; *Fr.* fôr' bȧ'yȧr'). See KWANGCHOWAN.

Fort Beau'fort (bō'fērt). Town, SE Cape Province, S Union of South Africa, 105 m. NE of Port Elizabeth; pop. 6101.

Fort Beau·sé'jour' National Historic Park (bō'sā'-zhōōr'). See CANADA, *National Historic Parks.*

Fort Bel'voir (bĕl'vôr); *formerly* **Fort Hum'phreys** (hŭm'frĭz). Military post, SE Fairfax co., NE Virginia, on the Potomac; Engineer School.

Fort Bend (bĕnd). County in Texas. See *Table* at TEXAS.

Fort Ben'ja·min Har'ri·son (bĕn'jȧ·mĭn hăr'ĭ·s'n). Military post 2030 acres, Indianapolis, Marion co., cen. Indiana; estab. 1903; airport.

Fort Ben'ning (bĕn'ĭng). Military post 97,000 acres, Muscogee co., W Georgia, 8 m. S of Columbus; largest infantry post in the U.S.; established during World War I, infantry school from 1919.

Fort Ben'ton (bĕn't'n; -tŭn). City, ⊗ of Chouteau co., N cen. Montana, on Missouri river, in early days head of navigation at low water; pop. 1887.

Fort Bliss (blĭs). Military post 50 sq. m., El Paso, El Paso co., W Texas; cavalry and antiaircraft artillery; air corps.

Fort Bragg (brăg). **1** City, Mendocino co., W California, on Pacific coast 96 m. S of Eureka; pop. 4433; founded 1850; army post founded 1857; redwood lumber.
2 Military reservation, Cumberland co., S cen. North Carolina, ab. 10 m. NW of Fayetteville; estab. 1918; field artillery training center; includes Pope Field, U.S. Air Force base; site of battle of Monroes Crossroads 1865.

Fort Branch (brănch). Town, Gibson co., SW Indiana, 18 m. N of Evansville; pop. 1983.

Fort Bridg'er (brĭj'ēr). Village, Uinta co., SW Wyoming; pop. (est.) 150; nearby is the site of trading post built 1843 by James Bridger, an important station on Oregon Trail and a U.S. Army post 1858-90, site now a state park.

Fort Brown (broun). Military reservation 288 acres just E of Brownsville, Cameron co., Texas; fort established 1846; military post 1865-1944.

Fort Capuzzo. See Fort CAPUZZO.

Fort Carillon. See TICONDEROGA.

Fort Car'o·line (kăr'ō·lĭn; -lĭn). Fortified settlement, NE Florida, on S side of mouth of St. Johns river; established by French Huguenots 1564, destroyed the next year by the Spanish under Menéndez de Avilés.

Fort Cham'bly National Historic Park (shăm'blĭ; *Fr.* shäⁿ'blē'). See CANADA, *National Historic Parks.*

Fort Chi'mo (chĭ'mō). Outpost station and airfield, NE Quebec, Canada, on Koksoak river near its mouth near S coast of Ungava Bay.

Fort Christiansborg. See ACCRA.

Fort Chris·ti'na (krĭs·tē'nȧ). Swedish settlement on site of Wilmington, Delaware; established by Peter Minuit 1638. See WILMINGTON.

Fort Clay'ton (klā't'n). Fort on E shore of Miraflores

Lake, Canal Zone, ab. 5 m. from Pacific terminus of Panama Canal.

Fort Col'lins (kŏl'ĭnz). Residential and industrial city, ⊗ of Larimer co., N Colorado, 40 m. NNE of Boulder; pop. 25,027; founded 1864, incorp. 1879; manufactures beet sugar, cement. Colorado State University (1870; coed.).

Fort Con'ger (kŏng'gēr). Arctic post on Hall Basin, Grant Land, Ellesmere I., N Canada, ab. 81°45'N; station used by A. W. Greely 1881-84; one of the poles of cold, a monthly average (Feb.) of 40° below zero having been recorded. Cf. VERKHOYANSK, OIMYAKON.

Fort Crève'cœur' (fôrt' krĕv'kûr'; -kōōr'; *Fr.* fôr' krâv'kûr'). **1** See ILLINOIS state.
2 See ACCRA.

Fort–Dau'phin (fôrt·dō'fĭn; *Fr.* fôr'dō'făN'). Town and fortified seaport, SE Madagascar; pop. 7100.

Fort Da'vis (dā'vĭs). Village, ⊗ of Jeff Davis co., W Texas; pop. (est.) 718.

Fort Dearborn. See CHICAGO.

Fort de Char'tres (fôrt dĕ chär'tērz). Old fort, SW Illinois, near Kaskaskia, on the Mississippi; founded 1720; in state park.

Fort–de–France' (fôr'dē·fräns'). City, ✱ of Martinique, French West Indies, on large **Fort–de–France Bay** on SW coast of island; pop. (1936) 52,051; partially destroyed by earthquake 1839 and by fire 1890.

Fort de Kock (fôrt' dĕ kŏk'; kôk'); *now* **Bu'kit·ting'gi** (bōō'kĭ·tĭng'gĕ). Inland town, W Sumatra, ab. 50 m. N of Padang, Indonesia, in Padang Highlands; pop. 14,657; important as a military post; original fortifications erected by Dutch 1825.

Fort De·pos'it (dĕ·pŏz'ĭt). Town, Lowndes co., S cen. Alabama, 30 m. SW of Montgomery; pop. 1466; established as military post c. 1813.

Fort Des Moines. See DES MOINES, Iowa.

Fort Dev'ens (dĕv'ĕnz). Military post, Ayer, Middlesex co., Massachusetts; WAC training center in World War II; headquarters, 13th U.S. Army Corps.

Fort Dix (dĭks). Military reservation 13½ sq. m. in Burlington and Ocean cos., S cen. New Jersey, ab. 10 m. NNE of Mount Holly, near Wrightstown.

Fort Dodge (dŏj). City, ⊗ of Webster co., N cen. Iowa, 68 m. NW of Des Moines; pop. 28,399; railroad center; near gypsum deposits from which the Cardiff giant was carved (see CARDIFF, N.Y.).

Fort Don'el·son National Military Park (dŏn'l-s'n). See UNITED STATES, *National Historical Parks.*

Fort Drum (drŭm). See CORREGIDOR.

Fort Duf'fer·in (dŭf'ēr·ĭn). See MANDALAY.

Fort Du·quesne' (dōō·kān'). French fort on site of modern Pittsburgh, Pennsylvania; captured by British 1758 and renamed Fort Pitt.

Fort E'ben E'mael (ā'bĕn ā'mȧl). Fort, N of Liège, Belgium, on Albert Canal; captured by Germans May 11, 1940.

Fort Ed'ward (ĕd'wērd). Village, Washington co., E New York, on Hudson river 38 m. N of Troy; pop. 3737; on site of colonial Fort Edward; pulp and paper mills.

Fort E'rie (ēr'ĭ). Town, Welland co., SE Ontario, Canada, on Lake Erie as it empties into Niagara river; pop. 7572; connected with Buffalo, N.Y., by International Bridge (railroad), by Peace Bridge (dedicated 1927), and by ferries; manufactures aircraft, parachutes, and paint; gold refineries. Formed 1932 by amalgamation of Bridgeburg town and Fort Erie village; on site of old Fort Erie, which was captured by American forces July 13, 1813, besieged by British Aug. 7 to 14, and destroyed by American troops Nov. 1814.

For'tes·cue (fôr'tĕs·kū). River ab. 350 m. long, North West Region, W Western Australia; in flood seasons flows NW to Indian Ocean near Dampier Archipelago.

Fort Es·te'ros (ås·tā'rōs). Former Bolivian post in the Chaco, on Pilcomayo river, long. 60°W; now in Paraguay.

Fort E'than Al'len (ē'thăn ăl'ĕn; -ĭn). See ESSEX JUNCTION, Vermont.

Fort Fair'field (fâr'fēld). Town and village, Aroostook co., N Maine, on Aroostook river 10 m. NE of Presque Isle; pop. 5876; port of entry.

Fort Fish'er (fĭsh'ēr). Fort, S New Hanover co., SE North Carolina, near Cape Fear; designed to protect port of Wilmington; captured by Union forces Jan. 15, 1865.

Fort Fran'ces (frăn'sĕs; -sĭs). Town, ⊗ of Rainy River dist., SW Ontario, Canada, on Rainy river across from International Falls, Minnesota; pop. 8038; lumber and paper mills, large power plant.

Fort Fran'cis E. War'ren (frăn'sĭs ē wŏr'ĕn; -ĭn). Military post, Laramie co., SE Wyoming, adjoining Cheyenne; maneuver reservation, 52,000 acres, largest in the U.S.; U.S. Air Force base (U.S. Air Force Technical School); estab. ab. 1867.

Fort Frank (frăngk). See CORREGIDOR.

Fort Fred'er·i'ca National Monument (frĕd'ēr-ē'kà; frĕd·rē'kà). See UNITED STATES, *National Monuments.*

Fort Fron'te·nac (frŏn't'n-ăk; *Fr.* frôNt'nàk'). French fort on site of modern Kingston (*q.v.*), Ontario, Canada; captured by British 1758.

Fort Gaines (gānz). City, ⊗ of Clay co., SW Georgia; pop. 1320.

Fort Gar'ry (găr'ĭ). Fort and post of Hudson's Bay Co. established 1821 at junction of Assiniboine and Red rivers; now Winnipeg (*q.v.*).

Fort George (jôrj). River 520 m. long, cen. and W Quebec, Canada; flows W into lower James Bay.

Fort George G. Meade (jôrj jē mēd). Military reservation 7500 acres, NW Anne Arundel co., Maryland; estab. 1917; during World War II site of a WAC training school.

Fort Good Hope *or* **Good Hope.** Trading station on lower Mackenzie river, NW Mackenzie District, Northwest Territories, Canada, ab. 130 m. NW of Norman Wells.

Forth (fôrth). River ab. 114 m. long in S cen. Scotland; rises on NE slope of Ben Lomond, flows E into **Firth of Forth,** *anc.* **Bo·do'tri·a** (bŏ·dō'trĭ·à), an estuary extending inland from North Sea 48 m. and varying in width from 1½ to 17½ m. The Firth is spanned by a cantilever bridge 5330 ft. long from Dalmeny (on S side ab. 9 m. W of Edinburgh) to Queensferry.

Fort Hall (hôl). **1** Former fort at a junction point on the Oregon Trail, on Snake river N of Pocatello, SE Idaho; original fort built 1834. Present village of Fort Hall nearby (to E) is seat of Fort Hall Indian Reservation agency. **2** Town and post, S cen. Kenya, E Africa, on Tana river 56 m. NE of Nairobi; alt. 4410 ft.; weather station.

Fort Hen'ry (hĕn'rĭ). Locality, Stewart co., NW Tennessee, on Tennessee river S of Fort Donelson National Military Park; site of Fort Henry, captured by Grant Feb. 6, 1862.

Fort Hertz (hûrts) *or* **Pu'ta·o** (pōō'tä·ō). Government post in extreme N of Burma, S of Namni Pass.

Fort Hua·chu'ca (wà·chōō'kà). Town, Cochise co., SE Arizona, in Fort Huachuca Military Reservation.

Fort Hughes (hūz). See CORREGIDOR.

Fort Humphreys. See FORT BELVOIR.

For·tín' Bo'que·rón' (fôr·tēm' bō'kà·rôn'). Fort in S Boquerón dept., W Paraguay, in the Chaco Boreal.

Fort Jame'son (jām's'n). Town, ✳ of East Luangwa prov., E Northern Rhodesia, S cen. Africa, 290 m. ENE of Lusaka; pop. 1782.

Fort Jef'fer·son National Monument (jĕf'ēr·s'n). See UNITED STATES, *National Monuments.*

Fort John'ston (jŏn'stŭn; -s'n). Town, S Nyasaland, SE Africa, on Shire river 6 m. from S end of Lake Nyasa, ab. 65 m. N of Zomba.

Fort Kent (kĕnt). Town, Aroostook co., N Maine, on St. John river across from New Brunswick, Canada;

pop. 4761; port of entry; Fort Kent State Normal School (1878; coed.).

Fort Knox (nŏks). Military reservation 33,000 acres, N Hardin co., N cen. Kentucky; established 1917 as training camp, permanent military post since 1932; cavalry; Godman Air Force Base; location since 1936 of U.S. Gold Bullion Depository.

Fort-La'my' (fôr'là'mē'). Town, ✳ of Chad Republic, N cen. Africa, on Chari river in SW part of country; pop. 24,000.

Fort Lar'a·mie National Monument (fôrt lăr'à·mĭ). See UNITED STATES, *National Monuments.*

Fort Lau'der·dale (lô'dēr·dāl). City, ⊗ of Broward co., SE Florida, on Atlantic Ocean 25 m. N of Miami; pop. 83,648; established as a military post 1837; yachting and fishing resort. Deepwater harbor of Port Everglades is just S.

Fort Leav'en·worth (lĕv'ĕn·wûrth). Military reservation 8000 acres, Leavenworth co., E Kansas, adjoining Leavenworth; one of oldest military posts W of the Mississippi, estab. 1827; Federal penitentiary; Command and General Staff School; Sherman Air Force Base.

Fort Le·Boeuf' (fôrt lē·bŭf'; -bŏŏf'; *Fr.* fôr' lē·bŭf'). Fort erected by the French 1753 on site of Waterford, Pennsylvania, just S of Erie; visited 1753 by Washington with message from Gov. Dinwiddie of Virginia.

Fort Lee (lē). Borough, Bergen co., NE corner of New Jersey, on Hudson river 10 m. NNE of Jersey City; pop. 21,815; site of fort built, with Fort Washington, to defend West Point in Revolutionary War, and abandoned after fall of Fort Washington 1776; one of the cradles of motion picture industry; manufactures motion picture film; George Washington Bridge (completed 1931).

Fort Len'nox National Historic Park (lĕn'ŭks). See CANADA, *National Historic Parks.*

Fort Lew'is (lū'ĭs; lōō'-). Military post, Pierce co., W cen. Washington, SW of Tacoma; 62,000 acres; established 1917.

Fort Li'ard *or* **Liard** (lē'ärd). Trading post, SW Mackenzie District, Northwest Territories, Canada, on the Liard river ab. 130 m. SSW of Fort Simpson.

Fort Lou'doun Dam (lou'd'n). See *Table* at TENNESSEE VALLEY AUTHORITY.

Fort Lup'ton (lŭp'tŭn). Town, Weld co., N Colorado, on South Platte river 25 m. N of Denver; pop. 2194.

Fort Mc·Clel'lan (mà·klĕl'ăn). Military reservation 20,000 acres, Calhoun co., NE Alabama; infantry; National Guard.

Fort Mc·Hen'ry National Monument (măk·hĕn'rĭ; mà·kĕn'rĭ). See UNITED STATES, *National Monuments.*

Fort Mc·Mur'ray (măk·mûr'ĭ). Post, NE Alberta, W Canada, on Athabaska river; port.

Fort Mc·Pher'son *or* **McPherson** (măk·fûr's'n). Trading station, NW Mackenzie District, Northwest Territories, Canada, on Peel river S of Aklavik.

Fort Mad'a·le'na (măd'dä·lā'nä). Village and fortified post, NE Cyrenaica, Libya, N Africa, S of Sidi Omar; battles nearby 1941–42.

Fort Mad'i·son (măd'ĭ·s'n). Industrial city, a ⊗ of Lee co., SE corner of Iowa, on the Mississippi; pop. 15,247.

Fort Mal'den National Historical Park (môl'dĕn). See CANADA, *National Historic Parks.*

Fort Man'ning (măn'ĭng). Trading post, SW Nyasaland protectorate, SE Africa, near Mozambique border.

Fort Mar'i·on National Monument (măr'ĭ·ŭn; mâr'-). See *Castillo de San Marcos National Monument* at UNITED STATES, *National Monuments.*

Fort Ma·tan'zas National Monument (mà·tăn'zàs). See UNITED STATES, *National Monuments.*

Fort Max'im Gor'ki (măk'sĭm gôr'kĭ). One of the defense forts of Sevastopol, Crimea, Soviet Russia, Europe; after fierce fighting taken by Germans June 17, 1942.

Fort Meade (mēd). **1** City, Polk co., cen. Florida penin., 25 m. S of Lakeland; pop. 4014; site of military post during Seminole War.

2 Military reservation 7842 acres, Meade co., W South Dakota, just E of Sturgis; contains Fort Meade, post established 1878.

Fort Meigs (mĕgz). Former fort at rapids in Maumee river, NW Ohio; besieged unsuccessfully May 1–9, 1813 by force of British and Indians.

Fort Mill (mĭl). Town, York co., N South Carolina, 7 m. NNE of Rock Hill; pop. 3315; textile mills.

Fort Mills (mĭlz). Fort on Corregidor I. at entrance to Manila Bay, Phil. Is.

Fort Mims (mĭmz). Temporary stockade erected near junction of Alabama and Tombigbee rivers, Alabama; scene of a massacre of settlers by Creek Indians under their chief, William Weatherford, Aug. 30, 1813.

Fort Mon'mouth (mŏn'mŭth). Military post, E Monmouth co., E cen. New Jersey, SE of Red Bank; Signal School.

Fort, or **Fortress, Mon·roe'** (mŭn·rō'). Military post and post office, Hampton, SE Virginia, at Old Point Comfort at entrance to Hampton Roads; before 1946 site of coast artillery school; Jefferson Davis held prisoner here 1865–67 after Civil War.

Fort Mor'gan (môr'găn). City, ⊗ of Morgan co., NE Colorado, on South Platte river 70 m. ENE of Denver; pop. 7379; refines beet sugar.

Fort Moul'trie (mōōl'trĭ). Fort in Charleston harbor, SE South Carolina, on N side of entrance, on Sullivans I.; evacuated by Federal garrison Dec. 26, 1860 to strengthen Fort Sumter; seized by state authorities Dec. 27.

Fort My'er Heights (mī'ēr). Village, ⊗ of Arlington co., N Virginia, 6 m. N of Alexandria; seat of **Fort Myer,** U.S. military reservation.

Fort My'ers (mī'ērz). City, ⊗ of Lee co., SW Florida, on estuary of Caloosahatchee river just S of Charlotte Harbor; pop. 22,523; fort established 1850 and used as a Federal base in Civil War.

Fort Nas'sau (năs'ô). **1** Fort built 1623 by the Dutch on left bank of Delaware river opp. site of Philadelphia; used as trading post; abandoned 1651.
2 Fort built 1614 by the Dutch on Hudson river just S of present city of Albany; destroyed 1617 by flood; replaced by Fort Orange 1624 (see ALBANY, N.Y.).

Fort–Na'tio·nal' (fôr'nà'syō'nàl'). Commune, Alger dept., N Algeria; pop. 12,461; in hilly region ab. 64 m. E of Algiers.

Fort Necessity. Small fortification erected 1754 by English colonial expeditionary force under Major George Washington in Great Meadows (*q.v.*); attacked by French and Indians, forced to surrender July 3, 1754; site has been set aside as **Fort Necessity Battlefield Site:** see UNITED STATES, *National Historic Parks.*

Fort Nel'son (nĕl's'n). **1** River ab. 260 m. long, N British Columbia, Canada; has several headstreams rising on E slopes of Rocky Mts. in N Brit. Columbia; flows NW into Liard river.
2 Station, NE British Columbia, Canada, 225 m. N of Dawson Creek on Fort Nelson river, 58°46′N, 123°20′W; formerly a Hudson's Bay Co. post, now an important station on Alaska Highway.

Fort Ni·ag'a·ra (nī·ăg'rà; -ăg'à·rà). Fort at mouth of Niagara river, New York; successively French, British, and American; again captured by British 1813 and returned to United States 1815.

Fort Nor'man or **Norman** (nôr'măn). Trading station on right bank of Mackenzie river, W Mackenzie District, Northwest Territories, Canada, at mouth of Great Bear river SE of Norman Wells.

Fort O'gle·thorpe (ō'g'l·thôrp). Military reservation 810 acres, Catoosa co., NW Georgia; established 1903; cavalry; during World War II site of WAC Officer Candidate School and WAC training center.

Fort Olimpo. See FUERTE OLIMPO.

Fort Or'ange (ŏr'ĕnj; -inj). Former Dutch fort on site of modern Albany, N.Y. (*q.v.*).

Fort Payne (pān). City, ⊗ of De Kalb co., NE Alabama, 35 m. NE of Gadsden; pop. 7029.

Fort Peck Dam *and* **Reservoir** (pĕk). See UNITED STATES, *Dams and Reservoirs.*

Fort Pepperrell. See QUIDI VIDI.

Fort Pick'ens (pĭk'ĕnz). Fort on Santa Rosa I. at entrance to Pensacola harbor, Florida; held by Federals during Civil War (1861–65).

Fort Pierce (pērs). City, ⊗ of St. Lucie co., E Florida, on Indian River 30 m. NE of Lake Okeechobee; pop. 25,256; fort built originally 1838 as a defense against Indians; amphibious training base in World War II.

Fort Pierre (pēr). City, ⊗ of Stanley co., cen. South Dakota; pop. 2649; settled 1817 (see SOUTH DAKOTA).

Fort Pil'low (pĭl'ō). Fort on Mississippi river 40 m. N of Memphis, Tennessee; scene of Federal defeat Apr. 12, 1864.

Fort Pitt (pĭt). Name given Fort Duquesne after capture by British 1758. See PITTSBURGH.

Fort Plain (plān). Village, Montgomery co., E New York, on Mohawk river 23 m. W of Amsterdam; pop. 2809; settled by German Palatines 1722; textiles; site of Fort Plain (1776) nearby.

Fort Pontchartrain. See DETROIT.

Fort Por'tal (pōr't'l; pôr'-). Town, ✳ of Western Province, British protectorate of Uganda, E Africa, 160 m. W of Entebbe near Congo border.

Fort Presque Isle (prĕsk' ēl'; ĭl'). French fort on site of Erie, Pennsylvania; built 1753, burned by Indians 1763.

Fort Prince of Wales National Historic Park (wālz). See CANADA, *National Historic Parks.*

Fort Prov'i·dence or **Providence** (prŏv'ĭ·dĕns). Trading post, S Mackenzie District, Northwest Territories, Canada, on Mackenzie river at its outlet from Great Slave Lake.

Fort Pu·las'ki National Monument (pụ·lăs'kĭ; pụ-). See UNITED STATES, *National Monuments.*

Fort Ran'dolph (răn'dŏlf; -d'lf). U.S. fort at Caribbean terminus of Panama Canal, Canal Zone, on E side of entrance to Limon Bay.

Fort Re·cov'er·y (rē·kŭv'ēr·ĭ). Village, Mercer co., W Ohio, 41 m. SW of Lima; pop. 1336; on site of Gen. Arthur St. Clair's defeat by Indians 1791 and of Gen. Anthony Wayne's "recovery" of the area 1793.

Fort Re'no (rē'nō). Military post and reservation, Canadian co., cen. Oklahoma; estab. 1874.

Fort Res'o·lu'tion or **Resolution** (rĕz'ō·lū'shŭn). Trading post, S Mackenzie District, Northwest Territories, Canada, at mouth of Slave river on S shore of Great Slave Lake; formerly a fort of Hudson's Bay Co.

Fortress Monroe. See FORT MONROE.

Fortress Mountain. Peak 12,073 ft., cen. Park co., NW Wyoming.

Fortress of Lou'is·bourg National Historic Park (lōō'is·bûrg). See CANADA, *National Historic Parks.*

Fort Ri'ley (rī'lĭ). Military reservation 24,000 acres, Riley and Geary cos., E Kansas; Cavalry School, organized 1891; Marshall Air Force Base.

Fort Rose'ber'y (rōz'bĕr'ĭ; *Brit.* -bēr·ĭ, -brĭ). Town, ✳ of Mweru-Luapula prov., N Northern Rhodesia, 110 m. E of Elisabethville, Congo; pop. ab. 1000.

Fort Saint Da'vid (sānt dā'vĭd). Ruins of British fort on Coromandel Coast, Madras state, SE India, just N of town of Cuddalore; at first a small fort (Tegnapatam) built by a Hindu merchant; 1677 became possession of Marathas, who sold it to the English 1690; 1746 became British headquarters for southern India; Clive appointed its governor 1756; captured by French 1758, 1782; finally passed to British 1785.

Fort Sainte Anne (fôrt' sånt ăn'; *Fr.* fôr' săn'tàn'). Fort built by the French 1666 on Isle La Motte, Lake Champlain, NW Vermont; first settlement in Vermont (only temporary).

Fort Saint Frédéric. See CROWN POINT.

Fort Saint George. See MADRAS.

Fort Saint John (fôrt' sånt jŏn'). Station, NE Brit. Columbia, Canada, ab. 40 m. NW of Dawson Creek on Peace river; terminal construction camp on Alaska Highway.

Fort San'de·man (săn'dĕ·măn). Military post, ✳ of Zhob dist., NE Baluchistan, in Zhob valley 65 m. SW of the Gumal Pass; pop. 4228; established 1890.

Fort San Lo·ren'zo (săn' lô·rĕn'zō). United States fort at mouth of Chagres river, Canal Zone, W of Limon Bay.

Fort Schuy'ler (skī'lēr). **1** Military post estab. 1856 at Throgs Neck, New York, one of N defenses of New York harbor.
2 See FORT STANWIX.

Fort Scott (skŏt). Industrial city, ⊗ of Bourbon co., SE Kansas, 85 m. S of Kansas City; pop. 9410.

Fort Sel'kirk *or* **Selkirk** (sĕl'kûrk). Village, W cen. Yukon Territory, Canada, at junction of Lewes and Pelly rivers.

Fort Sher'i·dan (shĕr'ĭ·d'n). Village in Lake co., Illinois, on Lake Michigan 27 m. N of Chicago; U.S. military post; in World War II WAC Training School.

Fort Sher'man (shûr'măn). U.S. fort at Caribbean terminus of Panama Canal, Canal Zone, on W side of entrance to Limon Bay.

Fort Shev·chen'ko (shĭf·chĕn'kŭ); *formerly* **Fort A·le·ksan'drovsk** (ŭ·lyĭ·ksăn'drŭfsk). Russian military station, SW Kazakh S.S.R., Soviet Central Asia, at tip of Mangyshlak Penin. on NE shore of Caspian Sea.

Fort Sill (sĭl). Military post and reservation, Comanche co., SW Oklahoma, ab. 5 m. N of Lawton; estab. 1869; field artillery school; scene of surrender of the Comanches and Kiowa Indians c. 1875.

Fort Simp'son *or* **Simpson** (sĭm[p]'s'n). Trading post, SW Mackenzie District, Northwest Territories, Canada, on Mackenzie river where it is joined by the Liard.

Fort Slo'cum (slō'kŭm). Military station on Davids I. in Long Island Sound, near New Rochelle, New York; formerly a U.S. Air Force base.

Fort Smith (smĭth). **1** City, a ⊗ of Sebastian co., W Arkansas, at confluence of Arkansas and Poteau rivers on Oklahoma border; pop. 52,991; manufacturing and trading center for agricultural and coal and gas region. U.S. Army post 1817–71; incorp. as city 1851.
2 Fort in S Mackenzie District, Northwest Territories, Canada, on Slave river at Alberta boundary; former headquarters of Northwest Territories.

Fort Snel'ling (snĕl'ing). Military post in Minnesota, bet. Minnesota and Mississippi rivers S of Minneapolis; site acquired by Zebulon Pike 1805; fort, called Fort St. Anthony until 1825, built by Josiah Snelling 1820.

Fort Stan'wix (stăn'wĭks). Fort built 1756, rebuilt 1758 on site of Rome, New York, by Gen. John Stanwix; called **Fort Schuy'ler** (skī'lēr) from 1776; treaty with Iroquois Indians signed here 1784.

Fort Stock'ton (stŏk'tŭn). City, ⊗ of Pecos co., W Texas, 73 m. SSW of Odessa; pop. 6373; resort.

Fort Stot'sen·burg (stŏt's'n·bûrg). American camp and army station, NW Pampanga prov., Luzon, Phil. Is., NW of Angeles and 60 m. N of Manila; to the E is Clark Field, U.S. military airport; in 1947 leased to U.S. for period of 99 years.

Fort Sum'ner (sŭm'nēr). Village, ⊗ of De Baca co., E cen. New Mexico, 58 m. W of Clovis; pop. 1809.

Fort Sum'ter (sŭm'tēr). Fort on S side of entrance to Charleston harbor, South Carolina; object of Confederate attack Apr. 12–13, 1861 which began the Civil War; **Fort Sumter National Monument** established 1948: see UNITED STATES, *National Monuments*.

Fort Thom'as (tŏm'ăs). Residential city, Campbell co., N Kentucky, 5 m. SE of Covington; pop. 14,896.

Fort Ticonderoga. See TICONDEROGA.

Fort Tot'ten (tŏt'n). Military post on W end of Long I., New York, on East river near Whitestone; established 1862; School of Submarine Defense.

For·tu'na Bay (fôr·tū'nȧ). Bay S of W end of St. Thomas I., Virgin Is., West Indies.

For'tu·nate Islands (fôr'tụ̄·nĭt); *anc.* **For'tu·na'tae In'su·lae** (fôr'tụ̄·nā'tē ĭn'sụ̄·lē). Literally "Islands of the Blessed"; in early times a name applied to Canary Is.

For'tune (fôr'tụ̄n). Seaport, S Newfoundland, on S shore at mouth of Fortune Bay; pop. 867.

Fortune Bay. Inlet ab. 80 m. long of Atlantic Ocean in S Newfoundland; extensive fishing grounds; scene 1878 of conflict bet. Newfoundland and Gloucester fishermen.

Fortune Island. See LONG CAY.

Fort Un'ion (ūn'yŭn). **1** Trading post, site in NE Montana on Missouri river near mouth of the Yellowstone; built 1828 by Kenneth McKenzie of the American Fur Company and orig. called Fort Floyd; dismantled 1868.
2 Ruined fort, S Mora co., NE New Mexico, N of Watrous; established 1851, became one of most important military posts in SW United States; a Confederate objective (not reached) in Civil War; evacuated 1891.

Fort' Val'ley. City, ⊗ of Peach co., cen. Georgia; pop. 8310; Fort Valley State Coll. (1895; coed.).

Fort Van·cou'ver (văn·koo'vēr). Western terminal of Oregon Trail, now the city of Vancouver, Washington, on Columbia river.

Fort Victoria. See VICTORIA, Southern Rhodesia.

Fort Wads'worth (wŏdz'wûrth; -wērth). Military post on Staten I. at entrance to New York Bay; estab. 1827.

Fort Wag'ner (wăg'nēr). Fort on Morris I. in Charleston harbor, South Carolina; attacked by Union forces July 11 and 18, 1863; captured Sept. 7, 1863.

Fort Wal'ton Beach (wôl't'n; -tŭn). City, Okaloosa co., NW Florida, E of Pensacola; pop. 12,147.

Fort Wash'ing·ton (wŏsh'ing·tŭn). Military post during American Revolution, on upper Manhattan I., New York, on Hudson; captured by British Nov. 16, 1776.

Fort Wayne (wān). City, ⊗ of Allen co., NE Indiana, 105 m. NE of Indianapolis; pop. 161,776; 3d largest city in state; railroad center; manufactures electrical equipment, hosiery, gasoline filling-station equipment, car wheels, motor trucks. Indiana Technical Coll. (1930; men); Saint Francis Coll. (1890; women). Site originally occupied by Miami Indians and visited by La Salle 1670; French fur-trading post 1680; French fort built 1686, seized by British 1760, and lost to Indians under Pontiac; new fort built 1794 by Gen. Anthony Wayne, abandoned 1819; city chartered 1840.

Fort Wel'ling·ton (wĕl'ing·tŭn). Town, NE British Guiana, in Berbice co., 51 m. by rail SE of Georgetown.

Fort Wellington National Historic Park. See CANADA, *National Historic Parks*.

Fort Wil'liam (wĭl'yăm). **1** Industrial city, Thunder Bay dist., SW Ontario, Canada, on NW shore of Lake Superior only 3 m. from Port Arthur (the two being known as the "Twin Cities"); pop. 34,947; on both Canadian trunk railroad lines; one of most important transshipment ports on Great Lakes; huge grain elevators and large coal depot. A French trading post in 17th cent., later abandoned; 1801 became port for Hudson's Bay Company, the fort then built being still in existence.
2 Town, Inverness co., NW Scotland, on Loch Linnhe; pop. 2527; tourist center.

Fort Wood (wŏod). The Statue of Liberty National Monument on Bedloe's I., New York harbor, New York.

Fort Worth (wûrth). City, ⊗ of Tarrant co., N Texas, on Trinity river ab. 33 m. W of Dallas; pop. 356,268; commercial and transportation center of stock-raising, agricultural, and oil-producing area; manufactures flour, feed, oil-field equipment, metal products, airplanes, clothing; Carswell Air Force Base. Texas Christian Univ. (1873; coed.); Texas Wesleyan Coll. (1890; coed.); Southwestern Baptist Theological Seminary (1910; coed.). Settled around military post founded 1849.

Fort Yates (yāts). Township, Sioux county, extreme S

North Dakota, on Missouri river 50 m. S of Bismarck; pop. 1100 (white and Indian); Indian Agency headquarters for North and South Dakota.

For′ty Fort (fôr′tĭ). Residential borough, Luzerne co., E Pennsylvania, on Susquehanna river 3 m. N of Wilkes-Barre; pop. 6431. See WYOMING VALLEY.

For′ty·mile′ (fôr′tĭ-mīl′). Trading station, W Yukon Territory, Canada, ab. 40 m. WNW of Dawson on Yukon river where it receives **Fortymile River** (ab. 120 m. long, rises in Alaska).

Fort Yu′kon (yōō′kŏn). Village and old trading station, E A′aska, at junction of Porcupine river with the Yukon; pop. (1950) 446.

Fort Zea·lan′di·a (zē-lăn′dĭ-à). Fort built by the Dutch near Tainan on SW coast of Formosa; besieged and captured by Koxinga 1662.

Forum Alieni. See FERRARA commune.

Forum Julii. 1 Commune, SE France. See FRÉJUS. 2 Former duchy, NE Italy. See FRIULI. 3 Commune, NE Italy. See CIVIDALE DEL FRIULI

Forum Livii. See FORLÌ.

Fossa Claudia. See CHIOGGIA.

Fos·sa′no (fôs-sä′nō). Commune, Cuneo prov., Piedmont, NW Italy, on Stura river 13 m. NE of Cuneo; pop. 19,627; episcopal see; mineral baths.

Fosse, or **Foss, Way** (fŏs). Ancient Roman road in Britain; extended from Lincoln in E cen. part to Exeter in SW, passing through Leicester and Bath and intersecting Watling Street in S cen. Britain.

Fos′sil (fŏs′'l). Town, ⊗ of Wheeler co., N cen. Oregon, ab. 17 m. N of Condon; pop. 672.

Fossil Mountain. Peak 10,912 ft. in Teton Range, W Teton co., NW Wyoming.

Fos·som·bro′ne (fôs·sôm·brō′nâ). Commune, Pesaro e Urbino prov., Marches, cen. Italy, near Metauro river 16 m. S by E of Pesaro; pop. 10,650; episcopal see.

Fos·tat′ (fŏos-tät′). Anglicized form of al-Fustât: see CAIRO city, Egypt.

Fos′ter (fŏs′tẽr). County in North Dakota. See Table at NORTH DAKOTA.

Fos·to′ri·a (fŏs-tōr′ĭ-à). 1 Manufacturing city, Hancock and Seneca cos., NW Ohio, 15 m. NE of Findlay; pop. 15,732; stockyards, stone quarries; Fostoria glass first made here 1887 (company moved soon after its founding to Moundsville, West Virginia). 2 Town, Montgomery co., E Texas, ab. 38 m. NNE of Houston; pop. (est.) 666.

Foth′er·in·ghay′ (fŏth′ẽr·ĭng·gā′; fŏth′rĭng-). Village, Northamptonshire, England; castle where Mary, Queen of Scots was imprisoned Sept. 1586 to her execution Feb. 8, 1587.

Fou·gères′ (fōō′zhâr′). Manufacturing city, Ille-et-Vilaine dept., NW France, 29 m. NE of Rennes; pop. 40,432; granite quarries; one of chief centers of the Chouans during the Revolution.

Fou·ge·rolles′ (fōōzh′rôl′). Town, Haute-Saône dept., E France, SW of Remiremont; pop. 1654; manufactures kirsch.

Fou′la (fōō′lä). One of Shetland Is., NE of N Scotland; Old Norse language survived here until the early 19th cent.

Foul Bay (foul). Inlet of Red Sea on E coast of Egypt, at Tropic of Cancer.

Foul′ness′ Point (foul′nĕs′). Cape on **Foulness Island**, Essex, SE coast of England, N of entrance to the Thames estuary.

Foul′wind′, Cape (foul′wĭnd′). Cape on NW coast of South I., New Zealand, forming S side of Karamea Bight.

Foum Ta·ta′houine (fōōm tŏ·tä′wĭn). Town, SE Tunisia, N Africa, S of S end of Mareth Line (q.v.).

Foun′tain (foun′t'n). County in Indiana. See Table at INDIANA.

Fountain City. Urban community (unincorp.), Knox co., E Tennessee, 6 m. N of Knoxville; pop. 10,365.

Fountain Hill. Borough, Lehigh co., E Pennsylvania, on Lehigh river 4 m. E of Allentown; pop. 5428.

Four Corners. Locality in SW United States, the point of intersection of 37°N with 109°W, the only place in U.S. where boundaries of four states—Colorado, New Mexico, Arizona, and Utah—come together.

Four Forest Cantons, Lake of the. See Lake of LUCERNE.

Four Forest Cantons, the. See the Four FOREST CANTONS.

Four Lakes. Chain of 4 connected lakes in Dane co., S Wisconsin, named Mendota (or Fourth Lake), Monona (or Third Lake), Waubesa (or Second Lake), and Kegonsa (or First Lake).

Four League Bay (lēg). Inlet of Gulf of Mexico on W coast of Terrebonne parish, SE Louisiana.

Four′mies′ (fōōr′mē′). Commune, Nord dept., N France, SE of Lille; pop. 13,787; manufacturing of glass, textiles, shoes.

Four Mountains, Islands of the. See ISLANDS OF THE FOUR MOUNTAINS.

Four Peaks. Mountain 7645 ft. in NE Maricopa co., S cen. Arizona.

Fou′ta′ Djal′lon′ (fōō′tä′ jà′lôn′), also **Fu′ta′ Jal′-lon′.** Mountainous district, W Guinea, West Africa, highest point Tamgué ab. 4200 ft.; source of many streams, esp. the Niger and Senegal; inhabitants chiefly Fulahs; chief towns Labé and Timbo.

Foux, Cap à (kȧp′ à fōō′). Cape at NW tip of Hispaniola, on SE side of Windward Passage.

Fo′veaux′ Strait′ (fō′vō′). Channel 18 to 20 m. wide bet. South I. and Stewart I., New Zealand.

Fowchow. See FOWLING.

Fow′ey (foi; fō′ĭ). Seaport village, Cornwall, SW England, on S coast W of Plymouth; pop. 2344; U.S. naval training base in World War II.

Fowl′er (foul′ẽr). 1 Town, Fresno co., S cen. California, 10 m. SE of Fresno; pop. 1892; fruit drying and packing. 2 Town, ⊗ of Benton co., W Indiana, 25 m. NW of Lafayette; pop. 2491.

Fow′liang′ (fōō′lĕ·äng′; fō′-); formerly **King′teh′chen′** (jing′dŭ′jŭn′). Town, NE Kiangsi prov., SE China, near Anhwei border, E of Poyang Hu and ab. 75 m. SE of Kiukiang; pop. over 100,000; famous porcelain industry, established in Ch′ên dynasty (557–589 A.D.), became famous under the Sungs.

Fow′ling′ (fō′lĭng′) or **Fow′chow′** (fō′jō′). Town, SE Szechwan, S cen. China, on S bank of Yangtze where it is joined by the Wu, ab. 50 m. E of Chungking.

Fox (fŏks). 1 River ab. 220 m. long in SE Wisconsin and NE Illinois; flows S to the Illinois river at Ottawa in La Salle co., N Illinois. 2 River ab. 175 m. long, SE cen. Wisconsin; rises in N Columbia co., flows SW to a point ab. 1½ m. from Wisconsin river with which it is connected by canal (see PORTAGE, Wis.), then N and NE into Lake Winnebago and out of N end of lake into Green Bay at city of Green Bay.

Fox Basin. See FOXE BASIN.

Fox′bor′o (fŏks′bûr′ô). Town, Norfolk co., E Massachusetts, 11 m. W of Brockton; pop. 10,136; manufactures time recording and controlling devices.

Fox Channel = FOXE CHANNEL.

Foxe Basin (fŏks), formerly **Fox Basin.** Large body of water bet. Melville Penin. and W Baffin I., E Franklin District, Northwest Territories, Canada; connects with N end of Hudson Bay by **Foxe Channel** (ab. 110 m. wide), bet. Southampton I. and **Foxe Peninsula,** SW part of Baffin I.

Fox Islands. 1 Two islands, **North Fox Island** and **South Fox Island,** in N Lake Michigan, forming part of Leelanau co., NW Michigan. 2 Island group off SW tip of Alaska Penin., E Aleutian Is.; includes Unimak, Akutan, Unalaska, and Umnak Is.; chief settlements Unalaska and Dutch Harbor (q.v.).

Fox Peninsula. = FOXE PENINSULA.

Foyle (foil). River ab. 20 m. long in N Ireland; formed by confluence of Finn and Mourne rivers on border bet. Eire and Northern Ireland; flows N past Londonderry and expands into the estuary **Lough Foyle** (lŏk), 18 m. long, on boundary bet. co. Derry, Northern Ireland, and co. Donegal, Eire.

Foynes (foinz). Town, NW coast of co. Limerick, SW Eire, on S shore of Shannon estuary 22 m. W of Limerick; pop. 497; former airfield, now largely superseded for transatlantic flights by Shannon airfield at Rineanna.

Frack'ville (frăk'vil). Borough, Schuylkill co., E cen. Pennsylvania, 7 m. N of Pottsville; pop. 5654.

Fra·go'so Cay (frä·gō'sō). Island off NE coast of Las Villas prov., W cen. Cuba.

Fraile, El. See EL FRAILE.

Fra·me·ries' (fràm'rē'). Commune, Hainaut prov., SW Belgium, ab. 5 m. SSW of Mons; pop. 13,301.

Fram'heim' (främ'hām'). = LITTLE AMERICA.

Fra'ming·ham (frā'mǐng·hăm). Manufacturing town, Middlesex co., NE Massachusetts, 18 m. WSW of Boston; pop. 44,526; Massachusetts State College (1839; women); Cushing General Hospital.

Fran'ca (frăɴɴg'kȧ). City, NE São Paulo state, SE Brazil, on railroad 160 m. N of Campinas; pop. (1940 est.) 21,022.

Fran'çaise', Pointe (pwăɴt' frä̀ɴ'sâz'). Cape extending into Atlantic Ocean from NW tip of French Guiana.

Fran'ca·vil'la Fon·ta'na (fräng'kä·vēl'lä fôn·tä'nä). Commune, Brindisi prov., Apulia, SE Italy, 20 m. WSW of Brindisi; pop. 22,140; cathedral; imperial palace.

France (frȧns); *earlier* **Gaul** (gôl), *Fr.* **Gaule** (gōl), *Lat.* **Gal'li·a** (gǎl'ǐ·ȧ): see GAUL. Country of W cen. Europe; 212,655 sq. m.; pop. 41,907,056; ✻ Paris; bounded on N by English Channel, on NE by Belgium, on E by Germany, Switzerland, and Italy, on S by the Mediterranean Sea and Spain, and on W by Bay of Biscay; geographically includes the independent republic of Andorra (in the Pyrenees) and the principality of Monaco (on the Riviera). Divided into the following 90 departments (for pronunciation of their names, see their individual entries); since Jan. 1, 1947 former colonies of Martinique, Guadeloupe, Réunion, and French Guiana (Guyane) have been established as overseas departments:

DEPART-MENT	LOCA-TION	AREA[1]	POP.[1]	CAPITAL
Ain	E	2,248	316,710	Bourg
Aisne	N	2,866	484,647	Laon
Allier	cen.	2,848	368,778	Moulins
Alpes-Maritimes	SE	1,443	513,714	Nice
Ardèche	SE	2,144	272,698	Privas
Ardennes	NE	2,027	288,632	Mézières
Ariège	S	1,892	155,134	Foix
Aube	NE	2,326	239,563	Troyes
Aude	S	2,448	285,115	Carcassonne
Aveyron	S	3,385	314,682	Rodez
Bas-Rhin	NE	1,848	711,830	Strasbourg
Basses-Alpes	SE	2,697	85,090	Digne
Basses-Pyrénées	SW	2,977	413,411	Pau
Belfort, Terri-toire de	E	235	99,497	Belfort
Bouches-du-Rhône	SE	2,025	1,224,802	Marseilles
Calvados	NW	2,197	404,901	Caen
Cantal	S cen.	2,229	190,888	Aurillac
Charente	W	2,305	309,279	Angoulême
Charente-Maritime[2]	W	2,791	419,021	La Rochelle
Cher	cen.	2,819	288,695	Bourges
Corrèze	S cen.	2,272	262,770	Tulle
Corse[3]		3,367	322,854	Ajaccio
Côte-d'Or	E	3,391	334,386	Dijon
Côtes-du-Nord	NW	2,786	531,840	Saint-Brieuc
Creuse	cen.	2,163	201,844	Guéret
Deux-Sèvres	W	2,337	308,841	Niort
Dordogne	SW cen.	3,550	386,963	Périgueux
Doubs	E	2,052	304,812	Besançon
Drôme	SE	2,532	267,281	Valence
Eure	N	2,330	303,829	Évreux
Eure-et-Loir	N cen.	2,291	252,690	Chartres
Finistère	NW	2,729	756,793	Quimper
Gard	S	2,270	395,299	Nîmes
Gers	SW	2,428	192,451	Auch

DEPART-MENT	LOCA-TION	AREA[1]	POP.[1]	CAPITAL
Gironde	SW	4,140	850,567	Bordeaux
Haute-Garonne	S	2,457	458,647	Toulouse
Haute-Loire	S cen.	1,930	245,271	Le Puy
Haute-Marne	NE	2,420	188,471	Chaumont
Hautes-Alpes	SE	2,178	88,210	Gap
Haute-Saône	E	2,074	212,829	Vesoul
Haute-Savoie	E	1,774	259,961	Annecy
Hautes-Pyrénées	SW	1,750	188,604	Tarbes
Haute-Vienne	W cen.	2,119	333,589	Limoges
Haut-Rhin	NE	1,354	507,551	Colmar
Hérault	S	2,402	502,043	Montpellier
Ille-et-Vilaine	NW	2,697	565,766	Rennes
Indre	cen.	2,664	245,622	Châteauroux
Indre-et-Loire	NW cen.	2,377	343,276	Tours
Isère	SE	3,178	572,742	Grenoble
Jura	E	1,951	220,797	Lons-le-Saunier
Landes	SW	3,604	251,436	Mont-de-Marsan
Loire	SE cen.	1,852	650,226	Saint-Étienne
Loire-Atlantique[4]	NW	2,693	659,428	Nantes
Loiret	N cen.	2,629	343,865	Orléans
Loir-et-Cher	N cen.	2,478	240,908	Blois
Lot	S cen.	2,017	162,572	Cahors
Lot-et-Garonne	SW	2,078	252,761	Agen
Lozère	S	1,996	98,480	Mende
Maine-et-Loire	W	2,811	477,690	Angers
Manche	NW	2,475	438,539	Saint-Lô
Marne	NE	3,167	410,238	Châlons-sur-Marne
Mayenne	NW	1,986	251,348	Laval
Meurthe-et-Moselle	NE	2,036	576,041	Nancy
Meuse	NE	2,408	216,934	Bar-le-Duc
Morbihan	NW	2,738	542,248	Vannes
Moselle	NE	2,403	696,246	Metz
Nièvre	cen.	2,658	249,673	Nevers
Nord	N	2,228	2,022,167	Lille
Oise	N	2,272	402,569	Beauvais
Orne	NW	2,371	269,331	Alençon
Pas-de-Calais	N	2,606	1,179,467	Arras
Puy-de-Dôme	S cen.	3,090	486,103	Clermont-Ferrand
Pyrénées-Orientales	S	1,598	233,347	Perpignan
Rhône	E cen.	1,104	1,028,379	Lyons
Saône-et-Loire	E cen.	3,330	525,676	Mâcon
Sarthe	NW	2,410	388,519	Le Mans
Savoie	E	2,388	239,010	Chambéry
Seine[5]	N	185	4,962,967	Paris
Seine-Maritime[6]	N	2,448	915,628	Rouen
Seine-et-Marne	N	2,275	409,311	Melun
Seine-et-Oise	N	2,184	1,413,472	Versailles
Somme	N	2,443	467,479	Amiens
Tarn	S	2,231	297,871	Albi
Tarn-et-Garonne	S	1,440	164,629	Montauban
Var	SE	2,333	398,662	Draguignan
Vaucluse	SE	1,381	245,508	Avignon
Vendée	W	2,690	389,211	La Roche-sur-Yon
Vienne	W cen.	2,711	306,820	Poitiers
Vosges	NE	2,303	376,926	Épinal
Yonne	NE cen.	2,892	271,685	Auxerre

[1] Area in sq. m. Pop. from 1936 Census.
[2] Formerly called Charente-Inférieure.
[3] Constitutes island of Corsica.
[4] Formerly called Loire-Inférieure.
[5] Enclave in Seine-et-Oise dept.
[6] Formerly called Seine-Inférieure.

Chief mountains: Alps (*q.v.*) on SE (Italian border), Pyrenees on S (Spanish border), Jura Mts. on E (Swiss border), Vosges in NE, Massif Central and Auvergne Mts. in SE cen. part; highest point Mont Blanc 15,781 ft., in the Alps. *Chief rivers:* Seine, with its tributaries the Yonne, Marne, and Oise, flowing into English Channel; Loire, Garonne, and Adour, flowing into Bay of Biscay; Rhone, with its chief tributary the Saône, flowing S into Mediterranean Sea. *Islands:* Ushant (Île d'Ouessant) off tip of Brittany; Belle-Île, Noirmoutier, Yeu, Ré, and Oléron in Bay of Biscay; Hyères Is. in Mediterranean Sea; Channel Is. in English Channel belong to Great Britain. *Chief products:* Mostly agricultural, country almost self-sustaining; produces grains, wines, fruits; has coal and iron; fishing; manufactures esp. silk goods. *Chief cities:* Paris, Marseilles, Lyons, Bordeaux, Nice, Toulouse, Lille.

History: S part (Gallia Narbonensis) Roman province from 121 B.C.; N and cen. part conquered by Julius Caesar 58–51 B.C.; almost all came under kingdom established 481 A.D. by Salian Franks under Clovis (Mero-

FRANCE

Statute Miles

0 20 40 60 80 100

⊛ Capitals

PUBLISHED BY G. & C. MERRIAM COMPANY
SPRINGFIELD, MASS.
PREPARED BY J. W. CLEMENT CO., BUFFALO, N.Y.

2 Longitude East from Greenwich 4

CORSICA (CORSE)
Same Scale as Main Map

vingians); as Frankish empire under Charlemagne (768–814) included much of Saxon lands to E, but after his death new conquests given up by Partition of Verdun 843. During medieval feudal period, in which central authority was merely nominal, divided into domains (Normandy, Aquitaine, Burgundy, Flanders, etc.); after Norman Conquest 1066 lost duchy of Normandy to king of England and later also lost (to English Angevin kings, 1154–1399) Maine, Brittany, and most of Aquitaine; in course of Hundred Years' War (1337–1453) regained all of these lands except Calais (regained 1558); at end of Thirty Years' War (Treaty of Westphalia 1648) territory did not include Netherlands and Franche-Comté (both Spanish), Lorraine or Savoy; power decreased by Treaty of Paris ending Seven Years' War 1763. Royal government overthrown by French Revolution 1789, country becoming in turn a republic (First Republic 1792–99), the Consulate (1799–1804), an empire (First Empire 1804–15); during period of Napoleonic Wars (1796–1815), acquired by conquest most of W and cen. Europe, but lost all after final defeat of Napoleon at Waterloo 1815. Again became monarchy under Bourbons, but monarchy overthrown by revolution of 1848 and succeeded in turn by Second Republic (1848–52), Second Empire (1852–70), and Third Republic, established 1870, a result of French defeat in Franco-Prussian War (1870–71); N part of country ravaged by fighting in World War I (1914–18). In World War II conquered and controlled 1940–44 by Germans who divided it into "occupied" (N and W) and "unoccupied" (S) zones, the latter nominally under a French government with capital at Vichy, repudiated by the Fighting French (called Free French prior to July 14, 1942) under Charles de Gaulle, head of the French National Committee, which actively continued resistance to Axis forces and assumed authority over liberated French territories; country invaded by Allies (in Normandy June 6, 1944, on Mediterranean coast Aug. 15, 1944) and completely liberated by Sept. 1944; under provisional government until establishment of Fourth Republic 1945; Fifth Republic established under the constitution of Oct. 4, 1958 (see FRENCH COMMUNITY, FRENCH UNION).

Fran·cés', Cape (frän·sās'). Cape on SW coast of Pinar del Río prov., W Cuba, S of Cortés Bay.

Francés, Point. Cape on SW coast of Isle of Pines, Caribbean Sea; encloses Siguanea Bay.

Fran·cés' Vie'jo, Cape (frän·sās' vyĕ'hŏ). Cape, N coast of Hispaniola I., in Dominican Republic.

France'ville (fräns'vĭl; *Fr.* fräNs'vēl'). Town, SE Congo Republic, in former French Equatorial Africa on a tributary of the Ogooué river ab. 200 m. NW of Brazzaville.

Franche–Com'té' (fräNsh'kôN'tā'). Historical region of E cen. France; bounded anciently on N by Lorraine, E by Swiss Confederation, W by duchy of Burgundy and S by Savoy; ✳ Besançon; included in original kingdom of Burgundy founded 5th cent. A.D.; later became county of Burgundy as distinct from duchy of Burgundy; part of kingdom of Arles; belonged to Holy Roman Empire from 12th cent.; brought under control of duchy of Burgundy by Philip the Bold 1384; passed to Spanish Hapsburgs by marriage; occupied 1667 and 1674 by Louis XIV of France to whom Spain finally ceded it 1678; a province of France until the Revolution.

Franchise. See ARRAS.

Fran'ci·a. 1 (frän'shĭ·à) The kingdom of the Franks (Austrasia, Neustria, and Aquitaine), from c. 481 to 768. 2 (frän'shĭ·à) Duchy of N cen. France, c. 1000; chief towns Paris, Orléans, and Tours. 3 (*Ital.* frän'chä; *Span.* frän'thyä, -syä) Italian and Spanish for FRANCE.

Franciade. See SAINT-DENIS commune, France.

Fran'cis, Cape (frän'sĭs); *also* **Cape Saint Francis.** Cape, SE Newfoundland, E of entrance to Conception Bay N of St. John's.

Fran·cis'co Mo'ra·zán' (frän·sēs'kŏ mō'rä·sän'); *formerly* **Te·gu'ci·gal'pa** (tĕ·gōō'sĭ·gäl'på; *Span.* tä·gōō'sĕ·gäl'pä). Department, S cen. Honduras; 3870 sq. m.; pop. (1945 est.) 174,224; ✳ Tegucigalpa.

Fran'cis·town (frän'sĭs·toun). Chief town of N Bechuanaland Protectorate, S Africa, near Southern Rhodesia border 110 m. SW of Bulawayo.

Fran'co·fon'te (fräng'kŏ·fôn'tā). Commune, Siracusa prov., Sicily, 21 m. WNW of Syracuse; pop. 12,089.

Fran·co'ni·a (fräng·kō'nĭ·à; -kōn'yà). 1 Resort village, Grafton co. W New Hampshire, in Franconia Mts. ab. 5 m. S of Littleton.

2 *Ger.* **Fran'ken** (fräng'kĕn). Old duchy of S cen. Germany, now included chiefly in Bavaria, Baden-Württemberg, and Hesse states; chief cities Frankfurt am Main, Würzburg, Speyer, Worms, Bayreuth, Ansbach, Nürnberg. A medieval Frankish duchy, part of Austrasia (*q.v.*) and, after 843 A.D. (see FRANCE), of German part of former Carolingian empire; its dukes, of whom Conrad was raised to German throne, founded Franconian (or Salian) line of German emperors 1024–1137 and their descendants, the Hohenstaufen emperors 1138–1254; divided into Rhenish (west) and East Franconia, the latter alone retaining name of Franconia after 12th cent.; Franconian circle of empire formed 1512; name abolished 1806 but revived 1837 by kingdom of Bavaria in its subdivisions (government districts) of Upper, Middle, and Lower Franconia (see *Table* at BAVARIA).

Franconia Mountains. Western range of White Mts., in Grafton co., W New Hampshire; highest peak Mount Lafayette 5249 ft., on E side of **Franconia Notch** through which Pemigewasset river flows and which is flanked on W by Cannon Mt. (*q.v.*).

Fra'ne·ker (frä'nĕ·kēr). Commune, Friesland prov., N Netherlands; pop. 8103; university (1585–1811) suppressed by Napoleon I.

Franken. See FRANCONIA.

Fran'ken·berg (fräng'kĕn·bûrg; *Ger.* fräng'kĕn·bĕrk); *also* **Fran'ken·berg in Sach'sen** (fräng'kĕn·bĕrк ĭn zäk'sĕn). Industrial city, Saxony, Germany, 10 m. NE of Chemnitz; pop. 13,646.

Frankenstein, Frankenstein in Schlesien. See ZĄBKOWICE.

Fran'ken·thal (fräng'kĕn·täl). Manufacturing city, Rhineland-Palatinate state, W Germany, 28 m. SSW of Darmstadt; pop. 24,647; railroad junction. First mentioned 8th cent.; destroyed by French 1688–89 and later rebuilt; under French rule 1796–1816.

Frank'ford (frăngk'fērd). District, E Philadelphia city, Pennsylvania; U.S. government arsenal.

Frank'fort (frăngk'fērt). 1 City, ⊗ of Clinton co., cen. Indiana, 20 m. WSW of Kokomo; pop. 15,302.

2 City, ✳ of Kentucky and ⊗ of Franklin co., N cen. Ky., on Kentucky river 28 m. E of Louisville; pop. 18,365; became capital when state admitted to Union 1792. Kentucky State College (1886; coed.).

3 City, Benzie co., NW Michigan, on Lake Michigan at mouth of Betsie river 28 m. N of Manistee; pop. 1690; fishing center.

4 Industrial village, Herkimer co., NE cen. New York, 10 m. ESE of Utica; pop. 3872; forms single community with Mohawk, Ilion, and Herkimer; settled 1723.

5 Anglicized form of FRANKFURT, as in **Frankfort on the Main** and **Frankfort on the Oder.**

Frank'furt (frăngk'fērt; *Ger.* frängk'fŏŏrt). 1 Government district, E Brandenburg, eastern Germany; 7413 sq. m.; part E of the Oder to Poland 1945.

2 *in full* **Frank'furt am Main** (frängk'fŏŏrt äm mīn'); *Eng.* **Frank'fort on the Main** (frăngk'fērt). Manufacturing and commercial city, Hesse, Germany, on Main river 17 m. N of Darmstadt; pop. 647,623; notable buildings include Römer (old town hall), Saalhof and Taxis imperial palaces, cathedral, the museum, and academy of art. On site of Roman military establishment; important center under Caro-

lingian empire; free imperial city 1245 ff.; scene of coronation of most emperors 1152–1806; after French occupation, restored to autonomy 1815; seat of Frankfurt Parliament 1848–49; a partisan of Austria, it was occupied by Prussia 1866; scene of final peace of Franco-Prussian War 1871. In 20th cent. became important industrially; several times bombed in World War I and occupied for brief time by French troops 1920; in World War II specialized in manufacture of aircraft, motor vehicles, chemicals; frequently bombed by Allies and greatly damaged; occupied Mar. 30, 1945, became headquarters of American occupation forces and in 1948 of Bizonia. Birthplace of Goethe and of Meyer Amschel Rothschild.

3 *in full* **Frank′furt an der O′der** (frängk′fŏŏrt än dĕr ō′dĕr); *Eng.* **Frank′fort on the O′der** (frängk′fẽrt, ō′dĕr). Manufacturing city, * of Frankfurt govt. dist., Brandenburg, eastern Germany, on the Oder river 50 m. ESE of Berlin; pop. 70,884; university (founded here 1506) removed to Breslau 1811; Austrian and Russian victory over Frederick the Great nearby 1759; in World War II center of severe fighting in Russian advance on Berlin, taken Apr. 24, 1945. See Słubice.

Fränkische Saale. See Fränkische Saale.

Frank′lin (frängk′lĭn). **1** Name of a parish in Louisiana and of counties in twenty-four states of the U.S. See *Tables* at Louisiana, Alabama, Arkansas, Florida, Georgia, Idaho, Illinois, Indiana, Iowa, Kansas, Kentucky, Maine, Massachusetts, Mississippi, Missouri, Nebraska, New York, North Carolina, Ohio, Pennsylvania, Tennessee, Texas, Vermont, Virginia, Washington.

2 City, ⊗ of Heard co., W Georgia; pop. 603.
3 City, ⊗ of Johnson co., cen. Indiana, 20 m. S of Indianapolis; pop. 9453; Franklin College of Indiana (1834; coed. from 1842; Baptist).
4 City, ⊗ of Simpson co., S Kentucky, 21 m. S of Bowling Green; pop. 5319; tobacco market.
5 Town, ⊗ of St. Mary parish, S Louisiana; pop. 8673.
6 Town, Norfolk co., E Massachusetts, 19 m. W of Brockton; pop. 10,530; textile mills.
7 City, ⊗ of Franklin co., S Nebraska; pop. 1194.
8 Industrial city, Merrimack co., S cen. New Hampshire, on Merrimack river (*q.v.*) 10 m. SW of Laconia; pop. 6742; settled as part of Salisbury 1764 on site of former Abnaki Indian village; incorp. 1895.
9 Borough, Sussex co., N corner of New Jersey, 10 m. ENE of Newton; pop. 3624; as source of important zinc ores franklinite and willemite, the eastern U.S. center of zinc-mining industry.
10 Town, ⊗ of Macon co., SW North Carolina, on Little Tennessee river 55 m. WSW of Asheville; pop. 2173.
11 Manufacturing city, Warren co., SW Ohio, on Miami river 15 m. S of Dayton; pop. 7917.
12 Borough, Cambria co., SW cen. Pennsylvania, 2 m. NE of Johnstown; pop. 1352.
13 City, ⊗ of Venango co., NW Pennsylvania, 8 m. WSW of Oil City; pop. 9586; founded 1795; manufactures petroleum, oil well equipment, railroad supplies.
14 Town, ⊗ of Williamson co., cen. Tennessee, 19 m. S of Nashville; pop. 6977; scene of two battles in Civil War: (1) in Apr. 1863; (2) Nov. 30, 1864, important battle in which Union forces under Gen. Schofield defeated Confederates under Gen. Hood.
15 Town, ⊗ of Robertson co., E cen. Texas; pop. 1065.
16 Town, Southampton co., SE Virginia, on Blackwater river 21 m. W of Suffolk; pop. 7264; lumber, paper.
17 Town, ⊗ of Pendleton co., E West Virginia; pop. 758.
18 City, Milwaukee co., SE Wisconsin, SSW suburb of Milwaukee; pop. 10,000.
19 District, N Northwest Territories, Canada; area including water 549,253 sq. m.; includes Baffin I., all other Arctic islands and Boothia and Melville Penins.; pop. comprises only a few Eskimos; administered from Ottawa. Formed 1895, boundaries defined 1918.

Franklin, Mount. 1 Peak 5028 ft. of White Mts., in S Coos co., N New Hampshire, SSW of Mt. Washington.
2 Peak 7674 ft. in N South I., New Zealand.

Franklin, State of. A temporary state organized 1784 in W lands of North Carolina (now part of E Tennessee) which she had ceded to the United States (act of cession repealed 1785); first legislative sessions at Jonesboro; capital established at Greeneville 1785; last legislative session 1787; ceased to exist Feb. 1788.

Franklin Bay. Inlet of Amundsen Gulf, coast of Northwest Territories, Canada.

Franklin D. Roo′se·velt Lake (dē′ rō′zĕ·vĕlt; -vĕlt). Lake 151 m. long, cen. Washington; formed in Columbia river by Grand Coulee Dam, N end near Canada border; named Apr. 18, 1945.

Franklin Falls Dam (fôlz). Dam completed 1942 across Pemigewasset river near Franklin, S cen. New Hampshire; height 130 ft.; impounds water for flood control.

Franklin Lake. Shallow lake in S Elko co., NE Nevada; slightly brackish; no outlet.

Franklin Mountains. Range in W cen. Mackenzie District, Northwest Territories, Canada, W of Great Bear Lake; highest Mt. Clark 4733 ft.

Franklin Park. Village, Cook co., NE Illinois, suburb of Chicago; pop. 18,322.

Franklin Roosevelt Islands. = Roosevelt Island, Antarctica, formerly believed to be an island group.

Franklin Square. Urban community, Nassau co., New York, in SE Long I. W of Hempstead; pop. 32,483.

Franklin Strait. Channel bet. SE Prince of Wales I. and Boothia Penin., S Franklin District, Northwest Territories, Canada.

Frank′lin·ton (frängk′lĭn·tŭn). **1** Town, ⊗ of Washington parish, E Louisiana, N of New Orleans; pop. 3141.
2 See Columbus, Ohio.

Franklin Tunnel. Railroad tunnel 5600 ft. long ab. 30 m. E of San Francisco, California.

Frank′lin·ville (frängk′lĭn·vĭl). Village, Cattaraugus co., SW New York, 16 m. N of Olean; pop. 2124.

Franks Peak (frängks). Highest peak 13,140 ft. in the Absaroka Mts., at S end in S Park co., NW Wyoming.

Fran′tiš·ko′vy Láz′ně (frän′tyĭsh·kô′vĭ läz′nyĕ); *Ger.* **Fran′zens·bad′** (frän′tsĕns·bät′). Village, NW Bohemia, Czechoslovakia; mineral baths and springs.

Franz Jo′sef Fjord (tränts jō′zĕf [-zĭf] fyôrd; *Ger.* fränts yō′zĕf fyôrt); *also* **Kej′ser Franz Jo′sephs Fjord** (kī′sēr fränts yō′sĕfs fyôr). Inlet of Greenland Sea, NE coast of Greenland, ab. 73°15′N; 125 m. long.

Franz Jo′sef Land (fränts jō′zĕf [-zĭf] länd; *Ger.* fränts yō′zĕf länt); *Russ.* **Zem·lya′ Fran′tsa Io′si·fa** (zyĭm·lyȧ′ frän′tsȧ yō′syĭ·fȧ). *Also* **Fridt′jof Nan′sen Land** (frĭt′yôf nän′sĕn länd). Archipelago in Arctic Ocean, 80° to 82°N, 43° to 65°E, N of Novaya Zemlya, a part of Arkhangelsk Region, Soviet Russia, Europe; ab. 8000 sq. m.; consists of ab. 70 islands, largest: Aleksandra Land, George Land, Wilczek Land, and Graham Bell I.; most northerly land of Eastern Hemisphere; covered with ice. Discovered 1873 by Austrian expedition of Payer and Weyprecht; visited by several explorers since 1881, esp. by F. G. Jackson and Fridtjof Nansen 1896, Walter Wellman 1898, and the duke of the Abruzzi 1899; after Revolution 1917 explored by Russians, who claimed and renamed it 1928; has world's most northern meteorological station (estab. 1929 by U.S.S.R.). See Arctic Regions.

Franz Jo′sef–Spit′ze (fränts yō′zĕf shpĭt′sĕ). = Gerlsdorfer Spitze.

Fra·sca′ti (fräs·kä′tĕ). Commune, Roma prov., Latium, cen. Italy, on NW side of Alban Hills 11 m. SE of Rome; pop. 11,763; cathedral; summer resort; ancient Roman ruins, including villa of Cicero; near ruins of ancient Tusculum.

Fra′ser (frā′zēr; -zhēr). **1** River ab. 700 m. long, S cen. British Columbia, Canada; rises in Rocky Mts. near

Yellowhead Pass, flows NW bet. Rocky and Cariboo ranges, then in sharp turn S around N end of Cariboo Mts. nearly to U.S. border and finally W, breaking through Coast Mts. in long canyon, to empty into Strait of Georgia just S of Vancouver; navigable for ab. 90 m.; chief tributaries the Nechako, Chilcotin, Thompson, Blackwater, and Lillooet. Discovered by Alexander Mackenzie 1793, explored by Simon Fraser 1808.

2 Town, Grand co., N Colorado, NNW of Berthoud Pass; alt. 8568 ft.; often called "the Nation's icebox"; pop. 253.

3 City, Macomb co., SE Michigan, NE suburb of Detroit; pop. 7027.

Fra·ser·burgh (frā′zēr·bûr′ȯ; frā′zhēr-; *Brit. also* -bŭ·rŭ, -brŭ). Seaport burgh, Aberdeen co., NE Scotland, near Kinnairds Head on NE coast 57°40′N, 2°W; pop. 10,444; herring fisheries.

Fraser, *or* **Great Sandy, Island**. Island off SE coast of Queensland, Australia; 70 m. long; 66 sq. m.

Frat. See EUPHRATES.

Frat′ta·mag·gio′re (frät′tä·mäd·jō′rȧ). Commune, Napoli prov., Campania, S Italy, 7 m. N by E of Naples; pop. 19,168; resort.

Frau′en·burg (frou′ĕn·bo͞orκ); *Pol.* **From′bork** (frôm′-bôrk). Town, in former East Prussia, now in NW Mazury dept., N Poland, on the Frisches Haff ab. 40 m. E of Gdańsk; pop. 2288; seat of bishops of Ermeland; monument to Copernicus who was canon of cathedral here.

Frau′en·feld (frou′ĕn·fĕlt). Commune, ✳ of Thurgau canton, NE Switzerland, 21 m. NE of Zurich; pop. (1930) 8795; old castle; armory; manufactures machinery, beer. Became city in middle of 13th cent.

Fray Ben′tos (frī vän′tȯs; frä′ē̇). Town and river port, ✳ of Río Negro dept., W Uruguay, on E bank of Uruguay river ab. 175 m. NW of Montevideo; pop. ab. 9500; has large frigorífica and a meat-extract plant (estab. 1864).

Fray′ser's Farm (frā′zērz; -zhērz; *or* **Glen′dale** (glĕn′dāl). Battlefield near Richmond, Virginia, where Longstreet and A. P. Hill lost 3000 men in an encounter with Federals June 30, 1862.

Fre′chen (frĕκ′ĕn). Commune, W Germany, in North Rhine-Westphalia, SW suburb of Cologne; pop. 10,550.

Fred′er·i′ci·a (frĕd′ēr·ĭsh′ĭ·ȧ; *Dan.* frĭth·rē′tsē·ȧ). Seaport, Vejle co., SE Jutland Penin., Denmark; pop. (1945) 22,963; manufactures metal products; scene of battle July 6, 1849 in which Danes defeated Prussians.

Fred′er·ick (frĕd′rĭk; -ēr·ĭk). **1** Name of counties in two states of the U.S. See *Tables* at MARYLAND and VIRGINIA.

2 City, ⊗ of Frederick co., N Maryland, 24 m. SE of Hagerstown; pop. 21,744; in agricultural section; canneries; residence of Francis Scott Key and Barbara Fritchie; Hood College (1893; women). See MONOCACY battlefield.

3 City, ⊗ of Tillman co., SW Oklahoma, 25 m. SE of Altus; pop. 5879; cotton.

Frederick Henry. See FREDERIK HENDRIK.

Fred′er·icks·burg (frĕd′rĭks·bûrg; -ēr·ĭks-). **1** Town, ⊗ of Gillespie co., cen. Texas; pop. 4629; granite, limestone.

2 Industrial city, NE Virginia, in Spotsylvania co. but politically independent, on Rappahannock river 41 m. SW of Alexandria; 2 sq. m.; pop. 13,639; settled 1671; incorp. as city 1879; scene of battle Dec. 11–15, 1862, when Federal army under Burnside was defeated by Confederates under Robert E. Lee. Mary Washington College (1908; women) of the Univ. of Virginia.

Fredericksburg and Spot′syl·va′nia National Military Park (spŏt′s′l·vān′yȧ; -vä′nĭ·ȧ). See UNITED STATES, *National Historical Parks.*

Fred′er·ick·town′ (frĕd′rĭk·toun′; frĕd′ēr·ĭk-). City, ⊗ of Madison co., SE Missouri, 45 m. WNW of Cape Girardeau; pop. 3484; near lead deposits.

Fred′er·ick Wil′liam IV Falls (frĕd′rĭk [-ēr·ĭk] wĭl′-yȧm). Falls on Courantyne river on boundary bet. British Guiana and Surinam.

Fred′er·ic·ton (frĕd′rĭk·tŭn; -ēr·ĭk-). City, ✳ of New

Brunswick prov., SE Canada, and ⊗ of York co., in SW part at head of navigation of St. John river 55 m. NNW of St. John; pop. 16,018; trades extensively in lumber; railroad center; Univ. of New Brunswick (1800). Laid out as provincial capital 1785 across river from village of **Sainte Anne's Point** (sȧnt ănz′), which was settled by French 1740, earliest settlement in region, and received many Acadian refugees.

Fre′de·rik Hen′drik (frā′dĕ·rĭk hĕn′drĭk); *Eng.* **Frederick Henry**. Island in Arafura Sea, off S coast of island of New Guinea; ab. 110 m. by 55 m.; 3000 sq. m.; administratively a part of South New Guinea prov., S Neth. New Guinea; low, covered with swamps and jungles.

Fred′er·iks·berg (frĕd′rĭks·bûrg; frĕd′ēr·ĭks-; *Dan.* frĭth′rĭks·bărκ). City, Copenhagen co., Sjælland I., Denmark; 3 sq. m.; pop. (1945) 113,584; a suburb of Copenhagen.

Fre′de·riks·borg (frĭth′rĭks·bȯrκ). **1** County of Denmark. See *Table* at DENMARK.

2 Town, Frederiksborg co., N Sjælland, Denmark; pop. ab. 3000.

Fre′de·riks·haab (frĭth′rĭks·hôp). Danish settlement on S coast of Greenland, NNW of Ivigtut.

Fre′de·riks·havn (frĭth′rĭks·houn′). Seaport, Hjørring co., NE Jutland Penin., Denmark, on the Kattegat 37 m. NE of Aalborg; pop. (1945) 16,827; exports meat and fish.

Frederiksnagar. See SERAMPORE.

Fred′er·ik·sted (frĕd′rĭk·stĕd; frĕd′ēr·ĭk-). City on W coast of St. Croix I., Virgin Islands of the United States, West Indies; pop. 2177.

Fre·do′nia (frė·dō′nyȧ; -dō′nĭ·ȧ). **1** City, ⊗ of Wilson co., SE Kansas, N of Independence; pop. 3233; oil, gas.

2 Village, Chautauqua co., SW corner of New York, near Lake Erie 23 m. N of Jamestown; pop. 8477; manufactures grape juice, wine, shovels, coal-handling machinery; State Univ. of New York College of Education (1867; coed.).

Fredrikshald. See HALDEN.

Fredrikshamn. See HAMINA.

Fred′rik·stad (frĕd′rĭk·stä). Seaport, Østfold co., SE Norway, on E shore of Oslo Fjord at mouth of Glomma river; pop. 14,053; shipping point for lumber, chemicals, granite, feldspar.

Free′born′ (frē′bȯrn′). County in Minnesota. See *Table* at MINNESOTA.

Free′burg (frē′bûrg). Village, St. Clair co., SW Illinois, 18 m. SE of East St. Louis; pop. 1908.

Free′dom (frē′dŭm). Borough, Beaver co., W Pennsylvania, on Ohio river 21 m. NW of Pittsburgh; pop. 2895; founded 1832.

Free′hold′ (frē′hōld′). Industrial borough, ⊗ of Monmouth co., E cen. New Jersey, 18 m. S of Perth Amboy; pop. 9140; first white settlement 1650; settled by Scots 1715, called Monmouth Court House, later (1795) Monmouth, changed to Freehold 1801; incorp. 1869. See MONMOUTH COURT HOUSE.

Free′land (frē′lănd). Borough, Luzerne co., E Pennsylvania, S of Wilkes-Barre; pop. 5068; coal, textiles.

Freels, Cape (frēlz). Cape on E coast of Newfoundland, marking NW point of Bonavista Bay, 49°15′N.

Freels Peak. Mountain 10,900 ft., E El Dorado co., E California.

Free′man Lake (frē′măn). Lake, NW cen. Indiana, formed in Tippecanoe river by Oakdale Dam (completed 1925). Cf. SHAFER LAKE.

Free′mans·burg (frē′mănz·bûrg). Borough, Northampton co., E Pennsylvania, on Lehigh river; pop. 1652.

Free′man's Farm (frē′mănz). Locality near Bemis Heights on W bank of Hudson river bet. villages of Saratoga and Stillwater, Saratoga co., New York; center of fighting in two battles of Saratoga (*q.v.*) 1777.

Free′port (frē′pȯrt). **1** City, ⊗ of Stephenson co., N Illinois, 28 m. W of Rockford; pop. 26,628; settled 1835; chartered 1855; varied manufactures; scene of Lincoln-

Douglas debate (1858) in which Douglas expounded his "Freeport Doctrine" that local legislation could be effective against slavery despite the Supreme Court's Dred Scott decision.

2 Town, Cumberland co., SW Maine, 16 m. NNE of Portland; pop. 4055; incorporated 1789; final papers for separation of Maine from Massachusetts signed here 1820, establishing Maine as an independent state.

3 Residential village, Nassau co., SE New York, on S shore of Long I. 25 m. ESE of New York; pop. 34,419; fisheries, esp. oysters.

4 Borough, Armstrong co., W Pennsylvania, on Allegheny river 24 m. NE of Pittsburgh; pop. 2439; coal.

5 City and port of entry, Brazoria co., SE Texas, at mouth of Brazos river on Gulf of Mexico 40 m. WSW of Galveston; pop. 11,619; mines, processes, and ships sulfur; Dow Chemical Co. plant, built 1940, for extracting magnesium from sea water.

Freer (frēr). City, Duval co., S Texas, 60 m. ENE of Laredo; pop. 2724.

Free′stone′ (frē′stōn′). County in Texas. See *Table* at TEXAS.

Free Territory of Trieste. See TRIESTE.

Free′town′ (frē′toun′). **1** Town, Bristol co., SE Massachusetts, 10 m. N of New Bedford; pop. 3039.

2 Seaport town on N shore of Sierra Leone Penin., W Africa, ✳ of British dominion (until 1961 colony and protectorate) of Sierra Leone; pop. (1956 est.) 100,000; best harbor in West Africa, at mouth of Sierra Leone river; terminus of railroad branching at Bauya to SE and N cen. parts of protectorate; college, cathedral, museum. Founded 1788 chiefly by freed or rescued Negro slaves who were granted land by a native chieftain.

Fre·gel′lae (frĕ·jĕl′ē). Ancient Volscian town, Latium, Italy; a few ruins near modern Ceprano; near the Liris (mod. Liri); Latin colony established 328 B.C.; revolted against Rome 125 B.C.; destroyed, but existed as a village under the empire.

Fre·ge·nal′ de la Sier′ra (frē′hä·näl′ dä lä syĕr′rä). Commune, Badajoz prov., SW Spain, 47 m. SSE of Badajoz; pop. 10,806.

Fré′hel′, Cape (frā′ĕl′). Cape on coast of Côtes-du-Nord dept., NW France, 15 m. W by N of Saint-Malo.

Frei′berg (frī′bûrg; *Ger.* -bĕrк). Manufacturing and silver-mining city, Dresden dist., eastern Germany, 21 m. SW of Dresden near W bank of Mulde river; pop. 34,742; mining academy (founded 1765); 15th-cent. Gothic cathedral; 13th-cent. relic called the Golden Portal. Founded 12th cent. as silver-mining camp; scene of victory of Prussians over Austrians and Saxons 1762.

Frei′burg (frī′bŏŏrg; -bûrg; *Ger.* -bŏŏrк). **1** District of Baden. See *Table* at BADEN.

2 *Also* **Freiburg im Breis′gau** (ĭm brīs′gou). Manufacturing city, Baden-Württemberg state, W Germany, at W foot of Black Forest 80 m. SW of Stuttgart; pop. (1939) 111,860; fine Gothic cathedral, university (founded 1457, has excellent library, ducal palace. Scene of close battle Aug. 3 and 5, 1644 in which French under Enghien and Turenne were defeated by Bavarians under General Mercy.

3 See FRIBOURG, Switzerland.

Frei′en·wal′de (frī′ĕn·väl′dĕ), *also called* **Bad Freienwalde** (bät) *or* **Freienwalde an der O′der** (än dĕr ō′dĕr). City, in Frankfurt-an-der-Oder dist., Brandenburg, E Germany, near Oder river 33 m. NE of Berlin; pop. 10,328; health resort; warm mineral springs.

Frei′sing (frī′zĭng). City, Upper Bavaria dist., Bavaria, West Germany, 20 m. NNE of Munich; pop. 14,974; 12th-cent. cathedral; manufactures agricultural machines, pottery, glass. Founded by Romans; episcopal see 724–1803.

Frei′tal (frī′täl). Industrial city, Dresden dist., East Germany, 6 m. SW of Dresden; pop. 36,558; manufactures iron, leather, and glass goods; coal mining.

Fré′jus′ (frā′zhüs′); *anc.* **Fo′rum Ju′li·i** (fōr′ŭm jōō′lĭ·ī). Commune, Var dept., SE France; pop. 3577; Roman remains; cathedral; founded by Julius Caesar.

Fréjus, Mas′sif′ du (ma′sēf′ dü). Mountain mass at SW end of Graian Alps bet. France and Italy; crossed by **Col de Fréjus** (kōl′ dē), pass ab. 16 m. SW of Mont Cenis Pass, pierced by Mont Cenis Tunnel (see ALPS).

Fre·man′tle (frē·măn′t'l). Municipality, SW Western Australia, on Indian Ocean at mouth of Swan river 10 m. SW of Perth; pop. 17,006, with suburbs (1940) 28,171; founded 1829; seaport for Perth; exports chiefly wool, wheat, and gold. Suburbs are **East Fremantle** (pop. 5118) and **North Fremantle** (pop. 3109).

Fre′mont (frē′mŏnt). **1** Name of counties in four states of the U.S. See *Tables* at COLORADO, IDAHO, IOWA, WYOMING.

2 City, Alameda co., W California, SSE of Oakland; pop. 43,790.

3 City, Newaygo co., W Michigan, 22 m. NE of Muskegon; pop. 3384.

4 City, ⊗ of Dodge co., E Nebraska, on Platte river 33 m. WNW of Omaha; pop. 19,698; flour mills, canneries; Midland College (1887; coed.; Lutheran).

5 Manufacturing city, ⊗ of Sandusky co., N Ohio, 21 m. WSW of Sandusky; pop. 17,573; on site of Fort Stevenson (built 1812), scene of Maj. Croghan's defeat of English and Indians 1813; sugar beet and cannery center.

Fre·mont′ Peak (frē·mŏnt′). See SAN FRANCISCO PEAKS, Arizona.

Fre′mont Peak (frē′mŏnt). Mountain 13,730 ft. in Wind River Range, W cen. Wyoming.

French (frĕnch). River 60 m. long, bet. Sudbury and Parry Sound dists., SE Ontario, Canada; outlet of Lake Nipissing to Georgian Bay.

French Broad (frĕnch brôd). River 210 m. long, E United States; formed by junction of north and west forks in Transylvania co., SW North Carolina, flows NW through Great Smoky Mts. across Tennessee border, turns W to unite with Holston river near Knoxville and form Tennessee river; near this junction is Douglas Dam, one of dams of Tennessee Valley Authority (*q.v.*).

French′burg (frĕnch′bûrg). City, ⊗ of Menifee co., E Kentucky; pop. 296.

French Community; *Fr.* **Com′mu′nau′té′ fran′çaise′** (kô′mü′nō′tā′ frän′sâz′). The federation comprising metropolitan France, its overseas departments and territories, and the former African territories that, on becoming republics, chose to maintain their ties with France, formed under the Constitution of the Fifth Republic promulgated Oct. 5, 1958, and superseding the French Union.

French Congo. See FRENCH EQUATORIAL AFRICA.

French Creek (frĕnch). River ab. 140 m. long, flowing from SW New York SW and SE into Allegheny river at Franklin, cen. Venango co., NW Pennsylvania.

French Equatorial Africa; *earlier* **French Congo.** Former French overseas territory, NW Africa; bounded on N by Libya, E by (Anglo-Egyptian) Sudan, S by (Belgian) Congo, SW by Atlantic Ocean, W by Río Muni, Cameroun, Nigeria, and Niger; included Gabon, Middle Congo, Ubangi-Shari, and Chad territories (*qq.v.*), which in 1958 became autonomous republics in French Community; 959,256 sq. m.; pop. (1936) 3,418,066; ✳ Brazzaville; densely forested in S, in N mostly desert but included fertile Bodele region. Natives of region are Negroes, Semitic and Arab strains among those of Chad region, pygmies in forests. *Mountains:* Tibesti Mts. in NW (highest 11,201 ft.), Ennedi Mts. in NE (highest 4756 ft.). *Rivers:* Ogooué, in S, flows into Atlantic Ocean; Chari in N flows into Lake Chad; Sanga in Middle Congo flows into the Congo below Lake Tumba; Bomu, Ubangi and Congo rivers form the S boundary. *Chief towns:* Brazzaville, Fort-Lamy, Bangui, Libreville, Port Gentil, Pointe Noire, and Loango.

History: Coast discovered by Portuguese 1470; Lake

Chad explored by English 1823; not settled by Europeans until French settled on Gabon river 1841 and founded Libreville 1849; after settlement of Brazzaville 1880 French penetrations inland extended to Ubangi region and finally to Lake Chad 1897; borders of French possessions determined by series of agreements with Powers from 1885; three colonies, Gabon, Middle Congo, and Ubangi-Shari-Chad, designated 1910 divisions of the region whose name was changed from French Congo (Chad made a separate colony 1920); ab. 100,000 sq. m. which were ceded to Germany in return for her agreement on Morocco (Agadir crisis) 1911 were recovered 1919; declared its independence of Vichy government 1940; Brazzaville became center of operations of Free French (after July 1942 called Fighting French) in Africa; by the new French constitution of Oct. 1946 status of the colonies changed to that of territories within the French Union abolished 1958.

French Frig'ate Shoal (frĭg'ĭt). Group of islets, Hawaiian Is., 100 m. W of Necker I.; near lat. 23°50′N, long. 166°12′W.

French Gui·a'na (gḗ·ȧ'nȧ; -ăn'ȧ); *Fr.* **Guy'ane' fran'çaise'** (gü·ē'yȧn' frȧn'sâz'). French overseas department on NE coast of South America, having Surinam on the W and Brazil on E and S; by decree of July 6, 1930 divided into colony of **Guiana** (a coastal strip, 7720 sq. m., pop. 30,906) and **Territory of I'ni'ni'** [ē'nē'nē'] (hinterland, 27,020 sq. m., pop. 6099); Jan. 1, 1947 administratively reunited and entire area (34,740 sq. m., pop. [1936] 37,005) made a department of France; ✳ Cayenne; for many years has included a large penal settlement in NW on the Maroni and another on Devil's I. off coast NW of Cayenne, but convict population gradually being sent back to France. Chief mountains the Tumuc-Humac range on the S border separat-

ing it from Brazil; Inini hinterland largely plateau. Chief rivers the Maroni, forming boundary with Surinam on W, the Oyapock, forming boundary with Brazil on E, and the Mana and Sinnamarie rivers. Chief products rice, maize, manioc, sugar, cocoa, bananas (on the coast) and cabinet woods, gold, balata, hides (from Inini).

History: First French settlement at Cayenne 1604; neglected until 18th cent. when French made unsuccessful attempts to settle; occupied by British 1809 but restored to France after 1815; development hindered because of presence of penal colony since 19th cent.; boundary with Brazil settled by arbitration 1900; reorganized according to new French constitution of 1946.

French Guin'ea (gĭn'ĭ); *Fr.* **Gui'née' fran'çaise'** (gē'nā' frȧn'sâz'). Former French territory, French West Africa; became (as **Guinea**) independent Oct. 1, 1958; 96,886 sq. m.; pop. (1946 est.) 2,124,972; ✳ Conakry, on Tombo I.; bounded on N by Senegal, on N and NE by Mali, and on E and SE by Ivory Coast, on S by Liberia and Sierra Leone, on W by Atlantic Ocean, and on NW by Portuguese Guinea; includes Los Is. group opp. Conakry. Has marshy seacoast, ab. 170 m. long, the coastal plain rising to hilly and plateau regions in the interior which form a tableland that is source of upper tributaries of Niger and Senegal rivers, also of many streams flowing SW to Atlantic. In N is Fouta Djallon tableland and on S borders are ranges that reach 3500 ft. near coast and 6000 ft. on Liberia border. Chief products palm oil and nuts, gums, rubber, rice, coffee, and tropical fruits. Inhabitants are many different Negro tribes, some quite primitive; esp. important are the Baga, Fulah, Mandingo, and Susu. Chief towns Conakry, Boké, Labé, Kankan, Dubréka, and Kindia.

History: Once part of Senegal and called **Ri'vières' du Sud** (rē'vyâr' dü süd') because it comprised region of

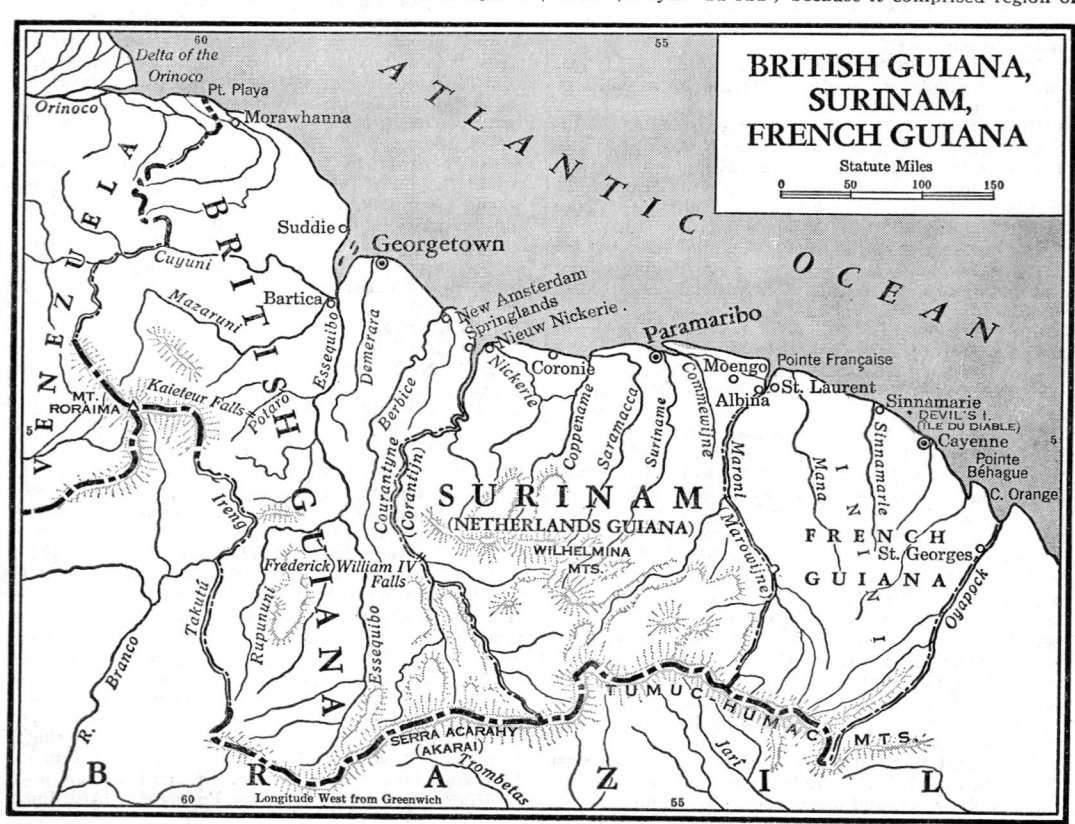

rivers S of the Senegal; proclaimed French protectorate ab. 1860; boundaries settled by treaties 1882 and 1886; after long struggle with native rulers formally established as colony of French Guinea 1893; made part of French West Africa (*q.v.*) 1904; status changed to that of territory 1946; became independent Oct. 1, 1958 by plebiscite; joined Sudanese Republic in Mali Federation 1959; withdrew 1960.

French India, *officially* **É'ta'blisse'ments' fran'-çais' dans l'Inde** (ā'tȧ'blēs'mäN' fräN'sĕ' däN länd'). Five settlements in India that formerly constituted a territory of France: Chandernagor, Pondichéry, Karikal, Yanaon, on E coast, Mahé on W coast; 197 sq. m.; pop. (1941) 323,295; ✱ Pondichéry. French stations in India founded by French East India Co. (chartered 1664); under leadership of Dupleix and La Bourdonnais, Deccan and Carnatic (*qq.v*) came to be controlled by France 1751 until Clive's victory at Plassey 1757 gave British ascendancy in India (see INDIA, 1); Pondichéry and other ports captured and restored several times, until by treaties of 1814 and 1815 French possessions in India were returned and (1816 and 1817) permanently established; restored to India 1949-54.

French In'do·chi'na (ĭn'dȯ·chī'nȧ); *Fr.* **In'do'chine' fran'çaise'** (ăN'dȯ'shēn' fräN'sâz'); *frequently called* **Indochina.** The E part of the peninsula of Indochina (*q.v.*), SE Asia, bordering on China on the N, Burma on NW, Thailand on the W; 291,119 sq. m.; pop. 23,236,000; ✱ Hanoi; before 1946 consisted of the following political divisions:

POLITICAL DIVISION[1]	LOCATION	AREA[2]	POP.[2]	CAPITAL
Annam[3]	E	56,974	5,656,000	Hué
Cambodia	SW	69,866	3,046,000	Pnompenh
Cochin China[3]	S	29,974	4,616,000	Saigon
Kwangchowan[4]	SE China	325	206,000	Fort Bayard
Laos	W & NW	89,320	1,012,000	Vientiane
Tonkin[3]	N	44,660	8,700,000	Hanoi

[1] Cochin China was a colony, while Annam, Cambodia, Laos, and Tonkin were protectorates and Kwangchowan French leased territory.
[2] Area = land area in sq. m. Pop. from 1936 Census.
[3] Annam, Tonkin, and Cochin China now constitute the state of Vietnam.
[4] Returned to China 1946.

For further geographical description, see entries of these political divisions. See *Map* at BURMA.

Corresponds approximately to empire of Annam as it existed at beginning of 19th cent., then owing suzerainty to China. French-controlled Cochin China, Cambodia, Annam, and Tonkin (*qq.v.*) were united for administration 1887, Laos and Kwangchowan added 1893 and 1898; occupied by Japanese 1940; clashed with Siamese forces; forced to cede territory in Cambodia and Laos to Siam 1941; after World War II occupied for a time by British and Chinese troops until French control re-established Mar. 4, 1946; scene of warfare 1946-54 as extreme nationalist group sought independence from France (see VIETNAM); by 1955 Vietnam had become divided at 17th parallel into two states and Cambodia and Laos were independent.

French Lick (frĕnch lĭk). Resort town, Orange co., S Indiana, SSW of Bedford; pop. 1954; sulfur springs.

French'man Bay (frĕnch'măn). Inlet of Atlantic Ocean on SE coast of Maine, E of Mt. Desert I.

French Morocco. See MOROCCO.

French Pol'y·ne'sia (pŏl'ĭ·nē'zhȧ; -zhĭ·ȧ; -shȧ; -shĭ·ȧ), *Fr.* **Po'ly'né'sie' fran'çaise'** (pȯ'lē'nä'zē' fräN'sâz'); *formerly* **French O'ce·an'i·a** (ō'shē·ăn'ĭ·ȧ; -ā'nĭ·ȧ), *Fr.* **É'ta'blisse'ments' (fran'çais) de l'O'cé'a'nie'** (ā'tȧ'blēs'mäN' [fräN'sĕ'] dē lō'sā'ȧ'nē'). French settlements in South Pacific Ocean, comprising Marquesas, Society, Gambier, and Tubuaï Is. and Tuamotu Archipelago, together classified as a territory of the French Community; 1575 sq. m.; pop. (1956) 79,000, (1946) 55,734; ✱ Papeete on Tahiti, Society Is.; covers wide area, approx. from 7°S to 29°S and 132°W to 156°W.

History: Tahiti explored by Louis de Bougainville 1766 and Marquesas visited by French missionaries in late 18th cent.; Oceania visited by Dumont d'Urville 1837-40; annexation of Marquesas and protection of Society group accomplished by French in 1842 and remainder taken over by close of 19th cent.; placed under single administration 1903; administration reorganized 1946.

French River. See FRENCH.

French Shore. Neutralized territory on W and N coasts of Newfoundland, from Cape Ray in SW to Cape St. John (50°N); established 1713 when Newfoundland ceded to British with certain rights granted to French fishermen, esp. that of drying fish on land; above limits defined 1783; source of much friction 19th cent. bet. England and France and of trouble with American fishermen (settled by convention 1909).

French So·ma'li·land' (sȯ·mä'lē·lănd'); *Fr.* **Côte fran'çaise' des So'ma'lis'** (kōt' fräN'sâz' dā sȯ'-mä'lē'). French territory, E Africa, on Gulf of Aden at entrance to Red Sea, bet. Eritrea (on NW) and Somalia (on SE) and Ethiopia (on W); 8492 sq. m.; pop. (1936) 46,391; ✱ Djibouti; mostly desert country, flat along coast, in interior hilly, low plateau. Exports salt, the country's chief industry, and coffee and hides.

History: Obock acquired by French 1862; small bit of hinterland added to establish French protectorate of Somaliland 1884-85; capital transferred to Djibouti on trade route to Ethiopia 1892; rail connection with Addis Ababa completed during World War I; by treaty with Italy 1935, France ceded 309 sq. m. to Eritrea; had status of a colony until 1946 when it became a territory within French Union.

French Su·dan' (soō·dăn'); *Fr.* **Sou'dan' fran'çais'** (soō'däN' fräN'sĕ'). Republic, former French territory, W Africa, *called 1958-60* **Su'da·nese' Republic** (soō'-dȧ·nēz'; -nēs'), *since 1960 known as* **Ma'li** (mä'lē), comprising W part of Sahara and Sudan; 464,873 sq. m.; pop. (1959) 4,300,000; ✱ Bamako; bounded on N by Southern Territories of Algeria, on E and SE by Niger Republic, on S by Upper Volta and Ivory Coast, and on W by Guinea, Senegal, Mauritania. Mostly desert; highland areas in E and S; crossed in S by Upper Niger which expands into lake and marsh region SW of Tombouctou; traversed in SW by headstreams of the Senegal. Through Kayes has rail connection with Dakar and to the NW by motor highway with Morocco. Exports include ground nuts, hides, gum, cotton, wool, wax. Chief towns Bamako, Kayes, Sikasso, Ségou, Tombouctou.

History: By 1899 agreement with Great Britain after Fashoda (Kodok) crisis, E Sudan region recognized as open to French; territories of Senegambia and Niger formed into colony 1904; known as Upper Senegal-Niger until 1920; frontier with Anglo-Egyptian Sudan settled 1924; included part of Upper Volta (*q.v.*) 1933-47; had status of a colony until reorganized as a territory of the French Union 1946; became a republic within French Community 1958; joined Senegal in Mali Federation 1959; union dissolved 1960.

French Togo. See TOGO.

Frenchtown. See MONROE, Michigan.

French Union; *Fr.* **U'nion' fran'çaise'** (ü'nyŏN' fräN'sâz'). The French federation formed by the Constitution of the Fourth Republic of Sept. 29, 1946 (confirmed by referendum of Oct. 13, 1946), comprising the French Republic with its overseas departments and territories and the associated states; superseded 1958 by the French Community (*q.v.*).

French'ville (frĕnch'vĭl). Town, Aroostook co., N Maine, on St. John river E of Fort Kent; pop. 1421.

French West Africa. Former French overseas territory in W Africa, comprising Mauritania, Senegal, Ivory Coast, Dahomey, French Guinea, French Sudan, Upper Volta, and Niger territories; 1,815,768 sq. m.; pop. (1945) 15,996,000; ✱ Dakar; organized 1895, reorganized 1946; abolished 1958.

French West Indies. Islands of the Lesser Antilles, West Indies, which belong to France; comprise Martinique and Guadeloupe (formerly colonies, since 1946 overseas departments) and the five dependencies of Guadeloupe: Désirade, Les Saintes, Marie Galante, Saint Barthélemy, and part of Saint Martin; total area 1073 sq. m.; pop (1936 est.) 550,951. See *Map* at LESSER ANTILLES.

Fresh′wa′ter (frĕsh′wô′tẽr; -wŏt′ẽr). Village, W Isle of Wight, England; watering place; site of Farringford estate, Lord Tennyson's home from 1853.

Freshwater Lake. See SWEETWATER LAKE.

Fres·nil′lo, *in full* Fresnillo de Gon·zá′lez E′che·ver·rí′a (fräz-nē′yō thä gôn·sä′läs ā′chä·vĕr·rē′ä). City, Zacatecas state, cen. Mexico; pop. 24,614; school of mines, founded 1853; near silver mines.

Fres′no (frĕz′nō). 1 County in California. See *Table* at CALIFORNIA.

2 City, its ⊗, S cen. California, 155 m. SE of San Francisco; pop. 133,929; in San Joaquin valley; marketing and shipping center; fruit packing (esp. raisins). Founded 1872, made ⊗ 1874, incorp. as city 1900. Fresno State College (1911; coed.).

Fresno Dam. Dam completed 1939 across Milk river, N Montana; height 109 ft.; impounds water for irrigation.

Fretum Gaditanum. See Strait of GIBRALTAR.

Fretum Gallicum. See Strait of DOVER.

Frey′ci·net′ Peninsula (frä′sĕ·nā′). Peninsula ab. 20 m. long on E coast of Tasmania, Australia, 42°10′S.

Fri′ant Dam (frī′ănt). See UNITED STATES, *Dams and Reservoirs;* SAN JOAQUIN river.

Friaul. See FRIULI.

Fri′bourg (frē′bŏŏr; *Fr.* frē′bŏŏr′); *Ger.* **Frei′burg** (frī′bŏŏrg; -bûrg; *Ger.* -bŏŏrᴋ). 1 Swiss canton; see *Table* at SWITZERLAND. In ancient times inhabited by the Helvetii; conquered by Franks in 6th cent.; to Holy Roman Empire 1032; remained Catholic during Reformation; under French rule 1798–1814.

2 Commune, its ✱, on peninsula in Saane river 17 m. SW of Bern; pop. (1941) 26,045; 13th-cent. cathedral; university (founded 1889); manufactures machinery, fertilizer, chocolate. Founded as military post in 12th cent.; became member of Swiss confederation 1481.

Fri′court′ (frē′kŏŏr′). Village, Somme dept., N France, near Albert; destroyed in World War I.

Fri′day Harbor (frī′dĭ). Town and resort, ⊗ of San Juan co.. NW Washington; pop. 706.

Frid′ley (frĭd′lĭ). City, Anoka co., E Minnesota, SE of Anoka; pop. 15,173.

Fridtjof Nansen Land. See FRANZ JOSEF LAND.

Fried′berg (frēd′bûrg; *Ger.* frēt′bĕrk). City, Hesse, Germany, near Usa river 15 m. N of Frankfurt am Main; pop. 11,048; varied manufactures.

Friedek. See FRÝDEK.

Friedland. See PRAVDINSK.

Fried′ling·en (frēt′lĭng·ĕn). Battlefield in SW corner of Baden, Germany, on the Rhine N of Basel and SE of Mulhouse; scene of victory of duc de Villars over Louis William of Baden 1702 (War of Spanish Succession).

Frie′drichs·ha′fen (frē′drĭᴋs·hä′fĕn); *before 1811 called* **Buch′horn** (bŏŏᴋ′hôrn). City, SE Baden-Württemberg state, Germany, on Lake Constance 14 m. E of Konstanz; pop. 11,289; important harbor; summer resort; varied manufactures. Passed to Bavaria 1802, to Württemberg 1810. Chief center of manufacture of Zeppelins during and for some years after World War I.

Frie′drichs·ruh′ (frē′drĭᴋs·rŏŏ′). Village, Schleswig-Holstein, Germany, 15 m. SE of Hamburg; home of Bismarck on his retirement.

Friedrichstadt. See YAUNYELGAVA.

Frie′drichs·thal (frē′drĭᴋs·täl). Mining and manufacturing town, Saarland, Germany, ab. 8 m. N of Saarbrücken; pop. ab. 14,000.

Friedrich–Wilhelmshafen. See MADANG.

Friendly Islands. See TONGA ISLANDS.

Friend′ship (frĕn[d]′shĭp). Village, ⊗ of Adams co., cen. Wisconsin; pop. 560.

Fri′ern Bar′net (frī′ẽrn bär′nĕt). Urban district, Middlesex, SE England, 10 m. NNW of London; pop. 29,164; part of Greater London.

Fries (frēz). Town, Grayson co., SW Virginia, 26 m. SSW of Pulaski; pop. 1039.

Friesche Eilanden. See FRISIAN ISLANDS.

Fries′land (frēz′lănd; -länd′; frēs′-; *Du.* frēs′länt). Province, N Netherlands, 1431 sq. m.; pop. (1939) 424,274; ✱ Leeuwarden; dairy farming, livestock raising.

Frim′ley and Cam′ber·ley (frĭm′lĭ, kăm′bẽr·lĭ). Urban district, Surrey, S England, N of Aldershot; pop. 20,376; nearby is Bisley (*q.v.*), well-known rifle range.

Fri′o (frē′ō). County in Texas. See *Table* at TEXAS.

Fri′o, Cape. 1 (frē′ōō) Cape extending into Atlantic Ocean from coast of Rio de Janeiro state, SE Brazil.

2 (frē′ōō; frē′ō) Cape extending into Atlantic Ocean on NW coast of South-West Africa, S of Angola boundary.

Fri·ol′ (frē·ôl′). Commune, Lugo prov., NW Spain, 11 m. W of Lugo; pop. 10,667.

Fri′sches Haff (frĭsh′ĕs häf; *Pol.* **Mie·rze′ja Wiś·la′na** (myĕ·zhĕ′yä vĕsh·lä′nä); *Russ.* **Fri′shes Gaf** (fryĕ′shĕs gäf′). Lagoon 56 m. long, 4 to 12 m. wide on SW coast of Baltic Sea, formerly in East Prussia, separated from Gulf of Danzig by long, narrow spit of land (**Fri′sche Neh′rung** [frĭsh′ĕ nā′rŏŏng]) which has an opening at N end; receives the Pregel at NE; divided 1945 bet. Poland and U.S.S.R. Cf. KURISHES GAF.

Fri′si·a (frĭzh′ĭ·à). Country along SE coast of North Sea at time of Frankish empire; corresponded approximately to modern Netherlands.

Fri′sian Islands (frĭzh′ăn); *Du.* **Frie′sche Ei′lan·den** (frē′sĕ ī′län·dĕn). Chain of islands in North Sea, bet. 3 and 20 m. from European mainland, including: (1) **North Frisian Islands** off NW coast of Schleswig-Holstein, NW Germany, and the SW coast of Denmark; chief islands (German) Sylt, Föhr, Nordstrand, Pellworm, and Amrum; (Danish) Römö, Fanö, and Manö. (2) **East Frisian Islands** off Lower Saxony state, NW Germany; chief islands Borkum, Juist, Norderney, Langeoog, Spiekeroog, and Wangerooge. (3) **West Frisian Islands** off Wadden Zee and N Netherlands coast; chief islands Texel, Vlieland, Terschelling, Ameland, and Schiermonnikoog. Helgoland (*q.v.*) belongs to German group of North Frisian Is.

Fris·sell′, Mount (frĭ·zĕl′). Mountain 2380 ft. in town of Salisbury, NW Connecticut; highest point in state.

Fritz′lar (frĭts′lär). Town, N Hesse state, W Germany, on the Eder; pop. (1933) 4240; church of St. Peter and monastery, both founded 732 by Boniface.

Fri′u·li (frē′ōō·lē; frē·ōō′lē). 1 *Ger.* **Fri·aul′** (frē·oul′); *anc.* **Fo′rum Ju′li·i** (fōr′ŭm jōō′lĭ·ī). Former duchy in NE Italy; became Lombard duchy 6th cent.; made Charlemagne's Friulian March; at close of 11th cent., part of patriarchate of Aquileia (*q.v.*); W part occupied by Venice in 15th cent.; E part (under Gorizia) acquired 1500 by Austria who received rest 1797; in Napoleon's Illyrian Provinces (*q.v.*); Venetian part returned to Italy during unification and rest after World War I; now mostly in Friuli prov., Venezia Euganea, and in Gorizia prov. (see *Table* at ITALY).

2 Province of Italy. See *Table* at ITALY.

Fro′bish·er Bay (frō′bĭsh·ẽr; frŏb′ĭsh-). Inlet extending NW in SE Baffin I., E Franklin District, Northwest Territories, N Canada, S of Hall Penin.; first entered by Martin Frobisher 1576; airfield at its head.

Frombork. See FRAUENBURG.

Frome (frōm). 1 River, Dorsetshire, S England; flows SE into Poole harbor.

2 River ab. 20 m. long, Herefordshire, W England; flows into the Lugg.

3 Urban district, Somersetshire, SW England, on the **Frome** (tributary of the Avon) 20 m. SSE of Bristol; pop. 11,116; wool, paper, art metal work.

Frome, Lake (frōm). Shallow lake ab. 60 m. long, E South Australia, E of Lake Torrens.

Fron'te·nac (frŏn't'n·ăk). **1** City, Crawford co., SE Kansas, 4 m. N of Pittsburg; pop. 1713.
2 (*Fr.* frônt'nak') County, Ontario, Canada. See *Table* at ONTARIO.
3 County, Quebec, Canada. See *Table* at QUEBEC.

Frontenac, Lac. See Lake ONTARIO.

Frontera. See ÁLVARO OBREGÓN.

Fron·tier' (frŭn·tēr'; frŭn'tēr). County in Nebraska. See *Table* at NEBRASKA.

Fron'tier Il·la'qas (frŭn'tēr ?ĭ·lä'kȧz; frŏn'tēr). Group of frontier districts (*illaqas*) N and W of Gilgit, NW Kashmir, India; 12,355 sq. m.; pop. (1941) 76,526.

Fron·ti'gnan' (frôn'tē'nyän'). Commune, Hérault dept., S France, on a narrow lagoon just E of Étang de Thau; pop. 3517; manufactures muscatel.

Front Range (frŭnt). A range of Rocky Mts. in N cen. Colorado; highest peak Grays Peak 14,274 ft.

Front Roy'al (roi'ăl). Town, ⊗ of Warren co., N Virginia, 20 m. S of Winchester; pop. 7949; scene of capture of Union troops by Confederates 1862.

Fröschwiller. See WÖRTH.

Fro·si·no'ne (frō·zē·nō'nä). **1** Province of Italy. See *Table* at ITALY.
2 *anc.* **Fru'si·no** (frōō'sĭ·nō). Commune, its ✱, Latium, cen. Italy, 48 m. ESE of Rome; pop. 18,447; remains of ancient Volscian town.

Frost'burg (frôst'bûrg). Town, Allegany co., NW Maryland, 9 m. W of Cumberland; pop. 6722; Maryland State Teachers College (1902; coed.).

Frost'proof' (frôst'prōōf'). Town, Polk co., cen. Florida penin., 35 m. SE of Lakeland; pop. 2664; citrus fruit.

Fro'ward, Cape (frō'[w]ērd). South tip of Brunswick Penin., Chile, on N side of Strait of Magellan; most S point of mainland of South America; in 53°53'43''S.

Fröy'a (frû'ĭ·ä). Island in Norwegian Sea off W coast of Norway, W of Trondheim Fjord and N of Hitra I.; pop. 4077.

Frun'ze (frōōn'zĕ; *Russ.* frōōn'zyĕ); *formerly* **Pish·pek'** (pĭsh·pĕk'; *Russ.* pyĭsh·pyĕk'). City, ✱ of Kirgiz S.S.R., Soviet Russia, Asia, on Chu river on Kazakh border 300 m. NE of Tashkent; pop. 92,659; cotton. Birthplace of Gen. Mikhail V. Frunze, for whom it was renamed.

Frusino. See FROSINONE.

Frý'dek (frē'dĕk); *Ger.* **Frie'dek** (frē'dĕk). Town, Silesia prov., cen. Czechoslovakia, just S of Moravská Ostrava; pop. (1930) 11,893.

Frye'burg (frī'bûrg). Town, Oxford co., W Maine, on border 38 m. W of Lewiston; pop. 1874; Fryeburg Academy (founded 1791).

Fu·cec'chio (fōō·chāk'kyō). Commune, Firenze prov., Tuscany, cen. Italy, on Arno river 23 m. W by S of Florence; pop. 12,830; textiles.

Fuchau. Var. of *Foochow:* see MINHOW.

Fuchow. Var. of *Fowchow:* see FOWLING.

Fu'chun' (fōō'chōōn') *or* **Tsien Tang** (chyĕn' täng'). Navigable river ab. 140 m. long, Chekiang prov., E China, flowing NE into Hangchow Bay; remarkable for its tidal bore.

Fu'ci·no (fōō'chē·nō); *anc.* **Fu'ci·nus** (fū'sĭ·nŭs); *mod.* **Ce·la'no** (chā·lä'nō). Former lake in Aquila prov., cen. Italy; 60 sq. m.; drained 1854–75, providing 42,000 acres for cultivation (vineyards).

Fue'go (fwä'gō). Volcano 12,582 ft. in Guatemala, SW of Guatemala city; eruption 1880.

Fuen'te de Can'tos (fwän'tä thä kän'tōs). Commune, Badajoz prov., SW Spain, 53 m. SE of Badajoz; pop. 10,982.

Fuente O'be·ju'na (ō'vĕ·hōō'nä); *formerly* **Fuen'te·o've·ju'na**. City, Córdoba prov., S Spain, 46 m. NW of Córdoba; pop. 17,639; coal, lead, and mica mines. Formerly seat of Knights of Calatrava.

Fuen'ter·ra'bia (fwän'tĕr·rä'vyä); *Eng.* **Fon'ta·ra'-bi·a** (fŏn'tȧ·rä'bĭ·ȧ). Town, Guipúzcoa prov., N Spain, at mouth of Bidassoa just N of Irún; pop. 6181; medieval town with interesting ruins; often a scene of conflict 12th to 19th cents.

Fuer'te, Rí'o del (rē'ō thĕl fwēr'tä). River ab. 180 m. long, SW Chihuahua and N Sinaloa states, Mexico; flows into Gulf of California.

Fuer'te O·lim'po (fwēr'tä ō·lēm'pō); *Eng.* **Fort O·lim'po** (ō·lĭm'pō). Town, ✱ of Olimpo dept., N Paraguay, on Paraguay river, in 21°S; pop. 2888.

Fuer'te·ven·tu'ra (fwēr'tä·vän·tōō'rä). One of the Canary Is. (*q.v.*), Las Palmas prov., Spain, 75 m. ENE of Grand Canary I.; 665 sq. m.; pop. (1930) 14,069; extinct volcanoes; chief port Puerto de Cabras.

Fu'ga (fōō'gä). Island in Babuyan group, N of Luzon, Phil. Is.; 36 sq. m.; pop. 556; fine anchorage.

Fu'ji (fōō'jĭ; fū'-; *Jap.* fōō·jĕ) *or* **Fu'ji·ya'ma** (fōō'jĭ-yä'mȧ; fū'-; *Jap.* fōō·jĕ·yä·mä); *more correctly* **Fu·ji-no–Ya·ma** (fōō·jĕ·nō·yä·mä) *or* **Fu·ji·san** (fōō·jĕ·sän). Sacred mountain 12,388 ft. in S cen. Honshu, Japan, ab. 70 m. WSW of Tokyo; an isolated peak, highest in Japan; almost a perfect cone; its crater has diameter of nearly 2000 ft.; a quiescent volcano, last eruption 1649.

Fû'ka (fōō'kä; -kä). Village on coastal road, NW Egypt, E of Matrûh and W of El Daba.

Fu·ka·e (fōō·kä·ĕ; *Angl.* fōō'kī). **1** Largest island of Goto Archipelago, off W coast of Kyushu, Japan; 1342 sq. m.; pop. (1945) 65,813.
2 Town on NE coast of the island, ✱ of Goto Archipelago.

Fu'kien' (fōō'kyĕn'), *also* **Fuh'kien'**. Maritime province, SE China; 61,259 sq. m.; pop. (1936 est.) 11,755,625; ✱ Minhow; bounded on N by Chekiang prov., on E and SE by East China Sea and Formosa Strait, on SW by Kwangtung, and on W by Kiangsi; chief river the Min flowing SE to East China Sea near Minhow; bordered on W by Tachin Shan (Mts.). Important agriculturally, tea and rice the chief crops; extensive forests from which in earlier times camphor was an important product. Chief cities Minhow, Amoy, Tsinkiang, Lungki, Nanping, Changting. In early times home of barbaric tribes; part of Southern Sung empire in 5th cent. A.D. and under Liang dynasty in 6th cent.; under Kublai Khan (13th cent.), according to Marco Polo, it had an immense trade through the port of Zayton (*q.v.*).

Fu·ku·i (fōō·kōō·ĕ). **1** Prefecture of Japan. See *Table* at JAPAN.
2 City, its ✱, Honshu, near the coast ab. 70 m. NNW of Nagoya; pop. 75,273; in feudal period seat of a daimio; after restoration became large industrial center, producing textiles, esp. habutai (a thin, soft, Japanese silk), and paper. Destroyed by earthquake June 28, 1948.

Fu·ku·o·ka (fōō·kōō·ō·kä; *Angl.* fōō'kōō·ō'kä). **1** Prefecture of Japan. See *Table* at JAPAN.
2 Seaport city, its ✱, N Kyushu, on Hakata Bay; pop. (1945) 252,282; manufactures iron and steel, electrical equipment, rubber, ordnance; shipbuilding. In ancient times one of the three trade ports of Japan; at time (1274–81) of attempted invasions of Kublai Khan, the scene of much fighting; heavily bombed 1945.

Fu·ku·shi·ma (fōō·kōō·shē·mä; *Angl.* fōō·kōō·shē'mȧ, fōō·kōō'shĭ·mä). **1** Prefecture of Japan. See *Table* at JAPAN.
2 City, its ✱, N cen. Honshu; pop. (1945) 47,047; railroad junction; trade center (agricultural products, silk and silk goods). In feudal times the castle town of a daimio.

Fu·ku·ya·ma (fōō·kōō·yä·mä; *Angl.* fōō'kōō·yä'mȧ). **1** City, Hiroshima prefecture, SW Honshu, Japan, on Inland Sea 33 m. W of Okayama; pop. (1945) 49,060.
2 Town, Hokkaido, Japan. See MATSUMAE.

Fulah Empire. See SOKOTO.

Ful'da (fōōl'dȧ; *Ger.* fōōl'dä). **1** River ab. 90 m. long, W cen. Germany; flows N from E Hesse state to unite with Werra river at Münden in former Hannover prov., Prussia, and form the Weser river.
2 Manufacturing city, in E Hesse state on Fulda river 54 m. NE of Frankfurt am Main; pop. 26,057; cathedral

(a smaller-scale replica of St. Peter's in Rome); abbey (founded 8th cent.; in 10th cent. abbot became primate of Germany); formerly seat of university (1734–1803). Passed to Prussia 1866; in World War II taken by American army Apr. 4, 1945.

Fulginium. See FOLIGNO.

Fulham. Metropolitan borough of London. See *Table* at LONDON.

Ful′ler·ton (fŏŏl′ẽr·t'n; -tŭn). **1** City, Orange co., SW California, 17 m. NE of Long Beach; pop. 56,180; oil. **2** City, ⊗ of Nance co., E cen. Nebraska; pop. 1475.

Ful′ton (fŏŏl′t'n). **1** Name of counties in eight states of the U.S. See *Tables* at ARKANSAS, GEORGIA, ILLINOIS, INDIANA, KENTUCKY, NEW YORK, OHIO, PENNSYLVANIA. **2** City, Whiteside co., NW Illinois, on Mississippi river 35 m. N of Rock Island; pop. 3387; hardware. **3** City, Fulton co., SW corner of Kentucky, on Tennessee border 23 m. SW of Mayfield; pop. 3265; railroad center. **4** Village, ⊗ of Itawamba co., NE Mississippi; pop. 1706. **5** City, ⊗ of Callaway co., cen. Missouri, 25 m. NNE of Jefferson City; pop. 11,131; shoe factory; mineral springs. Westminster College (1853; men; Presbyterian). **6** Manufacturing city, Oswego co., cen. New York, 24 m. NNW of Syracuse; pop. 14,261; cheese.

Fulton Chain Lakes. Chain of small lakes in NE cen. New York, chiefly in Herkimer co.

Ful′wood (fŏŏl′wŏŏd). Urban district, Lancashire, NW England, NE suburb of Preston; pop. 13,087.

Fu′na·fu′ti (fōō′nȧ·fōō′tĭ; fū′nȧ·fū′tĭ). Atoll, cen. Ellice Is., W Pacific Ocean, ab. 8°30′S lat. and 179°20′E long.; pop. (1936) 352; 30 islets; contains chief village and government headquarters of the group. Occupied by U.S. Marines Apr. 23, 1943 and converted into a U.S. base.

Fun·chal′ (fōōN·shäl′). **1** District of Portugal. See *Table* at PORTUGAL. **2** Seaport commune, its ✳, at head of large bay on SE coast of Madeira I.; pop. (1940) 54,033; winter resort; 15th-cent. cathedral; tomb of Zarco, discoverer of island.

Fun·dão′ (fōōN·douN′). Commune, Castelo Branco dist., E cen. Portugal, 24 m. N of Castelo Branco; pop. (1920) 3580; insurrection 1903.

Fundi. See FONDI.

Fun′dy, Bay of (fŭn′dĭ). Inlet of Atlantic Ocean in SE Canada, extending bet. S New Brunswick and Nova Scotia; ab. 145 m. long, 48 m. wide at its mouth; at upper end branches into Chignecto Bay and Minas Basin; remarkable for swift tidal currents; in places, tide sometimes rises 40 to 50 ft. St. John, New Brunswick on it.

Fünen. See FYN.

Fünfkirchen. See PÉCS.

Fung, El. See EL FUNG.

Fu Niu Shan (fōō′ nū′ shän′). Mountain range in E cen. China, chiefly in N Honan prov., an E extension of Chin Ling Shan; includes peaks ab. 9000 ft. high.

Fun′za (fōōn′sä). River in W cen. Colombia; flows into Magdalena river near Bogotá. See TEQUENDAMA FALLS.

Fuo′ri·grot′ta-Ba·gno′li (fwô′rĕ·grôt′tä·bä·nyô′lē). Suburb of Naples, Napoli prov., NW Campania, S Italy; pop. (1931) 39,933.

Füred. See BALATONFÜRED.

Fur′ka Pass (fŏŏr′kä; *Ger.* fŏŏr′kä). Mountain pass 7990 ft., bet. Uri and Valais cantons, S cen. Switzerland.

Fur′nas (fûr′nȧs). County in Nebraska. See *Table* at NEBRASKA.

Fur′neaux Islands (fûr′nō). Island group off NE Tasmania, Australia, at E end of Bass Strait; separated from Tasmania by Banks Strait; 1031 sq. m.; pop. ab. 1000; largest Flinders I. and Cape Barren I. Discovered 1773 by Capt. T. Furneaux in command of the *Adventure*, one of Capt. Cook's ships.

Furnes (fürn). Commune, West Flanders prov., NW Belgium; pop. 7818; Belgian headquarters in World War I, 6 m. behind the Yser front.

Fur′ness (fûr′nĕs; -nĭs). District, NW Lancashire, NW England, N of Morecambe Bay; S portion a peninsula with Barrow in Furness the chief town, N portion in Lake District; iron ore in SW; famous abbey, founded 1127 by a Benedictine order which joined Cistercian order 1148, became largest Cistercian abbey in England.

Fur Seal Islands. See PRIBILOF ISLANDS.

Für′sten·wal′de (für′stĕn·väl′dĕ). Industrial city, Brandenburg, eastern Germany, on Spree river 24 m. ESE of Berlin; pop. 23,168; cathedral. Received municipal privileges 1285; episcopal see 1385–1571; bombed during World War II.

Fürth (fürt). Manufacturing city, NW cen. Bavaria, Germany, at confluence of Regnitz and Pegnitz rivers 5 m. NW of Nürnberg; pop. 73,693; railroad junction; in World War II had airplane factories; bombed by Allies 1944–45.

Fu′ry and Hec′la Strait (fūr′ĭ, hĕk′lä). Passage ab. 100 m. long from Gulf of Boothia to Foxe Basin, bet. Melville Penin. and NW Baffin I., Canada.

Fu·san (fōō·sän) *or* **Pu·san** (pōō-). City, ✳ of South Keisho prov., S Korea, on Chosen Strait ab. 140 m. NW of Shimonoseki, Japan; pop. (1960) 1,163,671; fine harbor; large export and import business.

Fu·sa′ro (fōō·sä′rō); *anc.* **Pa′lus Ach′e·ru′si·a** (pā′lŭs ăk′ĕ·rōō′zhĭ·ȧ [-zĭ·ȧ]). Small lake, Campania, Italy, on peninsula bet. Gulf of Gaeta and Bay of Pozzuoli; oyster cultivation, hydrobiological station.

Fushih. See YENAN.

Fu′shi·mi (fōō′shĭ·mē; *Jap.* fōō·shē·mē). City, W cen. Honshu, Japan, in Kyoto prefecture, a S suburb of Kyoto; pop. 29,700; historically important as residence (1594–98) of the shogun Toyotomi Hideyoshi.

Fu′shun′ (fōō′shōōn′). City, Liaoning prov., NE China, on S bank of Hun river 30 m. E of Mukden; pop. (1957 est.) 985,000; on rich bituminous coal field. Mines known to Chinese since 13th cent. A.D.; modern development begun by Russians; divided into New Town (modern Japanese, estab. 1907) and Old Town (developed from Chinese village).

Fu′sin′ (fōō′shĭn′). City, Liaoning prov., NE China, WNW of Mukden; pop. 188,600.

Füs′sen (fü′sĕn). Commune, SW Bavaria Germany, near Tirol border; pop. (1933) 6721; castle; treaty signed Apr. 22, 1745 bet. Elector Maximilian III Joseph of Bavaria and Maria Theresa.

Fustât, al-. See CAIRO city, Egypt.

Futa Jallon. See FOUTA DJALLON.

Futa, *or* **La Futa, Pass.** See APENNINES.

Fu·tu′na (fōō·tōō′nä), *or* **Hoorn** (hōrn), **Islands.** Island group in SW Pacific Ocean, NE of Fiji Is.; a part of Wallis and Futuna Islands group, a territory of the French Commonwealth; before 1958 a dependency of the French overseas territory of New Caledonia; comprises Futuna (8 m. by 5 m.) and Alofi (6 m. by 3 m.) Is.; 58 sq. m.; pop. ab. 4000; annexed by France 1887.

Fu′yu′ (fōō′yü′) *or* **Pe·tu′na** (pĕ·tōō′nä; *Chin.* bô-dōō·nä). Town, Kirin prov., NE China, on Sungari river 100 m. SW of Harbin; pop. 57,065.

Fyn (fün); *Ger.* **Fü′nen** (fü′nĕn). One of islands of Denmark, bet. Sjælland on E and lower Jutland Penin. on W; comprises counties of Svendborg and Odense; 1149 sq. m.; pop. (1925) 298,721.

Fyne, Loch (lŏk fīn′). Inlet ab. 40 m. long of Firth of Clyde, W Scotland, in Argyll co.; herrings.

Fyz′a·bad′. **1** (fīz′ȧ·băd′; *native* fīz′ä·bäd′) Town, Afghanistan. See FAIZABAD. **2** (fīz′ȧ·băd′; *native* fâz′ä·bäd′). District of E cen. Uttar Pradesh. N Indian Union. **3** (*same as* 2) *or* **Fyzabad–cum–A·jodh′ya** (-kŭm′ȧ-yŏd′yä). City, E cen. Uttar Pradesh, N India, on Gogra river 75 m. E of Lucknow; pop. (1941) 55,215; rail center; refines sugar. Founded 1730; later became residence of the begums of Oudh; station for troops. Includes nearby Ajodhya (*q.v.*). **4** (fīz′ȧ·băd′) Village, SW Trinidad, on border of **Pitch** Lake; produces oil.

G

Gab′a·rus′ Bay (găb′a·rōōs′). Inlet of Atlantic Ocean, E coast of Cape Breton I., Nova Scotia, Canada, SW of Louisburg.

Gabelhorn. = OBER-GABELHORN.

Gabe Rock (gāb). Height 5006 ft. in SW Banner co., W Nebraska.

Ga′be·ro′nes (gä′bĕ·rō′nĕs). Town, SE Bechuanaland, Africa, 90 m. NNE of Mafeking; * of Bechuanaland Protectorate; pop. 3849.

Ga′bès (gä′bĕs; *Fr.* gȧ′bĕs′); *anc.* **Tac′a·pe** (tăk′a·pē). Seaport town and oasis (including Menzel and Jara) in SE Tunisia, on the **Gulf of Gabès** (*anc.* **Syr′tis Mi′nor** [sûr′tĭs mī′nēr]); pop. (1936), with oasis, 18,611; export trade in dates, skins, wool, and oil.

Ga′bi·i (gā′bĭ·ī). Ancient city, Latium, Italy, 12 m. E of Rome, on shore of a lake which has dried up; well-known baths; temple of Juno; medieval fortress.

Ga′ble, Great (gā′b′l). Mountain 2949 ft. in W Cumberland, NW England, in the Lake District.

Gable Mountain. Peak 9200 ft. in Glacier National Park, NW Montana.

Gablonz. See JABLONEC.

Ga′bon′ (gȧ·bôn′) *or* **Ga·bun′** (gȧ·bōōn′); *Eng.* **Gaboon′** (gȧ·bōōn′). 1 River, Gabon Republic, W equatorial Africa, just N of the equator; an estuary 7 m. wide extending ab. 40 m. inland where it becomes a stream ab. 2 m. wide; Libreville is at its mouth. Discovered by Portuguese at end of 15th cent.
2 *Fr.* **Ré′pu′blique′ Ga′bo′naise′** (rā′pü′blēk′ gȧ′bô′nâz′). Republic, W equatorial Africa: 102,300 sq. m ; pop. (1959 est.) 421,000; * Libreville; bounded on NW by Río Muni, on N by Cameroun, on E and S by Congo Republic, on W by Atlantic Ocean. Hilly in S and on N border; highest point Mt. Tembo 3936 ft. in N. Chief rivers Gabon and the Ogooué, whose basin covers most of territory. Chief towns Libreville, Port Gentil. First part of French Equatorial Africa to be settled by the French (1841); Libreville founded 1849; became a colony 1903 and part of French Equatorial Africa 1910; changed to a territory 1946; became a republic of the French Community 1958.

Ga′bro·vo (gä′brŏ·vŏ). Town, S Pleven dept., N cen. Bulgaria, on upper Yantra river 50 m. SE of Pleven, at N end of Shipka Pass; pop. (1926) 10,483; textiles, leather; first Bulgarian national school opened here 1835.

Gadadhar. See MACHU.

Ga′dag (gŭ′dŭg). Town (joint municipality), SW Maharashtra state, W India, 310 m. SE of Bombay; pop. (1941) 56,223; important rail junction; old Hindu temples with beautiful carving, especially the Temple of Trimbakeshwar and a temple to Vishnu.

Ga·da′mes *or* **Gha·da′mes** (gȧ·dăm′ĕs; -dä′mĕs; *Arab.* gŏ·dä′măs). Oasis and town, Fezzan, NW Libya, near Algerian boundary; pop. (town) ab. 8000.

Gad′a·ra (găd′a·rȧ). Greek town of the Decapolis, NE Palestine, ab. 6 m. SE of Sea of Galilee; gave its name to the Gadarenes (*Mark* v. 1; *Luke* viii. 26).

Gades, Gadir. See CÁDIZ.

Ga·dire′ (gȧ·dīr′), *also* **Ga·dier′** (gȧ·dēr′). Vars. of *Gadir*, ancient name of CÁDIZ.

Gaditanum, Fretum; Gaditan Strait. See Strait of GIBRALTAR.

Gads′den (gădz′dĕn). 1 County in Florida. See *Table* at FLORIDA.
2 Industrial city, ⊗ of Etowah co., NE Alabama, on Coosa river 60 m. ENE of Birmingham; pop. 58,088; settled c. 1840; in area rich in manganese, iron ore, coal, limestone, bauxite, sandstone, timber.

Gadsden Purchase. A tract of land 29,640 sq. m., now in New Mexico and Arizona, purchased 1853 by U.S. from Mexico for $10,000,000 after negotiations conducted by James Gadsden, U.S. minister to Mexico.

Gads′hill′ (gădz′hĭl′). Low hill in Kent, SE England, 3 m. WNW of Rochester; home of Charles Dickens.

Ga·e′ta (gä·ā′tä); *anc.* **Ca·ie′ta** (kȧ·yē′tȧ). Fortified seaport, Littoria prov., Latium, cen. Italy, on Gulf of Gaeta 41 m. ESE of Littoria; pop. 18,332; fisheries; ancient ruins, including a Roman theater, a Roman amphitheater, and a campanile. Center of commercial prosperity after dissolution of Roman and Eastern Empires; withstood numerous invasions, esp. by Lombards and Saracens; fell to Norman Sicily 1134; papal refuge 1848-50 from Roman revolutions; last stronghold of Neapolitan Bourbons in Italy; fell to General Cialdini after long siege 1861.

Gaeta, Gulf of. Inlet of Tyrrhenian Sea on W coast of Italy, N of Bay of Naples and E of Pontine Is.; its coast occupied by Allies May 1944.

Gae·tu′li·a (jē·tū′lĭ·ȧ; -tūl′yȧ). Ancient district, N Africa, N part of Libya and of Sahara region; inhabited by nomad tribes which belonged to Numidian Berber race.

Gaff′ney (găf′nĭ). City, ⊗ of Cherokee co., N South Carolina, 19 m. ENE of Spartanburg; pop. 10,435; textile mills; limestone. Limestone College (1845; women).

Gäfle, Gäfleborg. Vars. of GÄVLE, GÄVLEBORG.

Gaf′sa (găf′sȧ); *anc.* **Cap′sa** (kăp′sȧ). Town and oasis, W cen. Tunisia, ab. 115 m. W of Sfax; pop. ab. 5000; French garrison; thermal springs; prehistoric discoveries nearby have given name (*Capsian*) to a paleolithic culture of N Africa and S Europe regarded as contemporaneous with the Aurignacian. In World War II scene of some of first fighting by American troops in African campaign; taken by Germans last week of Feb. 1943 (cf. KASSERINE PASS), retaken by Americans Mar. 17, 1943.

Gage (gāj). County in Nebraska. See *Table* at NEBRASKA.

Gage′town (gāj′toun). Town (unincorporated), ⊗ of Queens co., S New Brunswick, Canada, on St. John river 36 m. N of St. John; pop. 899.

Ga′gny (gȧ′nyē′). Commune, Seine-et-Oise dept., N France, 6 m. ENE of Paris; pop. 13,495.

Gai′da·ro (*Gr.* gī′thä·rô; *Ital.* gī′dä·rô). Small island in the E Aegean Sea, S of Samos; included in the Dodecanese group.

Gail (gāl). Town, ⊗ of Borden co., NW Texas; pop. (1950) 138.

Gail·lac′ (gȧ′yȧk′). Manufacturing commune, Tarn dept., S France, on Tarn river ab. 12 m. W of Albi; pop. (1931) 7440; Benedictine abbey founded 960; noted for sparkling white wine.

Gail·lard′ Cut (gĭl·yärd′); *formerly* **Cu·le′bra Cut** (kṳ·lā′brȧ; -lĕb′rȧ; *Span.* kōō·lā′vrä). Southeast section of Panama Canal, Canal Zone, ab. 8 m. through Culebra Mt., from Gamboa to locks at Pedro Miguel; 45 ft. deep, width at bottom 300 ft.; name changed by Pres. Wilson in honor of David Du Bose Gaillard (d. 1913) who had charge of excavation of this most difficult part in construction of the canal.

Gaines (gānz). County in Texas. See *Table* at TEXAS.

Gaines′bor′o (gānz′bûr′ŏ). Town, ⊗ of Jackson co., N Tennessee; pop. 1021.

Gaines′ Mill (gānz). Battlefield just ENE of Richmond, Virginia; scene June 27, 1862 of defeat of Union forces under General Fitz-John Porter by Lee's Confederates; sometimes known as Cold Harbor (*q.v.*).

Gaines′ville (gānz′vĭl; *Sou.* also -v′l). 1 City, ⊗ of Alachua co., N Florida penin., 65 m. SW of Jacksonville; pop. 29,701; sawmills, naval stores; University of Florida (1853; coed.).
2 City, ⊗ of Hall co., N Georgia, 35 m. NW of Athens; pop. 16,523; incorporated 1821; textile mills; Brenau College (1878; women).

3 City, ⊗ of Ozark co., S Missouri; pop. 266.

4 City, ⊗ of Cooke co., N Texas, 30 m. W of Sherman; pop. 13,083; settled c. 1851 on route of the 1849 gold seekers; chartered as city 1879; processes agricultural products, refines oil.

5 Village, Prince William co., NE Virginia; battle Aug. 28, 1862, a part of second battle of Bull Run.

Gains'bor'ough (gānz'bûr'ō; *esp. Brit.*, -bŭ·rŭ, -brŭ). Urban district, Parts of Lindsey, Lincolnshire, E England, on the Trent 30 m. SW of Hull; pop. 17,509; the St. Ogg's of George Eliot's *Mill on the Floss;* Sweyn Forkbeard landed here 1013 with his Danish marauders.

Gaïon. See PAXOS.

Gaird'ner, Lake (gârd'nẽr). Lake ab. 90 m. long, S South Australia, N of Eyre Penin.

Gair Loch (gâr' lŏk'). Inlet of Atlantic Ocean on NW coast of Scotland, in Ross and Cromarty co.; the village of **Gair'loch'** is at its head.

Gai'thers·burg (gā'thẽrz·bûrg). Town, Montgomery co., W Maryland, 20 m. NW of Washington; pop. 3847; site of International Latitude Observatory, on 39°8'N lat., one of five such observatories in the world: see KITAB, Uzbek S.S.R.; MIZUSAWA, Japan; SAN PIETRO I., Sardinia (Carloforte); UKIAH, California.

Gajac. See VILLENEUVE-SUR-LOT.

Ga'la *or* **Gala Water** (gä'lä). River 21 m. long in SE Scotland; rises in Moorfoot Hills, S of Edinburgh; flows SSW into the Tweed near Abbotsford.

Ga·la'na (gȧ·lä'nȧ). River ab. 350 m. long in E Africa; rises in S Kenya, flows SE across S Kenya into Indian Ocean S of Formosa Bay.

Ga·lá'pa·gos Islands (gȧ·lä'pá·gŭs; -lăp'ȧ-) *or* **Co·lón' Archipelago** (kô·lōn'); *Span.* **Ar'chi·pié'la·go de Co·lón'** (är'chē·pyä'lä·gô thȧ kô·lōn'). Island group comprising Colón prov., Ecuador, in Pacific Ocean on the equator 600 m. W of mainland; ✳ San Cristóbal; 3029 sq. m.; pop. (1944 est.) 661; comprises many small islands and ab. 15 large ones, only two inhabited: San Cristóbal (*Eng.* Chatham) and Isabela (Albemarle). See *Map* at ECUADOR. Interesting specimens of wild life peculiar to the islands, on which exploration without official permission is prohibited; noted esp. for species of giant tortoise (*Span.* galápago), now almost extinct, which include perhaps the largest living form now known (*Testudo vicina*, syn. *gigantopus*) found on Isabel (Albemarle) I. During World War II one of islands, Seymour, site of air base established by U.S. forces Dec. 1941, evacuated July 1946.

Gal'a·shiels' (găl'ȧ·shēlz'). Burgh, Selkirk co., SE Scotland; pop. 12,496; manufactures tweeds.

Gal'a·ta (găl'ȧ·tȧ; *Turk.* gä'lä·tä'). Seaport suburb, chief business section of İstanbul, Turkey, on the Golden Horn S of Pera; in 1265 assigned by Michael Palaeologus to Genoese merchants; fortified by them but taken over by the Turks 1453.

Ga·la'ţi (gä·läts'; gä·lä'tsĕ) *or* **Ga'latz** (gä'läts). City, E Romania, on lower Danube ab. 115 m. NE of Bucharest; pop. (1939 est.) 102,232; port, exporting esp. timber and grain.

Ga·la'ti·a (gȧ·lā'shĭ·ȧ; -shȧ). Ancient country of cen. Asia Minor, originally including parts of Phrygia and Cappadocia; settled by Gauls in 3d cent. B.C.; expanded by them until checked by Attalus I of Pergamum c. 230 B.C.; became dependent upon Romans in 2d cent. B.C. and Roman province 25 B.C.; visited by St. Paul (*Epistle to the Galatians*). See ANKARA.

Ga'la·ti'na (gä'lä·tē'nä). Commune, Lecce prov., Apulia, SE Italy, 10 m. S of Lecce; pop. 20,794.

Ga'la·to'ne (gä'lä·tō'nä). Commune, Lecce prov., Apulia, SE Italy, 13 m. SSW of Lecce; pop. 11,595; cathedral.

Galatz. See GALAŢI.

Ga'lax (gā'lăks). City, SW Virginia, in Carroll and Grayson cos. but politically independent; pop. 5254; small manufactures; ships galax.

Gald'hö·pig'gen (gäl'hû·pǐg'ĕn). Peak 8097 ft. in the Jotunheimen, S cen. Norway, S of Glittertind.

Ga·le'ka·land' (gȧ·lä'kȧ·länd'). A district of Transkei (*q.v.*), Union of South Africa, along the coast bet. Great Kei and Umtata rivers, inhabited by the Galeka (or Gcaleka).

Ga·le'la (gä·lä'lä). See HALMAHERA.

Ga·le'na (gȧ·lē'nȧ). **1** City, ⊗ of Jo Daviess co., NW corner of Illinois, on Mississippi river; pop. 4410; in zinc and lead mining section; marble and granite works; home of Ulysses S. Grant.

2 City, Cherokee co., SE corner of Kansas, 22 m. S of Pittsburg; pop. 3827; lead and zinc deposits; smelters.

3 City, ⊗ of Stone co., SW Missouri; pop. 389.

Galena Park. City, Harris co., SE Texas; pop. 10,852.

Ga'len·stock' (gä'lĕn·shtôk'). Peak 11,805 ft. in Valais and Uri cantons, S cen. Switzerland.

Ga·le'ra Point (gȧ·lẽr'ȧ). Cape at NE tip of island of Trinidad.

Galeras, El. See EL GALERAS.

Gales'burg (gālz'bûrg). Industrial city, ⊗ of Knox co., W Illinois, 45 m. WNW of Peoria; pop. 37,243; settled 1836 by pioneers from Whitesboro, N.Y.; incorporated as city 1857; Knox College (1837; coed. from 1870).

Gales Ferry (gālz). Subdivision of town of LEDYARD, Connecticut.

Gale'ton (gāl'tŭn; -t'n). Borough, Potter co., N Pennsylvania, 47 m. NW of Williamsport; pop. 1646.

Ga·li'ci·a (gȧ·lĭsh'ĭ·ȧ; -lĭsh'ȧ); *Russ.* **Ga'lich** (gä'lyǐch), **Ga·li'tsi·ya** (gŭ·lyē'tsyĭ·yȧ). Former Austrian crownland in E cen. Europe, including N slopes of Carpathian Mts. and the valleys of upper Vistula and of upper Dniester, Bug, and Seret rivers; 30,645 sq. m. From 6th cent. A.D., inhabited by Slavs; medieval principalities of Halicz and Lodomeria emerged about 12th cent. and were united in 13th cent.; E part, once attached to principality of Kiev, separated from Russian territory by Mongol invasion; ultimately became part of Poland 1386; in partitions of Poland 1772 and 1795, annexed to Austria; Western Galicia included in grand duchy of Warsaw 1809; scene of rising after which Kraków (*q.v.*) returned to Austria (1846); in World War I scene of fighting bet. Russians and Austrians and Germans; ceded by Austria 1919; after the war Poland conquered E part which had joined Ukraine, and in 1923, was confirmed in her possession of it; became Polish departments of Kraków, Lwów, Stanisławów, and Tarnopol (*qq.v.*); divided bet. Germany and Soviet Union 1939 until outbreak of German war against Russia 1941; E half returned to Russia and made part of Ukraine after World War II.

Ga·li'ci·a (gȧ·lĭsh'ĭ·ȧ; -lĭsh'ȧ; *Span.* gä·lē'thyä, -syä); *anc.* **Gal·lae'ci·a** (gă·lē'shĭ·ȧ; -shȧ). Region and ancient kingdom, NW Spain; 11,256 sq. m.; bounded N and W by Atlantic Ocean, S by Portugal, SE by León, NE by Asturias; comprises modern provinces of La Coruña, Lugo, Orense, Pontevedra; deeply indented coast line with good harbors; mountainous; chief river the Miño; lead, tin, iron pyrites, and copper mines. Independent kingdom under the Suevi 411–585; overthrown first by Visigoths, later by Moors; became part of kingdom of Asturias and later of León and Castile.

Gal'i·lee (găl'ĭ·lē). **1** Hilly region of N Palestine, bounded on E by Jordan river and Sea of Galilee, and extending S to Plain of Esdraelon; in early times corresponded to land of tribe of Naphtali; in 1st cent. B.C. a Roman province, divided into Upper Galilee and Lower Galilee, and forming a tetrarchy under rule of Herod family; chief scene of Christ's ministry. Ancient capital Sepphoris. Roman capital Tiberias, other important town Nazareth.

2 *also* **Galilee and A'cre** (ä'kẽr; ā'kẽr; ä'krẽr; äk'ẽr; äk'rẽr). District in N Palestine, including the subdistricts Acre, Nazareth, Beisan, Safad, Tiberias; 1082 sq. m.; pop. 155,545, (1942 est.) 207,164.

Galilee, Sea of; *usual name in Gospels for mod.* **Bahr Ta'ba·ri'ya** (bä'h'r tŏ'bū·rē'yä; -yä). *In Bible also called* Sea of **Chin'ne·reth** (kĭn'ĕ·rĕth) [*Deut.* iii. 17], **Lake of Gen·nes'a·ret** (gĕ·nĕs'á·rĕt) [*Luke* v. 1], and **Sea of Ti·be'ri·as** (tĭ·bēr'ĭ·ǎs) [*John* vi. 1]. A freshwater lake 14 m. long by 8 m. wide, N Palestine; 686 ft. below sea level; chief towns on its shores Tiberias and Magdala (W), Capernaum and Bethsaida (N).

Ga·li'na Point (gä·lē'nä). Cape on NE coast of island of Jamaica, West Indies.

Gal'ion (găl'yŭn; găl'ĭ·ŭn). Manufacturing city, Crawford co., N cen. Ohio, 15 m. W of Mansfield; pop. 12,650; settled 1831; railroad center.

Gal'la (găl'á); *also* **Gal'la·land'** (-lǎnd'). Region, W Ethiopia; chief town Gambela; inhabited chiefly by Gallas.

Gal'la·bat (găl'á·băt; *Arab.* kŏl'lä·băt'). Town, S Kassala prov., E Sudan, on Ethiopian border NNW of Lake Tana; pop. ab. 3000.

Gallaecia. See GALICIA.

Gal'la·ra'te (gäl'lä·rä'tä). Industrial commune, Varese prov., Lombardy, N Italy, 10 m. S of Varese; pop. 24,505; produces cotton cloth.

Gal'la·tin (găl'á·t'n; -tĭn). **1** River ab. 125 m. long, S Montana; rises in NW corner of Wyoming, flows N to unite with Jefferson and Madison rivers and form the Missouri river; has formed a deep narrow canyon ab. 70 m. long, at entrance to which is a small village **Gallatin Gateway**, cen. Gallatin co., the canyon being one of the entrances to Yellowstone National Park.
2 Name of counties in three states of the U.S. See *Tables* at ILLINOIS, KENTUCKY, MONTANA.
3 City, ⊗ of Daviess co., NW Missouri, 25 m. WNW of Chillicothe; pop. 1658.
4 City, ⊗ of Sumner co., N Tennessee, 26 m. NE of Nashville; pop. 7901; burley tobacco market.

Gallatin Peak *or* **Mountain.** Peak 10,967 ft., S cen. Gallatin co., S Montana.

Gallatin Range. Mountains, Gallatin and Park cos., S Montana, bet. the Gallatin and Yellowstone rivers; highest point Electric Peak 11,155 ft., in NW corner of Yellowstone National Park.

Galle (gäl; găl), *formerly* **Point de Galle** (point dĕ). Town, ✳ of Southern Province, Ceylon, on Indian Ocean 66 m. SSE of Colombo; pop. 38,424; fortified seaport on rocky promontory. Occupied by Portuguese 1597; taken 1643 by Dutch, who erected fort; many curious old Buddhist monasteries.

Gal·le'gos (gä·yā'gŏs; gä·zhä'-). **1** River 180 m. long, S Argentina; flows E across S Santa Cruz territory into **Gallegos Bay** opp. Falkland Is.
2 *or* **Rí'o Gallegos** (rē'ō); *also* **Puer'to Gallegos** (pwĕr'tô). River port, ✳ of Santa Cruz territory, S Argentina, near mouth of Gallegos river; pop. (est.) 6325.

Gal'ley·head' (găl'ĭ·hĕd'). Cape on SW coast of Ireland, E of Cape Clear; lighthouse.

Gal'li·a (găl'ĭ·á). County in Ohio. See *Table* at OHIO.

Gallia, Gallia Cisalpina, Gallia Cispadana, etc. See GAUL.

Gal·lia'te (gäl·lyä'tä). Commune, Novara prov., Piedmont, NW Italy, 5 m. NE of Novara; pop. 10,284.

Gallim. See BEIT JALA.

Gal·li'nas, Point (gä·yē'näs). Northernmost point of South America, Guajira Penin., N Colombia; 12°15'N.

Gal·lip'o·li (gä·lĭp'ō·lĭ; *Ital.* gäl·lē'pō·lē). Fortified seaport and manufacturing commune, Lecce prov., Apulia, SE Italy, on E shore of Gulf of Taranto 21 m. SSW of Lecce; pop. 13,048.

Gallipoli. See GELÍBOLU.

Gal·lip'o·li Peninsula (gä·lĭp'ō·lĭ); *anc.* **Cher'so·ne'-sus Thrac'i·ca** (kûr'sō·nē'sŭs thrăs'ĭ·ká). Narrow tongue of land 63 m. long, extending SW from S coast of Turkey in Europe, bet. the Dardanelles on the SE and Saros Gulf and Aegean Sea on the NW and W. Scene of

battles 1915–16 in Allied campaign in World War I, in conjunction with naval bombardment of Dardanelles forts; troops, mainly Anzacs, landed Apr. 25, 1915; severe fighting at Krithia, Sari Bair, Suvla Bay, etc.; unsuccessful issue led to withdrawal (last troops left Jan. 8, 1916).

Gal'li·po·lis' (găl'ĭ·pō·lēs'). Industrial city, ⊗ of Gallia co., S Ohio, on Ohio river 30 m. NE of Ironton; pop. 8775; settled by French colonists 1790.

Gal·li'tzin (gä·lĭt's'n; -sĭn). Borough, Cambria co., SW cen. Pennsylvania, 10 m. W of Altoona; pop. 2783; railroad tunnel at crest of Alleghenies above Altoona.

Gäl'li·va're (yĕl'lĭ·vä'rĕ). Village, Norrbotten prov., N Sweden, in the Arctic Circle; pop. 2272; hydroelectric power plant; iron mines.

Gal'lo, Cape (găl'lō). **1** *anc.* **A·kri'tas** (á·krī'tǎs). Cape on SW coast of Peloponnesus, S Greece, on W side of Gulf of Messenia.
2 Point on NW coast of Sicily, NW of Palermo.

Gal'lon Head (găl'ŭn). Cape on W coast of island of Lewis with Harris in the Outer Hebrides, off NW coast of Scotland.

Gal'loo Island (găl'ōō). Island in NE Lake Ontario, off W cen. coast of Jefferson co., N New York.

Gal'lo·way (găl'ō·wā). District in SW Scotland, comprising Wigtown and Kirkcudbright cos.

Galloway, Mull of (mŭl). Cape on SW extremity of Scotland, projecting into Irish Sea W of entrance to Luce Bay; lighthouse.

Gal'lup (găl'ŭp). Town, ⊗ of McKinley co., NW New Mexico, bet. Southern Navajo and Zuñi Indian Reservations; pop. 14,089; incorporated 1891; made ⊗ 1901; railroad division point; coal mines; wool combing and packing, sheep and cattle raising.

Gal'lups Island (găl'ŭps). One of the smaller and outer islands in Boston Harbor, Massachusetts; U.S. radio training school.

Ga·loeng'goeng *or* **Ga·lung'gung** (gä·lōōng'gōōng). Volcanic peak 7221 ft., W Java, Indonesia, ab. 10 m. E of Garut; destructive eruption 1822.

Ga·lo'fa·lo (gä·lô'fä·lô); *anc.* **Cha·ryb'dis** (ká·rĭb'dĭs). Famous whirlpool near Cape Faro, Sicily.

Galt (gôlt). City, Waterloo co., SE Ontario, Canada, on Grand river 11 m. SE of Kitchener; pop. 19,207; in rich farming section; varied manufactures. Founded as Shade's Mills 1816; many early settlers were Scottish; renamed 1827 after John Galt, Scottish novelist.

Gal'ty (gôl'tĭ), *or* **Gal'tee, Mountains.** Range ab. 15 m. long extending E to W in cos. Tipperary and Limerick, S Ireland; highest peak **Gal'ty·more'** (gôl'tĭ·môr'), 3015 ft., in SW co. Tipperary.

Gal'va (găl'vá). City, Henry co., NW Illinois, 35 m. SE of Rock Island; pop. 3060.

Gal'ves·ton (găl'vĕs·tŭn). **1** County in Texas. See *Table* at TEXAS.
2 City and port of entry, its ⊗, SE Texas, on E end of **Galveston Island** (30 m. long) at S side of entrance to **Galveston Bay** (inlet of Gulf of Mexico) 48 m. SSE of Houston; pop. 67,175; connected with mainland by causeway and bridge; extensive port facilities, exports esp. cotton, sulfur, oil, grain; manufactures wire and nails, food products, cement, clothing; fisheries. Used as rendezvous by Jean Laffite 1817–21; made naval base during Texas revolt against Mexico 1835; temporary capital of the republic before and after battle of San Jacinto 1836; incorporated as city 1839; scene of Civil War battle 1863; suffered from severe hurricanes and floods (esp. 1900); first city to adopt (1901) commission plan of municipal government, later called Galveston plan.

Gal'way (gôl'wā). **1** County, W Eire, in Connacht prov.; 2293 sq. m.; pop. 168,198; ⊗ Galway; mountainous; chief river the Shannon; agriculture, fishing, quarrying (marble), manufacturing linen and woolen goods.
2 Municipal borough and seaport, its ⊗, at head of

Galway Bay (extends inland ab. 20 m. on border bet. cos. Galway and Clare); pop. 18,294; noted transatlantic passenger port; black marble quarrying, distilling, iron founding, fishing. Ruins of a 13th-cent. Franciscan friary; seat of University College.

Gam·be′la (găm·bā′lȧ; *Ethiopian* găm·bā·lä); *or* **Gam-bei′la.** Enclave in W Ethiopia, in Galla region; leased as a trading station to the Sudan government; pop. (1938) 15,013.

Gam′bell (găm′b'l). Village on coast at NW point of St. Lawrence I. in Bering Sea, Alaska; pop. (est.) 339.

Gam′bi·a (găm′bĭ·ȧ). **1** River ab. 460 m. long, W Africa; rises in Fouta Djallon, Guinea; flows NW through Senegal and W into Atlantic Ocean at Bathurst; lower 200 m., which are navigable at all seasons, are in Republic of Gambia.
2 Republic in British Commonwealth, NW Africa, formerly a British crown colony and protectorate; area 3977 sq. m., pop. 315,486; a strip of land extending ab. 6 m. on each side of the Gambia river and ab. 200 m. inland from river mouth, surrounded by Senegal; ✱ Bathurst, on Island of St. Mary at mouth of river; produces peanuts.
History: River mouth discovered by Portuguese in 15th cent. and river ascended by agent of English trading company 1618–19; Fort James, built on small island ab. 20 m. from mouth of Gambia, established 1664; Gambia settlement placed under government of Sierra Leone 1807–43 and 1866–88; crown colony 1843–66 and since 1888; boundaries of protectorate settled 1889; became independent Feb. 18, 1965.

Gam′bier (găm′bēr). Village, Knox co., cen. Ohio, ab. 5 m. E of Mount Vernon; pop. 1418; Kenyon College (1824; men).

Gambier Islands. Island group, French Polynesia, S Pacific Ocean, SE of Tuamotu Archipelago; lat. 23°15′S and long. 134°55′W; 12 sq. m.; pop. (1936) 1579; chief island Mangareva; nearly enclosed by great barrier reef 40 m. in circumference; generally considered a part of the Tuamotu Archipelago.

Gam·bo′a (găm·bō′ȧ; *Span.* gäm·bō′ä). Village on Panama Canal at SE corner of Gatun Lake, Canal Zone; channel (8 m.) of canal in arm of Gatun Lake W of Gamboa known as **Gamboa Reach.**

Ga′me·lei′ra, *or* **Ga′mel·lei′ra,** Cape (gȧ′mĕ·lā′ĕ·rȧ). Cape extending into Atlantic Ocean on NE coast of Rio Grande do Norte state, NE Brazil.

Gam′ka (găm′kȧ). River ab. 140 m. long in Great Karroo region of Cape Province, Republic of South Africa; unites with the Groote river to form the Gouritz.

Ga·mo·da, Cape (gä·mō·dä). Cape on E coast of Shikoku, Japan, projecting into Kii Channel.

Gam·toos′ (găm·tōōs′). River in S Cape Province, Republic of South Africa; including Groote river, its main headstream, ab. 300 m. long; flows SE to Indian Ocean.

Ga·mu′ (gä·mōō′). Municipality, W cen. Isabela prov., Luzon, Phil. Is., 7 m. S of Ilagan; pop. 18,201.

Gana. See GHANA.

Ga·na′le Dor′ya (gȧ·nä′lä dôr′yä). River ab. 225 m. long, S Ethiopia, flows SE, then S to join the Webbe and Dawa and form the Juba.

Gan′a·noq′ue (găn′ȧ·nŏk′wĕ). Town, Leeds co., SE Ontario, Canada, on St. Lawrence river 20 m. E of Kingston; pop. 4572; adjacent to the Thousand Is.

Gand. See GENT.

Gan′dak (gŭn′dŭk). River ab. 400 m. long in Nepal and N India; formed by union of several streams in cen. Nepal W of Katmandu, flows SW and SE through NW Bihar to the Ganges opp. Patna.

Gan′der (găn′dēr). River ab. 100 m. long, E Newfoundland; rises in S cen. section of the island, flows NE into **Gander Bay,** inlet of Atlantic Ocean W of Cape Freels; flows through **Gander Lake** on N shore of which at town of **Gander** (pop. 5725), 215 m. NW of St. John's, is British air base, take-off point for transatlantic flights

of land planes, one of the largest air bases in North America.

Gan·dha′ra (gŭn·där′ȧ). Region, NW Punjab, NW India, and part of E Afghanistan—loosely so called from ab. 6th cent. B.C. to 5th cent. A.D.; name preserved in modern *Kandahar.*

Gan·dí′a (gän·dē′ä). Seaport commune, Valencia prov., E Spain, on Mediterranean 38 m. SSE of Valencia; pop. 19,975; manufactures silk, velvet, leather.

Gandja. Var. of *Gandzha:* see KIROVABAD.

Gan′do (gän′dō) *or* **Gwan′du** (gwän′dōō). Emirate chiefly in Sokoto prov., NW Nigeria; 6208 sq. m.; pop. 287,000; originally included territory now in Niger and Dahomey republics; established c. 1819, came under control of Nigeria 1903; chief town Gando (pop. ab. 7000) ab. 60 m. SW of Sokoto. See SOKOTO.

Gandzha. Old name of KIROVABAD.

Gan′ges (găn′jēz); *Sanskrit and Hind.* **Gan′ga** (gŭng′gä). Sacred river of N and NE India ab. 1557 m. long; rises in the Himalayas near Gangotri on NE Tehri border, flows S through the state as the Bhagirathi, then out into the plain of India at Hardwar in NW Uttar Pradesh, thence SE through Uttar Pradesh, Bihar, and Bengal to merge with the Brahmaputra river and flow into the Bay of Bengal through the vast Ganges Delta (*q.v.*). Unites with the Jumna at Allahabad; receives from the S the Son and from the N the tributaries Gumti, Gogra, and Gandak; in upper course is source of extensive irrigation canals. On its banks are the sacred cities of Allahabad and Benares.

Ganges, *or* **Gan′ges–Brah′ma·pu′tra** (-brä′mȧ·pōō′trȧ), **Delta.** Region 80 to 200 m. wide E to W, ab. ⅓ of Bengal, NE India, covered by the streams forming the mouths of the Ganges and Brahmaputra rivers. On entering Bengal the Brahmaputra is joined by the Tista from the NW and from there to Goalanda in cen. Bengal is known as the **Ja′mu·na** (jŭ′mōō·nä). The main

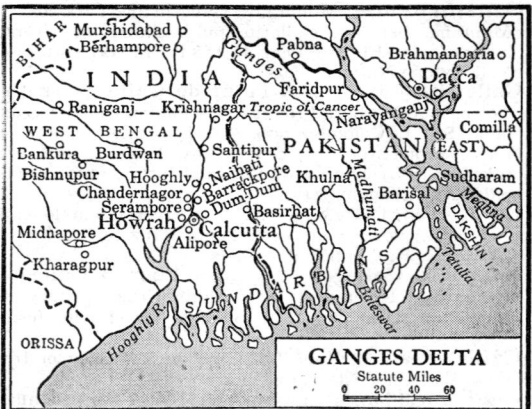

GANGES DELTA
Statute Miles
0   20   40   60

streams, Ganges and Jamuna, united at Goalanda form the **Pad′ma** (pŭd′mä), which below Dacca is joined by the Meghna; from this point to the Bay of Bengal the E mouth of the delta is known as the Meghna; the W outlet of the Meghna, W of Dakshin I., is the **Te·tu′li·a** (tĕ·tōō′lĭ·ä). Above Goalanda the **Mad′hu·ma′ti** (mŭd′hōō·mŭ′tĕ) leaves the Ganges entering the Bay of Bengal at the **Ba·les′war** (bȧ·lĕs′wēr) mouth. The stream farthest W is the Hooghly which leaves the Ganges near Murshidabad, passing Calcutta (90 m. from the sea) and entering the Bay of Bengal by the largest mouth of the delta; its upper course above Santipur is an old channel of the Ganges, generally known as the **Bha·gi′ra·thi** (bä·gē′rȧ·tĭ). Many smaller streams of the delta bet. the Tetulia and Hooghly mouths form a great swamp region (6526 sq. m.) known as the **Sun′dar·bans** (sōōn′dēr·bŭns).

Gan'gi (gän'jĕ); *anc.* **En'gy·um** (ĕn'jĭ·ŭm). Commune, Palermo prov., NW cen. Sicily, 52 m. ESE of Palermo; pop. 11,022; castle.

Gan'go·tri (gŭng'gô·trē). Mountain temple, 10,319 ft. above the sea, NW Uttar Pradesh, N India, near source of Bhagirathi river.

Gang'pur (gŭng'poŏr). Former Indian state, Eastern States, NE Indian Union; 2477 sq. m.; pop. (1941) 398,171, * Suadi.

Gangra. See ÇANKIRI.

Gang'tok (gŭng'tŏk). Commercial town, * of Sikkim, NE India, 28 m. NE of Darjeeling; on trade route bet. India and Tibet.

Ganja. Var. of *Gandzha*: see KIROVABAD.

Gan'nett Peak (găn'ĕt; -ĭt). Mountain 13,785 ft., Fremont co., cen. Wyoming, in Wind River Range; highest point in the state.

Gann·val'ley (găn·văl'ĭ). Village, ⊗ of Buffalo co., S cen. South Dakota; pop. (1950) 180.

Ga·nong'ga (gȧ·nŏng'gȧ). Small island of the New Georgia Is., cen. Solomon Is., W Pacific Ocean; S of Vella Lavella I.

Ga·o' (gä·ō'). Town on Niger river, E Sudan, West Africa; pop. (1940) 6923; military air base and station.

Gap (găp), *anc* **Va·pin'cum** (vȧ·pĭng'kŭm). Commune, * of Hautes-Alpes dept., SE France, 96 m. NNE of Marseilles; pop. 13,600; episcopal see; manufactures gloves.

Ga·pan' (gä·pän'). Municipality, S Nueva Ecija prov., Luzon, Phil. Is., S of Cabanatuan; pop. 23,324.

Gapsal. Var. of KHAPSALU.

Garaet–Achkel. See Lake ACHKEL.

Ga'ra Gor·fu' (gä'rä gôr·foō'). Peak 11,482 ft., cen. Ethiopia, N of Addis Ababa.

Ga'ra·ka'yo (gä'rä·kä'yō). Island, S Palau Is., SW Pacific Ocean, near Peleliu, 1 m. in diameter; occupied by U.S. forces Oct. 9, 1944.

Garam. See HRON.

Ga·ram Bi, Cape (gä·räm bē). Cape at S end of Formosa, on Bashi Channel.

Ga·ra·nhuns' (gä'rȧ·nyoōns'). City, Pernambuco state, E Brazil, 120 m. SW of Recife; pop. (1940 est.) 16,440.

Gar'a·pan' (gär'ȧ·pän'; gär'ȧ·pän'). Former town on W coast of Saipan, Mariana Is., W Pacific Ocean; administrative center of the Marianas under Japanese mandate. Captured by American forces July 1944.

Garbieh. See GHARBÎYA.

Garches (gärsh). Commune, Seine-et-Oise dept., N France, near Versailles; pop. (1931) 7377; Lafayette Escadrille monument in memory of American aviators killed in World War I.

Gar·cí'a Caves (gär·sē'ä). Large natural caves, with stalactites and an underground lake, near Monterrey, Nuevo León state, Mexico.

Gar'ci–Cres'po (gär'sĕ·krãs'pô). Town, Puebla state, SE cen. Mexico, 155 m. E of Mexico City; alt. 5550 ft.; thermal mineral springs.

Gard (gàr). Department of France. See *Table* at FRANCE.

Gar'da, Lake (gär'dä); *anc.* **La'cus Be·na'cus** (lā'kŭs bĕ·nā'kŭs). Lake in E Lombardy, N Italy, its E shore on Venezia Euganea boundary; 35 m. long and 2 to 10 m. wide; 143 sq. m.; drains S through Mincio river into the Po.

Gardaia. Var of GHARDAÏA.

Gar'den (gär'd'n). County in Nebraska. See *Table* at NEBRASKA.

Gar·de'na (gär·dē'nȧ). City, Los Angeles co., SW California, S suburb of Los Angeles, pop. 35,943.

Gar·de'na, Val di (väl' dĕ gär·dä'nä); *Ger.* **Gröd'·ner·tal'** (grŭd'nĕr·täl'). Picturesque valley 18 m. long in Venezia Tridentina, NE Italy.

Gar'den City (gär'd'n). **1** Town, Chatham co., SE Georgia, 2 mi. N of Savannah; pop. 5451.

2 City, ⊗ of Finney co., W Kansas, on Arkansas river; pop. 11,811.

3 City, Wayne co., SE Michigan, 15 m. W of Detroit; pop. 38,017.

4 Residential village, Nassau co., SE New York, on Long I. 18 m. E of New York; pop. 23,948. Protestant Episcopal Cathedral of the Incarnation; Adelphi Coll. (coed.; founded 1896 in Brooklyn); Mitchel Field (U.S. Air Force base; closed 1960); Roosevelt Field, airport from which Charles A. Lindbergh took off in 1927; printing and publishing center.

5 Village, ⊗ of Glasscock co., W Texas; pop. (1950) 118.

Garden Grove. City, Orange co., SW California, S of Anaheim; pop. 84,238.

Garden Island. Island in N Lake Michigan N of Beaver I.; part of Charlevoix co., NW Michigan.

Garden of the Gods. A region of ab. 500 acres near Colorado Springs, Colorado, noted for the numerous strange rock formations of red and white sandstone.

Garden Reach. SW suburb of Calcutta, NE Indian Union, on E bank of Hooghly river; pop. (1941) 85,188.

Garden Wall. Mountain 8600 ft. in Glacier National Park, NW Montana; a narrow ridge with glaciers on either side.

Gardinas. See GRODNO.

Gar'di·ner (gärd'nĕr; gär'd'n·ẽr). **1** City, Kennebec co., SW Maine, on Kennebec river 8 m. S of Augusta; pop. 6897; shoe factories, paper mills, wood-working shops.

2 Town, S Park co., S Montana; N entrance to Yellowstone National Park; pop. (est.) 400; alt. 5287 ft.; nearby are **Gardiner River** and **Gardiner Canyon.**

Gar'di·ners Bay (gärd'nẽrz; gär'd'n·ẽrz). Inlet of Long Island Sound on E end of Long I., New York.

Gardiners Island. Island in Gardiners Bay, E Long I., New York, W of Montauk Point; settled 1639; made part of Long I. and of East Hampton township 1683; reputed burial place of pirate loot by Captain Kidd.

Gard'ner (gärd'nĕr). **1** City, Worcester co., cen. Massachusetts, 9 m. W of Fitchburg; pop. 19,038; manufactures chairs, upholstered furniture, silverware.

2 One of the Phoenix Is. (*q.v.*), cen. Pacific Ocean, 4°40'S lat. and 174°30'W long.; ab. 2 m. long; large coconut plantations.

Gardner Canal *or* **Channel.** Inlet of Pacific Ocean ab. 80 m. long, W British Columbia, Canada, joining Douglas Channel at its mouth.

Gardner Lake. Lake in W cen. New London co., SE Connecticut.

Gardner Pinnacles *or* **Island.** Group of islets of Leeward Is., Hawaiian Is., in cen. Pacific Ocean 168°W; consists of lava rock columns 170 ft. high; in Hawaiian Is. Bird Reservation.

Gare Loch (gâr' lŏk'). Branch 7 m. long of the Firth of Clyde, SW Scotland.

Garenne–Colombes, La. See LA GARENNE-COLOMBES.

Gar'field (gär'fēld). **1** Name of counties in six states of the U.S. See *Tables* at COLORADO, MONTANA, NEBRASKA, OKLAHOMA, UTAH, WASHINGTON.

2 Industrial city, Bergen co., NE corner of New Jersey, on Passaic river 5 m. SE of Paterson; pop. 29,253; textiles, chemicals, clothing, paper products, rubber goods.

3 Town, Salt Lake co., N Utah, ab. 15 m. W of Salt Lake City; pop. (1950) 2079; copper mining and smelting.

Garfield, Mount. 1 Peak 13,072 ft. in San Juan co., SW Colorado.

2 Peak 4488 ft. in Franconia Mts., N cen. New Hampshire, in N Grafton co.

Garfield Heights. City, Cuyahoga co., N Ohio, 6 m. SSE of Cleveland; pop. 38,455; manufactures iron, steel, abrasives; oil refineries.

Garfield Mountain. 1 Peak 13,800 ft. in Chaffee and Pitkin cos., W cen. Colorado.

2 Highest peak 10,961 ft. in Bitterroot Range on Idaho-Montana state boundary.

Gar·ga'no, Mount (gär·gä'nõ); *anc.* **Gar·ga'nus Mons** (gär·gā'nŭs mŏnz'). Promontory extending 30 m. into Adriatic Sea from E coast of Foggia prov., Apulia, SE Italy; highest point 3465 ft.; easternmost point is **Te'sta del Gargano** (tĕs'tä däl).

Garh·wal' (gŭr·wäl'). **1** District, Kumaun division, N Uttar Pradesh, N Indian Union; 5628 sq. m.; pop. (1941) 602,115; * Pauri; includes some of highest peaks of the Himalayas: Kamet, Trisul, Badrinath, and Nanda Devi on its E border.
2 Former Indian state. See TEHRI.

Gar·ian' (gŭr·yän'). Town, NW Tripolitania, NW Libya, N Africa, ab. 40 m. S of Tripoli.

Gar·i·bal'di Park (gär'ĭ·bôl'dĭ). Canadian provincial park in SW British Columbia, N of Vancouver; 973 sq. m.; peaks, glaciers, snowfields.

Ga·ri·glia'no (gä'rē·lyä'nõ). River ab. 100 m. long in SE Latium, cen. Italy; flows SE, then SW on Campania border to Gulf of Gaeta; its main headstream the Liri, which receives an E tributary, the Rapido; in World War II formed German defense line 1943–44; crossed by Allies May 1944 after long and severe fighting.

Ga'rin (gä'rēn). Town, Buenos Aires prov., E Argentina, ab. 25 m. NW of Buenos Aires.

Gar'land (gär'lănd). **1** County in Arkansas. See *Table* at ARKANSAS.
2 City, Dallas co., NE Texas, 14 m. NE of Dallas; pop. 38,501.

Garm (gärm). Town, W cen. Tadzhik S.S.R., Soviet Central Asia, on Vaksh river 75 m. NE of Stalinabad.

Gar'misch–Par'ten·kir'chen (gär'mĭsh·pär'tĕn·kĭr'kĕn). Adjacent towns, Bavaria, Germany, in foothills of Bavarian Alps near Oberammergau; pop. Garmisch 5275, Partenkirchen 4832; noted as resort and center for winter sports; scene of winter Olympics Feb. 7–16, 1936. In World War II supposed to be a last retreat for Nazi leaders; taken by Allies Apr. 30, 1945.

Garmo Peak. See STALIN PEAK.

Gar'ner (gär'nẽr). Town, ⊗ of Hancock co., N Iowa, 21 m. W of Mason City; pop. 1990; in farming and dairying section.

Gar'nett (gär'nĕt; -nĭt). City, ⊗ of Anderson co., E Kansas, 42 m. NW of Fort Scott; pop. 3034; flour mills; oil wells.

Ga'roet (gä'rŏōt) *or* **Ga'rut** Town, West Java prov., Indonesia, ab. 32 m. SE of Bandung; pop. 24,219; on plateau (alt. 2300 ft.) surrounded by mountains; resort.

Ga'ro Hills (gä'rõ). Western spurs of hills of Assam, NE Indian Union, in bend of Brahmaputra; highest ab. 4670 ft.

Ga·ronne' (gȧ·rŏn'; *Fr.* gȧ'rôn'); *anc.* **Ga·rum'na** (gȧ·rŭm'nȧ). River ab. 355 m. long in SW France; rises on slopes of the Pyrenees, in Spain; flows NW past Toulouse and Bordeaux to unite with Dordogne river 13 m. N of Bordeaux and form Gironde estuary.

Ga·ronne', Haute– (ōt'gȧ'rôn'). Department of France. See *Haute-Garonne* in *Table* at FRANCE.

Ga·rou'a *or* **Ga·ru'a** (gȧ·rŏō'ȧ). Commercial town, Adamawa, N Cameroun, on the Benue at head of navigation in the summertime; pop. 15,000; belonged to Germany 1894–1915; besieged and captured by British and French 1915.

Gar'rard (gär'ăd). County in Kentucky. See *Table* at KENTUCKY.

Gar'rett (gär'ĕt). **1** County in Maryland. See *Table* at MARYLAND.
2 City, De Kalb co., NE Indiana, 20 m. N of Fort Wayne; pop. 4364.

Gar'ri·son (gär'ĭ·s'n). City, McLean co., W cen. North Dakota, 40 m. S of Minot; pop. 1794; lignite mines, wheat raising.

Garrison Dam. Dam in Missouri river near Garrison, North Dakota; earth embankment over 2 m. long, 210 ft. high; for flood control, irrigation, power; completed 1954; forms **Garrison Reservoir** (ab. 200 m. long).

Gar'ron Point (gär'ŭn). Headland in co. Antrim, NE Northern Ireland, on the Irish Sea.

Gar'ry, Lake (gär'ĭ). Lake 980 sq. m. in NW Keewatin District, Northwest Territories, Canada; traversed by Back river.

Gar'ston (gär'stŭn). Seaport, Liverpool borough, Lancashire, England, on the Mersey 6 m. SE of Liverpool; pop. 17,262; ships coal.

Gar'tok (gär'tŏk). Market town, SW Tibet, Outer China, on upper Indus at W end of Kailas Range; alt. 15,200 ft.; in summer a busy trading center; opened 1904.

Garua. See GAROUA.

Garumna. See GARONNE.

Garvelloch Isles. See ISLES OF THE SEA.

Gar'vin (gär'vĭn). County in Oklahoma. See *Table* at OKLAHOMA.

Gar'wood (gär'wŏŏd). Manufacturing borough, Union co., NE New Jersey, 6 m. W of Elizabeth; pop. 5426.

Gar'y (gâr'ĭ). Industrial city, Lake co., NW corner of Indiana, on Lake Michigan; pop. 178,320; site purchased and laid out by U.S. Steel Corp. 1905 (see also FAIRFIELD, Ala.); incorporated 1906; greatest steel-producing center in the world; scene of origin and development of the platoon school (*Gary plan*).

Gar'za (gär'zä). County in Texas. See *Table* at TEXAS.

Garza Dam *or* **Lake Dal'las Dam** (dăl'ăs; *Sou. also* -ĭs). Dam completed 1926 across Elm Fork of Trinity river, Denton co., N Texas; height 80 ft.; impounds water, **Lake Dallas,** for water supply of Dallas.

Ga·san' (gȧ·sän'). Municipality, SW coast of Marinduque I., Phil. Is., 11 m. S of Boac; pop. 10,794; an old town.

Gasc. See MAREB.

Gas City (găs). Industrial city, Grant co., N cen. Indiana, 5 m. SSE of Marion; pop. 4469; manufactures glass.

Gas'con·ade' (găs'kŭn·ād'). **1** River 250 m. long, S cen. Missouri; rises in Ozark Plateau, flows N into Missouri river in N Gasconade co.
2 County in Missouri. See *Table* at MISSOURI.

Gas'co·ny (găs'kŏ·nĭ); *Fr.* **Gas'cogne'** (gȧs'kôn'y'); *Lat.* **Vas·co'ni·a** (văs·kō'nĭ·ȧ; -kŏn'yȧ). Historical region of SW France; bounded anciently on N by Guienne, E by Languedoc, SE by Countship of Foix, S by Béarn and Pyrenees, W by Atlantic Ocean; * Auch. Part of Roman Aquitania Tertia; settled in 6th cent. A.D. by Basques from S of Pyrenees; conquered by Franks who erected duchy of Gascony; became attached to Aquitaine (*q.v.*) in 11th cent., and was long a stronghold of English allegiance on Continent; up to 1789, formed, with Guienne (*q.v.*), part of French *gouvernement* of Guienne and Gascony.

Gascony, Gulf of; *Fr.* **Golfe de Gas'cogne'** (gôlf' dē gȧs'kôn'y'). The SE portion of the Bay of Biscay.

Gas'coyne (găs'koin). River ab. 400 m. long, North West Region, W Western Australia; upper course in desert, flows W to Geographe Channel; nearly dry except in flood time.

Gash. See MAREB.

Ga'sher·brum (gŭ'shẽr·brŏŏm), *also* **Gu'shar·brum** (gŏŏ'-). Peak 26,470 ft. in the Karakoram Range of the Himalayas, N Kashmir, N India, just SE of Mt. Godwin Austen.

Gash'iun Nor (gäsh'yŏōn nŏr'). Large salt lake, W Gobi Desert, NW Ningsia prov., W Inner Mongolia, N China, lat. 42°10′N and long. 100°45′E; receives Etsin river.

Gas·ma'ta (gäz·mä'tȧ). Coastal town and government station, S New Britain I., Bismarck Archipelago, 200 m. SW of Rabaul; Japanese base in World War II; often bombed by Allies 1943–44.

Gas'pa·ril'la Island (găs'pȧ·rĭl'ȧ). Island in Gulf of Mexico, at N of entrance to Charlotte Harbor, off W coast of Charlotte co., SW Florida.

Gas'par Strait (găs'pẽr). Channel ab. 45 m. wide bet. Bangka and Billiton Is., Indonesia, E of S Sumatra.

Gas'pé (găs'pā; găs·pā'; *Fr.* gȧs'pā'); *also* **Gas'pe** (găs'pĕ), *for bay, cape. etc., as well.* County at end of Gaspé Penin., SE Quebec, Canada, bounded on N by St. Lawrence river and on E by Gulf of St. Lawrence; divided into: **East Gaspé** (*Fr.* **Gas'pé'–Est'** [găs'pā'-ĕst']), 2348 sq. m., pop. 37,442, ⊗ Percé; **West Gaspé** (*Fr.* **Gas'pé'–Ouest'** [-wĕst']), 2198 sq. m., pop. 15,089, ⊗ Sainte Anne des Monts; Magdalen Islands (*q.v.*). See *Table* at QUEBEC.

Gaspé, Cape. East tip of Gaspé Penin., at NE of entrance to Gaspé Bay, SE Quebec, Canada.

Gaspé Bay. Inlet of Gulf of St. Lawrence at E end of Gaspé Penin., SE Quebec, Canada; ab. 18 m. long.

Gaspé, *or* **Gas·pe'sian** (găs·pē'zhăn), **Park.** Canadian provincial park, West Gaspé co., N cen. Gaspé Penin., SE Quebec; 350 sq. m.; Mt. Jacques Cartier, fishing lakes and streams, and last herds of caribou S of the St. Lawrence.

Gaspé Peninsula. Peninsula in SE Quebec prov., Canada, N of New Brunswick and Chaleur Bay and S of mouth of St. Lawrence river; ab. 11,390 sq. m., 170 m. long; comprises Gaspé, Bonaventure, and Matane cos.; a tableland (highest ab. 4500 ft.), thickly forested with many lakes and rivers; excellent hunting and fishing; famous for its scenery.

Ga·stein' (gä·stīn'); *also* **Bad'ga·stein'** (bät'gä·stīn'). Village, Salzburg prov., Austria, 47 m. S of Salzburg in N foothills of Hohe Tauern on the Gasteiner Ache; pop. 2670; watering place. By Convention of Gastein Aug. 14, 1865, Schleswig-Holstein difficulties bet. Prussia and Austria temporarily adjusted.

Ga·stein'er A'che (gä·stīn'ẽr ä'кĕ). Stream ab. 25 m. long, Salzburg prov., Austria; flows N from Hohe Tauern to Salzach river through beautiful valley (alt. 3000–3500 ft.) noted for its mineral springs; contains two notable waterfalls: **Upper Gastein** 207 ft. and **Lower Gastein** 279 ft.

Gas'ti·neau (găs'tĭ·nō). Short channel, SE Alaska, bet. mainland and Douglas I. Both Juneau and Douglas are situated on it.

Gas'ton (găs'tŭn). County in North Carolina. See *Table* at NORTH CAROLINA.

Gas·to'ni·a (găs·tō'nĭ·ȧ; -tōn'yȧ). Industrial city, ⊗ of Gaston co., SW North Carolina, 20 m. W of Charlotte; pop. 37,276; manufactures textiles, plaster, mill machinery.

Gat *or* **Ghat** (gŏt). Town and oasis in SW Fezzan, Libya, N Africa; pop. ab. 8000.

Ga'ta, Cape (gä'tȧ; -tä). Southern point of Cyprus, tip of peninsula W of Akrotiri Bay.

Ga'ta, Cape (gä'tä); *Span.* **Ca'bo de Ga'ta** (kä'vð thä gä'tä). Cape on SE coast of Spain, forming E side of Gulf of Almería; naval engagement 1643 bet. French and Spanish.

Gata, Sierra de. See SIERRA DE GATA.

Gat'chi·na (gȧt'chĭ·nȧ); *formerly* **Kras·no·gvar'deisk'** (krȧs·nŭ·gvŭr·dyȧ'ĭsk) *or* (*1923–29*) **Trots'ko·e** (trŏts'kŭ·yĕ). Town, Leningrad Region, NW Soviet Russia, Europe, 25 m. SSW of Leningrad; pop. ab. 19,000; originally a Swedish estate; has castle and palace, summer residence of tsars. A military base during Revolution 1917–19; held by Germans in World War II.

Gate City (gāt). Town, ⊗ of Scott co., SW Virginia, 24 m. W of Bristol; pop. 2142.

Gates (gāts). County in North Carolina. See *Table* at NORTH CAROLINA.

Gates'head (gāts'hĕd). County borough, Durham, N England, on the Tyne opp. Newcastle; pop. 122,447, (1951) 115,017; has shipbuilding yards, locomotive works, glass and chemical manufactures; coal mines, grindstone quarries.

Gates'ville (gāts'vĭl). **1** Town, ⊗ of Gates co., NE North Carolina; pop. 460.

2 Industrial city, ⊗ of Coryell co., cen. Texas, 35 m. W of Waco; pop. 4626; cotton-processing and feed plants.

Gath (găth). City of ancient Philistia, Palestine, ab. 12 m. E of Ashdod; one of five Philistine city-kingdoms; residence of Goliath and the Anakim.

Ga·ti'co (gä·tē'kŏ); *formerly* **Co·bi'ja** (kŏ·vē'hä). Port, Antofagasta prov., N Chile; pop. 449; formerly belonged to Bolivia and was its only seaport; damaged by earthquake and tidal wave 1877; ceded to Chile 1883; exports copper.

Gat'i·neau (găt'n·ō; *Fr.* gȧ'tē'nō'). **1** River ab. 240 m. long, SW Quebec prov., Canada; rises in chain of lakes S of the height of land, flows S through Lake Baskatong and Gatineau co. into the Ottawa river at Hull opp. Ottawa; source of water power.

2 County, part of Hull co., SW Quebec, Canada. See HULL.

3 Village, Hull co., SW Quebec, Canada, just NE of Hull near mouth of Gatineau river; pop. 5771.

Ga·too'ma (gȧ·tōō'mȧ). Town, SW Mashonaland, NE Southern Rhodesia, 85 m. SW of Salisbury; pop. 1737; center of richest gold-mining section of Rhodesia.

Gat'ta·ran' (gä'tä·rän'). Municipality, W cen. Cagayan prov., Luzon, Phil. Is., on Cagayan river 20 m. S of Aparri; pop. 19,889.

Ga'tu·ka'i (gä'tōō·kä'ē; -kī'). Small island of the New Georgia Is., cen. Solomon Is., W Pacific Ocean, off SE coast of Vangunu I.

Ga·tun' (gȧ·tōōn'); *Span.* **Ga·tún'** (gä·tōōn'). Town, Cristobal dist., Canal Zone, 7 m. S of Colón; pop. 2477; nearby are the **Gatun Locks** and **Gatun Dam** (across Chagres river; completed 1912; maximum height 115 ft.; length of crest 8324 ft.), the latter forming **Gatun Lake** (area 164 sq. m.).

Ga'tun·cil'lo (gä'tōōn·sē'yð). River in Panama E of the Panama Canal; flows S into the Canal Zone, joins Chagres river near Madden Dam.

Gaua. See SANTA MARIA.

Gau'ga·me'la (gô'gȧ·mē'lȧ). Ancient village in Assyria, ab. 18 m. NE of Nineveh and ab. 32 m. W of Arbela (see ERBIL); scene of battle 331 B.C. in which Alexander the Great defeated Persians under Darius, erroneously called the battle of Arbela.

Gau·ha'ti (gou·hä'tĭ). Commercial town, NW Assam, NE Indian Union, on Brahmaputra river 335 m. NE of Calcutta; pop. 21,797; nearby temple of Kamakhya and the island of Umananda in the Brahmaputra are places of Hindu pilgrimage. Ceded to British 1826; British seat of administration for Assam 1826–74.

Gauja. See GAUYA.

Gaul (gôl); *Fr.* **Gaule** (gōl); *Lat.* **Gal'li·a** (găl'ĭ·ȧ). Ancient country of Europe, commonly the part S and W of the Rhine, W of Alps, and N of Pyrenees, inhabited from ab. 600 B.C. by Celtic race (Lat. *Galli*); in earliest times also N Italy.

Early divisions: **1 Cis·al'pine Gaul** (sĭs·ăl'pĭn; -pĭn); *Lat.* **Gallia Cis'al·pi'na** (sĭs'ăl·pī'nȧ), *also* **Gallia Ci·te'ri·or** (sĭ·tēr'ĭ·ẽr; sī-; -ôr). N Italy in valley of Po N of Apennines; settled by Celts c. 4th–3d cents. B.C.; conquered by Rome c. 222 B.C.; made Roman province c. 42 B.C., its SE boundary being the Rubicon (*q.v.*). Divided **c.** 1st **cent.** B.C. into: (a) **Cis'pa·dane Gaul** (sĭs'pȧ·dān; sĭs·pā'dăn); *Lat.* **Gallia Cis'pa·da'na** (sĭs'pȧ·dā'nȧ). Region S of lower Po, ab. coextensive with modern Emilia compartimento. (b) **Trans'pa·dane Gaul** (trăns'pȧ·dān; trăns·pā'dăn); *Lat.* **Gallia Trans'pa·da'na** (trăns'pȧ·dā'nȧ). Region N of upper Po, ab. coextensive with modern W Lombardy and N Piedmont. See CISALPINE REPUBLIC, CISPADANE REPUBLIC, TRANSPADANE REPUBLIC.

2 Trans·al'pine Gaul (trăns·ăl'pĭn; -pĭn); *Lat.* **Gallia Trans'al·pi'na** (trăns'ăl·pī'nȧ), *also* **Gallia Ul·te'ri·or** (ŭl·tēr'ĭ·ẽr; -ôr). = *Gallia* proper. See below.

3 Gallia Nar'bo·nen'sis (när'bð·nĕn'sĭs) *or* **Narbonensis.** SE part of Gallia proper, formed as Roman

province c. 121 B.C., with chief settlement at Narbo Martius (see NARBONNE); later named **Pro·vin′ci·a Ro·ma′na** (prô·vĭn′shĭ·ȧ rô·mā′nȧ), which became Provence (q.v.).

Gallia proper; Fr. **Gaule**; earlier **Gallia Trans·alpina** (see 2, above), later **Gallia Cel′ti·ca** (sĕl′tĭ·kȧ). Practically all of region of modern France including Gallia Narbonensis. Conquered by Julius Caesar 58–51 B.C.; divided into three parts according to native peoples inhabiting the regions—Aquitania (in SW), Gallia (W and center), Belgica (NE)—which under Augustus and Tiberius were re-formed into 5 administrative areas: Narbonensis, Aquitania, Lugdunensis, Belgica, and Rhine Military Frontier dist. (Germania Inferior and Germania Superior).

Gau′la·ni′tis (gô′lȧ·nī′tĭs). District of Decapolis, NE ancient Palestine, along E shore of Sea of Galilee.

Gau′ley (gô′lĭ). River ab. 120 m. long, cen. West Virginia; rises in Pocahontas co., flows W and S, joins New river in N Fayette co. to form Kanawha river.

Gaulus. See GOZO.

Gaunt (gônt; gänt). Medieval English corruption of GENT (Ghent), as in John of Gaunt (1340–99).

Gaur (gour) or **Lakh·nau′ti** (lŭk·nou′tĭ). Ancient city, former ✳ (c. 1200–1340, 1455–1563) of Bengal, in West Bengal, NE Indian Union, 8 m. S of English Bazar and ab. 163 m. N of Calcutta. As Mohammedan seat of government, famed for its size and splendor. Now has ruins of mosques, citadel, towers, etc.

Gau′ri San′kar or **Gau′ri·san′kar** (gou′rĭ·sŭng′kẽr). Peak 23,440 ft. in the Himalayas, N Nepal, 35 m. W of Mount Everest.

Gauss (gous), **Mount.** Extinct volcano ab. 1150 ft. on Wilhelm II coast, Antarctica, at 66°48′S, 89°19′E; discovered Feb. 1902 by expedition under Dr. Erich Drygalski and named for its ship, the Gauss.

Gau′sta (gou′stä). Peak over 6000 ft. in Telemark co., S Norway.

Gau′ya (gou′yä); Lettish **Gau′ja** (gou′yä); formerly **Aa** (ä). River 200 m. long, cen. Latvia; rises SE of Tsesis, flows in wide bend to Gulf of Riga NE of Riga.

Ga′var′nie′ (gȧ·vȧr′nē′). Village, Hautes-Pyrénées dept., SW France, near the Spanish border at head of the Gave de Pau whose valley here forms the **Cirque de Gavarnie** (sẽrk′ dē), most famous of the characteristic cirques of the Pyrenees, a vast amphitheater 2 m. wide with steep wall, in places reaching 5600 ft., over which the gave (mountain torrent) comes in a spectacular waterfall 1385 ft. high.

Gav′dos (gäv′thôs); anc. **Cau′da** (kô′dȧ) or **Clau′da** (klô′dȧ). Small island, 22 m. S of W end of Crete, E Mediterranean Sea; belongs to Greece; refuge of St. Paul's ship during tempest (Acts xxvii. 16).

Gave de Pau. See Gave de PAU.

Gäv′le (yâv′lĕ). Seaport city, ✳ of Gävleborg prov., E Sweden, NNW of Stockholm; pop. 40,988; exports iron ore and wood pulp; textile mills, chemical factories.

Gäv′le·borg (yâv′lĕ·bôr′y′). See Table at SWEDEN.

Ga′vor·ra′no (gä′vôr·rä′nô). Commune, Grosseto prov., Tuscany, cen. Italy, 16 m. NW of Grosseto; pop. 13,994.

Ga′vrelle′ (gȧ·vrĕl′). Village, Pas-de-Calais dept., NE France, E of Arras; pop. (1931) 363; taken by British naval division Apr. 1917 in battle of Arras.

Ga·vu′tu (gȧ·vōō′tōō). Small island in SE Solomon Is., in W Pacific Ocean, off S coast of Florida I. just E of Tulagi I. Key point (principal seaplane base) in Japanese defense of S Solomon Is.; seized by U.S. Marines Aug. 7–8, 1942. See TANAMBOGO.

Gawd–i–Zir′reh (gôd′ĕ·zir′ĕ). Lake and morass, SW Afghanistan, near Baluchistan and Iran borders; in wet season connected through Lake Helmand to NW.

Gaw′ler (gô′lẽr). Town, SE South Australia, 20 m. NNE of Adelaide; pop. 1676; wheat; gold, silver, copper, and lead mines.

Ga·ya′ (gȧ·yä′). City, Patna division, cen. Bihar, NE Indian Union, 57 m. S of Patna; pop. (1941) 105,223; large trade with Calcutta; numerous Hindu temples; ab. 7 m. S is Buddh Gaya (q.v.), one of the holiest sites of Buddhism.

Gay Head (gā). Promontory, W end of Martha's Vineyard.

Gay′lord (gā′lôrd). **1** City, ⊗ of Otsego co., N Michigan, 43 m. S of Cheboygan; pop. 2568; in potato-growing section.
2 City, ⊗ of Sibley co., S cen. Minnesota, 30 m. NNW of Mankato; pop. 1631.

Ga′za (gä′zȧ); Arab. **Ghaz′ze** (gȧz′zĭ′). **1** District in S Palestine, including Beersheba and Gaza subdists.; 5284 sq. m.; pop. 145,716, (1942 est.) 169,607; ✳ Gaza; formerly part of Southern District.
2 Subdistrict, Gaza dist., S Palestine; 429 sq. m.; pop. 94,634, (1938 est.) 105,596.
3 Commercial seaport, ✳ of district and subdistrict, near coast, with small harbor 3 m. distant; pop. (1944 est.) 30,327. Most southerly of the five city-kingdoms of the Philistines, in early times a junction point of trade routes; a base for campaign of Egyptian king, Thutmose III, against Syria c. 1480 B.C.; seat of Philistine worship of Dagon, whose temple Samson overthrew (Judges xvi. 23–31); taken by Sargon 720 B.C. and by Alexander the Great 332 B.C. after five months' siege; prominent in Wars of the Maccabees and several times captured or devastated by Syrians, Romans, Jews, and Arabs (634 A.D.); taken by Napoleon 1799. In World War I scene of three battles: Mar. 26–27, 1917, Apr. 19, 1917 (both British defeats), and Nov. 7, 1917 when Gen. Allenby forced evacuation of Turks.

Ga′za (gä′zȧ) or **Ga′za·land′** (-lănd′). District, N part of Lourenço Marques dist., Manica and Sofala prov., S Mozambique.

Gaz′a·ca (găz′ȧ·kȧ). Ancient city of Media, ✳ of Media Atropatene, in mountains SE of Lake Matianus (mod. Urmia) and W of Zenjan—exact location not known.

Gazala, El. See EL GAZALA.

Ga·zelle′ Peninsula (gȧ·zĕl′). Peninsula at NE end of New Britain I., Bismarck Archipelago, W Pacific Ocean; site of Rabaul.

Ga′zi·an·tep′ or **Gazi Antep** (gä′zĕ·än·tĕp′). **1** Vilayet, S Turkey in Asia; 4584 sq. m.; pop. 278,566.
2 formerly **Ain·tab′** (īn·täb′). Town, its ✳, ab. 60 m. N of Alep; pop. (1940) 57,314; strong castle in time of Crusades; base for successful campaign of Ibrahim Pasha against Turks 1839; center of Turkish resistance against French 1920–21; educational and mission center.

Gaz′zi (gäd′dzĕ). Town, suburb of Messina, Sicily; pop. (1931) 21,456.

Gdańsk (g′dän′y′sk). **1** See DANZIG.
2 New department, N Poland, borders on Baltic Sea and Gulf of Danzig; ✳ Sopot; formed after 1945 from Free City of Danzig, part of Polish department of Pomorze, and E part of former German Pomerania.

Gdy′ni·a (gȧ·dĭn′ĭ·ȧ; -dĭn′yȧ; Pol. g′dĭ′nyä); Ger. **Gding′en** (g′dĭng′ĕn). Seaport city, N Gdańsk prov., Poland, on Gulf of Danzig 10 m. NNW of Danzig; pop. (1938–39 est.) 125,000; chief port of Poland and largest port on Baltic; naval base; trades esp. in coal. Until 1920 an insignificant fishing village (pop. ab. 300); developed by Poland into modern, well-equipped port; made city 1926; pop. (1921) 3164; (1931) 30,210. Overcome by Germany Sept. 1939; restored to Poland 1945.

Gé·ant′, Ai′guille′ du (ā′gü·ē′y′ dü zhä′än′). Peak 13,170 ft. in the Savoy Alps, Haute-Savoie dept., E France, NE of Mont Blanc; nearby is the **Col du Géant** (kôl), mountain pass, alt. 11,145 ft., through the Alps from Chamonix SE to Italy.

Gea′ry (gẽr′ĭ). **1** County in Kansas. See Table at KANSAS.
2 City, Blaine and Canadian cos., W cen. Oklahoma, 49 m. W of Oklahoma City; pop. 1416; in wheat section.

Ge·au′ga (jḗ·ô′ga̤). County in Ohio. See *Table* at OHIO.
Ge′ba (gä′ba̤). River ab. 190 m. long, flowing WSW through Portuguese Guinea, W Africa, into the Atlantic Ocean; has wide estuary.
Gebal See DJEBEÏL.
Gebala. See YEBALA.
Gebel. See JEBEL.
Geb·ze′ (gĕb·zĕ′). Town, Kocaeli vilayet, NW Turkey in Asia, on NE coast of Sea of Marmara ab. 30 m. SE of İstanbul; pop. 2876.
Ge·da′ref (gĕ·dä′rĕf). Town, S Kassala prov., E Sudan; on Port Sudan-Sennar railroad.
Gedda. See JIDDA.
Ged′ding·ton (gĕd′ĭng·tŭn). Village, N Northampton-shire, cen. England; Eleanor Cross marking a stage of the funeral procession of Eleanor, queen of Edward I.
Ge′de or **Ge′deh** (gä′dĕ). Volcano 9705 ft., W Java, Indonesia, 45 m. SE of Djakarta; many eruptions since 1832, the most severe in 1840; twin peak of Mt. Pan-gerango (*q.v.*).
Gedi. See MALINDI.
Ge·diz′ (gĕ·dēz′) or **Sa′ra·bat′** (sä′rä·bät′); *anc.* **Her′-mus** (hûr′mŭs). River nearly 200 m. long in W Turkey in Asia; rises in mountains S of Kütahya, flows W into Gulf of İzmir.
Ge·dro′si·a (jḗ·drō′zhĭ·a̤; -zha̤). Ancient country of SW Asia, a subdivision of Ariana and a province of the Persian and Alexandrian empires; bounded on N by Drangiana and Arachosia, on E by India, on S by Arabian Sea, and on W by Carmania; largely desert; known in history chiefly for the hardships experienced by Alexander's army crossing it on his return from India 325–324 B.C.; corresponds nearly to modern Makran prov., SE Iran, and Baluchistan.
Geel or **Gheel** (kāl). Commune, Antwerp prov., N Belgium; pop. 18,638; colony where a model system for dealing with the insane is applied; scene 7th cent. of murder of the Irish princess Saint Dympna.
Gee·long′ (jḗ·lông′). Seaport, S Victoria, SE Australia, at W end of Port Phillip Bay 50 m. SW of Melbourne; pop. 16,931, with suburbs 39,225; important esp. for manufacture and shipping of wool.
Geelong West. Town, S Victoria, SE Australia, suburb of Geelong; pop. 13,738.
Geel′vink Bay (kāl′vĭngk). Bay on N coast of Nether-lands New Guinea; ab. 250 m. wide at mouth, Cape d'Urville to Manokwari, extends ab. 150 m. inland; con-tains the Schouten Is. and Japen and Numfoor Is.
Geelvink Channel. Channel bet. W Western Australia and Houtman Rocks.
Gee′raards·ber′gen (kā′rärts·bĕr′kĕ[n]) or **Gram′-mont′** (grȧ·môN′). Commune, East Flanders prov., NW cen. Belgium, 22 m. W of Brussels; pop. 12,130.
Gee′ste·mün′de (gā′stĕ·mün′dĕ). Former city (pop. ab. 25,000), Stade govt. dist., Hannover prov., Prussia, Germany; since 1924 part of Wesermünde (*q.v.*).
Gefle, Gefleborg. Vars. of GÄVLE, GÄVLEBORG.
Gehenna. See HINNOM.
Gei′len·kir′chen (gī′lĕn·kĭr′kĕn). Town, W Germany, just N of Aachen; pop. 5226; in line of Allied advance 1944–45.
Geis′ling·en an der Stei′ge (gīs′lĭng·ĕn än dĕr shtī′gĕ). Manufacturing city, Baden-Württemberg, Germany, 34 m. ESE of Stuttgart; pop. 13,762; metal goods, ma-chinery, cotton goods.
Ge′la (jä′lä); *before 1927* **Ter′ra·no′va di Si·ci′lia** (tĕr′rä·nô′vä dĕ sĕ·chĕ′lyä); *anc.* **Ge′la** (jē′la̤). Com-mune, Caltanissetta prov., Sicily, on S coast 30 m. SSE of Caltanissetta; pop. 32,885; fisheries; remains of an-cient city nearby. Founded 689 B.C. by Greek colonists from Rhodes and Crete; flourished under the tyrant Hippocrates; home of the poet Aeschylus; destroyed by Carthaginians; rebuilt by Timoleon 340 B.C. and again destroyed 282 B.C. In World War II scene of American landings July 11, 1943.

Gel′der·land (gĕl′dĕr·lă̇nd; *Du.* kĕl′dĕr·länt). Prov-ince, E Netherlands; 1965 sq. m.; pop. (1939) 923,210; ✻ Arnhem; livestock raising. The larger part of the county including Zutphen, Nijmegen, Arnhem (3 divi-sions known as Lower Gelderland) and Roermond (Up-per Gelderland) which had grown up around the county of Gelder (or Gelre) of the Holy Roman Empire and which became duchy 1339, united with Jülich 1379, was held by Charles the Bold of Burgundy 1472–77, and in-herited by Charles V of Spain; province originated when Lower Gelderland joined revolt of Netherlands (*q.v.*) 1579, while Upper Gelderland remained Spanish; Upper Gelderland claimed by Frederick of Prussia, awarded to Prussia 1713, and divided between kingdom of Nether-lands and Prussia 1815.
Gel′dern (gĕl′dĕrn). Town, in the Ruhr district, W Germany, 28 m. NW of Düsseldorf; pop. (1933) 7006; manufactures metalware, shoes. Seat of counts and dukes of Gelder (see GELDERLAND) to 1371; to Prussia 1713.
Gel′drop (kĕl′drôp). Commune, North Brabant prov., SE Netherlands, 4 m. SE of Eindhoven; pop. 8950; woolen manufacturing.
Ge·leen′ (kĕ·lān′). Commune, Limburg prov., SE Netherlands, NE of Maastricht; pop. 12,411.
Ge′li·bo·lu′ (gĕ′lĕ·bô·lōō′); *Angl.* **Gal·lip′o·li** (ga̤·lĭp′-ô·lĭ); *anc.* **Cal·lip′o·lis** (ka̤·lĭp′ô·lĭs). Seaport and manufacturing town, Çanakkale vilayet, Turkey in Europe, at entrance to Sea of Marmara on narrow neck of Gallipoli Penin.; pop. 12,442. Ancient Callipolis colo-nized by Greeks; medieval trading center; first European conquest of Turks 1354; see GALLIPOLI PENINSULA.
Gel′i·do′nya, Cape (gĕl′ĭ·dōn′ya̤; -dô·nyä′); *Turk.* **Ge′li·do·nya′ Bu·run′** (gĕ′lĕ·dô·nyä′ bōō·rōōn′). Cape on S coast of Turkey in Asia, on W side of entrance to Gulf of Antalya.
Gel′li·gaer′ (gĕ′hlĕ·gīr′; *Angl.* gĕl′ĭ-). Urban district, Glamorganshire, SE Wales; pop. 36,159; manufacturing and coal-mining center.
Gellivare. = GÄLLIVARE.
Gel′sen·kir′chen (gĕl′zĕn·kĭr′kĕn). Industrial city, North Rhine-Westphalia state, W Germany, 15 m. W of Dortmund; pop. (1939) 313,003; in Ruhr coal-mining region, largest coal-producing city on Continent; in-cludes since 1928 the city of Buer and the commune of Horst an der Emscher; Buer town hall, 16th-cent. Horst castle; manufactures iron and steel, glass, flour, chemi-cals, soap. Incorporated as city in Arnsberg govt. dist. 1875; often bombed 1943–45.
Gem′. County in Idaho. See *Table* at IDAHO.
Ge·mas′ (gĕ·mäs′). Town, SE Negri Sembilan state, Federation of Malaya, near border of Johore 35 m. NE of Malacca; pop. 2475; railroad junction. Severe fighting bet. Japanese and British Jan. 1942.
Gem′bloux′ (zhän′blōō′). Commune, Namur prov., S Belgium, 10 m. NW of Namur; pop. 5198; manufactures cutlery; State institute of agriculture; scene Jan. 31, 1578 of defeat of Dutch by Don John of Austria.
Gem′i·ni Peaks (jĕm′ĭ·nī). Mountain 13,900 ft. in Lake and Park cos., cen. Colorado.
Gem·lik′ Gulf (gĕm·lēk′). Inlet of SE Sea of Mar-mara, Turkey in Europe; Mudanya is on it.
Gem′mi Pass (gĕm′ĕ). Mountain pass 7640 ft. in the Bernese Alps, SW cen. Switzerland, 5 m. S of Thun.
Ge·mo′na (jä·mō′nä). Commune, Friuli prov., Venezia Euganea, NE Italy, 18 m. NW of Udine; pop. 11,570; 13th-cent. cathedral, 16th-cent. town hall.
Ge·na′den·dal (gĕ·nä′d'n·däl). Town, SW Cape Province, Union of South Africa, 68 m. E of Capetown; pop. ab. 3500; Moravian mission station founded 1737, oldest mission station in dominion.
Ge·nappe′ (zhĕ·nȧp′; *Angl.* jĕ·nǎp′) or **Ge·ne′pi·ën** (kȧ·nā′pĕ·ĕn). Town, Brabant prov., Belgium, SSE of Brussels on the Dyle; pop. 1887; ab. 2½ m. S is Quatre Bras (*q.v.*).

Genck. See GENK.

Gen′dring·en (kĕn′drĭng·ĕn). Commune, Gelderland prov., E Netherlands, 20 m. ESE of Arnhem on German border; pop. 10,184.

Geneina, El. See EL GENEINA.

Genepiën. See GENAPPE.

Ge′ne·ral′ Al′va·ra′do (hä′nä·räl′ äl′vä·rä′thô), or **Mi′ra·mar′** (mē′rä·mär′). Seaside resort, E Buenos Aires prov., E Argentina, S of Mar del Plata.

Ge′ne·ral′ Bel·gra′no (hä′nä·räl′ vĕl·grä′nô). Town, Buenos Aires prov., E Argentina, 80 m. S of Buenos Aires.

Gen′er·al Grant National Park (jĕn′ĕr·ăl gränt′). Former national park, SE cen. California; 4 sq. m.; included two groves of giant sequoias; estab. 1890; since 1940 known as **General Grant Grove Section** of Kings Canyon National Park (see UNITED STATES, *National Parks*).

General J. F. U′ri·bu′ru (*Eng.* jĕn′ĕr·ăl jā ĕf ōōr′ĭ·bŏŏr′ōō; *Span.* hä′nä·räl′ hō′tä ā′fä ōō′rĕ·vōō′rōō); *formerly* **Zá′ra·te** (sä′rä·tä). Town, N Buenos Aires prov., E Argentina, on Paraná river 56 m. NW of Buenos Aires; pop. (est.) 37,843; frigoríficos, paper factories.

Ge′ne·ral′ Ma·cha′do (hä′nä·räl′ mä·chä′thô). Municipality, Camagüey prov., E cen. Cuba; pop. 17,138.

General Pi′co (pē′kô). Town, La Pampa territory, S cen. Argentina, 290 m. WSW of Buenos Aires; pop. (est.) 14,500.

General San Mar·tín′ (sän′ mär·tēn′), *also* **San Martín.** City, Buenos Aires prov., E Argentina, a suburb of Buenos Aires; pop. 269,514.

General Sar·mien′to (sär·myān′tô), *also* **Sarmien·to.** Town, Buenos Aires prov., E Argentina, ab. 15 m. W of Buenos Aires; pop. 269,514.

General Tri′as (trē′äs). Municipality, NE Cavite prov., Luzon, Phil. Is., 7 m. S of Cavite; pop. 16,611.

Gen′e·see (jĕn′ĕ·sē; jĕn′ĕ·sē′). **1** River 144 m. long, W New York; rises in Potter co., N Pennsylvania, flows N into Lake Ontario near Rochester.

2 Name of counties in two states of the U.S. See *Tables* at MICHIGAN and NEW YORK.

Gen′e·se′o (jĕn′ĕ·sē′ô). **1** City, Henry co., NW Illinois, 24 m. E of Rock Island; pop. 5169.

2 Village, ⊗ of Livingston co., W New York, on Genesee river 26 m. SSW of Rochester; pop. 3284; fruit and vegetable raising, manufacturing; State Univ. of New York College of Education (1867; coed.).

Ge·ne′va (jĕ·nē′vȧ). **1** County in Alabama. See *Table* at ALABAMA.

2 City, ⊗ of Geneva co., SE Alabama, 2 m. N of Florida border; pop. 3840.

3 City, ⊗ of Kane co., NE Illinois, 36 m. W of Chicago; pop. 7646; founded ab. 1835, incorp. as city 1887; manufactures automobile parts, foundry products; ships livestock.

4 City, ⊗ of Fillmore co., SE Nebraska, 44 m. E of Hastings; pop. 2352.

5 City, Ontario co., W New York, at N end of Seneca Lake; pop. 17,286; vegetable and fruit canning; manufactures stoves, furnaces, radiators, cutlery, enamelware, optical goods. Hobart College for Men (founded 1822) and the co-ordinated William Smith College for Women (1908), the two known as "The Colleges of the Seneca." Settled c. 1785 on site of Indian village.

6 City, Ashtabula co., NE corner of Ohio, 8 m. WSW of Ashtabula; pop. 5677; manufactures farm implements, builders'-hardware; winery; greenhouses, apiaries.

7 *Fr.* **Ge·nève′** (zhĕ·nâv′). Swiss canton; see *History* and *Table* at SWITZERLAND.

8 *Fr.* **Ge·nève′** (zhĕ·nâv′). City, ✳ of Geneva canton, SW Switzerland, at S tip of Lake of Geneva on Rhone river; pop. (1941) 124,431; cultural center; tourist resort; buildings include those of the League of Nations, 10th–12th-cent. Gothic cathedral, university (see below); manufactures clocks, watches, jewelry, precision

instruments, iron goods, chemicals, scientific and surgical appliances.

History: A center of Allobroges, a Celtic-speaking people conquered by Romans; seat of Burgundian kingdom until latter conquered by Franks c. 500 A.D.; obtained privileges as result of struggle bet. bishop and Savoyards who constantly threatened the city's independence; in 16th cent., alliance with Bern and Fribourg protected it from Savoy; home of John Calvin, who established a theocratic state (1541) and made 16th-cent. Geneva the intellectual center of Protestant Europe; Calvin's Academy, founded 1559, became university 1873; united with France 1798; in 1815, with expanded territory, joined Swiss Confederation as canton of Geneva; scene of conference which drew up Geneva (Red Cross) Convention 1864; from 1920 to Apr. 18, 1946 seat of League of Nations, its buildings later taken over by UN.

Geneva, Lake of, or **Lake Le′man** (lē′mǎn; lĕm′ǎn; lê·mǎn′); *anc.* **Le·man′nus** (lê·mǎn′ŭs) or **Le·ma′nus** (lê·mä′nŭs). Lake in SW Switzerland and E France, extending in an arc along the boundary, only its S shore in France; 45 m. long, 1½ to 9 m. wide; 225 sq. m.; traversed E to W by Rhone river.

Ge·nè′vre, Col de (kôl′ dē zhĕ·nâ′vr′). Mountain pass 6102 ft., N part of Cottian Alps, bet. France and Italy, E of Briançon.

Genf (gĕnf). German form of GENEVA.

Ge·nil′ or **Je·nil′** (hä·nēl′). River ab. 150 m. long in S Spain; flows into Guadalquivir river 33 m. SW of Córdoba.

Ge′ni·tsa′ (yä′nyĕ·tsä′) or **Gia′ni·tsà′** (yä′nyĕ·tsä′) or **Yan′ni·tsa′** (yä′nyĕ·tsä′); *Serb.* **Ja′ni·ca** (yä′nĭ·tsä). City, Pella dept., W Macedonia, N Greece, ab. 20 m. E of Edessa; pop. 9128.

Genk or **Genck** (kĕngk). Commune, Limburg prov., NE Belgium, 11 m. N of Liége; pop. (1938 est.) 27,021.

Gen·nar·gen′tu (jän·när·jĕn′tōō). Mountain group, highest point 6017 ft., in E cen. Sardinia.

Gennesaret, Lake of. See Sea of GALILEE.

Gen′ne·vil′liers′ (zhĕn′vē′lyä′). Commune, Seine dept., N France, NNW suburb of Paris; pop. 29,369. Site of large U.S. camp in World War II.

Ge·no′a (jĕ·nô′ȧ). **1** Town, Douglas co., W Nevada, 12 m. SSW of Carson City; pop. (est.) 115; oldest permanent settlement in Nevada.

2 Village, Ottawa co., N Ohio, 12 m. SE of Toledo; pop. 1957; limestone quarries.

Gen′o·a (jĕn′ô·ȧ; *occasionally* jĕ·nô′ȧ); *Ital.* **Ge′no·va** (jā′nô·vä); *anc.* **Gen′u·a** (jĕn′ū·ȧ). Seaport, Genova prov., Liguria, NW Italy, at head of Gulf of Genoa at foot of Apennines 71 m. SSW of Milan; pop. 634,646; archiepiscopal see; one of most important Italian seaports; exports chiefly rice, wine, olive oil, silk goods, coral, paper, macaroni, marble; manufactures include textiles, paper, leather and leather goods, furniture; cathedral of San Lorenzo, 16th-cent. church of Sant'Ambrogio, 16th-cent. Palazzo Doria, the Doges' palace; university (founded 1243); Academy of Fine Arts (1751), Verdi Institute of Music. Birthplace of Christopher Columbus.

History: Ancient settlement on Ligurian coast, first mentioned by Romans 218 B.C.; trading center of Liguria even in Roman times; captured by Burgundians 539 A.D. and by Lombards 670; as independent city, soon became chief commercial city of Mediterranean and Levant, defeating its rival, Pisa, 1284; early European banking center (Bank of St. George); in return for its assistance against Venice 1261, rewarded by Palaeologi (see BYZANTINE EMPIRE) with special privileges at Constantinople and colonies at Chios, Lesbos, Samos, Kaffa (see FEODOSIYA), and Azov; in War of Chioggia 1378–81, lost century-long struggle with Venice for control of Levant; declined commercially, but became object of French rivalry with Milan (*q.v.*); under Andrea Doria

threw off French rule 1528; lost Chios 1566 and sold Corsica (*q.v.*) 1768; with surrounding coastal strip set up as Ligurian Republic by Napoleon 1797 and incorporated with France 1805; given to kingdom of Sardinia 1815; scene of international conference which failed to settle Russian debt question 1922; in World War II badly damaged by Allied bombings 1942–44; entered by Allies Apr. 25, 1945.

Genoa, Gulf of. Inlet on Ligurian coast, NW Italy; N part of Ligurian Sea.

Ge'no·va (jä'nō·vä). **1** Province of Italy. See *Table* at ITALY.
2 See GENOA.

Ge'no·ve'sa (hä'nō·vä'sä); *also* **Tow'er Island** (tou'-ēr). One of the Galápagos Is. (*q.v.*).

Gensan. See GENZAN.

Gent (Kĕnt); *Eng.* **Ghent** (gĕnt); *Fr.* **Gand** (gäN). Commercial and manufacturing fortified city, NW cen. Belgium, ✳ of East Flanders prov.; pop. (1938 est.) 162,858; at confluence of Schelde and Lys rivers and at junction of several canals; occupies a number of islands connected by bridges; important port; a center of flower-seed and bulb market; university. Scene of signing of Pacification of Gent Nov. 8, 1576, which united the provinces against Spain, and of a treaty Dec. 24, 1814 marking end of War of 1812 bet. Great Britain and United States; occupied by Germans in both World Wars.

Gent'brug'ge (Kĕnt'brü'g'ĕ). Commune, East Flanders prov., NW cen. Belgium; pop. 16,349.

Gen'te Her·mo'sa (hän'tä ĕr·mō'sä). = SWAINS island.

Gen'til'ly' (zhäN'tē'yē'). Commune, Seine dept., N France, S suburb of Paris; pop. 18,179.

Gen'tof'te (gĕn'tŭf'tĕ). City, Copenhagen co., island of Sjælland, Denmark; pop. 68,718.

Gen'try (jĕn'trĭ). County in Missouri. See *Table* at MISSOURI.

Genua. See GENOA.

Gen·zan (gĕn·zän) *or* **Gen·san** (gĕn·sän); *now* **Won·san** (wûn·sän). Seaport, South Kankyo prov., NE Korea, on East Chosen Bay 115 m. NNE of Seoul; pop. (1938 est.) 67,363; treaty port (opened 1891); fine harbor.

Ge·og'ra·phe Bay (jē·ŏg'rá·fĕ). Inlet of Indian Ocean, SW Western Australia, just E of Cape Naturaliste.

Géographe Channel. Passage bet. Bernier I. and mainland, W Western Australia; connects with Shark Bay on S.

Geok Te·pe' *or* **Gök–Té·pé'** (gûk'tĕ·pā'). Town, S Turkmen S.S.R., Soviet Central Asia, ab. 40 m. NW of Ashkhabad; scene of victory of Russians over Tekke tribe of Turkmen 1881.

George (jôrj). **1** County in Mississippi. See *Table* at MISSISSIPPI.
2 River 365 m. long, NE Quebec, Canada; flows N to Ungava Bay.
3 Town, S Cape Province, Republic of So. Africa, 235 m. E of Cape Town; pop. 9070; founded 1811; residential.

George, Cape. Cape on N Nova Scotia, Canada, at W entrance to George Bay.

George, Lake. 1 Lake in SE Putnam co., NE Florida penin.; an expansion of St. Johns river.
2 Lake bet. Warren and Washington cos., E New York; ab. 33 m. long, ¾ to 3 m. wide; outlet to N into Lake Champlain; scene of a number of engagements in French and Indian War 1754–63. Called **Lake Hor'i·con** (hŏr'ĭ·kŭn) by James Fenimore Cooper.
3 Small lake, SW Uganda, SE cen. Africa; NE of Lake Edward.

George Bay. Inlet of Gulf of St. Lawrence, NE Antigonish co., N Nova Scotia, Canada, bet. Nova Scotia and SW Cape Breton I.

George Daw'son (dô's'n), **Mount.** = Mount WADDINGTON.

George V Coast. Section of coast of Antarctica E of Wilkes Land; 142°20' to 153°E and bet. 67° and 71°S. For location of South Magnetic Pole, see VICTORIA LAND.

George Hill. Elevation 3004 ft. in Garrett co., NW corner of Maryland.

George Land. See FRANZ JOSEF LAND.

Georg'es (jôr'jĕz; -jĭz). River, SE New South Wales, SE Australia; flows into Botany Bay S of Sydney.

Georges Island. Island in outer Boston Harbor, Massachusetts, NNW of Hull; Fort Warren on it.

Georges Islands. Group of small islands at mouth of Muscongus Bay, S Maine; in Knox co.

George'town (jôrj'toun). **1** County in South Carolina. See *Table* at SOUTH CAROLINA.
2 Town, ⊗ of Clear Creek co., N cen. Colorado; pop. 307.
3 Town, ⊗ of Sussex co., S Delaware, 33 m. S of Dover; pop. 1765.
4 Former town in District of Columbia (*q.v.*), now part of city of Washington. Settled as early as 1665; town laid out 1751, incorp. 1789; lost charter 1871, annexed to Washington 1878. Georgetown Univ. (1789; men).
5 Village, ⊗ of Quitman co., SW Georgia; pop. 554.
6 City, Vermilion co., E Illinois, 10 m. S of Danville; pop. 3544; agriculture; coal mining.
7 City, ⊗ of Scott co., N cen. Kentucky, 12 m. N of Lexington; pop. 6986; horse breeding. Georgetown Coll. (1829; coed.; Baptist).
8 Town, Essex co., NE Massachusetts, NE of Lowell; pop. 3755.
9 Village, ⊗ of Brown co., SW Ohio, 35 m. ESE of Cincinnati; pop. 2674; manufactures shoes. Boyhood home of Ulysses S. Grant.
10 City and port of entry, ⊗ of Georgetown co., E South Carolina, at head of Winyah Bay 57 m. NE of Charleston; pop. 12,261; ships esp. naval stores, fish, lumber, cotton; fisheries. Settled 1735.
11 City, ⊗ of Williamson co., cen. Texas, 27 m. N of Austin; pop. 5218; cotton; mineral springs, limestone quarries; Southwestern Univ. (1840; coed.; Methodist).
12 Settlement on W coast of Ascension I.
13 City, N Guyana, at mouth of Demerara river; ✳ of Guyana and ⊗ of Demerara co.; pop. (1964 est.) 162,000; chief port of Guyana; cathedral. Founded by English 1781; called Stabroek during Dutch occupation when it was made seat of government of combined colonies of Essequibo and Demerara 1784; renamed Georgetown 1812.
14 Town on Grand Cayman I., Brit. West Indies; ✳ of Cayman Is.; pop. (1943) 1462.
15 Town on island of St. Vincent, Windward Is., Brit. West Indies; pop. 943.
16 Town, Halton co., SE Ontario, Canada, 28 m. W of Toronto; pop. 3452; manufactures shoes, paper. Founded 1837.
17 Coast town, ⊗ of Kings co., E Prince Edward I., Canada; pop. 762.
18 Town, Gambia, near mouth of the Gambia river, W Africa.

George Town (jôrj' toun). **1** Municipality and town, N Tasmania, Australia, near mouth of Tamar river 35 m. NNW of Launceston; pop. (municipality) 1071; resort; harbor.
2 Town on Exuma I., Bahama Is., Brit. West Indies; pop. 190; good harbor.
3 *or* **Pe·nang'** (pĕ·näng'). Seaport city, ✳ of Penang settlement, Federation of Malaya, on NE shore of Penang I.; pop. 149,408, (1937 est.) 165,411; in area noted for fine scenery, has hill (2066 ft.) just back of the town; inhabitants mostly Chinese.

George Wash'ing·ton Birthplace National Monument (jôrj' wŏsh'ĭng·tŭn). See UNITED STATES, *National Monuments;* WAKEFIELD.

George West. City, ⊗ of Live Oak co., S Texas; pop. 1878.

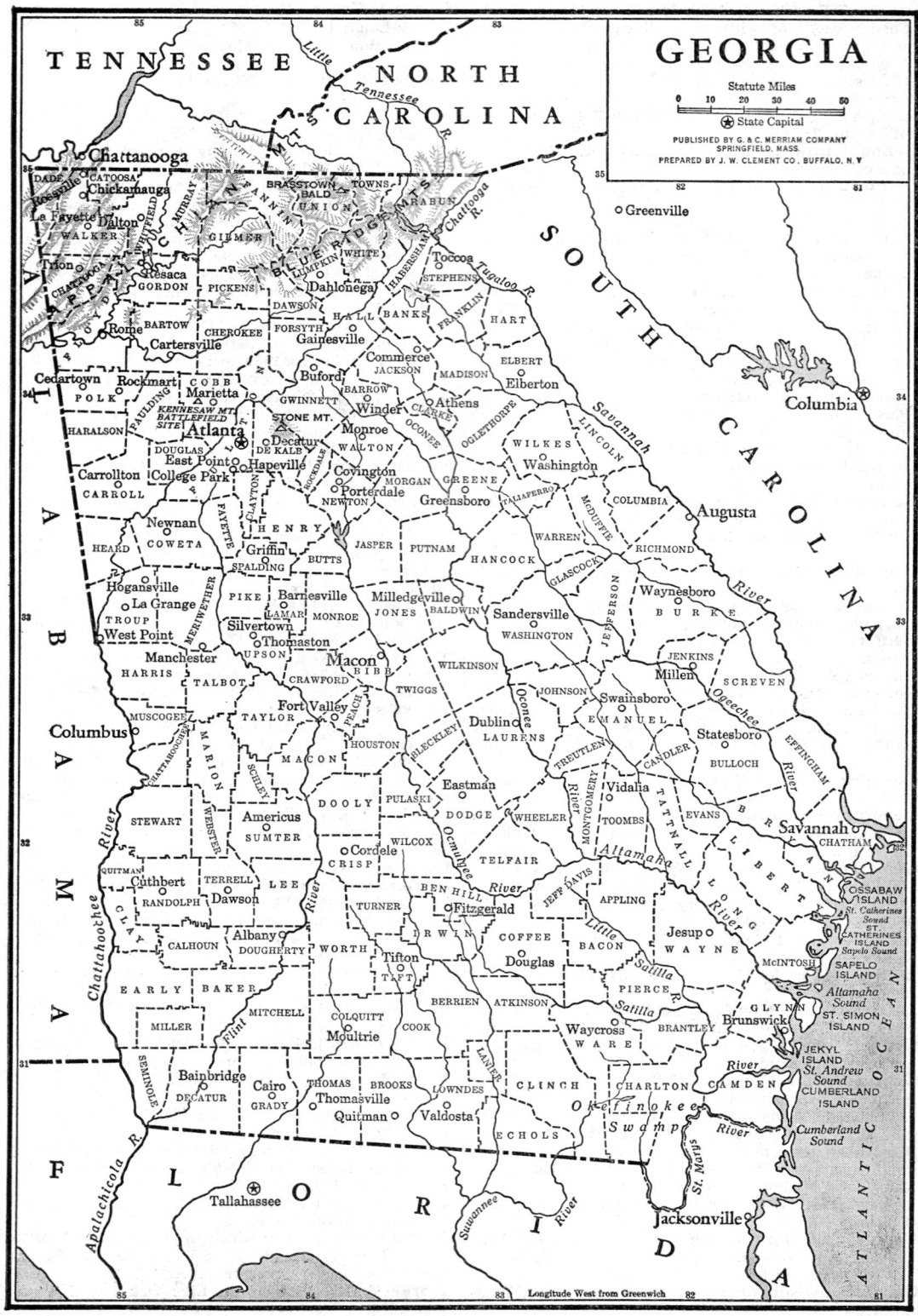

GEORGIA

Statute Miles

0　10　20　30　40　50

⭐ State Capital

PUBLISHED BY G. & C. MERRIAM COMPANY
SPRINGFIELD, MASS.
PREPARED BY J. W. CLEMENT CO., BUFFALO, N. Y.

TENNESSEE

NORTH CAROLINA

SOUTH CAROLINA

FLORIDA

ATLANTIC OCEAN

Longitude West from Greenwich

Geor'gia (jôr'jȧ; -jyȧ; -jĭ-ȧ). A southern state of U.S.A., an original state of the Union; bounded on N by Tennessee and North Carolina, on E by South Carolina and the Atlantic Ocean, on S by Florida, and on W by Alabama; 21st state in area, 58,876 sq. m. (land area 58,483 sq. m.); 16th state in population, 3,943,116; ✳ Atlanta. See *Table of States* at UNITED STATES. Divided into the following 159 counties (for pronunciation of their names, see their individual entries):

NAME	LOCATION	AREA[1]	POP.[1]	CO. SEAT
Appling	SE	514	13,246	Baxley
Atkinson	S	318	6,188	Pearson
Bacon	SE	293	8,359	Alma
Baker	SW	355	4,543	Newton
Baldwin	cen.	265	34,064	Milledgeville
Banks	NE	231	6,497	Homer
Barrow	N	171	14,485	Winder
Bartow	NW	463	28,267	Cartersville
Ben Hill	S cen.	255	13,633	Fitzgerald
Berrien	S	466	12,038	Nashville
Bibb	cen.	251	141,249	Macon
Bleckley	cen.	219	9,642	Cochran
Brantley	SE	447	5,891	Nahunta
Brooks	S	492	15,292	Quitman
Bryan	SE; coastal	439	6,226	Pembroke
Bulloch	E	684	24,263	Statesboro
Burke	E	832	20,596	Waynesboro
Butts	cen.	185	8,976	Jackson
Calhoun	SW	289	7,341	Morgan
Camden[2]	SE corner; coastal	656	9,975	Woodbine
Candler	E cen.	251	6,672	Metter
Carroll	W	495	36,451	Carrollton
Catoosa	NW	167	21,101	Ringgold
Charlton	SE	799	5,313	Folkston
Chatham[2]	SE; coastal	441	188,299	Savannah
Chattahoochee	W	253	13,011	Cusseta
Chattooga	NW	317	19,954	Summerville
Cherokee	NW	414	23,001	Canton
Clarke	NE	125	45,363	Athens
Clay	SW	224	4,551	Fort Gaines
Clayton	NW cen.	149	46,365	Jonesboro
Clinch	S	796	6,545	Homerville
Cobb	NW	346	114,174	Marietta
Coffee	S	613	21,953	Douglas
Colquitt	S	563	34,048	Moultrie
Columbia	E	306	13,423	Appling
Cook	S	226	11,822	Adel
Coweta	W	443	28,893	Newnan
Crawford	cen.	313	5,816	Knoxville
Crisp	SW cen.	296	17,768	Cordele
Dade	NW corner	165	8,666	Trenton
Dawson	N	213	3,590	Dawsonville
Decatur	SW	612	25,203	Bainbridge
De Kalb	NW cen.	269	256,782	Decatur
Dodge	S cen.	499	16,483	Eastman
Dooly	SW cen.	394	11,474	Vienna
Dougherty	SW	326	75,680	Albany
Douglas	W	201	16,741	Douglasville
Early	SW	526	13,151	Blakely
Echols	S	425	1,876	Statenville
Effingham	E	480	10,144	Springfield
Elbert	NE	362	17,835	Elberton
Emanuel	E cen.	686	17,815	Swainsboro
Evans	SE cen.	186	6,952	Claxton
Fannin	N	396	13,620	Blue Ridge
Fayette	W	199	8,199	Fayetteville
Floyd	NW	514	69,130	Rome
Forsyth	N	243	12,170	Cumming
Franklin	NE	269	13,274	Carnesville
Fulton	NW cen.	523	556,326	Atlanta
Gilmer	N	439	8,922	Ellijay
Glascock	E cen.	142	2,672	Gibson
Glynn[2]	SE; coastal	423	41,954	Brunswick
Gordon	NW	358	19,228	Calhoun
Grady	SW	467	18,015	Cairo
Greene	NE cen.	404	11,193	Greensboro
Gwinnett	N	437	43,541	Lawrenceville
Habersham	NE	283	18,116	Clarkesville
Hall	N	426	49,739	Gainesville
Hancock	cen.	485	9,979	Sparta
Haralson	W	285	14,543	Buchanan
Harris	W	465	11,167	Hamilton
Hart	NE	257	15,229	Hartwell
Heard	W	301	5,333	Franklin
Henry	NW cen.	331	17,619	McDonough
Houston	cen.	379	39,154	Perry
Irwin	S	372	9,211	Ocilla
Jackson	NE	337	18,499	Jefferson
Jasper	cen.	373	6,135	Monticello
Jeff Davis	SE cen.	331	8,914	Hazlehurst
Jefferson	E cen.	532	17,468	Louisville
Jenkins	E	351	9,148	Millen
Johnson	cen.	313	8,048	Wrightsville
Jones	cen.	402	8,468	Gray

NAME	LOCATION	AREA[1]	POP.[1]	CO. SEAT
Lamar	W cen.	181	10,240	Barnesville
Lanier	S	167	5,097	Lakeland
Laurens	cen.	811	32,313	Dublin
Lee	SW	355	6,204	Leesburg
Liberty[2]	SE; coastal	510	14,487	Hinesville
Lincoln	E	253	5,906	Lincolnton
Long	SE	403	3,874	Ludowici
Lowndes	S	506	49,270	Valdosta
Lumpkin	N	292	7,241	Dahlonega
McDuffie	E	263	12,627	Thomson
McIntosh[2]	SE; coastal	431	6,364	Darien
Macon	SW cen.	399	13,170	Oglethorpe
Madison	NE	281	11,246	Danielsville
Marion	W	365	5,477	Buena Vista
Meriwether	W	499	19,756	Greenville
Miller	SW	287	6,908	Colquitt
Mitchell	SW	511	19,652	Camilla
Monroe	cen.	399	10,495	Forsyth
Montgomery	SE cen.	235	6,284	Mount Vernon
Morgan	N cen.	356	10,280	Madison
Murray	N	342	10,447	Chatsworth
Muscogee	W	220	158,623	Columbus
Newton	N cen.	273	20,999	Covington
Oconee	NE cen.	186	6,304	Watkinsville
Oglethorpe	NE	432	7,926	Lexington
Paulding	NW	318	13,101	Dallas
Peach	cen.	151	13,846	Fort Valley
Pickens	N	225	8,903	Jasper
Pierce	SE	342	9,678	Blackshear
Pike	W	230	7,138	Zebulon
Polk	NW	312	28,015	Cedartown
Pulaski	S cen.	254	8,204	Hawkinsville
Putnam	cen.	350	7,798	Eatonton
Quitman	SW	170	2,432	Georgetown
Rabun	NE corner	369	7,456	Clayton
Randolph	SW	436	11,078	Cuthbert
Richmond	E	325	135,601	Augusta
Rockdale	N cen.	128	10,572	Conyers
Schley	SW cen.	162	3,256	Ellaville
Screven	E	651	14,919	Sylvania
Seminole	SW corner	274	6,802	Donalsonville
Spalding	W cen.	201	35,404	Griffin
Stephens	NE	180	18,391	Toccoa
Stewart	W	463	7,371	Lumpkin
Sumter	SW cen.	491	24,652	Americus
Talbot	W	390	7,127	Talbotton
Taliaferro	NE cen.	195	3,370	Crawfordville
Tattnall	SE cen.	493	15,837	Reidsville
Taylor	W cen.	400	8,311	Butler
Telfair	S cen.	440	11,715	McRae
Terrell	SW	329	12,742	Dawson
Thomas	S	540	34,319	Thomasville
Tift	S	266	23,487	Tifton
Toombs	SE cen.	369	16,837	Lyons
Towns	N	166	4,538	Hiawassee
Treutlen	E cen.	194	5,874	Soperton
Troup	W	447	47,189	La Grange
Turner	S	293	8,439	Ashburn
Twiggs	cen.	365	7,935	Jeffersonville
Union	N	319	6,510	Blairsville
Upson	W cen.	333	23,800	Thomaston
Walker	NW	448	45,264	La Fayette
Walton	N cen.	330	20,481	Monroe
Ware	SE	912	34,219	Waycross
Warren	E cen.	284	7,360	Warrenton
Washington	cen.	674	18,903	Sandersville
Wayne	SE	646	17,921	Jesup
Webster	W	195	3,247	Preston
Wheeler	SE cen.	306	5,342	Alamo
White	NE	243	6,935	Cleveland
Whitfield	NW	281	42,109	Dalton
Wilcox	S cen.	383	7,905	Abbeville
Wilkes	NE	472	10,961	Washington
Wilkinson	cen.	458	9,250	Irwinton
Worth	S	580	16,682	Sylvester

[1] Area = land area in sq. m. Pop. from 1960 Census.
[2] Includes islands of Sea Islands chain.

Nickname: Empire State of the South; also Peach State. *State flower:* Cherokee rose. *Motto:* Wisdom, Justice, Moderation. *Chief cities:* Atlanta, Savannah, Columbus, Augusta, Macon. *Rivers:* Chattahoochee and Flint, uniting in SW to form the Apalachicola; Ocmulgee and Oconee, uniting in SE to form the Altamaha; Savannah, forming E boundary bet. Georgia and South Carolina. *Highest point:* Brasstown Bald 4784 ft. on boundary of Towns and Union cos. *Other important natural feature:* Okefinokee Swamp 660 sq. m. in SE. *Chief industries:* Agriculture, esp. cotton growing.

History: Discovered by Spanish and penetrated by Spanish missions; English colony, last of original 13 colonies to be founded, chartered 1732 and settled 1733 at

Savannah by Oglethorpe as refuge for debtors and buffer state bet. Spanish Florida and the Carolinas; surrendered charter to crown 1754; Savannah held by British 1778–82; chartered University of Georgia 1785, the oldest state university; first southern state to ratify federal constitution Jan. 2, 1788; ceded claims to western lands (now Alabama and Mississippi) 1802; in dispute over southern boundary from colonial days until 1866 when it accepted line based upon Joseph Ellicott's points; seceded from Union Jan. 19, 1861; scene of battle of Chickamauga 1863, campaign bet. Chattanooga and Atlanta, and Sherman's "March to the Sea" 1864; ordinance of secession repealed Oct. 30, 1865 and slavery abolished; last state to be readmitted to Union July 15, 1870; adopted present constitution 1877.

Georgia; *Georgian* **Sa·kart′ve·lo** (sä·kärt′vĕ·lô); *Russ.* **Gru′zi·ya** (grōō′zyĭ·yȧ); *officially* **Georgian Soviet Socialist Republic**; *anc.* **I·be′ri·a** (ī·bēr′ĭ·ȧ). Ancient and medieval kingdom; now a constituent republic of the U.S.S.R., W Transcaucasia; 26,875 sq. m.; pop. 3,542,289, (1941 est.) 3,722,252; * Tiflis; includes Abkhazian and Adzhar Autonomous Republics and South Ossetian Autonomous Region. Separated from R.S.F.S.R. on N and NE by main range of Caucasus Mts.; bounded on SE by Azerbaidzhan, on S by Armenian S.S.R. and Turkey, and on W by Black Sea; comprises mainly the S slopes of W and cen. Caucasus, and valleys of the Rion and upper Kura rivers. Chief industry agriculture; principal crops grains, cotton, tobacco, tea, and fruits; raises domestic animals, poultry, and bees; has coal and manganese mines. Predominant ethnic strain Japhetic (Caucasian); chief nationalities Georgian 67.7%, Armenian 11.6%, and Turkic 5%. Chief towns Tiflis, Batum, Kutais, Sukhumi.

History: Region contained ancient kingdoms of Colchis and Iberia; dependent upon Rome after 1st cent. B.C. but retained autonomy; Christianized in 4th cent. A.D.; E part, esp. under Sassanidae, became Persian, and, in 8th cent., was conquered by Arabs; reunited with W part 11th cent.; expanded to include region from Black Sea to Caspian and parts of Armenia and Persia before its disintegration under impact of Mongol and Turkish invasions; under Armenian, Turkish, and Persian control until it sought Russian protection in 18th cent.; annexation to Russia 1801 caused Russian war with Persia 1804–13 (see GULISTAN); when Russia collapsed 1917, entered short-lived Transcaucasian Republic; declared independent republic 1918; established Soviet government 1921; in 1922 joined Transcaucasian S.F.S.R. and entered U.S.S.R.; became constituent republic 1936.

Georgia, Strait of. Channel in SW Canada and NW U.S.; has Vancouver I. on the W and mainland of SW British Columbia and Whatcom co., Washington on the E; ab. 240 m. long, 30 m. wide at its widest part; connects by Johnstone Strait with Queen Charlotte Strait and extends S to Haro Strait (*q.v.*); forms part of inland steamship passage from U.S. to Alaska.

Geor·gi·an′a (jôr′jĭ·ăn′ȧ). Town, Butler co., S Alabama, 60 m. SW of Montgomery; pop. 2093.

Geor′gi·an Bay (jôr′jĭ·ăn; -jăn; -jyăn). Inlet ab. 125 m. long by 50 m. wide of Lake Huron, SE Ontario prov., Canada; has entrance ab. 20 m. wide bet. E Manitoulin I. and Cape Hurd. Thirty islands in **Georgian Bay Islands National Park** (see CANADA, *National Parks*).

Geor′gia·ville (jôr′jȧ·vĭl; -jyȧ). Village, Providence co., N Rhode Island, ab. 7 m. W of Central Falls; pop. (est.) 1247; governmental center of Smithfield town.

Ge·or′gi·evsk (gĭ·ôr′gĭ·yĕfsk). Town, S Stavropol Territory, Soviet Russia, Europe, 18 m. E of Pyatigorsk; pop. 21,629; on Rostov-Baku railroad; trade center for agricultural and cattle products; has annual fairs. Founded 1777; taken by Germans 1942, recaptured by Russians Jan. 10, 1943.

Geor·gi′na (jôr·jē′nȧ). River ab. 400 m. long in Arunta Desert region, E Northern Territory and W Queensland, Australia; in some seasons flows to the Warburton.

Ge′ra (gā′rä). Industrial city, Thuringia, E Germany, on the Weisse Elster 47 m. ESE of Erfurt; pop. 81,402; railroad junction; castle, old church (Trinitatiskirche), 16th-cent. town hall; manufactures textiles (esp. woolens), iron and steel products, vehicles, machinery, leather. Destroyed by fire 1639, 1686, and 1780; formerly capital of Reuss-Schleiz-Gera principality.

Geral, Serra. See SERRA GERAL.

Ger′ald·ton (jĕr′ăl[d]·tŭn). **1** Town, W Western Australia, 210 m. NNW of Perth; pop. 4985; good harbor. **2** Town, Thunder Bay dist., SW Ontario, Canada, 55 m. E of Lake Nipigon; pop. 3227; incorporated 1937.

Gé′rard′mer′ (zhā′rär′mā′). Commune, Vosges dept., NE France, on a lake in the Vosges Mts. 20 m. SE of Épinal; pop. (1931) 8512; summer and winter resort.

Gerasa. See JERASH.

Ger·bi′ni (jĕr·bē′nē). Town, E Sicily, W of Catania.

Ger′go′vie′ (zhĕr′gô′vē′). Plateau, Puy-de-Dôme dept., S cen. France, S of Clermont-Ferrand; above village of **Gergovie**; site of **Ger·go′vi·a** (jûr·gō′vĭ·ȧ), ancient settlement of the Arverni where Vercingetorix repulsed Julius Caesar's forces 52 B.C., later destroyed by Caesar.

Ge′ring (gē̞r′ĭng). City, ⊗ of Scotts Bluff co., W Nebraska, on No. Platte river opp. Scottsbluff; pop. 4585.

Ger′i·zim, Mount (gĕr′ĭ·zĭm; gĕ·rī′zĭm); *Arab.* **Je′bel et Tur** (jä′băl ăt tōōr′). Mountain 2849 ft. just S of Nablus, Palestine; sacred place for Samaritans.

Gerls′dor′fer Spit′ze (gĕrls′dôr′fĕr shpĭt′sĕ); *Czech* **Ger′la·chov′ka** (gĕr′lȧ·kôf′kȧ); *in 1949 renamed* **Stalin Peak.** Peak 8737 ft. in Tatra Mts., Carpathians, N Slovakia, Czechoslovakia.

Ger′man Coast (jûr′măn); *Fr.* **Côte des Al′lemands′** (kōt′ dā-zăl′măn′). District extending ab. 40 m. along right bank of Mississippi river from a point ab. 30 m. above New Orleans, Louisiana; settled 1721 by Alsatians who had come to America under inducements of John Law's Mississippi Scheme, which collapsed 1720.

German East Africa. See TANGANYIKA.

Ger·ma′ni·a (jûr·mā′nĭ·ȧ; -mān′yȧ; jĕr-). Ancient region of cen. Europe rather more extensive than modern Germany, comprising territory E of the Rhine and N of the Danube which never became part of Roman Empire. Areas just W of Rhine conquered by Romans became: **Germania In·fe′ri·or** (ĭn·fēr′ĭ·ẽr; -ôr), a Roman province of E Gallia (mod. NE France and part of Belgium and Netherlands); and **Germania Su·pe′ri·or** (sū̇·pēr′ĭ·ẽr; -ôr; sŭ-), Roman province of NE Gallia (nearly equivalent to Alsace-Lorraine).

Germanicopolis. See ÇANKIRI.

Germanicum, Mare. See NORTH SEA.

German New Guinea. = Territory of NEW GUINEA.

German Ocean. See NORTH SEA.

German Southwest Africa. See SOUTH-WEST AFRICA.

Ger′man·town (jûr′măn·toun). **1** Village, Montgomery co., SW cen. Maryland, NW of Rockville; pop. (est.) 125; U.S. Atomic Energy Commission headquarters. **2** Village, Montgomery co., SW Ohio; pop. 3399; tobacco products, flour, concrete products. **3** Residential section of Philadelphia, Pennsylvania, located principally in ward 22, on Wissahickon Creek; originally settled as township by German colonists 1683–84; battle of Germantown Oct. 4, 1777 in which Washington tried unsuccessfully to dislodge British troops stationed there under Sir Wm. Howe; consolidated with Philadelphia (*q.v.*) 1854; early printing and publishing center; textile manufactures.

German Vol′ga Republic (vŏl′gȧ; *Russ.* vôl′-); *officially* **Volga German Autonomous Soviet Socialist Republic.** Former autonomous republic, SE Soviet Russia, Europe; 10,885 sq. m.; pop. 605,542; * Engels; on E bank of the Volga river, except for a small

area, which was W of the Volga river; surrounded on W, N, and E by Saratov Region and bounded on S and SW by Stalingrad Region; mainly level steppe land; chief occupation agriculture. Region settled 1760–61 by 27,000 Germans invited by special decree of Empress Catherine II. At first granted special privileges, lost all autonomy by 1870; Revolution of 1917 prevented transfer of colonists to Siberia which had been ordered 1915. Chief nationalities: German 67%, Russians 20%, Ukrainians 12%. Organized as a district 1918 and in 1924 as an autonomous republic; suffered greatly in famine of 1921–22; republic abolished Sept. 24, 1941, its territory divided bet. Saratov and Stalingrad Regions.

Ger'ma·ny (jûr'mȧ·nĭ); *Ger.* **Deutsch'land'** (doich'-länt'); *officially* **Deut'sches Reich** (doi'chĕs rīk'). Country, cen. Europe; 182,426 sq. m.; pop. (1939) 69,622,483; including Austria, Sudetenland, and Memel, then (1939) parts of Germany, 226,289 sq. m., pop. 79,410,095; ✽ Berlin. Bounded on N by Denmark and Baltic Sea, on E by Poland, on E and S by Czechoslovakia, on SE by Austria, on SW by Switzerland, on W by France, Luxembourg, Belgium, and Netherlands, and on NW by the North Sea. See *Map*, pp. 398, 399. Before World War II divided into the following 16 states (for pronunciation of their names, see their individual entries), which under the National Socialist regime were reorganized into 17 administrative units:

ENGLISH NAME	GERMAN NAME	LOCA-TION	AREA[1]	POP.[1]	CAPITAL
Anhalt	Anhalt	cen.	893	436,213	Dessau
Baden	Baden	SW	5,817	2,518,103	Karlsruhe
Bavaria	Bayern	S	30,046	8,280,090	Munich
Bremen	Bremen	NW	99	400,086	Bremen
Brunswick	Braun-schweig	cen.	1,417	599,208	Bruns-wick
Hamburg	Hamburg	N	288	1,682,220	Hamburg
Hesse	Hessen	SW	2,969	1,469,909	Darm-stadt
Lippe	Lippe	NW	469	188,598	Detmold
Mecklen-burg[2]	Mecklen-burg	N	6,068	910,826	Schwerin
Oldenburg	Oldenburg	NW	2,083	582,400	Oldenburg
Prussia[3]	Preussen	N and cen.	113,545	41,762,040	Berlin
Saarland[4]	Saarland	SW	743	863,736	Saar-brücken
Saxony	Sachsen	cen.	5,788	5,206,861	Dresden
Schaum-burg-Lippe	Schaum-burg-Lippe	NW	131	54,162	Bücke-burg
Thuringia	Thüringen	cen.	4,540	1,760,595	Weimar
Württem-berg	Württem-berg	S	7,530	2,907,166	Stuttgart

[1] Area is in sq. m. Pop. is from 1939 Census.
[2] Formed Jan. 1, 1934 from former states of Mecklenburg-Schwerin and Mecklenburg-Strelitz.
[3] Annexed Waldeck Apr. 1, 1929.
[4] Returned to Germany by plebiscite Jan. 13, 1935.

The states of the Federal Republic of Germany are: Baden-Württemberg, Bavaria, Berlin (not formally incorporated), Bremen, Hamburg, Hesse, Lower Saxony, North Rhine-Westphalia, Rhineland-Palatinate, Saarland, and Schleswig-Holstein (*qq.v.*). *Mountains:* Generally level in N, mountainous in W and SW, hilly in cen. parts (Harz Mts.); bordered on S and E by Erz Gebirge and Bohemian Forest and on S by Bavarian Alps; highest point Zugspitze 9719 ft. in Bavarian Alps. *Chief rivers:* Rhine (lower part in Netherlands), Ems, Weser, and Elbe flowing to North Sea; Oder river flowing to the Baltic; in S the upper Danube flowing E into Austria and eventually to the Black Sea. *Lakes:* Largest Lake Constance on Swiss border; many lakes in NE (Pomerania), N (Mecklenburg), and SE (Bavaria). *Chief islands:* In the Baltic Sea Rügen, Usedom, Wollin, Fehmarn; in the North Sea the North Frisian and East Frisian Is. *Chief cities:* Berlin, Hamburg, Munich, Cologne, Leipzig, Essen, Düsseldorf, Frankfurt am Main, Dortmund. *Chief economic products:* Agricultural products (grains, potatoes, sugar beets, grapes, domestic animals, and poultry), timber, minerals (esp. coal, iron, lignite, potash), manufactured articles (iron and steel, electrical and chemical products, fertilizers, rayon, cotton and woolen yarn, textiles, earthenware, automobiles, cement, beer, wine).

History: Region E of Rhine and N of Danube (ancient Germania), inhabited from early times by Teutonic peoples, never included in Roman Empire; began as political entity with the division of Carolingian empire (see FRANCE) allotted to Louis the German 843 A.D.; Germany, with N Italy, included in Holy Roman Empire (*q.v.*); even at height of Emperor's influence divided into numerous secular and ecclesiastical feudal units which increased their power during papal-imperial struggle; accession of first ruler of Hapsburg line, Rudolf I, 1273; expanded eastward, Prussia being conquered 13th cent. by Teutonic Knights; weakness and political dissolution of Empire accelerated by Reformation which began with Lutheran revolt 1517; Germany split into Catholic and Protestant states which suffered greatly from disastrous Thirty Years' War 1618–48 (see BOHEMIA); Empire yielded territory to France, Sweden, Brandenburg, and recognized practical sovereignty (Ger. *Landeshoheit*) of its separate states 1648; in 18th cent. Prussia under the Hohenzollerns prospered and soon became strongest military state and weakened Austria in Silesian Wars; on dissolution of Holy Roman Empire 1806, German states became dependents of France. Formed *Germanic Confederation* under Austrian hegemony 1815–66; by 1866 most German states included in customs union (Ger. *Zollverein*) sponsored by Prussia; failed to achieve unity in Frankfurt National Assembly 1848–49; as victor in Seven Weeks' War against Austria 1866, Prussia became leader of German unification; *German Empire*, a federal state dominated by Prussia, proclaimed at close of Franco-Prussian War 1871 with Bismarck first Chancellor (1871–90); acquired Alsace-Lorraine (*q.v.*); allied with Austria 1879 and with Italy 1882, thus forming Triple Alliance; adopted policy of colonial expansion 1884 and engaged in Kulturkampf 1872–87. Supported Austria in the quarrel with Serbia (*q.v.*) which precipitated World War I 1914; forced Kaiser's abdication and proclaimed republic 1918; by Versailles Treaty 1919 lost Alsace-Lorraine, Moresnet, Eupen, and Malmédy, most of Posen and West Prussia (including Danzig), Memel, and all her colonies in Africa and in the Pacific; adopted Weimar Constitution 1919; Ruhr (*q.v.*) region occupied by French 1923; signed Locarno (*q.v.*) treaties 1925; member of League of Nations Council 1926–33. Ceased to be federal republic 1933 and became, under Chancellor Hitler, centralized, unitary, totalitarian state dominated by National Socialist party; recovered the Saar by plebiscite 1935; reoccupied Rhineland and formed Rome-Berlin Axis and alliance with Japan 1936; annexed Austria and Sudeten Germans 1938, rest of Czechoslovakia (*q.v.*) 1939. In pact with U.S.S.R. 1939–41, began war (World War II) with Poland and with Great Britain and France Sept. 1939; conquered Norway Apr. 1940; overran Netherlands and Belgium May–June 1940; forced surrender of France June 1940; attacked Russia June 22, 1941, defeated at Stalingrad Jan. 1943, gradually forced out of Russia 1943–44; driven out of North Africa May 1943; driven out of France and finally forced to surrender to Allies May 8, 1945; by Potsdam Conference July 17–Aug. 2, 1945, lost to Poland territory in E (see EAST PRUSSIA). Divided 1945 into four zones of occupation: American comprising Bavaria and SW Germany; British including NW Germany, chiefly Prussian territory; French including Baden, W Württemberg, Saarland, and S Rhineland (bounded on NW in part by lower Elbe) comprising Mecklenburg, the E part of Prussia, Saxony, and Thuringia; in 1949 the American, British, and French zones formed West German Federal Republic, ✽ Bonn (*q.v.*) and in Soviet zone was set up the East German Democratic Republic, ✽ East Berlin.

GERMANY
As of March 31, 1938

Statute Miles

0 20 40 60 80 100

⊛ Capitals

PUBLISHED BY G. & C. MERRIAM COMPANY
SPRINGFIELD, MASS.
PREPARED BY J. W. CLEMENT CO. BUFFALO, N.Y.

RUHR VALLEY

Statute Miles

0 5 10 15

Ger′mers·heim (gĕr′mērs·hīm); *anc.* **Vi′cus Ju′li·i** (vī′kŭs jōō′lǐ·ī). Commune, SE Rhineland-Palatinate, Germany, on the Rhine 8 m. SSW of Speyer; pop. 3310; bet. 1644 and 1815 belonged alternately to France and the Palatinate.

Ger′mis·ton (jûr′mĭs·tŭn). City, S Transvaal, NE Union of South Africa, 9 m. E of Johannesburg; pop. 79,440; gold fields; world's largest gold refinery; airport, one of largest in South Africa.

Ge′rol·stein (gā′rōl·shtīn). Village, W Germany, 28 m. N of Trier; health resort.

Ge·ro′na (hā·rō′nä). **1** Municipality, NE cen. Tarlac prov., Luzon, Phil. Is., 10 m. N of Tarlac; pop. 20,982. **2** Province of Spain. See *Table* at SPAIN. **3** *anc.* **Ge·run′da** (jē·rŭn′dà). Fortified commune, * of Gerona prov., NE Spain, 52 m. NE of Barcelona; pop. 29,632; 14th-cent. Gothic cathedral, 13th-cent. collegiate church; under Moorish rule c. 713–785 and 795–1015; became principality under kingdom of Aragon; often besieged, esp. by French 1809.

Ger′ra *or* **Ger′rha** (jĕr′à). Ancient port, E Arabia, on SW coast of Sinus Persicus (Persian Gulf); mentioned by Strabo and Pliny; site probably at modern Oqair.

Gers (zhâr). **1** River ab. 75 m. long SW France; flows N into Garonne river near Agen. **2** Department of France. See *Table* at FRANCE.

Ger′sau (gĕr′zou). Village, Schwyz canton, E cen. Switzerland, on Lake of Lucerne; pop. (1930) 1870; resort; independent state 1390–1817.

Ger·sop′pa, Falls of (jĕr·sŏp′à). Cataract 830 ft. high in small stream (Sharavati) ab. 18 m. from its mouth, on border bet. S Bombay prov. and NW Mysore, India.

Ger′the (gĕr′tĕ). Former commune (pop. 20,956), Arnsberg govt. dist., Westphalia prov., Prussia, Germany; since 1929 part of Bochum (*q.v.*).

Gerunda. See GERONA.

Ge′se·rich, Lake (gā′zĕ·rĭк). Lake, formerly in SW East Prussia prov., Prussia, Germany; now in Olsztyn dept., N Poland.

Ge′shur (gē′shĕr). Region in ancient Palestine from NE shore of Sea of Galilee E to Bashan; in the time of David an Aramaean kingdom (*2 Sam.* xiii. 37).

Gesoriacum *or* **Gessoriacum.** See BOULOGNE.

Geth·sem′a·ne (gĕth·sĕm′à·nē). The enclosure or garden on the Mount of Olives outside of Jerusalem which was the scene of the agony and arrest of Jesus (*Matt.* xxvi. 36–47).

Get′tys·burg (gĕt′ĭz·bûrg). **1** Manufacturing borough, ⊗ of Adams co., S Pennsylvania, 30 m. WSW of York; pop. 7960; iron mines, granite quarries; Lutheran Theological Seminary (1826; men), Gettysburg Coll. (1832; coed.). Laid out in 1780's, became ⊗ 1800, incorp. 1806; scene of battle July 1–3, 1863, in which Federals under Meade defeated Confederates under Lee, stopping Lee's invasion of the North (see CEMETERY RIDGE), site now comprising **Gettysburg National Military Park** (see UNITED STATES, *National Historical Parks*). **2** City, ⊗ of Potter co., N cen. South Dakota; pop. 1950.

Ge′vels·berg (gā′fĕls·bĕrк). City, W Germany, in North Rhine-Westphalia state 32 m. NE of Cologne; pop. 20,704; iron products, stoves.

Gex (zhĕks; zhĕ). Town, Ain dept., E France, 10 m. NNW of Geneva, Switzerland; pop. (1931) 1341; in the **Pa′ys′ de Gex** (pā′ē′ dĕ), region bet. Alps and Jura Mts., at different times under control of counts of Savoy, Geneva, and Switzerland, belongs to France since 1601.

Ge·yik′ Da·ği′ (gĕ·yēk′ dä·ī′). Peak 10,270 ft. in SW Turkey in Asia, E of Gulf of Antalya.

Gey′sir (gī′zĕr; -sĕr; *Brit. also* gā′-, gē′-; *Icelandic* gyä′-sĭr); *Eng.* **Great Gey′ser** (gī′zĕr; -sĕr; gā′-; gē′-). Inactive geyser in SW cen. Iceland; active for short while following earthquake 1896.

Ge′zer (gē′zēr). Ancient Canaanite city; site S of Lydda, WNW of Jerusalem, at Tell Jezar; excavations have revealed many cultures.

Ge·zi′ra (jĕ·zē′rà); *Arab.* **El Je·zi′ra** (ăl jă·zē′rŏ). **1** District bet. Blue Nile and White Nile rivers, E cen. Republic of the Sudan. **2** Province, Republic of the Sudan. See BLUE NILE.

Ghadames. See GADÂMES.

Gha′na (gä′nà). **1** *or* **Ga′na.** Ancient and medieval Sudanese kingdom in W Sahara, Africa. **2** *or* **Ga′na** (gä′nà). Former city, its *, ab. 350 m. WNW of Tombouctou; exact location uncertain. **3** A republic of the British Commonwealth. See GOLD COAST.

Ghanayim, El. See EL GHANAYIM.

Ghan′si (gän′sē) *or* **Ghan′si·land′** (-lănd′); *also* **Khan′zi** (kän′zē). Plateau region, NW Kalahari Desert, Bechuanaland Protectorate, S Africa; on NE is Lake Ngami, on W South-West Africa; settled by Cecil Rhodes as buffer state against German colonization from South-West Africa.

Gharapuri. See ELEPHANTA.

Gharaq es Sultani, El. See EL GHARAQ ES SULTANI.

Ghar·bî′ya *or* **Gar·bi′eh** (gär·bē′yà; *Arab.* gŭr·bē′yä). Province, N Lower Egypt. See *Table* at EGYPT.

Ghar·da′ïa (gär·dä′yà). **1** Territory of Algeria. See *Table* at ALGERIA. **2** Commune, its *, 300 m. S of Algiers; pop. 45,533.

Ghâ′rib, Ge′bel (gä′băl gä′rĭb). Mountain 5745 ft., E Egypt, near S end of Gulf of Suez SW of **Ras Ghârib** (räs), point on the gulf; petroleum.

Ghat. See GAT.

Ghats, Eastern *and* **Western** (gôts). Two mountain ranges in S India: **Eastern Ghats** (average height 1500–2000 ft.) extending for ab. 500 m. along SE and E coast as far N as mouth of Mahanadi river; **Western Ghats** (average height 3000–5000 ft.) extending 800 m. along SW and W coast as far N as mouth of Tapti river; bet. them is the Deccan (*q.v.*).

Ghaza. Var. of GAZA, Palestine.

Gha′zi·pur (gä′zĭ·pŏŏr). Town SE Uttar Pradesh, N India, on Ganges river 40 m. ENE of Benares; pop. 27,498; former licensed center for collecting and processing opium; has scent distilleries. Founded 1330.

Ghaz′ni (gäz′nē). Commercial city, E cen. Afghanistan, 92 m. SW of Kabul; pop. ab. 10,000. Became Moslem in 9th cent.; made capital of Ghaznevid dynasty by Subuktigin 977; its most famous ruler was Mahmud of Ghazni (997–1030) who conquered neighboring regions and made the city capital of a kingdom extending from the Tigris to the Ganges which endured until 1173 when it was finally overcome by Mohammed of Ghor; taken by Ogadai, son of Genghis Khan, c. 1235. Declined politically under the Moguls of India until 1737 when it became part of new Afghan kingdom; in Afghan Wars of 19th cent. captured by British July 23, 1839; later besieged for four months by Afghans and surrendered Mar. 6, 1842; retaken and partly destroyed by British Sept. 1842.

Ghazze. See GAZA.

Gheel. See GEEL.

Ghe′lu·velt (gā′lü·vĕlt). Small commune, West Flanders prov., NW Belgium, 5 m. E of Ieper (Ypres); pop. 1388; battlefield 1914, 1917.

Ghent. See GENT.

Ghe′ri·ah (gā′rī·à). Locality, Maharashtra state, India, S of Bombay; site of pirate stronghold reduced by Clive 1756.

Ghilan. See GILAN.

Ghor (gôr) *or* **Ghur** (gŏŏr). Ancient kingdom, SW Asia, in what is now NW Afghanistan; its princes, first mentioned in 11th cent. A.D., closely connected with Ghaznevid dynasty; their greatest ruler Mohammed of Ghor, who captured Ghazni 1173 and conquered all northern India (1186–1206).

Ghor, the (gôr). The valley of the Dead Sea and lower Jordan, Palestine and Jordan; 4 to 12 m. wide, ab. 65 m. long.

Gia'lo (jä'lô). Oasis, S Cyrenaica, NE Libya.

Gianitsà. See GENITSA.

Gian·nu'tri (jän·nŏŏ'trĕ). Small island in Tyrrhenian Sea off SW coast of Tuscany, cen. Italy.

Gi'ant Mountain (jī'ănt). Peak 4622 ft. in the Adirondack Mts., Essex co., NE New York.

Giant Mountains. = RIESEN GEBIRGE.

Gi'ant's Castle (jī'ănts). Peak 9657 ft. in Drakensberg Mts., E Union of South Africa, on border bet. Basutoland and Natal.

Giant's Causeway. Formation of prismatic basaltic columns on N coast of co. Antrim, Northern Ireland, making a rough platform extending for 300 yards along coast and at one point ab. 500 ft. into the sea.

Gia·ra·bub' or **Ja·ra·bub'** (jär'à·bŏŏb'); Arab. **Jaghbub'** (jŭg·bŏŏb'). Oasis, E Cyrenaica, Libya; African * of the Senusi, ceded to Italy by Egypt 1925; occupied by British Nov. 1941.

Giar're (jär'rä). Commune, Catania prov., E Sicily, at E foot of Mt. Etna; pop. 18,501.

Gia·ve'no (jä·vâ'nô). Commune, Torino prov., Piedmont, NW Italy 17 m. SW of Turin; pop. 9441.

Gi·ba'ra (hĕ·vä'rä). Municipality and town, N coast of Oriente prov., E Cuba; pop. (town) 8045; exports esp. bananas; port opened to commerce 1827. See HOLGUÍN.

Gib'bon Falls (gĭb'ŭn). Waterfall 84 ft. high on **Gibbon River,** Yellowstone National Park, NW Wyoming.

Gib'e·ah (gĭb'ê·à). Town, S ancient Palestine, ab. 4 m. N of Jerusalem; political capital of Saul, first king of Israel (1 Sam xxii. 6).

Gib'e·on (gĭb'ê·ŭn). **1** City of Canaan, Palestine, 6 m. NW of Jerusalem; the modern village of El Jib (pop. 643); its inhabitants (Gibeonites) made an alliance with Joshua but were made slaves.
2 Town, S cen. South-West Africa, on Great Fish river 180 m. SSE of Windhoek; pop. 5107; scene of fighting bet. German and South African forces during World War I.

Gi·bral'tar (jĭ·brôl'tẽr; Span. hê'vräl·tär'). Town and fortress on Rock of Gibraltar, Brit. colony, S Spain; ab. 2 sq. m.; British naval base and fine harbor. Captured 711 A.D. and fortified by Tariq, Moorish invader of Spain; finally taken by Spanish 1462; captured by British 1704 during War of Spanish Succession and retained by treaty 1713; unsuccessfully besieged by French and Spanish 1779–83.

Gibraltar, Bay of. = Bay of ALGECIRAS.

Gibraltar, Rock of; anc. **Cal'pe** (kăl'pê). Peninsula of S Spain, 2¾ m. long by ¾ m. wide, at E end of Strait of Gibraltar, since 1940 separated from the mainland by a canal; highest point 1396 ft.; one of the Pillars of Hercules (q.v.).

Gibraltar, Strait (also often **Straits**) **of;** Lat. **Fre'tum Gad'i·ta'num** (frē'tŭm găd'ĭ·tā'nŭm), **Gad'i·tan Strait** (găd'ĭ·tăn); Arab. **Bab al·Za·kak'** (bäb' ăz·zŭ·käk') "narrow gate." Passage 32 m. long connecting Mediterranean Sea and Atlantic Ocean, bet. Spain and Africa (Span. Morocco), with Gibraltar and Ceuta on either side at E end, Capes Trafalgar and Spartel at W end; ab. 8 m. in narrowest part, ab. 23 m. in widest. See PILLARS OF HERCULES.

Gi·bral'tar Point (jĭ·brôl'tẽr). Cape on N side of entrance to The Wash, E cen. England, S of Skegness.

Gib'son (gĭb's'n). **1** Name of counties in two states of the U.S. See Tables at INDIANA and TENNESSEE.
2 or **Gibson City.** City, ⊗ of Glascock co., E cen. Georgia; pop. 479.
3 Residential city, Ford co., NE cen. Illinois, 32 m. E of Bloomington; pop. 3453.

Gib'son·burg (gĭb's'n·bûrg). Village, Sandusky co., N Ohio, 20 m. SSE of Toledo; pop. 2540; flour mills; oil and gas wells.

Gibson Desert. Desert ab. 250 m. by 520 m., cen. and E Western Australia, S of Great Sandy Desert; salt lakes.

Gibson Peak. Mountain 13,729 ft. in Custer and Saguache cos., S cen. Colorado.

Gib'son·ville (gĭb's'n·vĭl). Town, Alamance and Guilford cos. N cen. North Carolina; pop. 1784; food-processing plants, cottonseed oil and feed mills.

Gid'dings (gĭd'ingz). City, ⊗ of Lee co., cen. Texas, 30 m. W of Brenham; pop. 2821.

Gid'e·on (gĭd'ê·ŭn). City, New Madrid co., SE Missouri, 24 m. NNW of Caruthersville; pop. 1411.

Gien (zhyăN). Commune, Loiret dept., N cen. France, on the Loire 38 m. ESE of Orléans; pop. (1931) 8257; castle, rebuilt 1494 by Anne of Beaujeu; manufactures faïence.

Giens (zhyăN). Peninsula on SE coast of Var dept., S France, S of Hyères, which forms E side of the **Gulf of Giens,** the E end of inlet on which Toulon is located.

Giess'bach (gēs'bäk). Waterfall 980 ft., E of Lake of Brienz, SE Bern canton, Switzerland.

Gies'sen (gē'sĕn). City, cen. Hesse state, Germany, on Lahn river 35 m. N of Frankfurt am Main; pop. 33,600; two 16th-cent. castles; university (founded early 17th cent.); manufactures tobacco and machine, iron, and rubber goods. Chartered as city 1248; passed to Hesse 1265; in World War II entered by American troops Mar. 28, 1945.

Gif'fard' (zhē'fär'; Angl. zhĕ'fär'). Village, Quebec co., S Quebec, Canada, on St. Lawrence river 2 m. N of Quebec; pop. 8097.

Gi·fu (gē·fŏŏ). **1** Prefecture of Japan. See Table at JAPAN.
2 City, its *, cen. Honshu, 20 m. NNW of Nagoya on Nagara river; pop. (1945 est.) 142,543; manufactures paper wares (umbrellas, lanterns, fans, napkins, crape, etc.). A castle town in medieval Japan; captured 1564 by Oda Nobunaga; a center of civil conflict until about 1600; famous as scene of cormorant fishing on the Nagara.

Gi·gan'te (hê·hän'tâ). Mountain 10,653 ft., Guanajuato state, cen. Mexico.

Gi'gha (gē'à). Small island of the Inner Hebrides, ab. 3½ m. W of Kintyre Penin., SW Scotland.

Gi'glio (jē'lyô); anc. **I·gil'i·um** (ĭ·jĭl'ĭ·ŭm). Italian island in Mediterranean Sea off SW coast of Tuscany, cen. Italy; ab. 15 sq. m.; highest point 1634 ft.; has two towns: **Giglio Ca·stel'lo** (käs·tĕl'lô), pop. (1931) 1004, on the height, and the port of **Giglio Por'to** (pôr'tô), pop. 944; granite quarries since Roman times.

Gi·hei'na (jĭ·hā'nà; -nä). Town, Girga prov., Upper Egypt, near Nile NW of Sohâg; pop. 17,000.

Gi·hulng'an (hê·hŏŏlng'än). Municipality, NE Negros Oriental, Negros, Phil. Is., on Tañon Strait; pop. 53,582; largest town in province; founded 1800.

Gi·jón' (hē·hôn'). Seaport, Oviedo prov., NW Spain, on Bay of Biscay 16 m. NE of Oviedo; pop. (1941 est.) 101,517; fine harbor (founded 1552 by Charles V); commercial fishing; manufactures glass, pottery, soap, chocolates, tobacco. Founded before Roman times; captured by Moors, 8th cent.; port of refuge of Spanish Armada after its defeat by British 1588.

Gi'la (hē'là). **1** River ab. 630 m. long flowing from SW New Mexico W across S Arizona to Colorado river near Yuma, SW corner of Arizona; its valley is chief habitat of the Gila monster, a large poisonous lizard.
2 County in Arizona. See *Table* at ARIZONA.

Gi'la (jē'là). River, SW Ethiopia; flows NW into the Pibor river on border of Sudan below Akobo Post.

Gila Cliff Dwellings National Monument (hē'là). See UNITED STATES, *National Monuments.*

Gi·lan' *or* **Ghi·lan'** (gē·län'). Province, NW Iran, SW of Caspian Sea; 5473 sq. m.; ✱ Resht.

Gil'bert (gĭl'bẽrt). **1** City, St. Louis co., NE Minnesota, 3 m. ESE of Virginia; pop. 2591; former iron-mining center.
2 River ab. 250 m. long, N Queensland, Australia; flows NW into Gulf of Carpentaria.

Gilbert and El'lice Islands Colony (ĕl'ĭs). British colony in W Pacific Ocean, consisting of the Gilbert Is., Ellice Is., Ocean I., three islands (Fanning, Washington, and Christmas) of the Line Is., and the Phoenix Is., 316 sq. m.; pop. (1936) 34,443; ✱ Tarawa. The two main groups proclaimed a British protectorate 1892 and made a colony 1915; Fanning I., Washington I., and Ocean I. added 1916, Christmas I. in 1919, and the Phoenix group 1937.

Gilbert Grosvenor Range. See GROSVENOR RANGE.

Gilbert Islands. Island group containing 16 atolls in the W Pacific Ocean on the equator, SSE of Marshall Is. and NE of Solomon Is.; 166 sq. m.; pop. 26,340, with Ocean I. 29,131; forms main part of British Gilbert and Ellice Islands Colony; most important islands Tarawa (largest), Makin, Abaiang, Abemama, Tabiteuea, Nonouti, and Beru. Islands have long been densely populated; natives, of Melanesian race, have been noted for warlike nature. Probably first sighted by Mendaña in 1567; various islands visited by British navigators bet. 1767 and 1824; visited by Commander Wilkes 1846; scene of missionary labors of Hiram Bingham 1857–64, 1873–75. Proclaimed a British protectorate 1892, made part of Gilbert and Ellice Islands Colony 1915; occupied by Japanese Dec. 1941–Nov. 1943 (see TARAWA).

Gil'ber·ton (gĭl'bẽr·t'n; -tŭn). Borough, Schuylkill co., E cen. Pennsylvania, 8 m. N of Pottsville; pop. 1712; coal mining.

Gil'bert Peak (gĭl'bẽrt). Mountain 13,422 ft., NE Utah, bet. Summit and Duchesne cos.; in Uinta Mts.

Gil·bo'a, Mount (gĭl·bō'à). Mountain 1696 ft., Samaria, Palestine, W of the Jordan and S of the Valley of Jezreel near source of the Qishon; place where Saul was defeated by the Philistines and slew himself (*1 Sam.* xxxi. 1, 4).

Gil'christ (gĭl'krĭst). County in Florida. See *Table* at FLORIDA.

Gil'e·ad (gĭl'ē·ăd; -ăd). **1** Mountainous region E of Jordan river in ancient Palestine, extending approximately from the Yarmuk to the Arnon; now in NW Jordan.
2 Ancient city of the Gilead, S of the Jabbok.

Gilead, Mount. Peak 3597 ft., NNE of the Dead Sea, in Jordan; in ancient Palestine in cen. Gilead.

Giles (jīlz). Name of counties in two states of the U.S. See *Tables* at TENNESSEE and VIRGINIA.

Gil'gal (gĭl'găl). Name of several places in ancient Palestine, some yet unidentified; esp. village near Jericho, the first encampment of the Israelites W of Jordan (*Josh.* iv. 19–24).

Gil'git (gĭl'gĭt). **1** Frontier district, NW Kashmir state, N India; 3118 sq. m.; pop. 31,902; in NW Himalayas, forming part of Dardistan; formerly an agency (1889–1901), SE part now a tributary of Kashmir; the region known in early Indian history.
2 Former agency, NW Kashmir state, N India, N and NW of the district; contained the Frontier Illaqas (*q.v.*) and Hunza dist.
3 Town on Gilg't River (tributary of the Indus, ab. 150 m. long) at elevation of 4890 ft.; once a Buddhist center, now an important strategic station on the highway from Kashmir to Chitral on W and to Hunza and Hindu Kush passes on N.

Gil·les'pie (gĭ·lĕs'pĭ). **1** County in Texas. See *Table* at TEXAS.
2 City, Macoupin co., SW cen. Illinois, 27 m. NE of Alton; pop. 3569; coal mining.

Gil·lette' (jĭ·lĕt'). Town, ⊗ of Campbell co., NE Wyoming, 80 m. ESE of Sheridan; pop. 3580; grain, livestock; coal.

Gil'li·am (gĭl'ĭ·ăm). County in Oregon. See *Table* at OREGON.

Gil'ling·ham (gĭl'ĭng·ăm). Agricultural parish near Shaftesbury, Dorsetshire, S England; pop. 3274.

Gil'ling·ham (jĭl'ĭng·ăm). Municipal borough, Kent, SE England, on the Medway 30 m. ESE of London; pop. 60,983, (1951) 68,099; fruit growing; manufactures brick, cement.

Gillis Island. See WHITE ISLAND.

Gil'ly (zhē'yē'). Commune, Hainaut prov., SW Belgium, on the Sambre just E of Charleroi; pop. 26,094; mining.

Gil'man (gĭl'măn). City, Iroquois co., E Illinois, 27 m. S of Kankakee; pop. 1704.

Gil'mer (gĭl'mẽr). **1** Name of counties in two states of the U.S. See *Tables* in GEORGIA and WEST VIRGINIA.
2 City, ⊗ of Upshur co., NE Texas, 34 m. NE of Tyler; pop 4312; oil; farming.

Gi·lo'lo (jĭ·lō'lō). = HALMAHERA.

Gil'pin (gĭl'pĭn). County in Colorado. See *Table* at COLORADO.

Gilpin Peak. Mountain 13,682 ft. in Ouray and San Miguel cos., SW Colorado.

Gil'roy (gĭl'roi). City, Santa Clara co., W California, 30 m. SE of San Jose; pop. 7348; fruits, vegetables, livestock, poultry.

Gim'ma (ĭm'à). Town in E Galla region, W Ethiopia, ab. 170 m. SW of Addis Ababa; pop. ab. 5000.

Gin'chy' (zhăn'shē'). Village, Somme dept., N France, 25 m. NE of Amiens; captured by British in battle of the Somme Sept. 9, 1916.

Gi·ne'vra (jē·nĕv'rä). Italian form of GENEVA.

Gin·go'og (hĕng·gō'ôg). Municipality, E Misamis Oriental prov., N Mindanao, Phil. Is.; pop. 16,746; on S shore of **Gingoog Bay,** inlet of Mindanao Sea ab. 22 m. wide at mouth.

Gin'ne·ken, *in full* **Ginneken en Ba'vel** (kĭn'ĕ·kĕn ĕm bä'vĕl). Commune, North Brabant prov., S Netherlands, just S of Breda; pop. 13,111.

Gi·no'sa (jē·nō'sä). Commune, Ionio prov., Apulia, SE Italy, 26 m. WNW of Taranto; pop. 13,139.

Gin'seng Mountain (jĭn'sĕng; *locally* jĕn'sĭng). Peak 3790 ft. in the Catskill Mts., SE New York.

Gio'fra (jô'frä). Oasis, NW cen. Libya; chief town Socna.

Gio'ia del Col'le (jô'yä dĕl kôl'lä). Commune, Bari prov., Apulia, SE Italy, 20 m. SE of Bari; pop. 24,312; Norman castle.

Gio·io'sa Io'ni·ca (jô·yō'sä yô'nē·kä). Commune, Reggio di Calabria prov., S Calabria, S Italy, on Ionian Sea; pop. 14,518; sea bathing.

Gior'ni·co (jôr'nē·kô). Village, Ticino canton, SE Switzerland, on Ticino river; pop. ab. 800; scene of victory of greatly outnumbered Swiss forces over the Milanese Dec. 28, 1478.

Gio·vi·naz'zo (jô·vē·nät'tsô). Fortified seaport, Bari prov., Apulia, SE Italy, on Adriatic 10 m. WNW of Bari; pop. 12,664; episcopal see (from 951).

Giovi Pass. See APENNINES.

Gipps'land (gĭps'lănd). Region ab. 14,000 sq. m., SE coast of Victoria, SE Australia; chief town Sale; fertile, rich in minerals; includes **Gippsland Lakes.**

Gipps Town (gĭps). Former town, on S bank of Parramatta river, New South Wales, Australia; now entirely within city of Sydney.

Gi·ran (gē·rän). Town, NE coast of Formosa; pop. 21,379.

Gi·rard' (jĭ·rärd'). **1** City, Macoupin co., SW cen. Illinois, 22 m. SSW of Springfield; pop. 1734.

2 City, ⊗ of Crawford co., SE Kansas, 10 m. NW of Pittsburg; pop. 2350.

3 City, Trumbull co., NE Ohio, NW of Youngstown; pop. 12,997; manufactures steel, iron, leather, oilcloth.

4 Borough, Erie co., NW corner of Pennsylvania, on Lake Erie 16 m. WSW of Erie; pop. 2451.

Gi'rar·dot' (hē'rär·thôt'). City, Cundinamarca dept., cen. Colombia, near Bogotá; pop. 22,557.

Gi·rard'ville (jĭ·rärd'vĭl). Borough, Schuylkill co., E cen. Pennsylvania, 9 m. NNW of Pottsville; pop. 2958; coal mining.

Gir'dle Ness (gûr'd'l nĕs). Headland on E cen. coast of Scotland, 2 m. S of Aberdeen; lighthouse.

Gi·re·sun' (gĕ·rĕ·soon') or **Ke·ra·sun'** (kĕ·rä·soon'). **1** Vilayet, NE Turkey in Asia; 2513 sq. m.; pop. 260,154.

2 anc. **Cer'a·sus** (sĕr'å·sŭs), later **Phar·na'ci·a** (fär·nā'shǐ·å; -shà). Seaport, its ✴, on the Black Sea 70 m. W of Trabzon; pop. 14,897; site of Byzantine fortress. From ancient Cerasus the wild cherry was introduced into Italy c. 100 B.C., hence reputed source of English word cherry (Greek kerasos cherry tree, Latin cerasus, French cerise); Pharmacia was founded on or near site of Cerasus by Pharnaces I, king of Pontus (c. 183-170 B.C.).

Gir'ga or **Gir'geh** (gĭr'gä; Arab. -gä). **1** Province, cen. Upper Egypt. See Table at EGYPT.

2 City, its ✴, on the Nile SE of Sohâg; pop. ab. 20,000; noted for pottery; ancient Roman Catholic monastery.

Girgenti. See AGRIGENTO.

Gi'ri·dih (gĭr'ĭ·dĭ). Town, E Bihar state, NE India, 170 m. NW of Calcutta; pop. 21,122.

Girin. Var. of KIRIN.

Gi·rishk' (gĭ·rĭshk'). Town, S cen. Afghanistan, on Helmand river 75 m. WNW of Kandahar; center of rich agricultural district.

Gir·nar' (gĭr·när'). Mountain, India. See JUNAGARH.

Gi·rón' (hē·rōn'). Town, Azuay prov., S Ecuador; pop. (1944 est.) 12,224.

Gi·ronde' (jĭ·rŏnd'; Fr. zhē'rônd'). **1** Estuary on W coast of France, formed by confluence of Garonne and Dordogne rivers near Bordeaux; extends 45 m. inland.

2 Department of France. See Table at FRANCE.

Gir'van (gûr'văn). Seaport burgh, Ayr co., SW Scotland, 17 m. SSW of Ayr at mouth of Firth of Clyde; pop. 5990; watering place; fishing port.

Gis'borne (gĭz'bĕrn). Seaport borough, Hawke's Bay provincial dist., E North I., New Zealand, on Poverty Bay; pop. (1941 est.) 16,200; nearby is place where Capt. Cook landed 1769.

Gi·shu (gē·shoo) or **Wi·ju** (wē·joo). Town, North Heian prov., NW Korea, on the Yalu ab. 10 m. NW of Shingishu; pop. 9766.

Gi'sors' (zhē'zôr'). Commune, Eure dept., N France, 20 m. NW of Paris; pop. (1931) 5868; as medieval capital of the Vexin dist. on frontier of Normandy was subject of many disputes bet. English and French; ruins of castle begun 1097 by William Rufus.

Gitschin. See JIČÍN.

Giuba. See JUBA.

Giu·dec'ca or **La Giu·dec'ca** (lä joo·dĕk'kä). Long, narrow island, forming S part of city of Venice, Italy; separated from main island by channel, **Ca·na'le del'la Giudecca** (kä·nä'lä däl'lä); in early times inhabited by Jews (hence its name); later made a pleasure resort, now suburb for workers.

Giu·lia'no in Cam·pa'nia (joo·lyä'nō ēng käm·pä'nyä). Commune, Napoli prov., Campania, S Italy, 6 m. NNW of Naples; pop. 21,474.

Giu·lia·no'va (joo·lyä·nō'vä). Commune, Teramo prov., Abruzzi e Molise, cen. Italy, on Adriatic Sea 16 m. ENE of Teramo; pop. 10,873.

Giur'giu (joor'joo); Bulg. **Giur'ge·vo** (zhoor'zhå·vō). City, S Romania, in Muntenia on the Danube; pop. 30,348; river port, ships esp. grain and oil.

Gi'ven'chy'–en–Go'helle' (zhē'vän'shē'än·gô'ĕl'). Commune, Pas-de-Calais dept., N France, 7 m. NNW of Arras; pop. (1931) 1229; fighting Sept.–Nov. 1915, taken by Canadians Apr 12, 1917.

Gi'vet' (zhē'vě'). Commune, Ardennes dept., NE France, near Belgian frontier; pop. 5553; divided by the Meuse into **Grand–Givet** (grän'–), with church built 1682 by Vauban, and **Pe·tit'–Givet** (pē·tē'–); formerly an important fortress; occupied by Germans Aug. 1914–Nov. 1918.

Gi'vors' (zhē'vôr'). Commune, Rhône dept., E cen. France, on Rhone river 13 m. S of Lyons; pop. 13,378; metal, glass, and dye works.

Gi'za or **Gi'zeh** (gē'zà). Province, Upper Egypt. See Table at EGYPT.

Giza or **El Gizeh** (äl; ĕl). City, ✴ of Giza prov., Upper Egypt, on W bank of the Nile near Cairo; pop. (1937) 37,779; formerly an important city, with magnificent palaces, now in ruins; 5 m. W lie the great pyramids and famous Sphinx. See PYRAMIDS.

Gi'zhi·ga (gē'zhǐ·gà). Town, Koryak National District, NE Soviet Russia, Asia, at head of W inlet of Shelekova Gulf.

Gi'zo (gē'zō). Small island of the New Georgia Is., cen. Solomon Is., W Pacific Ocean, bet. Ganongga I. and Kolombangara I.; government station for the New Georgia Is.

Gi·życ'ko (gē·zhĭts'kô); Ger. **Löt'zen** (lû'tsĕn). City, E Olsztyn dept., N Poland, at S end of Lake Mamry; pop. (1946) 10,500.

Gji'no·kas·tër (gyē'nô·käs'tër); Gr. **Ar'gy·ro·ka·stron** (är'yē·rô'käs·trôn); Ital. **Ar'gi·ro'ca·stro** (är'jē·rô'käs·trô). **1** Prefecture, S Albania; 1599 sq. m.; pop. 143,926.

2 Town, Gjinokastër prefecture; pop. 10,836; under Turkish rule 1420–1913; held by Greeks Dec. 1940–Apr. 1941 in war with Italy.

Gjö'vik (yû'vĕk). Town, Opland co., S cen. Norway, on Lake Mjösa; pop. 5072; dairy farming.

Glace Bay (glās). Town, Cape Breton co., E Nova Scotia, Canada, on Atlantic Ocean 12 m. E of Sydney; pop. 25,586; fair harbor; produces coal.

Gla'cier (glā'shēr). County in Montana. See Table at MONTANA.

Glacier Bay. Narrow inlet of Pacific Ocean ab. 60 m. long in N part of SE Alaska, NE extension of Cross Sound; in center of **Glacier Bay National Monument** (see UNITED STATES, National Monuments).

Glacier National Park. **1** See UNITED STATES, National Parks.

2 See CANADA, National Parks.

Glacier Peak. Mountain 10,436 ft. in E Snohomish co., NW cen. Washington.

Gla'ciers', Ai'guille' des (ā'gĭī·ē'y' dā glå'syā'). Mountain 12,517 ft. in the French Alps, just SW of Mont Blanc.

Glad'bach–Rheydt (glät'bäk·rīt'). Former city in the Rhine Province of Prussia, Germany, 15 m. W of Düsseldorf; pop. 193,530; formed by incorporation (1929–33) of cities of München-Gladbach, Odenkirchen, and Rheydt, and surrounding territory. Area has 10th-cent. church, 17th-cent. town hall (München-Gladbach); 16th-cent. castle (Rheydt); center of Rhenish textile industry; also manufactures metal and electrical goods, machinery. In World War II captured by Allies Mar. 2, 1945. See MÜNCHEN-GLADBACH.

Glad'beck (glät'běk). City, W Germany, in North Rhine-Westphalia state, 22 m. WNW of Dortmund; pop. 60,043; coal mining.

Glades (glādz). County in Florida. See *Table* at FLORIDA.

Glade'wa'ter (glād'wô'tēr; -wŏt'ēr). City, Gregg and Upshur cos., NE Texas, 25 m. ENE of Tyler; pop. 5742; oil; timber.

Glad'stone (glăd'stōn). 1 City, Delta co., S Michigan penin., on W side of Little Bay de Noc 8 m. N of Escanaba; pop. 5267; harbor; makes sporting goods.

2 City, Clay co., NW Missouri, N of Kansas City; pop. 14,502.

3 City, Clackamas co., NW Oregon, on Clackamas river 9 m. S of Portland; pop. 3854.

Glad'stone (glăd'stōn; -stŭn). Town, E Queensland, Australia, on Pacific Ocean 270 m. NNW of Brisbane; pop. 3039; port; founded on site of unsuccessful colony sponsored by Gladstone.

Glad'stone Peak (glăd'stōn). Mountain 13,900 ft. in Dolores and San Miguel cos., SW Colorado.

Glad'win (glăd'wĭn). 1 County in Michigan. See *Table* at MICHIGAN.

2 City, ⊗ of Gladwin co., cen. Michigan, 30 m. NNE of Mt. Pleasant; pop. 2226.

Gla'mis (glä'mĭs; glăm'ĭs; *Scot.* glämz). Village, S Angus co., E Scotland, in by Dundee; pop. 879; 17th-cent. castle on site of an 11th-cent. structure.

Gla·mor'gan·shire (glá·môr'găn·shīr; -shēr) *or* **Glamor'gan**. County, SE Wales; 813 sq. m.; pop. (1951) 1,201,989; ⊗ Cardiff; rivers Taff, Neath, Tawe; coal and iron mining, iron and steel manufacture, livestock.

Gla'mu·jö'kull (glou'mü·yû'küt·l'). Glacier in NW Iceland.

Gla'rus (glä'rōos). 1 Swiss canton. See *Table* at SWITZERLAND.

2 Commune, its ✳, E cen. Switzerland, 36 m. E of Lucerne; pop. (1930) 5269; destroyed by fire May 1861; textiles. Zwingli parish priest here 1506–16.

Glas'cock (glăs'kŏk). County in Georgia. See *Table* at GEORGIA.

Glas'gow (glăs'kō; -gō). 1 City, ⊗ of Barren co., S Kentucky, 30 m. E of Bowling Green; pop. 10,069; agriculture; petroleum.

2 City, ⊗ of Valley co., NE Montana, 15 m. NNW of Fort Peck Dam on Missouri river; pop. 6398; ships cattle, sheep, and grain.

Glas'gow (glăs'kō; -gō; glăz'gō; *Brit. also* gläs'-, gläz'-). Royal burgh, geographically in Lanark co., W cen. Scotland, on both banks of the Clyde; forms county of a city; pop. (1951) 1,089,555; the largest city in Scotland; seaport, extensive docks; famous for shipbuilding; manufactures heavy iron and steel products, textiles, chemicals; ships coal; 13th-cent. cathedral, university (1450); Art Gallery and home of "Glasgow School of Art."

History: Although date of origin uncertain, probably had been settled for some centuries when its bishop received rights of royal burgh 1175–78; as prominent Scottish ecclesiastical center, declined for a time after the Reformation; became free royal burgh 1636; prosperous commercial center from 18th cent., developed shipbuilding and iron industries 19th cent.

Glass'bor'o (glăs'bûr'ô). Borough, Gloucester co., SW New Jersey, 17 m. S of Camden; pop. 10,253; settled by German glassmakers 1775; Glassboro State Coll. (1922; coed.).

Glass'cock (glăs'kŏk). County in Texas. See *Table* at TEXAS.

Glass Mountains. Range, N Brewster co., W Texas; highest peak 6523 ft.

Glass'port (glăs'pōrt). Borough, Allegheny co., SW Pennsylvania, on Monongahela river 10 m. SSE of Pittsburgh; pop. 8418; manufactures glass, steel hoops, tools.

Glas'ten·bur'y Mountain (glăs'těn·bĕr'ĭ; glăs''n-). Mountain 3764 ft., Bennington co., SW Vermont.

Glas'ton·bur'y (glăs'tŭn·bĕr'ĭ; glăs''n-). Town, SE Hartford co., N Connecticut, 5½ m. SE of Hartford; pop. 14,497; manufactures soap, silverware, plastics, textiles, paper. Settled 1650, incorp. 1690.

Glas'ton·bur'y (glăs'tŭn·bĕr'ĭ; glăs''n-; *esp. Brit.*, -bĕr·ĭ, -brĭ). Municipal borough, Somersetshire, SW England; pop. 5081; ancient abbey, ancient Celtic settlement, extensive finds of pre-Roman metal objects.

Glatz. See KŁODZKO.

Glatzer Neisse. See NYSA river.

Glau'chau (glou'kou). Manufacturing city, Karl-Marx-Stadt dist., E Germany, on Mulde river 16 m. W of Karl-Marx-Stadt; pop. 27,318; two 16th-cent. castles.

Gla'zov (glä'zŭf). Town, N Udmurt Republic, Soviet Russia, Europe, 200 m. E of Kirov; pop. 12,430; on Kirov-Molotov railroad.

Glebe (glēb). City, E New South Wales, SE Australia, SW suburb of Sydney; pop. 19,886.

Gleiwitz. See GLIWICE.

Glen'brook (glĕn'brŏŏk). Subdivision of town of STAMFORD, Connecticut; residential.

Glen Can'yon (glĕn kăn'yŭn). Gorge along the Colorado river, S Utah and N Arizona, above Marble Canyon; site of **Glen Canyon Dam** in Colorado river.

Glen'coe (glĕn'kō). 1 Residential village, Cook co., NE Illinois, 22 m. N of Chicago; pop. 10,472.

2 City, ⊗ of McLeod co., S cen. Minnesota, 45 m. WSW of Minneapolis; pop. 3216; dairying; ships cattle.

3 Town, Natal, South Africa, NW of Durban; pop. 3339.

Glen·coe' (glĕn·kō'). Glen in northern Argyll co., W Scotland; site of notorious massacre of Macdonalds of Glencoe by soldiers of Campbell of Glenlyon 1692.

Glen Cove (glĕn kōv). Residential city, Nassau co., SE New York, on N shore of Long I. 22 m. ENE of New York; pop. 23,817.

Glen'dale (glĕn'dāl). 1 City, Maricopa co., SW cen. Arizona, 8 m. NW of Phoenix; pop. 15,696; cotton ginning; cottonseed oil, flour, feed.

2 City, Los Angeles co., SW California, 6 m. N of Los Angeles; pop. 119,442; occupies part of first Spanish land grant in California (Rancho San Rafael 1784); founded 1886; manufactures airplanes, airplane engines, tools and dies, furniture, pottery and tile, and medical supplies.

3 City, St. Louis co., E Missouri, 11 m. SW of St. Louis; pop. 7048.

4 Village, Hamilton co., SW corner of Ohio, 12 m. N of Cincinnati; pop. 2823.

5 See FRAYSER'S FARM.

6 City, Milwaukee co., SE Wisconsin; pop. 9537.

Glen'da·lough', **Vale of** (glĕn'dá·lŏk'). Valley in co. Wicklow, E Ireland, containing two small lakes; ruins of several ecclesiastical structures, esp. the monastery founded by St. Kevin 6th cent.

Glen'dive (glĕn'dīv). City, ⊗ of Dawson co., E Montana, on Yellowstone river 72 m. NE of Miles City; pop. 7058; sugar beets, grain, forage; lignite, natural gas.

Glen·do'ra (glĕn·dōr'á). City, Los Angeles co., SW California, 22 m. ENE of Los Angeles; pop. 20,752.

Glen·elg' (glĕn·ĕlg'). 1 River 281 m. long, W Victoria, SE Australia; flows into Discovery Bay just over the border in South Australia.

2 Town, SE South Australia, on Gulf of St. Vincent 6 m. SW of Adelaide; pop. 10,412; watering place; South Australia first declared a British colony here 1836.

3 Town, Inverness co., NW Scotland, on Sound of Sleat.

Glen El'lyn (glĕn ĕl'ĭn). Village, Du Page co., NE Illinois, 23 m. W of Chicago; pop. 15,972.

Glen'field (glĕn'fēld). Town, New South Wales, SE Australia, 18 m. SW of Sydney.

Glen·gar'riff (glĕn·găr'ĭf). Town, SW co. Cork, SW Eire, on N inlet of Bantry Bay; resort.

Glen·gar'ry (glĕn·găr'ĭ). 1 County, Ontario, Canada. See *Table* at ONTARIO.

2 Narrow beautiful valley in Inverness co., NW Scotland; fine lake and castle.

Glen In'nes (glĕn ĭn'ĕs). Town, NE New South Wales, SE Australia, in New England Range; pop. 5356.

Glen·ly'on (glĕn·lī'ŭn). **1** Urban community (unincorporated), Luzerne co., E Pennsylvania, ab. 11 m. SW of Wilkes-Barre; pop. 4173.
2 Narrow valley over 30 m. long in Perth co., cen. Scotland, N of Loch Tay; near E end is Glenlyon House, ancient seat of the Campbells of Glenlyon.

Glenn (glĕn). County in California. See *Table* at CALIFORNIA.

Glenn Highway. Highway ab. 170 m. long in S Alaska, running ENE from Anchorage to Copper Center on Richardson Highway.

Glenn'ville (glĕn'vĭl; *Sou.* also -v'l). City, Tattnall co., SE cen. Georgia, 50 m. W of Savannah; pop. 2791.

Glen·ol'den (glĕn·ōl'dĕn). Borough, Delaware co., SE Pennsylvania, 8 m. WSW of Philadelphia; pop. 7249.

Glen·or'chy (glĕn·ôr'kĭ). Town, SE Tasmania, Australia, N suburb of Hobart; pop. 9898.

Glen Ridge (glĕn' rĭj). Residential borough, Essex co., NE New Jersey, 5 m. NNW of Newark; pop. 8322.

Glen'rock (glĕn'rŏk). Town, Converse co., E Wyoming, on North Platte river; pop. 1584.

Glen Rock. Borough, Bergen co., NE corner of New Jersey, 4 m. NNE of Paterson; pop. 12,896; residential.

Glen Rose. City, ⊗ of Somervell co., N cen. Texas, 40 m. SSW of Fort Worth; pop. 1422; mineral wells.

Glen Roy (glĕn' roi'). Narrow valley in Inverness co., NW Scotland, N of Fort William; noted for its *parallel roads*, a geological formation.

Glens Falls (glĕnz fôlz). City, Warren co., E New York, at falls (60 ft.) in Hudson river 38 m. NE of Amsterdam; pop. 18,580; manufactures paper and pulp, clothing, cement and brick, chemicals; limestone and black marble quarries. Settled c. 1763; destroyed by British 1780. Cooper's Cave (at foot of falls), named for James Fenimore Cooper, setting for an episode of his *Last of the Mohicans.*

Glen'side (glĕn'sīd). Locality, Montgomery co., SE Pennsylvania, ab. 10 m. N of Philadelphia; pop. (est.) 9000; manufactures paints, toys, rubber and wood products; stone quarries.

Glens (glĕnz), also **Glynns** (glĭnz), **of An'trim** (ăn'trĭm). Series of valleys on NE coast of co. Antrim, Northern Ireland.

Glen'view (glĕn'vū). Village, Cook co., NE Illinois, 18 m. NNW of Chicago; pop. 18,132; U.S. Naval Air Station.

Glen'ville (glĕn'vĭl). **1** Subdivision of town of GREENWICH, Connecticut.
2 Town, ⊗ of Gilmer co., cen. West Virginia; pop. 1828; Glenville State Coll. (1872; coed.).

Glenville Dam. See *Table* at TENNESSEE VALLEY AUTHORITY.

Glen'wood (glĕn'wŏŏd). **1** City, ⊗ of Mills co., SW Iowa, 18 m. SSE of Council Bluffs; pop. 4783; granite quarries.
2 City, ⊗ of Pope co., W cen. Minnesota, at N end of Lake Minnewaska; pop. 2631; resort.

Glenwood Springs. City, ⊗ of Garfield co., W Colorado, on Colorado river; pop. 3637; thermal mineral springs.

Glevum. See GLOUCESTER, England.

Glit'ter·tind' (glĭt'ĕr·tĭn'). Peak 8048 ft. in the Jotunheimen, S cen. Norway.

Gli·wi'ce (glĕ·vē'tsĕ); *Ger.* **Glei'witz** (glī'vĭts). Manufacturing city, cen. Śląsk dept., SW Poland, formerly in Silesia prov., Prussia, Germany, 14 m. W of Katowice; pop. (1946) 114,048; blast furnaces, coal mines. Chartered as city 1276; passed to Prussia 1742; in World War II taken by Russians Jan. 25, 1945; assigned to Poland by Potsdam Conference 1945.

Globe (glōb). City, ⊗ of Gila co., E cen. Arizona, 70 m. E of Phoenix; pop. 6217; incorp. 1907; important copper mines; also silver, gold, asbestos, manganese, vanadium, and tungsten in vicinity.

Gloces'ter (glŏs'tēr). Town, Providence co., N Rhode Island, near Connecticut border; pop. 3397; governmental center Chepachet.

Gło'gów (glō'goof); *Ger.* **Glo'gau** (glō'gou). Manufacturing city, N Wrocław dept., SW Poland, formerly in Silesia prov. Prussia, Germany, on Odra (Oder) river 32 m. N of Legnica; pop. (1946) 15,533; cement, clay pipe, hats, furniture, vehicles, tower clocks. In World War II taken by Russians Feb. 1945; assigned to Poland by Potsdam Conference 1945.

Glom'ma (glŏm'ä). River 375 m. long, E Norway; rises in Dovrefjell plateau; flows S into Skagerrak at Fredrikstad.

Glo'rieuses', **Îles** (ēl' glô'ryûz'); *Eng.* **Glo'ri·o'so Islands** (glôr'ĭ·ō'sō). Group of small French islands in Indian Ocean WNW of N Madagascar.

Glossa, Cape. See Cape LINGUETTA.

Glos'sop (glŏs'ŭp). Municipal borough, Derbyshire, N cen. England, 16 m. ESE of Manchester; pop. 18,014; cotton mills, paper mills.

Glouces'ter (glŏs'tēr; glŏs'-). **1** Counties in two states of the U.S. See *Tables* at NEW JERSEY and VIRGINIA.
2 City, Essex co., NE Massachusetts, on coast of Cape Ann 27 m. NE of Boston; pop. 25,789; port of entry; summer resort; artist colony; one of great fishing ports of North America; granite quarries. Visited by Champlain 1605, settled 1623; chartered as city 1874. Has bronze statue, "Fisherman at the Wheel," by Leonard Craske.
3 Village, ⊗ of Gloucester co., E Virginia; pop. (est.) 500.
4 County, New Brunswick, Canada. See *Table* at NEW BRUNSWICK.
5 County in England. See GLOUCESTERSHIRE.
6 *anc.* **Gle'vum** (glē'vŭm). County borough, ⊗ of Gloucestershire, SW cen. England, on the Severn 94 m. WNW of London; pop. 52,937, (1951) 67,268; has cathedral, on site of an abbey founded 681. Founded by Nerva (emperor 96–98 A.D.); began early to trade in iron and cloth; scene of first Sunday School, founded by Robert Raikes 1780.

Gloucester, Cape. Cape at NW corner of New Britain I., Bismarck Archipelago, on Dampier Strait; landing place of U.S. Marines Dec. 26, 1943.

Gloucester City. Manufacturing city, Camden co., SW New Jersey, on Delaware river 3 m. S of Camden; pop. 15,511. Settled by Irish Quakers 1682; scene of skirmishes during Revolution; incorporated 1868.

Glouces'ter·shire (-shĭr; -shēr) *or* **Gloucester.** County, SW cen. England; area 1257 sq. m.; pop. (1951) 938,618; ⊗ Gloucester; other towns Bristol, Tewkesbury, Cheltenham, Stroud; rivers Severn, Avon, Wye; agriculture, sheep grazing, manufacturing (hardware, pottery, woolen goods, tobacco, chocolate, chemicals).

Glous'ter (glŏs'tēr; glŏs'-). Village, Athens co., SE Ohio, 30 m. S of Zanesville; pop. 2255; brickmaking.

Glov'ers·ville (glŭv'ērz·vĭl). City, Fulton co., E New York, 12 m. NW of Amsterdam; pop. 21,741; settled c. 1760 by Scots; glovemaking center of U.S.; leather, silks, knit goods, wood products.

Glo'zel (glô'zĕl'). Village, Allier dept., cen. France, SE of Vichy; site of discovery 1924–26, by local farmer, of bricks and tablets bearing inscriptions and apparently belonging to antiquity, which aroused a controversy still not settled.

Głub·czy'ce (gloop·chĭ'tsĕ); *Ger.* **Le'ob·schütz** (lā'ŏp·shüts). City, SW Śląsk dept., SW Poland, NW of Racibórz; pop. (1946) 13,452; formerly in Germany.

Glück'stadt (glük'shtät). Town, Schleswig-Holstein, north Germany, on the Elbe river NW of Altona; pop. 6820; founded 1616 and fortified by Christian IV of Denmark; fortifications destroyed 1814; fishing.

Glu'khov (gloo'kŭf). Town, NE Ukraine, U.S.S.R., ab. 40 m. NE of Konotop; pop. 15,363.

Gly'der Fach (glĭd'ēr väk). Mountain 3262 ft. in Caernarvonshire, NW Wales.

Gly'der Fawr (glĭd'ẽr vour). Mountain 3279 ft. in Caernarvonshire, NW Wales.

Glynn (glĭn). County in Georgia. See *Table* at GEORGIA.

Glynns of Antrim. See GLENS OF ANTRIM.

Gmünd (g'münt); *also* **Schwä'bisch–Gmünd** (shvä'-bĭsh-). Manufacturing city, Baden-Württemberg state, Germany, 28 m. E of Stuttgart; pop. 20,406; clocks, machinery, cigarettes. Chartered as city 1162; free city until 1803 when it passed to Württemberg.

Gmun'den (g'mōōn'dĕn). Commune, Upper Austria, on Lake Traun at outlet into Traun river; pop. 7780; summer resort.

Gna'den·hut'ten (jĕ·nä'd'n·hŭt"n). Village, Tuscarawas co., E Ohio, on Tuscarawas river; pop. 1257; founded 1772 under leadership of Moravians by Christian Indians who had to move to Sandusky 1781; scene Mar. 7, 1782 of massacre by white men of a group of the Indians who had returned.

Gniez'no (g'nyĕz'nô); *Ger.* **Gne'sen** (g'nā'zĕn). Commune, Poznań dept., Poland, 28 m. ENE of Poznań; pop. (1938–39 est.) 32,985; manufactures cloth, iron goods, sugar, leather, beer, oil; important horse markets; ancient cathedral containing relics of St. Adalbert (*Pol.* Wojciech), patron saint of Poland. First king of Poland (Boleslav the Mighty) crowned here 1025 for second time; coronation place of kings of Poland to 1320.

Gnossus. See KNOSSOS.

Go'a (gō'ä); *Port.* **Gô'a** (gō'ä). 1 Former Portuguese territory, W India, 250 m. S of Bombay; 1301 sq. m.; ✳ Pangim; comprises four districts taken in early 16th cent. known as Velhas Conquistas (Old Conquests), seven districts acquired later, Novas (New) Conquistas, and island of Angediva; 62 miles of coast line; traversed by a spur of the Western Ghats ab. 4000 ft. high, from which several short but navigable streams flow to the marshy coast, the two largest the Mandavi and the Juari. Exports copra, iron, wood, spices, rice, and poultry. Annexed by India 1962.
2 *or* **Old Goa.** Seaport, its former ✳; founded 1440; at first under Bahmani dynasty (see DECCAN); under king of Bijapur 1482–1510; taken by Portuguese under Albuquerque 1510 and made capital of Portuguese India; scene of beginning of St. Francis Xavier's missionary labors 1542; besieged by ruler of Bijapur 1570; a city of 200,000 at height of its prosperity (1575–1625); blockaded by Dutch fleets 1603, 1639; site abandoned for New Goa (see PANGIM) by most Portuguese inhabitants early 18th cent. as result of cholera epidemics; now mostly in ruins but has cathedral (founded 1511) and several churches and convents still standing.

Go'a (gō'ä). Municipality, E Camarines Sur prov., Luzon, Phil. Is., near head of Lagonoy Gulf; pop. 13,411; at foot of Mt. Isarog.

Goajira, Goagira. See GUAJIRA.

Go'a·lan'da (gō'ä·lŭn'dä) *or* **Raj·ba'ri** (räj·bä'rĭ). Town, on right bank of Ganges at its junction with the Jamuna, East Bengal, NE Pakistan; often destroyed by shifting courses of the rivers.

Go'al·pa'ra (gō'äl·pä'rä). Town, NW Assam, NE Indian Union, on S bank of Brahmaputra; pop. 6415; a district capital before 1879.

Goat' Haunt' Mountain. Peak 8306 ft. in Glacier National Park, NW Montana.

Goat Island. 1 Island in Niagara river, W New York, just above Niagara Falls; ¾ m. long; divides Niagara Falls (*q.v.*) into American Fall and Horseshoe Fall.
2 See NEWPORT, Rhode Island.
3 = *Santa Clara:* see JUAN FERNÁNDEZ Is.
4 See YERBA BUENA ISLAND.

Goat Mountain. 1 Peak 8816 ft. in Glacier National Park, NW Montana.
2 Peak 8600 ft. in Culberson co., W Texas.

Go·ba'bis (gô·bä'bĭs). Town, E South-West Africa, 130 m. E of Windhoek; pop. 5325; alt. 4740 ft.; airport; in pastoral region.

Gobannium. See ABERGAVENNY.

Gö'bels·berg' (gû'bĕls·bĕrk'). Highest peak 2625 ft. in the Hausruck Mts., Upper Austria, Austria.

Go'bi, the (gō'bē; -bǐ); *Chin.* **Sha'mo'** (shä'mō'). Desert, ab. 500,000 sq. m., cen. Asia, mostly in Mongolia; a broad depression (average alt. 3000 to 5000 ft.) in plateau region, bounded on S by ranges of N Tibetan plateau (Nan Shan in Tsinghai and Ala Shan in Ningsia), on W and NW by Altai Mts., on E by mountains of Chahar and E Outer Mongolia; in S includes the Ordos, S of the bend of the Hwang Ho; SW part entirely sand but on other borders is steppe land; by some, taken to include Tarim basin also. See HAN-HAI.

Goch (gôк). City NW North Rhine-Westphalia state, W Germany, on Dutch border 66 m. WSW of Münster; pop 11,798; manufactures margarine, oil, cigars, tobacco, shoes, leather. Chartered 1291; belonged to dukes of Gelder (see GELDERLAND); in World War II scene of severe fighting Feb. 18–21, 1945.

God'al·ming (gŏd'l·mǐng). Municipal borough, Surrey, S England, on the Wey 30 m. SW of London; pop. 14,239; manufactures paper, leather, hosiery. Became borough 1574; since 1872 seat of Charterhouse School, founded in London in 17th cent.

Go·da'va·ri (gō·dä'vä·rē). River ab. 900 m. long, cen. India; rises in NW Maharashtra state, flows SE across the Deccan, crossing N Andhra Pradesh, and thence SE into Bay of Bengal through several mouths; its chief tributaries Dudna, Pranhita, Indravati, and Sabari on the N and Manjra on the S; navigable in lower course; source of reservoirs, canals, and irrigation systems; a sacred river of the Hindus.

God'dard, Mount (gŏd'ẽrd). Peak 13,555 ft. in Sierra Nevada, in E Fresno co., S cen. California.

Gode'rich (gŏd'rĭch). Resort town, ⊗ of Huron co., SE Ontario, Canada, on SE shore of Lake Huron 65 m. NNE of Sarnia; pop. 4934; harbor; lumbering; makes salt, road machinery; grain elevator. Founded 1828.

Go'des·berg (gō'dĕs·bĕrk), *also* **Bad Godesberg** (bät). Commune, in North Rhine-Westphalia state, West Germany, on left bank of the Rhine 4 m. S of Bonn; pop. 20,396; mineral springs; ruins of castle (called the Godesburg, founded 1213, destroyed 1583 by Bavarians) nearby; manufactures pharmaceutical goods, motorcycles. Scene of conference Sept. 22, 1938 bet. Neville Chamberlain and Hitler, prior to that at Munich, in regard to Czechoslovakia.

God'havn (gŏd'hä'vĕn; *Dan.* gôth·houn'). Town, W Greenland, on Davis Strait on S coast of Disko I. in 69°15'N lat., 53°30'W long.; pop. 415; an administrative center; formerly important in whaling industry; has radio and other scientific stations.

Godh'ra (gŏd'rä; *native* gŏd'hrä). Town, N Andhra Pradesh, W India, 68 m. ESE of Ahmadabad; pop. 35,110; tanneries; trades in timber.

Göding. See HODONÍN.

Gö'döl·lö (gû'dûl·lû). Commune, 12 m. NE of Budapest, cen. Hungary; pop. 10,993; former royal palace and summer residence.

Go·doy' Cruz (gô·thoi' krōōs'). Town, Mendoza prov., W Argentina; pop. (est.) 12,000; S suburb of Mendoza; wine making.

Gods Lake (gŏdz). Lake 319 sq. m., E Manitoba, Canada; its outlet is **Gods River,** a tributary of Hayes river.

Godt'haab' (gôt'hôp'). Town, ✳ of Greenland, on SW coast in 64°10'N lat., 51°32'W long.; pop. 1313; oldest Danish settlement in Greenland, founded 1727; has radio and other scientific stations.

God'win Aus'ten (gŏd'wǐn ôs'tĕn; -tǐn) *or* **Dap'sang** (dŭp'sŭng) *or* **K²** (kä'tōō'). Highest peak 28,250 ft. in Karakoram Range, and 2d highest mountain in the world, in N Kashmir, N India, near Sinkiang border.

Godwin Island. Island in Atlantic Ocean, SE coast of Northampton co., Virginia.

Goe·de·ree′de (kōō′dě·rä′dě). Island, South Holland prov., Netherlands, in estuary of the Maas (Meuse) river; 83 sq. m.; pop. 31,361. W section is called **Goe·ree′** (kōō·rā′) and E section **O′ver·flak·kee′** (ō′vēr-flä·kā′).

Goe′noeng (gōō′nŏong). Dutch form of Malay *gunung*, "mountain," used with proper names, as **Goenoeng A′woe** (ä′wōō). See GUNUNG.

Goe′noeng A′pi (gōō′nŏong ä′pē) *or* **Gu′nung Api** (gōō′nŏong). Volcanic island, one of the Banda Is.. Malay Archipelago, Indonesia; with Great Banda (*q.v.*) and Bandanaira I. forms harbor of Bandanaira; an active volcano, 1858 ft. high; eruptions 1820, 1852.

Goe′noeng·si·to′li (gōō′nŏong·sě·tô′lě; -stô′lě) *or* **Gu′nung·si·to′li.** Chief village of Nias I. off W coast of Sumatra, Indonesia.

Goen·toer′ (gŏon·tŏor′) *or* **Gun·tur′.** Volcano 7377 ft. in W cen. Java, Indonesia, NW of Garut.

Goeree. See GOEDEREEDE.

Goes (kōōs). Commune, Zeeland prov., SW Netherlands, on South Beveland I.; pop. 9124.

Goffs′town (gôfs′toun). Town, Hillsboro co., S New Hampshire, 5 m. WNW of Manchester; pop. 7230.

Go·ge′bic (gŏ·gē′bĭk). County in Michigan. See *Table* at MICHIGAN.

Gogebic Lake. Lake ab. 12 m. long in NW Michigan penin, in Ontonagon and Gogebic cos.

Gogebic Range. Iron range, N Wisconsin and W Upper Peninsula of Michigan, extending E-W in Gogebic co., Michigan, and Bayfield, Ashland, and Iron cos., Wisconsin; highest point 1823 ft., in Gogebic co.

Gog′ra (gôg′rä). River ab. 570 m. long, N India; rises near Lake Manasarowar in SW Tibet, flows S through the Himalayas in Nepal, then SE in Uttar Pradesh into the Ganges near Chapra on NW Bihar border. In Nepal called the **Kar·na′li** (kär·nä′lĭ).

Goi·â′ni·a (goi·ä′ně·à), *formerly* **Goy·a′ni·a.** City in SE cen. Brazil; ✳ of Goiaz state; pop. (1940 est.) 15,406.

Goi·ás′, *also* **Goi·az′** *or* **Goy·az′** (goi·äs′). 1 State of Brazil. See *Table* at BRAZIL.
2 Town, Goiás state, cen. Brazil, 75 m. NW of Goiânia; pop. (1940 est.) 5991.

Goil, Loch (lŏĸ goil′). Inlet of Firth of Clyde in Argyll co., W cen. coast of Scotland, an arm of Loch Long.

Going-to-the-Sun Mountain. Peak 9594 ft. in Glacier National Park, NW Montana, N of **Going-to-the-Sun Highway** which crosses the park.

Goj′jam (gō′jăm; *Ethiopian* gwŏ′dyäm), *also* **Go′jam.** Former kingdom in Ethiopia, later a province, now a region in N cen. Ethiopia; chief town Debra Markos.

Gök (gûk). River in N Turkey in Asia; flows E into Kızıl Irmak.

Gökcha. See SEVAN.

Gök·su′ (gûk·sōō′). 1 *anc.* **Cal′y·cad′nus** (kăl′ĭ·kăd′-nŭs). River ab. 150 m. long in S Turkey in Asia (Cilicia); flows into Mediterranean at ruins of ancient Seleucia (Tracheotis) SW of Mersin; the river in which Frederick Barbarossa drowned 1190.
2 River ab. 100 m. long in E cen. Turkey in Asia; rises in Anti-Taurus Mts.; flows SW into Seyhan river; by some considered the main stream of the Seyhan.

Gök-Tépé. See GEOK TEPE.

Go·la·sec′ca (gŏ·lä·sěk′kä). Village, W Lombardy, N Italy, near S end of Lake Maggiore; nearby lived a prehistoric group of Iron Age people.

Gol′borne (gōl′bĕrn). Urban district, Lancashire, NW England, 15 m. W of Manchester; pop. 16,876.

Gol′car (gō′kẽr). Former urban district, West Riding, Yorkshire, N England, near Huddersfield.

Gol′chi·ka (gôl′chĭ·kà). Village, Taimyr National District, Soviet Russia, Asia, on E shore of Yenisei estuary.

Gol·con′da (gŏl·kŏn′dà). 1 City, ✳ of Pope co., SE corner of Illinois; pop. 864; fluorite deposits.
2 Ruined town and fortress, W Andhra Pradesh, S cen. India, 5 m. W of Hyderabad city. Capital 1512-

1687 of ancient kingdom ruled by Kutb Shahi dynasty, one of the five Mohammedan kingdoms of the Deccan (*q.v.*); conquered by Aurangzeb 1687–88 and annexed to Delhi empire; famous for its diamonds.

Gold Beach (gōld). City, ⊗ of Curry co., SW corner of Oregon, on Pacific Ocean; pop. 1765.

Gold Coast. 1 *now* **Gha′na** (gä′nà). Republic of the British Commonwealth, W Africa, consisting of former Gold Coast and Ashanti colonies, Northern Territories protectorate, and Togoland trust territory; 92,100 sq. m.; pop. (1963 est.) 7,100,000; ✳ Accra; bounded on W by Ivory Coast, on N by Upper Volta, on E by Togo, and on S by Gulf of Guinea. Generally level with some hills; covered with forests; traversed by the Volta. Chief products cocoa, rubber, palm oil, gold, diamonds, and manganese ore. Natives are Negroes, chiefly of Ashanti, Fanti, and Akim tribes. Chief towns Accra, Kumasi, Sekondi.

History: Visited by Portuguese traders who founded Elmina 1482; Portuguese holdings captured by Dutch 1637 and abandoned as price of return of Brazil 1642; a center for slave trade which was carried on by rival Dutch, English (English Royal African Co. chartered 1672), French, Danish companies; acquired by British by purchase of Danish (1850) and Dutch (1871) settlements; British colony, alternately under Sierra Leone (*q.v.*) and separate, finally became separate 1874; frontier with Togoland determined by treaties with Germany 1886, 1899; took over Ashanti (*q.v.*) and Northern Territories 1901; in 1922, British mandate of Togoland placed under Gold Coast administration. Became (as Ghana) a dominion of the British Commonwealth Mar. 6, 1957; became a republic in the Commonwealth 1960.
2 Coast of the Gulf of Guinea along shore of Ghana, W of the Slave Coast—so called from large quantities of gold formerly taken from sands and mines along the coast.

Gold Coast Colony. Former British colony on the Gold Coast; now in Ghana and divided into two territories, the West Region and the East Region; ✳ Accra; on N bordered on Ashanti and on W on Ivory Coast.

Gold Dust Peak. Mountain 13,500 ft. in Eagle co., NW cen. Colorado.

Gold′en (gōl′děn). 1 City, ⊗ of Jefferson co., cen. Colorado, 10 m. W of Denver; pop. 7118; founded 1859 as mining camp; capital of Colorado Territory 1862–67; summer resort; in region producing coal, gold, clay, wheat, sugar beets. Colorado School of Mines (1874; coed.).
2 Town, SE Brit. Columbia, Canada, on Canadian Pacific R.R. and on Columbia river; alt. 2585 ft.

Golden Bay. West arm of upper Tasman Bay on N coast of South I., New Zealand.

Golden Chersonese. See MALAY PENINSULA.

Gold′en·dale (gōl′děn·dāl). City, ⊗ of Klickitat co., S Washington, 57 m. SSW of Yakima; pop. 2536.

Golden Fall. See GULLFOSS.

Golden Gate. Strait ab. 2 m. wide leading from Pacific Ocean into San Francisco Bay; San Francisco on its S shore; named 1849 during the gold rush; crossed by bridge, central span 4200 ft. (second longest in world), built 1933–37.

Golden Horn. 1 Peak 13,600 ft. in San Juan and San Miguel cos., SW Colorado.
2 Harbor of Vladivostok, Maritime Territory, Soviet Russia, Asia, an inlet of Amur Bay.
3 *Turk.* **Ha·liç′** (hä·lēch′). Inlet of the Bosporus, ab. 5 m. long, Turkey in Europe, forming harbor of İstanbul; separates Pera and Galata from older part of city.

Golden Throne. Peak 23,600 ft. in Karakoram Range of the Himalayas, N Kashmir, N India, SE of Godwin Austen.

Golden Valley. 1 Name of counties in two states of the U.S. See *Tables* at MONTANA and NORTH DAKOTA.
2 Village, Hennepin co., SE cen. Minnesota, 5 m. W of Minneapolis; pop. 14,559.

Gold'field' (gōld'fēld'). Village, ⊗ of Esmeralda co., SW Nevada, 26 m. S of Tonopah; pop. 184; formerly active (esp. 1910–11) gold-mining center.

Goldingen. See KULDIGA.

Golds'bor'o (gōldz'bûr'ȯ). City, ⊗ of Wayne co., E North Carolina, on Neuse river 46 m. SE of Raleigh; pop. 28,873; tobacco auction; processes tobacco, manufactures textiles, furniture, brick.

Gold'stone' Mountain (gōld'stōn'). Peak 9892 ft. on NE boundary of Lemhi co., E cen. Idaho.

Gold'thwaite (gōld'thwāt). City, ⊗ of Mills co., cen. Texas; pop. 1383.

Go·le'niów (gȯ·lĕ'nyōof); Ger. **Goll'now** (gôl'nō). Manufacturing city, W Szczecin dept., NW Poland, formerly in Pomerania prov., Prussia, Germany, 16 m. NE of Stettin (Szczecin); pop. (1946) 5000; cement, sandstone, wooden goods; livestock market. In World War II taken by Russians Mar. 8, 1945; assigned to Poland by Potsdam Conference 1945.

Goletta. See LA GOULETTE.

Golgotha. See CALVARY.

Go'li·ad' (gō'lĭ·ăd'). **1** County in Texas. See *Table* at TEXAS.

2 City, its ⊗, S Texas, 22 m. W of Victoria; pop. 1782; historic resort, built up around mission and presidio estab. by Spaniards in 1749; figured in the Mexican revolt against Spain 1812–13, and in the revolt of Texas 1835 ff.

Goll'ling·er (gôl'ĭng·ẽr). Waterfall 202 ft. in Salzach river, Salzburg, Austria, ab. 10 m. S of Salzburg near village of **Goll'ling** (gôl'ĭng).

Gollnow. See GOLENIÓW.

Go·lod'na·ya Step (gŭ·lôd'ná·yȧ styäp'y'); or **Hun'ger·steppe'** (hŭng'gẽr·stĕp'). Steppe region ab. 300 m. wide in SE Kazakh S.S.R., Soviet Central Asia, W of Lake Balkhash; bordered on NW by Sary Su.

Gomal, Gomal Pass. See GUMAL, GUMAL PASS.

Gombroon. See BANDAR ABBAS.

Go'mel (gô'myĭl·y'; *Angl.* gō'mĕl). City, ✱ of Gomel Region, SE White Russia, U.S.S.R., on the Sozh 140 m. N of Kiev; pop. 144,169; railroad junction; trades in wool, flax, lumber, agricultural machinery; has steamer traffic connections with towns on the Dnieper. A historical and cultural center, founded as early as 12th cent.; alternately a possession of Poland and Russia, finally becoming Russian 1772; held by Germans Aug. 21, 1941 to Nov. 25, 1943.

Gomel Region. Region, SE White Russia, U.S.S.R.; bounded on S by the Ukraine; ✱ Gomel.

Go·me'ra (gȯ·mā'rä). One of Canary Is. (*q.v.*), 22 m. W of Tenerife I.; 144 sq. m.; pop. (1930) 25,405; in Santa Cruz de Tenerife prov., Spain; chief town and port San Sebastián.

Gó'mez (gō'mås). Town, Buenos Aires prov., E Argentina, ab. 35 m. SE of Buenos Aires.

Gómez Pa·la'cio (pä·lä'syȯ). City, Durango state, NW cen. Mexico, 195 m. W of Monterrey; pop. 25,558.

Gom'me·court' (gôm'kōōr'). Village, Pas-de-Calais dept., N France, 9 m. N of Albert; pop. (1931) 128; scene of much fighting 1916–18.

Go·mor'rah (gȯ·môr'ȧ). See SODOM.

Go'na (gō'nȧ). Settlement and mission station on N coast of E Papua, New Guinea, on Holnicote Bay just NNW of Buna; scene of much fighting 1942–43; see BUNA.

Go·na'ïves' or **Les Gonaïves** (lā gô·nä'ēv'). Commercial town, W Haiti, on **Gulf of Gonaïves** 68 m. NNW of Port-au-Prince; pop. (1936 est.) 10,500; fine harbor; exports cotton, coffee, cabinet woods. Independence of Haiti proclaimed here Jan. 1, 1804.

Go'nave' Island (gô'nàv'), also **Go'na'ïve' Island** (gō'nà'ēv'). Island of the West Indies, in Gulf of Gonaïves, Haiti; 287 sq. m.; highest point 984 ft.

Gon'da (gōn'dä). Town, E Uttar Pradesh, N India, 65 m. ENE of Lucknow; pop. 17,450.

Gon'dal (gōn'dȧl). **1** Former Indian state, cen. Kathiawar, Western India States, India; 1024 sq. m.; pop. (1941) 244,514.

2 Town, its ✱, now in Gujarat state, on tributary of the Bhadar ab. 250 m. NNW of Bombay; pop. 24,573.

Gon'dar (gōn'dẽr; *Ethiopian* gwōn'-). City, NW Ethiopia, 21 m. N of Lake Tana; ✱ of Amhara prov.; pop. 22,000; alt. 7300 ft.; made Abyssinian capital early 16th cent., reached height of power middle 18th cent., afterward sacked several times; has castles and other royal buildings which through Portuguese influence resemble European medieval fortresses.

Gon·do'ko·ro (gôn·dō'kȯ·rō). Town, Equatoria prov., S Sudan; on right bank of Nile (White Nile) just S of Mongalla; unhealthy site; became ivory and slave-trading center after first visit by Europeans 1841; occupied by British after 1898, made part of Uganda protectorate; made part of Anglo-Egyptian Sudan 1914.

Gond·wa'na (gŏnd·wä'nȧ). Region of India, now a part of Madhya Pradesh, inhabited chiefly by the Gonds, a Dravidian (or pre-Dravidian) people, formerly noted for the practice of human sacrifices, who formed several kingdoms 12th–18th cents.; in geology has given its name to the hypothetical land area, **Gondwana Land** or **Gond·wa'na·land'** (-lănd'), believed to have connected South Africa and India at one time.

Gon·za'ga (gŭn·zä'gȧ; *Ital.* gōn·dzä'gä). Commune, Mantova prov., Lombardy, N Italy, 14 m. S of Mantua; pop. 10,088.

Gon·zal'es (gŭn·zăl'ĕs). **1** County in Texas. See *Table* at TEXAS.

2 City, its ⊗, S cen. Texas, 60 m. E of San Antonio; pop. 5829; clay pits; cotton. Scene of first battle in Texas Revolution 1835.

Gooch'land (gōōch'lănd). **1** County in Virginia. See *Table* at VIRGINIA.

2 Village, its ⊗, E cen. Virginia; pop. (est.) 200.

Good'e·nough (gōōd'n·ŭf) or **Mo·ra'ta** (mȯ·rä'tȧ). Island, W D'Entrecasteaux Is., in W Pacific Ocean off E coast of Papua, New Guinea; ab. 20 m. long and 10 to 12 m. wide; has central peak, **Mount Goodenough,** 8419 ft.; chief village Bwaidoga.

Goodenough Bay. Inlet at NW end of Ward Hunt Strait (Solomon Sea), on N coast of SE Papua, New Guinea.

Good Harbor Bay. Inlet of Lake Michigan on N shore of Leelanau co., NW Michigan.

Good Hope. See FORT GOOD HOPE.

Good Hope, Cape of. 1 Most northerly point of Vogelkop Penin., NW Neth. New Guinea, ab. 20′S.

2 *Port.* **Ca'bo da Bo'a Es·pe·ran'ça** (kȧ'vōō thȧ vō'ȧ êsh·pĕ·rän'sȧ). Cape on SW coast of Cape Province, S Republic of So. Africa, W of False Bay and 30 m. S of Cape Town, in 34°21′S; alt. 840 ft. First rounded 1488 by Bartholomeu Dias who named it **Cabo Tor·men·to'so** [tōōr·männ·tō'zōō] ("Cape of Storms"); passed by Vasco da Gama 1497 on voyage to India; first Dutch settlement at Table Bay nearby 1652.

Good'hue (gōōd'hū). County in Minnesota. See *Table* at MINNESOTA.

Good'ing (gōōd'ĭng). **1** County in Idaho. See *Table* at IDAHO.

2 City, its ⊗, S Idaho, ab. 12 m. E of junction of Big Wood river with the Snake; pop. 2750; founded 1883 as Toponis, name changed to Gooding 1896; creamery, cannery, potato storage facilities.

Good'land (gōōd'lănd). City, ⊗ of Sherman co., NW Kansas, 20 m. E of Colorado border; pop. 4459; wheat growing, livestock raising.

Good'news' Bay (gōōd'nūz'). Village, SW Alaska, on inlet of Bering Sea just S of Kuskokwim Bay; pop. (est.) 159; airport.

Good'well (gōōd'wĕl). Town, Texas co., NW Oklahoma, in panhandle ab. 12 m. SW of Guymon; pop. 771; Panhandle Agricultural and Mechanical Coll. (1909; coed.).

Good'win Sands (good'wĭn). Dangerous shoals 10 m. long in N Strait of Dover, ab. 7 m. E of Deal, England; encloses the Downs, famous roadstead where Dutch fleet under van Tromp was defeated by English 1652.

Goole (gool). Urban district, West Riding, Yorkshire, N England, at confluence of Ouse and Don rivers 25 m. W of Hull; pop. 19,227; shipbuilding and shipping center.

Goose (goos). River ab. 85 m. long, E North Dakota; formed by confluence of forks in Steele co., flows E into Red river in E Traill co.

Goose Bay. Air base for transatlantic route, ab. 120 sq. m., Hamilton Inlet, Labrador; built (1941) and operated during World War II jointly by Canada and U.S.

Goose Creek. Former city, Harris co., SE Texas, on Galveston Bay; now part of Baytown.

Goose Creek Dam *and* **Reservoir.** See OAKLEY DAM.

Goose Island. Island in Long Island Sound off SE coast of New Haven co., Connecticut.

Goose Lake. Dry lake on Oregon-California boundary; once ab. 30 m. long by 10 m. wide.

Goos'port (gŏs'pōrt). Urban community (unincorporated), Calcasieu parish, SW Louisiana, NE suburb of Lake Charles; pop. 16,778.

Goo'ty (goo'tĭ; goot'ĭ). Town, Anantapur dist., SW cen. Andhra Pradesh, S India, 48 m. E of Bellary; pop. 9712; has citadel, a Maratha stronghold in 18th cent.

Göp'ping·en (gûp'ĭng·ĕn). City, Baden-Württemberg state, Germany, 24 m. ESE of Stuttgart; pop. 22,017; 15th-cent. church, 16th-cent. castle; varied manufactures. Burned 1782 and later rebuilt.

Go'rakh·pur (gō'rãk·pŏŏr). **1** Former division, NE United Provinces, N Indian Union; 9563 sq. m.; pop. (1941) 7,972,108.
2 City, its ✳, now in SE Uttar Pradesh, on Rapti river 100 m. N of Benares; pop. (1941) 84,650; railroad divisional point, railroad workshops. Founded c. 1400.

Gör'bers·dorf (gûr'bērs·dôrf). Village, now (since 1945) in Poland, formerly in Breslau govt. dist., Lower Silesia, Prussia, Germany; pop. 1210; in Sudeten Mts. S of Wałbrzych (Waldenburg); alt. 1900 ft.; health resort.

Gor'da, Pun'ta (pōōn'tä gôr'thä). Cape on W tip of Zapata Penin., SW Matanzas prov., W cen. Cuba, at S of entrance to Broa Bay.

Gör·des' (gûr·dĕs'). Town, Manisa vilayet, W Turkey in Asia, 25 m. E of Akhisar; pop. 3089; rug industry.

Gor'di·um (gôr'dĭ·ŭm). Ancient city, ✳ of Phrygia; according to tradition founded by Gordius, mythical king of Phrygia; scene of episode of the cutting of the Gordian knot by Alexander; now ruins on right bank of the Sakarya 50 m. WSW of Ankara, Turkey in Asia.

Gor'don (gôr'd'n). **1** County in Georgia. See *Table* at GEORGIA.
2 Town, Wilkinson co., cen. Georgia, 20 m. E of Macon; pop. 1793.
3 City, Sheridan co., NW Nebraska; pop. 2223.
4 River ab. 85 m. long, SW Tasmania; rises in central highlands, flows S, then W, to Macquarie Harbour.

Gor'dons Bay (gôr'd'nz). Inlet of South Pacific Ocean, New South Wales, SE Australia, on SE edge of Sydney.

Gor'dy·e·ne (gôr'dĭ·ē'nĕ); *also* **Cor'du·e·ne** (kôr'dū̇-). Mountainous region of ancient Armenia, in S part S of Lake Thospitis (Van); its inhabitants were the Gordyaeans, probably ancestors of the modern Kurds.

Gore (gōr). Borough, Southland subdivision, S South I., New Zealand, 30 m. NE of Invercargill; pop. 4090.

Gore, the. NE tip of Vermont, E of Halls stream; 1 sq. m.; projects E into New Hampshire ab. 2 m.

Gore Bay. Town, ⊗ of Manitoulin dist., S Ontario, Canada, on N shore of Manitoulin I.; pop. 752.

Go'rée' (gō'rā'). Island and town, Senegal, West Africa, formerly in the circumscription of Dakar and Dependencies, which was united with Senegal 1946; in the harbor formed by peninsula of Cape Vert; pop. (town) ab. 1000; first capital of French West Africa; first occupied by Dutch; captured by French in behalf of Senegal

Co. 1677; slave-trading center; held by British during Napoleonic Wars but restored to France 1817; lost importance with foundation of Dakar (*q.v.*).

Gore Mountain (gōr). Peak 3595 ft. in the Adirondack Mts., Warren co.. E New York.

Gor·go'na (gôr·gō'nä). Italian island in Ligurian Sea bet. Leghorn and N tip of Corsica; ab. 2 sq. m.

Gor'gon·zo'la (gôr'gŭn·zō'lä; *Ital.* gôr·gŏn·dzō'lä). Town, Milano prov., SW cen. Lombardy, N Italy, NE of Milan; pop. (1931) 5708; produces Gorgonzola cheese.

Gor'ham (gôr'ăm). **1** Town, Cumberland co., SW Maine, 10 m. W of Portland; pop. 5767; Maine State Teachers College (1878; coed.).
2 Town, N New Hampshire, in Coos co., at confluence of Androscoggin and Peabody rivers 5 m. S of Berlin; pop. 3039; tourist center; lumbering; lead and galena mines.

Go'ri (gō'rĭ). Town, E cen. Georgia, U.S.S.R., on Kura river ab. 40 m. NW of Tiflis; pop. ab. 12,000; altitude 2010 ft.; center of a district known for its corn, wine, and lumber; summer resort; birthplace of Josef Stalin. Founded in 12th cent. as a fortress for Armenian refugees; destroyed by Nadir Shah in 18th cent.; in recent years has suffered from earthquakes.

Go'ri·ca (gō'rē·tsä). = KORRÇE.

Go'rin·chem (kō'rĭng·kĕm) *or* **Gor'kum** (gôr'kŭm). Commune, South Holland prov., SW Netherlands, at confluence of the Waal and Maas (Meuse) rivers; pop. 14,033; nearby is castle where Hugo Grotius was imprisoned 1619–21.

Go·ri'zia (gō·rē'tsyä). **1** Province of Italy. See *Table* at ITALY.
2 *Ger.* **Görz** (gûrts). Commune, its ✳, NW Venezia Giulia, NE Italy, on Isonzo river on new Yugoslav border, 74 m. ENE of Venice; pop. 46,640; 14th-cent. Gothic cathedral; tourist resort; manufactures silks, cotton, leather goods, pottery, furniture. Capital of former Austrian crownland of Görz and Gradisca; strategic point in Isonzo campaign in World War I; captured by Italians 1916; recaptured by German-Austrian offensive 1917; ceded to Italy by Treaty of St-Germain 1919.

Gor'ki (gôr'kĭ; *Russ.* gôr'y'·kĭ); *before 1932* **Nizh'ni Nov'go·rod** (nĭzh'nĭ nŏv'gŏ·rŏd; *Russ.* nyēsh'nyĭ nŏf'-gŭ·rŭt). City, ✳ of Gorki Region, Soviet Russia, Europe, on S bank of Volga at its confluence with the Oka 250 m. E of Moscow; 6th city in size in U.S.S.R.; pop. 644,116; one of the great industrial cities of Russia; manufactures esp. automobiles, radio sets, airplanes; railroad center.
History: First established as a fort 1221 by Prince Yuri Vsevolodovich; as Nizhni Novgorod famous for centuries for its fair, held (Aug. and Sept.) at irregular intervals from 1817 to 1914, which was market for barter trade with the Orient through Siberia and Turkistan; contains memorials of early Russia from 13th and 14th cents.: the ancient citadel (kremlin), cathedrals, convents, and palace of ruling family. Plundered by Tatars 1377–78; annexed to Moscow 1417; in 17th cent. a center of political and religious disturbance; in 18th and 19th cents. became a cultural center.

Gorki Region. Region, E cen. Soviet Russia, Europe, crossed by the Volga; 34,431 sq. m.; pop. 3,876,274; ✳ Gorki. N part along the Vetluga covered with pine forests; S part fertile black-earth area; rich in iron, phosphorite, peat; highly developed local peasant industries.

Gorkum. See GORINCHEM.

Gor·li'ce (gôr·lē'tsĕ). Commune, SW Rzeszów dept., SE Poland, 58 m. ESE of Kraków; pop. (1938–39 est.) 6730; center of petroleum industry. Battle May 1915 of the Dunajec campaign in which Russians were driven back by Austro-German armies.

Gör'litz (gûr'lĭts). City in eastern Germany, 54 m. E of Dresden chiefly on W bank of the Neisse river; pop. (1946) 93,697; manufactures machinery, textiles. Since 1945 the small part, pop. (1946) 6800, on E bank of the river belongs to Poland (Wrocław dept.) and is called **Zgor·ze'lec** (zgôr·zĕ'lĕts).

Gor·lov′ka (gŭr·lôf′kà). City, E Stalino Region, E Ukraine, U.S.S.R., just N of Stalino; pop. 108,693; in the Donbas.

Gor′ner Grat (gôr′nēr grät′). Ridge 10,289 ft., Valais canton, SW cen. Switzerland, 3 m. SE of Zermatt; affords one of the finest views in the Alps, including Monte Rosa, the Matterhorn, the Weisshorn, and the Dom.

Gor′no–Ba·dakh·shan′ (gôr′nŭ·bà·dŭk·shàn′) *or* **Mountain–Badakhshan.** Autonomous region, a province of SE Tadzhik S.S.R., Soviet Central Asia; 25,784 sq. m.; pop. 41,769; ✳ Khorog; in the Pamirs bordering on Afghanistan and Sinkiang; very cold; its inhabitants are Iranian (87%) and Kirghiz (13%).

Go·ro·dok′ Ya·gel′lon·ski (gŭ·rŭ·dôk′ yŭ·gĕl′lŭn·skĭ); *Pol.* **Gró′dek Ja′giel·loń′ski** (grōō′dĕk yä′gyĕl·lôn′-y′·skĕ). Town, W Ukraine, U.S.S.R., 16 m. WSW of Lvov (formerly in Lwów dept., Poland); pop. (1938–39 est.) 15,015; trades in flax, grain. Important Russian fortification in World War I; battle June 12, 1915 in which Russians were defeated.

Go′rong Islands (gō′rŏng). See CERAM.

Go′ron·ta′lo (gō·rôn·tä′lō). Town on S coast of N peninsula (Minahassa) of Celebes I., Indonesia; pop. 15,603; harbor; important trade center.

Gorontalo, Gulf of. See Gulf of TOMINI.

Gor·ty′na (gôr·tī′nà). Ruins of ancient town, S cen. Crete, SW of Candia and ancient Knossos near S coast; many temples; long a rival of Knossos; its legal code, longest existing Greek inscription, found here 1884.

Go′ryn (gô′rĭn); *Pol.* **Ho′ryń** (hô′rĭn·y′). River ab. 485 m. long, formerly in E Poland, now in W Ukraine and cen. White Russia; flows N into Pripyat river in the Pripet Marshes.

Góry Tarnowskie. = TARNOWSKIE GÓRY.

Görz. See GORIZIA commune.

Gor′zów (gôr′zōōf); *Ger.* **Lands′berg** (länts′bĕrk), *also* **Landsberg an der War′the** (än dĕr vär′tĕ). Industrial city, NW Poznań dept., W Poland, on Warta river, formerly in Brandenburg prov., Prussia, Germany, 78 m. ENE of Berlin; pop. (1946) 46,559; 13th-cent. church; 18th-cent. church; manufactures textiles, jute, nets, cables, machinery, shoes, brewery and distillery products, tile. Founded 1257; battle Feb. 1813 in which French and Poles were defeated by Russians; assigned to Poland by Potsdam Conference 1945.

Go′sain·than′ (gō′sīn·tän′). Peak 26,291 ft. in the Himalayas, in S Tibet near border of Nepal, ab. 55 m. NE of Katmandu.

Gösch′e·nen (gûsh′ĕ·nĕn). Village, Uri canton, cen. Switzerland; pop. (1930) 860; at N entrance to St. Gotthard Tunnel.

Go′schen Strait (gō′shĕn). Channel ab. 10 m. wide bet. East Cape, SE Papua, New Guinea, and Normanby I. of the D'Entrecasteaux Is., SE of Ward Hunt Strait.

Gos′forth (gŏz′fôrth; -fĕrth). Urban district, Northumberland, N England, N suburb of Newcastle; pop. 24,424.

Go′shen (gō′shĕn). **1** County in Wyoming. See *Table* at WYOMING.

2 City, ⊗ of Elkhart co., N Indiana, 22 m. ESE of South Bend; pop. 13,718; manufactures flour, and wood and rubber products. Goshen Coll. (1894; coed.; Mennonite).

3 Village, ⊗ of Orange co., SE New York, 18 m WSW of Newburgh; pop. 3906; racing center for harness horses. While teaching school here 1782 Noah Webster worked on his "blue-backed" spelling book (pub. 1783).

4 District of ancient Egypt E of the Nile delta; granted to Jacob and his family by the king of Egypt; place where Jacob's descendants lived until the Exodus (*Gen.* xlvi–xlvii).

5 Boer republic in Bechuanaland, S Africa, established in W Transvaal 1882 as part of westward expansion of Boers; became part of British Bechuanaland 1885. See STELLALAND.

Goshen Point. Point, New London co., SE Connecticut, W of mouth of Thames river.

Gos′lar (gôs′lär). Manufacturing city, SE Lower Saxony state, W Germany, 23 m. S of Brunswick in N Harz Mts.; pop. 20,854; railroad junction; iron mining. Founded in 10th cent.; joined Hanseatic League c. 1350; promulgated *Goslar statutes*, a famous code of laws, in middle of 14th cent.; passed to Prussia 1802, to Westphalia 1807; again became part of Prussia 1866.

Gos′per (gŏs′pēr). County in Nebraska. See *Table* at NEBRASKA.

Gos′pić *or* **Gos′pich** (gŏs′pĭch; *Yugo.* gŏs′pĕt·y′). Commune, W Yugoslavia, 70 m. SE of Rieka (Fiume); pop. 10,600.

Gos′port (gŏs′pōrt). Municipal borough, Hampshire, S England, on Portsmouth harbor opp. Portsmouth; pop. 58,246; royal victualing yard and naval barracks.

Gos′sau (gôs′ou). Commune, St. Gallen canton, Switzerland, 6 m. W of St. Gallen; pop. (1930) 7914; embroidery and lace.

Gos′se·lies′ (gôs′lē′). Commune, Hainaut prov., SW Belgium, 4 m. N of Charleroi; pop. 10,150; manufactures linen, nails, enamelware; coal mining, foundries.

Gö′ta (yû′tà). Navigable river 58 m. long in S Sweden; drains Lake Vänern and flows SSW into the Kattegat; locks at the falls of Trollhättan (*q.v.*); part of **Göta Canal** connecting Göteborg on the W with Stockholm on the E, 58 locks, highest point 300 ft., uses many lakes (total distance ab. 360 m., constructed part ab. 54 m.).

Gö′ta·land′ (yû′tà·länd′) *or* **Gö′ta·ri′ke** (-rē′kĕ). The southern division of Sweden; land area 33,515 sq. m.; pop. 3,202,350; comprises the 12 provinces of Älvsborg, Blekinge, Göteborg and Bohus, Gotland, Halland, Jönköping, Kalmar, Kristianstad, Kronoberg, Malmöhus, Östergötland, and Skaraborg.

Gö′te·borg′ (yû′tĕ·bôr′y′) *or* **Goth′en·burg** (gŏth′n·bûrg; gŏt′′n-). Seaport, ✳ of Göteborg and Bohus prov., SW Sweden, at mouth of Göta river on the Kattegat; pop. 296,289; 2d largest city in Sweden; founded 1619 by Gustavus Adolphus; shipbuilding; manufactures textiles, matches, porcelain, timber and wood products, iron and steel products; originated 1865 what is known as the Gothenburg system for the regulation of the sale of intoxicating liquors.

Göteborg and Bo′hus (bōō′hōōs). Province of Sweden. See *Table* at SWEDEN.

Go′tha (gō′tä; *Angl.* gō′thà, -tà). City, Thuringia, E Germany, 15 m. W of Erfurt; pop. 45,780; 13th-cent. church, 16th-cent. town hall; manufactures airplanes, machinery, precision instruments, rubber products, soap, sausage. Dates back to 9th cent.; noted for its insurance companies, first one organized 1821, and for its extensive book trade, esp. the geographical house of Justus Perthes. Often bombed during World War II.

Go′tham. 1 (gō′tăm; gŏt′ăm) Village, Nottinghamshire, England, 7 m. SW of Nottingham; inhabitants obtained the name "the wise men of Gotham" for their reputed simplicity, since according to tradition when King John visited the village to select a site for a palace, the people not wishing to support such a royal residence, feigned stupidity.

2 (gŏth′ăm; gō′thăm) The city of New York—first popularly so called in *Salmagundi* (1807–08), a humorous work by Washington Irving, William Irving, and James Kirke Paulding, because the inhabitants were such wiseacres.

Goth′en·burg. 1 (gŏth′′n·bûrg) City, Dawson co., S cen. Nebraska, on Platte river 36 m. ESE of North Platte; pop. 3050.

2 (gŏth′′n-; gŏt′′n-) See GÖTEBORG.

Goth′ic Line (gŏth′ĭk). German defense line in World War II, in N cen. Italy, extending from Pisa to Rimini along heights above the Arno, 150 m. N of Rome; attacked by Allies Sept. 1944; penetrated after severe fighting by Dec. 1944.

Gothic Mountain. Peak 4738 ft. in the Adirondack Mts., Essex co., NE New York.

Goth'land' (gŏth'lănd'; -lănd). = GOTLAND.

Got'land *or* **Gott'land'** (gŏt'lănd'; -lănd; *Swed.* gôt'-länd'). Island in Baltic Sea off SE coast of Sweden; with islands of Fårö, Karlsö, etc., constitutes a province of Sweden, 1225 sq. m., pop. 59,609, ✲ Visby; agriculture, sheep raising, fisheries, cement works. Center of trade since early times as evidenced by large number of Roman, Byzantine, and Arabic coins found; belonged to Sweden in 13th cent., at height of importance 14th cent. when Visby (*q.v.*) belonged to Hanseatic League; attacked by Danish 1361; became abode of pirates; to Denmark by Peace of Stettin 1570; to Sweden by Treaty of Brömsebro 1645; occupied temporarily by Danes 1676–79, 1808.

Go'to Archipelago (gō'tō); *Jap.* **Go-to Ret-to** (gō·tō rĕt·tō). Literally "five-island chain or group"; chain of islands extending for ab. 100 m. SW from NW Kyushu, Japan; five main islands Fukae, Uku, Nakadori, Naru, Hisaga; part of Nagasaki prefecture; ✲ Fukae.

Got'tes-berg (gŏt'ĕs-bĕrк); *Pol.* **Bo-gu'szów** (bô-gōō'shōōf). Mining and manufacturing city, S Wrocław dept., SW Poland, formerly in Silesia prov., Prussia, Germany, 47 m. SW of Wrocław; pop. (1946) 8000; coal; assigned to Poland by Potsdam Conference 1945.

Göt'ting-en (gût'ĭng-ĕn). Manufacturing city, S Lower Saxony state, W Germany, on the Leine river 55 m. SSW of Brunswick; pop. 41,514; university; beer, aluminum goods, scientific instruments, pianos, textiles. First mentioned in 10th cent.

Gottland. See GOTLAND.

Got'torp (gŏt'ôrp). Castle just NW of the city of Schleswig, Schleswig-Holstein, northwestern Germany; gave its name to Gottorp or Holstein-Gottorp line of Oldenburg family, founded 1586 by Duke Adolf, a younger son of King Frederick I of Denmark.

Gottschee. See KOČEVJE.

Gottwaldov. See ZLÍN.

Gou'da (gou'dȧ; *Dutch* кou'dȧ). Commune, South Holland prov., SW Netherlands, NE of Rotterdam; pop. (1939) 33,258; manufactures pottery; cheese market (Gouda cheese); Groote Kerk, known esp. for its 40 stained glass windows, mostly made by Dirck Crabeth.

Gough, *or* **Gough's, Island** (gŏf, gŏfs). Small island in South Atlantic Ocean, one of the Tristan da Cunha group, 39°20′S, 11°10′W; a British claim, attached Jan. 12, 1938 to St. Helena I.

Gou-in' Reservoir (gwăn). Lake in SW Quebec, Canada, NW of city of Quebec; its outlet St. Maurice river.

Goul'burn (gōl'bĕrn). **1** River 280 m. long, E cen. Victoria, SE Australia, flows NW to Murray river.
2 City, SE New South Wales, SE Australia, 50 m. NE of Canberra; pop. 14,851; made a city 1864.

Gould, Mount (gōold). Peak 9541 ft. in Glacier National Park, NW Montana.

Goulds'bor'ough (gōolz'bûr'ō). Town, Hancock co., SE Maine, on inlet 10 m. NE of Mt. Desert I.; pop. 1100; resort.

Goulette, La. See LA GOULETTE.

Gou'li'mine' (gōō'lē'mēn'). Town, SW Morocco, NW Africa, near SE border of Ifni.

Goumenitsa. See HEGOUMENITSA.

Goun'dam' (gōon'dàm'). Town, Mali (formerly French Sudan), West Africa, near Lake Faguibine SW of Tombouctou; pop. (1940) 6344.

Gou'rin' (gōō'răn'). Commune, Morbihan dept., NW France, 25 m. NE of Quimper; pop. (1931) 5909; 16th-cent. Gothic church and chapel.

Gou'ritz (gou'rĭts; gō'rĭts). River ab. 40 m. long, Cape Province, Union of South Africa; formed by confluence of Groote and Olifants rivers, flows S into Indian Ocean near Mossel Bay.

Gour'ni-a (gōor'nĭ-ȧ). Ancient town, NE Crete, at head of Mirabella Bay; on a low hill, streets 5 ft. wide, some with steps; ruins of palace and shrine.

Gour'ock (gōor'ŭk). Burgh, Renfrew co., SW Scotland,

on S shore of Firth of Clyde; pop. 9107; seaport; summer resort, yachting center. During World War II debarkation point for U.S. forces (in 2½ years after May 1942, ab. 1,317,000 Americans landed here).

Gouv'er-neur' (gŭv'ēr-nŏŏr'; gōō'vēr-; -nûr'). Village, St. Lawrence co., N New York, 24 m. S of Ogdensburg; pop. 4946; talc, lead, and zinc mines; marble works; manufactures wood pulp, silk, hosiery.

Gou-yave' (?gōō-yäv') *or* **Char'lotte Town** (shär'lŭt). Town, W coast of Grenada I., Windward Is., Brit. West Indies; pop. ab. 2000.

Gov'an (gŭv'ăn). Former suburb of Glasgow, Scotland, now part of the city; shipyards.

Gove (gōv). **1** County in Kansas. See *Table* at KANSAS.
2 *or* **Gove City.** City, its ⊗, W Kansas; pop. 228.

Gov'er-na-dor' Island (gō'vēr-nȧ-thôr'). Island in Guanabara Bay, N of Rio de Janeiro, Brazil.

Gov'ern-ment Mountain (gŭv'ērn-mĕnt). Peak 8347 ft., cen. Coconino co., N cen. Arizona.

Gov'er-nor s Harbour (gŭv'ēr-nērz). Town on Eleuthera I. in Bahama Is., Brit. West Indies; pop. 578.

Governors Island. **1** Island in inner part of Boston Harbor, Massachusetts; site of Ft. Winthrop.
2 Fortified island in New York Bay, off S end of East river; U.S. Military Reservation; old fort, Castle William, built 1807–11.

Go-wan'da (gō·wŏn'dȧ). Village, Cattaraugus and Erie cos., SW New York, 28 m. S of Buffalo; pop. 3352; settled 1810, called Lodi until 1848; leather, glue, carbonated beverages, gelatin. State Homeopathic Hospital in nearby **Hel'muth** (hĕl'mŭth) in Erie co.

Go-wa'nus Bay (gō·wŏn'ŭs). Inlet of Upper New York Bay extending into S Brooklyn, W Long I., New York.

Gow'er (gou'ēr). Peninsula extending S into Bristol Channel from S cen. coast of Wales.

Go'ya (gō'yä). Town, Corrientes prov., NE Argentina, on E bank of Paraná river 112 m. S of Corrientes; pop. (est.) 23,170.

Goyaz. See GOIAZ.

Go'zo (gô'tsō); *anc.* **Gau'lus** (gô'lŭs). Island of Malta group in Mediterranean Sea 58 m. S of Sicily; ab. 25 sq. m.; pop. 23,796; chief town Victoria. See MALTA.

Graaff Rei'net (gräf rī'nĕt). Town, S Cape Province, S Union of South Africa, on Sunday river 135 m. NNW of Port Elizabeth, in center of the Great Karroo; pop. 11,983; produces fine quality wool and angora hair. Founded by the Dutch in 1786.

Graasten. See GRAVENSTEIN.

Gra'cias (grä'syäs). **1** See LEMPIRA.
2 Town, ✲ of Lempira dept., W Honduras, on the Ulúa river 100 m. WNW of Tegucigalpa; pop. (1935) 2294.

Gra'cias a Dios (grä'syäs ä thyōs'), **Cape (Ca'bo** [kä'vô]). Northeast extremity of Nicaragua, extending into Caribbean Sea near Honduras border.

Gra-cio'sa (grȧ-syô'zȧ). Island in cen. Azores, NW of Terceira; 24 sq. m.; pop. ab. 8000; in Angra do Heroísmo dist.; chief town Santa Cruz da Graciosa.

Gra-cio'sa Bay (grä-thyô'sä, -syô'-). Inlet on NW coast of Ndeni I., Santa Cruz Is., SW Pacific Ocean; good harbor. Mendaña died here 1595.

Gra-di'sca (*Ital.* grä-dēs'kä; *Ger.* -dís'-). Commune, Gorizia prov., NW Venezia Giulia, NE Italy, SW of Gorizia on opp. side of the Isonzo; pop. ab. 5000; Venetian fortress ceded to Austria 1511 and became part of Austrian crownland of Görz and Gradisca (see GORIZIA); taken by Italians June 1915 and made part of Italy 1918.

Gra'do (grä'dō). Commune, Venezia Giulia, NE Italy, on a small island in NW part of Gulf of Trieste, N Adriatic Sea; pop. ab. 6000; resort; founded by refugees from Aquileia in time of Attila; has fine cathedral, rebuilt 571–586, with a mosaic pavement.

Gra'do (grä'thō). Commune, Oviedo prov., NW Spain, 12 m. WNW of Oviedo; pop. 17,318; iron founding; ordnance works.

Gra'dy (grā'dĭ). Name of counties in two states of the U.S. See *Tables* at GEORGIA and OKLAHOMA.

Graecia Magna. = MAGNA GRAECIA.

Gra'fen·berk (grä'fĕn·bĕrk); *Ger.* **Grä'fen·berg** (grä'-fĕn·bĕrk). Village, N Silesia, Czechoslovakia, NW of Opava; first water cure introduced here 1826 by Vincenz Priessnitz, founder of hydrotherapy.

Gra'fen·wöhr' (grä'fĕn·vûr'). Village, Upper Palatinate, Bavaria, Germany, ab. 21 m. SE of Bayreuth; pop. 2002; Nazi concentration camp.

Gräf'rath (grâf'rät). Former city (pop. 10,582), Düsseldorf govt. dist., Rhine Province, Prussia, Germany; since 1929 part of Solingen (*q.v.*).

Graf'ton (grăf'tŭn). **1** County in New Hampshire. See *Table* at NEW HAMPSHIRE.

2 Town, Worcester co., cen. Massachusetts, 6 m. ESE of Worcester; pop. 10,627; residential. Site of an Indian village established by John Eliot 1654.

3 City, ⊗ of Walsh co., NE North Dakota, 38 m. NNW of Grand Forks; pop. 5885; settled 1877; wheat-growing region.

4 City, ⊗ of Taylor co., N West Virginia, on Tygart river 12 m. SSE of Fairmont; pop. 5791; railroad terminus.

5 Town, NE New South Wales, SE Australia, on Clarence river 45 m. from its mouth and 150 m. S of Brisbane; pop. 6412; port.

Gra·gna'no (grä·nyä'nô). Commune, Naples prov., Campania, S Italy, 18 m. SE of Naples; pop. 16,548; macaroni factories.

Gra'ham (grā'ăm). **1** Name of counties in three states of the U.S. See *Tables* at ARIZONA, KANSAS, NORTH CAROLINA.

2 Town, ⊗ of Alamance co., N cen. North Carolina, 21 m. E of Greensboro; pop. 7723; textile center.

3 City, ⊗ of Young co., N Texas, 57 m. S of Wichita Falls; pop. 8505; oil refineries, flour and feed mills.

Graham, Mount. **1** See GRAHAM PEAK.

2 Peak 3890 ft. in Catskill Mts., Ulster co., SE New York.

Gra'ham Bell Island (grā'ăm bĕl'). See FRANZ JOSEF LAND.

Graham Coast, *formerly* **Graham Land.** Part of the Falkland Islands Dependencies (*q.v.*) in Antarctica, due S of Tierra del Fuego extending from ab. 65°S to 66°15'S; once known as **North Graham Island** and **South Graham Island** but on later exploration found to be part of the mainland; now considered W part of Palmer Penin. Annexed to Great Britain by John Biscoe 1831–32.

Graham Island. Northernmost and largest of the Queen Charlotte Is., off W British Columbia, Canada.

Graham Peak, *or* **Mount Graham.** Peak 10,750 ft. in Pinaleno Mts., Graham co., SE Arizona.

Gra'hams·town (grā'ămz·toun). Residential town, SE Cape Province, S Republic of So. Africa, 75 m. ENE of Port Elizabeth; pop. 32,000; summer resort; the Republic's most important educational center: Rhodes University (1904, before 1951 part of Univ. of South Africa), St. Andrew's Coll. (1855; Anglican), St. Aidan's Coll. (Roman Catholic), Kingswood Coll. (Wesleyan), Diocesan Coll., Anglican Training Coll. for Women. Has been called the most English town in South Africa. Founded 1812 as a British military outpost in a region which for many years was scene of almost constant struggle bet. whites and natives; besieged by Kafirs in 1819; chief town of British settlers of 1820.

Gra'ian Alps (grā'yăn; grī'ăn). See *Table* at ALPS.

Grain Coast (grān). Section of coast of Upper Guinea, W Africa, now Liberia, from Cape Palmas to Sierra Leone border—so called from the old trade in grains of paradise (*Amomum melegueta*), a kind of pepper (melegueta pepper).

Grain'ger (grān'jĕr). County in Tennessee. See *Table* at TENNESSEE.

Gra'ja·ú' (grä'zhá·ōō'). River ab. 450 m. long, Maranhão state, NE Brazil; flows NNE to Mearim river.

Grajaú, Lake. Lake in N cen. Maranhão state, NE Brazil, bet. the Pindaré and Grajaú rivers.

Gram'mi·che'le (gräm'mē·kâ'lā). Commune, Catania prov., E Sicily, 32 m. SW of Catania; pop. 14,014; stone quarries; on site of Occhialà, which was destroyed 1693 by earthquake.

Grammont. See GEERAARDSBERGEN.

Gram'pi·ans, the (grăm'pĭ·ănz). **1** Mountain range, W Victoria, SE Australia; highest Mt. William 3029 ft.

2 *or* **Gram'pi·an Hills** (-ăn). Mountain system of Scotland, extending NE to SW across cen. Scotland, forming a natural boundary bet. the Scottish Highlands and the Scottish Lowlands; highest peak Ben Nevis 4406 ft., highest mountain in Great Britain. See Mount GRAUPIUS.

Gran. **1** See HRON river, Czechoslovakia.

2 See ESZTERGOM city, Hungary.

Gra·na'da (grä·nä'dá; *Span.* grä·nä'thä). **1** Department, SW Nicaragua; 541 sq. m.; pop. (1943 est.) 55,462; ✲ Granada.

2 City, ✲ of Granada dept., SW Nicaragua, on NW shore of Lake Nicaragua; pop. (1943 est.) 26,214; oldest city in Nicaragua, founded by Córdoba 1523; produces sugar, coffee, cacao, hides, indigo.

3 Ancient kingdom, Upper Andalusia, S Spain; 11,100 sq. m.; divided 1833 into modern provinces of Granada, Almería, and Málaga. For its history, see GRANADA city, below, and ANDALUSIA.

4 Province of Spain. See *Table* at SPAIN.

5 City, ✲ of Granada prov., S Spain, in Sierra Nevada Mts. 80 m. SE of Córdoba; pop. (1941 est.) 155,827; divided into three sections: Antequeruela (founded 1410), Albaicín, and Granada; manufactures paper, soap, woolens, liqueurs; archiepiscopal see (from 1493); university (1531); the Alhambra (built 1248–1354), one of finest examples of Moorish architecture in Spain; Renaissance cathedral (begun 1529), containing tombs of Ferdinand and Isabella of Castile; the Cartuja, a Carthusian monastery; Moorish remains, among them the Alcazaba (citadel).

History: Founded by Moors in 8th cent.; part of Caliphate of Córdoba 1031–1229; became capital 1238 of independent Moorish kingdom of Granada founded by Nasrid dynasty; attained greatest prosperity in 13th cent.; after Spanish reconquest, remained for 250 years the last Moorish stronghold in Spain; captured 1492 by Ferdinand and Isabella of Castile, completely destroying Moorish power in Spain.

Gran'bur'y (grăn'bĕr'ĭ; -bĕr·ĭ; grăm'-). City, ⊗ of Hood co., N cen. Texas; pop. 2227.

Gran'by (grăn'bĭ; grăm'bĭ). **1** Town, NW Hartford co., N Connecticut; pop. 4968; settled 1664, incorp. 1786.

2 Industrial city, Shefford co., S Quebec, Canada, 45 m. E of Montreal, pop. 21,989; furniture and woodworking industries; rubber goods, bricks, plumbing supplies.

Gran Canaria. See GRAND CANARY.

Gran Chaco. See CHACO.

Gran Colombia. See GREAT COLOMBIA.

Grand (grănd). **1** Former name of Colorado river from its source to its junction with Green river in SE Utah.

2 River in Iberville parish, S Louisiana; empties into Atchafalaya river.

3 River 260 m. long, SW Michigan; flows from Jackson co. N and W into Lake Michigan at Grand Haven; furnishes water power; navigable 40 m. from mouth.

4 River 300 m. long, NW Missouri; rises in Adair co., SW cen. Iowa, flows SE across NW Missouri into Missouri river.

5 River 140 m. long, W Missouri; flows SE across Henry co. into the Lake of the Ozarks in Benton co.

6 River ab. 200 m. long, N South Dakota; formed by confluence of North and South Forks in N Perkins co., flows E into Missouri river.

7 The lower course of the Neosho river (*q.v.*) in Oklahoma. See GRAND RIVER DAM

8 Name of counties in two states of the U.S. See *Tables* at COLORADO and UTAH.

9 River 140 m. long, SE Ontario, Canada; rises in Grey co. and flows S and SE to Lake Erie.

10 The HAMILTON river, Labrador.

Grand Andely, Le. See LES ANDELYS.

Grand Atlas (grănd). See ATLAS MOUNTAINS.

Grand Ba·ha′ma (bȧ·hä′mȧ; *in U.S.*, *also* -hä′-). One of the Bahama Is., West Indies; 430 sq. m.; pop. 4095.

Grand Bank. **1** Shoal or banks in Atlantic Ocean E and S of Newfoundland; extends ab. 500 m. from W to E, ab. 200 m. wide; average depth 50 fathoms; crossed by the Labrador Current from the N mingling with the Gulf Stream along its E edge; greatest cod-fishing region in the world, for centuries has been frequented by fishing fleets of Canada, Great Britain, France, and U.S.; made dangerous by fog, icebergs, and the fact that it is in the path of the transatlantic liners.

2 Seaport, S Newfoundland, on S shore and near mouth of Fortune Bay; pop. (1951) 2148; is a supply depot for fishing fleets.

Grand Bas′sa (băs′ȧ), *or* **Bu·chan′an** (bŭ·kăn′ăn; bŭ-). Seaport, W Liberia, ab. 70 m. SE of Monrovia.

Grand Bas′sam′ (bȧ·săm′), *or* **Bassam.** Seaport, Ivory Coast republic, West Africa, adjoining Bingerville and just E of Abidjan; pop. 5743; customs station.

Grand Bourg *or* **Grand′-Bourg′** (grän′boōr′). Commune, ✱ of Marie Galante I., Guadeloupe dept., French West Indies; pop. 13,833; on SW coast of the island.

Grand Caicos (grănd). See TURKS AND CAICOS ISLANDS.

Grand Caillou Bayou. See CAILLOU LAKE.

Grand Canal (grănd). **1** Inland waterway, NE China, ab. 1000 m. long, from Tientsin, Hopeh prov., to Hangchow, Chekiang prov. (air-line distance ab. 650 m.). Central part from the Yangtze (at Chinkiang) to Hwang Ho finished 486 B.C.; extended S to Hangchow 605-618 A.D.; N section finished by Kublai Khan 1282-92; later extended to Tungchow (Tunghsien) and Peking. Called by the Chinese "Imperial river" (*Yu-ho*) or "Transport river" (*Yun-ho*). Now silted up in part and superseded somewhat by coast transport and the Tientsin-Pukow railroad.

2 *Ital.* **Il Ca·na′le Gran′de** (ēl kä·nä′lā grän′dā). Main water thoroughfare of Venice, in winding course, 80 to 175 ft. wide; crossed by Rialto and other bridges; lined with palaces and fine buildings.

Grand Ca·nar′y (grănd kȧ·nâr′ĭ); *Span.* **Gran Ca·na′ria** (gräng′ kä·nä′ryä). One of the Canary Is. (*q.v.*), 40 m. ESE of Tenerife I.; in Las Palmas prov., Spain; 523 sq. m.; pop. (1930) 216,853; chief city Las Palmas.

Grand Can′yon (grănd kăn′yŭn). **1** Gorge in the Colorado river where it flows across NW corner of Arizona; usually taken as extending from mouth of Little Colorado river to Grand Wash Cliffs near Arizona-Nevada boundary but sometimes taken as also including Marble Canyon, above, and when measured thus, ab. 280 m. long; 4-18 m. wide, in places more than a mile deep; many peaks and smaller canyons within the main canyon; surrounding plateau 5000 to 9000 ft. above sea level; an area mostly N of the canyon in NE Mohave co. set aside 1932 as **Grand Canyon National Monument** (see UNITED STATES, *National Monuments*); E of the National Monument in Coconino co. is **Grand Canyon National Park** (see UNITED STATES, *National Parks*).

2 Village, Coconino co., N Arizona, in Grand Canyon National Park; pop. (est.) 1000; park administration building.

Grand Canyon of the Snake = HELL'S CANYON, Idaho.

Grand Canyon of the Tuolumne. See TUOLUMNE river.

Grand Canyon of the Yellowstone. See YELLOWSTONE river.

Grand Cayman (grănd). See CAYMAN ISLANDS.

Grand Cess (grănd sĕs). Coastal town, SE Liberia, W Africa, 40 m. WNW of Cape Palmas.

Grand′-Combe, La. See LA GRAND′-COMBE.

Grand Com′bin′ (grän′ kôN′băN′). Peak 14,164 ft. in Pennine Alps, S Switzerland.

Grand Cor′nier′ (grän′ kôr′nyā′). Peak 13,020 ft. in Pennine Alps, S Switzerland.

Grand Cou′lee (grănd koō′lĭ). **1** Valley bet. ranges of cliffs in cen. Washington, extending N to S in Douglas co.

2 City, Grant co., cen. Washington, at site of Grand Coulee Dam on Columbia river 78 m. WNW of Spokane; pop. 1058; comprised of former towns of Coulee Heights, Coulee Center, and Grand Coulee.

Grand Coulee Dam. See UNITED STATES, *Dams*.

Grand Coulee Reservoir. = FRANKLIN D. ROOSEVELT Lake.

Grand Cou′ron′né′ (grän′ koō′rô′nā′). Wooded heights E and NE of Nancy, France; battle Sept. 5-12, 1914 in which Germans attempted to capture Nancy but were driven back by Castelnau.

Grand′court′ (grän′koōr′). Village, Somme dept., N France, N of Albert; pop. (1931) 198; severe fighting during battle of the Somme 1916; taken by British Feb. 7, 1917.

Gran′de, I′lha (ē′lyȧ grănn′dĕ). **1** Island in Atlantic Ocean off NE coast of Brazil, at mouth of Parnaíba river.

2 Island 15 m. long and 8 m. wide in Atlantic Ocean off S coast of Rio de Janeiro state, SE Brazil.

Grande, Ri′o (rē′ŏ grănd′; grän′dĕ; rī′ŏ grănd′). River in S United States. See RIO GRANDE.

Gran′de, Ri′o (rē′ŏ grănn′dŏ). **1** River ab. 250 m. long, W Africa; rises in Fouta Djallon, W French Guinea, flows by winding course W into Geba estuary, Portuguese Guinea; lower course sometimes called **Co·ru·bal′** (′koō·roō·väl′), upper course in French Guinea, the **Kom′ba** (kôm′bȧ).

2 River ab. 300 m. long, W Baía state, E Brazil; flows NE into São Francisco river.

3 River ab. 680 m. long in SW Minas Gerais state, E Brazil; flows W to unite with Paranaíba river and form Paraná river; forms section of boundary bet. Minas Gerais and São Paulo states.

Gran′de, Rí′o (rē′ŏ grän′dȧ). **1** River ab. 170 m. long, Mendoza prov., W cen. Argentina; rises near Chilean border, flows SE to unite with Barrancas river and form Colorado river.

2 A name of the Mamoré (*q.v.*) in its upper course, Bolivia.

3 *or* **Río Grande de Santiago.** River, Mexico. See SANTIAGO.

4 River ab. 200 m. long, Nicaragua; flows E to Caribbean Sea.

Gran′de A·ñas′co (grän′dȧ ä·nyäs′kŏ). River in W Puerto Rico; flows W into Añasco Bay.

Grande Baie. See SAINT ALEXIS DE LA GRANDE BAIE.

Grande Casse (gränd′ käs′). Peak 12,668 ft., W Graian Alps, Savoie dept., E France.

Grande Chartreuse, La. See LA GRANDE CHARTREUSE.

Grande–Comore. See GREAT COMORO.

Gran′de de A′re·ci′bo (grän′dȧ thä ä′rā·sē′vŏ). River in N Puerto Rico; flows N through Arecibo municipality into Atlantic Ocean.

Grande de Lo·í′za (thä lō·ē′sä). River in NE Puerto Rico; flows N and NE into Atlantic Ocean.

Gran′de Island (grän′dȧ). Island ab. ½ sq. m. in center of entrance to Subic Bay (*q.v.*), S Zambales prov., Luzon, Phil. Is.; strongly fortified; retaken from Japanese Feb. 1, 1945.

Grande Prai′rie (grănd′ prâr′ĭ). Town, W Alberta, Canada, 235 m. WNW of Edmonton; pop. 2664; airport.

Grand Erg Occidental, Grand Erg Oriental. See El ERG.

Grande Ronde (grănd rŏnd′). River 175 m. long, NE Oregon; rises in SW Union co., flows NE across Washington border and into Snake river.

Grandes Jo′rasses′ (gränd′ zhô′ràs′). Two peaks (higher one 13,806 ft.), NE of Mont Blanc, in Pennine Alps, S Switzerland.

Grande Sou′fri′ère′ (gränd′ sōō′frē′âr′). Volcano 4869 ft. in S Basse-Terre, Guadeloupe, French West Indies.

Grande Terre (grän′ târ′; *Fr.* grän′ târ′). Island forming E part of Guadeloupe, French West Indies.

Grand Falls (grănd fôlz). **1** Town, Victoria co., W New Brunswick, Canada, on St. John river 35 m. SE of Edmundston; pop. 2365; close by are the Grand Falls of the St. John, ab. 75 ft.; resort. **2** *now* **Churchill Falls.** Falls 200 ft. wide, 316 ft. high, in Churchill river, W Labrador, **ab.** 225 m. from Lake Melville; just above McLean canyon, 12 m. long, through which river drops another 300 ft.; discovered 1839, forgotten, and rediscovered 1891. **3** Town, cen. Newfoundland, on N bank of Exploits river; pop. (1942 est.) 5200; large pulp and paper mills.

Grand Forks (grănd fôrks). **1** County in North Dakota. See *Table* at NORTH DAKOTA. **2** City, ⊗ of Grand Forks co., E North Dakota, on Red river 73 m. N of Fargo; pop. 34,451; railroad and industrial center in hard wheat belt; manufactures flour, feed, beet sugar; meat packing. Univ. of North Dakota (1883; coed.; in nearby suburb, University) and its affiliate, Wesley College (1892; coed.). Established as fur-trading post 1801; settled 1871; incorporated as city 1881.

Grand Haven. City, ⊗ of Ottawa co., W Michigan, on Lake Michigan at mouth of Grand river 12 m. S of Muskegon; pop. 11,066; summer resort; port of entry; varied manufactures.

Grand Island. 1 Island 8 m. long in upper Niagara river; part of Erie co., W New York. **2** City, ⊗ of Hall co., SE cen. Nebraska, on Platte river 90 m. W of Lincoln; pop. 25,742; railroad center; flour mills, beet-sugar refineries, packing houses, dairies.

Grand Isle (grănd īl). **1** Island at SW entrance to Barataria Bay, off coast of SE Louisiana; in Jefferson parish. **2** Island ab. 10 m. long in Lake Champlain, Grand Isle co., NW corner of Vermont. **3** County in Vermont. See *Table* at VERMONT. **4** Town, Aroostook co., N Maine, on St. John river 22 m. E of Fort Kent; pop. 978.

Grand Junction. City, ⊗ of Mesa co., W Colorado, at junction of Gunnison and Colorado rivers; pop. 18,694; incorporated 1881; trade center and distributing point for irrigated valley; peach orchards.

Grand Lac. See TONLE SAP.

Grand La′hou′ (grän′ là′ōō′). Seaport, Ivory Coast, West Africa, 70 m. W of Abidjan, pop. 4402.

Grand Lake (grănd). **1** Lake, NE Grand co., N Colorado, on SW border of Rocky Mountain National Park; the town of **Grand Lake** (pop. 170) is on it. **2** Lake in NE Cameron parish, SW Louisiana; outlet SW into Gulf of Mexico. **3** Lake chiefly in Iberia and St. Mary parishes, S Louisiana; ab. 30 m. long, 9 m. wide; drains through Atchafalaya river into Atchafalaya Bay. **4** *or now* **West Grand Lake.** Lake in E Maine, near W boundary of Washington co. **5** *or* **Grand Reservoir.** See Lake ST. MARYS, Ohio. **6** See GRAND RIVER DAM, Oklahoma. **7** Lake 74 sq. m., Queens co., S New Brunswick, Canada; outlet St. John river. **8** *or formerly* **East Grand Lake.** Largest of the Chiputneticook Lakes on SW border of York co., SW New Brunswick, Canada; borders on Maine. **9** Lake 192 sq. m., ab. 56 m. long, N Newfoundland; outlet through Humber river; coal deposits.

Grand Lake Met′a·scou·ac′ (mĕt′à·skwăk′; -skōō-yăk′). Lake in S Quebec prov., Canada, in NW Laurentides Park.

Grand Lebanon. = *Great Lebanon:* see LEBANON.

Grand Ledge (grănd lĕj). Industrial city, Eaton co., S Michigan, W of Lansing; pop. 5165; clay products.

Grand Liban. See LEBANON.

Grand Ma·nan′ Island (grănd′ mà·năn′). Island ab. 20 m. long at entrance to Bay of Fundy and S of Passamaquoddy Bay, off SW coast of New Brunswick, SE Canada; pop. ab. 3000; separated from coast of Maine by **Grand Manan Channel** (ab. 8 m. wide), which has strong currents; fine cliff scenery; summer resort; chief village North Head; fishing.

Grand Manitoulin. = MANITOULIN ISLAND.

Grand Ma·rais′ (grănd′ mà·rā′). Village, ⊗ of Cook co., NE corner of Minnesota, on Lake Superior 23 m. S of Canadian border; pop. 1301.

Grand′′Mère′ (grän′mâr′). City, Champlain co., S Quebec, Canada, on St. Maurice river 20 m. NNW of Three Rivers; pop. 11,089; paper and pulp mills; manufactures shirts, shoes, textiles.

Grand Monadnock. See MONADNOCK.

Grand–Montrouge, Le. See MONTROUGE.

Grand Paradis. See GRAN PARADISO.

Grand Pass (grănd). Narrow strait connecting Barataria Bay, SE Louisiana, with Gulf of Mexico.

Grand Po′po (grănd pō′pō; *Fr.* grän′ pô′pō′). Seaport, SW Dahomey, West Africa, at mouth of the Mono river; pop. ab. 1000; on coastal railroad bet. Porto-Novo and Lomé.

Grand Prai′rie (grănd prâr′ĭ). City, Dallas co., NE Texas, 13 m. W of Dallas; pop. 30,386.

Grand′pré′ (grän′prā′). Village, Ardennes dept., NE France, on Aire river 10 m. SE of Vouziers; pop. 670; center of fighting Oct. 1918 in the Meuse-Argonne offensive (see ARGONNE).

Grand Pré (grän′ prā′; *Fr.* grän′ prā′). Village, Kings co., N Nova Scotia, Canada, on S shore of Minas Basin near Wolfville; founded c. 1675; early home of the Acadians; scene of Longfellow's *Evangeline.* See ACADIA.

Grand Rap′ids (grănd răp′ĭdz). **1** City, ⊗ of Kent co., W Michigan, on Grand river 61 m. WNW of Lansing; pop. 177,313; manufactures esp. furniture, also metal products, foods, chemicals, paper products, textiles; petroleum refineries. Calvin College (1876; coed.; Christian Reformed Church); Aquinas College (1886; coed.). Originally site of an Ottawa Indian village; trading post 1826; became lumbering center; chartered as city 1850. **2** Village, ⊗ of Itasca co., N Minnesota, 32 m. WSW of Hibbing; pop. 7265; paper mills.

Grand River. See GRAND.

Grand River, *or* **Pen′sa·co′la** (pĕn′sà·kō′là), **Dam.** Dam completed 1940 across Grand (Neosho) river, NE Oklahoma; height 147 ft.; impounds water for power; forms lake 64 sq. m. variously known as **Lake of the Cher′o·kees′** (ŭv thĕ chĕr′ô·kēz′), **Grand Lake,** and **Pensacola Reservoir.**

Grand–Saint–Ber′nard′ (grän′săn′bĕr′nàr′). Alpine pass. See ALPS.

Grand Sa·line′ (sà·lēn′). City, Van Zandt co., NE Texas, 30 m. NW of Tyler; pop. 2006; salt mining and processing.

Grands Cou′loirs′, Pointe des (pwănt′ dā grän′ kōō′-lwàr′). Peak 12,665 ft. in Graian Alps, Savoie dept., E France.

Grand Sen′ti·nel (sĕn′tĭ·nĕl; -n'l; -t'n·'l). Peak 8514 ft. in Sierra Nevada, E Fresno co., S cen. California.

Grand′son′ (grän′sôn′) *or* **Granson.** Commune, Vaud canton, W Switzerland, SW of Neuchâtel; pop. (1930) 1663; manufactures cigars; castle, 12th-cent. church; garrison surrendered and put to death Feb. 1476 by Charles the Bold who with heavy loss was defeated in battle Mar. 2 by Swiss Confederates.

Grand Terre Island (grănd′ tĕr′; târ′; *Fr* grän′ târ′). Island at entrance to Barataria Bay off coast of SE Louisiana; in Jefferson parish; Barataria lighthouse.

Grand Te'ton (grănd tē'tŏn). Peak 13,766 ft. in cen. Grand Teton National Park, Teton co., NW Wyoming; highest point in Teton Range.

Grand Teton National Park. See UNITED STATES, *National Parks.*

Grand Trav'erse (grănd trăv'ērs). County in Michigan. See *Table* at MICHIGAN.

Grand Traverse Bay. Inlet of Lake Michigan bet. Leelanau and Antrim cos., NW Michigan.

Grand Trianon. See VERSAILLES.

Grand Turk. Island 7 m. long and town, * of Turks and Caicos Is. dependency of Jamaica; pop. (1938 est.) 1578.

Grand'view' (grănd'vū'). City, Jackson co., W Missouri, 5 mi. S of Kansas City; pop. 6027.

Grand'view' Heights (grănd'vū'). City, Franklin co., cen. Ohio, 6 m. NW of Columbus; pop. 8270.

Grand'ville (grănd'vĭl). City, Kent co., W Michigan, 5 m. SW of Grand Rapids; pop. 7975.

Grand Wash Cliffs (wŏsh). Chain of cliffs in NW Mohave co., NW Arizona, along E bank of **Grand Wash River** flowing SSW to Lake Mead.

Grange'mouth (grānj'mŭth; -mouth). Seaport burgh, Stirling co., cen. Scotland, on Forth estuary at terminus of the Forth and Clyde Canal 3 m. NE of Falkirk; pop. 15,305; shipbuilding yards.

Gran'ger (grān'jēr). City, Williamson co., cen. Texas, 26 m. S of Temple; pop. 1339.

Granges. See GRENCHEN.

Grange'ville (grānj'vĭl). City, ⊗ of Idaho co., N cen. Idaho; pop. 3642; lumber, wheat, livestock; gold mines.

Gra·ni'cus (gra-nī'kŭs). Small river in Mysia, NW Asia Minor, flowing N into the Propontis (Sea of Marmara); near its mouth Alexander defeated the Persians 334 B.C.

Gran'ite (grăn'ĭt). County in Montana. See *Table* at MONTANA.

Granite City. Industrial city, Madison co., SW Illinois, 7 m. N of East St. Louis; pop. 40,073; sheet steel, tin plate, graniteware.

Granite Dome. Peak 10,300 ft. in Sierra Nevada, in NE Tuolumne co., cen. California.

Granite Falls. 1 Waterfall 350 ft. in Mount Rainier National Park, W cen. Washington.
2 City, Chippewa and Yellow Medicine cos., ⊗ of Yellow Medicine co., SW Minnesota, on Minnesota river 13 m. SE of Montevideo; pop. 2728; hydroelectric power plant.
3 Town, Caldwell co., W North Carolina, 10 m. SSE of Lenoir; pop. 2644; textiles, hosiery, lumber.

Granite Peak. 1 Mountain 12,850 ft. in SE Park co., S Montana; highest point in state.
2 Mountain 8990 ft. in cen. Washoe co., NW Nevada.

Gran'ite·ville (grăn'ĭt·vĭl; *Sou. also* -v'l). Village, Aiken co., W South Carolina, ab. 5 m. NW of Aiken; pop. 1017; textiles.

Granja, La. See SAN ILDEFONSO.

Gran Ma'lin·dang' (grän mä'lēn·däng'). Mountain 7961 ft., Misamis prov., N Mindanao, Phil. Is., 12 m. NW of Misamis.

Gra·nol·lers' (grä'nŏ·[l]yĕrs'). Commune, Barcelona prov., NE Spain, 16 m. NNE of Barcelona; pop. 13,960.

Gran Pa'ra·di'so (gräm pä'rä·dē'zō); *Fr.* **Grand Pa'-ra'dis'** (grän' pá'rá'dē'). Peak 13,324 ft., highest of the Graian Alps, in NW Piedmont, NW Italy.

Gran Piedra, La. See LA GRAN PIEDRA.

Gran Qui·vi'ra National Monument (grăn kĭ-vēr'á). See QUIVIRA; UNITED STATES, *National Monuments.*

Gran Salar de Uyuni. = SALAR DE UYUNI.

Gran Sas'so d'I·ta'lia (grän säs'sō dē·tä'lyä). Mountain group, N Abruzzi e Molise, cen. Italy; includes Monte Corno 9560 ft., highest peak in the Apennines.

Gran Sir'te (grän sēr'tä). = Gulf of SIDRA.

Granson. See GRANDSON.

Grant (grănt). 1 Name of a parish in Louisiana and of counties in fourteen states of the U.S. See *Tables* at LOUISIANA, ARKANSAS, INDIANA, KANSAS, KENTUCKY,

MINNESOTA, NEBRASKA, NEW MEXICO, NORTH DAKOTA, OKLAHOMA, OREGON, SOUTH DAKOTA, WASHINGTON, WEST VIRGINIA, WISCONSIN.
2 Village, ⊗ of Perkins co., SW Nebraska; pop. 1166.

Grant, Mount (grănt). 1 Peak 8620 ft. in Flathead co., NW Montana.
2 Peak 9965 ft. in E Churchill co., W Nevada.
3 Peak 11,303 ft., W Mineral co., SW Nevada; highest in Wassuk Range.

Grant City. City, ⊗ of Worth co., NW Missouri; pop. 1061.

Gran'tham (grăn'tăm; -thăm; grän'tăm). Municipal borough, Parts of Kesteven, Lincolnshire, E England, on the Witham 23 m. E of Nottingham; pop. 23,405; malt; agricultural implements; battlefield where Oliver Cromwell won his first victory (Mar., 1643) over Royalists.

Grant Land (grănt). North section of Ellesmere I., N Franklin District, Northwest Territories, Canada—a former designation.

Grant Peak. Mountain 11,015 ft. in Yellowstone National Park, on E boundary, NW Wyoming.

Grants (grănts). Railroad town, Valencia co., W New Mexico, ab. 70 m. NW of Belen; pop. 10,274.

Grants'burg (grănts'bûrg). Village, ⊗ of Burnett co., NW Wisconsin; pop. 900.

Grants Pass (grănts). City, ⊗ of Josephine co., SW Oregon, on Rogue river 25 m. WNW of Medford; pop. 10,118; fruit growing, dairying, lumbering (fir, pine), mining (gold, silver, copper, platinum, chromium), salmon fishing and canning.

Grants'ville (grănts'vĭl). Town, ⊗ of Calhoun co., cen. West Virginia; pop. 866.

Gran Valira. See VALIRA.

Gran'ville (grăn'vĭl; *Sou. also* -v'l). 1 County in North Carolina. See *Table* at NORTH CAROLINA.
2 Village, Washington co., E New York, on Vermont border 50 m. NNE of Troy; pop. 2715; slate quarries.
3 Village, Licking co., cen. Ohio, 6 m. W of Newark; pop. 2868; Denison Univ. (1831; coed.).
4 Town, E New South Wales, SE Australia, 13 m. W of Sydney; pop. 19,717; railroad and manufacturing center.

Gran'ville' (grän'vēl'). Fortified seaport and manufacturing commune, Normandy, in Manche dept., NW France, on Gulf of Saint-Malo 30 m. SW of Saint-Lô; pop. 10,329; 12th-cent. church. Besieged by Vendeans 1793 and by English 1808; in World War II taken by Americans July 30, 1944.

Gran'ville Lake (grăn'vĭl). Lake 392 sq. m., NW Manitoba, Canada; an expansion of Churchill river.

Gran Zebrù. See KÖNIGSPITZE.

Grap'pa, Mount (gräp'pä); *Ital.* **Mon'te Grappa** (mōn'tä). Peak 5835 ft. in S Dolomites, NE Italy, 10 m. N of Bassano; severe fighting Oct. 24–30, 1918.

Gras, Lac de (lăk' dē grä'). Lake 674 sq. m. in cen. Mackenzie District, Northwest Territories, Canada; a source of the Coppermine river.

Graslitz. See KRASLICE.

Gras'mere (grăs'mẽr). 1 Lake 1 m. long in the Lake District, NW England, in Westmorland.
2 Former urban district on the lake, now in Lakes urban district; Wordsworth's home for many years.

Gras'moor (grăs'mŏŏr; -mōr) *or* **Grasmoor Hill.** Mountain 2791 ft. in Cumberland, NW England, in Lake District.

Gräs'ö' (grăs'ŭ'). Island off SE coast of Sweden, in Gulf of Bothnia N of Väddö I.; 34 sq. m.

Grasse (gräs). Manufacturing commune, Alpes-Maritimes dept., SE France, 17 m. W of Nice; pop. 20,481; winter resort; manufactures perfumes and essences. Independent republic in 12th cent.; became part of countship of Provence 1227.

Grass Valley (grăs). City, Nevada co., E California, 45 m. W of Lake Tahoe; pop. 4876; in gold-mining region.

Grass'y Bay (grăs'ĭ). Bay off NW coast of Bermuda I.

Grassy Knob. Peak 4768 ft. in Union co., N Georgia.

Gratianopolis. See GRENOBLE.

Gra'tiot (grăsh'ŭt). County in Michigan. See *Table* at MICHIGAN.

Gratz. See GRAZ.

Grau·bün'den (grou·bün'děn); *Fr.* **Gri'sons'** (grē'-zôN'). Largest canton of Switzerland; see *Table* at SWITZERLAND. In Alps (Rhaetian Alps in E); includes Engadine valley and sources of Rhine and Inn rivers; numerous mountain passes (Bernina, Oberalp, etc.). Formed largest part of ancient Roman province of Raetia (*q.v.*); conquered by Franks 6th cent.; became part of Germany early 10th cent.; accepted Reformation 1526; joined Swiss Confederation 1803.

Graudenz. See GRUDZIĄDZ.

Grau'pi·us, Mount (grô'pĭ·ŭs); *Lat.* **Mons Graupius** (mŏnz'). Mountain in ancient Caledonia, of uncertain location; scene of battle in which Galgacus was defeated 84 A.D. by Romans under Agricola, mentioned by Tacitus in his *Agricola;* has been also called, erroneously, Mount Grampius, the name which became applied to the Grampians of Scotland.

Grave Creek Mound. See MOUNDSVILLE.

Gra've·lines' (gràv'lēn'). Seaport commune, Nord dept., N France, 15 m. SW of Dunkerque; pop. 1844; produces paper, sugar, salt; cans vegetables, cures fish.

Grav'el Mountain (grăv'ĕl; -'l). Peak 13,600 ft. in Hinsdale co., SW Colorado.

Gra've·lotte' (gràv'lôt'). Village, Moselle dept., NE France, near Metz; pop. (1931) 365; scene of one of most important battles of Franco-Prussian War 1870 in which the French under Marshal Bazaine were forced to retreat into Metz by the Germans under King William.

Gravenhage, 's. See The HAGUE.

Gra'ven·hurst (grā'vĕn·hûrst). Town, Muskoka dist., SE Ontario, Canada, at foot of Lake Muskoka 10 m. SSW of Bracebridge; pop. 3005; center for campers and sportsmen.

Grav'en·stein (grăv'ĕn·stīn; *Ger.* grä'vĕn·shtīn); *Dan.* **Graa'sten** (grô'stĕn). Village, Aabenraa-Sönderborg co., SE Denmark, SSE of Aabenraa; pop. ab. 1000; formerly in Schleswig-Holstein, Germany.

Graves (grāvz). County in Kentucky. See *Table* at KENTUCKY.

Graves (gràv). District, Gironde dept., SW France; extends ab. 25 m. along the Garonne W and S of Bordeaux; gravelly soil, hence the name; famous red and white wines; adjoining on the SE is Sauternes (*q.v.*).

Graves'end' (gràv'zĕnd'; grāv'zĕnd'). Municipal borough, Kent, SE England, on Thames estuary 22 m. E of London; pop. 45,043; shipbuilding yards, fisheries, iron foundries; exports coal, lumber, lime; here (1617) Pocahontas died and was buried.

Graves'end' Bay (gràv'zĕnd'). Inlet of Lower New York Bay, SW Long I.

Gra'ville'-Sainte Ho'no'rine' (gràv'vĕl'sǎn'-tô'nô'-rēn'). Former commune, Seine-Inférieure dept., N France; pop. (1931) 37,853; now part of Le Havre.

Gra·vi'na in Pu'glia (grä·vē'nä ēm pōo'lyä). Commune, Bari prov., Apulia, SE Italy, 30 m. SW of Bari; pop. 23,208; cathedral; catacombs; castle built by Frederick II; limestone quarries.

Gray (grā). 1 Name of counties in two states of the U.S. See *Tables* at KANSAS and TEXAS.

2 Town, ⊗ of Jones co., cen. Georgia; pop. 1320.

3 Commune, Haute-Saône dept., E France, river port on Saône 30 m. SW of Vesoul; pop. (1931) 5826; founded in 7th cent.; gave its name to distinguished English family of Grey, or de Grey; church of 13th–15th cents., 17th-cent. château.

Gray'ling (grā'lǐng). City, ⊗ of Crawford co., N Michigan, 45 m. S of Traverse City; pop. 2015.

Gray Peak. 1 Mountain 4902 ft. in Adirondack Mts., Essex co., NE New York.

2 Mountain 10,300 ft. in Yellowstone National Park, NW Wyoming.

Grays Harbor (grāz). 1 Inlet of Pacific Ocean on SW coast of Grays Harbor co., W Washington.

2 County in Washington. See *Table* at WASHINGTON.

Grays Lake. Lake bet. Bonneville and Caribou cos., SE Idaho.

Grays Landing. Locality, Fayette co., SW Pennsylvania, on Monongahela river ab. 12 m. SW of Uniontown; pop. (1950) 3090.

Gray'son (grā's'n). 1 Name of counties in three states of the U.S. See *Tables* at KENTUCKY, TEXAS, VIRGINIA.

2 City, ⊗ of Carter co., NE Kentucky; pop. 1692.

Grays Peak (grāz). Mountain 14,274 ft. in Clear Creek and Summit cos., cen. Colorado; highest peak in Front Range.

Grays Thur'rock (thûr'ŭk) or **Grays.** Former urban district, Essex, SE England, on the Thames 18 m. E of London; pop. (1931) 18,173.

Gray'ville (grā'vǐl; -'l). City, Edwards and White cos., SE Illinois, on Wabash river; pop. 2280.

Graz (gräts); *earlier* **Gratz** (gräts). City, ✳ of Styria prov., Austria, on left bank of Mur river 87 m. SSW of Vienna; pop. (1939) 207,867; in Styrian Alps; medieval fortifications converted into promenades; 11th-cent. castle, 16th-cent. university buildings, 15th-cent. Gothic cathedral, 17th-cent. arsenal; important railroad center; railroad shops; manufactures iron and steel, paper, scientific and optical instruments, chemicals. Residence of early rulers of Styria.

Great Abaco. See ABACO.

Great Ad'mi·ral·ty Island (ăd'mǐ·rǎl·tǐ). = MANUS.

Great American Desert. Originally, a vaguely defined region, W United States, W of the Missouri river and sometimes including region W of the Rocky Mts.— so named from reports of early explorers to whom the territory appeared uninhabitable; later, the semiarid region bet. the Sierra Nevada and the Rockies, including the Great Basin; now, the region of deserts in SW Arizona and SE California.

Great Artesian Basin. = ARTESIAN BASIN.

Great Atlas. = *Grand Atlas:* see ATLAS MOUNTAINS.

Great Australian Bight. Bay ab. 600 m. wide on S coast of Australia; part of Indian Ocean.

Great Bahama. = GRAND BAHAMA island.

Great Bahama Bank. See BAHAMA BANKS.

Great Ban'da (băn'dà) or **Lon'tor** (lôn'tôr). Largest of the Banda Is., Indonesia; 7½ m. long; pop. 3155; volcanic in origin; with Bandanaira and Gunung Api encloses a small inland sea that forms the harbor of Bandanaira, one of best in the Malay Archipelago.

Great Banjak. See BANJAK ISLANDS.

Great Bar'ri·er Island (băr'ĭ·ĕr) or **O·te'a** (ô·tā'à). Island off E coast of N extension of North I., New Zealand, at E entrance to Hauraki Gulf.

Great Barrier Reef. Coral reef, the largest deposit of coral in the world, off NE coast of Queensland, Australia, ab. 1250 m. long; N end close to coast, S end ab. 150 m. out to sea; shallow waters inside reef strewn with coral islets or atolls, outside in Coral Sea waters of great depth; high tides and tremendous surf on outer edge.

Great Bar'ring·ton (băr'ǐng·tŭn). Town, Berkshire co., W Massachusetts, on Housatonic river 18 m. S of Pittsfield; pop. 6624; summer resort; William Cullen Bryant town clerk here 1815–25.

Great Ba'sin (bā's'n). Elevated region bet. the Wasatch and Sierra Nevada Mts., including most of Nevada and parts of Utah, California, Idaho, Wyoming, and Oregon; ab. 210,000 sq. m.; chief rivers the Humboldt, N Nevada, and the Sevier, SW cen. Utah; has no drainage to the ocean, chief drainage center Great Salt Lake; includes Great Salt Lake Desert, Carson Sink, Mojave Desert (*qq.v.*) and Death Valley (see UNITED STATES, *National Monuments*).

Great Bay. Inlet at extreme S tip of Ocean co., E New Jersey; connecting with Atlantic Ocean through Little Egg Inlet.

Great Bear Lake (bâr). Lake 12,200 sq. m. in NW cen. Mackenzie District, Northwest Territories, Canada; of very irregular shape, with several long arms, its greatest length ab. 175 m.; its outlet is **Great Bear River** (ab. 100 m. long), flowing W to the Mackenzie; frozen ab. 8 months in the year; abounds in fish. Discovered ab. 1800 and explored by Sir John Franklin 1825; radium ores discovered on its E shore 1929.

Great Belt (bĕlt). Strait bet. Sjælland and Fyn Is., connecting the Kattegat with the Baltic Sea; 40 m. long, averages 10 m. wide. Cf. LITTLE BELT.

Great Bend (bĕnd). City, ⊗ of Barton co., cen. Kansas, on Arkansas river 53 m. WNW of Hutchinson; pop. 16,670; on old Santa Fe trail; Coronado's Quivira (q.v.) generally located nearby.

Great Benin. See BENIN province, Nigeria.

Great Berg (bûrg). River, SW Cape Province, S Union of South Africa; rises E of Cape Town, flows N and W into St. Helena Bay.

Great Berk'hamp·stead (bûr'kăm[p]·stĕd; -stĭd; bär'-). Urban district, Hertfordshire, SE England, on Grand Junction Canal 26 m. NW of London; pop. 10,777; straw plaiting; chemical works; remains of 11th-cent. castle. Birthplace of William Cowper.

Great Bermuda. See BERMUDA.

Great Bitter Lake. See BITTER LAKES.

Great Black (blăk). River ab. 40 m. long, NW Maine; formed by junction of branches in NW Aroostook co., flows NE into St. John river.

Great Blasket. See BLASKET ISLANDS.

Great Brit'ain (brĭt'n). Largest island in Europe and kingdom coextensive with the island, comprising England, Scotland, and Wales; 88,619 sq. m.; pop. (1931) 44,795,357, (1951) 48,840,893. For the natural features, chief cities, and other data, see ENGLAND, SCOTLAND, WALES.

History: (1) *Britain:* Inhabited in pre-Roman times by Celtic-speaking peoples whose early religion was druidism (see STONEHENGE), its chief tribe in the S being the Britons (*Lat.* Brittones); invaded by Julius Caesar 55 and 54 B.C. but not subjugated until Roman conquest in 1st cent. A.D. (first attack by Claudius 43 A.D., last serious opposition the revolt 61 A.D. under Boadicea, Queen of the Iceni). In Roman times divided into southern Britain (corresponding to modern England and Wales), part of Roman Empire as province of Britannia, and northern Britain (see SCOTLAND) by Hadrian's Wall, constructed 120–123 A.D., extending from Solway Firth to mouth of the Tyne; southern Britain saw building of roads (see FOSSE WAY; WATLING STREET), establishment of cities, and introduction of Christianity; attacked by various barbarian tribes; gradually abandoned by Romans during first half of 5th cent., garrisons being withdrawn 410; invaded by Nordic tribes, the Angles, Saxons, and Jutes, who drove Celtic inhabitants into SW and W parts (Cornwall and Wales) and into Armorica (q.v.) on the Continent.

(2) *England:* After Anglo-Saxon invasions of 5th cent., southern Britain (except Wales in W and Strathclyde in NW) became divided into seven petty kingdoms, the Heptarchy (q.v.), which, beginning with Kent in 6th cent., were converted to Christianity; by end of 8th cent. dominated by Wessex, whose king Egbert (775?–839) was first to bring all English peoples under one overlord and whose king Alfred the Great (849–899) defeated the Danes under Guthrum. By Peace of Wedmore 878 Danes left only in NE part of England N of Watling Street (the Danelaw, reconquered by c. 954); English kingdom part of empire of Canute of Denmark 1017–35. Conquered 1066 by William of Normandy, who introduced centralized government; began conquest of Ireland under Henry II; by inheritance of its Norman rulers and by marriage 1152 of Henry II with Eleanor of Aquitaine acquired holdings in France, which, beginning with John's forfeiture of Normandy 1204 and ending with

fall of Calais 1558, were gradually lost during a period of many conflicts with the French including the Hundred Years' War 1337–1453 (see CRÉCY, POITOU, AGINCOURT, ORLÉANS); medieval England saw foundation of political and personal liberty in Magna Charta, signed June 15, 1215 by King John, and establishment of parliamentary system by Edward I, who summoned first parliament Nov. 27, 1295; subdued Wales 1284; torn by Wars of the Roses 1455–85 bet. houses of Lancaster and York, terminated with accession of Henry VII, first of the Tudor sovereigns. Broke with Rome under Henry VIII and established Church of England as state church; entered period of maritime and colonial expansion (see BRITISH EMPIRE) accelerated by defeat of Spanish Armada 1588; with exception of years as a Commonwealth (1649–60) ruled 1603–1714 by the Stuarts, who were rulers also of Scotland; effected formal union with Scotland 1707, *Great Britain* being adopted as official name of both island and kingdom.

(3) *Great Britain:* In 18th cent. completed evolution of modern party system and cabinet government, engaged in series of wars with Spain and France which resulted in imperial gains (esp. Canada and India), led in developments of Industrial Revolution, and lost American colonies. In 19th cent. enacted legislative union with Ireland 1801, thus forming the **United Kingdom of Great Britain and Ireland;** participated in wars to liberate Continent from French control 1793–1815 (see the PENINSULA; WATERLOO); passed 1832 first of series of Reform Bills (others 1867, 1884–85, 1918) leading to universal suffrage; repealed Corn Laws 1846, removing last barrier to free trade; as an ally of Turkey fought in Crimean War 1854–56; put down Sepoy Mutiny 1857–58 in India; fought Boer War 1899–1902 with the Transvaal and Orange Free State. Participated as one of the Allies in World War I Aug. 4, 1914–Nov. 11, 1918. Granted dominion status to Ireland 1922, establishing Irish Free State, and forming with Northern Ireland the **United Kingdom of Great Britain and Northern Ireland;** as result of Imperial Conferences, esp. of 1918, 1926, and 1930, agreed 1931 to the Statute of Westminster granting to the self-governing dominions equality of status within the British Commonwealth of Nations (q.v.); abandoned policy of free trade 1932. Participated as one of the Allies in World War II Sept. 3, 1939–Aug. 14, 1945; after the fall of France 1940, threatened by invasion by the Germans until German defeat in air war ("Battle of Britain") Aug. 8–Oct. 31, 1940; base for the Allied invasion of Normandy, NW France, June 1944. Gave up rule over India Aug. 15, 1947 and Burma Jan. 4, 1948.

Great Cataract. See CUNENE.

Great Central Plain. An area in the interior of the United States including a large portion of the upper Mississippi drainage basin; bounded on E by the Appalachian Plateau, on S by Gulf Plain and the Interior Highlands, on W by the Great Plains, and on N by Laurentian Highlands.

Great Cha·zy' (shā·zē'). River, Clinton co., NE corner of New York; flows out of Chazy Lake NE into Lake Champlain.

Great Co'co (kō'kō). Small island of the Andaman Is., separated from North Andaman I. by Coco Channel.

Great Co·lom'bi·a (kō·lŭm'bĭ·à); *Span.* **Gran Co·lom'bia** (gräng' kō·lôm'byä). Country of NW South America, 1819–30; formed as result of wars of Latin American states against Spain for independence, chiefly by activities of Gen. Simón Bolívar. Created by proclamation of Congress of Angostura Aug. 17, 1819; comprised what is now Colombia, Panama, Venezuela, and Ecuador (not completely independent of Spain until May 1822); at first known as Republic of Colombia but soon after as Great Colombia; ✳ Bogotá; terminated by secession of Venezuela 1829 and by establishment of Ecuador as independent state 1830. See COLOMBIA.

Great Com′o·ro (kŏm′ô·rō); *Fr.* **Grande′–Co′-more′** (gräɴd′kô′môr′). Largest of the Comoro Is., N Mozambique Channel; 38 m. long, ab. 12 m. wide; N part a plateau, alt. ab. 2000 ft.; in S is Karatala volcano; chief town Moroni.

Great Corn Island. See CORN ISLANDS.

Great Crag′gy Mountains (krăg′ĭ). Range, W North Carolina; includes **Craggy Dome** 6105 ft., Buncombe co., and nearby **Craggy Pinnacle** 5944 ft. Extending 10 m. along crest of the range are the **Craggy Gardens,** a dense stand of purple rhododendron.

Great Crosby. See CROSBY.

Great Dayak. See KAHAJAN.

Great Divide. See CONTINENTAL DIVIDE.

Great Dividing Range *or* **Eastern Highlands.** Entire extent of mountain ranges along E border of Australia, in Queensland, New South Wales, and Victoria; from 100 to 200 m. wide; includes Australian Alps (*q.v.*) in southeast part, with highest summits in Australia; at N end is Atherton Plateau (*q.v.*).

Great Doab. See DOAB.

Great Drif′field (drĭf′ēld). Urban district, East Riding, Yorkshire, N England; pop. 6888.

Great East. An extensive administrative unit of the Netherlands Indies 1938–49 including all islands of the archipelago E of Borneo and Lombok, i.e., Celebes, the Moluccas, the Lesser Sunda Is. from Soembawa eastward, and all Neth. New Guinea and adjacent islands; 293,020 sq. m.; pop. 8,585,365.

Great Egg Inlet (ĕg). Narrow strait leading from Atlantic Ocean into **Great Egg Bay**, bet. Cape May and Atlantic cos., S New Jersey, which receives the **Great Egg**, *or* **Great Egg Harbor, River** (ab. 40 m. long, flows SE, lower part in Atlantic co.).

Great Elobey. See ELOBEY.

Great End. Mountain 2984 ft. in Cumberland, NW England, in Lake District.

Greater Antilles. See WEST INDIES.

Greater Armenia. See Greater ARMENIA.

Greater Berlin. See BERLIN.

Greater Copenhagen. See COPENHAGEN.

Greater London. See LONDON.

Greater Mont′re·al′ (mŏn′trè·ôl′; mŭn′-). The urban area on the St. Lawrence, Quebec, Canada, consisting of the island of Montreal, pop. 1,320,232, including the city proper (pop. 1,021,520) and the enclosed municipalities (cities of Verdun, Outremont, and Westmount, and town of Mount Royal), the city of Lachine, and the remaining towns and villages on Montreal I., and the cities of Longueuil and St. Lambert and adjacent towns in Chambly co.; total pop. 1,395,400.

Greater New York. See NEW YORK city.

Greater Phrygia. See PHRYGIA.

Greater Shanghai. See SHANGHAI.

Greater Sunda Islands. See SUNDA ISLES.

Greater Walachia. See MUNTENIA.

Greater Win′ni·peg (wĭn′ĭ·pĕg). The urban district in S Manitoba, Canada, formed by Winnipeg (pop. 235,710) and St. Boniface and various suburbs; total pop. 354,069.

Great Exuma. See EXUMA.

Great Falls (fôlz). **1** See CUMBERLAND FALLS.
2 Cataract 35 ft. high in the Potomac river on boundary bet. Maryland and Virginia; in a series of rapids ab. 15 m. above Washington where the river descends ab. 90 ft.
3 Dam in Caney Fork river, forming **Great Falls Lake** bet. White, Van Buren, and Warren cos., cen. Tennessee. See *Table* at TENNESSEE VALLEY AUTHORITY.
4 City, ⊗ of Cascade co., cen. Montana, on Missouri river 12 m. N of the **Great Falls of the Missouri** (92 ft.); pop. 55,357; copper refining and smelting; coal, natural gas, silver, and lead deposits; U.S. Air Force base. College of Great Falls (1932; coed.).
5 Town, Chester co., N South Carolina, ab. 22 m. SE of Chester; pop. 3030; textile manufactures.

Great Fish (fĭsh). **1** River in Canada. See BACK RIVER.
2 River ab. 300 m. long, South-West Africa; rises S cen. part, flows S into Orange river.
3 River ab. 230 m. long in SE Cape Province, Union of South Africa; flows SSE into Indian Ocean NE of Port Alfred.

Great Gable. See Great GABLE.

Great Geyser. See GEYSIR.

Great Grimsby. = GRIMSBY, Lincolnshire, England.

Great Gua′na Cay (gwä′nả). One of the Bahama Is., in Atlantic Ocean bet. SE Andros I. and Cat I.

Great Har′wood (här′wŏŏd). Urban district, Lancashire, NW England, 22 m. N of Manchester; pop. 10,738.

Great Inagua. See INAGUA.

Great Indian Desert. = *Indian Desert* (see THAR DESERT).

Great I′saacs (ī′zȧks; -zĭks). Lighthouse (estab. 1859) on small cay in NW Bahama Is., NE of the Bimini.

Great Island. Island in Cork Harbour, S coast of Ireland; site of city of Cobh (Queenstown).

Great Kai Island. See KAI ISLANDS.

Great Kanawha. See KANAWHA.

Great Kapela. See KAPELA.

Great Karimata. See KARIMATA ISLANDS.

Great Karimoen. See KARIMOENDJOWO.

Great Karroo. See KARROO.

Great Kei (kā). River ab. 150 m. long, Cape Province, S Union of South Africa, W boundary of Transkeian Territories; flows SE to Indian Ocean.

Great Khingan Mountains. See KHINGAN mountains.

Great Lake, the. Largest lake in Tasmania, Australia, in cen. part S of the Great Western Mts.; 50 sq. m., ab. 15 m. long; 2880 ft. above sea level; drained by Ouse river, a tributary of the Derwent; dam and hydroelectric plant.

Great Lakes. **1** Chain of five lakes, Superior, Michigan, Huron, Erie, and Ontario (*qq.v.*), in cen. North America; through the chain (except for Lake Michigan, which is wholly within the U.S.) runs the U.S.-Canada boundary; drained by St. Lawrence river. Discovered and explored in 17th cent. by French, Champlain being probably first to reach upper lakes 1615; Lake Michigan explored by Nicolet 1634; founding of Detroit (*q.v.*) 1701 assured French control of region until Canada was ceded to British 1763; Lakes Ontario and Erie scenes of naval warfare bet. U.S. and British during War of 1812; disarmament effected under terms of Rush-Bagot Agreement 1817; came to be of great importance as commercial link bet. eastern and northwestern U.S., especially after building of steamships and of Erie Canal 1825.
2 Group of large lakes chiefly in Great Rift Valley, E cen. Africa, including esp. Lakes Rudolf, Albert, Victoria, Tanganyika, and Nyasa.

Great Lakes Naval Training Station. See WAUKEGAN, Illinois.

Great Lyakhov. See LYAKHOV ISLANDS.

Great Mal′vern (môl′vẽrn; mô′vẽrn). Town in urban district of Malvern, Worcestershire, W cen. England; pop. 21,681.

Great Mar′low (mär′lō). Parish, part of Marlow urban dist., Buckinghamshire, S cen. England, near Windsor; residence of Shelley and Peacock.

Great Meadows. Level area on the Youghiogheny river, ab. 10 m. E of present Uniontown, SW Pennsylvania; site of Fort Necessity, built 1754 under Washington's supervision in campaign against French at Fort Duquesne.

Great Miami. See MIAMI river.

Great Miquelon. See MIQUELON ISLAND.

Great Natoena. See NATOENA ISLANDS.

Great Neck (nĕk). Residential village, Nassau co., SE New York, on N shore of Long I.; pop. 10,171.

Great Neck Estates. Residential village, Nassau co., SE New York, on N shore of Long I.; pop. 3262.

Great Neck Plaza. Residential village, Nassau co., SE New York, on N shore of Long I., near Great Neck; pop. 4948.

Great Nethe. See NETHE.

Great Nic'o·bar (nĭk'ō·bär). One of the Nicobar Is. (*q.v.*).

Great Novgorod. See NOVGOROD city.

Great Ormes Head (ôrmz). Cape extending into Irish Sea on N coast of Wales, E of Anglesey I.; lighthouse.

Great Ouse. See OUSE.

Great Pamir. = PAMIR.

Great Pat'er·nos'ter Point (păt'ẽr·nŏs'tẽr; pä'tẽr-). Cape on W coast of Cape Province, Union of South Africa, S of Saint Helena Bay.

Great Peconic Bay. See PECONIC BAY.

Great Pee Dee. = PEE DEE.

Great Plains. The continental slope of cen. North America (United States and Canada) extending E from the Rocky Mts. to the margin of the Central Plains in the U.S. and to the margin of the Laurentian Highlands in Canada; N to S extent is from delta of Mackenzie river to S Texas; characterized by smooth, treeless plains traversed by broad, shallow valleys of rivers rising in Rocky Mts., but in some sections with sand hills (esp. in NW Nebraska), buttes, and badlands.

Great Point. Northeastern point of Nantucket I., Massachusetts.

Great Rann of Cutch. See Rann of CUTCH.

Great Re'dang *or* **Redang** (rä'däng). Island off E coast of Malay Penin. in South China Sea.

Great Rift Valley (rĭft). A great depression extending from valley of the Jordan in Palestine S to Mozambique, SE Africa—a geological rather than a geographical term, marking a series of geological faults which are the result of great volcanic action; includes Dead Sea, Gulf of 'Aqaba, Red Sea, the chain of lakes in S Ethiopia, Lake Rudolf and the chain of small lakes S of it in Kenya and Tanganyika which are in eastern rift valley. and Lakes Albert, Edward, Kivu, Tanganyika, and Nyasa in western rift valley. Below sea level at Dead Sea but in Africa in some places at over 6000 ft. (as at Lake Naivasha in the eastern rift which has elevation of 6135 ft.); esp. marked in cen. Kenya in the eastern rift valley bet. 1°N and 1°S where it has perpendicular cliffs several thousand feet high.

Great Saint Ber·nard' (sânt bẽr·närd'). Alpine pass. See ALPS.

Great Salt Desert (sôlt). = DASHT-I-KAVIR.

Great Salt Lake. Lake in Great Basin of United States, N Utah, in Box Elder, Tooele, Salt Lake, Davis, and Weber cos.; ab. 80 m. long, 35 m. wide; 2360 sq. m.; greatest depth 60 ft.; waters strongly saline; elevation, 4218 ft.; receives Bear, Jordan, and Weber rivers from E; no outlet; has a number of islands, including Antelope Island (15½ m. long). Discovered by James Bridger 1824.

Great Salt Lake Desert. Broad, flat, low area SW of Great Salt Lake, N Utah; barren and uncultivated.

Great Salt Plains Dam. Dam across Salt Fork of Arkansas river in Grant co., N Oklahoma, forming reservoir 10 m. long for flood control and conservation.

Great Sand Dunes National Monument. See UNITED STATES, *National Monuments.*

Great Sandy Desert. 1 = RUB' AL KHALI.
2 Tract 300 by 500 m. of waterless country, N cen. Western Australia.

Great Sandy Island. See FRASER ISLAND.

Great Sangir. See SANGIHE ISLANDS.

Great Scheidegg. See SCHEIDEGG.

Great Schütt (shüt); *Czech.* **Vel'ký Žit'ný** (vĕl'y·kē zhĭt'nē); *Hung.* **Csal'ló·köz'** (chŏl'lō·kûz'). Island in SW Slovakia, Czechoslovakia, formed by arms of Danube river to the N of the main stream extending from Bratislava to Komárom; 53 m. long, bet. 9 and 18 m. wide.

Great Sea, the. The Mediterranean—esp. in Biblical usage (as in *Num.* xxxiv. 6).

Great Ser'pent Mound (sûr'pĕnt). Prehistoric earthwork, Adams co., S Ohio; ab. 1330 ft. long; curls like a snake; 20 ft. wide at base, averages ab. 3 ft. high; walls indicate possibility it was used for defense; probably mostly used in religious worship; in Serpent Mound State Park.

Great Sit'kin (sĭt'kĭn). Small island NE of Adak I. in Andreanof Is., Aleutian Is.

Great Skellig. See SKELLIGS.

Great Slave Lake (slāv). Lake in S Mackenzie District, Northwest Territories, Canada; 10,719 sq. m.; ab. 300 m. long, 50 m. wide; of irregular shape, with several long arms; outlet the Mackenzie, flowing from its W end; on S receives Slave river, the outlet of Lake Athabaska, and on SW the Hay river. Discovered 1771.

Great Slave River. See SLAVE river.

Great Smok'y Mountains *or* **Great Smok'ies** (smōk'ĭ, -ĭz). Range of the Appalachian Mts. extending along North Carolina-Tennessee boundary; highest peak Clingmans Dome 6642 ft.; remarkable for its flora, includes largest tract of hardwood in America and largest virgin forest of red spruce. Has been set aside as **Great Smoky Mountains National Park:** see UNITED STATES, *National Parks.*

Great Sound. Body of water enclosed by curve at W end of Bermuda I.

Great South Bay. Long narrow inlet of Atlantic Ocean bet. Fire I. and S shore of Long I., New York.

Great Trail. Indian trail from Fort Pitt at junction of Allegheny and Monongahela rivers to present site of Detroit; used by white men until Cumberland Road opened.

Great Tupper Lake. See TUPPER LAKES.

Great Vic·to'ri·a Desert (vĭk·tōr'ĭ·å). Desert region ab. 450 m. E to W in SE Western Australia and W South Australia; average height 500 to 1000 ft. sloping to Nullarbor Plain on S.

Great, *or* **Chinese, Wall;** *Chin.* **Chang–chêng** (jäng'-chŭng'). Famous defensive wall 20 to 50 ft. high, 15 to 25 ft. thick, with towers at intervals, extending for 1250 m. bet. Mongolia and China Proper, built in the 3d cent. B.C. (completed 204 B.C.) by the emperor Shih Huang Ti; actual length, including branches and windings, more than 2000 m.; built by 300,000 men, mostly criminals; now of value only as marking a geographical boundary. Had four important gates: Shanhaikwan, now Linyu (at E end), Nankow (leading to Wanchuan), Yen Mên (N Shansi), and Kiayukwan (at extreme W, in Kansu).

Great Wass (wŏs). Island in Atlantic Ocean off coast of Washington co., SE Maine.

Great Western Mountains. Mountain range in N cen. Tasmania, Australia, extending NW and SE along N border of the lake region; highest ab. 4200 ft.

Great Whale (hwāl). River 365 m. long, cen. and W Quebec prov. Canada; flows W into SE Hudson Bay; outlet of Bienville Lake.

Great Yarmouth. See YARMOUTH.

Great Zab. See Great ZAB.

Gre'co, Cape (grä'kō; grĕk'ō; grē'kō). Southeastern point of Cyprus, at S end of Famagusta Bay.

Gre'co Mi·la·ne'se (grâ'kō mē·lä·nā'sâ). Town, Milan commune, Italy, suburb of Milan; pop. (1931) 27,610.

Gredos, Sierra de. See SIERRA DE GREDOS.

Greece (grēs); *Gr.* **Hel'las** (hĕl'ās); *Mod. Gr.* **El·las'** (â·läs'). Kingdom, SE Europe, SW part of Balkan Penin.; with Ionian Is. and Crete 50,147 sq. m.; pop. (1938 est.) 7,108,814. (1940 est.) 7,535,000; ✱ Athens; bounded on N by Albania, Yugoslavia, and Bulgaria, on NE by Turkey in Europe, on E by Aegean Sea, on S by Mediterranean, and on W by Ionian Sea; forms a peninsula of irregular shape, with many deep indentations in coast line and two large peninsulas projecting from it: in NE Chalcidice with its three long projections, in S the Peloponnesus (in medieval times Morea), joined to N

GREECE

Statute Miles

0   25   50   75   100

⊛ Capitals

PUBLISHED BY G. & C. MERRIAM COMPANY
SPRINGFIELD, MASS.
PREPARED BY J. W. CLEMENT CO., BUFFALO, N.Y.

Longitude East from Greenwich

part by Isthmus of Corinth and ending in three long peninsulas, the cen. one ending in Cape Matapan, the southernmost point of the mainland. Divided into 10 geographical divisions which are in turn divided into the following departments (for pronunciation of their names, see their individual entries):

NAME	LOCATION	AREA[1]	POP.[1]	CAPITAL
Achaea and Elis	NW Peloponnesus	2,065	361,845	Patras
Aetolia and Acarnania	W Central Greece and Euboea	3,004	255,862	Mesolóngion
Arcadia	cen. Peloponnesus	1,686	187,327	Tripolis
Argolis and Corinth[2]	NE Peloponnesus	1,942	190,184	Nauplia
Arta	S Epirus	670	62,462	Arta
Attica and Boeotia[3]	E Central Greece and Euboea	2,514	1,144,330	Athens
Canea	W Crete	921	126,654	Canea
Cephalonia[4]	Ionian Is.	342	72,140	Argostolion
Chalcidice	S Macedonia	1,267	77,222	Polygyros
Chios[5]	Aegean Is.	355	82,914	Chios
Corfu[6]	Ionian Is.	244	114,620	Corfu
Cyclades	Cyclades	966	146,987	Hermoupolis
Drama	N cen. Macedonia	1,349	139,583	Drama
Euboea[7]	Central Greece and Euboea	1,586	179,523	Chalcis
Evros[8]	Western Thrace	1,643	151,260	Alexandroúpolis
Florina	W Macedonia	1,412	152,809	Florina
Hérákleion	E cen. Crete	993	162,978	Candia
Ioannina	N Epirus	2,317	159,020	Ioannina
Kavalla[9]	NE Macedonia	858	139,309	Kavalla
Kozánē	W Macedonia	2,456	202,849	Kozánē
Laconia	SE Peloponnesus	1,595	148,499	Sparta
Larissa	E Thessaly	2,922	312,272	Larissa
Lasithion	E Crete	732	75,914	Hagios Nikólaos
Lesbos[10]	Aegean Is.	825	177,214	Mytilene
Messenia	SW Peloponnesus	1,315	297,191	Kalamata
Mount Athos	Acte penin., Macedonia	111	4,858	Karyai
Pella	W Macedonia	1,039	117,990	Edessa
Phthiotis and Phocis	cen. Central Greece and Euboea	2,547	219,454	Lamia
Preveza[11]	W Epirus	624	77,368	Preveza
Rethýmnē	W cen. Crete	553	76,141	Rethymnon
Rhodope	Western Thrace	1,719	203,629	Komotinē
Samos[12]	Aegean Is.	306	77,858	Vathy
Serrai	cen. Macedonia	1,622	216,569	Serrai
Thessalonike	W cen. Macedonia	3,358	539,697	Salonika
Trikkala	W Thessaly	2,226	249,748	Trikkala
Zante[13]	Ionian Is.	156	44,750	Zante

[1] Area in sq. m. Pop. is 1938 est.
[2] Includes Antikýthēra, Cerigo, Hydra, and Spetsai Is.
[3] Includes Aegina, Poros, and Salamis Is.
[4] Comprises Cephalonia and Ithaca Is.
[5] Comprises Chios I.
[6] Comprises Corfu and Paxos Is.
[7] Comprises Euboea I. and the Northern Sporades.
[8] Includes Samothrace.
[9] Includes Thasos I.
[10] Comprises Lesbos, Lemnos, and Hagios Evstrátios Is.
[11] Includes Leukas I.
[12] Comprises Samos and Ikaria Is.
[13] Comprises Zante I.

Islands: Near coast the Ionian Is. on W and S and Euboea on E; in Aegean Sea the large groups of Cyclades, North and South Sporades, and Dodecanese (*q.v.*); Thasos, Samothrace, and Lemnos in N Aegean; Lesbos, Chios, and Samos in E Aegean off W coast of Turkey in Asia; Crete to the SE in the Mediterranean. *Mountains:* Pindus Mts. in Epirus; peaks of Olympus and Ossa on E coast; Othrys range, Oeta and Parnassus in cen. part; and Cyllene and Erymanthus, with many ranges, in the Peloponnesus. *Chief rivers:* Peneus, Achelous, Arakhthos, Cephisus, and Alpheus; most rivers short. *Chief products:* Mainly agricultural; grains, tobacco, cotton, fruits (esp. currants), wine. *Chief cities:* Athens (Athēnai), Salonika (Thessaloníkē), Patras (Patrai), Kavalla, Candia (Hérákleion).

Divided in ancient times into regions which were at times independent kingdoms: Thrace, Macedonia, Epirus, Thessaly, Peloponnesus, and which were, esp. in S Greece, made up of many subdivisions (provinces or states), some of great historical importance in the classic period, as, Attica, Boeotia, Phocis, Aetolia, Achaea,

Corinth, Elis, Arcadia, Laconia, and Messenia. *Chief ancient cities:* Athens, Sparta, Corinth, Thebes, Piraeus. [In modern Greece many names are somewhat changed in form because of difference in transliteration systems of ancient and modern Greek. In this book the form preferred for the more important ancient names is generally the common, well-known spelling.]

History: Mainland site of early civilizations of Aegean origin (see MYCENAE, TIRYNS); c. 1500–1000 B.C. invaded by Greeks, a people from NW of Balkan Mts., who soon formed many small independent city-kingdoms; in age of commercial and industrial advance c. 750–550 B.C., Greek city-states founded colonies in N Aegean, on shores of Black Sea, in S Asia Minor and Cyprus, in Nile delta and near Cyrene, in N shores of W Mediterranean, and, most important, in S Italy (see MAGNA GRAECIA) and Sicily; ancient Greece never achieved political unity, but Sparta in Peloponnesus and Athens in Attica became predominant states while all states participated in shifting and loosely organized leagues; finally repulsed Persian invasions at Plataea in 479 B.C.; Athenian empire developed in 5th cent. B.C. and was broken by Peloponnesian Wars 460–404 B.C.; in 4th cent. B.C., Greek states became dependent upon Macedon until liberated by Rome at Cynoscephalae 197 B.C.; gradually conquered by Rome which set up provinces of Epirus, Achaea, and Macedonia; part of Byzantine Empire until 1204 when Constantinople was captured at end of Fourth Crusade and Baldwin I became first of the Latin emperors; again part of Byzantine Empire (*q.v.*) 1261 until its fall 1453; became part of Ottoman Empire when conquered by Turks 1456; modern Greek kingdom won independence from Turkey in war 1821–29; received Ionian Is. 1864, Thessaly and part of Epirus 1881; defeated by Turkey in brief war over Crete (*q.v.*) which Greece finally annexed 1913; as result of Balkan Wars 1912–13, gained several islands in Aegean and territory in Macedonia; declared war on Germany 1916; at close of war with Turkey 1920–22, gave back E Thrace, İmroz, and Bozcaada and claim to Dodecanese (former gains by Treaty of Sèvres 1920); exchanged population with Turkey 1923–30; republic 1924–35; joined Balkan Pact 1934; restored monarchy 1935; invaded by Italy 1940 and conquered by Germany 1941; liberated by Greek and British troops Sept. 24–Oct. 30, 1944; recalled King George to throne by plebiscite 1946; received Dodecanese 1947.

Gree'ley (grē'li). **1** Name of counties in two states of the U.S. See *Tables* at KANSAS and NEBRASKA.
2 Manufacturing city, ⊗ of Weld co., N Colorado; pop. 26,314; Colorado State College (1889; coed.).
3 *or* **Greeley Center.** Village, ⊗ of Greeley co., E cen. Nebraska; pop. 656.

Green (grēn). **1** River 120 m. long, N Illinois; flows SW out of Lee co. to Rock river.
2 Navigable river 360 m. long, flowing from cen. Lincoln co., E cen. Kentucky, W and NW into Ohio river.
3 River, W cen. Washington; flows W through S King co. to unite with White river and form Duwamish river.
4 River 730 m. long in W United States; flows from Wind River Mts., NE Sublette co., W Wyoming, S into Utah where it turns E, makes a loop in NW corner of Colorado, then turns SW and S in Utah to enter Colorado river on boundary bet. Wayne and San Juan cos., SE Utah.
5 Name of counties in two states of the U.S. See *Tables* at KENTUCKY and WISCONSIN.

Green Bank. Locality, Pocahontas co., E West Virginia, ab. 20 m. NE of Marlinton; site of National Radio Astronomy Observatory.

Green Bay. **1** Inlet of NW Lake Michigan, on shore of S Michigan penin. and NE Wisconsin; ab. 120 m. long, 10 to 20 m. wide, average depth ab. 100 ft.; from early visits by French explorers (see WISCONSIN) was head of important portage route bet. Great Lakes and Mississippi river by way of Fox and Wisconsin rivers (*qq.v.*).

2 City, ⊗ of Brown co., E Wisconsin, on S end of Green Bay at mouth of Fox river; pop. 62,888; port for river and lake steamers; meat-packing plants, fisheries, shipyard, limestone quarries; manufactures paper, iron and steel, cheese, building materials. Visited by Jean Nicolet 1634; settled by Langlade 1745, oldest settlement in Wisconsin; in region controlled by British 1763; ceded to U.S. 1783; fur-trading center; occupied by British in War of 1812; Fort Howard, U.S. military post, built 1816; incorp. as city 1854.

Green'belt' (grēn'bĕlt'). City, Prince Georges co., S cen. Maryland; pop. 7479; built 1935-38 by U.S. government to provide low-priced housing for families of moderate income.

Green'bri'er (grēn'brī'ẽr). **1** River ab. 175 m. long, SE West Virginia; rises in N Pocahontas co., flows SW into New river near Hinton.
2 County in West Virginia. See *Table* at WEST VIRGINIA.

Green'cas'tle (grēn'kås''l). **1** City, ⊗ of Putnam co., W cen. Indiana, 32 m. ENE of Terre Haute; pop. 8506; agriculture; lumbering. DePauw Univ. (1837; coed., Methodist).
2 Borough, Franklin co., S Pennsylvania, 12 m. S of Chambersburg; pop. 2988; textiles, machinery.

Green Cove Springs (kōv). City, ⊗ of Clay co., NE Florida, on St. Johns river 25 m. S of Jacksonville; pop. 4233; sulfur spring.

Green'dale (grēn'dāl). **1** Town, Dearborn co., SE Indiana, suburb of Lawrenceburg on Ohio river; pop. 2861; distilleries.
2 Residential village, Milwaukee co., SE Wisconsin; pop. 6843; built by U.S. government as experiment in city planning and low-cost housing; incorp. 1938.

Greene (grēn). Name of counties in fourteen states of the U.S. See *Tables* at ALABAMA, ARKANSAS, GEORGIA, ILLINOIS, INDIANA, IOWA, MISSISSIPPI, MISSOURI, NEW YORK, NORTH CAROLINA, OHIO, PENNSYLVANIA, TENNESSEE, VIRGINIA.

Greene'ville (grēn'vĭl). Town, ⊗ of Greene co., NE Tennessee, 30 m. WSW of Johnson City; pop. 11,759; burley tobacco market; Tusculum Coll. (1794; coed.). Capital of State of Franklin 1785-87; home of Andrew Johnson, his homestead, tailor shop, and burial place now set aside as national monument (see *Andrew Johnson National Monument* at UNITED STATES, *National Monuments*).

Greeneville Dam. See *Table* at TENNESSEE VALLEY AUTHORITY.

Green'field (grēn'fēld). **1** City, ⊗ of Hancock co., cen. Indiana, 20 m. E of Indianapolis; pop. 9049; cans tomatoes; birthplace of James Whitcomb Riley.
2 City, ⊗ of Adair co., SW cen. Iowa, 50 m. WSW of Des Moines; pop. 2243.
3 Town, ⊗ of Franklin co., NW Massachusetts, on Connecticut river 34 m. N of Springfield; pop. 17,690; manufactures taps and dies and other hardware, leather goods, silverware. Founded 1686, originally part of Deerfield.
4 City, ⊗ of Dade co., SW Missouri; pop. 1172.
5 Industrial village, Highland co., S Ohio, 21 m. W of Chillicothe; pop. 5422; stone quarries.
6 Town, Weakley co., NW Tennessee, 30 m. WSW of Paris; pop. 1779.
7 Town, La Crosse co., W Wisconsin, SE of Winona, Minnesota; pop. 17,636.

Greenfield Park. Town, Chambly co., S Quebec, Canada, 4 m. E of Montreal on opp. side of St. Lawrence; pop. 3379.

Green Harbor. Settlement on harbor, W end of Ice Fjord, West Spitsbergen I.

Green'hills' (grēn'hĭlz'). Village, Hamilton co., SW corner of Ohio, near Cincinnati; pop. 5407; completed 1937 as a federal government project in low-cost housing.

Green Island. Industrial village, Albany co., E New York, on an island in Hudson river 8 m. N of Albany; pop. 3533; automobile assembling plant, iron factories.

Green Islands. Group of small islands in extreme N Solomon Is., W Pacific Ocean, 45 m. NNW of Buka I.; largest Nissan I.; ab. 30 sq. m.; pop. (1930) 1548; belong to Kieta dist. of Territory of New Guinea.

Green Lake. 1 Lake ab. 7 m. long in Green Lake co., cen. Wisconsin, 25 m. W of Fond du Lac.
2 County in Wisconsin. See *Table* at WISCONSIN.
3 Village and resort, ⊗ of Green Lake co., cen. Wisconsin, at NE end of Green Lake; pop. 953.

Green'land (grēn'lănd; -lånd'); *Dan.* **Grön'land'** (grûn'lån'). Island, largest in the world (considering Australia as a continent), NE of North America and generally considered as belonging to that continent; 839,800 sq. m. (ice sheet ab. 707,900 sq. m., coast 114,600 sq. m., coast islands 17,300 sq. m.); pop. 16,630, (1953) 25,302; length 1660 m. from Cape Farewell to Cape Morris Jesup, width ab. 800 m. at widest part; largely within Arctic Circle. A Danish possession; formerly administered as a colony; by revised constitution of 1953 made an integral part of Danish kingdom; ✻ Godthaab, secondary administrative center Godhavn. Ice sheet at least 1000 ft. thick; highest points of land 5000 to 9000 ft. Coast line much indented with deep, long fiords, some having steep walls 4000 ft. high. Has many islands along shores and many glaciers on both E and W coasts. Inhabitants chiefly Eskimos, with a few hundred Danish settlers and officials; natives engaged in hunting, sealing, whaling, and fishing; cryolite mines near Ivigtut largest in world. Chief settlements, in addition to two divisional capitals, Julianehaab, Upernavik, Sukkertoppen, Frederikshaab, Angmagssalik, Narsarssuak.

History: Discovered and colonized in 10th cent. A.D. by Eric the Red, Norse leader, whose son, Leif Ericson, was traditional discoverer of North America; visited by Davis, Hudson, Baffin ab. end of 16th cent.; from 19th cent., explored by Kane, Hall, Nordenskjöld, by Nansen who made first crossing of Greenland 1888, Peary, and other expeditions of Danish, American, Norwegian, German, and British nationality; visited by Danish expedition of Mylius-Erichsen 1902-07; Danish East Greenland Co., founded 1919, established posts; made crown colony 1924 by Denmark who claimed full sovereignty 1921; eastern Greenland, annexed by Norway 1931, awarded to Denmark by decision of World Court 1933; after occupation of Denmark by Germans in 1940, subject of an agreement Apr. 9, 1941 (ratified by Danish Rigsdag May 1945) by which U.S. was permitted to establish air bases, weather stations, etc., necessary for protection of the island and preservation of Danish sovereignty there during World War II.

Greenland Sea. Section of Arctic Ocean off NE coast of Greenland; now generally considered as part of Norwegian Sea.

Green'lawn' (grēn'lôn'). Urban community (unincorporated), Suffolk co., New York, on Long I. E of Huntington; pop. 5422.

Green'lee (grēn'lē; -lē). County in Arizona. See *Table* at ARIZONA.

Green Lowther. See The LOWTHERS.

Green'ly (grēn'lĭ). Small island in Quebec prov., Canada, at W end of Strait of Belle Isle opp. the Labrador line.

Green Mountain. 1 Peak 5101 ft. in Lawrence co., W South Dakota.
2 See ASCENSION island.

Green Mountain Dam *and* **Reservoir.** See UNITED STATES, *Dams and Reservoirs.*

Green Mountains. A range of the Appalachian system, extending from Canada through Vermont into W Massachusetts; highest peak Mount Mansfield 4393 ft.

Green'ock (grĭn'ŭk; grēn'-; grēn'-). Seaport and manufacturing burgh, Renfrew co., SW Scotland, on S shore of the Firth of Clyde; pop. (1951) 76,299; shipbuilding; iron foundries, distilleries, sugar refineries, textile and paper mills. Birthplace of James Watt.

Green'point' (grēn'point'). District, N Brooklyn borough, New York City, bounded on W by the East river; formerly a shipbuilding center, place where *Monitor* was built (launched Jan. 30, 1862).

Green' Point'. Town, W suburb of Cape Town, Cape Province, Republic of South Africa. See Sea Point.

Green'port (grēn'pōrt). Village, Suffolk co., SE New York, on N extension of Long I. bet. Long Island Sound and Gardiners Bay; pop. 2608; summer resort; oyster and fishing industries; shipbuilding.

Green River. 1 See Green, above.

2 Town, ⊗ of Sweetwater co., SW Wyoming, on Green river 15 m. W of Rock Springs; pop. 3497; lumbering, coal mining; livestock.

Green River Mountain. Peak 10,175 ft. in N Sublette co., W Wyoming.

Greens'bor'o (grēnz'bûr'ō). 1 Town, ⊗ of Hale co., W Alabama, 35 m. S of Tuscaloosa; pop. 3081; settled 1816, incorp. 1823; former site (1856–1918) of Southern Univ. (now Birmingham-Southern Coll. at Birmingham); ante bellum mansions.

2 City, ⊗ of Greene co., NE cen. Georgia, 29 m. SSE of Athens; pop. 2773; cotton mills.

3 City, ⊗ of Guilford co., N cen. North Carolina, 26 m. E of Winston-Salem; pop. 119,574; made ⊗ 1808; textile mills, terra cotta works, foundries, machine shops, lumber mills. Greensboro College (1838; coed.), Woman's College of the Univ. of N.C. (1891), Agricultural and Technical College of N.C. (1891; coed.), Bennett College (1873; women). Guilford Courthouse National Military Park (see United States, *National Historical Parks*) nearby.

Greens'burg (grēnz'bûrg). 1 City, ⊗ of Decatur co., SE cen. Indiana, 18 m. SE of Shelbyville; pop. 6605.

2 City, ⊗ of Kiowa co., S Kansas; pop. 1988.

3 City, ⊗ of Green co., cen. Kentucky; pop. 2334.

4 Town, ⊗ of Saint Helena parish, E Louisiana; pop. 512.

5 City, ⊗ of Westmoreland co., SW Pennsylvania, 27 m. ESE of Pittsburgh; pop. 17,383; founded 1785; coal and coke industries; manufactures metal products, glass, electric power equipment; Seton Hill College (1883; women).

Greens'fork' (grēnz'fôrk'). Township, Randolph co., E Indiana; pop. 1303; elevation 1240 ft., highest point in state.

Greens Peak (grēnz). Mountain 10,115 ft. in S Apache co., E Arizona.

Greens Reservoir (grēnz). Reservoir in SW Pinal co., S cen. Arizona.

Greens'ville (grēnz'vĭl; *Sou.* also -v'l). County in Virginia. See *Table* at Virginia.

Green'tree' (grēn'trē'). Borough, Allegheny co., SW Pennsylvania, 4 m. W of Pittsburgh; pop. 5226.

Green'up (grēn'ŭp). 1 County in Kentucky. See *Table* at Kentucky.

2 City, its ⊗, NE Kentucky; pop. 1240.

Green'ville (grēn'vĭl; *Sou.* also -v'l). 1 County in South Carolina. See *Table* at South Carolina.

2 Commercial city, ⊗ of Butler co., S Alabama, 42 m. SW of Montgomery; pop. 6894; settled 1819, incorp. 1889; cotton, pecans.

3 City, ⊗ of Meriwether co., W Georgia; pop. 726.

4 City, ⊗ of Bond co., SW cen. Illinois, 47 m. ENE of East St. Louis; pop. 4569; Greenville College (1892; coed.).

5 City, ⊗ of Muhlenberg co., W Kentucky, 30 m. NNE of Hopkinsville; pop. 3198; tobacco; coal mining.

6 Town, Piscataquis co., N cen. Maine, on Moosehead Lake 60 m. NW of Bangor; pop. 2025.

7 City, Montcalm co., cen. Michigan, 25 m. ENE of Grand Rapids; pop. 7440.

8 City, ⊗ of Washington co., W Mississippi, on Mississippi river; pop. 41,502; cotton.

9 City, ⊗ of Wayne co., SE Missouri; pop. 282.

10 City, ⊗ of Pitt co., E North Carolina, 33 m. SE of Rocky Mount; pop. 22,860; market for tobacco, cotton, corn. East Carolina Coll. (1907; coed.).

11 City, ⊗ of Darke co., W Ohio, 32 m. NW of Dayton; pop. 10,585; railroad center; manufactures stoves, knit goods, machinery. On site of Fort Greenville (built 1793) where Anthony Wayne's treaty with Indians was signed 1795, and of Shawnee Indian village, home of Tecumseh; became county seat 1809.

12 Borough, Mercer co., W Pennsylvania, 27 m. N of New Castle; pop. 8765; settled 1796; manufactures railroad cars, steel products, machinery; Thiel College (1866; coed.).

13 City, ⊗ of Greenville co., NW South Carolina, 100 m. NW of Charleston; pop. 66,188; textile center; manufactures cotton, rayon, and worsted goods, textile machinery, clothing, cottonseed oil, peanut products; chemicals and patent medicines; tourist resort in piedmont region of Blue Ridge; U.S. Air Force base. Furman Univ. (1826; coed.); Bob Jones Univ. (1927; coed.).

14 City, ⊗ of Hunt co., NE Texas, 43 m. NE of Dallas; pop. 19,087; manufactures cottonseed oil, flour, foundry products; oil refinery, cotton compress.

15 See Sino, Liberia.

Green'wa'ter Lake Park (grēn'wô'tẽr; -wŏt'ẽr). Canadian provincial park, E cen. Saskatchewan prov., SE of Prince Albert; 35 sq. m.; virgin forests, many lakes.

Greenway. See Charles City.

Green'wich (grēn'wĭch; grĭn'wĭch; grēn'ĭch). Residential town, SW Fairfield co., SW Connecticut, on Long Island Sound on New York border; pop. 53,793; settled 1640; annexed to Connecticut 1656.

Green'wich (grēn'wĭch). Village, Washington co., E New York, 27 m. NNE of Troy; pop. 2263; manufactures paper, thread, farm machinery.

Green'wich (grĭn'ĭj; *less often* grēn'-, -ĭch). Metropolitan borough, SE London, England, on S bank of the Thames; pop. 91,492; site of Royal Naval College and formerly of the Royal Greenwich Observatory, at lat. 51°28'38''N, long. 0°0'0'', established 1675 and after World War II removed to Herstmonceux castle in East Sussex, 45 m. SE of London, where the atmosphere is clearer than in the great metropolitan area. The Greenwich meridian still serves as the basis for standard time throughout the world and for reckonings of longitude. See *Table* at London.

Green'wich (*variously pronounced; see other* Greenwich *entries*). Island in South Shetland Is. (*q.v.*).

Green'wich Village (grĕn'ĭch; *less often* grĭn'-, -ĭj). Formerly a village on Manhattan I., now a part of Manhattan borough, New York City, bounded approximately by W 14th St., Spring St., Broadway, and the Hudson river; long frequented by authors, artists, and students.

Green'wood (grĕn'wŏŏd). 1 Name of counties in two states of the U.S. See *Tables* at Kansas and South Carolina.

2 Town, a ⊗ of Sebastian co., W Arkansas; pop. 1558.

3 Town, Johnson co., cen. Indiana, 10 m. S of Indianapolis; pop. 7169.

4 City, ⊗ of Leflore co., W Mississippi, 50 m. E of Greenville; pop. 20,436; long-staple cotton.

5 City, ⊗ of Greenwood co., W South Carolina, 36 m. SE of Anderson; pop. 16,644; railroad center; manufactures cottons, cheese, clothing, lumber, foundry and machine shop products. Lander College (1872).

Greenwood Lake. Lake ab. 9 m. long in N Passaic co., N New Jersey, and Orange co., SE New York; summer resort.

Greer (grēr). 1 County in Oklahoma. See *Table* at Oklahoma.

2 Town, Greenville and Spartanburg cos., NW South Carolina, 12 m. ENE of Greenville; pop. 8967; textile mills.

Gregg (grĕg). County in Texas. See *Table* at Texas.

Greg'o·ry (grĕg'ô·rĭ; grĕg'rĭ). **1** County in South Dakota. See *Table* at SOUTH DAKOTA.
2 City, Gregory co., S South Dakota; pop. 1478.
Gregory, Lake. Shallow salt lake, NE South Australia, ESE of Lake Eyre.
Greifenberg. See GRYFICE.
Greifs'wald (grīfs'vält; *sometimes Anglicized* -wôld). City, East Germany, in the former Pomerania province, Prussia, 19 m. SE of Stralsund; pop. 26,695; university (1456). Incorporated as city 1250.
Greiz (grīts). City, East Germany, 14 m. WSW of Zwickau; pop. 37,490; old castle, residence of former prince of Reuss; textile manufactories. Until 1918 capital of principality of Reuss-Greiz.
Gre·na'da (grĕ·nā'dá). **1** County in Mississippi. See *Table* at MISSISSIPPI.
2 City, ⊗ of Grenada co., N cen. Mississippi, 28 m. NE of Greenwood; pop. 7914; cotton growing.
3 Territory of West Indies Federation, in Windward Is.; comprises Grenada I. and the southern Grenadines (including Carriacou); 133 sq. m.; pop. (1939 est.) 90,085; ✻ St. George's on Grenada I.
4 Island, southernmost of the Windward Is., West Indies, 90 m. N of Trinidad; 120 sq. m.; pop. (1939 est.) 80,727; ✻ St. George's on SW coast; of volcanic origin; has many short streams; mountainous, highest point Mt. St. Catherine 2749 ft.; chief exports cocoa, nutmegs, lime oil, bananas, cotton. Discovered 1498 by Columbus, who named it Concepción; colonized by French governor of Martinique 1650; finally passed to French crown 1674; captured by British 1762 and ceded to them 1763; held by French 1779–83; scene of native rising suppressed by British 1795.
Gren'a·dier' Island (grĕn'á·dēr'). Island in NE Lake Ontario, NW of Sackets Harbor, Jefferson co., N New York.
Gren'a·dines' (grĕn'á·dēnz'; grĕn'á·dēnz). Group of 600 small islands, Windward Is., at E end of Caribbean Sea, bet. Grenada and St. Vincent; 30 sq. m.; pop. ab. 13,000; largest Carriacou; S part (13 sq. m.; pop., 1939 est., 9358) to Grenada, N part (17 sq. m.; pop. 3683, including Bequia and Union Is.) to St. Vincent.
Gren'chen (grĕn'ĸĕn); *Fr.* **Granges** (gränzh). Commune, Solothurn canton, NW Switzerland, 7 m. W of Solothurn; pop. (1941) 10,939; manufactures clocks.
Gre·no'ble (grĕ·nō'b'l; *Fr.* grĕ·nô'bl'); *anc.* **Cu'la·ro** (kū'lá·rō), *later* **Gra'ti·an·op'o·lis** (grā'shĭ·ăn·ŏp'ô·lĭs; grā'shăn-). Commercial and manufacturing city, ✻ of Isère dept., SE France, on Isère river 133 m. NNE of Marseilles; pop. 95,806; 10th-cent. cathedral; fine Renaissance law court; university (1339); tourist center; manufactures gloves (for which it is noted), cement, paper, chemical products. La Grande Chartreuse ab. 12½ m. N of here. Capital of the Dauphiné till 1450.
Gren'ville (grĕn'vĭl). **1** Town, E coast of Grenada I., Brit. West Indies; pop. ab. 3000.
2 County, Ontario, Canada. See *Table* at ONTARIO.
Grenz'mark Po'sen–West'preus'sen (grĕnts'märk pō'zĕn·vĕst'proi'sĕn). Former Prussian province, E Germany, on border of Poland; formed 1919 out of parts of former Posen and West Prussia provs.; in 1922 made equivalent to Schneidemühl govt. dist. (see PIŁA); since 1945 divided among several departments of W Poland.
Gresh'am (grĕsh'ăm). City, Multnomah co., NW Oregon, 14 m. E of Portland; pop. 3944.
Gret'na (grĕt'ná). **1** Industrial city, ⊗ of Jefferson parish, SE Louisiana, on Mississippi river opp. New Orleans; pop. 21,967; molasses, industrial alcohol, cottonseed oil, petroleum products.
2 Parish, Dumfries co., S Scotland, on English border; pop. 3036; 1 m. SE of **Gretna Green,** village, on the Sark, long famous as marrying place of runaway couples from England.
Gre've (grā'vā). Commune, Firenze prov., Tuscany, cen. Italy, 15 m. SE of Florence; pop. 14,789.

Gre've·ling'en (ĸrā'vĕ·lĭng'ĕ[n]). Inlet on SW coast of the Netherlands bet. Schouwen and Goedereede Is.
Gre'ven·broich' (grā'vĕn·brōĸ'). Town, North Rhine-Westphalia state, W Germany, 10 m. SE of München-Gladbach; pop. 4041; railroad junction; aluminum products. Taken by Allies Mar. 1945.
Grey (grā). **1** County, Ontario, Canada. See *Table* at ONTARIO.
2 River ab. 70 m. long in NW South I., New Zealand; flows SW into Tasman Sea at Greymouth.
Grey'beard' (grā'bĕrd'). Mountain 5448 ft., Buncombe co., W North Carolina.
Grey'bull' (grā'bōōl'). **1** River ab. 100 m. long, NW Wyoming; rises in S Park co., flows NE into Bighorn river.
2 Town, Big Horn co., N Wyoming, on Bighorn river 33 m. N of Worland; pop. 2286; petroleum deposits; oil refineries.
Greyerz. See GRUYÈRES.
Grey'lock', Mount (grā'lŏk'). Peak 3491 ft. in Berkshire Hills, Berkshire co., NW Massachusetts; highest point in state; memorial tower 105 ft. high on summit dedicated to soldiers and sailors of Massachusetts.
Greylock Mountain. **1** Peak 13,578 ft. in La Plata co., SW Colorado.
2 Peak 9317 ft. in N Elmore co., SW cen. Idaho.
3 Peak 7850 ft. in SW Klamath co., S Oregon.
Grey'mouth (grā'mouth). Seaport borough, N Westland provincial dist., W South I., New Zealand, at mouth of Grey river 138 m. SW of Nelson; pop. (1941 est.) 8460; exports coal and timber.
Greys (grāz). River ab. 65 m. long, W Wyoming; flows N in N Lincoln co. into Snake river.
Grey'town (grā'toun). **1** Seaport, Nicaragua. See SAN JUAN DEL NORTE.
2 Town, cen. Natal, E Republic of South Africa, 58 m. NNW of Durban; pop. 4408; sheep and cattle; wattle.
Grid'ley (grĭd'lĭ). City, Butte co., N California, 55 m. N of Sacramento; pop. 3343.
Gridley Mountain. Mountain 2200 ft. in Salisbury, extreme NW Connecticut.
Gries'heim am Main (grēs'hīm äm mīn'). Former commune (pop. 12,357), Wiesbaden govt. dist., Hesse-Nassau prov., Prussia, Germany; since 1928, part of Frankfurt am Main (*q.v.*).
Gries Pass (grēs). Mountain pass 8089 ft. in Alps bet. Piedmont, NW Italy, and Valais canton, Switzerland.
Grif'fin (grĭf'ĭn). City, ⊗ of Spalding co., W cen. Georgia, 42 m. SSE of Atlanta; pop. 21,735; textile mills.
Grif'fith (grĭf'ĭth). Town, Lake co., NW corner of Indiana, 8 m. S of Lake Michigan; pop. 9483.
Griggs (grĭgz). County in North Dakota. See *Table* at NORTH DAKOTA.
Gri·jal'va (grē·häl'vä). River ab. 350 m. long in Chiapas and Tabasco states, SE Mexico; flows N into Bay of Campeche.
Grim, Cape (grĭm). Northwest point of Tasmania, Australia.
Gri·mal'di (grē·mäl'dē). Caves in commune of Ventimiglia, Imperia prov., W Liguria, NW Italy, just across the border from Menton, France; remains of a prehistoric race of men (Grimaldi race, a Negroid type, late paleolithic) have been discovered here.
Grimes (grīmz). County in Texas. See *Table* at TEXAS.
Grim'ma (grĭm'ä). Manufacturing city, Saxony, E Germany, on left bank of the Mulde river 16 m. SE of Leipzig; pop. 11,334; 13th-cent. castle; 15th-cent. town hall; machinery, paper, chemical apparatus.
Grims'by (grĭmz'bĭ). **1** Town, Lincoln co., SE Ontario, Canada, on SW shore of Lake Ontario 18 m. E of Hamilton; pop. 2773; cans fruit.
2 County borough, Parts of Lindsey, Lincolnshire, E England, near mouth of the Humber 18 m. SSE of Hull; pop. 92,458, (1951) 94,527; has harbor; fisheries, shipbuilding yards, breweries.

Grim'sel Pass (grĭm′zĕl). Mountain pass 7159 ft. in Bernese Alps, SW cen. Switzerland.

Gríms'ey (grĕms′ā). Island in Arctic Ocean, NE of Eyja Fjord, N Iceland.

Grin'del·wald' (grĭn′dĕl·vält′; *sometimes Anglicized* -wôld′). Valley and town in cen. Switzerland, in Bernese Alps, N of the Wetterhorn and E of Interlaken; pop. (town) ab. 3000; cattle raising; tourist resort; elevation of valley 3400–3500 ft., town at 3468 ft.

Grin·nell' (grĭ·nĕl′). City, Poweshiek co., SE cen. Iowa, 23 m. SSE of Marshalltown; pop. 7367; glove-manufacturing center. Grinnell College (1846; coed.). Settled 1854; incorp. as town 1865, as city 1882.

Grinnell, Mount. Peak 8838 ft. in Glacier National Park, NW Montana.

Grinnell Land. Central section of Ellesmere I., N Franklin District, Northwest Territories, Canada.

Grinnell Peninsula. Northwest portion of Devon I., Franklin District, Northwest Territories, Canada, SW of Ellesmere I.

Gri'qua·land' East (grē′kwȧ·lănd′; grĭk′wȧ-). One of Transkeian Territories, E Cape Province, S Union of South Africa; 6602 sq. m.; pop. 328,504; chief town Kokstad; fine agricultural and sheep-raising country. Settled 1862 by Griquas, a people of Bushman and Hottentot descent, under their leader, Adam Kok.

Griqualand West. Region in N Cape Province, S Union of South Africa, N of Orange river and W of Orange Free State; 15,197 sq. m.; chief town Kimberley; bounded on N by British Bechuanaland; dry, desert country, noted for its diamond fields. After their discovery 1867, region, settled earlier by Griquas, became subject of dispute bet. Orange Free State and British, who annexed it 1871; joined to Cape Colony 1880.

Gri'qua·town (grē′kwȧ·toun; grĭk′wȧ-). Town, N cen. Cape Province, Union of South Africa, 90 m. W of Kimberley; pop. 1644; in district yielding diamonds, asbestos, galena, crocidolite, wool, mohair, and cereals. Occupied several times by Boers during Boer War; remains of old fort.

Gris–Nez, Cape (grē′nā′). Literally "Gray Nose"; headland, Pas-de-Calais dept., N France, extending into Strait of Dover 15 m. SW of Calais; point nearest to Great Britain; lighthouse. Cf. BLANC-NEZ.

Grisons. See GRAUBÜNDEN.

Gris'see, *formerly* **Gri'see** (grē′sā). Seaport, Bodjonegoro residency, East Java prov., Indonesia, ab. 8 m. NW of Surabaja; pop. 25,621; on Surabaja Strait opp. Madura I.; airport.

Gris'wold (grĭz′wŭld). Town, NE New London co., SE corner of Connecticut, on E bank of Quinebaug river; pop. 6472; incorporated 1815; agriculture, dairying; includes borough of Jewett City (*q.v.*).

Gri'va (grē′vä); *Russ.* **Gri'va** (gryē′vȧ). Town, E Zemgale prov., S Latvia, U.S.S.R.; pop. (1935) 5546; on Dvina river opp. Daugavpils.

Gri've·gnée' (grēv′nyā′). Manufacturing commune, Liège prov., E Belgium, a suburb of Liège; pop. 14,357; coal mines; metallurgical works.

Griz'zly Mountain (grĭz′lĭ). **1** Peak 13,800 ft. in Chaffee co., cen. Colorado.
2 Peak 14,020 ft. in Pitkin and Chaffee cos., W cen. Colorado.
3 Peak 9070 ft. in Glacier National Park, NW Montana.

Grizzly Peak. 1 Mountain 10,369 ft. in Sierra Nevada, on boundary bet. Tuolumne and Mono cos., E cen. California.
2 Peak 13,738 ft. in Dolores and San Juan cos., SW Colorado.
3 Peak 13,702 ft. in La Plata co., SW Colorado.

Gro'chów (grô′kŏŏf). Village, an E suburb of Warsaw, Poland, on right bank of the Vistula; scene of drawn battle Feb. 20, 1831 bet. Poles and Russians under Diebitsch, in Polish Revolution.

Gródek Jagielloński. See GORODOK YAGELLONSKI.

Gro·de'ko·vo (grŭ·dyĕ′kŭ·vŭ). Town, SW Maritime Territory, Soviet Russia, Asia, 95 m. NNW of Vladivostok; border town opp. Suifenho in Manchuria.

Grödnertal. See Val di GARDENA.

Grod'no (grôd′nô); *Lithuanian* **Gar·di'nas** (gär·dĭ′näs). City, * of Grodno Region, W White Russia, U.S.S.R., on Neman river 47 m. NE of Białystok, Poland; pop. (1938–39 est.) 57,281; manufactures textiles, tobacco, leather; trades in lumber, agricultural products. At various times in its history under Lithuanian, Russian, and Polish rule; capital of Lithuania in 14th cent.; seat of Polish Sejm 1795 which ratified third Partition of Poland; captured by Germans Sept. 1915, and again, in World War II, in June 1941; retaken by Russians July 16, 1944.

Grodno Region. Region of NW White Russia, U.S.S.R., bounded on N by Lithuanian S.S.R. and on W by Poland; * Grodno.

Gro'dzisk Ma'zo·wiec'ki (grô′jĕsk mä′zô-vyĕts′kĕ). Commune, Warszawa dept., Poland, 12 m. SW of Warsaw; pop. (1938–39 est.) 18,737.

Groes'beck (grōs′bĕk). City, ⊗ of Limestone co., E cen. Texas, 33 m. E of Waco; pop. 2498; farming; oil and clay deposits.

Groes'beek (krōōs′bāk). Commune, Gelderland prov., E Netherlands, near German border; pop. 7816; frontier and customs station.

Groix, Île de (ēl′ dĕ grwä′). Island in Bay of Biscay off Morbihan dept., NW France, 9 m. S of Lorient; 6 sq. m.; pop. (1931) 4716; sea caves, dolmens; fishing.

Grom·bal'ia (grŏm·băl′yȧ). Town, NE Tunisia, at base of Cape Bon Penin. ab. 25 m. SE of Tunis.

Gro'nau (grō′nou); *also* **Gronau in West'fa'len** (ĭn vĕst′fä′lĕn). City, North Rhine-Westphalia state, W Germany, near Dutch border 32 m. NW of Münster; pop. 14,159; agriculture.

Gron'gar Hill (grŏng′gẽr). Hill in Carmarthenshire, S Wales; celebrated by John Dyer, English poet.

Gro'ning·en (grō′nĭng·ĕn; *Du.* ᴋʀō′nĭng·ĕ[n]). **1** Province, NE Netherlands; 923 sq. m.; pop. (1939) 423,329; * Groningen; agriculture, dairy farming, livestock raising.
2 City, * of Groningen prov., NE Netherlands; pop. (1939) 121,632; commercial center; university (1614); Church of St. Martin, dating in part from 13th cent.; Museum van Oudheden. Place of internment of British Royal Naval Brigade after fall of Antwerp Oct. 1914; in World War II taken by Allies Apr. 1945.
3 Town, N Surinam, on Saramacca river ab. 22 m. W of Paramaribo.

Grönland. See GREENLAND.

Grön'sund (grŭn′sŏŏn). Channel bet. Falster and Möen Is., SE Denmark.

Groo'te (ᴋʀōō′tĕ). **1** River, Cape Province, Union of South Africa; joins Olifants river to form Gouritz river.
2 River, Cape Province, South Africa, main headstream of the Gamtoos (*q.v.*).

Groote Ey'landt (grōōt ī′länd). Island 950 sq. m. in W Gulf of Carpentaria, Northern Territory, Australia.

Groot'fon·tein' (ᴋʀōōt′fŏn·tān′; *Angl.* grōōt′-). Town, N South-West Africa, 220 m. NNE of Windhoek; pop. 35,006; copper and lead mining center. World's largest known meteorite is on nearby farm.

Gros Is'let Bay (grōs ī′lĕt; -līt). Inlet of Caribbean Sea, NW coast of Saint Lucia I., West Indies, ab. 5 m. N of Castries; seaplane base 120 acres leased for 99 years to U.S. by Great Britain Sept. 3, 1940.

Gros'sa, I'so·la (ē′zō·lä grôs′sä). = DUGI OTOK.

Gross·bee'ren (grōs·bā′rĕn). Village just S of Berlin, eastern Germany; pop. ab. 2000; scene of battle Aug. 23, 1813 in which French were defeated by Prussians under von Bülow and Berlin was thereby saved.

Gros'sen·hain (grōs′ĕn·hīn). City, Saxony, E Germany, 19 m. NNW of Dresden; pop. 12,893; manufactures machinery, tinware, paper, cloth.

Grosse Pointe (grōs' point'; point'). Residential city, Wayne co., SE Michigan, on Lake St. Clair 9 m. E of Detroit; pop. 6631.

Grosse' Pointe' Farms. Residential city, Wayne co., SE Michigan, on Lake St. Clair 10 m. E of Detroit; pop. 12,172.

Grosse Pointe Park. Residential city, Wayne co., SE Michigan, on Lake St. Clair; pop. 15,457.

Grosse Pointe Woods. Village, Wayne co., SE Michigan; pop. 18,580; residential suburb of Detroit.

Grosser Belchen. See Ballon de GUEBWILLER.

Gros'ser Feld'berg (grō'sēr fĕlt'bĕrK). Highest peak 2886 ft. in Taunus range, W Germany.

Grosse Scheidegg. See *Great Scheidegg* at SCHEIDEGG.

Gros·se'to (grôs·sā'tô). **1** Province of Italy. See *Table* at ITALY.

2 Commune, its *, Tuscany, cen. Italy, 94 m. NW of Rome; pop. 26,428; 13th-cent. Gothic cathedral; fortified citadel; museum of Etruscan antiquities; ruins of **Ru·sel'lae** (rōō·sĕl'ē), an ancient Etruscan city deserted in 12th cent.; sulfur baths.

Gross Fiescherhorn. See Gross FIESCHERHORN.

Gross·glock'ner (grōs·glôk'nēr). Peak 12,461 ft. of the Hohe Tauern in the Tirol Alps, bet. E Tirol and Carinthia, S Austria; highest point in Austria.

Gross·gör'schen (grōs·gûr'shĕn). Village, E Germany, formerly in Saxony prov., Prussia, near Lützen; battle, often called battle of Lützen (*q.v.*), May 2, 1813.

Gross–Jä'gers·dorf (grōs-yä'gērs-dôrf) *or* **Gross–Jä'gern·dorf** (-gērn-). Village, W Gumbinnen govt. dist., former East Prussia prov., Prussia, near Pregel river W of Insterburg (Chernyakhovsk); pop. 400; scene of battle July 30, 1757 in which Russians under Apraksin defeated Prussians under Lehwald; assigned to U.S.S.R. by Potsdam Conference 1945.

Gross Ot'ters·le'ben *or* **Gross-ot'ters·le'ben** (grōs-ôt'ērs-lā'bĕn). Commune, E Germany, in what was formerly Saxony prov., Prussia, SW suburb of Magdeburg; pop. 10,408.

Gross Ro'sen (grōs rō'zĕn). Town, in former Silesia, Prussia, Germany, SSE of Liegnitz (Legnica); site of concentration camp in World War II; now **Ro'goź·ni'ca** (rô'gôzh-nē'tsä), Wrocław dept., SW Poland.

Gross Schreckhorn. See Gross SCHRECKHORN.

Gross Strehlitz. See STRZELCE OPOLSKIE.

Gross Ve·ne'di·ger (grōs vā·nā'dĭ·gēr; -yēr). Peak 12,008 ft. in Hohe Tauern range in the Tirol Alps, bet. E Tirol and Carinthia, Austria, and near Italian border.

Grosswardein. See ORADEA.

Gros've·nor Dale (grōv'nēr). Subdivision (est. pop. 530) of town of THOMPSON, Connecticut; textile mills.

Gros've·nor Range, *formerly* **Gil'bert Grosvenor Range** (gĭl'bērt grōv'nēr). Mountain range, Antarctica, S of Ross Shelf Ice, bet. it and the South Pole; 86°S lat., crossed by 178th meridian; on the W touches Queen Alexandra Range and on E the Queen Maud Range.

Gros Ventre (grō' vänt'). River ab. 100 m. long, W Wyoming; rises in Wind River Range, N Sublette co., flows W into Snake river in cen. Teton co.

Grot'on (grŏt'n). **1** Town, S New London co., SE corner of Connecticut, on Long Island Sound at mouth of Thames river opp. New London; pop. 29,937; settled 1649, incorp. 1704; agriculture, commercial fishing; manufactures submarine engines, submarines, ships; U.S. submarine base; site of Fort Griswold which was attacked and taken by British under Benedict Arnold 1781. Includes borough of **Groton** (pop. 10,111).

2 Town, Middlesex co., NE Massachusetts, 11 m. E of Fitchburg; pop. 3904; Groton School (boys preparatory school; 1884).

3 Industrial village, Tompkins co., S cen. New York, 26 m. SSE of Auburn; pop. 2123; typewriters.

Grot·ta'glie (grŏt·tä'lyä). Commune, Ionio prov., Apulia, SE Italy, 11 m. ENE of Taranto; pop. 16,010; pottery.

Grouse Hill (grous). Peak 7401 ft. in W Klamath co., S Oregon, N of Crater Lake.

Grouse Mountain. Peak 10,132 ft. in SW Catron co., W New Mexico.

Grove City (grōv). **1** Village, Franklin co., cen. Ohio, 8 m. SSW of Columbus; pop. 8107.

2 Borough, Mercer co., W Pennsylvania, 18 m. ENE of New Castle; pop. 8368; settled 1798; manufactures gas engines, carriages; Grove City College (1876; coed.).

Grove Hill. Town, ⊗ of Clarke co., SW Alabama; pop. 1834.

Grove'land (grōv'lănd). Town, Essex co., NE corner of Massachusetts, 16 m. ENE of Lowell; pop. 3297.

Gro'ver (grō'vēr). City, San Luis Obispo co., SW California, S of San Luis Obispo; pop. 5210.

Groves (grōvz). City, Jefferson co., SE coastal Texas, E of Port Arthur; pop. 17,304.

Grove'ton (grōv'tŭn). **1** Town in Northumberland township, Coos co., N New Hampshire, ab. 19 m. NW of Berlin; pop. 2004; paper and pulpwood mills.

2 City, ⊗ of Trinity co., E Texas; pop. 1148.

3 See BULL RUN.

Groyne, The (groin). Former English name of La Coruña commune, Spain.

Groz'ny (grôz'nĭ). City, * of Grozny Region and of former Chechen-Ingush Republic, Soviet Russia, Europe, on a tributary of the Terek river 70 m. ENE of Dzaudzhikau; pop. 172,468; oil center, connected by pipelines with Makhachkala on the Caspian and with Tuapse and Rostov to the NW; second only to Baku in petroleum production. Originally a Russian frontier fortress, established 1818; oil discovered 1893; goal, but never reached, of German drive in Caucasus 1942.

Grozny Region. Subdivision of Russian Soviet Federated Socialist Republic, SE Russia in Europe, N of cen. Caucasus Mts. and NW of Dagestan; newly formed 1945, including most of former Chechen-Ingush Republic and E part of former Ordzhonikidze Territory; on NE borders on the Caspian; * Grozny.

Grubeshov. See HRUBIESZÓW.

Gru'dziądz (grōō'jŏnts); *Ger.* **Grau'denz** (grou'dĕnts). City, Pomorze dept., Poland, on Vistula river 30 m. N of Toruń; pop. (1938–39 est.) 58,461; important agricultural center; manufactures iron goods, machinery, tile, shoes. Founded by Teutonic Knights 1291; to Poland 1466; seized by Prussia 1772, and in 1920 again assigned to Poland; held by Germany in World War II.

Gruin'ard Bay (grĭn'yērd). Bay on NW coast of Ross and Cromarty co., N Scotland.

Grullo, El. See EL GRULLO.

Gru'mo Ap'pu·la (grōō'mô äp'pōō·lä). Commune, Bari prov., Apulia, SE Italy, SW of Bari; pop. 11,415.

Grünberg, Grünberg in Schlesien. See ZIELONA GÓRA.

Grun'dy (grŭn'dĭ). **1** Counties in four states of the U.S. See *Tables* at ILLINOIS, IOWA, MISSOURI, TENNESSEE.

2 Town, ⊗ of Buchanan co., SW Virginia; pop. 2287.

Grundy Center. City, ⊗ of Grundy co., NE cen. Iowa, 25 m. WSW of Waterloo; pop. 2403.

Grütli. See RÜTLI.

Gru'yère' (grü'yâr'). District, SE Fribourg canton, W cen. Switzerland; 192 sq. m.; pop. ab. 25,000; noted esp. for its cheese (Gruyère cheese) originally made here.

Gru'yères' (grü'yâr'); *Ger.* **Grey'erz** (grī'ērts). Commune, Gruyère dist., Switzerland, 16 m. SW of Fribourg; pop. (1930) 1465; old castle, seat of counts of Gruyère.

Gruziya. See GEORGIA.

Gry·fi'ce (grĭ-fē'tsĕ); *Ger.* **Grei'fen·berg** (grī'fĕn·bĕrk). Town, NW Szczecin dept., NW Poland, NE of Stettin; pop. (1946) 10,426.

Gry·nei'on (grĭ-nī'ŏn). Ancient Aeolian town on NW coast of Asia Minor, near Cyme; a religious center, noted for its worship of Apollo.

Gryt'vi'ken Harbour (grüt'vē'kĕn). See SOUTH GEORGIA.

Gua·ca·na·ya′bo Bay (gwä′kä·nä·yä′vô). Bay in W coast of Oriente prov. and S coast of Camagüey prov., E Cuba.

Gua′chi·rí′a (gwä′chê·rē′ä). River ab. 110 m. long in NE cen Colombia, flows E into Meta river.

Gua′da·la·ja′ra (gwä′thä·lä·hä′rä; *Angl.* gwŏd′ä·lä·här′ä) t Province of Spain. See *Table* at SPAIN.

2 *anc.* **Ar′ri·a′ca** (?är′i·ä′kä). Commune, ✻ of Guadalajara prov., cen. Spain. 34 m NE of Madrid; pop. 23,508; manufactures woolens, leather, soap. palace of Mendoza family; Roman bridge and aqueduct; held by Moors 714–1081

3 City, W cen. Mexico, ✻ of Jalisco state, 280 m. WNW of Mexico City, pop. 229,235; altitude 5200 ft.; fine cathedral (built 1561–1618); university (1792); center of rich agricultural and industrial area; important mining center; noted for its pottery, clay figures, and drawn work. See MEXICO republic.

Gua′da·la·viar′ (gwä′thä·lä·vyär′). River ab. 150 m. long in E Spain; flows S and SE into Mediterranean Sea 3 m. E of Valencia.

Gua′dal·ca·nal′ (gwŏd″l·kà·năl′; *Span.* gwä′thäl·kä-näl′: *local pron* kä′lä·kä′nä). Island in SE Solomon Is., W Pacific Ocean, ab. 300 m. SE of Bougainville, 100 m. SE of New Georgia, and 35 m. SW of Malaita; 92 m. long and 33 m. wide at its widest part; 2509 sq. m.; chief village Aola; part of British Solomon Is. protectorate. Has no good harbors and only a few at all usable; traversed lengthwise by Kavo Mts.; highest peak Popomanasiu 8005 ft.; many short streams are along coast, the best known the Matanikau, Lunga, and Tenaru rivers in N. Has many coconut plantations; in some of the low coast regions mangrove swamps. First visited by English navigator 1788; gradually settled by white traders after 1860; taken as part of protectorate by British 1893. In World War II occupied 1942 by Japanese who built airfield on N coast which was seized by U.S. Marines Aug. 7, 1942 (see HENDERSON FIELD), the first episode in the "Battle of Guadalcanal" (Aug 7–Nov. 13, 1942) which included several naval battles (see SAVO) and several bitterly contested land battles (see MATANIKAU, TENARU, LUNGA POINT); evacuated by Japanese Feb. 1943.

Gua′da·le′te (gwä′thä·lä′tä). River ab. 75 m long in SW Spain. flows SW into Gulf of Cádiz through 2 mouths

Gua′da·li·mar′ (gwä′thä·lê·mär′). River ab. 90 m. long in S Spain. flows into the Guadalquivir, 14 m. N of Jaén.

Gua′dal·quiv′ir (gwŏd″l kwǐv′ẽr; *Span.* gwä′thäl·kê-vẽr′); *Arab.* **Wa′di el Ke·bir′** (wä′dẽl kä·bẽr′); *anc.* **Bae′tis** (bē′tĭs). River 374 m. long, in S Spain; flows W and SW into Gulf of Cádiz at Sanlúcar de Barrameda.

Gua′da·lu′pe (*for places in Span.-speaking countries*: gwä′thä·lōō′pä, *or Anglicized as follows; for places in U S.*: gwŏd″l·ōōp, gô′d′l-, wŏd′′l-, gwŏd″l·ōō′pê).

1 River ab. 300 m. long, SE Texas; rises in Kerr co., flows SE into San Antonio river ab 9 m. from its mouth.

2 Name of counties in two states of the U.S. See *Tables* at NEW MEXICO and TEXAS.

3 Island 80 sq. m. in Pacific Ocean 180 m. off coast of W cen. Lower California; an extinct volcano, height ab. 4500 ft, set aside ab 1923 by Mexican government as a game reservation, esp. for protection of elephant seals.

4 Town in Uruguay See CANELONES.

Gua′da·lu′pe Hi·dal′go (gwä′thä·lōō′pä ê·thäl′gō; *Angl.* gwŏd″l·ōōp, *etc.*, hi·däl′gō), *officially* **Gus·ta′vo A. Ma·de′ro** (gōōs·tä′vô ä′ mä·thä′rō). City, Federal District, cen. Mexico; pop. 25,934; large church containing a portrait of the Virgin Mary, object of pilgrimage for many Indians in Mexico Treaty signed here Feb. 2, 1848 terminating Mexican War.

Guadalupe Mountains. 1 Mountain range, S New Mexico and SW Texas; highest Guadalupe Peak 8751 ft.

2 *or* **Sier′ra de Gua′da·lu′pe** (syěr′rä thä gwä′thä-

lōō′pä). Range in SW cen. Spain, mostly in S Cáceres prov.; highest peak Cabeza del Moro 5110 ft.

Guadalupe Peak. Mountain 8751 ft. in Culberson co., W Texas; in Guadalupe Mts.; highest point in Texas.

Gua′dar·ra′ma (gwä′thär·rä′mä), **Sierra de.** See SIERRA DE GUADARRAMA.

Guadarrama Pass. Mountain pass ab. 4151 ft. in the Sierra de Guadarrama, cen. Spain, S of Segovia.

Gua′de·loupe′ (*Fr.* gwäd′lōōp′; *Angl.* gwŏd″l·ōōp, gô′d′l-). Name applied to 2 islands in E West Indies, Basse-Terre (or Guadeloupe proper) and Grande Terre, separated by a narrow channel; 583 sq. m.; with dependencies Marie Galante, Désirade, Les Saintes, St. Barthélemy, and part of St. Martin, constitutes **Guadeloupe** department of France, 688 sq. m., pop. (1936) 304,239; ✻ Basse-Terre.

History: Discovered by Columbus 1493; occupied by French 1635; held by British 1759–63, 1794, 1810–13; transferred to Sweden 1813 and restored to France 1816; in World War II held under Vichy control until July 1943; in reorganization of France and possessions 1946 status changed from colony to overseas department.

Gua·dia′na (*Span.* gwä·thyä′nä; *Port.* gwä·thyä′nä); *anc.* **A′nas** (ä′năs). River 515 m. long in Spain and Portugal; rises in S cen. Spain; flows W to Portuguese border; turns S, forming 2 sections of the boundary bet. Spain and Portugal, and empties into Gulf of Cádiz.

Gua·dia′na Bay (gwä·thyä′nä). Bay in N coast of W tip of Pinar del Río prov., W Cuba, E of Cape San Antonio.

Gua·dia′na Me·nor′ (gwä·thyä′nä mà·nôr′). River ab. 30 m. long, S Spain; unites with the Guadalquivir 4 m. ESE of Úbeda.

Gua·dia′ro (gwä·thyä′rô). River ab. 40 m. long in S Spain; flows S into Mediterranean Sea 11 m. NE of Gibraltar.

Gua·dia′to (gwä·thyä′tô). River ab. 70 m. long in S Spain; flows into the Guadalquivir 17 m. WSW of Córdoba.

Gua·dix′ (gwä·thēk′). City, Granada prov., S Spain, 26 m. ENE of Granada; pop. 26,023; manufactures brandy, pottery, hemp, hats. Roman remains, Moorish castle, 18th-cent. cathedral; one of oldest episcopal sees in Spain.

Gua′fo (gwä′fô). Island off SW coast of Chile, SW of Chiloé I. and W of Gulf of Guafo.

Gua′gua (gwä′gwä). Municipality, S cen. Pampanga prov., Luzon, Phil. Is., on N edge of Pampanga delta 7 m. SW of San Fernando; pop. 22,331.

Guahan. See GUAM.

Guái′ma·ro (gwi′mä·rô). Municipality, E Camagüey prov., E cen. Cuba, 44 m. SE of Camagüey near border of Oriente prov.; pop. 17,543.

Guai·ní′a (gwi·nē′ä). Upper course of Rio Negro in E Colombia; joined to Orinoco river through Casiquiare river.

Guai·rá′ (gwi·rä′). Department of Paraguay. See *Table* at PARAGUAY.

Guai′ra (gwi′rä) *or* **Se′te Que′das** (sâ′tě kâ′thäsh); *formerly* **Guay′ra** (gwi′rä). Cataract, "Seven Falls," in the Paraná river on boundary bet. Brazil and Paraguay; formed by a narrowing of the river bed into a gorge ab. 200 ft. wide through which the water plunges 56 ft.; total descent 374 ft.

Guaira, La. See LA GUAIRA.

Guai·te′cas, *or* **Guay·te′cas, Islands** (gwi·tä′käs). Group of islands in Pacific Ocean off SW coast of Chile, comprising N part of Chonos Archipelago.

Gua·ja′ba Cay (gwä·hä′vä). Island, Camagüey Archipelago, off N coast of Camagüey prov., E cen. Cuba.

Gua·ji′ra (gwä·hē′rä); **Goa·ji′ra** *or* **Goa·gi′ra** (gwä-). Commissary of Colombia. See *Table* at COLOMBIA. Forms a peninsula ab. 80 m. long by 30 to 60 m. wide bet. Gulf of Venezuela and the Caribbean; its N point is Point Gallinas.

Gua'la·ce'o (gwä'lä·sä'ô). Town, Azuay prov., S Ecuador, 15 m. E of Cuenca; pop. (1944 est.) 9334; manufactures straw hats.

Gua·lán' (gwä·län'). Town, Zacapa dept., E Guatemala, on the Motagua NE of Zacapa; pop. 5478.

Gual'do Ta·di'no (gwäl'dô tä·dē'nô). Commune, Perugia prov., Umbria, cen. Italy, 20 m. ENE of Perugia; pop. 12,701; cathedral; pottery.

Gua'le·guay' (gwä'lä·gwī'; -gwä'ĕ). **1** River ab. 300 m. long in Entre Ríos prov., E Argentina; flows S into the Paraná.
2 Town, Entre Ríos prov., E Argentina, 80 m. ESE of Rosario; pop. (est.) 24,457.

Gua'le·guay·chú' (gwä'lä·gwī·chōō'). Town, Entre Ríos prov., E Argentina, near Uruguay river 125 m. E of Rosario; pop. (est.) 32,015.

Guam (gwŏm) *or* **Gua·han'** (gwä·hän'). Largest and southernmost of Mariana Is., W Pacific Ocean, 1589 m. E of Manila; 32 m. long, bet. 4 and 10 m. wide; 206 sq. m.; pop. 67,044; ✱ Agana; in S half are hills (highest 1334 ft.) with several streams and fertile areas, N half mainly plateau ab. 500 ft.; has reef along much of the coast; on W coast is best anchorage, Apra Harbor, bet. Orote Penin. and Cabras I.; visited occasionally by earthquakes and typhoons; chief crop coconuts, also exports sugar, cocoa, and tropical fruits. Natives are Chamorros. Discovered by Magellan 1521; occupied by Spain 1565 but not completely subjected until 130 years later; ceded to U.S. by Spain Dec. 1898 and occupied 1899; developed by U.S. as naval station and in 1936 as civil aviation stop; seized by Japanese Dec. 11, 1941; retaken by American forces July 20–Aug. 10, 1944; made headquarters of U.S. Navy in the Pacific Jan. 28, 1945.

Gua'ma·ca'ro (gwä'mä·kä'rô). Municipality, Matanzas prov., W cen. Cuba, SW of Cárdenas; pop. 11,729.

Gua'na·ba·co'a (gwä'nä·vä·kō'ä). Municipality and town, La Habana prov., W Cuba, just E of Havana; pop. (town) 21,999.

Gua'na·ba'ra (gwä'nä·vä'rä). State of Brazil, ✱ Rio de Janeiro; 451 sq. m.; formed 1960 of former Federal District.

Guanabara Bay *also* **Rio de Janeiro Bay.** Inlet of Atlantic Ocean in SE Brazil; the city of Rio de Janeiro is on its SW shore; 16½ m. long, 11 m. wide, entrance ab. 1 m. wide.

Gua'na·cas'te (gwä'nä·käs'tä). Province, NW Costa Rica; 4270 sq. m.; pop. (1943 est.) 84,536; ✱ Liberia.

Guanacaste, Cor'dil·le'ra (kôr'thĕ·yä'rä). Range in NW Costa Rica; highest ab. 5100 ft.

Gua'na·ha'ni (gwä'nä·hä'nē). Native (Lucayan) name of the island which was Columbus's first landfall in New World. See SAN SALVADOR island, Bahama Is.

Gua'na·ja (gwä·nä'hä) *or* **Bo·nac'ca** (bô·nä'kä). One of the Bay Is. in the Caribbean Sea N of N cen. Honduras.

Gua'na·jay' (gwä'nä·hī'). Municipality and town, Pinar del Río prov., W Cuba, 25 m. SW of Havana; pop. (town) 10,473.

Gua'na·jua'to (gwä'nä·hwä'tô). **1** State, cen. Mexico. See *Table* at MEXICO.
2 City, its ✱, cen. Mexico, 170 m. NW of Mexico City; pop. 23,521; altitude 6550 ft.; in mountainous region noted for centuries for its gold and silver mines, still being worked; famous for its catacombs.

Gua·nal', Point (gwä·näl'). Cape on S coast of Isle of Pines, West Indies.

Gua·na're (gwä·nä'rä). **1** River in W Venezuela; flows ESE to join the Portuguesa river.
2 Town, ✱ of Portuguesa state, W cen. Venezuela, ab. 75 m. SSW of Barquisimeto; pop. (1941 est.) 3681.

Gua'ne (gwä'nä). Municipality, Pinar del Río prov., 28 m. SW of Pinar del Río, W Cuba; pop. 27,502.

Guá'ni·ca (gwä'nē·kä). Municipality (pop. 13,767) and town (pop. 4100) SW Puerto Rico; town is on Guánica Harbor 25 m. W of Ponce.

Guánica Harbor. Bay on S coast of Mayagüez municipality, W Puerto Rico; landing place of American troops in Spanish-American War 1898.

Gua'ni·quil'la Point (gwä'nĕ·kē'yä). Cape on SW coast of Puerto Rico, N of Boquerón Bay.

Gua'no (gwä'nô). Town, Chimborazo prov., cen. Ecuador, just N of Riobamba; pop. (1944 est.) 11,871.

Guan·tá'na·mo (gwän·tä'nä·mô). Municipality and town, SE Oriente prov., E Cuba; town, ab. 10 m. N of Guantánamo Bay, pop. (1943) 42,445; sugar center; municipality includes seaport barrio Caimanera on W side of Guantánamo Bay.

Guantánamo Bay. Bay on SE coast of Oriente prov., E Cuba; 30 sq. m.; site of U.S. naval station (leased 1903); in Spanish-American War its shores landing place of U.S. naval units June 1898.

Guapay. See MAMORÉ.

Gua'po·ré' (gwä'pōō·rä'). **1** *or* **I·té'nez** (ê·tä'nâs). River ab. 950 m. long in W cen. South America; rises in W Mato Grosso state, SW Brazil, flows NW, forming section of Brazil-Bolivia boundary, to join the Mamoré river.
2 Territory of Brazil. See *Table* at BRAZIL.

Gua'qui (gwä'kē). Lake port, La Paz dept., W Bolivia, at S end of Lake Titicaca near mouth of Desaguadero river; railroad terminus 61 m. from La Paz.

Gua·ram·ba·ré' (gwä'räm·bä·rä'). Town, Central dept., SW cen. Paraguay; pop. ab. 6400.

Gua·ran'da (gwä·rän'dä). City, ✱ of Bolívar prov., W Ecuador, 72 m. NE of Guayaquil; pop. (1944 est.) 15,606; cinchona bark.

Gua'ra·pua'va (gwä'rä·pwä'vä). Town, S cen. Paraná state, S Brazil, 140 m. W of Curitiba.

Gua'ra·tin'gue·tá' (gwä'rä·tēng'gĕ·tä'). City, São Paulo state, SE Brazil, 125 m. W of Rio de Janeiro; pop. (1940 est.) 15,654; commercial center of agricultural district producing esp. coffee.

Guar'da (gwär'thä). **1** District of Portugal. See *Table* at PORTUGAL.
2 Commune, its ✱, NE Portugal, 65 m. ENE of Coimbra; pop. 8150; cathedral.

Guar'da·fui', Cape (gwär'dä·fwē'; -fōō'ĭ); *Arab.* **Ras As·sir'** (räs ä·sēr'); *anc.* **A·ro'ma·ta** (á·rō'má·tä). Cape extending into Indian Ocean from NE tip of Somalia, S of entrance to Gulf of Aden.

Guard'house', the (gärd'hous'). Mountain 9300 ft. in Glacier National Park, NW Montana.

Guar'dia·gre'le (gwär'dyä·grä'lä). Commune, Chieti prov., Abruzzi e Molise, cen. Italy, 12 m. S of Chieti; pop. 12,243; summer resort.

Guard'i·an, the (gär'dĭ·ǎn). Peak 13,624 ft. in San Juan co., SW Colorado.

Guá'ri·co (gwä'rê·kô). **1** River ab. 225 m. long in W Venezuela; flows SW and S into Apure river.
2 State of Venezuela. See *Table* at VENEZUELA.

Gua'ri·ti'co (gwä'rê·tê'kô). River ab. 160 m. long, in W Venezuela; flows ENE into Apure river.

Gua'ru·já' (gwä'rōō·zhá'). See SANTOS.

Guásimas, Las. See LAS GUÁSIMAS.

Guaso Nyiro. See WASO NYIRO.

Gua·stal'la (gwäs·täl'lä); *anc.* **War'da·stal'la** (wôr'dá·stäl'á). Commune, Reggio nell'Emilia prov., Emilia, N Italy, on Po river 14 m. NE of Reggio; pop. 13,723; cathedral; palace of Gonzaga family; produces spun silk, leather, cheese. Founded by Lombards in 7th cent.; belonged successively to Reggio, Cremona, and Milan; became center of countship of same name 1406; to Gonzaga family 1538; made center of duchy 1621; to Spanish duke of Parma 1748; joined Cisalpine Republic 1796; ruled by members of Napoleonic family 1805–47, by duke of Modena 1847–60; became part of kingdom of Italy 1860.

Gua'ta·vi'ta (gwä'tä·vē'tä). Town, Cundinamarca dept., cen. Colombia, near Bogotá; ancient city of the Chibchas.

Gua′te·ma′la (gwä′tĕ·mä′là; *Span.* gwä′tå·mä′lä). **1** Republic, Central America; 42,044 sq. m.; pop. (1940) 3,283,209; ✳ Guatemala; bounded on W and N by Mexico, on E by British Honduras and the Gulf of Honduras, on the SE by Honduras and El Salvador, and on S by the Pacific Ocean. Mountainous; main range the SE extension of the Sierra Madre of Mexico, roughly parallel with Pacific coast ab. 40 m. distant, including Tajumulco 13,816 ft., Tacaná 13,333 ft., Acatenango 12,980 ft., Santa María 12,300 ft., Atitlán 11,562 ft.; interior is extensive tableland 2000 to 5000 ft.; regions on both Pacific and Atlantic coasts are hot lowlands. Chief rivers the Usumacinta in NW on Mexican border, the Sarstoon flowing E into Honduras Bay, the Polochic (through Lake Izabal) and Motagua flowing to Gulf of Honduras. Chief lakes Lake Izabal in E, Petén in N, and Atitlán in SW cen. part. Chief crop coffee; other products sugar, grains, bananas, chicle, cinchona, hardwoods. Chief cities Guatemala, Quezaltenango, Cobán, Zacapa, Antigua, Escuintla, and Puerto Barrios, the Atlantic port.

History: Conquered by Alvarado 1524; Guatemala city founded and captaincy general of Guatemala established (included present Guatemala, El Salvador, Honduras, Nicaragua, Costa Rica) 1527; revolted from Spain 1821 and joined Iturbide's Mexican empire; withdrew from United Provinces (see CENTRAL AMERICA) and became independent republic 1839; dominated by Carrera 1840–65; under President Barrios 1873–85, tried to form by force a union of Central American states; ruled by Estrada Cabrera 1898–1920; declared war on Germany 1918; in 1933 settled century-old boundary dispute with Honduras; in World War II declared war on Axis powers 1941. **2** Department, S cen. Guatemala; 821 sq. m.; pop. 319,197; ✳ Guatemala. **3** *or* **Guatemala City.** City, ✳ of Guatemala dept. and of Guatemala; pop. 163,826; largest city in Central America; altitude ab. 5000 ft., in volcanic area; center of fertile agricultural region. Founded by Alvarado 1527 as Santiago de los Cabelleros, destroyed 1541 by floods; capital moved to Antigua, which was destroyed by earthquake 1773; rebuilt on present site 1776, became capital 1779; severely damaged 1917–18 by earthquakes.

Guatemala Antigua. = ANTIGUA, Guatemala.

Guaura. See HUAURA.

Gua·via′re (gwä·vyä′rå). River ab. 450 m. long in Colombia; flows E from its source in Andes Mts. in SW cen. Colombia; empties into Orinoco river on Colombia-Venezuela boundary.

Gua·ya′ma (gwä·yä′mä). Municipality (1950 pop. 30,511) and town (1950 pop. 16,913), SE Puerto Rico; near coast 32 m. E of Ponce; its port is Arroyo.

Gua·ya′na (gwä·yä′nà). Var. of GUIANA.

Gua′ya·ne′co Islands (gwä′yä·nä′kō). Group of small islands in Pacific Ocean off SW coast of Chile, S of Gulf of Peñas.

Gua′ya·nil′la (gwä′yä·nē′yä). Municipality (pop. 17,396) and town (pop. 3067), SW Puerto Rico; town on coast 12 m. W of Ponce on **Guayanilla Harbor.**

Gua′ya·quil′ (gwä′yä·kēl′; *Angl.* gwī′å·kēl, -kwĭl); *officially* **San·tia′go de Gua′ya·quil′** (sän·tyä′gồ thả gwä′yä·kēl′). Seaport, ✳ of Guayas prov., SW Ecuador, on Guayas river ab. 40 m. from the coast and 170 m. SW of Quito; pop. (1944 est.) 172,948; chief port of Ecuador; exports balsa wood, cocoa, coffee, ivory nuts, rubber, hides; cathedral, university, military aviation school. Founded July 25, 1535, St. James's day, hence its official name; attacked by pirates 1624, 1683, and 1709; has often been burned; scene of historic meeting bet. Bolívar and San Martín 1822.

Guayaquil, Gulf of. Inlet of Pacific Ocean in SW coast of Ecuador, and bounded on S by tip of NW Peru; receives Guayas river from the N; contains many islands in inner part, the largest Puná I.

Gua′yas (gwä′yäs). **1** River ab. 180 m. long in Guayas prov., W Ecuador; an arm of Gulf of Guayaquil and the estuary of Bodegas river; with Bodegas river navigable for ab. 200 m. **2** Province of Ecuador. See *Table* at ECUADOR.

Guay′mas (gwī′mäs; gwä′ĕ-). Town, Sonora state, NW Mexico; pop. 8796; port on Gulf of California; railroad terminus; the port of Hermosillo.

Guay·na′bo (gwī·nä′vồ). Municipality (pop. 39,718) and town (pop. 3343), NE Puerto Rico; town 8 m. S of San Juan.

Guayra. See GUAÍRA.

Guaytecas Islands. See GUAITECAS ISLANDS.

Gua′za·ca·pán′ (gwä′sä·kä·pän′). Town, Santa Rosa dept., S Guatemala, near coast S of Guatemala City; pop. 6438.

Gu′ban (gōō′bän). Plateau region, NW Somalia.

Gu′bat (gōō′bät). Municipality, NE Sorsogon prov., Luzon, Phil. Is., port on Pacific coast ab. 10 m. ESE of Sorsogon; pop. 22,880.

Gub′bio (gōōb′byồ); *anc.* **Eu·gu′bi·um** (û·gū′bĭ·ŭm) *and* **I·gu′vi·um** (ĭ·gū′vĭ·ŭm; ĭ-). Commune, Perugia prov., Umbria, cen. Italy, 23 m. N by E of Perugia; pop. 32,727; 13th-cent. cathedral, 13th-cent. church of St. Francis, 14th-cent. Palazzo dei Consoli, and 15th-cent. ducal palace; ancient Roman theater and mausoleum; manufactures majolica. See UMBRIA.

Gu′bin (gōō′bēn); *Ger.* **Gu′ben** (gōō′bĕn). Manufacturing city, SW Poznań prov., W Poland, on Nysa river 27 m. S of Frankfurt an der Oder; formerly in Brandenburg prov., Prussia; pop. (1946) 43,914; manufactures esp. textiles and hats. In origin a Wendish town; successively a possession of Brandenburg 1311, Bohemia 1367, Saxony 1635, and Prussia 1815; in World War II in area of considerable fighting Feb.–Apr. 1945; assigned to Poland by Potsdam Conference 1945.

Gud′brands·dal (gōō′bräns·däl′). Valley ab. 140 m. long in Opland co., S cen. Norway; extends NW and SE above Lake Mjösa and Lillehammer, N part bet. the Jotunheimen and Dovrefjeld; scene of severe fighting Apr. 1940 when British were driven N by Germans.

Gu′den (gōō′thĕn). Longest river in Denmark, 98 m. long; rises in N cen. Jutland, empties into Randers Fjord, an inlet of the Kattegat on E coast.

Gu′di·ya′tam (gōō′dĭ·yä′tàm). Town, N Madras, S Indian Union, near Palar river 100 m. W of Madras; pop. 24,688.

Gueb′wil′ler′ (gĕb′vē·lâr′); *Ger.* **Geb′wei′ler** (gāp′vī-lēr). Commune, Haut-Rhin dept., NE France, 15 m. SSW of Colmar; pop. 10,577.

Gueb′wil′ler′, Bal′lon′ de (bȧ′lôɴd′ gĕb′vē·lâr′); *Ger.* **Gros′ser** (grồ′sēr), *or* **Sul′zer** (zōōl′tsēr), **Bel′chen** (bĕl′kĕn). Mountain 4667 ft. in Haut-Rhin dept., NE France, W of Guebwiller; highest in Vosges Mts.

Gue′cho (gwä′chồ). Commune, Vizcaya prov., N Spain, on Bay of Biscay 8 m. NW of Bilbao; pop. 17,795.

Guelderland. Var. of GELDERLAND.

Guel′ma′ (gĕl′mä′). Commune, Constantine dept., NE Algeria, ab. 40 m. E of Constantine; pop. 12,607.

Guelph (gwĕlf). Manufacturing city, ⊗ of Wellington co., SE Ontario, Canada, 15 m. ENE of Kitchener; pop. 27,386; railroad junction; manufactures iron and steel products, pianos, organs, woolen goods, carpets, cotton and linen goods; has several foundries; Ontario Agricultural Coll. (1874), an affiliate of Toronto Univ.; Ontario Veterinary Coll.; Ontario Reformatory. Founded 1827.

Gué′mappe′ (gā′màp′). Village, Pas-de-Calais dept., N France, 7 m. ESE of Arras; pop. (1931) 211; battles in region Apr.–May 1917 and Mar. 1918.

Gué′rande′ (gā′ränd′). Commune, Loire-Inférieure dept., NW France, ab. 10 m. W of St-Nazaire; pop. (1931) 6164; greater part of stone walls built by John V of Brittany 1431 still preserved; 12th–16th cent. church.

Gué′ret′ (gā′rĕ′). Commune, ✳ of Creuse dept., cen. France, 124 m. S of Orléans; pop. 6119.

Guer·ni′ca (gĕr·nḗ′kä). Town, N Spain, in E viscaya prov. ENE of Bilbao; once seat of a Basque parliament; bombed 1937 by German planes in Spanish civil war; its destruction the subject of a noted painting by Pablo Picasso.

Guern′sey (gûrn′zĭ). **1** County in Ohio. See *Table* at OHIO.
2 One of the Channel Is., in the English Channel; 25 sq. m.; pop. 40,588; constitutes, with Alderney, Sark, and adjacent islands, a bailiwick with area 30 sq. m., pop. 42,743, and ✻ St. Peter Port; market gardening, cattle breeding (the *Guernsey* breed of cattle originating here).

Guernsey Dam. Dam across North Platte river, NE Platte co., SE Wyoming, forming **Guernsey Reservoir** or **Lake**.

Guer·re′ro (gĕr·rĕ′rō). State, S Mexico. See *Table* at MEXICO.

Guettar, El. See EL GUETTAR.

Gueu′de·court′ (gûd′kōōr′). Village, Somme dept., N France, 3 m. SSW of Bapaume; pop. (1931) 159; taken by British Sept. 1916.

Guey′dan (gā′dän). Town, Vermilion parish, S Louisiana, 35 m. WSW of Lafayette; pop. 2156.

Gü′fer·horn (gü′fēr·hôrn). Peak 11,132 ft. in the Adula group, on Swiss-Italian border.

Gu′gu (gōō′gōō). Mountains, cen. Ethiopia, E of Addis Ababa; highest peak **Gugu** 11,886.

Gu·guan′ (gōō·gwän′). Island, cen. Mariana Is., W Pacific Ocean; ab. 2½ m. by 1 m.

Guí′a (gē′ä). Commune, N coast of Grand Canary I., Canary Is.; pop. (1930) 8393.

Gui·a·na (gē·ä′nà; -än′à). **1** Region bet. the Orinoco, Negro, and Amazon rivers and the Atlantic Ocean, in N South America, including Surinam, British Guiana, French Guiana, S and E Venezuela, and N Brazil; ab. 690,000 sq. m. Coast discovered by Spanish explorers 1499–1500; originally name Guiana referred to region extending farther west than present boundaries and was thought to include El Dorado; see BRITISH GUIANA, FRENCH GUIANA, and SURINAM.
2 Coastal strip of French Guiana. See FRENCH GUIANA.

Guiana Mas′sif (măs′ĭf; -ēf; *Fr.* mȧ′sēf′) or **Highlands.** Highland area in N South America, extending from E Venezuela E across British Guiana, Surinam, and French Guiana.

Guibray. See FALAISE.

Gui·enne′ or **Guy·enne′** (gü·ē′yĕn′; gē′-); *Lat.* **Aq′ui·ta′nia** (ăk′wĭ·tān′yà; -tā′nĭ·à). Historical region of SW France; bounded anciently on N by Limousin, NE by Auvergne, E and SE by Languedoc, S by Gascony, W by Atlantic Ocean, NW by Angoumois; ✻ Bordeaux; old duchy near Garonne and Dordogne rivers, part of Aquitaine (*q.v.*); name, Guienne, often used interchangeably with Aquitaine; after French crown recovered it from English at close of Hundred Years' War, re-established as duchy separate from Gascony, etc.; from 17th cent. to 1789, part of French *gouvernement* of Guienne and Gascony. See AQUITANIA SECUNDA.

Gui′ja (gē′hä). Lake 20 m. long on border bet. El Salvador and Guatemala; traversed by Lempa river.

Guilan. Var. of GILAN.

Guild′ford (gĭl′fērd). Municipal borough, Surrey, S England, on the Wey 28 m. SW of London; pop. 47,484; sheep and cattle fairs; ruins of Norman castle; grammar school founded 1509; Anglican cathedral (begun 1936, consecrated 1961).

Guild′hall (gĭld′hôl). Town, ⊗ of Essex co., NE corner of Vermont; pop. 248.

Guil′ford (gĭl′fērd). **1** County in North Carolina. See *Table* at NORTH CAROLINA.
2 Town, SE New Haven co., S Connecticut; on Long Island Sound E of New Haven; pop. 7913; settled 1639.
3 Town, Piscataquis co., N cen. Maine; pop. 1880.
4 Town, Chenango co., S cen. New York, ab. 30 m. NE of Binghamton; pop. 2368.

Guilford College. Town, Guilford co., N cen. North Carolina; ab. 6 m. NW of Greensboro; pop. (est.) 1700; settled by Quakers 1750; Guilford College (1834; coed.).

Guilford Courthouse. Locality, Guilford co., N cen. North Carolina, near Greensboro; scene of battle Mar. 15, 1781 in which Americans under Greene defeated British troops under Cornwallis, ending British control of the Carolinas; area now set aside as **Guilford Courthouse National Military Park** (see UNITED STATES, *National Historical Parks*).

Guil′le·mont′ (gē′y′·môN′). Village, Somme dept., N France; pop. (1931) 193; captured by Germans 1914, became center of German resistance; taken by British Sept. 3, 1916.

Güí′mar (gwē′mär). Village, E coast of Tenerife, Canary Is.; pop. (1930) 8513; resort.

Gui·ma·rães′ (gē·mȧ·rãēnsh′). Commune, Braga dist., NW Portugal, 12 m. SE of Braga; pop. 9023; birthplace of Alfonso, first king of Portugal; besieged and taken 1127 by Alfonso VII of León.

Gui′ma·ras′ (gē′mä·räs′). Island off S coast of Panay I., cen. Phil. Is., separated from it by narrow Iloilo Strait; 223 sq. m.; pop. 38,547; chief town Jordan; part of Iloilo prov.

Guimaras Strait. Channel, generally 15 to 20 m. wide but only 7 m. wide opp. Guimaras I.; extending NE and SW bet. SE Panay I. and NW Negros I., cen. Phil. Is.; connects Visayan Sea with Sulu Sea.

Guim·ba′ (gēm·bä′). Municipality, W Nueva Ecija prov., Luzon, Phil. Is., ab. 17 m. NW of Cabanatuan; pop. 27,681; on main highway bet. Pangasinan and Nueva Ecija provs.

Gui·na·yang′an (gē′nä·yäng′än). Municipality, SE Tayabas prov. SE Luzon, Phil. Is., on coast at head of Ragay Gulf; pop. 15,948.

Guin′ea (gĭn′ĭ); *Fr.* **Gui·née′** (gē′nā′); *Span.* **Gui·ne′a** (gḗ·nā′ä; *Port.* **Gui·né′** (gḗ·nā). **1** Coast region in W Africa, from Gambia river to Gabon river; bet. Gambia and Cameroun (**Upper Guinea**) and bet. Cameroun and S Angola (**Lower Guinea**); name, from an ancient kingdom, not in general European use until after 1500. See FRENCH GUINEA, PORTUGUESE GUINEA, SPANISH GUINEA. Various sections of coast of Upper Guinea given different names by early traders: Slave Coast, Gold Coast, Ivory Coast, Grain Coast (*qq.v.*).
2 Republic, W Africa. See FRENCH GUINEA.

Guinea, Gulf of. Great inlet of Atlantic Ocean on W cen. coast of Africa, bet. Upper Guinea and Lower Guinea and including Benin and Biafra bights.

Guinea Current. A current in the Atlantic Ocean flowing E along the Guinea coast, W Africa.

Guinée française. See FRENCH GUINEA.

Gui′ne·gate′ or **Gui′ne·gaste′** (gēn′gȧt′); *now* **En′gui·ne·gatte′** (äN′-). Commune, Pas-de-Calais dept., N France, S of St-Omer; pop. (1931) 441; scene of two battles: (1) bet. Louis XI and Emperor Maximilian Aug. 7, 1479 and (2) bet. Henry VIII and France Aug. 16, 1513 in which the French were defeated, known as "Battle of the Spurs" from hasty flight of the French.

Güí′nes (gwē′nȧs). Municipality and town, La Habana prov., W Cuba; pop. (town) 22,669; railroad junction 30 m. SE of Havana; center of large plantation district producing esp. tobacco; terminus of first railroad built in Cuba (1835–38).

Guînes (gēn). Commune, Pas-de-Calais dept., N France, 7 m. SE of Calais; pop. (1931) 4223; held by English 1352–1558; residence of Henry VIII in 1520 during meeting of "Field of the Cloth of Gold" bet. him and Francis I. See ARDRES.

Guin′gamp′ (găN′gäN′). Commune, Côtes-du-Nord dept., NW France, 17 m. WNW of St-Brieuc; pop. (1931) 8644; tourist center; former capital of county, later the duchy, of Penthièvre; ruins of 15th-cent. castle and of town walls; noted for church (14th–16th cents.) where annual pardons are granted to pilgrims.

Gui'no·ba'tan (gē'nȯ·bä'tän). Municipality, E cen. Albay prov., Luzon, Phil. Is., ab. 9 m. WNW of Legaspi; pop. 26,419; in region producing much hemp (abacá).

Guio'nes, Point (gyō'nās). Cape on W coast of Nicoya Penin., W Costa Rica.

Gui·púz'co·a (gē·pōōth'kȯ·ä; -pōōs'-). Province of Spain. See *Table* at SPAIN.

Guir, Cape (gēr). Cape on SW coast of Morocco.

Güi'ra de Me·le'na (gwē'rä thä mä·lā'nä). Municipality and town, La Habana prov., W Cuba, 25 m. SSW of Havana; pop. (town) 10,824.

Güi'ria (gwē'ryä). Town, Sucre state, N Venezuela, on Gulf of Paria on S coast of Paria Penin.; pop. 5283.

Guis'bor·ough (gĭz'bŭ·rŭ; -brŭ). Urban district, North Riding, Yorkshire, N England, 10 m. ESE of Middlesbrough; pop. 8609; remains of a priory founded by Robert de Bruce (an ancestor of Robert the Bruce) 1119.

Guis'card' (gēs'kär'). Commune, Oise dept., N France, 19 m. NNE of Compiègne; pop. (1931) 1076; held by Germans Aug. 1914–Mar. 1917; again lost, but finally freed Sept. 1918.

Guise (*Angl.* gēz or, *less often*, gwēz; *Fr.* gü·ēz' or gēz). Commune, Aisne dept., N France, on the Oise 23 m. N of Laon; pop. (1931) 7110; ruins of 16th-cent. castle from which ducs de Guise derived their title 1528; noted for its co-operative ironworks with a *familistère* constructed 1859 by J. B. A. Godin for the association founded by him here in 1846. In World War I much damaged.

Guise'ley (gīz'lĭ). Former urban district, West Riding, Yorkshire, N England; pop. (1931) 5607; since 1937 in Ilkley.

Gui'uan (gē'wän). Municipality, SE tip of Samar, Phil. Is., on NE coast of Leyte Gulf 76 m. SE of Catbalogan; pop. 23,110; good anchorage; in World War II during American reoccupation of Visayan Is. an important base and post office 1944–45.

Gu'ja·rat' (gōōj'jä·rät') *or* **Gu'je·rat'** (gōōj'jĕ-); *also* **Gu'ze·rat'** (gōōj'zĕ·rät').
1 Region, W India, in widest use includes Gujarati-speaking regions of Kathiawar, Cutch, Baroda, Palanpur, and other former Indian states geographically located in or near the N part of former Bombay prov.
2 Usually restricted to level region N of Narbada river and in NE part of Kathiawar, W India; officially established 1937-39 as **Gujarat States Agency** and Baroda (*q.v.*) in charge of Resident at Baroda; comprised Baroda and 11 other states (Balasinor, Bansda, Baria, Cambay, Chota Udaipur, Dharampur, Jawhar, Lunawada, Rajpipla, Sachin, and Sant) and the Rewa Kantha Agency (many small states and estates including The Dangs, Sankheda Mewas, and Pandu Mewas); excluding Baroda 7352 sq. m., pop. (1941) 1,458,702. Annexed to Sultanate of Delhi 1297; its Mohammedan governor founded independent kingdom, 1401; territory extended by Ahmad I (1411–41) who built Ahmadabad; annexed 1572–73 by Mogul Emperor Akbar; in 18th cent., overrun by Marathas who later ceded to British much of old kingdom of Gujarat. Formerly these states were grouped in the old Rewa Kantha Agency, Kaira Agency, Surat Agency, Nasik Agency, and Thana Agency; on July 7, 1947 several of the states (including Bansda, Lunawada, Rajpipla, and Sant) joined a new confederation of Indian states; after Aug. 15, 1947, within the Indian Union.
3 A state of the Republic of India, comprising the Gujarati-speaking NW portion of the former Bombay state; formed May 1, 1960; 72,245 sq. m.; pop. (1961) 20,633,350; ✷ Ahmadabad. See MAHARASHTRA.

Guj'ran·wa'la (gōōj'răn·wä'lä). **1** District, Lahore division, E West Punjab, Pakistan; 2311 sq. m.; pop. (1941) 912,234.
2 Town, state ✷, 40 m. N of Lahore; pop. (1941) 84,545; grain trade. Birthplace of Ranjit Singh; capital of Sikh power in its early period; included in territory annexed by British after Second Sikh War (1848–49).

Guj'rat (gōōj'rät). Town, Rawalpindi division, N West Pakistan, near Chenab river 68 m. N of Lahore; pop. 59,608; known for work in gold and silver inlay; ceramics, electric fans. Present town founded c. 1500, traditionally the third in a series on this site; scene of battle 1849 in which Sikh power was broken.

Gul'bar·ga (gōōl'bĕr·gä'). Town N cen. Mysore state, S cen. India, 120 m. W of Hyderabad; pop. 41,083; manufactures cotton, flour, paint, and oil. Seat of Bahmani kings of the Deccan 1347–1422; many interesting remains of this era, notably a mosque patterned after that of Córdoba in Spain.

Gülek Boğaz. See CILICIAN GATES.

Gulf (gŭlf). **1** County in Florida. See *Table* at FLORIDA. **2** Unincorporated town, Matagorda co., SE Texas, near Matagorda Bay, ab. 18 m. S of Bay City; pop. (1950) 1650; sulfur mining, processing, and shipping.

Gulf In'tra·coast'al Waterway (ĭn'trȧ·kōs't'l). System of inland waterways including rivers, bays and canals from Carrabelle, Florida, E of the Apalachicola river, to Brownsville, Texas; includes Mobile Bay and Mississippi Sound, goes through New Orleans, takes in the Sabine-Neches Waterway (*q.v.*) and the ship canal at Houston, Texas.

Gulf Plain. Lowland bordering the Gulf of Mexico, S United States.

Gulf'port (gŭlf'pōrt). **1** City Pinellas co., W Florida penin.; pop. 9730; suburb of St. Petersburg. **2** City, ⊗ of Harrison co., SE Mississippi, on Gulf of Mexico; pop. 30,204; resort; ships cotton, lumber.

Gulf States. The states of the United States bordering on the Gulf of Mexico: Florida, Alabama, Mississippi, Louisiana, and Texas.

Gulf Stream. Warm ocean current in North Atlantic Ocean; flows out of Gulf of Mexico through Straits of Florida, where it is a current 50 m. wide and more than 2000 ft. deep, continues NE along coast of United States to Nantucket I. and thence eastward; in N mid-Atlantic (40°N, 45°W) merges with North Atlantic Drift Current, a warm current flowing NE to the Barents Sea and influencing climate of W Europe as far as Norway; at ab. 30°W sends off Southeast Drift Current touching coasts of Iberian Penin. and NW Africa; rate of flow, more than 4 m. an hour in the S and between 10 and 15 m. a day farther N. Strictly, the term *Gulf Stream* does not apply beyond 60°W.

Gu'lis·tan' (gōō'lĭs·tän'). **1** Village, West Pakistan, in N Baluchistan, 40 m. NW of Quetta. **2** Village, cen. Azerbaidzhan S.S.R., U.S.S.R.; treaty bet. Russia and Persia signed here Oct. 12, 1813 by which Persia gave up Georgia and neighboring districts.

Gul·kan'a (gŭl·kăn'ȧ). Village on Copper river, SE Alaska; pop. (1950) 25; on Richardson and Glenn Highways; junction for cutoff to Tanacross on Alaska Highway.

Gull'foss' (gŭt'l'·fôs'); *Eng.* **Golden Fall.** Waterfall 150 ft. in Hvítá river, SW Iceland, near Geysir.

Gull Island (gŭl). Island at E end of Long Island Sound, New York, just NE of Plum I.; fixed light.

Gull Lake. Lake, Cass and Crow Wing cos., N cen. Minnesota; resort.

Gul'marg (gŭl'märg). Village, SW Kashmir, N India, 30 m. W of Srinagar.

Gul'pai·gan' (gōōl'pī·gän'). Town, W cen. Iran, 90 m. NW of Isfahan; pop. ab. 8000; wood carving; many orchards in surrounding area.

Gu·mal' (gŭ·mŭl') *or* **Go·mal'** (gȯ·mŭl'). River, S North-West Frontier Province, NW Pakistan; flows from E Afghanistan E and SE to the Indus near Dera Ismail Khan; chief tributary the Zhob.

Gumal, *or* **Gomal, Pass.** Mountain pass 7500 ft. at N end of Sulaiman Range, NW border of Pakistan, in S North-West Frontier Province WNW of Dera Ismail Khan; most important pass on W frontier of India bet. the Khyber and Bolan Passes.

Gum·bin′nen (gŏŏm·bǐn′ĕn). **1** Former government district, East Prussia prov., Prussia, Germany; 3628 sq. m. **2** See GUSEV.

Gum·ma (gŏŏm·mä). Prefecture of Japan. See *Table* at JAPAN.

Gum′mers·bach (gŏŏm′ĕrs·bäк). City, North Rhine-Westphalia state, West Germany, 28 m. E of Cologne; pop. 17,338; manufactures textiles, leather, lumber.

Gumry. See LENINAKAN.

Gum′ti (gŏŏm′tĕ). River ab. 500 m. long, N India; rises in NE Uttar Pradesh, flows SE past Lucknow to the Ganges below Benares; navigable for small vessels.

Gümüljina. See KOMOTINĒ.

Gü′müş·a·ne′ (gü′müsh·ȧ·nĕ′) or **Gü′müsh Kha-neh′** (gü′müsh kä·nĕ′). **1** Vilayet, NE Turkey in Asia; 3899 sq. m.; pop. 162,667. **2** Town, its ✳, 40 m. SSW of Trabzon; pop. 3174; noted for its silver mines.

Gu′na (gŏŏ′nȧ). Peak 13,880 ft. in N cen. Ethiopia, E of Lake Tana.

Gun Cay (gŭn). Island in the Bahama Is., S of the Biminis; lighthouse on S end (estab. 1836).

Gun′flint′ (gŭn′flǐnt′). Village, Cook co., NE Minnesota, at W end of **Gunflint Lake** on the U.S.-Canada boundary; iron ore in the region to the S, first to be discovered in the state but never mined because of its high titanium content.

Gu·nib′ (gŏŏ·nǐb′). Village, W Dagestan, SE Soviet Russia, Europe, in E Caucasus Mts.; scene of capture 1859 of the Caucasian leader, Shamyl, which ended resistance of mountain tribes to Russian domination.

Gun′ni·son (gŭn′ǐ·s′n). **1** River 150 m. long, W cen. Colorado; rises in SE Gunnison co., flows W and NW into Colorado river in cen. Mesa co. Black Canyon of the Gunnison is a National Monument (see UNITED STATES, *National Monuments*). See also BLACK CANYON. **2** Island in NW Great Salt Lake, Utah; bird rookery. **3** County in Colorado. See *Table* at COLORADO. **4** Town, ⊗ of Gunnison co., W cen. Colorado, on Gunnison river 50 m. W of Salida; pop. 3477; founded 1879 as mining center; resort; Western State College of Colorado (1911; coed.).

Gunong. See GUNUNG.

Gun′pow′der (gŭn′pou′dĕr). River ab. 60 m. long, N Maryland; rises in NE Carroll co., flows SE into upper Chesapeake Bay.

Gun·san (gŏŏn·sän). Var. of GUNZAN.

Gun′sight′, Mount (gŭn′sīt′). Peak 9250 ft. in Glacier National Park, NW Montana.

Gun′ters·ville (gŭn′tĕrz·vĭl). Industrial city, ⊗ of Marshall co., NE Alabama, on Tennessee river, 30 m. NW of Gadsden; pop. 6592; river port.

Guntersville Dam. See *Table* at TENNESSEE VALLEY AUTHORITY.

Gun·tur′ (gŏŏn·tŏŏr′). City, cen. Andhra Pradesh, E India, NW of mouths of Kistna river, 220 m. N of Madras; pop. (1941) 83,599; important cotton and tobacco trade. Apparently founded in 18th cent. by French; ceded to British 1788, cession confirmed 1823.

Guntur. See GOENTOER.

Günük. See XANTHUS.

Gu′nung (gŏŏ′nŏong) or **Gu′nong** (gŏŏ′nông). Malay term meaning "mountain," *Dutch* **Goe′noeng** (gŏŏ′-noŏng); as in **Gunong Ta·han′** (tä·hän′), **Gunong Ker·bau′** (kĕr·bou′), **Goenoeng A′woe** (ä′wŏŏ). See second element of the name.

Gunung Api. See GOENOENG API.

Gunungsitoli. See GOENOENGSITOLI.

Gun·zan (gŏŏn·zän) or **Kun·san** (kŏŏn·sän). Seaport, North Zenra prov., SW Korea, 110 m. S of Keijo; pop. (1938 est.) 44,284; exports much rice.

Gur, Lough (lŏк gŏŏr′). Small lake, co. Limerick, S Eire, S of Limerick; prehistoric stone monuments; castle ruins.

Gu·ra′bo (gŏŏ·rä′vȯ). Municipality (pop. 16,603) and town (pop. 3957), E Puerto Rico; town 17 m. SE of San Juan.

Gur·das′pur (gŏŏr·däs′pŏŏr). **1** District, formerly entirely in Lahore division, N Punjab, NW India; 1889 sq. m.; pop. (1941) 1,153,511; divided 1947 with ab. 1240 sq. m. (pop. ab. 769,000) in Punjab state, Indian Union, and ab. 649 sq. m. (pop. ab. 385,000) in West Punjab, Pakistan. **2** Town, formerly ✳ of the district, bet. Beas and Ravi rivers 75 m. NE of Lahore; pop. 12,094; now in Punjab state, Indian Union.

Gur′don (gûr′d′n). City, Clark co., SW Arkansas, 15 m. SSW of Arkadelphia; pop. 2166; railroad junction; cotton, lumber.

Gu′rev or **Gu′ryev** (gŏŏ′ryĕf). Seaport town, ✳ of Gurev Region, SW Kazakh S.S.R., Soviet Central Asia, at N end of Caspian Sea at mouth of Ural river; terminus of oil pipeline NE to Aktyubinsk and Orsk.

Gurev, or **Guryev, Region.** Subdivision of Kazakh S.S.R., Soviet Central Asia, in SW part; bounded on S by Turkmen S.S.R. and on W by Caspian Sea and Astrakhan Region of R.S.F.S.R.; ✳ Gurev; largely marsh and desert; has long coast line on the Caspian, including Buzachi Penin. and Mangyshlak Penin. crossed by lower courses of Ural and Emba rivers.

Gur·gan′ (gŏŏr·gän′). **1** River ab. 180 m. long in N Iran; flows W into SE Caspian Sea N of Bandar Shah. **2** See ASTERABAD province and city.

Gurhwal. Var. of GARHWAL.

Gurk (gŏŏrk). River ab. 75 m. long in Carinthia prov., S Austria; flows E and S into Drau (Drava) river 10 m. E of Klagenfurt.

Gur′kha (gŏŏr′kȧ). Village, E cen. Nepal, 50 m. WNW of Katmandu; former capital of the Gurkha race.

Gur′la Man·dha′ta (gŏŏr′lȧ mänd·hä′tä). Peak 25,355 ft. in the Himalayas, in SW Tibet near border of Nepal.

Gur′nards Head (gûr′nĕrdz). Promontory on SE coast of Cornwall, SW England, N of Lands End.

Gur′net Point (gûr′nĕt; -nĭt). Cape on N side of Plymouth Bay, Massachusetts; 2 fixed lights.

Gu′ru·pi′ (gŏŏ′rŏŏ·pē′). River ab. 350 m. long, NE Brazil; flows N from W Maranhão state, forming boundary bet. Pará and Maranhão; empties into Atlantic Ocean.

Guryev. See GUREV.

Gu·sa′u (gŏŏ·zä′ŏŏ). Town, Sokoto prov., Northern Region, NW Nigeria, 130 m. W of Kano; pop. ab. 15,000; lumber.

Gu′sev (gŏŏ′syĕf); *Ger.* **Gum·bin′nen** (gŏŏm·bǐn′ĕn). Manufacturing city, Kaliningradsk Region, R.S.F.S.R., 68 m. E of Kaliningrad; pop. 19,002; agricultural machinery, steam and water mills, electrical goods. Scene of Russian victory over Germans Aug. 19–20, 1914; assigned to U.S.S.R. by Potsdam Conference 1945.

Gusharbrum. See GASHERBRUM.

Gus′tav Line (gŏŏs′täf). In World War II the main German defense line across Italy S of Rome; its key position Cassino with the Liri valley behind it; reached by Allies Feb. 1944, not taken until May 1944.

Gustavo A. Madero. See GUADALUPE HIDALGO.

Gus·ta′vus (gŭs·tä′vŭs; -tä′-). Village, SE Alaska, on Cross Sound N of Chichagof I. and W of Juneau; entrance to Glacier Bay National Monument; airport.

Gü′strow (güs′trō). Manufacturing city, East Germany, 50 m. SW of Stralsund; pop. 19,084; 13th-cent. cathedral; 16th-cent. ducal castle; steel, machinery, doors and windows, chemicals.

Gu′ta (gŏŏ′tä; *Slovak* gŏŏ′tà); *Hung.* **Gú′ta** (gŏŏ′tŏ); *Ger.* **Gut′ta** (gŏŏt′ä). Town, SW Slovakia prov., E cen. Czechoslovakia; pop. (1930) 10,827; N of the Danube; included in Hungary 1938–45.

Gü′ters·loh (gü′tĕrs·lō). City NE North Rhine-Westphalia state, W Germany, 31 m. E of Münster; pop. 22,174; manufactures foodstuffs, textiles, iron goods.

Guth′rie (gŭth′rĭ). **1** County in Iowa. See *Table* at IOWA.
2 City, ⊗ of Logan co., cen. Oklahoma, 28 m. N of Oklahoma City; pop. 9502; manufactures steel, concrete, wooden products; oil wells; railroad terminus. Founded 1889; capital of Oklahoma territory and state 1890–1910.
3 Village, ⊗ of King co., NW Texas; pop. (1950) 111.
Guthrie Center. City, ⊗ of Guthrie co., SW cen. Iowa, 50 m. W of Des Moines; pop. 2071.
Guti. Var. of GOOTY.
Gutta. See GUTA.
Gut′ten·berg (gŭt′′n·bûrg). **1** Town, Clayton co., NE Iowa, on Mississippi river 30 m. NW of Dubuque; pop. 2087; settled 1834, colonized by German immigrants 1845.
2 Town, Hudson co., NE New Jersey, on Hudson river 5 m. N of Jersey City; pop. 5118.
Guyana. See BRITISH GUIANA.
Guy′an·dot (gī′ăn·dŏt). River ab. 150 m. long, SW West Virginia; rises in Wyoming co., flows NW into Ohio river near Huntington.
Guyane française. See FRENCH GUIANA.
Guyenne. See GUIENNE.
Guy′mon (gī′mŭn). City, ⊗ of Texas co., NW Oklahoma; pop. 5768.
Guy′ot, Mount (gē′ō; -yō). **1** Mountain 12,305 ft. on E boundary of Tulare co., California, near Mt. Whitney.
2 Peak 4589 ft., N cen. New Hampshire, in N Grafton co.
3 Peak 6621 ft. in Great Smoky Mts., on boundary bet. Tennessee and North Carolina.
Guys′bor′ough (gĭz′bûr′ō; -bŭ·rŭ; -brŭ). **1** County, Nova Scotia, Canada. See *Table* at NOVA SCOTIA.
2 Town (unincorporated), its ⊗, E Nova Scotia, Canada, at head of Chedabucto Bay; pop. (district) 8577.
Guzerat. See GUJARAT.
Gwa′dar or **Gwa′dur** (gwô′dẽr). Port on Makran coast, SW Baluchistan; pop. 4730; with ab. 300 sq. m. of adjoining territory belonged to Oman from beginning of 19th cent. until ceded to Pakistan 1958.
Gwa′li·or (gwä′li·ôr). **1** Former state, N Central India, Indian Union; 26,367 sq. m.; pop. (1941) 4,006,159; ✱ Lashkar; one of the five chief Indian states, the dominion of the Sindhia family of Marathas; larger part bet. Rajputana on W and United Provinces and Central India on E, with Chambal river forming its N and NW boundary; other smaller sections in SW Central India; now in Madhya Pradesh.
2 Town, N Madhya Pradesh, N cen. India, 60 m. S of Agra; pop. 21,999; old part of city, which has many fine Mogul architectural remains, overlooked by famous medieval Hindu fort of Gwalior, on a sandstone cliff 300 ft. high and including within its walls the beautiful palace of Man Singh, the citadel, temples, and reservoirs. Fort annexed by Mahadaji Sindhia, Maratha leader of 18th cent. who expanded his territory from vicinity of Ujjain to include large part of cen. India; fort lost to English as result of Maratha Wars, the Maratha kingdom, reduced in territory, being allowed to stand; fort restored to ruler by Lord Dufferin 1886. To the S is the new city, **Lash′kar** (lŭsh′kẽr), founded c. 1800.
Gwandu. See GANDO.
Gwa′tar (gwô′tẽr). Coastal town, SE Iran, on border of Baluchistan.
Gwatar Bay. Inlet of Arabian Sea on SW coast of Baluchistan, on Iranian border.
Gwee·bar′ra Bay (gwē·băr′à). Inlet of Atlantic Ocean in W co. Donegal, N Eire, N of Donegal Bay.
Gwee·dore′ (gwē·dōr′). Town, co. Donegal, N Eire, 20 m. NW of Letterkenny; pop. ab. 2000; tourist resort; fishing.
Gwe′lo (gwā′lō). Town, Matabeleland, SW Southern Rhodesia, S Africa, 90 m. ENE of Bulawayo; pop. 3256; center for district producing gold, chrome ore, asbestos fiber, and some diamonds.
Gwin·nett′ (gwĭ·nĕt′). County in Georgia. See *Table* at GEORGIA.
Gwy′dir (gwī′dẽr). River 450 m. long, NE New South Wales, SE Australia, flows W into Barwon river.
Gwyn′edd or **Gwyn′eth** (gwĭn′ĕth). Ancient region in NW Wales, now included in Caernarvonshire, Denbighshire, and Merionethshire.
Gyang′tse′ or **Gyan′tse′** (gyäng′tsĕ′). Town, SE Tibet, Outer China, 100 m. SW of Lhasa; pop. ab. 5000; junction point for caravan routes W to Ladakh, NE to Lhasa, and S to Sikkim and India; famous for manufactures of woolen cloth and carpets; first opened to trade by treaty of 1904.
Gy′a·ros (yē′à·rôs). Mountainous island, NW Cyclades, S Aegean Sea, NW of Syros; 7 sq. m.; in Cyclades dept., Greece.
Gym′pie (gĭm′pĭ). Town, E Queensland, Australia, 90 m. N of Brisbane; pop. 7749; in region producing gold, silver, coal, antimony, and copper.
Gyo′ma (dyŏ′mŏ). Commune, SE Hungary, 55 m. SW of Debrecen; pop. 12,474.
Gyön′gyös (dyûn′dyûsh). City, N cen. Hungary, NE of Budapest; pop. 20,058; trade center in area producing wool and wines.
Györ (dyûr); *Ger.* **Raab** (räp). Autonomous city, NW Hungary, 67 m. WNW of Budapest; 21 sq. m.; pop. 68,000; 12th-cent. cathedral, 15th-cent. episcopal palace.
Gy′-Pa′ra·ná′ (zhē′pà′rà·nà′). River ab. 500 m. long (with longest headstream) in W cen. Brazil; rises in W Mato Grosso state, flows N and NW into Madeira river.
Gyth′i·um (jĭth′ĭ·ŭm; jĭ·thī′ŭm); *Mod. Gr.* **Gý′thei·on** (yē′thyôn). Seaport town, S Laconia dept., SE Peloponnesus, Greece, near head of Gulf of Laconia; pop. 6701; important Spartan base in Greek wars.
Gyu′la (dyōō′lŏ). City, SE Hungary, NE of Szeged near Romanian border; pop. 23,938.
Gyulafehérvár. See ALBA IULIA.
Gzhatsk (gzhàtsk). Town, NE Smolensk Region, Soviet Russia, Europe, 90 m. W of Moscow, on main Moscow-Smolensk highway and railroad; pop. ab. 7000; in World War II held a few months of 1941–42 by the Germans.

H

Ha'a·bai' (hä'à·bī') *or* **Ha'a·pai'** (-pī'). Island group in cen. Tonga Is. (*q.v.*), SW cen. Pacific Ocean, ab. 60 m. S of Vavau group; ab. 50 islands, including Haano, Foa, Lifuka, Uiha, and Tofua; pop. (1937) 6856; chief village Pangai on Lifuka I.

Haa'kon (hăk'ŭn). County in South Dakota. See *Table* at SOUTH DAKOTA.

Haan (hän). City, North Rhine-Westphalia state, W Germany, NW suburb of Solingen; pop. 10,670; manufactures steel, tools, silk goods, woolens.

Ha·a'no (hä·ä'nô). Island in NE Haabai group, Tonga Is., SW cen. Pacific Ocean.

Haapai. See HAABAI.

Haapsalu. See KHAPSALU.

Haar'lem (här'lĕm; *Du.* här'-). City, * of North Holland prov., W Netherlands, 12 m. W of Amsterdam; pop. (1939) 140,469; center of tulip-growing and exporting section; 15th-cent. Groote Kerk of St. Bavo; Frans Hals Museum; Teyler Museum (science). Forced to yield to Spaniards after siege of 7 months 1572–73; recaptured 1577 by William of Orange.

Haar'lem·mer·meer' (här'lĕm·ĕr·mār'; *Du.* här'-). Commune, North Holland prov., W Netherlands, built on land reclaimed from the former **Haarlem Lake**, a branch of Zuider Zee; pop. (1939) 33,174.

Hab (hŭb). River ab. 220 m. long, E and SE Baluchistan; flows S into Arabian Sea, in its lower course forming boundary bet. Baluchistan and Sind, Pakistan.

Habana, La. See LA HABANA and HAVANA.

Habarovsk. Var. of KHABAROVSK.

Hab·ba'ni·ya, Lake (hăb·bă'nĭ·yà; -yă). Lake along S bank of the Euphrates, cen. Iraq, 50 m. W of Baghdad; scene of brief fighting Apr.–May 1941 for control of large British airfield established near its N shore during World War II.

Hab'er·sham (hăb'ĕr·shăm; -shăm). County in Georgia. See *Table* at GEORGIA.

Habesha, El. See ETHIOPIA.

Ha'bor (hā'bôr). Biblical name (*2 Kings* xvii. 6) for the Khabur river.

Habs'burg (hăps'bûrg; *Ger.* häps'bŏͅoͅrK). Hamlet in Aargau canton, N cen. Switzerland, NE of Aarau; pop. (1930) 170; original seat of the Hapsburgs (*Ger.* Habsburg).

Ha·chi·jo (hä·chē·jō). **1** Group of islands off SE Honshu, Japan, S of the O Shima group at S end of Izu Shichito; forms an administrative unit of Tokyo prefecture; ab. 32 sq. m.; pop. (1945) 6214; consists of Hachijo I. and three islets. **2** Chief island of the group, 180 m. S of Tokyo; 27 sq. m.; pop. (1945) 5919; sericulture, stock raising.

Ha·chi·no·he (hä·chē·nô·hĕ). Coastal town, Aomori prefecture, N Honshu, Japan; pop. (1945) 77,506.

Ha·chi·o·ji (hä·chē·ō·jĕ). City, Tokyo prefecture, SE cen. Honshu, Japan, 27 m. W of Tokyo; pop. (1945) 63,192; since early 18th cent. noted for its weaving industry, esp. of silk fabrics for Japanese wear; produces habutai, pongee, and silk-cotton mixtures.

Hack'en·sack (hăk'ĕn·săk). **1** River ab. 40 m. long, flowing from Rockland co., SE New York, S across New Jersey border and into Newark Bay. **2** City, ⊗ of Bergen co., NE corner of New Jersey, on Hackensack river 7 m. ESE of Paterson; pop. 30,521; manufactures bricks, cement, haberdashery, wallpaper, paperboard, silk, chemicals, airplane parts. Settled by Dutch 1647, by English 1668; served as Revolutionary camping ground in turn for Americans and British; incorp. 1868, chartered as city 1921.

Hack'etts·town (hăk'ĕts·toun). Town, Warren co., NW New Jersey, 19 m. W of Morristown; pop. 5276; manufactures silk goods, leather, agricultural implements.

Hackney. Metropolitan borough of London. See *Table* at LONDON.

Ha'da·mar (hä'dä·mär). Town, Hesse state, W Germany, 27 m. N of Wiesbaden; site of concentration camp during World War II.

Ha·dar'ba, Ras (räs hä·där'bà; -bă); *or* **Cape El'ba** (ĕl'bà). Cape extending into Red Sea, NE Sudan.

Hadd, Cape (hăd); *Arab.* **Ras al Hadd** (räs ăl hăd). East extremity of Oman, SE Arabia, projecting into the Arabian Sea, 22°35'N.

Had'dam (hăd'ăm). Agricultural town, cen. Middlesex co., S Connecticut, on Connecticut river; pop. 3466; incorporated 1668.

Had'ding·ton (hăd'ĭng·tŭn). **1** *or* **Had'ding·ton·shire** (-shĭr; -shēr). See EAST LOTHIAN. **2** Burgh, ⊗ of East Lothian co., SE Scotland; pop. 4497; includes Giffordgate, birthplace of John Knox.

Had'don (hăd'ʼn). Urban township, Camden co., SW New Jersey, SSE of Camden; pop. 17,099.

Had'don·field (hăd'ʼn·fēld). Residential borough, Camden co., SW New Jersey, 6 m. SE of Camden; pop. 13,201; founded c. 1710 by Elizabeth Haddon, an English Quaker; scene of Revolutionary skirmishes; meeting place of New Jersey's first legislature 1777.

Had'don Heights (hăd'ʼn). Borough, Camden co., SW New Jersey, 5 m. SSE of Camden; pop. 9260.

Ha·de'ji·a (hä·dā'jĭ·à). **1** River 375 m. long N Nigeria; rises W of Kano and flows ENE to the Yobe on Nigerian border. **2** Town, Kano prov., Northern Region, Nigeria, on Hadejia river 110 m. E of Kano; chief town of former emirate of Katagum.

Ha·de'ra (hä·dā'rä). Town, W Palestine, in part assigned to Israel, near coast 26 m. S of Haifa.

Ha'ders·lev (hä'thĕrs·lĭv); *Ger.* **Ha'ders·le'ben** (hä'dĕrs·lā'bĕn). **1** County of Denmark. See *Table* at DENMARK. **2** Seaport, its ⊗, SE Jutland; pop. (1945) 17,583; railroad center; iron foundries, breweries, tanneries, fisheries; under German rule 1864–1920; 13th-cent. cathedral.

Hadhr, Al. See HATRA.

Ha·dhra·maut' *or* **Ha·dra·maut'** (hŏ·drŏ·mōͅōͅt'; -mout'). Coastal region of S Arabia, E of Aden, part of Aden Protectorate; ab. 58,500 sq. m.; pop. ab. 150,000; boundaries vague; large areas desert; in cen. part is fertile valley along **Wadi Hadhramaut** (ab. 400 m. long); parallel to coast is mountain range 4000 to 8000 ft. with plateau and oases inland; chief town port of Mukalla. In ancient times had advanced civilization as indicated by extensive ruins; little known before end of 19th cent. as the inhabitants (Hadhramautians or Hadhrumi) have resisted entry by foreigners; divided into several sultanates with the more important of which the British have resident advisers (since 1866, by treaty).

Hadibu. See TAMRIDAH.

Ha·di'tha (hä·dē'thä; -thä). Town, W cen. Iraq, on W bank of the Euphrates above Hit.

Had'ley (hăd'lĭ). Town, Hampshire co., W Massachusetts, on Connecticut river 16 m. N of Springfield; pop. 3099; birthplace of Gen. Joseph Hooker. Settled 1659, incorporated 1661.

Hadley Falls Dam. See HOLYOKE DAM.

Hadranum. See ADRANO.

Hadria. See ADRIA.

Hadrianopolis. See EDIRNE.

Hadria Picena. See ATRI.

Hadrumetum. See SOUSSE.

Haeju. See KAISHU.

Hae'len (hä'lĕ[n]). Commune, Limburg prov., NE Belgium; pop. 2755; scene of Belgian victory over Germans Aug. 12, 1914.

Haemus. See BALKAN MOUNTAINS.

Haf'fe (hăf'fȧ; -fă). Town, N Latakia, Syria, ab. 15 m. NE of Latakia.

Haf'nar·fjör'dur (häp'när·fyûr'thŭr). Town, SW Iceland, ab. 10 m. S of Reykjavík; pop. (1942) 3783.

Haft Kel (häft kĕl). Town and oil well, in foothills of S Zagros Mts., SW Iran, ab. 50 m. E of Ahwaz; connected by pipelines with Abadan.

Ha·fun' (hä·fōōn'), **Bay of**. Inlet of Indian Ocean on NE coast of Somalia, S of Cape Hafun.

Hafun, Cape; *Arab.* **Ras Hafun** (räs). Cape on coast of NE Somalia; the E extremity of Africa, 10°25′N and 51° 25′ E.

Ha'ga·ry (hŭ'gȧ·rĭ). River ab. 125 m. long, S cen. India, rises in W Mysore and flows N to the Tungabhadra.

Ha'gen (hä'gĕn). Industrial city, North Rhine-Westphalia state, W Germany, 30 m. ENE of Düsseldorf; pop. (1939) 151,870; iron goods, tools, light machinery, railroad cars, chemicals. Since 1929 includes former city of Haspe.

Ha'gers·town (hä'gĕrz·toun). **1** Town, Wayne co., E Indiana, 15 m. WNW of Richmond; pop. 1730.
2 City, ⊗ of Washington co., N Maryland, 68 m. WNW of Baltimore; pop. 36,660; manufactures organs, furniture, flour, cement, aircraft.

Ha·gi (hä·gē). Coastal town, Yamaguchi prefecture, SW Honshu, Japan, in N part on Sea of Japan; pop. (1945) 38,388 former ✻ of Yamaguchi prefecture.

Ha·gi'a Tri·a'da (ä·yē'ä trē·ä'thä). Ruins of ancient town, near Tympákion and shore of Bay of Messara, S Crete; important archaeological site.

Hagion, Hagios. See SAINT.

Hagion Oros. **1** See MOUNT ATHOS.
2 See SINGITIC GULF.

Ha'gi·os E·li'as, *or* **Ha'gi·os I·li'as** (ä'yôs ê·lyē'äs), **Mount**. Name of several mountains in Greece, including: (1) a peak 7904 ft. in the Taygetus Mts., W Laconia, SE Peloponnesus; (2) *anc.* **O'cha** (ō'kȧ), a peak 4839 ft. in S Euboea I.; (3) a peak 5558 ft. in Othrys Mts., S Thessaly.

Ha'gi·os Ev·strá'ti·os (ä'yôs âf·strä'tyôs), *also* **Ha'gi·os Ey·strá'ti·os** (âf·strä'tyôs). Island in N cen. Aegean Sea, ab. 25 m. S of Lemnos; pop. ab. 1100; chief town Hagios Evstrátios, near NW tip of island; administered from Lemnos, a province of Lesbos dept., Greece.

Ha'gi·os Ni·kó'la·os (ä'yôs nyê·kô'lä·ôs). Seaport town, ✻ of Lasithion dept., E Crete, Greece; pop. 1543; on W shore of Mirabella Bay.

Ha'go·noy' (hä'gô·noi'). Municipality, SW Bulacan prov., Luzon, Phil. Is., in Pampanga delta 7 m. W of Malolos; pop. 29,734.

Hague, Cape La. See Cape LA HAGUE.

Hague, The (häg); *Du.* **'s Gra·ven·ha'ge** (skrä'vĕn·hä'ĸĕ). City, South Holland prov., SW Netherlands, 3 m. SW of Amsterdam and 4 m. inland from North Sea; pop. (1939) 504,264; chiefly residential; meeting place of the International Peace Conference 1899, and the Second International Peace Conference 1907; site of the international courts of arbitration and justice, housed in the Peace Palace (gift of Andrew Carnegie); Royal Palace, Groote Kerk, Municipal Museum, Mauritshuis. Originally a hunting seat of the counts of Holland, since 1250 the royal residence; in World War II occupied by Germans May 16, 1940.

Ha'gue·nau' (àg'nō'). Commune, Bas-Rhin dept., NE France, 11 m. N of Strasbourg; pop. 22,523; 13th-cent. church; 15th-cent. chancellery (now a municipal library); breweries, spinning mills. Built around hunting lodge of duke of Swabia 11th cent.; site of Hohenstaufen imperial tribunal (before which Richard the Lion-Hearted appeared); became free city 1255, French 1634; fortresses razed by Louis XIV; in World War II taken by Americans Mar. 1945.

Ha! Ha! Bay *or* **Ha Ha Bay** (hä' hä'). Inlet on S side of Saguenay river, S Quebec, Canada, ab. halfway bet. St. Lawrence river and Lake St. John.

Ha·ha Ji·ma (hä·hä jê·mä). **1** Island group of the Bonin Is., Japan.
2 Largest island of the group.

Hahn'ville (hän'vĭl). Village, ⊗ of Saint Charles parish, SE Louisiana; pop. 1297.

Hai *or* **Hai Ho** (hī' hŭ'). The lower course of the Pei river, China, from its junction at Tientsin with the Grand Canal to its mouth on Gulf of Po Hai.

Haichow. See TUNGHAI.

Haidarabad. See HYDERABAD.

Haidar Pasha. See HAYDARPAŞA.

Hai'ding·er (hī'dĭng·ēr). Mountain 10,059 ft., N of Aorangi, Southern Alps, South I., New Zealand.

Haï'dra (hī'drȧ), *anc.* **Am·moe'da·ra** (ȧ·mē'dȧ·rȧ). Town, W Tunisia, on boundary of Algeria; phosphates; ruins of ancient town include two arches and a mausoleum.

Hai'fa (hī'fȧ; *Arab.* hä'fă). **1** District, NW Palestine; 393 sq. m.; pop. 95,472, (1942 est.) 203,407; formerly a subdistrict of Haifa-Samaria dist.
2 *anc.* **Syc'a·mi'num** (sĭk'ȧ·mī'nŭm). Seaport, its ✻, at S end of Bay of Acre at foot of Mt. Carmel; pop. 50,403, (1944 est.) 125,493; not important historically, its growth recent; terminus of one of the oil pipelines from Iraq to the Mediterranean; important local industries, one of chief cities of new state of Israel.

Hai'fa-Sa·mar'i·a District (hī'fȧ·sȧ·mâr'ĭ·ȧ). Former district in N cen. Palestine; now divided into Haifa and Samaria dists.

Haifong. = HAIPHONG.

Hai'ku (hī'kōō; *Hawaiian* hä'ê·kōō'). Village, Makawao dist., Maui co., on N coast of Maui I. 4 m. E of Paia, Hawaii; pop. (est.) 800.

Hail *or* **Haïl** (hīl; *Arab.* hä'ĭl). Town and oasis, ✻ of Jebel Shammar prov., N Nejd, Saudi Arabia, ab. 240 m. NE of Medina; pop. ab. 20,000.

Hai'lar' (hī'lär'). **1** River ab. 240 m. long, NW Manchuria; flows W into Argun river just N of Hulun Nor.
2 Town. See HULUN.

Hai'ley (hā'lĭ). City, ⊗ of Blaine co., S cen. Idaho; pop. 1185.

Hai'ley·bur'y (hā'lĭ·bĕr'ĭ). Residential town, ⊗ of Timiskaming dist., SE Ontario, Canada, on W shore of Lake Timiskaming 80 m. N of North Bay; pop. 2346; airport. Founded c. 1873.

Hai'lun (hī'lōōn'). Town, SE cen. Heilungkiang prov., N Manchuria, ab. 110 m. N of Harbin.

Hai'nan (hī'nän'). Island in South China Sea off S coast of Kwangtung prov., SE China, and E of Gulf of Tonkin; a part of Kwangtung prov.; 13,000 sq. m.; pop. ab. 3,000,000 (ab. ⅔ Chinese); ✻ Kiungshan; separated from Luichow Penin. by **Hainan Strait** (15 m. wide). Mountainous (central range, 2500 to 5100 ft.), much of area thickly forested; resources undeveloped; chief towns Kiungshan and its port Hoihow. Chinese since 2d cent. B.C.; not closely controlled until Yüan dynasty (1280–1368); Kiungshan (*q.v.*) opened to foreign trade 1858; occupied by Japanese 1939–45.

Hai'nau (hī'nou). Var. of HAYNAU.

Hai'naut' (ĕ'nō'). **1** Medieval county in the Low Countries, now included in Belgium (Hainaut prov.) and N France (Nord dept.); erected in 9th cent. A.D.; united by marriage with county of Flanders and later with Holland; in 14th cent. came to be held by Wittelsbach house of Bavaria; taken by Philip of Burgundy 1433; became in turn part of Spanish and Austrian Netherlands and a province of kingdom of Belgium.
2 Province, SW Belgium; 1436 sq. m.; pop. (1941 est.) 1,214,101; ✻ Mons; agriculture, livestock raising, coal mining.

Hain'burg (hīn'bŏŏrĸ). Town, Lower Austria, on the Danube near its confluence with the March W of Bratislava; pop. 7545; manufactures tobacco. A very old town has many Roman remains including an aqueduct still in use.

Haine (ân). River 40 m. long, S Hainaut prov., Belgium, flowing W into Schelde river in France.

Haines (hānz). Town, SE Alaska, on W side of Lynn Canal ab. 20 m. S of Skagway; pop. 392; former U.S. Army base.

Haines City. City, Polk co., cen. Florida penin., 20 m. E of Lakeland; pop. 9135; incorporated 1920; citrus center.

Hai'phong' (hī'fông'); *Fr.* **Ha'ï'phong'** (à'ē'fôN'). Seaport, E Tonkin, N Vietnam, in the delta of the Coi river ab. 20 m. from the Gulf of Tonkin and ab. 60 m. E of Hanoi; pop. (1953) 188,600; harbor suffers from silting in its channels but has sizable export trade; manufactures cement, glass, and cotton and silk textiles; naval station; connected by railway with Kunming in Yunnan, China. Established 1874; occupied by Japanese Sept. 26, 1940–Aug. 1945.

Hai'ti (hā'tĭ). **1** Original name for HISPANIOLA island.
2 *Fr.* **Ha'ï'ti'** (à'ē'tē'). Republic occupying W third of Hispaniola I., West Indies; 10,850 sq. m.; pop. (1963 est.) 4,443,000; ✻ Port-au-Prince; sometimes called the Black Republic. On NW at Cap à Foux separated from E tip of Cuba by Windward Passage; coast line irregular with large indentation (Gulf of Gonaïves) on W coast enclosed by two peninsulas (the one on the S being the long, mountainous Tiburon Penin.) and containing the large island of Gonave; off N coast is Tortue I. Highest point in SE, in La Selle Mts., 8793 ft.; only large river the Artibonite; chief exports coffee, cotton, sugar, bananas, sisal. Chief towns Port-au-Prince, Cap Haitien, Cayes, Gonaïves. Population chiefly Negroes; official language French. See *Map* at HISPANIOLA.

History: West part of island of Hispaniola belonged to French from Treaty of Ryswick 1697; French rule not challenged until slave insurrection 1791 which was succeeded by stormy period under native rulers who at times dominated entire island, as did Toussaint L'Ouverture 1801–02, Dessalines 1804–06, and Boyer 1822–43; republic since 1820; because of financial and civil disorder, subject to occupation by American marines and a virtual protectorate of U.S. 1915–34; adopted present constitution 1935, amended it 1946, 1950, and 1957. See also HISPANIOLA.

Hai'yang' (hī'yäng'). Island in Korea Bay, China, SE of Liaotung Penin. and SW of mouth of Yalu river; naval battle Sept. 17, 1894 in which Japanese decisively defeated the Chinese.

Ha'ja·ra, Al (äl hä'jŭ·rŏ). Extensive desert region, S Iraq, bet. the Euphrates and border of Saudi Arabia.

Haj'du·bö'ször·mény (hoi'dōō·bû'sûr·mān'y'). City, E Hungary, 10 m. NW of Debrecen; pop. 31,467.

Haj'du·do'rog (hoi'dōō·dō'rôg). Commune, E Hungary, ab. 20 m. N of Debrecen; pop. 13,024.

Haj'du·had'ház (hoi'dōō·hŏd'häz). City, E Hungary, N of Debrecen; pop. 12,069.

Haj·du'ki No'we (hī·dōō'kĕ nô'vĕ); *Ger.* **Neu'hei'duk** (noi'hī'dōōk). Former commune, SW Poland; since 1934 part of Chorzów (*q.v.*).

Haj'du·ná'nás (hoi'dōō·nä'näsh). City, E Hungary, NNW of Debrecen; pop. 19,132.

Haj'du·szo'bosz·ló' (hoi'dōō·sô'bôs·lō'). City, E Hungary, 8 m. SW of Debrecen; pop. 19,392.

Ha'ka·la'u (hä'kä·lä'ōō). Village, South Hilo dist., Hawaii co., Hawaii, on E coast of Hawaii I. N of Hilo; pop. (est.) 800.

Ha·kâ·ri' (hä·kä·rē'). Vilayet, SE corner of Turkey; pop. (1945) 34,919.

Ha·ka·ta Bay (hä·kä·tä). Inlet of Sea of Japan, NW coast of Kyushu, Japan; forms outer harbor of Fukuoka.

Ha·ko·da·te (hä·kô·dä·tĕ). Seaport city, SW Hokkaido, Japan, on Tsugaru Strait; pop. (1945) 181,531; for many years chief city of the island and capital of Hokkaido prefecture, now replaced by Sapporo; built on rocky peninsula; excellent harbor; first opened to foreign trade 1854.

Ha·ko·ne (hä·kô·nĕ). Village and mountain resort in SE Honshu, Japan, in Kanagawa prefecture 20 m. SE of Fuji and ab. 40 m. SW of Yokohama; on a lake (**Hakone**); numerous hot springs; wonderful views of Fuji.

Ha·ku·rei (hä·kōō·rā). Island in Yellow Sea, off W coast of Korea, 70 m. SW of Chinnampo.

Ha·ku·san (hä·kōō·sän). Mountain 8865 ft., Ishikawa prefecture, on Gifu border, W Honshu, Japan; an extinct volcano, last eruption recorded 1554; comprises 5 peaks.

Hal (äl). Commune, S Brabant prov., cen. Belgium, ab. 10 m. S of Brussels; pop. 17,408; in flax-growing section.

Ha'la (hŭlá). Town, 30 m. N of Hyderabad, Pakistan, in Sind; pop. (1931) 5757; noted for its glazed pottery.

Halab. See ALEP.

Hala Mountains. = KIRTHAR RANGE.

Halas. See KISKUNHALAS.

Ha·la'wa Bay (hä·lä'vå). Bay on NE coast of Molokai I., Hawaii, W of Halawa Point.

Halawa Point. Cape at NE end of Molokai I., Hawaii.

Hal'ba (hăl'bá; -bä). Town, N Lebanon, on railroad 15 m. NE of Tripoli.

Hal'ber·stadt (häl'bĕr-shtät). City, E Germany, in the former Prussian prov. of Saxony, 33 m. SE of Brunswick; pop. 48,184; founded in 9th cent.; varied manufactures; in World War II center for manufacture of bombers.

Hal·con', Mount (häl·kôn'); *native name* **Mag-A·sa'wang-Tu'big** (mäg'ä·sä'wäng·tōō'bĭg). Highest peak 8481 ft. in Mindoro I., Phil. Is., in N part ab. 15 m. SW of Calapan.

Hal'cott, Mount (hôl'kŭt). Peak 3537 ft. in Catskill Mts., Greene co., SE New York.

Hal'den (häl'dĕn); *formerly* **Fred'riks·hald'** (frĕd'-riks·häl'). Seaport, Östfold co., SE Norway, on the Skagerrak near Swedish border; pop. 10,337; lumber-manufacturing center; quarrying, textile mills.

Hal'di·mand (hôl'dĭ·mănd). County, Ontario, Canada. See *Table* at ONTARIO.

Hal'dit·jok'ko (häl'dĭt·yôk'kô). = HALTIATUNTURI.

Hale (hāl). **1** Name of counties in two states of the U.S. See *Tables* at ALABAMA and TEXAS.
2 Urban district, Cheshire, NW England, 10 m. S of Manchester; pop. 12,155.

Ha'le·a'ka·la' (hä'lä-ä'kä-lä'). Volcanic mountain 10,025 ft. in E Maui I., Hawaii; largest extinct crater in the world, area 19 sq. m., depth 2720 ft. Area, formerly part of Hawaii National Park, was in 1961 made a separate park, **Haleakala National Park.** See UNITED STATES, *National Parks*.

Haleb. See ALEP.

Hale'don (hāl'dŭn). Borough, Passaic co., N New Jersey, 2 m. N of Paterson; pop. 6161.

Ha'le·i'wa (hä'lä·ē'vå). Village, Honolulu co., on Waialua Bay on N coast of Oahu, Hawaii; pop. 2504.

Ha'le·mau'mau (hä'lä·mou'mou). "The House of Everlasting Fire," the fire pit of Kilauea crater on the slope of Mauna Loa volcano, Hawaii I., Hawaii; when active, contains from 48 to 190 acres of red-hot lava.

Ha·le'pa (kä·lä'pä); *Gr.* **Kha·le'pa** (kä-). Eastern suburb of Canea, on island of Crete, Greece; by Pact of Halepa signed here Oct. 1878 the Sultan granted practical self-government to Crete.

Hales Bar (hālz). Dam across Tennessee river 33 m. below Chattanooga, Tennessee. See *Table* at TENNESSEE VALLEY AUTHORITY.

Hales Corners. Village, Milwaukee co., SE Wisconsin, SW of Milwaukee; pop. 5549.

Hales'ow'en (hālz'ō'ĕn). Urban district, Worcestershire, W cen. England, on the Stour 8 m. SW of Birmingham; pop. 39,884; manufactures iron and steel.

Ha'ley·ville (hā'lĭ·vĭl). City, Winston co., NW Alabama, 46 m. SW of Decatur; pop. 3740.

Hal'fa (hăl'fá; -fä). **1** Former province, N Anglo-Egyptian Sudan; now part of Northern Province, Sudan.
2 Town, Northern Province, Sudan. See WADI HALFA.

Hal·fa′ya Pass (hăl·fă′yȧ; -yă). Pass through the coast range of hills just S of Salûm, extreme NW Egypt; battles Jan. and Nov. 1942; called "Hellfire Pass" by British soldiers.

Half Dome. Peak 8852 ft. in Sierra Nevada, in E Mariposa co., cen. California.

Half Moon Bay. City, San Mateo co., W California, on Half Moon Bay (inlet); pop. 1957.

Haliacmon. See VISTRITSA.

Hal′i·ar′tus (hăl′ĭ·är′tŭs). Ancient town, Boeotia, Greece, 15 m. NW of Thebes; place where Spartan commander Lysander was killed 395 B.C.

Hal′i·bur′ton (hăl′ĭ·bûr′t'n). County, Ontario, Canada. See *Table* at ONTARIO.

Haliç. See GOLDEN HORN, 3.

Hal′i·car·nas′sus (hăl′ĭ·kär·năs′ŭs); *mod.* **Bo·drum′** (bŏ·drŏŏm′). Ancient city in SW Caria, Asia Minor, on S coast of a peninsula; site of tomb of Mausolus (Mausoleum of Halicarnassus), erected c. 350 B.C. by Queen Artemisia, which ranked among Seven Wonders of the World in ancient times (its remains in the British Museum); birthplace of Herodotus.

Ha′licz (hä′lēch; *Russ.* gȧ′lyĭch). **1** Polish name of GALICIA.

2 Medieval principality, E Galicia, 12th and 13th cents.; then part of Russia, comprising lands about the upper courses of Dniester and Prut rivers; chief town Halicz. United with Lodomeria in 13th cent., later belonged for varying periods to Poland, Austria, Russia, and Germany; now in SW Ukraine, U.S.S.R.

3 Town, SW Ukraine, U.S.S.R., on the Dniester ab. 60 m. SE of Stanislav (formerly in Stanisławów dept., Poland); pop. 4386; scene of fighting in both World Wars.

Hal′i·don Hill (hăl′ĭ·d'n; -dŭn). Hill near Berwick upon Tweed, N England; battle July 19, 1333 in which Edward III, assisting Edward de Baliol, claimant to the throne of David Bruce, defeated the Scots.

Hal′i·fax (hăl′ĭ·făks). **1** Counties in two states of the U.S. See *Tables* at NORTH CAROLINA and VIRGINIA.

2 Town, ⊗ of Halifax co., NE North Carolina, 29 m. NNE of Rocky Mount; pop. 370; settled c. 1723; scene of North Carolina's first constitutional convention.

3 Town, ⊗ of Halifax co., S Virginia; pop. 792.

4 County, Nova Scotia, Canada. See *Table* at NOVA SCOTIA.

5 Commercial city, ✳ of Nova Scotia, Canada, and ⊗ of Halifax co., on Atlantic Ocean in cen. part of S coast of province; pop. 85,589; natural harbor, dry docks, dockyards; in winter Canada's most active port; used by fishing fleets; iron foundries, soap, boot and shoe factories, machine shops, breweries; railroad terminus; one of most strongly fortified cities of Canada. Old fortress; Dalhousie College and University (1818); Saint Mary's College (1841; men). Founded 1749 as British stronghold to rival French Louisburg; made capital of Nova Scotia in place of Annapolis Royal 1750; incorporated as city 1842; garrisoned by British troops until its defense was taken over by dominion forces 1906; Canadian naval base since 1910; greatly damaged by an explosion caused by a harbor collision 1917; in World War II an important embarkation port.

6 County borough, West Riding, Yorkshire, N England, on the Hebble 22 m. NE of Manchester; pop. 98,115, (1951) 98,376; has manufactures of cotton, wool, and worsted goods, machinery, chemicals. Defoe is reputed to have written part of *Robinson Crusoe* at an inn here.

Halifax Bay. Inlet of Pacific Ocean on E coast of Queensland, Australia, 19°S, 147°E; Townsville on it.

Halifax Citadel National Historic Park. See CANADA, *National Historic Parks.*

Hall (hôl). Name of counties in three states of the U.S. See *Tables* at GEORGIA, NEBRASKA, TEXAS.

Hall (häl) *or* **Schwä′bisch–Hall** (shvâ′bĭsh·häl′). Town, Baden-Württemberg, Germany, 35 m. NE of Stuttgart; pop. (1939) 15,165; salt mines.

Hal′land (häl′länd). Province of Sweden. See *Table* at SWEDEN.

Hal′lan·dale (hăl′ăn·dāl). City, Broward co., SE Florida, on Atlantic Ocean 15 m. N of Miami; pop. 10,483.

Hal′la·ni′ya (hăl′lȧ·nē′yȧ; -yă). Largest of the Kuria Muria Is.; 22 sq. m.

Hall Basin (hôl). Expansion of passage at ab. 81°30′ bet. Ellesmere I. and NW Greenland; connects Kennedy Channel with Robeson Channel.

Hal′le (häl′ĕ), *also* **Halle an der Saa′le** (än dĕr zä′lĕ). Commercial and industrial city, E Germany, in what was formerly Saxony prov., Prussia, on the Saale 31 m. WNW of Leipzig; pop. (1939) 220,364; important railroad junction; medieval town hall; 15th-cent. tower; former archiepiscopal residence; university; manufactures include machinery, chemicals, oil, starch, beet sugar; printing establishments, extensive salt works. Existed in 9th cent.; member of Hanseatic League in 13th and 14th cents.; captured by French 1806; to Prussia 1813; in World War II frequently bombed 1944–45; taken by Allies Apr. 17–19, 1945.

Hal′letts·ville (hăl′ĕts·vĭl). City, ⊗ of Lavaca co., SE cen. Texas, 45 m. N of Victoria; pop. 2808; ships livestock, cotton, cottonseed oil.

Hal′li·gen (häl′ĭ·gĕn). Island group off W coast of Schleswig-Holstein, northwestern Germany, consisting of the southern islands of the North Frisian group; largest islands Nordstrand and Pellworm.

Hall Lake (hôl). See UNITED STATES, *Dams and Reservoirs* (Elephant Butte Dam).

Hal′lock (hăl′ŭk). Village, ⊗ of Kittson co., NW corner of Minnesota, 55 m. NW of Thief River Falls; pop. 1527.

Hal′lo·well (hŏl′ō·wĕl; -wĕl). City, Kennebec co., SW Maine, on Kennebec river 3 m. S of Augusta; pop. 3169; shoe factories.

Hall Peninsula (hôl). Peninsula N of Frobisher Bay, SE Baffin I., E Franklin District, Northwest Territories, Canada.

Halls (hôlz). Town Lauderdale co., W Tennessee, 11 m. S of Dyersburg; pop. 1890; cotton, lumber.

Halls Stream (hôlz). Tributary of the Connecticut river, running bet. province of Quebec, Canada, and state of New Hampshire, U.S.; 20 m. long.

Hall′statt (häl′shtät; *Angl.* hôl′stät). Village, Salzkammergut dist., Upper Austria prov., Austria; pop. 1360; on shore of **Hall′stät′ter Lake** (häl′shtĕt′ĕr); site of an early iron-age culture, known from discovery 1846–99 of more than 2000 graves from which many cultural and art objects were taken dating back to as early as 900 B.C.

Hal′luin′ (à′lü·ăN′). Commune, Nord dept., N France, on Belgian border 13 m. N of Lille; pop. 13,278.

Hall′wil (häl′vĭl), Lake; *Ger.* **Hall′wi·ler See** (häl′vĭlĕr zā). Lake 5 m. by 1 m. in N cen. Switzerland, in Aargau canton, formed by expansion of the Aa river.

Hal′ma·he′ra (hăl′mȧ·hĕr′à); *Du.* **Djai·lo′lo** (jī·lō′lō). Largest island of the Moluccas, in Indonesia, lying on the equator; formerly a part of Ternate division of Moluccas residency; 6928 sq. m.; pop., with Morotai, 83,743; no towns of importance; in NE is a steamer port Galela. Irregular in shape, resembling Celebes; on E has four peninsulas enclosing three large bays; on W coast are the small islands of Ternate and Tidore (*qq.v.*); much of island not yet well known; all peninsulas have mountains, 3000 to 5000 ft., those in W being volcanic; some trade in coconuts, dammar, spices. Known early to Spanish and Portuguese; under Sultan of Ternate who yielded it to Dutch 1683; in latter part of 19th cent. scene of insurrections and piracy; taken 1942 by Japanese whose bases were frequently bombed by Allies 1944.

Halm′stad (hȧlm′städ). Seaport, ✳ of Halland prov., SW Sweden, on the Kattegat; pop. 30,364; paper mills, shipbuilding yards, fisheries, breweries; granite quarries. Belonged to Denmark before 1658.

Hal′my·ros (hăl′mĭ·rŏs); *Mod. Gr.* **Hal′my·ròs′** (äl′-mĕ·rôs′). Town, Larissa dept., E Thessaly, Greece, W of Gulf of Volos; pop. 5760.

Häl′sing·borg′ *or* **Hel′sing·borg′** (hĕl′sĭng·bôr′y′). Seaport, Malmöhus prov., SW Sweden, on Öresund opp. Helsingör, Denmark; pop. 65,357; ships grain; sugar refineries, copper smelters, rubber factories, breweries, potteries; coal and clay deposits.

Hal′stead (hôl′stĕd; -stĭd; hăl′-). Urban district, Essex, SE England, on the Colne 46 m. NE of London; pop. 5995; 16th-cent. grammar school.

Hal′tia·tun′tu·ri (häl′tyä·tōōn′tōō·rĭ) *or* **Hal′tia** (häl′tyä). Peak 4344 ft. in NW Finland, on Norwegian border; highest point in Finland.

Hal′tom City. (hôl′tŭm). Village, Tarrant co., N Texas, NE of Fort Worth; pop. 23,133.

Hal′ton (hôl′t′n; -tŭn). County, Ontario, Canada. See *Table* at ONTARIO.

Halys. See KIZIL IRMAK.

Ham (ăm). Village, Somme dept., N France, on the Somme 35 m. SE of Amiens; pop. (1931) 2787; ruins of medieval castle which frequently served as state prison for political offenders, including Joan of Arc and esp. Louis Napoleon (imprisoned 1840–46); 12th–13th cent. church with ancient crypt; suffered greatly during World War I, esp. during German retreat Mar. 1917.

Ha′ma (hä′má; -mä). = TIHAMA.

Ha′ma (hä′má; hä·mä′); *Bib.* **Ha′math** (hā′măth); *classical* **Ep′i·pha·ni′a** (ĕp′ĭ·fá·nĭ′á). Commercial city, W Syria, on the Orontes 75 m. S of Alep; pop. (1935) 39,960; on railroad in a rich agricultural region; noted for its picturesque huge water wheels used in Middle Ages for irrigation. An old city of Hittite origin and frequently mentioned in the Bible as on the N boundary of Israel; several times captured by Assyrian kings (*2 Kings* xviii. 34; *Isaiah* xi. 11); also figured in Mohammedan conquest and wars of the Crusades; home of famous Arab historian Abulfeda, who was its prince 1310–31.

Hamad, El. See SYRIAN DESERT.

Ha′ma·dan (hăm′á·dăn; *native* hà′mä·dän′). 1 Province, NW Iran; 11,788 sq. m.; pop. 350,000.
2 *anc.* **Ec·bat′a·na** (ĕk·băt′′n·á). City, its ✳, W Iran, in plain at foot of Mt. Alwand ab. 180 m. WSW of Tehran; pop. ab. 104,000; important commercial city noted esp. for its leather goods and rugs; residence and burial place of Arab philosopher Avicenna. Ancient Ecbatana capital of Media Magna and summer residence of Persian and Parthian kings; taken by Cyrus from Astyages 550 B.C.; captured by Alexander 330 B.C., by Arabs 645 A.D. The **Ach·me′tha** (ăk·mē′thá) of the Bible (*Ezra* vi. 2), in the palace of which the decree of Cyrus was found; site of the traditional tomb of Mordecai and Esther.

Ha′ma·ku′a (hä′mä·kōō′ä). District, Hawaii co., Hawaii, NE Hawaii I.; chief village Honokaa.

Ha·ma·ma·tsu (hä·mä·mä·tsōō). Industrial city, Shizuoka prefecture, S Honshu, Japan, near coast 56 m. SW of Nagoya; pop. (1945) 81,497; chief products tea, musical instruments; an old daimio castle town; bombed by Allies May–June 1945.

Ha′mar (hä′mär). City, ✳ of Hedmark co., E Norway, on W shore of Lake Mjösa N of Oslo; pop. 5922; locomotive works, boiler factories, dairies; seat of a bishopric. Original town, destroyed by the Swedes 1567, founded 1152 by the English pope, Adrian IV; scene of fighting Apr. 1940.

Hamath. See HAMA, Syria.

Ham′bach (häm′bäk). Commune, Rhineland-Palatinate, Germany, 15 m. W of Speyer; pop. 2400; produces wine; to SW lie ruins of Hambach Castle, scene of the Hambacher Fest May 1832, a gathering of ab. 25,000 persons demanding a republic and national unity of Germany.

Ham′ber Park (hăm′bĕr). Canadian provincial park,

SE Brit. Columbia, on W slope of Rocky Mts. NW of Golden; 3800 sq. m.

Ham′blen (hăm′blĕn). County in Tennessee. See *Table* at TENNESSEE.

Ham·born′ (häm·bôrn′; häm′bôrn). Former city (pop. 126,618), Düsseldorf govt. dist., Rhine Province, Prussia, Germany; became part of Duisburg-Hamborn 1929. See DUISBURG.

Ham′burg (hăm′bûrg). 1 City, ⊗ of Ashley co., SE Arkansas; pop. 2904; sawmills.
2 City, Fremont co., SW corner of Iowa, on Missouri border 47 m. S of Council Bluffs; pop. 1647.
3 Village, Erie co., W New York, 10 m. S of Buffalo; pop. 9145; truck farming; manufactures optical goods.
4 Borough, Berks co., SE Pennsylvania, on Schuylkill river 15 m. N of Reading; pop. 3747; founded 1779; farming; manufactures.
5 (*Ger.* häm′bōōrK) State of the Federal Republic of Germany, N Germany; 288 sq. m.; pop. (1957 est.) 1,786,800; ✳ Hamburg.
6 (*Ger.* häm′bōōrK) Maritime commercial city, NW Germany, on right bank of Elbe river at junction of two small streams, the Alster and Bille, ab. 93 m. SE of mouth of Elbe and ab. 178 m. by rail NW of Berlin; pop. (1939) 1,682,220; great seaport; has extensive harbor and dock installations and outport at Cuxhaven at mouth of Elbe river; noteworthy buildings included the Exchange, commercial library, modern Rathaus in Renaissance style, theater, 14th-cent. church, 19th-cent. Gothic church, and an 18th-cent. Renaissance church; university (1919); Johanneum institution (college, museums, city library); an international air-traffic center; traded esp. in raw materials, coffee, sugar, tobacco, cotton, wine, ironware, hosiery, machinery, paper; manufactures include wrought metal, precision tools, optical instruments, machinery, distillery products, tobacco, felt, airplanes; shipbuilding works. Birthplace of Brahms and Mendelssohn.
History: Founded by Charlemagne who built citadel here against Slavs bet. 808 and 811; made episcopal see 831, archiepiscopal see 834; served as missionary center for northern Europe; alliance with Lübeck 1241 and 1249 led to formation of Hanseatic League; became independent 1292; made imperial city 1510; accepted Reformation 1521–29; joined Schmalkaldic League 1536; under French rule 1806–15; became member of German Federation as free city 1815; devastated by fire 1842; received new constitution 1861 and 1921; scene of Communist rioting 1923; lost special privileges as free state 1933; by decree of Jan. 26, 1937 reorganized along lines making it a geographical unit, including large strip of land on the left (south) bank of the Elbe river and incorporating the cities of Altona, Harburg-Wilhelmsburg, and Wandsbek; laid waste by numerous bombing attacks by Allies in World War II; taken by British forces on May 3, 1945.

Ham′den (hăm′dĕn). Suburban residential town, cen. New Haven co., S Connecticut; pop. 41,056.

Hä′me (hä′mĕ). Department of Finland. See *Table* at FINLAND.

Hä′meen·lin′na (hä′mân·lĭn′nä); *Swedish* **Ta·vas′te·hus** (tä·väs′tĕ·hōōs). City, Häme dept., SW Finland; pop. (1939 est.) 9200; developed around a castle built 1249 by Birger of Bjälbo; incorporated 1638; fortress held by Russians 1918 until recovered by Finnish troops with German aid.

Ham′e·lin (hăm′lĭn; -ĕ·lĭn). = HAMELN.

Ha′meln (hä′mĕln). Manufacturing city, Lower Saxony, W Germany, in what was formerly Hannover prov , Prussia, on Weser river 25 m. SW of Hannover; pop. 25,649. Famous as scene of legend of *Pied Piper of Hamelin*.

Hamhung. See KANKO.

Hami. See QOMUL.

Ha·mid′ (hä·mēt′). District of the Ottoman Empire, S Asia Minor, W of Karaman; roughly equivalent to modern Isparta vilayet and W Konya.

Ham′il·ton (hăm′ĭl·tŭn; -t′n). **1** Counties in ten states of the U.S. See *Tables* at FLORIDA, ILLINOIS, INDIANA, IOWA, KANSAS, NEBRASKA, NEW YORK, OHIO, TENNESSEE, TEXAS.
2 Town, ⊗ of Marion co., NW Alabama; pop. 1934.
3 City, ⊗ of Harris co., W Georgia; pop. 396.
4 City, Hancock co., W Illinois, on Mississippi river 33 m. N of Quincy; pop. 2228.
5 Town, Essex co., NE corner of Massachusetts, 21 m. NE of Boston; pop. 5488.
6 City, Caldwell co., NW Missouri, 28 m. W of Chillicothe; pop. 1701; grain and livestock center.
7 City, ⊗ of Ravalli co., W Montana, 45 m. S of Missoula; pop. 2475; lumber mills, creamery, cannery.
8 *or* **Hamilton Square.** Urban township, Mercer co., W cen. New Jersey, E of Trenton; pop. 65,035.
9 Village, Madison co., cen. New York, 26 m. SW of Utica; pop. 3348; settled 1792; canning and quarrying industries. Colgate University (chartered 1819; men).
10 Industrial city, ⊗ of Butler co., SW Ohio, 20 m. N of Cincinnati; pop. 72,354; manufactures paper and fiber products, safes and vaults, diesel engines, stoves. On site of Fort Hamilton, built by St. Clair 1791, used as garrison post in Wayne's campaign of 1793–94; settled c. 1803, and became ⊗; incorporated 1810.
11 City, ⊗ of Hamilton co., cen. Texas, 47 m. E of Brownwood; pop. 3106; cotton gins, flour and cottonseed-oil mills; clay and limestone deposits.
12 City, E New South Wales, SE Australia, suburb of Newcastle; pop. 18,975.
13 Town, Queensland, NE Australia, a suburb of Brisbane; pop. 15,235.
14 Town, SW Victoria, SE Australia, 160 m. W of Melbourne; pop. 5786; freezes and exports mutton. Hamilton and Western District College; Hamilton Academy.
15 Seaport town, ✳ of Bermuda Is., on Bermuda I.; pop. (1939) 3217; founded 1790, made capital 1815; has landlocked harbor.
16 City, ⊗ of Wentworth co., SE Ontario, Canada, at W end of Lake Ontario ab. 40 m. SW of Toronto; pop. 208,321; important transportation center: harbor, railroad terminus, airport; manufactures steel, iron, electrical equipment, textiles. McMaster University (1887; coed.) in nearby Westdale; Royal Botanical Gardens. Visited by La Salle 1669; first settled 1813.
17 *or now* **Churchill.** River ab. 600 m. long, S cen. Labrador; in its upper course called Ashuanipi; rises in Ashuanipi Lake near Canada border, flows N to Dyke Lake, then SE through Dyke Lake and Lobstick Lake and finally NE into Lake Melville (*q.v.*); just below outlet from Lobstick Lake are Churchill Falls (see GRAND FALLS).
18 Borough, Auckland provincial dist., cen. North I., New Zealand; on Waikato river 70 m. SSE of Auckland; pop. (1941 est.) 20,900; center of farming, cattle, and sheep district.
19 Burgh, Lanark co., S cen. Scotland; pop. (1951) 40,173; coal and iron mines, quarries, iron foundries.
Hamilton, Lake. 1 Lake in S Garland and NW Hot Spring cos., SW cen. Arkansas, formed by **Car′pen·ter Dam** (kär′pĕn·tēr) across Ouachita river.
2 Lake in cen. Texas, in San Saba, Llano, and Burnet cos.
Hamilton, Mount. Peak 4209 ft., Santa Clara co., W California, 13 m. E of San Jose; site of Lick Observatory.
Hamilton Dam. See BUCHANAN DAM.
Hamilton Inlet. Inlet of Atlantic Ocean, SE Labrador, estuary of Hamilton river; with Lake Melville ab. 150 m. long; one of the largest fiords on the Labrador coast, 14 to 25 m. wide. Visited by early explorers (John Davis, 1586); site of French and English trading posts in 18th cent.; at its head Rigolet was established 1837 by Hudson's Bay Co.
Hamilton Square. Township, New Jersey. See HAMILTON.

Ha′mi·na (hä′mĭ·nả); *Swedish* **Fre′driks·hamn′** (frä′drĭks·hȧm′′n). Town, Viipuri dept., SE Finland, on Gulf of Finland; pop. ab. 4000; scene of signing of treaty of peace 1809 by which Sweden ceded Finland to Russia.
Ha·mir′pur (hȧ·mēr′pŏŏr). Town, Jhansi division, SW Uttar Pradesh, N Indian Union, on the Jumna 38 m. SSW of Cawnpore; pop. 7195; traditionally founded by a Rajput chieftain in 11th cent.
Ham′let (hăm′lĕt; -lĭt). Town, Richmond co., S North Carolina, 48 m. WSW of Fayetteville; pop. 4460; railroad center for peach and tobacco region.
Ham′lin (hăm′lĭn). **1** County in South Dakota. See *Table* at SOUTH DAKOTA.
2 City, Jones co., NW cen. Texas, 40 m. NNW of Abilene; pop. 3791; railroad division point; gypsum, sand, gravel deposits.
3 Town, ⊗ of Lincoln co., W West Virginia; pop. 850.
Hamm (häm), *also* **Hamm in West′fa′len** (ĭn vĕst′-fä′lĕn). Commercial and manufacturing city, North Rhine-Westphalia state, W Germany, on Lippe river 21 m. SSE of Münster; pop. 50,040; 15th-cent. town hall; iron and wire mills; manufactures machinery; in World War II a traffic, power, and supply center. Founded 1226; one of Hanse Towns 1417 ff.; passed to Brandenburg 1666; frequently bombed by Allies 1944–45, taken Apr. 3–4, 1945.
Hamma, El. See EL HAMMA.
Ham·ma′da el Ham′ra (hăm·mä′dả [-dä] ăl hăm′rȯ). Plateau and desert region, W Tripolitania, NW Libya, on border of Algeria; ab. 40,000 sq. m.; explored by J. Richardson and H. Barth 1850–55.
Hammâm, El. See EL HAMMÂM.
Ham·mam′–bou–Ha′djar (hăm·măm′bŏŏ·hăj′är). Commune, Oran dept., NW Algeria, SW of Oran; pop. 10,106.
Ham′ma·met′ (hăm′ȧ·mĕt′; *Arab.* hăm′mȧ·măt′). Coastal town, NE Tunisia, on the **Gulf of Hammamet,** an inlet of the Mediterranean, at S base of peninsula ending in Cape Bon; seized May 10, 1943 by British in pursuit of German forces retreating into the peninsula.
Ham·mam′ Mes′kou·tine′ (hăm·măm′ mĕs′kŏŏtēn′). Hot springs (*Arab.* "accursed baths"), Constantine dept., NE Algeria, 10 m. W of Guelma; limestone deposits in form of cascades, cones, etc.
Ham′mar, Hor al (hôr ăl hȧ′mŭr). Lake or marshland region ab. 70 m. long by 15 m. wide, SE Iraq, S of the Euphrates before it joins the Tigris at Al Qurna; has connection with the Euphrates and with the Shatt-al-Arab above Basra.
Ham′me (häm′ĕ). Commune, East Flanders prov., NW cen. Belgium, 14 m. SW of Antwerp; pop. 14,801.
Ham′me·ren, Cape (häm′ĕ·rĕn). Cape on N tip of Bornholm I., Denmark; lighthouse.
Ham′mer·fest′ (häm′fĕr·fĕst′). Northernmost city in Europe, ⊗ of Finnmark co., N Norway; located on Kvalöy I., 70°38′N; pop. 3649; manufactures cod-liver oil; exports furs, eiderdown, and smoked and salted fish; home port for Arctic sealing and whaling fleets. Has uninterrupted daylight May 13 to July 29; sees no sun Nov 18 to Jan. 23.
Hammersmith. Metropolitan borough of London. See *Table* at LONDON.
Ham′mo·nas′set (hăm′ȧ·năs′ĕt; -ĭt). River ab. 18 m. long, S Connecticut; forms S part of boundary bet. New Haven and Middlesex cos. and empties into Long Island Sound just E of **Hammonasset Point.**
Ham′mond (hăm′ŭnd). **1** Industrial city, Lake co., NW corner of Indiana, on Illinois border adjacent to Calumet City; pop. 111,698; manufactures railroad equipment and supplies, steel, hospital supplies; oil refineries, packing plants; incorporated as city 1884.
2 City, Tangipahoa parish, SE Louisiana, 45 m. E of Baton Rouge; pop. 10,563; strawberries. Southeastern Louisiana College (1925; coed.).

Ham′monds·port (hăm′ŭndz·pōrt). Village, Steuben co., S New York, at S end of Keuka Lake 25 m. E of Hornell; pop. 1176; vineyards; wine and champagne making center; manufactures aircraft; birthplace of Glenn H. Curtiss.

Ham′mon·ton (hăm′ŭn·tŭn). Town, Atlantic co., SE New Jersey, 27 m. SE of Camden; pop. 9854; ships fruit.

Hamp′den (hăm′dĕn). **1** County in Massachusetts. See *Table* at MASSACHUSETTS.

2 Town, Penobscot co., E cen. Maine, on Penobscot river 7 m. S of Bangor; pop. 4583.

Hamp′den–Syd′ney (hăm′dĕn·sĭd′nĭ). Town, Prince Edward co., S cen. Virginia, ab. 5 m. SW of Farmville; pop. (est.) 200; Hampden-Sydney Coll. (1776; men).

Hampi. See VIJAYANAGAR.

Ham′pole (hăm′pōl). Village, West Riding, Yorkshire, N England, 6 m. NW of Doncaster; home of Richard Rolle de Hampole, the hermit (d. 1349).

Hamp′shire (hăm[p]′shēr; -shĭr). Counties in two states of the U.S. See *Tables* at MASSACHUSETTS and WEST VIRGINIA.

Hampshire *or* **Hants** (hănts). **1** Formerly, a county in S England, comprising the modern administrative counties of Hampshire (see **2**, below) and the Isle of Wight (*q.v.*); 1650 sq. m.; pop. (1938 est.) 1,166,650.

2 *officially* **Southampton.** The popular and postal name of an administrative county, S England, mainland part of former county of Hampshire (see **1**, above); 1503 sq. m.; pop. (1951) 1,196,617; ⊗ Winchester; other towns Portsmouth, Southampton, Bournemouth, Gosport, Aldershot, Eastleigh.

Hamp′stead (hăm[p]′stĕd; -stĭd). **1** Residential town, Montreal I., S Quebec, Canada, W of Montreal city; pop. 3260.

2 Metropolitan borough of London; includes **Hampstead Heath.** See *Table* at LONDON.

Hamp′ton (hăm[p]′tŭn). **1** County in South Carolina. See *Table* at SOUTH CAROLINA.

2 City, ⊗ of Calhoun co., S Arkansas; pop. 1011.

3 City, ⊗ of Franklin co., N cen. Iowa, 27 m. S of Mason City; pop. 4501; corn canneries.

4 Town, Rockingham co., SE New Hampshire, on Atlantic Ocean 10 m. S of Portsmouth; pop. 5379; shoe manufacturing. Incorporated 1639; outpost of Massachusetts Bay Colony. **Hampton Beach** (resort on Atlantic) nearby.

5 Town, ⊗ of Hampton co., SW South Carolina; pop. 2486.

6 Independent city, SE Virginia, on Hampton Roads 7 m. NE of Newport News; pop. 89,258; fisheries, packing plants (oysters, crabs). Hampton Institute (1868; coed.); Langley Field (*q.v.*), Old Point Comfort, and Fort Monroe in environs. Settled by colonists from Jamestown 1610 (oldest continuous English community in America); burned by British in War of 1812 and by its own inhabitants to prevent occupation by Federals 1861; incorp. as city 1908; consolidated with Elizabeth City co. 1952.

7 Town (unincorporated), ⊗ of Kings co., S New Brunswick, Canada, 22 m. NNE of St. John; pop. 1832.

8 Former urban district, Middlesex, SE England, SW of London on the Thames; pop. 13,061; part of Greater London; nearby is Hampton Court Palace, one of largest of the royal residences, built by Cardinal Wolsey 1515, and given to Henry VIII 1526.

Hampton Bay. Inlet of Atlantic Ocean on S side of E Long I., New York.

Hampton Roads. Channel 40 ft. deep and 4 m. wide through which the James, Elizabeth, and Nansemond rivers flow into Chesapeake Bay; naval battle bet. *Merrimac* and *Monitor* Mar. 9, 1862. The **Port of Hampton Roads,** comprising harbors of Newport News, Norfolk, and Portsmouth, is under local jurisdiction of State Port Authority of Virginia, created 1926.

Ham·run′ (hăm·rōōn′). Town, E cen. Malta I., just W of Valletta; pop. ab. 12,000.

Ham Sud (ăm süd). Village (unincorporated), ⊗ of Wolfe co., S Quebec, Canada, 28 m. NE of Sherbrooke.

Ham·tramck′ (hăm·trăm′ĭk). City, Wayne co., SE Michigan, entirely within city of Detroit; pop. 34,137; automobile manufacturing.

Hamun–i–Helmand. See *Lake Helmand* at HELMAND.

Ha·mun′–i–Lo·ra′ (hä·mōōn′ĕ·lō·rä′). Large lake (*hamun*) with no outlet, Chagai, NW Baluchistan, Pakistan; receives the Pishin Lora.

Ha·mun′–i–Mash·kel′ (-măsh·kĕl′); *anc.* **Ar′i·a Pa′lus** (âr′ĭ·à [á·rī′á] pā′lŭs). Lake (*hamun*), morass, and desert region, Chagai, NW Baluchistan, Pakistan, on Iranian border; receives Mashkel river from the SE.

Han (hän). **1** River ab. 900 m. long in Shensi and Hupeh provs., E cen. China, flowing SE into Yangtze river at Hankow; navigable for large vessels for ab. 370 m.

2 Lower course of river system, ab. 100 m. long, E Kwangtung prov., SE China; flows S past Chaoan to South China Sea at Swatow.

3 River in Korea. See KAN.

Ha′na (hä′nä). **1** District, Maui co., Hawaii, E end of Maui I.; pop. 1073.

2 Village in district, on E coast of Maui I. near Kauiki Head; pop. (est.) 547.

Ha′na·le′i (hä′nä·lā′ē). District, N Kauai I., Kauai co., Hawaii; pop. 1312.

Hanalei Bay. Bay on N coast of Kauai I., Hawaii.

Ha′na·ma′ni·o′a, Cape (hä′nä·mä′nĕ·ō′ä). Cape on S coast of Maui I., Hawaii, on Alalakeiki Channel opp. Kahoolawe I.

Ha′na·ma′u·lu (hä′nä·mä′ŏŏ·lōō). Village, Lihue dist., E coast of Kauai I., Hawaii, N of Nawiliwili Bay; pop. (est.) 1031.

Ha′na·pe′pe (hä′nä·pā′pä). Village, Waimea dist., S coast of Kauai I., Hawaii; pop. 1383; on **Hanapepe Bay** (W of Wahiawa Bay) adjoining Port Allen.

Ha′nau (hä′nou). City, Hesse, Germany, formerly in Hesse-Nassau prov., Prussia, on Main river 11 m. E of Frankfurt am Main; pop. 38,670; railroad junction; old Gothic church; 16th-cent. town hall; 17th-cent. church; 18th-cent. castle; diamond polishing; manufactures jewelry, rubber goods, chemicals, electrical appliances, tobacco, machinery. Became city 1303; Napoleonic victory over Bavarians and Prussians under Wrede nearby 1813.

Hanchung. See NANCHENG.

Han Cities. See WUHAN.

Han′cock (hăn′kŏk). **1** Counties in ten states of the U.S. See *Tables* at GEORGIA, ILLINOIS, INDIANA, IOWA, KENTUCKY, MAINE, MISSISSIPPI, OHIO, TENNESSEE, WEST VIRGINIA.

2 City, Houghton co., NW Michigan penin., 70 m. NW of Marquette; pop. 5022; copper mines; manufactures mining machinery, iron and brass products.

3 Village, Delaware co., S New York, on Delaware river 35 m. ESE of Binghamton; pop. 1830; summer resort, fishing.

Hancock, Mount. Peak 10,100 ft. near S boundary of Yellowstone National Park, NW Wyoming.

Hand (hănd). County in South Dakota. See *Table* at SOUTH DAKOTA.

Han′degg Falls (hän′dĕk); *Ger.* **Han′deck–Fall** (hän′dĕk·fäl′). Cataract ab. 150 ft. high in Aare river, SE Bern canton, Switzerland, NE of the Finsteraarhorn in upper Hasli valley.

Han′dies Peak (hăn′dĭz). Peak 14,013 ft. in Hinsdale co., SW Colorado.

Han′dlo·vá (hän′dlô·vä); *Hung.* **Nyi′tra·bán′ya** (nyĭ′trŏ·bän′yŏ). Town, W Slovakia prov., E cen. Czechoslovakia, in mountains 90 m. NE of Bratislava; pop. (1930) 10,448.

Hand′öl′ (hän′dŭl′). Waterfall 148 ft., W Jämtland, W Sweden, in a small river flowing N into Lake Ann.

Hands'worth (hăndz'wûrth; -wêrth). Former urban district, West Riding, Yorkshire, N England; since 1921 incorporated in Sheffield; manufacturing, collieries.

Han'ford (hăn'fĕrd). **1** City, ⊗ of Kings co., SW cen. California, 30 m. S of Fresno; pop. 10,133; fruit canneries; oil refineries. Settled 1871.
2 Village, part of Richland town, Benton co., S Washington, on Columbia river ab. 20 m. N of Richland center; made site 1943 of industrial plant (Hanford Engineer Works) of the Manhattan District (q.v.). See RICHLAND.

Hang'chow' (hăng'chou'; *Chin.* häng'jō'). City and treaty port, ✳ of Chekiang prov., E China, at mouth of Fuchun river at head of Hangchow Bay ab. 110 m. SW of Shanghai; pop. (1936 est.) 485,100; important coastal trade; center of rice culture and silk manufacture; S terminus of Grand Canal; E of the famous Lake Si Hu; for centuries considered one of finest cities of China. Founded 606 A.D.; capital of China during later Sung dynasty (12th cent.). Known to Marco Polo as **Kin'-sai'** (kĭn'sä'; *Pekingese* jĭng'shĭr'). Devastated in Taiping Rebellion 1861; opened to foreign trade 1896.

Hangchow Bay. Funnel-shaped bay at mouth of the Fuchun (Tsien Tang) river, Chekiang prov., E China; 60 m. wide at entrance, extends inland 70 m.; famous for its bore. Chu Shan archipelago lies across S entrance.

Hang'klip', Cape (hăng'klĭp'). Cape on SW coast of Cape Province, Union of South Africa, on SE side of entrance to False Bay.

Hang'ö' (häng'û'); *Finnish* **Han'ko** (häng'kô'). Seaport and peninsula, Uusimaa dept., S Finland, on Baltic Sea; pop. (1939 est.) 7900; resort; exports lumber, fish, dairy products; Russians defeated Swedish fleet nearby 1714; ceded to U.S.S.R. as a military base Mar. 12, 1940; regained by Finns and Germans 1941; after World War II relinquished by Russia in exchange for Porkkala Penin.

Han–hai (hän'hī'). Chinese name for the vast Gobi and Sinkiang desert area in cen. Asia.

Hanka. See KHANKA.

Han Kiang (hän' jĭ·äng'). = HAN river.

Han'kin·son (hăng'kĭn·s'n). City, Richland co., SE corner of North Dakota, 56 m. S of Fargo; pop. 1285; manufactures mattresses.

Han'kow' (hăng'kou'; *Chin.* hän'kō'). Literally "Mouth of the Han river"; often called the "Pittsburgh of China." Former city, SE Hupeh prov., E cen. China; pop. (1936 est.) 804,500; on N bank of the Yangtze E of the Han and opp. Wuchang, 585 m. by river from Shanghai; largest of the three Han Cities (including also Hanyang and Wuchang) now incorporated in the city of Wuhan (q.v.); commercially a rival of Shanghai; banking center; iron and steel works, textile manufactures, rice and flour mills; extensive river trade. For centuries during prominence of Wuchang a neglected fishing village; opened to trade 1861; grew rapidly after 1900; in Revolution 1911 burned by Imperialist troops; captured by Nationalists Dec. 1926, by Japanese Oct. 1938.

Han'ley (hăn'lĭ). Former county borough, Staffordshire, W cen. England, since 1910 part of Stoke on Trent; manufactures earthenware and porcelain; birthplace of Arnold Bennett. See the POTTERIES.

Hann, Mount (hän). Mountain 2800 ft. in Kimberleys, NE Western Australia.

Han'na (hăn'á). **1** Town, Carbon co., S Wyoming, 38 m. E of Rawlins; pop. 625; Union Pacific R.R. coal camp.
2 Town, SE Alberta, Canada, 100 m. ENE of Calgary; pop. 2027.

Han'na, Ůmm al (ŏŏm'măl hăn'ná; -ná). Village, SE Iraq, on the Tigris 15 m. E of Kut-al-Imara; fighting Jan. and Apr. 1916 bet. British and Turks.

Han'nas·town (hăn'áz·toun). Locality, Westmoreland co., SW Pennsylvania, ab. 5 m. NNE of Greensburg; coal mining; pre-Revolutionary capital of W Pennsylvania.

Han'ni·bal (hăn'ĭ·bắl). City, Marion co., NE Missouri, on Mississippi river; pop. 20,028; railroad center, river port; manufactures shoes, stoves, railroad-car wheels; boyhood home of Mark Twain.

Han·no'ver (hä·nō'vēr; -fēr). **1** Province of former Prussia. See *Table* at PRUSSIA.
2 Government district, cen. Hannover prov., former Prussia, Germany; 2233 sq. m.
3 *Eng.* **Han'o·ver** (hăn'ō·vēr). Commercial and industrial city, ✳ of Lower Saxony and of the former Hannover province, Germany, on the Leine river 35 m. WNW of Brunswick; pop. (1939) 472,527; 17th-cent. palace; 15th-cent. town hall; varied manufactures; railroad shops, bridge works; in World War II specialized in rubber, ordnance, and aircraft manufacture and in oil refining.

History: First mentioned 1163; became residence 1636 of dukes of Brunswick-Lüneburg, the duke being raised to rank of elector of Hannover 1692, the elector succeeding to English throne as George I 1714 (first of House of Hanover); acquired Bremen and Verden from Sweden 1719; in Seven Years' War supported by England as ally of Prussia; occupied by French 1803 and made part of Napoleon's kingdom of Westphalia 1807–13; with accession of Victoria to English throne 1837, became separate from England with which it had had a personal union since 1714; received 1833 constitution which was suspended by King Ernest Augustus (1837–51); kingdom extinguished and incorporated with Prussia as result of Austro-Prussian War 1866; frequently bombed in World War II.

Hannoversch–Münden. See MÜNDEN.

Han'ö' Bay (hän'û'). Inlet of Baltic Sea on SE coast of Sweden.

Ha·noi' (hä·noi'); *Fr.* **Ha'no'ï'** (à'nô'ē'). City, SE Tonkin, Indochina, on Coi river ab. 75 m. from the sea; ✳ of North Vietnam, formerly ✳ of French Indochina and of Tonkin; pop. 149,000; its port is Haiphong; European (French) quarter on lake, native quarter, old citadel; railroad terminus. Dates back to era before Chinese invasions; occupied by French 1882 and made capital of Tonkin, became capital of French Indochina 1887; after occupation by Japanese frequently bombed by Allies 1943–45; became capital of the Communist-dominated Democratic Republic of Vietnam 1954.

Han'o·ver (hăn'ō·vēr). **1** County in Virginia. See *Table* at VIRGINIA.
2 Town, Jefferson co., SE Indiana, on Ohio river; pop. 1170; Hanover College (1827; coed.; Presbyterian).
3 Town, Plymouth co., SE Massachusetts, 10 m. E of Brockton; pop. 5923.
4 Town, Grafton co., W New Hampshire, on Connecticut river 5 m. NNW of Lebanon; pop. 7329; chartered 1761; settled 1765; Dartmouth College (chartered 1769; opened 1770; men).
5 Borough, York co., S Pennsylvania, 18 m. SW of York; pop. 15,538; manufactures shoes, wire cloth, jute products; settled 1733; battle bet. Federal and Confederate cavalry 1863.
6 Village, ⊗ of Hanover co., E cen. Virginia; pop. (est.) 250; home of Patrick Henry, Henry Clay, Thomas Nelson Page.
7 Town, Grey co., SE Ontario, Canada, 30 m. S of Owen Sound; pop. 3533.
8 English form of HANNOVER, Prussian city and ✳ of former electorate whose elector, succeeding to English throne as George I, established the English royal house of Hanover (1714–1901).

Hanover Island. Island off SW coast of Chile, S of Concepción Strait.

Han'sa Bay (hăn'sá). Inlet on N coast of North-East New Guinea, halfway bet. Madang and Wewak, 145°E; occupied by Australian forces June 15, 1944.

Han'ság (hŏn'shäg). Marshy region 147 sq. m. in E Austria and W Hungary, SE of Neusiedler Lake.

Han'sen Dam (hăn's'n). See UNITED STATES, *Dams.*

Hanse Towns (hăns) *or* **Han'se·at'ic League** (hăn'-sē·ăt'ĭk). A defensive commercial confederacy in the Middle Ages, originating in a league of merchants of various free Germanic cities trading abroad; earliest date of any union 1241 when Lübeck and Hamburg made agreements for mutual defense in trading; at first meeting 1256 included Lübeck, Hamburg, Lüneburg, Wismar, Rostock, and Stralsund; joined later by other towns, the league reached height of its power 14th and 15th cents. when it contributed to defeat of Waldemar IV of Denmark 1367-68 and secured control of Baltic trade by Peace of Stralsund 1370; included such widely separated places as Novgorod, Reval, Riga, Danzig, Magdeburg, Cologne, Bruges, and London; gave trading privileges to merchants of many other towns; held last general assembly 1669; name of Hanseatic towns retained by Lübeck, Hamburg, and Bremen as long as they were free cities.

Hans'ford (hănz'fẽrd). County in Texas. See *Table* at TEXAS.

Hans Lol'lik Island (hănz lŏl'ĭk). One of the Virgin Islands of the United States, West Indies, N of St. Thomas and separated from it by Leeward Passage.

Han'son (hăn's'n). **1** County in South Dakota. See *Table* at SOUTH DAKOTA.
2 Town, Plymouth co., SE Massachusetts, 8 m. ESE of Brockton; pop. 4370; cranberry bogs.

Han'tha·wad'dy (hăn'thȧ·wŏd'ĭ). District, Pegu division, Lower Burma; 1931 sq. m.; pop. 408,831; marshland; produces rice.

Hants (hănts). **1** County in Nova Scotia, Canada. See *Table* at NOVA SCOTIA.
2 See HAMPSHIRE, England.

Han'well (hăn'wĕl; -wĕl). Former urban district, Middlesex, SE England, 10 m. W of St. Paul's, London, now part of Ealing; residential suburb of London.

Han'yang' (hän'yäng'). Former city, SE Hupeh prov., E cen. China, on N bank of the Yangtze W of Han river mouth and opp. Hankow and Wuchang; pop. ab. 450,000; now incorporated in city of Wuhan (*q.v.*); has grown rapidly since 1900 as part of industrial development of Hankow; iron and steel works; government arsenal.

Ha'o (hä'ō); *also* **Bow Island** (bō). Atoll 30 m. long, 5 to 9 m. wide in cen. Tuamotu Archipelago, French Oceania, S Pacific Ocean, 18°S and 141°W; called Bow Island by Captain Cook 1769.

Ha'par (hä'pẽr). Var. of HAPUR.

Ha'pa·ran'da (hȧ'pȧ·rän'dȧ). Seaport, Norrbotten prov., N Sweden, at mouth of Torne river on Gulf of Bothnia opp. Finnish town of Tornio; pop. 2951; exports lumber products, tar, and articles made by the Lapps. Founded 1812.

Hape'ville (hāp'vĭl; *Sou. also* -v'l). Residential city, Fulton co., NW cen. Georgia, 8 m. S of Atlanta; pop. 10,082.

Hap'sal (găp'säl). = KHAPSALU.

Ha'pur (hä'pŏor). Town, W Uttar Pradesh, N Indian Union, on Kali Nadi river 35 m. E of Delhi; pop. 25,116; supposedly founded in 10th cent.; trades in bamboo, sugar, grain, brassware, timber, cotton.

Har'a·han (hăr'ȧ·hăn). City, Jefferson parish, SE Louisiana, W of New Orleans; pop. 9275.

Har'al·son (hăr'ăl·s'n). County in Georgia. See *Table* at GEORGIA.

Ha'ra·muk (hŭ'rȧ·mŏok). Peak 16,015 ft. in the Himalayas, in Kashmir, N India, 25 m. N of Srinagar.

Ha·ran' (hä·rän'); *anc.* **Car'rhae** (kăr'ē). Town, Urfa vilayet, SE Turkey in Asia, ab. 22 m. SSE of Urfa; pop. 620. In ancient times an important city (**Char'ran** [kăr'ăn] in *Acts* vii. 2) of N Mesopotamia, on the main trade routes from Babylonia to the Mediterranean; residence of Terah and Abraham (*Gen.* xi. 31, 32). Scene of two Roman defeats: (1) 53 B.C., Crassus defeated and killed by Parthians; (2) 296 A.D., Galerius defeated by the Persians.

Ha·rap'pa (hȧ·răp'ȧ). Locality, Multan division, S West Punjab, Pakistan, in the Indus valley; site of an early (chalcolithic) culture, perhaps dating back to 3300 B.C., and indicating in its archaeological remains an early connection bet. Indian and Sumerian culture. See MOHENJO-DARO.

Ha'rar *or* **Har'rar** (hä'rẽr). **1** Region and province, E Ethiopia; a government (province) 1936-41 of Italian East Africa; 79,844 sq. m.; pop. (1939 est.) 1,600,000.
2 Commercial city, its ✳, E Ethiopia, SSE of Diredawa; pop. ab. 25,000; trades esp. in coffee; enclosed by a stone wall.

Har'bin (här'bĭn); *Chin.* **Pin'kiang'** *or* **Ping'kiang'** (bĭn'jĭ·äng'). City, ✳ of Sungkiang prov., cen. Manchuria, and ✳ of former Pinkiang prov., E cen. Manchukuo, on Sungari river 145 m. NNE of Changchun; pop. (1940 est.) 661,984; almost in exact center of Manchuria, the junction point of all the great railroads; one of the great trade marts of the Far East. Only a village in 1896, began to grow rapidly with completion 1898 of railroad to Port Arthur. Russian administrative headquarters 1898-1905; Chinese 1905-32, part of the time under war lords; seized by Japanese 1932; taken by Russians Aug. 1945.

Har'bor Beach (här'bẽr). City, Huron co., E Michigan, on Lake Huron 20 m. S of mouth of Saginaw Bay; pop. 2282; fishing; summer resort.

Har bour Grace (här'bẽr grās'). Seaport, SE Newfoundland, on W shore of Conception Bay 27 m. W of St. John's; pop. (1951) 2331; has been the take-off point for several important transatlantic airplane flights.

Harbour Island. One of the Bahama Is., Brit. West Indies, just off N Eleuthera I.; 2 sq. m.; pop. (1943) 769.

Har'burg–Wil'helms·burg (här'bŏorк·vĭl'hĕlms-bŏorк). Former city in Lüneberg govt. dist., Hannover prov., Prussia, Germany, on Elbe river opp. Hamburg; pop. (1939) 118,193; formed 1927 by consolidation of city of Harburg and commune of Wilhelmsburg (an island in the Elbe opp. Hamburg); incorporated in Hamburg 1937.

Har·dang'er Fjord (här·däng'ẽr fyôrd; *Norw.* fyŏr). Inlet of North Sea on SW coast of Norway, in Hordaland co.; extends inland NE and E 114 m.

Har·dang'er·vid'da (-vĭd'ȧ). Large plateau in S Norway, E of Hardanger Fjord.

Har'dee (här'dē). County in Florida. See *Table* at FLORIDA.

Har'de·man (här'dĕ·măn). Name of counties in two states of the U.S. See *Tables* at TENNESSEE and TEXAS.

Har'den·berg (här'dĕn·bĕrк). Two communes in Overijssel prov., E Netherlands, near German border: **Ambt'–Har'den·berg** (ämpt'-), pop. 13,123; **Stad'–Har'den·berg** (stät'-), pop. 2639.

Har'den·berg-Ne'vi·ges (här'dĕn·bĕrк·nā'vē·gĕs). City, SW cen. North Rhine-Westphalia state, W Germany, 4 m. NW of Wuppertal; pop. 13,299; 16th-cent. pilgrimage church; textiles, iron goods.

Har'der·wijk (här'dẽr·vĭk). Commune and seaport, Gelderland prov., E Netherlands, on the IJsselmeer (*q.v.*); pop. 8661; formerly one of Hanse Towns; has declined in importance since start of planning for reclamation of the Zuider Zee.

Har'din (här'd'n; -dĭn). **1** Name of counties in six states of the U.S. See *Tables* at ILLINOIS, IOWA, KENTUCKY, OHIO, TENNESSEE, TEXAS.
2 Village, ⊗ of Calhoun co., W Illinois; pop. 356.
3 City, ⊗ of Big Horn co., S Montana, 45 m. E of Billings; pop. 2789.

Har'ding (här'dĭng). Counties in two states of the U.S. See *Tables* at NEW MEXICO and SOUTH DAKOTA.

Har'dins·burg (här'd'nz·bûrg; -dĭnz-). City, ⊗ of Breckenridge co., NW cen. Kentucky; pop. 1377.

Har'doi (hŭr'doi). Town, Lucknow division, cen. Utter Pradesh, N Indian Union, 60 m. NW of Lucknow; pop. 17,069.

Har′dwar (hŭr′dwär). Town, Meerut division, NW Uttar Pradesh, N Indian Union, on the Ganges where it leaves the Siwalik Range and enters the great plain, 110 m. NNE of Delhi; pop. 33,287; railroad center; place where the main Ganges canal begins; the temple of Gangadwara and the bathing ghat with its footprint of Vishnu, visited annually by over 2 million pilgrims; every twelve years scene of an especially large bathing festival, the Kumbh-Mela, attracting more than 500,000 pilgrims; very old, has had many names.

Hard′wick (härd′wĭk). **1** Town, Worcester co., cen. Massachusetts, 21 m. WNW of Worcester; pop. 2340; in agricultural and livestock-raising section.
2 Village in Hardwick town (pop. 2349), Caledonia co., NE Vermont, 20 m. NNE of Montpelier; pop. 1521; settled 1797; granite, lumber; manufactures furnaces.

Hard′wicke Bay (härd′wĭk). Inlet in Yorke Penin., SE Spencer Gulf, South Australia.

Har′dy (här′dĭ). **1** County in West Virginia. See *Table* at WEST VIRGINIA.
2 Town, a ⊗ of Sharp co., N Arkansas, on Spring river; pop. 555; resort.

Hardy Dam. Dam completed 1931 across Muskegon river, W Michigan; height 120 ft.; impounds water for water power, forming **Hardy Pond** in Newaygo and Mecosta cos.

Hare Bay (hâr). Inlet of Atlantic Ocean near N tip of Newfoundland on E side.

Hare Island. Island in St. Lawrence river opp. Rivière du Loup, S Quebec prov., Canada.

Ha·rel·be·ke (hä·rĕl·bā′kĕ) *or* **Har′le·beke′** (Fr. árl′-bȧk′). Commune, West Flanders prov., NW Belgium, on Lys river 22 m. SW of Gent; pop. 10,446; in tobacco-growing section.

Har·fleur′ (här·flûr′; Fr. àr′-). Seaport, Seine-Maritime dept., N France, 4 m. E of Le Havre; pop. (1931) 5012; before rise of Le Havre, a chief port of France; captured by Henry V 1415, retaken by French 1435, again held by English 1445–49 but recovered by Dunois; pillaged by Huguenots 1562; has late 15th-cent. church.

Har′ford (här′fẽrd). County in Maryland. See *Table* at MARYLAND.

Har·gei′sa (här·gā′sȧ). Town, N Somalia, formerly ✻ of British Somaliland, 50 m. SW of Berbera; pop. varies bet. 15,000 and 20,000 according to season.

Har′gi′court′ (àr′zhē′kōōr′). Village, Aisne dept., N France, 9 m. NW of St-Quentin; pop. 890; fighting in 1917, destroyed by Germans Mar. 21, 1918.

Ha′ri (hä′rē); *formerly* **Djam′bi** (jäm′bē). River ab. 450 m. long, S cen. Sumatra, Indonesia; rises in Barisan Mts., flows E to Berhala Strait.

Ha′ri·a′na *or* **Ha′ry·a′na** (här′ī·ä′nȧ). State, NE India, formed 1966 from southern districts of former Punjab state; 17,600 sq. m.; pop. 7,000,000; ✻ Chandigarh.

Ha·ri·ma Sea (hä·rē·mä). Body of water at E end of Inland Sea bet. S Honshu and N Shikoku, Japan; bounded on E by Awaji I. and on W by Shodo I.

Ha·ri·mu·ko·tan (hä·rē·mōō·kō·tän). Small island of the Kuril Is., S of Onnekotan; transferred to Russia 1946.

Har·ing·vliet (här′ĭng·vlēt). Inlet ab. 2½ m. wide of North Sea on SW coast of Netherlands; the W extension of Hollandsch Diep to the sea.

Ha′ri Rud (här′ī rōōd′), *also* **He′ri Rud** (hĕr′ī); *anc.* **Ar′i·us** (âr′ĭ·ŭs; ȧ·rī′ŭs). River 650 m. long, NW Afghanistan and S Turkmen S.S.R.; rises in mountains (Koh-i-Baba) W of Kabul, flows W through fertile valley at Herat, turns N forming part of boundary bet. Afghanistan and Turkmen S.S.R. on E and Iran on W, and then is lost in sands of Kara Kum desert of S Turkmen S.S.R. By Russians its lower course called by the Turkmenian name, Tedzhen (q.v.).

Har′ju (här′yōō). Province of Estonia. See *Table* at ESTONIA.

Har′kány (hŏr′kän·y′). Town, S Hungary, S of Pécs and SW of Mohács; pop. (1920) 750; mineral springs;

scene of battle (often called "Second battle of Mohács") Aug. 12, 1687 in which Charles of Lorraine defeated the Turks.

Har′lan (här′lȧn). **1** Name of counties in two states of the U.S. See *Tables* at KENTUCKY and NEBRASKA.
2 City, ⊗ of Shelby co., W Iowa, 40 m. NE of Council Bluffs; pop. 4350; agriculture; livestock raising.
3 City, ⊗ of Harlan co., SE Kentucky, 28 m. NE of Middlesborough; pop. 4177; coal mining.

Harlebeke. See HARELBEKE.

Har′lech (här′lĕk; -lǐ). Village, W Wales, on coast 8 m. N of Barmouth; pop. 1096; ancient capital of Merionethshire. Harlech Castle an excellent example of Edwardian concentric fortification, founded by Edward I 1285, captured by Glendower 1404; last Welsh fortress to be held for King Charles until its fall 1647.

Har′lem (här′lĕm). **1** River channel NE of Manhattan I., New York; with Spuyten Duyvil creek connects the Hudson and East rivers.
2 City, Blaine co., N Montana, E of Havre; pop. 1267.
3 District of Manhattan borough, New York City, N of Central Park bet. Eighth Ave. and the East and Harlem rivers; a former village created 1658 and named New Haarlem; annexed to New York City 1731; small group of Negroes settled here 1900; now the chief Negro quarter of New York; includes also Italian and Spanish (Latin American) sections.
4 Var. of HAARLEM.

Har′lin·gen (här′lĭn·jĕn). City, Cameron co., S Texas, 21 m. NNW of Brownsville; pop. 41,207; ships fruits (esp. citrus fruit), vegetables; cotton processing.

Har′ling·en (här′lĭng·ĕn). Commune and seaport, Friesland prov., N Netherlands, on Wadden Zee 16 m. W of Leeuwarden; pop. 10,443; ships dairy products.

Har′low·ton (här′lō·toun [*sic*]). City, ⊗ of Wheatland co., cen. Montana, 48 m. SSW of Lewistown; pop. 1734.

Har′mon (här′mŭn). County in Oklahoma. See *Table* at OKLAHOMA.

Har′mo·ny (här′mō·nĭ). Borough, Butler co., W Pennsylvania, NW of Pittsburgh; pop. 5106.

Harmozia. See HORMUZ.

Harnes (àrn). Commune, Pas-de-Calais dept., N France, 11 m. NNE of Arras; pop. (1931) 12,181; coal mines.

Har′nett (här′nĕt; -nǐt). County in North Carolina. See *Table* at NORTH CAROLINA.

Har′ney (här′nĭ). County in Oregon. See *Table* at OREGON.

Harney Basin. Former lake bottom 2500 sq. m. in Harney co., S Oregon.

Harney Lake. Lake ab. 10 m. long, Harney Basin, cen. Harney co., SE Oregon; connected with Malheur Lake.

Harney Peak. Mountain 7242 ft. in Black Hills, in Pennington co., SW South Dakota; highest point in state and highest point in United States E of Rocky Mts., although by some the Black Hills are considered a part of the Rocky Mountain system.

Härn′ö·sand *or* **Hern′ö·sand′** (hâr′nŭ·sánd′). Seaport, ✻ of Västernorrland prov., E Sweden, at mouth of Ångerman river; pop. 13,316; ships forest products, as tar, timber, cellulose, wood pulp; plundered and burned by Russians 1721.

Har′o Strait (här′ō). Strait SE of Vancouver I., in W part of Washington Sound, connecting Juan de Fuca Strait with Strait of Georgia, the three straits being traversed by the United States-Canadian boundary.

Har′pen·den (här′pĕn·dĕn). Urban district, Hertfordshire, SE England, 25 m. NNW of London; pop. 14,236; site of the Rothamsted Experimental Station (founded 1843), noted for biological and agricultural research.

Har′per (här′pẽr). **1** Name of counties in two states of the U.S. See *Tables* at KANSAS and OKLAHOMA.
2 City, Harper co., S Kansas, 52 m. S of Hutchinson; pop. 1899.
3 Commercial seaport, extreme SE Liberia, W Africa, at Cape Palmas; pop. 1600.

Har'pers Ferry (här'pĕrz). Residential town and tourist resort, Jefferson co., NE West Virginia, in Blue Ridge Mts. at confluence of Potomac and Shenandoah rivers ab. 55 m. NW of Washington, D.C.; pop. 572; settled c. 1747; site of U.S. arsenal estab. 1796 and seized in John Brown's raid 1859; strategic base in Civil War.

Har'per Woods (här'pĕr). City, Wayne co., SE Michigan, NE of Detroit; pop. 19,995.

Har'peth (här'pĕth; -pĭth). River ab. 90 m. long, W cen. Tennessee; rises in SW Rutherford co., flows NW into Cumberland river.

Harps'well (härps'wĕl; -wĕl). Town, Cumberland co., SW Maine, 22 m. NE of Portland; pop. 2032; seaside resort.

Har·put' (här-pŏot'; ᴋär-); *formerly* **Khar·put'.** Town, Elâziz vilayet, E cen. Turkey in Asia, near banks of upper Euphrates; pop. ab. 5000; trades in cotton, oil, wine; bazaars, Jacobite convent, ancient church; scene of Armenian massacre 1895.

Harran. = Haran.

Harrar. See Harar.

Harrat ar Raha. See Harrat ar Raha.

Har'ri·can'aw (här'ĭ-kăn'ô). River 250 m. long, SW Quebec, Canada; rises in lakes at ab. 48°N, flows NNW to S end of James Bay in Ontario.

Har'ri·man (här'ĭ-măn). City, Roane co., E Tennessee, 38 m. W of Knoxville; pop. 5931; hosiery, woolens, farm implements; coal and iron ore deposits; railroad center.

Harriman, Mount. Peak 7950 ft. in SW Klamath co., S Oregon.

Harriman Dam. See Lake Whitingham.

Har'ring·ton (här'ing·tŭn). City, Kent co., cen. Delaware, 17 m. S of Dover; pop. 2495; canneries, sawmills.

Harrington Harbour. Village, SE Quebec, Canada, on shore of Gulf of St. Lawrence; hospital of the Grenfell Mission.

Harrington Sound. Body of water in NE cen. Bermuda I.

Har'ris (här'ĭs). **1** Name of counties in two states of the U.S. See *Tables* at Georgia and Texas.

2 Southern section of island of Lewis with Harris in Outer Hebrides, off NW coast of Scotland; 195 sq. m.; pop. 3121; a part of Inverness co.; place where Harris tweed was originally made.

Harris, Sound of. Channel bet. Lewis with Harris I. and North Uist I. in the Outer Hebrides, NW Scotland.

Har'ris·burg (här'ĭs·bûrg). **1** City, ⊗ of Poinsett co., NE Arkansas; pop. 1481.

2 City, ⊗ of Saline co., SE Illinois, 22 m. E of Marion; pop. 9171; coal mining; flour and lumber mills.

3 Village, ⊗ of Banner co., W Nebraska; pop. (1950) 140.

4 City, ✳ of Pennsylvania and ⊗ of Dauphin co., SE cen. Pennsylvania, on Susquehanna river 98 m. WNW of Philadelphia; pop. 79,697; railroad center; manufactures steel and iron products, machinery, meat and lumber products, building materials, textiles, clothing. Settled c. 1712; known as Harris's Ferry until 1785 when it became ⊗; scene of noted conventions, esp. Harrisburg Convention of 1788; became borough 1791, state capital 1812, city 1860; site of Camp Curtin, first camp for Union forces during Civil War.

Har'ri·smith (här'ĭ·smĭth). Town, NE Orange Free State, E cen. Republic of So. Africa, 153 m. NW of Durban; pop. 9208; important trade center; health resort; Bushman paintings in nearby caves.

Har'ri·son (här'ĭ·s'n). **1** Name of counties in eight states of the U.S. See *Tables* at Indiana, Iowa, Kentucky, Mississippi, Missouri, Ohio, Texas, West Virginia.

2 City, ⊗ of Boone co., N Arkansas, ab. 64 m. ENE of Fayetteville; pop. 6580; incorporated 1876; ships lumber; deposits of lead, zinc, marble, silicon. Diamond Cave (stalactite and stalagmite cavern) in vicinity.

3 City, ⊗ of Clare co., cen. Michigan; pop. 1072.

4 Village, ⊗ of Sioux co., NW Nebraska; pop. 448.

5 Industrial town, Hudson co., NE New Jersey, on Passaic river opp. Newark; pop. 11,743; steelworks, foundries; manufactures pumps, elevators, electron tubes.

6 Village, Hamilton co., SW corner of Ohio, on Indiana border 18 m. WNW of Cincinnati; pop. 3878; iron castings, shoes, pottery.

7 Urban township, Allegheny co., SW Pennsylvania, NE suburb of Pittsburgh; pop. 15,710.

Harrison Bay. Inlet of Arctic Ocean on N coast of Alaska, E of Point Barrow; 70°30′N, 152°W.

Har'ri·son·burg (här'ĭ·s'n·bûrg). **1** Village, ⊗ of Catahoula parish, cen. Louisiana; pop. 594.

2 Industrial city, N Virginia, ⊗ of Rockingham co. but politically independent, 23 m. NNE of Staunton; 2 sq. m.; pop. 11,916; estab. 1780; manufactures shoes, rayon, stone products; Madison Coll. (1908; coed.).

Harrison Lake. See Lillooet.

Harrison's Landing. See Berkeley.

Harrison Stickle. See Langdale Pikes.

Har'ri·son·ville (här'ĭ·s'n·vĭl). City, ⊗ of Cass co., W Missouri, 30 m. S of Independence; pop. 3510.

Har'ris·ville (här'ĭs·vĭl). **1** City, ⊗ of Alcona co., NE Michigan; pop. 487.

2 Village, Providence co., N Rhode Island, ab. 17 m. NW of Providence; pop. 1024; administrative center of Burrillville town; woolen goods.

3 Town, ⊗ of Ritchie co., NW West Virginia; pop. 1428.

Har'rods·burg (här'ŭdz·bûrg). City, ⊗ of Mercer co., cen. Kentucky, 9 m. NNW of Danville; pop. 6061; founded 1774, settled 1775, oldest city in the state; site of cabin in which Nancy Hanks and Thomas Lincoln were married. See Springfield, Kentucky.

Har'ro·gate (här'ō·gāt). Village, Claiborne co., NE Tennessee, on Kentucky border ab. 48 m. NE of Knoxville; pop. (1950) 247; formerly a summer resort; Lincoln Memorial Univ. (1897; coed.).

Har'ro·gate (här'ō·gĭt; -gāt). Municipal borough, West Riding, Yorkshire, N England, 13 m. N of Leeds; pop. 50,454; fashionable resort; many mineral springs.

Har'row (här'ō). Urban district, Middlesex, SE England, 12 m. NW of London; pop. 219,463; part of Greater London; includes parish of **Harrow on the Hill,** seat of a famous school for boys, founded 1571 by John Lyon.

Har'språng' (här'sprông'); *Lapp* **Njom'mel·sas'ka** (nyôm'mĕl·säs'kä). Waterfall 110 ft. high in Lule river, Norrbotten prov., N Sweden.

Hart (härt). **1** Name of counties in two states of the U.S. See *Tables* at Georgia and Kentucky.

2 City, ⊗ of Oceana co., W Michigan, 18 m. S of Ludington; pop. 1990; fruit growing; canneries.

Hart'ford (härt'fĕrd). **1** County in Connecticut. See *Table* at Connecticut.

2 Industrial and commercial city, ✳ of Connecticut and ⊗ of Hartford co., N Connecticut, at head of navigation on Connecticut river 36 m. NNE of New Haven; largest city in the state; pop. 162,178; port of entry; one of great insurance centers of the world; varied manufactures; printing and bookbinding industry; numerous parks with excellent recreational facilities; State Capitol, Old State House, State Arsenal and Armory, Atheneum, Colt and Morgan memorials; Trinity College (1823; men); Univ. of Hartford (1877; coed.).

History: Established as trading post and fort by Dutch 1633; settled by band of colonists from Massachusetts Bay 1635–36; given present name 1637; first constitution of Connecticut Colony drawn up 1639; according to tradition royal charter protected from Governor Andros in famous Charter Oak incident 1687; capital of Connecticut (*q.v.*) although shared honor with New Haven 1701–1875; during Revolution important and rich military supply depot; incorporated as city 1784; home of the "Hartford wits" in 18th cent.; site of Hartford Convention 1814. The town (incorporated 1784) and the city were made coextensive 1881 and consolidated 1896.

3 Village, Madison co., SW Illinois, on Mississippi river 15 m. N of East St. Louis; pop. 2355.

4 City, ⊗ of Ohio co., W cen. Kentucky; pop. 1618.

5 Village, Van Buren co., SW Michigan, 32 m. W of Kalamazoo; pop. 2305; fruit growing.

6 Unincorporated village (in town of Hartford, pop. 6355), Windsor co., E Vermont, residential suburb of White River Junction; founded 1761.

7 City, Washington co., SE Wisconsin, 30 m. NW of Milwaukee; pop. 5627; manufactures automobile parts.

Hartford City. City, ⊗ of Blackford co., E Indiana, 17 m. ESE of Marion; pop. 8053; natural gas and oil fields.

Hart′heim (härt′hīm). Town, Baden-Württemberg, Germany, SW of Freiburg near French border; site of concentration camp during World War II.

Har·ting·ton (här′tǐng·tǔn). City, ⊗ of Cedar co., NE Nebraska, 42 m. N of Norfolk; pop. 1648.

Hart, *or* **Hart′s, Island** (härt, härts). Island in Long Island Sound off E coast of the Bronx, New York City; attached to Bronx borough; New York City's potter's field; United States naval prison.

Hart′land Point (härt′lǎnd). Cape on W coast of Devonshire, SW England, on S side of entrance to Bristol Channel W of Barnstaple Bay; lighthouse.

Har′tle·pool (här′t'l·pōōl; härt′lē-). Municipal borough, Durham, N England, on North Sea 26 m. SSE of Newcastle; pop. 17,217; extensive docks; ships coal, timber; shipbuilding; manufactures iron, steel, and cement.

Hart′ley (härt′lĭ). **1** County in Texas. See *Table* at TEXAS.

2 Town, O'Brien co., NW Iowa, 28 m. N of Cherokee; pop. 1738.

3 Town, SW Mashonaland, NE Southern Rhodesia, 70 m. WSW of Salisbury; center of agricultural and gold-mining district.

Hart′manns·wei′ler·kopf′ (härt′mäns·vī′lĕr·kôpf′). Commanding height 3700 ft. in the Vosges Mts., Haut-Rhin dept., NE France, 8 m. NW of Mulhouse; severe fighting for its control 1915.

Hart′selle (härt′sĕl). City, Morgan co., N Alabama, 11 m. S of Decatur; pop. 5000; founded 1870; cotton ginning.

Harts′horne (härts′hôrn). City, Pittsburg co., SE Oklahoma, 15 m. ESE of McAlester; pop. 1903; coal mining, lumbering.

Harts′ville (härts′vĭl; *Sou.* also -v'l). **1** Town, Darlington co., NE South Carolina, 21 m. NW of Florence; pop. 6392; manufactures cotton, rayon, and silk textiles; Coker College (1908; women).

2 City, ⊗ of Trousdale co., N Tennessee; pop. 1712.

Hart′ville (härt′vĭl). City, ⊗ of Wright co., S Missouri; pop. 486.

Hart′well (härt′wĕl; -wĕl). City, ⊗ of Hart co., NE Georgia, 37 m. NE of Athens; pop. 4599; incorporated 1856; textile mills.

Haru. See MOEN.

Harun, Jebel. See Mount HOR.

Har′vard (här′vĕrd). **1** City, McHenry co., N Illinois, 28 m. ENE of Rockford; pop. 4248; in lake region.

2 Town, Worcester co., cen. Massachusetts, 11 m. ESE of Fitchburg; pop. 2563; Harvard Astronomical Observatory; in vicinity are remains of New Eden, the Utopian community established 1844 by Bronson Alcott.

Harvard, Mount. Peak 14,399 ft. in Sawatch Range, in Chaffee co., cen. Colorado.

Har′vey (här′vĭ). **1** County in Kansas. See *Table* at KANSAS.

2 Industrial city, Cook co., NE Illinois, 18 m. S of Chicago; pop. 29,071; diesel engines, railroad equipment, machinery.

3 City, Wells co., cen. North Dakota, 58 m. WSW of Devils Lake (city); pop. 2365; railroad division point.

Har′well (här′wĕl; -wĕl). Village, Berkshire, S England, ab. 12 m. S of Oxford; pop. 821; airfield in World War II; site of first chain-reacting pile established in England.

Har′wich (här′wĭch). Town, Barnstable co., SE Massachusetts, 12 m. E of Barnstable; pop. 3747; summer resort.

Har′wich (här′ĭj; -ĭch). Municipal borough, Essex, SE England, on North Sea 68 m. ENE of London; pop. 13,488; British naval station.

Har′wich Port (här′wĭch). Village, Barnstable co., SE Massachusetts, on Atlantic Ocean; pop. (est.) 1000; summer resort.

Har′wood Heights (här′wo͝od). Village, Cook co., NE Illinois, NW suburb of Chicago; pop. 5688.

Harz (härts). Mountain group in cen. Germany, bet. Elbe and Weser rivers S of Brunswick; highest peak Brocken 3747 ft.; has many summer resorts; well forested; profitable mines of varied kinds; region, long a stronghold of paganism, has been source of many legends.

Harz′burg *or* **Bad Harzburg** (bät härts′bo͝ork). Town, Brunswick, N Germany, in Lower Saxony state N of the Harz Mts.; pop. 6198; mineral springs.

Ha′sa, al– (ăl hä′să); *Angl.* **El Ha′sa** (ĕl hăs′à). District or province of Nejd, Saudi Arabia, in E part on W coast of Persian Gulf; ab. 22,500 sq. m.; pop. ab. 160,000; chief town Hofuf; a steppe region with oases, producing dates, wheat, and rice, and noted for its donkeys and camels; chief towns Hofuf and Mubarraz and the ports of Qatif and Jubail. In early times a semi-independent principality; Turkish 1875 to 1914 when it was taken by the Wahabis.

Ha′san Dag (hä′sän dä′). Peak 10,673 ft. in cen. Turkey in Asia, SE of Tuz Lake.

Has′be·ya (hăs′bĕ·yà; -yä). Town, Lebanon, just W of Mt. Hermon; castle held for a time by the Crusaders; nearby is a sanctuary of the Druses.

Has′brouck Heights (hăz′bro͝ok). Residential borough, Bergen co., NE corner of New Jersey, 7 m. SE of Paterson; pop. 13,046; founded 1685.

Has′kell (hăs′kĕl). **1** Name of counties in three states of the U.S. See *Tables* at KANSAS, OKLAHOMA, TEXAS.

2 Village, Passaic co., N New Jersey, ab. 10 m. NW of Paterson; pop. (est.) 1500.

3 Town, Muskogee co., E Oklahoma, on Arkansas river 19 m. W of Muskogee; pop. 1887.

4 City, ⊗ of Haskell co., N Texas, 50 m. N of Abilene; pop. 4016; ships cotton and livestock.

Has′ko·vo (kȧs′kô·vô). Var. of KHASKOVO.

Ha′sle·mere (hā′z'l·mēr). Urban district, Surrey, S England, 11 m. S of Aldershot; pop. 11,992; in high valley bet. two ridges: Hindhead, on N side of which is "Devil's Punch Bowl," a curious depression, and Blackdown, on E slope of which is Aldworth, a house built by Tennyson 1868–69 and in which he died 1892.

Has′li (häs′lē). Valley, SE Bern canton, W cen. Switzerland, E of the Grindelwald, through which passes upper course of the Aare (*q.v.*).

Has′ling·den (hăz′lǐng·dĕn). Municipal borough, Lancashire, NW England, 17 m. N of Manchester; pop. 14,505; bricks, cotton textiles.

Ha′spe (häs′pĕ). Former city (pop. 25,688), Arnsberg govt. dist., Westphalia prov., Prussia, Germany; became part of Hagen (*q.v.*) 1929.

Has′san (hŭs′săn). Town, S Mysore state, S Indian Union, 63 m. NW of Mysore; pop. 10,544

Has′selt (häs′ĕlt). Commune, ✱ of Limburg prov., NE Belgium, 42 m. E of Brussels; pop. (1938 est.) 26,828; distilleries; scene of septennial fete on Assumption Day, Aug. 15, when it is visited by throngs of pilgrims; battle Aug. 6, 1831 in which Dutch defeated Belgian nationalists.

Has·su′na (hăs·so͝o′nä; -nä). Archaeological site, N Iraq, on W bank of Tigris 25 m. S of Mosul; village uncovered (1945) is one of oldest in the world, dating back probably to 5000 and 6000 B.C.

Hasta Colonia. See ASTI.

Hasta Pompeia. See ASTI.

Ha'sten·beck (häs'tĕn·bĕk). Village, west Germany, 3 m. SE of Hameln; scene of French victory over the English July 26, 1757 which led to convention of Kloster-Zeven (see ZEVEN).

Has'tings (hās'tǐngz). **1** City, ⊗ of Barry co., SW Michigan, 29 m. NE of Kalamazoo; pop. 6375.
2 City, ⊗ of Dakota co., SE Minnesota, on Mississippi river 20 m. SE of St. Paul; pop. 8965; manufactures flour-milling accessories, paper, clay products; dairy products.
3 City, ⊗ of Adams co., S Nebraska, 23 m. S of Grand Island; pop. 21,412; manufactures building materials, windmills, farm implements; flour and feed mills, creameries. Hastings College (1882; coed.).
4 Borough, Cambria co., SW cen. Pennsylvania, 20 m. WNW of Altoona; pop. 1751.
5 County, Ontario, Canada. See *Table* at ONTARIO.
6 County borough, East Sussex, S England, on English Channel at entrance to Strait of Dover; pop. 65,207, (1951) 65,506; one of the Cinque Ports; scene of the battle of Hastings Oct. 14, 1066 in which William the Conqueror defeated Saxons under King Harold.
7 Borough, Hawke's Bay provincial dist., E North I., New Zealand, near Napier 160 m. NE of Wellington; pop. (1941 est.) 19,000.

Hastings–on–Hud'son (-hŭd's'n). Residential village, Westchester co., SE New York, on Hudson river 18 m. N of New York, opp. the Palisades; pop. 8979; manufactures copper, chemicals, paving blocks; produced mustard gas for American troops in World War I.

Ha·tay' (hä·tī'). Vilayet, S Turkey in Asia, on Mediterranean coast; pop. (1940 est.) 246,138; coextensive with former Sanjak of Alexandretta (*q.v.*); created 1938 as a republic, an autonomous unit among the Levant States, with Turkish majority in its assembly; incorporated in Turkish republic June 23, 1939 by agreement bet. France and Turkey.

Hat'bor'o (hăt'bûr'ō). Borough, Montgomery co., SE Pennsylvania, 15 m. NNE of Philadelphia; pop. 7315.

Hatch'ie (hăch'ĭ). River ab. 180 m. long, flowing from N Mississippi NW into Mississippi river on NW boundary of Tipton co., Tennessee.

Hat'field (hăt'fēld). Town, Hampshire co., W Massachusetts, on Connecticut river 18 m. N of Springfield; pop. 2350; attacked by Indians 1675 and 1677; home of: Sophia Smith, founder of Smith College; Col. Ephraim Williams, founder of Williams College; Rev. Jonathan Dickinson, first president of the College of New Jersey (Princeton); and Elisha Williams, president of Yale 1726–39.

Ha'thras (hä'träs). Town, Aligarh dist., W Uttar Pradesh, N Indian Union, 85 m. SSE of Delhi; pop. 39,784; railroad center; has ruined Jat fort.

Ha'ti·a or **Ha'ty·a** (hä'tĭ·à). Island group, formerly one island, in main (E) mouth of the Ganges, Dacca division, East Bengal, Pakistan; 171 sq. m.; pop. ab. 85,000.

Ha·til'lo (ä·tē'yō). Municipality (pop. 20,238) and town (pop. 2582), NW Puerto Rico; town near coast just W of Arecibo.

Hat'ra (hăt'rà); *mod.* **Al Hadhr** (ăl hŏd'ēr). Ancient town and fortress, Mesopotamia, in desert W of the Tigris 55 m. SW of Mosul; now village and archaeological site in NW Iraq; Trajan repulsed by the Parthians 117 A.D.; scene of revolt 240 A.D. crushed by Shapur I.

Ha'tri·a (hä'trĭ·à). Var. of *Hadria*: see ADRIA.

Hatria Picena. See ATRI.

Hat'ten·heim (hät'ĕn·hīm). Village, W Hesse state, W Germany, in the Rheingau, noted wine-producing region; Steinberger white wine made nearby.

Hat'ter·as, Cape (hăt'ẽr·ăs). Cape, SE **Hatteras Island,** Dare co., North Carolina, a long, narrow sand bar, one of the chain of islands off E coast of North Carolina; extends into Atlantic Ocean at a dangerous navigation point; lighthouse, 193 ft. high, abandoned 1936 because the sea had come too close, replaced by new

light on a tower farther inland; much of area included in **Cape Hatteras National Seashore Recreational Area;** to the SW, near S tip of the island, is village of **Hatteras,** pop. (est.) 700.

Hatteras Inlet. Narrow strait leading from Atlantic Ocean into Pamlico Sound bet. S tip of Hatteras I. and Ocracoke I.; during Civil War guarded by two forts built by Confederates but captured by Federals Aug. 28–29, 1861.

Hat'ties·burg (hăt'ĭz·bûrg). Industrial city, ⊗ of Forrest co., SE Mississippi, 28 m. SSW of Laurel; pop. 34,989; railroad center; Mississippi Southern Coll. (1910; coed.).

Hat'ting·en (hät'ĭng·ĕn), *also* **Hattingen an der Ruhr** (än dēr rōōr'). Industrial city, cen. North Rhine-Westphalia state, W Germany, SE suburb of Essen on Ruhr river; pop. 14,402; machinery, flanges, rivets, screws, locomotives; ruins of 13th-cent. castle (Isenburg).

Hattushash. See BOGAZKÖY.

Ha·tu'tu (hä·tōō'tōō). Island 4 sq. m., Marquesas Is., S Pacific Ocean, 10 m. NE of Eïao I.

Hat'van (hŏt'vŏn). Commune, cen. Hungary, 30 m. E of Budapest; pop. 15,454.

Hatya. See HATIA.

Hatzfeld. See JIMBOLIA.

Hau·bour'din' (ō'bōōr'dăn'). Commune, Nord dept., N France, 6 m. SW of Lille; pop. 11,001; textiles, foods.

Haud (houd). Region, SE Ethiopia and SW former British Somaliland (now Somalia); semidesert, also has grassy plains and thorn jungle.

Hau'dio'mont' (ō'dyō'môN'). Commune, Meuse dept., NE France, 8 m. SE of Verdun; pop. (1931) 287; held by Germans Feb. 1916–Sept. 1918.

Hau'ge·sund' (hou'gĕ·sōōn'). Seaport, Rogaland co., SW Norway, on a fiord opp. Stavanger; pop. 17,166; exports fish; shipbuilding yards, woolen mills; place where American ship *City of Flint* under a German crew anchored Oct. 20, 1939 when it was returned to Americans by the Norwegians.

Haul·bow'line (hôl·bō'lĭn). Small island, Cork Harbour, SE co. Cork, SW Eire; formerly an important British naval base.

Hau·rak'i Gulf (hou·răk'ĭ; -rä'kĭ). Large bay, inlet of Pacific Ocean, on N coast of North I., New Zealand; in SW has inlet, Waitemata Harbor, on which Auckland is situated.

Hau·ran' (hou·rän'). Plateau region in S Syria, S of Damascus and E of Jordan river; fertile, produces much grain. In Greco-Roman period a part of it known as Auranitis (*q.v.*).

Hauran, Wa'di (wă'dĭ). River (*wadi*) ab. 240 m. long in Syrian Desert, W Iraq; flows ENE to the Euphrates near Khan Baghdadi.

Hau'sa·land' or **Hausa Land** (hou'sà·lănd'). Strictly, an ethnological term; the region in Africa N of the Niger and Benue rivers, now corresponding to N Nigeria; chief town Kano; inhabited by the Hausa, a Negroid people of the Sudan. Early kingdom conquered 1801 by Mohammedan Fulah Empire (see SOKOTO sultanate); incorporated in Nigeria 1900.

Haus'ruck Mountains (hous'rŏōk). Range in Upper Austria prov., Austria, S of the Danube and SE of the Inn; highest peak Göbelsberg 2625 ft.

Hau'ta (hou'tō). Town, cen. Nejd, Saudi Arabia, on Tropic of Cancer 80 m. S of Riyadh; pop. ab. 12,000.

Haut–A'tlas' (ō'·tä'tläs'). French form of *High Atlas:* see ATLAS MOUNTAINS.

Haute–Ga'ronne' (ōt'gà'rôn'). Department of France. See *Table* at FRANCE.

Haute–Loire (ōt'lwär'). Department of France. See *Table* at FRANCE.

Haute–Marne (ōt'märn'). Department of France. See *Table* at FRANCE.

Hautes–Alpes (ōt'-zàlp'). Department of France. See *Table* at FRANCE.

Haute–Saône (ōt'sōn'). Department of France. See *Table* at FRANCE.

Haute–Sa'voie' (ōt'sȧ'vwȧ'). Department of France. See *Table* at FRANCE.

Hautes–Py'ré·nées' (ōt'pē'rā'nā'). Department of France. See *Table* at FRANCE.

Haute–Vienne (ōt'vyĕn'). Department of France. See *Table* at FRANCE.

Haute–Volta. See UPPER VOLTA.

Haut'mont' (ō'môn'). Commune, Nord dept., N France, on Sambre river 46 m. SE of Lille; pop. 14,636; produces iron, steel, chemicals.

Haut–Rhin (ō'răn'). Department of France. See *Table* at FRANCE.

Havaiki. See HAWAIKI.

Ha·van'a (hȧ·văn'ȧ). **1** City, ⊗ of Mason co., cen. Illinois, on Illinois river 38 m. SW of Peoria; pop. 4363; manufactures flour, farm implements, gasoline engines. **2** *Span.* **La Ha·ba'na** (lä ä·vä'nä). Seaport on NW coast of Cuba, 90 m. SSW of Key West, Florida; ✳ of La Habana prov., and ✳ of Cuba; pop. (1960) 787,765; harbor (ab. 3 m. by 1½ m.), one of best in W hemisphere, its entrance through narrow channel having El Morro castle (erected 1589–97) and lighthouse on E and La Punta Fort (or castle) in old city on W; old city or commercial section on peninsula bet. harbor and ocean, new city, largely residential, on hills to W and S; railroad center; exports sugar, tobacco, cigars, and cigarettes; over 100 tobacco factories; cathedral (1704), palace of old captains general, Univ. of Havana (1670); fine squares and drives, esp. the Prado boulevard and the Malecón along N shore.

History: Founded by Diego Velásquez 1519 (removed from another site of 1515); burned 1528 but soon rebuilt; chief naval station of Spain in New World and suffered esp. in 16th cent. in wars bet. Spain and England; captured by English 1762, restored 1763; since 1700 its history the same generally as that of Cuba (*q.v.*); its outer harbor scene of blowing up of U.S. battleship *Maine* Feb. 15, 1898, immediate cause of Spanish-American War; since 1898 capital of independent Cuba.

Ha·van'nah (hȧ·văn'ȧ). Village on N coast of Etate I., New Hebrides, SW Pacific Ocean; good harbor.

Hav'a·su Lake (hăv'ȧ·sōō). See UNITED STATES, *Dams and Reservoirs* (Parker Dam).

Ha'vel (hä'fĕl). River ab. 225 m. long in NE cen. Germany; flows S out of Mecklenburg to Spandau, where it is joined by the Spree, and on into Elbe river.

Ha'vel·land (hä'fĕl·länt'). Former district in W Brandenburg prov., Prussia, later in Potsdam govt. dist.

Have'lock (hăv'lŏk). Former city, Lancaster co., SE Nebraska, now part of Lincoln; railroad repair works.

Have'lock Island (hăv'lŏk; -lŭk). See RITCHIE'S ARCHIPELAGO.

Hav'er·ford (hăv'ẽr·fẽrd). **1** Urban township, Delaware co., SE Pennsylvania; pop. 54,019. **2** Residential community in Lower Merion township (pop. 59,420), Montgomery co. SE Pennsylvania, NW of Philadelphia; settled by Welshmen in 1680's; Haverford College (1833; men; Society of Friends).

Hav'er·ford·west' (hăv'ẽr·fẽrd·wĕst'). Municipal borough and seaport, ⊗ of Pembrokeshire, SW Wales; pop. 7266; ruins of 12th-cent. castle and of 12th-cent. Augustinian priory.

Ha'ver·hill (hā'vrĭl; hā'vẽr·ĭl). **1** Industrial city, Essex co., NE corner of Massachusetts, on Merrimack river 15 m. NE of Lowell; pop. 46,346; shoe manufacturing; birthplace of John Greenleaf Whittier. **2** Town, Grafton co., W New Hampshire, on Connecticut river 22 m. SSW of Littleton; pop. 3127; chartered 1763; dairying, farming, granite quarrying.

Hav'er·straw (hăv'ẽr·strô). Village, Rockland co., SE New York, on W shore of Hudson river 32 m. N of New York; pop. 5771; traprock quarries, brick yards, cement works; textiles, hardware, leather; artists' colony.

Havlíčkův Brod. See NĚMECKÝ BROD.

Hav're (hăv'ēr). City, ⊗ of Hill co., N Montana, 108 m. NE of Great Falls; pop. 10,740; ships livestock, wheat, potatoes; Northern Montana College (1913; coed.).

Havre, Le. See LE HAVRE.

Ha'vre Au'bert' (ȧ'vrō'bâr'). Chief village of Magdalen Is. (part of Gaspé co.), Quebec, Canada, on Amherst I.

Hav're de Grace (hăv'ẽr dĕ grăs'; grās'). City, Harford co., NE Maryland, at mouth of Susquehanna river; pop. 8510; resort; duck hunting; race track.

Ha'vrin'court' (ȧ'vrăN'kōōr'). Village, Pas-de-Calais dept., N France, 19 m. SE of Arras; pop. (1931) 613; severe fighting Apr., May, and Sept. 1918.

Haw (hô). River ab. 130 m. long, N cen. North Carolina; formed by forks uniting in Alamance co., flows SE and unites with Deep river to form Cape Fear river.

Ha·wai'i (hȧ·wī'ē; -wô'yē; -wô'yä; -vī'ē). **1** *or* **Ha·wai'ian** (hȧ·wī'[y]ăn; -wô'yăn) **Islands**; *formerly* **Sand'wich Islands** (săn[d]'wĭch; *Brit. also* -wĭj). Chain of volcanic and coral islands in N cen. Pacific Ocean, 2090 m. WSW of San Francisco, comprising 20 islands; constitutes a state (**Hawaii**) of the United States, admitted 1959 as 50th state, including entire chain except Midway Is.; 47th state in area, 6424 sq. m.; 43d state in population, pop. 632,772; ✳ Honolulu on Oahu I. See *Table of States* at UNITED STATES. Divided into the following 4 counties (for pronunciation of their names, see their individual entries):

COUNTY	ISLAND	AREA[1]	POP.[1]	CO. SEAT
Hawaii	Hawaii	4,021	61,332	Hilo
Honolulu[2]	Oahu	607[2]	500,409	Honolulu
Kauai	Kauai Niihau	623	28,176	Lihue
Maui	Kahoolawe Lanai Maui Molokai[3]	1,173	42,855	Wailuku
		6,424	632,772	

[1] Area = land area in sq. m. Pop. from 1960 Census.
[2] Includes the uninhabited islands of the archipelago (Kaula, Kure, Necker, French Frigate Shoal, Gardner Pinnacles, etc.).
[3] Includes Kalawao district which, although officially designated as a county, consists only of Kalaupapa leper settlement and has no local government.

Islands have fine climate and fertile soil; produce esp. sugar and pineapples, other crops tobacco, coffee, rice, cotton, and bananas; remarkable for fine scenery, volcanoes, and the great varieties of bird and marine life; their location affords great trade advantages. *Nicknames:* Aloha State, Paradise of the Pacific. *State flower:* Red hibiscus. *Motto:* Ua Mau Ke Ea O Ka Aina I Ka Pono (The Life of the Land is Established in Righteousness). *Chief cities:* Honolulu and Hilo. *Highest point:* Mauna Kea 13,796 ft. on Hawaii I. See *Hawaiian Islands Bird Reservation* at LEEWARD ISLANDS and *Hawaii National Park* and *Haleakala National Park* at UNITED STATES, *National Parks.*

History: By tradition first reached by Polynesians when small group arrived from S ab. 500 A.D.; received other immigrants in 12th and 13th cents.; discovered and named Sandwich Is. 1778 by Capt. Cook who was killed here 1779; islands united under rule (1795–1819) of King Kamehameha I; frequented by American whalers from early 19th cent.; first visited by Christian missionaries (Americans) 1820; by 1844 recognized as independent by U.S., Great Britain, and France; when native dynasty founded by Kamehameha I terminated 1872 had made much progress; secured reciprocity treaty with U.S. 1875; under last two native rulers 1874–1893 subjected to misrule which led to deposition of Queen Liliuokalani and request for annexation to U.S. 1893 (annexation treaty withdrawn from U.S. Senate by Pres. Cleveland); set up

provisional government 1893, republic 1894; annexed to U.S. by joint resolution 1898; established as U.S. territory Apr. 30, 1900; began to use Pearl Harbor (*q.v.*) as coaling and repair station 1908; received jurisdiction over Midway Is. 1909; after 1920 extensively developed as U.S. Pacific naval and military base; scene of Japanese attack on Pearl Harbor Dec. 7, 1941; admitted as a state Aug. 21, 1959.

2 Largest of the Hawaiian Is., southernmost large island of the group, constituting a county of the state of Hawaii; 4021 sq. m.; pop. 68,350; ⊗ Hilo; top of a gigantic submarine mountain; contains four volcanic mountains: Mauna Kea, Hualalai, Mauna Loa, and Kilauea (the last two in Hawaii National Park). Chief villages Keaau, Kohala, Pahala, Papaikou, and Honokaa.

Hawaiian Islands Bird Reservation. See LEEWARD ISLANDS, Hawaiian Is.

Hawaii National Park. See UNITED STATES, *National Parks*.

Ha·wai′ki (hä·wī′kĭ) *or* **Ha·vai′ki** (hä·vī′kĭ). Mythical country, the fabled original homeland from which the Polynesians believe themselves to have come and to which their spirits return after death.

Ha·wa′ra (há·wä′rá). Site, SE of Birket Qârûn, Lower Egypt, of a pyramid, probably built by Amenemhet III of XIIth dynasty, and of remains of the Labyrinth, which was a huge funerary temple.

Ha′war·den (hä′wôr′d′n). City, Sioux co., NW Iowa, on Big Sioux river 35 m. N of Sioux City; pop. 2544; livestock shipping.

Haw′ar·den (hô′ẽr·d′n; här′d′n). Parish, Flintshire, N Wales, near Chester, England; site of the Hawarden Castle, built 1752 near ruins of medieval castle, long residence of Gladstone; St. Deniol's Library, founded by Gladstone 1895, in building erected 1902.

Ha′wash (hä′wäsh) *or* **A′wash** (ä′-). River ab. 500 m. long in E Ethiopia; flows NE into the Danakil Desert on border of French Somaliland.

Ha′we·a, Lake (hä′wĕ·á). Lake 48 sq. m. in S cen. South I., New Zealand.

Ha′we·ra (hä′wĕ·rá). Seaport, Taranaki provincial dist., W North I., New Zealand, on South Taranaki Bight 120 m. N of Wellington; pop. 4630.

Hawes′ville (hôz′vĭl; *Sou. also* -v′l). City, ⊗ of Hancock co., NW cen. Kentucky; pop. 882.

Hawes Water (hôz). Lake in Lake District, NW England, in Westmorland 5 m. N of Kendal; 3 m. long; maximum depth 103 ft.; provides part of Manchester water supply.

Ha′wi (hä′wē). Village, North Kohala dist., Hawaii co., Hawaii, near Upolu Point on N coast of Hawaii I.; pop. (est.) 800.

Ha′wick (hô′ĭk). Burgh, Roxburgh co., SE Scotland, on the Teviot 40 m. NE of Dumfries; pop. 16,718; manufactures tweeds and hosiery.

Hawke Bay (hôk). Large inlet of South Pacific Ocean on E cen. coast of North I., New Zealand; has Napier on SW shore.

Hawke's Bay (hôks). Provincial district of New Zealand. See *Table* at NEW ZEALAND.

Hawkes′bur′y (hôks′bĕr′ĭ; -bĕr·ĭ; -brĭ). **1** River 340 m. long, E New South Wales, SE Australia, flows E to Pacific Ocean N of Sydney; navigable for small boats for ab. 70 m.

2 Manufacturing town, Prescott co., SE Ontario, Canada, on Ottawa river 54 m. ENE of Ottawa; pop. 7194; pulp and paper, lumber; population largely French Canadian.

Haw′kins (hô′kĭnz). **1** County in Tennessee. See *Table* at TENNESSEE.

2 City, Wood co., NE Texas, ESE of Quitman; pop. 868; Jarvis Christian Coll. (1912; coed.).

Haw′kins·ville (hô′kĭnz·vĭl). City, ⊗ of Pulaski co., S cen. Georgia, 38 m. SSE of Macon; pop. 3967; cotton, peanuts, cheese.

Hawks′bill′ Mountain (hôks′bĭl′). Peak 4049 ft. in the Blue Ridge, Page co., N Virginia; highest point in Shenandoah National Park.

Haw′ley (hô′lĭ). Borough, Wayne co., NE corner of Pennsylvania, 27 m. E of Scranton and just N of Lake Wallenpaupack; pop. 1433; founded 1827.

Ha′worth (hô′ẽrth; hô′wûrth, -wẽrth; hou′ẽrth). Village in West Riding, Yorkshire, N England, WNW of Bradford; pop. 5911; home of the Brontë sisters, Charlotte, Emily, and Anne.

Haw River (hô). Town, Alamance co., N cen. North Carolina, on Haw river ab. 3 m. NE of Graham; pop. 1410; textile mills.

Haw′thorn (hô′thôrn). City, S Victoria, SE Australia, E suburb of Melbourne; pop. 33,761.

Haw′thorn′den (hô′thôrn′dĕn). Estate, 8 m. SE of Edinburgh, Midlothian, Scotland; home of Scottish poet William Drummond.

Haw′thorne (hô′thôrn). **1** Residential city, Los Angeles co., SW California, 12 m. SW of Los Angeles; pop. 33,035; incorporated 1922; in region producing oil and gas; aircraft manufacturing.

2 Village, ⊗ of Mineral co., SW Nevada, on S end of Walker Lake; pop. 2838.

3 Borough, Passaic co., N New Jersey, 2 m. NNE of Paterson; pop. 17,735; hosiery, textiles, paint, glass; dye works.

Hay (hā). **1** Town, S New South Wales, SE Australia, on Murrumbidgee river 230 m. WNW of Canberra; pop. 3156; railroad terminus in wool region.

2 River, NW Canada; ab. 320 m. long, with its headstream, the Chinchaga, ab. 380 m.; rises in NE Brit. Columbia, flows E and N through NW Alberta to SW Great Slave Lake; its valley affords highway N from Peace river to the lake.

Ha·ya·ma (hä·yä·mä). Village, Kanagawa prefecture, SE Honshu, Japan, ab. 30 m. SW of Tokyo; pop. (1945) 13,999; bathing resort.

Hay′ange′ (ĕ′yänzh′). Industrial commune, Moselle dept., NE France, 16 m. N of Metz; pop. (1931) 12,607; oldest iron-working city in Lorraine.

Hayasdan. See ARMENIAN SOVIET SOCIALIST REPUBLIC.

Hayasui Strait. See BUNGO STRAIT.

Hay Canyon Butte (hā). Isolated peak 3440 ft. in Fall River co., SW corner of South Dakota.

Hay′dar·pa·ṣa′ *or* **Hai′dar Pa·sha′** (hī′där·pä·shä′). Town, E end of Sea of Marmara, Turkey in Asia, a suburb of Istanbul.

Hay′den (hā′d′n). Town (unincorporated), Gila co., E cen. Arizona; pop. 1760; smelting plants.

Hay′dock (hā′dŏk). Urban district, Lancashire, NW England, 15 m. ENE of Liverpool; pop. 11,838.

Haye–du–Puits, La. See LA HAYE-DU-PUITS.

Hayes (hāz). **1** County in Nebraska. See *Table* at NEBRASKA.

2 River ab. 300 m. long, E Manitoba, Canada; rises in chain of lakes and flows NE to Hudson Bay at York Factory.

3 Town, Kent, SE England, ab. 13 m. S of London; pop. 1678.

4 = HAYES AND HARLINGTON.

Hayes, Mount. Mountain 13,740 ft., E Alaska, at E end of Alaska Range, ab. 63°40′N, 147°W.

Hayes and Har′ling·ton (här′lĭng·tŭn). Urban district, Middlesex, SE England, 14 m. W of London; pop. 65,608; part of Greater London.

Hayes Center. Village, ⊗ of Hayes co., S Nebraska; pop. 283.

Hayes Peninsula. Large projection of land, NW Greenland, bet. Baffin Bay on S and Kane Basin on N; Cape York its SW point, Thule its chief settlement; largely covered with glaciers.

Hayes′ville (hāz′vĭl; *Sou. also* -v′l). Town, ⊗ of Clay co., SW North Carolina; pop. 428.

Haynau. See CHOJNÓW.

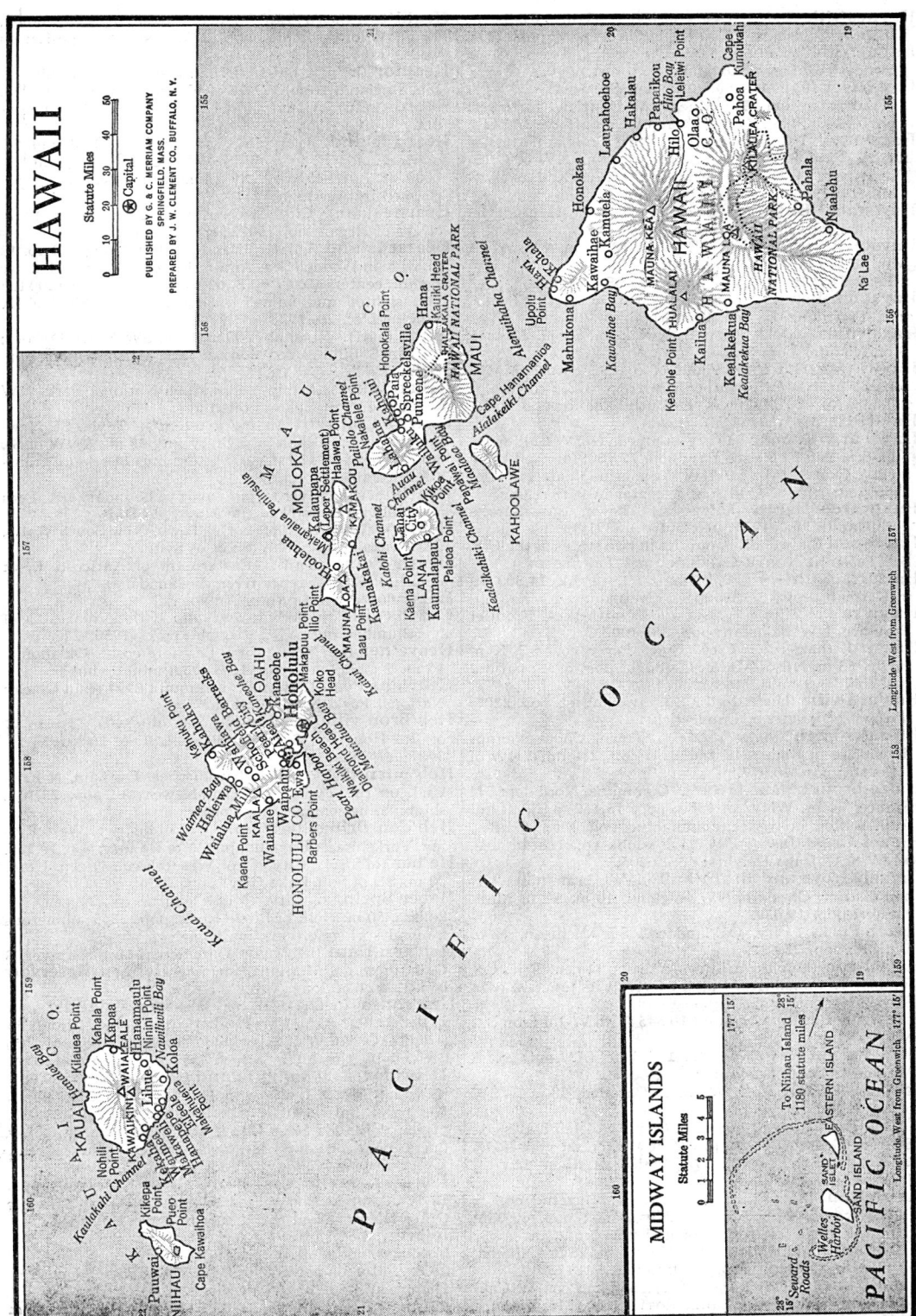

HAWAII

Statute Miles

⊗ Capital

0 10 20 30 40 50

PUBLISHED BY G. & C. MERRIAM COMPANY
SPRINGFIELD, MASS.
PREPARED BY J. W. CLEMENT CO., BUFFALO, N.Y.

PACIFIC OCEAN

MIDWAY ISLANDS

Statute Miles

0 1 2 3 4 5

PACIFIC OCEAN

To Niihau Island
1180 statute miles

Seward
Roads

Welles
Harbor

SAND ISLET

EASTERN ISLAND

SAND ISLAND

Longitude West from Greenwich

Haynes'ville (hānz'vĭl; *Sou. also* -v'l). Town, Claiborne parish, N Louisiana, 48 m. NE of Shreveport; pop. 1297.
Hayne'ville (hān'vĭl; *Sou. also* -v'l). Town, ⊗ of Lowndes co., S cen. Alabama; pop. (est.) 990.
Hay River (hā). **1** River, Canada. See HAY.
2 Trading station, SW Mackenzie District, Northwest Territories, Canada, on S shore of Great Slave Lake.
Hays (hāz). **1** County in Texas. See *Table* at TEXAS.
2 City, ⊗ of Ellis co., cen. Kansas, 48 m. NW of Great Bend; pop. 11,947; oil fields; Fort Hays Kansas State Coll. (1902; coed.).
Hay'stack' Butte (hā'stăk'). Peak 7405 ft. in Glacier National Park, NW Montana.
Haystack Mountain. 1 Peak 4918 ft. in Adirondack Mts., Essex co., NE New York.
2 Peak 3462 ft. in S Windham co., SE Vermont.
Haystack Peak. Mountain 9966 ft. in Sierra Nevada, in E Tuolumne co., cen. California.
Hays'ville (hāz'vĭl). City, Sedgwick co., S cen. Kansas, S of Wichita; pop. 5836.
Hay'ti (hā'tī). **1** City, Pemiscot co., SE corner of Missouri, 5 m. NW of Caruthersville; pop. 3737; cotton.
2 Town, ⊗ of Hamlin co., E South Dakota; pop. 425.
Hay'ti (hā'tī). Var. of HAITI.
Hay'ward (hā'wērd). **1** City, Alameda co., W California, 5 m. E of San Francisco Bay; pop. 72,700; founded 1854.
2 City, ⊗ of Sawyer co., NW Wisconsin, 38 m. N of Rice Lake (city); pop. 1540; resort center in lake region.
Hay'wards Heath (hā'wērdz). Town, East Sussex, S England; pop. (1931; urban dist.) 5391.
Hay'wood (hā'wŏod). Counties in two states of the U.S. See *Tables* at NORTH CAROLINA and TENNESSEE.
Ha·zar', Kuh'-i– (kōō'hē·hả·zär'). Peak 14,500 ft. in Kerman prov., SE Iran, S of Kerman.
Ha·za'ra (hả·zä'rả). Tribal area, North-West Frontier Province, NW Pakistan; pop. 352,400.
Haz'ard (hăz'ērd). City, ⊗ of Perry co., SE Kentucky, 53 m. NE of Middlesborough; pop. 5958; natural gas, coal; saw mills, steel mill.
Haz'ard·ville (hăz'ērd·vĭl). Subdivision (est. pop. 2200) of town of ENFIELD, Connecticut.
Ha·za'ri·bagh' (hả·zä'rĭ·bäg'). Town, Chota Nagpur division, cen. Bihar, NE Indian Union, 210 m. WNW of Calcutta; pop. 20,977.
Ha'ze·brouck' (ȧ'zē·brōōk'). Commune, Nord dept., N France, 24 m. WNW of Lille; pop. 15,462; agricultural trade center; breweries; manufactures oil, soap textiles.
Ha'zel Crest (hā'z'l). Village, Cook co., NE Illinois, NNW of Chicago Heights; pop. 6205.
Ha'zel Grove and Bram'hall (hā'z'l, brăm'hôl). Urban district, Cheshire, NW England, 10 m. SE of Manchester; pop. 19,659.
Hazel Park. City, Oakland co., SE Michigan, N of Detroit; pop. 25,631.
Ha'zel·ton (hā'z'l·tŭn; -t'n). Village, N cen. Brit. Columbia, W Canada, on Bulkley river at its junction with Skeena river; end of Cariboo Road.
Hazelton Peak. Mountain 10,545 ft. in W Johnson co., N Wyoming.
Ha'zel·wood (hā'z'l·wŏod). **1** Village, St. Louis co., E Missouri, NW of St. Louis; pop. 6045.
2 Town, Haywood co., W North Carolina, 28 m. WSW of Asheville; pop. 1925.
Ha'zle·hurst (hā'z'l·hûrst). **1** City, ⊗ of Jeff Davis co., SE cen. Georgia, 48 m. NNW of Waycross; pop. 3699.
2 City, ⊗ of Copiah co., SW Mississippi, 32 m. SSW of Jackson; pop. 3400.
Ha'zle·ton (hā'z'l·tŭn; -t'n). City, Luzerne co., E Pennsylvania, 20 m. S of Wilkes-Barre; pop. 32,056; coal; knit goods, clothing, iron and steel products.
Head'land (hĕd'lănd). City, Henry co., SE Alabama, 10 m. N of Dothan; pop. 2650; founded 1817.
Healds'burg (hēldz'bûrg). City, Sonoma co., W California, 14 m. NNW of Santa Rosa; pop. 4816; founded 1852; fruit growing.

Heald'ton (hēl[d]'tŭn). Town, Carter co., S Oklahoma, 22 m. W of Ardmore; pop. 2898; asphalt deposits; oil wells.
Hea'nor (hē'nēr; hā'-). Urban district, Derbyshire, N cen. England, 10 m. WNW of Nottingham; pop. 24,395.
Heard (hûrd). County in Georgia. See *Table* at GEORGIA.
Heard Island. Island in S Indian Ocean, ab. 310 m. SE of Kerguelen I., in 53°10'S, 74°35'E; highest point ab. 6000 ft. Discovered by American navigator 1853; claimed by Australia 1947.
Hearne (hûrn). City, Robertson co., E cen. Texas, 18 m. NNW of Bryan; pop. 5072; cotton; railroad center.
Hearst Island (hûrst). Island ab. 42 m. long and ab. 12 m. wide in Weddell Sea, Antarctica, off E coast of Palmer Penin.; centers ab. 69°30'S, 62°W; highest point 1200 ft.; first sighted and named Hearst Land by Sir Hubert Wilkins Dec. 20, 1928.
Heart (härt). River ab. 200 m. long, SW North Dakota; rises in S Billings co., flows E into Missouri river opp. Bismarck.
Heart Lake. Lake in Yellowstone National Park, NW Wyoming; S of Yellowstone Lake.
Heart's Con·tent' (härts' kŏn·tĕnt'). Town, SE Newfoundland, on E shore of Trinity Bay 35 m. WNW of St. John's; pop. (1942 est.) 1000; terminus of several transatlantic cables.
Heath (hēth). River forming part of boundary bet. Peru and Bolivia; flows N to the Madre de Dios.
Heath'cote (hēth'kŏt; kŭt). Town, New South Wales, SE Australia, ab. 18 m SSW of Sydney.
Heath Point (hēth). Eastern tip of Anticosti I., at mouth of St. Lawrence river, E Canada.
Heathrow. See LONDON AIRPORT.
Heaths'ville (hēths'vĭl; *Sou. also* -v'l). Village, ⊗ of Northumberland co., E Virginia; pop. (1950) 225.
Heave'ner (hēv'nēr). City, Le Flore co., E Oklahoma, 13 m. S of Poteau; pop. 1891; coal mines; timber.
Heav'ens Peak (hĕv'ĕnz). Mountain 8994 ft. in Glacier National Park, NW Montana.
Heb'bron·ville (hĕb'rŭn·vĭl; *Sou. also* -v'l). Town, ⊗ of Jim Hogg co., S Texas, 50 m. ESE of Laredo; pop. 3987; oil wells; cattle ranches.
Heb'burn (hĕb'ērn). Urban district, Durham, N England, on the Tyne 7 m. E of Newcastle; pop. 23,163; shipbuilding; engineering works.
Heb'den Bridge (hĕb'dĕn). Urban district, West Riding, Yorkshire, N England, just W of Halifax; pop. 10,233.
He'ber (hē'bēr). City, ⊗ of Wasatch co., N cen. Utah, 30 m. SE of Salt Lake City; pop. 2936.
Heber Springs. City, ⊗ of Cleburne co., N cen. Arkansas, 50 m. NNE of Little Rock; pop. 2265; numerous mineral springs of curative value.
Heb'gen Dam (hĕb'gĕn). Dam across Madison river, S Gallatin co., S Montana, forming **Hebgen Reservoir** *or* **Lake** 21 m. long.
Heb'ri·des (hĕb'rĭ·dēz), *or* **Western Islands;** *anc.* **E·bu'dae** (ê·bū'dē) *or* **He·bu'dae** (hē-). Islands in Atlantic Ocean W of Scotland; 2900 sq. m.; pop. 61,795; divided by the Little Minch into two groups: **Outer Hebrides** *or* the **Long Island** (lŏng), pop. ab. 39,000, principal islands Lewis with Harris, North Uist, South Uist, and Barra; **Inner Hebrides,** pop. ab. 21,000, principal islands Skye, Mull, and Islay. Scene of frequent incursions of Scandinavian settlers from 6th cent. A.D.; ceded by Norway to Scotland in 13th cent.
Hebrides, Sea of the; *also* **Gulf of the Hebrides.** Body of water off NW coast of Scotland, bet. S part of Outer Hebrides and the N part of Inner Hebrides.
He'bron (hē'brŭn). **1** City, ⊗ of Thayer co., S Nebraska, 47 m. W of Beatrice; pop. 1920.
2 City, Morton co., SW cen. North Dakota, 37 m. E of Dickinson; pop. 1340; clay deposits, brick plant.
3 *Arab.* **El Kha·lil'** (ĕl kŏ·lēl'). Subdistrict, Jerusalem dist., cen. Palestine; 797 sq. m.; pop. 76,879.

4 *anc.* **Kir'jath–Ar'ba** (kûr'jăth·är'bá; kĭr'-). Town, ✳ of Hebron subdist., Palestine, 20 m. SSW of Jerusalem; pop. (1944 est.) 23,133; on caravan route to Egypt; one of the four holy cities of the Talmud: believed to be one of oldest cities in the world; home of Abraham; contains the structure, the Haram, enclosing the mosque built over the **Cave of Mach·pe'lah** [măk·pē'lá] (*Gen.* xxv. 9-10) where tradition says Abraham and Sarah were buried. Taken by Joshua; for a time the home of David; captured by Judas Maccabaeus; figured in wars of the Romans, Moslems, and Crusaders.

Heb'ros (âv'rôs). Modern Greek form of *Evros* department of Greece: see *Table* at GREECE.

Hebrus. See MARITSA.

Hebudae. See HEBRIDES.

Hec'a·te Strait (hĕk'á·tē; -tē). Channel 35 to 80 m. wide bet. W Brit. Columbia, Canada, and the Queen Charlotte Is., connecting Dixon Entrance with Queen Charlotte Sound.

Hec'a·tom'py·los (hĕk'á·tŏm'pĭ·lŏs). Ancient city, for a time ✳ of kingdom of Parthia, at foot of S slope of E Elburz Mts.; center of ancient highways, hence, its name (literally, Greek, "hundred-gated"); ruins near modern Damghan, NW Khurasan prov., NE Iran.

Hech'ing·en (hĕk'ĭng·ĕn). Commune, cen. Baden-Württemberg state, southwestern Germany, 25 m. SSW of Stuttgart; pop. 5123.

Heck'mond·wike (hĕk'mŭnd·wīk). Urban district, West Riding, Yorkshire, N England, SW of Leeds; pop. 8648; manufactures blankets, carpets; coal mining; dyeworks, iron foundries.

Hecla. Var. of HEKLA.

Hec'la and Gri'per Bay (hĕk'lá, grī'pēr). Bay, Melville I., W Franklin District, Northwest Territories, Canada; 75°40′N, 111°W

Hecla Island. Island in S Lake Winnipeg, SE Manitoba prov., S Canada.

He'de·mar·ken (hā'dĕ·mär'kĕn). Former name of *Hedmark*. see *Table* at NORWAY.

Hedge'hope Hill (hĕj'ŭp). Peak 2348 ft. in Cheviot Hills along border bet. England and Scotland.

Hedjaz. Var. of HEJAZ.

Hed'mark' (hăd'märk'). See *Table* at NORWAY.

Hed'on (hĕd'n). Municipal borough, Yorkshire, N England, ab. 5 m. E of Hull; pop. 1991; in 13th cent. an important port; notable church of St. Augustine.

Heem'ste·de (hām'stā'dĕ). Commune, North Holland prov., W Netherlands, S suburb of Haarlem; pop. 14,417.

Hee'ren·veen (hā'rĕn·vān). Commune, Friesland prov., N Netherlands, 17 m. SSE of Leeuwarden; pop. (1939) 22,169.

Heer'len (hār'lĕ[n]). Commune, Limburg prov., SE Netherlands, just NE of Maastricht 5 m. from German border; pop. (1939) 50,502; industrial center of the province; coal mining.

Hef'lin (hĕf'lĭn). Town, ⊗ of Cleburne co., NE Alabama; pop. 2400; settled 1883; lumber.

He'gou·me·ni'tsa (ē'gōō·mâ·nyē'tsä) *or* **Gou'me·ni'tsa** (gōō'mâ·nyē'tsä). Commune, Ioannina dept., N Epirus, Greece; pop. 564; on coast opp. S Corfu I.

Heian Hoku. See NORTH HEIAN.

Heian-kyo. See KYOTO.

Heian Nan. See SOUTH HEIAN.

Hei'de (hī'dĕ), *also* **Heide in Hol'stein** (ĭn hôl'shtīn; *Angl.* hōl'stīn). City, Schleswig govt. dist., Schleswig-Holstein, northwestern Germany, 28 m. SW of Schleswig; pop. 10,621; important cattle market; produces furniture.

Hei'del·berg (hī'd'l·bûrg). **1** Borough, Allegheny co., SW Pennsylvania, 6 m. WSW of Pittsburgh; pop. 2118. **2** Town, S Transvaal, NE Union of South Africa, 30 m. ESE of Johannesburg; pop. 5828; peace treaty at close of Boer war of 1880 signed here. **3** (*Ger.* hī'dĕl·bĕrκ) City, Baden-Württemberg state, W

Germany, on Neckar river 11 m. ESE of Mannheim; pop. 73,034; manufactures cement, tobacco, scientific instruments, leather; famous university (1386); ruins of 13th-cent. castle around which city grew; capital of the Palatinate until 1719; center of German Calvinism in 16th cent. (*Heidelberg Catechism* 1563); passed to Baden 1802.

Hei'de·nau (hī'dĕ·nou). Industrial city, Saxony, Germany, SE suburb of Dresden on Elbe river; pop. 16,198.

Hei'den·heim (hī'dĕn·hīm). City, Baden-Württemberg state, Germany, 41 m. NW of Augsburg; pop. 19,363; partly ruined 11th-cent. castle (Hellenstein); manufactures machinery, textiles, medical supplies; place where Saint Walburga died 777.

Hei'ho' (hā'hŭ'). **1** Former province (1932–45), N Manchukuo; 42,388 sq. m.; pop. (1940 est.) 149,679; ✳ Taiheiho. **2** Town. See TAHEIHO.

Hei·jo (hā·jō); *now* **Pyong·yang** (pyŭng·yăng). City, ✳ of North Korea and of South Pyongan (South Heian) prov., NW Korea, on N bank of the Taedong 125 m. NW of Seoul; pop. (est.) 700,000; first city of North Korea in size and importance; a center of Korean culture going back to 1100 years B.C.

Heil'bron (hĭl'brŏn). Town, N Orange Free State, E cen. Republic of So. Africa, 73 m. S of Johannesburg; pop. 3999; center of republic's main maize district; capital of Orange Free State May 13-20, 1900.

Heil'bronn' (hĭl'brŏn'). Industrial city, Baden-Württemberg state, W Germany, on Neckar river 27 m. N of Stuttgart; pop. 45,520; railroad junction; old fortifications converted into promenades; manufactures machinery, metal goods, furniture, wooden goods, paper. Belonged to Frankish crownlands 8th cent.; became city 1350, passed to Württemberg 1802.

Heilsberg. See LIDZBARK WARMIŃSKI.

Hei'lung'kiang' (hā'lōong'jĭ·äng'). **1** River. See AMUR. **2** One of the three original provinces of Manchuria, in N part bordering Amur river; 174,554 sq. m.; pop. (1936 est.) 3,672,777; ✳ Lungkiang; under Japanese control (1932–45) included North and East Hsingan, Heiho, Lunkiang, Peian, and parts of Pinkiang and Sankiang provinces of Manchukuo; reorganized Sept. 1945 with 70,969 sq. m., pop. 2,469,000, ✳ Peian.

Heilungkiang–cheng. See AIGUN.

Hei'no·la (hā'nô·lá). Town, S Finland, in Mikkeli prov., 80 m. NNE of Helsinki; pop. 1793.

He·jaz' (hĕ·jăz'); *Arab.* **al-Hi'jaz** (ăl'hĭ·jăz'). Kingdom extending along Red Sea coast of W Arabia; ab. 150,000 sq. m., ab. 800 m. long and 100 to 200 m. wide; pop. ab. 2,000,000; ✳ Mecca; forms with Nejd the Kingdom of Saudi Arabia; bounded on the N by Jordan on E by Nejd, on S by Asir, and on W by Red Sea; NW coast extends along Gulf of 'Aqaba. Its coastal plain generally desolate; on its E edge is mountain range (highest point Harrat ar Raha in N 7000 ft.) with inland basins that have little drainage. Chief products grains and dates. Most fertile part in S around Mecca and Medina, its chief towns; other towns Taif and the ports of Jidda, Yenbo', and Wejh.

History: Seat of Mecca and Medina (*qq.v.*). original centers of Mohammedanism; as province of Arabia, fell under Egyptian domination after end of Abbasside caliphate 1258; became Ottoman dependency after conquest of Egypt 1517; restored to order 1811–20 by Mehemet Ali, viceroy of Egypt, after Wahabi revolt; resisted building of railroad by Turks before World War I; revolted and proclaimed independence under Husein ibn-Ali 1916; its independence guaranteed by Great Britain in contradiction to latter's promises to ibn-Saud; defeat of Husein by ibn-Saud 1919; independence guaranteed by Treaty of Sèvres 1920; consolidated as dual kingdom with Nejd 1926 after Husein driven out 1924; from 1932 part of single kingdom of Saudi Arabia (*q.v.*).

Hek′la (hĕk′lȧ; *Icelandic* hĕ′h′·klä). Volcano 4747 ft. in SW Iceland; largest crater ab. 1¼ m. in circumference and 200 to 300 ft. deep; 21 eruptions recorded since 12th cent.

Helder, Den. See DEN HELDER.

Hel′der·berg Mountains (hĕl′dẽr·bûrg). Range of hills ab. 1000 ft. high in Albany and Schoharie cos., E New York.

Hel′en, Mount (hĕl′ĕn; -ĭn). Peak 8540 ft. in Flathead and Glacier cos., NW Montana.

Hel′e·na (hĕl′ẽ·nȧ). **1** City, ⊗ of Phillips co., E Arkansas, on Mississippi river 88 m. ENE of Pine Bluff; pop. 11,500; river port and railroad terminus. Settled 1820; scene of battle July 4, 1863 won by Union forces under General B. M. Prentiss.
2 City, ✳ of Montana and ⊗ of Lewis and Clark co., W cen. Montana, 48 m. NNE of Butte; pop. 20,227; founded 1864 on a site where gold had been discovered; incorporated as town 1870, as city 1881; capital of Montana Territory 1875, and of the state 1889. Carroll College (1910; part coed.; Roman Catholic).
3 See MAKRONĒSI.

Hel′ens·burgh (hĕl′ĕnz·bûr′ō; -bŭ·rŭ; -brŭ). Coastal burgh, Dunbarton co., W cen. Scotland, on N shore of Firth of Clyde; pop. 8760; resort.

Hel′ford (hĕl′fẽrd). Short stream in S Cornwall, England; flows S and E to English Channel; marks N limit of The Lizard.

Hel′go·land (hĕl′gō·länd′; *Ger.* -länt′); *Eng.* **Hel′i·go·land′** (hĕl′ĭ·gō·länd′). Island in North Sea off W coast of Schleswig-Holstein, northwestern Germany, 28 m. from nearest mainland; ¼ sq. m.; pop. ab. 3000; attached to North Frisian Is. and a part of Schleswig-Holstein state. Danish to 1807 when it was seized by British (formal cession 1814); ceded to Germany 1890; fortifications dismantled after World War I but rebuilt by Hitler; in World War II surrendered to Allies May 5, 1945.

Helgoländer Bucht. See HELIGOLAND BIGHT.

Hel′i·ce (hĕl′ĭ·sē). Ancient city, one of chief cities of Achaea, N Peloponnesus, S Greece, in N part on shore of Gulf of Corinth; noted for its temple and worship of Poseidon; destroyed 373 B.C. by earthquake and tidal wave.

Hel′i·con (hĕl′ĭ·kŏn; -kŭn). Famous mountain 5738 ft. in SW Attica and Boeotia dept., E cen. Greece, near Gulf of Corinth; was in SW part of ancient Boeotia on border of Phocis; supposed by ancient Greeks to be the abode of Apollo and the Muses; on it were the fountains of Aganippe and Hippocrene.

Hel′i·go·land′ Bight (hĕl′ĭ·gō·länd′); *Ger.* **Hel′go·län′der Bucht** (hĕl′gō·lĕn′dẽr bŏŏĸt′). Arm of the North Sea extending S and E of the island of Helgoland; scene of naval battle Aug. 28, 1914 bet. British and German lighter craft, resulting in definite advantage to British.

He′li·op′o·lis (hē′lĭ·ŏp′ō·lĭs). **1** *Bib.* **On** (ŏn). Ancient holy city in Lower Egypt; its ruins lie 6 m. NE of Cairo; dedicated to worship of the sun god, Ra, who was supposed to be incarnate in the Mnevis, a black bull, its temple becoming depository for historical records; its obelisks taken by later Romans to decorate Rome and other cities in Egypt, two of these obelisks, Cleopatra's Needles, being removed (1) 1878 to the Thames Embankment, London, (2) 1880 to Central Park, New York City.
2 Ancient city of Egypt, said to be of the late Stone Age and destroyed ab. 5000 B.C.; its site recently discovered at the necropolis of Hilwân, on right bank of the Nile 15 m. S of Cairo; not the On of the Bible (see sense 1, above).
3 See BAALBEK.

Hellas. See GREECE.

Hel′lemmes′-Lille′ (ĕ′lĕm′lēl′). Commune, Nord dept., N France, E suburb of Lille; pop. (1931) 18,096; spinning mills; 17th-cent. pilgrimage church.

Hel′len·doorn (hĕl′ĕn·dōrn). Commune, Overijssel prov., E Netherlands, 17 m. SE of Zwolle; pop. 13,721; textile manufactures.

Hel′ler·town (hĕl′ẽr·toun). Borough, Northampton co., E Pennsylvania, 8 m. ESE of Allentown; pop. 6716.

Hel′les, Cape (hĕl′ēz). South tip of Gallipoli Penin., Turkey in Europe.

Hellespont, Hellespontus. See DARDANELLES.

Hell′fire′ Pass (hĕl′fīr′). See HALFAYA PASS.

Hell Gate (hĕl). A narrow part of the East River, New York City, bet. Long I. and Manhattan I., and also bet. Ward's I. and Long I. and bet. Ward's I. and Manhattan I.; made safe for navigation by removal, begun 1851, of rock reefs and by dredging; channel 200 ft. wide at narrowest part, 26 ft. deep; spanned by the Hell Gate Bridge (railroad, completed 1917) and the Triborough Bridge (highway, completed 1936).

Hel·lín′ (â-[]yēn′). Manufacturing commune, Albacete prov., SE Spain, 35 m. SSE of Albacete; pop. 25,643; sulfur mining and refining.

Hells Canyon (hĕlz). Canyon of the Snake river on Idaho-Oregon border; 40 m. long, deepest point over 7000 ft.

Hel′mand *or* **Hel′mund** (hĕl′mŭnd); *anc.* **Et′y·man′der** (ĕt′ĭ·măn′dẽr). River ab. 650 m. long in SW Afghanistan; flows SW and W into Lake Helmand (*Pers.* **Ha·mun′-i-Hel·mand′** [hȧ·mōōn′i·hĕl·mănd′]) morass on border bet. Iran and Afghanistan. See GAWD-I-ZIRREH.

Helmantica. See SALAMANCA.

Hel′mond (hĕl′mônt). Manufacturing commune, North Brabant prov., S Netherlands, 9 m. ENE of Eindhoven; pop. (1939) 28,787; fine castle, built 1402.

Helm′stedt (hĕlm′shtĕt). City, Lower Saxony, Germany, 21 m. E of Brunswick; pop. 17,166; 11th-cent. church; lignite mining; seat of university 1576–1810.

Helmund. See HELMAND.

Helmuth. See GOWANDA, New York.

Hel Peninsula (hĕl); *Ger.* **(Halb′in′sel) He′la** (hälp′in′zĕl hā′lä). Spit of land ab. 22 m. long, Gdańsk dept., N Poland, on W side of Gulf of Danzig.

Hel′per (hĕl′pẽr). City, Carbon co., E cen. Utah, on Price river 7 m. N of Price; pop. 2459; coal mining.

Helsingborg. See HÄLSINGBORG.

Hel′sing·ör′ (hĕl′sĭng·ûr′); *Eng.* **El′si·nore** (ĕl′sĭ·nōr). Seaport, Frederiksborg co., N Sjælland I., Denmark; pop. (1945) 18,930; shipbuilding; glass and textile manufacturing; site of Kronborg Castle, dating from 16th cent. and famous as scene of Shakespeare's *Hamlet*.

Hel′sin·ki (hĕl′sĭng·kĭ); *Swedish* **Hel′sing·fors** (hĕl′sĭng·fôrz; *Swedish* hĕl′sĭng·fôrs′, -fôsh′). Seaport, ✳ of Finland and ✳ of Uusimaa dept., S Finland, on Gulf of Finland on a peninsula surrounded by islands and protected by fortifications at Suomenlinna; pop. (1939 est.) 311,500; manufactures paper, sugar, tobacco products, carpets, machinery; university. Founded N of present site by Gustavus I of Sweden 1550; removed to present site 1640; fortified 1729; with Finland (*q.v.*) became Russian 1809; made Finnish capital instead of Turku (see ÅBO) 1812; damaged in bombings by Russians 1939–40.

Hel′ston (hĕl′stŭn). Market town, Cornwall, SW England, 11 m. WSW of Falmouth; pop. (1951) 5545; formerly a tin-mining center; tourist resort for visitors to the Lizard S of it; noted for annual holiday, May 8, when dancers perform in the streets and gardens.

Hel·vel′lyn (hĕl·vĕl′ĭn). Mountain 3118 ft. in SE Cumberland, NW England, in Lake District 9 m. SE of Keswick.

Helvetia. See SWITZERLAND.

Hel′vick Head (hĕl′vĭk). Cape on S coast of Ireland, P of entrance to Dungarvan Harbour.

Hel′ville (ĕl′vēl′). Town on French island of Nossi-Bé, off NW coast of Madagascar.

Helwân. See HILWÂN.

Hem′el Hemp′stead (hĕm′ĕl hĕm[p]′stĕd; -stĭd). Municipal borough, Hertfordshire, SE England, near the Gade 23 m. NW of London; pop. 23,523; paper mills.

He′me·ling′en (hā′mĕ·lĭng′ĕn). Industrial commune, NW Germany, in Bremen state on Weser river 7 m. SE of Bremen; pop. 10,042; silverware, machinery, aluminum, magnesium, porcelain, electrical appliances, chemicals.

Hem′et (hĕm′ĕt; -ĭt). City, Riverside co., SE California, 31 m. SE of San Bernardino; pop. 5416; ancient rock paintings and carvings.

He′mix·em (hā′mĭk·sĕm). Commune, Antwerp prov., N Belgium, a S suburb of Antwerp on the Schelde; pop. 9312; manufactures copper, brass, ceramic, and majolica ware.

Hem′lock Lake (hĕm′lŏk). Lake ab. 7 m. long, 1 m. wide in W New York, bet. Ontario and Livingston cos.; outlet from N end joins outlet from Honeoye Lake and flows into Genesee river.

Hemp′field (hĕmp′fēld). Urban township, Westmoreland co., SW Pennsylvania, SE of Pittsburgh; pop. 29,704.

Hemp′hill (hĕmp′hĭl). **1** County in Texas. See *Table* at TEXAS.
2 City, ⊗ of Sabine co., E Texas; pop. 913.

Hemp′stead (hĕm[p]′stĕd; -stĭd). **1** County in Arkansas. See *Table* at ARKANSAS.
2 Residential village, Nassau co., SE New York, on Long I. 20 m. E of New York; pop. 34,641; settled c. 1643; market gardening; manufactures cork insoles, phosphates. Hofstra University (1935; coed.; before 1940 an affiliate of N.Y. Univ.).
3 Town, ⊗ of Waller co., SE Texas, 20 m. E of Brenham; pop. 1505; nearby is Prairie View Agricultural and Mechanical College (1876; coed.).

Hems′worth (hĕmz′wûrth; -wĕrth). Urban district, West Riding, Yorkshire, N England, SE of Wakefield; pop. 13,654.

He·na′res (ā·nä′rās). River ab. 75 m. long in cen. Spain; flows SW into Jarama river 10 m. ESE of Madrid.

Hen′daye′ (äɴ′dā′y′). Commune, Basses-Pyrénées dept., SW France; pop. (1931) 6939; on the Bidassoa 13 m. SW of Biarritz; frontier town, resort.

Hen′der·son (hĕn′dēr·s′n). **1** Name of counties in five states of the U.S. See *Tables* at ILLINOIS, KENTUCKY, NORTH CAROLINA, TENNESSEE, TEXAS.
2 Commercial city, ⊗ of Henderson co., NW Kentucky, on Ohio river 10 m. S of Evansville, Indiana; pop. 16,892; manufactures furniture, clothing, and hardware. Settled 1784, became a city 1854.
3 City, Clark co., SE corner of Nevada, S of Las Vegas; pop. 12,525.
4 Industrial city, ⊗ of Vance co., N North Carolina, 40 m. NNE of Raleigh; pop. 12,740; cotton and tobacco market; manufactures cotton and tobacco products.
5 City, ⊗ of Chester co., W Tennessee, 17 m. SW of Jackson; pop. 2691.
6 City, ⊗ of Rusk co., E Texas, 31 m. ESE of Tyler; pop. 9666; oil wells and industries; manufactures cottonseed oil, foundry and lumber products.

Henderson Field. Airfield on N coast of Guadalcanal, SE Solomon Is., W Pacific Ocean; built originally by Japanese 1942, named by U.S. Marines who seized it Aug. 7, 1942. See GUADALCANAL.

Henderson, *or* **E·liz′a·beth** (ē·lĭz′á·bĕth), **Island.** British uninhabited coral island in S Pacific Ocean, SE of Tuamotu Archipelago; lat. 24°21′S and long. 128°18′W; ab. 120 m. NE of Pitcairn I.; attached to Pitcairn I. colony.

Henderson Lake. Lake ab. 2½ m. long in W Essex co., NE New York; a source of Hudson river.

Hen′der·son·ville (hĕn′dēr·s′n-vĭl). City, ⊗ of Henderson co., SW North Carolina, in Blue Ridge Mts. 21 m. SSE of Asheville; pop. 5911; summer and health resort; textile mills.

Hen′don (hĕn′dŭn). Urban district, Middlesex, SE

England, NW suburb of London; pop. 115,682, (1951) 155,835; part of Greater London; airfields.

Hen′dricks (hĕn′drĭks). County in Indiana. See *Table* at INDIANA.

Hen′dry (hĕn′drĭ). County in Florida. See *Table* at FLORIDA.

Hen Egg Mountain (hĕn′ ĕg′). Peak 5002 ft. in W Brewster co., W Texas.

Heng *or* **Heng Shan** (hŭng′ shän′); *also* **Nan Yo** (nän′ yô′). Sacred mountain of China, E cen. Hunan prov., N of Hengyang; 2953 ft.; has many Buddhist temples on its summit.

Heng′e·lo (hĕng′ĕ·lō). Commune, Overijssel prov., E Netherlands, near German border; pop. (1939) 41,476; industrial center; manufactures textiles, esp. cotton.

Heng′feng′ (hŭng′fŭng′). Town, NE Kiangsi prov., SE China, on railroad E of Nanchang.

Heng′yang′ (hŭng′yäng′), *formerly* **Heng′chow′** (-jō′). Town, S cen. Hunan prov., SE cen. China, on Siang river ab. 150 m. S of Changsha; pop. ab. 20,000; important rail and river junction point; American air base, scene of severe fighting 1944, taken by Japanese Aug. 8 but recovered.

Hé′nin′-Lié′tard′ (ā′näɴ′lyā′tàr′). Commune, Pas-de-Calais dept., N France, 4 m. N of Arras; pop. 21,946; coal mines; metal works; ancient capital of a principality erected 1579 by Charles of Alsace; damaged in World War I.

Hénin-sur-Co′jeul′ (-sür-kô′zhûl′). Village, Pas-de-Calais dept., N France, SE of Arras; pop. (1931) 333; battles Apr. 1917 and Aug. 1918.

Hen′kel Mountain (hĕng′kĕl). Peak 8700 ft. in Glacier National Park, NW Montana.

Hen′ley *or* **Henley on Thames** (hĕn′lĭ, tĕmz). Municipal borough, Oxfordshire, cen. England, 35 m. W of London; pop. 7970; known esp. as scene of annual Henley rowing regatta, estab. 1839.

Hen·lo′pen, Cape (hĕn·lō′pĕn). Cape on E coast of Sussex co., Delaware, at S of entrance to Delaware Bay.

Henna. See ENNA commune.

Hen′ne·bont′ (ĕn′bôɴ′). Commune, Morbihan dept., NW France, on the Blavet 6 m. NE of Lorient; pop. (1931) 8148; famous for its defense by Jeanne de Montfort when besieged by Charles de Blois 1342; Gothic church built 1513-30; nearby is Cistercian abbey founded 1270.

Hen′ne·pin (hĕn′ĕ·pĭn). **1** County in Minnesota. See *Table* at MINNESOTA.
2 Village, ⊗ of Putnam co., N cen. Illinois; pop. 391.

Hen′pan, Cape (hĕn′pän). Northernmost point of Buka I., NW Solomon Is., W Pacific Ocean; 5°S.

Hen·ri′co (hĕn·rī′kō). County in Virginia. See *Table* at VIRGINIA.

Hen′ri·et′ta (hĕn′rĭ·ĕt′á). Town, ⊗ of Clay co., N Texas, 19 m. ESE of Wichita Falls; pop. 3062; manufactures flour, lumber; oil and gas wells.

Henrietta Ma·ri′a, Cape (má·rī′á; -rē′á). Cape, N coast of Ontario prov., Canada, at W of entrance to James Bay.

Hen′ry (hĕn′rĭ). **1** Name of counties in ten states of the U.S. See *Tables* at ALABAMA, GEORGIA, ILLINOIS, INDIANA, IOWA, KENTUCKY, MISSOURI, OHIO, TENNESSEE, VIRGINIA.
2 City, Marshall co., N cen. Illinois, on Illinois river 30 m. N of Peoria; pop. 2278.

Henry, Cape. Cape on NE coast of Princess Anne co., Virginia, S of entrance to Chesapeake Bay, opp. Cape Charles.

Henry, Mount. 1 Peak 12,197 ft. in Sierra Nevada, in E Fresno co., S cen. California.
2 Peak 8870 ft. in Glacier National Park, NW Montana.

Hen′ry·et′ta (hĕn′rĭ·ĕt′á). City, Okmulgee co., E cen. Oklahoma, 13 m. S of Okmulgee; pop. 6551; manufactures glass, foundry products; zinc smelters; coal mines; gas and oil wells.

Hens′low, Cape (hĕnz′lō). Cape on SE extremity of Guadalcanal, Solomon Is., W Pacific Ocean.

Hen′za·da′ (hĕn′zȧ·dä′). **1** District, Irrawaddy division, Lower Burma; 2782 sq. m.; pop. 613,280.
2 Town, its ✱, on the Irrawaddy 75 m. NNW of Rangoon; pop. 28,542; at head of Irrawaddy delta; connected by rail with Bassein; center of rice and tobacco cultivation.

Hep′pen·heim (hĕp′ĕn·hīm). Commune, Starkenburg prov., SE Hesse, Germany, 18 m. S of Darmstadt; pop. 8880; nearby are ruins of Starkenburg castle built 1066 by the abbot Ulrich von Lorsch; stone quarries.

Hepp′ner (hĕp′nẽr). City, ⊗ of Morrow co., N Oregon, 45 m. WSW of Pendleton; pop. 1661.

Hep′ta·ne′sus (hĕp′tȧ·nē′sŭs). Literally "seven islands"; ancient name of the IONIAN ISLANDS.

Hep′tarch·y, the (hĕp′tär·kĭ). The seven Anglo-Saxon kingdoms of Britain: Kent, Sussex, Wessex, Essex, Northumbria, East Anglia, Mercia. See these names.

Her′a·cle′a (hĕr′ȧ·klē′ȧ). **1** Ancient city, Lucania, Italy, near Gulf of Taranto; founded by Greeks from Tarentum (mod. Taranto); battle 280 B.C. in which Pyrrhus, King of Epirus, defeated the Romans but with heavy losses, hence, a "Pyrrhic victory."
2 See AYVALIK.

Heraclea Lyncestis. See BITOLJ.

Heraclea Pontica. See EREĞLI.

Her′a·cle·op′o·lis (hĕr′ȧ·klē·ŏp′ō·lĭs). Ancient city in Egypt; site in Faiyûm prov. near the Nile; capital for one period in the Middle Kingdom in Egypt, IXth and Xth Dynasties ruling at this time (c. 2445–2160 B.C.) being called the Heracleopolitan Dynasties.

Heracleum. See CANDIA.

Hē·rá′klei·on (ē·rä′klĕ·ôn), *also* **He·rak′li·on** (hē·räk′lĭ·ŏn; hẽr′ȧ·klĭ′ŏn). **1** Department of Greece. See *Table* at GREECE.
2 City. See CANDIA.

Her′ald Island (hĕr′ăld). Small island, in Chuckchee Sea, Arctic Ocean, 40 m. E of Wrangel I.

He·rat′ (hĕ·rät′). **1** A major province, NW Afghanistan.
2 *anc.* **Ar′i·a** (âr′ĭ·ȧ; á·rī′ȧ). City, Herat prov., NW Afghanistan, on the Hari Rud; pop. ab. 85,000; remarkable for its huge earthworks and defense walls and for its palaces, mosques, and tombs, some partly in ruins. An old city, for centuries on trade route from India to Persia, Mesopotamia, and Europe; subject at different times to Khurasan, Seistan, Bukhara, and to Turkmen; obscured by Ghazni during Middle Ages and although recovered under rulers of Ghor practically destroyed twice by the Mongols, 1232 and 1398; rebuilt, prospered as independent Afghan kingdom; in modern times has undergone many revolutions; attacked by Persia 1856; taken by Dost Mohammed Khan 1863.

Hé′rault′ (ā′rō′). **1** River ab. 100 m. long in S France; rises in Cévennes Mts., flows SSW into Gulf of Lions near Agde.
2 Department of France. See *Table* at FRANCE.

Her′bert Hoo′ver Lake (hûr′bẽrt hōō′vẽr). Lake on border bet. Papua and Neth. New Guinea, New Guinea I., W of Fly river.

Her′ber·ton (hûr′bẽr·t′n). Town, near coast of NE Queensland, Australia, 55 m. SW of Cairns; mining, esp. for tin.

Her′berts·hö′he (hĕr′bẽrts·hŭ′ẽ). See KOKOPO.

Herceg Novi. Var. of ERCEGNOVI.

Hercegovina. See HERZEGOVINA.

Her′cu·la′ne·um (hûr′ků·lā′nē·ŭm). Ancient city, Campania, Italy, on coast SE of Neapolis, at NW foot of Mt. Vesuvius; with Pompeii, just S of the mountain, destroyed by eruption of 79 A.D. See RESINA.

Her′cu·les (hûr′ků·lēz). Town, Transvaal, NE Union of South Africa; suburb of Pretoria; pop. 16,119.

He·re′dia (ā·rā′thyä). **1** Province, cen. Costa Rica; 1132 sq. m.; pop. (1943 est.) 53,023; coffee, sugar, cattle, hides.

2 Town, its ✱, just NW of San José; pop. (1943 est.) 10,331; center of coffee industry.

Her′e·ford (hûr′fẽrd). City, ⊗ of Deaf Smith co., NW Texas, 40 m. SW of Amarillo; pop. 7652; ships cattle.

Her′e·ford (hĕr′ĕ·fẽrd). **1** County, W England. See HEREFORDSHIRE.
2 Municipal borough, ⊗ of Herefordshire, W England, on the Wye 47 m. SW of Birmingham; pop. 32,490; founded by West Saxons in 7th cent. as an outpost near Welsh marches; trade center of agricultural and livestock-raising section; 11th-cent. cathedral.

Her′e·ford Inlet (hĕr′ĕ·fẽrd; hûr′fẽrd). Narrow strait leading from Atlantic Ocean through barrier reefs in SE Cape May co., S New Jersey.

Her′e·ford·shire (hĕr′ĕ·fẽrd·shĭr; -shẽr) *or* **Hereford.** County, W England, on border of Wales; 842 sq. m.; pop. (1951) 127,092; ⊗ Hereford; another important town Leominster; rivers Wye, Teme, Frome; agriculture, livestock raising (Hereford cattle), quarrying.

Hé′rens′, Dent d′ (dän′ dä′rän′). Peak 13,715 ft. in Pennine Alps, on Swiss-Italian boundary.

He′rent·hals (hā′rĕnt·häls; -rĕn·täls). Manufacturing commune, Antwerp prov., N Belgium, 18 m. E of Antwerp; pop. 12,172.

Her′ford (hĕr′fôrt). Manufacturing city, North Rhine-Westphalia state, Germany, 43 m. ENE of Münster; pop. 35,940.

Hé′ri′court′ (ā′rē′kōōr′). Commune, Haute-Saône dept., E France, near Belfort; pop. (1931) 5811; battles: (1) 1474 in which the Swiss were victorious over Charles the Bold; (2) Jan. 1871, in Franco-Prussian War, in which Bourbaki tried unsuccessfully to raise the siege of Belfort.

He′rings·dorf (hā′rĭngs·dôrf). Town on N coast of Uznam (Usedom) I. off Pomerania, Prussia, Germany; now belongs to Poland; seaside resort 5 m. NW of Swinemünde (Świnoujście).

Her′ing·ton (hĕr′ĭng·tŭn). City, Dickinson co., E cen. Kansas, 40 m. ESE of Salina; pop. 3702.

Heri Rud. See HARI RUD.

He′ri·sau (hā′rē·zou); *Fr.* **Hé′ri·sau′** (ā′rē′zō′). Commune, ✱ of Appenzell Outer Rhodes demicanton, NE Switzerland, 5 m. SW of St. Gallen; pop. (1941) 12,789; railroad junction; textiles (esp. cotton goods), embroidery.

Héristal. See HERSTAL.

Her′je·da′len (här′yĕ·dä′lĕn). Former district, cen. Sweden; belonged to Norway before 1645 when it was ceded to Sweden as result of the war 1643–45.

Her′ki·mer (hûr′kĭ·mẽr). **1** County in New York. See *Table* at NEW YORK.
2 Industrial village, ⊗ of Herkimer co., NE cen. New York, on Mohawk river 14 m. ESE of Utica; pop. 9396; forms single community with Mohawk, Ilion, and Frankfort across river; manufactures office furniture, metal specialties, knit goods. Settled by Palatines c. 1725; raided in French and Indian War; site of Fort Dayton (1776), from which Gen. Herkimer marched to battle of Oriskany; attacked by Indians under Brant 1778.

Herm (hûrm). One of the Channel Is., 3 m. E of Guernsey; ½ sq. m.; in Guernsey bailiwick.

Her′mann (hûr′mȧn). City, ⊗ of Gasconade co., E cen. Missouri, on Missouri river 44 m. E of Jefferson City; pop. 2536; settled 1837 by colonists sent out by German Settlement Society of Philadelphia, Pa.

Hermannstadt. See SIBIU.

Hermanos, Los. See LOS HERMANOS.

Her·man′us (hûr·măn′ŭs). Town, SW Cape Province, S Union of South Africa, 60 m. ESE of Cape Town; pop. 1704; seaside resort, one of world's finest angling centers.

Her′mi·nie (hûr′mĭ·nĭ). Locality, Westmoreland co., SW Pennsylvania, ab. 8 m. SW of Greensburg; pop. 1571.

Her′mit·age (hûr′mĭ·tĭj). City, ⊗ of Hickory co., SW cen. Missouri; pop. 328.

Hermitage Bay. Inlet ab. 25 m. long of Atlantic Ocean, S coast of Newfoundland; has several long arms.

Her'mit Islands (hûr'mĭt). See NORTHWESTERN ISLANDS.

Her'mon, Mount (hûr'mŭn); *Arab.* **Je'bel esh Sheikh** (zhä'bǎl ǎsh shīk; shāk). Mountain 9232 ft., highest point in Anti-Liban Range, SW Levant States, on boundary bet. Lebanon and SW Syria 28 m. WSW of Damascus and just N of Palestine; has snow-covered crest; the N limit of Israelite conquests; figures in Hebrew poetry (*Ps.* lxxxix. 12; cxxxiii. 3).

Her·mon'this (hûr·mŏn'thĭs). Ancient city in Upper Egypt, on W bank of Nile near Thebes.

Hermopolis. See HERMOUPOLIS.

Hermopolis Magna. See EL ASHMÛNEIN.

Hermopolis Parva. See DAMANHÛR.

Her·mo'sa (ĕr·mō'sä; *Angl.* hēr·mō'så). Municipality, NE Bataan prov., Luzon, Phil. Is., 10 m. N of Balanga and ab. 2 m. from NW coast of Manila Bay; pop. 8821; severe fighting early in Bataan campaign Jan. 1942.

Her·mo'sa Beach (hēr·mō'så). Resort city, Los Angeles co., SW California, on Pacific Ocean 15 m. SSW of Los Angeles; pop 16,115.

Her·mo·sil'lo (ĕr'mō·sē'yô). Town, NW Mexico, ✲ of Sonora state, on Sonora river ab. 65 m. from Gulf of California; pop. 18,601; gold, copper, and silver mines.

Her·mou'po·lis (hēr·mōō'pô·lĭs; *Mod. Gr.* âr·mōō'pô·lyĕs), *also transliterated* **Her·mop'o·lis** (hēr·mŏp'ô·lĭs); *also called* **Sy'ros** (sī'rôs; *Mod. Gr.* sē'rôs). Commercial seaport city, ✲ of Cyclades dept., Cyclades Is., Greece, on E coast of Syros I.; pop. 21,156.

Hermsdorf. See SOBIĘCIN.

Hermus. See GEDIZ.

Her'nád (hĕr'näd). River ab. 118 m. long in Czechoslovakia and Hungary; rises in Slovakia, flows E and S into the Sajó (tributary of the Tisza).

Hernandarias. See TACURUPUCÚ.

Her·nan'do (hēr·nǎn'dō). **1** County in Florida. See *Table* at FLORIDA.

2 Town, ⊗ of De Soto co., NW corner of Mississippi; pop. 1898.

Her'ne (hĕr'nĕ). Industrial city, North Rhine-Westphalia state. Germany. in the Ruhr 33 m. SSW of Münster; pop 68,249; coal mines; chemicals, machinery. cable; hardware.

Herne Bay (hûrn). Urban district, Kent, SE England, on North Sea 53 m. E of London; pop. 18,298; seaside resort.

Her'ning (här'nĭng). Commercial city, Ringköbing co., W cen. Jutland, Denmark, E of Ringköbing; pop. (1945) 16,285.

Hernösand. See HÄRNÖSAND.

He·ro·op'o·lis (hē'rô·ŏp'ô·lĭs; hĕr'ô). Ancient town on E edge of Nile delta, N Egypt; terminus of canal from Bubastis on the Nile and port at head of **Gulf of Heroopolis** (now Bitter Lakes and Gulf of Suez).

Her·re'ra (ĕr·rĕ'rä). Former province on the Azuero Penin., S Panama; now included in Los Santos prov. (*q.v.*).

Her·re'ro (ĕr·rĕ'rô). Cape on E cen. coast of Yucatán penin., SE Mexico, at S of entrance to Espíritu Santo Bay.

Herreroland. See DAMARALAND.

Her'rin (hĕr'ĭn). City, Williamson co., S Illinois, 5 m. NE of Marion; pop. 9474; trading center in coal-mining section; scene of so-called Herrin Massacre during a miners' strike 1922.

Herrn'hut' (hĕrn'hōōt'). Village, NE Saxony, E Germany, 18 m. SE of Bautzen; pop. 1680; seat of a persecuted colony of Moravians, hence called Herrnhuters, who settled here 1722 on estate of Count von Zinzendorf.

Her'schel (hûr'shĕl). **1** Small island in NW Mackenzie Bay, off coast of N Yukon Territory, Canada.

2 Trading post on the island.

Hers'feld (hĕrs'fĕlt). City, in Hesse, Germany, on Fulda river 31 m. SSE of Kassel; pop. 11,297; railroad junction; manufactures cloth, jute, machinery, apparatus, cable; 14th-cent. Gothic church; ruins of 12th-cent. church of Benedictine abbey founded here c. 769.

Her'shey (hûr'shĭ). Unincorporated community, Dauphin co., SE cen. Pennsylvania, ab. 13 m. E of Harrisburg; pop. 6851; privately developed as workers' community by Hershey Chocolate Corp. 1903.

Her'stal (hĕr'stäl); *Fr.* **Hé·ris'tal** (ā'rēs'tål'). Commune, Liège prov., E Belgium; pop. (1938 est.) 26,885; manufactures iron and steel; birthplace of Pepin II (Pepin of Herstal) and often the residence of Charlemagne.

Herst'mon·ceux', *also* **Hurst'mon·ceux'** (hûrs[t]'-mŭn·sōō'; -sū'). Village, S England, in East Sussex 9 m. NE of Eastbourne; 15th-cent. castle, restored, now site of Royal Greenwich Observatory.

Her'ten (hĕr'tĕn), *also* **Herten in West'fa'len** (ĭn vĕst'fä'lĕn). Commune in what was formerly Westphalia prov., Prussia, Germany, 10 m. N of Essen; pop. 34,055; coal mining; manufactures machinery.

Hert'ford (hûrt'fẽrd). **1** County in North Carolina. See *Table* at NORTH CAROLINA.

2 Town, and port of entry, ⊗ of Perquimans co., NE North Carolina, on arm of Albemarle Sound 17 m. WSW of Elizabeth City; pop. 2068; manufactures lumber, cotton products; fisheries.

Hert'ford (här'fẽrd; härt'-). **1** County, SE England. See HERTFORDSHIRE.

2 Municipal borough, ⊗ of Hertfordshire, SE England, on the Lea 22 m. N of London; pop. 13,890; site of synod held 673 by Theodore of Tarsus.

Hert'ford·shire (här'fẽrd·shĭr; -shẽr; härt'-) *or* **Hertford** *or* **Herts** (härts; hûrts). County, SE England; 632 sq. m.; pop. (1951) 609,735; ⊗ Hertford; has other towns Watford, St. Albans, Hemel Hempsted, Hitchin; rivers Lea, Colne; agriculture.

Hertogenbosch, 's. See 's HERTOGENBOSCH.

Her'tsel·i·ya *or* **Her'zl·i·ya** (hĕr'ts'l·ē'yå). Town, W Palestine, in new state of Israel near coast 8 m. N of Tel Aviv; named after Theodor Herzl.

Her'vey Bay (hûr'vĭ). Inlet of Pacific Ocean in SE Queensland, Australia, N of Brisbane, bet. Fraser I. and mainland.

Her'vey Islands (hûr'vĭ; här'-). Island group in N Cook Is., S Pacific Ocean, comprising two small uninhabited islands Manuae and Te au o tu; a name formerly used for Cook Is. as a whole.

Her'ze·go·vi'na (hûr'tsĕ·gô·vē'nå; *Ger.* hĕr'tsä·gō'-vĕ·nä, -gô·vē'nä); *Serb.* **Her'ce·go'vi·na** (hĕr'tsĕ·gō'-vĕ·nä). Region, NW Balkan Penin.; 3531 sq. m., now part of the federated republic of Bosnia and Herzegovina, Yugoslavia. As principality of the Huns, independent, except for brief intervals, from 10th–14th cents.; conquered by Bosnia 14th cent.; became independent duchy (origin of name Herzegovina), early 15th cent.; overcome by Turks 1483; by Treaty of Berlin 1878, placed under control of Austria-Hungary which made it part of new province of Bosnia and Herzegovina; became part of Serb-Croat-Slovene State 1918 and part of Zetska co., Yugoslavia, 1929; made part of Bosnia and Herzegovina (*q.v.*) federated republic 1946.

Herzliya. See HERTSELIYA.

Hes'din' (ā'dăn'). Town. Pas-de-Calais dept., N France, NE of Abbeville; pop. 2616; founded by Charles V; birthplace of Abbé Prévost.

Hesh'bon (hĕsh'bŏn). A Moabite town ab. 20 m. E of the Jordan and just NE of Mt. Nebo; in Old Testament times in ancient Palestine, now (**Hes'ban** [*Arab.* hĭs'-bän]) in W Jordan.

Hes'pe·ler (hĕs'pĕ·lẽr). Town, Waterloo co., SE Ontario, Canada, 10 m. E of Kitchener; pop. 3862.

Hes'pe·rus Peak (hĕs'pẽr·ŭs). Mountain 13,225 ft. in NE Montezuma co., SW Colorado; highest in La Plata Mts.

Hesse (hĕs; hĕs'ĕ; *sometimes taken as a Ger. word and pron'd.* hĕs'ĕ; *but the Ger. word* Hesse *means Hessian, the Ger. place name being* Hessen); *Ger.* **Hes'sen** (hĕs'ĕn).
1 Region in SW Germany, comprising the state of Hesse and the former Prussian province of Hesse-Nassau.
2 Former German state, SW Germany; 2969 sq. m.; pop. 1,347,279, (1939) 1,469,909; ✳ Darmstadt; watered by Fulda, Lahn, and Weser rivers; agricultural products, wine, machinery, metal goods, earthenware, brick. Divided into the following three provinces (for pronunciation of their names, see their individual entries):

NAME	LOCA-TION	AREA[1]	POP.[1]	CAPITAL
Oberhessen[2]	N	1,269	328,490	Giessen
Rheinhessen	SW	531	384,168	Mainz
Starkenburg	SE	1,169	634,621	Darmstadt

[1] Area in sq. m. Pop. from 1925 Census.
[2] Sometimes Anglicized as **Upper Hesse.**

3 State of the Federal Republic of Germany, including larger part of Hesse-Darmstadt along with part of Hesse-Nassau; 8150 sq. m.; pop. (1957 est.) 4,599,700; ✳ Wiesbaden.
History: (1) Medieval landgraviate expanded from original holdings W to the Rhine and S to the Main; 1567, according to will of Landgrave Philip I, divided bet. four sons, two of whom founded surviving houses of **Hesse'-Darm'stadt** (-därm'stăt) and **Hesse'-Cas'-sel** (-käs''l); (2) Hesse-Darmstadt (*Ger.* **Hes'sen-Darm'stadt** [hĕs'ĕn·därm'shtät]) inherited by George I in 1567, extended its territory and became grand duchy of Hesse in Napoleon's Confederation of the Rhine 1806; joined Prussian customs union 1828; in 1866, after supporting Austria in Seven Weeks' War forced to cede to Prussia **Hesse'-Hom'burg** (-hŏm'bûrg) and part of Upper Hesse; joined North German Confederation 1867; republic 1918; came under (Ger.) *Statthalter* appointed by Hitler 1935; (3) Hesse-Cassel (*Ger.* **Hes'sen-Kas'sel** [hĕs'ĕn·käs'ĕl]), or electoral Hesse, came from line of William IV, eldest son of Landgrave Philip I; its ruler, as Frederick I King of Sweden 1720–51; part of kingdom of Westphalia 1807–13; restored as independent state 1815; joined Prussian customs union 1831; its liberal reforms of 1848 overthrown with aid of intervention 1850; occupied by and united with Prussia in 1866 as result of siding with Austria; (4) **Hesse'-Nas'sau** [-năs'ô] (*Ger.* **Hes'sen-Nas'sau** [hĕs'ĕn·näs'ou]) a former Prussian province (see *Table* at PRUSSIA) formed from territories annexed in 1866: electoral Hesse, duchy of Nassau, part of landgraviate of Hesse-Homburg, free city of Frankfurt am Main, etc., and since 1929, former republic of Waldeck; lost sovereignty at accession of National Socialists 1934, becoming mere administrative unit of German Reich.
Hes'sle (hĕs''l; hĕz''l). Former urban district, East Riding, Yorkshire, N England, just W of Hull.
Hest'mann·öy' (hĕst'män·û'ü). Small island in Norwegian Sea off W cen. coast of Norway at Arctic Circle.
Hes'ton and I'sle·worth (hĕs'tŭn [hĕs''n], ī'z'l·wûrth [-wĕrth]). Municipal borough, Middlesex, SE England, W suburb of London; pop. 75,460, (1951) 106,636; part of Greater London; chiefly residential.
Hetch Hetch'y Dam *and* **Reservoir** (hĕch' hĕch'ĭ). See UNITED STATES, *Dams and Reservoirs* (O'Shaughnessy Dam); TUOLUMNE river.
Het'ting·er (hĕt'ĭng·ẽr). **1** County in North Dakota. See *Table* at NORTH DAKOTA.
2 City, ⊗ of Adams co., SW North Dakota; pop. 1769.
Het'ton (hĕt''n). Urban district, Durham, N England, 13 m. SSE of Newcastle; pop. 18,511.
Heumar. See PORZ.
Heungshan. See MACAO island.
Heuvelton. See OGDENSBURG.
Hé'ver'lé' (ā'vẽr'lā'). Commune, Brabant prov., cen. Belgium, S of Louvain; pop. 10,141; market gardens.

He'ves (hĕ'vĕsh). Commune, E cen. Hungary, 56 m. E of Budapest; pop. 9985.
Hev'ros (âv'rôs). = *Evros* department of Greece: see *Table* at GREECE.
Hex'ham (hĕk'săm). Urban district, Northumberland, N England, on the Tyne 20 m. W of Newcastle; pop. 9715; present abbey church of St. Andrew dates from 13th cent.
Hex'ham·shire (-shĭr; -shēr). District around Hexham, S Northumberland, N England, one of original counties palatine till close of 16th cent.
Heydekrug. See ŠILUTĖ town.
Hey'sham (hā'shăm). Former urban district, Lancashire, NW England, on S shore of Morecambe Bay; pop. (1921) 5027; since 1928 part of Morecambe and Heysham; watering place; Norman church with ruins of ancient oratory nearby.
Heyst (hīst). Commune and seaside resort, West Flanders prov., NW Belgium, just NE of Zeebrugge; pop. 6001.
Heyst-op-den-Berg (hīst'ôp·dĕ·bĕrK'). Commune, Antwerp prov., N Belgium, 15 m. SE of Antwerp; pop. 9315.
Hey'wood (hā'wŏŏd). Municipal borough, Lancashire, NW England, 9 m. NNW of Manchester; pop. 25,193; cotton mills; coal mines.
Hi'a·le'ah (hī'à·lē'à). City, Dade co., SE Florida, 5 m. NW of Miami; pop. 66,972; incorporated 1925; airport. Hialeah Park race track.
Hi'a·was'see (hī'à·wŏs'ē). **1** Var. of HIWASSEE.
2 Town, ⊗ of Towns co., N Georgia; pop. 455.
Hi'a·wa'tha (hī'à·wô'thà). City, ⊗ of Brown co., NE Kansas, 28 m. NW of Atchison; pop. 3391; corn, wheat, apples.
Hib'bing (hĭb'ĭng). Village, St. Louis co., NE Minnesota, 58 m. NW of Duluth; pop. 17,731; site of largest open-pit iron mine in the world; in the Mesabi Range.
Hibernia. See IRELAND.
Hibernicus, Oceanus. See IRISH SEA.
Hi'bok·hi'bok (hē'bŏk·hē'bŏk). Native name of volcano on Camiguin I., N of Mindanao, Phil. Is.; 5620 ft.; in violent eruption Sept. 1948 and again in 1951.
Hick'man (hĭk'măn). **1** Name of counties in two states of the U.S. See *Tables* at KENTUCKY and TENNESSEE.
2 City, ⊗ of Fulton co., SW corner of Kentucky, on Mississippi river; pop. 1537.
Hick'o·ry (hĭk'ō·rĭ; hĭk'rĭ). **1** County in Missouri. See *Table* at MISSOURI.
2 City, Catawba co., W cen. North Carolina, 25 m. W of Statesville; pop. 19,328; manufactures wagons, cordage, cotton and knit goods, furniture. Lenoir-Rhyne College (1891; coed.). Annexed West Hickory 1931.
Hicks'ville (hĭks'vĭl). **1** Village, Nassau co., SE New York, on Long I NE of Mineola; pop. 50,405.
2 Village, Defiance co., NW Ohio, 50 m. NW of Lima; pop. 3116.
Hic'po·chee, Lake (hĭk'pō·chē). Lake in SE Glades co., S cen. Florida penin.; connected by canal with Caloosahatchee river on W and Lake Okeechobee on E, a link in the Cross-Florida Waterway.
Hi·da·ka Mountains (hē·dä·kä). Range in S Hokkaido, Japan; highest peak Horoshiri 6732 ft.
Hi·dal'go (hǐ·dăl'gō). **1** Counties in two states of the U.S. See *Tables* at NEW MEXICO and TEXAS.
2 (*Span.* ē·thäl'gō) State, cen. Mexico. See *Table* at MEXICO.
Hi·dal'go del Par·ral' (ē·thäl'gō thĕl pär·räl'). = PARRAL.
Hid'de·kel (hĭd'ē·kĕl). Biblical name of the Tigris.
Hi·ei·zan (hē·ā·zän). Mountain 2800 ft., Kyoto prefecture, W cen. Honshu, Japan, just N of Kyoto and near SW shore of Lake Biwa; place of pilgrimage; monastery built by Saicho.
Hien'ghène' (yĕn'gĕn'). Town on E coast of New Caledonia I., SW Pacific Ocean, near N end.

Hiera. See VULCANO.

Hi·e·ra·kon'po·lis (hī′ĕr·à·kŏn′pô·lĭs). Ancient city of Upper Egypt, on left bank of Nile, S of Thebes; important tombs and relics found in its ruins.

Hie·rá'pe·tra (yā·rä′pà·trä). Seaport town, Lasithion dept., E Crete; pop. 3611.

Hi'er·ap'o·lis (hī′ĕr·ăp′ô·lĭs). Ancient city of Phrygia, Asia Minor, near Maeander river just N of Laodicea; an early seat of Christianity.

Hierosolyma. See JERUSALEM.

Hier'ro (yĕr′rô); *formerly* **Fer'ro** (fĕr′rô). Westernmost of the Canary Is. (*q.v.*), 78 m. WSW of Tenerife I., in Santa Cruz de Tenerife prov., Spain; 107 sq. m.; pop. (1930) 8071; chief town Valverde; volcanic in origin; rocky, unfertile soil; warm springs; produces figs, wines, and brandies. Thought by ancient geographers to mark W limit of world and hence they reckoned longitude from it.

Hig'ga·num (hĭg′à·nŭm). Subdivision (est. pop. 900) of town of HADDAM, Connecticut; agricultural implements.

Hig'gins Lake (hĭg′ĭnz). Lake ab. 7 m. long in N Roscommon co., N cen. Michigan; has outlet into Houghton Lake to the S.

Hig'gins·ville (hĭg′ĭnz·vĭl). City, Lafayette co., W Missouri, 39 m. NW of Sedalia; pop. 4003; seed corn; coal; manufactures shoes, incubators, brick and tile.

High Atlas. See ATLAS MOUNTAINS.

High Bridge. Borough, Hunterdon co., NW cen. New Jersey, 15 m. E of Phillipsburg; pop. 2148; iron and steel.

High'gate (hī′gāt). Town, Franklin co., NW Vermont, near Canadian boundary; pop. 1608; settled 1787; customs station.

High'gate (hī′gĭt; -gĕt). North suburb of London, England, NE of Hampstead Heath in Hornsey; residence of Coleridge and Andrew Marvell; place where, the legend has it, Dick Whittington heard Bow bells and decided to go on to London.

High Island. Island in N Lake Michigan, NW of Beaver I., part of Charlevoix co., NW Michigan.

High Knob. Peak 4188 ft. in Wise co., SW Virginia.

High'land (hī′lănd). **1** Counties in two states of the U.S. See *Tables* at OHIO and VIRGINIA.
2 City, Madison co., SW Illinois, 27 m. ESE of East St. Louis; pop. 4943.
3 Town, Lake co., NW corner of Indiana, 7 m. S of Lake Michigan; pop. 16,284.
4 Village, Ulster co., SE New York, on W bank of Hudson river almost opp. Poughkeepsie and ab. 14 m. S of Kingston; pop. 2931.

Highland Falls. Village, Orange co., SE New York, on Hudson river 5 m. SW of Newburgh; pop. 4469; adjoins West Point; Ladycliff Coll. (1933; women).

Highland Lake. Lake in NE Litchfield co., NW Connecticut, W of Winsted.

Highland Park. 1 Residential city, Lake co., NE corner of Illinois, on Lake Michigan 25 m. N of Chicago; pop. 25,532.
2 City, Wayne co., SE Michigan, entirely within city of Detroit; pop. 38,063; automobile manufacturing; Lawrence Institute of Technology (1932; men).
3 Borough, Middlesex co., cen. New Jersey, on Raritan river 2 m. E of New Brunswick; pop. 11,049; nonmetallic station of U.S. Bureau of Mines.
4 Town, Dallas co., NE Texas, entirely within city of Dallas; pop. 10,411.

Highland Peak. Mountain 9395 ft. in N cen. Lincoln co., E Nevada.

High'lands (hī′lăndz). **1** County in Florida. See *Table* at FLORIDA.
2 Borough, Monmouth co., E cen. New Jersey, on Sandy Hook Bay 17 m. ESE of Perth Amboy; pop. 3536; fishing village, summer resort; first U.S. Navy wireless station erected on nearby Monmouth Hills 1903; place where Henry Hudson first landed 1609.

3 See GUIANA MASSIF.

Highlands, the. That portion of the mainland of Scotland in and N of the Grampians; more definitely, the area above an imaginary line drawn from mouth of the Nairn on Moray Firth SE to the Dee, S to a headstream of North Esk, and SW to the Clyde opp. Greenock. The area below this imaginary line is known as **the Low'lands** (lō′lăndz).

Highlands of Nav'e·sink (năv′ĕ·sĭngk; nā′vĕ-; nĕv′ĕ-); *also* **Navesink Highlands** *or* **Navesink Hills.** Range of hills in NE New Jersey, extending from near Sandy Hook to Raritan Bay.

Highlands of the Hud'son (hŭd′s'n). Hilly region on both sides of Hudson river in Rockland, Orange, Putnam, and Dutchess cos., SE New York.

High'more (hī′mōr). City, ⊗ of Hyde co., cen. South Dakota; pop. 1078.

High Peak. 1 Mountain 3660 ft. in the Catskill Mts., Greene co., SE New York.
2 Highest mountain 6683 ft. of Zambales Mts., in N cen. Zambales prov., Luzon, Phil. Is., ab. 17 m. NE of Iba.

High Plains. The Great Plains esp. from Nebraska southward.

High Point. 1 Elevation 1803 ft. in N Sussex co., N New Jersey; highest point in New Jersey, in High Point (State) Park; New Jersey War Memorial, stone tower 225 ft. high.
2 Industrial city, Guilford co., N cen. North Carolina, 14 m. WSW of Greensboro; pop. 62,063; in Piedmont Region; furniture-manufacturing center; High Point College (1924; coed.).

High Rock Lake. Reservoir for water power in Yadkin river (*q.v.*), bet. Rowan and Davidson cos., cen. North Carolina; formed by **High Rock Dam.**

High Sierra. The Sierra Nevada in California.

High'spire' (hī′spīr′). Borough, Dauphin co., SE cen. Pennsylvania, on Susquehanna river 7 m. SE of Harrisburg; pop. 2999.

High Springs. City, Alachua co., N Florida penin., 22 m. NW of Gainesville; pop. 2329; founded 1885; tobacco, corn, peanuts.

High Tatra Mountains. See TATRA MOUNTAINS.

High'tow'er Bald (hī′tou′ĕr bôld′). Peak 4517 ft. in Towns co., N Georgia.

Hights'town (hīts′toun). Borough, Mercer co., W cen. New Jersey, 13 m. ENE of Trenton; pop. 4317; founded 1721; market center for farming country; Peddie School for boys (1864).

High Will'hays (wĭl′īz). Highest point 2039 ft. in Dartmoor, Devonshire, SW England.

High'wood (hī′wŏod). City, Lake co., NE corner of Illinois, on Lake Michigan 12 m. S of Waukegan; pop. 4499.

High Wycombe. See CHEPPING WYCOMBE.

Higuera, La. Commune, cen. Chile. See CRUZ GRANDE.

Hiitola. See KHITOLA.

Hiiumaa. See KHIUMA.

Hijaz, al-. See HEJAZ.

Hi·ko·ne (hē·kô·nĕ). Town on E shore of Lake Biwa, W cen. Honshu, Japan, in Shiga prefecture; pop. (1945) 44,133; noted for its beautiful scenery. Castle town of a daimio 1623–1868, one of strongest supporters of the Tokugawas; residence in 19th cent. of Baron Ii Naosuke who signed Japan's first treaties with U.S., England, and Russia.

Hi'ko, *or* **Hy'ko, Range** (hī′kō). Small range in cen. Lincoln co., E Nevada.

Hi·kue'ru (hē·kwā′rōō). Island, cen. Tuamotu Archipelago, S Pacific Ocean, ab. 220 m. SE of Rotoava.

Hild'burg·hau'sen (hĭlt′bŏŏrK·hou′zĕn). Town, Thuringia, E Germany, on the Werra SE of Meiningen; pop. 6520; capital of a principality 1683 which was united to Saxe-Meiningen 1826; late 17th-cent. ducal palace.

Hil'den (hĭl′dĕn). Manufacturing city, North Rhine-Westphalia state, Germany, near Rhine river 7 m. SE of Düsseldorf; pop. 20,024; textiles, pipes, bicycles, varnish.

Hil′des·heim (hĭl′dĕs·hĭm). Manufacturing city, Lower Saxony state, W Germany, 18 m. SSE of Hannover; pop. 58,522; rubber goods, dairy and agricultural machinery; sugar refining; bell and iron founding.

Hill (hĭl). Name of counties in two states of the U.S. See *Tables* at MONTANA and TEXAS.

Hill 60. Height ab. 3 m. SE of Ieper (Ypres), West Flanders prov., NW Belgium; scene of bitter fighting Apr. 17–May 5, 1915.

Hill 70. Hill ab. 3 m. N of Lens, France; fighting Sept. 1915; captured by Canadians Aug. 15, 1917.

Hill 102 *or* **Ma·mai′ Kur′gan** (mŭ·mī′ kōōr′gȧn). Height in city of Stalingrad, SE Russia in Europe; severe fighting Sept. 14, 1942 in which Russians were unable to retake it from Germans.

Hill 192. Height in Normandy, NW France, N of Carentan, commanding road from St-Lô to Bayeux; taken by Americans July 11, 1944.

Hill 193. See CASTLE HILL.

Hill 295. See LE MORT HOMME.

Hill 304. Height 10 m. NW of Verdun and near Le Mort Homme, NE France; fighting May 1916 and Aug. 1917.

Hill 516. Height, Cassino, Italy; site of Monte Cassino (*q.v.*), Benedictine monastery.

Hill 609 *or* **Djeb′el Ta·hent′** (jĕb′ĕl tȧ·hĕnt′). Height commanding Mateur, N Tunisia; severe fighting Apr. 28–29, 1943; captured by Americans May 1, 1943.

Hill 660. See BORGEN BAY.

Hil′la (hĭl′ȧ; *Arab.* hĭl′lȧ, -lä). **1** Province (*liwa*), cen. Iraq; pop. (1935 est.) 211,666.

2 Town, in Hilla prov., cen. Iraq, near the Euphrates 58 m. S of Baghdad; near site of ancient Babylon.

Hill City. City, ⊗ of Graham co., NW cen. Kansas; pop. 2421.

Hil′le·gers·berg′ (hĭl′ĕ·ᴋᴇrs·bĕrᴋ′). Commune, South Holland prov., SW Netherlands, residential suburb of Rotterdam; pop. (1939) 23,321.

Hil′le·gom (hĭl′ĕ·ᴋôm). Commune, South Holland prov., SW Netherlands, 8 m. S of Haarlem; pop. 10,812.

Hil′le·röd (hĭl′ĕ·rûth). Town, ⊗ of Frederiksborg co., N Sjælland, Denmark, 19 m. NW of Copenhagen; pop. (1945) 8887.

Hil′lers, Mount (hĭl′ērz). Peak 10,650 ft. in E Garfield co., S Utah.

Hill′gard, Mount (hĭl′gärd). Peak 11,460 ft. in Sevier co., cen. Utah.

Hil′liard (hĭl′yērd). Village, Franklin co., cen. Ohio, NW of Columbus; pop. 5633.

Hill′man Peak (hĭl′mȧn). Mountain 8156 ft. in W Klamath co., S Oregon; highest point on rim of Crater Lake.

Hills′bor′o (hĭlz′bûr′ô). **1** *or* **Hills′bor′ough** (-bûr′ô). County in New Hampshire. See *Table* at NEW HAMPSHIRE.

2 City, ⊗ of Montgomery co., S cen. Illinois, 48 m. SSE of Springfield; pop. 4232; coal mining, zinc smelting.

3 City, Marion co., E cen. Kansas; pop. 2441; poultry.

4 Town, ⊗ of Jefferson co., E Missouri; pop. 457.

5 *or* **Hillsborough.** Manufacturing town, Hillsboro co., S New Hampshire, 18 m. WSW of Concord; pop. 2310; settled 1741; woolens, hosiery, underwear, lumber. Birthplace of Franklin Pierce, 14th president of U.S.

6 Village, Sierra co., SW New Mexico, 40 m. ENE of Silver City; pop. (1950) 216.

7 Industrial town, ⊗ of Orange co., N North Carolina, 13 m. WNW of Durham; pop. 1349; summer capital of the state in second half of 18th cent.; meeting place of Provincial Congress 1775 and of general assemblies 1778, 1780, 1783, 1784; center of Regulator disturbances 1768–71; occupied by Cornwallis 1781; raided by Tories 1781.

8 City, ⊗ of Traill co., E North Dakota; pop. 1278.

9 City, ⊗ of Highland co., S Ohio, 32 m. WSW of Chillicothe; pop. 5474; manufactures foundry products.

10 City, ⊗ of Washington co., NW Oregon, 15 m. W of Portland; pop. 8232; settled 1841; wheat, milk products.

11 City, ⊗ of Hill co., NE cen. Texas, 33 m. N of Waco; pop. 7402; stock raising; cotton.

Hillsboro Bay. Inlet of Northumberland Strait, in S Prince Edward I., SE Canada.

Hills′bor′ough (hĭlz′bûr′ô). **1** River, W Florida; flows SW into Tampa Bay.

2 County in Florida. See *Table* at FLORIDA.

3 Residential town, San Mateo co., W California, 10 m. S of San Francisco; pop. 7554.

4 See HILLSBORO county and town, New Hampshire.

Hills′dale (hĭlz′dāl). **1** County in Michigan. See *Table* at MICHIGAN

2 City, ⊗ of Hillsdale co., S Michigan, 25 m. SSW of Jackson; pop. 7629; Hillsdale College (1844; coed.; Baptist).

3 Borough, Bergen co., NE corner of New Jersey, 9 m. ENE of Paterson; pop. 8734.

Hill′side (hĭl′sīd). **1** Village, Cook co., NE Illinois, WSW of Oak Park; pop. 7794.

2 Township, Union co., NE New Jersey, 2 m. N of Elizabeth; pop. 22,304.

Hills′ville (hĭlz′vĭl; *Sou. also* -v′l). Town, ⊗ of Carroll co., S Virginia; pop. 905.

Hill Tippera. See TRIPURA.

Hill X (ĕks). Height on Attu I., Aleutian Is.; held by Japanese and captured by Americans after sharp fighting in May 1943.

Hi′lo (hē′lō). **1** District, Hawaii co., Hawaii. See NORTH HILO.

2 City, ⊗ of Hawaii co., Hawaii, on **Hilo Bay** on E coast of Hawaii I.; pop. 25,966; excellent harbor; exports sugar, coffee, fruits, orchids; tourist center for volcanoes Mauna Kea and Mauna Loa and Kilauea in Hawaii National Park. Important in early years of the kingdom; nearby in 1796 Kamehameha I crushed the last serious revolt on Hawaii I.; American mission established ab. 1820.

Hi′long·hi′long, Mount (hē′lông·hē′lông). Mountain 6027 ft., NE Agusan prov., Mindanao, Phil. Is., highest of Diuata Mts.

Hi·long′os (hē·lông′ôs). Municipality on SW coast of Leyte I., Phil. Is., 62 m. SSW of Tacloban; pop. 25,920.

Hil′ton·head′ Island (hĭl′t′n·hĕd′). Island in Atlantic Ocean off South Carolina coast S of mouth of Broad river.

Hil′ver·sum (hĭl′vĕr·sŭm). Commune, North Holland prov. W Netherlands. pop. 74,036; radio stations.

Hil·wân′ (hĭl·wăn′) *or* **Hel·wân′** (hĕl-). Town and baths on Nile river S of Cairo, Lower Egypt, opp. ruins of Memphis; pop. ab. 11,000. See HELIOPOLIS, 2.

Hi·ma′chal Pra·desh′ (hĭ·mä′chȧl prȧ·dāsh′). Territory of the Republic of India, NW India, in the Himalayas NW of Uttar Pradesh. bordering on Tibet; comprises two separate areas; a union of former Punjab hill states, formed 1948; administered from Simla (Punjab); area 10,904 sq m.; pop. 1,109,500.

Hi·ma′la·yas, the (hĭ·mä′lȧ·yȧz; -mäl′yȧz; *Anglicized* hĭm′ȧ·lā′ȧz), *or, more correctly,* **the Hi·ma′la·ya** (-[y]ȧ). Mountain system, S Asia, bordering the Indian subcontinent on the N in a 1500-mile long arc extending from Kashmir in the W to Assam in the E and covering most of Nepal, Sikkim, Bhutan, and the S edge of Tibet; separated from the Karakoram Range in the NW by the Indus river and bounded on the N and E by the Brahmaputra river; divided into three main ranges, the Greater Himalaya in the N, having an average elevation of 20,000 ft. and including Everest, 29,028 ft., the Lesser Himalayas in the center, and the Outer Himalayas in the S, including Siwalik Range. Besides Everest includes peaks of Kanchenjunga, Dhaulagiri, Nanga Parbat, Nanda Devi; crossed in E from Kalimpong to Gyangtse by pass through Chumbi valley and in W from Srinagar to Gilgit by Burzil Pass. In World War II ranges of E end, forming a barrier on air ferry route from India into China, became known as "the Hump."

Hi'ma·may'lan (hĕ'mä·mī'län). Municipality, W Negros Occidental, Negros, Phil. Is., at S end of Guimaras Strait 40 m. S of City of Bacolod; pop. 28,407; formerly capital of all Negros.

Hi·me·ji (hĕ·mĕ·jĕ). Industrial city, Hyogo prefecture, W Honshu, Japan, 34 m. WNW of Kobe near N shore of Inland Sea; pop. (1945) 83,167; army division headquarters; fine old castle, large Buddhist temple.

Him'er·a (hĭm'ēr·à). Ancient Greek city on N coast of Sicily; home of Greek lyric poet Stesichorus; scene of battle in which Gelon of Syracuse defeated the Carthaginians 480 B.C.; destroyed by Hannibal 408 B.C. and a new city founded at Termini Imerese.

Ḫimṣ. See HOMS.

Hi·na'tuan (hĕ·nä'twän). Municipality, SE Surigao prov., Mindanao, Phil. Is., on coast 115 m. SE of Surigao; pop. 14,722.

Hinatuan Passage. Channel ab. 8 m. wide bet. Bucas Grande I. and mainland of NE Mindanao, Phil. Is.; by some extended to include the channel bet. NE Mindanao and S Dinagat I.

Hin'chin·brook (hĭn'chĭn·brŏŏk). **1** Island on E side of entrance to Prince William Sound, S Alaska; on its W side is Nuchek village. **2** Island on NE coast of Queensland, Australia, bet. Townsville and Cairns.

Hinck'ley (hĭngk'lĭ). Urban district, Leicestershire, cen. England, 23 m. ENE of Birmingham; pop. 39,088; manufactures hosiery and shoes; coal; mineral springs.

Hindenburg, Hindenburg in Oberschlesien. Industrial city, formerly in Oppeln govt. dist., Silesia prov., Prussia, Germany, now in Poland. See ZABRZE.

Hin'den·burg Line (hĭn'dĕn·bûrg; *Ger.* -bŏŏrk). A line of defensive fortifications established 1916 by Germans across NE France, extending S from near Lille, past Cambrai and Saint-Quentin, turning E near Laon and reaching nearly to Metz; had many branch lines; scene of severe fighting in World War I, esp. 1917.

Hin·di'ya (hĭn·dē'yà; -yä). **1** River in S cen. Iraq; leaves the Euphrates river at **Hindiya Barrage** (dam in the Euphrates ab. 45 m. S of Baghdad) and after flowing SE past Babylon and Hilla returns to it lower in its course at ab. 31°20′N; flows through Shinafiya marsh region; important in ancient irrigation system. **2** Town, Iraq, on E bank of main stream of Euphrates ab. 10 m. S of Hindiya Barrage.

Hind'ley (hĭnd'lĭ). Urban district, Lancashire, NW England, 14 m. WNW of Manchester; pop. 19,414; cotton mills; coal mines.

Hind'man (hĭnd'măn). City, ⊗ of Knott co., SE Kentucky; pop. 793.

Hind'marsh (hĭnd'märsh). Town, SE South Australia, NW suburb of Adelaide; pop. 12,989.

Hindmarsh, Lake. Lake 47 sq. m., W Victoria, SE Australia; receives the Wimmera river.

Hin·dol' (hĭn·dŏl'). Former Indian state, Eastern States, NE Indian Union, N of Mahanadi river ab. 45 m. NW of Cuttack; 291 sq. m.; pop. (1941) 58,505; ✳ Hindol; area now in Orissa.

Hindostan. See HINDUSTAN.

Hinds (hĭndz). County in Mississippi. See *Table* at MISSISSIPPI.

Hin'du Kush (hĭn'dŏŏ kŏŏsh'; kŭsh'); *known to historians of Alexander's time as* **Par'o·pa·mi'sus** (păr'ō·pà·mī'sŭs) *or* **Cau'ca·sus In'di·cus** (kô'kà·sŭs ĭn'dĭ·kŭs). Mountain range, cen. Asia, extending ab. 500 m. along N Kashmir border and W and SW into Afghanistan to the Koh-i-Baba range W of Kabul; on E extends to the Pamirs and the Karakoram Range; watershed bet. Kabul river on S and tributaries of the Amu Darya on N. In cen. part peaks above 20,000 ft., highest Tirich Mir 25,263 ft.; crossed by passes (up to 17,500 ft.) from Chitral to Turkistan, one of most important being Baroghil Pass at 12,457 ft.

Hindur. See NALAGARH.

Hin'du·stan' (hĭn'dŏŏ·stăn') *or* **Hin'do·stan'** (-dō-). Literally "the place of the Hindus," the Persian name of India, variously applied to: **1** The whole Indian peninsula N of the Deccan (*q.v.*); *i.e.* the region bounded on N by the Himalayas and on S by the Vindhya Mts. and Narbada river, comprising Ganges valley from the Punjab to Assam; chief languages Hindi and its dialects Hindustani and Urdu. **2** A smaller area comprising E Punjab and Rajputana, and greater part of the United Provinces; *i.e.* the region where chief vernacular is Hindi. **3** Loosely, the whole of India. **4** An occasional name for the Indian Union.

Hines'ville (hīnz'vĭl; *Sou. also* -v'l). Town, ⊗ of Liberty co., SE Georgia; pop. 3174.

Hin'gan·ghat' (hĭng'găn·gät'). Town, NE Maharashtra state, cen. India, on tributary of Wardha river 50 m. S of Nagpur; pop. 22,601; cotton mills, presses, and ginning factories; has given its name to one of the best indigenous cotton staples of India.

Hing'ham (hĭng'ăm). Town, Plymouth co., SE Massachusetts, on Massachusetts Bay 11 m. SE of Boston; pop. 15,378; summer resort.

Hin'gol (hĭng'gōl). River ab. 320 m. long, cen. and S Baluchistan; flows S into Arabian Sea. Its upper course also known as the **Nal** (nŭl).

Hi'ni·ga'ran (hĕ'nĕ·gä'rän). Municipality, W Negros Occidental, Negros, Phil. Is., at S end of Guimaras Strait 40 m. S of City of Bacolod; pop. 27,438.

Hink'ley Reservoir (hĭngk'lĭ). Reservoir in W Herkimer co., NE cen. New York.

Hin'lo'pen Strait (hĭn'lō'pĕn). Channel bet. West Spitsbergen I. and Northeast Land, Spitsbergen.

Hin'nom (hĭn'ŭm). A valley near ancient Jerusalem; its identification uncertain, but believed to be the shallow wadi S of the city. In Old Testament times place where the refuse of the city was deposited and perpetual fires kept burning to Moloch; hence, later, its Greek form **Ge·hen'na** (gė·hĕn'à; gė-) became the New Testament word for "hell."

Hinn'öy' (hĭn'ŭ'ŭ). Largest island of the Vesterålen, in Norwegian Sea off NW coast of Norway; 848 sq. m.; pop. 20,420.

Hi'no·jo'sa del Du'que (ē'nō·hō'sä thĕl dŏŏ'kä). Commune, Córdoba prov., S Spain, 48 m. NNW of Córdoba; pop. 14,844; agricultural products; copper mines; manufactures textiles, metal products.

Hins'dale (hĭnz'dāl). **1** County in Colorado. See *Table* at COLORADO. **2** Village, Cook and Du Page cos., NE Illinois, 17 m. W of Chicago; pop. 12,859. **3** Manufacturing town, Cheshire co., SW corner of New Hampshire, on Ashuelot river near its junction with the Connecticut 14 m. SSW of Keene; pop. 2187; scene of Indian attack 1748.

Hinterpommern. = *Farther Pomerania:* see POMERANIA.

Hin'ter Rhein (hĭn'tĕr rīn'). River in SE Switzerland; rises in glaciers on the Rheinwaldhorn and flows NE to join the Vorder Rhein and form the Rhine river.

Hin'ton (hĭn't'n; -tŭn). City, ⊗ of Summers co., S West Virginia, on New river 20 m. ESE of Beckley; pop. 5197; railroad center; mineral springs.

Hiogo. See HYOGO.

Hip'per·holme (hĭp'ēr·hōm). Urban district, West Riding, Yorkshire, N England, just E of Halifax; pop. (1931) 5383; since 1937 part of Brighouse.

Hip'po (hĭp'ō) *or* **Hippo Re'gi·us** (rē'jĭ·ŭs). City in ancient Numidia; see BÔNE, Algeria.

Hipponiates, Gulf of. See Gulf of SANT' EUFEMIA.

Hipponium. See VIBO VALENTIA.

Hippo Zarytus. See BIZERTE.

Hips'well (hĭps'wĕl; -wĕl). Village, North Riding, Yorkshire, England, near Richmond; generally considered to be birthplace of John Wycliffe.

Hi′ra (hē′rà); *Arab.* **al-Ḥi′rah** (ăl-hē′rŏ-h′). Ancient kingdom of the Lakhmid dynasty (3d cent. A.D. to 602) comprising lower Euphrates valley and upper part of Persian Gulf, subordinate to the Sassanidae of Persia; its chief town **Hira**, 4 m. SE of modern An Najaf, Iraq, captured by Arabs under Khalid ab. 633 and declined rapidly after founding of Al Kufa 638.

Hi·ra·do (hē·rä·dŏ). Island off NW coast of Kyushu, Japan; ab. 66 sq. m., 19½ m. long and 6 m. wide; pop. (1945) 37,457; chief town and harbor Hirado. Important in feudal period; first trading port opened to foreign vessels: to Portuguese c. 1550–1639 when they were driven out by Iyemitsu; to Dutch 1610–41 when they were transferred to Deshima; to English, who had a factory 1613–24.

Hi′ram (hī′răm). Village in Hiram township (pop. 2151); Portage co., NE Ohio, ab. 30 m. SE of Cleveland; pop. 1011; Hiram College (1850; coed.).

Hirata Gunto. See PARACEL ISLANDS.

Hi·ra·tsu·ka (hē·rä·tsoŏ·kä). City, Kanagawa prefecture, SE Honshu, Japan, on N shore of Sagami Sea 18 m. SW of Yokohama; pop. (1945) 39,165.

Hi·ro·sa·ki (hē·rŏ·sä·kē). City, Aomori prefecture, N Honshu, Japan; pop. (1945) 57,592; in plain of the Iwaki river 23 m. SW of Aomori and near Mt. Iwaki; center for silk culture, fruit growing, and manufacture of a special kind of lacquer.

Hi·ro′shi·ma (*Jap.* hē·rôsh′mä; *Angl.* hē′rŏ-shē′mà, hē·rŏ′shī·mà). **1** Prefecture of Japan. See *Table* at JAPAN.
2 City, its ✳, at W end of Inland Sea; pop. (1938 est.) 334,600, (1945) 137,197; before World War II, one of the important commercial cities of Japan, beautifully situated with rail, river, and canal connections. Founded at end of 16th cent.; a military headquarters in wars of 1894–95, 1900, and 1904–05; about 60% destroyed Aug. 6, 1945 by explosion of first atomic bomb used in warfare (dropped by U.S. plane) which caused an estimated loss of 80,000 lives, this event being one of immediate causes of surrender of Japan Aug. 14, 1945. See also MIYAJIMA.

Hirschberg, Hirschberg in Schlesien *or* **im Riesengebirge.** See JELENIA GÓRA.

Hir′son′ (ēr′sôn′). Manufacturing commune, Aisne dept., N France, on Oise river 34 m. NE of Laon; pop. 11,203; foundries.

Hi·sa·ga (hē·sä·gä). Island in Goto Archipelago (*q.v.*), Japan.

Hispalis. See SEVILLE.

Hispania. See SPAIN.

Hispania Tarraconensis. See TARRACONENSIS.

His·pan′ic America (hĭs·păn′ĭk). = LATIN AMERICA.

His′pan·io′la (hĭs′păn·yō′là), *orig. Span.* **Es′pa·ño′la** (äs′pä·nyō′lä); *also* **Hai′ti** (hā′tĭ; *Fr.* à′ē′tē′). Island of the cen. West Indies, in N cen. Caribbean Sea E of Cuba and W of Puerto Rico; 29,979 sq. m.; pop. ab. 4,900,000; divided bet. republic of Haiti on W and Dominican Republic on E.

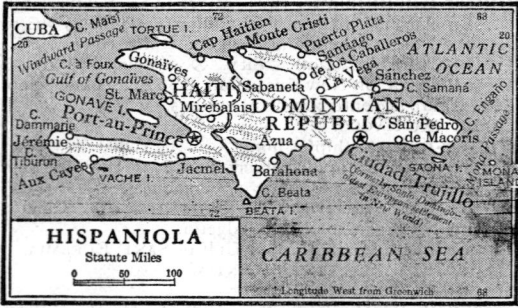

History: Visited by Columbus 1492 and settled 1493; became center of Spanish rule in West Indies (see also

History at WEST INDIES); natives soon exterminated by the Spanish and replaced by Negro slaves; W part of island, occupied in 17th cent. by buccaneers and ceded to France by Spain 1697, came to be known as colony of (Fr.) Saint Domingue, while E part (Santo Domingo) remained under the Spanish; island thus divided until latter part of 18th cent. when slave insurrection (1791) introduced period of conflict; occupied 1793–98 by British who were driven out by Toussaint L'Ouverture; entire island under Toussaint 1801–02; scene of struggle against domination of French 1802–04 when independence declared under Dessalines and the island became republic of Haiti; divided again 1807–21 with Spanish ruling E part; entire island ruled by Boyer from 1822 until E part revolted 1843 and formed the Dominican Republic 1844. See DOMINICAN REPUBLIC and HAITI.

His·sar′ (hĭ·sär′). **1** Town, E cen. Punjab state, NW Indian Union, on W Jumna canal 100 m. WNW of Delhi; pop. 25,179; founded 1356 by Firuz Shah III of Delhi; almost depopulated by famine 1783, but fort constructed shortly thereafter by Irish adventurer George Thomas and population restored.
2 Town, W Tadzhik S.S.R., Soviet Central Asia, just W of Stalinabad; once capital of an independent region, later incorporated in Bukhara.

His·sar·lik′ (hĭ·sär·lĭk′). Site of ancient Troy (*q.v.*), Canakkale vilayet, NW Turkey in Asia, 4 m. SE of mouth of the Dardanelles.

His·sar′ Mountains (hĭ·sär′). Mountain range 6500 to ab. 10,000 ft. in NW Tadzhik S.S.R., Soviet Central Asia, a branch of the Alai Mts.

Histonium. See VASTO.

Hit (hĭt); *anc.* **Is** (ĭs). Town, W cen. Iraq, on W bank of the Euphrates river at head of navigation ab. 90 m. W of Baghdad; pop. ab. 5500; in oil-producing region; in ancient times source of bitumen used in construction of walls and buildings of Babylon.

Hi·ta·chi (hē·tä·chē). Coastal city, NE Ibaraki prefecture, Honshu, Japan, 83 m. NE of Tokyo; pop. (1945) 38,525; center of important industrial area; bombarded by American fleet July 17–18, 1945.

Hitch′cock (hĭch′kŏk). **1** County in Nebraska. See *Table* at NEBRASKA.
2 City, Galveston co., SE Texas, NW of Galveston; pop. 5216.

Hitch′in (hĭch′ĭn). Urban district, Hertfordshire, SE England, on the Hiz 32 m. N of London; pop. 19,959.

Hither Pomerania. See POMERANIA.

Hit′ler Line (hĭt′lēr). In World War II a German defense line, W Italy, from Terracina on W coast to Aquino in mountains W of Cassino; a support for the Gustav Line; taken by Allies May 1944.

Hit′ra (hĭt′rä); *formerly* **Hit′te·ren** (hĭt′ĕ·rĕn). Island in Norwegian Sea off W coast of Norway, WSW of entrance to Trondheim Fjord; 210 sq. m.; pop. 3015.

Hi′u (hē′oō). Largest of the Torres Is. (*q.v.*).

Hi′va O′a *or* **Hi′va·o′a** (hē′và·ō′à). One of the Marquesas Is., French Polynesia, S Pacific Ocean; 23 m. long, 154 sq. m.; pop. ab. 1000; chief village Atuana, administrative center of the group. Of volcanic origin; has high central ridge, highest point Mt. Temetiu 4134 ft.; produces esp. copra, grows some cotton and sugar; place where Gauguin is buried.

Hi·was′see (hĭ·wŏs′ē) *or* **Hi′a·was′see** (hī′à·wŏs′ē). River ab. 150 m. long, rising in NE Georgia, flowing across W extremity of North Carolina and into SE Tennessee to empty into Tennessee river ab. 10 m. SW of Decatur; in its course are three great dams, Apalachia, Hiwassee, and Chatuge, of the Tennessee Valley Authority (*q.v.*).

Hiwassee Dam. See *Table* at TENNESSEE VALLEY AUTHORITY.

Hjäl′ma·ren′ (yĕl′mà·rŭn′). Lake 185 sq. m. in S cen. Sweden, in Örebro and Södermanland provs. E of N Lake Vänern and N of Lake Vättern.

Hjör′ring (yûr′ĭng). **1** County of Denmark. See *Table* at DENMARK.

2 City, its ⊗, NE Jutland; pop. 11,714; commercial and shipping center in agricultural section.

Hkamti Long. See MYITKYINA.

Hlaing. See RANGOON river.

Hlu′čín (hloo′chēn); *Ger.* **Hul′tschin** (hool′chēn). **1** District, NE Silesia, Czechoslovakia, just NW of Moravská Ostrava; 127 sq. m.; obtained by Czechoslovakia from Germany by Treaty of Versailles 1919— the only part of the Sudeten area originally German; population was 82 per cent Czechoslovak.

2 Town, its chief urban center, ab. 6 m. NW of Moravská Ostrava; pop. ab. 5000.

Ho (hō). Town, ✳ of S division (now Volta Region) of Togoland, Ghana, West Africa, 60 m. NW of Lomé; pop. 3549.

Hoang′hai′ (hwäng′hī′). Former name of KOKAI.

Hoang′ho′ (hwäng′hō′; -hŭ′) = HWANG HO.

Ho′back Peak (hō′băk). Mountain 10,864 ft. in NW Sublette co., W Wyoming.

Ho′bart (hō′bẽrt). **1** City, Lake co., NW corner of Indiana, 8 m. S of Lake Michigan; pop. 18,680; settled 1849, incorp. 1921.

2 City, ⊗ of Kiowa co., SW Oklahoma, 31 m. NNE of Altus; pop. 5132; cotton; dairying, poultry and stock raising.

Ho′bart (hō′bärt; -bẽrt). City, ✳ of Tasmania, Australia, in SE part on Derwent river 12 m. from the sea, at base of Mt. Wellington; pop. 47,056, with suburbs 60,408; deep sheltered harbor; exports fruit, grain, wool, timber, and minerals; has iron foundries, sawmills, flour mills, tanneries, and woolen mills; University of Tasmania. See RISDON. Founded in 1804 as a penal colony; made the capital of Tasmania 1812; called Hobart Town up to 1881, also, for a time, Hobarton; became a city 1857.

Hobbs (hŏbz). City, Lea co., SE corner of New Mexico, near Texas border ab. 18 m. N of Eunice; pop. 26,275; founded 1907; expanded following discovery of oil in 1927; headquarters for oil-well supplies.

Hobbs Coast. Section of coast of West Antarctica, lying along N Marie Byrd Land within lands claimed by United States, from ab. 131° to 140°30′W.

Hobe Sound (hōb). Town, Martin co., E Florida, 12 m. SE of Stuart; pop. (est.) 900; resort.

Hob′kirk′s Hill (hŏb′kûrks). Locality 2 m. N of Camden, South Carolina; battle Apr. 25, 1781 in which Continentals, during their strategic retreat under Nathanael Greene, were defeated by British under Francis Rawdon-Hastings who was in command of British post at Camden.

Ho′bo·ken (hō′bō′kĕn; *locally also* -bŭk′ĕn). City, Hudson co., NE New Jersey, on Hudson river 2 m. N of and adjoining Jersey City and opp. New York City (with which it is connected by ferries and tunnels); pop. 48,441; railroad center, with long waterfront; port of entry and departure for steamship lines; large coal and iron trade; varied manufactures; shipbuilding. Stevens Institute of Technology (1870; men). Land purchased from Indians by Dutch 1630 and named New Amsterdam; bought by Peter Stuyvesant 1658; sold to Samuel Bayard 1711; purchased 1784 by John Stevens, who laid out town 1804; became pleasure resort, esp. for New Yorkers; incorporated as town 1849, as city 1855.

Ho′bo·ken (hō′bō′kĕn). Commune, Antwerp prov., N Belgium, a suburb of Antwerp; pop. 30,552; shipbuilding yards.

Hoch′e·lag′a (hŏsh′ĕ·läg′ȧ). **1** Early name, given by Cartier 1535 on maps, of the St. Lawrence river and of the region above the village (see 2, below).

2 Indian (Huron) village, E end of island (now Montreal I.) in St. Lawrence river, Canada, found by Cartier 1535; it had disappeared, probably destroyed by hostile tribes, when place was visited by Champlain 1603.

3 County, S Quebec, Canada. See MONTREAL AND JESUS ISLANDS.

Hoch′fei′ler (hōк′fī′lẽr). Peak 11,555 ft., highest point of the Zillertaler Alps, S Tirol, Austria.

Hoch′heim (hōк′hīm; *Ger.* hōк′hīm, hôк′-). Commune, W Germany, in Hesse, on the Main near its confluence with the Rhine; pop. 4070; noted for its production of a white wine, called *Hochheimer*, or *hock*.

Ho′chih′ (hŭ′chĭr′). Town, NW Kwangsi prov., SE China, 95 m. W of Liuchow; terminus of railroad from Kweilin; held by Japanese through latter part of World War II; taken by Chinese May 21, 1945.

Hoch′kirch (hōк′kĭrк). Village, Dresden dist., Saxony, E Germany, NW of Löbau; pop. 505; in Seven Years′ War scene of victory Oct. 14, 1758 of Austrians over Prussians under Frederick the Great.

Höchst (hûкst; hûkst), *also* **Höchst am Main** (äm mīn′). Former city (pop. 31,534), Wiesbaden govt. dist., Hesse-Nassau prov., Prussia, Germany, on Main river; since 1928 part of Frankfurt am Main.

Höch′städt (hûк′shtĕt). Town, Swabia govt. dist., Bavaria, Germany, on Danube NE of Ulm; pop. 2160; scene of battles in War of the Spanish Succession in which the Imperialists were routed by the French and Bavarians Sept. 30, 1703 and in which the French and Bavarians were overwhelmed by Marlborough and Prince Eugene Aug. 13, 1704 (often called the battle of Blenheim, *q.v.*); in Napoleonic Wars scene of victory of Moreau′s army of the Rhine over the Austrians under Kray von Krajowa June 19, 1800.

Hoch′stuhl (hōк′shtool). Mountain 7334 ft. on border bet. S Austria and NW Yugoslavia; highest point in the Karawanken Alps.

Hoch′vo′gel (hōк′fō′gĕl). Peak 8492 ft. in the Algäu Alps, on the border bet. Germany and Austria E of Lake Constance.

Hock′ing (hŏk′ĭng). **1** River ab. 80 m. long, rising in Fairfield co., S cen. Ohio, and flowing SE into Ohio river below Parkersburg, West Virginia.

2 County in Ohio. See *Table* at OHIO.

Hock′ley (hŏk′lĭ). County, Texas. See TEXAS, *Table.*

Hoddes′don (hŏdz′dŭn). Urban district, Hertfordshire, SE England, at confluence of Lea and Stort rivers 19 m. N of London; pop. 13,728; a favorite angling place of Izaak Walton.

Ho·dei′da (hō·dā′dȧ; *Arab.* hoo·dā′dȧ, -dȧ, -dī′-). Industrial and commercial seaport, W Yemen, SW Arabia, on the Red Sea; pop. ab. 40,000; the port of San′a; has an exposed anchorage but an active trade with Aden, Suez, and Massaua; chief exports coffee and dates.

Hodge′man (hŏj′mȧn). County in Kansas. See *Table* at KANSAS.

Hodg′en·ville (hŏj′ĕn·vĭl; *Sou. also* -v′l). City, ⊗ of Larue co., cen. Kentucky, 47 m. S of Louisville; pop. 1985; location of Abraham Lincoln National Historical Park (see UNITED STATES, *National Historical Parks*).

Hód′me·zö·vá′sár·hely (hōd′mĕ·zŭ·vä′shär·hä). Autonomous city, SE Hungary, near Tisza river 13 m. NE of Szeged; 294 sq. m.; pop. (1939) 61,736.

Hod′na, Chott el (shŏt′ ĕl hŏd′nȧ); *Arab.* **Shatt el Hod′na** (shŏt′ ȧl hood′nȧ; -nȧ). Marshy saline lake in SW Constantine dept. NE Algeria.

Hodna Mountains. Range of the Little Atlas Mts. in W Constantine dept., NE Algeria.

Ho·do (hō·dō). Waterfall ab. 60 ft. high in Tochigi prefecture, cen. Honshu, Japan, near Nikko and E of Lake Chuzenji.

Ho′do·nín (hō′dô·nyēn); *Ger.* **Gö′ding** (gŭ′dĭng). Town, SW Moravia prov., cen. Czechoslovakia, on the March river 50 m. N of Bratislava; pop. 13,103.

Hoeksche Waard. See BEIJERLAND.

Hoek van Holland. See HOOK OF HOLLAND.

Hoek van Mandar. See Gulf of MANDAR.

Hoens′broek (hoons′brook). Commune, Limburg prov., SE Netherlands, NE of Maastricht; pop. 13,618.

Hoet'jes Bay (hōōt'yĕs). Village on N shore of Saldanha Bay, Cape Province, S Republic of So. Africa, 70 m. NNW of Cape Town; pop. 1537; fine harbor.

Hof (hōf). City, NE Bavaria, Germany, on Saale river 31 m. NNE of Bayreuth; pop. 41,377; railroad junction; airport; manufactures woolens, carpets, iron goods, machinery, porcelain, smoked meats.

Ho'fei' (hŭ'fā'); *formerly* **Lu'chow'** (lōō'jō'). City, ✳ of Anhwei prov., E China, N of Chao Hu.

Hoff'man Island (hŏf'mǎn). Island off E coast of Staten I., New York, in Lower New York Bay: part of Richmond borough.

Hoff'mann, Mount (hŏf'mǎn). Peak 10,836 ft. in Sierra Nevada, in E Tuolumne co., cen. California.

Hoffman Mountain. Peak 3715 ft. in Adirondack Mts., Essex co., NE New York.

Ho·fuf' (hōō-fōōf'). Oasis and chief town of al-Hasa, Nejd, Saudi Arabia, in S part on caravan route from Riyadh to Trucial Oman; pop. ab. 30,000; great mosque; active market.

Ho'gans·ville (hō'gănz-vĭl; *Sou. also* -v'l). City, Troup co., W Georgia, 10 m. NE of La Grange; pop. 3658; incorporated 1870; cotton mills.

Hog'back' Mountain (hŏg'băk'). Peak 4300 ft. in Banner co., W Nebraska.

Hogback Peak. Mountain 10,500 ft. in Sierra Nevada, in E Fresno co., S cen. California.

Hog'gar Mountains (hŏg'ẽr; hŏ·gär'). = AHAGGAR MOUNTAINS.

Hog Island (hŏg). **1** Island in N Lake Michigan, NE of Beaver I.; part of Charlevoix co., NW Michigan. **2** Island in Delaware river below Philadelphia, Pennsylvania; great shipyards. **3** Island in Atlantic Ocean, N Northampton co., Virginia.

Hog'land (hŏg'lănd) *or* **Suur'saa·ri** (sōōr'sä·rĭ). Island in Gulf of Finland, S of seaport of Kotka and ab. 110 m. W of Leningrad.

Ho'go·leu, *or* **Ho'go·lu, Islands** (hō'gŏ·lōō). Former name of TRUK ISLANDS.

Hogue, La. See LA HOGUE.

Ho'hen·frie·de·berg (hō'ĕn-frē'dĕ·bĕrK) *or* **Ho'hen-fried'berg** (-frēt'bĕrK); *Pol.* **Do·bro'mierz** (dô·brô'myĕsh). Village, Śląsk Dolny dept., SW Poland, near Strzegom; pop. 650; formerly in Silesia, Prussia, Germany: in Second Silesian War scene of victory of Prussians under Frederick the Great over Austrians and Saxons under Charles of Lorraine June 4, 1745.

Ho'hen·lim'burg (hō'ĕn-lĭm'bōōrK). City, North Rhine-Westphalia state, Germany, 40 m. NE of Cologne; pop. 15,490; rolling mills.

Ho'hen·lin'den (hō'ĕn-lĭn'dĕn). Village, Bavaria, Germany, 20 m. E of Munich; pop. 670; scene of battle Dec. 3, 1800 in which French under Moreau defeated Austrians under Archduke John, a victory which together with that of Napoleon at Marengo led to Peace of Lunéville 1801.

Hohenmauth. See VYSOKÉ MÝTO.

Hohensalza. See INOWROCŁAW.

Ho'hen·stau'fen (hō'ĕn-shtou'fĕn; *Angl.* hō'ĕn-stou'fĕn). Mountain 2240 ft. near Göppingen, cen. Baden-Württemberg state, S Germany; contains ruins of ancestral castle of Hohenstaufen family.

Ho'hen·stein–Ernst'thal (hō'ĕn-shtīn-ĕrnst'täl). Industrial city, Saxony, E Germany, on N edge of Erzgebirge 9 m. W of Chemnitz; pop. 16,754; textiles, metal goods.

Ho'hen·twiel' (hō'ĕn-tvēl'). Conical mountain 2260 ft. in S Baden-Württemberg state, near Singen, Germany; contains ruins of a fortress.

Ho'hen·wald (hō'ĕn-wôld). Town, ⊗ of Lewis co., SW cen. Tennessee; pop. 2194.

Ho'hen·zol'lern (hō'ĕn-tsŏl'ẽrn; *Angl.* hō'ĕn·zŏl'ẽrn). **1** Historical region and province of Prussia, S Germany; mountainous area; agriculture, forestry. See *Table* at PRUSSIA. Formed in 1849 from territories of Hohen-

zollern-Hechingen and Hohenzollern-Sigmaringen; derived from ancient family seat of Hohenzollerns of whom the Franconian branch were rulers of Prussia and emperors of Germany 1871–1918; ceded to Prussian king by their rulers. members of (Swabian) line of Hohenzollerns; since 1951 part of Baden-Württemberg. **2** Castle in this region of Hohenzollern, on Mount Zollern, near Hechingen.

Ho'hes Licht (hō'ĕs lĭKt). Peak 8649 ft. in the Algäu Alps, on border bet. Swabia and Tirol, N of Lech valley.

Ho'he Tau'ern (hō'ĕ tou'ẽrn). See *Table* at ALPS.

Ho'he Venn Mountains (hō'ĕ fĕn). Range in Liège prov., E Belgium; highest peak Baraque Michel 2200 ft.

Ho·ho'kus (hō·hō'kŭs). Borough, Bergen co., NE corner of New Jersey, on Hohokus river 7 m. NNE of Paterson; pop. 3988.

Höh'scheid (hû'shīt). Former city (pop. 15,853), Düsseldorf govt. dist., Rhine Province, Prussia, Germany; since 1929 part of city of Solingen (*q.v.*).

Hoi'how' (*Cantonese* hoi'hou'; *Pekingese* hī'kō'); *Fr.* **Hoï-Hao** (ô'yà'ō'). Port and roadstead of Kiungshan, 3 m. NW of it on NE coast of Hainan I., Kwangtung prov., SE China; pop. ab. 22,000; made an open port 1876.

Hoi'sing·ton (hoi'zĭng·tŭn). City, Barton co., cen. Kansas, 10 m. N of Great Bend; pop. 4248; wheat growing, livestock raising.

Hoke (hōk). County in North Carolina. See *Table* at NORTH CAROLINA.

Ho'kiang' (hŭ'jĭ·äng'). Former province, E Manchuria, NE China, on the lower Sungari river; 50,816 sq. m.; pop. (1945 est.) 1,298,000; ✳ Kiamusze.

Ho'ki·ang'a Harbor *or* **River** (hō'kĭ·äng'à). Broad inlet or harbor on W coast of N peninsula of North I., New Zealand, 125 m. NW of Auckland.

Ho'ki·ti'ka (hō'kĕ·tē'kä; hŏk'ĭ·tĭk'à). Borough, ✳ of Westland provincial dist., W South I., New Zealand, 160 m. SW of Nelson; pop. 2685; seaport; gold and coal in vicinity.

Hok·kai'do (hŏ·kī'dō; *Jap.* hŏk·kī·dō) *or* **Ye·zo** (yĕ·zō) *formerly* **E·zo** (ĕ·zō). **1** Northernmost of the four main islands of Japan, in Pacific Ocean off E coast of Asia, N of island of Honshu; 30,307 sq. m.; pop. (1930) 2,812,335, (1945) 3,518,389; separated from S Sakhalin on N by Soya Strait, from Honshu on S by Tsugaru Strait, and from the Kuril Is. on NE by Nemuro Strait. Has several high peaks. esp. Asahi Dake (formerly Ishikari Dake) 7513 ft., Horoshiri 6732 ft., and Tokachi 6814 ft.; rivers include Ishikari, largest in Japan, and the Tokachi. Main industry fishing; produces corn and potatoes; has great resources in timber and coal. Chief cities Sapporo (capital of Hokkaido prefecture), Hakodate, Otaru, and the naval bases, Muroran and Nemuro.
    History: In early times inhabited by Ainus; not made part of Japan until medieval period (ab. 1604); scene of conflicts bet. Shogun's representatives and Russian adventurers; its modern development begun 1871–81 when government was assisted by American engineers and agriculturists; after 1881 given over to private interests. **2** Prefecture, N Japan, including Hokkaido, adjacent small islands, and (formerly) the Kuril Is. (Chishima Retto); 30,307 sq. m.; pop. (1940) 3,272,718; ✳ Sapporo. In early times divided into 10 provinces. See *Table* at JAPAN. Since 1945 does not include Kuril Is. (pop. 6000), which were transferred to U.S.S.R.

Hoko *or* **Penghu.** Largest island of Pescadores (*q.v.*).

Hoko Shoto *or* **Hoko Gunto.** See PESCADORES.

Hokou. See HUKOW.

Ho'kow' (hō'kou'; *Chin.* hŭ'kō'). Frontier town and treaty port, SE Yunnan prov., S China, on Yuan river opp. Laokay in Tonkin; pop. ab. 4000; connected by rail with Hanoi.

Ho·ku·ro·ku·do (hō·kŏō·rŏ·kŏō·dō). Literally "northern land"; a division of Japan in cen. Honshu; comprises 7 of the old provinces, ab. 9670 sq. m.

Ho·ku·sei (hŏ·kŏŏ·sā). Town, South Kankyo prov., NE Korea, SW of Joshin ab. 12 m. from coast of Sea of Japan; pop. 19,756.

Ho·ku·to (hŏ·kŏŏ·tō). Town, N Formosa, ab. 7 m. from Taihoku; watering place.

Hol'bæk (hŭl'bĕk). **1** County of Denmark. See *Table* at DENMARK.
2 Town, ⊗ of Holbæk co., NW Sjælland, Denmark, 33 m. W of Copenhagen; pop. 14,708.

Hol'beach (hōl'bēch). Market town, Parts of Holland, Lincolnshire, E England, 51 m. ESE of Nottingham; pop. 6112.

Holborn. Metropolitan borough of London. See *Table* at LONDON.

Hol'brook (hōl'brŏŏk). **1** Town, ⊗ of Navajo co., NE Arizona; pop. 3438; helium field.
2 Town, Norfolk co., E Massachusetts, 5 m. N of Brockton; pop. 10,104.

Hol'burn Head (hŏl'bẽrn; hōl'-). Cape on NE coast of Scotland; lighthouse.

Hol'den (hōl'dĕn). **1** Town, Worcester co., cen. Massachusetts, 8 m. NNW of Worcester; pop. 10,117.
2 City, Johnson co., W Missouri, 36 m. SE of Independence; pop. 1951.

Hol'den·ville (hōl'dĕn·vĭl). City, ⊗ of Hughes co., E cen. Oklahoma, 28 m. NE of Ada; pop. 5712; oil and gas wells; coal deposits.

Hol'der·ness (hōl'dẽr·nĕs; -nĭs). Town, Grafton co., W New Hampshire, on Squam Lake; pop. 749; summer resort.

Hol'der·ness' (hōl'dẽr·nĕs'). Peninsula in SE East Riding, Yorkshire, N England, bet. Humber river and the North Sea; 309 sq. m.

Hol'drege (hōl'drĭj). City, ⊗ of Phelps co., S Nebraska, 24 m. SW of Kearney; pop. 5226; flour mill, creamery.

Hol·guín' (ôl·gēn'). Municipality and town, N cen. Oriente prov., E Cuba, in plateau region 65 m. NW of Santiago de Cuba; pop. (town) 35,865; through its port, Gibara, exports tobacco, maize, cattle products, cabinet woods. Settled c. 1720; insurgent center 1868–78 and 1895–98.

Holin. See KARAKORUM.

Hol'la (hŏl'à). Peak 12,092 ft., Kafa, SW Ethiopia, NW of Lake Abaya.

Hollabrunn. See OBERHOLLABRUNN.

Hol'land (hŏl'ănd). **1** City, Ottawa co., W Michigan, on Lake Michigan 25 m. WSW of Grand Rapids; pop. 24,777; summer resort; manufactures furnaces and furnace equipment, beet sugar, aniline dyes; ships poultry. Hope College (1851; coed.; Reformed Church in America).
2 Medieval county of Holy Roman Empire on North Sea coast, now in North and South Holland provs., Netherlands; established 1018 when it became independent of Lorraine; in 1247 its Count William II elected emperor during struggle against Frederick II; united with Zeeland and Hainaut in 14th cent.; ceded to Burgundy (*q.v.*) by Countess Jacqueline 1433; see NETHERLANDS.
3 Kingdom. See NETHERLANDS.

Holland, the Parts of. See LINCOLNSHIRE.

Hol·lan'di·a (hŏ·lăn'dĭ·à). **1** Former subdivision of Ternate division, Moluccas residency, Neth. Indies, comprising the NE part of Neth. New Guinea bet. Mamberamo river and North-East New Guinea (British) boundary and including N slopes of Snow Mts.; 36,501 sq. m.; pop. 165,323; administered from Tidore.
2 *now* (*Indonesian*) **Ko'ta·ba'ru** (kō'tà·bä'rŏŏ), its chief settlement, ✳ of West Irian (formerly Neth. New Guinea), on NE coast on Humboldt Bay 25 m. W of North-East New Guinea (British) boundary; good harbor; pop. 16,300. Seized from Japanese Apr. 22, 1944 by U.S. forces; its three Japanese airfields taken a short time later; became divisional headquarters July 6, 1944 and headquarters of Gen. MacArthur Sept. 8, 1944.

Hol'landsch Diep (hŏl'änts dēp'). ⁕Estuary of the Maas (Meuse) river in SW Netherlands, on border bet. South Holland and North Brabant provs.

Hol'land Tunnel (hŏl'ănd). Vehicular tunnel 9250 ft. long under Hudson river from Manhattan I., New York, to Jersey City, New Jersey.

Hol'le·be'ke (hŏl'ĕ·bā'kĕ). Commune, West Flanders prov., Belgium, near Ieper (Ypres); pop. 703; fiercely contested bet. British and Germans 1914–18, almost wholly destroyed.

Hol'li·days·burg' (hŏl'ĭ·dāz·bûrg'). Borough, ⊗ of Blair co., S cen. Pennsylvania, 6 m. S of Altoona; pop. 6475, coal and iron ore deposits, limestone quarries; boiler factories, machine works. Founded 1768; became railroad and canal terminus in 1830's.

Hol'li·days Cove (hŏl'ĭ·dāz). A former city in Brooke and Hancock cos., N West Virginia, 25 m. NNE of Wheeling; since 1947 part of Weirton.

Hol'lins College (hŏl'ĭnz). Post office, Roanoke co., W cen. Virginia, ab. 7 m. N of Roanoke; Hollins Coll. (1842; women).

Hol'lis (hŏl'ĭs). **1** Residential community in Queens borough of New York City, Queens co., SE New York, on Long I.
2 City, ⊗ of Harmon co., SW Oklahoma, 35 m. W of Altus; pop. 3006; cattle raising.

Hol'lis·ter (hŏl'ĭs·tẽr). City, ⊗ of San Benito co., W California, 20 m. E of Monterey Bay; pop. 6071; settled 1868; fruit and vegetable canning.

Hol'lis·ton (hŏl'ĭs·tŭn). Town, Middlesex co. NE Massachusetts, 18 m. ESE of Worcester; pop. 6222; shoe factories.

Holl'man, Cape (hŏl'măn). Cape at N end of Willaumez Penin., N New Britain, Bismarck Archipelago.

Holloman Air Force Base. See ALAMOGORDO.

Hol'ly (hŏl'ĭ). Village, Oakland co., SE Michigan, 16 m. S of Flint; pop. 3269.

Holly Hill. City, Volusia co., E Florida, on Atlantic Ocean 5 m. N of Daytona Beach; pop. 4182.

Holly Springs. City, ⊗ of Marshall co., N Mississippi, 54 m. NW of Tupelo; pop. 5621; ships cotton and dairy products. Rust Coll. (1866; coed.); Mississippi Industrial Coll. (1905; coed.).

Hol'ly·wood' (hŏl'ĭ·wŏŏd'). **1** District in city of Los Angeles, California, E of Beverly Hills; center of U.S. motion-picture industry.
2 City, Broward co., SE Florida, on Atlantic Ocean 18 m. N of Miami; pop. 35,237; founded 1921; winter resort.

Holmes (hōmz). Counties in three states of the U.S. See *Tables* at FLORIDA, MISSISSIPPI, OHIO.

Holmes, Mount. Peak 10,300 ft. in Yellowstone National Park, NW Wyoming.

Holmes'burg (hōmz'bûrg). Suburban district, NE Philadelphia, Pennsylvania, near Delaware river.

Holmes Reefs. Group of coral islets in W Coral Sea outside Great Barrier Reef, 16°50'S.

Holm'firth (hōm'fûrth). Urban district, West Riding, Yorkshire, N England, 6 m. S of Huddersfield; pop. 19,073; woolens, stone quarries.

Holm'ön' (hôlm'ûn'). Swedish island in Gulf of Bothnia off coast of Västerbotten prov., N Sweden.

Holm'sjön' (hôlm'shûn'). Lake, Västernorrland prov., E Sweden. drained by Ljungan river.

Hol'ni·cote Bay (?hŏl'nĭ·kōt). Inlet of Solomon Sea on N coast of E Papua, New Guinea I., ab. 8°30'S; Buna, Gona, and Sanananda are on it.

Hol'royd (hŏl'roid). Town, E New South Wales, SE Australia, suburb of Sydney; pop. 15,915.

Hol'ste·bro' (hŭl'stĕ·brō'). Town, Ringköbing co., W Jutland, Denmark, 24 m. NE of Ringköbing; pop. 15,580.

Hol'stein (hōl'stīn; *Ger.* hôl'shtīn). Historical region, NW Germany; hilly country with numerous lakes and extensive forests; gave name to fine breed of cattle. From ab. 800 A.D., part of German duchy of Saxony in

Carolingian empire; German duke of Holstein came to rule Schleswig (q.v.), a fief of Denmark; in 1460, in dynastic union with Schleswig under Oldenburg kings of Denmark; raised to a duchy 1474; thoroughly Germanized, but a Danish holding; duke of Holstein (king of Denmark) became member of German Confederation 1815; its status, as part of Schleswig-Holstein (q.v.), caused friction bet. Germanic Confederation and Denmark; by agreement bet. Austria and Prussia, after war with Denmark 1864, Holstein administered by Austria; incorporated by Prussia as part of Schleswig-Holstein 1866.

Hol'steins·borg (hŭl'stīns-bôrk). Danish settlement on W coast of Greenland, in North Greenland division just N of Arctic Circle; pop. 927.

Hol'ston (hōl'stŭn). River 140 m. long in E Tennessee; formed by junction of north and south forks in Sullivan co., flows SW to unite with French Broad river near Knoxville and form the Tennessee river, in its course are two great dams, Cherokee and South Holston, of the Tennessee Valley Authority (q.v.). See WATAUGA.

Holston Mountain. Peak 4350 ft. in Carter and Sullivan cos., NE Tennessee.

Holt (hōlt). Name of counties in two states of the U.S. See MISSOURI and NEBRASKA.

Hol'ton (hōl't'n; -tŭn). City, ⊗ of Jackson co., NE Kansas, 28 m. N of Topeka; pop. 3028; corn, fruit.

Holt'ville (hōlt'vĭl). City, Imperial co., SE corner of California, 10 m. E of El Centro; pop. 3080; ships dairy products, fruits, and vegetables.

Holtz Bay (hōlts). Inlet, NE Attu I., Aleutian Is.; one of landing places of American forces May 11, 1943 (see also MASSACRE BAY).

Ho'lung'kiang' (hō'lŏong'jǐ·äng'). = HEILUNGKIANG.

Holwan. See SAR-I-PUL.

Ho'ly Cross (hō'lǐ krôs'). Village, W Alaska, on lower Yukon 115 m. NNE of Bethel; pop. (est.) 262.

Holy Cross, Mount of the. Peak 13,996 ft. in Sawatch Range, in Eagle co., NW cen. Colorado.

Hol'y·head' (hŏl'ǐ·hĕd'). **1** Island 8 m. long by 3½ m. wide in NE St. George's Channel, off W coast of island of Anglesey, NW Wales; in Anglesey co.; connected with Anglesey by a long causeway; mostly barren rock. **2** Welsh **Caer Gy'bi** (kīr gû'bǐ). Urban district and seaport on N coast of Holyhead I.; pop. 10,700; fine harbor protected by breakwater more than a mile long; nearest British port to Dublin (61 m.); church, reputedly founded 7th cent. by one St. Gybi.

Ho'ly Island (hō'lǐ) or **Lin'dis·farne** (lǐn'dǐs·färn). Peninsula, which becomes an island at high water, off NE coast of Northumberland, N England; 3 m. long by 1¾ m. wide; site of monastery founded 635 by St. Aidan and destroyed by Danes 793; ruins of late 11th-cent. priory; 16th cent. castle.

Holy Land. Palestine—so called first in Zech. ii. 12.

Holy Loch (lŏk). Small inlet on W shore of Firth of Clyde, W Scotland, opp. mouth of Clyde river; U.S. submarine base.

Hol'yoke (hōl'yōk). **1** Town, ⊗ of Phillips co., NE Colorado; 48 m. E of Sterling; pop. 1555. **2** Industrial city, Hampden co., SW Massachusetts, on Connecticut river 8 m. N of Springfield; pop. 52,689; textile mills; leading manufacturing city in the U.S. in fine writing and envelope papers. Originally part of Springfield and of West Springfield after 1774; incorporated as town 1850; large power dam (see HOLYOKE DAM).

Holyoke, Mount. Peak 954 ft. in Hampshire co., near Holyoke, W Massachusetts.

Holyoke, or **Had'ley Falls, Dam** (hăd'lǐ). Dam completed 1900 (replacing earlier dams of 1848-49) at Hadley Falls across Connecticut river above Holyoke, SW Massachusetts; impounds water for water power.

Holy Roman Empire. A realm of cen. Europe in medieval and modern periods, originating 800 A.D. when Charlemagne was crowned Emperor of the West (some-

times called the First Reich); revived as Roman Empire of the German Nation with coronation 962 of Otto the Great as emperor of an area including Germany and N Italy; at its height in mid-11th cent. before emperors began great struggle with Papacy for dominance; under Hohenstaufens 1138-1254, imperial power drained by renewed struggle with popes over control of Italy; had no emperor 1254-73 (Great Interregnum) when German unity collapsed and seeds of later particularism of princes were planted; under Rudolf of Hapsburg 1273-91 who consolidated dynastic monarchy (see AUSTRIA) at expense of imperial strength; seven imperial electors set up by Golden Bull 1356: archbishops of Mainz, Trier, Cologne, king of Bohemia, count Palatine of Rhine, duke of Saxony, and margrave of Brandenburg; lost most Italian holdings by 16th cent. (see ITALY); from 15th cent. to 1806, emperor's crown almost hereditary in Hapsburg family; formally dissolved during Napoleonic Wars 1806 (see GERMANY).

Hol'y·rood' (hŏl'ǐ·rōōd'). Royal palace, E Edinburgh city, Scotland; residence of Mary, Queen of Scots, 1561-67; not much used by royalty since ascension of James VI to throne of England 1603; adjoining the palace is abbey which was scene of coronations of James II of Scotland and Charles I of England, and of Mary's marriage to Darnley 1565 and which contains burial vault of Scottish kings and burial places of Darnley and Rizzio.

Holy See. See VATICAN CITY.

Hol'y·well (hŏl'ǐ·wĕl; -wĕl). Manufacturing urban district, Flintshire, NE Wales; pop. 8196; site of St. Winifred's Well, reputed to have burst forth on spot where her head fell when St. Winifred was beheaded by the pagan prince Caradoc (c. 634), now a place of pilgrimage for Roman Catholics and sometimes called "the Lourdes of Wales."

Hol'y·wood (hŏl'ǐ·wōōd). Urban district, co. Down, SE Northern Ireland; pop. 6316; on Belfast Lough 6 m. NE of Belfast.

Holz'min'den (hōlts'mǐn'dĕn). City, Lower Saxony, Germany, on Weser river 55 m. SW of Brunswick; pop. 12,192; manufactures chemicals, lumber, glass, machinery; ships colored sandstone.

Homalig. = JOMALIG.

Ho'ma·lin (hō'má·lĭn). Town, Upper Chindwin dist., W Upper Burma, on Chindwin river near Manipur border.

Hom'berg (hŏm'bûrg; Ger. hôm'bĕrK), also **Hom'berg am Nie'der·rhein'** (hôm'bĕrK äm nē'dĕr·rīn'). Manufacturing town, North Rhine-Westphalia state, Germany, on Rhine river opp. Duisburg; pop. 26,290; coal mining; dyes, refractory goods, machinery; iron founding.

Hom'burg (hŏm'bûrg; Ger. hôm'bōōrK), also called **Bad Hom'burg** (bät hôm'bōōrK) or **Homburg vor der Hö'he** (fōr dĕr hü'ĕ). City, SW Hesse state, Germany, 18 m. ENE of Wiesbaden; pop. 16,325; mineral baths; health and tourist resort; 17th-cent. castle with fine tower; manufactures leather goods, hats (first Homburg hats made here), machinery, chocolates, synthetic oil. Ruled by landgraves of Hesse-Homburg 1622-1866; bombed during latter part of World War II.

Homel. Var. of GOMEL.

Ho'mer (hō'mĕr). **1** Unincorporated town, S Alaska, on Cook Inlet SW of Seward; pop. 1247; seaport. **2** Town, ⊗ of Banks co., NE Georgia; pop. 612. **3** Town, ⊗ of Claiborne parish, N Louisiana, 47 m. ENE of Shreveport; pop. 4665; trading center of timber section; petroleum deposits. **4** Village, Cortland co., cen. New York, 28 m. S of Syracuse; pop. 3622; settled 1791; in dairying region; bean canneries.

Homer City. Borough, Indiana co., W cen. Pennsylvania, 20 m. NW of Johnstown; pop. 2471.

Ho'mer·ville (hō'mĕr·vĭl; Sou. also -v'l). City, ⊗ of Clinch co., S Georgia; pop. 2634.

Home′stead (hōm′stĕd). **1** City, Dade co., SE Florida, 28 m. SW of Miami; pop. 9152; incorporated 1923; trade center for region producing citrus fruits, vegetables. **2** Industrial borough, Allegheny co., SW Pennsylvania, on Monongahela river 6 m. ESE of Pittsburgh; pop. 7502; steel, iron products, glass, machinery. Settled 1871, incorp. 1880; scene of serious strike 1892.

Homestead National Monument. See UNITED STATES, *National Monuments.*

Home′town (hōm′toun). City, Cook co., NE Illinois, SW suburb of Chicago; pop. 7479.

Home′wood (hōm′wŏŏd). **1** City, Jefferson co., cen. Alabama, 2 m. SE of Birmingham; pop. 20,289.

2 Village, Cook co., NE Illinois, 22 m. S of Chicago; pop. 13,371.

Hom′il·don (hŏm′ĭl·dŭn), or **Hum′ble·don** (hŭm′b'l-dŭn), **Hill.** Small hill, N Northumberland, N England, SE of Flodden; scene of victory of Sir Henry Percy (Hotspur) and George Dunbar, Earl of March, over the Scots 1402.

Hom′i·ny (hŏm′ĭ·nĭ). City, Osage co., N Oklahoma, 30 m. NW of Tulsa; pop. 2866; cotton, livestock, poultry; oil and gas wells.

Ho′mon·hon′ (hō′mŏn·hŏn′) or **Jo′mon·jol′** (hō′-mŏn·hŏl′) or **Mal·hon′** (mäl·hŏn′). Island, S of Samar, Phil. Is., in entrance to Leyte Gulf; 40 sq. m.; pop. 550; belongs to Guiuan municipality of Samar prov.; place of first landing of Magellan on Philippine Is. Mar. 17, 1521; also, with Suluan (*q.v.*), first landing of MacArthur and Americans on invasion of Philippines Oct. 19, 1944.

Homs (hôms) or **Ḥimṣ** (ĸĭmsh); *anc.* **Em′e·sa** (ĕm′ĕ·sȧ). City, W Syria, on the Orontes 85 m. N of Damascus; pop. 132,637; in fertile area with fine gardens and orchards; manufactures silk goods; on ancient highway N from Egypt; nearby is battleground of Kadesh (*q.v.*). As Emesa devoted to worship of Sun god (Elagabal) and birthplace of Heliogabalus, one of its priests who became Roman emperor 218 A.D.; scene of defeat of Zenobia 272 by Emperor Aurelian; seized by Arabs 638; its walls destroyed 1099 in revolt against the Ommiad caliph Marwan II; held by Egyptians under Ibrahim Pasha 1831–40 and scene of a revolt 1832; taken by British and Arabs Oct. 15, 1918.

Homs or **Khoms** (ĸōms). Seaport, N Tripolitania, Libya, halfway bet. Tripoli and Misurata; pop. 2500; ruins of ancient Leptis Magna, an important Roman walled city, ab. 2 m. to the E.

Hon (hŭn). Town, N cen. Libya; in oasis ab. 220 m. S of Misurata.

Ho′nan′ (hō′nän′; *Chin.* hŭ′nän′). **1** Province, E cen. China; 66,676 sq. m.; pop. (1936 est.) 34,289,848; ✻ Chengchow; bounded on N by Shansi, Hopei, and Shantung provs., on E by Kiangsu and Anhwei, on S by Hupei, and on W by Shensi; one of most densely populated provinces. Rivers the Hwang Ho, forming NW boundary and flowing SE, the Lo in NW, and the upper course of the Hwai. In the SW are the most easterly spurs of the Kunlun Mts. with highest point at 7800 ft. Has rich agricultural regions; produces coal, silk, cotton. Chief cities Kaifeng, Loyang, Chengchow, Nanyang. Region of earliest settlements in China from which its culture spread; its geographical location controlled movements of early tribes; Loyang (or Honan) capital of China in the Eastern Han, Chin, and T'ang dynasties and Kaifeng of the Sung dynasty (10th cent. A.D.).

2 See LOYANG.

Hon′da (hŏn′dä; *Span.* ôn′dä). Town, Tolima dept., W cen. Colombia, NW of Bogotá; pop. 12,424.

Honda Rapids. Rapids in Magdalena river in NW cen. Colombia, stopping navigation at that point.

Hon′do (hŏn′dō). **1** City, ⊗ of Medina co., S cen. Texas, 37 m. W of San Antonio; pop. 4992.

2 (*Jap.* hŏn·dō) Island of Japan. See HONSHU.

3 (*Span.* ôn′dō) River ab. 150 m. long rising in N Guate-mala and flowing NE into Chetumal Bay; forms boundary bet. British Honduras and Mexico (Quintana Roo territory).

Hon·du′ras (hŏn·dŏŏr′ȧs; -dūr′-; *Span.* ôn·dōō′räs). Republic, Central America; 59,160 sq. m.; pop. (1940) 1,105,504, (1945 est.) 1,201,310; ✻ Tegucigalpa; bounded on N by Gulf of Honduras and Caribbean Sea, on E by Caribbean Sea, on S by Nicaragua and Gulf of Fonseca, on SW by El Salvador, and on W by Guatemala. Coast line ab. 400 m. on the Caribbean and ab. 40 m. on the Pacific (Gulf of Fonseca) bet. El Salvador and Nicaragua; most easterly point Cape Gracias a Dios; off N coast are Bay Is. Generally mountainous with many ranges much varied in extent and direction; highest in S above 10,000 ft. Chief rivers Chamelecón and Ulúa in W, Aguán in N, Patuca in E, Choluteca in S; the Segovia (*q.v.*) claimed as the border with Nicaragua; only large inland lake Yojoa in W with outlet to Ulúa river. Chief economic resources bananas, coconuts, cabinet woods, coffee, silver. Chief cities Tegucigalpa, San Pedro Sula, La Ceiba, Tela, Puerto Cortés. ·

History: Coast discovered by Columbus 1502; Trujillo and Puerto Cortés founded c. 1525; included in captaincy general of Guatemala 1539; proclaimed independence 1821; in United Provinces of Central America 1823 until its secession 1838; from 1842, participant in several unsuccessful efforts to federate Honduras, Nicaragua, and El Salvador; 1859 received Bay Is., former subject of dispute with Great Britain; scene of incessant civil war and of intervention of U.S. on several occasions; in World War I declared war on Germany July 19, 1918 and in World War II on Axis powers Dec. 1941. Coco (Segovia) river confirmed as SE boundary by International Court of Justice 1961 in settlement of dispute with Nicaragua.

Honduras, British. See BRITISH HONDURAS.

Hon·du′ras, Cape (hŏn·dŏŏr′ȧs; -dūr′-); *Span.* **Ca′bo de Hon·du′ras** (kä′vô thä ôn·dōō′räs). Cape on N coast of Honduras, extending into Caribbean Sea.

Hon·du′ras, Gulf of (hŏn·dŏŏr′ȧs; -dūr′-). Inlet of Caribbean Sea bet. S British Honduras, E Guatemala, and N Honduras.

Honduras Bay. Inlet of Gulf of Honduras, with British Honduras on N and Guatemala on W and S.

Hon′ea Path (hŭn′ĭ). Town, Abbeville and Anderson cos., W South Carolina; pop. 3453; textile manufactures.

Hon′e·oye Lake (hŭn′ē·oi). Lake ab. 5 m. long in W Ontario co., W New York; outlet from N end flows into Genesee river.

Hones′dale (hōnz′dāl). Borough, ⊗ of Wayne co., NE corner of Pennsylvania, 25 m. ENE of Scranton; pop. 5569; coal mining and shipping; manufactures silk and woolen goods, shoes, electric elevators, glassware; starting point of trial run of first locomotive in U.S. Aug. 9, 1829.

Hon′ey Grove (hŭn′ĭ). City, Fannin co., NE Texas, 20 m. W of Paris; pop. 2071.

Honey Island or **Honey Island Swamp.** Swamp in SE Louisiana and SW Mississippi, in delta of Pearl river; in 19th cent. a hide-out for pirates and during Civil War for deserters from Confederate Army.

Honey Lake. Lake in SE Lassen co., NE California; ab. 20 m. long; altitude 3949 ft.; no outlet.

Hon′fleur′ (ôN′flûr′). Seaport, Calvados dept., NW France, on Seine estuary opp. Le Havre; pop. 8158; founded in 11th cent.; frequently taken and retaken in wars bet. France and England and not finally acquired by France until 1449; center for exploration in 16th and 17th cents.; in 18th cent. supplanted by Le Havre in commercial importance; shipbuilding; iron and copper foundries. Had several fine churches and other buildings, all destroyed in fighting during World War II.

Hon′ga River (hŏng′gȧ). Inlet of Chesapeake Bay on SW shore of Dorchester co., SE Maryland.

Hongkew. See SHANGHAI.

Hong Kong (hŏng'kŏng'). *also, unofficially,* **Hongkong.**
1 British crown colony, SE China, E of mouth of the
Pearl river. ab. 90 m. S of Canton; 391 sq. m.; pop. (1931)
849,003 (est. 1958 pop. 2,806,000, including refugees
from Communist-controlled areas of China); ✱ Victoria.
Comprises (1) *British owned:* (a) **Hong Kong Island;**
32 sq. m.; pop. (1931) 410,921, irregular with broken
ridge; highest point Victoria Peak 1810 ft. in NW; coast
much indented; separated (1 m. across) from British
Kowloon by spacious Hong Kong harbor and from mainland farther E by Lyemun Pass; on NW shore is Victoria
(*q.v.*) city. (b) **Kow'loon' Peninsula** (kou'loon'),
part of mainland opp. Hong Kong I.; 3 sq. m.; chief town
Kowloon (*q.v.*) with pop. (1931) of 264,675. (c) Floating
population, mostly Chinese (1931) 75,250 (est. 1940 as
100,000). (2) *Leased:* **New Territories,** enclave of
Kwangtung prov. comprising area N of Kowloon Penin.
from Mirs Bay on E to Deep Bay, inlet of Pearl river, on
W; 356 sq. m.; pop. (1931) 98,157 (outside Kowloon
urban area); includes also Lantao, Lamma, and other
islands, divided into Northern District, pop. (1931)
73,678, ✱ Taipo, and Southern District, pop. (1931)
24,479, ✱ Victoria. Colony a great center of world commerce in the Far East; has steamship connections with
all principal ports of the world; tobacco and other manufacturing, shipbuilding, sugar refining.
2 = VICTORIA (Hong Kong).
History: Island occupied by British 1839, ceded to
them by Chinese in 1841, cession confirmed by Treaty of
Nanking 1842; Kowloon Penin. ceded by China to British 1860; New Territories leased to Great Britain for 99
years 1898; bombed by Japanese, December 18 to 24,
1941 and surrendered Dec. 25. Reoccupied by British
forces Sept. 1945.
Ho'ni·a'ra (hō'nĭ·ä'rá). Town, SE Solomon Is., on NW
Guadalcanal I.; ✱ of British Solomon Is.
Hon'is·ter Hause (hŏn'ĭs·tẽr hôs') *or* **Pass.** Mountain
pass 1190 ft. near Keswick, Cumberland, NW England.
Hon'i·ton (hŏn'ĭ·t'n; *locally* hŭn'-). Municipal borough, Devonshire, SW England, 16 m. NE of Exeter;
pop. 4614; famous for its manufacture of Honiton lace,
introduced by refugees from Flanders under Queen
Elizabeth; has a school for lace making.
Ho'no·ka'a (hō'nō·kä'ä). Village, Hamakua dist., Ha-
waii co., Hawaii, on NE coast of Hawaii I.; N of Mauna
Kea; pop. 1247.
Ho'no·ka'la Point (hō'nō·kä'lä). Point on NE coast of
Maui I., Hawaii.
Ho'no·ka·o'pe Bay (hō'nō·kä·ō'pä). Bay on NW coast
of Hawaii I., bet. Keawaiki Bay and Kawaihae Bay.
Hon'o·lu'lu (hŏn''l·ōō'lōō; *native* hō'nō·lōō'lōō). **1** County,
Hawaii; 590 sq. m.; pop. 500,409; ⊗ Honolulu; its legal
designation established by Municipal Act of 1907, is
City and County of Honolulu; comprises Oahu I.
and the small uninhabited islands of the Hawaiian
group.
2 Seaport city, SE Oahu I., Hawaii, forming a district of
City and County of Honolulu; ✱ of the state of Hawaii
and ⊗ of Honolulu co.; pop. 294,179; has fine protected
harbor; its unique position in center of North Pacific
Ocean (2098 naut. m. from San Francisco, 4711 m. from
Panama, 4483 m. via Suva from Sydney, 4767 m. from
Manila, 3380 from Yokohama, and 1304 statute m. by
air from Midway) makes it a port of exceptional importance; at mouth of Nuuanu valley with mountains
immediately behind it (Punchbowl 498 ft. and Mt.
Tantalus 2013 ft.) and farther to NE the Koolau Range
with peaks above 3000 ft. (see NUUANU PALI); to SE is
suburb of Waikiki with excellent beach; government
executive building, former royal palace, finished 1882;
Univ. of Hawaii (1907); Bishop Museum. Harbor first
discovered 1794 by Capt. William Brown; city began
1816; became capital 1820.
Ho·no'pu Point (hō·nō'pōō). Cape on NW coast of
Lanai I., Hawaii.

Hon'shu (hŏn'shōō; *Jap.* hôn·shōō) *or* **Hon'do** (hŏn'dō;
Jap. hôn·dŏ). Largest of the four chief islands of Japan,
considered as the mainland of Japan; area with adjacent
small islands 87,293 sq. m.; pop. (1938 est.) 55,205,500,
(1945) 54,612,618; in early times divided administra-
tively into 7 divisions comprising 58 provinces; its mod-
ern subdivisions include 34 out of the 47 prefectures of
Japan. For physical features, chief cities, history, etc.,
see JAPAN.
Hon'te (hôn'tĕ). The West Schelde Estuary (*q.v.*), SW
Netherlands.
Hon'to (hŏn'tō; *Jap.* hôn·tô). Town on SW coast of
Karafuto, Sakhalin I., 45 m. W of Otomari; pop. (1939
est.) 16,607.
Hood (hood). County in Texas. See *Table* at TEXAS.
Hood, Mount. Peak 11,245 ft. in Cascade Range, in
Clackamas and Hood River cos., NW Oregon; highest
point in Oregon.
Hood Canal. Navigable inlet of Puget Sound, W Wash-
ington; ab. 80 m. long, bet. 2 and 3 m. wide; extends SW
of Admiralty Inlet.
Hood Island. See ESPAÑOLA island.
Hoo'doo Peak (hōō'dōō). Mountain 10,522 ft. in W
Park co., NW Wyoming.
Hood River. 1 County in Oregon. See *Table* at OREGON.
2 City, its ⊗, N Oregon, on Columbia river ab. 17 m.
NW of The Dalles; pop. 3657; settled 1854; ships fruits
(esp. apples, pears, cherries) and berries; fruit-packing
plants and canneries, distilleries (brandy).
Hoo'ge (hō'ĸĕ). Former château E of Ieper (Ypres),
West Flanders prov., NW Belgium; scene of several bat-
tles in World War I; liquid fire first used here in the
German attack of July 30, 1915.
Hoo'ge·veen (hō'ĸĕ·vän'). Commune, Drenthe prov.,
NE Netherlands; pop. 15,313; railroad and canal town 23
m. NE of Zwolle.
Hoo'ge·zand' (hō'ĸĕ·zänt'). Commune, Groningen
prov., NE Netherlands, on canal 9 m. ESE of Groningen;
pop. 11,429.
Hoogh'ly *or* **Hug'li** (hōōg'lĭ). **1** Most westerly and
commercially the most important channel of Ganges
river in Ganges Delta (*q.v.*), West Bengal, NE Indian
Union; ab. 120 m. long from Santipur to Bay of Bengal;
navigable to Calcutta; nearly 10 m. wide at mouth;
formed by confluence at Nadia and Santipur of its headwaters, several distributaries of the Ganges, the most
important being the Bhagirathi, an old channel of the
Ganges.
2 *or* **Hoogh'ly–Chin'su·ra** (hōōg'lĭ·chĭn'sōō·rá).
Town, Burdwan division, West Bengal, NE Indian Union, on Hooghly river 22 m. N of Calcutta; pop. 32,634;
joint municipality; trading post established by Portu-
guese 1537, by the Dutch at Chinsura 1642, and by the
English at Hooghly 1651; British forced out temporarily
1685 by Nawab of Bengal; sacked by Marathas 1742.
Hook'er (hōōk'ẽr). County in Nebraska. See *Table* at
NEBRASKA.
Hooker Island. Island in Arctic Ocean, S cen. Franz
Josef Land, U.S.S.R.; meteorological station.
Hook Head (hōōk). Cape on SE coast of Ireland, at E
of entrance to Waterford Harbour.
Hook of Hol'land (hōōk, hŏl'ănd); *Du.* **Hoek van
Hol'land** (hōōk' vän hôl'änt). **1** Cape on SW coast of
South Holland prov., SW Netherlands, N of mouth of
Nieuwe Maas river; scene of naval battle 1914.
2 Seaport on the cape ab. 6 m. NW of Rotterdam; pop.
2969; belongs to Rotterdam.
Hook'sett (hōōk'sĕt; -sĭt). Town, Merrimack co., S cen.
New Hampshire, on Merrimack river 7 m. S of Concord;
pop. 3713; manufactures furniture. Mount St. Mary
College (1934; women).
Hoole (hōōl). Urban district, Cheshire, NW England,
suburb of Chester; pop. 9054.
Ho·o'le·hu'a (hō·ō'lä·hōō'ä). Village, Molokai dist.,
Maui co., W cen. Molokai I., Hawaii; pop. (est.) 973.

Hoo′nah (hōō′nȧ). Town, SE Alaska, on NE coast of Chicagof I. 20 m. WSW of Juneau; pop. 686.

Hoo′per Islands (hōō′pēr; hōōp′ēr). Island group on E side of lower Chesapeake Bay, in SW Dorchester co., Maryland.

Hooper Strait. Strait bet. Bloodsworth I. and mainland of Dorchester co., SE Maryland.

Hoopes′ton (hōōps′tŭn; hōōps′-). City, Vermilion co., E Illinois, 25 m. N of Danville; pop. 6606; in agricultural section; canneries.

Hoorn (hōrn). Commune, North Holland prov., W Netherlands, on an inlet of IJsselmeer; pop. 12,049; important cheese and cattle market; has two medieval gates; scene of Dutch naval victory over Spanish 1573. Birthplace of Willem C. Schouten, mariner, first to double Cape Horn (named after this town), and of Abel J. Tasman, explorer and discoverer of Tasmania.

Hoorn Islands. See FUTUNA ISLANDS.

Hoo′sac Mountains (hōō′sak). A range of the Green Mts. in Berkshire co., W Massachusetts; highest peak Spruce Hill 2588 ft.

Hoosac Tunnel. Railroad tunnel 4¾ m. long, Berkshire co., W Massachusetts, in Hoosac Mts.; completed 1875 after 24 years of work.

Hoo′sic (hōō′sĭk). River ab. 90 m. long rising in N cen. Berkshire co., Massachusetts, flowing N and NW across SW extremity of Vermont into New York, and emptying into Hudson river 14 m. N of Troy, Rensselaer co., E New York.

Hoo′sick Falls (hōō′sĭk). Village, Rensselaer co., E New York, on Hoosic river near Vermont border 21 m. ENE of Troy; pop. 4023; manufactures paper and papermaking machinery, electrical appliances, agricultural implements; Bennington Battlefield (state park), site of British entrenchments at battle of Bennington 1777, nearby.

Hoo′sier Pass (hōō′zhēr). Mountain pass 11,542 ft., Park and Summit cos., cen. Colorado, in Park Range of the Rocky Mts.; highway.

Hoo′ver Dam (hōō′vēr). See UNITED STATES, *Dams and Reservoirs.*

Hop (hŏp). River, E cen. Connecticut; rises in W Tolland co., flows SE into the Willimantic river near Willimantic.

Hop, Mount. Peak 13,943 ft. in Chaffee co., cen. Colorado.

Ho Pa Shan (hō′ bä′ shän′). Mountain range on border bet. S Shensi and NE Szechwan provs., cen. China.

Ho·pat′cong, Lake (hō·păt′kŏng). Lake ab. 8 m. long on boundary bet. Morris and Sussex cos., N New Jersey; summer resort.

Hope (hōp). Commercial city, ⊗ of Hempstead co., SW Arkansas, 32 m. NE of Texarkana; pop. 8399; distributing point for truck-gardening, fruit-growing, and cotton region; county seat moved here from Washington 1939.

Hope, Point; *or* **Tig′a·ra** (ʔtĭg′ȧ·rȧ). Cape and village, NW Alaska, on Arctic Ocean N of Bering Strait, ab. 68°N; Eskimo center for whale catching. Nearby is Ipiutak, site of ancient city that flourished probably 2000 years ago, discovered 1939–40 by Department of Anthropology of Univ. of Alaska; tombs yielded skeletons buried with beautiful ivory carvings and many engraved implements of a culture definitely not Eskimo or Indian.

Hope′dale (hōp′dāl). **1** Town, Worcester co., cen. Massachusetts, 16 m. ESE of Worcester; pop. 3987; location of a Utopian religious community established 1841 by a joint-stock company under leadership of Adin Ballou, Universalist minister; experiment ended by Ballou's successor E. D. Draper, who bought 75% of the stock, dissolved the company 1856, and founded the Draper Corp., manufacturers of textile machinery and textiles.
2 Village and harbor, E coast of Labrador, 55°29′N.

Ho′pei′ *or* **Ho′peh′** (hō′pā′; *Chin.* hŭ′bā′); *formerly* **Chih′li′** (chē′lē′; *Chin.* jĭr′lē′). Province, NE China;

59,341 sq. m.; pop. (1936 est.) 28,644,437; ✳ Tientsin; one of the Five Northern Provinces, bounded on N by Jehol, on E by the Gulf of Po Hai and Shantung, on S by Honan, on W by Shansi, and on NW by Inner Mongolia; mostly a level plain; N and NW boundary closely coincides with E part of Great Wall; E part crossed by the Grand Canal, beginning at Tientsin. Produces much coal; its maritime situation has made it important in international trade. For centuries chief defense area against Mongols and Manchus to the N; its chief city Peking (modern Peiping) capital of China most of the time 1267–1928; other cities Tientsin, Tsingyuan, Linyu, Chinwangtao, Shihkiachwang.

Hope Island (hōp). Island 20 m. long in Barents Sea ab. 60 m. SE of Edge I., Spitsbergen, Svalbard, Norway.

Hopes Ad·vance′, Cape (hōps′ ăd·văns′). Cape, N Ungava Penin., N Quebec prov., Canada, on Hudson Strait at W side of entrance to Ungava Bay.

Hope′town (hōp′toun). Town, NE Cape Province, S Republic of So. Africa, on Orange river 70 m. SSW of Kimberley; pop. 2215; place where first South African diamonds were found 1867.

Hope Town. Town on small island off E coast of Great Abaco I., Bahama Is.; pop. 365.

Hope′well (hōp′wĕl; -wĕl). **1** Borough, Mercer co., W cen. New Jersey, 13 m. N of Trenton; pop. 1928; camping ground of Washington's army before battle of Monmouth.
2 City, SE Virginia, in Prince George co. but politically independent, at confluence of James and Appomattox rivers 10 m. NE of Petersburg; 5 sq. m.; pop. 17,895; manufactures synthetic textiles, pottery, chemicals.

Hopewell Cape. Town (unincorporated), ⊗ of Albert co., SE New Brunswick, Canada, at mouth of Petitcodiac estuary; pop. 1235.

Hop′kins (hŏp′kĭnz). **1** Counties in two states of the U.S. See *Tables* at KENTUCKY and TEXAS.
2 City, Hennepin co., SE cen. Minnesota, 8 m. WSW of Minneapolis; pop. 11,370; truck gardening; manufactures farm machinery.

Hop′kins·ville (hŏp′kĭnz·vĭl). City, ⊗ of Christian co., SW Kentucky, 68 m. S of Henderson; pop. 19,465; tobacco and livestock market; Campbell Air Force Base.

Hop′kin·ton (hŏp′kĭn·tŭn). **1** Town, Middlesex co., NE Massachusetts, 13 m. ESE of Worcester; pop. 4932; shoe manufacturing.
2 Agricultural town, Merrimack co., S cen. New Hampshire, 7 m. W of Concord; pop. 2225; chartered and settled 1735.
3 Town, Washington co., S Rhode Island, 23 m. W of Newport; pop. 4174; taken from Westerly and incorporated 1757.

Ho′qui·am (hō′kwĭ·ăm). Seaport city, Grays Harbor co., W Washington, on Grays Harbor adjacent to Aberdeen (*q.v.*) ab. 50 m. W of Olympia; pop. 10,762; lumber center, manufactures lumber products; salmon and tuna fisheries, fish and oyster canneries.

Hor, Mount (hōr); *Arab.* **Je′bel Ha·run′** (jă′băl hä·rōōn′). Mountain 4430 ft., E of Wadi el ʻAraba, SW Transjordan, highest of the Seir Mts. of ancient Edom; ruined city of Petra (*q.v.*) is on its NE slope; by tradition the mountain on which Aaron died and was buried (*Num.* xx. 22–29).

Hor′bur·y (hôr′bēr·ĭ). Urban district, West Riding, Yorkshire, N England, just SW of Wakefield; pop. 7966.

Hor′da·land′ (hôr′dä·län′). County of Norway. See *Table* at NORWAY.

Hör′de (hŭr′dĕ). Former city (pop. 34,694), Arnsberg govt. dist., Westphalia prov., Prussia, Germany; since 1928 part of city of Dortmund (*q.v.*).

Ho′reb (hōr′ĕb). Mountain, identity unknown, perhaps in Sinai Penin. See Mount SINAI.

Hor′gen (hôr′gĕn). Commune, Zurich canton, NE cen. Switzerland, on Lake of Zurich 9 m. SSE of Zurich; pop. (1930) 9358; manufactures silk.

Ho′ři·ce (hôr′zhǐ·tsě); *Ger.* **Hö′ritz** (hû′rǐts). Town, SW Bohemia, Czechoslovakia, 20 m. SW of České Budějovice; Passion play since 1816.

Hor′i·con (hôr′ǐ·kŏn). City, Dodge co., SE cen. Wisconsin, 25 m. S of Fond du Lac; pop. 2996; manufactures farm equipment, furniture.

Horicon, Lake. See Lake GEORGE.

Hor′mi·gue′ros (ôr′mě·gä′rōs). Municipality (pop. 7153) and town (pop. 1647), W Puerto Rico; town on railroad 4 m. S of Mayagüez.

Hor′muz (hôr′mŭz; *native* hôr·mōōz′, hôor-), *also* **Or′-muz** (ôr′mŭz; *native* ôr·mōōz′, ōor-); *anc.* **Har·mo′zi·a** (här·mō′zhǐ·a; -zǐ·a). Ancient town on coast of Persia, near modern Bandar Abbas on Strait of Ormuz, S Iran; scene of battle in which Parthian Empire was overthrown by Ardashir I (see PERSIA) 226 A.D.; conquered by Arabs and later the seat of small Arabian kingdom; trade center for overland route to India; removed to island (11 m. SE of Bandar Abbas), probably in 13th cent.; 14th–16th cents. the leading mart in Persian Gulf; held by Portuguese 1515–1622; captured by Persian ruler aided by forces of English East India Co. 1622; declined after removal of its trade to Bandar Abbas on mainland.

Hormuz, Strait of. = Strait of ORMUZ.

Horn (hôrn) *or* **North Cape.** Cape, NW Iceland, W of Húna Bay.

Horn, Cape; *Span.* **Ca′bo de Hor′nos** (kä′vô thä ôr′nôs); *often, colloquially,* **the Horn.** Cape, a rock 1390 ft. high, at S extremity of South America, 55°59′S, on **Horn Island** of Wollaston group, S Tierra del Fuego Archipelago (*q.v.*), projecting S into Drake Passage; first sighted by Sir Francis Drake 1578; named 1615 by Dutch navigators, J. Le Maire and W. C. Schouten, after Hoorn in Holland; further explored by Nodal brothers 1619.

Hor′na·fjör′thur (hôt′nä·fyûr′thür). Inlet of Atlantic Ocean on SE coast of Iceland; fine harbor.

Horn′a′van (hōōrn′ä′vän). Lake 97 sq. m. in Västerbotten prov., N Sweden; drained by Skellefte river.

Horn′cas·tle (hôrn′kås′'l). Urban district, the Parts of Lindsey, Lincolnshire, E England; pop. 3809; noted for its horse fairs.

Horn′church′ (hôrn′chûrch′). Urban district, Essex, SE England, 16 m. ENE of London; pop. 104,128.

Hor·ne′len (hôr·nā′lěn). Island off SW coast of Norway, near entrance to Nord Fjord; shores rise abruptly to a height of ab. 3000 ft.

Hor·nell′ (hôr·něl′). City, Steuben co., S New York, 56 m. S of Rochester; pop. 13,907; settled 1790; railroad center; manufactures textiles, hosiery, brick and tile, leather, wagons, farm tools, electrical machinery.

Horn Island (hôrn). 1 Island off SE Mississippi coast, bet. Mississippi Sound and Gulf of Mexico.
2 Small island off Cape York, N Queensland, Australia, E of Thursday I.

Hornos, Cabo de. See Cape HORN.

Horn Peak (hôrn). 1 Mountain 13,400 ft. in Custer and Saguache cos., S cen. Colorado.
2 Mountain 8922 ft. in Blue Mts., NE Oregon.

Horns′by (hôrnz′bǐ). Town, New South Wales, SE Australia, ab. 12 m. N of Sydney.

Horn′sey (hôrn′zǐ). Municipal borough, Middlesex, SE England, N suburb of London; pop. 95,523, (1951) 98,134; part of Greater London; residential.

Horn′sund·tind′ (hôrn′sōōn·tǐn′). Mountain 4960 ft. at S end of West Spitsbergen I., near **Horn Sound** (*Norw.* **Horn′sund** [hōrn′sōōn]), inlet on SW coast.

Hor′nu′ (ôr′nü′). Commune, Hainaut prov., SW Belgium, just W of Mons; pop. 11,847.

Hör′num (hûr′nŏŏm). Southern part of island of Sylt, off W coast of Schleswig-Holstein, northwest Germany; sandy region.

Ho·ro·den′ka (hô·rô·děng′kä). Town, SW Ukraine, U.S.S.R., 37 m. SE of Stanislav and S of the Dniester river; formerly in Stanisławów dept., Poland; pop. (1938–39 est.) 12,200; manufactures linen, brandy. In World War I scene of Russian victory over Germans May 1915; in World War II occupied by Russians Sept. 1939 but lost in German attack 1941.

Ho·ro·shi·ri (hô·rô·shē·rē). Mountain peak 6732 ft. in Hidaka Mts., S Hokkaido I., Japan.

Hor·que′ta (ôr·kä′tä). Town, SE Concepción dept., Paraguay, E of Concepción; pop. ab. 13,160.

Hor′ry (ō′rē). County in South Carolina. See *Table* at SOUTH CAROLINA.

Horse′head′ Lake (hôrs′hěd′). Lake in cen. Kidder co., S cen. North Dakota.

Horse′heads′ (hôrs′hědz′). Village, Chemung co., S New York, 5 m. N of Elmira; pop. 7207; manufactures bricks, optical goods.

Hör′sel Ber′ge (hûr′zěl běr′gě) *or* **Ve′nus·berg** (vē′nŭs·bûrg; *Ger.* vā′nŏŏs·běrк). Mountains, NW Thuringia, Germany, bet. Gotha and Eisenach; contains the cave in which, according to medieval legend, Venus held her court.

Horse Me′sa Dam (hôrs′ mā′så). See UNITED STATES, *Dams.*

Hor′sens (hôr′sěns). Seaport, Aarhus co., E Jutland, Denmark, at head of **Horsens Fjord;** pop. (1945) 32,400; ships dairy products; manufactures textiles, electrical equipment, tobacco and rubber products.

Horseshoe Bend *or* **To′ho·pe′ka** (tō′hô·pē′kå). Locality, Tallapoosa co., E Alabama, in a bend of the Tallapoosa river; scene Mar. 27, 1814 of defeat of Creek Indians by Andrew Jackson.

Horseshoe Curve. Construction and scenic feature of Pennsylvania Railroad just W of Altoona, Pennsylvania, of exceptional engineering interest; completed 1852; 2375 ft. long, and graded 91 ft. to the mile.

Horseshoe Fall. See NIAGARA FALLS.

Horseshoe Mountain. Peak 13,912 ft. in Park and Lake cos., cen. Colorado.

Horse Trough. Peak 4052 ft. in Union co., N Georgia.

Hors′forth (hôrs′fěrth). Urban district, West Riding, Yorkshire, N England, 5 m. NW of Leeds; pop. 14,105.

Hor′sham (hôr′shăm). 1 Locality in Horsham township (pop. 8933), Montgomery co., SE Pennsylvania, ab. 9 m. NE of Norristown; pop. (1950) 2174.
2 Town, W Victoria, SE Australia, 115 m. W of Bendigo; pop. 5272.
3 Urban district, West Sussex, S England; pop. 16,682; to NW is Field Place, birthplace of Percy Bysshe Shelley; Christ's Hospital (transferred from London 1902).

Horst *or* **Horst an der Em′scher** (hôrst′ än děr ěm′-shěr). Former commune, Westphalia prov., Prussia, Germany; became part of Gelsenkirchen (*q.v.*) 1928.

Hor′ta (hôr′tá; *Port.* ôr′tá). 1 District of Portugal. See *Table* at PORTUGAL.
2 Seaport commune, its ✳, in Azores on SE coast of Fayal I.; pop. (1930) 7643; radio station; telegraph center; exports wine, oranges, grain; air base.

Hor′ten (hôr′t'n). Seaport, Vestfold co., SE Norway, on W side of Oslo Fjord; pop. 10,788; fortified; headquarters of Norwegian fleet; shipbuilding yards, arsenal; naval academy. In World War II naval battle Apr. 9, 1940 occurred nearby in which the Norwegians sank some German transports and damaged the cruiser *Emden.*

Hor′ton (hôr′t'n). 1 City, Brown co., NE Kansas, 23 m. WNW of Atchison; pop. 2361; corn, apples.
2 River ab. 200 m. long, NW Mackenzie District, Northwest Territories, Canada, E of Anderson river; flows NW into W side of Franklin Bay.
3 Parish, Buckinghamshire, SE England, 3 m. ESE of Windsor; pop. 1156; residence 1632–38 of John Milton.

Hor′wich (hŏr′ĭch; -ĭj). Urban district, Lancashire, NW England, 15 m. NW of Manchester; pop. 15,552; locomotives, cotton textiles.

Ho′ry Kut′né (hô′řĭ kŏŏt′nâ). = KUTNÁ HORA.

Horyń. See GORYN.

Ho·ryu·ji (hō·ryōō·jē). Town, Nara prefecture, W cen. Honshu, Japan, ab. 7 m. SW of Nara; pop. (1945) 3734; site of oldest existing Buddhist temple in Japan, built ab. 607 A.D.

Ho·shang'a·bad (hô·shŭng'ả·bǎd; -ä·bäd). Town, cen. Madhya Pradesh, Indian Union, on Narbada river; pop. 12,332; bet. 1720 and 1818 scene of conflicts bet. Marathas and Bhopal rulers.

Ho'shi·ar'pur (hō'shĭ·är'pŏŏr). Town, cen. Punjab state, NW Indian Union, 95 m. E of Lahore; pop. 26,730; produces inlaid ivory, metal, and inlaid woodwork, cotton goods, shoes, and copperware. Founded early 14th cent.; occupied 1809 by Ranjit Singh; annexed by British 1849.

Hos'pet (hōsh'pĕt). Town, SW Andhra Pradesh, S Indian Union, on Tungabhadra river 37 m. W of Bellary; pop. 21,673.

Hos·pi·ta·let' (ōōs·pē·tả·lĕt'). City, Barcelona prov., NE Spain, SW suburb of Barcelona; pop. 51,249; textiles.

Hos'te (ōs'tả). Chilean island 90 m. long and 50 m. wide in Tierra del Fuego Archipelago (q.v.), S of W Tierra del Fuego I.

Hoth'am, Mount (hŏth'ăm). Mountain 6100 ft. in the Darg Plateau, E Victoria, SE Australia, SW of Mt. Kosciusko.

Hotien. See KHOTAN.

Ho·tin' (hô·tēn'). 1 Former department, N Bessarabia, Romania; 1460 sq. m.; pop. 395,345.
2 Town, its *. See KHOTIN.

Hot Spring. County in Arkansas. See *Table* at ARKANSAS.

Hot Springs. 1 County in Wyoming. See *Table* at WYOMING.
2 City, ⊗ of Garland co., W cen. Arkansas, in Ouachita Mts. 47 m. WSW of Little Rock; pop. 28,337; health and tourist resort noted for its 47 thermal springs. Settled 1807; made, with surrounding area, a U.S. Government reservation 1832, **Hot Springs National Park** 1921 (see UNITED STATES, *National Parks*).
3 *since 1950* **Truth or Consequences.** Town, ⊗ of Sierra co., SW New Mexico, on the Rio Grande 60 m. NNW of Las Cruces; pop. 4269; hot mineral springs.
4 City, ⊗ of Fall River co., SW corner of South Dakota, in foothills of Black Hills 48 m. S of Rapid City; pop. 4943; health resort; thermal and mineral springs; sandstone quarries; mica, feldspar, gold, silver mines.
5 Village, Bath co., western Virginia, 5 m. SW of Warm Springs; pop. (est.) 200; mineral springs; Japanese diplomats interned here 1942 at beginning of war with Japan; scene of United Nations Conference on Food and Agriculture 1943.

Hot Springs Peak. Mountain 7692 ft. in E Humboldt co., NW Nevada.

Hot Sul'phur Springs (sŭl'fẽr). Town, ⊗ of Grand co., N Colorado; pop. 237; hot sulfur springs.

Hotte, Mas·sif' de la (mả·sēf' dē lả ôt'). Highland on Tiburon Penin., SW Haiti, Hispaniola I., West Indies; highest point 7872 ft.

Hot'ten·tot Point (hŏt''n·tŏt). Cape on SW coast of South-West Africa, N of Lüderitz.

Hou'dain' (ōō'dăɴ'). Commune, Pas-de-Calais dept., N France, near Béthune; pop. (1931) 6730; coal; has church (12th and 16th cents.); destroyed in World War I and rebuilt.

Hou'dan' (ōō'dän'). Village, Seine-et-Oise dept., N France; pop. (1931) 2068; has 15th–16th cent. church and keep of an early 12th-cent. castle; noted for its poultry market, the Houdan breed of domestic fowl originating here.

Hou'deng'–Goe'gnies' (ōō'däɴ'gû'nyē'). Commune, Hainaut prov., SW Belgium, on a tributary of the Haine, E of Mons; pop. 9022; coal mines, smelting, woodworking, rope making, glassworks.

Houf'fa'lize' (ōō'fả'lēz'). Village, Luxembourg prov.,

SE Belgium, 10 m. N of Bastogne; pop. 1317; taken by Germans in early phase of Battle of the Bulge Dec. 1944; retaken by Allies Jan. 16, 1945.

Hough'ton (hō't'n). 1 County in Michigan. See *Table* at MICHIGAN.
2 Village, ⊗ of Houghton co., NW Michigan penin., 70 m. NW of Marquette; pop. 3393; in copper-mining section; distribution center for Keweenaw Penin. Michigan College of Mining and Technology (1885; coed.).
3 Village, Allegany co., SW New York, 65 m. SE of Buffalo; pop. (est.) 1200; Houghton College (1883; coed.).

Houghton Lake. Lake 16 m. long by 7 m. wide in cen. Roscommon co., N cen. Michigan; largest inland lake in the state; source of Muskegon river.

Hough'ton le Spring (hō't'n lĕ sprĭng'; hou't'n). Urban district, Durham, N England, 11 m. SSE of Newcastle; pop. 30,676; limestone quarrying, coal mining.

Hou'gou'mont' (ōō'gōō'môn'). Château on the battlefield of Waterloo, Belgium; held by British throughout the battle, June 18, 1815, against repeated attacks.

Hougue, La. See LA HOGUE.

Hou'illes (ōō'y'). Commune, Seine-et-Oise dept., N France, NW of Paris on Seine river; pop. 22,974.

Houl'ton (hōl't'n; -tŭn). Town, ⊗ of Aroostook co., N Maine, on Canadian border 22 m. N of Grand Lake; pop. 8289; ships potatoes, lumber; wood products.

Hou'ma (hō'mả). City, ⊗ of Terrebonne parish, SE Louisiana, 49 m. WSW of New Orleans on the Intracoastal Waterway; pop. 22,561; packing houses for shrimp, oysters, crabs; fisheries; sugar and molasses. Founded 1810, incorp. as city 1898.

Houns'low (hounz'lō). Town, Heston and Isleworth urban district, Middlesex, SE England; suburb of London; to W is **Hounslow Heath,** site of a Roman camp, once a resort of highwaymen.

Hou'plines' (ōō'plēn'). Commune, Nord dept., N France, on Belgian frontier just E of Armentières; pop. (1931) 5430; battle Apr. 9, 1918 when it was taken by British.

Hourn, Loch (lŏk hōŏrn'). Inlet of Sound of Sleat on NW coast of Scotland, in Inverness co.; extends inland ab. 13 m.

Hou·sa·ton'ic (hōō'sả·tŏn'ĭk). River 148 m. long, formed by junction of E and W branches S of Pittsfield, Berkshire co., W Massachusetts, and flowing S, across W Connecticut, into Long Island Sound at Stratford.

Hous'ton (hūs'tŭn). Name of counties in four states of the U.S. See *Tables* at ALABAMA, MINNESOTA, TENNESSEE, TEXAS.

Hous'ton (hous'tŭn). County in Georgia. See *Table* at GEORGIA.

Hous'ton (hūs'tŭn). 1 Town, a ⊗ of Chickasaw co., NE Mississippi, 30 m. SW of Tupelo; pop. 2557; dairying.
2 City, ⊗ of Texas co., S Missouri, 42 m. N of West Plains; pop. 1660.
3 Borough, Washington co., SW Pennsylvania, 19 m. SW of Pittsburgh; pop. 1865.
4 City and port of entry, ⊗ of Harris co., SE Texas, ab. 25 m. NW of Galveston Bay; connected with Gulf of Mexico by **Houston Ship Canal** or **Channel** (through former Buffalo Bayou and Galveston Bay, 57.3 m. long, 200 ft. wide, 34 ft. deep); largest city in the state and 7th largest in U.S., pop. 938,219; ships esp. petroleum products, cotton, sulfur, lumber, rice; petroleum refining, meat packing, printing and publishing, sugar and rice mills; manufactures chemicals, cement, cotton and cottonseed oil products, oil-well machinery; sulfur, salt, limestone deposits; Ellington Air Force Base. William Marsh Rice University (1912; coed.; name changed from Rice Institute 1960); Univ. of Houston (1934; coed.); Texas Southern Univ. (1927; coed.). Founded 1836; incorporated and became ⊗ 1837; capital of Republic of Texas 1837–39, 1842–45; developed rapidly since completion of ship canal 1914.

Hout'man Rocks (hout'măn) *or* **Houtman A·bro'-lhos** (å·brō'lyŏŏsh). Rocky islets, in Indian Ocean 140 m. W of Geraldton, W Western Australia.

Hove (hōv). Municipal borough. East Sussex, S England, W suburb of Brighton on English Channel; pop. 54,993, (1951) 69,435.

Ho'ven·weep National Monument (hō'věn·wēp). See UNITED STATES, *National Monuments*.

How'ard (hou'ĕrd). **1** Name of counties in seven states of the U.S. See *Tables* at ARKANSAS, INDIANA, IOWA, MARYLAND, MISSOURI, NEBRASKA, TEXAS.
2 City, ⊗ of Elk co., SE Kansas; pop. 1017.
3 City, ⊗ of Miner co., E South Dakota; pop. 1208.

Howe, Cape (hou). Extreme SE point of Australia, on border of New South Wales and Victoria.

How'ell (hou'ĕl). **1** County in Missouri. See *Table* at MISSOURI.
2 City, ⊗ of Livingston co., SE Michigan, 25 m. NNW of Ann Arbor; pop. 4861; cattle; dairy products.

Howe Sound (hou). Inlet of Strait of Georgia, extending N into British Columbia, N of Vancouver, Canada.

How'ick (hou'ĭk). Resort, Natal, E Union of South Africa, NW of Pietermaritzburg; pop. 1726; at the falls (364 ft. high) in the Umgeni river.

How'land Island (hou'lănd). Small island in cen. Pacific Ocean, near the equator NW of Phoenix Is.; 1 sq. m.; belongs to the United States; has airport, constructed 1937. Visited for guano bet. 1856 and 1890.

How'rah (hou'rà). City, West Bengal state, NE Indian Union, on Hooghly river opp. Calcutta; pop. (1941) 379,292; important industrial community and railroad terminus; jute and cotton mills, railroad workshops, paper factories; Bengal engineering school; Royal Botanic Garden (established 1787).

Howth (hōth; houth). Urban district and seaport, co. Dublin, E Eire, on a rocky peninsula N of Dublin Bay; pop. 4832; watering place.

Hox'ie (hŏk'sĭ). City, ⊗ of Sheridan co., NW Kansas; pop. 1289.

Hox'ne (hŏk's'n). Village, N Suffolk, England; Stone-Age deposits; scene of defeat of St. Edmund by the Danes in 870.

Hox'ton (hŏks'tŭn). District, metropolitan borough of Shoreditch, NE cen. London, England.

Hoy (hoi). One of the Orkney Is., off N coast of Scotland; 13 m. long; pop. 995; its highest point 1564 ft. is highest in the Orkneys.

Hoy'lake and West Kir'by (hoi'lāk, kûr'bĭ). Urban district, Cheshire, NW England, on Irish Sea 9 m. W of Liverpool; pop. 30,920; watering place; famous golf links, scene of many championship matches.

Hoy'land Neth'er (hoi'lănd nĕth'ĕr). Urban district, West Riding, Yorkshire, N England, near Barnsley; pop. 15,707; brickworks, coal mines.

Hoy·ran', Lake (hoi·rän'); *Turk.* **Hoyran Gö·lü'** (gû·lü'). Lake (*gölü*) in W Turkey in Asia, S of Afyon Karahisar; forms the N part of Eğridir Lake.

Hoy Sound (hoi). Body of water bet. islands of Pomona (Mainland) on N and Hoy on S in the Orkney Is., off N coast of Scotland.

Hoyt Peak (hoit). Mountain 10,248 ft. in S Summit co., NE Utah.

Ho·zu (hō·zŏŏ). River, Honshu, Japan; joins Uji river to form the Yodo river.

Hradec Králové. See KÖNIGGRÄTZ.

Hradiště Mnichovo. = MNICHOVO HRADIŠTĚ.

Hra'ni·ce (hrä'nyi·tsě); *Ger.* **Mäh'risch–Weiss'kir'-chen** (mâ'rĭsh·vis'kĭr'kĕn). Town, E Moravia prov., cen. Czechoslovakia, 24 m. E of Olomouc; pop. (1930) 10,818.

Hron (hrôn); *Hung.* **Ga'ram** (gŏ'rŏm); *Ger.* **Gran** (grän). River ab. 150 m. long in S Slovakia prov., Czechoslovakia; flows W, then S into Danube river opp. Esztergom.

Hru·bie'szów (hrŏŏ·byě'shŏŏf); *Russ.* **Gru·be·shov'** (grŏŏ·byĭ·shôf'). Commune, Lublin dept., Poland, 64 m. ESE of Lublin just W of the Bug; pop. (1938–39 est.) 13,500; agriculture; scene of battle July 1915 bet. Germans and Russians.

Hrvatska. See CROATIA.

Hsai'kwan' (sī'kwän'). Town, Yunnan, S China, on Burma Road near S end of Erh Hai (Tali Lake), now SIAKWAN.

Hsen'wi' (sĕn'wē'). Town, ✳ of North Hsenwi state, Northern Shan States, Burma, on Burma Road 25 m. NNE of Lashio.

Hsiang. See SIANG river, SE cen. China.

Hsiao Khingan Shan. = *Little Khingan Mountains:* see KHINGAN.

Hsien–Yang. See SIAN.

Hsikang. = SIKANG.

Hsin'chiang' (shĭn'jĭ·äng'). Var. of SINKIANG.

Hsin·chu (shĭn·chŏŏ). = SHINCHIKU.

Hsing'an' (shĭng'än'). **1** *formerly* **Khing'an'** (shĭng'-). Region, W section of Manchukuo (Manchuria), bordering on Mongolia; under Japanese comprised four provinces of East, North, South, and West Hsingan; 164,235 sq. m.; pop. (1940 est.) 2,123,170; inhabited chiefly by Mongols.
2 One of nine new provinces of Manchuria, in NW part; created Sept. 1945; 103,918 sq. m.; pop. 1,293,000; ✳ Hulun.

Hsing'an' Shan (shĭng'än' shän'). Mountain range, SW Jehol, NE China, roughly parallel with Chahar border; comprises S section of Great Khingan Mts.

Hsining. See SINING.

Hsin'king' (shĭn'jĭng'). See CHANGCHUN.

Hsinking Special Municipality. Former province (1932–45), S cen. Manchukuo, comprising the capital city Hsinking (Changchun); 169 sq. m.; pop. (1940 est.) 554,202.

Hsinmin. See SINMIN.

Hsi'paw' (sē'pô'). **1** State of the Northern Shan States, NE of Mandalay, E cen. Burma; 4591 sq. m.; pop. 148,731; ✳ Hsipaw.
2 Town, its ✳, on railroad ab. 90 m. NE of Mandalay; pop. 4849.

Hsu'chang' (sŏŏ'chäng'); *formerly* **Hsu'chow'** (sŏŏ'jō'). Town, N Honan prov., E cen. China, on Peiping-Hankow railroad just S of Chenghsien; scene of hard battle May 1938 after which Japanese gained control of Lunghai railroad.

Hua'cas Point (wä'käs). Cape on W cen. coast of Peru, S of Callao.

Hua'cho (wä'chŏ). Seaport, Lima dept., cen. Peru, 70 m. N of Callao; pop. (1940 est.) 13,320; shipping point for cotton and sugar district.

Hua·chu'ca Peak (wä·chŏŏ'kà). Mountain 8406 ft. in SW Cochise co., SE Arizona.

Hua'hi'né' (wä'ē'nā'). One of the Leeward Is. group of Society Is., French Polynesia, S Pacific Ocean, ab. 80 m. WNW of Tahiti; 7 m. N to S by 4 m. wide; pop. 1283; produces copra, tropical fruits, and vegetables; highest point 2231 ft.

Huail'las (wī'yäs). Peak 18,045 ft. in W Bolivia, N of Lake Poopó.

Huai'na Po'to·sí' (wī'nä pō'tō·sē'). Andean mountain peak 20,260 ft. in Bolivia, 20 m. N of La Paz.

Huaina–Putina. See OMATE.

Hu'a·la·lai' (hŏŏ'ä·lä·lī'). Volcano 8275 ft., W Hawaii I.; dormant since 1801.

Hual·cán' (wäl·kän'). Peak ab. 21,000 ft. in Cordillera Occidental, Peru.

Hual·la'ga (wä·yä'gä). River ab. 700 m. long in W and N Peru; rises in Andes Mts., flows N into Marañón river in N Peru.

Hual·la·ti'ri (wä·yä·tē'rē). Peak 19,883 ft. in Andes Mts. on boundary bet. Bolivia and Chile.

Hual'pai Peak (wäl'pī). Mountain 8266 ft. in **Hualpai Mountains,** S cen. Mohave co., W Arizona.

Hua·man'tla, *in full* **Huamantla de Juá'rez** (wä-män'tlä thä hwä'räs). Town, Tlaxcala state, cen. Mexico; pop. 7287.

Huam·blín' (wäm·blēn') *or* **So·cor'ro** (sô·kôr'rô). Island off SW coast of Chile, NW of Chonos Archipelago.

Huambo. See NOVA LISBOA.

Hua·mi'na (wä·mē'nä). Peak 14,435 ft. in Apurímac dept., S Peru.

Huan'ca·ve·li'ca (wäng'kä·vä·lē'kä). **1** Department of Peru. See *Table* at PERU.

2 Town, its ✳, 140 m. SE of Lima; pop. (1940 est.) 8139; altitude ab. 12,500 ft.; founded by Francisco de Toledo 1572; chief industry mining, esp. of quicksilver.

Huan·ca'yo (wäng·kä'yô). City, ✳ of Junín dept., cen. Peru, on Mantaro river ab. 122 m. E of Lima; pop. (1940 est.) 28,679; altitude 10,958 ft.; noted for its market place to which come Indians from surrounding districts; has observatory of terrestrial magnetism maintained by Carnegie Institution of Washington, D.C.

Huan·cha'ca (wän·chä'kä). Town, Potosí dept., SW Bolivia, ab. 20 m. NE of Uyuni; silver mining.

Huan·doy' (wän·doi'). Peak 21,088 ft. in Ancash dept., W Peru.

Huá'nu·co (wä'nōō·kô). **1** Department of Peru. See *Table* at PERU.

2 Town, its ✳, near Huallaga river ab. 170 m. NE of Lima; pop. (1940 est.) 12,877; altitude 6273 ft.; celebrated for its fruits; founded by Gómez Alvarado 1539; former capital of Junín dept. (until 1855); nearly destroyed by Chilean riots and massacres 1881, 1883; 35 m. to the W is Inca town **Huánuco Vie'jo** (vyě'hô), settled by Spanish 1535, now almost abandoned.

Hua'ra (wä'rä). Seaport commune, Tarapacá prov., N Chile, ab. 25 m. N of Iquique; pop. 11,257.

Hua·rás' (wä·räs'), *formerly spelled* **Hua·raz'** (wä·räs'). Town, ✳ of Ancash dept., W Peru, on Santa river 190 m. N of Lima; pop. (1940 est.) 12,099; altitude 9932 ft.; silver, cinnabar, copper, gold, coal.

Huas'ca·rán' (wäs'kä·rän') *or* **Huas·cán'** (wäs·kän'). Peak 22,205 ft. in Ancash dept., W Peru; highest mountain in Peru.

Huas'co (wäs'kô). Port, Atacama prov., N cen. Chile, midway bet. Coquimbo and Caldera; pop. 2311; exports copper, silver, gold, cattle, and hay.

Hua Shan. See HWA.

Hua'ta·bam'po (wä'tä·väm'pô). Town, S Sonora state, NW Mexico, near coast; pop. 5643.

Hua·tus'co, *in full* **Huatusco de Chi'cuel·lar'** (wä-tōōs'kô thä chē'kwä·yär'). Town, Veracruz state, E Mexico, ab. 50 m. W of Veracruz; pop. 6539.

Huau'chi·nan'go (wou'chē·näng'gô). Town, Puebla state, SE cen. Mexico, 45 m. E of Pachuca; pop. 5779.

Huau'ra (wou'rä) *or* **Guau'ra** (gwou'rä). River ab. 85 m. long in cen. Peru; flows W into Pacific Ocean N of Lima.

Huayhuash, Cordillera. See ANDES.

Hub'bard (hŭb'ērd). **1** County in Minnesota. See *Table* at MINNESOTA.

2 Village, Trumbull co., NE Ohio, 6 m. NE of Youngstown; pop. 7137; manufactures steel, slag products.

3 City and health resort, Hill co., NE cen. Texas, 28 m. NNE of Waco; pop. 1628; mineral springs.

Hubbard, Mount. Peak 14,950 ft. in St. Elias Range on Alaska-Yukon boundary, SE of Mt. Logan.

Hubbard Lake. Lake ab. 10½ sq. m. in N Alcona co., NE Michigan; outlet N into Thunder Bay.

Hub'bard·ton (hŭb'ērd·tŭn). Town, Rutland co., Vermont; pop. 238; scene of battle July 7, 1777 in which British defeated Gen. Fraser defeated Americans under Seth Warner.

Hu·ber'tus·burg (hŭ·bûr'tŭs·bûrg; *Ger.* hōō·bĕr'tōōs-bōōrκ) *or* **Hu'berts·burg** (hū'bĕrts·bûrg; *Ger.* hōō'bĕrts·bōōrκ). Castle near Oschatz, Saxony, Germany; here on Feb. 15, 1763 treaty was signed ending the Seven Years' War.

Hub'li (hōōb'lĭ). Town, W Mysore, W Indian Union, 300 m. SSE of Bombay; pop. (1941) 95,512.

Huchow. See WUHING.

Huck'ing·en (hōōk'ing·ĕn). Former commune (pop. 14,632), Düsseldorf govt. dist., Rhine Province, Prussia, Germany; since 1929 part of Duisburg (*q.v.*).

Huck'nall (hŭk'nᶁl; -n'l). Urban district, Nottinghamshire, N cen. England, 5 m. NNW of Nottingham; pop. 23,213; manufactures hosiery; coal mines; burial place of Lord Byron.

Hud'ders·field (hŭd'ērz·fēld). County borough, West Riding, Yorkshire, N England, 24 m. NE of Manchester; pop. 13,475, (1951) 129,021; has woolen mills, engineering plants, ironworks; coal deposits.

Hud'son (hŭd's'n). **1** River 306 m. long, E New York; rises in Essex co., in Adirondack Mts.; flows S into Upper New York Bay, at its S end forming boundary bet. New York and New Jersey; has New York City at its mouth; navigable to Troy. Explored 1609 by Henry Hudson.

2 County in New Jersey. See *Table* at NEW JERSEY.

3 Industrial town, Middlesex co., NE Massachusetts, 15 m. NE of Worcester; pop. 9666; rubber and leather products, wooden containers.

4 City, Lenawee co., S Michigan, 27 m. S of Jackson; pop. 2546; flour mills, pump factory.

5 Residential town, Hillsboro co., S New Hampshire, on Merrimack river opp. Nashua; pop. 5876.

6 Industrial city, ⊗ of Columbia co., SE New York, on E bank of Hudson river 28 m. S of Albany; pop. 11,075; cement, machinery, woolen goods. First permanently settled 1783; home port of schooners in whaling, seal, and West Indies ocean trade c. 1790.

7 Town, Caldwell co., W North Carolina, SE of Lenoir; pop. 1536.

8 City, ⊗ of St. Croix co., W Wisconsin, on St. Croix river 15 m. N of its confluence with Mississippi river; pop. 4325.

Hudson Bay. Inland sea 850 m. long and 600 m. wide, ab. 472,000 sq. m., in Keewatin District, E Northwest Territories, Canada, bounded on SW by Manitoba, on S by Ontario, and on E by Quebec prov.; average depth 420 ft., greatest depth ab. 1500 ft.; connected with Atlantic Ocean by Hudson Strait and with Foxe Basin to N by Foxe Channel; on S has large shallow extension, James Bay; contains islands, largest Southampton I. in N, all of which are administratively a part of Keewatin District; on its NW shore are two large inlets Wager Bay and Chesterfield Inlet. East coast navigated by Hudson 1610; explored bet. 1612 and 1632 by Button, Fox, and James; surrounding land, known as Rupert's Land (*q.v.*), controlled by Hudson's Bay Co. 1670–1869; definitely declared as within Keewatin by Order in Council 1918.

Hudson Bay Junction. Village, E Saskatchewan, W Canada; pop. 1115; W of N end of Lake Winnipegosis; railroad junction.

Hudson Falls. Village, ⊗ of Washington co., E New York, on Hudson river 40 m. N of Troy; pop. 7752; manufactures paper; settled in 1760's; in line of Burgoyne's march 1777; burned by Sir Guy Carleton 1780.

Hudson Strait. Strait 50 to 100 m. wide, 450 m. long, NE Canada, bet. S Baffin I. and N Quebec prov., connecting Atlantic Ocean with Hudson Bay. Entered by Frobisher 1576–78; navigated by Hudson 1607–11.

Hud'speth (hŭd'spĕth; -spĭth). County in Texas. See *Table* at TEXAS.

Hue *or* **Hué** (hṳ·ā'; *Fr.* ü·ā'). City, former ✳ of Annam, French Indochina, in cen. Vietnam; pop. 28,000; in flat alluvial region surrounded by hills; a native market town, trades esp. in rice. Has royal palace and tombs of Annamese kings; taken by French 1883.

Hue'chu·cui'cui, Point (wä'chōō·kwē'kwē). Cape on NW tip of Chiloé I. off SW coast of Chile.

Hue'co Mountains (wä'kô). Range in S New Mexico and W Texas; highest point 6717 ft.

Hue′hue·te·nan′go (wā′wȧ·tȧ·näng′gȯ). **1** Department, W Guatemala; 2857 sq. m.; pop. 176,480.

2 Town, its ✳; pop. (1938 est.) 7139; mining center (lead, silver, copper).

Huel′va (wĕl′vä). **1** Province of Spain. See *Table* at SPAIN.

2 Commune, its ✳, SW Spain, on Odiel river 10 m. from the Atlantic Ocean and 53 m. WSW of Seville; pop. (1941 est.) 57,509; fisheries, machine shops, shipyards; copper, manganese, and iron mining. Founded by Carthaginians; colonized by Romans; Roman aqueduct; monastery in which Columbus resided for a time; large statue of Columbus.

Hueneme. See PORT HUENEME.

Huér′cal–O·ve′ra (wĕr′käl·ȯ·vä′rä). Commune, Almería prov., SE Spain, 45 m. NE of Almería; pop. 13,030; agriculture; lead, copper, silver mines.

Huer′fa·no (ȯr′fȧ·nō; wûr′-; wâr′-). **1** River ab. 90 m. long, S Colorado; flows E and NE from Sangre de Cristo Range into Arkansas river.

2 County in Colorado. See *Table* at COLORADO.

Huertgen Forest. = *Hürtgen Forest:* see HÜRTGEN.

Hues′ca (wäs′kä). **1** Province of Spain. See *Table* at SPAIN.

2 *anc.* **Os′ca** (ŏs′kȧ). Commune, its ✳, NE Spain, 208 m. NE of Madrid; pop. 17,730; episcopal see; manufactures cloth, pottery, bricks, leather; 15th-cent. Gothic cathedral; 12th-cent. Romanesque church; episcopal palace and old palace of kings of Aragon; formerly site of university of Saragossa. Important Roman town; site of school for native chiefs founded by Quintus Sertorius c. 76 B.C.; taken and fortified by Moors 8th cent.; recaptured 1096 by Pedro I of Aragon; made capital of kingdom of Aragon 1096–1118.

Hu′ey·town (hū′ĭ·toun). City, Jefferson co., cen. Alabama, NW of Bessemer; pop. 5997.

Hufuf. = HOFUF.

Hughes (hūz). **1** River ab. 15 m. long, W West Virginia; formed by confluence of forks on W boundary of Ritchie co., flows W into Little Kanawha river.

2 Name of counties in two states of the U.S. See *Tables* at OKLAHOMA and SOUTH DAKOTA.

Hughesovka. See STALINO.

Hughes′town (hūz′toun). Borough, Luzerne co., E Pennsylvania, 9 m. NE of Wilkes-Barre; pop. 1615.

Hughes′ville (hūz′vĭl). Borough, Lycoming co., N cen. Pennsylvania, 17 m. E of Williamsport; pop. 2218.

Hugh Town (hū). See SCILLY ISLES.

Hugli. See HOOGHLY.

Hu′go (hū′gō). **1** Town, ⊗ of Lincoln co., E Colorado; pop. 811.

2 City, ⊗ of Choctaw co., SE Oklahoma, 54 m. E of Durant; pop. 6287; creosoting plant, cotton gins; manufactures lumber, cottonseed oil.

Hu′go·ton (hū′gȯ·t′n; -tŭn). City, ⊗ of Stevens co., SW Kansas; pop. 2912.

Huhohaote, Huhehot. See KWEISUI.

Hui′gra (wē′grä). Town, Chimborazo prov., cen. Ecuador, 72 m. by rail E of Guayaquil; alt. 4000 ft.

Hui′la (wē′lä). **1** Volcano 18,700 ft. in W cen. Colombia, ab. 60 m. NE of Popayán.

2 Department of Colombia. See *Table* at COLOMBIA.

Huix′tla (wēs′tlä). Town, S Chiapas state, SE Mexico, near Guatemala border; pop. 6828.

Hui′zen (hoi′zĕ[n]). Commune, North Holland prov., W Netherlands, on the IJsselmeer ESE of Amsterdam; pop. 7500; fishing; radio station.

Hu′kawng′ *or* **Hu′kong′** (hōō′kông′). Valley, loosely administered subdivision of NE Upper Chindwin dist., N Burma; 5586 sq. m.; lies in course of upper Chindwin river bet. Kumon Range and foothills of Patkai Range; amber mines. Scene of fierce fighting 1943–44 in World War II; crossed by Ledo Road (later Stilwell Road).

Hu′kow′ (hōō′kou′; *Chin.* -kō′) *or* **Ho′kou′** (hō′kou′). Town, N Kiangsi prov., SE China, on the Yangtze ab.

140 m. SSE of Hankow; pop. ab. 50,000; at outlet of **Hukow Canal** (90 m.) from Poyang Hu (lake).

Hu′kwang′ (hōō′gwäng′). Former political division of SE China set up under Yüan dynasty (1206–1368) and comprising territory of four modern provinces of Hupeh, Hunan, Kwangtung, and Kwangsi; ✳ Wuchang; first reduced under the Mings (1368–1644). See HUPEH.

Hu′lan′ (hōō′län′). Town, S Heilungkiang prov., N Manchuria, on a tributary of the Sungari ab. 20 m. N of Harbin; pop. ab. 25,000; trade center on Harbin-Aigun railroad.

Hule, Bahret el. See Waters of MEROM.

Hu′lin′ (hōō′lĭn′). Town, E Kirin prov., Manchuria, on Ussuri river opp. Iman.

Hull (hŭl). **1** Town, Plymouth co., SE Massachusetts, on point of peninsula in Massachusetts Bay 9 m. ESE of Boston; pop. 7055; summer resort.

2 County, SW Quebec, Canada; divided into **Ga′ti′neau′** (gȧ′tē′nō′) co., 2432 sq. m., pop. 35,264, ⊗ Maniwaki, and **Hull** co., 139 sq. m., pop. 57,318, ⊗ Hull. See *Table* at QUEBEC.

3 City, ⊗ of Hull co., Quebec, on Ottawa river opp. Ottawa, Ontario, and at mouth of Gatineau river; pop. 43,483; produces lumber, pulp, paper, and cement; mica, feldspar, and iron mines in vicinity; Hull Normal School. Founded 1800, incorporated 1875.

4 *or* **Kings′ton upon Hull** (kĭng′stŭn, hŭl′). County borough, East Riding, Yorkshire, N England, on the Humber where it is joined by the Hull river 157 m. N of London; pop. 313,544, (1951) 299,068; is an important seaport, forming outlet for products of Yorkshire and Lancashire; manufactures chemicals, flour, starch, soap, textiles, paper, iron and steel; shipbuilding; fisheries; Trinity House (charity for seamen). Known in 12th cent., received charter 1299; its grammar school founded 1486; repeatedly bombed by Germans in spring of 1941.

Hull Island. 1 One of the smaller islands of the Phoenix Is. (*q.v.*), in S part, cen. Pacific Ocean, 4°30′S and 172°10′W, SSW of Canton I.

2 See MARIA ISLAND, Tubuai Is.

Hüls (hüls). Town, former Rhine Province, W Germany, a NW suburb of Krefeld; pop. 6785; industrial center; heavily bombed by Allies Aug. 1943.

Hultschin. See HLUČÍN.

Hu′lun′ (hōō′lōōn′); *former Jap. name* **Hai′lar′** (hī′lär′). Town, ✳ of Hsingan prov., NW Manchuria, and ✳ of former North Hsingan prov., NW Manchukuo; on Hailar river ab. 240 m. NW of Lungkiang; pop. ab. 15,000; station on former Chinese Eastern Railway and trading center of Mongol nomads for horses and cattle.

Hu′lun′ Nor (hōō′lōōn′ nôr′); *formerly* **Da′lai′ Nor** (dä′lī′). Lake (*nor*), NW Manchuria, near Mongolia border; receives Kerulen river; source of Argun river, a headstream of the Amur; ab. 40 m. in circumference, alt. 4200 ft.

Hu′lu′tao′ (hōō′lōō′dou′). Town and seaport on Gulf of Liaotung, SE Jehol, NE China, ab. 25 m. S of Chinhsien.

Hu′ma·ca′o (ōō′mä·kä′ō). Municipality (pop. 33,381) and town (pop. 8005), E Puerto Rico; town near coast 28 m. SE of San Juan; in section producing sugar, coconuts, fruit, and tobacco.

Hu′mans·dorp (hū′mäns·dôrp). Town, near S coast of Cape Province, S Union of South Africa; pop. 2152; W of Port Elizabeth.

Hum′ber (hŭm′bẽr). **1** *anc.* **A′bus** (ā′bŭs). Estuary on E coast of England, formed by confluence of Ouse and Trent rivers 8 m. E of Goole; flows E and SE into North Sea; navigable for large vessels as far as Hull.

2 River 120 m. long, W Newfoundland; flows SW to the Bay of Islands at Corner Brook; one branch flows from Grand Lake.

Hum′ber·mouth (hŭm′bẽr·mouth; -mŭth). Town, W Newfoundland, at mouth of Humber river; pop. (1942 est.) 1500; adjoins Corner Brook on E.

Hum′ber·stone (hŭm′bẽr·stōn; -stŭn). Village, Welland co., SE Ontario, Canada, on Welland Ship Canal 5 m. S of Welland; pop. 3895.

Humbledon Hill. See HOMILDON HILL.

Hum′boldt (hŭm′bōlt). **1** River 290 m. long in N Nevada; rises in Elko co., flows W and SW into Humboldt Lake.

2 Counties in three states of the U.S. See *Tables* at CALIFORNIA, IOWA, NEVADA.

3 City, Humboldt co., NW cen. Iowa, 16 m. N of Fort Dodge; pop. 4031.

4 City, Allen co., SE Kansas, 8 m. N of Chanute; pop. 2285.

5 City, Gibson co., NW Tennessee, 15 m. NNW of Jackson; pop. 8482; manufactures canned foods, shoes, crates.

6 Town, S cen. Saskatchewan, Canada, 68 m. E of Saskatoon; pop. 2435; railroad divisional point.

Humboldt, Mount. Peak 5361 ft. on island of New Caledonia, SW Pacific Ocean, near SE coast.

Humboldt Bay. **1** Inlet of Pacific Ocean on W cen. coast of Humboldt co., NW California.

2 Bay on NE coast of Neth. New Guinea, near boundary of North-East New Guinea (British); site of Hollandia; scene of Allied landing Apr. 1944.

Humboldt Current. = PERUVIAN CURRENT.

Humboldt Lake *or* **Sink.** Lake in S Pershing and N Churchill cos., W Nevada; ab. 20 m. long, from 8 to 10 miles wide at greatest extent; receives Humboldt river from the N; no outlet.

Humboldt Peak. Mountain 14,100 ft. in Custer co., S cen. Colorado.

Humboldt Range. Range in cen. Pershing co., NW Nevada; in Great Basin.

Humboldt Salt Marsh. Marsh in NE Churchill co., W Nevada.

Hum′mels·town (hŭm′ĕlz·toun). Borough, Dauphin co., SE cen. Pennsylvania, 9 m. E of Harrisburg; pop. 4474.

Hump, the. See the HIMALAYAS.

Humphrey. See MANIHIKI.

Hum′phreys (hŭm′frĭz). Counties in two states of the U.S. See *Tables* at MISSISSIPPI and TENNESSEE.

Humphreys, Mount. **1** Peak 13,972 ft. in Sierra Nevada, on boundary bet. Fresno and Inyo cos., SE cen. California.

2 Peak 11,019 ft. in Yellowstone National Park, NW Wyoming.

Humphreys Peak. Highest point in Arizona, 12,611 ft. See SAN FRANCISCO PEAKS.

Hu·mu′ya (ōō·mōō′yä). River of W Honduras; an important tributary of the Ulúa river.

Hun (hŏon). **1** River, N Shansi prov., NE China. See YUNGTING.

2 River ab. 240 m. long, S Manchuria, mostly in Liaoning prov.; flows SW to the Liao near its mouth.

Hú′na Bay (hōō′nà). *Icel.* **Hú′na·fló′i** (hōō′nä·flō′ĭ). Inlet of Arctic Ocean on NW cen. coast of Iceland.

Hu′nan′ (hōō′nän′). Province, SE cen. China; 105,467 sq. m.; pop. (1936 est.) 28,293,735; ✷ Changsha; bounded on N by Hupeh prov., on E by Kiangsi, on S by Kwangtung and Kwangsi, and on W by Kweichow and Szechwan. Lies S of the Yangtze which forms part of its boundary on NE; in NE is Tungting Hu (lake) into which flow Yuan, Siang, and Tzu rivers; along its W and SW borders is the Nan Ling mountain range (highest ab. 5000 ft.); in E cen. part is Heng, one of the sacred mountains of China (2953 ft.). Important for its agriculture but more so for its mineral wealth, esp. coal and antimony. Chief cities Changsha, Changteh, Siangtan, Hengyang. Western mountainous part still inhabited by members of non-Chinese aboriginal tribes; central region of early kingdoms of S China, but has taken only small part in its history; invaded 1852 by Taiping rebels who failed to take Changsha; scene of much fighting 1944–45 in World War II. See HUPEH.

Hun′chun′ (hŏon′chŏon′). Treaty mart, SE Kirin prov., E Manchuria, near Tumen river not far from its mouth and 40 m. E of Yenki; pop. (1931 est.) 39,000; near point where Russian, Korean, and Manchurian boundaries meet, NW of Changkufeng (*q.v.*).

Hun′ga·ry (hŭng′gà·rĭ); *Hung.* **Ma′gyar·or′szág** (mŏ′dyŏr·ŏr′säg); *Ger.* **Un′garn** (ŏong′gärn). State, cen. Europe; bounded on N by Czechoslovakia, on NE by Carpatho-Ukraine, E by Romania, S by Yugoslavia, W by Austria; ✷ Budapest; area before World War II 35,875 sq. m.; pop. (1939) 9,106,252; acquisition of lands from Czechoslovakia (Ruthenia) and Romania (Transylvania) through Axis relationship increased area to ab.

66,000 sq. m. and pop. to ab. 15,000,000. Consists mainly of a plain, the Alföld, with fertile agricultural land that produces excellent grain; in N are S spurs of Carpathian Mts., highest point ab. 3300 ft.; bisected by the Danube flowing N to S; in W is Lake Balaton, largest lake in cen. Europe; in E is the Tisza, large tributary of the Danube, flowing across the Alföld N to S. Chief industry agriculture; produces wine (on NW shore of Lake Balaton and in NE hilly districts), coal and bauxite. Chief cities Budapest, Szeged, Debrecen, Kecskemét, Pécs, Hódmezővásárhely.

History: Valleys of mid-Danube and of Tisza, formerly Slavic, occupied by Magyars c. 893–901 A.D.; Magyar westward advance defeated by German Emperor Otto I 955; c. 1000 became independent kingdom and completed conversion to Latin Christianity; acquired Dalmatia, Slavonia, and Croatia in 11th cent.; received grant of Golden Bull, comparable to Magna Charta, 1222; invaded by Mongols 1241; after Árpád dynasty (997–1301) died out, crown became elective; ruled by house of Anjou 1308–82 and by Sigismund (Emperor of Germany) 1387–1437; under Hunyadi (d. 1456) resisted first wave of Turkish invasion; in reign of Matthias Corvinus (1458–90), who conquered Silesia, Moravia, and lower Austria (including Vienna), Hungary leading power of cen. Europe; broken by Turks at battle of Mohács 1526; in 16th cent., Transylvania (*q.v.*) became independent, and most of Hungary was divided bet. Turks (see OTTOMAN EMPIRE) and Austria (*q.v.*); recaptured Buda from Turks 1686; came under Hapsburgs 1687; with Slavonia and Transylvania, all Hungary except Banat ceded to Austrian crown 1699; scene of revolt under Lajos Kossuth 1848, revolt suppressed 1849; part of "dual monarchy" of Austria-Hungary (*q.v.*) 1867–1918; proclaimed independent republic 1918, soviet government under Béla Kun 1919, and monarchy with vacant throne under Regent Horthy 1920; lost about two thirds of territory by Treaty of Trianon 1920, including Slovakia, Western Hungary, Fiume, Croatia, Slavonia, Banat, Transylvania; received Sopron (*q.v.*) by plebiscite 1921; as sympathetic partner of the Axis, acquired

territory in S Slovakia and Ruthenia 1938, Carpatho-Ukraine 1939, and N half of Transylvania (see Ro-MANIA) 1940; lost these regions when Axis powers were defeated 1945; dissolved monarchy and established republic 1946.

Hungersteppe. See GOLODNAYA STEP.

Hungjao. See SHANGHAI.

Hung'shui' (hŏŏng'shwā'). River ab. 700 m. long, S China; rises in E Yunnan, flows S and E forming part of boundary bet. Kweichow and Kwangsi, then in E Kwangsi unites with Siang river at Kweiping to form Si river; navigable for small vessels only.

Hung'tze' Hu (hŏŏng'dzŭ' hŏŏ'). Lake (*hu* in Anhwei and Kiangsu provs., E China; traversed by the Hwang Ho.

Hunkyar İskelesi. See UNKIAR-SKELESSI.

Hun'se (hŭn'sĕ). River ab. 50 m. long in Netherlands; flows NW through Drenthe and Groningen provs. into Lauwer Zee.

Huns'rück (hŏŏns'rük). Mountainous region, W Germany, in North Rhine-Westphalia state bet. Moselle and Nahe rivers, extending SW from the Rhine to French border; highest peak 2677 ft. Occupied by Allies Mar. 1945.

Hunstanton, New. See NEW HUNSTANTON.

Hunt (hŭnt). County in Texas. See *Table* at TEXAS.

Hunt, Mount. Peak 10,775 ft. in S Grand Teton National Park, NW Wyoming.

Hun'te (hŏŏn'tĕ). River ab. 117 m. long in Lower Saxony state, Germany; rises in hills E of Osnabrück and flows into Weser river near Bremen.

Hun'ter (hŭn'tēr). Navigable river 300 m. long, E New South Wales, SE Australia, flows E to South Pacific Ocean at Newcastle.

Hunter, Cape. Cape on SW coast of Guadalcanal I., SE Solomon Is., W Pacific Ocean.

Hun'ter·don (hŭn'tēr·d'n; -dŭn). County in New Jersey. See *Table* at NEW JERSEY.

Hun'ter Island (hŭn'tēr). **1** Island off NW Tasmania. See HUNTERS ISLANDS.

2 Island off W coast of British Columbia, Canada, opp. mouth of Dean Channel.

3 Tract of land surrounded by rivers in W Ontario prov., Canada, on Minnesota border E of Rainy Lake; in Quetico Provincial Park.

Hunter Mountain. Peak 4025 ft. in Catskill Mts., Greene co., SE New York.

Hunter Peak. Mountain 8442 ft. on E boundary of Idaho co., N cen. Idaho.

Hun'ter's Bay (hŭn'tērz). Inlet of Bay of Bengal on W coast of Burma, SE of Akyab and E of Boronga Is.

Hunter's Hill. Town, E New South Wales, SE Australia, NW suburb of Sydney, N of Parramatta river; pop. 8988.

Hun'ter's Island (hŭn'tērz). Former island in Long Island Sound off E coast of the Bronx, New York City; attached to Bronx borough and now made part of mainland by filled-in area.

Hun'ters Islands (hŭn'tērz). Group of islands off Cape Grim, the NW point of Tasmania, Australia; comprises Hunter, Three Hummock, and Robbins Is. and many islets.

Hun'ting·burg (hŭn'tĭng·bûrg). Industrial city, Dubois co., SW Indiana, 38 m. ENE of Evansville; pop. 4146; clay deposits; pottery, wagons.

Hun'ting·don (hŭn'tĭng·dŭn). **1** County in Pennsylvania. See *Table* at PENNSYLVANIA.

2 Industrial borough, ⊗ of Huntingdon co., S cen. Pennsylvania, 22 m. E of Altoona; pop. 7234; platted 1767; machines, boilers, sewer pipe, radiators, stationery; Juniata College (1876; coed.).

3 Town, ⊗ of Carroll co., W Tennessee; pop. 2119.

4 County, Quebec, Canada. See *Table* at QUEBEC.

5 Town, ⊗ of Huntingdon co., S Quebec, Canada, 40 m. SW of Montreal; pop. 2806.

6 County, E cen. England. See HUNTINGDONSHIRE.

7 Municipal borough, ⊗ of Huntingdonshire, E cen. England, on the Great Ouse 58 m. N of London; pop. 5282; breweries, engineering works, market gardens; birthplace of Oliver Cromwell.

Hun'ting·don·shire (hŭn'tĭng·dŭn·shĭr; -shēr) *or* **Huntingdon** *or* **Hunts** (hŭnts). County, E cen. England; area 366 sq. m.; pop. (1951) 69,273; ⊗ Huntingdon; other towns St. Ives, Ramsey, Old Fletton; rivers Nene and Ouse; agriculture, livestock raising.

Hun'ting·ton (hŭn'tĭng·tŭn). **1** County in Indiana. See *Table* at INDIANA.

2 City, ⊗ of Huntington co., NE Indiana, 22 m. SW of Fort Wayne; pop. 16,185; grain elevators, limestone quarries; Huntington Coll. (1897; coed.; United Brethren in Christ).

3 Town, Hampshire co., W Massachusetts, 16 m. WNW of Springfield; pop. 1392.

4 Residential village (pop. 11,255), with **Huntington Station** (pop. 23,438) included in **Huntington** town (pop. 126,221; settled 1653), Suffolk co., SE New York, on N shore of Long I.; Nathan Hale captured near here by British 1776.

5 City, Cabell and Wayne cos., W West Virginia, ⊗ of Cabell co., on Ohio river ab. 50 m. W of Charleston; pop. 83,627; tobacco and agricultural (esp. apples) market; railroad terminus; coal mines, gas wells; manufactures nickel and nickel alloys, steel rails, stoves, glass, shoes; Marshall Univ. (1837; coed.).

Huntington Beach. City, Orange co., SW California, on Pacific Ocean 14 m. SE of Long Beach; pop. 11,492; oil wells.

Huntington Lake *and* **Huntington Lake Dam.** See SAN JOAQUIN river, California.

Huntington Park. Industrial city, Los Angeles co., SW California, 4 m. S of Los Angeles; pop. 29,920; incorporated as city 1906.

Huntington Woods. Residential city, Oakland co., SE Michigan, 11 m. from Detroit; pop. 8746.

Hunt Mountain (hŭnt). **1** Peak 8232 ft. in Blue Mts., Baker co., E Oregon.

2 Peak 10,151 ft. in E Big Horn co., N Wyoming.

Hunts (hŭnts). See HUNTINGDONSHIRE.

Hunts Peak. 1 Mountain 12,466 ft., Sangre de Cristo Mts., S Colorado, on boundary bet. Fremont and Saguache cos. S of Salida.

2 = OURAY PEAK.

Hunts'ville (hŭnts'vĭl). **1** City, ⊗ of Madison co., N Alabama, 23 m. NE of Decatur; pop. 72,365; varied manufactures; natural-gas wells; Marshall Space Flight Center nearby (to SW). Oakwood College (1896; coed.). Settled 1805 around Big Spring (now in center of city); chartered as town 1811, first settlement in Alabama to receive charter, and as city 1844; site of Alabama constitutional convention and temporary ✻ 1819; burned by Federal troops 1862.

2 City, ⊗ of Madison co., NW Arkansas; pop. 1050.

3 City, ⊗ of Randolph co., N cen. Missouri, 7 m. W of Moberly; pop. 1526.

4 Village, ⊗ of Scott co., N Tennessee; pop. (est.) 700.

5 City, ⊗ of Walker co., E Texas, 47 m. E of Bryan; pop. 11,999; manufactures cottonseed oil, lumber, furniture; Sam Houston State Teachers Coll. (1879; coed.). Home and grave of Gen. Sam Houston.

6 Town, Muskoka dist., SE Ontario, Canada, 20 m. N of Bracebridge; pop. 3286; fishing and summer resort.

Hun'za (hŏŏn'zȧ). **1** River ab. 90 m. long, N Kashmir, N India; flows W from E Karakoram Range, then S to join the Gilgit at Gilgit.

2 District, N Kashmir, N India, now in Gilgit; 8000 sq. m.; pop. 32,000; with Nagar constituted two small states that in frontier troubles with Russia (end of 19th cent.) were occupied by British (Hunza-Nagar expedition of 1891); inhabited by a Dard race.

3 Village in Hunza dist., on Hunza river.

4 Pass 8000 ft. from the Hunza valley over Karakoram Mts. to the Pamirs and Chinese Turkistan.

Hu'on (hū'ŏn). **1** River ab. 90 m. long, S Tasmania, Australia; flows E and S through wide estuary to D'Entrecasteaux Channel; navigable to Huonville; its banks the home of the Huon pine (*Dacrydium franklinii*). **2** Municipality, SE Tasmania. See HUONVILLE.

Huon Gulf. Large inlet of Solomon Sea on SE coast of North-East New Guinea, just N of boundary of Territory of Papua and S of Huon Penin.; site of Lae, Salamaua, and Morobe.

Huon Islands. Small group of barren islands in E Coral Sea, 170 m. NNW of New Caledonia; dependency of New Caledonia; guano deposits.

Huon Peninsula. Peninsula ab. 55 m. wide on SE coast of North-East New Guinea; bordered by Huon Gulf on S; scene of severe fighting, esp. around Finschhafen and Sattelberg, Sept.–Nov. 1943.

Hu'on·ville (hū'ŏn·vĭl). Town in Huon municipality, SE Tasmania, Australia, at head of navigation on Huon river 17 m. SW of Hobart; pop. (municipality) 5037; fruit-growing center.

Hu'pei' *or* **Hu'peh'** (hōō'pā'; *Chin.* hōō'bĕ'). Province, E cen China; 80,169 sq. m.; pop. 25,541,636; ✻ Wuhan; bounded on N by Honan, on E by Anhwei, on S by Kiangsi and Hunan, and on W by Szechwan and Shensi. In S crossed from W to E by the Yangtze; contains Yangtze Gorges (*q.v.*) in W; in center crossed by the Han flowing SE to the Yangtze. Hilly, with lakes and swamps in the two river valleys; bordered on N, W, and SW by mountain ranges 7000 to 10,000 ft. Has some coal and iron resources; because of its central location on the Yangtze, important industrially and politically. Chief cities the Wuhan group (Wuchang, Hankow, and Hanyang), Ichang, Shasi, Kiangling, and Siangyang. In early times roughly coextensive with state of Chu; later formed N part of Hukwang which was divided by the Emperor K'ang-hsi (reigned 1662–1722) into the modern provinces of Hupeh and Hunan.

Hurd, Cape (hûrd). Cape, SE Ontario prov., Canada, at end of Bruce Penin., on S side of channel connecting Georgian Bay and Lake Huron.

Hur'ley (hûr'lĭ). **1** Mining town, Grant co., SW New Mexico, ab. 9 m. SE of Silver City; pop. 1851. **2** City, ⊗ of Iron co., N Wisconsin, on Michigan border 32 m. ESE of Ashland; pop. 2763; formerly important logging town, locale for Edna Ferber's *Come and Get It*; ships iron ore.

Hur'ling·ham (hûr'lĭng·hăm; *Span.* ōōr'lĕng·än'). Town in Argentina, a suburb of Buenos Aires.

Hu'ron (hūr'ŭn). **1** River ab. 90 m. long, SE Michigan; flows from Oakland co. SW, then curves SE into Lake Erie at SE corner of Wayne co. **2** Name of counties in two states of the U.S. See *Tables* at MICHIGAN and OHIO. **3** Village and resort, Erie co., N Ohio, on Lake Erie 8 m. ESE of Sandusky; pop. 5197; ships coal, iron ore, fish. **4** City, ⊗ of Beadle co., E cen. South Dakota, 47 m. N of Mitchell; pop. 14,180; settled 1879; became city 1883; railroad division point; meat packing, food processing; Huron Coll. (1883; coed.). **5** County, Ontario, Canada. See *Table* at ONTARIO.

Huron, Lake. Lake in U.S. and Canada, 2d in size of the five Great Lakes (*q.v.*); bounded on N and E by province of Ontario, Canada, and on S and W by Michigan, the U.S.-Canada boundary passing through it; ab. 206 m. long, area 23,000 sq. m.; greatest depth 750 ft.; elevation 580 ft.; at NW end connected through Straits of Mackinac with Lake Michigan, and through St. Marys river with Lake Superior, and at SE end through St. Clair river, Lake St. Clair, and Detroit river with Lake Erie. See GEORGIAN BAY; NORTH CHANNEL; SAGINAW BAY.

Huron Bay. Inlet of Lake Superior in NE Baraga co., NW Michigan penin.

Hur'ri·cane (hûr'ĭ·kān; -kĭn). City, Washington co.,

SW corner of Utah, 38 m. S of Cedar City; pop. 1251.

Hurricane Mountain. Peak 3687 ft. in the Adirondack Mts., Essex co., NE New York.

Hurst (hûrst). City, Tarrant co., N Texas, NE of Fort Worth; pop. 10,165.

Hurstmonceux. See HERSTMONCEUX, village in East Sussex, England.

Hurst'ville (hûrst'vĭl). City, E New South Wales, SE Australia, S suburb of Sydney W of Botany Bay; pop. 22,667.

Hürt'gen (hürt'gĕn). Town, W Germany, E of Aachen W of the Rur river; nearby **Hürtgen Forest** scene of severe fighting Sept. 1944.

Hu'ru·nu'i (hōō'rōō·nōō'ē). River ab. 80 m. long in NE South I., New Zealand; flows E into South Pacific Ocean N of Pegasus Bay.

Hú'sa·vĭk' (hōō'sä·vēk'). Point on NE coast of Iceland.

Hu'şi (hōōsh; hōō'shĕ). City, Moldavia region, NE Romania, near Prut river; pop. 16,792; in a tobacco and grape-growing region; episcopal see; cathedral built 1441 by Stephen of Moldavia. By Treaty of Prut signed here July 21, 1711, Peter the Great gave Azov back to the Turks.

Hu'si·nec (hōō'sĭ·nĕts); *Ger.* **Hu'si·netz** (hōō'zĕ·nĕts). Village, SW Bohemia, Czechoslovakia, W of České Budějovice; birthplace of John Huss.

Hus'kvar'na (hōōs'kvär'nà). Town, Jönköping prov., S Sweden, at S end of Lake Vättern E of Jönköping; pop. 10,266.

Hus·sein'–Dey' (hōō-sĭn'dā'; -sän'-). Southeast suburb of city of Algiers, N Algeria; pop. 15,152.

Hu'sum (hōō'zōōm). Seaport and manufacturing town on W coast of Schleswig-Holstein, western Germany; pop. (1939) 14,549; ab. 2½ m. from the North Sea, its harbor formed by canalization of the **Hu'su·mer Au** (-zōō·mĕr ou'); trades in cattle; oyster fisheries.

Huszt. See KHUST.

Hutch'in·son (hŭch'ĭn·s'n). **1** Counties in two states of the U.S. See *Tables* at SOUTH DAKOTA and TEXAS. **2** Industrial city, ⊗ of Reno co., cen. Kansas, on Arkansas river 42 m. WNW of Wichita; pop. 37,574; flour mills, grain elevators, salt plants, oil wells and natural gas deposits; extensive salt mines. **3** City, McLeod co., S cen. Minnesota, 48 m. S of St. Cloud; pop. 6207; agriculture, dairying.

Hutch'in·sons Island (hŭch'ĭn·s'nz). Island in Atlantic Ocean, off coast of St. Lucie co., E cen. Florida.

Huth'waite (hōōth'wāt; hōōth'-; hŭth'-). Urban district, Nottinghamshire, N cen. England, SW suburb of Mansfield; pop. (1931) 5092; since 1935 part of Sutton in Ashfield urban district.

Hu–tsên. See SHANGHAI.

Huy (ü·ē'). Manufacturing commune, Liège prov., E Belgium, on Meuse river ab. 15 m. SW of Liège; pop. 14,155; paper mills; ruins of abbey of Neufmoustier founded by Peter the Hermit.

Huy'ton with Ro'by (hī't'n, rō'bĭ). Urban district, Lancashire, NW England, 7 m. E of Liverpool; pop. 55,783.

Hü·yük' (hü·yük'); *formerly* **Eu·yuk'** (ü·yük'). Ruins, Çorum vilayet, N cen Turkey; ab. 100 m. ENE of Ankara; remains of a large Hittite building include walls decorated with relief carvings and a gateway on each side of which is a huge block, its front face carved in the shape of a sphinx, its inner face bearing a relief carving of a two-headed eagle.

Hva'ler (vä'lĕr), *or* **Whale Islands** (hwāl). Group of small islands in Oslo Fjord, SE Norway.

Hvar (kvär); *Ital.* **Le'si·na** (lâ'zĭ·nä); *anc.* **Phar'us** (fär'ŭs). **1** Dalmatian island in Adriatic Sea off SW coast of Yugoslavia; formerly included in Primorje co., Yugoslavia; now (since 1945) in Bosnia and Herzegovina federated republic; area ab. 111 sq. m.; pop. ab. 21,000; grapes, olives, figs, dates; marble; chief towns Hvar, its ✻, and Stari Grad. Settled by Greeks ab. 390 B.C.; occu-

pied from 7th cent. by Slavs; has at different times been under rule of Venice, Hungary, France, and Austria; occupied for a time by Italians 1918 but later annexed to Yugoslavia; occupied again by Italians 1941.
2 Town and seaport, its ✳, at W end of the island; pop. (1921) 3568; bishopric; Franciscan monastery; beautiful Venetian buildings, including a fine loggia.

Hven or **Hveen** (vän). Swedish island in Öresund, off SW coast of Sweden; home of Tycho Brahe.

Hvít′á′ (hwē′tau′), or **White** (hwīt) **River.** River ab. 150 m. long in cen. and SW Iceland; flows SW into Atlantic Ocean.

Hwa, or **Hua, Shan** (hwä′ shän′). Mountain ab. 3000 ft. in S cen. Shensi prov., NE cen. China, E of Sian in the Chin Ling Shan; one of the five sacred mountains of China.

Hwai (hwī). River ab. 350 m. long in S Honan and NW Anhwei provs., E China; flows into the Hwang Ho above Hungtze Hu (lake); has many tributaries watering a rich agricultural region. See Hwang Ho.

Hwai′ning′ (hwī′nĭng′) or **An′king′** (än′kĭng′), also **Ngan′king′** (gän′kĭng′). City, ✳ of Anhwei prov., E China, on N bank of Yangtze bet. Hankow and Nanking, 280 m. WSW of Shanghai (370 m. by river); pop. ab. 110,000; ravaged by Taipings 1852; occupied by Japanese 1938; its Great Pagoda (7 stories) one of finest in Yangtze valley.

Hwai′yin′ (hwī′yĭn′). City, cen. Kiangsu prov., E China, just E of Hungtze Hu (lake) on the Grand Canal; important commercial center.

Hwa′jung′ (hwä′rŏong′). City, N Hunan, SE cen. China, on N shore of Tungting Hu (lake); scene of fighting bet. Japanese and Chinese Mar. 1943.

Hwang Hai. See Yellow Sea.

Hwang Ho (hwäng′ hō′; _Chin._ hǔ′) or **Yel′low River** (yĕl′ō). River (ho) ab. 2700 m. long, N cen. and E China, 2d largest in country; navigable as far as Lanchow; rises in Amne Machin Shan, SE Tsinghai, at ab. 14,000 ft.; flows E and NE across Kansu, then N as E boundary of Ningsia; at 40°N makes a great bend flowing E across Suiyuan, Inner Mongolia, then S bet. Shensi and Shansi, receiving the Fen tributary from the E; at Tungkwan in E Shensi receives the Wei and turns directly E through gorges along N Honan border. Its lower course across the Great Plains has shifted many times through the centuries, vitally affecting 35,000,000 acres of rich farmland; for more than 500 years before 1852 its outlet was Yellow Sea in Kiangsu; from 1852 to 1938 its course NE from near Kaifeng across Shantung past Tsinan to Gulf of Po Hai; in 1938 again diverted, this time by Chinese military action against the Japanese invaders, from near Chenghsien in Honan SE across Honan and Anhwei to unite with the Hwai, passing through Hungtze Hu (lake) to its old bed in Kiangsu and its new mouth 250 m. farther S; in 1947 turned back to its old bed through Shantung. Because of its frequent disastrous floods, called "China's Sorrow."

Hwangpoo. Var. of Hwang Pu.

Hwang Pu (hwäng′ pōō′), _formerly_ **Whang′poo′.** River ab. 100 m. long, S Kiangsu prov., E China; one of the outlets of Tai Hu; flows NE past Shanghai (q.v.) to enter mouth of the Yangtze at Woosung.

Hwei (hwā). River ab. 200 m. long in N China; a headstream of the Etsin (q.v.).

Hweichow. See Sihsien.

Hwei′li′ (hwā′lē′). Town, SE Sikang, S China, N of the Yangtze ab. 120 m. NNW of Kunming; station in mountainous region on highway from Tali to Chengtu.

Hwei′tseh′ (hwā′dzǔ′); _formerly_ **Tung′chwan′** (dŏong′chwän′). City, NE Yunnan, S China, near the Yangtze 100 m. N of Kunming; pop. ab. 20,000.

Hwic′ce (hwĭk′kĕ). Ancient Anglo-Saxon kingdom, SW cen. England; probably included Worcestershire, S Warwickshire, most of Gloucestershire (not extreme W part) and region around Bath, N Somersetshire.

Hy′a·lite Peak (hī′á·līt). Mountain 10,110 ft. in S cen. Gallatin co., S Montana.

Hy·an′nis (hǐ·ǎn′ǐs). **1** Town, S Barnstable co., SE Massachusetts; part of Barnstable town; pop. 5139; trading center for Cape Cod summer resorts.
2 Village, ⊗ of Grant co., W Nebraska; pop. 373.

Hyannis Port. Town, Barnstable co., SE Massachusetts, on Nantucket Sound; summer resort.

Hy′atts·ville (hī′ǎts·vĭl). City, Prince Georges co., S cen. Maryland, 7 m. NE of Washington; pop. 15,168.

Hya′ty (yä′tê). Town, Guairá dept., S cen. Paraguay; pop. ab. 5340.

Hy′bla or **Hybla Ma′jor** (hī′blá mā′jĕr). Ancient town in Sicily, on S slope of Mt. Etna; considered by many scholars to be the modern Paternò; famous for its honey.

Hybla Heraea. See Ragusa commune.

Hy′da·burg (hī′dá·bûrg). Town on W coast of Prince of Wales I., SE Alaska, opp. N end of Dall I.; pop. 251.

Hydaspes. See Jhelum.

Hyde (hīd). **1** Name of counties in two states of the U.S. See _Tables_ at North Carolina and South Dakota.
2 Municipal borough, Cheshire, NW England, on the Tame 9 m. ESE of Manchester; pop. 31,498; textile mills.

Hy′den (hī′d'n). City, ⊗ of Leslie co., SE Kentucky; pop. 348.

Hyde Park (hīd). **1** Former town, Norfolk co., E Massachusetts, since 1912 part of Boston.
2 Residential village, Dutchess co., SE New York, on E bank of Hudson river ab. 6 m. N of Poughkeepsie; pop. 1979; settled by Dutch 1741; Franklin D. Roosevelt Library (opened 1941); birthplace of Franklin Delano Roosevelt, 32d president of the U.S.
3 Village, ⊗ of Lamoille co., N Vermont; pop. 474.
4 Park in W cen. London, England; area ab. 364 acres; recreation center; known esp. as favorite place for open air meetings.

Hy′der·a·bad′ or **Hai′dar·a·bad′** (hī′dĕr·á·băd′; -băd′; _native_ hâ′dŭr·ä·bäd′). **1** _often called_ **Ni·zam′s′ Do·minions** (nǐ·zämz′; -zämz′). Former Indian state, since 1956 a part of Andhra Pradesh, cen. Deccan, S cen. India; bounded on N and NE by Berar, on S and SE by Madras, and on W by Bombay; mountainous in some parts, has many fertile plains; chief rivers Godavari, Wardha, Penganga, Kistna, and Tungabhadra. Chief products cereals, cotton, tobacco, fruits.
History: In ancient kingdom of Golconda (q.v.); on overthrow of Golconda by Aurangzeb 1687, became part of Mogul Empire; ruled since 1713 by nizams, beginning with Asaf Jah, Mogul governor of the Deccan, who founded independent kingdom in 1724; after 1748 scene of rivalry over succession in which British and French supported different candidates; ceded to British Northern Circars 1766 and, in 1853, the "Assigned Districts" which later became Berar (q.v.). Refused to enter Indian Union 1947 but yielded under threat of force 1948.
2 Walled city, its ✳, now ✳ of Andhra Pradesh, in NW part, on Musi river 310 m. NNW of Madras; pop. (1941) 739,159 (including Secunderabad and suburbs); pottery works, paper factories, and carpet and textile mills; nizam's palace, the Char Minar (or Four Minarets), and several mosques and tombs; Osmania Univ., Nizam Coll. (affiliate of Madras Univ.). At adjacent Secunderabad is a large military cantonment. Founded 1589 by ruler of Golconda; suffered a disastrous flood 1908 and serious depopulating pestilences and influenza epidemics since 1911.
3 City, Sind, SW Pakistan, on E bank of Indus river 120 m. N of its mouths and ab. 100 m. NE of Karachi; pop., with cantonment, (1941) 127,521; rail center; noted for handicrafts: silk, gold, and silver embroidery, lacquer and enamel ware, and pottery. In its fort are mosques, palaces, and the arsenal. Founded 1768 by Ghulam Shah Kalhora; capital of Sind till 1843 when it surrendered to the British.

Hy′dra (hī′drȧ; *Mod. Gr.* ē′t̤hrä); *anc.* **Hyd′re·a** (hĭd′-rê·ȧ). **1** Greek island in S Aegean Sea 4 m. off E coast of Peloponnesus; ab. 11 m. long, area 20 sq. m.; pop. 3729; belongs to Argolis and Corinth dept.; refuge in 16th and 17th cents. of persecuted peoples from the mainland, who developed shipbuilding and commerce; fleets and patriotism of Hydriotes in War of Independence (1821–29) of great value to Greek cause.
2 Its chief town, port on N coast of island; pop. 3547.

Hydraotes. See RAVI.

Hydruntum. See OTRANTO.

Hy·ères′ (yâr). Commune, Var dept., SE France, near the Mediterranean 32 m. S of Draguignan; pop. 26,378; winter resort; market gardens. Founded 10th cent.

Hyères Islands; *Fr.* **Îles d'Hy·ères′** (ēl′ dyâr′). French island group in the Mediterranean Sea off SE coast of France, SE of Toulon; group includes Port Cros, Île du Levant, and the fortified island of Porquerolles. Occupied by Allies Aug. 14–15, 1944.

Hyko Range. See HIKO RANGE.

Hy·met′tus (hī·mĕt′ŭs). Mountain ridge 3370 ft. just E and SE of Athens, Attica and Boeotia dept., Greece; famed for honey and for a marble used in building ancient Athens.

Hynd′man Peak (hīnd′mȧn). Mountain 12,078 ft. in S Custer co., cen. Idaho.

Hyo·go *or* **Hio·go** (hyō·gô). **1** Prefecture of Japan. See *Table* at JAPAN.
2 Town. See KOBE.

Hypanis. 1 River, SW Russia, Europe. See KUBAN.
2 River, SW Ukraine, U.S.S.R. See BUG.

Hyphasis. See BEAS.

Hypsas. See CRIMISUS.

Hypseloreitēs. See IDA.

Hyrcania. See ASTERABAD province.

Hyrcanum Mare. See CASPIAN SEA.

Hy′rum (hī′rŭm). City, Cache co., N Utah, 8 m. S of Logan; pop. 1728; farming.

Hy′sham (hī′shăm). Town, ⊗ of Treasure co., SE cen. Montana; pop. 494.

Hythe (hīt̤h). Municipal borough, Kent, SE England, on Strait of Dover 10 m. WSW of Dover; pop. 9218; one of the Cinque Ports; market town for agricultural section; summer resort.

I

Iadera. See ZADAR.

Ia'lo·mi'ţa (yä′lô·mē′tsä) *or* **Ia'lo·mi'tsa.** River ab. 140 m. long, SE Romania; rises in the Transylvanian Alps NW of Ploeşti and flows S and E into Danube river.

Ialpug. See YALPUKH.

I·al'y·sus (ĭ·ăl′ĭ·sŭs). Ancient city. N Rhodes, SE Aegean Sea; ruins just SW of town of Rhodes; a city of the Pentapolis of Asia Minor.

I'ao (ē′ou), *or* **Wai·lu'ku** (wī·lōō′kōō), **Valley.** Canyon ab. 5 m. long and 4000 ft. deep on slope of Mt. Puu Kukui, W Maui I., Hawaiian Is.

I'a·pyg'i·a (ī′à·pĭj′ĭ·à). Ancient Greek name of SE Italy, the part in the "heel" of the boot.

Ia'şi (yäsh; yä′shê) *or* **Jas'sy** (yäs′ê). Commercial city, NE Romania, in Moldavia, on a tributary of Prut river; pop. (1939 est.) 104,471; archbishopric; university; national theater. Capital of Romania before 1861 when government was moved to Bucharest; suffered in various wars; burned by Tatars 1513, by Turks 1538, and by Russians 1686; Treaty of Jassy ending Catherine the Great's second war with Turkey signed here Jan. 9, 1792; temporary capital of Romania in World War I; taken by Russians Aug. 25, 1944 in World War II.

I'ax·ar'tes (ĭ′ăk·sär′tēz). = JAXARTES.

I'ba (ē′bä). 1 Mountain 5265 ft., E Zambales prov., Luzon, Phil. Is.

2 Municipality, ✳ of Zambales prov., Luzon, Phil. Is., on coast 85 m. NW of Manila; pop. 8299; good anchorage at mouth of river.

I·ba'dan (ê·bä′dän). City, Oyo prov., W Western Region, Nigeria, ab. 70 m. NE of Lagos (ab. 120 m. by rail); pop. 387,133, (1959 est.) 500,000; ✳ of the Western Region; largest Negro city in Africa; inhabitants mostly Yorubas.

I·ba·gué' (ē′vä·gā′). City, ✳ of Tolima dept., W cen. Colombia; pop. 27,448; on high plain (alt. 4300 ft.) ab. 60 m. W of Bogotá; founded 1550.

I'ba·jay' (ē′bä·hī′). Municipality, NW Capiz prov., Panay, Phil. Is., on coast 43 m. WNW of Capiz; pop. 22,740.

Ibañeta, Puerto. See RONCESVALLES.

I'bar (ē′bär). River ab. 130 m. long, Serbia, cen. Yugoslavia; rises in North Albanian Alps in Montenegro and flows N to the Western Morava near Kraljevo.

I·ba·ra·ki (ê·bä·rä·kê). Prefecture of Japan. See *Table* at JAPAN.

I·bar'ra (ê·vär′rä). Town, ✳ of Imbabura prov., N Ecuador, 55 m. NNE of Quito; pop. (1944 est.) 13,798; alt. 7340 ft.; founded by Álvaro de Ibarra, president of Quito, 1597; has suffered from volcanic eruptions of Imbabura and from earthquakes; nearby Huayna Capac, father of Atahualpa, won two decisive victories, adding to his realm a large part of Ecuador.

I·be'ri·a (ī·bēr′ĭ·à). 1 Parish in Louisiana. See *Table* at LOUISIANA.

2 Ancient Hispania; the Iberian Penin.

3 Ancient region S of the Caucasus Mts., bordering Colchis on W, Albania on E, and Armenia on S; corresponds nearly with modern Soviet republic of Georgia. Iberians, as allies of Mithridates VI, were defeated by Pompey.

I·be'ri·an Peninsula (ī·bēr′ĭ·ăn). Peninsula, SW Europe, occupied by Spain and Portugal; in Roman times, Hispania; so called from name applied by early Greeks to people dwelling by the river Iberus (*mod.* Ebro) in Spain.

Iberus. See EBRO.

I'ber·ville (ī′bēr·vĭl; ē′bēr-; *Fr.* ē′bĕr′vēl′). 1 Parish in Louisiana. See *Table* at LOUISIANA.

2 County, Quebec, Canada. See *Table* at QUEBEC.

3 Town, ⊗ of Iberville co., on Richelieu river 23 m. SE

of Montreal; pop. 5185; agricultural implements, artificial silks, carriages.

I'bi·cuí' *or* **I'bi·cu·hy'** (ē′vê·kwē′). 1 River ab. 400 m. long, Rio Grande do Sul state, S Brazil; flows W to Uruguay river on Argentina boundary.

2 *or* **I'by·cuí'** (ē′vê·kwē′). Town, Paraguarí dept., S Paraguay; pop. ab. 14,350; mineral deposits of magnetic iron, hydric oxide, and brown hematite.

Ibiza. See IVIZA.

I'bo (ē′vōō). Small Portuguese island off NE coast of Mozambique; site of **Ibo,** former capital of Cabo Delgado dist., N Mozambique.

Ib'ra (ĭb′rà). Inland town, Oman, SE Arabia, WNW of Sur; pop. ab. 5000.

I·bu·su·ki (ê·bōō·sōō·kê). Town, Kagoshima prefecture, S Kyushu I., Japan, on W side of entrance to Kagoshima Bay; pop. (1945) 25,608.

I'ca (ē′kä). 1 River 120 m. long, Ica dept., SW Peru; flows SW into Pacific Ocean.

2 Department of Peru. See *Table* at PERU.

3 City, its ✳, on Ica river, 170 m. SE of Lima; pop. (1940 est.) 21,437; cotton, sheep, vineyards; original city founded 1563, twice destroyed by earthquakes.

I·çá' (ê·sà′). Name of Putumayo river in Brazil.

I·ca'cos Point (ê·kä′kôs). Tip of peninsula at SW corner of island of Trinidad.

I·ça'na (ê·sä′nà); *in Colombia* **I·sa'na** (ê·sä′nä). River rising in E Colombia and flowing E and SE into the Rio Negro, NW Brazil, above confluence of the Uaupés with the Rio Negro.

I·car'i·a (ī·kâr′ĭ·à). 1 Island. See IKARIA.

2 Ancient town, Attica, Greece; ruins on N slope of Mt. Pentelikon.

I·car'i·an Sea (ī·kâr′ĭ·ăn); *Lat.* **I·car'i·um Ma're** (ī·kâr′ĭ·ŭm mā′rē). The part of the Aegean Sea bet. the islands of Patmos and Leros and the coast of Asia Minor. According to legend Icarus fell into the sea here.

Ice Bay (īs). Inlet of Indian Ocean ab. 30 m. wide in coast of Antarctica, bet. Enderby Land on E and Queen Maud Land on W, in ab. 67°45′S and 50°E.

Ice Fjord. Inlet ab. 70 m. long of Arctic Ocean, W coast of West Spitsbergen. See ADVENT BAY.

I·çel' (ê·chĕl′) *or* **I·chi·li'** (ê·chê·lē′). 1 Vilayet, S Turkey in Asia, part of ancient Cilicia; 5582 sq. m.; pop. 244,236; ✳ Mersin.

2 City. See MERSIN.

Ice'land (īs′lănd); *Dan.* **Is'land** (ēs′län); *Icelandic* **Ís'land** (ēs′länt). Island bet. North Atlantic and Arctic Oceans, 155 m. SE of Greenland and 570 m. W of Norway; separated from Greenland by Denmark Strait and from Norway by Norwegian Sea; bet. lat. 63°24′ and 66°33′N and long. 13°31′ and 24°30′W; greatest length from E to W ab. 290 m.; area 39,709 sq. m.; pop. (1930) 108,861; ✳ Reykjavík. Roughly oval with coast line ab. 3730 m. long, indented by many long fiords; Faxa Bay on W coast and Húna Bay and Breidi Fjord on either side of base of large peninsula (average alt. 2000 ft.) on NW; mostly tableland, esp. in SE where great snow field of Vatnajökull (average elevation 2000–3000 ft.) covers 3300 sq. m.; highest point Öraefajökull 6429 ft.; more than 100 volcanoes, which have created great lava fields, most noted Mt. Hekla 4747 ft.; 120 glaciers; lowland forms ab. ¼ of area and is only part habitable and only ab. ½ of land is productive; has suffered from destructive earthquakes; many small streams, lakes, and hot springs; fisheries most valuable industry. Chief towns Reykjavík, Akureyri, Hafnarfjördur (near Reykjavík), Vestmannaeyjar (on island off S coast).

History: Settled by Norwegians in second half of 9th cent. A.D. (date usually given as 874); founded the Althing (national assembly) 930; adopted Christianity 1000; united with Norway 1262, with Denmark 1380; by

Act of Union 1918, became independent kingdom in personal union with Denmark; placed under British and American military occupation in World War II; British forces landed May 10, 1940, American marines July 7,

ICELAND
Statute Miles
0   50

1941, both with permission; American North Atlantic naval base for rest of war. Proclaimed intention not to renew 1918 Act of Union with Denmark, the action being voted in plebiscite May 24, 1944; independent republic proclaimed June 17, 1944.

I'chang' (ē'chäng'). Walled city, S Hupeh prov., E cen. China, at head of navigation of the Yangtze 1000 m. from the East China Sea and 170 m. W of Hankow (387 m. by river); pop. (1931 est.) 107,940; made treaty port by Chefoo Convention 1876; transshipment point for goods to and from Szechwan through Yangtze Gorges (*q.v.*); airport.

Ichang Gorges. = YANGTZE GORGES.

Ichili. See İÇEL.

I·chi·no·mi·ya (ē·chē·nō·mē·yä). Town, Aichi prefecture, SE Honshu, Japan, ab. 11 m. NNW of Nagoya; pop. 53,376; 7th-cent. Shinto shrine.

I·chin'ska·ya Sop'ka (ĭ·chēn'skà·yà sôp'kà). Volcano (*sopka*) 11,834 ft. in cen. part of Central Range, Kamchatka Penin., Khabarovsk Territory, Soviet Russia, Asia.

Ichow. See LINI.

Ick'nield Street (ĭk'nēld'). Ancient highway of S cen. England, probably a Roman road; extended W from near Bury St. Edmunds through Wantage to Cirencester and Gloucester.

I·cod' (ē·kôth'). Commune on NW Tenerife I., W Canary Is., 28 m. WSW of Santa Cruz de Tenerife; in Santa Cruz de Tenerife prov., Spain; pop. 13,263; agricultural products; silk.

Iconium. 1 See KONYA.
2 See RUM.

Icosium. See ALGIERS seaport city.

Iculisma. See ANGOULÊME.

I'cu·tú', Mount (ē'kōō·tōō'). Peak ab. 11,000 ft. in cen. Venezuela.

I'cy Bay (ī'sĭ). Inlet of Gulf of Alaska, SE Alaska, W of Yakutat Bay.

Icy Cape. Cape on NW coast of Alaska, ab. 161°30'W, 70°15'N.

Icy Strait. Strait, SE Alaska; joins Chatham Strait and Glacier Bay.

I'da (ī'dà). 1 County in Iowa. See *Table* at IOWA.
2 *mod.* **Kaz'da·ğı'** (käz'dä·ĭ'). Famous mountain in NW Asia Minor, SE of site of ancient Troy and along N shore of Gulf of Adramyttium; actually a range (**Ida Mountains**), highest point 5810 ft.; in Homeric legend an abode of the gods.
3 *mod.* **Psi'lo·ri'ti** (psē'lô·rē'tē); *Gr.* **Hy'pse·lo·rei'tēs** (ē'psĕ·lô·rē'tēs). Highest mountain in Crete, in cen. part, 8195 ft.; in early times closely connected with worship of Zeus.

I'da·bel (ī'dà·bĕl'). City, ⊗ of McCurtain co., SE corner of Oklahoma; pop. 4967; farming, lumbering.

I'da Grove (ī'dà). City, ⊗ of Ida co., W Iowa, 28 m. S of Cherokee; pop. 2265.

I'da·ho (ī'dà·hō). 1 A northwest state of U.S.A., 43d state admitted to Union (1890); bounded on N by British Columbia in Canada, on E by Montana and Wyoming, on S by Utah and Nevada, on W by Oregon and Washington; 13th state in area, 83,557 sq. m. (land area 82,769 sq. m.); 42d state in population, 667,191; ✳ Boise. See *Table of States* at UNITED STATES. Divided into the following 44 counties (for pronunciation of their names, see their individual entries):

NAME	LOCATION	AREA[1]	POP.[1]	CO. SEAT
Ada	SW	1,046	93,460	Boise
Adams	W	1,377	2,978	Council
Bannock	SE	1,124	49,342	Pocatello
Bear Lake	SE corner	988	7,148	Paris
Benewah	NW	791	6,036	St. Maries
Bingham	SE	2,072	28,218	Blackfoot
Blaine	S cen.	2,649	4,598	Hailey
Boise	W cen.	1,913	1,646	Idaho City
Bonner	N	1,736	15,587	Sandpoint
Bonneville	SE	1,846	46,906	Idaho Falls
Boundary[2]	N	1,275	5,809	Bonners Ferry
Butte	SE cen.	2,240	3,498	Arco
Camas	S cen.	1,057	917	Fairfield
Canyon	SW	580	57,662	Caldwell
Caribou	SE	1,747	5,976	Soda Springs
Cassia	S	2,544	16,121	Burley
Clark	E	1,751	915	Dubois
Clearwater	NE	2,522	8,548	Orofino
Custer	cen.	4,933	2,996	Challis
Elmore	SW cen.	3,062	16,719	Mountain Home
Franklin	SE	667	8,457	Preston
Fremont	E	1,819	8,679	St. Anthony
Gem	SW	555	9,127	Emmett
Gooding	S	722	9,544	Gooding
Idaho	N cen.	8,515	13,542	Grangeville
Jefferson	E	1,089	11,672	Rigby
Jerome	S	593	11,712	Jerome
Kootenai	N	1,256	29,556	Coeur d'Alene
Latah	NW	1,090	21,170	Moscow
Lemhi	E cen.	4,585	5,816	Salmon
Lewis	W	478	4,423	Nezperce
Lincoln	S	1,203	3,686	Shoshone
Madison	E	473	9,417	Rexburg
Minidoka	S	750	14,394	Rupert
Nez Perce	W	847	27,066	Lewiston
Oneida	S	1,191	3,603	Malad City
Owyhee	SW corner	7,648	6,375	Murphy
Payette	SW	403	12,363	Payette
Power	SE	1,411	4,111	American Falls
Shoshone	NE	2,609	20,876	Wallace
Teton	E	459	2,639	Driggs
Twin Falls	S	1,942	41,842	Twin Falls
Valley	W cen.	3,678	3,663	Cascade
Washington	W	1,475	8,378	Weiser
Yellowstone National Park (part)	E	58[3]		

[1] Area = land area in sq. m. Pop. from 1960 Census.
[2] Northernmost county, bordering Canada (Brit. Columbia) on N, Montana on E, Washington on NW.
[3] Main part of Yellowstone National Park is within Wyoming state boundaries (2930.8 sq. m.), with adjacent strips in Montana (258.9 sq. m.) and Idaho (57.6 sq. m.). Total area with inland water 3419 sq. m.

Nickname: Gem State, also Gem of the Mountains. *State flower:* Syringa. *Motto:* Esto Perpetua (May She Endure Forever). *Chief cities:* Boise, Idaho Falls, Pocatello, Twin Falls. *Rivers:* Snake, flowing from SE region W to Oregon border, then N forming boundary bet. Idaho and Oregon; Salmon, rising in cen. region, flowing N and then W across the state and emptying into the Snake. *Lakes:* Pend Oreille and Coeur d'Alene in N, American Falls Reservoir in SE. *Highest peak:* Borah 12,655 ft., in Custer co. *Chief industries:* Mining (esp. lead, silver, zinc), lumbering, sheep raising, agriculture (esp. potatoes and fruit).

History: First white exploration by Lewis and Clark expedition 1805; held by United States and Great Britain jointly until by treaty 1846 Great Britain gave United States sole possession south of 49th parallel; included in Oregon Territory 1848; part N of 46°, included in Washington Territory 1853; gold discovered 1860; crossed by

Oregon Trail; organized as separate territory 1863; admitted to Union July 3, 1890; early adopted woman suffrage.

2 County in Idaho. See *Table* at IDAHO.

Idaho City. Village, ⊗ of Boise co., W cen. Idaho; pop. 188; founded 1862 during a gold rush; said to have had at one time a population of 30,000, which declined as mining claims were worked out.

Idaho Falls. City, ⊗ of Bonneville co., SE Idaho, on Snake river 50 m. NNE of Pocatello; pop. 33,161; ships esp. potatoes, wheat, and sugar beets.

Idaho Springs. Resort city, Clear Creek co., N cen. Colorado, 30 m. W of Denver; pop. 1480; mining center; thermal mineral springs.

Idalia. See YALIAS river.

I·da'li·um (ĭ·dā'lĭ·ŭm); *mod.* **Da'li** (dä'lĕ). Village, E cen. Cyprus, on Yalias river; site of ancient temple, sacred to Aphrodite.

I'dar (ē'dẽr). **1** Former Indian state, NE Western India States, Indian Union; 1668 sq. m.; pop. (1941) 307,798; at one time in Mahi Kantha Agency; joined Union of Rajasthan June 26, 1947.

2 Town, its ✳, 55 m. NNE of Ahmadabad; pop. 5635.

Idar–Oberstein. See OBERSTEIN.

I'den·burg (ē'd'n·bûrg). **1** *Du.* **I'den·burg Top'pen** (ē'dĕn·bûrκ tôp'ĕn). Peaks (*toppen*) in Nassau Range of Snow Mts., W West Irian, Indonesia; highest 15,748 ft. **2** (*Du,* ē'dĕn·bûrκ) River, NE West Irian, Indonesia. See TARITATOE.

Id'fu (ĭd'fōō) *or* **Ed'fu** (ĕd'fōō). Town on Nile river, Upper Egypt, lat. 25°N; pop. ab. 15,000; ancient ruins; famous for its temple of Horus, almost wholly preserved, begun by Ptolemy III Euergetes 237 B.C. and not finally completed until 57 B.C.

I·djen' *or* **I·jen'** (ė·jĕn'). Old crater forming a plateau with many volcanoes on E end of Java, Indonesia; highest points Raung 10,932 ft. and Merapi, an active volcano, 9184 ft.

I'dle·wild' (ī'd'l·wīld'). Locality, SW Long I., in Queens co., New York, on NE shore of Jamaica Bay; world's largest airfield (now **John F. Kennedy International Airport**), 7 sq. m.; opened 1948.

Id'lib (ĭd'lĭb). Commercial town, NW Syria, 35 m. SW of Alep; pop. ab. 20,000.

I'dri·ja (ē'drė·yä); *Ital.* **I'dri·a** (ē'drė·ä). Mining commune, W Slovenia, NW Yugoslavia, 20 m. ENE of Gorizia; pop. 10,317; formerly in Venezia Giulia, Italy; 16th-cent. castle; mercury mines (discovered 1490); produces cinnabar.

Id·u·mae'a *or* **Id'u·me'a** (ĭd' û·mē'à; ĭ'dū-). Name given by Greeks and Romans to the country of the Edomites (see EDOM) who, after being driven westward by the Nabataeans c. 300 B.C., settled in S Judaea.

I'du·ty'wa Reserve (ē'dōō·tī'wà). A district of Transkei (*q.v.*), E Cape Province, S Republic of So Africa; pop. 36,392; chief town **Idutywa,** NE of Butterworth.

Ie *or* **Ie Shi·ma** (ė·yĕ shē·mä). Small island (*shima*) ab. 4 m. off W coast of cen. Okinawa I., Ryukyu Is., Japan; island and Japanese air field at Ie village occupied by U.S. forces Apr. 16–20, 1945; American war correspondent Ernie Pyle killed here Apr. 18.

Ie'per (yā'pẽr); *Fr.* **Y'pres** (ē'pr'; *popularly in World War I,* wi'pẽrz). Commune, West Flanders prov., NW Belgium; pop. 15,680; famous as a commercial center in medieval times, esp. in the cloth-weaving industry; said to have had a population of 200,000 in 13th cent., when the Cloth Hall (Les Halles) and church of St. Martin were built; a border town, subject to many sieges, and therefore gradually declined; in World War I in one of most fiercely contested areas of entire war and scene of three great battles: Oct. 19–Nov. 22, 1914, Apr. 22–May 25, 1915, and July 31–Nov. 1917; completely destroyed but rebuilt.

I·er'ne (ī·ûr'nė). Ancient name of Ireland, from the Greek.

Ie Shima. See IE.

Ie'si (yâ'zē); *anc.* **Æ'sis** (ē'sĭs). Commune, Ancona prov., Marches, cen. Italy, 16 m. WSW of Ancona; pop. (1931) 28,793; episcopal see; birthplace of Emperor Frederick II.

Ie'so·lo (yâ'zō·lô). Commune, Venezia prov., Venezia Euganea, NE Italy, on Gulf of Venice 20 m. E by N of Venice; pop. (1931) 10,438.

If (ĕf). Small island off S coast of France, near Marseilles; site of famous fortress prison Château d'If.

I'fa·lik (ē'fä·lēk). Island of the Caroline Is., W Pacific Ocean, ab. halfway bet. Truk and Yap.

I'fe (ē'fä). Town, Oyo prov., Western Region, Nigeria, E of Ibadan; pop. 24,170.

Iferten. See YVERDON.

If'ni (ĭf'nĭ). Coastal district, SW Morocco, NW Africa; 741 sq. m., pop. ab. 20,000; an overseas province of Spain, ✳ Sidi Ifni; occupied nominally by Spain from 1860; boundaries fixed 1912 by treaty with France; Spanish occupation became real 1934; limits reduced by French government 1935.

Iforas, Adrar des. See ADRAR.

I'fu·ga'o (ē'fōō·gä'ô). Subprovince, SE Mountain Province, Luzon, Phil. Is.; 975 sq. m.; pop. 68,598; ✳ Kiangan; western two thirds mountainous with some high peaks, esp. Pulog (*q.v.*); E third sloping to Magat river on SE border thinly inhabited; chief product rice; under Spaniards region known as Kiangan; part of Nueva Vizcaya prov. 1902–08; created a subprovince of Mountain Province 1908.

Igabrum. See CABRA.

I·gar'ka (ĭ·gär'kà). Town on Yenisei river, SW Taimyr National District, Soviet Russia, Asia, ab. 850 m. N of Krasnoyarsk; pop. ab. 18,000.

I'gi·di', Erg (ĕrg' ē'gē·dē'). Var. of *Erg Iguidi:* see El ERG.

Igilgili. See DJIDJELLI.

Igilium. See GIGLIO.

Iglau. See JIHLAVA.

I·gle'sias (ė·glä'zyäs). Commune, Cagliari prov., S Sardinia, near W coast 32 m. WNW of Cagliari; pop. 21,720.

Igló. See SPIŠSKÁ NOVÁ VES.

Ig'ri·dir' (ē'rĭ·dîr'; *Turk.* ē'ė·rė·dẽr'). Var. of EĞRIDIR.

I·gua·çú' (ė·gwà·sōō'). Temporary territory of S Brazil 1943–46.

I·gua'la (ė·gwä'lä). Town, Guerrero state, S Mexico, ab. 50 m. SSW of Cuernavaca in silver-mining district; pop. 12,756. Plan of Iguala, with the three guarantees: religion, independence, union, proclaimed here Feb. 24, 1821 by Agustín de Iturbide.

I'gua·la'da (ē'gwä·lä'thä). Manufacturing city, Barcelona prov., NE Spain, 32 m. WNW of Barcelona; pop. 15,603; textile mills, ironworks; ruins of ancient city walls; 12 m. to the E is the Montserrat (*q.v.*) with its famous monastery.

I·guas·su' *or* **Iguaçu** (ė·gwà·sōō'); *Span.* **I'gua·zú'** (ē'gwä·sōō'). River ab. 380 m. long, S Brazil; flows W in Paraná state and empties into the Alto Paraná on border of NE Argentina, forming small section of Argentina-Brazil boundary; ab. 16 m. from its junction with the Paraná are **Iguassu Falls,** ab. 2½ m. wide, composed of more than twenty cataracts averaging 200 ft. high and separated from each other by masses of rock and tree-covered islands; formerly called **Victo'ri·a Falls** (vĭk·tōr'ĭ·à).

Iguidi, Erg. See El ERG.

Iguvium. See GUBBIO.

I'hing' (ē'hĭng'). Town, S Kiangsu prov., E China, near W shore of Tai Hu (lake) 28 m. S of Wutsin; noted for a reddish-yellow pottery (boccaro) introduced into Europe by the Portuguese.

Ihú. See YHÚ.

Ii'sal·mi (ē'säl·mĭ). Town, S cen. Finland, in Kuopio dept., on railroad 50 m. N of Kuopio; pop. 3564; lumbering.

I·je'bu (ĕ·jä'bōō). **1** Province of Nigeria. See *Table* at NIGERIA.
2 *or* Ijebu–O'de (-ō'dä). Town, its *, 45 m. NE of Lagos; pop. 27,909.

Ijen. See IDJEN.

IJ·mui'den (ī·moi'dĕ[n]). Town, in Velsen commune, North Holland prov., W Netherlands, at mouth of North Sea Canal; pop. 27,939; noted in prewar times as fishing town; bombed during World War II; port for German torpedo boats.

IJs'sel (ī'sĕl); *Eng.* Ijs'sel *or* Ys'sel (ī'sĕl); *anc.* Sa'la (sä'lä). Navigable river in Netherlands, 70 m. long, the N mouth of the Rhine; flows N out of Neder Rijn in E Netherlands to IJsselmeer; its ancient name applied to inhabitants along its banks, the *Salian* Franks.

IJs'sel·meer' (ī'sĕl·mār'); *Eng.* Lake Ijssel *or* Ysel. The former Zuider Zee (*q.v.*), reduced in size as result of reclamation of Wieringermeer (*q.v.*) and the NE polder; eventually will comprise only N section of former Zuider Zee; receives IJssel river from the SE.

IJs'sel·mon'de (ī'sĕl·mȏn'dĕ); *also* Ijs'sel·mon'de. Island in Maas delta, South Holland prov., SW Netherlands; diked since 13th cent.

I'ka·ri'a (ē'kä·rē'ä) *or* Ni'ka·ri'a (nyē'-) *or* Ka'ri·ot' (kä'rē·ȏt'); *anc.* I·car'i·a (ī·kâr'ī·ȧ). Island in Aegean Is., ab. 13 m. WSW of Samos; by some included among Southern Sporades (see SPORADES); 99 sq. m.; pop. 11,913; administratively a part of Samos dept., Greece.

I·ki (ē·kē). Island in Tsushima Strait, bet. Tsushima and NW coast of Kyushu, Japan; 53 sq. m.; pop. (1945) 45,340; administratively a part of Nagasaki prefecture; chief town Mushozu; overrun by Mongols in 13th cent.

I'ki·run' (ē'kē·rōōn'). Town, Oyo prov., Western Region, Nigeria, just N of Oshogbo; pop. 23,874.

I·la'gan (ē·lä'gän). Municipality, * of Isabela prov., Luzon, Phil. Is., on Cagayan river where the Abuluan joins it, 84 m. S of Aparri; pop. 31,323.

I·la'la (ē·lä'lä). District, NE Zambia, S of Lake Bangweulu.

I-lan (ē'län'); *Jap. official name* San'hsing' (sän'-shǐng'). Treaty port, N Kirin prov., E Manchuria, on right bank of Sungari river where it is joined by the Mutan, ab. 190 m. NE of Harbin; pop. ab. 50,000; furs, lumber; steamer connections to Russian towns.

I·la'wa (ē·lä'vä); *Ger.* Deutsch–Ey'lau (doich'ī'lou). Town, Olsztyn dept., N Poland, formerly in East Prussia, Germany, 87 m. SSE of Kaliningrad (Königsberg); pop. (1946) 13,948; lumber, potato meal, machinery; cattle markets; railroad junction point.

Ilebo. See PORT FRANCQUI.

Île–de–France *or* Isle–de–France (ēl'dĕ·fräns'). Historical region of N cen. France; bounded anciently on N by Picardy, E by Champagne, S by Orléanais, W by Normandy; * Paris; political center of old France; made a province in middle of 15th cent.

Île de France. See MAURITIUS.

Île' de la Ci'té' (ēl' dĕ lä sē'tä'). Small island in Seine river, Paris, France, on which the city of Paris was first settled; Cathedral of Notre Dame, Palais de Justice.

Île des Pins. See KUNIE.

Île d'Orléans. See ORLEANS.

Île du Le·vant' (ēl' dül·vän'). One of the Hyères Is. (*q.v.*).

I·lek' (ī·lyĕk'). River ab. 300 m. long, Soviet Russia; rises in W Kazakh S.S.R. and flows NW to the Ural, its lower course forming part of S boundary of Chkalov Region.

Ile Per'rot' (ēl' pĕ'rō'); *Fr.* Île Per'rot' (ēl' pĕ'rō'). Island in St. Lawrence river SW of Montreal I., Quebec prov., E Canada; administratively a part of Vaudreuil co., Quebec; lies bet. Lake of Two Mountains and Lake St. Louis; connected by bridges with Montreal I. and with mainland at Vaudreuil.

Ilerda. See LÉRIDA.

Île Rouad. See ARWAD.

Île Rousse. = L'ÎLE ROUSSE.

Îles de la Madeleine. See MAGDALEN ISLANDS.

Îles de la Société. See SOCIETY ISLANDS.

Îles de Loos. See LOS ISLANDS.

Îles du Salut. See SAFETY ISLANDS.

Îles du Vent. See WINDWARD ISLANDS, Society Is.

I·le'sha (ĕ·lĕsh'ȧ). Town, Western Region, Nigeria, SE of Oshogbo; pop. 21,892.

Îles Loyauté. See LOYALTY ISLANDS.

Îles Marquises. See MARQUESAS ISLANDS.

Îles Scilly. See SCILLY ISLES, W Society Is.

Îles sous le Vent. See LEEWARD ISLANDS.

I·let'ska·ya Za·shchi'ta (ī·lyĕt'skä·yȧ zŭsh·chē'tȧ); *formerly* I·letsk' (ī·lyĕtsk'). Town, Chkalov Region, Soviet Russia, Europe, S of Chkalov; pop. (1926) 11,058; saltworks; health resort.

Il'ford (il'fẽrd). Municipal borough, Essex, SE England, NE suburb of London on the Roding; pop. 131,061, (1951) 184,707; is a part of Greater London; paper mills; photographic materials.

Il'fra·combe' (il'frä·kōōm'). Urban district, Devonshire, SW England, on Bristol Channel 57 m. N of Plymouth; pop. 9218; seaside resort.

I'lha Gran'de Bay (ē'lyä grȧnn'dĕ). Inlet of Atlantic Ocean on S coast of Rio de Janeiro state, SE Brazil.

Ilhas do Cabo Verde. See CAPE VERDE ISLANDS.

I·lha'vo (ĕ·lyä'vōō). Commune, Aveiro dist., NW Portugal, on coastal lagoon 3 m. SW of Aveiro; pop. 11,250; fisheries, saltworks; glass, china.

I·lhé'us (ĕ·lyâ'ōōs). City, SE coast of Baía state, E Brazil, 120 m. S of Baía; pop. (1940 est.) 15,707; exports large percentage of Brazil's cacao crop.

I'li (ē'lē). **1** River ab. 800 m. long, NW Sinkiang prov., W China, flowing into SW end of Lake Balkhash, Kazakh S.S.R.; formed by Kunges and Tekes rivers in N ranges of the Tien Shan; in China flows through fertile valley, settled since early times; in U.S.S.R. chief town on its banks is Ili, above which it is navigable for ab. 280 m. in rainy season.
2 Formerly a district, its E part now in Sinkiang; contested for by Russia and China but became Chinese by treaty 1881.

Il·i·am'na (il'ī·ȧm'nȧ). Village at NE end of Iliamna Lake, SW Alaska.

Iliamna Lake. Lake 80 m. long by 25 m. broad, SW Alaska, W of Cook Inlet.

Iliamna Peak. Volcano 10,085 ft., SW Alaska, on W side of Cook Inlet.

Ilici. See ELCHE.

I·li'gan (ĕ·lē'gän). Municipality, N Lanao prov., Mindanao, Phil. Is., on SE shore of Iligan Bay 17 m. N of City of Dansalan; pop. 28,273; chief port on N coast; scene of uprising in Philippine Revolution 1896.

Iligan Bay. Inlet 25 to 40 m. wide of S Mindanao Sea, N coast of Mindanao, Phil. Is.; its SW arm is the long Panguil Bay.

I·limsk' (ī·lyĕmsk'). Town, cen. Irkutsk Region, Soviet Russia, Asia, on I·lim' (ī·lyĕm') river (tributary of Angara, ab. 240 m. long); on N branch of Trans-Siberian R.R.

I·lin' Island (ĕ·lēn'). Island off SW coast of Mindoro, Phil. Is.; 30 sq. m.; pop. 1376; S of Mangarin Bay, where American forces made a landing Dec. 15, 1944.

I'li·ni'za (ē'lē·nē'sä). Peak 17,394 ft. in Andes Mts., Ecuador.

Il'i·on (il'ī·ǔn). Village, Herkimer co., NE cen. New York, on Mohawk river 11 m. ESE of Utica; pop. 10,199; forms single community with Mohawk, Herkimer, and Frankfort; firearms and ammunition, typewriters, office equipment.

Il'i·on (il'ī·ȏn). See TROY ancient city, Asia Minor.

I·li'o Point (ĕ·lē'ō). Point, NW Molokai I., Hawaii, on Kaiwi Channel.

Il'i·pa (il'ī·pȧ). Town of ancient Baetica, S Spain, ab. 60 m. N of Hispalis (*mod.* Seville); scene 206 B.C. of victory

of Scipio Africanus over the Carthaginians whose power in Spain was broken; battle famous for superb military tactics.

I·lis′sus (ĭ-lĭs′ŭs; ī-). Short river, Attica and Boeotia dept., E cen. Greece, S of Athens; flows into the Cephisus.

Ilium. See TROY ancient city, Asia Minor.

Il′kes·ton (ĭl′kĕs·tŭn). Municipal borough, Derbyshire, N cen. England, 8 m. WNW of Nottingham; pop. 33,674; lace, silk, hosiery, earthenware; iron and coal mines.

Ilk′ley (ĭlk′lĭ). Urban district, West Riding, Yorkshire, N England; pop. 17,265; health resort; Roman remains.

Il′ku·ri Shan (ĭl′kōō-rĭ shän′). Mountain range in N Manchuria connecting N ends of Great Khingan Mts. and Little Khingan Mts.; forms a watershed bet. Nonni and Kumara rivers.

Ill (ĭl). River ab. 40 m. long, Tirol-Vorarlberg prov., SW Austria, flowing NW into Rhine NW of Feldkirch.

Ill (ĭl). River 123 m. long, Haut-Rhin and Bas-Rhin depts., NE France, flowing into Rhine.

Il·lam′pu (ê-yäm′pōō). One peak 21,276 ft. of Mount Sorata, W Bolivia. Cf. ANCOHUMA.

Il·la′na Bay (ê-yä′nä). Inlet of Moro Gulf on W coast of Mindanao, Phil. Is.; ab. 45 m. wide at mouth; receives in SE the waters of the Rio Grande de Mindanao.

Il′la·pel′ (ē′yä-pĕl′). Inland town, Coquimbo prov., cen. Chile, 100 m. N of Valparaíso; pop. 6085.

Il′la·war′ra (ĭl′á·wŏr′á). District, SE New South Wales, SE Australia; extends along the coast 40 m. from ab. 30 m. S of Sydney; dairying; coal and iron; bet. its chief towns, Kiama and Wollongong, is **Illawarra Lake**, a salt lagoon 9 m. long and 3 m. wide, connected with the sea by narrow channel.

Ille (ēl). River, Ille-et-Vilaine dept., NW France, flowing S to the Vilaine at Rennes.

Il′le·cil′le·waet (ĭl′ê-sĭl′ê-wĭt). **1** Glacier in Selkirk Mts. in Glacier Park, Brit. Columbia, Canada; its ice field drops 3600 ft. into the valley.
2 River flowing from its foot into Columbia river near Revelstoke.

Ille′–et–Vi′laine′ (ēl′ā·vê′lĕn′). Department of France. See *Table* at FRANCE.

Il′ler (ĭl′êr). River ab. 100 m. long, S Germany; rises in Tirol and flows N through Bavaria and along boundary of Baden-Württemberg into the Danube near Ulm.

Illiberis. See ELNE.

Il′li·lou·ette′ Falls (ĭl′ĭ-lōō-ĕt′). Waterfall 370 ft. in Yosemite National Park, E cen. California.

Il′li·ma′ni (ē′yê·mä′nê). Mountain in W Bolivia, E of La Paz; highest peak 21,184 ft.

Il′li·nois′ (ĭl′ĭ-noi′; *less often*, -noiz′). **1** Navigable river 273 m. long, Illinois; formed by confluence of Des Plaines and Kankakee rivers in Grundy co., SW of Joliet, NE Illinois, flows diagonally SW across Illinois to empty into the Mississippi in W Illinois; upper waters (Des Plaines river) connected by ship canal with Lake Michigan (see ILLINOIS WATERWAY).
2 A north central state of U.S.A., 21st state admitted to Union (1818); bounded on N by Wisconsin, on E by Lake Michigan and Indiana, on SE and S by Kentucky, on SW by Missouri, and on W by Missouri and Iowa; 24th state in area, 56,400 sq. m., not including 1526 sq. m. of water of the Great Lakes (land area 55,935 sq. m.); 4th state in population, 10,081,158; ✳ Springfield. See *Table of States* at UNITED STATES. Divided into the following 102 counties (for pronunciation of their names, see their individual entries):

NAME	LOCATION	AREA[1]	POP.[1]	CO. SEAT
Adams	W	866	68,467	Quincy
Alexander	SW corner	224	16,061	Cairo
Bond	SW cen.	383	14,060	Greenville
Boone	N	283	20,326	Belvidere
Brown	W	307	6,210	Mount Sterling
Bureau	N	868	37,594	Princeton
Calhoun	W	259	5,933	Hardin
Carroll	NW	468	19,507	Mount Carroll
Cass	W cen.	370	14,539	Virginia

NAME	LOCATION	AREA[1]	POP.[1]	CO. SEAT
Champaign	E cen.	1,000	132,436	Urbana
Christian	cen.	709	37,207	Taylorville
Clark	E	505	16,546	Marshall
Clay	SE cen.	464	15,815	Louisville
Clinton	SW cen.	498	24,029	Carlyle
Coles	E cen.	507	42,860	Charleston
Cook	NE	954	5,129,725	Chicago
Crawford	E	442	20,751	Robinson
Cumberland	SE cen.	347	9,936	Toledo
De Kalb	N	636	51,714	Sycamore
De Witt	cen.	399	17,253	Clinton
Douglas	E cen.	420	19,243	Tuscola
Du Page	NE	331	313,459	Wheaton
Edgar	E	628	22,550	Paris
Edwards	SE	225	7,940	Albion
Effingham	SE cen.	483	23,107	Effingham
Fayette	S cen.	718	21,946	Vandalia
Ford	NE cen.	488	16,606	Paxton
Franklin	S	434	39,281	Benton
Fulton	W cen.	874	41,954	Lewistown
Gallatin	SE	328	7,638	Shawneetown
Greene	W	543	17,460	Carrollton
Grundy	NE	432	22,350	Morris
Hamilton	SE	435	10,010	McLeansboro
Hancock	W	797	24,574	Carthage
Hardin	SE	183	5,879	Elizabethtown
Henderson	W	381	8,237	Oquawka
Henry	NW	826	49,317	Cambridge
Iroquois	E	1,122	33,562	Watseka
Jackson	SW	603	42,151	Murphysboro
Jasper	SE cen.	495	11,346	Newton
Jefferson	S	574	32,315	Mount Vernon
Jersey	W	374	17,023	Jerseyville
Jo Daviess	NW corner	614	21,821	Galena
Johnson	S	345	6,928	Vienna
Kane	NE	516	208,246	Geneva
Kankakee	NE	680	92,063	Kankakee
Kendall	NE	320	17,540	Yorkville
Knox	W	728	61,280	Galesburg
Lake	NE corner	457	293,656	Waukegan
La Salle	N	1,153	110,800	Ottawa
Lawrence	SE	374	18,540	Lawrenceville
Lee	N	729	38,749	Dixon
Livingston	NE cen.	1,043	40,341	Pontiac
Logan	cen.	622	33,656	Lincoln
McDonough	W	582	28,928	Macomb
McHenry	N	611	84,210	Woodstock
McLean	cen.	1,173	83,877	Bloomington
Macon	cen.	577	118,257	Decatur
Macoupin	SW cen.	872	43,524	Carlinville
Madison	SW	731	224,689	Edwardsville
Marion	S cen.	580	39,349	Salem
Marshall	N cen.	395	13,334	Lacon
Mason	cen.	541	15,193	Havana
Massac	S	246	14,341	Metropolis
Menard	cen.	312	9,248	Petersburg
Mercer	NW	556	17,149	Aledo
Monroe	SW	380	15,507	Waterloo
Montgomery	S cen.	706	31,244	Hillsboro
Morgan	W cen.	565	36,571	Jacksonville
Moultrie	cen.	345	13,635	Sullivan
Ogle	N	757	38,106	Oregon
Peoria	NW cen.	624	189,044	Peoria
Perry	SW	443	19,184	Pinckneyville
Piatt	cen.	437	14,960	Monticello
Pike	W	829	20,552	Pittsfield
Pope	SE corner	381	4,061	Golconda
Pulaski	S	204	10,490	Mound City
Putnam	N cen.	166	4,570	Hennepin
Randolph	SW	594	29,988	Chester
Richland	SE	364	16,299	Olney
Rock Island	NW	420	150,991	Rock Island
Saint Clair	SW	670	262,509	Belleville
Saline	SE	384	26,227	Harrisburg
Sangamon	cen.	880	146,539	Springfield
Schuyler	W	434	8,746	Rushville
Scott	W	251	6,377	Winchester
Shelby	cen.	772	23,404	Shelbyville
Stark	NW cen.	291	8,152	Toulon
Stephenson	N	568	46,207	Freeport
Tazewell	cen.	653	99,789	Pekin
Union	SW	414	17,645	Jonesboro
Vermilion	E	898	96,176	Danville
Wabash	SE	221	14,047	Mount Carmel
Warren	W	542	21,587	Monmouth
Washington	SW	565	13,569	Nashville
Wayne	SE	715	19,008	Fairfield
White	SE	501	19,373	Carmi
Whiteside	NW	690	59,887	Morrison
Will	NE	845	191,617	Joliet
Williamson	S	429	46,117	Marion
Winnebago	N	520	209,765	Rockford
Woodford	N cen.	537	24,579	Eureka

[1] Area = land area in sq. m. Pop. from 1960 Census.

Nickname: Prairie State; also Sucker State. *State flower:* Violet. *Motto:* State Sovereignty—National Un-

ion. *Chief cities:* Chicago, Rockford, Peoria, Springfield, East St. Louis. *Rivers:* Mississippi, forming W boundary; Ohio, forming SE boundary; Wabash, forming lower section of E boundary; Illinois (see 1, above). *Highest point:* Charles Mound 1241 ft., in Jo Daviess co. *Chief industries:* Agriculture, meat packing, petroleum production, manufacturing (esp. iron and steel, agricultural implements).

History: Explored by Marquette and Jolliet 1673 and by La Salle who erected Fort Crèvecœur on Illinois river 1680; included in French Louisiana; ceded by France to England 1763 and by England to U.S. 1783; Virginia, Massachusetts, and Connecticut claims to territory given up by 1786; part of Northwest Territory 1787 and of Indiana Territory 1800; organized as separate territory which included present Wisconsin and eastern part of Minnesota 1809; admitted to Union as state Dec. 3, 1818 with capital at Kaskaskia (capital transferred to Vandalia 1820 and to Springfield 1837); adopted present constitution 1870.

Illinois Bayou. Bayou ab. 75 m. long in Pope co., NW cen. Arkansas, draining SW into Arkansas river; has three headstreams (middle, east, and west forks).

Illinois Waterway. Combined system of rivers, canals, and state recreation areas, NE Illinois, with Chicago at N end; comprises: **Illinois and Michigan Canal** 96 m. long, from Chicago river to La Salle on Illinois river, opened 1848, discontinued 1900; South Branch of Chicago river, connected by **Chicago Drainage Canal** 28 m. long with Lockport on Des Plaines river, opened 1900, by which current was reversed and the flow of sewage directed into the Illinois river; **Sanitary and Ship Canal,** new name of improved Chicago Drainage Canal after its acquisition 1930 by the Federal government.

Illiturgis. See ANDÚJAR.

Ill'kirch-Graf'fen·sta'den (ĭl'kĭrk·gräf'ĕn·shtä'dĕn). Commune, Bas-Rhin dept., NE France, on Ill river; pop. (1931) 7739; suburb of Strasbourg; scene of signing of capitulation of Strasbourg to Louis XIV 1681.

Íl'lo·ra (ē'[l]yô·rä). Commune, Granada prov., S Spain, 15 m. WNW of Granada; pop. 13,458; textiles, soap, liquors; Moorish castle.

Il·lyr'i·a (ĭ·lĭr'ĭ·à). Ancient country comprising E Adriatic coast and its hinterland; inhabited by Illyrians, a Balkan people, loosely united, who practiced piracy on Roman shipping; after series of wars beginning with one in 229–228 B.C., finally overthrown 35–33 B.C. by Romans who established large province of Illyricum; furnished many soldiers for the Roman legions, several of whom became emperor (Claudius II, Diocletian, etc.); prefecture of Illyricum (*q.v.*) erected by Diocletian (d. 313 A.D.); region occupied by south Slavs in 6th cent. (see BALKAN STATES); practically coextensive with Illyrian Provinces (*q.v.*); kingdom of Illyria, comprising Carinthia, Carniola, and Küstenland, a division of Austria 1816–49.

Illyrian Provinces. The division of the empire formed by Napoleon from the Austrian lands (beyond the Sava river) which France acquired by Treaty of Schönbrunn 1809; included Carinthia, Carniola, Gorizia, Istria, part of Croatia, Dalmatia, Ragusa (see DUBROVNIK), and the Ionian Is.; * Ljubljana; although reconquered by Austria in 1813 and formally restored to her in 1815, reformed government aroused Illyrian (later Yugoslav) nationalism.

Il·lyr'i·cum (ĭ·lĭr'ĭ·kŭm). **1** Roman province with shifting boundaries, in ancient Illyria; roughly coextensive with W Yugoslavia; established 9 A.D. by Tiberius. See ILLYRIA.
2 Roman prefecture of 4th cent. A.D. including most of the Balkan Penin. (Dacia, Macedonia, Epirus, Thessaly, Achaea) and Crete.

Il'men (ĭl'mĕn; *Russ.* ēl'y'·myĕn·y'). Shallow lake 300 to 700 sq. m., Novgorod Region, NW Soviet Russia, Europe; receives Lovat and Msta rivers; outlet the

Volkhov; in World War II came under control of Germans Aug. 21, 1941; recovered by Russians Jan.–Feb. 1944.

Il'me·nau (ĭl'mĕ·nou). City, Thuringia, E Germany, 24 m. S of Erfurt; pop. 13,612; resort; manufactures glass, thermometers, porcelain, wooden goods, toys, dyes; residence of Goethe.

I'lo (ē'lô). Port, Moquegua dept., S Peru, 53 m. SE of Mollendo; connected by railroad with Moquegua, 60 m. N.

I'lo·bas'co (ē'lô·väs'kô). City, El Salvador, 40 m. NE of San Salvador; pop. 21,225; cattle raising, coffee, sugar, and indigo.

I·lo'cos Nor'te (ē·lō'kôs nôr'tå). Province, NW Luzon, Phil. Is.; 1308 sq. m.; pop. 237,586; * Laoag; coast line regular with few good harbors; on N coast are Bangui and Pasaleng Bays and Cape Bojeador; in E is N end of Cordillera Central with highest point Mt. Sicapoo 7743 ft.; plains and low hills along W coast; only large river the Laoag; produces esp. rice; weaving, stock raising, fishing; plains inhabited mainly by Ilokanos, mountain region by Tinggian, Igorot, and Apayaos. Chief towns Laoag, Dingras, and Batac.

History: Region probably known in pre-Spanish times to Chinese and Japanese traders; all NW Luzon known as Ilocos by Spaniards and created as a province by them; explored as early as 1572 by Juan de Salcedo; N part detached 1818 and created as Ilocos Norte prov.; revolted many times against Spanish injustices, esp. 1589, 1660, 1788, and was active during 1898–99; civil government established Sept. 1901; region came under Japanese control Dec. 1941.

Ilocos Sur (sōōr'). Province, NW Luzon, Phil. Is., forming a narrow strip along coast of South China Sea widening at S end; 1037 sq. m.; pop. 271,532; * Vigan; has greatest density of population of all provinces of Phil. Is.; coast line fairly regular, but with frequent reefs; land comparatively level, except in SE; E boundary formed by coast range, a W part of Cordillera Central; highest point ab. 3600 ft.; only large river lower course of the Abra; little agriculture because of poor soil; best crop maguey; inhabitants mostly Ilokanos, engaged in manufacture and trade. Chief towns Vigan, Narvacan, Candon, and Cabugao.

History: See ILOCOS NORTE; created a province 1818 but of much larger area including parts of Abra and La Union; contains several old towns antedating Spanish times; revolts against Spanish authority, esp. in 1660 and 1763, successful for a time; civil government established Sept. 1901; came under control of Japanese Dec. 1941.

I'log (ē'lôg). Municipality, SW Negros Occidental, Negros, Phil. Is., near coast on **Ilog River** (ab. 40 m. long, flowing NNW from Negros Oriental) 45 m. S of City of Bacolod; pop. 20,957; an old town, settled 1584; center of sugar industry.

I'lo·i'lo (ē'lô·ē'lô). **1** Province, S and NE Panay I., Phil. Is.; 2048 sq. m.; pop. 744,022; * City of Iloilo; includes Guimaras I. (*q.v.*); one of most populous provinces of the Archipelago; coast line quite irregular, esp. in E and SE, with many small islands; cen. and E parts level, NE hilly, W mountainous; largest stream the Jalaur; chief industry agriculture with main crops sugar and rice; timber and other forest products; weaving; inhabitants Visayans. Chief towns Iloilo, Janiuay, Santa Barbara, Pototan, and Miagao.

History: Probably first settled on SW coast by Malay datos and their followers in pre-Spanish times; Spaniards made first visits about the time of Legaspi 1565; region suffered in 16th and 17th cents. from Moro raids; original province covered entire island; parts taken to form Capiz 1716 and Antique 1798; grew rapidly in 19th cent.; given up to Revolutionary government 1898; civil government established Apr. 1901.

2 *officially* **City of Iloilo.** Chartered city, * of Iloilo

ILLINOIS

Statute Miles

0 10 20 30 40 50

⊛ State Capital

PUBLISHED BY G & C MERRIAM COMPANY
SPRINGFIELD, MASS.
PREPARED BY J. W. CLEMENT CO., BUFFALO, N. Y.

Longitude West from Greenwich

prov., in SE part on Iloilo Strait; pop. 90,480; fifth city in size in Philippines and second to Manila in commercial importance; did not acquire a leading position until 1688; often raided by Moro pirates but because of prosperity of province declared a port for foreign trade 1855; manufacturing and cultural center; suffered much during Japanese occupation 1942–45.

Iloilo Strait. Narrow channel 1 to 5 m. wide bet. S Panay I. and N Guimaras I., Phil. Is.; at W end broadens out to ab. 25 m. wide; Iloilo and Jordan are on it.

I'lo·pan'go (ē'lô·päng'gô). Volcanic lake 5½ m. long, cen. El Salvador; islands have at times appeared in it.

I'lo·rin' (ē'lô·rēn'; ê·lô'rēn). **1** Province of Nigeria. See *Table* at NIGERIA.

2 Town, its ✳, ab. 170 m. NE of Lagos; pop. 47,590; surrounded by mud walls; Yoruba agricultural center; trades esp. in palm oil and rubber; capital of a Yoruba kingdom ab. 1800; overcome by Fulahs 1825; came under British control 1900.

Il'sen·burg (ĭl'zĕn·bŏŏrk). Village, E Germany, in former Saxony prov., Prussia, on N side of Harz Mts., NW of Blankenburg; pop. (1933) 5333; health resort; old castle.

I'lūk·ste (ĭ'lŏŏk·stĕ). Town, E Zemgale prov., S Latvia, on Dvina river just N of Daugavpils and near border of Lithuania; pop. (1930) 1202; acquired by Latvia Mar. 1. 1921.

Ilva. See ELBA.

I·ma·ba·ri (ê·mä·bä·rê) *or* **I·ma·ha·ru** (ê·mä·hä·rŏŏ). Town, Ehime prefecture, NW Shikoku, Japan; pop. (1945) 39,284; port on Inland Sea.

I·man' (ĭ·män'). City, W Maritime Territory, Soviet Russia, Asia, on Ussuri river 212 m. NNE of Vladivostok; pop. ab. 5000; on Trans-Siberian R.R.

I·man'dra (ĭ·män'drä). Lake 330 sq. m., ab. 65 m. long, W Kola Penin., Murmansk Region, Soviet Russia, Europe; outlet flows S to Kandalaksha Gulf.

Imataca, Sierra de. See SIERRA DE IMATACA.

Im'a·us (ĭm'å·ŭs). Ancient name of mountain range of W Himalayas.

Imaus Scyth'i·cus (sĭth'ĭ·kŭs; sĭth'-). The Tien Shan (Mts.).

Im·ba (êm·bä); *Jap.* **Im·ba·nu·ma** (êm·bä·nŏŏ·mä). Lake in SE Honshu, Japan, ab. 30 m. E of Tokyo; ab. 44 m. in circumference; 15 sq. m.

Im'ba·bu'ra (êm'bä·vŏŏ'rä). **1** Province of Ecuador. See *Table* at ECUADOR.

2 Volcano 15,028 ft., N Ecuador.

Imbros. See İMROZ.

Im'e·ri'ti·a (ĭm'ĕr·ĭsh'ĭ·å) *or* **Im'e·re'ti·a** (-ê'shĭ·å). District of W Georgia, U.S.S.R., formerly an independent kingdom, its ✳ Kutais; declared its independence c. 1424; in 18th cent. threatened by Turks and occupied by them 1750–70; came under Russian authority 1770 and finally annexed 1810. Imeritians now number ab. 500,000 and are thought to represent a very early branch of the Caucasians.

I'mi (ē'mê). Town, SE cen. Ethiopia, on the Webbe Shibeli.

Im·mac'u·la'ta (ĭ·măk'ů·lä'tå). Locality, Chester co., SE Pennsylvania, ab. 25 m. W of Philadelphia; Immaculata College (1920; women).

Im·na'ha (ĭm·nô'hô; ĭm'nå·hô). River ab. 75 m. long, NE Oregon; rises in S Wallowa co., and flows N into Snake river; its gorge averages 5500 ft. in depth for 40 m., one of the deepest and narrowest in U.S.

I'mo·la (ē'mô·lä). Commune, Bologna prov., Emilia, N Italy, on Santerno river 21 m. SE of Bologna; pop. 41,525; 12th-cent. cathedral; former Franciscan monastery.

I'mot·ski (ē'môt·skê) *or* **I·mo'schi** (ê·môs'kê). City, Bosnia and Herzegovina, W Yugoslavia, ab. 40 m. ESE of Split; pop. (1921) 41,367.

Im·pe'ria (êm·pâ'ryä). **1** Province of Italy. See *Table* at ITALY.

2 Seaport, its ✳, Liguria, NW Italy, on Ligurian Sea 60

m. SW of Genoa; pop. 28,540; formed 1923 by union of former communes Oneglia and Porto Maurizio; 18th-cent. church; health resort.

Im·pe'ri·al (ĭm·pêr'ĭ·ăl). **1** County in California. See *Table* at CALIFORNIA.

2 City, Imperial co., SE corner of California, in Imperial Valley 5 m. N of El Centro; pop. 2658; founded 1902; headquarters of Imperial Irrigation District; 67 ft. below sea level; grapefruit, cantaloupe, dates, strawberries, asparagus.

3 City, ⊗ of Chase co., S Nebraska; pop. 1423.

4 Locality, Allegheny co., SW Pennsylvania, ab. 14 m. W of Pittsburgh; pop. 1592.

Imperial Beach. City, San Diego co., SW California, on San Diego Bay near Mexican border; pop. 17,773.

Imperial Dam. Dam completed 1938 across Colorado river on S California-Arizona boundary, N of Yuma, Ariz.; height 85 ft.; impounds water for irrigation in **Imperial Reservoir** N of and adjoining Laguna Reservoir.

Imperial Valley. Valley in Imperial co., SE corner of California, and partly in Lower California; mostly below sea level; formerly desert, uninhabited, a part of Colorado Desert; includes Salton Sea; first irrigation project completed 1902; region now watered by the All-American Canal, 80 m. long, 200 ft. wide, which is fed by the Imperial Reservoir; market gardens; cotton and alfalfa.

Imp'hal (ĭmp'hŭl). City, ✳ of Manipur state, E Assam, NE Indian Union, 400 m. ENE of Calcutta; pop. (1941) 99 716; in **Imphal Plain** of cen. Manipur; has military cantonment; object of Japanese attack and siege Mar.–June 1944; siege raised June 30.

Im'pru·ne'ta (êm'prŏŏ·nä'tä). Commune, Firenze prov., Tuscany, cen. Italy, 6 m. S of Florence; pop. (1931) 10,420.

İm·roz' (ĭm·rôz'); *Gr.* **Im'bros** (ĭm'brŏs; *Gr.* êm'vrôs). Turkish island in NE Aegean Sea, W of Gallipoli Penin. and NW of entrance to Dardanelles; 110 sq. m.; pop. 6337; in ancient times a seat of worship of the Cabiri; Byzantine and Turkish island to 1912; occupied by Greece 1912–14 and then by British during Gallipoli campaign (see GALLIPOLI PENINSULA); given back to Turkey and demilitarized 1923.

I'mus (ē'mŏŏs). Municipality, NE Cavite prov., Luzon, Phil. Is., 7 m. SE of Cavite; pop. 18,039.

'Imwas. See EMMAUS.

I'na·bang'a (ê'nä·bäng'ä). Municipality on NW coast of Bohol I., Phil. Is., on Bohol Strait; pop. 23,855.

In'ac·ces'si·ble (ĭn'ăk·sĕs'ĭ·b'l). Westernmost of the Tristan da Cunha Is., S Atlantic Ocean.

In'a·chus (ĭn'å·kŭs). River ab. 75 m. long, a headstream of the Achelous in SE Epirus, NW Greece.

In'a·du Knob (ĭn'å·dŏŏ). Peak 5941 ft., Cocke co., E Tennessee.

I·na'gua (ĭ·nä'gwå). Either one of two islands of the Bahamas: **Great Inagua** (50 m. long and 25 m. wide; lighthouse on its SW point) or **Little Inagua** (8 m. long), both in Atlantic Ocean N of W Haiti; together constitute a district, 560 sq. m., pop. (1943) 890.

I'na·ri (ĭ'nå·rĭ). Town, N Finland, in Oulu dept., on SW shore of Lake Inari; pop. 1978.

Inari, Lake. Lake 549 sq. m., N Finland; receives Ivalo river from the S; outlet flows to Arctic Ocean.

I·na·wa·shi·ro (ê·nä·wä·shê·rô). Lake, Fukushima prefecture, N cen. Honshu, Japan, SW of Mt. Bandai; ab. 33 m. in circumference, alt. 1920 ft.

In'ca (ĭng'kä; *Span.* êng'kä). Commune, Baleares prov., Spain, N cen. Majorca I., 16 m. ENE of Palma; pop. 12,176.

In'ca, Pa'so del (pä'sô thĕl êng'kä). Andean pass 15,620 ft. on border bet. La Rioja prov., NE Argentina, and S Atacama prov., N cen. Chile.

In'ca·hua'si (êng'kä·wä'sê) *or* **In'ca·guas'si** (-gwä'sê). Peak 21,720 ft., NW Catamarca prov., NW Argentina, on border of Chile.

In·ce′, Cape (ĕn·jĕ′); *Turk.* **İn′ce·bu·run′** (ĕn′jĕ-bŏŏ·rōōn′). Cape (*burun*) on N coast of Turkey in Asia, projecting into Black Sea W of Sinop.

Ince in Ma′ker·field (ins, mā′kēr·fēld) *or* **Ince.** Urban district, Lancashire, NW England, 16 m. WNW of Manchester; pop. 20,414; coal mining, textiles, ironworks.

Inch′cape, *or* **Bell, Rock** (ĭnch′kāp, bĕl). Rock in North Sea, ab. 11 m. SE of Arbroath, Scotland, covered by sea at high tide; has lighthouse built 1807-11 by Robert Stevenson, grandfather of R. L. Stevenson; subject of legends.

Inch′colm (ĭnch′kŭm). Small island in Firth of Forth, E Scotland, NW of Leith; ruins of 12th-cent. abbey.

Inch′keith (ĭnch′kēth). Small island, Firth of Forth, E Scotland, N of Leith; lighthouse.

In′chon′ (ĭn′chŏn′). = JINSEN.

In′cu′dine′, Mont l′ (môn′ lăn′kü′dēn′). Mountain 7007 ft., S Corsica, ESE of Ajaccio.

In′dal (ĭn′däl); *Swed.* **In′dals·älv′** (ĭn′däls·ĕlv′). River (*älv*) 260 m. long, N cen. Sweden; flows SE into Gulf of Bothnia.

In·dan′ (ĕn·dän′). Municipality, E Camarines Norte, Luzon, Phil. Is., near coast 5 m. NNW of Daet; pop. 11,249; an early settlement.

In·dang′ (ĕn·däng′). Municipality, S cen. Cavite prov., Luzon, Phil. Is.; road center 21 m. S of City of Cavite; pop. 15,388.

In′daw (ĭn′dô). Town, Mandalay division, N cen. Burma, on railroad just W of Katha; taken by Allies Dec. 10, 1944.

In′daw·gyi′, Lake (ĭn′dô·jē′). Lake, N Burma, W of Myitkyina and Loipyet Hills.

Indefatigable Island. See SANTA CRUZ island, Galápagos Is.

In·de·pend′ence (ĭn·dē·pĕn′dĕns). **1** County in Arkansas. See *Table* at ARKANSAS.

2 Town, ⊗ of Inyo co., E California, 82 m. E of Fresno; pop. (est.) 875.

3 City, ⊗ of Buchanan co., E Iowa, 25 m. E of Waterloo; pop. 5498; agriculture, dairying.

4 City, ⊗ of Montgomery co., SE Kansas, 58 m. WSW of Pittsburg; pop. 11,222; oil wells, natural-gas fields; brick and cement plants.

5 City, a ⊗ of Kenton co., N Kentucky; pop. 309.

6 City, ⊗ of Jackson co., W Missouri, 9 m. E of Kansas City; pop. 62,328; home of Mormon colony 1831-34; now center of Reorganized Church of Jesus Christ of Latter Day Saints; starting point of Santa Fe and Oregon Trails during Gold Rush (1849); in Civil War scene of first phase of battle of Westport Oct. 21, 1864. Now chiefly a residential suburb of Kansas City. Home of Harry S. Truman.

7 Village, Cuyahoga co., N Ohio, 9 m. S of Cleveland; pop. 6868.

8 City, Polk co., NW Oregon, S of Salem; pop. 1930.

9 Town, ⊗ of Grayson co., SW Virginia, WSW of Galax; pop. 679.

Independence Fjord. Fiord 225 m. long, N Greenland, just SE of Peary Land, Arctic Ocean; longest in Greenland.

Independence Hill. Urban community (unincorporated), Lake co., NW Indiana, S of Gary; pop. 1824.

Independence Pass. Mountain pass 12,095 ft., Lake and Pitkin cos., W cen. Colorado, in Sawatch Range of the Rocky Mts.; highway, highest automobile pass in the state.

Independence Range. Range in N Nevada, chiefly in W Elko co.

Independence Rock. Granite boulder in S Natrona co., cen. Wyoming, on N bank of Sweetwater river; 1950 ft. long, 850 ft. wide, 193 ft. high at N end; a landmark on the old Oregon Trail.

In′de·pen·den′ci·a (ĭn′dē·pĕn·dĕn′shǐ·ȧ; -shä; *Span.* ēn′dā·pān·dān′syä). = FRAY BENTOS.

In′de·ra·gi′ri (ĭn′dĕ·rȧ·gǐ′rǐ) *or* **In′dra·gi′ri** (ĭn′drä-). **1** Navigable river ab. 225 m. long, cen. Sumatra, Indonesia; rises in Padang Highlands, flows E into N end of Berhala Strait.

2 Former district, E cen. Sumatra, forming a part of Riouw residency, Neth. Indies; 6589 sq. m.; pop. 114,644; chief town Rengat; interior highlands along coastal lowlands along Inderagiri river.

In′dex Mountain (ĭn′dĕks). Mountain 5639 ft., King co., W Washington, in Cascade Mts. ENE of Seattle.

Index Peak. **1** Mountain 11,977 ft., Carbon co., S Montana.

2 Mountain 11,500 ft. in the Absaroka Mts., NW Wyoming.

In′di·a (ĭn′dǐ·ȧ; *esp. Brit.*, -dyä). **1** Peninsula and country, S Asia, S of the Himalayas bet. the Arabian Sea and the Bay of Bengal; often termed a subcontinent. Cf. HINDUSTAN.

Chief mountains: The Himalayas (*q.v.*) in N, containing highest peaks in the world, and in NW the borders of the Hindu Kush, Safed Koh, and Sulaiban Range, this mountain barrier bet. India and the rest of Asia being crossed by some famous passes, esp. the Khyber, Bolan (5900 ft.), and Gumal (7500 ft.) Passes in NW; Vindhya Mts. bet. Ganges valley and the Deccan (*q.v.*); Eastern and Western Ghats along E and W coasts; Nilgiri Hills in S. *Chief rivers:* Ganges with its chief tributary, the Jumna, in extensive river plain of the N; Indus system in NW with tributaries (Chenab, Jhelum, Sutlej, Beas, and Ravi); Brahmaputra in the NE flowing into the Ganges delta; Narbada and Tapti in N Deccan; Godavari and Kistna in cen. Deccan. *Chief cities:* Calcutta, Bombay, Madras, Hyderabad, Lahore, Ahmadabad, Delhi, Cawnpore, Lucknow, and Karachi. Summer capitals and hill stations: Simla, Darjeeling, and Ootacamund. See also BHUTAN, CARNATIC, COROMANDEL COAST, GUJARAT, KATHIAWAR, MALABAR COAST, NEPAL.

History: Invaded from Iranian plateau c. 2000-1200 B.C. by Aryans, who pushed to S and SE the earlier Dravidian and Munda inhabitants; developed important religious systems: Brahmanism, with its accompanying social caste system, evolved from the Vedic religion of Aryan invaders, and Buddhism and Jainism, both founded in 6th cent. B.C.; invaded across Indus in NW (Punjab) by Alexander the Great 327-325 B.C. Northern part consolidated (with Afghanistan) into an empire by Chandragupta, Hindu founder of Maurya dynasty (c. 322-185 B.C.), whose grandson Asoka (d. 232 B.C.) extended his empire by addition of kingdoms of Bengal and Orissa to include over two thirds of peninsula, all but extreme S part; N part again united by rulers of Gupta dynasty (320-480 A.D.); divided politically into states of varying size and power. Mohammedan invasions begun ab. 1000 A.D. by raid in N by the Afghan Mahmud of Ghazni; earliest Mohammedan kingdom, Sultanate of Delhi, including N India and part of Coromandel Coast, founded 1206 by Mohammed Tughlak but soon split up; a Moslem dynasty the Bahmani, flourished in the Deccan from 14th cent.; for chief contemporary Hindu state, see VIJAYANAGAR; peninsula opened by Vasco da Gama's voyage 1497-98 to direct European trade, which Portuguese monopolized in 16th cent. and for which Dutch, English, and French competed in 17th cent. Gradually conquered 1526-1707 by Mogul emperors, of whom the first was Baber and the most famous Akbar (1556-1605), until their power was challenged in late 17th cent. by the Marathas, a Hindu people whose powerful confederacy was broken by Afghans at Panipat (*q.v.*) 1761; torn by dynastic conflicts with decline of Mogul power after 1707, thus opening way for European intervention and territorial acquisition.

Period of British control: Establishment of trading posts ("factories") in 17th cent. by rival British and

French East India Companies (chartered 1600 and 1664, respectively) led in 18th cent. to war bet. England and France culminating in French defeat at Plassey 1757 (see CALCUTTA, DECCAN, FRENCH INDIA); ascendancy of British East India Company resulted in first extensive territorial acquisitions (Bengal and Bihar 1765, the Circars 1766) but alleged misrule by Company caused British Parliament to pass Regulating Act 1773 and Pitt's Act 1784 establishing "dual control" of Company and Crown; after wars with Mysore (q.v.) and Marathas, British acquired Malabar Coast 1792, Kanara 1799, Carnatic 1801, Orissa 1803, and Maratha lands (see POONA); Company's monopoly of trade abolished 1813; annexed Burma 1826–86, Sind 1843, Punjab 1849, Berar and Nagpur 1853, Oudh 1856, and Baluchistan (qq.v.); by 1887 the parts of India not under direct British control were protected states, under native rulers, with varying degrees of dependence upon British; government modified (1861, 1909, 1919) in direction of limited self-rule. After World War I, scene of bitter struggle bet. British rulers and Indian Nationalists, under Gandhi's leadership; eventual federation of all India the goal of Act of 1935 which separated Burma and Aden from India, divided British India into 11 provinces each under a governor and provincial legislature, and provided for eventual membership of Indian States in central legislature at New Delhi. During World War II Manipur state in Assam invaded by Japanese Mar.–June 1944; NE Assam used by Allies as base for aid to China by air, for construction of Ledo Road (later Stilwell Road) through N Burma, and for campaign in N Burma; after war period 1945–47 marked by famines and by rioting bet. Hindus and Moslems. By Act of Parliament July 18, 1947, effective Aug. 15, 1947, British rule given up and India divided into the Indian Union (predominantly Hindu), Pakistan (predominantly Moslem), and Indian States originally with more or less independent status: see INDIAN UNION, PAKISTAN, INDIAN STATES.

2 *or* **In′di·an Empire** (ĭn′dĭ·ăn; -dyăn). Those parts of India formerly (until Aug. 15, 1947) under British rule or protection together with Baluchistan and the Andaman and Nicobar Islands but (since Apr. 1937) exclusive of Burma and Aden; 1,581,410 sq. m.; pop. (1941) 388,997,955; divided into British India (865 446 sq. m.; pop. 295,808,722) and 562 Indian States, some very small (715,964 sq. m.; pop. 93,189,233); ✻ New Delhi. Administered by a governor-general appointed directly by the British Crown, usually for 5 years, assisted by an Executive Council. British India divided 1935 for administrative purposes into 11 provinces each under a governor (Assam, Bengal, Bihar, Bombay, Central Provinces and Berar, Madras, North-West Frontier Province, Orissa, Punjab, Sind, United Provinces of Agra and Oudh) and 6 provinces each under a chief commissioner responsible directly to the governor-general (Ajmer-Merwara, Andaman and Nicobar Islands, British Baluchistan, Coorg, Delhi, Panth Piploda). The Indian States (q.v.), all subject in some degree to the British sovereign, had varying systems of government.

3 = INDIAN UNION. As now used in the political sense the name *India* does not include Pakistan.

In′dia, Bas′sas da (bȧ′sȧzh thȧ ēnn′dyȧ). Small French islands in cen. Mozambique Channel bet. SW Madagascar and SE Mozambique.

India, Farther. See INDOCHINA.

In′di·an′a (ĭn′dĭ·ăn′ȧ). **1** A north central state of U.S.A., 19th state admitted to Union (1816); bounded on N by Michigan and Lake Michigan, on E by Ohio, on S by Kentucky, and on W by Illinois; 38th state in area, 36,291 sq. m., not including 228 sq. m. of water of the Great Lakes (land area 36,205 sq. m.); 11th state in population, 4,662,498; ✻ Indianapolis. See *Table of States* at UNITED STATES. Divided into the following 92 counties (for pronunciation of their names, see their individual entries):

NAME	LOCATION	AREA[1]	POP.[1]	CO. SEAT
Adams	E	345	24,643	Decatur
Allen	NE	671	232,196	Fort Wayne
Bartholomew	S cen.	402	48,198	Columbus
Benton	W	409	11,912	Fowler
Blackford	E cen.	167	14,792	Hartford City
Boone	cen.	427	27,543	Lebanon
Brown	S cen.	324	7,024	Nashville
Carroll	NW cen.	374	16,934	Delphi
Cass	N cen.	415	40,931	Logansport
Clark	S	384	62,795	Jeffersonville
Clay	W	364	24,207	Brazil
Clinton	cen.	407	30,765	Frankfort
Crawford	S	312	8,379	English
Daviess	SW	433	26,636	Washington
Dearborn	SE	306	28,674	Lawrenceburg
Decatur	SE cen.	370	20,019	Greensburg
De Kalb	NE	365	28,271	Auburn
Delaware	E cen.	400	110,938	Muncie
Dubois	SW	433	27,463	Jasper
Elkhart	N	468	106,790	Goshen
Fayette	E	215	24,454	Connersville
Floyd	S	149	51,397	New Albany
Fountain	W	397	18,706	Covington
Franklin	E	394	17,015	Brookville
Fulton	N	367	16,957	Rochester
Gibson	SW	499	29,949	Princeton
Grant	N cen.	421	75,741	Marion
Greene	SW	549	26,327	Bloomfield
Hamilton	cen.	403	40,132	Noblesville
Hancock	cen.	305	26,665	Greenfield
Harrison	S	479	19,207	Corydon
Hendricks	cen.	417	40,896	Danville
Henry	E cen.	400	48,899	New Castle
Howard	N cen.	293	69,509	Kokomo
Huntington	NE	390	33,814	Huntington
Jackson	S	520	30,556	Brownstown
Jasper	NW	562	18,842	Rensselaer
Jay	E	386	22,572	Portland
Jefferson	SE	366	24,061	Madison
Jennings	SE	377	17,267	Vernon
Johnson	cen.	315	43,704	Franklin
Knox	SW	517	41,561	Vincennes
Kosciusko	N	538	40,373	Warsaw
Lagrange	N	379	17,380	Lagrange
Lake	NW corner	514	513,269	Crown Point
La Porte	N	608	95,111	La Porte
Lawrence	S	459	36,564	Bedford
Madison	cen.	453	125,819	Anderson
Marion	cen.	402	697,567	Indianapolis
Marshall	N	444	32,443	Plymouth
Martin	SW	345	10,608	Shoals
Miami	N cen.	380	38,000	Peru
Monroe	S cen.	412	59,225	Bloomington
Montgomery	W cen.	507	32,089	Crawfordsville
Morgan	cen.	406	33,875	Martinsville
Newton	NW	413	11,502	Kentland
Noble	NE	410	28,162	Albion
Ohio	SE	87	4,165	Rising Sun
Orange	S	405	16,877	Paoli
Owen	SW cen.	391	11,400	Spencer
Parke	W	451	14,804	Rockville
Perry	S	384	17,232	Cannelton
Pike	SW	335	12,797	Petersburg
Porter	NW	425	60,279	Valparaiso
Posey	SW corner	414	19,214	Mount Vernon
Pulaski	NW	433	12,837	Winamac
Putnam	W cen.	490	24,927	Greencastle
Randolph	E	457	28,434	Winchester
Ripley	SE	442	20,641	Versailles
Rush	E cen.	409	20,393	Rushville
Saint Joseph	N	467	238,614	South Bend
Scott	SE	193	14,643	Scottsburg
Shelby	cen.	409	34,093	Shelbyville
Spencer	SW	396	16,074	Rockport
Starke	NW	311	17,911	Knox
Steuben	NE corner	310	17,184	Angola
Sullivan	SW	457	21,721	Sullivan
Switzerland	SE	221	7,092	Vevay
Tippecanoe	W cen.	501	89,122	Lafayette
Tipton	cen.	261	15,856	Tipton
Union	E	168	6,457	Liberty
Vanderburgh	SW	241	165,794	Evansville
Vermillion	W	263	17,683	Newport
Vigo	W	415	108,458	Terre Haute
Wabash	N	421	32,605	Wabash
Warren	W	368	8,545	Williamsport
Warrick	SW	391	23,577	Boonville
Washington	S	516	17,819	Salem
Wayne	E	405	74,039	Richmond
Wells	NE	368	21,220	Bluffton
White	NW	497	19,709	Monticello
Whitley	NE	336	20,954	Columbia City

[1] Area = land area in sq. m. Pop. from 1960 Census.

Nickname: Hoosier State. *State flower:* Zinnia. *Motto:* The Crossroads of America. *Chief cities:* Indianapolis, Gary, Fort Wayne, Evansville, South Bend. *Rivers:*

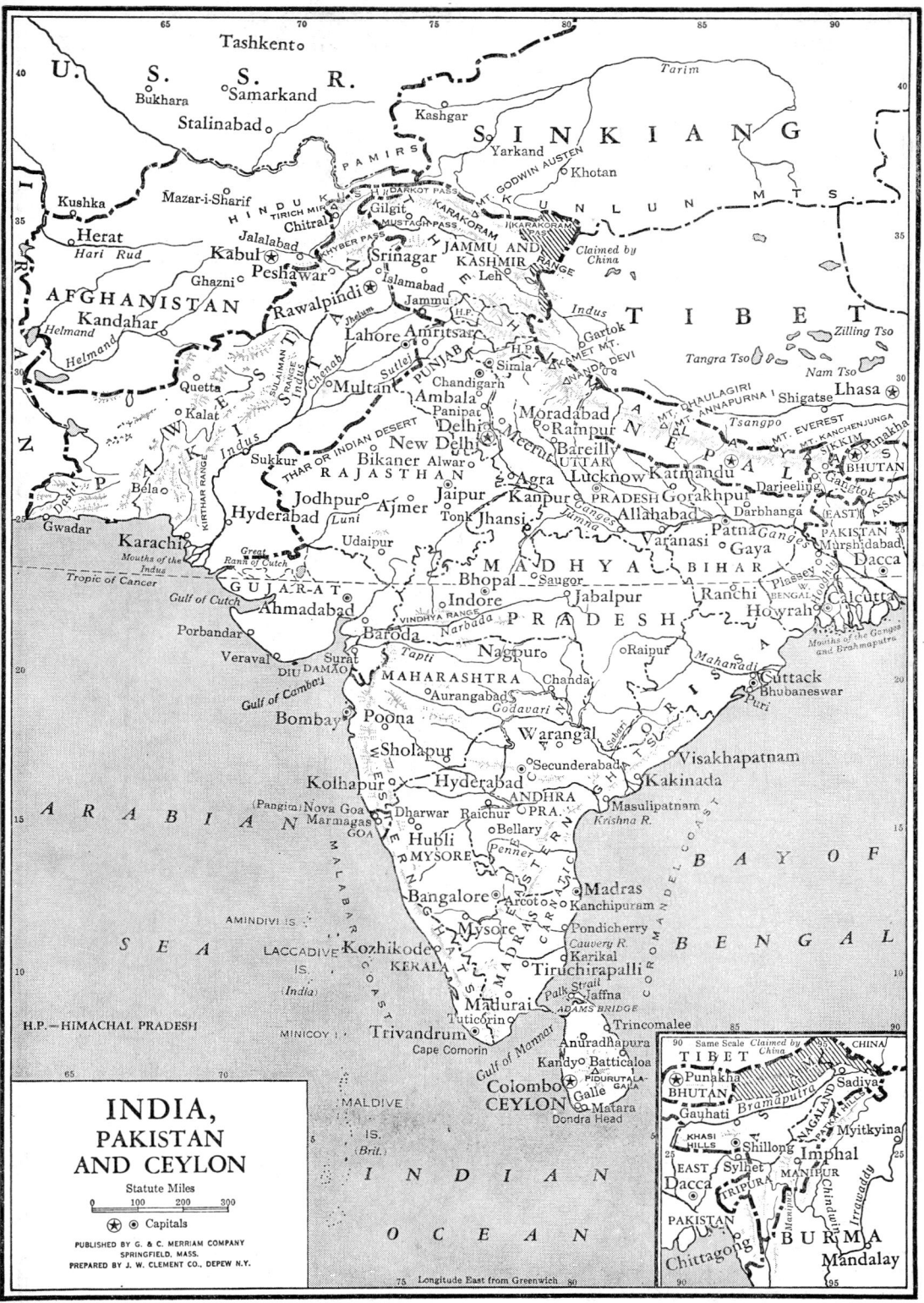

INDIA,
PAKISTAN
AND CEYLON

Statute Miles

0   100   200   300

⊛ ◉ Capitals

PUBLISHED BY G. & C. MERRIAM COMPANY
SPRINGFIELD, MASS.
PREPARED BY J. W. CLEMENT CO., DEPEW N.Y.

H.P.—HIMACHAL PRADESH

INDIANA

Statute Miles

0 10 20 30 40

✱ State Capital

PUBLISHED BY G. & C. MERRIAM COMPANY
SPRINGFIELD, MASS.
PREPARED BY J. W. CLEMENT CO., BUFFALO, N. Y.

Wabash, flowing from middle Ohio border W across state and then S to form lower section of boundary with Illinois; Ohio, forming SE and S boundary with Kentucky; White, with East and West Forks, flowing from central and S area SW into the Wabash. *Highest point:* Greensfork Township 1240 ft. in Randolph co. *Chief industries:* Agriculture, manufacturing.

History: French settlement at Vincennes c. 1700; included in territory ceded by France to England 1763; ceded by England to United States by Treaty of Paris 1783; included in Northwest Territory 1787 and 1800 in Indiana Territory (see NORTHWEST TERRITORY); admitted to Union Dec. 11, 1816; capital removed from Corydon to Indianapolis 1825; adopted present constitution 1851.

2 County in Pennsylvania. See *Table* at PENNSYLVANIA.
3 Borough, ⊗ of Indiana co., W cen. Pennsylvania, 25 m. NW of Johnstown; pop. 13,005; station on Underground Railroad; Indiana State College (1871; coed.).

Indiana Harbor. Harbor district, East Chicago, NW Indiana, on Lake Michigan.

In′di·an·ap′o·lis (ĭn′dĭ·ăn·ăp′ŏ·lĭs; -ăp′lĭs). City, Marion co., cen. Indiana; ✳ of Indiana; largest city in the state; pop. 476,258; settled 1820; made capital 1825; incorp. as town 1836, as city 1874; railroad center; meat-packing houses, flour mills, hosiery mills; beautiful War Memorial (buildings, parkways, plazas); Fort Benjamin Harrison (*q.v.*); Stout Field, with U.S. Air Force Reserve Training Center. Indiana Central College (1902; coed.; United Brethren Church); Indiana University Medical Center (1903); Butler University (1850; coed.).

Indian Countercurrent. The equatorial countercurrent in the N Indian Ocean.

Indian, *or* **Great Indian, Desert.** See THAR DESERT.

Indian Harbour. Settlement on island on N side of entrance to Hamilton Inlet, SE Labrador; one of earliest hospitals of Grenfell Mission located here 1894.

Indian Head. 1 Mountain 3585 ft. in Catskill Mts., Greene co., SE New York.
2 Market town, S Saskatchewan, Canada, 44 m. E of Regina; pop. 1569; Dominion experimental farm.

Indian Lake. 1 Lake ab. 7 m. long, E cen. Hamilton co., NE cen. New York; outlet N into Hudson river.
2 Lake, NW Logan co., W Ohio.

Indian Ocean; *anc.* **O·ce′a·nus In′di·cus** (ō·sē′à·nŭs ĭn′dĭ·kŭs). Body of water E of Africa, S of Asia, W of Australia, and N of Antarctica; ab. 28,375,000 sq. m.; greatest known depth 24,440 ft. off coast of Java.

In′di·a·no′la (ĭn′dĭ·à·nō′là). **1** City, ⊗ of Warren co., S cen. Iowa, 16 m. S of Des Moines; pop. 7062; Simpson College (1867; coed.; Methodist).
2 City, ⊗ of Sunflower co., W Mississippi, 23 m. E of Greenville; pop. 6714; cotton-processing plants.

Indianola Peak *or* **Elephant Tusk.** Mountain 5240 ft., S Brewster co., W Texas.

Indian Peak. Mountain 10,929 ft., W Park co., NW Wyoming.

Indian River. 1 Lagoon, E Florida, 165 m. long and of varying width; runs parallel with the coast in Brevard, Indian River, and St. Lucie cos. S to St. Lucie Inlet in Martin co., connecting with the ocean at Indian River Inlet; navigable for boats of shallow draft.
2 County in Florida. See *Table* at FLORIDA.

Indian River Bay. Inlet of Atlantic Ocean on SE coast of Sussex co., Delaware.

Indian River Inlet. Narrow strait leading from Atlantic Ocean through barrier reefs off E coast of St. Lucie co., E Florida.

Indian States. Various semi-independent areas in India ruled by native Indians, formerly subject in varying degrees to British authority, but in Aug. 1947 made nominally independent states (see INDIA, 1). There were 562 such states varying greatly in both area and population. Under British rule (see INDIA, 2) their systems of government varied, the larger states (such as Hydera-

bad, Gwalior, Baroda, Mysore, Cochin, Jammu and Kashmir, Travancore, Indore, Sikkim) were in direct relation with the governor-general through a resident, while many of the smaller states were grouped in Agencies (such as Central India, Eastern States, Rajputana, Punjab States, Gujarat, Western India, Kolhapur and Deccan, Madras States) administered by a resident assisted by political agents. By 1948 most of these states had been merged into adjacent provinces of the Indian Union or grouped into new administrative units.

Indian Territory. Former territory 31,000 sq. m. in U.S.A., now in Oklahoma. See OKLAHOMA.

Indian Union; *now usu.* **Republic of India.** A confederation of regions formerly in the Indian Empire (see INDIA, 2) having a predominantly Hindu population, established Aug. 15, 1947 by Act of Parliament (July 18, 1947) as a self-governing dominion of the British Commonwealth; ab. 1,290,000 sq. m.; pop. ab. 320,000,000; ✳ New Delhi. Comprises 11 of the 17 provinces of former British India (see INDIA, 2), namely Madras, Bombay, United Provinces, Bihar, Central Provinces and Berar, Orissa, Ajmer-Merwara, Andaman and Nicobar Islands, Coorg, Delhi, and Panth Piploda; parts of the Punjab (Jullundur and Ambala divisions, part of Lahore division, comprising East Punjab) and Bengal (Burdwan division, and parts of Presidency and Rajshahi divisions, comprising West Bengal); and all of Assam prov. except ⅝ of Sylhet dist.; on Nov. 26, 1949 adopted constitution establishing a republic which was inaugurated Jan. 26 1950. Reorganized 1956, divided into 14 states (15 states in 1960, 16 in 1963) and 6 (now 10) centrally administered territories.

Indicus, Oceanus. See INDIAN OCEAN.

In′dies (ĭn′dĭz; -dēz). Usually, the East Indies; the plural form of *Indie* or *Indy*, adapted from Latin *India* and applied originally to India and adjacent lands and islands in the Far East; later applied by writers to lands discovered by Europeans in 15th and 16th cents. in the Western Hemisphere, and supposed to be geographically the same region; later the two regions became known as EAST INDIES and WEST INDIES.

In′di·gir′ka (ĭn′dĭ·gĭr′kà; *Russ.* ĭn·dyĭ·gēr′kà). River ab. 850 m. long, NE Yakutsk Republic, Soviet Russia, Asia; rises on N slopes of Verkhoyansk Range, flows N, cutting a deep gorge through Cherskogo Range, to East Siberian Sea; navigable but frozen much of the year.

In′di·o (ĭn′dĭ·ō). City, Riverside co., SE California, SE of San Bernardino; pop. 9,745; founded 1876; resort; dates, cotton, alfalfa.

In′dis·pen′sa·ble Reefs (ĭn′dĭs·pĕn′sà·b'l). Reefs S of Rennell I., SE Solomon Is., W Pacific Ocean; ab. 11°S lat.

Indispensable Strait. Channel ab. 35 m. wide bet. NE Guadalcanal I. and SW Malaita I., SE Solomon Is., W Pacific Ocean.

In′do·chi′na (ĭn′dō·chī′nà) *or* **Farther India. 1** The SE peninsula of Asia, comprising Burma, Thailand, Laos, Cambodia, Vietnam, and the Federation of Malaya (see *Maps* at BURMA and Federation of MALAYA). Since ancient times culturally subject to Indian (Hindu) and Chinese civilization; for history of important kingdoms, see ANNAM, CAMBODIA, SIAM, and BURMA; after penetration by Europeans, E part controlled by French (see FRENCH INDOCHINA), center by independent Siam, and W and S part by British; occupied by Japanese 1940–45.
2 = FRENCH INDOCHINA.

Indochine française. See FRENCH INDOCHINA.

In′do·ne′sia (ĭn′dō·nē′zhà; -zhĭ·à; -shà; -shĭ·à). **1** Occasional name for the Malay Archipelago, meaning literally "The Islands of India"—a term introduced by Adolf Bastian, German ethnologist, and used since 1884; refers generally to all regions inhabited by peoples related to the Malays proper.
2 Republic, SE Asia. See NETHERLANDS INDIES.

Indonesia, East. See EAST INDONESIA.

Indonesia, Republic of. **1** Formerly, a state of the United States of Indonesia (see NETHERLANDS INDIES); ✳ Jogjakarta. First set up Aug. 17, 1945 at the end of World War II without sanction of the Dutch, who did not formally recognize it until the Linggadjati (Cheribon) Agreement, initialed Nov. 15, 1946, signed Mar. 25, 1947; as first recognized by the Dutch comprised Java, Madura, and Sumatra, but by Aug. 1947 its territory was reduced by the Dutch occupation forces chiefly to a small area in the S cen. part of Java; under auspices of UN Good Offices Committee signed truce with Netherlands aboard the U.S.S. *Renville* Jan. 17, 1948; attacked Dec. 18, 1948 by the Dutch who captured Jogjakarta on the 19th and interned the Republican leaders; re-established July 1949 when government was restored to Jogjakarta; became one of the states of the United States of Indonesia; in 1950 led in the development of the United States of Indonesia into a unitary state and formed the nucleus of the new Republic of Indonesia. **2** The Netherlands Indies—their name since 1950.

Indonesia, United States of. See NETHERLANDS INDIES.

In·dore' (ĭn·dōr'). **1** Former Indian state, cen. Indian Union; 9934 sq. m.; in valley of the Narbada, geographically in former Central India Agency; became 1948 part of Madhya Bharat, which in turn was merged 1956 in Madhya Pradesh. **2** City, cen. India, in W Madhya Pradesh, 340 m. NE of Bombay; ✳ of former Indore state and Central India Agency; pop 310,859; Daly College; cotton mills. City, founded 1715, grew rapidly under Maratha dynasty of Holkars which was established in 18th cent. by Malhar Rao Holkar, an officer of the peshwa; lost much of territory after defeat by Lord Lake 1804; accepted British protectorate 1818.

In'do·scyth'i·a (ĭn'dŏ·sĭth'ĭ·à; -sĭth'-). Ancient country, NW India, comprising valley of the Indus.

Indragiri. See INDERAGIRI.

In'dra·ma'joe (ĭn'drȧ·mä'yōō) *or* **In'dra·ma'yu.** Town on N coast of West Java prov., Indonesia, near **Cape Indramajoe;** pop. 21,190.

In'dra·poe'ra *or* **In'dra·pu'ra** (ĭn'drȧ·pōō'rȧ). **1** See KERINTJI. **2** Town, Sumatra, Indonesia, on coast 90 m. SSE of Padang; early Dutch settlement.

Indraprastha. See DELHI.

In·dra'va·ti (ĭn·drä'vȧ·tē). River ab. 330 m. long, S India; rises in Orissa, flows W through Madhya Pradesh, then S to the Godavari on border of Andhra Pradesh.

In'dre (ăN'dr'). **1** River 115 m. long in cen. France; flows NW in Indre and Indre-et-Loire depts. into the Loire river. **2** Department of France. See *Table* at FRANCE.

In'dre–et–Loire' (ăN'drȧ·lwȧr'). Department of France. See *Table* at FRANCE.

Indreville. See CHÂTEAUROUX.

Indur. See ENDOR.

In'dus (ĭn'dŭs). One of three great rivers of N India, 1700 to 1900 m. long; rises on N slopes of Kailas Range, SW Tibet, flows NW through Tibet and Kashmir ab. 680 m., cutting through Ladakh Range and receiving the Shyok from the E; turns and flows SW through Pakistan (West Punjab and Sind) to Arabian Sea; in several places its course forms provincial boundaries; only large tributary the Panjnad (*q.v.*); area of its basin estimated at 372,000 sq. m.; navigable for small steamers to Hyderabad; crossed by several bridges and in N Sind at Sukkur (*q.v.*) by great barrage that provides water for vast irrigation project. Important in Indian history: excavations at Mohenjo-Daro and Harappa indicate an advanced Indus culture ab. 2500 B.C.; its valley scene of many invasions and conflicts from time of Alexander the Great to Third Afghan War of 1919.

I'ne·bo·lu' (ē'nĕ·bô·lōō'); *formerly* **I'ne·bo·li'** (-lē'). Town, N Turkey in Asia, on Black Sea coast 70 m. W of Sinop; pop. 4302; birthplace of Alexander the Paphlagonian and location of his fraudulent oracle (2d cent. A.D.).

İ·ne·göl' (ê·nê·gûl'). Town, Bursa vilayet, NW Turkey in Asia, 25 m. ESE of Bursa; pop. 13,081.

Inessa. See BIANCAVILLA.

I'nez (ī'nĕz; -nĭz). City, ⊗ of Martin co., E Kentucky; pop. 566.

In·fan'ta (ĭn·fän'tȧ; *Span.* êm·fän'tä). **1** Former district along Pacific coast of E Luzon, Phil. Is., a dependency of Laguna; annexed to Tayabas 1902. **2** Municipality on Polillo Strait, E Tayabas prov., Luzon; pop. 20,331; in former Infanta dist.

In'gate·stone (ĭng'gȧt·stŭn). Village in civil parish of **Ingatestone and Fry'er·ning** (frī'ẽr·nĭng) [pop. 2352], Essex, SE England, 23½ m. NE of London.

In'ga·ví' *or* **Yn'ga·ví'** (ēng'gä·vē'). Mountain S of La Paz, Bolivia; scene of battle Nov. 20, 1841 in which Bolivians under José Ballivián defeated Peruvians under Agustín Gamarra who was killed.

In'gel·mun'ster (ĭng'gĕl·mün'stĕr). Commune, West Flanders prov., NW Belgium, E of Roeselare; pop. 7578; captured by Germans Oct. 1914, retaken by French Oct. 1918.

Ingermanland. See INGRIA.

In'ger·soll (ĭng'gĕr·sŏl; -s'l). Industrial town, Oxford co., SE Ontario, Canada, on Thames river 18 m. NE of London; pop. 6524; lumber, grain, dairy products.

Ing'ham (ĭng'ȧm). County in Michigan. See *Table* at MICHIGAN.

In'gle·bor'ough Mountain (ĭng'g'l·bûr'ŏ; -bŭ·rȧ; -brŭ). Peak 2373 ft., W Yorkshire, N England; ancient walled fort on summit; on S side is **Ingleborough Cave,** large cavern with stalactites and stalagmites.

In'gle·field Bay *or* **Gulf** (ĭng'g'l·fēld). Inlet of Smith Sound, W coast of Greenland.

In·gle'sa Bay (ĕng·glā'sä). Inlet of Pacific Ocean on W coast of Atacama prov., N cen. Chile.

In'gle·wood (ĭng'g'l·wŏŏd). **1** Residential and industrial city, Los Angeles co., SW California, 8 m. SW of Los Angeles; pop. 63,390; founded 1873, incorp. 1908; chinchilla farms; airplanes, furniture. **2** Urban community (unincorporated), Davidson co., N cen. Tennessee, near Nashville; pop. 26,527.

In'go·da (ĭng'gô·dä). River ab. 360 m. long, SW Chita Region, Soviet Russia, Asia; flows NE from S end of Yablonoi Mts. to unite with Onon river and form Shilka river.

In'gol·stadt (ĭng'gŭl·stät; *Ger.* ĭng'ôl·shtät). City, Bavaria, Germany, on left bank of Danube river 43 m. N of Munich; pop. 26,630; metal goods, lumber, brewery products; old ducal palace; ruins of Jesuit college (founded 1555); 15th-cent. Gothic church. Under Charlemagne 806; became city 1250, later capital of a dukedom; university founded here 1472 (transferred to Landshut 1800, to Munich 1826); fortifications built 1539, destroyed by French 1800, later rebuilt.

In'gram (ĭng'grăm). Borough, Allegheny co., SW Pennsylvania, 4 m. W of Pittsburgh; pop. 4730.

In'gri·a (ĭng'grĭ·à) *or* **In'ger·man·land'** (ĭng'gĕr·mȧn·länd'). District of early Russia, S of E end of Gulf of Finland, now in Leningrad Region, Soviet Russia, Europe; for several centuries nominally under Novgorod; fought for by Sweden and Russia 14th to 17th cents.; became Swedish 1617 to 1703; its chief fort on the Neva captured by Peter the Great 1703 who there founded St. Petersburg; permanently Russian by Treaty of Nystad (see UUSIKAUPUNKI) 1721.

In'grid Chris'ten·sen Coast (ĭng'grĭd krĭs'tĕn·s'n). Section of coast of Antarctica, on Indian Ocean, ab. 74° to 81°E, bet. Lars Christensen Coast and Leopold and Astrid Coast; discovered and claimed by Norway 1935.

In·gul' (ĭn·gōōl'). River ab. 200 m. long, S Ukraine, U.S.S.R., flowing S into Bug river near its mouth, at Nikolaev.

In·gu·lets' (ĭn·gōō·lyĕts'). River ab. 300 m. long, S Ukraine, U.S.S.R., flowing S into Dnieper river near its mouth.

In·gur' (ĭn·gōōr'). River ab. 110 m. long, NW Georgia, U.S.S.R., flowing SW from Caucasus Mts. to Black Sea; forms part of E boundary of Abkhazia. The Svanetians dwell along its upper course.

In·gush' (ĭn·gōōsh') or **In'gu·she'ti·a** (ĭng'gŭ·shē'-shĭ·à). Former autonomous area N of Caucasus Mts. and W of Chechen area, Soviet Russia, Europe; 1242 sq. m.; ✻ Ordzhonikidze; for a time part of Mountain Republic; in Nov. 1920 joined with Chechen area to form Chechen-Ingush Republic (*q.v.*) which was dissolved during World War II.

Ing'wa·vu'ma (ĭng'wá·vōō'má). District, N Zululand, NE Natal, Union of South Africa; ab. 1950 sq. m.; pop. 17,000; acquired by Great Britain 1895; chief town Ingwavuma, on Swaziland border. See TONGALAND.

I'nham·ba'ne (ĭn'yăm·bä'nĕ). **1** Former district, SE Mozambique, SE Africa; 21,000 sq. m.; pop. ab. 248,000; now belongs to Sul do Save prov.

2 Commercial seaport, Sul do Save prov., S Mozambique, SE Africa, on **Inhambane Bay,** inlet of Mozambique Channel; ✻ of former Inhambane dist.; pop. (1935 est.) 11,349.

Ining. See KULDJA.

I'ni'ni', Territory of (ē'nē'nē'). Inland section of French Guiana; see FRENCH GUIANA.

I·ní'ri·da (ê·nē'rê·thä). River, E Colombia; flows E and NE into Guaviare river near its confluence with the Orinoco on Venezuelan border.

Inisfail. Var. of INNISFAIL.

In'i·shere' (ĭn'ĭ·shĕr'). See ARAN ISLANDS.

In'ish·maan' (ĭn'ĭsh·män'). See ARAN ISLANDS.

In'ish·more' (ĭn'ĭsh·mōr'). Largest of the Aran Is., in Galway Bay, W Ireland; 9 m. long; on it is Kilronan, chief town of the Aran Is.

In'ish·ow'en Head (ĭn'ĭsh·ō'ĕn; -ĭn). Cape on N coast of Ireland, W of entrance to Lough Foyle.

In'ish·tra·hull' (?ĭn'ĭsh·trá·hŭl'). Island in Atlantic Ocean off N tip of Ireland, in co. Donegal; lighthouse.

In'ker·man (ĭng'kĕr·măn; *Russ.* ĭn·kĕr·män'). Village near mouth of Chernaya river, just E of Sevastopol, SW Crimea, Soviet Russia, Europe; scene of battle Nov. 5, 1854 during Crimean War in which English and French defeated Russians under Prince Menshikov, with heavy losses on both sides; in World War II taken by Germans June 28, 1942.

Ink'ster (ĭngk'stēr). Residential village, Wayne co., SE Michigan, 13 m. W of Detroit; pop. 39,097.

In'land Empire (ĭn'lănd). Region in NW United States bet. Cascade Range and Rocky Mts., including E Washington and NE Oregon, N Idaho, and extreme W Montana; lumbering, livestock raising, mining.

Inland Passage. See INSIDE PASSAGE.

Inland Sea; *Jap.* **Se·to Nai·kai** (sĕ·tō nī·kī) or **Seto no U·chi** (nō ōō·chē). Irregular-shaped body of water ab. 240 m. long, extending E and W bet. Honshu I. on N and Shikoku and Kyushu Is. on S, Japan; closed at E end by Awaji I.; connected with outer sea by 4 channels: Akashi Strait at NE, Naruto Strait at SE, Bungo Strait (formerly Hayasui) at SW, and Shimonoseki Strait at W end; noted for scenic beauty: studded with 300 islands and bordered on N and S by mountain chains, 3000 to 6000 ft. high; divided into 5 basins: Harima Sea, Bingo Sea, Mishima Sea, Iyo Sea, and Suwo Sea; comparatively shallow and marked by strong tidal movements.

Inland Waterway. = *Intracoastal Waterway;* see ATLANTIC INTRACOASTAL WATERWAY and GULF INTRACOASTAL WATERWAY.

In'le, Lake (ĭn'lā). Lake in cen. Burma, in state of Yawnghwe, Southern Shan States.

Inn (ĭn); *anc.* **Ae'nus** (ē'nŭs). River 320 m. long, Switzerland, Austria, and Germany; rises in lake in Rhaetian Alps, Graubünden, Switzerland, flows NE through Engadine valleys into Tirol, SW Austria; thence E past Innsbruck, then NE through Bavarian Alps to Bavaria, entering the Danube at Passau; in its lower course, boundary bet. Bavaria and Upper Austria, receives the Salzach.

Inner Hebrides. See HEBRIDES.

Inner Mongolia See Inner MONGOLIA.

Inner Rhodes. See APPENZELL.

Inner Sound. Body of water off NW coast of Scotland, bet. Raasay I. and Scottish mainland.

In'nes·dale (ĭn'ĕs·dāl). Town, S cen. Transvaal, NE Union of South Africa, N suburb of Pretoria; pop. ab. 10,000.

In'nis·fail' (ĭn'ĭs·fāl'; *Ir.* -ĭsh·fôl'). Ireland—poetical name.

Inniskilling. See ENNISKILLEN.

In'no·ko (ĭn'ō·kō). River, W Alaska, flowing SW, almost parallel to Yukon river which it enters at ab. 160°W.

Inns'bruck (ĭnz'brŏŏk; *Ger.* ĭns'-). Manufacturing city, ✻ of the Tirol province, W Austria, on Inn river 61 m. S of Munich; pop. (1939) 78,523; university (founded 1677); tourist resort; textiles, chemical and pharmaceutical goods, glass, mosaics, gloves; bell founding; made city 1232; residence 1363–1665 of collateral line of Hapsburgs; capital of the Tirol from c. 1420; center of uprising of Tirolese peasants 1809; occupied by Italians 1918.

In'ny (ĭn'ĭ). River, NE cen. Ireland, flowing SW from Lough Sheelin into Lough Ree.

I·nö·nü' (ĭ·nû·nū'). Village, Bilecik vilayet, NW Turkey in Asia, on railroad ab. 20 m. WNW of Eskişehir; here İsmet Paşa, Turkish general, twice defeated Greeks in war of 1919–22 and took name of village as last name (İsmet İnönü, president of Turkey 1938–50).

I'no·wroc'law (ē'nô·vrôts'läf); *Ger.* **Ho'hen·sal'za** (hō'ĕn·zäl'tsä), *before 1905* **I'no·wraz'law** (ē'nô·vräts'-läf). Commune, Pomorze dept., N cen. Poland, 62 m. NE of Poznań; pop. (1938–39 est.) 38,956; health resort; iron goods, machinery; under Prussian rule before World War I.

In Sa·lah' (ĭn sŏ·lä'h'). Oasis, cen. Southern Territories, Algeria, N Africa; pop. 1088; junction of highways and airways.

In'sein (ĭn'sān). **1** District, Pegu division, Lower Burma; 1914 sq. m.; pop. 331,452.

2 Town, its ✻, 10 m. N of Rangoon; pop. 20,487.

Inside, *or* **Inland, Passage.** Protected steamer route from Puget Sound, Washington, to Skagway, Alaska, following channels bet. the mainland and the many islands along the coast in this region; chief ports Ketchikan, Wrangell, Juneau.

Insterburg. See CHERNYAKHOVSK.

In'sti·tute (ĭn'stĭ·tūt). Village, Kanawha co., West Virginia, W of Charleston; pop. (est.) 3000; West Virginia State College (1891; Negro; coed.).

Insula. See LILLE.

In'sul·inde' (ĭn's'l·ĭnd'; -ĭnd'; ĭn's'l·ĭn'dĕ; *Du.* ĭn'sü-lĭn'dĕ). = NETHERLANDS INDIES.

Inter-American Highway. See PAN-AMERICAN HIGHWAY.

Interamna, Interamnia. See TERAMO commune.

Interamna Nahars. See TERNI.

In'ter·la'ken (ĭn'tĕr·lä'kĕn; ĭn'tĕr·lä'kĕn). Commune, Bern canton, Switzerland, on Aare river bet. Lake of Thun and Lake of Brienz 26 m. SE of Bern; pop. (1930) 3771; health resort; textiles, lumber, liquors; founded c. 1128; valley region famous for view of the Jungfrau.

In'ter·loch'en (ĭn'tĕr·lŏk'ĕn). Village, Grand Traverse co., Michigan, on Green Lake in NW southern penin.; National Music camp.

International Date Line. = DATE LINE.

In'ter·na'tion·al Falls (ĭn'tẽr-năsh'ŭn-ăl). City, ⊗ of Koochiching co., N Minnesota, on Rainy river near Rainy Lake; pop. 6778; railroad center; paper mills.

International Peace Garden. International park area, N North Dakota and SW Manitoba, Canada, near Whitewater Lake (Canada); 888 acres in U.S.

International Zone *or* **Tangier Zone.** See TANGIER.

Internum, Mare. See MEDITERRANEAN SEA.

In'ti·bu·cá' (ēn'tĕ-vōō-kä'). Department, W cen. Honduras; 1057 sq. m.; pop. (1945 est.) 54,882; ✳ La Esperanza.

In'tra (ēn'trä). Former commune; now subdivision (1931 pop. 14,135) of commune of VERBANIA, Italy.

In'tra·coast'al Waterway (ĭn'trȧ-kōs't'l). 1 See AtLANTIC INTRACOASTAL WATERWAY.
2 See GULF INTRACOASTAL WATERWAY.

I·nu·bo, Cape (ē-nōō-bō). Cape on SE coast of Honshu, Japan, in Chiba prefecture, E of Tokyo; lighthouse, 36°N, 141°E.

In·ú'til Bay (ēn-ōō'tēl); *Eng.* **Use'less Bay** (ūs'lĕs; -lĭs). Large inlet on NW coast of Tierra del Fuego I., Chile; opens into Strait of Magellan.

In'ver·ar'ay (ĭn'vẽr-âr'ĭ). Burgh, Argyll co., W Scotland; pop. 503; herring fishing; castle.

In'ver·car'gill (ĭn'vẽr-kär'gĭl). Seaport borough, ✳ of Southland subdivision of Otago provincial dist., S South I., New Zealand, on estuary of Foveaux Strait 110 m. WSW of Dunedin; pop. with suburbs 29,094; Bluff its port; wheat, oats, wool, meat, dairy products; woolen and lumber mills, foundries, breweries.

In'ver·ell' (ĭn'vẽr-ĕl'). Town, NE New South Wales, SE Australia, 280 m. N of Sydney; pop. 5304; wheat, grapes, corn; silver, tin, diamond mines.

In'ver·ness' (ĭn'vẽr-nĕs'). Town, ⊗ of Citrus co., W Florida penin.; pop. 1878.

In'ver·ness' (ĭn'vẽr-nĕs'; ĭn'vẽr-nĕs'). 1 County, Nova Scotia, Canada. See *Table* at NOVA SCOTIA.
2 Coastal town, Inverness co., NE Nova Scotia, Canada, on W coast of Cape Breton I. on Gulf of St. Lawrence; pop. 2360; coal, copper, gypsum, and clay deposits.
3 Village, ⊗ of Megantic co., S Quebec, Canada, 40 m. SSW of Quebec; pop. 278.
4 *or* **In'ver·ness'–shire** (ĭn'vẽr-nĕs'shĭr; -nĕsh'-; -shẽr). County, NW Scotland; 4211 sq. m., includes several of Inner and Outer Hebrides, as Harris, North Uist, South Uist, Skye, and Eıgg; pop. (1951) 84,924; ⊗ Inverness; mountainous region, including Ben Nevis 4406 ft., highest peak in British Isles; sheep grazing, fisheries, quarrying.
5 Burgh, ⊗ of Inverness co., NW Scotland, on the Ness at NE terminus of Caledonian Canal; pop. 28,115; shipbuilding plants, breweries, textile mills.

In·ves'ti·ga'tor Strait (ĭn-vĕs'tĭ-gā'tẽr). Channel bet. N Kangaroo I. and mainland, South Australia; forms SW entrance to Gulf of St. Vincent.

In'wood (ĭn'wŏŏd). Village, Nassau co., SE New York, on Long I. on shore of Jamaica Bay, ab. 12 m. E of Brooklyn; pop. 10,362; oyster industry.

In'yo (ĭn'yō). County in California. See *Table* at CALIFORNIA.

In'yo·kern' (ĭn'yō-kûrn'). Town, Kern co., E California, 30 m. W of Death Valley and NE of Bakersfield; pop. (est.) 450; naval ordnance research station.

In'yo Mountains (ĭn'yō). Range in W cen. Inyo co., E California.

Io·an'ni·na *or* **Io·án'ni·na** (yô-ä'nyĕ-nä). 1 Department of Greece. See *Table* at GREECE.
2 *also* **Yan'ni·na** (yä'nĕ-nä); *Serb.* **Ja'ni·na** (yä'nĕ-nä). City, its ✳, N Epirus, NW Greece, near Albanian frontier on **Lake Ioannina**; pop. 20,485; 11thcent. Byzantine city; captured by Turks 1431; famous as seat of Ali Pasha, the Lion of Janina; taken by Greeks 1913; held for short time by Italians in their attack on Greece Oct. 1940 but recaptured; taken by Germans Apr. 19, 1941.

I·o'la (ī-ō'lȧ). City, ⊗ of Allen co., SE Kansas, 15 m. N of Chanute; pop. 6885; cement works.

I·ol'cus (ī-ŏl'kŭs). Ruined city, SE Thessaly, NE Greece, near modern Volos; legendary home of Jason and port from which Argonauts set out.

I·o'na (ī-ō'nȧ). Island of the Inner Hebrides, Scotland, off SW tip of Mull I.; 6 sq. m.; early center of the Celtic church; St. Columba and his disciples landed here from Ireland c. 563.

I·o'ni·a (ī-ō'nĭ-ȧ; -ōn'yȧ). 1 County in Michigan. See *Table* at MICHIGAN.
2 City, its ⊗, S cen. Michigan, 32 m. E of Grand Rapids; pop. 6754; reed furniture, flour, pottery.
3 Ancient district on W coast of Asia Minor bordering on Aegean Sea and extending from a point near mouth of Hermus river S to the Halicarnassus Penin.; mountainous country 90 m. long and 20 to 30 m. wide; included some of islands of E Aegean Sea (Chios, Samos, etc.); its hinterland was Lydia and Caria; received name from Ionians, a branch of ancient Greeks, who probably migrated from Greek mainland to Asia Minor c. 1000 B.C.; never a political unit, had religious league of 12 **Ionian Cities** (N to S): Phocaea, Clazomenae, Erythrae, Teos, Lebedos, Colophon, Ephesus, Priene, Myus, Miletus, and the two island cities of Chios and Samos; became subject to Lydia (*q.v.*) and later, to Persia c. 547 B.C.; produced Ionic school of philosophy and architectural advances (Ionic order); revolt of Miletus (*q.v.*) brought on Greek wars with Persia; freed from Persia by Alexander of Macedon 334 B.C.; became part of the Roman province of Asia; ruined during the Turkish conquest of Asia Minor.

I·o'ni·an Islands (ī-ō'nĭ-ăn; ī-ōn'yăn); *anc.* **Hep'ta·ne'sus** (hĕp'tȧ-nē'sŭs). Group of 7 Greek islands in Ionian Sea: Corfu, Paxos, Leukas, Ithaca, Cephalonia, and Zante off W coast of Greece, and Cerigo off S coast of Peloponnesus; 853 sq. m.; pop. ab. 259,600; except Leukas which belongs to Preveza dept., Epirus, they form a geographical division of Greece including departments of Cephalonia, Corfu, and Zante (see *Table* at GREECE); generally mountainous; fruits (esp. currants), olive oil, grain, wine. Colonized by ancient Greeks; part of Roman and Byzantine Empires; Corfu occupied by Venetians 1386–1797; taken by French 1797 but surrendered to Russians 1799; organized as Septinsular Republic under Russian protection 1800–07; British protectorate 1815–64; annexed to Greece 1864.

Ionian Sea; *Lat.* **Ma're I·o'ni·um** (mä'rē ī-ō'nĭ-ŭm). Part of Mediterranean Sea bet. SE coast of Italy and W Greece, connected with Adriatic Sea by Strait of Otranto; along its E shore are the Ionian Is. and on NW is the Gulf of Taranto.

Io'nio (yô'nyô). Province of Italy. See *Table* at ITALY.

Io'ri·bai'wa (yô'rē·bi'wȧ). Village, SE Papua, New Guinea, in mountains 30 m. E of Port Moresby; Japanese advance from Buna and Gona stopped here by Australians Sept. 1942.

I'os (ī'ŏs; *Mod. Gr.* ē'ôs). 1 *or* **Ni'o** (nyē'ô). Island in Aegean Sea, in S cen. Cyclades; 46 sq. m.; pop. ab. 2000; belongs to Cyclades dept., Greece.
2 Town on W coast of island.

I·os'co (ī-ŏs'kō). County in Michigan. See *Table* at MICHIGAN.

Iosh·kar' O·la' (yôsh·kàr' ŭ·lȧ'); *also* **Yosh·kar' Ola** (yôsh·kàr'). Town, ✳ of Mari Republic, Soviet Russia, Europe, in cen. part, ab. 80 m. NW of Kazan.

I'o·wa (ī'ô·wȧ; *locally also* -wä). 1 River 291 m. long, formed by confluence of branches in N cen. Iowa and flowing SE into the Mississippi in SE Iowa.
2 A north central state of U.S.A., 29th state admitted to Union (1846); bounded on N by Minnesota, on E by Wisconsin and Illinois, on S by Missouri, and on W by Nebraska and South Dakota; 25th state in area, 56,290 sq. m. (land area 56,045 sq. m.); 24th state in population, 2,757,537; ✳ Des Moines. See *Table of States* at

UNITED STATES. Divided into the following 99 counties (for pronunciation of their names, see their individual entries):

NAME	LOCATION	AREA[1]	POP.[1]	CO. SEAT
Adair	SW cen.	569	10,893	Greenfield
Adams	SW	426	7,468	Corning
Allamakee	NE corner	639	15,982	Waukon
Appanoose	S	523	16,015	Centerville
Audubon	W	448	10,919	Audubon
Benton	E cen.	718	23,422	Vinton
Black Hawk	NE cen.	567	122,482	Waterloo
Boone	cen.	573	28,037	Boone
Bremer	NE	439	21,108	Waverly
Buchanan	E	569	22,293	Independence
Buena Vista	NW	573	21,189	Storm Lake
Butler	NE cen.	582	17,467	Allison
Calhoun	NW cen.	572	15,923	Rockwell City
Carroll	W cen.	574	23,431	Carroll
Cass	SW	559	17,919	Atlantic
Cedar	E	585	17,791	Tipton
Cerro Gordo	N	576	49,894	Mason City
Cherokee	NW	573	18,598	Cherokee
Chickasaw	NE	505	15,034	New Hampton
Clarke	S	429	8,222	Osceola
Clay	NW	571	18,504	Spencer
Clayton	NE	778	21,962	Elkader
Clinton	E	695	55,060	Clinton
Crawford	W	716	18,569	Denison
Dallas	S cen.	597	24,123	Adel
Davis	SE	509	9,199	Bloomfield
Decatur	S	530	10,539	Leon
Delaware	E	573	18,483	Manchester
Des Moines	SE	409	44,605	Burlington
Dickinson	NW	382	12,574	Spirit Lake
Dubuque	E	608	80,048	Dubuque
Emmet	N	395	14,871	Estherville
Fayette	NE	728	28,581	West Union
Floyd	N	503	21,102	Charles City
Franklin	N cen.	586	15,472	Hampton
Fremont	SW corner	523	10,282	Sidney
Greene	W cen.	569	14,379	Jefferson
Grundy	NE cen.	501	14,132	Grundy Center
Guthrie	SW cen.	596	13,607	Guthrie Center
Hamilton	N cen.	577	20,032	Webster City
Hancock	N	570	14,604	Garner
Hardin	N cen.	574	22,533	Eldora
Harrison	W	695	17,600	Logan
Henry	SE	440	18,187	Mount Pleasant
Howard	N	471	12,734	Cresco
Humboldt	NW cen.	435	13,156	Dakota City
Ida	W	431	10,269	Ida Grove
Iowa	E cen.	584	16,396	Marengo
Jackson	E	644	20,754	Maquoketa
Jasper	S cen.	736	35,282	Newton
Jefferson	SE	436	15,818	Fairfield
Johnson	E	620	53,663	Iowa City
Jones	E	585	20,693	Anamosa
Keokuk	SE cen.	579	15,492	Sigourney
Kossuth	N	979	25,314	Algona
Lee	SE corner	522	44,207	Keokuk & Fort Madison
Linn	E	713	136,899	Cedar Rapids
Louisa	SE	403	10,290	Wapello
Lucas	S	434	10,923	Chariton
Lyon	NW corner	588	14,468	Rock Rapids
Madison	S cen.	565	12,295	Winterset
Mahaska	SE cen.	572	23,602	Oskaloosa
Marion	S cen.	568	25,886	Knoxville
Marshall	cen.	574	37,984	Marshalltown
Mills	SW	445	13,050	Glenwood
Mitchell	N	467	14,043	Osage
Monona	W	697	13,916	Onawa
Monroe	S	435	10,463	Albia
Montgomery	SW	422	14,467	Red Oak
Muscatine	E	439	33,840	Muscatine
O'Brien	NW	575	18,840	Primghar
Osceola	NW	398	10,064	Sibley
Page	SW	535	21,023	Clarinda
Palo Alto	N	561	14,736	Emmetsburg
Plymouth	NW	863	23,906	Le Mars
Pocahontas	NW cen.	580	14,234	Pocahontas
Polk	S cen.	594	266,315	Des Moines
Pottawattamie	SW	964	83,102	Council Bluffs
Poweshiek	SE cen.	589	19,300	Montezuma
Ringgold	S	538	7,910	Mount Ayr
Sac	W	578	17,007	Sac City
Scott	E	453	119,067	Davenport
Shelby	W	587	15,825	Harlan
Sioux	NW	766	26,375	Orange City
Story	cen.	568	49,327	Nevada
Tama	E cen.	720	21,413	Toledo
Taylor	SW	528	10,288	Bedford
Union	S	426	13,712	Creston
Van Buren	SE	487	9,778	Keosauqua
Wapello	SE	437	46,126	Ottumwa
Warren	S cen.	572	20,829	Indianola
Washington	SE	568	19,406	Washington
Wayne	S	532	9,800	Corydon
Webster	NW cen.	718	47,810	Fort Dodge
Winnebago	N	402	13,099	Forest City
Winneshiek	NE	688	21,651	Decorah
Woodbury	W	871	107,849	Sioux City
Worth	N	401	10,259	Northwood
Wright	N cen.	577	19,447	Clarion

[1] Area = land area in sq. m. Pop. from 1960 Census.

Nickname: Hawkeye State. *State flower:* Wild rose. *Motto:* Our Liberties We Prize, and Our Rights We Will Maintain. *Chief cities:* Des Moines, Cedar Rapids, Sioux City, Davenport, Waterloo. *Rivers:* Des Moines, flowing diagonally across state NW to SE, forming in its lower course the boundary with Missouri, and emptying into the Mississippi; Mississippi, forming E boundary; Missouri, forming W boundary bet. Iowa and Nebraska; Big Sioux, forming W boundary bet. Iowa and South Dakota. *Highest point:* 1675 ft. on N boundary near Sibley in Osceola co. *Chief industries:* Agriculture (raises esp. corn, oats, and hay), stock raising (esp. hogs), meat packing.

History: Became part of U.S. by Louisiana Purchase 1803; part of Missouri Territory 1812–21, unorganized 1821–34, part of territories of Michigan 1834–36 and of Wisconsin 1836–38; first permanent settlement made 1833 at Dubuque; organized in 1838 as Iowa Territory which included parts of Minnesota, North Dakota and South Dakota; held first constitutional convention 1844; present constitution dates from 1851. Admitted to Union Dec. 28, 1846; capital removed from Iowa City to Des Moines 1857.

3 Name of counties in two states of the U.S. See *Tables* at IOWA and WISCONSIN.

Iowa City. City, ⊗ of Johnson co., E Iowa, 25 m. S of Cedar Rapids; pop. 33,443; settled 1838; capital of Iowa Territory 1839–57; State University of Iowa (1847; coed.).

Iowa Falls. City, Hardin co., N cen. Iowa, 37 m. NW of Marshalltown; pop. 5565.

Iowa Park. Town, Wichita co., N Texas, 10 m. W of Wichita Falls; pop. 3295.

I'pa·me·rí' (ē'pȧ·mĕ·rē'). Town, Goiaz state, cen. Brazil, 100 m. SE of Goiânia; pop. 7452.

Ipek. See PEĆ.

I'pel' (ĭ'pĕl·y'); *Hung.* **I'poly** (ĭ'poi); *Ger.* **Ei'pel** (ī'pĕl). River ab. 125 m. long, S Slovakia and N Hungary; flows SSW, forming section of boundary bet. Czechoslovakia and Hungary, empties into Danube river 10 m. below Esztergom, NW Hungary; in 1938–45 almost entirely within Hungary.

I·pia'les (ē·pyä'lås). Town, Nariño dept., SW Colombia; pop. 8343.

I'pin' (ē'pĭn'); *formerly* **Su'chow'** (sü'jō'; shü'-) *or* **Sui'fu'** (swā'fōō'). Commercial city, SW Szechwan prov., S cen. China, on Yangtze river at its junction with the Min, 140 m. SW of Chungking; pop. ab. 125,000; export center for Chinese wax, musk, cotton goods, medicinal herbs, and other products of Tibet, Yunnan, and Szechwan.

Ipiranga. See YPIRANGA.

I'poh (ē'pō). City, cen. Perak state, Federation of Malaya, 75 m. SE of George Town, Penang; pop. 53,183, (1937 est.) 64,343; on railroad trunk line; commercial center of Kinta Valley tin-mining region; captured by Japanese Dec. 29, 1941.

Ipoly. See IPEL'.

Ipsambul. See ABU SIMBEL.

Ipsara. See PSARA.

Ip'sus (ĭp'sŭs). Village in S Phrygia (NW of modern Akşehir), Asia Minor; scene of a decisive battle 301 B.C. in Wars of the Diadochi in which Lysimachus and Seleucus defeated Antigonus and his son Demetrius, precipitating the breakup of the Greco-Macedonian world; Antigonus was slain.

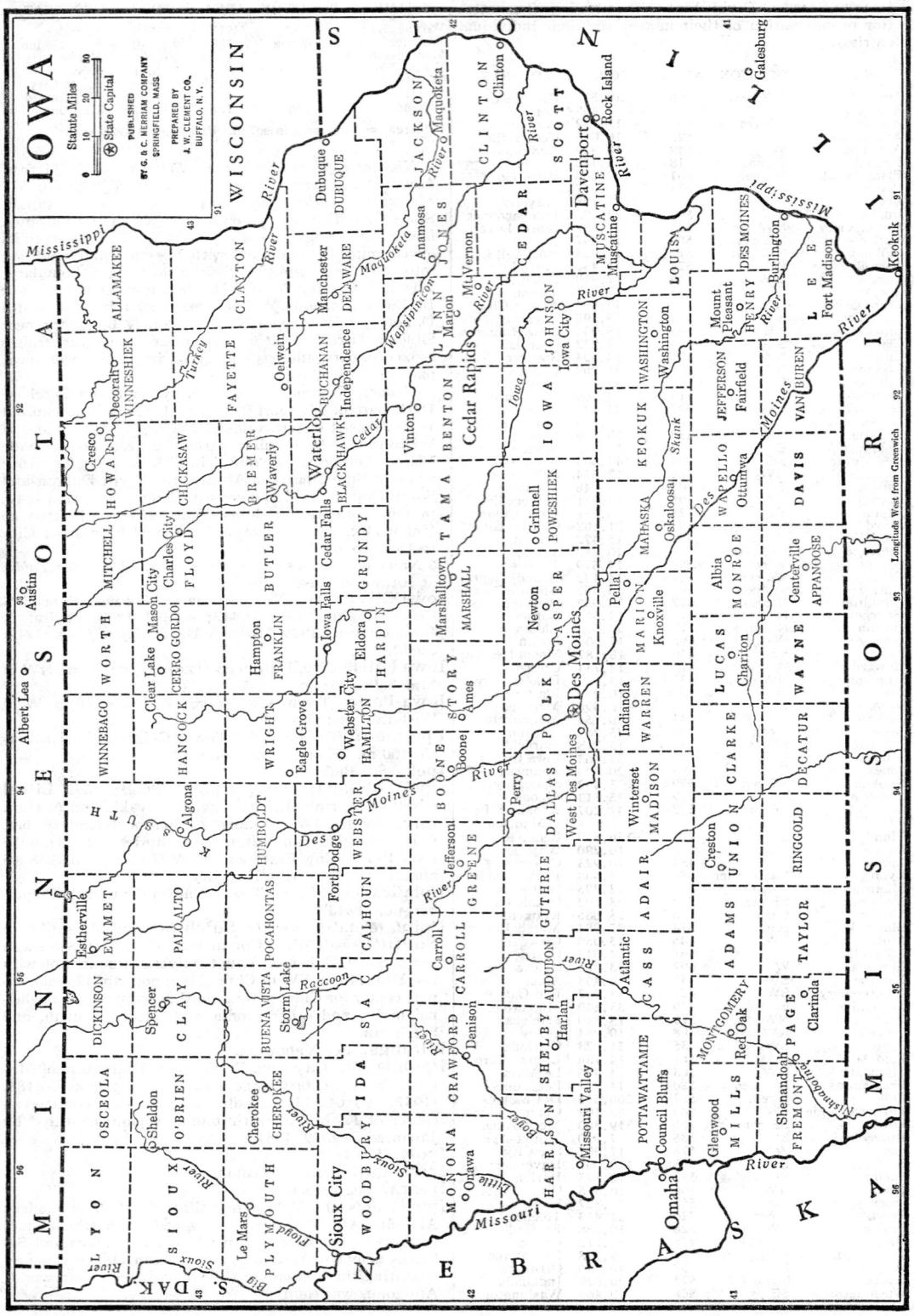

IOWA

Statute Miles

⊛ State Capital

PUBLISHED
BY G. & C. MERRIAM COMPANY
SPRINGFIELD, MASS.

PREPARED BY
A. W. CLEMENT CO.
BUFFALO, N. Y.

Ips′wich (ĭps′wĭch). **1** Town, Essex co., NE corner of Massachusetts, 23 m. E of Lowell; pop. 8544.
2 City, ⊗ of Edmunds co., N South Dakota; pop. 1131.
3 City, SE Queensland. Australia, 25 m. SW of Brisbane; pop. 22,499; founded 1829; coal mining, agriculture.
4 County borough, ⊗ of East Suffolk, E England, at head of Orwell estuary 64 m. ENE of London; pop. 87,502, (1951) 104,788; farm machinery; port, shipping center; birthplace of Cardinal Wolsey.

I·qui′que (ê·kē′kȧ). Seaport city, N Chile, ab. 235 m. N of Antofagasta; ✻ of Tarapacá prov.; pop. 38,094; nitrate export center; founded 16th cent.; partly destroyed by earthquake 1868 and 1877, and by fire 1875; occupied by Chileans in war with Peru 1879; ceded to Chile by treaty Oct. 23, 1883.

I·qui′tos (ê·kē′tôs). City and river port on upper Amazon, NE Peru, 1268 m. NE of Lima by overland route; ✻ of Loreto dept.; pop. (1940 est.) 34,231; commercial outlet for NE Peru by way of the Amazon; a Peruvian (not Indian) city, dating from 1863.

I′ra·an′ (ī′rȧ·ăn′). Town, Pecos co., W Texas, on Pecos river ab. 75 m. S of Midland; pop. 1255.

I·ra·já′ (ê·rȧ·zhä′). Town, NW suburb of Rio de Janeiro, Brazil.

Irak. See IRAQ.

Iraklion. = *Hērákleion:* see CANDIA.

I·ran′ (ê·rän′; *Angl.* ĭ·răn′, ī-); *formerly, and by some still called,* **Per′sia** (pûr′zhȧ; -shȧ). Modern kingdom, W Asia; ab. 628,000 sq. m.; pop. ab. 15,000,000; ✻ Tehran; bounded on N by Caspian Sea and the Turkmen S.S.R., on E by Afghanistan and Baluchistan, on S by Gulf of Oman and Persian Gulf, on W by Iraq, and on NW by the Soviet Socialist Republics of Armenia and Azerbaidzhan; a region of plateaus and mountains, esp. Elburz Mts. in N along Caspian Sea; W end of the Hindu Kush in NE; and many ranges (Zagros Mts.) in W with peaks above 10,000 ft.; highest point Mt. Demavend 18,600 ft., in Elburz Mts.; E half occupied by greater part of Plateau of Iran (*q.v.*); chief rivers Karun and Karkheh in W, Sefid Rud in NW, and Atrek on N border; only important island Qishm in the Strait of Ormuz; chief exports wool, carpets, gum tragacanth, almonds, opium, oil, and cotton; chief cities Tehran, Tabriz, Isfahan, Meshed, Hamadan; principal ports Bushire, Bandar Abbas, Bandar Shahpur on the Persian Gulf and Pahlevi and Bandar Shah on the Caspian; people are Aryans and their language one of the oldest of the Indo-European family.

History: The name *Ariana,* in ancient Greek and Roman usage, was variously applied to the geographical region (the Plateau of Iran) and to SE parts, excluding Persis; the plateau was the home of ancient civilizations of Elam, Media, and Persia; c. 2000 B.C., occupied by Iranian peoples among which were Medes and Persians. For history before 1935, see PERSIA. Iran adopted as official name of modern Persia Mar. 22, 1935; Riza Shah Pahlavi abdicated Sept. 16, 1941; treaty of alliance with Great Britain and U.S.S.R. signed Jan. 29, 1942; joined United Nations Sept. 14, 1943; conference of Churchill, Stalin, and Roosevelt held at Tehran Nov. 27–Dec. 2, 1943; internal troubles (revolt in Azerbaijan prov.) 1945–46.

Iran, Plateau of. Plateau, extensive highland area in W Asia, comprising cen. and E Iran and W sections of Afghanistan and Baluchistan; ab. 1,000,000 sq. m., of which ab. 600,000 are in Iran; average altitude 3000 to 5000 ft.; contains great salt deserts of Dasht-i-Lut and Dasht-i-Kavir.

I·ran′ Mountains (?ê·rän′). Mountain range running N and S bet. E Sarawak and N cen. Borneo; highest nearly 10,000 ft.

I′ra·pua′to (ē′rä·pwä′tô). City, Guanajuato state, cen. Mexico, in farming district; pop. 32,337; at altitude of ab. 5600 ft.

I·raq′ (ê·räk′; ĭ·răk′). **1** *also* **I·rak′**; *Arab,* **'I·raq′.** Republic, an Arab independent country in SW Asia, including most of Mesopotamia; bounded on N by Turkey, on E by Iran, on S by Kuwait and Saudi Arabia, and on W by Jordan and Syrian Republic; 116,600 sq. m.; pop. (1935 est.) 3,560,456, (1939 est.) 3,800,000; ✻ Baghdad; comprises for most part level country drained by Euphrates and Tigris rivers which unite ab. 120 m from Persian Gulf NNW of Basra to form the Shatt-al-Arab, and by tributaries of the Tigris from the E; river region fertile with many lakes; wide desert region in W (part of Syrian Desert) and SW; mountainous in Kurdistan region of NE; chief products dates, wool, grains, cotton, and hides; has extensive oil fields esp. around Kirkuk and Khanaqin; administratively divided into 14 provinces (*liwas*); chief cities Baghdad, Mosul, Basra, An Najaf, Karbala, Kirkuk, and Hilla.

History: Kingdom established 1921 after World War I out of former Turkish territory; under British mandate 1920 until Oct. 1932 when it became independent under King Faisal I; semi-independent state in alliance with Great Britain 1922; a limited monarchy according to organic law 1924; awarded Mosul (*q.v.*) by League of Nations 1925; independence and sovereignty recognized in treaties with Great Britain 1927 and 1930, the full result of which was admission to League 1932; in treaty with Saudi Arabia (*q.v.*) 1936; occupied by British Apr.–June 1941 to prevent Nazi control; joined United Nations 1943; republic established following army coup July 1958 during which King Feisal and Crown Prince Abdul Illah were assassinated. See MESOPOTAMIA, and for ancient history BABYLONIA and ASSYRIA.

2 *formerly* **Sul·tan′a·bad′** (sōōl·tän′ȧ·bäd′). City, W cen. Iran; pop. ab. 55,000; on highway N from Ahwaz, junction point ab. equally distant (80 m.) from Hamadan to NW and Qum to NE; pottery and metalwork.

'I·raq′ 'A′ra·bi (ĭ·räk′ ŭ′rŏ·bē). The region of lower Mesopotamia; the Tigris-Euphrates valley S of Baghdad, comprising Basra, Baghdad, and adjoining provinces in Iraq; nearly coextensive with ancient Babylonia.

'I·raq′-i-'A′jam (ĭ·räk′ĕ·ä′jȧm) *or* **I·raq′ A·je·mi′** (ĭ·räk′ ȧ·jȧ·mē′). Region and former province in W cen. Iran; as province, capital was Sultanabad (Iraq).

Irawadi. Var. of IRRAWADDY.

I′ra·zú′ (ē′rä·sōō′). Volcano 11,200 ft., cen. Costa Rica, near city of Cartago; active 1841 and 1910; only place on North American continent where on a clear day both the Atlantic and Pacific Oceans can be seen.

Ir′bid (ĭr′bĭd). Town, N Jordan; pop. 2750; road junction 42 m. N of Amman.

Ir·bit′ (ĭr·byēt′). Commercial town, Sverdlovsk Region, Soviet Russia, Asia, 110 m. NE of Sverdlovsk; pop. ab. 12,000; famous for its annual fair held from 1643.

Ire′dell (ĭr′dĕl). County in North Carolina. See *Table* at NORTH CAROLINA.

Ire′land (īr′lănd); *Lat.* **Hi·ber′ni·a** (hī·bûr′nĭ·ȧ). *Also known as the* **Em′er·ald Isle** (ĕm′ẽr·ăld) *and* (*in poetry*) **Er′in** (ĕr′ĭn; ēr′ĭn). **1** Island of the British Isles, W of England and separated from it by St. George's Channel and the Irish Sea; divided bet. the independent Republic of Ireland (see EIRE), which occupies the 26 counties in the S, cen., and NW part, and Northern Ireland (a division of the United Kingdom), which occupies the six counties in the NE part; total area 31,840 sq. m.; total pop. (Eire census of 1936; Northern Ireland census of 1937) 4,248,165. Consists of central plain with lakes (*loughs*) in N, cen., and W parts, esp. Erne, Neagh, Mask, Corrib, Conn, Ree, Derg, and the small and beautiful Lakes of Killarney in SW, and with groups of hills averaging 2000 to 3000 ft. on N, W, and S; highest point Carrantual 3414 ft. in SW. *Rivers:* Shannon in cen. part, Bann in N, Lagan in NE, Boyne and Liffey in E, Barrow, Nore, and Suir in SE, Blackwater and Lee in S. Coast line irregular; harbors include Lough Foyle, Belfast Lough, Donegal Bay, Sligo Bay, Galway Bay, Dingle

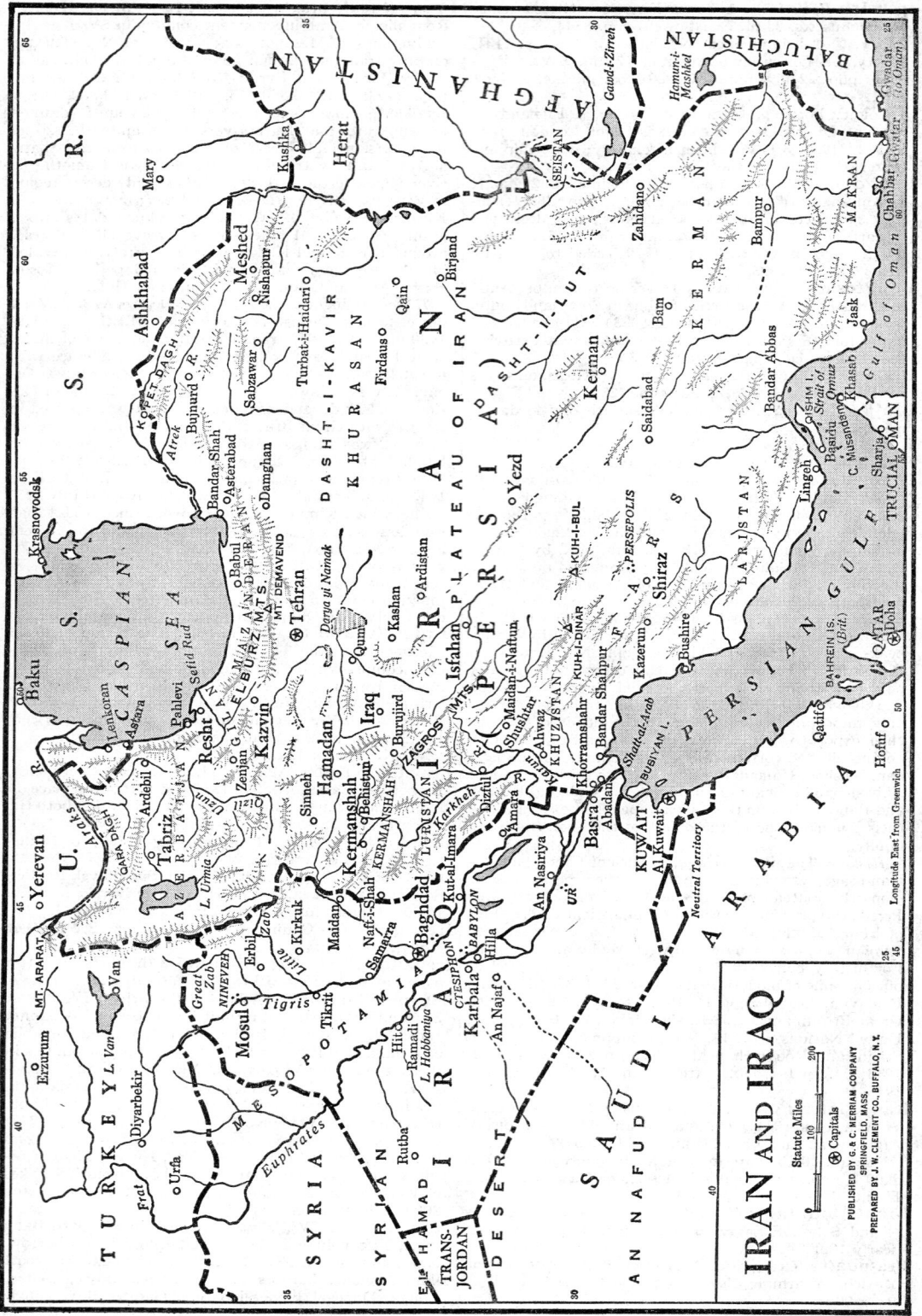

IRAN AND IRAQ

Statute Miles

PUBLISHED BY G. & C. MERRIAM COMPANY
SPRINGFIELD, MASS.
PREPARED BY J. W. CLEMENT CO., BUFFALO, N.Y.

⊛ Capitals

Bay, Bantry Bay, Dundalk Bay, and estuaries of the Shannon and Lee (Cork Harbour); numerous small islands, esp. Rathlin, Achill, Aran Is., Valencia, and Fastnet. *Chief industries:* Of Eire, agriculture, stock raising, and manufactures (textiles, clothing, tobacco, whiskies, flour, sugar beets); of Northern Ireland, textiles, esp. linen shipbuilding, and agriculture. *Chief cities:* In Eire, Dublin, Cork, Limerick, Dun Laoghaire, Waterford, Galway, Dundalk, and Drogheda; in Northern Ireland, Belfast, Londonderry, Armagh, and Enniskillen.

History: Invaded by Celts c. 500 B.C.; according to tradition, governed as kingdoms of Ulster, Leinster, Connaught, Munster, and Meath, under which were numerous warring tribal kings; in 5th cent. A.D., converted to Christianity by St. Patrick; Irish monasticism produced outstanding scholars and missionaries, 6th–9th cents.; raided by Vikings (see CLONTARF) who founded Dublin, Waterford, and Limerick as trading stations; conquered 1169–71 by Norman lords and Henry II who established English rule over strip of coast around Dublin (later known as the Pale); Irish Parliament restricted by Poynings's Law 1494; extent of Pale varied until Cromwell, after rebellion of 1641–42, subdued all of Ireland; colonized, especially in N by Scots, Welsh, and English; supported James II at battle of the Boyne (*q.v.*) 1690; united legislatively with Great Britain, forming United Kingdom of Great Britain and Ireland (see GREAT BRITAIN) 1801; in 19th cent., "Irish Question" (including problems of status of Catholics, land, self-government—Home Rule after 1886) became a key issue of British politics; unsuccessfully attempted to throw off British rule by Easter Rebellion (Easter Monday, Apr. 24, 1916); S Ireland refused Home Rule as provided by Act of 1920, and, after civil war 1919–21, was granted dominion status as Irish Free State 1921 (established 1922); 6 counties of Ulster formed Northern Ireland (*q.v.*) 1920.

2 The Republic of Ireland: see EIRE.

Ireland, Northern. See NORTHERN IRELAND.

Ireland Island. One of the Bermuda Is., W of Grassy Bay and N of Great Sound; British naval base.

I·reng' (ĭ·rĕng'). River ab. 180 m. long, British Guiana, tributary of the Takutú; flows S and forms section of boundary bet. W cen. British Guiana and Brazil.

Ir·giz' (ĭr·gēz'; *Russ.* -gēs'). **1** River ab. 270 m. long, W cen. Kazakh S.S.R., Soviet Central Asia, flowing SE into Chelkar Tengiz (lake), NE of Lake Aral.
2 Town, W cen. Kazakh S.S.R., on Irgiz river ab. 220 m. SE of Aktyubinsk; junction of caravan routes.
3 River ab. 300 m. long, SE Soviet Russia, Europe; rises in S Kuibyshev Region and flows W into Volga river opp. Volsk; navigable except at low-water season.

Iri. See EUROTAS.

Irian. See NEW GUINEA.

I·ri'ga (ê·rē'gä). **1** Extinct volcano 4023 ft., S Camarines Sur prov., Luzon, Phil. Is.
2 Municipality, S Camarines Sur prov., SW of Mt. Iriga and on railroad 22 m. SE of Naga; pop. 31,005; largest town in province; in rich agricultural region.

I·rin'ga (ê·rǐng'gä). **1** Former province, SW Tanganyika Territory, E Africa; 38,531 sq. m.; pop. 493,316.
2 Town, its *, 255 m. SW of Dar es Salaam.

I·ri·o·mo·te (ê·rê·ô·mō·tĕ). Island 57 m. in circumference, in Sakishima group, SW end of Ryukyu Is., Japan.

Ir'i·on (ĭr'ĭ·ŭn). County in Texas. See *Table* at TEXAS.

I·ri·rí' (ê·rê·rē'). River ab. 570 m. long, cen. Pará state, N Brazil; rises in N Mato Grosso and flows N into Xingú river.

Iris. See YEŞIL IRMAK.

I'rish Free State (ī'rĭsh); *Gaelic* **Saor'stat' Eir'eann** or **Saor'stát' Éir'eann** (sâr'stôt' âr'ĭn). Name of EIRE before 1937.

Irish Sea; *anc.* **O·ce'a·nus Hi·ber'ni·cus** (ô·sē'á·nŭs hī·bûr'nĭ·kŭs). Body of water bet. England on E and

Ireland on W, connected with Atlantic Ocean on N through North Channel and on S through St. George's Channel.

Ir·kutsk' (ĭr·kōōtsk'). City, * of Irkutsk Region, Soviet Russia, Asia, in S part on Angara river 45 m. from SW shore of Lake Baikal; pop. 243,380; one of chief cities on Trans-Siberian R.R.; cultural center; varied manufactures· market for furs and skins; established 1652 as government station; grew because of trade with China and Amur valley and connection with Lena gold fields and with fur trade; much damaged during Russian Civil War 1918–21.

Irkutsk Region. Region, S Soviet Russia, Asia; 387,274 sq. m.; pop. 1,286,696; * Irkutsk; Lake Baikal forms a large part of its E border; principal streams the Angara, the upper headstreams of the Lena, the Lower Tunguska, and the Uda, and the lower course of the Vitim; chiefly a mountain and plateau region with highest peaks in Sayan Mts. on SW boundary; most important resources mineral, esp. gold (at Bodaibo), coal, salt, mica, but timber, fishing, fur-bearing animals, and agricultural products also valuable; industrial centers Irkutsk and Cheremkhovo, both near or on the navigable Angara and the Trans-Siberian R.R., which traverses region from NW to SE; chief cities Irkutsk, Cheremkhovo, Tulun, Bodaibo Region began to be settled in latter half of 17th cent.; long used as place of banishment for political and other exiles; in 19th cent. received many voluntary settlers; became part of East Siberia region; reorganized as subdivision of Soviet Russia in Asia 1936.

Ir'lam (ûr'lăm). Urban district, Lancashire, NW England, at confluence of Mersey and Irwell rivers 7½ m. W of Manchester; pop. 15,063.

I·ro, Cape (ê·rō). Cape on SE coast of Honshu, Japan, bet. Suruga Bay and Sagami Sea.

I'ron (ī'ẽrn). Name of counties in four states of the U.S. See *Tables* at MICHIGAN, MISSOURI, UTAH, WISCONSIN.

I·ron'de·quoit (ĭ·rŏn'dĕ·kwoit; -kwŏt). Town, Monroe co., W New York; pop. 55,337; part of town annexed to Rochester 1932.

Irondequoit Bay. Inlet of Lake Ontario, E of Rochester, W New York; rendezvous 1687 of Marquis de Denonville in his sally against the Iroquois; French post 1710.

I'ron Gate *or* **Gates** (ī'ẽrn); *Romanian* **Por·ţi'le de Fier** (pôr·tsē'lĕ dĕ fyĕr'); *Ger.* **Ei'ser·nes Tor** (ī'zĕr·nĕs tōr'). Gorge 2 m. long, with rapids, in Danube river bet. Orşova and Turnu-Severin, Romania, on Yugoslav boundary.

Iron Mountain. **1** Elevation 325 ft., Polk co., cen. Florida penin.; highest point in state.
2 Mountain 1077 ft., St. Francois co., E Missouri, ab. 12 m. NE of Taum Sauk.
3 Peak 5500 ft., Custer and Pennington cos., SW South Dakota.
4 City, ⊗ of Dickinson co., S Michigan penin., 48 m. W of Escanaba; pop. 9299; former iron-mining center; distributing point for Menominee Range area.
5 *known also as* **El Cer'ro del Mer·ca'do** (ĕl sĕr'rô thĕl mĕr·kä'thô). Rounded hill ab. 700 ft. high N of city of Durango in Durango state NW cen. Mexico; composed chiefly of iron in various stages of oxidation.

Iron Mountains. Ridge ab. 80 m. long, extending along boundary bet. Smyth and Grayson cos. and bet. Grayson and Wythe cos., in Virginia, and SW into Tennessee; highest peak ab. 4200 ft.

Iron River. City, Iron co., SW Michigan penin., 34 m. WNW of Iron Mountain; pop. 3754; iron mining.

I'ron·ton (ī'ẽrn·tŭn). **1** City, ⊗ of Iron co., SE Missouri; pop. 1310.
2 City, ⊗ of Lawrence co., S Ohio, on Ohio river opp. Russell, Kentucky, 21 m. SE of Portsmouth; pop. 15,745; founded 1848; formerly iron-industry center; coke, cement, stoves, shoes, steel castings; railroad terminus.

I′ron·wood (ī′ẽrn·wŏŏd). City, Gogebic co., NW Michigan penin., on Wisconsin border 15 m. SE of Lake Superior; pop. 10,265; iron mining, lumbering.

Ir′o·quois (ĭr′ō·kwoi). **1** River ab. 120 m. long, rising in NW Indiana, and flowing W across Illinois border, then N into Kankakee river in NE Illinois.
2 County in Illinois. See *Table* at ILLINOIS.

Iroquois Falls. Mill town, Cochrane dist., E Ontario, Canada, 45 m. NE of Timmins; pop. 1342; on railroad W of Lake Abitibi; large pulp and paper mill.

Ir′ra·wad′dy (ĭr′á·wŏd′ĭ). **1** River ab. 1350 m. long in cen. Burma; formed by confluence of Mali and Nmai rivers just N of Myitkyina in Upper Burma, flows S through cen. Burma into Bay of Bengal through several mouths, near Rangoon; has extensive delta; navigable to Bhamo; main tributary the Chindwin which joins it 60 m. WSW of Mandalay; other branches the Shweli, Mu, and Myitnge; passes through three defiles where course is narrow and rapid; important towns on its banks Myitkyina, Bhamo, Katha, Mandalay, Myingyan, Prome, and Henzada.
2 Division of Lower Burma. See *Table* at BURMA.

Ir·tysh′ *or* **Ir·tish′** (ĭr·tĭsh′). River ab. 2200 m. long in NE Kazakh S.S.R., Central Asia, and W part of Soviet Russia in Asia (Omsk Region); rises on W slopes of Altai Mts. in N Sinkiang, flows W across Chinese border through Zaisan Lake and then NW to join Ob river at ab. 61°N; largest tributary of the Ob and navigable for most of its course; Semipalatinsk, Pavlodar, Omsk, and Tobolsk on its banks.

I·rún′ (ē·rōōn′). Commune, Guipúzcoa prov., N Spain, on Bidassoa river 9 m. E of San Sebastián near French border; pop. 14,368; port of entry; iron foundries, tanneries, paper mills, potteries, medicinal springs.

Ir′vine (ûr′vĭn). **1** City, ⊗ of Estill co., E Kentucky, 23 m. SSE of Winchester; pop. 2955.
2 Burgh, Ayr co., SW Scotland, on Irvine estuary 11 m. N of Ayr; pop. 14,741; ships coal; shipbuilding, chemical works.

Ir′ving (ûr′vĭng). City, Dallas co., NE Texas, NW of Dallas; pop. 45,985.

Ir′ving·ton (ûr′vĭng·tŭn). **1** Town, Essex co., NE New Jersey, 3 m. WSW of and adjoining Newark; pop. 59,379; manufactures toy trains, radio loud speakers, cutlery; metal refineries, foundries, dye works.
2 Residential and industrial village, Westchester co., SE New York, on Hudson river 22 m. N of New York and 3 m. S of Tarrytown; pop. 5494; forms one community with North Tarrytown, Elmsford, and Tarrytown; manufactures greenhouses, ventilating boilers; home of Washington Irving (*Wolfert's Roost*, renamed *Sunnyside*).

Ir′well (ûr′wĕl; -wẽl). River ab. 40 m. long, W England; flows in winding course S past Rochdale, Bury, and Manchester into the Mersey at Irlam.

Ir′win (ûr′wĭn). **1** County in Georgia. See *Table* at GEORGIA.
2 Borough, Westmoreland co., SW Pennsylvania, 18 m. ESE of Pittsburgh; pop. 4270; coal mining, ironworking.

Ir′win·ton (ûr′wĭn·tŭn). Town, ⊗ of Wilkinson co., cen. Georgia; pop. 673.

Is. See HIT.

I′sa (ē′sá). Town, Sokoto prov., NW Northern Region, Nigeria, ab. 150 m. NW of Kano; pop. ab. 16,000.

Isabel. See SANTA ISABEL.

Is′a·bel, Mount (ĭz′á·bĕl). Peak 10,154 ft., N cen. Lincoln co., W Wyoming.

I′sa·be′la (ē′sä·vā′lä; *Angl.* ĭz′á·bĕl′á). **1** Cape and port, N Dominican Republic, Hispaniola I.; Columbus's first settlement 1493.
2 Province, NE Luzon, Phil. Is., in upper valley of Cagayan river; 4069 sq. m.; pop. 219,864; ✳ Ilagan; third province in area on Luzon; on E along Pacific coast is part of Sierra Madre range (highest point 6188 ft.) and along W border are foothills of ranges in Mountain

Province; between is wide fertile valley of the upper Cagayan with its tributaries the Magat and Abuluan; along S border are NE ranges of Caraballo Mts.; chief tobacco province of the Philippines; other products corn, rice, sugar and coffee. Inhabitants chiefly Ibanags and Ilokanos. Chief towns Ilagan, Santiago, Cabagan, Gamu, and Cauayan.
History: Province created 1856 out of lands belonging to Cagayan and Nueva Vizcaya; old towns centers of missionary activities in 17th cent.; suffered from revolts 1763, 1785; civil government established Aug. 1901.
3 *or* **Isabela de Ba·si′lan** (ē′sä·vä′ä thä vä·sē′län). Former municipality on NW coast of Basilan I., Zamboanga prov., Mindanao, Phil. Is., ab. 14 m. S of Zamboanga across Basilan Strait; pop. 12,156; fine harbor; now a district of City of Zamboanga.
4 Municipality, cen. Negros Occidental, Negros, Phil. Is., 37 m. S of City of Bacolod; pop. 43,509; important communications center and sugar town.
5 Municipality (pop. 28,754) and town (pop. 7302), NW Puerto Rico; town on coast 10 m. NE of Aguadilla.

Isabela, *or* **Al′be·marle** (ăl′bĕ·märl), **Island.** Island, largest of Galápagos Is.; 1650 sq. m.; in W part of the group, 91°38′W, its N end crossed by equator. See GALÁPAGOS ISLANDS.

Is·a·bel′la (ĭz′á·bĕl′á). County in Michigan. See *Table* at MICHIGAN.

I′sach·sen Peninsula (ī′zăk·s'n; -zĭk-). Peninsula in NW Ellef Ringnes I., N Franklin District, Northwest Territories, Canada; formerly thought to be an island.

Ī′sa·fjör′dur (ē′sä·fyûr′thûr). Town at tip of peninsula of NW Iceland; pop. (1942) 2897.

Isana. See IÇANA.

I·san′ti (ĭ·săn′tĭ). County in Minnesota. See *Table* at MINNESOTA.

I′sar (ē′zär). River 219 m. long, Bavaria, S Germany; rises in Tirol and flows through Munich and past Landshut NW into the Danube; not navigable.

I·sar′co (ē·zär′kō). River ab. 70 m. long, South Tirol, N Italy, in Venezia Tridentina compartimento; flows into the Adige at Bolzano.

I′sa·rog′ (ē′sä·rôg′). Volcanic mountain 6483 ft., E cen. Camarines Sur prov., Luzon, Phil. Is., on isthmus bet. Lagonoy Gulf and San Miguel Bay; base ab. 36 m. in circumference; source of many streams.

I·sau′ri·a (ī·sô′rĭ·á). Ancient district in E Pisidia, Asia Minor, on N slope of W Taurus Mts.; in 1st cent. B.C. boundaries were changed so that it included a part of W Cilicia; furnished several rulers of Byzantine Empire, esp. Zeno (reigned 474–491) and Leo III, founder of the Isaurian dynasty, which ruled from 717 to 802.

Is·bar·ta′ (ĕs·bär·tä′). = ISPARTA.

Isca Damnoniorum. See EXETER.

Isca Silurum. See CAERLEON.

Is′chi·a (ĭs′kĭ·á; *Ital.* ēs′kyä); *anc.* **Ae·nar′i·a** (ē·nâr′ĭ·á). Island in Tyrrhenian Sea bet. Gulf of Gaeta and Bay of Naples; 18 sq. m.; pop. (1931) ab. 30,000; administratively a part of Napoli prov., Campania, S Italy; highest point the volcanic Monte Epomeo 2588 ft.; summer resort, mineral springs; suffered greatly from volcanic eruptions and earthquakes, esp. the earthquake of 1883; chief town Ischia.

Ischl (ĭsh′l); *also called* **Bad Ischl** (bät). Commune, Upper Austria prov., Austria, on Traun river S of Lake Traun 51 m. SW of Linz; pop. 10,227; trade center; tourist and health resort; mineral springs, salt mine.

Isdud. See ASHDOD.

I·se (ē·sĕ). Old province, S coast of Honshu, Japan, now part of Mie prefecture. Name also applied to the two sacred Shinto shrines to the Sun Goddess, located at Ujiyamada, in Mie prefecture; for centuries the mecca of pilgrims and of the emperor and his high officials.

Ise Bay *or* **A·tsu·ta Bay** (ä·tsŏŏ·tä); *formerly* **O·wa·ri Bay** (ō·wä·rē). Inlet of Pacific Ocean on S coast of Honshu, Japan, bet. Mie and Aichi prefectures.

I'se Fjord (ē′sĕ). Inlet of the Kattegat on N coast of Sjælland I., Denmark; extends S inland 20 m.; its E extension is Roskilde Fjord.

Iseghem. See IZEGEM.

I·sel′le (ê-zĕl′lȧ). Town, NE Piedmont, NW Italy, just NW of Domodossola; S terminal of Simplon Pass and Tunnel.

I·se′o, Lake (ê-zā′ô). Lake 14 m. long in Lombardy, N Italy, on border bet. Brescia and Bergamo provs.; 24 sq. m.

I′ser (ē′zēr); *Czech* **Ji′se·ra** (yĭ′sĕ·rȧ). River 94 m. long, N Bohemia Czechoslovakia, flowing S into Labe (Elbe) river.

I′se·ran′, Col de l′ (kôl′ dē lēz′rän′). Mountain pass 9084 ft. high, Graian Alps, E Savoie dept., E France; highway, completed 1937.

I′sère′ (ē′zâr′). **1** River 150 m. long, SE France; rises on slopes of Graian Alps near border of Italy, flows W and SW into Rhone river 4 m. NNW of Valence.

2 Department of France. See *Table* at FRANCE.

I′ser·lohn′ (ē′zēr·lōn′). City, North Rhine-Westphalia state, Germany, 15 m. W of Arnsberg; pop. 30,820; manufactures steel pens, needles, hardware; wire drawing; rolling mills.

I·ser′nia (ê-zĕr′nyȧ); *anc.* **Æ·ser′ni·a** (ê-zûr′nĭ·ȧ). Commune, Campobasso prov., Abruzzi e Molise, cen. Italy, 22 m. W by N of Campobasso; pop. 14,517; cathedral; manufactures lace; has ancient remains. Came under Romans 295 B.C.; became Roman colony 263 B.C.; took part in Social War 90 B.C. Suffered from earthquake 1805.

I′se·yin′ (ē′sà-yēn′). City, Oyo prov., W Western Region, Nigeria, NNW of Ibadan; pop. 36,805.

Is′fa·han (ĭs′fȧ·hăn; -hän; *Iranian* ĭs′fȧ·hän′); *formerly* **Is′pa·han** (ĭs′pȧ·hăn; -hän). **1** Province, cen. Iran; 20,971 sq. m.

2 *anc.* **As′pa·da·na** (ăs′pȧ·dā′nȧ). Industrial city, W cen. Iran; ✱ of Isfahan prov. and former ✱ of Persia; pop. ab. 205,000; on main highways S to Shiraz, N to Tehran, and E to Yezd; covers wide area; in center is Maidan-i-Shah, a great rectangular garden enclosing royal mosque, Masjid-i-Shah, built by Shah Abbas I at end of 16th cent.; has large bazaar; particularly noted for silver filigree and metal work, lacquered ware, weapons, brocades.

History: As Aspadana, ancient Median town; captured by Arabs during their conquest of Persia 641–650 A.D.; a seat of Seljuk power in late 11th cent.; invaded by Tamerlane 1387; reached height of prosperity during 17th cent. when it was residence of Shah Abbas I (see PERSIA); declined after capture by Afghans 1722; Persian capital soon moved to Shiraz.

Ish′a·wooa Cone (ĭsh′ȧ·wä). Mountain 11,840 ft. in Absaroka Range, SW Park co., NW Wyoming.

I·shi·ga·ki (ê-shē-gä-kê). Island in cen. part of Sakishima group, S Ryukyu Is., Japan.

I·shi·ka·ri (ê-shê-kä-rê). River 275 m. long, W Hokkaido I., Japan; longest river in Japan; flows W into Otaru Bay.

Ishikari Dake. See ASAHI DAKE.

I·shi·ka·wa (ê-shê-kä-wä). Prefecture of Japan. See *Table* at JAPAN.

I·shim′ (ĭ-shĭm′). **1** River ab. 1330 m. long in N cen. Kazakh S.S.R., Central Asia, and in W part of Soviet Russia in Asia (Omsk Region); rises in cen. steppe region of Kazakh Republic and flows N past Petropavlovsk to join the Irtysh at Ust Ishim, 57°40′N.

2 Town on lower Ishim river, Omsk Region, on railroad 85 m. N of Petropavlovsk; pop. 14 099.

I·shi·no·ma·ki (ê-shê-nô-mä-kê). Town, Miyagi prefecture, N Honshu on E coast, Japan; pop. (1945) 38,173; fair harbor; important port of call for small coastal steamers.

Ishinomaki Bay. Inlet of Pacific Ocean, Miyagi prefecture, NE coast of Honshu, Japan.

I·shi·zu·chi·ya·ma (ê·shê·zōō·chê·yä·mä). Peak 6500 ft., W Shikoku I., Japan; highest peak in Shikoku.

Ish′pe·ming (ĭsh′pĕ·mĭng). City, Marquette co., N Michigan penin., 15 m. W of Marquette; pop. 8857; iron mining.

Ishtib. See ŠTIP.

I′si′gny′ (ē′zē′gnē′), *in full* **I′si′gny′–sur–Mer′** (-sür-mâr′). Village NW Calvados dept., NW France, W of Bayeux and near Carentan; pop. (1931) 2834; watering place; captured by American forces June 6–10, 1944 in Normandy invasion of World War II.

Isin. See ISSIN.

I·sio′lo (ê-zyô′lô). Town, NE Kenya colony, E Africa, N of Mt. Kenya; ✱ of Northern Province.

I′sis (ī′sĭs). Local name for upper course of the Thames river, in England.

Iskandarîyah, al-. See ALEXANDRIA.

Is·kar′do (ĭs·kär′dō). = SKARDU.

Iskelib. See İSKİLİP.

İs′ken·de·run′ (ĕs′kĕn·dĕ·rōōn′) *or* **Is′ken·de·ron′**; *formerly* **Al′ex·an·dret′ta** (ăl′ĕg·zăn·drĕt′ȧ; ăl′ig-; *Brit. also* -zän-); *Fr.* **A′lex′an′drette′** (à′lĕk′sän′drĕt′). Seaport city on SE shore of Gulf of İskenderun (Alexandretta), Hatay, S Turkey in Asia, ab. 60 m. SE of Adana; pop. 13,997; chief town of former sanjak of Alexandretta and of republic of Hatay; on branch railroad and on coastal highway S of site of Issus (battle 333 B.C.); founded by Alexander and named by him ("Little Alexandria") to commemorate the battle; has good harbor but unhealthful location; chief port of Alep and formerly outlet for overland trade from Persia and India until opening of Suez Canal.

İskenderun, Gulf of; *Turk.* **İskenderun Kör·fe·zi′** (kûr·fĕ·zē′); *formerly* **Gulf of Alexandretta.** Inlet of E Mediterranean Sea on S coast of Turkey in Asia near Syrian boundary; its E coast is vilayet (former republic) of Hatay.

Is′ker (ĭs′kēr). **1** (*Russ.* ē′skēr) *Cossack name* **Si·bir′** (syĭ·byēr′y′). Ancient town, ✱ of a Tatar khanate in W Siberia in 16th cent., near site of city of Tobolsk, Soviet Russia, Asia; captured 1581 by Ermak Timofeev (or Yermak), a hetman of the Don Cossacks, an event which marked beginning of Russian conquest of N Asia; town gave its name to the region, Siberia.

2 *or* **Is′kr** (ĭs′kēr). River 249 m. long, NW cen. Bulgaria; rises in Rhodope Mts., flows N through Balkan Mts. into Danube river 22 m. W of Nikopol.

İs·ki·lip′ (ĕs·kĕ·lēp′) *or* **Is·ke·lib′** (ĭs·kĕ·lēp′). Town near left bank of the Kızıl Irmak, Çorum vilayet, N cen. Turkey in Asia, 103 m. NE of Ankara; pop. 10,547.

Is′la (ī′lȧ). River 48 m. long, chiefly in Angus co., E Scotland; flows S and SW to the Tay in Perth co.

Is′la Cris·ti′na (ēz′lä krēs-tē′nä). Seaport, Huelva prov., SW Spain, on the Mediterranean Sea 21 m. W of Huelva; pop. 10,499; fisheries, esp. for tuna, sardines.

Isla de León. 1 Island, SW Spain. See Isla de León.

Isla de los Estados. See STATEN ISLAND, Argentina.

Isla de Pinos. See ISLE OF PINES, Caribbean Sea.

Is·lam′a·bad′ (ĭs·läm′ȧ·bäd′; ĭz·läm′ȧ·bäd′). Projected (1959) capital of Pakistan; site just NE of Rawalpindi.

Is′land (ī′lănd). County in Washington. See *Table* at WASHINGTON.

Island, Ísland. See ICELAND.

Is′land Beach (ī′lănd). Narrow sand spit off E coast of Ocean co., E New Jersey, enclosing Barnegat Bay.

Island Lake. Lake 551 sq. m., E Manitoba prov., Canada; outlet through Gods Lake and Hayes river to Hudson Bay.

Island No. 10. Former island in Mississippi river, in New Madrid co., SE corner of Missouri; scene of Civil War engagements Apr. 7, 1862.

Island Park. Village on Long I., Nassau co., SE New York; on Atlantic Ocean 20 m. ESE of New York; pop. 3846.

Island Pond. Village, Essex co., NE Vermont, on **Island Pond,** ab. 19 m. SE of Newport; pop. 1319; port of entry from Canada; fishing resort.

Is′lands, Bay of (ĭ′lăndz). **1** Inlet of Gulf of St. Lawrence, W Newfoundland; estuary of Humber river.
2 Inlet of Pacific Ocean on NE coast of N extension of North I., New Zealand, W of Cape Brett.

Islands of the Four Mountains. Island group in E cen. Aleutian Is., Alaska, W of Umnak; chief islands Chuginadak, Kagamil, Carlisle, and Herbert.

Is′las de la Ba·hí′a (ēz′läz thä lä vä-ē′ä). Department of Honduras, comprising the Bay Is. off N coast; 144 sq. m.; pop. (1945 est.) 7314; * Roatán.

Is′las de O′ri·en′te (ēzh′läzh thē ō′rĕ-ānn′tĕ). Early Portuguese name of the Philippine Is.—literally "Eastern Islands," because lying to the E within the new lands assigned to Portugal by Treaty of Tordesillas (q.v.) 1494.

Is′las de Po·nien′te (ēz′läz thä pŏ·nyän′tä). Early Spanish name of the Phil'ppine Is.—literally "Western Islands," because lying to the W (beyond Mexico) within the lands of the Far East claimed by Spain because of Magellan's discovery.

Is′las Fi′li·pi′nas (ēz′läs fē′lĕ·pē′näs). Spanish for PHILIPPINE ISLANDS.

Is′lay (ī′lä; -lå). Most southerly island of the Inner Hebrides, off W coast of Scotland; 234 sq. m.; pop. 4266; in Argyll co.; farming, fishing, whisky distilling.

Isle (ēl). River ab. 100 m. long, SW cen. France; rises in Haute-Vienne dept., flows SW into Dordogne river.

Isle au Haut (ĭl′ ō hō′). Island at entrance to Penobscot Bay off S cen. Maine coast; included in Knox co.; half of it in Acadia National Park.

Isle–de–France. See ÎLE-DE-FRANCE.

Isle La Motte (ĭl′ lå mŏt′). Island ab. 6 m. long in Lake Champlain, Grand Isle co., NW Vermont; settled by French (Fort Sainte Anne) 1666; black-marble quarry.

Isle of Ely, Man, etc. See Isle of ELY, Isle of MAN, etc.

Isle of Pines (ĭl, pīnz). **1** *Span.* **Is′la de Pi′nos** (ēz′lä thä pē′nŏs). Island in NW Caribbean Sea, S of W Cuba; 1180 sq. m.; pop. 9450; administratively, a municipality of La Habana prov.; chief barrio Nueva Gerona.
2 French island in Pacific Ocean. See KUNIE.

Isle of Wight (ĭl, wīt). **1** County in Virginia. See *Table* at VIRGINIA.
2 Village, its ⊗, SE Virginia, 17 m. W of Newport News.
3 Island in English Channel. See Isle of WIGHT.

Isle Roy′ale (ĭl roi′ăl). Island in NW Lake Superior, ab. 44 m. long by 8 m. wide, N of, and a part of, Keweenaw co., N tip of upper Michigan penin.; copper deposits were mined by Indians, their pits still in evidence; with surrounding islands now constitutes **Isle Royale National Park:** see UNITED STATES, *National Parks.*

Isles Der′nieres′ (ēl dĕr′nyâr′). Small group of islands in Gulf of Mexico, in Terrebonne parish, SE Louisiana.

Isles of Shoals (ĭlz, shōlz). Group of 9 rocky islands 10 m. SE of Portsmouth, New Hampshire; ab. 1 sq. m.; most important Star and Appledore; resort; Maine-New Hampshire boundary passes through the group.

Isles of the Sea *or* **Gar·vel′loch Isles** (gär·vĕl′ŭκ). Island group in Firth of Lorne, W Scotland.

Islet, L'. See L'ISLET.

Is·le′ta (ĭz-lā′tå). Indian village and pueblo, Bernalillo co., cen. New Mexico, on the Rio Grande in Isleta Pueblo Indian Reservation, S of Albuquerque; pop. (est.) 900; inhabited by Indians chiefly of Tanoan stock.

Isle′ton (ĭl′t'n; -tŭn). City, Sacramento co., N cen. California, 30 m. S of Sacramento; pop. 1039.

Islington. Metropolitan borough of London. See *Table* at LONDON; SMITHFIELD.

I′slip (ī′slĭp). **1** Village in Islip town (pop. 172,959), Suffolk co., SE New York, on Long I. on Great South Bay, ab. 10 m. W of Patchogue; pop. (est.) 8000; oysters; resort.
2 Village, Oxfordshire, cen. England, ab. 6 m. N of Oxford; birthplace of Edward the Confessor.

Is′ly′ (ĕs′lē′). Short river, NE Morocco, N Africa.

Is′ma·il (ĭz′mä·ĭl; -mĭ-; *Romanian* ēs′mä-ēl′); *Russ.* **Iz′ma·il** (ĭz′mä·ĭl; -mĭ-; *Russ.* ĭs·mŭ·ēl′). **1** Former department, S Bessarabia, Romania, N of Danube delta; 1626 sq. m.; pop. 224,229; now Izmail Region of the Ukraine, U.S.S.R.
2 City, its *. See IZMAIL.

Is′ma·i·li′a (ĭz′mä·ĭ-lē′à; ĭz′mĭ-; *Arab.* ĭs·mä·ĭ-lē′yå, -yä). Town, Canal governorate, NE Egypt, on Lake Timsah; pop. ab. 16,000; halfway station on Suez Canal.

Ismailia Canal. Canal extending trom Nile river near Cairo to Suez Canal at Ismailia on Lake Timsah.

Ismid. See İZMİT.

Is′na (ĭs′nà) *or* **Es′na** (ĕs′nà). Commercial town on Nile river, Upper Egypt, S of the ruins of Thebes; pop. ab. 9000; pottery; Ptolemaic and Coptic ruins.

Isola Lunga. See DUGI OTOK.

Isole Egadi. See EGADI ISLANDS.

Isole Egee. See AEGEAN ISLANDS.

Isole Eolie. See LIPARI ISLANDS.

I·son′zo (ē·zôn′tsô); *anc.* **Son′ti·us** (sŏn′shĭ·ŭs; -shŭs). River 75 m. long, NW Yugoslavia and NE Italy (Venezia Giulia); flows S into Gulf of Trieste; area of severe fighting in World War I, esp. at Gorizia and Caporetto.

Ispahan. See ISFAHAN.

Is·par·ta′ (ĭs·pär·tä′). **1** Vilayet, SW Turkey in Asia; 3194 sq. m.; pop. 166,441.
2 Town, its *, 110 m. W of Konya; pop. 18,222.

Is′ra·el (ĭz′rĭ·ĕl; -rå·ĕl). **1** Ancient kingdom in Palestine; as first formed under Saul c. 1025 B.C. comprised the lands in Canaan (q.v.) which in 12th cent. B.C. were occupied by Hebrew tribes descended from the sons of Jacob (Israel) who had been led out of Egypt by Moses; consolidated by David who began to rule c. 1013 B.C. and made Jerusalem his capital and under whom it included also Galilee and land E of the Jordan; became prosperous trading nation under Solomon who erected temple at Jerusalem; after death of Solomon kingdom divided, the ten northern tribes seceding and forming c. 933 B.C. under Jereoboam the kingdom of **Israel** *or* **Northern Kingdom,** while the two tribes in the S under Solomon's son Rehoboam formed kingdom of Judah (q.v.); Northern Kingdom (capital first at Shechem, then Tirzah, finally at Samaria which was built by Omri c. 887 B.C.) weakened by rivalry with Judah and Damascus, finally overthrown by Assyrians, who under Sargon II captured Samaria 722 B.C.
2 Republic, W part of former British mandate of Palestine, bounded on N by Lebanon, on E by Syria and Jordan, on SW by United Arab Republic (Sinai Penin.), and on W by Mediterranean Sea; 7993 sq. m.; pop. 2,643,000; de facto * Jerusalem—see PALESTINE.

History: Established by decree of May 15, 1948, in the partition of Palestine between Jews and Arabs as recommended (1947) by a special committee of the United Nations. Its establishment intensified the state of civil war in Palestine bet. Arabs and Jews; invaded by Arab forces of neighboring countries; in offensive actions Oct. and Dec. 1948 regained positions in the S (the Negeb) which had been lost to Egyptian forces in July; occupied new city of Jerusalem early in 1948 and on Feb. 1, 1949 declared it to be a part of the state of Israel; signed armistice agreement with Arab states retaining new city of Jerusalem but yielding to Egypt the coastal region around Gaza; engaged in war with Arab countries 1956–57 (Sinai campaign); in the face of renewed Arab threats in 1967 occupied the immediately adjoining parts of Syria, the parts of Jordan W of the Jordan river, and the whole of the Sinai Peninsula in a lightning campaign June 6–10 ("the 6-day war") ending in a ceasefire but without withdrawal from occupied territories.

Issa. See VIS.

Is′sa·que′na (ĭs′à·kwē′nà). County in Mississippi. See *Table* at MISSISSIPPI.

Is'ser'ville' (ē'sĕr'vēl'). Commune, Alger dept., N Algeria, near Tizi-Ouzou; pop. 13,548.

Is'sin *or* **Is'in** (ĭs'ĭn). Archaeological site, a low mound with a large building on it, S Iraq, bet. the Euphrates and the Tigris 60 m. SE of Hilla; ancient city of Babylonia, of Semitic origin; conquered by Elamites 2126 B.C.; part of Babylonian empire of Hammurabi.

Issiq Köl. See ISSYK KUL.

Is'soire' (ē'swâr'). Commune, Puy-de-Dôme dept., S cen. France, 18 m. SSE of Clermont-Ferrand; pop. (1931) 6719; 12th-cent. Romanesque church.

Is'sou'dun' (ē'sōō'dŭN'); *anc.* **Ux·el'lo·du'num** (ŭk-sĕl'ō-dū'nŭm). City, Indre dept., cen. France, 19 m. NE of Châteauroux; pop. 11,511.

Is'sus (ĭs'ŭs). Ancient town, S Asia Minor, ab. 20 m. N of modern Iskenderun, in a narrow coastal plain S of passes through Taurus Mts.; scene of two battles: (1) Oct. 333 B.C., Alexander won victory over Darius and the Persians; (2) 194 A.D., Roman emperor L. Septimius Severus defeated his rival Pescennius Niger.

Is'syk Kul (ĭs'ĭk kûl'); *also* **Is'siq Köl** (ĭs'ĭk kûl'). **1** Lake (*kul*), NE Kirgiz Republic, Soviet Central Asia; 115 m. long by 38 m. wide; 2250 sq. m.; a brackish lake lying in a basin at alt. 5400 ft. bet. W spurs of the Tien Shan; mountain ranges to S and N have peaks 13,000 to 18,000 ft. high; sometimes receives waters from the Chu river at W end; in early times shores inhabited by Usuns and Yuechi, later by Kara Kirghiz tribes. **2** Region, one of the six subdivisions of the Kirgiz Republic, in NE part surrounding the lake.

Is'sy'-les-Mou'li'neaux' (ē'sē'lā-mōō'lē'nō') *or* **Issy.** Commune, Seine dept., N France, SW suburb of Paris on Seine river; pop. 44,091.

Is'tan·bul (ĭs'tăm·bōōl'; *Turk.* ĕ·stäm·bōōl'); *formerly* **Con'stan·ti·no'ple** (kŏn'stăn·t'n·ō'p'l; -tĭ·nō'-). **1** Vilayet, NW Turkey, on both sides of Bosporus; 2149 sq. m. (1293 sq. m. in Europe, bet. Black Sea and Sea of Marmara; 856 sq. m. in Asia, on Sea of Marmara); pop. 883,599; ✻ Istanbul.
2 *anc.* **By·zan'ti·um** (bĭ·zăn'shĭ·ŭm; bĭ-; -shŭm; -tĭ·ŭm). City, its ✻, on European side of Bosporus and NE shore of Sea of Marmara; chief city and former ✻ of Turkey; pop. (1940), including suburbs, 789,346; contains church of Saint Sophia, erected 532–562 in time of Justinian.
History: As ancient Byzantium founded c. 660 B.C. by Greeks from Megara and Argos under Byzas; destroyed in reign (521–486) of Darius Hystaspis but recolonized by Greeks from Sparta 479 B.C.; rose to great importance as trading port; often contended for by various states (Sparta, Macedonia, Rhodes, Rome) in 750 years bet. Peloponnesian War and time of Constantine; captured by Emperor Septimius Severus 196 A.D. Name changed 330 A.D. to Constantinople (Lat. *Constantinopolis*, fr. Gr. *Konstantinou polis* Constantine's city) by Constantine the Great, who chose its site for his new capital of Eastern Roman, or Byzantine, Empire (see BYZANTINE EMPIRE); official capital 395–1453; old city on Golden Horn, an arm of Bosporus, was greatly enlarged by Byzantine emperors and protected by walls; attacked many times, esp. by Alexius Comnenus 1081 and by Crusaders 1204; captured 1453 by Turks under Mohammed II; Mohammedan capital 1453–1922, and seat of government (Sublime Porte) of Ottoman sultans 1453–1922, when, after its occupation by Allies 1918–23 and deposition of sultan 1922, Ankara became 1923 capital of new Turkish Republic. Following a decree of the Grand National Assembly Nov. 1928, the use of the Latin alphabet became general and the name Istanbul was officially adopted 1930. For sections or suburbs of the city, see BEYOĞLU, GALATA, SAN STEFANO, ÜSKÜDAR.

Ister. See DANUBE.

Is·tib', Is·tip' (ĕsh·tēp'). Vars. of ŠTIP.

Is'tok·po'ga, Lake (ĭs'tŏk·pō'gȧ). Lake in cen. Highlands co., cen. Florida penin.

Is·tran'ca Mountains (ĭs·trän'jä; *Turk.* **Istranca Da'ğla·rı'** (dä'lä·rī'). Mountain range along Black Sea coast, Kirklareli and İstanbul vilayets, Turkey in Europe; highest point ab. 3360 ft.

Is'tri·a (ĭs'trĭ·ȧ; *Ital.* ês'trĕ·ä). **1** Former province of Italy. See *Table* at ITALY.
2 *or* **Is'tri·an Peninsula** (ĭs'trĭ·ăn). Peninsula, NE coast of Adriatic Sea, ab. 60 m. long from Trieste at its base to its S point; 1545 sq. m.; Pulj (Pola), its chief town, is near S end; Rieka (Fiume) is just E of its E border; on SE is Gulf of Veliki Kvarner.
History: Inhabited by Istrians who were overthrown by Romans in 177 B.C.; Carolingian march of Istria, erected c. 788 A.D., was united with duchy of Bavaria in 10th cent.; came to patriarchs of Aquileia and, in 13th cent., to Venice; N part was an Austrian crownland under the Hapsburgs, but S part was Venetian until 1797; part of Illyrian Provinces 1809–13; ceded by Austria 1919 and awarded to Italy, except for Fiume, 1920; after World War II E part claimed by Yugoslavia and all except region around Trieste (Free City of Trieste) assigned to it by treaty of 1946.

I·tá' (ê·tä'). City, Central dept., S Paraguay, just SE of Asunción; pop. ab. 16,892.

I'ta·ba·ia'na (ē'tȧ·vȧ·yä'nȧ). Town, Paraíba state, E Brazil, on railroad WSW of João Pessoa; pop. 8185.

I·ta·bi'ra (ê·tȧ·vē'rȧ); *now* **Pre'si·den'te Var'gas** (prä'zĕ·thänn'tĕ vȧr'gȧs). Town, Minas Gerais state, SE Brazil, on S slope of Mt. Caué (*q.v.*).

I·ta·bu'na (ê·tȧ·vōō'nȧ). City, SE Baía state, E Brazil, W of Ilhéus; pop. (1940 est.) 15,868.

I'ta·cu'ru·bí' (ē'tä·kōō'rōō·vē'). Town, S Cordillera dept., cen. Paraguay; pop. ab. 8600.

Itacurubí del Ro·sa'rio (thĕl rrō·sä'ryô). Town, San Pedro dept., cen. Paraguay; pop. ab. 9700.

I'ta·ja·í' (ē'tä·zhä·ē'). **1** River 140 m. long, Santa Catarina state, S Brazil, flowing E into Atlantic Ocean.
2 Port at mouth of river; pop. (1940 est.) 13,367.

I'ta·ju·bá' (ē'tä·zhōō·vä'). City, S Minas Gerais state, E Brazil, 110 m. NE of São Paulo; pop. 14,940.

Italia. See ITALY.

I·ta'lia ir·re·den'ta (ê·tä'lyä êr·râ·dĕn'tä). Literally, "unredeemed Italy"; name given by Italians to lands near Italy (as Trentino, Trieste, Istria, Fiume, Dalmatia) once belonging to Italy and having a large Italian population, sought by Irredentists for reincorporation in the kingdom. Movement began c. 1878 and was especially strong in 1887 and 1910.

I·tal'ian East Africa (ĭ·tăl'yăn); *Ital.* **A'fri·ca O·ri·en·ta'le I·ta·li·a'na** (ä'frê·kä ō·rê·ân·tä'lā ê·tä·lê·ä'nä). Former Italian possessions in East Africa, including Eritrea, Ethiopia, and Italian Somaliland.

Italian So·ma'li·land' (sô·mä'lê·lănd'); *Ital.* **So·ma'lia I·ta·li·a'na** (sô·mä'lyä ê·tä·lê·ä'nä). Former Italian colony, E Africa, extending S from Cape Guardafui to Dicks Head at the boundary of Kenya colony; ab. 194,000 sq. m.; pop. (1931) 1,021,572, (1939 est.) 1,150,000; ✻ Mogadiscio; coast line very regular with few bays; best harbor Chisimaio; N coast forming SE shore of Gulf of Aden, E coast (ab. 1250 m.) bordering on Indian Ocean; bounded by Kenya, Ethiopia, and British Somaliland on W; hinterland nearly all desert with some fertile areas along the Juba in S, highest point 3400 ft. in hills inland from Cape Guardafui; its two chief rivers, both with sources far inland in Ethiopia, the Juba in the S and the Webbe Shibeli in S cen. part; chief exports cotton, sesame oil, gum, hides, fruit; chief towns Mogadiscio, Brava, Obbia. Benadir coast granted to Italy by sultan of Zanzibar 1889; colony leased to a private company 1893–1905; incorporated as state in Italian East Africa 1936; invaded by British troops 1941; governed by the British after the war until in 1950 it became a trust territory under the Italians; united with former British Somaliland, it became (as Somalia) an independent republic 1960. See SOMALIA.

ITALY

Statute Miles

0 20 40 60 80 100

⊛ Capitals of Countries
⊙ Capitals of Provinces

PUBLISHED BY G. & C. MERRIAM COMPANY
SPRINGFIELD, MASS.
PREPARED BY J. W. CLEMENT CO., BUFFALO, N. Y.

ITALY—COMPARTIMENTI AND PROVINCES

COMPARTIMENTI

COMPAR-TIMENTI	PROVINCES	LOCA-TION	AREA (SQ. M.)	POP. (1943)
Abruzzi e Molise	Aquila, Campobasso, Chieti, Pescara, Teramo	cen.	5,955	1,677,146
Apulia	Bari, Brindisi, Foggia, Ionio, Lecce	SE	7,442	2,886,570
Calabria	Catanzaro, Cosenza, Reggio di Calabria	S	5,823	1,907,953
Campania	Avellino, Benevento, Napoli, Salerno	S	5,214	3,991,409
Emilia	Bologna, Ferrara, Forlì, Modena, Parma, Piacenza, Ravenna, Reggio nell'Emilia	N	8,547	3,472,017
Latium	Frosinone, Littoria, Rieti, Roma, Viterbo	cen.	6,627	3,063,203
Liguria[1]	Genova, Imperia, La Spezia, Savona	NW	2,099	1,535,976
Lombardy	Bergamo, Brescia, Como, Cremona, Mantova, Milano, Pavia, Sondrio, Varese	N	9,186	6,190,361
Lucania	Matera, Potenza	S	3,856	584,240
Marches	Ancona, Ascoli Piceno, Macerata, Pesaro e Urbino	cen.	3,743	1,330,774
Piedmont[2]	Alessandria, Aosta, Asti, Cuneo, Novara, Torino, Vercelli	NW	11,335	3,602,721
Sardinia[3]	Cagliari, Nuoro, Sassari		9,301	1,153,384
Sicily[3]	Agrigento, Caltanissetta, Catania, Enna, Messina, Palermo, Ragusa, Siracusa, Trapani		9,926	4,256,077
Tuscany	Apuania, Arezzo, Firenze, Grosseto, Livorno, Lucca, Pisa, Pistoia, Siena	cen.	8,861	3,088,511
Umbria	Perugia, Terni	cen.	3,282	765,711
Venezia Euganea	Belluno, Friuli, Padova, Rovigo, Treviso, Venezia, Verona, Vicenza	NE	9,858	4,483,891
Venezia Giulia e Zara[4]	Carnaro, Gorizia, Istria, Trieste, Zara	NE	3,457	1,030,231
Venezia Tridentina	Bolzano, Trento	NE	5,252	660,825

[1] Small area on W border ceded to France by treaty of Feb. 10, 1947.
[2] Several areas, especially those around Mont Cenis and the Briga-Tenda region, ceded to France by treaty of Feb. 10, 1947.
[3] Island in Mediterranean.
[4] All of this compartimento, except for city of Gorizia and small area W of the Isonzo, ceded to Yugoslavia by treaty of Feb. 10, 1947. See *Table of Provinces*, below.

PROVINCES

PROVINCES[1]	LOCATION (BY COMPARTIMENTI)	AREA (SQ. M.)	POP.[2] (1936)
Agrigento[3]	SW Sicily	1,172	418,265
Alessandria	SE Piedmont	1,376	493,698
Ancona	N cen. Marches; on Adriatic	748	372,229
Aosta	NW Piedmont	1,838	227,500
Apuania[4]	NW Tuscany	446	196,716
Aquila	NW Abruzzi e Molise	1,944	365,716
Arezzo	E Tuscany	1,236	316,380
Ascoli Piceno	S Marches	807	303,869
Asti	SE cen. Piedmont	584	245,764
Avellino	cen. Campania	1,109	451,466
Bari	cen. Apulia; on Adriatic	1,980	1,010,907
Belluno	N cen. Venezia Euganea	1,418	216,333
Benevento	NE Campania	998	349,707
Bergamo	cen. Lombardy	1,065	605,810
Bologna	S cen. Emilia	1,429	714,705
Bolzano	N Venezia Tridentina	2,736	277,720
Brescia	E Lombardy	1,834	744,571
Brindisi	SE Apulia; on Adriatic	709	254,062
Cagliari	S Sardinia	3,590	507,201
Caltanissetta	cen. Sicily	813	256,687
Campobasso	S Abruzzi e Molise	1,785	399,095
Carnaro[5]	E Venezia Giulia e Zara	433	109,018
Catania	E Sicily	1,377	713,160
Catanzaro	cen. Calabria	2,025	606,364
Chieti	S cen. Abruzzi e Molise	999	374,727
Como	W cen. Lombardy	798	501,752
Cosenza	N Calabria	2,566	587,025
Cremona	S cen. Lombardy	678	369,483
Cuneo	SW Piedmont	2,871	608,912
Enna	cen. Sicily	989	218,294

PROVINCES—Continued

PROVINCES[1]	LOCATION (BY COMPARTIMENTI)	AREA (SQ. M.)	POP.[2] (1936)
Ferrara	NE Emilia	1,015	381,299
Firenze	NE cen. Tuscany	1,497	853,032
Foggia	NW Apulia; on Adriatic	2,746	523,612
Forlì	SE Emilia	1,124	444,528
Friuli[6]	E Venezia Euganea	2,766	721,670
Frosinone	SE Latium	1,251	445,607
Genova	E cen. Liguria	700	867,162
Gorizia[7]	NW Venezia Giulia e Zara	1,052	200,152
Grosseto	SW Tuscany	1,738	185,801
Imperia[8]	W Liguria	457	158,565
Ionio[9]	S Apulia; on Gulf of Taranto	941	321,888
Istria[10]	S Venezia Giulia e Zara	1,436	294,492
La Spezia	E Liguria	345	222,080
Lecce	SE tip of Apulia	1,065	526,553
Littoria	SW Latium	795	227,218
Livorno	W Tuscany	471	249,468
Lucca	NW Tuscany	684	352,205
Macerata	S cen. Marches	1,071	290,057
Mantova	SE Lombardy	903	407,977
Matera	E Lucania	1,465	166,776
Messina	NE Sicily	1,253	627,093
Milano	SW cen. Lombardy	1,066	2,175,838
Modena	cen. Emilia	1,042	467,555
Napoli	NW Campania	1,206	2,192,245
Novara	NE Piedmont	1,393	395,730
Nuoro	E Sardinia	2,808	224,643
Padova	S cen. Venezia Euganea	827	668,025
Palermo	NW cen. Sicily	1,922	890,752
Parma	NW cen. Emilia	1,335	381,771
Pavia	SW Lombardy	1,144	492,096
Perugia	N Umbria	2,456	534,359
Pesaro e Urbino[11]	N Marches	1,117	311,916
Pescara	N cen. Abruzzi e Molise	472	211,561
Piacenza	NW Emilia	998	294,785
Pisa	NW Tuscany	946	341,428
Pistoia	N Tuscany	368	210,950
Potenza	W Lucania	2,391	376,486
Ragusa	SE Sicily	582	223,086
Ravenna	E Emilia	718	279,127
Reggio di Calabria	S Calabria	1,233	578,262
Reggio nell'Emilia	W cen. Emilia	885	375,288
Rieti	NE Latium	1,061	174,961
Roma	W Latium	2,113	1,562,580
Rovigo	S Venezia Euganea	697	336,807
Salerno	S Campania	1,901	705,277
Sassari	NW Sardinia	2,903	302,362
Savona	W cen. Liguria	597	219,108
Siena	SE Tuscany	1,473	268,459
Siracusa	SE Sicily	849	277,572
Sondrio	N Lombardy	1,235	142,919
Teramo	N Abruzzi e Molise	755	249,532
Terni	S Umbria	826	191,559
Torino	W cen. Piedmont	2,116	1,168,384
Trapani	NW Sicily	968	375,169
Trento	S Venezia Tridentina	2,516	391,309
Treviso	E cen. Venezia Euganea	956	570,580
Trieste[12]	W Venezia Giulia e Zara	494	351,595
Varese	W Lombardy	462	395,896
Venezia	SE cen. Venezia Euganea	948	629,123
Vercelli	E cen. Piedmont	1,157	366,146
Verona	SW Venezia Euganea	1,196	585,893
Vicenza	SW cen. Venezia Euganea	1,051	559,375
Viterbo	N Latium	1,408	236,722
Zara[13]	Venezia Giulia e Zara	43	22,000

[1] Unless otherwise noted, its capital city has the same name.
[2] 1943 population estimates, used for the compartimenti, not available for provinces.
[3] Formerly Girgenti.
[4] Formerly Massa e Carrara prov.; former capital Massa.
[5] Capital Fiume, now Rieka; province ceded to Yugoslavia by treaty of Feb. 10, 1947.
[6] Capital Udine. Formerly called Udine prov.
[7] *Ger.* Görz; included most of former Austrian crownland of Görz and Gradisca; all except city of Gorizia and small area W of the Isonzo ceded to Yugoslavia Feb. 10, 1947.
[8] Formerly Porto Maurizio prov.; former capital Porto Maurizio.
[9] Capital Taranto. Formerly called Taranto prov.
[10] Capital Pola, now Pulj; province ceded to Yugoslavia by treaty of Feb. 10, 1947.
[11] Capital Pesaro.
[12] City of Trieste and adjoining territory of ab. 320 sq. m. established as Free Territory of Trieste by treaty of Feb. 10, 1947; city to Italy, Istrian penin. to Yugoslavia Oct. 1954; pop. 270,164.
[13] Exclave on Dalmatian coast, comprising Lagosta I. (now Lastovo) and the commune of Zara (now Zadar); ceded to Yugoslavia by treaty of Feb. 10, 1947.

It'a·ly (ĭt″'l·ĭ; -á·lĭ); *Ital.* **I·ta'lia** (ē·tä′lyä); *Lat.* **I·tal'i·a** (ĭ·tăl′ĭ·á; -tăl′yá). Republic in S Europe, comprising the boot-shaped peninsula ab. 760 m. long and from 100 to 150 m. wide which extends S into the Mediterranean Sea, and the islands of Sicily and Sardinia (*qq.v.*), and a number of small islands, esp. Elba, Capri, Ischia, Capraia, Lipari Is. and Pontine Is.; bounded on N by Switzerland, on E by Yugoslavia and the Adriatic and Ionian Seas, on S and SW by the Tyrrhenian Sea (Mediterranean Sea), and on W by the Ligurian Sea and France; 119,764 sq. m.; pop. (1943) 45,681,000; ✻ Rome; divided into 18 compartimenti comprising 94 provinces (see *Tables* on p. 505; for pronunciation of their names, see their individual entries).

Mountains: Peninsula traversed entire length by the Apennines (*q.v.*) and bordered on NW, N, and NE by various ranges of the Alps (*q.v.*); highest points on N border Mont Blanc 15,781 ft. and Monte Rosa 15,217 ft., in the Apennines Monte Corno 9585 ft., and in Sicily Mt. Etna 10,741 ft. *Rivers:* Largest the Po, with its many tributaries forming a valley which constitutes the great plain of the N; other important streams the Tiber (Tevere) in cen. part, Arno, Volturno, and Liri in W, Adige in N, Piave and Tagliamento in NE, and Isonzo on NE border, and many shorter rivers on E side flowing to the Adriatic. *Lakes:* Large lakes in N noted for their beauty: Maggiore, Como, Garda; Trasimeno in N cen. part, Bolseno and Bracciano in W cen. part; many lagoons at N end of the Adriatic near mouths of the Po. *Coastal features:* E coast line fairly regular except for headland of Gargano near the S; separated from Albania by Strait of Otranto; in SE large Gulf of Taranto forms the "heel" (Apulia) and the "toe" (Calabria) of Italy; S tip separated from Sicily by Strait of Messina; W coast indented by Gulfs of Sant' Eufemia, Salerno, and Gaeta, and Bay of Naples. *Economic resources:* Cereal crops, livestock, vines, olives, sugar beets, vegetables; minerals (iron, sulfur, bauxite); textile industry, silk culture, chemicals. *Chief cities:* Rome, Milan, Naples, Turin, Genoa, Palermo, Bologna, Florence, Catania, Venice, Bari. Within its borders are two small independent states San Marino and Vatican City (*qq.v.*).

History: For earlier history, see ETRURIA, ROME, and ROMAN EMPIRE; after barbarian invasions of 4th and 5th cents. A.D., Germanic kingdoms established by Ostrogoths and by Lombards; S part remained longest under nominal Byzantine rule; in midst of disorder, Papacy at Rome founded its position as political arbiter of medieval Italy; part of Carolingian empire 774 and of Holy Roman Empire (*q.v.*) from 962; in course of struggle bet. papal and imperial authority (Guelph versus Ghibelline), the Italian communes (see MILAN, FLORENCE, etc.) obtained independence, built up petty states, and became commercial and political rivals; S Italy (see NAPLES and SICILY) ruled by foreign dynasties; c. 1000, Venice (*q.v.*) began her rise to career of territorial expansion; during period of marked political disunity, Italy produced cultural movements known as the Risorgimento (conventionally dated c. 1300–1500) and the Cinquecento (16th cent.); scene of Italian Wars 1494–1559, a struggle for power bet. Hapsburg (imperial and Spanish) and Valois (French) forces; Hapsburg predominance temporarily broken and territorial consolidation effected by Napoleon who erected kingdom of Italy (included Venice and Milan) 1805 and finally incorporated in France Piedmont, Genoa, Parma, Lucca, Tuscany, and States of the Church; from 1815–70, Lombardy and Venetia threw off Austrian rule, and with Modena, Parma, Lucca, kingdom of Naples, and States of the Church, were annexed to kingdom of Sardinia to form kingdom of Italy; member of Triple Alliance 1882–1915; undertook colonial expansion (see ERITREA, ETHIOPIA and ADUWA, ITALIAN SOMALILAND, LIBYA, TRIPOLI); at war with Turkey 1911–12; entered World War I on side of Allies 1915; government seized by Fascists under Mussolini in

"March on Rome" 1922; annexed Fiume (see RIEKA) 1924; abolished parliamentary institutions for rule by Fascist Grand Council 1928; made peace with Papacy (see VATICAN CITY) 1929; at war with Ethiopia 1935–36; occupied Albania (*q.v.*) 1939; became military and political ally of Germany 1939; entered World War II 1940; invaded by Allies 1943 and its Fascist government overthrown; German resistance strong in cen. part 1943–45 (battles of Salerno, Cassino, Anzio; Rome taken June 4, 1944); became republic June 10, 1946; lost Dodecanese to Greece 1945 and territory on borders to France and Yugoslavia by treaty of Feb. 10, 1947.

I'ta'ny' (ē′tà′nē′). Upper tributary of Maroni river, N South America, forming section of boundary bet. French Guiana and Surinam.

I'ta·pa·ri'ca (ē′tá·pá·rē′ká). Island in Atlantic Ocean off Baía state, Brazil, at entrance to All Saints Bay.

I'ta·pe'cu·rú' (ē′tá·pā′kōō·rōō′). River ab. 450 m. long, Maranhão state, NE Brazil, flowing N into São José Bay.

I'ta·pe·ru'na (ē′tá·pĕ·rōō′ná). City, Rio de Janeiro state, SE Brazil, 150 m. NE of Rio de Janeiro; pop. 6792.

I'ta·pe'ti·nin'ga (ē′tá·pā′tē·nēnng′gá). City, São Paulo state, SE Brazil, 85 m. W of São Paulo; pop. (1940 est.) 13,000.

I'ta·pi'cu·rú' (ē′tá·pē′kōō·rōō′). River 350 m. long, Baía state, E Brazil, flowing SE to Atlantic Ocean.

I·ta·pi'ra (ē·tá·pē′rá). City, São Paulo state, SE Brazil, ab. 30 m. N of Campinas; pop. 7975.

I'ta·pú'a (ē′tä·pōō′ä). Department of Paraguay. See *Table* at PARAGUAY.

I·ta·pu'ra (ē·tá·pōō′rá). Town, W São Paulo state, Brazil, at confluence of Tietê with the Alto Paraná.

I·tas'ca (ĭ·tăs′ká). 1 County in Minnesota. See *Table* at MINNESOTA.
2 City, Hill co., NE cen. Texas, 37 m. W of Corsicana; pop. 1383; textiles.

Itasca, Lake. Lake 2 sq. m., N Minnesota, in SE Clearwater co.; elevation 1460 ft.; discovered 1832 and established as source of Mississippi river; in **Itasca State Park** (35 sq. m.).

I·ta'ta (ē·tä′tä). River 110 m. long, S cen. Chile, N of Concepción, flowing into Pacific Ocean.

I'ta·tia·í'a, Mount (ē′tá·tyá·ē′á). Peak 9255 ft. in Mantiqueira range, SE Brazil, at junction of boundaries of the states of São Paulo, Minas Gerais, and Rio de Janeiro.

I'tau·guá' (ē′tou·gwä′). Town, Central dept., SW Paraguay, ab. 17 m. SE of Asunción; pop. ab. 11,300; lace making.

It·a·wam'ba (ĭt′á·wŏm′bá). County in Mississippi. See *Table* at MISSISSIPPI.

It·ba'yat (ĭt·bä′yät). Island, largest of Batan Is., N Phil. Is.; 33 sq. m.; pop. ab. 1600.

Iténez. See GUAPORÉ.

Ith'a·ca (ĭth′á·ká). 1 Village, ⊗ of Gratiot co., cen. Michigan, 24 m. S of Mt. Pleasant; pop. 2611.
2 City, ⊗ of Tompkins co., S cen. New York, on S end of Cayuga Lake 39 m. NE of Elmira; pop. 28,799; settled by whites c. 1788; became city 1888; firearms, salt products, electric clocks, cement; Cornell Univ. (1865; coed.) and State Colleges of Veterinary Medicine (1894), Agriculture (1904), and Home Economics (1925); Ithaca College (1892; coed.).

Ith'a·ca (ĭth′á·ká); *Gr.* **I·thá'kē** (ē·thä′kyē′). 1 One of the Ionian Is., in the Ionian Sea off W coast of Greece and just NE of Cephalonia; 36 sq. m.; pop. 8836; with Cephalonia I. forms Cephalonia dept., Greece: see *Table* at GREECE. Consists of two mountain groups (highest point 2650 ft.) with narrow isthmus between; chief products olive oil, currants, and wine; generally identified in Greek mythology as home of Homer's Odysseus; occupied by Germans 1941.
2 *also called* **Va·thy'** (vä·thē′). Its chief town, on E coast; pop. 3265.

Ithome, Mount. See Messene.

I·to′gon (ē·tō′gôn). Municipal district (pop. 35,179) and town, S cen. Benguet subprov., Mountain Province, Luzon, Phil. Is., ab. 6 m. SE of Baguio center.

Itonama. See San Miguel.

Itsukushima. See Miyajima.

It′ta Be′na (ĭt′á bē′ná). Town, Leflore co., W Mississippi, 9 m. W of Greenwood; pop. 1914.

I·tú′ (ē·tōō′). City, São Paulo state, SE Brazil, on Tietê river 45 m. NW of São Paulo; pop. (1940 est.) 13,977.

It′u·rae′a or **It′u·re′a** (ĭt′ū·rē′á). Country in NE part of ancient Palestine, S of Damascus; part conquered and annexed to Judaea 106 b.c. by Aristobulus I; later in 1st cent. a.d. formed part of Tetrarchy of Philip.

I·tur′be (ē·tōōr′vá). Town, Guairá dept., SE cen. Paraguay; pop. ab. 8300.

I·tu′ri (ē·tōōr′ē). River, Republic of Congo, cen. Africa; rises W of Lake Albert, flows SW and W into the Congo; called the Aruwimi in lower course.

Iturup. See Etorofu.

I′tu·zain·gó′ (ē′tōō·sĭng·gō′). Town, NE Argentina, on Paraná river ab. 50 m. W of Posadas; scene of battle Feb. 20, 1827 in which Brazilian forces under Barbacena were decisively defeated by Argentine and Uruguayan forces under Alvear.

It′ze·hoe (ĭt′sĕ·hō). City, Schleswig govt. dist., Schleswig-Holstein, northwestern Germany, 33 m. NW of Hamburg; pop. 19,637; nets, soap, machinery, lumber, cement, sugar; founded c. 810; became city 1238.

I·u′ka (ī·ū′ká). Town, ⊗ of Tishomingo co., NE corner of Mississippi, 20 m. ESE of Corinth; pop. 2010; scene of battle Sept. 19, 1862, when Gen. Rosecrans attacked a Confederate force under Gen. Price.

I·va·í′ (ē·vá·ē′). River ab. 300 m. long, S Brazil; flows NW in Paraná state into Paraná river.

Ivangorod. See Deblin.

I′van·hoe (ī′văn·hō). Village, ⊗ of Lincoln co., SW Minnesota, 22 m. W of Marshall; pop. 719.

I·va′nov Industrial Area (ĭ·vá′nŭf). Former subdivision of Soviet Russia in Europe, in cen. part NE of Moscow; divided 1936 into Ivanovo and Yaroslavl Regions.

I·va′no·vo (ĭ·vá′nŭ·vŭ); formerly **Ivanovo Voz·ne-sensk′** (vŭz·nyĭ·syěnsk′). Industrial city, ✻ of Ivanovo Region, Soviet Russia, Europe, S of the Volga, ab. 145 m. NE of Moscow; pop. 285,069; textile factories, esp. cotton; iron and other heavy industries; called the "Soviet Manchester"; formed 1861 by incorporating two villages, one of which (Ivanovo) dates from 16th cent.; large worker population active in revolutionary movement 1917–18.

Ivanovo Region. Region, cen. Soviet Russia, Europe, crossed by the Volga; 24,472 sq. m.; pop. 2,650,383; ✻ Ivanovo; N of the Volga is heavily forested, S of it is agricultural land; formerly part of Ivanov Industrial Area, in extensive plain of Volga, Oka, and Klyazma rivers; reorganized as separate region 1936.

I′vig·tut (ē′vĭg·tōōt). Danish settlement on SW coast of Greenland, 175 m. NW of Cape Farewell; important cryolite quarries.

I·vi·nhei′ma (ē·vē·nyā′má). River ab. 200 m. long, S Mato Grosso state, SW Brazil; flows SE into Paraná river.

I·vi′za (ē·vē′thä; -sä); Span. **I·bi′za** (ē·vē′-); anc. **Eb′u-sus** (ĕb′ũ·sŭs). 1 Third largest island of Balearic group, Baleares prov., Spain; in W Mediterranean SW of Majorca and ab. 80 m. E of coast of Spain; 230 sq. m.; pop. 33,961; agricultural products. See Balearic Islands. 2 Seaport, its ✻, 80 m. SW of Palma; pop. 9644; exports figs, raisins, pine lumber, salt.

I′vo·ry Coast (ī′vō·rĭ; ī′vrĭ); Fr. **Côte d′I′voire′** (kōt′ dē′vwär′). 1 Republic in the French Community, West Africa, W of Ghana; area 125,692 sq. m.; pop. (1965 est.) 3,500,000; ✻ Abidjan; bounded on NW by the Republic of Mali, on NE by Upper Volta, on E by Ghana, on S by Atlantic Ocean, and on W by Liberia and Guinea; coast line bordered with lagoons; no good harbors; coastal plain in the S part gradually sloping to plateau in cen. part, with hills and mountains in W and NW; watered by the Bandama and Sassandra rivers and upper tributaries of Volta and Niger; railroad runs through center from the NE; produces grain, tropical fruits, cotton, coffee; exports forest products. Chief towns Abidjan, Bouaké, Grand Bassam, and Grand Lahou.

History: From 1842 French had treaty with native rulers of Ivory Coast; occupied by French who were forced to fight native king of Mandingos in hinterland 1885–86; in 1889 formal French protectorate established and its boundary with Gold Coast delimited; made a colony 1893; included in reorganized French West Africa 1895; received larger part of Upper Volta (q.v.) 1933; given territorial status by French Constitution of 1946; lost Upper Volta 1947; voted 1958 to remain in French Community as an autonomous republic; granted full independence within the Community 1960.

2 Atlantic coast along Ivory Coast Republic, W of Ghana, ab. 2°30′W long. to 7°30′W—so called because in early years much frequented by traders for ivory.

I·vre′a (ē·vrâ′ä); anc. **Ep′o·re′di·a** (ĕp′ŏ·rē′dĭ·á). Commune, Aosta prov., Piedmont, NW Italy, 32 m. ESE of Aosta; pop. 14,473; 11th-cent. cathedral; 14th-cent. castle; scene of action in Napoleon's Italian campaign 1800; manufactures typewriters.

I′vry′–la–Ba′taille (ē′vrē′lä·bá′tä′y′). Commune, Eure dept., N France, on Eure river 40 m. W of Paris; pop. (1931) 1374; scene of decisive victory of Huguenots under Henry IV over Catholics under duke of Mayenne Mar. 14, 1590.

I′vry′–sur–Seine (ē′vrē′sür·sân′). Commune and river port, Seine dept., N France, SE suburb of Paris on Seine river; pop. 44,859; chemicals, metal goods, tiles.

Ivy Lea. See Thousand Islands.

I·wa·ki (ē·wä·kē). River ab. 50 m. long, Aomori prefecture, N Honshu, Japan, flowing N to Sea of Japan.

Iwaki, Mount. Peak 5331 ft. in Aomori prefecture, N Honshu, Japan, NW of Hirosaki.

I·wa·mi·za·wa (ē·wä·mē·zä·wä). Town, Hokkaido prefecture, W Hokkaido, Japan, 25 m. ENE of Sapporo; pop. (1945) 41,198; railroad junction and center of coal fields.

I·wa·nai (ē·wä·nī). Town, Hokkaido prefecture, on SW coast of Hokkaido, Japan, SW of Otaru; pop. (1945) 20,394; fisheries; sulfur, coal, and copper mines.

I·wa·te (ē·wä·tě). 1 or **I·wa·te·ya·ma** (ē·wä·tě·yä·mä). Mountain 6696 ft., Iwate prefecture, N Honshu, Japan, just N of Morioka; a dormant volcano with ancient crater in which are shrines often visited by pilgrims. **2** Prefecture of Japan. See *Table* at Japan.

I′wo (ē′wō). City, Oyo prov., W Western Region, Nigeria, on railroad just NE of Ibadan; pop. 57,191; a Yoruba city.

I′wo Islands (ē′wō); Jap. **I·wo Ret·to** (ē·wō rět·tō). See Volcano Islands.

I′wo Ji′ma (ē′wō jē′má; Jap. ē·wō jě·mä) or **Na·ka I·wo** (nä·kä ē·wō); commonly shortened to **I′wo** (ē′wō; Jap. ē·wō). Literally "Sulfur Island"; small volcanic island 5½ m. long by 2½ m. wide, 8 sq. m., center island of the three in the Volcano Is., 660 nautical m. S of Tokyo; an outer Japanese fortified station, including three airfields. Scene of one of severest campaigns in U.S. history; bombed by U.S. planes Dec. 1944, Jan. and Feb. 1945; invaded by U.S. marines Feb. 19; Mt. Suribachi at S end seized Feb. 23; Motoyama airfields taken Feb. 23–26, and island finally completely taken by Mar. 15.

Ix′elles′ (ēk′sěl′). Commune, Brabant prov., cen. Belgium, a suburb of Brussels; pop. (1938 est.) 89,317.

Ix′ta·cal′co (ēs′tä·käl′kō). Town, Federal District, cen. Mexico, 1 m. S of Mexico City; pop. 5249; site of "Floating Gardens."

Ixtacihuatl. See Iztaccihuatl.

Ix′ta·pa·la′pa (ēs′tä·pä·lä′pä). Town, Federal District, cen. Mexico, 5 m. SE of Mexico City; pop. 9223.

Ix′tla (ēs′tlä). Subdivision of plateau of Anáhuac (q.v.) in cen. Mexico; mean elevation 3320 ft.

I·yo Sea (ê·yô). Open body of water forming SW part of Inland Sea, bet. Shikoku and Kyushu, Japan; connected with Pacific Ocean by Bungo Strait.

I′za·bal′ (ē′sä·väl′). Department, E Guatemala; 2371 sq. m.; pop. 83,153; ✳ Puerto Barrios.

Izabal, Lake; or **Dul′ce Gulf** (dōōl′sä). Lake ab. 25 m. long, E Guatemala; drains through Dulce river (q.v.) NE into Honduras Bay.

I·zal′co (ê·säl′kô). **1** Volcano ab. 6200 ft., Sonsonate dept., El Salvador, ab. 10 m. N of Sonsonate; created 1770 by eruption from side of Santa Ana; continually active, its glow can be seen from the Pacific Ocean.
2 Town at foot of the volcano; pop. (1942 est.) 7709.

I′za·mal′ (ē′sä·mäl′). Town, Yucatán state, on Yucatán penin., SE Mexico, 38 m. E of Mérida; pop. 5305.

Iz′ard (ĭz′ẽrd). County in Arkansas. See *Table* at AR-KANSAS.

I′ze·gem (ē′zĕ·ĸĕm); *formerly* **I′se·ghem** (ē′sĕ·ĸĕm). Commune, West Flanders prov., NW Belgium, 25 m. SW of Gent; pop. 15,111; linens, tobacco.

I′zhevsk (ē′zhĕfsk). Town, ✳ of Udmurt Republic, Soviet Russia, Europe, 175 m. ENE of Kazan; pop. 175,740; on tributary of Kama river and on branch of Kazan-Sverdlovsk R.R.; founded 1760; steel mills and ammunition factories, established early in 19th cent.; also milling, brickmaking, and brewing plants.

Izh′ma (ēzh′má). Navigable river ab. 180 m. long, flowing N in cen. Komi Republic, Soviet Russia, Europe; a W tributary of the Pechora.

I′zieux′ (ē′zyû′). Commune, Loire dept., SE cen. France, 6 m. ENE of St-Étienne; pop. (1931) 10,095; coal mines.

Iz′ma·il (ĭz′mä·ĭl; -mĭ-; *Russ.* ĭz·mü·ēl′); *Romanian* **Is′ma·il** (ĭz′mä·ĭl; -mĭ-; *Romanian* ēs′mä·ēl′). City, ✳ of Izmail Region, on N side of Danube delta ab. 45 m. from Black Sea; pop. 26,123; a cosmopolitan trading town, formerly a Turkish fort; occupied by Russia 1770, 1790, and 1812; since 1812 transferred several times: Romanian 1856–78 and 1918–40; Russian 1878–1918 and since 1940 although from 1941 to 1944 held by Axis forces.

Izmail Region. Region, SW Ukraine, U.S.S.R., S part of former Bessarabia bordering on Black Sea SW of Odessa and on Danube delta; chief towns Izmail, its capital, and Belgorod-Dnestrovski; organized 1945.

Iz·mir′ (ĭz·mĭr′); *formerly* **Smyr′na** (smûr′ná). **1** Coastal vilayet, W Turkey in Asia; 4826 sq. m.; pop. 597,812.
2 Seaport city, its ✳, at head of Gulf of İzmir; pop. (1940) 184,362; second city of Turkey in size and its most important port in Asia with large and beautiful harbor; exports figs, tobacco, raisins, carpets, silk; connected by rail with Bandırma, İstanbul, Aydın, and through Konya with E Turkey; has large Greek population.

History: Ancient Smyrna an Aeolian and later Ionian town; destroyed 6th cent. B.C. by Alyattes, King of Lydia; new city built by Antigonus and improved by Lysimachus 3d cent. B.C.; taken by Romans, it belonged mostly to Byzantine Empire; held for a time by Knights of St. John prior to Turkish conquest in 15th cent.; occupied by Greeks 1919 and temporarily ceded to them 1920; recaptured by Turkish Nationalists 1922; nearly destroyed by fire Sept. 14–15, 1922 and badly damaged by earthquakes 1928.

İzmir, Gulf of; *formerly* **Gulf of Smyr′na** (smûr′ná); *anc.* **Si′nus Smyr·nae′us** (sī′nŭs smûr·nē′ŭs). Large irregular inlet of Aegean Sea, W Turkey in Asia, N of the peninsula opp. Chios I.; extends inland ab. 40 m.; breadth at entrance 13 m.; city of İzmir is at its head.

İz·mit′ or **Is·mid′** (ĭz·mĭt′); *anc.* **As′ta·cus** (ăs′tȧ·kŭs); *later* **Nic′o·me′di·a** (nĭk′ô·mē′dĭ·ȧ). Town on Gulf of İzmit, ✳ of Kocaeli vilayet, NW Turkey in Asia, on railroad 54 m. E of İstanbul; pop. 18,154; 16th-cent. mosque; seat of a Greek metropolitan and an Armenian archbishop; as Astacus, a celebrated city of Bithynia, destroyed by Lysimachus; on neighboring site Nicomedia built 264 B.C. by Nicomedes I as his new capital.

İzmit, or **Ismid, Gulf of.** Inlet of E Sea of Marmara on NW coast of Turkey in Asia.

Iz·ná′jar (ēth·nä′här; ĕs-). Commune, Córdoba prov., S Spain, 51 m. SE by S of Córdoba; pop. 12,345.

İz·nik′ (ĭz·nĭk′); *anc.* **Ni·cae′a** (nĭ·sē′ȧ), *Angl.* **Nice** (nīs). Village, Bursa vilayet, NW Turkey in Asia, at E end of İznik Lake, 39 m. ENE of Bursa; pop. 2495; of slight importance but located on site of Nicaea, a great city of the Byzantine Empire; founded by Antigonus c. 316 B.C.; rival of Nicomedia as chief city of Bithynia; grew in importance after Constantinople became capital of Eastern Roman Empire; seat of first Nicene Council 325 A.D. which condemned the Arian heresy and promulgated the Nicene Creed, and of the second (seventh Ecumenical) Council 787 that defined veneration due to images; made temporary capital by the Crusaders whose Nicaean emperors of the Lascaris family ruled 1206 to 1261; remained an important city during first years of Ottoman rule.

İznik Lake; *Turk.* **İznik Gö·lü′** (gû·lü′); *anc.* **As·ca′-ni·a** (ăs·kā′nĭ·ȧ; -kän′yȧ). Lake (göl*ü*) 14 m. long, NW Turkey in Asia, E of Sea of Marmara; outlet through a small stream into Sea of Marmara.

Iz′tac·ci′huatl (ēs′täk·sē′wä·t'l) or **Ix′ta·ci′huatl** (ēs′-tä·sē′wä·t'l). Mountain 16,883 ft. SE of Mexico City, Mexico, N of Popocatepetl; extinct volcano, has three summits, no crater.

I·zu (ê·zōō). Peninsula, S cen. Honshu, Japan, extending into Pacific Ocean bet. Suruga Bay and Sagami Sea.

Izúcar de Matamoros. See MATAMOROS.

I·zu Shi·chi·to (ê·zōō shê·chê·tō). Literally "Seven Isles of Izu"; a group of volcanic islands, seven main ones, in Pacific Ocean off Izu Penin. on SE coast of Honshu, Japan, S of Yokohama; comprises six islands of the O Shima group (most important Miyake, Mikura, Nii Jima) and the Hachijo group (qq.v.).

I·zyum′ (ĭ·zyōōm′). Town, E Ukraine, U.S.S.R., on the Donets 75 m. SE of Kharkov; pop. ab. 14,000; held by Germans May 1942–43.

J

Jabal. See JEBEL.

Jabalpur. See JUBBULPORE.

Jab'bok (jăb'ŏk); *Arab.* **Wa'di Zer·qa'** (wä'dĕ zŭr·kä'). River ab. 100 m. long, NW Jordan, flowing W into the Jordan at a point ab. 25 m. N of Dead Sea; in ancient Palestine it was in Gilead and formed N boundary of the Amorites (*Josh.* xii. 2).

Ja'besh–gil'e·ad (jā'bĕsh·gĭl'ĕ·ăd). Town of Gilead, ancient Palestine, in valley of the Jordan E of the river ab. 20 m. S of the Sea of Galilee; in days of the Judges destroyed by tribe of Benjamin (*Judges* xxi. 8–15); besieged by Ammonites and siege relieved by Saul (*1 Sam.* xi. 1–11).

Ja'blo·nec (yä'blô-nĕts); *Ger.* **Ga'blonz** (gä'blônts). City, N Bohemia prov., W Czechoslovakia; pop. (1930) 33,958; glass beads, ornaments.

Ja'blo·ni'ca Pass (yä'blô-nyĭ'tsà); *also* **De·la'tyn Pass** (dĕ·lä't'n; *Pol.* dĕ·lä'tĭn) *and* **Ta'tar Pass** (tä'tĕr). Pass through E Carpathian Mts. bet. Ukraine and Carpatho-Ukraine, ab. 30 m. SW of Kolomyya; through it passes railroad from U.S.S.R. to upper valley of the Tisza; used by Mongols (Tatars) in their invasion and conquest of Hungary 1241; scene of much fighting bet. Austrians and Russians Oct. 1914 to Feb. 1917; used by Russians 1944 in their attack on Hungary.

Ja'boa·tão' (zhá'vwà·touN'). City, Pernambuco state, E Brazil, a W suburb of Recife; pop. (1940 est.) 13,102.

Ja'bor (jä'bôr). Port and chief village on Jaluit I., Marshall Is., W Pacific Ocean, at SE pass into the lagoon; * of the Marshall Is.

Ja'bo·ti·ca·bal' (zhá'vōō·tē'kà·väl'). City, São Paulo state, SE Brazil, near Ribeirão Preto; pop. 11,938.

Ja'ca (hä'kä). Town, Huesca prov., N Spain, in S Pyrenees; pop. (1930) 7056; Gothic cathedral.

Ja'ca·re·í' (zhá'kà·rĕ·ē'). City, São Paulo state, SE Brazil, 50 m. ENE of São Paulo; pop. (1940 est.) 11,965.

Ja'ca·ré'pa·guá' (zhá'kà·rä'pá·gwä'). Town, Federal District, Brazil, suburb of Rio de Janeiro; pop. ab. 20,000.

Ja'ca·tra' (jä'kä·trä'). **1** Town on NW coast of Java, Indonesia; site of first European factory on the island 1610; chosen 1619 by Gov. Coen for first permanent Dutch settlement, with name changed to Batavia.
2 Japanese name for Batavia 1942–45.

Já'chy·mov (yä'kĭ·môf); *Ger.* **Sankt Jo'a·chims·thal'** (zängkt yō'ä·kĭms·täl'; yō·äk'ĭms-). Commune, NW Bohemia, Czechoslovakia, in Erz Gebirge 12 m. N of Karlovy Vary; pop. 7320; uranium mines.

Ja·cin'to City (já·sĭn'tō). City, Harris co., SE Texas, on Galveston Bay, E suburb of Houston; pop. 9547.

Jack (jăk). County in Texas. See *Table* at TEXAS.

Jack'field (jăk'fēld). Village, Shropshire, W England, E of Wenlock; pottery; esp. Jackfield ware, made in 18th cent., distinguished by its thick, brilliant black glaze applied over a common red clay.

Jacks'bor'o (jăks'bŭr'ô). **1** Village, * of Campbell co., N Tennessee; pop. (est.) 800.
2 City, * of Jack co., N Texas, 55 m. NW of Fort Worth; pop. 3816; rock-crushing plant, flour mill, oil refinery.

Jack'son (jăk's'n). **1** River, W Virginia; rises in Highland co., flows SW and then SE to unite with Cowpasture river in N Botetourt co. and form James river.
2 Name of a parish in Louisiana and of counties in twenty-three states of the U.S. See *Tables* at ALABAMA, ARKANSAS, COLORADO, FLORIDA, GEORGIA, ILLINOIS, INDIANA, IOWA, KANSAS, KENTUCKY, LOUISIANA, MICHIGAN, MINNESOTA, MISSISSIPPI, MISSOURI, NORTH CAROLINA, OHIO, OKLAHOMA, OREGON, SOUTH DAKOTA, TENNESSEE, TEXAS, WEST VIRGINIA, WISCONSIN.
3 City, Clarke co., SW Alabama, on Tombigbee river 50 m. N of Mobile Bay; pop. 4959.
4 Mining city, * of Amador co., cen. California, 40 m.

ESE of Sacramento; pop. 1852; settled 1849, incorp. 1906; gold-bearing quartz.
5 City, * of Butts co., cen. Georgia, 35 m. NW of Macon; pop. 2545; incorp. 1826; cotton mills, cannery.
6 City, * of Breathitt co., E Kentucky, 24 m. NNW of Hazard; pop. 1852.
7 Town, East Feliciana parish, E Louisiana, 27 m. N of Baton Rouge; pop. 1824.
8 Industrial city, * of Jackson co., S Michigan, 34 m. S of Lansing; pop. 50,720; railroad center; automobile accessories, machinery, radios, electrical equipment; scene of founding of the Republican party in a convention July 6, 1854.
9 City, * of Jackson co., S Minnesota, 25 m. W of Fairmont; pop. 3370.
10 City, * of Mississippi and a * of Hinds co., SW cen. Mississippi, on Pearl river; pop. 144,422; largest city in the state; railroad and cotton-shipping center; lumber, cottonseed oil, and textile mills. Millsaps College (1892; coed.; Methodist); Jackson College (1877; Negro); Belhaven College (1894; women). Originally a trading station known as Le Fleur's Bluff; selected as capital 1821; first session of legislature 1822; name changed to Jackson in honor of Andrew Jackson; scene of secession convention Jan. 1861; captured by Union army under Gen. Sherman July 16, 1863.
11 City, * of Cape Girardeau co., SE Missouri, 10 m. NW of Cape Girardeau; pop. 4875; trading and milling center in agricultural section.
12 City, Carroll co., E New Hampshire, near Pinkham and Carter Notches; pop. 315; resort.
13 Town, * of Northampton co., NE North Carolina; pop. 765.
14 City, * of Jackson co., S Ohio, 25 m. SE of Chillicothe; pop. 6980; coal and iron mines; deposits of sand, clay, quartz, shale; gas wells; blast furnaces.
15 City, * of Madison co., W Tennessee, on south fork of Forked Deer river 80 m. ENE of Memphis; pop. 33,849; settled 1819; incorp. as town 1823, as city 1845; railroad center; cotton, cottonseed oil, steel for bridges, store fixtures, furniture, veneer and lumber, flour. Union Univ. (1834; coed.); Lane College (1882; Negro; coed.); Lambuth College (1924; coed.).
16 Town, * of Teton co., NW Wyoming; pop. 1437.

Jackson, Mount. **1** Peak 13,687 ft. in Eagle co., NW cen. Colorado.
2 Peak 10,023 ft., on Continental Divide in Glacier National Park, NW Montana.
3 Peak 4012 ft., N cen. New Hampshire, on NE border of Grafton co. E of Crawford Notch, in the Presidential Range of the White Mts.

Jackson Heights. See QUEENS borough, New York City.

Jackson Hole. Valley, NW Wyoming, E of Teton Range, partly in Grand Teton National Park; formerly an important hunting and trapping ground.

Jackson Lake Dam. Dam completed 1916 across south fork of Snake river, Teton co., NW Wyoming; height 59 ft.; forms **Jackson Lake Reservoir.**

Jackson Peak. Mountain 10,707 ft. in S Teton co., NW Wyoming.

Jack'son·ville (jăk's'n·vĭl; *Sou.* also -v'l). **1** City, Calhoun co., NE Alabama, 18 m. SE of Gadsden; pop. 5678; settled 1822; near mining region; Alabama State College (1883; coed.).
2 City, Pulaski co., cen. Arkansas, 13 m. NE of Little Rock; pop. 14,488.
3 Seaport city, * of Duval co., NE Florida, near mouth of St. Johns river; pop. 201,030; 3d largest city in state; ships rosin, turpentine, lumber, citrus fruits, cotton; cigar making. Settled 1816, laid out and renamed 1822, incorp. 1832; charter repealed 1840, and replaced by new

charter 1851; base for Confederate blockade runners during Civil War; severely damaged by fire 1901.

4 City, ⊗ of Morgan co., W cen. Illinois, 30 m. W of Springfield; pop. 21,690; platted 1825, incorp. 1830; corn, wheat, oats, hay; textile mills, shoe factories. Illinois College (1829; coed.); MacMurray College (1846; coed.).

5 City, ⊗ of Onslow co., SE North Carolina; pop. 13,491; oyster beds; hunting and fishing resort.

6 City, Cherokee co., E Texas, 24 m. ENE of Palestine; pop. 9590; railroad center; ships tomatoes; basket, garment, and canning factories; cotton press.

Jacksonville Beach. City, Duval co., NE Florida, on Atlantic Ocean 15 m. ESE of Jacksonville; pop. 12,049.

Jac'mel' (zhȧk'měl'). Seaport, S Haiti, on coast ab. 25 m. SSW of Port-au-Prince; pop. ab. 12,000.

Ja'cob·a·bad' (jä'kŭb·a·băd'; -ȧ·bäd'). Town, N Sind, W Pakistan, 200 m. N of Hyderabad; pop. 15,748.

Ja·co'na (hä·kō'nä). Town, Michoacán state, SW Mexico, 75 m. WNW of Morelia; pop. 5750.

Jacques Car'tier' (zhäk' kȧr'tyä'). **1** River ab. 70 m. long, S Quebec, Canada; flows S out of **Jacques Cartier Lake** in Laurentides National Park into St. Lawrence river 22 m. WSW of city of Quebec.

2 County, S Quebec, Canada. See MONTREAL AND JESUS ISLANDS.

Jacques Cartier, Mount. Mountain 4350 ft., N Gaspé Penin., in West Gaspé co. and in Gaspé Park; highest point in Quebec prov., Canada.

Jac'qui·not Bay (zhȧk'i·nō). Large inlet of Solomon Sea on S coast of New Britain I., Bismarck Archipelago, W Pacific Ocean, near E end of the island in ab. 152°E; fine anchorage.

Ja·cuí' (zhȧ·kwē'). River ab. 300 m. long, Rio Grande do Sul state, S Brazil, flowing S and E to Lagoa dos Patos.

Ja'dar (yä'där). Small river in NW Serbia, Yugoslavia, a tributary of Drina river; battle Aug. 1914 in which the Serbs defeated the Austrians.

Ja'de Bay (yä'dě). Inlet of North Sea on N coast of Oldenburg region of Lower Saxony, NW Germany; on its W coast is Wilhelmshaven.

Ja'dot'ville (zhȧ'dō'vēl'). Industrial city, SE Katanga prov., SE Congo, 60 m. NW of Elisabethville; copper-mining center; pop. 76,877.

Ja·én' (hä·ān'). **1** Province of Spain. See *Table* at SPAIN.

2 Commune, its ✱, S Spain, 178 m. S of Madrid; pop. (1941 est.) 55,108; leather, soap, alcohol, linen; 16th-cent. cathedral; Moorish citadel.

Jaf'fa (jăf'a; yăf'a); *Arab.* **Ya'fa** (yä'fä; -fä). **1** Subdistrict, Lydda dist., S Palestine; 129 sq. m.; pop. 145,502, (1938 est.) 299,970.

2 *anc.* **Jop'pa** (jŏp'a). Commercial seaport in Jaffa subdistrict, Palestine, 35 m. NW of Jerusalem; part of Tel Aviv since 1950; pop. 51,866, (1944 est.) 93,443; poor harbor but long the pilgrim port for Jerusalem, with which it is now connected by rail. Ancient town, mentioned in Biblical history (2 *Chron.* ii. 16); destroyed by Vespasian 68 A.D.; seat of early Christian bishopric; twice captured by Crusaders, but lost to Mohammedans 1268; destroyed 1345 by Egyptian sultan; captured by Napoleon 1799; occupied by British 1917; center of postwar disturbance 1945–47.

Jaff'na (jäf'na). **1** Peninsula ab. 50 m. long, N extremity of Ceylon.

2 Town, ✱ of Northern Province, Ceylon, on Jaffna Penin.; pop. 45,708; good harbor and active trade; exports cotton, tobacco, timber, and fruits; includes old Dutch fort and Hindu shrines. Taken by Tamils 204 B.C. whose rajas ruled till ousted by Portuguese 1617, who in turn were succeeded by Dutch 1658; became British 1795; was last Portuguese possession in Ceylon; seat of American missions and Roman Catholic bishop.

Jaf'frey (jăf'rĭ). Town, SW New Hampshire, in Chesh-

ire co., 13 m. ESE of Keene; pop. 3154; summer resort on S shoulder of Grand Monadnock; its business center is **East Jaffrey.**

Jagannath. See PURI.

Jag'dal·pur (jŭg'dȧl·poor'). Town, former ✱ of Bastar state, in SE Madhya Pradesh, E India, 125 m. NW of Vizagapatam; pop. 10,128.

Jägerndorf. See KRNOV.

Ja'gers·fon·tein' (yä'kĕrs·fôn·tān'). Town, SW Orange Free State, E cen. Union of South Africa, 60 m. SW of Bloemfontein; pop. 2435; has most important diamond mine in state.

Jag'ged Mountain (jăg'ĕd; -ĭd). Peak 13,836 ft. in San Juan co., SW Colorado.

Jaghbub. See GIARABUB.

Jag'raon (jŭg'roun). Town, Punjab state, NW Indian Union, 90 m. SE of Lahore; pop. 27,108.

Jagst (yäkst). Circle of Württemberg. See *Table* at WÜRTTEMBERG.

Jagst'hau'sen (yäkst'hou'zĕn). Village, N Baden-Württemberg, S Germany, NE of Heilbronn; birthplace of Götz von Berlichingen.

Ja'gua·rão' (zhä'gwȧ·roun'). **1** *Span.* **Ya'gua·rón'** (yä'gwä·rôn'). River ab. 135 m. long, forming E section of boundary bet. Uruguay and S Brazil; empties into Lake Mirim.

2 City, S Rio Grande do Sul state, S Brazil, near mouth of river; pop. (1940 est.) 10,747.

Ja'gua·ri'be (zhä'gwȧ·rē'vě). River ab. 350 m. long, E Ceará state, NE Brazil; flows into Atlantic Ocean at Aracatí.

Ja'güey Gran'de (hä'gwě·ĕ [-gwä] grän'dȧ). Municipality, Matanzas prov., W cen. Cuba, 45 m. SE of Matanzas; pop. 10,665.

Jah·rum' (jȧ·hroom'). City, Fars prov., SW Iran, ab. 90 m. SE of Shiraz; pop. ab. 15,000; produces dates.

Ja·hú' (zhȧ·oo'). Var. of JAÚ.

Jainat. See CHAINAT.

Jain'ti·a Hills (jīn'tĭ·ä). Hill region in N cen. Assam, NE Indian Union. E of Khasi Hills; form part of Assam dist. of Khasi and Jaintia Hills.

Jai'pur (jī'poor; *native* jä'poor); *also* **Jey'pore** (jī'pōr; jä'-). **1** Former Indian state, E Rajputana, NW Indian Union; now in Rajasthan state; 15,610 sq. m.; pop. (1941) 3,040,876; hills and desert in N and W, fertile in E and S; founded in 12th cent. (probably 1128) by Rajput chief from Gwalior; furnished famous generals to Mogul emperors; came under British protection 1818; was ruled by a maharaja.

2 City, its ✱, now ✱ of Rajasthan, ab. 140 m. W of Agra; pop. (1951) 291,130; founded 1728 by Maharaja Jai Singh II; walled and fortified; only city in India laid out in rectangular blocks and wide streets; most important city in Rajputana; has lively trade, textile industry, glass manufacturing, enamel and metalworking, and jewel cutting and setting; noted for the Maharaja's palace with curious open-air observatories, and the Public Gardens. For the former capital of Jaipur state, see AMBER.

Jaipur Residency. Former division of Rajputana Agency, NW India, including Indian states of Alwar, Jaipur, Kishangarh, Shahpura, and Tonk. Since 1947 these states have either joined other groups or have been assimilated with administrative units of the Indian Union.

Jai'sal·mer (jī'sȧl·měr). **1** Former Indian state, W Rajputana, NW India, formerly in Western Rajputana States Agency; 15,980 sq. m.; pop. (1941) 93,246; on June 26, 1947 joined the Union of Rajasthan; almost entirely a sandy waste, forming part of Thar, or Indian, Desert; has practically no crops, but some grazing; founded 1156 by a Rajput chief; entered into political relations with British 1818.

2 Town, its ✱, in desert 140 m. WNW of Jodhpur; pop. 7120.

Jaj'ce (yī'tsĕ). Town, N cen. Bosnia and Herzegovina, Yugoslavia, on Vrbas river; pop. 7515; manufactures chemicals. Held by Hungarians against onslaughts of Turks 1463–1526; finally surrendered to Turks 1528 and held by them until 1908 when Bosnia and Herzegovina was annexed by Austria.

Jakarta. = DJAKARTA. See BATAVIA.

Jakko, Mount. See SIMLA.

Ja'kobs·havn' (yä'kôps·houn'). Danish settlement on Disko Bay, W coast of Greenland, in North Greenland division; pop. 681.

Jakobstad. See PIETARSAARI.

Jakobstadt. See YEKABPILS.

Jal (jäl). City, Lea co., SE corner of New Mexico, 37 m. S of Hobbs; pop. 3051; oil discovered 1927.

Ja·lal'a·bad or **Je·lal'a·bad** (jà-läl'à·bäd; native jà-läl'ä·bäd'). Town, E Afghanistan, W of Khyber Pass and on Kabul river near its junction with the Kunar; pop. ab. 6000; in strategic location in river plain 70 m. E of Kabul and 80 m. W of Peshawar; also commands Kunar valley N to Chitral; site chosen by Mogul emperor Baber and town built by Akbar 1560. Defended in First Afghan War by British under Sir Robert Sale Nov. 1841–Apr. 1842; winter residence of Afghan rulers.

Jalandhar. See JULLUNDUR.

Ja·la'pa (hä·lä'pä). **1** Department, SE Guatemala; 797 sq. m.; pop. 124,855.
2 Town, its ✳; pop. 9968; altitude 4526 ft.; corn, beans, livestock.
3 older **Xa·la'pa** (hä·lä'pä); in full **Jalapa En·rí'-quez** (ân·rē'kâs). City, E Mexico, ✳ of Veracruz state; pop. 39,530; mountain resort, altitude 4500 ft.; coffee, tobacco.

Ja'la·pa·har' (jŭ'lä·pà·här'). See DARJEELING.

Ja·la'ur (hä·lä'ōōr). River ab. 60 m. long, NW and cen. Iloilo prov., Panay, Phil. Is.; rises in mountains near Antique border, flows W and S to Iloilo Strait.

Jal'gaon (jäl'goun). Town, N Maharashtra state, W India, 235 m. NE of Bombay; pop. 34,375.

Ja·lis'co (hä·lēs'kō). State, W cen. Mexico. See *Table* at MEXICO.

Jal'lieu' (zhà'lyû'). Commune, Isère dept., SE France, 25 m. ESE of Lyons; pop. (1931) 5377; forms with Bourgoin an industrial center.

Jal'na (jäl'nà). Town, N cen. Maharashtra state, S cen. Indian Union, ab. 35 m. E of Aurangabad; pop. 22,408.

Jalomitsa. Var. of IALOMITA.

Ja·lón' (hä·lôn'). River ab. 120 m. long, NE cen. Spain, flowing NE into Ebro river 13 m. above Saragossa.

Ja·lo·sto·ti·tlán' (hä·lō'stō·tĕ·tlän'). Town, Jalisco state, Mexico, 68 m. NE of Guadalajara; pop. 6493.

Jal'pai·gu'ri (jŭl'pī·gōō'rē). **1** District, formerly entirely in Rajshahi division, N Bengal, NE Brit. India, on Bhutan frontier; 3050 sq. m.; pop. (1941) 1,089,513; divided 1947 with ab. ⅕ of area and ¼ of population assigned to East Bengal, Pakistan, the remainder to West Bengal, Indian Union.
2 Town, its ✳, in Indian Union on Tista river; pop. 18,962.

Jal'te·pec' (häl'tâ·pĕk'). River 160 m. long, on Isthmus of Tehuantepec, Mexico; rises in E Oaxaca state, flows NE into Bay of Campeche.

Ja·lud' (jă·lōōd'). River, Palestine; W tributary of the Jordan, N of Mt. Gilboa; its valley called the Valley of Jezreel (see Plain of ESDRAELON).

Jal'u·it (jäl'ōō·it). Largest of the Marshall Is., in Ralik Chain, in W Pacific Ocean; atoll 38 m. long by 21 m. wide; has ab. 50 islets; harbor at Jabor, on SE side; strongly garrisoned by Japanese; bypassed by American forces in attack on Kwajalein.

Ja·mai'ca (jà·mā'kà). **1** Former town, since 1898 part of borough of Queens in New York City, ⊗ of Queens co., SE New York, on Long I.; settled by English 1655; became ⊗ 1683; manufacturing and commercial center in market-gardening region.

2 Largest of the British islands in the West Indies, 95 m S of E Cuba; ab. 145 m. long; 4450 sq. m.; pop. (1960) 1,613,148; with its dependencies Morant Cays and Pedro Cays constitutes a British dominion, independent since 1962. Mountainous, with main ridge running E and W; highest point Blue Mt. Peak 7388 ft. in Blue

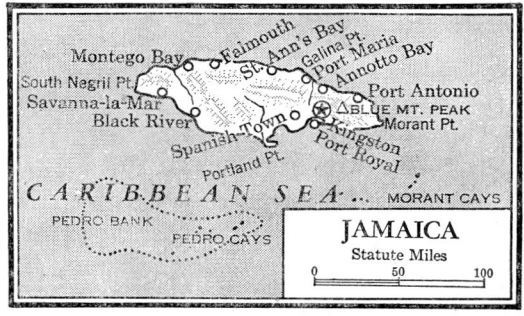

Mts. at E end; has many short streams; on coast are several bays with good anchorage, esp. Kingston harbor, Old Harbour Bay (or Portland Bight), Montego Bay, Port Antonio; exports sugar, rum, bananas, coffee, ginger, and cocoa; chief towns Kingston, Spanish Town, Montego Bay, Port Antonio.

History: Discovered by Columbus 1494; a Spanish colony 1509–1655; St. Iago de la Vega founded bet. 1520–26 (see SPANISH TOWN); captured by English under Penn and Venables 1655; governed by representative council 1661–1866 when Legislative Council was substituted; Port Royal, center of its flourishing slave trade, destroyed by earthquake, and Kingston built 1692; until 19th cent., when slavery was abolished, prospered as a producer of sugar; put down several Negro insurrections, notably in 1865; Kingston severely damaged by earthquake 1907; in World War II a fleet anchorage in Old Harbour Bay, several land areas on its shores, and use of Port Royal dockyard leased to United States. A British colony 1655–1958, a territory of West Indies Federation 1958–61, and a British dominion since 1961; became independent 1962.

Jamaica Bay. Inlet ab. 20 sq. m. of Atlantic Ocean at W end of Long I., New York; protected by the narrow peninsula on which Rockaway Beach is located.

Jamaica Plain. Former village in Suffolk co., Massachusetts, now a part of Boston; location of Arnold Arboretum.

Ja·mal' Ba·riz' (jà·mäl' bä·rēz'). Peak 13,000 ft. in S cen. Iran, SE of Kerman.

Ja·mal'pur (jà·mäl'pŏŏr). **1** Town, Mymensingh dist., NE East Bengal, Pakistan, near Jamuna river 190 m. NNE of Calcutta; pop. 23,077.
2 Town, NE Bihar, NE Indian Union near Ganges river 80 m. E of Patna; pop. 30,346.

Ja·may' (hä·mī'). Town, Jalisco state, W cen. Mexico, on NE shore of Lake Chapala; pop. 5892.

Jambes (zhänb). Commune, Namur prov., S Belgium, suburb of Namur; pop. 7954; glassworks.

Jambi. See DJAMBI.

Jam'bol (yäm'bŏl). = YAMBOL.

Jam·de'na or **Yam·de'na** (yäm·dā'nä). Largest of the Tanimbar group of islands in S Moluccas, Indonesia, E Malay Archipelago; 70 m. long by 28 m. wide; ab. 1100 sq. m.; pop. 15,684; chief village Saumlakki at S end.

James. **1** River, North Dakota and South Dakota; see DAKOTA river.
2 River 340 m. long, cen. Virginia; formed by confluence of Jackson and Cowpasture rivers in N Botetourt co., flows E into Chesapeake Bay through broad estuary at Hampton Roads; navigable to Richmond.

James Bay. Southern extension of Hudson Bay, bet. NE Ontario and W Quebec provs., Canada; ab. 280 m. long and 150 m. wide; contains Akimiski I. and several small islands; receives several large rivers, esp. the Fort George, Eastmain, Nottaway, and Harricanaw in Quebec, and the Moose, Albany. and Attawapiskat in Ontario.

James'burg (jāmz'bûrg). Borough, Middlesex co., cen. New Jersey, 10 m. S of New Brunswick; pop. 2853.

James City. County in Virginia. See *Table* at VIRGINIA.

James Island. See SAN SALVADOR.

Jame'son Bay (jām's'n). See JAN MAYEN ISLAND.

James Peak (jāmz). Mountain 13,259 ft. in Clear Creek, Grand, and Gilpin cos., N cen. Colorado; Moffat Tunnel goes through it.

James Ross Island. See ROSS ISLAND.

James'town (jāmz'toun). **1** City, ⊗ of Russell co., S Kentucky; pop. 792.

2 Manufacturing city, Chautauqua co., SW corner of New York, at S end of Chautauqua Lake 57 m. SSW of Buffalo; pop. 41,818; truck and dairy farms, orchards, vineyards; metal and wooden furniture, textiles, tools, voting machines, washing machines, office equipment; settled 1810, chartered as city 1886.

3 City, ⊗ of Stutsman co., SE cen. North Dakota, 95 m. W of Fargo; pop. 15,163; settled 1871; in wheat and livestock region; flour, processed cereal foods; stockyards, bottling works; Jamestown College (1883; coed.).

4 Residential town and summer resort, Newport co., SE Rhode Island, coextensive with Conanicut I., 3 m. W of Newport; pop. 2267.

5 City, ⊗ of Fentress co., N Tennessee; pop. 1727.

6 Ruined village, James City co., E Virginia, on peninsula (now Jamestown I.) of James river almost opp. Williamsburg; in Colonial National Historical Park; first permanent English settlement in America, founded May 13, 1607; capital of Virginia 1607–98; suffered famine ("Starving Time" 1609–10) and Indian attacks; meeting place of first legislative assembly in America 1619; almost entirely destroyed by Nathaniel Bacon 1676, rebuilt, but again declined following removal of capital to Williamsburg; site of Jamestown Exposition 1907.

7 Seaport town, ✻ of British island of St. Helena, S Atlantic Ocean; pop. (1942) 2381.

James W. Ellsworth Land. See ELLSWORTH HIGHLAND.

Jam·khan'di (jŭm·kŭn'dĭ). **1** Former Indian state in Deccan and Kolhapur States, W Indian Union, geographically in S Maharashtra; 522 sq. m.; pop. (1941) 126,272; formerly in Southern Maratha States.

2 Town, its ✻, 68 m. E of Kolhapur; pop. 15,523.

Jam'mu (jŭm'ōō); *also* **Jum'moo. 1** Region, Kashmir state, N India, formerly a province, occupying upper valley of Chenab river.

2 Town, S Kashmir state, N India, on Tawi river (tributary of the Chenab) 85 m. NNE of Lahore; pop. 38,613, with cantonment 42,794; winter residence of prince of Kashmir; has fort and a large palace of the raja; former seat of a Rajput dynasty, later acquired by the Sikhs.

Jammu and Kashmir. See KASHMIR.

Jam·na'gar (jŭm·nŭ'gĕr) *or* **Na'va·na'gar** (nŭ'vä·nŭ'-gĕr). City, formerly ✻ of Navanagar state, now in E Gujerat state, W India, on Gulf of Cutch 310 m. NW of Bombay; pop. (1941) 71,588; founded 1540.

Jam·rud' (jŭm·rōōd'). Fort and cantonment in former North-West Frontier Province, NW Pakistan, 9 m. W of Peshawar; important frontier outpost at mouth of Khyber Pass; scene of military operations at various times, esp. 1836–37, 1878–79, and 1897–98; headquarters of Khyber Rifles.

Jam'shed·pur (jŭm'shĕd·pōōr'). City, SE Bihar, NE Indian Union, at confluence of Subarnarekha and Karkhai rivers 140 m. W of Calcutta; pop. 218,162; founded 1909; center of metal industry; blast furnaces, coke ovens, steel and iron works, railroad shops, machine factories.

Jämt'land (yĕmt'länd). **1** Old province of Sweden, N of Herjedalen, in N cen. part bordering on Norway; ab. 20,000 sq. m.; Östersund is only important town; noted for its scenery; acquired by treaty from Norway 1645 during reign of Christina.

2 Modern province of Sweden. See *Table* at SWEDEN.

Ja'mu·na (jŭ'mōō·nä). River, main stream of Brahmaputra river from the Tista to the Ganges, India.

Ja'mun·dá' (zhä'mōōn·dä'). River, N Brazil; rises near British Guiana boundary, flows S into Amazon river, forming section of boundary bet. Pará and Amazonas states.

Ja·nau'cu (zhä·nou'kōō). Island in the mouth of the Amazon river, N of Caviana I., off NE coast of Pará state, Brazil.

Janes'ville (jānz'vĭl). Industrial city, ⊗ of Rock co., S Wisconsin, 12 m. N of Beloit; pop. 35,164; settled c. 1835; automobiles and automobile bodies, fountain pens, cotton and woolen goods, punch presses, awnings.

Janica. See GENITSA.

Ja·nic'u·lum (jå·nĭk'ů·lŭm); *called also* **Mons Au'-re·us** (mŏnz ô'rē·ŭs). A hill on right bank of the Tiber river opp. the seven hills of Rome.

Janina. See IOANNINA.

Jänisjärvi. See YANISYARVI.

Ja'ni·uay' (hä'nĕ·wī'). Municipality, W cen. Iloilo prov., Panay, Phil. Is., in the hill country on a tributary of the Jalaur 19 m. NNW of City of Iloilo; pop. 38,778; one of oldest towns on the island.

Jan'ji·ra (jŭn'jĭ·rå). **1** Former Indian state, Deccan and Kolhapur States. W Indian Union, geographically in E Maharashtra on coast 50 m. S of Bombay city; 326 sq. m.; pop (1941) 103,557; ✻ Murud.

2 Island and fort opp. Murud, at entrance to inlet.

Jankovácz. See JÁNOSHALMA.

Jan May'en Island (yän mī'ĕn). Norwegian volcanic island in Arctic Ocean 300 m. E of Greenland and 360 m. NNE of Iceland, 71°N, 8°W; 34 m. long and greatest width 9 m.; 144 sq. m.; highest point extinct volcano of Beerenberg 8347 ft.; meteorological station at Jameson Bay; discovered by Henry Hudson 1607; often visited by explorers; annexed to Norway May 8, 1929.

Jannabatain. See AJNADAIN.

Já'nos·hal·ma (yä'nōsh·hŏl'mŏ) *or* **Jan'ko·vácz** (yŏn'kŏ·väts). Commune, S Hungary, 40 m. W of Szeged; pop. 14,805.

Jao'ra (jou'rä). **1** Former Indian state, Malwa, W Central India. Indian Union; 601 sq. m.; pop. (1941) 110,953; founded 1808; its ruler had title of Nawab and was descended from an Afghan from Swat.

2 Town, its ✻, 160 m. ENE of Ahmadabad; pop. 20,998.

Jap (yäp). German var. of YAP.

Ja·pan' (jå·păn'); *Japanese* **Nip·pon** (nĭp·pŏn) *or* **Ni-hon** (nē·hŏn); *also* **Dai Nippon** (dī), *literally* "Great Japan." Empire, under new constitution of Nov. 3, 1946 (in force May 3, 1947), consisting of an island chain in W Pacific Ocean, off E coast of Asia, extending bet. lat. 46° and 24°N; 142,007 sq. m.; pop. (1945 survey) 72,598,077; ✻ Tokyo; comprises four main islands (Honshu, Shikoku, Kyushu, and Hokkaido) and the Ryukyu Is. to the S, the statistics breaking down as follows:

NAME	AREA[1]	POP.[1]
Honshu	87,293	54,612,618
Shikoku	7,246	3,836,378
Kyushu[2]	16,240	10,028,892
Hokkaido	30,307	3,518,389
Okinawa[3]	921	601,800
	142,007	72,598,077

[1] Area is in sq. m. Pop. is 1945 survey, except for Okinawa prefecture. which is 1938 est.
[2] Includes N part of Ryukyu Is. which is in Kagoshima prefecture.
[3] A prefecture comprising Okinawa and Sakishima groups in S Ryukyu Is.

Before World War II had indirect control over Manchukuo (*q.v.*) and included also the following:

NAME	AREA[1]	POP.[1]
Formosa (Taiwan)	13,808	5,747,000
Pescadores	49	70,000
Karafuto[2]	13,931	339,357
Korea (Chosen)	85,225	22,633,751
Kuril Is. (Chishima Retto)[3]	3,900	6,000
Kwantung Leased Territory[3]	1,444	1,750,000
South Sea Mandated Territory[4]	645	102,519
	119,062	30,648,627

[1] Area is in sq. m. Pop. is 1945 survey with exception of South Sea Mandated Territories which is 1935 Census.
[2] S part of Sakhalin I.
[3] S part of Liaotung Penin., S Manchuria.
[4] Called Nanyo by Japanese; included Marshall, Mariana, and Caroline Is., comprising ab. 760 small islands with capital at Koror in Palau Is.

The total area and population of the former Japanese Empire, exclusive of Manchukuo, was 261,069 sq. m. and pop. 103,246,704.

Japan is divided into the following 47 prefectures (for pronunciation of their names, see their individual entries):

NAME	LOCATION	AREA[1]	POP.[1]	CAPITAL
Aichi	S Honshu	1,961	2,857,338	Nagoya
Akita	N Honshu	4,502	1,211,962	Akita
Aomori	N Honshu	3,718	1,083,250	Aomori
Chiba	SE Honshu	1,960	1,966,873	Chiba
Ehime	NW Shikoku	2,187	1,361,484	Matsuyama
Fukui	W Honshu	1,551	724,856	Fukui
Fukuoka	N Kyushu	1,907	2,746,855	Fukuoka
Fukushima	N cen. Honshu	5,320	1,957,356	Fukushima
Gifu	W cen. Honshu	4,051	1,518,649	Gifu
Gumma	cen. Honshu	2,446	1,546,081	Maebashi
Hiroshima	SW Honshu	3,257	1,885,471	Hiroshima
Hokkaido[2]	N Japan	30,307	3,518,389	Sapporo
Hyogo	W Honshu	3,213	2,821,892	Kobe
Ibaraki	SE Honshu	2,351	1,944,573	Mito
Ishikawa	W Honshu	1,620	887,510	Kanazawa
Iwate	N Honshu	5,881	1,227,789	Morioka
Kagawa	NE Shikoku	718	863,553	Takamatsu
Kagoshima	S Kyushu	3,514	1,538,466	Kagoshima
Kanagawa	SE Honshu	908	1,865,667	Yokohama
Kochi	S Shikoku	2,742	775,578	Kochi
Kumamoto	W cen. Kyushu	2,871	1,556,351	Kumamoto
Kyoto	W cen. Honshu	1,603,797		Kyoto
Mie	S Honshu	2,225	1,394,286	Tsu
Miyagi	N Honshu	2,808	1,461,316	Sendai
Miyazaki	SE Kyushu	2,987	913,687	Miyazaki
Nagano	cen. Honshu	5,260	2,120,950	Nagano
Nagasaki	NW Kyushu	1,573	1,318,589	Nagasaki
Nara	W cen. Honshu	1,424	779,685	Nara
Niigata	NW Honshu	4,855	2,389,653	Niigata
Oita	NE Kyushu	2,445	1,124,513	Oita
Okayama	W Honshu	2,720	1,564,626	Okayama
Okinawa[3]	S Japan	921	601,800	Naha
Osaka	W cen. Honshu	700	2,800,958	Osaka
Saga	NW Kyushu	943	830,431	Saga
Saitama	SE cen. Honshu	1,468	2,047,090	Urawa
Shiga	W cen. Honshu	1,564	860,911	Otsu
Shimane	SW Honshu	2,555	860,275	Matsue
Shizuoka	S Honshu	2,999	2,220,358	Shizuoka
Tochigi	cen. Honshu	2,485	1,546,355	Utsunomiya
Tokushima	E Shikoku	1,599	835,763	Tokushima
Tokyo	SE cen. Honshu	828	3,488,284	Tokyo
Tottori	W Honshu	1,347	563,320	Tottori
Toyama	W Honshu	1,643	953,834	Toyama
Wakayama	SW Honshu	1,823	936,006	Wakayama
Yamagata	N Honshu	3,600	1,326,350	Yamagata
Yamaguchi	SW Honshu	2,348	1,356,540	Yamaguchi
Yamanashi	S cen. Honshu	1,724	839,057	Kofu

[1] Area in sq. m. Pop. is 1945 survey, except Okinawa which is 1938 est.
[2] Does not include the Kuril Is.
[3] Comprises the S part of the Ryukyu Is. (Okinawa and Sakishima groups).

All islands mountainous, including many high peaks (7000 to 10,000 ft.) and volcanoes; highest Fuji 12,388 ft., on S Honshu; lies in earthquake belt of W Pacific and has suffered from many destructive shocks, esp. Sept. 1923 and Dec. 21, 1946; islands indented with many bays, affording fine harbors; most important water area Inland Sea (*q.v.*); off shores of large islands are many smaller islands (Sado, Awaji, Tsushima) and groups (Oki, Goto, Izu Shichito, Bonin, Volcano); rivers short and rapid and only a few partly navigable; many beautiful lakes (Biwa, Chuzenji, Inawashiro). Economically poor in arable land; fishing, silk and textile production, smaller crafts, and in modern period iron and steel production and shipbuilding. Chief cities Tokyo, Osaka, Nagoya, Yokohama, Kyoto, Kobe, Kita-Kyushu.

History: Earlier inhabitants, the Ainu, were driven northward by invaders, probably of Manchu-Korean and Malayan stock; traditional history dates from 660 B.C., accession of Jimmu Tenno, ruler of Yamato (*q.v.*) and founder of the imperial line; written history began in 5th cent. A.D. when Japan entered contact with highly developed Chinese culture from which it adopted handwriting; Buddhism introduced 552; closely imitated Chinese institutions 6th–9th cents.; in 794, imperial capital moved to Heian-kyo (modern Kyoto) where it remained until 1869; from 9th–12th cents., court dominated by Fujiwara family; in 1192, Minamoto Yoritomo became shogun (military dictator) and founded first of the shogunates which controlled emperor 1192–1867; in Kamakura period 1192–1333, military feudalism, evolved since 9th cent., reached full development; invaded by Mongols 1274, 1281; in 15th cent. (Ashikaga shoguns 1338–1568), general breakdown of feudalism.

First visited by Europeans (Portuguese) 1542–43; Christianity introduced by St. Francis Xavier 1549–51; in late 16th cent. Japanese Empire united and outlying provinces conquered by Hideyoshi and Iyeyasu (first of Tokugawa shoguns 1603–1867); edicts of successors of Iyeyasu cut off Japanese contact with foreigners, including European traders and missionaries, except at Nagasaki (*q.v.*); in 1854, Commodore Perry, an American, secured first commercial treaty; Meiji era 1868–1912 began with emperor's resumption of direct rule 1868; rapidly adopted Occidental civilization, modified government (constitution of 1889) and extended foreign contacts; fought war with China over Korea (*q.v.*) 1894–95 (see SHIMONOSEKI); allied with Great Britain 1902; victorious in Russo-Japanese war 1904–05; annexed Korea 1910; made Twenty-one Demands on China 1915; for participation in World War I, secured former German possessions in Pacific, N of equator.

Occupied Manchuria (*q.v.*) 1931–32, Shanghai 1932, and began war with China gradually taking over all large coastal cities and many interior sections 1937–45. Signed military alliance with Germany and Italy 1940. Entered World War II Dec. 7, 1941 by surprise attack on Pearl Harbor, Hawaii; attacked Philippine Is. Dec. 8, 1941; occupied Manila Jan. 2, 1942 and after long and severe fighting on Bataan Penin. overwhelmed smaller American and Filipino force Apr. 9, 1942 and took Corregidor May 6. Seized Hong Kong Dec. 25, 1941; invaded Malay Penin. Dec. 8–9, 1941, and forced surrender of Singapore Feb. 15, 1942; invaded Siam Dec. 1941 and Burma Dec. 8, 1942, cutting Burma Road (*q.v.*). Seized Amboina, E coast of Borneo, and Sumatra, and Java Jan.–Mar. 1942. Received first setback in naval and air battles of Midway June 3–6, 1942 and Coral Sea May 7–8; defeated on land and sea at Guadalcanal Aug. 1942–Feb. 1943; driven out of SE New Guinea (Territory of Papua) Dec. 1942–Jan. 1943 and out of Aleutians Aug. 1943; defeated at Tarawa Nov. 21–24, 1943; lost Kwajalein Jan. 30–Feb. 6, 1944 and Eniwetok Feb. 17–22 in the Marshall Is. Driven back in Ledo Road campaign, N Burma, Feb.–May 1944 and defeated in Manipur Mar.–June 1944; lost Admiralty Is. Mar. 18, 1944, Saipan June 15–July 9, Tinian July 23–Aug. 1, and Guam July 20–Aug. 10, 1944; lost Manila Jan. 9–Feb. 23, 1945. Partly successful in China 1944–45 but with great losses of ships, planes, and material sources unable to hold Iwo Jima Feb.–Mar. 1945 and Okinawa Apr.–June; many large cities devastated by carrier planes; Hiroshima Aug. 6 and Nagasaki Aug. 9 practically destroyed by atomic bombs; attacked by Russia Aug. 8 in Manchuria; surrendered Aug. 14; mainland (first in Tokyo area) occupied by Allied troops in Sept.

Japan, Sea of. Branch of W Pacific Ocean lying bet. Japan on E, and Maritime Territory, Soviet Russia, and Korea on W; ab. 405,000 sq. m.; on N connects by Gulf of Tatary and Tatar Strait with Sea of Okhotsk; on NE by Soya Strait bet. Sakhalin and Hokkaido with Sea of Okhotsk; on E by Tsugaru Strait bet. Hokkaido and Honshu with the Pacific; and on SW by Korea Strait bet. Korea and Japan with East China Sea. For naval battle fought here 1905, see Tsushima Strait.

Japan Current *or* **Black Stream;** *Jap.* **Ku·ro·shi·o** (koō·rô·shē·ô). A branch of the equatorial current of the Pacific Ocean, flowing along the E coast of Formosa, thence NE along E coast of Honshu, Japan, and merging into the easterly drift of the North Pacific Ocean S of the Aleutian Is.; noticeable for its deep blue color (hence the name *Black Stream*); has influence on climate similar to that of the Gulf Stream (*q.v.*).

Japan Stream. = Japan Current.

Japan Trough. Any of several deeps of the Pacific Ocean off the E coast of Japan; several have been measured more than 30,000 ft. deep; deepest yet found is Ramapo Deep, 34,626 ft., in lat. 30°43′N, long. 142°28′E.

Japara, Japara–Rembang. See Djapara, Djapara-Rembang.

Ja′pen *or* **Jap′pen** (yä′pĕn). **1** Island 110 m. long in Geelvink Bay, on N coast of Neth. New Guinea, S of Schouten Is.; 936 sq. m.; has elevated central ridge; highest point 4908 ft.; chief settlements Seroei in cen. part of S coast, and Ansoes on S coast near W end. **2** A former administrative subdivision of Ternate division, Moluccas residency, including Japen I. and a large part of mainland of Neth. New Guinea on SE coast of Geelvink Bay; 10,905 sq. m.; pop. 28,684.

Ja′pu·rá′ (zhä′poō·rá′). River ab. 1750 m. long, NW South America; rises in SW Colombia, where it is known as the **Ca′que·tá′** (kä′kä·tä′), and flows SE across Brazilian border into Amazon river.

Jap′vo, Mount (jŭp′vō). Mountain 9826 ft. in Barail Range, S part of Naga Hills, on N boundary of Manipur; highest mountain in Assam, NE Indian Union.

Jaquemel. Var. of Jacmel.

Ja′qui·ra′na (zhä′kĕ·rä′ná). = Javarí.

Jara. See Gabès.

Jarabub. See Giarabub.

Ja·ra′ma (hä·rä′mä). River ab. 115 m. long, cen. Spain; joins Henares river 10 m. ESE of Madrid and empties into Tagus river a little below Aranjuez.

Jar·di′nes de la Rei′na (här·thē′nås thä lä rĕ′ĕ·nä). Chain of small islands in West Indies, extending NW to SE in Caribbean Sea S of cen. Cuba; belong to Cuba.

Jar′geau (zhär′zhō′). Town, Loiret dept., N cen. France, on the Loire 10 m. E of Orléans; pop. 1234; scene of victory of Joan of Arc over the English 1429.

Ja·rí′ *or* **Ja·ry′** (zhá·rē′). River 360 m. long, NE Brazil; rises in Tumuc-Humac Mts. and flows SSE from SW Surinam border into Amazon river near its mouth.

Jarls′berg (yärls′bĕr). Former name of *Vestfold:* see *Table* at Norway.

Jar′nac′ (zhär′näk′). Commune, Charente dept., W France, on the Charente 18 m. W of Angoulême; pop. (1931) 3796; scene of battle Mar. 13, 1569 in which Catholics under duke of Anjou (later Henry III) defeated the Huguenots under Prince of Condé and in which Condé was killed.

Ja′ro (hä′rô). **1** Municipality, N Leyte prov., Phil. Is., on E slope of mountains 15 m. W of Tacloban; pop. 23,914; taken by Americans Oct. 31, 1944. **2** Municipality, SE Iloilo prov., Panay, Phil. Is., on Jaro river 4 m. N of City of Iloilo; pop. 25,797; one of earliest Spanish settlements in the Philippines, founded 1584; made an episcopal see 1865.

Ja·ro′slaw (yä·rô′släf); *Ger.* **Ja′ro·slau** (yä′rô·slou); *Russ.* **Ya′ro·slav** (yär′ô·släv; *Russ.* yĭ·rŭ·släf′). City of E Galicia, E Rzeszów dept., SE Poland, near Ukraine border, on San river 28 m. E of Rzeszów; pop. (1938–39

est.) 22,195; agricultural center; scene of German defeat by Russians Oct. 1914; occupied by Germans and Austrians May 1915 and by Germans June 1941.

Jar′ra·hi′ (jär′rä·hē′). River ab. 165 m. long, SW cen. Iran; flows generally SW into head of Persian Gulf; seaport of Bandar Shahpur is at its mouth.

Jar′row (jär′ō). Municipal borough, Durham, N England, 6 m. E of Newcastle; pop. 28,541; chemical manufacturing, paper mills, shipbuilding yards, iron foundries; ships coal; ruins of 7th-cent. monastery where the Venerable Bede spent his life.

Ja·ru′co (hä·roō′kô). Municipality, La Habana prov., W Cuba, 23 m. ESE of Havana; pop. 25,692.

Jär′va (yär′vä); *Russ.* **Yar′va** (yär′vá). Province of Estonia. See *Table* at Estonia.

Jar′vis Island (jär′vĭs). One of the Line Is. (*q.v.*) just S of the equator in cen. Pacific Ocean, 190 m. SW of Christmas I.; long. 160°W; 1 sq. m.; worked by an American company for its guano 1857–79; annexed by Great Britain 1889; claimed by United States 1935; airfield and weather station.

Jary. See Jarí.

Jash′pur (jŭsh′poōr). Former Indian state in Eastern States, NE Indian Union; now geographically in Madhya Pradesh, 1955 sq. m.; pop. (1941) 223,612; **＊ Jash′pur·na′gar** (-nŭ′gēr).

Jasienica Dolna. See Nieder Hermsdorf.

Ja′sin (jä′sĭn). District, E Malacca, Federation of Malaya; pop. 48,173.

Jasiña. See Yasenya.

Jasiolda. See Yaselda.

Jask (jäsk). Seaport, S Iran, on Gulf of Oman ab. 130 m. SE of Bandar Abbas; was capital of former Makran prov.; formerly British.

Ja′slo (yä′slô). Commune, Rzeszów dept., Poland, 30 m. SE of Tarnów; pop. (1938–39 est.) 12,000; petroleum; pilgrimage chapel; battle 1914.

Jas′mund (yäs′moͤnt). Peninsula, NE Rügen I., Germany; in waters of Baltic Sea nearby occurred battle May 25, 1676 in which Danes under Niels Juel defeated the Swedes.

Ja′son·ville (jā′s′n·vĭl). City, Greene co., SW Indiana, 23 m. SSE of Terre Haute; pop. 2436.

Jas′per (jăs′pēr). **1** Name of counties in eight states of the U.S. See *Tables* at Georgia, Illinois, Indiana, Iowa, Mississippi, Missouri, South Carolina, Texas. **2** City, ⊗ of Walker co., NW cen. Alabama, 38 m. NW of Birmingham; pop. 10,799; settled 1815; coal mining, lumber mills, cotton mills. **3** City, ⊗ of Newton co., NW Arkansas; pop. 273. **4** City, ⊗ of Hamilton co., N Florida, 79 m. W of Jacksonville; pop. 2103; settled 1824; tobacco, lumber and lumber products, cotton. **5** City, ⊗ of Pickens co., N Georgia; pop. 1036. **6** City, ⊗ of Dubois co., SW Indiana, 36 m. ESE of Vincennes; pop. 6737; founded 1818; manufactures desks. **7** Town, ⊗ of Marion co., S Tennessee; pop. 1450. **8** City, ⊗ of Jasper co., E Texas, 58 m. N of Beaumont; pop. 4889; livestock, agricultural products; lumber and veneer mills. **9** Unincorporated village in Jasper National Park, Alberta prov., Canada, on Athabaska river, altitude 3472 ft.; pop. 1728; starting point for park excursions.

Jasper National Park. See Canada, *National Parks.*

Jassy. See Iași.

Jász′a′pâ·ti (yäs′ô′pä·tĭ). Commune, cen. Hungary, 50 m. E of Budapest; pop. 13,599.

Jász′á·rok·szál′lás (yäs′ä·rôk·säl′läsh). Commune, cen. Hungary, 42 m. E of Budapest; pop. 15,292.

Jász′be·ré·ny (yäs′bĕ·rān·y′). City, cen. Hungary, 37 m. E of Budapest; pop. 34,781.

Jath (jŭt). **1** Former Indian state, Deccan and Kolhapur states, W Indian Union, now geographically in S Maharashtra state; 972 sq. m.; pop. (1941) 107,036. **2** Town, its ＊, 70 m. ENE of Kolhapur; pop. 6055.

Ja'ti·bo·ni'co (hä'tĕ·vŏ·nē'kŏ).   Municipality and town, Camagüey prov., E cen. Cuba; pop. (town) 7409; town on railroad at Las Villas border.

Já'ti·va *or* **Já'ti·ba** (hä'tĕ·vä); *formerly* **Xá'ti·va** (hä'-); *anc.* **Se'ta·bis** (sē'tá·bĭs). Commune, Valencia prov., E Spain, 35 m. S of Valencia; pop. 18,263; agriculture; silk, paper, brandy, oil, pottery, leather, soap, flour. Roman colony; made episcopal see under Goths; captured and fortified by Moors; reconquered by James I of Aragon 1244; under attack 1522 and 1707.

Jatiwangi. See DJATIWANGI.

Ja·ú' (zhá·ōō'). City, cen. São Paulo state, SE Brazil, 150 m. NW of São Paulo; pop. (1940 est.) 18,665; coffee.

Jau'a·pe·rí' (zhou'á·pĕ·rē'). River ab. 240 m. long, NE Amazonas state, N Brazil, flowing SW and S into the Rio Negro.

Jauer. See JAWOR, Poland.

Jauf (jouf). Town, N Nejd, Arabia, in An Nafud region 250 m. E of Ma'an; pop. ab. 10,000.

Jau'ja (hou'hä). Town, Junín dept., cen. Peru, just N of Huancayo; pop. (1940 est.) 8276.

Jaunjelgava. See YAUNYELGAVA.

Jaunlatgale. See YAUNLATGALE.

Jaun'pur (joun'pŏŏr). City, SE Uttar Pradesh, N Indian Union, on Gumti river 60 m. ENE of Allahabad; pop. 37,675; railroad center; known for perfumes and papier-mâché articles; founded 1359 by Firuz Shah III, King of Delhi; has an old fort with gateway, splendid mosques, and a fine bridge over the Gumti; capital 1394–1478 of princes of so-called Sharki dynasty.

Ja'va (jä'vá; jăv'á). Island, Indonesia, in the Greater Sunda Is. group, SE of Sumatra and S of Borneo, between Java Sea and Indian Ocean; separated from SE Sumatra by Sunda Strait and from Bali on E by Bali Strait; 600 m. long by 125 m. at widest part; 48,830 sq. m.; pop. 39,755,992; with nearby island of Madura until 1947 formed the more directly administered part of the Netherlands Indies, comprising 3 provinces, East Java (including Madura), Middle Java, and West Java, and native states (Surakarta and Jogjakarta, 3554 sq. m., pop. 4,123,875); total area of **Java and Ma·du'ra** (má·dōōr'á) 50,942 sq. m.; pop. 41,718,364. Mountainous with 20 or more peaks above 8000 ft., mostly volcanic with about 13 active today; highest Semeru 12,060 ft.; N coast land generally low with several good harbors; S coast abrupt with only one harbor Tjilatjap; many short streams, most important Solo, Brantas, Tjiliwong; has extensive system of railroads and highways. One of most densely populated agricultural countries on the globe; chief crops sugar, coffee, tea, cocoa, rubber; before World War II produced 90% of world's supply of quinine; produces also teak and coal, and much rice for home consumption. Chief cities Djakarta, Surabaja, Semarang, Bandung, Surakarta, and Jogjakarta.

History: Conquered and occupied bet. 1st cent. A.D. and 700 A.D. by Hindu princes who introduced Brahmanism; little known of early history until 14th cent. when state of Madjapahit in E Java conquered Srivijaya empire of Sumatra and expanded to include almost all of Malay Archipelago 1335–80; Madjapahit lost its colonies by c. 1478, was conquered by Mohammedans and finally destroyed by 1518; when Europeans arrived in 16th cent., Bantam and Mataram were leading Mohammedan states; Batavia (*q.v.*) was founded by Dutch East India Co. 1619 which expelled English 1623 (see AMBOINA); Dutch gradually spread control eastward from Batavia; Bantam captured and annexed by Dutch 1808–09; held by British 1811–16; Dutch control, menaced by revolt 1825–30, afterwards became stronger; seized by Japanese by Mar. 1942 and after close of World War II scene of strong Indonesian independence movement, resulting in the Linggadjati Agreement and the establishment 1947 of the Republic of Indonesia (*q.v.*).

Java Head. Cape on extreme W end of Java at entrance to Sunda Strait from the Indian Ocean.

Ja'va·rí' (zhá'vá·rē') *or* **Ya'ca·ra'na** (yá'ká·rä'ná). River ab. 650 m. long, NW cen. South America; flows NE, forming large section of the boundary bet. Peru and Brazil, and empties into Amazon river on Brazilian border.

Java Sea. Part of the Pacific Ocean N of Java, S of Borneo, and E of S end of Sumatra; lat. 3° to 7°S, long. 106° to 116°E; a shallow sea, 300 ft. or less in depth; ab. 600 m. long by 200 m. wide; scene of battle SW of Bawean I. Feb. 26–28, 1942 in which Japanese fleet won victory over fleet of Allied Nations.

Java Trough; *called also* **Whar'ton Deep** (hwôr't'n). One of the deepest known parts of the Indian Ocean 22,968 ft., off S coast of island of Java, in 10°S lat. and 108°E long.

Ja·whar' (já·wär'). Former Indian state, Gujarat States, W Indian Union; 308 sq. m.; pop. (1941) 65,126; geographically in NW Maharashra in Western Ghats, 75 m. N of Bombay; ruler is a Koli chief.

Ja'wor (yä'vôr); *Ger.* **Jau'er** (you'ĕr). City, cen. Wrocław dept., SW Poland, 11 m. SSE of Legnica; pop. (1946) 13,817; formerly in Silesia, Germany; late-Gothic cathedral; manufactures sausage, agricultural machinery, furniture, cigars; raises sugar beets; assigned to Poland by Potsdam Conference 1945.

Ja·wo'rów (yä·vô'rōōf). Town, SW Ukraine, U.S.S.R. See YAVOROV.

Ja·worz'no (yä·vôzh'nô). Commune, W Kraków dept., Poland, 12 m. ESE of Katowice; pop. (1938–39 est.) 23,000; coal, calomine; zinc refineries, glass furnaces.

Jax·ar'tes (jăk·sär'tēz). River, Soviet Russia, Central Asia: see SYR DARYA.

Jay (jā). **1** County in Indiana. See *Table* at INDIANA.

2 Town, Franklin co., W Maine, 28 m. N of Lewiston; pop. 3247.

3 Town, ⊗ of Delaware co., NE Oklahoma; pop. 1120.

Jayabum. See CHAIYAPHUM.

Jay'a·nath' (chī'nät'). Var. of *Jainat:* see CHAINAT.

Jayhun. See AMU DARYA.

Jay Peak *or* **Big Jay Peak** (jā). Mountain 4018 ft. in NW Orleans co., N Vermont.

Ja·yu'ya (hä·yōō'yä). Municipality (pop. 14,633) and town (pop. 2344), cen. Puerto Rico; town is 15 m. N of Ponce.

Ja·zi'ra, Al (äl jä·zē'rŏ). Region of upper Mesopotamia; the Tigris-Euphrates valley NW of Baghdad.

Jaz'zi, Ci'ma di (chē'mä dė yät'tsē). Peak 12,527 ft. in Pennine Alps, on Swiss-Italian border.

Jean'er·ette' (jĕn'ĕr·ĕt'). Town, Iberia parish, S Louisiana, 32 m. SE of Lafayette; pop. 5568; sugar, pecans, rice.

Jean·nette' (jĕ·nĕt'). Industrial city, Westmoreland co., SW Pennsylvania, 22 m. ESE of Pittsburgh; pop. 16,565; settled 1888; glassware, rubber tires, plumbing supplies, cement, beer; coal mines, gas wells.

Jeb'ba (jĕb'á). Town, Ilorin prov., Northern Region, Nigeria, on railroad and on Niger river 50 m. N of Ilorin; important river port.

Jebeil. = DJEBEÏL.

Jeb'el (jĕb'ĕl); *Arab.* **Ja'bal** (jä'bắl; *in Lower Egypt*, gä'-; *in some parts of Syria*, zhä'-; *in Upper Egypt*, dyä'- *or* dä'-); *Egyptian* **Ge'bel** (gä'bắl); *French* **Dje'bel'** (jä'bĕl'). Forms from the Arabic word meaning "mountain, hill"; often used in place names in North Africa and SW Asia. For names of mountains containing this word, see the second element, as **Djebel Chélia**, **Jebel Sham**, etc., see at CHÉLIA, SHAM, etc.

Jeb'el Au'li·a (jĕb'ĕl ou'lĭ·á; *Arab.* jä'bắl ou'lĭ·yä; -yä) *also* **Ge'bel Aulia** (*Arab.* gä'bắl). Site of storage dam across the White Nile, 27 m. S of Khartoum in Sudan; completed 1937; holds back Nile flood waters July–October.

Jeb'el ed Druz (jĕb'ĕl ĕd drōōz'; *Arab.* jä'bắl ắd drōōz') *or* **Jeb'el Druze** (jĕb'ĕl drōōz'). **1** Subdivision of the Republic of Syria. Levant States, SW Asia, E of the

Sea of Galilee and bordering on N Jordan; 2700 sq. m.; pop. (1935) 51,780, (1938 est.) 71,000; ✳ Es Suweida. See *Map* at SYRIA. Plateau and mountainous region; highest point Jebel Druze 5791 ft.; inhabited by Druses, survivors of Mohammedan sect founded in 10th cent. A.D.; recognized 1921 as autonomous state within French mandate of Syria; led nationalist revolt in Syria against French 1925; incorporated in the Republic of Syria Jan. 12, 1942.

2 Mountain in this area. See Jebel DRUZE.

Jeb'el Sham'mar (jĕb'ĕl shăm'ẽr; *Arab.* jă'băl shăm'-mŭr). Northern province of Nejd, Saudi Arabia; pop. ab. 220,000; ✳ Hail; chiefly desert but with a number of fertile oases; formerly an emirate; its native dynasty overcome 1921 by the Wahabi leader ibn-Saud, and later the emirate made part of Saudi Arabia.

Jed'burgh (jĕd'bŭ·rŭ; -brŭ). Burgh, ⊗ of Roxburgh co., SE Scotland; pop. 4083; ruins of noted 12th-cent. abbey; the proverbial Jedburgh justice (punishing first and trying afterwards) is so called from an early 17th-cent. summary execution of a band of malefactors here.

Jedda. See JIDDA.

Jedida, El. See MAZAGAN.

Je·drze'jów (yĕn·jĕ'yŏof). Commune, Kielce dept., Poland, 27 m. SSW of Kielce; pop. 12,853.

Jeff Da'vis (jĕf' dā'vĭs). Name of counties in two states of the U.S. See *Tables* at GEORGIA and TEXAS.

Jef'fer·son (jĕf'ẽr·s'n). **1** River ab. 250 m. long (including its headstreams in Beaverhead co.), SW Montana; formed by confluence of branches in NW Madison co., flows N and E to unite with Madison and Gallatin rivers and form Missouri river.

2 Name of a parish in Louisiana and of counties in twenty-five states of the U.S. See *Tables* at ALABAMA, ARKANSAS, COLORADO, FLORIDA, GEORGIA, IDAHO, ILLINOIS, INDIANA, IOWA, KANSAS, KENTUCKY, LOUISIANA, MISSISSIPPI, MISSOURI, MONTANA, NEBRASKA, NEW YORK, OHIO, OKLAHOMA, OREGON, PENNSYLVANIA, TENNESSEE, TEXAS, WASHINGTON, WEST VIRGINIA, WISCONSIN.

3 City, ⊗ of Jackson co., NE Georgia; pop. 1746.

4 City, ⊗ of Greene co., W cen. Iowa, 33 m. SSW of Fort Dodge; pop. 4570; market center.

5 Town, Coos co., N New Hampshire, in White Mts.; pop. 600; summer resort.

6 Town, ⊗ of Ashe co., NW North Carolina; pop. 814.

7 Village, ⊗ of Ashtabula co., NE corner of Ohio, 8 m. S of Ashtabula; pop. 2774; granite and marble works.

8 Borough, Allegheny co., SW Pennsylvania, S of Pittsburgh; pop. 8280.

9 City, ⊗ of Marion co., NE Texas, near W end of Caddo Lake 15 m. N of Marshall; pop. 3082; agriculture, lumbering; oil field nearby; founded 1836 on route followed by Sam Houston and, later, by David Crockett.

10 City, ⊗ of Jefferson co., SE Wisconsin, 13 m. S of Watertown; pop. 4548; settled 1836; shoes, furniture.

Jefferson, Mount. 1 Peak 5725 ft. in Presidential Range of White Mts., in S Coos co., N New Hampshire.

2 Peak 10,495 ft. in W Jefferson co., N cen. Oregon.

Jefferson City. 1 City, ✳ of Missouri and ⊗ of Cole co., cen. Missouri, on Missouri river; pop. 28,228; selected as capital 1821, and occupied as such 1826 (see SAINT CHARLES); incorp. as town 1825, as city 1839; agriculture; coal and zinc deposits nearby; Lincoln University (1866; coed.).

2 Town, Jefferson co., E Tennessee, WSW of Morristown; pop. 4550; Carson-Newman College (1851; coed.).

Jefferson Da'vis (dā'vĭs). Name of a parish in Louisiana and of a county in Mississippi. See *Tables* at LOUISIANA and MISSISSIPPI.

Jefferson Heights. Urban community (unincorporated), Jefferson parish, SE Louisiana, W of New Orleans; pop. 19,353.

Jef'fer·son·ville (jĕf'ẽr·s'n·vĭl). **1** City, ⊗ of Twiggs co., cen. Georgia; pop. 1013.

2 City, ⊗ of Clark co., S Indiana, on Ohio river across from Louisville, Kentucky; pop. 19,522; shipyards; U.S. Army quartermaster depot.

Jehlam. Var. of JHELUM.

Je·hol' (jĕ·hōl'; *Chin.* rŏ'hŏ'). **1** Region, NE China, N of the Great Wall; 74,278 sq. m.; pop. (1936 est.) 2,054,305; long considered a part of Inner Mongolia; later, the N part of Chihli prov., China Proper, from which it was separated 1928 to become a province of SW Manchuria; from 1933 to 1945 with reduced area a province of the newly established Japanese state of Manchukuo (*q.v.*) with capital at Chengteh (Jehol). Later a province of China, bounded on E by Liaoning prov. of Manchuria, on S by Hopeh prov., China, and on W by Chahar prov., Inner Mongolia; mountainous, traversed by Lwan and upper Liao rivers.

2 City, its ✳. See CHENGTEH.

Je·hosh'a·phat, Valley of (jĕ·hŏsh'á·făt). A common name of the valley of the Kidron (*Joel* iii. 2, 12).

Je·juí' *or* **Je·juy'** (hĕ·hwē'). River in E cen. Paraguay, flowing W into Paraguay river.

Jēkabpils. See YEKABPILS.

Jek'yll Island (jĕk'ĭl). Island in Atlantic Ocean, off mainland of Glynn co., SE Georgia; formerly owned by the Jekyll Island Club, a group of wealthy men who maintained summer homes here; now a state park.

Je'lai (jā'lī). River, W headstream of the Pahang, NW Pahang state, Federation of Malaya; joins the Tembeling to form the Pahang at ab. 4°N; Kuala Lipis, ✳ of the state, is on its right bank.

Jelalabad. See JALALABAD.

Je·le'nia Gó'ra (yĕ·lĕ'nyä gōō'rä); *Ger.* **Hirsch'berg** (hĭrsh'bĕrк; *Angl.* hûrsh'bûrg), *also* Hirschberg in Schle'si·en (hĭrsh'bĕrк ĭn shlā'zĕ·ĕn) *or* im Rie'sen·ge·bir'ge (ĭm rē'zĕn·gĕ·bĭr'gĕ). Manufacturing city, W Wrocław dept., SW Poland, 29 m. SW of Legnica; pop. 28,673; formerly in Silesia, Germany; gateway to the nearby Riesen Gebirge; manufactures paper, iron, glass, textiles; assigned to Poland by Potsdam Conference 1945.

Je'lep·la' (jĕ'lĕp·lä'). Pass (*la*), alt. 14,390 ft., on border of Sikkim, NE India, leading into Chumbi valley, Tibet, Outer China, 45 m. NE of Darjeeling.

Jelgava. See YELGAVA.

Jel'li·co (jĕl'ĭ·kō). City, Campbell co., N Tennessee, on Kentucky border; pop. 2210; coal mining.

Je·mappes' (zhē·màp'). Commune, Hainaut prov., SW Belgium, just W of Mons; pop. 14,407; battlefield where the French under Dumouriez defeated the Austrians Nov. 6, 1792.

Jember. See DJEMBER.

Je·meppe' (zhē·mĕp'). **1** Commune, Liège prov., E Belgium, W suburb of Liège on Meuse river; pop. 13,905.

2 Commune, Namur prov., S Belgium, W of Namur; pop. 3848.

Je'mez Springs (hä'mĕs). Hamlet, Sandoval co., NW cen. New Mexico; pop. 223; S of it is the Jemez Indian Pueblo, established ab. 1700, on the **Jemez River** (tributary of the Rio Grande, ab. 50 m. long); N of it is the **Jemez State Monument** with ruins of early mission.

Jemtland. Former name of JÄMTLAND.

Je'na (jē'ná). Town, ⊗ of La Salle parish, cen. Louisiana; pop. 2038.

Je'na (yā'nä). City, Thuringia, Germany, on Saale river 25 m. E of Erfurt; pop. 52,649; famous university (founded 1558); remains of old fortifications; 11th-cent. church; 14th-cent. Gothic town hall; one of chief centers of glass industry in world; famous for its manufacture of lenses and other optical goods; first planetarium built here; first mentioned (under name Ja'ni [yä'nĕ]) bet. 881 and 899; became city 1284; scene of famous Napoleonic victory over Prussian and Saxon armies Oct. 14, 1806; original Burschenschaft organized here 1815.

Jenil. See GENIL.

Je·nin′ (jĕ·nēn′). **1** Subdistrict, Samaria dist., N cen. Palestine; 336 sq. m.; pop. 41,411, (1938 est.) 50,532.
2 *anc.* **En·gan′nim** (ĕn·găn′ĭm). Town, its ✳, at S end of Plain of Esdraelon; pop. 2774.

Jen′kins (jĕng′kĭnz). **1** County in Georgia. See *Table* at GEORGIA.
2 City, Letcher co., SE Kentucky, 22 m. SSW of Pikeville; pop. 3202; coal mining.

Jen′kin·town (jĕng′kĭn·toun). Residential borough, Montgomery co., SE Pennsylvania, 10 m. N of Philadelphia; pop. 5017; Beaver College (1853; women).

Jenné. See DJENNÉ.

Jen′nings (jĕn′ĭngz). **1** County in Indiana. See *Table* at INDIANA.
2 City, ⊗ of Jefferson Davis parish, SW Louisiana, 36 m. E of Lake Charles; pop. 11,887; agriculture, petroleum.

Je·quié′ (zhĕ·kyä′). City, SE cen. Baía state, E Brazil, 125 m. SW of Salvador; pop. (1940 est.) 13,403.

Je·qui′ti·nho′nha (zhĕ·kē′tē·nyō′nyȧ). River ab. 500 m. long, E Brazil; rises in cen. Minas Gerais state, flows NE and E through Baía state into Atlantic Ocean.

Je·ra·blus′ (jŭ·rŏ·bloos′); *Fr.* **Dje′ra′blous′** (jä′rȧ′-bloos′). Town, N Syria, on the Euphrates.

Je′rash (jŭ′rŏsh); *anc.* **Ger′a·sa** (jĕr′ȧ·sȧ). Town, N Jordan, ab. 20 m. N of Amman; ancient Gerasa a city of the Decapolis; ruins.

Je·rauld′ (jĕ·rôld′). County in South Dakota. See *Table* at SOUTH DAKOTA.

Jerba. See DJERBA.

Jé·ré′mie′ (zhā′rā′mē′). Seaport on NW Tiburon Penin., Haiti, 120 m. W of Port-au-Prince; pop. ab. 8000.

Je·rez′ *or* **Jerez de la Fron·te′ra** (hȧ·rāth′ [-rāz′] thä lä frôn·tā′rä); *formerly* **Xe′res** (old pron. shā′rȧs, shĕ′rĕs; *mod.* hā′rȧs). City, Cádiz prov., SW Spain, 13 m. NE of Cádiz; pop. (1941 est.) 89,784; commercial center; once noted esp. for its sherry (named for the town); Roman colony; believed by some to be scene of famous battle of Moors under Tariq with West Goths under Roderick 711 (see RÍO BARBATE); recaptured but lost by Ferdinand III and finally taken 1264 by Alfonso X.

Jerez de los Ca′bal·le′ros (lōs kä′vä·[l]yā′rōs). Manufacturing commune, Badajoz prov., SW Spain, 37 m. SSE of Badajoz; pop. 16,154; agricultural trade center; marble quarries; Moorish walls, gates, and fortress; birthplace of Balboa; thought to have been founded by Phoenicians; reconquered from Moors 1229; enlarged and given to Knights Templar 1232.

Jer′i·cho (jĕr′ĭ·kō). **1** Urban community (unincorp.), Nassau co., SE New York, on Long I.; pop. 10,795.
2 Subdistrict, Jerusalem dist., cen. Palestine; 132 sq. m.; pop. 3483, (1938 est.) 4227.
3 Arab. **E·ri′ha** (ä·rē′hä; -hä). Village in Jericho subdistrict, Palestine ab. 5 m. N of the Dead Sea and 17 m. ENE of Jerusalem; pop. 1693. Site of an important ancient city, a stronghold commanding the valley of the lower Jordan; captured c. 1400 B.C. by Joshua (*Josh.* vi). Later several times destroyed and rebuilt on a site at or near the modern village of Erīha; captured by British Feb. 21, 1918 in World War I.

Jerid, Shatt el. See Chott DJERID.

Jer′i·moth Hill (jĕr′ĭ·mŏth). Elevation 812 ft., Providence co., Rhode Island, W of Providence on Connecticut border; highest point in the state.

Jer′myn (jûr′mĭn). Borough, Lackawanna co., NE Pennsylvania, NE of Scranton; pop. 2568; coal.

Je·rome′ (jĕ·rōm′). **1** County in Idaho. See *Table* at IDAHO.
2 Town, Yavapai co., cen. Arizona; pop. 243; copper.
3 City, ⊗ of Jerome co., S Idaho, 14 m. N of Twin Falls; pop. 4761; in irrigated section; agriculture, dairying.

Jer′sey (jûr′zĭ). **1** Colloquial for NEW JERSEY.
2 County in Illinois. See *Table* at ILLINOIS.
3 One of the Channel Is., in the English Channel; 45 sq. m.; pop. 50,462; ✳ St. Helier; constitutes a bailiwick; resort; agriculture, stock raising.

Jersey Bay. Bay S of E end of St. Thomas I., Virgin Is., West Indies.

Jersey City. City and port, ⊗ of Hudson co., NE New Jersey, on Hudson river and Upper New York Bay, across from New York City; pop. 276,101; connected with New York by ferries and tunnels (railroad and vehicular); manufacturing; meat packing; St. Peter's College (1872; men); John Marshall College (1929; coed.); Jersey City State College (1929); coed.). Bought from Indians by Michael Pauw c. 1630; taken over by the British 1664; chartered as town 1668; scene of defeat of British by "Light Horse Harry" Lee 1779; chartered as City of Jersey 1820, as Jersey City 1838; became ⊗ 1840; important station on Underground Railroad; scene of Black Tom explosion 1916.

Jersey Shore. Borough, Lycoming co., N cen. Pennsylvania, on West Susquehanna river 13 m. W of Williamsport; pop. 5613; settled 1785; automobile parts.

Jer′sey·ville (jûr′zĭ·vĭl). City, ⊗ of Jersey co., W Illinois, 60 m. SW of Springfield; pop. 7420.

Je·ru·sa·lem (jĕ·rōō′sȧ·lĕm). **1** District, S cen. Palestine, including the subdistricts Bethlehem, Hebron, Jericho, Jerusalem, Ramallah; 1650 sq. m.; pop. 266,562, (1942 est.) 362,405.
2 Subdistrict, Jerusalem dist.; 199 sq. m.; pop. 132,661, (1938 est.) 176,560.
3 *Arab.* **El Quds esh She·rif′** (ăl kōōts′ ăsh shä·rēf′); *anc.* **Hi′er·o·sol′y·ma** (hī′ẽr·ō·sŏl′ĭ·mȧ). City, ✳ of district and subdistrict and ✳ of Palestine; pop. 90,503 (new city, pop. 65,320; old city, pop. 25,183), (1944 est.) pop. 155,314. Situated on two rocky hills at altitude of 2500 ft., 35 m. from the Mediterranean and ab. 13 m. W of N end of Dead Sea; connected by railroad with Jaffa on the coast and center of ancient highways N, E, S, and W. Holy City of Jews, Christians, and Moslems; called "City of David" and "City of the Great King" (*Ps.* xlviii. 2): see ZION; a walled city until 19th cent.; since 1858 and esp. since 1920 much modernized, with fine water supply, electric power, planned street development; Hebrew University; many churches, monasteries, synagogues, and mosques (third Holy City of Islam).

History: First mentioned in Tell el 'Amarna letters c. 1500 B.C.; fortress of Jebusites captured by David c. 1000 B.C. and made the capital of kingdom of Israel, and later, of Judah (qq.v.); walls of city were built and the Temple founded by Solomon c. 970 B.C.; destroyed by Nebuchadnezzar of Babylon 586 B.C.; restored to Jews by Cyrus (see PERSIA) 538 B.C.; in mid-5th cent. B.C., Nehemiah rebuilt its walls; as city of Palestine (q.v.) ruled by Alexander the Great, Ptolemies, Seleucids, and by Romans who ruled it during Christ's lifetime; partly destroyed by Titus 70 A.D. and by Hadrian in 135; rebuilt as Roman city, **Ae′li·a Cap′i·to·li′na** (ē′lĭ·ȧ kăp′ĭ·tȯ·lī′nȧ); held by Persians 614–629; taken by Moslem Arabs 638; its capture in 1077 by Seljuks who mistreated Christian pilgrims was immediate cause of Crusades; captured by Crusaders who erected Latin kingdom of Jerusalem (1099–1291); after its fall into hands of Saladin 1187, its recovery was goal of several Crusades; held continuously by Moslems 1244–1917; occupied by British in campaign against Turks Dec. 9, 1917; old city taken over by Transjordan Arabs 1948; new city captured by Israeli forces 1948, on Feb. 1, 1949 declared by the provisional government of Israel to be part of the new state, and in 1950 made ✳.

Jer′vaulx (jûr′vō). Hamlet, North Riding, Yorkshire, N England; noted for ruins of its abbey, ab. 4 m. SW, dating from 1156.

Jer′vis Bay (jär′vĭs; jûr′-). Inlet of South Pacific, 10 to 12 m. long, on E coast of New South Wales, SE Australia; equidistant (ab. 90 m.) SSW from Sydney and ENE from Canberra; 28 sq. m., including the fine harbor on S side of bay; a part of Australian Capital Territory (q.v.).

Jer′vis Island (jär′vĭs). = JARVIS ISLAND.

Je′si (yâ′zĕ). Var. of IESI.

Jes'sa·mine (jĕs′à·mĭn). County in Kentucky. See *Table* at KENTUCKY.

Jes'sel·ton (jĕs′′l·tŭn; -t′n). Seaport town, ✳ of West Coast residency, Brit. North Borneo; since 1947 ✳ of North Borneo (Sabah); pop. 21.497.

Jes·sore' (jĕ·sōr′). 1 District, Presidency division, formerly in SE Bengal, NE Brit. India; 2925 sq. m.; pop. (1941) 1,828,216; divided 1947 so that ab. ⅞ of it was assigned to East Bengal, Pakistan, the remainder to West Bengal, Indian Union.
2 Town, its ✳, 74 m. NE of Calcutta; pop. 11,356.

Jes'sup (jĕs′ŭp). Locality, Lackawanna co., NE Pennsylvania, ab. 8 m. NE of Scranton; pop. (est.) 6280.

Jes'up (jĕs′ŭp). City, ⊗ of Wayne co., SE Georgia, 40 m. NE of Waycross; pop. 7304; agricultural trade center; naval stores.

Je'sus Island (jē′zŭs); *Fr.* **Île Jé'sus'** (ēl′ zhā′zü′). Island 84 sq. m. in St. Lawrence river just W of Montreal I.; constitutes Laval co. (a part of Montreal and Jesus Islands co.), S Quebec prov., E Canada; pop. 37,843; separated from Montreal I. by Rivière des Prairies and from mainland by Rivière des Mille Îles; chief town Sainte Rose.

Je·sús' y Tri'ni·dad' (hā·sōōs′ ē trē′nē·thäth′). Town, Itapúa dept., SE Paraguay; pop. ab. 23,677.

Je·thou' (zhě·tōō′). One of the Channel Is., S of Herm; 44 acres; in Guernsey bailiwick.

Jet'more (jĕt′mōr). City, ⊗ of Hodgeman co., SW cen. Kansas; pop. 1028.

Jet'pur (jĕt′pŏor). Town, Gujerat state, W India, in cen. Kathiawar penin. on Bhadar river, 240 m. NW of Bombay; pop. 22,973.

Jette (zhĕt). Manufacturing commune, Brabant prov., cen. Belgium, a suburb of Brussels; pop. 22,226.

Jeu'mont' (zhû′mŏn′). Commune, Nord dept., N France, near Belgian frontier; pop. (1931) 6642; French customs frontier; manufactures esp. glass; partly destroyed in World War I.

Jew'el Cave National Monument (jōō′ĕl kāv). See UNITED STATES, *National Monuments*.

Jew'ell (jōō′ĕl). County in Kansas. See *Table* at KANSAS.

Jew'ett City (jōō′ĕt; -ĭt). Manufacturing borough (pop. 3608) in town of GRISWOLD, Connecticut; rayon, cotton textiles.

Jew'ish Autonomous Region (jōō′ĭsh); *also* **Bi'ro·bi·dzhan'** *or* **Bi'ro-Bi·djan'** (bē′rŏ·bĭ·jän′; *Russ.* byĭ·rŭ·byĭd·zhän′). Autonomous region, a subdivision of the R.S.F.S.R., geographically in Khabarovsk Territory, on Amur river, SE Soviet Russia, Asia; 14,085 sq. m.; pop. 108,419; ✳ Birobidzhan; territory set aside 1928 by Soviet Government for colonization by Jews; made an autonomous region 1934; largely agricultural, but has coal mines and forests; light industries and factories for consumer goods, esp. furniture; in World War II specialized in mass production of skis.

Jeypore. See JAIPUR.

Jezairi–Bahri-Sefid. See ARCHIPELAGO.

Jezira. = Al JAZIRA.

Jezira, El. See GEZIRA.

Jeziret ibn Omar. See CIZRE.

Jez're·el (jĕz′rē·ĕl; -rēl). Town, Samaria, ancient Palestine, in Valley of Jezreel NW of Mt. Gilboa; a capital of Ahab (*1 Kings* xviii. 45); scene of death of Jezebel (*2 Kings* ix. 30–35).

Jezreel, Valley of. See Plain of ESDRAELON.

Jha'bu·a (jä′bōō·à). Former Indian state, SW Central India, Indian Union, 80 m. W of Indore; 1265 sq. m., pop. (1941) 178,327; ✳ Jhabua; on July 7, 1947 joined a new confederation of states.

Jha'la·wan (jŭ′là·wän). Former division of Kalat state, E Baluchistan; 21,118 sq. m., pop. 224,000.

Jha'la·war (jä′là·wär). Former Indian state, Eastern Rajputana States, SE Rajputana, India; in two sections; 824 sq. m.; pop. (1941) 122,299; ✳ Jhalrapatan; its

Rajput ruler bore title of Maharajrana.

Jhal'ra·pa'tan (jäl′rà·pä′tăn). 1 *or* **Jhalrapatan Chhao'ni** (chou′nĭ). Town, ✳ of former Jhalawar state, SE Rajputana, India, 160 m. S of Jaipur; pop. 10,442.
2 *or* **Pa'tan** (pä′tăn). Old town, 4 m. S; pop. 6316.

Jhang (jŭng). District, Multan division, N cen. West Punjab, Pakistan; 3415 sq. m.; pop. (1941) 821,631; ✳ Jhang-Maghiana; Jhelum and Chenab rivers unite within its borders.

Jhang–Ma'ghi·a'na (jŭng′mŭ′gĭ·ä′nä). Town, ✳ of Jhang dist., West Punjab, N Pakistan, near left bank of Chenab river 120 m. WSW of Lahore; pop. (1941) 50,051; a joint municipality of which Maghiana is newer and more important part; trades in grain and cloth.

Jhan'si (jän′sĭ). 1 Former division, SW United Provinces, N Indian Union; 10,553 sq. m.; pop. (1941) 2,553,492.
2 City, its ✳, 130 m. S of Agra; pop. (1941) 103,254; has military cantonment; rail point with large railroad workshops; walled community with ancient Mogul fort, constructed 1613, conquered by Marathas 1742; capital of independent Maratha principality 1770–1853 when the last prince died without issue and sovereignty of British followed; scene of massacre during Sepoy Mutiny.

Jhe'lum (jā′lŭm); *anc.* **Hy·das'pes** (hī·dăs′pēz).
1 River ab. 450 m. long, N India, one of the "Five Rivers" of the Punjab; rises in Himalayas in W cen. Kashmir, flows NW through Vale of Kashmir, passing through Srinagar and Wular Lake, then SW out of Kashmir through Pir Panjal Mts. into N West Punjab, Pakistan, and unites with the Chenab; source of canals and irrigation systems in the Punjab; navigable except through the mountains.
2 District, Rawalpindi division, N West Punjab, Pakistan; 2774 sq. m.; pop. (1941) 629,658.
3 Town, its ✳, on Jhelum river 105 m. NNW of Lahore; pop. 23,499.

Jhind. See JIND.

Jibuti. See DJIBOUTI.

Ji'ca·rón' (hē′kä·rôn′). Island in Pacific Ocean off SW coast of Panama.

Ji'čín (yĭ′chĕn); *Ger.* **Gi·tschin'** (gĭ·chĕn′). Town, NE Bohemia prov., W Czechoslovakia; pop. (1930) 11,034; market center; founded 1302 by Wenceslaus II.

Ji'co (hē′kŏ). Town, Veracruz state, E Mexico; pop. 5804.

Jid'da (jĭd′à) *or* **Jed'da** (jĕd′à); *also* **Ged'da** (jĕd′à). Port on Red Sea, Hejaz, W Arabia, 46 m. W of Mecca and its seaport; pop. ab. 148,000; import center; walled city, ab. 300 years old; chief port for pilgrims to Mecca; resisted Wahabi attacks in early 19th cent.; Turkish until June 1916 when it yielded to British and became part of the Hejaz; after yearlong siege surrendered Dec. 23, 1925 to ibn-Saud.

Ji'gi·ley' (hē′hē·lĕ′ē; -lā′), *or* **Ji·güey'** (hē·gwĕ′ē; -gwä′), **Bay.** Bay on NW coast of Camagüey prov., E cen. Cuba, SW of Romano Cay.

Ji'gua·ní' (hē′gwä·nē′). Municipality and town, Oriente prov., E Cuba, 48 m. NW of Santiago de Cuba; pop. (town) 13,995.

Ji·güe'ro, Point (hē·gā′rŏ). Cape at NW end of Puerto Rico, SW of Point Borinquen and on E side of Mona Passage.

Jigüey Bay. See JIGILEY BAY.

Ji'hla·va (yĭ′hlà·và); *Ger.* **I'glau** (ē′glou). City, W Moravia prov., cen. Czechoslovakia; pop. (1930) 31,028; mining community, silver mines nearby having been worked since the Middle Ages; textiles and tobacco products.

Jihpen. See NIPPON.

Jihun. See CEYHAN.

Jijelli. See DJIDJELLI.

Ji'ji·ga (jē′jē·gä). Town, E Ethiopia, just E of Harar; taken by British Mar. 1941.

Jilolo. Var. of DJAILOLO.

Jim·bo'lia (zhĕm·bô'lyä); *Ger*. **Hatz'feld** (häts'fĕlt). Town, W Romania, W of Timișoara near border of Yugoslavia; pop. 13,200; formerly belonged to Hungary; to Yugoslavia 1920; part of Romania since 1923.

Ji·me'nez (hĕ·mä'nås). Municipality, W Misamis Occidental prov., Mindanao, Phil. Is., on W shore of Iligan Bay, 57 m. W of Cagayan; pop. 24,182.

Ji·mé'nez (hĕ·mä'nås). Town, Chihuahua state, N Mexico, on railroad 120 m. SE of Chihuahua; pop. 5175.

Jim Hogg (jǐm hŏg). County in Texas See *Table* at TEXAS.

Jim'ma (jǐm'à). Region, SW cen. Ethiopia; chief town Jiran.

Jim Thorpe (jǐm thôrp). Borough, Carbon co., E Pennsylvania, SSE of Wilkes-Barre; pop. 5945; formed 1954 from former boroughs of Mauch Chunk and East Mauch Chunk.

Jim Wells (jǐm wĕlz). County in Texas. See *Table* at TEXAS.

Jind *or* **Jhind** (jĭnd). **1** Former Indian state, one of the three Phulkian States, S Punjab, NW India; 1299 sq. m. in three separate tracts; pop. (1941) 361,812; ＊ Sangrur; founded by a Sikh raja 1763, recognized by Mogul emperor 1768; loyal to British in Mutiny of 1857; rendered service to British government in other wars, esp. World War I.
2 Town in state, 72 m. NW of Delhi; pop. 11,699; once (before 1827) capital of the state.

Jin'dři·chův Hra'dec (yǐn'dĕr·zhĭ·ко̄оf hrȧ'dĕts); *Ger*. **Neu'haus** (noi'hous). Town, SE Bohemia prov., W Czechoslovakia, 70 m. SSE of Prague; pop. 9099.

Jin'ja (jǐn'jä). Town on Lake Victoria just above Owen Falls Dam at beginning of Victoria Nile, Uganda, E Africa; pop. ab. 30,000.

Ji'no·te'ga (hē'nô·tä'gä). **1** Department, W cen. Nicaragua; 5869 sq. m.; pop. (1943 est.) 52,178.
2 Town, its ＊, NNW of Matagalpa; pop. (1943 est.) 5446.

Ji'no·te'pe (hē'nô·tä'på). Town, SW Nicaragua; ＊ of Carazo dept., 20 m. S of Managua; pop. (1943 est.) 9987.

Jin·sen (jĕn·sĕn); *now* **In·chon** (ĭn·chŏn) *or* **Chemul·po** (jĕ·mo̅o̅l·pô). Seaport city, W Korea, 24 m. W of Seoul; pop. 402,009; built on a promontory with fine harbor and scenery; originally a fishing hamlet, first opened 1883 as trading port; grew rapidly under Japanese exploitation 1894–1905.

Jin'to·to'lo Channel (hēn'tô·tô'lô). Passage ab. 19 m. wide bet. SW Masbate I. and NE Panay I., Phil. Is., connecting Visayan Sea with Sibuyan Sea.

Ji'pi·ja'pa (hē'pē·hä'pä). City, Manabí prov., W Ecuador, ab. 75 m. NW of Guayaquil; pop. 7605; famous for manufacture of Panama hats made of toquilla straw from the leaves of the jipijapa (*Carludovica palmata*).

Ji'qui·lis'co (hē'kē·lēs'kô). Town, Usulután dept., SE El Salvador; pop. (1942 est.) 5884.

Ji'quil·pán' de Juá'rez (hē'kēl·pän' dä hwä'rås). Town, Michoacán state, SW Mexico; pop. 7560.

Ji'ran (jē'rån) *or* **Ji'ren** (-rĕn). Town, SW cen. Ethiopia, ab. 165 m. SW of Addis Ababa; chief town of Jimma region.

Jisera. See ISER.

Jitomir. See ZHITOMIR.

Ji'u (zhē'o̅o̅) *or* **Schyl** (shēl). River ab. 200 m. long in Oltenia region, S Romania, flowing SSE past Craiova into the Danube.

Ji·wa'ni (jē·wä'nē) *or* **Ji·un'ri** (jē·o̅o̅n'rē), **Cape.** Cape, SW corner of Baluchistan, extending into Arabian Sea.

Joachimsthal. = JÁCHYMOV.

João Pes·so'a (zhwouɴm pĕ·sō'à); *sometimes called* **Pa'ra·i'ba** (pà'rȧ·ē'vȧ). City, E Paraíba state, E Brazil, ＊ of Paraíba state; pop. (1940 est.) 73,234; 11 m. from its port Cabedelo; trades in cotton with Recife to the S.

Joazeiro. See JUAZEIRO.

Job Peak (jōb). Mountain 8799 ft. in cen. Churchill co., W Nevada.

Jó'dar (hō'thär). Commune, Jaén prov., S Spain, 22 m. E of Jaén; pop. 12,315.

Jo Da'viess (jō dā'vĭs). County in Illinois. See *Table* at ILLINOIS.

Jodh'pur (jōd'pẽr; *native* jōd'po͞or). **1** *or* **Mar'war** (mär'wär). Former Indian state, Western Rajputana States, NW Rajputana, NW India; 36,120 sq. m.; pop. (1941) 2,555,904; ＊ Jodhpur; region borders on Thar Desert on W, touches Great Rann of Cutch on SW; traversed by Luni river flowing SW; irrigated sections produce wheat and cotton; breeds best camels in India.
2 City, India, in Rajasthan, 235 m. N of Ahmadabad; pop. 180,717; ivory carvings, lacquer ware, vegetable dyes, brass and iron utensils; seat of Jaswant College, affiliated with Univ. of Allahabad; ruins of Mandor, former capital of princes of Marwar, 5 m. N; a walled city, with large fort containing the maharaja's palace, founded 1459 by Rao Jodha; recognized English sovereignty 1818.

Jod'rell Bank (jŏd'rĕl). Locality, NE Cheshire, England, ab. 15 m. SSW of Manchester; site of radio telescope maintained by Univ. of Manchester.

Jo'en·suu (yô'ĕn·so͞o). Commercial city, Kuopio dept., S Finland; pop. (1939 est.) 5600; copper mining.

Jœuf (zhûf). Commune, Meurthe-et-Moselle dept., NE France, 37 m. N of Nancy; pop. (1931) 11,066; a principal metallurgical center of Lorraine.

Jof'fre, Mount (?zhŏf'ẽr). Peak 11,316 ft., SE Brit. Columbia, Canada, on Alberta border SW of Calgary.

Jog'gins (jŏg'ĭnz). Mining town, Cumberland co., N Nova Scotia, Canada, on Chignecto Bay 17 m. WSW of Amherst; pop. 1100; coal; widely known source of fossils.

Jog'ja·kar'ta (jŏg'yȧ·kär'tä; jŏg'-) *or* **Djok'ja·kar'ta** *or* **Jok'ya·kar'ta** (jŏk'yȧ·kär'tä; jŏk'-; *native* jōk'yä·kär'tä). **1** Former native (Mohammedan) sultanate on S coast of Java, Neth. Indies; 1223 sq. m.; pop. 1,559,027; ＊ Jogjakarta; constituted a government geographically within Middle Java prov., SW of Surakarta and E of Banjoemas residency; founded 1755 at breakup of Mataram sultanate; led revolt against Dutch 1825–30; occupied by Japanese 1942; center of activities of Republic of Indonesia (*q.v.*) from 1945.
2 City, S Java, Indonesia, at foot of Mt. Merapi 175 m. WSW of Surabaja; pop. 136,649; destroyed by earthquake 1867 and rebuilt.

Johanna. See ANJOUAN.

Jo·han'nes·burg (jō·hăn'ĭs·bûrg; -ĭz-; yô·hän'ĕs-). City, S Transvaal, NE Republic of South Africa, 300 m. NW of Durban; pop. (1960) 1,152,525; largest city in Africa S of Cairo; in the Witwatersrand just N of its cen. part; gold mining, with mines E, S, and W of it in municipal area (82 sq. m.); produce market; varied manufactures; municipal hospital claimed to be second largest in world; has own observatory and also branch observatories of Yale Univ. and Leiden Univ.; Univ. of Witwatersrand (founded 1903), St. John's College. Founded 1886 on discovery of gold; occupied by British during Boer War 1900; created a city 1928.

Jo·han'nis·berg (yô·hän'ĭs·bĕrк). Village, Hesse state, Germany, in the Rheingau on Rhine river; pop. 1520; to the S lies its castle, built 1759 and given to Prince Metternich 1816, surrounded by vineyards yielding the famous Johannisberger wine.

John Day (jŏn dā). River 281 m. long, N Oregon; rises in E Grant co. in E cen. part of state and flows W and N into Columbia river on boundary bet. Sherman and Gilliam cos.; principal tributaries the **South Fork** rising in N Harney co. and flowing N, and **Middle Fork** and **North Fork** which join in N Grant co. and flow SW; basin notable for fossil beds.

John o'Groat's House (jŏn ŭ·grōts'). Point on N coast of Caithness, N Scotland; popularly considered most northerly point of Great Britain (see DUNNET HEAD); the usual terminus of races the length of Great Britain from Land's End.

John'son (jŏn's'n). **1** Name of counties in twelve states of the U.S. See *Tables* at ARKANSAS, GEORGIA, ILLINOIS, INDIANA, IOWA, KANSAS, KENTUCKY, MISSOURI, NEBRASKA, TENNESSEE, TEXAS, WYOMING.

2 *or* **Johnson City.** City, ⊗ of Stanton co., SW Kansas; pop. 860.

John'son·burg (jŏn's'n-bûrg). Industrial borough, Elk co., NW cen. Pennsylvania, 25 m. N of Du Bois; pop. 4966; laid out 1888; paper, chemicals, iron goods, leather.

Johnson City. 1 Village, Broome co., S New York, 3 m. W of Binghamton; pop. 19,118; with Endicott and Binghamton, one of so-called Triple Cities; shoes, candy, photographic paper, felt; tanneries.

2 City, Washington co., NE Tennessee, 20 m. S of Virginia border; pop. 29,892; first settled c. 1777; incorp. 1869; shipping point for farming and lumbering area; iron foundries, tanneries; textiles and textile mill supplies, furniture, boxes; tourist center; East Tennessee State College (1911; coed.).

3 City, ⊗ of Blanco co., cen. Texas; pop. 611.

John'ston (jŏn'stŭn; jŏn's'n). **1** Name of counties in two states of the U.S. See *Tables* at NORTH CAROLINA and OKLAHOMA.

2 Town, Providence co., N Rhode Island, ab. 5 m. SW of Providence; pop. 17,160; administrative center Thornton village; settled 1650; originally part of Providence; became separate town 1759; worsted yarns; granite quarries.

3 Coral atoll, with two small islets (Johnston and Sand) and reef 12 m. in circumference, cen. Pacific Ocean; ab. 700 m. SW of Honolulu. 17°N lat., 168°30'W long.; belongs to the United States; naval air station; discovered 1807 by British sea captain; claimed by the U.S. 1858; worked for guano; made part of U.S. defense system 1934.

John'ston City (jŏn's'n). City, Williamson co., S Illinois, 8 m. N of Marion; pop. 3891; fruit, coal.

John'stone (jŏn'stŭn; -s'n). Manufacturing burgh, Renfrew co., SW Scotland; pop. 15,661; engineering works; cotton, thread, paper; coal and iron mines.

Johnstone, Lake. Lake 131 sq. m. in S Saskatchewan, Canada, ab. 20 m. SW of Moose Jaw.

Johnstone Strait. Narrow passage ab. 60 m. long along N coast of Vancouver I. SW Brit. Columbia, Canada, connecting Queen Charlotte Strait with Strait of Georgia.

Johns'town (jŏnz'toun). **1** City, ⊗ of Fulton co., E New York, 11 m. WNW of Amsterdam; pop. 10,390; founded 1762 by Sir William Johnson; gloves and mittens, knit goods, leather, gelatin; lumber mills, machine shops, tanneries.

2 Industrial city, Cambria co., SW cen. Pennsylvania, on Conemaugh river 60 m. E of Pittsburgh; pop. 53,949; center of iron ore and bituminous coal region; limestone quarries, clay pits; steel and iron, chemicals, textiles, brick, lumber, mining equipment. Incorporated as village 1800, as borough 1831, as city 1889; scene of many disastrous floods (esp. May 31, 1889, when Conemaugh Dam above city burst after heavy rains and more than 2200 were drowned).

3 See PRESCOTT, Ontario, Canada.

Jo·hore' (jŏ·hōr'). **1** One of the nine Malay States (see Federation of MALAYA) at the S extremity of the Malay Penin., SE Asia; 7500 sq. m.; pop. 505,311, (1940 est.) 737,590; ✳ Johore Bahru; lies bet. South China Sea and Strait of Malacca; much area covered with jungle; mountainous in E cen. part (3300 ft.) but highest point, Mount Ophir 4186 ft., is in NW near Malacca border; principal streams the Muar, Endau, and Johore; coast line ab. 250 m. long with numerous small islands; separated from it to the S by Johore Strait is island of Singapore, part of Singapore colony (*q.v.*); chief export rubber; others iron and tin ores, copra, fruits; chief towns Johore Bahru, Bandar Maharani, and Bandar Penggaram.

History: A Mohammedan-ruled state founded after 1511 by former sultan of Malacca (*q.v.*); came under British influence in 19th cent.; ceded Singapore 1819; its relations with Great Britain established by treaties 1885 and 1914; occupied by Japanese Jan. 1942; became part of Federation of Malaya, established 1948.

2 Short stream of SE Johore state, S Malay Penin., with long and wide estuary.

Johore Bah'ru (bä'rōō). Town, ✳ of Johore state, in S part on Johore Strait opp. Singapore I., Federation of Malaya; pop. 21,463, (1937 est.) 97,634; has fine palace, residence of the sultan.

Johore Strait; *Malay* **Se·lat' Te·brau'** (slät' tĕbrä'ōō). Channel ab. ¾ of a mile wide and 32 m. long, bet. Singapore I. and the mainland of Johore state, S Malay Penin.; crossed by causeway from Woodlands to Johore Bahru; large naval base at E end; scene of fierce fighting Feb. 1942.

Joi'gny' (zhwȧ'nyē'); *anc.* **Jo·vi·ni'a·cum** (jṓ'vĭ·nī'ȧ-kŭm). Commune, Yonne dept., NE cen. France, on Yonne river 15 m. NNW of Auxerre; pop. (1931) 6671; probably of Roman origin; seat of a countship in 10th cent.; unsuccessfully besieged by English 1429.

Join·vi'le (zhoin·vē'lĕ); *formerly spelled* **Join·vil'le** (-vē'lĕ). City, Santa Catarina state, S Brazil, 25 m. inland from port of São Francisco. (1940 est.) 16,883.

Join'ville Island (join'vĭl). Island ab. 40 m. by 20 m. long in West Antarctica off tip of Palmer Penin., Falkland Islands Dependencies, at NW point of Weddell Sea, ab. 63°S, 55°50'W.

Join'ville'-le-Pont' (zhwăn'vēl'lĕ-pôn'). Commune, Seine dept., N France, ESE suburb of Paris; pop. 14,151; photographic and cinematographic supplies; military school.

Jö'kuls·á' (yû'kûls-ou'). Name of three rivers in Iceland: (1) In N cen. part, flowing N into Skaga Fjord; over 100 m. long. (2) In NE, flowing N into Arctic Ocean (see DETTIFOSS). (3) In E, flowing NE into Norwegian Sea.

Jokyakarta. Var. of JOGJAKARTA.

Joliba. See NIGER river.

Jo'li·et (jṓ'lĭ·ĕt; jṓ'lĭ·ĕt'; *chiefly by outsiders* jŏl'ĭ-, jŏl'ĭ-). City, ⊗ of Will co., NE Illinois, 35 m. SW of Chicago; pop. 66,780; founded ab. 1830; railroad and industrial center; steel mills, railroad shops, automobile factories; coal deposits and limestone quarries nearby; state penitentiary; College of St. Francis (1925; women).

Jo'liette (zhṓ'lyĕt'). **1** County, Quebec, Canada. See *Table* at QUEBEC.

2 Manufacturing city, its ⊗, 35 m. N of Montreal; pop. 16,064; railroad junction; trades in lumber and farm products; paper and grist mills, sawmills, foundries, agricultural implement factories; founded 1841 by descendant of the explorer Jolliet, incorporated 1863.

Jolla, La. See LA JOLLA.

Jo·lo' (hṓ·lṓ'; *Angl.* hō'lō) *or* **Su'lu** (sōō'lōō). **1** Chief island, Sulu Archipelago, Sulu prov., Phil. Is., SW of Basilan I.; 345 sq. m.; pop. with adjacent small islands 132,155; chief town Jolo; lies bet. Sulu Sea and Celebes Sea; of volcanic origin, crossed by three parallel mountain chains with several peaks, highest 2894 ft.; good climate, fertile soil, agriculture well developed; thickly wooded. Inhabitants converted to Mohammedanism in 14th cent. See SULU province.

2 Municipality, ✳ of Sulu prov., on NW coast of Jolo I.; pop. 12,571; port of entry with considerable trade with Zamboanga, Manila, and Singapore; headquarters for pearl fishing; ancient residence of Sulu sultans but most traces of Moro town now gone; present town begun by Spaniards 1878; taken by American troops Apr. 9, 1945, giving them complete control of Sulu Archipelago.

Jo·ma'lig (hṓ·mä'lĭg). Island 20 sq. m., E Polillo group, Phil. Is., at NE corner of Lamon Bay E of Luzon; belongs to Tayabas prov.

Jomanes. See JUMNA.

Jomonjol. See HOMONHON.

Joms'borg (yŏms'bôrg). Viking fortified settlement built c. 970 near Julin on Wolin I. at mouth of the Oder, Germany; destroyed by Danes 1098.

Jones (jōnz). Name of counties in six states of the U.S. See *Tables* at GEORGIA, IOWA, MISSISSIPPI, NORTH CAROLINA, SOUTH DAKOTA, TEXAS.

Jones, Cape. Cape, W coast of Quebec prov., Canada, at E entrance to James Bay.

Jones'bor'o (jōnz'bûr'ṓ). **1** City, a ⊗ of Craighead co., NE Arkansas, 67 m. NNW of Memphis, Tennessee; pop. 21,418; trading center; wood products, cottonseed oil, flour; Arkansas State College (1½ m. E; opened 1910; coed.). Founded 1859 as seat of newly formed Craighead county; incorporated 1883.
2 City, ⊗ of Clayton co., NW cen. Georgia; pop. 3014.
3 City, ⊗ of Union co., SW Illinois, 30 m. SW of Marion; pop. 1636.
4 Town, Grant co., N cen. Indiana, 5 m. S of Marion; pop. 2260; electrical wire and cable factory.
5 Town, ⊗ of Jackson parish, N Louisiana, 41 m. WSW of Monroe; pop. 3848; lumbering.
6 Town, ⊗ of Washington co., NE Tennessee, 7 m. W of Johnson City; pop. 1148; meeting place of constitutional convention and first legislative sessions of State of Franklin until 1785.

Jones Mountain. Peak 13,851 ft., Hinsdale and San Juan cos., SW Colorado.

Jones'port (jōnz'pōrt). Town, Washington co., SE corner of Maine, on Atlantic Ocean bet. Englishman and Pleasant Bays; pop. 1563; fishing and sardine packing; summer resort.

Jones Sound (jōnz). Channel ab. 40 m. wide, bet. S Ellesmere I. and N Devon I., N Franklin District, Northwest Territories, Canada; opens into Baffin Bay.

Jones'ville (jōnz'vĭl; *Sou.* also -v'l). **1** Town, Catahoula parish, cen. Louisiana, 45 m. ENE of Alexandria; pop. 2347; fishing, lumbering.
2 Town, Yadkin co., NW cen. North Carolina, 36 m. W of Winston-Salem; pop. 1895.
3 Town, ⊗ of Lee co., SW tip of Virginia; pop. 711.

Jön'kö'ping (yûn'chû'pĭng). **1** Province of Sweden. See *Table* at SWEDEN.
2 City, its ✳, S Sweden, at S end of Lake Vättern; pop. 39,171; match factories, textile and paper mills, shoe factories, iron foundries. An old town, chartered 1284, important in early history of Sweden; destroyed 1612 but soon rebuilt; place where treaty was signed 1809 bet. Sweden and Denmark.

Jon'quière' (zhôN'kyâr'). Town, Chicoutimi co., S Quebec, Canada, 8 m. W of Chicoutimi, bet. the Saguenay and Lake Kenogami; pop. 21,618; pulp mills, large lumber interests, railroad shops; founded 1848.

Jop'lin (jŏp'lĭn). City, Jasper and Newton cos., SW Missouri, 72 m. W of Springfield; pop. 38,958; railroad center; ships grain and livestock; lead and zinc mines; founded 1839, chartered as city 1874.

Joppa. See JAFFA.

Jor'dan (jôr'd'n). **1** River 45 m. long, N cen. Utah, flowing from Utah Lake N into Great Salt Lake.
2 Town, ⊗ of Garfield co., Montana; pop. 557.
3 River ab. 200 m. long, Palestine; rises in Anti-Liban Mts. W of Mt. Hermon and flows S through the Waters of Merom and Sea of Galilee to N end of the Dead Sea; narrow and sluggish at its mouth; most of it S of Sea of Galilee forms boundary bet. Palestine and Jordan and lies in the great depression of the Ghor (ab. 65 m. long); not navigable; noted for associations with Old Testament and New Testament history.
4 *in full* **Hashemite Kingdom of Jordan.** See TRANSJORDAN.

Jor·dan' (hôr·thän'). Municipality, N coast of Guimaras I., Iloilo prov., Phil. Is., on Iloilo Strait opp. City of Iloilo; pop. 23,053.

Jor'dan, Mount (jôr'd'n). Peak 13,316 ft. in Sierra Nevada, N Tulare co., S cen. California.

Jor'ge Montt (hôr'hä̇ mônt'). Island off SW coast of Chile, S of Hanover I.

Jo·rul'lo (hȯ·rōō'yȯ) Volcanic peak 4331 ft. in Michoacán state, SW Mexico.

Jos (jŏs). Town, ✳ of Plateau prov., cen. Northern Region, Nigeria, ab. 143 m. S of Kano; tin mines.

Jo·se' Pañg'a·ni·ban' (hȯ·sā' päng'ȧ·nĕ̇·bän'). Municipality on N coast of Camarines Norte prov., Luzon, Phil. Is., W of Paracale; pop. 20,889.

Jo'seph (jō'zĕf; -zĭf; *Fr.* zhō'zĕf'). One of the Safety Is. (*q.v.*).

Jo'seph, Lake (jō'zĕf; -zĭf). Lake, NW Muskoka dist., SE Ontario, Canada, in the Muskoka Lake region, connected with Lakes Muskoka (*q.v.*) and Rosseau; summer vacation land.

Jo'seph Bo'na·parte Gulf (jō'zĕf [-zĭf] bō'nȧ·pärt). Inlet of Timor Sea in NE corner of Western Australia, SE of Cape Talbot.

Jo'se·phine (jō'zĕ·fēn). **1** County in Oregon. See *Table* at OREGON.
2 Locality, Indiana co., W cen. Pennsylvania, ab. 18 m. NW of Johnstown.

Jo'seph Peak (jō'zĕf; -zĭf). Mountain 10,300 ft. in Yellowstone National Park, NW Wyoming.

Jo·shin (jō·shĕn) *or* **Song·jin** (sŭng·jēn). Seaport town, South Kankyo prov., NE coast of Korea, 85 m. SW of Seishin; pop. 19,349.

Josh'u·a Tree National Monument (jŏsh'ṷ·ȧ). See UNITED STATES, *National Monuments*.

Jos'se·lin' (zhôs'lăN'). Town. Morbihan dept., NW France, W of Ploërmel; pop. (1931) 2099; once seat of countship held 13th cent. by Lusignan family; 16th-cent. castle.

Jos'te·dals·bre'en (yôs'tĕ·däls·brā'ĕn; yōōs'-). Plateau bet. 400 and 500 sq. m. in Sogn og Fjordane co., W Norway; highest point ab. 6800 ft.; contains largest ice field in Europe.

Jost Van Dyke (yŏst' văn dīk'). One of the British Virgin Is., West Indies, W of Tortola; mountainous.

Jo·tap'a·ta (jō·tăp'ȧ·tȧ). Ancient fortress, Galilee, N Palestine, N of Sepphoris, commanded by Josephus 67 A.D. when it was taken by Vespasian after siege of 47 days.

Jo'tun·hei'men (yō'tŏŏn·hā'mĕn) *or* **Jo'tun·fjell'** (-fyĕl'). Mountain region in Opland co., S cen. Norway, containing Galdhöpiggen (8097 ft.) and Glittertind (8048 ft.) peaks.

Jour'dan·ton (jûr'd'n·tŭn). City, ⊗ of Atascosa co., Texas; pop. 1504.

Joux (zhōō). Lake, Vaud canton, SW Switzerland, N of Lake of Geneva; 6 m. long and ⅔ m. wide, largest lake in Jura Mts.

Jouy–en–Jo'sas' (zhwē̇'äN·zhō'zäs'). Commune, Seine-et-Oise dept., N France, SE of Versailles; pop. (1931) 2029; site of workshop set up 1759 by Christophe Oberkampf which later became textile factory noted for manufacture of printed cloth (Jouy print).

Jo'vel·la'nos (hō'vä̇·yä̇'nōs). Municipality and town, Matanzas prov., W cen. Cuba; pop. (town) 13,324; transportation center 16 m. S of Cárdenas.

Joviniacum. See JOIGNY.

J. P. Coen Top (yà̇' pä' kōōn' tôp). Peak (Du. *top*) 15,075 ft., E end of Snow Mts. in Neth. New Guinea near 140°E; named after Jan Pieterszoon Coen, governor general of Dutch possessions in the East 1618–23, 1627–29.

Ju'ab (jōō'ăb). County in Utah. See *Table* at UTAH.

Jua'na (hwä'nä̇). An early name of Cuba.

Jua'na·ca·tlán (hwä'nä̇·kä̇·tlän'). Falls 72 ft. high in Santiago river, Jalisco state, W cen. Mexico, near Guadalajara; used for water power.

Jua'na Di'az (hwä'nä̇ thē̇'äs). Municipality (pop. 30,043) and town (pop. 4618), S Puerto Rico, town 7 mi. ENE of Ponce.

Juan Al·da'ma (hwän äl·dä'mä). Town, Zacatecas state, cen. Mexico, 115 m. N of Zacatecas; pop. 5506.

Juan de Fu′ca Strait (hwän′ dĕ foo̅′kȧ). Strait bet. Vancouver I., Canada, and Clallam co., NW Washington; 100 m. long and 15 to 20 m. wide.

Juan de la Luz En·rí′quez (hwän′ dä lä loos′ ȧn·rē′-kȧs). Town, Veracruz state, E Mexico; pop. 5392.

Juan de No′va (*Span.* hwän′ dä nō′vä). Small French island in N cen. Mozambique Channel bet. NE cen. Mozambique and NW cen. Madagascar.

Juan Fer·nán′dez (hwän′ fĕr·nän′dȧs; *Angl.* joo̅′ȧn fĕr·nän′dĕz). Group of 3 islands, Más Afuera, Más a Tierra, and Santa Clara or Goat I. belonging to Chile, in S Pacific Ocean ab. 400 m. W of Chile; 70 sq. m.; Alexander Selkirk, the original of Defoe's hero Robinson Crusoe, lived on Más a Tierra Oct. 1704 to Feb. 1709.

Juan-les-Pins (zhwän′lä′păn′). Village, Alpes-Maritimes dept., SE France, on Cap d'Antibes SW of Antibes; coastal resort.

Juárez. See CIUDAD JUÁREZ.

Jua·zei′ro (zhwȧ·zā′ē·roo) *formerly* **Joa·zei′ro** (zhwȧ-).
1 City, N border of Baía state E Brazil 275 m. NW of Salvador; pop. (1940 est.) 10,079.
2 City, Ceará state, NE Brazil; pop. (1940 est.) 23,761.

Ju′ba (joo̅′bä). **1** *Ital.* **Giu′ba** (joo̅′bä). River ab. 1000 m long, E Africa; rises in several headstreams (Dawa, Ganale Dorya, and Webhe) in mountains of S cen. Ethiopia, flows S across SW Somalia into Indian Ocean; the port of Chisimaio is at its mouth.
2 Town, ✴ of Equatoria prov., S Sudan, on Bahr el Jebel (Nile) river; pop. 10,660.

Ju·bail′ (joo̅·bīl′; -bāl′). Town, port of al-Hasa, E Nejd, Saudi Arabia, on Persian Gulf

Ju′ba·land (joo̅′bä·länd′) *or* **Trans–Ju′ba** (tränz-joo̅′bä); *Ital.* **Ol′tre Giu′ba** (ōl′trä joo̅′bä). Region, SW Somalia, E Africa, bet. Kenya colony and the Juba river; formerly a province of Kenya, ceded by Britain to Italy 1925; administered as separate colony until July 1, 1926 when it became a part of Italian Somaliland.

Ju·bayl′ (joo̅·bīl′; -bāl′); *Fr.* **Dje·beil′** (joo̅·bĭl′; -bāl′); *anc.* **Byb′los** (bĭb′lŏs). Coast village, Lebanon republic, 20 m. N of Beirut; as Byblos, a very old city of Phoenicia (the **Ge′bal** [gē′băl] of the Bible, *Ezek.* xxvii. 9), seat of the worship of Adonis; an early Phoenician inscription has been found here and excavations have uncovered remains of temple, citadel, tombs, etc.; exported papyrus to Egypt, hence the Greek *biblos* book, papyrus, and Eng. *Bible.*

Jub′bal (joob′ăl). Former Indian state, Punjab States, N East Punjab, NW Indian Union; 320 sq. m.

Jub′bul·pore (jŭb′ŭl·pōr) *or* **Ja′bal·pur** (jŭb′ăl·poor).
1 Former division, N Central Provinces and Berar, Indian Union; 25,730 sq. m.; pop. (1941) 3,691,112.
2 City, its ✴, near Narbada river 150 m. NNE of Nagpur; now in cen. Madhya Pradesh; pop. (1951) 256,998; in scenic region surrounded by rocky gorges and lakes; a trade and distribution point and rail junction; maintains large civil and military cantonment with a government gun-carriage factory.

Juby, Cape. See Cape YUBI.

Jú′car (hoo̅′kär). River ab. 300 m. long, E Spain; rises in N Cuenca prov., flows S, then turns E in N Albacete prov., and flows through cen. Valencia prov. into Mediterranean Sea 26 m. S of Valencia.

Ju·chi·tán′, *officially* **Juchitán de Za′ra·go′za** (hoo̅′-chē·tän′ dä sä′rä·gō′sä). Town, Oaxaca state, SE Mexico; pop. 14,550; port on S side of Isthmus of Tehuantepec on Gulf of Tehuantepec; supply depot for rich agricultural region.

Ju·cua′pa (hoo̅·kwä′pä). Town, Usulután dept., SE El Salvador, 11 m. from Usulután; pop. (1942 est.) 6196.

Ju·dae′a *or* **Ju·de′a** (joo̅·dē′ȧ). The southern division of Palestine under Persian, Greek, and Roman rule, succeeding the kingdom of Judah (*q.v.*); bounded on N by Samaria, its N boundary extending approximately from N of Joppa to the Jordan ab. 13 m. above the Dead Sea; on E bounded by the Jordan and Dead Sea, on SW by

Sinai (Egypt), and on W by the Mediterranean; became Roman province after conquests of Pompey; in late Roman years included Idumaea.

Ju′dah (joo̅′dȧ). Ancient kingdom in S Palestine, bet. the Mediterranean and the Dead Sea; ✴ Jerusalem; included Philistia on the W; the southern kingdom of the Jews after N part of Israel (*q.v.*) had broken away c. 933 B.C; passed under Babylonian rule 605 B.C.; kingdom came to an end with destruction of Jerusalem (*q.v.*) by Nebuchadnezzar 586 B.C. See JUDAEA.

Judah, Wilderness of. See WILDERNESS.

Ju′dith (joo̅′dĭth). River ab. 100 m. long, cen. Montana; flows NE and N through Judith Basin and Fergus cos. into the Missouri river.

Ju′dith, Point (joo̅′dĭth; *locally also* joo̅′dĭ). Southeast point, Washington co., Rhode Island, at W side of entrance to Narragansett Bay.

Ju′dith Basin (joo̅′dĭth). County in Montana. See *Table* at MONTANA.

Juf, El. See EL DJOUF.

Juggernaut. See PURI.

Jugoslavia, Jugoslavija. See YUGOSLAVIA.

Jui·gal′pa (hwĕ·gäl′pä). Town, S cen. Nicaragua, ✴ of Chontales dept., ab. 15 m. from NE shore of Lake Nicaragua; pop. (1943 est.) 3700.

Juist (yüst). Narrow island 9 m. long, East Frisian Is., off NW coast of Germany, NE of Borkum.

Juiz de Fo′ra (zhwēzh′ thĕ fô′rȧ). Manufacturing city, S Minas Gerais state E Brazil, on railroad ab. 80 m. N of Rio de Janeiro; pop. (1940 est.) 72,254; textiles.

Ju·juy′ (hoo̅·hwē′). **1** Province of Argentina. See *Table* at ARGENTINA.
2 Town, its ✴, NW Argentina; pop. (est.) 19,257; altitude ab. 4000 ft.

Jules′burg (joo̅lz′bûrg). Town, ⊗ of Sedgwick co., NE corner of Colorado, on South Platte river; pop. 1840; railroad division point, founded 1881; the fourth and only remaining town of that name in vicinity.

Julfa. See DZHULFA.

Ju·lia′ca (hoo̅·lyä′kä). Town, Puno dept., SE Peru, 189 m. by rail NE of Arequipa; pop. (1940 est.) 7002; altitude 12,550 ft.; railroad junction for Cuzco and Lake Titicaca; wool, hides.

Julia Joza, Julia Traducta. See TARIFA.

Jul′ian Alps (joo̅l′yăn); *Ger.* **Ju′li·sche Al′pen** (yoo̅′-li·shĕ äl′pĕn). See *Table* at ALPS.

Ju′li·an′a Top (joo̅′li·än′a [-ä′nä] tŏp; *Du* yü′lē·ȧ′nä tŏp). Peak (Du. *top*) 15,420 ft. E end of Snow Mts. in Neth. New Guinea, ab. 140°20′E 4°30′S, near source of Digoel river.

Ju′li·a′ne·haab′ (yoo̅′lē·ȧ′nĕ·hôp′). Danish settlement near S end of Greenland, in South Greenland division; pop. 3532; radio station; center for seal hunting.

Jul′ian March (joo̅l′yăn märch). The borderland region bet. NW Yugoslavia and NE Italy traversed by Julian Alps and Isonzo river; Trieste and Istrian Penin. lie to the S.

Julian Ve·ne′ti·a (vĕ·nē′shĭ·ȧ; -shȧ). = *Venezia Giulia:* see VENETIA modern region.

Jü′lich (yü′lĭк). **1** Region of W Germany bet. Cologne on the Rhine and Aix-la-Chapelle (Aachen), ab. 1600 sq. m.; chief town Jülich; county 11th to 14th cent.; became duchy 1356, associated with duchies of Berg and Cleve 1423-1592; possession contested in 17th cent. by Netherlands and Saxony; held by German counts until 1801; seized and held by France 1801-15; to Prussia 1815.
2 Town, North Rhine-Westphalia, Germany, on the Rur river 16 m. NE of Aachen; pop. 8596; chief town of county and duchy of Jülich; fortified in 17th cent. and several times captured; largely destroyed Jan.–Feb. 1945 in World War II.

Ju′lier′, Col du (kôl′ dü zhü′lyä′). Mountain pass, altitude 7504 ft., SW of St. Moritz, in Rhaetian Alps, Graubünden canton, E Switzerland.

Ju·lin′ (yōō·lēn′). Ancient Wendish trading town on S coast of Wolin I., off coast of Pomerania, Germany, identified with modern Wolin, since 1945 in NW Poland, and called **Vi·ne′ta** (vĕ·nā′tä) by the Germans; in 10th and 11th cents. was important center for trade bet. Scandinavia, Saxony, and Russia; Viking fortress of Jomsborg was nearby.

Juliobona. See LILLEBONNE.

Juliobriga. See LOGROÑO.

Juliomagus. See ANGERS.

Jul′lun·dur (jŭl′ŭn·dẽr) or **Ja′lan·dhar** (jä′lŭnd·hŭr). 1 Division, East Punjab, NW Indian Union; 18,992 sq. m.; pop. (1941) 5,438,581.

2 City, its ✳, 80 m. E of Lahore; pop. (1941) 135,283; former capital of ancient kingdom of **Jullundur** or **Tri·gar′ta** (trĭ·gär′tä; *native* -gŭr′tä); burned to ground by Sikhs 1757 and made part of the Sikh jurisdiction 1811; came under British sovereignty 1846.

Jum·bor (chōōm·p′hôn). = JUMPORN.

Ju′met′ (zhü′mĕ′). Commune, Hainaut prov., SW Belgium, 25 m. S of Brussels; pop. (1938 est.) 28,919; mining, smelting, glass-manufacturing center.

Ju·mil′la (hōō·mē′[l]yä). Commune, Murcia prov., SE Spain, 38 m. NNW of Murcia; pop. 21,165; vineyards, orchards; brandy, soap, oil; 15th-cent. church; castle.

Jummoo. See JAMMU.

Jum′na (jŭm′nä); *anc.* **Jom′a·nes** (jŏm′à·nēz). River 860 m. long, N cen. India; rises in Tehri dist. in the Himalayas, flows S and SE into the Ganges at Allahabad, in its upper course forming long section of W boundary of Uttar Pradesh; flows just E of Delhi and past Muttra and Agra; connects with numerous canals; navigable for most of its course for barges and small vessels; chief tributaries, all from S, the Chambal, Sind, Betwa, and Ken.

Jump (jŭmp). River ab. 100 m. long, NW cen. Wisconsin; rises in Price co., flows SW into Chippewa river in N Chippewa co.

Jump′off′ (jŭmp′ôf′). Mountain 6100 ft. in Sevier co., E Tennessee, in Great Smoky Mts.

Jumporn. See CHUMPHON.

Ju·na′garh (jōō·nä′gẽr) or **Ju·na′gadh** (-gŭd). 1 Former Indian state, Western India States, S cen. Kathiawar, W India; 3337 sq. m.; pop. (1941) 670,719; ruined temple of Somnath; entered into relations with British 1807; after division of India 1947 decided to join Pakistan, but since its people voted to join Indian Union its status referred 1948 to United Nations; area now part of Gujerat state, India.

2 Town, ab. 240 m. NW of Bombay; pop. (1941) 58,111; produces gold and silver embroideries and brass and copper ware; picturesquely placed at foot of sacred Girnar Mt. (3666 ft.); has an old fort, cave dwellings, temples, and other remains of early Hindu and Mohammedan times; seat of college of arts.

Ju′na·lus·ka, Mount (jōō′nà·lŭs′kà). Peak 6223 ft. in W North Carolina.

Jun·cal′ (hōōng·käl′). Peak 19,877 ft. in Andes Mts. on boundary bet. Chile and Argentina just S of Mt. Aconcagua.

Jun′cos (hōōng′kôs). Municipality (pop. 21,496) and town (pop. 6247), E Puerto Rico, SE of San Juan.

Junc′tion (jŭngk′shŭn). 1 City, ⊗ of Kimble co., W cen. Texas, on Llano river 113 m. W of Austin; pop. 2441; market center; hunting and fishing resort.

2 Town, ⊗ of Piute co., S cen. Utah; pop. 219.

Junction City. City, ⊗ of Geary co., NE cen. Kansas, 18 m. SW of Manhattan at junction of Republican and Smoky Hill rivers; pop. 18,700; in grain-producing and dairy section; limestone quarries nearby.

Junction Peak. Mountain 13,625 ft. in Sierra Nevada, NE Tulare co., S cen. California.

Jun′dia·í′ (zhōōɴɴ′dyà·ē′). City, SE São Paulo state, SE Brazil; pop. (1940 est.) 29,891; railroad junction point 25 m. NNW of São Paulo; textiles.

Ju′neau (jōō′nō). 1 County in Wisconsin. See *Table* at WISCONSIN.

2 City, ⊗ of Dodge co., SE cen. Wisconsin; pop. 1718.

3 Seaport city, SE Alaska, on mainland on Gastineau Channel opp. island and town of Douglas, ab. 90 m. NE of Sitka; ✳ of Alaska; pop. 6797; behind it mountains rise to 3000 ft.; has excellent harbor and steamer connections with Seattle and Vancouver; trading center of mining and lumbering region; salmon-canning industry. Founded ab. 1881; became seat of administration (transferred from Sitka) 1906; continued as capital of organized territory 1912 and of state 1959.

Jun·gar′i·a (jŏŏng·gär′ĭ·à; jŭng-). Var. of DZUNGARIA.

Jungbunzlau. See MLADÁ BOLESLAV.

Jung′frau′ (yŏŏng′frou′). Peak 13,642 ft., SW cen. Switzerland, in Bernese Alps, on border bet. Bern and Valais cantons S of Interlaken which is famous for its view of the Jungfrau.

Ju′ni·at′a (jōō′nĭ·ăt′à). 1 River ab. 150 m. long, S cen. Pennsylvania; formed by two branches in Huntingdon co., flows E through Mifflin, Juniata, and Perry cos. into Susquehanna river.

2 County in Pennsylvania. See *Table* at PENNSYLVANIA.

Ju·nín′ (hōō·nēn′). 1 District (pop. 58,469) and town (pop. ab. 20,000), Buenos Aires prov., E Argentina, on railroad 150 m. W of Buenos Aires; grain, cattle.

2 Small port, Tarapacá prov., N Chile, ab. 35 m. N of Iquique; pop. 14; exports nitrate.

3 or **Chin′chay·co′cha** (chēn′chī·kō′chä). Lake ab. 25 m. long and 8 to 10 m. wide, Junín dept., cen. Peru; altitude 12,225 ft.

4 Department of Peru. See *Table* at PERU.

5 Town, Junín dept., at S end of Lake Junín ab. 95 m. NE of Lima; pop. 7000; in wars of independence, scene of a decisive battle Aug. 6, 1824 in which Spaniards under the viceroy La Serna and Gen. Canterac were defeated by Bolívar and Sucre.

Junkseylon. See PHUKET.

Ju′pi·ter, Mount (jōō′pĭ·tẽr). Peak 5650 ft. in Jefferson co., W Washington.

Jupiter Inlet. Narrow strait leading from Atlantic Ocean through barrier reefs off NE coast of Palm Beach co., SE Florida.

Jupiter Island. Island in Atlantic Ocean, off coast of Martin co., SE Florida.

Jupiter Peak. Mountain 13,837 ft. in La Plata co., SW Colorado.

Jur (jŏŏr). River ab. 300 m. long, SW Sudan; flows N and NE in Equatoria prov. to join with the Bahr el Arab in Upper Nile prov. to form the Bahr el Ghazal.

Ju′ra. 1 (jŏŏr′à; *Fr.* zhü′rä′) Mountain range extending ab. 200 m. along boundary bet. France and Switzerland; highest peak Reculet 5642 ft. in Ain dept., France; the W slopes are source of the Doubs and Ain rivers of France.

2 Department of France. See *Table* at FRANCE.

3 (jŏŏr′à) Island 24 m. long of the Inner Hebrides, off W coast of Scotland; pop. 263; nearly cut in two by Loch Tarbert (*q.v.*); in S are the Paps of Jura, highest 2571 ft.; administratively a part of Argyll co.; fishing, agriculture, granite quarrying.

Ju′ra, Sound of (jŏŏr′à). Body of water off W coast of Scotland bet. island of Jura and Scottish mainland.

Juramento, Río del. See Río SALADO.

Jurjura. Var. of DJURDJURA.

Ju·ruá′ (zhōō·rwä′). River over 1200 m. long, NW cen. South America; rises in Andes Mts. in E cen. Peru, flows NE and empties into the Solimões, upper course of the Amazon, in NW Brazil.

Ju·rue′na (zhōō·rwä′nĭ). River ab. 600 m. long, W cen. Brazil; flows N in Mato Grosso state, receives the Arinos river from the E; forms part of boundary bet. Mato Grosso and Amazonas states; on border bet. Amazonas and Pará states is joined by the São Manoel to form the Tapajoz.

Ju′ru·pa·rí′ (zhōō′rōō·pȧ·rē′). Small island in mouth of Amazon river, off NE coast of Pará state, Brazil.

Justinianopolis. See KIRŞEHİR.

Justinopolis. See CAPODISTRIA.

Ju′ta·í′ (zhōō′tȧ·ē′), *formerly* **Ju′ta·hy′** (zhōō′tȧ·ē′). River 400 m. long, a S tributary of the Amazon in W Amazonas state, NW Brazil; flows NE and joins the Solimões (Amazon) above the Juruá.

Ju·tia′pa (hōō·tyä′pä). **1** Department, SE Guatemala; 1243 sq. m.; pop. 200,416.

2 Town, its ✳, 45 m. SE of Guatemala City; pop. 6480.

Ju′ti·cal′pa (hōō′tê·käl′pä). Town, E cen. Honduras, ✳ of Olancho dept., 70 m. NE of Tegucigalpa; pop. (1940) 3836; agriculture.

Jut′land (jŭt′lănd); *Dan.* **Jyl′land** (yül′ȧn); *anc.* **Cher′so·ne′sus Cim′bri·ca** (kûr′sṓ·nē′sŭs sĭm′brĭ·kȧ). Peninsula projecting N from NW cen. Germany and extending bet. the North Sea and the Kattegat, comprising Danish mainland and N part of Schleswig-Holstein prov., Germany. Politically the name applies only to the mainland of Denmark; including islands N of Lim Fjord, 11,411 sq. m., pop. 1,672,235; has given its name to great naval battle fought off its W coast in North Sea May 31–June 1, 1916, bet. British and German fleets; although British losses were greater, the battle in its results was a British victory.

Ju·togh′ (jōō·tōg′h′). See SIMLA.

Juvavum. See SALZBURG city.

Ju′ven·ti′no Ro′sas (hōō′vän·tē′nŏ rrô′säs). Town, Guanajuato state, cen. Mexico; pop 6831.

Ju′vi′sy′, *in full* **Juvisy–sur–Orge** (zhü′vē′zē′sür-ôrzh′). Commune, Seine-et-Oise dept., N France, S of Paris; pop. (1931) 8143; important railroad junction; observatory founded by Flammarion 1882.

Jylland. See JUTLAND.

Jy′väs·ky′lä (yü′väs·kü′lă). City, S cen. Finland, in Vaasa dept., at N end of Lake Päijänne; pop. (1939 est.) 8700; commercial center; paper mills.

K

K² (kā′ tōō′). See GODWIN AUSTEN.

Ka·a′la (kä·ä′lä). Peak 4030 ft. in Waianae Range, W Oahu I., Hawaii; highest peak on Oahu.

Kaapstad. See CAPE TOWN.

Kaa′ters·kill Creek (kä′tērz·kĭl; -tēr·skĭl; kô′-). Creek in Catskill Mts., New York; has beautiful waterfalls in its upper course; in lower course goes through a steep-sided, narrow ravine, **Kaaterskill Clove** (klōv).

Ka′ba·can′ (kä′bä·kän′). Town (municipal district), NE cen. Cotabato prov., Mindanao, Phil. Is., N of marsh region on left bank of Pulangi river; pop. 8659; communications center of S Mindanao, taken by American forces from Japanese Apr. 24, 1945.

Ka′ba·e′na (kä′bä·ā′nä). Island in N part of Flores Sea, off SE coast of Celebes I., Malay Archipelago, Indonesia; belongs to Celebes govt.

Ka·ba′lo (kä·bä′lō). Town on Lualaba river (upper Congo), SE Congo; terminus of railroad running 170 m. to Albertville on Lake Tanganyika.

Ka′ban·ka′lan (kä′bäng·kä′län). Municipality, S Negros Occidental, Negros, Phil. Is., on Ilog river ab. 50 m. S of City of Bacolod; pop. 29,315.

Kab′ar·di·no–Bal·kar′i·an Republic (käb′ĕr·dē′nō·bäl·kär′ĭ·ăn); *officially* **Kabardino–Balkarian Autonomous Soviet Socialist Republic.** Autonomous republic in cen. part of N slopes of Caucasus Mts., SE Soviet Russia, Europe; 4747 sq. m.; pop. 359,236, (1941 est.) 377,485; ✱ Nalchik; a subdivision of the R.S.F.S.R.; bounded on N by Stavropol Territory, on E and SE by North Ossetian Republic, on S and W by Georgia. Its component areas are **Ka·bar′di·a** (kà·bär′dĭ·à), mainly the N level part, and **Bal·kar′i·a** (bäl·kär′ĭ·à), the mountain area in the S. Chief river the Terek with many headstreams, all flowing NE. Chief mountains include some of the highest peaks of the Caucasus, such as Dykh Tau 17,085 ft., Shkara Tau 17,040 ft., and Koshtan Tau 16,875 ft. Chief occupations agriculture (maize, millet, vegetables, and the vine), raising of fine horses (in Kabardia), and raising of cattle, sheep, and goats; has good forests; well-developed peasant industries. Predominant ethnic strain Japhetic (Caucasian); chief nationalities Kabardian 60%, Balkarian 16% (both Mohammedan). Formerly part of Terek government under the tsars; after the Revolution became part of the Mountain Republic; two areas combined 1924 as one autonomous area; made a republic 1936.

Kab′ba (käb′à; käb′ä). Province of Nigeria. See *Table* at NIGERIA.

Ka·bin′da (kà·bĭn′dà; *Port.* kà·vēɴn′dà). **1** Portuguese territory and seaport, Angola. See CABINDA.
2 Town, Katanga prov., S Congo.

Kab′lac (käb′läk). Mountain 9580 ft., Indonesia, in cen. Timor; highest mountain on Timor I.

Ka′boe·roe′ang *or* **Ka′bu·ru′ang** (kä′bōō·rōō′äng). See TALAUD ISLANDS.

Ka·bou′di·a, Cape (kà·bōō′dĭ·à). Cape on E coast of Tunisia.

Ka·bu′ga·o (kä·bōō′gä·ō; -gou). Town (municipal district), ✱ of Apayao subprov., Mountain Province, Luzon, Phil. Is., in cen. part on Abulug river; pop. 4646.

Ka′bul (kä′bŏŏl; *often Anglicized* kà·bŏŏl′) **1** River ab. 360 m. long, E Afghanistan and NW India; rises on S slopes of Koh-i-Baba range W of Kabul; has several important tributaries including the Kunar from the N and the Swat in India; passes through gorges of Mohmand Hills N of Khyber Pass to the Indus near Attock, West Punjab, Pakistan.
2 A major province in E Afghanistan.
3 City, ✱ of Afghanistan, in Kabul prov. and on Kabul river at W end of its valley, alt. above 1 m.; pop. ab. 120,000; commands strategic routes through mountain passes into India from the W; for centuries has been in path of great invasions of the peninsula—as of Alexander the Great, Mahmud of Ghazni, Genghis Khan, Baber, Nadir Shah, and Ahmad Shah. For two centuries (1526-1738) included in the Mohammedan empire of Delhi; with Kandahar one of the two capitals under Ahmad Shah (1747-73) and made only capital 1774 under his successor; in First Afghan War occupied 1842 by British, who partially destroyed it; again occupied by Lord Roberts 1879; after 1880 rebuilt and modernized by the amir Abd-er-Rahman Khan; ruler's palace just outside the city.

Kabushia. See MEROË.

Ka·by′li·a, Great *and* **Little** (kà·bĭ′lĭ·à; -bĭl′ĭ·à). Two regions in N Algeria inhabited by Kabyles.

Kach′hi (käch′hē) *or* **Kach Gan·da′va** (käch gän·dä′và). Region, NE Baluchistan, Pakistan, a flat area E of mountains of N Kalat; ab. 5300 sq. m.; outlet is through Jacobabad in Sind.

Ka·chin′ State (kà·chĭn′). State, N Burma, comprising Bhamo and Myitkyina districts.

Ka′chug (kà′chŏŏk). Town in E Irkutsk Region, Soviet Russia, Asia, W of Lake Baikal on upper Lena river near its source.

Kadavu. See KANDAVU.

Ka′desh (kā′dĕsh). **1** Ancient city in W Syria, on Orontes river ab. 15 m. SW of modern Homs; in early times a kingdom, probably a survival of Hyksos power; seized by the Egyptian king Thutmose III, after Megiddo, c. 1471 B.C.; scene of indecisive battle bet. the Hittites 1288 B.C. and Ramses II of Egypt.
2 See KADESH-BARNEA.

Ka′desh–bar′ne·a (kā′dĕsh·bär′nē·à) *or* **Kadesh.** Ancient town in S Palestine, in the country of the Amalekites SW of the Dead Sea and on W edge of Wilderness of Zin; its location not exactly known; twice scene of encampments of Israelites (*Num.* xiii. 26; xx. 1; xxxiii. 36).

Kadesia. See KADISIYA.

Ka′dhi·main *or* **Al Kadhimain** (ăl kä′thĭ·mĭn′; -män′; kä′zĭ-). City, cen. Iraq, a N suburb of Baghdad; one of the three holy Shiite cities of Iraq.

Ka′di (kŭ′dĭ) Division of former Baroda state, W India, N of Ahmadabad

Ka·diak′ (*Russ.* kŭ·dyäk′). Var. of KODIAK.

Ka′di·köy′ (kä′dĭ·kü′ē); *anc.* **Chal′ce·don** (kăl′sĕ·dŏn; -dŭn; kăl·sē′d′n). City, Istanbul vilayet, Turkey in Asia, a suburb and district of the city of Istanbul, opp. the city on E side of entrance to Bosporus and S of Üsküdar; pop. 57,358. Ancient Chalcedon founded 685 B.C. by Greeks of Megaris; later a city of Bithynia, then of Pergamum; became Roman 133 B.C.; under Byzantine Empire seat of Fourth Ecumenical Council 451 A.D. which condemned the Eutychian heresy; suffered much in attacks by barbarians, Persians, and Turks.

Ka′di·si·ya (kä′dĭ·sē′yà) *or* **Ka′de·si′a** (kä′dĕ·sē′à); *Arab.* **al–Qa′di·si′yah** (äl·kä′dĭ·sē′yä·h′). Locality in medieval Persia (now in Iraq) on the Euphrates near Hilla and S of Baghdad; scene of battle 637 A.D. in which the caliph Omar I defeated the Persian forces of Yazdegerd III, last of the Sassanids.

Ka·di′yev·ka (kŭ·dyē′yĕf·kà); *formerly* **Ser′go** (syĕr′gŭ). Industrial town, W Voroshilovgrad Region, E Ukraine, U.S.S.R., 32 m. E of Artemovsk; pop. 68,360; in Donets Basin.

Ka·do′ka (kà·dō′kà). City, ⊗ of Jackson co., SW cen. South Dakota; pop. 840.

Ka·du′na (kà·dōō′nà). Town, ✱ of Northern Region, Nigeria, in Zaria prov., ab. 140 m. SW of Kano.

Ka·e′na Point (kä·ā′nä). **1** Cape on NW coast of Lanai I., Hawaii.
2 Cape on extreme NW point of Oahu I., Hawaii.

Kaesong. See KAIJO.

Kae′wi·eng′ (kä′vĭ·ĕng′). = KAVIENG.

Ka'fa or **Kaf'fa** (kăf'á; *native* kȧ·fä'). Region and former province, SW Ethiopia; chief town Bonga; reputed native home of the coffee plant; long an independent kingdom, partly Christianized; conquered by Mohammedans 16th cent. and by Ethiopians 1897.

Kaf'fa (käf'fä). See FEODOSIYA.

Kaf·frar'i·a (kă·frâr'ĭ·ȧ). Region of Cape Province, Republic of So. Africa, now officially called Transkeian Territories (*q.v.*); from Great Kei river on S to Natal on N bet. the Drakensberg Mts. and the coast; inhabited by the Kaffirs, South African natives of Bantu race, who fought serious wars with British 1846–47, 1850–53, and 1877–78; chief town formerly Kokstad. British Kaffraria is the region to the SW bet. the Great Kei and Great Fish rivers.

Kaf'i·ri·stan' (käf'ĭ·rĭ·stăn'; kȧ·fïr'ĭ·stăn'; kä'fĭ·rĭ·stăn'); *now called* **Nu'ri·stan** (nŏŏr'ĭ·stăn; nŏŏr'ĭ·stän'). Mountainous district in E Afghanistan S of Hindu Kush Mts.; ab. 5000 sq. m.; inhabited by Kafirs, a small remnant of a very early Iranian people.

Ka'fir·ni·gan' (kä'fĭr·nĭ·hän'). River, a N tributary of the Amu Darya, in SW Tadzhik S.S.R., Soviet Russia, Asia; flows SW near Uzbek border.

Ka·fu'e (kä·fŏŏ'ā). **1** River ab. 500 m. long, Kafue prov., Zambia; flows in winding course S, W, and E to the Zambezi river.
2 Province, S Zambia; 13,620 sq. m.; pop. 51,900; * Lusaka.

Ka·ga·wa (kä·gä·wä). Prefecture of Japan. See *Table* at JAPAN.

Ka·ge'ra (kä·gā'rä). River ab. 429 m. long in NW Tanganyika, E Africa; flows N, along boundary of Rwanda; turns E along boundary of Uganda and empties into Lake Victoria; known as the longest headstream of the Nile.

Ka·gi (kä·gē). City, W cen. Formosa, 35 m. N of Tainan; pop. (1935) 72,984.

Ka·go·shi·ma (kä·gō·shē·mä). **1** Prefecture of Japan. See *Table* at JAPAN.
2 Seaport city, its *, on W coast of **Kagoshima Bay,** a deep inlet on S coast of Kyushu, Japan; pop. (1938 est.) 191,200; well-protected harbor; center of manufacture of Satsuma ware. An ancient place, long the castle city of a powerful daimio of the Satsuma clan, esp. important at time of Restoration; bombarded by British warships 1863; destroyed by fire 1877; severely damaged by eruption of Sakurajima (on island in bay) 1914; in World War II severely bombed by Allies June–Aug. 1945.

Ka·gul' (kŭ·gŏŏl'); *Romanian* **Ca·hul'** (kä·hŏŏl'). Town, formerly in Bessarabia, Romania; pop. (1930) 10,437; now (since 1945) in S Moldavian S.S.R., U.S.S.R.

Ka·ha'jan (kä·hä'yän) or **Great Da'yak** (dä'yäk). River ab. 225 m. long, S Borneo, Indonesia; rises in E end of Schwaner Mts. and flows S to Java Sea.

Ka·ha·ku·lo'a Head (kä·hä'kŏŏ·lō'ä). Cape on NW coast of Maui I., Hawaii, on W side of Kahului Bay.

Ka·ha'la Point (kä·hä'lä). Cape on NE coast of Kauai I., Hawaii.

Ka·ha'na Bay (kä·hä'nä). Bay on NE coast of Oahu I., Hawaii.

Ka·hi'li (kä·hē'lē). Village, S end of Bougainville I., NW Solomon Is., W Pacific Ocean, just E of Buin on Tonolai Harbour; during World War II site of Japanese airfield.

Kah·lam'ba (kä·läm'bä). = *Quathlamba:* see DRAKENSBERG MOUNTAINS.

Kah'len·berg (kä'lĕn·bĕrK). Eminence 1584 ft. ab. 5½ m. NW of Vienna, Austria, in the Wienerwald.

Kahlur. See BILASPUR.

Ka·ho'ka (kȧ·hō'kȧ). City, ⊗ of Clark co., NE corner of Missouri, 54 m. NNW of Hannibal; pop. 2160; ships grain.

Ka·ho'o·la·we (kä·hō'ō·lä'vä). Island in S cen. Hawaii, W of S Maui I.; 45 sq. m.; a part of Maui co.

Ka·hu'ku (kä·hŏŏ'kŏŏ). Village, Koolauloa dist., Honolulu co., Hawaii, near **Kahuku Point,** the N point of Oahu I.; pop. 1238.

Ka·hu·lu'i (kä'hŏŏ·lŏŏ'ē). Village in Kahului dist. (pop. 4223), Maui co., Hawaii, on **Kahului Bay** on N coast of Maui I.

Kai'a·ka' Bay (kī'ä·kä'). Bay on N coast of Oahu I., Hawaii, at base of Kaena Point.

Kai'a·po'i (kī'ä·pō'ē). Borough, Canterbury provincial district, E South I., New Zealand, N of Christchurch at mouth of Waimakariri river; pop. 1700.

Kai'bab Plateau (kī'băb). Tableland in N Arizona, on N rim of Grand Canyon (*q.v.*); has beautiful forests, set aside as Kaibab National Forest.

Kai·bi'to Plateau (kī·bē'tō). Tableland in NE Coconino co., N cen. Arizona.

Kaieiewaho. See KAUAI channel.

Kai'e·teur' Falls (kī'ē·tŏōr'). Waterfall in Potaro river, cen. British Guiana; 741 ft. high, ab. 350 ft. wide.

Kai'feng' (kī'fŭng'). City, N Honan province, E cen. China, ab. 340 m. NW of Nanking; pop. ab. 223,000; in Hwang Ho valley and often menaced by Hwang Ho floods. One of most historic cities of China, an early settlement site and junction point of routes to the east and south; capital of the empire in period of the Five Dynasties (907–960 A.D.) and, as **Pien'–ching'** (byĕn'jĭng'), under Northern Sung dynasty (960–1127); site of a Jewish colony in early centuries of Christian era, as recorded on a famous inscription stone still in existence.

Kaiffa. Var. of HAIFA.

Kai·ga·ne (kī·gä·nĕ). See SHIRANE.

Kai (kī), or **Kei** (kī), **Islands.** Island group of SE Moluccas, Indonesia, Malay Archipelago, SE of Ceram I. and W of Aru Is., 565 sq. m.; pop. 50,648. Comprises **Noe'hoe·tjoet'** or **Nu'hu·tjut'** (nŏŏ'hŏŏ·chŏŏt') or **Great Kai Island,** 290 sq. m., 50 m. long, mountainous (volcanic), **Noe'hoe·ro'wa** or **Nu'hu·ro'wa** (-rō'wä) or **Little Kai,** and many small islets scattered over E end of Banda Sea. Inhabitants are fine boatbuilders.

Kai·jo (kī·jō), *now* **Kae·song** (kā·sông); *formerly also* **Song·do** (sông·dô). City, NW Keiki prov., W Korea, ab. 45 m. N of Seoul; pop. (1938 est.) 68,565; an old town, for several centuries capital of a ruling dynasty; noted for its ginseng and porcelain wares.

Kai·kou'ra Range (kī·kōr'ȧ). Mountain range in NE South I., New Zealand, N of Clarence river; from 4000 ft. to highest peak Tapuaenuku 9465 ft.

Kai·las' (kī·läs'). **1** Mountain range, SW Tibet; highest peak 23,165 ft.; contains sources of the Indus and Sutlej rivers and headstreams of the Brahmaputra.
2 Group of peaks ab. 22,000 ft., in cen. part of Kailas Range, 31°N, 81°E, N of Lake Manasarowar and SE of Gartok; sacred to Hindus and a favorite pilgrimage resort; famous in Sanskrit literature as Siva's paradise.

Kai·lu'a (kī·lŏō'ä). **1** City, Honolulu co., Hawaii, on Kailua Bay; pop. (with Lanikai) 25,622.
2 or **Kailua–Ko'na** (kō'nä; -nä). Village, Hawaii co., Hawaii, on W coast of Hawaii I. N of Kealakekua; pop. 466; chief town and port of old Kona dist.; residence of early kings of the islands; landing place of first missionaries to Hawaii 1820.

Kailua Bay. Bay on E coast of Oahu I., Hawaii, N of Makapuu Point.

Kai·ma'na (kī·mä'nä). Town, S coast of West Irian, 125 m. SE of Fakfak; important trading post.

Kai·ma'na·wa Range (kī·mä'nä·wä). Mountain range in cen. North I., New Zealand.

Kai'pa·ra Harbor (kī'pä·rȧ; kī'prȧ). Inlet of Pacific Ocean on W coast of N extension of North I., New Zealand, forming an excellent harbor.

Kai'ping' (kī'pĭng'). District and town, NE Hopei prov., NE China, N of Tientsin; large coal field.

Kai'ra (kī'rȧ). Town, SE Gujarat, W Indian Union, 20 m. S of Ahmadabad; pop. 8313; dates back to 5th cent.

K
L

Kair'ouan' (*Fr.* kĕr·wän'). *or* **Kair·wan'** (kĭr·wän'); *Arab.* **Qair·wan'** (kĭr·wän'). City, NE Tunisia, WSW of Sousse; pop. (1936) 22,991; trades in leather goods and carpets; a Holy City of the Moslems, has beautiful mosques; founded 670 A.D. by the Arab general, Okba, to whom one of the mosques is dedicated; capital of the Aghlabite dynasty 800–909. In World War II occupied by Allies Apr. 1943.

Kais. See QAIS.

Kaisargarh. See TAKHT-I-SULAIMAN.

Kaisaria, Kaisarieh. See KAYSERI.

Kai'se·rin Au·gu'sta (kī'zĕ·rĭn ou·gŏŏs'tä). German name of the SEPIK river, North-East New Guinea.

Kai'sers·lau'tern (kī'zĕrs·lou'tĕrn). Industrial city in the Palatinate, Bavaria, Germany, 43 m. NW of Karlsruhe; pop. 59,336; machinery, bicycles, iron goods, lumber, textiles, brewery products, tobacco. First mentioned 882; became city 1276; scene of French victory over Prussians 1793; capital of French department of Donnersberg 1801–14; passed to Bavaria 1816.

Kai'ser·stuhl' (kī'zĕr·shtŏŏl'). Mountain group, SW Baden-Württemberg, SW Germany, NW of Freiburg; highest peak 1827 ft.

Kai'sers·werth (kī'zĕrs·vĕrt'; *Ger.* kī'zĕrs·vārt'). Town, W Germany, 6 m. below Düsseldorf on Rhine river; since 1929 a part of Düsseldorf; grew up around a Benedictine monastery built 710; scene of activities of Theodor Fliedner, who became pastor here 1821 and opened refuge for discharged female convicts 1833 and later several other charitable institutions.

Kaiser Wilhelm Canal. See KIEL CANAL.

Kaiser Wilhelm II Land. See WILHELM II COAST.

Kai'ser–Wil'helms·land' (kī'zĕr·vĭl'hĕlms·länt'). Former German colony, now North-East New Guinea. See NORTH-EAST NEW GUINEA.

Kai·shu (kī·shōō) *or* **Hae·ju** (hī·jōō). Town, ✻ of Kokai prov., W Korea, 75 m. NW of Keijo ab. 4 m. from coast; pop. 29,688.

Kai'šia·do·ris (kī'shĕ·dô·rēs) *or* **Kai'sha·do·ris** (kī'·shĕ·dô·rēs). Town, ✻ of Trakai dist., E Lithuania, 15 m. E of Kaunas; pop. 7242; junction point on Kaunas-Vilnyus railroad.

Kai'thal (kīt'hăl). Town, Punjab state, NW Indian Union, 90 m. N of Delhi; pop. 19,418; an old town; connected with Hindu legends, esp. with the monkey god Hanuman. Held by Sikhs 1767 to 1843 when it became British.

Kai'wi (kī'wē). Channel 23 m. wide bet Oahu I. and Molokai I., Hawaii.

Kai'yuan' (kī'yü·än'). Town, E Liaoning prov., S Manchuria, on South Manchuria Railway ab. halfway bet. Mukden and Changchun; pop. 34,380; consists of walled town and new town around railroad station; a distribution center for soybeans.

Ka'jaa·ni (kä'yä·nĭ). City, cen. Finland, in Oulu dept.; pop. (1939 est.) 7750; on rapids just SE of Oulujärvi; trade and transportation center; sawmills, paper mills; manufactures cellulose.

Ka'jan (kä'yän). River ab. 250 m. long, E Borneo, Indonesia; rises in mountains of N cen. Borneo and flows E to Celebes Sea.

Ka'jang (kä'yäng). Town, E cen. Selangor, Federation of Malaya, on W coast railroad line 10 m. S of Kuala Lumpur; pop. 6060; center for rubber plantations.

Ka·je'li (kä·yā'lē). Village on bay on E coast of Buru I., Moluccas, Indonesia.

Kak'a·ton'ga, Lake (kăk'à·bŏng'gà). Lake 66 sq. m. in Pontiac co., SW Quebec, Canada; its outlet flows SE into Lake Baskatong.

Kakinada. See COCANADA.

Käkisalmi. See KEKSGOLM.

Kalaat Saman. See QAL 'AT SAMAN.

Ka'la·ba'hi (kä'lä·bä'hĕ). Chief town on Alor I., Lesser Sunda Is., Indonesia, at head of **Kalabahi Bay** at W end of island; excellent anchorage.

Ka'lach' (kŭ·lách'). Town, W cen. Stalingrad Region, SE Soviet Russia, Europe, on E bank of the Don at its nearest point to the Volga; head of navigation of the Don and W terminus of Volga-Don canal; an important bridgehead in World War II; taken by Germans after three weeks' fighting July 27, 1942; retaken by Russians Nov. 20 1942.

Ka'la·dan' (kŭ'lŭ·dŭn'). River ab. 300 m. long in Arakan division, Lower Burma; flows S from Chin Hills to Bay of Bengal at Akyab; known as **Boi'nu** (boi'nōō) river in its upper course; one upper tributary rises in the Lushai Hills in SE Assam; its valley scene of much fighting 1943–44.

Ka La'e (kä lä'à) *or* **South Cape** *or* **South Point.** Cape on S extremity of Hawaii I.; missile-tracking station.

Kalaeloa Point. See BARBERS POINT.

Ka'la·han'di (kä'lä·hŭn'dĕ); *formerly* **Ka·rond'** (kà·rŏnd'). Former Indian state, Eastern States, NE Indian Union; 3559 sq. m.; pop. (1941) 597,940; ✻ Bhawanipatna (pop. 7174), 185 m. WSW of Cuttack.

Ka'la·ha'ri Desert (kä'lä·hä'rĕ). Plateau and partly desert region, Bechuanaland Protectorate and W cen. Union of South Africa, N of the Orange river and S of Lake Ngami; S portion traversed by dry river beds, as the Molopo and the Kuruman; average elevation over 3000 ft.; vegetation mostly grass, dense scrub in W and N; big game; first crossed by David Livingstone and William C. Oswell 1849.

Kalakh. See CALAH.

Kalámai. See KALAMATA.

Ka'la·mas' (kä'lä·mäs'); *anc.* **Thy'a·mis** (thī'à·mĭs). River ab. 70 m. long. cen. Epirus, NW Greece; flows S and W to Ionian Sea opp. Corfu I.; marked N border of ancient Thesprotia.

Kal'a·ma'ta (kăl'à·mä'tà; *Gr.* kä'lä·mä'tä) *or* **Ka·lá'm:ai** (kä·lä'mà). Commercial seaport city, ✻ of Messenia dept., SW Peloponnesus, S Greece, at head of Gulf of Messenia; pop. 28,955; nearby is site of ancient Pharae; sacked by Ibrahim Pasha 1825.

Kalamata, Gulf of. See Gulf of MESSENIA.

Kal'a·ma·zoo' (kăl'à·mà·zōō'). **1** River 200 m. long, SW Michigan; rises in Hillsdale co., flows N, then W into Lake Michigan in Allegan co.

2 County in Michigan. See *Table* at MICHIGAN.

3 City, ⊗ of Kalamazoo co., SW Michigan, 47 m. S of Grand Rapids; pop. 82,089; manufactures paper, drugs, stoves and furnaces, gas heaters, caskets, clothing. Kalamazoo College (1833; coed.; Baptist); Western Michigan Univ. (1903; coed.).

Ka'la'shar' (kŭ'lä'shär'). = QARA SHAHR.

Ka·lat' *or* **Khe·lat'** (kà·lät'). **1** Former Indian state, N and cen. Baluchistan; 72,503 sq. m.; has rugged and barren mountains, but also wide, fertile valleys. Ruled by a Khan, probably of Arabic descent; in 1947 remained independent of newly formed Pakistan but joined the new state 1948; area now part of prov. of West Pakistan.

2 Walled town with citadel, its ✻ and ✻ of Baluchistan States, 88 m. S of Quetta; altitude 6780 ft.; occupied by British 1839; made site of British garrison 1854.

Ka·la'u·pa'pa (kä·lä'ŏŏ·pä'pä). Village and leper settlement, Kalawao dist., Maui co., Hawaii, on N coast of Molokai I. on Makanalua Penin. pop. (est.) 446; leper settlement most fully equipped in the world, covering some 8000 acres. See KALAWAO.

Kalaus. See MANYCH valley.

Ka'la·wa'o (kä'lä·wä'ŏ). **1** District, Maui co., N Molokai I., Hawaii; 14 sq. m.; called **Kalawao County** but area consists only of the Kalaupapa leper settlement and has no local government; represented in territorial legislature as part of Maui county.

2 Village, N Molokai, site of original leper settlement, where Father Damien began his work 1873.

Kalbe. See CALBE.

Ka·le' Sul'ta·ni·e' (kä·lĕ' sŏŏl'tä·nē·yĕ'). = ÇANAK-KALE town.

Ka·le′wa (kä·lä′wä). Town, Upper Chindwin dist., W Upper Burma, on Chindwin river 150 m. NW of Mandalay; scene of fighting in World War II Japanese campaign against India; taken by Allies Dec. 2, 1944.

Kalgan. See WANCHUAN.

Kal·goor′lie (kăl·gŏŏr′lĭ). Municipality, S Western Australia, 335 m. ENE of Perth; pop. 9091, with suburbs 17,332; in gold-mining section.

Ka′li (kä′lĭ). Upper course of Sarda river (q.v.), N India.

Ka′li′ (jĭ·ä′lē′) or **Lha′ri′guo′** (hlä′rē′gwô′). Village, W Sikang, S China, on highway from Lhasa to Chamdo, ab. 165 m. NE of Lhasa; nearby is large Buddhist convent and temple.

Kaliakra, Cape. See Cape CALIACRA.

Ka′li·an′ Point (kä′lē·än′). Cape on SW coast of Davao prov., Mindanao, Phil. Is.

Ka′li Bay (kä′lē). Inlet, W end of Manus I., Admiralty Is., W Pacific Ocean.

Ka·li′bo (kä·lē′vô); formerly **Ca·li′vo.** Municipality, NW Capiz prov., Panay, Phil. Is., near coast 28 m. WNW of Capiz; pop. 1o,095.

Ka′li·man′tan (kä′lē·män′tän). Indonesian name of BORNEO.

Ka′li Mas (kä′lē mäs′). River ab. 35 m. long, E Java, Indonesia; leaves the Brantas river (q.v.) near Modjokerto and flows NE and N through city of Surabaja to Surabaja Strait.

Ka′lim·pong (kä′lĭm·pông). Town, N West Bengal, NE Indian Union, ab. 8 m. ENE of Darjeeling; pop. 8776; hill sanatorium, alt. 3930 ft.; frontier market, Indian end of trade route through Sikkim to Tibet.

Ka′li Na′di (kä′lē nŭ′dē). River ab. 300 m. long, N India; rises near Saharanpur and flows SSE in W Uttar Pradesh, joining the Ganges N of Cawnpore.

Ka·lin′di (kä·lĭn′dē). River in NE India; flows S in Ganges-Brahmaputra Delta.

Ka·lin′ga (kä·lēng′gä). Subprovince, N cen. Mountain Province, Luzon, Phil. Is.; 1100 sq. m.; pop. 24,452; ✳ Lubuagan; comprises valley of Chico river entirely surrounded by mountains ranging from 5000 to 8400 ft.; has forests and much grass area; not well suited to agriculture but raises some rice, maize, and camotes.

Ka·li′nin (kä·lē′nĭn; Russ. kŭ·lyē′nyĭn); before 1932 **Tver** (tá·vĕr′; Russ. tvyĕr′y′). City, ✳ of Kalinin Region, Soviet Russia, Europe, in SE part of Region 100 m. NW of Moscow and on both banks of the Volga; pop. 216,131; on Moscow-Leningrad railroad; produces machinery, textiles, and leather goods. An old city, begun 1180 as a fort in W part of Suzdal principality; for two centuries capital of Tver principality; long a rival of Moscow for supremacy in Russia, but annexed to it 1490 under Ivan III; suffered 1570 a great massacre of its citizens under Ivan the Terrible; taken by Germans in autumn of 1941, recaptured by Russians Dec. 1941.

Ka·li′nin·grad (kä·lē′nĭn·grăd; Russ. kŭ·lyē′nyĭn·grät′); Ger. **Kö′nigs·berg** (kŭ′nĭks·bĕrk; Angl. kā′nĭgz·bûrg). Industrial and commercial seaport, ✳ and ✳ of Kaliningradsk Region, W Soviet Russia, Europe, and ✳ of former province of East Prussia, Germany, on Pregel river near the Frisches Haff 80 m. ENE of Danzig; pop. (1939) 368,433; connected with Bay of Danzig by ship canal; manufactures locomotives, machinery, iron castings, textiles, amber articles, copper, steel, chemicals, iron goods, earthenware, tobacco, brewery and distillery products, cement; 14th-cent. Gothic cathedral, palace, 17th-cent. citadel; university (1544) destroyed in World War II; birthplace of Immanuel Kant. Founded 1255; joined Hanseatic League 1365; fortified 1626; in World War I invested and bombed by Russians 1914; in World War II bombed by Russians after 1942, occupied by Russian armies Apr. 9, 1945 after long siege; assigned to U.S.S.R. by Potsdam Conference 1945; named Kaliningrad by Russians 1946; made a naval base.

Ka·li′nin·gradsk Region (kä·lē′nĭn·grätsk; Russ. kŭ·lyē′nyĭn·grätsk′). Region, W Soviet Russia, Europe, formerly part of East Prussia, Germany, comprising the area around Kaliningrad (Königsberg); ab. 3475 sq. m.; pop. (1945 est.) 400,000; ✳ Kaliningrad; includes cities of Sovetsk (Tilsit) and Chernyakhovsk (Insterburg).

Kalinin Region. Region, W cen. Soviet Russia, Europe, hilly country at source of Volga; area (1945) 41,070 sq. m.; pop. 3,211,439; ✳ Kalinin; reduced 1945 by creation of new regions; well drained by the upper Volga and its tributaries, esp. the Mologa; crossed by canal system connecting the Baltic with the Volga; has some agriculture (esp. grain) and dairying; manufacturing in the larger cities. Chief cities Kalinin, Vyshni-Volochek, and Rzhev.

Kalininsk. See PETROZAVODSK.

Kal′i·spell (kăl′ĭ·spĕl; -spĕl′). City, ⊗ of Flathead co., NW Montana, 8 m. NW of N end of Flathead Lake; pop. 10,151; market center in agricultural, lumber, and fruit section.

Ka′lisz (kä′lēsh); Ger. **Ka′lisch** (kä′lĭsh). Commune, Poznań dept., Poland, on Prosna river 58 m. W of Łódź; pop. (1938–39 est.) 80,216; railroad junction; manufactures textiles; sheep and goose breeding. An old and beautiful city; scene of Swedish defeat by combined army of Russians and Poles 1705; place where Prussia and Russia formed coalition against Napoleon Feb. 28, 1813; occupied by Germans Aug. 1914 and greater part destroyed; again under Germans in World War II.

Ka′li·woen′goe (kä′lē·wōōng′gōō) or **Ka′li·wun′gu.** Town, Central Java prov., Indonesia, just W of Semarang; pop. 17,357.

Ka′lix (kä′lĭks). River 267 m. long in N Sweden; flows SE and S into head of Gulf of Bothnia; many rapids.

Kal′ka (kăl′kä); mod. **Kal′mi·us** (kăl′mĭ·ŭs). Short river, SE Ukraine, U.S.S.R., flows S into the Gulf of Taganrog; scene of victory of the Mongols over Russians 1223.

Kal′ka (kăl′kä; native käl′-). Village, Punjab state, NW Indian Union; pop. 7937; border station on railroad from Ambala to Simla (23 m.).

Kalkandelen. See TETOVO.

Kal·kas′ka (kăl·kăs′kä). **1** County in Michigan. See Table at MICHIGAN.

2 Village, ⊗ of Kalkaska co., N Michigan; pop. 1321.

Kalk Bay (kôk). Seaside town, suburb of Cape Town, Cape Province, Union of South Africa, on W shore of False Bay; pop. ab. 4000.

Kalk′fon·tein′ (kälk′fŏn·tān′). Town, SE South-West Africa, on railroad 230 m. SE of Lüderitz.

Kal′la·ve′si (käl′lä·vĕ′sĭ). Lake in S cen. Finland, 100 m. E of Vaasa; W shore site of city of Kuopio.

Kal·lip′o·li (kä·lĭp′ŏ·lĭ; Gr. kä·lyē′pŏ·lyĕ). Modern Greek var. of GALLIPOLI.

Kal′li·the′a or **Cal′li·the′a** (kä′lyē·thä′ä). Commune, Attica and Boeotia dept., E Central Greece and Euboea division, Greece, S suburb of Athens; pop. 26,603.

Kal′lo·ní′, Gulf of (kä′lô·nē′); Mod. Gr. **Kól′pos Kal′lo·nís′** (kôl′pôs kä′lô·nēs′). Long inlet of Aegean Sea in S Lesbos I., Greek Aegean Is., widening out in center of island; town of Kalloní lies at head of it.

Kal′mar (käl′mär; Swed. käl′mär). **1** Province of Sweden. See Table at SWEDEN.

2 Seaport, its ✳, SE Sweden, on Kalmarsund opp. Öland I.; pop. 23,834; shipbuilding yards, match factories; ships timber; place where Union of Kalmar was formed 1397, uniting Denmark, Sweden, and Norway into a single monarchy (1397–1523).

Kal′mar·sund′ (käl′mär·sŭnd′; Swed. käl′mär-). Body of water separating Öland I. in Baltic Sea from Swedish mainland.

Kalmius. See KALKA.

Kal′myk (kăl′mĭk; käl·mĭk′; Russ. kŭl·mĭk′), or **Kal′muck** (kăl′mŭk; käl·mŭk′), **Republic;** officially **Kalmyk Autonomous Soviet Socialist Republic;** also **Kal·myk′i·a** (käl·mĭk′ĭ·ȧ). Former autonomous republic, SE Soviet Russia, Europe, on NW shore of

Caspian Sea and W of lower Volga; 28,641 sq. m.; pop. 220,723, (1941 est.) 231,935; ✻ Elista (now called Stepnoi); was a subdivision of the R.S.F.S.R.; largely steppe land, dry desert with hills along W border; no railroad except from Astrakhan S along the Caspian shore; chief occupations cattle raising and fishing (at Volga mouth). Region settled 1636 by Kalmucks, or Kalmyks, a nomadic, Buddhist people, western Mongols from cen. China, who became subject to Russia 1646 and later furnished fighting men for some of Peter the Great's armies; its present inhabitants (Kalmucks form 75.6% of population) descended from the western Kalmucks who were left behind when 300,000 of their people, fearing oppression, suddenly left Jan. 5, 1771 to return to China, undertaking a journey of terrible privations (see De Quincey's *The Revolt of the Tartars*) from both cold and heat and from attacks by Kirghiz and Bashkirs, barely a third of their number reaching the destination; badly hit by civil war and famine after the Revolution 1917; made a republic 1935; after recapture of Stalingrad by Russians 1943, republic liquidated and its territory distributed among Stavropol Territory, Stalingrad and Rostov Regions, and the newly formed Astrakhan Region, which received most of it.

Ka·lo·csa (kŏ′lŏ·chŏ). City, S Hungary, near Danube river 70 m. S of Budapest; pop. 12,776; in an agricultural region; archbishopric, founded c. 1135; cathedral; frequently attacked by Turks in 16th cent.

Ka·lo′hi (kä·lō′hē). Channel ab. 9 m. wide bet. Molokai I. on N and Lanai I. on S, Hawaii.

Kal′pi (käl′pē). Town, SW Uttar Pradesh, N Indian Union, on Jumna river 45 m. SW of Cawnpore; pop. 9843; ancient town important in early wars; captured by British 1803; scene of Sir Hugh Rose's defeat of rebels of Jhansi 1858.

Ka·lu′ga (kà·lōō′gà; *Russ.* kŭ-). City, E Kaluga Region, Soviet Russia, Europe, WNW of Tula and ab. 90 m. SW of Moscow; pop. 89,484; on left bank of Oka river and on several railroad lines; smelting works, sawmills; manufactures machinery. Dates back to 14th cent.; included in Moscow principality 1518; in early 17th cent. devastated by Cossacks, plague, and fire; in World War II overrun by first German offensive Nov. 1941, but retaken by Russians Jan. 1942.

Kaluga Region. Region, cen. Soviet Russia, Europe, in black earth area N of the Ukraine; ✻ Kaluga; crossed by Oka river; formerly part of Tula Region; newly created during World War II.

Ka·lu′shin (kŭ·lōō′shĭn); *Pol.* **Ka′łusz** (kä′łōōsh). Town, SW Ukraine, U.S.S.R., on a tributary of the Dniester 18 m. WNW of Stanislav (formerly in Stanisławów dept., Poland); pop. (1938–39 est.) 14,699; important potassium and salt mines; manufactures beer, liquors, leather; scene of battles bet. Russians and Germans July 1917.

Ka′lu·ta′ra (kŭ′lōō·tŭ′rà). Town, SW Western Province, Ceylon, on Indian Ocean 26 m. S of Colombo; pop. 14,280.

Kaluwawa. See FERGUSSON.

Kal·yan′ (kŭl·yän′). Town, W Maharashtra, W Indian Union, 33 m. NE of Bombay; pop. 26,291; important railroad junction point; trades in rice, brick, and tile; a commercial center in 17th cent.

Kal·ya′ni (kŭl·yä′nĭ). Town, N Mysore state, India, ab. 40 m. N of Gulbarga; formerly (10th to 12th cent.) seat of powerful Chalukya dynasty.

Ka′lym·nos (kä′lyĕm·nôs); *Ital.* **Ca·li′no** (kä·lē′nŏ) *or* **Ca·lim′no** (kä·lēm′nŏ); *anc.* **Ca·lym′na** (kà·lĭm′nà) *or* **Ca·lym′nos** (kà·lĭm′nôs). **1** An island of the Dodecanese (*q.v.*), off end of Bodrum Penin. N of Kos I.; 49 sq. m.; pop. (1936) 15,247.

2 *or* **Po·the′a** (pŏ·thē′à). Town, its ✻, on the S coast.

Kalyub, Kalyubiya. = QALYUB, QALYUBÎYA.

Ka′ma (kä′mà; *Russ.* kà′-). River ab. 1200 m. long in E Soviet Russia, Europe; rises in N border of Udmurt Republic, flows N in Kirov Region, then E and S in Molotov Region (in Asia) along W slope of Middle Urals, then S in SE Udmurt Republic and WSW in Tatar Republic to the Volga ab. 40 m. below Kazan; largest tributary of the Volga; navigable for ab. 1000 m.; important part of Russian water transportation system; chief tributaries Belaya, Vyatka, and Chusovaya.

Ka·mai′ki Point (kä·mī′kē). Cape on SE coast of Lanai I., Hawaii.

Ka′maing (kä′mīng). Town, N Burma, 20 m. NW of Mogaung near the Stilwell Road; taken by Chinese June 18, 1944.

Ka·ma·i·shi (kä·mä·ē·shē). Town, Iwate prefecture, N Honshu, Japan; pop. (1945) 24,475; site of large ironworks, which were largely destroyed by U.S. bombs and shells July 14, 1945.

Ka′ma·ko′u (kä′mä·kō′ōō). Mountain 4958 ft. in E Molokai I., Hawaii.

Ka·ma·ku·ra (kä·mä·kōō·rä). Town, Kanagawa prefecture, SE Honshu, Japan, on Sagami Sea ab. 10 m. S of Yokohama; pop. (1945) 47,545; historically one of most important towns of Japan; probably founded in 7th cent. A.D.; selected by Minamoto Yoritomo as his residence and on his assumption of the shogunate 1192 became seat of government of Japan to remain so until downfall of Hojo rulers 1333 when it was nearly destroyed; during Minamoto shogunate perhaps had population of 800,000 to 1,000,000; with rise of Tokyo to power 1603 declined to a fishing village. Since the Restoration 1868 has become a favorite resort; site of Daibutsu, the great bronze image of Buddha, cast in 1252, 50 ft. in height and 96 ft. in circumference; has a shrine of Hachiman (founded 1063) and several temples.

Ka′ma·ran′ *or* **Qa′ma·ran′** (kä′mŭ·rän′). British island in S Red Sea, off coast of Yemen, SW Arabia, 45 m. N of Hodeida; 22 sq. m.; pop. ab. 2200; administratively attached to Aden; site of a quarantine station for pilgrims to Mecca, under joint control of governments of India and Netherlands Indies.

Kamar Bay. See QAMR BAY.

Ka′mar·ha′ti (kä′mär·hä′tĭ). Town, West Bengal, NE Indian Union, on left bank of Hooghly river 12 m. N of Calcutta; pop. 30,334.

Kam·baeng·bejra (käm·p′häng·p′hĕt—*sic*). = KAMBAENG PETCH.

Kambaeng Petch. See KAMPHAENG PHET.

Kam·bo′dja (käm·bō′jä). Town on coast of Cochin China, S Vietnam, S of Saigon; former capital of Khmer kingdom of Cambodia (*q.v.*); founded c. 435 A.D.

Kambryk. See CAMBRAI.

Kam·chat′ka (käm·chät′kà). **1** Peninsula, NE Soviet Russia, Asia; 750 m. long, extending S bet. Sea of Okhotsk and Bering Sea to a point (Cape Lopatka) 7 m. from Shumushu, northernmost of Kuril Is.; 104,260 sq. m., width varies from 80 to 300 m.; formerly constituted major portion of Kamchatka dist. of Far Eastern Region; S two thirds now form a district of Khabarovsk Territory, while the N third (the isthmus) is part of Koryak National District; chief occupations hunting of fur-bearing animals and fishing. Its mountain system, the **Kamchatka Mountains,** consists of two main ranges: the Eastern Range, the shorter, along E coast, having many high volcanic peaks, including Klyuchevskaya 15,666 ft., highest in all Siberia; the Central Range (*Russ.* Sredinny Khrebet) extending length of the peninsula, average height 3000 ft. First visited by Russians 1696; explored in 18th cent.; developed slowly since 1850.

2 Chief river of the peninsula, ab. 350 m. long; rises in Central Range, flows N and E to Bering Sea.

3 Former district of Far Eastern Region, Soviet Russia, Asia, comprising Kamchatka Penin. and an area on mainland NW of Shelekova Gulf; pop. ab. 32,000; chief town Petropavlovsk-Kamchatski; included Komandorskie Is.

Kam′chi·a (kăm′chĕ·yä). River ab. 110 m. long in E Bulgaria; flows E into Black Sea S of Varna.

Ka′men (kä′mĕn). Industrial city, North Rhine-Westphalia state, W Germany, 9 m. NE of Dortmund; pop. 11,686; coal mining; manufactures shoes and pressed, stamped, and hammered ware.

Ka′men (kȧ′myĕn). Town, N Altai Territory, Soviet Russia, Asia, on Ob river ab. 110 m. SW of Novosibirsk.

Ka·me·nets′ Po·dol′ski (kȧ·myĭ·nyĕts′ pŭ·dôl′y′·skĭ). **1** Region, SW Ukraine, U.S.S.R., N of the Dniester; formerly bordered on Poland; ✳ Proskurov.
2 City its largest city and ✳ of former Podolia prov. and region; on a bluff on a small tributary of the Dniester 12 m. N of Khotin; pop. 33,035; some industrial plants. A border town with a long history; destroyed by Mongols 1240; a strong church city with cathedrals and monasteries dating from 14th cent.; became chief town of Podolia 1434; suffered much in 15th and 16th cents. from invasions of Tatars, Moldavians, and Turks; came under Turks 1672, restored to Poland 1699, and annexed to Russia 1795. In World War II held by Germans July 1941 to Mar. 1944.

Ka′me·nic′ký Še′nov (kȧ′mĕ·nyĭts′kē shĕ′nôf); *Ger.* **Stein′schö′nau** (shtīn′shŭ′nou). Commune, N Bohemia, W Czechoslovakia, E of the Labe (Elbe) and NE of Litoměřice; pop. (1930) 5330; makes crystal glass.

Ka′me·njak, Cape (kä′mĕ·nyäk); *Ital.* **Cape Promon·to′re** (prô·mŏn·tô′rä). Southern tip of Istria Penin., NW Yugoslavia.

Kamenskoe. See DNEPRODZERZHINSK.

Ka′mensk Shakh·tin′ski (kȧ′myĕnsk shŭк·tyĕn′skĭ), *formerly* **Kamensk.** Town, W Rostov Region, Soviet Russia, Europe, on Donets river; on trunk railroad line; an important distribution point, esp. for grain. In World War II within German lines July 1942–Feb. 1943.

Kamensk–U·ral′ski (ōō·räl′y′·skĭ), *formerly* **Kamensk.** Town, N Chelyabinsk Region, Soviet Russia, Asia, 100 m. N of Chelyabinsk; pop. 159,000.

Ka′menz (kä′mĕnts). City, Dresden dist., East Germany, in Saxony on the Schwarze Elster river 17 m. WNW of Bautzen; pop. 11,165; manufactures cloth, clay products, stoneware, glass, machinery; birthplace of Lessing. Founded c. 1200.

Kamerun. See CAMEROONS.

Ka′met (kŭ′mät). Peak 25,447 ft. in the Himalayas, in N Garhwal dist. of Uttar Pradesh, N Indian Union, on Tibet border; ascended June 1931, at that time the highest peak ever climbed.

Ka·mien′na Gó′ra (kä·myĕn′nä gōō′rä); *Ger.* **Lan′des·hut** (län′dĕs·hōōt), *also* **Landeshut in Schle′si·en** (ĭn shlä′zĕ·ĕn). City, S Wrocław dept., SW Poland, on Bobr river 52 m. WSW of Wrocław; pop. (1946) 13,688; formerly in Silesia, Germany; manufactures textiles, shoes. Scene of Prussian victory over Austrians 1745, and of Austrian victory over Prussians 1760; assigned to Poland by Potsdam Conference 1945.

Ka·mien′na Skar·ży′sko (kä·myĕn′nä skär·zhĭ′skô). Commune, Kielce dept., Poland, 15 m. NW of Kielce; pop. (1938–39 est.) 19,870; important railroad junction.

Ka·mi′ri (kȧ·mēr′ĕ). See NOEMFOOR.

Kam′loops (kăm′lōōps). City, S British Columbia, Canada, at confluence of N and S branches of Thompson river 160 m. NE of Vancouver; pop. 8099; railroad divisional point; center of supply for large mining (gold and copper) and grazing district; fruit canneries. Founded 1810 as Fort Thompson.

Kammer, Lake; *Ger.* **Kammersee.** See Lake ATTER.

Kam′ou·ras′ka (kăm′ōō·räs′kȧ). County, Quebec, Canada. See *Table* at QUEBEC.

Kam·pa′la (kăm·pä′lä). City, ✳ of Uganda and of the kingdom and province of Buganda, just N of Entebbe; pop. ab. 47,000.

Kam′par (kăm′pär). **1** Town, S cen. Perak state, Federation of Malaya, 20 m. SE of Ipoh; pop. 15,302; on E coast trunk line railroad in Kinta Valley tin region.

2 River ab. 200 m. long in cen. Sumatra, Indonesia; rises in Barisan Mts. N of Bukittingi, flows E into S end of Strait of Malacca.

Kam′pen (kăm′pĕn). Commercial commune, Overijssel prov., E Netherlands, on IJssel river; pop. (1939) 20,737; formerly a member of Hanseatic League; stadhouse; church of St. Nicholas.

Kam′per·duin (käm′pĕr·doin). = CAMPERDOWN.

Kam·phaeng Phet *or* **Kam·baeng Petch** (kämp′häng p′hĕt). **1** Province, W Thailand; 3431 sq. m.; pop. 57,184.
2 Town, its ✳, on left bank of Ping river 65 m. NW of Nakhon Sawan.

Kamp–Lintfort. See LINTFORT.

Kampo. See CAMPO.

Kam′pot′ (käm′pōt′). Seaport town, S Cambodia, Indochina, 75 m. SSW of Pnompenh; pop. ab. 3000; center of pepper culture.

Kamp′tee (kämp′tē) *or* **Kam′thi** (kämt′hē). Town, NE Maharashtra state, Indian Union, on Wainganga river 10 m. NNE of Nagpur; pop. 20,787; founded 1821 as military cantonment; a trade center of decreasing importance.

Kamranh Bay. Var. of CAMRANH BAY.

Kam′sack (käm′săk). Town, SE Saskatchewan, Canada, on Assiniboine river 35 m. NE of Yorkton; pop. 2327.

Ka′mu·e′la (kä′mōō·ā′lä). Village, South Kohala dist., Hawaii co., Hawaii, in N part of island of Hawaii; pop. (est.) 1500; post office for Waimea.

Ka·mu·i (kä·mōō·ē), **Cape.** Cape on W coast of Hokkaido, Japan, W of entrance to Otaru Bay.

Ka·my′shin (kŭ·mĭ′shĭn). Town, N Stalingrad Region, Soviet Russia, Europe, on the Volga opp. Nikolaevski ab. 110 m. NNE of Stalingrad; pop. ab. 23,000; river port; terminus of railroad from Tambov.

Kan (gän). River ab. 350 m. long in Kiangsi prov., SE China, flows N through Poyang Hu (lake) into the Yangtze.

Kan (kän) *or* **Han** (hän). River ab. 220 m. long in cen. Korea, flowing WNW into Yellow Sea N of Jinsen.

Ka·nab′ (kȧ·năb′). City, ⊗ of Kane co., S Utah; pop. 1654.

Ka·na′bec (kȧ·nä′bĕk; kȧ·nô′-). County in Minnesota. See *Table* at MINNESOTA.

Ka′nab Plateau (kä′năb). Tableland 6000 ft. high in N Mohave co., NW Arizona, on NW border of Grand Canyon National Monument.

Ka·na′ga (kȧ·nä′gȧ). One of the Andreanof Is. in Aleutian Is., W of Adak I., SW Alaska.

Ka·na·ga·wa (kä·nä·gä·wä). **1** Prefecture of Japan. See *Table* at JAPAN.
2 Town, Kanagawa prefecture, Honshu, Japan, N suburb of Yokohama; pop. ab. 18,000; formerly an important port, now incorporated with Yokohama; treaty signed here Mar. 31, 1854 bet. U.S. and Japan, opening two ports to trade. See URAGA.

Kananur. See CANNANUR.

Ka′na·ra (kä′nȧ·rȧ). **1** *formerly* **North Kanara.** Former district, S Southern division, Bombay prov., W India; 3961 sq. m.; pop. (1941) 441,157; ✳ Karwar.
2 Kanara, South. See SOUTH KANARA.

Ka′na·tak (?kä′nä·täk). Village, SW Alaska, in Aleutian Range, on E coast of Alaska Penin. at S end of Shelikof Strait.

Ka·nauj′ (kȧ·nouj′). Town, Farrukhabad dist., SW cen. Uttar Pradesh, N Indian Union, on Ganges river 50 m. NW of Cawnpore; pop. 20,360; noted for perfumes. An ancient city, famous in early times; mentioned by Ptolemy; in 7th cent. reached height of its magnificence as capital of Harsha's kingdom; captured by Mahmud of Ghazni 1019 and came under Mohammedan sovereignty 1194; memorials of the Hindu age have completely disappeared.

Ka·na′wha (kȧ·nô′[w]ȧ; *also, local and colloq.,* -nô′ĭ). **1**

or **Great Kanawha.** Navigable river 97 m. long, W West Virginia; formed by junction of New and Gauley rivers in Fayette co., flows NW into the Ohio river.

2 County in West Virginia. See *Table* at WEST VIRGINIA.

Ka·na·za·wa (kä-nä-zä-wä). Seaport city * of Ishikawa prefecture, W Honshu, Japan, near coast of Sea of Japan; pop. (1938 est.) 191,600; during 300 years of feudalism the seat of one of the most powerful of daimios; scene of victory of Nobunaga over rebellious priests 1575; declined in prosperity after 1868 but has now become important industrially esp. in manufacture of habutai, lacquer, pottery, bronze ware.

Kan·cha·na·bu·ri (kän-boo-rē—*sic*). **1** Province, SW Siam; 7288 sq. m.; pop. 114,392.

2 Town, its *, 70 m. WNW of Bangkok on Klong river; lead, sapphire mines.

Kan·chen·jun·ga (kŭn'chĕn-jŭng'gȧ) *or* **Kin·chin·jun·ga** (kĭn'chĭn-jŭng'gȧ). Peak 28,146 ft. in the Himalayas, on boundary bet. Nepal and Sikkim state in NE India; 3d highest mountain in the world; fine view of it from Darjeeling.

Kanchipuram. See CONJEEVERAM.

Kanchow. See KANHSIEN.

Kan·da·gach (kän-dŭ-gäch'). Town, W Kazakh S.S.R., Soviet Russia, Asia, ab. 55 m. SSE of Aktyubinsk; railroad junction.

Kan'da·har (kän'dȧ-här; *native* kȧn-dȧ-här'). **1** A major province in SE Afghanistan.

2 *anc.* **Al'ex·an'dri·a Ar'a·cho'si·o'rum** (ăl'ĕg-zăn'drĭ-ȧ [-ĭg-] ăr'ȧ-kō'sĭ-ōr'ŭm). Commercial city, its *, 300 m. SW of Kabul; pop. ab. 32,000, with suburbs ab. 60,000; second city in size in the country; at elevation of 3400 ft., connected with Quetta over the Chaman Pass; has long been a great trading center both for imports and exports.

History: Held by Mogul Empire of India (*q.v.*) after its capture by Baber; captured 1625 by Shah Abbas I of Persia; center of successful Afghan rising against Persia 1706–08; independent until 1737; under Ahmad Shah (1747–73), one of the capitals of Afghanistan (*q.v.*); held by British 1839–42 and 1879–81; during the latter period its garrison relieved 1880 by memorable march of Gen. Frederick Roberts (later created Earl Roberts of Kandahar). See ARACHOSIA.

Kan·da·lak'sha (kän'dȧ-läk'shȧ; *Russ.* kȧn-dŭ-läk'-shä). Coast town, SW Murmansk Region, Soviet Russia, Europe, at head of Kandalaksha Gulf and on Leningrad-Murmansk railroad; pop. 7799; chief occupation fishing; military base in attack on Finland 1939–40.

Kandalaksha Gulf *or* **Bay.** Inlet of NW White Sea on NW coast of Soviet Russia, Europe, S and SW of Kola Penin., Murmansk Region.

Kan'dang·haoer' (kän'däng-hour') *or* **Kan'dang·haur'.** Town, West Java prov., Indonesia, ab. 40 m. NW of Cheribon; pop. 11,623.

Kan·da'vu (kän-dä'voo) *or* **Ka·da'vu** (kä-dä'-). One of the Fiji Is., in SW part of group, in SW Pacific Ocean; 32 m. long, area 165 sq. m.; almost cut in two by narrow isthmus at center; mountainous and fertile, but undeveloped.

Kandavu Passage. Channel ab. 38 m. wide in Fiji Is., bet. Viti Levu I. on N and Kandavu I. on S.

Kan'der·steg (kän'dĕr-shtāк). Town, S Bern canton, Switzerland; pop. 3554; health resort, winter sports center.

Kan'dı·ra' (kän'dĭ-rä'). Town, Kocaeli vilayet, NW Turkey in Asia, near Black Sea coast 25 m. NW of Adapazari; pop. 2450.

Kan'di·yo·hi' (kän'dĭ-yȯ-hī'). County in Minnesota. See *Table* at MINNESOTA.

Kan'dy (kän'dĭ). Town, * of Central Province, Ceylon, on Mahaweli river 60 m. ENE of Colombo; pop. 37,147; in midst of beautiful mountain and lake scenery; last capital of ancient kings of Ceylon; contains Buddhist and Brahman temples, including Dalada Maligawa, the world's most sacred Buddhist temple; has official residence of governor of Ceylon, palaces of ancient kingdoms, and crypts and tombs of ancient rulers and heroes; famous botanical gardens at Peradeniya, 3 m. SW. Held briefly by Dutch 1763; taken over 1802 by British who gained permanent control 1814–15; in World War II became headquarters of Admiral Lord Louis Mountbatten Apr. 1944.

Kane (kān). **1** Name of counties in two states of the U.S. See *Tables* at ILLINOIS and UTAH.

2 Borough and resort, McKean co., N Pennsylvania, 23 m. SSW of Bradford; pop. 5380; founded 1859; manufactures wood products, toys, textiles, wire glass; oil, gas, silica deposits.

Kanea. = CANEA.

Kane Basin (kān). Section of the channel bet. E Ellesmere I. and NW Greenland, N of Baffin Bay, 79°N.

Ka'nem (kä'nĕm). Former protected state NE of Lake Chad, Chad territory, French Equatorial Africa; 22,000 sq. m.; pop. ab. 100,000; chief town Mao; a native state founded 9th cent.; became Mohammedan 11th cent. and reached height of its power 300 years later; became subject to Bornu 13th cent. forming with it a strong native empire until 19th cent.; for a time subject to Wadai; since 1958 part of Republic of Chad.

Ka'ne·o'he (kä'nȧ-ō'hȧ). Town, Koolaupoko dist., Honolulu co., Hawaii, on **Kaneohe Bay,** wide inlet on E coast of Oahu I. N of Honolulu; pop. 14,414; missile-tracking station.

Kanesh. See KANISH.

Kan'gar (käng'gär). Town, * of Perlis state, Federation of Malaya, near coast 25 m. NNW of Alor Star; pop. 2010.

Kan'ga·roo' Island (kăng'gȧ-roo'). Island S of Yorke Penin. at entrance to Gulf of St. Vincent, South Australia; 85 m. long, area 1970 sq. m.; pop. ab. 1000.

Kan'ga·var' (käng'gä-vȧr'). Town, W Iran, ab. 40 m. SW of Hamadan; pop. ab. 5000; on a main highway; in a fertile region at altitude of 6000 ft.

Kang'e·an (käng'ȧ-än). **1** Island group of Indonesia, in Java Sea 80 m. E of Madura; 258 sq. m.; pop. 40,743.

2 Largest island of the group; 188 sq. m.

Kan'gra (käng'grȧ). Town, NE Punjab state, NW Indian Union, ab. 14 m. SW of Dharmsala; important in early Indian history.

Kang'ting' (käng'dĭng'); *formerly* **Ta'tsien'lu'** (dä'-jĭ-ĕn'loo'). City, * of Sikang prov., S China, in a narrow valley of the Tatsienlu river (tributary of the Min), at altitude 8500 ft., 260 m. W of Chungking; pop. ab. 20,000; near the Szechwan border on trade routes from China to N Sikang and Kashgar and to Tibet and India; N of Minya Konka. Formerly a Chinese administrative center for Tibetan affairs; became capital of new province of Sikang 1928.

Kang'to' (käng'tō'). Mountain peak 23,260 ft., E Himalayas, on border bet. Assam and SE Tibet.

Kan'hsien' (gän'shĭ-ĕn'); *formerly* **Kan'chow'** (gän'-jō'). Town, S Kiangsi prov., SE China, on upper Kan river ab. 200 m. NNE of Canton; in World War II site of American air base; taken by Japanese 1945, retaken by Chinese July 15, 1945.

Kan'ia·pis'kau (kän'yȧ-pĭs'kou). River 445 m. long, New Quebec dist., N Quebec prov., Canada; flows from **Lake Kaniapiskau** (441 sq. m., in 54°N, 69°W) in cen. Quebec prov., N to unite with the Larch river and form Koksoak river.

Ka'ni·gu'ram (kŭ'nĭ-goor'ȧm). Chief town of the Wazirs, cen. South Waziristan, in former North-West Frontier Province, Pakistan, NE of Wana and ab. 80 m. NW of Dera Ismail Khan.

Ka'nin Peninsula (kȧ'nyĭn). Peninsula projecting into Barents Sea on N coast of Nenets National District, Soviet Russia, Europe, having Cheshskaya Bay on E and entrance to White Sea on W; its NW extremity is **Kanin Point.**

Ka'nish (kä'nĭsh) *or* **Ka'nesh** (-nĕsh). Ancient city of E cen. Asia Minor, home of a branch (Kaneshite) of the Hittites; now the village of **Kul'te·pe'** (kōōl'tĕ·pĕ'), an archaeological site SW of Kayseri and W of Erciyas Daği; mines of area supplied silver to Assyria 1900 B.C.

Kan'ka·kee' (kăng'kà·kē'). **1** River 225 m. long, rising in N Indiana and flowing SW and W to unite with the Des Plaines in NE Illinois and form the Illinois river. **2** County in Illinois. See *Table* at ILLINOIS. **3** City, ⊗ of Kankakee co., NE Illinois, 32 m. SSE of Joliet; pop. 27,666; ships grain and livestock; manufactures furniture, farm implements, stoves; limestone quarries; Olivet Nazarene College (1907; coed.).

Kan'kan' (kän'kän'). Town in E Guinea, W Africa; terminus of railroad from Conakry; highway junction point.

Kan'ker (käng'kĕr). Former Indian state, Eastern States, N of Bastar state, NE Indian Union; now in E Madhya Pradesh; 1413 sq. m.; pop. (1941) 149,471; ✳ Kanker (pop. 5305).

Kan·ko (kän·kō) *or* **Ham·hung** (häm·hōŏng). City, ✳ of South Kankyo prov., NE Korea, 10 m. from coast ab. 52 m. N of Genzan; pop. (1938 est.) 63,859; its port is Seikoshin.

Kankyo Hoku; Kankyo Nan. See NORTH KANKYO; SOUTH KANKYO.

Kan·nap'o·lis (kă·năp'ô·lĭs; -năp'lĭs). Unincorporated town, Cabarrus and Rowan cos., S cen. North Carolina, ab. 7 m. N of Concord; pop. 34,647; manufactures esp. towels, blankets, sheets.

Kannstatt. See CANNSTATT.

Ka'no (kä'nō). **1** Province of Nigeria. See *Table* at NIGERIA. **2** Commercial walled city, its ✳; pop. (with township) 97,031; on railroad in N cen. Nigeria 500 m. NE of Lagos; has extensive trade in native manufactured goods, agricultural products, and livestock; center of caravan routes; inhabitants chiefly Hausa, with a considerable number of Fulahs. Known to Arab geographers in 12th cent.; figured prominently as center of a Hausa state in Negro wars in 15th–16th cents.; early converted to Mohammedanism; conquered by Fulahs c. 1800; visited by H. Barth 1851 and 1854; became British 1903.

Ka·no·ya (kä·nō·yä). City, Kagoshima prefecture, S Kyushu, Japan, on E side of Kagoshima Bay 22 m. SE of Kagoshima; pop. (1945) 51,558.

Kan'pur (kän'pōōr). = CAWNPORE.

Kan·ra (kän·rä); *Jap.* **Kan·ra·san** (kän·rä·sän). An extinct volcano 6388 ft. on Saishu I., in East China Sea off S coast of Korea.

Kan·san'shi (kän·sän'shĕ). Town, N Kasempa prov., NW Northern Rhodesia, S cen. Africa, 260 m. NW of Lusaka near Congo border; pop. (white) 110; extensive copper deposits.

Kan'sas (kăn'zăs). **1** *in Kansas usu. called* **Kaw** (kô). River 169 m. long, E Kansas; formed by confluence of Republican and Smoky Hill rivers at Junction City, Geary co., flows E into Missouri river at Kansas City. **2** A central state of U.S.A., 34th state admitted to Union (1861); bounded on N by Nebraska, on E by Missouri, on S by Oklahoma, on W by Colorado; 14th state in area, 82,276 sq. m. (land area 82,108 sq. m.); 28th state in population, 2,178,611; ✳ Topeka. See *Map*, p. 535; also *Table of States* at UNITED STATES. Divided into the following 105 counties (for pronunciation of their names, see their individual entries):

NAME	LOCATION	AREA[1]	POP.[1]	CO. SEAT
Allen	SE	505	16,369	Iola
Anderson	E	577	9,035	Garnett
Atchison	NE	421	20,898	Atchison
Barber	S	1,146	8,713	Medicine Lodge
Barton	cen.	892	32,368	Great Bend
Bourbon	SE	639	16,090	Fort Scott
Brown	NE	578	13,229	Hiawatha
Butler	S	1,445	38,395	El Dorado
Chase	E cen.	774	3,921	Cottonwood Falls

NAME	LOCATION	AREA[1]	POP.[1]	CO. SEAT
Chautauqua	SE	647	5,956	Sedan
Cherokee	SE corner	587	22,279	Columbus
Cheyenne	NW corner	1,027	4,708	Saint Francis
Clark	S	984	3,396	Ashland
Clay	NE cen.	658	10,675	Clay Center
Cloud	N	711	14,407	Concordia
Coffey	E	655	8,403	Burlington
Comanche	S	800	3,271	Coldwater
Cowley	S	1,135	37,861	Winfield
Crawford	SE	598	37,032	Girard
Decatur	NW	899	5,778	Oberlin
Dickinson	E cen.	855	21,572	Abilene
Doniphan	NE corner	391	9,574	Troy
Douglas	E	468	43,720	Lawrence
Edwards	SW cen.	614	5,118	Kinsley
Elk	SE	647	5,048	Howard
Ellis	cen.	900	21,270	Hays
Ellsworth	cen.	718	7,677	Ellsworth
Finney	W	1,302	16,093	Garden City
Ford	S	1,083	20,938	Dodge City
Franklin	E	577	19,548	Ottawa
Geary	NE cen.	399	28,779	Junction City
Gove	W	1,070	4,107	Gove
Graham	NW cen.	891	5,586	Hill City
Grant	SW	568	5,269	Ulysses
Gray	SW	869	4,380	Cimarron
Greeley	W	783	2,087	Tribune
Greenwood	SE	1,150	11,253	Eureka
Hamilton	W	992	3,144	Syracuse
Harper	S	801	9,541	Anthony
Harvey	SE cen.	540	25,865	Newton
Haskell	SW	579	2,990	Sublette
Hodgeman	SW cen.	860	3,115	Jetmore
Jackson	NE	655	10,309	Holton
Jefferson	NE	549	11,252	Oskaloosa
Jewell	N	915	7,217	Mankato
Johnson	E	476	143,792	Olathe
Kearny	W	853	3,108	Lakin
Kingman	S cen.	865	9,958	Kingman
Kiowa	S	720	4,626	Greensburg
Labette	SE	654	26,805	Oswego
Lane	W	720	3,060	Dighton
Leavenworth	NE	465	48,524	Leavenworth
Lincoln	cen.	726	5,556	Lincoln
Linn	E	607	8,274	Mound City
Logan	W	1,073	4,036	Russell Springs
Lyon	E	852	26,928	Emporia
McPherson	cen.	895	24,285	McPherson
Marion	E cen.	959	15,143	Marion
Marshall	NE	911	15,598	Marysville
Meade	SW	976	5,505	Meade
Miami	E	592	19,884	Paola
Mitchell	N cen.	716	8,866	Beloit
Montgomery	SE	649	45,007	Independence
Morris	E cen.	707	7,392	Council Grove
Morton	SW corner	725	3,354	Richfield
Nemaha	NE	709	12,897	Seneca
Neosho	SE	587	19,455	Erie
Ness	W cen.	1,081	5,470	Ness City
Norton	N	880	8,035	Norton
Osage	E	721	12,886	Lyndon
Osborne	N cen.	898	7,506	Osborne
Ottawa	NE cen.	723	6,779	Minneapolis
Pawnee	cen.	749	10,254	Larned
Phillips	N	906	8,709	Phillipsburg
Pottawatomie	NE	850	11,957	Westmoreland
Pratt	S cen.	729	12,122	Pratt
Rawlins	NW	1,078	5,279	Atwood
Reno	cen.	1,255	59,055	Hutchinson
Republic	N	719	9,768	Belleville
Rice	cen.	721	13,909	Lyons
Riley	NE cen.	624	41,914	Manhattan
Rooks	N	893	9,734	Stockton
Rush	cen.	724	6,160	La Crosse
Russell	cen.	897	11,348	Russell
Saline	cen.	720	54,715	Salina
Scott	W	723	5,228	Scott City
Sedgwick	S cen.	999	343,231	Wichita
Seward	SW	639	15,930	Liberal
Shawnee	NE	545	141,286	Topeka
Sheridan	NW	893	4,267	Hoxie
Sherman	NW	1,055	6,682	Goodland
Smith	N	893	7,776	Smith Center
Stafford	cen.	794	7,451	Saint John
Stanton	SW	676	2,108	Johnson
Stevens	SW	729	4,400	Hugoton
Sumner	S	1,183	25,316	Wellington
Thomas	NW	1,070	7,358	Colby
Trego	W cen.	901	5,473	Wakeeney
Wabaunsee	E	791	6,648	Alma
Wallace	W	911	2,069	Sharon Springs
Washington	N	891	10,739	Washington
Wichita	W	724	2,765	Leoti
Wilson	SE	574	13,077	Fredonia
Woodson	SE	504	5,423	Yates Center
Wyandotte	NE	151	185,495	Kansas City

[1] Area = land area in sq. m. Pop. from 1960 Census.

Nickname: Sunflower State; also Jayhawker State. *State flower:* Sunflower. *Motto:* Ad Astra per Aspera (To the Stars by Hard Ways). *Chief cities:* Wichita, Kansas City, Topeka, Salina, Hutchinson. *Rivers:* in S the Arkansas, flowing from W border E to cen. area and then S across border into Oklahoma; in N, also flowing W to E, the Saline and Solomon rivers, tributaries of the Smoky Hill river which joins the Republican river from the N to form Kansas river (see 1, above). *Highest point:* 4135 ft., on W border in Wallace co. *Chief industries:* Agriculture, stock raising.

History: Probably entered by Coronado's expedition 1540; the greater part came to U.S. as part of Louisiana Purchase (*q.v.*) 1803; by Kansas-Nebraska Act 1854, organized as territory which was to become free or slave state on basis of popular sovereignty (repeal of Missouri Compromise of 1820); scene of virtual civil war bet. rival slave and free interests 1854-56; adopted constitution 1859; admitted to Union as free state Jan. 29, 1861.

Kansas City. 1 Industrial city, ⊗ of Wyandotte co., NE Kansas, at confluence of Kansas and Missouri rivers, separated from Kansas City, Missouri, by state line; 2d largest city in state; pop. 121,901; stockyards, packing houses, and large grain-storage facilities, soap factories, steel and flour mills, oil refineries; oil wells, sand and limestone deposits nearby; railroad center. First settled by Wyandot Indians 1843; sold to federal government 1855; settled by whites 1857; modern city formed 1886 by consolidation of a number of adjoining towns. **2** City, Jackson co., W Missouri, on S bank of Missouri river on Kansas-Missouri state line adjoining Kansas City, Kansas; pop. 475,539; 2d largest city in state; railroad, industrial, and commercial center; stockyards and packing houses; hay, grain, horse, and mule market; steel plants, oil refineries, flour and lumber mills, agricultural machinery works; University of Kansas City (1929; coed.), Rockhurst Coll. (1910; men). Permanent settlement dates from 1821 when trading post established within present boundaries of city by the Chouteaus, fur traders; city grew out of settlements of Westport, founded 1833, and Westport Landing (on the river 4 m. N), which became busy port for river traffic; Town of Kansas, laid out 1838, developed after 1846; name changed to City of Kansas 1853 and to Kansas City 1889.

Kansk (kånsk). Industrial city, S Krasnoyarsk Territory, Soviet Russia, Asia, on a tributary of the Yenisei and on Trans-Siberian R.R. 110 m. E of Krasnoyarsk; pop. 14,000; near lignite deposits and iron fields. Founded 1628.

Kan'su' (kän'sōō'; *Chin.* gän'sōō'). Province of N cen. China, the NW province of China Proper; 145,930 sq. m.; pop. (1936 est.) 6,705,446; ✳ Lanchow; forms a long narrow wedge bet. Ningsia on N and Tsinghai on S, touching Shensi on E, Szechwan on SE, and Sinkiang on W. Crossed by the upper Hwang Ho from SW to NE, whose tributaries and the Hwei (in N cen. part) afford valleys for highways. Mountainous, includes N ranges of Nan Shan in W (20,000 ft.) and E extension (Min Shan) of Kunlun Mts. in S (17,000 ft.); at lower levels characterized by sandy plains and (esp. in the E) by rich loess terraces. Great part of it traversed by W end of Great Wall, with its branches. Least Chinese in population of all the provinces; about ⅓ of inhabitants Moslems, many are of aboriginal tribes. For years chief opium-producing province; now has agricultural, cattle-raising, and mining potentialities. Chief towns Lanchow, Kiuchuan, Pingliang, Tienshui, Ansi. Served as corridor for great highway to the W, the old Silk Road (*q.v.*)—to Turkistan, India, Persia; much traveled in early and medieval times and in recent years the main war supply and trade route with Russia. In early times outside China Proper; for several centuries a part of the kingdom of Wei; came under Kublai Khan in 13th cent.; under the Mings a part of Shensi; made a separate province 1911; suffered from great earthquake 1920.

Kan'tang' (kän'täng'). Village and port on W coast of Malay Penin., SW Thailand, 85 m. SE of Phuket; port for Trang.

Kantara, El. See EL KANTARA.

Kan'ta·ra·wa'di (kän'tȧ·rȧ·wä'dē). Native state, E Karenni, E Burma; 3161 sq. m.; pop. 30,677.

Kan·tish'na (kǎn·tǐsh'nȧ). Village, S cen. Alaska, on N border of Mt. McKinley National Park.

Kan'ye or **Kan'ya** (kän'yȧ). Town, Bechuanaland Protectorate, cen. South Africa, 70 m. NNW of Mafeking; pop. ab. 12,000; capital of the Bangwaketsi tribe.

Kao'hsiung' (gou'shyŏong'). City, Formosa: see TAKAO.

Kao'ko·veld' (kou'kō·fĕlt'). Mountain range, NW South-West Africa, parallel to coast just E of Namib Desert.

Ka'o·lack or **Ka'o·lak** (kä'ō·lȧk; kou'lȧk). Town, W Senegal, West Africa, ab. 90 m. SE of Dakar on the Salum river; pop. (1942) 26,844.

Kaolan. See LANCHOW.

Kao Luang. See KHAO LUANG.

Kao'mi' (kou'mē'). Town, E cen. Shantung prov., NE China, on railroad 40 m. NW of Tsingtao.

Ka·pa'a (kä·pä'ä). Town, Kawaihau dist., E coast of Kauai I., Hawaii, N of Lihue; pop. 3439.

Kapaau–Halaula. See KOHALA.

Ká'pe·la, Cape (kä'pȧ·lä) Southern point of Cerigo, one of the Ionian Is. off the SE coast of Peloponnesus, Greece.

Ka·pe'la, Great *and* **Little** (kä·pĕ'lä). Mountain ranges in Croatia, Yugoslavia, extending from NW to SE parallel with the coast; on E edge of the Karst plateau; highest peak ab. 4600 ft.

Ka'pen·gu'ri·a (kä'pĕn·gōōr'ī·ȧ). Town, NW Kenya colony, E Africa, W of Lake Rudolf; ✳ of Turkana extra-provincial dist.

Kap'fen·berg (käp'fĕn·bĕrк). Commune, Styria prov., Austria, near Bruck 25 m. N of Graz; pop. 11,202; summer resort; manufactures iron goods, paper, chamotte ware, crucibles.

Kaphērevs. See CAPHAREUS

Kapıdağı. See CYZICUS peninsula.

Ka'pi·la·vas'tu (kŭ'pĭ·lȧ·vŭs'tōō). Principality and town in ancient India; site ab. 27°37'N, 83°11'E, near Paderia, S Nepal, and N of Gorakhpur, Indian Union; birthplace of Gautama Buddha, the Sakya Prince Siddhartha.

Ka'pi·ti Island (kä'pĭ·tē) Small island off SW coast of North I., New Zealand, at N end of Cook Strait; bird sanctuary.

Kap'lan (kăp'lăn). Town, Vermilion parish, S Louisiana, 23 m. SW of Lafayette; pop. 5267; rice mills; ships rice, cotton, poultry, eggs.

Ka'poe·as (kä'pōō·äs) or **Ka'pu·as.** River ab. 450 m. long in West Borneo, Indonesia; rises in mountains of N cen. Borneo and flows W into South China Sea at Pontianak near the equator; navigable for small steamers for over 300 m.

Kapoeas, or **Kapuas, Mountains.** Range in W cen. Borneo, Malay Archipelago, extending E and W along boundary bet. SE Sarawak and West Borneo; highest point ab. 5797 ft.

Ká'pol·na (kä'pōl·nŏ'). Town, cen. Hungary, SW of Eger; pop. (1920) 1840; scene of battle Feb. 26-27, 1849 in which Austrians under Windisch-Graetz defeated Hungarians under Dembiński.

Ka'pos·vár' (kŏ'pōsh·vär'). City, SW Hungary, 30 m. S of Lake Balaton; pop. 29,542; market center in livestock-raising region; cathedral.

Kap'pel (käp'ĕl). Village, Zurich canton, NE cen. Switzerland; scene of battle (bet. Zurichers and the Catholic cantons) in which Zwingli was killed Oct. 11, 1531.

Kaproncza. See KOPRIVNICA.

Ka'pu·dzhikh' (kä'pōō·jĭk'). Mountain 12,851 ft., SW Azerbaidzhan, U.S.S.R. on E border of Nakhichevan A.S.S.R.

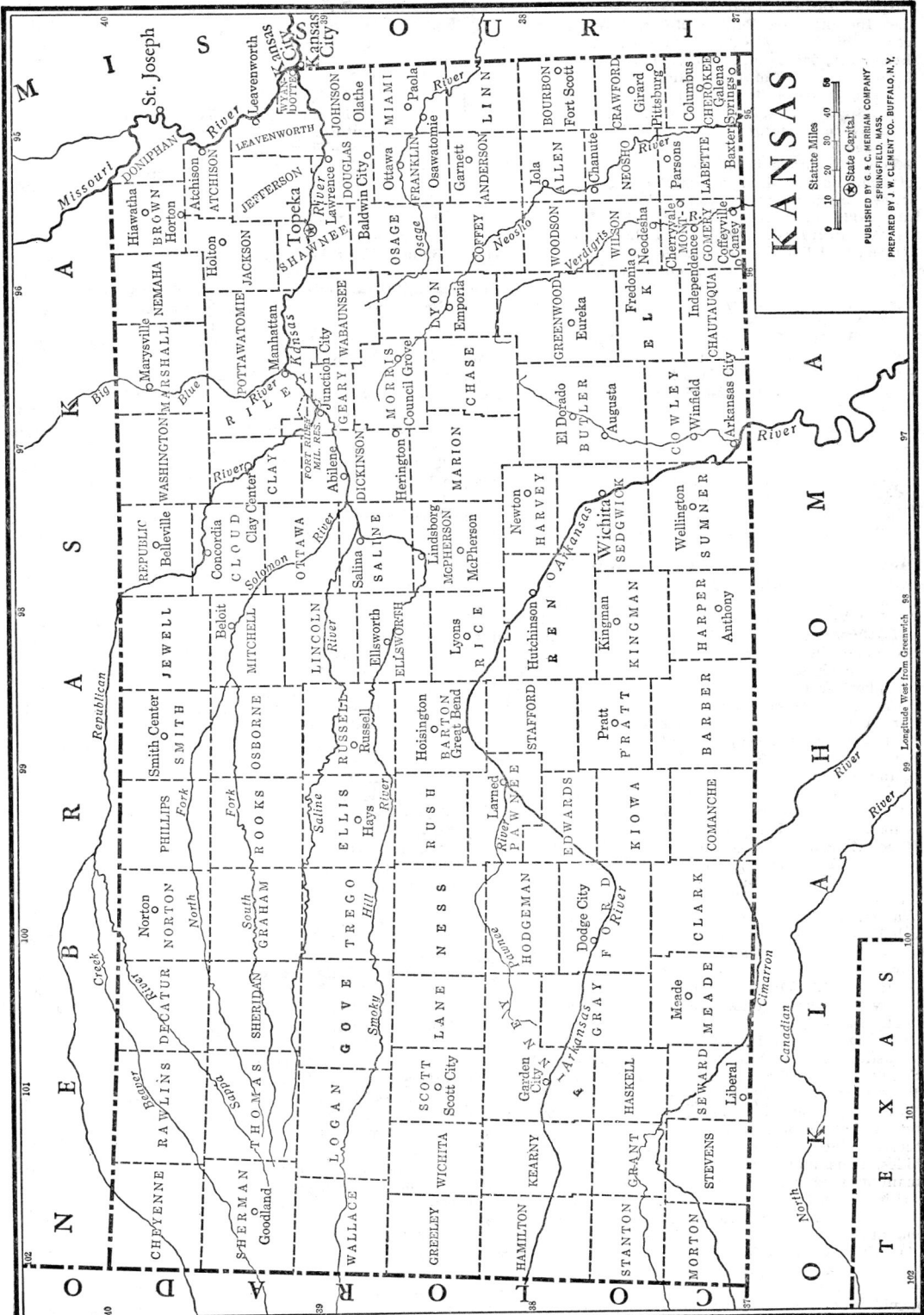

KANSAS

Statute Miles

⊛ State Capital

PUBLISHED BY G. & C. MERRIAM COMPANY
SPRINGFIELD, MASS.
PREPARED BY J. W. CLEMENT CO. BUFFALO, N.Y.

Ka·pur'tha·la (kā·pŏŏr'tȧ·lȧ; *native* -pŏŏrt'hȧ-). **1** Former Indian state, Punjab States, NW Indian Union, geographically in W Punjab state, India, on left bank of Beas river; 645 sq. m.; pop. (1941) 378,380.
2 Town, its ✱, 62 m. E of Lahore; pop. 20,210; includes spacious palace of the maharaja; seat of Rundhir College.
Kap'us·ka'sing (kăp'ŭs·kā'sĭng). **1** River ab. 180 m. long, N cen. Ontario prov., Canada; flows N to the Mattagami.
2 Town, Cochrane dist., E Ontario, Canada, 80 m. NNW of Timmins; pop. 4687; on transcontinental railroad; has large dominion experimental station.
Ka'ra (kä'rä). River in NW Iran. See QARA SU.
Ka'ra (kä'rä; *Russ.* kȧ'rȧ). River ab. 140 m. long, Soviet Russia, E of Pai Khoi Penin., flowing N from Ural Mts. into Kara Sea; in part forms boundary bet. the national districts of Nenets and Yamalo-Nenets.
Karabakh Mountain Area. See NAGORNO-KARABAKH AUTONOMOUS REGION.
Ka·ra' Bo·gaz' Gol (kä·rä' bô·äz' gûl'). Large shallow gulf, an inlet of E Caspian Sea, on coast of Turkmen S.S.R. Soviet Russia, Asia; ab. 100 m. long by 85 m. wide; almost entirely enclosed on W by narrow strip of sand.
Ka·ra' Bu·run' *or* **Ka·ra'bu·run'** (kä·rä'bŏŏ·rŏŏn'). Name of several capes or points (Turk. *burun* cape) on the coast of Turkey in Asia, esp.: (1) on SW shore of Sea of Marmara; (2) on E shore of Gulf of Antalya, S Turkey; (3) on Black Sea coast just E of the Bosporus (Karadeniz Boğazı).
Ka·ra·ca·dağ' (kä·rä·jä·dä'). Peak 6070 ft. in SE Turkey in Asia, SW of Diyarbekir.
Ka·ra·cha'ev (kä·rŭ·chä'yĕf), *or* **Ka·ra·chai'** (kä·rŭ·chī'), **Autonomous Region.** Former autonomous region, SE Soviet Russia, Europe, on N slope of Caucasus Mts. at W end; 3821 sq. m.; pop. 149,925, (1941 est.) 157,540; ✱ Mikoyan Shakhar (now Klukhori); a subdivision of the R.S.F.S.R.; bounded on S by Georgia and on W by Krasnodar Territory. Mountainous, along S boundary several peaks over 10,000 ft.; traversed by Kuban river whose headstreams are in mountains in S part. Chief occupation sheep raising; also some dairying. No towns except the capital, and no railroads. Predominant ethnic strain Turko-Tatar; its inhabitants chiefly Karachaevs (83% of population), who came from the Crimea 15th cent. and after much wandering and racial intermixture, esp. with the Cherkess, settled in upper Kuban valley. Part of Mountain Republic after the Revolution; united with the Cherkess Autonomous Region 1922–26; given separate administration 1926 and its new capital, Mikoyan Shakhar established 1927; made autonomous region 1936; abolished (1943) during World War II, N half incorporated in Stavropol Territory and S half absorbed by Georgian S.S.R.
Ka·ra·chev' (kä·rŭ·chôf'). Town, cen. Orel Region, Soviet Russia, Europe, on railroad bet. Bryansk and Orel; pop. 12,000; in World War II held by Germans nearly three years, retaken by Russians in fierce fighting Sept. 1943.
Ka·ra'chi (kȧ·rä'chĭ). City and seaport, SW Sind, W Pakistan, former ✱ of Pakistan, on arm of Arabian Sea just NW of the mouths of the Indus, 550 m. NW of Bombay; pop. 247,791, with military cantonment (1951) 1,126,400; principal seaport of Pakistan; important international airport; trade and distribution center for extensive hinterland; exports wheat, grain, raw cotton, hides, skins, and raw wool; imports steel goods, cotton manufactures, and sugar. Founded c. 1725; became British 1843.
Ka·ra·dağ' *or* **Ka'ra Dağ** (kä'rä·dä'). Name of several mountains (Turk. *dağ* mountain) in Turkey in Asia, esp.: (1) In S, peak 7451 ft. near W end of Taurus Mts. and SE of Konya. (2) In SE, peak 11,909 ft. in mountains of Kurdistan, SE of Lake Van. (3) Peak 9682 ft. in Armenia N of Aras (Araks) river and SE of Kars.

Karadeniz Boğazı. See BOSPORUS.
Karaferieh. See VEROIA.
Ka·ra'fu·to' (kä·rä'fŭ·tō'). **1** Japanese name of Sakhalin I.
2 Former Japanese possession comprising S half of Sakhalin I., S of 50°N lat.; ab. 13,931 sq. m.; pop. (1938 est.) 339,357; chief towns Toyohara (administrative center), Esutoru, Shikuka, Otomari; since 1946 belongs to Russia. See SAKHALIN island.
Ka'ra·gach' (kä'rä·[g]äch'). Town, NW Turkey in Europe, SW suburb of Edirne (Adrianople) S of Maritsa river.
Ka·ra·gan·da' (kä'rä·gän·dä'). City, ✱ of Karaganda Region, Kazakh S.S.R., Soviet Central Asia, on railroad 135 m. SSE of Akmolinsk; pop. 165,937; large coal beds in vicinity.
Karaganda Region. Large subdivision, cen. Kazakh S.S.R., Soviet Central Asia, NW of Lake Balkhash; ✱ Karaganda; extensive steppe region.
Ka·ra'gin (kŭ·rä'gĭn). Island, W Bering Sea, ab. 30 m. off E coast of N Kamchatka Penin., Soviet Russia, Asia; highest point 3140 ft.; formerly in Khabarovsk Territory, now attached to Koryak National District.
Ka·ra·his·sar' (kä'rä·hĭ·sär'); *mod.* **Şe·bin'ka·ra·hi·sar'** (shĕ·bēn'-). Town, Giresun vilayet, NE Turkey in Asia, ab. 63 m. NW of Erzincan; pop. 7667; altitude 4860 ft.; built around a citadel. In early days a Roman colony; later a Byzantine frontier station not taken by Turks until 1465.
Ka·rai'ku·di *or* **Ka·raik'ku·di** (kä·rī'kŏŏ·dĭ). Town, SE Madras, S Indian Union, 38 m. ESE of Madura; pop. 21,672.
Ka'ra–Kal'pak' (kä'rä–käl·päk'), *officially* **Kara-Kalpak Autonomous Soviet Socialist Republic.** An autonomous area in NW part of Uzbek S.S.R., SE of Lake Aral and N of the Khiva oasis along right bank of the Amu Darya and in the delta; 79,631 sq. m.; pop. 303,470; ✱ Nukus (former ✱ Chimbai). Much of it desert (SW part of the Kyzyl Kum) but has fertile regions along the river. About ⅓ of population is Kara-Kalpak, a tribe allied to the Kazak Kirghiz, an agricultural people. Chief towns Chimbai, Turtkul, Nukus. First became Russian 1867 as a part of Turkistan; made autonomous 1932.
Karakash. See QARA QASH.
Ka·ra·ke'long (kä'rä·kā'lŏng). Chief island of the Talaud Is., NE of Celebes, Indonesia; ab. 41 m. long by 15 m. wide; chief town Beo on W coast.
Ka'ra·kho'to (kä'rä·kō'tō) *or* **Kha'ra Kho'to** (kä'-). Ruined town, N Ningsia prov., W Inner Mongolia, N China, on E edge of Etsin river valley and on S edge of Gobi desert; discovered 1909, with its valuable library of 2500 volumes, by Russian scientist Pëtr Kozlov; formerly a great trade center, possibly the Etzina of Marco Polo.
Karakol. See PRZHEVALSK.
Kar'a·ko'ram Pass (kär'ȧ·kōr'ȧm). Pass through Karakoram Range, NE Kashmir, N India, E of Mount Godwin Austen; alt. 18,290 ft.; has long been the chief route over the Himalayas bet. Kashmir and China.
Karakoram, *or* **Karakorum, Range.** Mountain range in N Kashmir, N India, extending E into Tibet along S border of Sinkiang; highest peak Godwin Austen 28,250 ft.; has approximately 60 peaks at ab. 22,000 ft.
Kar'a·ko'rum (kär'ȧ·kōr'ŭm); *Chin.* **Ho'lin'** (hŭ'lĭn').
1 Ruins of ancient ✱ of Mongolia on right bank of upper Orkhon, ab. 47°N, 103°E, 200 m. WSW of Urga; at first a Mongol camp, established by Genghis Khan as his capital early in 13th cent.; rebuilt and palace erected by Ogadai, his son and successor (1229–41); deserted by Kublai Khan for new capital at Khanbalik (Marco Polo's Cambaluc, *mod.* Peiping) 1267; visited by Marco Polo c. 1275; later destroyed.
2 Ruins of earlier city, ✱ of Uigur kingdom 8th to 12th cent., 15 to 20 m. NW on left bank of the Orkhon.

Ka′ra Kul *or* **Qa′ra Kul** (kä′rä kûl′). Lake ab. 130 sq. m., alt. 13,200 ft., on Pamir plateau, NE Gorno-Badakhshan Region, E Tadzhik S.S.R., Soviet Central Asia.

Ka′ra Kum *or* **Qa′ra Qum** (kä′rä kŏŏm′). Literally "the Black Desert," a desert area 110,000 sq. m., S of Lake Aral, including most of Turkmen S.S.R. and stretching from the Caspian to the Amu Darya on the E, Soviet Central Asia.

Ka′ra·man′ (kä′rä·män′); *anc.* **La·ran′da** (lȧ·răn′dȧ). Town, SE Konya vilayet, SW cen. Turkey in Asia, on railroad 62 m. SE of Konya; pop. 9061; renowned for its castle and mosques; early history obscure; became seat of Isaurian pirates; in 13th cent. made capital of an independent Armenian state, **Karaman** or **Kar′a·ma′ni·a** (kăr′ȧ·mä′nĭ·ȧ; -män′yȧ), long at war with various Asiatic states, overcome by Ottoman Turks under Mohammed II 1473.

Ka′ra·me′a Bight (kä′rȧ·mā′ȧ). Wide gulf on NW coast of South I., New Zealand, bet. Rocks Point and Cape Foulwind.

Karan. See KHARAN.

Ka′rang (kä′räng). Mountain 5833 ft. of W Java, Indonesia, near Sunda Strait.

Ka′rang·sem·boeng′ (kä′räng·sĕm·bŏŏng′) *or* **Ka′rang·sem·bung′.** Town, West Java prov., Indonesia, just S of Cheribon; pop. 16,634.

Ka·ran′ja (kä·rŭn′jä). Island on E side of entrance to Bombay Harbor, on W coast of India.

Ka′ra Sea (kär′ȧ; *Russ.* kä′rȧ). Arm of Arctic Ocean extending E of Novaya Zemlya and off coasts of Taimyr, Yamalo-Nenets, and Nenets National Districts, Soviet Russia; has many small islands; frozen much of the year.

Karashahr. See QARA SHAHR.

Ka′ra·si (kä′rä·sē′). A sanjak or district of the Ottoman Empire, NW Turkey in Asia, bordering on Sea of Marmara and Aegean Sea.

Ka′ra Strait (kär′ȧ; *Russ.* kä′rȧ). Strait ab. 35 m. wide connecting Kara Sea with Barents Sea bet. Novaya Zemlya and Vaigach I., Nenets National District, Soviet Russia, Europe.

Ka′ra Su (kä′rä sŏŏ′). **1** River in SW Bulgaria and NW Greece. See MESTA.

2 *also* **Western Euphrates.** River in E Turkey in Asia, the main headstream of the Euphrates; rises in mountains of Armenia N of Erzurum and flows W and S to unite with the Murat Suyu (or Eastern Euphrates) and continue as the Euphrates river (*q.v.*).

Ka′ra·su′ba·zar′ (kä′rä·sŏŏ′bä·zär′). Town, S cen. Crimea, Soviet Russia, Europe, NE of Simferopol; pop. 7625.

Ka′ra·ta′la (kä′rȧ·tä′lȧ). Volcano 7874 ft. on S Great Comoro I., Comoro Is., N Mozambique Channel, NW of Madagascar; eruptions 1830, 1855, 1858, 1904.

Ka·ra·tsu (kä·rä·tsŏŏ). Seaport city, Saga prefecture, NW Kyushu, Japan; pop. (1945) 44,414; coal fields.

Ka·rau′li (kȧ·rou′lĭ). **1** Former Indian state, Eastern Rajputana States, India; 1227 sq. m.; pop. (1941) 152,413; bordered on Gwalior on NW and was separated from Gwalior on SE by Chambal river. Founded in 11th cent.; for a time under Mogul emperors and Marathas; taken under British protection 1817; joined Union of Rajasthan, 1947.

2 Town, its *, 85 m. SE of Jaipur; pop. 19,671.

Kara Usu Nur. = KHARA USU NUR.

Ka′ra·wan′ken (kä′rä·väng′kĕn). See *Table* at ALPS.

Kar′ba·la (kär′bȧ·lȧ; *Arab.* kŭr′bä·lä). **1** Province (*liwa*), cen. Iraq; pop. (1935 est.) 124,290.

2 *or* **Ker′be·la** (kŭr′bĕ·lä; *Arab.* kŭr′bĕ·lä). Town, cen. Iraq, 55 m. SSW of Baghdad, on edge of the desert W of Hindiya river; pop. (1935 est.) 65,000; Holy City for Moslems of the Shiite branch containing the shrine of Husain, slain here in 680 A.D. and commemorated in the Muharram; active trade center.

Kar′cag (kŏr′tsŏg). City, E Hungary, 35 m. WSW of Debrecen; pop. 24,565.

Kar′chi (kär′kê). Var. of KHALKĒ.

Kar·di′tsa; *Mod. Gr.* **Kar·dí′tsa** (kär·thē′tsä). Town, S Trikkala dept., W Thessaly, Greece; pop. 13,883.

Ka·rei′ma (kŭ·rä′mȧ; -mä. Town, Northern Province, N Republic of Sudan, on the Nile NNW of Merowe.

Ka·re′li·a (kȧ·rē′lĭ·ȧ; -rēl′yȧ); *officially* **Ka·re′lo-Finn′ish Soviet Socialist Republic** (kȧ·rē′lō·fĭn′ish). A constituent republic of the Union of Soviet Socialist Republics, in NW part of the Soviet Union in Europe; 64,220 sq. m., with added territory from Finland 77,720 sq. m.; pop. 469,145 (1941 est.) 892,977; * Petrozavodsk; bounded on N by Murmansk Region, on E by White Sea and Arkhangelsk Region, on S by Vologda and Leningrad Regions, and on W by Finland. Geologically similar to Finland with its low hills (highest ab. 1000 ft.) and numerous lakes, marshes, and streams; includes practically all of Lake Onega and N part of Lake Ladoga, also other smaller lakes as Seg, Kunto, and Top. Forests its chief wealth; agriculture much restricted by cold climate and poor soil; hunting and fishing important. Predominant ethnic strain Finno-Ugrian; chief nationalities Karelian and Finn 75%, Russian ab. 25%. Chief towns Petrozavodsk, Serdobol, Medvezhegorsk, Kem.

History: Karelians, one of the chief divisions of the Finns, first mentioned in history in 9th cent.; their folk tales and songs the source of the Finnish epic *Kalevala;* they formed in medieval times a strong independent state which in 17th cent. came under Swedish dominion and in 1721 was annexed by Russia; region formed into an autonomous republic July 25, 1923; territory much affected by Russian-Finnish War of 1939–40; after treaty of Mar. 15, 1940 by which certain border areas of Finland (ab. 13,500 sq. m.) were transferred to Russia, the Karelo-Finnish S.S.R. was constituted Mar. 31, incorporating the new territory; part of this new republic occupied 1941–43 by Nazis and Finns.

Ka·re′li·an Isthmus (kȧ·rē′lĭ·ăn; -rēl′yăn). The strip of land ab. 65 m. wide bet. W shore of Lake Ladoga and the Gulf of Finland, Soviet Russia, Europe, including region around Vyborg which was formerly part of Finland; in World War II scene of much fighting 1939–40 and again in 1944; taken by U.S.S.R. at end of war and added to Leningrad Region.

Ka·ren′ni (kȧ·rĕn′ĭ). District in E Burma, S of Southern Shan States, comprising a group of three feudatory states, Kantarawadi, Bawlake, and Kyebogyi; 4519 sq. m.; pop. 58,761; * Loikaw; country of the Karens, a group of Indo-Chinese tribes; not part of British Burma but administered by own chiefs under advice of Commissioner of Federated Shan States. See KAYAH STATE.

Ka·ren′ State (kȧ·rĕn′). State, S Burma, including parts of former Toungoo, Thaton, and Amherst districts.

Karfreit. See CAPORETTO.

Karghalik. See QARGHALIQ.

Kar′gil (kŭr′gĭl). Tahsil, SW Ladakh frontier dist., Jammu and Kashmir, N India; 7392 sq. m.; pop. 50,238; * Kargil.

Kar·go′pol (kŭr·gô′pŭl·y′). Town, Arkhangelsk Region, N Soviet Russia, Europe, on Onega river N of Lake Lacha, 170 m. N of Vologda.

Ka·ri′ba Dam (kȧ·rē′bȧ). Dam in Kariba Gorge of Zambezi river bet. SE Northern Rhodesia and N Southern Rhodesia, SE of Lusaka, completed Dec. 1958; maximum height 420 ft.; forms **Kariba Lake**, reservoir ab. 165 m. long.

Kar′i·bib′ (kär′ĭ·bĭb′). Town, W cen. South-West Africa, 90 m. WNW of Windhoek; pop. 5837; tin mines.

Ka′ri·kal′ (kä′rĭ·käl′). **1** Province of former French India, on Coromandel Coast E of Tanjore 150 m. S of Madras; 52 sq. m.; pop. (1941) 60,555; received by French 1739 from raja of Tanjore; changed hands several times but was established as French 1817; reorganized 1947 as one of the five free cities of French India within the French Union; transferred to India 1954.

2 Seaport town, its *, on one of mouths of Cauvery river; pop. (1941) 19,363.

Ka′ri·ma′ta Islands (kä′rĕ·mä′tä). Group of islands of Indonesia, in South China Sea W of island of Borneo, on NE side of Karimata Strait; 86 sq. m.; chief island **Karimata, or Great Karimata,** 70 sq. m; a part of West Borneo province.

Karimata Strait. Passage ab. 125 m. wide bet. SW Borneo and Billiton I., connecting South China Sea and Java Sea.

Ka·rim′na·gar (kȧ·rēm′nȧ·gĕr). Town, N Andhra Pradesh, S cen. Indian Union, 87 m. NE of Hyderabad; pop. ab. 10,000.

Ka′ri·moen·djo′wo (kä′rĕ·moon·jō′vō) or **Ka′ri - mun·dja′wa** (kä′rĕ·moon·jä′vä). Group of 27 islands in Java Sea ab. 55 m. N of Djapara, Java, Indonesia; 19 sq. m.; pop. 1231; only large island Great Karimun.

Ka′ri·moen, or **Ka′ri·mun, Islands** (kä′rĕ·moon). Island group, Indonesia, off E coast of Sumatra, at S end of Strait of Malacca and W of Riouw Archipelago.

Kariot. See IKARIA.

Kar′i·sim′bi (kär′ĭ·sĭm′bĭ). Peak 14,786 ft. on boundary bet. Ruanda and Kivu prov., E Congo, NE of Lake Kivu; a quiescent volcano; highest peak in the Virunga Mts.

Kar′kar (kär′kär). **1** Small island in Bismarck Archipelago, W Pacific Ocean, off N coast of NE New Guinea just N of Madang; occupied by Allies June 1944.

2 or **Qar′qar** (kär′kär). Unidentified place in W part of ancient Syria, perhaps Apamea on the Orontes river; scene of indecisive battle 854 (or 853) B.C. bet. Shalmaneser III, King of Assyria, and Ahab of Israel and his ally, Benhadad of Damascus.

Kar·ka′ra·linsk (kŭr·kȧ′rȧ·lyĭnsk). Town, E cen. Kazakh S.S.R., in steppe region N of Lake Balkhash ab. 110 m. ESE of Karaganda; highway junction point.

Karkenah. See KERKENNAH ISLANDS.

Kar·kheh′ (kȧr·kȧ′) or **Ker·kheh′** (kȧr·kȧ′); anc. **Cho·as′pes** (kō·ăs′pēz). River ab. 340 m. long in W Iran; rises S of Mt. Alwand, flows SW to marshlands E of the Tigris in SE Iraq.

Kar·ki′nit Bay (kŭr·kyē′nyĭt). Inlet of Black Sea on NW coast of the Crimea, S Soviet Russia, Europe; indents the Perekop isthmus.

Kar′li (kär′lĭ). Village, W Maharashtra state, W Indian Union, ab. 35 m. NW of Poona; celebrated caves containing Buddhist temples, some of the oldest and best preserved in India.

Karl-Marx-Stadt. City, Germany. See CHEMNITZ.

Karl′ö′ (kärl′ŭ′). Island, N Gulf of Bothnia, W of Oulu, Finland.

Karl′ó·cza (kŏr′lō·tsŏ). Hungarian form of KARLOVCI SREMSKI.

Kar′lo·vac (kär′lŏ·väts); Ger. **Karl′stadt** (kärl′shtät). Industrial city, Slovenia, N Yugoslavia, 30 m. SW of Zagreb; pop. 21,208; hydroelectric power plants.

Kar′lov·ci Srem′ski (kär′lŏv·tsĭ srĕm′skĭ); Ger. **Kar′-lo·witz** (kär′lŏ·vĭts). Town, N Serbia, NE Yugoslavia, on right bank of Danube river; pop. 5572; trade center in grape-growing region; cathedral; palace; scene of signing of Treaty of Karlowitz Jan. 26, 1699 by Austria, Poland, Turkey, Venice, marking suppression of power of Turkey in Europe and cession of lands to Austria and Poland.

Kar′lo·vy Va′ry (kär′lô·vĭ vȧ′rĭ); Ger. **Karls′bad** or **Carls′bad** (kärlz′băd; Ger. kärls′bät). Town, NW Bohemia prov., W Czechoslovakia, on the Ohře, an Elbe tributary ab. 15 m. from German border; pop. (1930) 24,029; watering place, with sulfur springs; scene of drawing up of the Carlsbad Decrees 1819 by ministers of the German states led by Prince Metternich, designed to suppress liberalism.

Karlsburg. See ALBA IULIA.

Karls′hamn (kärls′hȧm′n). Town, Blekinge prov., S Sweden, on Baltic coast just W of Karlskrona; pop. 10,206.

Karl·sko′ga (kärl·skoo′gȧ). Industrial city, Orebro prov., S cen. Sweden, 23 m. W of Örebro; pop. 29,161.

Karls·kro′na (kärls·kroo′nȧ). City * of Blekinge prov., S Sweden, built on the mainland and five nearby islands in Baltic Sea; pop. 32,341; excellent fortified harbor, used as Swedish naval base; dry docks; manufactures naval equipment, porcelain; breweries; granite quarries.

Karls′ru′he (kärls′roo′ĕ; kärls·roo′ĕ; Angl. kärlz′roo′ĕ). **1** District of former state of Baden. See Table at BADEN.

2 also **Carls′ru′he.** City, NW Baden-Württemberg, W Germany, * of former state of Baden, on the Rhine 35 m. S of Mannheim; pop. 231,472; manufactures machinery, foodstuffs, beer, majolica. Founded and laid out 1715 by Margrave Karl Wilhelm von Baden-Durlach; in World War I devastated by French air raid 1916; in World War II the center of considerable fighting in latter part of 1944 and beginning of 1945.

Karl′stad′ (kärl′stä[d]′). City, * of Värmland prov., SW Sweden, on Lake Vänern; pop. 31,369; engineering works, iron foundries, textile mills, sawmills, match factories; mineral springs; scene of signing of treaty 1905 which ended the union of Sweden and Norway.

Karlstadt. City in Yugoslavia. See KARLOVAC.

Karm′öy′ (kärm′mü′ü). Island 18 m. long in North Sea, a part of Rogaland co., SW Norway; 67 sq. m.; pop. 14,286.

Kar′nak (kär′năk). Village on the right (E) bank of the Nile in Upper Egypt; N part (Luxor is S part) of site of ancient Thebes (q.v.); site of early temple of Amen, perhaps prehistoric; later temple of Middle Kingdom replaced by great structure of Amenhotep III, which with additions by kings of Diospolite dynasties, esp. by Seti I and Ramses II, with its great hall, pylons, statues, obelisks, etc., is still well preserved and represents the greatest temple ever built.

Kar·nal′ (kĕr·näl′). Town, Ambala division, Punjab state, NW Indian Union, on Jumna canal 7 m. from Jumna river, 75 m. N of Delhi; pop. 26,610; said to have been founded by Raja Karna, mythical champion of the Kauravas.

Kar·na′li (kär·nä′lĭ). The name of the GOGRA river in Nepal.

Kar′na·phu′li (kär′nȧ·poo′lĭ; native kŭr′năp·hoo′lĭ). River, S East Bengal, Pakistan, flows W into Bay of Bengal; navigable to Chittagong.

Karnatik. See CARNATIC.

Karnes (kärnz). County in Texas. See Table at TEXAS.

Karnes City. Town, ⊗ of Karnes co., S Texas, 52 m. SSE of San Antonio; pop. 2693; oil and gas wells.

Kar Nicobar. See CAR NICOBAR.

Kar′ni·sche Al′pen (kär′nĭ·shĕ äl′pĕn). = Carnic Alps: see Table at ALPS.

Kar′no·bat′ (kär′nŏ·bät′). Town, Burgas dept., SE Bulgaria 18 m. WNW of Burgas; pop. 10,225.

Kärn′ten (kĕrn′tĕn). Province of Austria. See Carinthia in Table at AUSTRIA.

Karnul. Var. of KURNOOL.

Ka·ro·li′nen (kä′rŏ·lē′nĕn). German name of the CARO-LINE ISLANDS, W Pacific Ocean, a former German possession.

Ká′roly·vá′ros (kä′roi·vä′rŏsh). = KARLOVAC.

Karond. See KALAHANDI.

Ka·ron′ga (kȧ·rông′gȧ). Town, and lake trading port, Nyasaland protectorate, SE Africa, at N end of Lake Nyasa on W side, 22 m. S of the frontier; important in World War I as military headquarters.

Karoo. Var. of KARROO.

Kar′pa·thos (kär′pȧ·thŏs); Ital. Scar′pan·to (skär′pän·tŏ); anc. **Car′pa·thus** (kär′pȧ·thŭs) or **Car′pa·thos** (-thŏs). An island of the Dodecanese (q.v.), bet. Rhodes and the E end of Crete; 118 sq. m.; pop. (1936) 7770; largest of the Dodecanese proper and next in size to Rhodes with which its history has long been closely connected; under Venetian rule 1306 to 1540 when it

passed to the Turks; ceded to Italy 1912; returned to Greece Mar. 31, 1947.

Karpathos, *or* **Scarpanto, Strait.** Channel ab. 30 m. wide in S Dodecanese, separating islands of Rhodes and Karpathos.

Kar'pe·ni'sion (kär′pả·nyē′syôn); *also* **Car'pe·ni'si** (kär′pả·nyē′sẻ). Town, Aetolia and Acarnania dept., W Greece, at S end of Pindus Mts. and NE of Agrinion; battle nearby Aug. 20, 1823 with Turks, in which the Greek leader, Marco Bozzaris, was killed.

Kar·roo' (kả·rōō′). A dry tableland region of Cape Province Union of South Africa, of more than 100,000 sq. m., divided into three parts: (1) **Great,** *or* **Central, Karroo,** in S cen. part, ab. 350 m. from E to W and from 2000 to 3000 ft. above sea level, characterized by dry air and little rain, no grass, only vegetation being karroo bush (*Acacia horrida*); chief towns Beaufort West, Graaff Reinet, Somerset East, Willowmore. (2) **Little,** *or* **Southern, Karroo,** in S along coast, ab. 200 m. long, 1000 to 2000 ft. altitude; separated from Great Karroo by Zwartberg Mts.; some fertile sections; chief towns Worcester Oudtshoorn, Robertson. (3) **North Karroo** in N part along Orange river; largely desert; formerly haunt of vast numbers of game.

Kars (kärs). **1** Vilayet, NE Turkey in Asia; 6709 sq. m.; pop. 305,536; ✳ Kars; a mountainous region; formerly part of Armenia, after Middle Ages occupied or invaded by Turks, Kurds, Kabardians, Circassians, and others; as a result of Russo-Turkish War 1877–78 transferred to Russia; returned to Turkey by treaty 1921.
2 City, its ✳ on railroad and highway 42 m. W of Leninakan, U.S.S.R.; pop. 18,049; built on a mountain spur, its citadel (built in 16th cent.) long a strong military post. Capital of an independent Armenian principality in 9th and 10th cents.; captured by Seljuk Turks in 11th cent., by Mongols in 13th cent., and by Tamerlane in 1387; stormed and captured by Russians 1828, 1855, and 1878.

Kar'shi (kär′shǐ) *or* **Bek–Bu'di** (běk–bōō′dǐ). Town, ✳ of Kashka-Darya dist., SE Uzbek S.S.R., Soviet Central Asia, ab. 90 m. SE of Bukhara; pop. 14,150; fine mosque; on railroad; junction point of several important highways; residence of Tamerlane.

Karst. See CARSO.

Kar·ta'bo (kär·tä′bō). Village, British Guiana, ab. 40 m. SW of Georgetown on lower Essequibo river; jungle laboratory.

Ka·run' (kả·rōōn′). River ab. 450 m. long in W Iran; flows W and S in Khuzistan prov. and empties into the Shatt-al-Arab at Khorramshahr at N end of Abadan I.; has winding course through mountains, navigable in its lower course; chief tributary the Ab-i-Diz from the N.

Kar'vin·ná' (kär′vĭn·nä′) *Ger.* and *Pol.* **Kar'win** (kär′-vēn) City, Silesia prov., cen. Czechoslovakia, just E of Moravská Ostrava; pop. (1930) 22,330; in a lumbering and coal-mining area; held by Poland 1938–45.

Kar'war (kär′wär). Town, ✳ of Kanara dist., W Mysore state, W Indian Union, on coast 50 m. S of Pangim, Goa; pop. 16,122.

Ka·ry·ai' (kả·ryâ′). Commune, ✳ of Mount Athos dept, Macedonia Greece; pop. 305; near E coast in cen. part of Acte Penin.

Ka·saan' (kả·sän′). Settlement, Prince of Wales I., Alaska. See *Old Kasaan National Monument* at UNITED STATES, *National Monuments.*

Kasaba. See TURGUTLU.

Ka·sai' (kä·sī′); *Port.* **Cas·sai'** (kả·sī′). **1** River ab. 1200 m. long in SW Africa; rises in cen. Angola, flows E, then N, forming section of Angola-Congo boundary; continues N and NW through S cen. and W Congo to empty into Congo river on border of Congo Republic (formerly part of French Equatorial Africa); chief S tributary of the Congo. See KWAMOUTH.
2 Province, Republic of Congo (formerly Belgian Congo). See LUSAMBO.

Ka·sa'ma (kả·sä′mả). Town, ✳ of Awemba prov., NE Northern Rhodesia, in N part 100 m. S of S end of Lake Tanganyika; pop. 695.

Ka'sa·man'sa (kä′sả·män′sả). = CASAMANCE.

Kasan. Var. of KAZAN, Russia.

Ka·san'ga (kả·säng′gả); *formerly* **Bis'marck·burg** (bĭs′märk·bŏŏrk). Port at S end of Lake Tanganyika, SW Tanganyika, E Africa.

Ka·sar', Cape (kả·sär′). Cape on NE coast of Africa, extending into the Red Sea; marks N limit of Eritrea.

Ka'sa·ri (kä′sả·rĭ). River ab 60 m. long, W Estonia; flows SW to an inlet of Baltic Sea.

Kasbek. See KAZBEK.

Kaschau. See KOŠICE.

Ka·sem'pa (kả·sĕm′pả). Province, NW Northern Rhodesia, S cen. Africa; 38,855 sq. m.; pop. 62,053; ✳ Kasempa.

Kas'ganj (käs′gŭnj). Town, W Uttar Pradesh, N Indian Union, on affluent of Ganges river 100 m. SE of Delhi; pop. 23,100.

Ka·shan' (kä·shän′). City cen Iran, N of Isfahan, on railroad 65 m. from Qum; pop. ab. 45,000; an old town formerly famous for its velvets and brocades and for its faience; now produces excellent carpets and is known for its melons and figs.

Kash'gar (käsh′gär; *native* käsh′kä′). **1** River ab. 200 m. long, W Sinkiang prov, W China, flowing E toward the Yarkand river but is lost in the desert.
2 *Chin.* **Shu'fu'** (shōō′fōō′) Chief commercial town of W Sinkiang, W China, at oasis on Kashgar river; pop. ab. 80,000; in fertile region but dependent on irrigation; alt. ab. 4000 ft.; W terminus of N and S caravan and motor highways across Sinkiang from China; starting point for routes N to Kirgiz S.S.R., W to Fergana region, U.S.S.R., and S to Hunza and Kashmir in India; chief exports raw wool, cotton and cotton goods, tea, sheep, and dyes. Occupied in 2d cent. B.C. by the Yuechi; later held by Chinese, Turkish tribes, and Mongols; conquered by Genghis Khan and Tamerlane; visited and described by Marco Polo c. 1275; from 14th cent. to 1759 suffered many changes (completely destroyed 1514); Chinese since 1759 but at times under Russian influence; chief city of Chinese Turkistan (Kashgaria).

Kashgaria. See CHINESE TURKISTAN.

Ka'shing' (kä′shĭng′) *or* **Chia'hsing'** (jǐ·ä′shĭng′). Commercial city, N Chekiang, E China on Grand Canal ab. 53 m. SW of Shanghai; pop. ab. 60,000; trades chiefly in eggs poultry, rice, beans, and oil.

Ka·shi'ra (kŭ·shī′rả). Town, Moscow Region, cen. Soviet Russia, Europe, on Oka river 48 m. NNE of Tula; severe fighting Dec. 1941.

Ka·shi·wa·ba·ra (kä·shē·wä·bä·rä). See PARAMUSHIRO.

Kash'ka–Dar'ya' (kàsh′kả·dŭr·yả′). District, S Uzbek S.S.R., Central Asia; ✳ Karshi.

Kash'mir (kăsh′mǐr; kàsh·mǐr′; *native* kŭsh′mēr), *formerly* **Jam'mu and Kashmir** (jŭm′ōō): *Eng.* **Cash'mere** (kăsh′mēr; kàsh·mēr′). **1** Indian state, N India, on Sinkiang and Tibet frontier; 82,258 sq. m. (includes Kashmir proper and Frontier Illaqas in Gilgit); pop. (1941) 4,021,616; ✳ Srinagar; mountainous, includes W end of Himalayas and Karakoram Range.
2 Division of Kashmir state, N India; 69,903 sq. m.; pop. (1941) 3,945,090; includes districts of Ladakh, Baltistan, Gilgit, Hunza (*qq.v.*).
3 District, formerly a province, the cen. part of Kashmir state. 8555 sq. m.; pop 1,569,218; ✳ Srinagar; almost entirely mountainous, with "Vale," or "Happy Valley," of Kashmir (elevation at Srinagar 5250 ft.) in center, watered by the Jhelum and its tributary the Kishenganga; to N the W Himalayas form great ranges (highest point Nanga Parbat 26,660 ft.) and on the NE and E are peaks 16,000 to 18,000 ft.; in SW is the Pir Panjal range. Chief crops rice, maize, wheat, barley, fruits and vegetables. Srinagar famous for its Cashmere shawls and wood carvings. Became part of Mogul Empire (see IN-

DIA) under Akbar 1587; in second half of 18th cent. included in Ahmad Shah's Afghan empire; annexed to Sikh kingdom by Ranjit Singh 1819; after Sikh wars, held by Raja of Jammu as part of British India 1846; after Aug. 15, 1947 an area of dispute bet. Indian Union and Pakistan.

Kashmir North, or **Ba'ra·mu'la** (bä'rȧ·mōōl'ȧ). District, Kashmir N India; 3326 sq. m.; pop. 559,828; ✳ Baramula.

Kashmir South, or **Sri·na'gar** (srē·nŭg'ēr). District, Kashmir, N India; 2822 sq. m.; pop. 771,943.

Kasi. See BENARES.

Ka·si'mov (kȧ·sē'môf; *Russ.* kŭ·syē'mŭf). Town, Ryazan Region, Soviet Russia, on Oka river 70 m. ENE of Ryazan; pop. ab. 13,000; a trading town with annual fairs; founded 1152 and an important Tatar city from 15th cent. to 1667.

Ka·si·roe'ta (kä'sĕ·rōō'tä). See BATJAN.

Kas·kas'ki·a (kȧs·kȧs'kǐ·ȧ). **1** River 300 m. long, SW Illinois, partly navigable; rises in Champaign co., flows SW into Mississippi river in SW cen. Randolph co.

2 Village, Randolph co., SW Illinois, at junction of the Kaskaskia river with the Mississippi; pop. 97; site of oldest town in the West, founded 1703 as an Indian village, passed to the British 1765, made capital of territory of Illinois 1809, capital of state of Illinois 1818–20; by 1910 town completely destroyed as result of flood 1844 and further encroachments of the Mississippi 1881 and later.

Kas'ki·nen (käs'kǐ·nĕn) or **Kask'ö'** (kȧs'kû'). Seaport town, SW Finland, in Vaasa dept., on small coastal island ab. 50 m. S of Vaasa; pop. 1755.

Ka'sos (kä'sôs); *Ital.* **Ca'so** (kä'sŏ). An island of the Dodecanese (*q.v.*), SW of Karpathos and NE of E end of Crete; 27 sq. m.; pop. (1936) 1890.

Kasr, El. Var. of EL QASR.

Kasr el Kebir, El. Var. of *El Qsar el Kbir:* see ALCÁZARQUIVIR.

Kassa. See KOŠICE.

Kassai. = KASAI.

Kas'sa·la (käs'ȧ·lȧ). **1** Province, NE Sudan; 76,495 sq. m.; pop. 941,039.

2 Town, ab. 250 m. E of Khartoum near border of Eritrea; pop. 40,612; built on a plain at ab. 1700 ft.; founded by Egyptians as a fort 1840; held by Mahdists 1885–94; retaken by Italian force after battle of July 17, 1894 and restored to Egypt 1897; in World War II held briefly by Italians 1940–41.

Kassandra. See PALLENE.

Kassandra, Gulf of. See TORONAIC GULF.

Kas'sel (käs'ĕl; *Angl.* kăs''l). **1** Government district in former Hesse-Nassau prov., Prussia, Germany.

2 *also* **Cas'sel.** City, its ✳ and ✳ of the former Hesse-Nassau prov., now in Hesse state, on Fulda river 71 m. WNW of Erfurt; pop. (1939) 217,085; iron goods, machinery, aircraft, locomotives; scientific instruments, pianos; palace of former elector of Hesse-Cassel, 14th-cent. church. Founded before 913 A.D.; became city in 13th cent.; captured by French in Seven Years' War; supplied mercenaries to aid British against American colonies; capital of kingdom of Westphalia 1807; passed to Prussia 1866; in World War II frequently bombed 1943-45, taken by Americans Apr. 4, 1945.

Kas'se·rine (käs'ēr·ēn; *Arab.* käs'rĭn). Village on railroad and at mountain pass (**Kasserine Pass,** 2 m. wide with mountains ab. 4000 ft. high on either side) in cen. Tunisia, ab. 80 m. SW of Kairouan; taken from Americans in German raid Feb. 14, 1943 but recovered Feb. 25.

Kas'ta·mo·nu' (käs'tä·mŏ·nōō') or **Kas'ta·mu·ni'** (-mōō·nē'). **1** Vilayet, N Turkey in Asia; 5639 sq. m.; pop. 367,881.

2 Town, its ✳, on a tributary of the Kızıl Irmak 110 m. NNE of Ankara; pop. 14,158; near copper mines, noted for its manufacture of copper utensils; became Turkish **1393.**

Kas'tav (käs'täv); *Ital.* **Ca'stua** (käs'twä). Commune, SW Slovenia, Yugoslavia, ab. 6 m. W of Rieka (Fiume) on the coast; pop. 10,535; Roman remains; on 1946 Italian border.

Ka'ste·lor'ri·zon (käs·tä·lô'rĕ·zôn); *Angl.* **Ca'stel·lo'ri·zo** (käs·tä·lô'rĕ·zō); *Ital.* **Ca·stel'ros'so** (käs·tĕl'rôs'sō); *anc.* **Me·gis'te** (mĕ·jĭs'tē). Island in E Mediterranean Sea, 80 m. E of Rhodes and 2 m. off SW coast of Turkey in Asia; 4 sq. m.; pop. (1936) 2238; included in the Dodecanese, ceded by Turkey to Italy 1923; population entirely Greek; retroceded to Greece 1947.

Ka'sto·ri'a (käs·tô·rē'ä). Commune, Florina dept., W Macedonia, N Greece, 20 m. SSW of Florina on Lake Kastoria (20 sq. m.); pop. 11,736.

Kastro. 1 See KÁSTRON.

2 See MYTILENE city.

Kastron. See CHIOS city.

Ká'stron (käs'trôn) or **Ka'stro** (käs'trô). Seaport commune on W coast of Lemnos I., Aegean Sea; ✳ of the island; in Lesbos dept., Greece; pop. 3726.

Kastrop–Rauxel. See CASTROP-RAUXEL.

Ka·su·mi·ga·u·ra or **Kasumiga Ura** (kä·sōō·mē·gä·ōō·rä). Lagoon, Ibaraki prefecture, SE Honshu, Japan, on lower course of the Tone river ab. 50 m. NE of Tokyo; ab. 18 m. long and 17 m. wide at its broadest part; 89 sq. m.; resort and naval air station.

Ka·sur' (kȧ·sōōr'). Town, E West Punjab, Pakistan, near Sutlej river 34 m. SSE of Lahore; pop. (1941) 53,101; settled comparatively late by a Pathan colony from beyond the Indus.

Kasvin. Var. of KAZVIN.

Ka'ta·ghan'–Ba'dakh·shan' (kȧ'tȧ·gän'bȧ'dȧκ·shän'). A major province in NE Afghanistan, on the frontier; ✳ Faizabad; includes old province of Badakhshan and former district of Kataghan to the W of it.

Ka·ta'gum (?kȧ·tä'gōōm). Region, N Nigeria, N Africa, E of Kano on the borders of Bornu; formerly an independent emirate, taken over by British 1903; chief town Hadejia.

Ka·tah'din, Mount (kȧ·tä'd'n; -dǐn). Peak 5268 ft. in E Piscataquis co., N cen. Maine; highest point in the state.

Ka·tá'ko·lon (kä·tä'kô·lôn). Town, W coast of Elis, Achaea and Elis dept., NW Peloponnesus, S Greece, W of Pyrgos.

Ka·tan'ga (kȧ·täng'gȧ; kȧ·tăng'gȧ). Province, S Republic of Congo (formerly Belgian Congo); ✳ Elisabethville; noted esp. for its rich deposits of copper, uranium, chrome, cobalt, tin, iron, gold, and other minerals. See ELISABETHVILLE.

Ka·tang'lad, Mount (kä·täng'läd). Highest point 7804 ft. of a mountain group in W cen. Bukidnon prov., N cen. Mindanao, Phil. Is.

Katar. See QATAR.

Katch'all (kăch''l). One of the Nicobar Is. (*q.v.*).

Ka·te'na (kȧ·tä'nȧ). Village on W coast of Okinawa, near S end ab. 12 m. N of Naha, Ryukyu Is., Japan; airport, taken with little fighting by American forces Apr. 1, 1945.

Ka'te·rí'nē (kä'tȧ·rē'nyĕ). Town, Thessalonike dept., W cen. Macedonia, Greece, on W shore of Gulf of Salonika SSW of Salonika; pop. 10,138.

Ka'tern·berg (kä'tĕrn·bĕrκ). Former city (pop. 22,381), Düsseldorf govt. dist., Rhine Province, Prussia, Germany; since 1929 part of Essen (*q.v.*).

Kates Needle (käts). Mountain 10,002 ft. on boundary bet. SE Alaska and W Brit. Columbia, Canada; NE of Wrangell.

Ka·tha' (kȧ·thä'). **1** District, Sagaing division, Upper Burma; 7593 sq. m.; pop. 254,170.

2 Town, its ✳, on right bank of the upper Irrawaddy 155 m. N of Mandalay; port for river steamers; railroad terminus.

Ka'tha·ri'nen·stadt (kä'tä·rē'nĕn·shtät). Var. of *Ekaterinenstadt,* a former name of MARKSSHTADT.

Kath·er·i′na, Geb′el (jĕb′ĕl kăth′ĕr·ē′nȧ); *or* **Mount Cath′er·ine** (kăth′ĕr·ĭn; kăth′rĭn). Mountain 8652 ft., highest part of Gebel Musa mountain group, Sinai Penin.

Kath′er·ine (kăth′ĕr·ĭn; kăth′rĭn). Post station, N Northern Territory, Australia, on Daly river and on railroad ab. 170 m. SE of Darwin.

Ka′thi·a·war′ (kä′tĭ·ȧ·wär′). Peninsula, W Gujerat state, W coast of India; 23,432 sq. m.; pop. 3,484,222; bounded on N by Rann of Cutch, on E by Ahmadabad dist., and on S and W by Arabian Sea; formerly included two British agencies—Eastern Kathiawar and Western Kathiawar—later subdivisions of the Western India States Agency—comprised also 188 Indian states, including 16 larger and independent states, formerly under a resident at Rajkot, but after 1947 semi-independent or associated with the Indian Union; also parts of Baroda (Amreli and Okhamandal) and part of Ahmadabad dist. Home of many important old Hindu races, with notable antiquities. The states of Jetpur, Wankaner, Morvi, Palitana, Gondal, Wadhwan, Porbandar, and Navanagar joined a new confederation July 7, 1947.

Kathmandu. See KATMANDU.

Katia. See QATIA.

Katif. = QATIF.

Ka′ti·pu·nan′ (kä′tĕ·pōō·nän′); *formerly* **Lu·bung′an** (lōō·bōōng′än). Municipality, N Zamboanga prov., Mindanao, Phil. Is.; pop 35,355; port on S side of passage bet. Sulu Sea and Mindanao Sea.

Kat′mai, Mount (kăt′mī). Volcano 7000 ft. in **Katmai National Monument** (see UNITED STATES, *National Monuments*), at N end of Alaska Penin. on Shelikof Strait, S Alaska; main crater one of largest in world; top of mountain blown off by great eruption of June 1912; region of importance to volcanologists because phenomena exist on scale of great magnitude. See VALLEY OF TEN THOUSAND SMOKES.

Kat′man·du′ (kät′män·dōō′), *also* **Kath′man·du′** (kät′man-). City, ✳ of Nepal, in valley of Himalayas ab. 75 m. from Indian frontier; pop. (est.) 108,805.

Ka·toom′ba (kȧ·tōōm′bȧ). Town, E New South Wales, SE Australia, 60 m. W of Sydney; pop 6439.

Ka′to·wi′ce (kä′tô·vē′tsĕ); *Ger.* **Kat′to·witz** (kät′ō-vĭts). Industrial city, ✳ of Śląsk dept., S Poland, 45 m. WNW of Kraków; pop. (1938–39 est.) 134,500; Roman Catholic episcopal see; one of most important coal-producing centers in Europe; manufactures iron, steel, zinc, brass, bronze, machinery, tools, chemicals, tile, cement blocks. Became city 1865; reverted to Poland 1921 after World War I; seized by Germans Sept. 5, 1939; retaken by Russians Jan. 1945.

Kat′rine, Loch (lŏk kăt′rĭn). Lake in SW Perth co., cen. Scotland, 5 m. E of Loch Lomond; ab. 9½ m. long, 2 m. wide; maximum depth 495 ft.; scene of Scott's *Lady of the Lake.* See ELLEN'S ISLE.

Ka′tri′ne·holm′ (kȧ′trē′nĕ·hôlm′). Town, Södermanland co., SE Sweden, 70 m. WSW of Stockholm; pop. 12,038.

Ka′tsi·na (kä′tsĭ·nȧ). Town, Zaria prov., Northern Region, Nigeria, 85 m. NW of Kano; pop. 22,620; ✳ of ancient kingdom of **Katsina,** one of earliest of the Hausa states; ancient seat of learning; probably had population of ab. 100,000 in 17th and 18th cents.; still a cultural as well as commercial center; seized by the Fulahs in early 19th cent.; taken over by British 1904; Mohammedan teachers college; hospital.

Kat′te·gat (kăt′ĕ·găt; kät′ĕ·gät). Broad arm of North Sea, bet. Sweden on E and Jutland, Denmark, on W, connecting with North Sea through the Skagerrak and with Baltic Sea through Öresund, the Great Belt, and the Little Belt; bet. 40 and 70 m. wide.

Kattowitz. See KATOWICE.

Ka·tun′ (kŭ·tōōn′). River ab. 400 m. long, W and S Oirot Autonomous Region, Soviet Russia, Asia; flows N, joins the Biya to form the Ob.

Kat′wijk *or* **Katwijk aan Zee** (kät′vīk än zā′). Commune, South Holland prov., SW Netherlands, at mouth of the Oude Rijn; pop. 15,637; fishing town and seaside resort 4 m. NW of Leiden.

Katzbach. See KOCABA.

Kat′zen·buck′el (kät′sĕn·bŏŏk′ĕl). Mountain 2057 ft., N Baden-Württemberg, Germany; highest point in the Odenwald.

Ka·u′ (kä·ōō′). District, Hawaii co., Hawaii, S part of Hawaii I.; pop. 3368; chief village Pahala.

Kau′ai (kou′ī). **1** *formerly also* **Ka·i′e·i′e·wa′ho** (kä-ē′ä·ē′ä·wä′hō). Channel 63 m. wide bet. the islands of Oahu and Kauai, Hawaii.
2 Island in NW Hawaii, WNW of Oahu; 551 sq. m.; pop. 27,922; with Niihau forms Kauai co.; mountainous, its two chief peaks, Kawaikini and Waialeale, in the center; has several short streams, being the only island of the Hawaiian group that may be said to have rivers; its more important anchorages Nawiliwili, Hanalei, and Hanapepe Bays; chief town Lihue; principal industry raising sugar.
3 County, NW Hawaii; comprises Kauai and Niihau Is.; 623 sq. m., pop. 28,176, ⊗ Lihue on Kauai I.

Kauf′man (kôf′măn). **1** County in Texas. See *Table* at TEXAS.
2 City, its ⊗, NE Texas, 30 m. ESE of Dallas; pop. 3087.

Kaufmann Peak. See LENIN PEAK.

Kau·i′ki Head (kou·ē′kĕ). Cape and promontory on E end of Maui I., Hawaii.

Kau Kau Bay (kou′ kou′). Bay on N side of E end of Guadalcanal I., SE Solomon Is., W Pacific Ocean.

Kau·kau′na (kô·kô′nȧ). City, Outagamie co., E Wisconsin, pop 10,096; settled c. 1790, made city 1885; manufactures paper, lumber, cheese, foundry products.

Kau′kau Veld (kou′kou fĕlt′). Barren region NW of the Kalahari Desert, S Africa, extending over NE South-West Africa and NW Bechuanaland Protectorate W of the Okovanggo Basin.

Kau′ke·nau (kou′kĕ·nou). Settlement on S coast of Neth New Guinea, ab. 315 m. ESE of Fakfak at 4°40′S; adjacent to Mimika which has airport.

Ka·u′la (kä·ōō′lä) *or* **Ta·hu′ra** (tä·hōō′rä). Small barren uninhabited rock in Pacific Ocean 23 m. WSW of Niihau I., Hawaii, alt 550 ft.

Kau′la·ka′hi (kou′lä·kä′hĕ). Strait bet. islands of Niihau and Kauai, Hawaii.

Kaulun *or* **Kaulung.** See KOWLOON.

Kau′ma·la′pau (kou′mä·lä′pou). Village, Lanai dist., Maui co., Hawaii, on W coast of Lanai I.

Kau′na·ka′kai (kou′nä·kä′kī). Village, Molokai dist., Maui co., Hawaii, on S coast of Molokai I.; pop. (est.) 1500.

Kau′nas (kou′näs). **1** District of Lithuania. See *Table* at LITHUANIA.
2 *Russ.* **Kov′no** (kôv′nȯ); *Pol.* **Kow′no** (kôv′nō). City, ✳ of Kaunas dist. and 1920 to 1940 ✳ of Lithuania, at confluence of Neris with Neman river 130 m. E of Kaliningrad (Königsberg); pop. (1938 est.) 152,365; breweries, wire and nail factories; important railroad junction point; several notable old buildings, esp. the Lithuanian-Gothic church of Vytautas (15th cent.); seat of national university. Founded in 11th cent.; in medieval times often attacked and partially destroyed; in World War I captured by Germans 1915; became capital of Lithuania after Poland's second seizure of the former capital, Vilnyus (Wilno), Oct. 9, 1920; in World War II occupied by Russians 1940 and by Germans 1941, retaken by Russians 1944.

Kau′ra Na·mo′da (kou′rä nȧ·mō′dȧ). Town, Sokoto prov., Northern Region, N Nigeria, 100 m. E of Sokoto; pop ab. 13,000.

Kau′ri·a′la (kou′rĭ·ä′lä). Earlier name of the Karnali. See GOGRA.

Ka·va′jë (kä·vä′yĕ). Town, Durrës prefecture, W Albania, on coast S of Durrës; pop. 8308; tobacco.

Ka·val′la (kȧ·văl′ȧ); *Mod. Gr.* **Ka·vál′la** (kä·vä′lä).
1 Department of Greece. See *Table* at GREECE.
2 Seaport city, ✳ of Kavalla dept., NE Macedonia, NE Greece, at head of **Gulf of Kavalla** opp. Thasos I.; pop. 49,980; exports tobacco; near site of ancient Neapolis where St. Paul landed on way to Philippi; center of revolution 1935. Birthplace of Mehemet Ali.
Kavalli. See CAVALLY.
Kaveri. See CAUVERY.
Ka′vi·eng′ (kä′vǐ·ĕng′). Town with good harbor on North Cape, NW tip of New Ireland, Bismarck Archipelago, ab. 162 m. NW of Rabaul; chief port on the island and ✳ of the New Ireland administrative district; shipping point of many coconut plantations. Seized by Japanese Jan. 23, 1942; frequently bombed by Allies 1943–44.
Kavir. = DASHT-I-KAVIR.
Kav·kaz′ski Khre·bet′ (kŭf·kȧs′skǐ ᴋryǐ·byĕt′). Russian name for CAUCASUS MOUNTAINS.
Ka′vo Mountains (kä′vō). Range extending lengthwise of the island of Guadalcanal, SE Solomon Is., W Pacific Ocean; highest peak Popomanasiu 8005 ft.
Ka·wa·go·e (kä·wä·gō·ĕ). City, Saitama prefecture, SE cen. Honshu, Japan, ab. 20 m. NW of Tokyo; pop. (1945) 47,160.
Ka·wa·gu·chi (kä·wä·gōō·chê). **1** Lake in S Honshu, Japan, near Fuji; ab. 10 m. in circumference; altitude 2700 ft.
2 City, Saitama prefecture, SE Honshu, Japan, just N of Tokyo; pop. (1945) 97,709.
Kaw (kô). River, Kansas. See KANSAS.
Ka′wai·ha′e (kä′wǐ·hä′ȧ). Village, South Kohala dist., Hawaii co., Hawaii, on **Kawaihae Bay** on NW coast of Hawaii I.; pop. (1950) 123; interisland steamer landing.
Ka′wai·ha′u (kä′wǐ·hä′ōō). District, NE Kauai I., Kauai co., Hawaii; pop. (1950) 6512; chief town Kapaa.
Ka′wai·ho′a, Cape (kä′wǐ·hō′ä); *or* **Kawaihoa Point.** Cape on S end of Niihau I., Hawaii.
Kawaihoa Point. See KOKO HEAD, SE Oahu, Hawaii.
Ka′wai·ki′ni (kä′wǐ·kē′nê). Mountain 5170 ft., cen. Kauai I., Hawaii.
Ka′wa·ka′wa (kä′wä·kä′wä). Village, Auckland provincial dist., N North I., New Zealand, near Russell on Bay of Islands on E coast.
Ka·war′dha (kȧ·wûrd′hä). **1** Former Indian state, NE India; 794 sq. m.; pop. (1941) 77,284.
2 Town, its ✳, now in Madhya Pradesh, 140 m. NE of Nagpur; pop. ab 5000.
Ka·war′tha Lakes (kȧ·wôr′thȧ). A series of lakes in Peterborough and Victoria cos., SE Ontario, Canada, forming a chain E and W in region N of Peterborough and Lindsay; traversed by Trent Canal system.
Ka·wa·sa·ki (kä·wä·sä·kê). City, Kanagawa prefecture, Honshu, Japan, a S suburb of Tokyo on W coast of Tokyo Bay; pop. (1955) 445,500; has temple founded in 12th cent.; manufacturing center of heavy electrical equipment, chemicals, and aircraft.
Ka·we′ah Peaks (kȧ·wē′ȧ). Four mountains: Black Kaweah 13,752 ft., Red Kaweah 13,754 ft., Gray Kaweah 13,728 ft., and Big Kaweah 13,816 ft., in Sierra Nevada, in Tulare co., S cen. California.
Ka·we′li·ko′a Point (kȧ·wā′lê·kō′ä). Cape on SE coast of Kauai I., Hawaii.
Ka′whi·a Harbor (kä′hwê·ä; *colloq.* käf′wê·ä). Inlet of Pacific Ocean on NW cen. coast of North I., New Zealand.
Ka′wi (kä′wê). Mountain group, E Java, Indonesia; highest point 9409 ft.; includes Mt. Kelut and adjoins Mt. Ardjuno on the N.
Ka′wich Range (kä′wǐch). Range in S cen. Nye co., S Nevada; highest point **Kawich Peak** 9500 ft.
Kay (kā). County in Oklahoma. See *Table* at OKLAHOMA.
Ka′yah State (kī′ȧ). State, E Burma, comprising the Karenni district.

Kay′ak (kī′ăk). Island off coast of SE Alaska, E of Prince William Sound; islet at its S end is Cape St. Elias.
Kayan. See KEN.
Kayes (kāz). Town, SW Republic of Mali, West Africa, on Senegal river; pop. (1940) 15,894; on railroad from Dakar and Thiès in Senegal to Bamako and Koulikoro.
Kay′lor (kā′lẽr). Locality, Armstrong co., W Pennsylvania, ab. 14 m. NW of Kittanning; pop. (1950) 2575.
Kay′ser (kī′zẽr). Peak 3020 ft. in SW Surinam.
Kay′se·ri′ (kī′sĕ·rē′) *or* **Kai′sa·ri·a′** (kī′sä·rê·yä′).
1 Vilayet, cen. Turkey in Asia; 5840 sq. m.; pop. 310,458.
2 *anc.* **Cae′sa·re′a Maz′a·ca** *or* **Mazaca** (sē′zȧ·rē′ȧ [sĕs′ȧ-; sĕz′ȧ-] măz′ȧ·kȧ). City, its ✳, at foot of Erciyas Daği; pop. (1940) 53,908; for centuries an important trade center. Caesarea Mazaca was chief city of ancient Cappadocia.
Ka·zakh′ Soviet Socialist Republic (kä·zäk′; *Russ.* kŭ·zȧk′) *or* **Ka′zakh·stan′** (kä′zäk·stän′; *Russ.* kȧ·zŭᴋ·stȧn′) *or* **Ka′zak·stan′** (kä′zäk·stän′). A constituent republic of the Union of Soviet Socialist Republics, Central Asia; 1,059,700 sq. m.; pop. 6,145,937, (1941 est.) 6,458,175; ✳ Alma Ata; second largest unit in area in the U.S.S.R.; bounded on N by Chelyabinsk, Kurgan, Omsk, and Novosibirsk Regions, on NE by Altai Territory and Oirot Autonomous Region of Soviet Russia in Asia, on E by Sinkiang, China, on S by Kirgiz, Uzbek, and Turkmen S. S. Republics, on W by Caspian Sea and Astrakhan and Stalingrad Regions and on NW by the Saratov and Chkalov Regions, all four in Soviet Russia in Europe. Occupied in cen. part by great Kirgiz Steppe and in S by desert regions: in SW the Ust Urt and in SE the Muyun Kum. Includes N half of Lake Aral, all of Lake Balkhash, and the smaller lakes Zaisan, Tengiz, and Chelkar Tengiz. Chief rivers the Syr Darya in S, upper Irtysh in NE, the lower Ural in W; other important streams the Ishim, Tobol, Ili, and Emba. In E, N of Lake Balkhash, plateau lands rise to the lofty Tien Shan and W Altai Mts. on Chinese boundary. Predominant ethnic strain Turko-Tatar; chief nationalities Kazakh 57%, Russian 20%, Ukrainian 13%. Chief crops grains, cotton, flax, hemp; its rich mineral resources largely undeveloped; in E crossed by famous Turk-Sib R.R. from Semipalatinsk to Alma Ata and Tashkent; in W has oil pipeline from Gurev on the Caspian to Aktyubinsk and Orsk. Chief towns Alma Ata, Semipalatinsk, Karaganda, Petropavlovsk, Akmolinsk, Uralsk.
History. Region came under the Mongols in 13th cent. and fragments of the Golden Horde long settled here; gradually 1730-1819 came under Russian rule and formed large part of Russian Turkistan; an autonomous republic erected by the Kazakh Kirghiz 1920; admitted to U.S.S.R. as constituent republic 1936.
Ka·zan′ (kȧ·zän′). River ab. 450 m. long, cen. Canada; rises in SE Mackenzie District, Northwest Territories, flows NNE through Yathkyed and other lakes to enter Baker Lake on S. in Keewatin District; one of main streams of the Barren Grounds.
Ka·zan′ (kȧ·zän′; *Russ.* kŭ·zȧn′y′). **1** Former government in E Russia in Europe, now included in Mari, Chuvash, and Tatar Autonomous Republics, Soviet Russia, Europe.
2 City, ✳ of Tatar Republic, E Soviet Russia, Europe, on short tributary 3 m. from the Volga where it turns S, 200 m. E of Gorki; pop. 401,665; on Moscow-Sverdlovsk railroad ab. 40 m. above the junction of the Kama with the Volga; a key city, commercially and industrially, of the Middle Volga Area; trades in textiles, leather goods, soap, toilet articles, felt boots, and machinery; many of its fine old buildings—kremlin, cathedral, tower, monastery, etc.—are still standing, although some were damaged during the Revolution; university (founded ab. 1804), many technical schools; formerly its fairs were visited by peoples of E Russia and W Asia. Original Kazan, not far from present city, under Black Bulgarian empire; converted to Mohammedanism in 10th cent.;

conquered by Tatars in 13th cent.; new city founded 1437 and made capital of kingdom 1438 by khan of the Golden Horde; captured by Ivan the Terrible 1552; center of Tatar national movement Oct. 1917; suffered during Revolution and subsequent famine 1921–22; captured by Czechs Aug. 1918.

Ka′zan·lik′ (kä′zän·lĭk′). Town, Stara Zagora dept., cen. Bulgaria, in Tundzha valley on S slope of Balkan Mts. S of Shipka Pass; pop. (1926) 11,598; center of attar of roses industry; taken by Russians Jan. 7, 1878 in war with Turkey.

Ka·zan Ret·to (kä·zän rĕt·tō). See VOLCANO ISLANDS.

Kaz·bek′ (kŭz-byĕk′), also **Kas·bek′** (kŭz-). Peak 16,541 ft. in cen. Caucasus Mts., Soviet Russia, Europe, bet. the South Ossetian Autonomous Region (in Georgia) and the North Ossetian A.S.S.R.; an extinct volcano with steep slopes, towering above Daryal Pass; eight glaciers; first climbed 1868; subject of many legends.

Kazdaği. See IDA.

Ka′ze·run′ (kä′zĕ·rōōn′). Town, Fars prov., SW Iran, ab. 70 m. W of Shiraz; pop. ab. 7000; fine orange groves; produces cotton, opium, rice, and almonds.

Kaz·vin′ or **Qaz·vin′** (kȧz·vēn′). **1** Province, NW Iran; 9826 sq. m.

2 City, its ⊛, NW Iran, ab. 90 m. NW of Tehran; pop. ab. 60,000; important communications center S of W end of Elburz Mts., having connections with Tehran, Resht, Tabriz, and Hamadan; trades esp. in silk, carpets, and rice. Founded by Shapur II in 4th cent. A.D.; favored by Harun al-Rashid, who built a mosque here; influential under Moslems, became capital under Tahmasp I in 16th cent.; capital transferred to Isfahan by Abbas I; has suffered much from earthquakes.

Kéa. See KEOS.

Ke′a·u (kā′ä·ä′ōō). Town, Puna dist., Hawaii co., Hawaii, E Hawaii I., S of Hilo; pop. 1334; its post office is Olaa.

Ke′a·ho′le Point (kā′ä·hō′lȧ). Cape on W coast of Hawaii I.

Ke·a′lai·ka·hi′ki (kȧ·ä′lī·kä·hē′kȧ). Channel ab. 20 m. wide bet. Lanai and Kahoolawe Is., Hawaii.

Ke·a′la·ke·ku′a (kȧ·ä′lä·kȧ·kōō′ä). Village, in North Kona and South Kona dists., Hawaii co., Hawaii, on **Kealakekua Bay** on W coast of Hawaii I.; pop. (est.) 325; landing place of Capt. James Cook on his second visit to Hawaiian Is. Jan. 1779 and place where he was killed in quarrel with natives Feb. 14; a favorite place of anchorage for visiting foreign vessels in early years of kingdom; has monument to Cook erected 1874 by Lord Byron.

Keans′burg (kēnz′bûrg). Borough, Monmouth co., E cen. New Jersey, on Raritan Bay; pop. 6854; resort and port of call for pleasure and fishing craft.

Kear′ney (kär′nĭ). **1** County in Nebraska. See *Table* at NEBRASKA.

2 City, ⊗ of Buffalo co., S cen. Nebraska, on Platte river 45 m. WSW of Grand Island; pop. 14,210; wheat, livestock. Nebraska State Teachers College (1905; coed.).

Kearn Peak (kûrn). Mountain 11,493 ft. in Sierra Nevada in E Tulare co., S cen. California.

Kearns (kûrns). Urban community (unincorporated), Salt Lake co., N Utah, SW of Salt Lake City; pop. 17,172.

Kear′ny (kär′nĭ). **1** County in Kansas. See *Table* at KANSAS.

2 Town, Hudson co., NE New Jersey, bet. Passaic and Hackensack rivers at head of Newark Bay, 2 m. N of Newark; pop. 37,472; shipbuilding, oil refining; manufactures machinery, thread, linoleum, metal goods, truck bodies, chemicals, paints and varnishes.

Kear′sarge (kĕr′särj). See PEQUAWKET.

Kearsarge, Mount. Peak 2937 ft. in Merrimack co., S cen. New Hampshire.

Kears′ley (kĕrz′lĭ). Urban district, Lancashire, NW England, 8 m. NW of Manchester; pop. 10,675.

Ke′a·wai′ki Bay (kā′ä·wī′kȧ). Bay on NW coast of Hawaii I., bet. Kiholo Bay and Honokaope Bay.

Ke·bil′li (kĕ·bĭl′ĭ). Town, S cen. Tunisia, on SE corner of Chott Djerid.

Ke·bir′, Wa′di el (wä′dĕl kȧ·bēr′). **1** River in NE Algeria, flowing NNE through city of Constantine into Mediterranean Sea near Philippeville; not navigable; in its upper course sometimes known as the **Rum′mel** (rōōm′ĕl) river.

2 See GUADALQUIVIR river, Spain.

Keb′ne·kai′se (kĕb′nĕ·kī′sĕ). Highest peak 6963 ft. in the Kjölen Mts., N Sweden.

Ke·boe′men (kȧ·bōō′mĕn) or **Ke·bu′men.** Town, Central Java prov., Indonesia, on railroad near S coast 50 m. W of Jogjakarta; pop. 14,102.

Kecs′ke·mét′ (kĕch′kĕ·māt′). Autonomous city, cen. Hungary, 52 m. SE of Budapest; 362 sq. m.; pop. (1939) 83,732; market center for agricultural, fruit-growing, and livestock-raising region; important annual cattle fair.

Ke′dah (kā′dä). A state in the Federation of Malaya, S Malay Penin.; formerly one of the five Unfederated Malay States under British protection; 3660 sq. m.; pop. 429,691, (1940 est.) 515,758; ⊛ Alor Star; bounded on NE by Thailand, on SE and S by Perak, on SW by Province Wellesley, on W by Andaman Sea, and on NW by Perlis; includes large island of Langkawi off NW coast; generally level with short streams; has mountain range on E border (3000 to 6100 ft.). Chief exports rubber, rice, tapioca, and tin; inhabitants Malays, Chinese, and Indians. Chief towns Alor Star and Sungei Patani.

History: Goes back to 400 A.D. according to Sanskrit and Arab records; converted to Islam in 15th cent.; held captive by king of Achin in 17th cent.; leased Penang to British East India Co. 1786; subject to Siam 1821–1909, transferred to Great Britain 1909; overrun by Japanese Dec. 1941; became part of the Federation of Malaya (*q.v.*), established 1948.

Ke·dai′nyai (kĕ·dī′nyī; -nĕ·ī). **1** District of Lithuania. See *Table* at LITHUANIA.

2 Town, its ⊛, cen. Lithuania, 30 m. N of Kaunas; pop. (1938 est.) 8602.

Ke·dar′nath (kȧ·där′nät; *native* -nät·h′). Peak 23,420 ft. in the Himalayas, on NW border of Garhwal dist., India, W of Badrinath; place of pilgrimage.

Ke·da′woeng (kȧ·dä′ōong) or **Ke·da′wung.** Town, West Java prov., Indonesia; pop. 18,617; suburb of Tjirebon.

Ke′desh (kē′dĕsh) or **Kedesh–naph′ta·li** (-näf′tȧ·lī). Town, Galilee, N Palestine, ab. 5 m. NW of the Waters of Merom; a city of refuge, frequently mentioned in the Bible.

Kedg′es Straits (kĕj′ĕz; -ĭz). Strait bet. South Marsh I. and Smith I. in Chesapeake Bay, Maryland, connecting Tangier Sound with Chesapeake Bay.

Ke·di′ri (kȧ·dē′rĕ). **1** River in Java. See BRANTAS.

2 Former residency, S Java, in East Java prov., Neth. Indies; 2718 sq. m.; pop. 2,469,955; ⊛ Kediri; fertile plain region in valley of the Brantas bet. the Wilis and Kelut mountain groups; center of sugar industry; rice, cotton, coffee. In early times the region of a Hindu kingdom.

3 City, its ⊛, now in Indonesia, on Brantas river 65 m. SW of Surabaja; pop. 48,567.

Ked′le·ston (kĕd′l'stŭn; kĕl′s'n). Parish, Derbyshire, N cen. England, 3½ m. NW of Derby; home of Marquis Curzon.

Ke′doe (kā′dōō) or **Ke′du.** Former residency. Middle Java prov., Neth. Indies; 1799 sq. m.; pop. 2,129,894; ⊛ Magelang; bordered Banjoemas on W, Semarang on N, and Jogjakarta and Soerakarta principalities on E; area includes or is bordered by some of the highest mountains of Java; has no harbors on S coast; one of most densely populated areas on the globe; agriculturally highly developed.

Ke'doeng·woe'ni (kä'dŏŏng·wōō'nĕ) *or* **Ke'dung-wu'ni.** Town, Central Java prov., Indonesia, just S of Pekalongan; pop. 10,677.

Kedron. See KIDRON.

Kedu. See KEDOE.

Keele (kēl). River 230 m. long, Northwest Territories, Canada; flows E from Mackenzie Mts. to Mackenzie river above Fort Norman.

Keele Peak. Peak 9750 ft. in Mackenzie Mts., NW Canada, on boundary bet. Yukon Territory and Mackenzie District, Northwest Territories.

Kee'ler, Cape (kē'lẽr). Promontory 1700 ft. high on E coast of Palmer Penin., Antarctica, in 68°47'S, 63°15'W; discovered 1928.

Keeling Islands. See COCOS ISLANDS.

Keelung. See KIRUN.

Keene (kēn). **1** City, ⊗ of Cheshire co., SW corner of New Hampshire, on Ashuelot river 40 m. W of Manchester; pop. 17,562; market center in farming area; mica quarries; manufactures woolen goods, shoes, chairs, machinery; Keene State College (1909; coed.). First permanent settlement 1750; incorporated as city 1873. **2** See KEENE VALLEY, N.Y.

Keene Valley. Village and resort, Essex co., NE New York, ab. 39 m. SSW of Plattsburgh; summer home of eminent landscape painters and scholars; ab. 3 m. S of resort village of **Keene,** pop. (est.) 500, and with it included in Keene town (pop. 726).

Keese'ville (kēz'vĭl). Village, Clinton and Essex cos., NE New York, 12 m. S of Plattsburgh; pop. 2213; manufactures furniture, radio cabinets.

Keet'mans·hoop (kāt'mäns·hōōp). Town, S South-West Africa, 270 m. SSE of Windhoek; pop. (1936) 2604; in sheep country; railroad engineering shops.

Kee·wa'tin (kĕ·wä't'n; -tĭn). Village, Itasca co., N Minnesota, 8 m. WSW of Hibbing; pop. 1651; iron.

Kee·wa'tin (kĕ·wä't'n; -tĭn). **1** District, SE Northwest Territories, Canada; area including water 228,160 sq. m.; includes E part of mainland of N Canada NW of Hudson Bay and the islands in Hudson and James Bays; administered from Ottawa. Created 1876 when it included a much larger area (ab. 516,000 sq. m.); has several times been reorganized with parts of it added to Manitoba and Ontario provs. **2** Town, Kenora dist., W Ontario, Canada, on N shore of Lake of the Woods at source of Winnipeg river across from Kenora; pop. 1634; large power plant, flour mills, and sawmills.

Kef, Le; *or* **El Kef.** See LE KEF.

Kefe. Tatar form of Kaffa, Genoese name of Feodosiya (*q.v.*).

Kef'la·vík' (kyĕp'lä·vēk'). Village, SW Iceland, ab. 22 m. WSW of Reykjavík on SW shore of Faxa Bay; pop. ab. 800; location of **Keflavík Field,** international airport. See MEEKS FIELD.

Ke·gon-no-ta·ki (kĕ·gŏn·nŏ·tä·kĕ). Waterfall in Tochigi prefecture, cen. Honshu, Japan, near Nikko; ab. 323 ft. high and 18 ft. wide.

Ke·gon'sa, Lake (kĕ·gŏn'så). See FOUR LAKES.

Kehl (kāl). Commune, Baden-Württemberg, Germany, on the Rhine opp. Strasbourg; pop. (1939) 12,138.

Kei, Great. See GREAT KEI.

Keigh'ley (kēth'lĭ). Municipal borough, West Riding, Yorkshire, N England, in the Aire valley 17 m. WNW of Leeds; pop. 40,441, (1951) 56,938; manufactures woolen goods, sewing machines, washing machines, tools.

Kei Islands. See KAI ISLANDS.

Kei·jo (kā·jō), *now* **Seoul** (sōl; så·ōōl'; *Korean* sŭ'ōōl), *also* **Kyong·song** (kyông·sông). City, ✳ of S Korea and of Keiki prov., on Kan river near W coast 24 m. from its port, Inchon; pop. (1960) 2,445,402; formerly a walled city with eight stone gates, now mostly torn down although the finest, Nandaimon Gate, is still preserved; palaces, a bell tower, pagoda. Capital of Korean dynasty for 518 years 1392–1910.

Kei·ki (kā·kē); *Jap.* **Keiki-do** (kä·kĕ·dō). Province of Korea. See *Table* at KOREA.

Keil'berg (kĭl'bĕrк). Highest peak 4080 ft. in the Erzgebirge, on boundary bet. Saxony and Bohemia.

Kei'ser (kī'zẽr). Locality, Northumberland co., E cen. Pennsylvania, near Mount Carmel; pop. (1950) 1854.

Kei·shin Port (kā·shĕn). Name given 1941 to the amalgamated Tokyo-Yokohama harbor after completion of extensive improvements.

Keisho Hoku; Keisho Nan. See NORTH KEISHO; SOUTH KEISHO.

Kei'te·le (kā'tĕ·lĕ). Lake, S cen. Finland.

Keith (kēth). County in Nebraska. See *Table* at NEBRASKA.

Kei'zer (kī'zẽr). Urban community (unincorporated), Marion co., NW Oregon, N of Salem; pop. 5288.

Kejser Franz Josephs Fjord. See FRANZ JOSEF FJORD.

Ke·ka'ha (kĕ·kä'hä). Town, Waimea dist., on SW coast of Kauai I., Hawaii, W of Waimea; pop. 2082.

Ke'kri (kā'krĭ). Town, SE Rajasthan, NW India, 50 m. SE of Ajmer; pop. 7179.

Keks'golm (kĕks'gōm; *Russ.* kĕks'gŭl·y'm); *Finnish* **Kä'ki·sal'mi** (kä'kĭ·säl'mĭ); *Swed.* **Kex'holm** (kĕks'hōm; *Swed.* chĕks·hôlm'). Town, SW Karelia, U.S.S.R., on W shore of Lake Ladoga 75 m. N of Leningrad; pop. ab 5000; has rail connection with Leningrad; principal trade in lumber and granite. Built as a Swedish fortress 1293–95; changed hands several times bet. Swedes and Russians; became Finnish 1811; ceded to Soviet Union by treaty of Mar. 12, 1940; retaken by Germans and Finns 1941 but again became Russian 1944.

Ke'la·ni *or* **Kelani Gan'ga** (kä'lá·nē gŭng'gä). River (*ganga*) ab. 90 m. long W Ceylon, flows W to Indian Ocean near Colombo.

Ke·lan'tan (kĕ·lăn'tăn; *native* -län'tän). **1** River ab. 150 m. long in Kelantan state, Malay Penin.; rises in the mountains on the SW border, flows NNE into the South China Sea; navigable for much of its course; has many tributaries. **2** A state of the Federation of Malaysia, S Malay Penin., formerly one of the five Unfederated Malay States under British protection; 5750 sq. m.; pop. 362,517, (1940 est.) 390,332; ✳ Kota Bahru; bounded on N by Thailand, on NE by South China Sea, on E by Trengganu, on S by Pahang, on W by Peak; level and fertile in N, hilly in S, with mountains on Pahang border (see Gunong TAHAN); almost entirely in basin of Kelantan river; produces chiefly rice, also rubber, coconuts, betel nuts, livestock raising, fishing. In 14th cent. under Java; later under Malacca, and at end of 19th cent. under Siam; became a British dependency 1909; overrun by Japanese Dec. 1941; became part of the Federation of Malaya (*q.v.*), established 1948.

Kelat. Var. of KALAT.

Ke·layres' (kĕ·lârz'). Locality, Schuylkill co., E cen. Pennsylvania, ab. 4 m. SSW of Hazleton; pop. (1950) 1059; coal mining.

Kel'heim (kāl'hĭm). Town, E Bavaria, Germany, on the Danube where the Altmühl joins it ab. 12 m. SW of Regensburg; pop. 3954.

Ke·li'bi·a (kĕ·lē'bĭ·à). Town, NE Tunisia, on E coast of Cape Bon Penin. S of Cape Bon.

Kel·kit' (kĕl·kēt'). River ab. 180 m. long in NE Turkey in Asia; flows generally W into the Yeşil Irmak near its mouth.

Kel'ler·wand (kĕl'ẽr·vänt); *Ital.* **Mon'te Co·glians'** (mŏn'tä kŏ·lyäns'). Mountain 9217 ft., on border bet. Austria and Italy; highest peak in Carnic Alps.

Kel'leys Island (kĕl'ĭz). Island in Lake Erie, off NE coast of Ottawa co., N Ohio; a part of Erie co., Ohio.

Kel'logg (kĕl'ŏg; -ŭg). City, Shoshone co., NE Idaho, 35 m. ESE of Coeur d'Alene; pop. 5061; silver, lead mines.

Kellogg, Mount. Peak 8385 ft. in NE Pima co., S Arizona.

Kells (kělz); *anc.* **Ce′a·nan′nus** (sē′á·năn′ŭs). Town, W co. Meath, E Eire, 25 m. W of Drogheda; pop. of urban district (1936) 2304; site of monastery, founded c. 550 by Saint Columba, dissolved 1551, where was produced the Book of Kells, an elaborately illuminated manuscript of the Gospels in Latin, with certain local records, in the Irish Celtic style of the 7th to 9th cents., preserved in library of Trinity College, Dublin.

Kel′ly Field (kĕl′ĭ). U.S. Air Force base, Bexar co., S Texas, near San Antonio; established Apr. 1917; Air Corps Advanced Flying School (until 1942); air matériel depot.

Ke·loet′ *or* **Ke·lut′** *or* **Ke·lud′** (klŏot). Volcano 5678 ft. East Java prov., Indonesia, SE of Kediri.

Ke·low′na (kĕ·lō′ná). City, S Brit. Columbia, Canada, on E shore of Okanagan Lake 60 m. N of U.S. border; pop. 8517; fruit, tobacco, timber.

Kel′so (kĕl′sō). **1** City, ⊗ of Cowlitz co., SW Washington, on Cowlitz river just NE of Longview; pop. 8379; smelt fishing, lumbering, dairy farming.
2 Burgh (pop. 4119) and manufacturing town, Roxburgh co., SE Scotland, on the Tweed; ruined abbey; place where Sir Walter Scott attended school.

Keltsy. See KIELCE.

Kem (kĕm). **1** River ab. 250 m. long, Karelia, U.S.S.R.; flows E to White Sea opp. Solovetski Is.; outlet of Lake Kunto and other lakes of N cen. Karelia.
2 Seaport town, N Karelia, U.S.S.R., on Kem river ab. 10 m. above its mouth, 185 m. W of Arkhangelsk; pop. 2600; lumbering, fishing; station on Murmansk R.R.

Kemarat. See KHEMMARAT.

Ke′me·ro′vo (kĕm′ĕ·rō′vo; *Russ.* kä′myĕ·rŭ·vŭ). City, ✳ of Kemerovo Region, Soviet Russia, Asia, in Kuznetsk Basin 125 m. E of Novosibirsk; pop. 132,978; new industrial city on the Tom river, a tributary of the Ob, above Tomsk; important mining interests.

Kemerovo Region. Region of the Russian Soviet Federated Socialist Republic in Asia; ✳ Kemerovo; newly established during World War II from the SE part of Novosibirsk Region; Kuznetsk Basin in cen. part; mountainous in S; watered by Tom and Chulym rivers and their tributaries.

Ke′mi (kĕ′mĭ). **1** River ab. 300 m. long in Oulu dept., N Finland; flows S into head of Gulf of Bothnia.
2 Seaport, Oulu dept., N Finland, on Gulf of Bothnia; pop. (1939 est.) 19,300; sawmills; rail connections to the NE through Kemijärvi to Kandalaksha in Murmansk and to the SE with Oulu.

Ke′mi·jär′vi (kĕ′mĭ·yär′vĭ). **1** Lake in N cen. Finland, formed by expansion of Kemi river.
2 Town, N cen. Finland, in Oulu dept.; pop. 8357; 110 m. NE of Kemi. By treaty of Mar. 12, 1940 railroad to be built from it eastward to Kandalaksha in Murmansk Region.

Kemiö. See KIMITO.

Kem′mel′, Mont (môn′ kĕ′mĕl′). Height 5 m. SW of Ieper (Ypres), Belgium; scene of desperate battles in 1918, taken by Germans Apr. 24–27 and recaptured by British Aug. 31.

Kem′merer (kĕm′ẽr). Town, ⊗ of Lincoln co., SW Wyoming, 45 m. NNE of Evanston; pop. 2028; coal, livestock.

Kemp, Lake (kĕmp). See WICHITA FALLS DAM.

Kemp Coast, *formerly* **Kemp Land.** Section of coast of Antarctica W of Mac-Robertson Coast in ab. long. 56° to 59°40′E, lat. 66° to 68°S; on shore of Indian Ocean.

Kem′pen (kĕm′pĕn). Commune, western Germany, in North Rhine-Westphalia 40 m. NW of Cologne; pop. (1933) 8445; birthplace of Thomas a Kempis.

Kem′per (kĕm′pẽr). County in Mississippi. See *Table* at MISSISSIPPI.

Kemp′ston (kĕm[p]′stŭn). Urban district, Bedfordshire, SE cen. England, suburb of Bedford on the Ouse; pop. 8641.

Kemp′ten (kĕmp′tĕn). City, Swabia govt. dist., Bavaria, Germany, on Iller river 65 m. WSW of Munich;

pop. 21,874; important railroad center; dairy products, textiles, paper.

Ken (kän) *or* **Ka′yan** (kä′yȧn). River 230 m. long, N cen. India; flows N out of Bundelkhand into S Uttar Pradesh to the Jumna W of Allahabad.

Kena. Var. of QENA.

Ke′nai (kē′nĭ). Village, S Alaska, on Cook Inlet on NW coast of Kenai Penin.; pop. (est.) 900; airfield.

Kenai Mountains. Mountain range on Kenai Penin., S Alaska; highest 5684 ft.

Kenai Peninsula. Peninsula, S Alaska, bet. Cook Inlet on W and Prince William Sound on E; ab. 160 m. long by 130 m. wide; location of Seward and Seldovia.

Ke′nans·ville (kē′nănz·vĭl; *Sou. also* -v′l). Town, ⊗ of Duplin co., SE North Carolina; pop. 724.

Ken′dal. **1** Municipal borough, ⊗ of Westmorland, NW England, on the Kent 62 m. NNW of Manchester; pop. 18,543; has manufactured woolen goods since 14th cent.; also manufactures boots and shoes, paper, farm machinery. Ruins of a castle which was birthplace of Catherine Parr, 6th wife of Henry VIII.
2 (?kĕn·däl′) Town, Central Java prov., Indonesia, 15 m. W of Semarang near coast; pop. 13,804.

Ken′dall (kĕn′d′l). Counties in two states of the U.S. See *Tables* at ILLINOIS and TEXAS.

Ken′dall·ville (kĕn′d′l·vĭl). City, Noble co., NE Indiana, 27 m. N of Fort Wayne; pop. 6765; manufactures refrigerators, windmills, pumps.

Ken·da′ri (kĕn·dä′rē). Town and port, Celebes I., Indonesia, on E coast of the SE peninsula 240 m. ENE of Makassar; exports rattans, varnish resins, and native silverware; unimportant before 1941; seized Feb. 1, 1942 by Japanese who developed it as naval and air base for their operations against Amboina and Java.

Ken′drick Peak (kĕn′drĭk). Mountain 10,418 ft. in cen. Coconino co., N cen. Arizona.

Ken′e·dy (kĕn′ĕ·dĭ). **1** County in Texas. See *Table* at TEXAS.
2 City and health resort, Karnes co., S Texas, 49 m. W of Victoria; pop. 4301; hot mineral wells; cotton and food processing plants.

Keneh. Var. of KENA.

Kenesaw Mountain. Var. of KENNESAW MOUNTAIN.

Keng′tung (kĕng′tŏong). **1** Former state, largest of Southern Shan States, in E part, N Burma; 12,405 sq. m.; pop. 225,894; ✳ Kengtung; since 1947 part of Shan State; **Kengtung Hills** in cen. part rise to above 6500 ft.
2 Town, its ✳, on a tributary of the Mekong river and on main highway to Thailand 230 m. ESE of Mandalay; pop. 5508.

Ken′horst (kĕn′hôrst). Borough, Berks co., SE Pennsylvania; pop. 2815.

Kenia. Var. of KENYA.

Ke′nigs·berg (kyô′nyĭks·byẽrk). Russian form of *Königsberg*, now officially named KALININGRAD.

Ken′il·worth (kĕn′l·wûrth; -wẽrth). **1** Village, Cook co., NE Illinois, 17 m. N of Chicago; pop. 2959.
2 Borough, Union co., NE New Jersey, 4 m. W of Elizabeth; pop. 8357.
3 Urban district, Warwickshire, cen. England; pop. 10,738; ruins of great castle (celebrated by Sir Walter Scott in his novel *Kenilworth*) founded by Geoffrey de Clinton c. 1120, and the property of Simon de Montfort in 13th cent. and of John of Gaunt in middle 14th cent., presented by Queen Elizabeth to Robert Dudley, Earl of Leicester, who entertained the queen there in 1575 (as described in Scott's novel).

Kénitra. See PORT LYAUTEY.

Ken′mare (kĕn′mâr). City, Ward co., NW cen. North Dakota, 50 m. NW of Minot; pop. 1696; lake resort.

Ken·mare′ (kĕn·mâr′). Village and summer resort, co. Kerry, SW Eire; pop. ab. 1000; at head of **Ken′mare Riv′er** (kĕn′mâr rĭv′ẽr), a deep narrow inlet of Atlantic Ocean N of Bantry Bay, 5 m. wide at mouth.

KENTUCKY
AND
TENNESSEE

Statute Miles
0   10   20   30   40

⊛ State Capital

PUBLISHED BY G. & C. MERRIAM COMPANY
SPRINGFIELD, MASS.
PREPARED BY J. W. CLEMENT CO., BUFFALO, N. Y.

Ken′more (kĕn′mōr). Residential village, in town of Tonawanda, Erie co., W New York, on Niagara river 7 m. N of Buffalo; pop. 21,261.

Ken·more′ (kĕn·mōr′). Village and parish, Perth co., cen. Scotland, at NE end of Loch Tay near where river Tay flows out of it; pop. (1951) 873.

Ken′ne·bec (kĕn′ĕ·bĕk). **1** River 164 m. long, W cen. and S Maine; flows S from Moosehead Lake to Atlantic Ocean; navigable for large vessels to Bath.
2 County in Maine. See *Table* at MAINE.
3 Town, ⊗ of Lyman co., S cen. South Dakota; pop. 372.

Ken′ne·bunk (kĕn′ĕ·bŭngk; kĕn′ĕ·bŭngk′). Town, York co., SW Maine, 8 m. S of Biddeford; pop. 4551.

Ken′ne·bunk·port′ (kĕn′ĕ·bŭngk·pōrt′). Town, York co., SW Maine, on Atlantic Ocean 9 m. S of Biddeford; pop. 1851; summer resort.

Ken′ne·dy, Cape (kĕn′ĕ·dĭ). See Cape CANAVERAL.

Kennedy, Mount. Mountain 13,095 ft. NW Canada in Yukon Territory in Saint Elias Range SE of Mt. Logan.

Kennedy Channel. Channel ab. 110 m. long, NW coast of Greenland, bet. Washington Land and NE coast of Ellesmere I.; connects Kane and Hall basins.

Ken′ner (kĕn′ĕr). City, Jefferson parish, SE Louisiana, on Mississippi river 12 m. W of New Orleans; pop. 17,037.

Ken′ne·saw Mountain (kĕn′ĕ·sô). Isolated peak 1809 ft. in Cobb co., NW Georgia, near Atlanta; scene of battle June 27, 1864 in which Sherman made an unsuccessful frontal attack on Confederate troops in his campaign against Atlanta; set aside 1917 as Kennesaw Mountain Battlefield Site (648 acres), battlefield site abolished 1947; now part of **Kennesaw Mountain National Battlefield Park.**

Ken′net (kĕn′ĕt; -ĭt). River ab. 44 m. long in S England; flows ENE through Wiltshire and Berkshire into the Thames at Reading.

Ken′nett (kĕn′ĕt; -ĭt). City, ⊗ of Dunklin co., SE Missouri, 22 m. W of Caruthersville; pop. 9098; in cotton-growing section.

Kennett Square. Borough, Chester co., SE Pennsylvania, 33 m. WSW of Philadelphia; pop. 4355; settled 1705; ships mushrooms.

Ken′ne·wick (kĕn′ĕ·wĭk). City, Benton co., S Washington, on Columbia river 5 m. W of its confluence with Snake river; pop. 14,244; fruit, grapes, dairy products, wheat.

Ke·nog′a·mi (kĕ·nŏg′à·mĭ). **1** River ab. 200 m. long, cen. Ontario, Canada; flows NE and N from its chief source, Long Lake, just N of Lake Superior, to the Albany.
2 Lake, Lake St. John and Chicoutimi cos., S Quebec prov., Canada; receives the Chicoutimi river, which flows out of it NE into Saguenay river.
3 Town, Chicoutimi co., S Quebec, Canada, on Saguenay river 8 m. W of Chicoutimi and near Jonquière; pop. 9895; settled 1912 as a model town with pulp and paper mills.

Ke·no′ra (kĕ·nōr′à). **1** District, Ontario, Canada. See *Table* at ONTARIO.
2 Town, administrative center of Kenora dist., W Ontario, Canada, on Winnipeg river just N of Lake of the Woods; pop. 8695; flour, lumber, and pulp mills; important fisheries in lake and nearby streams; summer resort; railroad divisional point and commercial air base. Founded 1879 as Rat Portage; contested in boundary dispute bet. Manitoba and Ontario, with serious riots, July 1883; name changed 1904 to Kenora.

Ke·no′sha (kĕ·nō′shà). **1** County in Wisconsin. See *Table* at WISCONSIN.
2 Industrial city, ⊗ of Kenosha co., SE corner of Wisconsin, on Lake Michigan 10 m. S of Racine; pop. 67,899; manufactures automobiles, beds and bedsprings, brass and copper goods, hosiery and knit goods, machinery. Settled 1835.

Ke·no′va (kĕ·nō′và). City, Wayne co., SW West Virginia, at mouth of Big Sandy river 8 m. W of Hunting-

ton; pop. 4577; railroad center; ships petroleum products, cement, chemicals; manufactures electric insulators.

Ken·si·co Dam *and* **Reservoir** (kĕn′sĭ·kō; kĕn′zĭ-). See UNITED STATES, *Dams and Reservoirs.*

Ken′sing·ton (kĕn′sĭng·tŭn; -zĭng-). Subdivision (est. pop. 4500) of town of BERLIN, Connecticut; metal and paper goods.

Ken′sing·ton (kĕn′zĭng·tŭn). Metropolitan borough of London; includes **South Kensington.** See *Table* at LONDON.

Ken′sing·ton and Nor′wood (kĕn′zĭng·tŭn, nôr′wŏŏd). Joint municipality, SE South Australia, E suburb of Adelaide; pop. 14,402.

Kent (kĕnt). **1** Counties in five states of the U.S. See *Tables* at DELAWARE, MARYLAND, MICHIGAN, RHODE ISLAND, TEXAS.
2 Town, W Litchfield co., NW Connecticut, on New York border; pop. 1686; watered by Housatonic river; incorporated 1739; hydroelectric plant; resort and art colony; Kent School (preparatory school for boys).
3 Manufacturing city, Portage co., NE Ohio, on Cuyahoga river 8 m. ENE of Akron; pop. 17,836; buses, electric motors, automobile parts, air compressors, locks. Kent State Univ. (1910; coed.); Davey Institute of Tree Surgery.
4 City, King co., W cen. Washington, 16 m. S of Seattle; pop. 9017; hop culture; condensed milk, canned and frosted foods, cheese.
5 County, New Brunswick, Canada. See *Table* at NEW BRUNSWICK.
6 County, Ontario, Canada. See *Table* at ONTARIO.
7 River ab. 20 m. long, Westmorland, NW England; flows S into Morecambe Bay.
8 County, SE England; area 1525 sq. m.; pop. (1951) 1,563,286; ⊗ Maidstone; other towns Canterbury, Dover, Folkestone, Chatham, Ramsgate, Sheerness; agriculture, sheep grazing, dairying, fisheries, manufacturing (paper, pottery, iron products), shipbuilding. Territory occupied by the Cantii, a people of Britain, when Caesar arrived; settled by Anglo-Saxons, probably by Jutes, 5th cent. A.D.; first kingdom of Anglo-Saxon Heptarchy (*q.v.*) to attain under Ethelbert (560–616) supremacy S of the Humber; converted to Roman Christianity in 597 by Augustine, first archbishop of Canterbury; maintained its identity as subkingdom although it was soon ruled by Mercia (*q.v.*) and later by Wessex (*q.v.*).

Ken′tei′ Shan (gĕn′tā′ shän′). Mountain range, N Outer Mongolia, NE of Urga, in part parallel with U.S.S.R. border; highest 8494 ft.

Kent Island (kĕnt). Island 15 m. long in upper Chesapeake Bay, W Queen Annes co., E Maryland; largest island in the bay; site of trading station established 1631 by William Claiborne.

Kent′land (kĕnt′lǎnd). Town, ⊗ of Newton co., NW Indiana, 37 m. NW of Lafayette; pop. 1783; cheese factory.

Ken′ton (kĕn′t′n; -tŭn). **1** County in Kentucky. See *Table* at KENTUCKY.
2 City, ⊗ of Hardin co., NW cen. Ohio, on the Scioto river 26 m. E of Lima; pop. 8747; manufactures electric cranes, hoists, welders, foundry products, toys and games, food products; limestone quarries; in agricultural section producing esp. onions.

Kent Point. South tip of Kent I., Chesapeake Bay, Maryland.

Ken·tuck′y (kĕn·tŭk′ĭ; kĭn-). **1** Navigable river 259 m. long, N cen. Kentucky; formed by confluence of forks in Lee co., flows NW into Ohio river in N Carroll co.
2 An east central state of U.S.A., 15th state admitted to Union (1792); bounded on N by Illinois, Indiana, and Ohio, on E by West Virginia and Virginia, on S by Tennessee, and on W by Missouri; 37th state in area, 40,395 sq. m. (land area 39,864 sq. m.) 22d state in population, 3,038,156; ✴ Frankfort. See *Map,* pp. 546–547; also

Table of States at UNITED STATES. Divided into the following 120 counties (for pronunciation of their names, see their individual entries):

NAME	LOCATION	AREA[1]	POP.[1]	CO. SEAT
Adair	S cen.	393	14,699	Columbia
Allen	S	364	12,269	Scottsville
Anderson	cen.	206	8,618	Lawrenceburg
Ballard	W	259	8,261	Wickliffe
Barren	S	486	28,303	Glasgow
Bath	NE	287	9,114	Owingsville
Bell	SE	370	35,336	Pineville
Boone	N	252	21,940	Burlington
Bourbon[2]	NE	300	18,178	Paris
Boyd	NE	159	52,163	Catlettsburg
Boyle	cen.	182	21,257	Danville
Bracken	NE	206	7,422	Brooksville
Breathitt	E	494	15,490	Jackson
Breckinridge	NW cen.	566	14,734	Hardinsburg
Bullitt	cen.	300	15,726	Shepherdsville
Butler	W cen.	443	9,586	Morgantown
Caldwell	W	357	13,073	Princeton
Calloway	SW	381	20,972	Murray
Campbell	N	151	86,803	Alexandria & Newport
Carlisle	SW	196	5,608	Bardwell
Carroll	N	131	7,978	Carrollton
Carter	NE	402	20,817	Grayson
Casey	cen.	435	14,327	Liberty
Christian	SW	726	56,904	Hopkinsville
Clark	E cen.	259	21,075	Winchester
Clay	SE	474	20,748	Manchester
Clinton	S	191	8,886	Albany
Crittenden	W	365	8,648	Marion
Cumberland	S	307	7,835	Burkesville
Daviess	NW	466	70,588	Owensboro
Edmonson[3]	SW cen.	304	8,085	Brownsville
Elliott	NE	240	6,330	Sandy Hook
Estill	E	260	12,466	Irvine
Fayette[4]	NE cen.	280	131,906	Lexington
Fleming	NE	350	10,890	Flemingsburg
Floyd	E	402	41,642	Prestonsburg
Franklin	N cen.	211	29,421	Frankfort
Fulton	SW corner	205	11,256	Hickman
Gallatin	N	100	3,867	Warsaw
Garrard	E cen.	236	9,747	Lancaster
Grant	N	250	9,489	Williamstown
Graves	SW	560	30,021	Mayfield
Grayson	W cen.	514	15,834	Leitchfield
Green	cen.	282	11,249	Greensburg
Greenup	NE	350	29,238	Greenup
Hancock	NW cen.	187	5,330	Hawesville
Hardin	cen.	616	67,789	Elizabethtown
Harlan	SE	469	51,107	Harlan
Harrison	N	308	13,704	Cynthiana
Hart[3]	cen.	425	14,119	Munfordville
Henderson	NW	440	33,519	Henderson
Henry	N	289	10,987	New Castle
Hickman	SW	248	6,747	Clinton
Hopkins	W	555	38,458	Madisonville
Jackson	SE	337	10,677	McKee
Jefferson	N cen.	375	610,947	Louisville
Jessamine	E cen.	177	13,625	Nicholasville
Johnson	E	264	19,748	Paintsville
Kenton	N	165	120,700	Covington & Independence
Knott	SE	356	17,362	Hindman
Knox	SE	373	25,258	Barbourville
Larue[5]	cen.	260	10,346	Hodgenville
Laurel	SE	443	24,901	London
Lawrence	E	425	12,134	Louisa
Lee	E	210	7,420	Beattyville
Leslie	SE	412	10,941	Hyden
Letcher	SE	339	30,102	Whitesburg
Lewis	NE	485	13,115	Vanceburg
Lincoln	E cen.	340	16,503	Stanford
Livingston	W	317	7,029	Smithland
Logan	S	563	20,896	Russellville
Lyon	W	254	5,924	Eddyville
McCracken	W	251	57,306	Paducah
McCreary	SE	408	12,463	Whitley City
McLean	W	257	9,355	Calhoun
Madison	E cen.	446	33,482	Richmond
Magoffin	E	303	11,156	Salyersville
Marion	cen.	343	16,887	Lebanon
Marshall	W	303	16,736	Benton
Martin	E	231	10,201	Inez
Mason	NE	239	18,454	Maysville
Meade	NW cen.	308	18,938	Brandenburg
Menifee	E	210	4,276	Frenchburg
Mercer	cen.	256	14,596	Harrodsburg
Metcalfe	S	296	8,367	Edmonton
Monroe	S	334	11,799	Tompkinsville
Montgomery	E	204	13,461	Mount Sterling
Morgan	E	369	11,056	West Liberty
Muhlenberg	W	482	27,791	Greenville
Nelson	cen.	437	22,168	Bardstown
Nicholas	NE	204	6,677	Carlisle

NAME	LOCATION	AREA[1]	POP.[1]	CO. SEAT
Ohio	W cen.	596	17,725	Hartford
Oldham	N	184	13,388	La Grange
Owen	N	351	8,237	Owenton
Owsley	E	197	5,369	Booneville
Pendleton	N	279	9,968	Falmouth
Perry	SE	343	34,961	Hazard
Pike	E	786	68,264	Pikeville
Powell	E	173	6,674	Stanton
Pulaski	SE cen.	630	34,403	Somerset
Robertson	NE	101	2,443	Mount Olivet
Rockcastle	SE cen.	311	12,334	Mount Vernon
Rowan	NE	290	12,808	Morehead
Russell	S	242	11,076	Jamestown
Scott	N cen.	284	15,376	Georgetown
Shelby	N cen.	384	18,493	Shelbyville
Simpson	S	239	11,548	Franklin
Spencer	cen.	193	5,680	Taylorsville
Taylor	cen.	284	16,285	Campbellsville
Todd	SW	376	11,364	Elkton
Trigg	SW	457	8,870	Cadiz
Trimble	N	146	5,102	Bedford
Union	W	343	14,537	Morganfield
Warren	S	546	45,491	Bowling Green
Washington	cen.	307	11,168	Springfield
Wayne	S	440	14,700	Monticello
Webster	W	339	14,244	Dixon
Whitley	SE	458	25,815	Williamsburg
Wolfe	E	227	6,534	Campton
Woodford	E cen.	193	11,913	Versailles

[1] Area = land area in sq. m. Pop. from 1960 Census.
[2] The term *Bourbon whisky* was originally applied to corn whisky made in this county.
[3] Mammoth Cave National Park in Edmonson co. (E cen. and E; major portion of park, including Mammoth Cave itself) and Hart co. (W).
[4] Center of the "Bluegrass" region and of race-horse breeding.
[5] Central portion contains Abraham Lincoln National Historical Park.

Nickname: Bluegrass State. *State flower:* Goldenrod. *Motto:* United We Stand, Divided We Fall. *Chief cities:* Louisville, Lexington, Covington. Owensboro, Paducah. *Rivers:* Ohio, forming N boundary of the state, and receiving in W the waters of the Tennessee and the Cumberland, and in N cen. region the waters of the Kentucky and the Licking. *Highest point:* Big Black Mountain 4150 ft., in Harlan co. *Chief industries:* Agriculture (corn, wheat, tobacco), whisky distilling, horse raising, coal mining.

History: First entered by English 1750; included in territory ceded by French 1763; explored by expeditions under Daniel Boone from 1769; first permanent English settlement at Boonesborough made by Transylvania Co. 1775; because of its many Indian wars known as the "Dark and Bloody Ground"; organized as county of Virginia 1776; included in territory of U.S. by Treaty of Paris 1783; received consent of Virginia to statehood 1789; admitted to Union June 1, 1792; despite an attempt to be neutral in American Civil War, invaded by Confederate troops 1862.

Kentucky Dam. See *Table* at TENNESSEE VALLEY AUTHORITY.

Kent'ville (kĕnt'vĭl). Agricultural town, ⊗ of Kings co., W Nova Scotia, Canada, 55 m. NW of Halifax; pop. 4240; near early Acadian settlements; noted for its fine apples. Settled by New Englanders in 1760.

Kent'wood (kĕnt'wŏŏd). Town, Tangipahoa parish, SE Louisiana, 54 m. NE of Baton Rouge; pop. 2607; cotton, lumber.

Ken'ya (kĕn'yȧ; kēn'yȧ); *formerly* **East Africa Protectorate.** Republic; former Brit. crown colony and protectorate, E Africa; area 224 960 sq. m.; pop. (1966 est.) 9,200,000; ✳ Nairobi; divided into seven provinces (Central, Coast, Eastern, Nyanza, North East, Rift Valley, and Western) and one extraterritorial district (Nairobi). Kenya Protectorate, comprising the coast islands and a coastal strip 10 m. wide from S boundary to Tana river, leased from Sultan of Zanzibar, administered as a part of Coast Province. Bounded on N by Ethiopia, on E by Somalia, on SE by Indian Ocean, on S by Tanganyika, on W by Lake Victoria and Uganda, and on NW by Sudan. Mountainous in W half, having two

N–S ranges with the Great Rift Valley bet. them; highest peaks Mt. Kenya 17,040 ft., in center nearly on the equator, and Mt. Elgon 14,176 ft., on Uganda border. Lowland strip along coast extends gradually up into wide level plain which in the N is high and arid. Noted for its abundance of big game and also for its numerous forest and bush animals. Rivers are Tana and Waso Nyiro in the E and many short streams in the W flowing into Lakes Victoria on SW and Rudolf, a large long lake in NW; many small lakes in Great Rift Valley (*q.v.*). Agriculture is important, high levels at the equator allowing great variety of products; chief exports coffee, sugar, tea, cotton sisal and other fibers, and tin. Chief towns Nairobi, Mombasa, Kisumu, Nakuru.

History: East African coast frequented by British traders from early 19th cent.; coastal strip belonging to ruler of Zanzibar (*q.v.*) leased 1887 to British East Africa Co. which soon extended its holdings into the interior; boundaries with German East Africa (see TANGANYIKA) fixed 1886, 1890; region organized as British East Africa Protectorate 1895; except for the coastal strip, which together with its islands was named Kenya Protectorate (see above), region made crown colony 1920; became independent member of Brit. Commonwealth 1963.

Kenya, Mount. Extinct volcano 17,040 ft. in cen. Kenya colony, E Africa, near the equator.

Ken'yon (kĕn'yŭn). Village, Goodhue co., SE Minnesota, 13 m. E of Faribault; pop. 1624.

Ken–zan–fu. See SIAN.

Ke'o·kuk (kē'ŏ·kŭk). **1** County in Iowa. See *Table* at IOWA.

2 City, a ⊗ of Lee co., SE Iowa, on Mississippi river at extreme SE corner of state; pop. 16,316; manufactures cereal products, steel products, tires, clothing; site of **Keokuk Dam** (completed 1913 across Mississippi river, height 53 ft.), which impounds water, **Lake Keokuk,** for water power.

Ke·on'jhar (kå·ōn'jĕr). **1** Former Indian state, E Eastern States, NE Indian Union; 3206 sq. m.; pop. (1941) 529,786; once in Orissa Feudatory States.

2 Town, its ✳, 83 m. N of Cuttack; pop. ab. 5000.

Ke·on'thal (kå·ōnt'hȧl). Former Indian state, Punjab States, N East Punjab, NW India, one of the group of Simla Hill States; 116 sq. m.

Ke'os (kē'ŏs) *or* **Ze'a** (*Ital.* tsâ'ä); *Mod. Gr.* **Ké'os** (kyâ'ôs); *anc.* **Ce'os** (sē'ŏs). Island, NW Cyclades, in Aegean Sea; belongs to Cyclades dept., Greece; 12 m. long, area 67 sq. m.; pop. ab. 4000; chief town **Ké'a** (kyâ'ä); ab. 13 m. SE of Cape Colonna, the S point of Attica; birthplace of the poets Simonides and Bacchylides.

Ke'o·sau'qua (kē'ŏ·sô'kwȧ). Town, ⊗ of Van Buren co., SE Iowa; pop. 1023.

Keowee. See SENECA river.

Keph'al·lē·ni'a (kyâ'fä·lyĕ·nyē'ä). See CEPHALONIA island, Ionian Is., Greece.

Kep'hart, Mount (kĕp'härt). Peak 6400 ft. in Great Smoky Mts., on boundary bet. Tennessee and North Carolina 8 m. NE of Clingmans Dome.

Keppel's Island. See NIUATOBUTABU.

Ke'rak (kŭ'rŏk). **1** Ancient emirate, N Arabia, E of the Jordan river; region now in Jordan.

2 See EL KERAK.

Ke'ra·la (kā'rȧ·lȧ). State, SW India, bordering on Arabian Sea; formed 1956 from Travancore and Cochin state and part of Madras state; ✳ Trivandrum; area 15,035 sq. m.; pop. 15,000,000.

Ke·ra·ma Islands; *Jap.* **Kerama Ret·to** (kĕ·rä·mä rĕt·tō). Group of small islands off SW coast of Okinawa I., Ryukyu Is., Japan; largest Tokashiki; first landings in Okinawa campaign made here by U.S. forces Mar. 26–27, 1945.

Kerasun. See GİRESUN.

Ker·bau', Gu'nong (gōo'nông kĕr·bou'). Mountain (*gunong*) 7159 ft. in Federation of Malaya, S Malay Penin., on boundary bet. NW Pahang and E Perak; second highest peak in Malay Penin.

Kerbela. See KARBALA.

Kerch (kĕrch). **1** Peninsula ab. 70 m. long extending E from the Crimea; consists of low land with salt lakes and mud springs; considerable mineral resources.

2 City, E Crimea, Soviet Russia, at E end of Kerch Penin. on Kerch Strait; pop. 104,471; an active seaport; exports iron ore; railroad terminus; mining and metallurgical industries; church of St. John the Baptist, founded 717; archaeologically of special interest because of antiquities found in vicinity. One of oldest cities of S Russia; as Greek colony of **Pan'ti·ca·pae'um** (păn'tĭ-kå-pē'ŭm), founded by Milesians c. 600 B.C.; with surrounding territory formed kingdom of the Cimmerian Bosporus (*q.v.*) which was later conquered by Pontus; held by Huns, Khazars, and other invaders of Crimea (*q.v.*); trading port held by Genoese from 14th to 15th cent. when Turks captured it; its conquest by Russia confirmed 1774; damaged in Crimean War. In World War II although peninsula overrun by Germans when Crimea was invaded 1941, city not captured until May 16, 1942; saw much violent fighting before its recapture by Russians Apr. 1944.

Kerch, *or* **E'ni·ka·le'** (ā'nĕ·kä·lĕ'), **Strait;** *anc.* **Bos'po·rus Cim·me'ri·us** (bŏs'pŏ·rŭs sĭ·mēr'ĭ·ŭs). Shallow strait connecting Sea of Azov with Black Sea; 25 m. long, 2 to 9 m. wide; lies E of Kerch Penin.

Ke'rem·pe' Cape (kĕ'rĕm·pē'); *Turk.* **Kerempe Burun'** (bōo·rōon'). Cape on NW coast of Turkey in Asia, on the Black Sea bet. Zonguldak and Sinop.

Keren. See CHEREN.

Ker'gue·len (kûr'gĕ·lĕn; -lĕn) *or* **Des'o·la'tion Island** (dĕs'ō·lā'shŭn); *Fr.* **Ker'gué'len'** (kĕr'gā'lĕn'). French island in S Indian Ocean, lat. 49°S and long. 70°E; area 1318 sq. m.; a French dependency; mountainous, highest point Mt. Ross 6429 ft.; irregular coast line with deep fiords; snow fields in center, many lakes and pools in lower outer portion; Kerguelen cabbage (*Pringlea antiscorbutica*) not so abundant as formerly. Discovered by French navigator Kerguélen-Trémarec Feb. 13, 1772; annexed by France Jan., 1893.

Ke·rin'tji (kĕ·rĭn'chē) *or* **Ko·rin'tji** (kŏ-). **1** Lake in Barisan Mts., W Sumatra, 115 m. SSE of Padang.

2 *formerly* **In'dra·poe'ra** (ĭn'drȧ·pōo'rȧ). Volcanic peak 12,467 ft. in W cen. Sumatra, in Barisan Mts. 80 m. SSE of Padang; highest mountain in Sumatra.

Ke'ri'ya' (kŭ'lē'yä'). **1** River ab. 300 m. long, SW Sinkiang, W China; rises in Astin Tagh and flows N into Takla Makan (desert).

2 *or* **Ki'ri'a'** (kŭ'lē'yä'); *Chin.* **Yu'tien'** (yü'tĭ·ĕn'). Town on Keriya river, S Sinkiang prov., W China, 95 m. ESE of Khotan; pop. ab. 16,000; on S caravan and motor highway across Sinkiang; starting point for route S to W Tibet.

Ker'ka (kĕr'kä; *Angl.* kûr'kȧ); *Serbo-Croat.* **Kr'ka** (kûr'kä; *Angl.* -kȧ); *anc.* **Ti'ti·us** (tĭsh'ĭ·ŭs; tĭsh'ŭs). River ab. 40 m. long, N Dalmatia, in Bosnia and Herzegovina, W Yugoslavia; flows S into Adriatic Sea a little below Šibenik; has a long, wide estuary and is noted for several beautiful waterfalls bet. Knin and Šibenik.

Ker·ken'nah Islands (kĕr·kĕn'ä), *also* **Kar·ken'ah** (kär·kĕn'ä); *anc.* **Cer·ci'na** (sĕr·sī'nä). Group of islands in cen. Mediterranean Sea, off E coast of Tunisia, at N side of entrance to Gulf of Gabès; to Tunisia.

Kerkheh. See KARKHEH.

Ker·ki' (kĕr·kē'). Town, SE Turkmen S.S.R., Central Asia, on left bank of Amu Darya near Afghanistan border, 170 m. SW of Samarkand; pop. ab. 7000; a caravan and trade center.

Kerkinitis. See Lake AKHINOU.

Kerk'ra'de (kĕrk'rä'dĕ). Commune, Limburg prov., SE Netherlands, on German frontier 18 m. E of Maastricht; pop. (1939) 37,564; in coal-mining region.

Kerkuk. Var. of KIRKUK.

Kérkyra. See Corfu.

Ker·mad′ec Islands (kẽr·măd′ĕk; -ĭk). Uninhabited island group in SW cen. Pacific Ocean, ab. 600 m. NNW of New Zealand and ab. 500 m. S of S Tonga Is.; 13 sq. m.; annexed to New Zealand 1887; largest island Raoul, or Sunday, I.

Ker·man′ (kẽr·män′). **1** *anc.* **Car·ma′ni·a** (kär·mā′-nĭ·à; -män′yà). Province, SE Iran; 167,612 sq. m.; ✱ Kerman; the largest province of modern Iran, covering SW part of Plateau of Iran; ancient Carmania a subdivision of Ariana and a province of Persian Empire and of Alexander's Empire, bounded on N by Parthia, on E by Drangiana and Gedrosia, on S by water (mod. Persian Gulf and Gulf of Oman), and on W by Persis.
2 *anc.* **Car·ma′na** (kär·mā′nà). City, its ✱; pop. ab. 50,000; on motor road from Isfahan and Yezd extending SE to Zahidan (Duzdab); manufactures shawls and carpets; its ancient mosque dates from 11th cent.; most of city destroyed 1794 by an earthquake.

Ker·man′shah′ (kẽr·män′shä′; *native* -shä′h′). **1** Province, W Iran; 10,617 sq. m.; one of most productive regions of Iran.
2 City, its ✱, ab. 90 m. W of Hamadan; pop. ab. 89,000; on ancient trade and caravan route from Hamadan to the Tigris; connects by rail with Khanaqin in Iraq; large Kurd population.

Ker·mi·an′ (kẽr′mê·än′). Sanjak or district, SW cen. Anatolia, Ottoman Empire; comprises region SW of Akshehr.

Ker′mit (kûr′mĭt). City, ⊗ of Winkler co., W Texas, 43 m. NNE of Pecos; pop. 10,465.

Kern (kûrn). **1** River ab. 150 m. long, S cen. California; rises in NE Tulare co. and flows SW through Bakersfield into Buena Vista Lake.
2 County in California. See *Table* at California.

Ker′ners·ville (kûr′nẽrz·vĭl; *Sou. also* -v′l). Town, Forsyth co., N cen. North Carolina, 9 m. E of Winston-Salem; pop. 2942; manufactures silk, hosiery.

Kerns′town (kûrnz′toun). Village, Frederick co., N Virginia, 4 m. S of Winchester; battle Mar. 23, 1862 in which Federal forces under Gen. Nathan Kimball defeated Gen. Jackson's Confederate troops.

Ké′ro·man′ (kā′rô′män′). Village and fishing port of Brittany, NW France, adjacent to Lorient; after 1920 developed by French government as port for trawlers and during World War II by Germans as U-boat base.

Kerr (kûr). County in Texas. See *Table* at Texas.

Kerr′ville (kûr′vĭl; *Sou. also* -v′l). City, ⊗ of Kerr co., SW cen. Texas, 55 m. NNW of San Antonio; pop. 8901; livestock, cotton; market for wool and mohair; resort.

Ker′ry (kĕr′ĭ). County, SW Eire, in Munster prov.; 1815 sq. m.; pop. 139,834; ⊗ Tralee; mountainous area, with many lakes (Lakes of Killarney, etc.); agriculture, dairy farming, fishing, quarrying (limestone, slate).

Kerry Head. Cape on SW coast of Ireland, on S side of mouth of Shannon river.

Ker·shaw′ (kẽr·shô′). County in South Carolina. See *Table* at South Carolina.

Ker′to·so′no(kẽr′tô·sō′nō). Town, East Java prov., Indonesia, 55 m. SW of Surabaja; pop. 12,249.

Ker′u·len (kẽr′ōō·lĕn). **1** River 650 m. long, NE Outer Mongolia; rises in Kentei Shan, flows S then E to Hulun Nor in NW Manchuria; a headstream of the Amur.
2 *or* **Ba′yan Tu·men′** (bä′yän tōō·mĕn′). Town, NE Outer Mongolia, on Kerulen river; station on caravan and motor highway from Hulun in Manchuria to Urga, also junction for road to Borzya in U.S.S.R.

Ke·run′, Lake (kĕ·rōōn′). = Birket Qârûn.

Ke·she′na (kĕ·shē′nà). Village, ⊗ of Menominee co., NE Wisconsin, on Wolf river; pop. (est.) 400.

Kes′sel-Loo′ (kĕs′ĕl-lō′). Commune, Brabant prov., cen. Belgium, adjacent to Louvain 7 m. E of Brussels; pop. 12,324.

Kes′te′ven, the Parts of (kĕs′tē′vĕn; kĕs·tē′vĕn). See Lincolnshire.

Kes′wick (kĕz′ĭk). Urban district, Cumberland, NW England, near N end of Derwentwater; pop. 4868; lead pencils from locally mined graphite; village is 3½ m. S of Skiddaw and is cen. point for various expeditions in the Lake District; home of Coleridge 1800–09 and of Southey 1803–43. Scene of first Keswick Convention 1875 and headquarters of Keswick Movement.

Keszt′hely (kĕst′hā). Commune, W Hungary, at W end of Lake Balaton; pop. 10,122.

Ket (kĕt). Navigable river ab. 500 m. long, S Siberia, Soviet Russia, Asia; rises N of Krasnoyarsk in SW Krasnoyarsk Territory, flows W into Ob river at Kolpashevo.

Ke′ta (kē′tà) *or* **Kwit′ta** (kwĭt′à). Seaport, E Ghana, W Africa, on Keta Lagoon; pop. ab. 6000.

Ke·ta′pang (kĕ·tä′päng). Seaport town, West Borneo prov., SW Borneo, Indonesia; pop. 4385; on Karimata Strait and only port of importance on Borneo coast bet. Pontianak and Bandjermasin.

Ketch′i·kan′ (kĕch′ĭ·kăn′). Town and seaport on SW coast of Revillagigedo I., SE Alaska; pop. 6483; well-built modern town, the first Alaskan port of call from U.S.; salmon fishing, mining, fur raising; timber.

Ketch′um (kĕch′ŭm). Village and precinct (pop. 746), Blaine co., cen. Idaho, SE of Sawtooth Mts.; just N of it is Sun Valley (*q.v.*).

Ke·toi (kĕ·toi). One of the Kuril Is., NE of Shimushiru.

Kęt′rzyn (kĕnt′shĭn); *Ger.* **Ra′sten·burg** (räs′tĕn-bŏŏrk). City, NE Olsztyn dept., N Poland, W of Lake Mamry; pop. (1946) 10,200; formerly in East Prussia.

Ket′ter·ing (kĕt′ẽr·ĭng). **1** City, Montgomery co., SW Ohio, S of Dayton; pop. 54,462.
2 Urban district, Northamptonshire, cen. England, 50 m. E of Birmingham; pop. 36,799.

Ket′tle (kĕt′'l). River ab. 160 m. long, British Columbia and NE Washington; rises in British Columbia, flows S across Washington border, bends NE and enters British Columbia for a short distance, then turns S across border and joins Columbia river in E Ferry co., Washington.

Kettle Dome. Peak 9452 ft. in Sierra Nevada, E Fresno co., S cen. California.

Kettle Peak. Mountain 10,038 ft. in Sierra Nevada, N Tulare co., S cen. California.

Kettle River Range. Range in N Ferry co., NE Washington, extending N into British Columbia.

Keu′ka (kū′kà; kà·ū′kà), *or* **Crook′ed** (krŏŏk′ĕd; -ĭd) **Lake.** Lake in W New York, extending across boundary bet. Yates and Steuben cos.; one of the Finger Lakes; ab. 18 m. long and 1½ m. average width; outlet from N end into Seneca Lake; vineyards along its shores.

Keuka Park. Village, Yates co., W New York, on Keuka Lake; Keuka College (1890; women).

Keunjhar. Var. of Keonjhar.

Ke′ve·laer (kā′vĕ·lär). Town, North Rhine-Westphalia, W Germany, NW of Düsseldorf; pop. ab. 9000; area to S scene Mar. 3, 1945 of contact bet. American and Canadian forces.

Kew (kū). **1** City, S Victoria, SE Australia, NE suburb of Melbourne; pop. 25,487.
2 Parish, Surrey, S England, suburb of London on right bank of Thames opp. Brentford; pop. 4362; Royal Botanic Gardens, largest and finest in the world, originating in 1759 and adopted as a national establishment 1840; Gardens have 25,000 varieties, area with adjoining pleasure grounds 288 acres.

Ke·wa′nee (kê·wŏn′ê). City, Henry co., NW Illinois, 38 m. ESE of Rock Island; pop. 16,324; agriculture, coal mining; farm implements, boilers, mine chutes.

Ke·wau′nee (kê·wô′nê). **1** County in Wisconsin. See *Table* at Wisconsin.
2 City, its ⊗, E Wisconsin, on Lake Michigan 25 m. E of Green Bay (city); pop. 2772; founded as fur-trading post 1795; manufactures school, office, and church furniture, aluminum ware, machinery.

Ke′wee·naw (kē′wê·nô). County in Michigan. See *Table* at Michigan.

Keweenaw Bay. Inlet of Lake Superior, SE of Keweenaw and upper Houghton cos. and extending S into Baraga co., NW Michigan penin.

Keweenaw Peninsula. Peninsula, NW part of Michigan penin., including Keweenaw co. and part of Houghton co., extending into Lake Superior; tip end is called **Keweenaw Point.** The **Keweenaw Waterway** crosses the peninsula from Keweenaw Bay, through Portage Lake to Lake Superior, shortening the route to Duluth, Minnesota.

Kew Gardens (kū). Residential community in Queens borough of New York City, Queens co., SE New York, on Long I.

Kexholm. See KEKSGOLM.

Key'a Pa'ha (kē'á pä'hä). County in Nebraska. See Table at NEBRASKA.

Key Bis·cayne' (kē' bis·kān'). Island off coast of Dade co., SE Florida, bet. N Biscayne Bay and Atlantic Ocean.

Key Islands (kī). Var. of Kei Islands: see KAI ISLANDS.

Key Lar'go (kē' lär'gō). One of the larger of the Florida Keys, 30 m. long, less than 2 m. wide; traversed by the first island link of the Overseas Highway (see FLORIDA KEYS).

Key'port (kē'pōrt). **1** Borough, Monmouth co., E cen. New Jersey, on Raritan Bay 7 m. SSE of Perth Amboy; pop. 6440; boat-building and fishing center; airplanes, rubber goods, furniture. **2** Village, Kitsap co., W Washington, on arm of Puget Sound N of Bremerton; pop. (est.) 500; site of a naval torpedo station.

Key'ser (kī'zēr). City, ⊗ of Mineral co., NE West Virginia, on North Branch of the Potomac river 58 m. W of Martinsburg; pop. 6192; agriculture; supply point and battleground in Civil War.

Key'stone' (kē'stōn'). City, McDowell co., S West Virginia, 8 m. E of Welch; pop. 1457.

Keystone Dam. See UNITED STATES, Dams and Reservoirs.

Keytes'ville (kēts'vil). City, ⊗ of Chariton co., N cen. Missouri; pop. 644.

Key Vac'a (kē' văk'á). See FLORIDA KEYS.

Key West (kē' wĕst'). City, ⊗ of Monroe co., SW corner of Florida, on **Key West** (island less than 4 m. long by 2 m. wide at SW extremity of Florida keys) 60 m. SW of S tip of Florida; pop. 33,956; southernmost city of U.S. excluding Hawaii; sponge and turtle fisheries; cigar making; U.S. naval station and fort (Fort Taylor); winter resort. Became bankrupt 1934 and was subject of government planned experiment to make the city a popular resort; success of plan prevented by hurricane 1935 which destroyed the railroad and highway approaches; now within five hours of Miami by motor since completion of Overseas Highway 1938 (see FLORIDA KEYS).

Kha·ba'rovsk (kŭ·bä'rŭfsk). City, ✳ of Khabarovsk Territory, on right bank of Amur river 29 m. below Ussuri tributary; pop. 199,364; former capital of Far Eastern Region; junction station on Trans-Siberian R.R.; market for products of the Ussuri valley; center in the fur trade; in recent years has made rapid industrial advancement; oil refinery, radio station. Site of fort established 1652; settled by Russian colonists under Count N. Muraviëv-Amurski 1858.

Khabarovsk Territory. A territory of Soviet Russia, Asia, along Pacific coast of Siberia from Amur river to Bering Strait; 1,067,444 sq. m.; pop. 1,430,875; ✳ Khabarovsk; since 1945 has been reduced by formation in N of Chukot and Koryak National Districts and has been increased by addition of S Sakhalin (Karafuto) and the Kuril Is. Bounded on W and NW by Yakutsk A.S.S.R., on NE by Koryak National District, on E by Pacific Ocean, on SE by Maritime Territory (Primorski Krai), on S by Manchuria, and on SW by Chita Region; almost entirely encloses the Sea of Okhotsk; includes the S two thirds of Kamchatka Penin., Komandorskie Is.,

Sakhalin I. and Kuril Is., and (geographically) the Jewish Autonomous Region. Rivers: S part lies in basin of the lower Amur, which forms for ab. 700 m. the boundary with China (Manchuria); other rivers are the Zeya and Amgun, tributaries of the Amur, and the upper courses of the Maya and Kolyma. Mountains: Traversed by numerous ranges, running generally NE and SW, esp. E end of the Stanovoi Mts. and the Kolyma range; in Kamchatka are the highest peaks in Siberia and the only active volcanoes. Natural resources, industries, etc.: Has great mineral resources, esp. in coal and iron; steel industry at Komsomolsk and other cities; many new power plants, oil refineries, mills and factories; fishing and agriculture; has section of double-tracked Trans-Siberian R.R. along the Amur to Khabarovsk and thence S to Vladivostok, a branch N to Komsomolsk, and the new BAM transcontinental to Komsomolsk (q.v.) from the NW. Chief cities: Khabarovsk, Blagoveshchensk, Komsomolsk, Petropavlovsk, Magadan, Aleksandrovsk.

History: First settlements were forts at Okhotsk and on Kamchatka, established by Cossacks in latter half of 17th cent.; settlements along the Amur began in 19th cent. and Amur made the boundary by Treaty of Aigun 1858; Trans-Siberian R.R. completed 1915; much confusion in region 1917–20 but independent Far Eastern Republic set up 1920. See FAR EASTERN REGION.

Kha·bur' or **Kha·bour'** (kä·boor'); anc. **Ha'bor** (hā'bôr). River ab. 200 m. long, SE Turkey in Asia and NE Syria, rising in S slopes of Karacadağ mountain and flowing S into the Euphrates river just below the town of Deir-ez-Zor.

Kha·bu'ra (kä·boo'rô). Coastal town, Oman, SE Arabia, on Gulf of Oman ab. 100 m. WNW of Masqat.

Khaf. See RU-I-KHAF.

Kha'fa·je (kä'fä·yä). Site of ancient Sumerian city, Mesopotamia, on E bank of Diyala river just E of Baghdad, E Iraq; has revealed archaeological objects, esp. Sumerian stone statuettes dating ab. 3000 B.C.

Khaibar. See KHYBER.

Khaifa. Var. of HAIFA.

Khai'ra·garh (kī'rä·gär'; native -gŭr'h'). **1** Former Indian state, Eastern States, NE Indian Union, W of Nandgaon state; 931 sq. m.; pop. (1941) 173,713. **2** Town, its ✳, 107 m. E of Nagpur; pop. 4159.

Khair'pur (kīr'poor). **1** Former Indian state, NE Sind, Pakistan, E of the Indus river; 5989 sq. m.; pop. (1941) 305,787; geographically in Sind, once administered under the Punjab States Agency; under ruler of a Baluch family; loyal to British in Afghan campaigns of 19th cent. **2** Town, its ✳, 15 m. S of Sukkur; pop. 11,582.

Kha·kass' Autonomous Region (kä·käs'; Russ. кŭ-käs'). An autonomous region of the R.S.F.S.R., S Siberia, geographically in SW Krasnoyarsk Territory; 19,161 sq. m.; pop. 270,655, (1941 est.) 284,404; ✳ Abakan; mountainous, with valuable mines and forests; agriculture, cattle raising. Predominant ethnic strain Turkic and Mongol; chief nationalities Khakass ab. 52%, Russian 48%.

Khalepa. See HALEPA.

Kha'li·fat (kŭ'lē·fát). Peak 11,440 ft. in Quetta-Pishin dist., N Baluchistan, Pakistan, E of Quetta.

Khalil, El. See HEBRON.

Khal'ka (käl'kä). River ab. 240 m. long, NW Manchuria; flows NW to Hulun Nor and forms section of boundary bet. Manchuria and Outer Mongolia; is outlet of Bor Nor; fighting on its banks 1939.

Khal'kē (käl'kyĕ). Ital. **Cal'chi** (käl'kē). An island of the Dodecanese (q.v.), W of Rhodes; 12 sq. m.; pop. (1936) 1461.

Khalkidikē. See CHALCIDICE.

Khalkis. See CHALCIS.

Kham'gaon (käm'goun). Town, N Maharashtra state, cen. Indian Union, 166 m. W of Nagpur; pop. 23,462; cotton market.

Kham·seh′ or **Kham·se′** (ḵăm·sȧ′). Province, NW Iran; 10,825 sq. m.; * Zenjan.

Khan′a·bad′ (ḵăn′ä·bäd′). Town, Kataghan-Badakhshan prov., NE Afghanistan, on highway WSW of Faizabad.

Kha′na·qin′ (kä′nŭ·kēn′). Town on E frontier of Iraq, 90 m. NE of Baghdad on a tributary of the Diyala; pop. ab. 5000; center of rich oil fields recently discovered.

Khan Bagh·da′di (ḵăn′ bŭg·dä′dē). Town, W cen. Iraq, on W bank of Euphrates 20 m. NW of Hit; battle Mar. 26–27, 1918 in World War I in which Turks were defeated by British.

Khan′ba·lik′ or **Khan′ba·liq′** (ḵăn′bä·lēk′). Mongol name ("City of the Great Khan") of Kublai Khan's capital of China, rebuilt by him 1264–67 on the site of the earlier Yen, corresponding to the modern Peiping (*q.v.*); called Cambaluc by Marco Polo who described it as a magnificent city; its Chinese name was Ta-tu ("great capital").

Khand·pa′ra (kŭnd·pä′rä). **1** Former Indian state, Eastern States, NE Indian Union; 229 sq. m.; pop. (1941) 87,341.
2 Town, its *, now in Orissa state, S of the Mahanadi and 50 m. W of Cuttack; pop. ab. 5000.

Khand′wa (kŭnd′wä). Town, Jubbulpore division, S Madhya Pradesh, Indian Union, 185 m. WNW of Nagpur; pop. 34,622; rail junction and cotton center.

Khanh′hoa′ (kän′y′·hwä′). Coastal town, S Annam, 45 m. N of Phanrang.

Khania. See CANEA.

Khanikin. = KHANAQIN.

Khan′ka (kăng′kȧ; *Russ.* ḵȧn′kȧ) or **Han′ka** (hăng′kȧ; *Russ.* ḵȧn′kȧ). Lake ab. 1700 sq. m. on boundary bet. Manchuria and Maritime Territory, Soviet Russia, Asia, N of Vladivostok; ab. S three quarters in Russian territory; shallow, unnavigable for large vessels; well stocked with fish; outlet is a W tributary of the Ussuri.

Khan Tengri. = TENGRI KHAN.

Khan′ty–Man′si (ḵȧn′tĭ·mȧn′sĭ). National district, W Siberia, Soviet Russia, Asia; a large area of marshland traversed by Ob and Irtysh rivers, erected into a subordinate unit of the R.S.F.S.R. during World War II out of part of Omsk Region; ab. 294,000 sq. m. (1941 est.) 102,200; * **Khan′ty–Man′sisk** (-sĭsk), town at junction of the Ob and Irtysh. Previous to the war known as the **O·styak′–Vo·gul′ National District** (ŭ·styȧk′vŭ·gōōl′), established 1930.

Khan Yu′nis (ḵăn yōō′nĭs). Frontier town, SW Palestine, on coast at Egyptian border near Rafa and ab. 15 m. SSW of Gaza.

Khanzi. See GHANSI.

Khao, or **Kao, Lu′ang** (k′hou lōō′äng). Isolated peak 5860 ft., SW Thailand, in cen. Malay Penin. W of Nakhon Si Thammarat.

Khap′sa·lu (ḵăp′sȧ·lōō); *Estonian* **Haap′sa·lu** (häp′sȧ·lōō). Town, * of Lääne prov., W Estonia, 55 m. SW of Tallin; pop. (1937) 4955; seaport on Baltic Sea opp. Vormsi I.; founded 1228.

Kha′rag·pur (kŭ′rȧg·pōōr) or **Kha′rak·pur** (kŭ′rȧk·pōōr). City, West Bengal, NE Indian Union, on Kasai river 65 m. W of Calcutta; pop. 129,636.

Khara Khoto. See KARAKHOTO.

Kha′ran (kä′rän) or **Ka′ran.** State of former Baluchistan States, NW of Kalat, Pakistan; 18,508 sq. m.; pop. (1941) 33,832; bordered Chagai on N and Iran on W.

Kha′ra Nur (ḵä′rä nōōr′). Salt lake (*nur*), W Outer Mongolia, just E of the larger lake Khara Usu Nur.

Kha′ra U′su Nur (ḵä′rä ōō′sōō nōōr′). Salt lake (*nur*) 40 m. long, W Outer Mongolia; E of Dzhirgalantu; lat. 48°N, long. 92°E.

Kharbin. Var. of HARBIN.

Kharg (ḵärg). Small island in NE Persian Gulf, off SW coast of Iran, NW of Bushire; important as last Dutch foothold in Persian Gulf, given up 1766 after destruction of factory by Persians.

Khâr′ga (kär′gȧ; *Arab.* ḵär′gȧ; -gȧ). Valley and oasis in Southern Desert prov., Egypt, lat. 25°N and long. 31°E; pop. ab. 8000; chief town El Khârga.

Khârga, El. See EL KHÂRGA.

Khar′kov (kär′kôf; *Russ.* ḵȧr′y′·kŭf); *Ukrainian* **Khar′kiv** (kär′kĭf). **1** Region, NE Ukraine, U.S.S.R. crossed by Donets river.
2 City, its *, on small tributaries of the Donets, 400 m. S of Moscow; pop. 833,432; fourth largest city in U.S.S.R.; one of the great railroad and industrial centers of the Soviet Union; its proximity to the coal of the Donbas and the iron of Krivoi Rog has made it a center for manufacture of heavy metal products; has airport with services to Moscow, Kiev, Odessa, and Baku; university (founded 1805), now the Institute of People's Education. Founded 1654 as an outpost fortress of Moscow; kept by Cossacks in allegiance to Russian tsars during 17th cent. and made capital of the Ukraine 1765; increased rapidly with development of the Donbas; in World War I seized by Germans Apr. 1918; suffered considerably in civil war period until 1920; capital of new Ukrainian S.S.R. 1921–34; in World War II captured by Germans Oct. 1941, made object of extended conflict Jan.–June 1942 and again in 1943; finally retaken by Russians Aug. 23, 1943, after much had been laid waste.

Kharput. See HARPUT.

Khar·sa′wan (ḵȧr·sä′wȧn). Former Indian state, Eastern States, S border of Bihar prov., NE Indian Union; 157 sq. m.; pop. (1941) 50,580; once an Orissa state.

Khar′ta·phu′ (kär′tä·pōō′; *native* k′här′tä·p′hōō′). Peak 23,800 ft. in the Himalayas, NE of Mt. Everest.

Khar′ti·chang′ri (kär′tĕ·chäng′rĕ). Peak 23,420 ft. in the Himalayas, NE of Mt. Everest.

Khar·toum′ or **Khar·tum′** (kär·tōōm′; *Arab.* ḵŏr-). **1** Province, NE cen. Sudan (republic), NE Africa; 8097 sq. m.; pop. 504,923.
2 City, its * and * of the Sudan, at junction of White Nile and Blue Nile; pop. 93,103; Gordon College; transportation and trading city for large area. Founded under Mehemet Ali 1823; abandoned after its seizure by the Mahdi 1885; reoccupied by British 1898 and rebuilt.

Khartoum, or **Khartum, North.** Suburb of the city of Khartoum; pop. (1938 est.) 107,720; under siege by the Mahdi's army 1885; Gordon killed and city captured; recovered by Anglo-Egyptian army 1898.

Kha·ruf′, Je′bel (ḵä′bȧl ḵŏ·rōōf′). Mountain 3280 ft. on boundary bet. SW Palestine and NE Sinai Penin.

Kha′sav Yurt (ḵä′säv yōōrt′). Town, NW Dagestan, Soviet Russia, Europe, 45 m. WNW of Makhachkala; pop. 6893; on railroad in hilly region; under Soviets has developed an important agricultural experiment station; village practically destroyed during civil war 1917–21.

Kha′si and Jain′ti·a Hills (kä′sĭ, jīn′tĭ·ȧ). District, Surma Valley and Hill division, cen. Assam, NE Indian Union; 2353 sq. m.; pop. (1941) 118,665; * Shillong.

Khasi Hills. Hill region, highest 6440 ft., NW cen. Assam, NE Indian Union, bet. the Brahmaputra and Surma rivers; with Jaintia Hills constitutes the district of Khasi and Jaintia Hills.

Khasi States. Group of 25 former Indian states in Khasi Hills, Assam, NE Indian Union; 3788 sq. m.; pop. (1941) 213,586; chief town Shillong; largest are Khyrim and Mylliem; surrounded on three sides by Assam; on S borders on East Bengal, Pakistan.

Khas′ko·vo (käs′kŏ·vŏ). City, Stara Zagora dept., S cen. Bulgaria; pop. (1934) 26,516; S of Maritsa river and on N slope of Rhodope Mts.; agriculture, rose growing, tobacco.

Kha·tan′ga (kȧ·täng′gȧ; *Russ.* kŭ·tän′gȧ). **1** River ab. 800 m. long, E Taimyr National District, Soviet Russia, Asia; rises in highlands N of Arctic Circle in NE Krasnoyarsk Territory, flows SE and N through broad estuary (**Khatanga Bay**) to Laptev Sea.
2 Town on right bank of Khatanga river ab. 150 m. from its mouth.

Khatmandu. Var. of KATMANDU.

Khat′ti (kät′tĕ). = *Hattushash:* see BOGAZKÖY.

Kha·wak′ Pass (kä·wäk′). Pass, altitude 11,640 ft., in E Hindu Kush Mts., Afghanistan.

Kha·zar′i·a (kȧ·zär′ĭ·ȧ). Region of SE Russia in Europe inhabited c. 200 A.D.–950 A.D. by the Khazars or Chozars, probably of Turkish origin. At first their home was in the Caucasus but later they controlled the lands bet. the Caucasus Mts. and the Volga and Don rivers and even beyond to the Dnieper and the Crimea (**Little Khazaria**) and organized the trade routes bet. the Black Sea and the Caspian; in 8th cent. the majority embraced Judaism; conquered by Russians in 10th and 11th cents.

Khelat. See KALAT.

Khem–Belder. See KYZYL.

Khem′ma·rat *or* **Ke′ma·rat** (kĕm′ȧ·rät; *Siamese* k′hĕm·mä·rät). Town on Mekong river, E Thailand.

Khe′ri (kā′rĕ). Town, N India, in Uttar Pradesh, 73 m. N of Lucknow; pop. 7071.

Kher·son′ (kĕr·sôn′). 1 Region, S Ukraine, U.S.S.R.; borders on Black Sea and Sea of Azov and connects on S with the Crimea Penin.; crossed by lower Dnieper river. 2 Seaport city, W Kherson Region, on the Dnieper ab. 19 m. from its mouth; pop. 97,186; has rail connection with Nikolaev 35 m. to the NW; harbor closed by ice Dec. to early March. Named from the probable site of an early Greek colony, the Chersonesus Heracleotica; founded 1778 by Potëmkin as a naval station and fortress; in World War II held by Germans 1941 to Mar. 1944.

Khe′ta (kĕ′tȧ). River nearly 500 m. long, chief tributary of the Khatanga in Taimyr National District, Soviet Russia, Asia; flows N and NE.

Khiakhta, Khiakta. Vars. of KYAKHTA.

Khil′chi·pur (kĭl′chĭ·pŏŏr). Former state, central India, NW of Bhopal state; 274 sq. m.; ✳ Khilchipur (pop. 5779).

Khi·lok′ (kĭ·lôk′). River ab. 350 m. long, SW Chita Region and S Buryat-Mongol Republic, Soviet Russia, Asia; rises in Yablonoi Mts., flows SW into Selenga river above Ulan Ude.

Khing′an′ (shĭng′än′). 1 Former name of region in W Manchuria. See HSINGAN. 2 Two mountain ranges of E Asia: **Great Khingan Mountains** or **Ta Khingan Shan** (dä′, shän′), range running N and S in Hsingan region of Manchuria, E Chahar and W Jehol, averaging 3000 to 5000 ft.; forms a barrier bet. Mongolia and Manchuria. **Little Khingan Mountains** or **Hsiao Khingan Shan** (shyou′), in E Heilungkiang prov., N Manchuria, W of Amur river, separating it from the Sungari valley; highest point ab. 3600 ft. See HSINGAN SHAN.

Khíos. See CHIOS.

Khir·bat′ Qum·ran′ (kĭr·bät′ kŏŏm·rän′). Locality, Palestine, in NW Jordan on Wadi Qumran near NW shore of the Dead Sea; site of an ancient religious community (c. 100 B.C.–A.D. 68) of a Jewish sect, probably Essenes. Nearby is a series of caves in which have since 1947 been found manuscripts left by this group and known as the Dead Sea scrolls.

Khir′gis Nur (kĭr′gĭs nŏŏr′). Large lake, W Outer Mongolia, NNE of Khara Usu Nur.

Khi·tai′ (kĭ·tī′). Persian name of China; see CATHAY.

Khi′to·la (kĕ′tŭ·lȧ; *Finnish* **Hii′to·la** (hē′tô·lä). Town, formerly in Viipuri dept., SE Finland; pop. 8509; now in SW Karelia, U.S.S.R. ab. 45 m. NNE of Vyborg.

Khi′u·ma (kĕ′ŏŏ·mä; *Estonian* **Hii′u·maa** (hē′ŏŏ·mä); *Swed.* **Dag′ö′** (däg′ȗ). Island in Baltic Sea off W coast of Estonia, U.S.S.R., N of Sarema I.; 371 sq. m.

Khi′va (kē′vȧ; *Russ.* кē′vȧ; *Iranian* кē·vä′). 1 *anc.* **Cho·ras′mi·a** (kȯ·răz′mĭ·ȧ), *later* **Khwa·rizm′** (kwȯ·rĕz′·m; *Iranian* кvä·răz′·m). Former khanate, W Asia, on left bank of the lower Oxus (Amu Darya); after its conquest by the Russians 1873 incorporated as subject territory in the empire; declared a republic 1920 and included in Uzbek S.S.R. 1924, now forming a section (Khoresm) of N part; lies S of Lake Aral and except for

region along the Amu Darya and oases is chiefly desert. 2 Town in oasis region W of lower Amu Darya, former ✳ of Khiva khanate and of Khoresm exclave; now in NW Uzbek S.S.R., Soviet Central Asia; pop. 19,866; a flourishing city 7th–12th cents., but later suffered much from invasions; has a citadel and many mosques and Moslem schools.

Khobdo. See DZHIRGALANTU.

Khob′do (kȯb′dō) *or* **Kob′do** (kȯb′dō). River ab. 300 m. long in extreme W Outer Mongolia; rises on N slope of Altai Mts., flows NE and SE to salt lakes Khara Usu Nur and Khara Nur.

Kho′i (kō′ē). Town, Azerbaijan prov., NW Iran; pop. ab. 60,000; important trade and communications center in mountains N of Lake Urmia on highway from Tabriz to Erzurum; because of its nearness to Turkish and Russian boundaries, strongly fortified, esp. since ab. 1800; has several times been object of fighting.

Kho′jak Pass (kō′jȧk). Pass in a W ridge of the Sulaiman Mts. bet. Quetta and Chaman, N Baluchistan, Pakistan; altitude ab. 7400 ft.

Khojend, Khodzhent. See LENINABAD.

Khokand. Var. of KOKAND.

Kholm (kôlm). 1 See CHEŁM commune, Poland. 2 Town, NW Kalinin Region, Soviet Russia, Europe, on left bank of Lovat river 60 m. N of Velikie Luki; pop. 5007; in World War II held by Germans from Aug. 1941 to spring of 1943.

Khol·mo·go′ry (kŭl·mŭ·gô′rĭ). Town, Arkhangelsk Region, NW Soviet Russia, Europe, on left bank of Northern Dvina river 50 m. SE of Arkhangelsk city; pop. 1000; important, esp. in time of Peter the Great, as center for cattle raising and for shipping.

Khoms. See HOMS.

Khong (kȯng; *native* kŭm). Town and island in the Mekong river, S Laos, on the Cambodia boundary, Indochina.

Khon Kaen (k′hôn kän). 1 Province, E cen. Thailand; 6138 sq. m.; pop. 473,475. 2 Town, its ✳, on railroad 100 m. N of Nakhon Ratchasima.

Kho·per′ (kŭ·pyôr′). River ab. 560 m. long, SE Soviet Russia, Europe; rises in Penza Region and flows generally S through Saratov, Voronezh, and Stalingrad Regions into the Don; navigable most of the year to Borisoglebsk.

Khoqand. Var. of KOKAND.

Khorasan, Khorassan. Vars. of KHURASAN.

Khorat. See NAKHON RATCHASIMA.

Kho·resm′ (kȯ·rĕz′′m; *native* kō·răz′′m). District in Russian Turkistan, along the lower Amu Darya, comprising a part of former khanate of Khiva, 1890 sq. m., with ✳ at Khiva; formerly an exclave of Uzbek S.S.R., now incorporated in Uzbek S.S.R. See KHWARIZM.

Kho·rog′ (kȯ·rōg′). Town, ✳ of Gorno-Badakhshan Autonomous Region, SE Tadzhik S.S.R., Soviet Central Asia, on the Ab-i-Pandj; pop. ab. 1000.

Khor′ram·shahr′ (kōōr′răm·shȧr′; *native* -shȧ′h′r); *formerly* **Mo·ham′me·rah′** (mŏŏ·hȧm′mȧ·rȧ′). Town, W Iran, on the Karun at its junction with the Shatt-al-Arab, NNW of Abadan, ✳ of Khuzistan prov.; pop. ab. 30,000; during World War II developed considerably as a trading port and oil-refinery town.

Khors′a·bad (kôr′sȧ·bȧd; *native* kôr′sȧ·bȧd′). Village, N Iraq, ab. 12 m. N of Mosul E of the Tigris; extensive ruins uncovered here are believed to be the ancient city Dur Sharrukin, with palace and temple, of Sargon II, King of Assyria, 722–705 B.C.

Kho′tan′ (kō′tän′). 1 River, W Sinkiang prov., W China; joins the Yarkand to form Tarim river, but dry much of the year. 2 *Chin.* **Ho′tien′** (hō′tyĕn′). Town and oasis on Khotan river, SW Sinkiang, W China, 160 m. SE of Yarkand; pop. ab. 30,000; at foot of Kunlun Mts. and on S caravan and motor highway across Sinkiang; raises cereal crops,

cotton, fruits; has been from earliest times on the Silk Road and the largest and most important oasis supply base on S edge of Takla Makan Desert; through it Buddhist culture introduced from India; has experienced many political changes; Chinese since 1878.

Kho·tin′ (kŭ·tyēn′); *Romanian* **Ho·tin′** (hô·tēn′); *also* **Cho′cim** (kŏ′tsēm) *or* **Cho·tin′** (kŭ·tyēn′). Town, SW Ukraine, U.S.S.R., on right bank of the Dniester 30 m. NE of Chernovtsy; pop. 15,287; formerly in Bessarabia; has some manufacturing and local trading activity but more important for its location, a former military post at a much-used crossing of the Dniester. In medieval times a Genoese colony; belonged successively to Moldavians, Poles, Russians, Turks, and Romanians; scene of Turkish defeat 1621 by Poles under Chodkiewicz and Stanisław Lubomirski and again in 1673 by John III Sobieski; seized by Russia 1739 and with Bessarabia incorporated in Russian Empire 1812; under Romania 1918–40; held by Germans 1941–44; retaken by Russians Mar. 1944.

Khu′a Kem (kōō′wä kĕm′). See YENISEI.

Khu Khan (kōō kän; *Siamese* k′hōō k′hän). **1** Province, SE Thailand; 3374 sq. m.; pop. 365,036.
2 Village, its ✱, 55 m. SW of Ubon near the Cambodia border.

Khulm (kōŏlm). See TASHKURGHAN.

Khul′na (kōŏl′nä). **1** District, Presidency division, formerly in S Bengal, now (since 1947) in East Bengal, Pakistan; 4805 sq. m.; pop. (1941) 1,943,218; forms large part of swampy forested islands (Sundarbans) of Ganges Delta.
2 Town, its ✱, 80 m. E of Calcutta; pop. 19,120.

Khun·sar′ (kōōn·sär′). Town, W cen. Iran, ab. 80 m. NW of Isfahan and on highway from Isfahan to Iraq (Sultanabad); pop. ab. 10,000; fruit.

Khu′ra·san (kōŏr′à·sän; *Iranian* kōŏ·rä·sän′) *or* **Kho′ra·san** (kōr′à·sän; *Iranian* kō·rä·sän′). Province, NE Iran; 124,949 sq. m.; ✱ Meshed; second province in size in modern Iran; in early times under Arab rulers covered much more area; forms part of Plateau of Iran; its population comprises many different races; overrun by Moslems c. 650; scene of widespread unrest and revolts in 8th cent.; rise of the Veiled Prophet (al-Mokanna) c. 774–780; conquered 1220 by Genghis Khan and 1380 by Tamerlane.

Khur′ja (kōŏr′jà). Town, W Uttar Pradesh, N Indian Union, on Kali Nadi river 50 m. SE of Delhi; pop. 31,279; trades in grain, indigo, sugar, and ghee; has a modern Jain temple.

Khur·ram′a·bad′ (kōŏr·räm′ä·bäd′). Town, Luristan prov., W Iran; pop. ab. 4000; distributing center on highway running N from Persian Gulf ports through Ahwaz and Dizful to Iraq and Hamadan.

Khust (kōōst); *Czech* **Chust** (kōōst); *Hung.* **Huszt** (hōōst). Town, Zakarpatskaya Region of W Ukraine, U.S.S.R., in foothills of E Carpathian Mts.; pop. (1930) 17,897; before 1945 in Carpathian Ruthenia, E Czechoslovakia.

Khuwa·rizm′ (kwŏ·rĭz′′m). Var. of KHWARIZM.

Khu′zi·stan′ (kōō′zĭ·stän′); *formerly* **A′ra·bi·stan′** (ä′rà·bĭ·stän′); *anc.* **Su′si·a′na** (sū′zĭ·ä′nà; -än′à). Province, SW Iran; 34,027 sq. m.; ✱ Khorramshahr; a fertile region, with lowlands bordering on Persian Gulf; rich oil fields; its extent closely corresponds to the ancient country of Elam and to the later Susiana, a province of the Persian and Alexandrian empires, at the head of the gulf and bordered by Media on N, Persis on E, and Babylonia on W.

Khva·lynsk′ (kvŭ·lĭnsk′). Town and river port, N Saratov Region, Soviet Russia, Europe, on the Volga ab. 110 m. NE of Saratov; pop. 8802; has grain trade largely controlled by a religious sect, the Raskolniks.

Khwa·rizm′ (kwŏ·rĭz′′m); *also* **Khwa·rezm′** (kwŏ-rĕz′′m; *Iranian* kwä·räz′′m) *and* **Khwa·razm′** (kwŏ-räz′′m; kwä·räz′′m). The region corresponding roughly with Chorasmia, a N province of ancient Persia; covered valley of lower Oxus and extended across steppes W to Caspian Sea and E to Bukhara. In 12th cent. an empire, founded by a slave in service of Seljuk sultan Malik Shah; extended conquests in Transoxiana, making Samarkand its capital; overwhelmed 1220 by Mongols under Genghis Khan and again by Tamerlane 1378. Under Russians approximately same region known as Khoresm (*q.v.*). See KHIVA.

Khy′ber (kī′bẽr); *also* **Khai′bar.** Former agency, North-West Frontier Province, India; 962 sq. m.

Khyber Pass. Pass ab. 33 m. long in Safed Koh range and S of Mohmand Hills on border bet. Afghanistan and Pakistan, 10½ m. W of Peshawar (see JAMRUD); ravine and water course, from 50 to 450 ft. wide, in places bet. cliffs (600 to 1000 ft. high) and mountains (1400 to 3000 ft. high); former British forts **A′li Mas′jid** (ŭ′lĭ mŭs′-jĭd), in center of pass, and **Lan′di Ko′tal** (lŭn′dĭ kō′-tŭl), at Afghan border (the highest point, ab. 3370 ft.); probably not used by Alexander the Great, but has been traversed for centuries by armies and peoples invading India; scene of sharp fighting in Afghan Wars 1839–42 and 1878–80 and with Afridis; now a strategic military road.

Khy′rim (kī′rĭm). See KHASI STATES.

Ki′a (kē′à). Settlement on **Kia Passage,** NW end of Santa Isabel I., E cen. Solomon Is., W Pacific Ocean.

Kiach′ta *or* **Kyakh′ta** (kyäк′tä) *or* **Al′tan Bu′lak** (äl′tän bōō′läk); *formerly* **Mai′ma′chin′** (mī′mä′-chēn′). Commercial town, N Outer Mongolia, opp. Kyakhta in Buryat-Mongol A.S.S.R. and just E of Orkhon river; on caravan and motor highway 150 m. N of Urga.

Kiakhta. See KYAKHTA.

Kia′ling′ (jĭ·ä′lĭng′). River ab. 500 m. long, rising in the Min Shan in Kansu and Szechwan provs., cen. China, and flowing S into Yangtze river at Chungking; has important headstream tributary in Shensi prov.

Ki·a′ma (?kĭ·ä′mà). Town, E New South Wales, Australia, on Pacific Ocean 50 m. SSW of Sydney; pop. 2426; agriculture, coal mining; has artificial port.

Kiambone, Ras. Var. of *Ras Chiambone:* see DICKS HEAD.

Ki·a·mich′i (kī′à·mĭsh′ĭ). River ab. 100 m. long, SE Oklahoma; rises in E Le Flore co., flows SW into Red river in SE Choctaw co.

Kia′mu′sze′ (jĭ·ä′mōō′sōō′); *Jap. official name* **Chia′-mus′su′** (jĭ·ä′mōō′sōō′). City, ✱ of Hokiang prov., E Manchuria, on lower Sungari river 185 m. NE of Harbin; pop. (1940 est.) 128,667.

Ki′an′ (jē′än′); *also* **Lu′ling′** (lōō′lĭng′). Town, S cen. Kiangsi prov., SE China, on Kan river ab. 125 m. SSW of Nanchang; pop. ab. 52,000; on great trade highway from Canton N to Yangtze valley.

Kiang·an′ (kyäng·än′); *formerly* **Quiang·an′** (kyäng-). **1** Name under Spanish rule of Ifugao subprov., Mountain Province, Luzon, Phil. Is.
2 Town (municipal district), ✱ of Ifugao subprov., in SW cen. part; pop. 16,146.

Kiang′ling′ *or* **Chiang′ling′** (jĭ·äng′lĭng′); *formerly* **King′chow′** (jĭng′jō′). Walled city on N bank of Yangtze, S Hupei prov., E cen. China, 2 m. W of Shasi (*q.v.*); pop. ab. 15,389; one of the oldest of Chinese cities, called by various names in different periods; once the capital of kingdom of Chu (8th–5th cent. B.C.); under the Manchus was a great garrison town; has many temples; enclosed by a wall 30 ft. high.

Kiang′mai′ (chĭ·äng′mī′). Var. of CHIANG MAI.

Kiang–nan (jĭ·äng′nän′). Province of China in Ming period. See ANHWEI.

Kiang–ning. See NANKING.

Kiang′si′ (jĭ·äng′sē′). Province, SE China; 77,281 sq. m.; pop. (1936 est.) 15,820,403; ✱ Nanchang; bounded on N by Hupei and Anhwei provs., on E by Chekiang and Fukien, on S by Kwangtung, and on W by Hunan;

for the most part coincides with basin of Kan river; watered by many tributaries of the Kan, has very fertile soil; chief crops rice, wheat, beans, tobacco, and, formerly, sugar and tea. Hilly, esp. in S half; bordered by mountain ranges, highest Tachin Shan on E; has mineral wealth, esp. coal in Pingsiang mines in W, most of which is shipped to industrial Wuhan cities; for centuries has produced at Fowliang (Kingtehchen) some of finest porcelain of China; chief cities Nanchang, Kiukiang, Hukow, Linchwan, Kian, and Kanhsien. In early times a N and S corridor for migrations and communication; for varying periods a part of Wei kingdom and under the Western Chin, Southern Sung, and T'ang dynasties; under the Mongol dynasty (1206–1368) included W half of Kwangtung.

Kiang'su' (jǐ·äng'sōō'). Province, E China; 41,818 sq. m.; pop. (1936 est.) 36,469,321; ✳ Chinkiang; bounded on N by Shantung prov., on E by Yellow Sea and East China Sea, on S by Chekiang, and on W by Anhwei; one of smallest and most thickly populated provinces of China, constituting for most part a deltaic plain, the mouth of the Yangtze; traversed also since 1938 by the Hwang Ho following in part its old course of 1852 and by the Grand Canal; covered with numerous lakes, largest Tai Hu; S part rich agriculturally; chief products rice, cotton, wheat, mulberry, peanuts, and melons; because of Shanghai the leading industrial province; chief cities Shanghai, Nanking, Chinkiang, Wuhsien (treaty ports), and Wutsin and Wusih. Under Ming dynasty (1368–1644) a part of Nanking prov.; under Manchus E part of Kiang-nan; set up as separate province in 18th cent.; headquarters 1853–54 during Taiping Rebellion; with growth of Shanghai (*q.v.*) increased rapidly in importance.

Kiang'tu' (jǐ·äng'dōō'); *formerly* **Yang'chow'** (yäng'jō'). City, cen. Kiangsu, E China, on Grand Canal 15 m. N of Chinkiang and the Yangtze; pop. ab. 100,000; old walled city, capital of China under Sui dynasty (589–618 A.D.); noted for its wealth; a literary and cultural center; Marco Polo appointed as its governor 1282–85 by Kublai Khan.

Kiang'yin' (jǐ·äng'yǐn'). Town, S Kiangsu prov., E China, on the Yangtze 80 m. NW of Shanghai; center of large junk traffic on the river.

Kiao'chow' (jǐ·ou'jō'). **1** District or territory, SE Shantung prov., NE China, of ab. 200 sq. m. surrounding **Kiaochow Bay** (area 200 sq. m.); leased by Germany 1898; chief town Tsingtao (*q.v.*).
2 Town, now Kiaohsien (*q.v.*), NW of the bay.

Kiao'hsien' (jǐ·ou'shyěn'); *formerly* **Kiao'chow'** (jǐ·ou'jō'). Town, NW of Kiaochow Bay and ab. 25 m. NW of Tsingtao (45 m. by rail), Shantung prov., NE China; once prosperous but has now lost much of its trade.

Kiating. See LOSHAN.

Ki'awah Island (kē'wô). Island in Atlantic Ocean, in Charleston co., South Carolina, ab. 15 m. SW of Charleston.

Kia'yu·kwan' (jǐ·ä'yü'gwän'). See GREAT WALL.

Ki'bo (kē'bō). Highest peak 19,317 ft. of Mt. Kilimanjaro in E Africa, and the highest point in Africa.

Kick'a·poo (kǐk'à·pōō). River ab. 100 m. long, SW Wisconsin; rises in Monroe co., flows S into Wisconsin river in S Crawford co.

Kick'ing Horse Pass (kǐk'ǐng hôrs'). Mountain pass, Canadian Rockies, on boundary bet. SE British Columbia and Banff National Park in Alberta.

Kid'der (kǐd'ēr). County in North Dakota. See *Table* at NORTH DAKOTA.

Kid'der·min'ster (kǐd'ēr·mǐn'stēr). Municipal borough, Worcestershire, W cen. England, on the Stour 18 m. WSW of Birmingham; pop. 37,423; worsteds, metalware; Kidderminster carpets (manufactured since 1735).

Kid'nap'pers, Cape (kǐd'nǎp'ērz). Cape on SE cen. coast of North I., New Zealand, forming S side of Hawke Bay.

Kid'ron (kǐd'rŏn; kī'drŏn) *or* **Ked'ron** (kĕd'rŏn; kē'drŏn). Valley, or wadi, in Palestine, source of stream (**Kidron**) rising on E side of Jerusalem, separating it from Mount of Olives and flowing E to Dead Sea.

Kids'grove' (kǐdz'grōv'). Urban district, Staffordshire, W cen. England; pop. 16,231.

Kid·wel'ly (kǐd·wĕl'ǐ). Town, Carmarthenshire, S Wales, near coast of Carmarthen Bay; pop. (1951) 3007; 13th-cent. church and castle (original structure built 1094).

Kiel (kēl). **1** City, Calumet and Manitowoc cos., E Wisconsin, 18 m. NW of Sheboygan; pop. 2524.
2 Seaport city and naval base, Schleswig govt. dist., ✳ of Schleswig-Holstein, N Germany, at head of Kiel Harbor 40 m. NW of Lübeck; pop. (1939) 272,311; chief German naval port on Baltic; naval arsenal, dockyards; site of largest German naval hospital; NE entrance to famous Kiel Canal (*q.v.*) is just N of the city; university (founded 1665) includes medical school; manufactures soap, machinery, woolens, leather; produces also sugar, tobacco, smoked fish. Became city 1242; joined Hanseatic League 1284; part of kingdom of Denmark 1773; Peace of Kiel signed here 1814; passed to Prussia 1866; headquarters of German Imperial fleet in World War I; scene of mutiny of German sailors which preceded German revolution of 1918; in World War II many times bombed and much damaged 1943–45.

Kiel Bay; *Ger.* **Kie'ler Bucht** (kē'lēr bōōĸt'). Part of the Baltic Sea on the E coast of Schleswig-Holstein, north Germany, extending E to Fehmarn I.; in SW is **Kiel Harbor**, *Ger.* **Kieler För'de** (fûr'dě), the inlet at the head of which is the port of Kiel.

Kiel Canal *or* **Kai'ser Wil'helm Canal** (kī'zēr vǐl'hělm). Canal 61 m. long extending from the Baltic Sea to the North Sea, NE to SW across Schleswig-Holstein in north Germany, from city of Kiel past Rendsburg

to Brunsbüttelkoog at the mouth of the Elbe; constructed 1887–95 and owned by the German Reich; alterations made 1914; surface width 335 ft., bottom width 144 ft., depth 36 ft.; has no locks except those at either end, necessary because of tides; frequently bombed in World War II.

Kiel'ce (kyěl'tsě; *Russ.* **Kel'tsy** (kěl'tsǐ). **1** Department of S Poland; 8570 sq. m.; pop. 2,936,976; in reorganization of administrative units of Poland 1946, area somewhat reduced.
2 City, its ✳, 90 m. S of Warsaw; pop. (1938–39 est.) 68,827; railroad junction; episcopal see; agricultural center; copper mines nearby; marble quarries. Founded 1173; scene of battles bet. Russians and Germans 1914, 1915 in World War I; occupied by Germans in World War II; recaptured by Russians Jan. 1945.

Kien'ow' (jǐ·ěn'ō') *or* **Kien'ning'** (jǐ·ěn'nǐng'). Town, N cen. Fukien prov., SE China, on tributary of Min river 95 m. NW of Minhow; in World War II had American air base; captured by Japanese 1944.

Ki·e′ta (kē·ā′tà). **1** District of the Territory of New Guinea; comprises Bougainville, Buka, and adjacent small islands in Solomon Is., W Pacific Ocean; 3720 sq. m.; pop. (1930) 56,087; chief town Kieta. See SOLOMON ISLANDS.
2 Chief town of the Solomon Is., on E coast of Bougainville I. on Rawa Harbour, W Pacific Ocean, and administrative center of Kieta dist.; trading center; has radio station and airfield; taken by Japanese Jan. 23, 1942.

Ki′ev (kē′yĕf; *Angl.* kē′ĕf). **1** Region, NW Ukraine, U.S.S.R.; crossed by Dnieper river.
2 City, its ✷ and ✹ of the Ukrainian S.S.R. since 1934, on right bank of the Dnieper 470 m. SW of Moscow; pop. 846,293; before World War II third largest city in U.S.S.R.; a junction of several railroads; the new part of the city the commercial center where many great industries have been established, esp. smelting works, tobacco factories, flour mills, refineries, machinery, glass, and leather factories; distributing point for a wide area, its trading activity having grown out of its great annual fair, the Kiev Contract Fair; in its Old Town were many old buildings famous in its long history, among them: the cathedral of St. Sophia (11th cent.), oldest in Russia; monastery of St. Michael (1108); church of St. Andrew (1750), built by Rastrelli; and the Pechersky, or Cave, Monastery, an ancient (founded probably in 11th cent.) and sacred place of pilgrimage.
History: One of the oldest cities in Russia and so long prominent that it is known to Russians as "the Mother of Cities." As the town of Kiev, 9th cent. A.D., became capital of a Varangian principality, which, under Prince Oleg (c. 880–912), was chief of a number of small Russian states; center for trade down the Dnieper to Black Sea and on the route from Scandinavia to Constantinople; became seat of the metropolitan of Russian Christianity 988; its power and wealth declined in 12th cent.; became object of rivalry among other princes, captured by prince of Suzdal 1169; overrun and ruined by Mongol invasion 1240; became part of Lithuania in 14th cent. and Poland in 16th cent.; finally incorporated by Russia 1686. Capital of independent Ukrainian republic 1917–19, when it was fought over by Bolsheviki and German expeditionary force; again made capital of the Ukraine 1934; in World War II seized by Germans Sept. 19, 1941; recovered Nov. 6, 1943, but much of it destroyed.

Ki·ga′li (kē·gä′lē). Town, ✷ of Rwanda, in cen. part E of Lake Kivu.

Ki·go′ma (kē·gō′mà). **1** Former province, Tanganyika, E Africa, now part of Western Province.
2 Port, Western Province, Tanganyika, on Lake Tanganyika 4 m. N of Ujiji; terminus of railroad from Dar-es-Salaam; pop. ab. 14,000.

Ki·ho′lo Bay (kē·hō′lō). Bay on NW coast of Hawaii I., S of Keawaiki Bay.

Ki·i (kē·ē). Old province, cen. part of S coast of Honshu, Japan, now Wakayama prefecture and part of Mie prefecture.

Kii Channel. Strait ab. 25 m. wide bet. E coast of Shikoku I. and S coast of Honshu I., Japan, and connecting Harima Sea and Osaka Bay (through Kitan Strait) with the Pacific Ocean.

Kiirun. Var. of KIRUN.

Ki·kai Shi·ma (kē·kī shē′·mä) or **Kikai Ji·ma** (jē·mä). Island, NE Amami Is., N Ryukyu Is., Japan; 23 sq. m.; pop. (1945) 18,184.

Ki′ke′pa Point (kē·kā′pä). Point, N end of Niihau I., Hawaii, 22°N lat.

Ki·ko′a Point (kē·kō′ä). Point on SE coast of Lanai I., Hawaii, on Kealaikahiki Channel.

Ki·ko′ri (kē·kōr′ē). **1** River ab. 200 m. long, cen. Papua, New Guinea; flows SE to Gulf of Papua.
2 Settlement in delta of Kikori river (ab. 8°S, 144°E) at head of Gulf of Papua, S Territory of Papua; has rainfall of ab. 230 inches annually.

Ki·ku′yu (kē·kōō′yōō). Village in Central Province,

Kenya colony, E Africa, near Nairobi.

Ki′lau·e′a (kē′lou·ā′ä). Crater 2 m. wide and at a height of 4088 ft. on E side of Mauna Loa, in Hawaii National Park, S cen. Hawaii I., Hawaii; largest active crater in the world. See HALEMAUMAU.

Kilauea Point. Point on N coast of Kauai I., Hawaii, 22°14′N lat.

Kil·bren′nan (kĭl·brĕn′ăn), or **Kil·bran′nan** (-brăn′ăn), **Sound.** Channel bet. Kintyre Penin. and Arran I., off SW coast of Scotland; ab. 14 m. long and 4 m. wide.

Kil·col′man (kĭl·kŭl′măn). Castle N of Mallow, N co. Cork, SW Eire; home of Edmund Spenser; ruins.

Kil·dare′ (kĭl·dâr′). **1** County, E Eire, in Leinster prov.; 654 sq. m.; pop. 57,892; ⊗ Naas; rivers Liffey, Boyne, Barrow; agriculture, stock raising, textile manufacture, brewing and distilling.
2 Town, co. Kildare, E Eire, 30 m. SW of Dublin; pop. 1758; Protestant cathedral; remains of 13th-cent. castle; the Curragh is just E of it.

Kil′gore (kĭl′gōr). City, NE Texas, in Gregg and Rusk cos., 24 m. E of Tyler; pop. 10,092; oil-production center.

Ki·lid′ Bahr (kē·lēd′ bä′h′r); *Turk.* **Ki·lid′i·ba·hir′** (kē·lēd′ē·bä·hir′). Fortified town on Gallipoli Penin., Turkey in Europe, on W bank of Dardanelles nearly opp. Çanakkale.

Ki·li′fi (kē·lē′fē). Coastal town, E Kenya protectorate, E Africa, ab. 40 m. N of Mombasa.

Ki′lik Pass (kē′lĭk). Pass in range bet. E Hindu Kush and W Karakoram, Hunza dist., N Kashmir, N India, near Afghan border; alt. 15,600 ft.

Kilimane. Var. of QUELIMANE.

Kil′i·man·ja′ro, Mount (kĭl′ĭ·măn·jä′rō). Mountain in NE Tanganyika, near Kenya border, E Africa; highest peak Kibo 19,317 ft., the highest point in Africa; next highest peak Mawenzi 16,892 ft.

Ki′li·na′i·la′u Islands (kē′lē·nä′ē·lä′ōō). Group of islets N of Bougainville I., NW Solomon Is., W Pacific Ocean; part of Kieta dist. of the Territory of New Guinea.

Kil′in·di′ni (kĭl′ĭn·dē′nē). Town on SW side of Mombasa I., off S coast of Kenya protectorate, E Africa; **Kilindini Harbor,** the finest landlocked and sheltered harbor on E African coast, forms modern part of Mombasa harbor.

Ki·lis′ or **Kil·lis′** (kē·lēs′). Town, Gaziantep vilayet, S Turkey in Asia, 36 m. N of Alep, near Syrian border; pop. 24,632; center of olive cultivation.

Ki′li·ya (kē′lyĭ·yà). **1** *Romanian* **Chi′lia** (kē′lyä). River ab. 65 m. long, the N branch of the Danube delta, E Romania; borders Letea I. on N and marks boundary bet. Romania and U.S.S.R.
2 *Romanian* **Chi′lia–Nou′ă** (kē′lyä-nou′à). Town, Izmail Region, S Ukraine, U.S.S.R., on the Kiliya branch of the Danube delta; pop. 17,049.

Kil·ken′ny (kĭl·kĕn′ĭ). **1** County, SE Eire, in Leinster prov.; 796 sq. m.; pop. 68,614; ⊗ Kilkenny; rivers Suir, Nore, Barrow; coal mining, quarrying (marble, slate), brewing and distilling.
2 Municipal borough, its ⊗; pop. 10,237; marble quarrying, coal mining, brewing; College of St. John (founded in 16th cent.) which had as students Swift, Congreve, Farquhar, Bishop Berkeley; noted 12th-cent. castle and 13th-cent. cathedral. Site of convention 1342 at which Anglo-Irish drew up a remonstrance to Edward III protesting a discriminatory proclamation; scene of parliament 1367 which passed famous statute to curb the growing lawlessness of the Anglo-Irish; scene of a synod of Irish Catholic bishops and clergy, 1642, which tried to overcome the hostility bet. the old Irish and Anglo-Irish.

Kil·kís′ (kyĕl·kyēs′). Commune, Thessaloníkē dept., W cen. Macedonia, N Greece, ab. 24 m. N of Salonika; pop. 7957.

Kil·lal′a Bay (kĭ·lăl′à). Inlet of Atlantic Ocean on NW coast of Ireland; bet. cos. Sligo and Mayo, Eire; Moy river flows into it at its head.

Kil·lar′ney (kĭ·lär′nĭ). **1** Town, SW Manitoba, Canada, 47 m. SSE of Brandon; pop. 1262; grain elevators, lumber yards, manufactures farm implements.
2 Urban district, co. Kerry, SW Eire, near Lakes of Killarney; pop. 5609; tourist center; ruins of an ancient castle and two ancient abbeys nearby.

Killarney, Lakes of. Three beautiful lakes, co. Kerry, SW Eire; lowest and largest (ab. 8 sq. m.) is Lough Leane; all are studded with islands and famous for their scenery; on Ross I. in Lough Leane is Ross Castle· other ruins nearby (see MUCKROSS).

Kil′la·ry Harbour (kĭl′à·rĭ). Inlet of Atlantic Ocean on W coast of Ireland, S of Clew Bay.

Kill Dev′il Hill (kĭl′ dĕv′'l). See KITTY HAWK.

Kil·leen′ (kĭ·lēn′). City, Bell co., cen. Texas, N of Austin; pop. 23,377.

Kil′lie·cran′kie (kĭl′ĭ·krăng′kĭ). Mountain pass, Perth co., cen. Scotland, in SE part of the Grampians; nearby occurred battle July 17, 1689 in which John Graham of Claverhouse, 1st Viscount Dundee, defeated the Scots at the cost of his own life.

Kil′li·nek (kĭl′ĭ·nĕk); *formerly* **Kil′li·nik** (-nĭk). Small island off N tip of Labrador, S of E entrance to Hudson Strait, in Quebec prov., Canada; Port Burwell is on it and Cape Chidley is its N point; separated from mainland by McLelan Strait.

Kil′ling·ly (kĭl′ĭng·lĭ). Town, E Windham co., NE corner of Connecticut, on Quinebaug river and Rhode Island border; pop. 11,298; settled 1693, incorp. 1708; includes borough of Danielson (*q.v.*); cottons and woolens.

Kil′ling·ton Peak (kĭl′ĭng·tŭn). Mountain 4241 ft., E cen. Rutland co., W Vermont.

Kil′ling·worth (kĭl′ĭng·wûrth). Village, Northumberland, England, 6 m. NE of Newcastle; place where George Stephenson tried his first locomotive 1814.

Killis. See KILĬS.

Kill van Kull (kĭl′ văn kŭl′). Channel bet. New Jersey and Staten I., New York; connects Newark Bay with Upper New York Bay.

Kil·main′ (kĭl·mān′). = QUELIMANE.

Kil·mar′nock (kĭl·mär′nŭk). Burgh, Ayr co., SW Scotland, 12 m. NE of Ayr; pop. (1951) 42,120; coal mining; locomotives, woolens, leather, china.

Ki′lo·sa (kē′lô·sä). Town, E cen. Tanganyika, E Africa, 150 m. W of Dar es Salaam; pop. ab. 4500.

Kil·ro′nan (kĭl·rō′năn). Chief town in Aran Is., co. Galway, W Eire, on Inishmore; pop. 376; region noteworthy for ancient remains.

Kil·rush′ (kĭl·rŭsh′). Urban district on Shannon estuary, SW coast of co. Clare, W Eire; pop. 3426; fishing, flagstone quarrying; on nearby Scattery I. are remains of 6th-cent. monastery.

Kil·syth′ (kĭl·sīth′). Burgh, Stirling co., cen. Scotland; pop. 9915; coal mining, ironworking, stone quarrying; scene of victory of Montrose and his Cavaliers over the Covenanters under Baillie Aug. 15, 1645.

Kilung. Var. of *Keelung*: see KIRUN.

Kil′wa, *in full* **Kilwa Ki·vin′je** (kĭl′wä kē·vĭn′jä). Coastal town, SE Tanganyika, British East Africa; pop. ab. 3000; very poor harbor. Probably founded 1830 by people from **Kilwa** or **Kilwa Ki·si·wa′ni** (kē′sĕ·wä′nĕ) 25 m. to the S; an ancient town with an excellent harbor, on a small island off the coast; founded 975 A.D. by a Persian prince; many remains of its early times; capital of Zanguebar (*q.v.*); occupied by Portuguese 1505, abandoned by them 1512; became center of the slave trade; Germans, ruling from 1885, laid out modern town; under British as part of Tanganyika since 1919.

Kil·win′ning (kĭl·wĭn′ĭng). Burgh, Ayr co., SW Scotland; pop. 6553; ruined abbey (founded c. 1140); according to tradition, birthplace of freemasonry (said to have been brought in by foreign craftsmen who built the abbey) in Scotland.

Kim′ball (kĭm′b'l). **1** County in Nebraska. See *Table* at NEBRASKA.

2 City, ⊗ of Kimball co., W Nebraska, 43 m. S of Scottsbluff; pop. 4384; shipping point for wheat and potatoes.
3 City, McDowell co., S West Virginia, 5 m. E of Welch; pop. 1175.

Kimball, Mount. Mountain 9690 ft., N Wrangell Mts., SE Alaska, S of the Alaska Highway and E of the Richardson Highway.

Kim′be Bay (kĭm′bĕ). Large inlet of Bismarck Sea on N coast of New Britain, Bismarck Archipelago; bordered on W by Willaumez Penin.

Kim′ber·ley (kĭm′bĕr·lĭ). Town, N Cape Province, Republic of So. Africa, 86 m. WNW of Bloemfontein, near Orange Free State border; pop. 40,231; world's diamond center with Kimberley, De Beers, and other famous mines nearby; horse breeding. Founded 1870 shortly after discovery of diamonds in region; capital 1873–80 of Griqualand West before it became part of Cape Colony; besieged by Boers for four months during Boer War Oct. 14, 1899–Feb. 15, 1900. Scenery remarkable for immense pits and heaps of earth, the aftermath of mining operations. See BEACONSFIELD.

Kim′ber·leys (kĭm′bĕr·lĭz). Plateau region, N Western Australia; includes all territory N of 19°30′S lat.; ab. 144,000 sq. m.; chief town Wyndham; gold fields.

Kim′ber·ly (kĭm′bĕr·lĭ). Village, Outagamie co., E Wisconsin, 4 m. E of Appleton; pop. 5322; paper.

Kim′ble (kĭm′b'l). County in Texas. See *Table* at TEXAS.

Ki′mi·to (chĭ′mĭ·tô) or **Ke′mi·ö** (kĕ′mĭ·û). **1** Finnish island in Gulf of Bothnia off SW Finland.
2 Town, Turku-Pori dept., SW Finland, on Kimito I.; pop. ab. 6000.

Kímolos. See CIMOLUS.

Kimpolung. See CÂMPULUNG.

Kim′ry (kēm′rĭ). Town, SE Kalinin Region, Soviet Russia, Europe, at NE end of new reservoir lake, E of Kalinin and 75 m. N of Moscow; pop. 18,520; a center of Russian shoe and leather industry.

Kin (kēn). River ab. 250 m. long, SW Korea, flowing SW into the Yellow Sea.

Kin′a·ba·lu′ (kĭn′à·bà·lōō′); *formerly* **Kin′i·ba·lu′** (kĭn′ĭ·bà·lōō′). Mountain 13,455 ft. in N cen. British North Borneo; highest peak on island of Borneo.

Kin′a·ba·tang′an (kĭn′à·bà·täng′än). River 350 m. long, E British North Borneo, flowing E into the Sulu Sea; navigable for ab. 200 m.

Kin′a·bu·lu′ (kĭn′à·bŭ·lōō′). Var. of KINABALU.

Kin·caid′ (kĭn·kād′). Village, Christian co., cen. Illinois, 22 m. SE of Springfield; pop. 1544.

Kin·car′dine (kĭn·kär′d'n; -dĭn; kĭng-). **1** Resort town, Bruce co., SE Ontario, Canada, on S shore of Lake Huron 47 m. SW of Owen Sound; pop. 2672; saltworks, knitting mills, extensive fisheries; center for trading in agricultural products.
2 or **Kin·car′dine·shire** (-shĭr; -shēr); *formerly* **The Mearns** (mûrnz). County, E Scotland; 382 sq. m.; pop. (1951) 47,341; ⊗ Stonehaven; livestock grazing, fishing, quarrying.

Kin′che·loe Point (kĭn′chĕ·lō). Point on W coast of Tillamook co., NW Oregon.

Kinchinjunga. See KANCHENJUNGA.

Kinchow. See CHINCHOW.

Kin′der·hook (kĭn′dĕr·hŏŏk). Village, Columbia co., SE New York, E of Hudson river; pop. 1078; birthplace of Martin Van Buren, 8th president of the U.S.

Kinder Scout. See PEAK DISTRICT.

Kin′di·a (kĭn′dĭ·à). Town, W Guinea, W Africa, on railroad 60 m. NE of Conakry.

Kin′du (kĭn′dōō). Town, W Kivu prov., E Congo, on upper Congo river; pop. (1938) 7361.

Ki·nel′ (kĭ·nĕl′; *Russ.* kĭ·nyĕl′y). River ab. 220 m. long, E Soviet Russia, Europe; rises in N Chkalov Region and flows W to join the Samara just E of Kuibyshev.

Kin′e·o, Mount (kĭn′ĕ·ō). Peak 1806 ft. on E shore of Moosehead Lake, NW cen. Maine; composed of flint.

Ki′nesh·ma (kē′nyĭsh·må). Industrial city on right bank of the Volga, N Ivanovo Region, Soviet Russia, Europe, on railroad 50 m. NE of Ivanovo; pop. 75,378; the Volga port of Ivanovo.

King (kĭng). 1 Name of counties in two states of the U.S. See *Tables* at TEXAS and WASHINGTON.
2 Name of several islands: see KING ISLAND.

King *or* **Ching** (jĭng). River ab. 200 m. long, rising in NE Kansu prov., N cen. China, and flowing SE to the Wei in cen. Shensi.

King and Queen (kĭng, kwēn). County in Virginia. See *Table* at VIRGINIA.

King and Queen Courthouse. Village, ⊗ of King and Queen co., E Virginia, 34 m. ENE of Richmond.

Kingchow. See KIANGLING.

King City (kĭng). City, Monterey co., W California, on Salinas river 90 m. SE of San Jose; pop. 2937; settled 1868, incorp. 1912; agricultural trade center.

King Edward VIII Falls. Waterfall 840 ft., in a tributary of the Mazaruni river, W British Guiana, in Serra Pacaraima; NW of Kaieteur Falls in 5°30′N.

King Edward VII Land. See EDWARD VII PENINSULA.

King′fish′er (kĭng′fĭsh′ēr). 1 County in Oklahoma. See *Table* at OKLAHOMA.
2 City, its ⊗, cen. Oklahoma, 36 m. NW of Oklahoma City; pop. 3249; flour and feed mills; ships wheat.

Kingfisher Peak. Mountain 11,100 ft., SW Park co., NW Wyoming.

King Fred′er·ik VIII Land (frĕd′ēr·ĭk; frĕd′rĭk; *Dan.* frĭth′rĭk). Coastal region in NE Greenland.

King George (jôrj). 1 County in Virginia. See *Table* at VIRGINIA.
2 Village, its ⊗, E Virginia; pop. (est.) 240.

King George, Mount. 1 Peak 11,226 ft., SE British Columbia, Canada, near Alberta border.
2 Peak 12,300 ft. in St. Elias Range, SW Yukon, Canada, E of Mt. Logan.

King George V Land. = GEORGE V COAST.

King George Island. See SOUTH SHETLAND ISLANDS.

King George′s Falls (jôr′jĭz). = AUGHRABIES FALLS.

King George Sound. Inlet of Indian Ocean, S coast of Western Australia, 35°6′S lat., 118°E long.; forms outer harbor of Albany.

Kin′gi·sepp′ (kĭng′gĭ·sĕp′; *Russ.* kĭn·gĭ·syĕp′); *formerly* **Yam′burg** (yăm′bŏŏrk) *or* **Ya′ma** (yà′må). Frontier railroad town, NW Leningrad Region, Soviet Russia, Europe, 20 m. E of Narva; one of oldest towns in Russia, founded as Yama in 9th cent. and important later in 14th cent. in Baltic wars; a Bolshevik base in 1917 for Yudenich's army; in 1944 after being under German control for 3 years retaken by Russians; name changed in 1922 from Yamburg to Kingisepp in honor of Revolutionary leader V. E. Kingisepp.

King Island (kĭng). 1 Steep rocky island at S end of Bering Strait off W coast of Seward Penin., Alaska, and ab. 65 m. SE of the Diomede Is.; Eskimo pop. ab. 180; discovered by Capt. Cook 1778; center for walrus hunting.
2 Island ab. 42 m. long, at W end of Bass Strait, 50 m. NW of Tasmania, Australia.
3 Island in N Mergui Archipelago (*q.v.*), Burma.

King′man (kĭng′măn). 1 County in Kansas. See *Table* at KANSAS.
2 City, ⊗ of Mohave co., NW corner of Arizona, 65 m. ESE of Boulder Dam; pop. 4525; unincorporated.
3 City, ⊗ of Kingman co., S cen. Kansas, 30 m. SSW of Hutchinson; pop. 3582; in agricultural section.

Kingman Reef. Reef in cen. Pacific at N end of Line Is., 6°N, 162°W, 920 m. S of Honolulu; triangular in shape, 9 m. by 5 m., enclosing a deep lagoon; discovered 1798; annexed by U.S. May 1922; bet. 1934 and 1938 used as an experimental aviation station.

Kings (kĭngz). 1 River ab. 75 m. long, NW Arkansas; rises in SE Madison co., flows N across Missouri boundary and empties into White river.

2 River, S cen. California; rises in E Fresno co., flows W and disappears in region formerly covered by Tulare Lake; upper canyon forms part of Kings Canyon National Park.
3 Name of counties in two states of the U.S. See *Tables* at CALIFORNIA and NEW YORK.
4 Name of counties in three provinces of Canada. See *Tables* at NEW BRUNSWICK, NOVA SCOTIA, PRINCE EDWARD ISLAND.

King′s (kĭngz). Former name of co. OFFALY, Eire.

Kings Bay. Inlet on NW coast of West Spitsbergen I., S of Cross Bay.

Kings′burg (kĭngz′bûrg). City, Fresno co., S cen. California, 20 m. SE of Fresno; pop. 3093; settled c. 1875; peaches, grapes, oranges.

Kings′bur′y (kĭngz′bĕr′ĭ; -bĕr·ĭ). County in South Dakota. See *Table* at SOUTH DAKOTA.

Kings′bur·y (kĭngz′bĕr·ĭ; -brĭ). Former urban district, Middlesex, SE England, on the Brent 8 m. WNW of London; now part of Wembley municipal borough.

Kings Canyon National Park. See UNITED STATES, *National Parks.*

Kings′ford (kĭngz′fērd). City, Dickinson co., S Michigan penin., 3 m. W of Iron Mountain; pop. 5084; sawmill, chemical plant, hydroelectric power plant.

Kings′ley Dam (kĭngz′lĭ). See UNITED STATES, *Dams.*

King′s Lynn (kĭngz lĭn) *or* **Lynn Re′gis** (rē′jĭs) *or* **Lynn.** Municipal borough, Norfolk, E England, on the Ouse near the Wash 90 m. NNE of London; pop. 26,173; formerly one of chief ports in England; fisheries, flour mills, shipbuilding yards, engineering and metalworking plants.

Kings′mill′ (kĭngz′mĭl′). 1 Early name of Gilbert Is., W Pacific Ocean.
2 Island group comprising 7 islands in S part of Gilbert Is. group S of the equator.

King′s Mill. See MOLINO DEL REY.

Kings Mountain. 1 Ridge in NW York co., N South Carolina, and SE Cleveland co., S North Carolina; the part in South Carolina is scene of an American victory over the British Oct. 7, 1780 and has been set aside as **Kings Mountain National Military Park** (see UNITED STATES, *National Historical Parks*).
2 City in Kings Mountain township (pop. 14,724), Cleveland co., SW North Carolina, at foot of Kings Mt. 11 m. W of Gastonia; pop. 8008; textile mills.

King Sound. Inlet, N Western Australia, SE of Cape Leveque; connected by Sunday Strait with Timor Sea; receives Fitzroy river.

King′s Peak. Peak 13,498 ft. in the Uinta Mts., NE Utah; highest point in Utah.

Kings Point. Town, near Great Neck, Long Island, New York; pop. 5410; United States Merchant Marine Academy (1938; men).

Kings′port (kĭngz′pōrt). Industrial city, Sullivan co., NE Tennessee, on Holston river 22 m. NW of Johnson City; pop. 26,314; settled 1761; manufactures cellulose acetate, paper, cement, plastics, glass, cotton goods, book cloth, hosiery, brick; printing and binding.

Kings′ton (kĭng′stăn). 1 Town, Plymouth co., SE Massachusetts, on Plymouth Bay 16 m. ESE of Brockton; pop. 4302.
2 City, ⊗ of Caldwell co., NW Missouri; pop. 311.
3 City, ⊗ of Ulster co., SE New York, on Hudson river 15 m. N of Poughkeepsie; pop. 29,260; summer resort in Catskill Mts. region; railroad repair shops, brickyards; clothing, hats, refrigerators, hotel equipment, iron and bronze castings, road machinery, cement. Established as Dutch trading post c. 1615; passed into English hands 1667; played important role in Revolution; meeting place of first state government, court, and legislature 1777; burned by British 1777; rebuilt, and incorporated as village 1805; chartered as city 1872.
4 Borough, Luzerne co., E Pennsylvania, 3 m. N of Wilkes-Barre; pop. 20,261; incorporated 1850; coal min-

ing, railroad shops; silk, cigars; figured in Wyoming Valley Indian massacre of 1778.

5 Village in South Kingstown town (*q.v.*), Washington co., S Rhode Island, 17 m. NE of Westerly; pop. 2616; ⊗ 1752–1900. University of Rhode Island (chartered 1892; coed.).

6 Village, ⊗ of Roane co., E Tennessee; pop. 2010.

7 Seaport town, SE South Australia, 145 m. SSE of Adelaide.

8 City, ⊗ of Frontenac co., SE Ontario, Canada, on NE shore of Lake Ontario near head of St. Lawrence river; pop. 33,459; important transshipment point for Welland Ship Canal and outlet for traffic on Rideau Canal; has locomotive works, grain elevators, and various factories. Seat of Queen's Univ. (founded 1841) and Royal Military College. Fort Frontenac erected here by French 1673 and shortly thereafter destroyed by Iroquois Indians; restored 1695, it became key to Upper St. Lawrence; present city founded 1783 by Loyalist refugees; used as base for British naval force on Lake Ontario during War of 1812; capital of Canada 1841–44.

9 Commercial seaport, SE Jamaica, West Indies; ✱ of Jamaica; pop. (1960) 123,213; built on an excellent harbor; has library, museum, old parish church, and suburban areas noted for their natural beauty. Founded in 1692 after earthquake had destroyed Port Royal; became seat of government in 1872; has suffered much from fires and earthquakes, almost destroyed by earthquake 1907.

Kingston on Thames (tĕmz). Municipal borough, ⊗ of Surrey, S England, 12 m. WSW of London; pop. 40,168; part of Greater London; pleasure resort.

Kingston upon Hull. See HULL.

Kings'town (kĭngz'toun; kĭng'stŭn). **1** Seaport on island of St. Vincent, Windward Is., British West Indies; ✱ of British colony of St. Vincent; pop. 4269; on SW coast at head of **Kingstown Bay** at foot of the mountains; has government buildings, cathedral church, and a fine botanic garden (estab. 1763), oldest institution of its kind in Western Hemisphere. It was to order breadfruit plants for this garden that Capt. Wm. Bligh made his famous voyage 1787 on the *Bounty* to Tahiti.

2 See DUN LAOGHAIRE, Eire.

King's Town. See NEWCASTLE, Australia.

Kings'tree (kĭngz'trē). Town and winter resort, ⊗ of Williamsburg co., E South Carolina, on Black river 35 m. S of Florence; pop. 3847; settled 1732; timber, tobacco; furniture, veneer.

Kings'ville (kĭngz'vĭl). **1** Village in Kingsville township (pop. 3706), Ashtabula co., NE corner of Ohio, ab. 7 m. NE of Ashtabula; pop. (est.) 900.

2 City, ⊗ of Kleberg co., S Texas, 34 m. SW of Corpus Christi; pop. 25,297; headquarters of King Ranch (ab. 2000 sq. m.); ships dairy cattle, cotton, olives, dates, winter vegetables; manufactures cottonseed oil, butter, brooms. Texas Coll. of Arts and Industries (1917; coed.).

3 Town, Essex co., SE Ontario, Canada, on Lake Erie 25 m. SE of Windsor; pop. 2631; summer resort.

Kings'wood (kĭngz'wŏŏd). Urban district, Gloucestershire, SW cen. England, NE suburb of Bristol; pop. 18,921.

Kingtehchen. See FOWLIANG.

King·us'sie (kĭng·ū'sĭ). Burgh, E Inverness co., N cen. Scotland, on the Spey; pop. (1951) 1067; health resort; across the river is **Ruth'ven** (rŭth'vĕn), birthplace of James Macpherson, self-alleged translator of *The Poems of Ossian*.

King Wil'helms Land (vĭl'hĕlmz). Coastal region, NE Greenland, ab. 76°N.

King Wil'liam (kĭng wĭl'yăm). **1** County in Virginia. See *Table* at VIRGINIA.

2 Village, its ⊗, E Virginia; pop. (1950) 50.

King William Island. Island 6200 sq. m., S Franklin District, Northwest Territories, Canada, SW of Boothia Penin.

King'wil'liams·town (kĭng'wĭl'yămz·toun) *or* **King Williams Town.** *Also* **King William's Town;** *called* **King** *locally.* Town, SE Cape Province, S Union of South Africa, on Buffalo river 130 m. ENE of Port Elizabeth; pop. 10,660; trade center for farming and lumbering region; cotton textiles; in vicinity is large group of German settlers and also one of dominion's largest Kaffir farming communities. Founded 1835 and named after William IV; abandoned 1836–46 during unsettled conditions; after first Kaffir War made capital of British Kaffraria 1847–65.

King'wood (kĭng'wŏŏd). Town, ⊗ of Preston co., N West Virginia, 19 m. SE of Morgantown; pop. 2530.

Kin'hwa' (jĭn'hwä'). City, cen. Chekiang prov., E China, ab. 80 m. S of Hangchow; important railroad junction; modern airfield, used by Americans in World War II; captured after severe fighting by Japanese 1942.

Kinibalu. See KINABALU.

Kin'loch (kĭn'lŏk). City, St. Louis co., E Missouri, NW of St. Louis; pop. 6501.

Kin·nairds' Head (kĭ·nârdz'). Headland projecting into North Sea on NE coast of Scotland, NE Aberdeen co.; lighthouse.

Kin'ney (kĭn'ĭ). County in Texas. See *Table* at TEXAS.

Kin·ross' (kĭn·rôs'). **1** *or* **Kin·ross'-shire** (-rôs'shĭr; -shĕr; -rŏsh'-). County, E cen. Scotland; 82 sq. m.; pop. (1951) 7418; sheep raising; woolens and linen.

2 Burgh, its ⊗, 12 m. NW of Kirkcaldy; pop. 2525.

Kinsai. See HANGCHOW.

Kin·sale' (kĭn·sāl'). Urban district and seaport, S co. Cork, SW Eire, at head of **Kinsale Harbour;** pop. 2422; watering place; fisheries; scene of short-lived landing of Spanish expeditionary force to assist Irish insurrectionaries 1601 and of James II and his French auxiliaries 1690.

Kinsale, Old Head of. Cape on S coast of Ireland, S of Kinsale; lighthouse.

Kin'sha' *or* **Kin'sha'-kiang** (jĭn'shä'jĭ·äng'). "Golden sand river," Chinese name for the upper course of Yangtze river down to Ipin (Suchow), junction point with the Min.

Kinshasa. See LÉOPOLDVILLE.

Kins'ley (kĭnz'lĭ). City, ⊗ of Edwards co., SW cen. Kansas, 38 m. ENE of Dodge City; pop. 2263; trade center in wheat-producing section.

Kins'man Mountain (kĭnz'măn). Two peaks (north) 4275 ft., (south) 4363 ft., in Grafton co., New Hampshire, W of Franconia Notch.

Kin'ston (kĭn'stŭn). City, ⊗ of Lenoir co. E North Carolina 25 m. ESE of Goldsboro; pop. 24,819; tobacco and cotton center; stock raising, truck farming.

Kin'ta Valley (kĭn'tä). Area in SE Perak state, Federation of Malaya; center of tin-producing region, one of the richest in the world; formed by the **Kinta River,** an E tributary of the Perak.

Kint'la Lake (kĭnt'lȧ). Lake 6 m. long, at alt. 4000 ft. Flathead co., NW Montana, in Glacier National Park.

Kintla Peak. Mountain 10,100 ft., Flathead co., NW Montana, in Glacier National Park.

Kin·tyre' (kĭn·tīr') *or* **Can·tyre'** (kăn-). Peninsula ab. 40 m. long and 6½ m. average width, extending S on coast of SW cen. Scotland, in Argyll co., with the North Channel and the Atlantic Ocean on W and Kilbrennan Sound (an arm of the Firth of Clyde) on E.

Kintyre *or* **Cantyre, Mull of** (mŭl). Cape on S extremity of Kintyre Penin., off SW Scotland, projecting into North Channel; lighthouse.

Kin·zu'a Dam (kĭn·zōō'ȧ). Dam completed 1965 across Allegheny river, Warren co., N Pennsylvania; will form reservoir 27 m. long extending into S New York.

Kioga. See KYOGA.

Kion'ga (kyông'gȧ). District 400 sq. m., known as the **Kionga Triangle,** NE Mozambique, SE Africa, S of Ruvuma river; formerly a part of German East Africa, transferred to Portugal 1919 after World War I.

Kioto. See KYOTO.

Ki'o·wa (kī'ō·wä). **1** Name of counties in three states of the U.S. See *Tables* at COLORADO, KANSAS, OKLAHOMA. **2** Town, ⊗ of Elbert co., E cen. Colorado; pop. 195.

Kip'a·wa (?kĭp'à·wä). Lake 117 sq. m., SE of Lake Timiskaming in Timiskaming co., SW Quebec, Canada.

Kipp, Mount (kĭp). Peak 8800 ft., in Glacier National Park, NW Montana.

Kip·pure' (kĭ·pūr'). Mountain range on boundary bet. cos. Dublin and Wicklow, E Ireland; highest peak 2473 ft.

Ki'ra Ki'ra (kēr'à kēr'à). Settlement on N cen. coast of San Cristobal I., SE Solomon Is., W Pacific Ocean; site of government station.

Kirch'heim un'ter Teck (kĭrk'hīm ŏŏn'tēr tĕk'). City, cen. Baden-Württemberg, Germany, 16 m. ESE of Stuttgart; pop. 10,057.

Kirch'hör'de (kĭrк'hûr'dĕ). Former commune (pop. 14,661), Arnsberg govt. dist., Westphalia prov., Prussia, Germany; since 1929 part of Dortmund.

Ki·rensk' (kĭ·rĕnsk'; *Russ.* kĭ·ryĕnsk'). Town, E cen. Irkutsk Region, Soviet Russia, on right bank of Lena river 425 m. NE of Irkutsk; a commercial and trading center on the proposed N Trans-Siberian R.R. (Baikal-Amur-Magistral).

Kiresün. = GIRESUN.

Kir·ghiz' *or* **Qir·ghiz'** (kĭr·gēz'). Former name of Kazakh S.S.R., Soviet Russia, Asia—so called because the Kazakhs are an important branch of the Kirghiz people.

Kir·giz', *or* **Kir·ghiz'**, **Range** (kĭr·gēz'); *formerly* **A·le·ksan'dr Range** (ŭ·lyĭ·ksàn'dēr). Mountain range, N Kirgiz S.S.R., Soviet Central Asia, extends W from Issyk Kul; its highest peak at E end, Mt. Semenov 15,350 ft.; crossed by passes 6550 to 11,825 ft.

Kirgiz, *or* **Kirghiz, Soviet Socialist Republic**; *also* **Kir·gi'zi·a** (kĭr·gē'zĭ·à; -zhĭ·à; -zhà). A constituent republic of the Union of Soviet Socialist Republics, Central Asia; 75,950 sq. m.; pop. 1,459,301, (1941 est.) 1,533,439; ✳ Frunze. Bounded on N by Kazakh S.S.R., on E and SE by Sinkiang, China, on SW by Tadzhik S.S.R., and on W by Uzbek and Kazakh S.S. Republics; entirely mountainous with Tien Shan range along Chinese boundary and Alai Mts. in SW part, high peaks ranging from 16,000 to 23,620 (Tengri Khan) ft.; many glaciers and lakes at high altitudes (largest Issyk Kul); its chief river, the Naryn, a tributary of the Syr Darya, runs W in a high valley. Chief occupation stock raising, but cotton, hemp, wheat, and other grains are raised. Predominant ethnic strain Turko-Tatar. Chief towns Frunze, Przhevalsk, Osh, Dzhalal Abad. Region inhabited, probably earlier than 13th cent., by the Kirghiz, a people of Turkic speech and Mongolian race; annexed to Russia 1864 as part of Russian Turkistan; after 1917 nominally a Kara-Kirghiz autonomous area, which was reorganized 1926 and made a constituent republic of the U.S.S.R. 1936.

Kirgiz Steppe (stĕp) *or* **the Steppes** (stĕps). Steppe region of cen. Kazakh S.S.R., Soviet Central Asia.

Kiria. See KERIYA.

Ki'rin' (kē'rĭn'; *Pekingese* jē'lĭn'). **1** One of the three original provinces of Manchuria, in cen. and E part; 109,384 sq. m.; pop. (1936 est.) 7,135,542; ✳ Yungki. Within its borders under Japanese control 1932–45 it included the following provinces of Manchukuo: Kirin, Mutankiang, parts of Sankiang, Pinkiang, and Chientao. **2** Former province 1932–45, SE cen. Manchuo; 34,284 sq. m.; pop. (1940 est.) 5,865,024; ✳ Kirin (Yungki). **3** One of nine new provinces of Manchuria created Sept. 1945, in cen. part; 34,616 sq. m.; pop. 5,122,000; ✳ Changchun. **4** City. See YUNGKI.

Ki·ri·shi·ma (kē·rē·shē·mä). Mountain 5574 ft., NE Kagoshima prefecture, S Kyushu I., Japan; regarded as sacred because, according to legend, the god Ninigi de-

scended on its E summit (Takachihodake) as the forerunner of Jimmu, the first Japanese sovereign.

Ki'ri·wi'na (kēr'ē·wē'nà). **1** Largest of the Trobriand Is., W Solomon Sea, 50 m. N of Fergusson I.; ab. 25 m. long and bet. 3 and 6 m. wide; chief town Losuia, near N end. Occupied by Americans and Australians July 2, 1943 and used as air base. **2** Former name of Trobriand Is. group.

Kirjath–Arba. See HEBRON.

Kirk'by in Ash'field (kûr'bĭ, ăsh'fēld). Urban district, Nottinghamshire, N cen. England, 12 m. NNW of Nottingham; pop. 20,131.

Kirk·cal'dy (kûr·kô'dĭ; kûr·kä'dĭ). Seaport burgh, Fife co., E Scotland, on the Firth of Forth 26 m. N of Edinburgh; pop. (1951) 49,037; linoleum and oilcloth, iron and steel goods, linens, pottery; near coal deposits; birthplace of Adam Smith.

Kirk·cud'bright (kûr·kōō'brĭ). **1** *or* **Kirk·cud'-bright·shire** (-shĭr; -shēr). County, S Scotland; 899 sq. m.; pop. (1951) 30,742; agriculture and stock raising, quarrying (granite). **2** Burgh, its ⊗, at head of Dee estuary 30 m. SW of Dumfries; pop. 2498; 16th-cent. ruined castle; ruins of Dundrennan Abbey nearby; at St. Mary's Isle Burns first said the well-known grace "Some hae meat...."

Kir'kee (kĭr'kē). Town, suburb of Poona (*q.v.*), Maharashtra state, W Indian Union; pop. 16,302; scene of British victory 1817 over Baji Rao, the last peshwa of the Marathas.

Kir'ke·nes' (kĭr'kĕ·nās'). Seaport town, Finnmark co., N Norway, at head of inlet on S side of Varanger Fjord near Finland border; developed as tourist resort before World War II; held by Germans as base during the war.

Kirk'in·til'loch (kûr'kĭn·tĭl'ŏк). Burgh, Dunbarton co., W cen. Scotland, on Forth and Clyde Canal 8 m. NE of Glasgow; pop. 14,824; coal and iron mining, muslin weaving, chemicals.

Kirk'land (kûrk'lănd). City, King co., W cen. Washington, on inlet of Puget Sound 8 m. NE of Seattle; pop. 6025; in agricultural section.

Kirk'lar·e·li' (kĭrk'lär·ĕ·lē'). **1** Vilayet, NE Turkey in Europe, bordering on Black Sea on the E; 2185 sq. m.; pop. 172,697. **2** *formerly* **Kirk-Ki·lis·sa'** (kĭrk'kĕ·lē·sä'). Town, its ✳, on highway and branch railroad 35 m. E of Edirne; pop. 20,740; has many mosques and Greek churches; large proportion of its inhabitants are Bulgarians and Jews; has considerable trade with İstanbul. Scene of defeat of Turks by Bulgarians Oct. 25, 1912.

Kirk·pat'rick, Mount (kûrk·păt'rĭk). Peak 14,600 ft. in S Victoria Land, Antarctica, S of Mt. Markham, long. 167°E, lat. 84°20'S; one of the highest in Queen Alexandra Range.

Kirks'ville (kûrks'vĭl). City, ⊗ of Adair co., N Missouri, 55 m. N of Moberly; pop. 13,123; in grain-growing, poultry, and livestock-raising section; coal deposits nearby. Northeast Missouri State Teachers College (1867; coed.); Kirksville College of Osteopathy and Surgery (1892).

Kir·kuk' (kĭr·kōōk'). **1** Province (*liwa*), NE cen. Iraq; pop. (1935 est.) 223,634. **2** Town, Kirkuk prov., NE Iraq, 90 m. SE of Mosul; pop. ab. 30,000; agricultural and market center, noted especially for its sheep industry; inhabitants mainly Kurds; terminus of railroad from Baghdad. Its great oil fields, discovered 1927, are directly connected by pipelines across Syrian Desert with Haifa and Tripoli. Seized by Arab forces Apr. 1941 but retaken by British before June 1, 1941.

Kirk'wall (kûrk'wôl; -wăl). Burgh, on Pomona I. in the Orkney Is., ⊗ of Orkney co., NE Scotland; pop. 4348; good harbor; fisheries, boat building; cathedral.

Kirk'wood (kûrk'wŏŏd). City, St. Louis co., E Missouri, 13 m. W of St. Louis; pop. 29,421; business and residential suburb of St. Louis.

Kirlibaba. = CÂRLIBABA.

Kirman, Kirmanshah. Vars. of KERMAN, KERMAN-SHAH.

Kirmasti. See MUSTAFA KEMAL PAŞA.

Kir Moab *or* **Kir of Moab.** Ancient name of EL KERAK, Jordan.

Ki'rov (kē'rŭf); *formerly* **Vyat'ka** (vyȧt'kȧ). City, ✱ of Kirov Region, Soviet Russia, Europe, on left bank of Vyatka river 265 m. NE of Gorki; pop. 143,181; on railroads and trade routes to N, E, and W; has many industries and is a cultural center with research and technical institutes. Founded 1181 as a colony of Novgorod; capital of a medieval principality; plundered twice by Tatars in 14th and 15th cents.; came under Moscow 1489; name changed from Vyatka to Kirov 1934.

Ki·ro'va·bad (kĭ·rō'vȧ·bȧd; *Russ.* kĭ·rŭ·vŭ·bȧt'); *formerly* **Gan'dzha** (gän'jä); *known as* **E·li'sa·vet·pol'** (ê·lĭz'ȧ·vĕt·pôl'; *Russ.* yĭ·lyĭ·sŭ·vyĕt'pŭl·y') *1813 to 1920.* City, W Azerbaidzhan, U.S.S.R., S of Kura river and on railroad and oil pipeline 110 m. SE of Tiflis; pop. 98,743; on N spur of Armenian plateau at altitude of ab. 1440 ft.; has extensive calico mills; manufactures also wool and silk textiles and wines; nearby are important mines, esp. manganese and copper. An old Armenian town, its inhabitants now represent many races; controlled variously in medieval times; annexed by Russia 1813; scene of Persian defeat by Russians 1826; name changed from Gandzha ab. 1935. Birthplace 1141 of Persian poet Nizami.

Ki·ro'vo·grad (kĭ·rō'vô·grȧd; *Russ.* kĭ·rŭ·vŭ·grȧt').
1 Region, S cen. Ukraine, U.S.S.R., S of the Dnieper.
2 *formerly* **Zi·nov'ievsk** (zĭ·nōv'yĕfsk; *Russ.* zyĭ·nôf'-yĕfsk) *and* **E·li'sa·vet·grad'** (ê·lĭz'ȧ·vĕt·grȧd'; *Russ.* yĭ·lyĭ·sŭ·vyĕt'grȧt). City, its ✱, on E bank of Ingul river 155 m. SE of Kiev; pop. 100,331; primarily an agricultural center in the black-earth region of S Ukraine, but as a railroad town near the Donbas it has developed many industrial enterprises; founded as a fortress 1754 and named after Empress Elizabeth; in 1917, after the Revolution, Elisavetgrad renamed in honor of the Bolshevik leader G. E. Zinoviev, who was born here; again renamed 1935 after Sergei Kirov; in World War II held by Germans 1941–44.

Ki'rov Region (kē'rŭf). Region, E Soviet Russia, Europe, plateau country W of the Ural Mts.; 40,723 sq. m.; pop. 2,226,109; ✱ Kirov; occupies large part of Vyatka river basin; thickly forested, extensive peat beds.

Ki'rovsk (kē'rŭfsk). Town, W cen. Murmansk Region, Soviet Russia, Europe, at base of Kola Penin.; new commercial town on railroad 85 m. S of Murmansk and E of Lake Imandra; uranium deposits nearby.

Kir'rie·muir' (kĭr'ĭ·mūr'). Burgh, Angus co., E Scotland; pop. 4998; linen weaving; birthplace ("Thrums") of Sir James M. Barrie.

Kir·sa'nov (kĭr·sȧ'nŭf). Town, E Tambov Region, Soviet Russia, Europe, on Tambov-Saratov R.R.; pop. 25,043; in iron-mining area; important for its smelting works; also has flour mills.

Kır'şe·hir' (kĭr'shĕ·hēr'). **1** Vilayet, cen. Turkey in Asia; 3509 sq. m.; pop. 141,450.
2 *anc.* **Jus·tin'i·an·op'o·lis** (jŭs·tĭn'ĭ·ȧn·ŏp'ô·lĭs). Town, its ✱, on highway N of the Kızıl Irmak and ab. 85 m. SE of Ankara; pop. 13,778; noted for its carpets; important in Byzantine period; enlarged and renamed by Emperor Justinian.

Kir·thar' Range (kĭr·tär'; *native* kĭrt·hŭr'). Mountain range bet. Baluchistan and Sind prov., NW Pakistan; highest peak ab. 7000 ft.

Ki·run (kē·rōōn) *or* **Kee'lung** (kē'lōōng') *or* **Chi'-lung'** (jĭ'lōōng'). Seaport, N Formosa; pop. 145,000; one of the two ports of the capital Taihoku; has best harbor in the island; nearby are valuable gold, silver, and copper mines.

Ki'ru·na (kē'rŭ·nȧ'). Town, Norrbotten prov., N Sweden, SE of Torne Träsk, on railroad bet. Narvik,

Norway, and Luleå, Sweden; pop. 10,718; a mining town near rich deposits of high iron content.

Kir·yu (kĕr·yōō). Town, Gumma prefecture, Honshu, Japan, ab. 55 m. NNW of Tokyo; pop. (1945) 85,180; a center of weaving industry.

Kis'–Al'föld *or* **Kis'al'föld** (kĭsh'ŏl'fŭld). = Little ALFOLD.

Kisangani. See STANLEYVILLE.

Ki·sar' (kĭ·sär'). Small island ab. 15 m. N of E tip of Timor, S Malay Archipelago; ab. 8 m. in diameter; pop. ab. 8000; attached to Amboina division of Indonesia.

Kish (kĭsh). One of most important of the ancient cities of Sumer and Akkad; its ruins lie ab. 8 m. E of site of Babylon and in early times was on the Euphrates whose course changed later; ruins are very extensive and different strata give valuable archaeological information of different eras: near the surface were found ruins of great temple of the time of Nebuchadnezzar II and Nabonidus 605–539 B.C., below it the palace of Sargon I c. 2600 B.C., and at lowest level remains of Sumerian culture of 4th millennium B.C.; according to legend the ruling city after the Flood.

Ki'shan·garh *or* **Ki'shen·garh** (kĭsh'ȧn·gär; *native* kī'shȧn·gŭr'h). **1** Former Indian state, once in Jaipur Residency, Rajputana, NW India, SW of Jaipur; 837 sq. m.; pop. (1941) 104,127; made treaty with British government 1818; became member of Union of Rajasthan June 26, 1947.
2 Town, its ✱; pop. 11,929; founded 1611.

Ki·shen'gan'ga (kĭ·shän'gŭng'gä). River ab. 130 m. long, in the Himalayas, W Kashmir; flows W through mountains N of the valley of Kashmir, then SW to join the Jhelum.

Ki'shi·nev (kĭsh'ĭ·nĕf; *Russ.* kĭ·shĭ·nyôf'); *Romanian* **Chi·şi·nău'** (kē'shĕ·nŭ'ōō). City, ✱ of Bessarabia under Russians and Romanians, on a tributary of the Dniester 90 m. NW of Odessa; pop. 112,500; commercial town on railroad from Iaşi to Odessa; exports fruit, tobacco, and wine; seat of a bishop, has a cathedral. Founded 1436; attacked by Turks; acquired 1812 by Russia from Moldavia; scene of massacre of Jews Apr. 1903 instigated by Russian official classes; as part of Bessarabia was under Romanians 1918–40; made capital of Moldavian Republic 1940; held by Axis powers 1941–44; entered by Russians Aug. 24, 1944.

Kishm. See QISHM.

Kishon. See QISHON.

Kis'ka (kĭs'kȧ). Island, most westerly and largest of Rat Is. group, W Aleutian Is., SW Alaska; mountainous; highest point above 4000 ft.; Kiska Harbor is on E coast; seized by Japanese June 1942; reoccupied by American and Canadian forces Aug. 15, 1943.

Kis'ki·min'e·tas (kĭs'kĭ·mĭn'ê·tȧs). River ab. 20 m. long, SW Pennsylvania; formed by confluence of Conemaugh river and Loyalhanna Creek in SW Indiana co., flows NW into Allegheny river.

Kis'kö·rös (kĭsh'kŭ·rŭsh). Commune, S Hungary, 65 m. S of Budapest; pop. 13,756.

Kis·kun·do'rozs·ma (kĭsh'kŏŏn·dô'rôzh·mô) *or* **Do'rozs·ma** (dô'rôzh·mô). Commune, S Hungary, NW of Szeged; pop. 20,575.

Kis'kun·fé'legy·há'za (kĭsh'kŏŏn·fā'lĕd·y'·hä'zŏ) *or* **Fé'legy·há'za** (fā'lĕd·y'·hä'zŏ). City, cen. Hungary, 66 m. SE of Budapest; pop. 41,404; market center for livestock, tobacco, fruits, and wines; dates from ab. 1743.

Kis'kun·ha'las (kĭsh'kŏŏn·hŏ'lŏsh) *or* **Ha'las** (hŏ'lŏsh). City, S Hungary, 35 m. NW of Szeged; pop. 28,339.

Kis'kun·maj'sa (kĭsh'kŏŏn·moi'shŏ). Commune, S Hungary, 25 m. NW of Szeged; pop. 19,369.

Kis'lo·vodsk (kĭs'lô·vŏtsk; *Russ.* kĭs·lŭ·vôtsk'). City, S Stavropol Territory, Soviet Russia, Europe, on a tributary of the Kuma; pop. 51,289; in foothills of N Caucasus Mts. (alt. 2690 ft.) at end of branch railroad ab. 15 m. SW of Pyatigorsk; health resort; mineral springs.

Kismayu. See CHISIMAIO.

Ki·so (kē·sŏ̄). River 144 m. long, SW cen. Honshu, Japan; rises in Nagano prefecture and flows SW into the head of Ise Bay.

Kis'pest' (kĭsh'pĕsht'); *Ger.* **Klein–Pest** (klīn'pĕst'). City, cen. Hungary; pop. (1939) 62,797; a SE suburb of Budapest.

Kis'se·raing (kĭs'ĕ·rīng; *native* kĭ'thĕ·rīn). Island in E cen. Mergui Archipelago (q.v.), Burma.

Kis·sim'mee (kĭ·sĭm'ē). **1** River ab. 150 m. long, S cen. Florida; flows S from Lake Tohopekaliga through **Lake Kissimmee** (ab. 12 m. long) into Lake Okeechobee. **2** City, ⊗ of Osceola co., cen. Florida penin., on Tohopekaliga Lake 18 m. S of Orlando; pop. 6845; commercial center of cattle-raising region; fruits and vegetables; hunting and fishing resort.

Kis'sing·en *or* **Bad Kissingen** (bät kĭs'ĭng·ĕn). Town, W Germany, in Lower Franconia, Bavaria, on Fränkische Saale river ab. 62 m. E of Frankfurt; pop. 9517; mineral waters.

Kist'na (kĭst'nȧ); *also, formerly,* **Krish'na** (krĭsh'nȧ). River of the Deccan, S India, ab. 800 m. long; rises near Mahabaleshwar in Maharashtra in the Western Ghats within 40 m. of the Arabian Sea, flows ESE into Hyderabad, continues ENE, forming large section of S boundary of Hyderabad, turns SE and flows into Bay of Bengal through several mouths S of Masulipatam.

Kis'új·szál'lás (kĭsh'ōō·y'·säl'läsh). City, E Hungary, 12 m. SW of Karcag; pop. 15,015.

Ki·su'mu (kē·sōō'mōō). Town, ✻ of Nyanza prov., Kenya, E Africa; nonnative pop. ab. 2000; port on Homa Gulf, NE Lake Victoria, and on railroad ab. 160 m. NW of Nairobi.

Kis'vár'da (kĭsh'vär'dŏ). Commune, NE Hungary, 60 m. NE of Miskolc; pop. 12,841.

Ki'ta (kē'tȧ). **1** Town, W Mali (former French Sudan), West Africa, on Bamako-Dakar railroad 100 m. W of Bamako; pop. ab. 4000. **2** = KETA, Ghana, W Africa.

Ki·tab' (kĭ·täb'). Town, N suburb of Shakhrisyabz, SE Uzbek S.S.R., Soviet Central Asia, ab. 40 m. S of Samarkand; site of International Latitude Observatory on 39°8′N lat.; one of five such observatories in the world: see GAITHERSBURG, Maryland; MIZUSAWA, Japan; SAN PIETRO Island, Sardinia (Carloforte); UKIAH, California.

Ki·tai'. **1** (kĭ·tī') Modern Russian name of China: see CATHAY. **2** (chĭ'tī') See KUCHENGTZE.

Kita Iwo. See VOLCANO ISLANDS.

Ki·ta·ka·mi (kē·tä·kä·mē). River 152 m. long, Iwate and Miyagi prefectures, N Honshu, Japan; flows S into Ishinomaki Bay at Ishinomaki.

Ki·ta'–Kyu'shu (kē·tä'kyōō'shōō). City, Fukuoka prefecture, N Kyushu, Japan, formed 1963 by amalgamation of Kokura, Moji, Tobata, Wakamatsu, and Yawata (qq.v.); pop. 1,056,381.

Ki·ta'le (kē·tä'lȧ). Town, W Kenya, E Africa, near Uganda border and just E of Mt. Elgon.

Ki·tan Strait (kē·tän); *formerly* **Yu·ra Strait** (yōō·rä). Strait bet. S Honshu I., Japan, and SE Awaji I., connecting Osaka Bay (a branch of the Inland Sea) with Kii Channel and the Pacific Ocean.

Kit Car'son (kĭt kär's'n). County in Colorado. See *Table* at COLORADO.

Kit Carson Peak. Mountain 14,100 ft. in Saguache co., S Colorado.

Kitch'e·ner (kĭch'ĕ·nẽr); *formerly* **Ber·lin'** (bûr·lĭn'; bẽr-). Industrial city, ⊗ of Waterloo co., SE Ontario, Canada, 62 m. WSW of Toronto; pop. 44,867; rubber goods, furniture. Seat of St. Jerome's College (founded 1864). First settled 1806 by Pennsylvania Dutch, then by Germans 1825 who named it Berlin; name changed 1916 in honor of Lord Kitchener.

Kithairōn. See CITHAERON.

Ki'tha·reng (kĭth'ȧ·rĕng). Var. of KISSERAING.

Kit'i·mat (kĭt'ĭ·măt). Seaport, W British Columbia, Canada, at head of Douglas Channel; aluminum plant.

Kit'sap (kĭt'săp). County in Washington. See *Table* at WASHINGTON.

Kit·tan'ning (kĭ·tăn'ĭng). Borough, ⊗ of Armstrong co., W Pennsylvania, on Allegheny river 37 m. NE of Pittsburgh; pop. 6793; settled after 1796; coal, iron, limestone; clay pits; oil and gas wells; plate glass.

Kit'ta·tin'ny Mountain (kĭt'ȧ·tĭn'ĭ). Ridge of the Appalachian Mts., extending from Ulster co., SE New York, SW through Sussex and Warren cos. in NW New Jersey, and into Pennsylvania where it forms boundary bet. Monroe, Carbon, and Schuylkill cos. on the NW and Northampton, Lehigh, and Berks cos. on the SE, and continuing SW to the Maryland border; average height ab. 2000 ft.; frequently called Shawangunk in New York and Blue Mts. in Pennsylvania.

Kit'ter·y (kĭt'ẽr·ĭ). Town, York co., SW Maine, across bay from Portsmouth, New Hampshire; pop. 10,689; site of Portsmouth Navy Yard (established 1806). See PORTSMOUTH, New Hampshire.

Kittery Point. Extreme S point, York co., SW Maine.

Kittim. See CITIUM.

Kit'ti·tas (kĭt'ĭ·tăs). County in Washington. See *Table* at WASHINGTON.

Kitt'son (kĭt's'n). County in Minnesota. See *Table* at MINNESOTA.

Kit'ty Hawk (kĭt'ĭ hôk'). Small village, Dare co., E North Carolina, on narrow sand barrier opp. Albemarle Sound; pop. (1950) 250; nearby is Kill Devil Hill (now a national memorial) where Wright brothers performed experiments, making first airplane flight in U.S. Dec. 17, 1903.

Kit'yang' (kĭt'yäng'). Town, E Kwangtung prov., SE China, ab. 24 m. NW of Swatow.

Kitz'bühel (kĭts'bü[ĕ]l). Resort town, Tirol, W Austria, ENE of Innsbruck; pop. 7221.

Kit'zing·en (kĭt'sĭng·ĕn). City, Bavaria, Germany, on Main river; pop. 10,272.

Kiu'chuan' (jĭ·ō'chü·än'); *formerly* **Su'chow'** (sōō'jō'). Town, NW Kansu prov., N cen. China, on highway to Turkistan ab. 375 m. NW of Lanchow; pop. ab. 25,000; partially destroyed in Mohammedan uprising 1865–72; center of fertile agricultural region.

Kiu'kiang' (jĭ·ōō'jĭ·äng'). City and treaty port, N Kiangsi prov., SE China, N of Poyang Hu (lake) and on S bank of Yangtze, 450 m. by boat from Shanghai; pop. (1931 est.) 80,166; rivals Hankow and Minhow in shipments of tea and is principal market for Kingtehchen (Fowliang) pottery; also exports rice, paper, and grass cloth. Opened as treaty port 1862.

Kiung'shan' (chĭ·ōōng'shän'); *formerly* **Kiung'chow'** (-jō'). City and treaty port, ✻ of Hainan I., on NE coast, SW Kwangtung prov., SE China; pop. (1931 est.) 45,757; most important town on island; opened to foreign trade 1858 by Treaty of Tientsin but not actually used until 1876; its outport is Hoihow (q.v.).

Kiushu. See KYUSHU.

Ki'vi·jär'vi (kĭ'vĭ·yăr'vĭ). Lake, SW cen. Finland, in Vaasa dept.

Ki'vu (kē'vōō). Province, Republic of Congo (formerly Belgian Congo). See COSTERMANSVILLE.

Ki'vu, Lake (kē'vōō). Lake 1025 sq. m. in cen. Africa, on E border of Republic of Congo bet. Kivu and Rwanda, N of Lake Tanganyika and S of Lake Edward; chief town on its shores Bukavu (Costermansville) at S end; center of volcanic region: Karisimbi, Mikeno, Nyamlagira, and Nyiragongo, all above 10,000 ft., nearby.

Ki'yang' (kē'yäng'). Town, S Hunan prov., SE cen. China, on tributary of the Siang 50 m. S of Hengyang; in World War II an American outpost captured by Japanese Sept. 5, 1944.

Ki'yiv (kē'yĭv). Ukrainian form of KIEV.

Kı·zıl' A·da·lar' (kĭ·zĭl' ä·dä·lär'). See PRINCES ISLANDS.

Ki·zil′ Ar·vat′ (kĭ·zĭl′ är·vät′). Town, SW Turkmen S.S.R. Soviet Central Asia, on railroad; pop. 6615.
Ki·zil′ Ir·mak′ (kĭ·zĭl′ ĭr·mäk′); *anc.* **Ha′lys** (hā′lĭs). River ab. 600 m. long, in cen. and N cen. Turkey in Asia; rises in the mountains E of SIVAS and flows in a great curve SW, W, N, and NE into the Black Sea bet. Samsun and Sinop; the largest river of Asia Minor; its main tributaries are the Delice from the E and the Gök from the W.
Kizil Khoto. See KYZYL.
Kizil Kum. = KYZYL KUM.
Kizil Uzen. See QIZIL UZUN.
Kiz·lyar′ (kĭs·lyär′; *Angl.* kĭz′lĭ·är′). Town, E Grozny Region, Soviet Russia, Europe, at head of Terek delta ab. 40 m. from the Caspian Sea; pop. 9514; formerly in Dagestan; on the Astrakhan-Makhachkala railroad ab. 75 m. NNW of the latter. Surrounded by gardens and vineyards and famous for its wines; has active trade in wheat, maize, and fruits; fishing an important industry. An old town; now has Georgian, Tatar, Armenian, and Persian inhabitants; first became prominent 1715; its citadel or fortress dates from 1736.
Ki·zu (kē·zōō) *or* **Ki·zu·ga·wa** (-gä·wä). River, S Honshu, Japan, rising in Mie prefecture; a tributary of the Yodo, joining it S of Kyoto.
Ki·zu·ga·wa (kē·zōō·gä·wä). **1** See KIZU.
2 See YODO river.
Kjö′ben·havn′ (kŭ′p′n·houn′). = COPENHAGEN.
Kjöge Bight. See KÖGE BIGHT.
Kjö′len Mountains (chû′lĕn). Range along boundary bet. NE Norway and NW Sweden; highest peak Kebnekaise 6963 ft.
Kla′bat (klä′bät). Volcanic peak 6545 ft., on NE tip of Celebes I., Indonesia, just E of Manado.
Klabat Bay. Inlet of South China Sea, N coast of Bangka I., Indonesia.
Klad′no (klăd′nō; *Czech* klád′nô). Industrial city, NW cen. Bohemia prov., W Czechoslovakia, 15 m. W of Prague; pop. (1930) 20,751; coal and iron mines.
Kla′gen·furt (klä′gĕn·fōŏrt). City, ✳ of Carinthia prov., Austria, near Yugoslav border just N of Karawanken Mts. and 62 m. WSW of Graz; pop. (1939) 57,462; 16th-cent. cathedral; manufactures metal goods, chemicals, paper. Became city 1279; at height of commercial importance in 18th cent.; occupied by Yugoslav troops 1919; center of plebiscite area in 1920.
Klaipeda. See MEMEL.
Klam′ath (klăm′ăth). **1** River 250 m. long, S Oregon and NW California; rises in Lake Ewauna, Klamath co., S Oregon, flows SW across NW extremity of California into the Pacific Ocean.
2 County in Oregon. See *Table* at OREGON.
Klamath Falls. Industrial city and tourist resort, ⊗ of Klamath co., S Oregon, at S end of Upper Klamath Lake and on E slope of Cascade Range, 15 m. N of California border; pop. 16,949; estab. c. 1867; lumber mills, meat-packing plants; grows potatoes, alfalfa, grain; hot mineral springs.
Klamath Lakes. Two connected lakes, **Upper Klamath Lake** in SW Klamath co., S Oregon, and **Lower Klamath Lake** (now dry) extending into Siskiyou co., N California; length of combined lakes ab. 44 m.
Klamath Mountains. Mountain range of the Coast Ranges in NW California, extending from Siskiyou co. N into Oregon; includes, in N part, the **Sis′ki·you Mountains** (sĭs′kĭ·yōō).
Klang (kläng; *Angl.* klăng). Town near the coast, W Selangor state, Federation of Malaya; pop. 20,913, (1937 est.) 27,498; on Kuala Lumpur-Port Swettenham R.R.; formerly noted for its coffee, now raises rubber.
Klar (klär). River 215 m. long, SE cen. Norway and W Sweden; rises in SE cen. Norway, flows S across Swedish border into Lake Vänern.
Kla′ten (klä′t′n). Town, W Surakarta govt., S cen. Java, Indonesia, 20 m. SW of Surakarta; pop. 12,039.

Kla′to·vy (klä′tô·vĭ); *Ger.* **Klat′tau** (klät′ou). Town, SW Bohemia prov., W Czechoslovakia, ab. 70 m. SW of Prague; pop. (1930) 14,088; market center in rose-growing region; has fine 13th-cent. church.
Klausenburg. See CLUJ.
Klau′sen Pass (klou′zĕn). Alpine pass 6437 ft., Uri canton, cen. Switzerland, E of Altdorf.
Klausthal–Zellerfeld. See CLAUSTHAL-ZELLERFELD.
Kla′wak (klä′wŏk). Seaport, W Prince of Wales I., S Alexander Archipelago, SE Alaska; pop. 251.
Kle′berg (klā′bûrg). County in Texas. See *Table* at TEXAS.
Kleine Scheidegg. See *Little Scheidegg* at SCHEIDEGG.
Klein–Pest. See KISPEST.
Kleinrosseln. See PETITE-ROSSELLE.
Klerks′dorp (klĕrks′dôrp; *Angl.* klûrks′-). Town, S Transvaal, NE Union of South Africa, 10 m. N of Vaal river and 100 m. WSW of Johannesburg; pop. 8953; in gold and diamond district; founded 1838, first Boer settlement in Transvaal.
Kleve. See CLEVE.
Klick′i·tat (klĭk′ĭ·tăt). **1** River, S Washington; flows S in Yakima co. and through Klickitat co. into Columbia river.
2 County in Washington. See *Table* at WASHINGTON.
Klin (klēn; klĭn; *Russ.* klyēn). Town, Moscow Region, Soviet Russia, Europe, on Moscow-Leningrad R.R. 31 m. NW of Moscow; pop. ab. 5000; farthest point E in German drive on Moscow reached Nov. 25, 1941.
Klin′tsy (klĭnt′sĭ; *Russ.* klyĭn·tsĭ′). Town, W Bryansk Region, SW Soviet Russia, Europe, on railroad ab. 85 m. WSW of Bryansk; pop. 27,677; founded in 18th cent.
Klip′heu′vel (klĭp′hû′vĕl). Town, SW Cape Province, S Union of South Africa, 22 m. (30 m. by rail) NE of Cape Town; has largest wireless, telegraph, and telephone transmitting station in Africa.
Kłodz′ko (klôts′kô); *Ger.* **Glatz** (gläts). Manufacturing city, S Wrocław dept., SW Poland, on Nysa river 52 m. SSW of Wrocław in Sudeten Mts.; pop. (1946) 20,000; formerly in Silesia prov., Prussia, Germany; fortified place; iron foundries; varied manufactures. Assigned to Poland by Potsdam Conference 1945.
Klofajökull. See VATNAJÖKULL.
Klon′dike (klŏn′dīk). Region, cen. Yukon Territory, Canada, in Yukon river basin S of Ogilvie Range; ab. 800 sq. m.; lies on both sides of **Klondike River,** ab. 90 m. long, a tributary of the Yukon flowing W to join it near Dawson; has very severe winter climate. Rich gold-bearing gravel occurs along the small creeks; gold discovered Aug. 16, 1896 on Bonanza Creek, ab. 3 m. from Dawson; news reached U.S. Jan. 1897 and was followed by rush 1897–99 of 30,000 persons by way of Lynn Canal, Chilkoot and White Passes, and the Yukon; peak of production reached in 1900 ($22,000,000); total production 1885 to 1929 was more than $175,000,000.
Klong (klông) *or* **Me·klong** (mă·klông). River ab. 300 m. long, W Thailand; rises at S end of Dawna Range, flows S and SSE to head of Gulf of Siam; Samut Songkhram is the port at its mouth.
Klo′ster·neu′burg (klō′stēr·noi′bōŏrκ). City, Lower Austria prov., Austria, on Danube river 17 m. NW of Vienna; pop. 14,083; chemical factory.
Kloster–Zeven. See ZEVEN.
Klu·ane′ (klōō·än′). Station at S end of Kluane Lake, SW Yukon, Northwest Territories, Canada; now a post on the Alaska Highway.
Kluane Lake. Lake 184 sq. m., largest in Yukon Territory, Canada, in SW part along N slope of St. Elias Range; its outlet is **Kluane River,** ultimately discharging into White and Yukon rivers; the Alaska Highway extends along its S and W shores through the stations of Kluane and Burwash Landing.
Klu·ang′ (klōō·äng′; klwäng). Town on railroad and on Endau river, N Johore state, Federation of Malaya; pop. 6473; airfield.

Klucz·bo′rk (klōŏch·bô′rĕk); *Ger.* **Kreuz′burg** (kroits′bŏŏrk); *also* **Kreuzburg in O′ber·schle′si·en** (ĭn ō′bĕr·shlä′zĕ·ĕn). Town, N Śląsk dept., SW Poland, 30 m. NNE of Opole; pop. (1946) 11,000; formerly in Silesia, Germany. Assigned to Poland by Potsdam Conference 1945.

Klu·kho′ri (klōō·kô′ryĭ); *formerly* **Mi·ko·yan′ Sha·khar′** (myĭ·kŭ·yȧn′ shŭ·kȧr′). Town, ✶ of former Karachaev Autonomous Region, SE Russia, Europe; on right bank of Kuban river 165 m. SE of Krasnodar; a village rebuilt as Karachaev capital 1927 and given name Mikoyan Shakhar; on abolition of Karachaev Autonomous Region (*q.v.*), renamed Klukhori and relocated in Georgian S.S.R. From it the **Klu·khor′** (klōō·kôr′) **Pass** (8400 ft.) leads through the Caucasus Mts. W of Mt. Elborus to Sukhumi.

Kly·az′ma (klĭ·ăz′mȧ; *Russ.* klyȧs′y′·mȧ). River ab. 425 m. long, W cen. Soviet Russia, Europe; rises just N of Moscow, flows E to join the Oka W of Gorki.

Klyu·chev′ska·ya Sop′ka (klyōō·chĕf′skȧ·yȧ sôp′kȧ). Volcano (*sopka*) 15,666 ft. in Eastern Range, Kamchatka Penin., Khabarovsk Territory, Soviet Russia, Asia; highest mountain in Siberia.

Knä′red (k′nä′rĕd). Town, S Sweden, SE of Halmstad; scene of signing of peace bet. Sweden and Denmark Jan. 28, 1613.

Knares′bor·ough (nârz′bŭ·rȧ; -brȧ). Urban district, West Riding, Yorkshire, N England; pop. 8393; ruins of ancient castle.

Kne′za (k′nĕ′zä). Town, Vrattsa dept., NW Bulgaria, 28 m. W of Pleven; pop. (1926) 10,554.

Knife (nīf). River ab 100 m. long, W North Dakota; rises in N Billings co., flows E into Missouri river at Stanton, in E Mercer co.

Knight Inlet (nīt). Narrow inlet ab. 70 m. long, SW British Columbia, Canada; opens into Queen Charlotte Strait.

Knights′bridge (nīts′brĭj). Locality near Bir Hacheim, N Cyrenaica, NE Libya, N Africa; scene of fighting 1942–43 during World War II, esp. at time of disastrous defeat of British tank force by Rommel June 13, 1943.

Knights′town (nīts′toun). Town, Henry co., E cen. Indiana, 28 m. SSW of Muncie; pop. 2496.

Knin (k′nēn). Town, W Bosnia and Herzegovina, W Yugoslavia, on Kerka river ab. 28 m. NNE of Šibenik; pop. 13,212.

Knit′tel·feld (k′nĭt′ĕl·fĕlt). Industrial city, Styria prov., Austria, on Mur river 30 m. WNW of Graz; pop. 11,920.

Knock′a·doon′ Head (nŏk′ȧ·dōōn′). Cape on S coast of Ireland, S of entrance to Youghal Bay.

Knockanaffrin. See COMERAGH MOUNTAINS.

Knock·meal′down (nŏk·mēl′doun). Mountain range in S Ireland, on boundary bet. cos. Tipperary and Waterford; highest peak Knockmealdown 2609 ft.

Knos′sos *or* **Cnos′sus** *or* **Gnos′sus** (nŏs′ŭs). Royal city of ancient Crete, near the N coast of the island; ruins of its great palace are a few miles SE of Candia. Center of Cretan Bronze Age culture; probably flourished c. 2000–1400 B.C., with period around 1800 B.C. the high point of the purely Cretan influence. Seat of legendary King Minos (or line of kings of that name) and site of the labyrinth of Daedalus.

Knott (nŏt). County in Kentucky. See *Table* at KENTUCKY.

Knot′ting·ley (nŏt′ĭng·lĭ). Urban district West Riding, Yorkshire, N England; pop. 9989.

Knowl′ton (nōl′t′n; -tŭn) Village, ⊗ of Brome co. S Quebec, Canada on Brome Lake 32 m. SW of Sherbrooke; pop. 1094; resort.

Knox (nŏks). **1** Name of counties in nine states of U.S. See *Tables* at ILLINOIS, INDIANA, KENTUCKY, MAINE, MISSOURI, NEBRASKA, OHIO, TENNESSEE, TEXAS.
2 City, ⊗ of Starke co., NW Indiana, 33 m. SW of South Bend; pop. 3458.

Knox Coast *or* **Land.** Section of coast of Wilkes Land, Antarctica, on Indian Ocean, 67°S and 104°E to 109°E; in Australian claim.

Knox′ville (nŏks′vĭl; *Sou. also* -v′l). **1** Town, ⊗ of Crawford co., cen. Georgia; pop. (1950) 602.
2 City, Knox co., W Illinois, 5 m. ESE of Galesburg; pop. 2560; in agricultural section.
3 City, ⊗ of Marion co., S cen. Iowa, 32 m. ESE of Des Moines; pop. 7817.
4 Commercial and industrial city, ⊗ of Knox co., E Tennessee, on Tennessee river ab. 105 m. NE of Chattanooga; pop. 111,827; manufactures textiles, furniture, flour and feed; iron, marble, and cement works; coal, iron, zinc, and copper mines; marble quarries; timber; tobacco warehouses; administrative center of TVA (1933 ff.). Univ. of Tennessee (1794; coed.); Knoxville College (1876; coed.). Settled 1786; became ⊗ 1792; served as 1st capital of Tennessee 1796–1812, again 1817–19; incorp. as city 1815; occupied by Union troops of Gen. Burnside 1863, besieged by Confederate army under Longstreet 1863.

Knud Ras′mus·sen Land (k′nōōth räs′mŏŏ·s′n). Region, N and NW Greenland, between Baffin Bay and Lincoln Sea.

Knuts′ford (nŭts′fẽrd). Urban district, Cheshire, NW England, near the Birken 13 m. SSW of Manchester; pop. 6619; the *Cranford* of Elizabeth Cleghorn Gaskell.

Knys′na (k′nĭs′nȧ). Town, S Cape Province, S Republic of So. Africa, on landlocked estuary of Knysna river 160 m. W of Port Elizabeth; pop. 2418; in great forest region.

Ko (kô), *also* **Koh.** Siamese word for "island." For names beginning with this word, see the second element, as **Ko Kut,** see KUT.

Ko′ba·rid (kô′bä·rēd). Yugoslav name for CAPORETTO.

Kobdo. **1** See KHOBDO river, Outer Mongolia.
2 See DZHIRGALANTU town, Outer Mongolia.

Ko′be (kō′bĕ; kō′bä; *Jap.* kō·bĕ). Seaport and commercial city, ✶ of Hyogo prefecture, S coast of W Honshu, Japan; pop. (1964 est.) 1,196,000; built partly along the N shore of Osaka Bay and partly on the hillsides; has close connections with city of Osaka ab. 20 m. to the E; fine port facilities, second only to Yokohama in importance; shipbuilding, manufacture of heavy electrical equipment, rubber, and aircraft; many foreign consulates and representatives of foreign business firms. Until the Restoration 1868 only a fishing village; has absorbed the old town of Hyogo; in World War II severely bombed by Allied forces during last months of conflict.

København. See COPENHAGEN.

Ko′blenz *or* **Co′blenz** (kō′blĕnts; *sometimes Anglicized* kŏ·blĕnz′). **1** Government district, former Rhine Province, Prussia, Germany; 2397 sq. m.
2 *anc.* **Con′flu·en′tes** (kŏn′flōō·ĕn′tēz). Commercial and manufacturing city, N Rhineland-Westphalia, formerly ✶ of the Rhine Province, Prussia, at confluence of Moselle and Rhine rivers 50 m. SSE of Cologne; pop. 58,322; 14th-cent. bridge over Moselle river; 10th and 11th-cent. churches; manufactures beverages, foodstuffs, cigars, pianos, shoes, paper, clay products; active trade in wines. Originally a Roman station; became city 1254; besieged by French 1688; principal place of refuge for French émigrés during Revolution; occupied by French 1794; became capital 1801 (Treaty of Lunéville) of French department of Rhin-et-Moselle; to Prussia 1815; capital of Rhine Province (Prussia) 1822; fortified; occupied by American troops 1919–23 and by French troops 1923–29; in World War II scene of battle Mar. 16, 1945 in which it was taken by Americans.

Kob′rin (kôb′rĭn; *Russ.* ·ryĭn); *Pol.* **Kob′ryń** (kôb′rĭn·y′). Town, SW White Russia, U.S.S.R., 28 m. ENE of Brest (formerly in Polesie dept., Poland); pop. 10,101.

Ko′bro·or′ *or* **Ko′bro·ör′** (kō′brô·ûr′). Island, forming the central section of Tanahbesar, Aru Is., Indonesia.

Ko·buk′ (kô·bŏŏk′). River ab. 275 m. long, NW Alaska, S of Baird Mts.; flows W to Kotzebue Sound.

Koca. See XANTHUS river.

Ko·ca′ba (kṓ·tsä′bä); *Ger.* **Katz′bach** (käts′bäĸ). River ab. 60 m. long in Śląsk Dolny dept., SW Poland, flowing NE past Lignica into the Odra (Oder) river; scene of battle of Katzbach Aug. 26, 1813 in which one of Napoleon's armies was defeated by Germans under Blücher.

Ko′ca·e·li′ (kṓ′jä·ĕl·ē′). Vilayet, NW Turkey in Asia; 3229 sq. m.; pop. 335,492; * İzmit.

Ko′čev·je (kō′chĕv·yĕ); *Ger.* **Gott′schee** (gôt′shā). Town in Carniola, NW Yugoslavia, in mountains NE of Rieka; pop. 3079.

Ko′cher (kôĸ′ĕr). River ab. 100 m. long, in Baden-Württemberg, S Germany; flows into Neckar river 6 m. N of Heilbronn.

Ko′chi (kō′chĕ). **1** Prefecture of Japan. See *Table* at JAPAN.
2 Seaport city, its *, on S coast of Shikoku I. on inlet of Tosa Bay; pop. (1945) 111,630.

Kochiu. Var. of *Kokiu*: see MENGTSZ.

Koch Peak (kŏch). Mountain 11,293 ft. in W Gallatin co., S Montana.

Kocs (kŏch). Village, NW Hungary, SSE of Komárom; the coach (English word derived from name of the village) said to have originated here.

Ko·dai′ka·nal (kō·dī′kȧ·năl). Sanatorium, W Madras state, Indian Union, 50 m. NW of Madura; pop. (1931) 6523; government meteorological observatory, alt. ab. 7000 ft.

Ko′di·ak (kō′dĭ·ăk). **1** Island in Gulf of Alaska SE of Alaska Penin., S Alaska; 3465 sq. m.; chief industry fishing, esp. for salmon, which is more abundant here than anywhere else in Alaska; fur raising. Habitat of Kodiak bear. Site of first Russian colony in America (founded 1784); headquarters of Russian Trading Co. until 1805.
2 Town on NE coast of island; pop. 1710; incorporated 1940; a naval air and submarine base (estab. 1939).

Ko′dok (kō′dŏk); *formerly* **Fa·sho′da** (fȧ·shō′dȧ). Town, N Upper Nile prov., SE Sudan, N of Malakal; pop. ab. 3000; its seizure by a French force created serious international crisis 1898 almost causing war bet. Great Britain and France.

Koe′does (kōō′dōōs) or **Ku′dus.** Town, Central Java prov., Indonesia, on railroad 35 m. NE of Semarang; pop. 54,524.

Koe′kel·berg (kōō′kĕl·bĕrĸ). Commune, Brabant prov., Belgium, suburb of Brussels; pop. 13,906.

Koenigsberg. = *Königsberg:* see KALININGRAD.

Koe′pang (kōō′päng) or **Ku′pang.** Town, * of Indonesian Timor, on **Koepang Bay** at SW end of Timor I., Indonesia; pop. 7171; has good harbor except in northwest monsoon; airfield is stopover point on Java-Australia line. Founded by Dutch 1618.

Koesfeld. See COESFELD.

Koetai. See MAHAKAM.

Koe′ta·ra′dja (kōō′tä·rä′jä) or **Ku′ta·ra′ja.** Seaport, * of Atjeh govt., NW Sumatra, Indonesia; pop. 10,724; typical Malay city with good harbor at Uleelheue, active trade, and cosmopolitan population; railroad terminus. Capital city for several centuries (see ACHIN) of powerful Malay sultanate.

Koe′to·ar′djo (kōō′tō·är′jō) or **Ku′to·ar′dyo** (-jō). Town, Central Java prov., Indonesia, 30 m. W of Jogjakarta; pop. 11,496.

Kof′fy·fon·tein′ (kôf′ĭ·fôn·tān′). Town, SW Orange Free State, E cen. Republic of So. Africa, on Riet river 45 m. SSE of Kimberley; pop. 2521; diamond mines.

Ko′fo·ri·du′a (kō′fōr′ĕ·dōō′ȧ). Town, S Ghana, W Africa, on railroad ab. 38 m. N of Accra; pop. 10,529, (1942 est.) 13,957.

Ko′fu (kō′fōō). City, S cen. Honshu, Japan; * of Yamanashi prefecture, 65 m. W of Tokyo; pop. (1945) 82,685; important market for cocoons, raw silk, and silken fabrics; agricultural center for vegetables and fruits, esp. grapes; produces fine crystals. In former times the seat of several powerful feudal lords.

Kog′a·rah (kŏg′ȧ·rȧ). City, E New South Wales, SE Australia, S suburb of Sydney, W of Botany Bay; pop. 27,937.

Kö′ge, or **Kjö′ge, Bight** (kû′gĕ). Bay on E cen. coast of Sjælland I., Denmark; scene of battle June 30, 1677 in which Danes under Niels Juel defeated superior Swedish naval force under Evert Horn.

Ko·gen (kō·gĕn); *Jap.* **Ko·gen-do** (kō·gĕn·dō). Province of Korea. See *Table* at KOREA.

Ko·gur·yu (kō·gōōr·yōō). See *History* at KOREA.

Koh. 1 (kō′h′) Persian word for "mountain." For names beginning with this word, see the second element.
2 (kō) See Ko.

Ko·ha′la (kō·hä′lä). **1** Districts, Hawaii. See NORTH KOHALA, SOUTH KOHALA.
2 Village, North Kohala dist., Hawaii co., Hawaii, near coast at N end of Hawaii I.; pop. (est.) 1000; officially **Kapa′au-Ha·lau′la** (kä·pä′ou·hä·lou′lä), formerly Kapaau, combined since census of 1930. Birthplace and burial place of Kamehameha I, first Hawaiian king, and his headquarters during the struggle for control of the islands.

Kohala Mountains. Range in N end of Hawaii I., Hawaii; highest ab. 5500 ft.

Ko·hat′ (kō·hät′). **1** District of former North-West Frontier Province, Pakistan; 2707 sq. m.; pop. 289,404.
2 Town, its *, on affluent of Indus river 37 m. S of Peshawar; pop. 25,100, with cantonment 34,350; in midst of Pathan country; military base for southern Afridi frontier. Connected with Peshawar by **Kohat Pass** (ab. 13 m. long and 400 yd. to 1¼ m. wide).
3 Tribal area, NW of district; 1493 sq. m.; pop. 128,900; inhabited chiefly by Afridis and Orakzai.

Ko′hi·ma (kō′hē·mä). Town, * of Nagaland state, NE Indian Union; pop. 2759; near N Manipur border and 30 m. SE of the railroad at Dimapur; taken by Japanese in Manipur campaign Mar.–June 1944; recaptured by Anglo-Indian troops June 30, 1944.

Koh-i-nuh. See ARARAT.

Koh′ler (kō′lĕr). Residential village, Sheboygan co., E Wisconsin, 5 m. W of Sheboygan; pop. 1524; "model" community of Kohler Mfg. Co.

Kohl′scheid (kōl′shīt). Commune, North Rhine-Westphalia state, W Germany, N suburb of Aachen; pop. 10,752; coal mining; metal founding.

Ko Hu (gŭ′ hōō′; *Angl.* kō′). Lake, S Kiangsu prov., E China, NW of Tai Hu and W of the Grand Canal at Wusih.

Koil, Koil-Aligarh. See ALIGARH.

Koi′vis·to (koi′vĭs·tô). Town, formerly in SE Finland, in Viipuri dept., opp. **Koivisto Island** at E end of Gulf of Finland; pop. 11,748; port of Viipuri (now Vyborg) ab. 20 m. S of it on Karelian Isthmus. In war bet. Russia and Finland 1939–40 forts on island marked W end of Mannerheim Line; scene of severe fighting; captured by Russians Mar. 1940; now in Leningrad Region, U.S.S.R. See BJÖRKÖ.

Ko·ka (kō·kä). Large bay, inlet of Yellow Sea, in cen. part of W coast of Korea; Inchon is on it.

Ko·kai (kō·kī); *Jap.* **Ko·kai-do** (kō·kī·dō). Province of Korea. See *Table* at KOREA.

Ko·kand′ or **Kho·kand′** (kō·känd′). **1** Region around towns of Kokand and Fergana, E Uzbek S.S.R., Soviet Central Asia; became powerful khanate in 18th cent.; ab. 1760 recognized Chinese sovereignty; after 1800 came into conflict with other Turkic peoples of Turkistan and finally with the Russians; last Central Asian khanate to be conquered by Russia 1875–76; made a province of Turkistan (*q.v.*) under ancient name of Fergana; became part of newly formed Uzbek S.S.R. 1924.
2 City, E Uzbek S.S.R., Soviet Central Asia, ab. 100 m. SE of Tashkent; pop. 84,665; a modernized city, important rail and trade center in a fertile oasis region; cotton growing. Its early history obscure; town founded 1732, chief town of Kokand khanate.

Kok·che·tav′ Region (kŭk·chĕ·tȧf′). **1** Subdivision of Kazakh S.S.R., Soviet Central Asia; in N part bet. North Kazakhstan and Akmolinsk Regions; established 1945. **2** Chief town in region, on railroad 115 m. S of Petropavlovsk.

Kokiu. See MENGTSZ.

Kok′ko·la (kôk′kô·lä). Seaport, Vaasa dept., W Finland, on Gulf of Bothnia 70 m. NNE of Vaasa; pop. (1949 est.) 12,826; exports timber.

Ko·ko′da (kô·kō′dȧ). Settlement in SE Territory of Papua, New Guinea, WSW of Buna on E side of Owen Stanley Range; connected with Port Moresby by highway ab. 100 m. long over the mountains; used by Japanese as base for attacks Sept.–Oct. 1942; occupied by Australians Nov. 3, 1942.

Ko′ko Head (kō′kō) or **Ka′wai·ho′a Point** (kä′wī·hō′ä). Promontory on SE coast of Oahu I., Hawaii, on E side of Maunalua Bay.

Ko·ko′le Point (kô·kō′lä). Cape on W coast of Kauai I., Hawaii.

Ko′ko·mo (kō′kô·mō). Industrial city, ⊗ of Howard co., N cen. Indiana, 50 m. N of Indianapolis; pop. 47,197; metal goods, farm equipment, radios, stoves and furnaces; founded ab. 1843 on site of an Indian trading post; home of the inventor Elwood Haynes.

Koko Nor. See TSINGHAI; TSING HAI.

Ko′ko·po (kō′kô·pō). Town, NE New Britain I., Bismarck Archipelago, W Pacific Ocean, on SE coast of Blanche Bay 14 m. SE of Rabaul; formerly Herbertshöhe, and former German capital of New Britain (Neu-Pommern).

Kok′so·ak (kôk′sô·ăk). River 110 m. long, N Quebec prov., Canada; formed by confluence of Kaniapiskau and Larch rivers, flows NE into S Ungava Bay.

Kok′stad (kôk′städ). Town, NE Cape Province, S Union of South Africa, 110 m. SW of Durban; the chief town of Griqualand East (q.v.) in the Transkeian Territories; pop. 5627; center of farming district, esp. for sheep and cattle raising; important cheese industry; fine climate and high altitude (4500 ft.), health resort.

Ko′kum·bo′na (kō′kŭm·bō′nȧ). Coastal village, NW Guadalcanal I., SE Solomon Is., W Pacific Ocean, W of the Matanikau river and 7 m. W of Henderson Field; scene of severe fighting Aug. and Oct. 1942; not captured by Americans until Jan. 25, 1943.

Ko·ku·ra (kô·kōō·rä). Seaport, Fukuoka prefecture, N Kyushu I., Japan, at S end of Shimonoseki Strait; pop. (1945 est.) 131,688; in 1963 incorporated in new city of Kita-Kyushu (q.v.).

Kol. See ALIGARH.

Ko′la (kō′lä; Russ. kô′lä). **1** South tributary of the Tuloma river, W Murmansk Region, Soviet Russia, Europe, joining it at Kola. **2** Town on railroad ab. 12 m. S of Murmansk and at junction of Kola river with the Tuloma; one of oldest towns in extreme N of Russia; several times destroyed by Swedes and British.

Ko·la′ba (kô·lä′bä). District, SW Maharashtra state, W Indian Union; 2212 sq. m.; pop. (1941) 668,922; ✵ Alibag.

Ko′la Bay (kō′lä; Russ. kô′lä). Inlet of Barents Sea, ab. 22 m. long, NW Murmansk Region, Soviet Russia, Europe; Murmansk is at its head; receives Tuloma river.

Ko′lam·bu′gan (kō′läm·bōō′gän). Municipality, NW Lanao prov., Mindanao, Phil. Is., on coast on S side of entrance to Panguil Bay opp. Misamis; pop. 39,647.

Ko′la Peninsula (kō′lä; Russ. kô′lä). Peninsula projecting E on NW coast of Soviet Russia, Europe, bet. the White Sea and the Arctic Ocean (Barents Sea); forms Murmansk Region (q.v.).

Ko·lar′ (kô·lär′). Town, E Mysore, S Indian Union, 140 m. W of Madras; pop. 16,161.

Kolar Gold Fields. City, E Mysore, S Indian Union, 145 m. W of Madras; pop. (1941) 133,859; gold mines.

Kolarovgrad. See SHUMEN.

Kolberg. See KOŁOBRZEG.

Kolchugino. See LENINSK-KUZNETSKI.

Kold′ing (kŭl′ing). Seaport, Vejle co., SE Jutland, Denmark, on inlet of Little Belt; pop. (1945) 27,660; exports cattle, fish, grain. Dates back to 10th cent.; scene of two battles in Danish history: (1) 1644 in victory over Swedes; (2) Danish defeat in Schleswig-Holstein troubles Apr. 22, 1849; has oldest stone church in Denmark (13th cent.).

Kol·gu′ev (kŭl·gōō′yĕf). Island in Barents Sea, 50 m. off the mainland, NE of Kanin Penin., Nenets National District, N Soviet Russia, Europe; ab. 1300 sq. m.; chiefly tundra; its inhabitants Samoyeds with a few herds of reindeer.

Kol′ha·pur (kō′lȧ·pŏŏr). **1** Former Indian state, chief state of the Deccan and Kolhapur States, geographically in SW Maharashtra state, W India; 3219 sq. m.; pop. (1941) 1,092,046; formerly in Southern Maratha States. In heart of Western Ghats with E part sloping into plain of the Deccan; ruling family traces descent from younger son of Sivaji, founder of Maratha power; invaded by British expeditions 1765 and 1792; came under control of British in 1812. **2** City, its ✵ and headquarters of Deccan and Kolhapur States, 180 m. SSE of Bombay; pop. (1941) 93,032; trade center; many old Buddhist temples.

Kolhapur and Deccan States. See DECCAN AND KOLHAPUR STATES.

Kolima, Kolima Range. See KOLYMA, KOLYMA RANGE.

Ko·lim′ski Ridge (kŭ·lim′ski). = KOLYMA RANGE.

Ko′lín (kô′lēn); Ger. **Ko·lin′** (kô·lēn′). Town, cen. Bohemia prov., W Czechoslovakia, on Labe (Elbe) river E of Prague; pop. (1930) 18,509; nearby is battlefield where Frederick the Great was defeated June 18, 1757 by Austrian marshal Daun.

Ko′li Point (kō′lē). Point on N coast of Guadalcanal I., SE Solomon Is., W Pacific Ocean, on W side of mouth of Malimbiu river and ab. 3 m. E of Lunga Point; American base for fighting along the Malimbiu and Metapona rivers Nov. 1942.

Kollam. See QUILON.

Kölln (kûln). A 13th-cent. Wendish village which with village of Berlin united under name Berlin. See History at BERLIN, Germany.

Kolmar. See COLMAR.

Köln (kûln). **1** Government district, former Rhine Province, Prussia, Germany; 1536 sq. m. **2** See COLOGNE.

Ko′ło (kō′lô). Commune, Łódź dept., Poland, on Warta river 44 m. WNW of Łódź; pop. (1938–39 est.) 14,211; cigars.

Ko·lo′a (kô·lō′ä). **1** District, S Kauai I., Kauai co., Hawaii. **2** Village in district, near S coast of Kauai I. SW of Lihue; pop. 1426; had first sugar plantation in Hawaii (estab. 1835).

Koloa Bay. Bay on S coast of Kauai I., Hawaii, E of Lawai Bay.

Ko·łob′rzeg (kô·lôb′zhĕk); Ger. **Kol′berg** (kôl′bĕʀk). City and port on Gulf of Pomerania, N Szczecin prov., NW Poland, 25 m. W of Koszalin; pop. (1946) 33,580; formerly in Pomerania prov., Prussia, Germany; manufactures cosmetics; trades in grain, lumber, coal, fertilizer; beach resort. Captured by the Russians Mar. 19, 1945; assigned to Poland by the Potsdam Conference 1945.

Ko′lom·bang′a·ra (kō′lŏm·băng′ȧ·rȧ). Island off W end of New Georgia I., cen. Solomon Is., W Pacific Ocean; circular shaped, ab. 17 m. in diameter, with volcanic cone 5856 ft.; bet. it and New Georgia is Kula Gulf (naval battles July 1943); on S shore Japanese had airfield at Vila (q.v.); object of air attacks, but bypassed in Allied advance northward (see VELLA LAVELLA).

Kolomea. See KOLOMYYA.

Ko·lom'na (kŭ·lôm'nȧ). City, Moscow Region, Soviet Russia, Europe, on railroad near confluence of Moskva and Oka rivers, 65 m. SE of Moscow; pop. 75,139; an old town with several churches and ruins of a fort of early construction; suffered much in Tatar invasions; recently has become important because of railroad shops, munitions and other factories.

Ko·lo·my'ya (kŭ·lŭ·mĭ'yȧ); *Pol.* **Ko'ło·my'ja** (kô'lô-mĭ'yä); *Ger.* **Ko'lo·me'a** (kō'lô·mā'ä). City, SW Ukraine, U.S.S.R., on Prut river 30 m. SSE of Stanislav (formerly in Stanisławów dept., Poland); pop. (1938–39 est.) 40,000; at E end of gateway through E Carpathian Mts. via Jablonica Pass and in rail communication with Stanislav and Chernovtsy; agricultural trade center; manufactures pottery, chemicals, textiles. Captured Feb. 1915 by Germans; held by both Russians and Germans in World War II.

Ko'lo'shan' (kō'lō'shän'). Suburb of Chungking, Szechwan prov., S cen. China; contained certain government headquarters offices during air raids of 1938–45.

Kolozsvár. See CLUJ.

Kol·pa·she'vo (kŭl·pŭ·shô'vŭ). Town, cen. Tomsk Region, Soviet Russia, Asia, on right bank of the Ob where the Ket joins it.

Kol'pi·no (kôl'pyĭ·nŭ). Town, Leningrad Region, NW Soviet Russia, Europe, a SE suburb of Leningrad; pop. ab. 17,000.

Kol'ski Po·lu·os'trov (kôl'skĭ pŭ·lōō·ôs'trŭf). Russian name of KOLA PENINSULA.

Ko·ly'ma *or* **Ko·li'ma** (kô·lē'mȧ; *Russ.* kŭ·lĭ'mȧ). River 1110 m. long, NE Yakutsk Republic, Soviet Russia, Asia; rises in Kolyma Range in Khabarovsk Territory, flows generally N and NE into Arctic Ocean; navigable to Verkhne Kolymsk; gold diggings worked along its course; its chief tributaries the Omolon and Anyui.

Kolyma, *or* **Kolima, Range;** *Russ.* **Ko·lym'ski Khre·bet'** (kŭ·lĭm'skĭ ĸryĭ·byĕt'). Mountain range in NE Khabarovsk Territory, Soviet Russia, Asia, N of the Sea of Okhotsk and nearly parallel to coast line.

Ko·ma·ga·ta·ke (kô·mä·gä·tä·kĕ). Name of several mountain peaks in Japan: (1) Active volcano 3740 ft. on SW shore of Uchiura Bay, SW Hokkaido I. (2) Volcanic peak 4349 ft., W Kanagawa prefecture, SE Honshu, near Hakone. (3) Peak 9666 ft., S cen. Nagano prefecture, cen. Honshu. (4) Peak 9843 ft., W Yamanashi prefecture, S cen. Honshu.

Ko·man·dor'ski·e Islands (kŭ·mŭn·dôr'skĭ·yĕ; *Angl.* kŏm'ȧn·dôr'skĭ); *Eng.* **Com·mand'er Islands** (kô·mȧn'dēr). Island group E of Kamchatka Penin., in SW Bering Sea; 850 sq. m.; administered as part of Khabarovsk Territory; chief islands Bering or Beringa (on which the explorer Vitus Bering died 1741) and Medny; chief settlement Nikolskoe; former hunting ground for the fur seal, but by 1911 practically all animals slaughtered; now a radio and naval station.

Ko'mâr·no (kô'mär·nô); *Ger.* **Ko'morn** (kō'môrn); *Hung.* **Ko'má·rom** (kô'mä·rôm). Town, S Slovakia prov., E cen. Czechoslovakia, at confluence of the Váh with the Danube opp. Komárom; pop. (1930) 21,137; commercial and shipping center; transferred from Hungary to Czechoslovakia 1920 by Treaty of Grand Trianon; birthplace of the Hungarian novelist Jókai.

Ko'má·rom (kô'mä·rôm). **1** See KOMÁRNO.
2 *Ger.* **Ko'morn** (kō'môrn). Autonomous city, NW Hungary, on Danube river opp. Komárno, Czechoslovakia; 10 sq. m.; pop. 26,267.

Ko·ma'rów (kô·mä'rōōf). Town, Lublin dept., E Poland, ab. 56 m. SE of Lublin; pop. (1921) 2900; scene of a battle Aug. 26–Sept. 2, 1914 in which the Austrians under Baron Auffenberg von Komarów defeated the Russians.

Ko·ma'ti (kô·mä'tĕ). River ab. 500 m. long, S Africa; rises in N Drakensberg Mts., SE Transvaal, N Union of South Africa, flows E, curves through N Swaziland,

turns N; joined by Crocodile river; ab. a mile below junction flows through a cleft 600 ft. deep at Komati Poort; crosses boundary bet. Union of South Africa and Mozambique and flows in a wide curve N then S, into Delagoa Bay.

Ko·ma'ti Poort (kô·mä'tĕ pōōrt). Frontier railroad town. E Transvaal, NE Union of South Africa, ab. 48 m. NW of Lourenço Marques, on Komati river.

Komba. See Rio GRANDE, W Africa.

Ko'mi–Perm'iak (kô'mĭ·pûrm'yăk; *Russ.* kô'myĭ-pyĕrm'yȧk), *or* **Ko'mi–Perm** (kô'mĭ·pûrm'; *Russ.* kô'-myĭ·pyĕrm'), **National District.** National district, NW Siberia, Soviet Russia, Asia, W of the Ural Mts.; 8916 sq. m.; pop. (1926) 201,000; ✳ Kudymkar; in basin of upper Kama river; formed 1925 from area S of Komi A.S.S.R.; geographically the NW part of Molotov Region.

Ko'mi Republic (kô'mĭ; *Russ.* kô'myĭ); *formerly* **Zyr'i·an Autonomous Area** (zĭr'ĭ·ȧn). *Officially* **Komi Autonomous Soviet Socialist Republic.** Autonomous republic, NE Soviet Russia, Europe, W of the Northern Urals; 145,221 sq. m.; pop. 318,969, (1941 est.) 335,172; ✳ Syktyvkar; a subdivision of the R.S.F.S.R. Bounded on N by Nenets National District, on E by the Yamalo-Nenets and Khanty-Mansi National Districts, on SE by Molotov Region, on S by Komi-Permiak National District and Kirov Region, and on W Arkhangelsk Region. Mostly level country, with tundra in N, mountain slopes of Urals in E, and the Timan height of land in NW; lies chiefly in the basins of the Pechora and upper Vychegda rivers. Two thirds of area is covered by forests; has some agriculture, now rapidly being modernized, and some cattle raising and dairying; few industries except those connected with lumbering; no railroads until 1943 when 700 m. of Northern Pechora R.R. completed NE from Kotlas; has big deposits of coal, iron, oil, and manganese, as yet little developed; no large towns. Predominant ethnic strain is Finno-Ugrian. An autonomous area created 1921; N strip along the Arctic transferred 1929 to Nenets National District; reorganized 1936 as a republic.

Ko·mo'do (kô·mô'dô). Small island ab. 25 m. long by 12 m. wide, E of Sumbawa I. and W of Flores I., in the Lesser Sunda Is., Indonesia; wild and rugged and little known until giant lizards (dragon lizard, *Varanus komodoensis*) were discovered on it in 1912.

Komorn. See KOMÁRNO, KOMÁROM.

Komotau. See CHOMŮTOV.

Ko'mo·ti·nē' (kô'mô·tĕ·nyē'); *Turk.* **Gü'mül·ji·na'** (gü'mül·jē·nä'). City, ✳ of Rhodope dept., Western Thrace, NE Greece, E of Xanthe; pop. 30,136.

Kom'so·mo'lets (kŏm'sô·mô'lĕts; *Russ.* kŭm·sŭ·mô'-lyĕts). Northernmost of the large islands of the Severnaya Zemlya group, in Arctic Ocean, Taimyr National District, Soviet Russia, Asia; N of 80° lat.

Kom'so·molsk' (kŏm'sô·môlsk'; *Russ.* kŭm·sŭ·môl'-y'sk). City, S Khabarovsk Territory, Soviet Russia, Asia, on left bank of Amur river 165 m. NNE of Khabarovsk; pop. 70,746; an entirely new city, begun 1932 by 4000 volunteers of the Young Communist League (Russ. *Komsomol*—hence the name); has had very rapid growth; on Trans-Siberian R.R. extension from Khabarovsk to Nikolaevsk and terminal of N transcontinental line (the BAM—Baikal-Amur-Magistral; *Eng.* Main Baikal-Amur Line); has great steelworks and one of largest shipyards in the Far East; also oil refinery, power plants, mills, factories; ski school.

Ko'na (kô'nȧ; *Hawaiian* -nä). Districts, Hawaii. See NORTH KONA, SOUTH KONA.

Ko'na·hu'a·nu'i (kô'nä·hōō'ä·nōō'ĕ). Peak 3105 ft. in Koolau Range, E Oahu I., Hawaii.

Konakri. See CONAKRY.

Kon'a·wa (kŏn'ȧ·wä). Town, Seminole co., cen. Oklahoma, 14 m. N of Ada; pop. 1555; shipping point for farming area.

Kon′da·pal′li (kŏn′dá·pŭl′lĭ). Town and hill fortress, NE Andhra Pradesh, SE Indian Union, 48 m. NW of Masulipatam; pop. 4554; important in Bahmanid conquests of latter part of 15 cent.

Kon·do′a I·rang′i (kŏn·dō′á ĭ·räng′ĭ). Town, N Central Province, Tanganyika, E Africa, 250 m. NW of Dar es Salaam.

Kong (kŏng). **1** District, E cen. Ivory Coast Republic, West Africa; home of a tribe of the Mandingo, formerly a native kingdom of some importance.
2 Chief town of district, on highway 100 m. N of Bouaké.

Kön′gä·mä (kûn′gä·mä′) or **Kön′kä·mä** (-kä-). River in N extremity of Sweden, forming its extreme N boundary with Finland; flows SE to join the Muonio river.

Kongju. See KOSHU.

Kong′moon′ (kŏng′mōōn′) or **Kong′moon′fow′** (-fō′). Town, cen. Kwangtung prov., SE China, in W part of Si delta, ab. 45 m. above Macao; pop. (1931 est.) 32,200; formerly a trading port of much importance but has lost in competition with Hong Kong and Pakhoi; made a treaty port 1904.

Kongo. Var. of CONGO.

Kon·go′lo (kŏng·gō′lō). Town on Lualaba river, N Katanga prov., SE Congo.

Kongosan. See DIAMOND MOUNTAINS.

Kongs′berg (kŏngs′bĕr). Town, Buskerud co., S Norway, WSW of Oslo; pop. 7274; hydroelectric power plant, arms and munitions factory; formerly a silver-mining center.

Konia. See KONYA.

Konieh. Var. of KONYA.

Kö′nig·grätz′ (kû′nĭk·grâts′); *Czech* **Hra′dec Krá′-lo·vé** (hrä′dĕts krä′lô·vä). Town, E Bohemia prov., W Czechoslovakia, on Labe (Elbe) river; pop. (1930) 17,818; battle (also known as Sadowa) July 3, 1866, in which Prussians under Count von Moltke decisively defeated the Austrians under Gen. Benedek in Austro-Prussian War.

Königinhof. See DVŮR KRÁLOVÉ NAD LABEM.

Königliche Weinberge. See VINOHRADY KRÁLOVSKÉ.

Kö′nigs·berg (kû′nĭks·bĕrк; *Angl.* kā′nĭgz·bûrg).
1 Former government district, NW East Prussia prov., Prussia, Germany; 5076 sq. m.; since 1946 the greater part of it has formed Kaliningradsk Region, Soviet Russia, Europe.
2 City. See KALININGRAD.

Königshütte. See KRÓLEWSKA HUTA.

Kö′nig·spit′ze (kû′nĭк·shpĭt′sĕ); *Ital.* **Gran Ze·brù′** (grän′ dzä·brōō′). Peak 12,661 ft. in Ortler Mts., NW Venezia Tridentina, NE Italy.

Kö′nigs·see′ (kû′nĭкs·zā′). Small lake picturesquely located in E end of Bavarian Alps, S of Berchtesgaden in extreme SE corner of Bavaria, Germany; called one of the most beautiful lakes in the Reich.

Kö′nigs·win′ter (kû′nĭкs·vĭn′tĕr). Town, S North Rhine-Westphalia, Germany, on the Rhine SE of Bonn; pop. (1933) 4724; summer resort.

Ko′nin (kô′nēn). Commune, Łódź dept., Poland, on Warta river 60 m. WNW of Łódź; pop. 10,390; textiles, leather; agricultural products; trades in grain.

Ko′ning·in′ne Bay (kô′nĭng·ĭn′ĕ). Inlet of Indian Ocean, W coast of Sumatra, Indonesia; on its NW shore is Emmahaven, port of Padang.

Kó′ni·tsa (kô′nyê·tsä). Commune, Ioannina dept., N Epirus, NW Greece, near Albanian border ab. 27 m. N of Ioannina; pop. 1959.

Konitz. See CHOJNICE.

Kö′niz (kû′nĭts). Commune, Bern canton, W cen. Switzerland, SW suburb of Bern; pop. (1941) 14,399; old church and castle.

Könkämä. See KÖNGÄMÄ.

Kon′kan (kŏn′kán). Coast region of Maharashtra state, W Indian Union, extending from Goa N to Damão; a humid, fertile plain.

Kon′kou′ré′ (kôn′kōō′rä′). River, Guinea, West Africa; rises in Fouta Djallon, flows SW into Atlantic Ocean N of Conakry.

Ko·no·top′ (kŭ·nŭ·tôp′; *Angl.* kŏn′ô·tŏp′). City, W Sumy Region, NE Ukraine, U.S.S.R., 125 m. NE of Kiev; pop. 36,186; railroad junction point in rich farming area, on main line from Kiev to Moscow; raises and exports much grain; flour mills; manufactures farm machinery. In World War II taken by Germans 1941; retaken by Russians Aug. 26, 1943.

Koń′skie (kôn′y′·skyĕ). Commune, Kielce dept., Poland, on a tributary of Pilica river 18 m. NNW of Kielce; pop. 11,102; iron mines nearby.

Kon′stan·ti′nov·ka (kŏn′stän·tē′nŭĭ·kà; *Russ.* kŭn-stŭn·tyē′nŭĭ·kà). City, E Ukraine, U.S.S.R., SW of Artemovsk, in the Dnieper bend; pop. ab. 25,000; large steel mills.

Kon′stanz (kôn′stänts). **1** District of Baden. See *Table* at BADEN.
2 *Eng.* **Con′stance** (kŏn′stăns); *less commonly* **Con′-stanz** (kôn′stänts); *anc.* **Con·stan′ti·a** (kŏn·stăn′-shĭ·à; -shà). *In Middle Ages sometimes called* **Kost′nitz** (kôst′nĭts). Lake port, Baden-Württemberg, Germany, on Lake Constance 75 m. S of Stuttgart; pop. 31,252; cathedral, grand-ducal residence, and the Kaufhaus (in which Council of Constance met); textiles, chemicals, carpets. Supposed to have been founded by Constantius Chlorus c. 300 A.D.; seat of famous Council of Constance (partly ecumenical) 1414–18 in which three antipopes were deposed and the doctrines of Huss, Wycliffe, and Jerome of Prague were condemned as heretical; annexed to Austria 1548, to Baden 1805.

Kon·ya′ or **Kon·ia′** (kŏn·yä′). **1** Vilayet, SW cen. Turkey in Asia; 18,910 sq. m.; pop. 569,684.
2 *anc.* **I·co′ni·um** (ĭ·kō′nĭ·ŭm). City, its *, on SW edge of the anc. Turkish plateau; pop. (1940) 56,698; in midst of famous fruit orchards; declined in prosperity in 19th cent., but has grown rapidly since coming of the railroad ab. 1895; contains mosque of the dancing dervishes. Ancient Iconium in Phrygia later became capital of Lycaonia; visited by Paul on his first missionary journey; ab. 1100 became capital of Seljuk sultans of Rum, later seized by Crusaders; in 13th cent. a cultural center under Ala-ad-Din I; in 15th cent. a secondary city of Karaman; became part of Ottoman Empire 1472.

Koo′chi·ching (kōō′chĭ·chĭng). County in Minnesota. See *Table* at MINNESOTA.

Koochiching Falls. Falls in the Rainy river, S Ontario, Canada, near Fort Frances and International Falls.

Ko′o·la′u·lo′a (kō′ô·lä′ōō·lō′ä). District, Honolulu co., NE Oahu I., Hawaii; pop. 8043; chief locality Kahuku village.

Ko′o·la′u·po′ko (kō′ô·lä′ōō·pō′kō). District, Honolulu co., SE Oahu I., Hawaii; pop. 60,238; chief locality Kaneohe village.

Ko′o·la′u Range (kō′ô·lä′ōō). Mountain range extending along E side of Oahu I., Hawaii; highest peak Konahuanui 3105 ft.

Kooringa. See BURRA.

Koo′te·nai (kōō′t′n·à; kōōt′nā). **1** County in Idaho. See *Table* at IDAHO.
2 See KOOTENAY.

Kootenai Mountain. Peak 8300 ft. in Glacier National Park, NW Montana.

Koo′te·nay (kōō′t′n·à; kōōt′nā); *in U.S. known as the* **Koo′te·nai.** River 400 m. long in SW Canada and NW U.S.; rises on SW slopes of Rocky Mts N of Kootenay National Park, SE Brit. Columbia, flows S through the park into NW Montana where it turns W and N through Idaho; again crosses border into Brit. Columbia and enters Kootenay Lake (narrow lake 65 m. long, 221 sq. m.) at its S end; issues from W side of lake to flow N past Nelson to the Columbia river. Explored by David Thompson in 1807.

Kootenay National Park. See CANADA, *National Parks.*

Kopaïs. See COPAIS.

Ko′pa·o·nik′ (kō′pä·ȯ·nēk′). Mountain range, S cen. Yugoslavia, in cen. Serbia E of the Ibar river; highest peak Suvo Rudišta 7020 ft.

Kopar; Koper. See CAPODISTRIA.

Köpenick. See CÖPENICK.

Ko′pet Dagh (kō′pĕt dä′). Mountain range extending ab. 450 m. NW to SE along border bet. NE Iran and the Turkmen S.S.R., E of S end of Caspian Sea; highest point 9813 ft.

Kö′ping′ (chû′pǐng′). Town, Västmanland co., E Sweden, at W end of Lake Mälaren; pop. 10,041.

Kop′par·berg′ (kôp′pȧr·bǎr′y); *formerly* **Dal′e·car′- li·a** (dǎl′ĕ·kär′lǐ·ȧ). Province of Sweden. See *Table* at SWEDEN.

Köprili. See VELES.

Ko′priv′ni·ca (kō′prēv′nĕ·tsä); *Hung.* **Ka′pron·cza** (kŏ′prŏn·tsȯ); *Ger.* **Ko·prei′nitz** (kȯ·prī′nǐts). Town, NE Croatia, N Yugoslavia, S of the Drava and NE of Zagreb; pop. (1921) 8096.

Kora. See KURA.

Korat. = *Khorat:* see NAKHON RATCHASIMA.

Korçë. See KORRÇE.

Kor′ču·la (kôr′cho͞o·lä); *Ital.* **Cur′zo·la** (ko͞or′tsȯ·lä; ko͞or·tsȯ′lä). **1** *anc.* **Cor·cy′ra Ni′gra** (kôr·sī′rȧ nǐ′grȧ; nĭg′rȧ). Yugoslav island in Adriatic Sea off Dalmatian coast; 107 sq. m.; pop. ab. 28,000; formerly a part of Zetska co., now attached to Bosnia and Herzegovina federated republic.

2 Town on E end of the island; pop. 6563; cathedral; 15th-cent. monastery; originally settled by Greeks; under Austrian rule 1815–1918; passed to newly organized Yugoslavia 1918.

Kor′do·fan′ (kôr′dȯ·fän′). Province, cen. Sudan, NE Africa; 146,930 sq. m.; pop. 1,761,968; ✱ El Obeid.

Ko·re·a′ (kȯ·rä·ä′). Former Indian state, Eastern States, NE Indian Union; 1647 sq. m.; pop. (1941) 126,874; ✱ Sonhat; inhabitants chiefly aboriginal tribes.

Ko·re′a (kȯ·rē′ȧ); *Japanese official name* **Cho·sen** (chō·sĕn). Former kingdom, from 1910 to 1945 a Japanese dependency, on E coast of Asia, E of China; area 85,225 sq. m.; pop. (1938 est.) 22,633,751; forms a peninsula 600 m. long by 135 m. wide extending S from Manchuria bet. Sea of Japan and Yellow Sea. Its name to its own people is Chosen, "Land of Morning Calm." Its S coast separated from Japan by Korea Strait and its N boundary marked by the Tumen river on E, the Yalu river on W, and the Chang Pai Shan range in the center. Almost entirely covered with mountains, some (as Diamond Mts.) noted for scenic beauty; E coast has few harbors, W and S coasts have many islands (largest Saishu To) and estuaries. Mainly agricultural but has great undeveloped water power for industrial growth. Chief products rice, grains, soybeans; has valuable deposits of coal, iron, and gold. Chief cities Seoul, Pyongyang, Pusan, Taegu, Inchon. See *Map* at CHINA, Divided into 13 provinces (for statistics previous to World War II, see *Table*, below; for pronunciation of their names, see their individual entries):

NAME	LOCA-TION	AREA[1]	POP.[1]	CAPITAL
Keiki	W cen.	4,949	2,528,829	Keijo
Kogen	E	10,138	1,566,375	Shunsen
Kokai	W	6,463	1,695,858	Kaishu
Chusei, North	S cen.	2,863	905,284	Seishu
Chusei, South	W	3,129	1,518,552	Taiden
Heian, North	NW	10,978	1,648,041	Shingishu
Heian, South	NW	5,766	1,507,579	Heijo
Kankyo, North	NE	7,854	860,191	Ranan
Kankyo, South	NE	12,344	1,662,369	Kanko
Keisho, North	SE	7,330	2,479,662	Taikyu
Keisho, South	SE	4,750	2,225,467	Fusan
Zenra, North	SW	3,301	1,553,106	Zenshu
Zenra, South	SW	5,360	2,482,438	Koshu

[1] Area is in sq. m. Pop. is 1938 est.

History: Kingdom of Chosen established in N part of peninsula by Chinese perhaps as early as 12th cent. B.C.; in 3d cent. B.C. a vassal of Yen; N kingdom conquered and annexed by Chinese 108 B.C.; by 1st cent. B.C., had developed into three independent kingdoms of Silla, Koguryu, and Pakche; introduced to Buddhism 4th cent. A.D. which Koreans later carried to Japan (*q.v.*); in period of predominance of kingdom of Silla 670–935, Chinese culture flourished; under Koryo (from 935), a state founded in W cen. Korea, most of Korea united as one kingdom under Chinese suzerainty; invaded by Mongols 1231; kingdom of Chosen with capital at Seoul (Keijo) ruled by Li dynasty 1392–1910; invaded by Japanese under Hideyoshi 1592–98; from c. 1637, shut out foreign contacts; forced to grant treaty opening ports to Japan 1876 which recognized Korean independence; in period of internal disorder, forced to unite with Japan in resisting Chinese interference (Korea considered Chinese vassal), thus bringing on Chinese-Japanese war 1894–95; Russo-Japanese rivalry over Korea a cause of war 1904–05; became Japanese protectorate 1907; formally annexed to Japan as province of Chosen 1910; freed from Japanese control on defeat of Japan Aug. 1945; after the war divided at 38th parallel into two zones of occupation, Russian in N and American in S, in which were set up (1948) the North Korean People's Republic, ✱ Pyongyang (Heijo), and the South Korean Republic, ✱ Seoul (Keijo); scene of warfare bet. North Korean Republic and allied forces of the United Nations 1950–53.

Korea Bay. Northeast arm of Yellow Sea bet. Liaotung Penin. and NW Korea; receives the Yalu river.

Korean Archipelago. See CHOSEN ARCHIPELAGO.

Korea Strait. Channel ab. 120 m. wide, bet. S Korea and SW Japan, divided into Chosen Strait on NW and Tsushima Strait on SE by the island of Tsushima in its center; connects SW Sea of Japan with East China Sea.

Koriak National District. See KORYAK NATIONAL DISTRICT.

Korinchi. Var. of *Korintji:* see KERINTJI.

Kórinthos. See CORINTH.

Korintji. See KERINTJI.

Koritsa. Var. of *Korytsa:* see KORRÇE.

Ko·ri·ya·ma (kō·rē·yä·mä). **1** City, Fukushima prefecture, N cen. Honshu, Japan, 25 m. S of Fukushima; pop. (1945) 54,699; commercial and industrial center, with many silk mills; bombed by Allies Apr. 1945.

2 Town, Nara prefecture, W cen. Honshu, Japan, 3 m. SW of Nara; pop. (1945) 22,252.

Kor′ma·ki·ti′, Cape (kôr′mä·kė·tē′). Cape near cen. part of N coast of Cyprus, in E Mediterranean Sea.

Kor′man·tine (kôr′măn·tǐn). Coastal village and remains of Dutch fort ab. 3 m. W of Saltpond, Ghana, W Africa; first slaves for British West Indies were taken from this port.

Körmöczbánya. See KREMNICA.

Ko′ro (kō′rō). Island of the Lomai Viti group, Fiji Is., SW Pacific Ocean, in cen. part S of Vanua Levu on NW border of Koro Sea; 58 sq. m.; produces cotton, copra, arrowroot, tortoise shell.

Ko·ro′li Desert (kō·rō′lǐ). Desert area in N Kenya, SE Africa, E of S end of Lake Rudolf.

Ko·rom′ba (kȯ·rŏm′bȧ), *or* **Ku·ram′ba** (ko͞o·räm′bȧ), **Mount.** Peak 3528 ft. in W Viti Levu I., Fiji Is., SW Pacific Ocean.

Korónē, Gulf of. See Gulf of MESSENIA.

Ko′ror *or* **Kor′ror** (kȯ′rôr). Town on small island of same name off S tip of Babelthuap I. in Palau Is., W Pacific Ocean; has good harbor and was trading center under German regime; from 1921 to 1945 administrative capital of all Japanese mandated islands (called Nanyo by the Japanese) in the Pacific.

Kö′rös (kû′rûsh). River in E Hungary; formed by confluence of streams which rise in W Romania, flows SW into Tisza river at Csongrád.

Ko′ro Sea (kô′rō). Open sea in cen. area of the Fiji Is., SW Pacific Ocean; Nanuku Passage on NE is steamship lane to the NE.

Ko·ros′ko (kŏ·rôs′kŏ) *or* **Ku·rus′ku** (kōō·rōōs′kōō). Town, Upper Egypt, on Nile, 118 m. S of Aswân by river; terminus of an old caravan route.

Körösmezö. See YASENYA.

Ko′ro·sten′ (kōr′ŏ·stĕn′; *Russ.* kŭ·rŭ·styän′y′). Town, NE Zhitomir Region, W Ukraine, U.S.S.R., in steppe region 90 m. WNW of Kiev; a key railroad junction of five lines, on the N-to-S line from White Russia to Berdichev and on the E-to-W line from Kiev to Kovel and Lublin. Scene of bitter fighting Nov.–Dec. 1943 during Russian advance W of Kiev; taken by Russians Dec. 29, 1943.

Ko·ro′vin (?kŏ·rō′vĭn). **1** Volcano 4852 ft. in N part of Atka I., Aleutians, SW Alaska.
2 Bay, inlet on N coast of Atka I.

Korr′çë (kôr′chĕ); *Gr.* **Ko′ry·tsa′** (kô′rĕ·tsä′); *Ital.* **Co·riz′za** (kô·rĕt′tsä). **1** Prefecture, SE Albania; 1279 sq. m.; pop. 147,536.
2 Town, its ✳, near Greek border; pop. 22,787; industrial and commercial center in agricultural region; manufactures esp. textiles and carpets; flour mills. In World War II used 1940 as advanced base by Italians in operations against Greece; captured by Greeks Nov. 22, 1940.

Kor·sör′ (kôr·sûr′). Seaport, Sorö co., SW Sjælland, Denmark, 62 m. WSW of Copenhagen; pop. (1945) 10,667; trading center; fisheries.

Kor·sun′ (kŭr·sōōn′y′). Town, S Kiev Region, N Ukraine, U.S.S.R., 80 m. SSE of Kiev; on main railroad line of cen. Ukraine; scene of fierce battle 1648 in which Bogdan Chmielnicki, Cossack hetman, defeated the Poles; in World War II held by Germans 1941–44; taken by Russians Feb. 1944.

Kort′rijk (kôrt′rīk); *Fr.* **Cour′trai′** (kōōr′trā′). Commune, West Flanders prov., NW Belgium, on Leie (Lys) river 15 m. NNE of Lille; pop. (1938 est.) 40,979; linens and lace. In Middle Ages a populous commercial city of Flanders; scene of battle of the Golden Spurs July 11, 1302 in which Flemish burghers defeated French barons and knights; also a battleground in later wars.

Ko·ryak′, *or* **Ko·riak′, National District** (kŭ·ryák′). National district of Soviet Russia in Asia, comprising chiefly the mountainous region on coast of Bering Sea at the base, in the isthmus, and the NW third of Kamchatka Penin. and the region of the Penzhina basin NE of the Sea of Okhotsk; includes also Karagin I.; 119,968 sq. m.; pop. (1941 est.) 12,500; ✳ Palana. Borders Chukot National District on N and Khabarovsk Territory on SW; inhabitants are Koryaks, recently renamed the Nymylans, a Palaeo-Asiatic people; their chief industry is fishing. Originally a part of the Far Eastern Region; established 1930 as a national district but for many years considered geographically as a part of Khabarovsk Territory; important in recent years in air communications routes of E Siberia.

Ko·ryak′ska·ya Sop′ka (kŭ·ryàk′skå·yå sôp′kå). Volcano (*sopka*) 11,342 ft. at S end of Eastern Range, Kamchatka Penin., Khabarovsk Territory, Soviet Russia, Asia.

Korytsa. See KORRÇË.

Kos (kŏs; *Mod. Gr.* kôs) *or* **Cos** (kŏs); *Ital.* **Co′o** (kô′ŏ). **1** An island of the Dodecanese (*q.v.*), off end of Bodrum Penin., SW Turkey in Asia; 111 sq. m.; pop. (1936) 19,731; ancient Cos settled in very early times by Dorians, had celebrated temple of Aesculapius, and belonged to the Pentapolis of Asia Minor; birthplace of Hippocrates.
2 Town on NE coast of the island.

Ko′sa·la (kō′så·là). An Aryan kingdom in N India (modern Oudh) c. 550–320 B.C.; ✳ Ajodhya (*q.v.*); the chief state in time of Buddha.

Ko′ścian (kôsh′chän); *Ger.* **Ko′sten** (kôs′tĕn). Commune, Poznań dept., Poland, 22 m. SSW of Poznań; pop. 10,275.

Kos′ci·us′ko (kŏs′ĭ·ŭs′kō). **1** County in Indiana. See *Table* at INDIANA.
2 City, ⊗ of Attala co., cen. Mississippi, 46 m. SE of Greenwood; pop. 6800; dairy products.

Kos′ci·us′ko, Mount (kŏz′ĭ·ŭs′kō). Mountain 7328 ft. of Australian Alps, SE New South Wales; highest peak in Australia and highest point of the highland region (**Kosciusko Plateau**) on border bet. New South Wales and Victoria at source of Murray river.

Kosel. See KOŹLE.

Ko·shi·ki Archipelago (kŏ·shē′kĕ); *Jap.* **Koshiki Ret·to** (rĕt·tō). Group of small islands off SW coast of Kyushu, Japan.

Kosh′ko·nong, Lake (kŏsh′kŏ·nŏng). Lake ab. 8 m. long and 4 m. wide in SW Jefferson co., SE Wisconsin; an expansion of Rock river.

Kosh′tan Tau (kŏsh′tän tou′). Mountain (*tau*) 16,875 ft. in Caucasus Mts. near Dykh Tau, in S Kabardino-Balkarian Republic, Soviet Russia, Europe.

Ko·shu (kō·shōō). **1** *or* **Kong·ju** (gŏng·jōō). Town, South Chusei prov., W Korea, 80 m. S of Seoul; pop. 11,478; important in early Korean history.
2 *or* **Kwang·ju** (gwäng·jōō). Town, ✳ of South Zenra prov., SW Korea, 115 m. W of Pusan; pop. 52,674.

Ko′si (kō′sē) *or* **Ku′si** (kōō′sē). River ab. 304 m. long in E Nepal and N India; formed by confluence of three streams in E Nepal, flows S across border into India and through N Bihar prov. into the Ganges E of Bhagalpur.

Ko′ši·ce (kŏ′shĭ·tsĕ); *Hung.* **Kas′sa** (kŏsh′shŏ); *Ger.* **Ka′schau** (käsh′ou). City, SE Slovakia prov., Czechoslovakia, on the Hernád river 135 m. NE of Budapest; pop. (1930) 70,117; has fine 14th-cent. Gothic cathedral; a modern city with excellent buildings, streets, and parks; has many industries, esp. wine manufacture. Originally a city of N Hungary; became part of Czechoslovakia 1918; held by Hungary 1938–45 but returned to Slovakia.

Ko′si Lake (kō′sē). Lake, Tongaland, N Natal, NE Union of South Africa; near coast, just S of border of Mozambique; in NE corner has an outlet by way of a short river, **Kosi River**, which flows NE into the Indian Ocean at **Kosi Bay.**

Ko′ší·ře (kŏ′shēr·zhĕ). Southwest suburb of Prague, Bohemia, Czechoslovakia, W of the Vltava river; pop. ab. 16,000.

Kös·lin′ (kûs·lēn′). **1** Former government district, E Pomerania prov., Prussia, Germany; 5447 sq. m.; since 1945 in NW Poland.
2 City. See KOSZALIN.

Ko′so Gol *or* **Kos′so-gol** (kŏ′sŏ gŭl′). Lake, N Outer Mongolia, near U.S.S.R. border of Tuva Autonomous Region, at elevation 5620 ft.; Dzhibkhalantu-Irkutsk highway passes along its E shore.

Ko′so·va (kŏ′sŏ·vä). Prefecture, NE Albania; 824 sq. m.; pop. 49,081; ✳ Kukës.

Ko′so·vo *or* **Kos′so·vo** *or* **Kosovo Po′lje** (kô′sŏ·vŏ pô′lyĕ). Elevated plain, formerly in SW Moravska and N Vardarska cos., S Yugoslavia, W of Priština; now (since 1946) in Kosovo-Metohija autonomous province. Site of important battle in Balkan history June 20, 1389 in which Serbs, Albanians, and Bosnians were defeated by Turks under Murad I; as a result Serbian Empire was crushed, and Serbia (*q.v.*) became vassal of Ottoman Empire; in a second battle Oct. 17, 1448 John Hunyadi was defeated by Sultan Murad II; on Nov. 20–25, 1915 the scene of final defeat of Serbians by Bulgarian army in World War I.

Kosovo–Me·to′hi·ja (-mĕ·tō′hĕ·yä). Autonomous province, S Yugoslavia, in W part of republic of Serbia; newly formed subdivision under constitution of 1946.

Kosovska Mitrovica. See MITROVICA.

Kosseir. See EL QUSEIR.

Kosso–gol. See KOSO GOL.

Kossovo. 1 Var. of KOSOVA, Albania.
2 See KOSOVO, Yugoslavia.

Kos·suth′ (kŏ·sōōth′). County in Iowa. See *Table* at IOWA.

Kosten. See KOŚCIAN.

Kö′sten·dil′ (kū′stĕn·dĭl′). Var. of KYUSTENDIL.

Kos′ti (kôs′tĭ). Town, Blue Nile prov., E Sudan, S of Ed Dueim; pop. (1938 est.) 15,000.

Kostnitz. See KONSTANZ.

Ko·stro·ma′ (kŭ·strŭ·má′). **1** River 250 m. long, N cen. Soviet Russia, Europe, navigable for 200 m.; rises in NE corner of Kostroma Region, flows SSW to the Volga at Kostroma.
2 City, SW Kostroma Region, Soviet Russia, Europe, on left bank of Volga where it is joined by the Kostroma, ab. 45 m. ENE of Yaroslavl; pop. 121,205; has suburbs on opp. side of Volga; an important lumber center; manufactures woodenware, machinery, cotton goods, shoes, and esp. linen, for which it has been noted since 16th cent. Has cathedral, originally built 1239, a fine example of early Russian architecture. One of oldest towns in Russia, founded 1152; in 13th cent. in Rostov-Suzdal principality, later, in 15th cent., absorbed by Moscow principality; frequently plundered by Tatars.

Kostroma Region. New region, N cen. Soviet Russia, Europe, created for economic reasons during World War II out of E half of Yaroslavl Region; * Kostroma.

Kos′trzyn (kôs′chĭn); *Ger.* **Kü·strin′** or **Cü·strin′** (kūs·trēn′). Industrial city, NW Poznań dept., W Poland, on the Oder at its confluence with the Warta 53 m. E of Berlin; pop. (before World War II) ab. 20,000; formerly in Brandenburg prov., Prussia; 16th-cent. castle in which Frederick the Great was held prisoner Sept.– Nov. 1730; manufactures potato meal, agricultural machinery, stamped and enamel work; saw milling, fisheries, cattle markets. First mentioned 1232; passed to Brandenburg 1262; made seat of margravate 1535 and fortified; held by French 1806–14; fortifications expanded and improved in 19th cent.; in World War II an important German defense post in campaign of Russians for Berlin 1945; taken by Russian armies Mar. 29; assigned to Poland by Potsdam Conference 1945.

Koswig. See COSWIG.

Ko·sza′lin (kô·shä′lēn); *Ger.* **Kös·lin′** (kûs·lēn′). City, NE Szczecin dept., NW Poland, near Baltic Sea 88 m. NE of Stettin (Szczecin); pop. (1946) 31,937; formerly in Pomerania prov., Prussia; 14th-cent. Gothic church; manufactures paper, preserved fish, beer. Founded at end of 12th cent.; became city 1266; in World War II taken by Russians Feb. 14, 1945; assigned to Poland by Potsdam Conference 1945.

Kö′szeg (kû′sĕg). Town, W Hungary, N of Szombathely near Austrian border; pop. (1930) 8537; in fruit and wine-producing region.

Ko′ta Bah′ru (kō′tá bä′rōō); *also* **Kota Bha′ru** (bä′-rōō). Town, * of Kelantan state, Federation of Malaya, in N near coast at head of delta of Kelantan river; pop. 14,843; has been much improved in buildings, streets, etc., in last 25 years; has modern airport. One of the first places seized (Dec. 10, 1941) by Japanese in campaign against Singapore.

Kotabaru. See HOLLANDIA.

Ko′tah (kō′tá). **1** Former Indian state, Eastern Rajputana States, SE Rajputana, NW India; 5714 sq. m.; pop. (1941) 777,398; drained by the Chambal and its tributaries; formed from Bundi state ab. 1625; on June 26, 1947 became a member of the Union of Rajasthan.
2 Town, its *, on right bank of Chambal river 120 m. S of Jaipur; pop. 37,876; muslins and carpets; includes old city walls, palaces of the maharao, and temples.

Ko′ta Ko′ta (kō′tá kō′tá). Town on W shore of Lake Nyasa, Nyasaland Protectorate, SE Africa.

Ko·tel′nich (kô·tĕl′nĭch; *Russ.* kŭ·tyäl′nyĭch). Railroad and commercial town, W Kirov Region, Soviet Russia, Europe, on Vyatka river 50 m. SW of Kirov; pop. 10,664.

Ko·tel′ni·kov′ski (kô·tĕl′nĭ·kôf′skĭ; *Russ.* kŭ·tyäl′nyĭ-

kŭf·skĭ). Town, Volgograd Region, SE Soviet Russia, Europe, ab. 90 m. SSW of Volgograd; in World War II taken by Germans Aug. 1942; retaken by Russians Dec. 29, 1942.

Ko·tel′ny or **Ko·tel′ni** (kô·tĕl′nĭ; *Russ.* kŭ·tyäl′y′·nyĭ). Island 110 m. long, largest of the New Siberian Is., in W part of group; belongs to Yakutsk Republic, Soviet Russia, Asia.

Kö′then or **Cö′then** (kû′tĕn). City, Anhalt, Germany, 12 m. SW of Dessau; pop. 26,595; railroad junction; 15th-cent. Gothic church; varied manufactures; mineral waters; lignite mining nearby.

Kot′ka (kŏt′ká; *Finn.* kôt′ká). Seaport, * of Viipuri dept., SE Finland, on a small island in the Gulf of Finland E of Helsinki; pop. (1943 est.) 21,704; ships lumber; hydroelectric power plant; manufactures paper, cellulose, sugar.

Kot·las′ (kŭt·läs′). Town, SE Arkhangelsk Region, Soviet Russia, Europe, on right bank of Northern Dvina; pop. 4258; a river and railroad junction point with rapid growth in recent years; at head of Northern Dvina navigation; important grain-shipping point.

Kot′lik (kŏt′lĭk). Village on the W coast of Alaska, on S shore of Norton Sound and at N end of the Yukon delta.

Kot′lin (kŏt′lĭn; *Russ.* kôt′lyĭn). Island in Kronshtadt Bay, E end of Gulf of Finland. See KRONSHTADT.

Kotonu. See COTONOU.

Ko′tor (kō′tôr) or **Cat′ta·ro** (kät′tä·rô). Seaport and commercial center, formerly in Zetska co., S Yugoslavia, on the **Gulf of Kotor,** an inlet of Adriatic Sea; pop. 5011; since 1946 in Montenegro republic, Yugoslavia; excellent harbor, formerly a base of Austro-Hungarian navy; under Venetian rule 1420–1797; passed to Austria 1797, to France 1807–14, back to Austria 1814–1918, to newly organized Yugoslavia 1918.

Ko·to·sho or **Koto Sho** (kō·tō·shô). Island in Pacific Ocean, ab. 40 m. E of the S tip of Formosa.

Ko·tovsk′ (kŭ·tôfsk′). Industrial city, Tambov Region, cen. Soviet Russia, Europe; formerly a part of Tambov, made a separate city 1944.

Ko′tri (kō′trĭ). Town, S Sind, Pakistan, on right bank of the Indus opp. Hyderabad; pop. 7617; important railroad and river transportation center.

Kot′ta·yam (kŏt′á·yám). Town, W Kerala state, S India, on inlet of Arabian Sea 30 m. SSE of Cochin; pop. 25,236; noted as site of an old Syrian Christian community.

Kottbus. See COTTBUS.

Kot′to (kŏt′ō). River 400 m. long, cen. Africa; flows S through E Central African Republic, N cen. Africa, into Ubangi river on the border of Congo.

Kot′ze·bue (kŏt′sĕ·bū). Village in NW Alaska, at tip of long neck of land (Baldwin Penin.) in Kotzebue Sound; pop. 1290; U.S. air base.

Kotzebue Sound. Large inlet from 40 to 65 m. wide, of Chuckchee Sea, NW Alaska, just NE of Bering Strait; receives Noatak and Kobuk rivers.

Kötz′schen·bro′da (kû′chĕn·brō′dä). City, Saxony, Germany, NW suburb of Dresden on Elbe river; pop. 17,425.

Kouang–Tchéou–Wan. See KWANGCHOWAN.

Kou′li·ko′ro (kōō′lĭ·kōr′ō). Town, Mali, West Africa, on the Niger just NE of Bamako; terminus of a railroad from Kayes on the Senegal; founded 1884.

Koulouri. See SALAMIS.

Koun·rad′ski (kōōn·rät′skĭ). Town, SE Karaganda Region, Kazakh S.S.R., Soviet Central Asia; railroad terminus just N of Balkhash and near N shore of Lake Balkhash; copper-mining center.

Kountze (kōōnts). City, ⊗ of Hardin co., E Texas; pop. 1768.

Kour·nine′, Jeb′el (jĕb′ĕl kōōr·nēn′). Hill in N Tunisia, NE of Sebkret el Kourzia and W of Zaghouan; scene of severe fighting Apr. 29–May 2, 1943.

Kou·rous'sa (kōō·rōō'sà). Town, E cen. Guinea, W Africa, on railroad from Conakry to Kankan and on left bank of upper Niger.

Kou'vo·la (kō'vô·là). Town, S Finland, in Viipuri dept.; pop. 5124; railroad junction point.

Ko'vel (kô'vĕl; *Russ.* kô'vyïl·y'); *Pol.* **Ko'wel** (kô'vĕl). City, NW Ukraine, U.S.S.R., 43 m. NW of Lutsk; pop. (1938–39 est.) 35,000; formerly in Wołyń dept., Poland; important railroad junction and agricultural center; captured by Austrians Aug. 17, 1915; in battles following, from Aug. to Sept. 1915, Russians were unable to retake it; held by Germans in World War II until July 1944.

Kovno. See KAUNAS.

Kov·rov' (kŭv·rôf'). Town on Klyazma river, cen. Ivanovo Region, Soviet Russia, Europe, 150 m. E of Moscow; pop. 67,163; railroad junction.

Kov'zha (kôv'zhà). Stream ab. 50 m. long, NW Vologda Region, Soviet Russia, Europe; flows SSE to Lake Beloe; forms part of the Mariinsk Canal System.

Koweit. See KUWAIT.

Kowel. See KOVEL.

Ko·wie' (?kô·vē'). Short river, Cape Province, S Union of South Africa; flows into Indian Ocean at Port Alfred.

Kow'loon' (kou'lōōn'), *also* **Kau'lun'** (kou'lōōn') *or* **Kau'lung'** (*Pekingese* jï·ô'lōong'). 1 Peninsula. See HONG KONG.
2 Town on W shore of Kowloon Penin., SE China, separated from Victoria on Hong Kong I. by Hong Kong harbor, 1 m. wide at narrowest point; urban area 18 sq. m., pop. (1931) 264,675, extends N into leased New Territories (see HONG KONG) and includes Kowloon, New Kowloon, and Kowloon City; much of area is modern development; connected by rail with Canton; important commercial center. Ceded to British 1860.

Kowno. See KAUNAS.

Koy'u·kuk (ki'û·kŭk). River ab. 425 m. long, W Alaska; flows SW from Brooks Range to Yukon river.

Ko·zá'nē (kô·zä'nyĕ). 1 Department of Greece. See *Table* at GREECE.
2 City, its ✻, ab. 67 m. SW of Salonika; pop. 12,702; held by Germans Apr. 1941 to Oct. 1944.

Kozhikode. City, India. See CALICUT.

Koź'le (kôzh'lĕ); *Ger.* **Co'sel** *or* **Ko'sel** (kō'zĕl). Town, W Śląsk dept., SW Poland, on the Odra (Oder) W of Zabrze; pop. (1946) 13,321; formerly in Germany.

Kozlov. See MICHURINSK.

Kra, Isthmus of (krä). Narrow section in N cen. Malay Penin., lat. 10°N, in SW Thailand; ab. 40 m. wide at its narrowest part. Pakchan river flows S in the isthmus forming S end of boundary bet. Lower Burma and Thailand; Ranong is Thai port at its mouth; range of hills at narrowest part ab. 2000 ft. high.

Kra'bi (krä'bē). 1 Province, SW Thailand; 1520 sq. m.; pop. 55,683.
2 Town, its ✻, a port on W coast of Malay Penin. 40 m. E of Phuket.

Kra'ger·ö' (krä'gĕ·rû'). Seaport town, Telemark co., S Norway, 40 m. NE of Arendal; pop. 4314; lumber.

Kra'gu·je·vac' *or* **Kra'gu·ye·vats'** (krä'gōō·yĕ·väts'). Town, N cen. Serbia, NE Yugoslavia, 60 m. SE of Belgrade, in Šumadija region; pop. 27,208; a residence of Serbian princes to 1842; usual meeting place of Serbian legislature 1868–80; captured by Bulgarians and Germans Nov. 1, 1915 in World War I; had iron foundry and ammunition factory and was long chief arsenal and garrison town of Serbia.

Krain. See CARNIOLA.

Kra'ka·tau' (krä'kà·tou') *or* **Kra'ka·to'a** (krä'kà·tō'à); *also* **Kra'ka·tao'** (-tou'); *local Malay name* **Ra·ka'ta** (rä·kä'tä). Island volcano in center of Sunda Strait, between Sumatra and Java, Indonesia. Its eruption Aug. 26–28, 1883 was the most tremendous of modern times. Before the eruption ab. 2620 ft. high; its top blown off by an explosion, which caused tidal wave ab. 50 ft. high, killing 36,000 people in W Java; dust, ashes, and smoke rose to height of ab. 17 m. and the sound of the explosion was heard in Constantinople, Australia, Philippines, and Japan; atmospherical effects encircling the globe caused strange sunrise and sunset conditions for months afterward. Now only a low island with crater lake.

Kra'ków (krä'kōōf); *Eng.* **Cra'cow** (krä'kō); *Ger.* **Kra'kau** (krä'kou). 1 Department, S Poland; 6795 sq. m.; pop. 2,296,842; in reorganization of administrative units of Poland 1946, area somewhat reduced.
2 City, its ✻, on Vistula river 156 m. SSW of Warsaw; pop. (1938–39 est.) 251,451; railroad junction; principal educational center in Poland: university (founded 1364; most ancient in Central Europe), seat of Polish academy of science; principal public library of Poland; 14th-cent. Gothic cathedral; manufactures machinery, agricultural implements, chemicals, oil, leather goods, beer; trades in lumber, salt, cattle, and dairy and poultry products.
History: Polish town, in 10th cent. part of territory under Boleslav I of Bohemia (*q.v.*); captured by Boleslav I of Poland 999; established as capital of Polish kingdom and an hereditary principality by Boleslav III (1102–38); invaded by Mongols 1241; received municipal rights (Magdeburg rights) 1257; made Polish capital by Ladislas I Lokietek 1305 and remained capital to 1609 (see WARSAW); captured by Swedes 1655, 1702; coronation and burial place of Polish kings to 1764; taken by Austria in Third Partition of Poland 1795; included in Napoleon's Grand Duchy of Warsaw 1809–15; independent buffer state; republic of Kraków erected 1815; restored to Austria 1846; belonged to independent Poland after World War I; held by Germans in both World War I and II; taken by Russians Jan. 19, 1945.

Kra'len·dijk (krä'lĕn·dīk). Chief town on Bonaire I., Neth. West Indies, on W coast.

Krá'lic·ká' (krä'lĭts·kä'); *Ger.* **Kra'litz** (krä'lĭts). Town, NE Moravia, Czechoslovakia, just E of Prostějov; here was printed 1579–93 the Kralitz or Brothers' Bible, the most important Bohemian version.

Kraljevina Srba, Hrvata i Slovenaca. = *Kingdom of the Serbs, Croats, and Slovenes:* see YUGOSLAVIA.

Kra'lje·vo (krä'lyĕ·vô). Town, NW Serbia, E Yugoslavia, at junction of the Ibar with Western Morava river; pop. ab. 4000.

Kra·ma·torsk' (krà·mŭ·tôrsk'). City, N Stalino Region, E Ukraine, U.S.S.R., in cen. Donbas on a tributary of the Donets ab. 25 m. W of Artemovsk; pop. 93,350; an industrial city of recent development, had one of the largest plants in the world for metallurgical equipment; held by Germans from 1941 to Sept. 1943.

Krapotkin. See KROPOTKIN.

Kras. See CARSO.

Kras'li·ce (kräs'lĭ·tsĕ); *Ger.* **Gras'litz** (gräs'lĭts). Town, NW Bohemia prov., W Czechoslovakia, ab. 20 m. NNE of Cheb; pop. (1930) 13,953; manufactures musical instruments.

Kraś'nik (kräsh'nĭk; *Pol.* kräs'y'·nĕk). Commune, Lublin dept., Poland, 28 m. SSW of Lublin; pop. 11,615; agriculture; scene of Austrian defeat by Russians Aug. 1914.

Kras'no·dar (kräs'nô·där; *Russ.* krås·nŭ·dàr'); *formerly* **E·ka'te·ri'no·dar** (ê·kät'ēr·ē'nô·där; *Russ.* yĭ·kȧ·tyï-ryē'nŭ·dàr'). City, ✻ of Krasnodar Territory, in W cen. part, S Soviet Russia, Europe, 160 m. S of Rostov; pop. 203,946; on right bank of Kuban river and on railroad from Rostov to Novorossisk; one of most important industrial and cultural cities of the Caucasus region; also coal mining, fishing; Workers' Scientific Institute, museum, and art gallery. Founded 1794 as a small fort by Empress Catherine II; occupied by Germans Aug. 9, 1942 and retaken Feb. 12, 1943.

Krasnodar Territory. Territory, a subdivision of the R.S.F.S.R., S Soviet Russia, Europe; 34,200 sq. m.; pop. 3,172,885; ✻ Krasnodar; W part of former North Caucasus region; bounded on N by Rostov Region, on E by

Stavropol Territory and Cherkess Autonomous Region, on SE by Abkhazia A.S.S.R. (in Georgia), on S and SW by Black Sea, and on W by Sea of Azov; separated from E Crimea (Kerch Penin.) by Kerch Strait; includes the Adygei Autonomous Region and the lower and middle course of the Kuban river. In S contains mountains and foothills of W Caucasus; much of it is fertile plain with marshland along the Azov shore; crossed by several railroad lines; essentially an agricultural region but has oil fields, rich mineral resources, forests in S; cattle raising and fishing also important. Chief towns Krasnodar, Armavir, Novorossisk, and Tuapse. In medieval period under Tatar khanates; came under Russian control for the most part in 18th cent. See NORTH CAUCASUS. Territory created 1936; largely overrun by German armies 1942–43.

Kras'no·grad (kräs′nô·gräd; *Russ.* krás·nŭ·grát′). Town, Kharkov Region, NE Ukraine, U.S.S.R., 55 m. SW of Kharkov; pop. 12,710; railroad and highway junction point; recaptured by Russians Feb. 1943.

Krasnogvardeisk. See GATCHINA.

Kras·no·kok·shaisk′ (krás·nŭ·kŭk·shĭsk′). = IOSH-KAR OLA.

Krasnostav. See KRASNYSTAW.

Kras'no·u·ralsk′ (kräs′nô·û·rälsk′; *Russ.* krás·nŭ·ōō-rál′y′sk). Town, W Sverdlovsk Region, Soviet Russia, Asia, 45 m. N of Sverdlovsk; pop. ab. 25,000; industrial town on E slope of Ural Mts.

Kras'no·vodsk (kräs′nô·vôtsk; *Russ.* krás·nŭ·vôtsk′). Seaport town on **Krasnovodsk Gulf,** NW Turkmen S.S.R., Soviet Central Asia; pop. 10,022; chief town of Krasnovodsk Region, across Caspian Sea from Baku; railroad terminus, important in cotton and fruit trade with E Turkmen and W Uzbek Republics. Dates from a fort built in 1717.

Krasnovodsk Region. Subdivision, W Turkmen S.S.R., Soviet Central Asia, chief town Krasnovodsk; borders on SE Caspian Sea and includes the Kara Bogaz Gol (gulf); bounded by Ashkhabad Region on E and by Iran on S; largely a desert region.

Kras'no·yarsk (kräs′nô·yärsk; *Russ.* krás·nŭ·yársk′). Town, ✳ of Krasnoyarsk Territory, in S part, Soviet Russia, Asia, on left bank of upper Yenisei river and on Trans-Siberian R.R., 420 m. E of Novosibirsk; pop. 189,999; has grown rapidly since construction of the railroad and is now cultural as well as commercial and manufacturing city; center of gold-mining district. Founded as a fort by Cossacks 1628; in later 17th cent. frequently attacked by Tatars and Kirghiz.

Krasnoyarsk Territory. A territory of Soviet Russia, Asia, in W cen. Siberia; 827,507 sq. m.; pop. 1,940,002; ✳ Krasnoyarsk. Geographically includes the two national districts of Taimyr and Evenki (*qq.v.*), both established in 1930. Bounded on N by Arctic Ocean (Laptev and Kara Seas), on E by Yakutsk A.S.S.R. and Irkutsk Region, on S by Tuva Autonomous Region, and on W by Kemerovo and Tomsk Regions and the Khanty-Mansi and Yamalo-Nenets National Districts. In SW includes Khakass Autonomous Region which is politically independent. Includes Yenisei river and the greater part of the valleys of its tributaries (see TUNGUSKA), and also the Khatanga (in Taimyr National District); largely tundra in the Taimyr and lower Yenisei region, hilly in cen. part, and quite mountainous in S, containing foothills of Sayan Mts. Crossed by the Trans-Siberian R.R., passing through Achinsk and Krasnoyarsk, also by a parallel trunk line farther S, recently completed, reaching the rich mining and agricultural lands about Minusinsk. Chief towns Krasnoyarsk, Minusinsk, Achinsk, Artemovsk, Yeniseisk, Igarka. Colonized by Russians from middle of 17th cent. but developed slowly; long a place of exile; after completion of Trans-Siberian R.R. (1891–98) from Moscow to Vladivostok, marked by rapid growth; originally part of West Siberia Region, made subdivision of R.S.F.S.R. in Asia 1936.

Kras'no·ye Se·lo′ (krás′nŭ·yĕ syĕ·lô′). Town, Leningrad Region, Soviet Russia, Europe, just SSW of Leningrad and N of Krasnogvardeisk (Gatchina); taken by Germans in assault on Leningrad Sept. 4, 1941.

Krasny. See KYZYL.

Kras'ny Luch (krás′nĭ lōōch′). City, Voroshilovgrad region, Ukrainian S.S.R., in the Donbas; pop. 50,829; coal mining.

Kras·ny'staw (kräs·nĭ′stäf); *Russ.* **Kras·no·stav′** (krás·nŭ·stáf′). Commune, Lublin dept., Poland, 32 m. SE of Lublin; pop. 10,435; cordage; captured by Russians in battle, July 18, 1915.

Kra'tié′ (krá′tyä′). Commercial town on the Mekong, E Cambodia, Indochina, 105 m. NE of Pnompenh.

Kra·wang′ (krä·wäng′). Town, Batavia dist., West Java prov., Indonesia, on railroad 35 m. E of Batavia; pop. 18,227.

Kray (krī). Former commune (pop. 25,405), Düsseldorf govt. dist., Westphalia prov., Prussia, Germany; since 1929 part of Essen (*q.v.*).

Kre'feld, *formerly also* **Kre'feld-Uer'ding·en** (krä′-fĕlt-ür′dĭng·ĕn). City, W North Rhine-Westphalia state, Germany, on Rhine river 19 m. WSW of Essen; pop. (1939) 169,485; formed 1929 by incorporation of former cities of Krefeld (or Crefeld) and Uerdingen am Rhein; center of silk-spinning, silk-dyeing, and velvet-making industries; varied manufactures. Bombed by Allies June 1943–45; taken Mar. 3, 1945.

Kre'men·chug (krĕm′ĕn·chōōg; *Russ.* kryĭ·myĭn-chōōk′). City, S Poltava Region, E cen. Ukraine, U.S.S.R., on the Dnieper 160 m. SE of Kiev; pop. 89,553; an industrial city in black-earth region with large trade in grain and lumber and manufactured tobacco products; has rail connections N to Moscow and Kharkov and S across the Dnieper with Kirovograd by a long tubular bridge; also an ecclesiastical (Greek-Catholic) center with many churches. Founded 1571; capital of New Russia 1765–89; in the Revolution and succeeding civil war 1917–21, suffered much damage; in World War II seized by Germans Sept. 1941 but retaken in great Russian drive Sept.–Dec. 1943.

Kre'me·nets′ (krĕm′ĕ·nĕts′; *Russ.* kryĭ·myĭ·nyĕts′); *Pol.* **Krze·mie'niec** (kshĕ·myĕ′nyĕts). City, W Ukraine, U.S.S.R., 47 m. SSE of Lutsk; pop. (1938–39 est.) 22,465; formerly in Wołyń dept., Poland; episcopal see; trades in grain. Formerly site of a famous lyceum (transferred 1833 to Kiev and combined with university there).

Krem'lin′–Bi'cê'tre (krĕm′län′bē′sâ′tr′). Commune, Seine dept., N France, S suburb of Paris; pop. 17,038.

Krem'ni·ca (krĕm′nyĭ·tsä); *Ger.* **Krem'nitz** (krĕm′-nĭts); *Hung.* **Kör'möcz·bá'nya** (kûr′mûts·bä′nyô). Commune, cen. Slovakia, E cen. Czechoslovakia, NW of Zvolen; pop. 5389; formerly produced much gold and silver. Belonged to Hungary until 1920.

Krems (krĕms). City, ✳ of Lower Danube prov., Austria, on Danube river 38 m. WNW of Vienna; pop. (1939) 28,035; machinery, metal goods; active trade in wine and fruit. In World War II taken by Russians Apr. 1945.

Kremsier. See KROMĚŘÍŽ.

Krētē. See CRETE.

Krētikòn Pélagos. See Sea of CANDIA.

Kre'tin·ga (krĕ′tĭng·gä). **1** District of Lithuania. See *Table* at LITHUANIA.
2 Town, its ✳, ab. 10 m. N of Memel; pop. 9861.

Kreuzburg, Kreuzburg in Oberschlesien. See KLUCZBORK.

Kreuz'ling·en (kroits′lĭng·ĕn). Commune, Thurgau canton, NE Switzerland, near W end of Lake Constance, adjoining Konstanz; pop. (1930) 8615.

Kreuz'nach (kroits′näk); *also called* **Bad Kreuznach** (bät). City, W Germany, in NE Rhineland-Palatinate state, on Nahe river 37 m. SSE of Koblenz; pop. 24,928; mineral springs and baths; health resort; manufactures leather, tobacco, glass, combs, marble goods.

Kri'an District (krē'än). Area in NW Perak state, Federation of Malaya, just S of Province Wellesley; center of rice-growing region.

Kri'bi (krē'bē). Port, French Cameroun, NW Africa, on the Bight of Biafra 80 m. S of Douala.

Krim. See CRIMEA.

Krimmitschau. See CRIMMITSCHAU.

Krimm'ler Falls (krĭm'lēr). Falls in **Krimmler River,** an upper tributary of the Salzach flowing N from the Hohe Tauern, SW Austria; in three parts with total drop of 1246 ft.

Kri·o', Cape (krē·ō'). 1 or **Cape Kri·os'** (krē·ōs'); *Mod. Gr.* **Kri·oú' Me'to·pon** (krē·ōō' mä'tô·pôn). Southwest point of the island of Crete, E Mediterranean Sea.
2 Cape at W end of long narrow peninsula on SW coast of Turkey in Asia, projecting into the Aegean Sea near island of Kos, S of Bodrum Penin.; site of ancient Cnidus.

Krishna. See KISTNA.

Krish'na·gar (krĭsh'nȧ·gēr). Town, ✻ of Nadia dist., West Bengal, NE Indian Union, on Hooghly river 58 m. N of Calcutta; pop. 24,284; contains residence of the maharaja of Nadia.

Kristiania. See OSLO.

Kris'tian·sand' or **Chris'tian·sand'** (krĭs'chăn·sănd'; *Norw.* krĭs'tyän·sän'). Seaport, ⊗ of Vest-Agder co., SW Norway, on the Skagerrak SW of Oslo; pop. 18,781; shipping point for fish and lumber; flour mills, sawmills, dairies, woolen mills; 17th-cent. Gothic cathedral; has airport and resort beaches. Founded 1641; in World War II captured by Germans Apr. 9, 1940 after brief resistance in which German cruiser *Karlsruhe* was sunk.

Kris'tian·stad' (krĭs'chăn·städ'; *Swed.* krĭs'tĭ·än'stä[d], krĭ·shän'stä). **1** Province of Sweden. See *Table* at SWEDEN.
2 Seaport, its ✻, on Helge river near Baltic Sea; pop. 22,807; trade center in agricultural section; flour mills, woolen mills, sugar refineries, distilleries; exports granite and wood pulp. Founded 1614 by Christian IV of Denmark; ceded to Sweden 1658; captured by Danes 1676, recaptured by Swedes 1678.

Kris'tian·sund' or **Chris'tian·sund'** (krĭs'chăn·sōōnd'; *Norw.* krĭs'tyän·sōōn'). Seaport, ⊗ of Möre og Romsdal co., W Norway, WSW of Trondheim; pop. 14,646; built on three small islands enclosing a harbor; exports fish, butter, and lumber; shipbuilding yards.

Kris'tii·na' (krĭs'tē·nä') or **Kris·ti'ne·stad** (krĭs·tē'ne·stä[d]). Coastal town, W Finland, in Vaasa dept., on Gulf of Bothnia 60 m. S of Vaasa; pop. 3431.

Kris'ti·ne·hamn' (krĭs'tē·ne·häm'n). Lake port, Värmland prov., SW Sweden, on Lake Vänern; pop. 15,236; machine factories.

Kri·thia' (krē·thyä'). Village near tip of Gallipoli Penin., Turkey in Europe; early objective of Anzac troops in Gallipoli campaign Apr.–June 1915.

Kri·voi' Rog (kryĭ·voi' rôk'; *Angl.* krĭv'oi rōg'). City, W Dnepropetrovsk Region, SE cen. Ukraine, U.S.S.R., on the Ingulets river ab. 80 m. SW of Dnepropetrovsk; pop. 197,621; railroad and industrial city, important chiefly for its location in midst of rich iron mines and on W edge of the Donets Basin, which produces coal; metallurgical plants, foundries, mills, and chemical works. As an urban center it is of recent growth; city and mines seized by Germans 1941; held as a salient by them after Kiev and Dnepropetrovsk had fallen; retaken by Russians Feb. 22, 1944.

Krk (kûrk); *Ital.* **Ve'glia** (vě'lyä). **1** Island in the Mali Kvarner at head of the Adriatic Sea, Croatia, NW Yugoslavia; 165 sq. m.; pop. 20,013; occupied by d'Annunzio 1920.
2 Town on S coast of island; pop. 2473; 11th-cent. cathedral; settled by Greeks, and successively under rule of Rome, Croatia, Venice, Austria 1797–1809, France 1809–13, Austria again 1813–1918.

Krka. See KERKA.

Kr'nov (kûr'nôf); *Ger.* **Jä'gern·dorf** (yä'gērn·dôrf). Town, Silesia prov., cen. Czechoslovakia, on Oppa river 30 m. NW of Moravská Ostrava; pop. (1930) 23,465; textile mills.

Kro'če·hla'vy (krô'chě·hlä'vĭ). Town, NW Bohemia prov., W Czechoslovakia, ab. 14 m. W of Prague; pop. (1930) 11,414.

Kro'ja (krô'yä). = KRUJË.

Kro·le'vets (krŭ·lyä'vyěts; *Angl.* krŏ·lā'věts). Town, Sumy Region, N Ukraine, U.S.S.R., ab. 23 m. N of Konotop; pop. ab. 12,000; fairs.

Król·lew'ska Hu'ta (krōō·lĕf'skä hōō'tä); *Ger.* **Kö'-nigs·hüt'te** (kū'nĭks·hüt'ě). Former city (pop. 80,734), Śląsk dept., Poland; since 1934 part of Chorzów (*q.v.*).

Kro'mě·říž (krô'myěr·zhēsh); *Ger.* **Krem'sier** (krĕm'-zēr). Town, N Moravia prov., cen. Czechoslovakia, on Morava river 35 m. E of Brno; pop. (1930) 18,583; industrial and commercial center; meeting place of Austrian Reichstag 1848–49.

Kronenberg. See CRONENBERG.

Kro'no·berg (krōō'nōō·bär'y'). Province of Sweden. See *Table* at SWEDEN.

Kro·nots'ka·ya Sop'ka (krŭ·nôts'kȧ·yȧ sôp'kȧ). Volcano (*sopka*) 11,909 ft., in Eastern Range, Kamchatka Penin., Khabarovsk Territory, Soviet Russia, Asia.

Kro·nots'ki, Cape (krŭ·nôts'kĭ). Point extending into Bering Sea, E coast of Kamchatka Penin., Soviet Russia, Asia, at ab. 54°50'N lat., 162°E long.

Kron'shtadt or **Kron'stadt** (krŏn'stät; *Russ.* krŭn-shtät'). Fortress on Kotlin I. in **Kronshtadt Bay** (E end of Gulf of Finland), NW Leningrad Region, Soviet Russia, Europe, ab. 25 m. W of Leningrad. Island seized by Peter the Great 1703 and fortress founded 1710; town well laid out; has exceptionally fine harbor but blocked by ice for ab. 5 months yearly; given name of Kronshtadt 1823; was strong defense point for Russian Empire and is now most important Soviet naval station; scene of mutinies 1825, 1882, 1905; took active part in Revolution of 1917; in 1921 navy mutiny against Soviets was ruthlessly put down.

Kronstadt. 1 See BRAŞOV, Romania.
2 See KRONSHTADT, Soviet Russia, Europe.

Kroon'stad (krōōn'stät). Town, N Orange Free State, E cen. Union of South Africa, 120 m. NE of Bloemfontein; pop. with suburbs 13,629; center of rich farm district; railroad junction; has excellent educational system; popular resort.

Kro·pot'kin, *formerly* **Kra·pot'kin** (krŭ·pŏt'kĭn; *Russ.* krŭ·pôt'kĭn). Town, E Krasnodar Territory, Soviet Russia, Europe, on Kuban river 80 m. ENE of Krasnodar; pop. 31,019; railroad junction, a center for grain trade; flour mills, elevators, machine factories.

Kros'no (krôs'nô). Commune, Lwów dept., Poland; pop. (1938–39 est.) 13,738; textiles; petroleum and natural-gas industries; on railroad near foot of East Beskids ab. 40 m. SE of Tarnów.

Kro·to'szyn (krô·tô'shĭn); *Ger.* **Kro'to·schin** (krō'tô-shēn). Commune, Poznań dept., Poland, 50 m. SSE of Poznań; pop. (1938–39 est.) 14,000; railroad junction near former German border N of Wrocław; machinery, cement. Legendary residence of first Piast ruler.

Kroub or **Le Kroub** (lĕ krōōb'). Commune, Constantine dept., NE Algeria, just SE of Constantine; pop. 10,217.

Kru Coast (krōō). That section of the SE coast of Liberia NW of Cape Palmas inhabited by Krumen.

Kru'ger National Park (krōō'gēr; *Afrikaans* krü'[g]ēr). Park and game reserve, E Transvaal, NE Union of South Africa, 200 m. long by 40 m. wide, 8652 sq. m., on Mozambique frontier; crossed by Olifants river; has great numbers of wild animals native to South Africa. Established 1926 by Act of Parliament; had its origin in President Kruger's game sanctuary established 1898, then known as the Sabi reserve and including country bet. Limpopo and Sabi rivers.

Kru′gers·dorp (krōō′gĕrz·dôrp; *Afrikaans* krü′[g]ĕrs-dôrp). Town, S Transvaal, NE Union of South Africa, 20 m. W of Johannesburg; pop. 54,810; in manganese and gold mine region. Founded 1887; separated from Randfontein 1929. The Pardekraal monument, commemorative of victory of Boers over Zulu chieftain Dingaan, Dec. 16, 1838, is object of annual pilgrimage.

Kru′jë (krōō′yĕ); *Ital.* **Cro′ia** (krô′yä). Town, cen. Albania, NNW of Tiranë; pop. ab. 4000.

Krum′lov (krōōm′lôf); *Ger.* **Kru′mau** (krōō′mou). Town, in the Bohemian Forest, SW Bohemia, W Czechoslovakia, SSW of České Budějovice; pop. (1930) 8589; produces textiles, paper; castle.

Krung Thep. See BANGKOK.

Kru′še·vac (krōō′shĕ·väts). Town, N cen. Serbia, E Yugoslavia, on Western Morava river 34 m. NW of Niš; pop. 11,054; market town in fruit-growing and cattle-raising region; munitions factories. Capital of Serbia 1839–42; occupied by Germans 1941.

Kruš′né Ho′ry (krōōsh′nâ hô′rï). Czech name of ERZ GEBIRGE mountain range bordering Bohemia on NW.

Kru′town (krōō′toun). Native settlement, suburb of Monrovia, Liberia, W Africa.

Kru′zof (krōō′zôf). Small island in Alexander Archipelago, SE Alaska, W of Baranof I. and opp. Sitka; naval air base; Mt. Edgecumbe at its S end.

Krzemieniec. See KREMENETS.

Ksar-el–Kebir, El. = *El Qsar el Kbir:* see ALCÁZAR-QUIVIR.

Ksour Mountains (ksōōr). Range of the Atlas Mts. in N Aïn-Sefra territory, NW Algeria.

Ktaa′dn (kȧ·tä′d′n). Var. of KATAHDIN.

Kti′ma (k′tē′mä). Town, ✳ of Paphos dist., W Cyprus, near the coast and just N of the site and ruins of ancient Paphos.

K² (kä′tōō′). See GODWIN AUSTEN.

Ku–. For many Chinese names beginning thus, see Kw-.

Kua′la Kang′sar (kwä′lȧ kŭng′sẽr). Town, N cen. Perak state, Federation of Malaya, on Perak river and on W coast railroad; pop. 6030; N of Ipoh and ab. 12 m. SE of Taiping; residence of sultan of Perak.

Kuala Ku′bu (kōō′bōō). Town, NE Selangor state, Federation of Malaya, on main railroad line 25 m. N of Kuala Lumpur; pop. 5333; starting point of highway NE to Pahang state.

Kuala Li′pis (lē′pĭs). Town, ✳ of Pahang state, in NW cen. part, on Jelai river, Federation of Malaya; pop. 4111; on the central and E coast railroad of Malay Penin. ab. 75 m. N of Kuala Lumpur.

Kuala Lum′pur (lōōm′pŏŏr). City, ✳ of Selangor state and of Federation of Malaysia; pop. 111,418, (1937 est.) 136,068; on main W coast railroad line ab. 200 m. NW of Singapore (246 m. by rail) and junction point for branch to Port Swettenham; the most important Malay city on the peninsula, noted for its fine buildings, roads, gardens, etc.; tin mines and rubber plantations in surrounding districts. In Singapore campaign 1942 abandoned by British Jan. 11.

Kuala Pi′lah (pē′lä). Town, cen. Negri Sembilan state, Federation of Malaya; pop. 3999; terminus of branch railroad line.

Kuala Se·lang′or (sĕ·läng′ôr). Coastal town on Strait of Malacca, NW Selangor state, Federation of Malaya, 25 m. N of Port Swettenham; fishing center. Occupied by Japanese troops Jan. 5, 1942.

Kuala Treng·ga′nu (trĕng·gä′nōō). Town, ✳ of Trengganu state, Federation of Malaya, in NE part, at mouth of Trengganu river; pop. 13,972.

Kuan′tan (kwän′tän). Town on E coast of Pahang state, Federation of Malaya, N of the mouth of the Pahang river; pop. 5482; has fair harbor at river mouth and was a key point on E coast seized by Japanese in their invasion of Malay Penin. Dec. 1941–Jan. 1942. British warships *Prince of Wales* and *Repulse* lost in naval battle Dec. 10, 1941 off this coast.

Ku·ba′ (kōō·bä′). Town, NE Azerbaidzhan, U.S.S.R., on E slopes of Caucasus Mts. 95 m. NW of Baku; pop. ab. 14,000; silk goods, carpets.

Ku·ban′ (kōō·bän′; *Russ.* kōō·bán′y′). **1** *anc.* **Hyp′a·nis** (hïp′ȧ·nĭs). River 512 m. long in region NW of Caucasus Mts., SE Soviet Russia, Europe; rises in the Caucasus in Georgian S.S.R., flows N and NW into a wide marshy delta with three mouths—two on the Sea of Azov and one on the Black Sea; navigable for less than 100 m.; its main headstream rises on slopes of Mt. Elborus.
2 Former government of SE Russia, NE of the Black Sea; since the Revolution has been reorganized into Krasnodar Territory and several autonomous regions.

Ku·ban′go (kōō·bäng′gō). = OKOVANGGO.

Ku′ben·sko·e, Lake (kōō′byĕn·skŭ·yĕ). Lake ab. 40 m. long, W cen. Vologda Region, Soviet Russia, Europe; outlet the Sukhona river, a tributary of the Northern Dvina; connected by canal with the Sheksna river, thus joining the Northern Dvina and the Leningrad-Volga systems (see MARIINSK CANAL SYSTEM).

Ku′cha′ (kōō′chŭ′) *or* **Ku′che′** (-chŭ′). Town and oasis, W cen. Sinkiang, W China, S of Tien Shan range on early Silk Road (*q.v.*) and midway bet. Aqsu and Qara Shahr on modern caravan and motor highway; pop. ab. 15,000; an old city, apparently an early Aryan colony; praised by travelers for its wealth and productiveness; in medieval times under the Uigurs.

Kuchan. See QUCHAN.

Ku′cheng′tze′ (kōō′chŭng′dzō′) *or* **Ki′tai′** (chï′tï′). Town, cen. Sinkiang, W China, ab. 85 m. E of Urumchi, on N highway from Qomul to Urumchi.

Ku′ching (kōō′chïng) *or* **Sa·ra′wak** (sȧ·rä′wäk, -wä). Seaport, ✳ of Sarawak, Borneo, on Sarawak river ab. 10 m. from its mouth; pop. ab. 30,000; has considerable trade, with weekly steamer service to Singapore. Seized by Japanese Dec. 26, 1941.

Ku·chuk′ Kai′nar·ji′ (kü·chük′ kï′när·jï′); *Romanian* **Cai·nar′gea-Mi′că** (kï·när′jä·mē′kȧ). Village, Bulgaria, a few miles SE of Silistra; scene of treaty July 21, 1774, terminating Russo-Turkish War, by which Russia gained: (1) territory on the Bug and Kuban rivers and Kerch on the Crimea (*q.v.*); (2) freedom for Russian shipping on Black Sea; (3) right of intervention in Danubian Principalities; (4) protection of Orthodox Christians in Ottoman Empire.

Ku·da·ma·tsu (kōō·dä·mä·tsōō). City, Yamaguchi prefecture, SW Honshu, Japan, 53 m. E of Shimonoseki on N shore of Inland Sea; pop. 34,045; oil refineries.

Ku′dat (kōō′dät). Town, N Brit. North Borneo, on W side of Marudu Bay near N tip of island of Borneo.

Kudus. See KOEDOES.

Ku·dym′kar *or* **Ku·dim′kar** (kōō·dïm′kẽr). Town, ✳ of Komi-Permiak National District, Soviet Russia, Asia, on a tributary of the Kama river 100 m. NW of Molotov, Soviet Russia, Asia.

Kuenlun Shan. See KUNLUN SHAN.

Kufa, Al. See AL KUFA.

Kufara. See Oases of CUFRA.

Ku′fow′ (chü′fōō′) *or* **Chü′fou′** (chü′fōō′). Town, W Shantung prov., NE China, ab. 65 m. S of Tsinan and near the Tientsin-Pukow railroad. Residence of Confucius during most of his life and of his descendants (K′ung family) to the present day; 1 m. N is cemetery (600 acres) containing tomb of Confucius and graves of thousands of his descendants. Town has great Confucian temple; original small structure built 478 B.C., but has been rebuilt or renovated by successive emperors.

Kufra. See Oases of CUFRA.

Kuft. Var. of QIFT.

Kuh (kōō′h). Var. of KOH—Persian word for "mountain."

Kuh-i-Alwand. See Mount ALWAND.

Kuh′i·stan′ (kōō′hē·stän′). Former province in E cen. Iran, now a district of Kerman prov.

Kui′by·shev (kōō′ĭ·bĭ·shĕf; *Angl.* kwē′bĭ·shĕf). **1** Town, W Novosibirsk Region, Soviet Russia, Asia, just N of the Trans-Siberian R.R. 190 m. W of Novosibirsk.
2 *before 1935* **Sa·ma′ra** (sŭ·má′rá; *Angl.* sȧ·mär′ȧ). City and river port, ✻ of Kuibyshev Region, Soviet Russia, Europe, on left bank of Volga at loop where it reaches farthest point E and where Samara river joins it, 550 m. SE of Moscow; pop. 390,267; university (founded 1919); a trading center since end of 18th cent. with the Kirgiz Steppe region and cities of Turkistan. Established 1586; scene of Pugachev's rebellion against Catherine II 1774; in World War II became temporary capital of U.S.S.R. Oct. 16, 1941 when Moscow was threatened by German advance.
Kui′by·shev·ka (kōō′ĭ·bĭ·shĕf·kȧ; *Angl.* kwē′bĭ·shĕf′-kȧ); *formerly* **Boch·ka·re′vo** (bŭch·kŭ·rô′vŭ). Town, Khabarovsk Territory, E Siberia, Soviet Russia, Asia, just NE of Blagoveshchensk; junction point on Trans-Siberian R.R. for Blagoveshchensk.
Kuibyshev Region. Region, E Soviet Russia, Europe, at bend of middle Volga; 33,582 sq. m.; pop. 2,767,562; ✻ Kuibyshev; traversed by the Volga which here makes great bend to the E; tableland region W of river, flat steppes to E. Chief occupations stock raising and agriculture; has rich soil but because of scant rainfall often suffers from bad harvest and famine as in 1921. Chief cities Kuibyshev, Syzran, and Chapaevsk.
Kuisui. Var. of KWEISUI.
Ku′iu (kōō′yōō). Island, SE Alaska, W of Kupreanof I. and separated from Baranof I. by Chatham Strait.
Ku·ju (kōō·jōō) *or* **Ku·ju·san** (-sän). Mountain 5866 ft., Oita prefecture, NE Kyushu, Japan.
Ku′ka (kōō′kȧ) *or* **Ku′ka·wa** (-wä). Town, Bornu prov., NE Northern Region, Nigeria, near W edge of Lake Chad; formerly a populous town and capital of a native Bornu kingdom.
Ku′ke·na′äm (?kōō′kĕ·nä′äm). Mountain 8620 ft., W British Guiana; near Roraima and like it is flat-topped; has a waterfall 2000 ft. high.
Ku′kës (kōō′kĕs); *also* **Kuk′si** (kōōk′sĕ). Town, ✻ of Kosova prefecture, NE Albania, on Drin river E of Shkodër.
Ku′kong′ (kōō′kông′; *Chin.* chü′jĭ·äng′); *formerly* **Shiu′chow′** (shĭ·ōō′jō′). City, N Kwangtung, SE China, 125 m. N of Canton on Peh river; pop. ab. 40,000; trading and coal-mining center. Captured by Japanese Jan. 31, 1945.
Kuku–khoto. Mongol name of KWEISUI.
Ku′kum (kōō′kōōm). Village on NW coast of Guadalcanal I., SE Solomon Is., W Pacific, just W of Lunga Point; used 1942 by Japanese as landing base, then by Americans as naval operating base.
Ku′ku Nor (kōō′kōō nôr′). = *Koko Nor:* see TSING HAI.
Ku·la′ (kōō·lä′). Town, Manisa vilayet, W Turkey in Asia, near the Gediz river ab. 15 m. N of Alaşehir; pop. 8612; rugmaking.
Ku′la Gulf (kōō′lä). Body of water 17 m. long by ab. 10 m. wide, bet. NW New Georgia I. and Kolombangara I. in the Solomon Is.; closed by small Arundel I. at SW. Scene of two Japanese-American naval engagements July 5 and 13, 1943, both victories for Americans.
Ku′la·ma′dau (kōō′lȧ·mä′dou). Village, port of Bonagai and chief settlement on Woodlark I. (*q.v.*) in Solomon Sea.
Ku′lam·bang′a·ra (kōō′läm·băng′ȧ·rȧ). Var. of KoLOMBANGARA.
Ku′lang′su′ (kōō′läng′shü′). See AMOY.
Kul′di·ga (kōōl′dĭ·gä); *Ger.* **Gol′ding·en** (gôl′dĭng·ĕn). **1** Administrative district, cen. Kurzeme prov., W Latvia, U.S.S.R.; 1211 sq. m.
2 Town in district, on Venta river 80 m. W of Riga; pop. (1935) 7180; varied manufactures.
Kul′dja *or* **Kul′ja** (kōōl′jä); *Chin.* **I′ning′** (ē′nĭng′); *also formerly* **Ning′yuan′** (nĭng′yü·än′). Town, NW

Sinkiang, W China, on Ili river 320 m. W of Urumchi; pop. ab. 15,000; in mountain region bet. the Tien Shan and the Ala Tau ranges; chief crops cereals; formerly an important trade center and still connected by routes to Issyk Kul and Alma Ata in U.S.S.R. Seized by Russia in 1871, but restored by treaty 1881.
Ku′li·ko′vo (kōō′lĭ·kō′vō; *Russ.* kōō·lyĭ·kô′vŭ). Plain in E Tula Region, Soviet Russia, Europe, near source of the Don; battle Sept. 8, 1380 in which Dimitri Donskoi and Russian princes decisively defeated the Tatars.
Ku′ling′ (gōō′lĭng′). Village, N Kiangsi prov., SE China, in mountains 13 m. S of Kiukiang; alt. 3500 ft.; pop. ab. 2000; best known summer resort in cen. China Proper, with superb scenery and healthful climate.
Kulja. See KULDJA.
Kulm. See CHEŁMNO.
Kulm′bach (kōōlm′bäk). City, Bavaria, Germany, on Main river 13 m. NNW of Bayreuth; pop. 11,874; 15th-cent. Gothic church, 17th-cent. baroque monastery; 13th-cent. Plassenburg (Hohenzollern fort) overlooks city; noted chiefly for its beer. First mentioned 966 A.D.; passed to Prussia 1791, to Bavaria 1810.
Kulmsee. See CHEŁMŻA.
Kulpa. See KUPA.
Kulp′mont (kŭlp′mŏnt). Borough, Northumberland co., E cen. Pennsylvania, 17 m. WNW of Pottsville; pop. 4288; founded 1875; coal mines.
Kultepe. See KANISH.
Ku′lu (kōō′lōō). Valley, N Punjab state, NW Indian Union, in Himalayas SE of Chamba; forms mountain basin of upper Beas river; chief town Sultanpur (alt. 4584 ft.); higher villages at 9000 ft.; in ancient times a Rajput principality.
Kulun. See URGA.
Kulun Nor. = HULUN NOR.
Ku·lyab′ (kōō·lyȧb′). Town, SW Tadzhik S.S.R., Soviet Central Asia, in mountains N of the Amu Darya and ab. 55 m. SE of Stalinabad; chief town of Kulyab Region.
Kulyab Region. Subdivision of Tadzhik S.S.R. in SW part, Soviet Central Asia.
Kum. See QUM.
Ku·ma′ (kōō·mä′). River ab. 400 m. long, SE Soviet Russia, Europe; rises in Stavropol Territory, flows E to the Caspian Sea, reaching the sea only in flood season; its lower course forms part of boundary bet. Astrakhan and Grozny Regions.
Ku·ma·ga·ya (kōō·mä·gä·yä). Town, Saitama prefecture, SE cen. Honshu, Japan, 35 m. NW of Tokyo; pop. (1945) 56,505; trades in cocoons, textiles, and grain.
Ku·ma·mo·to (kōō·mä·mô·tô). **1** Prefecture of Japan. See *Table* at JAPAN.
2 City, its ✻, Kyushu I., on Shirakawa river near its mouth on the W coast and in an extensive plain; pop. (1945 est.) 181,128; founded in 16th cent. at time of building of its great castle; confiscated 1632 and given to the daimio Hosokawa, whose family retained town and castle until 1868. During feudal period the castle was one of strongest in all Japan; partly destroyed 1877. Town has a Buddhist temple that attracts many pilgrims.
Ku·ma·no Sea (kōō·mä·nô). Inlet of W Pacific Ocean on S coast of Honshu, Japan, SW of Totomi Sea.
Ku′ma·no·vo (kōō′mä·nô·vô). Town, N Macedonia, S Yugoslavia, 15 m. NE of Skoplje; pop. 16,949; trade center, esp. in fruits, liquor, and cattle; battlefield 1912 where Serbians defeated the Turks; occupied 1941 by Bulgarians.
Ku·maon′ (kōō·moun′). Var. of KUMAUN.
Ku·ma′ra (kōō·mär′ȧ). River ab. 230 m. long, N Manchuria; flows E into Amur river N of the Ilkuri Shan.
Ku·ma′si (kōō·mä′sĭ); *formerly* **Coo·mas′sie** (kōō-mäs′ĭ). City, cen. Ghana, formerly ✻ of Ashanti colony, W Africa, 118 m. NW of Accra; pop. 35,829, (1942 est.) 43,413; connected by rail with Accra and Takoradi; a commercial center with modern buildings, roads,

schools. Capital of tribe which in 18th cent. became leading Ashanti people and established Ashanti confederation or kingdom (see ASHANTI); first entered by British under Wolseley 1874 during Second Ashanti War; captured by Sir Francis Scott 1896 in Fourth Ashanti War; as capital of British protectorate, besieged by natives in rising Apr.–July 1900.

Ku·maun' (kŏō·moun'). Division, N Uttar Pradesh N Indian Union; 13,757 sq. m.; pop. (1941) 1,581,262; administrative headquarters Naini Tal.

Kum'ba·ko'nam (kŏōm'bȧ·kŏ'năm) or **Com'ba·co'num** (kŏm'bȧ·kŏ'nŭm). City, SE Madras, S Indian Union, 22 m. NE of Tanjore; pop. (1941) 67,008; has metal and silk industries; a stronghold of Brahmanism, one of southern India's most famed temple cities with splendid pagodas, gopuras, and tanks; every twelve years scene of festival of purification held in the temple lake, attended by thousands of pilgrims. Once capital of the Chola kingdom.

Ku·me (kŏō·mě). Small island of Okinawa group, S Ryukyu Is., Japan, ab. 55 m. W of Naha; seized by U.S. forces June 1945 in Okinawa campaign.

Kumilla. See COMILLA.

Kum Ka·le' (kŏōm' kä·lě'). Turkish fort on S side of Dardanelles at its W end, Turkey in Asia; scene of action in World War I when its guns were silenced by British fleet and landings made by French Apr. 1915.

Ku'mon Range (kŏō'mŏn). Mountain range in N Burma, E of Hukawng valley; source of Chindwin river.

Ku'mu·ka'hi, Cape (kŏō'mŏō·kä'hě). Cape on E extremity of Hawaii I., Hawaii.

Ku'na Peak (kŏō'nȧ). Mountain 12,951 ft. in Sierra Nevada, E Tuolumne co., cen. California.

Ku·nar' (kŏō·när'). The lower course of the Chitral river in E Afghanistan.

Ku·na·shi·ri (kŏō·nä·shě·rě). One of the Kuril Is. (q.v.); the second in size and the one nearest Hokkaido, Japan.

Kunchinjunga. Var. of KANCHENJUNGA.

Kun'dar (kŏōn'där). River in NE Baluchistan; flows NE into Gumal river, in its lower course forming a section of the Baluchistan-Afghanistan boundary.

Kun·duz' (kŏōn·dŏōz'). **1** River ab. 225 m. long, NE Afghanistan; flows N from Hindu Kush Mts. to Amu Darya and forms in part W boundary of Badakhshan. **2** Town and former khanate, E of the river.

Kuneitra, El. See EL KUNEITRA.

Kunene. See CUNENE.

Kunersdorf. See KUNOWICE.

Kung'hit Island (kŭng'hĭt). Southern island of the Queen Charlotte Is. off W Brit. Columbia, W Canada.

Kun·grad' (kŏōn·grät'). Town, Kara Kalpak A.S.S.R., Soviet Central Asia, in delta of Amu Darya; pop. 3000; on caravan and motor highway trade routes.

Kun'gur or **Qun'gur** (kŏōn'gŏōr). Mountain 25,146 ft., W Sinkiang, China, SW of Kashgar; highest point in Muztagh Ata Range.

Kun·gur' (kŏōn·gŏōr'). Town, SE Molotov Region, Soviet Russia, Europe (politically, in Asia; see SIBERIA), at foot of W slope of Ural Mts. on railroad ab. 50 m. SSE of Molotov; pop. 19,803; center of an agricultural district, rich also in gypsum and kaolin; handles large amount of local trade and is noted throughout Russia for its leather goods. Founded in middle of 17th cent.; scene of much tribal conflict; because of its favorable location early became important in trade with Far East.

Kun'he'gyes (kŏōn'hě'dyěsh). Commune, E Hungary, ab. 10 m. NW of Karcag; pop. 11,685.

Ku'nie (kŏō'nyä); Fr. **Île des Pins** (ēl' dā păn'); Eng. **Isle of Pines** (īl' ŭv pīnz'). Island in SW Pacific Ocean, 32 m. SE of S end of New Caledonia I.; 62 sq. m.; pop. ab. 1500; used as French convict station, attached to New Caledonia territory.

Kun'lun', or **Kuen'lun', Shan** (kŏōn'lŏōn' shän'). Mountain ranges (shan), cen. Asia, on N edge of Tibetan plateau and S of Sinkiang, extending from Pamirs and Karakoram Range on W to SE Tsinghai and lesser ranges in cen. China (W China Proper); highest Ulugh Muztagh 25,340 ft.; has many subsidiary ranges.

Kun'ming' (kŏōn'mǐng'); formerly **Yun·nan'** (yŏō-năn'; Chin. yün'nän'). City, ✱ of Yunnan prov., S China, in E part of province 380 m. SW of Chungking; pop. ab. 90,000; chief city of SW China, advantageously situated on fertile plain at elevation of 6400 ft. on N shore of a large lake (Tien); as a trade center exports tin, precious stones, furs, tea, salt, and has increased in importance since opening 1910 as terminus of railroad to Tonkin, Indochina; a cen. station on the Burma Road (q.v.). In World War II of great importance as transportation center, American air base, and Chinese military headquarters; frequently bombed by Japanese.

Ku'no·wi'ce (kŏō'nō·vē'tsě); Ger. **Ku'ners·dorf** (kŏō'něrs·dôrf). Village, W Poznań dept., W Poland, 4 m. E of Frankfurt; pop. (1946) 1372; formerly in Brandenburg, Germany; battle of Kunersdorf fought here Aug. 12, 1759, during Seven Years' War, in which Frederick the Great suffered ruinous defeat by Russians and Austrians.

Kunsan. See GUNZAN.

Kun'szent·már'ton (kŏōn'sěnt·mär'tŏn). Commune, SE Hungary, on Körös river N of Csongrád; pop. 11,251.

Kun'to (kŏōn'tŭ). Lake, NW Karelia, U.S.S.R.; its outlet is Kem river.

Ku·nu'a (kŏō·nŏō'ȧ). Settlement on NW coast of Bougainville I., NW Solomon Is., W Pacific Ocean.

Kuo'la·yar'vi; Finnish Kuo'la·jär'vi (kwô'lȧ·yär'vǐ). Town, NW Karelia, U.S.S.R., on railroad from Kemi to Kandalaksha; pop. 6016; in region ceded by Finland to Russia 1940.

Kuo'pio (kwô'pyô). **1** Department of Finland. See Table at FINLAND.
2 City, its ✱, S Finland, on W shore of Lake Kallavesi; pop. (1939 est.) 25,100; lumber center; sawmills, match factories.

Ku'pa (kŏō'pä) or **Kul'pa** (kŏōl'pä). River ab. 235 m. long, Croatia, NW Yugoslavia, flowing E into Sava river.

Kupang. See KOEPANG.

Kup'fer·dreh' (kŏōp'fěr·drä'). Former commune (pop. 13,390), Düsseldorf govt. dist., Rhine Province, Prussia, Germany; since 1929 part of Essen (q.v.).

Ku'pre·a'nof (kŏō'prě·ä'nôf; -ăn'ôf). Island, E Alexander Archipelago, SE Alaska; chief town Kake.

Ku·pyansk' (kŏō·pyänsk'). Town, E Kharkov Region, NE Ukraine, U.S.S.R., on Oskol river 60 m. E of Kharkov; railroad junction point.

Ku·ra' (kŏō·rä'); anc. **Cy'rus** (sī'rŭs). River 825 m. long, the largest river of Transcaucasia; rises in NE Turkey (where it is called **Ko·ra'** [kô·rä']) in mountains NW of Kars, flows N into Georgia then ESE through Azerbaidzhan to the Caspian Sea S of Baku. Has large delta, just above which it is joined by its largest tributary the Araks from the S; the largest on the N is the Alazan. Fed by many mountain streams and has rapid current in upper course; furnishes hydroelectric power at Tiflis.

Kuramba, Mount. See Mount KOROMBA.

Kur'di·stan' (kŏōr'dǐ·stän'; Angl. kûr'dǐ·stăn'). Mountainous country with indefinite boundaries forming a nonpolitical region in SE Turkey in Asia, and in adjoining areas of NW Iran and NE Iraq, inhabited by Kurds; ab. 74,000 sq. m.; pop. est. at 1,500,000 to 2,500,000; lies chiefly in Turkey S of Armenia and N of the Tigris, extending from the Euphrates on W to the mountains of Iran W of Hamadan and including Lake Van; chief towns Diyarbekir, Bitlis, and Van in Turkey, Mosul and Kirkuk in Iraq, and Kermanshah in Iran. There are also many Kurds in Soviet Armenia. A Kurdish autonomous state was provided for in Treaty of Sèvres 1920 but terms never carried out.

Ku′re (kŏŏr′ĕ; kōō′rä; *Jap.* kōō·rĕ). City, Hiroshima prefecture, SW Honshu, Japan, on N shore of Inland Sea at its W end, 12 m. SE of Hiroshima; pop. (1945 est.) 152,184; has fine, spacious harbor and is one of the large naval stations of Japan; dockyard, arsenal, steel factories, and a naval academy. Bombed by Allies 1945.

Ku′re (kōō′rä), *or* **O′cean** (ō′shăn), **Island.** Uninhabited islet of Leeward Is., Hawaiian Is., in cen. Pacific Ocean ab. 1500 m. NW of Niihau; 500 acres; included in state of Hawaii and in Hawaiian Islands Bird Reservation.

Ku′res·sa′re (kōō′rĕs·sä′rĕ); *Estonian* **Ku′res·saa′re** (kōō′rĕs·sä′rĕ); *Ger.* **A′rens·burg** (ä′rĕns·bŏŏrK). Seaport on S shore of Sarema I., * of Saare prov., W Estonia, U.S.S.R.; pop. (1937) 4675; seaside resort; in World War I held by Germans 1917–18 and by Bolsheviks 1918–19; in World War II held by Germans.

Kurg. See Coorg.

Kur·gan′ (kŏŏr·gän′). City, * of Kurgan Region, Soviet Russia, Asia, on Trans-Siberian R.R. 140 m. E of Chelyabinsk; pop. 53,224; on the Tobol river in a rich agricultural plain E of the Urals; trade center for farm products, esp. butter, cattle, and grain; machine shops, mills, and factories. In a region long settled; its name means "tumulus" or "barrow" and it is so called from the many ancient burial mounds in the vicinity.

Kurgan Region. Newly formed region of Soviet Russia, Asia, established during World War II out of E half of Chelyabinsk Region; * Kurgan; bounded on E and S by Kazakh S.S.R.

Kur·gan′ Tyu·be′ (kŏŏr·gän′ tü·bĕ′; *Russ.* kŏŏr·gän′ tyŏō·byĕ′). Town, SW Tadzhik S.S.R., Soviet Central Asia, on left bank of Vaksh river 40 m. S of Stalinabad.

Ku′ri·a Mu′ri·a Islands (kŏŏr′ĭ·à mŏŏr′ĭ·à). Group of five rocky islets in the Arabian Sea off SW coast of Oman, bet. Capes Nus and Sharbatat, SE Arabia; 28 sq. m.; pop. ab. 2200; attached to Persian Gulf Residency. Largest is Hallaniya. Ceded by the sultan of Masqat to Great Britain 1854 for a cable station.

Ku·ri·ha·ma (kōō·rĕ·hä·mä). Small coastal town, Kanagawa prefecture, SE Honshu, Japan, ab. 1 m. S of Uraga; place where Commodore Perry landed to meet the representative of the shogunate 1853.

Ku′ril, *or* **Ku′rile, Islands** (kŏŏ′rēl; -rĭl; kŏŏ·rēl′); *also* **Ku′rils** *or* **Ku′riles** (kŏŏ′rēlz; -rĭlz; kŏŏ·rēlz′); *Jap.* **Chi·shi·ma Ret·to** (chĕ·shĕ·mä rĕt·tō). Group of ab. 32 islands extending 730 m. N and S bet. S tip of Kam-

KURIL ISLANDS
(U.S.S.R.)
Statute Miles
0   100   200

chatka Penin. to NE coast of island of Hokkaido, Japan, off E coast of Asia; 3960 sq. m.; pop. (1945) 6000; ad-

ministratively a former province of Hokkaido prefecture, Japan. The 8 most important islands, named from N to S, are Shumushu, Paramushiro, Onnekotan, Shasukotan, Shimushiru, Uruppu, Etorofu, Shikotan (SE of Kunashiri), and Kunashiri. All islands of volcanic origin, some having active volcanoes today; highest point on Araito I. 7674 ft.; many peaks bet. 3000 and 6000 ft.; no really good harbors; only a few islands inhabited, some aboriginal Ainus still found. Islands discovered 1634 by Dutch navigator Martin de Vries; N part of chain occupied by Russians in 18th cent.; given to Japan 1875 in exchange for N Sakhalin I.; after end of World War II, returned to Russia Sept. 1945.

Kuril, *or* **Kurile, Strait;** *Jap.* **Chi·shi·ma Kai·kyo** (chĕ·shĕ·mä kī·kyō). Channel ab. 7 m. wide, separating Kuril Is. from S end of Kamchatka Penin. (Cape Lopatka) and connecting the sea of Okhotsk with Bering Sea.

Ku–ring′–gai (kōō·rĭng′gī). City, E New South Wales, SE Australia, N suburb of Sydney; pop. 27,937.

Ku′ri·sche Neh′rung (kōō′rĭ·shĕ nā′rŏŏng). Long spit of land separating the Kurishes Gaf from the Baltic Sea; now in U.S.S.R., formerly in East Prussia, Germany.

Ku′ri·shes Gaf (kōō′rĭ·shĕs häf); *Ger.* **Ku′ri·sches Haff** (kōō′rĭ·shĕs häf). Lagoon, an inlet of the Baltic Sea in the U.S.S.R.; 625 sq. m.; N part in Lithuania (see Memel), S part in Kaliningradsk Region, R.S.F.S.R.; receives the Neman (Memel) river.

Kur′la (kŏŏr′lä). Town, cen. Sinkiang, W China, on N edge of Takla Makan desert and just SW of Qara Shahr and Bagrach Kol; a junction point on early Silk Road and on modern N highway.

Kur′la (kŏŏr′lä). Town, W Maharashtra, W India, suburb 8 m. NNE of Bombay; pop. 30,311.

Kur′land *or* **Cour′land** (kŏŏr′länd). **1** Former Russian government on E Baltic shore, now constituting Kurzeme and Zemgale provs. of Latvia. See Baltic Provinces. In 1237, duchy, inhabited by Lettish people, Cours or Kurs, conquered by Teutonic Knights; given up to Poland and Lithuania and transformed into duchy under Polish suzerainty 1561; after 1737 its duke in close relation to Russian throne; placed self under Russian rule 1795; scene of bitter campaigns of Germans against Russians 1914–15; became part of Latvia (*q.v.*) 1918. **2** The modern province of Kurzeme, Latvia.

Kurna. = Al Qurna.

Kur·nool′ (kĕr·nōōl′). Town, W Andhra Pradesh, S Indian Union, on Tungabhadra river 240 m. NW of Madras; pop. 35,314; trade center with manufactures of cotton cloth and carpets; has remains of old Hindu fort.

Kuroshio. See Japan Current.

Kur′ram (kŏŏr′ăm). **1** River ab. 200 m. long, NW Pakistan; rises in the Safed Koh, flows E and SE in North-West Frontier Province to the Indus river W of Mianwali.

2 Former agency, North-West Frontier Province, Pakistan, W of Kohat; 739 sq. m.; pop. 63,352; comprises beautiful valley of Kurram river S of the Safed Koh, inhabited chiefly by Turi.

Kursk (kŏŏrsk). City, * of Kursk Region, Soviet Russia, Europe, in cen. part, on N bank of Seim river; pop. 119,972; main railroad center of the region; before World War I had important annual fair; has developed some local industries and is a trade and agricultural center. Taken by Germans 1941; a front-line stronghold 1942, but recovered by Russians Jan. 8, 1943.

Kursk Region. Region, S cen. Soviet Russia, Europe, in cen. Russian plateau; 21,153 sq. m.; pop. 3,130,114; * Kursk; bounded on S by Kharkov Region of the Ukraine, and on the W by Sumy Region, Ukraine; crossed by Seim river and is source of Donets and tributaries of Donets and Dnieper. In N part of black-earth (chernozem) area, produces crops of rye and oats, also some sugar beets, wheat, millet, potatoes; has forests in N. Lack of educational facilities, poor transportation, World War I, and famine of 1921 retarded its progress.

Ku·ru·man (kŏŏ′rŏŏ·män). Town, British Bechuanaland, N Cape Province, S Union of South Africa, just SE of the Kalahari Desert, ab. 120 m. NW of Kimberley; pop. 2596; mission station of Robert Moffat 1825 ff.; nearby in a dolomite cave is a spring yielding 5 million gallons of water a day; it is the source of the **Kuruman River** which formerly flowed W into the Molopo river but has disappeared over most of its lower course in S part of the Kalahari Desert (see also MOLOPO).

Ku·ru·me (kŏŏ·rŏŏ·mĕ). City, Fukuoka prefecture, N Kyushu, Japan, 55 m. NE of Nagasaki; pop. (1945) 75,778; a military station; known widely for its chief industrial product Kurume-Gasuri, a durable blue-figured cotton fabric.

Ku·ru·ne′ga·la (kŏŏr′ŏŏ·nĕg′à·là). Town, ✱ of North-Western Province, in SE part, W Ceylon, 52 m. NE of Colombo; pop. 10,467; trade and distribution center for important agricultural region growing rice, coconuts, tea, coffee, and cacao beans.

Kurusku. See KOROSKO.

Kur′ze·me (kŏŏr′zĕ·mĕ) or **Kur′land** (kŏŏr′lănd). Province, W Latvia, U.S.S.R., along coast of Baltic Sea and SW shore of Gulf of Riga; 5099 sq. m.; pop. (1938 est.) 297,453; ✱ Lepaya; includes the administrative districts of Aizpute, Kuldiga, Lepaya, Talsi, Ventspils. Chiefly lowland, drained by Venta river; chief occupations agriculture and livestock raising. Often a battlefield in World War I; ceded to Germany by Treaty of Brest Litovsk 1918; became a part of newly organized Latvia 1918; Bolshevik forces driven out Oct. 1919.

Kuş′a·da·sı or **Kush A·da·si′** (kŏŏsh′ä·dä·sĭ′). Seaport on Kuşadası Gulf, İzmir vilayet, W Turkey in Asia, 40 m. S of İzmir and near ruins of Ephesus; pop. 5843.

Kuşadası Gulf. Inlet of E Aegean Sea on W coast of Turkey in Asia, NE of island of Samos; extends inland ab. 45 m., average width 20 m.

Ku·sai′e (kŏŏ·sī′à). Island ab. 9 m. long and 6 m. wide in E part of the Caroline Is., W Pacific Ocean 330 m. ESE of Ponape I.; has several mountains (highest 2064 ft.) and two good harbors, esp. Lele on E coast; well provided with timber sought for shipbuilding. Bombed by Americans but left in Japanese control 1942–44.

Kush. See CUSH.

Ku·shi·ro (kŏŏ·shĕ·rŏ). Seaport, Hokkaido prefecture, on SE coast of Hokkaido I., Japan; pop. (1945) 50,652; exports sulfur and lumber.

Kushk (kŏŏshk). Town, NW Afghanistan, 40 m. N of Herat and N of Paropamisus Mountain range; on the **Kushk River** (see KUSHKA) ab. 30 m. from the Russian frontier post of Kushka.

Kush′ka (kŏŏsh′kà; Russ. kŏŏsh′kȧ). Russian military post and railhead, SE Turkmen S.S.R., on Afghan border 66 m. N of Herat; on the **Kushka River** (Kushk in Afghanistan), ab. 135 m. long, a tributary of the Murgab.

Kusi. See KOSI.

Ku′si·ya′ra (kŏŏ′sĭ·yä′rä). River, S branch of the Surma, chiefly in Sylhet dist., East Bengal, Pakistan; flows W to the Meghna on Bengal border.

Kus′ko·kwim (kŭs′kŏ·kwĭm). River ab. 550 m. long, SW Alaska, S of the Yukon; flows SW to **Kuskokwim Bay,** an inlet of Bering Sea; its two upper tributaries North Fork and South Fork rise in Alaska Range near Mt. McKinley National Park.

Küs′nacht (küs′näкt). Commune, Zurich canton, Switzerland, on Lake of Zurich just SSE of Zurich; pop. 6084.

Küss′nacht (küs′näкt). Village, Schwyz canton, Switzerland, at NE corner of Lake of Lucerne just E of Lucerne; pop. (1930) 4430; nearby is scene, according to legend, of William Tell's shooting of Gessler.

Ku·sta·nai′ (kŏŏ·stŭ·nī′). Town, ✱ of Kustanai Region, Kazakh S.S.R., Soviet Central Asia, in N part on left bank of Tobol river 170 m. E of Magnitogorsk; on

railroad from Troitsk; market for grains of surrounding fertile black-earth area; industrial center of rapid growth, with electric plants, flour mills, leather manufactories. Established 1871.

Kustanai Region. Subdivision of Kazakh S.S.R., Soviet Central Asia, in N part; ✱ Kustanai; bounded by Kurgan Region of the R.S.F.S.R. on N, by North Kazakhstan, Kokchetav, and Akmolinsk Regions on E, by Karaganda Region on S, and by Aktyubinsk Region of the Kazakh S.S.R. and Chkalov and Chelyabinsk Regions of the R.S.F.S.R. on W.

Küstendil. See KYUSTENDIL.

Küstenja. See CONSTANȚA.

Kü′sten·land (küs′tĕn·länt′); Eng. **Coast′land′** (kōst′lănd′). Former administrative district (province) of Austria, including the crownlands Istria and Görz and Gradisca, now largely in NW Yugoslavia.

Küstrin. See KOSTRZYN.

Kut (kŏŏt). **1** Province (liwa), SE Iraq; pop. (1935 est.) 138,200.

2 Short for KUT-AL-IMARA.

Kut or **Ko Kut** (kō kŏŏt). Island (Thai ko) in NE Gulf of Siam off SE coast of Thailand.

Kü′tah·ya′ or **Ku′ta·iah′** (kü′tä·yä′). **1** Vilayet, W Turkey in Asia; 5564 sq. m.; pop. 347,682.

2 Commercial town, its ✱, on railroad 65 m. SE of Bursa; pop. 17,939.

Kutai, Kutei. Vars. of Koetai: see MAHAKAM.

Ku·ta′i·si (kŏŏ·tä′ĭ·sĭ) or **Ku·ta·is′** (kŏŏ·tŭ·ēs′; Angl. kŏŏ·tīs′). City, W Georgia, U.S.S.R., on both banks of Rion river ab. 65 m. NE of Batum; pop. 81,479; on a branch of the Tiflis-Poti railroad, an important trading center, with tobacco and textile factories; produces coal; much fruit raised in vicinity. Chief town, under the name Ae′a (ē′à), of ancient Colchis; later capital of Imeritia; occupied by Russians 1773; suffered much in wars bet. Persians, Mongols, Turks, and Russians.

Kut–al–I·ma′ra or **Kut–el–A·ma′ra** (kŏŏt′ăl[ĕl]·à-mär′à; Arab. kŏŏt′äl·à·mä′rŏ). Town, SE cen. Iraq, on the Tigris 100 m. SE of Baghdad; pop. ab. 6000; has some importance as a grain market. Captured by British after battle of Sept. 28, 1915; besieged by Turks from Dec. 8, 1915 until they finally forced British surrender Apr. 29, 1916; recaptured by new British expeditionary force under Gen. Maude Feb. 23, 1917. Cf. ʿAMARA.

Kutaraja or **Kuta Raja.** See KOETARADJA.

Kutch. See CUTCH.

Kutenai. = KOOTENAY.

Kut′ná Ho′ra (kŏŏt′nä hô′rȧ); Ger. **Kut′ten·berg** (kŏŏt′ĕn·bĕrк). Town, E cen. Bohemia prov., W Czechoslovakia, 45 m. SE of Prague; pop. (1930) 13,900; built up near silver mines, worked from 13th cent.; suffered during severe fighting of the Hussite struggles 1420–33 and the Thirty Years' War 1618–48; the flooding of the mines aided its decline.

Kut′no (kŏŏt′nô). Commune, Warszawa dept., Poland, 71 m. W of Warsaw; pop. (1938–39 est.) 25,113; railroad junction; manufactures textiles, sugar; produces grain. Scene of German defeat of Russians Nov. 1914, in the battle for control of Łódź; in World War II scene of capture of Polish army by Germans Sept. 15, 1939.

Kutoardyo. See KOETOARDJO.

Kuttenberg. See KUTNÁ HORA.

Kutz′town (kŏŏts′toun). Borough, Berks co., SE Pennsylvania, 15 m. NE of Reading; pop. 3312; founded 1771; manufactures textiles, foundry products; Kutztown State College (1860; coed.).

Ku·wait′ (kŏŏ·wīt′; -wät′) or **Ku·weit′**; also **Ko·weit′** (kō·wīt′; -wät′). **1** Principality, NW coast of Persian Gulf, forming wedge of desert territory bet. Iraq and Saudi Arabia; 6178 sq. m.; pop. 468,389; ✱ Al Kuwait; has trade in pearls, wool, horses, and, recently, in oil. At Al Kuwait important caravan routes converge. Ruled by descendants of a dynasty founded in 18th cent.; independence under British protection recognized

by Great Britain 1914; oil discovered 1938; became fully independent of Great Britain June 1961. See BUBIYAN and BAHREIN ISLANDS.
2 Seaport. See AL KUWAIT.

Ku·wa·na (kōō·wä·nä). Coastal city, Mie prefecture S Honshu, Japan, ab. 15 m. SW of Nagoya near mouth of Kiso river; pop. (1945) 28,952; in rice-growing area.

Kuweit. See KUWAIT.

Kuy′by·shev (kōō′ǐ·bǐ·shĕf; *Angl.* kwē′bǐ·shĕf). = KUI-BYSHEV.

Ku′yun·jik′ (kōō′yōŏn·jǐk′). Mound on E bank of the Tigris, N Iraq, the site of ancient Nineveh (*q.v.*); discovered 1820, excavations begun by Layard 1845.

Kuz′bas *or* **Kuz′bass** (kōōz′băs; *Russ.* kōōz·bás′). Short for Kuznetsk Basin (*q.v.*).

Kuz·netsk′ (kōōz·nĕtsk′; *Russ.* kōōz·nyĕtsk′). City, E Penza Region, Soviet Russia, Europe, near source of Sura river and on Tula-Kuibyshev railroad ab. 65 m. E of Penza; pop. 29,647; important trade center.

Kuznetsk Basin. Basin of Tom river, cen. Kemerovo Region, Soviet Russia, Asia, extending from Tomsk to Stalinsk with immense coal deposits around and S of Kemerovo; has been converted into great independent industrial area because of recent discovery of rich iron-ore deposits at Temir Tau, S of Stalinsk.

Kuz·netsk′ Si·bir′ski (kōōz·nĕtsk′ sǐ·bǐr′skǐ; *Russ.* kōōz·nyĕtsk′ syǐ·byĕr′skǐ). = *Novo Kuznetsk:* see STALINSK.

Kvae′nang·en Fjord (kvä′näng·ĕn). Inlet of Arctic Ocean on NW coast of Norway.

Kval′öy (kväl′û′ü). Name of two islands in Arctic Ocean off N coast of Norway: **North Kvalöy**, in Finnmark co., 127 sq. m., pop. 4218, chief town Hammerfest; **South Kvalöy**, in Troms co., 284 sq. m., pop. ab. 3000. Tromsö is on islet bet. South Kvalöy and mainland.

Kvarner. See MALI KVARNER; VELIKI KVARNER.

Kwa′ja·lein (kwǒj′ȧ·līn; -lān). Island (atoll) in cen. part of Ralik Chain, W Marshall Is., W Pacific, 2415 m. SW of Pearl Harbor, 9°N lat. and 167°E long.; ab. 78 m. long, with 18 islets and fine large anchorage in the lagoon; chief islets Kwajalein at SE and Roi and Namur at N. Strongly fortified by Japanese; taken Jan. 30-Feb. 6, 1944 by Americans; site of missile-tracking station.

Kwa′koe·gron (kwä′kōō·krôn). Town, N Surinam, 50 m. by rail S of Paramaribo on the Saramacca river.

Kwa′mouth (kwä′mouth). River port on Congo river, Congo, at mouth of Kasai river, the confluence being called the **Kwa** mouth.

Kwan′cheng′tze′ (kwän′chĕng′tsĕ′). = CHANGCHUN.

Kwan′do (kwän′dō); *Port.* **Cuan′do** (kwănn′dōō). River ab. 600 m. long in S Africa; rises in cen. Angola, flows SE, forming S section of boundary bet. Angola and Northern Rhodesia, continues E along NE boundary of Bechuanaland, and empties into Zambezi river just above Victoria Falls.

Kwangchow. See CANTON.

Kwang′cho′wan′ (gwäng′jō′wän′) *or* **Kwang′chow′** (gwäng′jō′); *Fr.* **Kouang′-Tché′ou′-Wan′** (kwänn′-chä′ōō′wän′). Former French leased territory, SW coast of Kwangtung prov., SE China, on E side of Luichow Penin. ab. 270 m. W of Hong Kong; 325 sq. m.; pop. (1936 est.) 206,000; Fort Bayard (now called Siying), an excellent harbor with pop. of ab. 12,000. Nearby is Chinese commercial city Tche Kam (pop. 35,000). Narrow coast land, two large islands and many small ones, and adjacent waters acquired by France 1898 by lease for 99 years; was attached to French Indochina but during World War II was held by Japanese 1942-45; returned to China by France 1946.

Kwangju. See KOSHU.

Kwan′go (kwäng′gō); *Port.* **Cuan′go** (kwǎnng′gōō). River in S cen. Africa; rises in cen. Angola, flows N, forming a section of Angola-Congo boundary, and empties into Kasai river in W Congo ab. 100 m. above its junction with the Congo river.

Kwang′si′ (gwäng′sē′). Province, SE China; 83,985 sq. m.; pop. (1936 est.) 13,385,215; Yungning; bounded on N by Kweichow and Hunan provs., on E and S by Kwangtung, on SW by Tonkin, Indochina, and on W by Yunnan. Wildest and least developed of provinces of China; covered with hills and traversed by the Siang (Yu), Hungshui, and Kwei rivers, all tributaries of the Si; produces much rice in the river valleys and also has valuable forest products, as cassia, camphor, cinnamon, and wood oil. Chief cities Yungning, Kweilin, Tsangwu, Liuchow, and Lungchow. In former times the refuge of bandits and insurrectionists.

Kwang′teh′ (gwäng′dĕ′). Town, SE Anhwei prov., E China, ab. 65 m. NW of Hangchow; an important transportation center and scene of considerable fighting in World War II, esp. in 1943.

Kwang′tung′ (gwäng′dŏong′). **1** Province, SE China; 83,918 sq. m.; pop. (1936 est.) 32,289,805; Canton; bounded on N by Hunan and Kiangsi provs., on NE by Fukien, on E and S by South China Sea, and on W by Kwangsi; bordered on N by Meiling (Mts.) which separate it from Kiangsi prov.; lies largely in the tropics and has both mountain and plain regions, with four large rivers, Si, Peh, Tung, and Han. Has varied agricultural products, esp. rice, tea, sugar, tobacco, and fruit; also trades in silk, tung oil, salt, fish. Coast line almost 800 m. long, provides several excellent harbors; has many islands, esp. Hainan (*q.v.*) and those in the Si delta. Chief cities Canton, Swatow, Namhoi, Chaoan, Samshui, Kityang, Kongmoon, and Pakhoi.

History: In early centuries was too far from ruling dynasties in the north to have any marked influence; created under Ming dynasty (1368-1644); after 1757 was center of Chinese contact with foreign countries, esp. through Canton (*q.v.*) which was for nearly a century the only port opened to trade. Illicit importation of Indian opium into it brought on first war with Great Britain 1841-42 with resulting cession of Hong Kong and Treaty of Nanking 1842 providing for establishment of five treaty ports; ceded Kowloon to British 1860 and 1898, and Macao to Portugal 1887; Kwangchowan (*q.v.*) leased to France 1898 (restored 1946). The province most disaffected with imperial control and since 1900 it has developed a strong nationalist feeling; marked by much unrest at time of revolution 1911 and the formation of the Kuomintang under Sun Yat-sen 1912; occupied by Japanese 1938; in World War II in 1944 and 1945 had several important American air bases and was scene of much fighting.
2 Erroneous spelling for KWANTUNG.

Kwan′tung′ (gwän′dŏong′) *or* **Kwantung Leased Territory;** *also* **Kwan′to′** (gwän′dō′) *and, erroneously,* **Kwang′tung′** (gwäng′dŏong′). Territory, S part of Liaotung Penin., S Manchuria; 1444 sq. m.; pop. (1935) 1,656,726, (1938 est.) 1,750,000; Dairen. Mountainous peninsula with two ports Dairen and Port Arthur and customs border station Chinchou; connected by South Manchuria Railway with Mukden, Harbin, and Chinese and Russian railroad systems. Leased to Russia by China 1898 by compulsion; taken over by Japan 1905 by Treaty of Portsmouth and lease extended in 1915 to 99 years; again leased to U.S.S.R. by treaty 1945.

Kwanza. See CUANZA.

Kwathlamba. Var. of *Quathlamba:* see DRAKENSBERG MOUNTAINS.

Kwei (gwä). River ab. 200 m. long, E Kwangsi prov., S China, flowing S to join the Si at Tsangwu.

Kwei′chow′ (gwä′jō′). **1** Province, S China; 69,278 sq. m.; pop. (1936 est.) 9,043,207; Kweiyang; bounded on N by Szechwan prov., on E by Hunan, on S by Kwangsi, and on W by Yunnan. A plateau region bet. the tributaries of the Yangtze and Si rivers; contains many aboriginal peoples, chiefly the Miao; chief occupation agriculture but forestry important; chief exports timber, tung oil, hides; has rich mercury deposits. Has no rail-

roads but one from Kwangsi prov. to Kweiyang is planned; communications have improved since outbreak of World War II· crossed by Burma Road from Kunming through Kweiyang to Chungking. Chief towns Kweiyang, Anshun, Tsunyi. Has not played a significant part in Chinese history but in World War II was important as Chinese and Allied base.

2 City, S Szechwan, China. See FENGKIEH.

Kweichu. See KWEIYANG.

Kwei′hwa′ (gwä′hwä′); *also* **Kwei′hwa′ting′** (-tĭng′) *and* **Kwei′hwa′cheng′** (-chŭng′). City, formerly in N Shansi prov., NE China; now part of Kweisui.

Kweihwa–Suiyuan. See KWEISUI.

Kwei′lin′ (gwä′lĭn′). City, NE Kwangsi prov., SE China, on right bank of Kwei river 235 m. NW of Canton; pop. ab. 100,000; former capital of Kwangsi, an old city dating back to Sui dynasty (c. 589 A.D.); has trade connections by river with Tsangwu and Canton; exports silk, skins. Has very grotesque rock formations in vicinity. In World War II again made capital and developed 1944–45 as great American air base; attacked by Japanese Sept. 1944; abandoned by U.S. Air Force Sept. 17 and destroyed Oct. 28; retaken July 27, 1945 after a six-week battle.

Kwei′ping′ (gwä′pĭng′); *formerly* **Sun′chow′** (shŭn′-jō′). Town, E Kwangsi, SE China, at 110°4′E; here the Hungshui and Siang rivers unite to form the Si.

Kwei′sui′ (gwä′swä′) *or* **Hu′ho·hao′te** (hōō′hô·hou′tä) *or* **Hu′he·hot′** (hōō′hä·hôt′); *formerly* **Kwei′hwa′-Sui′yuan′** (gwä′hwä′swä′yü·än′); *Mongol.* **Ku′ku·kho′to** (kü′kü·kô′tô). Commercial town, ✻ of Suiyuan prov., cen. Inner Mongolia, N China, in S part of province on Peiping-Suiyuan R.R. 155 m. W of Wanchuan; pop. ab. 65,000. Formerly a sacred city of the Mongols and since 11th cent. a Chinese trading center with them; of increased importance since completion of railroad 1921 from Kalgan (Wanchuan); E terminus of trade routes to W Outer Mongolia and to Sinkiang. Consists of two towns **Kweihwa** or **Kweihwating** and **Suiyuan**, recently united. After occupation of E Inner Mongolia by Japanese 1937–38 made capital (as Hohohoto) of new buffer state of Mêng Chiang.

Kwei′yang′ (gwä′yäng′) *or* **Kwei′chu′** (-jōō′). City, ✻ of Kweichow prov., S China, 220 m. S of Chungking ab. halfway on highway (Burma Road extension) bet. Kunming and Chungking; pop. 116,598; on plateau at 3400 ft. elevation; administrative and route center of the province. In World War II developed as an American air base.

Kwen′lun′ Shan (kŏŏn′lŏŏn′ shän′). = KUNLUN SHAN.

Kwi′dzyń (kvē′jĭn·y′); *Ger.* **Ma·ri′en·wer′der** (mä·rē′-ĕn·vĕr′dēr). Manufacturing town, SE Gdańsk dept., N Poland, ab. 70 m. SSE of Danzig; pop. (1946) 45,578; formerly in East Prussia, Germany; military station; dyeworks; manufactures clay products, tobacco, preserved foodstuffs; trades in agricultural products, cattle, horses. Founded 1233 by the Teutonic Order; center of plebiscite 1920 by which people of town and vicinity voted to remain in East Prussia; in section of East Prussia assigned to Poland by Potsdam Conference, 1945.

Kwitta. See KETA.

Kwo′ka (kwô′kä). Mountain 9842 ft., highest point in Arfak range, NW Neth. New Guinea.

Kworra. See NIGER river.

Kyakh′ta (kyäк′tä). **1** See KIACHTA.

2 *or* **Kiakh′ta.** Market and customs town, S Buryat-Mongol Republic, Soviet Russia, Asia, at Outer Mongolia border E of the Selenga river; pop. 8903; connected with Ulan Ude by branch of Trans-Siberian R.R.

Kya′ring Tso (kyä′rĭng tsô′). Lake ab. 40 m. long, E cen. Tibet, Outer China, lat. 31°N, long. 88°30′E.

Kyauk′pa·daung′ (chouk′pả·doung′). Town, Myingyan dist., Upper Burma, E of Irrawaddy river 100 m. SW of Mandalay; oil fields.

Kyauk′pyu′ (chouk′pyōō′). **1** District, Arakan division, Lower Burma; 4767 sq. m.; pop. ab. 220,292.

2 Town, its ✻, on Combermere Bay at N end of Ramree I.; pop. 4232; port of call for steamers bet. Calcutta and Rangoon.

Kyauk′se (chouk′sĕ). **1** District, Mandalay division, Upper Burma; 1245 sq. m.; pop. 151,320.

2 Town, its ✻, on railroad 25 m. S of Mandalay; pop. 7353.

Kyauk′taw (chouk′tô). Town, Arakan division, W Burma, on the Kaladan river N of Akyab; in region of severe fighting 1943–44; taken by British Feb. 25, 1944.

Ky·bar′tai (kē·bär′tī). City, Vilkavishkis dist., SW Lithuania, U.S.S.R., on the Kaunas-Kaliningrad railroad at the former East Prussian frontier; pop. (1938 est.) 7274.

Kye′bo·gyi′ (châ′bō·jē′). Native state in Karenni dist., E Burma; 790 sq. m.; pop. 14,282.

Kyi (kyē) *or* **Kyi′chu′** (kyē′chōō′). River ab. 200 m. long, N tributary of the Tsangpo, SE Tibet, Outer China, on which Lhasa is situated.

Kyklades. See CYCLADES.

Kyle (kīl). District, cen. Ayrshire, SW Scotland; celebrated in poetry of Robert Burns.

Kyl·lē′nē (kĭ·lē′nĕ; *Gr.* kyĕ·lyē′nyĕ). **1** See CYLLENE.

2 Commune, Achaea and Elis dept., NW Peloponnesus, S Greece; pop. 976.

Ký′mē (kē′mĕ; *Gr.* kyē′mĕ). Seaport commune on E coast of Euboea I., Euboea dept., Greece; pop. 4205.

Ky′nance Cove (kī′năns). Inlet of Atlantic Ocean on SW coast of England, 1½ m. W of Lizard Head.

Kynosura. See CYNOSURA.

Kyo′ga *or* **Kio′ga** (kyō′gả). Lake ab. 1000 sq. m., S cen. Uganda, E Africa; Victoria Nile flows through it.

Kyo·ga, Cape (kyō·gä). Cape on N coast of W extension of Honshu I., Japan, W of Wakasa Bay.

Kyo′mon′ (kyō′môn′); *formerly* **Port Ham′il·ton** (hăm′ĭl·tŭn; -t′n). Island group off S Korea, 44 m. NE of Saishu I.; fine harbor, occupied by Great Britain 1885–87.

Kyŏng′gi′ (kyông′gē′). = KEIKI.

Kyŏng′sang′ (kyông′säng′), **North** *and* **South.** = NORTH KEISHO, SOUTH KEISHO.

Kyongsong. See KEIJO.

Kyo·sai (kyô·sī). Island in Chosen Strait, off SE coast of Korea near Fusan.

Kyo′to *or* **Kio′to** (kyō′tô). **1** Prefecture of Japan. See *Table* at JAPAN.

2 Manufacturing city, its ✻, and ancient ✻ of Japan, W cen. Honshu; pop. (1938 est.) 1,159,800; on a plain with mountain ranges on all sides except the S, 6 m. W of S end of Lake Biwa and ab. 26 m. NNE of Osaka; center of Japanese art, having many factories turning out porcelain, lacquer ware, embroidery, brocades, bronzes, etc.; in recent years has become part of the Osaka-Kobe industrial area, manufacturing light electrical equipment, aircraft parts, chemicals, etc. Residence for more than 1000 years of the imperial family; some palace buildings remain and there are many fine Buddhist and Shinto temples, shrines, and other structures. Seat of Imperial University (founded 1897) and Doshisha, a Christian college. City founded as **Hei·an·kyo** (hä·än·kyō) and established as capital of Japan in 794 by Emperor Kwammu; at times superseded as actual seat of government (see KAMAKURA, capital of shogunate 1192–1333), but remained the classical capital till 1869, when government was removed to Tokyo.

Ky·ra′ Pa′na·gia′ (kyĕ·rä′ pä′nä·yä′). Island, Northern Sporades, NW Aegean Sea, NE of Alonēsos; in Euboea dept., Greece.

Ky·re′ni·a (kī·rē′nĭ·ả; *Gr.* kyĕ·rē′nyä). **1** District, N Cyprus, E Mediterranean Sea; 245 sq. m.; pop. (1931) 22,659.

2 Seaport, its ✻, in cen. part of N coast; pop. (1942 est.) 2394.

Ky·syl′cho′to (kĭ·zĭl′ᴋô′tô). = Kyzyl.
Ký′the·ra (kyē′thĕ·rä). **1** See Cerigo.
2 Town, ✻ of Cerigo, in cen. part of the island, Ionian Is., Greece.
Kyth′nos (kĭth′nŏs) or **Cyth′nos** (sĭth′nŏs); *Mod. Gr.*
Kýth′nos (kyēth′nôs); *also* **Ther·mia′** (thär·myä′). Island, NW Cyclades, Aegean Sea, ab. 8 m. SSE of Keos; belongs to Cyclades dept., Greece; ab. 18 sq. m.; pop. ab 5000; chief town **Kýthnos** on NE coast, pop. 1190; level and fertile; has thermal springs.
Kyu′shu (kyōō′shōō); *also* **Kiu′shu.** Southernmost of the four main islands of Japan, in Pacific Ocean off E coast of Asia, separated on N from SW Honshu by Shimonoseki Strait and on E from Shikoku by Bungo Strait; 16,240 sq. m.; pop. (1938 est.) 9,802,300, (1945 survey) 10,028,892; a mountainous island with several famous peaks, ranging from 5000 ft. to 6500· Aso, Kuju, Kirishima, Sakurajima. Its coast line irregular with fine harbors; chief cities Nagasaki, Moji, Kagoshima, Fukuoka, Kumamoto, Yawata, and Sasebo; was first part of Japanese Empire opened to foreigners (see Deshima, Hirado).

Kyu′sten·dil′ (kū′stĕn·dĭl′) or **Kü′sten·dil′** (kū′-). City, Sofia dept., W Bulgaria. 43 m. SW of Sofia; pop. (1934) 16,241; hot mineral springs; trades in wine, fruit, tobacco. Dates from Roman times; in 14th cent. was seat of independent Macedonian principality.
Ky·zyl′ or **Ki·zil′ Kho′to** (kĭ·zĭl′ ᴋô′tô); *Russ.* **Kras′ny** (krȧs′nĭ); *formerly* **Khem–Bel′der** (ᴋĕm′bĕl′dĕr). Town, ✻ of Tuva Autonomous Region, N cen. Asia, in cen. part at junction of the Bei Kem and Khua Kem (Mongol *kem* river); pop. ab. 10,000.
Ky·zyl′ Kum or **Qi·zil′ Qum** (kĭ·zĭl′ kōōm′). Desert 88,000 sq m., SE of Lake Aral, in Uzbek and Kazakh Republics, Soviet Central Asia; covers a great area bet. Amu Darya and the Syr Darya rivers.
Kzyl–Or·da′ (kȧ·zĭl′ôr·dä′; k′sĭl′-); *formerly* **Pe·rovsk′** (pyĕ·rôfsk′). Town, ✻ of Kzyl-Orda Region, S Kazakh S.S.R., Soviet Central Asia, 315 m. NW of Tashkent on N bank of Syr Darya and on Chkalov-Tashkent R.R.
Kzyl–Orda Region. Subdivision of Kazakh S.S.R., Soviet Central Asia, in S part E of Lake Aral; ✻ Kzyl-Orda; bounded on S by the Kara-Kalpak A.S.S.R. in the Uzbek S.S.R.; traversed by lower course of the Syr Darya.

L

L.A. See Los Angeles city, California.

Laa′gen (lô′gĕn). = Lågen.

La A·gue′ra (lä ä·gä′rä). Region and Spanish administrative post, S Río de Oro, NW Africa, on coast S of Cape Yubi.

Laaland. See Lolland.

La Al·bue′ra (lä äl·vwä′rä). Commune, Badajoz prov., SW Spain, 15 m. SE of Badajoz; pop. 1946; scene of defeat May 16, 1811 of French under Marshal Soult by British, Portuguese, and Spanish under Viscount Beresford in Peninsular War.

Lää′ne (lä′nĕ). Province of Estonia. See *Table* at Estonia.

La A′sun·ción′ (lä ä′sŏŏn·syôn′). Town, ✻ of Nueva Esparta state, Venezuela, located on E Margarita I., in Caribbean Sea off N coast of Venezuela; pop. (1941 est.) 4041.

Laatokka. See Ladoga.

La·a′u Point (lä·ä′ŏŏ). Cape on SW extremity of Molokai I., Hawaii.

La Ban′da (lä vän′dä). Town, Santiago del Estero prov., N Argentina; pop. (est.) 15,889; NE suburb of Santiago del Estero.

La Bar′ca (lä vär′kä). Town, Jalisco state, W cen. Mexico, near E end of Lake Chapala; pop. 13,427; center of region raising much grain and sugar.

La Bas·sée′ (lä bä·sā′). Commune, Nord dept., N France, 13 m. SW of Lille; pop. 4109; in World War I captured by Germans Sept. 1914; subjected to many attacks by British but not retaken until Oct. 3, 1918.

La Baule. See Escoublac.

Labe. See Elbe.

La′bé′ (lä′bā′). Town, W cen. Guinea, W Africa, 170 m. NE of Conakry; pop. ab. 10,000; chief town of the Fulah in the Fouta Djallon dist.

La·belle′ (lá·bĕl′). County, Quebec, Canada. See *Table* at Quebec.

La Belle (lá bĕl′). City, ⊗ of Hendry co., S Florida; pop. 1262.

La Belle-Al′liance′ (lá bĕl′á′lyäNs′). Hamlet in Belgium, battlefield of Waterloo.

La·berge′ (?lá·bĕrzh′). Lake, S Yukon, NW Canada, N of Whitehorse; Lewes river flows through it.

La·bette′ (lá·bĕt′). County in Kansas. See *Table* at Kansas.

La Biche (lá bĭsh′); *Fr.* **Lac la Biche** (läk′ lä bĭsh′). Lake, E Alberta, Canada; outlet is short stream, **La Biche River,** a tributary of the Athabaska.

La Bi·coc′ca (lä bĕ·kôk′kä). **1** Village, Lombardy, N Italy, bet. Milan and Monza; scene of battle Apr. 27, 1522, in which the French under Francis I were defeated by Emperor Charles V and allies.
2 Village, Lombardy, just SE of Novara; sometimes gives its name to the battle of Novara, fought here Mar. 23, 1849.

La′bin (lä′bēn); *Ital.* **Al·bo′na** (äl·bō′nä). Commune, W Croatia, NW Yugoslavia, on Istria Penin. 21 m. NE of Pulj; pop. 16,973.

La·bine′ Bay (lá·bēn′). Inlet, E end of Great Bear Lake, Mackenzie District, NW Territories, Canada; village of Port Radium, former pitchblende-mining center, on its shore.

La′bin·ska·ya (lá′byĭn·ská·yá; *Angl.* läb′ĭn·skä′yá). Town, SE Krasnodar Territory, Soviet Russia, Europe, ab. 40 m. E of Maikop; pop. 28,830; manganese and coal deposits in vicinity.

La·bo′ (lä·bō′). Mountain 3094 ft. in SE Camarines Norte, Luzon, Phil. Is., at point where boundary bet. Tayabas and Camarines Sur joins Camarines Norte border.

La Bo′ca (lá bō′kä; *Span.* lä vō′kä). Pacific coast seaport, Balboa dist., Canal Zone.

L′A′bord′ à Plouffe (lá′bôr′-tä plŏŏf′). Village, Jesus I., S Quebec, Canada, on Rivière des Prairies 10 m. WNW of Montreal; pop. 4604.

La·bo′u·la′ye (lä·vō′ŏŏ·lä′yá). Town, S Córdoba prov., N cen. Argentina, 200 m. SSE of Córdoba; pop. (est.) 14,911.

Lab′ra·dor (läb′rá·dôr). **1** Large peninsula, NE North America, divided bet. Newfoundland and Quebec provs., Canada; ab. 530,000 sq. m. See New Quebec, Ungava.
2 Mainland section of Newfoundland prov., Canada, ab. ⅓ of Labrador Penin. E of height of land; area 112,630 sq. m. (land area 107,435 sq. m.); pop. 7890. Borders on Atlantic on E and on Quebec prov. on S and W; its N point, Cape Chidley on Killinek I. is at entrance to Hudson Strait. Only large river is the Churchill (formerly Hamilton, *q.v.*) in the S, which enters Lake Melville; in it are Churchill Falls and it and its tributaries drain several large lakes in SW part (Ashuanipi, Dyke, Lobstick, Mishikamau). A plateau region, little explored, but its highest mountains are above 5000 ft.; along its S border (1000–2000 ft.) rise several streams of E Quebec flowing into the Gulf of St. Lawrence. Coast much indented with long fiords and lined with many small islands. Rich in minerals; chief resources furs and fish. Its inhabitants mainly Eskimos and Algonquian Indians. Has good harbors; from S to N chief ports are Battle Harbour, Cartwright, Indian Harbour, Hopedale, Nain, and Nachvak. Coast known to Norsemen as early as 10th cent.; visited by John Cabot (1498), Corte-Real (1500), and Jacques Cartier. Boundary with Canada, under dispute since 1809, settled by decision of Committee of British Privy Council Mar. 1927.

Labrador Current. Ocean current flowing S along W Greenland and Labrador coasts and E of Newfoundland, uniting with Gulf Stream in the area of the Grand Bank; its cold waters meeting with the warm waters of the Gulf Stream cause the frequent fogs of this part of the N Atlantic.

Lá′bre·a (lá′vrĕ·á). Town on right bank of Purus river, Amazonas state, W Brazil, 130 m. W of Crato, to which it is joined by railway.

La Bre′a (lä vrä′ä). Village and port on S shore of Gulf of Paria, W Trinidad; location of Brighton Pier whence the pitch from Pitch Lake just S of the port is shipped to all parts of the world.

Lab′ro·foss′ (läb′rŏ·fôs′). Waterfall 140 ft. in Lågen river, S Norway, 3 m. below Kongsberg.

La·bu′an (lá·bŏŏ′ăn). Island on N side of Brunei Bay, off NW coast of Borneo, 725 m. NE of Singapore; constitutes with adjacent small islands a settlement attached to North Borneo (Sabah), Malaysia; 35 sq. m.; pop. 7507, (1947 est.) 9253; chief town Victoria, which has excellent harbor and is shipping and distributing point for much of N Borneo; well cultivated; chief products rice, sago, rubber, and fruits.
History: At suggestion of James Brooke ceded 1846 to Great Britain by Sultan of Brunei; made crown colony 1848 and for a time (1889–1905) administered by British North Borneo; transferred to Straits Settlements 1905 with which it was incorporated 1907 as part of Singapore; constituted a separate settlement 1912 under governor of Straits Settlements; seized by Japanese Dec. 1941; made part of colony of North Borneo 1946.

La·buk′ (lä·bŏŏk′). River ab. 210 m. long, E North Borneo, Malaysia; flows ENE to **Labuk Bay,** large inlet of Sulu Sea.

Lab′y·rinth, the (läb′ĭ·rĭnth). Fortified position S of Neuville-Saint-Vaast and near Vimy Ridge, in Pas-de-Calais dept., N France; scene of series of battles May 30–June 19, 1915.

La Calamine. See Moresnet.

La Ca·le′ra (lä kä·lā′rä). = Calera.

La Calle (là kȧl′). Seaport, NE Constantine dept., NE Algeria, 10 m. from Tunisia border; pop. 5323; coral fishing. Lost by French and burned 1827, rebuilt 1836.

La Ca′margue′ (là kȧ·märg′) Marshy island in delta of the Rhone river, S France.

La Ca·nad′a (là kȧ·nyăd′ȧ). Urban community (unincorporated), Los Angeles co., SW California, NW of Pasadena; pop. (with Flintridge) 18,338; Descanso Gardens.

La Car·lo′ta (lä kär·lō′tä). Municipality, W cen. Negros Occidental prov., Negros, Phil. Is., 18 m. S of City of Bacolod; pop. 26,084.

La Ca′ro·li′na (lä kä′rô·lē′nä). Commune, Jaén prov., S Spain, on S slope of the Sierra Morena 32 m. N of Jaén; pop. 14,875; trades in minerals, oil, wine; lead mining; silk factories. Settled by Swabian colonists 1769 through efforts of Charles III to encourage exploitation of the Sierra Morena.

La Cas′tel·la′na (lä käs′tȧ·yä′nä). Municipality, cen. Negros Occidental prov., Negros, Phil. Is., 24 m. S of City of Bacolod; pop. 16,861.

Lac au Sau′mon′ (läk′ ō sō′môn′). Village, Matane co., on Gaspé Penin., SE Quebec, Canada, on Matapédia river 28 m. SSE of Matane; pop. 1703.

Lac′ca·dive Islands (läk′ȧ·dĭv). Group of islands and coral reefs in Arabian Sea, lat. 10°–12°20′ N and long. 72°–74°E, 200 m. off SW coast of India; 11 sq. m.; pop. 16,046; administratively were included in Madras prov., British India, the S group being assigned to the Malabar dist. and the N group (sometimes called the **A′min·di′vi Islands** [ŭ′mĭn·dē′vĭ]) to the South Kanara dist.; since 1956 forms **Laccadive and Amindivi Islands** territory of Republic of India. There are 14 islands; the inhabitants are Moslems; their language is Malayalam. Chief industry manufacture of coir.

Lac du Flam′beau (läk′ dü̇ flăm′bō). Lake in Vilas co., N Wisconsin; a source of Flambeau river.

Lacedaemon. See SPARTA, 7.

La Cei′ba (lä sē′ė̇·vä; sā′vä). Caribbean seaport, ✻ of Atlántida dept., N Honduras; pop. 11,293; bananas.

La′cha, Lake (lä′chȧ; *Russ.* lȧ′chȧ). Lake ab. 141 sq. m. in SW Arkhangelsk Region, Soviet Russia, Europe; one of the sources of Onega river.

La Chaux–de–Fonds (là shōd′fôn′). Industrial commune, Neuchâtel canton, W Switzerland, in Jura Mts. 31 m. WNW of Bern; pop. (1941) 30,943; watchmaking.

Lach Dera. See WASO NYIRO.

La·chine′ (lȧ·shēn′). Manufacturing city, Montreal I., S Quebec, Canada, on St. Lawrence river 8 m. SW of Montreal; pop. 27,773; serves as winter resort and summer residence. Active as port, upper terminus of **Lachine Canal** (Lachine to Montreal, 8¾ m., 5 locks constructed 1821–24; opened 1825) around the **Lachine Rapids** (ab. 3 m.) of the St. Lawrence, below Lake St. Louis and S of Montreal I. First settled as estate of Robert La Salle 1668 and named (Fr. *La Chine* China) in mockery of his dream that it was a westward passage to China; later settled as a town 1675; destroyed by Iroquois 1689 and nearly all inhabitants massacred.

La′chish (lä′kĭsh). Ancient fortified city, W Judah, Palestine, W of Hebron; its ruins now marked by a mound, Tell ed-Duweir, ab. 16 m. E of Gaza. An inhabited place probably as early as 2500 B.C.; at time of Israelite conquest of Canaan overcome by Joshua; later besieged by Sennacherib 701 B.C., and by Nebuchadnezzar c. 586 B.C.

Lach′lan (läk′lȧn). River 800 m. long, tributary of Murrumbidgee, cen. New South Wales, SE Australia; flows W from Blue Mts. but volume small in dry seasons.

La Chor·re′ra (lä chôr·rĕ′rä). Town, cen. Panama, 19 m. W of Panama; pop. 4345.

La·chute′ (lȧ·shōōt′; *Fr.* là′shüt′). Mill town, ⊗ of Argenteuil co., SW Quebec, Canada, 40 m. WNW of Montreal; pop. 6179; shipping center for farm and dairy products; receives water power from falls (Fr. *chute*) in North river and has cotton, paper, and pulp mills.

Lacinium Promontorium. See Cape COLONNE.

La Cio′tat′ (là syô′tä′); *anc.* **Cith′a·ris′ta** (sĭth′ȧ·rĭs′tȧ). Commune, Bouches-du-Rhône dept., SE France, on Mediterranean 12 m. SE of Marseilles; pop. 13,428; naval constructions.

La Cisa Pass. See APENNINES.

Lack′a·wan′na (lăk′ȧ·wŏn′ȧ). **1** County in Pennsylvania. See *Table* at PENNSYLVANIA.
2 Industrial city, Erie co., W New York, on Lake Erie 5 m. S of Buffalo; pop. 29,564; bridgeworks, shipyards; manufactures steel, cement, abrasives, refractories.

La·clede′ (lȧ·klēd′). County in Missouri. See *Table* at MISSOURI.

Lacobriga. See LAGOS.

La·combe′ (lȧ·kōm′). Town, S cen. Alberta, Canada, 74 m. S of Edmonton; pop. 2277; has a Dominion experimental station.

La′con (lä′kŏn). City, ⊗ of Marshall co., N cen. Illinois, on Illinois river 25 m. N of Peoria; pop. 2175.

La Con′cep·ción′ (lä kŏn′sĕp·syôn′). Town, W Panama, W of David; pop. 2162.

La Con′da·mine′ (lä kôn′dȧ·mēn′). Commune, Monaco; pop. (1939) 11,339; bathing resort.

La·co′ni·a (lȧ·kō′nĭ·ȧ; -kōn′yȧ). **1** Manufacturing city, ⊗ of Belknap co., cen. New Hampshire, 22 m. N of Concord; pop. 15,288; Lakes Paugus, Winnisquam, and Opechee S of city; summer and winter resort; trading center. Settled 1761 (long known as Meredith Bridge); incorporated as town 1855, as city 1893.
2 Tract of land of indefinite limits around Lake Champlain, extending N to the St. Lawrence; granted 1629 to John Mason and Sir F. Gorges.
3 *or* **La·con′i·ca** (lȧ·kŏn′ĭ·kȧ). Ancient country occupying SE Peloponnesus, Greece; ✻ Sparta. Bounded on N by Arcadia and Argolis, on E by Aegean Sea, on S by Mediterranean (Gulf of Laconia), and on W by Gulf of Messenia and Messenia. Lofty Taygetus Mts. are along its W coast and border, containing highest peak in the Peloponnesus (7904 ft.); Parnon range is in the E. Drained by Eurotas river. Its two peninsulas on the S enclosing Gulf of Laconia are long rugged promontories terminating in Capes Malea and Matapan. Off Cape Malea is Cerigo I., administered as one of the Ionian Is. Central part of river valley is fertile and productive but agriculture is restricted by general mountainous character. Chief towns Sparta, Gythium, Monemvasia. Its history is that of Sparta (*q.v.*).
4 Department of Greece. See *Table* at GREECE.

Laconia, Gulf of. Inlet of the Mediterranean Sea on the S coast of Peloponnesus, S Greece, bet. Capes Matapan and Malea.

La Co·ru′ña (lä kô·rōō′nyä). **1** Province of Spain. See *Table* at SPAIN.
2 *Eng.* **Co·run′na** (kô·rŭn′ȧ); *anc.* **Ca·ro′ni·um** (kȧ·rō′nĭ·ŭm) Seaport commune, ✻ of La Coruña prov., NW Spain, on Atlantic Ocean 127 m. W of Oviedo; pop. (1941 est.) 105,402; trades in livestock, fruits, vegetables, wine, hams, sardines, leather; manufactures cigars, cordage, paper, lumber, linen goods, canvas, barrels; lighthouse (Torre de Hércules) thought to have been built by Carthaginians.
History: Believed to antedate Roman times; reached height of prosperity in Middle Ages; part of caliphate of Córdoba; captured by Portugal 1370; point of departure for Spanish Armada 1588; sacked by Drake 1589; scene of English naval victories over French 1747 and 1805; noted esp. for victory of English under Sir John Moore over French under Marshal Soult 1809; captured by French 1823 and by Carlists 1836.

La·cos′ta Island (lȧ·kŏs′tȧ). Island in Gulf of Mexico, at S entrance to Charlotte Harbor, off W coast of Lee co. SW Florida.

La Cour′neuve′ (là kōōr′nûv′). Commune, Seine dept., N France; NNE suburb of Paris; pop. 17,390; manufactures chemicals, railroad supplies.

Lac qui Parle (lä′kĕ pärl′). **1** Small lake, W Minnesota, an expansion of the Minnesota river; forms part of boundary bet. Lac qui Parle and Chippewa cos. **2** County in Minnesota. See *Table* at MINNESOTA.

La Crosse (lá krôs′). **1** County in Wisconsin. See *Table* at WISCONSIN.
2 City, ⊗ of Rush co., cen. Kansas; pop. 1767.
3 City, ⊗ of La Crosse co., W Wisconsin, at junction of Black and Mississippi rivers; pop. 47,575; settled 1841; trade and shipping center of agricultural region; manufactures agricultural implements, rubber footwear gauges, heating and air-conditioning equipment; Wisconsin State Coll. (1909; coed.).

Lac–Saint–Jean. See LAKE SAINT JOHN.

La Cumbre. = *Uspallata Pass:* see ANDES.

Lacus Asphaltites. See DEAD SEA.

Lac Vieux De·sert′ (läk vū′ dĕ·zâr′). Lake on boundary bet. Vilas co., N Wisconsin, and Gogebic co., NW corner of Michigan penin.; source of the Wisconsin river.

La·dakh′ (lá·däĸ′) *or* **La·dak′** (lá·däk′). **1** Frontier district, E Kashmir state, N India, including the entire E half of the state; 45,762 sq. m.; pop. 192,138; * Leh; includes Baltistan (sometimes called *Little Tibet*). Contains W Himalayas (Ladakh Range) and Karakoram Range, also valley of upper Indus river.
2 Tahsil, E Ladakh dist.; 29,848 sq. m.; pop. 34,423; * Leh.

Ladakh, *or* **Ladak, Range.** Mountain range in E Kashmir N India, NE of Indus river; average height 19,000 ft.

La Digue (lá dēg′). See SEYCHELLES.

La′do En′clave (lä′dō ĕn′klāv). A territory, area 15,000 sq. m., on the W bank of the Nile river N of Lake Albert, now in Uganda and in Equatoria prov. of SE Sudan; explored by British 1870 and later, and claimed for Great Britain 1894; leased to Belgium 1894–1910. Chief town was Lado, on the Nile just S of Mongalla.

Lad′o·ga (lăd′ô·gá; *Russ.* lá′dŭ·gá); *Russ. also* **La′-dozh·sko·e O′ze·ro** (lä′dŭsh·skŭ·yĕ ô′zyĭ·rŭ); *Finnish* **Laa′tok·ka′** (lä′tôk·ká′). Lake, largest in Europe, formerly divided bet. Soviet Russia and Finland, N Europe; ab. 7000 sq. m., 130 m. long by 75 m. wide; now entirely in U.S.S.R. divided bet. SW Karelia and N Leningrad Region. Fed by ab. 70 streams mostly in Finland and Karelia on N and W; on the S in Russia by the Volkhov and Syas, on the E by the Svir, the outlet of Lake Onega. Its outlet is the Neva, from the SW corner through Leningrad to the Gulf of Finland. Frozen from October to April. Has abundance of fish and has canal system along its S and E shores. Chief towns on its shores are Shlisselburg (now Petrokrepost) and Novaya Ladoga in Leningrad Region and Serdobol (Sortavala) and Keksgolm (Käkisalmi) in Karelia (formerly in Finland). Approximately northwestern two thirds and adjacent lands taken by Soviet Russia as result of treaty of 1940; S part held by Germans 1941–44 in World War II but regained 1944; during siege of Leningrad railroad built across ice of lake brought supplies to city in the winter.

La Dôle (lá dōl′). See DÔLE peak.

La Do·ra′da (lä thô·rä′thä). River port, Caldas dept., W cen. Colombia, on Magdalena river 613 m. from Barranquilla and 109 m. from Puerto Berrio; pop. 5965.

La′dril·le′ro Gulf (lä′thrĕ·yä′rô). Inlet of Pacific Ocean W of Wellington I., off SW coast of Chile.

La·drone′ Islands (lá·drōn′). **1** Island group in China Sea, opp. entrance to the Pearl river.
2 See MARIANA ISLANDS.

La·drones′ (lá·drōnz′; *Span.* lä·thrō′nâs). Group of small islands in Pacific Ocean off extreme SW coast of Panama.

La·due′ (lá·dōō′; -dū′). City, St. Louis co., E Missouri, 10 m. W of St. Louis; pop. 9466.

La′dy·brand (lä′dĭ·bränd). Town, E Orange Free State, E cen. Union of South Africa, on Caledon river 80 m. E of Bloemfontein; pop. 4749.

La′dy·smith (lä′dĭ·smĭth). **1** City, ⊗ of Rusk co., NW Wisconsin, at falls of Flambeau river 30 m. E of Rice Lake (city); pop. 3584; wood processing; creamery; canning plant.
2 City, SE Vancouver I., Brit. Columbia, Canada, on Strait of Georgia 43 m. NNW of Victoria; pop. 2094; terminus of ferry from mainland and shipping port for adjacent mining region; center of extensive logging industry. Incorporated 1904 and named after Ladysmith, South Africa.
3 Town, W Natal, E Union of South Africa, on a tributary of the Tugela river 115 m. NW of Durban; pop. 9701; active center of trade with N Natal, Orange Free State, and Transvaal; industrial community. Scene of most famous siege of Boer War; occupied by British troops and invested by Boers Oct. 1899–Feb. 28, 1900. See COLENSO.

La′e (lä′å). Town on SE coast of North-East New Guinea, 7°S lat., on Huon Gulf at mouth of Markham river ab. 200 m. directly N of Port Moresby. After partial destruction of Rabaul by volcanoes, made capital of Territory of New Guinea 1941. Seized by Japanese Feb. 1942 and used as major supply base; frequently bombed by Allies 1942–43; occupied by Australians Sept. 16, 1943.

Lae′ken (lä′kĕ[n]). Former commune in Brabant prov., cen. Belgium, now part of Brussels.

Læs′ö′ (lĕs′û′). Island forming a part of Denmark, lying in the upper Kattegat off NE coast of Jutland Penin.; 43 sq. m.; pop. (1925) 3161.

La Es′pe·ran′za (lä ĕs′pĕ·rän′zá; *Span.* äs′pä·rän′sä). Town, * of Intibucá dept., SW Honduras; pop. (1935) 1078.

La Es·tra′da (lä äs·trä′thä). City, Pontevedra prov., NW Spain, 20 m. NNE of Pontevedra; pop. 27,240; in rich agricultural and stock-raising region; mineral springs.

La′fay·ette′ (lä′fĭ·ĕt′; läf′ĭ-; lä′fĭ-; *in sou. U.S., often* lá·fā′ĕt, lá·fät′, lá·fĕt′). **1** Name of a parish in Louisiana and of counties in five states of the U.S. See *Tables* at LOUISIANA, ARKANSAS, FLORIDA, MISSISSIPPI, MISSOURI, WISCONSIN.
2 City, ⊗ of Chambers co., E Alabama; pop. 2605.
3 City, Boulder co., N cen. Colorado, 18 m. NNW of Denver; pop. 2612; coal.
4 City, ⊗ of Tippecanoe co., W cen. Indiana, on Wabash river 58 m. NW of Indianapolis; pop. 42,330; in agricultural section; market center for grain and livestock; manufactures flour, lumber, electrical appliances, safes. Purdue Univ. (1869; coed.). The battlefield of Tippecanoe, in which General William Henry Harrison defeated the Indians 1811, is on the edge of the city.
5 City, ⊗ of Lafayette parish, S Louisiana, 55 m. WSW of Baton Rouge; pop. 40,400; market and distributing center for cotton, cottonseed oil, sugar, lumber, livestock. Univ. of Southwestern Louisiana (1900; coed.).
6 City, ⊗ of Macon co., N Tennessee; pop. 1590.

La Fay′ette (*for pron., see preceding entry*). City, ⊗ of Walker co., NW Georgia, 18 m. WSW of Dalton; pop. 5588; agricultural trading center; textile mills; scene of local engagements (1864) in the Civil War.

Lafayette, Mount. Peak 5249 ft. in Franconia Mts., N cen. New Hampshire, in N Grafton co.

Lafayette National Park. Former name (1919–29) of *Acadia National Park:* see UNITED STATES, *National Parks.*

La Fère (lá fâr′). Commune, Aisne dept., N France; pop. 2534; important point on Hindenburg Line during World War I, occupied by Germans Sept. 3, 1914–Oct. 10, 1918.

La Fe′ri·a (lá fĕr′ĭ·á). City, Cameron co., S Texas, 25 m. NW of Brownsville; pop. 3047; in agricultural section.

La Fer·té′ (lá fĕr′tä′). Name applied to many French towns which were originally fortified places; derived from *fermeté*, meaning "stronghold."

La Fer′té′–Ber′nard′ (là fĕr′tā′bĕr′nàr′). Commune, Sarthe dept., NW France, 27 m. NE of Le Mans; pop. 3859; captured by English 1424 after siege of 4 months; belonged to Guise family in 16th cent.

La Fer′té′–Mi′lon′ (-mē′lôɴ′). Commune Aisne dept., N France, 47 m. SW of Reims; pop. (1931) 1560; birthplace of Jean Racine; partially destroyed in World War I.

La Flèche (là flĕsh′). Commune, Sarthe dept., NW France, on Loir river 24 m. SSW of Le Mans; pop. 10,101; manufactures gloves and hats; 16th-cent. castle (once a Jesuit college in which Descartes studied).

La Fol′lette (là fŏl′ĕt; -ĭt). City, Campbell co., N Tennessee, 31 m. NNW of Knoxville; pop. 6204; coal and iron mines nearby.

La For·tu′na, Point (lä fôr·tōō′nȧ). Point on SE coast of St. Bernard parish, SE Louisiana, extending into Breton Sound.

La·fourche′ (là·fōōrsh′; *Fr.* là′fōōrsh′). **1** Bayou, SE Louisiana; an outlet of Mississippi river, ab. 150 m. long; navigable by steamboats.
2 Parish in Louisiana. See *Table* at LOUISIANA.

La Futa Pass. See APENNINES.

Lag′an (làg′ăn). River ab. 35 m. long in NE Ireland; rises in co. Down, SE Northern Ireland; flows NNE into Belfast Lough at Belfast.

La′gan (là′gän). River 180 m. long, S Sweden; flows S and W into the Kattegat S of Halmstad.

La Ga′renne′–Co′lombes′ (là gà′rĕn′kô′lôɴb′). Commune, Seine dept., N France; NW suburb of Paris; pop. (1931) 23,167; manufactures chemicals.

La′ga·ri′na (là′gä-rē′nä). Valley of the Adige river in Venezia Tridentina compartimento, NE Italy, E of Lake Garda from above Rovereto to the Venetian boundary; ab. 50 m. long.

La·gar′to (lä·gär′tō). River in cen. Panama, W of the Canal Zone; flows NW into the Caribbean Sea.

La′gash (là′gäsh) or **Shir·pur′la** (shîr·pōōr′là). Sumerian city and city-state in S Babylonia, bet. the Euphrates and Tigris rivers ab. lat. 31°30′N and long. 46°9′E. Flourished c. 3000 B.C. to c. 2300 B.C.; its classical period, esp. in sculpture and literature was under its ruler Gudea, c. 2350 B.C.; excavations (at modern village of Telloh) have revealed ruins of palace and temple and many inscribed tablets.

Lå′gen (lô′gĕn) or **Nu′me·dals·lå′gen** (nōō′mĕ·däls-lô′gĕn). River 185 m. long in S Norway; flows S into Skagerrak at Larvik.

Lag′gan, Loch (lŏk làg′ăn). Lake in Perth co., cen. Scotland.

Laggan Bay. Inlet of Atlantic Ocean on S coast of Islay I., off W coast of Scotland.

La′ghou·at′ (là·gwät′; là′gwät′). Oasis and commune, N Ghardaia territory, Southern Territories, Algeria, in the Atlas Mts.; pop. 23,062.

La Giudecca. See GIUDECCA.

La′go (*Span.* là′gō; *Port.* là′gō). Spanish and Portuguese for "lake"; in such names as **Lago Puyehue, Lago Rupanco,** etc., see Lago PUYEHUE, Lago RUPANCO.

La·go′a (là·gō′ȧ). Portuguese for "lagoon" or "lake"; in such names as **Lagoa dos Patos,** etc., see Lagoa dos PATOS.

La·go·noy′ (là′gó·noi′). Municipality, E Camarines Sur prov., Luzon, Phil. Is., NE of Mt. Isarog and near head of Lagonoy Gulf; pop. 18,852.

Lagonoy Gulf. Large inlet of the Pacific Ocean in SE Luzon, Phil. Is.; its N and W shores formed by Camarines Sur prov. and its S shore by Albay prov. and the chain of four islands: San Miguel, Cagraray, Batan, and Rapu-Rapu; on the NE is Catanduanes I.

Lagoon Islands. See ELLICE ISLANDS.

La′gos (là′gôs), *in full* **La′gos de Mo·re′no** (là′gôz thä mō·rā′nō). Town, Jalisco state, W cen. Mexico; pop. 12,490; on railroad 45 m. NW of Guanajuato; alt. 6000 ft. Founded c. 1540.

La′gos (là′gŭs; là′gŏs). **1** Island off low and marshy coast of SW Nigeria, West Africa; named in 15th cent. by Portuguese explorers because of its many lagoons or lakes (Port. *lagos*); 5 sq. m.; pop. 90,193.
2 Former British colony, West Africa, consisting of Lagos I. and strip of mainland opposite; now equivalent to the Colony (see *Table* at NIGERIA), a province of Nigeria. Bought by Great Britain 1861; see NIGERIA, *History*.
3 Seaport, * of Colony prov. and * of Nigeria, on Lagos I. at W end of a large lagoon, S Colony prov., Western Region, SW Nigeria; pop. of municipal area 126,108, (1939 est.) 167,000; connected by rail with Kano in N Nigeria; has extensive wharfage; has several fine modern buildings. In early times a resort of slave hunters.

La′gos (là′gōosh); *anc.* **Lac′o·bri′ga** (làk′ô·brī′gȧ). Seaport commune, Faro dist. S Portugal, on Atlantic Ocean 41 m. W by N of Faro; pop. 9443; sardine and tunny fisheries; naval battle in **Lagos Bay** Aug. 18, 1759, in which French fleet was defeated by English under Admiral Boscawen.

Lagosta. See LASTOVO.

La Gou′lette′ (là gōō′lĕt′); *Ital.* **Go·let′ta** (gò-lĕt′ȧ; *Ital.* -lät′tä). Seaport town, the port of Tunis, NE Tunisia, N Africa, on strip of sand which separates Lake of Tunis from Gulf of Tunis; pop. ab. 4000.

La Grand′′–Combe′ (là grän′kôɴb′). Mining and manufacturing commune, Gard dept., S France, on Gardon d'Alès river 31 m. NNW of Nîmes; pop. 12,343; coal.

La Grande (là grånd′). City, ⊗ of Union co., NE Oregon, on Grande Ronde river at foot of Blue Mts. 40 m. N of Baker; pop. 9014; sawmills, creameries, cold-storage and meat-packing plants, flour mills. Eastern Oregon College (1929; coed.). First settled on old Oregon Trail 1861.

La·grange′ (là·grånj′). **1** County in Indiana. See *Table* at INDIANA.
2 Town, ⊗ of Lagrange co., N Indiana, 40 m. E of South Bend; pop. 1990; dairy center.

La Grange (là grånj′). **1** City, ⊗ of Troup co., W Georgia, 40 m. N of Columbus; pop. 23,632; incorporated 1828; textile mills. La Grange Coll. (1831; women).
2 Village, Cook co., NE Illinois, 13 m. W of Chicago; pop. 15,285; suburb of Chicago; prehistoric Indian burial mounds nearby.
3 City, ⊗ of Oldham co., N Kentucky; pop. 2168.
4 Town, Lenoir co., E North Carolina, 13 m. ESE of Goldsboro; pop. 2133; manufactures hardware.
5 City, ⊗ of Fayette co., SE cen. Texas, on Colorado river 32 m. WSW of Brenham; pop. 3623; in section growing cotton and corn.

La Grange Park. Village, Cook co., NE Illinois; pop. 13,793; a W suburb of Chicago.

La Granja. See SAN ILDEFONSO.

La Gran Pie′dra (là gräm′ pyä′thrä). Peak 4920 ft. near Santiago de Cuba, Cuba.

La Guai′ra (là gwī′rä). Seaport town in the Federal District, N Venezuela; port for Caracas; pop. 16,279; one of most important commercial towns in Venezuela with good harbor, dry dock, and shipbuilding plant; in direct line 8 m. N of Caracas but 23 m. by railroad in winding line up the mountains to the capital at 3020 ft. Founded 1588; destroyed by earthquake of 1812 and damaged during war for independence.

La Guayra. = LA GUAIRA.

La·gu′na (*Span.* là·gōō′nä; *Eng. and Port.* là·gōō′nȧ). Spanish and Portuguese for "lake" or "lagoon"; in such names as **Laguna Blanca, Laguna del Perro, Laguna Madre,** etc., see BLANCA, PERRO, MADRE.

La·gu′na (là·gōō′nȧ). **1** Indian village and pueblo, Valencia co., W New Mexico, in Laguna Indian Reservation, ab. 42 m. W of Albuquerque; pop. (est.) 500.
2 Seaport city, Santa Catarina state, S Brazil, 60 m. S of Florianópolis; pop. 8571.

La·gu′na (là·gōō′nä). Province of irregular shape, S cen. Luzon, Phil. Is.; 465 sq. m.; pop. 279,505; * Santa Cruz;

smallest province on Luzon. On N and NE borders on Laguna de Bay and its NE portion N of the lake borders on Rizal prov.; bounded on E and SE by Tayabas prov., on SW by Batangas, and on W by Cavite: mountainous in the NE and S parts; highest points Maquiling 3750 ft., and San Cristobal on the Tayabas border ab. 4900 ft.; well watered by many short streams from the mountain ranges to the lake, some of which are remarkable for waterfall (see PAGSANJAN), grottoes, or mineral springs. Its most notable physical feature the Lake of Bay (Laguna de Bay), which abounds in fish. Has fertile soil and produces coconuts, rice, sugar cane, abacá, and corn chiefly for Manila markets; varied and important industries. Inhabitants mostly Tagalogs. Chief towns Santa Cruz, San Pablo City, Calamba, Biñan, and Santa Rosa.

History: Region well populated when visited by Spaniards 1571; scene of uprising of Chinese 1639; invaded by British 1763; scene of revolt 1840; boundaries changed several times in latter part of 19th cent.; active in 1896 revolt; civil government established July 1902.

Laguna, La. See LA LAGUNA.

La·gu′na Beach (là·gōō′nà). City, Orange co., SW California, 27 m. SE of Long Beach; pop. 9288; resort and artists' colony in rugged coastal area.

La·gu′na Dam (là·gōō′nà). Dam across Colorado river on S California-Arizona boundary N of Yuma, Arizona; forms **Laguna Reservoir** S of and adjoining Imperial Reservoir.

Laguna de Bay. See Laguna de BAY.

Laguna de Flores. See PETÉN lake.

La′gu·nil′las (lä′gōō·nē′yäs). Town, Zulia state, NW Venezuela, on E shore of Lake Maracaibo 40 m. SE of Maracaibo; pop. (1941 est.) 6850.

La Ha·ba′na (lä ä·vä′nä). **1** Province, W Cuba. See *Table* at CUBA.

2 See HAVANA.

La Ha′bra (là hä′brà). City, Orange co., SW California, 19 m. NE of Long Beach; pop. 25,136; incorporated 1925; in oil-producing region.

La Hague, Cape (là häg′); *Fr.* **Cap de la Hague** (kàp′ dĕ là àg′). Headland on the coast of Manche dept., NW France, W of Cherbourg, projecting into the English Channel.

La·hai′na (là·hī′nà; lä·hī′nä). **1** District, Maui co., Hawaii, W end of Maui I.; pop. 4844.

2 City in district, on NW coast of Maui on Auau Channel, the channel at this point being known as **Lahaina Roadstead**, an important anchorage of U.S. Pacific fleet; pop. 3423; long a place of royal residence of Hawaiian kings and an early mission station; in 1840 rival of Honolulu as a leading town; importance decreased after 1875.

La Haye–du–Puits (là ā′dü·pü·ē′). Commune, Manche dept., NW France, on W side of Cotentin Penin. S of Cherbourg; pop. (1931) 1480; captured by Americans July 5–6, 1944.

La′hej (lä′hĭj). Town in Aden colony, SW Arabia, ab. 15 m. N of the city of Aden; pop. ab. 12,000; a sultanate under British protection.

La Hi·gue′ra (lä ē·gā′rä). Commune, cen. Chile; see CRUZ GRANDE.

La′hi·la′hi Point (lä′hē·lä′hē). Cape on W cen. coast of Oahu I., Hawaii.

Lahn (län). River 135 m. long in Hesse state, Germany; flows S and SW into Rhine river 4 m. SE of Koblenz; navigable to Giessen.

La Hogue (là hōg′; *Fr.* là ôg′) *or* **La Hougue** (là hōōg′; *Fr.* là ōōg′). Roadstead off Point Barfleur on the E coast of Cotentin Penin., Manche dept., NW France; naval battle May 19–23, 1692 in which French under de Tourville were defeated by the combined English and Dutch fleets under Adm. Edward Russell.

La·hore′ (là·hōr′). **1** Former division of the Punjab, NW Brit. India; 12,203 sq. m.; pop. (1941) 7,218,001; in 1947 divided: Gujranwala, Sheikhupura, and Sialkot dists.

and parts of Gurdaspur and Lahore dists. assigned to West Punjab, Pakistan; Ambala and Jullundur dists. and remainders of Gurdaspur and Lahore assigned to East Punjab, Indian Union.

2 District of division; 2595 sq. m.; pop. (1941) 1,695,375; divided 1947 bet. East Punjab and West Punjab.

3 City, ✻ of district and division and ✻ (since 1955) of West Pakistan, near Ravi river ab. 270 m. NW of Delhi; pop. (1941) 671,659; important rail junction and trade center; large railroad workshops. The modern city includes the old walled native city, the former European quarter, several suburbs, and the large cantonment of Mian Mir; especially notable among the fine architectural remains are the Fort and the mosque of Wazir Khan, the tomb of Emperor Jahangir in nearby Shahdara (across the Ravi), the famous suburban Shalamar Gardens of Shah Jahan with magnificent terraces and fountains, and the tomb of Sikh prince Ranjit Singh. An ancient city, but not prominent until the time of the Moguls; capital of Ghazni and Ghuri sultans in 11th and 12th cents. and often the residence of the Great Mogul— 1584–98 under Akbar and 1622–27 under Jahangir; became part of Sikh kingdom in 1767 and flourished anew under Ranjit Singh; conquered by British troops 1846, placed under British sovereignty 1849. Punjab Univ. (founded 1882); Aitchison Chiefs' College for sons of noblemen.

Lahr (lär). Manufacturing city, Baden-Württemberg, Germany, 22 m. N of Freiburg; pop. 14,075; 13th-cent. church; manufactures cigars, leather, lumber. First mentioned 1250; made city 1366; passed to Baden by Peace of Lunéville 1801.

Lah′ti (lä′tĭ). City, Häme dept., S Finland, NNE of Helsinki; pop. (1939 est.) 26,700; lumber center.

Lahu, Grand. = GRAND LAHOU.

Laibach. See LJUBLJANA.

Laichow. See YEHSIEN.

Laigue, Fo·rêt′ de (fô′rĕd′ lĕg′). Woods near Compiègne, N France. See RETHONDES.

Lail·la′hue (lī·yä′wä). Peak 16,995 ft. on Peru-Bolivia boundary SW of Lake Titicaca.

Laings′burg (lăngz′bûrg). Town, S Cape Province, S Union of South Africa, NW of Oudtshoorn; pop. 1829.

Laing's Nek (lăngz nĕk) *or* **Lang's Nek.** Mountain pass, cen. Drakensberg Mts., Natal, E Republic of So. Africa; railroad bet. Durban and Pretoria goes through a tunnel here; scene Jan. 28, 1881 of Boers' defeat of a British force which attempted to enter the Transvaal.

Lainsitz. See LUŽNICE.

Lai′yang′ (lī′yäng′). City, E Shantung prov., NE China, 50 m. SW of Chefoo; pop. 40,000; silk trade.

La′ja (lä′hä). **1** A lake in cen. Chile, in the Andes Mts.

2 River ab. 150 m. long in S cen. Chile, flowing W from Laja lake into Bío-Bío river; **Laja Falls** are a short distance from the city of Concepción.

La′jas (lä′häs). Municipality (pop. 15,375) and town (pop. 914), SW Puerto Rico; town in railroad junction point ab. 12 m. SE of Mayagüez.

La′jes (là′zhĕs). City, S cen. Santa Catarina state, S Brazil, 110 m. W of Florianópolis; pop. 7633; highway junction point.

Lajes do Pico. See PICO.

La Jol′la (là hoi′à). A NW section of San Diego, California; pop. (est.) 24,000; site of University of California, San Diego.

La′jos·mi′zse (lŏ′yŏsh·mĭ′zhĕ). Commune, cen. Hungary, 40 m. SE of Budapest; pop. 12,489.

La Jun′ta (là hŭn′tà). City, ⊗ of Otero co., SE Colorado, on Arkansas river 63 m. ESE of Pueblo; pop. 8026; founded 1875, incorporated as town 1881, as city 1901; trade center for irrigated agricultural region.

Lake (lāk). **1** Name of counties in twelve states of the U.S. See *Tables* at CALIFORNIA, COLORADO, FLORIDA, ILLINOIS, INDIANA, MICHIGAN, MINNESOTA, MONTANA, OHIO, OREGON, SOUTH DAKOTA, TENNESSEE.

2 Province, N Tanganyika, E Africa, on the shores of Lake Victoria; 39,096 sq. m.; pop. 1,249,892; ✳ Mwanza; comprises former Bukoba and Mwanza provs.

3 River ab. 35 m. long, E cen. Tasmania, Australia; flows N to join the South Esk at Longford.

Lake An'des (ăn'dēz). City, ⊗ of Charles Mix co., S South Dakota; pop. 1097.

Lake Ar'thur (är'thẽr). Town, Jefferson Davis parish, SW Louisiana. 37 m. ESE of Lake Charles; pop. 3541; in rice and sugar-producing section; fishing and hunting.

Lake Bluff (blŭf). Village, Lake co., NE corner of Illinois, on Lake Michigan 8 m. S of Waukegan; pop. 3494.

Lake But'ler (bŭt'lẽr). City, ⊗ of Union co., NE Florida; pop. 1311.

Lake Charles (chärlz). Commercial and industrial city, ⊗ of Calcasieu parish, SW Louisiana, 13 m. NNE of Calcasieu Lake; pop. 63,392; ships cotton, sugar, rice, fruit; sulfur and petroleum deposits nearby: petroleum refineries, chemical manufactories.

Lake City. **1** Town, a ⊗ of Craighead co., NE Arkansas; pop. 850.

2 Town, ⊗ of Hinsdale co., Colorado, 43 m. SE of Montrose; pop. 106.

3 City, ⊗ of Columbia co., N Florida, 44 m. NNW of Gainesville; pop. 9465; resort; trades in lumber and naval stores; headquarters for Ocala National Forest.

4 City, Calhoun co., NW cen. Iowa; pop. 2114.

5 City, ⊗ of Missaukee co., NW cen. Michigan; pop. 718.

6 City, Wabasha co., SE Minnesota, on Mississippi river 31 m. NNE of Rochester; pop. 3494.

7 Town, Florence co., E South Carolina, 22 m. S of Florence; pop. 6059; stock, poultry, and truck farms.

8 Town, Anderson co., E Tennessee, 9 m. W of Norris Dam; pop. 1914.

Lake Dallas Dam. See GARZA DAM, Texas.

Lake District. Mountainous region in NW England, comprised within Cumberland, Westmorland, and Furness dist., Lancashire, containing many well-known lakes and peaks. Among the lakes are Bassenthwaite, Buttermere, Coniston Water, Crummock Water, Derwentwater, Ennerdale Water, Grasmere, Hawes Water, Lowes Water, Rydal Water, Thirlmere, Ullswater, Wast Water, Windermere. A favorite resort of English poets, especially since Wordsworth's long residence here and his association with the other Lake Poets Southey and Coleridge; see GRASMERE, KESWICK.

Lake'field (lāk'fēld). Village, Jackson co., S Minnesota, 20 m. ENE of Worthington; pop. 1789.

Lake For'est (fŏr'ĕst; -ĭst). City, Lake co., NE corner of Illinois, on Lake Michigan 10 m. S of Waukegan; pop. 10,687. Lake Forest Coll. (1857; coed; Presbyterian); Barat Coll. of the Sacred Heart (1917; women).

Lake Ge·ne'va (jĕ·nē'vá). **1** City and resort, Walworth co., S Wisconsin, on shore of Lake Geneva 30 m. W of Kenosha; pop. 4929; Yerkes Observatory nearby.

2 = Lake of GENEVA.

Lake George (jôrj). Village, ⊗ of Warren co., E New York, on S end of Lake George 40 m. NE of Amsterdam; pop. 1026; year-round sports center.

Lake Harbour. Post of the Royal Canadian Mounted Police, on inlet of Hudson Strait, S Baffin I.

Lake'hurst (lāk'hûrst). Borough, Ocean co., E New Jersey, 8 m. NW of Toms River; pop. 2780; U.S. Naval Air Station; estab. 1919; here *Graf Zeppelin* started and finished 21-day around-the-world trip 1929 and the *Hindenburg* was destroyed by fire May 6, 1937.

Lake Jack'son (jăk's'n). City, Brazoria co., SE Texas, S of Houston; pop. 9651.

Lake'land (lāk'lănd). **1** City, Polk co., cen. Florida penin., 30 m. E of Tampa; pop. 41,350; winter resort; citrus fruit packing plants. Florida Southern Coll. (1886; coed.; Methodist).

2 City, ⊗ of Lanier co., S Georgia, 20 m. NE of Valdosta; pop. 2236; agricultural market.

Lake Lin'den (lĭn'dĕn). Village, Houghton co., NW Michigan penin., 67 m. NW of Marquette; pop. 1314; copper ore stamping mill.

La·kem'ba (lá·kĕm'bá). **1** Island group, ab. 33 islands, S end of Lau group, SE Fiji Is., SW Pacific Ocean.

2 Chief island of the Lakemba group, bet. 4 and 5½ m. in diameter, 12 sq. m., in 18°10'S lat.; long a meeting place bet. Fijians and Tonga islanders; produces copra and tropical fruits. Here first Wesleyan missionaries settled 1835.

Lake Mills (mĭlz). **1** Town, Winnebago co., N Iowa, 26 m. NW of Mason City; pop. 1758.

2 City, Jefferson co., SE Wisconsin, 23 m. E of Madison; pop. 2951; shoes, dairy equipment, dehydrated milk.

Lake'more (lāk'mōr). Village, Summit co., NE Ohio, 8 m. SE of Akron; pop. 2765.

La'ken·heath (lā'kĕn·hēth). Village, NW Suffolk, E England, 9 m. W of Thetford; U.S. air base.

Lake of the Ozarks. See Lake of the OZARKS.

Lake of the Woods. **1** Lake in N Minnesota and extending into Canadian provinces of Manitoba (on the W) and Ontario (on the E); ab. 65 m. long and from 10 to 60 m. wide; area 1851 sq. m., of which 466 sq. m. are in U.S. territory; elevation 1060 ft.; receives Rainy river from the SE and drains N into Lake Winnipeg.

2 County in Minnesota. See *Table* at MINNESOTA.

Lake O'ri·on (ōr'ĭ·ŭn). Village, Oakland co., SE Michigan, 10 m. NNE of Pontiac; pop. 2698; summer resort.

Lake of the Cherokees. See GRAND RIVER DAM.

Lake Plac'id (plăs'ĭd). Village, Essex co., NE New York, in Adirondack Mts. on Mirror Lake, near Lake Placid (*q.v.*), 40 m. SW of Plattsburg; pop. 2998; summer and winter resort, scene of international winter sports events; site of Lake Placid Club, founded 1895 by Melvil Dewey.

Lake Pleas'ant (plĕz''nt). Village and resort, ⊗ of Hamilton co., NE cen. New York, 50 m. ENE of Utica; pop. 718.

Lake Pleasant Dam. Dam completed 1927 across Agua Fria river on boundary of Yavapai and Maricopa cos., W cen. Arizona; height 256 ft.; impounds water, **Lake Pleasant,** for irrigation and water power.

Lake'port (lāk'pōrt). **1** City, ⊗ of Lake co., W California, on W side of Clear Lake; pop. 2303.

2 Village, Belknap co., cen. New Hampshire; suburb of Laconia on Lake Paugus.

Lake Prov'i·dence (prŏv'ĭ·dĕns). Town, ⊗ of East Carroll parish, NE corner of Louisiana, on Mississippi river 60 m. ENE of Monroe; pop. 5781.

Lake Saint John (sānt jŏn'). **1** See Lake SAINT JOHN.

2 *Fr.* **Lac-Saint-Jean** (lák'săN'zhäN'). County, S Quebec, Canada; divided into **East Lake Saint John** (*Fr.* Lac-Saint-Jean-Est [-ĕst']), 905 sq. m., pop. 31,128, ⊗ Saint Joseph d'Alma, and **West Lake Saint John** (*Fr.* Lac-Saint-Jean-Ouest [-wĕst']), 22,813 sq. m., pop. 50,878, ⊗ Roberval. See *Table* at QUEBEC.

Lake Spaul'ding Dam (spôl'dĭng). Dam completed 1919 across S Yuba river, N cen. California; height 275 ft.; impounds water for water power.

Lake Suc·cess' (sŭk·sĕs'). Village, Nassau co., SE New York, W Long Island, near N shore E of Flushing and ab. 4½ m. NW of Mineola; pop. 2954; headquarters of United Nations Security Council 1946-51.

Lake'view' (lāk'vū). **1** Urban area, Calhoun co., S Michigan, SW of Battle Creek; pop. 10,384.

2 Town, ⊗ of Lake co., S Oregon, 6 m. N of Goose Lake; pop. 3260; lumber, dairy products.

Lake Village. City, ⊗ of Chicot co., SE corner of Arkansas, 80 m. SSE of Pine Bluff; pop. 2998; resort on Lake Chicot; cotton gins, barrel-stave mills.

Lake'ville (lāk'vĭl). **1** Subdivision (est. pop. 1500) of town of SALISBURY, Connecticut; trade center.

2 Town, Plymouth co., SE Massachusetts, 15 m. S of Brockton; pop. 3209; in agricultural section.

Lake Wales (wālz). City, Polk co., cen. Florida penin., 25 m. ESE of Lakeland; pop. 8346; winter resort; Edward W. Bok's Mountain Lake bird sanctuary with Singing Tower nearby. See MOUNTAIN LAKE.

Lake Wash′ing·ton Ship Canal (wŏsh′ĭng·tŭn). See Lake WASHINGTON.

Lake′wood (lāk′wŏŏd). **1** City, Los Angeles co., SW coastal California, NE of Long Beach; pop. 67,126.
2 Urban community (unincorporated), Jefferson co., cen. Colorado, W of Denver; pop. 19,338.
3 Town, Ocean co., E New Jersey, 14 m. SW of Asbury Park; pop. 13,004; health and winter resort in pine forest and lake region. Georgian Court Coll. (1908; women).
4 Village, Chautauqua co., SW corner of New York, on Chautauqua Lake 5 m. W of Jamestown; pop. 3933.
5 City, Cuyahoga co., N Ohio, on Lake Erie 5 m. W of Cleveland; pop. 66,154; residential suburb of Cleveland.

Lake Worth (wûrth). **1** See Lake WORTH.
2 City, Palm Beach co., SE Florida, on Lake Worth (lagoon) 6 m. S of West Palm Beach; pop. 20,758; incorporated 1923.

La′khim·pur (lŭk′hēm·pŏŏr). Town, E Uttar Pradesh, 75 m. N of Lucknow; pop. 17,497.

Lakhnauti. See GAUR.

Lakhon. See NAKHON PHANOM.

La′kin (lā′kĭn). City, ⊗ of Kearny co., W Kansas; pop. 1432.

Lakki Bay. See LEROS.

La·ko·ni′a (*Mod. Gr.* lä′kô·nyē′ä). = *Laconia* department of Greece: see *Table* at GREECE.

La′kor (lä′kôr). Small island 10 m. by 6 m. in E part of Leti Is., Indonesia; pop. 1576.

La·ko′ta (là·kō′tà). City, ⊗ of Nelson co., E North Dakota; pop. 1066.

Lak′se Fjord (läk′sĕ). Inlet of Arctic Ocean on NE coast of Norway, bet. Porsanger Fjord and Tana Fjord.

La La·gu′na (lä lä·gŏŏ′nä). Commune, Santa Cruz de Tenerife prov. (W Canary Is.), Spain, NE Tenerife I., 2 m. NNW of Santa Cruz de Tenerife; pop. 33,042; former capital, and former seat of the Univ. of San Fernando; 16th-cent. cathedral; brandy, tobacco, leather.

La′leh·zar, Kuh′–i– (kŏŏ′hĕ·lä′lĕ·h′·zär′). Peak 14,350 ft. in Kerman prov., SE Iran, S of Kerman.

La Li′ber·tad′ (lä lē′vĕr·täth′). **1** Seaport on N shore of Santa Elena Penin., Guayas prov., W Ecuador, 55 m. W of Guayaquil; oil fields.
2 Department, SW El Salvador; 843 sq. m.; pop. (1942 est.) 146,238; ✳ Nueva San Salvador.
3 Seaport, La Libertad dept., SW El Salvador, 23 m. SSW of San Salvador; pop. 3500; coffee, sugar, sisal.
4 Department of Peru. See *Table* at PERU.
5 Municipality, NE Negros Oriental prov., Negros, Phil. Is., on Tañon Strait, 51 m. N of Dumaguete; pop. 17,795.

La′lin′ (lä′lĭn′). River ab. 200 m. long in Kirin prov., cen. Manchuria, flowing NW and W into Sungari river.

La·lín′ (lä·lēn′). Commune, Pontevedra prov., NW Spain, 28 m. NE of Pontevedra; pop. 18,620; agriculture; tanneries; paper mills.

La Lí′ne·a (lä lē′nä·ä). Commune, Cádiz prov., SW Spain, on Bay of Algeciras and Gibraltar frontier 56 m. SE of Cádiz; pop. 38,188; military garrison.

La Loche (là lōsh′). Small lake, NW Saskatchewan, Canada, source of Churchill river, its immediate outlet in short stream to Churchill lake. At its N end is **La Loche Portage**, ab. 12 m. long to Clearwater river, a headstream of the Athabaska and Mackenzie river system; much used by trappers and hunters.

La′lo Point (lä′lō). Cape at S end of Tinian I., Mariana Is., W Pacific, ab. 14°N; last stand of Japanese on the island Aug. 1, 1944.

La Lou·vière′ (là lŏŏ·vyâr′). Manufacturing commune, Hainaut prov., SW Belgium, 27 m. S of Brussels; pop. 23,852.

Lama. See LAMMA.

La Mad′da·le′na (lä mäd′dä·lä′nä). Seaport, Sassari prov., NW Sardinia, on Maddalena I. in Strait of Bonifacio 54 m. NE of Sassari; pop. 10,968.

La Ma′de·leine′ (lä mà′dlĕn′). **1** Rock shelter on the Vézère river above Les Eyzies (see Les EYZIES), Dordogne dept., SW France; type station, from primitive implements and carvings found here, of the Magdalenian period representing the highest paleolithic culture in Europe.
2 Commune, Nord dept., N France, NE suburb of Lille; pop. 22,831; metalworks, spinning mills, potteries.

La Mag′da·le′na Con·tre′ras (lä mäg′thä·lä′nä kôn·trā′räs). Town, N Federal District, cen. Mexico; pop. 7823.

La Mal′baie′ (là màl′bā′). Resort village, ⊗ of East Charlevoix co., S Quebec, Canada, at confluence of Malbaie and St. Lawrence rivers; pop. 2466; summer resort. Visited 1608 by Champlain who gave it its name because of poor anchorage; settled chiefly by Scots; American war prisoners confined here during American Revolution. Vicinity geologically interesting.

La Man′cha (lä män′chä). Geographical region, S cen. Spain; comprises Ciudad Real, S Toledo, NW Albacete, and SW Cuenca provs.; formerly the southernmost division of New Castile; high (ab. 2000 ft.), level, arid, treeless plateau, producing chiefly esparto grass and, in lesser quantity, grain and wine; celebrated in Cervantes' novel *Don Quijote de la Mancha*.

La Manche. See ENGLISH CHANNEL.

La·mar′ (là·mär′). **1** Name of counties in four states of the U.S. See *Tables* at ALABAMA, GEORGIA, MISSISSIPPI, TEXAS.
2 City, ⊗ of Prowers co., SE Colorado, on Arkansas river 50 m. E of La Junta; pop. 7369; trade center.
3 City, ⊗ of Barton co., SW Missouri, 32 m. NNE of Joplin; pop. 3608. Birthplace of Harry S. Truman, 33d president of the U.S.

La·marck′, Mount (là·märk′). Peak 13,302 ft. in Sierra Nevada, in E Fresno co., S cen. California.

La Marque (là märk′). City, Galveston co., SE coastal Texas, SE of Houston; pop. 13,969.

La′mas (lä′mäs). Town, San Martín dept., N Peru, 45 m. SE of Moyobamba; pop. (1940 est.) 5625.

Lamb (lăm). County in Texas. See *Table* at TEXAS.

Lambaesis. See LAMBESSA.

Lam′balle (län′bàl′). Commune, Côtes-du-Nord dept., NW France, ESE of St-Brieuc; pop. (1931) 4775; capital of the counts of Penthièvre 1134–1420.

Lam′ba·ré′né′ (län′bà′rā′nä′). Town, W Gabon, W equatorial Africa, on lower Ogooué river; hospital and medical settlement.

Lam′ba·ye′que (läm′bä·yā′kå). **1** Department of Peru. See *Table* at PERU.
2 Town, Lambayeque dept., NW Peru, near the coast just N of Chiclayo; pop. (1940 est.) 6846.

Lam′bel, Mount (läm′bĕl). Mountain 7054 ft. at S end of New Ireland, Bismarck Archipelago; highest point on island.

Lam′ber′sart′ (län′bĕr′sàr′). Commune, Nord dept., N France, NW suburb of Lille; pop. (1931) 14,377; spinning mills.

Lam′bert·ville (läm′bĕrt·vĭl). City, Hunterdon co., NW cen. New Jersey, on Delaware river 14 m. NNW of Trenton; pop. 4269; in agricultural region; varied manufactures; connected by bridge with New Hope, Pennsylvania, across the river.

Lam·bes′sa (läm·bĕs′à) or **Lam′bèse′** (län′bâz′); *anc.* **Lam·bae′sis** (läm·bē′sĭs). Commune, S Constantine dept., Algeria, N Africa, SW of Constantine and 17 m. W of ruins of Timgad; pop. 2264; center of agricultural district and site of a large convict establishment (built c. 1850). Ancient Lambaesis an important Roman town of S Numidia; its numerous ruins of special interest as being the remains of great Roman camp.

Lambeth. Metropolitan borough of London. See *Table* at LONDON.

Lam′bé′zel′lec′ (län′bā′zĕ′lĕk′). Commune, Finistère dept., NW France, N suburb of Brest; pop. (1931) 16,761; metalworks.

Lamb′ton (lăm[p]′tŭn). County, Ontario, Canada. See *Table* at ONTARIO.

Lam·bu′nao (läm-bōō′nou). Municipality, NW Iloilo prov., Panay, Phil. Is., in foothills of W range 26 m. NNW of City of Iloilo; pop. 23,249.

La′meng′ (lä′mĕng′). Town, W Yunnan, S China, on Burma Road just W of the Salween and NE of Lungling; fighting June 1944.

La·me′sa (lȧ·mē′sȧ). City, ⊗ of Dawson co., NW Texas, 43 m. NNW of Big Spring; pop. 12,438; raises cotton, cattle, corn; egg-drying plant.

La Me′sa (lä mā′sȧ). Residential city, San Diego co., SW corner of California, 8 m. NE of San Diego; pop. 30,441.

La′mi·a (lä′mĭ·ȧ; *Mod. Gr.* lä·mē′ä); *formerly in modern times* **Zi·tu′ni** (zē·tōō′nē; *Gr.* -nyē̇). Inland town, * of Phthiotis and Phocis dept., Greece, near head of Gulf of Lamia; in ancient times in Malis and nearer the shore line; pop. 14,205. Antipater besieged here by confederate Greeks under Leosthenes for several months (Lamian War, 4th cent. B.C.)

Lamia, Gulf of; *anc.* **Ma·li′a·cus Si′nus** (mȧ·lī′ȧ·kŭs sī′nŭs). Inlet of Aegean Sea on E coast of Greece; a W extension of the Atalante channel; on its S shore is the Pass of Thermopylae (*q.v.*).

Lam·lash′ (lăm·lăsh′). Village, E coast of Arran I., Bute co., SW Scotland; on **Lamlash Bay,** an inlet of the Firth of Clyde; fine harbor.

Lam′ma′ (lä′mä′) *or* **La′ma′.** Island, S part of New Territories, Hong Kong colony, China, just SW of Hong Kong I.; pop. ab. 2000.

Lam′me Fjord (lăm′ĕ). W extension of Ise Fjord on N coast of Sjælland, Denmark.

Lam′mer·muir′ (lăm′ẽr·mūr′), *or* **Lam′mer·moor′** (-mŏŏr′), **Hills.** Range of hills in East Lothian and Berwick cos., SE Scotland; highest point Says Law 1749 ft.

La·moille′ (lȧ·moil′). **1** River ab. 75 m. long, NW Vermont; flows W through Lamoille and S Franklin cos., S and W into Lake Champlain in NW Chittenden co.

2 County in Vermont. See *Table* at VERMONT.

La·mon′ Bay (lä·môn′). Large landlocked bay, an inlet of the Pacific on E coast of Luzon, Phil. Is.; ab. 60 m. each way, N to S and E to W; chiefly in Tayabas prov., its SE shore in Camarines Norte; protected on N by the islands of Polillo, Patnanongan, and Jomalig and contains the large island of Alabat in the S. Japanese landed here Dec. 22–28, 1941.

La·mong′an (lä·mông′än). Town, East Java prov., Indonesia, on railroad 25 m. WNW of Surabaja; pop. 11,012.

La·mo′ni (lȧ·mō′nĭ). Town, ⊗ of Decatur co., S Iowa, 68 m. SSW of Des Moines; pop. 2173.

La Mon′ja (lä mông′hä). Rocky islet, outer part of entrance to Manila Bay, part of Corregidor Is., Phil. Is., nearly 3 m. W of Corregidor I.

La·motte′ Peak (lȧ·mŏt′). Mountain 12,723 ft. in cen. Summit co., NE Utah.

La Moure (lȧ mŏŏr′). **1** County in North Dakota. See *Table* at NORTH DAKOTA.

2 City, ⊗ of La Moure co., SE North Dakota; pop. 1068.

Lam·pang (läm·päng). **1** Province, NW Thailand; 4827 sq. m.; pop. 308,384; * Lampang.

2 Town, its *, on left bank of Wang river and on railroad 45 m. SE of Chiang Mai; connected by highway with Chiang Rai.

Lam·pas′as (lăm·păs′ȧs). **1** County in Texas. See *Table* at TEXAS.

2 City, its ⊗, cen. Texas, 45 m. W of Temple; pop. 5061; shipping point for livestock, pecans, wool, mohair, furs, poultry; tourist resort, with mineral springs nearby.

Lam′pe·du′sa (läm′pĕ·dōō′sȧ; -zȧ; *Ital.* läm′pä·dōō′zä); *anc.* **Lop′a·du′sa** (lŏp′ȧ·dū′sȧ). One of the Pelagian Is. in Mediterranean Sea midway bet. Malta and Tunisia; 8 sq. m.; pop. in 1931 (including Linosa) ab. 4000; politically attached to Agrigento prov. SW Sicily, Italy; has one village, the port of Il Porto; Italian prison colony. Continuously bombarded for one day by Allied fleet June 12, 1943; taken June 13; according to peace treaty of 1947 its fortifications to be destroyed.

Lam′pert·heim (läm′pĕrt·hīm). Commune, Hesse state, Germany, near Rhine river 22 m. SSW of Darmstadt; pop. 11,580; manufactures cigars, furniture; electrical works.

Lampeti. See LETRINOI.

Lam·phun (läm·p′hōōn) *or* **Lam·pun** (läm·pōōn). **1** Province, NW Thailand; 1740 sq. m.; pop. 170,891; * Lamphun.

2 Town, its *, on railroad 15 m. S of Chiang Mai.

Lam·pio′ne (läm·pyō′nä). See PELAGIAN ISLANDS.

Lamp′sa·cus (lămp′sȧ·kŭs); *mod.* **Lap′se·ki** (läp′-sĕ·kē′). Ancient Greek colony in Mysia on the Hellespont opp. Callipolis (Gallipoli); famous for its wine. Under Persia early in 5th cent. B.C.; ally of Athens 479 B.C., later of Rome. Home of Strato of Lampsacus, Greek peripatetic philosopher.

Lam′pung (läm′pōōng), *or* **Lam′pong** (-pông), *or* **Lam′poeng** (-pōōng), **Bay.** Bay at the S end of the island of Sumatra, Indonesia, opening into Sunda Strait. Port of Telukbetung is at its head.

Lampung, *or* **Lampong, Districts;** *Du.* **Lam′-pong·sche District′en** (läm′pông·sĕ dĭs·trĭk′tĕ[n]). Region formerly a Dutch residency (area 11,111 sq. m., pop. 361,563, * Telukbetung), S Sumatra I., Indonesia. Low lands bordering on Sunda Strait and W Java Sea with S end of Barisan Mts. in the W; has two bays on the S: Semangka and Lampung; its rivers all flow eastward. Exports much rubber; raises also rice, tobacco, pepper, and coconuts. Has had in recent years many immigrants from Java. Occupied by Japanese, Feb. 1942.

Lamta. See LEPTIS MINOR.

La′mu (lä′mōō). **1** Island off the E coast of Kenya, E Africa, SW of Dicks Head and 150 m. N of Mombasa.

2 Seaport on the island of Lamu; pop. ab. 7000.

3 Town, Arakan division, W Lower Burma, near coast opp. Ramree I.

La·na′i (lä·nä′ē). Island in cen. Hawaii, W of Maui I.; 141 sq. m.; pop. 2115, a district of Maui co., state of Hawaii; separated from Molokai on the N by Kalohi Channel, from Maui on the E by Auau Channel, and from Kahoolawe on the SE by Kealaikahiki Channel. A single mountain, highest point 3480 ft.; pineapple plantations.

Lanai City. Town in Lanai dist. in center of Lanai I.; pop. 2056.

La·nal′hue, Lake (lä·näl′wȧ). Lake in S Chile, 23 m. S of the port of Lebu on the Pacific Ocean.

La·na′o (lä·nä′ō; -nou′). Province, W cen. Mindanao, Phil. Is.; 2574 sq. m.; pop. 243,437; * City of Dansalan. Bounded on N by Iligan Bay, on E by Bukidnon prov., on SE by Cotabato prov., on SW by Illana Bay, on W by Zamboanga prov., and separated on NW from Misamis Occidental by Panguil Bay; its W end an isthmus ab. 13 m. wide bet. Illana Bay and the long Panguil Bay on the N. A plateau region with mountains surrounding the large Lake Lanao in center. Little agriculture; chief industry fishing. Inhabitants chiefly Moros. Chief towns City of Dansalan and Kolambugan and Iligan municipalities.

History: From early times a Moro stronghold; some Spanish control established 1891–99; became part of Moro prov. 1903 and received civil government 1914.

Lanao, Lake. Lake in cen. Lanao prov., Mindanao, Phil. Is.; 91 sq. m., 22 m. long by 16 m. at widest; in plateau region N of range of active volcanoes; outlet is Agus river, flowing N to Iligan Bay.

Lan′ark (lăn′ẽrk). **1** County, Ontario, Canada. See *Table* at ONTARIO.

2 *or* **Lan′ark·shire** (-shǐr; -shẽr). County, S cen. Scotland; area 892 sq. m.; pop. (1951) 1,614,125; ⊗ Lanark; other towns Glasgow, Hamilton, Motherwell and Wishaw, Airdrie; chief river Clyde; shipbuilding (esp. at Glasgow), textile and machinery manufacture, coal and iron mining, engineering, livestock raising.

3 Burgh, ⊗ of Lanark co., S cen. Scotland, on the river Clyde 30 m. SE of Glasgow; pop. 6219; cotton mills. **New Lanark,** founded (1784) by David Dale and Richard Arkwright 1 m. SW, was the scene of some of Robert Owen's social and industrial experiments.

Lan′ca·shire (lăng′kȧ·shǐr; -shẽr) *or* **Lan′cas·ter** (lăng′kȧs·tẽr). Maritime, manufacturing, and mining county, NW England; area 1875 sq. m.; pop. (1951) 5,116,013; ⊗ Preston; industrial centers Liverpool, Manchester; watering places Blackpool, Fleetwood, Morecambe and Heysham, Southport; rivers include the Mersey and Ribble; large deposits of coal, iron, lead, copper, limestone; mining, manufacturing of textiles (esp. cotton), chemicals, machinery, glass, and rubber; shipbuilding.

History: Region part of Anglo-Saxon kingdom of Northumbria and of the Danelaw; honor of Lancaster an important medieval fief which in late 14th cent. became a county palatine; Lancastrian line of English kings the heirs of John of Gaunt, Duke of Lancaster; esp. in Industrial Revolution in 18th cent. Lancashire became noted manufacturing center (see MANCHESTER, LIVERPOOL, etc.).

Lan′cas·ter (lăng′kȧs·tẽr; *in U.S.,* also -kăs′tẽr; lăn′-kȧs′tẽr). **1** Name of counties in four states of the U.S. See *Tables* at NEBRASKA, PENNSYLVANIA, SOUTH CAROLINA, VIRGINIA.

2 Urban area, Los Angeles co., SW coastal California, NE of Los Angeles; pop. 26,012.

3 City, ⊗ of Garrard co., E cen. Kentucky, 13 m. E of Danville; pop. 3021.

4 Town, Worcester co., cen. Massachusetts, 10 m. SE of Fitchburg; pop. 3958; Atlantic Union Coll. (1882; coed.) at South Lancaster.

5 City, ⊗ of Schuyler co., N Missouri; pop. 740.

6 Industrial town, ⊗ of Coos co., N New Hampshire, on Connecticut river 18 m. W of Berlin; pop. 3138; summer resort and skiing center.

7 Village, Erie co., W New York, 11 m. E of Buffalo; pop. 12,254; residential suburb of Buffalo.

8 City, ⊗ of Fairfield co., S cen. Ohio, 27 m. SE of Columbus; pop. 29,916; in natural-gas belt; manufactures glassware, machinery. Birthplace of William T. Sherman.

9 City, ⊗ of Lancaster co., SE Pennsylvania, 35 m. ESE of Harrisburg; pop. 61,055; tobacco, livestock, and agricultural center; manufactures cork, linoleum, textiles (silk), watches, umbrellas, iron and steel products; Franklin and Marshall Coll. (1787; men); Theological Seminary of the Evangelical and Reformed Church. Founded c. 1721; became gunmaking center; played important part in French and Indian War, and, later, in Revolution; capital of U.S. briefly in 1777 and capital of Pennsylvania for 10 years before 1812; became W terminus of Philadelphia and Lancaster turnpike 1794.

10 Town, ⊗ of Lancaster co., N South Carolina, 21 m. SE of Rock Hill; pop. 7999; manufactures textiles, cottonseed oil, fertilizer.

11 City, Dallas co., NE Texas, S of Dallas; pop. 7501.

12 Village, ⊗ of Lancaster co., E Virginia; pop. (1950) 150.

13 City, ⊗ of Grant co., SW corner of Wisconsin, 13 m. WNW of Platteville; pop. 3703; farming and dairying.

14 See LANCASHIRE.

15 Municipal borough, NW Lancashire, England, on the Lune 46 m. N of Liverpool; pop. 51,650; textile mills, furniture factories, dyeing works; ancient castle. Norman with traces of Roman and Saxon construction.

Lancaster Sound. Channel ab. 50 m. wide bet. Devon I. and N Baffin I., E Franklin District, Northwest Territories, N Canada; opens into NW Baffin Bay.

Lan′chi′ (län′chē′). City, cen. Chekiang prov., E China, on railroad a few miles NW of Kinhwa.

Lan′chow′ (län′jō′) *or* **Kao′lan′** (kou′län′). City, ✳ of Kansu prov., N cen. China, on right bank of Hwang Ho and near Great Wall; pop. ab. 500,000; connected by highway with Sian to the ESE (310 m. by air); the last large Chinese city on the W highway to Turkistan and Russia; ab. 475 m. NW of Chungking; has many large industries and is trade center of extensive region.

Lan·cia′no (län-chä′nō). Commune, Chieti prov., Abruzzi e Molise, cen. Italy, 14 m. ESE of Chieti; pop. 23,367; cathedral; remains of 11th-cent. walls.

Lan′dau (län′dou), *also* **Landau in der Pfalz** (ĭn dẽr pfälts′). Manufacturing and commercial city, Bavaria, Germany, 18 m. NW of Karlsruhe; pop. 14,486; 13th-cent. early-Gothic church; 15th-cent. late-Gothic church; manufactures shoes, machinery, furniture, soap, brushes, pastry; trades in wine, fruit, cattle.

Lan′deck (län′dĕk). Town, in western Tirol province, SW Austria, on the Inn river ab. 40 m. W of Innsbruck; pop. 4749; E terminal of the Arlberg pass and tunnel route to Voralberg.

Lan′der (län′dẽr). **1** County in Nevada. See *Table* at NEVADA.

2 Town, ⊗ of Fremont co., cen. Wyoming, at SE corner of Shoshone Indian Reservation; pop. 4182; trade center in livestock-raising and mining section.

Lan′der′neau′ (län′dẽr·nō′). Commune, Finistère dept., NW France, ENE of Brest; pop. (1931) 8004.

Landes (länd). Department of France. See *Table* at FRANCE.

Landes, Les. See LES LANDES.

Landes de Lan′vaux′ (dē län′vō′). Strip of rocky, desolate land, S Morbihan dept., Brittany, France, near coast; studded with megalithic monuments. Cf. CARNAC.

Landeshut, Landeshut in Schlesien. See KAMIENNA GÓRA.

Lan′di Kha′na (lŭn′dĭ k′hä′nȧ). Fort and village, E Afghanistan, on the border in Khyber Pass just W of Landi Kotal.

Landi Kotal. See KHYBER PASS.

Lan′dis (lăn′dĭs). Town, Rowan co., cen. North Carolina, 13 m. SW of Salisbury; pop. 1763.

Land of Promise. See PROMISED LAND.

Lands′berg (länts′bẽrк). **1** *also* **Landsberg am Lech** (äm lĕк′). Commune, Bavaria, Germany, on Lech river ab. 20 m. S of Augsburg; pop. 7728.

2 *also* **Landsberg an der Warthe.** See GORZÓW.

Lands End *or* **Land's End** (lăndz ĕnd); *anc.* **Bo·le′-ri·um** (bō·lēr′ĭ·ŭm). Cape on SW coast of Cornwall, SW England; westernmost land of England.

Lands′hut (länts′hoōt). City, Bavaria, Germany, on Isar river NE of Munich; pop. 26,105; 12th-cent. castle (Burg Trausnitz; before 1555 called Burg Landshut); 17th-cent. church; 14th-cent. town hall; manufactures foodstuffs, brewery products, iron goods. Became city 1279; residence of dukes of Bavaria-Landshut 1255–1340, 1392–1503; site of a university 1800–26; scene of Napoleon's defeat of Archduke Charles 1809; capital of former government district of Lower Bavaria.

Lands·kro′na (länts·krōō′nȧ). Seaport, Malmöhus prov., SW Sweden; pop. 22,602; shipbuilding yards, sugar refineries, flour mills, chemical works; Swedes won naval victory off this port 1677 over the Danes.

Lane (lān). Name of counties in two states of the U.S. See *Tables* at KANSAS and OREGON.

Lane Cove. Town, E New South Wales, SE Australia; NW suburb of Sydney; pop. 15,134.

La·nett′ (lȧ·nĕt′). City, Chambers co., E Alabama, on Georgia border 40 m. E of Martin Lake; pop. 7674; known as Bluffton until its incorporation 1893; has cotton mills.

Lan·ga′na, Lake (läng·gä′nä). Lake in cen. Ethiopia, bet. Lakes Zwai and Shala, S of Addis Ababa.

Lan′ga·nes′, Cape (loung′gä·nâs′). Cape on NE extremity of Iceland.

Lang′chung′ (läng′ĭoöng′); *formerly* **Pao′ning′** (bou′-nĭng′). City, N Szechwan prov., S cen. China, on right bank of Kialing river ab. 135 m. N of Chungking; pop. ab. 100,000.

Lang′dale Pikes (lăng′dāl pīks′). Two mountain peaks, **Har′ri·son Stick′le** (hăr′ĭ·s'n stĭk′'l) 2401 ft. and **Pike o′ Stickle** (pīk′ ŭ) 2323 ft., in NW Westmorland, NW Eng.and in the Lake District.

Lang′don (lăng′dŭn). City, ⊗ of Cavalier co., NE North Dakota, 49 m. NNE of Devils Lake (city); pop. 2151; in agricultural section.

Lang′e·land′ (läng′ĕ·län′). Island ab. 33 m. long and 3 m. wide forming a part of Denmark, in Baltic Sea off SE coast of Fyn I. and bet. Fyn and Lolland; 110 sq. m.; pop. (1925) 21,212; chief town Rudköbing.

Langeland Belt (bĕlt). Strait in the Baltic Sea, S of the Great Belt, and bet. Langeland I. and Lolland I., Denmark.

Lang′e·marck (läng′ĕ·märk). Commune, West Flanders prov., NW Belgium, 5 m. NE of Ieper (Ypres); pop. 4360; destroyed during World War I and rebuilt since that time. First successful poison gas attack said to have been made here Apr. 22, 1915; lost to Allies but recovered Aug. 16, 1917.

Langenbielau. See BIELAWA.

Lang′en·dreer′ (läng′ĕn·drār′). Former commune (pop. 27 566), Arnsberg govt. dist., Westphalia prov., Prussia, Germany· since 1929 part of Bochum (q.v.).

Lang′en·sal′za (läng′ĕn·zäl′tsä). City, in the former Saxony province, Prussia, Germany, 19 m. WNW of Erfurt; pop. 11,979· sulfur spring; health resort. Scene of battles in Seven Years′ War 1761 and in Seven Weeks′ War 1866, when the Prussians defeated the Hanoverians; joined to Prussia 1815.

Lang′en·thal (läng′ĕn·täl). Commune, Bern canton, Switzerland, E of Solothurn; pop 7257.

Lang′e·oog (läng′ĕ·ōk). Narrow island 9 m. long in cen. part of East Frisian Is., off NW coast of Germany; W of Spiekeroog.

Lang′ford, Mount (läng′fĕrd). Peak 10,600 ft. in Yellowstone National Park, NW Wyoming.

Lang·ka′wi, Pu′lau (poō′lou läng·kä′wĕ). Island (*pulau*) in Andaman Sea off NW coast of Kedah state, W side of Malay Penin.; well cultivated and populous. Has peak 2888 ft.

Lan′glade (lăng′glād; lăn′glād; läng′lād). County in Wisconsin. See *Table* at WISCONSIN.

Lan′glade′ (län′glád′) See MIQUELON ISLAND.

Langlade, Isthmus of. Isthmus 7 m. long connecting the former islands of Great Miquelon and Little Miquelon (Langlade); has been created by the accumulation of sand on the reef bet. the two islands which were very close together and now comprise a single island (see MIQUELON ISLAND)

Lang′ley (läng′lĭ). Village, Aiken co., W South Carolina, ab. 8 m. SW of Aiken; pop. 1216.

Langley, Mount. Peak 14,042 ft. in Sierra Nevada, in E Tulare co., S cen. California.

Langley Field. U.S. Air Force base, Elizabeth City co., SE Virginia, just N of Hampton; Headquarters Tactical Air Command; research station of the National Advisory Council for Aeronautics; founded 1917.

Lang′lu La (läng′loō lä′). Mountain pass (*la*) 15,000 ft. in NE Tibet, ab. 90 m. N of Lhasa; in range that is the watershed bet. the Salween and Brahmaputra rivers.

Lang′nau (läng′nou). Town, Bern canton, Switzerland; in the valley of the Emme river, E of Bern; pop. 8376; ships Emmenthal cheese.

Lang′öy (läng′ŭ′ü). Westernmost island of the Vesterålen, in the Norwegian Sea off NW coast of Norway; 332 sq. m.; pop. 12,920.

Lan·gre′o (läng·grä′ō), *now* **Sa′ma** (sä′mä). Commune, Oviedo prov., NW Spain, 14 m. SE of Oviedo; in region producing fruit, wheat, hemp; iron and coal mining; manufactures ironware.

Lan′gres (län′gr′); *anc.* **An′de·ma·tun′num** (ăn′dĕ-mà tŭn′ŭm); *later* **Lin′go·nes** (lĭng′gö·nēz). Commune, Haute-Marne dept., NE France, ab. 38 m. NNE of Dijon on a high part (ab. 1550 ft.) of **Langres Plateau**; pop. (1931) 7558. Has fine view and in earlier times was important point strategically; cathedral and Church of St. Martin; remains of Roman town.

Lang′side′ (läng′sīd′). South suburb of Glasgow, Scotland; scene of the defeat of Mary, Queen of Scots, May 13, 1568.

Lang′s Nek. See LAING′S NEK.

Lang′son′ (läng′sŏn′; *Fr.* län′sôn′). Town, NE Tonkin, N Vietnam, on Chinese frontier of Kwangsi prov. 85 m. NE of Hanoi; most important town on northeastern frontier; connected by rail with Hanoi and with terminus of the line at Nacham. Occupied by French 1885.

Langs Point (längz). Elevation 4460 ft. in Cheyenne co., W Nebraska.

Lang′ston (läng′stŭn). Town, Logan co., cen. Oklahoma; pop. 136; founded 1890. Langston Univ. (1897; coed.).

Lang Su′an *or* **Lang·su′an** (läng·soō′än). Town, SW Thailand, on railroad along E coast of Malay Penin. (on Isthmus of Kra) 55 m. N of Surat Thani.

Lan′gue·doc′ (läng′dŏk′; läng′gwĕ·dŏk′; *Fr.* läng′dôk′). Historical region of S cen. France; bounded anciently on N by Auvergne and Lyonnais, E by Dauphiné, Comtat Venaissin, and Provence, SE by Mediterranean Sea, S by Roussillon, SW by Countship of Foix, W by Gascony, NW by Guienne; capitals Toulouse and Montpellier; Cévennes Mts. in E.

History: Region without unity except that based on a common language (*Fr.* langue d'oc) until 13th cent. when it was brought under influence of the counts of Toulouse; home of the Albigenses, exterminated in wars of religion in 13th cent.; region from Carcassonne to the Rhone passed to Louis IX of France 1229; western part left to counts of Toulouse until seized 1271 by Philip III; from 16th to 18th cents. scene of persecution of Protestants terminating in War of the Camisards 1702–05.

La·nier′ (là·nēr′). County in Georgia. See *Table* at GEORGIA.

La·nín′ (lä·nēn′). Volcanic peak 12,270 ft. on Argentina-Chile border, bet. SW Neuquén territory, W Argentina, and NE Valdivia prov., S cen. Chile.

Lan′ka·da′, Lake (läng′gä·thä′). Lake, N Chalcidice, Macedonia, NE Greece, W of Lake Bolbē and ENE of Salonika.

Lan′nion′ (là·nyôn′). Town, Côtes-du-Nord dept., NW France, NW of St-Brieuc; pop. 5540; small, active port on a river that flows into the English Channel; ruins of 15th-cent. castle of Tonguédec ab. 6 m. to the SE.

Lans′dale (lănz′dāl). Borough, Montgomery co., SE Pennsylvania, 21 m. N of Philadelphia; pop. 12,612; clothing, textiles, leather goods, tile, metal products.

Lans′downe (lănz′doun). **1** Residential borough, Delaware co., SE Pennsylvania, 5 m. W of Philadelphia; pop. 12,601; suburb of Philadelphia.

2 Cantonment and hill station, N Uttar Pradesh, N Indian Union, 120 m. NE of Delhi; pop. ab. 4000.

L′Anse (lăns). Village, ⊗ of Baraga co., NW Michigan penin., on Lake Superior 52 m. WNW of Marquette; pop. 2397.

Lans′ford (lăns′fĕrd; lănz′-). Borough, Carbon co., E Pennsylvania, 28 m. S of Wilkes-Barre; pop. 5958; coal mining; manufactures dresses, children's clothing.

Lan′sing (lăn′sĭng). **1** Village, Cook co., NE Illinois, on Indiana border 24 m. S of Chicago; pop. 18,098.

2 City, ✱ of Michigan, in Ingham co., S Michigan, 50 m. WSW of Flint; pop. 107,807; automobile manufacturing center and trading point for agricultural section; manu-

factures also agricultural implements, wheelbarrows, gas engines, boilers, chemicals, automobile accessories. Settled before 1840; succeeded Detroit as capital of Michigan 1847; site of first agricultural college in U.S., Michigan State College (authorized 1855, opened 1857; coed.), now in East Lansing.

Lan·tan'a (lăn·tăn'á). Town, Palm Beach co., SE Florida, S of Lake Worth; pop. 5021.

Lan'tao' (län'dou'). Island 58 sq. m., 16 m. long, SW part of New Territories, Hong Kong colony, China, across E part of mouth of Pearl river W of Hong Kong I., thinly populated (pop. ab. 8000).

Lan'tsang' (län'tsäng') **1** See MEKONG.
2 Town, SW Yunnan prov., S China.

La·nús' (lä·nōōs'). City, Buenos Aires prov., E Argentina, S suburb of Buenos Aires; pop. 286,400.

La·nu'vi·um (lá·nū'vĭ·ŭm). City in ancient Latium, Italy, *modern* **La·nu'vio** (lä·nōō'vyô), *formerly* **Ci'vi·ta La·vi'nia** (chē'vĕ·tä lä·vē'nyä), near Albanus Mons, 20 m. SE of Rome.

La·nu'za Bay (lä·nōō'sä). Inlet of Pacific on E coast of Surigao prov., Mindanao, Phil. Is., ab. 13 m. wide at entrance; Cauit Point marks its SE corner.

Lan'za·ro'te (län'thä·rō'tĕ; län'sä-). One of the Canary Is. (*q.v.*), 109 m. NE of Grand Canary I. and northeasternmost island of the group; in Las Palmas prov., Spain; 326 sq. m.; pop. (1930) 22,430; bold and precipitous coast; basaltic cliffs; volcanic in origin; chief town Arrecife.

La·oag' (lä·wäg'). **1** River ab. 60 m. long, largest of Ilocos Norte prov., Luzon, Phil. Is.; has many tributaries in upper course spreading out fanwise in mountains to N and S; lower course flows W to South China Sea.
2 Municipality on right bank of Laoag river, ab. 5 m. above its mouth, ✷ of Ilocos Norte prov., Luzon, Phil. Is.; pop. 41,842; center of local commerce.

La·oang' (lä·wäng'). Municipality, NE coast of Samar on **Laoang Island** (12 sq. m.), Phil. Is., 57 m. N of Catbalogan; pop. 19,736.

La·od'i·ce'a (lä·ŏd'ĭ·sē'á; lä'ŏd·ĭ-). Name of several Greek cities in Asia Minor or SW Asia; esp.: (1) City of Phrygia. See DENIZLI. (2) *or* **Laodicea ad Mare.** See LATAKIA, 2.

Laoet, Poe'lau (pōō'lou lout'); *also* **Laut** (lout). Island (*poelau*) in the Java Sea, off SE coast of Borneo, Indonesia, 50 m. long by 35 m. wide, 744 sq. m.; pop. 29,526; coal mines.

Lao'ho'kow' (lou'hō'kō'). City, N Hupeh prov., E cen. China, ab. 200 m. NW of Hankow; in World War II American air base, scene of considerable fighting in 1945.

Lao'igh, Ben (bĕn lū'ĭ). — BEN LUI.

Laoigh'is (lā'ĭsh) *or* **Leix** (lāks); *formerly* **Queen's** (kwēnz). County, cen. Eire, in Leinster prov.; 664 sq. m.; pop. 50,109; ⊗ Maryborough; rivers Barrow, Nore; agriculture, dairy farming, textile manufacture.

Lao'kay' (lou'kī'). Border town, N Tonkin, Vietnam, on Coi river 155 m. NW of Hanoi, on railroad leading from Hanoi into Yunnan prov., China; has many modern improvements. Only large town in region; strategically important, has long been subject to conflict bet. Chinese and Annamese; came under French control 1886.

Laon (läN) *anc.* **Lau·du'num** (lô·dū'nŭm). Commercial and manufacturing commune, ✷ of Aisne dept., N France, 77 m. NE of Paris; pop. 20,254; railroad center; 12th-cent. Gothic cathedral, old episcopal palace (now the palace of justice). 12th-cent. church. 13th-cent. gates; to the SW is the Abbey of Prémontré, founded 1119; agricultural and normal schools; manufactures metal goods, sugar; noted for production of artichokes, asparagus, fruits.
History: Probably the *Bibrax* of the Gauls; fortified by Romans in 5th cent.; episcopal see 5th–18th cents.; checked invasions of Franks Vandals, Huns etc.; held successively by Burgundians, English, French in Hundred Years' War; scene of Napoleon's defeat by Blücher 1814; occupied by Germans in Franco-Prussian War and

both World Wars; taken by Americans Aug. 1944.

La O'ro·ta'va (lä ō'rō·tä'vä). Commune, Santa Cruz de Tenerife prov. (W Canary Is.), Spain; includes **Puer'to Orotava** (pwĕr'tô), N cen. Tenerife I., 20 m. WSW of Santa Cruz de Tenerife, and **Vil'la Orotava** (bē'[l]yä), 4 m. SE of Puerto Orotava; pop. 17,682; health resort.

La O·ro'ya (lä ō·rō'yä). Town, Junín dept., cen. Peru, 137 m. by rail E of Callao; pop. (1940 est.) 14,492; altitude 12,180 ft.; lead refinery, large copper smelter.

Laos (lous; lä'ōs). **1** Region in cen. Indochina, with indefinite boundaries, inhabited by the Laos; includes the valley of the middle Mekong and those of the upper tributaries of the Chao Phraya; by some the Shan States are also included.
2 Kingdom, N and NW Indochina, formerly (1949–54) an independent state within the French Union; before 1949, a protectorate; area 91,428 sq. m.; pop. (1963 est.) 2,500,000; ✷ Vientiane. Bounded by the province of Yunnan, China on the N, by Vietnam on the E, by Cambodia on the S, by Thailand on the SW and W, and by Burma on the NW. In the NW occupies the valley of the Mekong but most of its N and S extent lies E of that river which forms boundary with Thailand. Mountainous, with peaks in the N above 9000 ft. and in the S ab. 5000; thickly forested. As a protectorate was the least developed part of French Indochina. Population is much mixed; chiefly Thais (including Laos), aboriginal races, and people from China, Burma, etc. Chief towns Vientiane, Luang Prabang, Thakhek. Suffered from many invasions in early times; Vientiane destroyed and annexed by Siamese 1828; came under French administration 1893 as a protectorate; ceded small strip to Siam 1941 but received it again 1946; became autonomous 1946.

Lao'shan' (lou'shän'). Bay and hills (**Laoshan Hills**) on shore of bay, E Shantung, NE China, ab. 20 m. NE of Tsingtao; famous for scenic beauty.

Laoyao. See LIENYUNKANG.

La·pac' (lä·päk'). Island in Tapul group, cen. Sulu Archipelago, Phil. Is., just W of Siasi I.; 16 sq. m.; pop. 5804; forms part of Siasi municipality.

La Pal'lice' (lä pȧ'lēs'). Port, NW Charente-Maritime dept., W France, ab. 3 m. WSW of La Rochelle; built to accommodate large vessels which cannot get into the harbor of La Rochelle; German submarine base during World War II

La Pal'ma (lä päl'mä; *Angl.* lȧ päl'mȧ). **1** Town and port, E Panama, ✷ of former Darien prov.; pop. 1103; on an inlet of Gulf of Panama 100 m. SE of Panama
2 *originally* **San Mi·guel' de la Pal'ma** (sän mĕ·gĕl' dĕ lä päl'mä). One of the Canary Is. (*q.v.*), 53 m. WNW of Tenerife I., in Santa Cruz de Tenerife prov., Spain; 280 sq. m.; pop. 51,784; mountainous; chief town Santa Cruz de la Palma. Occupied by Alonzo de Lugo 1491.

La Pam'pa (lä päm'pä; *Angl.* lȧ päm'pȧ). Territory of Argentina. See *Table* at ARGENTINA.

La Parida. See Cerro BOLÍVAR.

La Paz (lä päs'; *Angl.* lȧ päz'). **1** Town, Entre Ríos prov., E Argentina, on left bank of the Paraná ab. 85 m. NNE of Paraná; pop. (est.) 15,431.
2 Department of Bolivia. See *Table* at BOLIVIA.
3 *in full* **La Paz de A'ya·cu'cho** (lä päz' thä ä'yä·kōō'chō). City, ✷ of La Paz dept., W Bolivia, and a ✷ of Bolivia (the actual seat of government), E of Lake Titicaca; pop. (1943 est.) 301,000; altitude 11,910 ft.; highest capital in the world, located in valley at foot of Illimani; principal industrial and distributing center of Bolivia; exports bar tin, quinine bark, wolfram, antimony lead, and silver; cathedral, university, National Institute of Bacteriology Founded 1548 by Alonso de Mendoza as Pueblo Nuevo de Nuestra Señora de la Paz; twice besieged by 40,000 Indians in revolt 1781–82; joined Chuquisaca (Sucre) in revolt against Spanish (July 1809) which was later suppressed, became part of independent Bolivia 1825 and name changed to La Paz

de Ayacucho (literally. The Peace of Ayacucho) to commemorate the battle of Ayacucho; made capital of republic 1898.

4 Department, S El Salvador; 909 sq. m.; pop. (1942 est.) 113,890; ✳ Zacatecoluca.

5 Department, SW Honduras; 1247 sq. m.; pop. (1945 est.) 48,658; ✳ La Paz.

6 Town, ✳ of La Paz dept., SW Honduras, 33 m. W of Tegucigalpa; pop. (1935) 3174; mining and agricultural center.

7 Town, SE Lower California, NW Mexico, on S shore of **La Paz Bay**; ✳ of Lower California South District; pop. 10,401; has trade connections with chief Pacific ports of North America; center for pearl fishing, silver mining, and agriculture.

8 Town, San Luis Potosí state, cen. Mexico; pop. 5071.

La·peer′ (lȧ·pēr′). **1** County in Michigan. See *Table* at MICHIGAN.

2 City, ⊗ of Lapeer co., E Michigan, 20 m. E of Flint; pop. 6160; makes cabinets, cedar chests, bookcases.

La Pe·rouse′ Bay (lä′ pē·rōōz′). Bay on S coast of Maui I., Hawaii.

La Pérouse Island. See VANIKORO.

La Pérouse Strait. See SOYA STRAIT.

La Pie·dad′, in full **La Piedad Ca·va′das** (lä pyȧ-thäth′ kä·vä′thäs). Town, Michoacán state, SW Mexico, on Lerma river and on railroad 110 m. W of Querétaro; pop. 12,369.

Lapin. See LAPPI.

La′pi·nin′ (lä′pē·nēn′). Long flat island off N E Bohol on W side of Canigao Channel, Phil. Is.; 20 sq. m.; pop. 5350; mangrove-covered.

Lap′land (lăp′lănd; -lănd); *Norw.* **Lap′land** (läp′län); *Swed.* **Lapp′land** (läp′länd); *Finnish* **Lap′pi** (läp′pĭ). A region extending over N Norway, N Sweden, N Finland, and the Kola Penin. in NW Russia, all above the Arctic Circle; total area ab. 150,000 sq. m., with larger parts in Sweden and Russia; pop. ab. 30,000 Lapps (two thirds in Norway), a Mongoloid race, largely nomadic; mountains, tundra, swamps, forests, and many lakes (Torne, Inari, Imandra) and rivers; chief industries fishing and reindeer raising; has several mining towns, esp. Kiruna and Gällivare in Sweden. Lapps known from earliest times but have usually been held subject by stronger peoples (Swedes, Norwegians, Finns, or Russians); since 19th cent. they have been treated with much more consideration by the controlling governments.

La Pla′ta (lȧ plä′tȧ). **1** County in Colorado. See *Table* at COLORADO.

2 Town, ⊗ of Charles co., S Maryland; pop. 1214.

La Pla′ta (lȧ plä′tȧ; *Span.* lä plä′tä). **1** or **Buenos Aires.** Viceroyalty in Spanish South America, established 1776, including modern Argentina, Uruguay, Paraguay, and Bolivia (then known as Upper Peru); ✳ Buenos Aires; unsuccessfully attacked by British 1806, 1807; divided into self-governing units during wars for independence of Latin American states c. 1812–28.

2 Seaport, ✳ of Buenos Aires prov., E Argentina, 35 m. ESE of Buenos Aires; pop. (est.) 256,378; founded 1882 as the new capital of the province at village of Ensenada, now part of it; laid out like Washington, D.C.; National University.

3 River ab. 35 m. long in E cen. Puerto Rico; flows N into Atlantic Ocean.

la Plata, Río de. See RÍO DE LA PLATA.

La Pla′ta Mountains (lȧ plä′tȧ). A range of the Rocky Mts. in SW Colorado; highest peak Hesperus Peak 13,225 ft.

La Plata Peak. Mountain 14,340 ft. in Chaffee co., cen. Colorado.

La Pointe (lȧ point′). Settlement on Madeline I., one of the Apostle Is. (*q.v.*).

La·porte′ (lȧ·pōrt′). Borough and mountain resort ⊗ of Sullivan co., NE Pennsylvania; pop. 195.

La Porte (lȧ pōrt′). **1** County in Indiana. See *Table* at INDIANA.

2 Industrial city, ⊗ of La Porte co., N Indiana, 25 m. W of South Bend; pop. 21,157; manufactures road-building machinery, steel-tube furniture, farm implements.

3 City, Harris co., SE Texas, on Galveston Bay 20 m. ESE of Houston; pop. 4512.

La Porte City. Town, Black Hawk co., NE cen. Iowa, 16 m. SE of Waterloo; pop. 1953.

Lap′pa′ (läp′pä′). Customs port on SE coast of **Lappa**, or **Pa·te′ra** (pä·târ′ȧ), **Island** opp. Macao, Kwangtung prov., SE China, on W side of mouth of Pearl river; serves as station for Chinese supervision of junk traffic in Canton-Hong Kong area.

Lap′peen·ran′ta (läp′pân·rän′tä). Town, Viipuri dept., SE Finland, near Karelian border; pop. (1939 est.) 13,100.

Lap′pi (läp′pĭ). **1** See LAPLAND.

2 or **La′pin** (lä′pĭn). Department of N Finland, the Finnish part of the region of Lapland. See *Table* at FINLAND.

Lappland. See LAPLAND.

Lapp′mark (lăp′märk; *Swed.* läp′märk). General name for the N districts of Sweden (see LAPLAND), inhabited by Lapps.

La·prai′rie (lȧ·prâr′ĭ). **1** County, Quebec, Canada. See *Table* at QUEBEC.

2 Town, its ⊗, S Canada, on St. Lawrence river ab. 8 m. SSE of Montreal across the river; pop. 4058; summer resort; has an old fort which was attacked 1691 by New England troops; starting point of first railroad in British North America 1832.

Lapseki. See LAMPSACUS.

Lap′te·va Strait (läp′tyĕ·vȧ). Passage ab. 27 m. wide bet. mainland of N Yakutsk Republic, Soviet Russia, Asia, and Bolshoi I. of the Lyakhov Is.; connects East Siberian Sea and Laptev Sea.

Lap′tev Sea (läp′tyĕf); *Russ.* **Lap′te·vykh** (läp′tyĕ-vĭk); *formerly* **Nor′den·skjöld′ Sea** (nōōr′dĕn·shŭld′). Part of Arctic Ocean along N coast of Soviet Russia, Asia, bet. Severnaya Zemlya on W and New Siberian Is.

La′puan (lä′pwȧn). River ab. 100 m. long, Vaasa dept., W Finland; flows N into Gulf of Bothnia.

La Puen′te (lä pwĕn′tē). City, Los Angeles co., SW California, NNE of Long Beach; pop. 24,723.

La Pun·til′la (lä pōōn·tē′yä) Cape on SW coast of Ecuador, the tip of Santa Elena Penin.

Lapurdum. See BAYONNE, France.

Lap′wai (läp′wā). Village, Nez Perce co., W Idaho, ab. 12 m. E of Lewiston on S tributary of the Clearwater river; pop. 500; first white settlement in Idaho 1836; abandoned 1847 after Whitman massacre; reopened 1871. Site of U.S. Indian agency.

La Quia′ca (lä kyä′kä). Town, N Jujuy prov., NW Argentina, on border of Bolivia 175 m. from Jujuy; altitude over 10,000 ft.; railroad terminus; on the Pan American Highway.

La·quin′horn (lä·kvēn′hôrn). Peak 13,140 ft. in the Pennine Alps, S Switzerland, S of Simplon Pass.

Lar (lär). Town, S Iran, on caravan route 125 m. WNW of Bandar Abbas; former ✳ of Laristan prov.; pop. ab. 12,000.

La′ra (lä′rä). State of Venezuela. See *Table* at VENEZUELA.

La·ra′cha (lä·rä′chä). Commune, La Coruña prov., NW Spain, 11 m. WSW of La Coruña; pop. 11,459.

La′rache′ (*Fr.* lȧ·räsh′; *Span.* lä·rä′chä; *Arab.* **El A·raish′** (ăl ŭ·rīsh′); *anc* **Lix′us** (lĭk′sŭs). Seaport on Atlantic coast, N Morocco; pop. (1936) 29,477, ancient city of importance under the Phoenicians and as a Roman colony; belonged to Spain 1610–89 and from 1912.

La·raish′ (lŭ·rīsh′). Var. of LARACHE.

Lar′a·mie (lăr′ȧ·mĭ). **1** River ab. 200 m. long, SE Wyoming, rises in N Colorado, flows N across Wyoming border, turns NE and empties into North Platte river.

2 County in Wyoming. See *Table* at WYOMING.

3 City, ⊗ of Albany co., SE Wyoming, 45 m. WNW of Cheyenne; pop. 17,520; trade center in livestock-raising section; coal, iron, gold, silver, and petroleum deposits nearby; oil refineries, cement factories, stockyards. Univ. of Wyoming (1887; coed.).

Laramie Mountains *or* **Range.** Range in SE Wyoming and N Colorado; highest point **Laramie Peak** 10,272 ft.

Laranda. See KARAMAN.

La·ran·toe′ka *or* **La′ran·tu′ka** (lä′rän·tōō′kä). Town and port on NE coast of Flores I., Lesser Sunda Is., Indonesia; seat of important native state in early times.

La′rat (lä′rät). Island 20 m. long by 7 m. wide in N part of Tanimbar Is., E Malay Archipelago, Indonesia.

L'Ar′ba′ (lär′bä′). Commune, Alger dept., N Algeria, just S of Algiers; pop. 12,253.

Larch (lärch). River ab. 300 m. long (with longest headstream) in N Quebec prov., Canada; flows NE to unite with the Kaniapiskau river and form the Koksoak river.

Larch′mont (lärch′mŏnt). Residential village, Westchester co., SE New York, on Long Island Sound 20 m. NE of New York City; pop. 6789.

La·re′do (lá·rā′dō). City and port of entry, ⊗ of Webb co., S Texas, on Rio Grande opp. Nuevo Laredo, Mexico; pop. 60,678; railroad center; shipping point for onions, grapefruit, limes, oil, cattle; produces cannel coal, natural gas, oil; manufactures straw hats, foundry products, shoes and clothing; oil refineries, antimony smelter, brickworks, stockyards. Established by Spanish settlers 1755; occupied by Texas Rangers 1846 and by forces of Gen. Lamar 1847; chartered as city 1852.

Laredo, Nuevo. See NUEVO LAREDO.

La′res (lä′räs). Municipality (pop. 26,922) and town (pop. 4216), W cen. Puerto Rico.

Lar′go (lär′gō). City, Pinellas co., W cen. Florida, S of Clearwater; pop. 5302.

Lar′go Cay (lär′gō). Island in N Caribbean Sea, E of Isle of Pines and S of W Cuba.

Largs (lärgz). Seaport burgh, Ayr co., SW Scotland; pop. 8606; watering place; scene of victory of King Alexander III over Haakon IV of Norway 1263.

La Ri′ca′ma′rie′ (lä rē′kà′mà′rē′). Commune, Loire dept., SE cen. France, 2 m. SSE of Saint-Étienne; pop. (1931) 10,246; coal mining.

La Riège. See ARIÈGE.

Lar′i·mer (lär′ĭ·mẽr). County in Colorado. See *Table* at COLORADO.

Lar′i·more (lär′ĭ·mōr). City, Grand Forks co., E North Dakota, 28 m. W of Grand Forks; pop. 1714.

La Rio′ja (lä ryô′hä). **1** Province of Argentina. See *Table* at ARGENTINA.

2 Town, ✳ of La Rioja prov., NW Argentina, in Andine region 80 m. SSW of Catamarca; pop. (est.) 15,312.

3 A region of N Spain, chiefly in Logroño prov.; a winegrowing district along the upper Ebro; ab. 1690 sq. m.

La·ris′sa (lá·rĭs′á); *Gr.* **La′ri·sa** (lä′rē·sä). **1** Department of Greece. See *Table* at GREECE.

2 City, ✳ of Larissa dept., E Thessaly, Greece, on Salambria river ENE of Trikkala; pop. 23,899; railroad center. Anciently capital of the Pelasgians; supported Athens in Peloponnesian War; headquarters of Ali Pasha in Greek War of Independence; scene of severe fighting bet. Germans and army of Greeks and British Apr. 1941.

La′ri·stan′ (lä′rē·stän′). Province, S Iran, on the Persian Gulf; 21,020 sq. m.; ✳ Bandar Abbas; has mountains, arid upland, and swampy coastal strip.

Larius, Lacus. See Lake COMO.

Lark *or* **Larke** (lärk). River ab. 26 m. long in Suffolk and Cambridge, E England; flows ENE into the Ouse near Ely.

Lar·ka′na *or* **Lar·kha′na** (lär·kä′nà). Town, NW Sind prov., Pakistan, near W bank of Indus river 200 m. NNE of Karachi; pop. 26,841; manufactures cotton, silk, leather, metalware.

Lark′spur (lärk′spûr). City, Marin co., W California, ab. 10 m. NW of San Francisco; pop. 5710.

Larks′ville (lärks′vĭl). Borough, Luzerne co., E Pennsylvania, 3 m. W of Wilkes-Barre; pop. 4390; coal mining.

Lar′na·ca (lär′nà·kà). **1** District, SE Cyprus, E Mediterranean Sea; 397 sq. m.; pop. (1931) 42,208.

2 Seaport, its ✳, 23 m. SE of Nicosia; pop. (1942 est.) 14,220; exports barley, wheat, fruits, gypsum, and asbestos. On part of site of ancient Citium (*q.v.*).

Larne (lärn). Municipal borough, co. Antrim, NE Northern Ireland, seaport at head of Lough Larne; pop. 11,976; trade center and watering place; linen manufacture. Edward Bruce landed nearby 1315 on his journey to accept Irish throne.

Lar′ned (lär′nĕd; -nĭd). City, ⊗ of Pawnee co., cen. Kansas, at confluence of Arkansas and Pawnee rivers 24 m. SW of Great Bend; pop. 5001; on Santa Fe Trail.

La Ro′chelle′ (lä rô′shĕl′); *anc.* **Ru·pel′la** (rōō·pĕl′à). Fortified seaport, ✳ of Charente-Maritime dept., W France, on Bay of Biscay 124 m. SW of Tours; pop. 47,737; 15th-cent. Gothic town hall, 18th-cent. cathedral, old episcopal palace (now library and museum), 16th-cent. "House of Henry II"; important fisheries; manufactures porcelain, tile, sugar, glass. Anciently capital of Aunis; made commune 1199; became chief Huguenot stronghold in 16th cent.; besieged by Richelieu 1627–28 and forced through famine to capitulate. See LA PALLICE.

La Roche′–sur–Yon′ (lä rôsh′sür·yôɴ′). Commune, ✳ of Vendée dept., W France, 37 m. S of Nantes; pop. 16,073; agricultural trade center; horse breeding. Founded by Napoleon 1804 to serve as capital of Vendée dept.; called **Na′po·lé′on′–Ven′dée′** (nà′pô′lā′ôɴ′-väɴ′dā′) 1804–14, 1848–70, and **Bour′bon′–Ven′dée′** (bōōr′bôɴ′-) 1814–48.

La Ro′da (lä rrô′thä). Commune, Albacete prov., SE Spain, 21 m. NW of Albacete; pop. 11,602; agricultural products.

La Ro·ma′na (lä rrô·mä′nä). Seaport, Seibo prov., E Dominican Republic, 23 m. E of San Pedro de Macorís; pop. (commune, 1941) 28,868, (city, 1944 est.) 13,814; sugar, coffee, cacao.

la Ronge, Lac. See Lac la RONGE.

Lar′rey Point (lär′ĭ). Cape on NW coast of Western Australia in 20°S lat.

Lar′sa (lär′sà); *Bib.* **El·la′sar** (ĕl·lā′sär). Ancient city of S Babylonia, on left bank of the Euphrates river bet. Erech and Ur. Known in time of Abraham (*Gen.* xiv. 1) and flourished in period of Sumerian decline c. 2200 to c. 1950 B.C.

Lars Chris′ten·sen Coast (lärz krĭs′tĕn·s'n). Section of coast of Antarctica, E of Mac-Robertson Coast on the Indian Ocean; lat. ab. 68°S; long. 69°30′ to 74°E; discovered by Norwegian whalers Jan. 1931 and claimed by Norway.

Lar′sen Shelf Ice (lär′s'n). Shelf ice in NW Weddell Sea, along E coast of Palmer Penin., Antarctica, from 64°30′S to ab. 69°S; explored and named 1893.

La·rue′ (lá·rōō′). County in Kentucky. See *Table* at KENTUCKY.

Lar′vik′ (lär′vēk′). Seaport, ⊗ of Vestfold co., SE Norway, at head of **Larvik Fjord**; pop. 10,471; lumber, granite quarries, distilleries; manufactures small arms.

La Sa′gra (lä sä′grä). Mountain 7818 ft. in E Andalusia, S Spain, in Granada prov.

La Sal (lá säl′). Mountain group, Grand and San Juan cos., E Utah; highest Mt. Peale 13,089 ft.

La Salle (lá säl′). **1** Name of a parish in Louisiana and of counties in two states of the U.S. See *Tables* at LOUISIANA, ILLINOIS, TEXAS.

2 City, La Salle co., N Illinois, 13 m. W of Ottawa; pop. 11,897; coal mines, zinc.

3 Town on S shore of Montreal I., S Quebec, Canada; part of Greater Montreal; pop. 11,633; N terminus of railroad bridge.

La Sa·lud′ (lä sä·lōō̆th′). Municipality, La Habana prov., W Cuba, 18 m. S of Havana; pop. 6225.

Las An′i·mas (läs än′i·mäs). **1** County in Colorado. See *Table* at COLORADO.
2 City, ⊗ of Bent co., SE Colorado, on Arkansas river 20 m. E of La Junta; pop. 3402; founded 1869; farming, dairying, poultry raising.

La Sarre (lá sär′; *Fr.* lȧ sȧr′). Village, Abitibi co., SW Quebec, Canada; pop. 2744.

Las Be′la (lŭs bā′lȧ). Former state, SE Baluchistan States, Pakistan; 7043 sq. m.; pop. (1941) 69,067; ✳ Bela; formerly under suzerainty of Kalat. Hab river formed most of E boundary with Sind; valley and delta of Purali river occupy cen. and W part.

Las Cas·ca′das (läs käs·kä′thäs). Village, Balboa dist. SE Canal Zone, on W side of Panama Canal just NW of Gaillard Cut; pop. 124.

Las′caux′ Cave (läs′kō′). See MONTIGNAC.

Las Charcas. See CHARCAS Spanish audiencia.

Las Con′chas (läs kôn′chäs). Town, Buenos Aires prov., E Argentina, on E shore of Río de la Plata ab. 18 m. NW of Buenos Aires; pop. (est.) 23,540.

Las Cru′ces (läs krōō′sĕs; -sĭs). Town, ⊗ of Dona Ana co., S New Mexico, near the Rio Grande 42 m. NNW of El Paso, Texas; pop. 29,367; in irrigated agricultural region (cotton, sugar beets, fruit, alfalfa); livestock; silver, lead, and fluorspar deposits in vicinity. New Mexico State Univ. of Agriculture, Engineering, and Science (1888; coed.) in nearby University Park.

La Selle (lȧ sĕl′). Mountain group in SE Haiti, Hispaniola I., West Indies; highest peak **La Selle** 8793 ft.

La′sem (läsĕm). Town, Central Java prov., Indonesia, near coast just E of Rembang; pop. 15,731.

La Se·re′na (lä sȧ·rā′nä). City, cen. Chile, ab. 220 m. N of Valparaíso; ✳ of Coquimbo prov.; pop. 21,742; bishopric; court of appeals. Founded 1544; destroyed by Indians; rebuilt 1549; sacked by English pirates 1680; scene of Chilean Declaration of Independence Feb. 12, 1818.

Lasēthion. = *Lasithion* department of Greece: see *Table* at GREECE.

La Seyne–sur–Mer (lä sân′sür·mâr′). Seaport commune, Var dept., S France, on Mediterranean Sea 4 m. SW of Toulon; pop. 27,073; shipbuilding works; sawmills.

Las Flo′res (läs flō′räs). Town, Buenos Aires prov., E Argentina, 110 m. S of Buenos Aires.

Las Guá′si·mas (läz gwä′sĕ·mäs). Locality in S Oriente prov., E Cuba, ESE of Santiago de Cuba; scene of engagement June 24, 1898, won by Americans, which was preliminary to battle of El Caney and taking of Santiago.

La·shio′ (lä·shō′). Town, ✳ of Shan State (formerly in Northern Shan States), E cen. Burma, 130 m. NE of Mandalay; pop. 4638; terminal of railroad from Mandalay and starting point of the Burma Road (*q.v.*), 260 m. by air to Kunming, 700 m. by road. Taken by Japanese Apr. 26, 1942.

Lash′kar (lŭsh′kĕr). City, Madhya Pradesh, N cen. Indian Union; pop. (1941) 113,718; formerly ✳ of Gwalior state; trade center; constitutes the new part of Gwalior town (*q.v.*), and lies a few miles S of the old city; originally the camp site (Hindustani *lashkar* the camp) of the maharaja's army.

La Sila. = *Silagian Mountains:* see APENNINES.

La·si′thi Mountains (lä·sē′thĕ). Mountains, E Crete; highest point Diktē (*q.v.*) 7170 ft.

La·si′thi·on (lä·sē′thyôn). Department of Greece. See *Table* at GREECE.

Las Ma·rí′as (läz mä·rē′äs). Municipality (pop. 9237) and town (pop. 511), W Puerto Rico; town is inland 10 m. ENE of Mayagüez.

Las Na′vas de To·lo′sa (läz nä′väz thä tô·lō′sä). Village, Jaén prov., NE Andalusia, S Spain; scene of battle July 16, 1212 in which Alfonso VIII defeated the Moors.

Läsö. = LÆSÖ.

La So·la′na (lä sô·lä′nä). Commune, Ciudad Real prov., S cen. Spain, 39 m. E by S of Ciudad Real; pop. 13,462; agricultural products.

La Sou′fri·ère′ (lä sōō′frē′âr′) *or* **Soufrière.** Volcano 4048 ft. at N end of St. Vincent I. in the Windward Is., West Indies; violent eruption May 7, 1902, resulting in loss of 2000 lives; remained active until Mar. 1903.

Las Pal′mas (läs päl′mäs). **1** Province of Spain. See *Table* at SPAIN.
2 Seaport city, ✳ of Las Palmas prov. (E Canary Is.), Spain, in NE Grand Canary I., 57 m. SE of Santa Cruz de Tenerife; pop. (1941 est.) 123,691; exports sugar, potatoes, tomatoes, almonds, bananas; manufactures glass, leather, hats, woolen goods; commercial fishing; shipbuilding; governor's palace, an 18th-cent. cathedral, town hall; year-round bathing resort.

La Spe′zia (lä spä′tsyä). **1** Province of Italy. See *Table* at ITALY.
2 Fortified seaport, its ✳, Liguria, NW Italy, on **Gulf of La Spezia** 51 m. ESE of Genoa; pop. 106,119; naval arsenal; largest and best harbor in Italy; became chief naval station of Italy 1861; shipbuilding works; summer and winter resort. In World War II surrendered by Germans Apr. 23, 1945.

Las Pie′dras (läs pyä′thräs). Municipality (pop. 17,047) and town (pop. 3147), E Puerto Rico; town is inland just NW of Humacao.

Las Ro′sas (lär rô′säs). Town, Chiapas state, SE Mexico; pop. 5712.

Lassa. Var. of LHASA.

Las′sen (läs′n). County in California. See *Table* at CALIFORNIA.

Lassen Peak. Volcano 10,453 ft. at S end of Cascade Range; in Shasta co. near border of Plumas co., NE California; only active volcano in U.S. proper; cinder cone 6913 ft.; sudden spectacular eruption 1914–16 after 200 years' quiescence; principal feature in **Lassen Volcanic National Park:** see UNITED STATES, *National Parks.*

Las′si′gny′ (lȧ′sē′nyē′). Village, Oise dept., N France, near Compiègne; pop. (1931) 763; fighting 1914 and Mar. 1917; captured by French Aug. 21, 1918.

Las·si′thi (lä·sē′thĕ). = *Lasithion* department of Greece: see *Table* at GREECE.

L'As′somp′tion′ (lȧ′sôNp′syôN′). **1** River ab. 100 m. long, chiefly in Joliette and L'Assomption cos., S Quebec, Canada; flows generally S; empties in St. Lawrence river opp. N end of Montreal I.
2 County, Quebec, Canada. See *Table* at QUEBEC.
3 Town, its ⊗, 23 m. NNE of Montreal on L'Assomption river; pop. 2688.

Lass·wade′ (läs·wād′). Village, Midlothian co., SE Scotland, SE of Edinburgh; residence 1798–1804 of Sir Walter Scott; De Quincey established his daughters here 1840 and lived with them at intervals until his death 1859.

Las Ta′blas (läs tä′vläs). Town, S Panama, ✳ of Los Santos prov.; pop. 2127; near coast on W side of Gulf of Panama.

Last Mountain Lake (låst). Long narrow lake 98 sq. m. in S cen. Saskatchewan, Canada; S end ab. 20 m. NW of Regina; discharges into Qu'Appelle river.

La′sto·vo (lä′stô·vô); *Ital.* **La·go′sta** (lä·gôs′tä; *Ital.* lä·gôs′tä). Island in Adriatic Sea off Dalmatian coast, lat. 42°47′N; 24 sq. m.; pop. (1931) ab. 2000; administratively a part of Bosnia and Herzegovina federated republic, W Yugoslavia; formerly Italian; as commune includes nearby small island of Sušac.

La′stra a Si′gna (läs′trä ä sēn′yä). Commune, Firenze prov., Tuscany, cen. Italy, on Arno river 8 m. W of Florence; pop. 13,228; church with 14th-cent. frescoes; 14th-cent. walls.

Las Tres Vír′ge·nes (läs träz vĕr′hä·nås). Mountain 6545 ft. in E cen. Lower California, NW Mexico.

Las Ve′gas (läs vā′gȧs). **1** City, ⊗ of Clark co., SE corner of Nevada, 22 m. NW of Hoover Dam; pop. 64,405; distributing center for mining and stock-raising section; travel and recreationa center; hot springs NW of city; housed offices for Hoover Dam project until 1932. Occupied by Mormons 1855–57; bought by railroad for townsite and division point 1903; became ⊗ 1909; created City of Las Vegas 1911.
2 Urban community, San Miguel co., NE cen. New Mexico, ab. 40 m. E of Santa Fe; constitutes two municipalities separated from each other by Gallinas river: City of Las Vegas, sometimes called East Las Vegas or New Town (pop. 7790), ⊗ of San Miguel co.; and Town of Las Vegas, sometimes called West Las Vegas or Old Town (pop. 6028); total pop. 13,818. Old Town settled on Santa Fe Trail by Spaniards 1823–33; taken for U.S. by Gen. Stephen W. Kearny 1846; became seat of military operations 1851 following establishment of military post. Shipping point and supply depot in cattle and sheep country; manufactures bricks, dairy products, flour. New Mexico Highlands Univ. (1893; coed.); health resort and hot springs nearby; Conchas Dam (1939) to the E.
Las Vil′las (läz vē′yäs); *formerly* **San′ta Clar′a** (sän′tȧ klär′ȧ; *Span.* sän′tä klä′rä). Province of Cuba. See *Table* at CUBA.
Las Vil·luer′cas (läz vĕ·[l]ywĕr′käs). Peak 4920 ft. in Guadalupe Mts., W cen. Spain.
Las·wa′ri (läs·wä′rĭ). Village, Rajasthan, NW India, in former Alwar state, 12 m. E of Alwar and ab. 78 m. SSW of Delhi; scene of Lord Lake's defeat of Marathas Nov. 1, 1803 in Second Maratha War.
La·ta·cun′ga (lä′tä·kōōng′gä). City, ✳ of Cotopaxi prov., cen. Ecuador, 50 m. S of Quito; pop. (1944 est.) 20,357; founded by Spanish 1534; on plateau ab. 9150 ft. above sea level; ab. 25 m. S of the great volcano Cotopaxi; has suffered repeatedly from eruptions and earthquakes.
La′tah (lä′tô; lä′tô′). County in Idaho. See *Table* at IDAHO.
Lat′a·ki′a (lăt′ȧ·kē′ȧ; *Arab.* lȧ′thĭ·kē′yȧ; -yă; lȧ′dĭ-). **1** Former republic, originally a territory now a part of Syria (region of United Arab Republic), N of Lebanon; 2310 sq. m.; pop. (1958 est.) 4,420,587; ✳ Latakia; coastal region bet. N extension of Lebanon Mts. (Djebel Ansariya) and the Mediterranean Sea and opp. island of Cyprus; the Orontes forms part of its E boundary. Chief towns Latakia, Tartus, and Baniyas. See *Map* at SYRIA. Before World War I a part of Turkey; became a territory of the French mandate of Syria 1920, known as Alawiya or the Territory of the Alaouites; made a state 1922 and in 1926 an autonomous part of Syria; incorporated Jan. 12, 1942 in the Syrian Republic.
2 *Fr.* **Lat′ta·quié′** (lȧ′tȧ′kyä′); *anc.* **La·od′i·ce′a** *or* **Laodicea ad Ma′re** (lȧ·ŏd′ĭ·sē′ȧ ȧd mä′rē; lȧ′ŏd·ĭ-). Seaport, formerly ✳ of Latakia, W Syria; pop. (1935) 21,404; in antiquity had several other names; became an important and wealthy city during the Crusades; captured by Tancred 1102 and retaken by Saladin 1188; declined in importance but revived in 17th cent. by its cultivation of and trade in (Latakia) tobacco, which is still its chief industry.
La Tène (lȧ tân′). Shallows at E end of Lake of Neuchâtel, Switzerland; site of discovery of Iron-Age remains; name now applied to a period of the Iron Age assumed to date from 500 B.C. to 100 A.D.
La·ter′za (lä·tĕr′tsä). Commune, Ionio prov., Apulia, SE Italy, 27 m. NW of Taranto; pop 10,364.
La Teste (lȧ tĕst′); *formerly* **La Teste-de-Buch** (lȧ tĕs′tĕ-dĕ-büsh′). Town, Gironde dept., SW France, SSE of Arcachon; pop. 5331; ancient capital of the *Pays de Buch.*
Lat′ga·le (lăt′gä·lĕ) *or* **Lat·gal′ia** (lăt·găl′yȧ; -găl′ĭ·ȧ); *Russ.* **Lat·ga′li·ya** (lŭt·gä′lyĭ·yȧ). Province, E Latvia; 6053 sq. m.; pop. (1938 est.) 588,871; ✳ Daugavpils; includes the administrative districts of Daugavpils, Yaunlatgale, Ludza Rezekne. Region of lakes and farm lands; became part of newly organized Latvia 1918.
La′thom and Burs′cough (lä′thŭm bûrs′kō). Former urban district, Lancashire, NW England, NE of Liverpool and WNW of Manchester; site of **Lathom House,** formerly seat of the Stanley family (earls of Derby) and object of siege by Parliamentarians Feb.–May 1644 when it was defended by the Countess of Derby, Charlotte de la Trémoille.
La Thuile (lȧ tü·ēl′). Town, Aosta prov., NW Piedmont, NW Italy; terminal of Little Saint Bernard Pass.
La·tia′no (lä·tyä′nô). Commune, Brindisi prov., Apulia, SE Italy, 13 m. SW of Brindisi; pop. (1931) 10,010.
Lat′i·mer (lăt′ĭ·mẽr). County in Oklahoma. See *Table* at OKLAHOMA.
Latina. See LITTORIA.
Latin America. Spanish America (*q.v.*) and Brazil.
Latin Empire. Part of the Byzantine Empire ruled by the Crusaders 1204–61; ✳ Constantinople; included lands on W, N, and NE shores of the Aegean Sea (except Euboea) and around the Sea of Marmara. See BYZANTINE EMPIRE.
Latin Way; ** *Lat.* **Vi′a La·ti′na (vī′ȧ lȧ·tī′nȧ). Ancient Roman road running SE from Rome past Tusculum and joining the Appian Way near Capua, or. as some state, at Beneventum.
La′ti·um (lä′shĭ·ŭm). **1** Ancient country of Italy in cen. part of W coast on Tyrrhenian Sea, bounded by Etruria on NW and by Campania on SE; inhabited by Latins whose cities (Ardea, Lavinium, Tusculum, Laurentum, Alba Longa, etc.) had formed Latin League by 500 B.C.; dominated by Rome from 5th cent. B.C.; Latins revolted and Latin League dissolved after its defeat in Latin War 340–338 B.C.; after Social War 90–88 B.C. Latin cities received rights of Roman citizenship.
2 *Ital.* **La′zio** (lä′tsyô). Compartimento of cen. Italy; for provincial divisions, area, and pop. see *Table* at ITALY; lies bet. Tyrrhenian Sea and Apennines and bet. Tuscany and Campania; includes the Campagna di Roma (*q.v.*) and the Pontine Marshes (*q.v.*); watered chiefly by Tiber river.
La Tor·tu′ga (lä tôr·tōō′gä). Venezuelan island in the Caribbean Sea off N cen coast of Venezuela, 55 m. W of the island of Margarita; 85 sq. m.
La Trappe. Monastery. See SOLIGNY-LA-TRAPPE.
La Tri′ni·dad′ (lä trē′nē·thäth′). Town (municipal district), ✳ of Benguet subprov., Mountain Province, Luzon, Phil. Is., ab. 3 m. N of Baguio; pop. 6554; at elevation of ab. 8000 ft., has cool climate; fruits and vegetables of temperate zone raised in surrounding gardens. Became capital after 1909.
La Tri′ni·té′ (lä trē′nē′tā′). Commune, E coast of Martinique, French West Indies; pop. (1936) 39,173.
La·trobe′ (lȧ·trōb′). **1** Borough, Westmoreland co., SW Pennsylvania, 26 m. W of Johnstown; pop. 11,932; coal and iron mines; manufactures iron and steel, coke, textiles; St. Vincent Coll. (1846; men).
2 Town, N Tasmania, Australia, near mouth of Mersey river 5 m. S of Devonport; pop. 1676
La·trun′ (?lȧ·trōōn′). Village, S Palestine, on highway 15 m. W of Jerusalem; site of British detention camp 1946.
Lattaquié. See LATAKIA seaport.
Lat′ti·mer Mines (lăt′ĭ·mẽr). Locality Luzerne co., E Pennsylvania, near Hazleton; pop. (1950) 1540.
La′tu·kan′, Mount (lä′tōō·kän′). Active volcano 7078 ft. in SE Lanao prov., Mindanao, Phil. Is., on Cotabato boundary.
La Tuque (lä tük′). Town, Champlain co., S Quebec, Canada, on St Maurice river 77 m. N of Three Rivers; pop. 9538; chief industries paper manufacture and power; hunting and fishing resort.
La·tur′ (lä·tōōr′). Town, SE Maharashtra state, S cen. India, 140 m. NW of Hyderabad; pop. 30,760.

Lat′vi·a (lăt′vĭ·à); *Lettish and Lithuanian* **Lat′vi·ja** (lät′vĭ·yä). Republic N Europe, at E end of Baltic Sea; annexed by U.S.S.R. 1940 and incorporated into the Soviet Union as the **Lat′vi·an Soviet Socialist Republic** (lăt′vĭ·ăn); 25,399 sq. m.; pop. (1938 est.) 1,994,506; ✳ Riga. Bounded on N by Estonia, on E by Pskov and Velikie Luki Regions of R.S.F.S.R., on SE by White Russia and Poland, on S by Lithuania, and on W by the Baltic Sea. For administrative purposes, divided into 4 provinces: Kurzeme in W, Latgale in E, Vidzeme in N, and Zemgale in S. Northern half of its W coast indented by Gulf of Riga, large inlet of Baltic Sea. A lowlying plain, with no part above 1000 ft. Chief river the Dvina, flowing from SE to Gulf of Riga near Riga; other streams the Venta, Lielupe, and Gauya. Has great forests; main industries agriculture, lumbering, dairying, and livestock raising. Chief exports timber, flax, plywood, butter. Predominant ethnic strain Baltic; chief nationalities Latvian 75.6%, Russian 13.3%. Has three good ports Riga, Lepaya, and Ventspils, the two latter being ice-free all the year. Other towns Daugavpils, Yelgava, Rezekne, and Tsesis.

History: See BALTIC PROVINCES, KURLAND, LIVONIA, and BALTIC STATES. Proclaimed an independent republic Nov. 1918; chiefly from the former Russian provinces of Kurland and southern Livonia; recognized by Russia 1920; joined League of Nations 1921; ratified nonaggression treaty with U.S.S.R. 1932; established nationalist dictatorship 1934; signed mutual assistance treaty with Russia and met German problem by repatriation 1939; annexed by U.S.S.R. Aug. 3, 1940; overrun by German army 1941, but retaken 1944–45; incorporation in U.S.S.R. not recognized by United States.

Lauban. See LUBAŃ.

Lau′der·dale (lô′dēr·dāl). Name of counties in three states of the U.S. See *Tables* at ALABAMA, MISSISSIPPI, TENNESSEE.

Laudunum. See LAON.

Lau′en·burg (lou′ĕn·bŏŏrK). 1 Region, SE Schleswig-Holstein, Germany; a former duchy, 456 sq. m., on the Elbe just E of Hamburg; under German rulers 1260–1689; during next two cents. to 1864 belonged for varying periods to France, Hannover, Prussia, and Denmark; became part of Prussia 1865 but retained its constitution and special privileges; entered North German Confederation 1866 and German Empire 1870; incorporated in Prussia 1876; ceased as duchy 1918.
2 *also* **Lauenburg in Pommern.** See LĘBORK.

Lauf′feld *or* **Lauf′feldt** (louf′fĕlt); *also* **Law′feld** (lou′fĕlt). Village in NE Belgium, just W of Maastricht, Netherlands; scene of victory of Marshal Saxe over Allies July 2, 1747.

Lauis. See LUGANO.

Lau (lou), *or* **Eastern, Islands.** Group of many small islands in E part of Fiji Is., SW Pacific Ocean; ab. 45 sq. m.; comprises two main groups, Exploring Is. in N and Lakemba Is. in S.

Laun. See LOUNY.

Laun′ces′ton (lôn′sĕs′tŭn; län′-); *orig.* **Pat′er·so′nia** (păt′ĕr·sōn′yà; -sō′nĭ·à). City, NE Tasmania, Australia, at confluence of North and South Esk rivers to form Tamar river 40 m. from Bass Strait; pop. 27,532; trade and distribution center of mining and farming region; wheat and potatoes main regional crops; exports hardwood, oil, and gold; port made accessible to larger oceangoing vessels by a floating dock; maintains woolen mills, smelters, and pottery works.

Launces′ton (lôn′stŭn; län′-; -s′n); *anc.* **Dun′he′ved** (dōōn′hĕ′vĕd). Municipal borough, Cornwall, SW England, 52 m. WSW of Exeter near the Tamar river; pop. 4467; ruins (chiefly the circular keep) of old Norman castle, seat of the earls of Cornwall.

La U·nion′ (lä ōō·nyôn′). Narrow coastal province, NW Luzon, Phil. Is., along South China Sea; 530 sq. m.; pop. 207,701; ✳ San Fernando. Mostly mountainous with narrow strip of lowland along the coast; mountain range along E border averages 1500 to 2000 ft. Well watered by many short streams. Has several fine ports, esp. San Fernando. Produces sugar, coconuts, tobacco, rice, sisal hemp; makes cloth, pottery, baskets, hats, mats, lace, embroidery. Inhabitants mainly Ilokanos. Chief towns San Fernando, Bauang, Naguilian, Luna, and Agoo.

History: Province created 1854 from the "union" of towns and districts formerly parts of Pangasinan and Ilocos Sur—hence the name. Region explored by Spanish as early as 1572; experienced a short-lived successful rebellion 1661; joined the Filipino revolutionary movement of 1896; civil government established Aug. 1901; invaded by Japanese Dec. 1941.

La U·nión′ (lä ōō·nyôn′). 1 Town, Valdivia prov., S cen. Chile; pop. 7234.
2 Department, E El Salvador; 883 sq. m.; pop. (1942 est.) 105,628; ✳ La Unión.
3 Town, E El Salvador, ✳ of La Unión dept., on Gulf of Fonseca; pop. (1942 est.) 5969; commercial port.
4 Commune, Murcia prov., SE Spain, 28 m. SE of Murcia; pop. 10,079; iron, sulfur, manganese mines nearby.

La′u·pa·ho′e·ho′e (lä′ōō·pä·hō′à·hō′à). Village, North Hilo dist., Hawaii co., Hawaii, on E coast of Hawaii I. ab. 22 m. NNW of Hilo; pop. (est.) 500.

Lau′rel (lô′rĕl; lŏr′ĕl). 1 County in Kentucky. See *Table* at KENTUCKY.
2 Town, Sussex co., S Delaware, 15 m. SW of Georgetown; pop. 2709; shipping point for watermelons, cucumbers, sweet potatoes, cantaloupes; manufactures boxes, baskets, crates.
3 Town, Prince Georges co., S cen. Maryland, 18 m. NNE of Washington; pop. 8503.
4 City, a ⊗ of Jones co., SE Mississippi, 53 m. SW of Meridian; pop. 27,889; lumbering, vegetable canning.
5 City, Yellowstone co., S cen. Montana, on Yellowstone river 17 m. SW of Billings; pop. 4601.

Lau′rel·dale (lô′rĕl·dāl, lŏr′ĕl-). Borough, Berks co., SE Pennsylvania, 5 m. N of Reading; pop. 4051.

Laurel Hill. Ridge in SW Pennsylvania, extending along boundary bet. Somerset co. on E and Fayette and Westmoreland cos. on W, and N into Cambria and Indiana cos.; coal deposits

Laurel Mountain. Peak 2603 ft. in E Preston co., N West Virginia.

Lau′rens (lô′rĕnz; lŏr′ĕnz). 1 Name of counties in two states of the U.S. See *Tables* at GEORGIA and SOUTH CAROLINA.
2 City, ⊗ of Laurens co., NW South Carolina, 23 m. NNE of Greenwood; pop. 9598; cotton goods, glass.

Lau·ren′tian Highlands *or* **Upland** (lô·rĕn′shăn); *also* **Canadian Shield.** Plateau region, E Canada and NE U.S., extending E from the Mackenzie basin to Davis Strait and S to S Quebec, S Ontario, NE Minnesota, N Wisconsin, NW Michigan, and NE New York including the Adirondack Mts.

Laurentian, *or* **Lau′ren·tide** (lô′rĕn·tīd; *Fr.* lô′räN′tēd′), **Hills** *or* **Mountains.** Range in Quebec prov., Canada, N of the St. Lawrence river on S edge of the Laurentian Highlands; highest point Les Éboulements in Charlevoix co. 2551 ft.

Lau′ren·tides Park (lô′rĕn·tīdz; *Fr.* lô′räN′tēd′). Canadian provincial park, N of Quebec city, SE Quebec prov.; 4000 sq. m.; in Laurentian Highlands S of Lake St. John; contains many lakes and streams with fine fishing; game preserve.

Lau·ren′tum (lô·rĕn′tŭm). Ancient city of Latium, cen. Italy, near coast NW of Lavinium with which it became united.

Lau·ri′a (lou·rē′ä). Commune, Potenza prov., Lucania, S Italy, 42 m. S of Potenza; pop. 11,097.

Lau′rier′–Ou′tre·mont′ (lô′ryā′ōō′trĕ·môn′). Former county, Quebec prov., E Canada, on Montreal I.; in 1941 a district including part of Montreal and Outremont city, pop. 72,680.

Lau′rin·burg (lô′rĭn·bûrg; lŏr′ĭn-). City, ⊗ of Scotland co., S North Carolina, 39 m. WSW of Fayetteville; pop. 8242; farming.

Lau′ri·um (lô′rĭ·ŭm; lŏr′ĭ·ŭm). Residential village, Houghton co., NW Michigan penin., 70 m. NW of Marquette; pop. 3058; near Calumet, copper-mining center.

Lau′ri·um (lô′rĭ·ŭm; lŏr′ĭ-) *or* **Lau′ri·on** (-ŏn); *Mod. Gr.* **Láv′rei·on** (läv′ryŏn). Seaport town on E coast of S end of Attica and Boeotia dept., Greece; pop. 6393; near **Mount Laurium,** famous in ancient Greece for its silver mines.

Lau·sanne′ (lô·zăn′; *Fr.* lō′zän′). Commune, * of Vaud canton, W Switzerland, on N shore of Lake of Geneva 32 m. NE of Geneva; pop. (1941) 92,541; railroad junction; 13th-cent. castle (former episcopal palace), 13th-cent. cathedral, university (founded 1890; as academy 1537); manufactures iron goods, beer, tobacco, chocolates. Made episcopal see in late 6th cent. (bishopric removed to Fribourg 1663); Reformation introduced 1536; treaties concluded here 1912, 1923; Lausanne Pact concluded here 1932 reducing German war reparations about 90%.

Lausitz. See LUSATIA.

Lau′sit·zer Ge·bir′ge (lou′zĭt·sĕr gĕ·bir′gĕ). See SUDETEN.

Lausitzer Neisse. See NEISSE.

Laut. See Poelau LAOET.

Lau·ta′ro (lou·tä′rō). Town, Cautín prov., S cen. Chile, ab. 363 m. S of Santiago; pop. 9602.

Lau′ter·brun′nen (lou′tĕr·broŏn′ĕn). Valley in Bern canton, SW cen. Switzerland, S of Interlaken and NW of the Jungfrau; pop. ab. 2600; lace making; numerous waterfalls.

Lau·to′ka (lou·tō′kȧ). Seaport, W coast of Viti Levu, Fiji Is., SW Pacific Ocean; center of sugar industry.

Lau′wers Zee (lou′vĕrs zā′). Inlet of North Sea on N coast of Netherlands, on border bet. Friesland and Groningen provs.

Lau′zon′ (lō′zôn′). Residential town, Levis co., S Quebec, Canada, on right bank of St. Lawrence river opp. Quebec; pop. 9643; shipbuilding.

La′va, Mount (lä′vȧ; läv′ȧ). Peak 10,400 ft. in Uinta co., SW Wyoming.

Lava Beds National Monument. See UNITED STATES, *National Monuments.*

La·vac′a (lȧ·văk′ȧ). 1 River ab. 110 m. long, SE Texas; rises in Lavaca co., flows S into **Lavaca Bay** in Calhoun co., an arm of Matagorda Bay.
2 County in Texas. See *Table* at TEXAS.

La′va·do′res (lä′vä·t͟hō′rȧs). Commune, Pontevedra prov., NW Spain, 14 m. SSW of Pontevedra; pop. 38,462; manufactures paper, leather, tile; fish-salting works.

Lava Hot Springs. Village, Bannock co., SE Idaho, 25 m. SE of Pocatello; pop. 593; hot mineral waters; interesting rock formations.

La·val′ (lȧ·väl′; *Fr.* lȧ′vȧl′). 1 County, Quebec, Canada. See MONTREAL AND JESUS ISLANDS.
2 Manufacturing commune, * of Mayenne dept., NW France, 44 m. E of Rennes; pop. 28,380; 16th-cent. cathedral; castle with 12th-cent. donjon; 16th-cent. bridge; manufactures cotton and linen cloth (since 14th cent.), foundry products, flour, shoes, leather; trades in marble, grain. Founded before 9th cent. A.D.; Vendeans defeated Republicans here 1793.

La′val′ des Ra′pides (lȧ′vȧl′ dā rȧ′pēd′). Town, Jesus I., Laval co., S Quebec, Canada, on Rivière des Prairies 8 m. WNW of Montreal; pop. 4998.

La′val·le′ja (lä′vä·yĕ′hä); *formerly* **Mi′nas** (mē′näs). Department of Uruguay. See *Table* at URUGUAY.

La′van·saa′ri (lä′vän·sä′rĭ). Small island in Gulf of Finland, E of Hogland.

La′va·pié′, Point (lä′vä·pyä′). Cape on coast of Bío-Bío prov., S cen. Chile, S of Gulf of Arauco.

La′vaur′ (lȧ′vôr′). Commune, SW Tarn dept., S France; pop. (1931) 6045; an old town of Languedoc, taken by Simon de Montfort 1211 during his campaign against the Albigenses; seat of bishopric until the Revolution.

La Ve′ga (lä vā′gä). 1 Province, cen. Dominican Republic. See *Table* at DOMINICAN REPUBLIC.
2 *formerly* **Con′cep·ción′ de la Vega** (kôn′sĕp·syôn′ dä). Commune, its *; pop. (1944 est.) 11,683.

La·vel′lo (lä·vĕl′lō). Commune, Potenza prov., Lucania, S Italy, 29 m. N of Potenza; pop. 11,453.

La Ven′dée′ (lä vän′dā′). = VENDÉE dept.

La Ven′ta (lä vän′tä). Village, W Tabasco state, SE Mexico, near Tonalá river; on an island ab. 4 m. wide in mangrove swamps of the coast; site of recent excavations by the National Geographic Society and the Smithsonian Institution; among the finds were some excellent jade and five huge heads carved of basalt, representing "La Venta culture" of a people flourishing c. 500 to 800 A.D.

La Vé′ren′drye′ Provincial Park (lä vā′rän′drē′). Canadian provincial park in SW Quebec NW of Ottawa; 4948 sq. m.; numerous lakes and rivers.

La Verne (lä vûrn′). City, Los Angeles co., SW California, 25 m. E of Los Angeles; pop. 6516; citrus-packing center; La Verne Coll. (1891; coed.).

La Ve′ta Pass (lä vē′tä). Mountain pass 9378 ft., Costilla co., S Colorado, in Sangre de Cristo Range of the Rocky Mts.; westernmost branch of the Santa Fe Trail passed through it; highway.

La·via′na (lä·vyä′nä). Commune, Oviedo prov., NW Spain, 15 m. ESE of Oviedo; pop. 12,455.

La Vic·to′ria (lä vĭk·tōr′ĭ·ȧ; *Span.* vĕk·tō′ryä). Town, Aragua state, N Venezuela; pop. (1941 est.) 9078.

Lavinia, Civita. See LANUVIUM.

La·vin′i·um (lȧ·vĭn′ĭ·ŭm). Ancient town in NW Latium, cen. Italy, near the coast 19 m. S of Rome; sacred to the Penates and to Vesta; said to have been founded by Aeneas and named for his wife Lavinia.

Lavongai. See NEW HANOVER.

La·vo′ni·a (lȧ·vō′nĭ·ȧ; -vŏn′yȧ). City, Franklin co., NE Georgia, 37 m. NNE of Athens; pop. 2088.

La′vras (lä′vräs). City, S cen. Minas Gerais state, E Brazil, 150 m. NW of Rio de Janeiro; pop. 12,257.

Lávreion. See LAURIUM.

La·wa′i Bay (lä·wä′ē). Bay on S coast of Kauai I., Hawaii, bet. Koloa Bay and Wahiawa Bay.

Lawers, Ben. See BEN LAWERS.

Lawfeld. See LAUFFELD.

Lawk′sawk′ (lôk′sôk′). Former state, W Southern Shan States, E cen. Burma; 2365 sq. m.; pop. 30,102; chief town Lawksawk, 30 m. N of Taunggyi.

Lawn′dale (lôn′dāl). City, Los Angeles co., SW California, E of Manhattan Beach; pop. 21,740.

Lawn′side (lôn′sīd). Borough, Camden co., SW New Jersey, 7 m. SSE of Camden; pop. 2155; incorporated 1926; Negro-owned and Negro-governed borough.

La′woe (lä′woō) *or* **La′wu.** Mountain 10,712 ft. bet. Surakarta and Madiun, E cen. Java, Indonesia.

Law′ra (lô′rȧ). Town, NW Ghana, W Africa, near Ivory Coast border 160 m. NW of Tamale.

Law′rence (lô′rĕns; lŏr′ĕns). 1 Name of counties in eleven states of the U.S. See *Tables* at ALABAMA, ARKANSAS, ILLINOIS, INDIANA, KENTUCKY, MISSISSIPPI, MISSOURI, OHIO, PENNSYLVANIA, SOUTH DAKOTA, TENNESSEE.
2 Town, Marion co., cen. Indiana, NE of Indianapolis; pop. 10,103.
3 City, ⊗ of Douglas co., E Kansas, on Kansas river 25 m. E of Topeka; pop. 32,858; a residential and industrial center; flour mills, organ factory, cannery, poultry-packing plant. Univ. of Kansas (1863; coed.). Founded 1854 by New England Emigrant Aid Co.; center of Free State activities in pre-Civil War years; raided by Quantrill's guerrillas Aug. 21, 1863.
4 Industrial city, a ⊗ of Essex co., NE corner of Massachusetts, on Merrimack river 9 m. ENE of Lowell; pop. 70,933; textiles (esp. worsted cloth), textile machinery, paper, hard-rubber products; has many parks and play-

grounds, and an athletic stadium; incorporated as a city 1853.

5 Residential village, Nassau co., SE New York, on Long I., 16 m. ESE of New York; pop. 5907.

Law'rence·burg (lô'rĕns·bûrg; lŏr'ĕns-). **1** City, ⊗ of Dearborn co., SE Indiana, on Ohio river 55 m. SE of Shelbyville; pop. 5004; distilleries. Founded 1801; flooded 1937.

2 City, ⊗ of Anderson co., cen. Kentucky, 12 m. S of Frankfort; pop. 2523; in bluegrass section; distilleries.

3 City, ⊗ of Lawrence co., S Tennessee, 31 m. SSW of Columbia; pop. 8042; manufactures woolens, cheese; phosphate mining.

Law'rence·ville (lô'rĕns·vĭl; lŏr'ĕns-; *Sou. also* -v'l). **1** City, ⊗ of Gwinnett co., N Georgia, 26 m. ENE of Atlanta; pop. 3804; became ⊗ 1821.

2 City, ⊗ of Lawrence co., SE Illinois, 55 m. N of Evansville, Indiana; pop. 5492; oil refineries.

3 Town, Mercer co., W cen. New Jersey, ab. 6 m. N of Trenton, pop. (est.) 1056; named in honor of Capt. James Lawrence; Lawrenceville School (1810).

4 Town, ⊗ of Brunswick co., S Virginia, SW of Petersburg; pop. 1941; St. Paul's Coll. (1888; coed.).

Law'ton (lô't'n). City, ⊗ of Comanche co., SW Oklahoma, 80 m. SW of Oklahoma City; pop. 61,697; founded 1901; farming (esp. cotton); manufactures cottonseed oil, flour, dairy products; hematite, granite, limestone deposits nearby; oil wells. Wichita National Forest and Game Preserve in vicinity, Fort Sill (*q.v.*) 5 m. N.

Law·ton'ka, Lake (lô·tŏng'ká). Lake ab. 2 sq. m. in N Comanche co., SW Oklahoma; formed by dam (60 ft. high, 375 ft. long) across Medicine Bluff creek; water supply for Fort Sill and Lawton to the S.

Lawu. See LAWOE.

Lay'san (lī'sän). Islet of the Leeward Is., Hawaiian Is., cen. Pacific Ocean, ab. 750 m. NW of Niihau I., ab. 26°N lat., 172°W long.; included in Hawaiian Islands Bird Reservation.

Lay'ton (lā't'n). City, Davis co., N Utah, N of Salt Lake City; pop. 9027.

Laz·di'yai (läz·dĭ'yī). Town, ✻ of Seinai dist., S Lithuania, 50 m. S of Kaunas; pop. 6698.

La'zi (lä'sĕ). Municipality, S coast of Siquijor I., Siquijor subprov. of Negros Oriental, Negros, Phil. Is., 25 m. SE of Dumaguete; pop. 15,157; has good harbor.

Lazio. See LATIUM.

Lea (lē). **1** County in New Mexico. See *Table* at NEW MEXICO.

2 River 46 m. long, SE England; rises in Bedfordshire, flows SE through Hertfordshire and S bet. Essex and Middlesex cos. into the Thames.

Lead (lēd). City, Lawrence co., W South Dakota, 33 m. WNW of Rapid City; pop. 6211; settled 1876; site of Homestake Mine, one of largest gold mines in world.

Lead'bet'ter Point (lĕd'bĕt'ẽr). Point on NW coast of Pacific co., SW Washington, at S of entrance to Willapa Bay.

Lead'gate (lĕd'gĭt; -gāt). Urban district, Durham, N England, 11 m. SW of Newcastle; pop. (1931) 6395; since 1937 in Consett.

Lead'ville (lĕd'vĭl). Mining city, ⊗ of Lake co., cen. Colorado, in Rocky Mts. (alt. 10,190 ft.) 75 m. WSW of Denver; pop. 4008; founded 1860 as gold camp; one of principal centers of early American mining history; mines gold, silver, lead, zinc, copper, bismuth, manganese, and molybdenum.

Leaf (lēf). **1** River ab. 200 m. long, SE Mississippi; rises in S Scott co., flows SE to unite with Chickasawhay river in N George co. and form the Pascagoula river.

2 River 295 m. long, N Quebec prov., Canada; flows NE from Lake Minto into Ungava Bay.

League Island (lēg). District, S Philadelphia city, Pennsylvania; U.S. Navy Yard.

Leake (lēk). County in Mississippi. See *Table* at MISSISSIPPI.

Leakes'ville (lēks'vĭl; *Sou. also* -v'l). Town, ⊗ of Greene co., SE Mississippi; pop. 1014.

Lea'key (lā'kĭ). City, ⊗ of Real co., SW cen. Texas; pop. 587.

Leaks'ville (lēks'vĭl; *Sou. also* -v'l). Town, Rockingham co., N North Carolina, 30 m. N of Greensboro; pop. 6427; one industrial community with adjoining town of **Spray** [sprā] (pop. 5542); manufactures bedding, curtains, woolen goods, rugs.

Le'a·lu'i (lē'á·lōō'ĭ). Town, native ✻ of Barotse prov., Northern Rhodesia, on E bank of Zambezi river.

Leam *or* **Leame** (lĕm). River 25 m. long in cen. England, flowing into the Avon near Warwick.

Lea'ming·ton (lē'mĭng·tŭn). Town, Essex co., SE Ontario, Canada, 30 m. ESE of Windsor, near Lake Erie shore; pop. 6950; center of rich tobacco-growing district.

Leam'ing·ton (lĕm'ĭng·tŭn); *officially* **Royal Leamington Spa** (spä). Municipal borough, Warwickshire, cen. England, on the Leam river 2 m. NE of Warwick; pop. 36,345; health resort, with mineral springs.

Leane, Lough (lŏĸ lān). Largest of the Lakes of Killarney (*q.v.*).

Lea'side (lē'sīd). Residential town, York co., SE Ontario, Canada, N suburb of Toronto; pop. 16,233.

Leath'er·head' (lĕth'ẽr·hĕd'). Urban district, Surrey, S England; pop. 27,203.

Leav'en·worth (lĕv'ĕn·wûrth). **1** County in Kansas. See *Table* at KANSAS.

2 City, ⊗ of Leavenworth co., NE Kansas, on Missouri river 22 m. NW of Kansas City; pop. 22,052; railroad, trading, and industrial center; coal deposits; manufactures furniture, stoves, mining machinery, washing machines, structural iron; Saint Mary College (1923; women) in S suburb of Xavier. Settled 1854 by proslavery emigrants from Missouri; oldest city in Kansas. See FORT LEAVENWORTH.

3 City, Chelan co., cen. Washington, on Wenatchee river 20 m. NW of Wenatchee; pop. 1480; fruit packing.

Leav'itt Peak (lĕv'ĭt). Mountain 11,575 ft. in Sierra Nevada, on boundary bet. Mono and Tuolumne cos., E cen. California.

Lea'wood (lē'wŏŏd). City, Johnson co., E Kansas, S of Kansas City; pop. 7466.

Leb'a·de'a (lĕb'á·dē'á); *Mod. Gr.* **Le·vá'dei·a** (lá·vä'-thyä). Commune, Attica and Boeotia dept., E Central Greece and Euboea division, Greece, ab. 60 m. NW of Athens; pop. 12,585.

Lebanese Republic. See LEBANON, 15.

Leb'a·non (lĕb'á·nŭn). **1** County in Pennsylvania. See *Table* at PENNSYLVANIA.

2 Agricultural town, N New London co., SE corner of Connecticut, 5 m. S of Willimantic; pop. 2434.

3 City, St. Clair co., SW Illinois, 20 m. E of East St. Louis; pop. 2863; McKendree College (1828; coed.; Methodist).

4 City, ⊗ of Boone co., cen. Indiana, 25 m. NW of Indianapolis; pop. 9523; shipping point for grain, livestock, and dairy products.

5 City, E Smith co., N Kansas; pop. 583; former geographical center of U.S. (until admission of Alaska) ab. 4 m. NW, at lat. 39°50'N long. 98°35'W.

6 City, ⊗ of Marion co., cen. Kentucky, 28 m. W of Danville; pop. 4813; in bluegrass section; tobacco market.

7 City, ⊗ of Laclede co., S cen. Missouri, 25 m. S of E end of Lake of the Ozarks; pop. 8220; ships grain and dairy products.

8 Industrial city, Grafton co., W New Hampshire, 19 m. N of Claremont; pop. 9299; recreational center.

9 Village, ⊗ of Warren co., SW Ohio, 18 m. E of Hamilton; pop. 5993; canning, shoe manufacturing; prehistoric mounds and earthworks nearby.

10 City, Linn co., W Oregon, 20 m. E of Corvallis; pop. 5858; produces strawberries, fruits, nuts; paper milling, fruit canning.

11 Industrial city, ⊗ of Lebanon co., SE cen. Pennsylvania, 25 m. E of Harrisburg; pop. 30,045; limestone and brownstone quarries; iron mines; manufactures iron and steel, textiles (esp. silk), tobacco and food products, shoes and rubbers. Laid out 1756, incorp. as city 1868. **12** City, ⊗ of Wilson co., N cen. Tennessee, 31 m. E of Nashville; pop. 10,512; manufactures woolen blankets, tool handles, barrel staves, flour; dairy farms; timber. Cumberland Univ. (1842; coed.).
13 Town, ⊗ of Russell co., SW Virginia, NNE of Bristol; pop. 2085.
14 *anc.* **Lib·a·nus** (lĭb′*à·nŭs*). Mountain range in Republic of Lebanon, Levant States, parallel with and close to the Mediterranean coast; ab. 100 m. long; highest peak Dahr el Qadib 10,131 ft. near N end.
15 *or* **Leb′a·nese′ Republic** (lĕb′*à·*nēz′; -nēs′), *Fr.* **Ré′pu′blique′ li′ba′naise′** (rā′pü′blēk′ lē′bà′nâz′). Independent republic at E end of Mediterranean Sea, N of Palestine, and enclosed by Syria on E and N; 4105 sq. m.; pop. (1935) 862,618, (1965 est.) 2,250,000; ✳ Beirut; one of the Levant States. Comprises region of Lebanon Mts.; bounded on E by Anti-Liban range; valley bet. the two ranges, known as El Bika (*anc.* Coele-Syria), watered by the Litani river in S and by the upper Orontes in N. Mt. Hermon on SE border. Has good motor roads and active trade; produces silk, tobacco, olives, fruits, and cereals. Chief towns Beirut, Tripoli, Zahle, and Saïda. See *Map* at SYRIA.
History: Inhabited by Maronites, members of a Syrian Christian sect established in 7th cent. A.D. and subject to Rome from 12th cent.; in 1841 and 1860, Maronites massacred by the Druses (see JEBEL ED DRUZ); under pressure of European powers especially France, **Great Lebanon** (*Fr.* **Grand Li′ban′** [grän′ lē′bän′]) established as autonomous government under Christian governor appointed by the Porte 1861–1914; declared autonomous under French mandate 1920; reorganized as Lebanese Republic 1926 (see SYRIA, 2); after treaty with France 1936, its constitution, previously suspended, was restored 1937; passed under control of the British and Free French July 1941; independence established Jan. 1, 1944.
Lebanon Springs. Village and health resort, Columbia co., SE New York, near Massachusetts border ab. 22 m. SE of Albany; pop. (1950) 424; mineral springs.
Leb′be·ke (lĕb′*ĕ·*kĕ). Commune, W cen. Belgium, in East Flanders prov. ab. 15 m. NW of Brussels; pop. 10,536.
Lebda. See LEPTIS MAGNA.
Le Bec–Hel′louin′ (lĕ bĕk′ĕ′l′wăn′). Commune, Eure dept., N France, ab. 25 m. NW of Évreux; pop. (1931) 436; remains of the Benedictine Abbey of Bec, founded 1034, which became famous under Lanfranc (prior 1045–62) and Anselm (prior 1063–78, abbot 1078–93).
Leb′e·dos (lĕb′*ĕ·*dŏs). Ancient city, one of the 12 Ionian Cities, situated on coast of Asia Minor bet. Teos and Ephesus.
Le Blanc–Mes′nil′ (lĕ blän′mā′nēl′). Commune, Seine-et-Oise dept., N France, NE suburb of Paris; pop. (1931) 19,343.
Le·bong′ (lĕ·bông′). See DARJEELING.
Le′bork (lĕnm′bôrk); *Ger.* **Lau′en·burg** (lou′ĕn-bōᴏʀk), *also* **Lauenburg in Pom′mern** (in pôm′ĕrn). City, N Gdańsk dept., N Poland, 68 m. ENE of Koszalin; formerly in Pomerania prov., Prussia, Germany; pop. (1946) 19,108; railroad junction; 14th-cent. late-Gothic church; 14th-cent. castle; astronomical observatory; manufactures tile, lumber, machinery, stoves, barrels, liqueurs, beer. Founded 1341; in World War II taken by Russians Mar. 11, 1945; assigned to Poland by Potsdam Conference 1945
Le Boucau. See BOUCAU.
Le Bour·get′ (lĕ bōᴏr·zhä′; *Fr.* bōᴏr′zhĕ′). Commune, Seine dept., N France, 6 m. NE of Paris; pop. (1931) 7598; airport, one of the largest and most important in France, the one at which Charles Lindbergh landed May 21, 1927 from the first solo nonstop transatlantic flight.
Le Bous′cat′ (lĕ bōᴏs′kà′). Commune, Gironde dept., SW France, NNW suburb of Bordeaux; pop. (1931) 16,128.
Le·bri′ja (lâ·vrē′hä); *older* **Le·bri′xa** (lâ·vrē′shä), **Ne·bri′ja** (nâ·vrē′hä), *or* **Ne·bri′xa** (nâ·vrē′shä); *anc.* **Na·bris′sa** (*nà·*brĭs′*à*) *or* **Ne·bris′sa** (nĕ·brĭs′*à*). Commune, Sevilla prov., SW Spain, on Guadalquivir river 33 m. S of Seville; pop. 14,536; agricultural trading center; clay deposits; manufactures aluminum products; cathedral. Settled by Greeks; reconquered from Moors by Ferdinand III 1248 and Andrew the Wise 1264. Birthplace of Elio Antonio de Nebrija (1444–1532), leader of the revival of learning in Spain.
Le′bu (lā′vōō). Seaport and coal-mining center, S cen. Chile, ab. 330 m. S of Valparaíso; ✳ of Arauco prov.; pop. (commune) 8239.
Le Calabrie. See CALABRIA.
Le Can′net′ (lĕ kà′nĕ′). Commune, Alpes-Maritimes dept., SE France, NNE suburb of Cannes; pop. (1931) 10,016; produces flowers and perfume essences.
Le Cap. See CAP HAITIEN.
Le Ca′teau′ (lĕ kà′tō′); *formerly* **Le Cateau–Cam′-bré′sis′** (-kän′brā′zē′). Commune, Nord dept., N France, 13 m. ESE of Cambrai; pop. 8427; treaty (Cateau-Cambrésis) Apr. 2–3, 1559, bet. France, England, and Spain, confirmed French possession of Calais and surrendered French conquests in Italy; suffered much during religious conflicts of 16th cent. (1562–1598), again during the Revolution, and in World War I: battle Aug. 26, 1914 when British suffered loss in retirement from Mons; captured by British Oct. 10, 1918 and suffered heavy bombardment.
Le Ca′te·let′ (lĕ kà′tlĕ′). Village, Aisne dept., N France, 11 m. N of St-Quentin; pop. 259; battle Sept. 29, 1918 when small force of Americans was cut off; has American cemetery.
Lec′ce (lât′châ). **1** Province of Italy. See *Table* at ITALY. **2** Commune, its ✳, Apulia, SE Italy, in the "heel" of the boot near Adriatic Sea 207 m. E by S of Naples; pop. 49,261; 12th-cent. cathedral; ancient Roman amphitheater; manufactures textiles.
Lec′co (lâk′kô). Manufacturing commune, Como prov., Lombardy, N Italy, at S end of SE branch (**Lake Lecco**) of Lake Como at mouth of Adda river, 16 m. E by N of Como; pop. 36,973; metallurgy.
Le Cen′ter (lĕ sĕn′tēr). Village, ⊗ of Le Sueur co., S Minnesota, 20 m. NNE of Mankato; pop. 1597.
Lech (lĕk); *anc.* **Li′cus** (lī′kŭs). River 177 m. long in Austria and Bavaria, S Germany; rises in Vorarlberg, SW Austria, flows N through Tirol and S cen. Bavaria past Augsburg into the Danube river.
Le Cham′bon–Feu′ge·rolles′ (lĕ shän′bôn′ fûzh′rôl′). Commune, Loire dept., SE cen. France, 4 m. SW of St-Étienne; pop. (1931) 15,106; metalworks.
Le Châ′te·lard′ (lĕ shä′tlàr′). Commune, Vaud canton, W Switzerland, near E shore of Lake of Geneva 15 m. ESE of Lausanne; pop. (1930) 11,996. See MONTREUX.
Lech′feld (lĕk′fĕlt). Field or plain on Lech river in E Swabia, Bavaria, Germany, S of Augsburg; scene of battle 955 in which Otto I defeated the Magyars.
Lech′lade (lĕch′lād). Parish, Gloucestershire, SW cen. England, on the Thames; terminus of Thames and Severn Canal.
Le·comp′ton (lĕ·kŏmp′tŭn). City, Douglas co., E Kansas; pop. 304; scene of framing of the Lecompton Constitution Oct.–Nov. 1857, a proslavery constitution for the state of Kansas which was overwhelmingly defeated by the voters.
Le Conte, Mount (lĕ kŏnt′). **1** Mountain 13,960 ft., Tulare co., S cen. California, on E boundary of Sequoia National Park.
2 Peak 6593 ft. in Sevier co., E Tennessee, in Great Smoky Mts.

Le Crac. See EL KERAK.

Le Creu'sot' (lĕ krŭ'zō'). Commune, Saône-et-Loire dept., E cen. France, 39 m. NNW of Mâcon; pop. 29,417; mining; site of the great ironworks of the Schneider Co.

Lec'toure' (lĕk'tŏōr'). Commune, N Gers dept., SW France; pop. (1931) 4218; dates from pre-Roman times; capital of Armagnac from 1325; bishopric suppressed 1790; church (15th–17th cents.), formerly the cathedral.

Lectum, Cape. See Cape BABA.

Lę̣·czy'ca (lĕn·chĭ'tsä); *Russ.* **Len·chi'tsa** (lyĭn·chē'tsȧ); *Ger.* **Len·tschi'za** (lĕn·chē'tsä). Commune, Łódź dept., Poland, on Bzura river 20 m. NNW of Łódź; pop. 10,553; manufactures textiles, beet sugar; agricultural products.

Ledang, Gunong. See Mount OPHIR.

Le'de·berg (lā'dĕ·bĕrK). Commune, East Flanders prov., NW cen. Belgium, just SE of Gent; pop. 12,897.

Ledi, Ben. See BEN LEDI.

Ledja. See EL LEDJA.

Le'do (lē'dō; lā'-). Town, Assam state, Indian Union, ab. 35 m. S of Sadiya; branch railhead of Bengal-Assam railroad and starting point of **Ledo Road,** strategical military highway begun in Dec. 1942 by U.S. Army engineers to connect with Burma Road (q.v.); road built under great difficulties across Patkai Range through Hukawng valley to Mogaung, Myitkyina (Ledo to Myitkyina 262 m.), and Bhamo in N Burma; name changed to Stilwell Road (q.v.) Jan. 1945.

Ledo Salinarius. See LONS-LE-SAUNIER.

Led'yard (lĕd'yẽrd; lĕj'ẽrd). Agricultural town, New London co., SE Connecticut, E of Thames river 7 m. NE of New London; pop. 5395; incorporated 1836.

Lee (lē). **1** Name of counties in twelve states of the U.S. See *Tables* at ALABAMA, ARKANSAS, FLORIDA, GEORGIA, ILLINOIS, IOWA, KENTUCKY, MISSISSIPPI, NORTH CAROLINA, SOUTH CAROLINA, TEXAS, VIRGINIA.

2 Town, Berkshire co., W Massachusetts, 9 m. S of Pittsfield; pop. 5271; paper manufacturing.

3 River ab. 50 m. long in SW Ireland; flows from W to E across co. Cork into Cork Harbour; noted for the scenery along its shores.

Leech'burg (lēch'bûrg). Industrial borough, Armstrong co., W Pennsylvania, 25 m. ENE of Pittsburgh; pop. 3545; coal mining, strip-steel manufacturing.

Leech Lake (lēch). Lake in N Cass co., N cen. Minnesota; ab. 20 m. long and from 4 to 15 m. wide; altitude 1297 ft.; outlet E into Mississippi river.

Leeds (lēdz). **1** City, Jefferson and St. Clair cos., cen. Alabama, 15 m. ENE of Birmingham; pop. 6162; barite mined in vicinity.

2 County, Ontario, Canada. See *Table* at ONTARIO.

3 City and county borough, West Riding, Yorkshire, N England, on the Aire 36 m. ENE of Manchester; pop. 482,809, (1951) 504,954; an industrial center; manufactures woolen goods, metalwares, locomotives, farm implements, airplane parts, pottery and glassware, leather goods, furniture, and chemicals; University of Leeds.

Leek (lēk). Urban district, Staffordshire, W cen. England; pop. 19,358; market town; ruins of 13th-cent. Cistercian abbey.

Lee'la·nau (lē'lȧ·nô). County in Michigan. See *Table* at MICHIGAN.

Leer (lār); *also* **Leer in Ost'fries'land** (ĭn ôst'frēs'länt). Commercial and manufacturing city, NW Lower Saxony state, W Germany, near right bank of lower Ems river 34 m. WNW of Oldenburg; pop. 12,238; manufactures paper, distillery products, machinery. In World War II taken by Allies Apr. 23, 1945.

Leer·dam' (lār·däm'). Commune, South Holland prov., SW Netherlands; pop. 8950; glass manufactures.

Lees'burg (lēz'bûrg). **1** City, Lake co., cen. Florida penin., 36 m. WNW of Orlando; pop. 11,172; founded 1856; fishing resort; manufactures grape juice, wine, jelly, jam; kaolin deposits.

2 City, ⊗ of Lee co., SW Georgia; pop. 774.

3 Town, ⊗ of Loudoun co., N Virginia, 38 m. NW of Alexandria; pop. 2869.

Lees Ferry (lēz). Locality, N Coconino co., N Arizona, on Colorado river near Marble Canyon; ferry established 1872, only crossing of the Colorado river for many miles; now site of Navajo Bridge (sometimes called Marble Canyon or Grand Canyon Bridge) 467 ft. above the river, ab. 800 ft. long, completed 1929.

Lee's Summit. City, Jackson co., W Missouri, 18 m. SE of Kansas City; pop. 8267.

Lees'ville (lēz'vĭl; *Sou.* also -v'l). Town, ⊗ of Vernon parish, W Louisiana, 53 m. W of Alexandria; pop. 4689; trade center for lumbering, farming, and livestock-raising section.

Lee·to'ni·a (lė̄·tō'nĭ·ȧ; -tōn'yȧ). Village, Columbiana co., E Ohio, 16 m. SSW of Youngstown; pop. 2543; coal mining.

Leets'dale (lēts'dāl). Borough, Allegheny co., SW Pennsylvania, on Ohio river 14 m. WNW of Pittsburgh; pop. 2153; metal manufactures.

Leeu'war'den (lā'vär'dĕ[n]). Commercial and industrial commune, ✻ of Friesland prov., N Netherlands, on the Ee river; pop. (1939) 54,971; formerly noted for its manufactures in gold and silver; now trade and market center of a livestock-raising and dairy-farming section; Groote Kerk (built ab. 1480), Frisian Museum, stadhouse, Kanselarij (chancellery).

Leeu'win, Cape (lŏō'ĭn). The extreme SW point of Australia.

Lee'ward Islands (lē'wẽrd; *by some,* lū'ẽrd, lŏō'-). **1** *Fr.* **Îles sous le Vent** (ēl' sŏōl' vän'). Western group of the Society Is., French Polynesia, S Pacific Ocean; pop. (1941) 11,891; chief islands Huahiné, Raïatéa, and Tahaa.

2 The chain of small islets, rocks, and shoals, some composed of lava rock, some of coral and sand, extending 1250 m. WNW from main islands of the Hawaiian Is., ab. 162°W to 178°25'W; all except Midway are uninhabited and seldom visited, and constitute the **Hawaiian Islands Bird Reservation,** set aside 1909 by U.S. government as a bird sanctuary; islets include Nihoa, Necker, Gardner Pinnacles, Laysan, Lisianski, Pearl and Hermes Reef and Kure, or Ocean. Since discovery 1859 considered as belonging to the Hawaiian Is.; under the jurisdiction of Honolulu co.

3 Geographically, the northern chain of islands in the Lesser Antilles, E West Indies—so called because of their more sheltered position than the Windward Is. from the prevailing northeasterly winds. The chain extends from Dominica on the S to Virgin Is. on the N; administratively divided bet. the U.S. (St. Thomas, St. Croix, and St. John in the Virgin Is.), Netherlands (Saba, St. Eustatius, and S part of St. Martin), France (Guadeloupe, Marie Galante, Désirade, Les Saintes, St. Barthélemy, and N part of St. Martin) and Great Britain (see LEEWARD ISLANDS colony, below). For geographical descriptions and history, see sense 4, below, entries for individual islands, and VIRGIN ISLANDS.

4 Government division, West Indies Federation, in Leeward Is.; administratively divided into 3 territories (until 1956 called presidencies): Antigua (Antigua, Barbuda, and Redonda islands), Montserrat (Montserrat I.), and St. Kitts-Nevis (St. Kitts, Nevis, Anguilla, and Sombrero Is.); does not include the British Virgin Is.; formerly included also presidency (and island) of Dominica, transferred 1940 to Windward Is.; 414 sq. m.; pop. (1942 est.) 98,135; ✻ St. Johns on Antigua.

History. First British settlement, on St. Kitts, 1625, followed by period of conflict with Spanish (17th cent.) and French (17th and 18th cents.); islands united under a common legislature early in 18th cent. and, after a lapse of this form of government, reunited under a common council 1871. For further details, see entries for individual islands.

Leeward Passage. Channel bet. Hans Lollik I. and N St. Thomas I., Virgin Is., West Indies.

Le·flore' (lĕ·flōr'). County in Mississippi. See *Table* at MISSISSIPPI.

Le Flore (lĕ flōr'). County in Oklahoma. See *Table* at OKLAHOMA.

Le·froy', Lake (lĕ·froi'). Lake, S Western Australia, N of Lake Cowan and near Boulder.

Le·gas'pi (lä·gäs'pĕ; *Angl.* lĕ·gäs'pĭ). Municipality, ✳ of Albay prov., Phil. Is., at head of Albay Gulf, near S base of Mt. Mayon; pop. 41,468; comprises original municipalities of Legaspi on the coast, Albay ab. 2 m. inland, and 18 barrios; two municipalities merged in 1907 and name of Albay changed to Legaspi 1925. Founded ab. 1636; partly destroyed by eruption of Mayon 1814; held by Japanese Dec. 12, 1941 to Apr. 1, 1945.

Leg'horn (lĕg'hôrn); *Ital.* **Li·vor'no** (lė·vôr'nô). Seaport commune, ✳ of Livorno prov., Tuscany, cen. Italy, on Tyrrhenian Sea 160 m. NW of Rome; pop. 124,963; episcopal see; 17th-cent. cathedral; 16th-cent. synagogue; royal castle; royal naval academy; trade center and port; manufactures straw hats (the original Leghorns), leather, chemicals, paper, soap, iron products, glass; shipbuilding. Under Florentine rule 1421; made free port by Cosimo I; for three centuries most important harbor of Tuscany; under Napoleon, capital of French department of La Méditerranée; strongly defended by Germans in World War II but taken by Americans July 19, 1944.

Le·gna'go (lā·nyä'gô). Commune, Verona prov., Venezia Euganea, NE Italy, on Adige river 23 m. SE of Venice; pop. 21,771; connected by canal with Po river. Venetian and Austrian fortified stronghold.

Le·gna'no (lä·nyä'nô). Commune, Milano prov., Lombardy, N Italy, 11 m. NW of Milan; pop. 31,952; manufactures machines; Frederick Barbarossa defeated here 1176 by Lombard League.

Leg·ni'ca (lĕg·nē'tsä); *Ger.* **Lieg'nitz** (lēg'nĭts). City, cen. Wrocław dept., SW Poland, 39 m. WNW of Wrocław; pop. (1946) 46,900; formerly in Germany; railroad junction; 14th-cent. Gothic church, 12th-cent. castle; manufactures textiles, machinery, pianos. Scene of victory of Frederick the Great over Austrians Aug. 15, 1760; in World War II taken by Russians Feb. 10, 1945; assigned to Poland by Potsdam Conference 1945.

Le Grand Andely. See LES ANDELYS.

Le Grand–Montrouge. See MONTROUGE.

Le'guan (?lā'gwän). Island at mouth of the Essequibo river, off NE coast of British Guiana.

Leh (lā). Town, ✳ of Ladakh frontier dist. and of tahsil, E Kashmir, N India; pop. 3093; on N bank of Indus at altitude of 11,500 ft., 160 m. E of Srinagar; by road 482 m. via Leh Pass from Yarkand; great trade center of W Himalayas on routes connecting India, Chinese Turkistan, and Tibet; starting point of many expeditions; has most elevated meteorological observatory in Asia.

Le Ha'vre (lĕ à'vr'; *Angl.* hȧ'vr', -vrĕ, -vĕr); *Eng.* **Havre;** *formerly* **Le Ha'vre–de–Grâce** (lĕ à'vrĕ-dĕ-gräs'). Commercial seaport, Seine-Maritime dept., N France, on English Channel on N side of Seine estuary 110 m. WNW of Paris; pop. 164,083; church of Notre Dame, town hall (former gubernatorial palace), round tower of Francis I, arsenal, barracks, exchange, and theater; fine seaside resort adjacent on NW; port for transatlantic steamers; import and export center for Paris and NW France; important market for coffee and cotton; varied manufactures. Base for American and British troops in World War I; in World War II taken by Germans June 14, 1940; sealed off by Allied advance in France Sept. 1, 1944 and taken Sept. 8–11, 1944.

Le'he (lā'ĕ). Former city, Hannover prov., Prussia, Germany; since 1924 part of Wesermünde (*q.v.*).

Le'hi (lē'hī). City, Utah co., N cen. Utah, on Utah Lake 16 m. NNW of Provo; pop. 4377; farming (sugar beets, fruit); canning and sugar-refining industries.

Le'high (lē'hī). **1** River ab. 100 m. long in E Pennsylvania; rises in S extremity of Wayne co., flows SW, then turns SE to empty into the Delaware river at Easton. **2** County in Pennsylvania. See *Table* at PENNSYLVANIA.

Le·high'ton (lē·hī't'n). Borough, Carbon co., E Pennsylvania, on Lehigh river 21 m. NW of Allentown; pop. 6318; locomotive shops; textile mills. Settled by Moravians 1746; destroyed by Indians 1755; resettled 1794; incorporated as borough 1866.

Leh'man Caves National Monument (lē'măn). See UNITED STATES, *National Monuments.*

Lehr'te (lār'tĕ). City, Lower Saxony, Germany, 10 m. E of Hannover; pop. 10,714.

Le·hu'a (lȧ·hōō'ä), *or* **Egg** (ĕg), **Island.** Small barren uninhabited rock off N tip of Niihau I., NW Hawaii; lighthouse, 702 ft. above the sea.

Lei (lā). River ab. 185 m. long, E Hunan, SE cen. China, flows W and N to the Siang.

Leices'ter (lĕs'tēr). **1** Town, Worcester co., cen. Massachusetts, 6 m. W of Worcester; pop. 8177; textiles. **2** County of England. See LEICESTERSHIRE. **3** City and county borough, ⊗ of Leicestershire, cen. England, on the Soar 35 m. ENE of Birmingham; pop. 239,169, (1951) 285,061; chief industries are the manufacture of hosiery and boots and shoes; ruins of an ancient Norman castle, and of an abbey founded in 1143. Place where Richard III spent the night before he was killed in the battle of Bosworth Field, and to which his body was brought for burial.

Leices'ter·shire (lĕs'tēr·shĭr; -shēr) *or* **Leices'ter** (lĕs'tēr). County, cen. England; 832 sq. m.; pop. (1951) 630,893; ⊗ Leicester; other towns are Loughborough, Ashby de la Zouch, Hinckley; rivers include the Soar and Wreak; grazing (esp. sheep), agriculture, quarrying (limestone, slate), woolen hosiery.

Leich'hardt (līk'härt). **1** River ab. 220 m. long in NW Queensland, Australia, flows N to Gulf of Carpentaria. **2** City, E New South Wales, SE Australia, SW suburb of Sydney; pop. 15,134.

Lei'den *or* **Ley'den** (lī'd'n; *Du. usu.* lä'ė·yĕ); *anc.* **Lug·du'num Bat'a·vo'rum** (lŭg·dū'nŭm băt'ȧ·vōr'ŭm). Industrial commune, South Holland prov., SW Netherlands, on Oude Rijn river; pop. (1939) 78,198; birthplace of Rembrandt and of John of Leiden; residence of the Pilgrims for 11 years before they sailed 1620 for America; famous for its heroic defense May–Oct. 1574 against Spanish siege; University of Leiden (founded 1575); home of the Elzevir family of printers, and still a printing and publishing center.

Lei'dy, Mount (lī'dĭ). Peak 10,317 ft. in E cen. Teton co., NW Wyoming.

Leidy Peak. Mountain 12,015 ft. in N Uintah co., E Utah.

Leie. See LYS.

Leigh (lē). Municipal borough, Lancashire, NW England, 11 m. W of Manchester; pop. 48,714; coal mines, iron foundries, textile mills, glassworks.

Leigh'lin (lē'lĭn). Town, co. Carlow, Eire, ab. 8 m. S of Carlow; site of monastery founded 7th cent.

Leigh'ton Buz'zard (lā't'n bŭz'ĕrd). Urban district, Bedfordshire, SE cen. England, on the Ouzel 38 m. NW of London; pop. 9023.

Lei'ne (lī'nĕ). River 120 m. long, W cen. Germany; rises in the Eichsfeld and flows W and N past Göttingen and Hannover to the Aller SE of Verden.

Lein'ster (lĕn'stēr; *Ir.* lĭn'-). Province, SE Eire; 7581 sq. m.; pop. 1,220,411; includes cos. Carlow, Dublin, Kildare, Kilkenny, Laoighis, Longford, Louth, Meath, Offaly, Westmeath, Wexford, Wicklow. One of the early provinces of Ireland; its N part, Meath, made a separate kingdom in 2d cent. A.D.; remainder independent in 12th and 13th cents., and cos. Carlow and Wexford independent until 16th cent.

Leinster, Mount. Peak 2610 ft. on boundary bet. cos. Carlow and Wexford, SE Ireland.

Leip'sic (lĭp'sĭk). Village, Putnam co., NW Ohio, 17 m. WNW of Findlay; pop. 1802.

Leip'zig (līp'sĭg; -sĭk; *Ger.* līp'tsĭk). **1** Circle of Saxony. See *Table* at SAXONY.

2 *also* **Leip'sic** (lĭp'sĭk); *Latin* **Lip'si·a** (lĭp'sĭ·à). Manufacturing and commercial city, Saxony, E Germany, at confluence of Weisse Elster, Pleisse, and Parthe rivers 94 m. SSW of Berlin; pop. (1939) 701,606, (1958) 593,902; old fortifications replaced by streets and promenades; numerous churches of the 11th and following cents., in one of which (St. Thomas) Bach was organist; 16th-cent. town hall, old Gewandhaus (scene of celebrated Gewandhaus concerts), modern town hall (Rathaus) on site of old Pleissenburg castle; third largest university (founded 1409) in Germany; three annual fairs (held since 12th cent.); one of leading publishing centers of the world.

History: First mentioned c. 11th cent.; chartered in 12th cent., its fair became important commercially; scene of famous debate bet. Luther, Karlstadt, and Eck 1519; in Thirty Years' War, two battles (sometimes called battles of Breitenfeld) won by Swedes nearby, 1631 and 1642; in 17th cent., supplanted Frankfurt as center of German book trade; scene of "Battle of the Nations" (*Ger.* Völkerschlacht) Oct. 16–19, 1813, when Napoleon's power in Germany was broken by the Allies. In World War II taken by American forces, Apr. 20, 1945; site of concentration camp.

Lei·ri'a (lā·ė·rē'à). **1** District of Portugal. See *Table* at PORTUGAL.

2 Commune, its *, W cen. Portugal, on Lis river 73 m. N by E of Lisbon; pop. 6147; first Portuguese printing press 1466.

Leitch'field (lĭch'fēld). City, ⊗ of Grayson co., W cen. Kentucky; pop. 2982.

Leith (lēth). Former burgh, Midlothian co., SE Scotland, now united to Edinburgh; a great seaport and shipbuilding center, with many industries.

Lei'tha (lī'tä). River 112 m. long in E Austria; flows NE across Hungarian border and enters the Rába near its junction with the Danube; historically, formed section of boundary bet. Austria and Hungary until transfer of Burgenland to Austria 1922. See CISLEITHANIA and TRANSLEITHANIA.

Leith Hill. See NORTH DOWNS.

Leitmeritz. See LITOMĚŘICE.

Lei'trim (lē'trĭm). County, N Eire, in Connacht prov.; 589 sq. m.; pop. 50,908; ⊗ Carrick on Shannon; livestock grazing, agriculture.

Leix. County, Leinster prov., Eire. See LAOIGHIS.

Lei·xõ'es (lā·ė·shōn'ĕsh). Seaport, NW Portugal, in parish of Matozinhos; artificial harbor, main port of Oporto.

Lek (lĕk). The northern branch of the Lower Rhine in Netherlands, a continuation W of the Neder Rijn; unites with Merwede river to form the Nieuwe Maas; scene of fierce fighting in World War II esp. Sept. 17–25, 1944, during Allied airborne attack near Arnhem.

Le Kef (lĕ kĕf') *or* **El Kef** (ăl kăf'); *anc.* **Sic'ca Ve·ne'-ri·a** (sĭk'à vė·nēr'ĭ·à). Town, N Tunisia, ab. 90 m. SSW of Tunis; pop. 7362; built on a steep rock at a junction of main highways; made a Roman colony by Augustus; modern town smaller and less important than Roman town; remains of Roman temple and baths.

Le Kroub. See KROUB.

Le'land (lē'lănd). **1** Village, ⊗ of Leelanau co., NW Michigan; pop. (est.) 400.

2 City, Washington co., W Mississippi, 10 m. E of Greenville; pop. 6295; in section producing cotton, alfalfa, vegetables, pecans.

Le·le' (lĕ·lŭ'; -lā'). Village and harbor on E coast of Kusaie I., E Caroline Is., W Pacific Ocean; has remarkable ruins nearby; formerly a rendezvous for whaling vessels.

Le'le·i'wi Point (lā'lā·ē'wĕ). Point on E coast of Hawaii I., Hawaii, S of Hilo Bay.

Le'les (lā'lĕs). Plain, West Java prov., Indonesia, just N of Garut; noted for its extensive cultivation of rice.

Le Lo'cle (lĕ lô'kl'). Commune, Neuchâtel canton, W Switzerland, on French border 5 m. SW of La Chaux-de-Fonds; pop. (1941) 11,336; watch-making center.

Lelupe. See LIELUPE.

Le Madonie. See MADONIE MOUNTAINS.

Le'ma·ha'bang (lā'mä·hä'bäng). Town, West Java prov., Indonesia, just SSE of Cheribon; pop. 12,940.

Le Maine. See MAINE.

Le Maire' Strait (lĕ mâr'). Strait ab. 20 m. wide bet. Staten I. and SE Tierra del Fuego I., S Argentina.

Le'man (lē'măn; lĕm'ăn; lĕ·män'). Name of Vaud canton, W Switzerland, under the Helvetic Republic 1798–1803.

Leman, Lake; *anc.* **Le·man'nus** (lė·măn'ŭs) *or* **Le·ma'nus** (lė·mā'nŭs). See Lake of GENEVA.

Le Mans (lĕ män'). Commercial and manufacturing city, * of Sarthe dept., NW France, on Sarthe river 117 m. SW of Paris; pop. 84,525; railroad center; 11th-cent. Gothic cathedral; Roman ruins; manufactures metal goods, canned goods, chemicals, leather, textiles, tobacco, railroad cars. French defeated here by Prussians during Franco-Prussian War 1870–71. Birthplace of Henry II, the first Plantagenet.

Le Marche. See MARCHES.

Le Mars (lĕ märz'). City, ⊗ of Plymouth co., NW Iowa, 25 m. NNE of Sioux City; pop. 6767; Westmar College (1900; coed.).

Le Mas d'A'zil (lĕ màs' dà'zēl'). Commune, N Ariège dept., S France, ab. 40 m. SW of Toulouse; pop. (1931) 1720; in 1887 nearby cave scene of discovery of prehistoric human remains representative of culture now called *Azilian* belonging to a period of the Stone Age immediately preceding the neolithic.

Lem'bang (lĕm'bäng). Village, W Java, Indonesia, N of Bandung at foot of Tangkuban Prahu; health resort; alt. 4000 ft.

Lemberg. See LVOV.

Le'me·ry' (lā'mà·rē'). Municipality, Batangas prov., Luzon, Phil. Is., on right bank of Pansipit river opp. Taal and near E shore of Balayan Bay; pop. 19,207.

Lemessus. See LIMASSOL.

Lem'go (lĕm'gō). City, West Saxony, Germany, 44 m. SW of Hannover; pop. 11,489; manufactures furniture, cigars, linen, lumber.

Lem'hi (lĕm'hī). **1** River 75 m. long, E cen. Idaho; rises in SE Lemhi co., flows N into Salmon river at Salmon.

2 County in Idaho. See *Table* at IDAHO.

Lemhi Range. Range in E cen. Idaho, chiefly in Lemhi and Butte cos.; highest point 11,324 ft.

Lem'mon (lĕm'ŭn). City, Perkins co., NW South Dakota, on North Dakota border 14 m. N of Grand river; pop. 2412; grain and livestock; lignite coal mines.

Lemmon, *also* **Lem'on, Mount** (lĕm'ŭn). Mountain 9180 ft., highest peak in Santa Catalina Mts., in NE corner of Pima co., S Arizona.

Lem'nos (lĕm'nŏs); *Mod. Gr.* **Lēm'nos** (lyēm'nôs). Island in N Aegean Sea off W coast of Turkey in Asia; 175 sq. m.; pop. 24,397; * Kástron; administratively constitutes a province in the department of Lesbos, Greece; mountainous and fertile; has some grazing and fruit growing; has fine harbor at Moudros on S coast; produces a medicinal earth (Lemnian bole or earth) long sold in Europe as an astringent. Important in Greek mythology, esp. as sacred to Hephaestus.

History: Occupied by ancient Greeks; held by Persians at beginning of 5th cent. B.C.; in Delian League and important part of Athenian Empire; in Roman, Byzantine, and Ottoman Empires; taken from Ottoman Empire by Greece 1912; base of British fleet in Dardanelles campaign of World War I.

Lem'on Grove (lĕm'ŭn). Urban community (unincorporated), San Diego co., S California, E of San Diego; pop. 19,348.

Lem'on Rock (lĕm'ŭn). See SKELLIGS.
Le·mont' (lĕ·mŏnt'). Village, Cook co., NE Illinois, on Illinois river 25 m. SW of Chicago; pop. 3397.
Le·moore' (lĕ·mōr'). City, Kings co., SW cen. California, 29 m. S of Fresno; pop. 2561; trade center for dairy and fruit region.
Le Mort Homme (lĕ môr'-tôm') *or* **Hill 295.** Height ab. 6 m. NW of Verdun, NE France; scene of violent battle when captured by Germans May 29, 1916; recaptured by French Aug. 20, 1917.
Le Moule (lĕ mōōl'). Seaport, Grande Terre I., E part of island of Guadeloupe, French West Indies; pop. (1931 est.) 17,159.
Le Mous'tier' (lĕ mōōs'tyā'). Cave, Dordogne dept., SW France, on right bank of the Vézère above Les Eyzies (see LES EYZIES); from important archaeological finds here, including a human skeleton and flint points, gives its name to the *Mousterian* period of paleolithic culture marking culmination of Neanderthal race.
Lemovices. See LIMOGES.
Le·moyne' (lĕ·moin'). Residential borough, Cumberland co., S Pennsylvania, on Susquehanna river across from Harrisburg; pop. 4662.
Lem'pa (lăm'pä). River ab. 200 m. long in El Salvador; flows through Lake Guija E and S into the Pacific Ocean.
Lem·pi'ra (lăm·pē'rä); *formerly* **Gra'cias** (grä'syäs). Department, W Honduras; 1295 sq. m.; pop. (1945 est.) 81,182; ✱ Gracias.
Lem'ro' (lĕm'rō'). River ab. 175 m. long, Arakan division, W Lower Burma; rises in Chin Hills and flows S into Hunter's Bay, inlet of Bay of Bengal, E of Akyab.
Le'na (lē'nà; *Russ.* lyĕ'-). River ab. 3000 m. long, E cen. Siberia, Soviet Russia, Asia, with drainage basin estimated at 100,000 sq. m.; rises on W slopes of Baikal Mts. W of Lake Baikal, flows NE in Irkutsk Region through wooded mountain ranges, then E forming part of S boundary of Yakutsk Republic; from ab. 117°E flows in great bend E and N entirely within the Yakutsk Republic to enter Laptev Sea in delta 250 m. wide at ab. 72°N. Has many tributaries (estimated by some at 1000), chief of which on right are Vitim, Olekma, and Aldan, on left Vilyui; land along upper course and on tributaries rich in minerals. In lower 1200 m. of course fall is slight and width is 4 to 20 m. Yakutsk is only large town on its entire course. Delta first reached 1637; scene of death 1881 of members of expedition of American explorer, George W. De Long.
Le'na (lā'nä). Commune, Oviedo prov., NW Spain, 13 m. S of Oviedo; pop. 15,532; iron, cinnabar, and coal mining; meat-packing plants.
Len'a·wee (lĕn'à·wē). County in Michigan. See *Table* at MICHIGAN.
Lenchitsa. See LĘCZYCA.
Len·di·na'ra (lân·dē·nä'rä). Commune, Rovigo prov., Venezia Euganea, NE Italy, 10 m. W of Rovigo; pop. 15,717; manufactures silk.
Lendum. See LENS.
Len'gua de Va'ca, Point (lāng'gwä thä vä'kä). Cape on W coast of Coquimbo prov., cen. Chile, S of city of Coquimbo.
Len'in·a·bad' (lĕn'ĭn·à·bäd'; *Russ.* lyä'nyĭ·nŭ·bàt'); *formerly* **Kho·jend'** (kŏ·jĕnd'), *Russ.* **Kho·dzhent'** (kŏ·jĕnt'; *Russ.* kŭ-). Town, ✱ of Leninabad Region, NW Tadzhik S.S.R., Soviet Central Asia, on left bank of Syr Darya river 90 m. S of Tashkent; pop. 37,258; occupied by Russians 1866; has several manufactures.
Leninabad Region. Subdivision of Tadzhik S.S.R., in NW part; ✱ Leninabad.
Le'nin·a·kan' (lĕ'nĕ·nä·ᴋän'); *formerly* **A'le·ksan'-dro·pol** (ăl'ĕg·zăn'drŏ·pôl; ăl'ĭg-; *Brit. also* -zän'-; *Russ.* ŭ·lyĭ·ksŭn·drŏ'pŭl·y') *and* **Gum·ry'** (gŏŏm·rē'). City, NW Armenian S.S.R., Soviet Union, on a tributary of the Araks 55 m. NW of Yerevan; pop. 67,707; an industrial city on the Tiflis-Tabriz railroad manufacturing especially carpets and textiles, machinery, soap, copper

articles; has recently advanced development of irrigation and agriculture in its vicinity; contains remains of Turkish fortresses. Suffered from a severe earthquake 1926.
Len'in·grad (lĕn'ĭn·gräd; *Russ.* lyä'nyĭn·grát'). City, ✱ of Leningrad Region and (as **St. Pe'ters·burg** [sânt pē'tĕrz·bûrg]) ✱ of Russian empire 1712 to 1917; second largest city in U.S.S.R., at E end of Gulf of Finland (Kronshtadt Bay), built on the Neva delta; pop. 3,191,304; intersected by many canals, crossed by more than 600 bridges; has long been cultural center of Russia; many fine buildings (Academy of Sciences, The Hermitage, Winter Palace, Palace of Art, Cathedral, Peter Paul fortress, and museums, universities, and institutes).
History: Town of St. Petersburg founded in 1703 by Peter the Great as "a window into Europe" and in 1712 made capital of Russia; a scene of Decembrist revolt 1825 and of incident known as Red Sunday in 1905 revolution; renamed **Pet'ro·grad** (pĕt'rŏ·gräd; *Russ.* pyĭ·trŭ·grát') 1914; original center of Russian Revolution of 1917 (Kerenski government and Petrograd Soviet), but capital of Soviet Russia soon moved to Moscow; renamed Leningrad 1924; besieged by German armies Sept. 1941 to Jan. 1944.
Leningrad Area. Former subdivision of Soviet Russia, Europe, in NW part; 127,473 sq. m.; ✱ Leningrad; included several provinces whose centers were Leningrad, Novgorod, Pskov, Cherepovets, and the exclave of the Murmansk dist. and Kola Penin.
Leningrad Region. Region, NW Soviet Russia, Europe; 52,843 sq. m.; pop. 6,435,076; ✱ Leningrad; bounded on N by Karelo-Finnish Soviet Socialist Republic and on the W by Estonia; approximately two thirds of Lake Ladoga lies within its borders. On the NW penetrated by Kronshtadt Bay, the E end of the Gulf of Finland. Its principal streams are the Neva (outlet of Lake Ladoga), Svir (outlet of Lake Onega), and Volkhov (outlet of Lake Ilmen). Level country with forests and some marsh lands; has considerable agricultural development. Its manufacturing industries widely varied, esp. in Leningrad. Chief cities, besides Leningrad, Vyborg, Volkhov, Pavlovsk, Pushkin, and Tikhvin. Region early settled by Finnish tribes; for several centuries nominally subject to Novgorod but contended for by Swedes; part included in Ingria (*q.v.*) 1617–1703 but with capture of Swedish fort on the Neva by Peter the Great 1703, history of region centers on St. Petersburg (see LENINGRAD). After World War II extended to include all of Karelian Isthmus, N part of which was formerly in Finland.
Len'in (lĕn'ĭn; *Russ.* lyä'nyĭn), *or* **Kauf'mann** (kouf'mán), **Peak.** Mountain 23,386 ft., highest in Trans Alai range, bet. Kirgiz S.S.R. and the Gorno-Badakhshan Region, NE Tadzhik S.S.R., Soviet Central Asia; second highest peak in the U.S.S.R., Stalin Peak (*q.v.*) being the highest.
Len'insk (lĕn'ĭnsk; *Russ.* lyä'nyĭnsk). **1** Town, Leningrad Region, Soviet Russia. See PETRODVORETS.
2 *formerly* **Pri·shib'** (prĭ·shĭb'; *Russ.* pryĭ·shĭp'). Town, E Stalingrad Region, Soviet Russia, Europe, 35 m. E of Stalingrad on an E arm of the lower Volga; pop. ab. 15,000; near site of Sarai (*q.v.*).
3 *or* **Leninsk–Turk·men'skii** (-tŏŏrk·mĕn'skĭ; *Russ.* -myĕn'-). See CHARDZHOU.
Leninsk–Kuz·nets'ki (-kŏŏz·nĕts'kĭ; *Russ.* -kŏŏs·nyĕts'-); *formerly* **Kol·chu'gi·no** (kŭl·chŏŏ'gĭ·nŭ). Mining town in center of Kuznetsk Basin, W Kemerovo Region, Soviet Russia, Asia, on Tom river 75 m. NW of Stalinsk; pop. 81,980.
Leninsk–Om'skii (-ôm'skĭ). Suburb of Omsk, Omsk Region, W Soviet Russia, Asia; pop. 35,000.
Len'ko·ran' (lĕng'kŏ·rän'). Seaport town, SE Azerbaidzhan, U.S.S.R., on SW shore of Caspian Sea near the Iranian border; pop. 11,878; has fair harbor but no rail connections; trades chiefly in lumber, fish, and fruit. Taken from Persia by the Russians 1813.

Len'nep (lĕn'ĕp). Former city (pop. 14,155), Düsseldorf govt. dist., Rhine Province, Prussia, Germany; since 1929 part of Remscheid (*q.v.*).

Len'nox (lĕn'ŭks). **1** Urban area, Los Angeles co., SW California, SE of Santa Monica; pop. 31,224.

2 City, Lincoln co., SE South Dakota, 18 m. SSW of Sioux Falls; pop. 1353.

Lennox and Ad'ding·ton (ăd'ĭng·tŭn). County, Ontario, Canada. See *Table* at ONTARIO.

Lennox Hills. Range of hills in Dunbarton and Stirling cos., SW cen. Scotland; highest point **Earl's Seat** (ûrlz) 1894 ft.

Len'nox·ville (lĕn'ŭks·vĭl). Town, Sherbrooke co., S Quebec, Canada, 4 m. SSE of Sherbrooke; pop. 2895; seat of Bishop's Univ. (1843; coed.; Anglican).

Le·noir' (lĕ·nôr'). **1** County in North Carolina. See *Table* at NORTH CAROLINA.

2 Town, ⊗ of Caldwell co., W North Carolina, near Blue Ridge Mts. 38 m. W of Statesville; pop. 10,257; in summer resort region; furniture, veneer, cotton yarn.

Lenoir City. City, Loudon co., E Tennessee, on Tennessee river; pop. 4979; ships agricultural products (hay, grain); hosiery, railroad cars, foundry products.

Le·nore' Lake (lĕ·nôr'). Lake 8 m. long in NW Grant co., cen. Washington.

Len'ox (lĕn'ŭks). Town, Berkshire co., W Massachusetts, 7 m. S of Pittsfield; pop. 4253; summer resort; estate including site of Hawthorne's cottage and Tanglewood where summer concerts of Boston Symphony Orchestra are given.

Lens (läns); *anc.* **Len'ti·um** (lĕn'shĭ·ŭm) *or* **Len'dum** (lĕn'dŭm). Industrial city, Pas-de-Calais dept., N France, 11 m. NNE of Arras; pop. 32,730; coal-mining center; iron, steel, and engineering works. Scene of French victory over Spaniards Aug. 2, 1648; in World War I occupied by Germans 1914–18, scene of battle Aug. 15, 1917 in which Canadians attacked successfully, and again on Oct. 3, 1918 when it was retaken by Allies.

Lentia. See LINZ.

Len·ti'ni (lån·tē'nė); *anc.* **Le·on·ti'ni** (lē'ŏn·tī'nī). Commune, Siracusa prov., SE Sicily, 22 m. NW of Syracuse; pop. 23,830; oldest Greek settlement in Sicily.

Lentium. See LENS.

Lentschiza. See LĘCZYCA.

Léo. See LÉOPOLDVILLE.

Le·o'ben (lå·ō'bĕn). City, Styria prov., Austria, on Mur river 27 m. NW of Graz; pop. 11,890; railroad junction; manufactures metal goods; iron and lignite mining; preliminary peace treaty bet. France and Austria signed here Apr. 18, 1797.

Leobschütz. See GŁUBCZYCE.

Le·o'la (lĕ·ō'lå). City, ⊗ of McPherson co., N South Dakota; pop. 833.

Leom'in·ster. 1 (lĕm'ĭn·stẽr) Industrial city, Worcester co., cen. Massachusetts, 5 m. SSE of Fitchburg; pop. 27,927; furniture, combs, textiles, paper and paper boxes. Part of Lancaster until 1740; chartered as city 1915.

2 (lĕm'stẽr, *less often* lĕm'ĭn·stẽr) Municipal borough, Herefordshire, W England, on the Lugg 40 m. WSW of Birmingham; pop. 5707.

Le'on (lē'ŏn). **1** Name of counties in two states of the U.S. See *Tables* at FLORIDA and TEXAS.

2 City, ⊗ of Decatur co., S Iowa, 60 m. S of Des Moines; pop. 2004.

Le·on' (lå·ôn'). Municipality, SW Iloilo prov., Panay, Phil. Is., 14 m. WNW of City of Iloilo; pop. 20,797.

Le·ón' (lå·ôn'). **1** Former name of COTOPAXI prov., Ecuador.

2 City, Guanajuato state, cen. Mexico, 32 m. WNW of Guanajuato; pop. 74,155; altitude 5850 ft.; textile mills; center of agricultural area. Founded 1576.

3 Department, W Nicaragua; 2355 sq. m.; pop. (1943 est.) 96,846; ✳ León.

4 City, W Nicaragua, ✳ of León dept. and 2d largest city in Nicaragua, on railroad near Pacific coast ab. 50 m. NW of Managua; pop. (1943 est.) 33,269; founded by Córdoba 1523 on the shore of Lake Managua; destroyed 1609 by violent eruption of Momotombo and earthquake, and rebuilt on its present site 1610; former capital of Nicaragua; agricultural, cattle-raising, commercial, and industrial center; has had long political and commercial rivalry with city of Granada.

5 Region and ancient kingdom, NW Spain; 14,884 sq. m.; bounded on N by Asturias, E by Old Castile, S by Estremadura, SW by Portugal, NW by Galicia; comprises modern provinces of León, Salamanca, Zamora; traversed by Duero river and its affluents, the Esla and Tormes; central subtropical valley rises to severely cold mountain ranges on N and S borders; produces oranges, lemons, wine, olives, wheat, flax, cereals; extensive walnut, oak, chestnut forests; coal, iron, copper mines; stock raising; manufactures flour, textiles iron products.

History: Independent Christian kingdom, ruled 910–14 by Garcia, son of Alfonso III of Asturias, after Asturian reconquest of town of León from Moors in 8th cent.; ruled 999–1027 by Alfonso V, the Restorer of León; reconquest of León from Moors completed in 11th cent.; united with Castile 1037–1157, independent kingdom 1157–1230, and permanently reunited with Castile 1230; its chief city after union with Castile was Burgos.

6 Province of Spain. See *Table* at SPAIN.

7 City, ✳ of León prov., NW Spain, 82 m. NW of Valladolid; pop. 44,755; manufactures leather, linen, brandy, lumber; 13th-cent. Gothic cathedral, 12th-cent. convent, and the 11th-cent. church of San Isidoro containing burial place of the early kings and queens of León and Castile. Ancient Roman military station; capital of ancient kingdom of León.

León, Is'la de (ēz'lä thä lå·ôn'). **1** Island 10 m. long and 2 m. wide in Cádiz prov., SW Spain.

2 See SAN FERNANDO.

Le·o'na, Point (lĕ·ō'nå; *Span.* lå·ō'nä). Cape, NW Spanish Morocco, W of Ceuta.

Leon'ard Mur'ray, Mount (lĕn'ẽrd mûr'ĭ). Mountain 7808 ft., W cen. Papua, New Guinea, E of Strickland river basin and NW of Kikori; source of several rivers.

Leon'ard·town (lĕn'ẽrd·toun). Town, ⊗ of Saint Marys co., S Maryland, on an inlet of the Potomac river estuary; pop. 1281.

Le'on Creek (lē'ŏn). River in S cen. Texas; unites with Medina river in Bexar co. to form San Antonio river.

Le·o'ne, Mon'te (mŏn'tå lå·ō'nå). Highest peak 11,684 ft. of the Lepontine Alps, bet. Switzerland and Italy, oɐ SW side of Simplon Pass.

Le·on·for'te (lå·ôn·fôr'tå). Commune, Enna prov., cen. Sicily, 7 m. NNE of Enna; pop. 16,144; in agricultural and mining district.

Le·o'ni·a (lĕ·ō'nĭ·å; -ōn'yå). Residential borough, Bergen co., NE New Jersey, 10 m. N of Jersey City; pop. 8384.

Le'o·nine City (lē'ō·nĭn). Section of Rome, Italy, W of the Tiber river; includes the Vatican.

Leontini. See LENTINI.

Le·on·top'o·lis (lē'ŏn·tŏp'ō·lĭs). City of ancient Egypt, in Nile delta 17 m. N of Cairo; site of the Temple of Onias supposed to have been built during 2d cent. B.C. by the Jewish high priest Onias III; residence of Hieracas and the Hieracites 4th cent. A.D.

Léopol. French form of *Lemberg:* see LVOV.

Le'o·pold and As'trid Coast (lē'ō·pōld, ås'trĭd). Section of Antarctica coast on Indian Ocean, W of Wilkes Land, ab. 67°S and ab. 81° to 86°E long.; discovered 1934; in Australian claim.

Leopold Coast. See LUITPOLD COAST.

Le'o·polds·berg' (lā'ō·pôlts·bĕrκ'; *Angl.* lē'ō·pōldz·bûrg'). Eminence 1387 ft. high ab. 5½ m. NW of Vienna, Austria, in the Wienerwald.

Le'o·pold II, Lake (lē'ō·pōld); *Fr.* **Lac Lé'o'pold' II** (låk' lā'ō'pôl' dū'). Lake in W Congo; 900 to 3200 sq. m. according to the season; drains S into Fini river (*q.v.*) and on into the Congo.

Léo′pold′ville′ (lā′ô′pôld′vēl′; *Angl.* lē′ô·pōld·vĭl). Province, SW Republic of Congo (formerly Belgian Congo); 136,505 sq. m.; native pop. (1938) 1,997,796; ✲ Léopoldville.

2 *now* **Kin′sha′sa** (kēn′shä′så; kĕn·shä′-). Commercial city, ✲ of Republic of Congo, on W border at outlet of the Stanley Pool in the Congo river; urban district 40 sq. m.; pop. (1964) ab. 1,000,000; connected by rail with Matadi, port on lower Congo; in recent years has become a center of African air services, having connections in Rhodesia with British lines and via Brazil with Miami, Fla.

Le·o′ti (lē·ō′tĭ). City, ⊗ of Wichita co., W Kansas; pop. 1401.

Le·pan′to (lå·pän′tô). Former Spanish comandancia of NW Luzon, Phil. Is.; became part of **Lepanto–Bontoc′** (-bôn·tôk′) prov. 1902, which was redivided 1908 into two subprovinces of Mountain Province; united 1920 with Amburayan subprov. to form **Lepanto–Am′bu·ra′yan** (-äm′bōō·rä′yän) subprov., which was divided 1939 bet. Bontoc subprov. and Ilocos Sur and La Union provs.

Le·pan′to (lē·păn′tō; *Ital.* lâ′pän·tô). See NÁVPAKTOS.

Lepanto, Gulf of. See Gulf of CORINTH.

Le·pan′to Strait (lē·păn′tō; *Ital.* lâ′pän·tô). Narrow channel connecting Gulfs of Patras and Corinth and separating N Peloponnesus from cen. mainland of Greece. For battle of Lepanto see NÁVPAKTOS.

Le′pa·ya (lyĕ′pä·yä) *or* **Li·ba′va** (lyĭ·bá′và); *Latvian* **Lie′pā·ja** (lyĕ′pä·yä). **1** Administrative district, SW Kurzeme prov., W Latvia; 1162 sq. m.

2 *Ger.* **Li′bau** (lē′bou). Seaport city, its ✲ and ✲ of Kurzeme prov., W Latvia, on Baltic Sea; pop. (1935) 57,098; Latvian naval base with four harbors; manufactures metal products, heavy machines, linoleum; exports grain, wool, skins, linseed, and wood products. Founded by Teutonic Knights 1263; under Lithuanian rule 1418, and Prussian rule 1560; captured by Charles XII of Sweden 1701, and in 1795 by the Russians, who developed its port 1893–1906. In World War I became a German base; provisional Latvian government established here Dec. 1918 when Bolshevik army attacked Riga; under German occupation from Apr. to June 1919 and in World War II 1941–44.

Le Per′reux′–sur–Marne′ (lē pĕ′rû′sür·màrn′). Commune, Seine dept., N France, ESE suburb of Paris on Marne river; pop. (1931) 23,808; shipbuilding.

Le Petit Andely. See LES ANDELYS.

Le Pe·tit′–Que·vil′ly (lēp·tē′kĕ·vē′yē′). Industrial commune, Seine-Inférieure dept., N France, WSW suburb of Rouen on Seine river; pop. (1931) 18,910.

Le·pi′ni Mountains (lå·pē′nē); *Ital.* **Mon′ti Lepini** (mōn′tē). Mountain range in SE Roma prov., Latium, cen. Italy, the ancient Volscian Mts.; drain into Pontine Marshes; highest peak Semprevista 5040 ft.

L′É′pi′pha′nie′ (lā′pē′fá′nē′). Village, L′Assomption co., S Quebec, Canada, 27 m. N of Montreal; pop. 2462.

Lepontine Alps. See *Table* at ALPS.

Le Pré–Saint′–Ger′vais′ (lē prā′săN′zhĕr′vĕ′). Industrial commune, Seine dept., N France, NE suburb of Paris; pop. 14,790; foundries; paints, varnishes.

Lep′tis Mag′na (lĕp′tĭs măg′nà); *mod.* **Leb′da** (lĕb′då). Ancient seaport in Roman Africa, a suburb of Homs, Libya; founded by Phoenicians from Sidon; one of three chief cities of Tripolis (see TRIPOLI region); under Masinissa after Second Punic War, from 201; made a Roman colony by Trajan; birthplace of L. Septimius Severus who was largely responsible for present plan of the city; ruins of the forum, baths, and a basilica.

Leptis Mi′nor (mī′nēr; -nôr) *or* **Leptis Par′va** (pär′và); *mod.* **Lam′ta** (lăm′tà). Ancient town, Byzacium, N Africa, SE of Hadrumetum (*mod.* Sousse, Tunisia); loyal to Rome from end of Second Punic War; prosperous under the empire; ruins of docks along the coast; amphitheater, Byzantine fort.

Le Puglie. See APULIA.

Le Puy (lē pü·ē′), *formerly* **Le Puy′–en–Ve·lay′** (-äNv·lā′); *medieval* **A·ni′ci·um** (à·nĭsh′ĭ·ŭm) *or* **Po′di·um An′i·cen′sis** (pō′dĭ·ŭm ăn′ĭ·sĕn′sĭs). Manufacturing city, ✲ of Haute-Loire dept., S cen. France, 65 m. SE of Clermont-Ferrand; pop. 21,660; in a mountainous volcanic region; has 12th-cent. Romanesque cathedral and 10th-cent. Gothic church; manufactures lace, tulle, woolens, bells, clocks.

Le Ques′noy′ (lē kĕ′nwà′). Commune, Nord dept., N France, 9 m. SE of Valenciennes; pop. (1931) 3268; many times besieged, esp. by Austrians 1793; in World War I captured by New Zealand troops Nov. 5, 1918.

Lera. See Îles de LÉRINS.

Le Rain′cy′ (lē răN′sē′). Manufacturing commune, Seine-et-Oise dept., N France, NNE suburb of Paris; pop. 12,145; made commune 1869; produces hardware, plaster.

Ler·ca′ra Frid′di (lår·kä′rä frēd′dē). Commune, Palermo prov., NW cen. Sicily, 29 m. ESE of Palermo; pop. 12,255; sulfur mining.

Ler′do *or* **Ciu·dad′ Lerdo** (syōō·thäth′ lĕr′thô). Town, Durango state, NW cen. Mexico, just S of Gómez Palacio; pop. 9349.

Le′ri·ci (lā′rē·chē). Seaport, La Spezia prov., Liguria, NW Italy, on Gulf of La Spezia 6 m. SE of La Spezia; pop. 11,448; 12th-cent. castle; sea bathing.

Lé′ri·da (lā′rē·thä). **1** Province of Spain. See *Table* at SPAIN.

2 *anc.* **I·ler′da** (ĭ·lûr′då). Commune, ✲ of Lérida prov., NE Spain, on Segre river 77 m. E of Saragossa; pop. (1941 est.) 41,858; manufactures leather, glass, woolens, silk, cotton; two cathedrals, palaces, convents. Scene of defeat of Pompey's generals by Caesar 49 B.C.; made episcopal see during Visigoth occupation; seat of medieval university; captured by Ramón Berenguer IV 1149 and by French 1707 and 1808.

Lerin. See FLORINA.

Le·ri′nae In′su·lae (lē·rī′nē ĭn′sū·lē). = Îles de LÉRINS.

Lé′rins′, Îles de (ēl′ dē lā′răNs′). Two islands, **Sainte-Mar′gue·rite′** (săNt′màr′gē·rēt′] (*anc.* **Le′ra** [lē′rá]) and **Saint–Ho′no′rat′** [săN′-tô′nô′rà′] (*anc.* **Le·ri′na** [lē·rī′nà]), in the Mediterranean Sea off Cannes, SE France.

Ler′ma (lĕr′mä). The upper course of the Santiago river, SW Mexico. See SANTIAGO.

Ler′na (lûr′nà) *or* **Ler′ne** (lûr′nē). Marsh and stream in ancient Argolis, E Peloponnesus, S Greece, near Argos; celebrated in Greek legend as the place where Hercules killed the Lernaean Hydra.

Le Roncole. See RONCOLE.

Le′ros (lē′rŏs); *Ital.* **Le′ro** (lâ′rô). An island of the Dodecanese (*q.v.*), N of Kalymnos; 28 sq. m.; pop. (1936) 13,657; large bay, Lakki Bay, on SW coast developed by Italians as submarine base.

Le·roy′ (lĕ·roi′; lē-; lē′roi). City, McLean co., cen. Illinois, 15 m. SE of Bloomington; pop. 2088.

Le Roy (lē roi′; lē; lē′roi). Village, Genesee co., W New York, 24 m. WSW of Rochester; pop. 4662; produces stringless beans, fruit; manufactures gelatin, farm implements, medicines.

Ler′wick (lûr′wĭk; lĕr′ĭk; lĕr′wĭk). Burgh, ⊗ of Zetland co., Shetland Is., N Scotland; pop. 5538; fishing.

Les An′de·lys′ (lā-zäN′dlē′). Commune, Eure dept., N France, on right bank of Seine river 20 m. NE of Évreux; pop. 3947; formed from two small settlements, **Le Grand An′de·ly′** (lē gräN′-tän′dlē′) and **Le Pe·tit′ An′de·ly′** (lēp·tē′-tän′dlē′), the former dating from 526 A.D., the latter from 1196; 13th-cent. cathedral; site of Château Gaillard built by Richard Cœur de Lion; manufactures textiles and imitation pearls.

Le Sars (lē sàr′). Village, Pas-de-Calais dept., N France, just SW of Bapaume; battle Sept.–Oct. 1916, a phase of the battle of the Somme.

Les Baux, *formerly* **Les Beaux** (lā bō′). Commune, Bouches-du-Rhône dept., SE France, 9 m. NE of Arles; pop. (1931) 204; important in Middle Ages, now has many ruins; bauxite first discovered here 1821.

Les′bos (lĕz′bŏs; *Mod. Gr.* lâz′vŏs) *or* **Myt′i·le′ne** (mĭt″l-ē′nė); *Mod. Gr.* **My′ti·li′ni** (mē′tė-lyē′nyė). Island in E Aegean Sea off NW coast of Turkey in Asia, by some included among the Southern Sporades (see SPORADES); 623 sq. m.; pop. ab. 137,000; with Lemnos and Hagios Evstrátios, forms Lesbos dept., Aegean Is. division, Greece (see *Table* at GREECE). Hilly, with highest point 3080 ft.; cut from S into center by Gulf of Kalloni. Chief export olives; chief town Mytilene. Has suffered much from earthquakes.

History: Peopled by Aeolians and became chief Aeolian settlement on Asiatic coast; active in commerce; in 7th cent. B.C. famous for its lyric poets, esp. Alcaeus and Sappho; declined in influence in 6th cent. B.C.; yielded to Persians; member of Delian League; off its shores 406 B.C. the Athenian Conon defeated in naval battle; frequently involved in wars before beginning of Christian Era. Held by Byzantines, Seljuks, Venetians, and after 1462 by Turks; annexed by Greece 1913; held by Germans Apr. 1941 to Oct. 1944. See AEGEAN ISLANDS.

Les Cayes (lā kå′y′; lā kā′). = CAYES.

Les É′boule′ments′ (lā-zā′bŏŏl′män′). Mountain 2551 ft., Charlevoix co., S Quebec prov., Canada; highest point in Laurentian Highlands.

Les É′parges′ (lā-zā′pàrzh′). Village, Meuse dept., NE France, 7 m. SE of Verdun; scene of bitter fighting bet. French and Germans June 1915.

Les Eyzies. See LES EYZIES.

Les Gonaïves. See GONAÏVES.

Lesh (lĕsh); *Ital.* **A·les′sio** (ä·lĕs′syŏ); *anc.* **Lis′sus** (lĭs′ŭs). Town, NW Albania, at mouth of Drin river; founded by Dionysius of Syracuse 385 B.C.

Le′si·na (lā′zė-nä). See HVAR.

Le·si·na, Lake (lā-zē′nä). Small lake on N coast of Mount Gargano, SE Italy.

Les′ko·vac (lĕs′kŏ-väts) *or* **Les′ko·vats.** Town, S cen. Serbia, SE Yugoslavia, on the Southern Morava river; pop. 17,632; manufactures hemp, furniture, soap; brick kilns; thermal springs; in a region growing flax and hemp. Occupied by Germans 1941.

Les′ko·vik (lĕs′kŏ-vēk). Town, SE Albania, in Pindus Mts. on Greek border, NW of Kónitsa.

Les Landes (lā länd′). Sandy coastal region, Gironde and Landes depts., SW France, bet. the Gironde and Adour; lagoons near the seashore; pine forests inland.

Les′lie (lĕs′lĭ). County in Kentucky. See *Table* at KENTUCKY.

Les Li′las′ (lā lē′lä′). Industrial commune, Seine dept., N France, NW suburb of Paris; pop. (1931) 19,500; produces metal goods, chemicals, glassware.

Les Martigues. See MARTIGUES.

Lesotho. See BASUTOLAND.

Les Pa′vil′lons′-sous-Bois′ (lā på′vē′yôN′sŏŏ·bwä′). Commune, Seine dept., N France, ENE suburb of Paris; pop. (1931) 14,334.

Les Planches (lā plänsh′). Commune, Vaud canton, W Switzerland, at E end of Lake of Geneva; pop. (1930) 5666. See MONTREUX.

Les Sa′bles–d′O′lonne′ (lā så′blė-dô′lôn′). Commune, Vendée dept., W France, on Bay of Biscay 21 m. SW of La Roche-sur-Yon; pop. 14,536; fishing port; shipbuilding; produces canned sardines and anchovies.

Les Saintes (lā săNt′). Island group in Guadeloupe overseas dept., French West Indies, S of Guadeloupe I.; 5½ sq. m.; pop. (1938 est.) 2044.

Les′say′ (lĕ′sā′). Village, Normandy, Manche dept., NW France, 12 m. NNW of Coutances; pop. 448; occupied by U.S. troops July 16, 1944 in advance on St-Lô.

Les′se (lĕs′ė). River 50 m. long in SE Belgium; flows W through rocky gorges, partly underground, into Meuse river.

Lesser Antilles. One of the three divisions of the West Indies (*q.v.*) comprising the islands stretching in an arc from Puerto Rico to the NE coast of South America and

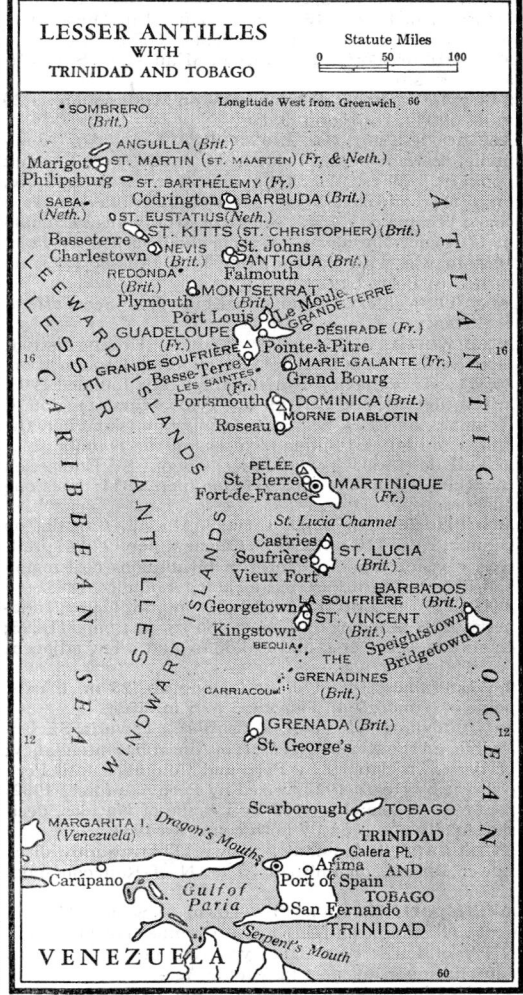

LESSER ANTILLES WITH TRINIDAD AND TOBAGO

Statute Miles

the islands N of Venezuela; includes Virgin Is., Leeward Is., Windward Is., and the islands of the Netherlands West Indies, and is generally considered to include Barbados, Trinidad, and Tobago.

Lesser Armenia. 1 Region of E Pontus, Asia Minor, 1st cent. B.C., on W border of Armenia.
2 = LITTLE ARMENIA, Cilicia.
3 See CILICIA (modern region in Turkey).

Lesser Phrygia. = *Phrygia Minor:* see PHRYGIA.

Lesser Slave Lake (slāv). Lake 480 sq. m., cen. Alberta, Canada; its outlet is **Lesser Slave River,** a tributary of the Athabaska.

Lesser Sunda Islands. See SUNDA ISLES.

Lesser Walachia. = OLTENIA.

Les′sines′ (lĕ′sēn′). Manufacturing commune, Hainaut prov., SW Belgium, on Dender river 25 m. SW of Brussels; pop. 10,386; porphyry quarries.

Les·si′ni Mountains (läs-sē′nė); *Ital.* **Mon′ti Lessini** (mōn′tė). Mountain group, SW Dolomites, NE Italy, E of Lake Garda.

Lessö. Var. of LAESÖ.

Les Trois–É′vê′chés′ (lä trwä′-zä′vě′shä′). Literally "the three bishoprics," ancient district in duchy of Lorraine; comprised the three bishoprics of Verdun, Toul, and Metz (the cities and some surrounding territory) which belonged to Germany in Middle Ages; taken by Henry II of France 1552; now included in Meuse, Moselle, and Meurthe-et-Moselle depts., NE France.

Le Sueur (lě sōŏr′). **1** County in Minnesota. See *Table* at MINNESOTA.
2 City, Le Sueur co., S Minnesota, on Minnesota river 20 m. N of Mankato; pop. 3310.

Lesz′no (lěsh′nô); *Ger.* **Lis′sa** (lĭs′á; *Ger.* lĭs′ä). Commune, Poznań dept., Poland, 41 m. SSW of Poznań; pop. (1938–39 est.) 20,881; manufactures iron furniture, machinery, alcohol, cigars. Settled by Moravians 16th cent.; became city 1547; center of Moravians in Poland in 17th cent.; residence of Comenius; burned by Poles 1656 in war with Sweden; ceded to Prussia 1793; returned to Poland 1920.

Letch′er (lěch′ẽr). County in Kentucky. See *Table* at KENTUCKY.

Letch′worth (lěch′wûrth; -wẽrth). Urban district, Hertfordshire, SE England, 34 m. N of London; pop. 20,321; site of the first British garden city, founded 1903.

Le′tea (lě′tyä); *also* **Lu′tea** (lōō′tyä). Marshy region, E Romania, on Black Sea coast forming an island bet. the Kiliya (on N) and Sulina branches of the Danube.

Le Teil (lě tâ′y′). Town, Ardèche dept., SE France, on the Rhone 42 m. NNW of Avignon; pop. 3823; limestone quarries.

Leth′bridge (lěth′brĭj). City, S Alberta, Canada, on Oldman river 110 m. SSE of Calgary; pop. 22,947; railroad divisional point; center of bituminous coal region and irrigated farm district; airport. Founded 1885.

Le′ti (lět′ě) *or* **Let′ti**. **1** Island group, Moluccas, Indonesia, in S part NE of Timor; 466 sq. m.; pop. 11,295; comprises Leti, Moa, and Lakor Is. and a few adjacent islets.
2 Westernmost island of Leti group ab. 25 m. E of E point of Timor; 9 m. long by 3 to 5 m. wide.

Le·ti′cia (lä-tē′syä; *Angl.* lě-tĭsh′ĭ-á). Town in SE Colombia, on the Amazon river; ✳ of Amazonas intendancy; border town claimed by Peru and Colombia until Peru ceded it by treaty 1922; seized by Peruvian forces 1932; restored to Colombia 1933 by League of Nations, decision finally accepted by both countries 1934.

Let′pa·dan′ (lět′pá·dän′). Town, Tharrawaddy dist., Lower Burma, on railroad 75 m. N of Rangoon; pop. 12,160.

Le Tré′port′ (lě trā′pôr′). Town, N Seine-Inférieure dept., N France, on the English Channel 114 m. by rail NNW of Paris; pop. 5168; watering place; 16th-cent. church; important port in Middle Ages.

Le·tri′noi (lä-trē′nyě). City, Achaea and Elis dept., NW Peloponnesus, S Greece, on coast E of S tip of Zante I.; pop. 20,496; formed by **Pyr′gos** [pěr′gôs] (pop. 19,336) and **Lam·pe′ti** [läm-bá′tě] (pop. 1160); sacked by Turks 1825 (Greek War of Independence).

Lette (lět). = AILETTE.

Let′ter·ken′ny (lět′ẽr-kěn′ĭ). Urban district, cen. co. Donegal, N Eire, near S end of Lough Swilly; pop. 2649; market town; ropemaking.

Letti. See LETI.

Lett′land (lět′länd; *Ger.* lět′länt), **Let′to·nie′** (*Fr.* lĕ′tô′nē′). = LATVIA.

Leu·ca′di·a (lū·kā′dĭ·á). Ancient name of LEUKAS I.; the **Leu·ca′di·an Rock** (-án) was Leucates, or modern Cape Doukato (*q.v.*).

Leucas. See LEUKAS.

Leucates. See Cape DOUKATO.

Leu′ca·yec′ (lā′ōō·kä·yěk′). Island in N section of Chonos Archipelago, in Pacific Ocean off SW coast of Chile.

Leu′co·si′a (lū′kô·sē′á; *Gr.* läf′kô·sē′ä). Var. of *Levkosia:* see NICOSIA.

Leuc′tra (lūk′trá). Ancient village in Boeotia, E cen. Greece, 10 m. SW of Thebes; scene of battle 371 B.C. in which Thebans under Epaminondas defeated Spartans under Cleombrotus I, breaking Spartan supremacy.

Leuk (loik). Town, Valais canton, SW cen. Switzerland, on the Rhone NE of Sion; pop. 1966; hot mineral springs.

Leu′kas (lū′kǎs) *or* **Lev·kás′** (lâf·käs′); *anc.* **Leu·ca′di·a** (lû·kā′dĭ·á); *Ital.* **San′ta Mau′ra** (sän′tä mou′rä). One of the Ionian Is., in the Ionian Sea off W coast of Greece, S of the entrance to the Ambracian Gulf; 111 sq. m.; pop. 28,331; chief town **Leu′cas** (lū′kǎs); a province in Preveza dept., W Epirus, Greece. Mountainous (highest ab. 3000 ft.), with little level ground; produces much olive oil, currants, and wine. Southern point is Cape Doukato (*q.v.*). Early settled by Corinthians; has ancient cyclopean walls and remains of temple to Apollo Leukates, and several Turkish forts; by some scholars thought to be the Ithaca of the *Odyssey*, rather than nearby Ithaca itself.

Leu′then (loi′těn); *Pol.* **Lu·ty′nia** (lōō-tĭ′nyä). Village, cen. Śląsk Dolny dept., SW Poland, near Wrocław (Breslau); formerly in Silesia prov., Prussia, Germany; pop. (1925) 970; scene of battle Dec. 5, 1757 in which Frederick the Great defeated the Austrians.

Leuven. See LOUVAIN.

Leuze (lûz). Manufacturing commune, Hainaut prov., SW Belgium, 11 m. E of Tournai; pop. 6202; scene of battle Sept. 20, 1691 in which forces of Louis XIV under the duc de Luxembourg defeated the army of the Grand Alliance under Prince of Waldeck.

Léva. See LEVICE.

Levádeia. See LEBADEA.

Le Val d'A′jol′ (lě väl′ dä′zhôl′). Commune, Vosges dept., NE France, comprising many hamlets in the Vosges Mts.; pop. (1931) 6615.

Le·val′lois′–Per′ret′ (lě-vä′lwä′pě′rě′). Industrial commune, Seine dept., N France, NW suburb of Paris on Seine river; pop. 65,186; river port; produces automobiles, machinery, perfumes.

Le·vang′er (lě-väng′ẽr). Town, ⊗ of Nord-Tröndelag co., N cen. Norway, at head of Trondheim Fjord; pop. 1616.

Le·vant′ (lě-vănt′). Name given to the E shores of the Mediterranean Sea, W Greece to W Egypt.

Levante, Riviera di. See RIVIERA.

Levant State. Any country in the Levant; specif.,
Levant States, the divisions of the mandate of Syria as first established in 1920: Syria, Lebanon, Latakia (or Territory of the Alaouites), and the Jebel ed Druz. See SYRIA, former French mandate. Reduced to two after establishment of independent republics of Syria and Lebanon Jan. 1, 1944.

Lev′el·land′ (lěv′ěl·lǎnd′). City, ⊗ of Hockley co., NW Texas, 26 m. W of Lubbock; pop. 10,153; farming, stock raising.

Le′ven (lē′věn). **1** River ab. 7 m. long, Dunbarton co., W Scotland; flows out of S end of Loch Lomond into Clyde river at Dumbarton.
2 River 16 m. long in Kinross and Fife cos., E Scotland; flows E out of Loch Leven into Firth of Forth.
3 Seaport burgh, Fife co., E Scotland, on Firth of Forth at mouth of the Leven; pop. 8868; summer resort. Nearby is Largo, birthplace of Alexander Selkirk.

Leven, Loch. 1 Arm of Loch Linnhe, W Scotland, extending along boundary bet. Argyll and Inverness cos.
2 Lake in Kinross co., E cen. Scotland; has island on which are the ruins of Lochleven Castle.

Le·veque′, Cape (lě·věk′). Cape at N tip of Dampier Land on N coast of Western Australia.

Le′ver·ku′sen (lā′věr·kōō′zěn). Industrial city, North Rhine-Westphalia state, W Germany, on Rhine river 16 m. SE of Düsseldorf; pop. 42,470; formed 1930 by consolidation of former city of Wiesdorf and surrounding communes; manufactures chemicals, iron goods, machinery, tile.

Le Vé'si·net' (lē vā'zē'nĕ'). Commune, Seine-et-Oise dept., N France, WNW suburb of Paris; pop. 11,222.

Le·vi'a·than Peak (lĕ·vī'à·thăn). Mountain 13,535 ft. in San Juan co., SW Colorado.

Le'vi·ce (lĕ'vĭ·tsĕ); *Hung.* **Lé'va** (lā'vŏ); *Ger.* **Le'wenz** (lā'vĕnts). Town, S Slovakia prov., E cen. Czechoslovakia, 75 m. E of Bratislava; pop. (1930) 12,552.

Le'vi·co (lā'vĕ·kŏ). Commune, S Trento prov., S Venezia Tridentina, NE Italy; pop. 5857; in the Dolomites just E of Trent; mineral springs.

Le·vin' (lĕ·vēn'). Borough, Wellington provincial dist., SW North I., New Zealand; pop. 2635.

Le'vis (lē'vĭs); *Fr.* **Lé'vis'** (lā'vē'). 1 County, Quebec, Canada. See *Table* at QUEBEC.

2 *formerly* **Pointe Le'vi'** (pwănt' lā'vē'). City, Levis co., S Quebec, Canada, on St. Lawrence river opp. Quebec; pop. 13,162; railroad terminus and landing place for transatlantic passengers; has large dry dock; produces lumber; overlooked by heights occupied by four large forts. Founded 1679; incorporated as a city 1916.

Le·vi'sa Bay (lå·vē'sä). Bay in N coast of Oriente prov., E Cuba, E of and adjoining Nipe Bay.

Le·vi'sa Fork (lĕ·vī'så). River ab. 160 m. long, E Kentucky; rises in NW Buchanan co., SW Virginia, flows N into Kentucky and unites with Tug Fork to form the Big Sandy river (*q.v.*).

Lev'it·town (lĕv'ĭt·toun). 1 Urban township, Burlington co., S cen. New Jersey, NE of Camden; pop. 11,861. 2 Urban community (unincorporated), Nassau co., SE New York, on Long I. E of New York; pop. 65,276.

Lev'ka (lâf'kä). Mountain 7907 ft. in W cen. Crete, S of Canea; second highest peak in the island.

Levkás. See LEUKAS.

Levkosia. See NICOSIA town, Cyprus.

Lé'vri'er' Bay (lā'vrē'ā'). Inlet of Atlantic Ocean on W coast of West Africa, E of Cape Blanc.

Le·vu'ka (lå·vōō'kå). Town, E coast of Ovalau I., W cen. Fiji Is., SW Pacific Ocean; important trade center in early days and ✻ of Fiji Is. under British 1874–82.

Le'vy (lē'vĭ). County in Florida. See *Table* at FLORIDA.

Lewenz. See LEVICE.

Lew'es (lū'ĭs; lōō'-). 1 Seaport town, Sussex co., S Delaware, on S end of Delaware Bay 15 m. NW of Georgetown; pop. 3025; settled 1631 by Dutch; bombarded by British 1813. Port of entry; fishing port; canneries; makes tinware. Delaware Breakwater (built 1818–90). 2 River 338 m. long, S cen. Yukon, Canada; rises in Tagish and Atlin Lakes on S border and flows NW through Lake Laberge to unite with Pelly river and form the Yukon river; now usually considered the upper course of the Yukon. 3 Municipal borough, ⊗ of East Sussex, S England, on the Ouse 6 m. N of English Channel and 43 m. S of London; pop. 13,104; scene of battle May 14, 1264 in which Simon de Montfort defeated Henry III.

Lew'ey, Mount (lū'ĭ; lōō'ĭ). Peak 3740 ft. in Adirondack Mts., Hamilton co., NE cen. New York.

Lewey Lake Mountain. Peak 3903 ft. in the Adirondack Mts., NE New York.

Lew'is (lū'ĭs; lōō'-). 1 Early name of Snake river, Idaho. 2 River ab. 80 m. long, SW Washington; rises in NE Skamania co., flows WSW into Columbia river forming boundary bet. Cowlitz and Clark cos. 3 Name of counties in seven states of the U.S. See *Tables* at IDAHO, KENTUCKY, MISSOURI, NEW YORK. TENNESSEE, WASHINGTON, WEST VIRGINIA. 4 *or* **the Lews** (lūz; lōōz). North section of the island of Lewis with Harris, in the Outer Hebrides off NW coast of Scotland; pop. 23,345; belongs to Ross and Cromarty co.

Lewis, Butt of (bŭt). Headland on N tip of island of Lewis with Harris, in the Outer Hebrides off NW coast of Scotland; lighthouse.

Lewis and Clark (klärk). County in Montana. See *Table* at MONTANA.

Lewis and Clark Cavern; *also* **Mor'ri·son Cave** (mŏr'ĭ·s'n). Limestone cave in SE Jefferson co., cen. Montana; state park.

Lewis Bay. Inlet of Nantucket Sound on S coast of Barnstable co., Massachusetts.

Lew'is·burg (lū'ĭs·bûrg; lōō'ĭs-). 1 Borough, ⊗ of Union co., cen. Pennsylvania, 21 m. SSE of Williamsport; pop. 5523; agriculture; coal fields; manufactures furniture, textiles. Bucknell Univ. (1846; coed.). 2 Town, ⊗ of Marshall co., S cen. Tennessee, 18 m. SE of Columbia; pop. 6338; ships livestock; condensed milk, dairy products, stoves, pencils. Home of James K. Polk. 3 Town, ⊗ of Greenbrier co., SE West Virginia; pop. 2259.

Lewisham. Metropolitan borough of London. See *Table* at LONDON.

Lewis Lake. Lake in Yellowstone National Park, NW Wyoming, SW of Yellowstone Lake.

Lewis Range. A range of the Rocky Mts., in W Montana, along E side of Glacier National Park N into Canada; according to some authorities extends SE through Flathead and Lewis and Clark cos.

Lew'is·ton (lū'ĭs·tŭn; lōō'-). 1 City, ⊗ of Nez Perce co., W Idaho, at confluence of Clearwater and Snake rivers across from Washington 95 m. SSE of Spokane; pop. 12,691; first incorporated town in Idaho Territory, and first capital of the Territory (1863); wheat, fruit, lumber; gold, silver, and lead mines. Northern Idaho College of Education (1893; coed.). 2 Commercial and industrial city, Androscoggin co., SW Maine, on Androscoggin river 30 m. N of Portland; pop. 40,804; 2d largest city in Maine; manufactures cotton, woolen, and rayon goods; Bates College (1864; coed.). Settled 1770. 3 Village, Niagara co., W New York, on Niagara river 7 m. N of Niagara Falls; pop. 3320; first white settlement c. 1800; burned by British and Indians 1813. 4 City, Cache co., N Utah, on Idaho border 16 m. N of Logan; pop. 1336; farming, dairying; beet sugar.

Lew'is·town (lū'ĭs·toun; lōō'-). 1 City, ⊗ of Fulton co., W cen. Illinois, 37 m. SW of Peoria; pop. 2603; prehistoric Indian burial mounds; home of Edgar Lee Masters. 2 City, ⊗ of Fergus co., cen. Montana, ESE of Great Falls; pop. 7408; trade center in agricultural section. 3 Industrial borough, ⊗ of Mifflin co., cen. Pennsylvania, 45 m. WNW of Harrisburg; pop. 12,640; manufactures viscose, tools, locomotive parts, woolens, hosiery; iron and glass sand deposits in vicinity. Laid out 1790; incorporated 1811.

Lew'is·ville (lū'ĭs·vĭl; lōō'-; *Sou.* also -v'l). City, ⊗ of Lafayette co., SW Arkansas; pop. 1373.

Lewis with Har'ris (hăr'ĭs). Most northerly island of the Outer Hebrides off NW coast of Scotland; 770 sq. m.; pop. 26,466; the larger N section (see LEWIS) is administratively part of Ross and Cromarty co.; the smaller S section (see HARRIS) a part of Inverness co.

Lews, the. See LEWIS, N section of Lewis with Harris I.

Lex'ing·ton (lĕk'sĭng·tŭn). 1 County in South Carolina. See *Table* at SOUTH CAROLINA. 2 Town, ⊗ of Oglethorpe co., NE Georgia; pop. 376. 3 City, ⊗ of Fayette co., NE cen. Kentucky, 23 m. ESE of Frankfort; pop. 62,810; tobacco market; breeding of thoroughbred horses; home of Henry Clay from 1797 until his death 1852. Transylvania College (1780), oldest educational institution W of the Alleghenies; University of Kentucky (1865; coed.). Founded 1779, incorp. 1782. 4 Residential town, Middlesex co., NE Massachusetts, 10 m. NW of Boston; pop. 27,691; scene of battle Apr. 19, 1775 in which a force of minutemen offered armed resistance to a British contingent marching to seize stores at Concord (*q.v.*), the opening engagement of the American Revolution. 5 City, ⊗ of Holmes co., W cen. Mississippi, 29 m. S of Greenwood; pop. 2839; lumbering; ships cotton.

6 City, ⊗ of Lafayette co., W Missouri, on Missouri river 33 m. E of Independence; pop. 4845; coal deposits; scene of Confederate victory Sept. 18-20, 1861.
7 City, ⊗ of Dawson co., S cen. Nebraska, on Platte river 37 m. W of Kearney; pop. 5572.
8 Manufacturing city, ⊗ of Davidson co., cen. North Carolina, 19 m. WSW of High Point; pop. 16,093; became ⊗ 1824; flour, cotton and rayon goods, furniture.
9 Town, ⊗ of Lexington co., cen. South Carolina; pop. 1127.
10 City, ⊗ of Henderson co., W Tennessee, 26 m. E of Jackson, pop. 3943; battle of Parker's Crossroads fought nearby 1863.
11 Town, ⊗ of Rockbridge co., W cen. Virginia, 30 m. NW of Lynchburg; pop. 7537; sulfur deposits; limestone quarries; tourist center. Washington and Lee Univ. (1749; men); Virginia Military Inst. (1839; men). Burial place of Stonewall Jackson and of Robert E. Lee. Natural Bridge nearby. Became town 1777; rebuilt following destruction by fire in 1796; bombarded during Civil War.
Leyden. See LEIDEN.
Ley′land (lā′lănd). Urban district, Lancashire, NW England, 22 m. NNE of Liverpool; pop. 14,722.
Ley′te (lā′tĕ; *Span.* -tâ). Island, one of the Visayan Is., E Phil. Is.; 2785 sq. m.; constitutes with adjacent islands a province 3084 sq. m.; pop. 915,853, ✳ Tacloban. Of irregular shape, having many bays, some of which form good harbors; 121 m. long from NW to SE, varies in width from 14 m. at center to ab. 45 m. in the N. Separated from Samar on NE by very narrow San Juanico Strait; off its N end is Biliran I. and off S end Panaon I. Mountainous, with long range N to S through the center, highest peak 4426 ft.; many peaks are extinct volcanoes; has many streams but few large ones. Raises hemp, rice, cotton, corn, sugar, and tobacco; also produces timber, coal, sulfur, and iron. Chief towns Tacloban, Ormoc, Baybay, Abuyog, Burauen, and San Isidro.
    History: Discovered Mar. 1521 by Magellan, who celebrated Mar. 31 first Mass in the Philippines on Limasawa, at S end; visited by Villalobos 1543 and by Legaspi 1565; in early years of Spanish government under jurisdiction of Cebu; scene of revolts 1622, 1649; its administration separated from that of Samar 1768; civil government established by Americans Apr. 22, 1901. In World War II occupied by Japanese 1942 but scene of continued opposition by guerrilla forces; invaded Oct. 20, 1944 by Americans, who defeated Japanese fleet Oct. 21–26 in Leyte Gulf (*q.v.*) and completely conquered the island by Dec. 1944 after severe fighting around Ormoc.
Leyte Gulf. Inlet of Pacific Ocean E of Leyte and S of Samar, E Phil. Is.; on S connects by Surigao Strait with Mindanao Sea. Offers good anchorage for large fleet; partially shut off from Pacific on E by Homonhon I.; entered Oct. 19, 1944 by American invasion fleet under Gen. MacArthur which protected landings on E Leyte shore; scene of air and naval battle (Japanese defeat) Oct. 25–26, 1944.
Ley′ton (lā′t'n). Municipal borough, Essex, SE England, NE suburb of London; pop. 128,313, (1951) 105,183; part of Greater London; chiefly residential.
Lhariguo. See KALI.
Lha′sa (lä′sà; läs′à); *also* **Las′sa** (lăs′à). Buddhist sacred city, ✳ of Tibet, Outer China, in SE part ab. 250 m. NE of Darjeeling near the Indian border; pop. ab. 50,000; altitude 11,830 ft.; located in a level plain on a tributary (Kyi) of the Tsangpo, surrounded by hills, on one of which is the **Po′ta·la** (pō′tä·lä), the great palace (oldest part built ab. 12 cents. ago) of the Dalai Lama, religious and political head of the country. Has many temples, monasteries, convents, esp. the Jokhang temple, said to have been founded 652, the religious center of Tibet; nearby are several other great monasteries (Sera, Debung, Galdan); the center of national pilgrimages and great festivities, esp. at New Year's; for centuries the seat of Tibetan kings. Because of its inaccessibility and

the religious exclusiveness and hostility of the lamas, long closed to all foreign visitors, hence its name, the "Forbidden City." First visited by Europeans (except for a few pilgrims) by the British expedition 1904 of Col. Francis E. Younghusband.
Lho′tse (hlô′tsĕ). Southern peak 27,923 ft. of Mount Everest massif, in the Himalayas.
Li (lē); *formerly* **Wu** (wōō). River ab. 150 m. long, SE China, a S tributary of the Siang in Kwangsi prov. which it joins just above Yungning.
Liakhov Islands. Var. of LYAKHOV ISLANDS.
Liákoura. See PARNASSUS.
Li·an′, Cape (lē·än′). Cape on S shore of Thailand proper projecting into the Gulf of Siam, SSE of Bangkok.
Liang·a′ Bay (lyäng·ä′). Inlet of Pacific on SE coast of Surigao prov., Mindanao, Phil. Is., ab. 20 m. wide at its mouth; at its head is **Lianga** (pop. 15,770).
Liangchow. See WUWEI.
Liao (li·ou′). River ab. 700 m. long, S Manchuria, chiefly in Liaoning and Jehol provs.; rises in S Jehol, flows NE, then turns SW to the Gulf of Liaotung just below Yingkow; navigable for ab. 400 m.
Liao′ning (li·ou′nĭng′). **1** *formerly* **Feng′tien′** (fŭng′-ti·ĕn′) *and* **Sheng′king′** (shŭng′jĭng′). Former province, S Manchuria; 124,224 sq. m.; pop. (1936 est.) 16,465,303; ✳ Mukden (Shenyang); under Japanese control 1932–45 included the provinces of Fengtien, South Hsingan, Antung, Tunghua, and parts of Chinchow and Chientao; area reduced 1945, see 2, below.
2 One of nine new provinces (since Sept. 1945), S Manchuria; 29,200 sq. m.; pop. 12,460,000; ✳ Mukden.
Liao′peh′ (li·ou′bä′). One of nine new provinces (since Sept. 1945), SW Manchuria; 40,498 sq. m.; pop. 4,030,000; ✳ Szepingkai.
Liao′tung′, Gulf of (li·ou′dŏong′). North part of the Gulf of Po Hai, W of Liaotung Penin., S Manchuria.
Liaotung Peninsula. Literally "East of the Liao"; peninsula, S part of Liaoning prov., S Manchuria, in Yellow Sea; includes Kwantung Leased Territory. See KWANTUNG.
Liao′yang′ (li·ou′yäng′). City and treaty mart, S Liaoning prov., S Manchuria, on a tributary of the Hun river 35 m. S of Mukden; pop. (1940 est.) 100,165; in a rich cotton district on the South Manchuria Railway; an ancient town, important as a district center under early dynasties; site of great battle, a victory of the Japanese under Oyama over the Russian armies under Kuropatkin Aug. 25–Sept. 4, 1904.
Liao′yuan′ (li·ou′yü·än′); *Jap.* **Cheng′chia′tun′** (jŭng′ji·ä′dōon′). Town, Liaoning prov., SW Manchuria, on right bank of Liao river ab. 115 m. N of Mukden; pop. ab. 50,000; formerly an important market city for E Mongolia; rapid growth in modern times began ab. 1876.
Li′ard (lē′ärd). **1** River 550 m. long, W Canada; rises in Stikine Mts. in SE Yukon, flows E across N Brit. Columbia and turns NW to empty into Mackenzie river in SW Mackenzie District, Northwest Territories. The Alaska Highway follows its N bank for many miles in N Brit. Columbia.
2 Trading post on the Liard. See FORT LIARD.
Li′ba·cao′ (lē′bä·kä′ô; -kou′). Municipality, W Capiz prov., Panay, Phil. Is., on river at foot of the mountains 32 m. WSW of Capiz; pop. 20,253.
Li′ban′ (lē′bän′). French form of LEBANON.
Lí′ba·no (lē′vä·nô). Town, Tolima dept., W cen. Colombia, 33 m. ESE of Manizales; pop. 7659.
Libanus. See LEBANON.
Libau, Libava. See LEPAYA.
Lib′by (lĭb′ĭ). City, ⊗ of Lincoln co., NW corner of Montana, on Kootenai river 60 m. WNW of Kalispell; pop. 2828; lumbering; vermiculite deposits nearby.
Li′benge′ (lē′bänzh′). Town, NW Congo, S cen. Africa, on the Ubangi river S of Bangui, Central African Republic.

Lib′er·al (lĭb′ẽr·ăl). City, ⊗ of Seward co., SW Kansas, on Oklahoma border 73 m. SW of Dodge City; pop. 13,813; in natural-gas section; oil refineries, flour mills, farm-implement manufactory.

Liberalitas Julia. See ÉVORA.

Li′be·rec (lĭ′bĕ·rĕts); *Ger.* **Rei′chen·berg** (rī′Kĕn-bĕrK). City, N Bohemia prov., W Czechoslovakia; pop. (1930) 38,568; woolen and cotton manufactures; cloth industry here dates from 16th cent.; a center of the German Sudeten movement 1938.

Li·be′ri·a (lī·bẽr′ĭ·à). Republic in West Africa, extending ab. 350 m. along the coast SE of Sierra Leone; ab. 43,000 sq. m.; pop. (est.) 1,250,000; ✻ Monrovia. Bounded on NE by Guinea, on NE and E by Ivory Coast Republic, on SW by the Atlantic, and on NW by Sierra Leone. Its coast is known as the Grain Coast (*q.v.*) and the SE section is called the Kru Coast; its SE point on Ivory Coast border is marked by Cape Palmas; has no good natural harbors. A plateau country well watered and densely forested; chief rivers Mano, St. Paul, St. John, Cess, and Cavally; excessive rainfall and large forest areas prevent much agriculture; chief exports rubber and forest products (piassava, palm kernels). Native inhabitants are of various tribes, chiefly Mandingo, Kru, Vai. Chief towns Monrovia, Robertsport, Marshall, Sino, and Harper.

History: Project for settlement of freed American Negroes begun by American Colonization Society 1817; settled at Monrovia 1822; named by Robert G. Harper from the Latin *liber* "free"; established as Free and Independent Republic of Liberia 1847; separate republic of Maryland, founded 1833, united with Liberia 1857; because of bankruptcy and internal disorder 1909 placed virtually under U.S. protection 1911; declared war on Germany 1917; Firestone Co. of U.S. granted 1925 concession of one million acres for rubber plantation.

Li·be′ria (lĕ·vā′ryä). Town, ✻ of Guanacaste prov., NW Costa Rica; pop. ab. 3000.

Libertad, La. See LA LIBERTAD.

Li′ber·ta·dor′ (lē′vĕr·tä·thôr′). Province, NW Dominican Republic. See *Table* at DOMINICAN REPUBLIC.

Lib′er·ty (lĭb′ẽr·tĭ). 1 Name of counties in four states of the U.S. See *Tables* at FLORIDA, GEORGIA, MONTANA, TEXAS.

2 Town, ⊗ of Union co., E Indiana, 13 m. S of Richmond; pop. 1745.

3 City, ⊗ of Casey co., cen. Kentucky; pop. 1578.

4 Town, ⊗ of Amite co., SW Mississippi; pop. 642.

5 City, ⊗ of Clay co., NW Missouri, 13 m. NNE of Kansas City; pop. 8909. William Jewell College (1849; coed.; Baptist).

6 Village, Sullivan co., SE New York, 45 m. W of Poughkeepsie; pop. 4704; year-round resort.

7 Town, Pickens co., NW South Carolina, in Blue Ridge foothills 18 m. W of Greenville; pop. 2657.

8 City, ⊗ of Liberty co., E Texas, on Trinity river 39 m. ENE of Houston; pop. 6127; in farming and ranching section; oil wells nearby.

Liberty, Mount. Peak 4460 ft. in Grafton co., New Hampshire.

Liberty Island. See BEDLOE'S ISLAND.

Lib′er·ty·ville (lĭb′ẽr·tĭ·vĭl). Village, Lake co., NE corner of Illinois, 10 m. SW of Waukegan; pop. 8650.

Libia. See LIBYA.

Libian Desert. See LIBYAN DESERT.

Libian Sahara. Former (Italian) administrative and military territory, cen. and S Libya; 465,362 sq. m.; pop. (1936) 48,165; ✻ Hon; part of Sahara Desert.

Lib·ma′nan (lĕb·mä′nän). Municipality, W cen. Camarines Sur prov., Luzon, Phil. Is., on tributary of lower Bicol river 11 m. NW of Naga; pop. 23,000; has large hemp and rice industries.

Li′bourne′ (lē′bōōrn′). Commune, Gironde dept., SW France, on Dordogne river 17 m. ENE of Bordeaux; pop. 19,491; shipbuilding; preserved foods, wines.

Li′brar′y (lī′brĕr′ĭ). Locality, Allegheny co., SW Pennsylvania, ab. 10 m. S of Pittsburgh; pop. (1950) 2124.

Li′bre·ville′ (lē′brĕ·vĕl′). Seaport town, ✻ of Gabon Republic, W equatorial Africa, on N side of mouth of Gabon river; pop. 17,900; occupied by Free French Nov. 1940.

Li·bur′ni·a (lī·bûr′nĭ·à; -bûrn′yà). District on the coast of the Adriatic Sea in ancient Illyria; included in modern Croatia, Yugoslavia; its inhabitants, the Liburni, inventors of the Liburnian galley, noted for their skill in navigation.

Lib′y·a (lĭb′ĭ·à). **1** Ancient Greek name for N Africa, outside of Egypt; later, for that part of Africa immediately W of Egypt which was afterwards divided into Marmarica and Cyrenaica and became part of the Roman colony of Africa.

2 or **Lib′i·a** (lĭb′ĭ·à; *Ital.* lē′byä); *Ital.* **Li′bia I·ta·l·a′na** (lē′byä ē·tä·lē·ä′nä). Former colony of Italian Colonial Empire on coast of N Africa, originally comprising Tripolitania and Cyrenaica; bounded on N by Mediterranean Sea, on E by Egypt, on SE by Republic of Sudan, on S by republics of former French Equatorial Africa and French West Africa, on W by Algeria, and on NW by Tunisia; 679,358 sq. m.; pop. 1,091,830; ✻ Tripoli; includes former Turkish vilayet of Tripoli. Largely desert, forming NE section of Sahara; agricultural areas developed along the coast, in the Barca Plateau, and in the oases; highland areas in N cen. part and along S border; in the interior are the Hammada el Hamra (desert in NW), Fezzan (desert and oases region in SW), Murzuch (dunes in SW), and the oases of Giofra, Fezzan, Cufra, and Giarabub. Caravan and motor highways pass through these oases from Lake Chad and N Equatorial Africa to ports of Tripoli and Bengasi on the Mediterranean; coast is marked by wide indentation of Gulf of Sidra. Chief products grains (wheat and barley) and fruits (dates, olives, and grapes). Chief towns Tripoli, Misurata, Bengasi, Derna, and Homs, and in the interior, Gadâmes and Murzuch.

History: Divided for administration into provinces of Tripolitania and Cyrenaica (*qq.v.*) 1919; in 1934, divided into four provinces of Tripoli, Misurata, Bengasi, and Derna, and a military territory in the S (Libyan Sahara territory); incorporated in national territory of Italy 1939; scene of several extended campaigns bet. Great Britain and Italy in World War II which were of great importance: victory of British under Wavell over Graziani Sept. 1940–Feb. 1941; Rommel's advance into Egypt Feb.–Mar. 1941; British offensive, driving back the Germans, Nov. 1941–Jan. 1942; Rommel's second offensive into Egypt May–July 1942; battle of El Alamein and Rommel's retreat to Tunisia Oct.–Nov. 1942; capture of Tripoli Jan. 24, 1943. After World War II Italian claims to the colony renounced by the peace treaty of Feb. 1947; became an independent federal state (kingdom) at end of 1951, with three principal subdivisions Tripolitania, Cyrenaica, and the Fezzan, and two capitals Tripoli and Bengasi.

Lib′y·an Desert (lĭb′ĭ·àn). Desert area of the eastern Sahara W of the Nile in N Africa, in Libya, Egypt, and Republic of Sudan.

Li·can·cá′bur (lē′käng·kä′vōōr) or **Li′can·caur′** (lē′-käng·kour′). Volcano 19,456 ft. in N Chile, NE of Antofagasta and near SW Bolivian border.

Li·ca′ta (lē·kä′tä); *anc.* **Phin′ti·as** (fĭn′tĭ·ăs). Seaport commune, Agrigento prov., SW Sicily, on Mediterranean 26 m. SE of Agrigento; pop. 31,611; exports asphalt and sulfur; in World War II a beachhead for the landing of American forces July 11, 1943.

Lich′field (lĭch′fēld). Municipal borough, Staffordshire, W cen. England, on affluent of the Trent 15 m. NNE of Birmingham; pop. 10,624; brewing; cathedral, dating in part from 13th cent.; grammar school, founded 1495, numbers among its pupils Samuel Johnson, Joseph Addison, David Garrick.

Lich·ten·burg. 1 (lĭK′tĕn·bŏŏrK) Village, Saxony, cen. Germany, on the Elbe just N of Torgau; Nazi concentration camp in World War II.
2 (lĭk′tĕn·bûrg) Town, SW Transvaal, NE Union of South Africa, 120 m. W of Johannesburg; pop. 5811; diamonds in vicinity; experimental dry farming.

Lich′ten·stein–Calln′berg (lĭK′tĕn-shtīn-käln′bĕrK). City, Saxony, Germany, 14 m. WSW of Chemnitz; pop. 11,829; 16th-cent. castle; textiles, gloves, stockings.

Lick′ing (lĭk′ĭng). 1 River 350 m. long, NE Kentucky; rises in Magoffin co., flows NW into Ohio river at Covington.
2 County in Ohio. See *Table* at OHIO.

Li·co′sa, Cape (lē·kō′sä). Promontory on S end of Gulf of Salerno, Campania, S Italy.

Licus. See LECH.

Li′da (lē′dà; *Russ.* lyē′dà). City, W White Russia, U.S.S.R., 25 m. NW of Novogrudok (formerly in Nowogródek dept., Poland); pop. (1938–39 est.) 26,257; important railroad junction; tobacco factories.

Lid′combe (lĭd′kŭm). Town, E New South Wales, SE Australia, W suburb of Sydney; pop. 17,378.

Lidd. See LYDDA.

Lidg′er·wood (lĭj′ĕr·wŏŏd). City, Richland co., SE corner of North Dakota, ab. 30 m. WSW of Wahpeton; pop. 1081.

Li′di·ce (lĭd′ĭ·sĕ; -ĭt·sĕ; *Czech* lĭ′dyĭ·tsĕ). 1 Village, W cen. Bohemia, Czechoslovakia, near Kladno and ab. 10 m. WNW of Prague; its male inhabitants (ab. 200) killed, its women sent to concentration camps, its children placed in German institutions, and all buildings completely destroyed June 9–10, 1942 by Nazi Gestapo in revenge for killing of Reinhard Heydrich, German Deputy Reich Protector in Bohemia and Moravia.
2 Village, Will co., NE Illinois, just N of Joliet, formerly **Stern Park Gardens** (stûrn), a small Czech-American community, renamed July 12, 1942 in ceremonies in memory of Lidice, Czechoslovakia; pop. (est.) 2820.

Li′ding·ö′ (lē′dĭng·û′). City, Stockholm prov. SE Sweden, residential suburb NE of Stockholm; pop. 12,769.

Lid′kö′ping (lēd′chû′pĭng). City, Skaraborg prov., Sweden, on Lake Vänern; pop. 12,733.

Li′do (lē′dô); *in full,* **Lido di Ma′la·moc′co** (dē mä′lä-môk′kô). Literally, Italian *lido* "shore, beach"; the island reef outside the Lagoon of Venice, Venezia prov., NE Italy, separating the lagoon from the Gulf of Venice; esp., **the Lido,** town at N end of island, pop. (1931) 8676, the most fashionable sea-bathing resort in Italy, with many fine hotels, villas, etc.

Lidz′bark War·min′ski (lēts′bärk vär·mēn′y′·skĕ); *Ger.* **Heils′berg** (hīls′bĕrK). Town, N cen. Olsztyn dept., N Poland, 25 m. N of Olsztyn (Allenstein) on the Łyna river; pop. (1946) 5000; formerly in East Prussia, Germany; 13th-cent. castle; tanning, dyeing, brewing industries; assigned to Poland by Potsdam Conference 1945.

Liech′ten·stein (lĭK′tĕn·shtīn). Independent principality on E bank of the Rhine bet. Saint Gallen and Graubünden cantons in NE Switzerland and alpine province of Vorarlberg in W Austria; 62 sq. m.; pop. (1941) 11,102; ✻ Vaduz. Narrow strip of lowland along the Rhine; peaks of spur of Rhaetian Alps in S are above 8400 ft. Chief products corn, wine, fruit; chief industries cotton, pottery, and leather goods.
History: In 1719, counties of Schellenberg and Vaduz, in hands of branch of house of Liechtenstein, were erected as principality of Liechtenstein in the Holy Roman Empire; part of Confederation of the Rhine 1806; in Germanic Confederation (see GERMANY) 1815–66; belonged to Austrian customs union before collapse of Hapsburg monarchy 1918; entered Swiss customs union 1923.

Li·ège′ or **Li·ége′** (lē·āzh′; lē·ĕzh′; *Fr.* lyäzh, lyâzh, *locally* lyäsh). 1 Province, E Belgium; 1525 sq. m.; pop. (1941 est.) 870,447; ✻ Liège; varied industries, manu-

facturing, coal mining. Formerly, an independent church state, governed by the prince-bishops of Liège; passed to the kingdom of Netherlands 1815, and to Belgium 1830.
2 *Flemish* **Luik** (loik). City, its ✻, located at the confluence of Ourthe and Meuse rivers; pop. (1938 est.) 162,229; heavily fortified; manufactures firearms and motor cars; center of large coal-mining and industrial region; has extensive suburbs on the high land to the N. Its great cathedral of St. Lambert destroyed 1794; later, the church of St. Paul, dating from 10th cent., made the cathedral; university (founded 1817). First mentioned in historical records in 558; residence of St. Hubert in 8th cent.; became bishopric 930; noted center of learning in Middle Ages; seized by Napoleon and became part of France 1794–1815; assigned to Netherlands by Congress of Vienna 1815 and took active part in revolt of 1830; in World War I attacked by Germans Aug. 4, 1914, surrendered Aug. 7 but its forts held out longer, delaying German advance; in World War II captured by Germans by surprise attack May 11, 1940; retaken by American army Sept. 8, 1944.

Lieg′nitz (lēg′nĭts) 1 Former government district, NW Silesia, Prussia, Germany; 5257 sq. m.
2 City, its ✻. See LEGNICA.

Lie′lu·pe (lyĕ′lŏŏ·pĕ) or **Aa** (ä); *Russ.* **Le′lu·pe** (lyĕ′lŏŏ·pyĕ). River 70 m. long, N Lithuania and S Latvia; formed by two tributaries rising in N Lithuania, flows N past Yelgava to Gulf of Riga W of Riga.

Lien′yun′kang′ (lĭ·ĕn′yŏŏn′käng′); *formerly* **Lao′yao′** (lou′you′). Town on coast of N Kiangsu prov., E China; starting point of Lunghai railroad running W to Shensi prov.

Li′enz (lē′ĕnts). 1 Political district. = EAST TIROL.
2 Commune, East Tirol, SW Austria, on Drava river; pop. 6197; tourist resort.

Liepāja. See LEPAYA.

Lier (lēr) or **Lierre** (lyĕr). Commune, Antwerp prov., N Belgium, at confluence of Great and Little Nethe rivers just SE of Antwerp; pop. (1938 est.) 28,631; manufactures lace. In World War I captured by the Germans Oct. 5, 1914.

Lies′tal (lēs′täl). Commune, ✻ of Basel-Land demicanton, Basel canton, NW Switzerland, 8 m. SE of Basel; pop. (1930) 6698; 15th-cent. town hall; museum of Roman antiquities; manufactures textiles, iron goods; produces wine; made city in latter half of 13th cent.

Lietuva. See LITHUANIA.

Lié′vin′ (lyä′văn′). Commune, Pas-de-Calais dept., N France, 9 m. N of Arras; pop. 25,127; coal; completely destroyed in World War I.

Liè′vre (lyâ′vr′). River 205 m. long, SW Quebec prov., Canada; flows S through Labelle and Papineau cos. into the Ottawa river below Hull; outlet of many lakes.

Lif′fey (lĭf′ĭ). River 50 m. long in E Ireland; rises among the Wicklow Mts. in co. Wicklow, curves NW and NE into Dublin Bay (an inlet of the Irish Sea) at Dublin.

Lif′ford (lĭf′ĕrd). Town, ⊗ of co. Donegal, N Eire; pop. 478; on Foyle river opp. Strabane in Northern Ireland.

Li·fu′ (lē·fŏŏ′) or **Li′fou** (lē′fŏŏ′). Largest and most important island of the Loyalty Is., New Caledonia territory (French), ab. 60 m. E of New Caledonia, SW Pacific Ocean; 50 m. long and 10 to 15 m. wide; 640 sq. m.; pop. (1936) 5439; irregular in shape and flat, with no hills or rivers; very fertile.

Li·fu′ka (lē·fŏŏ′kà). Island in NW part of Haabai group, Tonga Is., SW cen. Pacific Ocean; contains the only considerable village (Pangai) in the group, with the former king's palace.

Li·ga′o (lē·gä′ô). Municipality, cen. Albay prov., Luzon, Phil. Is., on railroad 16 m. NW of Legaspi; pop. 27,927; in fine hemp-growing district, W of Mt. Mayon.

Liger. See LOIRE.

Light′house′ Point (līt′hous′). E tip of Franklin co., NW Florida, at W entrance to Apalachee Bay.

Li′gny′ (lē′nyē′). Commune, Namur prov., S Belgium, 14 m. NW of Namur; pop. 2030; battlefield where Napoleon defeated the Prussians June 16, 1815 just before the battle of Waterloo.

Ligny-en-Bar′rois′ (-äṉ-bȧ′rwȧ′). Commune, S Meuse dept., NE France, SE of Bar-le-Duc; pop. (1931) 5031; 13th–17th cent. church; ancestral castle of Marshal Luxemburg.

Lig′o·nier′ (lĭg′ô·nēr′). **1** City, Noble co., NE Indiana, 35 m. NW of Fort Wayne; pop. 2595.
2 Borough and mountain resort, Westmoreland co., SW Pennsylvania, 19 m. WSW of Johnstown; pop. 2276; founded 1816 on site of Fort Ligonier (1758); mining, dairying, farming center.

Li·gu′ri·a (lĭ·gūr′ĭ·ȧ; *Ital.* lê·gōō′ryä). **1** Ancient geographical region inhabited by Ligurians, people of pre-Indo-European stock, who lived in SW Europe; the Ligurians E of Rhone river were gradually subdued by Romans during 2d cent. B.C.; an Augustan region in Roman Empire; in 1797 a strip of coast surrounding Genoa was erected as Ligurian Republic which France annexed 1805.
2 Compartimento of NW Italy; for provincial divisions, area, and pop., see *Table* at ITALY; on Ligurian Sea bet. France and Tuscany; consists of extremely fertile coastal strip—the Italian Riviera—famous for its scenery and climate, and an inland mountainous region; produces citrus fruits, wine, olives, nuts; shipbuilding, iron, and machine-making works; famous as resort. Small area (the S end of Briga-Tenda, *q.v.*) on W border ceded to France by treaty of Feb. 10, 1947.

Li·gu′ri·an Alps (lĭ·gūr′ĭ·ăn). See *Table* at ALPS.

Ligurian Apennines; *Ital.* **Appennino Ligure.** See APENNINES.

Ligurian Sea; *anc.* **Si′nus Li·gus′ti·cus** (sī′nŭs lĭ·gŭs′tĭ·kŭs). Branch of Mediterranean Sea enclosed by the Italian compartimenti of Liguria and Tuscany on N and E, and the French island of Corsica on the S; includes the Gulf of Genoa.

Li′hir (lē′hĭr). Small island in the Bismarck Archipelago, W Pacific Ocean, off NE coast of New Ireland.

Li′hou (lē′hōō). One of the Channel Is., just W of Guernsey; 38 acres.

Li′hou Reefs and Cays (lē′hō). Coral reefs in SW Coral Sea off NE Queensland, Australia; mark E limit of Great Barrier Reef formations.

Li·hu′e (lê·hōō′ā). **1** District, SE Kauai I., Kauai co., Hawaii; pop. 4106.
2 Town in district, ⊗ of Kauai co., SE Kauai I.; pop. 3908; has steamer connection with Honolulu via Nawiliwili Bay.

Liim Fjord. Var. of LIM FJORD.

Likh′vin (lĭk′vĭn; *Russ.* lyĭk′vyĭn). Town, W Tula Region, Soviet Russia, Europe, 56 m. W of Tula; head of navigation of Oka river. In World War II held a few months by Germans in Moscow offensive 1941–42.

Li′kiang′ (lē′jĭ·äng′). Town, NW Yunnan prov., S China, near the Yangtze 80 m. N of Tali.

Li′ki·ep (lē′kê·ĕp). Island (atoll), cen. part of Ratak Chain, N cen. Marshall Is., W Pacific Ocean, 10°N lat.; has 44 islets.

Li·ko′ma (lê·kō′mȧ). Island in E cen. Lake Nyasa, Nyasaland protectorate, SE Africa; site of a fine cathedral, built by native Christians.

Lilas, Les. See LES LILAS.

L′Île Rousse (lēl′ rōōs′). Seaport, NW Corsica; pop. 2226; exports citron; founded 1758 by Pasquale di Paoli, the Corsican patriot.

Lilibeo, Cape. See Cape BOĔO.

Lille (lēl); *formerly* **Lisle** (lēl; *Angl.* lĭl), *sometimes* **L′Isle;** *Lat.* **In′su·la** (ĭn′sû·lȧ); *Flemish* **Rys′sel** (rĭs′ĕl). Manufacturing and commercial city, ✱ of Nord dept., N France, 130 m. NNE of Paris; pop. 200,575; two 15th-cent. churches, a 16th-cent. church, and the 17th-cent. exchange; university; frontier trade center; manufactures include textiles, beet sugar, soap, oil, tobacco, machinery, foundry products, and brewery and distillery products.
History: Founded c. 1030; destroyed by Philip Augustus 1213; rebuilt by Joanna, Countess of Flanders; retaken 1297; medieval capital of Flanders; given to king of France 1312; passed to Burgundian possessions, Austria, Spain, and recaptured 1667 by Louis XIV; captured 1708; restored to France by Treaty of Utrecht 1713; one of principal elements in N French fortifications at beginning of World War I; under German occupation Oct. 1914 to Oct. 1918, formed an important link in the Hindenburg Line; conscription of French labor by Germans for work in Germany known as the "Lille deportations"; in World War II occupied by Germans June 1940–Sept. 1944.

Lille′bonne′ (lēl′bôn′); *anc.* **Ju′li·o·bo′na** (jōō′lĭ·ô·bō′nȧ). Commune, Seine-Inférieure dept., N France, near the mouth of the Seine; pop. (1931) 5334; remains of Roman theater and baths.

Lil′le·ham′mer (lĭl′ĕ·häm′ẽr). Town, ⊗ of Opland co., S cen. Norway, 85 m. N of Oslo; pop. 5375; in valley of the Lågen at N end of Lake Mjösa and on railroad from Oslo to Trondheim; center of grain and potato-farming country; has sawmills, flour mills, and machinery factories.

Lil′lers′ (lē′lâr′). Commune, E cen. Pas-de-Calais dept., N France; pop. (1931) 8364; 12th-cent. Romanesque church, restored.

Lil′ling·ton (lĭl′ĭng·tŭn). Town, ⊗ of Harnett co., cen. North Carolina; pop. 1242.

Lil′loo·et (lĭl′ōō·ĕt; -ĭt). River ab. 150 m. long, SW Brit. Columbia, Canada; rises in Coast Mts., flows SE through Lakes Lillooet and Harrison (123 sq. m.) into Fraser river E of Vancouver.

Lil′ly (lĭl′ĭ). Borough, Cambria co., SW cen. Pennsylvania, 15 m. WSW of Altoona, pop. 1642.

Li·long′we (lê·lông′wâ). Town, W Nyasaland protectorate, SE Africa, 50 m. W of S end of Lake Nyasa; has airdrome on Rhodesian and Nyasaland airway bet. Blantyre and Fort Jameson.

Lilybaeum. See MARSALA.

Lim (lēm). River ab. 120 m. long, Montenegro and Bosnia, S cen. Yugoslavia; rises in North Albanian Alps and flows N into Drina river.

Li′ma (lī′mȧ). Industrial city, ⊗ of Allen co., NW Ohio, 68 m. SSW of Toledo; pop. 51,037; formerly important oil center; manufactures locomotives, steel products, automobile bodies, electrical refrigerators, cigars, electric signs; oil refinery.

Li′ma (lē′mȧ; *Span.* -mä). **1** Department of Peru. See *Table* at PERU.
2 City, its ✱ and ✱ of Peru, on Rimac river ab. 8 m. E from its port Callao; pop. (1940 est.) 533,645; altitude 512 ft.; center of Peruvian economic, political, and intellectual life. Called "City of the Kings," because its site was chosen on Jan. 6, the feast of the Wise Men or the Three Kings. Buildings include 16th-cent. cathedral, government palace, and the university of San Marcos (founded 1551, the oldest university in America). Founded by Pizarro 1535; audiencia established 1542; capital of viceroyalty of Peru (*q.v.*); ruined by earthquake 1746; occupied by Chilean forces during War of the Pacific 1881–83.

Li′ma, Point (lē′mȧ; *Span.* -mä). Cape on E coast of Puerto Rico.

Li′man (lē′män). Mountain 8409 ft., highest point of Wilis mountain group, E cen. Java, SE of Madioen.

Li′ma Reservoir (lī′mȧ). Reservoir in Red Rock Creek, SE Beaverhead co., SW Montana.

Li·ma·sa′wa (lē′mä·sä′wä). Long, narrow island 3 sq. m., ab. 2 m. off S end of Leyte I., Phil. Is.; has two small barrios. Site of Magellan's second landing in the Philippines Mar. 25, 1521; here on Easter Sunday, Mar. 31, first Mass celebrated in the islands.

Li'mas·sol' *or* **Li'ma·sol'** (lĭm'ȧ·sôl'). **1** District, S Cyprus, E Mediterranean Sea; 540 sq. m.; pop. (1931) 57,841.

2 *anc.* **Le·mes'sus** (lê·měs'ŭs). Seaport, its ✳, on Akrotiri Bay, S coast of Cyprus; pop. (1942 est.) 17,630; trades in wine.

Li·may' (lê·mī'). River ab. 250 m. long, SW cen. Argentina; flows NE out of Lake Nahuel Huapí in Andes Mts. on W boundary bet. Neuquén and Río Negro territories; unites with Neuquén river to form Río Negro.

Lim'bach (lĭm'bäĸ). Residential and manufacturing city, Saxony, Germany, 7 m. W of Chemnitz; pop. 17,044; embroidered goods, machinery.

Lim'bang (lĭm'bäng) *or* **Bru'nei** (broo'nĭ). Navigable river ab. 120 m. long, NW Borneo; flows NW and N through N Sarawak into Brunei Bay near Brunei.

Limb'di (lĭm'dĭ). Former Indian state, NE Kathiawar, Western India States, Indian Union, SE of Wadhwan; 344 sq. m.; pop. (1941) 44,024.

Lim'be (lĭm'bā). Town, S Nyasaland protectorate, SE Africa, E suburb of Blantyre (*q.v.*).

Lim·bo'to, Lake (lĭm·bō'tō). Small lake, cen. part of N peninsula of Celebes, Indonesia, just W of Gorontalo; resort with hot springs.

Lim'burg (lĭm'bûrg; *Dutch and Flemish* -bûrk). **1** Region of W Europe, originally part of Lower Lorraine on E bank of the Meuse E of the duchy of Brabant and at times joined with it; in 17th cent. formed part of Spanish Netherlands and in 1815 became a province of new kingdom of Netherlands; later divided bet. Netherlands and Belgium (see below).

2 *or* **Lim'bourg** (lĭm'boorg; *Fr.* lăn'boor'). Province, NE Belgium; 929 sq. m.; pop. (1941 est.) 427,740; ✳ Hasselt; coal mining. Limburger cheese originally produced in this province near Liège.

3 Province, SE Netherlands; 851 sq. m.; pop. (1939) 608,274; ✳ Maastricht; agriculture, livestock raising, dairy farming, coal mining.

Lim'burg an der Lahn (lĭm'bûrg [*Ger.* -boorĸ] än dẽr län'). City, Hesse state, W Germany, on Lahn river 23 m. NNW of Wiesbaden; pop. 11,501; railroad junction; manufactures machinery, metal and paper goods, soap, brewery products; horse and cattle market; trades in leather; 13th-cent. cathedral and castle. Became city in 13th cent.

Lime'house' (līm'hous'; *locally sometimes* lĭm'ŭs). Parish, Stepney borough, E London, England, on Thames river; pop. ab. 31,000.

Li·mei'ra (lê·mā'ê·rȧ). Town, São Paulo state, SE Brazil, 80 m. NW of São Paulo; pop. (1940 est.) 17,542; center of orange cultivation and silkworm culture.

Limen Vatheos. See VATHY.

Lim'er·ick (lĭm'ẽr·ĭk; lĭm'rĭk); *Gaelic* **Luim'neach** (līm'năĸ). **1** County, SW Eire, in Munster prov.; 1037 sq. m.; pop. 141,153; ⊗ Limerick; chief river Shannon; agriculture, livestock raising, dairy farming, salmon fishing.

2 City or county borough, its ⊗, seaport on the Shannon; pop. 41,061; flour milling, bacon curing, dairy products, distilling; salmon fisheries; castle erected under King John; 12th-cent. cathedral. Important Danish settlement in 9th and 10th cents.; object of many sieges, notably by Oliver Cromwell 1651 and, as the last important stronghold of the Jacobites, by William of Orange 1691.

Li'mes Ger·man'i·cus (lī'mēz jẽr·măn'ĭ·kŭs). A part of the Roman defense system against the tribes of the N, built c. 74 A.D. E of the Rhine and along NE border of Germania Superior.

Lime'stone' (līm'stōn'). **1** Name of counties in two states of the U.S. See *Tables* at ALABAMA and TEXAS.

2 Town, Aroostook co., N Maine, 18 m. NNE of Presque Isle; pop. 13,102.

Lim Fjord (lĕm). Fiord in N section of Jutland, Denmark, extending from North Sea ENE across the penin-

sula to the Kattegat, and cutting off Vendsyssel-Thy; wide section (ab. 13 m.) in center of fiord known as Lögstör Bredning.

Lim'it, Point (lĭm'ĭt). Point of land, Cavite prov., S Luzon, Philippine Is., S of entrance to Manila Bay.

Lim'mat (lĭm'ät). River, Zurich and Aargau cantons, Switzerland; flows NW from NW end of Lake of Zurich to Aare river; the city of Zurich is on the lake and on both sides of the river. See LINTH.

Lim'men Bight (lĭm'ĕn). Shallow inlet in W part of Gulf of Carpentaria on E coast of Northern Territory, NE Australia, to the SW of Groote Eylandt.

Li·mo·ei'ro (lê·mwä'ê·rōō). City, NE Pernambuco state, E Brazil; pop. (1940 est.) 12,601; on railroad 40 m. NW of Recife.

Li·moges' (lê·mōzh'; *Fr.* lê'môzh'); *anc.* **Au·gus'to·ri'tum Lem'o·vi·cen'si·um** (ô·gŭs'tô·rī'tŭm lĕm'ô·vī·sĕn'shĭ·ŭm); *later* **Lem'o·vi'ces** (lĕm'ô·vī'sēz). Manufacturing and commercial city, ✳ of Haute-Vienne dept., W cen. France, on Vienne river 110 m. NE of Bordeaux; pop. 95,217; chief seat of porcelain industry in France (begun 1736); as important center of enamel art work, which flourished here in 12th cent., produced series of artists noted for paintings in enamel; 13th-cent. Romanesque-Gothic cathedral; old fortified city walls converted into fine promenades; meteorological observatory; manufactures include cotton and wool goods, paper, shoes, books; trades in cereals, wine, cattle, lumber. Depopulated by pestilence in 10th cent. and 1630–31.

Li·mon' (lê·môn'). Village near N coast of Leyte I., Phil. Is., ab. 31 m. W of Tacloban; pop. 1300; scene of severe fighting during American invasion, captured by Americans Nov. 23, 1944.

Li·món' (lê·môn'). **1** Province, E cen. Costa Rica; 3379 sq. m.; pop. (1943 est.) 38,793; ✳ Puerto Limón; bananas, cacao, timber.

2 City. See PUERTO LIMÓN.

Li·mon' Bay (lê·môn'); *Span.* **Ba·hí'a de Li·món'** (bä·ē'ȧ thȧ lê·môn'). Inlet of the Caribbean Sea, at the N end of the Panama Canal, in the Canal Zone.

Limonum. See POITIERS.

Li'mou·sin' (lē'moo'zăn'; *Angl.* lĭm'ŭ·zēn'). Historical region of cen. France; a plateau bounded anciently on N by Marche, E by Auvergne, S by Guienne, W by Angoumois, NW by Poitou; ✳ Limoges.

History: Inhabited by ancient Gallic tribe of Lemovices; conquered by Romans; devastated by Normans 9th cent. A.D.; part of Aquitaine and included in dowry given by Eleanor of Aquitaine to Henry II of England on her marriage to him 1152; captured by Philip Augustus 1208; given 1259 to Henry III of England who renounced claims to Normandy, Maine, and Poitou; united to France by Charles V 1369; viscountship passed to Albret family in 15th cent.; returned to the French crown under Henry IV and was province of France until Revolution.

Li'moux' (lē'moo'). Commune, Aude dept., S France; pop. (1931) 7797; produces wine.

Lim'pio (lēm'pyȯ). Town, a suburb of Asunción, in Central dept., S Paraguay; pop. ab. 7730.

Lim·po'po (lĭm·pō'pō) *or* **Croc'o·dile** (krŏk'ô·dĭl). River ab. 1000 m. long, SE Africa; rises near Johannesburg in Transvaal prov., South Africa, flows N and NE, forming the NW and N boundary of the Transvaal, turns SE across S Mozambique and empties into Indian Ocean. Both its entire course and its headstream sometimes called the Crocodile.

Lin (lĭn). River ab. 180 m. long, N Hunan prov., SE cen. China, flowing E to Tungting Hu; crosses cen. part of China's "rice bowl"; scene of much fighting during Chinese-Japanese War 1937–45.

Li'na·pa'can (lē'nä·pä'kän). Island 40 sq. m., Palawan prov., Phil. Is., N of Palawan I. in the channel connecting Sulu Sea with South China Sea; pop. 1245; chief barrio San Miguel on NE coast.

Linard, Piz. See SILVRETTA.

Li·na'res (lĕ·nä'räs). **1** Province of Chile. See *Table* at CHILE.

2 City, its ✻, S cen. Chile, ab. 173 m. S of Santiago; pop. 17,108; trading and distributing center.

3 Town, Nuevo León state, NE Mexico, on railroad 75 m. SE of Monterrey; pop. 9918.

4 Mining commune, Jaén prov., S Spain, 24 m. N of Jaén; pop. (1941 est.) 47,723; lead, silver, and copper mines; trades in grain, oil, and manufactured products. Carthaginians defeated nearby by Scipio Africanus 208 B.C.

Lin'chwan' (lĭn'chwän'). City, E cen. Kiangsi prov., SE China, S of Poyang Hu (lake) and ab. 55 m. SE of Nanchang.

Lin'coln (lĭng'kŭn). **1** Name of a parish in Louisiana and of counties in twenty-three states of the U.S. See *Tables* at LOUISIANA, ARKANSAS, COLORADO, GEORGIA, IDAHO, KANSAS, KENTUCKY, MAINE, MINNESOTA, MISSISSIPPI, MISSOURI, MONTANA, NEBRASKA, NEVADA, NEW MEXICO, NORTH CAROLINA, OKLAHOMA, OREGON, SOUTH DAKOTA, TENNESSEE, WASHINGTON, WEST VIRGINIA, WISCONSIN, WYOMING.

2 City, Placer co., E California, 25 m. N of Sacramento; pop. 3197; incorporated 1890; grain and fruit.

3 City, ⊗ of Logan co., cen. Illinois, 30 m. NNE of Springfield; pop. 16,890; in agricultural and coal-mining section; ships dairy products; crockery, chinaware.

4 *or* **Lincoln Center.** City, ⊗ of Lincoln co., cen. Kansas, on Saline river 32 m. WNW of Salina; pop. (est.) 1708.

5 Town, Penobscot co., E cen. Maine, 42 m. N of Bangor; pop. 4541; woolen factory.

6 Town, Middlesex co., NE Massachusetts, 13 m. WNW of Boston; pop. 5613.

7 City, ✻ of Nebraska and ⊗ of Lancaster co., SE Nebraska, 52 m. WSW of Omaha; pop. 128,521; railroad and commercial center in grain and livestock-raising section; shipping point for grain, poultry, and farm machinery; packing houses, canneries, creameries, brick and tile works. University of Nebraska (1869; coed.); Nebraska Wesleyan University (1887; coed.; Methodist); Union College (1891; coed.). Originally called Lancaster; chosen capital of state 1867 and name changed to Lincoln; home of William Jennings Bryan.

8 Town, Grafton co., W New Hampshire, 18 m. SSE of Littleton; pop. 1228; summer resort.

9 Town, Providence co., N Rhode Island, ab. 9 m. SE of Woonsocket; pop. 13,551; administrative center Lonsdale village (*q.v.*); taken from Smithfield and incorporated 1871; includes several villages; limestone quarries.

10 Town, Ontario, Canada. See *Table* at ONTARIO.

11 County in England. See LINCOLNSHIRE.

12 *anc.* **Lin'dum** (lĭn'dŭm). City and county borough, ⊗ of Parts of Lindsey, Lincolnshire, E England, on the Witham 39 m. ESE of Sheffield; pop. 66,243; (1951) 69,412; transportation center; engineering works, flour mills; manufactures farm implements and armored tanks; cathedral, built bet. 1075 and 1501; site of Roman, Saxon, Danish settlements, and of castle built by William the Conqueror in 1068.

Lincoln Heights. 1 City, Hamilton co., SW Ohio, N of Cincinnati; pop. 7798.

2 Urban area, Richland co., N cen. Ohio; pop. 8004.

Lincoln, Mount. 1 Peak 14,284 ft. in Park co., cen. Colorado; highest peak of Park Range of the Rocky Mts.

2 Peak 5108 ft. in the Franconia Mts., N cen. New Hampshire, in N Grafton co.

3 Peak 4013 ft. in E Addison co., W Vermont.

Lincoln Highway. Former highway 3332 m. long, from New York City to San Francisco, California; laid out 1913, completed 1927; now a local name for sections of the route still in use.

Lincoln Park. 1 Residential city, Wayne co., SE Michigan, 9 m. SW of Detroit; pop. 53,933.

2 Borough, Morris co., N New Jersey, 7 m. W of Paterson; pop. 6048.

Lin'coln's Birthplace (lĭng'kŭnz). = *Abraham Lincoln National Historical Park*: see UNITED STATES, *National Historical Parks.*

Lincoln Sea. Part of Arctic Ocean N of Ellesmere I. and Greenland, 82° to 85°N; connects by Robeson and Kennedy Channels with Kane Basin and Baffin Bay.

Lin'coln·shire (lĭng'kŭn·shĭr; -shēr) *or* **Lincoln.** Maritime county, E England; area 2664 sq. m.; pop. (1951) 706,574; comprises three administrative counties: the Parts of Holland (420 sq. m.; pop. 101,545; ⊗ Boston), the Parts of Kesteven (724 sq. m.; pop. 131,566; ⊗ Sleaford) the Parts of Lindsey (1520 sq. m.; pop. 473,463; ⊗ Lincoln); other towns Grimsby, Grantham, Louth, Stamford, Gainsborough; chief rivers Trent and Witham; fisheries along the coast, agriculture in inland area.

Lin'coln·ton (lĭng'kŭn·tŭn). **1** Town, ⊗ of Lincoln co., E Georgia; pop. 1450.

2 Town, ⊗ of Lincoln co., SW cen. North Carolina, 15 m. NNW of Gastonia; pop. 5699; became ⊗ 1785; cotton products, furniture.

Lincoln Tunnel. Vehicular tunnel ab. 8000 ft. long under the Hudson river from Manhattan I., New York City, to Weehawken, New Jersey; south tube opened 1937, north tube 1945.

Lincoln University. Locality, Chester co., SE Pennsylvania, ab. 20 m. SW of West Chester borough. Lincoln Univ. (1854; men).

Lin'coln·wood (lĭng'kŭn·wŏŏd). Village, Cook co., NE Illinois, N of Chicago; pop. 11,744.

l'Incudine, Mont. See Mont l'INCUDINE.

Lin'dau (lĭn'dou); *also* **Lindau im Bo'den·see'** (ĭm bō'dĕn·zā'). City, Bavaria, W Germany, partly on island in Lake Constance 25 m. ESE of Konstanz; pop. 13,582; Renaissance town hall, 10th-cent. church; seaplane base; resort; trade center for agricultural and dairy products.

Lin'den (lĭn'dĕn). **1** Town, ⊗ of Marengo co., W Alabama; pop. 2516; agricultural trading center.

2 Industrial city, Union co., NE New Jersey, 4 m. SSW of and adjoining Elizabeth; pop. 39,931; oil refineries, chemical works, motor-vehicle assembly plants, gin distilleries; paint, varnish, clothing, knit goods.

3 Town, ⊗ of Perry co., W Tennessee; pop. 1086.

4 Town, ⊗ of Cass co., NE Texas; pop. 1832.

5 Former city, Prussia, Germany; now part of Hannover; pop. ab. 82,000.

Lin'den–Dahl'hau'sen (lĭn'dĕn·däl'hou'zĕn). Former commune (pop. 21,695), Westphalia prov., Prussia, Germany; since 1929 part of Bochum (*q.v.*).

Lin'den Harbour (lĭn'dĕn). **1** Inlet of Solomon Sea on S coast of New Britain I., Bismarck Archipelago, W Pacific Ocean, E of Gasmata; good harbor.

2 Village on the inlet.

Lin'den·hurst (lĭn'dĕn·hûrst). Industrial village, Suffolk co., SE New York, on Long I., on Great South Bay 35 m. E of New York City; pop. 20,905.

Lin'den·wold (lĭn'dĕn·wōld). Borough, Camden co., SW New Jersey, 12 m. SSE of Camden; pop. 7335.

Lin'des·nes' (lĭn'dĕs·nās') *or* **the Naze** (nāz). Cape on S extremity of Norway, projecting into the North Sea, 57°59'N.

Lin'di (lĭn'dĭ). **1** River ab. 400 m. long, NE Congo; rises W of Lake Edward, flows NW and then curves toward the S; enters the Congo at Stanleyville.

2 Province, SE Tanganyika, E Africa; 41,825 sq. m.; pop. 429,392.

3 Seaport, its ✻, at mouth of Lukuledi river; pop. ab. 3500.

Lindisfarne. See HOLY ISLAND.

Lin'dos (lĭn'dŏs); *anc.* **Lin'dus** (-dŭs). Town on E coast of Rhodes off SW Turkey in Asia; ancient city one of the Pentapolis of Asia Minor.

Lind′say (lĭn′zĭ). **1** City, Tulare co., S cen. California, 52 m. SE of Fresno; pop. 5397; incorporated 1910; in citrus-fruit and olive-growing region.
2 City, Garvin co., S cen. Oklahoma, on Washita river 27 m. SE of Chickasha; pop. 4258; agriculture.
3 Town, ⊗ of Victoria co., SE Ontario, Canada, on Scugog river 24 m. W of Peterborough; pop. 9603; in fertile farm region, raising wheat and livestock; also produces lumber products, woolen goods, and railroad equipment; summer resort in a scenic lake region.

Lindsay, Mount. Mountain, highest point 5512 ft. in Macpherson Range bet. Queensland and New South Wales, Australia, near coast.

Linds′borg (lĭnz′bûrg). City, McPherson co., cen. Kansas, on Smoky Hill river 20 m. S of Salina; pop. 2609; railroad and trade center in section producing wheat, corn, livestock, and dairy products. Bethany College (1881; coed.; Lutheran).

Lind′sey, the Parts of (lĭn′zĭ). See LINCOLNSHIRE.

Lindum. See LINCOLN city, England.

Lindus. See LINDOS.

Línea, La. See LA LÍNEA.

Line Islands (lĭn). Group of islands in cen. Pacific Ocean S of the Hawaiian Is., N and S of the equator, extending from Kingman Reef ab. 6°N to Flint I. 11°26′S. Kingman Reef and Palmyra I. at N belong to U.S.; Washington I., Fanning I., and Christmas I., also N of the equator, 255 sq. m., pop. ab. 1000, are attached to British colony of Gilbert and Ellice Islands; S of the equator Jarvis, Malden, Starbuck, Caroline, Vostok, and Flint, 40 sq. m., are in area claimed by both Great Britain and United States.

Lin′fen′ (lĭn′fŭn′). Town on Fen river, S cen. Shansi prov., NE China, 140 m. SSW of Yangku.

Lin′ga·yen′ (lĭng′gä·yĕn′; -yän′). Municipality, ✳ of Pangasinan prov., Luzon, Phil. Is., in N part, on S shore of Lingayen Gulf W of Dagupan (terminus of railroad to Manila); pop. 30,655; one of chief cities of Luzon and important since early times; situated on an island in the Agno delta. Landing place of the Japanese forces in their invasion of Dec. 1941 and also of American forces in Jan. 1945.

Lingayen Gulf. Large inlet of South China Sea on NW coast of Luzon, Phil. Is., ab. 35 m. long and 23 m. across its entrance from Santiago I. to San Fernando Point; affords good anchorage for large number of vessels. Borders on La Union prov. on E and on Pangasinan on S and W and receives Agno and Bued rivers. Lingayen, Dagupan, San Fabian, and Sual are chief ports of Pangasinan on its shores. Scene of major naval and landing operations by Japanese Dec. 1941 and by Americans Jan. 1945.

Lin·geh′ (lĭng·gĕ′h′). Seaport town, S Laristan prov., S Iran, on the Persian Gulf; pop. ab. 15,000; opp. W end of Qishm I. and ab. 100 m. SW of Bandar Abbas. Old trading port, formerly a center for export of pearls; products now chiefly carpets, fruits, tobacco, hides. Held by Arabia from latter part of 18th cent. to 1887.

Ling′en (lĭng′ĕn); *also* **Lingen an der Ems** (än dĕr ĕms′). City, Lower Saxony state, NW Germany, on Ems river 42 m. NNW of Münster; pop. 10,914; textiles; trades in grain, cattle, horses.

Ling′ga (lĭng′gȧ). Chief island of the Lingga Archipelago, Indonesia; 40 m. long; 319 sq. m.; pop. 14,519.

Lingga Archipelago. Island group in Indonesia, off the E coast of Sumatra, S of Riouw Archipelago; 841 sq. m.; pop. 30,524; formerly a division of Riouw residency. Comprises Lingga I. and Singkep I. and many small islands, mainly of coral growth and in shallow water; separated from Sumatra by Berhala Strait.

Ling′ga·dja′ti (lĭng′gȧ·jä′tĕ). Town, N coast of Java, a suburb of Cheribon; agreement bet. Dutch and representatives of Republic of Indonesia initialed here Nov. 15, 1946.

Ling′ling′ (lĭng′lĭng′). Town, S Hunan prov., SE cen.

China, on Siang river and on Kweilin-Hengyang highway; in World War II important American air base, seized by Japanese Sept. 7, 1944; approached by Chinese just as war ended Aug. 1945.

Ling′mell (lĭng′mĕl). Mountain 2649 ft. in Cumberland co., NW England, 9 m. SW of Keswick, in the Lake District.

Lingones. See LANGRES.

Lin·gua·glos′sa (lēng·gwä·glôs′sä). Commune, Catania prov., E Sicily, just N of Mt. Etna; pop. 8371.

Lin·guet′ta (lĭng·gwĕt′ȧ; *Ital.* lēng·gwät′tä); *or* **Glos′sa** (glôs′ȧ; *Gr.* glôs′sä). Cape. Cape and promontory, SW Albania, 40°28′N. See ACROCERAUNIA.

Lin′i′ (lĭn′ē′); *formerly* **I′chow′** (ē′jō′). Town, SW Shantung prov., NE China, on small stream E of the Grand Canal.

Lin′kö′ping (lĭn′chû′pĭng). City, ✳ of Östergötland prov., SE Sweden, near S shore of Lake Roxen 110 m. SW of Stockholm; pop. 46,617; iron foundries, sugar refineries, textile mills, tobacco factories; cathedral, Romanesque-Gothic structure begun 1230; city suffered destructive fire 1700.

Lin·lith′gow (lĭn·lĭth′gō). **1** County in Scotland. See WEST LOTHIAN.
2 Burgh, ⊗ of West Lothian co., SE Scotland; pop. 3929; ruins of palace, residence of Scottish kings and birthplace of James V of Scotland and Mary, Queen of Scots.

Linlithgowshire. See WEST LOTHIAN.

Linn (lĭn). **1** Name of counties in four states of the U.S. See *Tables* at IOWA, KANSAS, MISSOURI, OREGON.
2 City, ⊗ of Osage co., cen. Missouri, ESE of Jefferson City; pop. 1050.

Lin′ne·us (lĭn′ē·ŭs). City, ⊗ of Linn co., N Missouri; pop. 471.

Linn′he, Loch (lŏκ lĭn′ē). Inlet of Atlantic Ocean on W coast of Scotland, extending NE 20 m. from the head of the Firth of Lorne, in Argyll co.

Li·no′sa (lē·nō′sä); *anc.* **Ae·gu′sa** (ė·gū′sȧ). One of the Pelagian Is. (*q.v.*), N of Lampedusa; taken by Allies June 13, 1943.

Lins (lēns). City, W cen. São Paulo state, SE Brazil, on railroad 230 m. NW of São Paulo; pop. (1940 est.) 17,403; coffee, lumber.

Lin′si′ (lĭn′sē′). Town, W Jehol, NE China, near Inner Mongolia (Chahar) border and ab. 260 m. NNE of Peiping; former Japanese key military post.

Lint′fort (lĭnt′fôrt); *now* **Kamp–Lint′fort** (kämp-). Coal-mining commune, North Rhine-Westphalia state, W Germany, WNW of Oberhausen; pop. 24,315.

Linth (lĭnt). River ab. 26 m. long, E cen. Switzerland; rises in S Glarus canton, flows N into W end of Lake Wallen; as the **Linth Canal** it connects Lake Wallen with the Lake of Zurich; the Limmat, flowing from the Lake of Zurich to the Aare, is sometimes considered as the lower course of the Linth.

Lin′thwaite (lĭn′thwāt). Former urban district, West Riding, Yorkshire, N England; pop. (1931) 9688; now part of Huddersfield county borough.

Lin′ton (lĭn′t′n; -tŭn). **1** City, Greene co., SW Indiana, 32 m. SSE of Terre Haute; pop. 5736; coal-mining center. By 1930 census it was within 3 m. of the center of population of the U.S.
2 City, ⊗ of Emmons co., S North Dakota, 46 m. SSE of Bismarck; pop. 1826; agriculture; sandstone quarries nearby.

Lin′tsing′ (lĭn′chĭng′). City, W Shantung prov., NE China, on the Grand Canal W of Tsinan; pop. ab. 48,000.

Lin′yu′ (lĭn′yōō′); *formerly* **Shan′hai′kwan′** (shän′hī′gwän′). Town on Gulf of Liaotung, NE Hopeh prov., NE China, on Manchuria boundary at E end of Great Wall; pop. ab. 30,000; ab. halfway bet. Peiping and Mukden (260 m. from either) and for centuries an important border town; first Chinese city occupied by the Manchus 1644 and scene of great activity in Boxer Rebellion 1900.

Linz (lĭnts). **1** anc. **Len′ti·a** (lĕn′shĭ·à; -shà). Commercial and manufacturing city, ✳ of Upper Austria prov., Austria, on Danube river 95 m. W of Vienna; pop. (1939) 128,006; two cathedrals, episcopal palace, town hall; extensive river trade; varied manufactures; shipbuilding. Became city 1324; seized by Bavaria 1741 and besieged by Napoleon 1805 and 1809; in World War II surrendered to American forces May 6, 1945.
2 Town, N Rhineland-Palatinate state, West Germany, on the Rhine 19 m. NNW of Koblenz; pop. 5017.

Li′ons, Gulf of (lī′ŭnz); Fr. **Golfe du Lion** (gôlf′ dü lyôN′); anc. **Si′nus Gal′li·cus** (sī′nŭs găl′ĭ·kŭs). Inlet of Mediterranean Sea on S coast of France, extending from peninsula of Giens, near Hyères, E of Marseilles, to Cape Creus on NE coast of Spain.

Li·pa′ (lė·pä′). Municipality, E cen. Batangas prov., Luzon, Phil. Is., E of Lake Taal and on railroad and highway 15 m. N of Batangas; pop. 45,175; second largest town in province, an active inland trade center.

Lípa, Česká. See ČESKÁ LÍPA.

Lip′a·ri Islands (lĭp′à·rĭ; Ital. lē′pä·rē); Ital. **I′so·le E·o′lie** (ē′zṓ·lȧ ā·ô′lyȧ); anc. **Ae·o′li·ae In′su·lae** (ē·ō′lĭ·ē ĭn′sů·lē). Group of small volcanic islands in the SE Tyrrhenian Sea off N coast of Messina prov., Sicily; 45 sq. m.; pop. (1931) ab. 15,000; includes the islands Salina, Vulcano, Stromboli, and the chief island **Lipari**, anc. **Lip′a·ra** (lĭp′à·rȧ), 13 sq. m., on which is located the town of **Lipari** (pop. 6298). According to legend the island on which Aeolus kept the winds confined in caves was one of this group.

Li′petsk (lē′pĕtsk; Russ. lyē′pyĕtsk). Town, N Voronezh Region, Soviet Russia, Europe, 65 m. N of Voronezh; pop. 66,625; resort town on railroad E from Yelets, noted since early 18th cent. for its chalybeate mineral springs and baths; leather works; flour mills.

Lip′no (lēp′nô). Commune, Warszawa dept., Poland, 87 m. NW of Warsaw; pop. 10,415; agriculture.

Lip′pe (lĭp′ĕ). **1** River ab. 150 m. long, W Germany; rises in the Teutoburger Wald and flows W in North Rhine-Westphalia into Rhine river at Wesel.
2 Former German state, NW Germany, bet. Teutoburger Wald and Weser river; 469 sq. m.; pop. (1939) 188,598; ✳ Detmold; agricultural products, tobacco, lumber, cattle. Originally settled by the Cherusci, a German tribe, whose leader Arminius defeated the Romans at Teutoburger Wald in 9 A.D.; appeared as separate state in 12th cent.; became principality of Holy Roman Empire 1720; in Confederation of Rhine 1807, Germanic Confederation 1815-66; joined North German Confederation 1866; became republic 1918; lost sovereign rights to Reich 1933-35; incorporated 1945 in North Rhine-Westphalia state.

Lipp′stadt (lĭp′shtät). Industrial city, North Rhine-Westphalia state, West Germany, on Lippe river 38 m. SE of Münster; pop. 18,498; 13th-cent. church, 18th-cent. town hall; manufactures twine, brewery and distillery products. Junction point of two Allied armies encircling the Ruhr Apr. 1, 1945.

Lips′comb (lĭps′kŭm) **1** County in Texas. See Table at TEXAS.
2 City, Jefferson co. cen. Alabama, 8 m. SW of Birmingham; pop. 2811.
3 Village, ⊗ of Lipscomb co. NW Texas; pop. (1950) 224.

Lipsia. See LEIPZIG city.

Lip′sos (lĭp′sŏs; Mod. Gr. lyē·psôs′); Ital. **Lis′so** (lēs′sồ) or **Lip′so** (lēp′sồ). An island of the Dodecanese (q.v.) N of Leros and E of Patmos; 7 sq. m.; pop (1936) 977.

Lip′tov·ský Svä′tý Mi′ku·láš (lĭp′tôf·skē svä′tē mĭ′kŏ̄·läsh); Hung. **Lip′tó·szent′mi′klós** (lĭp′tō·sĕnt′-mĭ′klōsh) Town, N Slovakia, E cen. Czechoslovakia on the Váh river E of Ružomberok; pop. 6866.

Li′ra (lē′rȧ). Town, Northern Province, N Uganda, E Africa, N of Lake Kyoga.

Li′ri (lē′rē); anc. **Li′ris** (lī′rĭs). River ab. 100 m. long, cen. Italy; rises near Avezzano E of Rome, flowing SE bet. parallel ranges of cen. Apennine Mts. and forming valley of the Liri; joined by the Sacco near Frosinone and farther E near Cassino by the Rapido after which it turns S to enter Gulf of Gaeta (Tyrrhenian Sea) near Minturno; its lower course also known as the Garigliano. In World War II its valley invaded by Allies May 1944 after fierce fighting Feb.–Mar. in effort to take Cassino (q.v.), key point on the Gustav Line, which barred Allied advance on Rome.

Lis (lēsh) or **Liz** (lēsh). River, cen. Portugal; flows N near Leiria, then W into Atlantic Ocean.

Lis·bo′a (lēzh·vṓ′ȧ). **1** District of Portugal. See Table at PORTUGAL.
2 See LISBON city, Portugal.

Lis′bon (lĭz′bŭn). **1** Town, Androscoggin co., SW Maine, 8 m. SE of Lewiston; pop. 5042.
2 Manufacturing town, Grafton co., N New Hampshire, 9 m. SW of Littleton; pop. 1788; summer and winter sports; township includes **Sug′ar Hill** (shŏŏg′ẽr), a hilltop settlement, center of Millerism in 19th cent.
3 City, ⊗ of Ransom co., SE North Dakota, 38 m. SSE of Valley City; pop. 2093; grain and dairy farms.
4 Village, ⊗ of Columbiana co., E Ohio, 23 m. S of Youngstown; pop. 3579; shipping point for region producing coal and clay; manufactures porcelain ware, china, sewer pipe, coal and clay products. Site of Morgan's surrender 1863 nearby.
5 Port. **Lis·bo′a** (lēzh·vṓ′ȧ); anc. **O·lis′i·po** (ṓ·lĭs′ĭ·pō) and **Fe·lic′i·tas Ju′lia** (fė·lĭs′ĭ·tăs jŏŏl′yȧ; jŏŏ′lĭ·ȧ). Commercial seaport city, ✳ of Portugal, of Estremadura prov., and of Lisboa dist., W Portugal; pop. (1940) 709,179; on estuary of the Tagus river (q.v.), has one of finest harbors in Europe; built on terraced hills; ancient fortress, cathedral (former Moorish mosque), two aqueducts, Ajuda palace, castle of St. George; Univ. of Lisbon (founded 1910); manufactures textiles, chemicals, paper, tobacco, soap, pottery, iron products; sugar refineries; birthplace of Camões.
History: Ancient Iberian settlement; held by Phoenicians and Carthaginians; became Roman municipium; captured by Visigoths and 716 by Moors; reconquered 1147 by Portuguese; sacked by Castile in 14th-cent. wars; during period of Portuguese voyages and colonial expansion, flourished as a leading European commercial center; began to lose prosperity at end of 16th cent.; held by Spain 1580-1640; devastated by earthquake 1755 with loss of life exceeding 50,000; occupied by French 1807-08. See PORTUGAL.

Lis′burn (lĭz′bẽrn; lĭs′-; -bûrn). Urban district, co. Antrim, NE Northern Ireland, on Lagan river 8 m. SW of Belfast; pop. 14,778; in agricultural section; linen manufacturing.

Lis′burne, Cape (lĭz′bẽrn; -bûrn). Cape on NW coast of Alaska, on Chuckchee Sea, 166°W.

Lis·can′nor Bay (lĭs·kăn′ẽr). Inlet of Atlantic Ocean on W coast of Ireland, S of Galway Bay.

Li′shui′ (lē′shwä′); formerly **Chu′chow′** (chŏŏ′jō′). City, S cen. Chekiang prov., E China, ab. 55 m. WNW of Yungkia. Scene of fighting bet. Chinese and Japanese 1942.

Lis′i·an′ski (lĭs′ĭ·ăn′skĭ; lĭs·yăn′skĭ). Islet of Leeward Is., Hawaiian Is., in cen. Pacific Ocean 860 m. NW of Niihau I.; included in Hawaiian Islands Bird Reservation. Discovered 1805.

Li′sieux′ (lē′zyü′); anc. **No′vi·om′a·gus** (nō′vĭ·ŏm′à·gŭs). City, Calvados dept., NW France, 27 m. E of Caen; pop. 16,032; manufactures textiles; 12th- and 15th-cent. churches; tourist resort. Named for its ancient inhabitants, the Lexovii; captured by Caesar; taken subsequently by Normans 877 A.D., Bretons 1130, Geoffrey Plantagenet 1141; episcopal see until Revolution. St. Thérèse, the Little Flower, lived in Carmelite convent here.

Lis·keard' (lǐs·kärd'). Town and municipal borough, Cornwall, SW England, WNW of Plymouth; pop. ab. 4391; nearby are the hurlers, prehistoric stone circles. An important manor in 11th cent., made a free borough 1240.

Lisle (līl). Village, Du Page co., NE Illinois, ab. 5 m. S of Wheaton; pop. 4219; Saint Procopius College (1885; men).

Lisle, L'Isle (lēl; *Angl.* līl). See LILLE.

L'Is'let' (lē'lě'). County, Quebec, Canada. See *Table* at QUEBEC.

Lis'more (lĭz'mōr). Town and river port, NE New South Wales, SE Australia, 100 m. S of Brisbane; pop. 11,763; dairying; sugar cane.

Lis·more' (lĭz·mōr'; lĭz'mōr). Island 9 m. long. at entrance to Loch Linnhe, Argyll co., W Scotland; site of remains of a castle and a cathedral.

Lissa. 1 See LESZNO commune, Poland.

2 See VIS island, Yugoslavia.

Lisso. See LIPSOS.

Lis·so'ne (lēs·sō'nå). Commune, Milano prov., Lombardy, N Italy, 7 m. N of Milan; pop. (1931) 14,266.

Lissus. See LESH.

Lis'ter og Man'dals (lĭs'tĕr ô män'däls). Former name of *Vest-Agder;* see *Table* at NORWAY.

List Land (lĭst' länt'). Northern part of the island of Sylt, off W coast of Schleswig-Holstein, northern Germany.

Lis·tow'el (lĭs·tō'ĕl). **1** Industrial town, Perth co., SE Ontario, Canada, 26 m. N of Stratford; pop. 3469.

2 Market town and urban district, N co. Kerry, SW Eire; pop. 3098; remains of old castle.

Li'su·land' (lē'sōō·länd'). Name given to region of NW Yunnan and S Sikang, S China, inhabited in part by the Chinese tribe Lisu; lies in the very mountainous country (peaks 12,000 to 25,000 ft.) cut by the four great rivers of SE Asia—the Yangtze, Mekong, Salween, and Irrawaddy—flowing through gorges two miles deep within 60 m. of one another.

Li·ta'ni (lē·tä'nĭ). River ab. 90 m. long, S Lebanon; rises at N end of El Bika near Baalbek, flows S bet. the Lebanon and Anti-Liban mountain ranges, turns SW and empties into Mediterranean Sea 6 m. N of Sour (ancient Tyre); in its lower course called the **Nahr el Qa'si·mi'ye** (nä'h'r ăl kä'sĭ·mē'yĕ).

Litch'field (lĭch'fēld). **1** County in Connecticut. See *Table* at CONNECTICUT.

2 Town, cen. Litchfield co., NW Connecticut; pop. 6264; incorporated 1719; summer resort; agriculture, lumbering; manufactures electrical devices; important trading center and strategic military depot in Colonial and Revolutionary times; site of first law school in America (1782); birthplace of Ethan Allen, Henry Ward Beecher, and Harriet Beecher Stowe. Includes borough of **Litchfield** (⊗ of Litchfield co.; pop. 1363; incorporated 1879).

3 City, Montgomery co., S cen. Illinois, 45 m. S of Springfield; pop. 7330; in agricultural and coal-mining area.

4 City, ✳ of Meeker co., S cen. Minnesota, 35 m. SSW of St. Cloud; pop. 5078; trading and industrial center in agricultural section; creameries, woolen mill; shipping point for livestock and poultry.

Lith'er·land (lĭth'ēr·lånd). Urban district, Lancashire, NW England, 4½ m. N of Liverpool; pop. 22,197.

Lith'gow (lĭth'gō). Town, E New South Wales, SE Australia, 65 m. WNW of Sydney; pop. 13,444; industrial community in extensive coal region; iron and steel foundries and mills, arms factory, pipe works.

Li·tho'nia (lĭ·thōn'yå; -thō'nĭ·å). City, De Kalb co., NW cen. Georgia, 16 m. E of Atlanta; pop. 1667; granite quarries.

Lith'u·a'ni·a (lĭth'ů·ā'nĭ·å; -ān'yå); *Lithuanian* **Lie·tu'va** (lyĕ·tōō'vä); *Russ.* **Lit·va'** (lyĭt·vä'). **1** A medieval principality, expanded from region E of Baltic, occupied before 12th cent. by heathen Lithuanians; their

attack on Poles caused latter to seek aid of Teutonic Knights; united as grand duchy to oppose the Teutonic Order ab. 1250; expanded 1316–40 by Gedimin into large state including Polotsk, Minsk, and area W of mid-Dnieper; under Olgierd (d. 1377) domain extended along Dnieper to Black Sea; by marriage of Jagello to Jadwiga of Poland formed personal union 1386 with Poland (*q.v.*); became predominantly Roman Catholic; merged with Poland by Union of Lublin 1569; acquired by Russia in three partitions of Poland 1772, 1793, 1795; administered by Russia separately from Poland; joined Polish revolt 1863; demanded self-government 1905. For later history as republic, see 2, below.

2 Republic, N Europe, at E end of Baltic Sea; annexed by U.S.S.R. 1940 and incorporated into the Soviet Union as the **Lith'u·a'ni·an Soviet Socialist Republic** (lĭth'-ů·ā'nĭ·ăn; -ān'yăn); 21,330 sq. m. (before loss of Memel); pop. (1938 est.) 2,575,363, (1941 est.) 3,134,070; ✳ Vilnyus. Bounded on N by Latvia, on E and SE by White Russia, on S by Poland, on SW by Kaliningradsk Region, R.S.F.S.R., and on W by the Baltic Sea. Before annexation by Soviet Union, divided into the following 23 districts (for pronunciations, see their individual entries):

NAME	LOCA-TION	AREA[1]	POP.[1]	CAPITAL
Alitus	S	1,070	139,562	Alitus
Birzhai-Pasvalys	N	1,051	110,426	Birzhai
Kaunas	cen.	1,007	233,057	Kaunas
Kedainyai	cen.	929	101,656	Kedainyai
Kretinga	W	1,017	114,892	Kretinga
Mariyampole	SW	880	118,964	Mariyampole
Mazheikyai	NW	757	83,590	Mazheikyai
Memel	W	329	73,079	Memel
Pagegiai	SW	362	42,138	Pagegiai
Panevezhis	NE cen.	1,694	178,058	Panevezhis
Raseinyai	W cen.	1,188	129,275	Raseinyai
Rokishkis	NE	836	95,459	Rokishkis
Seinai	S	482	48,029	Lazdiyai
Shakyai	SW	668	76,484	Shakyai
Shaulyai	N	2,335	238,892	Shaulyai
Šilutė	W	251	38,576	Šilutė
Taurage	W	1,266	136,279	Taurage
Telshai	NW	1,014	96,631	Telshai
Trakai	E	828	99,388	Kaišiadoris
Ukmerge	E	1,185	148,540	Ukmerge
Utena	E	1,165	127,955	Utena
Vilkavishkis	SW	510	93,578	Vilkavishkis
Zarasai	NE	506	50,855	Zarasai

[1] Area is in sq. m. Pop. is 1938 est.

Mostly low-lying land with many lakes and swamps; formerly heavily forested; highest point is not above 1000 ft.; crossed in S part by Neman river (in *Lithuanian*, Nemunas); also drained in N by upper courses of Venta and Lielupe; has only ab. 15 m. of coast on the Baltic with no good port. Chief occupation agriculture, much poultry and livestock raised; other industries lumbering, dairying, tanning, woodworking, and some iron manufacture; exports meat, butter, timber, flax, peat. Predominant ethnic strain Baltic; chief nationalities Lithuanian 85%, Russian 2.5%. Chief towns Kaunas, Shaulyai, Panevezhis.

History: Occupied by Germans during World War I; proclaimed independent republic Feb. 16, 1918; recognized by U.S.S.R. 1920; seizure of Vilnyus (*q.v.*) by Poland 1920 caused rupture of relations which lasted 1922–38; joined League of Nations 1921; invaded Memel (*q.v.*) 1923; established dictatorship under Smetona 1923; forced by Polish ultimatum to re-establish relations 1938; Memel taken by Germany and Vilnyus by Russians 1939; signed mutual assistance pact with U.S.S.R. which prepared way for annexation Aug. 3, 1940 as Lithuanian S.S.R.; overrun by German army 1941; recovered 1944; incorporation in U.S.S.R. not recognized by United States.

Lit'itz (lĭt'ĭts). Industrial borough, Lancaster co., SE Pennsylvania, 8 m. N of Lancaster; pop. 5987; settled by Moravians 1757; manufactures pretzels, animal traps, hosiery, underwear, paper products; music center.

Li′to·mě′ři·ce (lǐ′tô·myěr′zhǐ·tsě); *Ger.* **Leit′me·ritz** (līt′mě·rǐts). Town, N Bohemia prov., W Czechoslovakia, on the Labe (Elbe) river at head of steamer navigation, 35 m. NNW of Prague; pop. (1930) 18,509; manufacturing and commercial center in agricultural section; 17th-cent. cathedral; in last century became strongly German.

Lit′tle (līt′'l). **1** River, N cen. Louisiana; formed by the confluence of streams on SE boundary of Winn parish; flows SE into Catahoula Lake and from N end of lake E across Catahoula parish into Black river S of Harrisonburg.
2 River 80 m. long in E North Carolina; rises in Wake co., flows SE into Neuse river near Goldsboro.
3 River ab. 150 m. long, rising in Le Flore co., SE Oklahoma, and flowing S, then E across Arkansas border to empty into Red river on SW boundary of Hempstead co., SW Arkansas.

Little Abaco. See ABACO.

Little Alföld. See ALFÖLD.

Little America. Settlement of the Byrd Antarctic Expedition (1928–30) near the outer edge of Ross Shelf Ice on Bay of Whales, Ross Sea, Antarctica; used also as base of Byrd's second expedition (1933–35), by later explorers, and by Byrd's expedition of 1946–47.

Little Andaman. One of the Andaman Is. (*q.v.*).

Little Armenia. Medieval feudal kingdom, 13th and 14th cents., of Armenians in Cilicia (*q.v.*); few Armenians survived Turkish massacres.

Little Atlas. = *Maritime Atlas:* see ATLAS MOUNTAINS.

Little Bahama Bank. See BAHAMA BANKS.

Little Bald (bôld). Peak 5000 ft. in Unicoi co., NE Tennessee.

Little Barrier Island. Small island off E coast of N extension of North I., New Zealand, in entrance to Hauraki Gulf.

Little Bear Peak (bâr). Mountain ab. 14,000 ft. in Costilla co., S Colorado.

Little Belt (bělt). Strait bet. Fyn I. and the mainland of Denmark, connecting the Kattegat with the Baltic Sea; 30 m. long, varies from ab. 700 yds. to 18 m. in width. Cf. GREAT BELT.

Little Belt Mountains. A range of the Rocky Mts. in cen. Montana, chiefly in Cascade and Judith Basin cos.

Little Big′horn′ (bĭg′hôrn′); *also* **Little Horn.** River ab. 80 m. long, S Montana; rises in N Wyoming, flows N through Big Horn co., S Montana, into Bighorn river; on its banks Gen. Custer and his command were defeated and slain by Indians June 25, 1876; site of battle now Custer Battlefield National Monument (see UNITED STATES, *National Monuments*).

Little Bitter Lake. See BITTER LAKES.

Little Black. River, N Maine; formed by junction of branches in NW Aroostook co., flows SE into St. John river.

Little Blue. River rising in S Nebraska and flowing SE across Kansas border into Big Blue river below Marysville, Marshall co., NE Kansas.

Lit′tle·bor′ough (līt′'l·bûr′ō; -bŭ·rŭ; -brŭ). Urban district, Lancashire, NW England, on the Roch 13 m. NE of Manchester; pop. 10,982.

Little Bras d'Or. See BRAS D'OR.

Little Carpathian Mountains, *also* **Little Carpathians.** Mountain range, a SW extension of the Carpathian Mts., SW Slovakia, Czechoslovakia, N of Bratislava; highest point ab. 2500 ft.

Little Cayman. See CAYMAN ISLANDS.

Little Chief Mountain. Peak 9542 ft. in Glacier National Park, NW Montana.

Little Chute (shōot). Village, Outagamie co., E Wisconsin, on rapids in Fox river 8 m. E of Appleton; pop. 5099.

Little Co′co (kō′kō). Small island of the Andaman Is., separated from North Andaman I. by Coco Channel.

Little Colorado. River 300 m. long, NE Arizona; rises in S Apache co., flows NW into the Colorado river on E edge of Grand Canyon National Park.

Little Comp′ton (kǒmp′tŭn). Town, Newport co., SE Rhode Island, 8 m. E of Newport; pop. 1702; its center Little Compton Common; agriculture; fisheries.

Little Corn Island. See CORN ISLANDS.

Little Creek Peak. Mountain 10,010 ft. in E Iron co., SW Utah.

Little Current. Town, Manitoulin dist., S Ontario, Canada, on N Manitoulin I. bet. Georgian Bay and North Channel; pop. 1397; a lake port and fishing center.

Little Cuyahoga. See CUYAHOGA river, Ohio.

Little Diomede. See DIOMEDE ISLANDS.

Little Dunmow. See DUNMOW.

Little Egg Harbor. Inlet of Barnegat Bay, on SE coast of Ocean co., E New Jersey.

Little Egg Inlet. Narrow strait leading from Atlantic Ocean into Great Bay, on extreme S tip of Ocean co., E New Jersey.

Little Elobey. See ELOBEY.

Little Exuma. See EXUMA.

Little Falls. 1 City, ⊗ of Morrison co., cen. Minnesota, on Mississippi river 25 m. S of Brainerd; pop. 7551; trade center in agricultural and dairying section.
2 Town, Passaic co., N New Jersey, on Passaic river 5 m. SW of Paterson; pop. 9730; site of laundry said to be largest in world.
3 Industrial city, Herkimer co., NE cen. New York, 20 m. E of Utica; pop. 8935; in dairying region; manufactures cheese, dairy machinery, felt products, knit goods, bicycles. Settled c. 1725; burned by Tories and Indians 1782; incorporated as city 1895. The Mohawk river near here passes through **Little Falls Gorge** and falls ab. 45 ft. in one mile of its course.

Little Ferry. Borough, Bergen co., NE New Jersey, on Hackensack river 9 m. N of Jersey City; pop. 6175; brickyards, shipyards, machine shops, oil refineries.

Lit′tle·field (līt′'l·fēld). City, Lamb co., NW Texas, in the panhandle, 33 m. NW of Lubbock; pop. 7236; in stock-raising and agricultural (esp. cotton) region.

Little Fork. River, N Minnesota; rises in N cen. St. Louis co., flows NW into Rainy river on United States-Canada boundary.

Lit′tle·hamp′ton (līt′'l·hăm[p]′tŭn). Urban district, West Sussex, S England, on the coast at the mouth of the Arun river; pop. 13,948; watering place.

Little Hay′stack′ Mountain (hā′stăk′). Peak 4700 ft. in the Adirondack Mts., Essex co., NE New York.

Little Horn. See LITTLE BIGHORN river.

Little Hul′ton (hŭl′t'n; -tŭn). Town in Worsley urban district, Lancashire, NW England; pop. (1931) 7874.

Little Inagua. See INAGUA.

Little Jay Peak (jā). Mountain 3202 ft. in NW Orleans co., N Vermont.

Little Kai Island. See KAI ISLANDS.

Little Kanawha. River ab. 150 m. long in cen. and W West Virginia; rises in S Upshur co., flows W and NW into Ohio river at Parkersburg; navigable by small boats for 48 m.

Little Kapela. See KAPELA.

Little Karroo. See KARROO.

Little Khingan Mountains. See KHINGAN.

Little Lake. Lake on boundary bet. Jefferson and Lafourche parishes, SE Louisiana.

Little Le′ver (lē′vēr). Urban district, Lancashire, NW England, 3 m. SE of Bolton; pop. 4703.

Little Loch Broom. See LOCH BROOM.

Little Lyakhov. See LYAKHOV ISLANDS.

Little Miami. River ab. 140 m. long, Ohio; rises in Clark co., flows S to Ohio river just E of Cincinnati.

Little Minch (mĭnch). Strait SW of the North Minch, off NW coast of Scotland, extending bet. Skye I. of the Inner Hebrides and the cen. islands of the Outer Hebrides; varies in width bet. 14 and 20 m.

Little Miquelon. See MIQUELON ISLAND.

Little Missouri. 1 River ab. 150 m. long, SW Arkansas; rises in Pike co. and flows SE into the Ouachita river. 2 River 560 m. long, flowing from NE Wyoming NE across SE corner of Montana and NW corner of South Dakota into North Dakota, and continuing N into McKenzie co., where it turns E to empty into Missouri river in NE Dunn co., W North Dakota.

Little Monadnock. See Mount MONADNOCK.

Little Moose Mountain (mōōs). Peak 3630 ft. in Adirondack Mts., Hamilton co., NE cen. New York.

Little Neck Bay. Inlet of Long Island Sound, Queens borough, W Long I.; formerly source of saddle-rock oysters and littleneck clams, beds condemned 1909 because of pollution of the water.

Little Nemaha. See NEMAHA.

Little Nethe. See NETHE.

Little Nicobar. One of the Nicobar Is. (q.v.).

Little Paternosters. See BALABALAGAN ISLANDS.

Little Peconic Bay. See PECONIC BAY.

Little Pee Dee. River 145 m. long, flowing from Scotland co., S North Carolina, S across South Carolina border into Pee Dee river near its mouth.

Little Pow'der (pou'dĕr). River 100 m. long, flowing from cen. Campbell co., NE Wyoming, N into Powder river in Powder River co., SE Montana.

Little Rann of Cutch. See Rann of CUTCH.

Little Red. River ab. 120 m. long, Arkansas; formed by two branches in Van Buren co., flows SE into the White river on E boundary of White co., E Arkansas.

Little River. 1 See LITTLE. 2 County in Arkansas. See *Table* at ARKANSAS.

Lit'tle Rock'. Commercial city, * of Arkansas and ⊗ of Pulaski co., cen. Arkansas, on S bank of Arkansas river; largest city in the state; pop. 107,813; manufactures cottonseed oil, lumber products, furniture; railroad repair shops; in fertile region producing esp. cotton, grains, timber; large bauxite deposits, also coal, natural gas, marble, oil, clay. University of Arkansas Medical School (1879); Philander Smith College (1868; coed.); Little Rock University (1927; coed.). Founded 1820; made territorial capital 1821 and state capital on admission of Arkansas to the Union 1836; incorporated as city 1835; held by Confederate forces 1861–63.

Little Ross. Small island off S coast of Kirkcudbright co., S Scotland, E of entrance to Wigtown Bay; lighthouse.

Little Russia. Indefinite area including Carpatho-Ukraine (formerly Carpathian Ruthenia), E Poland, Ukraine, and W shores of Black Sea, inhabited chiefly by Ukrainians, who are also called Little Russians or Ruthenians. The term Ruthenians is sometimes restricted to the peoples of Carpathian Ruthenia and E Poland.

Little Sa'ble Point (sā'b'l). Point on W coast of Oceana co., W Michigan, extending into Lake Michigan.

Little Saint Bernard. Alpine pass. See ALPS.

Little Salkehatchie. River ab. 50 m. long, S South Carolina; rises in Bamberg co., flows SE to unite with Salkehatchie river and form Combahee river.

Little Sandy. River ab. 45 m. long, NE Kentucky; rises in S Elliott co., flows NE into the Ohio river in NE Greenup co.

Little Satilla. River ab. 60 m. long, SE Georgia; rises in Jeff Davis co., flows SE into Satilla river in Brantley co.

Little Scheidegg. See SCHEIDEGG.

Little Schütt (shüt); *Hung.* **Szi'get·köz'** (sǐ'gĕt·kûz'). Island in NW Hungary, formed by arms of the Danube river near Györ; ab. 28 m. long and 7 m. wide.

Little Sil'ver (sǐl'vēr). Borough, Monmouth co., E cen. New Jersey, SE of Perth Amboy; pop. 5202.

Little Sioux. River ab. 236 m. long, flowing from Jackson co., S Minnesota, S into Missouri river in W Harrison co., W Iowa.

Little Skellig. See SKELLIGS.

Lit'tles·town (lǐt''lz·toun). Borough, Adams co., S Pennsylvania, near Maryland border 25 m. SW of York; pop. 2756.

Little Tennessee. River ab. 150 m. long, rising near N boundary of Georgia and flowing N through Macon co., SW North Carolina, N and W across Tennessee border, and into Tennessee river in Loudon co., E Tennessee. In its course in North Carolina near Tennessee border is Fontana Dam, one of the dams of the Tennessee Valley Authority (q.v.).

Little Tibet. See BALTISTAN.

Little Tobago. Small British island in Atlantic Ocean off NE coast of Venezuela, E of Tobago; 1 sq. m.

Lit'tle·ton (lǐt''l·tŭn). 1 Town, ⊗ of Arapahoe co., NE cen Colorado. 8 m. S of Denver; pop. 13,670; in irrigated farming area. 2 Town, Middlesex co., NE Massachusetts, 12 m. SW of Lowell; pop 5109; dairy products, poultry, apples. 3 Town. Gratton co., W New Hampshire, 30 m. WSW of Berlin. pop. 5003; summer and winter resort; manufactures esp. gloves. Active in antislavery movement.

Little Traverse Bay. Inlet of Lake Michigan on SW coast of Emmet co., N Michigan.

Little Tupper Lake. See TUPPER LAKES.

Little Valley. Village, ⊗ of Cattaraugus co., SW New York; pop. 1244.

Little Wabash. River ab. 180 m. long, SE Illinois; rises in Coles co., flows SE into the Wabash river 8 m. from its mouth.

Little Walachia. See OLTENIA.

Little Zab. See ZAB.

Lit'to·ral (lǐt'ō·răl). = PRIMORJE, former county of Yugoslavia.

Lit·to'ri·a (lǐ·tōr'ǐ·à); *Ital.* lêt·tô'ryä); *since 1947 called* **La·ti'na** (lä·tē'nä). 1 Province of Italy. See *Table* at ITALY. 2 Commune, its *, Latium, cen. Italy, 35 m. SE of Rome; pop. 19,654; built c. 1929 on reclaimed land in Pontine Marshes; made capital of new province 1934.

Litva. See LITHUANIA.

Litz'mann·stadt (lǐts'män·shtät). German name of Łódź during World War II.

Liu'chow' (lǐ·ōō'jō'); *formerly* **Ma'ping'** (mä'pǐng'). Commercial city, cen. Kwangsi prov., SE China, on S bank of Lung river above its junction with the Hungshui, 90 m. S of Kweilin; on railroad. In World War II site of American air base and scene of much fighting 1944–45.

Liu'kiu', Liu–Kiu (lǐ·ōō'kǐ·ōō'). Vars. of RYUKYU.

Liu'kung' (lǐ·ōō'gŏong'), **Liu'kung'tao'** (-dou'). See WEIHAIWEI.

Li·vad'i·a (lǐ·văd'ǐ·à). 1 (*Gr.* lyê·vä'thyä) Var. of LEBADEA, Greece. 2 (*Russ.* lyǐ·vä'dyǐ·yà) Suburb of Yalta, Crimea; imperial palaces; residence of former tsars; buildings now used as Soviet sanitariums, hotels, etc.

Li'ven·good (lǐ'vĕn·gŏod). Village, E cen. Alaska, ab. 25 m. N of Fairbanks; pop. (1950) 40.

Li·ven'za (lê·vĕn'tsä). River 70 m. long in Venezia Euganea, NE Italy, N of Piave river; flows from the Alps SE into Adriatic Sea.

Live Oak (lĭv). 1 County in Texas. See *Table* at TEXAS. 2 City, ⊗ of Suwannee co., N Florida, 62 m. NW of Gainesville; pop. 6544; tobacco market.

Liv'er·more (lǐv'ēr·mōr). 1 City, Alameda co., W California, 23 m E of San Francisco Bay; pop. 16,058; magnesite mines in vicinity. 2 City, McLean co., W Kentucky, 18 m. S of Owensboro, pop. 1506; chair factories.

Livermore, Mount; *or* **Bald'y Peak** (bôl'dǐ). Mountain 8382 ft. in Jeff Davis co., W Texas, one of Davis Mts.

Livermore Falls. Town, Androscoggin co., SW Maine, 26 m. N of Lewiston; pop. 3343; paper mills.

Liv′er·pool (lĭv′ẽr·pōōl). **1** Village, Onondaga co., cen. New York, 5 m. N of Syracuse; pop. 3487; manufactures airplane and truck motors; salt deposits.
2 Town, E New South Wales, SE Australia, ab. 16 m. WSW ,of Sydney; pop. 6315.
3 Town, ⊗ of Queens co., SW Nova Scotia, Canada, on Atlantic Ocean 74 m. SW of Halifax; pop. 3535; trades in fish and lumber; shipbuilding, tanning, and leather manufacturing, iron founding, granite milling. Founded 1759 by New England settlers; base of operations for British privateers during American Revolution and War of 1812.
4 County borough and city, Lancashire, NW England, on the Mersey river estuary; pop. 855,688, (1951) 789,532; port and shipping point, second only to London in commercial importance; extensive docks; known especially for its flour mills, and formerly also for its pottery; the cathedral (started 1904 and still under construction; as planned will be the largest in England). Liverpool University (1881). In World War II repeatedly bombed 1940–41 by German planes.
Liverpool Range. Mountains, NE New South Wales, SE Australia; highest point Oxleys Peak 4500 ft.; extends W from Great Dividing Range, SW of New England Plateau.
Liv′ing·ston (lĭv′ĭng·stŭn). **1** Name of a parish in Louisiana and of counties in five states of the U.S. See *Tables* at LOUISIANA, ILLINOIS, KENTUCKY, MICHIGAN, MISSOURI, NEW YORK.
2 Town, ⊗ of Sumter co., W Alabama; pop. 1544; Livingston State College (1883; coed.).
3 Village, ⊗ of Livingston parish, SE Louisiana, 27 m. E of Baton Rouge; pop. 1183.
4 City, ⊗ of Park co., S Montana, 95 m. SE of Helena; pop. 8229; in agricultural and livestock-raising section.
5 Town, Essex co., NE New Jersey, 9 m. NW of Newark; pop. 23,124; in dairy, poultry, and truck-farming section.
6 Town, ⊗ of Overton co., N Tennessee, 20 m. NNE of Cookeville; pop. 2817.
7 Town, ⊗ of Polk co., E Texas, 45 m. SSW of Lufkin; pop. 3398; sawmills; oil, livestock, farm products.
Lí′ving·ston (lĭv′ĭng·stŭn; *Span.* lē′vĕn·stôn). Port, Izabal dept., E Guatemala, on Honduras Bay 14 m. NW of Puerto Barrios; pop. 5151; bananas, coffee.
Liv′ing·stone (lĭv′ĭng·stŭn). **1** Island in center of Victoria Falls, Zambezi river, bet. Northern Rhodesia and Southern Rhodesia.
2 Town, S Northern Rhodesia, near Victoria Falls on Zambezi river 250 m. WNW of Bulawayo; pop. 9526; ✳ of Batoka prov. and former ✳ of Northern Rhodesia until 1931; retains some of the colony's administrative posts. Seat of Rhodes-Livingstone Institute of Central African Studies (1937).
Livingstone Mountains. Range on NE border of Lake Nyasa, S Tanganyika, E Africa; highest point ab. 7000 ft.
Liv′ing·sto′ni·a (lĭv′ĭng·stō′nĭ·ȧ). Settlement, N Nyasaland protectorate, SE Africa, on NW shore of Lake Nyasa; mission headquarters, founded 1875, of United Free Church of Scotland.
Liv′ing·ston Island (lĭv′ĭng·stŭn). Island, W end of South Shetland Is., Falkland Islands Dependencies, on S side of Drake Passage; 37 m. long by 5 to 19 m. wide, in 62°35′S, 60°35′W. Discovered 1819; sealing station in international usage since 1820.
Liv′ny (lĭv′nĭ; *Russ.* lyēv′-). Town, SE Orel Region, cen. Soviet Russia, Europe, 28 m. SW of Yelets; pop. 21,000.
Li·vo′ni·a (lĭ·vō′nĭ·ȧ; -vōn′yȧ). City, Wayne co., SE Michigan, W of Detroit; pop. 66,702.
Li·vo′ni·a (lĭ·vō′nĭ·ȧ; -vōn′yȧ) *or* **Liv′land** (lĭv′lănd; -lănd; *Ger.* lēf′länt; *Russ.* **Li·vo′ni·ya** (lyĭ·vô′nyĭ·y·ȧ). Former government in Russia's Baltic Provinces in region E of the Baltic Sea, now included in Latvia and Estonia. Inhabited originally by Livs, a Finnish people, neighbors of the Letts and Esths; in 13th cent. conquered

and converted to Christianity by Livonian Brothers of the Sword, who in 1237 united with Teutonic Knights; eastern expansion and Christianization continued through 14th and 15th cents.; region disputed by Poland, Sweden, and Russia in Livonian War 1557–82; except for Tartu, which Russia took, became Polish 1561 and grand master of former order became duke of Kurland (*q.v.*); conquered by Gustavus Adolphus of Sweden 1629 and cession confirmed by Treaty of Oliva 1660. Ceded to Russia 1721 (as result of Great Northern War); freed from Russia, N part became part of Estonia and S part joined to Latvia 1918 (Vidzeme prov.).
Li·vor′no (lē·vôr′nô). **1** Province of Italy. See *Table* at ITALY.
2 See LEGHORN.
Li·vra·men′to (lē·vrȧ·mäNn′tŏō); *formerly* **Sant′·An′na do Livramento** (săNn·tȧ′nȧ thŏō). City, Rio Grande do Sul state, S Brazil, on Uruguay border opp. Rivera; livestock, dried meat and fruit center; pop. (1940 est.) 27,048.
Li′vry′-Gar′gan′ (lē′vrē′gȧr′gäN′). Commune, Seine-et-Oise dept., N France, ENE suburb of Paris; pop. (1931) 21,366.
Lixus. See LARACHE.
Liz. See LIS.
Liz′ard, the (lĭz′ẽrd). Peninsula, S Cornwall, SW England, extending S from Helston and Helford river; its S end is extreme S point of Great Britain, **Lizard Point** or **Lizard Head**, 49°57′30″N, 5°12′W; fine scenery; lighthouses and signal station for ships.
Lju′blja·na (lyōō′blyä·nä); *Ger.* **Lai′bach** (lī′bäк); *anc.* **E·mo′na** (ē·mō′nȧ). City, ✳ of Slovenia, NW Yugoslavia, on Sava river; pop. 79,056; railroad, industrial, and commercial center; iron foundries, machine shops, paper mills; cathedral, university, museum, art gallery. Ancient city of Emona founded by Augustus 34 B.C.; besieged by Alaric 400 A.D. and left in ruins by the Huns 451. Became part of Carinthia 12th cent.; came under rule of Hapsburgs 1277; capital of Illyrian Provinces 1809–13; capital of kingdom of Illyria 1816–49; meeting place 1821 of a congress of European powers (Congress of Laibach) which authorized Austria to use force to crush liberal revolutionary movements in Italy.
Ljung′an (yŭng′ȧn). River 234 m. long, Västernorrland prov., E Sweden; flows SE to the Gulf of Bothnia near Sundsvall.
Ljus′nan (yōōs′nän). River 267 m. long, cen. Sweden; rises on Norway border and flows SE into the Gulf of Bothnia S of Söderhamn.
Llan·ber′is (lăn·bĕr′ĭs; hlăn-). Village and parish, Caernarvonshire, NW Wales, S of Bangor near the foot of Mt. Snowdon; pop. (parish) 2373; at entrance to the **Pass of Llanberis**, 1169 ft., narrow, rocky defile.
Llan′daff (lăn′dăf; lăn·dăf′; hlăn[′]-). Suburb of Cardiff, Glamorganshire, SE Wales; cathedral.
Llan·do′ve·ry (lăn·dŭ′vrĭ; hlăn-). Town, Carmarthenshire, S Wales, NE of Carmarthen; pop. 1856; remains of Norman castle; school, founded 1848; noted for printing press in early 19th cent.
Llan·drin′dod Wells (lăn·drĭn′dŏd wĕlz; hlăn-). Urban district, ⊗ of Radnorshire, E Wales; pop. 3213; mineral springs; health resort.
Llan·dud′no (lăn·dĭd′nō; -dŭd′-; hlăn-). Urban district, NE Caernarvonshire, NW Wales; pop. 16,712; on the small peninsula terminating in Great Ormes Head; watering place.
Lla·nel′ly (lă·nĕl′ĭ; hlă·nĕ′hlĭ). Municipal borough and commercial seaport, Carmarthenshire, S Wales; pop. 34,329; exports coal; tin-plate and steel works, chemical plants, potteries.
Lla·ne′ra (lyä·nā′rä; yä-). Commune, Oviedo prov., NW Spain, 6 m. from Oviedo; pop. 11,424; fruits, vegetables, coal.
Lla′nes (lyä′nȧs; yä′-). Seaport commune, Oviedo prov., NW Spain, on Bay of Biscay 58 m. ENE of Oviedo; pop.

20,421; large coastal trade; fish-salting works; 14th-cent. Gothic cathedral.

Llan′fair (lăn′fâr; *Welsh* hlăn′vīr) *or* **Llan′fair·pwll-gwyn′gyll** (hlăn′vīr·pōō′h'l·gwin′gĭ·h'l). Village, SE Anglesey I., NW Wales, on Menai Strait; its full name (variously spelled) has 54 to 58 letters.

Llan·gef′ni (lăn·gĕv′nĭ; hlăn-). Urban district, ⊗ of Anglesey, NW Wales; pop. 2225.

Llan·gol′len (lăn·gŏl′ĕn; hlăn·gŏ′hlĕn). Town and urban district, SE Denbighshire, N Wales; pop. (urban district) 3275; summer resort; manufactures flannel.

Llan·id′loes (lăn·ĭd′lois; hlăn-). Town and municipal borough, Montgomeryshire, cen. Wales, on the Severn; pop. 2341; market center for an agricultural region; formerly had important publishing industry, was center for lead-mining district (esp. 1860–80), and manufactured shawls and tweeds until 1918.

Llanitos, Los. See Los LLANITOS.

Llan′o (lăn′ō). **1** River ab. 175 m. long, cen. Texas; rises in Sutton co., flows E into Colorado river on E boundary of Llano co.
2 County in Texas. See *Table* at TEXAS.
3 City, ⊗ of Llano co., cen. Texas, on Llano river 62 m. NW of Austin; pop. 2656; railroad terminus; granite quarries; trade in wool, mohair, livestock.

Lla′no de la Mag′da·le′na (yä′nō thä lä mäg′thä-lā′nä). Extensive plain in SW Lower California, NW Mexico.

Llan′o Es′ta·ca′do (lăn′ō ĕs′tä·kä′dō) *or* **Staked Plain** (stākt). Extensive plateau bet. 1000 and 5000 ft. high in SE New Mexico and W Texas.

Lla′nos (lä′nōz; *Span.* yä′nōs). Vast plains in N South America adjacent to and drained by the Orinoco river and its tributaries; ab. 40,000 sq. m.

Llan·qui′hue (yäng·kē′wä). Province of Chile. See *Table* at CHILE.

Llanquihue, Lake. Lake in S cen. Chile, in Llanquihue prov. just N of Puerto Montt; ab. 240 sq. m.; drains directly into Pacific Ocean.

Llan·tar′nam (lăn·tär′năm; *Welsh* hlăn·târ′năm). Former urban district, Monmouthshire, W England, 21 m. NW of Bristol; pop. (1931) 7283.

Llan′twit Major (lăn′twĭt; hlăn′-). Village and parish, S Glamorganshire, SE Wales, on Bristol Channel; pop. (parish) ab. 1500; site of monastery, estab. 6th cent. by St. Illtyd, a native of Brittany, famous as a school; church of St. Illtyd, with remains of early Celtic Christianity; ruins of a Roman villa.

Llay′–Llay (yī′yī′). Commune, Valparaíso prov., cen. Chile; on railroad midway bet. Valparaíso and Santiago; pop. 9245.

Lle·re′na, Point (yä·rā′nä). Cape on W coast of Osa Penin., S Costa Rica.

Llew·el′lyn Park (lōō·ĕl′ĭn). Suburb of West Orange, New Jersey.

Lleyn Peninsula *or* **Promontory** (līn; hlīn). Headland extending SW into St. George's Channel from NW coast of Wales, 24 m. long, 5 to 10 m. wide; encloses Cardigan Bay on N.

Llo′bre·gat′ (lyō′vrä·gät′; yō′-). River ab. 90 m. long in NE Spain; flows S into Mediterranean Sea 3 m. S of Barcelona.

Lloyd′min′ster (loid′mĭn′stēr). Town, Saskatchewan, Canada, on Alberta-Saskatchewan border 82 m. WNW of North Battleford; pop. (Sask.) 2232, (Alta.) 1706, (total) 3938; in fine farming region; headquarters of "all-British" colony established 1903.

Lloyd Shoals Reservoir (loid shōlz). Reservoir over 4½ sq. m. in NW Jasper co., cen. Georgia; formed by dam (built 1910) in Ocmulgee river.

Llul′lail·la′co (yōō′yī·yä′kō). Volcano 22,057 ft. in Andes Mts., N Chile, just W of Argentina boundary.

Llw′chwr (lōō′kōōr; hlōō′-) *or* **Lou′ghor** (lŭ′кēr). Urban district, Glamorganshire, SE Wales; pop. 25,737.

Lo (lō). River ab. 140 m. long, E cen. China; rises in E

Shensi prov. and flows ENE to the Hwang Ho E of Loyang in N Honan.

Lo′a (lō′à). Town, ⊗ of Wayne co., S cen. Utah; pop. 359.

Lo′a (lō′ä). River ab. 275 m. long in Antofagasta prov., N Chile, flowing into the Pacific Ocean.

Loanda. See LUANDA.

Lo·an′ge (lō·äng′gĕ); *Port.* **Lu·an′gue** (lwäNng′gĕ). River ab. 425 m. long in the Congo basin, S cen. Africa; rises in NE cen. Angola, flows N into Kasai river in SW Congo, forming boundary bet. Léopoldville and Lusambo provs.

Lo·an′go (lō·äng′gō). **1** Former African kingdom N of Congo river, part of the ancient kingdom of Congo. **2** Seaport, S Congo Republic (formerly Middle Congo territory), equatorial Africa, ab. 100 m. N of the mouth of the Congo; pop. ab. 12,000.

Lo·ang′wa (lō·äng′wä). = LUANGWA.

Lo·a′no (lō·ä′nō). Commune, Savona prov., Liguria, NW Italy, on Italian Riviera 17 m. SW of Savona; pop. (1931) 5134; scene of victory of French over Austrians Nov. 23–24, 1795.

Lö′bau (lû′bou). Industrial city, Dresden dist., East Germany, in Saxony 40 m. E of Dresden; pop. 12,635; textiles, shoes, pianos, rubber goods, sugar.

Lo·be·to′la (lō′bĕ·tō′lä). Mountain 5394 ft. at S end of Lomblen I., Lesser Sunda Is., Indonesia; an active volcano.

Lo·bi′to (lō·vē′tōō). Seaport on **Lobito Bay,** W cen. Angola; pop. 13,592.

Lob Nor. See LOP NOR.

Lo′bos (lō′vōs). Island in Gulf of Mexico off coast of N Veracruz state, Mexico.

Lobos, Cape. Cape on coast of W cen. Sonora state, Mexico, extending into the Gulf of California.

Lo′bos, Cay (kē′ lō′bŭs) *or* **Lobos Cay.** Small island of S Bahama Is., separated by Old Bahama Channel from NE cen. Cuba; lighthouse (estab. 1860).

Lo′bos, Point (lō′bōs). **1** Point, San Francisco, California, on S side of entrance to Golden Gate. **2** Promontory, Monterey co., California, on Carmel Bay SW of Carmel; state park.

Lo′bos Islands (lō′vōs); *sometimes called* **Seal Islands** (sēl). Two groups of small islands in Pacific Ocean off N coast of Peru, including **Lo′bos de Tier′ra** (lō′vōz thä tyĕr′rä) and **Lobos de A·fue′ra** (ä·fwä′rä); rich deposits of guano.

Lobositz. See LOVOSICE.

Lob′stick′ Lake (lŏb′stĭk′). Large lake of irregular shape, W Labrador, SE of Dyke Lake; forms part of course of Hamilton river.

Loburi. See LOP BURI.

Lo·car′no (lō·kär′nō); *Ger.* **Lug·ga′rus** (lōō·gä′rōōs). Commune, Ticino canton, SE cen. Switzerland, on N shore of Lake Maggiore 11 m. W of Bellinzona; pop. (1930) 6575; winter and health resort; site of old castle of dukes of Milan (now seat of government buildings). First mentioned 749 A.D.; passed to dukes of Milan 1342; taken by Swiss 1512; part of former Swiss canton of Lugano 1798–1803; scene of signing Dec. 1, 1925 of Locarno Pact, a series of five treaties and arbitration conventions bet. Germany, on the one hand, and Belgium, France, Great Britain, Italy, Poland, and Czechoslovakia on the other, designed to guarantee the continuation of peace and existing territorial boundaries.

Loch·a′ber (lŏĸ·ä′bēr; -ăb′ēr). Mountainous district in SW Inverness co., NW Scotland, at W end of the Grampians and NE of Loch Linnhe; includes Ben Nevis.

Loch′ar Moss (lŏĸ′ēr mŏs). Tract of moorland 10 m. long in Dumfries co., S Scotland.

Loch·gel′ly (lŏĸ·gĕl′ĭ). Burgh, Fife co., E Scotland, W of Kirkcaldy; pop. 9102; ironworks, collieries.

Loch·gilp′head (lŏĸ·gĭlp′hĕd). Burgh, ⊗ of Argyll co., W Scotland, at head of arm of Firth of Clyde 15 m. N of Greenock; pop. 1229; herring fishing.

Loch·iel' (lŏκ·ēl'; lŏk-). A district in Argyll and Inverness cos., Scotland.

Loch·ma'ben (lŏκ·mā'bĕn). Royal burgh and parish, Dumfries co., S Scotland, 8 m. NE of Dumfries; pop. (1951) 1127; several lakes in district; resort; ruins of castle; associated with Robert Bruce.

Loch Ra'ven (lŏk rā'vĕn). Urban community (unincorporated), Baltimore co., N Maryland, N of Baltimore; pop. 23,278.

Loch'y, Loch (lŏк lŏκ'ĭ). Lake 9 m. long, N cen. Scotland, in Inverness co.

Locke, Mount (lŏk). Peak 6828 ft. in Davis Mts., Jeff Davis co., W Texas; on its top McDonald Observatory, 3d largest in the world, opened May 5, 1939.

Lock'hart (lŏk'härt). **1** Village, Union co., NW South Carolina, on Broad river ab. 9 m. NE of Union; pop. 128; textile mills; hydroelectric power. **2** City, ⊗ of Caldwell co., S cen. Texas, 29 m. S of Austin; pop. 6084; cotton, livestock, poultry; oil fields.

Lock Ha'ven (lŏk hā'vĕn). City, ⊗ of Clinton co., cen. Pennsylvania, on West Branch of Susquehanna river 25 m. WSW of Williamsport; pop. 11,748; manufactures paper, brick, textiles, chemicals, metal products; Lock Haven State College (1877; coed.). Settled 1769; lumber center in 19th cent.

Lock'land (lŏk'lănd). City, Hamilton co., SW corner of Ohio, 9 m. N of Cincinnati; pop. 5292; manufactures paper products, chemicals, fertilizers, mattresses.

Lock'port (lŏk'pōrt). **1** City, Will co., NE Illinois, 30 m. SW of Chicago; pop. 7560; site of a lock and dam marking the end of the Chicago Sanitary and Ship Canal in the Illinois Waterway system; oil refinery. **2** Manufacturing city, ⊗ of Niagara co., W New York, 20 m. ENE of Niagara Falls; pop. 26,443; on N.Y. State Barge Canal; in agricultural and fruitgrowing region; sandstone and limestone quarries.

Locle, Le. See LE LOCLE.

Lo'cri (lō'krī; lŏk'rī). Ancient city in Magna Graecia, on E coast of SW extremity of Italy; founded ab. 683 B.C.; the Locrian code, framed by Zaleucus, said to be earliest written system of Greek legislation.

Lo'cris (lō'krĭs; lŏk'rĭs). Region in cen. part of ancient Greece, comprising: **Eastern Locris**, divided into two parts: **Locris Ep'ic·ne·mid'i·a** (ĕp'ĭ[k]·nē·mĭd'ĭ·à), along S shore of Gulf of Lamia extending E from Pass of Thermopylae and bordering on Malis, Doris, and Phocis; separated by narrow strip of Phocis from **Locris O·pun'ti·a** (ô·pŭn'shĭ·à) on Euboean Sea (mod. Atalante channel) opp. Euboea, E of Phocis and N of Boeotia; chief town Opus. **Western Locris, or Locris Oz'o·lis** (ŏz'ô·lĭs) (ŏz'ô·lĭs), mountainous region along N shore of strait joining Gulfs of Calydon (mod. Gulf of Patras) and Corinth, S of Aetolia and W of Phocis; chief town Amphissa. Locrians were probably early inhabitants of Greece, long subject to Phocians.

Lo'cust Gap (lō'kŭst). Locality, Northumberland co., E cen. Pennsylvania, ab. 6 m. E of Shamokin; pop. (1950) 1041.

Locust Grove. Urban community (unincorporated), Nassau co., SE New York, on Long I.; pop. 11,558.

Locust Mountain. Ridge in Schuylkill co., E cen. Pennsylvania; contains rich coal deposits.

Lod. See LYDDA.

Lo'de·lin'sart' (lôd'lăn'sàr'). Commune, Hainaut prov., SW Belgium, N suburb of Charleroi; pop. 11,220.

Lo'dève' (lô'dâv'); anc. **Lu·te'va** (lû·tē'và). Commune, N Hérault dept., S France, in S Cévennes; pop. (1931) 7020; cathedral, founded 950; manufactures woolens. Dates from pre-Roman times.

Lodge'pole' Creek (lŏj'pōl'). River ab. 150 m. long, SE Wyoming and W Nebraska, flowing E into South Platte river near Nebraska-Colorado boundary.

Lo'di (lō'dī). **1** City, San Joaquin co., cen. California, 12 m. N of Stockton; pop. 22,229; vineyards, grain, poultry; fruit and vegetable packing.

2 Industrial borough, Bergen co., NE corner of New Jersey, 5 m. SE of Paterson; pop. 23,502; manufactures dyes, chemicals.

Lo'di (lō'dē). Manufacturing commune, Milano prov., Lombardy, N Italy, on Adda river 20 m. SE of Milan; pop. 30,636; 12th-cent. cathedral; episcopal palace; majolica, dairy products. Built 1158 by Barbarossa 4 m. from the ancient Lodi destroyed by the Milanese in 1111; scene of defeat of Austrians by Napoleon May 10, 1796.

Lod'o·me'ri·a (lŏd'ô·mēr'ĭ·à). Principality of 12th and 13th cents. in Volhynia—also known as **Vlad'i·mir in Vol·hyn'i·a** (vlăd'ĭ·mĭr ĭn vŏl·hĭn'ĭ·à; vô·lĭn'-); joined with Halicz in 13th cent. to become part of Poland and later (1772) a division of Galicia. See VLADIMIR VOLYNSK.

Lo·dore' (lô·dōr'). Waterfall in the Lake District, Cumberland, NW England, near head of Derwentwater.

Łódź (lŏŏj); Russ. **Lodz** (lôts'y'). **1** Department in cen. Poland; 7876 sq. m.; pop. 2,633,050. **2** Industrial city, its *, 70 m. WSW of Warsaw; pop. (1938–39 est.) 672,000; episcopal see; most important textile center (esp. cotton) of Poland. Before World War I belonged to Russians, who in 19th cent. developed it from small village into large industrial city; occupied by Germans Nov. 11–25, 1914 after severe fighting; became part of Poland 1918; in World War II occupied by Germans Sept. 1939.

Loe'i or **Loe'y** (lû'ĭ). **1** Province, N Thailand; 4339 sq. m.; pop. 113,187; * Loei. **2** Town, its *, 20 m. S of the Mekong 90 m. E of Uttaradit.

Loe'ma·djang' (lōō'mä·jäng') or **Lu'ma·jang'**. Town, East Java prov., Indonesia, in plain E of Mt Semeru and S of Probolinggo; pop. 18,838.

Lo'fo'ten (lō'fō't'n, almost lōō'fōō't'n). Island group in Norwegian Sea off NW coast of Norway, in Nordland co. SW of Vesterålen; 475 sq. m.; pop. 24,884; principal islands Austvågöy, Vestvågöy, Moskenes; valuable fisheries.

Lof'tus (lŏf'tŭs). **1** Town in suburban area of Sydney, New South Wales, Australia, ab. 15 m. S of center of city. **2** Urban district, North Riding, Yorkshire, N England; pop. 7423.

Lo'gan (lō'găn). **1** Counties in ten states of the U.S. See Tables at ARKANSAS, COLORADO, ILLINOIS, KANSAS, KENTUCKY, NEBRASKA, NORTH DAKOTA, OHIO, OKLAHOMA, WEST VIRGINIA. **2** Town, ⊗ of Harrison co., W Iowa, 25 m. N of Council Bluffs; pop. 1605. **3** City, ⊗ of Hocking co., S cen. Ohio, 16 m. SE of Lancaster; pop. 6417; oil and gas wells, coal and clay deposits; manufactures shoes, brick, tile, pottery, furniture. Founded 1816. **4** City, ⊗ of Cache co., N Utah, 36 m. N of Ogden; pop. 18,731; dairying, canning; manufactures condensed milk, textiles, beet sugar. Mormon Tabernacle and Mormon Temple; Utah State Univ. of Agriculture and Applied Science (1888; coed.). Settled by Mormons c. 1855, incorp. 1886. **5** City, ⊗ of Logan co., SW West Virginia, 20 m. NE of Williamson; pop. 4185; coal mining, farming, lumbering.

Logan, Mount. 1 Peak 7700 ft. in N Mohave co., NW Arizona. **2** Peak 19,850 ft. in St. Elias Range in SW Yukon Territory, Canada, near Alaska boundary; 2d highest mountain in North America.

Logan Mountain. Peak 9252 ft. in Glacier National Park, NW Montana.

Lo'gans·port (lō'gănz·pōrt). City, ⊗ of Cass co., N cen. Indiana, 22 m. NNW of Kokomo; pop. 21,106; shipping center for corn and hogs; manufactures furniture, farm implements, automobile accessories.

Lo'gone' (lô'gôn'). River in NW equatorial Africa, bet. Chad and Cameroun; flows N into Chari river.

Lo·gro'ño (lô·grō'nyô). **1** Province of Spain. See *Table* at SPAIN.

2 *anc.* **Ju'li·ob'ri·ga** (jōō'lĭ·ŏb'rĭ·gà), *later* **Lu·cro'ni·us** (lŭ·krō'nĭ·ŭs). Commune, its ✱, N Spain, on Ebro river 155 m. NNE of Madrid; pop. (1941 est.) 47,635; manufactures and trades in wine, esp. Spanish burgundy; ancient city walls, bridge (built 1138). Captured by Moors 8th cent.; unsuccessfully besieged by French 1521; occupied by French 1808–13.

Lög'stör Bred'ning (lûg'stûr brĕd'nĭng). Wide section (ab. 13 m.) in cen. part of Lim Fjord, N Jutland, Denmark.

Lo·gu'no, Cape (lō̄·gōō'nō̄). Cape extending into NW Mozambique Channel on NE coast of Mozambique, SE Africa.

Lo·ha'ru (lō·hä'rōō). Former Indian state, Punjab States, SE East Punjab, W of Jind, NW India; 226 sq. m.; pop. (1941) 27,892; ✱ Loharu (pop. 2956).

Loheiya. See LUHAIYA.

Loibl (loi'b'l). Pass 4480 ft. high over the Karawanken Alps, connecting with fine highway Klagenfurt in Carinthia, Austria, and Ljubljana in NW Yugoslavia.

Loi'kaw' (loi'kô'). Town, ✱ of Karenni dist., E Burma, on a railway branch of the Salween ab. 70 m. NE of Toungoo.

Loi'pyet' Hills (loi'pyĕt'). Range of hills in N Burma, S of Kumon Range and W of upper Irrawaddy.

Loir (lwär; *Fr.* lwàr). River 195 m. long in NW cen. France; rises in Eure-et-Loir dept., flows W into Sarthe river 5 m. N of Angers.

Loire (lwär; *Fr.* lwàr). **1** *anc.* **Li'ger** (lī'jer). Longest river in France, 625 m. long; rises in Ardèche dept., SE France, flows N and NW to Orléans, then turns W and flows through Blois, Tours, and Nantes and empties into Bay of Biscay by a wide estuary below Saint-Nazaire; navigable.

2 Departments of France: **Haute'–Loire'** (ōt'lwàr'); **Loire;** and **Loire'–At'lan'tique'** (-àt'län'tēk'), *formerly* **Loire'–In'fé'rieure'** (-ăn'fā'ryûr'). See *Table* at France.

Loi'ret' (lwà'rĕ'). Department of France. See *Table* at FRANCE.

Loir–et–Cher (lwàr'ā·shâr'). Department of France. See *Table* at FRANCE.

Lo·i'za (lō·ē'sä); *formerly* **Ca·nó'va·nas** (kä·nō'vänäs). Municipality (pop. 28,131) and town (pop. 3007), NE Puerto Rico; town is on railroad ab. 17 m. ESE of San Juan.

Loíza Al·de'a (äl·dā'ä). Village in Loíza municipality, NE Puerto Rico; pop. 2330.

Lo'ja (lō'hä). **1** Province of Ecuador. See *Table* at ECUADOR.

2 City, its ✱, SW Ecuador, on Zamora river ab. 133 m. SSE of Guayaquil; pop. (1944 est.) 20,776; founded 1546; gold, silver, and copper mined in vicinity.

3 *earlier* **Lo'xa** (lō'hä). Commune, Granada prov., S Spain, on Genil river 21 m. W of Granada; pop. 23,998; manufactures textiles, leather, chocolates, pottery, paper; ancient churches, ducal palace, Moorish citadel. As important strategic point in defense of Granada, strongly fortified by Moors; reconquered by Ferdinand III 1226 and by Ferdinand and Isabella 1486.

Lo'ke·ren (lō'kĕ·rĕ[n]). Commune, East Flanders prov., NW cen. Belgium, 23 m. NW of Brussels; pop. (1938 est.) 25,398; scene of fighting Oct. 9, 1914, resulting in forced withdrawal of the British across Dutch frontier.

Lo·ko'ja (lō·kō'jà). Town, ✱ of Kabba prov., S Northern Region, Nigeria, on Niger river at mouth of Benue river; pop. ab. 8000. Founded 1860; formerly capital of Northern Nigeria.

Lok'tak Lake (lŏk'tăk). Marshy lake ab. 25 sq. m. in S Manipur state, NE India; its outlet is the Manipur river.

Lol'land (lŏl'ånd; *Danish* lō'lån) *or* **Laa'land** (lō'län). Island of Denmark, lying in Baltic Sea S of Sjælland and W of Falster; 477 sq. m.; pop. (1925) 86,657; with Falster forms Maribo co., Denmark.

Lo'lo·bau (lō'lō·bou). Small island in Bismarck Sea off N coast of E end of New Britain I., Bismarck Archipelago.

Lom *or* **Lom–Pa·lan'ka** (lôm'pä·läng'kä). Town, Vrattsa dept., NW Bulgaria, on Danube river; pop. (1926) 14,417.

Lo'mai Vi'ti (lō'mī vē'tĕ). Literally "Middle Fiji"; group of scattered islands on W side of Koro Sea bet. Vanua Levu and Kandavu, Fiji Is., SW Pacific Ocean; chief islands Koro, Ovalau, Ngau, Moala, Makongai, Nairai, and Batiki.

Lo'ma·lo'ma (lō'må·lō'må). Chief town of the Exploring Is., E Fiji Is., SW Pacific Ocean, on S shore of Vanua Mbalavu I.; has good harbor.

Lo·ma'mi (lō·mä'mĕ). River ab. 900 m. long in Congo; rises in S cen. part, flows N parallel with and W of the Lualaba and the upper Congo and empties into the Congo below Stanleyville.

Lo'mas (lō'mäs) *or* **Lo'mas de Za·mo'ra** (lō'mäz sä·mō'rä). City, Buenos Aires prov., E Argentina, a suburb of Buenos Aires (city); pop. 125,943.

Loma Tina. See Monte TRUJILLO.

Lom'bard (lŏm'bärd). Residential village, Du Page co., NE Illinois, 20 m. W of Chicago; pop. 22,561.

Lom'bar·dy (lŏm'bĕr·dĭ; -bär'dĭ; lŭm'-); *Ital.* **Lombar·di'a** (lōm·bär·dē'ä). Compartimento of N Italy; for provincial divisions, area, and pop. see *Table* at ITALY; in Italian Alps bet. Piedmont and Venezia Tridentina and Venezia Euganea; contains numerous Alpine peaks and glaciers and beautiful lakes; descends to richly fertile valley of Po river; important both agriculturally and industrially.

History: Center of kingdom founded in Po valley by Lombards, a German people who invaded Italy in 6th cent. A.D.; kingdom extended rule over almost all of Italy (except south) until it was crushed by Charlemagne 773–774; became part of Carolingian empire and of Holy Roman Empire; cities of Lombard plain formed 1167 Lombard League against Emperor Frederick I whom they defeated 1176 at Legnano; cities received independence by peace signed 1183; Lombard territory came to be scene of rise of duchy of Milan (*q.v.*) which became Spanish 1535; ceded to Austria 1713; became part of Napoleon's Cisalpine Republic 1797 and kingdom of Italy 1805; restored to Austria as part of Lombardo-Venetian kingdom 1815; ceded to Napoleon III of France who turned it over to Piedmont 1859 (see ITALY).

Lom'bart·zy'de (lôm'bärt·zī'dĕ). Commune, West Flanders prov., NW Belgium, near Nieuwpoort; pop. 903; scene of battles Oct. and Nov. 1914 and July 10, 1917 during World War I.

Lom·blen' (lŏm·blĕn'). Island of the Lesser Sunda Is., Indonesia, E of Flores I. and separated from Pantar I. by Alor Strait; 468 sq. m.; ab. 50 m. long by 22 m. wide, of irregular shape. Has numerous mountains, highest Lobetola 5394 ft., an active volcano.

Lom·bok' (lŏm·bŏk'). Island of the Lesser Sunda Is., Indonesia, E of Bali I.; ab. 70 m. long by 50 m. at widest point; 1825 sq. m.; pop. 701,290; ✱ Mataram. Separated on W from Bali by Lombok Strait, and on E from Sumbawa by Alas Strait. Has two mountain ranges, one along N coast and the other along the S, with wide valley between; in N range is the volcano Rindjani 12,224 ft., one of highest mountains in Indonesia. Mountain regions forest-clad and undeveloped, lowlands highly cultivated. Its fauna and flora of great interest because the island, situated on Wallace's line, marks a meeting point of Asian and Australian forms. In early times under Sultan of Makassar; suffered from piracy in 17th cent. and later subject to Bali; began relations with Dutch 1843 and came entirely under their control by 1894.

Lom'bok' Strait (lŏm'bŏk'). Channel ab. 22 m. wide bet. E Bali I. and W Lombok I., Indonesia, connecting W Flores Sea with the Indian Ocean; of interest to scien-

tists as an important part of Wallace's line. In its SW branch, Badung Strait, bet. SE Bali and the small island of Nusa Besar was fought Feb. 19, 1942 an important naval engagement of World War II in which a Dutch fleet inflicted considerable damage on the Japanese fleet, also sometimes called the battle of Lombok Strait.

Lo·mé′ (lō′mā′). Seaport town, ✳ of Republic of Togo, W Africa; pop. (1958) 64,000; former ✳ of French Togo and of German protectorate of Togo; connected by rail with inland towns and with other coast towns.

Lo·me′la (lō′mā′là). **1** River 290 m. long in cen. Congo; flows NW into Tshuapa river. **2** Town, N Lusambo prov., S cen. Congo, on the Lomela river N of Lusambo; air terminus.

Lo·mié′ (lō′myā′). Town, SE Cameroun.

Lo·mi′ta (lō-mē′tà). Urban community (unincorporated), Los Angeles co., SW California, SE of Torrance; pop. 14,983.

Lomme (lôm). Commune, Nord dept., N France, WNW suburb of Lille; pop. (1931) 20,684; spinning mills; clothing, hats, partially destroyed in World War I.

Lom′mel (lôm′ĕl). Commune, N Limburg prov., Belgium; pop. 9666.

Lomond, Ben. See BEN LOMOND.

Lo′mond, Loch (lŏk lō′mŭnd). Lake in Stirling and Dunbarton cos., S cen. Scotland; 27¼ sq. m., 24 m. long by ¾ to 5 m. wide, largest lake in Great Britain; surrounded by many mountains (Ben Lomond, Ben Vorlich); S part expands and contains many islets; Luss on W side and Balloch at S end are chief towns on its shores; on its E shore near Ben Lomond is the region made famous by Rob Roy, 18th-cent. outlaw of the clan Macgregor.

Lom–Palanka. See LOM.

Lom′po·ba′tang (lôm′pō·bä′täng); *formerly* **Bonthain′** (bôn·tīn′). Peak 9419 ft., SW Celebes, Indonesia, E of Makassar.

Lom′poc (lôm′pōk). City, Santa Barbara co., SW California, near Pacific Ocean 45 m. WNW of Santa Barbara; pop. 14,415; founded 1874; seed growing; Vandenberg Air Force Base (to the W).

Łom′ża (lôm′zhä); *Russ.* **Lom′zha** (lôm′zhà). City, W Białystok dept., NE Poland, on the Narew river 80 m. NE of Warsaw; pop. (1938–39 est.) 27,262; founded before the 9th cent.; long a prosperous commercial town, esp. in 16th cent.; later suffered in wars; in partition of Poland 1795 came under Prussian rule, then Russian 1807 to 1918. In World War II taken by Russians 1939, and by Germans 1941; retaken and included in White Russia 1944 but ceded back to Poland Aug. 1945.

Lo′na·co′ning (lō′nà·kō′nĭng). Town, Allegany co., NW Maryland, WSW of Cumberland; pop. 2077; coal.

Lo·na′to (lō·nä′tō). Commune, Brescia prov., Lombardy, N Italy, ab. 15 m. W of Brescia near S end of Lake Garda, pop. 9251; scene of an early victory of Napoleon over the Austrians Aug. 3, 1796.

Lon·co′che (lông·kō′chă). Town, Cautín prov., S cen. Chile; pop. 5109.

Lon′don (lŭn′dŭn). **1** City, ⊗ of Laurel co., SE Kentucky, 43 m. NW of Middlesborough; pop. 4035; trade center for agricultural section.
2 Manufacturing and agricultural city, ⊗ of Madison co., SW cen. Ohio, 23 m. W of Columbus; pop. 6379.
3 Industrial city, ⊗ of Middlesex co., SE Ontario, Canada, on Thames river 23 m. N of Lake Erie; pop. 95,343; founded 1826; Univ. of Western Ontario (1878); normal school; conservatory of music. Its port is Port Stanley on Lake Erie.
4 Administrative county in SE England, ✳ of the United Kingdom and of the British Empire; area 117 sq. m.; pop. 4,397,003, (1951) 3,348,336; lies on both sides of the Thames ab. 40 m. from its mouth. It comprises the **City of London,** *anc.* **Lon·din′i·um** (lŏn·dĭn′ĭ·ŭm), known as **the City** (the older part, now included in its financial and business district; 675 acres; pop. [1931]

10,999, [1951] 5268) and 28 metropolitan boroughs (see *Table,* p. 628), each with mayor, aldermen, and councilmen. The City is on N bank of the Thames in center of

LONDON
AND VICINITY
Statute Miles

the administrative county; governed by the City of London Corporation through its Lord Mayor, Courts of Aldermen, and Common Council; includes Fleet St., Newgate St., Cannon St., Cheapside, and many famous buildings, as St. Paul's Cathedral, the Temple (badly damaged 1941), Guildhall (damaged Dec. 1940), St. Bartholomew's Hospital, Post Office, Bank of England, etc.; its E border marked by the Tower; connected with S bank by five bridges (Tower, London, Cannon Street Railway, Southwark, and Blackfriars). The greatest commercial, industrial, and manufacturing center of the kingdom; has docks that cover 730 acres of water and quays 33 m. long; in the great railroad stations of the administrative county all the trunk lines of England converge; area served by extensive underground railroads (including "the tubes") which cross the Thames by several tunnels. Site of the Univ. of London (1836), with headquarters in Bloomsbury, having some 30 colleges or branches in Greater London including University College and the London School of Economics and Political Science, Queens College (1848; women), and many technical and professional institutions.

The administrative county and the **Outer Ring** (Middlesex and parts of Essex, Kent, Surrey, and Hertfordshire; area 576 sq. m.; pop. 3,806,939, [1951] 4,997,801) form **Greater London,** the metropolitan police area; total area 693 sq. m.; total pop. 8,203,942, (1951) 8,346,137, the largest city in the world.

History: From 43 to 409 A.D. a Roman town, Londinium; scene of revolt of Boadicea, Queen of Iceni (see GREAT BRITAIN, *History*) 61 A.D.; its fortifications, which had been destroyed by Danes 851, restored by Alfred the Great; from Anglo-Saxon times, grew as trade center of England; received charter privileges from 11th cent.; one of the Hanse Towns; city proper, governed by Lord Mayor and Aldermen of trade guilds, came to be the commercial center; Westminster (*q.v.*) the seat of English government; scene of Wat Tyler's rebellion 1381; in Wars of the Roses generally supported Yorkists; in Civil War (17th cent.) opposed to king and later to the Army; after the setbacks of severe plague 1665 and great fire 1666, grew to be the most populous city and most important trade center of the world; violently opposed James II; in 18th cent. Whig headquarters; scene of Gordon Riots 1780; by act of 1888 London area placed under London County Council; City of London and 28 self-governing metropolitan boroughs regulated according to act of 1899; in World War I raided by German planes and dirigibles 1915–18; in World War II suffered esp. 1940–41 from bombings by German planes and June–Sept. 1944 from robot bombs.

Treaties, etc.: Conference 1827–32 on establishment of kingdom of Greece; Treaty May 1852 determined suc-

LONDON—METROPOLITAN BOROUGHS

NAME	SQ. M.	POP. (1951)	LOCATION	BUILDINGS, LANDMARKS, ETC.
Bat'ter·sea (băt'ēr·sĭ)	3.38	117,130	SW; on S bank of Thames	Manufacturing; Battersea Park; 3 bridges across to Chelsea; St. Mary's Church (rebuilt 1776).
Ber'mond·sey (bûr'mŭn[d]·zĭ)	2.35	60,661	E cen.; on S bank of Thames	Tanners and saddlers. At NW corner connects by London Bridge with the City. Site of Bermondsey Abbey (1082).
Beth'nal Green (bĕth'n'l)	1.19	58,374	E; N of Stepney & Whitechapel	Manufacturing; Bethnal Green Museum (founded 1872); Victoria Park.
Cam'ber·well (kăm'bēr·wĕl; -wĕl)	7.00	179,729	S	Camberwell Green; St. Giles's Church; South London Art Gallery.
Chel'sea (chĕl'sĭ)	1.03	50,912	SW; on N bank of Thames	Residential; home of Thomas Carlyle (1795–1881); Chelsea Hospital; Chelsea Old Church; Crosby Hall; painters' quarter; Cheyne Walk; Chelsea Embankment.
Dept'ford (dĕt'fērd)	2.44	75,694	SE; on S bank of Thames	Dockyards. Royal Victualling Yard. Residence of John Evelyn. Christoper Marlowe killed and buried here.
Fins'bur·y (fĭnz'bēr·ĭ; -brĭ)	.92	35,347	E cen.; N of the City	Business offices. Finsbury Square; Bunhill Fields (cemetery); Wesley's Chapel; Charterhouse.
Ful'ham (fŏŏl'ăm)	2.67	122,047	SW; in bend N of Thames, S of Kensington	Chiefly residential. Fulham Palace; Hurlingham Club Grounds (polo).
Green'wich (grĭn'ĭj; grĕn'-; -ĭch)	6.03	91,492	SE; on S bank of Thames	Greenwich Hospital (since 1873 the Royal Naval College); Greenwich Park 188 acres, including Royal Observatory.
Hack'ney (hăk'nĭ)	5.14	171,337	NE; on boundary of London co.	Formerly fashionable suburb. Much of area covered by Hackney Marsh and Victoria Park.
Ham'mer·smith (hăm'ēr·smĭth)	3.57	119,317	W; N of Thames, W of Kensington	St. Paul's School (founded by John Colet 1509); Kelmscott House (Wm. Morris); Shepherd's Bush.
Hamp'stead (hăm[p]'stĕd; -stĭd)	3.54	95,073	NW; on boundary of London co.	Residential section of writers, artists, etc.; Keats Memorial House; Hampstead Heath (745 acres).
Hol'born (hō'bērn; hōl'-)	.63	24,806	W cen.; N of Thames, W of the City	Bloomsbury residential district and Square; British Museum; Gray's Inn and Lincoln's Inn; Staple Inn; Holborn Viaduct.
Is'ling·ton (ĭz'lĭng·tŭn)	4.83	235,645	N cen.; NW of the City	Industrial district. Canonbury Square and Tower; Agricultural Hall.
Ken'sing·ton (kĕn'zĭng·tŭn) [Royal Borough]	3.58	168,054	W; N of Thames	Residences of well to do. Kensington Palace and Gardens; Imperial Institute; Holland House; Museums; Royal Albert Hall; Campden Hill.
Lam'beth (lăm'bĕth; -bĕth)	6.38	230,105	SW cen.; on S bank of Thames	Lambeth Palace; Vauxhall; Bethlem Hospital; Waterloo Station; 4 bridges across Thames to Westminster.
Lew'i·sham (lū'ĭ·shăm; lū'ĭs·ăm; lŏŏ'-)	10.96	227,551	SE; S of Thames and Greenwich	Residential and gardening. Blackheath, Forest Hill and Sydenham sections. Blackheath (Common, 267 acres); Morden College.
Pad'ding·ton (păd'ĭng·tŭn)	2.12	125,281	NW; N of Kensington	Chiefly residential. Kensal Green (cemetery); Bayswater section; Paddington railroad station.
Pop'lar (pŏp'lēr)	3.64	73,544	E; on N bank of Thames	Shipping. Isle of Dogs with East and West India Docks. Blackwall and Bromley sections.
St. Mar'y·le·bone' [commonly Marylebone] (sănt mâr'ĭ·lĕ·bōn'; without 'St.,' măr'[ĕ·]lĕ·bŭn, măr'ĭ·bŭn)	2.30	75,764	W cen.; N of Hyde Park	Chiefly residential. Regent's Park (Royal Botanic and Zoological Gardens); Marylebone Station. St. John's Wood Road.
St. Pan'cras (sănt păng'krăs)	4.21	138,364	NW; NE of Regent's Park	Railroad center (3 great terminal stations). University College; Kentish Town and Camden Town.
Shore'ditch' (shōr'dĭch')	1.03	44,885	N cen.; N of the City	Industrial. First theater in London (James Burbage's, 1576). Hoxton and Moorfields sections.
South'wark (sŭth'ērk; south'wērk)	1.77	97,191	Cen.; on S bank of Thames	One of oldest parts of London. Site of Elizabethan Bear and Paris Gardens and of Globe Theater (Shakespeare) and of Tabard Inn (Chaucer). Cathedral.
Step'ney (stĕp'nĭ)	2.76	98,581	E; on N bank of Thames, E of the City	Industries, shipping. Tower of London; Whitechapel (London Hospital) and Spitalfields; along the Thames Wapping (London Docks), Shadwell, and Limehouse.
Stoke New'ing·ton (stōk nū'ĭng·tŭn)	1.35	49,137	N; on boundary of London co.	Residential; includes Clapton. St. Mary's Church (16th cent.).
Wands'worth (wŏn[d]z'wûrth; -wērth)	14.23	330,328	SW; S of the Thames	Industrial and residential. Includes Putney and Clapham wards. Wandsworth Common, Putney bridge to Fulham.
West'min·ster, City of (wĕs[t]'mĭn'stēr)	3.91	98,895	W cen.; on N bank of Thames, SW of the City	See WESTMINSTER, in Vocab.
Wool'wich (wŏŏl'ĭj; -ĭch)	12.94	147,824	E; on S bank of Thames	Woolwich Arsenal; Royal Dockyard; Royal Military Academy.

cession to Danish crown; Treaty May 11, 1867 Luxembourg neutralized; Declaration Feb. 1909 attempted to determine maritime law in time of war; Treaty May 20, 1913 ended First Balkan War; Pact Sept. 1914 by which France, Russia, and Great Britain agreed not to make a separate peace; Treaty Apr. 26, 1914, secret agreement of Allies with Italy; Declaration 1922 on reparations; Conference 1930 on naval affairs (unsuccessful); Conference 1933 on World Monetary and Economic affairs (unsuccessful).

London Airport or **Heath'row** (hēth'rō). International airport, S England, W of London in Heston and Isleworth municipal borough, Middlesex.

Lon'don·der'ry (lŭn'dŭn·dĕr'ĭ; *in Ireland, usu.* lŭn'dŭn·dĕr'ĭ) or **Der'ry** (dĕr'ĭ). **1** County, NW Northern Ireland, 804 sq. m.; pop. 155,520 (including Londonderry county borough); ⊗ Londonderry; agriculture, fishing, brewing, manufacturing (esp. linen and woolen goods). **2** County borough and seaport, its ⊗, NW Northern Ireland, on Foyle river near head of Lough Foyle 95 m. NW of Belfast; pop. 50,099; good harbor; shipbuilding yards; trading center for agricultural products; fisheries, tanneries, breweries; manufactures flour, textiles (linens, woolens), iron and brass wares. Began with an abbey founded by St. Columba 546; an ecclesiastical settlement until 16th cent.; scene of defeat 1566 of earl of Tyrone in rebellion against the English; burned in 1608; unsuccessfully besieged and blockaded for 105 days 1689 by army of James II; has two cathedrals (Anglican and Roman Catholic), Foyle College (1617). In World War II a U.S. convoy supply base.

Londonderry, Cape. Northernmost point of Western Australia, on Timor Sea; lat. 13°45′S.

Lon·dri'na (lōn·drē'nȧ). Town, Paraná state, S Brazil; pop. (1940 est.) 10,719.

Lone Mountain (lōn). **1** Peak 11,194 ft. in SW Gallatin co., S Montana.
2 Peak 9046 ft. in W cen. Elko co., NE Nevada.
3 Peak 9114 ft. in E Esmeralda co., SW Nevada.

Lone Pine Peak. Mountain 9652 ft. in cen. Custer co., cen. Idaho.

Long (lông). County in Georgia. See *Table* at GEORGIA.

Long, Loch (lŏ**к**). Inlet ab. 16 m. long in Argyll co., W coast of Scotland; a N extension of Firth of Clyde.

Lon'ga·ví' (lông'gä·vē'). Peak 10,597 ft. in E Linares prov., S cen. Chile.

Long Bay (lông). **1** Bay off S coast of North Carolina and NE coast of South Carolina, extending SW from Cape Fear.
2 Bay on W end of island of Jamaica, Brit. West Indies.

Long Beach. 1 Narrow sandy island, SE Ocean co., E New Jersey.
2 Industrial and resort city, Los Angeles co., SW California, on San Pedro Bay 20 m. S of Los Angeles; pop. 344,168; excellent harbor and 7-mile-long beach; oil industries, steelworks, fisheries, canneries. Founded 1880; discovery of oil nearby 1920 caused rapid growth of city.
3 City, Nassau co., SE New York, on an island in Atlantic Ocean off S shore of Long I. 21 m. ESE of New York City; pop. 26,473; residential suburb and shore resort; fisheries and lobster beds.

Long'ben'ton (lông'bĕn't'n; -tŭn). Urban district, Northumberland, N England, 3 m. NE of Newcastle; pop. 28,071.

Long Branch. 1 City, Monmouth co., E cen. New Jersey, on Atlantic Ocean 21 m. SE of Perth Amboy; pop. 26,228; seaside health and pleasure resort (begun 1788); summer residence of Grant while president of U.S.
2 Village, York co., SE Ontario, Canada, on Lake Ontario 9 m. W of Toronto; pop. 8727.

Long Cay. One of the SE Bahama Is., SW of Crooked I.; 8 sq. m.; pop. (1943) 101; lighthouse. As a former rendezvous of wreckers, known also as **Fortune Island**.

Long'champ' (lôn'shäN'). See BOIS DE BOULOGNE.

Long Ea'ton (lông ē't'n). Urban district, Derbyshire, N cen. England, 7 m. WSW of Nottingham; pop. 28,638; railroad rolling stock; lacemaking.

Long'fel'low Peak (lông'fĕl'ō). Mountain 8890 ft. in Glacier National Park, NW Montana.

Long'ford (lông'fērd). **1** Town, N Tasmania, Australia, at junction of South Esk and Lake rivers 15 m. S of Launceston; pop. 1259; one of earliest settlements in Tasmania; dairying and farming.
2 County, E cen. Eire; 403 sq. m.; pop. 37,847; ⊗ Longford; chief river Shannon; agriculture, livestock raising, dairying, marble quarrying.
3 Urban district, ⊗ of co. Longford, Eire; pop. 3807; processes bacon, butter; leather tanning; fine 19th-cent. cathedral.

Long Island. 1 See FLORIDA KEYS.
2 Island in Atlantic Ocean in Hancock co., SE coast of Maine; pop. 57.
3 Island along SE approach to harbor of Boston, Massachusetts.
4 Island, SE of New York and S of Connecticut, lying bet. Long Island Sound on N and Atlantic Ocean on S; 118¼ m. long, 23 m. at greatest width; 1401 sq. m. (including water, 1723 sq. m.); pop. 6,403,852; comprises Suffolk, Nassau, Queens, and Kings cos. of New York

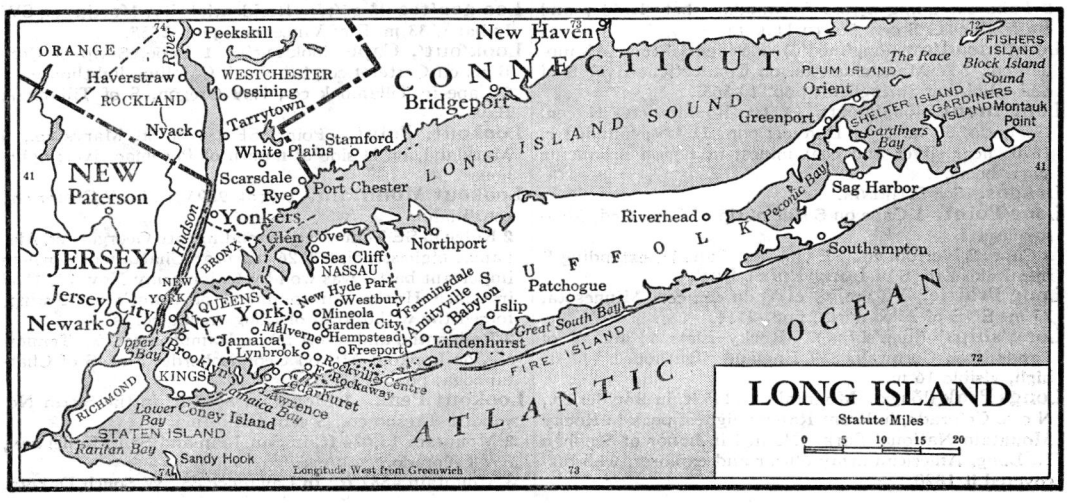

LONG ISLAND
Statute Miles
0   5   10   15   20

state; borough of Brooklyn (Kings co.) at its SW extremity. At W end separated from the Bronx and Manhattan by East river and from Staten I. by the Narrows. Has 280 m. of coast line indented by numerous inlets and bays, esp. Peconic and Gardiners Bays at E end and Great South and Jamaica Bays on S shore. Hilly along N shore; has many fine beaches along the S (Rockaway, Jones, Fire Island, Coney Island). At its E end is Montauk Point with several large islands in adjacent waters (Shelter, Gardiners, Plum, etc.). Has grown to be great residential district for New York City.

History: Included in grant to Plymouth Co. by James I 1620; conveyed to William Alexander, Earl of Stirling, 1635; became part of British colony of New York by treaty 1674; earliest settlement by Dutch 1623, and by English ab. 1640; scene of battle of Long Island (at Brooklyn Heights) in Revolutionary War Aug. 27, 1776 in which Lord Howe defeated Americans under Washington, who, however, successfully withdrew his forces across the river.

5 Island in S end of Willapa Bay, Pacific co., SW Washington.

6 Island in SW Lake Superior, Wisconsin; see APOSTLE ISLANDS.

7 One of the SE Bahama Is., in Atlantic Ocean SW of San Salvador; 130 sq. m.; pop. (1943) 4564.

8 Island in Bismarck Archipelago off NE coast of North-East New Guinea, WNW of Umboi I. and separated from mainland by Vitiaz Strait; occupied by Allied forces Dec. 27, 1943.

9 See HEBRIDES.

10 See BERMUDA.

Long Island City. Former city, since 1898 part of Queens borough of New York City, on Long I. and East river, SE New York; settled by Dutch c. 1640; industrial center; manufactures foods, machinery, furniture, cut stone, shoes, pianos. Former village of Astoria now a part of it.

Long Island Sound. Body of water 110 m. long and from 10 to 25 m. wide, bet. S shore of Connecticut and N shore of Long I., New York, connecting with East river on W and with Block Island Sound on E.

Long·ju'meau' (lôṅ'zhü'mō'). Commune, Seine-et-Oise dept., N France, ab. 11 m. S of Paris; pop. 2503; truce in wars of religion signed here Mar. 23, 1568 bet. Charles IX and Protestant leaders, but did not last long.

Long Key (lŏng). See FLORIDA KEYS.

Long Lake. **1** Lake in NE Hamilton co., NE cen. New York; ab. 14 m. long and 1 m. wide; elevation 1615 ft.; receives water from Raquette Lake to the SW and drains through Raquette river flowing N.

2 Lake extending across S boundary bet. Kidder and Burleigh cos., S cen. North Dakota.

Long'mead'ow (lŏng'mĕd'ō). Residential town, Hampden co., SW Massachusetts, on Connecticut river S of and adjoining Springfield; pop. 10,565.

Long'mont (lŏng'mŏnt). City, Boulder co., N cen. Colorado, 30 m. N of Denver; pop. 11,489; founded c. 1870; near silver and coal mines; in region producing sugar beets.

Longos. See SITHONIA.

Long Point. **1** Cape on S side of tip of Cape Cod, Massachusetts.

2 Cape, S Norfolk co., SE Ontario, Canada, extending E into Lake Erie S of **Long Point Bay.**

Long Prairie. Village, ⊗ of Todd co., cen. Minnesota, 23 m. ENE of Alexandria; pop. 2414.

Long'ships' (lŏng'shĭps'). Rocky islets 1¼ m. W of Lands End, Cornwall, SW England; lighthouse, 117 ft. high, visible 16 m.

Longs Peak (lôṅgz). Mountain 14,255 ft. in Boulder co., N cen. Colorado, in Front Range; highest peak in Rocky Mountain National Park. Named in honor of Stephen H. Long, American army officer and explorer, who discovered it 1820.

Long'ton (lŏng'tŭn). See the POTTERIES.

Lon·gueuil' (lôṅ·gāl'; *Fr.* lôṅ'gû'y'). Residential city, ⊗ of Chambly co., S Quebec, Canada, on St. Lawrence river across from Montreal; pop. 11,103; part of Greater Montreal; popular boating center.

Longue'val' (lôṅg'vàl'). Village, Somme dept., N France, 7 m. ENE of Albert; pop. (1931) 370; in center of territory gained by the British in the battle of the Somme July–Nov. 1916.

Long'view' (lŏng'vū'). **1** City, ⊗ of Gregg co., NE Texas, 20 m. W of Marshall; pop. 40,050; oil wells, refineries.

2 City, Cowlitz co., SW Washington, at confluence of Cowlitz and Columbia rivers 37 m. N of Vancouver; pop. 23,349; founded as model city on site of old Monticello 1922; incorp. 1924; market and shipping center of lower Columbia valley; connected with Oregon by large cantilever bridge 1930.

Longvilliers. See NOAILLES commune, Oise dept., France.

Long'wy' (lôṅ'wē'). Commune, Meurthe-et-Moselle dept., NE France, 60 m. N of Nancy; pop. 14,131; iron mines; steel mills. Fortified by Vauban; battles 1815 and 1870; destroyed and taken by Germans 1914; recaptured by American forces 1918.

Long'xuyên' (loung'swē'ŭn). Town, SW Cochin China, S Vietnam, on S side of Mekong delta 100 m. W of Saigon; pop. ab. 148,000; prosperous market town in extensive agricultural area.

Long'year' City (lŏng'yẽr'); *Norw.* **Long'year·by'en** (lŏng'yẽr·bü'ĕn). Village on Advent Bay, Ice Fjord, West Spitsbergen I.; pop. ab. 1000; coal mines.

Lo·ni'go (lô·nē'gō). Commune, Vicenza prov., Venezia Euganea, NE Italy, 13 m. SSW of Vicenza; pop. 12,393.

Lon'ne·ker (lôn'ĕ·kēr). Commune, Overijssel prov., E Netherlands, suburb of Enschede 3 m. to NE, near German border.

Lo'noke (lō'nōk). **1** County in Arkansas. See *Table* at ARKANSAS.

2 City, ⊗ of Lonoke co., cen. Arkansas, ab. 22 m. ENE of Little Rock; pop. 2359.

Lons'dale (lŏnz'dāl). Village, Providence co., N Rhode Island, ab. 7 m. SE of Woonsocket; seat of government for town of Lincoln.

Lons'-le-Sau'nier' (lôṅ'lĕ-sō'nyā'); *anc.* **Le'do Sal'i-nar'i·us** (lē'dō săl'ĭ-nâr'ĭ-ŭs). Commune, * of Jura dept., E France, 44 m. NW of Geneva (Switzerland); pop. 14,661; produces fine wines; warm saline springs; salt mines in a W suburb.

Lontor. See GREAT BANDA.

Loochoo Islands. See RYUKYU ISLANDS.

Loo·goo'tee (lô·gō'tē). Residential city, Martin co., SW Indiana, 33 m. E of Vincennes; pop. 2858.

Look'out', Cape (lŏŏk'out'). **1** Cape, S tip of Core Bank off Carteret co., SE North Carolina; lighthouse.

2 Cape in Tillamook co., NW Oregon, S of Tillamook Bay.

Lookout, Point. Point, SE tip of St. Marys co., S Maryland, on N side of mouth of Potomac river; lighthouse.

Lookout Mountain. **1** Peak 9893 ft., in W Custer co., cen. Idaho.

2 Ridge in SE Tennessee, extending into Georgia and Alabama; highest point 2126 ft., near Chattanooga, where important battle was won by Union army Nov. 24, 1863 in which Hooker, in command of Grant's right wing, forced the withdrawal of Longstreet's corps.

3 Residential and resort town, Hamilton co, SE Tennessee, on Lookout Mt. on Georgia border 5 m. S of Chattanooga; pop. 1817.

Lookout Peak. **1** Mountain 8547 ft. in the Sierra Nevada, E Fresno co., S cen. California.

2 Mountain 13,674 ft. in San Juan and San Miguel cos., SW Colorado.

3 Mountain 4887 ft., in Lawrence co., W South Dakota.

Lo·on′ (lỏ·ôn′). Municipality, W coast of Bohol I., Phil. Is., NNW of Tagbilaran, largest in the province; pop. 28,797; important trade center with good harbor.

Loon op Zand (lōn′ ôp zänt′). Commune, North Brabant prov., S Netherlands, 4 m. N of Tilburg; pop. 10,258.

Loop Head (lōōp). Cape on W coast of Ireland, on N shore of mouth of the Shannon; lighthouse.

Lo·os′ (lỏ·ôs′). 1 Manufacturing commune, Nord dept., N France, 4 m. W of Lille; pop. 14,362.
2 Commune, Pas-de-Calais dept., N France, ab. 3 m. NNW of Lens; pop. (1931) 6045; in battle Sept. 15 to Oct. 13, 1915, part of Marshal Joffre's offensive in Champagne, village captured by British with heavy losses. Nearby are 14 British cemeteries.

Loos, Îles de. See LOS ISLANDS.

Loos·dui′nen (lōs·doi′nĕ[n]). Suburb, S part of The Hague commune on the coast, South Holland prov., SW Netherlands; pop. 10,686.

Lopadusa. See LAMPEDUSA.

Lo·pat′ka, Cape (lỏ·păt′ká; *Russ.* lŭ·pàt′ká). Cape on S extremity of Kamchatka Penin., Khabarovsk Territory, Soviet Russia, Asia, projecting into Kuril Strait opp. Shumushu I.

Lop Bu·ri *or* **Lo·bu·ri** (lŭp·bōō·rē). 1 Province, SW cen. Thailand; 1392 sq. m.; pop. 157,906; ✲ Lop Buri.
2 Village, its ✲, on the Chao Phraya river 30 m. N of Ayudhya.

Lo·pe′vi (lỏ·pā′vě). Volcano 4747 ft. on island of same name, S cen. New Hebrides group, SW Pacific Ocean.

Lo·pez′, Cape (lỏ·pĕz′). Cape extending into Gulf of Guinea on W coast of Gabon, equatorial Africa.

Lo′pez Island (lō′pĕz). See SAN JUAN ISLANDS.

Lop Nor *or* **Lob Nor** (lôp nôr). Salt, marshy depression at E end of Tarim basin, N of the Astin Tagh, SE Sinkiang, W China, ab. 39°30′N, 89° to 90°E; divided into two lake basins which receive the Tarim river but have no outflow. The old Lop Nor (lake) of early Chinese geographers no longer exists.

Lo·po′ri (lỏ·pōr′ĕ). River ab. 340 m. long, NW cen. Congo; flows NW and W nearly parallel with the Congo to join the Maringa and form the Lulonga.

Lora, Hamun-i–. See HAMUN-I-LORA.

Lo′ra del Rí′o (lō′rä thĕl rē′ỏ). Commune, Sevilla prov., SW Spain, 29 m. NE of Seville; pop. 11,465; agriculture and mining.

Lo·rain′ (lỏ·rān′). 1 County in Ohio. See *Table* at OHIO.
2 City and lake port, Lorain co., N Ohio, on Lake Erie 25 m. W of Cleveland; pop. 68,932; permanently settled 1807; chartered as city 1895; shipbuilding yards; fisheries; manufactures steel, clothing, metal toys.

Lo′ra·lai (lỏ′rá·lī). 1 District, N Baluchistan, Pakistan; 7375 sq. m.; pop. (1941) 83,685; ✲ Loralai.
2 Town, former cantonment, its ✲, 100 m. E of Quetta; pop. 2695.

Lor′ca (lôr′kä); *anc.* **E′li·o·cro′ca** (ē′lĭ·ỏ·krō′ká). Commune, Murcia prov., SE Spain, 34 m. SW of Murcia; pop. 69,639; silver, sulfur, lead mines; manufactures flour, textiles; Moorish castle.

Lorch (lôrк). Town, E cen. Baden-Württemberg, S Germany, 6 m. N of Göppingen; pop. (1933) 3421; 12th-cent. church containing tombs of the Hohenstaufens.

Lord Howe Island (hou). 1 Island of volcanic origin in SW Pacific Ocean, off E coast of New South Wales 436 m. ENE of Sydney, Australia; lat. 31°30′S and long. 159°E; 5 sq. m.; pop. ab. 150; belongs to New South Wales. Highest point 2840 ft.
2 Small island off S coast of Ndeni I., Santa Cruz Is., SW Pacific Ocean.

Lord Howe Islands *or* **Lord Howe's Group.** See ONTONG JAVA.

Lords′burg (lôrdz′bûrg). Mining city, ⊗ of Hidalgo co., SW corner of New Mexico, 38 m. SW of Silver City; pop. 3436; tourist center, in mountainous region; airport and radio station.

Lo′re·lei (lōr′ĕ·lī) *or* **Lur′lei** (lōōr′lī). Rock on right bank of Rhine, near Sankt Goar bet. Bingen and Koblenz; ab. 440 ft. above river; in German legend, said to be haunted by a siren (Lorelei or Lurlei) who by her beauty and singing enticed sailors to destruction on the reef below.

Lo·re′na (lōō·rā′ná). City, São Paulo state, SE Brazil, 115 m. NE of São Paulo; pop. (1940 est.) 10,262.

Lo′reng·au′ (lōr′ĕng·ou′); *also* **Lo′rung·au′.** Seaport on E tip of Manus I., Admiralty Is., Bismarck Archipelago, W Pacific Ocean; ✲ of Manus administrative dist., Territory of New Guinea; occupied by Japanese Apr. 8, 1942 retaken by Americans Mar. 18, 1944.

Lo·ren′zo (lỏ·rĕn′zō). Village, Jefferson co., E Idaho; pop. (1950) 318.

Lo′re·o (lō′rä·ỏ). Commune, Rovigo prov., Venezia Euganea, NE Italy, 21 m. E of Rovigo; pop. 11,468.

Lo·re′to (lỏ·rā′tỏ; *Angl.* -rĕt′ỏ). 1 Commune, Ancona prov., Marches, cen. Italy, near the coast 15 m. S of Ancona; pop. (1931) 6796; place of pilgrimage, famous for its Holy House (Santa Casa), said to be that in which Jesus lived, brought by angels from Nazareth. The Loretto, or Loreto, nuns, or Ladies of Loretto, though named after it, were founded near Dublin, Ireland, 1822. Cf. LORETTO.
2 Extensive department, NE Peru (see *Table* at PERU); includes territory N of Marañón river which was in dispute, claimed by both Peru and Ecuador (*qq.v.*), until settlement of July 1945; 119,301 sq. m.; pop. (1940 est.) 321,341; ✲ Iquitos; forested region, watered by tributaries of the Amazon; separated from coastal departments by Andes Mts.; chief products rubber, salt, tobacco, fruits.
3 Town, Concepción dept., E Paraguay; pop. ab. 4360.

Lo·rette′ville (lỏ·rĕt′vĭl; *Fr.* lỏ′rĕt′vēl′). Village, ⊗ of Quebec co., S Quebec, Canada, on St. Charles river 7 m. WNW of Quebec; pop. 4382; suburb of Quebec, formerly site of Huron village (**Lorette**), established 1697; church, erected c. 1750, a reproduction of Santa Casa of Loreto, Italy. Nearby in St. Charles river are **Falls of Lorette,** ab. 100 ft. high.

Lo·ret′to (lỏ·rĕt′ỏ). 1 Village, Marion co., cen. Kentucky, 8 m. NW of Lebanon; pop. (est.) 500; place where the Lorettine order of nuns (or Sisters of Loretto) was founded 1812. Cf. LORETO, Italy.
2 Borough, Cambria co., SW cen. Pennsylvania, ab. 20 m. NE of Johnstown; pop. 1338; founded 1799; St. Francis College (1845; men).

Lo′ri·an Swamp (lōr′ĭ·ăn). Swamp, E Kenya, E Africa; traversed by the Waso Nyiro river.

Lo·ri′ca (lỏ·rē′kä). Seaport town, Bolívar dept., N Colombia, at mouth of Sinú river; pop. 6146.

Lo′rient′ (lỏ′ryäN′), *formerly* **L′O′rient′** (lỏ′ryäN′). Fortified seaport commune, Morbihan dept., NW France, on the Bay of Biscay 29 m. WNW of Vannes; pop. 45,817; harbor 4 m. from the sea formed by junction of Blavet and Scorff rivers; naval station and marine arsenal; shipbuilding; oyster breeding nearby. Founded 1664 by French East India Co. (Compagnie de l'Orient); became military fort 1690. Used as submarine base by Germans in World War II; frequently bombed by Allied airplanes 1943–44; taken by Allies May 1945. See KÉROMAN.

L′O′ri′gnal′ (lỏr·nĕl′; *Fr.* lỏ′rē′nyál′). Village, Prescott co., SE Ontario, Canada, on Ottawa river 50 m. ENE of Ottawa; ⊗ of Prescott and Russell co.; pop. 967; has sawmills and port facilities.

Lorne, Firth of (lôrn). Strait bet. Mull I. and mainland (Argyll co.) of W Scotland.

Lör′rach (lûr′äк). City SW Baden-Württemberg, W Germany, near Black Forest, 28 m. SSW of Freiburg and on Swiss border near Basel; pop. 16,011; manufactures textiles, hardware, chocolate, cigars; ruins of castle (Rötteln) nearby.

Lor·raine′ (lŏ·rān′; lô-; *Fr.* lô′rân′); *anc.* **Lo′tha·rin′-gi·a** (lŏ′thȧ·rĭn′jĭ·ȧ); *Ger.* **Lo′thring·en** (lō′trĭng·ĕn). Region of W Europe of varying limits, in early times approximately the valleys of the Rhine, Meuse, and Moselle, extending S to the Alps:
1 Medieval kingdom, originally part of Austrasia; by Treaty of Verdun 843 became part of realm (sometimes known as Middle Kingdom) of Emperor Lothair I; inherited by his son Lothair II 855–869, from whom it received name Lotharingia (Lat. *Lotharii regnum*); controlled by Germany, esp. King Louis the Child, until 911.
2 Duchy, formed by division of kingdom of Lorraine 959 (see *Color Plate* IV) into 2 duchies: **Lower Lorraine**, bet. Rhine and Schelde (later developing into separate duchies of Brabant, Limburg, etc.) and **Upper Lorraine**, commonly called **Lorraine**, region of upper Meuse and Moselle; French claim to it relinquished by Hugh Capet 987; ruled from 11th cent. continuously by a ducal family until its union 1740 with Hapsburgs; gradually reduced in size as French kingdom expanded; bishoprics (Les Trois-Évêchés) of Metz, Toul, and Verdun seized 1552 by Henry II of France; at times entirely held by French sovereigns; ruled 1737–66 by Stanislas I Leszczyński, dethroned king of Poland and father-in-law of Louis XV; permanently French from 1766; its chief cities Metz and Nancy; a province in Revolutionary France, divided later into departments of Meuse, Moselle, Meurthe-et-Moselle, and Vosges; after Franco-Prussian War 1871 ceded to Germany as part of Alsace-Lorraine (*q.v.*).

Los Al′a·mos (lŏs ăl′ȧ·mōs). **1** County of New Mexico. See *Table* at NEW MEXICO.
2 Town on a mesa in Jemez Mts. (alt. ab. 7400 ft.), Los Alamos co., New Mexico, ab. 35 m. NW of Santa Fe; pop. 12,584; chosen 1942 as site for research and development of nuclear weapons, place where U 235 and plutonium were first assembled into bombs.
Los Al′tos (lŏs ăl′tōs). City, Santa Clara co., W California, SSE of Palo Alto; pop. 19,696.
Los An′des (lŏs än′dās). **1** See ANDES.
2 Former territory, NW Argentina, in the Andes Mts.; practically coextensive with the Puna de Atacama region. See *Table* at ARGENTINA.
3 Town, Aconcagua prov., cen. Chile, ab. 40 m. N of Santiago; pop. 12,409; terminus of Transandine R.R. 65 m. E of Valparaíso (83 m. by rail); alt. 2675 ft.
Los An′ge·les (lŏs ăn′jĕ·lĕs; ăng′gĕ·lĕs; -lēz) **1** County in California. See *Table* at CALIFORNIA.
2 *often called* **L.A.** City, its ⊗, SW California, at its center ab. 15 m. from the Pacific Ocean although ex-

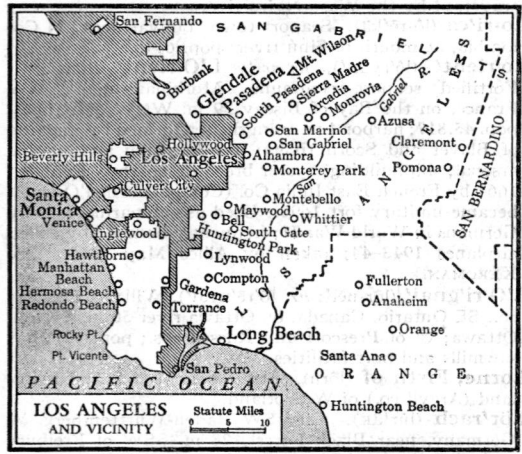

LOS ANGELES AND VICINITY
Statute Miles

tending to the coast in several places; pop. 2,479,015; 452 sq. m.; largest city in the state and 2d largest in U.S. in

area, and 3d largest in population; excellent harbor at San Pedro Bay ab. 25 m. S of center of city; industrial and resort city in agricultural and oil-producing section. The city area has in recent years absorbed many towns and villages and now completely surrounds independent cities of Santa Monica, Beverly Hills, Culver City, Redondo Beach, etc.; encloses Hollywood (*q.v.*). Has many parks and fine public and business buildings; also several small structures of the early Spanish period. Its water supply is brought from the Colorado river by an aqueduct (completed 1939) ab. 300 m. long. Univ. of Southern California (1879; coed.); Univ. of California at Los Angeles (1919; coed.); Occidental Coll. (1887; coed.); Loyola Univ. of Los Angeles (1865; coed.; Rom. Cath.); Pepperdine College (1937; coed.); Immaculate Heart College (1916); women; Rom. Cath.); Mount St. Mary's Coll. (1925; women; Rom. Cath.); Southwestern Univ. (1913; coed.). Founded 1781 on a Spanish grant, and named Nuestra Señora Reina de los Angeles; captured by Commodore Stockton, U.S. Navy, 1846; incorporated 1850; growth accelerated by arrival of Southern Pacific R.R. 1876, discovery of nearby petroleum deposits 1894, and improvement of the harbor 1912.
Los Án′ge·les (lôs äng′hä·lās). City, ✱ of Bío-Bío prov., S cen. Chile, 58 m. SE of Concepción in valley of Bío-Bío river; pop. 20,979.
Los A·ra′bos (lôs ä·rä′vŏs). Municipality, Matanzas prov., W cen. Cuba, on railroad 38 m. SE of Cárdenas; pop. 8295.
Los Ba′nos (lŏz vä′nŏs). City, Merced co., cen. California, 60 m. WNW of Fresno; pop. 5272.
Los Ba′ños (lŏz vä′nyŏs). Literally "the baths"; municipality, cen. Laguna prov., Luzon, Phil. Is., on S shore of Laguna de Bay 15 m. SW of Santa Cruz; pop. 9612; on provincial highway 34 m. SE of Manila. Finest mineral springs in the Philippines; seat of College of Agriculture of the Univ. of the Philippines. American air base 1941; Japanese concentration camp captured Feb. 23, 1945.
Loser, Mount. See Mount SINOBONG.
Los Estados, Isla de. See STATEN ISLAND.
Los Gat′os (lŏs găt′ŭs). City, Santa Clara co., W California, 8 m. SW of San Jose; pop. 9036.
Lo′shan′ (lō′shän′); *formerly* **Kia′ting′** (jĭ·ä′dĭng′). City, SW Szechwan prov., S cen. China, on right bank of Min river 77 m. S of Chengtu; pop. ab. 150,000; starting point for sacred mountain, Omei, ab. 30 m. to the W.
Los Her·ma′nos (lŏs ĕr·mä′nŏs). Group of small Venezuelan islands in Caribbean Sea off NE cen. coast 50 m. NNW of Margarita I.
Lo′šinj (lō′shĕn·y′); *Ital.* **Lus·si′no** (lōōs·sē′nŏ). Small island, formerly Italian, in the Veliki Kvarner (Gulf of Quarnero), S of Cres I., NW Yugoslavia; 24 m. long; 29 sq. m.; pop. (1931) ab. 11,000; administratively a part of Croatia.
Losinoostrovsk. See BABUSHKIN.
Los Islands (lŏs) *or* **Îles de Lo′os′** (ēl′ dē lô′ôs′). Group of small islands off Conakry, part of Guinea off SW coast, W Africa; 6 sq. m.; pop. ab. 1500; largest Tamara, with good harbor. Came into British possession 1818; ceded to France 1904.
Los Lla·ni′tos (lŏs yä·nē′tōs). Mountain 10,013 ft., W Guanajuato state, cen. Mexico.
Los Lu′nas (lŏs lōō′nȧs). Village, ⊗ of Valencia co., W New Mexico, on the Rio Grande 18 m. S of Albuquerque; pop. 1186.
Los Mo′chis (lŏz mō′chēs). Town, Sinaloa state, W Mexico, just N of Topolobampo; pop. 12,937.
Los Ne′gros (lŏz nā′grŏs). Group of small islands off E coast of Manus I., Admiralty Is., Bismarck Archipelago; on one of islands is Momote airfield; in World War II occupied by Americans in surprise attack Feb. 29, 1944.
Losoncz. See LUČENEC.
Los Pa·la′cios (lŏs pä·lä′syŏs). Municipality, Pinar del Río prov., W Cuba; pop. 18,270.

Los Pa′tos (lŏs pä′tōs). Mountain pass 11,700 ft. in the Andes Mts. near Aconcagua, W Argentina.

Los Re′yes (lôr rĕ′yås), *in full* **Los Re′yes de Sal-ga′do** (lôr rĕ′yåz thä säl·gä′thō). Town, Michoacán state, SW Mexico, S of Lake Chapala; pop. 5452.

Los Rí′os (lôr rē′ōs). Province of Ecuador. See *Table* at ECUADOR.

Los Ro′ques (lôr rō′kås). Group of small Venezuelan islands in Caribbean Sea off N cen. coast of Venezuela; produce salt and phosphates.

Los San′tos (lôs sän′tōs). Province, cen. Panama, on Pacific coast; 1979 sq. m.; pop. 87,739; * Las Tablas; includes former Herrera prov.

Los′ser (lôs′ēr). Commune, Overijssel prov., E Nether-lands, 6 m. NE of Enschede on German border; pop. 14,762.

Los′sie·mouth (lôs′ĭ·mouth). Burgh, Moray co., NE Scotland, on North Sea at mouth of the Lossie, 5 m. N of Elgin; pop. 5596; port and seaside resort; interesting caves in nearby cliffs.

Löss′nitz (lûs′nĭts). District, Saxony, Germany, on right bank of the Elbe NW of Dresden; ab. 5 m. long; pop. (1933) 7762; market gardens.

Lost City (lŏst). See OVERTON, Nevada.

Los Te′ques (lôs tā′kås). Town, * of Miranda state, N Venezuela, ab. 15 m. SW of Caracas; pop. (1941 est.) 10,326.

Los Tes·ti′gos (lôs tås·tē′gōs). Group of small Venezue-lan islands in Caribbean Sea N of NE Venezuela, ab. 50 m. NE of Margarita I.

Lost Mine Peak (mīn). Mountain 7550 ft. in S Brew-ster co., W Texas.

Lost River Range. Range in E cen. Idaho, chiefly in Custer and Butte cos.

Lost·with′i·el (lŏst·wĭth′ĭ·ĕl; -wĭth′-). Town and mu-nicipal borough, Cornwall, SW England, ab. 30 m. W of Plymouth; pop. (1951) 2165; railroad workshops; castle of Restormel nearby; scene of battle Sept. 2, 1644 in which Charles I defeated earl of Essex.

Lo·su′ia (lô·sōō′yà). Chief town of Trobriand Is. off SE Papua, New Guinea, on W coast of Kiriwina I. near N end.

Lot (lŏt). **1** *anc.* **Ol′tis** (ŏl′tĭs). Navigable river ab. 300 m. long in S France; rises in Lozère dept. on slopes of the Lozère Mts.; flows W into Garonne river W of Agen. **2** Department of France. See *Table* at FRANCE.

Lo′ta (lō′tä). Seaport, Concepción prov., S cen. Chile, 21 m. S of Concepción; pop. 31,087; coal-mining center; copper smelters; nearby is the famous Cousiño Park, containing plants and trees from all over the world.

Lot′bi·nière′ (lō′bē·nyâr′). County, Quebec, Canada. See *Table* at QUEBEC.

Lot′-et–Ga′ronne′ (lôt′ā·gà′rôn′). Department of France. See *Table* at FRANCE.

Lotharingia. See LORRAINE.

Lo′thi·an (lō′thĭ·ăn). Region of S Scotland; in early times, c. 547 to 1018, a district of N Northumberland extending from the Tweed to the Firth of Forth; later divided into 3 counties, the **Lo′thi·ans** (lō′thĭ·ănz), East Lothian, Midlothian, and West Lothian.

Lothringen. See LORRAINE.

Löt′schen Pass (lûch′ĕn). Mountain pass 8840 ft. in the Bernese Alps bet. Bern and Valais cantons, SW cen. Switzerland; under it is the **Lötsch′berg** (lûch′bĕrĸ) railroad tunnel, 9 m. long, at an altitude of 4080 ft.

Lötzen. See GIŻYCKO.

Lualaba. See LUALABA.

Lou′don (lou′d′n). **1** County in Tennessee. See *Table* at TENNESSEE.
2 Town, ⊗ of Loudon co., E Tennessee, on Tennessee river 30 m. SW of Knoxville; pop. 3812; manufactures hosiery, chairs.

Lou′don Hill (lou′d′n). Locality, Ayr co., SW Scotland, E of Kilmarnock; scene of victory of Robert Bruce over the English 1307.

Lou′don·ville (lou′d′n·vĭl). Village, Ashland co., N cen. Ohio, 15 m. SE of Mansfield; pop. 2611; manufactures buses, ambulances, airplane parts.

Lou′doun (lou′d′n). County in Virginia. See *Table* at VIRGINIA.

Lou′dun′ (lōō′dûn′). Commune, NW Vienne dept., W cen. France, 40 m. SW of Tours; pop. (1931) 5059; a Protestant community, suffered much after revocation of the Edict of Nantes; has traces of Roman times.

Lough′bor·ough (lŭf′bŭ·rŭ; -brŭ). Municipal borough, Leicestershire, cen. England, 13 m. SSW of Nottingham; pop. 34,731; before 1861 a lacemaking center; known esp. for its bell foundries; cast the great bell for St. Paul's, London, 1881. Site of a technical college.

Loughor. See LLWCHWR.

Lough·rea′ (lŏĸ·rā′). Market town SE co. Galway, W Eire, on N shore of Lough Rea 18 m. SW of Ballinasloe; pop. 2891; remains of Norman castle and Carmelite friary; a cromlech is nearby.

Lough′ton (lou′t′n). Former urban district, Essex, SE England, 12 m. NNE of London; pop. (1931) 7390; part of Greater London.

Lou·i′sa (lōō·ē′zà; *Iowa* -ĭ′zà). **1** Name of counties in two states in the U.S. See *Tables* at IOWA and VIRGINIA.
2 City, ⊗ of Lawrence co., E Kentucky, on Big Sandy river 25 m. S of Ashland; pop. 2071.
3 Town, ⊗ of Louisa co., cen. Virginia; pop. 576.

Lou′is·burg (lōō′ĭs·bûrg). **1** Town, ⊗ of Franklin co., N North Carolina, 30 m. NE of Raleigh; pop. 2862; manufactures lumber, wagons, flour.
2 *or* **Lou′is·bourg** (-bûrg). Town, Cape Breton co., E Nova Scotia, Canada, on Atlantic Ocean 18 m. SE of Sydney; pop. 1120; coal-shipping port and anchorage for fishing fleet. Founded by French 1713; strongly fortified (1720–40) to maintain its strategic control of entrance to the Gulf of St. Lawrence; besieged and captured by American colonials under Sir William Pepperell 1745; returned to the French by Treaty of Aix-la-Chapelle 1748; again taken by the English under Gen. Jeffrey Amherst and Admiral Boscawen 1758 and its fortifica-tions destroyed. Site of the fort and its remains now pre-served as a national historic park (**Fortress of Louis-bourg:** see CANADA, *National Historic Parks*).

Lou·ise′, Lake (lōō·ēz′). Lake 1½ m. by ¾ m. near Banff, SW Alberta, Canada; altitude 5670 ft.; in Banff National Park, at foot of high peaks; its outlet is short stream flowing into Bow river. Noted for its magnificent scenery.

Louise Island. Island, cen. Queen Charlotte Is. off W Brit. Columbia, Canada, on Hecate Strait.

Lou·ise′ville (lōō·ēz′vĭl). Town, ⊗ of Maskinongé co., S Quebec, Canada, on Lake St. Peter 20 m. WSW of Three Rivers; pop. 4088; mineral springs.

Lou·is′ Gen′til′ (lwē′ zhäɴ′tē′). Town, W cen. Mo-rocco, E of Safi; junction point on railroad connecting the port of Safi with Casablanca and Marrakesh; phos-phate mines in region.

Lou′i·si·ade′ Archipelago (lōō′ĭ·zĭ·äd′; -ăd′; lōō′ĭ·zĭ-; lōō·ē′zĭ-). Island group in Solomon Sea SE of E end of New Guinea; ab. 600 sq. m.; pop. ab. 3000; attached to the Territory of Papua; chief village, Bwagaoia, on E end of Misima I.; comprises large islands of Misima, Tagula, and Rossel, and many small islands and reefs; gold mines on Tagula I. Natives are Papuans, formerly cannibals. Discovered 1768 by French explorer d'Entre-casteaux, and named in honor of Louis XV of France; used early in 1942 by Japanese as seaplane base but given up after battle of Coral Sea May 1942.

Lou·i·si·an′a (lōō′ĭ·zĭ·ăn′à; lōō′ĭ·zĭ-; lōō′zĭ-; *chiefly by outsiders*, lōō·ē′zĭ-). **1** A southern state of U.S.A., 18th state admitted to Union (1812); bounded on N by Ar-kansas, on E and SE by Mississippi and the Gulf of Mexico, on S by the Gulf of Mexico, and on W by Texas; 31st state in area, 48,523 sq. m. (land area 45,162 sq. m.); 20th state in population, 3,257,022; * Baton Rouge.

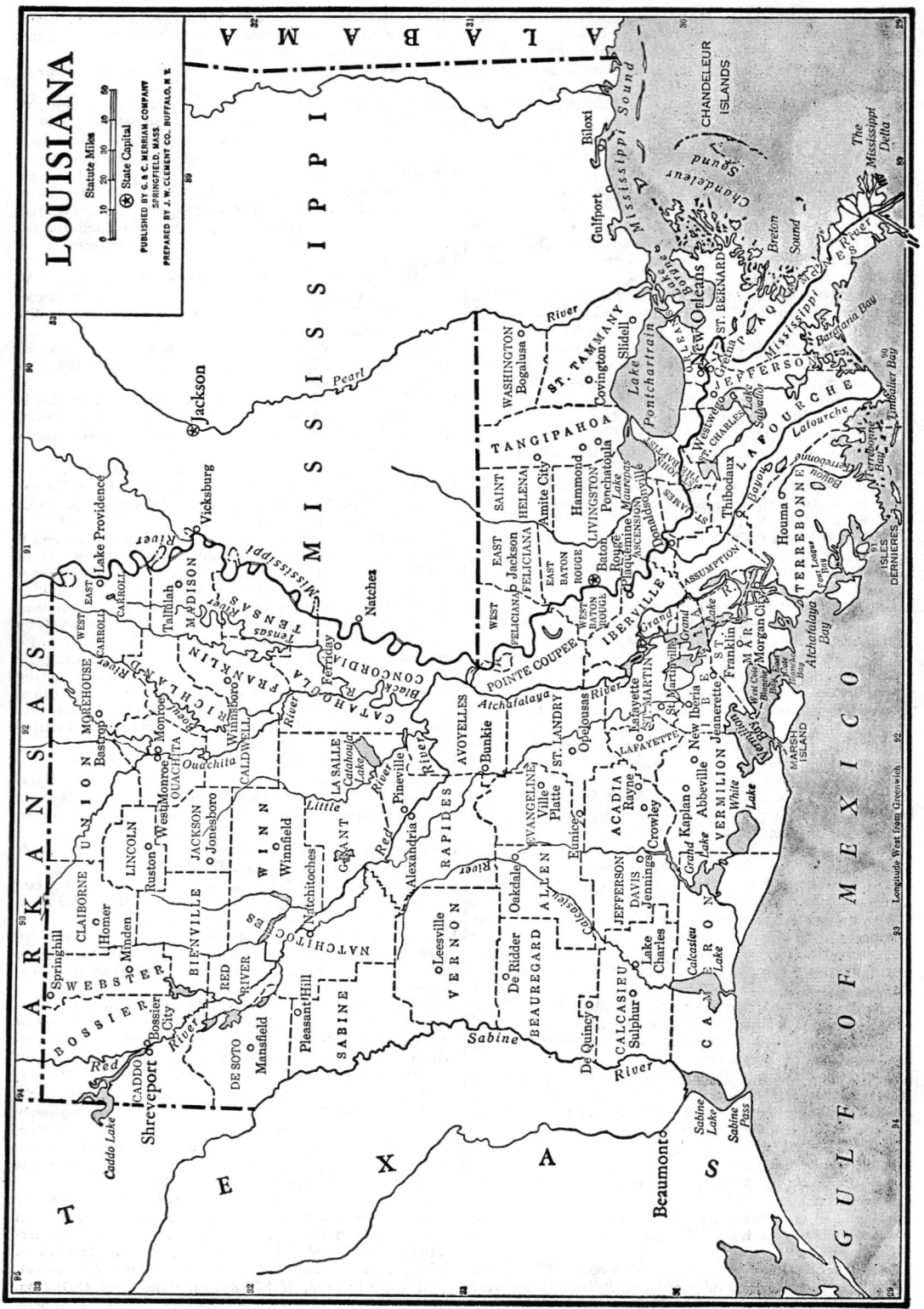

LOUISIANA

Statute Miles

PUBLISHED BY G. & C. MERRIAM COMPANY
SPRINGFIELD, MASS.
PREPARED BY J. W. CLEMENT CO. BUFFALO, N. Y.

⊛ State Capital

See *Table of States* at UNITED STATES. Divided into the following 64 parishes (for pronunciation of their names, see their individual entries):

NAME	LOCATION	AREA[1]	POP.[1]	PAR. SEAT
Acadia	S	662	49,931	Crowley
Allen	SW	775	19,867	Oberlin
Ascension	SE	300	27,927	Donaldsonville
Assumption	SE	357	17,991	Napoleonville
Avoyelles	cen.	826	37,606	Marksville
Beauregard	SW	1,184	19,191	De Ridder
Bienville	NW	826	16,726	Arcadia
Bossier	NW	841	57,622	Benton
Caddo	NW corner	891	223,859	Shreveport
Calcasieu	SW	1,104	145,475	Lake Charles
Caldwell	N cen.	550	9,004	Columbia
Cameron	SW corner[2]	1,444	6,909	Cameron
Catahoula	cen.	732	11,421	Harrisonburg
Claiborne	N	766	19,407	Homer
Concordia	E cen.	709	20,467	Vidalia
De Soto	NW	893	24,248	Mansfield
East Baton Rouge	SE cen.	462	230,058	Baton Rouge
East Carroll	NE corner	432	14,433	Lake Providence
East Feliciana	E	454	20,198	Clinton
Evangeline	S cen.	672	31,639	Ville Platte
Franklin	NE	648	26,088	Winnsboro
Grant	cen.	670	13,330	Colfax
Iberia	S[2]	588	51,657	New Iberia
Iberville	S	628	29,939	Plaquemine
Jackson	N	583	15,828	Jonesboro
Jefferson	SE[2]	409	208,769	Gretna
Jefferson Davis	SW	658	29,825	Jennings
Lafayette	S	283	84,656	Lafayette
Lafourche	SE[2]	1,157	55,381	Thibodaux
La Salle	cen.	638	13,011	Jena
Lincoln	N	469	28,535	Ruston
Livingston	SE	665	26,974	Livingston
Madison	NE	662	16,444	Tallulah
Morehouse	N	804	33,709	Bastrop
Natchitoches	NW cen.	1,297	35,653	Natchitoches
Orleans	SE[2]	199	627,525	New Orleans
Ouachita	N	642	101,663	Monroe
Plaquemines	SE[2,3]	984	22,545	Pointe a la Hache
Pointe Coupee	SE cen.	564	22,488	New Roads
Rapides	cen.	1,329	111,351	Alexandria
Red River	NW	413	9,978	Coushatta
Richland	NE	576	23,824	Rayville
Sabine	W	1,029	18,564	Many
Saint Bernard	SE[2]	510	32,186	Saint Bernard
Saint Charles	SE	304	21,219	Hahnville
Saint Helena	E	420	9,162	Greensburg
Saint James	SE	249	18,369	Convent
Saint John the Baptist	SE	225	18,439	Edgard
Saint Landry	S cen.	930	81,493	Opelousas
Saint Martin[4]	S	721	29,063	Saint Martinville
Saint Mary	S[2]	605	48,833	Franklin
Saint Tammany	SE	908	38,643	Covington
Tangipahoa	SE	803	59,434	Amite City
Tensas	NE	623	11,796	St. Joseph
Terrebonne	SE[2]	1,391	60,771	Houma
Union	N	906	17,624	Farmerville
Vermilion	S[2]	1,224	38,855	Abbeville
Vernon	W	1,360	18,301	Leesville
Washington	E	665	44,015	Franklinton
Webster	NW	626	39,701	Minden
West Baton Rouge	SE cen.	201	14,796	Port Allen
West Carroll	NE	356	14,177	Oak Grove
West Feliciana	E cen.	410	12,395	St. Francisville
Winn	SW	950	16,034	Winnfield

[1] Area = land area in sq. m. Pop. from 1960 Census.
[2] Parishes in extreme S and SE of state, bordering Gulf of Mexico, are largely composed of swampland intersected by bayous.
[3] Forms peninsula in extreme SE of state; bisected by Mississippi river whose delta is at SE end of parish.
[4] Area in SE separated from rest of parish by cen. part of Grand Lake and part of Iberia parish.

Nickname: Pelican State, also Creole State. *State flower:* Magnolia. *Motto:* Union, Justice, Confidence. *Chief cities:* New Orleans, Shreveport, Baton Rouge, Lake Charles, Monroe. *Rivers:* Mississippi, forming NE and E cen. boundary and flowing SE into Gulf of Mexico; Sabine, forming W cen. and SW boundary, and flowing into Gulf of Mexico; Red, flowing from NW diagonally SE across state and into the Mississippi. *Highest point:* 469 ft., in S Claiborne parish. *Chief industries:* Agriculture (cotton, corn, rice, sugar), lumbering, petroleum production.

History: Name originally applied to entire Mississippi river basin, claimed for France by La Salle 1682; first settlement in region at Biloxi, Mississippi, 1699, there being no successful settlement within area of present state until foundation of New Orleans (*q.v.*) 1718; region E of Mississippi river ceded by France to Great Britain 1763 and, except West Florida (see FLORIDA), by British to U.S. 1783; region W of Mississippi river sold by France to U.S. 1803 (see LOUISIANA PURCHASE) and out of this region Territory of Orleans organized 1804, admitted to Union Apr. 30, 1812 as state of Louisiana, the first to be carved out of Louisiana Purchase; part of state E of Mississippi river N of Lake Pontchartrain acquired with occupation of West Florida by U.S. 1813; passed ordinance of secession Jan. 26, 1861; repealed ordinance of secession, abolished slavery 1864; readmitted to Union July 18, 1868; adopted new constitution 1913.

2 City, Pike co., E Missouri, on Mississippi river 25 m. SE of Hannibal; pop. 4286; ships cattle, hogs, grain, vegetables, and fruit.

Louisiana Point. Point at SW extremity of Louisiana, on E side of entrance to Sabine Pass.

Louisiana Purchase. The vast territory 885,000 sq. m. purchased Apr. 30, 1803 for $15,000,000 by the United States from France, extending from the Mississippi to the Rocky Mts. and from Gulf of Mexico to British America, including the basin of the Missouri river and the major part of the Great Plains drained by western tributaries of the Mississippi; out of it were later formed four states (Arkansas, Iowa, Missouri, and Nebraska) and parts of nine others (Louisiana, Minnesota, Oklahoma, Kansas, Colorado, Wyoming, Montana, North Dakota, and South Dakota); with ill-defined boundaries, had been acquired by Spain from France 1762 and was retroceded to France by Treaty of San Ildefonso Oct. 1, 1800.

Lou'is Trich'ardt (lōō'ĭ[s] trĭch'ärt). Town, N Transvaal, NE Union of South Africa, 225 m. NE of Pretoria; pop. 4527; on S slope of Zoutpansberg Mts.; in fertile agricultural section (esp. cotton).

Lou'is·ville (lōō'ĭs·vĭl; *Sou.* also -v'l). **1** Town, Boulder co., N cen. Colorado, 18 m. NW of Denver; pop. 2073; coal.

2 City, ⊗ of Jefferson co., E cen. Georgia, 40 m. SW of Augusta; pop. 2413; townsite laid out 1786; capital of Georgia 1796–1805.

3 Village, ⊗ of Clay co., SE cen. Illinois; pop. 906.

4 (lōō'ĭ·vĭl, *Sou.* also -v'l) City, ⊗ of Jefferson co., N cen. Kentucky, on Ohio river; largest city in the state; pop. 390,639; laid out 1779, incorp. as city 1828; important market, distributing point, and railroad center; tobacco warehouses, distilleries, stockyards and packing houses, flour mills. University of Louisville (1798; coed.; oldest municipal university in U.S.); Louisville Presbyterian Seminary (1901); Southern Baptist Theological Seminary (1859); Jefferson School of Law (1905); Louisville College of Pharmacy (1870); Nazareth College (1920; women; Rom. Cath.). See CHURCHILL DOWNS.

5 City, ⊗ of Winston co., E cen. Mississippi, 45 m. SW of Columbus; pop. 5066; lumbering, dairy farming.

6 Village, Stark co., NE Ohio, 7 m. ENE of Canton; pop. 5116; makes steel, clay-working machinery; coal mines.

Lou·lé' (lō·lâ'). Commune, Faro dist., S Portugal, 10 m. NNW of Faro; pop. 18,585; manufactures leather, porcelain, esparto-grass and palm products; silver and copper mines.

Lou'ny (lō'ŏŏ·nĭ); *Ger.* **Laun** (loun). Town, NW Bohemia prov., W Czechoslovakia, 35 m. NW of Prague on the Ohře river; pop. (1930) 11,884.

Loup (lōōp). **1** River ab. 300 m. long (including North Loup river), E cen. Nebraska; rises in three branches, North Loup, Middle Loup, and South Loup rivers, and flows E into Platte river at Columbus in SE Platte co. **2** County in Nebraska. See *Table* at NEBRASKA.

Loup City. City, ⊗ of Sherman co., cen. Nebraska, 42 m. NW of Grand Island; pop. 1415.

Lourdes (loord; *Fr.* loord). Commune, Hautes-Pyrénées dept., SW France, on the Gave de Pau 11 m. SSW of Tarbes; pop. 11,529; marble and slate quarries; one of chief shrines of pilgrimage in Europe, having become famous 1858 through reputed apparitions of the Virgin (Our Lady of Lourdes) to a peasant girl (Bernadette of Lourdes) in a grotto here; magnificent church erected at grotto.

Lou·ren'ço Mar·ques' (lō-rän'sōō mĕr·käsh'). **1** Southernmost district of Mozambique, SE Africa; 28,800 sq. m.; pop. ab. 474,000; belongs to Sul do Save prov. **2** Seaport on Delagoa Bay, extreme S Mozambique, SE Africa; ✻ of Sul do Save prov. and ✻ of Mozambique; pop. (1935 est.) 47,390; has excellent harbor; airport. Founded by Portuguese; undeveloped until opening of hinterland around Delagoa Bay (*q.v.*) and completion of Delagoa Bay R.R. 1895.

Louth (louth; louⱨ). County, NE Eire, in Leinster prov.; 317 sq. m.; pop. 64,339; ⊗ Dundalk; rivers Dee, Boyne, Glyde; agriculture, fishing (esp. oyster fishing), livestock raising, linen manufacture.

Louth (louth). Municipal borough, Parts of Lindsey, Lincolnshire, E England, on the Lud 28 m. SSE of Hull; pop. 11,128; trade center in agricultural section.

Loutro. See PHOENIX.

Lou'vain' (lōō'văn'); *Flem.* **Leu'ven** (lû'vĕ[n]). Commune, Brabant prov., cen. Belgium, on the Dyle river 15 m. E of Brussels; pop. (1938 est.) 37,141; has Gothic town hall and several fine churches. Residence of dukes of Brabant 11th cent.; capital of Brabant and at height of prosperity as center of wool trade 14th cent.; decreased in importance because of civil wars 1379–83, but later became seat of learning; its university (founded 1425) had great library which was destroyed when town was captured and sacked by Germans Aug. 1914, and rebuilt (1921–28) by gifts from citizens of U.S. and other countries, only to be again destroyed May 1940.

Louvière, La. See LA LOUVIÈRE.

Lou'viers' (lōō'vyä'). Commune, Eure dept., N France, on Eure river 14 m. N of Évreux; pop. 10,239; agricultural trade center; manufactures textiles. Taken by English 1418 and 1431; recaptured 1440 by Charles VII.

Lo·vat' (lō·văt'; *Russ.* lŭ·vàt'y'). River 320 m. long, W Soviet Russia, Europe, flowing N through Velikie Luki and Novgorod Regions into Lake Ilmen.

Lov'cen (lōv'tyĕn) *or* **Lov'chen** (-chĕn). Mountain 5771 ft. in SW Montenegro, Yugoslavia, just W of Cetinje.

Love (lŭv). County in Oklahoma. See *Table* at OKLAHOMA.

Lo'vech (lō'vĕch). Town, Pleven dept., N cen. Bulgaria, 18 m. S of Pleven; pop. (1926) 9135.

Love'land (lŭv'lănd). **1** Commercial city, Larimer co., N Colorado, 12 m. S of Fort Collins; pop. 9734; founded 1877; beet-sugar refineries, vegetable and fruit canneries; a gateway to Rocky Mountain National Park. **2** Village, Clermont, Hamilton, and Warren cos., SW Ohio, 16 m. NE of Cincinnati; pop. 5008.

Loveland Mountain. Peak 13,624 ft. in Park co., cen. Colorado.

Loveland Pass. Mountain pass 11,992 ft., Clear Creek and Summit cos., N cen. Colorado, in Front Range of the Rocky Mts.; in winter sports area; highway.

Lov'ell (lŭv'ĕl). Town, Big Horn co., N Wyoming, on Shoshone river 43 m. NE of Cody; pop. 2451; beet sugar.

Lovell Island. Island in Boston Bay, off Boston, Massachusetts.

Love'lock (lŭv'lŏk). City, ⊗ of Pershing co., NW Nevada; pop. 1948; considerable Basque population.

Lo·ve'ni·a, Mount (lō·vē'nï·à; -vĕn'yà). Peak 13,227 ft. in E Summit co., NE Utah.

Love Point (lŭv). Point at N end of Kent I. in upper Chesapeake Bay, Maryland.

Loves Park (lŭvz). City, Winnebago co., N Illinois, NE of Rockford; pop. 9086.

Lov'ing (lŭv'ĭng). County in Texas. See *Table* at TEXAS.

Lov'ing·ston (lŭv'ĭng·stŭn). Village, ⊗ of Nelson co., cen. Virginia; pop. (est.) 375.

Lov'ing·ton (lŭv'ĭng·tŭn). Town, ⊗ of Lea co., SE corner of New Mexico, 23 m. NNW of Hobbs; pop. 9660.

Lo·von'gai (lō-vōng'gī). Var. of *Lavongai*: see NEW HANOVER.

Lo'vo·si'ce (lō'vô·sï'tsĕ); *Ger.* **Lo'bo·sitz** (lō'bô·zĭts). Town, NW Bohemia prov., W Czechoslovakia, on Labe (Elbe) river; pop. (1930) 5926; battle Oct. 1, 1756 in which Frederick the Great defeated the Austrians.

Low Archipelago. See TUAMOTU ARCHIPELAGO.

Low Countries. Low region bordering on the North Sea, comprising modern Netherlands, Belgium, and Luxembourg.

Lowe, Mount (lō). Peak 5601 ft., Los Angeles co., SW California; scenic railway; tourist resort.

Low'ell (lō'ĕl). **1** Industrial city, a ⊗ of Middlesex co., NE Massachusetts, 23 m. NW of Boston on Merrimack river at Pawtucket Falls (32 ft.), its chief source of power; pop. 92,107; since mid-19th cent. its chief industry has been manufacture of textiles; known as the "City of Spindles"; lost half of its textile factories after 1929 but has recovered by diversifying its industries. Birthplace of James A. M. Whistler. Lowell Technological Institute (1895; coed.); Massachussetts State College (1894; coed.). **2** City, Kent co., W Michigan, 17 m. E of Grand Rapids; pop. 2545; manufactures tools and buttons. **3** Town, Gaston co., SW North Carolina; pop. 2784.

Lowell, Lake. See DEER FLAT DAM, Idaho.

Low'ell·ville (lō'ĕl·vĭl). Village, Mahoning co., NE Ohio, 7 m. SE of Youngstown; pop. 2055.

Lö'wen·burg (lû'vĕn·bŏŏrĸ). Highest peak 1506 ft. of the Siebengebirge (*q.v.*), in W Germany.

Lower Andalusia. See ANDALUSIA.

Lower Apennines. Subsidiary ranges of the Apennines, situated in the triangular space bet. the Apennines proper and the W coast of Italy, including: (1) the Tuscan highland, bounded on the S by the lower Tiber; (2) the plain of Maremma; (3) the Alban Hills and Lepini Mts. (bet. the Tiber and Garigliano rivers); (4) the S section from the Garigliano to the mountains of Castellammare di Stabia and Sorrento Penin., including Vesuvius (3877 ft.).

Lower Arrow Lake. See ARROW LAKE.

Lower Austria; *Ger.* **Nie'der·ö'ster·reich'** (nē'dĕr·û'stĕr·rīĸ'; -û'strĭĸ). Province in NE Austria; see *Table* at AUSTRIA. Crossed by the Danube from W to E; bordered on NE by the March and has the Leitha forming part of boundary on SE. Hilly in N with higher mountains of E Alps on the S, crossed by the Semmering Pass. The city of Vienna, separate administratively, forms a district geographically in E part. Formerly an archduchy and crownland of Austrian Empire.

Lower Bann. See BANN.

Lower Bavaria. Bavarian government district. See *Table* at BAVARIA.

Lower Burgundy. See BURGUNDY.

Lower Burma. See BURMA.

Lower Bur'rell (bûr'ĕl). City, Westmoreland co., SW Pennsylvania, NE of Pittsburgh; pop. 11,952.

Lower California; *Span.* **Ba'ja Ca'li·for'nia** (bä'hä kä'lē·fôr'nyä). Peninsula extending SSE bet. the Pacific Ocean and the Gulf of California, NW Mexico; divided into 2 sections: a state, **Baja California,** to the N, ✻ Mexicali, area 27,653 sq. m.; pop. (1950) 226,965; and a territory, **Baja California Sur** (sōōr'), to the S, ✻ La Paz, area 27,976 sq. m., pop. 72,465. Discovered by Spanish 1533–34; most successfully settled by Jesuit missions (from late 17th cent.); separated from Alta (Upper) California 1772.

Lower Canada. Quebec province, Canada, 1791 to 1841. See QUEBEC province.

Lower Chateaugay Lake. See CHATEAUGAY LAKES.

Lower Chindwin. District, Sagaing division, W Upper Burma; 3681 sq. m.; pop. 383,434; ✻ Monywa.

Lower Danube. German name 1938–45 of *Lower Austria:* see *Table* at AUSTRIA.

Lower Egypt. See EGYPT.

Lower Fort Gar′ry National Historic Park (găr′ĭ). See CANADA, *National Historic Parks.*

Lower Franconia. Bavarian government district. See *Table* at BAVARIA.

Lower Gastein. See GASTEINER ACHE.

Lower Guinea. See GUINEA.

Lower Hutt (hŭt). Borough, suburb of Wellington, Wellington provincial dist., S North I., New Zealand; pop. 12,860.

Lower Klamath Lake. See KLAMATH LAKES.

Lower Lorraine. See LORRAINE.

Lower Mat′e·cum′be Key (măt′ē·kŭm′bē). See FLORIDA KEYS.

Lower Merion. Urban township, Montgomery co., SE Pennsylvania, NW of Philadelphia; pop. 59,420.

Lower New York Bay. See NEW YORK BAY.

Lower Palatinate. See Lower PALATINATE.

Lower Peninsula. Southern part of Michigan, S of Straits of Mackinac.

Lower Rhine; Ger. Nie′der·rhein′ (nē′dĕr·rīn′); *Du.* **Ne′der Rijn** (nā′dĕr rīn′). The section of the Rhine river bet. Bonn, Germany, and the North Sea; in Netherlands the general name for its various sections.

Lower Saranac Lake. See SARANAC LAKES.

Lower Saxony; Ger. Nie′der·sach′sen (nē′dĕr·zäk′-sĕn). State of Federal Republic of Germany, including former states of Brunswick, Oldenburg, and Schaumburg-Lippe; ✻ Hannover; 18,284 sq. m.; pop. 6,496,100.

Lower Silesia. Former province of Prussia. See *Silesia,* in *Table* at PRUSSIA.

Lower South·amp′ton (sou·thăm[p]′tŭn; south-·hăm[p]′-). Urban township, Bucks co., SE Pennsylvania, NE of Philadelphia; pop. 12,619.

Lower Tunguska. See TUNGUSKA.

Lower Volga Area. Former region, SE Soviet Russia, Europe; ab. 127,000 sq. m.; included territory on both sides of the lower Volga, the cities of Saratov, Stalingrad, Astrakhan, Volsk, and the German Volga Republic and Kalmyk A.S.S.R. Established 1928, divided 1936.

Lowes′toft (lōs′tŏft; -tŭf). Municipal borough, East Suffolk, E England, on North Sea 23 m. ESE of Norwich; pop. 42,837; fishing port, yachting center; formerly noted for its chinaware (Lowestoft ware).

Lowes Water (lōz). Lake in the Lake District, NW England, in Cumberland 6 m. SSE of Cockermouth.

Ło′wicz (lô′vĕch). Commune, Warszawa dept., Poland, on Bzura river 47 m. WSW of Warsaw; pop. (1938–39 est.) 17,613; manufactures leather, clay goods; horse and cattle market. In World War I taken by Germans Nov.–Dec. 1914 after fall of Łódź.

Lowlands, the. See the HIGHLANDS.

Lowndes (loun[d]z). Counties in three states of the U.S. See *Tables* at ALABAMA, GEORGIA, MISSISSIPPI.

Low′ther Hill (lou′thēr). Mountain 2377 ft. in the Lowthers, S Scotland.

Low′thers, the (lou′thĕrz). Mountain range in S Scotland, along boundary bet. Lanark and Dumfries cos.; highest peak **Green Lowther** 2403 ft.

Low′ville (lou′vĭl). Village, ⊗ of Lewis co., N cen. New York, 26 m. ESE of Watertown; pop. 3616; lumbering.

Loxa. See LOJA, Spain.

Loy′al·han′na Creek (loi′ăl·hăn′ă). River ab. 40 m. long, SW Pennsylvania; flows NW through Westmoreland co. to unite with Conemaugh river in SW Indiana co. and form Kiskiminetas river.

Loy′all (loi′ăl). City, Harlan co., SE Kentucky, 28 m. NE of Middlesborough; pop. 1260.

Loy′al·ty Islands (loi′ăl·tĭ) or **Loy′al·ties** (-tĭz); *Fr.* **Îles Loy′au′té′** (ēl′ lwȧ′yō′tā′). Island group in SW Pacific Ocean, in E part of New Caledonia territory

(French), forming a chain 60 m. E of New Caledonia and ab. 160 m. SW of the S end of the New Hebrides group; 1059 sq. m.; pop. (1936) 10,113; administrative center Chépénéhé. Chief islands Lifu, Maré, and Uvéa. Mostly low coral upheavals; copra, rubber, taro.

Lo′yang′ (lō′yäng′); *also* **Ho′nan′** (hō′nän′; *Chin.* hŭ′nän′). City, N Honan prov., E cen. China, ab. 120 m. W of Kaifeng S of the Hwang Ho near its confluence with the Lo; pop. ab. 500,000; in early history of China successively the capital of the Eastern Han, Chin, Northern Wei, and Sui dynasties; also the east capital under the T'ang dynasty and the west capital under the Sung dynasty.

Lo′zère′ (lô′zâr′). **1** Range in Cévennes Mts., S France; highest peak Pic de Finiels ab. 5585 ft.

2 Department of France. See *Table* at FRANCE.

Lu. See TO.

Lu′a·la′ba (lōō′ȧ·lä′bȧ); *Fr.* **Lou·a·la′ba′** (lwȧ′lȧ′bȧ′). River in SE Congo; flows N and joins the Luapula to form the Congo river; ab. 400 m. long to confluence with Luapula; from this point to Stanley Falls, 1000 m., the upper Congo often called the Lualaba.

Luan. See CHANGCHIH.

Lu·an′da (lōō·än′dȧ) or **Lo·an′da** (lô·än′dȧ; *Port.* lwän′dȧ). **1** District, NW Angola, SW Africa.

2 *also* **São Pau′lo de Lo·an′da** (souⁿм pou′lōō thĕ lwän′dȧ). Commercial city and seaport, W Luanda dist., on Bay of Bengo; ✻ of the district and of Angola; pop. (1934) ab. 40,000; founded by Portuguese 1575.

Luang′pra·bang′ (lwäng′prä·bäng′). **1** Native Lao state (kingdom), N Laos, Indochina; pop. ab. 198,000. Formerly under French protection, declared its independence of the French Apr. 1945; amalgamated with rest of Laos 1946; now forms a province.

2 Town, ab. 15,000, on the left bank of the Mekong river; pop. ab. 15,000; connected by highway with Vientiane; limit of navigation on the Mekong. Has large pagoda on hill above the town. Residence of king of Laos.

Luangue. See LOANGE.

Lu·ang′wa (lōō·äng′wä). **1** River ab. 400 m. long in E Northern Rhodesia; flows SSW into Zambezi river, in its lower course forming a section of the W boundary of Mozambique.

2 Province, cen. Northern Rhodesia; 38,060 sq. m.; pop. 134,687; ✻ Broken Hill.

Lu·an′shya (lōō·än′shyä). Town, Luangwa prov., cen. Northern Rhodesia; pop. ab. 6000; laid out 1928; copper.

Lu′a·pu′la (lōō′ȧ·pōō′lȧ). River in cen. Africa; outlet of Lake Bangweulu through the large swamp S of the lake, actually a continuation of the Chambezi; flows N along boundary bet. NW Northern Rhodesia and SE Congo through Lake Mweru and joins Lualaba to form Congo river.

Luar′ca (lwär′kä). Seaport, Oviedo prov., NW Spain, on Bay of Biscay 37 m. WNW of Oviedo; pop. 25,200; metal products, paper, fireworks; meat-salting plants.

Lu′ba·an′tun (lōō′vä·än′tōōn). Site, S British Honduras, 15 m. NW of Punta Gorda; Mayan ruins, discovered 1924.

Lu′bań (lōō′bän·y′); *Ger.* **Lau′ban** (lou′bän). City, W Wrocław dept., SW Poland, 38 m. WSW of Legnica; pop. (1946) 17,353; formerly in Silesia, Germany; 16th-cent. town hall; manufactures handkerchiefs; horse and cattle market. Made city in 13th cent.; assigned to Poland by Potsdam Conference 1945.

Lu·bang′ (lōō·bäng′). **1** Group of islands, Mindoro prov., Phil. Is., off NW coast of Mindoro I. 46 m. SW of entrance to Manila Bay and separated from Luzon by Verde Island Passage; 95 sq. m.; pop. 12,676; chief town Lubang. Comprises Lubang I. and the small islands of Ambil, Golo, and Cabra. Inhabitants are Tagalogs. Occupied by American forces Mar. 1945.

2 Largest island of group; 74 sq. m.; 17 m. long; pop. 10,606.

3 Municipality on N coast of the island; pop. 8702.

Lu·ba'o (lōō·bä'ô). Municipality, S Pampanga prov., Luzon, Phil. Is., on NW edge of Pampanga delta 9 m. SW of San Fernando; pop. 29,154.

Lub'bock (lŭb'ŭk). **1** County in Texas. See *Table* at TEXAS.

2 Industrial city, its ⊗, NW Texas; pop. 128,691; cottonseed-oil and feed mills; packs meat and poultry, processes dairy products and peanuts; railroad center. Texas Technological Coll. (1923; coed.).

Lu·bec' (lōō·bĕk'). Town, Washington co., SE corner of Maine, on Passamaquoddy Bay across from Campobello I.; pop. 2684; fishing, sardine canning.

Lü'beck (lü'bĕk; *Angl.* lōō'-). **1** Former district of Oldenburg. See *Table* at OLDENBURG.

2 Commercial and manufacturing city, Schleswig-Holstein, Germany, on two small streams connecting with Lübeck Bay 35 m. NE of Hamburg; pop. 230,562; important port; entered by four gates; fine 12th-cent. cathedral, a Gothic church, Gothic town hall, 13th-cent. hospital; manufactures iron goods, cement and cement goods, machinery, ships, preserved foodstuffs, furniture, tile.

History: Probably settled in 11th cent., refounded 1143 by duke of Holstein; taken by Henry the Lion (see SAXONY) 1158, secured final privileges of imperial city 1226; became leading center for medieval German trade in Baltic region and "Queen of the Hanse" (see HANSE TOWNS); declined from 16th cent.; by Treaty of Lübeck 1629, Denmark withdrew from Thirty Years' War; captured by French 1810; its autonomy restored 1815, joined (*Ger.*) Zollverein and North German Confederation; lost its status as autonomous free state 1933 (see GERMANY). In World War II taken by Allied forces May 4, 1945.

Lübeck Bay. Inlet of SW Bay of Mecklenburg on N coast of Germany.

Lu·be'fu (lōō·bā'fōō). River ab. 200 m. long in the Congo basin; flows W in cen. Congo into the Sankuru river shortly before its junction with Kasai river.

Lu·bi'lash (lōō·bē'läsh). River, the upper course of the Sankuru, S cen. Congo.

Lu'bin (lōō'bēn); *Ger.* **Lü'ben** (lü'bĕn). Town, N cen. Wrocław dept., SW Poland; pop. (1946) 2200; formerly in Silesia, Germany.

Lu'blin (lōō'blēn); *Russ.* **Lyu'blin** (lyōō'blĭn). **1** Department in E Poland; 10,269 sq. m.; pop. 2,467,266; slightly larger after reorganization of Polish departments 1946.

2 City, its ✳, 95 m. SE of Warsaw; pop. (1938–39 est.) 122,000; railroad junction; 16th-cent. cathedral; university (1918); Jewish rabbinical school; manufactures textiles, leather, agricultural machinery, beer. Once seat of several old Polish diets, and later of High Polish Law Courts; captured by Austrians Aug. 1914 and July 1915; seat of Austrian-Hungarian military government in Poland during World War I. In World War II taken by Germans Sept. 1939 and retaken by Russians July 25, 1944.

Lub'ny (lōōb'nǐ). Town, N Poltava Region, N cen. Ukraine, U.S.S.R., 110 m. E of Kiev; pop. 23,332.

Lub'sko (lōō'skô); *Ger.* **Som'mer·feld** (zôm'ẽr·fĕlt). Town, SW Poznań dept., W Poland, SE of Gubin; pop. (1946) 10,578; formerly in Brandenburg, Germany.

Lu·bua'gan (lōō·bwä'gän). Town (municipal district), ✳ of Kalinga subprov., Mountain Province, Luzon, Phil. Is., in SW part on Chico river; pop. 7366.

Lubumbashi. See ELISABETHVILLE.

Lubungan. See KATIPUNAN.

Luca. See LUCCA.

Lu·ca'ni·a (lṳ·kā'nĭ·à; -kän'yà; *Ital.* lōō·kä'nyä). **1** Ancient district of S Italy including modern Lucania compartimento and part of Salerno prov. in S Campania.

2 *formerly* **Ba·si'li·ca'ta** (bä·zē'lē·kä'tä). Compartimento of S Italy; for provincial divisions, area, and pop., see *Table* at ITALY; on Gulf of Taranto N of Calabria

bet. Campania and Apulia.

Lu·ca'ni·a, Mount (lṳ·kā'nĭ·à; -kän'yà). Peak 17,150 ft. in St. Elias Range in SW Yukon Territory, Canada, N of Mt. Logan near Alaska border.

Lucanian Apennines. See APENNINES.

Lu'cas (lū'kàs). Name of counties in two states of the U.S. See *Tables* at IOWA and OHIO.

Lu·ca'yas (lōō·kä'yäs). Early Spanish name of the BAHAMA ISLANDS.

Luc·ban' (lōōk·bän'). Municipality, S Tayabas prov., Luzon, Phil. Is., near Laguna border 15 m. NNW of Lucena; pop. 13,976; in mountainous district; center of rice growing.

Luc'ca (lōōk'kä). **1** Province of Italy. See *Table* at ITALY.

2 *anc.* **Lu'ca** (lū'kà). Commune, its ✳, Tuscany, cen. Italy, 38 m. W by N of Florence; pop. 82,300; early 13th-cent. cathedral; 7th-cent. church of San Frediano; 8th-cent. church of San Michele; ducal palace; aqueduct; ancient Roman remains; manufactures silk, jute.

History: Ancient town founded as Roman colony in territory conquered from Ligurians 180 B.C.; on ancient Cassian Way; chief town in Tuscany before rise of Florence (*q.v.*); early in 14th cent. lost freedom and came to be ruled as duchy by Castruccio Castracani 1327; sold to Florence and later achieved independence as republic ruled by an oligarchy; occupied by French 1799 and given as a principality to Napoleon's sister 1805; awarded to member of Spanish Bourbon family 1815; reunited with Tuscany 1847 and thus became part of kingdom of Italy 1860.

Luce (lūs). County in Michigan. See *Table* at MICHIGAN.

Luce (lüs). Small river in N France, an E tributary of Avre river, ab. 10 m. SE of Amiens; battles 1918.

Luce Bay (lūs). Inlet of Irish Sea on extreme SW coast of Scotland; enclosed by Mull of Galloway on W.

Luce'dale (lūs'dāl). Town, ⊗ of George co., SE Mississippi; pop. 1977.

Lu·ce'na (lōō·sā'nä). Municipality, ✳ of Tayabas prov., Luzon, Phil. Is.; on N shore of Tayabas Bay 63 m. SE of Manila; pop. 21,675; made capital 1901.

Lu·ce'na (lōō·thā'nä; -sā'-). Commune, Córdoba prov., S Spain, 39 m. SE of Córdoba; pop. 32,687; horse breeding; mineral waters; manufactures copper and zinc products, glassware, pottery, linens, shoes, iron products, chemicals.

Lu'če·nec (lōō'chě·nĕts); *Hung.* **Lo'soncz** (lô'shônts). Town, S Slovakia prov., Czechoslovakia, on the Ipel' 65 m. NE of Budapest; pop. (1930) 15,449.

Lucentum. See ALICANTE.

Lu·ce'ra (lōō·chä'rä). Commune, Foggia prov., Apulia, SE Italy, 12 m. WNW of Foggia; pop. 18,447; early 14th-cent. cathedral; ruins of castle built by Frederick II.

Lu·cerne' (lṳ·sûrn'; *Fr.* lü'sĕrn'); *Ger.* **Lu·zern'** (lōō·tsĕrn'). **1** Swiss canton; see *History* and *Table* at SWITZERLAND.

2 Commune, its ✳, cen. Switzerland, on W shore of Lake of Lucerne 25 m. SSW of Zurich; pop. (1941) 54,716; near Mounts Pilatus and Rigi; famous tourist center; medieval circular walls and watch towers, 14th-cent. Kapellbrücke, 15th-cent. Mühlenbrücke (covered bridges with notable paintings, including a *Danse macabre*), Renaissance town hall, 17th-cent. cathedral, Jesuit church, and many monuments, including esp. the famous Lion of Lucerne carved in rock. Developed around monastery of St. Leodegar (8th cent.); joined Swiss Confederation 1332; stronghold of Catholicism during Reformation; took part in Sonderbund War (see SWITZERLAND); occupied by Federals 1847.

Lucerne, *or* **the Four Forest Cantons, Lake of;** *Ger.* **Vier'wald'stät'ter·see'** (fēr'vält'shtĕt'ẽr·zā'). Lake in cen. Switzerland, enclosed by Schwyz, Uri, Unterwalden, and Lucerne cantons; 24 m. long and bet. ½ m. and 2 m. wide; 44 sq. m.

Lu·cerne′mines (lū·sûrn′mīnz). Locality, Indiana co., W cen. Pennsylvania, ab. 4 m. S of Indiana (borough); pop (est.) 1073.

Lu′chow′ (lōō′jō′). **1** City, Anhwei, E China. See HOFEI.

2 City, Szechwan, S cen. China. See LUHSIEN.

Luchu Islands. See RYUKYU ISLANDS.

Łuck. See LUTSK.

Luck′au (lōōk′ou). Commune, Brandenburg, eastern Germany, in Lower Lusatia 45 m. SSE of Berlin; pop. 4394; scene of defeat of Oudinot by Count von Bülow 1813.

Luck′en·wal′de (lōōk′ĕn·väl′dĕ). City, Brandenburg, eastern Germany, 31 m. SSW of Berlin; pop. 24,791; manufactures cloth, hats, metal and paper goods, machinery, furniture, pianos. Site of Cistercian monastery in 12th cent.

Luck′now (lŭk′nou). **1** Division, Oudh, cen. Uttar Pradesh (formerly United Provinces), N India.

2 City, ✱ of Uttar Pradesh, on Gumti river 270 m. ESE of Delhi; pop. (1941) 387,177; important rail center with extensive railroad workshops; paper and metal factories, printing presses, pottery works, and native handicrafts. Has many fine old buildings including the white marble Imambara, Pearl Palace with its famed collection of Oriental manuscripts, palaces of Chhattar Manzil, spacious Kaisar Bagh, unfinished great mosque with the mausoleum of Mohammed Ali Shah, and the suburban palace of Bibiapur; chief place of interest the residency, where in the Sepoy Mutiny the British were besieged from June 1857 till relieved by Gen. Campbell in Nov.; forced to abandon the city, the British retook it Mar. 1858. Lucknow University, Canning College; former large British military cantonment. First gained prominence under the Great Moguls and in 18th cent. as capital of Oudh, a position held until Oudh and Agra were joined as United Provinces 1902.

Lu′çon′ (lü′sôn′). Commune, S Vendée dept., W France; pop. (1931) 6648; connected with sea by canal ab. 8 m. long; bishopric; had among its bishops Richelieu 1607–14.

Lu·cre′ci·a, Point (lū·krē′shǐ·å; -shå; Span. lōō·krā′syä). Cape on N coast of Oriente prov., E Cuba.

Lu′crine, Lake (lū′krǐn; -krīn; Ital. La′go Lu·cri′no (lä′gō lōō·krē′nō); anc. La′cus Lu·cri′nus (lā′kŭs lū·krī′nŭs). Small lake, Campania, S Italy, near shore of Bay of Pozzuoli W of Pozzuoli, N of Baia; noted for its oysters since ancient times; a resort of the Romans, was surrounded with villas.

Lucronius. See LOGROÑO.

Lucus Augusti. See LUGO.

Lud (lŭd). Small river in Lincolnshire, E England, flowing N into the Humber.

Lü′den·scheid (lü′dĕn·shīt). **1** Industrial city, North Rhine-Westphalia state, W Germany, 37 m. E of Düsseldorf; pop. 32,758; manufactures aluminum, metal goods, wire; health and winter resort.

2 Commune, North Rhine-Westphalia state, W Germany, near city of Lüdenscheid; pop. 12,148.

Lü′de·ritz (lü′dĕ·rĭts); formerly **An′gra Pe·que′na** (äng′grå pĕ·kwē′nå). Town, SW South-West Africa, on Atlantic Ocean 520 m. NNW of Cape Town; pop. (1936) 2465; well-sheltered and active harbor which is seaboard terminus for rail line; center for important diamond region. See SOUTH-WEST AFRICA.

Lu′dhi·a′na (lōōd′hǐ·ä′nå). Town, Jullundur division, Punjab state, NW Indian Union, near Sutlej river 100 m. ESE of Lahore; pop. (1941) 111,639; important wheat, grain, and wool market; manufactures shawls, carriages, furniture, turbans, and scarves. Founded 1840. Seat of medical school for women.

Lud′ing·ton (lŭd′ǐng·tŭn). City, ⊗ of Mason co., W Michigan, on Lake Michigan 51 m. N of Muskegon; pop. 9421; lake port, ships lumber and farm products; market center in summer-resort area.

Lud′low (lŭd′lō). **1** Industrial city, Kenton co., N Kentucky, NW suburb of Covington; pop. 6233; furniture, electrical apparatus, brass products, compressing machines.

2 Town, Hampden co., SW Massachusetts, 7 m. NE of Springfield; pop. 13,805; cordage mills. Part of Springfield until 1775.

3 Residential locality, McKean co., N Pennsylvania, ab. 14 m. SE of Warren; pop. (est.) 619.

4 Village in Ludlow town (pop. 2386), Windsor co., E Vermont, on Black river 13 m. WNW of Springfield; pop. 1658; woolen mills.

5 Municipal borough, Shropshire, W England, on the Teme 37 m. WSW of Birmingham; pop. 6455; here Samuel Butler wrote *Hudibras*, and in the 11th-cent. Norman castle Milton's *Comus* was first performed (1634).

Ludlow, Mount. Peak 3372 ft., S cen. Vermont, on boundary bet. Windsor and Rutland cos.

Lu′do·wic′i (lōō′dô·wǐs′ǐ). City, ⊗ of Long co., SE Georgia; pop. 1578.

Lud′wigs·burg (lōōt′vǐks·bŏŏrk; lōōd′-). City, Baden-Württemberg state, Germany, W of the Neckar and 8 m. N of Stuttgart; pop. 28,994; 18th-cent. baroque church; two 18th-cent. castles; military station; manufactures metal goods, machinery, surgical instruments, wire, celluloid goods; a former residence of princes of Württemberg.

Lud′wigs·ha′fen am Rhein (lōōt′vǐks·hä′fĕn [lōōd′-] äm rīn′). Commercial and manufacturing city, SE Rhineland-Palatinate state, W Germany, on W bank of Rhine river opp. Mannheim; pop. 156,583; important railroad junction and river port; founded 1843, made city 1859; in recent years site of important chemical and engineering works; frequently bombed in World War II; taken by American armies Mar. 22, 1945.

Lud′za (lōōd′zä). **1** Administrative district, E Latgale prov., E Latvia; 905 sq. m.

2 Town, its ✱, 65 m. NE of Daugavpils near Russian border; pop. (1935) 5546.

Lu·e′bo (lōō·ā′bō). Town, W cen. Lusambo prov., S cen. Congo, on the Lulua river; airport.

Lu·em′be (lōō·ĕm′bå). River ab. 300 m. long in the Congo basin, S cen. Africa; rises in NE Angola, flows N into Kasai river.

Lu′feng′ (lōō′fŭng′). Town, cen. Yunnan, S China, on Burma Road 65 m. W of Kunming.

Luf′kin (lŭf′kĭn). Commercial and industrial city, ⊗ of Angelina co., E Texas, 115 m. NE of Houston; pop. 17,641; paper, lumber, machinery, processed foods.

Lug. See LUGG.

Lu′ga (lōō′gå). Town, W Leningrad Region, Soviet Russia, Europe, 80 m. S of Leningrad on railroad to Pskov; pop. 24,200; held by Germans 1941–44; retaken by Russians Feb. 13, 1944.

Lu·ga′no (lōō·gä′nō); Ger. **Lau′is** (lou′ĭs). Commune, Ticino canton, SE cen. Switzerland, on N shore of Lake Lugano 13 m. S of Bellinzona; pop. (1941) 17,030; episcopal see; famous tourist and health resort; manufactures silk, chocolate, furniture, tobacco. First mentioned in 6th cent.; taken from duke of Milan by Swiss Confederation 1512; capital of former Swiss canton of Lugano, became part of Ticino canton 1803.

Lu·ga′no, Lake (lōō·gä′nō); Ital. **La′go di Lu·ga′no** (lä′gō dē lōō·gä′nō) or **La′go Ce·re′sio** (chä·rā′syô); anc. **La′cus Ce·re′si·us** (lā′kŭs sĕ·rē′zhǐ·ŭs; -zhŭs). Lake in S Ticino canton, S Switzerland and N Italy, bet. Lakes Maggiore and Como; ab. 19 sq. m.

Lugansk. See VOROSHILOVGRAD.

Lu′gan·ville (lōō′gån·vǐl). Town, SE coast of Espíritu Santo I., New Hebrides Is., SW Pacific Ocean; chief settlement on the island.

Lu′gau (lōō′gou). Industrial city, Saxony, E Germany, at N foot of Erz Gebirge 10 m. SW of Karl-Marx-Stadt; pop. 10,619; coal mining; iron founding; manufactures gloves, stockings, chemicals.

Lug′du·nen′sis (lŭg′dǔ·nĕn′sĭs). One of the five administrative divisions of Gaul established by Augustus 27 B.C. comprising the cen. and N part and named from its capital, Lugdunum (Lyons); later Armorica formed its NW part; in 5th cent. A.D. most of it passed to the Franks.

Lugdunum. See LYONS.

Lugdunum Batavorum See LEIDEN.

Lu·gen′da (lōō·jĕn′dȧ). River in N Mozambique, SE Africa; flows out of Lake Chiuta NE into Ruvuma river.

Lugg or **Lug** (lŭg). River ab. 50 m. long in E Wales and W England; rises in Radnorshire, Wales, flows SE across English border into the Wye 5 m. below Hereford.

Luggarus. See LOCARNO.

Lugnaquilla. See WICKLOW MOUNTAINS.

Lu′go (lōō′gô). **1** Commercial commune, Ravenna prov., Emilia, N Italy, 15 m. W of Ravenna; pop. 30,125; trade center, esp. for cattle and silk cocoons.
2 Province of Spain. See Table at SPAIN.
3 anc. **Lu′cus Au·gus′ti** (lū′kǔs ô·gǔs′tī). Commune, ✳ of Lugo prov., NW Spain, on Miño river 48 m. SE of La Coruña; pop. 42,805; trade center, esp. in cattle and preserved meats; manufactures leather, linens, hats; sulfur spring; ancient Roman walls; 12th-cent. Gothic cathedral; a former capital of Galicia; several times captured and destroyed.

Lu′goj (lōō′gôzh). Commercial city, W Romania, in Banat region on Timiş river; pop. 23,674.

Luguvallium, Luguvallum. See CARLISLE, England.

Lu·hai′ya or **Lo·hei′ya** (lōō·hī′yȧ; -hā′-; -yă). Seaport, NW Yemen, on Red Sea coast NW of San'a.

Lu′hit (lōō′hĭt). River rising in SW Sikang prov., China, and flowing SW into the Brahmaputra at the great bend in NE Assam, NE India. Sadiya on its N bank near its mouth.

Lu′hsien′ (lōō′shĭ·ĕn′); formerly **Lu′chow′** (lōō′jō′). City, S Szechwan prov., S cen. China, on N bank of the Yangtze below Ipin, 146 m. SSE of Chengtu; pop. ab. 100,000; chief market in W China in salt trade.

Lui, Ben. = BEN LUI.

Lui′chow′ Peninsula (lā′jō′). Peninsula of SW Kwangtung prov., SE China, separated from Hainan I. by Hainan Strait; on its E coast is Kwangchowan, a former French leased territory.

Luik. See LIÈGE.

Luimneach. See LIMERICK.

Lui′no (lwē′nô). Commune, Varese prov., Lombardy, N Italy, on E shore of Lake Maggiore 14 m. NNW of Varese; pop. (1931) 12,507; scene of battle bet. Garibaldi and Austrians Aug. 14, 1848.

Lu′it·pold Coast (lōō′ĭt·pôlt); formerly **Le′o·pold Coast** (lē′ô·pôld). Section of coast of Antarctica, from ab. 29°W to 37°W, on SE coast of Weddell Sea, a part of Coats Land; included in Falkland Islands Dependencies (q.v.).

Lu·ján′ (lōō·hän′). Short river in NE Buenos Aires prov., E Argentina; flows E into Río de la Plata 23 m. NW of the city of Buenos Aires.

Lu·kan′ga Swamp (lōō·käng′gȧ). Large marsh area in cen. Northern Rhodesia, S cen. Africa.

Lukchun. = TURFAN depression.

Lu·ke′nie (lōō·kā′nyȧ). River more than 450 m. long in cen. Congo (formerly Belgian Congo); flows W into Kasai river when it joins the Congo; in its lower course, after being joined by waters from Lake Leopold II, known as Fini river.

Lu Kiang. See SALWEEN.

Lu′kou′chiao′ (lōō′gō′chĭ·ou′). City, N Hopeh prov., NE China, on E bank of the Yungting 9 m. SW of Peiping; river crossed here by the Marco Polo Bridge (q.v.); scene July 7, 1937 of the clash bet. Chinese and Japanese troops which began the Chinese-Japanese War (1937–45); after several demands by both governments China rejected the Japanese ultimatum of July 26, and Peiping surrendered July 28.

Łu′ków (lōō′kōōf). Commune, Lublin dept., Poland, 49 m. N of Lublin; pop. 13,971; leather, oil.

Lu·ku′ga (lōō·kōō′gȧ). River ab. 200 m. long in E Congo; flows W from Lake Tanganyika into the Lualaba (upper course of the Congo).

Lu·ku′la (lōō·kōō′lȧ). River ab. 150 m. long in E Congo; flows W into Ulindi river shortly before it joins the Lualaba.

Lu′le (lōō′lĕ). River 280 m. long in Norrbotten prov., N Sweden; issues from Stora Luleträsk, flows SE into the Gulf of Bothnia.

Lu′le·å′ (lōō′lĕ·ô′). Seaport, ✳ Norrbotten prov., N Sweden, on Gulf of Bothnia at mouth of Lule river; pop. 16,553; exports iron ore, timber, wood pulp.

Lü′le·bur·gaz′ (lü′lĕ·bōōr·gäz′; -gäs′) or **Lüle Burgas**. Town, S Kırklareli vilayet, Turkey in Europe, 86 m. WNW of İstanbul; pop. 11,530; scene of decisive battle of the First Balkan War Oct. 28–30, 1912 in which Turks were defeated, causing their retirement to Constantinople.

Lu′ling′ (lōō′lĭng′). See KIAN.

Lu′ling (lū′lĭng). City, Caldwell co., S cen. Texas, 42 m. S of Austin; pop. 4412; center of large oil-producing area.

Lu·lon′ga (lōō·lông′gȧ). River in NW Congo; formed by junction of the Maringa and Lopori rivers, flows W into the Congo.

Lu·lu′a (lōō·lōō′ȧ). River ab. 600 m. long in S Congo; flows N into Kasai river.

Lu·lu′a·bourg′ (lōō·lōō′ȧ·bōōr′). Town, ✳ of Kasai prov., S cen. Republic of Congo (formerly Belgian Congo), on Lulua river; pop. 60,758.

Lumajang. See LOEMADJANG.

Lum′ber (lŭm′bēr). River 125 m long, rising near boundary bet. Montgomery and Moore cos., cen. North Carolina, and flowing SE across South Carolina border, then S into Little Pee Dee river.

Lum′ber·ton (lŭm′bēr·t'n; -tǔn). City, ⊗ of Robeson co. S North Carolina, 32 m. S of Fayetteville; pop. 15,305; textiles, lumber.

Lump′kin (lŭm[p]′kĭn). **1** County in Georgia. See Table at GEORGIA.
2 City, ⊗ of Stewart co., W Georgia; pop. 1348.

Lumut. See DINDINGS.

Lu′na (lū′nȧ). **1** County in New Mexico. See Table at NEW MEXICO.
2 mod. **Lu′ni** (lōō′nē). Ancient town, Etruria, N Italy, on boundary bet. Etruria and Liguria; modern town site is W of Apuania, Tuscany; near the famous Carrara marble quarries. Destroyed by Saracens 1016. Gave its name to the district, **Lu·nig′i·a′na** (lū·nĭj′ĭ·ä′nȧ; -än′ȧ).

Lu′na·va′da (lōō′nä·vä′dä) or **Lu′na·wa′da** (-vä′dä). **1** Former Indian state, E Gujerat States, W Indian Union; 419 sq. m.; pop. (1941) 105,318.
2 Town, its ✳, 65 m. E of Ahmadabad; pop. 11 896.

Lund (lŭnd). City, Malmöhus prov., SW Sweden; pop. 30,665; publishing houses; iron foundries, brick kilns, sugar refineries, furniture factories; university, chartered by Charles XI 1666. Made bishopric 11th cent., archbishopric 1103, its archbishop becoming primate of Scandinavia 1163; reduced to bishopric 1536; scene of signing of a treaty 1679 bet. Sweden and Denmark.

Lundenburg. See BŘECLAV.

Lundi. See SAVE.

Lun′dy Isle (lŭn′dĭ). Island in Bristol Channel, 12 m. off coast of NW Devonshire, SW England; 2 sq. m.; lighthouse; once a pirate stronghold. Prehistoric remains; also ruins of chapel and castle.

Lun′dy's Lane (lŭn′dĭz). Roadway near Niagara Falls, Ontario prov., Canada, indecisive battle July 25, 1814 in which Americans and British both lost heavily.

Lü′ne·burg (lü′nĕ·bōōrk). **1** Government district of former Hannover prov., Prussia, Germany; 4379 sq. m.
2 City, Lower Saxony, SE of Hamburg; pop. 28,899; railroad junction; manufactures iron, lumber, chemicals,

paper, cement, lime, carpets. Became city 1247; member of Hanseatic League from 2d half of 13th cent.; in World War II taken by Allies Apr. 1945.

Lü'ne·bur'ger Hei'de (lü'nĕ·bōōr'gĕr hī'dĕ). Heath ab. 50 m. long bet. the Elbe and Aller rivers in NW cen. Germany.

Lu'nel' (lü'nĕl'). Commune, E Hérault dept., S France, SW of Nîmes; pop. (1931) 8435; wine.

Lü'nen (lü'nĕn), *also* **Lünen an der Lip'pe** (än dĕr lĭp'ĕ). Industrial city, N cen. North Rhine-Westphalia state, West Germany, on Lippe river 25 m. S of Münster; pop. 23,782; coal mining; blast furnaces.

Lu'nen·burg (lōō'nĕn·bûrg). **1** County in Virginia. See *Table* at VIRGINIA.

2 Town, Worcester co., cen. Massachusetts, 4 m. E of Fitchburg; pop. 6334.

3 Village, ⊗ of Lunenburg co., S Virginia; pop. (1950) 104.

4 County, Nova Scotia, Canada. See *Table* at NOVA SCOTIA.

5 Fishing town, ⊗ of Lunenburg co., S Nova Scotia, Canada, on Atlantic Ocean 37 m. SW of Halifax; pop. 2816; home port of America's greatest fishing fleet. Founded 1753 by Germans (from Lüneburg, Hannover) and Swiss on site of old French village; now largely retains its German character. Seized by privateers 1782 and plundered.

Lu·né'ville' (lü'nā'vēl'). Manufacturing city, Meurthe-et-Moselle dept., NE France, on Meurthe river 18 m. SE of Nancy; pop. 23,665; textiles, lace, yarn, gloves, hosiery, pottery, brewery products. Capital of 10th-cent. countship; fell to dukes of Lorraine 1344; residence 1735 ff. of Stanislas Leszczyński, former king of Poland; Peace of Lunéville signed 1801 bet. Germany and French Republic; suffered during German invasion 1914–18.

Lun'ga (lōōng'gȧ). Village at mouth of Lunga river on NW coast of Guadalcanal, SE Solomon Is., W Pacific Ocean, ab. 25 m. E of Cape Esperance on **Lunga Point.** The point, landing place of U.S. Marines Aug. 7, 1942, and **Lunga Lagoon** are at NW corner of Henderson Field, which is bounded on W by **Lunga River;** just E of the river and S of Henderson Field is a ridge of hills, **Lunga Ridge,** scene of a severe battle Sept. 12–13, 1942, which the Americans finally won. Off Lunga Point a naval battle won by the Americans Nov. 30, 1942.

Lun'ga, I'so·la (ē'zô·lä lōōng'gä). See DUGI OTOK.

Lung'ching'tsun' (lōōng'jĭng'tsōōn'). Treaty port, S Kirin prov., E Manchuria, just S of Yenki near Korea border; pop. 24,429.

Lung'chow' (lōōng'jō'). Town and treaty port, SW Kwangsi prov., SE China, on left bank of the Li, tributary of the Siang, ab. 190 m. above Yungning and on Tonkin border; pop. (1931 est.) 13,600; in direct connection with Langson in Tonkin; has large import trade for Yunnan and Kwangsi provs.; made treaty port 1889.

Lung'ern, Lake of (lōōng'ĕrn). Small lake in cen. Switzerland, S of Lake of Sarnen; traversed by Aa river.

Lung'hai' (lōōng'hī'). Name given to the railroad in N cen. China running W from the coast town of Lienyunkang in N Kiangsu prov. through Kaifeng in Honan prov. to Sian in Shensi prov. and beyond; continuous fighting for control of it during Chinese-Japanese war 1937–45.

Lung'ki' (lōōng'kē') *or* **Chang'chow'** (jäng'jō'). City, S Fukien prov., SE China, on left bank of Saikoe river 30 m. W of Amoy; pop. ab. 100,000; partially destroyed by Taiping rebels but now a thriving commercial center. Residence of Chu Hsi (1130–1200), philosopher and expounder of Confucianism, under the Southern Sung dynasty.

Lung'kiang' (lōōng'jĭ·äng'). **1** Former province (1932–45), N cen. Manchukuo; 25,904 sq. m.; pop. (1940 est.) 2,087,092; ✳ Lungkiang.

2 *Jap.* **Tsi'tsi·har** (tsē'tsĕ·här; *native* chī·chī·hä·ĕr). City and treaty port, former ✳ of Heilungkiang prov., N

Manchuria, and Japanese ✳ of Lungkiang prov., N cen. Manchukuo, on left bank of Nonni river 170 m. NW of Harbin; pop. (1940 est.) 133,495; 17 m. N of important junction point on former Chinese Eastern Railway; has large fairs each autumn with exchange market of European goods for regional furs, grain, etc.

Lung'kow' (lōōng'kō'). Treaty port, Shantung prov., NE China, on N coast of Shantung Penin. W of Chefoo; pop. (1931) 10,676.

Lung'ling' (lōōng'lĭng'). Town, W Yunnan prov., S China, on Burma Road bet. the Salween and Shweli rivers 85 m. NE of Wanting; alt. ab. 4500 ft.; 523 m. by road from Kunming. Taken by Japanese May 1942 and made into strong air base; threatened by Chinese June 1944 and captured Nov. 3, 1944.

Lu'ni (lōō'nĕ). **1** River ab. 200 m. long, NW India; rises on W slopes of Aravalli Range, flows SW in cen. and SW Rajputana to the Great Rann of Cutch.

2 Town in Italy. See LUNA.

Lunigiana. See LUNA town, Italy.

Lu·ni'nets (lōō·nyē'nyĕts); *Pol.* **Łu·ni'niec** (lōō·nē'-nyĕts). Town, White Russia, U.S.S.R., in Pripet Marshes 32 m. ENE of Pinsk (in former Polesie dept., E Poland); pop. 8715.

Lupatia. See ALTAMURA.

Lu'pin' (lōō'pĭn'); *Jap.* **Man'chou'li'** (män'chōō'lē'). Town, W Heilungkiang prov., N Manchuria, on former Chinese Eastern Railway at U.S.S.R. border; pop. 8782; a Mongol trading town, opened 1905.

Lup'ków (lōōp'kōōf). Pass 2135 ft. in the East Beskids, Carpathian Mts., on highway from Sanok, Poland, to E Slovakia; used by Russian and German armies in winter fighting of 1915–16.

Lu'que (lōō'kȧ). City, Central dept., S Paraguay, 9 m. E of Asunción; pop. ab. 23,470; founded 1635; 2d capital of the republic during war against the Triple Alliance 1865–70.

Lu·quil'lo (lōō·kē'yō). Municipality (pop. 8582) and town (pop. 2107), NE Puerto Rico; town on coast and on railroad 27 m. E of San Juan.

Luquillo Mountains. Range in E Puerto Rico; highest peak El Yunque 3496 ft.

Lu'ray (lōō'rā). Town and tourist resort, ⊗ of Page co., N Virginia, in Blue Ridge Mts. 30 m. NE of Harrisonburg; pop. 3014; manufactures flour, corn meal, work clothes; **Luray Caverns** (discovered 1878) nearby.

Lure (lür). Commune, E Haute-Saône dept., E France; pop. (1931) 6062; abbey founded c. 610 by a disciple of St. Columban.

Lur'gan (lûr'gȧn). Municipal borough, co. Armagh, S Northern Ireland, 20 m. SW of Belfast; pop. 16,181; linen factories.

Lu'ri·stan' (lōō'rĭ·stän'). Province, W Iran; 15,893 sq. m.; chief town Burujird; mountainous region, including the Zagros Mts. and the Pusht-i-Kuh; watered by the Karkheh and Karun. Independent 12th–15th cents.; its inhabitants chiefly Bakhtiaris.

Lurlei. See LORELEI.

Lu·sa'ka (lōō·sä'kȧ). Town, ✳ of Northern Rhodesia and of Kafue prov. in SE part, 240 m. NW of Salisbury; pop. 2396; in farm and mining (bismuth, gold, and copper) district. Made capital of Northern Rhodesia 1932.

Lu·sam'bo (lōō·säm'bō). **1** *now called* **Ka·sai'** (kä·sī'). Province, S cen. Republic of Congo (formerly Belgian Congo); 136,222 sq. m.; native pop. (1938) 1,953,931; ✳ Luluabourg.

2 Town, its former ✳, on the Sankuru (Lubilash) river, 5°S; pop. (1938) 5921.

Lu·sa'ti·a (lü·sā'shĭ·ȧ; -shȧ); *Ger.* **Lau'sitz** (lou'zĭts). Region of E Germany bet. the Elbe and Oder (modern Silesia); in 10th cent. became a margraviate of the Holy Roman Empire, in 1303 part of Brandenburg, and in 1368 part of Bohemia; in 15th cent. divided into Upper and Lower Lusatia; annexed to Saxony 1635. Its inhabitants, Lusatians, originally a Slavic tribe (the Wends).

Lu'shai Hills (lōō'shĭ). **1** Hilly region, S Assam, NE Indian Union; highest ab. 7000 ft.; part of N Arakan Yoma system. Inhabited by Lushais, an Indo-Chinese tribe, whose predatory raids 1840–90 made them very troublesome in E Assam; came under British control 1895.
2 District, Surma Valley and Hill division, Assam, comprising the hill region; 8142 sq. m.; pop. (1941) 152,786; administrative ✳ **Ai'jal** (ī'jȧl).

Lüshunkow. See PORT ARTHUR.

Lu'si'gnan' (lü'zē'nyäN'). Commune, Vienne dept., W cen. France, 15 m. SW of Poitiers; pop. (1931) 2048; ancient town, original seat of Lusignan family, rulers of Cyprus 1192–1474, and of Jerusalem and Armenia.

Lu'si·ta'ni·a (lū'sĭ·tā'nĭ·ȧ; -tān'yȧ). **1** Region of W Hispania, corresponding approximately to the greater part of modern Portugal and the Spanish provinces of Salamanca and Cáceres; from 27 B.C. until end of 4th cent. A.D. a province of the Roman Empire.
2 The classical name of Portugal (q.v.).

Lusk (lŭsk). Town, ⊗ of Niobrara co., E Wyoming, 50 m. N of Torrington; pop. 1890; grain, potatoes.

Lussino. See LOŠINJ.

Lut. = DASHT-I-LUT.

Lutch'er (lŭch'ẽr). Town, St. James parish, SE Louisiana, on Mississippi river 40 m. W of New Orleans; pop. 3274; sugar, rice, tobacco.

Lutea. See LETEA.

Lutetia or **Lutetia Parisiorum.** See PARIS.

Luteva. See LODÈVE.

Lüt'gen·dort'mund (lüt'gĕn·dôrt'mŏŏnt). Former commune (pop. 15,311), Arnsberg govt. dist., Prussia, Germany; coal mining; since 1928 part of Dortmund (q.v.).

Lu'ther·ville (lū'thẽr·vĭl). Village, Baltimore co., Maryland; pop. (est.) 9000.

Lu'ton (lū't'n). Municipal borough, Bedfordshire, SE cen. England, on the Lea 28 m. NNW of London; pop. 68,523, (1951) 110,370; center of hat and straw-plaiting industry in England; also manufactures automobiles, chemicals, dyes, and felt hats.

Lutsk (lōōtsk); *Pol.* **Łuck** (lōōtsk). City, NW Ukraine, U.S.S.R., on Styr river 125 m. ESE of Lublin; (formerly ✳ of Wołyń dept., Poland); pop. (1938–39 est.) 42,553; episcopal see; manufactures textiles, leather. An important town of medieval Volhynia, esp. wealthy in 15th cent.; declined much in wars bet. Russia and Poland 1557–82; taken by Russia 1791. In World War I center of Brusilov's offensive operations June–Aug. 1916; became part of Poland 1918. In World War II occupied by Russians 1939 and by Germans 1941; recovered 1944.

Lut'ter am Ba'ren·ber'ge (lōōt'ẽr äm bä'rĕn·bĕr'gĕ). Town, Brunswick cen. Germany, 23 m. SW of Brunswick; pop. ab. 1000; during Thirty Years' War scene of battle Aug. 17–27, 1626 in which the forces of the Catholic League under Field Marshal Tilly defeated the Protestants under King Christian IV of Denmark and Norway.

Lüt'tich (lüt'ĭK). Ger. for LIÈGE.

Lüt'tring·hau'sen (lüt'rĭng·hou'zĕn). Former city (pop. 13,671), Düsseldorf govt. dist., Rhine Province, Prussia, Germany; since 1929 part of Remscheid (q.v.).

Lutynia. See LEUTHEN.

Lüt'zel·burg (lüt'sĕl·bŏŏrK). Former Ger. name of LUXEMBOURG.

Lüt'zen (lüt'sĕn). Commune in former Saxony prov., Prussia, Germany, SW of Leipzig; pop. 4977; scene of two battles: (1) Nov. 16, 1632 in which the Swedes under Gustavus Adolphus defeated the Imperialists led by Wallenstein and in which Gustavus Adolphus was killed and (2) May 2, 1813 in which Napoleon overcame the Russians and Prussians (also called battle of Grossgörschen).

Lu·uk' (lōō·ōōk'). Town (municipal district), E Jolo I., Sulu prov., Phil. Is., 22 m. ESE of Jolo; pop. 27,878.

Lu·verne' (lů·vûrn'). **1** Town, ⊗ of Crenshaw co., S Alabama; pop. 2238; agricultural trade center.
2 City, ⊗ of Rock co., SW corner of Minnesota, 30 m. W of Worthington; pop. 4249; livestock, creamery, and grain co-operatives; granite quarries.

Lu·vu'a (lōō·vōō'ȧ). Name given to the Luapula river, cen. Africa, from where it leaves Lake Mweru to its junction with the Lualaba (upper Congo river) in E Congo.

Lux'em·bourg (lŭk'sĕm·bûrg; lōōk'sĕm·bŏŏrg; *Fr.* lük'-säN'bŏŏr') or **Lux'em·burg** (lŭk'sĕm·bûrg; lōōk'sĕm-bŏŏrg; *Ger.* lōōk'sĕm·bŏŏrK). **1** Medieval county and duchy, now largely in the grand duchy of Luxembourg and the Belgian province of Luxembourg.
2 Province, SE Belgium; 1705 sq. m.; pop. (1941 est.) 217,721; ✳ Arlon; rivers Ourthe, Semois; crossed by Ardennes forest; iron mining, quarrying (slate), agriculture.
3 Grand duchy, W Europe, bet. SE Belgium and W Germany; 999 sq. m.; pop. (1935) 296,913; ✳ Luxembourg; forms part of plateau of Ardennes; hilly and well-forested; watered by Sauer and Alzette rivers of the Moselle basin. Chief occupations agriculture, cattle raising, and iron mining. Inhabitants of German origin but French is widely spoken. Chief towns Luxembourg, Esch-sur-Alzette, Differdange, Dudelange. See *Map* at BELGIUM.

History: County of Luxembourg (in Holy Roman Empire) emerged in 10th cent. A.D.; beginning with Henry VII (1308–13), house of Luxembourg produced four German emperors (see also BOHEMIA); raised to rank of duchy 1354; through Burgundian house which secured it 1451, duchy passed to Spanish and later, to Austrian, Hapsburgs as part of Netherlands (q.v.); occupied by French 1794; grand duchy of Luxembourg, erected by Congress of Vienna, part of kingdom of Netherlands 1815–30; after Belgian revolt, W half given to Belgium, but rest remained grand duchy of Luxembourg in personal union with Netherlands 1839; joined German Zollverein 1842; neutrality and independence of Luxembourg guaranteed and Prussian garrison of town of Luxembourg withdrawn after Franco-German crisis 1867; with accession of Adolph of Nassau as grand duke 1890, broke connection with Netherlands; occupied by Germany in World War I; concluded economic union with Belgium 1922; occupied by Germans May 1940 to Sept. 1944; formed customs union with Belgium and the Netherlands 1947.
4 Manufacturing and commercial city, ✳ of grand duchy of Luxembourg; pop. (1935) 57,740; on a rocky height with steep cliffs on three sides on the Alzette in S part.

Lu'xeuil', *in full* **Luxeuil-les-Bains** (lük'sû'y'·lä-bäN'). Commune, Haute-Saône dept., E France; pop. (1931) 5695; thermal springs. Dates from pre-Roman times; often devastated, esp. by Attila 451, by Saracens in 8th cent., and by Normans in 9th cent.; noted for its abbey, founded 590 by St. Columban, suppressed during the Revolution.

Lux'or (lŭk'sôr; lōōk'-); *Arab.* **El Uq'sor** (ăl ŏŏk'sôr) or **El Qu'sur** (ăl kŏŏ'sôr). Town on E bank of the Nile, Qena prov., Upper Egypt; pop. ab. 15,000; S part of site of ancient Thebes; tombs of kings; ruins of a magnificent ancient temple built by Amenhotep III (reigned c. 1411–1375 B.C.) and of other structures by Ikhnaton and Ramses II. See KARNAK.

Luz (lüz). Village, SW Hautes-Pyrénées dept., SW France; pop. (1931) 1292; on the Gave de Pau opp. **Saint–Sau'veur'** (säN'sō'vûr'), village with thermal springs; has church of 12th and 13th cents. built by the Knights of St. John of Jerusalem.

Luzern. See LUCERNE.

Lu·zerne' (lů·zûrn'). **1** County in Pennsylvania. See *Table* at PENNSYLVANIA.
2 Borough, Luzerne co., E Pennsylvania, 3 m. NNW of Wilkes-Barre; pop. 5118; coal mining.

Luž′ni·ce (lōōzh′nyĭ·tsĕ); *Ger.* **Lain′sitz** (līn′zĭts). River ab. 160 m. long, S Bohemia prov., W Czechoslovakia; rises in Austria, flows N to Tabor, then turns abruptly SW and empties into the Vltava.

Lu·zon′ (lōō·zŏn′; *Span.* lōō·sôn′). Chief island of Philippine Is., in N part; 40,420 sq. m.; pop. 3,800,000; comprises cities of Manila and Baguio, 23 provinces, and Mountain Province which contains 5 subprovinces. Of irregular shape, coast line much indented forming many good anchorages, esp. Manila Bay, Lingayen Gulf, Lamon Bay, and Lagonoy Gulf. Has many islands and islets off its shores, esp. Babuyan Is. to the N, Catanduanes and Polillo off E coast. Separated on S from Visayan Is., Marinduque and Mindoro by San Bernardino Strait, Sibuyan Sea, and Verde Island Passage. Principal mountain group, Cordillera Central, in NW; Sierra Madre range along NE coast; in S are active volcanoes Taal and Mayon. Chief rivers Pampanga, Cagayan, Agno, and Pasig; only large lakes Laguna de Bay and Taal. Produces esp. rice, sugar, coconuts, tobacco, and hemp (abacá); has much undeveloped mineral wealth. Inhabitants mainly Tagalogs, Bikols, Ilokanos, Pangasinans, Pampangans. For *History*, see PHILIPPINE ISLANDS.

Luzon Strait. Name sometimes given to wide passage bet. N Luzon, Phil. Is., and S Formosa; connects the Pacific Ocean with the South China Sea and includes Bashi Channel, Balintang Channel, Babuyan Channel.

Luz·za′ra (lōōt·tsä′rä). Commune, Reggio nell'Emilia prov., Emilia, N Italy, 18 m. N of Reggio nell'Emilia; pop. 9946; scene of victory of Prince Eugene over Spanish and French army 1702.

Lvov (lȧ·vôf′; *Russ.* ly′vôf). **1** Region, W Ukraine, U.S.S.R., formerly in SE Poland.
2 *Pol.* **Lwów** (lȧ·vōōf′); *Ger.* **Lemberg** (lĕm′bûrg; *Ger.* lĕm′bĕrκ); *Ukrainian* **Lwiw** (ly′vēf). Commercial city, W Ukraine, U.S.S.R., 115 m. SW of Lutsk; (formerly ✻ of Lwów dept., Poland); pop. (1938–39 est.) 318,144; railroad junction; seat of three (Roman, Greek, Armenian) Catholic archbishops; university; 15th-cent. Roman Catholic cathedral, 15th-cent. Armenian Catholic cathedral, 18th-cent. Greek Catholic cathedral; manufactures agricultural machinery, metal goods, sugar, beer, liquors.
History: Founded 1270 by Ukrainian prince; captured by Poles 1340; became city 1352, Roman Catholic episcopal see 1412; one of the great trading towns of medieval Europe; passed to Austria after first partition of Poland 1772 and made capital of Austrian province of Galicia. In World War I center of two great battles bet. Russia and German allies: Aug. 26 to Sept. 1, 1914, and June 3 to 22, 1915; occupied by Ukrainians 1918 who set up republic (Western Ukrainia); Ukrainians subdued by Poles Nov. 1918. Occupied in World War II by Russians 1939, by German armies July 1941; retaken by Russians July 27, 1944.

Lwan (lȧ·wän′). River ab. 400 m. long, S Jehol and Hopeh prov., NE China; rises in Chahar, E Inner Mongolia, flows N, then E, then SE to Gulf of Po Hai. Chengteh on its N bank.

Lwiw. See LVOV.

Lwów (lȧ·vōōf′). **1** Former Polish department; 10,960 sq. m.; pop. 3,127,311. After World War II greater part (E and cen.) transferred to Ukraine, U.S.S.R. Smaller W part now in Rzeszów dept., SE Poland.
2 City. See LVOV.

Lya′khov Islands (lyä′κȧf). Two islands, **Bol·shoi′** [bŏl·shoi′; bōl-; *Russ.* bŭl·y′·shoi′] (Great Lyakhov) and **Ma′ly** [mä′lĭ] (Little Lyakhov), S of New Siberian Is., Soviet Union, Asia, E of Laptev Sea, belonging to Yakutsk A.S.S.R.; Bolshoi separated from mainland by Lapteva Strait. The group considered by some to be a part of New Siberian Is. Has great deposits of animal and vegetable remains of Ice Age. Discovered and described 1770 by a Russian merchant, Lyakhov.

Ly′all·pur (lī′ăl·pŏŏr). Town, Multan division, West Punjab, Pakistan, 75 m. W of Lahore; pop. (1941) 69,930; cotton industry.

Lyc′a·bet′tus (lĭk′ȧ·bĕt′ŭs; lī′kȧ-); *Gr.* **Ly′ka·bet·tos′** (*Mod. Gr.* lyē′kä·vĕ·tôs′). Mountain 909 ft. in NE part of Athens, Greece.

Ly·cae′us (lī·sē′ŭs). Mountain in ancient Arcadia, Greece, NW of Megalopolis; on border bet. present departments of Arcadia and Messenia; sacred to Zeus.

Lyc′a·o′ni·a (lĭk′ȧ·ō′nĭ·ȧ; lī′kȧ-; -ōn′yȧ). Ancient district and Roman province in S Asia Minor, an interior elevated region, in Bible times bounded on N by Galatia, on E by Cappadocia, on S by Cilicia, and on W by Pisidia and Phrygia, but its boundaries varied greatly; successively under Persia, Syria, and Rome, becoming a separate province 371 A.D. Its cities of Lystra, Iconium, and Derbe visited by Paul (*Acts* xiv).

Ly·ce′um (lī·sē′ŭm). A locality on the Ilissus in E part of ancient Athens, Greece, comprising an enclosure dedicated to Apollo and adorned with fountains and buildings erected by Pisistratus, Pericles, and Lycurgus; frequented by Athenian youths for exercise and by philosophers for teaching, esp. Aristotle and his followers (Peripatetics).

Lychnidus. See OHRID lake and town.

Lychnitis. 1 See OHRID lake.
2 See Lake SEVAN.

Ly′ci·a (lĭsh′ĭ·ȧ; lĭsh′ȧ). Ancient district in S Asia Minor, a mountainous coastal region watered by the Xanthus; bounded on NW by Caria and on NE by Pamphylia; chief towns Myra and Patara. Settled in early times, came under Persia and Syria and in 1st cent. A.D. annexed by Rome; as a Roman province ultimately united with Pamphylia, Pisidia, etc. (**Lycia et Pam·phyl′i·a** [ĕt păm·fĭl′ĭ·ȧ; -fĭl′yȧ]).

Lyck. See ELK.

Ly·com′ing (lī·kŭm′ĭng; -kō′mĭng; -kŏm′ĭng). County in Pennsylvania. See *Table* at PENNSYLVANIA.

Lycoming Creek. River ab. 35 m. long, N cen. Pennsylvania; rises in Bradford co., flows S and SW into the West Branch of Susquehanna river in S Lycoming co. near Williamsport.

Ly·cop′o·lis (lī·kŏp′ô·lĭs). Ancient city of Upper Egypt, its site near modern Asyût (*q.v.*).

Lyc′o·re′a (lĭk′ô·rē′ȧ; lī′kô-). **1** Southernmost peak of Mount Parnassus, Phocis, cen. Greece.
2 Ancient town at its foot.

Lyc′o·su′ra (lĭk′ô·sŏŏr′ȧ; lī′kô-). Ancient city of S Arcadia, cen. Peloponnesus, Greece, WSW of Megalopolis, said by Pausanias to be the oldest city of Greece; some ruins remain.

Lydd (lĭd). Municipal borough, SE Kent, SE England, NW of Dungeness on coast of Strait of Dover; pop. 2774; military camp nearby where the explosive *lyddite* was first developed.

Lyd′da (lĭd′ȧ); *Arab.* **Lidd** (lĭd); *Heb.* **Lod** (lōd). **1** District, W Palestine, including the subdistricts of Er Ramle and Jaffa; 487 sq. m.; pop. 216,081, (1942 est.) 454,688; ✻ Jaffa; formerly part of the Southern District.
2 City in Lydda dist., W Palestine, 9 m. SE of Jaffa on the road to Jerusalem; pop. (1944 est.) 17,616; an important railroad junction point. The ancient city, Lod (*1 Chron.* viii. 12), in Judaea in the Plain of Sharon, had long history; visited by Peter (*Acts* ix. 32); destroyed by Romans 66 and 70 A.D.; rebuilt and became a bishopric; by some supposed to be birthplace of St. George, patron saint of England; destroyed by Saladin 1191 and rebuilt by Richard of England.

Ly′den·burg (lī′d'n·bûrg). Town, E cen. Transvaal, NE Union of South Africa, 145 m. ENE of Pretoria; pop. 3845; agriculture, sheep farming; platinum mined in vicinity. Founded 1846 by Boers and made center of a district which they proclaimed a republic; became part of Utrecht dist. 1858 but remained in Transvaal when Utrecht (*q.v.*) was ceded to Natal 1903.

Lyd′i·a (lĭd′ĭ·á). Ancient country in W part of Asia Minor; bounded on N by Mysia, on E by Phrygia, on S by Caria, and on W by the Aegean; ✻ Sardis; included the valleys of the Hermus and Caÿster; important towns Magnesia, Philadelphia, and Thyatira. Its early dynasties legendary, but under the Mermnadae (685–546 B.C.) it became a powerful and cultured kingdom, contributing notably to ancient industrial progress, esp. in coinage; conquered by Persians under Cyrus 546 B.C., later passed to Syria and Pergamum, and under the Romans became a part of the province of Asia.

Lye and Wolles′cote (lī, wŏŏlz′kŭt). Former urban district, Worcestershire, England; pop. (1931) 12,237.

Ly′ell, Mount (lī′ĕl). Peak 13,090 ft. in Sierra Nevada, near junction point of Madera, Mariposa, and Tuolumne cos., E cen. California.

Lyell Island. Island, cen. Queen Charlotte Is., off W Brit. Columbia, Canada, on Hecate Strait.

Ly′e′mun′, or **Ly′ee′moon′, Pass** (lē′yü′mŭn′). Strait ¼ m. wide bet. NE Hong Kong I. and mainland; E end of Hong Kong harbor.

Lykabettos. See LYCABETTUS.

Ly′kens (lī′kĕnz). Borough, Dauphin co., SE cen. Pennsylvania, 23 m. NNE of Harrisburg; pop. 2527; first settled 1732; coal mining; manufactures shirts, hosiery, paper boxes.

Ly′man (lī′măn). **1** County in South Dakota. See *Table* at SOUTH DAKOTA.
2 Town, Spartanburg co., NW South Carolina, ab. 11 m. W of Spartanburg; pop. 1261.

Lyme Bay (līm). Widemouthed inlet of the English Channel on S coast of Somersetshire, SW England.

Lyme Re′gis (līm rē′jĭs). Municipal borough, Dorsetshire, S England; pop. 3191; seaside resort; manufactures cement. Monmouth landed here with some of his rebels 1685.

Lym Fjord. Var. of LIM FJORD.

Lym′ing·ton (lĭm′ĭng·tŭn). Municipal borough, Hampshire, S England, on the Lymington near English Channel 6 m. SW of city of Southampton; pop. 22,674; yacht-building yard. Before 18th cent. manufactured salt; became a port in 12th cent.

Lymm (lĭm). Urban district, Cheshire, NW England, 12 m. SW of Manchester; pop. 6410.

Lympne (lĭm); *anc.* **Por′tus Le·ma′nis** (pôr′tŭs lē-mā′nĭs). Village, Kent, SE England, 2 m. W of Hythe; 15th-cent. castle, now a modern mansion.

Ły′na (lī′nä). Polish name of the upper Alle river, now in Olsztyn dept., N Poland.

Lyn′brook (lĭn′brŏŏk). Village, Nassau co., SE New York, on S shore of Long I. 18 m. E of New York City; pop. 19,881; residential suburb and resort.

Lynch′burg (lĭnch′bûrg). **1** Town, ⊗ of Moore co., S Tennessee; pop. 396.
2 City, S cen. Virginia, in Campbell co. but politically independent; on James river in foothills of Blue Ridge Mts., 48 m. ENE of Roanoke; 13 sq. m.; pop. 54,790; dark-leaf tobacco market; manufactures shoes, tannin extract, foundry products, textiles, lumber, paper. Lynchburg Coll. (1903; coed.); Randolph-Macon Woman's Coll. (1893). Founded 1786; incorp. as town 1805, as city 1852; Confederate supply base in Civil War.

Lynch′es (lĭn′chĕz; -chĭz). River 140 m. long rising in S North Carolina and flowing SE into Pee Dee river on SE boundary of Florence co., South Carolina.

Lyn′den (lĭn′dĕn). City, Whatcom co., NW Washington, 14 m. N of Bellingham; pop. 2542.

Lynd′hurst (lĭnd′hûrst). **1** Township, Bergen co., NE New Jersey, 6 m. N of Newark; pop. 21,867; manufactures synthetic aromatic compounds.
2 City, Cuyahoga co., N Ohio, 11 m. E of Cleveland; pop. 16,805.

Lyn′don (lĭn′dŭn). **1** City, ⊗ of Osage co., E Kansas; pop. 953.
2 Town in Vermont. See LYNDON CENTER.

Lyndon Center. Village in Lyndon town (pop. 3425), Caledonia co., NE Vermont, ab. 8 m. N of St. Johnsbury; pop. 274; Lyndon Teachers College (1911; coed.).

Lyn′don·ville (lĭn′dŭn·vĭl). Village, Caledonia co., NE Vermont, 13 m. N of St. Johnsbury; pop. 1477.

Lyn·do′ra (lĭn-dôr′á). Locality, Butler co., W Pennsylvania; pop. 3232.

Lyngs Fjord (lŭngs). Inlet of Arctic Ocean on NW coast of Norway, E of Tromsö.

Lynmouth. See LYNTON.

Lynn (lĭn). **1** County in Texas. See *Table* at TEXAS.
2 City, Essex co., NE corner of Massachusetts, on Lynn Harbor 10 m. NE of Boston; pop. 94,478; one of leading shoe-manufacturing centers in U.S.; manufactures include also electrical appliances. Originally known as Saugus, settled 1629, incorp. as town 1631, renamed 1637; incorp. as city 1850; manufacture of shoes began 1635, reached its height in 19th cent.
3 See KING'S LYNN, England.

Lynn Canal. Deep fiord 80 m. long by 6 m. wide, SE Alaska, leading N from Juneau; near its head divides into Chilkat Inlet on W and Chilkoot Inlet on E; Taiya Inlet, at entrance to which is Skagway, is an upper arm of Chilkoot Inlet. Important S gateway to Klondike region.

Lynn′field (lĭn′fēld). Town, Essex co., NE corner of Massachusetts, 10 m. NNE of Boston; pop. 8398.

Lynn Harbor. Inlet of Massachusetts Bay on S shore of Essex co., NE corner of Massachusetts; the city of Lynn is at its N end.

Lynn Regis. See KING'S LYNN.

Lyn′ton (lĭn′t'n; -tŭn). Village, N Devonshire, SW England, NE of Barnstaple; on a cliff ab. 430 ft. high above **Lyn′mouth** (lĭn′mŭth; lĭm′ŭth), village on shore of Bristol Channel; both popular resorts; nearby is Doone Valley (*q.v.*).

Lyn′wood (lĭn′wŏŏd). Industrial city, Los Angeles co., SW California, 8 m. S of Los Angeles; pop. 31,614; manufactures oil tools, gas appliances, thermostats, traffic signals, tanks.

Ly′on (lī′ŭn). **1** Counties in five states of the U.S. See *Tables* at IOWA, KANSAS, KENTUCKY, MINNESOTA, NEVADA.
2 River ab. 38 m. long in Perth co., cen. Scotland, flowing into the Tay river.

Ly′on′ (lē′ôn′; *Fr.* lyôn). See LYONS.

Lyonais. See LYONNAIS.

Ly′on Mountain (lī′ŭn). Peak 3830 ft. in the Adirondack Mts., Clinton co., NE corner of New York.

Ly′on·nais′ or **Ly′o·nais′** (lē′ô-nā′; *Fr.* lyô′nĕ′). Historical region of SE cen. France; bounded anciently on N by Burgundy, SE by Dauphiné, S by Languedoc, SW by Auvergne, NW by Bourbonnais; equivalent to modern departments of Rhône and Loire; ✻ Lyons. Ancient territory of the Segusiavi; ruled by counts of Forez 11th–13th cents. A.D., later by the count-archbishops of Lyons; passed to house of Bourbon 1371; confiscated by French crown 1527; made province of France and appanage of crown under the Valois.

Ly′ons (lī′ŭnz). **1** City, ⊗ of Toombs co., SE cen. Georgia, 72 m. W of Savannah; pop. 3219; tobacco, cotton, sweet potatoes.
2 Residential village, Cook co., NE Illinois, 8 m. W of Chicago; pop. 9936; located at an old portage bet. the Des Plaines river and the Chicago river, which was used by Marquette and other early French explorers and by the Indians.
3 City, ⊗ of Rice co., cen. Kansas, 27 m. NNW of Hutchinson; pop. 4592; trading center on old Santa Fe trail.
4 Village, ⊗ of Wayne co., W New York, 24 m. WNW of Auburn; pop. 4673; railroad and transshipment point in agricultural region; manufactures machinery, furniture, brandy.

Ly′ons′ (lē′ôn′; lī′ŭnz); *Fr.* **Ly′on′** (lē′ôn′; *Fr.* lyôn);

anc. **Lug·du′num** (lŭg·dū′nŭm). Manufacturing and commercial city, ✻ of Rhône dept., E cen. France, at confluence of Rhone and Saône rivers 58 m. NW of Grenoble; pop. 471,270; 3d largest city of France and 2d in industrial and military importance; railroad center; 13 bridges over Saône river, 11 bridges over Rhone river, extensive quays; 12th-cent. Gothic cathedral (with four towers), 15th-cent. archiepiscopal palace, university (1808), a free Catholic university; most important center of manufacture of silk in world; other industries include foundries, glassworks, dye works, potteries, tanneries, printeries, breweries, chemical works.

History: Founded c. 40 B.C.; sometime residence of Roman emperors; made episcopal see 2d cent. A.D. (Irenaeus bishop of Lyons 177); sacked by Huns and Visigoths; held by Saracens 8th cent.; became capital of kingdom of Provence on dissolution of Charlemagne's empire; site of ecumenical church councils 1245, 1274; united to French crown 1312; received municipal charter 1320; suffered during French Revolution; site of revolts 1831, 1834, 1849, 1871. Birthplace of Caracalla, St. Irenaeus, Ampère. In World War II occupied by Free French forces Sept. 3, 1944.

Lys (lēs); *Flemish* **Lei′e** (lī′ĕ). River ab. 120 m. long in France and Belgium; flows NE, forming a section of the French-Belgian boundary, and joins the Schelde river at Gent; navigable for ab. 100 m.

Ly′se Fjord (lü′sĕ). Inlet of North Sea on SW coast of Norway, E of Stavanger.

Lys′kamm′ (lēs′käm′). Peak 14,888 ft. in Pennine Alps, in the Monte Rosa group on Swiss-Italian border; separated from Dufourspitze, highest peak of Monte Rosa, by **Lys Pass** (lēs), 13,934 ft.

Ly′so Gó′ry (lī′sô gŏŏ′rĭ). Eminence 2005 ft. in the department of Kielce, S cen. Poland, E of Kielce.

Lys′tra (lĭs′trà). Town in ancient Lycaonia, Asia Minor; its site is ab. 20 m. SSW of Konya; visited by Paul (*Acts* xiv. 6–21).

Lys′va (lĭs′và). City, Molotov Region, W Soviet Russia, Asia, on railroad 50 m. E of Molotov; pop. 51,192.

Lyth′am St. Anne′s (lĭth′ăm sánt ănz′). Municipal borough, Lancashire, NW England, on Irish Sea at mouth of the Ribble 22 m. N of Liverpool; pop. 30,298; seaport and watering place.

Lyt′tel·ton (lĭt″l·tŭn); *formerly* **Port Coo′per** (kŏŏ′pẽr; kŏŏp′ẽr). Borough, port and suburb of Christchurch, Canterbury provincial dist., E South I., New Zealand, on Port Lyttelton; pop. 3720; exports wool, meat, wheat.

Lyublin. See LUBLIN.

Lyublyana. Var. of LJUBLJANA.

M

M'-, Mc-. Abbreviated forms of Mac-. Names beginning with this prefix are all alphabetized as if spelled Mac-. M' is sometimes written M', esp. in British references.

Ma·a'la·e'a Bay (mä·ä'lä·ä'ä). Bay on SW side of Maui I., Hawaii.

Ma·'an' (mä·än'). Town, SW Jordan, ab. 60 m. SSE of the Dead Sea; on railroad S from Damascus and Amman and on highway S to 'Aqaba.

Maa'rian·ha'mi·na (mä'ryàn·hä'mĭ·nà) *or* **Ma·rie'-hamn'** (mà·rē'hàm'n). Seaport on Ahvenanmaa I., * of Ahvenanmaa dept., Finland, in the Gulf of Bothnia; pop. 1653.

Maas (mäs). The Dutch name of the Meuse river; after its entrance into Netherlands near Maastricht and again near Roermond, it flows N parallel to the German boundary past Venlo; its N branch flows W to unite with the Waal at Gorinchem, its S branch flows direct to the Hollandsch Diep; its estuary anastomoses with the Waal and Lek. See Rhine, Merwede, Nieuwe Maas, and Oude Maas.

Maas'bree (mäs'brä). Commune, Limburg prov., SE Netherlands, W of the Maas near Venlo; pop. 13,216.

Ma·a'sin (mä·ä'sĭn). Municipality on SW coast of Leyte I., Phil. Is., 78 m. S of Tacloban; pop. 29,264; a hemp port and has active coastwise trade.

Maas·sluis' (mäs·slois'). Commune, South Holland prov., SW Netherlands; pop. (1940) 9244; W of Rotterdam on the Nieuwe Maas.

Maas·tricht' (mäs·trĭkt') *or* **Maes·tricht'** (mäs-). Commune, * of Limburg prov., SE Netherlands, on Maas (Meuse) river near the frontier of Belgium; pop. (1939) 67,902; sandstone quarries nearby; church of St. Servatius, dating from 6th cent., oldest church in Netherlands; a Romanesque church dating from 11th cent.; has active trade in various manufactured articles with Belgian towns. Founded on site of Roman town; its location as a border town has subjected it frequently to siege or capture in various wars, esp. in 1579 when 8000 of its inhabitants were massacred by Spaniards, and in 1673, 1748, and 1794; withstood siege in 1830; occupied by Germans 1940; retaken by Americans Sept. 15, 1944.

Ma·ba·la'cat (mä'bä·lä'kät). Municipality, N Pampanga prov., Luzon, Phil. Is., on Manila-Dagupan R.R. 15 m. NNW of San Fernando; pop. 20,560.

Ma·bi'ri, Cape (mä·bē'rē). Cape on E cen. Bougainville I., NW Solomon Is., W Pacific Ocean.

Ma'ble·ton (mā'b'l·tŭn; -t'n). Urban area, Cobb co., NW Georgia, W of Atlanta; pop. 7127.

Ma·cá' (mä·kä'). Peak 9710 ft. in S Chile, E of Melchor I. and N of Aysén.

Ma'ca·be'be (mä'kä·bā'bä). Municipality, SE Pampanga prov., Luzon, Phil. Is., on edge of Pampanga delta 8 m. S of San Fernando; pop. 20,149. For many years furnished recruits for Spanish civil guard in the archipelago later for Philippine scouts of Amer. army.

Mc'A·doo (măk'à·dōō). Borough, Schuylkill co., E cen. Pennsylvania, 18 m. NE of Pottsville; pop. 3560; coal mining; manufactures textiles, paper boxes.

Ma'ca·é' (mä'kà·ä'). Coastal city, Rio de Janeiro state, SE Brazil, 95 m. ENE of Rio de Janeiro; pop. 9719.

Ma'ca·ja·lar' Bay (mä'kä·hä·lär'). Inlet of S Mindanao Sea in Misamis Oriental prov., N Mindanao, Phil. Is., ab. 19 m. across its mouth; Cagayan at its head.

Mc·Al'es·ter (măk·ăl'ĕs·tẽr). City, ⊗ of Pittsburg co., SE Oklahoma, 50 m. S of Okmulgee; pop. 17,419; coal mines; cotton gins; woodworking, food processing.

Mc·Al'len (măk·ăl'ĕn; -ĭn). City, Hidalgo co., S Texas, 50 m. WNW of Brownsville; pop. 32,728; raises citrus fruits, winter vegetables; canneries.

Ma·cao' (mà·kou'; -kä'ō̇); *Port.* **Ma·cau'** (mà·kou'). **1** Island in Si delta W of mouth of Pearl river, Kwang-

tung prov., SE China; now usually known by its Chinese name, **Heung'shan'** (shĭ·äng'shän').

2 Portuguese colony on peninsula of SE Macao I., enclave of Kwangtung prov., SE China, at SW entrance of Pearl river ab. 40 m. W of Hong Kong; 6 sq. m.; pop. (1940) 374,737; includes small islands of Taipa (pop. in 1927, 5595) and Colôane (pop. in 1927, 3124).

3 Its chief town; ab. 2 sq. m.; pop. (1927) 148,456; its harbor now somewhat silted up; healthful climate makes it a popular resort; chief gambling center of the Far East; exports rice, tea, fish, anise, and cassia.

History: Settled by Portuguese 1557; from 1717 until 19th cent., Macao and Canton were the only Chinese ports open to European trade; its independence declared by Portuguese 1849 but not recognized by China as Portuguese territory until 1887. For many years a haven for missionaries and traders; burial place of Robert Morrison and nearby is place where St. Francis Xavier died and was buried; residence c. 1558–59 of the Portuguese poet Camoëns, who wrote part of *The Lusiad* here.

Ma'ca·pá' (mä'kà·pä'). City, * of Amapá Territory, N Brazil; port, N of Amazon delta; pop. 9748.

Ma'ca·rá' (mä'kä·rä'). Town, Loja prov., SW Ecuador, on Peruvian border; pop. (1944 est.) 10,006.

Mc·Ar'thur (măk·är'thẽr). Village, ⊗ of Vinton co., S Ohio, 26 m. E of Chillicothe; pop. 1529; clay deposits.

MacArthur. See Ormoc.

Ma'cas (mä'käs). Town, E Ecuador, on Santiago river 123 m. E of Guayaquil; * of Santiago-Zamora prov.

Macassar. See Makassar.

Macau. See Macao.

Mac·bride' Head (măk·brīd'). Promontory extending into South Atlantic Ocean from NE coast of East Falkland I., Falkland Is., off SE South America.

Maccaluba. See Aragona.

Mc·Ca'mey (mà·kā'mĭ). City, Upton co., W Texas, 38 m. ENE of Fort Stockton; pop. 3375; oil, cattle.

Mc·Cau'ley Peak (mà·kô'lĭ). Mountain 13,558 ft. in La Plata co., SW Colorado.

Mc·Cays'ville (mà·kāz'vĭl; *Sou. also* -v'l). City, Fannin co., N Georgia, on Tennessee border; pop. 1871.

Mc·Clain' (mà·klān'). County in Oklahoma. See *Table* at Oklahoma.

Mac·clen'ny (mà·klĕn'ĭ). Town ⊗ of Baker co., NE Florida; pop. 2671.

Mac'cles·field (măk''lz·fēld). Municipal borough, Cheshire, NW England, on the Bollin 17 m. S of Manchester; pop. 35,981; center of silk manufacture in England; Jodrell Bank Experimental Station (radio telescope) nearby (to W).

M'·Clin'tock Channel (mà·klĭn'tŭk). Passage 50 to 120 m. wide bet. E Victoria I. and W Prince of Wales I., Franklin District, Northwest Territories, Canada.

Mc·Clin'tock Peak (mà·klĭn'tŭk). Mountain 8200 ft. in Glacier National Park, NW Montana.

Mc·Cluer' Gulf (mà·klōōr'). Inlet 125 m. long by 15 to 30 m. wide on NW coast of New Guinea I. Neth. New Guinea; almost cuts off Vogelkop Penin. from rest of New Guinea, being separated on E from Geelvink Bay by isthmus only ab. 15 m. wide.

M'·Clure', *or* Mc·Clure', Strait (mà·klōōr'). Channel bet. Banks I. and Melville I., Franklin District, Northwest Territories, Canada; opens on W into Arctic Ocean and on E into Viscount Melville Sound.

Mc·Clus'ky (mà·klŭs'kĭ). City, ⊗ of Sheridan co., cen. North Dakota; pop. 751.

Mc·Coll' (mà·kŏl'). Town, Marlboro co., NE South Carolina, 10 m. ENE of Bennettsville; pop. 2479.

Mc·Comb′ (må·kōm′). City, Pike co., S Mississippi, 60 m. ESE of Natchez; pop. 12,020; cotton and rayon mills; shipping point for truck-farm products.

Mc·Con′au·ghy, Lake (må·kŏn′å·gǐ). See UNITED STATES, *Dams and Reservoirs* (Kingsley Dam).

Mc·Cone′ (må·kōn′). County in Montana. See *Table* at MONTANA.

Mc·Con′nells·burg (må·kŏn′′lz·bûrg). Borough, ⊗ of Fulton co., S Pennsylvania; pop. 1245.

Mc·Con′nels·ville (må·kŏn′′lz·vǐl). Village, ⊗ of Morgan co., SE Ohio, on Muskingum river 21 m. SSE of Zanesville; pop. 2257; manufactures smoked meats, lumber, feed; coal mines and gas and oil wells nearby.

Mc·Cook′ (må·kŏok′). **1** County in South Dakota. See *Table* at SOUTH DAKOTA.
2 City, ⊗ of Red Willow co., S Nebraska, 65 m. S of North Platte; pop. 8301; trade center in agricultural and livestock-raising section; home of George W. Norris, U.S. senator 1913–43.

Mc·Cor′mick (må·kôr′mǐk). **1** County in South Carolina. See *Table* at SOUTH CAROLINA.
2 Town, its ⊗, W South Carolina; pop. 1998.

Mc·Crack′en (må·krăk′ĕn). County in Kentucky. See *Table* at KENTUCKY.

Mc·Crea′ry (må·krē̱r′ǐ). County in Kentucky. See *Table* at KENTUCKY.

Mc·Cro′ry (må·krōr′ǐ). City, Woodruff co., NE cen. Arkansas; pop. 1053; until 1931 a county seat (with Augusta and Cotton Plant).

Mc·Cul′loch (må·kŭl′ŭ). County in Texas. See *Table* at TEXAS.

Mc·Cur′tain (må·kûr′t′n). County in Oklahoma. See *Table* at OKLAHOMA.

Macdhui, Ben. See BEN MACDHUI.

Mc·Don′ald (măk·dŏn′′ld). **1** County in Missouri. See *Table* at MISSOURI.
2 Village, Trumbull co., NE Ohio, 6 m. NW of Youngstown; pop. 2727.
3 Borough, Allegheny and Washington cos., SW Pennsylvania; pop. 3141; coal mines, oil wells.

Mac·don′ald, Lake (măk·dŏn′′ld). Lake in desert region of cen. Australia, on Tropic of Capricorn just W of boundary bet. Western Australia and Northern Territory.

Mac·don′nell Ranges (măk·dŏn′′l). A series of parallel ridges and valleys of hard folded Paleozoic rocks, running east and west, S Northern Territory, Australia; highest Mt. Ziel 4955 ft.

Mc·Don′ough (măk·dŏn′ŭ). **1** County in Illinois. See *Table* at ILLINOIS.
2 City, ⊗ of Henry co., NW cen. Georgia; pop. 2224.

Mac·dou′gall (măk·dōō′găl). Lake 318 sq. m., NW Keewatin District, Northwest Territories, Canada; its outlet is Back river.

Mc·Dow′ell (măk·dou′ĕl). **1** Name of counties in two states of the U.S. See *Tables* at NORTH CAROLINA and WEST VIRGINIA.
2 Town, Highland co., western Virginia; pop. 127; scene of Confederate victory during Civil War, battle May 8, 1862, Confederate leaders Gens. Jackson and Edward Johnson.

Mc·Duf′fie (măk·dŭf′ǐ). County in Georgia. See *Table* at GEORGIA.

Mac·e·do′ni·a (măs′ĕ·dō′nǐ·å; -dōn′vå). **1** A region in cen. Balkan Penin., NW of the Aegean Sea, with somewhat indefinite boundaries but including Macedonia division of Greece, most of middle Vardar valley in SE Yugoslavia, and SW Bulgaria W of Mesta river; ab. 32,000 sq. m.; pop. ab. 2,500,000.
2 or **Mac′e·don** (măs′ĕ·dŏn). Ancient country and kingdom in the Macedonia region; ✳ Pella. Ancient kingdom originally located N of Thessaly and NW of Aegean Sea; under Philip II (359–336 B.C.) who developed the Macedonian phalanx, it came to include Thrace, Chalcidice, Thessaly, and Epirus; attained final

hegemony over Greece in battle of Chaeronea 338 B.C.; Macedonian Empire, comprising Macedonia and countries conquered by Alexander III (the Great) 336–323 B.C., reached from Macedon beyond eastern boundaries of former Persian Empire into upper India; empire soon broke up (see IPSUS), and Macedon sought to retain its power in Greece and Aegean Sea; decisively defeated 197 B.C. at Cynoscephalae by Rome after a series of wars; opposition to Rome finally suppressed and the empire ended when Perseus, last king of the Macedonians, was defeated at Pydna 168 B.C.; made a Roman province 148 B.C.; division of Byzantine Empire, lying W of Mesta river, when invaded by Slavic peoples 6th cent. A.D.; included successively in medieval Bulgarian and Serbian empires; gradually came under Ottoman Empire (Salonika held out to 1430) which held it until 1912; with rise of Bulgarian nationalism after 1878, "Macedonian question," i.e. independence of Macedonia from Turkey and rival Bulgarian, Serb, and Greek claims to Macedonia, finally led to Balkan Wars 1912–13; as result of Second Balkan War 1913 and of Bulgarian participation in World War I on side of Central Powers, Macedonia was partitioned bet. Yugoslavia and Greece, to exclusion of Bulgaria 1919; after 1919, revolutionary activity in Macedonia threatened relations of Bulgaria with other Balkan powers.
3 *Mod. Gr.* **Ma′ke·do·ni′a** (mä′kâ·thô·nyē′ä). Geographical division of modern Greece; includes all of N Greece except Western Thrace; 13,472 sq. m.; pop. (1938 est.) 1,590,886; forms Greek departments of Chalcidice, Drama, Florina, Kavalla, Kozánē, Mount Athos, Pella, Serrai, and Thessalonike (see *Table* at GREECE). Mountainous in W where it is drained by Vistritsa river; in E crossed by Vardar and Struma rivers; includes peninsula of Chalcidice; has increasing agricultural activity and a number of successful local industries. Chief towns Salonika, Kavalla, Serrai, and Drama.
4 Federated republic, SE Yugoslavia, comprising the Yugoslav section of the region of Macedonia; 10,227 sq. m.; pop. (1931) 949,958; created 1946; equivalent to S part of former Vardarksa co.; chief towns Skoplje, Bitolj, and Prilep.

Ma′cei·ó′ (mä′sā·ô′). City, ✳ of Alagoas state, E Brazil, ab. 270 m. NE of Salvador; pop. (1940 est.) 85,949; cotton and sugar port; has foundries, mills, and factories.

Ma′ce·que′ce (mä′sĕ·kä′sĕ) or **Ma′si·ke′si** (mä′sĕ·kä′sĕ). Chief town in Manica dist., W cen. Mozambique; pop. (1935 est.) 9284.

Ma′ce·ra′ta (mä′chä·rä′tä). **1** Province of Italy. See *Table* at ITALY.
2 Commune, its ✳, Marches, cen. Italy, 110 m. NNW of Rome; pop. 26.708; university; art museum.

Mc·Gehee′ (må·gē′). Commercial city, Desha co., SE Arkansas, near Mississippi river 56 m. SE of Pine Bluff; pop. 4448; trade and railroad center.

Mc·Gill′ (må·gǐl′). Town, White Pine co., E Nevada, ab. 13 m. NNE of Ely; pop. 2195; owned by Nevada Consolidated Copper Co.; smelter (1906).

Mac·gil′li·cud′dy's Reeks (må·gǐl′ǐ·kŭd′ǐz rēks′). Mountain range, co. Kerry, SW Eire; highest peak Carrantual 3414 ft., highest mountain in Ireland.

Mc·Grath′ (må·gràth′). Village, SW cen. Alaska, on upper Kuskokwim river W of Mt. McKinley; pop. (est.) 223; has airport on line bet. Fairbanks and Bethel.

Mc·Greg′or (må·grĕg′ēr). City, McLennan co., cen. Texas. 13 m. SSW of Waco; pop. 4642; railroad junction; center of livestock and agricultural area (cotton, grain).

Mc·Guire′, Mount (må·gwīr′). Peak 10,070 ft. in NW Lemhi co., E cen. Idaho.

Ma·cha′chi (mä·chä′chē). Resort town, Pichincha prov., N cen. Ecuador, in Andes Mts. at alt. 10,118 ft., just S of Quito; pop. (1944 est.) 8165; mineral-water springs.

Ma·chae′rus (må·kē̱r′ŭs). Fortified village of ancient Moab, in N part E of Dead Sea; its citadel built on the

spur of a hill surrounded by deep valleys; place where John the Baptist was beheaded.

Ma·cha'la (mä-chä'lä). Town, ✳ of El Oro prov., SW Ecuador, 75 m. S of Guayaquil; pop. (1944 est.) 7730; produces cacao, coffee, hides; gold mining in vicinity; its port is Puerto Bolívar.

Mc·Hen'ry (măk·hĕn'rĭ; mȧ·kĕn'-). **1** Name of counties in two states of the U.S. See *Tables* at ILLINOIS and NORTH DAKOTA.
2 City, McHenry co., N Illinois, 23 m. W of Waukegan; pop. 3336; in lake region, summer resort headquarters.

Ma·chi'as (mȧ·chī'ăs). **1** River ab. 70 m. long, SE Maine; rises in NE Hancock co., flows SE across Washington co. into Machias Bay.
2 Town, ⊗ of Washington co., SE corner of Maine, adjacent to Machias Bay 33 m. S of Calais; pop. 2614; port of entry; lumber and shipbuilding center. Washington State Teachers College (1909; coed.).

Machias Bay. Inlet of Atlantic Ocean on S coast of Washington co., SE Maine; receives Machias river on N.

Machias Seal Island. Island in Atlantic Ocean off SE Maine coast.

Ma'chi·cha'co, Cape (mä'chĕ·chä'kô). Cape extending into Bay of Biscay from Vizcaya prov., N coast of Spain, NE of Bilbao.

Ma·chi·na·to (mä·chē·nä·tô). Village, W coast of Okinawa I., Ryukyu Is., Japan, just N of Naha; important airfield, captured by Americans Apr. 29, 1945.

Machpelah, Cave of. See HEBRON.

Ma'chu (mä'chōō). River, W cen. Bhutan; flows S through the Himalayas across Indian border, where as the **Ga·da'dhar** (gȧ·däd'hēr) it joins the Brahmaputra. Punakha is on it.

Ma'chu Pic'chu (mä'chōō pēk'chōō). Site of ancient Inca city on a mountain in the Andes, NW of Cuzco, Peru; fairly extensive ruins include a temple; citadel was surrounded by terraced gardens; discovered by Hiram Bingham 1911.

Ma·chyn'lleth (mȧ·kûn'lĕth; -hlĕth). Village and urban district, W Montgomeryshire, Wales, on the Dyfi (Dovey) river; pop. (urban district) 1875; tourist resort; fishing (salmon).

Ma'cie·jo·wi'ce (mä'tsyĕ·yô·vē'tsĕ). Commune, N Lublin prov., E Poland, near E bank of the Vistula 43 m. SE of Warsaw; scene, Oct. 10, 1794, of Russian victory over rebelling Polish forces under Kosciusko who was wounded and captured.

Ma·ciel' (mä·syĕl'). Town, Caazapá dept., SE Paraguay; pop. ab. 5780.

Mc'In·tosh (măk'ĭn·tôsh). **1** Name of counties in three states of the U.S. See *Tables* at GEORGIA, NORTH DAKOTA, OKLAHOMA.
2 City, ⊗ of Corson co., N South Dakota; pop. 568.

Mac'In·tyre Mountain (măk'ĭn·tīr). Peak 5112 ft. in the Adirondack Mts., Essex co., NE New York.

Mac·kay' (mȧ·kī'). Town, E Queensland, Australia, on Pacific Ocean within Great Barrier Reef 180 m. NNW of Rockhampton; pop. 10,660; port facilities; in fertile agricultural region devoted largely to sugar and fruits, also to grazing and mining.

Mackay, Lake. Lake in desert region, cen. Australia, on boundary bet. Western Australia and Northern Territory.

Mc·Kay' Dam (mȧ·kī'). Dam completed 1926 across McKay Creek (tributary of Umatilla river), S of Pendleton, Umatilla co., NE Oregon; height 165 ft.; impounds water for irrigation.

Mac·Kay' Lake (mȧ·kī'). Lake 250 sq. m. in E cen. Mackenzie District, Northwest Territories, Canada; connected with Lake Aylmer.

Mc·Kean' (mȧ·kēn'). **1** County in Pennsylvania. See *Table* at PENNSYLVANIA.
2 One of the smaller islands of the Phoenix Is. (*q.v.*) group, in W part, WSW of Canton I., cen. Pacific Ocean, 3°30'S lat. and 174°20'W long.; 1 sq. m.

Mc·Kee' (mȧ·kē'). City, ⊗ of Jackson co., SE Kentucky; pop. 234.

Mc·Kees'port (mȧ·kēz'pōrt). Industrial city, Allegheny co., SW Pennsylvania, at confluence of Youghiogheny and Monongahela rivers 10 m. ESE of Pittsburgh; pop. 45,489; coal mines, gas fields; manufactures steel pipes and tubes, sheet steel and tin plate, boilers and radiators; meat-packing plants. Settled 1755; center of conflict during Whisky Insurrection 1794.

Mc·Kees' Rocks (mȧ·kēz'). Borough, Allegheny co., SW Pennsylvania, near Ohio river 4 m. WNW of Pittsburgh; pop. 13,185; industrial suburb of Pittsburgh. Settled 1764 on site of trading post (1743) and fort (1753).

Mc·Ken'zie (mȧ·kĕn'zĭ). **1** River 80 m. long, W Oregon; rises in SE Linn co., flows W into Willamette river near Eugene.
2 County in North Dakota. See *Table* at NORTH DAKOTA.
3 City, Carroll co., W Tennessee, 17 m. SSW of Paris; pop. 3780; railroad junction; manufactures lumber, cheese. Bethel Coll. (1842; coed.).

Mac·ken'zie (mȧ·kĕn'zĭ). **1** River, 1120 m. long from Great Slave Lake, in W Mackenzie District, Northwest Territories, Canada; flows NNW into Mackenzie Bay; when considered as including Slave river, Peace river, and Finlay river, ab. 2525 m. long, second longest river in North America; navigable for greater part of its length (rapids in Slave river); its valley is rich in forests and mineral resources. Discovered and descended by Alexander Mackenzie 1789. Trading posts of Hudson's Bay Company established along its course; these forts are now settlements, esp. Fort McPherson, Fort Good Hope, Fort Norman, Fort Simpson, and Fort Providence. Aklavik is chief settlement in delta and Fort Resolution on Great Slave Lake.
2 District, cen. and W Northwest Territories, Canada; area including water 527,490 sq. m.; includes the greater part of N mainland of Canada bet. Yukon Territory and Keewatin District and also most of the Mackenzie river valley, Great Bear Lake, Great Slave Lake, the Yellowknife Preserve, and many other lakes. Administered from Edmonton. Created 1895; boundaries redefined 1918. Extensive oil fields and uranium deposits.

McKenzie, Mount. Peak 3872 ft. in the Adirondack Mts., Essex co., NE New York.

Mackenzie Bay. Widemouthed inlet of Beaufort Sea, N of Yukon Terr. and NW Mackenzie Dist., Northwest Territories, Canada; receives Mackenzie river.

Mackenzie Mountains. Range in E Yukon Territory and W Mackenzie District, Northwest Territories, Canada; highest point Keele Peak 9750 ft. Watershed of tributaries of Mackenzie and Yukon rivers.

Mack'i·nac (măk'ĭ·nô; *esp. for straits & isl.*, -năk). County in Michigan. See *Table* at MICHIGAN.

Mackinac, Straits of. Straits 4 m. wide at narrowest point, connecting Lake Huron and Lake Michigan; site of Mackinac Bridge, completed 1957, connecting upper and lower Michigan peninsulas.

Mackinac Island. Island 3 m. long in Straits of Mackinac, in Mackinac co., SE Michigan penin.; coextensive with Mackinac Island city; pop. 572; state park; resort.

Mack'i·naw (măk'ĭ·nô). River ab. 100 m. long, cen. Illinois; flows W, from E McLean co. into the Illinois river a few miles below Pekin.

Mc·Kin'ley (mȧ·kĭn'lĭ). County in New Mexico. See *Table* at NEW MEXICO.

McKinley, Mount; *Russ.* **Bol·sha'ya** (bŭl·y'·shȧ'yȧ); *also* **De·na'li** (dĕ·nä'lĕ). Mountain 20,320 ft., S cen. Alaska, 63°N, 151°W, in Mount McKinley National Park (see UNITED STATES, *National Parks*); highest mountain in North America.

McKinley Park Station. Station for Mount McKinley National Park on railroad SSW of Fairbanks, E cen. Alaska, at NE end of Alaska Range.

Mc·Kin′ney (mȧ·kĭn′ĭ). City, ⊗ of Collin co., NE Texas, 30 m. N of Dallas; pop. 13,763; cotton, flour, oil mills; cotton compresses, cement works.

Mc·Lean′ (mȧ·klān′). Name of counties in three states of the U.S. See *Tables* at ILLINOIS, KENTUCKY, NORTH DAKOTA.

Mc·Leans′bor′o (mȧ·klānz′bûr′ō). City, ⊗ of Hamilton co., SE Illinois, SE of Mount Vernon; pop. 2951.

Mac·lear′ (mȧ·klēr′). Town, E Cape Province, S Union of South Africa, ab. 140 m. NNE of East London; pop. 2379; center of agricultural and stock-raising region.

Mc·Lel′an Strait (mȧ·klĕl′ȧn). Strait separating Killinek I. from the mainland of Labrador, ab. 60°10′N.

Mc·Len′nan (mȧ·klĕn′ȧn). County in Texas. See *Table* at TEXAS.

Mc·Leod′ (mȧ·kloud′). County in Minnesota. See *Table* at MINNESOTA.

Mac·leod′ (mȧ·kloud′). Town, S Alberta, Canada, on Oldman river 24 m. W of Lethbridge; pop. 1860; railroad divisional point on Canadian Pacific Ry.; center of rich farm district; trades in grain; coal mines and stone quarries in the vicinity.

Mc·Lough′lin, Mount (mȧ·klŏk′lĭn). Peak 9493 ft. in E Jackson co., SW Oregon.

Mc·Mech′en (măk·mĕk′ĕn). Residential city, Marshall co., N West Virginia, on Ohio river 5 m. N of Moundsville; pop. 2999.

McMillan Dam *and* **Lake**. See CARLSBAD, New Mexico.

Mc·Minn′ (măk·mĭn′). County in Tennessee. See *Table* at TENNESSEE.

Mc·Minn′ville (măk·mĭn′vĭl). **1** City, ⊗ of Yamhill co., NW Oregon, 21 m. NNW of Salem; pop. 7656; estab. 1844; manufactures lumber, condensed milk, brick and tile, gloves. Linfield Coll. (1857; coed.).
2 Town, ⊗ of Warren co., cen. Tennessee, 53 m. NW of Chattanooga; pop. 9013; settled c. 1800; manufactures hosiery, silk, blankets, flour, hardwood flooring; marble quarries; timber.

Mc·Mul′len (măk·mŭl′ĕn). County in Texas. See *Table* at TEXAS.

Mc·Mur′do Sound (măk·mûr′dō). Inlet of SW Ross Sea, bet. Ross I. and the coast of Victoria Land, Antarctica, in 77°30′S, 165°E.

McMurray. = FORT MCMURRAY.

Mc·Nair′y (măk·nâr′ĭ). County in Tennessee. See *Table* at TENNESSEE.

Mac·Naugh′ton, Mount (măk·nô′t′n). Peak 3976 ft. in Adirondack Mts., Essex co., NE New York.

Mc·Neill′ Peak (măk·nēl′). Mountain 6788 ft. in Yakima co., S Washington.

Ma·comb′ (mȧ·kōm′). **1** County in Michigan. See *Table* at MICHIGAN.
2 City, ⊗ of McDonough co., W Illinois, 37 m. SSW of Galesburg; pop. 12,135; Western Illinois University (1899; coed.).

Macomb Mountain. Peak 4371 ft. in the Adirondack Mts., Essex co., NE New York.

Ma′con (mā′s′n), *originally* **Ma′çon′** (mä′sŏn′). Bayou 150 m. long, NE Louisiana, rising near the Arkansas boundary and flowing S to the Tensas river in SE Franklin parish; part of its course forms boundary bet. Madison and Richland parishes; navigable.

Ma′con (mā′kŭn). **1** Name of counties in six states of the U.S. See *Tables* at ALABAMA, GEORGIA, ILLINOIS, MISSOURI, NORTH CAROLINA, TENNESSEE.
2 City, ⊗ of Bibb co., cen. Georgia, on Ocmulgee river 78 m. SE of Atlanta; pop. 69,764; commercial and industrial center; textile, flour, and lumber mills; canneries and meat-processing plants; kaolin deposits; Robins Air Force Base. Mercer Univ. (1833; coed.); Wesleyan Coll. (1836; women).
3 City, ⊗ of Noxubee co., E Mississippi, 28 m. SSW of Columbus; pop. 2432; in cotton-growing, lumbering, and dairy-farming section.

4 City, ⊗ of Macon co., N Missouri, 23 m. N of Moberly; pop. 4547; trading and shipping center in agricultural section; coal deposits nearby.

Ma′con′ (mä′kôN′); *anc.* **Ma·tis′co Æ′du·o′rum** (mȧ·tĭs′kō ē′dụ̇·ōr′ŭm; ĕd′ụ̇-). Manufacturing city, * of Saône-et-Loire dept., E cen. France, on Saône river 22 m. WNW of Bourg; pop. 19,324; railroad center; manufactures machinery, tools, paper, copper products; trades principally in Burgundy wines; remains of 12th-cent. cathedral. Episcopal see, 6th cent. until Revolution; Huguenot stronghold in 16th cent.

Macoraba. See MECCA.

Macorís. Short form of SAN PEDRO DE MACORÍS.

Ma·cou′pin (mȧ·kōō′pĭn). County in Illinois. See *Table* at ILLINOIS.

Mc·Part′land Mountain (măk·pärt′lănd). Peak 8400 ft. in Glacier National Park, NW Montana.

Mc·Pher′son (măk·fûr′s′n). **1** Name of counties in three states of the U.S. See *Tables* at KANSAS, NEBRASKA, SOUTH DAKOTA.
2 City, ⊗ of McPherson co., cen. Kansas, 27 m. NE of Hutchinson; pop. 9996; shipping and refining point for cen. Kansas oil fields. McPherson Coll. (1887; coed.).
3 See FORT MCPHERSON.

Mac·pher′son Range (măk·fûr′s′n). Short range of mountains forming E end of boundary bet. New South Wales and SE Queensland, Australia; highest Mt. Lindsay 5512 ft.

Mac·quar′ie (mȧ·kwŏr′ĭ). **1** River 750 m. long, E cen. New South Wales, Australia; flows NNW from Blue Mts. to Darling river.
2 River ab. 65 m. long, an E tributary of Lake river, E Tasmania, Australia.

Macquarie Harbour. Large inlet of Indian Ocean on W coast of Tasmania, Australia, ab. 20 m. long; receives Gordon river at S end. Cape Sorell is at W of entrance and town of Strahan is situated at N end.

Macquarie Islands. Group of small islands in S Pacific Ocean ab. 850 m. SE of Tasmania, Australia, and 700 m. SW of New Zealand, 53°30′S lat., 159°E long. Administered by Tasmania. Largest island (89 sq. m.) of group is crest of submarine mountain. Discovered 1810; home of seals, sea elephants, penguins, etc., but now seals practically exterminated. Base of Mawson polar expedition 1911–14; has weather, relief, and radio stations.

Mc·Rae′ (mȧ·krā′). City, ⊗ of Telfair co., S cen. Georgia, 78 m. NE of Albany; pop. 2738; turpentine.

Mac·Rob′ert·son Coast (măk·rŏb′ērt·s′n). Section of Antarctica coast on Indian Ocean, 70°S lat., 59°40′ to 69°30′E long.; E of Enderby Land in Australian claim.

Mc·Sher′rys·town (măk·shĕr′ĭz·toun). Borough, Adams co., S Pennsylvania, 20 m. WSW of York; pop. 2839.

Mac·tan′ (mäk·tän′). Island off E coast of Cebu in front of City of Cebu, Phil. Is.; 24 sq. m.; pop. 40,103; separated from Cebu I. by channel 1 m. wide. Has mangrove swamps, coconut groves, and some cultivated area; chief town Opon. Here on Apr. 27, 1521, Ferdinand Magellan was slain treacherously on an expedition in behalf of a native sovereign.

Mactaris. See MAKTAR.

Ma·cui′ra (mä·kwē′rä). Peak 2625 ft. on N tip of Colombia, SE of Point Gallinas.

Ma′cu·ri′jes, Point (mä′kōō·rē′häs). Cape extending W from S coast of Camagüey prov., E cen. Cuba, S of the mouth of the San Pedro river.

Ma·cu′to (mä·kōō′tō). Coastal watering place on N coast of Venezuela, adjoining La Guaira.

Mad (măd). River 100 m. long, W cen. Ohio; flows S and SE, from Logan co., to Miami river at Dayton.

Mad′a·gas′car (măd′ȧ·găs′kẽr). Island in the Indian Ocean 240 m. off E coast of S Africa; 227,678 sq. m.; pop. (1957) 5,065,372; a territory 1946–58 within the French Union (with dependencies Amsterdam, Saint Paul, Crozet, and Kerguelen Is.) and, as the **Mal′a·gas′y**

Republic (măl′å·găs′i) or **Mal′gache′ Republic** (mål′gàsh′), Fr. **Ré′pu′blique′ Mal′gache′** (rā′pü′blēk′), an autonomous republic 1958-60 and an independent republic in the French Community from 1960; ✳ Tananarive. Excluding Australia, the fourth largest island in the world, 980 m. long from Cape Amber (Cap d'Ambre) at N end to Cape Sainte-Marie at S end, and 360 m. broad at widest point; separated from Africa by the Mozambique Channel. Plateau and mountainous regions cover practically all the island; Ankaratra group (volcanic) in the center, and Tsaratanana Massif in the N (highest point 9449 ft.). Has many short streams, most of them flowing E to W; among the more important are the Betsiboka and the Mangoky. Only large inlet is Antongil Bay on NE coast; numerous small islands along the coast, notably Sainte-Marie on the E and Nossi-Bé on NW. Chief products are rice, sugar, coffee, manioc, maize, and sisal; forests are extensive and there is output of some minerals (graphite, mica, phosphates, precious stones). Inhabitants are mainly Malagasy tribes. Chief towns Tananarive, Antsirabe, and the ports of Tamatave, Majunga, Tuléar, and in the N Diégo-Suarez (fine harbor).

History: Discovered by Portuguese 1500; short-lived French stations established in 17th cent., reopened in 18th cent.; French posts held by British 1810-11; tribes of Madagascar in 19th cent. came to be ruled by Hovas, a native group, who had almost expelled Europeans before accession of a Christian ruler 1861; concluded treaty with France 1868; declared a French protectorate 1882, but resisted in war in 1883 and 1894-96; made French colony 1896 and gradually subdued; the Comoro Is. placed under government of Madagascar 1914 and French Australasian territories in 1924; in World War II occupied by British May 5, 1942 and Vichy administration taken over completely by Sept.

Ma′dame′ Island (ma′dàm′). Island off S coast of Cape Breton I., Nova Scotia, Canada; belongs to Richmond co., Nova Scotia. Arichat is on its S shore.

Ma′dang (mä′däng). **1** Administrative district of North-East New Guinea, Territory of New Guinea; 21,400 sq. m.; pop. (1930) 54,600.

2 *formerly* **Frie′drich–Wil′helms·ha′fen** (frē′drĭk-vĭl′hĕlms·hä′fĕn). Seaport town, its ✳, on Astrolabe Bay, E North-East New Guinea; in ab. 5°10′S; good harbor. Object of Australian drive along the coast Sept. 1943 to Feb. 1944; captured by Australian and U.S. forces Apr. 24, 1944.

Ma·da′ras Mountains (mä·thä′räs). Mountain range, W Crete, near S coast; highest point 7907 ft.

Ma·da′ri·pur (mä·dä′rê·pŏŏr). Town, East Bengal, Pakistan, on Ganges ENE of Calcutta; pop. 26,894.

Ma·dau′ros (må·dô′rŏs). Ancient city, Numidia, N Africa; near modern **Mdaou′rouch′** (′m·dou′rōŏsh′), ab. 50 m. N of Tebessa, Algeria; celebrated for its schools; birthplace of Apuleius; ruins of Roman baths and mausoleum, and of Byzantine basilica and fortress.

Mad′a·was′ka (măd′å·wŏs′kå). **1** Town, Aroostook co., N Maine, on St. John river 17 m. ENE of Fort Kent; pop. 5507; port of entry; wood-pulp and paper mills.

2 River 130 m. long, SE Ontario, Canada; rises in lakes in Haliburton co. and flows SE and NE in Renfrew co. into the Ottawa river at Arnprior above Ottawa.

3 County, New Brunswick, Canada. See *Table* at NEW BRUNSWICK.

Mad′da·le′na (mäd′dä·lā′nä). **1** Fortified post, E Cyrenaica, NE Libya, on Egyptian border on highway bet. Giarabub and Fort Capuzzo.

2 Island in Tyrrhenian Sea off extreme NE coast of Sardinia; pop. 10,968; administratively, a commune in Sassari prov., compartimento of Sardinia, Italy.

Maddalena, La. See LA MADDALENA.

Mad′da·lo′ni (mäd′dä·lō′nê) Commune, Napoli prov., Campania, S Italy, 15 m. NNE of Naples; pop. 23,366; castle, ancient towers; Ponti della Valle aqueduct (built

by Vanvitelli 1753-64) nearby.

Mad′e·ba (mäd′ĕ·bà; *Arab.* mä′dă·bà, -bǎ); *anc.* **Med′e·ba** (mĕd′ĕ·bà). Town, N cen. Jordan, E of N end of the Dead Sea and SSW of Amman; ancient Moabite town; fighting here during Wars of the Maccabees.

Ma·dei′ra (må·dēr′à). Village, Hamilton co., SW corner of Ohio, NE suburb of Cincinnati; pop. 6744.

Ma·dei′ra (må·dēr′à; *Port.* må·thä′ê·rà -thä′ê-). **1** River 2100 m. long (with the Mamoré) in W Brazil, most important tributary of Amazon river; formed by confluence of Bolivian rivers Mamoré and Beni at the Brazilian border; flows NE into Amazon below Manaus.

2 Island group in E Atlantic Ocean off coast of Morocco, N of the Canary Is. and SE of the Azores, 32°3′N lat. to 33°7′ and 16°13′W long. to 16°38′; comprises two inhabited islands, Madeira and Porto Santo, and two groups of barren islets, the Desertas and Salvages; constitutes the Funchal dist. of Portugal; 302 sq. m.; pop. (1940) 250,124; ✳ Funchal on Madeira I.

History: Porto Santo sighted by João Goncalves Zarco 1418; Madeira discovered 1420 by Zarco who founded Funchal 1421; British occupied Madeira for a short time in 1801 and again 1807-14.

3 Largest island of the group ab. 440 m. W of Morocco, ab. 34 m. long and ab. 12 m. wide; ✳ Funchal; has deep ravines and rugged mountains, with highest Pico Ruivo 6056 ft. in center of island; N coast is steep and very wild. Produces wine (*madeira*).

Madeira Falls. Waterfall in the Madeira river, W Brazil, near junction of Mamoré and Beni rivers on the Bolivian border.

Mä′de·le·ga′bel (mä′dĕ·lĕ·gä′bĕl). Peak 8689 ft. in the Algäu Alps, on the border bet. Bavaria and the Tirol.

Mad′e·leine, Cape (măd′′l·ĭn; -än; Fr. má′dlĕn′). Cape, N Gaspé Penin., at the mouth of St. Lawrence river, E Canada.

Madeleine, Îles de la. See MAGDALEN ISLANDS.

Madeleine, La. See LA MADELEINE.

Ma′de·leine′, Ri′vière′ de la (rē′vyâr′ dē lá má′dlĕn′). River ab. 70 m. long on Gaspé Penin., SE Quebec prov., Canada; flows NE and N into St. Lawrence river.

Ma·de′lia (må·dēl′yà; -dē′lĭ·à). Village, Watonwan co., S Minnesota, 21 m. WSW of Mankato; pop. 2190.

Mad′e·line Island (măd′′l·ĭn). See APOSTLE ISLANDS.

Ma·de′ra (må·dâr′à). **1** County in California. See *Table* at CALIFORNIA.

2 City, its ⊗, cen. California, 20 m. NW of Fresno; pop. 14,430; founded 1876; lumber; wines.

3 (*Span.* mä·thä′rä) Volcano 4960 ft., Nicaragua; one of two peaks (see CONCEPCIÓN) on the island of Ometepe in Lake Nicaragua.

Ma′dhya Bha′rat (mŭ′dyå bä′råt). Former state, cen. India; a union of 20 princely states, including Gwalior and Indore, formed 1948; since 1956 part of Madhya Pradesh.

Madhya Pradesh. See CENTRAL PROVINCES AND BERAR.

Madhumati. See GANGES DELTA.

Ma·di′di (mä·thē′thê). River ab. 190 m. long, NW Bolivia; flows NE into the Beni river.

Ma·dill′ (må·dĭl′). City, ⊗ of Marshall co., S Oklahoma, 22 m. ESE of Ardmore; pop. 3084.

Madina, al–. See MEDINA.

Ma′di·oen′ (må′dĕ·yōon′) or **Ma′di·un′** (må·dĕ·yōon′). **1** Former residency, East Java prov., Neth. Indies; 2348 sq. m.; pop. 1,909,801; ✳ Madioen. Bounded by Surakarta govt. on W, by Djapara-Rembang and Bodjonegoro residencies on N, and by Kediri residency on E. Region extends to S coast of island but has no port. Has fertile and well-watered plains in the N and lies bet. Mts. Lawu and Wilis. Raises esp. rice and sugar; produces teak.

2 City, its ✳, on railroad in cen. plain 90 m. WSW of Surabaja; pop. 41,872; site of principal repair shops of state railroads. Held by Communist forces for a time in Sept. 1948; taken by Dutch troops Dec. 25, 1948.

Mad′i·son (măd′ĭ·s'n). **1** River ab. 180 m. long, SW Montana; rises in S Gallatin co., flows W and N through Madison co. to unite with Jefferson and Gallatin rivers and form the Missouri river.
2 Name of a parish in Louisiana and of counties in nineteen states of the U.S. See *Tables* at LOUISIANA, ALABAMA, ARKANSAS, FLORIDA, GEORGIA, IDAHO, ILLINOIS, INDIANA, IOWA, KENTUCKY, MISSISSIPPI, MISSOURI, MONTANA, NEBRASKA, NEW YORK, NORTH CAROLINA, OHIO, TENNESSEE, TEXAS, VIRGINIA.
3 Town, SE New Haven co., S Connecticut, on Long Island Sound and Hammonasset river; pop. 4567; settled 1639, incorporated 1826; beach resort.
4 City, ⊗ of Madison co., N Florida, 52 m. E of Tallahassee; pop. 3239; settled 1838, trade center for agricultural region; hogs, poultry, lumber.
5 City, ⊗ of Morgan co., N cen. Georgia, 25 m. S of Athens; pop. 2680; trading center.
6 City, Madison co., SW Illinois, 5 m N of East St. Louis; pop. 6861; steel mill, railroad-car works.
7 City, ⊗ of Jefferson co., SE Indiana, on Ohio river 38 m. NE of New Albany, pop. 10,097; center of tobacco-growing section.
8 Town, Somerset co., W Maine, on Kennebec river 20 m. NW of Waterville; pop. 3935; woolen, wood-pulp, and paper mills.
9 City, ⊗ of Lac qui Parle co., W Minnesota, 22 m. W of Montevideo; pop. 2380; livestock and creamery co-operatives, flour mills, grain elevators, nurseries.
10 City, ⊗ of Madison co., NE Nebraska, 14 m. S of Norfolk; pop. 1513; flour mills, creameries.
11 Borough, Morris co., N New Jersey, 4 m. SE of Morristown; pop. 15,122, residential suburb; headquarters of Anthony Wayne during American Revolution. Drew Univ. (1867; coed.).
12 Town, Rockingham co., N North Carolina, 25 m. NNE of Winston-Salem; pop. 1912.
13 City, ⊗ of Lake co., E South Dakota, 38 m. NNW of Sioux Falls; pop. 5420; in agricultural section; grain elevators, flour mills, creamery, packing plant. General Beadle State Teachers College (1881; coed.).
14 Urban community (unincorporated), Davidson **co.**, N cen. Tennessee, NNE of Nashville; pop. 13,583
15 Town, ⊗ of Madison co., N Virginia; pop. 510.
16 Town, ⊗ of Boone co., SW West Virginia; pop. 2215.
17 City, ⊗ of Wisconsin and ⊗ of Dane co., S Wisconsin, on isthmus between Lake Monona and Lake Mendota; pop. 126,706; large wholesale and retail trade; manufactures farm machinery, machine tools, tin containers, flashlights and batteries, hospital and air-conditioning equipment; limestone quarries; tourist center and summer resort. Univ. of Wisconsin (1848, coed.); Edgewood Coll. (1927; women). Site chosen for capital of Wisconsin Territory 1836; incorp. as village 1846, as city 1856.
Madison, Mount. Peak 5363 ft. in the Presidential Range, White Mts., in S Coos co. N of Mt. Washington, N New Hampshire.
Madison Heights. 1 City, Oakland co., SE Michigan, N suburb of Detroit; pop. 33,343.
2 Town, Amherst co., cen. Virginia, on James river ab. 2 m. E of Lynchburg; pop. (1950) 2830.
Mad′i·son·ville (măd′ĭ·s'n·vĭl; *Sou.* also -v'l). **1** City, ⊗ of Hopkins co., W Kentucky, 33 m. N of Hopkinsville; pop. 13,110; tobacco and hardwood timber market.
2 Town, ⊗ of Monroe co., SE Tennessee; pop. 1812.
3 City, ⊗ of Madison co., E cen. Texas, 33 m. NE of Bryan; pop. 2324; lumbering, farming.
Madiun. See MADIOEN.
Ma′dja·pa′hit (mä′jä·pä′[h]ĭt). Malay kingdom in the East Indies 1293–1518 with its center in E Java and controlling most of Sumatra, coastal regions of Borneo and Celebes, and the Lesser Sunda Is.; finally overcome by Mohammedans.
Ma·doe′ra (mä·dōōr′ä) *or* **Ma·du′ra.** Island ab. 100

m. long by 24 m. wide off NE coast of Java, Indonesia; area 1760 sq. m.; a part of East Java prov.; formerly, with adjacent islands (Kangean Is., Sapudi, etc.), a Dutch residency, 2112 sq. m., pop. 1,962,462, ✱ Pamekasan. Hilly, highest point 1545 ft. Chief industries cattle breeding, fishing, and salt production; raises esp. maize, cassava, and rice. Chief towns Sumenep, Pamekasan, Sampang, and Bangkalan. Under Mataram 1624–74; Dutch influence established at end of 17th cent.; attached to Java as a residency 1885.
Madoera, *or* **Madura, Strait.** Arm of the Java Sea, extending S of Madura I. and N of E end of Java I., Indonesia; connects with Java Sea to the N by narrow Surabaja Strait W of Madura. Naval battle here Feb. 4, 1942 in which U.S.S. *Marblehead* took important part.
Ma′do·na (mä′dwŭ·nä). **1** Administrative district, SE Vidzeme prov., N Latvia; 1532 sq. m.
2 Town, its ✱, on railroad 80 m. E of Riga; pop. (1930) 2182.
Ma′do·ni′e Mountains (mä′dô·nē′ā); *Ital.* Le (lā), *or* **Mon′ti** (mōn′tē), **Madonie.** Mountain range in Palermo prov., NW cen. Sicily, highest peak Pizzo Antenna 6780 ft.
Mad′ra·ka, Cape (măd′rä·kä); *Arab.* **Ras Mad′ra·ka** (räs măd′rō·kä, -kä). Cape on E coast of Oman, SE Arabia, extending into the Arabian Sea at ab. 19°N.
Mad′ras (măd′räs). City, ⊗ of Jefferson co., N cen. Oregon; pop. 1515.
Ma·dras′ (mä·drăs′; -dräs′). **1** State (formerly a presidency), SE India, on Coromandel Coast; area 50,110 sq. m.; pop. (1956) 29,974,200; ✱ Madras. Borders on Andhra Pradesh on N, Mysore on NW, and Kerala on W. Reorganized 1956; formerly comprised a much larger area extending as far N as Orissa and including Laccadive Is. and part of Malabar Coast on W. Eastern Ghats extend from NE border to Nilgiri Hills in W; Cauvery river traverses the state. Region is agricultural but rainfall is irregular and irrigation developed only in some sections. Chief crops rice, millet, sugar, cotton, oil seed. Chief cities Madras, Madura, Trichinopoly, Salem.
History: In early times region occupied by Tamil kingdoms of Pandya, Chola, and Chera; then in the NE by the kings of Kalinga, and later in 14th cent. by Mohammedan invaders. South of the Kistna the Hindu kingdom Vijayanagar existed 1336–1565; Vasco da Gama reached Calicut 1498; Portuguese driven out by Dutch in 16th cent.; English made first settlement in 1611 at Masulipatam; after founding of Madras city 1640 English extended conquests; territory made a separate presidency 1653; captured by French 1746 but retroceded 1748 (Treaty of Aix-la-Chapelle); under the British received additional territory until early in 19th cent. Made autonomous province 1937, but privileges temporarily suspended 1939; part of Indian Union 1947.
2 City, its ✱, on Coromandel Coast; pop. (1951) 1,416,056, the main port on India's southeastern coast although harbor is wholly artificial; rail center; exports hides and skins, oil seeds, cotton, chrome, magnesite, coffee, and tea. Founded 1640 by Francis Day of the British East India Company; grew by process of accretion to original fort (**Fort St. George** [sānt jôrj′]); blockaded by Daud Khan 1702; unsuccessfully attacked by Marathas 1741; captured by French 1746 but returned by Treaty of Aix-la-Chapelle 1748; besieged by French 1758 and relieved by English fleet; successfully defended against Haidar Ali 1769 and 1780. St. Thomé, now part of city, founded by Portuguese 1504, ceded to English 1749, held by French 1672–74. Seat of Madras Univ. (founded 1857) and Presidency Coll. Traditional burial place of the apostle Thomas.
Madras States. Former agency, S India, including 5 Indian states: Travancore, Cochin, Pudukkottai, Banganapalle, and Sandur, the last three being enclaves of Madras prov.; 10,757 sq. m.; pop. (1941) 7,991,647; ✱ Triandrum. All states now in Indian Union.

Mad're, La·gu'na (lá·gōō'nä măd'rĕ; *Span.* lä·gōō'nä mä'thrä). **1** Long inlet of Gulf of Mexico bet. Padre I. and the mainland of S Texas S of Corpus Christi. **2** Long narrow inlet of the Gulf of Mexico on coast of NE cen. Mexico, state of Tamaulipas.

Madre, María. See MARÍA MADRE.

Ma'dre de Dios (mä'thrä thä thyōs'). **1** River ab. 900 m. long in Peru and Bolivia; rises in SE Peru, flows E across Bolivian border into Beni river in N Bolivia. **2** Department of Peru. See *Table* at PERU.

Madre de Dios Archipelago. Group of islands in S Pacific Ocean, off SW coast of Chile, N of Archipelago of Reina Adelaida, and S of Wellington I.

Mad'rid (măd'rĭd). City, Boone co., cen. Iowa, 22 m. NNW of Des Moines; pop. 2286; mining.

Ma·drid' (má·drĭd'; *Span.* mä·thrē[th]'). **1** Province of Spain. See *Table* at SPAIN. **2** City, * of Spain and of Madrid prov., cen. Spain, on Manzanares river 40 m. NNE of Toledo and 34 m. WSW of Guadalajara; pop. (1941 est.) 1,101,831; principal railroad junction in Spain; archiepiscopal see; commercial center for interior provinces; manufactures leather goods, machinery, electrical supplies, furniture, porcelain, jewelry, paper, tobacco, chocolates, shoes, plated ware, gloves; famous university (founded in 16th cent. at Alcalá de Henares); formerly surrounded by 20-foot wall, three of the gates of which still remain; built around a central plaza, the Puerta del Sol; royal palace on site of old Moorish alcazar; numerous art galleries including esp. the Prado museum; national library; numerous parks, among them the famous Buen Retiro gardens; bull ring; the Escorial, often associated with Madrid, is 27 m. NW of the city.

History: Moorish fortress captured in 932 A.D. by Ramiro II of León; again taken from Moors by Alfonso VI of Castile c. 1083; made capital of Spain 1560; occupied by French 1808–12 during Peninsular War; in Spanish Civil War held by Loyalists 1936–39; surrendered to Insurgents Mar. 29, 1939.

Mad River. See MAD.

Ma·driz' (mä·thrēs'). Department, Nicaragua; 531 sq. m.; pop. (1943 est.) 35,800; * Somoto.

Ma·dru'ga (mä·thrōō'gä). Municipality, La Habana prov., W Cuba, 20 m. WSW of Matanzas; pop. 9155.

Mad'u·ra. **1** (măd'ụ̆·rà; má·dōōr'à) *or* **Ma'du·rai'** (mü'dōō·rī'). City, S Madras state, S India, 270 m. SSW of Madras; pop. 361,781; muslin weaving, brasswork, wood carving. Noted for its great temple with colonnades and nine massive gate towers or gopuras adorned with elaborate carving and enclosing a quadrangle, the "Tank of the Golden Lilies"; also has several fine palaces; government industrial school. Capital of old Pandya dynasty from c. 4th cent. B.C. to end of 11th cent. A.D.; came under Vijayanagar in 14th cent.; under Nayak dynasty from middle 16th cent. to 1739 when taken by Nawab of Carnatic; taken over by British East India Company 1801. **2** (má·dōōr'à) See MADOERA.

Maeander. See MENDERES.

Ma·e·ba·shi (mä·yĕ·bä·shĕ). City, * of Gumma prefecture, cen. Honshu, Japan; pop. (1945) 79,732; in mountainous region with soil of volcanic origin favorable to the mulberry; hence one of the leading centers in growing silkworms and producing silk.

Mae Hong Son *or* **Mae·hong·son** (mă hông sôn); *also* **Mu·ai To** (mōō·ī tō). **1** Province, NW Thailand; 5899 sq. m.; pop. 70,203; * Mae Hong Son. **2** Town, its *, near Burma border 75 m. NW of Chiang Mai.

Mae Klong (mă klông). Var. of *Meklong;* see KLONG; SAMUT SONGKHRAM.

Mael'strom (mäl'strŏm); *Norwegian* **Mal'ström** (mäl'strūm). Whirlpool in the Norwegian Sea off the NW coast of Norway just S of Moskenes I., formerly supposed to suck in all vessels within a long radius.

Mae·o'ni·a (mê·ō'nĭ·à; -ōn'yà). Earlier name of Lydia, Asia Minor; later, a small district in NE Lydia.

Maeotis, Palus. See Sea of AZOV.

Maes (mäs). = MEUSE.

Maes'eyck (mäs'īk). Commune, Limburg prov., NE Belgium, on the Meuse river; pop. 5791; reputed birthplace of Hubert and Jan van Eyck.

Maes·teg' (mīs·tāg'). Urban district, Glamorganshire, SE Wales, 12 m. E of Swansea; pop. 23,124; coal mining.

Maestra, Sierra. See SIERRA MAESTRA.

Maestricht. See MAASTRICHT.

Ma·e'wo (?mä·ā'wō) *or* **Au·ro'ra** (ô·rōr'à; ụ̆·rōr'à). One of the New Hebrides Is., SW Pacific Ocean, in NE part of the group 65 m. E of Espíritu Santo I.; 29 m. long and 4 m. wide. Has long central range of mountains, thickly wooded; has small population.

Maf'e·king (măf'ĕ·kĭng). Town, N Cape Province, S Republic of So. Africa, 160 m. W of Pretoria, near W Transvaal border; pop. 6870; until 1965 seat of administration of Bechuanaland Protectorate although outside its borders. Native (Barolong) town distinct from white section—administered by own chiefs and free from European control. Trade and business center for vast region devoted to dairying, cattle, horses, and sheep. Founded 1885. Starting point for the Jameson Raid 1895; scene of famous siege during Boer War lasting 217 days, Oct. 12, 1899 to May 17, 1900.

Ma·fi'a (mä·fē'ä). Island in the Indian Ocean off E coast of Tanganyika, opp. mouth of Rufiji river, E Africa, S of Zanzibar; 170 sq. m.; pop. ab. 6000; administratively a part of Tanganyika.

Ma'fra (mä'frà). **1** City, Santa Catarina state, S Brazil, on a headstream of the Iguassú river 130 m. NW of Florianópolis; pop. 7379. **2** Commune, Lisboa dist., W Portugal, near Atlantic Ocean 16 m. NNW of Lisbon; pop. 4256; famous 18th-cent. monastery containing a fine church and over 800 rooms, built in imitation of the Escorial, now used as barracks and prison.

Maf'rak *or* **Maf'raq** (măf'rŏk), *in full* **Qal''at el Mafraq** (kŏl'ăt ăl). Town, N Jordan, ab. 35 m. NE of Amman, on railroad and oil pipeline; airfield, a Royal Air Force base 1948–49.

Ma·ga·dan' (má·gŭ·dán'). Port on N shore of Sea of Okhotsk, Khabarovsk Territory, Soviet Russia, Asia; pop. 62,000. Its twin town across a small peninsula is **No·ga'e·vo** (nŭ·gà'yĕ·vŭ); mining and industrial town; starting point of highways northward to head of navigation on the Kolyma and to Penzhina region; airport.

Ma'ga·dha (mŭ'gà·dà). Ancient kingdom, India, including Bihar S of the Ganges; * Pataliputra (mod. Patna); scene of many incidents in life of Gautama Buddha; especially powerful under the Maurya dynasty (c. 322–185 B.C.) founded by Chandragupta and extended by Asoka (273–232 B.C.) and by the later Gupta dynasty; declined ab. 5th cent. A.D.

Ma·ga'di (má·gä'dĕ). Town, S cen. Kenya, E Africa, SSW of Nairobi; terminus of railroad branch line.

Magadi, Lake. Lake ab. 30 m. long in S Kenya, E Africa, near Tanganyika border; has large soda deposits. Cf. Lake NATRON.

Mag'a·la·kwin' *or* **Mag'a·la·queen'** (măg'á·là·kwēn'). River 130 m. long, N Transvaal, NE Republic of South Africa; flows N into Limpopo river.

Ma'gal·la'nes (mä'gä·yä'nås). **1** Province of Chile. See *Table* at CHILE. **2** See PUNTA ARENAS.

Magallanes, Estrecho de. See Strait of MAGELLAN.

Ma'gan·gué' (mä'gäng·gä'). Town, Bolívar dept., N Colombia, at the junction of the Cauca and Magdalena rivers 90 m. SE of Cartagena; pop. 9770.

Mag-Asawang-Tubig. See Mount HALCON.

Ma·gat' (mä·gät'). River ab. 90 m. long, an important left tributary of the upper Cagayan river, NE Luzon, Phil. Is.; rises in Caraballo Mts. in SW Nueva Vizcaya

prov. and flows generally NE to the Cagayan in W cen. Isabela prov. above Ilagan. For part of its course it forms the SE boundary of Ifugao subprovince.

Mag′a·zine′ Mountain (măg′à·zēn′). Peak 2800 ft. in Logan co., NW cen. Arkansas, in Ouachita Mts.; highest point in state.

Mag′da·la (măg′dà·là) *or* **Mak′da·la** (măk′dà·là). Fortified town, Wallo region, N cen. Ethiopia; pop. 4000; altitude 9110 ft.; destroyed by British 1868; rebuilt.

Mag′da·la (măg′dà·là); *Heb.* **Mig·dal′** (mĭg·däl′); *Arab.* **El Maj′dal** (ăl mäj′dăl). Ancient town on the W shore of the Sea of Galilee, Palestine; now a small village just N of Tiberias, but not surely identified. Supposed home of Mary Magdalene (*Luke* viii. 2).

Mag′da·le′na (măg′dà·lē′nà; *Span.* mäg′thä·lā′nä).
1 Village, Socorro co., cen. New Mexico, 74 m. SSW of Albuquerque; pop. 1211; trading and shipping point for cattle ranchers.
2 Island off SW coast of Chile, NE of Chonos Archipelago.
3 River ab. 1060 m. long in S cen. and N Colombia; rises on E slopes of Andes in S Colombia, flows N into the Caribbean Sea near Barranquilla (*q.v.*); navigable for over 930 m.; with its many tributaries provides ab. 2500 m. of navigable waterways.
4 Department of Colombia. See *Table* at COLOMBIA.
5 Island in Pacific Ocean, off SW Lower California.
6 See FATU HIVA.

Magdalena, María. See MARÍA MAGDALENA.

Magdalena Bay. Inlet of Pacific Ocean on SW coast of Lower California.

Mag′da·len Islands (măg′dà·lĕn); *Fr.* **Îles de la Ma′de·leine′** (ēl′ dē là má′dlĕn′). Island group in S cen. part of the Gulf of St. Lawrence, E Quebec prov., Canada; 102 sq. m.; pop. 9999; chief village Havre Aubert; comprises 13 islands (largest are Coffin, Amherst, Grindstone). About 50 m. N of East Point, Prince Edward Island and ab. 100 m. SW of Newfoundland. Most of inhabitants are Acadians; chief occupation fishing; in former years considerable gypsum was mined. Administered as part of Gaspé co.

Mag′de·burg (măg′dĕ·bûrg; *Ger.* mäk′dĕ·bŏōrк). **1** Government district of former Saxony prov., Prussia, Germany; 4449 sq. m.
2 Fortified manufacturing and commercial city, ✳ of Magdeburg govt. dist. and of former Saxony prov., Germany, on Elbe river 82 m. WSW of Berlin; pop. (1939) 334,358; river port; 10th-cent. Benedictine convent, 13th-cent. cathedral; chief sugar market of Germany; manufactures beet sugar, iron, steel, machinery, locomotives, chocolate, chicory. First mentioned 805 A.D.; made archiepiscopal see 962; member of Hanseatic League for nearly 200 years; captured by Tilly 1631 (Thirty Years' War), by French 1806; to Prussia 1814. In World War II a great industrial center in the war effort; repeatedly bombed by Allies and taken Apr. 18–19, 1945.

Ma·ge·lang′ (mä′gà·läng′). City, Central Java prov., Indonesia, 37 m. S of Semarang; pop. 52,944; almost in exact geographical center of Java on railroad bet. Semarang on the N and Jogjakarta on the S; in fertile plain (alt. 1100 ft.) with high mountains on E and W. Formerly important as a military base; starting point for Borobudur and Mendut (*qq.v.*).

Ma·gel′lan, Strait of (má·jĕl′ăn; *Brit.* -gĕl′-); *Span.* **Es·tre′cho de Ma′gal·la′nes** (ăs·trā′chō thä mä′gä-yä′näs). Strait ab. 370 m. long at S extremity of South America, passing in a winding course bet. the mainland (Magallanes prov., Chile) and Tierra del Fuego Archipelago (*q.v.*); it connects S Atlantic with S Pacific Ocean, both its entrance and exit being 52°30′S. Dungeness Point (on N) and Cape Espíritu Santo (on S) mark entrance from the Atlantic; Cape Pilar at NW extremity of Desolación I. marks entrance from the Pacific. Punta Arenas (formerly Magallanes) is only town of impor-

tance on its course. Discovered Oct.–Nov. 1520 by Ferdinand Magellan.

Ma′gens Bay (mä′gĕnz). Bay in N coast of St. Thomas I., Virgin Is., West Indies.

Ma·gen′ta (má·jĕn′tà; *Ital.* mä·jĕn′tä). Commune, Milano prov., Lombardy, N Italy, 14 m. W of Milan; pop. 13,021; scene of famous victory of French and Sardinian army over Austrian forces June 4, 1859; magenta dye named in honor of battle.

Ma′ger·öy′ (mä′gĕr·û′ĭ). Island in Arctic Ocean off extreme N coast of Norway; 111 sq. m.; pop. 3728; its N tip is North Cape (*q.v.*).

Ma′gers·fon·tein′ (mä′gĕrs·fôn·tān′). Battlefield, W Orange Free State, E cen. Union of South Africa; here Cronje checked British in their advance to relief of Kimberley Dec. 1899.

Ma·ge′tan (mä·gĕ′tän). Town, East Java prov., Indonesia, a few miles W of Madiun at foot of Mt. Lawu; pop. 15,152.

Mag′gia (mäd′jä). River ab. 35 m. long, Ticino canton, SE cen. Switzerland; rises in Lepontine Alps, flows SE into N end of Lake Maggiore near Locarno.

Mag′gio·ra′sca, Mon′te (mŏn′tä mäd′jō·räs′kä). = *Monte Bue:* see APENNINES.

Mag·gio′re, Lake (mäd·jō′rå); *anc.* **Ver·ba′nus La′-cus** (vûr·bā′nŭs lā′kŭs). Lake 40 m. long and ab. 2 m. wide in N Italy and S Switzerland; 81 sq. m.; traversed (N to S) by Ticino river; Locarno, Ticino canton, Switzerland, is at N end. Has many village resorts on its shores and is nearly surrounded by mountains of S Lepontine Alps. See BORROMEAN ISLANDS.

Maghiana. See JHANG-MAGHIANA.

Maghreb el Aqsa, El. See MOROCCO.

Ma′ghrib *or* **Ma′ghreb** (mŭ′grĭb). Arabic name for NW Africa and, during the Moorish occupation, Spain; now used to include Morocco, Algeria, Tunisia, and, sometimes, Libya.

Ma′gi′ *or* **Ma′ji′** (mä′jē′). Town, SW Ethiopia, N of Lake Rudolf and near Sudan border.

Ma′gi′cienne′ Bay (má·zhē′syĕn′; *Angl.* má·jĭs′ĭ·ĕn, má·jĭsh′ĕn). Inlet on SE coast of Saipan I., Mariana Is.

Ma·gil′li·gan Point (má·gĭl′ĭ·găn). Cape on N coast of Ireland, on E side of entrance to Lough Foyle.

Ma′gi·not Line (măzh′ĭ·nō; *Fr.* má·zhē′nō′). A line of defensive fortification built 1930–34 by France to protect her eastern border—named after André Maginot (1877–1932), French minister of war; extended nearly 200 m. from S of Belfort to the Belgian border; effective during first few months of World War II but yielded with little fighting after German invasion of Belgium and collapse of French armies 1940.

Ma·gio′ne (mä·jō′nä). Commune, Perugia prov., Umbria, cen. Italy, 11 m. WNW of Perugia; pop. 10,611.

Mag′le·mo′se (măg′lĕ·mō′sĕ; mou′lĕ-; măg′lĕ-). Locality on W coast of Sjælland, Denmark, NW of Slagelse; archaeological site yielding bone and stone implements.

Ma′glie (mäl′yä). Commune, Lecce prov., Apulia, SE Italy, 15 m. SSE of Lecce; pop. 11,279.

Mag′na (măg′nà). Town, Salt Lake co., N Utah, ab. 12 m. WSW of Salt Lake City; pop. 6442; ore-concentrating plants (gold, silver, lead, copper, etc.).

Mag′na Char′ta Island (măg′nà kär′tà). See RUNNYMEDE.

Mag′na Grae′cia (măg′nà grē′shà; -shĭ·à). Collective name for the ancient Greek seaport colonies in S Italy; chief cities Tarentum (mod. Taranto), Sybaris (the oldest; founded c. 720 B.C.), Crotona (mod. Crotone), Heraclea (*qq.v.*).

Mag·ne′sia (măg·nē′zhà; -zhĭ·à). **1** Narrow coastal district in ancient Thessaly, Greece, extending along the Aegean Sea from Peneus river S to and including the peninsula enclosing the Sinus Pagasaeus (Gulf of Volos) on the E; according to tradition its inhabitants founded both cities of the same name in Asia Minor.
2 *or* **Magnesia ad Mae·an′drum** (ăd mē·ăn′drŭm).

Ancient city on the Maeander near its mouth, SE of Ephesus and just NE of modern Turkish town of Söke, W Asia Minor. Destroyed by Cimmerians c. 700 B.C. but rebuilt by Ionian colonists; site of beautiful temple to Artemis.

3 or **Magnesia ad Sipylum.** See MANISA city.

Mag·net'ic Pole (măg·nĕt'ĭk). Either of two spots on the earth's surface towards which the compass needle points from any direction throughout adjacent regions (except in their immediate vicinity where the horizontal intensity is so small that the compass cannot be used to determine direction) and at which the needle dips vertically. The **North Magnetic Pole** was formerly located on W shore of Boothia Penin., Canada, at approximately 71°N lat., 96°W long. (British Admiralty charts 70°40'N, 96°5'W), this location differing by nearly a degree from that found by Sir James C. Ross in 1831; according to calculations made in 1948 it was located in the NW part of Prince of Wales I., at 73°N lat., 100°W long.; according to scientists cannot be exactly fixed because of variations due to several causes. The **South Magnetic Pole** is at approximately 70°S lat. and 148°E long. (see VICTORIA LAND).

Mag·ni'to·gorsk (măg·nē'tŏ·gôrsk; Russ. măg·nyĭ·tŭ·gôrsk'). City, SW Chelyabinsk Region Soviet Russia, Asia, on the left bank of the Ural river 160 m. SSW of Chelyabinsk; pop. 145,870; chief iron and steel producing city of the Soviet Union. For centuries a village on steppe E of the Urals, inhabited by Bashkirs and Kirghiz engaged in cattle raising; named **Mag·nit'na·ya** (mŭg·nyēt'ná·yá) in early 18th cent. after discovery that two small mountains (Aider-Ly and Atach) nearby consisted of magnetized iron; began to be developed 1928 by the Soviet Government; by 1933 a large city, with plants built largely by American engineers and workers; in World War II poured more than 3,000,000 tons of iron and steel a year into tanks and guns.

Mag·no'lia (măg·nōl'yá; -nō'lĭ·á). **1** City, ⊗ of Columbia co., SW Arkansas, 35 m. W of El Dorado; pop. 10,651; incorporated as town 1853; in farming, lumbering, gas, and oil region.

2 City, ⊗ of Pike co., S Mississippi, 7 m. S of McComb; pop. 2083; cotton mills.

3 Borough, Camden co., SW New Jersey, 8 m. SSE of Camden; pop. 4199; agricultural center.

Ma·gof'fin (má·gŏf'ĭn). County in Kentucky. See Table at KENTUCKY.

Ma'gog (mā'gŏg). Industrial town, Stanstead co., S Quebec, Canada, on N end of Lake Memphremagog 17 m. SW of Sherbrooke; pop. 12,423; manufactures textiles. Founded 1776 by Loyalist emigrants from the United States.

Ma'gon·ti'a·cum (mā'gŏn·tī'á·kŭm). Var. of Mogontiacum: see MAINZ.

Ma'gra (mä'grä). River ab. 40 m. long, NW Italy; rises near the Cisa Pass and marks approximately the line bet. the Ligurian and Tuscan Apennines; flows S into Ligurian Sea near La Spezia.

Ma·gua·rí', Cape (má·gwá·rē'). Cape on NE extremity of Marajó I. at the mouth of the Amazon river, NE Brazil.

Maguntiacum. See MAINZ.

Ma·gwe' (má·gwā'). **1** Division of S Upper Burma. See Table at BURMA.

2 District of Magwe division; 3724 sq. m.; pop. 499,573; ✻ Magwe; includes Yenangyaung oil field.

3 Town, ✻ of district and division, on left bank of Irrawaddy 145 m. SW of Mandalay; pop. 8209. Taken by Allies May 1945.

Magyarkanizsa. See STARA KANJIŽA.

Magyarország. See HUNGARY.

Ma'gyar·ó'vár (mŏ'dyŏr·ō'vär); Ger. **Al'ten·burg** (äl'tĕn·bòòrk). Town, W Hungary, on the Leitha NW of Györ; pop. 8589.

Mahabad. See SAUJBULAGH.

Ma·ha'ba·lesh'war (má·hä'bá·lāsh'vĕr). Village and hill station, Satara dist., cen. Maharashtra, W Indian Union, ab. 90 m. SE of Bombay; pop. 4543; on summit of a ridge of Western Ghats, alt. 4500 ft.; rainfall excessive, often 300 to 400 in. per year; site of sanatorium established 1828 by Sir John Malcolm. Near source of the Kistna river, sacred to the Hindus.

Maha Chai. See SAMUT SAKHON.

Ma'ha·jam'ba Bay (mä'há·jäm'bá). Inlet of Mozambique Channel on, NW coast of the island of Madagascar.

Ma·ha'kam (mä·hä'käm) or **Ku·tai'** (kōō·tī'). River ab. 400 m. long, E Borneo, in South and East Borneo prov., Indonesia; rises in mountains of cen. Borneo and flows ESE to Makassar Strait in wide delta ab. 1°S of the equator. Navigable for most of its course; ab. 100 m. from its mouth joined in a region of marsh and lakes by the Belajan and Telen. Samarinda is the port near its mouth.

Ma·hal'la el Ku'bra (má·hăl'á ĕl kōō'brá). City, Gharbîya prov., Lower Egypt, in Nile delta W of Damietta branch 16 m. NE of Tanta; pop. (1960) 178,000.

Ma·ha'na·di (má·hä'ná·dĭ). River 512 m. long in E India; rises in mountains of S Madhya Pradesh, flows N, turns E, and flows S and E through Orissa to the Bay of Bengal through several mouths E of Cuttack; its chief tributary is the Seonath. Has great volume in flood season; its waters source of irrigation system.

Ma'ha·noy City (mä'[h]á·noi). Borough, Schuylkill co., E cen. Pennsylvania, 12 m. NE of Pottsville; pop. 8536; coal mining; manufactures clothing, shirts, beer.

Mahanoy Mountain. Ridge in Schuylkill and Northumberland cos., E cen. Pennsylvania; highest point 1745 ft.; forms N boundary of Mahanoy coal basin and contains rich deposits of anthracite.

Mahanuddy. Var. of MAHANADI.

Ma·ha'rash'tra (má·hä'räsh'trá). **1** Region of W cen. India marking the original land of the Marathas; it lay S of the Narbada and extended from E of Nagpur westward to the coast bet. Damão and Goa; its chief cities were Poona and Satara.

2 State, Republic of India, comprising the Marathi-speaking SE portion of former Bombay state; 118,717 sq. m.; pop. (1961) 39,553,718; ✻ Bombay; formed May 1, 1960. See GUJARAT.

Ma'ha·rès' (má·[h]á·rĕs'; Arab. mă·hä'rĭs). Coastal town, E Tunisia, N Africa, on Gulf of Gabès SW of Sfax.

Ma·ha Sa·ra·kham or **Ma·ha·sa·ra·gam** (mä·hä sä·rä·k'häm); also **Ta·lat** (tä·lät). **1** Province, E cen. Thailand; 5743 sq. m.; pop. 571,211; ✻ Maha Sarakham.

2 Town, its ✻, on Si river, 16 m. NW of Roi Et.

Ma·has'ka (má·hăs'ká). County in Iowa. See Table at IOWA.

Ma·ha'we'li or **Mahaweli Gan'ga** (má·hä'wä'lĭ gŭn'gä). Chief river (ganga) of Ceylon, ab. 208 m. long; flows N from Central Province to Bay of Bengal S of Trincomalee.

Mah·bub'na·gar (má·bōōb'ná·gĕr). Town, S Andhra Pradesh, S cen. India, 55 m. SSW of Hyderabad; pop. ab. 10,000.

Mah·di'a or **Meh·di'a** (má·dē'á). Seaport town, E Tunisia, N Africa, SE of Sousse; pop. ab 8000.

Ma'hé' (má·[h]ā'). **1** Chief island, Seychelles, Indian Ocean; 55 sq. m.; pop. ab. 22,000; chief town Victoria; mountainous, highest point 2993 ft.

2 formerly **May·ya'li** (mī·yä'lĭ). Free city, once a province, of former French India, in SW India, on Malabar Coast ab. 40 m. N of Calicut; 23 sq. m.; pop. (1941) 14,092; has no trade or industry of importance, the only French settlement on W coast of India. Occupied by French 1725; pawn in French-English wars, restored to France 1817; administration reorganized 1947; transferred to India 1954.

Ma'he'bourg' (má·[h]ā'bōōr'). Town on the SE coast of the British island of Mauritius; pop. (1931) 7698.

Ma·hen′ge (mä·hĕng′gå). **1** Province, S Tanganyika, E Africa, NE of Lake Nyasa; 31,968 sq. m.; pop. 209,293; ✳ Mahenge.
2 Town, its ✳, on a tributary of the Rufiji 220 m. SW of Dar es Salaam; pop. ab. 3000.
Ma′hi (mŭ′hĭ). River 300 m. long, W India; rises in NW Madhya Pradesh, flows NW and SW through S Rajputana and Gujerat into a wide estuary at the head of the Gulf of Cambay, E of the mouth of the Sabarmati river.
Ma′hi·a Peninsula (mä′hē·å). Peninsula projecting S from E cen. coast of North I., New Zealand, forming E side of Hawke Bay.
Ma′hi Kan′tha (mŭ′hĭ känt′hå). Formerly an agency, consisting of a group of Indian states, later in Sabar Kantha Agency, in the Western India States, W India.
Mah·no′men (mô·nō′mĕn). **1** County in Minnesota. See *Table* at MINNESOTA.
2 Village, its ⊗, NW Minnesota, 47 m. NE of Moorhead; pop. 1462.
Ma·hón′ (mä·ôn′); *Eng.* **Port Ma·hon′** (må·hōn′); *anc.* **Por′tus Ma·go′nis** (pōr′tŭs må·gō′nĭs). Seaport, Baleares prov., Spain, ✳ of Minorca I., 89 m. ENE of Palma; pop. 17,459; fortified harbor; coasting trade, exporting brandy, wine, agricultural produce, dried fruits, and importing grain, tobacco, sugar, coffee, and manufactured articles. Believed to have been founded by Carthaginian general Mago; held by Moors 8th–13th cents.; sacked by Barbarossa II 1535; occupied by English 1708–56 and 1763–82, by French 1756–62; captured by Spain 1782 and 1798; given to Spain by Treaty of Amiens 1802.
Ma·hone′ Bay (må·hōn′). Inlet of Atlantic Ocean in Lunenburg co., S Nova Scotia prov., Canada; the city of Lunenburg is located at its S entrance.
Ma·ho′ning (må·hō′nĭng). **1** River ab. 95 m. long, NE Ohio; rises in Columbiana co., E Ohio, flows NE then SE through Youngstown into Pennsylvania and joins Shenango river 4 m. SW of New Castle to form Beaver river.
2 County in Ohio. See *Table* at OHIO.
Ma′ho·pac (mä′ô·păk). Village, Putnam co., SE New York, on Lake Mahopac, ab. 12 m. NE of Peekskill; pop. 1337 trading center for resort community.
Mah′ra (mä′rà; *Arab.* mä′hrŏ). Sultanate in E Hadramaut on S coast of Arabia; mainly desert; chief town is port of Qishn, 200 m. ENE of Mukalla.
Mahratta States, Southern. = SOUTHERN MARATHA STATES.
Mähren. See MORAVIA.
Mährisch-Ostrau. See MORAVSKÁ OSTRAVA.
Mährisch-Schönberg. See ŠUMPERK.
Mährisch-Weisskirchen. See HRANICE.
Ma′hu·ko′na (mä′hŏŏ·kō′nä). Village, North Kohala dist., Hawaii co., Hawaii, on NW coast of Hawaii I. S of Upolu Point, pop. (1950) 147, its small harbor is port of call for interisland steamers.
Maiao. See TUBUAÏ MANU.
Mai′da (mī′då; *Arab.* mä′ĭ·då, -då). Coastal town, NW Yemen, SW Arabia, on the Red Sea N of Hodeida.
Mai·dan′ (mī·dăn′; mä-). Town, NE Iraq, on upper Diyala near Iranian border, NNE of Baghdad.
Mai·dan′-i-Naf·tun′ (mī·dän′ē·nåf·tōōn′). Town, SW Iran, on a tributary of the upper Karun river ab. 55 m. NE of Ahwaz; center for the oil fields of Masjid-i-Sulaiman.
Maid′en (mād′′n). Manufacturing town, Catawba co., W cen. North Carolina, 22 m. N of Gastonia; pop. 2039; produces furniture, textiles, flour.
Mai·de′nek (mī·dĕ′nĕk). Concentration camp of World War II near Lublin, Poland.
Maid′en·head (mād′′n·hĕd). Municipal borough, Berkshire, S England, on the Thames 27 m. W of London; pop. 27,125; chiefly a residential section and resort.
Maid′ens (mād′′nz). Group of rocks in the Irish Sea off E coast of co. Antrim, NE Northern Ireland; lighthouse.

Maid′stone (mād′stŏn; *Brit. usu.* -stŭn). Municipal borough, ⊗ of Kent, SE England, on the Medway 30 m. ESE of London; pop. 54,026; hop market; grammar school dating from 1549.
Maidstone Lake. Lake in E Essex co. NE corner of Vermont.
Mai·du′gu·ri (mī·dōō′gŏŏ·rė). Town, ✳ of Bornu prov., NE Northern Region, Nigeria; pop. (including Yerwa) 24,575; in Lake Chad region ab. 315 m. E of Kano.
Mai′har (mī′hēr). **1** Former Indian state, Baghelkhand, E cen. India, 412 sq. m.; pop. (1941) 79,558.
2 Town, its ✳, now in NE Madhya Pradesh, ab. 95 m. NNE of Jubbulpore; pop. 7678.
Mai′ka·la Range (mī′kå·là). Mountain range in cen. India, extending NE to SW chiefly in NE Madhya Pradesh; highest point ab. 3200 ft.
Mai·kop′ (mī·kôp′). City, ✳ of Adygei Autonomous Region, S Soviet Russia, Europe, 65 m. SE of Krasnodar; pop. 67,302; on railroad bet. Armavir and Tuapse; has mineral springs and is center of oil fields and region rich in minerals; has grown rapidly in recent years as industrial city. Occupied by the Germans from Aug. 1942 to Feb. 1943.
Maimachin. See KIACHTA.
Mai′ma·na′ (mī′må·nä′). **1** A minor province, NW Afghanistan.
2 Chief town of province, ab. 180 m. NE of Herat near Russian border.
Maimansingh. Var. of MYMENSINGH.
Main. **1** (mān; *Ger.* mīn); *anc.* **Moe′nus** (mē′nŭs). River 305 m. long in W cen. Germany; rises in the Fichtel Gebirge in N Bavaria, flows W into the Rhine opp. Mainz, passing through Wurzburg, Aschaffenburg, and Frankfurt in its course; navigable for ab. 240 m.
2 (mān) River in co. Antrim, NE Northern Ireland, flowing into Lough Neagh.
Maine (mān). A northeast state of U.S.A., 23d state admitted to Union (1820); bounded on N and E by Canadian province of New Brunswick, on S by Atlantic Ocean, on W by New Hampshire and Canadian province of Quebec; 39th state in area, 33,215 sq. m. (land area 31,040 sq. m.); 36th state in population, 969,265; ✳ Augusta. See *Table of States* at UNITED STATES; *Map*, p. 657. Divided into the following 16 counties (for pronunciation of their names, see their individual entries):

NAME	LOCATION	AREA[1]	POP.[1]	CO. SEAT
Androscoggin	SW	478	86,132	Auburn
Aroostook	N[2]	6,805	106,064	Houlton
Cumberland	SW; coastal	881	182,751	Portland
Franklin	W	1,717	20,069	Farmington
Hancock[3]	SE; coastal	1,542	32,293	Ellsworth
Kennebec	SW	865	89,150	Augusta
Knox	S; coastal	362	28,575	Rockland
Lincoln	S; coastal	457	18,497	Wiscasset
Oxford	W	2,085	44,345	South Paris
Penobscot	E cen.	3,408	126,346	Bangor
Piscataquis[4]	N cen.	3,948	17,379	Dover-Foxcroft
Sagadahoc	S; coastal	257	22,793	Bath
Somerset[4]	W	3,948	39,749	Skowhegan
Waldo	S; coastal	734	22,632	Belfast
Washington	SE corner; coastal	2,553	32,908	Machias
York	SW; coastal	1,000	99,402	Alfred

[1] Area = land area in sq. m. Pop. from 1960 Census.
[2] Northernmost point of E U.S.A.
[3] Includes Mount Desert Island, containing Acadia National Park.
[4] Includes part of Moosehead Lake.

Nickname: Pine Tree State, also Lumber State. *State flower:* White pine cone and tassel. *Motto:* Dirigo (I Direct). *Chief cities:* Portland, Lewiston, Bangor, Auburn, Augusta. *Rivers:* St. Croix, forming lower section of E boundary; Penobscot, flowing from cen. area S to Atlantic Ocean; Kennebec, flowing from W cen. region S to Atlantic Ocean; Salmon Falls forming section of extreme SW boundary. *Lakes:* Has ab. 1600; the largest Moosehead, Sebago, Chesuncook, Chamberlain, Grand, and the Rangeley Lakes. *High point:* Mount Katahdin

5268 ft. in Piscataquis co. *Chief industries:* Agriculture (esp. potatoes), fishing, lumbering, quarrying (granite).

History: Coast visited by Gosnold 1602 and other Englishmen just before it was included in grant to Plymouth Company 1606; first settlement by English at mouth of the Sagadahoc (Kennebec) 1607 failed, but Saco and Monhegan I. were settled c. 1622; through series of grants, beginning in 1622 and 1628, claimed by Massachusetts colony and Gorges; annexed to Massachusetts (1652) which bought out Gorges's claim 1678; northern parts frequently attacked by French who ceased active claims after 1713; a district of Massachusetts until 1820; admitted to Union as free state Mar. 15, 1820; boundary with Canada settled by treaty with Great Britain 1842.

Maine (mān; *Fr.* mân). **1** River 8 m. long in NW cen. France; formed by confluence of Sarthe and Mayenne rivers near Angers, flows S into Loire river.
2 *or* **Le Maine** (lĕ). Historical region of NW France; bounded anciently on N by Normandy, E by Orléanais, S by Touraine and Anjou, W by Brittany; * Le Mans.
History: Inhabited by Aulerci Cenomani; became countship in 10th cent. A.D.; united with countship of Anjou through marriage of heiress with count of Anjou 1126; became English when Henry Plantagenet became king of England 1154; taken by Philip Augustus 1204; passed to house of Anjou; reunited to French crown 1584; made duchy under Louis XIV.
Maine'-et-Loire' (mān'ā·lwâr'; *Fr.* mân'ā·lwár'). Department of France. See *Table* at FRANCE.
Maing'kwan' (mĭng'kwän'). Town, N Burma, on upper Chindwin river, near the Stilwell Road in Hukawng valley; amber mines; taken by Chinese from Japanese Mar. 4, 1944.
Ma·i'nit, Lake (mä·ē'nĭt). Lake 67 sq. m., NE Mindanao, Phil. Is., on boundary bet. NE Agusan prov. (42 sq. m.) and NW Surigao prov. (25 sq. m.); ab. 14 m. long.
Main'land' (mān'lănd'; -lＲnd). **1** Chief island of Japan. See HONSHU.
2 See POMONA, Orkney Is.
3 Chief island of the Shetland Is., NE of N Scotland; ab. 225 sq. m.; pop. 15,172; chief town Lerwick.
Main Pass (mān). One of the channels at the mouth of the Mississippi river (*q.v.*).
Main'pu·ri (mīn'pŏŏ·rē). Town, Agra division, W Uttar Pradesh, N Indian Union, 63 m. E of Agra; pop. 16,483.
Main'ti·ra'no (mīn'tē·rä'nō). Coastal town, W Madagascar, in cen. part on Mozambique Channel.
Mainz (mīnts); *Fr.* **Ma'yence'** (mȧ'yäNs'). Fortified manufacturing and commercial city, * of Rhineland-Palatinate and of Rheinhessen division, Germany, on Rhine at mouth of Main river 20 m. WSW of Frankfurt am Main; pop. (1957) 123,000; river port; manufactures include leather, furniture, hardware, carpets, tobacco, beer, chemicals, machinery, soap, hats, gold and silver ware; center of Rhenish wine industry; 11th-cent. Romanesque cathedral; 17th-cent. electoral palace; old citadel on site of Roman camp (see below); residence of Gutenberg; famous pedagogical institute.
History: Settled near Roman fort **Mo'gon·ti'a·cum** (mō'gŏn·tĭ'ȧ·kŭm), also **Ma'gun·ti'a·cum** (mä'gŭn-), founded by Drusus; made seat of archbishop 747 A.D.; attained self-government and became in 13th cent. head of Rhenish League; archbishop made an imperial elector 1356; city later lost privileges, and declined economically; held by French 1792–93 and 1798–1814; Hesse, Nassau, and Prussia received some of former territory 1814; headquarters of French army of occupation 1918–30; in World War II seized by American forces Mar. 21, 1945.
Ma'io *or* **Ma'yo** (mȧ'yōō). One of the Cape Verde Is.; 82 sq. m.; pop. ab. 2000; occupied by British until end of 18th cent.
Mai'po (mī'pô) *or* **Mai·pú'** (mī·pŏŏ'). River ab. 155 m.

long in Santiago prov., cen. Chile; flows W into Pacific Ocean. On its banks a few miles S of Santiago, in a battle Apr. 5, 1818, San Martín gained a victory over the Spanish forces that had been sent to regain Chile after its independence had been proclaimed (Feb. 12, 1818).
Mai·pú' (mī·pŏŏ') *or* **Mai'po** (mī'pô). Peak 17,356 ft. on Chile-Argentina boundary SE of Santiago, Chile.
Maipú, *or* **Maipo, Pa'so de** (pä'sô thä). Andean mountain pass on Argentina-Chile border, bet. W Mendoza prov., W Argentina, and E Santiago prov., cen. Chile; altitude 11,230 ft.
Mai'que·tí'a (mī'kä·tē'ä). Coastal town and watering place in Federal District, N Venezuela; pop. (1941 est.) 13,216; has large airport having connections with Miami, New York, and Montreal.
Maire Strait, Le. See LE MAIRE STRAIT.
Mai·sí' *or* **May·sí'**, **Cape** (mī·sē'). Cape at E extremity of Cuba, projecting into Windward Passage.
Mais'khal Island (mĭsk'häl). Island, Chittagong division, East Bengal, Pakistan, off extreme NE coast of India, separated from the mainland by **Maiskhal Channel.**
Mai'son'–Car'rée' (mā'zôn'kȧ'rā'). Commune, N Alger dept., N Algeria, just E of Algiers; pop. 24,341.
Mai'son'neuve' (mā'zô'nûv'). Eastern suburban residential section of the city of Montreal, Canada.
Mai'sons'–Al'fort' (mā'zôn'ȧl'fôr'). Commune, Seine dept., N France, SE suburb of Paris on Marne river; pop. 34,384.
Mai'sons'–La'fitte' (mā'zôn'lȧ'fēt'). Commune, Seine-et-Oise dept., N France, on Seine river 7 m. NW of Paris; pop. 13,040; racecourse.
Maisur. See MYSORE.
Mait'land (māt'lănd). Town, SW Cape Province, S Union of South Africa, E suburb of Cape Town; pop. (white) ab. 3000.
Maitland, East and West. Town, E New South Wales, SE Australia, on Hunter river 20 m. NW of Newcastle; pop. 12,329; in fertile agricultural, grazing, and bee-raising region; coal fields in vicinity.
Mai·zu·ru (mī·zōō·rōō). City and seaport, Kyoto prefecture, N coast of SW Honshu, Japan, NNW of Kyoto; pop. 29,303; made a naval base 1939.
Ma'ja (mä'yä). Large island S of estuary of Kapuas river, West Borneo prov., Indonesia.
Ma·ja'gua Bay (mä·hä'gwä). Bay in NE coast of Humacao municipality, E Puerto Rico.
Majdal, El. See EL MAJDAL.
Maji. See MAGI.
Maj'ma·'a (mäj'mä·ä). Town at N end of Jabal Tuwaiq, E Nejd, Saudi Arabia, ab. 90 m. E of Anaiza; pop. ab. 18,000.
Ma'jor (mā'jẽr). County in Oklahoma. See *Table* at OKLAHOMA.
Ma·jor'ca (mȧ·jôr'kȧ); *Span.* **Mal·lor'ca** (mä·[l]yôr'kä); *anc.* **Bal'e·ar'is Ma'jor** (băl'ê·âr'ĭs mā'jẽr). Largest island of the Balearic group, Baleares prov., Spain, in W Mediterranean 145 m. E of Spanish coast; 1352 sq. m.; pop. (1930) 292,447; * Palma; irregularly shaped with deeply indented coast line, esp. in NE; extremely mountainous in NW, gently rolling and fertile in S and E; picturesque scenery; produces wine, olives, grain, oranges, lemons, figs, almonds, flax; marble, iron, lead, and coal deposits; sheep raising; manufactures wine, olive oil, brandy, woolens, linens; trades in bricks, plaster, lime, brandy, oil, wines, silk, wool.
History: See also BALEARIC ISLANDS; kingdom of Mallorca erected by James I of Aragon (1213–76), included Minorca, Iviza, Roussillon, and Cerdagne; united to Aragon in mid-14th cent.; with Palma as port, was most prosperous of Balearic Is. until internal strife and advance of Italian cities brought decline in trade in 15th cent.; its peasants rose in revolt 1521–23; in Spanish Civil War 1936–39, joined Insurgents and was a base of Italian aid against Loyalists.

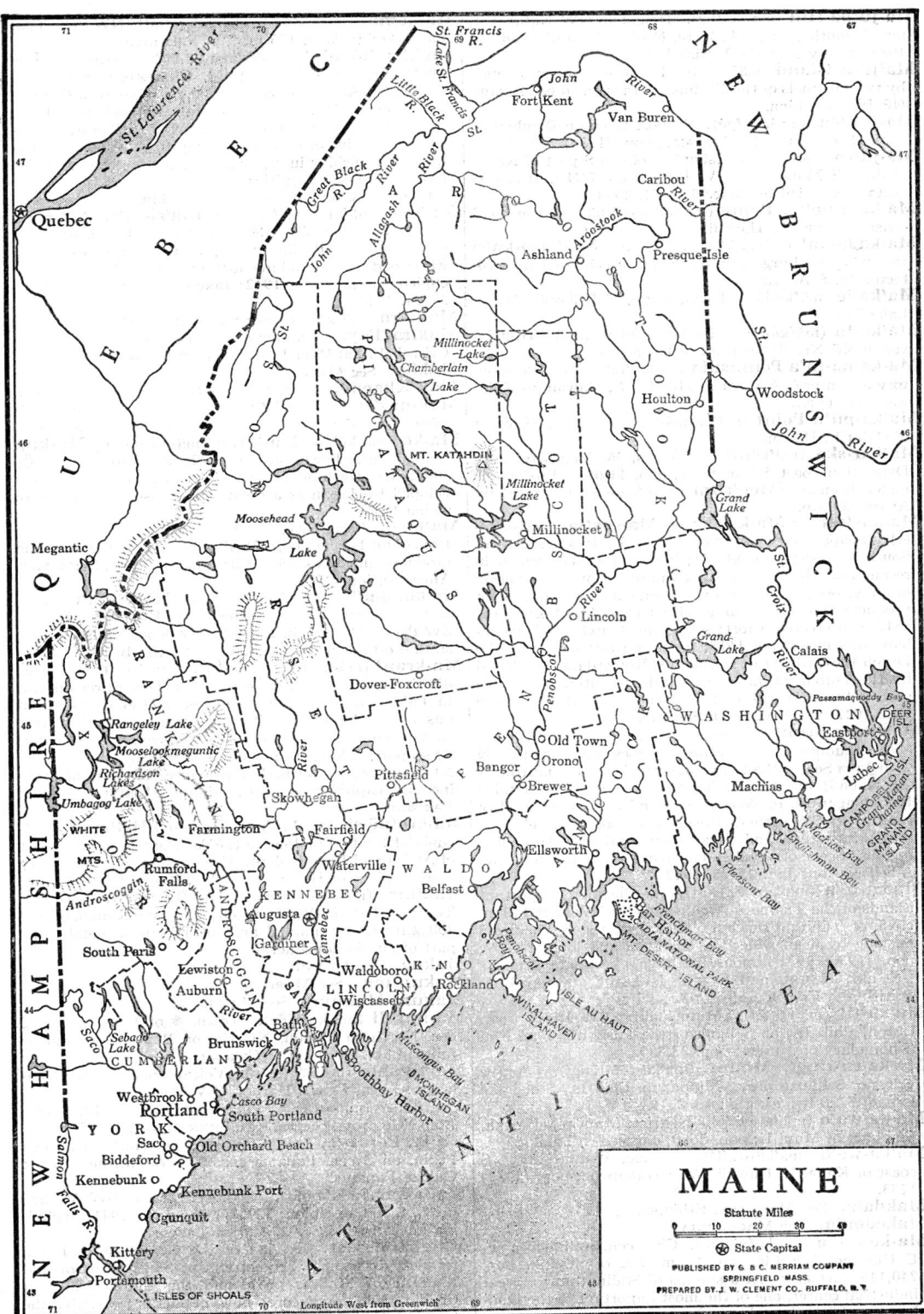

MAINE

Statute Miles

0   10   20   30   40

⊛ State Capital

PUBLISHED BY G. & C. MERRIAM COMPANY
SPRINGFIELD, MASS.
PREPARED BY J. W. CLEMENT CO., BUFFALO, N. Y.

Ma·ju′ba Hill (má·jōō′bá). Height in NW Natal, Union of South Africa, ab. 75 m. N of Ladysmith; scene of Boer victory over the British Feb. 27, 1881.

Ma′ju·li Island (mä′jōō·lǐ). Island 485 sq. m. formed by two channels of the Brahmaputra river in NE Assam, NE Indian Union.

Ma·jun′ga (má·jŭng′gá). Seaport town on Bombetoka Bay, NW coast of Madagascar; pop. (1936) 23,684.

Ma·ju′ro (má·jōōr′ō). Island (atoll) in S part of Ratak chain, SE Marshall Is., W Pacific, ab. 7°N lat.; has 33 islets. Occupied by Allies Jan. 31, 1944.

Ma·ka′hu·e′na Point (mä·kä′hōō·ā′nä). Cape on S coast of Kauai I., Hawaii.

Ma·ka′la·ka′ri (mä·kä′lä·kä′rě) or **Ma·ka′ri·ka′ri** (mä·kä′rě). Large salt basin, NE Bechuanaland Protectorate, S Africa.

Ma′ka·le (mä′kä·lā). Town, Tigre, N Ethiopia, NE of Lake Tana.

Ma′ka·lu (mŭ′kä·lōō). Peak 27,790 ft. in the Himalayas in NE Nepal; SE peak of Everest group.

Ma·ka′na·lu′a Peninsula (mä·kä′nä·lōō′ä). Promontory in center of N coast of Molokai I., Hawaii, in Kalawao dist. (q.v.).

Ma′ka·pu′u Point (mä′kä·pōō′ōō). Cape on SE coast of Oahu I., Hawaii.

Ma′kar·ska (mä′kär·skä). Town, W Yugoslavia, on Dalmatian coast SE of Split; pop. 11,685. Prosperous under Romans (**Moc′rum** [mŏk′rŭm]); destroyed by Avars 639 A.D.

Ma·kas′sar or **Ma·kas′ar** or **Ma·cas′sar** (má·kás′ēr). Seaport city on SW Celebes I., Indonesia, ✳ of South Celebes; pop. 84,855; has poor harbor which in recent years has been greatly improved by construction of quay, breakwater, and wharves; exports copra, forest products, spices, rice, co ee. First visited by Portuguese 1512 who erected a fort; settled by Dutch 1607; its inhabitants massacred 1618; town and fort seized by the Dutch 1667, when fort was named Rotterdam; developed by the Dutch as important trading center, made free port 1848; in World War II occupied by the Japanese Feb. 1942 (see MAKASSAR STRAIT).

Makassar Strait. Passage bet. E Borneo and W Celebes, Indonesia, connecting Celebes Sea on the N with Java Sea on the S; average width 155 m., narrowest (at N end) ab. 65 m., length ab. 450 m. Contains Balabalagan Is. in W cen. part and the large island of Laut at its SW corner. Forms a part of Wallace's line, separating fauna and flora of Oriental and Australian regions. Scene of naval and air battles bet. Japanese and Allied Nations Jan. 23–25, 1942.

Ma′ka·té′a (mä′kä·tā′ä). One of the more important islands of the Tuamotu Archipelago, in NW part 140 m. NNE of Tahiti, French Polynesia, in the S Pacific; 5 m. long by 3 m. wide; lat. 16°S and long. 148°W; pop. (1936) 992; famous for large phosphate deposits (see also NAURU and OCEAN ISLAND); developed by British and French since 1908.

Ma′ka·ti′ (mä′kä·tē′). Municipality, SW Rizal prov., Luzon, Phil. Is., on S bank of the Pasig ab. 1 m. E of E boundary of Manila; pop. 33,530.

Ma′ka·tu·ring′, Mount (mä′kä·tōō·rēng′). Active volcano, S Lanao prov., Mindanao, Phil. Is., S of Lake Lanao; 5720 ft.; eruption 1872.

Ma′ka·wa′o (mä′kä·wä′ō). District, Maui co., Hawaii, cen. part of Maui I.; pop. 5680; chief town Paia.

Ma′ka·we′li (mä′kä·wä′lě). Village, Waimea dist., S coast of Kauai I., Hawaii, W of Hanapepe; pop. (1950) 1283.

Makdala. See MAGDALA, Ethiopia.

Makedonia. See MACEDONIA.

Ma·ke′ev·ka (mŭ·kā′yěf·ká). City, cen. Stalino Region, E Ukraine, U.S.S.R., ab. 12 m. NE of Stalino; pop. 240,145; formerly just a suburb of Stalino; now a great industrial center, one of the most important in the Donbas, esp. in steel production.

Ma·ke′mo (mä·kā′mō). Island (atoll), NW cen. Tuamotu Archipelago, 125 m. E of Fakarava.

Ma′khach·ka·la′ (mä′ĸäch·kä·lä′); formerly **Pe·trovsk′** (pě·trôfsk′; Russ. pyǐ-). City, ✳ of Dagestan Republic, SE Soviet Russia, Europe, on W coast of Caspian Sea; pop. 86,847; on railroad from Astrakhan to Baku and terminus of railroad running NW to Rostov; transshipment point of oil from Grozny to the Volga; important for its fishing industry and cotton factories and also has cold storage facilities.

Ma′kian (mä′kyän). See TIDORE island.

Ma′kin (mä′kǐn; mä′-) or **Bu·ta′ri·ta′ri** (bōō·tä′rě·tä′rě). Island (atoll) at N end of Gilbert Is. ab. 100 m. N of Tarawa, W Pacific Ocean, 11 m. at greatest width with good lagoon and anchorage; pop. (1936) 1643. Occupied by Japanese 1942; taken by U.S. Army Nov. 20–24, 1943.

Ma·ki′ra (mä·kē′rä). See SAN CRISTOBAL.

Makira Bay. Widemouthed inlet on S coast of San Cristobal I., at W end, SE Solomon Is., W Pacific Ocean.

Makka. See MECCA.

Mak Khaeng. = Ban Mak Khaeng: see UDON THANI.

Mak·nas′sy (mäk·näs′ǐ). Town, cen. Tunisia, Africa, ab. 65 m. W of Sfax; battles Mar.–Apr. 1943.

Ma·ko (mä·kō) or **Ma·kung** (mä·gōong) or **Ma·kun** (mä·gōong). Town, on Penghu I., Pescadores; pop. ab. 3000; chief town of the island group, in recent years developed by Japan as a great naval base; transferred to China 1946.

Ma′kó (mŏ′kō). City, SE Hungary, on Mureş river near Romanian border; pop. 38,495; market center for farm products and livestock. Birthplace of Joseph Pulitzer, American journalist.

Ma′kong·a′i (mä′kông·ä′ě) or **Ma′kog·a′i** (mä′kông·ä′ě). Small island in the Lomai Viti group, Fiji Is., SW Pacific Ocean, ab. 28 m. SW of Koro I.; site of leper station established and equipped by the British.

Ma·kran′ (má·krän′) or **Me·kran′** (mě-). **1** Southwest division of former Kalat state, Baluchistan; region now in Pakistan; ab. 26,000 sq. m.; pop. 71,860; mountainous and arid; chief cultivated area is in Kej river (upper tributary of Dasht) valley in cen. part. Gwadar, its seaport, belonged to Oman until 1958. **2** Coastal region, formerly a province, SE Iran; as province its capital was Jask; adjoins Makran region of Pakistan.

Ma·kro′nē·si (mä·krô′nyě·sě); anc. **Hel′e·na** (hěl′ě·ná). Island 10 m. long in the Aegean Sea, off SE coast of Attica and Boeotia dept., Greece; 7 sq. m. Legendary landing place of Helen after fall of Troy.

Mak′tar (mäk′tŭr); anc. **Mac′ta·ris** (mäk′tá·rǐs). Town, N Tunisia, W of Ousseltia; became Roman colony 200 A.D.; has triumphal arch of Trajan, a temple, and part of an old aqueduct.

Makua. See UBANGI.

Makumma. See MORONA.

Makun, Makung. See MAKO.

Ma·kur′di (mä·kōōr′dě). Town, ✳ of Benue prov., S cen. Northern Region, Nigeria, on Benue river and on railroad ab. 170 m. N of Calabar.

Ma·ku′shin (má·kōō′shǐn). Volcano 6680 ft., NE Unalaska I., near Dutch Harbor, SW Alaska.

Mak·war′ (mäk·wär′). Village and dam on Blue Nile, Blue Nile prov., Sudan. See SENNAR town.

Ma′la, Point (mä′lä). Cape on E extremity of Azuero Penin. on S cen. Panama coast, at W entrance to the Gulf of Panama.

Mal′a·bar (mäl′á·bär). Former district, SW Madras prov., S Indian Union; 5790 sq. m.; pop. (1941), including Laccadive Is., 3,929,425; ✳ Calicut.

Malabar Coast. Region of the SW coast of India, formerly including the districts of South Kanara and Malabar of Madras prov. and the Indian states of Cochin and Travancore; now in Kerala; strictly, the territory bet. the Western Ghats and the Arabian Sea.

Chief ports Calicut, Tellicherry, Cannanore, and Cochin; also former French possession of Mahé. Its inhabitants, of Dravidian stock, speak Malayalam.

Mal'a·ba'ta, Point (măl'á·bä'tá). Point, N Morocco, NW Africa, E of Tangier.

Ma'la·bon' (mä'lä·bôn'). Municipality, NW Rizal prov., Luzon, Phil. Is., 2 m. inland from shore of Manila Bay just N of Manila; pop. 33,285.

Malaca. See MÁLAGA.

Ma·lac'ca (má·lăk'á). 1 State of Federation of Malaya, on W coast of S Malay Penin.; formerly a settlement of Straits Settlements; 637 sq. m.; pop. 186,711, (1941 est.) 236,087; * Malacca. Almost entirely agricultural with much of the acreage devoted to rubber.
2 Seaport municipality, its *, on Strait of Malacca 118 m. by sea from Singapore; pop. 38,042, (1937 est.) 43,258; connected by rail with Tampin in Negri Sembilan; chiefly coastal trade.
History: Founded in 14th cent. by Srivijaya refugees from Sumatra; in process of developing a Mohammedan empire when it was taken for Portuguese by Albuquerque 1511; early center of East Indian spice trade; its capture by Dutch (1641) secured Dutch predominance in Indies; held by British 1795–1802 and 1811–18; ceded to Great Britain in exchange for Benkoelen 1824; occupied by Japanese Jan. 1942.

Malacca, Strait of; *sometimes* **Straits of Malacca.** Channel bet. the S Malay Penin. and the island of Sumatra, connecting the Indian Ocean with the South China Sea; ab. 500 m. long and varies in width bet. 35 and 185 m.

Malacca Central. District, Malacca Federation of Malaya, on Strait of Malacca, comprising the environs of Malacca municipality; pop. 45,465.

Ma·lad' City (má·lăd'). City, ⊗ of Oneida co., S Idaho; pop. 2274.

Ma·lade' (má·lăd'). River ab. 90 m. long, N Utah; rises in N Oneida co., S Idaho, flows S across Utah border into Bear river in E Box Elder co., N Utah.

Ma'la·det'ta (mä'lä·dä'tä) *or* **Ma'la·de'ta.** Mountain range in the Pyrenees, in NE Spain near the French border; highest peak Pico de Aneto 11,169 ft.

Má'la·ga (măl'á·gá; *Span.* mä'lä·gä). 1 Town, Santander dept., N cen. Colombia, ab. 45 m. SE of Bucaramanga; pop. 5210.
2 Province of Spain. See *Table* at SPAIN.
3 *anc.* **Mal'a·ca** (măl'á·ká). Commercial, manufacturing, and seaport city, * of Málaga prov., S Spain, on Mediterranean 66 m. NE of Gibraltar; pop. (1941 est.) 238,264; produces and exports olive oil, fruits (esp. grapes, raisins, and oranges), almonds, lead, wine, cotton, sugar; iron mines nearby; manufactures metalware, soap, cottons, linens, machinery; winter resort; 13th-cent. citadel, called the Gibralfaro; 16th-cent. cathedral on site of old Moorish mosque. Founded by Phoenicians; held by Romans and Visigoths; taken by Moors 711; reconquered by Ferdinand and Isabella 1487.

Ma·la'ga·ra'si (má·lä'gá·rä'sē). River ab. 100 m. long in W Tanganyika, E Africa, flowing S and W into Lake Tanganyika.

Malagasy Republic. See MADAGASCAR.

Ma·lai'ta (má·lä'tá). Long, narrow island in SE Solomon Is. in the SW Pacific Ocean, 50 m. SE of Santa Isabel I. and NE of Guadalcanal; ab. 100 m. long; area ab. 2500 sq. m.; pop. (1931) ab. 40,000; chief village Auki. Part of British Solomon Is. protectorate. Second to Bougainville in population; has many coastal villages. Interior unexplored, inhabited by tribes still savage. Has no good harbors; highest point 4275 ft.

Ma·la'ka (mä·lä'kä; *Du.* má·lä'kä). Malay and Dutch forms of MALACCA.

Ma'la·kal (mä'lä·kăl). Town, * of Upper Nile prov., SE Sudan, on right bank of White Nile 410 m. S of Khartoum.

Ma'la·kand (mŭ'lá·kŭnd). Former agency, N North-

West Frontier Province, Brit. India; 11,383 sq. m.; pop. 902,075; now a region of Pakistan, includes tribal areas of Dir, Swat, and Chitral.

Malakand Pass. Mountain pass in S Swat, 40 m. NNE of Peshawar. Important in Chitral campaign 1895 and in frontier operations in Swat 1897–98.

Ma·la'khov (mŭ·lá'ĸŭf; *Angl.* măl'á·kŏf); *also* **Ma·la'-koff.** Fortification, SE part of Sevastopol, Crimea, S Soviet Russia, Europe; captured by the French Sept. 8, 1855 after a long siege; in World War II captured by the Germans July 1942.

Malakka. Var. of MALACCA.

Mal'a·koff (măl'á·kŏf). City, Henderson co., NE Texas, ab. 42 m. SW of Tyler; pop. 1657; lignite coal mines.

Ma'la'koff' (má'lä'kôf'), *sometimes* **Malakoff-la-Tour** (-lá·tōōr'). Commune, Seine dept., N France, S suburb of Paris; pop. 28,439; manufactures chemicals, metal goods, precision instruments.

Malaku. See MOLUCCAS.

Ma'lan'court' (má'län'kōōr'). Village, Meuse dept., NE France, NW of Verdun; battles Mar. 1916.

Ma·lang' (mä·läng'). 1 Former residency, cen. East Java prov., Neth. Indies; 3411 sq. m.; pop. 2,741,105; * Malang. Bounded on N by Surabaja and Madura Strait, on E by Besuki, on S by Indian Ocean, and on W by Kediri. Region has two ports on Madura Strait—Pasuruan and Probolinggo—but none on S coast. Comprises the mountain groups of Kawi on the W and Tengger on the E with fertile plains in between. Center of co*f*fee production.
2 City, Indonesia, ab. 60 m. SW of Surabaja; pop. 86,646; on upper Brantas river at foot of Mt. Kawi.

Ma·lan'je (má·län'jĕ) *or* **Ma·lan'ge** (-jĕ). Inland town, N cen. Angola; railroad terminus E of Luanda.

Ma'la Pas'cua, Point (mä'lä päs'kwä). Cape on SE extremity of Puerto Rico.

Mala Prespa, Lake. See Lake PRESPA.

Mä'lar·en (mä'lär·ĕn). Lake 440 sq. m. in SE Sweden; extends from the Baltic Sea W inland 70 m.; the city of Stockholm is situated on both sides of the strait connecting the lake with the Baltic Sea.

Ma'lar'tic' (má'lär'tēk'). Town, Abitibi co., SW Quebec, Canada; pop. 5983.

Ma'la·si'qui (mä'lä·sē'kē). Municipality, cen. Pangasinan prov., Luzon, Phil. Is., on Manila-Dagupan R.R. 14 m. SE of Lingayen; pop. 33,660; on a branch of the Agno river.

Malaskirt. = MALAZKIRT.

Malaspina. See Mount CANLAON.

Mal'a·spi'na Glacier (măl'á·spē'ná). Glacier ab. 90 m. long on S coast of Alaska, S from Mt. St. Elias to Yakutat Bay; covers 1500 sq. m. with front of ab. 60 m. on the Pacific; more than 1000 ft. thick.

Ma'la·tya' (mä'lä·tyä'). 1 Vilayet, E Turkey in Asia; 8208 sq. m.; pop. 385,388.
2 *anc.* **Mel'i·te'ne** (mĕl'i·tē'nē). City, its *, on railroad just W of the Euphrates ab. 112 m. NE of Gaziantep; pop. (1940) 38,009; at NE end of Taurus Mts.; has fine orchards and gardens; many ruined mosques, relics of the city built 756 by caliph al-Mansur. As Melitene an important Roman military post, enlarged and improved under Justinian; bet. 6th and 12th cents. as a frontier town changed hands many times and suffered much; became Turkish 1102. Birthplace of famous Syrian scholar Bar-Hebraeus 1226.

Malawi. See NYASALAND.

Malaya. See MALAY PENINSULA; BRITISH MALAYA; Federation of MALAYA.

Ma·lay'a, Federation of (má·lā'á). A federation of the 9 Malay States of the Malay Penin. (the former Federated Malay States of Negri Sembilan, Pahang, Perak, and Selangor, and the former Unfederated Malay States of Johore, Kedah, Kelantan, Perlis, and Trengganu) and two of the Straits Settlements (Malacca and Penang); 50,841 sq. m.; pop. 4,779,683; * Kuala

Lumpur. Formerly comprised the larger part of British Malaya; set up Apr. 1, 1946 as constitutional **Union of Malaya** (first proposed Oct. 1945); reorganized and established Feb. 1, 1948 as the Federation of Malaya (first proposed Dec. 1946, finally approved by British government July 1947); became a dominion of the Brit-

MALAYA
AND BRITISH CROWN COLONY OF
SINGAPORE
Statute Miles

ish Commonwealth 1957; joined Fed. of Malaysia Sept. 16, 1963. For physical features, see MALAY PENINSULA, MALACCA, PENANG, and the names of the various states. The subdivisions are given in the *Table* below (for pronunciation of their names, see individual entries):

POLITICAL DIVISION[1]	LOCATION[1]	AREA[2]	POP.[2]	CAPITAL
		STATES		
Johore	S end	7,500	737,590	Johore Bahru
Kedah	NW	3,660	515,758	Alor Star
Kelantan	N	5,750	390,332	Kota Bahru
Negri Sembilan	SW coast	2,580	296,009	Seremban
Pahang	E coast	13,820	221,800	Kuala Lipis
Perak[3]	W coast	7,980	992,691	Taiping
Perlis	NW	316	57,776	Kangar
Selangor	W coast	3,160	701,552	Kuala Lumpur[4]
Trengganu	E	5,050	211,041	Kuala Trengganu
		49,816	4,124,549	
		STRAITS SETTLEMENTS[5]		
Malacca	W coast	637	236,087	Malacca
Penang[6]	off W coast	388	419,047	George Town
		1,025	655,134	

[1] In S end of Malay Penin.
[2] Area = land area in sq. m. Pop. from 1940 and 1941 estimates.
[3] Since 1935 includes Dindings.
[4] Also * of Federation of Malaya.
[5] Does not include Singapore settlement, which became a separate British crown colony Apr. 1, 1946.
[6] Includes Province Wellesley.

Ma·lay′ Archipelago (mȧ·lā′; mä′lä) *or* **Ma·lay′sia** (mȧ·lā′zhȧ; -zhĭ·ȧ; -shȧ; -shĭ·ȧ). The largest of island groups in the world, off SE coast of Asia bet. the Pacific and Indian Oceans, comprising the islands of the East Indies, including Sumatra, Java, Lesser Sunda Is.,

Moluccas, Timor, New Guinea, Borneo, Celebes, Philippine Is.

History: Southern Malay Penin., Sumatra, cen. Java, and eastern Borneo were colonized from c. 1st cent. B.C. by Hindu Pallavas from SE India; later influenced by Buddhism; Sumatra, united under ruler of Srivijaya, by 12th cent. ruled empire including Philippines, Moluccas, Borneo, western Java, Ceylon, and southern Malay Penin.; Srivijaya empire conquered by kingdom of Singhasari and state of Madjapahit in Java (*q.v.*) 13th–14th cents.; in early 15th cent., Malay states came under Chinese influence, but later, Mohammedan traders gained ascendancy in several states (see MALACCA); after 1511, dominated by Portuguese who were succeeded by Dutch (see NETHERLANDS INDIES) and, on mainland, by British (see BRITISH MALAYA and Federation of MALAYA).

Ma′lay·ba′lay (mä′lī·bä′lĭ). Municipality, * of Bukidnon prov., Mindanao, Phil. Is.; pop. 18,816.

Ma·lay′ Peninsula (mȧ·lā′; mä′lä) *or* **Ma·lay′a** (mȧ·lā′ȧ); *anc.* **Cher′so·ne′sus Au′re·a** (kûr′sō·nē′sŭs ô′rē·ȧ); *Eng.* **Golden Cher′so·nese** (kûr′sō·nēz; -nēs). An extension of SE Asia S of lat. 10°N, the S tip of the Asiatic mainland, comprising the Federation of Malaya and SW part of Thailand; ab. 70,000 sq. m. Has range of mountains extending its entire length, dividing it on E and W unequally; highest known peaks are Kerbau 7159 ft. and Tahan 7185 ft. on border bet. Kelantan and Pahang. Noted for wealth of its tin mines.

Malaysia. 1 See MALAY ARCHIPELAGO.
2 *or* **Federation of Ma·lay′sia** (mȧ·lā′zhȧ; -shȧ). Country SE Asia formed Sept. 16, 1963 by union of Fed. of Malaya, Sabah, Sarawak, and Singapore; a limited constitutional monarchy; area 128,318 sq. m.; pop. 9,136,641; * Kuala Lumpur. Singapore withdrew from Federation 1965.

Malay States. The native states of the Malay Penin., esp. those under British protection in S part comprising most of the Federation of Malaya: Pahang, Perak, Selangor, and Negri Sembilan (former Federated Malay States) and Johore, Kedah, Kelantan, Perlis, Trengganu (former Unfederated Malay States); 49,816 sq. m.; pop. (1940–41 est.) 4,124,549. Formerly included, in cen. and N part of the peninsula, a group of semi-independent states inhabited chiefly by Malays and governed by Malay rulers, the chief of these states being Patani and Setul (ab. 7000 sq. m.; pop. 375,000); these states, now part of Thailand, have recently been reorganized into provinces, esp. Pattani, Satun, and Yala (*qq.v.*). See *Map* at Federation of MALAYA.

Ma′laz·kirt′ (mä′läz·kĭrt′); *formerly* **Man′zi·kert′** (män′tyĕ·kĕrt′). Armenian village, Ağrı vilayet, E Turkey in Asia, ab. 25 m. NW of Lake Van; pop. 1213. Scene of defeat and capture of Emperor Romanus IV Diogenes by Seljuk Turks under Alp Arslan who thus crushed power of Byzantine Empire (*q.v.*) in Asia Minor 1071.

Mal′baie′ (mȧl′bā′). River ab. 80 m. long in Charlevoix co., S Quebec, Canada; flows in wide curve, finally to the SE into the St. Lawrence river at La Malbaie.

Malbaie, La. See LA MALBAIE.

Mal′bork (mäl′bôrk); *Ger.* **Ma·ri′en·burg** (mä·rē′ĕn·bŏŏrk; *Angl.* mȧ·rē′ĕn·bûrg); *also* **Marienburg in West′preus′sen** (ĭn vĕst′prois′sĕn). City, E Gdańsk dept., N Poland, on Nogat river 25 m. SE of Danzig; pop. (1946) 38,968; formerly in East Prussia, Germany; railroad junction; manufactures rubber goods, chemicals, soap, sugar, cigars; cattle and horse market. Assigned to Poland by Potsdam Conference 1945.

Mal′da (mäl′dȧ). District, formerly in Rajshahi division, Bengal, NE Brit. India, E of the Ganges; 2004 sq. m.; pop. (1941) 1,232,618; * English Bazar; in 1947 divided bet. East Bengal, Pakistan (ab. ⅔ of the area) and West Bengal, Indian Union (ab. ⅓).

Mal′de·gem (mäl′dĕ·ĸĕm). Commune, East Flanders prov., NW cen. Belgium, just E of Brugge; pop. 10,843.

Mal′den (môl′dĕn). **1** City, Middlesex co., NE Massachusetts, 5 m. N of Boston; pop. 57,676; manufactures rubber boots, shoes, knit goods, drugs and chemicals; residential suburb. Founded 1640.
2 City, Dunklin co., SE Missouri, 28 m. ESE of Poplar Bluff; pop. 5007; cotton-ginning center.
3 Island of the Line Is. in cen. Pacific Ocean S of Hawaii and 275 m. SE of Jarvis I.; 4°S and 155°W; 35 sq. m.; yields guano; stone structures of unknown origin, now believed to be of comparatively recent Polynesian origin. In area claimed by Great Britain and U.S.

Mal′dens and Coombe, The (môl′dĕnz, kōōm). Urban district, Surrey, S England; pop. 45,559; part of Greater London.

Mal′dive Islands (măl′dīv; môl′-). Group of 13 clusters of coral islands (atolls) in Indian Ocean ab. 400 m. SW of Ceylon; 115 sq. m.; pop. ab. 70,000; a sultanate, formerly under British protection but independent since 1965; chief island and ✱ Male.

Mal′don (môl′dŭn). Municipal borough, Essex, SE England, on Blackwater estuary 38 m. ENE of London; pop. 9721; scene of battle 991 A.D. bet. the East Saxons and the Danes, and celebrated in an Old English poem.

Mal′do·na′do (mäl′dṓ·nä′thṓ). **1** Cape on SW extremity of Guerrero state, S Mexico.
2 Town, Peru. See PUERTO MALDONADO.
3 Department of Uruguay. See *Table* at URUGUAY.
4 Seaport town and resort, S Uruguay, ab. 65 m. E of Montevideo; ✱ of Maldonado dept.; pop. ab. 8000.

Ma′le (mä′lå). Chief atoll and ✱ of the Maldive Islands, in central part; actually two groups of islets: North, 32 m. by 23 m., and South, 20 m. by 12 m.

Ma·le′a, Cape (mȧ·lē′ȧ; *Mod. Gr.* mä·lä′ä). Cape at extremity of the E peninsula of Peloponnesus, S Greece.

Ma′le·gaon′ (mä′lå·goun′). Town, NW India, in Maharashtra 160 m. NE of Bombay; pop. 32,462.

Mal′e·ku′la (măl′ĕ·kōō′lȧ) or **Mal′li·co′lo** (măl′ĭ-kō′lō). An island of the New Hebrides in the SW Pacific Ocean 25 m. SE of Espíritu Santo; second in size of the group, ab. 50 m. long by 23 m. wide; 980 sq. m.; pop. (native; 1938 est.) 7000. Mountainous, highest point Mt. Penot 2925 ft., in cen. part; several good harbors, esp. Port Sandwich in SE and Port Stanley in NE.

Ma′le·me (mä′lå·mĕ). Village and large airport on NW coast of Crete, in Canea dept., Greece; taken from British by airborne German force May 20–25, 1941.

Ma′ler Kot′la or **Ma′ler·kot′la** (mä′lår·kŏt′lå).
1 Former Indian state, East Punjab, NW India; 165 sq. m.
2 Town, its ✱, 155 m. NNW of Delhi; pop. 25,240.

Ma′le·tsun·ya′ne (mä′lå·tsōōn·yä′nå). River, Basutoland, E Republic of So. Africa; flows S into the Sinqu river, headstream of the Orange river; has notable waterfall **Maletsunyane Falls** which drops 630 ft.

Maleventum. See BENEVENTO commune.

Mal′fa (mäl′fä). See SALINA.

Malgache Republic. See MADAGASCAR.

Mal′heur (măl′hūr). **1** River, E Oregon; rises in S Grant co., flows S, then turns NE into Snake river on NE boundary of Malheur co.
2 County in Oregon. See *Table* at OREGON.

Malheur Lake. Lake in cen. Harney co., SE Oregon.

Malhon. See HOMONHON.

Ma′li or **Mali Kha** (mä′lĕ k′hä′). River (*kha*) ab. 200 m. long in Upper Burma; flows S from the slopes of the hills on N boundary and unites with Nmai to form the Irrawaddy river above Myitkyina.

Ma′li (mä′lĕ). **1** or **Mali Federation.** Federation, 1959–60, of Senegal and Sudanese Republic; ✱ Dakar; dissolved by withdrawal of Senegal.
2 Republic, W Africa. See SUDANESE REPUBLIC.

Maliacus Sinus. See Gulf of LAMIA.

Ma·ligne′ (mȧ·lēn′). Lake 18 sq. m. in E cen. part of Jasper National Park, W Alberta, Canada; altitude ab. 5500 ft.; its outlet is **Maligne River**, tributary of the Athabaska. Largest glacier-fed lake in Canadian Rockies.

Ma·ligne′, Isle (ēl′ mȧ′lēn′y′). See SAINT JOSEPH D'ALMA.

Ma′lik-Si·ah′, Koh-i- (kō′hĕ·mä′lĕk·sĕ·yä′). Peak 5390 ft. in extreme SW Afghanistan, at junction of Iran-Afghanistan-Baluchistan boundaries.

Ma′li Kvar′ner (mä′lĕ kvär′nĕr); *Ital.* **Quar′ne·ro′lo** (kwär′nä·rō′lō). Gulf or channel, NE Adriatic Sea, bet. Cres I. and Lošinj I. on W and Pag I. and Rab I. on E.

Ma·lim′biu (mä·lĭm′byōō). Short stream E of Henderson Field on N coast of Guadalcanal I., SE Solomon Is., W Pacific Ocean; flows N; W side of its mouth marked by Koli Point. Fighting here Nov. 5 and 6, 1942.

Ma·li′nao (mä·lē′nou). Municipality on NE coast of Albay prov., Luzon, Phil. Is., at entrance to Tabaco Bay 17 m. N of Legaspi; pop. 15,089; in hemp region.

Ma·lin′che (mä·lēn′chä) or **Ma·lin′tzi** (-chĕ). Mountain 14,636 ft. in S Tlaxcala on border of Puebla, Mexico. Native name is **Ma′tlal·cue′yatl** (mä′tläl·kwä′yät·′l).

Ma′lin·dang′, Mount (mä′lĕn·däng′). Mountain 7956 ft., S Misamis Occidental prov., Mindanao, Phil. Is., 16 m. WNW of Misamis; highest point in province.

Ma·lin′di (mȧ·lĭn′dĭ). Seaport town, SE Kenya, E Africa; pop. ab. 2000; early capital of Portuguese East Africa; reached 1498 by Vasco da Gama who erected a monument, still standing. Nearby are ruins of ancient Gedi, possibly of Persian origin; consist of mosque, tombs, palace, and encircling wall (ab. 6 m.).

Malines. See MECHELEN.

Mal′in Head (măl′ĭn). Cape on N coast of co. Donegal, N Eire; the northernmost point of Ireland, 55°25′N.

Malintzi. See MALINCHE.

Ma′lis (mä′lĭs). District of ancient Greece, S of Thessaly and Othrys Mts. and extending along N and W shores of Gulf of Lamia. Its inhabitants were Dorians.

Ma·li′ta (mȧ·lē′tȧ; *Span.* mä·lē′tä). Municipality, SW Davao prov., Mindanao, Phil. Is., on SW coast of Davao Gulf 46 m. S of City of Davao; pop. 30,775.

Ma·lit′bog (mä·lēt′bôg). Municipality on W shore of Sogod Bay, S Leyte I., Phil. Is.; pop. 22,259.

Mal·la′wi (mä·lä′wĭ). Town, Asyût prov., Upper Egypt, on the Nile ab. 50 m. NNW of Asyût; pop. ab. 20,000.

Mal·le′co (mä·yä′kō). Province of Chile. See *Table* at CHILE.

Mal′lee (măl′ĕ). Regions in Australia covered with the dense brushwood or thicket formed by the eucalypts (esp. *Eucalyptus dumosa* and *E. oleosa*); esp. an area **(the Mallee)** in NW Victoria along the Murray river, formerly covering 14,000,000 acres, now under farms.

Mallicolo. See MALEKULA.

Mallorca. See MAJORCA.

Mal′low (măl′ō). Urban district, N cen. co. Cork, SW Eire, on Blackwater river; pop. 4948; ruins of castle; has mineral springs; formerly a noted spa; salmon angling.

Mal′lus (măl′ŭs) or **Mal′los** (măl′ŏs). Town, ancient Cilicia, near coast of modern Gulf of İskenderon; home of Crates of Mallus, Stoic philosopher of 2d cent. B.C.

Mal′mai′son′ (mäl′mā′zôn′). Château ab. 7 m. W of Paris, France; residence (1809–14) of Empress Josephine and later of Maria Christina of Spain, and of the Empress Eugénie.

Malmasia. See MONEMVASIA.

Mal′mé′dy′ (mȧl′mā′dē′). Commune, E Liège prov., E Belgium; pop. 5321. See EUPEN.

Malmes′bur·y (mämz′bĕr·ĭ; -brĭ). **1** Municipal borough, Wiltshire, S England; pop. 2509; William of Malmesbury was a monk at the ancient abbey here, and Aldhelm was the first abbot (c. 673).
2 Town, SW Cape Province, S Republic of So. Africa, 35 m. NNE of Cape Town; pop. 4865; mineral springs.

Malm′ö′ (mȧl′mŭ′). Fortified seaport, ✱ of Malmöhus prov., SW Sweden, on Öresund opp. Copenhagen, Denmark; pop. 167,885; 3d largest city in Sweden; exports farm products, chemicals, lumber; imports coal, oil, machinery; shipbuilding yards, beet-sugar refineries, textile mills, rubber works, fisheries; former center of her-

ring fisheries; under Danish rule until 1658; conquered and made a part of Sweden by Charles X; 16th-cent. town hall; 14th-cent. Gothic church.

Malm'ö·hus' (mäl'mû·hōōs'). Province of Sweden. See *Table* at SWEDEN.

Ma'lo·e·lap' (mä'lō·å·läp'). Island (atoll), cen. part of Ratak chain, E Marshall Is., W Pacific Ocean, ab. 8°20'N lat.; has 64 islets. One of the 5 Japanese air bases in the Marshalls; raided by U.S. Navy fleet 1942; bypassed Feb. 1945 in advance toward Japan.

Ma'lo'-les-Bains (må'lō'lä·bǎN'). Commune, Nord dept., N France, NE suburb of Dunkerque on North Sea; pop. (1931) 10,296; seaside resort.

Ma·lo'los (mä·lō'lōs). Municipality, ✻ of Bulacan prov., Luzon, Phil. Is., in SW part at head of delta of the Pampanga; pop. 33,384; important center in the rice trade. Chosen as capital of Philippine Republic 1898; meeting place of the revolutionary congress. Constitution of the republic framed here in the Barasoain Church Sept.–Nov. 1898 and proclaimed on Jan. 23, 1899. Taken by Americans Feb. 1945.

Ma·lone' (må·lōn'). Village, ⊗ of Franklin co., NE New York, 45 m. WNW of Plattsburg; pop. 8737; port of entry near boundary bet. U.S. and Canada; paper, pulp, and lumber mills, tanneries, foundry and machine shops, powder mills, woolen mills; selected by Irish-American Fenians as base for invasion of Canada 1866.

Ma'lo·ya·ro·sla'vets (må'lŭ·yå·rŭ·slå'vyĕts). Town, Kaluga Region, Soviet Russia, Europe, N of Kaluga; pop. 5450; scene of battle Oct. 24, 1812 in which the Russians prevented Napoleon's army from retreating southward. In World War II, an outer defense of Moscow, taken by Germans Oct. 17, 1941; retaken in 1942.

Mal·pe'lo Island (mäl·pā'lō). Island, E Pacific Ocean, W of Buenaventura, Colombia; belongs to Colombia.

Mal'peque Bay (môl'pĕk); *formerly* **Rich'mond Bay** (rĭch'mŭnd). Inlet of Gulf of St. Lawrence, in NE Prince Edward Island, SE Canada.

Mal'pla·quet' (mäl'plå·kā'; *Fr.* mäl'plå'kĕ'). Hamlet in Nord dept., N France; scene of Marlborough's victory over the French Sept. 11, 1709.

Malström. See MAELSTROM.

Mal'ta (môl'tå). **1** City, ⊗ of Phillips co., N Montana, 62 m. WNW of Glasgow; pop. 2239.

2 *anc.* **Mel'i·ta** (mĕl'ĭ·tå). British island 17½ m. long in Mediterranean Sea 58 m. S of Sicily; 95 sq. m.; pop. 235,000; chief island of a group known as **Malta**, *or* **Mal'tese'** (môl'tēz'; -tēs') **Islands,** including besides Malta the islands of Gozo and Comino, and constituting a former British colony, since 1964 an independent republic; total area 122 sq. m., pop. (1931) 241,621, ✻ Valletta. Has excellent harbors, esp. Valletta, one of the strongest naval bases of Great Britain; island is limestone formation, having thin but fertile soil and no trees. Agriculture is main occupation; chief products wheat, barley, vegetables, grapes, cotton. Chief towns Valletta, the "Three Cities" on S side of Valletta harbor (Senglea, Vittoriosa, and Cospicua), and the old capital Città Vecchia. See COSPICUA.

History: Phoenician and Carthaginian colony; captured by Romans 218 B.C.; part of Byzantine holdings when overrun by Saracens 870 A.D.; taken by Norman kingdom of Sicily (*q.v.*) 1090; given to Knights of St. John by Emperor Charles V 1530; held out against Turkish siege 1565; held by Napoleon 1798–1800; captured by British 1800 and retained by them 1814; received dominion government 1921; its status reverted to that of crown colony 1933, after the church-state controversy of 1930–32. In 19th cent. developed as powerful naval base; in World War II became world's most bombed spot, undergoing more than 1200 air raids.

Malta Channel. Part of Mediterranean Sea ab. 58 m. wide constituting the passage bet. SE Sicily and Malta.

Malt'by (môlt'bĭ). Urban district, West Riding, Yorkshire, N England; pop. 12,485.

Maltese Islands. See MALTA.

Małujowice. See MOLLWITZ.

Mal'van (mäl'vån). Town, S Maharashtra, W Indian Union, on Arabian Sea 200 m. S of Bombay; pop. 29,817.

Malvasia, Napoli di. See MONEMVASIA.

Mal'vern (mäl'vern). **1** City, ⊗ of Hot Spring co., SW cen. Arkansas, 15 m. SE of Hot Springs; pop. 9566; incorporated 1872; railroad and trade center; processes titanium ore; manufactures wood and cotton products.

2 Borough, Chester co., SE Pennsylvania, 22 m. WNW of Philadelphia; pop. 2268.

3 (môl'vern) City, S Victoria, SE Australia; SE suburb of Melbourne; pop. 43,250.

4 (môl'vern; mô'-) Urban district, Worcestershire, W cen. England; pop. 21,681; mineral springs.

Mal'verne (mäl'vern). Village, Nassau co., SE New York on Long I., 17 m. E of New York; pop. 9968; residential suburb of New York.

Mal'vern Hill (mäl'vern). Plateau on the James 14 m. SE of Richmond, Virginia; battle July 1, 1862, the last of the Seven Days' Battles of the Peninsular Campaign; Confederate attack repulsed but Federal troops withdrew the next day.

Mal'vern Hills (môl'vern; mô'-). Hills in W England extending bet. Worcestershire and Herefordshire; highest point 1395 ft.

Malvinas, Islas. See FALKLAND ISLANDS.

Mal'wa (mäl'wä). **1** Tableland, cen. India, mostly N of the Vindhya Mts. but extends S to include part of Narbada valley. Seat of ancient kingdom with capital at Ujjain; invaded by Mohammedans 1235; an independent kingdom 1401–1531; annexed to Mogul Empire 1561; in 18th and 19th cents. battleground of rival Maratha powers.

2 Former agency, W Central India, including a few larger Indian states (Jaora, Ratlam, and the Dewas; also parts of Indore and Tonk) and many minor states and estates; 2704 sq. m.; pop. 439,138.

Maly. See LYAKHOV ISLANDS.

Mamai Kurgan. See HILL 102.

Ma·mar'o·neck (må·mär'ō·nĕk). Residential village, Westchester co., SE New York, on Long Island Sound 22 m. NE of New York; pop. 17,673; partly in town of Mamaroneck (pop. 29,107), partly in town of Rye; manufactures woolen cloth, raincoats, perfume oils, motor oils. See RYE.

Mam·ba'jao (mäm·bä'hou). Municipality on N coast of Camiguin I., Misamis Oriental prov., Phil. Is.; pop. 21,414.

Mam'be·ra'mo (mäm'bä·rä'mō) *or* **Ta'ri·kai'ke·a** (tä'rĕ·kī'kä·ä). Largest river of West New Guinea, ab. 500 m. long; flows NW into Pacific Ocean near Cape d'Urville; formed near 3°10'S by junction of two large streams, the Tarikoe from the W and the Taritatoe from the E. Navigable for 100 m. by large vessels; junction point of two tributaries is in extensive marshy region S of mountain range, but sources of streams are on N slopes of Snow Mts.

Mam·bu'sao (mäm·bōō'sou). Municipality, cen. Capiz prov., Panay, Phil. Is., on W tributary of Panay river, 17 m. SW of Capiz; pop. 15,723. Established ab. 1605.

Ma'metz' (må'mĕts'). Village, Somme dept. N France, 4 m. SSE of Albert; battle July 1, 1916 in which British were victors.

Ma·mi·son' Pass (må·myĭ·zōn'). Mountain pass over cen. Caucasus Mts. just S of Adai Khokh and on boundary bet. North Ossetia and South Ossetia; alt. 9230 ft. Ossetian Military Road (built 1889) passes through it.

Mam'mo·la (mäm'mō·lä). Commune, Reggio di Calabria prov., Calabria, S Italy 38 m. NE of Reggio di Calabria; pop. 10,426.

Mam'moth (mäm'ŭth). **1** Mountain 6885 ft. in Grant co., E cen. Oregon.

2 Locality, Westmoreland co., SW Pennsylvania, ab. 9 m. SE of Greensburg; pop. (est.) 100.

Mammoth Cave. Cave in Edmonson co., SW cen. Kentucky, ab. 28 m. ENE of Bowling Green; series of large irregular chambers in five levels with many miles of avenues; shafts have been cut forming so-called pits or domes, as Bottomless Pit and Mammoth Dome which is 540 ft. long, 200 ft. wide, and 120 ft. high. Discovered probably c. 1799; source of saltpeter in War of 1812; Frozen Niagara (onyx cascades, gypsum flowers, stalactites and stalagmites) discovered 1923; new caverns remarkable for gypsum crystals and a 7000 ft. avenue discovered 1938; set aside as **Mammoth Cave National Park:** see UNITED STATES, *National Parks.*

Mammoth Hot Springs. Hot springs, ab. 70 in number, in Yellowstone National Park, Wyoming; 60° to 175°F.; remarkable for terraces of calcareous deposits covering ab. 200 acres. Administrative headquarters of Yellowstone National Park.

Mammoth Spring. Town, Fulton co., N Arkansas; pop. 825; site of one of largest springs in the world, source of hydroelectric power.

Ma·mo·ré' (mä′mŏ·rā′). River ab. 1200 m. long in N cen. Bolivia; rises in W cen. Bolivia and is known as **Rí′o Gran′de** (rē′ō grän′dā) or **Gua·pay′** (gwä·pä′ĕ; -pī′) in its upper course; flows SE, then turns NW and N through cen. Bolivia; forms section of boundary bet. NE Bolivia and Brazil; unites with Beni river to form Madeira river.

Mam′ry (mäm′rĭ); *Ger.* **Mau′er** (mou′ĕr). Lake, NE Olsztyn dept., N Poland, NE of Olsztyn, formerly in East Prussia prov., Germany; ab. 40 sq. m.; Węgorzewo is at its N end.

Mam Soul (màm soul). Peak 3862 ft. in Ross and Cromarty co., N Scotland.

Man, Calf of (măn). Small island in the Irish Sea off SW coast of the Isle of Man.

Man, Isle of; *anc.* **Mo·na′pi·a** (mŏ·nā′pĭ·à) or **Mo′na** (mō′nà). Island in the Irish Sea off NW coast of England; 221 sq. m.; pop. 49,308; ✳ Douglas; held by Norse (9th–13th cents.), Scotch (13th–14th cents.), English (from 14th cent.); has own language (Manx, now virtually extinct), legislature, and laws; tourist center.

Ma′na′ (mà′nà′). **1** River 170 m. long in cen. and N French Guiana; flows N into Atlantic Ocean near the Surinam boundary.
2 Coastal town, N French Guiana, at mouth of Mana river; pop. 1873.

Ma′na, Web′be (wĕb′à mä′nä; *native* wûb·bä mä·nä). River ab. 140 m. long, S Ethiopia, a tributary of the Ganale Dorya; flows SE.

Ma′na·bí′ (mä′nä·vē′). Province of Ecuador. See *Table* at ECUADOR.

Ma′na·cor′ (mä′nä·kôr′). Commune, Baleares prov., Spain, E Majorca I., 30 m. E of Palma; pop. 19,060; agricultural produce; manufactures leather, brandy, tile, pottery; 13th-cent. palace; resort, noted esp. for the underground lakes and stalactite caves nearby.

Ma·na′do (mä·nä′dō) or **Me·na′do** (mā-). **1** Former residency, N Celebes I., Neth. Indies; 34,191 sq. m., pop. 1,138,655; ✳ Manado; comprised the E peninsula, N half of cen. part of island, the long N peninsula (Minahassa), and adjacent island groups, esp. Banggai, Schildpad, Sangihe, and Talaud. Enclosed on three sides the Gulf of Tomini. Mountainous, many peaks above 5000 ft.; highest Nokilalaki 10,863 ft. and Waukara 10,259 ft., in SW part (N cen. part of island); volcanic (Mt. Klabat) in extreme NE; no rivers of importance. Chief crop of region coffee; produces also rice, maize, tobacco, sugar; exports various forest products. Inhabitants mainly Minahassa and Toraja.
2 Commercial seaport, Indonesia, at the NE end of Celebes I. (on Minahassa Penin.), on W slopes of Mt. Klabat; pop. 27,544; has airport and good harbor; directly on sea routes from Hong Kong and Manila to Australia. Established by Dutch 1657. Taken by Japanese Jan. 11, 1942.

Ma·na′gua (mä·nä′gwä; *Span.* mä·nä′gwä). **1** Department, W Nicaragua; 1332 sq. m.; pop. (1943 est.) 144,812; ✳ Managua.
2 City, its ✳ and ✳ of Nicaragua; located on S shore of Lake Managua; pop. (1943 est.) 93,032; largest city in Nicaragua; suffered from earthquake and fire 1931; rebuilt on modern plan. Made capital 1855.

Managua, Lake. Lake 38 m. long in W Nicaragua; area 575 sq. m.; drains S through Tipitapa river into Lake Nicaragua.

Manahiki. = MANIHIKI.

Ma′na·ka′ra (mä′nä·kä′rä). Coastal town, SE Madagascar; railroad terminus.

Ma′na′kha (mä·nä′kŏ). Town, cen. Yemen, SW Arabia, SW of San'a.

Ma·na′ma (mä·nä′mà; -mä). Town, ✳ of Bahrein Is., Persian Gulf, on N coast of Bahrein I.; pop. ab. 28,000; headquarters of British political agent and staff (see PERSIAN GULF RESIDENCY). Connected by causeway with Muharraq on adjacent island.

Ma′nan·ja′ry (mä′nän·zhä′rē). Coastal town, E Madagascar, E of Fianarantsoa; pop. ab. 11,000.

Ma·na′oag (mä·nä′wäg). Municipality, E cen. Pangasinan prov., Luzon, Phil. Is., 17 m. E of Lingayen; pop. 29,030.

Manáos. See MANAUS.

Ma′na·pia′ri (mä′nä·pyä′rē). River ab. 100 m. long in S cen. Venezuela; flows S into Ventuari river.

Ma′na·pi′re (mä′nä·pē′rä). River 130 m. long in N Venezuela; flows S into Orinoco river.

Ma·na′pla (mä·nä′plä). Municipality, NW Negros Occidental prov., Negros, Phil. Is., on Guimaras Strait 24 m. NE of City of Bacolod; pop. 19,490.

Ma′na·pou′ri Lake (mä′nä·pōōr′ĭ). Lake 48 sq. m. in SW South I., New Zealand; a source of the Waiau river.

Manar. = MANNAR.

Ma·nas′ (mä·näs′). River, E Bhutan; flows S across Indian border and into the Brahmaputra near Goalpara.

Man′a·sa·ro′war (mŭn′à·sà·rō′ĕr). Lake in Himalayas, SW Tibet, Outer China, at 15,000 ft. elevation, near source of the Sutlej S of Kailas Peak; place of pilgrimage for Hindus.

Man′a·squan (măn′à·skwŏn). Borough, Monmouth co., E cen. New Jersey, on Atlantic Ocean 8 m. S of Asbury Park; pop. 4022; summer resort.

Ma·nas′sas (mà·năs′ăs). Town, ⊗ of Prince William co., NE Virginia, 25 m. W of Alexandria; pop. 3555; battles of Bull Run (called Manassas by Confederates) fought here July 21, 1861 and Aug. 29 and 30, 1862.

Manassas Park. Town, Prince William co., NE Virginia, SW of Alexandria; pop. 5342.

Ma′na·ta′ra (mä′nä·tä′rä). Peak 12,140 ft. in NW Venezuela, W of Lake Maracaibo.

Man′a·tee (măn′à·tē′; măn′à·tē). **1** County in Florida. See *Table* at FLORIDA.
2 Former town, Manatee co., W Florida penin., 12 m. N of Sarasota; pop. (1940) 3595; founded 1842; became part of city of Bradenton 1944.

Ma′na·tí′ (mä′nä·tē′). **1** Town, Atlántico dept., N Colombia; pop. 5426; just E of Cartagena.
2 River 25 m. long in cen. and N cen. Puerto Rico; flows N into Atlantic Ocean.
3 Municipality (pop. 29,354) and town (pop. 9682), N Puerto Rico; town is on Manatí river and on railroad 25 m. W of San Juan.

Ma′na·tí′, Point (mä′nä·tē′). Cape on SE coast of Las Villas prov., N cen. Cuba.

Ma·naus′ (mà·nous′) or **Ma·ná′os** (mä·nous′). City, ✳ of Amazonas state, W Brazil, on left bank of Rio Negro 12 m. above its junction with the Amazon; pop. (1940 est.) 67,866; trading port for products of vast area of the Amazon basin (cacao, rubber, Brazil nuts, lumber, fruits); 1000 m. from the mouth of the Amazon but accessible to ocean steamers; museum, notable botanic gardens. Founded 1660; made provincial capital 1850.

Ma′na·wa′tu (mä′nä·wä′tōō). River 100 m. long, SW North I., New Zealand; flows SW and W into Cook Strait.

Mancha, La. See LA MANCHA.

Manche (mänsh). Department of France. See *Table* at FRANCE.

Manche, La. See ENGLISH CHANNEL.

Man′ches′ter (măn′chĕs′tẽr; -chĭs·tẽr). **1** Manufacturing town, E Hartford co., N Connecticut; pop. 42,102; settled 1672, incorporated 1823; manufactures paper, silk, velvet, woolens, machine tools, cutting machines, insulation, electrical appliances, friction clutches.
2 Industrial city, Meriwether and Talbot cos., W Georgia, 32 m. NE of Columbus; pop. 4115.
3 City, ⊗ of Delaware co., E Iowa, 35 m. NNE of Cedar Rapids; pop. 4402; trade center in agricultural section; makes bricks, flour, woolen goods, dairy products. U.S. govt. fish hatchery nearby.
4 City, ⊗ of Clay co., SE Kentucky, 38 m. N of Middlesborough; pop. 1868.
5 Town, Essex co., NE Massachusetts, on Atlantic Ocean 21 m. NE of Boston; pop. 3932; summer resort.
6 Manufacturing and industrial city, a ⊗ of Hillsboro co., S New Hampshire, on Merrimack river 18 m. N of Massachusetts border; largest city in the state; pop. 88,282; supplied with water power by Amoskeag Falls; manufactures cotton and woolen goods, cigars, shoes. St. Anselm's Coll. (1889; men); State industrial school. Grenier Field, U.S. Air Force base. Settled 1722; incorporated as Derryfield 1751; changed name to Manchester 1810; chartered as city 1846; former rendezvous of Pennacook Indians.
7 Village, Ontario co., W New York, 24 m. ESE of Rochester; pop. 1344; in Finger Lakes resort region.
8 Village, Adams co., S Ohio, on Ohio river 32 m. W of Portsmouth; pop. 2172.
9 City, ⊗ of Coffee co., S cen. Tennessee, 33 m. SSE of Murfreesboro; pop. 3930.
10 Village in Manchester town (pop. 2470), a ⊗ of Bennington co., SW corner of Vermont, 21 m. N of Bennington; pop. 403; summer resort (Equinox Mt. nearby); manufactures fishing rods and tackle.
11 County borough and city, Lancashire, NW England, on the Irwell 30 m. ENE of Liverpool; pop. 766,378, (1951) 703,175; the leading textile-manufacturing city in England and foremost cotton city in the world; chemical and dye factories, extensive machinery and engineering works; manufactures also rubber, paper, and paper products; important seaport (importing oil, timber, fruit, grain), made accessible to ocean steamers by the Manchester Ship Canal (*q.v.*); cathedral (originally a parish church, bishopric estab. 1847); Victoria Univ. (founded 1880), a grammar school (1515).
History: Woolen and linen manufacture introduced 14th cent., first cotton mill opened 1781; strong center of Puritanism 17th cent., in 18th cent. became strongly Jacobite; at beginning of 19th cent. without representation in Parliament despite its growing size and importance as industrial city, became center of reform agitation initiated by the Peterloo Massacre Aug. 16, 1819, when a crowd gathered on St. Peter's Fields to voice their grievances was dispersed by cavalrymen, with several killed and many injured; became a city 1853; severely affected by cotton famine during American Civil War; frequently bombed by Germans in spring of 1941. Birthplace of David Lloyd George.

Manchester Ship Canal. Canal from Eastham, NW Cheshire, NW England, to Manchester, by which Manchester was made a port accessible to large ocean steamers; 35½ m. long; 28 ft. deep; 120 ft. wide at the bottom; commenced in 1887 and formally opened in 1894; rise of 60½ ft. divided among 5 sets of locks; water supply provided from the Mersey and Irwell rivers.

Manchouli. See LUPIN.

Manchow. See MANCHURIA.

Man′chu′kuo′ (măn′chōō′kwō′; măn·chōō′kwō; *Chin.* män′jō′kwô′); *also* **Man′chou′kuo′.** A former state (empire) of E Asia, 1932–45, set up under Japanese influence, comprising the 3 provinces of old Manchuria (*q.v.*) and Jehol; 482,440 sq. m.; pop. 29,327,927, (1940 est.) 43,233,954; ✳ Hsinking (Changchun); old provinces subdivided and reorganized 1934 into 18 provinces and the special municipality of Hsinking, but their boundaries were changed several times. (For physical features, etc., see MANCHURIA and JEHOL.) Set up as independent republic Feb. 1932 after Japanese occupation of Manchuria 1931; created an empire 1934 with puppet Manchu emperor K'ang Tê as nominal ruler; Jehol occupied by Japanese and added to it 1933; its boundary with Outer Mongolia subject to dispute with Russia from 1931; dissolved 1945 at end of World War II.

Manchuli. Var. of *Manchouli*: see LUPIN.

Man·chu′ri·a (măn·chōōr′ĭ·à); *Chin.* **Man′chow′** (män′jō′). Territory, NE China, comprising originally the 3 provinces of Liaoning, Kirin, and Heilungkiang; in 1945 redivided into 9 provinces; 408,162 sq. m.; pop. (1936) 27,273,622; old ✳ Mukden; bounded on NW, N, and E by the U.S.S.R. (separated from it by the Amur and its tributaries, the Argun and Ussuri), on the S by Korea and inlets of the Yellow Sea, and on the W by Jehol, Chahar, and Outer Mongolia; on the SE it has no coast line on the Sea of Japan. Its N two thirds is watered by the tributaries of the Amur, esp. the Sungari which covers with its tributaries all the central and N area; in the S is the Liao and on the Korea border the Yalu. Much of its area is mountainous, of especial importance being the Great Khingan Mts. in the NW and the Chang Pai Shan on the Korea border. In the S the wide Liaotung Penin. projects into the Gulf of Po Hai, separating the Gulf of Liaotung on the W from Korea Bay; at its extremity is Kwantung (*q.v.*), territory leased to Japan and not considered politically a part of Manchuria. Primarily an agricultural country with large extent of very fertile soil; principal crops soybeans, kaoliang, wheat, millet, maize; also produces much live stock, has great timber resources, and is rich in minerals, particularly coal, iron, magnesite, gold, petroleum. Chief cities Changchun, Mukden, Harbin, Yungki, Lungkiang, Yingkow, and Antung. About 95% of the population are Chinese and Mongols. See *Map* at CHINA.
History: Included at various times in Chinese Empire; under Khitans and other Mongol peoples to N and W of Manchuria; original home of Manchus, of Mongol stock, who built a strong state under Nurhachu (d. 1627); conquered China and began Chinese Manchu dynasty (1644–1912); from 17th cent., when Russia began eastward advance, its N boundary came to be established at the Amur (*q.v.*); under loose Chinese control, coveted by Russia and Japan, the rivalry bet. these two countries over Manchuria being a partial cause of Russo-Japanese War 1904–05; Chinese civil administration set up 1907; increasingly the destination of Chinese immigration; adhered to Chinese Nationalist government 1928; annexed Jehol as a province 1928; after Mukden (*q.v.*) incident 1931, occupied by Japanese troops; despite action of League of Nations in Manchurian affair, set up by Japan puppet state of Manchukuo (*q.v.*) 1932, dissolved 1945 at end of World War II; scene of fighting bet. Chinese Nationalist and Communist troops 1946–48; came under complete control of Communists with their occupation of Mukden Nov. 1, 1948.

Man·chu·ti·kuo (män·chōō·tê·kwô). = MANCHUKUO.

Man′cos (măng′kŭs). **1** River, Montezuma co., SW Colorado; flows S and SE into San Juan river in NW New Mexico; Mesa Verde National Park on W bank.
2 Town, Montezuma co., SW Colorado; pop. 832; near Mesa Verde National Park.

Mand (mänd) *or* **Mund** (mōond). River ab. 300 m. long in SW Iran; flows W and SW into E cen. Persian Gulf S of Bushire.

Man'da (măn'dȧ). Town, S Tanganyika, East Africa, on good harbor on NE shore of Lake Nyasa.

Man'da·la'gan, Mount (măn'dä·lä'gän). Mountain 6222 ft. in N cen. Negros Occidental, Negros, Phil. Is.

Man'da·lay' (măn'dȧ·lā'). **1** Division in cen. Upper Burma. See *Table* at BURMA.
2 District, Mandalay division; 2115 sq. m.; pop. 371 636; * Mandalay.
3 City, * of division and district and chief town of Upper Burma, in cen. part 650 m. up the Irrawaddy river; pop. 134,950, including cantonment 147,932; a trade center with railroad and steamer connections; many bazaars; religious center for Burmese Buddhists; at foot of Mandalay Hill are the 450 Pagodas. Its cantonment, a moated citadel known as Fort Dufferin, was old city built 1856–57 and containing palace, halls, and other buildings of King Thebaw; capital of kingdom of Burma 1860–85. Bombed and largely destroyed Apr. 1942 by Japanese, who entered the city May 1; retaken by British Mar. 1945.

Man'dan (măn'dăn). City, ⊗ of Morton co., SW cen. North Dakota, across Missouri river from Bismarck; pop. 10,525; incorporated as city 1883; railroad division point: distribution center for wheat-growing and livestock area; lignite coal mines, clay pits.

Man'dar, Gulf of (măn'där). Inlet of Makassar Strait on SW coast of Celebes I., Indonesia, N of Makassar; its NW point is **Tan'djung Ran·ga'sa** (tän'jŏong räng·gä'sȧ), *Du.* **Hoek van Mandar** (hōōk' vȧn).

Man'da·vi (mŭn'dȧ·vē). See GOA.

Man'deure' (män'dûr'). Commune, NE Doubs dept., E France; pop. (1931) 5180; Roman remains.

Man'de·ville (măn'dĕ·vĭl; *Sou.* also -v'l). Town, St. Tammany parish, SE Louisiana; pop. 1740.

Man'di (mŭn'dĭ). Former Indian state, Punjab States, NE East Punjab, N Indian Union; 1139 sq. m.; pop. (1941) 232,593; * Mandi Nagar (pop. 7538).

Man·din'ga (män·dēng'gä). Port, NE cen. Panama, on N shore of the **Bay of Mandinga,** the inner part (W end) of Gulf of San Blas.

Man·dio'li (män·dyō'lē). See BATJAN.

Mand'la (mŭnd'lä). Town, cen. Madhya Pradesh, India, ab. 40 m. SE of Jubbulpore.

Man'dor (mŭn'dōr). See JODHPUR.

Man·du'ri·a (măn·dŏōr'ĭ·ȧ; *Ital.* män·dōō'ryä). Commune, Ionio prov., Apulia, SE Italy, ESE of Taranto; pop. 19,594; cathedral; pre-Roman remains of walls.

Mand'vi (mänd'vĭ). Seaport town, S coast of Cutch, Gujerat state, W India, on Gulf of Cutch 210 m. W of Ahmadabad; pop. 25,342.

Man·fre·do'ni·a (män·frĕ·dō'nĭ·ȧ; *Ital.* män'frā·dô'nyä). Seaport, Foggia prov., Apulia, SE Italy, on Gulf of Manfredonia 22 m. NE of Foggia; pop. 20,960; cathedral; 13th-cent. church; castle; built 1256 by King Manfred.

Manfredonia, Gulf of. Inlet of Adriatic Sea on SE coast of Italy, in NE Apulia compartimento.

Mang·a'ia (mäng·ä'yä). Island in SE part of the Cook Is., in S Pacific Ocean 110 m. ESE of Rarotonga; pop. (1936) 1459; chief village Oneroa, on W side of island. Remarkable geologically as a fine example of "makatea" formation—a circular island with broad coastal strip of coral limestone and completely encircled by a reef.

Man'gal·dan' (mäng'gäl·dän'). Municipality, N cen. Pangasinan prov., Luzon, Phil. Is., near coast on Bued river and on Dagupan-San Fernando R.R.; pop. 18,997.

Man'ga·lore (mäng'gȧ·lōr). City, NW Kerala state, S India, on Malabar Coast 190 m. W of Bangalore; pop. (1941) 81,069; fair harbor; exports pepper, coffee, sandalwood, and fish. Seat of a Catholic bishop and a Lutheran mission. Has two colleges and a training school. Site of Portuguese factory erected 1596; conquered by Haidar Ali of Mysore 1763; captured by British 1783 but the British garrison forced by Tipu Sahib to capitulate 1784; restored to British authority 1799.

Mangan. See PANGKIANG.

Mang'a·re'va (mäng'ä·rā'vä). Chief island of the Gambier Is., French Polynesia, S Pacific Ocean; 5 m. long, area ab. 7 sq. m.; pop. ab. 1000; has high central ridge covered with much vegetation.

Man'ga·rin' Bay (mäng'gä·rēn'). Inlet on SW coast of Mindoro I., Phil. Is.; San Jose is on its N shore. Occupied by Americans Dec. 15, 1944.

Man'ga·ta'rem (mäng'gä·tä'rĕm). Municipality, S Pangasinan prov., Luzon, Phil. Is., near left bank of the Agno 16 m. S of Lingayen; pop. 18,658.

Man'ger·ton (mäng'gĕr·t'n; -tŭn). Mountain 2756 ft. in cen. co. Kerry, SW Eire.

Mangishlak. Var. of MANGYSHLAK.

Mang'ka·li·hat', Cape (mäng'kä·lē·hät'). Cape on E coast of the island of Borneo, Malay Archipelago; projects into Celebes Sea at N entrance to Makassar Strait.

Man·gla'res or **Man'gles, Cape** (mäng·glä'räs, mäng'gläs). Cape extending into Pacific Ocean at SW extremity of Colombia.

Manglun. See MONGLON.

Mang'o (mäng'ō). One of the Fiji Is., SW Pacific Ocean, SW of Vanua Mbalavu I. in the Exploring Is., ab. 3 m. in diameter.

Man·go'ky (män·gō'kĭ). River, S Madagascar, flowing W into Mozambique Channel.

Mang·o'le (mäng·ô'lä). One of the Sula Is., Indonesia, Malay Archipelago, E of Taliabu I. and N of Sanana; 63 m. long by ab. 13 m. wide; pop. 3598; borders on Molucca Sea to the N.

Mang'o·nu'i (mäng'ô·nōō'ē). Village, Auckland provincial dist., on E coast of N extension of North I., New Zealand.

Man'gots·field (măng'gŭts·fēld). Urban district, Gloucestershire, SW cen. England; pop. 17,871.

Man'grove Lagoon (măn[g]'grōv). Inlet of Jersey Bay in SE St. Thomas I., Virgin Is. of the U.S., West Indies.

Mang'shih' (mäng'shĭr'). Town, SW Yunnan prov., S China, on Burma Road 72 m. NE of Wanting; alt. 3500 ft.; chief town of the Shan States of China.

Man·guei'ra, La·go'a da (lá·gō'ȧ thä männg·gä'ĕ·rȧ; -gä'ĕ·rȧ). Lake 62 m. long, S Rio Grande do Sul, S Brazil; along coast in strip of land bet. Lake Mirim and the Atlantic Ocean.

Man'gue·ni', Plateau of (män'gĕ·nē'). Elevated region, in NE Republic of Niger, West Africa, on Libyan border; 500 m. E to W by 400 m. N to S.

Man·gui'to (mäng·gē'tȯ). Municipality and town, Matanzas prov., W cen. Cuba, 35 m. SE of Cárdenas; pop. (town) 6340.

Man'gum (mäng'gŭm). City, ⊗ of Greer co., SW Oklahoma, 20 m. NNW of Altus; pop. 3950; cottonseed oil and flour mills; cotton gins; granite quarries nearby.

Man·gun'ça (männg·gōōn'sȧ). Island in Atlantic ocean off N coast of Maranhão state, Brazil, at the entrance to Cabelo da Velha Bay.

Man'gysh·lak' (mäng'gĭsh·läk'). Peninsula on the E coast of N Caspian Sea, SW Kazakh S.S.R., Soviet Central Asia, lat. 44°30'N; S of Buzachi Penin.

Man·has'set Bay (măn·hăs'ĕt; -ĭt). Inlet of Long Island Sound on N coast of Nassau co., Long I., New York.

Man·hat'tan (măn·hăt''n; cen.; măn·). **1** Island at N end of New York Bay, 13½ m. long and 2¼ m. wide, 22 sq. m. in area, bounded on N and NE by Spuyten Duyvil Creek and Harlem river, on E by East river, on S by New York Bay, and on W by Hudson river. Forms New York co. of New York state, and Manhattan borough (see below) of New York City. See history of NEW YORK state and city.
2 Borough, SE New York, coextensive with New York co. (area 22 sq. m.) and Manhattan I., part of New York City bet. Hudson and East rivers; pop. 1,698,281; separated from Long I. by East river and from mainland by Harlem river and Spuyten Duyvil Creek; includes islands: Welfare (Blackwells), Randall's, and Ward's, all

in East river; chartered as one of 5 boroughs comprising city of New York Jan. 1, 1898; contains main financial and commercial and important residential sections of the city. Columbia University (chartered 1754 as King's College; coed.); New York University (1831; coed.); City College of the City of New York (estab. as the Free Academy in 1848; incorporated under its present name in 1853; coed.); Hunter College (1870; women); General Theological Seminary (1817; Protestant Episcopal); Union Theological Seminary (1836; interdenominational); Barnard Coll. (1889; women; affiliated with Columbia Univ.); Cooper Union (1859; coed.); Juilliard School of Music (1926); Cornell Medical Coll. (1898); New York Public Library; Metropolitan Museum of Art; American Museum of Natural History; Museum of Modern Art; Metropolitan Opera House; Rockefeller Center (including Radio City). Governed as part of New York City by a mayor and city council; has a borough president, with local and county functions conducted independently of central municipal government. See also NEW YORK city.
3 City, ⊗ of Riley co., NE cen. Kansas, on Kansas river 50 m. W of Topeka; pop. 22,993; settled 1854; creameries, packing plants, planing mills. Kansas State Univ. of Agriculture and Applied Science (1863; coed.).

Manhattan Beach. 1 City, Los Angeles co., SW California, on Pacific Ocean 13 m. SW of Los Angeles; pop. 33,934; seaside resort.
2 Bathing beach and amusement resort, E end of Coney I., Brooklyn borough, New York City.

Manhattan District; *also* **Manhattan Engineer District.** A United States Government secret military organization, established Aug. 13, 1942 as a new district in the Corps of Engineers, U.S. Army, to develop atomic energy, esp. the atomic bomb; labeled for security reasons the "DSM Project" (Development of Substitute Materials). Geographically the district included: offices in Washington, D.C. (under Gen. Leslie R. Groves) and Oak Ridge, Tennessee; scientific groups in the Universities of California, Chicago, Columbia, and Princeton, and in the laboratory at Los Alamos (*q.v.*), New Mexico; industrial groups at Clinton Engineer Works, Oak Ridge, and at Richland and Hanford, Washington; and many smaller groups and units in U.S. Taken over by the U.S. Atomic Energy Commission, Jan. 1, 1947 (received Senate confirmation Apr. 9, 1947) and formally dissolved Aug. 1947. See ALAMOGORDO AIR BASE.

Man′heim (măn′hĭm). Borough, Lancaster co., SE Pennsylvania, 10 m. NNW of Lancaster; pop. 4790; former glassmaking center.

Ma·ni′ca (mȧ·nē′kȧ). Former district, W cen. Mozambique, SE Africa; chief town Macequece; Portuguese part of **Ma·ni′ca·land′** (-lănd′), territory in E Southern Rhodesia and W Mozambique; region has valuable gold fields. With Sofala, district formerly administered by Mozambique Company (see MOZAMBIQUE); now part of Manica and Sofala prov.

Manica and So·fa′la (sȯ·fä′lȧ). Province, W and S cen. Mozambique, SE Africa; comprises former districts of Manica, Sofala, and Tete; as now constituted is divided into districts Beira and Tete; * Beira.

Manich. = MANYCH.

Ma′ni·hi′ki (mä′nĭ·hē′kĭ); *formerly* **Hum′phrey** (hŭm′frĭ). Chief island (atoll) of the Manihiki Is., 650 m. N of Rarotonga; 2 sq. m.; pop. (1936) 487; chief villages Tuko on N end, and Tauhunu on W coast; produces copra and pearl shell.

Manihiki Islands; *sometimes called* **Northern Cook Islands** (kʊok). Group of 7 islands in cen. Pacific Ocean N of Cook Is.; 14 sq. m.; pop. ab. 2000; administered with Cook Is. by New Zealand; more important (inhabited) islands of the group include Manihiki, Danger Is., Tongareva, and Rakahanga.

Man′i·kua′gan (măn′ĭ·kwŏg′ăn). River 310 m. long, W Saguenay co., SE Quebec prov., Canada; rises in

height of land at ab. 53°N and flows S into St. Lawrence river near its mouth. One branch flows through **Lake Manikuagan** (ab. 51°N), 88 sq. m.

Ma·nil′a (mȧ·nĭl′ȧ). Town, ⊗ of Daggett co., NE Utah; pop. 329.

Ma·nil′a (mȧ·nĭl′ȧ; *Span.* mä·nē′lä). **1** Former province, Phil. Is., E of Manila Bay and N of Laguna de Bay; E two thirds taken 1853 to form part of Morong prov.; W portion and Morong united 1901 to form Rizal prov.
2 Commercial and manufacturing city, SW Luzon, Phil. Is., on E shore of Manila Bay, seat of government and chief port of Phil. Is.; 14 sq. m.; pop. 623,492; on N, E, and S surrounded by Rizal prov.; practically divided into two parts by the Pasig river; Intramuros or Walled City, the original Spanish fortified settlement, surrounded until recent years by a thick stone wall 25 ft. high and ab. 2½ m. in circumference; known as the "Pearl of the Orient" because of its beauty and importance. Univ. of Santo Tomas (1619; coed.), Univ. of Philippines (1908; coed.), and other educational institutions. Cosmopolitan population, largest element the Tagalogs.
History: Founded by Legaspi 1571; under early Spanish rule, became important commercial center; occupied by British 1762–63; captured by American forces Aug. 13, 1898 during Spanish-American War, after Admiral Dewey's defeat of the Spanish fleet (see MANILA BAY). In World War II captured by Japanese Jan. 2, 1942; retaken by American forces Feb. 1945; much of Intramuros and many buildings in other sections destroyed during the conflict. See City of QUEZON.

Manila Bay. Large inlet of South China Sea in W Luzon, Phil. Is., forming a landlocked sea of 770 sq. m., 120 m. in circumference, 28 m. across from Manila to Corregidor I. and 32 m. from the NW corner to Cavite shore. Finest landlocked harbor in the Orient and one of the finest in the world. Its entrance is through North and South Channels on either side of Corregidor I.

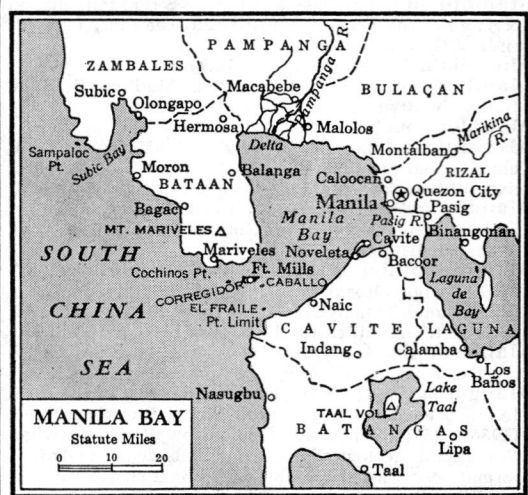

Surrounded by provinces of Bataan, Pampanga, Bulacan, Rizal, and Cavite. Scene of decisive naval battle of the Spanish-American War on May 1, 1898, when American Admiral George Dewey's fleet destroyed the Spanish fleet off Cavite, with no losses to the Americans. In World War II American shipping bombed and destroyed Dec. 1941–Jan. 1942; Japanese vessels similarly attacked and destroyed by American airplanes 1944–45. Came again under complete American control Feb.–Mar. 1945.

Ma·nin′djau (mȧ·nĭn′jou). Crater lake in Padang Highlands, W Sumatra, Indonesia, W of Bukittinggi, ab. 11 m. long by 6 m. wide.

Ma·ni'pa Strait (mà·nē'pà). Channel bet. Buru and Ceram Is. in the Moluccas, E Malay Archipelago; connects Ceram Sea with Banda Sea.

Ma'ni·pur (mä'nĭ·poŏr). **1** River ab. 210 m. long, W Upper Burma; flows S out of Loktak Lake, S Manipur state, NE Indian Union; crosses border into W Upper Burma; bends E and N to empty into Chindwin river. **2** Territory, NE Indian Union, in Assam States, SE of Assam on Burma border; 8620 sq. m.; pop. (1941) 512,069; * Imphal. Consists of wide valley with surrounding hills and mountains. Inhabited chiefly by Manipuris and Meithei. Had first relations with British 1762; scene of serious uprising 1890; government reorganized 1907; invaded Mar.–June 1944 by Japanese, who were driven out by Aug. 1944.

Ma'ni·sa' or **Ma'nis·sa'** (mä'nĕ·sä'). **1** Vilayet, W Turkey in Asia; 5346 sq. m.; pop. 425,275. **2** anc. **Mag·ne'sia** (măg·nē'zhà; -zhĭ·à). Manufacturing city, its *, 20 m. NE of İzmir; pop. (1940) 37,701; in Gediz valley and on main railroad line E to Afyon Karahisar; has buildings from Seljuk and early Osmanli period. Made seat of Byzantine government 1204 under Nicaean emperors and later (1313) the capital of a Turkoman emirate; conquered by Bajazet I 1398. Nearby are ruins of **Magnesia (ad Sip'y·lum)** [ăd sĭp'ĭ·lŭm] where in 190 B.C. the Romans defeated Antiochus the Great.

Man'is·tee' (măn'ĭs·tē'; măn'ĭs·tē). **1** River 150 m. long, NW Michigan; rises in W Crawford co., flows SW into Lake Michigan at Manistee, in Manistee co.; navigable for a short distance. **2** County in Michigan. See *Table* at MICHIGAN. **3** City, ⊗ of Manistee co., NW Michigan, on Lake Michigan at mouth of Manistee river 20 m. N of Ludington; pop. 8324; salt deposits; manufactures wood products; summer resort.

Man'is·tique' (măn'ĭs·tēk'; măn'ĭs·tēk). **1** River, S Michigan penin.; flows from Manistique Lake in SW Luce co. SW into N Lake Michigan at Manistique. **2** City, ⊗ of Schoolcraft co., S Michigan penin., on Lake Michigan at mouth of Manistique river, 43 m. ENE of Escanaba; pop. 4875; summer resort; fishing center; manufactures hardwood products and paper.

Manistique Lake. Lake in E Michigan penin., in Luce and Mackinac cos.; outlet, Manistique river.

Man'i·to'ba (măn'ĭ·tō'bà). Province, cen. Canada, easternmost of the Prairie Provinces; land area 219,723 sq. m.; pop. 776,541; * Winnipeg; has no counties but is subdivided into 16 census divisions. Bounded on N by Keewatin dist., on NE by Hudson Bay, on E by Ontario, on S by U.S.A. (Minnesota and North Dakota), and on W by Saskatchewan. Mostly low level country with many lakes and rivers, all draining to Hudson Bay. Has three large lakes—Winnipeg (larger than Lake Ontario), Winnipegosis, and Manitoba—in cen. part; these are fed by Red, Winnipeg, and Saskatchewan rivers and have the Nelson as their outlet; the Churchill and Seal are farther N. The port of Churchill at mouth of Churchill river has direct connection in summer months with Liverpool (2936 m.). Has one large national park (Riding Mountain), one national historic park (Fort Prince of Wales), and one provincial park (Whiteshell Forest Reserve). Chiefly an agricultural province with wheat the main crop; its large mineral resources only slightly developed. Chief cities Winnipeg, St. Boniface, Brandon, Portage la Prairie, Transcona.

History: Region first visited along the shore of Hudson Bay in early 17th cent.; Hudson's Bay Co. post established at Port Nelson 1670; S part explored by La Vérendrye and site of Winnipeg reached 1738; title to region surrendered by French 1763; Red River Settlement (q.v.) founded by Lord Selkirk 1811; became part of Assiniboia region; scene of Riel's Rebellion 1869–70; nucleus of province established 1870; enlarged 1881 and 1912; its growth accelerated by completion of railroads 1878–86.

Manitoba, Lake. Lake 1817 sq. m., ab. 120 m. long, S Manitoba prov., Canada, SW of Lake Winnipeg; outlet through Dauphin river to Lake Winnipeg.

Man'i·tou, Lake (măn'ĭ·tōō). See ROCHESTER, Indiana.

Manitou Island. Island in Lake Superior, the NE extremity of Keweenaw co., N tip of Michigan penin.

Manitou Island, North. Island in N Lake Michigan, in Leelanau co., NW Michigan.

Manitou Island, South. Island in N Lake Michigan, in Leelanau co., NW Michigan.

Man'i·tou'lin (măn'ĭ·tōō'lĭn). District, Ontario, Canada. See *Table* at ONTARIO.

Manitoulin Island. Island 80 m. long in N Lake Huron, separated from the mainland by North Channel, in S Ontario prov., Canada; with Cockburn and other small adjacent islands forms Manitoulin dist.

Man'i·tou Springs (măn'ĭ·tōō). Town, El Paso co., E cen. Colorado, at foot of Pikes Peak 3 m. NW of Colorado Springs; pop. 3626; resort; mineral springs; Garden of the Gods and Cave of the Winds in vicinity.

Man'i·to·woc' (măn'ĭ·tō·wŏk'). **1** County in Wisconsin. See *Table* at WISCONSIN. **2** Commercial and industrial city and port of entry, ⊗ of Manitowoc co., E Wisconsin, on Lake Michigan 25 m. N of Sheboygan; pop. 32,275; fur-trading post 1795; settled 1835; extensive coal trade; shipbuilding and repair yards; grain elevators; fisheries; manufactures aluminum ware, flour, malt products, canned vegetables.

Man'i·wa'ki (măn'ĭ·wô'kĭ). Village, ⊗ of Gatineau co. (part of Hull co.), SW Quebec, Canada, on Gatineau river 67 m. N of Hull; pop. 3835; in lumber region.

Man'i·za'les (măn'ĭ·zä'lĕs; -zäl'ĕs; *Span.* mä'nē·sä'läs). City, * of Caldas dept., W cen. Colombia, 110 m. W of Bogotá; pop. 51,025; important coffee center in the Cordillera Central of the Andes, alt. 7064 ft.; has direct rail connection with Buenaventura.

Manj'ra (mŭnj'rä). River ab. 320 m. long in cen. SE Maharashtra, S cen. India; rises on W border, flows SE, then turns N at border of Andhra Pradesh to join the Godavari NW of Nizamabad.

Man·ju'yod (mäng·hōō'yôd). Municipality, E Negros Oriental, Negros, Phil. Is., on Tañon Strait near its S end, 28 m. NNW of Dumaguete; pop. 25,581.

Man·ka'to (măn·kä'tō). **1** City, ⊗ of Jewell co., N Kansas; pop. 1231. **2** City, ⊗ of Blue Earth co., S Minnesota, on Minnesota river 65 m. SSW of Minneapolis; pop. 23,797; brick, cement, flour, leather goods; market for hogs, poultry, dairy products. Mankato State Coll. (1866; coed.).

Man'li·us (măn'lĭ·ŭs). Village, Onondaga co., cen. New York, 10 m. E of Syracuse; pop. 1997; military academy (1869).

Man'ly (măn'lĭ). City, E New South Wales, SE Australia, NE suburb of Sydney on Port Jackson; pop. 23,258; beach noted for surf bathing.

Man·ma'noc, Mount (măn·mä'nŏk). Peak 6634 ft. in Cordillera Central, N Luzon, Phil. Is., on E border of Abra prov.

Man·nar' (mà·när'). **1** Island in W Northern Province, Ceylon, at the E end of Adam's Bridge. **2** Town on island; pop. ab. 4000.

Mannar, Gulf of. Part of Indian Ocean W of Ceylon and SE of the S point of India; extends NE to Adam's Bridge; important pearl fisheries.

Man·nar'gu·di (mà·när'gōō·dē). Town, E Madras state, S Indian Union, ESE of Tanjore; pop. 22,764.

Man'ner·heim Line (măn'ĕr·hām; *Finnish* mán'nĕr·hām). Finnish fortified line across Karelian isthmus, extending from the Gulf of Finland to Lake Ladoga, ab. 80 m. long and with deep defenses reaching back nearly to the Finnish city of Viipuri (Vyborg); forts on Koivisto I. marked its W end. Begun 1939, never completely finished; broken by Russians Feb. 1940; retaken later by Finns and Germans but taken a second time by Russians June 18, 1944. Area now entirely in U.S.S.R.

Mann'heim (măn'hīm; *Ger.* män'hīm). **1** Former district of Baden, Germany. See *Table* at BADEN.
2 Commercial and manufacturing city, Baden-Württemberg state, on Rhine at confluence of Neckar river, 44 m. S by W of Frankfurt am Main; pop. 300,490; river port; 18th-cent. electoral palace; manufactures include iron castings, machinery, chemicals, cigars, woolens, carpets, paper, tile, rubber goods. Founded 1606; taken by Tilly 1622 (Thirty Years' War); completely destroyed by French 1689; rebuilt 1697; seat of Rhine Palatinate 1719–77; captured by French 1795, by Austrians 1799; to Baden 1803; bombed by Allies, World Wars I and II. In World War II captured by American forces ab. Mar. 30, 1945.

Man'ning (măn'ĭng). **1** Town, Carroll co., W cen. Iowa, 62 m. NE of Council Bluffs; pop. 1676.
2 Village, ⊗ of Dunn co., W North Dakota.
3 Town, ⊗ of Clarendon co., E cen. South Carolina, 17 m. SSE of Sumter; pop. 3917; lumbering, dairying.

Manning Provincial Park. Canadian provincial park in S British Columbia, in Cascade Mts. E of Vancouver; 280 sq. m.

Manning Strait. Channel ab. 35 m. wide bet. SE Choiseul and NW Santa Isabel Is., cen. Solomon Is., W Pacific Ocean; contains many small islands.

Man'ning·ton (măn'ĭng·tŭn). City, Marion co., N West Virginia, 12 m. W of Fairmont; pop. 2996; oil and gas wells; pottery, glassware, tools, cement blocks.

Ma'no (mä'nō). River ab. 110 m. long in W Africa; flows SW through N and NW Liberia, forming in its lower course a section of the boundary bet. Liberia and Sierra Leone.

Man'ö' (mä'nû'). Island, North Frisian Is., Denmark, S of Esbjerg.

Ma·no'kin River (mȧ·nō'kĭn). Inlet of Tangier Sound on W shore of Somerset co., SE Maryland.

Ma'nok·wa'ri (mä'nŏk·wä'rē). **1** Subdivision of Neth. New Guinea comprising the coastal strip of N and E Vogelkop Penin. and the area S and SE of Geelvink Bay; 14,716 sq. m.; pop. 31,352.
2 Its chief town, on NE coast of Vogelkop Penin., Neth. New Guinea, forming NW point of entrance to Geelvink Bay; has good harbor but is unhealthful; bypassed by Allies in World War II.

Ma·nom'bo (mȧ·nŏm'bō). Coastal town, SW Madagascar, N of Tuléar.

Man'or·bier' (măn'ĕr·bēr'). Village, Pembrokeshire, SW Wales, on coast of Bristol Channel; ruins of castle, birthplace of Giraldus de Barri, Welsh ecclesiastical geographer and historian.

Man·re'sa (män·rā'sä). Manufacturing commune, Barcelona prov., NE Spain, 30 m. NNW of Barcelona; pop. 36,381; manufactures textiles, brandy; ancient fortifications; cathedral.

Mans, Le. See LE MANS.

Man'sel Island (măn's'l). Island 70 m. long in NE Hudson Bay, Keewatin District, Northwest Territories, Canada; crossed by 62°N, 80°W.

Mans'field (măns'fēld; mănz'-). **1** Agricultural and manufacturing town, E Tolland co., N Connecticut, on Willimantic river; pop. 14,638; incorporated 1703; silk mills; fiberboard. Univ. of Connecticut at Storrs (1881; coed.); Mansfield State Training School and Hospital.
2 City, ⊗ of De Soto parish, NW Louisiana, 33 m. S of Shreveport; pop. 5839; nearby, at Sabine Crossroads, Union forces under Gen. Banks were defeated Apr. 8, 1864 by Confederate forces under Gen. Kirby-Smith and Gen. Taylor.
3 Industrial town, Bristol co., SE Massachusetts, WSW of Brockton; pop. 7773; textiles, tools, chocolate.
4 Industrial city, ⊗ of Richland co., N cen. Ohio, 54 m. WSW of Akron; pop. 47,325; manufactures brass, sheet steel and tin plate, electrical appliances and motors, gas ranges, rubber tires and tubes, farm implements; coal deposits and gas wells nearby.
5 Borough, Tioga co., N Pennsylvania, on Tioga river 39 m. N of Williamsport; pop. 2678; coal mines; gas wells. Mansfield State Coll. (1858; coed.).
6 Municipal borough, Nottinghamshire, N cen. England, on the Maun 15 m. N of Nottingham; pop. 51,343; trade center in coal-mining section; manufactures iron, shoes, and hosiery; grammar school founded 1561.

Mansfield, Mount. Peak 4393 ft. in Lamoille co., N Vermont; highest point in Vermont and Green Mts.

Mansfield Dam. See UNITED STATES, *Dams*.

Mansfield Wood'house (wŏŏd'hous). Urban district, Nottinghamshire, N cen. England; N suburb of Mansfield; pop. 17,819.

Man·sour', Jeb'el (jĕb'ĕl män·sōōr'; *Arab.* jä'băl mŏn·sōōr'). Mountain 2224 ft., N cen. Tunisia, WSW of Zaghouan; fighting Apr. 1943.

Mansûra, El. See EL MANSÛRA.

Man'ta (män'tä). Seaport on S shore of Manta Bay, Manabí prov., W Ecuador, 100 m. NW of Guayaquil; pop. (1944 est.) 14,248; port for Montecristi, Portoviejo, and Jipijapa.

Manta Bay. Inlet of Pacific Ocean on W coast of Ecuador, NW of Guayaquil.

Man·ta·ling·a'jan, Mount (män'tä·ling·ä'hän). Highest point on Palawan I., Phil. Is., at S end, 6839 ft.

Man·ta'ro (män·tä'rō). River ab. 280 m. long, S cen. Peru; flows E to Apurímac river.

Man·te'ca (män·tē'kȧ). City, San Joaquin co., cen. California, 10 m. S of Stockton; pop. 8242.

Man·te'no (män·tē'nō). Village, Kankakee co., NE Illinois, 10 m. N of Kankakee; pop. 2225.

Man·te·o (măn'tē·ō). Town and resort, ⊗ of Dare co., E North Carolina, on Roanoke I. bet. Albemarle and Pamlico Sounds; pop. 587.

Mantes'–Gas'si'court' (mäNt'gä'sē'kōōr'), *formerly* **Mantes'–sur–Seine'** (mäNt'sür·sân') *or* **Mantes'-la–Jo'lie'** (-lä·zhȯ'lē') ; *Lat.* **Me·dun'ta** (mē·dŭn'tȧ). Commune, Seine-et-Oise dept., N France, on Seine river 32 m. WNW of Paris; pop. 13,978; trades in agricultural products. Captured by Americans Aug. 18, 1944.

Man'ti (män'tī). City, ⊗ of Sanpete co., cen. Utah, 48 m. WSW of Price; pop. 1739; center for raising livestock and poultry; Mormon Temple.

Man·til'las, Lake (män·tē'yäs). Lake in cen. Tabasco state, SE Mexico.

Man'ti·ne'a (măn't'n·ē'ȧ) *or* **Man'ti·nei'a** (-ī'ȧ). Ancient village in E Arcadia, near Argolis border, E Peloponnesus, S Greece; scene of three battles: 418 B.C. in the Peloponnesian War in which Agis, King of Sparta, defeated the Argives and Mantineans; 362 B.C. in which Epaminondas was killed; and 207 B.C. in which Spartans were defeated by Philopoemen, Greek general of the Achaean League.

Mantiqueira, Serra da. See SERRA DA MANTIQUEIRA.

Man'tor·ville (măn'tĕr·vĭl). Village, ⊗ of Dodge co., SE Minnesota, 13 m. WNW of Rochester; pop. 498.

Man'to·va (män'tō·vä). **1** Province of Italy. See *Table* at ITALY.
2 See MANTUA, Italy.

Man'tua (män'twä). Municipality, Pinar del Río prov., W Cuba, 37 m. W of Pinar del Río; pop. 12,855.

Man'tu·a (män'tụ·ȧ); *Ital.* **Man'to·va** (män'tō·vä). Fortified manufacturing commune, ✳ of Mantova prov., Lombardy, N Italy, on Mincio river 80 m. WSW of Venice; pop. 40,467; machine works, oil and flour mills, breweries, tanneries; buildings include cathedral (designed by Giulio Romano), ducal palace and castle of Gonzaga family, home of Giulio Romano, Vergilian Academy of Sciences and Fine Arts.

History: Ancient town probably of Etruscan origin; Roman municipium, near which Vergil was born; taken by Lombards (see LOMBARDY) 568 A.D.; in 11th cent. belonged to margrave of Canossa, but became independent 1115; member of Lombard League; ruled by Gonzaga family 1328–1708; became duchy in 16th cent.; in War

of Mantuan Succession 1627–31, France and German emperor backed rival claimants to duchy; ceded to Austria 1714; taken in 1797 by Napoleon after a siege; duchy belonged to Cisalpine Republic 1797 and to Italian kingdom 1805; restored to Austria 1814; one of the forts of the famous Quadrilateral by which Austria controlled northern Italy; ceded to Italian kingdom 1866.

Ma'nu·a'e (mä'nŏō-ä'ă). See HERVEY ISLANDS.

Ma·nu'a Islands (má·nŏō'á). Group of 3 islands, Tau (area 17 sq. m.; pop. ab. 1000), Ofu, and Olosega, in Samoa, in SW Pacific Ocean, 65 m. E of the island of Tutuila; total area 22 sq. m.; pop. 2597; constitute an administrative district of American Samoa (*q.v.*).

Ma'nu·ka'u Harbor (mä'nŏō·kä'ŏō; mä'nŏō·kou). Inlet of Tasman Sea on NW coast of North I., New Zealand, forming an excellent harbor; suburbs of Auckland on its N shore.

Ma'nus (mä'nŏōs). **1** Administrative district of the Territory of New Guinea, comprising the Admiralty Is. and adjacent islands (the Northwestern Is.); 800 sq. m.; pop. (1930) 13,217; ✱ Lorengau. See LOS NEGROS.
2 Largest of the Admiralty Is. and chief part of Manus administrative district; ab. 55 m. long and 12 m. wide; area 600 sq. m.; terrain mountainous, and interior largely unexplored; has harbor at Lorengau at its E tip; has many coconut plantations. Seized by Japanese Apr. 1942; occupied by Allies and Lorengau captured Mar. 18, 1944; made into a major fleet repair station. Taken over by Australia as a base Dec. 1947.

Man'ville (măn'vil). **1** Borough, Somerset co., N cen. New Jersey, 9 m. WNW of New Brunswick; pop. 10,995; manufacturing; farming; stone quarries.
2 Village in Lincoln town, Providence co., N Rhode Island, ab. 3 m. SE of Woonsocket; pop. (est.) 3600; manufactures cotton, rayon, silk.

Man'y (măn'ĭ). Town, ⊗ of Sabine parish, W Louisiana; pop. 3164.

Man·ya'ra, Lake (män-yär'á). Small lake, NE Tanganyika, E Africa; SSW of Mt. Kilimanjaro.

Man·yas' Lake (män·yäs') *Turk.* **Manyas Gö·lü'** (män·yäs'gü·lü'). Lake, NW Turkey in Asia, near S shore of Sea of Marmara, S of Bandırma.

Ma·nych' (mŭ·nĭch'). **1** Valley or depression 330 m. long extending SE and NW from the lower Don to the lower Kuma river, SE Soviet Russia, Europe; crosses S Rostov Region and forms S boundary of Astrakhan Region; usually a series of salt lakes but when flooded in spring season, two rivers are formed flowing in opposite directions from a high point ab. long. 44°E. The Kalaus river (ab. 160 m. long) flows from the S to join the Eastern Manych river.
2 A lake in Manych valley, in SW Astrakhan Region, long. 43°E.
3 *or* **Western Manych.** River in Manych valley, a tributary of the lower Don, entering it near its mouth; receives the waters of Manych lake during spring seasons. Another stream, the **Eastern Manych,** flows E at high water to the Kuma.

Man·za'la (män·zä'lá). Town on SW shore of Lake Manzala, Lower Egypt.

Manzala, Lake. Large lagoon, Lower Egypt, SE of Damietta; N part of Suez Canal passes along its E edge. See TANIS.

Man·za'nar (măn·zä'nēr). Station, Inyo co., E California, ab. 12 m. N of Owens Lake; during World War II a Japanese relocation center.

Man'za·na'res (män'thä·nä'räs; män'sä-). **1** River 50 m. long in Madrid prov., cen. Spain; flows past Madrid into Jarama river, a tributary of the Tagus river.
2 Manufacturing commune, Ciudad Real prov., S cen. Spain, on Manzanares river 30 m. E of Ciudad Real; pop. 18,451; textiles, soap, wine, oil; medieval castle.

Man'za·nil'lo (män'sä·nē'yŏ). **1** Municipality and seaport on SW coast of Oriente prov., E Cuba, on Guacanayabo Bay; pop. (seaport) 35,730; exports sugar, molasses, tobacco, hardwood; mangrove swamps. Founded 1784.
2 Seaport, Colima state, SW Mexico, on Manzanillo Bay 38 m. WSW of Colima; pop. 6831; very old town; exports coffee, hides.

Manzanillo, Point. N extremity of Panama, extending into the Caribbean Sea NE of Colón.

Manzanillo Bay. 1 Inlet of Caribbean Sea, N Canal Zone; separated from Limón Bay to the W by peninsula on which Colón is located.
2 Bay in N coast of the island of Hispaniola, West Indies, on boundary bet. Haiti and the Dominican Republic.

Man·zan'o Peak (măn·zăn'ō; -zä'nō). Mountain 10,103 ft. in W Torrance co., cen. New Mexico; highest point in the **Manzano Range;** on boundary bet. Valencia and Torrance cos.

Manzikert. See MALAZKIRT.

Ma'o (mä'ō). Town, W Chad, N cen. Africa, NE of Lake Chad; pop. ab. 4000; chief town of Kanem.

Ma·o·ka (mä·ō·kä). Town, W coast of S Sakhalin I., Soviet Russia, Asia, on Gulf of Tatary; pop. (1939 est.) 17,879; an ice-free port; connects with Toyohara by railroad and highway. Until 1945 Japanese.

Ma'pi·a (mä'pĭ·á) *or* **Saint Da'vid** (sånt dä'vĭd). Group of three small islands and several islets in Pacific Ocean 150 m. N of Numfoor I. off N coast of Neth. New Guinea, 134°20'E and 1°N of equator. Occupied by American forces Nov. 15, 1944.

Ma·pi·mí', Bol·són' de (bôl·sôn' dâ mä'pē·mē'). Rocky depression ab. 50,000 sq. m. in N cen. Mexican plateau region, in Coahuila and Chihuahua states.

Maping. See LIUCHOW.

Ma'ple Creek (mä'p'l). Town, SW Saskatchewan, Canada, 80 m. WSW of Swift Current; pop. 1638.

Maple Heights. City, Cuyahoga co., N Ohio, 10 m. SE of Cleveland; pop. 31,667; residential suburb of Cleveland.

Maple Peak. Mountain 8302 ft. in N Greenlee co., E Arizona.

Maple Shade. Urban township, Burlington co., S cen. New Jersey, ab. 7 m. E of Camden; pop. 12,947; manufacturing; truck and grain farms.

Ma'ple·ton (mä'p'l·t'n; -tŭn). Town, Monona co., W Iowa, 38 m. ESE of Sioux City; pop. 1686.

Ma'ple·wood (mä'p'l·wŏŏd). **1** Village, Ramsey co., E Minnesota, N suburb of St. Paul; pop. 18,519.
2 Residential city, St. Louis co., E Missouri, 7 m. W of St. Louis; pop. 12,552.
3 Township, Essex co., NE New Jersey, S of South Orange and 6 m. W of Newark; pop. 23,977; residential suburb of New York and Newark.

Ma·po'cho (mä·pō'chō). River ab. 75 m. long in cen. Chile; flows into Maipo river 32 m. SW of Santiago.

Map'po Harbour (mäp'ō). Village and anchorage on S end of Maramasike I., SE Solomon Is., W Pacific Ocean.

Ma·pue'ra (má·pwä'rá). River 270 m. long in N Brazil; rises near S border of British Guiana; flows SE into Trombetas river NW of Lake Erepecú.

Ma·pu'to (má·pōō'tō). Navigable river 50 m. long, S Mozambique, formed by the Usutu and Pongola rivers; flows E to Delagoa Bay.

Ma·que'da Bay (mä·kā'thä). Inlet on W coast of Samar, Phil. Is., partly enclosed on W by Buad I.

Ma·qui'ling, Mount (mä·kē'lĕng). Mountain 3750 ft., S Laguna prov., Luzon, Phil. Is., near Batangas border S of Los Baños.

Ma·quo'ke·ta (má·kō'kĕ·tá). **1** River ab. 150 m. long, E cen. Iowa; rises in S Fayette co., NE Iowa, flows SE into Mississippi river in E Jackson co., E Iowa.
2 City, ⊗ of Jackson co., E Iowa, 30 m. S of Dubuque; pop. 5909.

Mar, Serra do. See SERRA DO MAR.

Ma'ra·cá' (má'rá·kà'). Island in Atlantic Ocean off NE coast of Pará state, Brazil.

Mar·a·cai'bo (măr'á·kī'bō; *Span.* mä'rä·kī'vô). City, ✱ of Zulia state, NW Venezuela, on W side of channel bet.

Lake Maracaibo and the Gulf of Venezuela; pop. (1941 est.) 135,582; one of the most important petroleum export centers in the world; shipbuilding; manufactures leather goods, coffee, beer, chocolate; exports coffee. Founded 1571; after 1668 a center for inland trade.

Maracaibo, Gulf of. = Gulf of VENEZUELA.

Maracaibo, Lake. South extension of Gulf of Venezuela, in NW Venezuela; 6300 sq. m.; receives Catatumbo river from SW; in region of rich oil fields, some wells having been sunk on the bottom of the lake through 50 ft. of water.

Maracanda. See SAMARKAND.

Ma′ra·cay′ (mä′rä·kī′). City, ✳ of Aragua state, N Venezuela, on highway 50 m. WSW of Caracas; pop. (1941 est.) 30,051; alt. 1500 ft.; coffee, cacao.

Ma′ra·dals·fos′ (mä′rä·däls·fôs′). Waterfall 650 ft., cen. Norway, just W of the Dovrefjell plateau.

Ma′ra·gheh′ (mä′rä·gå′) or **Ma′ra·gha′.** Town, Azerbaijan prov., NW Iran, ab. 18 m. E of Lake Urmia; pop. ab. 16,000; in fertile valley S of Kuh-i-Sahand; orchards and vineyards. Seat of government of Hulagu, Mongol ruler who conquered the region in 13th cent.

Ma′rah (mā′rá; mâr′á). Locality on E coast of Gulf of Suez, Sinai Penin., NE Egypt; first halting place of the Israelites after passing through the Red Sea and entering the wilderness; the waters were bitter (*Exod.* xv. 23–25).

Ma′rais′ (mȧ′rĕ′). Marshy district in S Vendée dept., W France; once partly covered by the sea.

Mar′ais des Cygnes (mĕr′(ē) dĕ sēn′; zēn′). River ab. 150 m. long, E Kansas and Missouri, flowing from S Wabaunsee co. E and SE to Osage river on boundary bet. Bates and Vernon cos., Missouri. See OSAGE.

Ma′ra·jó′ (mä′rä·zhō′). Island 14,000 sq. m. in the Amazon delta, NE Brazil, bet. the Amazon and Pará rivers; low-lying and often largely flooded; few inhabitants.

Marakesh. = MARRAKESH.

Má′ra·ma′ros (mä′rŏ·mŏ′rōsh). Former Hungarian county.

Má′ra·ma′ros·szi′get (-sĭ′gĕt). See SIGHET.

Ma′ra·ma·si′ke (mä′rä·mä·sē′kä). Narrow island ab. 32 m. long off SE coast of Malaita I., SE Solomon Is., W Pacific Ocean. Mappo Harbour is at its S end.

Ma′ra·nhão′ (mȧ′rȧ·nyoun′). **1** or **São Luiz** (soun lwēs′) or **São Luiz do Maranhão** (lwēzh′ thŏŏ). Island 28 m. long off N coast of Maranhão state, NE Brazil, bet. São Marcos Bay on the W and São José Bay on the E; site of the provincial capital, São Luiz. **2** State of Brazil. See *Table* at BRAZIL.

Mar′a·no′a (mär′á·nō′á). River 200 m. long, SE Queensland, Australia; flows S and joins the Condamine to form the Culgoa.

Ma·ra′no di Na′po·li (mä·rä′nŏ dĕ nä′pŏ·lĕ). Commune, Napoli prov., Campania, S Italy, 9 m. NW of Naples; pop. 17,368.

Ma′ra·ñón′ (mä′rä·nyôn′). River ab. 800 m. long in Peru; rises in the Andes Mts. in W cen. Peru; flows NW to N Peru; bends E and joins the Ucayali river to form the Amazon river (*q.v.*).

Ma′ra·pí′ (mȧ′rä·pē′). River in N Brazil; rises in Tumuc-Humac Mts.; flows S to unite with Parú (Oeste) river and form Erepecurú river.

Ma·ras′ (mä·räsh′) or **Ma·rash′.** **1** Vilayet, S cen. Turkey in Asia; 4327 sq. m.; pop. 188,877. **2** City, its ✳, at foot of E Taurus Mts. and near Ceyhan river 96 m. NE of Adana; pop. (1940) 30,695; has large Armenian population; center for trade in Kurdish carpets and embroideries. In very early times a Hittite town; under Moslem control c. 700 A.D.–1097, when it was captured by Crusaders. Became Turkish in 16th cent.; held for a short time by Egyptians 1832.

Mă·ră·şeş′ti (mȧ·rä·shĕst′; -shĕs′tĕ). Commune, Moldavia, Romania, N of Focşani; battle Aug. 1917.

Mar′a·thon (mär′á·thŏn; -thŭn). **1** County in Wisconsin. See *Table* at WISCONSIN. **2** A plain 5 m. long by 2 m. wide in E Attica and Boeotia

dept., Greece, ab. 24 m. NE of Athens; borders on **Bay of Marathon** (inlet of Aegean Sea) and ends in marsh at N. **3** Ancient town on this plain, probably located S of the modern town (pop. 2023); scene of battle in Sept. 490 B.C., in which Miltiades and 10,000 Greeks (mostly Athenians) completely defeated Datis and Artaphernes with a larger army of Persians.

Marathus. See 'AMRIT.

Mar·bel′la (mär·vä′[l]yä). Commune, Málaga prov., S cen. Spain, on Mediterranean SW of Málaga; pop. 9301.

Mar′ble Canyon (mär′b′l). Gorge along the Colorado river, N Arizona, extending from Lees Ferry (*q.v.*) S to the Little Colorado; often considered the upper part of Grand Canyon.

Mar′ble·head′ (mär′b′l-hĕd′; -hĕd′). Town, Essex co., NE Massachusetts, on Atlantic Ocean 15 m. NE of Boston; pop. 18,521; built on a rocky promontory (**Marblehead Neck**); noted as a yachting center; boat building, fishing. Founded ab. 1629, until 1649 a part of Salem; important in early history of American navy.

Mar′ble Hill (mär′b′l). **1** City, ⊗ of Bollinger co., SE Missouri; pop. 497. **2** Small section of Manhattan borough, New York City, on mainland N of Spuyten Duyvil Creek, bounded on N, W, and E by the Bronx.

Marble Point. Peak 6672 ft. in Baker co., E Oregon.

Mar′burg (mär′boŏrk; *Angl.* mär′bûrg). **1** *also* **Marburg an der Lahn** (än dĕr län′). City, Hesse, Germany, on Lahn river 46 m. N of Frankfurt; pop. 23,299; 13th-cent. church; university (founded 1527); manufactures machinery, leather, pottery, carpets, tobacco; founded in 12th cent.; passed to Prussia 1866. **2** See MARIBOR.

Mar′ca·ri′a (mär′kä·rē′ä). Commune, Mantova prov., Lombardy, N Italy, 13 m. W of Mantua; pop. 11,050.

Mar′ce·line′ (mär′sĕ·lēn′). City, Linn co., N Missouri, 35 m. NW of Moberly; pop. 2872; coal deposits nearby.

March (märk; *Czech* **Mo′ra·va** (mô′rä·vä). River 180 m. long in Moravia prov., Czechoslovakia; flows SW and S, forming a section of the boundary bet. Slovakia and Lower Austria; empties into Danube river 8 m. W of Bratislava; navigable for 78 m.

March (märch). Urban district, ⊗ of Isle of Ely, E England, on the Nene 52 m. E of Leicester; pop. 12,993.

Marche (mȧrsh); *Lat.* **Mar′chi·a** (mär′kĭ·á). Historical region of cen. France; bounded anciently on N by Touraine, NE by Berry and Bourbonnais, SE by Auvergne, S by Limousin, W by Poitou; ✳ Guéret (from 15th cent.). Became countship in 10th cent.; in possession of Lusignan family in 13th cent.; acquired by dukes of Bourbon, later confiscated by Francis I; province of France until Revolution.

Mar·che′na (mär·chā′nä). Commune, Sevilla prov., SW Spain, 32 m. E of Seville; pop. 19,859; woolens, pottery; stock raising, esp. for the bull ring; sulfur baths.

Mar·che′na (mär·chā′nä), or **Bind′loe** (bĭnd′lō), **Island.** One of the Galápagos Is. (*q.v.*).

March′es (mär′chĕz; -chĭz) *Ital.* **Le Mar′che** (lä mär′kä). Compartimento of cen. Italy; for provincial divisions, area, and pop., see *Table* at ITALY; lies bet. Adriatic Sea and Umbria and bet. Emilia and Abruzzi e Molise; produces grain, wine, tobacco. Formerly part of States of the Church (*q.v.*) against whom they voted in favor of union with Italy 1860.

March′feld (märk′fĕlt). Plain ab. 328 sq. m. lying N of the Danube at Vienna, Austria, and W of the March; scene of battle Aug. 1278 bet. Ottokar II, King of Bohemia, and Rudolf of Hapsburg, in which Ottokar was killed; in Napoleonic Wars scene of battles of Aspern (*q.v.*), Essling, and Wagram (*q.v.*).

Marchia. See MARCHE.

Mar′chienne′–au–Pont′ (mȧr′shyĕn′ō·pôN′). Commune, Hainaut prov., SW Belgium, on the Sambre near Charleroi; pop. 23,678; foundries and machine works.

Mar Chi·qui′ta (mär′ chḗ·kē′tä). **1** Lake 45 m. long in Córdoba prov., N cen. Argentina.
2 Town, Buenos Aires prov., E Argentina.

Mar′cia·ni′se (mär′chä·nē′zå). Commune, Napoli prov., Campania, S Italy, N of Naples; pop. 21,571.

Mar′ci′nelle′ (mär′sē′nĕl′). Commune, Hainaut prov., SW Belgium; suburb of S Charleroi; pop. 21,358.

Marcodurum. See DÜREN.

Mar′coing′ (mår′kwăN′). Commune, Nord dept., N France, on the Schelde canal near Cambrai; pop. (1931) 1929; in World War I destroyed during fighting around Cambrai Nov. 20–Dec. 7, 1917.

Mar′co Po′lo Bridge (mär′kō pō′lō). A beautiful marble bridge, 900 ft. long, with many arches, pillars, and sculptured lions, across the Yungting at Lukouchiao (q.v.), NE China, 9 m. SW of Peiping. So named from Marco Polo's description of it in his chronicle.

Mar′cos Juá′rez (mär′kŏs hwä′räs). Town, Córdoba prov., N cen. Argentina, 87 m. W of Rosario; pop. (est.) 12,912.

Marcos Paz (päs′). Town, Buenos Aires prov., E Argentina, 26 m. W of Buenos Aires.

Marcq′–en–Ba′rœul′ (mår′–käN·bå′rûl′). Commune, Nord dept., N France, NNE suburb of Lille; pop. (1931) 19,163; weaving and spinning mills; iron foundry.

Mar′cus Hook (mär′kŭs). Industrial borough and port, Delaware co., SE Pennsylvania, on Delaware river 18 m. WSW of Philadelphia; pop. 3299; oil refineries; manufactures rayon and rayon yarn, linoleum. Settled by Swedes in 1640's.

Marcus Island; *Jap.* **Mi·na·mi To·ri Shi·ma** (mĕ·nä·mē̇ tō·rē̇ shē̇·mä). Small, triangular-shaped island in W Pacific Ocean, NE of the Marianas and ab. 725 m. NW of Wake I., 24°18′N lat., 153°58′E long.; settlement on S coast. Developed with airfield, meteorological and radio stations as Japanese naval base; bombarded by American task force Feb.–Mar. 1942 and bombed by Allied planes Sept. 1943, but bypassed in attack on Japan. Administered by the United States.

Mar′cy, Mount (mär′sĭ). Peak 5344 ft. in the Adirondack Mts., NE New York; highest peak in the Adirondacks, and in New York State.

Mar′dan (mär′dăn; *native* mŭr′dän). Town, West Pakistan, 30 m. NE of Peshawar; pop. 45,358.

Mar del Pla′ta (mär′ thĕl plä′tä). Coastal city, Buenos Aires prov., E Argentina, S of Buenos Aires; pop. (est.) 114,729; seaside resort, known as the "Brighton of Argentina;" fishing, stone quarrying.

Mar·din′ (mär·dēn′). **1** Vilayet, SE Turkey in Asia, 4568 sq. m.; pop. 230,782.
2 Town, its ✳, on branch railroad near Syrian border 53 m. SE of Diyarbekir; pop. 20,982; a Kurdish town with mixed population; trades esp. in grain.

Ma′re (mā′rē; -rĕ). Latin meaning "sea"; used in classical names of bodies of water, as **Mare Adriaticum, Mare Ionium,** etc. See the second element of these names, or its Anglicized form.

Ma′ré′ (må·rā′). One of the Loyalty Is., at SE end of chain, ab. 22 m. long and 10 m. wide; pop. (1936) 2892; low coral formation.

Mare Adriatico; *Lat.* **Mare Adriaticum.** See ADRIATIC SEA.

Ma·reb′ (mä·rĕb′). River ab. 250 m. long in E Africa; rises in N Ethiopia; flows NW, forming a section of the Ethiopia-Eritrea boundary; crosses W Eritrea into E Republic of Sudan, and during high-water seasons empties into the Atbara river; known as the **Gasc** (găsk) or **Gash** (gäsh) in its lower course.

Mare Cantabricum. See Bay of BISCAY.

Ma·ree′, Loch (lŏk må·rē′). Lake 12½ m. long in Ross and Cromarty co., N Scotland; connected with Loch Ewe by a short river.

Mare Germanicum. See NORTH SEA.

Mare Internum. See MEDITERRANEAN SEA; cf. MARE NOSTRUM.

Mare Island (mär). Island in E San Pablo Bay, W cen. California; separated from Vallejo by narrow **Mare Island Strait.** U.S. Navy Yard, estab. 1853; now an extensive repair and maintenance naval base.

Ma·rem′ma (må·rĕm′å; *Ital.* mä·râm′mä). Marshy region in W Italy, chiefly in Grosseto prov., SW Tuscany.

Ma·ren′go (må·rĕng′gō). **1** County in Alabama. See *Table* at ALABAMA.
2 City, McHenry co., N Illinois, 25 m. E of Rockford; pop. 3568.
3 Town, Crawford co., S Indiana; pop. 803; nearby is **Marengo Cave,** a stalactite cave.
4 City, ⊗ of Iowa co., E cen. Iowa, 25 m. WSW of Cedar Rapids; pop. 2264.
5 (må·rĕng′gō; *Ital.* mä·rĕng′gŏ) Village, Alessandria prov., SE Piedmont, NW Italy; scene of battle June 14, 1800 in which Napoleon defeated the Austrians.

Ma′re Nos′trum (mā′rē [-rĕ] nŏs′trŭm). Literally "our sea"; occasionally used of the Mediterranean Sea: by the British to point out its importance as their life line to the Near and Middle East, and by the Italians to emphasize its significance in their national security.

Mar′e·o′tis, Lake (mär′ē·ō′tĭs); *Arab.* **Mar·yût′** (mŭr·yōōt′). Lake in the Nile delta, Lower Egypt, W of Rosetta mouth of the Nile; Alexandria is situated on narrow strip of land bet. it and the Mediterranean Sea.

Mare Rubrum. See ERYTHRAEAN SEA.

Ma·res′cot, Mount (må·rĕs′kŏt). Peak ab. 3900 ft., SE Santa Isabel I., E cen. Solomon Is., W Pacific Ocean; highest point on the island.

Mare Suevicum. See BALTIC SEA.

Mar′eth (mär′ĕth; *Arab.* mŭ′rĭth). Town, SE Tunisia, N Africa, SSE of Gabès; anchor point at N end of French defense line (**Mareth Line**); held by Germans 1942–43; broken by the British Mar. 27, 1943.

Mare Tirreno. See TYRRHENIAN SEA.

Ma·ret′ti·mo (mä·rät′tē·mô). One of the Egadi Is. (q.v.).

Mare Tyrrhenum. See TYRRHENIAN SEA.

Mar′fa (mär′fȧ). City, ⊗ of Presidio co., W Texas, 40 m. E of the Rio Grande; pop. 2799; hunting and summer resort; ships cattle and mohair.

Mar·ga·ri′ta (mär′gȧ·rē′tȧ; *Span.* -gä·rē′tä). Venezuelan island in the Caribbean Sea; ab. 444 sq. m.; pop. ab. 69,000; forms chief part of the Venezuelan state of Nueva Esparta (island group); **✳** La Asunción, chief town Porlamar; discovered by Columbus 1498.

Mar′gate (mär′gĭt), *formerly* **Mer′gate.** Municipal borough, Kent, SE England, on coast of Isle of Thanet 65 m. E of London; pop. 42,487; popular watering place.

Mar′gate City (mär′gāt; -gĭt). City, Atlantic co., SE New Jersey, on Atlantic Ocean 5 m. WSW of Atlantic City; pop. 9474.

Mar′ge·lan′ (mär′gĕ·län′). Town, E Uzbek S.S.R., Soviet Central Asia, E of Kokand and adjoining Fergana; pop. (1926) 44,000; an old city; mosques and bazaars; an agricultural center; also has important trade in cotton and silk goods. Known as **Old Margelan** to distinguish it from **New Margelan,** now Fergana (q.v.).

Margherita, Mount. See Mount RUWENZORI.

Mar′ghe·ri′ta di Sa·vo′ia (mär′gȧ·rē′tä dĕ sä·vô′yä); *before 1879 called* **Sa·li′ne di Bar·let′ta** (sä·lē′nä dĕ bär·lät′tä). Commune, Foggia prov., Apulia, SE Italy, on Adriatic Sea 31 m. ESE of Foggia; pop. 10,644; important sea-salt works.

Mar′go·sa·tu′big (mär′gô·sä·tōō′bĕg). Municipality, SE Zamboanga prov., Mindanao, Phil. Is., on an inlet of Moro Gulf 87 m. NE of City of Zamboanga; pop. 23,536.

Mar′gra′ten (mär′grä′tĕ[n]). Locality, Netherlands; largest temporary war cemetery in Europe for U.S. soldiers killed in World War II.

Mar′gum (mär′gŭm) *or* **Mar′gus** (-gŭs). Ancient town, Moesia Superior, at mouth of the Margus (*mod.* Morava) on the Danubius (Danube); scene of battle 285 A.D. in which Carinus defeated Diocletian.

Margus. 1 See MORAVA river.

2 See MARGUM town.

Mari, *or* **Mari Autonomous Soviet Socialist Republic.** See MARI REPUBLIC.

Ma·rí′a A′gui·lar′ (mä·rē′ä ä′gĕ·lär′). Cape on S coast of Las Villas prov., W cen. Cuba.

Ma·rí′a Cle′o·fás′ (mä·rē′ä klä′ō·fäs′). Island of the Tres Marías group (*q.v.*) in the Pacific Ocean off W coast of cen. Mexico.

Ma·rí′a E·le′na (mä·rē′ä ā·lā′nä). Town and commune, Antofagasta prov., N Chile, ab. 100 m. N of Antofagasta; pop. (commune) 9215; nitrate-processing plant.

Ma·rí′a Island (mä·rī′ä). **1** Small island 13 sq. m., W Gulf of Carpentaria, Australia, in Limmen Bight.

2 Island ab. 37 sq. m. off SE coast of Tasmania, Australia, N of Tasman Penin.; cement industry.

Ma·ri′a (mä·rī′ä), *or* **Hull** (hŭl), **Island.** Island, NW Tubuai Is., S Pacific Ocean.

Ma·rí′a Ma′dre (mä·rē′ä mä′thrä). Island of the Tres Marías group (*q.v.*) in Pacific Ocean off W coast of cen. Mexico.

Ma·rí′a Mag′da·le′na (mä·rē′ä mäg′thä·lā′nä). Island of the Tres Marías group (*q.v.*) in Pacific Ocean off W coast of cen. Mexico.

Mar′i·an′a Deep (mär′ĭ·ăn′ä; măr′-; -ä′nä). Ocean depth 32,177 ft., W Pacific Ocean, SE of Guam near the Nero Deep.

Mariana Islands, *commonly* **Marianas;** *formerly* **Ladrone′ Islands** (lä·drōn′). Island group in W Pacific Ocean, ab. 1500 m. E of the Philippine Is. and 1350 m. S of Honshu I., Japan; lat. 13° to 21°N and long. ab. 146°E; comprises 15 islands, area 246 sq. m. (including Guam, 452 sq. m.) and pop. 8414 (including Guam, 75,458); chief port and former ✱ Garapan, on Saipan I. Guam belongs to U.S.A.; remaining important islands are Saipan, Tinian, Rota, Pagan, Guguan, Agrihan, Aguijan. Discovered by Magellan 1521; called *Islas de los Ladrones* by ship's crew because natives pilfered articles from the boat; named *Las Marianas* 1668 in honor of Mariana of Austria, widow of Philip IV of Spain; sold (except for Guam) by Spain to Germany 1899 and assigned as Japanese mandate 1919 after World War I; under Japanese developed large sugar production and before 1941 were fortified to become "stationary island aircraft carriers." Saipan and Tinian (see also GUAM) attacked and seized by American forces June 15–Aug. 9, 1944; became part of Trust Territory of the Pacific Islands, assigned to U.S. 1947.

Ma·ria·na′o (mä′ryä·nä′ō). Municipality and city, La Habana prov., W Cuba; pop. (city) 114,743; residential suburb 6 m. W of Havana, with beach resorts.

Mar′i·an′na (mär′ĭ·ăn′ä; măr′-). **1** City, ⊗ of Lee co., E Arkansas, 12 m. W of Mississippi river SW of Memphis, Tennessee; pop. 5134; cotton.

2 City, ⊗ of Jackson co., NW Florida, 62 m. WNW of Tallahassee; pop. 7152; founded 1829; center of region producing corn, cotton, pecans, peanuts, fruit, esp. Satsuma oranges; limestone quarries and caves nearby.

Ma′rián·ské Láz′ně (mä′ryän·skä läz′nyĕ); *Ger.* **Ma·ri′en·bad** (mä·rē′ĕn·bät). Town, NW Bohemia, W Czechoslovakia, SE of Cheb; pop. 7177; mineral springs; ab. 7 m. E is the abbey of Tepl, founded 1193.

Ma·ri′as (mä·rī′äs). River 250 m. long, NW Montana; rises in Glacier co., NW Montana, flows E and SE into Missouri river in cen. Chouteau co., N cen. Montana.

Marías, Las. See LAS MARÍAS.

Ma·ri′as Pass. (mä·rī′äs). Mountain pass 5216 ft., NW Montana, in Lewis Range of Continental Divide at SE corner of Glacier National Park; discovered 1889; railroad, highway.

Maria–Theresiopel. See SUBOTICA.

Ma·ria′to, Point (mä·ryä′tō). Cape on SW extremity of Azuero Penin., S Panama.

Ma·ri′a van Die′men, Cape (mä·rē′ä văn dē′mĕn). Cape on NW extremity of North I., New Zealand.

Ma′rib (mär′ĭb); *Arab.* **Ma′′rib** (mä′rĭb). Ruins of ancient city of the Sabaeans, 60 m. ENE of San'a in E Yemen SW Arabia; a chief city of ancient Sheba; a great trading center; esp. famous for its great dam, constructed c. 7th cent. B.C. and destroyed in 6th cent. A.D., an event of importance in early Arab chronicles.

Ma′ri·bo (mä′rē·bō′). **1** See *Table* at DENMARK.

2 Town, ⊗ of Maribo co., Denmark, located on Lolland I.; pop. 4399; sugar refineries.

Ma′ri·bor (mä′rē·bôr); *Ger.* **Mar′burg** (mär′bōōrk; *Angl.* -bûrg). City, Slovenia, NW Yugoslavia, on Drava river near Austrian border 55 m. N of Zagreb; pop. 33,131; commercial and industrial center in fruit-growing and wine-making area; summer resort; 12th-cent. cathedral; 16th-cent. town hall.

Ma′ri·ca·ban′ (mä′rē·kä·bän′). Island off S Batangas prov., Luzon, Phil. Is.; 12 sq. m., ab. 7 m. long; pop. 4795; in Verde Island Passage off the point that separates Balayan Bay from Batangas Bay. Its barrios belong to Bauan municipality.

Ma′ri·ca′o (mä′rē·kä′ō). Municipality (pop. 1475) and town (pop. 6990), W Puerto Rico; town is inland on highway 11 m. E of Mayagüez.

Ma·ri′co (mä·rē′kō). River, ab. 130 m. long, a headstream of the Limpopo, W Transvaal, Union of South Africa; flows N through fertile Marico valley, producing citrus fruits, wheat, oats, and cotton; chief town Zeerust.

Mar′i·co′pa (mär′ĭ·kō′pä). County in Arizona. See *Table* at ARIZONA.

Maricopa Mountains. Small range in SE Maricopa co., SW cen Arizona.

Ma·rie′ Byrd Land (mä·rē′ bûrd′). Large section of Antarctica E of Ross Shelf Ice and Ross Sea and extending E to Ellsworth Highland; lat ab. 73° to 85°S and long. 100°–150°W; claimed for the U.S. by Richard E. Byrd 1929.

Ma·rie′ Ga·lante′ *or* **Ma·rie′–Ga′lante′** (mä·rē′gä′länt′). Island in E West Indies, a dependency of the French overseas territory of Guadeloupe 16 m. SE of Guadeloupe; 60 sq. m.; pop. (1938 est.) 29,746; ✱ Grand Bourg. Discovered by Columbus Nov. 3, 1493. Chief industry production of sugar.

Mariehamn. See MAARIANHAMINA.

Ma·riel′ (mä·ryĕl′). Municipality, Pinar del Río prov., W Cuba; pop. 11,106.

Marienbad. See MARIÁNSKÉ LÁZNĚ.

Marienburg. See MALBORK.

Ma·ri′en·dorf (mä·rē′ĕn·dôrf). Former commune, Germany, now a S suburb of Berlin.

Ma·ri′en·tal (mä·rē′ĕn·täl). Town, S cen. South-West Africa, on railroad S of Windhoek.

Marienwerder. See KWIDZYŃ.

Mar′ies (mär′ēz). County in Missouri. See *Table* at MISSOURI.

Ma·rie′stad (mä·rē′stä[d]). Town, ✱ of Skaraborg prov., S Sweden, on Lake Vänern; pop. 6871.

Mar′i·et′ta (mär′ĭ·ĕt′ä, mär′ĭ-). **1** Residential city, ⊗ of Cobb co., NW Georgia, 20 m. NW of Atlanta; pop. 25,565; U.S Air Force base; incorporated 1834, in Civil War held by Confederates for a time against Sherman's advance on Atlanta; at Kennesaw Mt. nearby Federals repulsed in bitter contest June 27, 1864; has large national cemetery.

2 City, ⊗ of Washington co., SE Ohio, on Ohio river 45 m. SE of Zanesville; pop. 16,847; pioneer city in Northwest Territory and oldest permanent settlement in Ohio (1788); developed as river port and shipbuilding center; coal, iron, oil, natural gas deposits; sandstone quarries; in agricultural region (fruits vegetables); manufactures furniture, paints and varnishes, grindstones, steel safes, silos. Marietta Coll. (1835; coed.).

3 City, ⊗ of Love co., S Oklahoma, 17 m. S of Ardmore; pop. 1933; farm center.

4 Borough, Lancaster co., SE Pennsylvania, on Susquehanna river 15 m. W of Lancaster; pop. 2385.

Ma·rie′ville (mȧ·rē′vĭl; *Fr.* mȧ′rē′vĭl′). Town, ⊗ of Rouville co., S Quebec, Canada, 23 m. ESE of Montreal; pop. 3117.

Ma′ri·glia′no (mä′rē·lyä′nô). Commune, Napoli prov., Campania, S Italy, 11 m. NE of Naples; pop. 15,444; castle; damaged by eruptions of Vesuvius 1631 and 1793.

Marignano. See MELEGNANO.

Ma′ri′got′ (ma′rē′gō′). See SAINT MARTIN.

Mariguana. See MAYAGUANA.

Ma·ri·insk′ Canal System (mȧ·ryĭ-ēnsk′). A series of navigable rivers and canals, forming one of the connections for barges and small vessels bet. Leningrad and the Volga, and thence to the Caspian Sea. Its course is: (a) the Neva, (b) canal along S shore of Lake Ladoga, (c) the Svir (canalized in part), (d) canal along S shore of Lake Onega to Vytegra, (e) the Vytegra, a connecting canal (the **Mariinsk**), and the Kovzha, (f) canal along W and S shores of Beloe Ozero, and (g) the Sheksna past Cherepovets through the Rybinsk Reservoir to Shcherbakov. Total length ab. 740 m.; first built 1808–10 but improved and in part reconstructed in recent years. See Lake KUBENSKOE.

Ma·ri·ki′na (mä′rē·kē′nä). **1** River ab. 30 m. long in Rizal prov., Luzon, Phil. Is.; rises in Montalban reservoir system; flows into Pasig river near Pasig. **2** Municipality, W cen. Rizal prov., Luzon, Phil. Is., on Marikina river 5 m. N of Pasig; pop. 15,166.

Ma·rí′lia (mä·rē′lyȧ). City, W cen. São Paulo state, SE Brazil, 230 m. NW of São Paulo; pop. (1940 est.) 24,794.

Ma·rin′ (mȧ·rĭn′). County in California. See *Table* at CALIFORNIA.

Ma·rín′ (mä·rēn′). Seaport commune, Pontevedra prov., NW Spain, on inlet of Atlantic Ocean 6 m. SSW of Pontevedra; pop. 16,294; commercial fisheries; fish-salting works; manufactures textiles.

Ma·ri′na (mȧ·rē′nȧ). Waterfall 500 ft. in a tributary of the Essequibo river, W British Guiana, in the Serra Pacaraima NW of Kaieteur Falls.

Ma·ri′na (mä·rē′nä). See ESPÍRITU SANTO island, New Hebrides Is.

Ma·rin·du′que (mä′rĕn·dōō′kå). Island and province, cen. Phil. Is., separated from S coast of Tayabas prov. by Mompog Pass; 355 sq. m.; pop 81,768; ✲ Boac. NW coast borders on Tayabas Bay and S coast on Sibuyan Sea. Covered with hills; produces hemp (abacá) and coconuts for export and has considerable mineral wealth. Inhabitants are Tagalogs. Chief town in addition to Boac is Santa Cruz. Formerly a subprovince of Tayabas but set up as a separate province 1920. Occupied by Americans Jan. 1945.

Ma·rine′ City (mȧ·rēn′). City, St. Clair co., SE Michigan, on St Clair river 16 m. S of Port Huron; pop. 4404.

Mar′i·nette′ (măr′ĭ·nĕt′). **1** County in Wisconsin. See *Table* at WISCONSIN. **2** City, ⊗ of Marinette co., NE Wisconsin, on Green Bay 44 m. NNE of Green Bay (city); pop. 13,329; port of entry; manufactures wooden and paper boxes, paper, chemicals; fishing and boating center.

Ma·rin′ga (mȧ·rĭng′gä). River 270 m. long in S cen. Africa; flows WNW in NW Congo and joins the Lopori river to form the Lulonga river.

Ma·ri′no (mä·rē′nô). Commune, Roma prov., Latium, cen. Italy, 12 m. SE of Rome; pop. 13,248.

Mar′i·on (măr′ĭ·ŭn; măr′-). **1** Name of counties in seventeen states of the U.S. See *Tables* at ALABAMA, ARKANSAS, FLORIDA, GEORGIA, ILLINOIS, INDIANA, IOWA, KANSAS, KENTUCKY, MISSISSIPPI, MISSOURI, OHIO, OREGON, SOUTH CAROLINA, TENNESSEE, TEXAS, WEST VIRGINIA. **2** City, ⊗ of Perry co., W cen. Alabama, 45 m. SSE of Tuscaloosa; pop. 3807, agricultural trade center; Judson Coll. (1838; women); federal fish hatchery nearby. **3** City, ⊗ of Crittenden co., E Arkansas; pop. 881. **4** City, ⊗ of Williamson co., S Illinois, 45 m. S of Mt. Vernon; pop. 11,274; fruit growing; coal mining.

5 City, ⊗ of Grant co., N cen. Indiana, 28 m. NW of Muncie; pop. 37,854; manufactures foundry products, radios, furniture, glass, and electrical appliances. Marion Coll. (1920; coed.). **6** City, Linn co., E Iowa, 7 m. ENE of Cedar Rapids; pop. 10,882. **7** City, ⊗ of Marion co., E cen. Kansas, 48 m. NNE of Wichita; pop. 2169; agriculture, poultry raising. **8** City, ⊗ of Crittenden co., W Kentucky, 35 m. ENE of Paducah; pop. 2468; mines of fluorspar. **9** Town, Plymouth co., SE Massachusetts, on Buzzards Bay 9 m. ENE of New Bedford; pop. 2881; summer resort. **10** Town, Wayne co., W New York, ab. 21 m. E of Rochester; pop. 2785. **11** Town, ⊗ of McDowell co., W North Carolina, 32 m. E of Asheville; pop. 3345; textiles, furniture. **12** Industrial city, ⊗ of Marion co., cen. Ohio, 43 m. N of Columbus; pop. 37,079; settled c. 1820; railroad and agricultural center; railroad shops, foundries; manufactures esp. steam shovels, tractors, and road rollers, also farm implements, automobile parts. Home of Warren G. Harding. **13** Town, ⊗ of Marion co., E South Carolina, 24 m. E of Florence; pop. 7174; in cotton, tobacco, timber region; manufactures cotton yarn, cottonseed oil, veneer. **14** Town, ⊗ of Smyth co., SW Virginia, 42 m. ENE of Bristol; pop. 8385; manufactures furniture, flour, leather, brick; lime and manganese deposits. Settled 1750.

Marion, Lake. See SANTEE DAM.

Marion Heights. Borough, Northumberland co., E cen. Pennsylvania, near Shamokin; pop. 1132.

Marion Reef. Circular coral atoll in Pacific off cen. part of Great Barrier Reef, Queensland, Australia, 19°S.

Mar′i·po′sa (măr′ĭ·pō′sȧ; -zȧ). **1** County in California. See *Table* at CALIFORNIA. **2** Village, ⊗ of Mariposa co., California; pop. (est.) 550.

Ma′ri·qui′na (mä′rē·kē′nä). Var. of MARIKINA.

Ma′ri Republic (mä′rĭ; *Russ.* mȧ′ryĭ), *officially* **Mari Autonomous Soviet Socialist Republic.** Autonomous republic, E cen. Soviet Russia, Europe; 8994 sq. m.; pop. 579,456, (1941 est.) 607,874; ✲ Ioshkar Ola; a subdivision of the R.S.F.S.R. Bounded on N and NE by Kirov Region, on SE by Tatar Republic, on S by Chuvash Republic, and on W by Gorki Region. Level country N of the Volga with lakes and peat bogs and large forest area. Region unhealthful with few roads and only one railroad (branch from Kazan to Ioshkar Ola). Since Revolution considerable progress has been made economically and culturally. Predominant ethnic strain is Finno-Ugrian; chief nationalities Mari 51%, Russian ab. 44%. The Mari speak a Finnish dialect and are akin to the Mordvinians and Permiaks; the Russians call them the Cheremiss. Region annexed in 16th cent., but people were not assimilated. Created an autonomous area 1920 and made a republic 1936.

Ma′ris·cal′ Es′ti·gar·ri′bia (mä′rĕs·käl′ ās′tē·gär·rē′vyä). Town, ✲ of Boquerón dept., NW Paraguay, in the Chaco.

Ma′ris·cal Mountain (märʹĭs·kôl; märʹ-). Peak 3940 ft. in S Brewster co., W Texas.

Ma·ris′sa (mȧ·rĭs′ȧ). Village, St. Clair co., SW Illinois, 33 m. SE of East St. Louis; pop. 1722.

Ma·rí′ti·ma, Cor′dil·le′ra (kôr′thĕ·yä′rä mä·rē′tē·mä). The Cordillera Occidental in Peru. See ANDES.

Maritima Avaticorum. See MARTIGUES.

Maritime Alps. See *Table* at ALPS.

Maritime Atlas. See ATLAS MOUNTAINS.

Mar′i·time Province (măr′ĭ·tĭm, -tĭm; -tĕm). Former province of Soviet Russia, Asia, comprising the coastal region of Siberia from Bering Strait to Vladivostok, with coast line of ab. 2300 m.; the Russian Far East; organized after region became Russian by Peking Convention 1860; became a part of the Far Eastern Region (*q.v.*) 1920. See MARITIME TERRITORY.

Maritime Provinces, *often* the **Mar'i·times** (măr'ĭ-tīmz; -tĭmz; -tēmz). The Canadian provinces of New Brunswick, Nova Scotia, and Prince Edward Island.

Maritime Territory; *Russ.* **Pri·mor'ski Krai** (prĭ-môr'skĭ [*Russ.* pryĭ-] krī). A territory of Soviet Russia, Asia, on SE coast of Siberia bordering on Sea of Japan; 72,877 sq. m.; pop. 907,220; ✱ Vladivostok. Bounded on NW by Khabarovsk Territory and on SW by Manchuria; this W border formed in part by the Ussuri river and Lake Khanka. At the extreme S along the Tumen river it touches NE Korea, and along its entire coast stretch the Sikhote Alin Mts. At its S end on Peter the Great Bay is Vladivostok, the finest Soviet seaport on the Pacific littoral; to the N along the Ussuri valley is rich agricultural country and timberland. Voroshilov is an important industrial center and at the N on Tatar Strait is Sovetskaya Gavan, a rail terminal and rapidly growing port. Part of Maritime Province (*q.v.*) 1860–1920; part of Far Eastern Region 1920–36; made a territory 1936.

Ma·ri'tsa (mä·rē'tsä); *Turk.* **Me·riç'** (mě·rēch'); *Gr.* **Ev'ros** (ěv'rŏs; *Gr.* âv'rôs); *anc.* **He'brus** (hē'brŭs). River ab. 320 m. long in SE Europe; flows E in S Bulgaria, then turning S at Edirne, flows as the Meriç bet. Eastern Thrace (Turkey in Europe) and Western Thrace (Greece) to empty into the Aegean Sea; receives the Tundzha at Edirne.

Maritzburg. See PIETERMARITZBURG.

Mariupol. See ZHDANOV.

Ma·ri·ve'les (mä·rē·vā'lās). Municipality at S end of Bataan, Luzon, Phil. Is., WNW of Corregidor I., on **Mariveles Bay** (inlet of North Channel); pop. 4444; important telegraph, military, and quarantine station. Scene of severe fighting in Bataan campaign Apr. 1942; retaken by American forces Feb. 15, 1945.

Mariveles, Mount. Mountain 4700 ft., an extinct volcano, at S end of Zambales Mts. at S end of Bataan Penin., Luzon, Phil. Is.; highest peak on Bataan.

Ma·ri·yam'po·le (mä'rĭ·yäm'pô·lě). **1** District of Lithuania. See *Table* at LITHUANIA.

2 Town, its ✱, ab. 30 m. SW of Kaunas; pop. 15,652.

Mark (märk). Medieval county, W Germany, in Westphalia S of Münster; belonged to Brandenburg in 17th cent.

Mar'ka·gunt Plateau (mär'kà·gŭnt). Elevated region, SW Utah, in which is located Cedar Breaks National Monument (see UNITED STATES, *National Monuments*).

Marked Tree (märk[t] trē). City, Poinsett co., NE Arkansas, at confluence of St. Francis and Little rivers, 26 m. SE of Jonesboro; pop. 3216.

Mar'ken (mär'kě[n]). Island, North Holland prov., W Netherlands, in SW part of IJsselmeer off Monnikendam and ab. 10 m. NE of Amsterdam; will eventually be in reclaimed SW polder; has 7 small hamlets frequently visited by tourists; connected since 1959 with mainland by dike carrying a highway.

Mar'ket Har'bor·ough (mär'kět [-kǐt] här'bŭ·rŭ [-brŭ]). Urban district, Leicestershire, cen. England, on the Welland 15 m. SE of Leicester; pop. 10,401; fox-hunting center; textiles, farm implements, rubber goods.

Mark'ham (mär'kăm). **1** River ab. 200 m. long, E North-East New Guinea; rises in mountains in NE, flows S and SE to Huon Gulf at Lae; an upper tributary of the Bulolo (*q.v.*); its valley scene of fighting during campaign for Lae 1943.

2 Village, Cook co., NE Illinois, S suburb of Chicago; pop. 11,704.

Markham, Mount. Peak 15,100 ft. in Victoria Land, Antarctica, bet. Mt. Albert Markham and Mt. Kirkpatrick, at lat. 83°S and long. 160°30'E.

Markirch. See SAINTE-MARIE-AUX-MINES.

Mark'lee·ville (märk'lē·vǐl). Town, ⊗ of Alpine co., E California; pop. (1950) 199.

Marks (märks). Town, ⊗ of Quitman co., NW Mississippi; pop. 2572.

Marks (märks; *Russ.* märks). Short form of MARKS-SHTADT, used esp. after abolition of the German Volga Republic 1941.

Marks·shtadt' (mŭrks·shtät'); *Ger.* **Marx'stadt** (märks'shtät); *formerly* **E·ka'te·ri'nen·stadt** (ĕ·kăt'-ĕr·ē'něn·stät; *Russ.* yĭ·kà·tyĭ·ryē'nyĭn·shtät'). Town, Soviet Russia, Europe, on left bank of Volga 35 m. NNE of Saratov; pop. 12,457; center of a German agricultural area; formerly in N German Volga Republic. Founded 1795; originally named after Empress Catherine II, renamed 1922 in honor of Karl Marx.

Marks'ville (märks'vĭl; *Sou. also* -v'l). Town, ⊗ of Avoyelles parish, cen. Louisiana; pop. 4257.

Marl (märl). Commune, North Rhine-Westphalia state, W Germany, N of Gelsenkirchen; pop. 58,400; coal.

Marl'bor'o (märl'bûr'ŏ). **1** County in South Carolina See *Table* at SOUTH CAROLINA.

2 *or* **Marl'bor'ough** (märl'bûr'ŏ; môl'bŭ·rŭ, -brŭ) City, Middlesex co., NE Massachusetts, 13 m. ENE of Worcester; pop. 18,819; manufactures shoes and shoe machinery, oil burners, paper boxes.

Marl'bor·ough (môl'bŭ·rŭ; -brŭ; märl'-). **1** Coastal town, N British Guiana, in Essequibo co.

2 Municipal borough, NE cen. Wiltshire, S England; pop. (1951) 4556; grammar school (founded 1551).

3 Provincial district of New Zealand. See *Table* at NEW ZEALAND.

Marles–les–Mines (mär'lä·mēn'). Commune, Pas-de-Calais dept., N France, 19 m. NW of Arras; pop. (1931) 13,391; coal mines.

Mar'lin (mär'lĭn). City and health resort, ⊗ of Falls co., cen. Texas, 20 m. SSE of Waco; pop. 6918; hot-water artesian wells; cotton; cottonseed oil, brick.

Mar'lin·ton (mär'lĭn·tǎn; -t'n). Town, ⊗ of Pocahontas co., E cen. West Virginia; pop. 1586; hunting resort.

Mar'low (mär'lō). **1** City, Stephens co., S Oklahoma, 26 m. E of Lawton; pop. 4027; ships corn, watermelons.

2 Urban district, Buckinghamshire, SE cen. England, on the Thames 30 m. W of London; pop. 6480.

Mar'ly'–le–Roi' (mär'lē'lě·rwä'). Suburb of Versailles, Seine-et-Oise dept., N France; pop. 1794; castle ruins.

Marmagão. See MORMUGÃO.

Mar'mande' (mär'mänd'); *anc.* **Mar·man'da** (mär-mǎn'dà). Commune, Lot-et-Garonne dept., SW France, on Garonne river 32 m. NW of Agen; pop. 10,481.

Mar'ma·ra (mär'mà·rà) *or* **Mar'mo·ra** (mär'mŏ·rà); *anc.* **Proc'on·ne'sus** (prŏk'ŏ·nē'sŭs). Island in the Sea of Marmara; 11 m. long; area 50 sq. m.; has quarries of white marble with black streaks.

Mar'ma·ra, Sea of (mär'mà·rà); *Turk.* **Mar'ma·ra' De'ni·zi'** (mär'mä·rä' dě'ně·zē'); *anc.* **Pro·pon'tis** (prŏ·pŏn'tĭs). Sea in NW Turkey, bet. Europe and Asia; 172 m. long; area 4250 sq. m.; connected with the Black Sea through the Bosporus, and with the Aegean Sea through the Dardanelles. Has several islands, esp. Marmara in the W and Princes Is. near İstanbul, a large promontory, Kapıdağı (Cyzicus), on the S coast, and two long inlets on the E. See *Map* at TURKEY IN EUROPE.

Mar·mar'i·ca (mär·măr'ĭ·kà). Desert plateau region of N Africa along the Mediterranean Sea bet. ancient Cyrenaica and Egypt; by some authorities extended into NW Egypt nearly to Alexandria; in ancient times fought over in many wars by Romans, Egyptians, Libyans, Arabs. In modern times the name has been given by Italians to the NE section of Cyrenaica; scene in World War II of much fighting 1942–43.

Mar'me·nor' *or* **Mar Me·nor'** (mär'mà·nôr'). Lagoon on SE coast of Spain, extending N from Cape Palos ab. 14 m.; greatest width ab. 6 m.

Mar·met' (mär·mět'). Town, Kanawha co., W cen. West Virginia, on Kanawha river 8 m. SSE of Charleston; pop. 2500.

Mar'mo·la'da (mär'mŏ·lä'dä). Highest peak 10,965 ft. in the Dolomites, NE Italy, bet. Venezia Euganea and Venezia Tridentina.

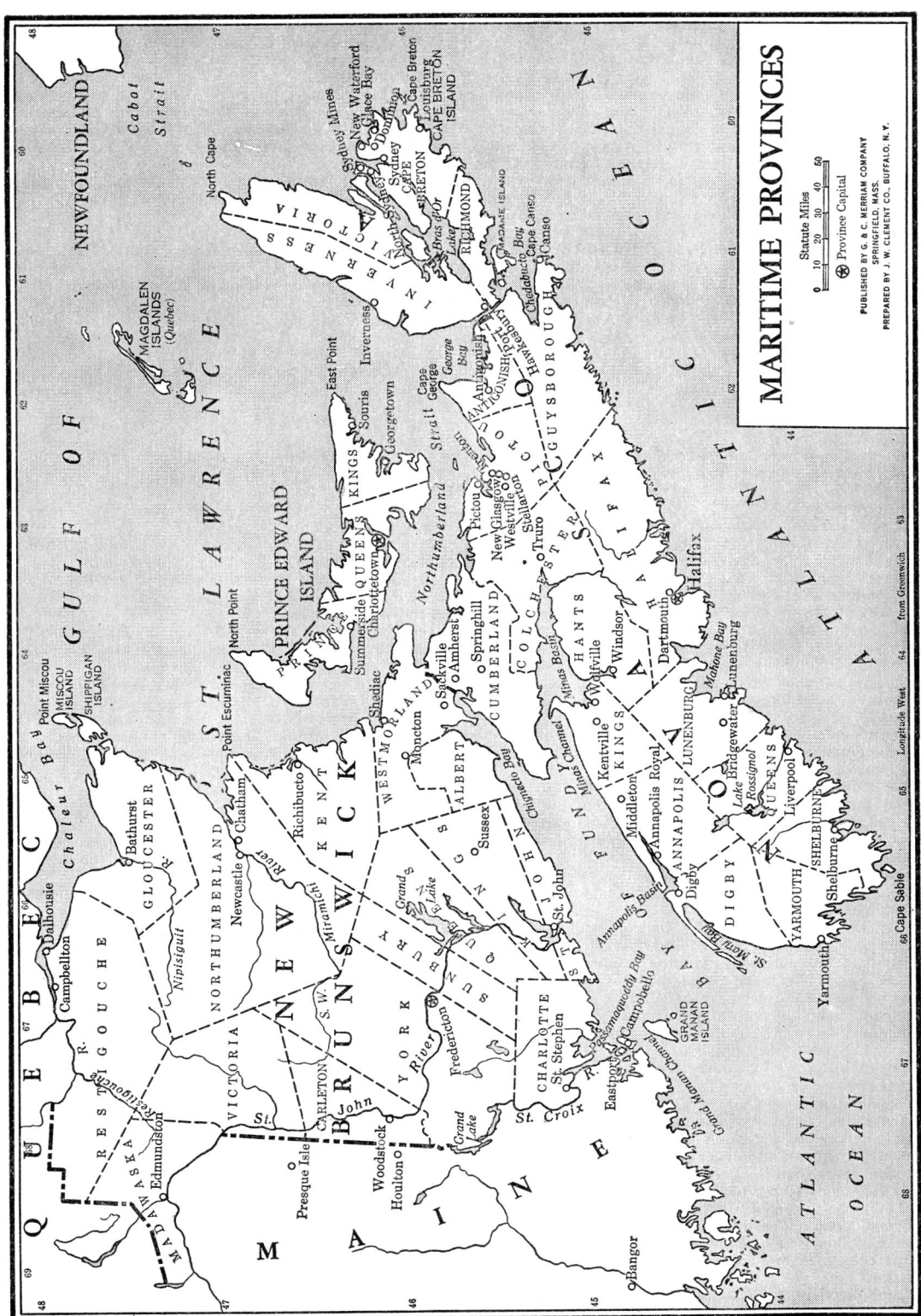

MARITIME PROVINCES

Statute Miles

0 10 20 30 40 50

⊕ Province Capital

PUBLISHED BY G. & C. MERRIAM COMPANY
SPRINGFIELD, MASS.

PREPARED BY J. W. CLEMENT CO., BUFFALO, N.Y.

Marmora. Var. of MARMARA.

Marmore, Cascate delle. See VELINO.

Marne (märn; *Fr.* márn); *anc.* **Mat'ro·na** (măt'rô·nà). River ab. 325 m. long in NE France; rises in NE cen. France; flows NW and W into Seine river at Charenton-le-Pont, near Paris; navigable for ab. 220 m.; scene of battles in World War I: Sept. 6–9, 1914 in which the Allies were victorious; and July 15–Aug. 4, 1918 in which after preliminary successes of Germans around Reims, the French and Americans made a successful counterattack at Château-Thierry under Foch, resulting in German defeat. In World War II reached by Americans Aug. 27–28, 1944.

Marne. Departments of France: **Haute-Marne** (ōt'-märn') and **Marne.** See *Table* at FRANCE.

Maroc. See MOROCCO.

Ma·ro'ni (mà·rō'nĭ); *Du.* **Ma'ro·wij'ne** (mà'rô·vī'nĕ). River ab. 420 m. long in N South America; with its tributary, the Itany, forms boundary bet. Surinam and French Guiana; empties into Atlantic Ocean.

Ma·roon' Peak (mà·rōōn'). Mountain 14,126 ft. in Pitkin co., W cen. Colorado.

Ma'ro Reef (mä'rō). A rocky islet of the Leeward Is., Hawaiian Is., 170°35'W.

Maros. See MUREŞ.

Maros-Vásárhely. See TÂRGU-MUREŞ.

Ma·rou'a (mà·rōō'à). Town, SW Chad, N cen. Africa; highway center.

Ma·ro'vo (mà·rō'vō). Lagoon. See NEW GEORGIA.

Marowijne. See MARONI.

Mar'pi Point (mär'pē). Northern point of Saipan I., Mariana Is., W Pacific Ocean.

Mar'ple (mär'p'l). **1** Urban township, Delaware co., SE Pennsylvania, W suburb of Chester; pop. 19,722.
2 Urban district, Cheshire, NW England, on the Goyt 9 m. SE of Manchester; pop. 13,068.

Mar·que'sas Islands (mär·kā'zàs), *also* **Mar·que'zas** (-zàs); *Fr.* **Îles Mar'quises'** (ēl' már·kēz'). Group of 13 islands of French Oceania, S Pacific Ocean, bet. ab. lat. 8° to 11°S and long. 140°W, N of Tuamotu Archipelago and 2000 m. SSE of Honolulu; 480 sq. m.; pop. 2699; ✳ Atuana on Hiva Oa I. The more important islands are in three groups: Nuku Hiva, Ua Pu, and Ua Huka in the center; Hiva Oa, Tahuata, and Fatu Hiva in the SE, and the small islands of Eïao and Hatutu in the NW. Rocky and mountainous islands of volcanic origin; highest point on Hiva Oa 4134 ft.; have fertile and well-watered valleys. First discovered by Álvaro de Mendaña in 1595; rediscovered by Capt. Cook 1774; taken by France 1842; French settlement not complete until after 1870.

Mar·que'sas (mär·kēz') **Keys.** Small group of islands W of the SW end of Florida Keys, at N of entrance to Gulf of Mexico, a part of Monroe co., Florida.

Mar·quette' (mär·kĕt'). **1** Counties in two states of the U.S. See *Tables* at MICHIGAN and WISCONSIN.
2 City, ⊗ of Marquette co., N Michigan penin., on Lake Superior; pop. 19,824; shipping point for iron ore; manufactures wood products, chemicals, machinery. Northern Michigan Coll. (1899; coed.).

Mar·ra'kesh *or* **Mar·ra'kech** (mà·rä'kĕsh; *Arab.* mŭr·rä'kōōsh); *formerly also* **Mo·roc'co** (mô·rŏk'ō). City, W cen. Morocco, NW Africa, one of the traditional capitals of sultanate of Morocco; pop. 215,312; beautifully situated in N foothills of W end of the Grand Atlas; many mosques, fountains; palace; has modern European town, founded 1913. Founded 1062 by Yusuf ibn-Tashfin as African capital of Almoravides dynasty; later (1147) also capital of the Almohades; in medieval period one of great cities of Islam; chief residence of Saadi rulers; taken by French Sept. 7, 1912.

Mar'ree' (mär'ē'). Town, E cen. South Australia, SE of Lake Eyre.

Mar'rick·ville (măr'ĭk·vĭl). City, E New South Wales, SE Australia, S suburb of Sydney; pop. 45,384.

Mar'ro·quí', Point (mär'rô·kē'). Southernmost point of Spain, at Tarifa, on the Strait of Gibraltar; also southernmost point of Europe, 36°2'N.

Marruecos. See MOROCCO.

Mar·sa'la (mär·sä'lä); *anc.* **Lil'y·bae'um** (lĭl'ĭ·bē'ŭm). Fortified seaport, Trapani prov., Sicily, on Mediterranean 18 m. S of Trapani; pop. 62,171; cathedral, theater, walls, catacombs; exports Marsala wine, grain, salt, soda; Garibaldi and volunteer forces landed here 1860.

Marsan. See MONT-DE-MARSAN.

Mar·scia'no (mär·shä'nō). Commune, Perugia prov., Umbria, cen. Italy, 15 m. S of Perugia; pop. 17,129.

Mars'den (märz'dĕn). Former urban district, West Riding, Yorkshire, N England; pop. (1931) 5723.

Mars Diep (märs dēp). Strait ab. 2 m. wide separating island of Texel from mainland of N North Holland prov., W Netherlands; outlet of Wadden Zee to North Sea.

Mar·seilles' (mär·sālz'). **1** City, La Salle co., N Illinois, on Illinois river 8 m. E of Ottawa; pop. 4347; paper mills; manufactures building and roofing material.
2 *Fr.* **Mar·seille'** (mär·sā'; *Fr.* már·sâ'y); *anc.* **Mas·sil'i·a** (mă·sĭl'ĭ·à; -sĭl'yà). Seaport, ✳ of Bouches-du-Rhône dept., SE France, on NE shore of Gulf of Lions 98 m. WSW of Nice; pop. 661,492; episcopal see; 2d largest city and principal commercial seaport of France; military and naval station; manufactures soap (esp. the variety called Marseilles soap), chemical products (esp. soda), machinery, sugar, olive oil, iron and brass goods, glass, hosiery, matches, candles; shipbuilding works; modern Byzantine cathedral (1893), Romanesque church of Notre Dame de la Garde, Palais des Arts de Longchamp in Renaissance style, mint.
History: Ancient Massilia colonized by Phocaeans (Ionian Greeks) c. 600 B.C.; developed vigorous trade up the Rhone valley and in the Mediterranean; planted several colonies on Gallic and Spanish coasts; aided by Rome in conflict with Carthage; deprived of its colonies when Caesar took it 49 B.C.; early seat of Christian bishopric; overrun by Visigoths, Ostrogoths, and Franks, 5th and 6th cents.; in 879 belonged to kingdom of Arles, and in 10th cent. to Provence; became independent 13th cent.; passed to French crown 1481; became important again in 19th cent. with development of French colonial empire and opening of Suez Canal. In World War II taken by U.S. troops Aug. 23, 1944.

Mar'shall (mär'shăl). **1** Counties in twelve states of U.S. See *Tables* at ALABAMA, ILLINOIS, INDIANA, IOWA, KANSAS, KENTUCKY, MINNESOTA, MISSISSIPPI, OKLAHOMA, SOUTH DAKOTA, TENNESSEE, WEST VIRGINIA.
2 City, ⊗ of Searcy co., N Arkansas; pop. 1095.
3 City, ⊗ of Clark co., E Illinois, 18 m. S of Danville; pop. 3270; trading center in oil-producing section.
4 City, ⊗ of Calhoun co., S Michigan, 12 m. ESE of Battle Creek; pop. 6736; in agricultural section.
5 City, ⊗ of Lyon co., SW Minnesota, 35 m. S of Montevideo; pop. 6681; in agricultural section.
6 City, ⊗ of Saline co., W cen. Missouri, 28 m. N of Sedalia; pop. 9572; wheat and corn shipping center. Missouri Valley Coll. (1888; coed.; Presbyterian).
7 Town, ⊗ of Madison co., W North Carolina, 15 m. NNW of Asheville; pop. 926.
8 City, ⊗ of Harrison co., NE Texas, 54 m. ENE of Tyler; pop. 23,846; manufactures wood pulp, car wheels, foundry products, brick and tile, pottery; oil, gas, lignite, clay, and glass-sand deposits nearby; in resort region. Bishop Coll. (1880; coed.; Negro); Wiley Coll. (1873; coed.; Negro); East Texas Baptist Coll. (1914; coed.). Settled 1841; incorp. as city 1848; served (in Texas) as temporary active capital of Missouri in administration of Confederate affairs during the Civil War.
9 Coastal town, W Liberia, W Africa, 30 m. SE of Monrovia; port for shipping rubber.

Marshall Ford Dam. See UNITED STATES, *Dams.*

Marshall Islands. Group of 32 atolls and more than 850 reefs in W Pacific Ocean, E of the Caroline Is. and

NNW of the Gilbert Is., 5° to 15°N lat. and 162° to 173°E long.; comprise the Ratak and Ralik chains of islands; land area 66 sq. m., including lagoons 176 sq. m.; pop. (1935) 10,446; ✳ Jaluit. Probably first sighted by Spanish navigator 1529; explored by English captains Gilbert and Marshall 1788; for next century uncontrolled; claimed by Germany 1885 and all rights to islands purchased by her from Spain 1899; invaded and seized by Japan 1914 and granted to Japan as mandate 1920; held with absolute sovereignty by Japan from 1935; invaded Jan.–Feb. 1944 by Americans, who seized Kwajalein and Eniwetok; became part of U.S. Trust Territory of the Pacific Islands 1947.

Mar·shall·town (mär′shăl·toun). City, ⊗ of Marshall co., cen. Iowa, 48 m. NE of Des Moines; pop. 22,521; railroad center in agricultural and livestock-raising section; manufactures furnaces, engines.

Marsh′field (märsh′fēld). **1** Town, Plymouth co., SE Massachusetts, 15 m. E of Brockton; pop. 6748; residence of Daniel Webster during latter part of his life. **2** City, ⊗ of Webster co., S Missouri, 24 m. ENE of Springfield; pop. 2221; ships grain, poultry, tomatoes. **3** See COOS BAY. **4** City, Wood co., cen. Wisconsin, 25 m. NW of Wisconsin Rapids; pop. 14,153; dairying, cheese making; manufactures veneer panels and doors, steel and sheet-metal products, shoes, mattresses, farm equipment.

Mars Hill (märz). **1** Isolated mountain with two peaks, 1350 ft. and 1500 ft., in Aroostook co., N Maine, near E Maine boundary. **2** Town, Aroostook co., N Maine, 12 m. SSE of Presque Isle; pop. 2062.

Mars′ Hill. See AREOPAGUS.

Marsh Island (märsh). Island off S coast of Louisiana, at entrance to Vermilion Bay; a game preserve.

Marsh Peak. Mountain 12,219 ft. in N Uintah co., E Utah.

Mar·sin′ (mär·sēn′). = MERSIN.

Marsivan. See MERZIFON.

Mars–la–Tour (märs′lä·tōōr′). Village, Meurthe-et-Moselle dept., NE France, SW of Metz; pop. (1931) 740; with Vionville scene of battle Aug. 16, 1870 in which French under Marshal Bazaine were defeated.

Mars′ton Moor (märs′tŭn). Moor 7 m. W of York, N England, scene of battle July 2, 1644 in which Parliamentarians under Fairfax, Cromwell, and Leslie defeated Royalists under Prince Rupert and Goring.

Mart (märt). City, McLennan co., cen. Texas, 12 m. E of Waco; pop. 2197; railroad division point; cotton ginning.

Mar′ta (mär′tä). River ab. 25 m. long in W cen. Italy; flows from Lake Bolsena into the N Tyrrhenian Sea.

Mar′ta·ban′ (mär′tá·bän′). Town, Thaton dist., SE Lower Burma, at mouth of the Salween river opp. Moulmein.

Martaban, Gulf of. Inlet of Bay of Bengal on coast of Lower Burma, bet. 16° and 17°N lat. and 96° and 98°E long.; receives waters of the Salween river, the Sittang river, and part of the Irrawaddy river.

Mar′ta·poe′ra or **Mar′ta·pu′ra** (mär′tä·pōō′rä). River ab. 100 m. long, SE Borneo, Indonesia, an E tributary of the Barito, joining it just below Bandjermasin.

Mar′ten (mär′tĕn). Former commune (pop. 12,298), Prussia, Germany; since 1928 part of Dortmund.

Mar′tha′s Vine′yard (mär′tház vĭn′yĕrd). Island ab. 20 m. long in Atlantic Ocean off SW coast of Cape Cod, SE Massachusetts, bet. Elizabeth Is. to the W and Nantucket to the E; part of Dukes co., Mass.; summer resort. Chief town Edgartown, on E coast.

Mar·tí′ (mär·tē′). Municipality and town, Matanzas prov., W cen. Cuba, near N coast 19 m. E of Cárdenas; pop. (town) 5060.

Mar′ti·gny′ (mär′tē′nyē′); Ger. **Mar′ti·nach** (mär′tē·näk′). Two communes, Valais canton, SW cen. Switzerland, near the Rhone where it makes a sharp turn

from SW to NW: (1) **Mar′ti·gny′–Ville′** (-vēl′); Ger. **Mar′ti·nach–Fleck′en** (-flĕk′ĕn); anc. **Oc′to·du′rus** (ŏk′tô·dūr′ŭs). Commune, 16 m. SW of Sion; pop. (1930) 2757; ancient aqueduct (remodeled 1882); ruins of 13th-cent. episcopal castle; made episcopal see in 4th cent. (later suppressed). (2) **Mar′ti·gny′–Bourg′** (-bōōr′); Ger. **Mar′ti·nach–Burg′** (-bōōrк′). Commune, just SW of Martigny-Ville; pop. (1930) 1555.

Mar′tigues′ (mär′tēg′) or **Les Martigues** (lā); anc. **Ma·rit′i·ma A·vat′i·co′rum** (má·rĭt′ĭ·má á·vǎt′ĭ·kôr′ŭm). Commune, Bouches-du-Rhône dept., SE France, on Mediterranean 18 m. NW of Marseilles; pop. 10,489; manufactures chemicals. Important during Middle Ages; formerly important fishing port; sometimes called "la Venise provençale," i.e., the Provençal Venice.

Mar′tin (mär′t′n; -tĭn). **1** Name of counties in six states of the U.S. See *Tables* at FLORIDA, INDIANA, KENTUCKY, MINNESOTA, NORTH CAROLINA, TEXAS. **2** City, ⊗ of Bennett co., S South Dakota; pop. 1184. **3** City, Weakley co., NW Tennessee, 31 m. W of Paris; pop. 4750; in agricultural section.

Martinach. See MARTIGNY.

Mar·ti′na Fran′ca (mär·tē′nä fräng′kä). Commune, Ionio prov., Apulia, SE Italy, 21 m. NNE of Taranto; pop. 32,629; baroque palace (built 1668).

Mar′tin Dam (mär′t′n; -tĭn). Dam completed 1926 across Tallapoosa river, E cen. Alabama; height 180 ft.; impounds water for power, forming **Martin Lake** in Elmore, Tallapoosa, and Coosa cos.

Mar·ti′nez (mär·tē′nĕs). Industrial city, ⊗ of Contra Costa co., W California, on Suisun Bay 18 m. NE of Oakland; pop. 9604; settled 1849; made ⊗ 1850; petroleum refineries; copper-smelting works; vertical lift bridge across Suisun Bay (horizontal clearance 291.5 ft.).

Mar·tín′ Gar·cí′a (mär·tēng′ gär·sē′ä). Island in the mouth of the Río de la Plata, off SW coast of Uruguay.

Mar′ti·nique′ (mär′t′n·ēk′; Fr. mår·tē′nēk′). Island, Windward Is., E West Indies; 385 sq. m.; pop. (1936) 246,712; constitutes a department of France; ✳ Fort-de-France. Mountainous; volcano of Mt. Pelée (q.v.) in N and Carbet (3960 ft.) in NW cen. part; has many rivers; large inlet, Fort-de-France Bay, on N shore of which is the capital Fort-de-France. Exports sugar (chief industry), rum, bananas, cacao. Probably discovered by Columbus; became French colony 1635; attacked by Dutch and British in 17th cent.; captured by Rodney 1762 but restored; by French constitution of 1946 made an overseas department of France. Birthplace of Empress Josephine.

Mar′tin′puich′ (mår′tǎn′pü·ēsh′). Village, Pas-de-Calais dept., N France, 6 m. NE of Albert; battle Sept. 15, 1916.

Mar′tins·burg (mär′t′nz·bûrg; -tĭnz-). Industrial city, ⊗ of Berkeley co., NE West Virginia, in E panhandle; pop. 15,179; fruit growing and packing (esp. apples, peaches); limestone quarries. Chartered as town 1778, as city c. 1859; important point in Shenandoah valley military operations (1861–63) during Civil War.

Mar′tins Ferry (mär′t′nz; -tĭnz). City, Belmont co., E Ohio, on Ohio river 19 m. S of Steubenville; pop. 11,919; settled before 1785; steel and soft-coal center.

Mar′tins·ville (mär′t′nz·vĭl; -tĭnz-). **1** City, ⊗ of Morgan co., cen. Indiana, 28 m. SW of Indianapolis; pop. 7525; health resort, with therapeutic artesian springs. **2** Industrial city, ⊗ of Henry co., S Virginia, but politically independent, 32 m. W of Danville; 2 sq. m.; pop. 18,798; founded as county seat 1793; manufactures furniture, textiles and knit goods.

Már′ti·res del Rí′o Blan′co y E. Za·pa′ta (mär′tē·räz thĕl rē′ô vläng′kô ē ä′ sä·pä′tä). Town, Federal District, cen. Mexico; pop. 6150.

Mar′ton (mär′t′n). Borough, Wellington provincial dist., S North I., New Zealand, 90 m. NNE of Wellington; pop. ab. 3000.

Mar′tos (mär′tŏs). Commune, Jaén prov., S Spain, 14 m. SW of Jaén; pop. 27,131; mineral baths; manufactures textiles, wax, flour, pottery; stock raising.

Mar′tre, Lac la (låk′ lä mär′tr′). Lake 1225 sq. m., S cen. Mackenzie District, Northwest Territories, Canada; its outlet flows SE to Great Slave Lake.

Ma·ru′du Bay (mä·rōō′dōō). Inlet, N Brit. North Borneo, S of Balabac Strait; airport at its S end.

Ma·ru·ga·me (mä·rōō·gä·mĕ). City, Kagawa prefecture, Shikoku I., Japan, on N coast on Inland Sea W of Takamatsu; pop. 30,304.

Ma′ru·té′a (mä′rōō·tā′ä). Large atoll of the Tuamotu Archipelago, S Pacific Ocean, ab. 125 m. E of Fakarava.

Mar′vine, Mount (mär′vĭn). Peak 11,002 ft. in Sevier co., cen. Utah.

Marwar. See JODHPUR.

Marxstadt. See MARKSSHTADT.

Mar′y Island (mâr′ĭ). See CANTON ISLAND.

Ma·ry′ (mä·rĭ′). **1** Region, subdivision in SE part of Turkmen S.S.R., Soviet Central Asia.

2 *formerly* **Merv** (mĕrv). Town, its ✻, in an oasis on Murghab river 180 m. E of Ashkhabad; pop. 19,099; center of rich cotton-producing region. A town of great antiquity, in Hindu, Parsi, and Arab tradition believed to be the ancient Paradise, hence the original home (Mouru) of the Aryan families and hence of the human race; center of a province (Margiana) of ancient kingdoms; under Arabs (646–874); overrun by Turks 1040, and conquered by Mongols 1221; occupied by Russians 1883.

Mar′y·bor·ough (mâr′ĭ·bŭ·rŭ, -brŭ). **1** Town, SE Queensland, Australia, on Mary river 140 m. N of Brisbane; pop. 11,414; markets coal, timber, cattle, sheep, grains, and sugar; foundries, railroad shops.

2 Town, cen. Victoria, SE Australia, 85 m. NW of Melbourne; pop. 5631; center of gold-mining region.

3 *or* **Port Laoigh′i·se** (pôrt lā′ĭ·shĕ). Town, ⊗ of co. Laoighis, cen. Eire, on Triogue river; pop. 3396; remnant of old castle.

Mar′y Hen′ry, Mount (mâr′ĭ hĕn′rĭ). Peak 9500 ft. in Rocky Mts., N British Columbia, Canada, S of Liard river.

Mar′y·land (mĕr′ĭ·lănd). **1** A middle Atlantic state of U.S.A., one of original states of the Union, the 7th to ratify the Federal Constitution (Apr. 28, 1788); bounded on N by Pennsylvania, on E by Delaware and the Atlantic Ocean, on S by Virginia and West Virginia, and on W by West Virginia; 42d state in area, 10,577 sq. m. (land area 9881 sq. m.); 21st state in population, 3,100,689; ✻ Annapolis. See *Table of States* at UNITED STATES. Divided into the following 23 counties (for pronunciation of their names, see their individual entries):

NAME	LOCATION	AREA[1]	POP.[1]	CO. SEAT
Allegany	NW	426	84,169	Cumberland
Anne Arundel	cen.	417	206,634	Annapolis
Baltimore	N	610[2]	492,428	Towson
Baltimore city[3]		79	939,024	
Calvert	S	219	15,826	Prince Frederick
Caroline	E	320	19,462	Denton
Carroll	N	456	52,785	Westminster
Cecil	NE corner	352	48,408	Elkton
Charles	S	458	32,572	La Plata
Dorchester	SE	580	29,666	Cambridge
Frederick	N	664	71,930	Frederick
Garrett	NW corner	662	20,420	Oakland
Harford	NE	448	76,722	Bel Air
Howard	cen.	251	36,152	Ellicott City
Kent	NE	284	15,481	Chestertown
Montgomery	cen.	494	340,928	Rockville
Prince Georges	S cen.	485	357,395	Upper Marlboro
Queen Annes	E	373	16,569	Centreville
Saint Marys	S	367	38,915	Leonardtown
Somerset	SE	332	19,623	Princess Anne
Talbot	E	279	21,578	Easton
Washington	N	462	91,219	Hagerstown
Wicomico	SE	380	49,050	Salisbury
Worcester	SE; coastal	483	23,733	Snow Hill

[1] Area = land area in sq. m. Pop. from 1960 Census.
[2] Exclusive of city of Baltimore which is administratively independent of the county.
[3] Administratively independent of Baltimore co. and has itself the status of a county.

Nickname: Old Line State, also Cockade State. *State flower:* Blackeyed Susan. *Motto:* Fatti Maschii, Parole Femine (Deeds Masculine, Words Feminine). *Chief cities:* Baltimore, Hagerstown, Cumberland. *Rivers:* Potomac, forming S boundary; Patuxent, flowing SE into Chesapeake Bay; Susquehanna, flowing across NE corner into headwaters of Chesapeake Bay. *Highest point:* Backbone Mt. 3360 ft. in Garrett co. *Chief industries:* Agriculture, clothing manufacture, fishing.

History: Granted to George Calvert (Lord Baltimore) as proprietary colony 1632; first American colony to achieve religious freedom; first settled at St. Marys 1634, which was its capital 1634–94; a royal colony 1689–1715; its boundary with Pennsylvania, in dispute from 1681, settled by drawing of Mason and Dixon's Line 1763–69; first constitutional convention Aug. 14–Nov. 11, 1776; adopted Articles of Confederation 1781; ceded territory for District of Columbia (*q.v.*); invaded by Confederate forces 1862; abolished slavery 1864; adopted present constitution 1867. See BALTIMORE.

2 The southernmost county of Liberia, W Africa; set up as an independent African state 1833 by Negroes from the United States; annexed to Liberia 1857.

Marylebone. = *Saint Marylebone* metropolitan borough of London: see *Table* at LONDON.

Mar′yl·hurst (mär′ĭl·hûrst). Suburb of Oregon City, Oregon; Marylhurst Coll. (1893; women; Rom. Cath.).

Mar′y·port (mâr′ĭ·pōrt). Urban district, Cumberland, NW England, on Solway Firth at mouth of the Ellen, 28 m. SW of Carlisle; pop. 12,237.

Mar′ys·vale Peak (mâr′ĭz·vāl). Mountain 10,359 ft. in Piute co., S cen. Utah.

Mar′ys·ville (mâr′ĭz·vĭl). **1** City, ⊗ of Yuba co., N cen. California, 42 m. N of Sacramento; pop. 9553; fruit and vegetable processing. Trading post 1842; incorporated as city 1851.

2 City, ⊗ of Marshall co., NE Kansas, 45 m. N of Manhattan on Big Blue River; pop. 4143; on the old Oregon Trail; now a railroad center in a grain, livestock, and dairy section.

3 City, St. Clair co., SE Michigan, on St. Clair river 5 m. S of Port Huron; pop. 4065; manufactures motor boats and automobile parts; salt deposits.

4 Village, ⊗ of Union co., Ohio, 27 m. NW of Columbus; pop. 4952; ships grass seed, cattle, sheep, hogs.

5 Borough, Perry co., S cen. Pennsylvania, on Susquehanna river 8 m. N of Harrisburg; pop. 2580.

6 Town, Snohomish co., NW cen. Washington, on Puget Sound 5 m. N of Everett; pop. 3117; manufactures boats, shingles, lumber; supply center for fishing resorts.

7 Town, York co., SW New Brunswick, Canada, 5 m. N of Fredericton; pop. 2152; cotton and lumber mills.

Maryût. See Lake MAREOTIS.

Mar′y·ville (mâr′ĭ·vĭl; *Sou. also* -v′l). **1** City, ⊗ of Nodaway co., NW Missouri, 42 m. N of St. Joseph; pop. 7807; Northwest Missouri State College (1905; coed.).

2 City, ⊗ of Blount co., E Tennessee, near Great Smoky Mts. National Park 15 m. S of Knoxville; pop. 10,348; lumber, hosiery; marble, limestone, slate, dolomite, sandstone quarries. Maryville Coll. (1819; coed.).

Mar′zo, Cape (mär′sŏ). Cape on NW coast of Colombia, extending into Pacific Ocean.

Ma·sa′da (må·sä′då). Fortified town on W shore at S end of Dead Sea, SE Judaea, Palestine; last stand of Jews against Romans 72 A.D.

Más A·fue′ra (mäs ä·fwä′rä). An island of the Juan Fernández group. See JUAN FERNÁNDEZ.

Ma·sai′ (må·sī′). Extraprovincial district, S Kenya, E Africa; 15,232 sq. m.; pop. 48,945; ✻ Ngong; native reserve.

Ma·san (mä·sän); *formerly* **Ma·sam·po** (mä·säm·pō). Seaport city, South Keisho prov., SE Korea, at head of an inlet of Chosen Strait 26 m. W of Pusan; pop. 29,858; a commercial and industrial center; opened to foreign trade 1899.

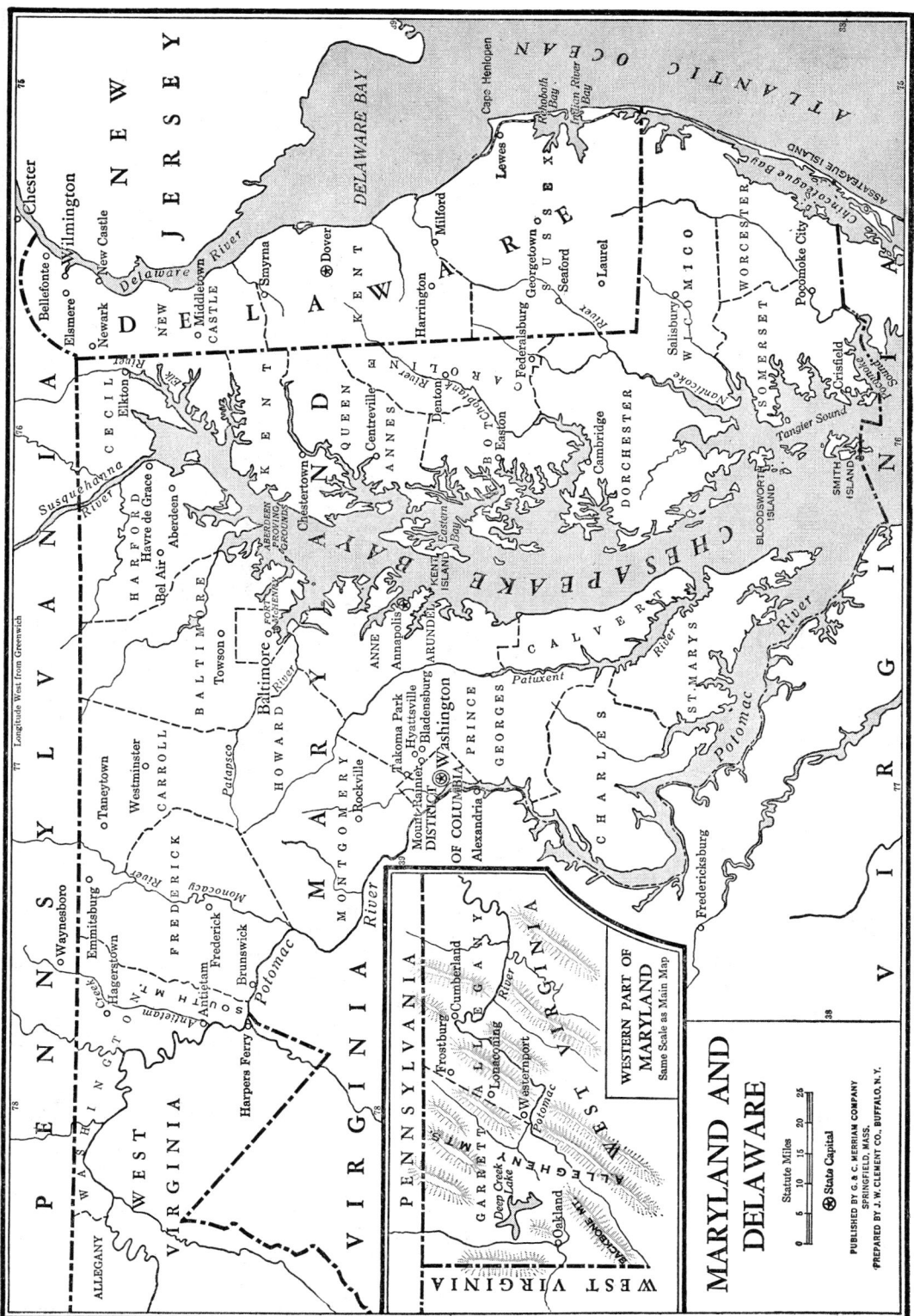

MARYLAND AND DELAWARE

PUBLISHED BY G. & C. MERRIAM COMPANY
SPRINGFIELD, MASS.
PREPARED BY J. W. CLEMENT CO., BUFFALO, N.Y.

Statute Miles
5 10 15 20 25

⊕ State Capital

WESTERN PART OF
MARYLAND
Same Scale as Main Map

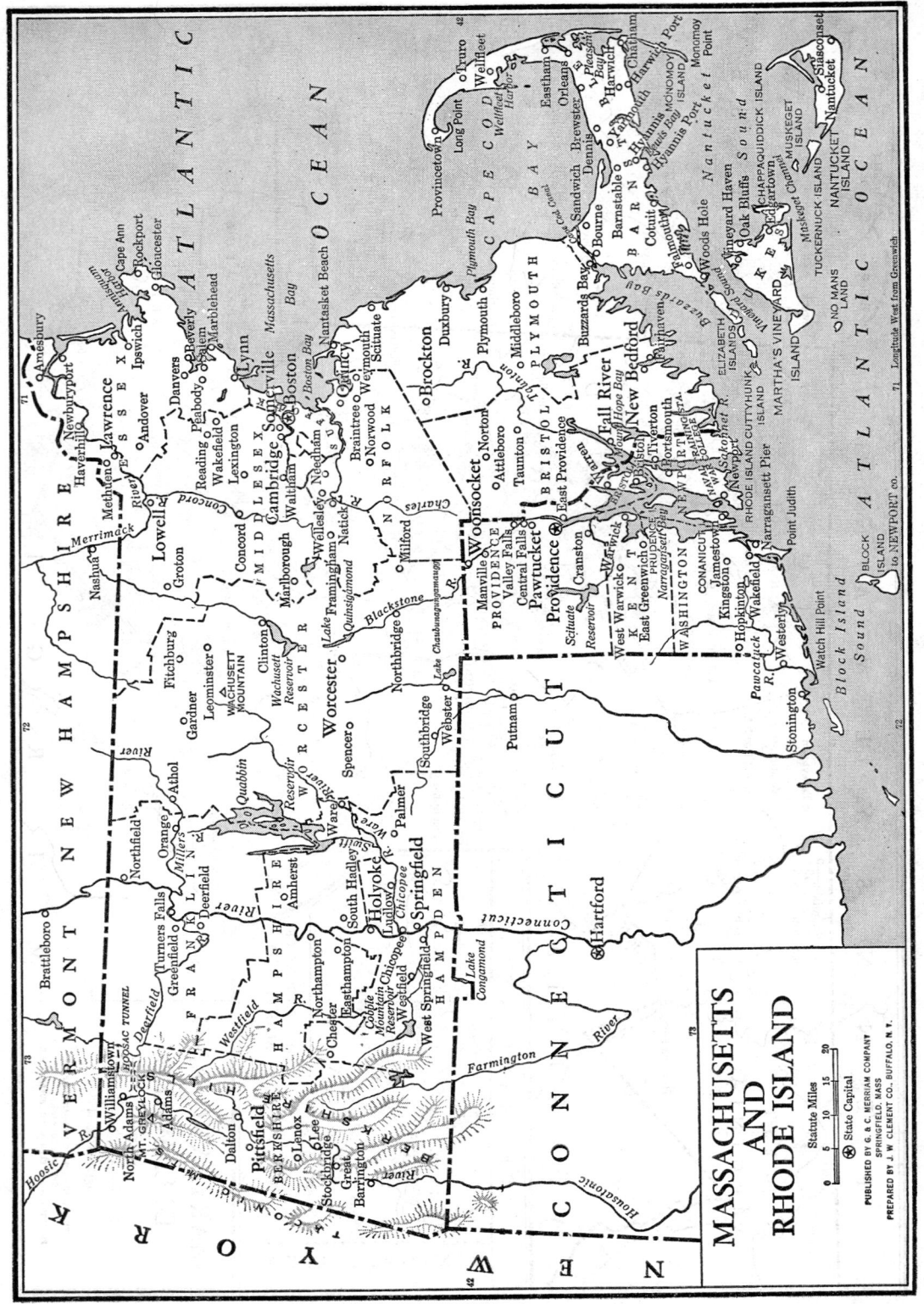

MASSACHUSETTS
AND
RHODE ISLAND

Statute Miles

⊛ State Capital

PUBLISHED BY G. & C. MERRIAM COMPANY
SPRINGFIELD, MASS.
PREPARED BY J. W. CLEMENT CO. BUFFALO, N.Y.

Masandam, Ras. See Cape MUSANDAM.

Mas'a·ryk Peak (măs'à·rĭk; *Czech* má'sá-). = GERLS-DORFER SPITZE.

Más a Tier'ra (más' ä tyĕr'rä). An island of the Juan Fernández group. See JUAN FERNÁNDEZ.

Ma·sa'ya (mä·sä'yä). **1** Department, SW Nicaragua; 232 sq. m.; pop. (1943 est.) 75,680.

2 Town, its *; pop. (1943 est.) 22,722; 4th largest city in Nicaragua; center of rich agricultural district; tobacco-growing center; known as the "City of Flowers."

Mas·ba'te (mäs·bä'tå). **1** Island and province in Visayan Is., cen. Phil. Is., S of SE Luzon; 1571 sq. m.; pop. 182,483; * Masbate. Formerly a subprovince of Sorsogon from which it is separated by Ticao Pass and Ticao I.; on the E borders on Samar Sea, on the S on Visayan Sea, and on the W on Sibuyan Sea; separated from NE Panay by Jintotolo Channel. Covered with mountains ranging from 1200 to 2000 ft. As province includes Burias I. and Ticao I. Produces sugar cane, cotton, hemp, and some rice; noted for its cattle and horses. Chief towns Masbate, Cataingan, Aroroy, Milagros, Dimasalang.

History: Explored by Spaniards in latter half of 16th cent.; long a part of Albay prov.; made separate comandancia 1846; under Americans received civil government Mar. 1901 and made subprovince of Sorsogon; created a province 1939; invaded by Americans Apr. 1945.

2 Municipality, * of Masbate prov., Phil. Is., on E coast of Masbate I. opp. Ticao I.; pop. 23,312; port of entry.

Mas·ca·ra (mäs'kå·rå: *Arab.* -kŭ·rö). Commune, N cen. Oran dept., NW Algeria, 60 m. SE of Oran; pop. (1936) 31,842; built on a mountain slope at alt. 1800 ft.; chief industry making of wine; has trade in grains and oil. Importance increased when it became headquarters of Abd-el-Kader 1832; captured twice by French, 1835 and 1841, and considerably damaged.

Mas·ca·rene Islands (mäs'kå·rēn). Group of islands in the Indian Ocean, bet. 400 and 500 m. E of Madagascar, comprising Réunion, Mauritius, and Rodriguez (qq.v.).

Mas'co·ma Lake (mäs'kŏ·má). Lake in SW Grafton co., W New Hampshire.

Mas'cot (mäs'kŏt). **1** Town, Knox co., E Tennessee, ab. 10 m. NE of Knoxville; pop. (est.) 1500; zinc mines.

2 Town, E New South Wales, SE Australia, on N shore of Botany Bay; S suburb of Sydney; pop. 14,363.

Mas·cou'tah (mäs·kōō'tá). City, St. Clair co., SW Illinois, 23 m. ESE of East St. Louis; pop. 3625.

Mas d'Azil, Le. See LE MAS D'AZIL.

Mas'e·ru (măz'ĕr·ōō). Town, * of Basutoland, South Africa, on Caledon river just S of Ladybrand, Orange Free State, and ab. 82 m. E of Bloemfontein; pop. 3712.

Mash·ad'–i–Murgh·ab' (mäsh·häd'ē·mōōr·gäb') ; *formerly* **Murghab.** Town, N Fars prov., SW Iran; site of Pasargadae (q.v.).

Ma'sher·brum (mŭ'shĕr·brōōm). Peak 25,660 ft. in the Karakoram Range of the Himalayas, N Kashmir, N India, SW of Mt. Godwin Austen (K²).

Mashhad. See MESHED.

Mash·kel' (mäsh·kĕl'). River in SE Iran and W Baluchistan region of West Pakistan; rises in SE Iran, flows in a curve E across Baluchistan boundary, NE, and finally NW into Hamun-i-Mashkel.

Mashkel Lake. = HAMUN-I-MASHKEL.

Ma·sho'na·land' (mä·shō'nå·länd'). Province, NE Southern Rhodesia, S Africa; 80,236 sq. m.; pop. (white) 26,130; * Salisbury. Region is open plain and fertile tableland, rich in gold, inhabited by Mashonas, a Bantu race; acquired by British South Africa Company 1890; became part of colony of Southern Rhodesia 1923. Chief towns Salisbury, Hartley, Gatooma, Umtali.

Ma·sia'ti (mä·syä'tĕ). Peak ab. 4900 ft. in S cen. Venezuela, near Brazil border.

Masikesi. See MACEQUECE.

Ma·sin'di (má·sĭn'dĭ). Town, W cen. Uganda, E Africa, E of Lake Albert.

Ma'sin·loc' (mä'sĕn·lôk'). Town on coast, W Zambales prov., W Luzon, Phil. Is., ab. 16 m. N of Iba; in foothills of W slope of Zambales Mts. behind the town is one of the richest chromite deposits in the world.

Ma·si'rah (mä·sē'rŏ). Island 44 m. long in the Arabian Sea, off E coast of Oman, SE Arabia, 150 m. S of Cape Hadd; administratively attached to Oman.

Masis. See ARARAT.

Mas·jid'–i–Su'lai·man' (mäs·jĭd'ĕ·sōō'lĭ·män'). Locality, one of the important oil fields of W Iran, in S Zagros Mts. ab. 60 m. NE of Ahwaz and near Maidan-i-Naftun; has oil pipeline to Ahwaz.

Mask, Lough (lŏk mäsk'). Lake 35 sq. m. in S co. Mayo, W Ireland.

Maskat. Var. of MASQAT.

Mas'ki·non'gé' (mäs'kē'nôn'zhā'). County, Quebec, Canada. See *Table* at QUEBEC.

Ma'son (mā's'n). **1** Name of counties in six states of the U.S. See *Tables* at ILLINOIS, KENTUCKY, MICHIGAN, TEXAS, WASHINGTON, WEST VIRGINIA.

2 City, ⊗ of Ingham co., S Michigan, 12 m. S of Lansing; pop. 4522.

3 City, ⊗ of Mason co., cen. Texas; pop. 1910.

Mason and Dix'on's Line (dĭk's'nz), *also* **Ma'son-Dix'on Line** (-dĭk's'n). The S boundary line of Pennsylvania, run (except for its westernmost 36 m.) by two English astronomers, Charles Mason and Jeremiah Dixon, bet. 1763 and 1767 to settle an old boundary dispute bet. proprietors of Pennsylvania and Maryland; its W part accepted 1784 as boundary bet. Virginia and Pennsylvania; became famous at time of Missouri Compromise 1820 as part of boundary bet. free and slave states; name later popularly applied to boundary bet. northern and southern states.

Mason City. 1 City, Mason co., cen. Illinois, 28 m. N of Springfield; pop. 2160; coal and clay deposits.

2 City, ⊗ of Cerro Gordo co., N Iowa, 62 m. NW of Waterloo; pop. 30,642; railroad and industrial center in agricultural section; manufactures brick, cement, tiles, beet sugar, meat products.

3 Former town, Okanogan co., N Washington, on right bank of Columbia river at Grand Coulee Dam; consolidated with town of Coulee Dam 1943.

Ma'sons Island (mā's'nz). Island in the harbor of Mystic, Connecticut, off SE coast of New London co.

Ma'son·town (mā's'n·toun). Borough, Fayette co., SW Pennsylvania, on Monongahela river 11 m. W of Uniontown; pop. 4730.

Mas'qat (mŭs'kăt; *Arab.* mŏs'kŏt) *or* **Mus'cat.** Seaport town, SE Arabia, on the S coast of the Gulf of Oman and on Tropic of Cancer; * of Oman; pop. ab. 4200; on a small peninsula with steep mountain range behind it; its N suburb Matrah is starting point for land routes. Exports dates, dried fish, and mother-of-pearl. From early 16th cent. to 1622 an unimportant Portuguese port, but became their Arabian headquarters 1622–48 after loss of Hormuz; held by Persians 1650–1741; then became a sultanate, esp. powerful during middle of 19th cent.; its capital 1832–56 was at Zanzibar. See PERSIAN GULF RESIDENCY.

Masqat and Oman. See OMAN.

Mas'sa (mäs'sä). Former commune, * of Massa e Carrara (now Apuania) prov., Tuscany, Italy; now part of commune of Apuania (q.v.).

Mas'sac (măs'ăk). County in Illinois. See *Table* at ILLINOIS.

Mas·sa·chu'setts (mäs'å·chōō'sĕts; -sĭts; -zĕts; -zĭts). A northeast state of U.S.A., one of original states of the Union, the 6th to ratify the Federal Constitution (Feb. 6, 1788); bounded on N by Vermont and New Hampshire, on E by the Atlantic Ocean, on S by the Atlantic Ocean, Rhode Island, and Connecticut, and on W by New York; 45th state in area, 8257 sq. m. (land area 7867 sq. m.); 9th state in population, 5,148,578; * Boston. See *Table of States* at UNITED STATES. Divided into

the following 14 counties (for pronunciation of their names, see their individual entries):

NAME	LOCATION	AREA[1]	POP.[1]	CO. SEAT
Barnstable[2]	SE; coastal	399	70,286	Barnstable
Berkshire	W	942	142,135	Pittsfield
Bristol	SE; coastal	556	398,488	Fall River, Taunton, New Bedford
Dukes[3]	SE; insular	106	5,829	Edgartown
Essex	NE corner; coastal	500	568,831	Salem, Newburyport, Lawrence
Franklin	NW	707	54,864	Greenfield
Hampden	SW	621	429,353	Springfield
Hampshire	W	528	103,229	Northampton
Middlesex	NE	829	1,238,742	Lowell, Cambridge
Nantucket[4]	SE; insular	46	3,559	Nantucket
Norfolk[5]	E; coastal	398	510,256	Dedham
Plymouth	SE; coastal	664	248,449	Plymouth
Suffolk	E; coastal	55	791,329	Boston
Worcester	cen.	1516	583,228	Worcester, Fitchburg

[1] Area = land area in sq. m. Pop. from 1960 Census.
[2] Coextensive with Cape Cod (q.v.).
[3] Comprises Martha's Vineyard, Elizabeth Is., and other islands.
[4] Comprises Nantucket I. and a few islets.
[5] Comprises a main area whose NE corner borders Boston Bay and two smaller areas separated from main area: one on Massachusetts Bay and surrounded on landward side by Plymouth co., the other enclosed by Middlesex and Suffolk cos.

Nickname: Bay State, also Old Bay State, Old Colony State. *State flower:* Mayflower. *Motto:* Ense Petit Placidam Sub Libertate Quietem (With the Sword She Seeks Calm Repose under Liberty). *Chief cities:* Boston, Worcester, Springfield, Cambridge, New Bedford, Fall River. *Rivers:* Connecticut, flowing N to S across W cen. part of state; Taunton, in SE, flowing into arm of Narragansett Bay; Merrimack, in extreme NE, flowing into Atlantic Ocean. *Highest point:* Greylock 3491 ft. in Berkshire co. *Chief industries:* Manufacturing (boots, shoes, cotton and woolen fabrics, paper, electrical machinery), fishing (cod, haddock, mackerel).

History: Coast skirted by Verrazano 1524; Cape Cod discovered by Gosnold 1602 who made first (temporary) settlement within present limits of state; Plymouth (q.v.) settled by Pilgrims 1620; a charter colony, founded and governed by Massachusetts Bay Co. 1629–84; Harvard College founded 1636; joined New England Confederation 1643; acquired province of Maine 1652; after loss of first charter 1684, governed as part of Dominion of New England 1686; by its second charter 1691, received confirmation to Maine and to Plymouth (qq.v.) colonies; in 18th cent., gradually became a center of resistance to imperial colonial policy (see BOSTON); evacuated by British troops after Lexington and Concord 1775; battle of Bunker Hill 1775; gave up claims to western lands 1785–86; western Massachusetts scene of Shays' Rebellion 1786–87; eastern Massachusetts early center of American cotton manufacture (see WALTHAM). Maine became separate state 1820.

Massachusetts Bay. Inlet of Atlantic Ocean on E coast of Massachusetts, ab. 50 m. long by 25 m. wide, extending from Cape Ann on the N to Strawberry Point on the S; the city of Boston is situated at its W end.

Mas·sa·cre Bay (măs′á·kĕr). Inlet on SE coast of Attu I. in the Aleutians, Alaska; landing here of American troops led to defeat of Japanese May–June 1943.

Mas·sa e Car·ra·ra (mäs′sä ā kär·rä′rä). Former name of *Apuania* prov.: see *Table* at ITALY.

Mas·sa′fra (mäs·sä′frä). Commune, Ionio prov., Apulia, SE Italy, 9 m. NW of Taranto; pop. 13,388.

Mas′sa Ma·rit′ti·ma (mäs′sä mä·rêt′tē·mä). Commune, Grosseto prov., Tuscany, cen. Italy, 24 m. NNW of Grosseto; pop. 14,999; 13th-cent. cathedral and town hall; in mining region (copper, iron, lead, and silver).

Mas′sa·nut′ten, or **Mas′a·nut′ton, Mountain** (măs′á·nŭt′′n). Mountain ridge, N Virginia, in Blue Ridge, bet. North and South Forks of Shenandoah river.

Mas′sa·pe′qua (măs′á·pē′kwá). Village and resort, Nassau co., SE New York, on S shore of Long I., ab. 10 m. SE of Mineola; pop. 32,900.

Massapequa Park. Village, Nassau co., SE New York, on Long I.; pop. 19,904.

Mas′sa·ro′sa (mäs′sä·rô′zä). Commune, Lucca prov., Tuscany, cen. Italy, 9 m. W of Lucca; pop. 12,546.

Mas·sa′ua (má·sä′wá; -sou′á) or **Mas·sa′wa** (má·sä′wä). Fortified seaport, Eritrea, NE Africa, on the **Bay of Massaua** (inlet of the Red Sea), situated partly on an island, partly on the mainland; pop. 17,169; pearl fishing.

Mas·se′na (má·sē′ná). Manufacturing village, St. Lawrence co., N New York, in town of Massena (pop. 17,730) near St. Lawrence river 31 m. W of Malone; pop. 15,478; in farming, dairying region; ships milk and cream, esp. to New York City; produces aluminum and mica products, pulp and paper, silk, milk powder.

Mas·sén′ya (mä·sän′yá). Town, SW Chad, N cen. Africa, on a tributary of the Chari; * of Baguirmi before its destruction 1898.

Massiaf. See MASYAF.

Mas′si·cault′ (má′sē′kō′). Town, N Tunisia, N Africa, ab. 12 m. SW of Tunis on the road bet. Tunis and Medjez-el-Bab; taken by British May 6, 1943.

Mas′si·cus (măs′ĭ·kŭs); *Ital.* **Mas′si·co** (mäs′sē·kō). Mountain ridge bet. ancient Campania and Latium, Italy, NW of Capua near shore of Gulf of Gaeta; noted for wine (*Massic*).

Mas′sif′ Cen′tral′ (má′sēf′ säN′träl′). Plateau region ab. 33,000 sq. m. of SE cen. France; highest point Puy de Sancy 6185 ft. of the Monts Dore; centers in departments of Cantal, Haute-Loire, and Aveyron; source of many streams, esp. Loire, Allier, Cher, and Creuse.

Massilia. See MARSEILLES.

Mas′sil·lon (măs′′l·ŭn). City, Stark co., NE Ohio, 8 m. W of Canton; pop. 31,236; coal mines, clay and sand pits; steel, aluminum products, heating equipment.

Mas′sive, Mount (măs′ĭv). Mountain 14,418 ft. in Lake co., cen. Colorado, in Sawatch Range; 2d highest mountain in Colorado.

Mas·sow′a (má·sou′á). Var. of MASSAUA.

Mastanli. See MOMTCHILOVGRAD.

Mas′ter·ton (măs′tĕr·tŭn; -t′n). Borough, Wellington provincial dist., S North I., New Zealand, 50 m. ENE of Wellington; pop. (1941 est.) 9480.

Ma·su·ka·wa (mä·sŏō·kä·wä). See PARAMUSHIRO.

Ma′su·li·pa′tam (mŭ′sŭ·lĭ·pŭt′ám) or **Ma′su·li·pat′nam** (mŭ′sŭ·lĭ·pŭt′nám) or **Ban′dar** (bŭn′dĕr). Seaport city, NE Andhra Pradesh, India, on Bay of Bengal on one of the mouths of Kistna river, 215 m. NNE of Madras; pop. 77,953; the port only an open roadstead; Noble College of the Church Missionary Society. British agency established here 1611, earliest British settlement on Coromandel Coast; British expelled by French in wars of the Carnatic; retaken by British 1759; destroyed by a cyclone and flood 1864 with loss of 30,000 lives.

Ma·su′ri·a (má·zŏōr′ĭ·á; -sŏŏr′-); *Ger.* **Ma·su′ren** (mä·zŏō′rĕn). Region in S part of former East Prussia, Germany, mostly in Allenstein govt. dist.; includes **Ma·su′ri·an Lakes,** scene of battles in World War I resulting in defeats for the Russian armies: Sept. 6–12, 1914, and (Suwałki) Feb. 7–14, 1915. Lake region under Russian control Jan. 1945; assigned to Poland by Potsdam Conference 1945 (see MAZURY).

Mas·yaf′ or **Mas·siaf′** (mäs·yäf′). Mountain stronghold, E Latakia, Syria, at S end of Djebel Ansariya; in 12th cent. became chief seat of Syrian branch of the Assassins; taken 1272 by the Mameluke sultan Baybars.

Mat′a·be′le·land′ (măt′á·bē′lĕ·länd′). Province, SW Southern Rhodesia, S Africa; 70,118 sq. m.; pop. (white) 23,534; chief town Bulawayo. Lies bet. the Limpopo and Zambezi rivers; rich in gold. Inhabited by Matabele, a Zulu race of the Bantu nation driven out of Natal 1827 and from Transvaal 1837; came under British South Africa Co. 1889; became part of Southern Rhodesia 1923. Chief towns Bulawayo, Gwelo, Selukwe.

Mat'a Bi'a (măt'á bē'á). Mountain 7710 ft., E Portuguese Timor, Malay Archipelago.

Ma·ta'di (má·tä'dĭ). Port near mouth of Congo river, W Léopoldville prov., W Congo; pop. (1938) 9110; most important port in Congo.

Mat'a·dor (măt'á·dōr; -dôr). Town, ⊗ of Motley co., NW Texas; pop. 1217.

Ma'ta·fa'o, Mount (mä'tá·fä'ŏ). Highest point 2141 ft. on Tutuila I., American Samoa, SW cen. Pacific.

Mat'a·gal'pa (măt'á·găl'pá; Span. mä'tä·gäl'pä). **1** Department, cen. Nicaragua; 3378 sq. m.; pop. (1943 est.) 123,284.

2 Town, its *, ab. 60 m. NNE of Managua; pop. (1943 est.) 9196; center of coffee-raising region; alt. 3000 ft.

Mat'a·gam'on Lake (măt'á·găm'ŭn). Lake on upper E boundary of Piscataquis co., N cen. Maine.

Mat'a·gor'da (măt'á·gôr'dá). County in Texas. See *Table* at TEXAS.

Matagorda Bay. Inlet of Gulf of Mexico 30 m. long, S Matagorda co. and E Calhoun co., SE Texas, receiving the Colorado river (of Texas) on the NE.

Matagorda Island. Island in Calhoun co., S Texas, lying bet. San Antonio Bay and the Gulf of Mexico.

Matagorda Peninsula. Narrow spit of land lying bet. Matagorda Bay and the Gulf of Mexico in Matagorda co., SE Texas.

Ma'ta·le (mŭ'tá·lä). Town, cen. Central Province, Ceylon, 14 m. N of Kandy; pop. 10,415; Buddhist monastery and temple of Alu Vihara 2 m. distant; center of cacao-growing area.

Mat'a·mo'ras (măt'á·mŏr'ăs). Borough and resort, Pike co., NE Pennsylvania, on Delaware river 52 m. E of Scranton; pop. 2087.

Mat'a·mo'ros (măt'á·mŏr'ōs; Span. mä'tä·mō'rōs). **1** Town, Coahuila state, NE Mexico, just E of Torreón; pop. 7962.

2 in full **I·zú'car de Ma'ta·mo'ros** (ē·sōō'kär thä mä'tä·mō'rōs). Town, Puebla state, SE cen. Mexico; pop. 7065.

3 Town, Tamaulipas state, E Mexico, on the Rio Grande 25 m. from its mouth and opp. Brownsville, Texas; pop. 15,699; chief exports coffee and hides. Founded ab. 1810; taken by Americans May 18, 1846 in Mexican War.

Ma·ta'na, Lake (má·tä'ná). Lake in mountainous region of cen. Celebes, Indonesia, near Lake Towuti; has been sounded to a depth of 1500 ft.

Ma'tane' (má'tän'; Angl. má·tăn'). **1** County, Gaspé Penin., SE Quebec, Canada; divided into **Matane** co., 1631 sq. m., pop. 30,243, ⊗ Matane, and **Ma'ta·pé'dia'** (má·tá'pä'dyá'; Angl. măt'á·pē'dĭ·á) co., 1751 sq. m., pop. 33,939, ⊗ Amqui.

2 Town, ⊗ of Matane co., on Gaspé Penin. on St. Lawrence river; pop. 6345; lumbering; port facilities.

Ma·ta'ni·kau' (mä·tä'nē·kou'). Short stream, NW coast of Guadalcanal I., SE Solomon Is., W Pacific; flows N to a point just E of Point Cruz and ab. 3 m. W of Lunga Point. Scene of severe battles Oct. 8–10 and Oct. 21, 1942.

Mat'a·nus'ka (măt'á·nōōs'ká). Village, S Alaska, on railroad ab. 30 m. NE of Anchorage at foot of valley of **Matanuska River** (ab. 90 m. long). See PALMER.

Ma·tan'za (má·tăn'zá; Span. mä·tän'sä). River in NE Buenos Aires prov., E Argentina; flows NE into Río de la Plata on S side of the city of Buenos Aires.

Ma·tan'zas (má·tăn'zás; Span. mä·tän'säs). **1** Province, W cen. Cuba. See *Table* at CUBA.

2 Municipality and city, its *, in NW part ab. 60 m. E of Havana; pop. (city) 49,591; has fine harbor, exports sugar. Founded 1693.

Matanzas Inlet. Passage connecting the Atlantic Ocean with the **Matanzas River** (a lagoon, NE Florida, S of St. Augustine) at S end of Anastasia I.; the lagoon, separating Anastasia I. from the mainland, contains a small island on which is located Fort Matanzas, built of coquina ab. 1736 by the Spaniards, and forming part of Fort Matanzas National Monument (see UNITED STATES, *National Monuments*).

Ma'ta·pa'lo, Cape (mä'tä·pä'lŏ). Cape on S tip of Osa Penin., S Costa Rica, W of Gulf of Dulce.

Mat'a·pan, Cape (măt'á·păn); Mod. Gr. **Taí'na·ron** (tä'nä·rôn); anc. **Tae'na·rum** (tē'ná·rŭm). Southernmost point of mainland of Greece, 36°22′N, at tip of cen. peninsula of Peloponnesus. Naval battle nearby Mar. 28, 1941 in which British sank three Italian cruisers and two destroyers and damaged a battleship.

Ma'ta·pé'dia' (má·tá'pä'dyá'; Angl. măt'á·pē'dĭ·á). **1** River ab. 60 m. long in Matapédia and Bonaventure cos., W Gaspé Penin., SE Canada; flows SE out of **Lake Matapédia** into Restigouche river.

2 See MATANE.

Ma'ta·ra (mä'tá·rá). Town, S Southern Province, Ceylon, on Indian Ocean 24 m. E of Galle; pop. 18,893; in district rich in coconut palms and cinnamon trees; has old Portuguese fort.

Ma·ta'ram (mä·tä'räm). **1** See LOMBOK.

2 Mohammedan sultanate in Malay Archipelago, founded 1582 and at height of its power in 17th cent., controlling all of Java except Bantam and E tip, and SE Borneo. Overcome by Dutch by 1755 and divided bet. principalities of Surakarta and Jogjakarta.

Ma'ta·ra'ni (mä'tá·rä'nē). Seaport town, S Peru, ab. 8 m. NW of Mollendo.

Mataríya, El. See EL MATARÍYA.

Ma'ta·ró' (mä'tá·rō'). Manufacturing commune and seaport, Barcelona prov., NE Spain, on Mediterranean 15 m. NE of Barcelona; pop. 29,920.

Ma·ta'ta (má·tä'tá). Village on Bay of Plenty, W of mouth of Rangitaiki river, Auckland provincial dist., N North I., New Zealand.

Ma'ta·tie'le (mä'tá·tyä'lá). Town, NE Cape Province, S Union of South Africa, 138 m. WSW of Durban; pop. 2653.

Ma·tau'ra (má·tou'rá). **1** River 120 m. long in S South I., New Zealand; flows S into Foveaux Strait E of Invercargill.

2 Borough, Southland subdivision of Otago provincial dist., S South I., New Zealand, on Mataura river 27 m. NE of Invercargill; pop. 1290.

Mat'a·wan (măt'á·wŏn). Borough, Monmouth co., E cen. New Jersey, 7 m. S of Perth Amboy; pop. 5097; electroplating supplies, pottery.

Ma'te·hua'la (mä'tä·wä'lä). Town, San Luis Potosí state, cen. Mexico, 100 m. N of San Luis Potosí; pop. 16,548; mining center.

Ma·te'ra (mä·tä'rä). **1** Province of Italy. See *Table* at ITALY.

2 Commune, its *, Lucania, S Italy, 126 m. E by S of Naples; pop. 22,069; 13th-cent. cathedral; castle; museum of antiquities; prehistoric artifacts found nearby.

Matesian Mountains, Ital. **Matese.** Plateau region of the Neapolitan Apennines: see APENNINES.

Má'té·szal'ka (mä'tä·sŏl'kŏ). Commune, NE Hungary, 43 m. NE of Debrecen; pop. ab. 7000.

Ma'teur' (má'tûr'). Town, N Tunisia, N Africa, ab. 10 m. SSW of Ferryville; occupied by Germans Dec. 1942; taken by Americans May 3, 1943 in battle for Bizerte. See HILL 609.

Ma'the·ran' (măt'há·rän'). Hill sanatorium, cen. Maharashtra, W India, 30 m. E of Bombay; pop. 2734.

Math'ews (măth'ūz). **1** County in Virginia. See *Table* at VIRGINIA.

2 Village, its ⊗, E Virginia; pop. (est.) 500.

Math'ew Town (măth'ū). Town on SW coast of Great Inagua I., Bahama Is., West Indies.

Ma·thi'as Point (má·thī'ăs). Point at NE tip of King George co., E Virginia, extending into Potomac river.

Math'is (măth'ĭs). City, San Patricio co., S Texas, 33 m. NW of Corpus Christi; pop. 6075.

Mathura. See MUTTRA.

Matianus. See Lake URMIA.

Ma·tin'i·cus (má·tĭn'ĭ·kŭs). Island in Atlantic Ocean off S cen. coast of Maine.

Matisco Æduorum. See Mâcon.

Matlalcueyatl. See Malinche.

Mat'locks, The (măt'lŏks). Urban district, Derbyshire, N cen. England, on the Derwent 19 m. S of Sheffield; pop. 17,770; mineral springs; inland spa.

Mat·ma'ta (măt·mä'tá; Ar. mĭt·mä'tă·h'). Town, SE Tunisia, ab. 27 m. S of Gabès and W of Mareth. Nearby **Matmata Hills** (highest 2000 ft.), noted for centuries for their cave dwellers; formed German defense in World War II; taken by British Indian troops Mar. 1943.

Ma'toch·kin Shar (má'tŭch·kĭn shár). Channel 3 m. wide bet. the two islands of Novaya Zemlya (q.v.).

Ma'to Gros'so (má'tōō grō'sōō; Angl. măt'ŭ grŏ'sō); formerly spelled **Mat'to Grosso.** **1** State of Brazil. See Table at Brazil.

2 Town on Guaporé river, Mato Grosso state, SW Brazil; pop. ab. 5000.

Mato Grosso, Plateau of. Highland in E cen. Mato Grosso state, SW Brazil; source of the Araguaia, Xingú, and Paraguay rivers, of headstreams of the Tapajoz, and of many tributaries of the Alto Paraná.

Ma·to'po, or **Ma·top'po, Hills** (má·tô'pō). Mountain group, S Southern Rhodesia, SE Africa, S of Bulawayo; tomb of Cecil Rhodes (see World's View).

Ma·to·zi'nhos (má·tōō·zē'nyōōsh). Parish, NW Portugal, NW of Oporto on the coast; includes port of Leixões (q.v.).

Ma'trah (mä'trá; Arab. mŏ'trŏ·h'). Seaport town, SE Arabia, on the Gulf of Oman; N suburb of Masqat; pop. ab. 8500; trade center for land routes into the interior.

Matrona. See Marne.

Ma·trûh' (mä·trōō'; Arab. mŏ·trōō'h'); also **Mer·sa' Matrûh** (mĕr·sä'; Arab. mŭr·sä'); anc. **Par'ae·to'ni·um** (păr'ê·tō'nĭ·ŭm). Village on coastal road, NW Egypt, E of Sidi Barrâni and W of Fûka, 150 m. W of Alexandria; site of old Roman town; in World War II taken and retaken several times 1942–43.

Matsang. See Brahmaputra.

Ma'tsu' (mä'tsōō', măt'sōō). Island, SE China, on coast ENE of Minhow (Foochow).

Ma·tsu·e (mä·tsōō·yĕ) or **Ma·tsu·ye.** City, ✻ of Shimane prefecture, N coast of W Honshu, Japan; pop. (1945) 54,033; situated on a lake and river, has exceptional transportation facilities and notable scenery.

Ma·tsu·ma·e (mä·tsōō·mä·yĕ); formerly **Fu·ku·ya·ma** (fōō·kōō·yä·mä). Town at SW tip of Hokkaido, Japan, on Tsugaru Strait; pop. 6316; oldest town on Hokkaido I.; has citadel as monument of feudal days.

Ma·tsu·mo·to (mä·tsōō·mô·tô). City, Nagano prefecture, cen. Honshu, Japan, 95 m. NE of Nagoya; pop. (1945) 77,077; chief commercial city of the prefecture; silkworm culture. Prominent in feudal days.

Ma·tsu·shi·ma (mä·tsōō·shĕ·mä). Group of more than 800 small islands of soft, porous, volcanic rock worn by waves into fantastic shapes, in **Matsushima Wan** [wän] (bay), Miyagi prefecture, N Honshu, Japan, ab. 10 m. NE of Sendai.

Ma·tsu·wa (mä·tsōō·wä). One of the Kuril Is. in cen. part of chain N of Rashowa; now part of Soviet Russia, Asia. Bombed by American planes 1944.

Ma·tsu·ya·ma (mä·tsōō·yä·mä). City, ✻ of Ehime prefecture, near Inland Sea, W Shikoku I., Japan; pop. (1945) 117,396.

Matsuye. See Matsue.

Ma·tsu·za·ka (mä·tsōō·zä·kä). Town, Mie prefecture, S Honshu, Japan, ab. 50 m. SSW of Nagoya; pop. (1945) 37,386; near Ise Bay; chief product a cotton textile.

Mat'ta·gam'i (măt'á·găm'ĭ). River 275 m. long, E Ontario, Canada; rises in Mattagami Lake and other lakes in Cochrane dist., flows N to join the Missinaibi and form the Moose river.

Mattagami Lake. 1 Lake in Cochrane dist., Ontario, Canada; a source of the Mattagami river.

2 Lake 88 sq. m., Abitibi co., SW Quebec prov., Canada, with outlet N through Nottaway river into James Bay.

Mat'ta·mus'keet Lake (măt'á·mŭs'kēt). Lake in SE Hyde co., E North Carolina.

Mat·tan'che·ri (mát·tăn'chă·rĭ). Town, cen. Kerala state, S India, on Malabar Coast just S of Kozhikode; pop. (1941) 53,346.

Mat'ta·pan (măt'á·păn). Locality, S Suffolk co., E Massachusetts; part of Boston.

Mat'ta·poi'sett (măt'á·poi'sĕt; -sĭt). Town, Plymouth co., SE Massachusetts, on Buzzards Bay 6 m. E of New Bedford; pop. 3117; summer resort.

Mat'ta·po·ni' (măt'á·pô·nĭ'). River ab. 125 m. long, E Virginia; rises in Spotsylvania co., flows SE to unite with Pamunkey river at West Point and form York river.

Mat'ta·wa (măt'á·wô). **1** River ab. 45 m. long, SE Ontario, Canada; flows E out of Trout Lake into the Ottawa river.

2 Lumber town, Nipissing dist., SE Ontario, Canada, at confluence of Mattawa and Ottawa rivers 38 m. E of North Bay; pop. 3097; formerly a fur-trading post of the Hudson's Bay Co.

Mat'ta·wam'keag (măt'á·wŏm'kĕg). River ab. 50 m. long, E Maine; formed by confluence of forks in S Aroostook co., flows SW into Penobscot river in E cen. Penobscot co.

Mat'ta·win (măt'á·wĭn). River 100 m. long, S Quebec prov., Canada; flows E into the St. Maurice river.

Mat'tea·wan (măt'á·wŏn). Former village, Dutchess co., SE New York; part of Beacon since 1913.

Mat'ter·horn (măt'ĕr·hôrn; Ger. mät'-) or **Mont Cer'vin'** (môn' sĕr'vän'). Peak 14,780 ft. in the Pennine Alps on the Swiss-Italian border.

Mat'ter·horn Peak (măt'ĕr·hôrn). Mountain 13,585 ft. in Hinsdale co., SW Colorado.

Mat'ter·joch (mät'ĕr·yôk) or **Thé'o·dule' Pass** (tā·ô'dül'). Mountain pass 10,900 ft. in Pennine Alps bet. N Italy and Valais canton, Switzerland, just SE of the Matterhorn.

Mat'ti·tuck (măt'ĭ·tŭk). Village and resort, Suffolk co., SE New York, on Long I. on Great Peconic Bay ab. 8 m. NE of Riverhead; pop. 1274.

Matto Grosso. See Mato Grosso.

Mat·toon' (mă·tōōn'). City, Coles co., E cen. Illinois, 40 m. SE of Decatur; pop. 19,088; incorporated 1855.

Ma·tu'pi (má·tōō'pĭ). Volcano, one of a group nearly surrounding the town of Rabaul, on Blanche Bay, E New Britain I., Bismarck Archipelago; its sudden eruption May 29–30, 1937, together with that of the new volcano Mt. Vulcan, caused great destruction at Rabaul and on Gazelle Penin. See Mount Mother.

Ma·tu·rín' (mä'tōō·rēn'). Town, ✻ of Monagas state, NE Venezuela; pop. (1941 est.) 12,549.

Ma·tu'tum, Mount (mä·tōō'tōōm). Mountain 7524 ft., SE Cotabato prov., Mindanao, Phil. Is., near Davao boundary; highest peak entirely within the province.

Mau or **Mau Nat·bhan'jan** (mou' nät·b'hŭn'jàn). Town, E Uttar Pradesh, N Indian Union, on tributary of Ganges river 55 m. NE of Benares; pop. 21,354.

Mau·á' (mou·á'). Village on N shore of Guanabara Bay, SE Brazil, ab. 10 m. N of Rio de Janeiro.

Ma'u·ban' (mä'ōō·bän'; mou·bän'). Municipality, S Tayabas prov., Luzon, Phil. Is., near E coast of Lamon Bay 19 m. NNE of Lucena; pop. 14,832; important in coastal trade. Here Japanese landed Dec. 23, 1941.

Mau'beuge' (mō'bûzh'). Fortified city, Nord dept., N France, on Sambre river near Belgian border 49 m. NE of Lille; pop. 23,622; arsenal; manufactures firearms, iron and steel goods, leather. Built around monastery founded in 7th cent.; fell to France 1678; captured by Germans after disastrous siege 1914; recaptured 1918.

Ma·u'bin (má·ōō'bĭn). **1** District, Irrawaddy division, Lower Burma; 1642 sq. m.; pop. 371,509.

2 Town, its ✻, on the Irrawaddy 40 m. W of Rangoon; pop. 8897.

Mauch'berg (mouĸ'bĕrĸ). Peak 8725 ft. in E cen. Transvaal prov., Republic of South Africa.

Mauch Chunk (mô chŭngk'). Former borough, E Pennsylvania. See JIM THORPE.

Mauch Chunk Mountain. Peak ab. 1500 ft. in Carbon co., E Pennsylvania, near Mauch Chunk.

Mauch'line (môĸ'lĭn). Town, Ayr co., SW Scotland, 8 m. ESE of Kilmarnock; pop. 4160; ab. 1 m. N is **Moss-giel'** (?mŏs·gēl'), the farm where Robert Burns lived with his brother 1784–88.

Maud (môd). City, Pottawatomie and Seminole cos., cen. Oklahoma, 16 m. SSE of Shawnee; pop. 1137; oil wells; cotton, lumber.

Mau'er (mou'ĕr). **1** Village, Baden-Württemberg, Germany, SE of Heidelberg; Heidelberg jaw found here 1907. **2** See MAMRY lake.

Maug (moug). Small island, N Mariana Is., 140 m. N of Pagan, ab. 20°N; taken by U.S. troops Aug. 1945.

Mau'ga Si'li, Mount (mou'ga sē'lē). Peak 6094 ft. in center of Savaii I., Western Samoa.

Mau'i (mou'ē). **1** Island of S cen. state of Hawaii; 728 sq. m.; pop. (1950) 40,193; a part of the county of Maui; 2d largest island of the Hawaiian group; its E and W ends are high mountains with flat isthmus in center connecting them. In E is Haleakala National Park including Haleakala (q.v.) 10,025 ft. and in W Puu Kukui 5790 ft. and Eke Crater 4480 ft. Maalaea Bay is large inlet on S coast and Lahaina Roadstead in Auau Channel on NW is fine anchorage. Chief town Wailuku city; large sugar plantations. **2** County, Hawaii, comprising Maui, Molokai, Lanai, and Kahoolawe Is.; 1173 sq. m.; pop. 42,576; ⊗ Wailuku, on Maui.

Ma'u·ke' (mä'ŏŏ·kā'). One of the Cook Is. in S Pacific Ocean, 150 m. NE of Rarotonga; 2½ m. by 4 m.

Mau'le (mou'lā). **1** River ab. 140 m. long in Maule prov., S cen. Chile; flows into Pacific Ocean near the town of Constitución, S of Valparaíso. **2** Province of Chile. See Table at CHILE.

Maul·lín' (mou·yēn'). River in Chiloé prov., S cen. Chile; flows out of Llanquihue Lake into the Pacific Ocean; waterfalls.

Maul·main' (moul·mān'; -mīn'). = MOULMEIN.

Mau·mee' (mô·mē'; mô'mē). **1** River ab. 175 m. long, Indiana and Ohio; formed by confluence of St. Joseph and St. Marys rivers at Fort Wayne, Allen co., NE Indiana, flows E and NE into Lake Erie at Toledo, NW Ohio. Navigable for 12 m. from mouth. **2** Residential city, Lucas co., NW Ohio, 8 m. SW of Toledo; pop. 12,063; settled 1817 on site of Fort Miami (1764), where Wayne defeated the Indians Aug. 20, 1794 at battle of Fallen Timbers.

Mau'mee Bay (mô'mē). Inlet of Lake Erie in NE Lucas co., NW Ohio, N of Toledo.

Ma·un' (mä·ŏŏn'). Town, N Bechuanaland Protectorate, S Africa, NE of Lake Ngami; pop. 5000.

Mau·na'bo (mou·nä'vô). Municipality (pop. 10,785) and town (pop. 1027), SE Puerto Rico; town on coast 14 m. E of Guayama.

Mau'na Ke'a (mou'nä kā'ä). Extinct volcano 13,796 ft. in N cen. Hawaii I., Hawaii; highest island mountain in the world and, reckoning from its base on ocean floor 18,000 ft. down, it is highest mountain on earth's surface ab. 32,000 ft.

Mauna Lo'a (lō'ä). **1** Mountain 1382 ft. in W Molokai I., Hawaii. **2** Volcano 13,680 ft. on S cen. Hawaii I., Hawaii, in Hawaii National Park; largest mountain in the world in cubic content; central crater pit is sometimes active, but there has been no eruption from it in historic times; many great lava flows in recent years have burst from the sides at elevations from 7000 to 13,000 ft. See KILAUEA and MOKUAWEOWEO.

Mau'na·lu'a Bay (mou'nä·lŏŏ'ä). Bay on SE coast of Oahu I., Hawaii, W of Koko Head.

Mau Natbhanjan. See MAU.

Maung'daw' (moung'dô'). Town, Akyab dist., W Lower Burma, on coast near India border 60 m. NW of Akyab; scene of fighting in World War II.

Mau'per'tuis' (mō'pĕr'tü·ē'). Battlefield 7 m. SE of Poitiers, France, where the Black Prince defeated the French 1356. See POITOU.

Mau·pi'ti (mou·pē'tē). One of the Leeward Is., Society Is., S Pacific Ocean, ab. 30 m. W of Bora Bora; ab. 6 m. in circumference enclosing wide lagoon; pop. ab. 250.

Mau're·pas', Lake (mōr'ē·pä'). Lake in SE Louisiana; connected on the E, through a river ab. 2 m. long, with Lake Pontchartrain.

Maures, Monts des (môN'dä môr'). Mountain massif, Var dept., SE France, on the Mediterranean coast at W end of the Riviera; highest point ab. 2550 ft.

Mau're·ta'ni·a (mô'rĕ·tā'nĭ·ȧ; -tān'yȧ) or **Mau'ri·ta'-ni·a** (mô'rĭ-). Ancient country in N Africa, W of Numidia; included modern Morocco and part of Algeria.

History: Ancient region of North Africa, part of Carthaginian empire; Mauretanian kingdom received western part of Numidia (q.v.) after fall of Jugurtha 106 B.C.; c. 25 B.C. Roman provinces of **Mauretania Cae·sar'i·en'sis** [sĕ·zâr'ĭ·sĭs] (eastern) and **Mauretania Tin'gi·ta'na** [tĭn'jĭ·tä'nȧ] (western) were erected; in 5th cent. A.D. overrun by Vandals and later by Moslem Arabs; for later history, see BARBARY and MOROCCO.

Mau'rice (mô'rĭs; môr'ĭs). River ab. 40 m. long, SW New Jersey; flows S into Maurice River Cove of Delaware Bay.

Mau'ri·ta'ni·a (mô'rĭ·tā'nĭ·ȧ; -tān'yȧ). **1** Fr. **Mau'ri'-ta'nie'** (mô'rē'tá'nē'). Autonomous republic (the **Islamic Republic of Mauritania**) of the French Community, formerly a French territory, N of Senegal river, W Africa; ✻ Nouakchott; 419,229 sq. m.; pop. 725,000. Bounded on NW and N by Río de Oro, on NE by Algeria, on E by Mali, on S by Senegal, and on W by Atlantic Ocean; N boundary approximately 25°N; lies in W end of the Sahara Desert, with low ranges of hills crossing it from NE to SW; highest in Adrar. Has several wadis in coast region flowing SW; only fertile area is along the Senegal. Inhabitants mostly Moorish Moslems. Chief products cattle, gum, and salt.

History: Coast opened by Portuguese who discovered Arguin in 15th cent.; coastal territory disputed by traders of different European nations; although recognized as in French sphere from 1817 Senegal treaty, it was not occupied until after 1900; made protectorate 1903 and part of French West Africa 1904, but conquered only gradually; made colony 1920; became territory 1946, an autonomous republic of the French Community 1958; until 1958 administered from St. Louis, Senegal. **2** See MAURETANIA.

Mau·ri'ti·us (mô·rĭsh'ĭ·ŭs; -rĭsh'ŭs); *formerly* **Île de France** (ēl' dē fräNs'). Island of the Mascarene Is., in the Indian Ocean ab. 450 m. E of Madagascar; 720 sq. m.; pop. (1962) 681,619; ✻ Port Louis; a former British colony, with dependencies island of Rodrigues and Agalega Is.; since 1968 an independent country. Mountainous, with fertile valleys and coastal plains; highest point Piton de la Rivière Noire in SW 2730 ft.; chief industry is growing sugar cane; other products are rice, vanilla, coconut oil, spice.

History: Discovered by Portuguese 1505; occupied by Dutch 1598–1710; held by French 1715–1810 when British captured it; formally ceded to British 1814; became independent Mar. 12, 1968.

Mau'ry (mûr'ĭ). County in Tennessee. See *Table* at TENNESSEE.

Maus'ton (môs'tŭn). City, ⊗ of Juneau co., cen. Wisconsin, 35 m. WNW of Portage; pop. 3531; lumbering.

Maut'hau'sen (mout'hou'zen). Village, Upper Austria prov., Austria, on the Danube opp. the mouth of the Enns; pop. ab. 2000; site of concentration camp during World War II.

Mauvaises Terres. See BAD LANDS.

Mav′er·ick (măv′ĕr·ĭk; măv′rĭk). County in Texas. See *Table* at TEXAS.

Maverick, Mount. Peak 3495 ft. in Brewster co., W Texas.

Ma·wen′zi (mä·wĕn′zĕ). Second highest peak 16,892 ft. of Mount Kilimanjaro in E Africa.

Maw′laik′ (mô′lĭk′). Town, ✳ of Upper Chindwin dist., Sagaing division, Upper Burma, on the Chindwin NE of Tiddim and 165 m. NW of Mandalay; pop. 2278.

Má′xi·mo Gó′mez (mäk′sĕ·mŏ gō′mäs). Municipality and town, Matanzas prov., W cen. Cuba, on railroad 15 m. SE of Cárdenas; pop. (town) 5416.

Max′ton (măks′tŭn). Town, Robeson co., S North Carolina, 35 m. SW of Fayetteville; pop. 1755.

Max′well·town′ (măks′wĕl·toun′; măks′wĕl-). Former burgh in Kirkcudbright co., S Scotland, now a part of Dumfries in Dumfries co.

May, Cape (mā). 1 Cape at extreme S point of New Jersey, S tip of Cape May co., at entrance to Delaware Bay.
2 See CAPE MAY.

Ma′ya (mà′yà). River ab. 500 m. long chiefly in cen. Khabarovsk Territory, Soviet Russia, Asia; rises on NW slopes of the Stanovoi Mts. and flows SW and NW to the Aldan river in SE Yakutsk A.S.S.R.

Ma′ya, Point (mä′yä). Cape on NW coast of Matanzas prov., W cen. Cuba.

May′a·gua′na (mā′à·gwä′nà; -gwô′nà; *attributively, also* -′--′) *or* **Mar′i·gua′na** (măr′ĭ-). One of the Bahama Is. in Atlantic Ocean E of Acklins I.; ab. 25 m. long and bet. 3 and 5 m. wide; 96 sq. m.; pop. (1943) 591.

Mayaguana Passage. Channel in the Bahama Is., West Indies, ESE of Crooked I. and Acklins I. and NW of Mayaguana I.

Ma′ya·güez′ (mä′yä·gwäs′). Municipality (pop. 83,850) and commercial and seaport city (pop. 50,147), W Puerto Rico; founded 1763; exports sugar, coffee, tobacco, fruit; seat of a college of the University of Puerto Rico (Agriculture and Mechanics).

Ma′ya·rí′ (mä′yä·rē′). Municipality, Oriente prov., E Cuba, near Nipe Bay on N coast 45 m. N of Santiago de Cuba; pop. 45,126.

Ma·ya′va·ram (mä·yŭ′vȧ·rȧm). Town, E Madras state, S India 40 m. NE of Tanjore; pop. 31,887; its ancient temple a place of pilgrimage.

May′beur′y (mā′bĕr′ĭ). Town, McDowell co., S West Virginia, 13 m. SE of Welch; pop. (with Switchback) 1423; coal mining.

May·bole′ (mā·bōl′). Burgh, Ayrshire, SW Scotland, 8 m. S of Ayr; pop. 4766; Culzean Castle.

Mayebashi. = MAEBASHI.

May′en (mī′ĕn). Manufacturing city, N Rhineland-Palatinate state, W Germany, in the Eifel 44 m. SSE of Cologne; pop. 14,327; 13th-cent. church.

Mayence. See MAINZ.

Ma′yenne′ (mä′yĕn′). 1 River ab. 125 m. long in NW France; rises in Orne dept., flows S to unite with Sarthe river near Angers and form Maine river; navigable for ab. 75 m.
2 Department of France. See *Table* at FRANCE.
3 Commune, N Mayenne dept., NW France; pop. (1931) 8238; center of conflict in campaigns of William the Conqueror, in wars of religion 16th cent. (it belonged to Guise family), and in wars of the Vendée 18th cent.

May′ers·ville (mā′ĕrz·vĭl; *Sou. also* -v′l). Village, ⊗ of Issaquena co., W Mississippi; pop. (1950) 136.

Mayes (māz). County in Oklahoma. See *Table* at OKLAHOMA.

May′fair (mā′fâr). A fashionable district in West End, London, England, in Westminster metropolitan borough E of Hyde Park—so called from an annual fair (abolished 1708) formerly held there in May.

May′field (mā′fēld). 1 City, ⊗ of Graves co., SW Kentucky, 22 m. S of Paducah; pop. 10,762; tobacco market; creamery, clothing manufactories; clay deposits.

2 Borough, Lackawanna co., NE Pennsylvania, 11 m. NE of Scranton; pop. 1996; coal mining.

Mayfield Heights. City, Cuyahoga co., N Ohio, 13 m. E of Cleveland; pop. 13,478; residential suburb.

May′myo (mā′myō). Town, Mandalay dist., Lower Burma, in the hills (alt. 3500 ft.) on railroad 30 m. ENE of Mandalay; pop. of municipality 16,586, with cantonment 21,335; government summer capital.

May′nard (mā′nĕrd). Town, Middlesex co., NE Massachusetts, 16 m. SSW of Lowell; pop. 7695; woolen mills.

May′nard·ville (mā′nĕrd·vĭl; *Sou. also* -v′l). City, ⊗ of Union co., NE Tennessee; pop. 620.

May·nooth′ (mā·nōōth′; mā′nōōth). Town, NE co. Kildare, E Eire; pop. 634; site of National Coll. of St. Patrick, the most noted Irish Roman Catholic seminary.

May′o (mā′ō). 1 Town, ⊗ of Lafayette co., NW Florida penin.; pop. 687.
2 County, NW Eire, in Connacht prov.; 2084 sq. m.; pop. 161,349; ⊗ Castlebar; chief industry fishing.

Ma′yo (mä′yô). 1 Peak 7810 ft. in S Chile, on the Argentina border W of Lake Argentino.
2 River ab. 250 m. long in Sonora state, Mexico, flowing into the Gulf of California.

Ma′yo (mà′yōō). See MAIO.

May·o′dan (mā·ō′dăn). Town, Rockingham co., N North Carolina, 27 m. NNE of Winston-Salem; pop. 2366; cotton mills.

Ma·yon′, Mount (mä·yôn′). Active volcano 7943 ft., E Albay prov., SE Luzon, Phil. Is.; the most perfect volcanic cone known; crowned almost continuously with a halo of vapor which at night becomes a fiery glow; has had destructive eruptions, esp. 1814, 1897, and 1928.

Ma·yor′, Is′la (ēz′lä mä·yôr′). Island 25 m. long W of Guadalquivir river in a swamp S of Seville, Spain.

Ma′yotte′ (mà·yôt′). One of the Comoro Is. (*q.v.*), in SE part nearest Madagascar; 140 sq. m.; pop. (1936) 17,477; chief town Dzaoudzi; highest point 2106 ft.

Ma·youm′ba (mà·yōōm′bà). Seaport, S Gabon, W equatorial Africa.

May′ra·i′ra Point (mī′rä·ē′rä). Most northerly point of Ilocos Norte prov., Luzon, Phil. Is., and of the island of Luzon, 18°39′N; marks W point of Pasaleng Bay.

Maysí, Cape. See Cape MAISÍ.

Mays Landing (māz). Town, ⊗ of Atlantic co., SE New Jersey, on Great Egg river 17 m. WNW of Atlantic City; pop. 1404; early shipbuilding port; resort.

Mays′ville (māz′vĭl; *Sou. also* -v′l). 1 City, ⊗ of Mason co., NE Kentucky, on Ohio river 53 m. SE of Covington; pop. 8484; river port and trade and industrial center.
2 City, ⊗ of De Kalb co., NW Missouri; pop. 942.

Ma·yu′ (mà·yōō′). River ab. 70 m. long in Akyab dist., Lower Burma; flows S into Bay of Bengal just N of Akyab; the narrow tongue of land extending S bet. it and the Bay of Bengal forms the **Mayu Peninsula** where there was fighting 1943–44 in Japanese attack on India.

Mayu Range. Coastal range of the Arakan Yoma system, Burma, W of Mayu river and extending along the Mayu Penin.; scene of severe fighting Feb. 1944.

Ma·yur′bhanj (mà·yōōrb′hŭnj). Former Indian state, NE Eastern States, near coast W of Balasore, NE India; 4034 sq. m.; pop. (1941) 990,977; ✳ Baripada.

May′ville (mā′vĭl). 1 Village and resort, ⊗ of Chautauqua co., SW corner of New York; pop. 1619.
2 City, Traill co., E North Dakota; pop. 2168. State Teachers Coll. (1889; coed.).
3 City, Dodge co., SE cen. Wisconsin, 22 m. S of Fond du Lac; pop. 3607.

May′wood (mā′wŏŏd). 1 Residential city, Los Angeles co., SW California, 5 m. SE of Los Angeles; pop. 14,588; U.S. Air Force base.
2 Residential village, Cook co., NE Illinois, 12 m. W of Chicago; pop. 27,330.
3 Borough, Bergen co., NE corner of New Jersey, 6 m. ESE of Paterson; pop. 11,460.

Mayyali. See MAHÉ.

Mazaca. See KAYSERİ city.

Maz′a·gan′ (măz′á·găn′); *now* **El–Ja·di′da** (ăl jă-dē′dá; -dă). Seaport, W coast of Morocco, NW Africa; pop. (1936) 24,391; founded 1502 by Portuguese and held by them until 1769.

Ma·za′ma, Mount (má·zä′má). Prehistoric volcanic mountain of Cascade Mts., W Klamath co., S Oregon; its caldera now occupied by Crater Lake (*q.v.*).

Ma′za′met′ (má′zá′mě′). Commune, Tarn dept., S France, 35 m. SSE of Albi; pop. 15,447; manufactures textiles and clothing; foundries, tanneries.

Ma′zan·de·ran′ (mä′zán·dĕ·rän′). Province, N Iran, narrow coastal region bet. the Caspian Sea and the Elburz Mts.; 7518 sq. m.; ✻ Sari; no good harbors; connected by rail and highway with Tehran.

Ma·zar′ (má·zär′). A major province, N Afghanistan; chief town Mazar-i-Sharif.

Ma·za′ra del Val′lo (mä·tsä′rä dâl väl′lô). Seaport, Trapani prov., NW Sicily; pop. 26,028; cathedral.

Ma·zar′–i–Sha·rif′ (má·zär′ĕ·shá·rēf′). City, ✻ of Mazar prov., N Afghanistan, 190 m. NW of Kabul; pop. ab. 30,000; chief town of Afghan Turkistan, just E of ancient Balkh; mosque venerated by Shiite Mussulmans as the tomb of Ali, son-in-law of Mohammed.

Ma′zar·rón′ (mä′thär·rôn′; -sär-). Commune, Murcia prov., SE Spain, 3 m. from Mediterranean and 27 m. S of Murcia; pop. 11,569; copper, lead, and iron mines (once worked by Romans and Phoenicians).

Maz′a·ru′ni (măz′á·rŏŏ′nĭ). River ab. 270 m. long in British Guiana; flows in wide curve SE to NE into the Essequibo river near its mouth; just before entering the Essequibo joins the Cuyuni river; diamond fields.

Ma′za·te·nan′go (mä′sä·tĕ·näng′gô). Town, ✻ of Suchitepéquez dept., SW Guatemala; pop. 14,227; in district producing coffee, sugar, cocoa, and fruits.

Ma′za·tlán′ (mä′sä·tlän′). Seaport, Sinaloa state, W Mexico; pop. 32,117; largest Mexican seaport on the Pacific coast; chief exports precious metals, hides, tobacco, istle, bananas.

Ma′za·tzal′ Peak (mä′sä·tsäl′). Mountain 7888 ft. in **Mazatzal Mountains**, on boundary bet. Gila and Yavapai cos., cen. Arizona.

Ma·zhei′kyai (mä·zhā′kě·ê). **1** District of Lithuania. See *Table* at LITHUANIA.
2 Town, its ✻, 45 m. NW of Shaulyai; pop. 4300.

Ma′zin′garbe′ (má′zăn′gárb′). Commune, Pas-de-Calais dept., N France, near Béthune; pop. (1931) 9301; coal mines.

Ma·zoe′ (?mä·zŏŏ′). Town, NE cen. Southern Rhodesia, S Africa, 20 m. N of Salisbury; pop. (1926; white) 1849; mining and agricultural center in fertile valley.

Ma·zo′vi·a (má·zō′vĭ·á; -zōv′yá). Ancient principality, Poland, E of the Vistula; long semi-independent; in 14th–16th cents. sent many colonists into Masuria; completely united to Poland by 1529; from 16th cent. its capital was Warsaw, succeeding Płock; became the province of Warsaw.

Ma·zu′ri·a (má·zŏŏr′ĭ·á). Var. of MASURIA.

Ma·zu′ry (mä·zŏŏ′rĭ). The southern two thirds of former East Prussia prov. of Germany (Masuria), added to Poland 1945–46 after World War II; pop. ab. 500,000; established as a new department, now called **Olsz′tyn** (ôlsh′tĭn), ✻ Olsztyn (Allenstein).

Mazzara del Vallo. = MAZARA DEL VALLO.

Maz′za·ri′no (mät′tsä·rē′nô). Commune, Caltanissetta prov., cen. Sicily, 16 m. S of Caltanissetta; pop. 17,715.

Mba (′m·bä′) *or* **Ba** (bä). **1** River, NW Viti Levu I., Fiji Is., SW Pacific Ocean.
2 Town on river near its mouth.

Mba·bane′ (′m·bä·bän′). Town, ✻ of Swaziland, SE Africa, 93 m. WSW of Lourenço Marques; pop. 1600.

Mbau (′m·bou′). Town, former native ✻ of Viti Levu, Fiji Is., on small island off E coast N of the Rewa delta.

Mbo′ca·ya′ty (′m·bō′kä·yä′tĕ). Town, Guairá dept., S cen. Paraguay; pop. ab. 11,500.

Mbomu. See BOMU.

Mbu·ya′pey (′m·bŏŏ·yä′pě·ê). Town, Paraguarí dept., S Paraguay; pop. ab. 7300.

Mdaourouch. See MADAUROS.

Mead, Lake (mēd). Reservoir in Colorado river in Mohave co., NW Arizona, and Clark co., SE Nevada, formed by Hoover Dam (see UNITED STATES, *Dams and Reservoirs*); largest artificial lake in world; area 227 sq. m., length 119 m., depth over 500 ft. near the dam; has capacity of over 31,000,000 acre-feet of water, used for flood control, irrigation, and power.

Meade (mēd). **1** Name of counties in three states of the U.S. See *Tables* at KANSAS, KENTUCKY, SOUTH DAKOTA.
2 City, ⊗ of Meade co., SW Kansas, 37 m. SSW of Dodge City; pop. 2019; in livestock-raising section.

Meade Peak. Mountain 9953 ft. in Bear Lake co., SE Idaho.

Mead′ow (měd′ō). River ab. 50 m. long, S cen. West Virginia; flows NW from Greenbrier co. and forms boundary bet. Nicholas and Fayette cos. until it joins the Gauley river.

Meadow Lands. Locality, Washington co., SW Pennsylvania, ab. 4 m. N of Washington; pop. 1967.

Mead′ville (mēd′vĭl; *Sou. also* -v′l). **1** Town, ⊗ of Franklin co., SW Mississippi; pop. 611.
2 City, ⊗ of Crawford co., NW Pennsylvania, 33 m. S of Erie; pop. 16,671; settled 1788; manufactures slide fasteners, iron and steel, rayon yarn, stereoscopes, machinery and tools; oil fields. Allegheny Coll. (1815; coed.).

Mea′ford (mē′fĕrd). Town, Grey co., SE Ontario, Canada, on Nottawasaga Bay 20 m. E of Owen Sound; pop. 3178; has good harbor; active lake trade.

Mea′gher (mär). County in Montana. See *Table* at MONTANA.

Me′a·rim′ (mā′á·rēN′). River in Maranhão state, SE Brazil; flows N to São Marcos Bay; chief tributaries the Pindaré and the Grajaú.

Mearns, The. See KINCARDINE.

Meath (mēth; *Ir.* mĕth). County, E Eire, in Leinster prov.; 903 sq. m.; pop. 61,405; ⊗ Trim; rivers Boyne, Blackwater; agriculture, livestock raising, textile manufacture. Kingdom set up in 2d cent. B.C. more extensive than present county; made county 1296 but status and boundaries not definitely established until early 17th cent.

Meaux (mō). Manufacturing commune, Seine-et-Marne dept., N France, 32 m. NNE of Melun; pop. 14,429; chief town of Brie; episcopal see since 375 A.D.; 12th to 16th-cent. cathedral; 13th-cent. episcopal palace; flour, starch, steel, foundry products, machinery, lumber, sugar. German drive on Paris stopped here 1914.

Meb′ane (měb′ăn). Town, Alamance and Orange cos., N cen. North Carolina, 24 m. WNW of Durham; pop. 2364; tobacco market; furniture, bedsprings, cotton yarns.

Mec′a·ti′na *or* **Mec′ca·ti′na, Cape** (měk′á·tē′ná). Point, SE Quebec, Canada, on Strait of Belle Isle.

Mec′ca (měk′á); *Arab.* **Mak′ka** (mäk′ká; -kă); *anc.* **Mac′o·ra′ba** (măk′ô·rä′bá). City, S Hejaz, W Arabia; ✻ of Hejaz and a ✻ of Saudi Arabia; pop. ab. 80,000; in a valley surrounded by low hills ab. 70 m. from the coast; Holy City of Islam; birthplace of Mohammed 570 A.D.; contains the Great Mosque with the Kaaba and sacred Black Stone; its Red Sea port is Jidda; has great bazaars. A place of some importance before Mohammed whose home it was until 622, when he was forced to flee to Medina (*q.v.*); sacked by Karmathians c. 930; came under Ottoman Turks 1517; early in 19th cent. seized by Wahabis whom Mehemet Ali defeated; seat of Grand Sherif of Mecca who, in 1908, was Husein ibn-Ali; under Husein, declared independence of Turkey 1916 and became capital of kingdom of Hejaz (*q.v.*); in 1924 occupied by Wahabis under ibn-Saud who later erected kingdom of Saudi Arabia (*q.v.*).

Me·chan′ic Falls (mě·kăn′ĭk). Town, Androscoggin co., SW Maine, 10 m. W of Lewiston; pop. 2195; paper mills.

Me·chan′ics·burg (mě·kăn′ĭks·bûrg). **1** Village, Champaign co., W Ohio, 29 m. W of Columbus; pop. 1810; lumber, patent medicines.
2 Borough, Cumberland co., S Pennsylvania, 9 m. WSW of Harrisburg; pop. 8123; settled 1790; manufactures silk, shirts, flavoring extracts, automobile wheels, structural steel; clay pits nearby.
Me·chan′ics·ville (-vĭl; *Sou. also* -v′l). Locality in Hanover co., Virginia, ab. 7 m. NE of Richmond; pop. (est.) 500; battle June 26, 1862 in which Confederates under Hill and Longstreet were repulsed with great loss by Union forces; also known as the battle of **Beaver Dam Creek.**
Me·chan′ic·ville (mě·kăn′ĭk·vĭl). City, Saratoga co., E New York, on Hudson river 17 m. N of Albany; pop. 6831; manufactures paper and pulp, knit goods.
Me·chant′, Lake (mě·shŏn′; *Fr.* mā′shän′). Lake in S Terrebonne parish, SE Louisiana; connected through Caillou Lake with Gulf of Mexico.
Me′che·len (měk′ě·lě[n]); *Fr.* **Ma′lines′** (mȧ′lēn′; *Angl.* mȧ·lēn′); *Eng.* **Mech′lin** (měk′lĭn). Commune, Antwerp prov., N Belgium; pop. (1938 est.) 62,311; formerly famous for its laces; manufactures woolen goods, tapestries, linens; Gothic cathedral; taken by Germans 1914.
Mechili, El. See EL MECHILI.
Me′chum (mē′chŭm). River ab. 30 m. long, cen. Virginia; flows NE and SE in Albemarle co. to empty into Rivanna river.
Meck′len·burg (měk′lěn·bûrg). Name of counties in two states of the U.S. See *Tables* at NORTH CAROLINA and VIRGINIA.
Meck′len·burg (měk′lěn·bŏŏrк; mä′klěn-; *Angl.* měk′lěn·bûrg). Former German state, N Germany; 6068 sq. m.; pop. (1939) 910, 826; * Schwerin; included also cities of Rostock and Neustrelitz; agriculture, grazing.
History: Originally Germanic territory which was occupied c. 600 A.D. by Slavic peoples who were gradually driven back by German colonization carried out under Henry the Lion; ruled briefly in 13th cent. by Waldemar II of Denmark; became duchy 1348; because of participation (in first part of Thirty Years' War) on Danish side, lost lands to Wallenstein 1629; received bishoprics of Schwerin and Ratzeburg 1648; in 1701 divided into duchies of **Mecklenburg–Schwe·rin′** (-shvä·rēn′) and **Mecklenburg–Stre′litz** (-shträ′lĭts); both became grand duchies 1815 and joined North German Confederation 1867; republics in 1918; reunited in 1934; lost sovereign rights 1933–35. See GERMANY.
Mecklenburg, Bay of. Inlet of SW Baltic Sea on coast of Mecklenburg, N Germany; includes Lübeck Bay.
Me·cos′ta (mě·kŏs′tȧ). County in Michigan. See *Table* at MICHIGAN.
Me·dan′ (mȧ·dän′). Commercial city, NE Sumatra, Indonesia; pop. 310,600; largest city of Sumatra; on small Deli river ab. 15 m. from its mouth and from the port of Belawan; center of a rich agricultural region, with rubber and tobacco the principal products.
Me′da·no′sa, Point (mā′thȧ·nō′sä). Cape on N cen. coast of Santa Cruz territory, S Argentina.
Med′dy·bemps Lake (měd′ĭ·běmps). Lake in E cen. Washington co., E Maine.
Mé·dé′a′ (mā′dā′ä′). Commune, N Alger dept., N Algeria, just S of the city of Algiers; pop. 16,431.
Medeba. See MADEBA.
Me′del·lin (mā′thȧ·yěn′). Municipality on extreme NW coast of Cebu I., Phil. Is., at N end of Tañon Strait opp. Bantayan I.; pop. 18,637.
Me′del·lín′. **1** (mā′thȧ·yěn′; *Angl.* měd′l·ēn′, měd′l·ĭn) City, * of Antioquia dept., NW Colombia, NW of Bogotá; pop. 143,952; in a valley of the Andes on a tributary of the Cauca at alt. 5052 ft.; a coffee and mining center; manufacturing; Univ. of Antioquia.
2 (mā′thä·[l]yěn′) Village, Badajoz prov., Spain, on the Guadiana river; pop. 2016; in ancient Estremadura; birthplace of Hernando Cortes; ruined castle.

Mé′de·nine′ (mād′nēn′; *Arab.* mȧ·dȧ·nēn′). Town, SE Tunisia, near Mareth 45 m. SSE of Gabès.
Med′field (měd′fēld). Town, Norfolk co., E Massachusetts, 17 m. SW of Boston; pop. 6021; burned in King Philip's War 1675.
Med′ford (měd′fěrd). **1** City, Middlesex co., NE Massachusetts, 5 m. N of Boston; pop. 64,971; formerly shipbuilding center, and famous for its rum (Medford rum). Tufts Univ. (1852; coed.).
2 Town, ⊗ of Grant co., N Oklahoma; pop. 1223.
3 City, ⊗ of Jackson co., SW Oregon, 60 m. W of Klamath Falls; pop. 24,425; center of fruit-growing (esp. pears), lumbering, dairying, and mining region; summer resort.
4 City, ⊗ of Taylor co., N Wisconsin, 32 m. W of Merrill; pop. 3260; dairying, woodworking, canning.
Me′di·a (mē′dĭ·ȧ). **1** Borough, ⊗ of Delaware co., SE Pennsylvania, 15 m. W of Philadelphia; pop. 5803.
2 Ancient country, S Asia, originally the plateau region corresponding to NW part of modern Iran which was occupied by Medes, an Iranian people; in 8th cent. B.C. divided into small principalities; part of Assyrian Empire to 626 B.C.; independent kingdom under Cyaxares, aided Babylon in bringing about downfall of Assyria 612 B.C.; expanded territory to include part of Assyria, Armenia and Cappadocia on W, to the Oxus river on NE, and Persia in S, capital Rhages; conquered by Cyrus, founder of Persian Empire 550 B.C. As a province of Persia it was bounded on N by the Elburz Mts., on NE by Hyrcania, on E by Parthia, on S by Persis and Susiana, on SW by Babylonia, on W by Assyria, and on NW by Armenia. After the conquest of Persia by Alexander it was divided into **Media At′ro·pa·te′ne** (ăt′rō·pȧ·tē′ně) in the N (capital Gazaca) and **Media Mag′na** (măg′nȧ) in the S (capital Ecbatana, mod. Hamadan). See AZERBAIJAN.
Med′i·cal Lake (měd′ĭ·kȧl). Town, Spokane co., E Washington, 15 m. WSW of Spokane; pop. 4765; on a small salt lake.
Me·di·ci′na (mȧ·dě·chē′nä). Commune, Bologna prov., Emilia, N Italy, 15 m. E of Bologna; pop. 14,903.
Med′i·cine Bow (měd′ĭ·sĭn [-s′n] bō). River ab. 120 m. long, S Wyoming; formed by confluence of branches in E Carbon co., flows N and W into North Platte river.
Medicine Bow Peak. Mountain 12,005 ft., highest point in Medicine Bow Range, S cen. Wyoming.
Medicine Bow Range *or* **Mountains.** A range of the Rocky Mts., extending N and S in Colorado and Wyoming; highest peaks Medicine Bow Peak 12,005 ft. and Elk Mountain 11,162 ft. in S cen. Wyoming.
Medicine Creek. River ab. 60 m. long, S cen. South Dakota; rises in E Jones co., flows E, then N into Missouri river on N boundary of Lyman co.
Medicine Hat. City, SE Alberta, Canada, on South Saskatchewan river 94 m. ENE of Lethbridge; pop. 16,364; railroad divisional point; river port; flour mills, brickyards, grain elevators, foundries, planing and lumber mills, machine shops; coal mines, natural-gas wells; provincial experimental farm. Founded 1883.
Medicine Lake. Lake in S Sheridan co., NE Montana.
Medicine Lodge. City, ⊗ of Barber co., S Kansas, 64 m. SW of Hutchinson; pop. 3072.
Me·di′na (*Texas and Arabia:* mě·dē′nȧ; *New York and Ohio:* mě·dī′nȧ). **1** River, S cen. Texas; flows through Bandera and Medina cos. to join the San Antonio river below San Antonio. See MEDINA DAM.
2 Name of counties in two states of the United States. See *Tables* at OHIO and TEXAS.
3 Village, Orleans co., W New York, 41 m. W of Rochester on N.Y. State Barge Canal; pop. 6681; in fruit-growing (grapes, apples) area; canneries, furniture and textile factories, iron foundries, machine shops.
4 City, ⊗ of Medina co., N Ohio, 18 m. WNW of Akron; pop. 8235; bee culture; manufactures bee supplies and products, beeswax candles.

5 *Arab.* **al-Ma·di′na** (ăl′mä·dē′nȧ; -nȧ); *earlier* **Yath′-rib** (yăth′rĭb). Inland city, E cen. Hejaz, W Arabia, 210 m. N of Mecca; pop. ab. 30,000; in a fertile valley ab. 120 m. from the Red Sea coast, connected by highway with Damascus and Mecca; its port is Yenbo'. Holy City of Islam, containing the tomb of Mohammed; noted for its mosque enclosing the tomb, its beautiful palaces and fountains, and its fruit orchards; the refuge of Mohammed after his flight (hegira) from Mecca; date of his arrival Sept. 20, 622, later adopted as beginning of Mohammedan calendar. Capital of the caliphate 622–661; after its sack by Ommiads 683 declined in influence; later came under Turks, Egyptians, and Wahabis; city of the new kingdom of Hejaz 1919–24 when after a long siege it fell to ibn-Saud.

Medina–Arkosh. See ARCOS DE LA FRONTERA.

Me·di′na Dam (mĕ·dē′nȧ). Dam completed 1913 across Medina river, bet. Bandera and Medina cos., S cen. Texas; height 178 ft.; impounds water, **Medina Lake**, for irrigation.

Me·di′na del Cam′po (mä·thē′nä thĕl käm′pô). Commune, Valladolid prov., NW cen. Spain, 25 m. SSW of Valladolid; pop. 13,154; manufactures brandy, leather, flour; stock raising.

Me·di′na–Si·do′nia (mä·thē′nä-sĕ·thō′nyä). Commune, Cádiz prov., SW Spain, 19 m. ESE of Cádiz; pop. 12,486; cattle raising; Gothic church; ancestral palace of dukes of Medina-Sidonia.

Mé′dine′ (mä′dēn′). Town, Sudan Republic, West Africa, on upper Senegal river above Kayes; fort built here by Louis Faidherbe was object of siege 1857 by the Moslem Omar al-Haji.

Me·di′net el Faiyûm (mä·dē′nĭt). Var. of EL FAIYÛM.

Mediolanum. 1 See SAINTES city, France.

2 See MILAN city, Italy.

Mediomatrica. See METZ.

Med′i·ter·ra′ne·an Sea (mĕd′ĭ·tĕ·rā′nē·ăn; -răn′yăn); *anc.* **Ma′re In·ter′num** (mā′rē [-rĕ] in·tûr′nŭm). Inland sea 2330 m. long enclosed by S Europe on the W and N, W Asia on the E, and N Africa on the S; area, including Adriatic Sea, 1,145,000 sq. m.; greatest depth 14,436 ft. near Cape Matapan. Connected on W with the Atlantic Ocean by the Strait of Gibraltar, on SE with the Red Sea by the Suez Canal, and on NE with the Black Sea by the Dardanelles, Sea of Marmara, and Bosporus. Its main subdivisions are the Adriatic Sea, Aegean Sea, Tyrrhenian Sea, Ionian Sea, and Ligurian Sea; its chief islands Sicily, Sardinia, Corsica, Crete, Cyprus, Balearic Is., Dodecanese, Cyclades, Sporades, Ionian Is., Malta.

Me′di·um Lake (mē′dĭ·ŭm). Lake ab. 4 m. long in Palo Alto co., N Iowa.

Me·djer′da *or* **Me·jer′da** (mĕ·jĕr′dȧ); *anc.* **Bag′ra·das** (băg′rȧ·dăs). River ab. 230 m. long in N Africa; rises in NE Algeria, flows E across N Tunisia into the Gulf of Tunis; fighting along its course Apr.–May 1943.

Medjerda Mountains. Range of the Little Atlas Mts. in NE Constantine dept., NE Algeria, extending across border into NW Tunisia; highest ab. 3300 ft.

Me·djez′-el-Bab (mä·jäz′ăl·bäb′). Town and road junction, N Tunisia, N Africa, ab. 40 m. WSW of the city of Tunis; in front line of fighting in Tunisian campaign Nov. 1942–Apr. 1943.

Med′men·ham (mĕd′năm). Village, S Buckinghamshire, SE cen. England; site of ruined Cistercian abbey, scene of revels of the Hell-fire Club or the secret society of the "Mad Monks of Medmenham" founded c. 1755 by Sir Francis Dashwood.

Med′ny (mĕd′nĭ; *Russ.* myĕd′-). See KOMANDORSKIE ISLANDS.

Medoacus Major. See BRENTA.

Mé′doc′ (mä′dôk′). District ab. 50 m. long and 6–7 m. wide, NW Gironde dept., SW France, N of Bordeaux; vineyards.

Me·do′ra (mĕ·dōr′ȧ). Village, ⊗ of Billings co., W North Dakota; pop. 133.

Me·dud′da (mĕ·dŏŏd′ȧ). = Cape HAFUN.

Me·dûm′ (mĕ·dōōm′). Locality 40 m. S of Cairo, Egypt, bet. Memphis and El Faiyûm; site of step pyramid built by Snefru (fl. c. 2920 B.C.), last king of Memphite dynasty.

Medunta. See MANTES-GASSICOURT.

Med·ve′di·tsa (mĕd·vĕd′ĭ·tsȧ; *Russ.* myĭd·vyä′dyĭ·tsȧ). Unnavigable river ab. 425 m. long, SE Soviet Russia, Europe; rises in N Saratov Region and flows SSW to the Don river in Stalingrad Region.

Med·ve·zhe·gorsk′ (mĕd′vĕzh·ĕ·gôrsk′; *Russ.* myĭd·vyĭ·zhĕ·gôrsk′). Town, S cen. Karelia, U.S.S.R., at N end of Lake Onega; on Murmansk railroad 80 m. N of Petrozavodsk.

Medvezhi Ostrova. See BEAR ISLANDS.

Med′way (mĕd′wā). **1** Town, Norfolk co., E Massachusetts, 22 m. SW of Boston; pop. 5168; manufactures textiles, shoes, and needles.

2 River ab. 60 m. long in SE England; formed by confluence of branches in Kent, flows N into the Thames at Sheerness; its estuary extends W to Rochester.

Meeanee. See MIANI.

Meean Meer. Var. of MIAN MIR.

Mee′ker (mē′kĕr). **1** County in Minnesota. See *Table* at MINNESOTA.

2 Town, ⊗ of Rio Blanco co., NW Colorado; pop. 1655.

Meeks Field (mēks). United States Army air base at Keflavík, SW Iceland; built during World War II, turned over to Iceland Oct. 1946 and renamed **Kef′la·vík′ Field** (kyĕf′lä·vēk′); now an international airport.

Mee′nen (mā′nĕn); *Fr.* **Me·nin′** (mē·năɴ′). Industrial commune, West Flanders prov., NW Belgium, on Lys river at French border; pop. 20,484.

Mee·ra′ne (mä·rä′nĕ). Industrial city, Saxony, Germany, 21 m. W of Chemnitz; pop. 24,094.

Meerssen. See MERSEN.

Mee′rut (mā′rŭt). **1** Former division, NW United Provinces, N India; 9230 sq. m.; pop. (1941) 5,716,451.

2 City, its ✳, on a tributary of Ganges river 40 m. NE of Delhi; pop. (1941) 169,290; dates back to days of Buddhist emperor Asoka; fort destroyed by Tamerlane in 1399; scene of outbreak of Sepoy Mutiny May 10, 1857 (cf. BARRACKPORE); has large military cantonment.

Mee′ster Cor·ne′lis (mās′tĕr   kôr·nā′lĭs); *now* **Dja′ti·ne·ga′ra** (jä′tĕ·nĕ·gä′rä). City, suburb of Djakarta (formally annexed 1935), Indonesia, SE of Weltevreden; pop. 97,831; developed from the 17th-cent. private estate of Cornelis Seenen.

Me·ga′ (mĕ·gä′). Town, Boran, S Ethiopia; junction of highways S from Addis Ababa to Chisimaio and Nairobi.

Meg′a·lop′o·lis (mĕg′ȧ·lŏp′ô·lĭs; *Mod. Gr.* mä′gä·lô′pô·lyēs). City, S Arcadia dept., cen. Peloponnesus, Greece, just E of the Alpheus river; pop. 2373. Founded 370 B.C. as Arcadian federal capital at suggestion of Epaminondas after the battle of Leuctra; its inhabitants made up of persons taken from ab. 40 Arcadian towns; intended to be a defense against Sparta; usually an ally of Thebes and Macedon; joined Achaean League 234 B.C.; destroyed by Cleomenes III 222 B.C.

Me·gan′tic (mĕ·găn′tĭk); *Fr.* **Mé′gan′tic′** (mā′gäɴ′tēk′). **1** Lake 14 sq. m., S Frontenac co., S Quebec, Canada; its outlet is the Chaudière.

2 County, Quebec, Canada. See *Table* at QUEBEC.

3 Town, ⊗ of Frontenac co., S Quebec, Canada, on NE shore of Lake Megantic; pop. 6164; fishing resort.

Meg′a·ra (mĕg′ȧ·rȧ). **1** See CARTHAGE, Africa.

2 (*Mod. Gr.* mä′gä·rä) Seaport city, Attica and Boeotia dept., Greece, on N coast of Saronic Gulf W of Athens; pop. 10,441. Anciently capital of Megaris; flourished as maritime city under Dorians, establishing colonies on shores of Propontis and Euxine; ruined commercially in Peloponnesian War. Birthplace of Euclid, founder of the Megarian school of philosophy.

Meg′a·ra Hy·blae′a (mĕg′ȧ·rȧ hĭ·blē′ȧ). Ruins of town on E coast of Sicily near Augusta and just NW of Syr-

acuse; founded 728 B.C. by Dorians from Megara; came under control of Gelon in 5th cent. B.C.

Meg'a·ris (mĕg'á·rĭs). District in ancient Greece, bet. the Saronic Gulf and Gulf of Corinth; ab. 143 sq. m.; chief town Megara; formed E part of Isthmus of Corinth.

Megh'na (mäg'nä). River ab. 150 m. long, East Bengal, Pakistan; formed on E boundary of Mymensingh dist. by the Surma and its tributaries, flows S and is joined by the Padma (the merged Brahmaputra and Ganges) SE of Dacca; its wide lower course is the E mouth of the Ganges-Brahmaputra Delta (q.v.); navigable but dangerous at certain seasons because of the high bore.

Me·gid'do (mĕ·gĭd'ō). Ancient city, N Palestine, on S side of Plain of Esdraelon and the valley of the Kishon, 20 m. N of Samaria; modern excavations have shown that it was settled ab. 3500 B.C. A great battlefield of ancient history (see ARMAGEDDON): in 1479 B.C. Thutmose III of Egypt defeated here a Syrian army; in 13th cent. B.C. Deborah and Barak overcame Sisera (Judges iv); in 609 (608?) B.C. Josiah was killed by Necho II of Egypt. In World War I Gen. Allenby began here his great offensive against the Turks Sept. 18, 1918.

Megiste. See KASTELORRIZON.

Mehdia. See MAHDIA.

Me·her'rin (mĕ·hĕr'ĭn). River 160 m. long, S Virginia and NE North Carolina; flows E and SE across state border to the Chowan river.

Meh Klong (mä klông). = MEKLONG.

Meh·sa'na (mä·sä'ná). 1 Division of (NW) former Baroda state, W Indian Union; 3068 sq. m.; pop. 1,010,007.

2 Town in the division, now in Gujerat state, 40 m. N of Ahmadabad; pop. 14,762.

Me·hun'–sur–Yè'vre (mĕ·ûn'sür·yâ'vr'). Town, Cher dept., cen. France, NW of Bourges; pop. 4551; ruins of 14th-cent. castle where Charles VII was crowned 1422 and died 1461.

Mei'de·rich (mī'dĕ·rĭk). Former industrial city, Rhine Province, Prussia, Germany, on the Rhine N of the Ruhr; annexed to Duisburg 1905.

Meiggs (mĕgz). Peak 15,518 ft. in Lima dept., cen. Peru, NE of the city of Lima.

Meigs (mĕgz). Name of counties in two states of the U.S. See Tables at OHIO and TENNESSEE.

Meije (mĕzh). Mountain 13,081 ft. in the Dauphiné Alps, SE France, bet. Isère and Hautes-Alpes depts.

Meik'ti·la (mēk'tĭ·lá). 1 District, Mandalay division, S Upper Burma; 2238 sq. m.; pop. 309,999; ✲ Meiktila.

2 Town, with ✲, on railroad 75 m. S of Mandalay; pop. 9195; a Buddhist center. In World War II a Japanese headquarters station; taken by British Mar. 2, 1945.

Mei'ling' (mā'lĭng') or **Ta Yu Ling** (dä' yü' lǐng'). Short mountain range, N Kwangtung, SE China, and pass (ab. 1000 ft.) through the range leading N to Kan valley in Kiangsi, much used as north-to-south highway.

Mei'ning·en (mī'nĭng·ĕn). City, Thuringia, Germany, near Werra river 40 m. SW of Erfurt; pop. 18,221; military station; airfield; 17th-cent. castle; railroad workshops. First mentioned 982; became city 1344; until 1918 capital of dukes of Saxe-Meiningen.

Mei'rel·be·ke (mī'rĕl·bā'kĕ). Commune, East Flanders prov., NW cen. Belgium; pop. 8268; horticulture.

Meis'sen (mī'sĕn). Manufacturing city, Saxony, E Germany, on the Elbe river 14 m. NW of Dresden; pop. 41,516; 10th-cent. castle, Gothic cathedral; known particularly for its manufacture of Dresden china; royal porcelain factory founded by Böttger (produces Böttger ware). Founded by Henry I in 10th cent.; from 968 to 1581 seat of bishops who were princes of the empire.

Mej'del (mĕj'dĕl). = EL MAJDAL.

Mejerda. See MEDJERDA.

Me'ji·ca'nos (mĕ'hē·kä'nŏs). Town, San Salvador dept., S El Salvador; pop. (1942 est.) 7389.

Méjico. Spanish form for MEXICO.

Me'jil·lo'nes (mĕ'hē·yō'nås). Small port, Antofagasta

prov., N Chile, ab. 40 m. N of Antofagasta; pop. (commune) 2826; exports nitrate, borax, copper, tin.

Me'jil·lo'nes del Sur, Bay of (mĕ'hē·yō'nåz thĕl sōōr'). Inlet on N coast of Chile, 38 m. N of Antofagasta.

Mekili. See EL MECHILI.

Mekka. = MECCA.

Me·klong (mĕ·klông). 1 River, Thailand. See KLONG.

2 Seaport, Thailand. See SAMUT SONGKHRAM.

Mek·nes' (mĕk·nĕs'; Arab. mĭk·näs'); Fr. **Mek'nès'** (mĕk'nĕs'); Span. **Me'qui·nez'** (mā'kĕ·nās'; -näth'). City, N Morocco, NW Africa, 36 m. WSW of Fès; a former ✲ of Morocco; pop. 140,380. In Middle Ages an Almohade citadel; for many years from 17th cent. was the residence of the Moroccan sultan; has fine palace, mosques, gateway.

Me·kong (mā·kông); Tibetan **Dza–chu** (dzä'chōō'); Chin. **Lan'tsang'** (län'tsäng'). River ab. 2600 m. long of SE Asia; rises in Tanglha Range of E Tibet, flows SE through Sikang and Yunnan provs., S China, and through E Indochina, forming the boundary bet. Laos and Burma and a large part of the boundary bet. Laos and Thailand; continues S through Cambodia and South Vietnam, where it empties into the South China Sea through several mouths; receives the Yangpi from the E in cen. Yunnan. Navigable to Luangprabang; its wide delta forms a fertile rice-producing area. In Sikang and Yunnan passes through deep gorges and lies between and close to the upper courses of the Salween and the Yangtze.

Mekran. See MAKRAN.

Me·la'lap (mä·lä'lăp). Town, SW cen. British North Borneo; terminus of railroad (127 m.) from Jesselton.

Mel'a·ne'sia (mĕl'á·nē'zhá; -zhǐ·á). Collective name for the islands in the Pacific Ocean NE of Australia, including New Caledonia, New Hebrides, Solomon Is., Admiralty Is., Bismarck Archipelago, Fiji Is., etc.; a subdivision of Oceania. So called from the black color of the natives who are generally considered to be a cross bet. Negroid Papuans and the Polynesians or Malays. See Map at OCEANIA.

Mel'bourne (mĕl'bĕrn). 1 City, ⊗ of Izard co., N Arkansas; pop. 571.

2 City, Brevard co., E Florida, on Indian river 58 m. SE of Orlando; pop. 11,982; incorporated 1923; resort.

3 City, S Victoria, SE Australia; at N end of Port Phillip Bay at mouth of the Yarra river; pop. 92,120, with suburbs 992,048; metroplitan area (1959 est.) 1,777,700; fine harbor; exports wool, gold, meats; varied manufactures; seat of Melbourne Univ. and its associated colleges. Founded 1835 by settlers from Tasmania; capital of state from 1851 and 2d largest city in commonwealth; temporary capital of commonwealth 1901–27.

Mel·chor' (mĕl·chôr'). Island in Chonos Archipelago, in Pacific Ocean off SW coast of Chile.

Mel·chor' Múz'quiz (mĕl·chôr' mōōs'kēs). Town, Coahuila state, NE Mexico, N of Monclova; pop. 7040.

Mel'do·la (mĕl'dō·lä). Commune, Forlì prov., Emilia, N Italy, 6 m. S of Forlì; pop. 10,961; 13th-cent. castle.

Meleda. See MLJET.

Me·le·gna'no (mä·lā·nyä'nō); formerly **Ma·ri·gna'no** (mä·rē·nyä'nō). Commune, Milano prov., Lombardy, N Italy, 10 m. SE of Milan; pop. 9377; flax spinning. Destroyed by Frederick II 1239; victory of King Francis I over Swiss troops of duke of Milan 1515; French victory over Austrians June 8, 1859.

Me·le'na del Sur (mä·lā'nä thĕl sōōr'). Municipality, N cen. La Habana prov., W Cuba; pop. 12,098.

Mel'fi (mĕl'fē). Commune, Potenza prov., Lucania, S Italy, 26 m. NNW of Potenza; pop. 15,384; cathedral (built 1155); castle; ancient city walls; fine sarcophagus; notable grotto church (frescoes of 12th and 13th cents.) nearby; earthquake 1930.

Mel'fort (mĕl'fĕrt). Town, S cen. Saskatchewan, Canada, 55 m. ESE of Prince Albert; pop. 2919; trades in lumber; railroad divisional point.

Melghir, Shatt el. See Chott MELRIR.

Mel′i·boe′a (mĕl′ĭ·bē′à). Ancient town near the coast of Magnesia, Greece, bet. Mt. Pelion and Mt. Ossa.

Me′lik, Wa′di el (wä′dĭ ăl mä′lĭk). River bed, cen. Sudan; extends from W Kordofan prov. NE to Nile river at Ed Debba.

Me·lil′la (må·lē′[l]yä); *anc.* **Rus′ad·dir′** (rŭs′ăd·dĭr′). Spanish presidio and commercial city, N coast of Morocco, NW Africa; pop. (1940) 77,353; on SE coast of Cape Tres Forcas in Er Rif region. Conquered by Spain 1470; many times under siege; hinterland secured 1909; scene of Riffian revolt 1921 under Abd-el-Krim; reoccupied 1926; scene of revolt of army chiefs which led to Spanish Civil War 1936.

Me′li·mo′yu (mä′lē·mō′yōō). Peak 7900 ft. in S Chile, E of Moraleda Channel.

Me′li·pil′la (mä′lē·pē′yä). Town, Santiago prov., cen. Chile, 38 m. SW of Santiago; pop. 9316; dairy products.

Melita. 1 See MALTA.

2 See MLJET.

Melitene. See MALATYA.

Me′li·to′pol (mĕl′ĭ·tô′p′l; *Russ.* myĭ·lyĭ·tô′pŭl·y′). Town, S Zaporozhe Region, S Ukraine, U.S.S.R., near NW shore of Sea of Azov 70 m. S of Zaporozhe; pop. 75,735; on main rail line from Kharkhov to Sevastopol; center of an agricultural district; fishing also an important industry. In World War II held by Germans 1941–43; taken by Russians Nov. 6, 1943, after very bitter fighting; a key point for control of the Crimea.

Mel·la′ha (mĕ·lä′hå). Village, an E suburb of Tripoli, and small lake on coast of Libya; large airport.

Mel′len (mĕl′ĕn). City, Ashland co., N Wisconsin; pop. 1182; ships iron ore; gabbro quarry.

Mel·lette′ (mĕ·lĕt′). County in South Dakota. See *Table* at SOUTH DAKOTA.

Měl′ník (myĕl′nyēk); *Ger.* **Mel′nik** (mĕl′nĭk). Town, N Bohemia, W Czechoslovakia, 18 m. N of Prague at junction of Labe and Vltava rivers; pop. (1930) 11,549.

Me′lo (mä′lô). City, * of Cerro Largo dept., E Uruguay, 205 m. NE of Montevideo; pop. ab. 23,000; distributing center for NE Uruguay.

Melodunum. See MELUN.

Me·lo′nes Dam (mĕ·lō′nĕz). Dam completed 1926 across Stanislaus river, Tuolumne and Calaveras cos., N cen. California; height 222 ft.; impounds water for irrigation.

Me·lo′ria (må·lô′ryä). Small island 4 m. off Leghorn, Italy; naval battles 1241 in which Sardinian king defeated Genoese and 1284 in which Genoese destroyed Pisan fleet.

Me′los (mē′lŏs; *Mod. Gr.* -lôs); *Ital.* **Mi′lo** (mē′lô). 1 An island of the Cyclades; 14 m. long; 57 sq. m.; pop. ab. 5000; in Cyclades dept., Greece; chief town Plaka. Of volcanic origin, highest point 2533 ft.; has large harbor on N which nearly divides the island. In early period occupied by Dorians; attacked and conquered 416 B.C. by Athenians and its people either killed or enslaved.

2 Ruined city on Melos; here the famous statue of Venus (Venus of Milo) was discovered 1820 and is now in the Louvre museum in Paris.

Mel·rir′, Chott (shät mĕl·rĭr′); *Arab.* **Shatt el Melghir′** (shät′ ăl mĕl·gēr′). Marshy saline lake 80–100 m. long in N Touggourt territory, NE Algeria.

Mel′rose (mĕl′rōz). 1 Residential city, Middlesex co., NE Massachusetts, 7 m. N of Boston; pop. 29,619.

2 City, Stearns co., cen. Minnesota, 30 m. WNW of St. Cloud; pop. 2135.

3 Burgh, N Roxburgh co., SE Scotland; pop. 2146; the "Kennaquhair" of Scott's *Abbot* and *Monastery*. Ruins of a Cistercian abbey, founded 1136 by David I.

Melrose Park. Village, Cook co., NE Illinois, 15 m. W of Chicago; pop. 22,291; steel plants.

Mel′tham (mĕl′thăm). Urban district, West Riding, Yorkshire, N England; pop. 5107.

Mel′ton Mow′bray (mĕl′t′n [-tŭn] mō′brå [-brĭ]).

Urban district, Leicestershire, cen. England, 15 m. NE of Leicester; pop. 14,052; noted for its pork pies and Stilton cheese; fox-hunting center.

Me·lun′ (mē·lûn′); *anc.* **Mel′o·du′num** (mĕl′ô·dū′nŭm). Manufacturing city, * of Seine-et-Marne dept., N France, on Seine river 27 m. SSE of Paris; pop. 17,499; 12th-cent. Romanesque church; fine château nearby. Conquered by Romans 53 B.C.; taken by Normans; royal residence under Capetians; taken by English 1420 and retaken by Joan of Arc 1430.

Me·lu′sa (mä·lōō′sä). Town, N Morocco, NW Africa, 18 m. NW of Tetuán.

Mel′ville (mĕl′vĭl; *Sou. also* -v′l). 1 Town, St. Landry parish, S cen. Louisiana, 37 m. NNE of Lafayette; pop. 1939; in section producing cotton, sugar, and rice.

2 Town, SE Saskatchewan, Canada, 26 m. SW of Yorkton; pop. 4458; railroad divisional point.

Melville, Cape. 1 Cape, NE Queensland, Australia, on E coast of Cape York Penin.

2 Cape, S Balaboc I., Palawan prov., SW Philippine Is.

Melville, Lake. Lake 1298 sq. m. in SE Labrador; constitutes inner basin of Hamilton Inlet; at its SW corner receives the Hamilton river.

Melville Bay. Large inlet of NE Baffin Bay on NW coast of Greenland, E of Cape York.

Melville Island. 1 Island 2400 sq. m. off NW coast of Northern Territory, Australia; separated from mainland by Clarence Strait, near Darwin.

2 Island 16,164 sq. m., 200 m. long by 130 m. wide, in Parry Is., W Franklin District, Northwest Territories, Canada, N of Victoria I.

Melville Peninsula. Peninsula, S Franklin District, Northwest Territories, Canada, bet. Committee Bay on the W and Foxe Basin on the E.

Melville Sound. See VISCOUNT MELVILLE SOUND.

Mel′vin·dale (mĕl′vĭn·dāl). Residential city, Wayne co., SE Michigan, 8 m. WSW of Detroit; pop. 13,089.

Me Ma·o′ya, Mount (mä mä·ō′yä). Peak 4728 ft., cen. New Caledonia, SW Pacific Ocean.

Mem′ba Bay (mĕm′bå). Inlet of Mozambique Channel on NE coast of Mozambique, N of Cape Loguno.

Me′mel (mä′mĕl). 1 River. See NEMAN.

2 *Lithuanian* **Klai′pe·da** (klī′pĕ·dä); *Ger.* **Me′mel·ge·biet′** (mä′mĕl·gĕ·bēt′) *or* **Me′mel·land** (-länt′). Territory, E coast of Baltic Sea; 1092 sq. m.; pop. (1939) 147,569; includes N half of narrow tongue of land (Kurische Nehrung) enclosing the Kurishes Gaf, a long narrow region along N bank of the Neman, and the port of Memel. Šilutė and Pagegiai, Lithuanian towns, were in the Memelgebiet. Original Memel district of Lithuania had 329 sq. m. and 73,079 population in 1938. Formerly German territory, the district of Memel was placed under inter-Allied control 1919–23; for *History*, see 3 below.

3 *Lithuanian* **Klaipeda.** Commercial and manufacturing seaport city, * of Memel territory, W Lithuania, on the Baltic Sea at the mouth of Neman (Memel) river; pop. (1938) 47,189; exports lumber, agricultural products, fish; manufactures chemicals, soap, wood pulp, iron products. Formerly much Russian and Polish trade passed through it.

History: Founded as a fort 1252; later, as **Me′mel·burg** (mä′mĕl·boorĸ), acquired by the Teutonic Knights; an important trading town in Hanseatic League; in 17th cent. held by Sweden and occupied by Russian troops 1757 and 1813, but Prussian possession since 17th cent.; treaty bet. England and Prussia signed here 1807. Taken by Russia in World War I; after 1919 administered by France under the League of Nations; seized by Lithuanians Jan. 15, 1923 as their only good port; made part of autonomous Memel territory, created by Memel Statute of May 8, 1924; seized by Germany early in 1939 and held until taken by Russian armies Jan. 1945; made part of Lithuania under Russian control; population largely German.

Mem'ming·en (měm'ĭng·ĕn). Industrial city, Swabia, SW Bavaria, Germany, 42 m. SW of Augsburg; pop. 14,049. First mentioned 1010; became city 1286; took part in Tetrapolitan Confession; Austrians defeated by Moreau nearby 1800; passed to Bavaria 1802.

Mem'phis (měm'fĭs). **1** City, ⊗ of Scotland co., NE Missouri, 28 m. NE of Kirksville; pop. 2106.
2 Commercial and industrial city, ⊗ of Shelby co., SW corner of Tennessee, on Mississippi river 10 m. N of Mississippi border; largest city in the state; pop. 497,524; market for cotton, cottonseed products, and hardwood lumber, steel, grain, livestock, oil; railroad center; good port facilities; varied manufactures. Army supply depot; naval air station. Southwestern at Memphis (1848; coed.); Memphis State Univ. (1909; coed.); LeMoyne Coll. (1870; coed.); Christian Brothers Coll. (1871; men).
History: Former home of Chickasaw Indians; served as landing place for early explorers and missionaries (De Soto, Jolliet, Marquette, La Salle); forts erected by French, later by Spanish, and by U.S. in 1797; platted and settled in 1819 by colony sent by Andrew Jackson, John Overton, and James Winchester; incorp. as town 1826, as city 1849; made port of customs 1850; became Confederate military center at beginning of Civil War 1861; temporary state capital 1862; captured by Union forces after battle of Memphis 1862, and remained in Union control until after the war; suffered from yellow fever epidemics 1867, 1873, and, esp., 1878; became impoverished and surrendered charter to state 1879; rechartered as city 1893.
3 City, ⊗ of Hall co., NW Texas, in the panhandle 75 m. SE of Amarillo; pop. 3332; cotton processing.
4 *modern* **Mit Ra·hi'na** (mēt rä·hē'nä). Ancient city in Lower Egypt, now a village on W bank of the Nile 14 m. S of Cairo; traditionally the capital of Menes (3400 B.C.) and of most of the rulers of the Old Kingdom and of the Middle Kingdom down to the XVIIIth dynasty; superseded by Heracleopolis during IXth and Xth dynasties and later by Thebes at beginning of New Kingdom; lost its importance after the conquest of Egypt by Alexander. Sacred to the worship of Ptah. In its ruins are the great temple of Ptah, royal palaces, an extensive necropolis. Pyramids of Saqqara nearby and Pyramids of Giza just to the N; in the Old Testament called **Noph** [nŏf] (*Isaiah* xix. 13; *Jer.* ii. 16, and elsewhere).

Mem'phre·ma'gog, Lake (měm'frē·mä'gŏg). Lake extending across U.S.-Canada border from N Vermont into S Quebec; ab. 30 m. long (7 in Vermont) and from 1 to 4 m. wide; its outlet flows into the St. Francis river, Quebec.

Me'na (mē'nä). City, ⊗ of Polk co., W Arkansas, in Ouachita Mts. 70 m. W of Hot Springs; pop. 4388; summer resort; shipping point for lumber; cotton gins, sawmills, brick and tile works, flour and feed mills.

Menado. See MANADO.

Menaeum. See MINEO.

Men'ai Strait *or* **Straits** (měn'ī). Channel ab. 14 m. long and from 200 yds. to ¾ m. wide off NW coast of Wales, bet. Anglesey I. and the mainland; spanned by two bridges, tubular and suspension.

Me·nal'du·ma·deel' (mä·näl'dü·mä·dāl'). Commune, Friesland prov., N Netherlands, just W of Leeuwarden; pop. 10,369.

Me Nam *or* **Menam.** See CHAO PHRAYA.

Me·nands' (mē·nän[d]z'). Village, Albany co., E New York, on Hudson river 2 m. N of Albany; pop. 2314.

Me'nang·ka'bau (mä'näng·kä'bou). Former empire of cen. and W Sumatra, regarded as the original home of the Malay race; migrations to Malay Penin. and other parts of the Malay Archipelago began probably in middle of 12th cent. A.D. Became partially Moslemized in 15th cent.; overcome by Dutch in 18th cent.

Menar, El. See EL MENAR.

Me·nard' (mě·närd'). **1** Name of counties in two states of the U.S. See *Tables* at ILLINOIS and TEXAS.

2 Town, ⊗ of Menard co., W cen. Texas, 52 m. SE of San Angelo; pop. 1914; railroad terminus; ships wool and mohair; ruins of old Spanish mission (1757) nearby.

Me·nash'a (mě·năsh'ä). City, Winnebago co., E Wisconsin, on Lake Winnebago and Fox river 5 m. S of Appleton; pop. 14,647; forms continuous community with twin city of Neenah (*q.v.*); settled 1843; manufactures paper, paper products, woodenware, pulleys, pumps, wire; printing plants, boilerworks.

Mende (mäND; *anc.* **Mi·ma'tum** (mĭ·mä'tŭm). Commune, ✳ of Lozère dept., S France, 76 m. NW of Avignon; pop. 5785; 15th-cent. ogival cathedral. See CÉVENNES.

Men'den (měn'děn). City, cen. North Rhine-Westphalia state, W Germany, ESE of Dortmund; pop. 13,677; manufactures metal and electrical goods.

Men'den·hall (měn'děn·hôl). Town, ⊗ of Simpson co., S cen. Mississippi; pop. 1946.

Men'de·res' (měn'dě·rěs'). **1** *anc.* **Mae·an'der** (mě·ăn'děr). River ab. 240 m. long in W Turkey in Asia; rises in mountains W of Afyon Karahisar and flows SW and W into Aegean Sea S of the island of Samos; notable in ancient legend for its wanderings. Near the mouth of the modern stream is the large Lake Bafa; its fertile valley noted for production of olives. The ancient Maeander flowed across N Caria and on or near its banks were the ancient cities of Laodicea, Magnesia, and Miletus.
2 *anc.* **Sca·man'der** (skä·măn'děr). River 60 m. long, NW Turkey in Asia; rises in Kazdağı (Mt. Ida) and flows W and NW into the Dardanelles across the plain of ancient Troy. The ancient Scamander, flowing past Troy, is supposed in its lower course to have been E of the modern stream.

Men'des (měn'děz). Archaeological site in Nile Delta, N Egypt, E of Damietta branch and just SE of El Mansûra; seat of veneration of Osiris. Near here c. 378 B.C. Egyptians under Nectanebo I defeated the Persians.

Men'dip Hills (měn'dĭp). Range of hills ab. 18 m. long in NE Somersetshire, SW England; highest elevation **Black Down** 1068 ft.

Men'do·ci'no (měn'dô·sē'nō). County in California. See *Table* at CALIFORNIA.

Mendocino, Cape. Cape on W coast of Humboldt co., NW California; extreme W point of California, 124°8'W.

Men·doet' *or* **Men·dut'** (měn·dōōt'). Village, Central Java prov., Indonesia, S of Magelang and near Borobudur; has temple with large and remarkable statue of Buddha, built a little later than Borobudur.

Men·do'ta (měn·dô'tä). City, La Salle co., N Illinois, 20 m. NW of Ottawa; pop. 6154.

Mendota, Lake. See FOUR LAKES.

Mendota Heights. Village, Dakota co., SE Minnesota, S suburb of St. Paul; pop. 5028.

Men·do'za (měn·dô'zä; *Span.* mân·dô'sä). **1** River in W Argentina; rises on slopes of Aconcagua Mt., flows E and N into Lake Guanacache.
2 Province of Argentina. See *Table* at ARGENTINA.
3 City, its ✳, W Argentina, ab. 60 m. SE of Aconcagua Mt.; pop. (est.) 100,429; center of grape culture a 1 native wines; on railroad and highway from Argentina across the Andes to Santiago, Chile, at alt. 2320 ft. Founded 1559 by an expedition sent from Chile; in 1776 became part of the new viceroyalty of La Plata, later Argentina; destroyed by earthquake and fire 1861.

Me'ne·men' (mě'ně·měn'). Town, Izmir vilayet, W Turkey in Asia, 14 m. NNW of İzmir; pop. 14,006.

Mé'ner·ville' (mā'něr·věl'). Commune, Alger dept., N Algeria, on coastal railroad E of Algiers; pop. 11,070.

Menevia. See SAINT DAVID'S.

Men'fi (měm'fē). Commune, Agrigento prov., SW Sicily, 40 m. NW of Agrigento; pop. 10,879.

Mêng Chiang (mŭng' jĭ·äng'). Japanese buffer state bet. Manchukuo and Outer Mongolia erected 1937, comprising approximately the provinces of Chahar and Suiyuan of Inner Mongolia; ab. 220,000 sq. m.; pop.

(est.) 5,000,000; ✳ Kweisui (called Hohohoto by the Japanese); came to an end with defeat of Japan 1945. See *History* at Inner MONGOLIA.

Men·ge·de (mĕng′gĕ·dĕ). Former commune (pop. 13,794), Arnsberg govt. dist., Westphalia prov., Prussia, Germany; since 1928 part of Dortmund (*q.v.*).

Meng·ga′la (mĕng·gä′lä). Town, Lampong Districts, SE Sumatra, Indonesia, pop. 14,174.

Meng′ku′ (mŭng′kōō′). Chinese name of MONGOLIA.

Meng′ting′ (mŭng′dĭng′). Town, SW Yunnan prov., S China, near Burma border SE of Lungling and the Burma Road; held by Japanese 1942–43.

Meng′tsz′ (mŭng′dzŭ′); *Fr.* **Mong–tseu** (mŭng′dzŭ′); *also* **Meng′tseu′** *or* **Meng′tze′** (mŭng′dzŭ′). City and former treaty port, S Yunnan, S China, near Tonkin border SSE of Kunming; pop. (1931 est.) 193,004; on fertile plateau (alt. 4300 ft.); important shipping point for nearby (**Ko′kiu′** [gō′jĭ·ō′]) tin mines.

Men′i·fee (mĕn′ĭ·fē). County in Kentucky. See *Table* at KENTUCKY.

Menin. See MEENEN.

Meninx. See DJERBA.

Men′lo Park (mĕn′lō). 1 Residential city, San Mateo co., W California, 23 m. SE of San Francisco; pop. 26,957; settled c. 1861, incorporated 1930.

2 Village, Middlesex co., cen. New Jersey, ab. 6 m. SE of Plainfield; pop. (1950) 400; 129-ft. Memorial Tower (topped by huge electric-light bulb) near site of Edison's laboratory where he invented incandescent light 1879. See WEST ORANGE.

Me·nom′i·nee (mĕ·nŏm′ĭ·nē). 1 River 125 m. long, NE Wisconsin; formed by confluence of Michigamme and Brule rivers, flows SE on Wisconsin-Michigan boundary and empties into Green Bay; provides water power.

2 County in Michigan. See *Table* at MICHIGAN.

3 County in Wisconsin. See footnote in *Table* at WISCONSIN.

4 City, its ⊗, S tip of Michigan penin., on Green Bay; pop. 11,289; wood products, beet sugar, dairying.

Menominee Range. Low range in upper Michigan penin. and NE Wisconsin, noted for iron-ore production.

Me·nom′o·nee Falls (mĕ·nŏm′ō·nē). Village, Waukesha co., SE Wisconsin, NNW of Milwaukee; pop. 18,276.

Me·nom′o·nie (mĕ·nŏm′ō·nē). City, ⊗ of Dunn co., W Wisconsin, 21 m. W of Eau Claire; pop. 8624; makes processed dairy products, flour, feed, aluminum ware. Stout State College (1893; coed.).

Me′no·ni′tas (mā′nō·nē′täs). Town, Chihuahua state, N Mexico; pop. 8014.

Menorca. See MINORCA.

Men·ta′na (mĕn·tä′nä). Commune, Roma prov., W Latium, cen. Italy, NE of Rome; pop. (1931) 3705; scene of battle Nov. 3, 1867 in which Garibaldi was defeated by combined papal and French troops.

Men·ta′wai (mĕn·tä′wī). Island group of ab. 70 islands in the Indian Ocean off the W cen. coast of Sumatra; 2354 sq. m.; pop. 18,149; includes large islands of Siberut, Sipora, North Pagai, and South Pagai. Of volcanic origin and surrounded by reefs; inhabitants belong to very early indigenous peoples of Sumatra.

Mentawei, Mentawi. Vars. of MENTAWAI.

Men·teith′, Loch (lŏK mĕn·tēth′). Small lake in Perth co., cen. Scotland, near border of Stirling co.

Men′ton′ (män′tôn′); *Ital.* **Men·to′ne** (mĕn·tō′nĕ). Commune, Alpes-Maritimes dept., SE France, on Mediterranean Sea 12 m. ENE of Nice; pop. 21,703; famous health and winter resort. Founded in 10th cent.; under princes of Monaco from 14th cent. to 1848; independent republic 1848–60; to France 1860. Grimaldi (*q.v.*) caves nearby.

Men′tone (mĕn′tōn). Village ⊗ of Loving co., W Texas; pop. 226.

Men′tor (mĕn′tēr). Village, Lake co., NE Ohio, on Lake Erie 22 m. NE of Cleveland; pop. 4354.

Menufieh. = MINÛFÎYA.

Menzala, Lake. = Lake MANZALA.

Menzel. See GABÈS.

Meping. See PING.

Mep′pel (mĕp′ĕl). Commune, Drenthe prov., NE Netherlands, 14 m. NNE of Zwolle; pop. 12,133.

Mequinez. See MEKNES.

Meq′uon (mĕk′wŏn). City, Ozaukee co., E Wisconsin, S of Sheboygan; pop. 8543.

Mer′a·mec (mĕr′à·măk). River 174 m. long, SE cen. Missouri; rises in Dent co., flows NE into Mississippi river below St. Louis.

Merampelou, Kólpos. See MIRABELLA BAY.

Me·ra′no (mā·rä′nō); *Ger.* **Me·ran′** (mā·rän′). Commune, Bolzano prov., Venezia Tridentina, NE Italy, on S slope of the Alps 17 m. NW of Bolzano; pop. 25,902; tourist and health resort; castle (1450), Gothic church (1367), fine villas. Near site of 1st-cent. (A.D.) *Castrum Maiense;* first mentioned 857 A.D.; received city rights 1305; capital of the Tirol 12th cent. to c. 1420; under Austrian rule until ceded to Italy 1919 by treaty of St-Germain.

Me·ra′pi (mĕ·rä′pē). 1 Volcano 9548 ft. in cen. Java, Indonesia, just N of Jogjakarta.

2 See IDJEN.

3 Volcanic peak 9485 ft. in the Padang Highlands, W Sumatra, 40 m. NE of Padang and near Bukittinggi; a peak of the Barisan Mts.; violent eruptions 1867, 1876.

Me·rau′ke (mĕ·rou′kĕ). Seaport and chief town on S coast of Neth. New Guinea; pop. ab. 2000; at mouth of **Merauke River** (ab. 125 m. long) 60 m. from Papua border; has trade with Papua and Australia; chief product copra. Only town in Neth. Indies not occupied by Japanese in World War II.

Mer·ba′boe (mĕr·bä′bōō) *or* **Mer·ba′bu.** Volcano 10,308 ft. in cen. Java, Indonesia, N of Jogjakarta.

Mer·can′ Dağ′la·rı′ (mĕr·jän′ dä′lä·rĭ′). Peak 11,315 ft. in E cen. Turkey in Asia, S of Erzincan.

Mer·ca′ra (mĕr·kä′rá). Town, S India, formerly ✳ of Coorg prov.; now in S Mysore state; pop. 10,117.

Mer·ca·ti′no Ma·rec′chia (mâr·kä·tē′nō mä·rāk′kyä). Commune, Pesaro e Urbino prov., Marches, cen. Italy, 33 m. W of Pesaro; pop. (1931) 9994.

Mer·ca′to San Se·ve·ri′no (mâr·kä′tō sän sá·vå-rē′nō). Commune, Salerno prov., Campania, S Italy, 7 m. N of Salerno; pop. (1931) 12,506.

Mercato Sa·ra·ce′no (sä·rä·chä′nō). Commune, Forlì prov., Emilia, N Italy, 20 m. SSE of Forlì; pop. 10,238.

Mer·ced′ (mĕr·sĕd′). 1 River ab. 150 m. long, cen. California; rises in S Yosemite National Park, flows W through the 6-mile long Yosemite Valley (*q.v.*) and into the San Joaquin river.

2 County in California. See *Table* at CALIFORNIA.

3 City, its ⊗, cen. California, in valley of the San Joaquin and S of the Merced river 55 m. NW of Fresno; pop. 26,957; in dairy, fruit, hay, cotton, and livestock region; cement, lumber; canneries, nurseries. Castle Air Force Base (7 m. NW).

Mer·ce·da′rio (mĕr·sä·thä′ryō). Peak 22,210 ft. in San Juan prov., W Argentina, near Chilean border.

Mer·ce′des (mĕr·sā′dĕs). City, Hidalgo co., S Texas, 20 m. E of McAllen; pop. 10,943; cotton ginning and oil industries; packs citrus fruits and vegetables.

Mer·ce′des (mĕr·sā′thās). 1 Town, Buenos Aires prov., E Argentina, 55 m. W of Buenos Aires; pop. 39,991.

2 Town, cen. Corrientes prov., NE Argentina, 120 m. SSE of Corrientes; pop. (est.) 15,000.

3 City, San Luis prov., cen. Argentina, ab. 60 m. E of San Luis; pop. (est.) 37,666.

4 City and river port, ✳ of Soriano dept., SW Uruguay, on Río Negro 155 m. NW of Montevideo, pop. 24,719; ships wool, cattle, wheat.

Mer·ced′ Peak (mĕr·sĕd′). Mountain 11,722 ft. on S boundary of Yosemite National Park, E cen. California.

Mer′cer (mûr′sēr). 1 Name of counties in eight states of the U.S. See *Tables* at ILLINOIS, KENTUCKY, MIS-

SOURI, NEW JERSEY, NORTH DAKOTA, OHIO, PENNSYL-
VANIA, WEST VIRGINIA.

2 Borough, ⊗ of Mercer co., W Pennsylvania, 17 m.
NNE of New Castle; pop. 2800; settled 1795; formerly
important horse mart and merchandising center.

3 Village, Auckland provincial dist., N North I., New
Zealand, on Waikato river 32 m. SSE of Auckland. Near
here was old frontier bet. Maori and colonist; adjacent
terrain scene of numerous encounters bet. Maori warriors and British troops 1863–64. Seat of St. Stephen's
Maori Boys Coll. for Maori youths.

Mer′cers·burg (mûr′sērz-bûrg). Borough, Franklin co.,
S Pennsylvania, 17 m. WSW of Chambersburg; pop.
1759; settled c. 1730; manufactures leather, shirts, lumber, dairy products. Mercersburg Academy (1836;
boys); home 1796–1809 of James Buchanan, 15th president of the United States, who was born nearby.

Mer′chant·ville (mûr′chănt·vĭl). Borough, Camden
co., SW New Jersey, 3 m. E of Camden; pop. 4075; incorporated 1874.

Mer′ci·a (mûr′shĭ·à; -shà). Ancient Anglian kingdom in
cen. England, one of a group of seven Anglo-Saxon kingdoms, sometimes known as the Heptarchy (*q.v.*); in 633
A.D. its pagan ruler overthrew Christian king of Northumbria (*q.v.*); leading member of Heptarchy in 8th cent.;
conquered 828 by Egbert, ruler of Wessex (*q.v.*) [802–
839]; in 9th cent. English Mercia separated by Watling
Street from Danish Mercia to the NE in Danelaw; Danelaw reconquered in 10th cent.

Mer′e·dith (mĕr′ĕ·dĭth). Town, Belknap co., cen. New
Hampshire, on Lakes Winnipesaukee and Waukewan 9
m. N of Laconia; pop. 2434; summer and winter resort;
linen mills.

Merendón, Sierra de. See SIERRA DE MERENDÓN.

Me′re·va′ri (mā′rà·vä′rē). River in SE cen. Venezuela;
flows N into Caura river.

Mer′e·weth′er (mĕr′ĕ·wĕth′ēr). Town, E New South
Wales, SE Australia; suburb of Newcastle; pop. 8068.

Merg, El. See BARCA town, Cirenaica, Libia.

Mergate. See MARGATE.

Mer′gen′ (mĕr′gĕn′); *formerly* **Nun′kiang′** (nōōn′jĭ-
äng′). Town, * of Nunkiang prov., N Manchuria, China,
on left bank of Nonni river SW of Aigun.

Mer·gui′ (mûr·gwē′). **1** District, S Tenasserim division,
Lower Burma; 10,906 sq. m.; pop. 161,987; * Mergui;
includes Mergui Archipelago.

2 Seaport town, site *, on a coastal island opp. King I.;
pop. 20,405; has large export trade in tin ore and rubber.

Mergui Archipelago. Group of ab. 800 islands in
Andaman Sea off coast of Mergui dist. in S Lower
Burma; bet. ab. lat. 9° and 13°; largest is Tavoy I. at
N end; among other large islands (N to S) are King,
Elphinstone, Ross, Sellore, Bentinck, Kisseraing, Domel,
Sullivan, and St. Matthew. Sparsely inhabited, chiefly
by Selungs and Burmans.

Meriç. See MARITSA.

Mé′ri′court′ (mā′rē′kōōr′). Commune, Pas-de-Calais
dept., N France, 9 m. from Arras; pop. (1931) 10,496;
coal mines; destroyed in World War I.

Me′ri·da (mā′rĕ·thä). Municipality on W side of Ormoc
Bay, NW coast of Leyte I., Phil. Is., SW of Ormoc and
42 m. SW of Tacloban; pop. 26,794.

Mé′ri·da (mā′rĕ·thä). **1** City, Yucatán penin., SE Mexico, * of Yucatán state; pop. 98,852; center of henequen
or sisal industry; exports sisal, chicle, hides, and farm
products; its port is Progreso. Founded 1542 on a site
within the ancient Maya Empire.

2 *anc.* **Au·gus′ta E·mer′i·ta** (ô·gŭs′tà ē·mĕr′ĭ·tà).
Commune, Badajoz prov., SW Spain, on Guadiana river
33 m. ENE of Badajoz; pop. 25,501; textiles, leather,
soap, cork, hats; noted esp. for its Roman ruins, including an amphitheater, bridge, aqueduct, circus, temple,
arch by Trajan, and colonnaded theater. Founded 23
B.C. by Augustus; became Visigothic episcopal see; taken
by Moors 712 A.D.; reconquered 1228 by Alfonso IX.

3 State of Venezuela. See *Table* at VENEZUELA.

4 Town, * of Mérida state, W Venezuela; pop. (1941
est.) 14,440; in the Cordillera Mérida ab. 30 m. S of the
S end of Lake Maracaibo on highway to Colombia.

Mérida, Cordillera. See CORDILLERA MÉRIDA.

Mérida, Sierra Nevada de. See CORDILLERA MÉRIDA.

Mer′i·den (mĕr′ĭ·d'n; -dĕn). **1** Manufacturing city,
New Haven co., S Connecticut, 17 m. NE of New
Haven; pop. 51,850; industrial center of truck-farming
region; known esp. for manufacture of plated and sterling
silverware; state reform school for boys. Settled 1661;
incorporated 1867; consolidated 1922 with town (incorporated 1806) with which it is coextensive.

2 Village, Sullivan co., SW New Hampshire, ab. 12 m.
N of Claremont; bird sanctuary (estab. 1910).

Me·rid′i·an (mĕ·rĭd′ĭ·ǎn). **1** City, ⊗ of Lauderdale co.,
E Mississippi, 16 m. W of Alabama border; pop. 49,374;
railroad center; cotton, cottonseed-oil, and textile mills;
vegetable, poultry, and livestock market; military camp
and divisional headquarters in Civil War; temporary
capital of Mississippi 1863; largely destroyed by Sherman's army 1864, but rebuilt after the war.

2 City, ⊗ of Bosque co., cen. Texas; pop. 993.

Mé′ri·gnac′ (mā′rē·nyàk′). Commune, Gironde dept.,
SW France; suburb of Bordeaux; pop. (1931) 15,363;
cattle market; 13th-cent. dungeon (Tour de Veyrines).

Me′ri·kar′via (mĕ′rĭ·kàr′vyà). Coastal town, SW Finland, in Turku-Pori dept., S of Kristiina; pop. 8799.

Merín. See Lake MIRIM.

Mer′i·on·eth·shire (mĕr′ĭ·ŏn′ĕth·shĭr; -shēr) *or* **Mer′-
i·on′eth** (mĕr′ĭ·ŏn′ĕth). County, W Wales; area 660
sq. m.; pop. 41,456; ⊗ Dolgelley; hilly region; rivers
Dyfi, Dee, Mawddach; stock raising (esp. Welsh ponies),
quarrying (limestone, slate). In ancient times when a
center of resistance to the English, Harlech (*q.v.*) was its
capital; slate industry became important in 18th cent.,
declined since 1914.

Mer′i·on Station (mĕr′ĭ·ŭn). Locality, Montgomery
co., SE Pennsylvania; pop. (est.) 5000.

Me′ri·tí′ (mā′rē·tē′). City, Rio de Janeiro state, SE
Brazil, W of Guanabara Bay and ab. 10 m. N of Rio de
Janeiro; pop. (1940 est.) 38,645.

Mer′i·weth′er (mĕr′ĭ·wĕth′ēr). County in Georgia. See
Table at GEORGIA.

Meriwether Lew′is National Monument (lū′ĭs;
lōō′ĭs). See UNITED STATES, *National Monuments.*

Me·ri′zo (mĕ·rē′zō). Town, SW coast of Guam, Mariana Is.; pop. ab. 1000.

Mer′kel (mûr′kĕl). City, Taylor co., NW cen. Texas, 18
m. W of Abilene; pop. 2312.

Merk′sem *or* **Merx′em** (mĕrk′sĕm). Commune, Antwerp prov., N Belgium; N suburb of Antwerp; pop. (1938
est.) 29,870.

Mer′kus, Cape (mûr′kŭs). Cape on SW coast of New
Britain, Bismarck Archipelago; near Arawe, landing
place of American invasion forces Dec. 1943.

Mer′lo (mĕr′lô). Town, Buenos Aires prov., E Argentina, ab. 20 m. W of Buenos Aires.

Mer′o·ë (mĕr′ô·ē). Ancient city on E bank of the Nile,
lat. 17°N; capital of Ethiopian kings from c. 700 B.C., of
Nubia 500 to 300 B.C., and of the later kingdom of
Meroë (Meroitic kingdom) lasting until ab. 350 A.D.;
its extensive ruins (temples, palaces, necropolis) are near
modern **Ka·bu′shi·a** (kà·bōō′shĭ·à), Northern Province, N Anglo-Egyptian Sudan. The kingdom included
the **Isle of Meroë**, *anc.* **Meroe In′su·la** (ĭn′sū·là),
the region bet. the Nile, the Blue Nile, and the Atbara
rivers, notable as a great center of commerce and caravan trade and also for the language (Meroitic) of its
inhabitants, written in hieroglyphics, and about which
little is known.

Me′rom, Waters of (mē′rŏm); *Arab.* **Bah′ret el
Hu′le** (bä′h′-rŏt ăl hōō′lĕ). Lake 4 m. long by ab. 3½ m.
wide, N Palestine, ab. 11 m. N of the Sea of Galilee;
through it passes the upper Jordan.

Mer′o·we′ (mĕr′ô·wā′). **1** Town, Northern Province, N Sudan, on the Nile river near the Fourth Cataract; capital of former Dongala prov.
2 Var. of MEROË.

Mer′ri·am (mĕr′ĭ·ăm). City, Johnson co., E Kansas, suburb SSW of Kansas City; pop. 5084.

Mer′rick (mĕr′ĭk). **1** County in Nebraska. See *Table* at NEBRASKA.
2 Urban community (unincorporated), Nassau co., SE New York, on Long I., pop. 18,789.
3 Peak 2764 ft. in Kirkcudbright co., S Scotland.

Mer′rill (mĕr′ĭl). City, ⊗ of Lincoln co., N Wisconsin, on Wisconsin river 15 m. N of Wausau; pop. 9451.

Mer′ri·mac (mĕr′ĭ·măk). Town, Essex co., NE Massachusetts, on Merrimack river NE of Lowell; pop. 3261.

Mer′ri·mack (mĕr′ĭ·măk). **1** River 110 m. long, S New Hampshire and NE Massachusetts; formed by junction of Pemigewasset and Winnipesaukee rivers at Franklin, New Hampshire, flows S across Massachusetts border, then turns NE and empties into the Atlantic Ocean at Newburyport, NE Massachusetts.
2 County in New Hampshire. See *Table* at NEW HAMPSHIRE.

Mer′ri·man Dam (mĕr′ĭ·măn). Dam 200 ft. high completed 1942 across Rondout creek, SW of Kingston, Ulster co., SE New York; reservoir for water supply.

Mer′ritt, Mount (mĕr′ĭt). Peak 9944 ft. in Glacier National Park, NW Montana.

Merritt Island. Island ab. 40 m. long and 6 m. wide at N end off E coast of Brevard co., E cen. Florida; separated from the mainland by the Indian river and from Canaveral Penin. by Banana river.

Mer′rit·ton (mĕr′ĭ·t′n; -tŭn). Town, Lincoln co., SE Ontario, Canada, on Welland Ship Canal just S of St. Catharines; pop. 4714. Just to the E occurred on June 24, 1813 the battle of Beaver Dams in which a small British force of 40 soldiers and 200 Indians captured an American detachment of 650 men.

Mersa Matrûh. See MATRÛH.

Mer′se·burg (mĕr′zĕ·bŏͦrk). **1** Government district, former Saxony prov., Prussia, Germany; 3944 sq. m.
2 Manufacturing city, its ✻, on Saale river 18 m. W of Leipzig; pop. 25,630; 13th-cent. cathedral, 15th-cent. castle; in recent years specialized in manufacture of synthetic oil. Important frontier fortification in Carolingian times; made episcopal see 968; made city 1162; residence 1656–1738 of dukes of Sachsen-Merseburg; passed to Prussia through Congress of Vienna; in World War II bombed 1944–45; taken by Allied armies Apr. 1945.

Mers–el–Ke·bir′ or **Mers–el–Ka·bir′** (mĕrs′ĕl·kȧ·bēr′). Town, NW Algeria, on coast just W of Oran; French naval base; in naval battle here July 3, 1940 most of the French warships were destroyed by the British; seized by Allies Nov. 10, 1942.

Mer′sen or **Meers′sen** (mār′sĕ[n]). Commune, Limburg prov., SE Netherlands, just NNE of Maastricht; pop. 5409. Treaty signed here Aug. 8, 870 bet. Charles the Bald, Holy Roman emperor, and Louis the German, king of Germany, divided the kingdom of their nephew, Lothair II.

Mer′sey (mûr′zĭ). **1** River ab. 65 m. long, N Tasmania, Australia; flows generally N to Bass Strait at Devonport.
2 River 70 m. long in NW England; rises in N Derbyshire, flows NW and W bet. Cheshire and Lancashire into the Irish Sea through a large estuary that forms the harbor of Liverpool. See MANCHESTER SHIP CANAL. Mersey Road Tunnel, constructed 1925–30, 2¼ m. long, passes under the river from Birkenhead to Liverpool.

Mer·sin′ (mĕr·sēn′) or **I·çel′** (ē·chĕl′). Seaport city, ✻ of İçel vilayet, S Turkey in Asia, 40 m. WSW of Adana; pop. (1940) 30,193; American mission center.

Mer′thyr Tyd′fil (mûr′thĕr tĭd′vĭl). County borough, Glamorganshire, SE Wales; pop. (1931) 71,108, (1951) 61,093; coal-mining center; iron and steel manufacturing; Richard Trevithick's steam locomotive, the first to be tried on rails, successfully hauled a train of ten tons of iron and seventy men on the Merthyr Tydfil–Pontypridd tramway 1804.

Mer′ton and Mor′den (mûr′t′n, môr′d′n). Urban district, Surrey, S England, on the Wandle 7 m. SW of London; pop. 41,227, (1951) 74,602; a part of Greater London; ruins of an Augustinian priory founded in 1115, and scene 1236 of meeting of barons who passed the Statute of Merton amending the law about conflicting rights of the lords and their tenants to make profit of lands, wastes, woods, and pastures.

Mert′zon (mûr′tsŭn). Town, ⊗ of Irion co., W cen. Texas; pop. 584.

Me′ru, Mount (mä′rōō). Peak 14,954 ft. in N Tanganyika, E Africa, W of Mount Kilimanjaro.

Merv. See MARY.

Mer′ville′ (mĕr′vēl′). Industrial town, Nord dept., N France, on the Lys 18 m. W of Lille; pop. 3663.

Mer·wa′ra (mĕr·wä′rȧ). Subdivision of former Ajmer-Merwara prov., NW Indian Union; ✻ Beawar.

Mer′we′de (mĕr′vā′dĕ). The lower Maas (Meuse) river below the Waal, in Netherlands, until its junction with the Lek to form as its right branch the Nieuwe Maas river. The section of the Merwede from Dordrecht to the Lek is sometimes called the Noord. See OUDE MAAS.

Mer′win, Lake (mûr′wĭn). See UNITED STATES, *Dams and Reservoirs* (Ariel Dam).

Merxem. See MERKSEM.

Mer′zi·fon′ (mĕr′zĕ·fôn′) or **Mar′si·van′** (mär′sĕ·vän′). Town, Amasya vilayet, N Turkey in Asia, 22 m. NW of Amasya; pop. 13,095. Seat of Anatolia Coll. and an American mission center.

Mer′zig (mĕr′tsĭk). Commercial commune, Saarland, Germany, on the Saar 21 m. NW of Saarbrücken; pop. 10,030; blast furnaces; bombed by Allies 1944.

Me′sa (mā′sȧ). **1** County in Colorado. See *Table* at COLORADO.
2 City, Maricopa co., SW cen. Arizona, 15 m. E of Phoenix; pop. 33,772; founded 1878 by Mormons.

Me·sa′bi Range (mĕ·sä′bĭ). Range ab. 100 m. long in NE Minnesota, in St. Louis and Itasca cos.; average height 200–500 ft.; highest point ab. 2000 ft.; contains vast deposits of iron ore.

Me·sa′gne (mȧ·sän′yä). Commune, Brindisi prov., Apulia, SE Italy, 8 m. SW of Brindisi; pop. 18,795.

Me′sa Verde National Park (mā′sȧ vûrd′). See UNITED STATES, *National Parks.*

Mes′ca·le′ro Ridge (mĕs′kȧ·lā′rō). Ridge in SE New Mexico, extending from cen. Lea co. NW along the Lea-Chaves co. boundary.

Meseritz. See MIĘDZYRZECZ.

Me·shed′ (mĕ·shĕd′); *Iranian* **Mash·had′** (mȧsh-hȧd′). City, NE Iran; ✻ of Khurasan prov.; pop. ab. 176,000; situated in the valley of a tributary of the Hari Rud at ab. 3200 ft. elevation; has for centuries been an important trade center and junction point on caravan routes and highways from India to Tehran and from N to S bet. Turkistan towns and Gulf of Oman. Has Shiite shrine and is place of annual pilgrimage. In 19th and 20th cents. important strategically because of its proximity to Russian and Afghan borders.

Me·shed′–i–Sar (mĕ·shĕd′ē·sär′; *Iranian* mȧsh·hȧd′ē-sär′). See BABUL.

Me′shou Dagh (mĕ′shōō dä′). Mountain range in NW Iran, N of Lake Urmia; highest point 10,430 ft.

Me·sil′la (mȧ·sē′yȧ). Unincorporated town, Dona Ana co., S New Mexico, on the Rio Grande near Las Cruces; pop. 1264; founded after end of Mexican War, it was in Mexican territory until Gadsden Purchase 1853 made it part of U.S.

Mesilla Park. Village, Dona Ana co., S New Mexico, suburb of Las Cruces and E of Mesilla; pop. (with University Park) 4387; New Mexico State Univ. of Agriculture, Engineering, and Science (at University Park).

Me'so·la (mä'zô·lä). Commune, Ferrara prov., Emilia, N Italy, in Po delta 34 m. ENE of Ferrara; pop. 13,623.

Me'so·lón'gi·on (mä'sô·lông'gyôn) *or* **Mis'so·lon'ghi** (mĭs'ô·lŏng'gĭ). Commercial city, ✳ of Aetolia and Acarnania dept., W Central Greece and Euboea division, Greece, on N shore of Gulf of Patras; pop. 9270. Withstood first Turkish siege 1822–23, but fell in the second 1825–26. The poet Byron died here 1824.

Mes'o·po·ta'mi·a (mĕs'ô·pô·tä'mĭ·à; -tām'yà). Literally, from the Greek, "the country between two rivers"; the region in SW Asia bet. the Tigris and Euphrates rivers, extending from the mountains of Asia Minor on the N to the Persian Gulf on the S. First so called after the time of Alexander the Great; in the Bible known as Paddan-Aram (*Gen.* xxv. 20). Its N part called by Arabs Al Jazira (see Al JAZIRA); in modern usage region includes 'Iraq 'Arabi and whole Tigris-Euphrates valley.

History: The fertility and location of the region made it seat of early civilizations of Babylonia and Assyria (*qq.v.*) c. 3000–625 B.C.; Upper Mesopotamia the home of kingdom of the Mitanni c. 1475–1275 B.C.; part of Persian Empire from 538 B.C. until conquered by Alexander of Macedon c. 331 B.C.; prior to Arab conquest in mid-7th cent. A.D., formed part of Parthian, Roman, and Neo-Persian (Sassanid) empires; Basra, Al Kufa, and later, Baghdad the centers of Arab control; after Mongol invasion 1258, importance of region as political and commercial center declined; taken by Ottoman Turks 1638; regained strategic value for Great Britain in 19th cent., esp. after Germans proposed Berlin-Baghdad R.R. and after discovery of petroleum deposits; scene of British Mesopotamian campaign against Turks 1914–18 (see CTESIPHON, KUT-AL-IMARA, BAGHDAD, and SHARQAT); became British mandate 1920; kingdom of Iraq (*q.v.*) erected 1921.

Mes·quite' (mĕs·kēt'). City, Dallas co., NE Texas, E of Dallas; pop. 27,526.

Messana. See MESSINA seaport.

Mes·sa'pi·a (mĕ·sā'pĭ·à). In ancient geography, that part of SE Italy inhabited by the Messapii, later applied also to Calabria.

Mes'sa·ra', Bay of (mä'sä·rä'). Inlet of Mediterranean Sea on S coast of Crete, near cen. part.

Mes·se'ne (mĕ·sē'nē). **1** *Mod. Gr.* **Mes·sē'nē** (mâ·sē'-nyē). Commune, Messenia dept., SW Peloponnesus, Greece; pop. 6725. Ancient city founded c. 369 B.C. on site chosen by Epaminondas as new capital of Messenia and as a check against Sparta. Its acropolis was the peak **I·tho'me** (ĭ·thō'mē; *Mod. Gr.* ē·thô'mē) 2630 ft. and on it was a temple of Zeus.

2 See MESSINA seaport, Sicily.

Mes·se'ni·a (mĕ·sē'nĭ·à; -sēn'yà; *Mod. Gr.* mâ'sĕ·nyē'ä). **1** A division of ancient Greece in SW Peloponnesus; bounded on N by Elis, on N and NE by Arcadia, on E by Laconia (Taygetus Mts.) and Gulf of Messenia, and on S and W by Ionian Sea. Its S part forms westernmost of peninsulas of Peloponnesus, terminating in Cape Akritas. One of the most fertile districts of Greece.

History: Dorians, first colonizers, united with original inhabitants to form strong race, but unable to resist Sparta; overcome by Spartans in First Messenian War c. 736–716 B.C., and reduced to helots; completely subjugated after revolt led by Aristomenes in Second Messenian War c. 650–630 B.C.; revolted again in 464 B.C. (Third Messenian War) but many Messenians forced to leave their land 461; after Leuctra 371 B.C. city of Messene (*q.v.*) founded; later, a member of the Achaean League and after 146 B.C. under Romans.

2 Department of Greece. See *Table* at GREECE.

Messenia, *or* **Ko·ró'nē** (kô·rô'nyĕ), **Gulf of.** Inlet of Mediterranean Sea on SW coast of Peloponnesus, S Greece; its E shore formed by Laconia.

Mes·si'na (mĕ·sē'nà; *Ital.* mâs·sē'nä). **1** Province of Italy. See *Table* at ITALY.

2 *anc.* **Zan'cle** (zăng'klē); *later* **Mes·sa'na** (mĕ·sā'nà)

and **Mes·se'ne** (mĕ·sē'nē). Fortified seaport, ✳ of Messina prov., NE Sicily, Italy, on Strait of Messina; pop. 192,051; archiepiscopal see; defended by citadel and several forts; fine harbor; buildings include Gothic cathedral, viceroy's palace, archiepiscopal palace; university (founded 1549); manufactures silk goods; exports silks, olive oil, linseed, wine, grain; fisheries. Founded by Greeks c. 1004 B.C.; taken by Messenians 686 B.C.; Roman free city 241 B.C.; captured by Saracens 831 A.D.; occupied and sacked by Richard I of England and his Crusaders 1191; under Spanish rule 1282–1676 and 1678–1713; beset by plague 1743 and 1854; devastated by earthquake 1783 and, esp., 1908; under Italian rule from 1860. In World War II scene of last stand of Germans in Sicily; abandoned Aug. 7–16, 1943 and occupied by Allies.

3 Town, N Transvaal, NE Union of South Africa; pop. 7173; near S bank of Limpopo river and on one of main railroad lines to Rhodesia; site of large copper mines.

Messina, Strait of; *anc.* **Sic'u·lum Fre'tum** (sĭk'ū·lŭm frē'tŭm). Channel 2½ to 12 m. wide bet. S Italy and NE island of Sicily.

Mes'sines' (mĕ'sēn'). Village in West Flanders prov., NW Belgium, near Ieper (Ypres). **Messines Ridge** dominates the surrounding terrain; battles Nov. 1, 1914, in which Germans seized the ridge, and June 7–14, 1917, in which it was retaken by the British.

Mes·ta' (mĕs·tä'); *Turk.* **Ka'ra Su** (kä'rä sōō'); *called* **Nes'tos** (nĕs'tôs; *Gr.* nâs'tôs) *in Greece.* River ab. 130 m. long in SW Bulgaria and NE Greece; flows from W end of Rhodope Mts. SE into N Aegean Sea opp. the island of Thasos.

Me'stre (mĕs'trä). Town on mainland, Venezia prov., SE cen. Venezia Euganea, NE Italy, part of Venice commune; pop. 31,727.

Mes'u·ra'do, Cape (mĕs'ŭ·rä'dō). Cape on the W coast of Liberia, W Africa, near Monrovia.

Me'ta (mä'tà; *Span.* -tä). **1** River ab. 685 m. long in Colombia; rises in W cen. Colombia, flows NE and E forming a section of Colombia-Venezuela boundary, and empties into Orinoco river on the Colombia-Venezuela boundary.

2 Intendancy of Colombia. See *Table* at COLOMBIA.

Me'ta In·cog'ni·ta (mē'tà ĭn·kŏg'nĭ·tà). Name given by Sir Martin Frobisher to S part of Baffin I.

Met'a·po'na (mĕt'à·pō'nà). Short stream E of Koli Point on N coast of Guadalcanal I., SE Solomon Is., W Pacific Ocean; fighting here Nov. 8–10, 1942.

Met'a·pon'tum (mĕt'à·pŏn'tŭm). Ancient Greek city, Lucania, S Italy, on NW shore of Gulf of Tarentum; founded by colonists from Crotona and Sybaris c. 700 B.C.; Pythagoras died here 497 B.C.; location of Hannibal's headquarters after Cannae. Ruins include two temples and some of the walls.

Me·tau'ro (mâ·tou'rō); *anc.* **Me·tau'rus** (mĕ·tô'rŭs). Small river in E cen. Italy; flows E into Adriatic Sea N of Ancona; battle of Metaurus in Second Punic War 207 B.C. in which Roman consuls completely defeated the Carthaginians under Hasdrubal; ended Hannibal's hope of conquest of Rome.

Met'calfe (mĕt'kàf; -kàf). County in Kentucky. See *Table* at KENTUCKY.

Meteor Crater. See CRATER MOUND.

Me'te·pec' (mā'tä·pĕk'). Town, México state, cen. Mexico; SE suburb of Toluca; pop. 5075.

Met'how (mĕt'hou). River ab. 60 m. long, N Washington; flows S in Okanogan co. into Columbia river.

Me·thu'en (mĕ·thū'ĕn). Industrial town, Essex co., NE corner of Massachusetts, 9 m. NE of Lowell; pop. 28,114; manufactures shoes, yarn, worsted cloth, brooms. Settled ab. 1642; was part of Haverhill until 1725.

Meth'ven (mĕth'vĕn). Village, Perth co., Scotland, ab. 7 m. NW of Perth; pop. (civil parish) 1671; castle 1 m. E; scene of battle 1306 in which English defeated Robert Bruce.

Me·tin′ic (mê·tǐn′ĭk). Island in Atlantic Ocean off S cen. Maine coast.

Metis. See METZ.

Met′la·kat′la or **Met′la·kaht′la** (mĕt′lȧ·kăt′lȧ). Village on Annette I., S of Ketchikan, Revillagigedo I., SE Alaska; pop. (1950) 817; formerly had U.S. Air Force base. Settled 1887 by refugee Indians.

Me·to′hi·ja (mĕ·tō′hê·yä). District, SW Yugoslavia, forming part of new autonomous province Kosovo-Metohija.

Me·trop′o·lis (mê·trŏp′ô·lĭs). City, ⊗ of Massac co., S Illinois, on Ohio river NW of Paducah, Kentucky; pop. 7339.

Met′ter (mĕt′ēr). City, ⊗ of Candler co., E cen. Georgia, 16 m. W of Statesboro; pop. 2362.

Mett′mann (mĕt′män). City, North Rhine-Westphalia state, W Germany, E of Düsseldorf; pop. 12,416; manufactures silverware.

Met′tray (mĕ′trā′). Village, Indre-et-Loire dept., NW cen. France, ab. 5 m. NW of Tours; famous reformatory, founded 1839.

Me·tuch′en (mê·tŭch′ĕn). Borough, Middlesex co., cen. New Jersey, 5 m. WNW of Perth Amboy; pop. 14,041; residential suburb; roofing, chemicals, needles, rubber.

Metz (mĕts; Fr. mâs); anc. **Di′vo·du′rum** or **Divodurum Me′di·o·mat′ri·cum** (dĭ′vô·dūr′ŭm mē′dĭ·ô-măt′rĭ·kŭm); later **Me′di·o·mat′ri·ca** (mē′dĭ·ô·măt′rĭ·kȧ) and **Me′tis** (mē′tĭs). Fortified city, ✱ of Moselle dept., NE France, on Moselle river 178 m. ENE of Paris; pop. 83,119; center of coal and metal industries of Lorraine; manufactures woolens, cottons, hosiery, hats, glue, leather, muslin; 13th-cent. late-Gothic cathedral. Military roads and fine aqueduct built by Romans; sacked by Attila in 5th cent. A.D.; under Frankish rule became capital of Austrasia; reached peak of prosperity in 13th cent.; with Toul and Verdun (Les Trois-Évêchés, the three bishoprics) taken by French 1552; French rule acknowledged by Peace of Westphalia 1648; forced to capitulate by Germans after disastrous siege 1870; under German rule 1870–1918; reverted to France after World War I; in World War II scene of severe fighting Sept. and Oct. 1944; captured by Allies Nov. 20.

Meu′don′ (mû′dôN′). Commune, Seine-et-Oise dept., N France; SW suburb of Paris on Seine river; pop. 20,749; astronomical observatory; military aviation center. The Forest of Meudon (Fr. Forêt de Meudon) formerly surrounded a famous château built by Louis XIV; later the wood became a holiday resort for Parisians.

Meu′le·be′ke (mû′lĕ·bā′kĕ). Commune, West Flanders prov., NW Belgium, 9 m. E of Roeselare; pop. 9232.

Meurthe (mûrt). River ab. 100 m. long, Vosges and Meurthe-et-Moselle depts., NE France; rises in Vosges Mts., flows NW into the Moselle near Nancy.

Meurthe–et–Mo′selle′ (mûr′tä·mô′zĕl′). Department of France. See Table at FRANCE.

Meuse (mūz; Angl. mūz); Du. **Maas** (mȧs); anc. **Mo′sa** (mō′zȧ). 1 River 575 m. long in W Europe; rises in Haute-Marne dept., NE France, flows N across E Belgium, forming a section of the NE boundary of Belgium; enters Netherlands and as the Maas curves W uniting at Gorinchem with the Waal, entering the North Sea through Hollandsch Diep. See MAAS. It receives the tributaries Sambre and Ourthe in Belgium and in Netherlands the Rur from Germany. The chief towns on its banks are Verdun, Sedan, and Mézières in France, Namur and Liège in Belgium, and Maastricht in Netherlands; Rotterdam is on the Nieuwe Maas in the Rhine delta. Its valley, esp. in NE France, was scene of much severe fighting in World War I; held by Germans until 1918; in World War II overrun by German armies in May and June 1940 and in Jan. 1945 its course SW of Liège was almost reached by Germans in Battle of the Bulge.

2 Department of France. See Table at FRANCE.

Meu′sel·witz (moi′zĕl·vĭts). Industrial city, Thuringia, Germany, 22 m. S of Leipzig; pop. 11,571; coal mining; manufactures textiles, porcelain, machinery.

Me·war′ (mȧ·wär′). See UDAIPUR.

Mewar and Southern Raj′pu·ta′na States (räj′pŏŏ·tä′nȧ). Formerly, a group of Indian states in S Rajputana including Udaipur, Banswara, Dungarpur, Partabgarh, and Kushalgarh.

Mew Island (mū). Island in North Channel, off E coast of Northern Ireland, at entrance to Belfast Lough; lighthouse.

Mex′bor·ough (mĕks′bŭ·rȧ; -brȧ). Urban district, West Riding, Yorkshire, N England; pop. 18,965; iron, glass, and pottery works.

Mexcala. See Río de las BALSAS.

Me·xi′a (mě·hā′ȧ—sic). City, Limestone co., E cen. Texas, 37 m. ENE of Waco; pop. 6121; railroad center; manufactures cottonseed oil, textiles, machinery; oil industries.

Me′xi·a′na (mā′shê·ȧ′nȧ). Island in the mouth of the Amazon river, N of Marajó I., off Pará state, Brazil.

Mex′i·cal′i (mĕk′sĭ·kăl′ĭ; Span. mě·hě·kä′lě). Town on N Lower California penin., NW Mexico, adjacent to Calexico, California; ✱ of Baja California state; pop. (1960) 174,410.

Mex′i·co (mĕk′sĭ·kō); Span. **Mé′ji·co** (mě′hě·kô); Mex. Span. **Mé′xi·co** (mě′hě-). 1 officially **Es·ta′dos U·ni′-dos Me′xi·ca′nos** (âs·tä′thôs ōō·ně′thôz mě′hě·kä′-nôs). Republic, S North America; 761,830 sq. m. (including uninhabited islands 763,944 sq. m.); pop. (1960) 34,923,129; ✱ Mexico City; bounded on N by U.S., on W and S by the Pacific, on SE by Guatemala, British Honduras, and Caribbean Sea, and on E by Gulf of Mexico; separated from U.S. on the boundary by the Río Bravo (Rio Grande in U.S.); NW part (peninsula of Lower California) separated from rest of Mexico by Gulf of California; in SE is peninsula of Yucatán. Narrowest part, Isthmus of Tehuantepec 130 m. Comprises the following 29 states, one federal district (see FEDERAL DISTRICT), and 2 territories (for pronunciation of their names, see their individual entries):

POLITICAL DIVISION	LOCATION	AREA[1]	POP.[1]	CAPITAL
Federal District	cen.	573	1,773,627	México, D.F
STATES				
Aguascalientes	cen.	2,499	160,282	Aguascalientes
Baja California	NW	27,653	78,006	Mexicali
Campeche	SE	19,670	89,399	Campeche
Chiapas	SE	28,729	660,464	Tuxtla Gutiérrez
Chihuahua	N	94,822	613,696	Chihuahua
Coahuila	NE	58,062	543,209	Saltillo
Colima	SW	2,009	74,346	Colima
Durango	NW cen.	42,272	472,601	Durango
Guanajuato	cen.	11,804	1,048,359	Guanajuato
Guerrero	S	24,885	729,737	Chilpancingo
Hidalgo	cen.	8,057	750,827	Pachuca
Jalisco	W cen.	31,149	1,406,481	Guadalajara
México	cen.	8,057	1,123,780	Toluca
Michoacán	SW	23,200	1,166,533	Morelia
Morelos	S cen.	1,916	182,000	Cuernavaca
Nayarit	W	10,444	213,411	Tepic
Nuevo León	NE	25,134	525,000	Monterrey
Oaxaca	SE	36,371	1,191,692	Oaxaca
Puebla	SE cen.	13,124	1,286,520	Puebla
Querétaro	cen.	4,432	243,576	Querétaro
San Luis Potosí	cen.	24,415	668,836	San Luis Potosí
Sinaloa	W	22,580	486,353	Culiacán
Sonora	NW	70,477	368,853	Hermosillo
Tabasco	SE	9,782	285,659	Villahermosa
Tamaulipas	E	30,731	461,965	Ciudad Victoria
Tlaxcala	cen.	1,555	219,599	Tlaxcala
Veracruz	E	27,736	1,614,579	Jalapa
Yucatán	SE	23,926	416,378	Mérida
Zacatecas	cen.	28,122	553,276	Zacatecas
TERRITORIES				
Baja California (Sur)	NW	27,976	51,199	La Paz
Quintana Roo	SE	19,438	18,485	Chetumal

[1] Area = land area in sq. m. Pop. from 1940 Census.

Chief mountains: Sierra Madre (S extension of Rocky Mts. system) dividing into mountain chains on E (Oriental) and W (Occidental) sides of central plateau (see ANÁHUAC), which has average altitude of 6000 ft. and occupies over 50% of country; highest point Citlaltepetl (volcano) 18,700 ft. in cen. Veracruz state; other peaks Popocatepetl (volcano) 17,887 ft., Iztaccihuatl 16,883 ft., Nevado de Toluca (volcano) 15,026 ft., Malinzín 14,632 ft., and Colima (volcano) 12,782 ft. *Chief rivers:* Pánuco, Grijalva, Balsas, Santiago, Usumacinta, Conchos, Río Bravo (Rio Grande). *Chief lakes:* Chapala, Cuitzeo, Pátzcuaro, Texcoco. *Economic resources:* In mineral deposits one of richest countries in world; produces ab. 40% of world output of silver; a leading producer of antimony, molybdenum, lead, mercury, zinc, copper, and gold; stands seventh in production of petroleum; exports henequen fiber, coffee, chicle, sugar, fruits, nuts, rubber, and hardwoods. *Chief cities:* México, D.F., Guadalajara, Puebla, Monterrey, Mérida, Tampico, Aguascalientes, San Luis Potosí, Torreón, León, and Veracruz.

History: Central and southern part, from Gulf to Pacific, controlled by Aztecs, an aboriginal people of high culture whose capital, Tenochtitlán (*q.v.*), was founded 1325 A.D.; Yucatán (*q.v.*), home of Mayas, in decline by 15th cent. Yucatán discovered by Córdoba 1517, and coast (to site of Veracruz) by Grijalva 1518; Veracruz founded 1519 by Cortes, who conquered the country 1519–21 and established Mexico City, which became center of viceroyalty of New Spain; interior gradually subdued and Spanish authority extended north to California in 16th cent., though Texas and California not effectively occupied by Spanish until 18th cent.; audiencia of Guadalajara created 1548 (later included southwest of present U.S.). After successful second revolt from Spain 1821, ruled by Emperor Iturbide 1822–23; joined by Guatemala and other Central American states for brief period during 1822–23 (see CENTRAL AMERICA); established a federal republic 1824; defeated by independent republic of **Texas** 1836; fought war with United States over annexation of Texas 1846–48; ceded to United States Upper California, New Mexico, and northern parts of Mexico by Treaty of Guadalupe Hidalgo 1848 and Gadsden Purchase 1853; underwent invasions by Spain, Great Britain, and France 1861; ruled by Emperor Maximilian who was supported by France 1864–67; under dictatorship 1877–1911 of President Porfirio Díaz, whose overthrow inaugurated period of revolution; adopted revised constitution 1917; in policies of nationalization of resources, expropriation of church property and secularization of education, and subdivision of great estates, faced opposition of U.S. and Great Britain, Roman Catholicism, and Mexican Conservatives, respectively.

2 or **Mexico City;** *officially* **Mé′xi·co, D.F.** (mĕ′-hĕ·kō, dĕs-trē′tō fā′thä·räl′). City, cen. Mexico, ✱ of the Federal District (Distrito Federal) and of Mexico; pop. 1,448,422; located near S end of great cen. plateau at 7415 ft. alt. and ab. 200 m. WNW of Veracruz on the Gulf of Mexico; a few miles W of Lake Texcoco and NW of the Chalco and Xochimilco lakes. Regularly laid out with cathedral, national palace, and municipal building around a large square (Plaza Mayor) forming the political and commercial center. Has many churches, monasteries, government buildings, also museum, Univ. of Mexico founded 1551; has numerous industrial establishments but is not primarily a manufacturing city.

History: Before Spanish invasion, Mexico City was the site of the Aztec capital (Tenochtitlán); captured by Cortes 1521; seat of the viceroyalty of New Spain 1521–1821; captured by Mexican revolutionists under Gen. Iturbide 1821; captured by Gen. Winfield Scott 1847 in the Mexican War; held by the French 1863–67; greatly improved in modern times, esp. during the presidency of Porfirio Díaz 1876–80, 1884–1911.

Mex′i·co (mĕk′sĭ·kō). **1** Town, Oxford co., W Maine, 36 m. NNW of Lewiston; pop. 5043; paper mills.
2 City, ⊗ of Audrain co., NE cen. Missouri, 29 m. ENE of Columbia; pop. 12,889; mule market and horse-breeding center; manufactures clay products.
3 (*Span.* mĕ′hē·kō) Municipality, E cen. Pampanga prov., Luzon, Phil. Is., on a tributary of the Pampanga river ab. 3 m. NE of San Fernando; pop. 22,341.
Mé′xi·co (mĕk′sĭ·kō; *Span.* mĕ′hē·kō). State, cen. Mexico. See *Table* at MEXICO.
Mex′i·co, Gulf of (mĕk′sĭ·kō). Gulf on SE coast of North America; bounded on N by United States, on E by United States, Cuba, and Mexico, on S by Mexico, on W by Mexico and United States; connects with Atlantic Ocean through Straits of Florida, and with Caribbean Sea through Strait of Yucatán; extends 1000 m. E to W and 800 m. N to S, and covers ab. 716,000 sq. m. in area; greatest depth 12,425 ft. (Sigsbee Deep) in SW cen. part.
Mexico, Valley of. Subdivision of the plateau of Anáhuac (*q.v.*) in cen. Mexico; mean elevation 7470 ft.; a vast oval basin ab. 50 m. long by 40 m. wide; total area 1758 sq. m.; includes the city of Mexico.
Mey′ca·ua·yan′ (mĕ′ê·kä·wä·yän′). Municipality, S Bulacan prov., Luzon, Phil. Is., on Manila-Dagupan R.R. near Rizal border and on E outlet of Pampanga delta 13 m. SE of Malolos; pop. 16,082.
Mey′ers·dale (mī′ērz·dāl). Borough, Somerset co., S Pennsylvania, 35 m. S of Johnstown; pop. 2901; agriculture; coal mining nearby.
Mèze (mâz). Seaport, Hérault dept., S France; pop. (commune) 4984; near shore of the Étang de Thau opp. Sète.
Me′zen (mā′z′n; *Russ.* myä′zyĭn·y′). **1** River ab. 550 m. long in N Soviet Russia, Europe; rises in W Komi A.S.S.R. and flows generally NW through cen. Arkhangelsk Region into **Gulf of Mezen,** an arm (ab. 50 m. long) of the E White Sea.
2 Town on right bank of Mezen river near its mouth, Arkhangelsk Region, ab. 130 m. NE of Arkhangelsk; pop. 1900; a fishing and trading port.
Mé′zenc′, Mount (mā′zänk′). Volcanic peak 5753 ft. in the Cévennes Mts., S France, in Haute-Loire dept. near Ardèche border.
Mé′zières′ (mā′zyâr′). Commune, ✱ of Ardennes dept., NE France, on Meuse river 126 m. NE of Paris; pop. 10,861; connected by bridge with Charleville opposite; fortified until 1886; manufactures metal goods; 16th-cent. Gothic church. Taken by Germans 1815, 1871, and 1914; reverted to France 1918.
Me′zö·be′rény (mĕ′zû·bĕ′rān·y′). Commune 60 m. SW of Debrecen, SE Hungary; pop. 14,555.
Me′zö·kö′vesd (mĕ′zû·kû′vĕsht). Commune 72 m. NE of Budapest, NE cen. Hungary; pop. 21,871; produces fine embroideries.
Me′zö·túr′ (mĕ′zû·tōōr′). City 60 m. NE of Szeged, SE Hungary; pop. 29,614; potteries.
Mfini. See FINI.
Mfumbiro Mountains. See VIRUNGA MOUNTAINS.
Mhow (mou). Town, Madhya Pradesh, cen. India, formerly in state of Indore, Central India; 13 m. SSW of Indore city; pop. 31,177; formerly had large British cantonment.
Mia·ga′o (myä·gä′ō). Municipality, SW Iloilo prov., Panay, Phil. Is., on Iloilo Strait 22 m. W of City of Iloilo; pop. 30,179; nearby was traditional settlement of Bornean datos in pre-Spanish times.
Mi·am′i (mī·ăm′ĭ; -*à*). **1** *formerly* **Great Miami.** River 160 m. long in W Ohio; rises in Indian Lake, Logan co., and flows S into the Ohio river at the SW extremity of Ohio.
2 Name of counties in three states of the U.S. See *Tables* at INDIANA, KANSAS, OHIO.
3 Town, Gila co., E cen. Arizona, 68 m. E of Phoenix; pop. 3350; copper mining.

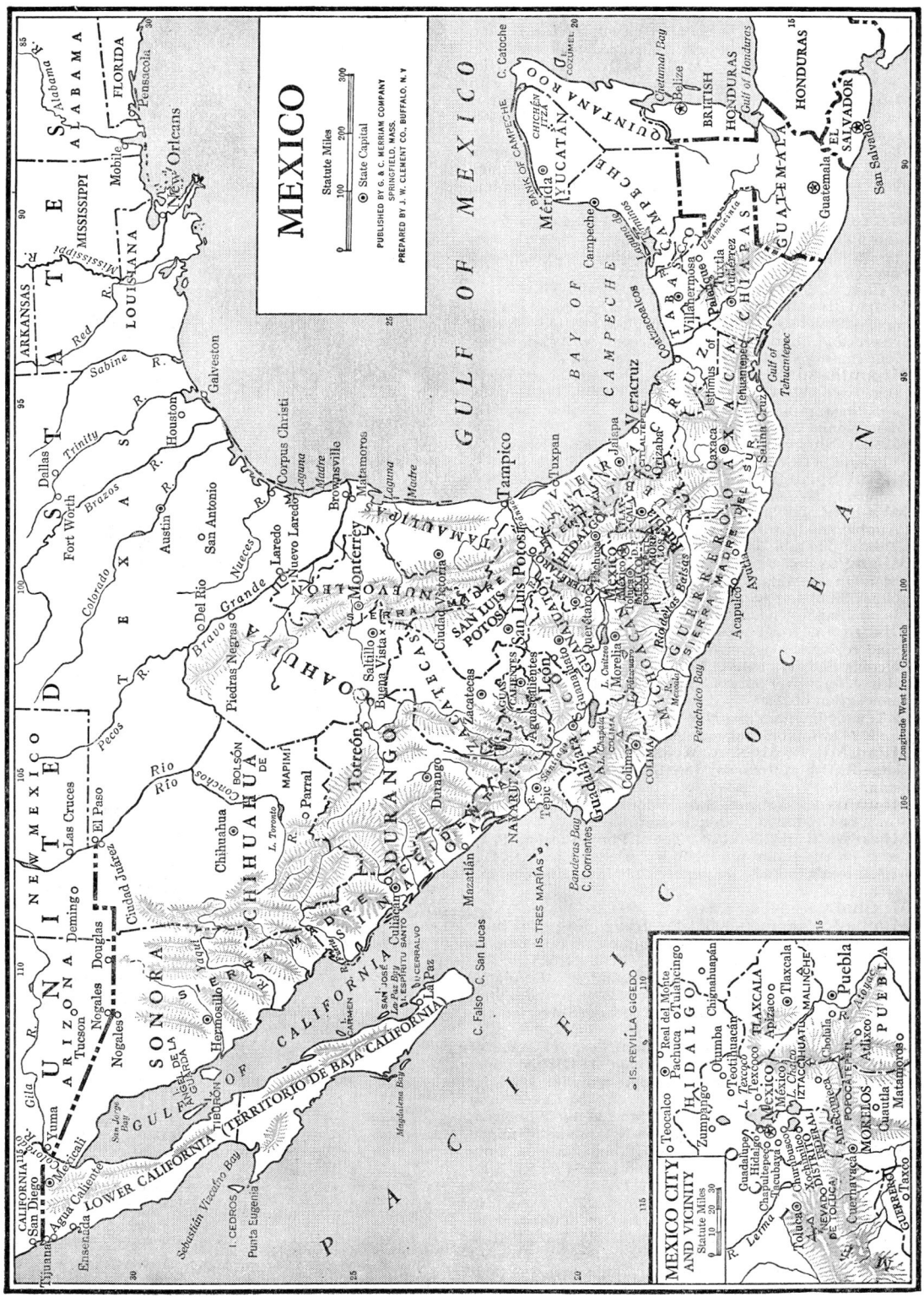

MEXICO

Statute Miles

⊛ State Capital

PUBLISHED BY G. & C. MERRIAM COMPANY
SPRINGFIELD, MASS.

PREPARED BY J. W. CLEMENT CO. BUFFALO, N.Y

MEXICO CITY
AND VICINITY

Statute Miles

4 City, ⊗ of Dade co., SE Florida, on Biscayne Bay; pop. 291,688; southernmost large city in the U.S., at lat. 25°46'S (cf. KEY WEST); alt. 11 ft.; center of winter resort area, including Miami Beach, Coral Gables, Hialeah; itself a great winter resort and sports center with bathing beach 7 m. long; one of largest aviation centers of U.S. with lines to Cuba, other parts of West Indies, and South America; army and navy bases. Barry College (1940; women). Built on site of old fort, begun in 1836, but modern city (incorporated July 1896 with pop. 260) began its rapid growth with coming of railroad and hotels 1896, developed by Henry M. Flagler.

5 City, ⊗ of Ottawa co., NE corner of Oklahoma, 66 m. E of Bartlesville; pop. 12,869; commercial center in area producing lead and zinc; cattle raising, dairying, meat packing; ships agricultural products.

6 City, ⊗ of Roberts co., NW Texas; pop. 656.

Miami Beach. City, Dade co., SE Florida, on island across Biscayne Bay from Miami; pop. 63,145; popular resort and tourist center, connected with Miami by four causeways.

Mi·am'is·burg (mī-ăm'ĭz-bûrg). Industrial city, Montgomery co., SW Ohio, on Miami river 10 m. S of Dayton; pop. 9893; in heart of tobacco-growing region; large Indian mound outside city.

Miami Shores. Village, Dade co., SE Florida, on Biscayne Bay 9 m. N of Miami; pop. 8865.

Miami Springs. Town, Dade co., SE Florida, NW suburb of Miami; pop. 11,229.

Mi'a·neh' (mē'ä-nä'; *Iranian* mě-yä-něj'). Town, Azerbaijan, NW Iran, on main highway 90 m. SE of Tabriz; pop. ab. 7000.

Mi·ang'as (mě-äng'äs) *or* **Pal'mas** (päl'mäs). Small island in the Malay Archipelago, in the Pacific Ocean ab. 60 m. SE of Cape San Agustin, Mindanao; N of Talaud Is. and nearest point of Indonesia to Philippine Is.

Mi·a'ni (mě-ä'nē; *also* **Mee·a'nee**. **1** Village, cen. Sind region, Pakistan, 6 m. N of Hyderabad; scene of victory Feb. 17, 1843 of Sir Charles Napier with small British force over mirs of Sind, which led to conquest and annexation of Sind.

2 Town, Shahpur dist., NW West Punjab, Pakistan, 100 m. NW of Lahore; pop. ab. 6000; large salt mines.

Mi'an Mir *or* **Mee'an Meer** (mē'än měr). Former large British cantonment 3 m. SE of Lahore (*q.v.*), Pakistan.

Mi·an'us (mī-ăn'ŭs). Subdivision (est. pop. 2100) of town of GREENWICH, Connecticut.

Mi·an'wa'li (mī-än'wä'lĭ). Town, Punjab region, Pakistan, on the Indus 105 m. S of Peshawar; pop. 15,412.

Mi'ca Peak (mī'kà). Mountain 5250 ft. in Kootenai co., N Idaho.

Mi Chai. See NONG KHAI.

Mi'cha·lov'ce (mī'kà·lôf'tsě); *Hung.* **Nagy'mi'hály** (nŏd'y'·mĭ'hĭ). Town, E Slovakia prov., E cen. Czechoslovakia, 29 m. E of Košice; pop. (1930) 11,688.

Mich'i·gam'me (mĭsh'ĭ-gä'mě; -găm'ě). River, W Michigan penin.; rises in Baraga co., flows E and S until it joins the Brule to form the Menominee river on the Wisconsin-Michigan boundary.

Mich'i·gan (mĭsh'ĭ-găn). A north central state of U.S.A., 26th state admitted to Union (1837); the upper peninsula is bounded on N by Lake Superior, on E by Whitefish Bay and St. Marys river, on S by Lake Huron and Lake Michigan, and on SW and W by Wisconsin; the lower peninsula is bounded on N by Lake Michigan and Lake Huron, on E by Lake Huron, Canadian province of Ontario, Lake St. Clair, and Lake Erie, on S by Ohio and Indiana, and on W by Lake Michigan; 23d state in area, 58,216 sq. m. (land area 57,022 sq. m.); in addition to this area has also 38,575 sq. m. of water of the Great Lakes; 7th state in population, 7,823,194; ✳ Lansing. See *Table of States* at UNITED STATES. Divided into the following 83 counties (for pronunciation of their names, see their individual entries):

NAME	LOCA-TION[1]	AREA[2]	POP.[2]	CO. SEAT
Alcona	NE	677	6,352	Harrisville
Alger	N penin.	913	9,250	Munising
Allegan	SW	829	57,729	Allegan
Alpena	NE	568	28,556	Alpena
Antrim	NW	477	10,373	Bellaire
Arenac	E	368	9,860	Standish
Baraga	NW penin.	904	7,151	L'Anse
Barry	SW	549	31,738	Hastings
Bay	E	446	107,042	Bay City
Benzie	NW	316	7,834	Beulah
Berrien	SW corner	580	149,865	St. Joseph
Branch	S	506	34,903	Coldwater
Calhoun	S	709	138,858	Marshall
Cass	SW	488	36,932	Cassopolis
Charlevoix[3]	NW	414	13,421	Charlevoix
Cheboygan	N	725	14,550	Cheboygan
Chippewa[3]	E and NE penin.	1,580	32,655	Sault Ste. Marie
Clare	cen.	572	11,647	Harrison
Clinton	S cen.	571	37,969	St. Johns
Crawford	N	563	4,971	Grayling
Delta[3]	S penin.	1,180	34,298	Escanaba
Dickinson	S penin.	757	23,917	Iron Mountain
Eaton	S	567	49,684	Charlotte
Emmet	N	461	15,904	Petoskey
Genesee	SE cen.	644	374,313	Flint
Gladwin	cen.	503	10,769	Gladwin
Gogebic	NW corner of penin.	1,112	24,370	Bessemer
Grand Traverse	NW	464	33,490	Traverse City
Gratiot	cen.	566	37,012	Ithaca
Hillsdale	S	601	34,742	Hillsdale
Houghton	NW penin.	1,030	35,654	Houghton
Huron	E	822	34,006	Bad Axe
Ingham	S	559	211,296	Mason
Ionia	S cen.	575	43,132	Ionia
Iosco	NE	547	16,505	Tawas City
Iron	SW penin.	1,197	17,184	Crystal Falls
Isabella	cen.	572	35,348	Mount Pleasant
Jackson	S	705	131,994	Jackson
Kalamazoo	SW	567	169,712	Kalamazoo
Kalkaska	N	564	4,382	Kalkaska
Kent	W	862	363,187	Grand Rapids
Keweenaw[4]	N tip of penin.	544	2,417	Eagle River
Lake	W	572	5,338	Baldwin
Lapeer	E	659	41,926	Lapeer
Leelanau[3]	NW	349	9,321	Leland
Lenawee	S	754	77,789	Adrian
Livingston	SE	571	38,233	Howell
Luce	NE penin.	914	7,827	Newberry
Mackinac[3]	SE penin.	1,014	10,853	St. Ignace
Macomb	SE	481	405,804	Mount Clemens
Manistee	NW	558	19,042	Manistee
Marquette	N penin.	1,841	56,154	Marquette
Mason	W	493	21,929	Ludington
Mecosta	cen.	563	21,051	Big Rapids
Menominee	S tip of penin.	1,032	24,685	Menominee
Midland	cen.	520	51,450	Midland
Missaukee	NW cen.	565	6,784	Lake City
Monroe	SE corner	562	101,120	Monroe
Montcalm	cen.	712	35,795	Stanton
Montmorency	NE	555	4,424	Atlanta
Muskegon	W	504	149,943	Muskegon
Newaygo	W	857	24,160	White Cloud
Oakland	SE	877	690,259	Pontiac
Oceana	W	536	16,547	Hart
Ogemaw	NE	574	9,680	West Branch
Ontonagon	NW penin.	1,321	10,584	Ontonagon
Osceola	cen.	581	13,595	Reed City
Oscoda	NE	565	3,447	Mio
Otsego	N	530	7,545	Gaylord
Ottawa	W	564	98,719	Grand Haven
Presque Isle	NE	654	13,117	Rogers City
Roscommon	N cen.	521	7,200	Roscommon
Saginaw	cen.	812	190,752	Saginaw
Saint Clair	SE	740	107,201	Port Huron
Saint Joseph	S	508	42,332	Centerville
Sanilac	E	961	32,314	Sandusky
Schoolcraft	S penin.	1,199	8,953	Manistique
Shiawassee	S cen.	540	53,446	Corunna
Tuscola	E	816	43,305	Caro
Van Buren	SW	607	48,395	Paw Paw
Washtenaw	SE	716	172,440	Ann Arbor
Wayne	SE	607	2,666,297	Detroit
Wexford	NW	563	18,466	Cadillac

[1] Counties in the upper peninsula (extending eastwards from Wisconsin boundary, bet. Lake Superior on N and Lakes Michigan and Huron on S and SE) are indicated by the addition of "penin." Counties in the lower peninsula are located with reference only to that part of the state, and are given no additional distinguishing term.
[2] Area = land area in sq. m. Pop. from 1960 Census.
[3] Includes islands.
[4] Includes Isle Royale, off Canadian shore NW of county proper.

ONTARIO
PASSAGE I.
Blake Pt.
ISLE ROYALE
Siskiwit Bay
Lake
Superior
TO
KEWEENAW CO.
Same Scale as Main Map

MICHIGAN

Statute Miles

0 10 20 30 40 50

⊛ State Capital

PUBLISHED BY G. & C. MERRIAM COMPANY
SPRINGFIELD, MASS.
PREPARED BY J. W. CLEMENT CO., BUFFALO, N.Y.

WESTERN PART OF
MICHIGAN
Same Scale as Main Map

LAKE SUPERIOR

KEWEENAW
Hancock Laurium
Houghton
HOUGHTON
Keweenaw Bay
PORCUPINE MTS.
ONTONAGON
BARAGA
Gogebic Lake
MARQUETTE
DICKINSON
Ironwood
GOGEBIC
IRON
Iron River
Brule River
Kingsford
Iron Mountain

LAKE SUPERIOR

KEWEENAW
BARAGA
Marquette
Ishpeming Negaunee
MARQUETTE
Escanaba
DICKINSON
Iron Mountain
Kingsford
MENOMINEE
DELTA
Manistique
Escanaba
Little Bay de Noc
Big Bay de Noc
Green Bay
MENOMINEE
Menominee River
ALGER
SCHOOLCRAFT
LUCE
CHIPPEWA
Whitefish Bay
Sault Ste. Marie
MACKINAC
St. Mary R.
DRUMMOND ISLAND
ONTARIO

LAKE HURON

Straits of Mackinac
MACKINAC ISLAND
BOIS BLANC ISLAND
BEAVER ISLAND
EMMET
Cheboygan
CHEBOYGAN
NORTH MANITOU ISLAND
Petoskey
Rogers City
PRESQUE ISLE
CHARLEVOIX
SOUTH MANITOU ISLAND
LEELANAU
ANTRIM
OTSEGO
MONTMORENCY
Alpena
ALPENA
Traverse City
BENZIE
GRAND TRAVERSE
KALKASKA
Grayling
CRAWFORD
OSCODA
Au Sable
ALCONA
Manistee R.
MANISTEE
MISSAUKEE
ROSCOMMON
River
OGEMAW
IOSCO
WEXFORD
Cadillac
Manistee
MASON
Ludington
LAKE
OSCEOLA
CLARE
GLADWIN
ARENAC
Lake River
Saginaw Bay
HURON
Bad Axe
OCEANA
NEWAYGO
MECOSTA
ISABELLA
Mount Pleasant
MIDLAND
Midland
Bay City
TUSCOLA
SANILAC
Muskegon
MUSKEGON
MONTCALM
Alma
GRATIOT
Saginaw
SAGINAW
Muskegon Heights
Grand Haven
KENT
Greenville
IONIA
Ionia
CLINTON
GENESEE
Owosso
SHIAWASSEE
Flint
LAPEER
Lapeer
ST. CLAIR
Port Huron
Sarnia
Grand Rapids
OTTAWA
Holland
Grand River
Hastings
Lansing
East Lansing
INGHAM
LIVINGSTON
OAKLAND
Pontiac
Birmingham
Royal Oak
MACOMB
Mount Clemens
St. Clair Shores
ALLEGAN
BARRY
Charlotte
EATON
South Haven
Kalamazoo R.
Kalamazoo
Battle Creek
Marshall
Albion
JACKSON
Jackson
Ann Arbor
Ypsilanti
WASHTENAW
WAYNE
Dearborn
Detroit
Lake St. Clair
Windsor
Wyandotte
VAN BUREN
St. Joseph
Benton Harbor
Dowagiac
CASS
Three Rivers
ST. JOSEPH
BRANCH
Coldwater
HILLSDALE
Hillsdale
Adrian
LENAWEE
MONROE
Monroe
Raisin R.
Detroit R.
BERRIEN
Niles
Sturgis
South Bend
Chicago

WISCONSIN
ILLINOIS
LAKE MICHIGAN
INDIANA
OHIO
Toledo
LAKE ERIE
ONTARIO

South Haven

88 87 86 85 84 Longitude West from Greenwich 83 82

Nickname: Wolverine State, also Lake State. *State flower:* Apple blossom. *Motto:* Si Quaeris Peninsulam Amoenam, Circumspice (If You Seek a Beautiful Peninsula, Look Around). *Chief cities:* Detroit, Flint, Grand Rapids, Dearborn, Lansing. *Rivers:* Montreal, Brule, and Menominee, forming W and SW boundary of upper peninsula; St. Clair, separating Michigan from Ontario bet. Lake Huron and Lake St. Clair; Detroit, separating Michigan from Ontario bet. Lake St. Clair and Lake Erie. *Highest point:* Porcupine Mountain 2023 ft. in Ontonagon co. *Chief industries:* Agriculture, mining (iron, copper, coal), lumbering and woodworking, manufacture of furniture and automobiles.

History: Shores of Lake Michigan explored by French from 1634; first settled at Sault Sainte Marie by Marquette 1668; military post of Detroit (*q.v.*) founded 1701; ceded to England 1763 and to U.S. 1783; nominally included in Northwest Territory 1787, but British retained control until 1796; became part of Indiana Territory (1800, 1803) until organized as Michigan Territory 1805; boundaries of Michigan Territory were extended 1818 and 1834; admitted as free state after settled boundary dispute with Ohio Jan. 26, 1837; Lansing became capital 1847; adopted present constitution 1908.

Michigan, Lake. Lake in NE cen. U.S., 3d in size of the 5 Great Lakes (*q.v.*) and the only one wholly within the U.S.; bounded on N and E by Michigan, on S by Indiana, on SW by Illinois, on W by Wisconsin; ab. 307 m. long; 22,400 sq. m.; greatest depth 923 ft.; elevation 580 ft.; at N end connected through Straits of Mackinac with Lake Huron; at its SW end is the city of Chicago; connected by means of the Chicago and Illinois rivers and connecting canals (see ILLINOIS WATERWAY), with the Mississippi river. See GREEN BAY.

Michigan City. City, La Porte co., N Indiana, on Lake Michigan; pop. 36,653; lake resort city, founded 1832; hosiery, furniture, railroad cars.

Michigan Island. See APOSTLE ISLANDS.

Mich′i·ka·mau′ Lake (mĭsh′ĭ·kȧ·mô′). = MISHIKAMAU LAKE.

Mich′i·li·mack′i·nac (mĭsh′ĭ·lĭ·măk′ĭ·nô). Old form of MACKINAC.

Mi′chin·má′hui·da (mē′chĕn·mä′wĕ·thä). Peak 8104 ft. in S cen. Chile, E of Corcovado Gulf.

Mich′i·pi·co′ten Harbour (mĭsh′ĭ·pĭ·kō′t′n). Port, SE Ontario, Canada, on NE shore of Lake Superior; ships ore.

Michipicoten Island. Island in NE Lake Superior off SW coast of Algoma co., S Ontario, Canada.

Mich′mash (mĭk′măsh); *mod.* **Mukh·mas′** (mŏŏk-mäs′). Town, NE Judaea, Palestine, N of Jerusalem; scene of Jonathan's victory over the Philistines (*1 Samuel* xiv).

Mi′cho·a·cán′ (mē′chō·ä·kän′). State, SW Mexico. See *Table* at MEXICO.

Mi·chu′rinsk (mĭ·chŏŏr′ĭnsk; *Russ.* myĭ·chŏŏ′ryĭnsk); *formerly* **Koz·lov′** (kŭz·lôf′). City, W Tambov Region, Soviet Russia, Europe, 35 m. WNW of Tambov and ab. 115 m. S of Ryazan; pop. 70,202; important industrial town and railroad junction point; trades in grain, cattle, and farm products. Began as a small monastery (founded 1627) in the forest; later became a frontier fort against the Tatars.

Mi′cro·ne′sia (mī′krŏ·nē′zhȧ; -zhĭ·ȧ). Islands of the W Pacific Ocean E of Phil. Is., widely scattered bet. 1° and 20°30′N lat. and 131° and 172°E long.; a subdivision of Oceania; total area ab. 1335 sq. m. See *Map* at OCEANIA. Includes the Mariana, the Palau, Caroline, Marshall, and Gilbert Is. which are all small; the Marianas, Palaus, and many of the Caroline Is. are of volcanic origin, some with peaks of 1000 to 2500 ft.; others of the Carolines and all of the Marshall and Gilbert Is. are low coral atolls. The Micronesians are a mixed race of Melanesian, Polynesian, and some Malaysian stock, but the interesting and unexplained ruins on several of the islands indicate a capable people of very early origin; their language is a subdivision of the Melanesian branch of Austronesian languages. All the island groups were placed under Japanese mandate 1919, except Guam, Wake, Nauru, and the Gilbert Is., which were taken over by the Japanese 1941–42 in World War II but for the most part retaken by American forces 1943–45.

Mid′del·burg (mĭd′′l·bûrg; *Dutch* -bŭrк). **1** Commune, ✳ of Zeeland prov., SW Netherlands, on Walcheren I. just N of Vlissingen; pop. 18,395; market town; frequented by artists; in Middle Ages a Hanse town. **2** Town, cen. Cape Province, S Union of South Africa, 170 m. N of Port Elizabeth; pop. 5341; cattle, sheep, and ostrich farming. **3** Town, S cen. Transvaal, NE Union of South Africa, 75 m. E of Pretoria; pop. 5778; a coal-mining community; copper, iron, and cobalt also found.

Midden–Java. See MIDDLE JAVA.

Mid′den–Pre·ang′er (mĭd′ĕ[n]·prä·äng′ĕr). = *Middle Preanger:* see PREANGER.

Middle America. Region including Mexico and Central America and, sometimes, the islands of the Caribbean.

Middle Andaman. One of the Andaman Is. (*q.v.*).

Middle Atlas. See ATLAS MOUNTAINS.

Middle Bass Island. See BASS ISLAND.

Mid′dle·bor′o, *officially* **Mid′dle·bor′ough** (mĭd′′l-bûr′ŏ). Town, Plymouth co., SE Massachusetts, 14 m. S of Brockton; pop. 11,065; manufactures shoes, metal products, hospital supplies, caskets.

Mid′dle·bourne (mĭd′′l·bōrn). Town, ⊗ of Tyler co., NW West Virginia; pop. 711.

Mid′dle·burg (mĭd′′l·bûrg). Borough, ⊗ of Snyder co., cen. Pennsylvania; pop. 1366.

Middleburg Heights. Village, Cuyahoga co., N Ohio, suburb of Cleveland; pop. 7282.

Mid′dle·bur′y (mĭd′′l·bĕr′ĭ; -bĕr·ĭ). **1** Town, NW New Haven co., S Connecticut, near Naugatuck river; pop. 4785; dairying, raising of saddle horses. **2** Village in Middlebury town (pop. 5305), ⊗ of Addison co., W Vermont, 30 m. NNW of Rutland; pop. 3688; marble, lumber; Middlebury Coll. (1800; coed.). Chartered 1761 as New Hampshire grant; became part of New York 1764; settled 1773; abandoned 1778–83; organized in state of Vermont 1786; incorporated 1832.

Middle Cascade. Waterfall 910 ft. in Yosemite Valley, California, in a tributary of the Merced river.

Middle Congo. Former French territory, W cen. Africa, in former French Equatorial Africa; as **Republic of Congo,** became an autonomous republic of the French Community Nov. 28, 1958; 132,012 sq. m.; pop. 759,724; ✳ Brazzaville.

Middle East. An extensive region comprising the countries of S and SW Asia and NE Africa—a term of British origin used to include the Near East (*q.v.*) and much more (Iraq, Iran, Afghanistan, Pakistan, India, and Burma) to the borders of the Far East (*q.v.*). ☞ *Middle East* is an indefinite and unofficial term; the U.S. Department of State does not officially employ it.

Middle Europe. See CENTRAL EUROPE.

Middle Fork Peak. Mountain 9130 ft. in W Lemhi co., E cen. Idaho.

Middle Franconia. Bavarian government district. See *Table* at BAVARIA.

Middle Island. = SOUTH ISLAND, New Zealand.

Middle Ja′va *or* **Central Ja′va** (jä′vȧ; jăv′ȧ); *Du.* **Mid′den–Ja′va** (mĭd′ĕ[n]·yä′vä). Province of Indonesia, comprising cen. Java; 10,873 sq. m.; pop. 11,141,-629; ✳ Semarang. Chief towns Semarang, Pekalongan, Magelang, Tegal, and Salatiga, and the two government capitals Surakarta and Jogjakarta.

Middle Kingdom. See CHINA.

Middle Loup. River ab. 220 m. long, cen. Nebraska; rises in S Cherry co., flows E and SE to unite with North Loup and South Loup rivers and form Loup river.

Middle Park. Plateau bet. 60 and 70 m. long in Grand co., N Colorado; crossed by the Colorado river; with North Park, South Park, and San Luis Park (*qq.v.*) forms a N–S chain of high, level, grassy areas enclosed by snow-capped mountains.

Mid′dle·port (mĭd′′l·pōrt). **1** Village, Niagara co., W New York, 30 m. ENE of Niagara Falls; pop. 1882. **2** Village, Meigs co., SE Ohio, on Ohio river 40 m. SW of Marietta; pop. 3373; coal and salt mines nearby.

Middle Preanger. See PREANGER.

Middle Rhine. The English name sometimes used of the section of the Rhine river bet. Mainz and Bonn.

Middle River. Urban area, Baltimore co., N Maryland, E suburb of Baltimore; pop. 10,825.

Middle Saranac Lake. See SARANAC LAKES.

Mid′dles·bor′ough *or* **Mid′dles·bor′o** (mĭd′′lz·bûr′ō). City, Bell co., SE Kentucky, at Cumberland Gap on Tennessee border; pop. 12,607; coal mining.

Mid′dles·brough (mĭd′′lz·brŭ). County borough, North Riding, Yorkshire, N England, on the Tees estuary 34 m. SSE of Newcastle; pop. 138,274, (1951) 147,336; iron and steel plants; in Cleveland dist. (*q.v.*).

Mid′dle·sex (mĭd′′l·sĕks). **1** Name of counties in four states of the U.S. See *Tables* at CONNECTICUT, MASSACHUSETTS, NEW JERSEY, VIRGINIA. **2** Borough, Middlesex co., cen. New Jersey, 6 m. N of New Brunswick; pop. 10,520. **3** County, Ontario, Canada. See *Table* at ONTARIO. **4** County, SE England, comprising NW part of London section; area 232 sq. m.; pop. (1951) 2,268,776; chief towns Brentford and Chiswick, Ealing, Hornsey, Harrow, Willesden, Tottenham, Uxbridge, Hampton; located largely in the Thames basin; chiefly a residential and market-gardening area.

Middle Teton. Peak 12,798 ft. in cen. Grand Teton National Park, NW Wyoming.

Mid′dle·ton (mĭd′′l·tŭn). **1** Town, Essex co., NE corner of Massachusetts, 15 m. ESE of Lowell; pop. 3718. **2** Town, Annapolis co., W Nova Scotia, Canada, 32 m. WSW of Kentville; pop. 1506; founded 1783. **3** Municipal borough, Lancashire, NW England, on the Irk 6 m. NNE of Manchester; pop. 32,602; ironworking.

Mid′dle·town (mĭd′′l·toun). **1** City, ⊗ of Middlesex co., S Connecticut, on Connecticut river 14 m. S of Hartford; pop. 33,250; settled 1650, incorporated 1784; coextensive with the town (incorporated 1651); commercial center for agricultural region producing tobacco, fruit, and dairy products; manufactures elastic webbing, rubber footwear, typewriters, brake lining, silks, marine hardware. Wesleyan University (1831; men). **2** Town, New Castle co., N Delaware, 23 m. SW of Wilmington; pop. 2191; flour milling, vegetable canning. **3** Town, Henry co., E cen. Indiana; pop. 2033. **4** City, Orange co., SE New York, 23 m. W of Newburgh; pop. 23,475; glassworks, foundries, tannery; manufactures wrapping and printing machinery, printers' supplies, machine tools, knives, leather goods. **5** Industrial city, Butler co., SW Ohio, 11 m. NE of Hamilton; pop. 42,115; incorporated as city 1833; manufactures tobacco, paper, steel, rolling-mill products. **6** Urban township, Bucks co., SE Pennsylvania; pop. 26,894. **7** Borough, Dauphin co., SE cen. Pennsylvania, on Susquehanna river 9 m. SE of Harrisburg; pop. 11,182 former boat-building and steel-manufacturing center. Olmsted Air Force Base. **8** Town and summer resort, Newport co., SE Rhode Island, on Narragansett Bay 5 m. N of Newport; pop. 12,675; center Middletown village; set off from Newport and incorporated as separate town 1743; pillaged by British fleet 1776.

Middle Urals. See URAL MOUNTAINS.

Middle Vol′ga Area (vŏl′gȧ). Former region, E cen. Soviet Russia, Europe, along the middle course of the Volga including part or most of Kuibyshev Region and

the Tatar, Mari, Chuvash, and Mordovian A.S.S. Republics; ab. 92,000 sq. m.; ✻ Samara (now Kuibyshev).

Mid′dle·wich (mĭd′′l·wĭch). Urban district, Cheshire, NW England, 21 m. SSW of Manchester; pop. 6734.

Mi′di′ (mē′dē′). The south, esp. of France.

Midi, Dent du. See DENT DU MIDI.

Mid′i·an (mĭd′ĭ·ăn). Ancient region of NW Arabia, E of the Gulf of 'Aqaba and bordered by Edom on the NW; the Midianites of Old Testament times were frequently at war with the Israelites.

Mid′land (mĭd′lănd). **1** Name of counties in two states of the U.S. See *Tables* at MICHIGAN and TEXAS. **2** City, ⊗ of Midland co., cen. Michigan, 18 m. W of Bay City; pop. 27,779; chemical works; salt and petroleum. **3** Borough, Beaver co., W Pennsylvania, on Ohio river 29 m. WNW of Pittsburgh; pop. 6425; steel, iron, coke. **4** City, ⊗ of Midland co., W Texas; pop. 62,625; cattle, oil. **5** Industrial town, Simcoe co., SE Ontario, Canada, on Georgian Bay 27 m. NNW of Barrie; pop. 7206; good harbor; iron and steel products, flour mills; resort.

Midland Junction. Town, SW Western Australia, suburb of Perth on Swan river; pop. 5410.

Midland Park. Manufacturing borough, Bergen co., NE corner of New Jersey, 5 m. N of Paterson; pop. 7543.

Mid′lands, the (mĭd′lăn[d]z). The central counties of England, esp. Derbyshire, Nottinghamshire, Leicestershire, Rutlandshire, Northamptonshire, Warwickshire, and Staffordshire; contains many of the large industrial cities: Birmingham, Coventry, Leicester, Derby, Walsall, Burton on Trent, Stoke on Trent; suffered severely from night air raids Nov. 1940 to Dec. 1941.

Mid·lo′thi·an. **1** (mĭd·lō′thĭ·ăn) Village, Cook co., NE Illinois, 18 m. S of Chicago; pop. 6605. **2** (mĭd·lō′thĭ·ăn; -thȳăn); *formerly* **Edinburgh** *or* **Edinburghshire**. County, SE Scotland; 366 sq. m.; pop. (1951) 565,746; ⊗ Edinburgh; the rivers Esk, Almond, Tyne; agriculture, livestock raising, dairying, fisheries, shipbuilding, manufacturing (paper, iron products, carpets), distilling.

Mid′na·pore (mĭd′nȧ·pōr) *or* **Mid′na·pur** (mĭd′nȧ·pōōr). Town, West Bengal, NE India, 68 m. W of Calcutta; pop. 32,021; noted for its silkworm culture.

Mid′sa·yap′ (mĭd′sä·yäp′). Municipality, NW cen. Cotabato prov., Mindanao, Phil. Is., on a N tributary of Mindanao river 20 m. E of Cotabato; pop. 23,033.

Mid′som′er Nor′ton (mĭd′sŭm′ēr nôr′t′n). Town, Somersetshire, SW England, 13 m. SSE of Bristol; pop. (1931) 7490; coal mining.

Mid′vale (mĭd′vāl). City, Salt Lake co., N Utah, 11 m. S of Salt Lake City; pop. 5802; ore smelters.

Mid′way′ (mĭd′wā′). Two small islands, Eastern I. and Sand I., parts of a low coral atoll in cen. Pacific Ocean, 1304 statute m. (1134 naut. m.) WNW of Honolulu; 177°20′W long.; 2 sq. m.; under administration of the U.S. Navy; not incorporated in state of Hawaii. See *Map* at HAWAII. Discovered and claimed by U.S. 1859; formally occupied for U.S. 1867; Sand I. made a submarine cable station 1905; China clipper transpacific station 1936; U.S. naval base. In World War II attacked unsuccessfully by Japanese Dec. 1941 and Jan. 1942; another Japanese attacking force defeated by American planes June 3–6, 1942.

Mid′way′–Hard′wick (mĭd′wā′härd′wĭk). Urban area, Baldwin co., cen. Georgia; pop. 16,909.

Midwest City. City, Oklahoma co., cen. Oklahoma, E suburb of Oklahoma City; pop. 36,058.

Mid′ye′ (mĕd·yĕ′). Town, Kırklareli vilayet, NE Turkey in Europe port on the Black Sea 64 m. NW of İstanbul.

Mi·e (mē·[y]ĕ). Prefecture of Japan. See *Table* at JAPAN.

Mie′cho·wi′ce (myĕ′κô·vē′tsĕ); *Ger.* **Mie′cho·witz** (mē′κô·vĭts). Commune, cen. Śląsk dept., SW Poland, W of Bytom; pop. 14,608; coal and iron mining; formerly

in Silesia, Germany, assigned to Poland by Potsdam Conference 1945.

Mię·dzy′rzec (myĕnn·dzĭ′zhĕts). Commune, Lublin dept., E Poland, 52 m. N of Lublin; pop. 16,837.

Mię·dzy′rzecz (myĕnn·dzĭ′zhĕch); *Ger.* **Me′se·ritz** (mä′zĕ·rĭts). Town, W Poznań dept., W Poland, on Odra river E of Frankfurt; pop. (1946) 10,848; formerly in Brandenburg, Germany.

Mie′res (myä′räs). Commune, Oviedo prov., NW Spain, 9 m. SSE of Oviedo; pop. (1941 est.) 51,704; iron, cinnabar, coal, and sulfur mines nearby.

Mierzeja Wiślana. See FRISCHES HAFF.

Miff′lin (mĭf′lĭn). County in Pennsylvania. See *Table* at PENNSYLVANIA.

Miff′lin·burg (mĭf′lĭn·bûrg). Borough, Union co., cen. Pennsylvania, 24 m. S of Williamsport; pop. 2476.

Miff′lin·town (mĭf′lĭn·toun). Borough, ⊗ of Juniata co., S cen. Pennsylvania; pop. 887.

Mif′jir, Nahr el (nä′h′r ăl mĭf′jĭr); *Eng.* **Dead River** (dĕd). River of Palestine, flowing W from Samaria through Plain of Sharon to Mediterranean Sea.

Migdal. See MAGDALA.

Migdal–Gad. See EL MAJDAL town, SW Palestine.

Migiurtinia. See MIJERTINS.

Mi·glia·ri′no (mē·lyä·rē′nŏ) Commune, Ferrara prov., Emilia, N Italy, 19 m. ESE of Ferrara; pop. 10,717.

Mi′gnon (mĭn′yŏn). City (unincorporated), Talladega co., Alabama; pop. 2271.

Mi·ha·ra (mē·hä·rä). See O SHIMA.

Mi·ja′res (mē·hä′räs) *or* **Mil·la′res** (mē·[l]yä′-). River ab 65 m. long, E Spain; flows SE, empties into Mediterranean Sea S of Castellón de la Plana.

Mij′er·tins (mĭj′ĕr·tĭnz) *or* **Mij′jar·ten** (mĭj′ĕr·tĕn); *Ital.* **Mi·giur·ti′nia** (mē·jōōr·tē′nyä). Region, NE Somalia, E Africa; includes Cape Guardafui; formerly a sultanate.

Mi·ka·ge (mē·kä·gĕ). Industrial town, Hyogo prefecture, W Honshu, Japan, on Osaka Bay just E of Kobe; pop. (1945) 8810.

Mi·ke′no (ʼmē·kā′nō). Quiescent volcano above 12,000 ft., Ruanda, cen. Africa, E of Lake Kivu.

Mi′kin·da′ni (mē′kĕn·dä′nĕ). Seaport, Lindi prov., SE Tanganyika, E Africa; pop. ab. 5000.

Mik′ke·li (mĭk′kĕ·lĭ). 1 Department of Finland. See *Table* at FINLAND.

2 *Swed.* **Sankt Mi′chel** (sångkt mē′kĕl). City, its ✳, S Finland; pop. (1939 est.) 10,500; commercial center in agricultural and fishing region.

Mi·ko′łów (mē·kô′lōōf). Commune, Śląsk dept., SW Poland, 7 m. SSW of Katowice; pop. (1938–39 est.) 14,030; not far from prewar Polish boundary.

Mikoyan Shakhar. See KLUKHORI.

Mi′kul·czy′ce (mē′kōōl·chĭ′tsĕ); *Ger.* **Mi′kult·schütz** (mē′kōōlt·shüts). Former commune (pop 17,745), Silesia, Germany; in 1927 made part of Hindenburg (see ZABRZE), which is now in Poland.

Mikulov. See NIKOLSBURG.

Mi′la (mē′lá). Commune, Constantine dept., NE Algeria, just NW of Constantine; pop. 11,565.

Mi·lac′a (mĭ·lăk′á). Village, ⊗ of Mille Lacs co., E cen. Minnesota, 28 m. ENE of St. Cloud; pop. 1821.

Mi·la′gro (mē·lä′grŏ). Town, Guayas prov., W Ecuador, 25 m. E of Guayaquil; pop. (1944 est.) 16,389; in rich agricultural district.

Mi·la′gros (mē·lä′grŏs). Municipality, S Masbate I. on Asid Gulf, Masbate prov., Phil. Is.; pop. 30,171.

Mi′lam (mĭ′lăm). County, Texas. See TEXAS, *Table*.

Mi′lan (mĭ′lăn). 1 Village, Monroe and Washtenaw cos., SE Michigan, 13 m. S of Ann Arbor; pop. 3616.

2 City, ⊗ of Sullivan co., N Missouri; pop. 1670.

3 Town, Gibson co., NW Tennessee, 21 m. N of Jackson; pop. 5208; fruit and vegetable shipping center.

Mi·lan′ (mĭ·lăn′; mĭ·län′); *Ital.* **Mi·la′no** (mē·lä′nŏ); *anc.* **Me′di·o·la′num** (mē′dĭ·ŏ·lä′nŭm; mĕd′ĭ-). Manufacturing and commercial commune, ✳ of Milano prov.,

Lombardy, N Italy, 76 m. N by E of Genoa; pop. 1,115,848; 2d largest city of Italy; in fertile plain bet. Adda and Ticino rivers; buildings include white-marble cathedral (begun 1387), castle, amphitheater, triumphal arch, basilica of St. Ambrose (founded 387), royal palace, archiepiscopal palace, Brera palace (including the Brera art gallery), Ambrosian library (earliest public library in Europe), La Scala theater (2d largest in Europe), the Ospedale Maggiore (founded 1456; hospital); manufactures silk, machinery, locomotives, automobiles, chemicals, electrical apparatus.

History: Ancient Gallic city captured by Romans 194 B.C.; in 4th cent. A.D. a chief city of Western Roman Empire from which Constantine issued Edict of Milan 313; seat of Archbishop Ambrose (d. 397); overrun by Huns, by Odoacer, and by Ostrogoths (539); under strong episcopal authority, it became semi-independent of the empire and took lead in defiance of Emperor Frederick I in his struggle with Lombard League (see LOMBARDY); rebuilt after its destruction by Frederick 1162; ruled by the Visconti as dukes of Milan 1311–1447 and under them expanded until the **Duchy of Milan,** *Ital.* **Du·ca′to di Mi·la′no** (dōō·kä′tŏ dē mē·lä′nŏ), *called also* **The Mil′a·nese′** (mĭl′á·nēz′; -nēs′), at its height included territory on both sides of middle Po and shared with Venice control of N Italy including Genoa; under Sforza family 1447–1535 duchy became pawn in Hapsburg-French rivalry in Italian wars of 16th cent.; duchy became Spanish 1535, ceded to Austria 1713; under Napoleon 1796–1814 city became capital of his Cisalpine Republic and kingdom of Italy (1805); as part of Lombardy 1815–59 duchy belonged to Austria and was included in cession of Lombardy to Piedmont 1859; became part of Italy 1860; nucleus of the duchy now the province of Milano; in World War II city reached by Allied forces Apr. 29, 1945.

Mi·la′no (mē·lä′nŏ). 1 Province of Italy. See *Table* at ITALY.

2 See MILAN, Italy.

Mi·las′ (mē·läs′); *anc.* **My·la′sa** (mī·lä′sá). Town, Muğla vilayet, SW Turkey in Asia, near coast; pop. 8322, fruit-growing center; formerly famous for its rugs (Melas rugs); ancient Mylasa was a flourishing city of Caria.

Mi·laz′zo (mē·lät′tsŏ); *anc.* **My′lae** (mī′lē). Fortified seaport, Messina prov., NE Sicily, on Tyrrhenian Sea 17 m. W of Messina; pop. 19,800; Spanish castle (now a prison); 17th-cent. cathedral; seaplane port. Scene of victory of Garibaldi over Bourbon forces 1860; waters off ancient Mylae scene of naval victory of Gaius Duilius over the Carthaginians 260 B.C. in First Punic War.

Milazzo, Gulf of. Inlet of the Mediterranean Sea 16 m. long on N coast of Sicily.

Mil′bank (mĭl′băngk). City, ⊗ of Grant co., NE South Dakota, 34 m. NE of Watertown; pop. 3500; manufactures trailers, dairy products; granite quarries.

Mil′den·hall (mĭl′dĕn·hôl). Town, West Suffolk, E England, 8 m. NE of Newmarket; Royal Air Force station; 15th-cent. market cross, 17th-cent. manor house.

Mil·du′ra (mĭl·dūr′á). Town, NW Victoria, SE Australia, on Murray river 15 m. above its junction with the Darling and ab. 300 m. NW of Melbourne; pop. 6614.

Mile 26. See EIELSON FIELD.

Miles City (mīlz). City, ⊗ of Custer co., SE Montana, on Yellowstone river 140 m. ENE of Billings; pop. 9665; horse and cattle market.

Mile′stone′ Mountain (mīl′stōn′). Peak 13,643 ft. in Sierra Nevada, N Tulare co., S cen. California.

Mi·let′to, Mon′te (mŏn′tā mē·lät′tŏ). Mountain, highest in Neapolitan Apennines (see APENNINES)

Mi·le′tus (mi·lē′tŭs; mĭ-). Ruined city (archaeological site) on W coast of Asia Minor, near the mouth of the Menderes in the modern vilayet of Aydın; one of the great cities of Asia Minor, on the coast of Caria and the southernmost and most important of the 12 Ionian

Cities; had four harbors and a large trade, founded colonies on the Black Sea and in Egypt and Italy, and for a time was the rival of Lydia; led Ionian revolt 500 B.C. but was overcome by Persia; later taken by Alexander; in Roman times yielded in influence to Ephesus; distinguished as a literary center.

Mil'ford (mĭl'fẽrd). **1** Residential and resort city, SW New Haven co., S Connecticut, on Long Island Sound and Housatonic river; pop. 41,662; settled 1639, incorporated 1640; oyster fisheries; manufactures brass fittings, hardware, electric motors, rubber substitutes. **2** Industrial city, Kent and Sussex cos., cen. Delaware, 18 m. S of Dover; pop. 5795; trade center for truck-garden and fruit-growing area; boatyards, flour mills. **3** Village, Iroquois co., E Illinois; pop. 1699. **4** Town, Worcester co., cen. Massachusetts, 16 m. ESE of Worcester; pop. 15,749; boots and shoes; granite. **5** Village, Oakland co., SE Michigan, 17 m. W of Pontiac; pop 4323; automobile parts, food products. **6** Manufacturing and fruit-growing town, Hillsboro co., S New Hampshire, 11 m. WNW of Nashua; pop. 4863; granite quarries nearby. **7** Village, Clermont and Hamilton cos., SW Ohio, 12 m. ENE of Cincinnati; pop. 4131. **8** Borough, ⊗ of Pike co., NE Pennsylvania, on Delaware river 47 m. E of Scranton; pop. 1198.

Milford Haven. Urban district and seaport, Pembrokeshire, SW Wales; pop. 11,717; excellent harbor on **Milford Haven** (large inlet of St. George's Channel); fisheries; Henry Tudor (afterwards Henry VII) landed here from France 1485 to conduct his successful campaign for English throne.

Milford Sound. Inlet of Tasman Sea on SW coast of South I., New Zealand; famous for its scenery.

Milh, Cape (mĭl); *Arab.* **Ras el Milh** (räs' äl mĭl'h'). Cape, NE Libya, near Egyptian border.

Milhau. See MILLAU.

Mi'li (mē'lē). Atoll at S end of Ratak Chain, SE Marshall Is., W Pacific Ocean; has 30 islets enclosing lagoon 23 m long; often bombed by Americans 1942-44.

Mil·ia'na (mĭl·yä'nȧ). Commune, N Alger dept., N Algeria, on railroad 60 m. WSW of Algiers; pop. 10,931.

Mi'li·ane' (mē'lyän'). Small river flowing NE across N cen. Tunisia, N Africa, and emptying into Mediterranean Sea just below and E of Tunis.

Mi·li·tel'lo in Val di Ca·ta'nia (mē·lē·tĕl'lō ĕm väl' dē kä·tä'nyä). Commune, Catania prov., E Sicily, 23 m. SW of Catania; pop. 11,314; earthquake 1693.

Milk (mĭlk). River 625 m. long, S Alberta prov. and N Montana; rises in Glacier co., NW Montana, flows NE across Canadian border and E along S Alberta prov., turns SE across Montana border and E along N Montana into Missouri river in S Valley co., NE Montana.

Milk'bosch Point (mĭlk'bôs). Cape on NW coast of Cape of Good Hope prov., South Africa.

Mil'lard (mĭl'ẽrd). County in Utah. See *Table* at UTAH.

Millares. See MIJARES.

Mil'lau (mē'yō'); *also* **Mil'hau'** (mē'yō'); *anc.* **Æ·mil'i·a'num** (ē·mĭl'ĭ·ā'nŭm). Commune, Aveyron dept., S France, 30 m. SE of Rodez; pop. 16,437; coal; tanneries, manufactures gloves, woolens.

Mill'brae (mĭl'brā). City, San Mateo co., W California, NW of San Mateo; pop. 15,873.

Mill'brook (mĭl'brōok). Residential village and summer resort, Dutchess co., SE New York, 13 m. ENE of Poughkeepsie; pop. 1717; artists' colony.

Mill'burn (mĭl'bẽrn). Township, Essex co., NE New Jersey, 7 m. W of Newark; pop. 18,799.

Mill'bur'y (mĭl'bĕr'ĭ; -bēr·ĭ). Town, Worcester co., cen. Massachusetts, 5 m. S of Worcester; pop. 9623; textiles.

Mill Creek (mĭl). Borough, Huntingdon co., S cen. Pennsylvania, ESE of Altoona; pop. 28,441.

Mil'ledge·ville (mĭl'ĭj·vĭl; *Sou.* also -v'l). City, ⊗ of Baldwin co., cen. Georgia, 30 m. NE of Macon; pop.

11,117; settled 1803; capital of Georgia 1805-68; bird sanctuary (from 1934). Georgia State College for Women (chartered 1889; opened 1891).

Mille Îles or **Mille Isles, Ri·vière' des** (rē·vyâr' dā mēl' ēl'). River ab. 24 m. long, a part of the course of the St. Lawrence river, NW and N of Jesus I., S Quebec, Canada; separates Jesus I. from the mainland; flows NE from Lake of Two Mountains to junction with Rivière des Prairies.

Mille Lacs (mĭl' lăks'). **1** Lake on boundary bet. Aitkin and Mille Lacs cos., E cen. Minnesota; ab. 16 m. in diameter; 198 sq. m. **2** County in Minnesota. See *Table* at MINNESOTA. **3** Lake 104 sq. m., W Ontario, Canada, NW of Port Arthur.

Mil'len (mĭl'ĕn). City, ⊗ of Jenkins co., E Georgia, 47 m. S of Augusta; pop. 3633; railroad junction.

Mil'ler (mĭl'ẽr). **1** Name of counties in three states of the U.S. See *Tables* at ARKANSAS GEORGIA, MISSOURI. **2** City, ⊗ of Hand co., E cen. South Dakota; pop. 2081.

Mil'le·ro'vo (mĭl'ē·rō'vō; *Russ.* myĭl·lyĕ·rô'vŭ). Town, W Rostov Region, Soviet Russia, Europe, on railroad N of Kamensk Shakhtinski, ab. 60 m. ENE of Voroshilovgrad; scene of much fighting when retaken from Germans by Russians Feb. 1943.

Mil'ler Peak (mĭl'ẽr). Mountain 9445 ft. in SW Cochise co., SE Arizona.

Mil'lers (mĭl'ẽrz). River ab. 60 m. long, N Massachusetts; rises in S New Hampshire, flows S across Massachusetts border, then W into Connecticut river in cen. Franklin co., NW Massachusetts.

Mil'lers·burg (mĭl'ẽrz·bûrg). **1** Village, ⊗ of Holmes co., NE cen. Ohio, 20 m. SE of Mansfield; pop. 3101; settled by Pennsylvania Dutch 1816; gas and oil wells, sandstone quarries in vicinity. **2** Borough, Dauphin co., SE cen. Pennsylvania, on Susquehanna river 20 m. N of Harrisburg; pop. 2984; manufactures shoes, machine tools; in dairying section.

Mil'lers·ville (mĭl'ẽrz·vĭl). Borough, Lancaster co., SE Pennsylvania, 4 m. SW of Lancaster; pop. 3883. Millersville State Coll. (1854; coed.).

Mil'ler·ton Lake (mĭl'ẽr·tŭn; -t'n). See UNITED STATES, *Dams and Reservoirs* (Friant Dam) and SAN JOAQUIN river.

Mil'ler·town (mĭl'ẽr·toun). Town, cen. Newfoundland, at NE end of Red Indian Lake; pop. 380.

Mill Hall (mĭl). Borough, Clinton co., cen. Pennsylvania, 28 m. WSW of Williamsport; pop. 1891.

Mil'li·gan College (mĭl'ĭ·găn). Village, Carter co., NE Tennessee, ab. 6 m. SW of Elizabethton; pop. (1950) 213; Milligan College (1882; coed.).

Mil'ling·ton (mĭl'ĭng·tŭn). Town, Shelby co., SW corner of Tennessee, N of Memphis; pop. 6059.

Mil'li·nock'et (mĭl'ĭ·nŏk'ĕt; -ĭt). Town, Penobscot co., E cen. Maine, 54 m. SW of Houlton; pop. 7453; paper mills.

Millinocket Lake. 1 Lake on W boundary of Penobscot co., E cen. Maine, SE of Mt. Katahdin and just NE of Pemadumcook Lake with which it is connected by a short stream. **2** Small lake, NE Piscataquis co., N cen. Maine.

Mil'lis (mĭl'ĭs). Town, Norfolk co., E Massachusetts, 20 m. SW of Boston; pop. 4374.

Mil'lom (mĭl'ŭm). Former urban district, Cumberland, NW England, on Duddon estuary 48 m. SSW of Carlisle; pop. (1931) 7405; ruins of Norman castle; iron smelting, hematite mining.

Mill'port (mĭl'pōrt). Burgh, Bute co., SW Scotland, at S end of Great Cumbrae I.; pop. 2012; resort.

Mills (mĭlz). Name of counties in two states of the U.S. See *Tables* at IOWA and TEXAS.

Mills, Fort. See FORT MILLS.

Mill Springs (mĭl). Village in Wayne co., S Kentucky, on Cumberland river; pop. (est.) 100; scene of battle Jan. 19, 1862 in which Confederates were defeated.

Mill′stät′ter Lake (mĭl′shtĕt′ẽr); *Ger.* **Millstätter See** (zā). Lake (*see*) ab. 7½ m. long in cen. Carinthia, S Austria, in Drau (Drava) valley ab. 33 m. W of Klagenfurt; resort.

Mill′town (mĭl′toun). **1** Borough, Middlesex co., cen. New Jersey, 3 m. S of New Brunswick; pop. 5435.
2 Town, Charlotte co., SW New Brunswick, Canada, on St. Croix river just above Calais, Maine; pop. 2267.

Mill′vale (mĭl′vāl). Borough, Allegheny co., SW Pennsylvania, on Allegheny river 3 m. N of Pittsburgh; pop. 6624; iron and steel products; meat-packing houses.

Mill Valley (mĭl). Residential city, Marin co., W California, NW of San Francisco; pop. 10,411; near Mt. Tamalpais and Muir Woods National Monument.

Mill′ville (mĭl′vĭl). **1** Town, Worcester co., cen. Massachusetts, SE of Worcester; pop. 1567; woolen mills.
2 Manufacturing city, Cumberland co., SW New Jersey, 10 m. ESE of Bridgeton on Maurice river; pop. 19,096; settled 1720; incorporated as town 1801, as city 1866; fishing and oyster industry; manufactures glass, cotton goods, hosiery, women's garments.

Milne Bay (mĭl[n]). Bay at SE extremity of the Territory of Papua, New Guinea; Samarai is near its SE point; occupied by Japanese Aug. 1942 but they were driven out by Australians Sept.–Oct. 1942.

Mil′ner·ton (mĭl′nẽr·tŭn; -t'n). Town, S Cape Province, S Union of South Africa, on coast 5 m. N of Cape Town of which it is a suburb; wireless station.

Miln·ga′vie (mĭl·gī′). Burgh, Dunbarton co., W cen. Scotland; pop. 7883; residential suburb of Glasgow.

Miln′row (mĭl[n]′rō). Urban district, Lancashire, NW England, SE suburb of Rochdale; pop. 8585.

Mi′lo. **1** (mī′lō) Town, Piscataquis co., N cen. Maine, 35 m. NNW of Bangor; pop. 2756; wood products, yarns.
2 (mē′lō) See MELOS, Greece.

Mil·pi′tas (mĭl·pē′tăs). City, Santa Clara co., W California, S of Palo Alto; pop. 6572.

Mil′spe (mĭl′spĕ). Commune, North Rhine-Westphalia state, W Germany, WNW of Wuppertal; pop. 11,291.

Mil′ton (mĭl′t'n; -tŭn). **1** Town, ⊗ of Santa Rosa co., NW Florida, 18 m. NE of Pensacola; pop. 4108; founded as trading post 1825; manufacture of naval stores.
2 Town, Norfolk co., E Massachusetts, 6 m. S of Boston; pop. 26,375; manufactures drugs, dyestuffs, chocolate; reputed site of first paper mill in New England 1728.
3 Town, Umatilla co., NE Oregon, 28 m. NE of Pendleton; pop. (with Freewater) 4110; cans and ships peas; grows wheat.
4 Borough, Northumberland co., E cen. Pennsylvania, 19 m. SSE of Williamsport; pop. 7972; manufactures metal products, textiles, furniture; clay pits.
5 Town, Cabell co., W West Virginia, 18 m. E of Huntington; pop. 1714; glass manufactures.
6 Village, Rock co., S Wisconsin, 8 m. NNE of Janesville; pop. 1671; Milton Coll. (1844; coed.).
7 Town, ⊗ of Halton co., SE Ontario, Canada, 29 m. WSW of Toronto; pop. 2451; produces flour, lumber, butter, screws, and rugs.
8 Former urban district, Hampshire, S England, E of Christchurch; pop. (1931) 5293.

Milton Re′gis (rē′jĭs). Former urban district in Kent, England, now part of SITTINGBOURNE AND MILTON.

Milvian Bridge. See SAXA RUBRA.

Mil·wau′kee (mĭl·wô′kê). **1** River 100 m. long, SE Wisconsin; rises in Fond du Lac co., flows into Lake Michigan at Milwaukee.
2 County in Wisconsin. See *Table* at WISCONSIN.
3 Commercial and industrial city and lake port, its ⊗, SE Wisconsin, on Lake Michigan; largest city in the state; pop. 741,324; excellent harbor, coal and grain port; metalworking, meat packing, tanning, printing and publishing industries; manufactures machinery (steam shovels, turbines, tractors, gears), motor vehicles, beer and malt products, silk hosiery, knit goods, boots and shoes. Marquette Univ. (1881; coed.); Milwaukee-

Downer Coll. (1851; women); Mount Mary Coll. (1915; women); University of Wisconsin, Milwaukee Campus (1885; coed.); Alverno Coll. (1887; women). Settled 1818 on site of Indian settlement; population increased by German immigrants 1838–45 and again in 1848; incorporated as city 1846.

Milwaukee Depth. See ATLANTIC OCEAN.

Mil·wau′kie (mĭl·wô′kê). City, Clackamas co., NW Oregon, on Willamette river 7 m. S of Portland; pop. 9099.

Mimatum. See MENDE.

Mim′bres (mĭm′brĕs). Village, Grant co., SW New Mexico, on the Mimbres river, W of Mimbres Mts.; pop. 1153; hot springs; pueblo ruins nearby.

Mimbres Mountains. Range in SW New Mexico, extending along boundary bet. Grant and Sierra cos.

Mim′i·co (mĭm′ĭ·kō). Residential town, York co., SE Ontario, Canada, on Lake Ontario 6 m. W of Toronto; pop. 11,342.

Mi′mi·ka (mē′mē·kä). See KAUKENAU.

Min (mĭn). **1** *or* **Min-kiang** (mĭn′jĭ·äng′). River (*kiang*) ab. 350 m. long, Szechwan prov., S cen. China, flowing SE through the Red Basin into Yangtze river at Ipin; navigable for most of its course.
2 *or* **Min-kong** (mĭn′kông′). Navigable river (*kong*) ab. 250 m. long, N cen. Fukien prov., SE China, flowing SE into East China Sea near Minhow.

Mi·nab′ (mē·näb′). Town, S Iran, 50 m. E of Bandar Abbas; pop. ab. 10,000; has extensive fruit orchards.

Mi′na·has′sa (mē′nä·häs′ä); *also* **Mi′na·ha′sa.** Peninsula forming NE end of Celebes I., Indonesia.

Mi·na·mi, Cape (mē·nä·mē). = Cape GARAN BI.

Minami Iwo. See VOLCANO ISLANDS.

Minami Tori Shima. See MARCUS ISLAND.

Minas. **1** See LAVALLEJA, Uruguay.
2 Town, Uruguay, ✻ of Lavalleja dept.; pop. 32,000.

Mi′nas Basin (mī′năs). Northeast extension of the Bay of Fundy, in cen. Nova Scotia, Canada; connected by **Minas Channel** with the Bay of Fundy.

Mi′nas de Rí′o·tin′to (mē′näz thä rē′ô·tēn′tô). Commune, Huelva prov., SW Spain, on Tinto river 36 m. NE of Huelva; pop. 9060; rich copper mines.

Mi′nas Ge·rais′ (mē′nä zhä·rīs′). State of Brazil. See *Table* at BRAZIL.

Mi′na·ti·tlán′ (mē′nä·tê·tlän′). Town, Veracruz state, E Mexico, head of navigation on the Coatzacoalcos river 24 m. from its mouth; pop. 18,539; petroleum refinery.

Min′bu′ (mĭn′boo′). **1** District, Magwe division, Upper Burma; 3594 sq. m.; pop. 277,876.
2 Town, its ✻, on right bank of Irrawaddy opp. Magwe, ab. 145 m. SW of Mandalay; pop. 6005; oil field.

Minch (mĭnch). Channel bet. the Outer Hebrides and the NW coast of Scotland; includes the North Minch and Little Minch (*qq.v.*).

Min′cio (mēn′chô); *anc.* **Min′ci·us** (mĭn′shĭ·ŭs; -shŭs). River 115 m. long, N Italy; issues from Lake Garda, flows S and E past Mantua and empties into Po river SE of Mantua; navigable up to Mantua.

Min′da·na′o (mĭn′dà·nä′ô; *Span.* mēn′dä-). **1** Island, S Phil. I.; including adjacent islands, 36,537 sq. m., pop. 1,997,304; comprises 9 provinces: Agusan, Bukidnon, Cotabato, Davao, Lanao, Misamis Occidental, Misamis Oriental, Surigao, and Zamboanga. Of irregular triangular shape, indented with many gulfs or bays. Basilan I. in SW is largest island attached to it (Zamboanga prov.) politically; other important islands are Dinagat, Siargao, Camiguin, Samal, and Bucas Grande. Separated from Visayan Is. to N by Mindanao Sea and bordered on E by Philippine Sea (part of Pacific), on S by Celebes Sea, and on W by Sulu Sea. Quite mountainous with many peaks above 5000 ft.; highest Apo 9689 ft. (highest in the archipelago). Has two great river systems, the Agusan in E and the Mindanao (with the Pulangi) in S and cen. parts. Chief industry agriculture;

finest abacá (hemp) in the world is raised around Davao Gulf. Inhabitants chiefly Moros in center and W, Visayans in N coast towns.

2 *or* **Ri'o Gran'de de Mindanao** (rē'ō grän'då thä); *formerly known as the* **Co'ta·ba'to** (kō'tä·vä'tō). River ab. 200 m. long, cen. Mindanao, Phil. Is.; known in its upper course as the Pulangi, rises in NE Bukidnon prov., flows S and SW to form the main stream in cen. Cotabato prov., whence it flows WNW to Illana Bay; navigable; with its many tributaries forms a wide fertile basin. Municipality of Cotabato is on N side of delta.

Mindanao Deep. Deepest known point of any ocean 35,400 ft., in Philippine Sea, W Pacific Ocean, off NE Mindanao, Phil. Is.; is just 50 m. ESE of Siargao I. in 9°30′N.

Mindanao Sea. Large interisland body of water, S Phil. Is., ab. 70 m. from N to S and 180 m. from E to W; bordered on N by islands of Negros, Cebu, Bohol, and Leyte, and on S by Mindanao. At W end opens into Sulu Sea and connects on NE with the Pacific by Surigao Strait and on N with Visayan Sea by Tañon Strait and with Camotes Sea by Bohol Strait and Canigao Channel. Contains the islands of Camiguin and Siquijor.

Mindello. See PORTO GRANDE.

Min'den (mĭn'děn). **1** City, ⊗ of Webster parish, NW Louisiana, 28 m. E of Shreveport; pop. 12,785; shipping point for cotton; petroleum and natural-gas deposits.
2 City, ⊗ of Kearney co., S Nebraska, 16 m. SSE of Kearney; pop. 2383.
3 Village, ⊗ of Douglas co., W Nevada, 14 m. S of Carson City; pop. (est.) 400.
4 Village, ⊗ of Haliburton co., SE Ontario, Canada, 30 m. ESE of Bracebridge; pop. of district 1272.
5 Former government district, Westphalia prov., Prussia, Germany; 2033 sq. m.
6 *anc.* **Min'thun** (mĭn'thŭn). Manufacturing city, N North Rhine-Westphalia state, W Germany, on Weser river 58 m. ENE of Münster; pop. 27,139; 11th-cent. churches, town hall with 13th-cent. façade, 13th-cent. early Gothic cathedral; manufactures beer, brandy, lead pipe, chemicals, glass, furniture, machinery; blueprinting, iron founding, sawmilling, shipyards.
History: Founded in Roman times; bishopric founded here by Charlemagne in 8th cent.; member of Hanseatic League; besieged several times during Thirty Years' War; to Brandenburg 1648 by Peace of Westphalia; French defeated near here by Duke Ferdinand of Brunswick Aug. 1, 1759; to kingdom of Westphalia 1807; to Prussia 1814; in World War II entered by Allied troops Apr. 6, 1945.

Min·do'ro (mĭn·dōr'ō). Island, cen. Phil. Is., SW of Luzon; 3759 sq. m., constituting with adjacent islands a province, 3891 sq. m., pop. 131,569, ✴ Calapan. Roughly of oval shape with long axis NW to SE, ab. 80 m. long by ab. 50 m. wide. Touches South China Sea on W and Sulu Sea on S, separated from Luzon on N by Verde Island Passage, from Tablas and other islands on E by Tablas Strait, and from Calamian Is. on SW by Mindoro Strait. Has fairly regular coast line with several good harbors; most important adjacent islands are Lubang Is. to NW, Semirara Is. to S, and Ilin I. off SW coast. Mountain range, with several high peaks, runs through center; highest are Halcon in N 8481 ft. and Baco in the center 8160 ft.; coastal plains on E and W sides are wide and fertile. Numerous rivers with falls and rapids. Main products rice, copra, abacá, corn, sugar, and fruits. Coal, marble, and sulfur exist and gold has been mined for many years; lumbering and fishing are important industries. Tagalogs live along coasts except at S end where Visayans are found; the pagan tribe of Mangyanes dwell in the interior. Chief towns, after Calapan, Naujan, Pinamalayan, and San Jose.
History: Known to Chinese before coming of Spaniards; first visited by Spaniards 1570; at first administered from Batangas; suffered from Moro raids in 17th

and 18th cents.; came under American control 1901 and organized into a province 1902; held by Japanese through World War II; invaded by Americans who landed near San Jose Dec. 15, 1944.

Mindoro Strait. Passage ab. 50 m. wide connecting South China Sea and N Sulu Sea, bet. SW Mindoro and Calamian Is.; much traveled by ships bet. Manila, Hong Kong, and other Asiatic ports on N and ports of S Philippines and Netherlands Indies on S.

Mind'szent (mĭnd'sĕnt). Commune on Tisza river 20 m. N of Szeged, S Hungary; pop. 10,926.

Mine'head' (mĭn'hĕd'). Urban district, Somersetshire, SW England, on Bristol Channel 43 m. WSW of Bristol; pop. 7400; seaside resort.

Mi·ne'o (mĕ·nâ'ō); *anc.* **Me·nae'um** (mĕ·nē'ŭm). Commune, Catania prov., E Sicily, 27 m. SW of Catania; pop. 8841; geophysical observatory, medieval crypts; terra cotta; mineral springs.

Min'e·o'la (mĭn'ê·ō'lå). **1** Village, ⊗ of Nassau co., SE New York, on Long I. 20 m. E of New York; pop. 20,519; suburb of New York City; packing plants, glass factory; polo fields nearby.
2 City, Wood co., NE Texas, 23 m. N of Tyler; pop. 3810; railroad junction; manufactures lumber products.

Mi'ner (mī'nĕr). County in South Dakota. See *Table* at SOUTH DAKOTA.

Min'er·al (mĭn'ĕr·ăl). Name of counties in four states of the U.S. See *Tables* at COLORADO, MONTANA, NEVADA, WEST VIRGINIA.

Mi'ne·ral' del Mon'te (mē'nâ·räl' dĕl mōn'tâ). See REAL DEL MONTE.

Min'er·al Point (mĭn'ĕr·ăl). City, Iowa co., SW Wisconsin, 17 m. ENE of Platteville; pop. 2385; formerly successively lead-mining and zinc-mining center.

Mineral Wells. City, Palo Pinto co., N cen. Texas, 42 m. W of Fort Worth; pop. 11,053; health and pleasure resort; mineral wells; manufactures mineral-water crystals.

Min'ers·ville (mĭn'ĕrz·vĭl). Borough, Schuylkill co., E cen. Pennsylvania, 4 m. WNW of Pottsville; pop. 6606; settled 1793; coal mining and shipping; manufactures garments, machine-shop products.

Mi·ner'va (mĭ·nûr'và). Village, Carroll and Stark cos., E Ohio, 15 m. ESE of Canton; pop. 3833; manufactures pottery, wax-paper products; coal mines and clay pits.

Mi·ner·vi'no Mur'ge (mĕ·når·vē'nō mōōr'jå). Commune, Bari prov., Apulia, SE Italy, 40 m. W of Bari; pop. 19,132.

Min'gan Islands (mĭng'găn). Group of islands in Gulf of St. Lawrence, N of Anticosti I., near mouth of Romaine river.

Min'gin' Range (mĭn'gĭn'). Mountain range in cen. Upper Burma, bet. Irrawaddy and Chindwin rivers.

Min'go (mĭng'gō). County in West Virginia. See *Table* at WEST VIRGINIA.

Mingo Junction. City, Jefferson co., E Ohio, on Ohio river 3 m. S of Steubenville; pop. 4987; steelworks; coal mines nearby.

Min·gre'li·a (mĭn·grē'lĭ·à; mĭng-; -grēl'yà). Region and former principality now included in NW Georgia, U.S.S.R.; lies within borders of ancient Colchis, partly in Caucasus Mts. and partly along Black Sea coast. Declared its independence early in 15th cent. but was subject to some extent to Persia and Turkey; came under Russian control 1803 and incorporated permanently 1867. Mingrelians, a Georgian people of Caucasian race, now number ab. 250,000.

Mingulay. See BARRA.

Mi'nho (mē'nyōō). **1** *Span.* **Mi'ño** (mē'nyō); *anc.* **Min'i·us** (mĭn'ĭ·ŭs). River 171 m. long, Spain and Portugal; rises in N Lugo prov., NW Spain, flows S and SW, forming boundary bet. Portugal and Spain, and empties into Atlantic Ocean on the boundary S of Vigo.
2 Province of Portugal. See *Table* at PORTUGAL.
3 Popular name for old province of ENTRE-MINHO-E-DOURO.

Min′how′ (mĭn′hō′) or **Foo′chow′** or **Fu′chau′** (fōō′jō′; -chou′). Seaport on Min river 34 m. from its mouth, ✻ of Fukien prov., SE China; pop. (1931 est.) 322,725; ab. halfway bet. Hong Kong (455 m. by sea) and Shanghai. Chief part is walled city ab. 2 m. from N bank of river; foreign settlement is at **Nan′tai′** (nän′tī′) on S bank opposite. Ocean steamers anchor at Pagoda I. ab. 10 m. downstream. For years famous as chief port for export of black tea (bohea); has developed several industries but trade now chiefly local or coastal. In the city and on nearby hills are beautiful examples of Chinese architecture—pagodas, temples, monasteries. First appeared in Chinese history during T′ang dynasty; one of the first five treaty ports opened to trade by Treaty of Nanking 1842; in World War II captured and recaptured several times 1944–45 by Japanese and Chinese.

Min′i·coy (mĭn′ĭ·koi). Small island, S Laccadive Is., off SW coast of India; belongs to Laccadive and Amindivi Islands territory of the Republic of India.

Min′i·do′ka (mĭn′ĭ·dō′ka). County in Idaho. See Table at IDAHO.

Minieh. = MINYA.

Minius. See MINHO.

Min–kiang. See MIN river, Szechwan prov., China.

Mink Mountain (mĭngk). Peak 3782 ft. in the Catskill Mts., SE New York.

Min–kong. See MIN river, Fukien prov., China.

Min′na (mĭn′à). Town, ✻ of Niger prov., W cen. Northern Region, Nigeria, on railroad ab. 65 m. N of the Niger river.

Min′ne·ap′o·lis (mĭn′ē·ăp′ō·lĭs; -ăp′lĭs). **1** City, ⊗ of Ottawa co., NE cen. Kansas, on Solomon river 20 m. N of Salina; pop. **2024**; in agricultural and livestock-raising section.

2 City, ⊗ of Hennepin co., SE cen. Minnesota, on Mississippi river at the Falls of Saint Anthony (q.v.); largest city in the state; pop. 482,872; twin city with St. Paul (q.v.); railroad center and important flour-milling center; has large trade in dairy products, linseed oil, and linseed cakes. University of Minnesota (1851; coed.); Augsburg College and Theological Seminary (1869; coed.). Site visited by Hennepin 1680; constituted part of Fort Snelling military reservation 1819; developed lumber industry which declined after 1900; milled first flour 1823; saw great increase in number of flour mills in 1850′s; incorporated as city 1867.

Min′ne·do′sa (mĭn′ē·dō′sá). Town, SW Manitoba, Canada, 29 m. N of Brandon; pop. **2085**; railroad divisional point in farming region; sash factory, grist mill.

Min′ne·ha′ha (mĭn′ē·hä′hä). County in South Dakota. See Table at SOUTH DAKOTA.

Minnehaha Creek. Small stream, Hennepin co., SE cen. Minnesota; outlet of Lake Minnetonka; flows through S part of Minneapolis (area set aside as a park); the falls, ab. 50 ft. high, celebrated by Longfellow′s use in his poem Hiawatha, occur just before the creek reaches the Mississippi river; natural flow of water small.

Min′nei, Mount (?mĭn′ā). Volcano 4380 ft., Ambrim I., New Hebrides, SW Pacific Ocean; eruption 1913.

Min′ne·so′ta (mĭn′ē·sō′tá). **1** River 332 m. long, S Minnesota; flows out of Big Stone Lake on South Dakota-Minnesota boundary, bends SE, then NE to join the Mississippi river at St. Paul.

2 A north central state of U.S.A., 32d state admitted to Union (1858); bounded on N by Canadian provinces of Manitoba and Ontario, on E by Lake Superior and Wisconsin, on S by Iowa, and on W by South Dakota and North Dakota; 12th state in area, 84,068 sq. m. (land area 80,009 sq. m.); in addition to this area Minnesota has also 2212 sq. m. of water of the Great Lakes; 18th state in population, 3,413,864; ✻ St. Paul. See Table of States at UNITED STATES. Divided into the following 87 counties (for pronunciation of their names, see their individual entries):

NAME	LOCATION	AREA[1]	POP.[1]	CO. SEAT
Aitkin[2]	E cen.	1,824	12,162	Aitkin
Anoka	E	425	85,916	Anoka
Becker	NW cen.	1,315	23,959	Detroit Lakes
Beltrami	N	2,517	23,425	Bemidji
Benton	cen.	404	17,287	Foley
Big Stone	W	510	8,954	Ortonville
Blue Earth	S	740	44,385	Mankato
Brown	S	613	27,676	New Ulm
Carlton	E	860	27,932	Carlton
Carver	SE cen.	358	21,358	Chaska
Cass[3]	N cen.	2,053	16,720	Walker
Chippewa	SW cen.	582	16,320	Montevideo
Chisago	E	419	13,419	Center City
Clay	W	1,050	39,080	Moorhead
Clearwater[4]	NW	1,005	8,864	Bagley
Cook	NE corner	1,403	3,377	Grand Marais
Cottonwood	SW	640	16,166	Windom
Crow Wing	cen.	999	32,134	Brainerd
Dakota	SE	571	78,303	Hastings
Dodge	SE	435	13,259	Mantorville
Douglas	W cen.	637	21,313	Alexandria
Faribault	S	713	23,685	Blue Earth
Fillmore	SE	859	23,768	Preston
Freeborn	S	702	37,891	Albert Lea
Goodhue	SE	758	33,035	Red Wing
Grant	W	557	8,870	Elbow Lake
Hennepin	SE cen.	565	842,854	Minneapolis
Houston	SE corner	565	16,588	Caledonia
Hubbard	N cen.	932	9,962	Park Rapids
Isanti	E	442	13,530	Cambridge
Itasca	N	2,663	38,006	Grand Rapids
Jackson	S	698	15,501	Jackson
Kanabec	E	525	9,007	Mora
Kandiyohi	SW cen.	824	29,987	Willmar
Kittson	NW corner	1,124	8,343	Hallock
Koochiching	N	3,129	18,190	International Falls
Lac qui Parle	W	773	13,330	Madison
Lake	NE	2,132	13,702	Two Harbors
Lake of the Woods[5]	N	1,308	4,304	Baudette
Le Sueur	S	441	19,906	Le Center
Lincoln	SW	540	9,651	Ivanhoe
Lyon	SW	713	22,655	Marshall
McLeod	S cen.	498	24,401	Glencoe
Mahnomen	NW	574	6,341	Mahnomen
Marshall	NW	1,800	14,262	Warren
Martin	S	707	26,986	Fairmont
Meeker	S cen.	620	18,887	Litchfield
Mille Lacs[2]	E cen.	568	14,560	Milaca
Morrison	cen.	1,136	26,641	Little Falls
Mower	S	703	48,498	Austin
Murray	SW	708	14,743	Slayton
Nicollet	S	459	23,196	St. Peter
Nobles	SW	712	23,365	Worthington
Norman	NW	885	11,253	Ada
Olmsted	SE	655	65,532	Rochester
Otter Tail[6]	W cen.	2,000	48,960	Fergus Falls
Pennington	NW	622	12,468	Thief River Falls
Pine	E	1,412	17,004	Pine City
Pipestone	SW	464	13,605	Pipestone
Polk	NW	2,012	36,182	Crookston
Pope	W cen.	681	11,914	Glenwood
Ramsey	E	160	422,525	St. Paul
Red Lake	NW	432	5,830	Red Lake Falls
Redwood	SW	874	21,718	Redwood Falls
Renville	SW cen.	980	23,249	Olivia
Rice	S	495	38,988	Faribault
Rock	SW corner	485	11,864	Luverne
Roseau	NW	1,676	12,154	Roseau
Saint Louis	NE	6,281	231,588	Duluth
Scott	SE	352	21,909	Shakopee
Sherburne	cen.	438	12,861	Elk River
Sibley	S cen.	581	16,228	Gaylord
Stearns	cen.	1,356	80,345	St. Cloud
Steele	S	425	25,029	Owatonna
Stevens	W	570	11,262	Morris
Swift	W	747	14,936	Benson
Todd	cen.	947	23,119	Long Prairie
Traverse	W	572	7,503	Wheaton
Wabasha	SE	521	17,007	Wabasha
Wadena	cen.	536	12,199	Wadena
Waseca	S	415	16,041	Waseca
Washington	E	390	52,432	Stillwater
Watonwan	S	433	14,460	St. James
Wilkin	W	752	10,650	Breckenridge
Winona	SE	623	40,937	Winona
Wright	S cen.	671	29,935	Buffalo
Yellow Medicine	SW	758	15,523	Granite Falls

[1] Area = land area in sq. m. Pop. from 1960 Census.
[2] Upper half of Mille Lacs Lake in Aitkin co., lower half in Mille Lacs co.
[3] Contains many lakes including Leech Lake.
[4] Includes Lake Itasca, source of Mississippi river.
[5] Includes part of Lake of the Woods and a section of land on W shore of the lake N of the 49th parallel.
[6] Contains many lakes, including Otter Tail Lake.

MINNESOTA

Nickname: Gopher State, also New England of the West, North Star State. *State flower:* Pink and white moccasin flower. *Motto:* L'étoile du Nord (Star of the North). *Chief cities:* Minneapolis, St. Paul, Duluth, Rochester, St. Cloud. *Rivers:* Mississippi, rising in N cen. region, flowing SE, and forming SE boundary of state; St. Croix, forming E cen. boundary and flowing into the Mississippi; Minnesota (see 1, above). *Highest point:* Peak 2230 ft. in Misquah Hills, in Cook co., N of Lake Superior. *Chief industries:* Agriculture, stock raising, iron mining, flour milling.

History: Probably visited by Radisson and Groseilliers 1654–60; Upper Mississippi valley explored by La Salle and Hennepin 1680; region W of Mississippi was part of Louisiana Purchase 1803; part E of Mississippi, ceded to British 1763 and to U.S. 1783, in part included in Northwest Territory 1787 and later in Indiana Territory 1800; Fort Snelling established 1820; N boundary settled by Ashburton Treaty 1842; included in various territories before erection of Minnesota Territory 1849 (included region W from Wisconsin to the Missouri and N from Iowa to Canada); admitted to Union as state May 11, 1858; Sioux uprising occurred in S Minnesota 1862.

Min′ne·ton′ka (mĭn′ĕ·tŏng′kȧ). Village, Hennepin co., SE Minnesota, W suburb of Minneapolis; pop. 25,037.

Min′ne·ton′ka, Lake (mĭn′ĕ·tŏng′kȧ). Lake ab. 12 m. long in Hennepin co., SE cen. Minnesota, ab. 10 m. W of Minneapolis; outlet is Minnehaha Creek (*q.v.*).

Min′ne·was′ka, Lake (mĭn′ĕ·wŏs′kȧ). Lake ab. 7 m. long in Pope co., W cen. Minnesota.

Min′ne·wau′kan (mĭn′ĕ·wô′kăn). City, ⊗ of Benson co., N cen. North Dakota; pop. 420.

Minni. See ARMENIA.

Miño. See MINHO.

Mi·nonk′ (mĭ·nŏngk′; -nŭngk′). City, Woodford co., N cen. Illinois, 33 m. ENE of Peoria; pop. 2001.

Mi·nor′ca (mĭ·nôr′kȧ); *Span.* **Me·nor′ca** (mā·nôr′kä). Second largest island of the Balearic group, Baleares prov., Spain, in W Mediterranean ab. 25 m. NE of Majorca; 264 sq. m.; pop. (1930) 41,490; ✻ Mahón; rugged and irregular coast with numerous bays; hilly and generally arid in N, fertile plateau in S; produces grapes, oranges, lemons, grain, flax, hemp, sweet potatoes; iron, copper, lead, marble, alabaster, and porphyry deposits; apiculture; wine, oil, dairy products.

History: See also BALEARIC ISLANDS; part of kingdom of Majorca (*q.v.*); in 1709 captured by British during War of Spanish Succession and retained by Treaty of Utrecht 1713; taken by France 1756 in Seven Years' War; ceded by French to British 1763; recovered by Spain by treaty terminating War of American Independence 1783; in Spanish Civil War 1936–39, remained Loyalist until forced to surrender Feb. 1939.

Mi′not (mī′nŏt). City, ⊗ of Ward co., NW cen. North Dakota, on Souris river 100 m. N of Bismarck; pop. 30,604; railroad center and distribution point for agricultural region; ships grain, lignite coal; manufactures flour, processed dairy and poultry products. North Dakota State Teachers Coll. (1913; coed.).

Mi′nots Ledge (mī′nŭts) *or* **Co·has′set Rocks** (kŏ·hăs′ĕt; -ĭt). Reef in Cohasset harbor 15 m. SE of Boston, Massachusetts; lighthouse.

Minsh. Var. of MINCH.

Min Shan (mĭn′ shän′). Mountain range in Kansu prov., along N boundary of Szechwan prov., cen. China; peaks ab. 14,000 ft.; E extension of Kunlun Mts.

Min′si, Mount (mĭn′sĭ). Peak ab. 1500 ft. in E Monroe co., E Pennsylvania, forming part of the W side of Delaware Water Gap.

Minsk (mĭnsk; *Russ.* myēnsk). City, ✻ of White Russia, in cen. part, U.S.S.R., and ✻ of Minsk Region, on a tributary of Berezina river near Polish border; pop. 238,772; largest Russian city on the main railroad line from Warsaw to Moscow and an important commercial and industrial city, producing especially machinery, lumber,

clothing, leather and wooden goods. Known as early as 11th cent., its location on the western border has caused many changes of rulers from 13th to 18th cents.—at times Lithuanian, Russian, Polish, or Swedish; ravaged by Tatars 1505; annexed by Russia 1793 but again partially destroyed by Napoleon 1812; a key point in the Revolution of 1917 but occupied by Germans 1918 and by Poles 1919; in World War II again seized by Germans July 1941 but retaken by Russians July 3, 1944.

Mińsk Ma′zo·wiec′ki (mēn′y'sk mä′zō·vyĕts′kĕ); *also* **No′wo–Mińsk′** (nō′vô–mēn′y'sk). Commune, Warszawa dept., Poland, 23 m. ESE of Warsaw.

Minsk Region. Region, cen. White Russia, U.S.S.R.; ✻ Minsk.

Min′ster (mĭn′stēr). Village, Auglaize co., W Ohio, 28 m. SSW of Lima; pop. 2193.

Minthun. See MINDEN city, Germany.

Min′to, Lake (mĭn′tō). Lake 235 sq. m., NW Quebec prov., Canada, having outlet NE through Leaf river into Ungava Bay.

Min·tur′no (mēn·tōōr′nō). Commune, Littoria prov., Latium, cen. Italy, 47 m. ESE of Littoria; pop. 13,650; 12th-cent. church (formerly cathedral); ruins nearby on Appian Way of ancient **Min·tur′nae** (mĭn·tûr′nē). In World War II Allied base in advance from coast May 1944.

Mi·nûf′ (mĭ·nōōf′). Town, Minûfîya prov., Lower Egypt, SW of Shibîn el Kôm; pop. ab. 20,000.

Mi·nû·fî′ya (mĭ·nōō·fē′yȧ). Province, Lower Egypt. See *Table* at EGYPT.

Mi′nu·sinsk′ (mĭn′ōō·sĭnsk′; *Russ.* myĭ·nōō·syēnsk′). Town, SW corner of Krasnoyarsk Territory, Soviet Russia, Asia, on the upper Yenisei river 160 m. S of Krasnoyarsk; pop. 20,403; in region that raises much wheat and is rich in minerals, esp. coal, copper, and antimony; flour mills, sawmills, sugar factory. Apparently, from remains discovered, a locality settled from prehistoric times.

Min′ya (mĭn′yȧ). Province, Upper Egypt. See *Table* at EGYPT.

Minya, El. See EL MINYA.

Min′ya Kon′ka (mĭn′yȧ kŏng′kȧ). Mountain 24,900 ft. in E Sikang prov., S China, 30 m. S of Kangting (Tatsienlu); highest mountain in China.

Mi′o (mī′ō). Village, ⊗ of Oscoda co., NE Michigan; pop. (est.) 500.

Miq′ue·lon Island (mĭk′ĕ·lŏn; *Fr.* mē′klôn′). Small island 83 sq. m., belonging to France, in Atlantic Ocean off S coast of Newfoundland; pop. (1936) 520; originally two islands, **Great Miquelon** and **Little Miquelon** *or* **Lan′glade′** (län′glȧd′), but now connected by narrow shingle bar, the Isthmus of Langlade (*q.v.*). See SAINT PIERRE AND MIQUELON.

Mi′ra (mē′rä). **1** River in N Ecuador; flows NW, forming a section of Ecuador-Colombia boundary, and empties into Pacific Ocean; navigable for ab. 30 m.
2 Commune, Venezia prov., Venezia Euganea, NE Italy, on Lagoon of Venice 10 m. W of Venice; pop. (1931) 20,011; site of the Palazzo Foscarino in which Byron resided 1817–19.

Mi′ra Bay (mē′rȧ). Inlet of Atlantic Ocean on NE coast of Cape Breton I., Canada, SE of Glace Bay.

Mir′a·beau (mĭr′ȧ·bō; *Fr.* mē′rȧ′bō′). Commune, Alger dept., N Algeria, 50 m. E of Algiers; pop. 10,117.

Mir′a·bel′la Bay (mĭr′ȧ·bĕl′ȧ); *Mod. Gr.* **Kól′pos Me′ra·mpe′lou** (kôl′pôs mä′rä·bä′lōō). Large inlet on N coast of Crete at E end; town of Hagios Nikólaos on its W shore.

Mi·ra′da Hills (mĭ·rä′dȧ). City, Los Angeles co., SW California, NW of Anaheim; pop. 22,444.

Mir′a·flo′res (mĭr′ȧ·flōr′ĕs; *Span.* mē′rä·flō′räs). **1** Village, lake, and double locks in the Canal Zone, ab. 5 m. NW of Panama; the locks lower vessels 54⅔ ft. to level of the Pacific.
2 Town, Peru, suburb of Lima; seaside resort.

Mi·ra'go'âne' (mē'rä'gô'än'). Port on N Tiburon Penin., SW Haiti.

Mi·raj' (mĭ·rŭj'). 1 Two former Indian states: **Miraj Senior** (368 sq. m., pop. [1941] 108,547) and **Miraj Junior** (194 sq. m., pop. [1941] 46,295) in Deccan and Kolhapur States, S Bombay, W Indian Union. Miraj Junior joined new United Deccan State Aug. 26, 1947. Area now in S Maharashtra state.
2 Town, former * of Miraj (Senior) state, near Kistna river 194 m. SE of Bombay; pop. 26,465; rail junction.

Mi'ra·mar' (mē'rä·mär'). 1 City, Broward co., SE Florida S of Fort Lauderdale; pop. 5485.
2 See GENERAL ALVARADO.

Mi'ra·mas' (mē'rä'mä'). Town, Bouches-du-Rhône dept., S France; pop. 4463; near shore of the Étang de Berre; proving track for racing cars.

Mir'a·mi·chi' Bay (mĭr'à·mĭ·shē'). Inlet of Gulf of St. Lawrence, in E Northumberland co., E New Brunswick, SE Canada; receives the **Miramichi River**, 135 m. long, rising in Victoria co. and flowing from the SW, the main stream sometimes known as the **South West Miramichi**.

Mi·ran'da (mĭ·răn'dä; *Port.* mē·răɴɴ'dà; *Span.* mē·rän'dä). 1 River 225 m. long, S Mato Grosso state, SW Brazil; flows NW into the Paraguay river.
2 Town, S Mato Grosso state, SW Brazil, on railroad and on right bank of Miranda river.
3 State of Venezuela. See *Table* at VENEZUELA.

Mi·ran'da de E'bro (mē·rän'dä thä ā'vrō). Commune, Burgos prov., N cen. Spain, on the Ebro 36 m. NE of Burgos; pop. 15,116; cereals, wine, fruit; garden truck; manufactures flour; mineral springs.

Mi·ran'do·la (mē·rän'dô·lä). Commune, Modena prov., Emilia, N Italy, 19 m. NNE of Modena; pop. 22,472; sarcophagi of 14th and 15th cents.

Mi·ra'no (mē·rä'nô). Commune, Venezia prov., Venezia Euganea, NE Italy, 12 m. WNW of Venice; pop. 15,354.

Mi'ras·sol' (mē'rä·sôl'). City, NW cen. São Paulo state, SE Brazil, 260 m. NW of São Paulo; pop. 7052.

Mi're·ba·lais' (mēr'bà·lĕ'). Town, E Haiti, SE of St. Marc.

Mir'field (mûr'fēld). Urban district, West Riding, Yorkshire, N England; pop. 11,885; woolens, esp. blankets and carpets.

Mir'go·rod (mĭr'gô·rŏd; *Russ.* myēr'gȧ·rŭt). Town, cen. Poltava Region, E cen. Ukraine, U.S.S.R., on railroad 50 m. WNW of Poltava; pop. 14,170.

Mi'ri (mē'rē). Seaport, NE Sarawak, Borneo, S of Baram Point; pop. ab. 11,000; has extensive oil fields.

Mi'rik', Cape (mē'rēk'). Cape extending into Atlantic Ocean on W coast of French West Africa, 19°30'N.

Mi·rim', Lake (mē·rēn'; *Span.* **Me·rín'** (mā·rēn'). Lake 108 m. long on E boundary of Uruguay, separating Uruguay from extreme S tip of Brazil.

Mir'ja·wa' (mēr'jä·wä'). Town, SE Iran, railroad junction ab. 140 m. NE of Bampur.

Mir'pur (mēr'pŏŏr). Town, Jammu prov., SW Jammu and Kashmir state, N India, near Jhelum river 85 m. SW of Srinagar; pop. 7274.

Mirpur Khas (käs'). See THAR AND PARKAR.

Mirs Bay (mĭrz). Bay on the coast of Kwangtung prov., SE China, E of New Territories, Hong Kong colony; its waters leased by China to Great Britain in 1898 for 99 years.

Mir'za·pur (mĭr'zä·pŏŏr). City, Benares division, SE Uttar Pradesh, N Indian Union, on right bank of Ganges river 45 m. ESE of Allahabad; pop. (1941) 70,944; formerly a great grain and cotton mart and seat of carpet manufacture; has mosques and Hindu temples. Now includes **Bin'dha'chal** (bĭnd'hä'chȧl), which has a shrine of Vindhyeshwari and is a center of pilgrimage.

Mi·sa'mis (mē·sä'mēs). 1 In Spanish times the province along N coast of Mindanao, now divided into Misamis Occidental and Misamis Oriental. Visited by Spanish missionaries 1622 and later; settlements made on Minda-

nao coast and on Camiguin; in early times a part of Cebu prov.; made a separate province 1818 but in 19th cent. its boundaries changed several times; also suffered from Moro raids; came under Americans 1899 and was granted civil government 1901; divided for 1939 census.
2 Municipality, Misamis Occidental prov., Mindanao, Phil. Is., at SW corner of Iligan Bay at entrance to Panguil Bay; pop. 36,313; has excellent anchorage.

Misamis Oc'ci·den·tal' (ôk'sē·thän·täl'). Province, N Mindanao, Phil. Is.; 802 sq. m.; pop. 210,057; * Oroquieta; coastal area W of Iligan Bay, NE of Zamboanga prov. and separated from NW Lanao prov. by Panguil Bay; mountainous with highest peak Mt. Malindang 7956 ft.; chief products hemp (abacá) and coconuts. Inhabitants mostly Visayans. Chief towns Oroquieta, Tangub, Misamis, Jimenez, and Plaridel. For *History*, see MISAMIS.

Misamis O'rien·tal' (ō'ryän·täl'). Province, N Mindanao, Phil. Is.; 1512 sq. m.; pop. 213,812; * Cagayan; long coastal strip E of Iligan Bay and Camiguin I. in S cen. Mindanao Sea; shuts off Bukidnon prov. from any coast line and contains two inlets Macajalar Bay and Gingoog Bay; touches Agusan prov. on the E and Lanao prov. on SW; has volcanic cone Hibokhibok 5620 ft. on Camiguin I.; has fertile soil; chief products hemp (abacá) and coconuts. Inhabitants mostly Visayans. Chief towns Cagayan, Mambajao, Balingasag, and Initao. For *History*, see MISAMIS.

Mi·sa·wa (mē·sä·wä). Town, Aomori prefecture, N Honshu, Japan, near coast ab. 14 m. N of Hachinohe; pop. (1945) 11,871; large airfield.

Misch'a'bel·hör'ner (mĭsh'ä'bĕl·hûr'nēr). Mountain mass in the Pennine Alps, Valais canton, SW cen. Switzerland; highest peak the Dom 14,942 ft.

Mis'cou Island (mĭs'kōō). Island off NE tip of New Brunswick, Canada, S of entrance to Chaleur Bay; its N tip is **Point Miscou**.

Mi·se'no (mē·zā'nô). Promontory NW of the Bay of Naples and S of ruins of Cumae, Italy; at its base to the N is Porto di Miseno, site of ancient town of **Mi·se'·num** (mī·sē'nŭm), a naval base under Augustus, constructed by Agrippa 31 B.C.

Mis'er·y, Mount (mĭz'ēr·ĭ). Peak 3711 ft. on the island of St. Kitts, West Indies.

Mish, Slieve. See SLIEVE MISH.

Mi·shaum' Point (mĭ·shôm'). Southern point of Bristol co., SE Massachusetts; extends into Buzzards Bay.

Mish'a·wa'ka (mĭsh'à·wô'kà). Industrial city, St. Joseph co., N Indiana, SE of South Bend; pop. 33,361; rubber goods, foundry equipment, structural steel.

Mish'i·ka·mau' Lake (mĭsh'ĭ·kà·mô'). Lake 612 sq. m. in W Labrador; drains E into Lake Melville.

Mi·shi·ma Sea (mē·shē·mä). One of the five basins of the Inland Sea, Japan, in W cen. part bet. Hiroshima prefecture on Honshu and Ehime prefecture on Shikoku.

Mi·sil·me'ri (mē·sēl·mä'rē). Commune, Palermo prov., Sicily, 8 m. SE of Palermo; pop. 12,176; castle.

Mi·si'ma (mē·sē'mà) or **Saint Ai'gnan'** (săn'·tā'·nyän'). Island ab. 30 m. long and bet. 1 and 4 m. wide in Louisiade Archipelago, Territory of Papua, 140 m. E of Milne Bay; ab. 100 sq. m.; pop. ab. 2500; at E end is Bwagaoia, chief village of the group; mountainous, with some peaks above 3000 ft.; has much gold.

Mi·sio'nes (mē·syō'nås). 1 Territory of Argentina. See *Table* at ARGENTINA.
2 Department of Paraguay. See *Table* at PARAGUAY.

Misiones, Sierra de. See SIERRA DE MISIONES.

Misis. See MOPSUESTIA.

Misithra. See MISTRA.

Miskish, Slieve. See SLIEVE MISKISH.

Mis'kolc (mĭsh'kôlts). Autonomous city, NE Hungary, 85 m. NE of Budapest on the Sajó river; 20 sq. m.; pop. (1939) 73,503; manufactures pottery and porcelain; center for large trade in cereals, wine, fruit, leather. Nearly destroyed by Mongols 1241–43.

Mi'so·öl (mē'sô·ôl) *or* **Mi'sol** (mē'sôl). Island ab. 50 m. long by 23 m. wide, Indonesia, N of Ceram and just W of Vogelkop Penin. of W New Guinea; 672 sq. m.; pop. 2450.

Misore Islands. See SCHOUTEN ISLANDS.

Mis'quah Hills (mĭs'kwô). Elevation 2230 ft. in Cook co., NE corner of Minnesota; highest point in the state.

Misr (mĭs'r'). Modern Arabic name of EGYPT.

Mis·sau'kee (mĭ·sô'kĭ). County in Michigan. See *Table* at MICHIGAN.

Mis'si·nai'bi (mĭs'ĭ·nī'bĭ). River 270 m. long, E cen. Ontario, Canada; rises in **Missinaibi Lake** and flows N and NE to join the Mattagami and form the Moose river.

Mis'sion (mĭsh'ŭn). **1** City, Hidalgo co., S Texas, near the Rio Grande 5 m. W of McAllen; pop. 14,081; produces citrus fruits, vegetables, cotton; brick and tile factories, machine shops, canning plant.
2 *formerly* **Mission City**. Village, SW Brit. Columbia, Canada, on right bank of Fraser river and on railroad 38 m. E of Vancouver; pop. 2668.

Mis'sion·ar'y Ridge (mĭsh'ŭn·ĕr'ĭ). Ridge extending NE to SW in Hamilton co., Tennessee, and Dade co., Georgia; a section of this ridge near Chattanooga was the site of a Union victory Nov. 25, 1863 in the Civil War.

Mission Range. A range of the Rocky Mts. in W Montana, chiefly in Lake and Missoula cos.; highest point McDonald Peak 10,300 ft.

Mis·sis'quoi (mĭ·sĭs'kwoi). **1** River ab. 90 m. long, NW Vermont; rises in Orleans co., flows N into Canada, thence S into Franklin co., Vermont, and W into Lake Champlain.
2 County, Quebec, Canada. See *Table* at QUEBEC.

Mis'sis·sa'gi (mĭs'ĭ·sä'gĭ). River ab. 130 m. long, SE Ontario, Canada; flows SW and S into North Channel.

Mississagi, Strait of. Strait bet. W Manitoulin I. and Cockburn I. in NE Lake Huron, SE Ontario prov., S Canada.

Mis'sis·sip'pi (mĭs'ĭ·sĭp'ĭ). **1** Called "Father of Waters." Navigable river, cen. United States; 2470 m. long to head of the Passes, or, if measured from headwaters of Missouri river, 3872 m. long; head of the Passes to Gulf of Mexico 17 m.; drainage area 1,257,000 sq. m.; rises in Lake Itasca, NW Minnesota, flows SE to form lower section of Minnesota-Wisconsin boundary, and the Iowa-Wisconsin and Iowa-Illinois boundaries, the Missouri-Illinois, Missouri-Kentucky, and Missouri-Tennessee boundaries, the Arkansas-Tennessee and Arkansas-Mississippi boundaries, and the N section of Louisiana-Mississippi boundary, thence continuing SE into the Mississippi river delta and into the Gulf of Mexico through several mouths, known locally as the Passes, as Main Pass, North Pass, South Pass, Southwest Pass.

History: Crossed by De Soto 1541; upper reaches explored by Marquette and Jolliet 1673; lower part traced by La Salle who laid claim for French to entire Mississippi valley (see LOUISIANA) 1682; after French cessions of 1762 and 1763, was boundary bet. Spanish on west and British on east; became western boundary of U.S. 1783, but its mouth was controlled by Spain which finally granted free navigation by treaty 1795; U.S. obtained control of western part of valley by Louisiana Purchase 1803; upper reaches explored by Pike 1805–06; after c. 1820, navigated by steamboats; during American Civil War, gradually opened by Federal forces until capture of Vicksburg 1863 destroyed Confederate hold on the river.

2 Southeastern state of U.S.A., 20th state admitted to Union (1817); bounded on N by Tennessee, on E by Alabama, on S by the Gulf of Mexico and Louisiana, and on W by Louisiana and Arkansas; 32d state in area, 47,716 sq. m. (land area 47,248 sq. m.); 29th state in population, 2,178,141; ✳ Jackson. See *Table of States* at UNITED STATES. Divided into the following 82 counties

(for pronunciation of their names, see their individual entries):

NAME	LOCATION	AREA[1]	POP.[1]	CO. SEAT
Adams	SW	448	37,730	Natchez
Alcorn	NE	405	25,282	Corinth
Amite	SW	729	15,573	Liberty
Attala	cen.	724	21,335	Kosciusko
Benton	N	412	7,723	Ashland
Bolivar	NW	917	54,464	Cleveland and Rosedale
Calhoun	N cen.	592	15,941	Pittsboro
Carroll	cen.	638	11,177	Vaiden and Carrollton
Chickasaw	NE	506	16,891	Houston and Okolona
Choctaw	cen.	417	8,423	Ackerman
Claiborne	SW	486	10,845	Port Gibson
Clarke	E	697	16,493	Quitman
Clay	E	414	18,933	West Point
Coahoma	NW	570	46,212	Clarksdale
Copiah	SW	781	27,051	Hazlehurst
Covington	S	416	13,637	Collins
De Soto	NW corner	443	23,891	Hernando
Forrest	SE	469	52,722	Hattiesburg
Franklin	SW	568	9,286	Meadville
George	SE	481	11,098	Lucedale
Greene	SE	728	8,366	Leakesville
Grenada	N cen.	447	18,409	Grenada
Hancock	S; coastal	485	14,039	Bay St. Louis
Harrison	SE; coastal	585	119,489	Gulfport
Hinds	SW cen.	877	187,045	Jackson and Raymond
Holmes	W cen.	764	27,096	Lexington
Humphreys	W	410	19,093	Belzoni
Issaquena	W	415	3,576	Mayersville
Itawamba	NE	541	15,080	Fulton
Jackson	SE corner; coastal	744	55,522	Pascagoula
Jasper	SE cen.	683	16,909	Bay Springs and Paulding
Jefferson	SW	520	10,142	Fayette
Jefferson Davis	S	414	13,540	Prentiss
Jones	SE	706	59,542	Ellisville and Laurel
Kemper	E	757	12,277	De Kalb
Lafayette	N	606	21,355	Oxford
Lamar	S	500	13,675	Purvis
Lauderdale	E	721	67,119	Meridian
Lawrence	S	433	10,215	Monticello
Leake	cen.	586	18,660	Carthage
Lee	NE	455	40,589	Tupelo
Leflore	W	588	47,142	Greenwood
Lincoln	SW	586	26,759	Brookhaven
Lowndes	E	508	46,639	Columbus
Madison	cen.	751	32,904	Canton
Marion	S	550	23,293	Columbia
Marshall	N	693	24,503	Holly Springs
Monroe	NE	769	33,953	Aberdeen
Montgomery	N cen.	403	13,320	Winona
Neshoba	E cen.	568	20,927	Philadelphia
Newton	E cen.	580	19,517	Decatur
Noxubee	E	695	16,826	Macon
Oktibbeha	NE cen.	454	26,175	Starkville
Panola	NW	685	28,791	Sardis and Batesville
Pearl River	S	828	22,411	Poplarville
Perry	SE	653	8,745	New Augusta
Pike	S	410	35,063	Magnolia
Pontotoc	N	501	17,232	Pontotoc
Prentiss	NE	418	17,949	Booneville
Quitman	NW	412	21,019	Marks
Rankin	S cen.	800	34,322	Brandon
Scott	cen.	615	21,187	Forest
Sharkey	W	436	10,738	Rolling Fork
Simpson	S cen.	587	20,454	Mendenhall
Smith	S cen.	642	14,303	Raleigh
Stone	SE	448	7,013	Wiggins
Sunflower	W	693	45,750	Indianola
Tallahatchie	NW	644	24,081	Charleston and Sumner
Tate	NW	383	18,138	Senatobia
Tippah	N	464	15,093	Ripley
Tishomingo	NE corner	451	13,889	Iuka
Tunica	NW	458	16,826	Tunica
Union	N	422	18,904	New Albany
Walthall	S	403	13,512	Tylertown
Warren	W	566	42,206	Vicksburg
Washington	W	728	78,638	Greenville
Wayne	SE	827	16,258	Waynesboro
Webster	N cen.	416	10,580	Walthall
Wilkinson	SW corner	675	13,235	Woodville
Winston	E cen.	606	19,246	Louisville
Yalobusha	N	504	12,502	Coffeeville and Water Valley
Yazoo	W cen.	938	31,653	Yazoo City

[1] Area = land area in sq. m. Pop. from 1960 Census.

MISSISSIPPI

Statute Miles

0   10   20   30   40

⊛ State Capital

PUBLISHED BY G. & C. MERRIAM COMPANY
SPRINGFIELD, MASS.
PREPARED BY J. W. CLEMENT CO., BUFFALO, N. Y.

Nickname: Magnolia State, also Bayou State. *State flower:* Magnolia. *Motto:* Virtute et Armis (By Valor and Arms). *Chief cities:* Jackson, Meridian, Biloxi, Greenville, Hattiesburg. *Rivers:* Mississippi, forming W boundary; Pearl, flowing SW and S and forming SW boundary bet. Mississippi and Louisiana; Big Black, flowing from N cen. area SW into the Mississippi; Tennessee, forming boundary in extreme NE area. *Highest point:* 806 ft. near Iuka in Tishomingo co. *Chief industries:* Agriculture (cotton, corn, oats, and hay).

History: Part of French Louisiana (*q.v.*); Biloxi settled by Iberville 1699; except for S part (British West Florida), region ceded to U.S. 1783; organized as territory 1798 comprising S half of present states of Mississippi and Alabama; enlarged 1804 and 1813 to include all of present states of Alabama and Mississippi; W part of this territory admitted to Union Dec. 10, 1817 as state of Mississippi; seceded Jan. 9, 1861; scene of important battles during Civil War; readmitted to Union Feb. 23, 1870; adopted present constitution 1890.

3 Name of counties in two states of the U.S. See *Tables* at ARKANSAS and MISSOURI.

4 River 105 m. long, SE Ontario, Canada; rises in Frontenac co. and flows NE and N through **Mississippi Lake** in Lanark co. into the Ottawa river.

Mississippi Sound. Inlet of Gulf of Mexico bet. mainland of S Mississippi and SW Alabama and an island chain off the coast; receives the Pascagoula river.

Missolonghi. See MESOLÓNGION.

Mis·sou′la (mĭ·zōō′lȧ). **1** County in Montana. See *Table* at MONTANA.

2 City, its ⊗, W Montana, near confluence of Bitterroot river and Clark Fork; pop. 27,090; copper and lead deposits nearby. Montana State University (1893; coed.).

Mis·sou′ri (mĭ·zŏŏr′ĭ; -zŏŏr′ȧ). **1** River, cen. and NW cen. United States; 2475 m. long (or 2723 m. including longest tributaries to ultimate source) to its junction with the Mississippi river; formed by confluence of Jefferson, Madison, and Gallatin rivers in Gallatin co., S Montana, flows E to cen. North Dakota, then S across South Dakota to form E section of South Dakota-Nebraska boundary, and the Nebraska-Iowa and Nebraska-Missouri boundaries, and the N section of the Kansas-Missouri boundary, turns E across cen. Missouri and joins the Mississippi river ab. 10 m. N of St. Louis. During high water, navigable by flat-bottomed boats nearly to Great Falls, Montana (*q.v.*). First explored by French traders; traced to its sources by Lewis and Clark 1804–06.

2 Central state of U.S.A., 24th state admitted to Union (1821); bounded on N by Iowa, on E by Illinois, Kentucky, and Tennessee, on S by Arkansas, on W by Oklahoma, Kansas, and Nebraska; 19th state in area, 69,674 sq. m. (land area 69,226 sq. m.); 13th state in population, 4,319,813; ✳ Jefferson City. See *Table of States* at UNITED STATES. Divided into the following 114 counties (for pronunciation, see their individual entries):

NAME	LOCATION	AREA[1]	POP.[1]	CO. SEAT
Adair	N	574	20,105	Kirksville
Andrew	NW	430	11,062	Savannah
Atchison	NW corner	549	9,213	Rockport
Audrain	NE cen.	692	26,079	Mexico
Barry	SW	800	18,921	Cassville
Barton	SW	594	11,113	Lamar
Bates	W	841	15,905	Butler
Benton	W cen.	742	8,737	Warsaw
Bollinger	SE	621	9,167	Marble Hill
Boone	cen.	683	55,202	Columbia
Buchanan	NW	411	90,581	St. Joseph
Butler	SE	714	34,656	Poplar Bluff
Caldwell	NW	430	8,830	Kingston
Callaway	cen.	835	23,858	Fulton
Camden	S cen.	655	9,116	Camdenton
Cape Girardeau	SE	576	42,020	Jackson
Carroll	NW cen.	694	13,847	Carrollton
Carter	SE	506	3,973	Van Buren
Cass	W	698	29,702	Harrisonville
Cedar	W	496	9,185	Stockton
Chariton	N cen.	759	12,720	Keytesville

NAME	LOCATION	AREA[1]	POP.[1]	CO. SEAT
Christian	SW	567	12,359	Ozark
Clark	NE corner	509	8,725	Kahoka
Clay	NW	413	87,474	Liberty
Clinton	NW	420	11,588	Plattsburg
Cole	cen.	385	40,761	Jefferson City
Cooper	cen.	563	15,448	Boonville
Crawford	SE cen.	760	12,647	Steelville
Dade	SW	504	7,577	Greenfield
Dallas	SW cen.	537	9,314	Buffalo
Daviess	NW	563	9,502	Gallatin
De Kalb	NW	423	7,226	Maysville
Dent	SE cen.	756	10,445	Salem
Douglas	S	809	9,653	Ava
Dunklin	SE	543	39,139	Kennett
Franklin	E	932	44,566	Union
Gasconade	E cen.	520	12,195	Hermann
Gentry	NW	488	8,793	Albany
Greene	SW	677	126,276	Springfield
Grundy	N	435	12,220	Trenton
Harrison	N	720	11,603	Bethany
Henry	W	737	19,226	Clinton
Hickory	SW cen.	410	4,516	Hermitage
Holt	NW	456	7,885	Oregon
Howard	N cen.	469	10,859	Fayette
Howell	S	920	22,027	West Plains
Iron	SE	554	8,041	Ironton
Jackson	W	603	622,732	Independence
Jasper	SW	642	78,863	Carthage
Jefferson	E	667	66,377	Hillsboro
Johnson	W	826	28,981	Warrensburg
Knox	NE	512	6,558	Edina
Laclede	S cen.	770	18,991	Lebanon
Lafayette	W	634	25,274	Lexington
Lawrence	SW	619	23,260	Mount Vernon
Lewis	NE	505	10,984	Monticello
Lincoln	E	629	14,783	Troy
Linn	N	624	16,815	Linneus
Livingston	N	533	15,771	Chillicothe
McDonald	SW corner	540	11,798	Pineville
Macon	N	814	16,473	Macon
Madison	SE	496	9,366	Fredericktown
Maries	S cen.	526	7,282	Vienna
Marion	NE	440	29,522	Palmyra
Mercer	N	456	5,750	Princeton
Miller	cen.	603	13,800	Tuscumbia
Mississippi	SE	411	20,695	Charleston
Moniteau	cen.	418	10,500	California
Monroe	NE	669	10,688	Paris
Montgomery	E cen.	533	11,097	Montgomery City
Morgan	cen.	596	9,476	Versailles
New Madrid	SE	679	31,350	New Madrid
Newton	SW	629	30,093	Neosho
Nodaway	NW	877	22,215	Maryville
Oregon	S	784	9,845	Alton
Osage	cen.	601	10,867	Linn
Ozark	S	750	6,744	Gainesville
Pemiscot	SE corner	488	38,095	Caruthersville
Perry	E	476	14,642	Perryville
Pettis	W cen.	679	35,120	Sedalia
Phelps	S cen.	677	25,396	Rolla
Pike	E	681	16,706	Bowling Green
Platte	NW	414	23,350	Platte City
Polk	SW	642	13,753	Bolivar
Pulaski	S cen.	551	46,567	Waynesville
Putnam	N	518	6,999	Unionville
Ralls	NE	478	8,078	New London
Randolph	N cen.	484	22,014	Huntsville
Ray	NW	574	16,075	Richmond
Reynolds	SE	822	5,161	Centerville
Ripley	S	639	9,096	Doniphan
Saint Charles	E	561	52,970	St. Charles
Saint Clair	W	699	8,421	Osceola
Sainte Genevieve	E	500	12,116	Sainte Genevieve
Saint Francois	E	457	36,516	Farmington
Saint Louis	E	497	703,532	Clayton
Saint Louis city		61	750,026	
Saline	W cen.	759	25,148	Marshall
Schuyler	N	306	5,052	Lancaster
Scotland	N	441	6,484	Memphis
Scott	SE	418	32,748	Benton
Shannon	S	999	7,087	Eminence
Shelby	NE	502	9,063	Shelbyville
Stoddard	SE	837	29,490	Bloomfield
Stone	SW	509	8,176	Galena
Sullivan	N	654	8,783	Milan
Taney	S	656	10,238	Forsyth
Texas	S	1,183	17,758	Houston
Vernon	W	838	20,540	Nevada
Warren	E	428	8,750	Warrenton
Washington	E	760	14,346	Potosi
Wayne	SE	741	8,638	Greenville
Webster	S	590	13,753	Marshfield
Worth	NW	267	3,936	Grant City
Wright	S	684	14,183	Hartville

[1] Area = land area in sq. m. Pop. from 1960 Census.
[2] Exclusive of city of St. Louis, which is politically independent of the county.

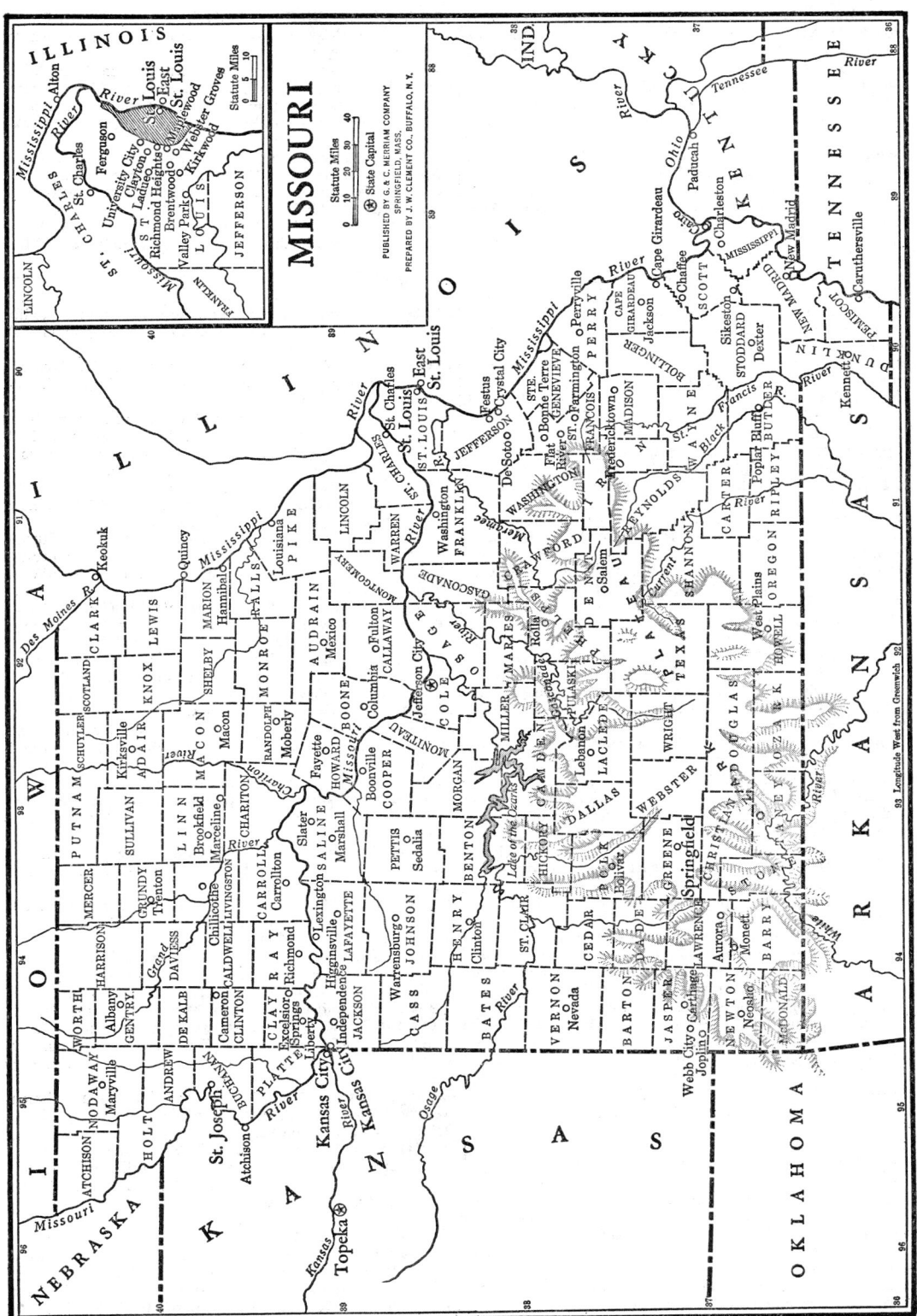

MISSOURI

Statute Miles
0 10 20 30 40

⊕ State Capital

PUBLISHED BY G. & C. MERRIAM COMPANY
SPRINGFIELD, MASS.
PREPARED BY J. W. CLEMENT CO., BUFFALO, N.Y.

Nickname: Show Me State, also Bullion State. *State flower:* Hawthorn. *Motto:* Salus Populi Suprema Lex Esto (Let the Welfare of the People Be the Supreme Law). *Chief cities:* St. Louis, Kansas City, Springfield, St. Joseph, Independence. *Rivers:* Missouri (see 1 above); Mississippi, forming E boundary; Des Moines, forming boundary at extreme NE tip of state and emptying into the Mississippi. *Highest point:* Taum Sauk Mountain 1772 ft. in Iron co. *Chief industries:* Agriculture (wheat, cotton), mining (lead, zinc).

History: Visited by Marquette 1673 and Jolliet 1683; probably first settled by French at Ste. Genevieve 1735; part of Louisiana Purchase 1803; after admission of state of Louisiana (*q.v.*) to Union, rest of former territory of Louisiana organized as Missouri Territory 1812; Missouri's application for admission as slave state 1817 caused bitter controversy which was settled by Missouri Compromise 1820 (Missouri admitted as slave state Aug. 10, 1821, Maine as free, no slavery above 36°30'— later repealed); did not secede from Union 1861; scene of fighting in American Civil War 1861–64; adopted present constitution 1945.

Missouri Valley. City, Harrison co., W Iowa, 20 m. N of Council Bluffs; pop. 3567; ships agricultural products.

Mis·tas·si·ni (mĭs′tă·sē′nĭ). **1** Lake ab. 100 m. long and 12 m. wide, 975 sq. m., S cen. Quebec, Canada; discharges through Rupert river into James Bay.
2 River ab. 185 m. long, S Quebec, Canada, flowing S into Lake St. John.
3 Village, Lake St. John co., S Quebec, Canada, opp. Dolbeau on Mistassini river 10 m. N of Lake St. John; pop. 2298.

Mi·ster·bian′co (mĕs·tăr·byäng′kô). Commune, Catania prov., E Sicily, on S slope of Mt. Etna 4 m. WNW of Catania; pop. 11,387.

Misti, El. See El Misti.

Mi·stra′ (mē·strä′). Ruined town, Laconia, SE Peloponnesus, Greece, W of Sparta; in 13th to 15th cents. a center of late-Byzantine culture; called also **Mi·si·thra′** (mē·sē·thrä′) from famous castle built 1249; capital of principality of Michael VIII Palaeologus 1261; later held by Greeks and Turks.

Mi·stret′ta (mēs·trät′tä); *anc.* **A·mes′tra·tus** (à·mĕs′-trà·tŭs). Commune, Messina prov., NE Sicily, 68 m. WSW of Messina; pop. 11,546; castle.

Mi·su·ra′ta (mĭ·sōō·rä′tà; -tä). **1** Former province (under Italian rule), NW Libya, N Africa, E of Tripoli prov. and W of Bengasi prov.; 38,191 sq. m.
2 Coastal city, its ✳, 125 m. E of Tripoli; pop. (1938 est.) 45,097; important Italian garrison town with considerable peacetime trade; taken by British Jan. 1943.

Misurata, Cape. Cape on N coast of Tripolitania, N Africa, W of entrance to the Gulf of Sidra.

Mi·tan′ni (mĭ·tăn′ĭ). Ancient kingdom of upper Mesopotamia, extending from the bend of the Euphrates nearly to the Tigris, covering parts of later regions of Assyria, Syria, and Armenia; among its cities were Carchemish and Aleppo. Founded by Hurrians c. 1475 B.C.; lasted until conquered by the Hittites c. 1275 B.C. Mitannians probably not of Indo-European stock.

Mi′ta Point (mē′tà; *Span.* -tä); *Span.* **Pun′ta Mi′ta** (pōōn′tä mē′tä). Cape off SW coast of Nayarit state, Mexico, at N side of entrance to Banderas Bay.

Mi′tar′ka′ (mē′tàr′kà′). Peak in Tumuc-Humac Mts. in S French Guiana.

Mitau. See Yelgava.

Mitch′am (mĭch′ăm). Municipal borough, Surrey, S England, on the Wandle 8 m. SSW of London; pop. 56,859, (1951) 67,273; part of Greater London; residential district, market gardening.

Mitch′ell (mĭch′ĕl). **1** Name of counties in five states of the U.S. See *Tables* at Georgia, Iowa, Kansas, North Carolina, Texas.
2 City, Lawrence co., S Indiana, 30 m. S of Bloomington; pop. 3552; manufactures cement.

3 City, Scotts Bluff co., W Nebraska, on North Platte river 10 m. WSW of Scottsbluff; pop. 1920; beet-sugar refinery; honey market.
4 City, ⊗ of Davison co., SE South Dakota, 72 m. W of Sioux Falls; pop. 12,555; incorp. as city 1883; railroad center in farming region; ships livestock, grain, frozen eggs; makes butter and cheese; meat and poultry packing. Dakota Wesleyan Univ. (1885; coed.).
5 River 300 m. long, cen. Cape York Penin., Queensland, Australia, flowing WNW to Gulf of Carpentaria.
6 Town, Perth co., SE Ontario, Canada, 13 m. WNW of Stratford; pop. 1979.

Mitchell, Mount. Peak 6684 ft. in Black Mts., Yancey co., W North Carolina; highest point E of Mississippi river.

Mitchell Peak. Mountain 10,375 ft. in Sierra Nevada, N Tulare co., S cen. California.

Mit′i·a′ro (mĭt′ĭ·ä′rō). One of the Cook Is. in S Pacific Ocean, 150 m. NE of Rarotonga; ab. 4 sq. m.; pop. (1936) 265; produces copra.

Mi′tla (mē′tlä). Village, Oaxaca state, SE Mexico; many Zapotec ruins, esp. long stone buildings with columns and frescoes.

Mi·to (mē·tô). Industrial and commercial city, ✳ of Ibaraki prefecture, SE Honshu, Japan, 60 m. NE of Tokyo; pop. (1945) 49,495; important historically, esp. since 1600 under the Tokugawa shogunate.

Mit Rahina. See Memphis Egypt.

Mi′tre Peninsula (mē′trä). Peninsula at SE extremity of Tierra del Fuego I. off S South America.

Mi′tro·vi·ca (mē′trô·vĕ·tsä). **1** *or* **Ko′sov·ska Mitrovica** (kō′sôv·skä). Town in Kosovo-Metohija autonomous prov., S Yugoslavia, on Ibar river 65 m. NW of Skoplje; pop. 11,301.
2 *or* **Srem′ska Mitrovica** (srĕm′skä); *Ger.* **Mi′trowitz** (mē′trô·vĭts). Town, Voivodina autonomous prov., Yugoslavia, on Sava river 42 m. WNW of Belgrade; pop. 13,840; river port and commercial center; Roman ruins of Sirmium nearby; suffered much destruction in wars of Middle Ages.

Mitrovitsa. Var. of Mitrovica.

Mit′ta·gong (mĭt′à·gŏng). Town, E New South Wales, SE Australia, 60 m. SW of Sydney; pop. 1747; coal and iron mines.

Mitteleuropa. See Central Europe.

Mit′tel·fran′ken (mĭt′ĕl·fräng′kĕn). Bavarian government district. See *Middle Franconia*, in *Table* at Bavaria.

Mitt′wei′da (mĭt′vī′dä). Manufacturing city, Saxony, Germany, 34 m. SE of Leipzig; pop. 19,278; textiles, furniture, metal goods.

Mi·tú′ (mē·tōō′). Town, ✳ of Vaupés commissary, SE Colombia, on Vaupés river near Brazilian border.

Mitylene. Var. of Mytilene.

Mi·u·ra (mē·ōō·rä). Peninsula, Kanagawa prefecture, SE Honshu, Japan, extending into Sagami Sea S of Yokohama and Tokyo Bay; Yokosuka and Uraga are on its NE coast and the village of Miura is at its S tip.

Mix′co·ac′ (mēs′kô·äk′). City, Federal District, cen. Mexico, 9 m. SW of Mexico City; nursery gardens.

Mi·ya·gi (mē·yä·gē). Prefecture of Japan. See *Table* at Japan.

Mi·ya·ji·ma (mē·yä·jē·mä) *or* **I·tsu·ku·shi·ma** (ē·tsōō·kōō·shē·mä). **1** Island ab. 5 m. long by 2½ m. wide in N inlet of the Inland Sea, Hiroshima prefecture, SW Honshu, Japan, ab. 12 m. SW of Hiroshima; highest point Misen 1800 ft. One of the most beautiful scenic spots in Japan, has many temples, shrines, a fine torii, pagoda, etc. Of very ancient origin.
2 Town on NW coast of island; pop. 4000.

Mi·ya·ko (mē·yä·kô). Small island in Sakishima group, S Ryukyu Is., Japan, ab. lat. 25°N; largest in **Miyako Islands** group, 70 sq. m., pop. (1945) 52,333.

Mi·ya·ko·no·jo (mē·yä·kô·nô·jō). Town, Miyazaki prefecture, SE Kyushu, Japan; pop. (1945) 59,279.

Mi·ya·no·shi·ta (mē·yä·nō·shĕ·tä). Village, Kanagawa prefecture, in the Hakone dist., SE Honshu, Japan, 6 m. W of Odawara; popular resort.

Mi·ya·za·ki (mē·yä·zä·kē). **1** Prefecture of Japan. See *Table* at JAPAN.
2 Seaport, its ✳, on SE coast of Kyushu; pop. (1945) 64,968.

Mi·ye (mē·yĕ). = MIE.

Miz'da (mĭz'dà). Oasis and caravan stop, NW Tripolitania, Libya, N Africa, S of the city of Tripoli.

Miz'en Head (mĭz'n). Cape on SW coast of Ireland bet. Long Island Bay and Dunmanus Bay; the southernmost point of Ireland, 51°27'N.

Miz'pah (mĭz'pä; -pà; *Heb.* mĭts·pä'). Name of several towns of ancient Palestine; literally "watchtower"; esp., the heap of stones erected in the mountains of Gilead N of the Jabbok by Jacob and Laban (*Gen.* xxxi. 44–49).

Miz'ra·im (mĭz'rà·ĭm; mĭz·rā'ĭm; *Heb.* mĭts·rä'yĭm). The Hebrew name of EGYPT.

Mi·zu·sa·wa (mē·zōō·sä·wä). Town, S Iwate prefecture, N Honshu, Japan, 60 m. N of Sendai; pop. (1945) 17,924; site of International Latitude Observatory, on 39°8'N lat., one of five such observatories in the world: see GAITHERSBURG, Maryland; KITAB, Uzbek S.S.R.; SAN PIETRO island, Sardinia (Carloforte); UKIAH, California.

Mjö'sa (myû'sä). Lake 62 m. long, 150 sq. m., SE Norway, in Opland and Hedmark cos.; largest lake in Norway.

Mko·a'ni ('m·kō·ä'nē). Township on Pemba I., N of Zanzibar, off NE coast of Tanganyika Territory, E Africa.

Mla'dá Bo'le·slav ('m·lä'dä bô'lĕ·slàf); *Ger.* **Jung·bunz'lau** (yŏong·bŏonts'lou). Town, N cen. Bohemia, W Czechoslovakia, 32 m. NE of Prague; pop. (1930) 19,604; railroad junction; dates from the 10th cent.; an ecclesiastical center closely associated with the Bohemian Brethren.

Mła'wa ('m·lä'vä). Commune, Warszawa dept., Poland, on railroad 65 m. NNW of Warsaw; pop. (1938–39 est.) 19,900; trades in grain; agricultural industries. Battles fought near here in World War I 1915.

Mljet ('m·lyĕt); *Ital.* **Me'le·da** (mâ'lä·dä); *anc.* **Mel'i·ta** (mĕl'ĭ·tà). Yugoslav island in the Adriatic Sea off the lower Dalmatian coast; 38 sq. m.; pop. ab. 2000; belongs to Bosnia and Herzegovina.

Mni'cho·vo Hra'diš·tĕ ('m·nyĭ'kō·vô hrá'dyĭsh·tyĕ); *Ger.* **Mün'chen·grätz'** (mün'kĕn·grâts'). Town, N Bohemia, W Czechoslovakia, 9 m. NNE of Mladá Boleslav; pop. (1930) 3992; meeting place of convention of Münchengrätz Sept. 18, 1833, where Austria, Prussia, and Russia agreed to guarantee the integrity of the Turkish Empire; scene of battle June 28, 1866 where Prussians invaded Bohemia and routed allied Austrian and Saxon army.

Mo'a (mō'à). Largest of the Leti Is., Indonesia, ENE of Timor, ab. 25 m. long by 9 m. wide; pop. 3641; central island of the group.

Mo'ab (mō'ăb). **1** City, ⊗ of Grand co., E Utah; pop. 4682.
2 Ancient kingdom in Syria, E of the Dead Sea, now the SW part of Jordan; bounded on S by Edom and on N separated by the Arnon from the country of the Amorites. Moabites were closely related to the Hebrews; sometimes at war with them, sometimes allied, esp. against the Assyrians. An important source of information about Moab is the Moabite stone, discovered 1868 at Dhiban (*q.v.*), which records the victories of Mesha, king of Moab, esp. those over Israel (*2 Kings* iii. 4, 5, 27).

Mo·a'la (mō·ä'lä). Island, one of the Lomai Viti group, S Fiji Is., SW Pacific Ocean; ab. 7 m. long by 6 m. broad; 28 sq. m.

Mo·ap'a (mō·ăp'à). Township, Clark co., SE Nevada, ab. 48 m. NE of Las Vegas; pop. 432; gypsum plants.

Mobangi. See UBANGI.

Mo'ber·ly (mō'bēr·lĭ). Industrial city, ⊗ of Randolph co., N cen. Missouri, 34 m. N of Columbia; pop. 13,170; shoe factory, hosiery mill; coal deposits nearby.

Mo·bile' (mô·bēl'; *when attributive,* mō'bēl'). **1** Navigable river 38 m. long, SW Alabama; formed by confluence of Tombigbee and Alabama rivers, flows S into Mobile Bay at Mobile.
2 County in Alabama. See *Table* at ALABAMA.
3 Commercial city and seaport, its ⊗, SW corner of Alabama, at mouth of Mobile river on NW shore of Mobile Bay; pop. 202,779; only seaport in Alabama; exports cotton, soft coal, lime, turpentine, resin, cement, lumber, agricultural products; shipbuilding; varied manufactures; Brookley Field, U.S. Air Force base. Spring Hill Coll. (1830; men); Barton Academy (1835–36; first public school in Alabama). Settled 1711; occupied by English, Spanish, and French; captured by Wilkinson 1813 for U.S.; incorporated as town 1814, as city 1819; battle of Mobile Bay (*q.v.*) 1864; taken by Federal troops under Canby 1865.

Mobile Bay. Inlet of Gulf of Mexico, 30 m. long and 10 to 12 m. wide, forming boundary bet. Baldwin co. on E and Mobile co. on W, SW Alabama, receiving the Mobile river on the N; scene of Civil War naval battle Aug. 5–23, 1864 in which Admiral Farragut ran a blockade of torpedoes (i.e., mines), dispersed the Confederate fleet, and secured surrender of the forts defending the bay (Aug. 7 and 23).

Mobile Point. Point at SW extremity of Baldwin co., Alabama, at S entrance to Mobile Bay.

Mo'bridge (mō'brĭj). City, Walworth co., N South Dakota, on Missouri river 30 m. S of North Dakota border; pop. 4391; in agricultural section; lignite coal mines.

Mo'ca (mō'kà; *Span.* -kä). **1** Commune (1941 pop. 75,937) and town (1944 est. pop. 8720), N cen. Dominican Republic, ✳ of Espaillat prov.; cacao raising.
2 Municipality (pop. 21,990) and town (pop. 1938), NW Puerto Rico; town is on highway near Aguadilla.

Moçambique. See MOZAMBIQUE.

Mo·ca'pra (mô·kä'prä). River ab. 100 m. long, N Venezuela; flows S into Guárico river.

Mo'cha (mō'kà); *Arab.* **Mu·kha'** (mŏŏ·kä'). Seaport, SW Yemen, SW Arabia, on the Red Sea; pop. ab. 2000; formerly noted for its export of coffee.

Mo'cha (mō'chä). Island 8 m. long in Pacific Ocean off cen. coast of Chile, ab. lat. 38°; belongs to Cautín prov.

Mochis, Los. See LOS MOCHIS.

Moch'los (mŏk'lŏs). Ruins, E Crete, on N coast on Mirabella Bay; tombs; jewels and pottery found here.

Mo'cho Mountains (mō'chō). Range in S cen. Jamaica, West Indies.

Mo·chu'di (mô·chōō'dē). Native town, SE Bechuanaland Protectorate, cen. South Africa, on railroad ab. 115 m. NNE of Mafeking; pop. ab. 8000.

Mocks'ville (mŏks'vĭl; *Sou. also* -v'l). Manufacturing town, ⊗ of Davie co., cen. North Carolina; pop. 2379.

Mo·co'a (mô·kō'ä). Town, ✳ of Putumayo commissary, S Colombia, 45 m. E of Pasto.

Mocrum. See MAKARSKA.

Mo'dane' (mō'dàn'). Town, SE Savoie dept., E France; pop. 3413; terminus of Mont Cenis Pass and Tunnel (see ALPS).

Mod'der (mŏd'ēr). River ab. 180 m. long in Orange Free State, Union of South Africa, a tributary of the Vaal; battle Nov. 28, 1899 in which British forces under Paul Methuen defeated Boers under Cronje. See also PAARDEBERG.

Mo'dé'liar'peth' (mô'dä'lyàr'pĕt'). Commune, Pondichéry settlement, in former French India; pop. (1941) 20,124.

Mo'de·na (mô'dà·nä; *Angl.* -d'n·à). **1** Province of Italy. See *Table* at ITALY.
2 *anc.* **Mu'ti·na** (mū't'n·à). Manufacturing commune, its ✳, Emilia, N Italy, 207 m. NNW of Rome; pop. 96,337; silks, woolens, leather, glass; 11th-cent.

Romanesque cathedral, 13th-cent. campanile, 17th-cent. ducal palace (now a military school), Palazzo dei Musei (art gallery; Estense library), university (1774).

History: Ancient Etruscan city; made Roman colony 183 B.C.; successfully defended against siege by Mark Antony 44–43 B.C.; destroyed and rebuilt under Constantine; to Este family 1288; made a duchy 1452; taken by French 1796 and made part of the Cisalpine Republic 1797 and of the Napoleonic kingdom of Italy 1805; lost by Este family on extinction of male line 1803 but reverted to descendant, Francis IV, 1815; to kingdom of Italy 1860.

Mo·des'to (mŏ-dĕs'tō). City, ⊗ of Stanislaus co., cen. California, on Tuolumne river 25 m. SE of Stockton; pop. 36,585; founded 1870; trade and shipping center; canneries, dairies, meat-packing plants.

Mo'di·ca (mô'dĕ-kä); *anc.* **Mo'ty·ca** (mŏ'tĭ·kȧ). Commune, Ragusa prov., SE Sicily, 5 m. SSE of Ragusa; pop. 37,936; 15th-cent. convent (now a prison); castle.

Mo'djo·ker'to (mō'jô-kĕr'tō) *or* **Mo'jo·ker'to.** Town, East Java prov., Indonesia, on Brantas river; pop. 23,600; railroad junction point 20 m. SW of Surabaja; center of sugar industry. Near here very early remains of fossil man were found 1934 and named *Homo modjokertensis;* probably much older than *Pithecanthropus erectus* (Java man).

Mo'dlin (mô'dlēn); *Russ.* **No'vo·geor'gievsk** (nō'vô-jôr'jĕfsk; *Russ.* nô'vŭ·gĭ·ôr'gĭ·yĕfsk). Fortified commune, Warszawa dept., Poland, at confluence of Vistula and Bug rivers 20 m. NW of Warsaw; pop. ab. 1200; founded as a fort built by Napoleon 1807; became important Russian military post in World War I; captured by Germans Aug. 12, 1915.

Möd'ling (mûd'lĭng). Manufacturing city, Lower Austria prov., Austria, 8 m. SSW of Vienna; pop. 18,695; enamel, metal goods, machinery, shoes.

Mo'doc (mō'dŏk). County in California. See *Table* at CALIFORNIA.

Mo·du'gno (mō·dōōn'yô). Commune, Bari prov., Apulia, SE Italy, 5 m. SW of Bari; pop. 11,433; Renaissance church.

Moe·a'ra·te'we (mōō·ä'rä·tä'wȧ) *or* **Mu·a'ra·te'we.** Town, South and East Borneo prov., on upper Barito river, Indonesia; pop. ab. 17,000.

Moeh'ne (mû'nĕ). = MÖHNE.

Moel Sych (moil' sĭκ'). Peak 2718 ft., highest in the Berwyn Mts., N Wales.

Mo'en (mō'ĕn) *or* **Ha'ru** (hä'rōō). Island ab. 5 m. long by 4 m. wide in NE part of Truk Is. (*q.v.*).

Mö'en (mû'ĕn). Island in Sjælland group, forming a part of Denmark, lying in the Baltic Sea E of S end of island of Sjælland and NE of Falster; 84 sq. m.; pop. (1925) 14,646; chief town Stege (pop. 2459).

Moe'na (mōō'nȧ) *or* **Mu'na.** Island off SE coast of Celebes I., Indonesia; ab. 60 m. long by 28 m. wide; 1124 sq. m.; by the census grouped with Butung.

Moeng'o (mōōng'ō). Town, NE Surinam, 104 m. up the Cottica river E of Paramaribo; pop. ab. 1400; bauxite deposits.

Mo'en·ko'pi Plateau (mō'ĕn·kō'pĭ). Tableland in E Coconino co., N cen. Arizona, along E boundary of the Painted Desert.

Moenus. See MAIN.

Moer·dijk' (mōōr·dĭk'). Village, North Brabant prov., S Netherlands, NW of Breda, on S bank of the Hollandsch Diep, here crossed by one of longest railroad bridges in Europe, partly destroyed by Germans May 1940.

Moe'ris, Lake (mē'rĭs). Large ancient lake occupying Faiyûm depression in Faiyûm prov., N Upper Egypt; extensively used to control flow of the Nile river. See BIRKET QÂRÛN.

Moers. See MÖRS.

Moe'si (mōō'sĕ) *or* **Mu'si.** River ab. 325 m. long, S Sumatra, Indonesia; rises in Barisan Mts. NE of

Benkulen, flows E and NE to Bangka Strait; has many tributaries. Palembang on it 56 m. from its mouth.

Moe'si·a (mē'shĭ·ȧ). Ancient country of SE Europe S of Danube river and extending from Drinus river to the Euxine (Black Sea), inhabited by a Thracian people and including part of early Thrace. Invaded by Romans 75 B.C. but not conquered until 29 B.C.; made Roman province c. 15 A.D. and later divided into two provinces: **Moesia Superior** (Upper Moesia, i.e., Serbia) and **Moesia Inferior** (Lower Moesia, i.e., N Bulgaria); occupied by Goths in 4th cent. A.D. and by Slavs and Bulgarians in 7th cent.

Moes'kroen (mōōs'krōōn); *Fr.* **Mous'cron'** (mōōs'-krôn'). Commune, West Flanders prov., NW Belgium, just S of Kortrijk; pop. (1938 est.) 35,722.

Mof'fat (mŏf'ăt). County in Colorado. See *Table* at COLORADO.

Moffat Tunnel. Railroad tunnel 6.1 m. long through James Peak, Gilpin and Grand cos., N cen. Colorado, ab. 50 m. NW of Denver.

Mof'fett Field (mŏf'ĕt; -ĭt). Air base, W California, at S end of San Francisco Bay; has dirigible hangar; laboratory of the National Advisory Committee for Aeronautics.

Mog'a·dish'u (mŏg'ȧ·dĭsh'ōō) *or* **Mog'a·di'sci·o** (mŏg'-ȧ·dĭsh'ĭ·ō; -dĭsh'ō). Seaport, ✳ of Somalia and former ✳ of Italian Somaliland, E Africa; pop. (1939 est.) ab. 55,000; captured by British Feb. 25, 1941.

Mog'a·dor (mŏg'ȧ·dôr). Fortified city and seaport, SW cen. coast of Morocco; pop. (1936) 15,166; has highway connections with Agadir, Casablanca, and Marrakesh. Founded ab. 1760 as rival to Agadir and Safi; landing place of U.S. forces Nov. 1942.

Mog'a·dore (mŏg'ȧ·dōr). Village, Portage and Summit cos., NE Ohio, 7 m. ESE of Akron; pop. 3851.

Mo·ga·mi (mô·gä·mē). River 134 m. long in Yamagata prefecture, N Honshu, Japan; flows N and NW into the Sea of Japan at Sakata.

Mo'gaung' (mō'goung'). Town, N Upper Burma, on railroad 30 m. W of Myitkina, on **Mogaung River,** a tributary of the upper Irrawaddy, and just S of the Stilwell Road which passes through the Mogaung valley; valley scene of fighting bet. Japanese and Allied forces Apr.–June 1944.

Moghreb el Aksa. Var. of *El Maghreb el Aqsa:* see MOROCCO.

Mo·gí' das Cru'zes (mōō-zhē' thȧs krōō'zĕs). City, São Paulo state, SE Brazil, on coast just E of São Paulo; pop. (1940 est.) 14,515.

Mo'gi·lev (mŏg'ĭ·lĕf; *Russ.* mŭ·gĭ·lyôf') *or* **Mogilev on the Dnieper.** City, ✳ of Mogilev Region, E White Russia, U.S.S.R., on both banks of the Dnieper 112 m. E of Minsk; pop. 99,440; an industrial and trading town; has several old churches and an ancient tower built by the Tatars. Founded probably in 13th cent.; often changed in ownership—Russian, Polish, or Swedish; suffered from church persecution and in 1708 was partly destroyed by Peter the Great; annexed to Russia 1772; near here Russian army under Bagration was defeated July 1812 by French; scene of much confusion in civil war period 1917–20; in World War II taken by Germans Aug. 1941 and reconquered by Russians June 28, 1944.

Mogilev Po·dol'ski (pô·dôl'skĭ; *Russ.* pŭ·dôl'y'·skĭ) *or* **Mogilev on the Dniester.** Town, SW Vinnitsa Region, W Ukraine, U.S.S.R., on the Dniester 60 m. S of Vinnitsa; pop. 22,271; connected by rail with Zhmerinka; has flour mill, sugar refinery; formerly more important as a trading center at a much used crossing of the Dniester on a main highway from Moldavia to Ukraine. Founded at end of 16th cent.; scene of much fighting bet. Cossacks, Poles, and Turks; suffered severely in World War I and the civil war that followed; in World War II held by Axis powers 1941–Mar. 1944.

Mogilev Region. Subdivision of White Russia, in E part; ✳ Mogilev on the Dnieper.

Mo·gí′ Mi·rim′ (mōō·zhē′ mĕ·rēṉ′). City, E São Paulo state, SE Brazil, 80 m. N of São Paulo; pop. 8449; railroad junction.

Mo·glia′no Ve′ne·to (mō·lyä′nṓ vâ′nä·tṓ). Commune, Treviso prov., Venezia Euganea, NE Italy 8 m. S of Treviso; pop. (1931) 12,177.

Mog′mog (mŏg′mŏg). See ULITHI.

Mo·go′cha (mŭ·gô′chȧ). Town, E cen. Chita Region, Soviet Russia, Asia, N of the Shilka on Trans-Siberian R.R. ab. 300 m. NE of Chita.

Mo′gok (mō′gŏk). Town, Katha dist., Upper Burma, on highway E of the Irrawaddy 70 m. NNE of Mandalay; pop. 6078; principal ruby mines of Burma.

Mo′gol·lon′ Mesa (mō′gŭ·yōn′; mŭg′ĭ·ōn′). Tableland in S Coconino co., Arizona; elevation ab. 8000 ft.

Mogollon Mountains *or* **Range.** Range in S Catron co., W New Mexico, extending across county boundary into Grant co.; highest point Whitewater Baldy 10,892 ft.; also includes **Mogollon Peak** 10,778 ft.

Mogontiacum. See MAINZ.

Mo·guer′ (mō·gĕr′). Commune, S Huelva prov., SW Spain, E of Huelva; pop. 7051; Columbus obtained some members of his crew from here.

Mo′hács (mō′häch). City, S Hungary, on Danube river near Yugoslavian border; pop. 16,276; commercial center; battlefield Aug. 29–30, 1526 where Turks completely defeated Hungarians; the "Second battle of Mohács" Aug. 12, 1687, in which Charles of Lorraine defeated the Turks, occurred at nearby Harkány (*q.v.*).

Mo′hall′ (mō′hôl′). City, ⊗ of Renville co., N North Dakota; pop. 956.

Mohammerah. See KHORRAMSHAHR.

Moharek. Var. of MUHARRAQ.

Mo·ha′ve (mō·hä′vĕ). County in Arizona. See *Table* at ARIZONA.

Mohave Desert. See MOJAVE DESERT.

Mo′hawk (mō′hôk). 1 River 148 m. long, largest tributary of the Hudson river, E cen. New York; formed by junction of east and west branches in Oneida co., flows S and E into Hudson river at Cohoes, above Troy; parallels the N.Y. State Barge Canal. See LITTLE FALLS, New York.
2 Village, Herkimer co., NE cen. New York, on Mohawk river 12 m. ESE of Utica; pop. 3533; forms single community with Frankfort, Ilion, and Herkimer; originally settled by Palatines; ravaged during French and Indian and Revolutionary Wars.

Mo′hé′li (mō′ä′lē′). One of the Comoro Is.; 89 sq. m.; pop. ab. 4000; chief town Fomboni.

Mo·hen′jo–Da′ro (mō·hĕn′jō·dä′rō). Prehistoric city, S Sind, Pakistan, a site of the chalcolithic epoch of Indus valley culture, c. 3000–2000 B.C., ab. 140 m. NE of Karachi; excavations of recent years have disclosed a large, well-planned city. Cf. HARAPPA.

Mo·hi′can (mō·hē′kăn). River ab. 40 m. long, cen. Ohio, flowing S to the Walhonding river.

Mo·hil′la (mō·hĭl′ȧ). = MOHÉLI.

Moh·mand′ Hills (mō·mănd′). Spur of Hindu Kush on border bet. North-West Provinces, Pakistan, and E Afghanistan, just N of Khyber Pass in the Safed Koh; through gorges in the range passes the Kabul river.

Möh′ne (mü′nĕ). River ab. 35 m. long in Westphalia, Germany; flows W to the Ruhr at Neheim. In its lower course is great reservoir dam, bombed and broken by the R.A.F. May 16, 1943; restored 1946.

Mohn′ton (mōn′t′n; -tŭn). Borough, Berks co., SE Pennsylvania, 6 m. SSW of Reading; pop. 2223.

Mo′hon′ (mō′ôn′). Commune, Ardennes dept., NE France, suburb of Mézières; pop. (1931) 7853; metallurgical works.

Mo·honk′, Lake (mō·hŏngk′). Lake in Ulster co., SE New York; resort W of New Paltz.

Moi′sie′ (mwȧ′zē′). River ab. 200 m. long, cen. Saguenay co., SE Quebec, Canada; flows S from border of SW Labrador to the St. Lawrence at its mouth.

Mois′sac′ (mwȧ′såk′). Town, Tarn-et-Garonne dept., S France, on Tarn river; pop. 3807; 15th-cent. church with 12th-cent. porch; cloisters adjoining the church.

Mois′son′ (mwȧ′sôṉ′). Village, Seine-et-Oise dept., N France, on the Seine 6 m. N of Mantes-Gassicourt; pop. (1931) 213; Boy Scout World Jamboree 1947.

Mo·ja′ve, *or* **Mo·ha′ve, Desert** (mō·hä′vĕ). Arid basin in S California, including parts of San Bernardino, Kern, and Los Angeles cos.

Mo·ji (mō·jē). Commercial seaport city, Fukuoka prefecture, N Kyushu I., Japan, on Shimonoseki Strait opp. the city of Shimonoseki with which it is connected by tunnel; pop. (1945) 94,229; exports coal; only a village in feudal times but here Japanese rulers received tribute from Korea; used as a base in wars with China and Russia. See KITA-KYUSHU.

Mojib, Wadi (el). See ARNON.

Mojokerto. See MODJOKERTO.

Mo′kai (mō′kī). Village, Auckland provincial dist., N cen. North I., New Zealand, just N of Lake Taupo.

Mo′kau (mō′kou). River ab. 70 m. long, W North I., New Zealand; flows SW to North Taranaki Bight.

Mo·kel′um·ne (mō·kĕl′ŭ·mĕ; -kŏl′-). River ab. 140 m. long, cen. California; rises in the Sierra Nevada and flows into San Joaquin river ab. 20 m. NW of Stockton.

Mo′kha (mō′kȧ). Var. of MOCHA seaport, Yemen.

Mok′mer (mŏk′mēr). Airfield on Biak I., Neth. New Guinea; captured by Americans June 17, 1944. See BOSNEK.

Mok′ni·ne (mŏk′nĭ·nĕ). Coastal town, E Tunisia, N Africa, SSE of Sousse; pop. (1936) 14,205.

Mokpo. See MOPPO.

Mok′sha (mŏk′shȧ). River ab. 380 m. long, E cen. Soviet Russia, Europe; rises near Penza and flows N and W through Mordovian Republic to the Oka above Murom; navigable for much of its course.

Mo·ku′a·we′o·we′o (mō·kōō′ä·wā′ō·wā′ō). The summit crater, 5 m. in circumference, 13,500 ft. high, of Mauna Loa in S cen. Hawaii I., Hawaii.

Mol (mōl), *formerly* **Moll.** Commune, Antwerp prov., N Belgium, 30 m. E of Antwerp; pop. 15,536; frequented by artists.

Mo′la di Ba′ri (mō′lä dē bä′rē). Commune, Bari prov., Apulia, SE Italy, on Adriatic 12 m. ESE of Bari; pop. 19,831; small harbor; 13th-cent. castle and cathedral.

Mola di Gaeta. See FORMIA.

Mold (mōld). Urban district, ⊗ of Flintshire, NE Wales; pop. 6436; in farming and coal-mining section; site of victory of native Christians under St. Germain over heathen Picts and Scots 430.

Mol′dau (môl′dou). 1 German name of MOLDAVIA.
2 German name of the VLTAVA river in Bohemia.

Mol·da·vi·a (mŏl·dā′vĭ·ȧ; -dāv′yȧ); *Romanian* **Mol·do′va** (môl·dô′vä); *Ger.* **Mol′dau** (môl′dou). Former principality E of Transylvania and N of E Walachia; included Bessarabia and Bucovina; later a province of Romania, area 14,690 sq. m. Founded in 14th cent. of Vlach and Hungarian elements; ruled by voivodes who were, from 1372, dependent upon Hungarian or Polish control; came under rule of Ottoman Turks in 16th cent.; united briefly to Walachia by Michael the Bold (d. 1601); from early 18th cent. governed for Turks by Greek Phanariots; Bucovina annexed to Austria 1774 and Bessarabia (*q.v.*) to Russia; for history after 1774, see DANUBIAN PRINCIPALITIES.

Mol·da′vi·an Carpathian Mountains (mŏl·dā′vĭ·ăn; -dāv′yăn). Southeast end of the Carpathians in Romania, forming boundary bet. Moldavia and Transylvania.

Moldavian Republic. 1 Independent Bessarabia 1917. See BESSARABIA province, Romania.
2 *officially* **Moldavian Autonomous Soviet Socialist Republic.** Former autonomous republic, U.S.S.R.; 3200 sq. m.; pop. (c. 1924) 572,300; ✳ Balta, later Tiraspol; a part of Ukrainian S.S.R. organized in

1924 from several districts of former Podolsk government (Podolia) of the U.S.S.R. Plain country along E bank of Dniester, with black soil; raises grains, fruit, and vegetables; produces sugar and wine. In 1940 merged with most of Bessarabia (*q.v.*) to form Moldavian S.S.R. (see 3, below).
3 *officially* **Moldavian Soviet Socialist Republic;** when organized called the **Moldavian Federal Soviet Republic.** A constituent republic of the U.S.S.R., formed 1940 from the former Moldavian A.S.S.R. and most of Bessarabia (*q.v.*); 13,200 sq. m.; pop. (1940) 2,400,000; ✻ Kishinev; its W boundary the Prut; does not include the districts around Izmail in S and Khotin in N which were made regions of the Ukraine. Predominant ethnic strain Romanian with 70% of the inhabitants Moldavian.
Mol'de (môl'dĕ). Town, Möre og Romsdal co., W Norway, on N shore of **Molde Fjord;** pop. 3229; resort, fishing port.
Mol·do'va (môl-dô'vä). **1** See MOLDAVIA.
2 River, NE Romania, in Moldavia region; flows SE into the Siret river near Roman.
Mo'len·beek–Saint–Jean (mō'lĕn-bāk-săn'zhän'). Commune, Brabant prov., cen. Belgium, a W suburb of Brussels; pop. (1938 est.) 62,606.
Mo'le·po·lo'le (mō'lä-pô-lō'lä). Town, SE Bechuanaland Protectorate, South Africa, on SE edge of Kalahari Desert; pop. ab. 9000.
Môle Saint Ni'co'las' (môl' săn' nē'kô'lä'). Town, NW Haiti, near tip of peninsula just N of Cap à Foux; Columbus landed here on first voyage.
Molesey. See EAST AND WEST MOLESEY.
Mo'lé'son' (mō'lä'zôn'). Peak 6581 ft., in the Alps, in Fribourg canton, W cen. Switzerland.
Mol·fet'ta (môl-fĕt'ä; *Ital.* môl-fāt'tä). Seaport, Bari prov., Apulia, SE Italy, on Adriatic 15 m. WNW of Bari; pop. 49,361; episcopal see; 12th-cent. and 18th-cent. cathedrals; cave dwellings nearby.
Mo·li'na (mô-lē'nä). Town, Talca prov., cen. Chile; pop. 5117.
Molina de Se·gu'ra (thä să-gōō'rä). Commune, Murcia prov., SE Spain, on Segura river 8 m. NNW of Murcia; pop. 13,721; manufactures paper.
Mo·line' (mô-lēn'). Industrial city, Rock Island co., NW Illinois, on Mississippi river just above Rock Island; pop. 42,705; manufactures tractors, agricultural machinery, esp. plows.
Mo·li·nel'la (mô-lē-nĕl'lä). Commune, Bologna prov., Emilia, N Italy, 26 m. ENE of Bologna; pop. 13,183.
Mo·li'no del Rey (mô-lē'nô thĕl rĕ'ĕ; rā'); *Eng.* **King's Mill.** Buildings SW of Mexico City, Mexico; scene of battle Sept. 8, 1847 in which Gen. Winfield Scott defeated superior forces of Santa Anna.
Molise, Abruzzi e. See ABRUZZI E MOLISE.
Moll. See MOL.
Molle, Ponte. See SAXA RUBRA.
Mol·len'do (mō-yän'dô). Seaport town and terminal of the Southern Railway, Arequipa dept., S Peru, 107 m. by rail SW of Arequipa; pop. (1940 est.) 12,628; import and export center for S Peru and Bolivia; open roadstead, largely replaced as a port by that of Matarani (*q.v.*).
Moll'witz (môl'vĭts); *Pol.* **Ma'łu·jo·wi'ce** (mä'lōō-yô-vē'tsĕ). Village, SE Wrocław dept., SW Poland, just W of Brzeg; formerly in Silesia, Prussia, Germany; scene of battle of Mollwitz Apr. 10, 1741 during First Silesian War (War of Austrian Succession) in which Frederick the Great defeated the Austrians.
Möln'dal (mûln'däl). City, Göteborg and Bohus prov., SW Sweden; pop. 17,124; paper and textile mills, margarine factories.
Mo·lo·dech'no (mŭ-lŭ-dyĕch'nŭ); *Pol.* **Mo'lo·decz'no** (mō'lô-dĕch'nô). Town, ✻ of Molodechno Region, NW White Russia, U.S.S.R., ab. 39 m. NW of Minsk; pop. ab. 2000; formerly in Wilno prov., Poland.
Molodechno Region. Region, NW White Russia,

U.S.S.R.; bounded on W and NW by Lithuanian Republic; ✻ Molodechno.
Mo·lo'ga (mŭ-lô'gà). **1** River ab. 340 m. long in Kalinin and Vologda Regions, W Soviet Russia, Europe, flowing into Volga river NW of Rybinsk; lower course now within the Rybinsk Reservoir.
2 Town, Yaroslavl Region, Soviet Russia, Europe, on W shore of Rybinsk Reservoir, NW of Rybinsk; pop. ab. 4000.
Mo·lo·ka'i (mō'lô-kä'ē; *Angl.* mŏl'ô-kī', mō'lô-). **1** Island ab. 40 m. long by 7 m. wide in cen. Hawaii; 259 sq. m.; pop. (1950) 5280; a part of Maui co. of state of Hawaii; has mountains at either end (Mauna Loa 1382 ft. at W and Kamakou 4958 ft. at E) with connecting saddle ab. 400 ft. high; on N coast is the Kalaupapa Leper Settlement. See KALAWAO.
2 District, Maui co., Hawaii, constituting all of Molokai I. except the small Kalawao dist.; pop. 4784; chief village Hoolehua.
Mo·lo'po (mô-lō'pō). River in S Africa, usually dry; forms S boundary of Bechuanaland Protectorate and Orange river in S near SE border of South-West Africa; lower course through Kalahari Desert. Cf. KURUMAN.
Mo·los'sis (mô-lŏs'ĭs) *or* **Mo·los'sia** (mô-lŏsh'à; -lŏsh'ĭ-à). District of ancient Epirus, NW Greece, extending along W bank of the Arachthus; noted for its breed of large hounds. The Molossians gradually became the most powerful people in Epirus.
Mo'lo·tov (mō'lŭ-tŭf; *Angl.* mŏl'ŭ-tŏf); *formerly, and since 1958,* **Perm** (pyĕrm). City, ✻ of Molotov Region, Soviet Russia, Asia (see MOLOTOV REGION), in S cen. part W of Ural Mts. on Kama river; pop. 255,196; on main rail line 265 m. E of Kirov and 180 m. WNW of Sverdlovsk, an important commercial and manufacturing city in the Ural Industrial Area; manufactures lumber products, leather, matches, cardboard, agricultural machinery. A village since early times; settlement added to by Russian merchant princes 1568; copper-smelting plant established here in early 18th cent.; received name of Perm 1781 when it was made district town; officially called Molotov 1942–58.
Molotov, Mount. Mountain 23,000 ft., N cen. Tadzhik S.S.R., Soviet Central Asia.
Molotov Region. Region, geographically in Soviet Russia, Europe, W of cen. Urals, but administered as part of Soviet Russia, Asia; 53,384 sq. m.; pop. 2,082,166; ✻ Molotov. Bounded on N and NW by Komi A.S.S.R. of Soviet Russia, Europe, on E by Sverdlovsk Region, on S by Bashkir A.S.S.R. and on W by Udmurt A.S.S.R. and Kirov Region of Soviet Russia, Europe. Traversed by the Kama and its tributary the Chusovaya, and along its E border by the W foothills of the Ural Mts. Rich in minerals. Chief cities Molotov, Berezniki, Kungur. In early times occupied by a Finnic people, the Permiaks, whence the former name of the capital city and of the national district (Komi-Permiak, estab. 1925) in NW part; settled by Russian merchant princes in 16th cent.; became part of Ural Area and is now in the Ural Industrial Area (*q.v.*); organized as a subdivision of the R.S.F.S.R. in 1936.
Mo·lo·tovsk (mô'lŭ-tŭfsk). Seaport town, NW Arkhangelsk Region, N Soviet Russia, Europe, on Dvina Gulf across the delta of the Northern Dvina from Arkhangelsk.
Mol·te'no (môl-tā'nô). Town, E cen. Cape Province, S Union of South Africa, 140 m. NW of East London; pop. 3686.
Mo·luc'ca Passage (mô-lŭk'à). Channel ab. 150 m. wide bet. NE Celebes I. and N section of Molucca Is., Malay Archipelago; connects Molucca Sea with Pacific Ocean.
Mo·luc'cas (mô-lŭk'àz) *or* **Ma·lu'ku** (mà-lōō'kŏō) *or* **Spice Islands** (spīs); *Du.* **Mo·luk'ken** (mô-lŭk'ĕ[n]). **1** Group of islands E Indonesia, bet. the islands of Celebes and New Guinea; ab. 32,300 sq. m.; pop.

560,013. They comprise (according to official census) three large islands: Halmahera, Ceram, Buru; several island groups, esp.: Sula Batjan, Obi, Kai, Aru, Tanimbar, Banda, Babar, Leti; many smaller islands, as Morotai, Wetar; and the much smaller but important islands of Amboina, Ternate, and Tidore. Several of the smaller groups to the SE (as Kai, Aru, Tanimbar) were not in former times considered a part of the Moluccas, but as attached to New Guinea. Most of the islands are mountainous, many volcanic; have dense forests with luxuriant vegetation; export sago, copra, cajuput oil, forest products, and the spices (esp. nutmegs, mace, and cloves) which in 16th cent. were sought by Portuguese, Dutch, and English for world trade.

History: Discovered by Portuguese 1512; in early 17th cent., c. 1605–21, captured by Dutch who thus were aided in securing virtual monopoly of spice trade; Amboina (*q.v.*) the early seat of Dutch control; held by British 1810–14. See also entries of separate islands.

2 Former residency of Outer Provinces in E part of Netherlands Indies, including the Moluccas and Netherlands New Guinea; 191,632 sq. m.; pop. 893,400; ✳ Amboina; comprises Amboina and Ternate divisions.

Mo·luc′ca Sea (mô·lŭk′à); *Du.* **Mo·luk′sche Zee** (mô·lûk′sĕ zā). Part of Pacific Ocean bet. NE Celebes I. on W and the Moluccas on E, Malay Archipelago; connected with the Pacific by Molucca Passage; by some extended to the S to include the Banggai and Sula Is. and the waters bet. SE Celebes and Buru I.

Molukken. See MOLUCCAS.

Mom·ba′sa (mŏm·bä′sà). **1** Island off the S coast of Kenya protectorate, E Africa, 150 m. N of Zanzibar at the mouth of a deep bay; 5 sq. m.; pop. ab. 43,000; its chief harbor is Kilindini at SW end, connected by bridge with mainland. Probably settled by Arabs in 11th cent.; mentioned as early as 1331 and visited by Vasco da Gama 1498; held by Portuguese 1529–1698; in 18th cent. subject to Oman whose local representative became independent ruler of Zanzibar (*q.v.*); in 1823 placed by its rulers under British protection but protectorate repudiated by British government; attached to Zanzibar until 1887; ✳ of East Africa Protectorate 1887–1907.

2 Municipality, including the island of Mombasa; ✳ of Coast Province, Kenya, and chief town and harbor of the protectorate; pop. ab. 178,000; an Oriental city with many narrow, irregular streets; remains of Portuguese buildings, esp. the fort.

Momein. See TENGCHUNG.

Mo·mence′ (mô·mĕns′). City, Kankakee co., NE Illinois, 12 m. E of Kankakee; pop. 2949.

Mo′ming (mō′mĭng). = ZINAL ROTHORN.

Mo·mo·ste·nan′go (mô′mō·stä·näng′gô). City, Totonicapán dept., W Guatemala; pop. 9635.

Mo·mo′te (mô·mō′tâ). Japanese airfield on one of the Los Negros Is. in the Admiralty Is., Bismarck Archipelago; seized by Americans Feb. 1944.

Mo′mo·tom′bo (mō′mô·tôm′bô). Volcano 4126 ft. in W Nicaragua, NW of Lake Managua; had violent eruption in 1609; active in 1902 and 1905.

Mom·pog′ Pass (môm·pôg′). Channel of interisland waters S of Luzon, Phil. Is., bet. mainland of Tayabas prov. and Marinduque I.; ab. 37 m. long by 12 m. wide.

Mom·pós′ (môm·pōs′). Town, N Bolívar dept., N Colombia, on the Magdalena 110 m. SE of Cartagena; pop. 6694.

Mom·tchi′lov·grad (mŏm·chē′lôv·grät); *formerly* **Ma′stan·li** (mäs′tän·lē). Town, S Stara Zagora dept., S Bulgaria, on tributary of Arda river; pop. (1926) 1137.

Mona. See MONA ISLAND.

Mon′a·ca (mŏn′à·kà). Borough, Beaver co., W Pennsylvania, on Ohio river 23 m. NW of Pittsburgh; pop. 8394; settled 1813; manufactures glass, iron and steel products, enamel and galvanized ware.

Mon′a·co (mŏn′à·kō; mô·nä′kō; *French* mô′nà′kō′).

1 Independent principality on the Mediterranean Sea near the French-Italian border; an enclave of SE France; ab. 370 acres; pop. (1939) 23,973; comprises communes of Monaco, La Condamine, and Monte Carlo; has gambling casino.

History: Town of Monaco, probably of Phoenician origin, in hands of Grimaldi family from 10th cent.; became independent principality in 13th cent.; annexed to France 1793–1814; under protection of Sardinia 1815–60; transferred to French protection and sold to France rights to towns of Menton and Roquebrune 1860; granted constitution 1911.

2 *anc.* **Mo·noe′cus** (mô·nē′kŭs). Commune, ✳ of the principality; pop. (1939) 1938; the oldest town, on a rocky headland projecting into the Mediterranean; contains cathedral, palace, oceanographical museum.

Mon′a·co Deep (mŏn′à·kō). Ocean depth 20,646 ft. in the Atlantic Ocean NW of the Canary Is.

Mo′nadh·li′ath Mountains *or* **Mo′nagh Le′a** (mō′nà·lē′à). Range of mountains, N cen. Scotland, in Inverness co., NW of the Cairngorm Mts.; highest peak **Carn Mairg** (kärn märg′) 3087 ft.

Mo·nad′nock, Mount (mô·năd′nŏk). Peak 3186 ft. in SE Cheshire co., SW New Hampshire; often called **Grand Monadnock** to distinguish from **Little Monadnock** 1890 ft. nearby.

Mo·na′gas (mô·nä′gäs). State of Venezuela. See *Table* at VENEZUELA.

Mon′a·ghan (mŏn′à·găn; -hăn; -kăn). **1** County, NE Eire, in Ulster prov.; 498 sq. m.; pop. 61,289; chief river Finn; agriculture, livestock grazing.

2 Urban district, its ⊗, NW of Dundalk; pop. 4780.

Monagh Lea. See MONADHLIATH MOUNTAINS.

Mon′a·hans (mŏn′à·hănz). City, ⊗ of Ward co., W Texas, 33 m. SW of Odessa; pop. 8567; oil wells.

Mo′na Island (mō′nà). **1** (*Span.* -nä) Island ab. 6 m. long and 4½ m. wide, West Indies; in S part of **Mona Passage** (80 m. wide), bet. Haiti on W and Puerto Rico on E; belongs to Puerto Rico; government reservation.

2 See ANGLESEY island, Wales.

3 See Isle of MAN.

Monapia. See Isle of MAN.

Mo·nash′ee Mountains (mô·năsh′ê). Range in SE British Columbia, Canada, W of the Selkirk Mts. and bet. the Columbia river valley on the E and Shuswap and Okanagan Lakes on the W; highest ab. 6000 ft.

Mon′as·tir′ (mŏn′ăs·tîr′). **1** (*Fr.* mô′nàs′tēr′); *anc.* **Rus′pi·na** (rŭs′pĭ·nà). Seaport town, NE Tunisia, N Africa, SSE of Sousse; pop. ab. 3000.

2 (*Turk.* mô·nä·stēr′) City in Yugoslavia. See BITOLJ.

Mon·ca·lie′ri (mŏng·kä·lyâ′rê). Commune, Torino prov., Piedmont, NW Italy, on Po river 7 m. S of Turin; pop. 21,181; 15th-cent. royal palace; meteorological observatory.

Mon′cay′ (*Fr.* môN′kä′) *or* **Mong Cai** (mông kī′). Town on coast, E Tonkin, N Vietnam, on Gulf of Tonkin near border of China.

Mon·ca′yo (mông·kä′yô). Peak 7593 ft. in NE cen. Spain, ab. 55 m. W of Saragossa, on the boundary bet. Aragon and Old Castile.

Mönch (mŭnK). Peak 13,465 ft. in the Bernese Alps, Bern canton, W cen. Switzerland.

Mön′chen–Glad′bach (mûn′kĕn·glät′bäK). = MÜNCHEN-GLADBACH.

Mon′chy′–le–Preux (môN′shē′lē·prû′). Village, Pas-de-Calais dept., N France, 5 m. E of Arras; held by Germans 1914–Apr. 11, 1917 and Mar.–Aug. 1918.

Moncks Corner (mŭngks). Town, ⊗ of Berkeley co., SE South Carolina; pop. 2030.

Mon·clo′va (mông·klō′vä). Town, Coahuila state, NE Mexico, 110 m. N of Saltillo; pop. 7181; altitude ab. 2000 ft.; copper, silver, zinc, and lead mines; coffee.

Mon′con′tour′ (môN′kôN′tōōr′). Village, Vienne dept., W cen. France, 27 m. NW of Poitiers; scene of battle Oct. 3, 1569 in which Huguenots were defeated by forces of duke of Guise.

Monc′ton (mŭngk′tăn). City, Westmorland co., SE New Brunswick, Canada, on Petitcodiac river at head of its estuary Chignecto Bay; pop. 27,334; railroad center; locomotive factories; manufactures woodenware, woolen goods; has airport. New Brunswick's second city in size, founded 1765.

Mon·de′go (mōnn·dā′gōō). River 130 m. long, cen. Portugal; flows SW into Atlantic Ocean at Cape Mondego, 40°12′N.

Mon′do·ñe′do (mōn′dō·nyā′t̸hō̸). Commune, Lugo prov., N Spain; pop. (1930) 9107; 17th-cent. cathedral; manufactures lace, leather, linen.

Mon·do′vi (mŏn·dō′vĭ). City, Buffalo co., W Wisconsin, 19 m. SSW of Eau Claire; pop. 2320.

Mon·do·vì′ (mōn·dō·vē′). Manufacturing commune, Cuneo prov., Piedmont, NW Italy, 13 m. ESE of Cuneo; pop. 19,621; 18th-cent. cathedral; ceramic products; scene of French victory over Austrians 1796.

Mon·dra·go′ne (mōn·drä·gō′nă). Commune, Napoli prov., Campania, S Italy, on Tyrrhenian Sea 27 m. NW of Naples; pop. 11,376.

Mon′em·va·si′a or **Mon′em·ba·si′a** (mō′năm·vä·sē′ä); Ital. **Na′po·li di Mal′va·si′a** (nä′pō·lē dē mäl′vä·zē′ä); Medieval Latin **Mal·ma′sia** (măl·mā′zhä; -zhĭ·à). Village on small island off coast of SE Laconia dept., SE Peloponnesus, Greece; pop. 638; an important commercial port and fortress in Middle Ages. Valued highly by Byzantine emperors; held by Venice 1463–1540; Turkish 1540–1690, when it again became Venetian; again Turkish 1715–1821; first town of Morea to be taken by Greeks in War of Independence; made seat of first national assembly. Noted for export of a special wine, known as malmsey or malvasia.

Mo·nes′sen (mō·nĕs′′n). City, Westmoreland co., SW Pennsylvania, on Monongahela river 20 m. S of Pittsburgh; pop. 18,424; metalworks, esp. steel and tin; coal mining.

Mo·nett′ (mō·nĕt′). City, Barry and Lawrence cos., SW Missouri, 35 m. SE of Joplin; pop. 5359; ships berries.

Mon·fal·co′ne (mōm·fäl·kō′nă). Commune, Venezia Giulia, NE Italy, near mouth of Isonzo river 17 m. NW of Trieste; pop. 19,634; shipbuilding; cotton mills; manufactures chemicals; almost destroyed in World War I.

Monferrato. See MONTFERRAT.

Mon·for′te de Le′mos (mōm·fôr′tă t̸hă lā′mōs). Commune, Lugo prov., NW Spain, 35 m. S of Lugo; pop. 21,264; agricultural products, wine; sawmills.

Mon·gal′a (mŏng·găl′à). River in S cen. Africa; flows SW from N Congo and empties into Congo river; with its headstream, the Ebola, ab. 400 m. long.

Mon·gal′la (mŏng·găl′à). 1 Former province, S Anglo-Egyptian Sudan, now part of Equatoria prov., Sudan. 2 Town, cen. Equatoria prov., S Sudan, on Bahr el Jebel (Nile) river N of Rejaf.

Mong Cai. See MONCAY.

Mon·ghyr′ (mŏng·gîr′). Town, Bhagalpur division, NE cen. Bihar, NE Indian Union, on right bank of the Ganges river 235 m. NNW of Calcutta; pop. (1941) 63,114; manufactures swords, firearms, ironware, and cigarettes; has walls of old Mogul fort. Captured by British 1763; here in 1766 Clive quelled "White Mutiny" of European officers.

Mon′gi·bel′lo (mŏn′jĭ·bĕl′ō; Ital. mōn·jĕ·bĕl′lō̸). Local name of Mt. ETNA, Sicily.

Mong′lon (mŏng′lŏn) or **Mang′lun** (mäng′lōōn). State of the Northern Shan States, E cen. Burma, on the Salween E of Mandalay; 3360 sq. m.; pop. 38,304; chief town Takut. Inhabitants Wa, Shan, Palaung, Chinese.

Mong′nai (mŏng′nī). Native state, S cen. Southern Shan States, E cen. Burma, crossed by the Salween; 3152 sq. m.; pop. 55,791; chief town Mongnai 55 m. ESE of Taunggyi.

Mon·go′lia (mŏn[g]·gōl′yà; -gō′lĭ·à). Vast territory with somewhat indefinite boundaries, E cen. Asia, N of China, comprising Outer Mongolia (Mongolian People's Republic), Inner Mongolia, and Tannu Tuva, now Tuva Autonomous Region of U.S.S.R.; formerly considered a part of Outer China.

History: Region inhabited since early times by nomadic peoples; lacks historical clarity until 13th cent. A.D. when Genghis Khan (1167–1227), the leader of one of the tribes, the Mongols, secured supremacy and began Mongol expansion; under Genghis and his successors, Mongol Empire, with its capital first at Karakorum and later at Peking, stretched from China to the Danube in eastern Europe; chief successors of Mongol Empire after it broke up were: khanate of the Golden Horde in Russia, Il-khans in Persia, Yüan dynasty in China; in the 14th cent., the descendant of Genghis Khan, Tamerlane, established a short-lived empire in western Asia; modern Mongolia loosely dependent upon China until Tannu Tuva (see TUVA) became a republic 1911 and Outer Mongolia, under Russian auspices, declared its independence. Outer Mongolia scene of struggle bet. Bolshevist and anti-Bolshevist forces which caused brief reincorporation with China 1919; under Soviet control, set up Mongolian People's Revolutionary Government 1924; independence guaranteed by Soviet Union 1936; declared independence by plebiscite 1945 as the Mongolian People's Republic (q.v.); independence recognized by China 1945. Inner Mongolia came under Chinese control, except Jehol (a part of Manchukuo 1933–45), until 1937 when the two eastern provinces, Chahar and Suiyuan, were overrun by the Japanese, who formed them into the Federated Council of the Mongol Border Land, or Mêng Chiang, renamed 1939 the Mongolian Federated Autonomous Government; all provinces again nominally Chinese at end of war 1945.

Mongolia, Inner. Region, SE part of Mongolia, stretching 1500 m. bet. Outer Mongolia (Mongolian People's Republic) and N China from NW Kansu to W Manchuria; 326,285 sq. m.; pop. (1936 est.) 5,142,793; comprises provinces of Chahar, Ningsia, and Suiyuan, and formerly included Jehol. Its N portion lies within the Gobi; its S border in certain sections marked by the Great Wall; crossed in center by the big bend of the Hwang Ho. Chief towns Wanchuan, Kweisui, Paotow, and Ningsia. See Map at CHINA. For History, see MONGOLIA.

Mongolia, Outer. See MONGOLIAN PEOPLE'S REPUBLIC.

Mon·go′lian People's Republic (mŏn[g]·gōl′yăn; -gōli·án) or **Outer Mongolia.** Autonomous republic occupying greater part of Mongolia, E cen. Asia; area 625,783 sq. m.; pop. (1936 est.) 2,077,669; ✳ Urga (Ulan Bator); bounded on NW and N by U.S.S.R. (Tuva Autonomous Region on NW, Irkutsk Region, Buryat-Mongol A.S.S.R., and Chita Region on N), on E by Manchuria, on SE and S by Inner Mongolia, and on W by Sinkiang. Mountainous in W part, with Altai Mts. (some peaks over 10,000 ft.) in SW and S, and Tannu Ola on Tuva border in NW; in N cen. part are the Kentei Mts. The desert of Gobi (q.v.) covers a wide tract in cen. and SE part. Chief rivers the Selenga and its tributary, the Orkhon, in N flowing into Lake Baikal, the Kerulen in E flowing into Hulun Nor in NW Manchuria, and the Khobdo in extreme W flowing to the lakes Khara Usu Nur and Khara Nur; other large lakes Ubsu Nur near the Tuva border and Koso Gol near border SW of Irkutsk. Inhabitants chiefly Khalkhas and other Mongolian nomad tribes, with some Chinese and Russians. Trade is in livestock and animal products; some gold is mined. Chief towns Urga (Ulan Bator), Dzhirgalantu (Kobdo), Dzhibkhalantu (Uliassutai), Kiachta. See Map at CHINA. For History, see MONGOLIA.

Mon′go·lo–Bur·yat′ Republic (mŏng′gŏ·lō·bŏŏr′yăt′). = BURYAT-MONGOL AUTONOMOUS SOVIET SOCIALIST REPUBLIC.

Mong'pan (mŏng'păn). **1** Native state, SE part of Southern Shan States, E cen. Burma, on Thai border; 2980 sq. m.; pop. 20,712; crossed by the Salween. **2** Town, its ✳, ab. 80 m. SE of Taunggyi.

Mong-tseu. See MENGTSZ.

Mon·gu' (mŏng·gōō'). Town, British ✳ of Barotse prov., W Northern Rhodesia, S cen. Africa; 7 m. E of Lealui, native ✳ of the province, pop. 714.

Mong'yu' (mŏng'yōō'). Town, SW Yunnan prov., S China, on Burma Road near Wanting; held by Japanese 1944 until they were driven out by Allies Jan. 27, 1945.

Mon·he'gan (mŏn·hē'găn). Island in Atlantic Ocean off S coast of S Maine, in Lincoln co.; settled c. 1622; lobster fishing.

Mon'i·teau' (mŏn'ĭ·tō'). County in Missouri. See *Table* at MISSOURI.

Mon'i·tor Peak (mŏn'ĭ·tēr). Mountain 13,710 ft. in La Plata co., SW Colorado.

Monitor Range. Range, cen. Nevada, chiefly in Nye co., extending N into Eureka co.

Monja, La. See LA MONJA.

Monk Bret'ton (mŭngk' brĕt''n). Former urban district, West Riding, Yorkshire, N England, now part of Barnsley; has Cluniac priory, founded 1157.

Monkchester. See NEWCASTLE.

Mon'key Point (mŭng'kĭ). Cape on SE coast of Nicaragua, extending into the Caribbean Sea.

Monk'wear'mouth (mŭngk'wēr'mŭth; -mouth). Suburb of Sunderland (*q.v.*), Durham, N England; Wearmouth monastery was the birthplace of Bede.

Mon'mouth (mŏn'mŭth; *in England, also* mŭn'-). **1** County in New Jersey. See *Table* at NEW JERSEY. **2** City, ⊗ of Warren co., W Illinois, 15 m. W of Galesburg; pop. 10,372; settled 1836, incorp. 1852; coal fields and clay deposits nearby; manufactures farm implements, sewer pipe, flour, dairy products. Monmouth College (1853; coed.; Presbyterian). **3** Town, Kennebec co., SW Maine, 12 m. NE of Lewiston; pop. 1884; trading center in apple-growing section. **4** Town, Polk co., NW Oregon, ab. 13 m. SW of Salem; pop. 2229. Oregon College of Education (1882; coed.). **5** County in England. See MONMOUTHSHIRE. **6** Municipal borough, Monmouthshire, W England, near junction of Monnow, Wye, and Trothy rivers 26 m. N of Bristol; pop. 5432; market town; ruins of a 12th-cent. castle in which Henry V was born.

Monmouth Court House. Now Freehold, New Jersey; scene of the battle of Monmouth June 28, 1778, and of the exploit of Molly Pitcher in taking her wounded husband's place as artilleryman in the course of the engagement.

Monmouth Junction. Town, Middlesex co., cen. New Jersey; pop. (est.) 700.

Mon'mouth·shire (mŏn'mŭth·shĭr; -shēr; mŭn'-) *or* **Monmouth.** County, W England, on the border of Wales; area 546 sq. m.; pop. (1951) 424,647; ⊗ Newport; other towns Monmouth, Abergavenny, Abertillery, Blaenavon, Caerleon; rivers Wye, Usk, Ebbw, Rhymney; coal and iron mining, limestone quarrying, livestock raising, and agriculture. Monmouthshire is sometimes regarded as a part of Wales.

Mon'ni·ken·dam' (mŏn'ĭ·kĕn·däm'). Commune, North Holland prov., W Netherlands; pop. 2416; 17th-cent. weighhouse, 15th-cent. church.

Mon'now (mŏn'ō; mŭn'ō) *or* **Mun'now** (mŭn'ō). Small river in SW cen. England, flowing into the Wye near Monmouth, in Monmouthshire.

Mo'no (mō'nō). **1** County in California. See *Table* at CALIFORNIA. **2** River 225 m. long, Togo, W Africa; lower course is boundary bet. Togo and Dahomey. **3** Island, largest of the Treasury Is. (*q.v.*), NW Solomon Is., W Pacific Ocean.

Mo·noc'a·cy (mō·nŏk'ȧ·sǐ). **1** River, N Maryland; rises in Adams co., S Pennsylvania, crosses state boundary and flows S through Frederick co., N Maryland, into Potomac river. **2** Battlefield along river near city of Frederick, where on July 4–5, 1864 Gen. Lew Wallace and Federal forces succeeded in delaying advance of Gen. Early's Confederates on Washington.

Monoecus. See MONACO.

Mo'no Lake (mō'nō). Lake ab. 14 m. long by 9 m. wide in cen. Mono co., E California; elevation 6730 ft.; water strongly saline; no outlet.

Mon'o·moy Point (mŏn'ō·moi). Narrow peninsula ab. 10 m. long extending S from Chatham on Cape Cod, Massachusetts; at certain times becomes an island.

Mo·no'na (mō·nō'nȧ). **1** County in Iowa. See *Table* at IOWA. **2** Village, Dane co., S Wisconsin, SE of Madison; pop. 8178.

Monona, Lake. See FOUR LAKES.

Mo·non'gah (mō·nŏng'gȧ). Town, Marion co., N West Virginia, 4 m. SW of Fairmont; pop. 1321; coal mining; scene of mine disaster 1907.

Mo·non'ga·he'la (mō·nŏng'gȧ·hē'lȧ; -hā'lȧ; mō·nŏng'-gȧ-). **1** River 128 m. long, N West Virginia and SW Pennsylvania; formed by junction of West Fork (rises in Lewis co.) and Tygart rivers in Marion co., N West Virginia, flows N across Pennsylvania border and unites with the Allegheny river to form the Ohio river at Pittsburgh. Navigable for 60 m. **2** City, Washington co., SW Pennsylvania, on Monongahela river 17 m. S of Pittsburgh; pop. 8388; settled 1792.

Mon'on·ga'li·a (mŏn'ŭn·gā'lĭ·ȧ). County in West Virginia. See *Table* at WEST VIRGINIA.

Mo'no Pass (mō'nō). Mountain pass in Sierra Nevada Mts., Mono co., E California; altitude 10,599 ft.

Mo·no'po·li (mō·nō'pō·lē). Seaport, Bari prov., Apulia, SE Italy, on Adriatic 25 m. ESE of Bari; pop. 28,856; early 12th-cent. cathedral; 11th-cent. Romanesque church; castle.

Mo'nor (mō'nōr). Commune, cen. Hungary, ab. 20 m. SE of Budapest; pop. 13,495.

Mon·re·a'le (mōn·rā·ä'lā). Commune, Palermo prov., NW cen. Sicily, 5 m. SW of Palermo; pop. 19,802; 12th-cent. cathedral; basilica with fine bronze doors (1186); sarcophagi of Norman kings William I and II.

Mon·roe' (mŭn·rō'). **1** Name of counties in seventeen states of the U.S. See *Tables* at ALABAMA, ARKANSAS, FLORIDA, GEORGIA, ILLINOIS, INDIANA, IOWA, KENTUCKY, MICHIGAN, MISSISSIPPI, MISSOURI, NEW YORK, OHIO, PENNSYLVANIA, TENNESSEE, WEST VIRGINIA, WISCONSIN. **2** Agricultural town, E Fairfield co., SW Connecticut, on Housatonic river; pop. 6402; incorporated 1923. **3** City, ⊗ of Walton co., N cen. Georgia, 23 m. SW of Athens; pop. 6826; cotton mills. **4** Industrial city, ⊗ of Ouachita parish, N Louisiana, 100 m. E of Shreveport; pop. 52,219; paper, wood products, carbon black, cottonseed oil; natural-gas deposits. **5** City, ⊗ of Monroe co., SE corner of Michigan, on Lake Erie at mouth of Raisin river 35 m. SW of Detroit; pop. 22,968; manufactures paper, fiberboard, packing boxes; commercial nurseries; Saint Mary Academy (1846). Settled by French Canadians 1780 and called **French'town** (frĕnch'toun); scene Jan. 22, 1813 of Raisin River Massacre which followed defeat of Americans by Col. Henry A. Proctor; renamed in honor of James Monroe 1817; chartered as city 1837. **6** Village in Monroe town (pop. 5965), Orange co., SE New York, 15 m. SW of Newburgh; pop. 3323. **7** City, ⊗ of Union co., S North Carolina, 24 m. SE of Charlotte; pop. 10,882; manufactures; marble works. **8** Town, Snohomish co., NW cen. Washington, 15 m. ESE of Everett; pop. 1901; condensed milk, lumber. **9** City, ⊗ of Green co., S Wisconsin, 30 m. W of Beloit; pop. 8050; trade and shipping center for area which produces Swiss and Limburger cheese.

Monroe, Lake. Lake on boundary bet. Volusia and Seminole cos., cen. Florida penin.

Monroe, Mount. Peak 5385 ft. in the White Mts., S Coos co., N New Hampshire.

Monroe City. City, Marion and Monroe cos., NE Missouri, 23 m. W of Hannibal; pop. 2337.

Monroe Peak. Mountain 11,600 ft. in SW Sevier co., cen. Utah.

Mon·roe'ville (mŭn·rō'vĭl; *Sou. also* -v'l). **1** City, ⊗ of Monroe co., SW Alabama; pop. 3632.

2 Borough, Allegheny co., SW Pennsylvania, E of Pittsburgh; pop. 22,446.

Mon·ro'vi·a (mŭn·rō'vĭ·à). **1** City, Los Angeles co., SW California, 14 m. ENE of Los Angeles; pop. 27,079; founded 1886; fruit-packing plants; manufactures paint, water heaters, textiles.

2 Seaport, ✳ of the republic of Liberia, W Africa, near the mouth of St. Paul river; pop. (including Krutown) ab. 60,000; site of a college maintained under the sponsorship of the Methodist Episcopal Church. Founded 1822 by the American Colonization Society and named by Robert G. Harper after Pres. James Monroe.

Mons (môns; *Angl.* mŏnz); *Flem.* **Ber'gen** (bĕr'κĕ[n]). Manufacturing commune, ✳ of Hainaut prov., SW Belgium; pop. (1938 est.) 26,417; coal-mining center; cathedral of St. Waudru and town hall. On site of Roman camp; made capital of Hainaut 804 by Charlemagne; became trading town with cloth market in 14th cent.; often besieged in wars of 17th and 18th cents.; scene of the first engagement fought Aug. 23, 1914 by the British Expeditionary Force in World War I.

Mons Aureus. See JANICULUM.

Mons Brisiacus. See BREISACH.

Mon'schau (môn'shou; *formerly* **Mont'joie'** (môN'-zhwä'). Town, North Rhine-Westphalia state, W Germany, SE of Aachen on French border; scene of fighting during World War II Dec. 1944 and Jan. 1945.

Mon·se'li·ce (mōn·sâ'lĕ·châ). Commune, Padova prov., Venezia Euganea, NE Italy, 13 m. SSW of Padua; pop. 16,447; 13th-cent. cathedral; ancient city walls.

Mon'se·ñor' de Me·ri'ño (mōn'sâ·nyôr' thä mā·rē'-nyô). Province, E cen. Dominican Republic. See *Table* at DOMINICAN REPUBLIC.

Mons Jo'vis (mŏnz jō'vĭs). See *Great Saint Bernard Pass* at ALPS.

Mon'son (mŭn's'n). Town, Hampden co., SW Massachusetts, 14 m. E of Springfield; pop. 6712; woolen mills.

Mons Rubicus. See MONTROUGE.

Mon'ster (môn'stĕr). Commune, South Holland prov., SW Netherlands, on North Sea coast just S of The Hague; pop. 10,478.

Mon·ta·gna'na (mōn·tä·nyä'nä). Commune, Padova prov., Venezia Euganea, NE Italy, 25 m. SW of Padua; pop. 12,702; medieval city walls; 24 medieval towers; cathedral.

Mon'ta·gu (mŏn'tà·gū). Town and health resort, SW Cape Province, S Union of South Africa, 100 m. E of Cape Town; pop. 3381; has fine climate and thermal springs, known by early Dutch settlers and natives.

Mon·tague' (mŏn·tāg'). **1** County in Texas. See *Table* at TEXAS.

2 Village, its ⊗, N Texas; pop. (with Forestburg) 1268.

Mon'ta·gue (mŏn'tà·gū). Town, Franklin co., NW Massachusetts, 5 m. SE of Greenfield; pop. 7836; hydroelectric generating station; manufactures fishing tackle.

Mon'ta·gue Island (mŏn'tà·gū). Island 50 m. long and 8 m. wide on W side of entrance to Prince William Sound, S Alaska, E of Kenai Penin.

Mont'al·ban' (mŏn'täl·vän'). **1** River, an upper tributary of the Marikina river, NE Rizal prov., Luzon, Phil. Is.; it and other streams have been developed into large reservoir furnishing water supply for Manila.

2 Municipality, N Rizal, on Montalban river W of reservoir; pop. 6402.

Mont·al·ci'no (mŏn·täl·chē'nô). Commune, Siena prov. Tuscany, cen. Italy, 22 m. SSE of Siena; pop. 10,216; 19th-cent. cathedral, early 14th-cent. church, 14th-cent. palace and art museum.

Mont·al'to (mŏn·täl'tô). Highest peak 6420 ft. in the Aspromonte ridge, S Apennines, Italy

Montalto Uf'fu·go (ōōf'fōō·gô). Commune, Cosenza prov., Calabria, S Italy, 10 m. NNW of Cosenza; pop. (1931) 17,747; settled by Waldensians in 14th cent.

Mon·tan'a (mŏn·tăn'à). Northwestern state of U.S.A., 41st state admitted to Union (1889); bounded on N by Canadian provinces of British Columbia, Alberta, and Saskatchewan, on E by North Dakota and South Dakota, on S by Wyoming and Idaho, and on W by Idaho; 4th state in area, 147,138 sq. m. (land area 145,878 sq. m.); 41st state in population, 674,767; ✳ Helena. See *Table of States* at UNITED STATES. Divided into the following 56 counties (for pronunciation of their names, see their individual entries):

NAME	LOCATION	AREA[1]	POP.[1]	CO. SEAT
Beaverhead	SW	5,556	7,194	Dillon
Big Horn	S	5,033	10,007	Hardin
Blaine	N	4,267	8,091	Chinook
Broadwater	SW cen.	1,243	2,804	Townsend
Carbon	S	2,070	8,317	Red Lodge
Carter	SE corner	3,313	2,493	Ekalaka
Cascade	cen.	2,659	73,418	Great Falls
Chouteau	N cen.	3,920	7,348	Fort Benton
Custer	SE	3,765	13,227	Miles City
Daniels	NE	1,443	3,755	Scobey
Dawson	E	2,358	12,314	Glendive
Deer Lodge	SW	738	18,640	Anaconda
Fallon	E	1,633	3,997	Baker
Fergus	cen.	4,244	14,018	Lewistown
Flathead[2,3]	NW	5,177	32,965	Kalispell
Gallatin	S	2,517	26,045	Bozeman
Garfield[4]	E cen.	4,595	1,981	Jordan
Glacier[2]	NW	2,974	11,565	Cut Bank
Golden Valley	cen.	1,178	1,203	Ryegate
Granite	W	1,733	3,014	Philipsburg
Hill	N	2,926	18,653	Havre
Jefferson	SW cen.	1,651	4,297	Boulder
Judith Basin	cen.	1,880	3,085	Stanford
Lake[3]	NW	1,500	13,104	Polson
Lewis and Clark	W cen.	3,477	28,006	Helena
Liberty	N	1,459	2,624	Chester
Lincoln	NW corner	3,715	12,537	Libby
McCone[4]	E	2,594	3,321	Circle
Madison	SW	3,530	5,211	Virginia City
Meagher	cen.	2,354	2,616	White Sulphur Springs
Mineral	W	1,223	3,037	Superior
Missoula	W	2,613	44,663	Missoula
Musselshell	cen.	1,886	4,888	Roundup
Park	S	2,627	13,168	Livingston
Petroleum	cen.	1,651	894	Winnett
Phillips	N	5,229	6,027	Malta
Pondera	NW	1,643	7,653	Conrad
Powder River	SE	3,285	2,485	Broadus
Powell	W	2,337	7,002	Deer Lodge
Prairie	E	1,727	2,318	Terry
Ravalli	W	2,384	12,341	Hamilton
Richland	E	2,065	10,504	Sidney
Roosevelt	NE	2,385	11,731	Wolf Point
Rosebud	SE	5,032	6,187	Forsyth
Sanders	NW	2,811	6,880	Thompson Falls
Sheridan	NE corner	1,700	6,458	Plentywood
Silver Bow	SW	716	46,454	Butte
Stillwater	S cen.	1,797	5,526	Columbus
Sweet Grass	S cen.	1,846	3,290	Big Timber
Teton	NW cen.	2,294	7,295	Choteau
Toole	N	1,965	7,904	Shelby
Treasure	SE cen.	984	1,345	Hysham
Valley[4]	NE	4,961	17,080	Glasgow
Wheatland	cen.	1,422	3,026	Harlowton
Wibaux	E	889	1,698	Wibaux
Yellowstone	S cen.	2,635	79,016	Billings
Yellowstone National Park (part)	S	269[5]	47	

[1] Area = land area in sq. m. Pop. from 1960 Census.
[2] Glacier National Park occupies NE part of Flathead co. and NW part of Glacier co.
[3] Upper (smaller) part of Flathead Lake in Flathead co., lower part in Lake co.
[4] Fort Peck Reservoir on boundaries of Garfield co. (along both sides of its NE corner), McCone co. (upper W boundary), and Valley co. (cen. boundary).
[5] Main part of Yellowstone National Park is within Wyoming state boundaries (2930.8 sq. m.), with adjacent strips in Montana (268.9 sq. m.) and Idaho (57.6 sq. m.). Total area with inland waters 3419 sq. m.

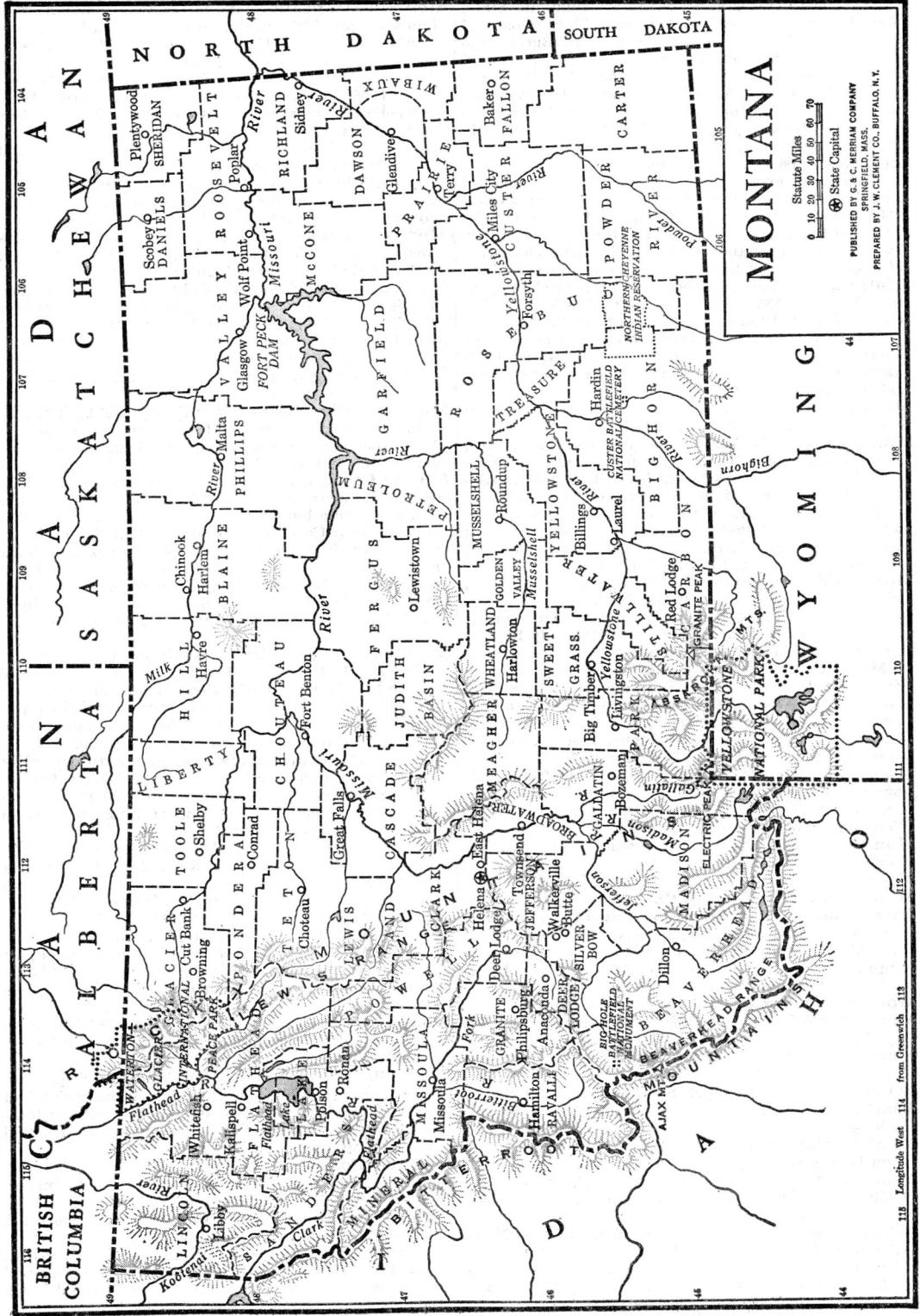

MONTANA

Statute Miles

⊕ State Capital

0 10 20 30 40 50 60 70

PUBLISHED BY G. & C. MERRIAM COMPANY
SPRINGFIELD, MASS.
PREPARED BY J. W. CLEMENT CO., BUFFALO, N.Y.

Nickname: Treasure State, also Mountain State. *State flower:* Bitterroot. *Motto:* Oro y Plata (Gold and Silver). *Chief cities:* Great Falls, Billings, Butte, Missoula. *Rivers:* Missouri, rising in S area and flowing N then E across state; Yellowstone, rising in NW Wyoming and flowing through Yellowstone National Park across the boundary into Montana and then N and NE into the Missouri. *Highest point:* Granite Peak 12,850 ft. in Park co. *Chief industries:* Mining (copper, gold, silver); stock raising (sheep, cattle, horses).

History: All except a small area in NW was part of Louisiana Purchase 1803; crossed by Lewis and Clark 1805–06; its boundary with Canada settled by treaties 1818 and 1846; part W of Rockies in the Oregon country, included in Washington Territory 1853 and 1859; part E of Rockies in territories of Nebraska 1854 and of Dakota 1861; part of Idaho Territory 1863; organized as Montana Territory 1864; first crossed by rail (Northern Pacific) 1883; admitted to Union Nov. 8, 1889.

Mon·ta'na (mŏn·tä'nä). Town, Valais canton, Switzerland; pop. 1485; health resort, winter sports; nearby is **Montana–Ver·ma'la** (-vâr·mä'lä), a resort for tuberculous patients.

Mon·ta'ña (mŏn·tä'nyä). Forested region of the E slope of the Andes, esp. that of N Peru.

Mon'tar'gis' (mōn'tàr'zhē'). Manufacturing commune, Loiret dept., N cen. France, 38 m. E of Orléans; pop. 13,885; remains of a castle which was long a royal residence; bronze statue of the "Dog of Montargis," the dog of Aubry de Montdidier, which, according to tradition, tracked down his master's murderer and vanquished him in a sort of judicial duel arranged by Charles V 1371; unsuccessfully besieged by English 1427.

Mon'ta'taire' (mōn'tà'târ'). Manufacturing commune, Oise dept., N France; pop. (1931) 7392.

Mont'au'ban' (mōn'tō'bäN'). **1** Village, Somme dept., N France, 6 m. E of Albert; scene of battle July 1, 1916, a phase of the battle of the Somme.

2 Manufacturing city, ✳ of Tarn-et-Garonne dept., S France, on Tarn river 31 m. N of Toulouse; pop. 32,025; cathedral, episcopal palace, town hall and bridge; manufactures silks, woolens, porcelain, starch, pottery, dyes. Ancient capital of Quercy; as Huguenot stronghold besieged 1580, 1621; taken by Richelieu 1629.

Mon·tauk' (mŏn·tôk'; *attributively, also* mŏn'tôk). Village and fishing resort, Suffolk co., SE New York, on Long I. near Montauk Point, and most easterly of New York state villages; pop. (est.) 1000.

Montauk Point. Point on E extremity of Long I., New York.

Mont aux Sources. See Mont Aux Sources.

Mont'bé'liard' (mōn'bā'lyàr'). Manufacturing commune, Doubs dept., E France, 43 m. ENE of Besançon; pop. 14,217; hardware, tools, clocks, cotton goods; trades in lumber, dairy products. Former capital of duchy of Burgundy; occupied by French 1674–97, 1723–48; given to France by Peace of Lunéville 1801.

Mont Blanc. See Mont Blanc.

Mont'bri'son' (mōn'brē'zōn'). Town, Loire dept., SE cen. France; pop. 6769; 13th–15th cent. church.

Mont·calm' (mŏnt·käm'). **1** County in Michigan. See *Table* at Michigan.

2 County, Quebec, Canada. See *Table* at Quebec.

Mont'ceau'–les–Mines (mōn'sō'lä·mēn'). Commune, Saône-et-Loire dept., E cen. France; pop. 26,902.

Mont Cenis; *Ital.* **Monte Cenisio.** Alpine pass and tunnel. See Alps.

Mont·clair' (mŏnt·klâr'; *attributively, also* mŏnt'klâr) **1** City, San Bernardino co., SE California, NE of Pomona; pop. 13,546.

2 Town, Essex co., NE New Jersey, 6 m. NNW of Newark; pop. 43,129; residential suburb of Newark and New York; settled c. 1666, incorporated 1868; Montclair State Coll. (1908; coed.) in nearby **Upper Montclair.** Washington's headquarters 1780.

Mont–de–Mar'san' (mōNd'màr'säN'). Commune, ✳ of Landes dept., SW France, 66 m. S of Bordeaux; pop. 13,009; metalworks. Capital of viscountship of Marsan; became part of Béarn 1256; to France 1589.

Mont'di'dier' (mōn'dē'dyā'). Commune, Somme dept., N France; pop. 4601; devastated in battles 1918.

Mont–Dore (mōn'dôr'). Commune, Puy-de-Dôme dept., S cen. France, on the Dordogne near its source; pop. (1931) 2629; watering place; thermal springs and baths, known since Roman times.

Mont·ea'gle (mŏnt·ē'g'l). Village and summer resort, Grundy co., S cen. Tennessee, ab. 35 m. NW of Chattanooga; pop. (est.) 700; annual Chautauqua assembly.

Mon'te·bel'lo (mŏn'tē·bĕl'ō). Residential city, Los Angeles co., SW California, 8 m. ESE of Los Angeles; pop. 32,097; incorporated 1920; oil wells nearby.

Mon'te·bel·lu'na (mŏn'tā·bäl·lōō'nä). Commune, Treviso prov., Venezia Euganea, NE Italy, 13 m. NW of Treviso; pop. 18,412; cathedral (built 1925).

Mon'te·bourg' (mōnt·bōōr'). Town, SE coast of Cotentin Penin., Manche dept., NW France; beachhead established nearby June 1944 by Americans in Normandy campaign of World War II.

Mon'te Car'lo (mŏn'tē kär'lō; *Fr.* mōn'tĕ' kär'lō'; *Ital.* mŏn'tä kär'lŏ). Commune, Monaco, on coast to the N of Monaco commune; pop. (1939) 10,681; gambling resort with casino and many hotels.

Mon'te Cas·si'no (mŏn'tē kà·sē'nō; *Ital.* mŏn'tä käs·sē'nŏ). Famous abbey in Frosinone prov., SE Latium, cen. Italy, on a hill (in World War II operations called Hill 516) near Cassino; founded c. 529 A.D. by St. Benedict of Nursia, who died here; since 1866 a national monument. Had to be four times rebuilt: after being sacked by the Lombards 589, destroyed by the Saracens 884, badly damaged by earthquake 1349, and destroyed by Allied bombing Feb.–May 1944 in World War II. See Cassino.

Mon'te·ca·ti'ni–Ter'me (mŏn'tä·kä·tē'nē·tĕr'mä). Commune, Pistoia prov., Tuscany, cen. Italy, 12 m. W by S of Pistoia; pop. 10,071; thermal mineral springs and baths; health resort. Nearby is **Montecatini di Val di Nie'vo·le** (dē väl' dē nyâ'vŏ·lä), commune, pop. 3211, seat of principal chemical plant in Italy.

Mon'te·cor·vi'no, *officially* **Montecorvino Ro·vel'la** (mŏn'tē·kôr·vē'nō rō·vĕl'à; *Ital.* mŏn'tä·kôr·vē'nŏ rō·vĕl'lä). Commune, Campania, S Italy, 11 m. E of Salerno; pop. 7966; airfield; scene of bitter fighting in Salerno campaign Sept. 1943.

Mon'te·cris'ti (mŏn'tē·krĭs'tĭ; *Span.* mŏn'tä·krēs'tĕ). **1** Province, NW Dominican Republic. See *Table* at Dominican Republic.

2 *formerly* **San Fer·nan'do de Monte Cristi** (sän' fĕr·nän'dō dĕ; *Span.* säm' fĕr·nän'dŏ thä). Commune, its ✳; pop. (1941) 8854; hides, cotton, hardwoods.

3 Town, Manabí prov., W Ecuador, 6 m. from its port Manta and ab. 90 m. NW of Guayaquil; pop. (1944 est.) 8614; center for copra industry and manufacture of Panama hats.

Mon'te·cris'to (mŏn'tē·krĭs'tō; *Ital.* mŏn'tä·krēs'tŏ). Italian island 4 sq. m. in Tyrrhenian Sea S of Elba.

Monte Croce. See Plöcken.

Mon'te·fia·sco'ne (mŏn'tä·fyäs·kō'nä). Commune, Viterbo prov., Latium, cen. Italy, in volcanic region E of Lake Bolsena 10 m. NNW of Viterbo; pop. 11,277; 16th-cent. cathedral and castle; Romanesque church; noted for its fine muscatel wine.

Mon'te·frí'o (mŏn'tä·frē'ŏ). Commune, Granada prov., S Spain, 22 m. WNW of Granada; pop. 13,246; manufactures textiles, brandy, soap; cattle raising.

Mon'te·gnée' (mōnt·nyä'). Commune, Liège prov., E Belgium, W suburb of Liège; pop. 10,555.

Mon·te'go Bay (mŏn·tē'gō). Seaport, NW Jamaica I., West Indies; pop. 11,500; resort; has good harbor and export trade in fruit. Originally site of large Arawak Indian village, visited by Columbus 1494.

Montego Bay Point. Cape on NW coast of the island of Jamaica, West Indies, just N of Montego Bay.

Monteleone di Calabria. See VIBO VALENTIA.

Mon·té′li·mar′ (môN′tā′lē′mȧr′); *anc.* **A·cu′num A·cu′si·o** (ȧ·kū′nŭm ȧ·kū′shĭ·ō), *later* **Mon·til′i·um Ad′he·ma′ri** (mŏn·tĭl′ĭ·ŭm ăd′hē·mā′rī). Mining and manufacturing commune, Drôme dept., SE France, on Rhone river 27 m. SSW of Valence; pop. 15,187; 12th-cent. dungeon; manufactures silk textiles, agricultural implements, alimentary pastes, nougat, hats. Destroyed by Visigoths in 5th cent.; made commune 1198; capital of state of Valdaine (joined to crown with the Dauphiné); besieged by Huguenots 1562, 1585, 1587; in World War II seized by Allies Aug. 25, 1944.

Mon′te Lir′i·o (mŏn′tē̇ lĭr′ĭ·ō). Town at N end of island in Gatun Lake, Panama Canal Zone; pop. ab. 250.

Mon·tel′lo (mŏn·tĕl′ō). **1** City, ⊗ of Marquette co., cen. Wisconsin; pop. 1021.
2 (*Ital.* mŏn·tĕl′lō) Plateau SW of Piave river and NE of Montebelluna, Venezia Euganea, NE Italy; battles in World War I, esp. in June 1918, an Italian victory; military key position in World War II.

Mon′te·mo·re′los (mŏn′tä·mô·rā′lôs). Town, Nuevo León state, NE Mexico, on railroad 45 m. SE of Monterrey; pop. 5579.

Mon′te·ne′gro (mŏn′tē̇·nē′grō). **1** (*Ital.* mŏn′tä·nā′-grō); *native* **Cr′na Go′ra** (tsûr′nä gō′rä), *literally* "Black Mountain." Former kingdom, SW Europe; area (1918) 3733 sq. m.; pop. ab. 200,000; ✳ Cetinje. Bounded on NW and N by Herzegovina, on E by Serbia, on S by Albania, and on SW by Dalmatia and the Adriatic Sea (coast line ab. 28 m. long). Mountainous, well-forested region including ranges of the North Albanian Alps; highest peak Durmitor 8294 ft. in cen. part; includes NW two thirds of Lake Scutari into which Morača river flows; other rivers are headstreams of the Drina and Ibar.
History: Originated after battle of Kosovo (*q.v.*) 1389, when defeated Serbs took refuge on "Black Mountain"; ruled by prince-bishops, it never yielded to Turkish authority; under Peter I (1782–1830), ally of Russia in her wars against Turkey, secured recognition of independence 1799; state became secular and modernized in 19th cent.; took part in war against Turkey 1876–78, and secured recognition of complete independence and additional territory 1878; kingdom after 1910; fought Turks in First and in Second Balkan Wars; took Shkodër but was forced to yield it to the powers who made it capital of Albania 1913; for help to Serbia, received one half of sanjak of Novi Pazar 1913; declared war on Austria-Hungary 1914 whose annexation of Bosnia and Herzegovina had frustrated Montenegrin territorial aims; voted union with Serbia, Croatia, and other Yugoslav territories to form Kingdom of the Serbs, Croats, and Slovenes 1918; region became part of Zetska co. 1929.
2 Federated republic of Yugoslavia, in S part in region of the former kingdom of Montenegro; created 1946 on establishment of the Federal People's Republic of Yugoslavia; ✳ Titograd (see PODGORICA).
3 (*Port.* mōֹN′tē̇·ä′grōō); *now* **A′ma·pá′** (ä′mä·pá′). Seaport, Amapá Territory, NE Brazil, opp. island of Maracá.

Mon′te Pla′ta (mŏn′tä plä′tä). Commune, ✳ of Monseñor de Meriño prov., E cen. Dominican Republic; pop. (1941) 17,303.

Mon′te·pul·cia′no (mŏn′tä·pōōl·chä′nô). Commune, Siena prov., Tuscany, cen. Italy, 29 m. SE of Siena; pop. 16,866; 16th-cent. cathedral, 13th-cent. church.

Mon′te·reau′-faut-Yonne (môN′trō′fō′yŏn′); *anc.* **Con·da′te** (kŏn·dā′tē̇). Manufacturing town, Seine-et-Marne dept., N France, at confluence of Yonne and Seine rivers; pop. 8917.

Mon′te·rey′ (mŏn′tē̇·rā′; *attributively, usu.* mŏn′tē̇·rā′).
1 County in California. See *Table* at CALIFORNIA.
2 Commercial city, Monterey co., W California, at S end of Monterey Bay; pop. 22,618; fishing center; winter and summer tourist resort; U.S. Army post. Site of city discovered 1542 by Juan Rodríguez Cabrillo, rediscovered 1602 by Sebastián Vizcaíno; first settled 1770 through founding of Franciscan mission; became social, military, and political center of Spanish California; capital of Spanish province of California 1774–1825, of Mexican province 1825–46; to U.S. 1846; site of first California constitutional convention 1849; incorporated 1850.
3 Town, Putnam co., N cen. Tennessee, 15 m. E of Cookeville; pop. 2069.
4 Town, ⊗ of Highland co., western Virginia; pop. 270.
5 See MONTERREY, Mexico.

Monterey Bay. Inlet of Pacific Ocean in Santa Cruz and Monterey cos., W cen. California.

Monterey Park. Suburban residential city, Los Angeles co., SW California, 8 m. E of Los Angeles; pop. 37,821.

Mon′te·rí′a (mŏn′tä·rē′ä). City, Bolívar dept., N Colombia, 120 m. SW of Cartagena; pop. 12,804.

Mon·te′ros (mŏn·tā′rôs). Town, Tucumán prov., N Argentina, just S of Tucumán; pop. 8500.

Mon′ter·rey′ (mŏn′tē̇·rā′; *Span.* mŏn′tĕr·rĕ̄′ĕ; -rā′); *sometimes, Anglicized,* **Mon′te·rey′** (mŏn′tē̇·rā′). City, NE Mexico, ✳ of Nuevo León state; pop. 333,422; in fertile valley at alt. 1624 ft.; iron and steel works, flour and textile mills; railroad and motor-road center; Topo Chico hot springs and García Caves (*q.v.*) nearby. Founded ab. 1560; in Mexican War scene of severe battle Sept. 21–23, 1846 in which city was finally taken by Gen. Taylor's American forces.

Mon′te San Gio·van′ni Cam·pa′no (mŏn′tä sän jô·vän′nē käm·pä′nô). Commune, Frosinone prov., Latium, cen. Italy, 9 m. E of Frosinone; pop. 10,984.

Monte San Giu·lia′no (jōō·lyä′nô); *anc.* **E′ryx** (ē′rĭks). Commune, Trapani prov., NW Sicily, on mountain 2465 ft. high 4 m. NE of Trapani; pop. (1931) 31,049. Base of Hamilcar Barca in First Punic War; medieval castle; ruins of Roman temple of Aphrodite.

Mon′te·sa′no (mŏn′tē̇·sā′nō). City, ⊗ of Grays Harbor co., W Washington, on Chehalis river 11 m. E of Aberdeen; pop. 2486; farming, lumbering, fishing industries.

Mon′te San·t′An′ge·lo (mŏn′tä sän·tän′jä·lô). Commune, Foggia prov., Apulia, SE Italy, 27 m. NE of Foggia; pop. 25,509; Norman castle; 13th-cent. campanile.

Mon′tes Cla′ros (mōֹNN′tĕsh klä′rōōs). City, N cen. Minas Gerais state, E Brazil, 225 m. N of Belo Horizonte; pop. (1940 est.) 13,972.

Mon·te·sper′to·li (mŏn·tä·spĕr′tō·lē). Commune, Firenze prov., Tuscany, cen. Italy, 10 m. SSW of Florence; pop. (1931) 12,061.

Mon′te·val′lo (mŏn′tē̇·văl′ō). Town, Shelby co., cen. Alabama, 32 m. S of Birmingham; pop. 2755; Alabama Coll. (founded 1896; coed.).

Mon′te·var′chi (mŏn·tä·vär′kē). Commune, Arezzo prov., Tuscany, cen. Italy, near Arno river 17 m. WNW of Arezzo; pop. 15,695; convent.

Mon′te·vid′e·o (mŏn′tē̇·vĭd′ē·ō). City, ⊗ of Chippewa co., SW cen. Minnesota, on Minnesota river 42 m. SE of Big Stone Lake; pop. 5693; in agricultural section.

Mon′te·vi·de′o (mŏn′tē̇·vĭ·dā′ō; -vĭd′ē·ō; *Span.* mŏn′-tä·vĕ·thä′ō). **1** Department of Uruguay. See *Table* at URUGUAY.
2 Seaport city, its ✳ and ✳ of Uruguay, in S part on N shore of La Plata estuary 135 m. E of Buenos Aires, Argentina; pop. (1956 est.) 922,885; chief port of the republic and the railroad terminus for all lines; principal industry meat packing; exports livestock, meat and meat extracts, wool, hides, grain, flour, fruit, and vegetables. University of the Republic (inaugurated 1849).
History: Settled by Spanish 1726 after they had expelled Portuguese; changed hands frequently as scene of conflict bet. Spanish and Portuguese, British and Spanish, Uruguayan patriots under Artigas and Argentina (see URUGUAY) over control of region of the Plata; held by Brazil 1817–28; became capital of independent Uruguay 1828.

Mon′te Vis′ta (mŏn′tĕ vĭs′tá). City, Rio Grande co., S Colorado, in San Luis Park 15 m. WNW of Alamosa; pop. 3385; founded 1887; vegetable-shipping point; center of large potato-growing area.

Mon′te·zu′ma (mŏn′tĕ·zōō′má). **1** County in Colorado. See *Table* at COLORADO.
2 City, Macon co., SW cen. Georgia, 45 m. SW of Macon; pop. 3744; shipping center for peaches and winter truck-garden produce; cottonseed-oil mill.
3 Town, of Poweshiek co., SE cen. Iowa; pop. 1416.

Montezuma Castle National Monument. See UNITED STATES, *National Monuments*.

Montezuma Peak. Mountain 13,131 ft. in Archuleta co., S Colorado.

Mont′fau′con′ (môN′fō′kôN′). Village, Meuse dept., NE France, 13 m. NW of Verdun; pop. 365; held by Germans throughout World War I; taken Oct. 4, 1918 by Americans in the Meuse-Argonne offensive.

Mont′fer′rand′ (môN′fĕ′räN′). Ancient city, now part of the city of Clermont-Ferrand, Puy-de-Dôme dept., S cen. France.

Mont′fer′rat′ (môN′fĕ′rá′); *Ital.* **Mon·fer·ra′to** (mŏn-fär·rä′tô). Former marquisate and duchy in Italy, S of Po river, now mostly in Alessandria prov., SE Piedmont.

Mont·gom′er·y (mŏn[t]·gŭm′ĕr·ĭ; -gŭm′rĭ; -gŏm′-).
1 Name of counties in eighteen states of the U.S. See *Tables* at ALABAMA, ARKANSAS, GEORGIA, ILLINOIS, INDIANA, IOWA, KANSAS, KENTUCKY, MARYLAND, MISSISSIPPI, MISSOURI, NEW YORK, NORTH CAROLINA, OHIO, PENNSYLVANIA, TENNESSEE, TEXAS, VIRGINIA.
2 Commercial city, ✳ of Alabama and of Montgomery co., SE cen. Alabama, on Alabama river ab. 85 m. SSE of Birmingham; pop. 134,393; central market for Black Belt; railroad center; coal and iron fields; manufactures cotton products, textiles, fertilizers, food products, brick and tile, creosote, wood products, drugs, machinery, boilers, farm implements, auto trailers, and furniture; stockyards and meat-packing plants. Huntingdon College (1909; coed.; previously founded at Tuskegee 1854 and 1872); Alabama State College (1874; coed.); U.S. Air Force Advanced School at Maxwell Field; U.S. Air Force Special Staff School at Gunter Field. Incorporated 1819; became state capital 1847; often called the "Cradle of the Confederacy"; site of signing of Articles of Secession 1861; first capital of the Confederacy Feb.–May 1861; taken by Union army 1865.
3 City, Le Sueur co., S Minnesota, 18 m. WNW of Faribault; pop. 2118; canneries, flour mill.
4 Borough, Lycoming co., N cen. Pennsylvania, 10 m. SE of Williamsport; pop. 2150.
5 City, SW cen. West Virginia, in Fayette and Kanawha cos., on Kanawha river 22 m. ESE of Charleston; pop. 3000; coal mining. West Virginia Institute of Technology (1895; coed.).
6 District, Multan division, West Punjab, Pakistan; 4204 sq. m.; pop. (1941) 1,329,103.
7 Town, ✳ of Montgomery dist., Pakistan, on Bari Doab Canal 92 m. SW of Lahore; pop. 26,164; founded 1864 and named after Sir Robert Montgomery, then lieutenant governor.
8 County in Wales. See MONTGOMERYSHIRE.
9 Municipal borough, Montgomeryshire, E Wales; pop. 904; cattle market.

Montgomery City. City, of Montgomery co., E cen. Missouri, 46 m. E of Columbia; pop. 1918.

Mont·gom′er·y·shire (-shĭr; -shẽr) *or* **Montgomery.** County, E Wales; area 797 sq. m.; pop. (1951) 45,989; Welshpool; hilly region; rivers Dyfi, Severn, Vyrnwy; agriculture, sheep raising, quarrying.

Mon′ti·cel′lo (mŏn′tĭ·sĕl′ō; *Va.*, -chĕl′ō). **1** City, of Drew co., SE Arkansas; pop. 4412; Arkansas Agricultural and Mechanical College (1909; coed.).
2 Town, of Jefferson co., N Florida, 28 m. ENE of Tallahassee; pop. 2490; trade center for area producing cotton, pecans, corn, fruit, and dairy products.

3 City, of Jasper co., cen. Georgia, 32 m. N of Macon; pop. 1931.
4 City, Piatt co., cen. Illinois, 25 m. NE of Decatur; pop. 3219; in agricultural and stock-raising section.
5 City, of White co., NW Indiana, 25 m. NNE of Lafayette on the Tippecanoe river bet. Shafer Lake and Freeman Lake (*qq.v.*); pop. 4035; resort.
6 City, Jones co., E Iowa, 30 m. ENE of Cedar Rapids; pop. 3190.
7 City, of Wayne co., S Kentucky, 22 m. SW of Somerset; pop. 2940; flour mills, pencil factories; oil field.
8 Town, Aroostook co., N Maine, 12 m. N of Houlton; pop. 1109.
9 Town, of Lawrence co., S Mississippi; pop. 1432.
10 Town, of Lewis co., NE Missouri; pop. 159.
11 Village, of Sullivan co., SE New York, 42 m. W of Poughkeepsie; pop. 5222; resort.
12 City, of San Juan co., SE corner of Utah; pop. 1845; founded by Mormons 1887; figured in San Juan river gold rush 1892.
13 Estate and residence of Thomas Jefferson, 3 m. SE of Charlottesville, Virginia.

Mon·ti·chia′ri (mŏn·tĕ·kyä′rē). Commune, Brescia prov., Lombardy, N Italy, SE of Brescia; pop. 11,650.

Mon·tiel′ (môn·tyĕl′). Town, SE Ciudad Real prov., SE cen. Spain; pop. 2740; just NW is battlefield where Peter the Cruel was defeated 1369 by Du Guesclin and Henry of Trastamara.

Mon′ti′gnac′ (môn′tĕ′nyák′). Town, E Dordogne dept., SW cen. France; nearby is Lascaux Cave with pictures of prehistoric interest.

Mon′ti′gnies′–sur–Sam′bre (môn′tĕ′nyē′sür·säN′br′). Commune, Hainaut prov., SW Belgium, just E of Charleroi; pop. 25,177; coal-mining center; manufactures ovens, machinery, and ironware.

Mon′ti′gny′–en–Go′helle′ (môn′tē′nyē′äN·gô′ĕl′). Commune, Pas-de-Calais dept., N France, just E of Lens; pop. 7707.

Mon′ti′gny′–lès–Metz′ (môn′tē′nyē′lĕ·mâs′). Commune, Moselle dept., NE France, 5 m. SSW of Metz; pop. 16,789; botanical garden; military airdrome; residential suburb of Metz.

Mon·ti′jo (môn·tē′hô). **1** Pacific coast port, SW cen. Panama, near the head of the Gulf of Montijo.
2 Town, Badajoz prov., W Spain, ab. 18 m. ENE of Badajoz; pop. 10,165; scene of battle May 26, 1644 in which Portuguese under Albuquerque defeated Spanish, who opposed reign of John IV.

Montijo, Gulf of. Inlet of Pacific Ocean on the SW coast of Panama, extending NE into Panama at the W base of Azuero Penin.

Montilium Adhemari. See MONTÉLIMAR.

Mon·til′la (môn·tē′[l]yä). Commune, Córdoba prov., S Spain, 22 m. SSE of Córdoba; pop. 22,527; agricultural products; wine, esp. amontillado; manufactures linen, woolens, pottery, soap, tile; ducal palace; Arab mosque (now a Christian church).

Mon′ti′vil′liers′ (môn′tē′vē′lyä′). Town, Seine-Inférieure dept., N France; pop. 5514; formerly noted for manufacture of cloth, esp. "musterdevillers," a woolen used for clothing 13th–16th cents.

Montjoie. See MONSCHAU.

Mont Jo′li′ (môN zhô′lē′). Village, Rimouski co., S Quebec, Canada, 18 m. ENE of Rimouski; pop. 4938; starting point and terminal of automobile loop highway around Gaspé Penin.

Mont Lau′ri·er (môN lô′rĭ·ā; lô′ryā′). Village, of Labelle co., SW Quebec, Canada, on Lièvre river 77 m. N of Ottawa; pop. 4701; terminus of branch of Canadian Pacific Railway from Montreal.

Mont′lu′çon′ (môN′lü′sôN′). Industrial city, Allier dept., cen. France, on Cher river 38 m. WSW of Moulins; pop. 42,515; foundries, steel mills; coal fields nearby. Founded in 11th cent.; became part of royal domain 1527.

Mont′ma′gny′ (môN′mà′nyē′). **1** County, Quebec, Canada. See *Table* at QUEBEC.
2 Industrial town, its ⊗, on S bank of St. Lawrence river 34 m. ENE of Quebec; pop. 5844; pulp mill, furniture factory; incorporated as town 1885.

Mont′mar′tre (môN′màr′tr′). Section in N part of Paris, France, occupying a hill above the Seine river; highest point 420 ft. Has large cemetery; an old town now within the city limits and noted for its cafés and night life; often figured in early battles and sieges.

Mont′mé′dy′ (môN′mā′dē′). Town, Meuse dept., NE France, near Belgian frontier 25 m. N of Verdun; pop. 1568; has citadel and old town, built 1235; became French 1659, fortified by Louis XIV.

Mont′mo·ren′cy (mŏnt′mô·rĕn′sĭ). **1** County in Michigan. See *Table* at MICHIGAN.
2 River ab. 60 m. long, Montmorency co., S Quebec, Canada; flows S into St. Lawrence river 6 m. below Quebec; has rapid current, fine scenery, and contains famous waterfalls (see 4, below).
3 County, Quebec, Canada. See *Table* at QUEBEC.
4 Village, Quebec co., S Quebec, Canada, on N bank of the St. Lawrence at mouth of Montmorency river (see 2, above) 6 m. NE of Quebec, at **Montmorency Falls** (265 ft. in one fall) which furnish light and power for Quebec city; pop. 5817.
5 (*Fr.* môN′mô′rän′sē′) Commune, Seine-et-Oise dept., N France, 9 m. N of Paris; pop. 10,535; 16th-cent. Gothic church. Formerly seat of Montmorency family; under Condé family (1689 ff.) and until the Revolution called **En′ghien′** (*Fr.* äN′gän′; *Belg.* -gyăn′); Rousseau resided in hermitage here 1756–57.

Mon·to′ne (mŏn·tō′nå). River 45 m. long, N cen. Italy; flows NE into Adriatic Sea 6 m. NE of Ravenna.

Mon·to′ro (môn·tō′rô). Commune, Córdoba prov., S Spain, on Guadalquivir river 22 m. ENE of Córdoba; pop. 14,980; produces olive oil, tropical fruits, timber.

Mon·tour′ (mŏn·tōōr′; *attributively,* mŏn′tōōr). County in Pennsylvania. See *Table* at PENNSYLVANIA.

Montour Falls. Village, Schuyler co., SW cen. New York, 16 m. N of Elmira; pop. 1533; in Finger Lakes region, near head of Seneca Lake; contains Shequaga Falls, 156-ft. waterfall; manufactures electric hoists.

Mon·tours′ville (mŏn·tōōrz′vĭl). Residential borough, Lycoming co., N cen. Pennsylvania, 5 m. E of Williamsport; pop. 5211; settled 1807; manufactures silk products, Venetian blinds.

Mont′par′nasse′ (môN′pàr′nàs′). Quarter in S cen. Paris, a center since late 19th century of Parisian artistic, student, and bohemian life; many noted cafés. Has Montparnasse Cemetery, 3d in size among Paris cemeteries, laid out 1824.

Mont·pe′lier (mŏnt·pēl′yēr). **1** City, Bear Lake co., SE Idaho, 70 m. SE of Pocatello; pop. 3146; railroad division point; settled 1864 by Mormons; phosphate rock.
2 Town, Blackford co., E cen. Indiana, 20 m. E of Marion; pop. 1954.
3 Village, Williams co., NW corner of Ohio, on St. Joseph river 55 m. W of Toledo; pop. 4131.
4 City, ✱ of Vermont and ⊗ of Washington co., N cen. Vermont, on Winooski river; pop. 8782. Settled c. 1788; became capital 1805, city 1895. Center of granite industry; manufactures granite monuments, maple sirup and sugar. Birthplace of Admiral George Dewey.

Mont′pel′lier′ (môN′pĕ′lyā′). Manufacturing and commercial city, ✱ of Hérault dept., S France, near Mediterranean 77 m. WNW of Marseilles; pop. 90,787; tourist, winter, and health resort; notable structures include a château, citadel, cathedral, palace of justice, Doric triumphal arch; university (founded 1289); oldest botanical garden in France (dating from 1593); manufactures cotton goods, soap, candles, verdigris, chemicals. Founded in 8th cent. around Benedictine abbey; Huguenot stronghold, captured 1622 by Louis XIII. Birthplace of the philosopher Comte.

Mont′re·al′ (mŏn′trē·ôl′; mŭn′-). **1** River ab. 40 m. long, N Wisconsin; rises in Iron co., flows NW and forms section of Wisconsin-Michigan boundary, empties into Lake Superior.
2 City, Iron co., N Wisconsin, 33 m. ESE of Ashland; pop. 1361; iron mining; ships iron ore.
3 *Fr.* **Mont′ré′al′** (môN′rā′àl′). City, ⊗ of Hochelaga co. (part of Montreal and Jesus Islands co.), on SE Montreal I., S Quebec, Canada, on the N bank of the St. Lawrence river; pop. (of city proper) 1,021,520. Named from Mount Royal, the hill in its center. Canada's largest city (see GREATER MONTREAL), main business and banking center and chief port of entry; its port is active terminal for both ocean-going and inland shipping, the latter via Lachine Canal (*q.v.*); largest seaport in the world at a distance from the ocean—1000 m. from the open sea, 870 m. from Belle Isle, and 180 m. above Quebec; great railroad and transportation center of E Canada; has three bridges over the St. Lawrence. Exports principally timber, grain, flour, cattle, butter,

MONTREAL
AND VICINITY
Statute Miles
0 1 2 3 4 5 6 7 8

cheese, furs; manufactures textiles, machinery, shoes, rubber, paints, electrical goods, and lumber. Population predominantly Roman Catholic and of French extraction (ab. 63%). Contains many churches (esp. St. James Cathedral and Notre Dame), religious institutions, libraries, museums, and many fine public parks. Seat of McGill Univ. (1821; coed.), Montreal Univ. (1878; coed.), and of College of Sainte Marie (1848; men), Loyola Coll. (1896; men).

History: Occupied by Indian town of Hochelaga (*q.v.*) when visited by Jacques Cartier 1535; permanent settlement made by Sieur de Maisonneuve 1642 and given the name **Ville-Ma′rie′ de Montréal** (vĭl′mà′rē′dē); its residents constantly embroiled with the Iroquois; the island abandoned by original company 1663 and turned over to Seminary of St. Sulpice; became center of fur trade and starting point for expeditions into the interior; last Canadian city held by the French, surrendering to the British in 1760; occupied briefly by American troops 1775–76; seat of Canadian government 1844–49.

Montreal and Je′sus Islands (jē′zŭs). County, S Quebec, Canada, formed from two islands on N side of the St. Lawrence river: Montreal I., also known as Mon-

treal co., subdivided into the counties of Hochelaga (⊗ Montreal) and Jacques Cartier (⊗ Pointe Claire), total area 201 sq. m., pop. 1,320,232, and Jesus I., equivalent to Laval co., 93 sq. m., pop. 37,843, ⊗ Sainte Rose.

Montreal East; *Fr.* **Montréal–Est** (-ěst′). Town, Montreal I., S Quebec, Canada, on St. Lawrence river 8 m. N of Montreal; pop. 4513.

Montreal Island. Island 32 m. long by 10 m. wide in St. Lawrence river, Quebec, E Canada; site of the city of Montreal and its residential suburbs; contains two counties, subdivisions of Montreal and Jesus Islands co.; Hochelaga in the N and Jacques Cartier in the S; pop. 1,320,232.

Montreal Lake. Lake 137 sq. m. in N cen. Saskatchewan, Canada; lower section is in Prince Albert National Park.

Montreal North; *Fr.* **Montréal–Nord** (-nôr′). Town, Montreal I., S Quebec, Canada, on Rivière des Prairies 8 m. N of Montreal; pop. 14,081; woodworking plant.

Montreal South; *Fr.* **Montréal–Sud** (-sü′). Town, Chambly co., S Quebec, Canada, on S bank of St. Lawrence river across from Montreal; pop. 4214.

Montreal West; *Fr.* **Montréal–Ouest** (-wěst′). Residential town, Montreal I., S Quebec, Canada, 6 m. SW of Montreal; pop. 3721.

Mon′treuil′ (môn′trû′y′); *also* **Montreuil–sous–Bois** (-sōō-bwä′). Commune, Seine dept., N France, E suburb of Paris; pop. 71,803; 12th-cent. church; manufactures chemicals, porcelain, rubber goods, furniture; produces fine fruit, esp. cherries and peaches.

Mon′treux′ (môn′trû′). Group of villages forming the communes of Le Châtelard and Les Planches in Vaud canton, W Switzerland; pop. ab. 19,795; a well-known resort at the E end of Lake of Geneva. Here in June 1936 a conference of European states met to revise the Straits Convention with Turkey.

Mon·trose′ (mǒn·trōz′; mǒn′trōz). **1** County in Colorado. See *Table* at COLORADO.
2 City, ⊗ of Montrose co., W Colorado, 57 m. SE of Grand Junction; pop. 5044; founded 1882; trade center for irrigated agricultural region; stock raising; radium mines nearby.
3 Borough and summer resort, ⊗ of Susquehanna co., NE Pennsylvania, 31 m. NNW of Scranton; pop. 2363.
4 Seaport burgh, Angus co., E Scotland, at mouth of the South Esk; pop. 10,760; fishing and shipbuilding center; popular resort; scene of John de Baliol's surrender 1296 to Edward I.

Mon·tross′ (mǒn·trǒs′; mǒn′trǒs). Town, ⊗ of Westmoreland co., E Virginia; pop. 394.

Mont′rouge′ (môn′rōōzh′); *also* **Le Grand–Mont′– rouge′** (lē grän′-); *anc.* **Mons Ru′bi·cus** (mǒnz rōō′-bĭ·kŭs). Commune, Seine dept., N France, S suburb of Paris; pop. 33,260; catacombs; manufactures paper, perfumery, precision instruments.

Mont Roy′al′ (môn rwä′yàl′). **1** See ROYAL, MOUNT.
2 See MOUNT ROYAL.

Monts, Pointe de (pwăňt′ dĕ môn′). Headland in Saguenay co., Quebec, Canada, on the St. Lawrence river; in 67°22′ W.

Mont–Saint–Amand. See SINT AMANDSBERG.

Mont–Saint–Jean (môn′săn′zhän′). Village in Belgium S of the village of Waterloo and N of the battlefield.

Mont–Saint–Mar′tin′ (môn′săn′mår′tăn′). Town, Meurthe-et-Moselle dept., NE France, on the frontier near meeting point of Belgian-Luxembourg-French boundaries; pop. 5146; steelworks, in a region of iron mines.

Mont–Saint–Mi′chel′ (môn′săn′mē′shĕl′). Fortified rock in **Mont–Saint–Michel Bay,** off the SW coast of Manche dept., NW France; remarkable ancient abbey and town on the summit of the rock.

Mont′sec′ (môn′sĕk′). Hill, Meuse dept., NE France,

near St-Mihiel; memorial on summit commemorates operations of American forces in St-Mihiel sector in World War I.

Mont·seny′ (mônt·sän′y′). Peak 5713 ft. in Barcelona prov., NE Spain, NE of Barcelona.

Mont′ser·rat′ (mŏnt′sĕ·rät′). **1** Island, a territory of the Leeward Islands, West Indies Federation, 27 m. SW of Antigua; area 33 sq. m.; pop. (1958) 14,465; ✻ Plymouth. Entirely volcanic, with three groups of mountains, the highest Soufrière 3002 ft.; mountains forested and much cultivated, giving island its name "Emerald Island of the West." Chief products cotton lint, cotton seed, fruits, and vegetables. Discovered by Columbus 1493; colonized by British from St. Kitts 1632; captured and held by French 1664–68 and 1782–84.
2 (*Span.* mônt′sĕr·rät′) Mountain 4072 ft. in Barcelona prov., NE Spain; has very jagged ridge, hence the name (*Lat.* Mons Serratus); site of a famous monastery dating according to legend from 880.

Mont–sur–Mar′chienne′ (môn′sür·mår′shyěn′). Commune, Hainaut prov., SW Belgium; pop. 10,901; S suburb of Charleroi.

Mont Trem′blant′ Park (môn trän′blän′). Canadian provincial park in S Quebec prov., N of Montreal.

Mon·tuo′sa (môn·twō′sä). Small island in Pacific Ocean off SW coast of Panama.

Mont Valérien. See Mont VALÉRIEN.

Mont′ville (mŏnt′vĭl). **1** Town, cen. New London co., SE Connecticut, on Thames river; pop. 7759; incorporated 1786; silk and cotton goods, paper products.
2 Village, Morris co., N New Jersey, 11 m. W of Paterson; pop. (est.) 1200.

Mon′u·ment Peak (mŏn′ů·mĕnt). Mountain 8956 ft. in N Adams co., W Idaho.

Monument Valley. Region in NE Arizona and SE Utah, a sandy plain from which rise monumentlike buttes 1000 ft. high, also mesas and arches, all of red sandstone; to the W of the valley is Rainbow Bridge National Monument and to the N Natural Bridges National Monument (see UNITED STATES, *National Monuments*).

Monviso. See Mount VISO.

Mon′ywa′ (mōn′yōō·wä′). Town, ✻ of Lower Chindwin dist., Burma, on left bank of lower Chindwin river 55 m. W of Mandalay; pop. 10,800. In World War II a Japanese communications center captured by British Jan. 22, 1945.

Mon′za (mŏn′tsä). Commune, Milano prov., Lombardy, N Italy, 10 m. NE of Milan; pop. 63,922; cathedral (founded 595 by Lombard queen Theodalinda; remodeled in 14th cent.); 13th-cent. town hall; palace of old Lombard kings; manufactures wool, carpets, silks, leather, brick and tile, hats. Ancient capital of Lombardy; scene of assassination of Humbert I of Italy 1900.

Monze, Cape. See Ras MUARI.

Moo′dus (mōō′dŭs). Subdivision of town of EAST HADDAM, Connecticut; pop. 1103.

Moo′dy (mōō′dĭ). County in South Dakota. See *Table* at SOUTH DAKOTA.

Mooltan. See MULTAN.

Moon. See MUHU.

Moon, Mountains of the. See Mount RUWENZORI.

Moo·nach′ie (mōō·năch′ê). Borough, Bergen co., NE corner of New Jersey, 8 m. SE of Paterson; pop. 3052.

Moor. See MÓR.

Moore (mōr; mŏor). Name of counties in three states in the U.S. See *Tables* at NORTH CAROLINA, TENNESSEE, TEXAS.

Moore, Lake. Lake in SW Salt Lake Region, Western Australia, NE of Perth.

Mo′o·ré′a (mō′ô·rā′å) *or* **Ei·me′o** (ī·mā′ō). One of E group (Windward Is.) of the Society Is., French Polynesia, S Pacific Ocean, 12 m. W of Papeete; 51 sq. m.; pop. (1941) 2279; mountainous, with highest peaks nearly 4000 ft.

Moore'field (mōr'fēld; mŏŏr'-). **1** River 50 m. long, E West Virginia; rises in SE Pendleton co., flows NE into South Branch of Potomac river at Moorefield in Hardy co.
2 Town, ⊗ of Hardy co., NE West Virginia; pop. 1434.
Moore Haven (mōr; mŏŏr). City, ⊗ of Glades co., S cen. Florida penin.; pop. 790.
Moores (mōrz; mŏŏrz). Locality, Delaware co., SE Pennsylvania, ab. 5 m. SE of Media.
Moores Creek National Military Park. See UNITED STATES, *National Historical Parks.*
Moores'town (mōrz'toun; mŏŏrz'-). Township, Burlington co., S cen. New Jersey, 9 m. E of Camden; pop. 12,497; Hessian headquarters 1776; truck and fruit farms.
Moores'ville (-vĭl; *Sou. also* -v'l). **1** Town, Morgan co., cen. Indiana, 15 m. SW of Indianapolis; pop. 3856.
2 Town, Iredell co., cen. North Carolina, 13 m. S of Statesville; pop. 6918; manufactures towels, cotton goods; tobacco and dairy farms.
Moor'foot' Hills (mōr'fŏŏt'; mŏŏr'-). Range of hills in SE Midlothian co. and along the border of Peebles co., SE Scotland; highest peak **Black'hope' Scar** (blăk'hōp' skär') 2136 ft.
Moor'head (mōr'hĕd; mŏŏr'-). **1** City, ⊗ of Clay co., W Minnesota, on Red River across from Fargo, North Dakota; pop. 22,934; important potato-growing section; dairy products, poultry. Concordia College (1891; coed.; Lutheran); Moorhead State College (1885; coed.).
2 Town, Sunflower co., W Mississippi, 19 m. W of Greenwood; pop. 1754; in cotton-growing section.
Moors'le'de (mōrs'lā'dĕ). Commune, West Flanders prov., NW Belgium, SW of Roeselare; pop. 5944; fighting during World War I.
Moos'burg (mōs'bŏŏrк). Town, Upper Bavaria govt. dist., Bavaria, Germany, on Isar river ab. 10 m. WSW of Landshut; pop. 4179; site of large prisoner-of-war camp in World War II, captured Apr. 29, 1945 by American forces and 110,000 prisoners liberated.
Moose (mŏŏs). River ab. 50 m. long, NE Ontario prov., Canada, flowing NE into James Bay; a wide stream, actually the estuary of the Abitibi, Mattagami, Missinaibi, and other rivers. Moosonee is near its mouth.
Moose Factory. Post adjacent to Moosonee (*q.v.*), on Moose river, NE Ontario, Canada; trading port of Hudson's Bay Co. on James Bay.
Moose'head Lake (mŏŏs'hĕd). Lake ab. 35 m. long and 10 m. wide on boundary bet. Piscataquis and Somerset cos., NW cen. Maine; elevation ab. 1000 ft.; resort for fishermen and sportsmen.
Moose Jaw (mŏŏs' jô'). City, S Saskatchewan, Canada, 43 m. W of Regina; pop. 24,355; important for its railroad connections; has grain elevators, mills, and extensive stockyards; lignite and clay deposits; flax is grown extensively; Saskatchewan Presbyterian College. Founded 1882.
Moose Lake. Lake 552 sq. m., W Manitoba, Canada; has several outlets to Saskatchewan river and Cedar Lake.
Moose'look·me·gun'tic Lake (mŏŏs'lŏŏk·mē·gŭn'tĭk). See RANGELEY LAKES.
Moose Mountain (mŏŏs). **1** Peak 3921 ft. in Adirondack Mts., Essex co., NE New York.
2 Peak 11,000 ft. in W Park co., NW Wyoming.
Moose Mountain Park. Canadian provincial park, SE Saskatchewan prov., SE of Regina; 192 sq. m.; fine scenery and fishing, with many lakes.
Moose Peak. Mountain 7521 ft. in W Flathead co., NW Montana.
Moo'sic (mŏŏ'sĭk). Borough, Lackawanna co., NE Pennsylvania, 5 m. SW of Scranton; pop. 4243; coal mining.
Moo'si·lauke, Mount (mŏŏ'sĭ·lôk'). Peak 4810 ft. in cen. Grafton co., W New Hampshire.
Moos'o·nee (mŏŏs''n·ē). Trading station and port on Moose river, Cochrane dist., Ontario, Canada; pop.

(with Moose Factory) 526; terminus of railroad from Cochrane.
Moo'sup (mŏŏ'sŭp). Subdivision of town of PLAINFIELD, Connecticut; manufacturing; pop. 2760.
Mop'po (mŏp'ō) *or* **Mok'po** (mŏk'pō). City, South Zenra prov., Korea; pop. (1938 est.) 65,572; has fine harbor; exports chiefly raw cotton and rice; opened to foreign trade 1897.
Mop'su·es'ti·a (mŏp'sŭ·ĕs'chĭ·à); *mod.* **Mi·sis'** (mĕsēs'). Ancient city in Cilicia, Asia Minor, on the Pyramus (Ceyhan) river, now a village in Seyhan vilayet, S Turkey in Asia. Birthplace of Theodore of Mopsuestia.
Mop'ti (mŏp'tē). Town on Niger river, cen. Sudan, cen. West Africa, on E edge of Niger depression area ab. 275 m. NE of Bamako; pop. (1940) 4790.
Mo·que'gua (mō·kā'gwä). **1** Department of Peru. See *Table* at PERU.
2 Town, its ✱, ab. 530 m. SE of Lima, and terminus of the railroad from the port of Ilo, 60 m. S; pop. ab. 5000; founded 1626; destroyed by earthquake 1868.
Mór (mōr); *Ger.* **Moor** (mōr). Commune, 43 m. W of Budapest, W Hungary; pop. 11,510.
Mo'ra (mōr'à). **1** County in New Mexico. See *Table* at NEW MEXICO.
2 Village, ⊗ of Kanabec co., E Minnesota, 47 m. ENE of St. Cloud; pop. 2329.
3 Village, ⊗ of Mora co., NE New Mexico, 40 m. NE of Santa Fe; pop. 4150.
4 (*Span.* mō'rä) Commune, Toledo prov., cen. Spain, 18 m. SE of Toledo; pop. 10,441; olive oil, wine.
Mo'ra Bay (mō'rä). Bay in SW coast of Oriente prov. E Cuba.
Mo'ra·ča (mō'rä·chä). Small river in S Yugoslavia, flowing S into Lake Scutari.
Mo·rad'a·bad (mō·räd'à·bäd; mō·rǎd'à·bǎd). City, Rohilkhand division, NW cen. Uttar Pradesh, N Indian Union, on right bank of Ramganga river 90 m. E of Delhi; pop. (1941) 142,414; founded 1625 by Rustam Khan; has impressive fort and fine mosque built by its founder; noted for its ornamental brassware; supports cotton industry.
Mo'ra·le'da Channel (mō'rä·lā'thä). Passage bet. Chonos Archipelago off SW coast of Chile and the Chilean mainland.
Mo'ra·man'ga (mō'rä·mäng'gä). Town, E cen. Madagascar; railroad junction 45 m. E of Tananarive.
Mo·ran', Mount (mō·rǎn'). Peak 12,594 ft. in N Grand Teton National Park, NW Wyoming.
Mo·rant' Bay (mō·rǎnt'). Town (pop. ab. 7000) and bay, SE coast of island of Jamaica, West Indies.
Morant Cays. Three small guano islands 33 m. SE of Morant Bay, off SE coast of Jamaica; a dependency of Jamaica from 1882.
Morant Point. Cape at E end of Jamaica, West Indies.
Mor'ar, Loch (lŏк mōr'ēr). Lake in W Inverness co., on coast of W cen. Scotland, 1½ m. S of Lake Nevis.
Mo'rat' (mō'rà'); *Ger.* **Mur'ten** (mŏŏr'tĕn). Commune, Fribourg canton, 'Switzerland, on E shore of Lake of Morat; pop. 2240; scene of Swiss victory over Charles the Bold of Burgundy June 22, 1476.
Morat, Lake of. Small lake ab. 5½ m. long and 2 m. wide in Switzerland, 2 m. SE of the Lake of Neuchâtel.
Morata. See GOODENOUGH.
Mo'ra·tal'la (mō'rä·tä'[l]yä). Commune, Murcia prov., SE Spain, 39 m. WNW of Murcia; pop. 14,536; manufactures brandy, soap, flour, textiles.
Mo·ra·tu·wa (?mō·rä'tŏŏ·wä). Town, W Western Province, Ceylon, on Indian Ocean 12 m. S of Colombo; pop. 32,409; fine woodcarving; seat of a college.
Mo'ra·va (*Czech* mō'rä·và; *Yugoslav* mō'rä·vä). **1** See MARCH river, Czechoslovakia.
2 See MORAVIA former province, Czechoslovakia.
3 *anc.* **Mar'gus** (mär'gŭs). River in E Yugoslavia, formed by confluence of **Southern Morava** and **Western Morava** at a point 33 m. NW of Niš; flows

NNW into Danube river near Smederevo; 100 m. long from point of confluence to the Danube; the Western Morava receives the Ibar from the S.

Mo·ra'vi·a (mô·rä'vĭ·à); *Czech* **Mo'ra·va** (mô'rà·và); *Ger.* **Mäh'ren** (mâ'rĕn). Former province, cen. Czechoslovakia, now part of the province of Moravia and Silesia.

History: Settled by a Slavic people, Moravians, from end of 6th cent. A.D.; became tributary to empire of Charlemagne (d. 843); introduced to Christianity by Cyril and Methodius; under Svatopluk, Great Moravia (including Bohemia and other territories in cen. Europe) revolted against German emperor and became independent kingdom 870; defeated by Magyars who settled in Tisza valley 893; conquered by Magyars (see HUNGARY) 906; in 10th cent., made part of Bohemian, and briefly, of Polish kingdoms; in 1029 reconquered by Bohemia (*q.v.*); in 1849 became a separate crownland of Austria, with capital at Brno, and in 1918 a part of Czechoslovakia. See MORAVIA AND SILESIA.

Moravia and Silesia; *Czech* **Mo'ra·va a Slez'sko** (mô'rà·và à slĕs'kô). Province, cen. Czechoslovakia, formed by uniting former provinces of Moravia (8627 sq. m.) and Silesia (1719 sq. m.) in the N; total area 10,346 sq. m.; pop. (1930) 3,565,010; ✻ of Moravia, Brno; ✻ of Silesia, Opava. Separated from Polish Silesia on N by Sudeten Mts., from Slovakia on E by White Carpathian Mts., and from Bohemia on W by Bohemian-Moravian Highlands; touches Austria on the S; occupies the larger part of the basin of the March (*Czech* Morava) which with its tributaries flows generally S; part of the March forms SE boundary; in Silesia is source of the Oder (*Czech* Odra). Agriculture, livestock raising, textile, steel, and machinery manufactures. Chief cities Brno, Moravská Ostrava, Olomouc, Prostějov, and Přerov, in Moravia, and Opava in Silesia. Both Moravia and Silesia (*qq.v.*) became provinces of Czechoslovakia 1918; united as one administrative unit 1927. All of Silesia and some sections in N and S Moravia became parts of German Sudetenland 1938; rest of Moravia joined with Bohemia as German protectorate 1939–45 of Bohemia-Moravia (*q.v.*).

Mo·ra'vi·an Gap *or* **Gate** (mô·rā'vĭ·ǎn). Mountain pass (alt. less than 1000 ft.) and ancient trade (amber) route in cen. Europe along upper courses of Oder and Vistula rivers bet. SE Sudeten and W Carpathian Mts. where former German Silesia, Poland, and Czechoslovakia meet. In modern history a strategic communications line bet. N and S.

Mo'rav·ska (mô'răv·skä). Former county (1929–45), E Yugoslavia; 10,120 sq. m.; pop. 1,452,967; ⊗ Niš; since 1945 part of the federated republic of Serbia.

Mo'rav·ská O'stra·va (mô'ràf·skä ô'strà·và); *Ger.* **Mäh'risch–Os'trau** (mâ'rĭsh·ôs'trou). City, N Moravia prov., cen. Czechoslovakia, near confluence of Oppa and Oder rivers near Moravian Gap; pop. (1930) 125,347; manufacturing center in coal-mining area; blast furnaces; has grown rapidly in recent years.

Mor'a·whan'na (môr'à·hwän'à). Town and small port, extreme N British Guiana, in Essequibo co., 150 m. NW of Georgetown, on the Barima river near Venezuela border; gold discovered in the vicinity c. 1889.

Mor'ay (mŭr'ĭ) *or* **El'gin** (ĕl'gĭn) *or* **El'gin·shire** (-shĭr; -shēr). County, NE Scotland; 476 sq. m.; pop. (1951) 48,211; ⊗ Elgin; the rivers Lossie, Spey, Findhorn; agriculture, livestock grazing, fishing, whisky distilling, sandstone quarrying.

Moray Firth. Deep inlet of the North Sea on NE coast of Scotland; extends inland 39 m.; the city of Inverness is near its head.

Mo·ra·zán' (mō·rä·sän'). Department, NE El Salvador; 909 sq. m.; pop. (1942 est.) 104,976; ✻ San Francisco.

Mor'bi·han' (môr'bē'äN'). Department of France. See *Table* at FRANCE.

Mor'di·al'loc (môr'dĭ·ăl'ŭk). Town, S Victoria, SE Australia, SE suburb of Melbourne on E shore of Port Phillip Bay; pop. 9219.

Mor·do'vi·an Republic (môr·dō'vĭ ǎn), *officially* **Mordovian Autonomous Soviet Socialist Republic.** Autonomous republic, cen. Soviet Russia, Europe, crossed by the Moksha river; 9843 sq. m.; pop. 1,188,598, (1941 est.) 1,248,982; ✻ Saransk; a subdivision of the R.S.F.S.R. Bounded on N by Gorki Region, on NE by Chuvash Republic, on E by Ulyanovsk Region, on S by Penza Region, and on W by Ryazan Region. In central plateau bordering on the black earth region, S and W of the Middle Volga; essentially an agricultural region, but some peasant industries, as woodworking, are well developed; many of the inhabitants follow hunting, fishing, and beekeeping; republic crossed by Moscow-Kuibyshev R.R. Predominant ethnic strain Finno-Ugrian; chief nationalities Mordovian, or Mordvinian, 37%, Russian 57%. The Mordovians, a people of the Finnic branch, are descendants of very early inhabitants of Russia, who have preserved national customs and dress and a literature of songs and legends; are nearly all Christians. Republic, established 1934, has made much progress since the Revolution.

More, Ben. See BEN MORE.

Morea. See PELOPONNESUS peninsula.

Mo·reau' (mô·rō'). River ab. 250 m. long, NW South Dakota; formed by confluence of north and south forks in SW Perkins co. flows E into Missouri river on E boundary of Dewey co.

More'cambe and Hey'sham (mor'kăm, hā'shăm). Municipal borough, Lancashire, NW England, on Morecambe Bay 46 m. N of Liverpool; pop. 37,000; watering place.

Morecambe Bay. Inlet of Irish Sea on NW coast of England; extends inland 16 m. in N Lancashire.

Mo·ree' (mô·rē'). Town, NE New South Wales, SE Australia, on Gwydir river 315 m. N of Sydney; pop. 4361; center of grazing and agricultural district.

More'head (mōr'hĕd). City, ⊗ of Rowan co., NE Kentucky, 37 m. SSE of Maysville; pop. 4170. Morehead State College (1923; coed.).

Morehead City. Town and ocean port, Carteret co., SE North Carolina, on Atlantic Ocean 33 m. SE of New Bern; pop. 5583; resort and fishing center; has 1000-ft. pier, the Ocean Shipping Port Terminal (erected 1935–37).

More'house (mōr'hous). **1** Parish in Louisiana. See *Table* at LOUISIANA.

2 City, New Madrid co., SE Missouri, 32 m. SSW of Cape Girardeau; pop. 1417; woodworking plant.

Mo·re'lia (mô·rā'lyä). City, SW Mexico, ✻ of Michoacán state; pop. 44,304; altitude 6200 ft.; first settled 1541; cathedral founded 1640; in cattle-raising and farming area.

Mo·re'los (mô·rā'lôs). State, S cen. Mexico. See *Table* at MEXICO.

Morena, Sierra. See SIERRA MORENA.

Mo·re'na Dam (mô·rē'nà). Dam completed 1930 across Cottonwood Creek, S San Diego co., SW California; height 279 ft.; impounds water for water supply.

Mo·ren'ci (mô·rĕn'sĭ). **1** Town, Greenlee co., SE Arizona; pop. 2431; copper mines.

2 City, Lenawee co., S Michigan, on Ohio border 38 m. S of Jackson; pop. 2053.

Mo·re'no (mô·rā'nô). Town, Buenos Aires prov., E Argentina, ab. 20 m. W of Buenos Aires.

Moreno Bay. Inlet of Pacific Ocean in W Antofagasta prov., N Chile; location of the city of Antofagasta.

Mö're og Roms'dal (mü'rĕ ô rŏms'däl; rōoms'-). County of Norway. See *Table* at NORWAY.

Mores'by Island (mōrz'bĭ). Central island of the Queen Charlotte Is. off W British Columbia, Canada.

Mo'res'net' (mô'rĕz'nĕ'). Former neutral territory bet. Belgium and Germany near Aachen; 11 sq. m.; since

1919 comprises the communes of Moresnet (pop. 1330), Neu-Moresnet (pop. 592), and La Calamine (pop. 4463), Liége prov., E Belgium.

More'ton Bay (môr't'n). Bay 65 m. long, inlet of Pacific Ocean on SE coast of Queensland, Australia, at mouth of Brisbane river, enclosed on E by **Moreton Island.**

Mo'rez' (mô'râz'). Town, SE Jura dept., E France; pop. 5020; manufactures clocks and spectacles; tourist resort, winter sports.

Mor'gan (môr'găn). 1 Name of counties in eleven states of the U.S. See *Tables* at ALABAMA, COLORADO, GEORGIA, ILLINOIS, INDIANA, KENTUCKY, MISSOURI, OHIO, TENNESSEE, UTAH, WEST VIRGINIA.

2 City, ⊗ of Calhoun co., SW Georgia; pop. 293.

3 City, ⊗ of Morgan co., N Utah; pop. 1299.

Morgan, Mount. 1 Peak 8700 ft. in Glacier National Park, NW Montana.

2 Peak 6144 ft. in Australian Capital Territory, Australia.

Morgan City. City, St. Mary parish, S Louisiana, 53 m. S of Baton Rouge; pop. 13,540; fishing and hunting center in a bayou section; muskrat, mink, and otter furs.

Mor'gan-field (môr'găn-fēld). City, ⊗ of Union co., W Kentucky, 22 m. WSW of Henderson; pop. 3741; in agricultural and livestock-raising section.

Mor'gan-ton (môr'găn-tŭn). Town, ⊗ of Burke co., W North Carolina, 15 m. SSW of Lenoir; pop. 9186; furniture, hosiery, textiles, lumber.

Mor'gan-town (môr'găn-toun). 1 City, ⊗ of Butler co., W cen. Kentucky; pop. 1318.

2 City, ⊗ of Monongalia co., N West Virginia, on Monongahela river 15 m. NE of Fairmont; pop. 22,487; coal mining and shipping, glassmaking; coal, oil, and gas fields, glass-sand pits, limestone quarries; manufactures coke, glass, concrete blocks, plumbing equipment, chemicals. West Virginia Univ. (1867; coed.).

Mor'gar'ten (môr'gär'tĕn). Mountain slope in Zug canton, N cen. Switzerland, on the border of Schwyz canton, just SE of Lake of Aegeri; battle Nov. 15, 1315 in which Swiss defeated greatly superior forces of Hapsburg Duke Leopold I.

Morges (môrzh). Commune, Vaud canton, W Switzerland, on Lake of Geneva; pop. (1930) 5047; famous view of Mont Blanc; birthplace of Fernán Caballero, Spanish novelist.

Mo·ri'ah (mô·rī'à). 1 Region and hill in S part of ancient Palestine on which Abraham prepared to sacrifice Isaac (*Gen.* xxii. 2); its location is unidentified.

2 Hill in E part of Jerusalem, on which Solomon built the Temple (*2 Chron.* iii. 1).

Moriah, Mount. Peak 4065 ft., SE Coos co., N New Hampshire, in E White Mts. N of Carter Dome.

Mo'ring·en (mō'rĭng·ĕn). Town, SE Lower Saxony state, W Germany, 12 m. N of Göttingen; pop. 2500; Nazi concentration camp 1939.

Mo·ri·o·ka (mô·rė·ō·kä). City, ✳ of Iwate prefecture, N Honshu, Japan, on the Kitakami river; pop. (1945) 95,748; trades in textiles and ironware. A daimio castle town since 1596.

Mor·lac'ca (môr·läk'kä; *Angl.* môr·läk'à). Channel along the coast of Croatia, N Yugoslavia, bet. Krk I. and the mainland.

Mor'laix' (môr'lĕ'). Commercial seaport, Finistère dept., NW France, on English Channel 42 m. NNE of Quimper; pop. 13,944.

Mor'lan·welz (môr'län·vĕlz). Commune, Hainaut prov., SW Belgium, NW of Charleroi; pop. 8258; ruins of abbey.

Mor'ley (môr'lĭ). Municipal borough, West Riding, Yorkshire, N England, 5 m SW of Leeds; pop. 39,783; woolen mills, glass factories, tanneries; coal deposits nearby.

Mor'mal' Forest (môr'màl'). Wooded region SE of Valenciennes, Nord dept., N France.

Mor'mon Flat' Dam' (môr'mŭn). Dam completed 1925 across Salt river below Horse Mesa Dam, E Maricopa co., S cen. Arizona; height 224 ft.; impounds water for power, forming **Canyon Lake** 10 m. long.

Mormon Lake. Lake 12 sq. m. in SE Coconino co., N cen. Arizona; did not exist before 1900; formed when underground drainage channels became filled with sediment.

Mormon Mountain. Peak 9545 ft. in NE Valley co., W cen. Idaho.

Mor'mu·gão' (môr'mōō·goun'); *formerly* **Mar'ma-gão'** (mär'mȧ·goun'). Seaport on peninsula, Goa, Portuguese India, 7 m. S of Pangim and ab. 225 m. S of Bombay; pop. 9500; fine harbor, opened 1887; railroad terminus; has steamer connections with Europe. Meeting place Oct. 1943 of *Teia Maru* and *Gripsholm*, Japanese and United Nations exchange ships.

Mor'ning·ton Island (môr'nĭng·tŭn). Island in Pacific Ocean off SW coast of Chile, W of S Wellington I.

Mo'ro (môr'ō). City, ⊗ of Sherman co., N Oregon; pop. 327.

Mo·ro'be (mô·rō'bȧ). 1 Administrative district, SE North-East New Guinea, on mainland of the Territory of New Guinea; 14,200 sq. m.; pop. (1930) 58,526. In the interior, in the Bulolo Valley near the town of Wau, is the Morobe gold field where in 1921 very rich gold deposits were discovered; region bet. Bulolo and the coast towns of Salamaua and Lae exceptionally mountainous and difficult so that practically all transport to and from mines is by air (ab. 46 m.) bet. Lae and Wau.

2 Seaport town, its ✳, on SE coast of Huon Gulf near Papua border, 95 m. SSE of Lae; has good harbor.

Mo·roc'co (mô·rŏk'ō). 1 *Arab.* **El Ma'ghreb el Aq'sa** [ăl mŭ'grĭb ăl ŭk'sä] (literally "the Far West"); *Fr.* **Ma'roc'** (mȧ'rôk'); *Span.* **Mar·rue'cos** (mär·rwä'kŏs). Sultanate, NW Africa, bounded on N by the Mediterranean Sea, on E and S by Algeria (SE boundary largely undetermined), on SW by Río de Oro, and on W by the Atlantic Ocean; area ab. 173,700 sq. m., pop. (est. 1960) 10,780,000; ✳ Rabat; traditional capitals, Fez and Marrakesh; from 1912 to 1956 comprised 3 zones: **French Morocco,** protectorate including most of Morocco, and having a long Atlantic coast line with no natural harbors; 153,870 sq. m., pop. (1936) 6,298,528 (1952 est.) 9,140,000; ✳ Rabat; **Spanish Morocco,** a protectorate on the N coast, 18,009 sq. m., pop. (1940) 991,000, ✳ Tetuán; and an international zone including city of Tangier and surrounding territory, 225 sq. m., pop. (1941 est.) 100,000; encloses on SW coast the small Spanish territory of Ifni (*q.v.*) and according to some included the Spanish Southern Protectorate of Morocco (see SOUTHERN PROTECTORATE OF MOROCCO). Physical features are the great mountain range of Grand Atlas and its smaller subsidiary ranges (see ATLAS MOUNTAINS) stretching from SW to NE, the mountainous Er Rif belt along the Mediterranean, the wide fertile plain along the Atlantic, and the plain, partly desert, in the SE beyond the Atlas range; highest point Toubkal 13,661 ft. Rivers of the Atlantic plain are numerous but short; chief are the Moulouya in N and the Tensift; many short streams on SE slopes of the Atlas are lost in the Sahara. Agriculture most important industry; chief products cereals, olives, grapes, citrus fruits, almonds; cattle raising also important. Chief cities: Casablanca, Fez, Marrakesh, Meknes, Rabat, Tangier, Tetuán. The cities of Ceuta and Melilla and several smaller garrisoned areas in the former Spanish zone were retained after 1957 by Spain.

History: Roman province of Mauretania (*q.v.*) underwent Moslem invasion 7th cent. A.D.; in 11th cent. founded independent kingdom under Almoravides, a Berber dynasty which conquered Spain and Portugal but was overthrown in 1147 by the Almohades; Ceuta taken by Portuguese 1415; Morocco invaded by Portuguese who were completely defeated 1578 (see ALCÁZARQUIVIR); Tangier held by England 1662-84; Mazagan, last

Portuguese stronghold, abandoned 1769; as one of Barbary States (see BARBARY), engaged in piracy until early 19th cent.; engaged in hostilities with French 1844 over Algerian boundary; in war against Spain 1859–73; control of Morocco became issue of European politics after Convention of Madrid (1880); with growth of internal disorder, independence question led to agreements bet. France and England (*Entente Cordiale* 1904) and bet. France and Spain, the latter reserving the northern Mediterranean coast for Spain; French rights in Morocco asserted in 1st and 2d Moroccan crises 1905 and 1911 (see TANGIER, ALGECIRAS, AGADIR); in 1912, larger part became French protectorate, north coast Spanish zone; Tangier internationalized 1923; in Spanish zone occurred bitter war of Abd-el-Krim 1921–26; Ifni under effective Spanish occupation 1934; Melilla scene of revolt of army chiefs which led to Spanish Civil War 1936; signed accords with both France and Spain 1956 by which it received independence.

2 City, one of traditional capitals of Morocco: see MARRAKESH.

Mo·ro·co·ca′la (mō′rō·kō·kä′lä). Peak 17,060 ft. in W Bolivia, E of N end of Lake Poopó.

Mo·ro·go′ro (mō′rō·gō′rō). Town, E Tanganyika, SE Africa; pop. ab. 6000; mica and uranium in vicinity; captured by British from Germans Aug. 26, 1916 during World War I.

Mo′ro Gulf (mōr′ō). Large inlet in N part of Celebes Sea, SW of Mindanao, Phil. Is.

Mo′ro·land′ (mōr′ō·lǎnd′). Popular name sometimes given to islands in S of Phil. Is. where the Moros live, esp. Mindanao and the Sulu Archipelago.

Mo·ro·le·ón′ (mō′rō·lâ·ôn′). Town, Guanajuato state, cen. Mexico, 60 m. S of Guanajuato; pop. 10,418.

Mo·ron′ (mô·rôn′). Municipality on W coast of Bataan prov., Luzon, Phil. Is., 20 m. W of Balanga on SE side of entrance to Subic Bay; pop. 3301; in World War II scene of strong attack by Japanese early in Bataan campaign; captured by Japanese Jan. 23, 1942.

Mo·rón′ (mô·rôn′). **1** City, Argentina: see SEIS DE SEPTIEMBRE.

2 Municipality and town, W Camagüey prov., E cen. Cuba; pop. (town) 17,023; town is on railroad 68 m. NW of Camagüey.

3 *in full* **Mo·rón′ de la Fron·te′ra** (mô·rôn′ dǎ lä frôn·tā′rä). Commune, Sevilla prov., SW Spain, 35 m. SE of Seville; pop. 26,575; olive oil; red-hematite mines; marble quarries; Gothic church.

Mo·ro′na (mô·rō′nä). River ab. 230 m. long in Ecuador and Peru; rises in E Ecuador where it is called the **Ma·kum′ma** (mä·kōō′mä), flows S across border into Peru; empties into Marañón river, headstream of the Amazon.

Mo′ron·da′va (mōr′ŭn·dä′và). Coastal town, W Madagascar, in cen. part on Mozambique Channel; pop. (1936) 4293.

Mo′rong (mō′rông). **1** Former Spanish military district, cen. Luzon, Phil. Is., created 1853 from portions of Manila and Laguna provs., N of Laguna de Bay; ❋ Morong; became part of Rizal prov. 1901.

2 Municipality, S Rizal prov., Luzon, Phil. Is., near coast of Laguna de Bay 11 m. ESE of Pasig; pop. 8623.

Moroni. See GREAT COMORO.

Mo·ron′vil′liers′ (mô·rôn′vē′lyä′). Heights ab. 13 m. E of Reims, France; held by Germans through World War I; scene of several battles 1917; taken by Allies Oct. 1918.

Mo′ro Province (mōr′ō). Former province of the Philippines under military government, 1903 to 1914, including most of Mindanao I. (except Misamis and Surigao), the Sulu Archipelago, and Palawan S of 10°. Reorganized 1914 with civil government as the Department of Mindanao and Sulu with seven provinces.

Mo·ro·tai′ (mō′rō·tī′). Island, Indonesia, in the N Moluccas N of Halmahera; ab. 50 m. long by 26 m. wide;

695 sq. m.; pop. 9170; highest point 4100 ft.; air base. Seized by Japanese Jan. 1942 but retaken by Gen. MacArthur's force Sept. 14, 1944.

Mo·ro′vis (mō·rō′vēs). Municipality (pop. 18,094) and town (pop. 2428), N cen. Puerto Rico; town ab. 23 m. SW of San Juan.

Mor′peth (môr′pĕth). Municipal borough, Northumberland, N England, on the Wansbeck 12 m. N of Newcastle; pop. 10,797; iron and brass founding, tanning.

Mor′phou (môr′fōō). Town, NW cen. Cyprus, in Nicosia dist., on railroad line from Famagusta.

Morphou Bay. Inlet of Mediterranean on NW coast of Cyprus; Cape Kormakiti marks its N limit.

Mor′rill (môr′ĭl). County in Nebraska. See *Table* at NEBRASKA.

Mor′ril·ton (môr′ĭl·tŭn; -t'n). City, ⊗ of Conway co., cen. Arkansas, near Arkansas river 40 m. NW of Little Rock; pop. 5997.

Mor′ris (môr′ĭs). **1** Name of counties in three states of the U.S. See *Tables* at KANSAS, NEW JERSEY, TEXAS.

2 City, ⊗ of Grundy co., NE Illinois, 20 m. SW of Joliet; pop. 7935; platted 1842, incorp. 1857.

3 City, ⊗ of Stevens co., W Minnesota, 33 m. SW of Alexandria; pop. 4199.

Mor′ris·burg (môr′ĭs·bûrg). Village, Dundas co., SE Ontario, Canada, on St. Lawrence river 22 m. WSW of Cornwall; pop. 1858.

Mor′ris Dam *and* **Reservoir** (môr′ĭs). See UNITED STATES, *Dams and Reservoirs*.

Morris Island. Island at S of entrance to the harbor of Charleston, South Carolina.

Morris Jes′up, Cape (jĕs′ŭp). Most northerly point of Greenland, in Peary Land on Arctic Ocean, and most northerly point of land known in entire Arctic Region, 83°39′N.

Mor′ri·son (môr′ĭ·s'n). **1** County in Minnesota. See *Table* at MINNESOTA.

2 City, ⊗ of Whiteside co., NW Illinois, 40 m. NE of Rock Island; pop. 4159; dairy products; stove factories.

Morrison, Mount. See NIITAKA.

Morrison Cave. See LEWIS AND CLARK CAVERN.

Mor′ris Plains (môr′ĭs). Borough, Morris co., N New Jersey, 2 m. N of Morristown; pop. 4703; incorporated 1926; manufactures powdered coffee.

Mor′ris·town (môr′ĭs·toun). **1** Town, ⊗ of Morris co., N New Jersey, 17 m. WNW of Newark; pop. 17,712; largely residential city in agricultural region; produces rubber goods, clothing, pharmaceuticals. Morristown National Historical Park (estab. 1933). Settled 1709–10; incorporated 1865; Washington's headquarters 1776–77, 1779–80; scene of electric telegraph experiments of Morse and Vail c. 1837.

2 Village in Morristown town (pop. 1776), St. Lawrence co., N New York, on St. Lawrence river ab. 11 m. SW of Ogdensburg and opp. Brockville, Ontario, Canada; pop. 541; fishing center.

3 City, ⊗ of Hamblen co., NE Tennessee, 42 m. ENE of Knoxville; pop. 21,267; tobacco market; ships poultry and dairy products; manufactures processed silk, lumber.

Morristown National Historical Park. See UNITED STATES, *National Historical Parks*.

Mor′ris·ville (môr′ĭs·vĭl). **1** Borough, Bucks co., SE Pennsylvania, on Delaware river across from Trenton, New Jersey; pop. 7790; manufactures rubber products.

2 Village, Lamoille co., N Vermont, on Lamoille river 20 m. N of Montpelier; pop. 2047; manufactures lumber, dairy products; tannery.

Mor′ro (môr′ō; *Span.* môr′rō). River, Sierra Leone, W Africa, tributary of the Mano.

Morro, Point. Cape extending into Pacific Ocean on W cen. coast of Atacama prov., N cen. Chile, S of Inglesa Bay.

Mor′ro Bay (môr′ō). Inlet of the Pacific, San Luis Obispo co., California, NW of San Luis Obispo; only landlocked harbor between San Francisco and Los Angeles.

Morro Castle. 1 Ancient fortification on E side of entrance to Havana harbor, Cuba; erected 1589–97; taken by English 1762, bombarded by Americans 1898. 2 Fort forming part of defenses of Santiago de Cuba (*q.v.*), SE Cuba, on E side of entrance to harbor.

Mor′ros·quil′lo, Gulf of (môr′rôs·kē′yō). Inlet of Caribbean Sea on NW coast of Colombia, NE of the Gulf of Darien.

Mor′row (mŏr′ō). Name of counties in two states in the U.S. See *Tables* at OHIO and OREGON.

Mörs *or* **Moers** (mûrs). Industrial city, North Rhine-Westphalia, W Germany, WNW of Duisburg; pop. 26,510; coal mining, iron founding; leather, tools, machinery.

Mor·shansk′ (mŭr·shȧnsk′). Town, N Tambov Region, Soviet Russia, Europe, 55 m. N of Tambov; pop. 27,758; industrial town on main railroad line from Tula E to Penza and Kuibyshev; railroad shops, flour mills.

Mors′ö′ (môrs′û′), *or* **Mors Island** (môrs). Island of Denmark, in Lim Fjord in Thisted co., NW Jutland Penin.; 142 sq. m.; pop. (1925) 26,539; chief town Nyköbing.

Mor′tagne′ (môr′tȧn′y′). Town, Orne dept., NW France, NE of Alençon; pop. 2947; noted for horse fairs, was capital of the Perche (*q.v.*); has church of Notre Dame (built 15th–16th cent.).

Mor′tain′ (môr′tăn′). Town, S Manche dept., NW France, E of Avranches; pop. 1340; 13th-cent. Gothic church. Scene of American breakthrough Aug. 3, 1944 and of German counterattacks Aug. 7–11.

Mor·ta′ra (môr·tä′rä). Commune, Pavia prov., Lombardy, N Italy, 22 m. WNW of Pavia; pop. 11,544; 14th-cent. Lombard-Gothic church; 11th-cent. convent; scene of Austrian victory over Piedmontese 1849.

Mor′te·ratsch, Piz (pēts môr′tĕ·räch). Peak 12,315 ft. in the S part of the Rhaetian Alps N of Piz Bernina, Switzerland; famous glacier.

Mort Homme, Le. See LE MORT HOMME.

Mor′ti·mer′s Cross (môr′tĭ·mērz). Village, Herefordshire, W England, ab. 5 m. W of Leominster on the Lugg; scene of battle Feb. 2, 1461 in which Edward IV defeated the Lancastrians.

Mort′lake (môrt′lāk). Parish, Barnes municipal borough, Surrey, S England; pop. 23,879; part of Greater London.

Mor′ton (môr′t′n). 1 Name of counties in two states in the U.S. See *Tables* at KANSAS and NORTH DAKOTA. 2 Village, Tazewell co., cen. Illinois, 10 m. SE of Peoria; pop. 5325. 3 Town, ⊗ of Cochran co., NW Texas; pop. 2731.

Morton Grove. Village, Cook co., NE Illinois, 15 m. N of Chicago; pop. 20,533.

Mort′sel′ (môr′sĕl′). Commune, Antwerp prov., N Belgium; pop. 13,557; S suburb of Antwerp.

Mor′van′ (môr′vän′). Mountain range in E cen. France, in departments of Nièvre, Yonne, Côte-d'Or, and Saône-et-Loire; highest peak Bois-du-Roi 2959 ft.

Mor′ven (môr′vĕn). 1 Peak 2860 ft., NE cen. Scotland, in Aberdeen co. 2 Peak 2313 ft., N Scotland, in Caithness co.

Mor′vi (môr′vē). 1 Former Indian state, N Kathiawar, Western India States, Indian Union; 822 sq. m.; pop. (1941) 141,761; area now in W cen. Gujerat state. 2 Town, its ✳, 40 m. N of Rajkot; pop. 18,934.

Mosa. See MEUSE.

Mos′ca Pass (mŏs′kȧ). Mountain pass 9713 ft., Huerfano and Saguache cos., S Colorado, in Sangre de Cristo Range of the Rocky Mts.; road and trail; used since 1850, one of important passes on Arkansas river route to California and New Mexico.

Mos′cow (mŏs′kō). City, ⊗ of Latah co., NW Idaho, on Washington border 25 m. N of Lewiston; pop. 11,183; agricultural market center; grain, beans, potatoes, melons; kaolin deposits. University of Idaho (1889; coed.).

Mos′cow (mŏs′kou; -kō); *Russ.* **Mos·kva′** (mŭs·kvä′). 1 *also known as* **Mus′co·vy** (mŭs′kō·vĭ). Principality, W cen. Russia in Europe, founded 1295 by Daniel, son of Alexander Nevski, with fortified village of Moscow as its center; united with Vladimir principality in 15th cent.; its ruler became Grand Duke, who extended its power. For later history, see 2 below, and RUSSIA.

2 City, ✳ of Moscow Region and of Russia, on both sides of the Moskva river; pop. 4,137,018; the largest city in the Soviet Union and its political, economic, and cultural center; known as the "Holy Mother of the Russians"; on navigable waterway formed by the Moscow-Volga canal (opened 1937) and the Moskva river; a manufacturing city, esp. in light goods, but even more important as a distribution point. Its most imposing structure is the Kremlin (*Russ.* "citadel"), a large triangular fortress on the Moskva, with Red Square to the W, for several centuries the residence of ruling family (to 1712) and under the Soviets the meeting place of administrative councils and headquarters of government officials; nearby is the Lenin Mausoleum; several cathedrals, palaces, museums (as the Tretyakov Gallery and Lenin Museum), many theaters (esp. the Moscow Art and Meyerhold), the old Kitaigorod (commercial bazaar), University of Moscow (founded 1755—largest in Russia); has one of the newest and finest subway systems in the world.

History: First mentioned by Russian chronicles 1147 but probably existed as a village for some time previously; capital of feudal principality of Moscow (*q.v.* above); became court town under Ivan I c. 1340; became seat of metropolitan of Russian Church; under Grand Duke Ivan III (1462–1505), subjugated leading rival principality of Novgorod (*q.v.*), defeated Tatars, and invaded Lithuania. Grand Duke Ivan IV first to formally assume title of Tsar of Russia (*q.v.*); became capital of grand duchy of Russia 1547–1712 (see LENINGRAD); occupied 1812 by Napoleon I whose retreat from Moscow helped to break First Empire (see FRANCE). Made capital of Soviet Russia 1917; goal of German armies 1941–43 but never reached.

Mos′cow Region (mŏs′kou; -kō). Region, cen. Soviet Russia, Europe; 19,146 sq. m.; pop. 8,918,389; ✳ Moscow. Traversed by the Moskva and in SE part by the Oka. Rolling country with many forests; produces agricultural and dairy products (grains, fruits, vegetables, butter, etc.) esp. for nearby city consumption. Has many fine roads and railroads. Chief towns Moscow, Orekhovo Zuevo, Kolomna, Yegorevsk, Noginsk, Serpukhov.

Mo·selle′ (mō·zĕl′; *Fr.* mō′zĕl′). 1 *Ger.* **Mo′sel** (mō′-zĕl); *anc.* **Mo·sel′la** (mō·zĕl′ȧ). River 320 m. long, W Europe; rises in Vosges dept., NE France, flows N, forming a section of the boundary bet. Germany and the grand duchy of Luxembourg, turns NE and enters the Rhine at Koblenz; navigable for most of its course. Chief tributaries the Orne and Seuer from left and the Meurthe and Saar from right. Passes the cities of Nancy, Metz, Thionville in France and Trier in Germany. 2 Department of France. See *Table* at FRANCE.

Mo′ses Lake (mō′zĭz; -zĭs). 1 Lake 16 m. long in S cen. Grant co., cen. Washington; its lower extension, **Pot′-holes′ Reservoir** (pŏt′hōlz′), formed by O'Sullivan Dam. 2 City, Grant co., cen. Washington, on E shore of Moses Lake; pop. 11,299.

Mo′shi (mō′shē). Town on S slope of Mt. Kilimanjaro, NE Tanganyika, E Africa; pop. ab. 3000.

Mos′kal·vo (môs′kȧl·vô). Oil port on Gulf of Sakhalin, NW Sakhalin I., Soviet Russia, Asia; rail connection with Okha on E coast of island; icebound for six months.

Mos′ke·nes′ (môs′kĕ·nās′; mōōs′-). Southernmost island of the larger Lofoten, in the Norwegian Sea off NW coast of Norway; ab. 15 m. long and 8 m. wide.

Mos·kva′ (mŭs·kvä′). 1 River 315 m. long in Moscow Region, Soviet Russia, Europe; flows E through Moscow city to join the Oka river just below Kolomna; navigable from Moscow. 2 See MOSCOW.

Mos'man (mŏs'măn). City, E New South Wales, SE Australia, NE suburb of Sydney, on Port Jackson; pop. 23,667.

Mos·que'ro (mŏs·kâr'ō). Village, ⊗ of Harding and San Miguel cos., NE New Mexico; pop. 310.

Mos·qui'ti·a (mŭs·kē'tĭ·à; *Span.* mŏs·kē'tyä). **1** Unexplored territory in E Honduras, N of Segovia river; claimed by Nicaragua.
2 See MOSQUITO COAST.

Mos·qui'to Cays (mŭs·kē'tō). Group of small islands in Caribbean Sea off NE coast of Nicaragua.

Mosquito Coast or **Mos·qui'ti·a** (mŭs·kē'tĭ·à; *Span.* mŏs·kē'tyä). Region ab. 40 m. wide extending ab. 300 m. along coast of E Nicaragua, now forming Zelaya dept., Nicaragua; a British protectorate 1655–1860 and later an autonomous Indian reserve; chief town Bluefields. See SAN JUAN DEL NORTE.

Mosquito Gulf; *Span.* **Gol'fo de los Mos·qui'tos** (gôl'fŏ thä lŏz mŏs·kē'tŏs). Widemouthed inlet of the Caribbean Sea on the N coast of Panama, W of the Panama Canal.

Mosquito Peak. Mountain 13,794 ft. in Park and Lake cos., cen. Colorado.

Moss (mŏs). Seaport, ⊗ of Östfold co., SE Norway, on E side of Oslo Fjord; pop. 8293; seaside resort; shipbuilding yards, iron foundries; manufactures glass, shoes, paper, furniture; scene of signing of agreement uniting Norway and Sweden Aug. 14, 1814.

Mos·sâ'me·des (mô·säm'ĕ·dēz). Seaport, SW Angola, SW Africa; pop. (1935) ab. 5000; has rail connections with interior towns and steamer lines to Oporto.

Mos'sel Bay (mŏs''l). Seaport on Mossel Bay (inlet of Indian Ocean), S Cape Province, S Union of South Africa, ab. 230 m. E of Cape Town; pop. 7220; harvests oysters and mussels of fine quality—whence its name; popular summer resort. First visited by Bartholomew Dias 1488; hermitage erected here 1501 by João da Nova, first Christian place of worship in South Africa.

Mossgiel. See MAUCHLINE.

Moss'ley (mŏs'lĭ). Municipal borough, Lancashire, NW England, on the Tame 10 m. NE of Manchester; pop. 10,415; cotton and woolen mills.

Mos'so·ró' (mŏō'sŏō·rô'). City, NW Rio Grande do Norte state, NE Brazil, 150 m. WNW of Natal; pop. (1940 est.) 13,643.

Moss Point (mŏs). City, Jackson co., SE corner of Mississippi, 20 m. E of Biloxi; pop. 6631; lumbering, shipbuilding.

Mos'su·ril' (mŏ'sŏō·rēl'). Coastal town, NE Mozambique colony, SE Africa, opp. Mozambique I.

Most (môst); *Ger.* **Brüx** (brüks). City, NW Bohemia prov., W Czechoslovakia, ab. 48 m. NW of Prague; pop. (1930) 28,211; manufacturing center in coal-mining area; salt springs.

Mos'ta·ga'nem' (mŏs'tà·gà'nĕm'). Seaport, NE Oran dept., NW Algeria, 44 m. ENE of Oran; pop. of commune (1936) 36,961; originated in time of Almoravides in 11th cent.; at height of commercial prosperity in 16th cent.

Mo'star (mō'stär). Town, Bosnia and Herzegovina, W Yugoslavia, on Neretva river halfway bet. Sarajevo and Dubrovnik; pop. 20,295; formerly capital of Herzegovina and still its chief town; has fine old stone bridge; trade and cultural center.

Mo·sul' (mō·sŏōl'; *Arab.* mō'sŏōl, mou'sĭl). **1** Province (*liwa*), N Iraq; pop. (1935 est.) 453,004.
2 City, Mosul prov., N Iraq, on the W bank of the Tigris 220 m. NNW of Baghdad; pop. (1935 est.) 60,000, (1938 est.) 260,000; on the Turkey-Baghdad railroad and formerly an important town on caravan route from Persia across N Mesopotamia; a trading center for grain, livestock, fruit; once famous for its manufacture of muslins; has cosmopolitan population and numerous mosques, shrines, and churches. Across the river from ruins of ancient Nineveh and other sites of ancient cities now par-

tially excavated, as Tepe Gawra, Calah, and Dur Sharrukin. An old Arabic town taken by Moslems 636; later under Mongols, Persians, and Turks; became part of Ottoman Empire 1638; not included at first in mandate of Iraq but awarded to it by decision of League of Nations 1925; oil wells seized during Arab revolt Apr. 1941 but soon retaken by British.

Mo·ta'gua (mō·tä'gwä). River ab. 340 m. long, S cen. Guatemala; flows E and NE into the Gulf of Honduras.

Moth'er, Mount (mŭth'ēr). Volcano at NE tip of New Britain I., Bismarck Archipelago, on a peninsula just E of and overshadowing Rabaul and Blanche Bay; its eruption and earthquakes in 1878 created Vulcan I. in the bay and in May 1937 Matupi (*q.v.*), a crater on its S slope, and Mt. Vulcan together caused great destruction at Rabaul and vicinity.

Mother Island. = HAHA JIMA.

Mother Lode. Principal belt of gold-bearing quartz along the W foothills of the Sierra Nevada, California.

Mother Mountain. Peak 6840 ft. in Pierce co., W cen. Washington, NW of Mt. Ranier.

Moth'er·well and Wish'aw (mŭth'ēr·wĕl [-wĕl], wĭsh'ô). Burgh, Lanark co., S cen. Scotland, on right bank of the Clyde 13 m. SE of Glasgow; pop. (1951) 68,137; coal and iron deposits; steel manufacturing. Two burghs united 1920.

Mo·ti'ti Island (mō·tē'tē). Small island in the Bay of Plenty, off N cen. coast of North I., New Zealand.

Mot'ley (mŏt'lĭ). County in Texas. See *Table* at TEXAS.

Mo·to·bu (mō·tō·bŏō). Town at W end of **Motobu Peninsula,** on W coast of Okinawa I., Ryukyu Is., Japan; occupied in Okinawa campaign by U.S. troops by Apr. 20, 1945.

Mo·to·vi'li·kha (mŭ·tŭ·vyē'lyĭ·ĸà). City, Molotov Region, W Soviet Russia, Asia, on Kama river; pop. 33,110; an industrial suburb of Molotov, manufacturing ordnance, motors, and tractors.

Mo·to·ya·ma (mō·tō·yä·mä). Village and airfields in cen. part of Iwo Jima (*q.v.*).

Mo·tril' (mō·trēl'). Commercial commune, Granada prov., S Spain, 2 m. from Mediterranean and 31 m. S of Granada; pop. 20,495.

Mott (mŏt). City, ⊗ of Hettinger co., SW North Dakota; pop. 1463

Mott'lau (mŏt'lou). Short river, W of Vistula delta, flowing N through the city of Danzig, N Poland.

Mot'to·la (mŏt'tō·lä). Commune, Ionio prov., Apulia, SE Italy, 16 m. NW of Taranto; pop. (1931) 11,297; 15th-cent. cathedral.

Mo'tu–a'ri (mō'tŏō·ä'rē). Small island of Gambier Is., S Pacific Ocean, SW of Mangareva I.

Mo·tul' (mō·tŏōl'), *in full* **Motul de Fe·li'pe Car·ril'lo Puer'to** (dä fâ·lē'pä kär·rē'yŏ pwĕr'tŏ). Town, N Yucatán state, on Yucatán penin. SE Mexico, just E of Mérida; pop. 5384.

Mo·tu'sa (mō·tŏō'sà). Chief village of Rotuma I., Fiji Islands colony, SW Pacific Ocean.

Mo'ty·a (mō'tĭ·à). Ruins of ancient Phoenician town on very small island **San Pan'ta·le'o** (säm pän'tä·lâ'ŏ) or **San Pan'ta·le·o'ne** (-lâ·ō'nä), off W coast of Sicily just N of Marsala; destroyed 397 B.C. by Dionysius the Elder of Syracuse.

Motyca. See MODICA.

Mou'choir Bank (mŏō'shwär). Bank in Atlantic Ocean off N coast of Hispaniola in the West Indies.

Mouchoir Passage. Channel in N cen. West Indies, SE of Turks Is. and NW of Mouchoir Bank.

Mou'dros or **Mu'dros** (mŏō'thrŏs). Town and seaport on S coast of Lemnos I. in N Aegean Sea; belongs to Lesbos dept., Greece; pop. 1795; has fine harbor, a part of **Moudros Gulf.**

Moukden. Var. of MUKDEN.

Moule, Le. See LE MOULE.

Mou'lins' (mŏō'lăn'). Manufacturing city, ✳ of Allier dept., cen. France, and anciently ✳ of Bourbonnais; on

Allier river 58 m. SE of Bourges; pop. 22,365; 15th-cent. Gothic cathedral; 15th-cent. campanile; town hall.

Moul·mein′ (mōōl·mān′; mōl-; -mīn′; *Burmese* mō′lŭ-myīn′). Commercial city, ✱ of Amherst dist. and of Tenasserim division, Lower Burma, at mouth of Salween on E shore of Gulf of Martaban; pop. 65,506; formerly a port and shipbuilding center of great importance; now has some export trade in tea and rice; port for steamers up the Salween. Captured by Japanese Feb. 1942.

Mou′lou′ya′ (mōō′lōō′yȧ′) *or* **Mu·lu′ya** (mōō·lōō′yȧ) *or* **Mul·wi′ya** (mōōl·wē′yȧ); *anc.* **Mu′lu·cha** (mū′lŭ·kȧ). River ab. 300 m. long, Morocco, NW Africa; rises in cen. Morocco, flows NE into Mediterranean Sea E of Melilla.

Moul′ton (mōl′t'n; -tŭn). Town, ⊗ of Lawrence co., N Alabama; pop. 1716; incorporated 1818.

Moul′trie (mōl′trĭ). **1** County in Illinois. See *Table* at ILLINOIS.
2 City, ⊗ of Colquitt co., S Georgia, 35 m. SE of Albany; pop. 15,764; ships watermelons; meat-packing plant.

Moultrie, Lake. See PINOPOLIS DAM.

Mound (mound). Village, Hennepin co., SE Minnesota, W of Minneapolis; pop. 5440.

Mound City (mound). **1** City, ⊗ of Pulaski co., S Illinois, on Ohio river 8 m. above its confluence with Mississippi river; pop. 1669; manufactures lumber products; foundries and machine shops, canneries. Site of a national military cemetery.
2 City, ⊗ of Linn co., E Kansas; pop. 661.
3 City, Holt co., NW Missouri, 34 m. NW of St. Joseph; pop. 1249; shipping point for livestock, grain, and fruit.
4 Town, ⊗ of Campbell co., N South Dakota; pop. 144.

Mound City Group National Monument. See UNITED STATES, *National Monuments.*

Mounds (moundz). City, Pulaski co., S Illinois, 10 m. N of confluence of Ohio and Mississippi rivers; pop. 1835.

Mounds View. Village, Ramsey co., E Minnesota, N suburb of Minneapolis; pop. 6416.

Mounds′ville (moundz′vĭl). City, ⊗ of Marshall co., N West Virginia, in N panhandle on Ohio river 12 m. S of Wheeling; pop. 15,163; manufactures glass (esp. Fostoria ware) zinc, and enamel products; coal mines. Named for Grave Creek Mound, a prehistoric, conical burial mound, 320 ft. in diameter at the base and 70 ft. high, which is in center of the city.

Mount, Cape (mount). Cape on SE coast of Liberia, Africa, a promontory 1000 ft. high.

Mount Abu. See ABU.

Moun′tain·air′ (moun't'n·âr′). Town and health resort, Torrance co., cen. New Mexico, 44 m. SSE of Albuquerque; pop. 1605; shipping center for pinto-bean industry; pueblo ruins in environs.

Mountain Ash. Industrial urban district, Glamorganshire, SE Wales, 5 m. S of Merthyr Tydfil; pop. 31,528.

Mountain–Badakhshan. See GORNO-BADAKHSHAN.

Mountain Brook. City, Jefferson co., cen. Alabama, E suburb of Birmingham; pop. 12,680.

Mountain City. Town, ⊗ of Johnson co., NE corner of Tennessee; pop. 1379.

Mountain Grove. City, Wright co., S Missouri, 38 m. NW of West Plains; pop. 3176; trade center.

Mountain Home. **1** City, ⊗ of Baxter co., N Arkansas; pop. 2105.
2 City, ⊗ of Elmore co., SW cen. Idaho; pop. 9344; shipping point for wool.

Mountain Lake. **1** Bird sanctuary 58 acres, near Lake Wales, Polk co., cen. Florida penin.; established by Edward Bok; has beautiful Singing Tower (dedicated 1929), 230 ft. high with carillon of 71 bells.
2 Village, Cottonwood co., SW Minnesota, 30 m. NW of Fairmont; pop. 1943; home of a Mennonite colony.

Mountain Lakes. Residential borough, Morris co., N New Jersey, 7 m. N of Morristown; pop. 4037; spread out around eight artificial lakes.

Mountain Mead′ows (mĕd′ōz). Valley in Iron and Washington cos., SW Utah; massacre of emigrants occurred Sept. 1857 in Washington co., ab. 40 m. SW of Cedar City.

Mountain Province. Province, N Luzon, Phil. Is., comprising 5 (formerly 7) subprovinces—Apayao, Kalinga, Bontoc, Ifugao, and Benguet—in the mountainous territory bet. Cagayan, Isabela, and Nueva Vizcaya provs. on E and Abra, the Ilocos provs. and La Union on W; 5458 sq. m.; pop. 296,874; ✱ Bontoc; includes geographically but not administratively the City of Baguio (*q.v.*). Largest province on Luzon, but has few towns. In S includes all of the Cordillera Central and in N its E slopes; highest point Mt. Pulog 9606 ft.; its E and cen. parts traversed by Chico and other tributaries of the Cagayan and in S by upper courses of the Abra and Agno rivers. Its inhabitants chiefly members of various pagan tribes, such as the Tinggian, Igorot, Bontok, Ifugao, Kalinga, Gaddang, etc. Agriculture primitive but the terraced rice cultivation, especially of the Ifugaos, has been developed to a remarkable degree; local industries include weaving, metal working, pottery making.

History: Region but little known in 17th and 18th cents., but various expeditions carried out by Spanish bet. 1829 and 1850; later divided under Spanish rule into several politico-military comandancias; Benguet first organized 1900 under American rule and Baguio made capital; other subprovinces created 1901–08; united and organized 1908 as separate province under present name; City of Baguio incorporated 1909 and separated administratively; in 1920 former subprovinces of Lepanto and Amburayan united and boundaries of several others changed and further reorganization made before 1939.

Mountain Republic. A temporary subdivision, c. 1921–27, of SE Soviet Russia, Europe, later replaced by the Chechen-Ingush, Kabardino-Balkarian, Karachaev, and North Ossetian Autonomous Republics on N slopes of Caucasus Mts.

Mountains of the Moon. See Mount RUWENZORI.

Mountain View. **1** City, ⊗ of Stone co., N Arkansas; pop. 983.
2 City, Santa Clara co., W California, 11 m. NW of San Jose; pop. 30,889; orchards, canneries, packing houses.

Mount Air′y (âr′ĭ). **1** Town and summer resort, Surry co., N North Carolina, in foothills of Blue Ridge Mts. 35 m. NW of Winston-Salem; pop. 7055; granite quarry.
2 District, NW cen. Philadelphia (city), Pennsylvania; pop. (est.) 100.

Mount Al′bert (ăl′bẽrt). Borough, Auckland provincial dist., N North I., New Zealand, SW suburb of Auckland; pop. 20,190.

Mount An′gel (ăn′jĕl). City, Marion co., NW Oregon, 15 m. NE of Salem; pop. 1428. Mount Angel College (1887; coed.).

Mount Apo National Park. See Mount APO.

Mount Ath′os (ăth′ŏs; ā′thŏs; *Mod. Gr.* ä′thŏs) *or* **Ha′gi·on O′ros** (ä′yŏn ŏ′rŏs). An autonomous republic, Acte Penin., Chalcidice, NE Greece, comprising 20 monasteries, 17 of them Greek (see ATHOS); constitutes a department of Greece (see *Table* at GREECE).

Mount Ayr (âr). Town, ⊗ of Ringgold co., S Iowa, 70 m. SW of Des Moines; pop. 1738.

Mount Ber′ry (bĕr′ĭ). Town, Floyd co., NW Georgia, NW of Rome; pop. (est.) 1000; site of Berry schools, including a college (Berry Coll., 1926, coed.), the Martha Berry School for Girls (1909), the Mount Berry School for Boys (founded 1902), and the Possum Trot Rural Community giving adult education.

Mount Car′mel (kär′mĕl). **1** City, ⊗ of Wabash co., SE Illinois, on Wabash river 30 m. SE of Olney; pop. 8594; settled 1817, incorp. as village 1824, as city 1865; trading center in farm products; paper mills; a center of the mussel shell industry.
2 Borough, Northumberland co., E cen. Pennsylvania, 15 m. WNW of Pottsville; pop. 10,760; coal mining.
3 Mountain in Palestine. See Mount CARMEL.

Mount Car′roll (kăr′ŭl). City, ⊗ of Carroll co., NW Illinois; pop. 2056; iron-ore deposits nearby.

Mount Clem′ens (klĕm′ĕnz). City, ⊗ of Macomb co., SE Michigan, 20 m. NE of Detroit; pop. 21,016; health resort, with mineral waters. Selfridge Field, U.S. Air Force base.

Mount Des′ert (dĕz′ẽrt; *older pron.* dĕ-zûrt′). **1** Island 14 m. long by 8 m. wide, in Hancock co., off SE Maine; summer resort; damaged by forest fire 1947. Acadia National Park (see UNITED STATES, *National Parks*).
2 Town, Hancock co., SE Maine, center of Mt. Desert I.; pop. 1663.

Mount Do′ra (dōr′à). Town, Lake co., cen. Florida penin., 22 m. NNW of Orlando; pop. 3756; founded 1882; yachting and motorboating.

Mount E′ba (ē′bà). Semiarid district, cen. South Australia, 100 m. NW of Port Augusta; proposed range head for rockets and supersonic aircraft; the range planned to extend NW across South Australia and Western Australia to Christmas I. in the Indian Ocean, 3000 m. distant.

Mount E′den (ē′d'n). Borough, Auckland provincial dist., N North I., New Zealand, S suburb of Auckland; pop. 19,770.

Mount Edge′cumbe (ĕj′kŭm). Urban community (unincorporated), on W coast of Baranof I., SE Alaska, SW of Juneau; pop. 1884.

Mount E′phra·im (ē′frā·ĭm; ē′frĭ·ŭm). Borough, Camden co., SW New Jersey, 5 m. S of Camden; pop. 5447.

Mount For′est (fŏr′ĕst; -ĭst). Industrial town, Wellington co., SE Ontario, Canada, 38 m. NW of Guelph; pop. 2291.

Mount Gam′bier (găm′bẽr). Town, SE corner of South Australia, near Victoria border 240 m. SSE of Adelaide; pop. 5539.

Mount Gil′e·ad (gĭl′ē·ăd). Village, ⊗ of Morrow co., cen. Ohio, 16 m. E of Marion; pop. 2788; settled 1817; pottery and foundry products, pumps, chemicals.

Mount Health′y (hĕl′thĭ). City, Hamilton co., SW corner of Ohio, 9 m. N of Cincinnati; pop. 6553.

Mount Hol′ly (hŏl′ĭ). **1** Town, ⊗ of Burlington co., S cen. New Jersey, 16 m. S of Trenton; pop. (est.) 11,300; manufactures shoes, clothing, upholstery fabrics, leather goods; site purchased by Quakers 1676; temporary capital of New Jersey 1779; occupied by British troops during Revolution; became ⊗ 1796.
2 Industrial town, Gaston co., SW North Carolina, 10 m. E of Gastonia; pop. 4037; textile mills.

Mount Holly Springs. Borough, Cumberland co., S Pennsylvania, 20 m. WSW of Harrisburg; pop. 1840; formerly popular resort; mineral springs.

Mount Hope (hōp). **1** City, Fayette co., S cen. West Virginia, 8 m. N of Beckley; pop. 2000; commercial center of coal-mining area.
2 Town adjacent to Silver City and S of Cristobal, E of the canal, Canal Zone, Panama; pop. 314.

Mount Hope Bay. Northeast arm of Narragansett Bay, E section in SE Massachusetts and W section in E Rhode Island; receives Taunton river at its NE extremity; city of Fall River, Mass., on its NE shore.

Mount I′da (ī′dà). **1** City, ⊗ of Montgomery co., W Arkansas; pop. 564.
2 See IDA.

Mount Joy (joi). Borough, Lancaster co., SE Pennsylvania, 12 m. WNW of Lancaster; pop. 3292; manufactures shoes, textiles, chocolate, iron castings.

Mount Kis′co (kĭs′kō). Village, Westchester co., SE New York, 36 m. NNE of New York; pop. 6805.

Mount′lake′ Terrace (mount′lāk′). City, Snohomish co., NW Washington, S of Everett; pop. 9122.

Mount Lau′ri·er-Senne′terre′ Highway Reserve (lô′rĭ·à·sĕn′târ′; *Fr.* lô′ryä′-). Canadian provincial park, SW Quebec prov.; 2600 sq. m.; comprises land on both sides of highway from Montreal to the Lake Abitibi region, passing through Mont Laurier, near Lake Baskatong N to Senneterre on Canadian National Rys.

Mount Lavinia. See DEHIWALA-MOUNT LAVINIA.

Mount Leb′a·non (lĕb′à-nŭn). Urban township, Allegheny co., SW Pennsylvania, SW suburb of Pittsburgh; pop. 35,361.

Mount McKinley National Park. See UNITED STATES, *National Parks*.

Mount Mor′gan (môr′gàn). Mining town, E Queensland, NE Australia, 25 m. S of Rockhampton; pop. 4404.

Mount Mor′ris (mŏr′ĭs). **1** Village, Ogle co., N Illinois, 25 m. SW of Rockford; pop. 3075.
2 City, Genesee co., SE cen. Michigan, 8 m. N of Flint; pop. 3484.
3 Village in Mount Morris town (pop. 4567), Livingston co., W New York, 34 m. SSW of Rochester; pop. 3250.

Mount of the Holy Cross. See Mount of the HOLY CROSS.

Mount Ol′ive (ŏl′ĭv). **1** City, Macoupin co., SW cen. Illinois, 36 m. NE of East St. Louis; pop. 2295; coal.
2 Town, Wayne and Duplin cos., E North Carolina, S of Goldsboro; pop. 4673; tobacco, truck farming.

Mount Ol′i·ver (ŏl′ĭ·vẽr). Borough, Allegheny co., SW Pennsylvania, 3 m. S of Pittsburgh; pop. 5980.

Mount Ol′i·vet (ŏl′ĭ·vĕt). City, ⊗ of Robertson co., NE Kentucky; pop. 386.

Mount O·lym′pus National Monument (ô·lĭm′pŭs). Former United States national monument, NW Washington; 467 sq. m.; estab. 1909, included 1938 in the newly created Olympic National Park (see UNITED STATES, *National Parks*).

Mount Or′ford Park (ôr′fẽrd). Canadian provincial park 9425 acres, Sherbrooke co., Quebec prov., on Orford Mt. 2860 ft.; sports center, esp. for skiing.

Mount Penn (pĕn). Borough, Berks co., SE Pennsylvania, 3 m. E of Reading; pop. 3574.

Mount Pleas′ant (plĕz′'nt). **1** City, ⊗ of Henry co., SE Iowa, 28 m. WNW of Burlington; pop. 7339. Iowa Wesleyan College (1842; coed.; Methodist).
2 City, ⊗ of Isabella co., cen. Michigan, 46 m. W of Bay City; pop. 14,875; oil fields nearby; manufactures beet sugar, wood products, condensed milk. Central Michigan Univ. (1892; coed.).
3 Borough, Westmoreland co., SW Pennsylvania, 21 m. NNE of Uniontown; pop. 6107; manufactures glassware.
4 Town, Charleston co., SE South Carolina, on Atlantic Ocean 5 m. E of Charleston; pop. 5116; resort.
5 Town, Maury co., W cen. Tennessee, 12 m. WSW of Columbia; pop. 2921; in phosphate-mining area.
6 City, ⊗ of Titus co., NE Texas, 48 m. SE of Paris; pop. 8027; lumber, cottonseed products, clay products.
7 City, Sanpete co., cen. Utah, 34 m. W of Price; pop. 1572; Rambouillet sheep center.

Mount Pros′pect (prŏs′pĕkt). Village, Cook co., NE Illinois, 21 m. NW of Chicago; pop. 18,906.

Mount′rail′ (mount′rāl′). County in North Dakota. See *Table* at NORTH DAKOTA.

Mount Rai′nier (rā′nẽr). City, Prince Georges co., S cen. Maryland, 4 m. NE of Washington; pop. 9855.

Mount Rai·nier′ National Park (rà-nẽr′; rā-nẽr′; răn′yẽr). See UNITED STATES, *National Parks*.

Mount Rev′el·stoke National Park (rĕv′'l-stōk). See CANADA, *National Parks*.

Mount Rob′son Park (rŏb′s'n). Canadian provincial park, E British Columbia, W Rocky Mts.; contains Mt. Robson.

Mount Roy′al (mount roi′ăl) *or* **Mont Roy′al′** (môn rwä′yàl′). Town, Montreal I., S Quebec, Canada, NW of the height Mount Royal; pop. 11,352; part of Greater Montreal.

Mount Saint Jo′seph (sȧnt jō′zĕf; -zĭf). Village, Hamilton co., SW corner of Ohio, on the Ohio river near Cincinnati; College of Mount St. Joseph-on-the-Ohio (1854; women; Roman Catholic).

Mounts Bay (mounts). Inlet of Atlantic Ocean on extreme SW tip of England, bet. Lands End on the W and Lizard Head on the E.

Mount Shas′ta (shăs′tá). Town, Siskiyou co., N California, at foot of Mt. Shasta, ab. 100 m. NE of Eureka; pop. 1936; tourist center; state fish hatchery.

Mount Ster′ling (stûr′lǐng). **1** City, ⊗ of Brown co., W Illinois, 34 m. E of Quincy; pop. 2262.

2 City, ⊗ of Montgomery co., E Kentucky, 15 m. ENE of Winchester; pop. 5370; prehistoric mounds nearby.

Mount Un′ion (ūn′yŭn). Borough, Huntingdon co., S cen. Pennsylvania, on Juniata river 24 m. SW of Lewistown; pop. 4091; manufactures clothing, creosote, bricks; coal grading, quarrying, lumbering.

Mount Ver′non (vûr′nŭn). **1** City, ⊗ of Montgomery co., SE cen. Georgia; pop. 1166.

2 City, ⊗ of Jefferson co., S Illinois, 20 m. SE of Centralia; pop. 15,566; settled 1819, incorp. as city 1872; coal fields nearby; manufactures freight cars, stoves, electrical machinery, textiles.

3 City, ⊗ of Posey co., SW corner of Indiana, on Ohio river 18 m. W of Evansville; pop. 5970; near oil field.

4 City, Linn co., E Iowa, 13 m. E of Cedar Rapids; pop. 2593. Cornell College (1852; coed.).

5 City, ⊗ of Rockcastle co., SE cen. Kentucky; pop. 1177.

6 City, ⊗ of Lawrence co., SW Missouri, 32 m. WSW of Springfield; pop. 2381.

7 City, Westchester co., SE New York, on Bronx river adjacent to New York City; pop. 76,010; residential suburb; manufactures clothing, chemicals and dyes, electrical and office equipment; present city laid out 1852 by Home Industrial Association (1850) as refuge from high rents of New York; chartered 1892.

8 Manufacturing city, ⊗ of Knox co., cen. Ohio, 25 m. S of Mansfield; pop. 13,284; produces steam, diesel, and gas engines, glass, bits for rock drills, fabricated steel, cellophane.

9 Town, ⊗ of Franklin co., NE Texas; pop. 1338.

10 Home and burial place of George Washington, in Fairfax co., Virginia, on Potomac river ab. 15 m. below Washington, D.C.; acquired by Washington 1752; has been restored and is maintained by Mount Vernon Ladies' Association which bought it 1859.

11 City, ⊗ of Skagit co., NW Washington, on Skagit river 25 m. S of Bellingham; pop. 7921; pea canneries, condensed milk plants.

Mourne (mōrn). River in N Ireland; flows NNW in W Northern Ireland to unite with the Finn on the Eire border and form the Foyle.

Mourne Mountains. Range in SE Northern Ireland, in co. Down bet. Dundrum Bay and Carlingford Lough; highest peak Slieve Donard 2796 ft.

Mouscron. See MOESKROEN.

Mouse. See SOURIS river.

Moustier, Le. See LE MOUSTIER.

Mou′vaux′ (mōō′vō′). Commune, Nord dept., N France; pop. (1931) 9488; a N suburb of Lille.

Mow′bray (mō′brà; -brǐ). Town, suburb of Cape Town, Cape Province, S Union of South Africa; pop. ab. 9000.

Mow′er (mou′ĕr). County in Minnesota. See *Table* at MINNESOTA.

Moy (moi). River ab. 40 m. long in NW Ireland; rises in co. Sligo, curves SW, W, and N through co. Mayo into Killala Bay; navigable for a short distance.

Mo·ya′le (mô·yä′lå). Town, N Kenya, E Africa, near border of Ethiopia; British base in attack on Italian East Africa 1941.

Moyen Atlas. = *Middle Atlas:* see ATLAS MOUNTAINS.

Mo′yeu′vre–Grande (mwà′yû′vrĕ·gränd′). Commune, Moselle dept., NE France, on Orne river 11 m. NNW of Metz; pop. 11,067; iron mines; steelworks.

Mo′yo·bam′ba (mō′yŏ·väm′bä). Town, ✳ of San Martín dept., N Peru, on Mayo river 420 m. N of Lima; pop. (1940 est.) 7497; manufactures Panama hats.

Moy·tu′ra (moi·tōōr′à). Two localities in Ireland (Eire) associated with legends of the Firbolg: **Northern Moytura,** near Sligo, Connacht, where the Firbolg met final defeat in battle; probable site now marked by a few cairns; **Southern Moytura,** near Cong bet. Lough Mask and Lough Corrib, where they had been defeated seven years earlier.

Moyun–Kum. See MUYUN KUM.

Mo′zam·bique′ (mō′zăm·bēk′; mō′zăm·bēk′); *Port.* **Mo·çam·bi′que** (mōō·sänm·bē′kĕ). **1** or **Portuguese East Africa.** Portuguese possession in SE Africa; 297,654 sq. m.; pop. (1940) 5,081,266; ✳ Lourenço Marques. Bounded on N by Nyasaland and Tanganyika on E and SE by the Indian Ocean (Mozambique Channel), on S by Natal, on W by Transvaal and Southern Rhodesia, and on NW by Northern Rhodesia. Divided into four provinces: Sul do Save, Manica and Sofala, Zambezia, and Niassa. Mountainous in N (highest 8200 ft.) and along Southern Rhodesia border (ab. 9000 ft.). Crossed in cen. part by lower course (ab. 480 m.) of Zambezi river flowing SE into Mozambique Channel at Chinde; other important rivers the Limpopo in S, Save in S cen. part, Lugenda in N, and many shorter streams in NE; coastal plain extensive; N boundary marked by Ruvuma river and Cape Delgado. Chief products sugar, maize, cotton, copra, and various minerals. Chief towns Lourenço Marques, Beira, Inhambane, Quelimane, Mozambique.

History: Town of Mozambique a Portuguese trading fort early in 16th cent.; in 1875, the disputed Delagoa Bay (*q.v.*) region awarded to Portugal; after efforts of Portuguese explorers to expand to interior, British secured agreement which defined its boundaries with British South and East Africa 1891; Mozambique Co. chartered 1891; boundary with German East Africa determined 1894; organized as colony 1907; until 1942 was in two parts: (1) territory under direct Portuguese administration; (2) territory (**Mozambique Company's Territory**) including Manica and Sofala dists. under administration of the Mozambique Company whose charter expired July 19, 1942, the territory reverting to the Portuguese government.

2 Former district, N Mozambique; 33,500 sq. m.; pop. 935,000; ✳ Mozambique; now part of Niassa prov.

3 Seaport on small coral island (**Mozambique Island**) in Mozambique Channel, off NE coast of Mozambique colony, SE Africa; pop. ab. 7000; opp. the mainland town of Mossuril; has good harbor; population chiefly Mohammedan natives of mixed descent; exports ground nuts, oil seeds, and timber. Site of flourishing Arab town when visited by Vasco da Gama in 1498; capital of the colony until 1907.

Mozambique Channel. Strait bet. the island of Madagascar and the SE African mainland (Mozambique); ab. 950 m. long, 250 m. wide at narrowest (central) part and ab. 625 m. at widest.

Mozambique Current. A warm ocean current flowing from the Indian Ocean S through Mozambique Channel, past Natal (hence also called the **Natal Current**) and along the coast of Cape Province, S Union of South Africa, where it is known as the **Agulhas Current;** off Cape Agulhas it is deflected to the left and flows SE toward Australia; considered to have a decided effect on the climate of Cape Province.

Moz·dok′ (mŭs·dôk′). Town, S Stavropol Territory, Soviet Russia, Europe, on Terek river 55 m. WNW of Grozny; pop. 14,008; on Rostov-Baku R.R. and on oil pipelines. Taken by Germans Aug. 1942 and held for a short time.

Mo·zhaisk′ (mŭ·zhīsk′). Village, Moscow Region, Soviet Russia, Europe, on railroad 65 m. W of Moscow. Taken by Germans Oct. 15, 1941; marks farthest advance of German armies in Nov. 1941 directly W of Moscow; regained by Russians in winter drive 1941–42.

Mo·zyr′ (mŭ·zîr′). Town, ✳ of Polesye Region, SE White Russia, U.S.S.R., on Pripyat river 75 m. SW of Gomel; pop. 11,400; in World War II held by Germans 1941–44; retaken by Russians Jan. 12, 1944.

Mpon'da ('m·pôn'dä). Town, S Nyasaland protectorate, SE Africa, at S end of Lake Nyasa near Fort Johnston; pop. ab. 3200.

Msta ('m·stä'). River ab. 270 m. long, cen. Novgorod Region, Soviet Russia, Europe, flowing NW and W into N end of Lake Ilmen; navigable and connected by canals with Volga through the Tvertsa at Vyshni Volochek.

Msus ('m·soōs'). Village in desert 68 m. SE of Bengasi, Cyrenaica, NE Libya; British tank brigades destroyed here by German forces Dec. 28, 1941 and Jan. 23, 1942.

Mtsensk ('m·tsyĕnsk'). Town, N Orel Region, Soviet Russia, Europe, 35 m. NE of Orel; pop. 10,045.

Mu (moō). River ab. 170 m. long, N cen. Burma; flows S through Katha and Shwebo dists. to the Irrawaddy W of Sagaing.

Muai To. See MAE HONG SON.

Muang–Thai. Official Thai name of THAILAND.

Mua'ni·va'tu, Mount (mwä'nē·vä'toō). Peak 3708 ft. in cen. Viti Levu I., Fiji Is., SW Pacific Ocean.

Muar (mwär). **1** River ab. 100 m. long in NW Johore state, S end of Malay Penin.; its headstreams rise in Negri Sembilan and Pahang; flows SSW into the Strait of Malacca at Bandar Maharani; navigable for native boats for much of its course.
2 See BANDAR MAHARANI.

Muaratewe. See MOEARATEWE.

Mu·a'ri, Ras (räs moō·ä'rē); or **Cape Mon'ze** (môn'-zä). Cape, W Pakistan, 22 m. W of Karachi on the boundary bet. Sind and Baluchistan.

Mu·bar'raz (moō·bŭr'rŏz). Town in Hofuf oasis, S al-Hasa prov., Nejd, Saudi Arabia; pop. ab. 20,000.

Mu'bo (moō'bō). Inland town, SE North-East New Guinea, ab. 12 m. SSW of Salamaua; in World War II a main Japanese base; attacked by Allied forces Jan. 1943; captured July 16, 1943.

Much Wenlock. See WENLOCK.

Muck'ish (mŭk'ĭsh). Mountain 2197 ft. in N co. Donegal, N Ireland.

Muck Island (mŭk). One of the Inner Hebrides, S of Rum I., off W coast of Scotland; ab. 2 m. long; administratively a part of Argyll co.

Muck'le Flug'ga (mŭk''l flŭg'à). Rock in the ocean 1 m. N of Unst I. in the Shetland Is.; lat. 60°50'9"; northernmost of the British islands.

Muck'ross (mŭk'rŏs). Peninsula in co. Kerry, SW Eire, bet. the upper and lower Lakes of Killarney; site of ruins of an ancient Franciscan abbey, founded 1440.

Mu'cu·ra'po (moō'kŭ·rä'pō). Town, suburb of Port of Spain, Trinidad, West Indies; pop. 9411.

Mu'cu·ri'pe, Point (moō'koō·rē'pĕ). Cape extending into Atlantic Ocean on coast of Ceará state, NE Brazil, 5 m. E of Fortaleza.

Mu·dan'ya (moō·dän'yä). Town on Gemlik Gulf, an inlet of the Sea of Marmara, Bursa vilayet, NW Turkey in Asia; pop. 5024; port of Bursa.

Mud'dy (mŭd'ĭ). River ab. 80 m. long, SE Nevada; rises in Lincoln co., flows S into Virgin river.

Muddy Bog'gy Creek (bŏg'ĭ). River ab. 100 m. long, SE Oklahoma; rises in Pontotoc co., flows SE into Red river in S Choctaw co.

Muddy Pass. Mountain pass 8772 ft., Jackson and Grand cos., N Colorado, in Park Range of the Rocky Mts.; highway.

Mu'dhol (moōd'hŏl). **1** Former Indian state, Deccan and Kolhapur States, S Bombay prov., W India; 350 sq. m.; pop. (1941) 72,447.
2 Town, its ✳, 70 m. SE of Kolhapur; pop. 6975.

Mud'ki (moōd'kē). Village, in Ferozepore dist., Punjab state, NW Indian Union, 18 m. SE of Ferozepore; pop. ab. 3000; scene of British victory Dec. 11, 1845 by Sir Hugh Gough over Sikhs.

Mud Lake (mŭd). Intermittent lake, E Washoe co., Nevada.

Mud Mountain Dam. See UNITED STATES, Dams.

Mudros. See MOUDROS.

Mu·fum'bi·ro Mountains (moō·foōm'bĕ·rō). Var. of *Mfumbiro Mountains:* see VIRUNGA MOUNTAINS.

Mug'gia (moōd'jä). Seaport, Free Territory of Trieste, on bay in Gulf of Trieste at N end of Adriatic Sea 4 m. S by W of Trieste; pop. 12,028; 15th-cent. cathedral; 9th-cent. basilica nearby; Austrian naval station to 1919.

Muğ·la' or **Mugh·la'** (moō·lä'). **1** Vilayet, SW Turkey in Asia; 4925 sq. m.; pop. 196,772.
2 Town, its ✳, near SW coast; pop. 10,855.

Mu·gu', Point (mŭ·goō'). Cape, Ventura co., SW California SE of Oxnard; site of Point Mugu Naval Air Missile Test Center.

Mu·ham'mad, Ras (räs mŭ·hăm'măd). Cape, S end of Sinai Penin., NE Egypt, extending S into Red Sea.

Muhammerah. Var. of MOHAMMERAH.

Mu·har'raq (moō·hŭr'rŭk). **1** Island 4 m. by 1 m., Bahrein Is., Persian Gulf, ab. 1½ m. NE of Bahrein I.
2 Town, on Muharraq I.; pop. ab. 20,000. See MANAMA.

Mühl'berg (mül'bĕrk). Town, E Germany, in what was formerly Saxony prov., Prussia, on the Elbe ab. 37 m. E of Leipzig; pop. 3549; scene of battle Apr. 24, 1547 in which the Elector John Frederick of Saxony was defeated by Emperor Charles V; in World War II taken by Russians Apr. 23, 1945.

Mühl'dorf (mül'dôrf). Town, Oberbayern govt. dist., Bavaria, Germany, on the Inn river ab. 45 m. E of Munich; pop. 6061; in World War II had subterranean jet-plane factory built 1944 by 5000 slave laborers.

Muh'len·berg (mū'lĕn·bûrg). County in Kentucky. See *Table* at KENTUCKY.

Muh'len·fels Point (mū'lĕn·fĕlz). Cape on S coast of St. Thomas I., Virgin Is. of U.S., West Indies.

Mühl'hau'sen in Thü'ring·en (mül'hou'zĕn ĭn tü'-rĭng·ĕn). Industrial city, E Germany, in what was formerly Saxony prov., Prussia, 29 m. NW of Erfurt; pop. 36,755; 17th-cent. Renaissance town hall; manufactures textiles, tobacco, machinery, wood, leather. First mentioned 775 A.D.; became city c. 1200; to Prussia 1802, to kingdom of Westphalia 1807, again to Prussia 1815.

Mu'hu (moō'hoō); *Ger.* **Moon** (mōn); *Russ.* **Mu'khu** (moō'koō). Island in Baltic Sea bet. Sarema I. and the mainland; 80 sq. m.; pop. ab. 6000; attached to Saare prov., Estonia.

Muich–dhui, Ben. See BEN MACDHUI.

Muil·rea' (mwēl·rä') or **Mweel·rea'.** Mountain, W Ireland, in SW co. Mayo; highest point 2688 ft.

Muir, Mount (mūr). Peak 14,025 ft. in Sierra Nevada, E Tulare co., S cen. California.

Muir Glacier. Glacier in Glacier Bay National Monument, SE Alaska (see UNITED STATES, *National Monuments*); covers ab. 350 sq. m.; crossed by 59°N, 136°W.

Muir Pass. Mountain pass 12,059 ft., Fresno co., S cen. California, in N part of Kings Canyon National Park on the John Muir Trail which extends from Yosemite National Park to Sequoia National Park.

Muir Woods National Monument. See UNITED STATES, *National Monuments*.

Mui'zen·berg (mū'z'n·bûrg; *Dutch* moi'zĕn·bĕrk). Town, SW Cape Province, S Union of South Africa, on NW shore of False Bay 14 m. SSE of Cape Town; pop. ab. 10,000; now included in municipality of Cape Town; favorite summer resort; cottage in which Cecil Rhodes died 1902.

Mu·je'res (moō·hā'rās). An island belonging to Mexico in the Caribbean Sea off NE coast of Yucatán penin.

Mu'ka·che'vo; *Czech* **Mu'ka·če'vo** (moō'kä·chĕ'vô); *Hung.* **Mun'kács** (moōng'käch). Town, W Ukraine, U.S.S.R., formerly in Carpathian Ruthenia, E Czechoslovakia; pop. (1930) 26,123; textile mills; trading center in lumber, cattle, and grain; iron deposits nearby. Transferred to Hungary 1938, to U.S.S.R. July 29, 1945.

Mu'kah (moō'kä). Coastal town, W Sarawak, NW Borneo, just NE of the Rajang delta.

Mu·kal'la (moō·kăl'à). Seaport and chief town of Hadhramaut, Aden Protectorate, S Arabia, 320 m. NE

of Aden; exports gums, hides, senna, and coffee; trades with India, Somaliland, Red Sea ports, and Masqat. Residence of sultan.

Muk'den' (mook'děn'; mook'-; -děn); *Chin.* **Shen'-yang'** (shŭn'yäng'); *formerly* **Feng'tien'** (fŭng'tyĕn'). City, * of Liaoning prov., S Manchuria (was * of Fengtien prov., S Manchukuo); pop. (1953) 2,299,900; strategically located on the Hun, tributary of Liao river, for control over north-to-south routes in plain of S Manchuria; built in 3 parts: old walled city, 4 m. in circumference; new town, originally Japanese concession; and commercial quarter between; railroad junction point with large trade (soybeans, kaoliang, grains, sugar beets, forest products, furs); Fushun coal fields nearby; educational center; as dynastic city for 250 years has notable palaces, mausoleums, monuments.

History: Capital of the Kin Tatars in 12th cent.; base for Manchu conquest of China 1644 and capital during rule (1644–1912) of Manchu dynasty; suffered much during Boxer uprising 1900; in Russo-Japanese War became a key position, first held by Russians; scene of great battle Feb. 19 to Mar. 10, 1905 when it was captured by Japanese; seat of "Mukden War Lord," Chang Tso-lin, during civil war 1924–27; seized by Japanese 1931; center of severe fighting in Chinese civil war 1947–48; occupied by Communist forces Nov. 1, 1948.

Mukha. See MOCHA.

Mukhmas. See MICHMASH.

Mukhu. See MUHU.

Mu·ko Ji·ma (moo·kŏ jĕ·mä). One of the Bonin Is., Japan.

Mu'la (moo'lä). Commune, Murcia prov., SE Spain, 18 m. WNW of Murcia; pop. 14,312; iron and sulfur thermal springs and baths; ruins of ancient castle.

Mulahacen. = MULHACÉN.

Mul'ber'ry (mŭl'běr'ĭ). **1** Urban community (unincorporated), Butte co., cen. California, N of Sacramento; pop. 2643.
2 City, Polk co., cen. Florida penin., 12 m. S of Lakeland; pop. 2922; phosphate mining.

Mul·chén' (mool·chän'). Town, Bío-Bío prov., S cen. Chile, ab. 305 m. S of Santiago; pop. 6829.

Mul'de (mool'dě). River ab. 156 m. long, E cen. Germany; rises in the Erz Gebirge and flows N past Chemnitz into Elbe river near Dessau.

Mule Ear Peaks. Mountain 3880 ft. in S Brewster co., W Texas.

Mule'shoe' (mŭl'shoo'). Town, ⊗ of Bailey co., NW Texas; pop. 3871.

Mul'grave (mŭl'grāv). Island in Torres Strait, N of Queensland, Australia, adjacent to Banks I. and N of Thursday I.

Mul'ha·cén' (moo'lä·thän'; -sän') *or* **Mu·ley'-Ha·cén'** (moo·lě'ĕ·ä-). Peak 11,420 ft. in the Sierra Nevada, Granada prov., S Spain; highest peak in Europe outside of the Alps and Caucasus.

Mülhausen. See MULHOUSE.

Mül'heim am Rhein (mŭl'hīm äm rīn'). Former town in Rhine Province, SW Prussia, Germany, on Rhine river; since 1914 part of Cologne.

Mülheim an der Ruhr (än děr roor'). Commercial and manufacturing city, North Rhine-Westphalia state, W Germany, on Ruhr river near its mouth 7 m. WSW of Essen; pop. (1939) 136,805; airfield; blast furnaces; manufactures steel, leather, tobacco, foodstuffs. Bombed by Allies 1943–45; taken with other cities that fell with surrender of the Ruhr May 1945.

Mul'house' (mü'looz'); *Ger.* **Mül·hau'sen** (mŭl·hou'-zĕn). Industrial and commercial commune, Haut-Rhin dept., NE France, on Ill river 22 m. S of Colmar; pop. 96,697; produces textiles, machinery, railroad material. First mentioned 717 A.D.; imperial free city 1273; allied with Swiss 15th–18th cents.; became French 1798; model workingmen's colony founded here 1853; under German rule 1871–1918; reverted to France 1918.

Mu'li·a'ma (moo'lĕ·ä'mȧ). Village on E coast of New Ireland, Bismarck Archipelago, W Pacific Ocean; has good harbor.

Mu'ling' (moo'lǐng'). River 260 m. long, Kirin prov., E Manchuria; flows NE into Ussuri river.

Mull (mŭl). Island of the Inner Hebrides, off W coast of Scotland; 351 sq. m.; pop. 2419; administratively a part of Argyll co.

Mull, Ross of (rŏs). Long SW peninsula of the island of Mull, off W coast of Scotland.

Mull, Sound of. Body of water bet. the NE coast of island of Mull and the Scottish mainland.

Mul'lagh·more' (mŭl'ȧ·mŏr'). Promontory extending N into Donegal Bay, NW Ireland, 13 m. N of Sligo.

Mul'lan (mŭl'ăn). Village, Shoshone co., NE Idaho, on Montana border 52 m. ESE of Coeur d'Alene; pop. 1477; lead and silver mines.

Mullan Trail. Wagon trail, NW United States, from Fort Benton, Montana, at head of navigation of Missouri river, across Bitterroot Range to Walla Walla, Washington; built 1859–62 under direction of Lt. John Mullan; helped to open rich mining region.

Mul'len (mŭl'ĕn; -ĭn). Village, ⊗ of Hooker co., W cen. Nebraska; pop. 811.

Mul'lens (mŭl'ĕnz; -ĭnz). City, Wyoming co., S West Virginia, 18 m. SSW of Beckley; pop. 3544; railroad and trading center of coal and lumber area.

Mul'ler Mountains (mŭl'ĕr). Range in cen. island of Borneo, Malay Archipelago, running N and S bet. the residencies of West Borneo and South and East Borneo; average height 4000 to 5000 ft.; highest point 7349 ft.; source of many of the streams of the island.

Mul'let (mŭl'ĕt; -ĭt). Peninsula on W coast of Ireland, in co. Mayo, S of Erris Head, enclosing Blacksod Bay on the W, and connected with the mainland by a narrow isthmus at the NE.

Mul'lett Lake (mŭl'ĕt; -ĭt). Lake in N Cheboygan co., N Michigan; outlet N into Straits of Mackinac.

Mul'li·ca (mŭl'ĭ·kȧ). River ab. 40 m. long, S New Jersey; flows from W Burlington co. SE into Great Bay.

Mul'lin·gar' (mŭl'ĭn·gär'). Town, ⊗ of co. Westmeath, N cen. Eire; pop. 5237; trade center in agricultural district; woolens, tanning, brewing; a haunt of anglers.

Mul'lins (mŭl'ĭnz). Town, Marion co., E South Carolina, 32 m. E of Florence; pop. 6229; tobacco market.

Mull of Galloway, Kintyre, Oa. See Mull of GALLOWAY, KINTYRE, OA.

Mul·roy' Bay (mŭl·roi'; mŭl'roi). Inlet of Atlantic Ocean on N coast of co. Donegal, N Eire, W of Lough Swilly.

Mul·tan' (mool·tän'), *also* **Mool·tan'.** **1** Division, S and SW West Punjab, NW Pakistan; 31,763 sq. m.; pop. (1941) 6,365,817.
2 City, W Pakistan, near Chenab river 200 m. WSW of Lahore; pop. 175,429; rail center and one of chief trade communities in the Punjab, with large horse market; cotton, silk, carpet, and shoe industries. An ancient city, probably one of the Indian cities taken by Alexander; seized by Mahmud of Ghazni 1005; under emperors of Delhi 1526–1779 and Afghans till 1818, when it was taken by the Sikhs under Ranjit Singh; under British sovereignty 1849. Includes surrounding wall and fort enclosing shrines of two Mohammedan saints and an ancient Hindu temple; large military cantonment.

Mult·no'mah (mŭlt·nō'mȧ). County in Oregon. See *Table* at OREGON.

Multnomah Falls. Waterfall 620 ft., Multnomah co., NW Oregon, E of Portland, in a small tributary of the Columbia river which rises near summit of Larch Mt., 4095 ft. high.

Mulucha, Muluya. See MOULOUYA.

Mul·vane' (mŭl·vān'). City, Sumner co., S Kansas, 16 m. SSE of Wichita; pop. 2981.

Mulvius, Pons. See SAXA RUBRA.

Mulwiya. See MOULOUYA.

Mun (mōōn). River ab. 350 m. long, E Thailand; rises in hills NE of Bangkok, flows E into the Mekong river on the border of Laos, Indochina, at 15°20'N; receives large tributary the Si ab. 50 m. from its mouth. Largest town on its banks is Nakhon Ratchasima. Navigable in wet season.

Muna. See MOENA.

Mün'chen (mün'ĸĕn). See MUNICH.

München–Glad'bach (-glät'bäĸ). City, W North Rhine-Westphalia state, W Germany, 15 m. WSW of Düsseldorf; taken by Allies Mar. 2, 1945. See GLAD-BACH-RHEYDT.

Münchengrätz. See MNICHOVO HRADIŠTĚ.

Mun'cie (mŭn'sĭ). City, ⊗ of Delaware co., E cen. Indiana, 50 m. ENE of Indianapolis; pop. 68,603; railroad and trading center for agricultural section; iron mills, glassworks, packing houses. Ball State Teachers College (1918; coed.).

Mun'cy (mŭn'sĭ). Borough, Lycoming co., N cen. Pennsylvania, 13 m. E of Williamsport; pop. 2830; manufactures machinery, textiles.

Mund. See MAND.

Mun'da. **1** (mōōn'dä; *Angl.* mŭn'då) Settlement on S side of NW end of New Georgia I., cen. Solomon Is., W Pacific Ocean. Site of Japanese air base 1942–43; taken by American forces Aug. 5, 1943.

2 (mŭn'då) Ancient town, S Baetica, S Spain; scene of Caesar's victory over Pompey's sons 45 B.C.

Mun'day (mŭn'dĭ). City, Knox co., N Texas, 55 m. SSW of Vernon; pop. 1978; farming; cattle.

Mun'de·lein (mŭn'dĕ·lĭn). Village, Lake co., NE Illinois, NW of Chicago; pop. 10,526.

Mün'den (mün'dĕn); *also* **Han·no'versch–Münden** (hä·nō'vĕrsh-). City, S Lower Saxony state, W Germany, at confluence of Werra and Fuida rivers 10 m. NE of Kassel; pop. 11,991; summer resort; river port; 11th-cent. castle; 14th-cent. stone bridge; 17th-cent. Renaissance town hall; manufactures emery, rubber goods, lumber.

Mun'ford·ville (mŭn'fĕrd·vĭl; *Sou. also* -v'l). City, ⊗ of Hart co., cen. Kentucky; pop. 1157.

Mun'hall (mŭn'hôl). Industrial borough, Allegheny co., SW Pennsylvania, on Monongahela river 7 m. E of Pittsburgh; pop. 17,312; steel manufactures.

Mu'ni (mōō'nĕ). River 50 m. long, Río Muni territory, Spanish Guinea, W Africa; empties into Corisco Bay.

Mu'nich (mū'nĭk); *Ger.* **Mün'chen** (mün'ĸĕn). Industrial city, ✳ of Bavaria, Germany, on Isar river; pop. (1958) 1,033,964; famous for its breweries and as an educational, cultural, and artistic center of Germany; manufactures stained glass, iron, brass, optical and mathematical instruments, lithographic productions; 12th-cent. church of St. Peter, 14th-cent. town hall, modern Gothic town hall, 15th-cent. cathedral of Notre Dame (Ger. *Frauenkirche*), 17th-cent. palace, the Glyptothek museum (19th-cent. Ionic), old and new Pinakotheken; famous university (founded at Ingolstadt 1472; transferred to Landshut, thence to Munich 1826). First mentioned 1158; capital of Bavaria from 1255; occupied by Sweden 1632, by Austria 1705 and 1742; site of unsuccessful revolt of Hitler ("Beer Hall Putsch") Nov. 8–9, 1923; birthplace of Nazi movement; scene Sept. 29, 1938 of four-power conference (Germany, Italy, Great Britain, France) leading to the partition of Czechoslovakia; in World War II frequently bombed; taken by Allies May 1, 1945.

Mu'ni·sing (mū'nĭ·sĭng). City, ⊗ of Alger co., N Michigan penin., on Lake Superior 37 m. E of Marquette; pop. 4228; manufactures paper, woodenware.

Munkács. See MUKACHEVO.

Mun'ko Sar'dik (mŭng'kŏ sär'dĭk). Highest peak 11,453 ft. in the Sayan Mts., on boundary bet. Buryat-Mongol A.S.S.R. and Outer Mongolia at the N end of Koso Gol.

Munnow. See MONNOW.

Mu·ñoz' (mōō·nyôs'). Municipality, N cen. Nueva Ecija prov., Luzon, Phil. Is., in plain watered by the Chico ab. 16 m. N of Cabanatuan; pop. 21,814.

Mun'ster (mŭn'stĕr). **1** Town, Lake co., NW corner of Indiana, 10 m. S of Lake Michigan; pop. 10,313.

2 Province, S Eire; 9317 sq. m.; pop. 942,272; includes cos. Clare, Cork, Kerry, Limerick, Tipperary (North Riding and South Riding), Waterford.

Mün'ster (mün'stĕr; *Angl.* mūn'-, mĭn'-). **1** Government district of former Westphalia prov., Prussia, Germany; 2802 sq. m.

2 *also* **Münster in West'fa'len** (ĭn vĕst'fä'lĕn). Manufacturing and commercial city, ✳ of former Westphalia prov., W Germany, near the Dortmund-Ems canal 78 m. NNE of Cologne; pop. (1939) 143,748; manufactures textiles, leather, paper, metal goods, precision instruments, beer; 13th-cent. cathedral, 14th-cent. Liebfrauenkirche, 14th-cent. Gothic town hall, 18th-cent. castle; university (founded 1788). Grew up in 12th cent. around a monastery or minster (Ger. *münster*); fell to Anabaptists 1532–35; Treaty of Westphalia signed here Oct. 24, 1648, ending Thirty Years' War; taken by Allies Apr. 3, 1945.

Mun'ta·fiq (mōōn'tă·fĭk). Province (*liwa*), S Iraq; pop. (1935 est.) 231,990.

Mun·te'ni·a (mŭn·tē'nĭ·å; *Romanian* mōōn·tĕ'nyä) or **Greater Wa·la'chi·a** (wŏ·lä'kĭ·å). Region, S Romania; E part of Walachia; 20,267 sq. m.; formerly a province.

Mun'tok (mōōn'tŏŏk). Seaport, NW Bangka I., Indonesia; pop. 6929; chief export center for tin mined in the island.

Munychia. See PIRAEUS.

Muong'sing' (mwông'sĭng'). Town, NW Laos, Indochina, near China border just E of the Mekong.

Muo'nio (mwô'nyô). River ab. 200 m. long, NW Finland; flows S into Torne river, forming a section of the boundary bet. Finland and Sweden.

Muqaiyir. See UR.

Mur (mōōr); *Slavic* **Mu'ra** (mōō'rä). River 230 m. long, Austria and N Yugoslavia; rises in E end of Hohe Tauern and flows E in Salzburg prov., E and NE across Styria, turns S and SE across Yugoslav border into Drava river 25 m. E of Varaždin.

Mu·rad' Su (mōō·rät' sōō'). = MURAT SUYU.

Mu·ra'no (mōō·rä'nŏ). North suburb of Venice, Italy, on five small islands in the lagoon of Venice; noted for its cathedral and for the manufacture of Venetian glass.

Mu·rat' Da·ği' (mōō·rät' dä·ĭ'). Peak 7313 ft., W Turkey in Asia, W of Afyon Karahisar.

Murat Su·yu' (sōō·yōō'); *also* **Eastern Euphrates**; *anc.* **Ar·sa'ni·as** (är·sä'nĭ·ăs). One of the two headstreams of the Euphrates river; rises in NE Turkey in Asia in the mountains SW of Mt. Ararat, and flows W to unite with the Kara Su and form the Euphrates river.

Mur'chi·son (mûr'chĭ·s'n). River 400 m. long, W Western Australia, flowing W to Indian Ocean.

Murchison Falls. **1** Waterfall 118 ft. high in the Victoria Nile, just above Lake Albert, in Uganda. See NILE.

2 Waterfall in the Shire river, Nyasaland, SE Africa, lat. 15°40'S.

Mur'ci·a (mûr'shĭ·å; -shå; *Span.* mōōr'thyä, -syä). **1** Region and ancient kingdom, SE Spain; 10,108 sq. m.; bounded N and NW by New Castile, SW by Andalusia, S by Mediterranean, and E by Valencia; comprises modern provinces of Albacete and Murcia; watered by the Segura and its affluents; climate varies from subtropical to temperate and its arid regions require irrigation for agricultural exploitation; produces principally wheat, barley, flax; lead, copper, zinc, sulfur, iron mines; manufactures textiles and esparto products; stock raising.

History: Center of Carthaginian colonization in Spain; conquered by Moors in 8th cent.; made province of Caliphate of Córdoba; became independent Moorish kingdom in early 11th cent.; conquered by Castile 1266.

2 Province of Spain. See *Table* at SPAIN.

3 Commune, ✳ of Murcia prov., SE Spain, on Segura river 47 m. SW of Alicante; pop. (1941 est.) 198,387; manufactures silks, esp. taffeta and plush, woolens, leather, soap, glass, saltpeter, gloves, hats, linens, baize, pottery; 14th-cent. Gothic-Romanesque cathedral, 18th-cent. episcopal palace; Moorish granary; city walls. First settled by Romans; reconquered from Moors in 13th cent.; capital of ancient kingdom of Murcia.

Mur·cié′la·gos, Gulf of (moor-syä′lä-gôs); *formerly* **Cu·le′bra Gulf** (kū-lā′brà; -lĕb′rà; *Span.* koo-lā′vrä). Inlet of Pacific Ocean on NW coast of Costa Rica.

Mur′do (mûr′dō). City, ⊗ of Jones co., S cen. South Dakota; pop. 783.

Mu′reş *or* **Mu′resh** (moo′rĕsh); *Hung.* **Ma′ros** (mŏ′-rōsh). River ab. 400 m. long, Hungary and Romania; rises in Transylvania among the Carpathian Mts. near the Moldavian frontier, flows W across N Romania, continues W across Hungarian border and into Tisza river opp. Szeged; navigable for small boats for over 200 m.

Mur′frees·bor′o (mûr′frēz-bûr′ô). **1** City, ⊗ of Pike co., SW Arkansas; pop. 1096.

2 Town, Hertford co., NE North Carolina, 50 m. WNW of Elizabeth City; pop. 1690.

3 Commercial city, ⊗ of Rutherford co., cen. Tennessee, on West Fork of Stone River 33 m. SE of Nashville; pop. 18,991; shipping point for cotton and dairy products; manufactures buckets, churns, rayon and silk; Middle Tennessee State College (1909; coed.). Made county seat 1811, capital of Tennessee 1819–25; during Civil War site of battle (also called battle of Stones River, *q.v.*) Dec. 31, 1862–Jan. 2, 1863 in which Federal forces under Rosecrans won a strategic victory over Confederates under Bragg.

Murgh (moorg). Pass 7480 ft., NE Afghanistan, N of Kabul, in the Hindu Kush Mts.

Murgh·ab′ (moor-gäb′). **1** *Russ.* **Mur·gab′** (moor-gáp′). River ab. 450 m. long, NW Afghanistan and SE Turkmen S.S.R.; rises in W slopes of the Hindu Kush and flows W and NW until lost in the sands of the Kara Kum Desert beyond Mary.

2 Town in SW Iran. See MASHAD-I-MURGHAB.

3 Plain, ancient Persia: see PASARGADAE.

4 *or* **Aq′su′** (äk′soo′). River of Tadzhik S.S.R.; flows W in Pamirs as headstream of Amu Darya (*q.v.*).

Mu′ria·é′ (moo′ryà-â′). City, SE Minas Gerais state, E Brazil, 75 m. NE of Juiz de Fora; pop. 9418.

Mu′ri·ci·tan·deu′a (moo′rē-sē-tăn-dâ′oo-à). Island off N coast of Maranhão state, Brazil, at entrance to Turiassú Bay.

Mü′ritz, Lake (mü′rĭts). Lake, Mecklenburg, Germany, W of Neustrelitz.

Mur·man′, *or* **Mur·mansk′, Coast** (moor-màn′, -mànsk′); *also, earlier* **Nor′man Coast** (nôr′măn). The N coast of Kola Penin., Murmansk Region, NW Soviet Russia, Europe, ab. 165 m. long from 36°E to 41°E; generally ice-free because of warm easterly ocean current; has many inlets and good harbors and in many places cliffs 300 to 1000 ft.; abounds with fish.

Mur·mansk′ (moor′mànsk′). City, ✳ of Murmansk Region, NW Soviet Russia, Europe, in NW part on Kola Bay, ab. 22 m. from the ocean, 69°10′N; pop. 117,054; terminus of railroad to Leningrad; ice-free port all the year round with spacious safe anchorage. Settlement begun 1915; since completion of railroad 1917 has been provided with extensive port facilities; although frequently bombed by German planes, remained throughout World War II a Russian receiving base of great strategic value.

Murmansk Region. Region, NW Soviet Russia, Europe, nearly coextensive with Kola Penin.; 53,615 sq. m.; pop. 291,188; ✳ Murmansk. Bounded on N and E by Barents Sea, on S by White Sea and Karelo-Finnish S.S.R., and on W by Finland. A plateau with average elevation of 600 to 700 ft., highest point ab. 4000 ft.; a

tundra region of many lakes (largest Imandra), small rivers, morasses; chief river the Tuloma, in the NW. Little agriculture; rich in forests; has some mineral wealth. Chief inhabitants Lapp, with some Russians and Finns; main occupations fishing, hunting, lumbering, and raising reindeer. Formerly a district attached to Leningrad; its shore controlled 1918–19 by British fleet; since 1944 has included in the NW Petsamo and surrounding territory acquired from Finland (see PECHENGA).

Mu′roc (mûr′ŏk). Locality, SE Kern co., S California, in Mojave Desert on **Muroc Dry Lake** SE of Bakersfield; site of Edwards Air Force Base.

Mu′ro Lu·ca′no (moo′rô loo-kä′nô). Commune, Potenza prov., W Lucania, S Italy; pop. (1931) 8295; castle, scene of death of Joanna I, Queen of Naples.

Mu′rom (moo′rŭm). Town, SE Vladimir Region, E cen. Soviet Russia, Europe, on the Oka 90 m. SW of Gorki; pop. 22,621; on railroad E from Moscow; industrial center; linen and cotton goods; also trades in grain.

Mu·ro·ran (moo-rô-rän). Seaport, SW Hokkaido I., Japan, on N side of Uchiura Bay; pop. (1945) 91,178; important naval base and shipping port for coal; iron and steel center of N Japan; has regular steamship services with Hakodate and Aomori.

Mu′ros (moo′rōs). Commune, La Coruña prov., NW Spain, on inlet of Atlantic Ocean 49 m. SW of La Coruña; pop. 10,475; agricultural products; manufactures flour, soap, textiles; commercial fisheries, fish-salting.

Mu·ro·to, Cape (moo-rô-tô). Cape on SE coast of Shikoku I., Japan; lighthouse.

Mur′phy (mûr′fĭ). **1** Town, ⊗ of Owyhee co., SW corner of Idaho; pop. (1950) 125; shipping point for livestock.

2 Town and mountain resort, ⊗ of Cherokee co., W tip of North Carolina, 5 m. N of Georgia border and 16 m. E of Tennessee border; pop. 2235; marble, talc, iron mines.

Mur′phys·bor′o (mûr′fĭz-bûr′ô). City, ⊗ of Jackson co., SW Illinois, 24 m. W of Marion; pop. 8673; settled 1850, incorp. 1867; trading center; lumber, coal.

Mur·ra′ça (moor-rä′sà). Town on Zambezi river, cen. Mozambique, SE Africa; terminus of railroad from Dondo.

Mur′ray (mûr′ĭ). **1** Counties of three states of the U.S. See *Tables* at GEORGIA, MINNESOTA, OKLAHOMA.

2 City, ⊗ of Calloway co., SW Kentucky, 22 m. ESE of Mayfield; pop. 9303. Site of Murray State College (1923; coed.).

3 City, Salt Lake co., N Utah, on Jordan river 8 m. S of Salt Lake City; pop. 16,806; suburb of Salt Lake City; lead-ore smelting and refining.

4 Chief river of Australia, ab. 1200 m. long; to the source of the Darling (*q.v.*) 2310 m. Rises in Kosciusko Plateau, E Victoria, flows NW as boundary bet. Victoria and New South Wales; ab. 1200 m. into SE South Australia where it turns S and flows into Encounter Bay through Lake Alexandrina (*q.v.*); at ab. 142°E it receives the Darling from the N and farther E at 143°13′E the Murrumbidgee. In the dry season often shallow; in the wet season navigable to Albury for smaller vessels; sand bars at its mouth prevent entrance of large vessels.

Murray, Lake. 1 See UNITED STATES, *Dams and Reservoirs* (Saluda Dam).

2 Lake extending across boundary bet. Carter and Love cos., S Oklahoma.

3 Large lake in swamp and lake region bet. Fly and Strickland rivers, W Papua, New Guinea.

Murray Bay. Village on the St. Lawrence, Quebec, Canada, now part of La Malbaie.

Murray Bridge. Town, SE South Australia, on Murray river near its mouth 40 m. WSW of Adelaide; pop. 3651.

Mur′ree (mûr′ē). Hill resort, N West Pakistan, in Himalayas 28 m. NE of Rawalpindi; summer seat of some government officials and embassies.

Mur′rum·bidg′ee (mûr′ŭm-bĭj′ē). River ab. 1000 m. long, S New South Wales, SE Australia; flows W from Great Dividing Range near Canberra to join Murray

river at ab. 143°E; navigable for small vessels for ab. 500 m. in rainy season.

Mursa. See OSIJEK.

Mur′shid·a·bad′ (mŏŏr′shĭd·ä·bäd′). Town, West Bengal, NE India, on left bank of the Bhagirathi (old channel of the Ganges); pop. 9483; founded 1704 by Murshid Kuli Khan as Mohammedan capital of Bengal; a populous city in 18th cent. and headquarters of Siraj-ud-daula at the time of Plassey 1757; contains fine palace of the Nawab of Bengal.

Murtana. See PERGA.

Murten. See MORAT.

Murua. See WOODLARK.

Mu·rud′ (mŏŏ·rŏŏd′). Seaport town, ✳ of former Janjira state, in E Maharashtra, W India, 45 m. S of Bombay; pop. 7177.

Mu′ru·ro′a (mŏŏ′rŏŏ·rō′å). Atoll, S Tuamotu Archipelago, S Pacific Ocean, ab. 550 m. SE of Fakarava.

Murviedro. See SAGUNTO.

Mur·wa′ra (mŏŏr·wȧ′rȧ). Town, cen. Madhya Pradesh, India, on the Son river ab. 200 m. NNE of Nagpur; pop. 21,959.

Mürz (mürts). River ab. 45 m. long, Styria, SE Austria; rises in N Styria and flows SW to the Mur at Bruck.

Mur′zuch (mŏŏr′zŏŏk); *Arab.* **Mur′zuq** (mŏŏr′zŏŏk). Oasis, in the Fezzan, SW Libya; pop. ab. 7000.

Muş (mŏŏsh) *or* **Mush. 1** Vilayet, E Turkey in Asia; 6247 sq. m.; pop. 65,985.
2 Town, its ✳, 45 m. W of Lake Van; pop. 4912; an old Armenian town on fertile plain.

Mu′sa, Geb′el (jĕb′ĕl mŏŏ′sȧ). Mountain group, S Sinai Penin., Egypt; name applied by some only to N peak 7497 ft.; highest in the group Gebel Katherina 8652 ft. On its N slope is St. Catherine's Monastery of Mt. Sinai which has fine library; in it was found by Tischendorf 1844–45 one of oldest Greek Biblical MSS. known, the *Codex Sinaiticus,* which became property of the tsar, then of U.S.S.R., and was sold to British Museum 1933 for £100,000. See Mt. SINAI; HOREB.

Mu′sa, Jeb′el (jĕb′ĕl mŏŏ′sȧ); *anc.* **Ab′i·la** *or* **Ab′y·la** (ăb′ĭ·lȧ). Mountain 2775 ft. at Ceuta, N Morocco, opp. Gibraltar. See PILLARS OF HERCULES.

Mu′sa·la′ (mŏŏ′sä·lä′). Highest peak 9595 ft. in the Rhodope Mts., in the Rila Dagh, SW Bulgaria, SSE of Sofia.

Mu·san′dam, Cape (mŭ·săn′dăm); *Arab.* **Ras Masan′dam** (räs mȧ·săn′dŏŏm). Cape, NE Trucial Oman, SE Arabia, extending N into the Strait of Ormuz.

Muscat. See MASQAT.

Mus′ca·tine (mŭs′kȧ·tēn; mŭs′kȧ·tēn′). **1** County in Iowa. See *Table* at IOWA.
2 City, its ✳, E Iowa, on Mississippi river 25 m. W of Davenport; pop. 20,997; trading and industrial center in agricultural section; produces melons and vegetables; manufactures pearl buttons, aluminum, steel cabinets; meat-packing and food-processing plants.

Mus′cle Shoals (mŭs′'l shōlz′). **1** Rapids extending ab. 37 m. in Tennessee river, in Lauderdale co., N Alabama; now submerged under at least 9 ft. of water by completion of Wilson Dam at W end and Wheeler Dam at E end. See TENNESSEE river.
2 Town, Colbert co., NW Alabama, near Wilson Dam 3 m. S of Tennessee river; pop. 4084.

Mus·co′gee (mŭs·kō′gē). County in Georgia. See *Table* at GEORGIA.

Mus·co·net′cong (mŭs′kŏ·nĕt′kŏng). River 50 m. long, N New Jersey; flows from Lake Hopatcong SW to Delaware river at SW extremity of Warren co.

Mus·con′gus Bay (mŭs·kŏng′gŭs). Inlet of Atlantic Ocean on SW coast of Knox co., S Maine.

Mus′co·vy (mŭs′kŏ·vĭ). An old name of Russia. See Moscow principality.

Mus′grave Ranges (mŭs′grāv). Mountain ranges along boundary bet. South Australia and Northern Territory; highest Mt. Woodroffe 4970 ft.

Mush. See MUŞ.

Mu·sho·zu (mŏŏ·shō·zŏŏ). See IKI.

Mu′si (mŏŏ′sē). **1** River, Andhra Pradesh, S cen. India; flows E and then S into Kistna river.
2 River, S Sumatra, Neth. Indies. See MOESI.

Mu′sic Pass (mū′zĭk). Mountain pass 11,800 ft., Huerfano and Saguache cos., S Colorado, in the Sangre de Cristo Range of the Rocky Mts.; used since c. 1878 by travelers on Arkansas river route to California and New Mexico; trail.

Musigny. See CHAMBOLLE-MUSIGNY.

Mus′keg Bay (mŭs′kĕg). Inlet of Lake of the Woods, N Minnesota, in NE Roseau co.

Mus·ke′get Channel (mŭs·kē′gĕt; -gĭt). Strait bet. Martha's Vineyard on the W and Muskeget I., Tuckernuck I., and Nantucket on the E, in SE Massachusetts, and connecting Nantucket Sound with the Atlantic Ocean.

Muskeget Island. Island in Atlantic Ocean at E entrance of Muskeget Channel S of Cape Cod, SE Massachusetts; a part of Nantucket co.

Mus·ke′gon (mŭs·kē′gŭn). **1** River 200 m. long, W cen. Michigan; rises in Houghton Lake, Roscommon co., flows SW into Lake Michigan at Muskegon, in Muskegon co.; navigable for a short distance.
2 County in Michigan. See *Table* at MICHIGAN.
3 City, its ⊗, W Michigan, on Lake Michigan at mouth of Muskegon river 35 m. WNW of Grand Rapids; pop. 46,485; lake port and railroad center; trading point for summer resort area; manufactures motors, motor accessories, aircraft engines and parts, machinery, and office equipment; former lumbering center.

Muskegon Heights. City, Muskegon co., W Michigan, S suburb of Muskegon; pop. 19,552.

Mus·kin′gum (mŭs·kĭng′[g]ŭm). **1** River 120 m. long, E Ohio; formed by confluence of Tuscarawas and Walhonding rivers in Coshocton co., E cen. Ohio, flows S and SE into Ohio river at Marietta, Washington co.; navigable for 90 m.
2 County in Ohio. See *Table* at OHIO.

Mus·ko′gee (mŭs·kō′gē). **1** County in Oklahoma. See *Table* at OKLAHOMA.
2 City, its ⊗, E Oklahoma, on Arkansas river 47 m. SE of Tulsa; pop. 38,059; founded 1872; chartered as city 1898. Railroad center; oil and gas wells, zinc fields, limestone deposits; oil refineries, cotton gins; canning, truck gardening; manufactures road machinery, oil-well equipment, cottonseed products, batteries, flour, packed meat.

Mus·ko′ka (mŭs·kō′kȧ). District, SE Ontario, Canada. See *Table* at ONTARIO.

Muskoka, Lake. Lake 54 sq. m., Muskoka dist., SE Ontario, Canada; with Lakes Rosseau and Joseph and several hundred small lakes forms **Muskoka Lake Region,** noted for its scenery, its hunting and fishing, and as a summer resort. Outlet is **Muskoka River,** ab. 100 m. long, with two headstreams rising in lakes of Haliburton co. and Muskoka dist. and flowing SW through Lake Muskoka to Georgian Bay. Bracebridge is on it.

Mus′li·mi′ya (mŏŏs′lĭ·mē′yȧ; -yȧ). Town, NW Syria, ab. 8 m. N of Alep; junction on railroads NW to Adana in Turkey and NE to Nusaybin in Turkey.

Mu·soc′co (mŏŏ·zôk′kô). Town in Milan commune, Lombardy, N Italy; pop. (1931) 25,440; NW suburb of Milan.

Mus·sau′ (mŏŏs·sou′). Island ab. 20 m. long by 10 m. wide in the W Pacific Ocean, N Bismarck Archipelago, in Saint Mathias group NNW of New Hanover; largest island in the group.

Mus′sel·burgh (mŭs′'l·bŭ·rȧ; -brȧ). Seaport burgh, Midlothian co., SE Scotland, at mouth of the Esk; pop. 17,012; a suburb of Edinburgh; paper mills, breweries. Loretto school. Nearby is site of battle of Pinkie Cleuch 1547 in which English forces of duke of Somerset and earl of Warwick defeated Scots under earl of Huntly.

Mus'sel·shell' (mŭs''l-shĕl'). **1** River 300 m. long, cen. Montana; rises in Meagher co., flows E, then N into Missouri river in NW Garfield co.
2 County in Montana. See *Table* at MONTANA.

Mus'so·li'nia (mōōs'sô-lē'nyä); *since 1945 called* **Ar-bo're·a** (är·bô'rä·ä). Town, W Sardinia, on Gulf of Oristano.

Mus'so·me'li (mōōs'sô-mâ'lê). Commune, Caltanissetta prov., cen. Sicily, 18 m. WNW of Caltanissetta; pop. 14,014; castle; sulfur mining.

Mus·soo'rie (mŭ·sōō'rê). Hill station and sanitarium, Dehra Dun dist., N Uttar Pradesh, N Indian Union, 135 m. NNE of Delhi; pop. 4966; formerly one of chief summer resorts of Europeans of N India; alt. 6600 ft.

Mus·ta·fa' Ke·mal' Pa·şa' (mōōs·tä·fä' kĕ·mäl' pä-shä'); *formerly* **Kir·mas·ti'** (kĕr·mäs·tē'). Town, W Bursa vilayet, NW Turkey in Asia, 37 m. WSW of Bursa; pop. 14,688.

Mustagh Ata. See MUZTAGH ATA.

Mus·tagh' Range (mōōs·tä'). Former name of Karakoram Range (*q.v.*).

Mus'tang Island (mŭs'tăng). Island in Nueces co., S Texas, bet. Corpus Christi Bay and the Gulf of Mexico; one of the chain of islands along the Texas coast including St. Joseph I. and Padre I. (*qq.vv.*).

Mus'ters, Lake (mŭs'tērz; mōōs'tērs). Lake in S Chubut territory, S Argentina, W of Gulf of San Jorge.

Mu'tan' (mōō'dän'). River ab. 310 m. long, E Kirin prov., Manchuria; flows NE and N to join the Sungari at I-lan.

Mu'tan'kiang' (mōō'dän'jĭ·äng'). **1** Former province (1932–45), E Manchukuo; 12,723 sq. m.; pop. (1940 est.) 689,113; * Mutankiang.
2 City, E cen. Kirin prov., E Manchuria, on Mutan river and on former Chinese Eastern Railway, ab. 160 m. SE of Harbin; pop. (1940 est.) 179,217; capital of former Mutankiang prov., E Manchukuo.

Mutina. See MODENA.

Mu·ton'do (mōō·tōnn'dōō). Town, Rio de Janeiro state, E Brazil, near E shore of Guanabara Bay ab. 11 m. NE of Rio de Janeiro.

Mu·tsu Bay (mōō·tsōō). Large bay in Aomori prefecture, N extremity of Honshu I., Japan.

Mut'tenz (mōōt'ĕnts). Commune, Basel-Land demicanton, Switzerland, SE of Basel; pop. (1930) 4966; ruined castle.

Mut'ton Bay (mŭt''n). Village, E Quebec prov., E Canada, on Cape Mecatina on Strait of Belle Isle; nursing station of Grenfell Mission.

Mut'tra (mŭ'trå); *earlier* **Ma'thu·ra** (mŭt'hŏō·rä). City, W Uttar Pradesh, N Indian Union, on the right bank of the Jumna river 30 m. NW of Agra; pop. (1941) 76,716; cotton and paper factories. Ancient city, one of the most important centers of Indian art (the Muttra school, sculptors in red sandstone, 3d cent. B.C. to 6th cent. A.D.), and revered by Hindus as birthplace of Krishna; in early Christian era a center of Buddhism and Jainism; has a mosque built by Aurangzeb and a museum of antiquities. Plundered by Mahmud of Ghazni c. 1018 and destroyed by the Lodi sultan Sikandar II c. 1500; the great temple demolished by Aurangzeb in 1667; sacked by Ahmad Shah in 1756; under British sovereignty 1803.

Mu·wai'lih, al– (ăl'mōō·wī'lĭ; *Arab*. -lī·h'). Port on the Red Sea, N Hejaz, W Arabia, 65 m. SE of entrance to Gulf of 'Aqaba.

Mu·yun' Kum (mōō·yōōn' kōōm'); *also* **Mo·yun'–Kum** (mô·yōōn'–). Sandy desert region, SE Kazakh S.S.R., Soviet Central Asia, bet. the Chu and Syr Darya rivers.

Mu·zaf'far·garh (mōō·zŭf'ēr·gär; *native* -gŭr·h'). **1** District, Multan division, West Punjab, Pakistan; 5605 sq. m.; pop. (1941) 712,849; area bet. the Indus and the Chenab above their junction.
2 Town, its *, ab. 25 m. SW of Multan; pop. ab. 6000.

Mu·zaf'far·na'gar (mōō·zŭf'ēr·nŭg'ēr). Town, Meerut division, NW Uttar Pradesh, N Indian Union, 63 m. NNE of Delhi; pop. 35,347.

Mu·zaf'far·pur (mōō·zŭf'ēr·pōōr). **1** District, Tirhut division, NW Bihar state, NE Indian Union: 3025 sq. m.; pop. (1941) 3,244,651.
2 Town, its * and * of Tirhut division, on affluent of the Gogra river 35 m. N of Patna; pop. (1941) 54,009; has active trade with Nepal.

Mu'zo (mōō'sô). Municipality, Boyacá dept., cen. Colombia, SW of Chiquinquirá; pop. ab. 3000; emerald mines.

Mu·zon', Cape (?mōō·zŏn'). Southern point of Dall I. on Dixon Entrance, SE Alaska.

Muz·tagh' A·ta' *or* **Mus·tagh' A·ta'** (mōōs·tä' ä·tä'). Mountain 24,388 ft. in Muztagh Ata Range, W Sinkiang prov., W China, near the border of Tadzhik S.S.R. and ab. 75 m. SW of Kashgar.

Muztagh Ata Range. Mountain range running N and S along E Tadzhik border in W Sinkiang, W China; by some considered part of the Pamirs; highest point Kungur, in N part of range, 25,146 ft.; many peaks above 20,000 ft.

Muztagh, *or* **Mustagh, Pass.** Mountain pass in Karakoram Range, N Kashmir, W of Mount Godwin Austen; altitude 19,030 ft.

Mwan'za (mwän'zä). **1** Former province in N Tanganyika, E Africa, now the E part of Lake prov.
2 Port on S shore of Lake Victoria, N Tanganyika, E Africa; * of Lake prov.; pop. ab. 6000; railroad terminus.

Mweelrea. See MUILREA.

Mwe'ru (mwā'rōō). Lake ab. 80 m. long in cen. Africa, on boundary bet. SE Congo and Northern Rhodesia, W of S tip of Lake Tanganyika; the Luapula, a headstream of the Congo river, flows through it.

Mweru–Lu'a·pu'la (-lōō'ä·pōō'lä). Province, N Northern Rhodesia, S cen. Africa; 20,110 sq. m.; pop. 128,094; * Fort Rosebery.

Mya, Wa'di (wä'dĭ myă'). Dry river course in NE cen. Algeria, S of Chott Melrir.

Myaung'mya' (myoung'myä'). **1** District, Irrawaddy division, SW Lower Burma, in Irrawaddy delta; 2815 sq. m.; pop. 444,784.
2 Town, its *, 22 m. SE of Bassein; pop. 7773.

Myc'a·le (mĭk'å·lē; -lê). Ancient name of promontory in the S of Ionia (NW Caria) on the coast of Asia Minor; a religious center with temple to Poseidon on N shore. Battle fought 479 B.C. on the shore of this promontory was a contest for the Persian ships and was a Greek victory.

My·ce'nae (mī·sē'nē; -nê). Ruined city in Argolis and Corinth dept., NE Peloponnesus, Greece, ab. 7 m. N of Argos. One of the most ancient cities of Greece; a natural rock citadel on N edge of Argive plain.
History: Flourished during Bronze Age; on basis of Minoan or Cretan culture (see CRETE), built a distinctive art and civilization known as Mycenaean (more accurately Late Helladic c. 1600–1100 B.C., corresponding to Late Minoan); at height of its supremacy in Aegean area c. 1400 B.C.; declined c. 1200 B.C. before invasion of Greeks from north; scene of Schliemann's great archaeological discoveries 1874, 1876, including "Treasury of Atreus," which revealed existence of pre-Greek civilization in Aegean; ruins include famous Lion Gate, beehive tombs, shaft grave tombs, etc. Legendary capital of King Agamemnon.

My'ers·town (mī'ērz·toun). Borough, Lebanon co., SE cen. Pennsylvania, 22 m. W of Reading; pop. 3268; manufactures textiles, cigars, pretzels, foundry products.

Myin'gyan (myĭn'jän). **1** District, Mandalay division, Upper Burma; 2710 sq. m.; pop. 472,557.
2 Town, its *, on the left bank of the Irrawaddy river at its confluence with the Chindwin 60 m. WSW of Mandalay; pop. 25,457.

Myit′kyi′na′ (myĭ′chē′nä′). **1** District, N Sagaing division, Upper Burma; now in Kachin State; 22,262 sq. m.; area covered by census 11,876 sq. m., with pop. 166,175; attached Shan States (**Hkam′ti Long** [käm′tĕ long′]) 296 sq. m., with pop. 5349.
2 Town, its *, on left bank of upper Irrawaddy near China border 260 m. NNE of Mandalay; pop. 7328; most important town in N Burma N of Bhamo with which it is connected by small steamers through the upper defile of the Irrawaddy; on the Stilwell Road; has two airfields. Captured by the Japanese Apr. 1942 but after severe fighting was retaken by Allied forces Aug. 3, 1944.

Myit′nge′ (myĭt′ngâ′). River ab. 250 m. long, E Upper Burma; flows SW and W through Northern Shan States to the Irrawaddy river just S of Mandalay.

Myk′o·nos (mĭk′ô·nŏs; mī′kŏ-); *Mod. Gr.* **Mý′ko·nos** (mē′kô·nôs). Island, NE Cyclades, Aegean Sea, SE of Tenos; in Cyclades dept., Greece; 35 sq. m.; pop. ab. 5000; chief village **Mykonos**, pop. 1665. Island of Delos is off its SW coast.

Mylae. See MILAZZO.

Mylasa. See MILAS.

Myl·liem′ (mĭl·lēm′). See KHASI STATES.

My·men·singh (mī′mĕn·sĭng; *native* -sĭng·h′). **1** District, Dacca division, East Bengal, NE Pakistan; 6156 sq. m.; pop. (1941) 6,023,758.
2 *formerly* **Na·sir′a·bad** (ná·sēr′ä·bäd). Town, its *, 200 m. NE of Calcutta; pop. (1941) 52,950.

My·nydd′is′lw·yn (mŭ·nĭth′ĭs′lŏŏ·ŭn). Urban district, Monmouthshire, W England, 28 m. WNW of Bristol; pop. 14,418.

My·nydd′ Ta′rw (mŭ·nĭth′ tä′rŏŏ). Peak 2230 ft. in the Berwyn Mts., N Wales.

My′ra (mī′rà). One of the chief cities of ancient Lycia, S Asia Minor, on the coast; site of ancient ruins and rock tombs.

Mýr′dals·jö′kull (mēr′däls·yû′küt·l′). Glacier in S Iceland.

My·ri′na (mĭ·rī′nà). Ancient town of Aeolis, NW Asia Minor, on the coast 5 m. W of Gryneion; excavations here have uncovered many small terra-cotta figures.

Myr′tle Beach (mûr′t′l). Town, Horry co., E South Carolina, on Atlantic Ocean 13 m. SE of Conway; pop. 7834; seaside resort.

Mys (mĭs). Russian word meaning "promontory"; for names including it, see the second element.

My′si·a (mĭsh′ĭ·à). Ancient country in NW Asia Minor, bounded on N by the Propontis, on E by Bithynia and Phrygia (E boundary varied with the fortunes of the kingdoms on that side), on S by Lydia, and on W by the Aegean; included regions of the Troad in the NW and Aeolis along SW coast; chief cities Pergamum and Cyzicus. Became subject of Croesus of Lydia, then of Persia and Syria; assigned to Pergamum by Rome 190 B.C.; became part of Roman province of Asia 130 B.C.

Mys′ła·cho·wi′ce (mĭs′łä·ᴋô·vē′tsĕ). Locality, S Poland, near Kraków; in hunting lodge formerly occupied by Hermann Göring, Cominform organized Oct. 1947 by representatives of nine European nations.

Mys′ło·wi′ce (mĭs′łô·vē′tsĕ); *Ger.* **Mys′lo·witz** (mĭs′-lô·vĭts). Industrial commune, E Śląsk dept., SW Poland, 8 m. ESE of Katowice; pop. (1938–39 est.) 24,619; metalworks; coal mines. Prussian until 1922.

My·sore′ (mī·sōr′) *or* **Mai·sur′** (mī·sŏŏr′). **1** Indian state, S Indian Union, S of Maharashtra; enlarged 1956; 74,326 sq. m.; pop. 19,399,300; * Bangalore; occupies plateau region of Southern Deccan with hills in W; has healthful climate; watered by tributaries of Kistna, Penner, and Cauvery rivers; prosperous state with large silk and gold-mining (Kolar Gold Fields) industries. From early times to c. 1400 for the most part ruled by Hindu dynasties (Cholas, Cheras, etc.); succeeded by Hindu rajas of Vijayanagar, who were overwhelmed 1565 by Moslems from the N; throne usurped by Haidar Ali 1761, who with his son Tipu Sahib ruled until 1799; period of Mysore Wars; administration taken over by British 1831; returned to native rule 1881; since 1947 in Indian Union.
2 City, S Mysore state, S of Cauvery river 85 m. SW of Bangalore; pop. (1941) 150,540; has European-style fort including within its walls the maharaja's palace with its famed ivory-and-gold throne. Seat of maharaja's college and a university (estab. 1916). Dynastic capital of Mysore state; occupied by British 1831.

Mys′tic (mĭs′tĭk). **1** Short river rising in **Mystic Lakes** (2 connected lakes), Middlesex co., NE Massachusetts; flows SE into Boston Harbor N of Charlestown; navigable as far as Medford.
2 Subdivision of town of STONINGTON, Connecticut, at mouth of Mystic river (short stream flowing S to Long Island Sound); pop. 2536; shipping and fishing center in Revolutionary times; famous as shipbuilding center during 1849 gold rush.
3 City, Appanoose co., S Iowa, 34 m. WSW of Ottumwa; pop. 761; coal mining.

My′then (mē′tĕn). Twin peaks, **Gros′se My′the** (grō′sĕ mē′tĕ), 6239 ft., and **Klei′ne Mythe** (klī′nĕ), 5955 ft., near Schwyz, Schwyz canton, E cen. Switzerland.

My′tho′ (mē′tō′). Town, E Cochin China, Vietnam, in the Mekong delta 45 m. SSW of Saigon; terminus of railroad from Saigon; former French naval base.

Myt′i·le′ne (mĭt′′l·ē′nĕ); *Mod. Gr.* **My′ti·li′ni** (mē′tĕ-lyē′nyĕ). **1** Island. See LESBOS.
2 *formerly called* **Ka′stro** (käs′trô). City, * of Lesbos dept., Aegean Is., Greece, and chief town on Lesbos I.; pop. 27,870; has good harbor.

Mýto Vysoké. = VYSOKÉ MÝTO.

My′us (mī′ŭs). Ancient city, one of the 12 Ionian Cities, near the mouth of the Maeander and just ENE of Miletus, Asia Minor.

N

Naab *or* **Nab** (näp). River ab. 100 m. long in S Germany; rises in the Fichtel Gebirge and flows S in E Bavaria to join the Danube above Regensburg.

Naald′wijk (nält′vīk). Commune, South Holland prov., SW Netherlands, near mouth of the Maas 9 m. SSW of The Hague; pop. 11,757.

Na′a·le′hu (nä′ä·lä′hōō). Village, Kau dist., Hawaii co., Hawaii, on S coast of Hawaii I. NE of Ka Lae; pop. (est.) 1500.

Naar′den (när′dĕ[n]). Commune, North Holland prov., W Netherlands, ab. 12 m. ESE of Amsterdam on S shore of Zuider Zee; pop. 5839; will eventually be on edge of reclaimed SE polder.

Naas (nās). Urban district, ⊗ of co. Kildare, E Eire; pop. 3290; notable fox-hunting center; once seat of kings of Leinster; sacked and burned by Owen McRory O′More 1597.

Nab. See NAAB.

Nabadwip. See NADIA.

Na′bal, Na′bel (nă′băl). Arabic forms of NABEUL.

Na·band′ (nä·bánd′). 1 Cape on SW coast of Iran, projecting into E cen. Persian Gulf.
2 Town at cape.

Nab′be·ru′, Lake (năb′ĕ·rōō′). Lake on W edge of Gibson Desert, cen. Western Australia.

Na′beul′ (nà′bûl′); *anc.* **Ne·ap′o·lis** (nē·ăp′ō·lĭs). Coastal town, NE Tunisia, at S of base of Cape Bon Penin.; pop. ab. 8000; ancient Phoenician ruins on the shore.

Na′bha (näb′há). 1 Former Indian state, Punjab States, comprising many small districts in East Punjab, NW India; 947 sq. m.; pop. (1941) 340,044; one of the Sikh states of the Phulkian group; established its independence c. 1763.
2 Town, its *, 37 m. W of Ambala; pop. 17,311.

Nab′lus (năb′lŭs; nä′blŭs; *Arab.* nä′blōōs). 1 Subdistrict, Samaria dist., N cen. Palestine; 633 sq. m.; pop. 68,706, (1938 est.) 80,285.
2 *anc.* **She′chem** (shē′kĕm); *later* **Ne·ap′o·lis** (nē·ăp′ō·lĭs). Town, its * and * of Samaria dist., 30 m. N of Jerusalem in a valley bet. Mts. Ebal and Gerizim; pop. (1944 est.) 23,250; has large Mohammedan population. Ancient Shechem in hill country of Ephraim important in early Biblical period; home of Jacob; Jacob's well and tomb of Joseph; scene of Jeroboam's rebellion and, as chief city of Samaria, became his capital of Israel; fell into decay; rebuilt and renamed Neapolis by Emperor Vespasian; suffered damage in Crusades and from Ibrahim Pasha 1834.

Nabrissa. See LEBRIJA.

Na′bua (nä′bwä). Municipality, S Camarines Sur prov., Luzon, Phil. Is., just W of Iriga; pop. 29,433.

Na′ca·o′me (nä′kä·ō′mä). Town, S Honduras, * of Valle dept., 22 m. NNE of Amapala; pop. (1935) 1843.

Na′cham (nä′chäm); *also* **Nam–quan** (näm′kwän). Town, NE Tonkin, Vietnam, just NW of Langson; terminus of railroad from Hanoi; on Chinese frontier opp. Pingsiang in Kwangsi prov.

Nach′es′ (nách′ĕz′). River ab. 60 m. long, S cen. Washington; flows SE through N Yakima co. into Yakima river at Yakima.

Ná′chod (nä′ĸôt). Town, NE Bohemia, W Czechoslovakia, in Sudeten foothills on Silesian border; pop. (1930) 13,532; battlefield June 1866 where Prussians defeated Austrians in Austro-Prussian War.

Nach′vak (näch′văk). Village and harbor on inlet of N coast of Labrador, ab. 59°N.

Na′ci·mien′to Peak (nä′sĕ·myĕn′tō). Mountain 10,045 ft. in S Rio Arriba co., N New Mexico.

Nac′og·do′ches (năk′ŭ·dō′chĕz; -chĭz). 1 County in Texas. See *Table* at TEXAS.
2 Industrial and commercial city, its ⊗, E Texas, 20 m.

N of Lufkin; pop. 12,674; clay and lignite; Stephen F. Austin State Coll. (1917; coed.). Outgrowth of Spanish mission established 1716 for the Indians; figured in Texan revolution 1819 ff.; battle 1832.

Nadezhdinsk. See SEROV.

Nadi. See NANDI.

Na′di·a (nŭ′dĭ·ä). 1 District, formerly in Presidency division, Bengal, NE India; 2879 sq. m.; pop. (1941) 1,759,846; * Krishnagar; divided 1947, ab. ⅜ of it being assigned to West Bengal, Indian Union, and ab. ⅝ to East Bengal, Pakistan.
2 *officially* **Na′bad·wip′** (nŭ′bád·wēp′). Town, Nadia dist., in part assigned to West Bengal, on Bhagirathi river; pop. 18,861; ancient seat of learning.

Na′di·ad′ (nŭ′dĭ·äd′). Town, N Gujarat state, W Indian Union, on tributary of Sabarmati river 30 m. SE of Ahmadabad; pop. 34,584.

Na·dor′ (*Span.* nä·thôr′). Town, N Morocco, on coast just S of Melilla.

Nad·vor′na·ya (nŭd·vôr′ná·yả); *Pol.* **Nad·wór′na** (näd·vōōr′nä). Commune, S cen. Stanislav Region, W Ukraine, U.S.S.R.; pop. ab. 9000; battle Feb. 15–21, 1915 bet. Austrians and Russians.

Nad′zab (näd′zäb). Village, SE North-East New Guinea, 19 m. NW of Lae; Japanese airdrome in World War II seized by American paratroopers Sept. 1943.

Næst′ved (nĕst′vĕth). City, Præstö co., SE Sjælland, Denmark; pop. (1945) 15,104; railroad center.

Na·fa (nä·fä). = NAHA.

Na·fa′da (ná·fä′dá). Town, Bauchi prov., E cen. Northern Region, Nigeria, NE of Bauchi; pop. 11,898.

Nä′fels (nâ′fĕls). Village, Glarus canton, Switzerland; pop. (1930) 2948; scene of battle Apr. 9, 1388 in which Swiss defeated Austrians.

Naft–i–Shah (näft′ĕ·shä′h′). Oil field, W Iran, at border W of Kermanshah; adjoins Naft Khaneh oil field of E Iraq.

Naft Kha·neh′ (näft′ ĸä·nĕ′). Oil field, E Iraq, on Iranian border NE of Baghdad.

Na′ga (nä′gä). 1 Municipality on E coast of Cebu I., Phil. Is., at N end of Bohol Strait 11 m. SW of City of Cebu; pop. 25,850; has coastwise trade.
2 *formerly* **Nue′va Ca′ce·res** (nwä′vä kä′sá·räs). Municipality, * of Camarines Sur, in cen. part, Luzon, Phil. Is., on Bicol river ab. 5 m. S of San Miguel Bay; pop. 22,505; visited by Spaniards as early as 1573; Spanish town of Nueva Caceres founded on its site; capital of united Camarines provs. (see CAMARINES NORTE) and later of Camarines Sur.

Na′ga Hills (nä′gà; *Burmese* ná·gä′). 1 Hill region, India and Burma, including Naga and Patkai Hills; part of N Arakan Yoma system. See BARAIL RANGE. 1 Inhabited by Nagas who were formerly head-hunting savages, overcome by British expeditions 1865–80.
2 Subdivision (unadministered) of N Upper Chindwin dist., Upper Burma, in Naga Hills region; 3785 sq. m.

Na′ga·land′ (nä′gá·länd′). State, NE Republic of India in the Naga Hills; * Kohima; 6236 sq. m.; pop. (1961) 369,072.

Na·ga·no (nä·gä·nŏ). 1 Prefecture of Japan. See *Table* at JAPAN.
2 City, its *, ab. 100 m. NW of Tokyo; pop. (1945) 89,923; a center of silk industry; site of Buddhist temple and monastery; founded in 7th cent. A.D. but has buildings of modern construction.

Na·ga·o·ka (nä·gä·ō·kä). City, Niigata prefecture, NW Honshu, Japan, 35 m. S of Niigata; pop. (1945) 38,274; important in feudal times; declined on downfall of the Tokugawa; later regained prosperity with discovery of oil fields in vicinity.

Nagapattinam. See NEGAPATAM.

Na′gar (nŭg′ēr). See HUNZA.

Na·ga·ra (nä·gä·rä). Tributary of Kiso river in SW cen. Honshu, Japan; flows past Gifu.

Na·ga·ra (nä·k'hôn—*sic*), **Na·gor** (nä·k'hôn—*sic*). For towns in Thailand having Nagara or Nagor as first element, see those beginning NAKHON (meaning "town").

Na'gar A·ve'li (nŭg'ẽr *à*·vĕl'ĭ). See DAMÃO.

Na'ga·sa'ki (nä'gá·sä'kĕ; *Jap.* nä·gä·sä·kĕ). 1 Prefecture of Japan. See *Table* at JAPAN.

2 Seaport and commercial city, its *, at head of inlet ab. 3 m. long; pop. (1945 est.) 142,748; first port of entry for ships from S or W; harbor one of most beautiful in the world; coaling station, shipbuilding yards; before World War II exported coal, cotton goods, raw silk, tea, native manufactured products, and manufactured aircraft parts and electrical equipment. Not important in Japanese history until it was opened to trade 1568 or 1570 and became chief center of intercourse with foreigners; served as entry point of Christianity into Japan; made an imperial city by Hideyoshi 1587; visited by Spanish, Dutch, and Portuguese ships; only port kept open (see DESHIMA) to Dutch and Chinese when rest of Japan closed 1637–41 to all foreigners by Iyemitsu for two and a quarter centuries; opened again to foreign trade 1859; in World War II nearly half the city completely destroyed by atomic bomb Aug. 9, 1945.

Na·ga·to (nä·gä·tô). Old province at SW tip of Honshu, Japan, now part of Yamaguchi prefecture.

Nag'car·lan' (näg'kär·län'). Municipality, SE cen. Laguna prov., Luzon, Phil. Is., 12 m. S of Santa Cruz; pop. 14,762.

Na'ger·coil (nä'gẽr·koil). City, SE Kerala state, India, 10 m. N of Cape Comorin, extreme S tip of India; pop. (1941) 51,657.

Na'gi·na (nä'gĭ·nà). Town, N India, on tributary of Ramganga river 95 m. NE of Delhi; pop. 25,427; trades in sugar.

Na·god' (nà·gôd'). 1 Former Indian state, Baghelkhand, cen. India; 532 sq. m.; pop. (1941) 87,911.

2 Town, its *, 100 m. SW of Allahabad; pop. (including Unchahra) 8518.

Nagore. See NEGAPATAM.

Na·gor'no-Ka·ra·bakh' Autonomous Region (nŭ-gôr'nà·kà·rŭ·bàk'); *formerly* **Karabakh Mountain Area.** An autonomous region within the Azerbaidzhan S.S.R., SW Transcaucasia; 1659 sq. m.; pop. (1941 est.) 180,063; * Stepanakert; chief nationalities Armenian 89%, Turkic 10%; a mountainous forested area, well watered by short tributaries of the Kura; chief industry agriculture; taken from Persia by Russia 1813.

Na·go·ya (nä·gô·yä). City, * of Aichi prefecture, S Honshu, Japan, ab. 75 m. E of Kyoto at head of Ise Bay; pop. (1938 est.) 1,224,100, (1945 est.) 597,941; in recent years has become Japan's first city in production of airplanes; manufactures automobiles, machine tools, glazed pottery, textile fabrics, clocks; first to produce Japanese cloisonné enamelware; fine Buddhist temple; castle, erected 1610, which has been preserved in fine condition and is a palace of the Imperial family. Bombed by Allies 1945 in last months of World War II.

Nag'pur (näg'pŏor). 1 Division of former Central Provinces and Berar, Indian Union; 27,294 sq. m.; pop. (1941) 3,924,985.

2 City, its * and * of Central Provinces and Berar, 265 m. N of Hyderabad; now in Maharashtra; pop. 449,099; rail center; textile mills, hand-weaving industry; Nagpur Univ. (1923). Located at foot of old Fort Sitabaldi, scene of famous repulse of Maratha army by British defenders in 1817; came under British rule 1853.

Na·gua'bo (nä·gwä'vô). Municipality (pop. 17,195) and town (pop. 3396), E Puerto Rico, town near coast 7 m. NE of Humacao.

Na'gui·li'an (nä'gĕ·lē'än). Municipality, cen. La Union prov., Luzon, Phil. Is., 9 m. SE of San Fernando; pop. 15,933.

Nagybánya. See BAIA-MARE.

Nagybecskerek. See PETROVGRAD.

Nagyenyed. See AIUD.

Nagy'ka'ni·zsa (nŏd'y'·kŏ'nĭ·zhŏ). Industrial and com. mercial city, SW Hungary; pop. 30,127; held by Turks 1600–90.

Nagykároly. See CAREI.

Nagykikinda. See VELIKA KIKINDA.

Nagy'kö'rös (nŏd'y'·kû'rûsh). City, cen. Hungary, 47 m. SE of Budapest; pop. 30,656; market center in grape-growing section.

Nagymihály. See MICHALOVCE.

Nagyszalonta. See SALONTA.

Nagyszeben. See SIBIU.

Nagyszentmiklós. See SÂNNICOLAUL-MARE.

Nagyszőllős. See VEL'KÝ SEVLUŠ.

Nagyszombat. See TRNAVA.

Nagyvárad. See ORADEA.

Na·ha (nä·hä) *or* **Na·wa** (nä·wä). Seaport, * of Okinawa prefecture, on W coast of S Okinawa I., Ryukyu Is., Japan; pop. (1945) 65,765; exports a fiber cloth; Japanese military base with airfield; scene of severe fighting in battle for the city May 17–June 7, 1945.

Na'han (nä'hán). 1 = SIRMUR state, Indian Union.

2 Town, * of former Sirmur state, East Punjab, NW India, 35 m. ENE of Ambala; pop. 6859.

Nahanni, South. See SOUTH NAHANNI.

Na·hant' (nà·hànt'). Town, Essex co., NE corner of Massachusetts, 9 m. ENE of Boston on a long narrow peninsula extending S from Lynn into Massachusetts Bay; pop. 3960; summer resort.

Nahant Bay. Inlet of Massachusetts Bay on S shore of Essex co., NE corner of Massachusetts, separated from Lynn Harbor by the peninsula on which Nahant is situated.

Nahawend. = NEHAVEND.

Na'he (nä'ě). River ab. 70 m. long in Saarland and Rhineland-Palatinate states, W Germany; flows NE into Rhine river at Bingen on SE border of the Hunsrück.

Nahr. Arabic word meaning "river"; for names including this word, see the second element.

Nahr·wan' (när·wän'). Ancient canal ab. 60 m. long E of the Tigris river near Baghdad, E Iraq.

Nahud, En. See EN NAHUD.

Na·huel' Hua·pí', Lake (nä·wĕl' wä·pē'). Lake in Andes Mts., in S Neuquén territory, SW Argentina, on boundary of Río Negro territory near Chilean border; alt. 2500 ft.; area ab. 300 sq. m.; depth nearly 1000 ft. in places; source of Limay river; surrounded by mountains, El Tronador to SW; one of best-known of Argentine resorts. In **Nahuel Huapí National Park.**

Na'hui·zal'co (nä'wĕ·säl'kô). Town, Sonsonate dept., SW El Salvador, 5 m. from Sonsonate; pop. (1942 est.) 6111.

Na·hun'ta (nà·hŭn'tà). City, ⊗ of Brantley co., SE Georgia; pop. 952.

Na'ic (nä'ēk). Municipality, N coast of Cavite prov., Luzon, Phil. Is., 18 m. SW of City of Cavite; pop. 13,813.

Nai·ha'ti (nī·hä'tĭ). Town, West Bengal, NE Indian Union, on Hooghly river 23 m. N of Calcutta; pop. 30,908.

Nain (nīn; *in sense 2,* nän). 1 Town, cen. Iran, 75 m. E of Isfahan; pop. ab. 5000; highway junction point; makes fine earthenware.

2 Village and harbor, E coast of Labrador, 56°32'N.

Na'in (nä'ĭn; nän). Village, Galilee, N Palestine, 5 m. SSE of Nazareth (*Luke* vii. 11–17).

Nai'ni Tal (nī'nē täl'). Town and hill station, * of Kumaun division, NE Uttar Pradesh, N Indian Union, 148 m. NE of Delhi; pop. 10,673; popular resort and sanatorium; summer capital of Uttar Pradesh; alt. 6400 ft.; suffered from severe landslide Sept. 1880.

Nairn (nârn). 1 Small river in Nairn co., NE Scotland; flows NE into Moray Firth.

2 *or* **Nairn'shire** (nârn'shĭr; -shēr). County, NE Scot-

land, S of Moray Firth; area 163 sq. m.; pop. (1951) 8719; ⊗ Nairn; rivers Nairn, Findhorn; agriculture, livestock grazing, fishing.

3 Burgh, ⊗ of Nairn co., on Moray Firth at mouth of the Nairn; pop. 4700; fishing center; seaside resort.

Nai·ro′bi (nī·rō′bĭ). City forming an extraprovincial district in S cen. Kenya; ✳ of Kenya; pop. (est. 1961) 297,000; trading center; meteorological station; Royal College of Univ. of East Africa; Nairobi National Park game reserve nearby.

Nais′sar (nī′sĕr); *Estonian* **Nais′saar** (nīs′sär). Island ab. 5 m. long in Gulf of Finland, ab. 12 m. off Tallin, N Estonia.

Naissus, Naïssus. See NIŠ.

Nai·va′sha (nī·vä′sha). Town on Lake Naivasha, SW cen. Kenya, E Africa, NW of Nairobi; pop. 20,596.

Naivasha, Lake. Lake 12 m. long and 9 m. wide in SW cen. Kenya, in the Great Rift Valley (*q.v.*); altitude 6135 ft.; has no known outlet.

Najaf, An. See AN NAJAF.

Na·ja′sa (nä·hä′sä). River ab. 50 m. long in SE Camagüey prov., E cen. Cuba; flows S into Caribbean Sea.

Najd. See NEJD.

Ná′je·ra (nä′hä·rä). Commune, Logroño prov., N Spain, W of Logroño; pop. (1930) 2856; scene of victory of Black Prince over Henry II (of Trastamara) 1367 in his campaign for Peter the Cruel; also called battle of Navarrete.

Na·jib′a·bad (nȧ·jēb′ȧ·bäd). Town, NW Uttar Pradesh, N Indian Union, E of Ganges river 98 m. NE of Delhi; pop. 28,473; trades in timber, sugar, grain; varied manufactures; founded in middle of 18th cent. by Rohilla chief and has several fine Rohilla architectural monuments.

Na·ka·do′ri (nä·kä·dō′rē). Island in Goto Archipelago (*q.v.*), Japan.

Na·ka·gu·su·ku (nä·kä·gŏŏ·sŏŏ·kŏŏ). Town on SE coast of Okinawa I., Ryukyu Is., Japan, on Buckner Bay; pop. (1945) 16,731; ancient castle; taken June 1945 by Americans.

Nakagusuku Wan. See BUCKNER BAY.

Naka Iwo. See IWO JIMA.

Na·ka·le′le Point (nä′kä·lā′lĕ). Point on N coast of Maui I., Hawaii, near W end on Pailolo Channel.

Na·ka·no Shi·ma (nä·kä·nŏ shĕ′mä). Volcanic island 3215 ft. high, Tokara Is., in N Ryukyu Is., Japan.

Na·ka Shi·re·to·ko, Cape (nä·kä shĕ·rĕ·tŏ·kŏ). Cape on Karafuto at SE extremity of Sakhalin I.

Na·ka·tsu (nä·kä·tsŏŏ). Seaport town, Oita prefecture, NE Kyushu, Japan, 27 m. SSE of Moji on S shore of Suwo Sea; pop. (1945) 44,929; birthplace of Yukichi Fukuzawa.

Na·kawn (nä·k'hôn), **Na·korn** (nä·k'hôn). Vars. of NAKHON (in entries of Siamese names).

Nakel. See NAKŁO.

Na′khi·che·van′ (nä′kĕ·chĕ·vän′). **1** *officially* **Nakhichevan Autonomous Soviet Socialist Republic.** Autonomous republic, Transcaucasia, U.S.S.R., in SW mountainous part in bend of Araks river 2277 sq. m.; pop. (1941 est.) 138,528; ✳ Nakhichevan; politically part of Azerbaidzhan S.S.R., from which it is separated by a strip of the Armenian S.S.R.; on S separated by the Araks river from Azerbaijan prov., NW Iran. An agricultural country on a high plateau; produces cotton, rice; vineyards, fruit orchards; silkworm breeding, cattle raising. Predominant ethnic strain Turko-Tatar; chief nationalities Turkic 84.5%, Armenian 10.8%; chief towns Nakhichevan, Dzhulfa. Republic established 1921.

2 *anc.* **Nax′u·a′na** (näk′shŏŏ·ä′nȧ). Town, its ✳, on Araks river 85 m. SE of Yerevan; pop. 8946; according to Armenian tradition founded by Noah. Ancient trading center; often plundered by Persians, Mongols, Armenians; ceded to Russia 1828.

3 *or* **Nakhichevan on Don.** Industrial town on Don

river, Rostov Region, Soviet Russia, Europe; pop. ab. 71,000; suburb of Rostov; founded by Armenians 1780.

Na·khod′ka (nŭ·kŏt′kȧ). Seaport town, S Maritime Territory, Soviet Russia, Asia 55 m. ESE of Vladivostok; railroad terminus.

Na·khon *or* **Na·kon** (nä·k'hôn). Thai word for "town" used in some compound names.

Nakhon Na·yok (nä·yŭk); *also* **Na·ga·ra Nayok** (nä·k'hôn—*sic*). **1** Province, S Thailand; 834 sq. m.; pop. 98,266.

2 Town, its ✳, on a tributary of the Chao Phraya and on highway to Cambodia 60 m. NE of Bangkok.

Nakhon Pa·thom′ (pä·t'hŭm) *or* **Na·ga·ra Pathom** (nä·k'hôn). **1** Province, SW Thailand; 861 sq. m.; pop. 225,677.

2 Town, its ✳, a few miles W of Bangkok; large temple.

Nakhon Pha·nom (p'hä·nŭm); *also* **Na·ga·ra Pa·nom** (nä·k'hôn p'hä·nŭm) *and* **La·khon** (lä·k'hôn). **1** Province, NE Thailand; 4802 sq. m.; pop. 247,860.

2 Town, its ✳, on Mekong river opp. Thakhek in Indochina.

Nakhon Rat·cha·si·ma (rät·chä·sē·mä) *or* **Kho·rat** (k'hō·rät). **1** Province, S Thailand; 7861 sq. m.; pop. 599,165.

2 Town, its ✳, on Mun river 110 m. E of Ayudhya; pop. ab. 12,000; railroad junction point; distributing and trading center for E part of Thailand; rich copper mines; an ancient walled town, formerly subject to Cambodia.

Nakhon Sa·wan (sä·wän); *also* **Na·ga·ra Svar·ga** (nä·k'hôn sä·wän—*sic*). **1** Province, W Thailand; 3773 sq. m.; pop. 300,586.

2 Commercial town, its ✳, on the Chao Phraya where it is formed by confluence of Nan and Ping rivers.

Nakhon Si Tham·ma·rat (sē t'häm·mä·rät); *also* **Na·ga·ra Sri·dhar·ma·raj** (nä·k'hôn sē·t'häm·mä·rät). **1** Province, SW Thailand; 3947 sq. m.; pop. 387,006.

2 Seaport town, its ✳, on E coast of Malay Penin. 100 m. N of Songkhla; railroad terminus; a very old town; noted for its niello work in silver.

Na′kło (nä′klô); *Ger.* **Na′kel** (nä′kĕl). Commune, SW Pomorze dept., N cen. Poland, 20 m. W of Bydgoszcz on Noteć river; pop. 10,303; agricultural industries.

Naknek Lake. See Lake COVILLE.

Nakon. See NAKHON.

Naksh-i-Rus·tam′ (näksh′ĕ·rŏŏs·tȧm′). See PERSEPOLIS.

Nak′skov (näk′skou). Seaport, Maribo co., on W coast of Lolland I., Denmark; pop. (1945) 15,506; sugar refineries, shipbuilding yards; St. Nicholas church, dating from the 15th cent.

Na·ku′ru (nä·kŏŏ′rŏŏ). Town, W cen. Kenya, E Africa; ✳ of Rift Valley prov.; pop. 22,481.

Nal. See HINGOL.

Na′la·garh (nä′lȧ·gär; *native* -gŭr·h′) *or* **Hin′dur** (hĭn′dŏŏr). Former Indian state, Punjab States, N East Punjab, NW Indian Union, W of Simla; 276 sq. m.; pop. 50,015; ✳ Nalagarh.

Nal′chik (näl′chĭk; *Russ.* näl′y′·chĭk). Town, ✳ of Kabardino-Balkarian Republic, SE Soviet Russia, Europe, 63 m. NW of Dzaudzhikau; pop. 12,200; railroad terminus; health resort beautifully situated in a mountain valley. In World War II taken by Germans Oct. 29, 1942; retaken by Russians early in 1943.

Nal·gon′da (nŭl·gŏn′dȧ). Town, cen. Andhra Pradesh, India, 55 m. ESE of Hyderabad; pop. 5889.

Na·mak′, Dar·ya′ yi (där·yä′ yĕ näk·mä′). Salt lake and swamp (*darya*), Qum prov., NW cen. Iran, S of Tehran.

Nam′a·ka′gon (năm′ȧ·kä′gŭn). River ab. 75 m. long, NW Wisconsin; flows out of **Namakagon Lake**, S Bayfield co., SW and W into St. Croix river in Burnett co.

Na′mak·zar′ (nȧ′mȧk·zär′). Swampy lake in SE cen. Iran.

Na′man·gan′ (nä′mäng·gän′). Town, NE Uzbek S.S.R., Soviet Central Asia, in the Fergana valley NE of Kokand; pop. 77,351; some manufacturing; trades in cotton, fruit, animal products.

Na·ma′qua·land′ (nȧ·mä′kwȧ·lănd′) *or* **Na′ma·land′** (nä′mȧ·lănd′). 1 Coast region, SW Africa, extending from ab. 23°S to 31°S and from 80 to 350 m. inland; divided by Orange river into **Great Namaqualand** to the N (in South-West Africa) and **Little Namaqualand** to the S (in Cape Province, Union of South Africa); sandy plains and bare hills; rich in copper; pop. ab. 30,000 (Nama Hottentots).
2 The administrative district of Little Namaqualand, Union of South Africa; ✱ Springbok.

Na′ma·ta·nai′ (nä′mȧ·tȧ·nī′). Village on NE coast of New Ireland, Bismarck Archipelago, W Pacific Ocean; good harbor.

Nam′ber (näm′bēr). See NOEMFOOR.

Nam′cha Bar′wa (näm′chä bär′wä). Peak 25,445 ft. at E end of the Himalayas, SE Tibet, in the bend of the Brahmaputra.

Nam′dinh′ (näm′dĕn′y′). Town, SE Tonkin, N Vietnam, in Coi river delta 45 m. SE of Hanoi; pop. ab. 40,000, in 1936, 27,000; a trade center; manufactures; connected by rail with Hanoi. Came under French control 1883.

Namh′kam (näm′käm). Town, North Hsenwi state, Northern Shan States, Burma, on Shweli river near China border 60 m. N of Lashio and 65 m. SE of Bhamo; important station on Stilwell Road near where it joins the Burma Road. Held by Japanese 1942–45 but retaken Jan. 15, 1945 by Chinese troops.

Nam′hoi′ (näm′hoi′) *or* **Fat′shan′** (fät′shän′). Commercial and industrial city, cen. Kwangtung prov., SE China, ab. 12 m. above Canton in Si delta; pop. ab. 122,500.

Na′mib Desert (nä′mĭb). Arid region ab. 60 m. wide along coast of South-West Africa.

Nam′le·a (näm′lȧ·ä). Village on bay on E coast of Buru I., Indonesia; port of call for steamers.

Namnetes. See NANTES.

Nam′ni Pass (näm′nē). Mountain pass 15,300 ft. on N border of Burma; leads from upper valley of Nmai river to SE Tibet.

Nam′oi (näm′oi). River 526 m. long in NW New South Wales, SE Australia; flows into Darling river.

Na′mo·nu·i′to (nä′mô·nŏŏ·ē′tō). Atoll group in cen. Caroline Is. in W Pacific Ocean, 9°N lat. and 149°47′E long., NW of Truk.

Na·mo′si Peak (nä·mō′sĕ). Mountain 3027 ft. in SE Viti Levu I., Fiji Is., SW Pacific Ocean.

Nam′pa (năm′pȧ). City, Canyon co., SW Idaho, 18 m. W of Boise; pop. 18,013; fruit, vegetable, and dairy center; manufactures beet sugar, flour, meat products; Northwest Nazarene Coll. (1913; coed.).

Nam Pawn (näm pôn). River ab. 160 m. long in E Burma; flows S out of Southern Shan States and empties into Salween river.

Nam·pu′la (näm·pŏŏ′lȧ). Town, N Mozambique, SE Africa; ✱ of Niassa prov., in E part; on automobile highway and railroad.

Nam–quan. See NACHAM.

Nam′sen (näm′sĕn). River ab. 110 m. long in N cen. Norway; flows SSW and W past Namsos into **Namsen Fjord,** an inlet of Norwegian Sea on W coast of Norway.

Nams′os′ (näm′sōs′). Seaport, Nord-Tröndelag co., N cen. Norway, on N shore at head of Namsen Fjord; pop. 3615; lumbering, fishing; textile mills; cannery; copper deposits. Occupied by British troops Apr. 14 to May 3, 1940 in unsuccessful expedition to aid Norway.

Nam Teng (näm′ tĕng′); *better* **Teng.** River (*nam*) ab. 225 m. long, tributary of Salween river, E cen. Burma; flows S in Southern Shan States and enters Salween river just N of Karenni dist. border.

Nam Tso (näm′ tsô′) *or* **Teng′ri Nor** (tĕng′rĕ nôr′). Salt lake 15,186 ft. above sea level in E Tibet, Outer China; 50 m. long and 25 m. wide at its greatest extent; area ab. 700 sq. m.; lat. 30°40′N and long. 90°30′E; hot springs nearby on the NW.

Nam′tu *or* **Nam′tu–Pang′hai** (näm′tŏŏ·päng′hĭ). Town, ✱ of Tawngpeng state, Northern Shan States, E Burma, 25 m. WNW of Lashio; pop. 12,780.

Na′mu (nä′mŏŏ). Islet in Bikini atoll.

Na·mu′li (nä·mŏŏ′lĭ). Mountain 8200 ft., N Mozambique, SE Africa, E of Lake Chilwa.

Na·mur′ (nä·mŏŏr′; nȧ-; *Fr.* nȧ′mür′). 1 Province, S Belgium; 1413 sq. m.; pop. (1941 est.) 352,173; ✱ Namur; rivers Meuse, Sambre; agriculture, coal and iron mining.
2 Fortified manufacturing commune, its ✱, at confluence of Sambre and Meuse rivers; pop. (1938 est.) 32,831; cutlery, brass and iron goods; tanneries. Often scene of conflict: besieged by Louis XIV 1692 and retaken 1695 by William of Orange; fortifications reduced by German artillery Aug. 20–25, 1914 and city captured by the Germans; scene of fighting again in World War II; goal of German drive in Battle of the Bulge but not reached.

Na′mur (nä′mŏŏr). Islet of Kwajalein atoll (*q.v.*), Marshall Is.; taken by Allies Feb. 1–3, 1944.

Nam′yung′ (näm′yŏŏng′). Town, N Kwangtung prov., SE China, ab. 150 m. NE of Canton; in important wolfram-mining district. In World War II American air base; captured by Japanese Feb. 1945, retaken by Chinese July 25, 1945.

Nan (nän). 1 River ab. 350 m. long, one of main tributaries of the Chao Phraya river, W Thailand; flows S from Indochina border to unite with Ping river to form the Chao Phraya near Nakhon Sawan.
2 Province, N Thailand; 5723 sq. m.; pop. 198,700.
3 Town. its ✱, on upper Nan river 90 m. NNE of Uttaradit.

Na·nai′mo (nȧ·nī′mō). City, SE Vancouver I., Brit. Columbia, Canada, on Strait of Georgia 38 m. W of Vancouver; pop. 7196; fine harbor; center of coal-mining region; sawmills, brickyards, lumber mills; home port of large herring fleet. Site of blockhouse erected by Hudson's Bay Co. 1833; founded 1853.

Na·nang′o (nȧ·näng′ō). Settlement on E coast near NW end of Choiseul I., Solomon Is., W Pacific Ocean.

Na·na·o (nä·nä·ô). Town, Ishikawa prefecture, W coast of Honshu, Japan, on E side of Noto Penin.; pop. ab. 12,000; has regular steamship service with Vladivostok and northern Japanese ports.

Nance (năns). County in Nebraska. See *Table* at NEBRASKA.

Nan′chang′ (nän′chäng′). Old walled city, ✱ of Kiangsi prov., SE China, on right bank of Kan river just SW of Poyang Hu (lake); pop. 398,200; has extensive commerce in agricultural products and fine porcelain ware; only slightly affected by foreign influence.

Nan′cheng′ (nän′jŭng′); *formerly* **Han′chung′** (hän′jŏŏng′). City, S Shensi prov., NE cen. China, on N bank of the Han 135 m. SW of Sian; important commercial center.

Nan·cow′ry (năn·kou′rĭ); *better* **Nan·kau′ri.** 1 Island 19 sq. m., cen. group of Nicobar Is., Bay of Bengal, Indian Union.
2 Town at S end of island; good harbor.

Nan′cy (năn′sĭ; *Fr.* näⁿ′sē′). Manufacturing city, ✱ of Meurthe-et-Moselle dept., NE France, on Meurthe river 178 m. E of Paris; pop. 121,301; episcopal see; near rich iron fields; fortified; fine Italian-style cathedral, Gothic church of St. Épyre, 15th-cent. church of the Cordeliers, 17th-cent. town hall, ducal palace; university (founded 1572 at Pont-à-Mousson; removed here 1768).
History: Capital of ancient Lorraine; scene of battle in which Charles the Bold, Duke of Burgundy, was defeated and slain by René II, Duke of Lorraine, 1477; residence (1737 ff.) of Stanislas Leszczyński, Duke of

Lorraine and Bar, former king of Poland; passed to French crown 1776; occupied by Germans 1870–73; important railroad center in World War I; unsuccessfully attacked by Germans 1914, suffered under heavy bombardment; in World War II reached by American forces Sept. 5, 1944 and taken Sept. 15.

Nan'da De'vi (nŭn'dä dā've). Peak 25,645 ft. in the Himalayas, Uttar Pradesh, N India, on border of Garhwal.

Nan'da·ru'a (nän'dả·rōō'ả). Peak ab. 12,900 ft. in cen. Kenya, E Africa.

Nan'der (nän'dẽr). Town, SE Maharashtra state, S cen. India, on Godavari river 140 m. NNW of Hyderabad; pop. 26,992.

Nand'gaon (nänd'goun). Former Indian state, Eastern States Agency, NE Indian Union, N of Bastar; 872 sq. m.; pop. (1941) 202,973; ✱ Rajnandgaon.

Nan'di *or* **Na'di** (nän'dẽ). **1** Small river on Viti Levu I., Fiji Is., W Pacific Ocean; flows W into **Nandi Bay,** inlet of Pacific Ocean. Coast near its mouth developed 1943–44 as American base in World War II. **2** Village, Fiji Is., on W Viti Levu I. at mouth of Nandi river; international airport.

Nan'di·droog (nŭn'dĩ·drōog). Fortified hill 4853 ft., E Mysore state, S Indian Union, 31 m. N of Bangalore; fort constructed by Haidar Ali and Tipu Sahib; taken by storm 1791 by British under Lord Cornwallis.

Nan·dyal' (nŭn·dyäl'). Town, W Andhra Pradesh, S Indian Union, on tributary of Northern Penner river 205 m. NW of Madras; pop. 22,608.

Nangal Dam. See BHAKRA DAM.

Nan'ga Par'bat (nŭng'gả pŭr'bȧt). Peak 26,660 ft. in the W Himalayas, NW Kashmir, N India, S of the Indus.

Nang·tud', Mount (näng·tōōd'). Mountain 6724 ft., W Panay, Phil. Is., in cen. part of range bet. Antique and Capiz provs.

Nan·kai (nän·kī). Island in Chosen Strait, off S coast of Korea.

Nan·kai·do (nän·kī·dō). Old division of Japan including Shikoku and Awaji Is. and Kii prov. on Honshu.

Nankauri. See NANCOWRY.

Nan'king' (nän'kĭng'; *Chin.* nän'jĭng'), *literally* "Southern Capital"; *formerly* **Chian-ning** (jĩ-äng'nĭng') *or* **Kiang-ning** (jĩ-äng'nĭng'). Commercial city and treaty port, W Kiangsu prov., E China, on S bank of Yangtze, 150 m. NW of Shanghai and ab. 200 m. above it by river; pop. (1953) 1,091,600; former ✱ of Kiangsu prov. and ✱ of China 1928–37 and 1946–49; manufactures esp. fine cloths of satin and cotton (*nankeen*), paper flowers, paper and ink, pottery.
  History: Founded 1368 in Ming dynasty although built on site of important cities known by various names for more than 2000 years; capital of empire under Mings 1368–1403; taken by British 1842; scene of treaty signed Aug. 29, 1842 which ceded Hong Kong to Great Britain and opened five treaty ports; covered wide extent and was surrounded by high walls; contained imperial tombs and fine buildings, esp. the porcelain tower (begun 1413); largely destroyed by Taiping rebels who held city as their headquarters 1853–64; declared a treaty port 1858 but not opened until 1899; chosen 1928 by the Kuomintang as capital; capital removed to Chungking 1937 after the looting of the city by the Japanese; became capital again 1946, occupied by Communist forces 1949.

Nan'kow' (nän'kō'). Town, N Hopeh prov., NE China, on Peiping-Wanchuan railroad, ab. 25 m. NW of Peiping; nearby to the E in valley 6 m. long are Ming Tombs (or Thirteen Tombs, a semicircle of tombs of 13 of the 16 rulers of Ming dynasty) reached by an avenue (Holy Way) under a great arch (*pailou*) and bordered by large stone animals. **Nankow Pass** is 5 to 12 m. NW of Nankow through hills and gate in Great Wall; highest point ab. 1900 ft.; four railroad tunnels.

Nan Ling (nän' lĭng') *or* **Nan Shan** (nän' shän'). Literally "Southern Range," mountain system in S

China, roughly separating Kwangtung and Kwangsi provs. from Hunan and Kweichow provs.

Nanning. See YUNGNING.

Nan'ping' (nän'pĭng'); *formerly* **Yen'ping'** (yĕn'ping'). City on Min river, N cen. Fukien prov., SE China, 85 m. WNW of Minhow; pop. ab. 35,000.

Nansei Islands. See RYUKYU ISLANDS.

Nan'se·mond (nän'sẽ·mŭnd). **1** Short stream in Nansemond co., SE Virginia; flows NNE into Hampton Roads. **2** County in Virginia. See *Table* at VIRGINIA.

Nan'sen Sound (nän's'n). Strait bet. W Grant Land, Ellesmere I. and Axel Heiberg I., Canada.

Nan Shan *or* **Nan'shan'** (nän'shän'). **1** Mountain range on border bet. Tsinghai and Kansu provs., cen. China, running NW to SE; forms NE rampart of Tibetan plateau; peaks 18,000 to more than 20,000 ft.; traversed by passes 12,000–14,000 ft.; long valleys 12,000–14,000 ft. high; has lake, Tsing Hai, at E end. **2** See NAN LING.

Nan'ta·ha'la (nän'tȧ·hä'lȧ). River, W North Carolina; rises near Georgia-North Carolina boundary and flows N through Nantahala National Forest into Little Tennessee river in Swain co.; noted for scenery and the deep Nantahala Gorge.

Nantahala Dam. See *Table* at TENNESSEE VALLEY AUTHORITY.

Nan'tai' (nän'tī'). **1** See MINHOW, China. **2** *or* **Nan'tai'san'** (nän'tī'sän'). Peak 8170 ft. in the Nikko Range, N cen. Honshu, Japan, W of Lake Chuzenji; has extinct crater 1000 ft. in diameter.

Nantao. See SHANGHAI.

Nan·tas'ket Beach (nän·tăs'kĕt; -kĭt). Summer resort on Massachusetts Bay, 10 m. SE of Boston, Massachusetts, in Plymouth co.

Nan'terre' (nän'târ'). Commune, Seine dept., N France; W suburb of Paris; pop. 46,065; manufactures chemicals; birthplace of the Revolutionary hero Hanriot.

Nantes (nänts; *Fr.* nänt; *anc.* **Con'di·vin'cum** (kŏn'dĩ-vĭng'kŭm); *later* **Nam·ne'tes** (năm-nē'tēz); *Breton* **Naoned.** Manufacturing and commercial city, ✱ of Loire-Atlantique dept., NW France, on Loire river 107 m. W of Tours; pop. 195,185; connected by ship canal with St-Nazaire; built partly on islands in Loire river; 15th-cent. cathedral, 13th-cent. Gothic church, 14th-cent. ducal castle, palace of justice, town hall; large foreign trade.
  History: Capital of ancient Namnetes before Roman conquest of Gaul; passed to Romans; unsuccessfully besieged by Huns 445 A.D.; captured and destroyed by Normans in 9th cent.; ravaged by fire 1118; held by dukes of Brittany; passed to France 1499 on marriage of Anne of Brittany to Louis XII; famous Edict of Nantes issued by Henry IV Apr. 30, 1598; scene of Noyades (mass drownings) during French Revolution; in World War II reached by Americans Aug. 10, 1944.

Nan'ti·coke (nän'tĩ·kōk). **1** River ab. 75 m. long, SE Maryland; rises in S cen. Delaware, flows SW into Chesapeake Bay, SE Maryland. **2** City, Luzerne co., E Pennsylvania, on Susquehanna river 8 m. W of Wilkes-Barre; pop. 15,601; coal-mining center; manufactures.

Nantou. See SHANGHAI.

Nan·tuck'et (nän·tŭk'ĕt; -ĭt). **1** Island ab. 14 m. long in Atlantic Ocean S of Cape Cod, Massachusetts, constituting with adjoining islands Nantucket co., SE Massachusetts; summer resort. **2** County in Massachusetts. See *Table* at MASSACHUSETTS. **3** Town, ⊗ of Nantucket co., SE Massachusetts, on Nantucket Sound in N cen. Nantucket I.; pop. 3559; former whaling center.

Nantucket Sound. Body of water bet. S coast of Cape Cod and Nantucket I., SE Massachusetts, connecting with Atlantic Ocean on the E and Vineyard Sound on the W.

Nan'tung' (năn'tŏong'); *formerly* **Tung'chow'** (tŏong'-jō'). Seaport city, SE Kiangsu prov., E China, on N side of Yangtze estuary 65 m. NW of Shanghai; pop. (1953) 260,400.

Nant'wich (nănt'wĭch). Urban district, Cheshire, NW England, on the Weaver 30 m. SE of Liverpool; pop. 8840; large salt deposits, no longer worked; inland spa (brine baths); tanneries; manufactures shoes, clothing; trade center for agricultural section.

Nan'ty–Glo (năn'tĭ-glō'). Borough, Cambria co., SW cen. Pennsylvania, 11 m. NNE of Johnstown; pop. 4608; coal mining.

Nan'ty·glo' and Blai'na (năn'tĭ-glō', blī'nà). Urban district, Monmouthshire, W England, 34 m. NW of Bristol; pop. 11,427; trade center in coal-mining and ironworking section.

Na·nu'ku Passage (nä-nōō'kōō). Channel ab. 30 m. wide bet. Taveuni I. on the W and islets of N Lau group on the E, NE Fiji Is., SW Pacific Ocean. Leads out of Koro Sea and at its NE end is Wailangi Lala islet to guide ships going from Suva NE to Samoa and U.S.

Na'nu·me'a (nä'nōō-mä'ä). Island (atoll) 6 m. long, at N end of Ellice Is., W Pacific Ocean; pop. (1936) 775; two islets with no sheltered anchorage. Taken over by U.S. Marines Sept. 1943 and developed as a base.

Nan'yang' (năn'yäng'). City, SW Honan prov., E cen. China, ab. 150 m. SW of Kaifeng on tributary of the Han river.

Nan·yo (nän-yō). Japanese name of the South Sea Mandated Territories (see JAPAN), the islands in the Pacific that were under Japanese mandate 1919–45; * Koror, in the Palau Is.

Nan Yo (nän' yô'). See HENG.

Nan·yu'ki (nän-yōō'kĕ). Town, cen. Kenya, E Africa, N of Nyeri; railroad terminus.

Na'o, Cape (nä'ō); *Span.* **Ca'bo de la Nao** (kä'vô thä lä). Cape on E coast of Spain, 47 m. NE of Alicante, 38°45′N.

Naoned. See NANTES.

Na'os (nä'ŏs). Small fortified island in the Bay of Panama, just off SE end of Panama Canal.

Naoua. See NAWA.

Naousa. See NIAOUSTA.

Nap'a (năp'à). **1** County in California. See *Table* at CALIFORNIA.
2 City, its ⊗, W cen. California, on Napa river 10 m. N of San Pablo Bay; pop. 22,170; manufactures leather (*napa* leather), shoes, gloves; petrified forests, mineral springs, redwoods in vicinity; settled 1847–48, incorp. 1863.

Nap'a·nee (năp'à-nē). Town, ⊗ of Lennox and Addington co., SE Ontario, Canada, 25 m. W of Kingston at E end of Bay of Quinte; pop. 3897.

Nap'a·ta (năp'à-tà). Ancient town on the Nile, Upper Egypt, below the Fourth Cataract near modern Merowe; capital 750 B.C. of the kingdom of Nubia.

Nap'a·tree' Point (năp'à-trē'). Southwest extremity of Washington co., S Rhode Island, on the Connecticut border.

Na'per·ville (nā'pēr-vĭl). City, Du Page co., NE Illinois, 28 m. W of Chicago; pop. 12,933; North Central Coll. (founded 1861; moved to Naperville 1870; coed.).

Na'pi·er (nā'pĭ-ēr). Borough, * of Hawke's Bay provincial dist., E North I., New Zealand, on Hawke Bay 170 m. NE of Wellington; pop. (1941 est.) 19,400; exports fruit, wool, frozen meats, dairy products.

Na'pi·er·ville (nā'pĭ-ēr-vĭl). **1** County, Quebec, Canada. See *Table* at QUEBEC.
2 Village, its ⊗, S Quebec, Canada, 24 m. SSE of Montreal near New York state border; pop. 1356.

Na·pi'li Bay (nä-pē'lĕ). Inlet of Pailolo Channel on W coast of Maui I., Hawaii.

Na'ples (nā'p'lz). **1** City, since 1962 ⊗ of Collier co., SW Florida, on Gulf of Mexico 35 m. S of Fort Myers; pop. 4655; founded c. 1887; resort.
2 Village, Ontario co., W New York, 24 m. NNE of Hornell; pop. 1237; center of grape-growing region.
3 *Ital.* **Na'po·li** (nä'pô-lĕ); *anc.* **Ne·ap'o·lis** (nĕ-ăp'ô-lĭs). Seaport and industrial commune, Napoli prov., Campania, S Italy, on N side of Bay of Naples 117 m. SE of Rome; pop. 865,913; manufactures armaments, steel, engines, textiles, chemicals, china; most important seaport of Italy; archiepiscopal see; near heights of Posilipo and Vesuvius; five medieval castles (among them Saint Elmo), Vergil's tomb, 13th-cent. Gothic cathedral, church of the Holy Apostles (said to have been founded by Constantine the Great), church of St. Paul (1817–31; in imitation of Pantheon at Rome), the royal palace, the Galleria Umberto I, and a national museum containing artifacts of ancient Pompeii and Herculaneum; university (1224); zoological station, and marine aquarium and laboratory; naval and military station, arsenal.

History: Founded on site of ancient Parthenope (hence its ancient name *Neapolis*, i.e. "new city") c. 600 B.C. by refugees from Cumae, an ancient Greek colony; conquered by Romans in 4th cent. B.C.; included successively in kingdoms of Ostrogoths, Byzantines, and Moslems; conquered by Norman ruler of Sicily and became part of Kingdom of The Two Sicilies (see SICILY); after 1282, when Sicily became Aragonese, kingdom of Naples (included Italy south of Papal States) remained under Angevin house 1268–1435; crown of Naples reunited with that of Sicily under Alfonso of Aragon 1442; in late 15th cent., succession to Neapolitan throne claimed by French (Valois) kings and thus was precipitated Hapsburg-Valois struggle in Italy; conquered by Spanish 1504; ceded to Austria 1713; with Sicily, retroceded to Spain which refounded Kingdom of Two Sicilies under house of Bourbon 1735; capital of Napoleon's Parthenopean Republic 1799 and Sicilian kingdom 1806; scene of revolt 1820 which was suppressed by Austrian intervention; as result of Garibaldi's expedition 1860, joined Italian kingdom. In World War II badly damaged in bombings and by Germans in Salerno campaign; captured by Allies Oct. 7, 1943.

Naples, Bay of. Inlet of Tyrrhenian Sea 22 m. long on SW coast of Italy, S of Gulf of Gaeta and N of Gulf of Salerno.

Na'po (nä'pô). River ab. 550 m. long in NW South America; rises near Cotopaxi Mt. in N cen. Ecuador, flows E and SE across Peruvian border, and empties into Amazon river.

Na·po'le·on (nà-pō'lĕ-ŭn; -pōl'yŭn). **1** City, ⊗ of Logan co., S North Dakota; pop. 1078.
2 City, ⊗ of Henry co., NW Ohio, 35 m. WSW of Toledo; pop. 6739; manufactures windmills, tanks, spray guns.

Napoléon–Vendée. See LA ROCHE-SUR-YON.

Na·po'le·on·ville (nà-pō'lĕ-ŭn-vĭl; -pōl'yŭn-; *Sou. also* -v'l). Town, ⊗ of Assumption parish, SE Louisiana; pop. 1148.

Napoletano, Appennino. = *Neapolitan Apennines:* see APENNINES.

Na'po·li (nä'pô-lĕ). **1** Province of Italy. See *Table* at ITALY.
2 See NAPLES, Italy.

Napoli di Malvasia. See MONEMVASIA.

Na'po–Pas·ta'za (nä'pô-päs-tä'sä). Province, E Ecuador, E of the Andes and N of the Pastaza river; * Tena; formed 1925; with the province of Santiago-Zamora, constitutes the Eastern Region (*Span.* Región Oriental) of Ecuador; total area and pop. of the two provinces: 50,416 sq. m.; pop. (1944 est.) 179,433. Represents part of the former larger province of the same name; boundaries settled 1942.

Nap'pa·nee (năp'à-nē). City, Elkhart co., N Indiana, 20 m. SE of South Bend; pop. 3895; in agricultural area (mint and onions); manufactures furniture.

Na·qa'da (nŭ-kä'dà; -dä). Village, archaeological site

on left bank of the Nile, cen. Egypt, just N of Karnak; excavations by Petrie 1895.

Naqura, En. See EN NAQURA.

Nar. See NERA.

Na·ra (nä·rä). **1** Prefecture of Japan. See *Table* at JAPAN.

2 City, its *, W cen. Honshu, Japan, 26 m. E of Osaka, on the slope of a range of hills; pop. (1945) 70,814; has very extensive and beautiful park, the largest in Japan, in which are temples, shrines, an imperial museum, and a great image of Buddha (*daibutsu*) slightly larger than that at Kamakura (*q.v.*). The oldest permanent capital of Japanese empire 710–784; chief Buddhist center of early Japan and when capital several times larger than today; suffered rapid decline after Emperor Kwammu removed the court to Nagaoka (784).

Na'ra (nä'rå). Water channel ab. 250 m. long, E Sind, Pakistan, probably a former bed of the Indus; has been transformed into an irrigation canal system with 631 m. of canals; main channel is E of the Indus and flows N across the desert, crossing Khairpur and entering the Indus at Sukkur.

Na·rad'a Falls (nå·räd'å). Waterfall 168 ft. in Mount Rainier National Park, W cen. Washington.

Naradhivas. See NARATHIWAT.

Narainganj. = NARAYANGANJ.

Na'ran·ji'to (nä'räng·hē'tō). Municipality (pop. 17,319) and town (pop. 2719), NE cen. Puerto Rico; town on highway 14 m. SW of San Juan.

Na·ran'jo (nä·räng'hō). Site of early Maya city near Tikal, N Guatemala.

Na·ra·thi·wat *or* **Na·ra·dhi·vas** (nä·rä·t'hĭ·wät). **1** Province, SW Thailand; 1611 sq. m.; pop. 146,550.

2 Town, its *, seaport on Gulf of Siam on E coast of Malay Penin. 100 m. SE of Pattani.

Na·ra'yan·ganj' (nä·rä'yản·gŭnj'). Town, Dacca dist., SE East Bengal, Pakistan, on Meghna river 12 m. E of Dacca; pop. (1941) 56,007.

Nar·ba'da (nĕr·bŭd'å) *or* **Ner·bud'da. 1** River ab. 800 m. long in cen. India; rises in the Maikala Range in Central Provinces, flows W bet. the Vindhya Mts. and the Satpura Range, through Central India, Gujarat, and Bombay into the Gulf of Cambay; forms traditional boundary bet. Hindustan and the Deccan; second only to the Ganges in sacredness to the Hindus; navigable only in its lower course.

2 Former division, NW Central Provinces, India, S of the Narbada river, later in Jubbulpore and Nagpur divisions.

Nar'berth (när'bĕrth). Residential borough, Montgomery co., SE Pennsylvania, 7 m. WNW of Philadelphia; pop. 5109.

Narbo Martius. See NARBONNE.

Nar'bo·nen'sis (när'bō·nĕn'sĭs) *or* **Gal'li·a Narbonensis** (găl'ĭ·å). Part of ancient Gallia (see GAUL); under Augustus and Tiberius made one of 5 administrative areas into which Gaul was divided; in SE part bet. the Alps and Cévennes, extending up the Rhone as far as Vienna (Vienne) and W as far as Tolosa (Toulouse); chief town Narbo Martius.

Nar·bonne' (när·bŏn'; *Fr.* nàr·bôn'); *anc.* **Nar'bo Mar'ti·us** (när'bō mär'shĭ·ŭs; -shŭs). Commune, Aude dept., S France, near Mediterranean 31 m. E of Carcassonne; pop. 30,047; white-heather honey, wines; sulfur refineries, brandy distilleries, brick and tile works, cooperage; 13th-cent. Romanesque church, town hall (formerly fortified archiepiscopal palace), former cathedral (13th cent.).

History: Said to be first Roman colony beyond Alps (founded 118 B.C.); became capital of Gallia Narbonensis (see GAUL) c. 309 A.D.; taken by Visigoths 412, Saracens 719, Pepin the Short 759; prosperous manufacturing city 11th and 12th cents.; archiepiscopal see suppressed 1790; medieval fortifications replaced by boulevards 1865.

Narborough Island. See FERNANDINA island.

Nar·dò' (när·dô'). Manufacturing commune, Lecce prov., Apulia, SE Italy, on E shore of Gulf of Taranto 12 m. SW of Lecce; pop. 21,714; 13th-cent. cathedral; baroque palace and church.

Narenta. See NERETVA.

Na'rew (nä'rĕf); *Russ.* **Na·rev'** (nŭ·ryôf'). River 285 m. long in NE Poland; rises SE of Białystok, flows generally W and SW into Bug river near its confluence with the Vistula; battles on its bank Mar.–Aug. 1915, resulting finally in German success; in World War II fighting on its banks Sept. 1939 and Sept. 1944.

Na·rin'da Bay (nå·rĭn'då). Inlet of Mozambique Channel on NW coast of the island of Madagascar.

Na·ri'ño (nä·rē'nyô). Department of Colombia. See *Table* at COLOMBIA.

Nar·naul' (nĕr·noul'). Town, S Punjab state in former Patiala state, NW Indian Union, 80 m. WSW of Delhi; pop. 21,905.

Nar'ni·a (när'nĕ); *anc.* **Nar'ni·a** (när'nĭ·å). Commune, Terni prov., Umbria, cen. Italy, on Nera river 8 m. SW of Terni; pop. 17,660; episcopal see; town built on a rock 787 ft. high; 12th-cent. cathedral; palaces of 12th and 14th cents.

Na'ro (nä'rō). Commune, Agrigento prov., SW Sicily, 12 m. E of Agrigento; pop. 18,057; ruins of castle and walls; early Christian necropolis nearby.

Na'ro (nä'rō; nâr'ō). See NERETVA.

Na'roch (nä'rŭch); *Pol.* **Na'rocz** (nä'rôch). Small lake 8 m. long, ab. 32 sq. m., in former Wilno dept., NE Poland, 62 m. NE of city of Vilnyus; now in N White Russia, U.S.S.R.; scene of battle on its shores in World War I, Mar. 18–Apr. 30, 1916, which resulted in disastrous defeat to Russians.

Na'ro Fo'minsk (nä'rŭ fô'myĭnsk). Industrial town, SW Moscow Region, cen. Soviet Russia, Europe, on railroad 40 m. SW of Moscow; pop. 15,850; held for a few months 1941–42 by Germans.

Na·rón' (nä·rôn'). Commune, La Coruña prov., NW Spain, near Atlantic Ocean 17 m. NE of La Coruña; pop. 13,319; produces cereals, potatoes, wine; stock raising in region.

Na·ro'va (*Russ.* nŭ·rô'vå) *or* **Nar'va** (*Angl.* när'vå; *Russ.* när'vå; *Estonian* nàr'và). River ab. 48 m. long, NE Estonia, the outlet of Lake Peipus, flowing N past city of Narva (8 m. from its mouth) to Gulf of Finland; navigable to Narva but has falls (20 ft.) just above the city capable of providing 60,000–80,000 horsepower.

Nar'ra·been (när'å·bēn). Coast town, New South Wales, SE Australia, NE suburb of Sydney ab. 10 m. distant.

Nar'ra·gan'sett (năr'å·găn'sĕt; -sĭt). Town and summer resort, Washington co., S Rhode Island, at entrance to Narragansett Bay 9 m. WSW of Newport; pop. 3444; includes summer resort of **Narragansett Pier.** Settled 1675; scene of engagement bet. colonists and Narragansett Indians 1675; set aside 1888 as special district in South Kingstown; incorporated as separate town 1901.

Narragansett Bay. Inlet of Atlantic Ocean, 28 m. long, in SE Rhode Island, containing a number of islands including Rhode I., Prudence I., and Conanicut I. The city of Providence is at its N extremity and the city of Newport is on Rhode I. at the E side of the entrance to the bay.

Nar'ro·gin (năr'ō·jĭn). Town, SW Western Australia, 110 m. SE of Perth; pop. 2464.

Nar'rows, the (năr'ōz). **1** Strait, minimum width 1¼ m., bet. W end of Long I. and Staten I., SE New York, and connecting Upper New York Bay with Lower New York Bay; spanned by Verrazano-Narrows Bridge (1964), longest suspension bridge in world.

2 Narrowest part of the Dardanelles, ab. ¾ m. wide and 10 m. from the Aegean.

3 Narrow channel in Virgin Is., West Indies, bet. N St. John I. (U.S.) and SW Tortola (British).

Nar′sars·su′ak (när′sĕr·sōō′ăk). Village at head of a fiord on SW coast near S tip of Greenland, ab. 61°10′N, E of Ivigtut; airport.

Nar′singh·garh (när′sĭng·gär; *native* nŭr′sĭng·h′·gŭr′h′). **1** Former Indian state, Bhopal, cen. Central India, India; 731 sq. m.; pop. (1941) 125,178; Rajput state founded ab. 1681.
2 Town, its *, ab. 38 m. NW of Bhopal; pop. 9241.

Nar′singh·pur (när′sĭng·pōōr; *native* nŭr′sĭng·h′·pōōr). **1** Former Indian state, E Eastern States, NE India, N of Mahanadi river, W of Cuttack; 204 sq. m. pop. (1941) 48,448.
2 Town, cen. Madhya Pradesh, cen. Indian Union, on railroad 50 m. WSW of Jubbulpore; pop. 11,233.

Na·ru (nä·rōō). Island in Goto Archipelago (*q.v.*), Japan.

Na·ru·to Strait (nä·rōō·tō). Strait 1 m. wide bet. NE Shikoku I., Japan, and Awaji I., connecting the Inland Sea with Kii Channel and the Pacific Ocean; remarkable for great velocity (7 to 11 knots an hour) of its tides, esp. in the spring.

Nar′va (*Angl.* när′và; *Russ.* når′và; *Estonian* når′và). **1** River in Estonia. See NAROVA.
2 City, Viru prov., NE Estonia, on Narova river ab. 8 m. from its mouth in Gulf of Finland; pop. (1937) 24,516; chief industrial center of Estonia; important cotton mills, also jute, woolen, and flax mills; fisheries, lumberyards. Its port and a summer resort on the Gulf of Finland is **Nar′va–Jōe′suu** (når′và·yû′ĕ·sōō), pop. 1635.
   History: Founded 1223 by Danes; a seat of the Livonian Knights and the Hanseatic League; seized by Ivan the Terrible of Russia 1558; captured by Swedes 1651; scene of battle Nov. 30, 1700 in which Swedes under Charles XII defeated Peter the Great of Russia; recaptured by Russians 1704; scene of battles in World War I; occupied by Bolshevik forces who were driven out by Latvians and Finns Jan. 1919; in World War II seized by Germans 1941 but retaken 1944.

Nar′va·can′ (när′vä·kän′). Municipality, cen. Ilocos Sur near coast, Luzon, Phil. Is., on main highway 13 m. SSE of Vigan; pop. 22,769; largest town in province.

Nar′vik (när′vĭk). Seaport, Nordland co., N Norway, on a peninsula in Ofoten Fjord opp. the Lofoten; pop. 9920; ice-free harbor; exports iron ore; terminus of railroad from Sweden. Occupied by Germans Apr. 9, 1940; scene of naval battle in harbor Apr. 10–13 in which two British destroyers and all German craft were lost; held by British May 28–June 9, 1940.

Na·ryan′–Mar (nŭ·ryän′mår′). Village on right shore of Pechora delta, * of Nenets National District, Soviet Russia, Europe, ab. 60 m. from the sea.

Na·rym′ (nŭ·rĭm′). Town on Ob river, cen. Tomsk Region, Soviet Russia, Asia, 60 m. NW of Kolpashevo.

Na·ryn′ (nŭ·rĭn′). Town, * of Tyan-Shan Region, SE Kirgiz S.S.R., Soviet Central Asia, on **Naryn River,** an upper tributary of the Syr Darya; in mountainous region at ab. 6800 ft.

Nas′ca (näs′kä). Town, Ica dept., SW Peru, 85 m. SE of Ica on Pan American Highway; archaeological site of early Inca culture.

Nase′by (nāz′bĭ). Parish, Northamptonshire, cen. England, 12 m. E by N of Rugby; pop. 399; scene of battle June 14, 1645 in which Fairfax and Cromwell′s Parliamentary army disastrously defeated Charles I and Prince Rupert′s Royalist forces, ending all chance of success for king′s cause.

Nash (năsh). County in North Carolina. See *Table* at NORTH CAROLINA.

Nash′a·we′na Island (năsh′à·wē′nà). Island in S part of Elizabeth Is., Dukes co., SE Massachusetts.

Nash′u·a (năsh′ū·à; *locally also* -à·wä). **1** River ab. 80 m. long, NE cen. Massachusetts and SE New Hampshire; flows N from Wachusett Reservoir, Worcester co., cen. Massachusetts, across the state border into Merrimack river at Nashua, New Hampshire.
2 Industrial city, a ⊗ of Hillsboro co., S New Hamp-

shire, on Merrimack river 15 m. S of Manchester; pop. 39,096; originally a fur-trading post known as Watanic; U.S. fish hatchery; manufactures cotton goods, paper, shoes; settled 1656; chartered as city 1853.

Nash′ville (năsh′vĭl; *Sou. also* -v′l). **1** City, ⊗ of Howard co., SW Arkansas, 37 m. N of Texarkana; pop. 3579; in truck-gardening and fruit-growing area.
2 City, ⊗ of Berrien co., S Georgia, 26 m. N of Valdosta; pop. 4070.
3 City, ⊗ of Washington co., SW Illinois, 20 m. SW of Centralia; pop. 2606; in agricultural and coal-mining section.
4 Town, ⊗ of Brown co., S cen. Indiana, 17 m. W of Columbus; pop. 489; artist and tourist center.
5 Town, ⊗ of Nash co., NE North Carolina; pop. 1423.
6 Commercial and industrial city and port of entry, * of Tennessee and ⊗ of Davidson co., N cen. Tennessee, on Cumberland river; pop. 170,874; railroad center; manufactures shoes, cotton, flour and feed, lumber, brick, tobacco products; foundries, meat-packing plants, stone and cement works; printing and publishing center; The Hermitage (nearby; home of Andrew Jackson); Vanderbilt University (1872; coed.); George Peabody College for Teachers (1875; coed.); Scarritt College for Christian Workers (1924; coed.); Fisk University (1865; coed.); Tennessee Agricultural and Industrial State University (1912; coed.); Belmont College (1951; coed.). Settled as Nashborough 1779–80; incorp. as town 1784 and renamed Nashville; chartered as city 1806; became permanent state capital 1843; scene of Nashville (Southern) Convention 1850; captured and held by Union Army in Civil War from 1862; scene of battle of Nashville Dec. 15–16, 1864 in which Federals under Thomas badly defeated Confederates under Hood.

Nash′wauk (năsh′wôk). Village, Itasca co., N Minnesota, 13 m. WSW of Hibbing; pop. 1712; iron mining.

Nä′si·jär′vi (nä′sĭ·yär′vĭ). Lake in SW Finland; the city of Tampere is situated on its S shore.

Na′sik (nä′sĭk). Town, cen. Maharashtra state, W India, on Godavari river 100 m. NE of Bombay; pop. (1941) 52,386; renowned pilgrimage city of the Hindus; nearby cavern temples and cloisters of Buddhists dating from centuries just before and after the birth of Christ.

Nasira, En. See NAZARETH.

Na·sir′a·bad (ná·sēr′à·bäd). **1** Town, cen. Rajasthan, NW Indian Union, 15 m. SSE of Ajmer; pop. 21,397.
2 See MYMENSINGH.

Nasiri. = *Bandar Nasiri:* see AHWAZ.

Nasiriya, An. See AN NASIRIYA.

Na′so Point (nä′sō). Southwestern point of Panay I., Phil. Is., at S end of Antique prov.

Nasratabad. See SHAHR-I-ZABUL.

Nass (năs). River 205 m. long, W Brit. Columbia, Canada; flows SW through the Coast Mts. into Pacific Ocean (Dixon Entrance) 30 m. N of Prince Rupert.

Nas′sau (năs′ô). **1** Name of counties in two states of the U.S. See *Tables* at FLORIDA and NEW YORK.
2 City on NE coast of New Providence I. in the Bahamas, West Indies; * of British colony of Bahama Is.; pop. (1943) 29,391; good harbor; popular winter resort. Settled in 17th cent.; rendezvous of pirates until 1718; several towns attacked by Spaniards, last occupation in 1782; a supply base for Confederate blockade runners 1861–65 and for rumrunners 1920–33.
3 (năs′ô; *Ger.* näs′ou) Region, SW Germany; former duchy, later Wiesbaden govt. dist. of Hesse-Nassau prov., Prussia, now in W Hesse and NE Rhineland-Palatinate states; chief city Wiesbaden; a thickly forested and hilly territory N and E of the Rhine, crossed by the Lahn river and Taunus Mts.
4 (năs′ô; *Du.* näs′ou) Coastal town, N Surinam, near mouth of Saramacca river 45 m. W of Paramaribo.

Nas′sau Bay (năs′ô). Inlet of Solomon Sea on SE coast of North-East New Guinea just S of Salamaua; taken by Americans June 29–30, 1943.

Nas'sau Gulf (năs'ô). Gulf in S Tierra del Fuego Archipelago (q.v.), extreme S Chile, bet. Navarino I. on N and Wollaston Is. on S.

Nas'sau Range (năs'ô; *Du.* näs'ou). Mountain range, cen. Neth. New Guinea, forming W end of Snow Mts.; highest point in Carstensz group 16,404 ft. Only 4°S of the equator but covered with ice and glaciers; has great precipices; not discovered until 1911 and northern slopes not explored until 1926.

Näss'jö' (něsh'û'). Town, Jönköping co., S Sweden, SE of Jönköping; pop. 11,422.

Na·su (nä·sōō) *or* **Na·su·da·ke** (nä·sōō·dä·kĕ). Volcanic peak 6290 ft. on border bet. Fukushima and Tochigi prefectures, N cen. Honshu, Japan, NE of the village of Nikko.

Na'sug·bu' (nä'sōōg·bōō'). Municipality on W coast of Batangas prov., Luzon, Phil. Is., 36 m. NW of Batangas on South China Sea S of entrance to Manila Bay; pop. 19,820; airport. American invasion forces landed here Jan. 31, 1945.

Na·tal' (nȧ·tăl'). **1** (*Port.* nȧ·täl') Seaport city, ✱ of Rio Grande do Norte state, NE Brazil; pop. (1940 est.) 51,896; ab. 2 m. above mouth of small river; well-developed harbor; port for coastwise steamers; trades in cotton, sugar, hides; rail connections to S; Brazilian naval depot; large transatlantic airport 8 m. from city, largely developed by U.S. during World War II, used in ferrying service 1820 m. to Freetown or 1870 m. to Dakar. Founded 1597; held by Dutch 1633–54.
2 Province, E Union of South Africa; 24,857 sq. m., including Zululand 35,284 sq. m.; pop. (1936) 1,946,468 (nearly 80% natives); ✱ Pietermaritzburg. Bounded on N by Transvaal, Swaziland, and Mozambique, on E by Indian Ocean, on S and SW by Cape Province, and on W by Basutoland and Orange Free State; has sea coast ab. 375 m. long; narrow coastal plain, wide central midlands from 2000–4000 ft. above sea level, and foothills of Drakensberg Mts. along W border. *Rivers:* Pongola along N border, Tugela in cen. part, and Umzimkulu and Umtamvuna along Cape Province border. *Chief products:* Sugar, cereals, fruit, coal. *Chief towns:* Durban, Pietermaritzburg, Ladysmith, Newcastle, Vryheid.
History: Coast at Durban first sighted by Vasco da Gama on Christmas Day 1497 and named *Terra Natalis;* first visited by English 1684 but no settlement until 1824 at port of Natal (renamed Durban 1835); reached by Boers on great trek 1836–38; at war with Zulus 1838–40 and with English 1840–43; made a British colony 1843 and annexed to Cape Colony 1844; given separate government 1845 and made separate colony 1856; granted responsible government 1893; annexed Zululand 1897 and other districts in N 1903 (see UTRECHT and VRYHEID); scene of battles in Boer War 1899–1900; joined Union of South Africa 1910.

Natal Current. See MOZAMBIQUE CURRENT.

Na·tan'ya (nȧ·tän'yȧ). Town on coast of Palestine, ab. halfway bet. Jaffa and Haifa; large Jewish settlement.

Na·tash'kwan (nȧ·tăsh'kwăn; -kwŏn). River ab. 250 m. long, S Labrador and E Saguenay co., Quebec, Canada; flows S to the St. Lawrence opp. E end of Anticosti I.

Nat·chaug' (nȧ·chôg'). River, NE Connecticut; rises in NW Windham co., flows S and joins the Willimantic to form the Shetucket river at Willimantic.

Natch'ez (năch'ĕz; -ĭz). City, ⊗ of Adams co., SW Mississippi, on Mississippi river; pop. 23,791; trade center in agricultural section; cotton and cottonseed-oil mills, canneries, meat-packing plants.
History: Originally site of a Natchez Indian village; visited by La Salle 1662; ceded by France to England 1763; seized by Spain 1779; yielded to U.S. 1798; capital of Territory of Mississippi 1798–1802; incorporated as city 1803; headquarters of Aaron Burr and Harman Blennerhassett in their colonization scheme; held by Union forces 1863–65.

Natchez Trace (trās). Old road over 500 m. long from Nashville, Tennessee, to Natchez, Mississippi; construction begun 1806; used in early 19th cent. by traders returning from Natchez after having floated produce down the Mississippi river.

Natch'i·toches (năk'ĭ·tŏsh). **1** Parish in Louisiana. See *Table* at LOUISIANA.
2 City, ⊗ of Natchitoches parish, NW cen. Louisiana, 52 m. NW of Alexandria; pop. 13,924; trading and distributing center for cotton-producing section; Northwestern State College of Louisiana (1884; coed.).

Na·te'wa Bay, Natewa Peninsula (nä·tā'wä). See VANUA LEVU.

Na'thi·a Ga'li (nät'hĭ·ȧ gä'lĭ). Town in former North-West Frontier Province, W Pakistan, in hills 38 m. NNE of Rawalpindi; it was the summer capital of North-West Frontier Province.

Na·tib', Mount (nä·tĭb'). Mountain 4222 ft. in Zambales range, cen. Bataan prov., Luzon, Phil. Is.

Na'tick (nā'tĭk). **1** Town, Middlesex co., NE Massachusetts, 15 m. WSW of Boston; pop. 28,831; manufactures shoes, saws, tools, paper boxes; founded 1651 by John Eliot, "Apostle of the Indians," as first of his Praying Towns.
2 Village, Kent co., cen. Rhode Island, ab. 5 m. SW of Cranston; cotton manufactures.

National City. City, San Diego co., SW corner of California, on San Diego Bay 5 m. S of San Diego; pop. 32,771.

National Old Trails Road. Former highway 3096 m. long, extending from Washington, D.C., to Los Angeles, California; following routes of the Cumberland Road and the Santa Fe Trail.

National Park. Borough, Gloucester co., SW New Jersey, on Delaware river 6 m. SSW of Camden; pop. 3380.

Native States. = INDIAN STATES—an unofficial name.

Na·toe'na (nȧ·tōō'nä), *or* **Na·tu'na, Islands.** Island groups, **North Natoena Islands** and **South Natoena Islands,** of Indonesia, in the South China Sea E of S Malay Penin. and W of Borneo; area of North Natoena Is., including **Great Natoena** (40 m. by 30 m.), 727 sq. m.; area of South Natoena Is., 89 sq. m.; total area, 815 sq. m.; pop. 14,832; administratively a part of Riouw residency.

Na'tron, Lake (nā'trŏn). Lake ab. 50 m. long in extreme N Tanganyika Territory, near Kenya border, E Africa; large soda deposits. Cf. Lake MAGADI and NATRON LAKES.

Na·tro'na (nȧ·trō'nȧ). County in Wyoming. See *Table* at WYOMING.

Natrona Heights. Locality, Allegheny co., SW Pennsylvania, ab. 19 m. NE of Pittsburgh; pop. (est.) 8000.

Na'tron Lakes (nā'trŏn). Seven soda lakes (Arabic *natrūn* "native sodium carbonate") in **Wa'di Na·trun'** (wä'dĭ ăl nŏ·trōōn'), a valley below sea level in N Egypt, 60 m. WNW of Cairo.

Na'tu La (nä'tōō lä'). Pass (*la*) over the Himalayas in SE Sikkim, NE India, E of Gangtok; alt. 13,500 ft.; on highway from India to Lhasa.

Natuna Islands. See NATOENA ISLANDS.

Natural Bridge. Village in S Rockbridge co., W cen. Virginia, 16 m. S of Lexington; site of a natural bridge (over Cedar Creek) 215 ft. high, 50–100 ft. wide, with a 90-ft. span.

Natural Bridges National Monument. See UNITED STATES, *National Monuments.*

Nat'u·ral·iste, Cape (năt'û·rȧl·ĭst). Cape, SW Western Australia, on W side of Geographe Bay.

Nauchampatepetl. See COFRE DE PEROTE.

Nau'cra·tis (nô'krȧ·tĭs). Greek city of ancient Egypt, in the Nile delta, W of Rosetta branch.

Nau'en (nou'ĕn). Commune, Brandenburg, eastern Germany, 25 m. WNW of Berlin; pop. (1939) 12,167; powerful radio station.

Nau′ga·tuck (nô′gá·tŭk). **1** River 65 m. long in W Connecticut; rises in N Litchfield co., flows S through W New Haven co. into the Housatonic river at Derby; furnishes water power for industrial plants. **2** Manufacturing borough, New Haven co., S Connecticut, on Naugatuck river 5 m. S of Waterbury; pop. 19,511; manufactures rubber footwear, druggists' sundries, chemicals, plastics, motion-picture cameras, glass, sheet metal and wire goods, airplane instruments; rubber regenerating plant. Incorporated 1893; consolidated 1895; coextensive with the town (settled 1702, incorporated 1844).

Nau′heim or **Bad Nauheim** (bät′ nou′hīm). Town, Hesse state, Germany, ab. 24 m. N of Frankfurt, NE of Taunus Mts.; pop. (1939) 12,981; saline thermal waters.

Nau·jan′ (nou·hän′). Municipality, NE coast of Mindoro I., Phil. Is., just N of **Lake Naujan** 13 m. SE of Calapan; pop. 19,170; important trade center.

Nau′lo·chus (nô′lô·kŭs). Ancient port and Roman naval station on N coast of Sicily at its E end E of Mylae; in naval battle 36 B.C. M. Vipsanius Agrippa defeated Sextus Pompeius Magnus.

Naum′burg (noum′bōōRK), also **Naumburg an der Saa′le** (än dĕr zä′lĕ). Manufacturing city, in former Prussian province of Saxony, Germany, on the Saale river 28 m. SW of Halle; pop. 29,337; 12th-cent. cathedral, 16th-cent. late-Gothic town hall, 16th-cent. church; became episcopal see 1029; treaties signed here 1457, 1554.

Naupactus. See NÁVPAKTOS.

Nau′pli·a (nô′plĭ·á); Gr. **Náv′pli·on** (näf′plyĕ·ôn). Fortified seaport city, ✳ of Argolis and Corinth dept., NE Peloponnesus, Greece, on Gulf of Argolis S of Corinth; pop. 7163; important commercial center in Middle Ages; changed masters several times during this period bet. Turks and Venetians; served as capital of Greece after War of Independence until 1834. One of the evacuation points of the British Apr. 24–30, 1941 in World War II.

Nauplia, Gulf of. See Gulf of ARGOLIS.

Na·u′ru (nä·ōō′rōō); formerly **Pleas′ant Island** (plĕz′′nt). Island in W Pacific Ocean 26 m. S of the equator, long. 167°E, W of the Gilbert Is.; highest point 225 ft.; area 8½ sq. m.; pop. (1965) 5561; has no harbor; site of radio station; a joint British, New Zealand, and Australian trust territory. Discovered 1798; annexed by Germany 1888, and made a part of Marshall Is. protectorate; valuable phosphate deposits (estimated at 42 million tons) discovered ab. 1900, developed by British Phosphate Company which began work 1906; island occupied by Australian Expeditionary Force 1914 and placed under mandate 1919; seized by Japanese Aug. 1942. Became an independent republic Jan. 31, 1968.

Nausari. See NAVSARI.

Nau·shon′ Island (nô·shŏn′). Island 7 m. long, largest of the Elizabeth Is., in Dukes co., SE Massachusetts; summer resort.

Nau·voo′ (nô·vōō′; nô′vōō). City, Hancock co., W Illinois, on Mississippi river 45 m. N of Quincy; pop. 1039, occupied by Mormons under Joseph Smith 1838–39; became prosperous city of 20,000 people under Smith's leadership; abandoned by Mormons who migrated to Utah 1846 after Smith was killed by a mob 1844; made site of Utopian communistic society established in 1849 by group of French Icarians under leadership of Étienne Cabet, settlement breaking up 1856 because of internal factional disagreements.

Na′va·cer·ra′da, Puer′to de (pwĕr′tô thä nä′vä·thĕr·rä′thä; -sĕr·rä′thä). Mountain pass 6053 ft. in the Sierra de Guadarrama, cen. Spain.

Nav′a·jo (năv′á·hō). County in Arizona. See Table at ARIZONA.

Navajo Mountain. Solitary peak 10,416 ft., San Juan co., SE Utah, near Rainbow Bridge National Monument.

Navajo National Monument. See UNITED STATES, National Monuments.

Navajo Peak. Mountain 13,406 ft. in Boulder and Grand cos., N cen. Colorado.

Nav′an (năv′ăn) or **An Uaimh.** Town, cen. co. Meath, E Eire, at confluence of Blackwater and Boyne rivers 16 m. SW of Drogheda; pop. 4123; farm implements, woolens, tanning.

Na′va·na′gar or **Na′wa·na′gar** (nŭ′vä·nŭg′ĕr); also **Now′a·nug′gur** (nou′á·nŭg′ĕr). **1** Former Indian state, N Kathiawar, on S shore of Gulf of Cutch, Western India States, India; 3791 sq. m.; pop. (1941) 504,006; ✳ Jamnagar. Ruled by a Rajput maharaja; on July 7, 1947 joined a new confederation of states in W India. **2** See JAMNAGAR.

Nav′a·rin, Cape (năv′á·rĭn). Point, Chukot National District, NE Soviet Russia, Asia; extends into Bering Sea just S of Gulf of Anadyr.

Na′va·ri′no (nä′vä·rē′nô; Angl. năv′á-). **1** Chilean island in Tierra del Fuego Archipelago (q.v.) S of E Tierra del Fuego I. **2** Italian name of Pylos (q.v.), seaport in SW Morea, Greece; scene of naval battle fought in nearby waters Oct. 20, 1827 in which British, French, and Russian fleets under Sir Edward Codrington defeated Turkish and Egyptian fleet.

Na·var′ra (nä·vär′rä). Province of Spain. See Table at SPAIN.

Na·varre′ (ná·vär′). **1** Span. **Na·var′ra** (nä·vär′rä); Fr. **Na′varre′** (ná′vár′). Ancient kingdom, N Spain; bordered on N by France, E and S by Aragon, SW by Old Castile, NW by Basque Provinces; now forms modern Spanish province of Navarra and W part of French department of Basses-Pyrénées; in Pyrenees and Cantabrian Mts.; watered by Ebro, Bidassoa, Arga, and Aragon rivers.

History: In early times inhabited by Vascones, progenitors of the Basques and Gascons; conquered by Romans, and subsequently, 470 A.D., by Visigoths; gained early importance through famous mountain pass of Roncesvalles (q.v.); conquered by Charlemagne 778; became independent kingdom 10th cent.; under Sancho III (970–1035), united with Castile and León, this domain being divided 1035 into three kingdoms of Navarre, Aragon, and Castile; reunited with Aragon 1076–1134; appanage of France 1235–1328; S part conquered by Ferdinand II of Aragon 1512 and incorporated with Castile 1515; N part (now in department of Basses-Pyrénées, France) passed by inheritance 1589 to Henry IV of Bourbon, king of France.

2 Village, Stark co., NE Ohio, 8 m. WSW of Canton; pop. 1698.

Na′var·re′te (nä′vär·rĕ′tä). Commune, Logroño prov., N Spain, bet. Logroño and Nájera (q.v.); pop. (1930) 1683.

Na·var′ro (ná·vär′ō). County in Texas. See Table at TEXAS.

Navas de Tolosa, Las. See LAS NAVAS DE TOLOSA.

Nav′a·so′ta (năv′á·sō′tá). **1** River ab. 170 m. long, E Texas; flows S into Brazos river at point where Brazos, Grimes, and Washington cos. meet. **2** City, Grimes co., E cen. Texas, 26 m. SSE of Bryan; pop. 4937; railroad center; farming, stock raising; cotton gins and compresses, oil mills.

Na·vas′sa (ná·văs′á). Island 2 m. long in Caribbean Sea bet. Jamaica and Hispaniola; belongs to United States; has lighthouse.

Nav′e·sink Highlands or **Navesink Hills** (năv′ĕ·sĭngk; nä′vĕ-; nĕv′ĕ-). See HIGHLANDS OF NAVESINK.

Navesink River. Estuary, NE Monmouth co., E cen. New Jersey, N of Shrewsbury River. Both estuaries are barred from flowing directly into the Atlantic Ocean by the peninsula at the N end of which is Sandy Hook extending into Lower New York Bay.

Navigators Islands. See SAMOA.

Na'vo·jo'a (nä'vô·hō'ä). Town, S Sonora state, NW Mexico; pop. 11,009; railroad junction point near the coast.

Na'vo·la'to (nä'vô·lä'tô). Town, Sinaloa state, W Mexico; pop. 5151; on railroad just W of Culiacán.

Na·vo'tas (nä·vō'täs). Municipality, NW Rizal prov., Luzon, Phil. Is., on coast of Manila Bay adjacent to Malabon just N of Manila; pop. 20,861.

Náv'pak·tos (näf'päk·tôs); *Ital.* **Le'pan·to** (lâ'pän·tô; *Angl.* lĕ·pǎn'tō); *anc.* **Nau·pac'tus** (nô·pǎk'tŭs). Seaport in Aetolia and Acarnania dept., Greece, on the strait connecting the Gulfs of Corinth and Patras; pop. 3101; peace treaty 217 B.C. bet. Aetolians and Philip V of Macedon; new home of Messenians after end of Third Messenian War (after 461 B.C.); in 16th cent. known as Lepanto and noted for naval battle in nearby strait Oct. 7, 1571, in which Turkish fleet was completely defeated by combined fleets of Holy League under Don John of Austria.

Návplion. See NAUPLIA.

Na·vron'go (nȧ·vrông'gō). Town, N Northern Region, Ghana, W Africa, 100 m. N of Tamale.

Nav·sa'ri (nȧv·sä'rē); *also* **Nau·sa'ri** (nou-). Town, SW Baroda state, W Indian Union, near Gulf of Cambay 135 m. N of Bombay; pop. 24,397.

Nawa. See NAHA.

Na'wa (nä'wȧ; *Arab.* nä'wä) *or* **Na'oua'** (nȧ·wä'). Town, SW corner of Syria, ab. 47 m. S of Damascus.

Na·wab'ganj (nȧ·wäb'gŭnj). Town, E Uttar Pradesh, N Indian Union, 17 m. E of Lucknow; pop. 16,743; scene of victory by Sir Hope Grant June 12, 1858 during the Sepoy Mutiny.

Na·wab'shah (nȧ·wäb'shä; *native* -shä·h'). Town, cen. Sind, Pakistan, 50 m. N of Hyderabad; pop. 7023.

Nawanagar. See NAVANAGAR.

Na·wi'li·wi'li Bay (nä·wē'lē·wē'lē). Bay on SE coast of Kauai I., Hawaii, S of Ninini Point.

Nax'os (năk'sŏs). **1** *Mod. Gr.* **Ná'χos** (nä'ksôs). Largest island of the Cyclades, Aegean Sea, E of Paros, in Cyclades dept., Greece; ab. 22 m. long by 16 m. wide; area 171 sq. m.; pop. ab. 20,000; chief town Naxos (on NW coast, pop. 2160). In early times famous for its wines and as a center for worship of Dionysius; seized by Persia 490 B.C.; member of Delian League, but revolted 471 and made subject to Athens; seat of a medieval duchy 1207–1566 (see AEGEAN ISLANDS) and since War of Independence has belonged to Greece.
2 Oldest Greek colony in Sicily, founded 735 B.C.; destroyed by Dionysius the Elder 403 B.C.; its ruins recently discovered in hills near Taormina on E coast.

Naxuana. See NAKHICHEVAN.

Na·ya'garh (nȧ·yä'gẽr; *native* -gŭr·h'). **1** Former Indian state, E Eastern States, NE India; 562 sq. m.; pop. (1941) 161,409.
2 Town, its *, now in Orissa, 55 m. WSW of Cuttack.

Na'ya·rit' (nä'yä·rēt'). State, W Mexico. See *Table* at MEXICO.

Na·zan' Bay (nȧ·zän'). Inlet, SE Atka I., Andreanof Is., Aleutian Is., SW Alaska.

Na'za·ré' (nȧ'zȧ·râ'); *formerly* **Na'za·reth** (-rât'). City, Baía state, E Brazil, near coast 35 m. W of Salvador; pop. (1940 est.) 13,482.

Naz'a·reth (năz'ȧ·rĕth; năz'rĕth). **1** Town near Kalamazoo, Michigan; Nazareth Coll. (1897; women; Rom. Cath.)
2 Borough, Northampton co., E Pennsylvania, 13 m. NE of Allentown; pop. 6209; settled by Moravians 1740; mountain resort; manufactures cement, paper boxes, musical instruments; coal fields nearby.
3 Subdistrict, Galilee dist., N Palestine; area now in Israel; 187 sq. m.; pop. 28,592, (1938 est.) 35,378.
4 *Arab.* **En Na'si·ra** (ăn nä'sĭ·rŏ). Town, * of Nazareth subdistrict, ab. 18 m. SE of Haifa; pop. (1944 est.) 12,609; junction point of highways from Haifa and Jerusalem NE to Tiberias on the Sea of Galilee and on N edge of Plain of Esdraelon. Home of Joseph and Mary and of Jesus in his childhood; site of St. Mary's Well; captured several times during the Crusades; its Christian inhabitants massacred by Baybars 1263; taken by Turks 1517 and by British cavalry Sept. 20, 1918.

Na·ze (nä·zĕ). Chief town of Amami Is., Japan, on N coast of Amami O Shima; naval base.

Naze, the (nāz). **1** Headland on E coast of Essex, SE England, 5 m. S of Harwich.
2 See LINDESNES.

Na'zil·li' (nä'zil·lē'). Town, Aydın vilayet, SW Turkey in Asia, on railroad and on N bank of Menderes river 26 m. E of Aydın; pop. 12,026.

Nde·be'le ('n·dĕ·bē'lĕ). = MATABELELAND.

Nde'ni ('n·dā'nē); *formerly* **San'ta Cruz** (săn'tä krōōth'; krōōs'). Chief island of the Santa Cruz Is., SW Pacific Ocean, 250 m. E of S Solomon Is.; 215 sq. m.; has good harbor at Graciosa Bay.

Ndo'la ('n·dō'lä). Town, N Northern Rhodesia, S cen. Africa, on railroad 100 m. N of Broken Hill; pop. 7935; center of copper-mining region and known as "capital of the copper belt."

Ndreketi. See DREKETI.

Neagh, Lough (lŏk nā'). Lake 17 m. long in SW co. Antrim, Northern Ireland; 153 sq. m.; largest lake in British Isles.

Ne'ah Bay (nē'ȧ). Village, NW Clallam co., NW Washington, on inlet of Juan de Fuca Strait; pop. (est.) 900; headquarters of Makah Indian Reservation; site of earliest white settlement (by Spanish, lasted only five months, 1791) in the state of Washington.

Ne·an'der·thal (nā·än'dẽr·täl'; *Angl.* nĕ·ăn'dẽr·thôl'). Valley just E of Düsseldorf, in North Rhine-Westphalia, W Germany, where parts of the skeleton of an early type of man were discovered 1856.

Ne·ap'o·lis (nĕ·ăp'ô·lĭs). **1** Ancient city, Macedonia, NE Greece, the port of Philippi where St. Paul landed on his second missionary journey (*Acts* xvi. 11). Its site is near the modern Kavalla.
2 See NAPLES, Italy.
3 See NABLUS, Palestine.
4 See NABEUL, Tunisia.

Neapolitan Apennines. See APENNINES.

Near East (nẽr). **1** The Balkan States—in earlier usage.
2 The Balkan States and the countries of SW Asia (Turkey, Lebanon, Syria, Palestine, Jordan, Saudi Arabia and other countries of the Arabian penin.); also, generally, by extension includes Egypt and the African lands S of Egypt; as officially used by the U.S. Department of State, includes all of the above, Libya, and all the Middle East (*q.v.*). See also EAST and FAR EAST.

Near'er Tibet (nẽr'ẽr). Old name of E Tibet, now in W China.

Near Islands (nẽr). Island group, farthest W of the Aleutian Is., SW Alaska, 173°E; E of international date line; includes Attu (*q.v.*), the chief island, and Agattu, and Semichi Is.; occupied by Japanese June 1942; retaken by Americans May–June 1943.

Neath (nēth). **1** River ab. 20 m. long in S Wales; flows S into Bristol Channel E of Gower Penin.
2 Municipal borough, Glamorganshire, SE Wales, on the Neath river; pop. 32,305; coal mining and manufacturing (tin plate and iron products, chemicals); site of ruins of Neath Abbey, founded in 1130.

Nebek. See EN NEBK.

Ne'bo (nē'bō). See Mount PISGAH.

Ne'bo, Mount (nē'bō). Peak 11,680 ft. in E Juab co., W Utah.

Ne·bras'ka (nĕ·brăs'kȧ). A central state of U.S.A., 37th state admitted to Union (1867); bounded on N by South Dakota, on E by Iowa and a corner of Missouri, on S by Kansas and Colorado, and on W by Wyoming; 15th state in area, 77,227 sq. m. (land area 76,663 sq. m.); 34th state in population, 1,411,330; * Lincoln. See *Table of States* at UNITED STATES. Divided into the following

93 counties (for pronunciation of their names, see their individual entries):

NAME	LOCATION	AREA[1]	POP.[1]	CO. SEAT
Adams	S	562	28,944	Hastings
Antelope	NE	853	10,176	Neligh
Arthur	W	705	680	Arthur
Banner	W	738	1,269	Harrisburg
Blaine	cen.	711	1,016	Brewster
Boone	E cen.	683	9,134	Albion
Box Butte	NW	1,066	11,688	Alliance
Boyd	N	538	4,513	Butte
Brown	N	1,218	4,436	Ainsworth
Buffalo	S cen	952	26,236	Kearney
Burt	E	484	10,192	Tekamah
Butler	E	582	10,312	David City
Cass	E	554	17,821	Plattsmouth
Cedar	NE	743	13,368	Hartington
Chase	S	894	4,317	Imperial
Cherry	N	5,982	8,218	Valentine
Cheyenne	W	1,186	14,828	Sidney
Clay	S	570	8,717	Clay Center
Colfax	E	405	9,595	Schuyler
Cuming	NE	571	12,435	West Point
Custer	cen.	2,562	16,517	Broken Bow
Dakota	NE	255	12,168	Dakota City
Dawes	NW	1,389	9,536	Chadron
Dawson	S cen.	979	19,405	Lexington
Deuel	W	435	3,125	Chappell
Dixon	NE	480	8,106	Ponca
Dodge	E	529	32,471	Fremont
Douglas	E	333	343,490	Omaha
Dundy	S	921	3,570	Benkelman
Fillmore	SE	577	9,425	Geneva
Franklin	S	578	5,449	Franklin
Frontier	S	966	4,311	Stockville
Furnas	S	722	7,711	Beaver City
Gage	SE	858	26,818	Beatrice
Garden	W	1,685	3,472	Oshkosh
Garfield	cen.	570	2,699	Burwell
Gosper	S	462	2,489	Elwood
Grant	W	762	1,009	Hyannis
Greeley	E cen.	570	4,595	Greeley
Hall	SE cen.	540	35,757	Grand Island
Hamilton	SE cen.	541	8,714	Aurora
Harlan	S	575	5,081	Alma
Hayes	S	711	1,919	Hayes Center
Hitchcock	S	722	4,829	Trenton
Holt	N	2,408	13,722	O'Neill
Hooker	W cen.	722	1,130	Mullen
Howard	E cen.	566	6,541	St. Paul
Jefferson	SE	577	11,620	Fairbury
Johnson	SE	377	6,281	Tecumseh
Kearney	S	512	6,580	Minden
Keith	W	1,072	7,958	Ogallala
Keya Paha	N	769	1,672	Springview
Kimball	W	953	7,975	Kimball
Knox	NE	1,124	13,300	Center
Lancaster	SE	845	155,272	Lincoln
Lincoln	SW cen.	2,523	28,491	North Platte
Logan	cen.	570	1,108	Stapleton
Loup	cen.	574	1,097	Taylor
McPherson	W cen.	855	735	Tryon
Madison	NE	572	25,145	Madison
Merrick	E cen.	467	8,363	Central City
Morrill	W	1,403	7,057	Bridgeport
Nance	E cen.	438	5,635	Fullerton
Nemaha	SE	399	9,099	Auburn
Nuckolls	S	579	8,217	Nelson
Otoe	SE	617	16,503	Nebraska City
Pawnee	SE	433	5,356	Pawnee City
Perkins	SW	885	4,189	Grant
Phelps	S	545	9,800	Holdrege
Pierce	NE	573	8,722	Pierce
Platte	E	672	23,992	Columbus
Polk	E	433	7,210	Osceola
Red Willow	S	716	12,940	McCook
Richardson	SE corner	548	13,903	Falls City
Rock	N	1,012	2,554	Bassett
Saline	SE	575	12,542	Wilber
Sarpy	E	236	31,281	Papillion
Saunders	E	756	17,270	Wahoo
Scotts Bluff	W	726	33,809	Gering
Seward	SE	572	13,581	Seward
Sheridan	NW	2,466	9,049	Rushville
Sherman	cen.	570	5,382	Loup City
Sioux	NW corner	2,063	2,575	Harrison
Stanton	NE	431	5,783	Stanton
Thayer	S	577	9,118	Hebron
Thomas	cen.	716	1,078	Thedford
Thurston	NE	388	7,237	Pender
Valley	cen.	570	6,590	Ord
Washington	E	387	12,103	Blair
Wayne	NE	443	9,959	Wayne
Webster	S	575	6,224	Red Cloud
Wheeler	NE cen.	576	1,297	Bartlett
York	SE	577	13,724	York

[1] Area = land area in sq. m. Pop. from **1960** Census.

Nickname: Cornhusker State, also Blackwater State, Tree Planters State. *State flower:* Goldenrod. *Motto:* Equality Before the Law. *Chief cities:* Omaha, Lincoln, Grand Island, Hastings. *Rivers:* Missouri, forming E boundary; North Platte and South Platte, uniting in SW cen. area to form the Platte, flowing E into the Missouri. *Highest point:* 5340 ft. in SW Banner co. *Chief industries:* Agriculture (corn, wheat, oats), meat packing, flour milling.

History: Part of Louisiana Purchase 1803 and later of the Territory of Orleans (see LOUISIANA) and of Missouri Territory; erected as separate territory by Kansas-Nebraska Act 1854 (originally included area bet. Missouri river and the Rockies from 40°N to Canadian border); lost part of land to Dakota and Colorado territories 1861; held 1st constitutional convention 1866; admitted to Union as free state Mar. 1, 1867; established one-house legislature 1937.

Nebraska City. City, ⊗ of Otoe co., SE Nebraska, on Missouri river 41 m. S of Omaha; pop. 7252; home of J. Sterling Morton, the originator of Arbor Day, his residence now in a state park.

Nebrija, Nebrixa, *or* **Nebrissa.** See LEBRIJA.

Ne·ca′xa (nä·kä′hä). River, cen. Mexico, in Puebla and Veracruz states (known as the **Te′ca·lu′tla** [tä′kä·lōō′tlä] in Veracruz); has falls 540 ft. high which furnish electrical power.

Ne·chak′o (nĕ·chăk′ō). River 255 m. long, cen. British Columbia, Canada; flows N and E into Fraser river.

Nech′es (nĕch′ĕz; -ĭz). River 280 m. long, E Texas; rises in Van Zandt co., NE Texas, runs S and SE into Sabine Lake. See SABINE-NECHES WATERWAY.

Neck′ar (nĕk′är; *Angl.* -ẽr). **1** River 246 m. long, SW Germany; rises in the Black Forest, S Baden-Württemberg, flows N and W into the Rhine at Mannheim; navigable up to Cannstatt, near Stuttgart.
2 Circle of Württemberg. See *Table* at WÜRTTEMBERG.

Neck′er (nĕk′ẽr). Islet of Leeward Is. group, Hawaii, in cen. Pacific Ocean ab. 300 m. NW of Niihau I., 164°42′W; included in Hawaiian Islands Bird Reservation.

Ne′co·che′a (nä′kŏ·chā′ä). Seaport town, Buenos Aires prov., E Argentina, 265 m. directly S of Buenos Aires; pop. ab. 24,000; one of finest sea-bathing places on Argentina coast.

Ne′der·land (nē′dĕr·lănd). City, Jefferson co., SE Texas, near Beaumont; pop. 12,036; oil refining, truck farming, dairying.

Ne′der·land (nā′dĕr·länt). See NETHERLANDS.

Nederlandsch–Indië. See NETHERLANDS INDIES.

Ne′der Rijn (nā′dĕr rīn′). The Lower Rhine in the Netherlands; from it the IJssel flows N into IJsselmeer, and the Lek river continues W into the Nieuwe Maas and the North Sea.

Nedjed. = NEJD.

Né′doun′ka′dou′ (nā′dōōn′kä′dōō′). Town, Karikal settlement, in former French India, on SE coast; pop. (1941) 6593.

Nee′bish Island (nē′bĭsh). Island in Chippewa co., E Michigan penin., in St. Marys river, S of Sault Sainte Marie.

Need′ham (nēd′ăm). Town, Norfolk co., E Massachusetts, 10 m. WSW of Boston; pop. 25,793; residential.

Nee′dle Mountain (nē′d'l). Peak 12,130 ft. in S Park co., NW Wyoming, in the Absaroka Mts.

Nee′dles (nē′d'lz). City, San Bernardino co., SE California, on Colorado river; pop. 4590.

Needles, the. Three pointed rocks in the English Channel W of the Isle of Wight; lighthouse.

Ne′em·bu·cú′ (nā′ăm·bōō·kōō′). Department of Paraguay. See *Table* at PARAGUAY.

Nee′nah (nē′nà). City, Winnebago co., E Wisconsin, on Lake Winnebago 7 m. S of Appleton; pop. 18,057; forms one community with its twin city, Menasha (*q.v.*); settled 1843; manufactures paper, machine-shop products, knit goods; stores and ships cheese.

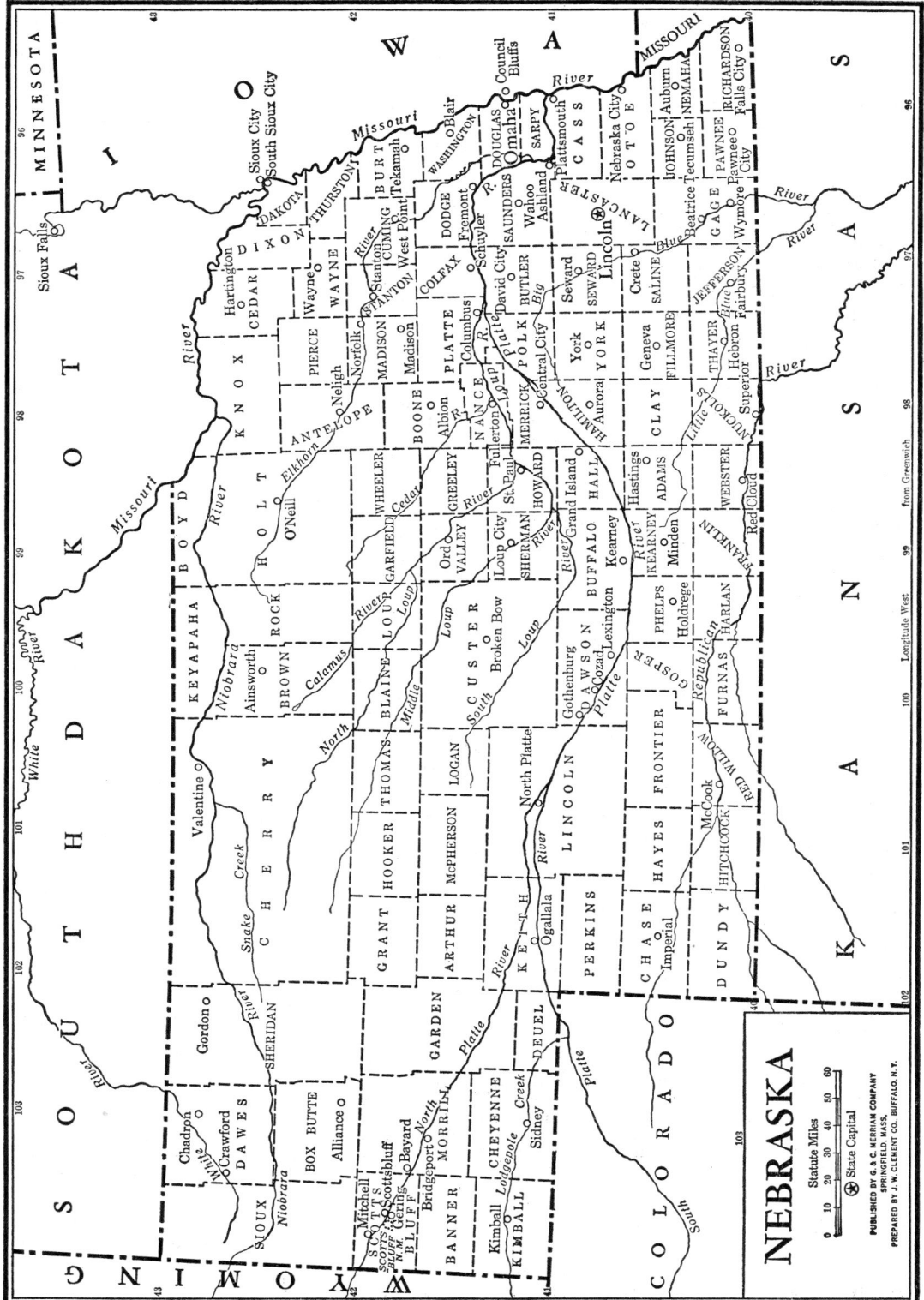

NEBRASKA

Statute Miles

⊕ State Capital

PUBLISHED BY G. & C. MERRIAM COMPANY
SPRINGFIELD, MASS.
PREPARED BY J. W. CLEMENT CO. BUFFALO, N. Y.

Nee′pa·wa (nē′på·wô; -wä). Town, SW Manitoba, Canada, 35 m. NE of Brandon; pop. 2895.

Neer·win′den (nār·vĭn′dĕ[n]). Village, Liège prov., E Belgium, 22 m. NW of Liège; scene of two battles: July 19, 1693, when William III of England was defeated by French under Marshal Luxembourg; Mar. 18, 1793, when General Dumouriez was defeated by Austrians.

Nef′ta (nĕf′tá). Town, W Tunisia, N Africa, on W shore of Chott Djerid; pop. (1936) 13,619.

Nefud. See AN NAFUD.

Ne′ga·pa′tam (nĕg′á·pŭt′ám) or **Na′ga·pat′ti·nam** (någ′á·pŭt′ĭ·nám) or **Ne′ga·pat′ti·nam** (nĕg′á·pŭt′-ĭ·nám). Seaport town, SE Madras state, S India, on Coromandel Coast 160 m. S of Madras; pop. 57,854; exports ground nuts, cotton goods, tobacco, vegetables; has large railroad workshops; depot for coolie emigration. Site of Portuguese factory at beginning of 16th cent.; occupied by Dutch 1660–71, by British 1799. Since 1866 forms joint municipality with **Na·gore′** (ná·gōr′), a port ab. 5 m. N.

Ne·gau′nee (nĕ·gô′nê). City, Marquette co., N Michigan penin., W of Marquette; pop. 6126; iron mining.

Neg′eb (nĕg′ĕb; nĕ·gĕb′) or **Neg′ev** (nĕg′ĕv; nĕ·gĕv′). Ancient region of the steppe region in S Judaea, Palestine; in modern times the desert area in S Palestine bordering on Egypt; assigned to Israel in proposed partition of Palestine 1948; scene of clashes bet. Jewish and Egyptian forces 1948–49.

Ne·goi′ (nĕ·goi′). Mountain 8346 ft., cen. Romania; highest peak in Transylvanian Alps.

Ne·gom′bo (nĕ·gŏm′bō). Seaport, urban district, NW Western Province, Ceylon, 19 m. N of Colombo; pop. 25,291. Taken by Dutch from Portuguese 1640; recovered 1641; retaken by Dutch 1644; taken by English 1796; fishing port.

Ne·grais′, Cape (nĕ·grīs′). Headland in Bassein dist., Lower Burma, projecting into Bay of Bengal SSW of city of Bassein; lat. 16°N and long. 94°10′E.

Ne′gra Point (nā′grä). Headland on NW coast of Ilocos Norte prov., Luzon, Phil. Is., bet. Cape Bojeador on W and Mayraira Point on E; marks W side of Bangui Bay.

Ne·gri′ Sem·bi′lan (nĕ·grē′ sĕm·bē′län). A union of native states, originally nine and now eleven, forming a state of the Federation of Malaya on the SW coast of S Malay Penin.; 2580 sq. m.; pop. 233,799, (1941 est.) 296,009; ✻ Seremban. Bounded on N and NE by Pahang, on SE by Johore, on S by Malacca settlement, on SW by the Strait of Malacca, and on W by Selangor. Hilly and well watered; has alluvial tin mines; produces rice, coconuts, rubber. Nine states united 1889; joined 1895 by Sungei Ujong and one other state and in the same year became one of the Federated Malay States. See Federation of MALAYA.

Ne′gro, Cape (nā′grô). Point, N Morocco, N Africa, NE of Tetuán.

Ne′gro, Mount (nā′grô). Peak 4429 ft. in cen. Panama, in the Tabasara Mts.

Ne′gro, Ri′o (*Port.* rē′oo nā′groo). 1 *Span.* **Rí′o Ne′gro** (rē′ô nā′grô). River ab. 1400 m. long in NW South America; rises in E Colombia, where it is known as the **Guai·ní′a** (gwī·nē′ä); flows E to the Venezuela boundary, and then S forming a section of the Colombia-Venezuela boundary; crosses into Brazil and continues SE into Amazon river at Manaus; is joined also to the Orinoco river through the Casiquiare river.

2 River, S Mato Grosso state, Brazil; flows SW and W through extensive marshland S of Taquarí river into Paraguay river.

Ne′gro, Rí′o (rē′ô nā′grô). 1 River ab. 630 m. long in Río Negro territory, S cen. Argentina; formed by confluence of Neuquén and Limay rivers, flows E into Atlantic Ocean N of Gulf of San Matías.

2 River ab. 290 m. long in cen. Uruguay; rises in S Brazil, flows SW across Uruguay into the Uruguay river.

Ne′gro Mountain (nē′grō) or **Da′vis Mountain** (dā′vĭs). Peak 3213 ft. in Somerset co., S Pennsylvania; highest point in the state.

Negro Overo. See SIERRA DE FAMATINA.

Negropont. 1 See CHALCIS.

2 *Ital.* **Negroponte.** See EUBOEA.

Ne′gros (nā′grôs). Island, one of the Visayan Is., cen. Phil. Is.; 4905 sq. m.; pop. (with adjacent small islands) 1,219,538; fourth in size in the archipelago, 134 m. long; divided into two provinces, **Negros Occidental** and **Negros Oriental** (*qq.v.*).

Negros, Los. See LOS NEGROS.

Ne′gros Oc′ci·den·tal′ (nā′grôs ôk′sĕ·thán·täl′). Province, N and W Negros I., Phil. Is.; 2989 sq. m.; pop. 824,858; ✻ City of Bacolod. Has fairly regular coast line, with few good harbors; broad coastal plains in N and W; separated on E from Negros Oriental by S two thirds of the mountain range which crosses center of the island N to S; highest peak Canlaon volcano 8087 ft. on boundary; many small streams; chief crops sugar, rice, hemp, tobacco, copra. Chief towns Bacolod, San Carlos, Escalante, Bago, Silay.

History: Long administered as part of Iloilo; became part of military province of Negros in 1856; made separate province 1890; granted civil government by Americans Apr. 1901. In World War II held by Japanese; invaded near Bacolod by Americans and occupied Mar. 29–Apr. 12, 1945.

Negros O′rien·tal′ (ō′ryán·täl′). Province, E and SE Negros I., cen. Phil. Is.; 2053 sq. m.; pop. 394,680; ✻ Dumaguete; includes subprovince of Siquijor (island SE of Negros). Separated from Negros Occidental by mountain range which in S curves toward coast W of Dumaguete; highest point Cuernos of Negros 6244 ft.; except for narrow coastal strip entire province mountainous or plateau; fine timber, some mining; produces sugar, kapok, coconuts. Chief towns Dumaguete, Gihulngan, Manjuyod, Tanjay, Bais. See SIQUIJOR.

History: Dumaguete probably only settlement before Spaniards came; other towns settled in 18th cent.; administered from Cebu until 1734 when it became part of new military district of Negros; suffered much from Moro pirates, but after 1856 increased in population and prosperity; made separate province 1890 and granted civil government by Americans May 1901.

Ne′ha·vend′ (ná′hä·vånd′). **1** Former province, W Iran; ✻ Burujird.

2 *Arab.* **Ni′ha·wand′** (nē′hä·vånd′). Town, W Iran, 42 m. S of Hamadan; pop. ab. 5000; battle 641 A.D. in which the Persians under Yazdegerd III were completely defeated by the Arabs.

Ne′heim-Hüs′ten (nā′hīm·hüs′tĕn). City, North Rhine-Westphalia state, W Germany, in the Ruhr dist. 23 m. ESE of Dortmund; pop. 32,300; metal goods.

Nei·a′fu (nā·á′foo). Town and port on Vavau I., N Tonga Archipelago, SW cen. Pacific Ocean; has completely landlocked harbor at head of picturesque sound.

Nei′ba or **Ney′ba** (nĕ′ĕ·vä; nā′vä). Commune, ✻ of Bahoruco prov., SW Dominican Republic; pop. (1941) 38,185.

Neiges, Pi′ton′ des (pē′tôn′ dä nâzh′). Peak 10,068 ft., cen. Réunion I.

Neills′ville (nēlz′vĭl). City, ⊗ of Clark co., W cen. Wisconsin, 21 m. WSW of Marshfield; pop. 2728; farm trade center.

Neis′se (nī′sĕ). **1** or **Lau′sit·zer Neisse** (lou′zĭt·sĕr) *Pol.* **Ny′sa Łu·życ′ka** (nī′sä loo·zhĭts′kä). River ab. 140 m. long; rises near Liberec in N Czechoslovakia, flows N in former Lower Silesia and Brandenburg provs., Prussia, past Zgorzelec and Gubin, and joins the Oder 21 m. SSE of Frankfurt; from the Czech border to its junction with the Oder forms, by decision of the Potsdam Conference 1945, part of the boundary bet. Poland and Germany. See POLAND.

2 See NYSA.

Neist Point (nēst). Cape on W coast of island of Skye in the Inner Hebrides, off NW Scotland; lighthouse.

Nei′va (nĕ′ê·vä; nā′vä). **1** Peak 12,100 ft. in Cordillera Oriental, cen. Colombia, SE of city of Neiva.

2 City, ✳ of Huila dept., S cen. Colombia, on the Magdalena river 150 m. SSW of Bogotá; pop. 15,096; produces cattle, coffee, Panama hats.

Nejd (nĕjd) *or* **Najd** (näjd). **1** The central tableland of Arabia.

2 Kingdom in cen. and E Arabia; 447,000 sq. m.; pop. ab. 4,000,000; ✳ Riyadh; forms with Hejaz the kingdom of Saudi Arabia (*q.v.*).

History: Before World War I a kingdom of Arabia (*q.v.*) nominally under Turkish suzerainty as Sultanate of Nejd; seat of ibn-Saud, Wahabi ruler since 1905, who declared Nejd an independent kingdom; made treaty of friendship with Great Britain 1915; declared wars against Husein of Hejaz (*q.v.*) and other parts of Arabia 1919–26; sultanate under ibn-Saud from 1926 and united with Hejaz as a dual kingdom; independence recognized by Great Britain 1927; after insurrection became a single kingdom under the name of Saudi Arabia (*q.v.*) 1932.

Ne·koo′sa (nĕ·kōō′sả). City, Wood co., cen. Wisconsin, on Wisconsin river 8 m. S of Wisconsin Rapids; pop. 2515.

Ne′ligh (nē′lĭ). City, ⊗ of Antelope co., NE Nebraska, on Elkhorn river 35 m. WNW of Norfolk; pop. 1776.

Nel·lore′ (nĕ·lōr′). Town, S Andhra Pradesh, S Indian Union, on Northern Penner river near its mouth 95 m. N of Madras; pop. (1941) 56,315; one of the chief ports of the Coromandel Coast; has Roman Catholic, American Baptist, and Lutheran missions.

Nel′son (nĕl′s'n). **1** Name of counties in three states of the U.S. See *Tables* at KENTUCKY, NORTH DAKOTA, VIRGINIA.

2 City, ⊗ of Nuckolls co., S Nebraska; pop. 695.

3 River 390 m. long, N cen. Manitoba, cen. Canada; flows out of N Lake Winnipeg through several lakes NE into Hudson Bay at Port Nelson; considered as including its headstreams, the Saskatchewan and Bow rivers, ab. 1660 m. long; navigable for part of its course. Its mouth discovered 1612 and first post of Hudson's Bay Company (Port Nelson) established there 1670; long used as a route inland for fur traders.

4 City, SE Brit. Columbia, Canada, on W arm of Kootenay Lake 33 m. NE of Trail; pop. 6772; railroad division point and supply center for extensive mining district; lumbering, fruit growing. Founded 1888.

5 Municipal borough, Lancashire, NW England, 28 m. W of Leeds; pop. 34,368; manufactures cotton, artificial silk.

6 Provincial district of New Zealand. See *Table* at NEW ZEALAND.

7 City, ✳ of Nelson provincial dist., N South I., New Zealand, at head of Tasman Bay 75 m. W of Wellington; pop. (1941 est.) 13,800; center of fruit district; has large and well-sheltered harbor. Founded 1841.

Nelson Reservoir. Reservoir in NE cen. Phillips co., N Montana.

Nel′son·ville (nĕl′s'n·vĭl). City, Athens co., SE Ohio, on Hocking river 25 m. SE of Lancaster; pop. 4834; manufactures brick and tile, shoes, woodworking products; coal mines, clay pits.

Nem′a·ha (nĕm′á·hô; nē′má-). **1** Two rivers, SE Nebraska: **Great,** *or* **Big, Nemaha,** ab. 150 m. long, flows from Lancaster co. SE to Missouri river near SE corner of the state; **Little Nemaha,** ab. 90 m. long, N of the Great Nemaha, flows SE into the Missouri in SE Nemaha co.

2 Name of counties in two states of the U.S. See *Tables* at KANSAS and NEBRASKA.

Ne′man (nĕm′ăn; *Russ.* nyĕ′măn); *Pol.* **Nie′men** (nē′mĕn); *Pol.* nyĕ′mĕn); *Lith.* **Ne′mu·nas** (nă′mŏŏ·näs). River, E cen. Europe, ab. 500 m. long and navigable for most of its length; rises in cen. White Russia S of Minsk,

flows W, then N into Lithuania, and W bet. Lithuania and Kaliningradsk Region into Kurishes Gaf; formerly known as the **Me′mel** (mā′mĕl) river in East Prussia, and as the **Russ** (rŏŏs) 22 m. from its mouth; connected by canal with the Pripyat. Battle Sept. 1914 in the region of the bend bet. Grodno and Kaunas (Kovno) in which Russians defeated Germans under Hindenburg.

Nemausus. See NÎMES.

Nem′by (näm′bĕ). Town, Central dept., S Paraguay, SE of Asunción; pop. ab. 5000.

Ne′me·a (nē′mē·á; *Mod. Gr.* nâ·mā′ä). **1** Valley in N Argolis, ancient Greece; site of present town of Nemea; in Greek mythology scene of the slaying of the Nemean lion by Hercules; had temple of Zeus in whose honor Nemean games, inaugurated 573 B.C., were held; scene of battle 394 B.C. in which Spartans defeated coalition forces in Corinthian War.

2 Town, Argolis and Corinth dept., NE Peloponnesus Greece, ab. 35 m. W of Corinth; pop. 3487.

Ně′mec·ký Brod (nyĕ′mĕts·kē brôt′); *since 1945* **Hav′líč·kův′ Brod** (häv′lĕch·kŏŏf′ brôt′), *Ger.* **Deutsch′-Brod′** (doich′brōt′). City, SE Bohemia, W Czechoslovakia, 60 m. SE of Prague; pop. (1930) 10,657.

Ne·men′cha Mountains (nĕ·mĕn′chá). Range of the Atlas Mts., in E Constantine dept., NE Algeria, extending to border of Tunisia.

Nemetocenna. See ARRAS.

Ne′mi, Lake (nā′mē; *Ital.* nâ′mē); *anc.* **Nem′o·ren′sis La′cus** (nĕm′ô·rĕn′sĭs lā′kŭs). Lake ⅔ sq. m. in the Alban Hills, SE of Lake Albano, Italy; nearby in ancient times were a grove and temple dedicated to Diana.

Ne·mours′ (nĕ·mŏŏr′). Town, Seine-et-Marne dept., N France, S of Melun; pop. 4801; seat of Nemours family, a countship created by Charles V in latter part of 14th cent.; dukedom held by Armagnac branch of the house of Orléans, by Gaston de Foix from 1505, and 1528–1659 by a branch of the house of Savoy.

Nemunas. See NEMAN.

Ne·mu·ro (nĕ·mŏŏ·rô). Town and naval base, E Hokkaido, at S end of Nemuro Strait; pop. (1945) 18,545; kelp export.

Nemuro Strait. Strait off E Hokkaido, Japan, separating Kunashiri I. (U.S.S.R.) from Hokkaido.

Nen. See NENE.

Ne′nagh (nē′ná; -năк). Urban district, co. Tipperary, S Eire, near river Nenagh; pop. 4902; trade center of agricultural area; ruins of castle erected under King John; burned by Jacobites (1688).

Ne·nan′a (nĕ·năn′á). City, E cen. Alaska, on S bank of Tanana river 50 m. WSW of Fairbanks; pop. 286; on the Seward-Fairbanks R.R.; airport.

Nene (nēn; nĕn) *or* **Nen** (nĕn). River 90 m. long in cen. and E England; rises in N Northamptonshire, flows NE into the North Sea through the Wash.

Ne·nets′ National District (nyĭ·nyĕts′). National district of the Samoyeds, part of Arkhangelsk Region, NE Soviet Russia, Europe, the tundra coast N of Komi A.S.S.R.; includes Vaigach I.; 82,797 sq. m.; pop. (1926) 28,125; ✳ Naryan-Mar; established 1929.

Ne·noe′sa, *or* **Ne·nu′sa, Islands** (nä·nŏŏ′sả). See TALAUD ISLANDS.

Ne·o′de·sha′ (nĕ·ō′dĕ·shā′; -ō′dĕ·shā′). City, Wilson co., SE Kansas, 13 m. N of Independence; pop. 3594; oil.

Ne·o′sho (nĕ·ō′shō; -shŭ). **1** River 460 m. long, SE Kansas and NE Oklahoma; rises in Morris co., E cen. Kansas, flows SE and S into Arkansas river in N Muskogee co., E Oklahoma. Called Grand river in Oklahoma.

2 County in Kansas. See *Table* at KANSAS.

3 City, ⊗ of Newton co., SW Missouri, 16 m. SSE of Joplin; pop. 7452; trade center in lumbering and agricultural section; lead deposit nearby.

Ne·pal′ (nĕ·pôl′). Independent state, a constitutional monarchy, on NE frontier of India; 54,000 sq. m.; 500 m. long, 90 to 140 m. broad; pop. 8,473,478; ✳ Katmandu. Bounded on N by Tibet, on E by Sikkim

and Darjeeling dist. of West Bengal, on S by Bihar and United Provinces, and on W by United Provinces from which it is separated by the Kali river. The S portion is level cultivated and forest land (Terai) the cen. and N parts are occupied by great Himalaya ranges; highest peaks Everest, Kanchenjunga, Dhaulagiri Gauri Sankar, and many others above 20,000 ft.; rivers flow southward and are upper tributaries of the Ganges system. Chief cities Katmandu in fertile valley in E cen. part, and Patan and Bhadgaon nearby. Ruler (maharajadhiraj) is of a Hindu Rajput family; people (Nepalese) represent many races of mixed Mongol origin; the most important is the Gurkha, of Hindu origin, which has been dominant since 1768. History goes back to a very early period; in medieval times under Rajput dynasties; first commercial treaty bet. India and Nepal signed 1792; scene of frontier attacks which led British to declare war in 1814; since peace of 1816 (Treaty of Segauli) relations have been friendly. In 1923 recognized by Great Britain as entirely independent. Form of government changed from military oligarchy to constitutional monarchy 1951.

Ne'paug (nē'pôg). River, NW Connecticut; rises in NE Litchfield co., flows SE into Farmington river.

Nepaug Reservoir. Reservoir in Nepaug river, Litchfield and Hartford cos., N Connecticut; water supply for Hartford.

Ne'phi (nē'fī). City, ⊗ of Juab co., W Utah, 38 m. S of Provo; pop. 2566; ships livestock and grain; manufactures flour, plaster; gypsum deposits. Settled 1851 and fortified with a wall; suffered in Indian raids; peace bet. Brigham Young and Chief Walker made nearby 1854.

Neph'in (nĕf'ĭn). Mountain 2646 ft., cen. co. Mayo, Connaught, NW Eire.

Neph'in·beg' (nĕf'ĭn·bĕg'). Mountain 2065 ft. in W co. Mayo, Connaught, NW Eire.

Nepigon, Nepissing. See Lakes NIPIGON and NIPISSING.

Nepisiguit. = NIPISIGUIT bay and river.

Nep'tune (nĕp'tūn). Urban township, Monmouth co., E cen. New Jersey, NW of Neptune City; pop. 21,487.

Nep'tune Beach (nĕp'tūn). Town, Duval co., NE Florida, ESE of Jacksonville; pop. 2868; resort.

Neptune City. Borough and ocean resort, Monmouth co., E New Jersey, SW of Asbury Park; pop. 4013.

Ne'ra (nā'rä); *anc.* **Nar** (när). River ab. 60 m. long in cen. Italy; flows out of the Apennines SW into Tiber river.

Né'rac' (nā'ràk'). Town, S Lot-et-Garonne dept., SW France, on the Baïse river; pop. 3597; center of Protestant activities during 16th cent., captured by Catholics 1562; peace bet. Catholics and Huguenots signed here 1579; headquarters of Henry IV 1580; taken by Louis XIII 1621 and subsequently ruined.

Nerbudda. See NARBADA.

Ner'chinsk (nĕr'chĭnsk; *Russ.* nyär'-). Town, S cen. Chita Region, Soviet Russia, Asia, near N bank of Shilka river ab. 135 m. E of Chita; pop. 6545; has active market for furs, tea, and cattle and important export trade with China in Russian manufactured goods. Founded as a fort 1654; for two centuries one of Russian outposts in Far East; Treaty of Nerchinsk 1689 with China, the first treaty concluded with that country by any European power, held up Russia's advance in Amur valley and was basis (as modified in 1727 and 1768) of relations with China until 1858.

Ner'chin·ski Za·vod' (nyär'chĭn·skĭ zŭ·vôt'). Town near left bank of the Argun, S Chita Region, Soviet Russia, Asia; pop. 3153; center of an extensive mining district, esp. rich in silver, gold, tin, and lead.

Ne'ret·va (nĕ'rĕt·vä); *Ital.* **Na·ren'ta** (nä·rĕn'tä); *anc.* **Na'ro** (nä'rō; nâr'ō). River ab. 140 m. long in SW Yugoslavia; rises E of Mostar, flows NNW, and ab. 28 m. N of Mostar turns S; flows past Mostar into Adriatic Sea; navigable for small vessels.

Ne·ris' (nē·rēz'). Var. of NIRIZ.

Ne·ris' (nĕ·rĭs') *or* **Ne·ries'** (nĕ·rēs'); *Pol.* **Wi'lja** (vē'lyä); *Russ.* **Ne·ris'** (nyĭ·ryēs'), *formerly* **Vi'li·ya** (vyē'lyĭ·yà). River ab. 280 m. long in NE Poland and E Lithuania; rises on E border of Poland and flows W into Neman river at Kaunas, Lithuania.

Nerium Promontorium. See Cape FINISTERRE.

Ne'ro Deep (nē'rō; nĕr'ō). Ocean depression ab. 31,614 ft. deep in the Pacific Ocean ab. 80 m. SE of Guam, in lat. 12°40′N and long. 145°40′E; discovered 1899.

Ne·ro'ne, Mon'te (mōn'tä nå·rō'nå). Highest mountain in the Umbrian Apennines. See APENNINES.

Ner'va (nĕr'vä). Commune, Huelva prov., SW Spain, 37 m. NE of Huelva; pop. 14,932.

Nes (nĕs). Town, E coast of Iceland; pop. (1944) 1177.

Nes'co·peck (nĕs'kô·pĕk). Borough, Luzerne co., E Pennsylvania, on Susquehanna river 22 m. WSW of Wilkes-Barre; pop. 1934.

Ne·sho'ba (nĕ·shō'bà). County in Mississippi. See *Table* at MISSISSIPPI.

Nesis. See NISIDA.

Nesle (nĕl). Town, Somme dept., N France, 7 m. WNW of Ham; pop. 2413; taken Mar. 1918 during World War I in German offensive.

Nēsoi Aigaiou. See AEGEAN ISLANDS division of modern Greece.

Ness (nĕs). **1** County in Kansas. See *Table* at KANSAS. **2** River 6 m. long. Inverness co., NW Scotland; flows NE out of Loch Ness into Moray Firth below Inverness.

Ness, Loch (lŏĸ). Lake in Inverness co., NW Scotland; 23 m. long, from NE to SW; forms part of Caledonian Canal.

Ness City. City, ⊗ of Ness co., W cen. Kansas; pop. 1653.

Nes'ton (nĕs'tŭn); *formerly* **Neston and Park'gate** (pärk'gāt; -gĭt). Urban district, Cheshire, NW England, on the Dee estuary 10 m. S of Liverpool; pop. 9727.

Nestos. See MESTA.

Nes'vizh (nyäs'vyĭsh); *Pol.* **Nieś'wież** (nyĕsh'vyĕsh). Town, W White Russia, U.S.S.R., 44 m. SE of Novogrudok; formerly in Nowogródek dept., Poland; pop. 7357; old castle of Polish-Lithuanian princes of Radziwill.

Net'cong (nĕt'kŏng). Borough, Morris co., N New Jersey, 14 m. WNW of Morristown; pop. 2765; center of summer resort area; ironworks and iron mines; manufactures silk and woolen goods.

Nethe (nĕt). River in Belgium; formed by the confluence of the **Great Nethe** and **Little Nethe** near Lier; flows WSW in Antwerp prov. to unite with the Dyle NW of Mechelen and form the Rupel river.

Neth'er·lands (nĕth'ẽr·lǎndz); *Dutch* **Ne'der·land** (nā'dẽr·länt); *called also* **Hol'land** (hŏl'ǎnd; *Du.* hôl'änt). Kingdom, NW Europe, on the North Sea, bounded on the S by Belgium and on the E by Germany; N part of former Low Countries; area (including inland water) 13,433 sq. m.; pop. (1939) 8,828,680; official ✳ Amsterdam, court residence and de facto ✳ The Hague; divided into the following 11 provinces (for pronunciation of their names, see their individual entries):

NAME	LOCA-TION	AREA[1]	POP.[1]	CAPITAL
Drenthe	NE	1,030	246,879	Assen
Friesland	N	1,431	424,274	Leeuwarden
Gelderland	E	1,965	923,210	Arnhem
Groningen	NE	923	423,329	Groningen
Limburg	SE	851	608,274	Maastricht
North Brabant	S	1,965	1,033,130	's Hertogenbosch
North Holland	W	1,163	1,690,965	Haarlem
Overijssel	E	1,318	576,723	Zwolle
South Holland	SW	1,212	2,167,299	Rotterdam
Utrecht	cen.	535	479,743	Utrecht
Zeeland	SW	1,040	254,854	Middelburg

[1] Area is in sq. m. and includes inland water. Pop. from 1939 Census.

Part of the plain of NW Europe with nearly a quarter of its area below sea level and no elevations higher than low hills; protected along part of the coast by dikes. All

NETHERLANDS

Statute Miles

0   10   20   30   40

⊛ ⊚ Capitals

PUBLISHED BY G. & C. MERRIAM COMPANY
SPRINGFIELD, MASS.
PREPARED BY J. W. CLEMENT CO., BUFFALO, N.Y.

WEST FRISIAN IS.

BORKUM

TERSCHELLING

SCHIERMONNIKOOG
AMELAND

Emden

Delfzijl

Vlie Stroom

VLIELAND

GRONINGEN

Ems

Dollart

Leeuwarden

Groningen

Hoogezand

Harlingen

Winschoten

TEXEL

FRIESLAND

Wildervank

Assen

NORTH

Den Helder

Sneek   Heerenveen

Odoorn

Wieringen

DRENTHE

N. E.
POLDER

Hoogeveen
Meppel

Emmen

Enkhuizen

Zuider

Alkmaar   Hoorn

SEA

NORTH

S. W.
POLDER

Zee

Kampen

Zwolle   Vecht

HOLLAND   Edam

Beverwijk   MARKEN

S. E.
POLDER

OVERIJSSEL

Harderwijk

Raalte   Almelo
Hellendoorn   Oldenzaal

Haarlem

Amsterdam

Deventer

Enschede

Hilversum   Apeldoorn

Leiden

Nijkerk

Zutphen

Baarn
Amersfoort   Barneveld

The Hague
('s Gravenhage)

Utrecht   Zeist

Ede   GELDERLAND

Oude

Rijn

Delft   Gouda

UTRECHT

Amerongen

Hook of Holland

SOUTH

Lek

Neder   Rijn

Arnhem

Doetinchem

Schiedam   Rotterdam

Tiel

Nijmegen

Haringvliet

HOLLAND   Gorinchem

Waal

Maas

GOEDEREEDE

Rhine   (Rijn)

Rhine

Dordrecht

SCHOUWEN

's Hertogenbosch

N. BEVELAND

NORTH   BRABANT

Dommel

WALCHEREN   THOLEN

Prinsenhage   Breda

Vlissingen
(Flushing)   Middelburg   Goes

Bergen op Zoom

Tilburg

Essen

S BEVELAND

Helmond

West   Scheldt

Deurne

MAAS

Eindhoven

Düsseldorf

Neuzen

Turnhout

Tegelen   Venlo

Antwerp
(Antwerpen)

Weert   Roermond

Gent
(Ghent)

Mechelen
(Malines)

Sittard

Cologne

Hasselt

Heerlen

Scheldt

Rur

Brussels   Louvain
(Leuven)

Maastricht

Aachen

BELGIUM

Bonn

Meuse

S part lies in plain and delta of the Neder Rijn and Maas (Meuse) rivers; N cen. part formerly occupied by large shallow inlet of North Sea, the Zuider Zee (*q.v.*), ab. 80 m. long, now partly reclaimed and separated from North Sea by dike from W Friesland prov. to Wieringermeer. Off N coast and enclosing large area of water is chain of West Frisian Is. (see FRISIAN ISLANDS) connecting on E with German East Frisian Is.; in SW (Zeeland prov.) are other large islands in combined delta of Schelde and Maas. Covered by many canals and canalized rivers connecting larger cities. Chief industries agriculture and horticulture; exports dairy products, livestock, vegetables, fruits, bulbs; some manufacturing (textiles, tobacco, beer, machinery, boots and shoes), fishing, and shipbuilding. Chief cities Amsterdam, Rotterdam, The Hague, Utrecht, Haarlem, Groningen, Eindhoven.

History: Region included in Charlemagne's empire; part of medieval kingdom of Lotharingia (see LORRAINE); split up into several counties and duchies (see BRABANT, FLANDERS, HOLLAND, etc.) which were first united in 14th cent. under dukes of Burgundy (*q.v.*); eventually passed to Spanish branch of Hapsburgs; in 1568, began revolt against repressive policy of duke of Alva; the 7 northern Protestant provinces, Holland, Zeeland, Utrecht, Gelderland, Groningen, Friesland, and Overijssel (the United Provinces) formed Union of Utrecht 1579 and declared independence 1581 (see BELGIUM for history of Spanish Netherlands, the provinces remaining loyal to Spain); independence finally recognized 1648; in 17th cent., the Dutch became leading commercial nation of Europe (see AMSTERDAM), expanded greatly its overseas territory (see NETHERLANDS INDIES, NEW NETHERLAND, NETHERLANDS WEST INDIES); engaged in numerous important wars of commercial and political rivalry, with the English 1652–54, 1665–67, with France 1689–97 and 1702–13; Spanish Netherlands awarded to Austria 1713; its ruler, William III and his wife, became co-rulers of England 1689; organized as Batavian Republic 1795–1806 and as kingdom of Holland 1806–10, both under French control; in 1814, received constitution, later revised; its ruler head of United Kingdom of Netherlands (1815–30) which was broken up by revolt of Belgium (*q.v.*) 1830; neutral in World War I; occupied by German forces 1940 and not freed until May 1945; granted independence to Netherlands Indies (*q.v.*) 1949.

Netherlands Antilles. See CURAÇAO territory.

Netherlands Guiana. See SURINAM.

Netherlands India. Occasional British term equivalent to NETHERLANDS INDIES.

Netherlands Indies *or* **Netherlands East Indies** *or* **Dutch East Indies;** *Du.* **Ne′der·landsch-In′di·ë** (nä′dĕr·länts·ĭn′dĕ·ĕ). Former possessions of the Netherlands in the Malay Archipelago, including Java, Sumatra, Bangka, Madura, Celebes, Ceram, Bali, Lombok, Flores, the Riouw Archipelago, the S and E parts of Borneo, the W parts of Timor and New Guinea, and many smaller islands; 735,006 sq. m.; pop. 60,727,233, (1947 est.) 76,360,000; ✱ Batavia (now Djakarta).

History: First visited by Dutch 1595–96; scene of activities of Dutch East India Co. 1602–1798; increasingly dominated by Dutch as they built Batavia (*q.v.*) 1619, drove out English competitors 1623 (see AMBOINA), and captured Malacca on mainland 1641; company territory turned over 1798 to government of French-controlled Netherlands from which most of it was seized by British during Napoleonic Wars; restored to Netherlands 1816; made step toward self-government when legislative assembly was established 1918; overrun by Japanese Jan.–Mar. 1942 and retaken by Allies at end of war 1945; became scene of Nationalist independence movement centered in new Republic of Indonesia (*q.v.*); made steps toward independence: in 1946 when Linggadjati Agreement (first formal proposal of a United States of Indonesia) was initialed Nov. 15 and the

state of East Indonesia proclaimed Dec. 25, in 1947 when the states of East Borneo and West Borneo (*qq.v.*) were established, in 1948 when a provisional federal government was set up, and in 1949 when a round-table conference at The Hague Aug. 25–Nov. 2 resulted in signing of an agreement establishing the **United States of Indonesia** (not including Netherlands New Guinea) as a sovereign republic; in 1950 abandoned federal setup and became unitary state, the **Republic of Indonesia.**

Netherlands New Guinea *or* **Dutch New Guinea;** *now* **West Irian** *or* **West New Guinea.** The western half of the island of New Guinea formerly belonging to the Netherlands, since 1963 to Indonesia; comprises all territory W of 141°E and adjacent islands of N and NW coasts, esp. Schouten Is., Japen, Numfoor, Salawati, and Waigeo, and Frederik Hendrik I. in the S; 159,334 sq. m.; pop. 333,387. Traversed by Snow Mts. (*q.v.*), highest point 16,404 ft. Coast line irregular, esp. in NW where indentations of Geelvink Bay and McCluer Gulf almost cut off large peninsula of Vogelkop. Has many rivers, Mamberamo largest in the N and Digoel in the S, also large areas of swamp land, esp. in the S. Many regions only partially explored; chief settlements on N and NW coasts: Hollandia (*Indonesian* Kotabaru) the capital, Manokwari, Sorong, Fakfak. See *Map* at NEW GUINEA.

History: Islands off NW first visited by Dutch in 17th cent.; coastal regions saw gradual extension of Dutch sovereignty in 18th cent.; NW New Guinea declared a dependency of Tidore 1828; in 1884 the meridian of 141°E agreed upon with British as frontier boundary and in 1885 defined as also the frontier of German New Guinea; this line slightly altered along course of Fly river by convention with Great Britain in 1895. In World War II the N coastal areas occupied by Japanese 1942 but retaken by Allies by seizure esp. of Hollandia, Wakde Is., Biak, and Noemfoor 1944; remained under Dutch control when rest of the Neth. Indies became independent 1949; relinquished to United Nations administration 1962 by the Dutch and transferred to Indonesia 1963.

Netherlands Ti′mor (tē′môr; tĕ·môr′). The western half of the island of Timor, Lesser Sunda Is., while under Dutch rule; ✱ Kupang; enclosed on its N shore the Portuguese exclave of Okusi Ambeno (*q.v.*); region has series of parallel mountain ranges, mainly on N side of central axis; highest point 7963 ft.; settlements chiefly along the coasts, undeveloped in the interior; main exports sandalwood, copra, hides, and livestock. First occupied by Portuguese; Kupang and vicinity seized by Dutch 1618 and W half of island claimed by them after Napoleonic Wars; occupied by Japanese Feb. 1942; transferred to Indonesia by the Dutch 1949.

Netherlands West Indies; *formerly* **Dutch West Indies.** Possessions in the West Indies, now called officially the Netherlands Antilles. See CURAÇAO overseas territory.

Neth′er Providence (nĕth′ẽr). Urban township, Delaware co., SE Pennsylvania; pop. 10,380.

Neth′er Stow′ey (nĕth′ẽr stō′ĭ). Village, Somersetshire, SW England, 7½ m. NW of Bridgwater, N of the Quantock Hills; residence 1796–98 of Samuel Taylor Coleridge who wrote *The Ancient Mariner* here.

Néthou, Pic de. See Pico de ANETO.

Net′ley (nĕt′lĭ). Village, Hampshire, S England, 3 m. SE of Southampton; ruins of Cistercian abbey, founded by Henry III; military hospital.

Net′til·ling Lake (nĕch′ĭ·lĭng). Lake in S cen. Baffin I., E Franklin District, Northwest Territories, Canada.

Net·tu′no (nät·tōō′nô). Commune, Roma prov., Latium, cen. Italy, on Tyrrhenian Sea 31 m. SSE of Rome; pop. 10,118; Treaty of Nettuno bet. Italy and Yugoslavia signed 1925; in World War II occupied by Americans Jan. 22, 1944 at same time as adjoining Anzio (*q.v.*).

Netum. See NOTO.

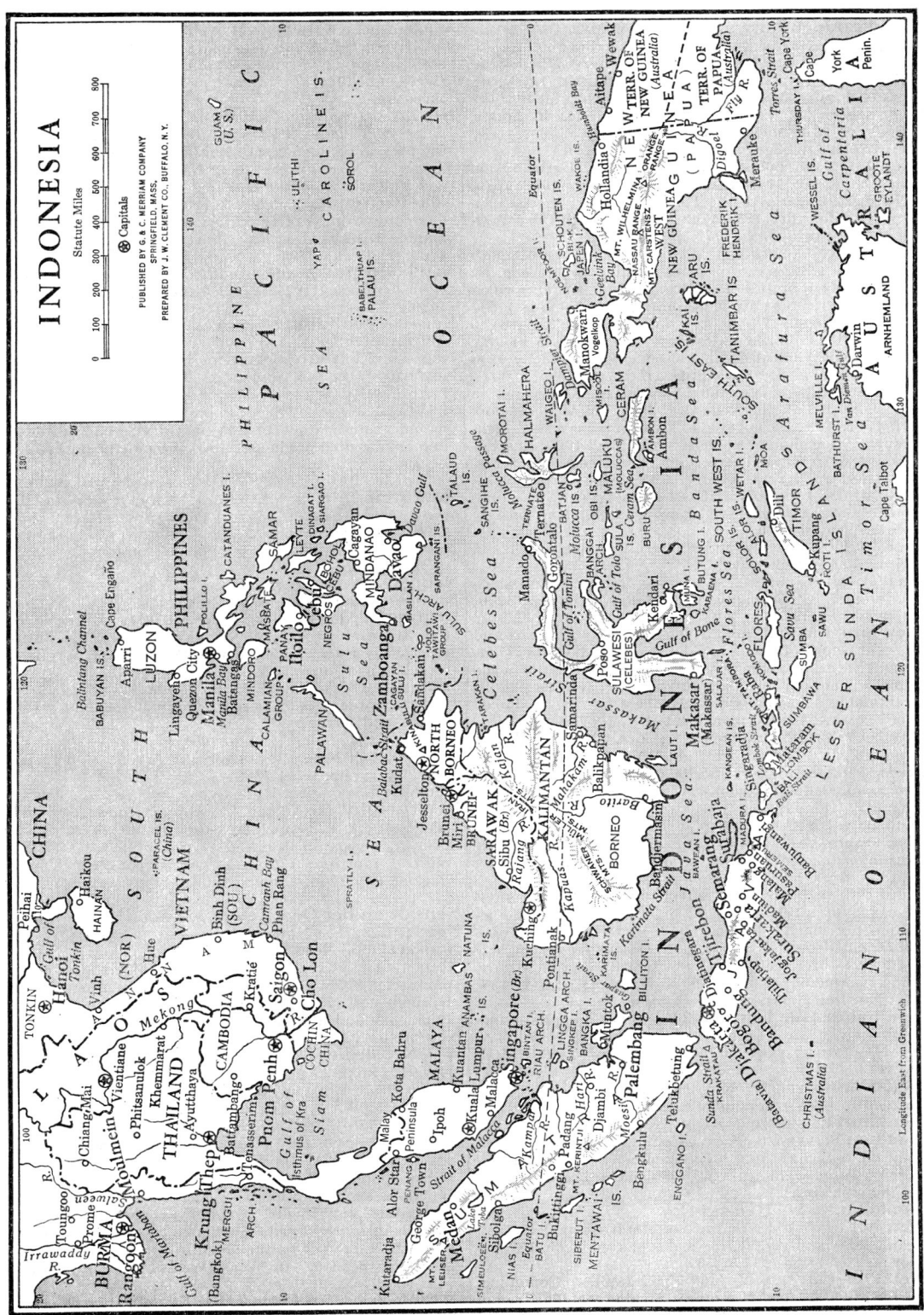

Netze. See NOTEĆ.

Neu'bran'den·burg (noi'brän'děn·bŏŏrk). City, Mecklenburg, Germany, 74 m. E of Schwerin; pop. 13,748; popular tourist resort; completely preserved 14th-cent. city walls; 14th-cent. early-Gothic church, 18th-cent. grand-ducal palace; manufactures agricultural machinery, chemicals, building materials; trades in horses. Founded 1248; to Mecklenburg 1292.

Neubreisach. See NEUF-BRISACH.

Neu'burg (noi'bŏŏrk). Town, Bavaria, Germany, on the Danube ab. 11 m. W of Ingolstadt; pop. (1933) 7670; ceded by Bavaria to the Palatinate 1507; capital of a small principality 1557–1742; reunited with the Palatinate 1742; to Bavaria 1777.

Neu'châ'tel' (nû'shä'těl'; Ger. also noi'-; Eng. also nŭ'-shä·těl'). **1** Swiss canton in the Jura Mts.; watered by numerous tributaries of the Rhine. Independent principality 1034; under French family of Longueville 1504–1707; to Prussia 1707–1806, France 1806–14; reverted to Prussia 1814; joined Swiss Confederation 1815 as only canton with monarchical government (monarchy suppressed 1848). See Table at SWITZERLAND. **2** Commune, ✳ of Neuchâtel canton, W Switzerland, on W shore of Lake of Neuchâtel 25 m. W of Bern; pop. (1941) 23,799; ancient castle, 12th-cent. town hall, 12th-cent. Gothic church; university (founded 1909; as academy 1866); railroad junction; manufactures watches, electrical appliances, jewelry.

Neuchâtel, Lake of. Lake 84 sq. m. in W Switzerland, on S border of Neuchâtel canton; largest lake entirely within Switzerland.

Neudorf. = Zipfer Neudorf, German name of SPIŠSKÁ NOVÁ VES, Czechoslovakia.

Neu'en·ahr' (noi'ĕn·är'). Town, N Rhineland-Palatinate state, W Germany, NW of Koblenz; pop. 5290; alkaline waters.

Neu'fahr'was'ser (noi'fär'väs'ẽr). Seaport town and port of Danzig, Poland, in Gdańsk dept., on Gulf of Danzig ab. 5 m. N of the city; adjoining it on the N is the small peninsula of **Wes'ter·plat'te** (věs'tẽr·plät'ĕ), containing a fortress which was held by a small Polish force against the Germans Sept. 1–7, 1939.

Neuf–Bri'sach' (nû'brē'zàk'); Ger. **Neu'brei'sach** (noi'brī'zäk). Town, NE Haut-Rhin dept., NE France, near German frontier ESE of Colmar; pop. 1775; fortress founded by Louis XIV 1699; held by Germans Nov. 10, 1870–1918.

Neuf'châ'teau' (nû'shä'tō'). Town, NW Vosges dept., NE France, ab. 35 m. NW of Épinal; pop. 3845; ruins of castle of dukes of Lorraine who owned the town during Middle Ages.

Neuf'châ'tel' or **Neufchâtel en Bray** (nû'shä'těl' [Eng. also nŭ'shä·těl'] äN brā'). Town, E Seine-Inférieure dept., N France, ab. 25 m. NE of Rouen; pop. 3825; chief town of Bray region; famous for its cheese.

Neu'gers·dorf (noi'gẽrs·dôrf). Industrial city, Saxony, East Germany, 35 m. ESE of Dresden; pop. 11,165; textiles, iron goods, weavers' looms.

Neu'hal'dens·le'ben (noi'häl'děns·lā'běn). Manufacturing city, Magdeburg dist., E Germany, 14 m. NW of Magdeburg; pop. 10,882; stoneware, terra cotta; gloves.

Neu–Hannover. See NEW HANOVER.

Neuhaus. See JINDŘICHŮV HRADEC.

Neuhäusel. See NOVÉ ZÁMKY.

Neu'hau'sen (noi'hou'zěn). Commune, S Schaffhausen canton, N Switzerland, just SW of Schaffhausen on border of Zurich canton; pop. (1930) 6355; has important aluminum works.

Neuheiduk. See HAJDUKI NOWE.

Neu'hof (noi'hōf). Name of Pestalozzi's farm in Aargau canton, Switzerland, where he established his first school for poor children c. 1776–80.

Neuil'ly'–Plai'sance' (nû'yē'plě'zäNs'). Commune, Seine-et-Oise dept., N France, E suburb of Paris; pop.

(1931) 12,148; manufactures machinery and electrical equipment; battles 1870–71.

Neuilly–sur–Marne (-sür·màrn'). Commune, Seine-et-Oise dept., N France, E suburb of Paris on Marne river; pop. (1931) 10,415; manufactures rubber products, furniture.

Neuilly–sur–Seine (-sür·sân'). Manufacturing commune, Seine dept., N France, a NW suburb of Paris near the Bois de Boulogne; pop. 56,938; automotive industry; Treaty of Neuilly signed here Nov. 27, 1919 bet. Allies and Bulgaria after World War I.

Neu–I'sen·burg (noi'ē'zěn·bŏŏrk). City, S Hesse state, Germany, 5 m. S of Frankfurt am Main; pop. 12,432; manufactures leather, machinery, furniture; founded 1700; made city 1894.

Neu'kölln' (noi'kûln'). Industrial suburb, SE Berlin, Germany; pop. (1925) 271,330; became part of Berlin 1920.

Neu–Langenburg. See TUKUYU.

Neumarkt. See NOWY TARG.

Neu–Mecklenburg. See NEW IRELAND.

Neu'mün'ster (noi'mün'stẽr). Commercial and manufacturing city, Schleswig-Holstein state, West Germany, SSW of Kiel; pop. 39,895; important railroad junction; manufactures leather, textiles, machinery, paper; trades in manufactured products, cattle. Founded before 1127; became city 1870.

Neun'kir'chen (noin'kĭr'kĕn). **1** in full **Neunkirchen am Stein'feld** (äm shtīn'fĕlt). City, Lower Austria prov., Austria, 35 m. SSW of Vienna; pop. 11,541. **2** Industrial city, Saarland, SW Germany, ab. 12 m. NE of Saarbrücken; pop. (1939) 39,866; iron foundry; coal-mining region.

Neupest. See ÚJPEST.

Neu–Pommern. See NEW BRITAIN island.

Ne'u·quén' (nā'ōō·kän'). **1** River ab. 375 m. long in W cen. Argentina; rises in W Neuquén territory; flows E to join Limay river on E border of Neuquén territory and form the Río Negro. **2** Territory of Argentina. See Table at ARGENTINA. On Chilean border, its W part mountainous, E part level; forests and fertile valleys in W; in S is Lake Nahuel Huapí (q.v.). **3** Town, ✳ of Neuquén territory, W Argentina, on Neuquén river; pop. (est.) 7500.

Neurode. See NOWA RUDA.

Neu'rup·pin' (noi'rŏŏ·pēn'). Manufacturing city and health resort, Potsdam govt. dist., Brandenburg prov., Prussia, Germany, 40 m. NNW of Berlin; pop. 18,187; railroad junction; 13th-cent. Gothic convent church. Became city 1256; almost completely destroyed by fire 1787.

Neusalz an der Oder. See NOWA SÓL.

Neusandez. See NOWY SĄCZ.

Neusatz. See NOVI SAD.

Neuse (nūs). River 260 m. long, E cen. North Carolina; navigable to New Bern; formed by junction of streams in Durham co., NE cen. North Carolina, flows SE into Pamlico Sound, E North Carolina.

Neu'sie'dler (noi'zē'dlẽr), Hung. **Fer'tö** (fĕr'tû), Lake; Ger. **Neusiedler See** (zā'). Shallow lake, E Austria and NW Hungary; 23 m. long by 7 m. broad; formerly entirely within Hungary, but in 1922 N two thirds transferred with Burgenland to Austria.

Neusohl. See BANSKÁ BYSTRICA.

Neuss (nois). **1** anc. **No·vae'si·um** (nǒ·vē'zhǐ·ŭm). Industrial city, W North Rhine-Westphalia state, W Germany, 5 m. W of Düsseldorf; pop. 44,890; railroad junction; manufactures paper and iron goods, textiles, agricultural implements, machinery, chemicals. Ancient Roman camp; besieged by Charles the Bold 1474; destroyed by duke of Parma 1586; taken by French 1794 and held to 1813. In World War II taken by Allies Mar. 2, 1945. **2** Commune in Switzerland. See NYON.

Neu′stadt (noi′shtät). = WIENER NEUSTADT city, Austria.

Neustadt an der Hardt (än dĕr härt′); anc. **No′va Civ′i·tas** (nō′vȧ sĭv′ĭ·tȧs); later **Nie′wen·stat** (nē′-vĕn·shtät). Industrial city, Rhineland-Palatinate state, W Germany, 18 m. SW of Mannheim; pop. 20,726; 14th-cent. Gothic church; 18th-cent. city hall; manufactures metal goods, textiles, paper, concrete; railroad junction; trades in wines. First mentioned 1235; became city 1275; during Thirty Years' War taken 1622, 1631, 1635, 1644; occupied by French 1688–97, 1793–95. Taken by Allied armies Mar. 22, 1945.

Neustadt in Oberschlesien. See PRUDNIK.

Neustettin. See SZCZECINEK.

Neu′stre′litz (noi′shtrȧ′lĭts). City, Mecklenburg, Germany, 61 m. NNW of Berlin; pop. 12,260; railroad junction; 18th-cent. grand-ducal palace; printing, sawmilling, iron founding. Founded 1733; capital of former free state of Mecklenburg-Strelitz.

Neus′tri·a (nūs′trĭ·ȧ). The western part of the dominions of the Franks after the conquest by Clovis in 511, comprising then the NW part of modern France bet. the Meuse, the Loire, and the Atlantic Ocean. See AUSTRASIA. After 912 the name was applied to Normandy.

Neuteich. See NOWY STAW.

Neutitschein. See NOVÝ JIČÍN.

Neutra. See NITRA.

Neutral Territory. Two triangular-shaped areas of desert land ab. 1100 sq. m. on NE boundary of Saudi Arabia; the inland area borders on S Iraq and the E section is on the Persian Gulf coast S of Kuwait. Apparently not included in any sovereignty due to incomplete boundary adjustments.

Neu–Ulm (noi′ŏŏlm′). City, Swabia govt. dist., Bavaria, Germany, on right bank of Danube river 2 m. SE of Ulm; pop. 11,919; railroad center.

Neuve–Cha′pelle′ (nûv′shȧ′pĕl′). Town, Pas-de-Calais dept., N France, 7 m. NE of Béthune; scene of battle Mar. 10–13, 1915, in which the British captured the town but failed in their objective of taking the ridge to the E; first use of artillery barrage during World War I, in which British lost 13,000 men.

Neuve–É′glise′ (nûv′ā′glēz′); Flem. **Nieuw′ker′ke** (nē′ŏŏ·kĕr′kĕ). Village, West Flanders prov., NW Belgium, S of Ieper (Ypres); pop. 2308; scene of heavy fighting Apr. 12–13, 1918 in World War I.

Neu′ville′–Saint–Vaast (nû′vēl′săN′väst′). Commune, Pas-de-Calais dept., N France, 4 m. N of Arras; pop. (1931) 872; battles 1915–16, esp. May 9–10, 1915.

Neu′wied′ (noi′vēt′). Industrial city, N North Rhine-Palatinate state, Germany, on the Rhine 7 m. NNW of Koblenz; pop. 20,322; river port; manufactures machinery, soap, cement, rolled metal; excavations of large Roman camp nearby. Founded 1653.

Neu′zen (nû′zĕ[n]) or **Ter·neu′zen** (tĕr-). Commune, Zeeland prov., SW Netherlands, on S shore of Schelde estuary ab. 25 m. WNW of Antwerp; pop. 10,458.

Ne′va (nē′vȧ; Russ. nyĕ·vä′). Navigable river ab. 40 m. long, NW Leningrad Region, Soviet Russia, Europe, flowing from SW corner of Lake Ladoga into the Gulf of Finland through several mouths; connected by canals and other waterways with the White Sea in the N and the Volga and Caspian Sea in the SE (see MARIINSK CANAL SYSTEM); usually frozen Nov. to April. Leningrad (q.v.) is in its delta.

Ne·vad′a (nĕ·văd′ȧ; -vä′dȧ). **1** A western state of U.S.A., 36th state admitted to Union (1864); bounded on N by Oregon and Idaho, on E by Utah and Arizona, and on SW and W by California; 7th state in area, 110,540 sq. m. (land area 109,789 sq. m.); 49th state in population, 285,278; ❋ Carson City. See Table of States at UNITED STATES; see also Map of California and Nevada at CALIFORNIA. Divided into the following 17 counties (for pronunciation of their names, see their individual entries):

NAME	LOCATION	AREA[1]	POP.[1]	CO. SEAT
Churchill	W	4,907	8,452	Fallon
Clark	SE corner[2]	7,927	127,0'6	Las Vegas
Douglas	W	724	3,481	Minden
Elko	NE corner	17,127	12,011	Elko
Esmeralda	SW	3,570	619	Goldfield
Eureka	cen.	4,182	767	Eureka
Humboldt	NW	9,702	5,708	Winnemucca
Lander	cen.	5,621	1,566	Austin
Lincoln	E	10,649	2,431	Pioche
Lyon	W	2,012	6,143	Yerington
Mineral	SW	3,734	6,329	Hawthorne
Nye	cen. and S	18,064	4,374	Tonopah
Ormsby	W	141	8,063	Carson City
Pershing	NW	5,993	3,199	Lovelock
Storey	W	262	568	Virginia City
Washoe	NW corner	6,281	84,743	Reno
White Pine	E	8,893	9,808	Ely

[1] Area = land area in sq. m. Pop. from 1960 Census.
[2] On SE separated from Ariz. by Colorado River, including Hoover Dam. Lake Mead in E part.

Nickname: Silver State; also Sagebrush State. *State flower:* Sagebrush. *Motto:* All for Our Country. *Chief cities:* Las Vegas, Reno. *Rivers:* Humboldt, rising in NE area, flowing W then SW and emptying into Humboldt Lake; Colorado river, forming extreme SE boundary. *Chief lakes, etc.:* Pyramid and Winnemucca Lakes in W, and Walker Lake in SW; many dry lakes (as Mud Lake) and marshy salt regions (Carson Sink and Humboldt Salt Marsh in W cen. part); Black Rock Desert in NW. *Highest point:* Boundary Peak 13,145 ft. in Esmeralda co. on California-Nevada boundary. *Chief industries:* Mining (gold, silver, copper), sheep ranching.

History: Explored by John C. Frémont 1843–45; part of region ceded by Mexico to U.S. 1848; in Utah Territory 1850–61; first permanent settlement made 1851 at Mormon Station (now Genoa); received increasing number of settlers after discovery of Comstock Lode 1859 (see VIRGINIA CITY); organized as separate territory 1861; held first constitutional convention 1863; admitted to Union as state Oct. 31, 1864.

2 Name of counties in two states of the U.S. See *Tables* at ARKANSAS and CALIFORNIA.

Ne·va′da (nĕ·vä′dȧ). **1** City, ⊗ of Story co., cen. Iowa, 30 m. N of Des Moines; pop. 4227; in agricultural section; poultry-distributing point.

2 City, ⊗ of Vernon co., W Missouri, 53 m. N of Joplin; pop. 8416; shipping point for livestock, grain, and poultry.

Ne·va′da (nĕ·vä′dȧ; Span. nȧ·vä′thä). Mountain 21,000 ft. in the Andes, in SW Los Andes territory, NW Argentina; near the Chilean border.

Nevada, Sierra. See SIERRA NEVADA.

Ne·vad′a City (nĕ·văd′ȧ; -vä′dȧ). City, ⊗ of Nevada co., E California, 45 m. W of Lake Tahoe; pop. 2353; gold mining.

Nevada de Chita. See SIERRA NEVADA DE COCUY.

Nevada de Cocuy, Sierra. See SIERRA NEVADA DE COCUY.

Nevada de Mérida, Sierra. See CORDILLERA MÉRIDA.

Nevada de Santa Marta, Sierra. See SIERRA NEVADA DE SANTA MARTA.

Ne·vad′a Falls (nĕ·văd′ȧ; -vä′dȧ). Waterfall 594 ft. in Yosemite National Park, E cen. California.

Ne·va′do (nȧ·vä′thō). For names of mountains beginning with this element see the distinguishing element.

Nevado de Famatina. See SIERRA DE FAMATINA.

Ne′vel (nā′vĕl; nĕv′ĕl; Russ. nyā′vyĭl·y′). Town, SW Velikie Luki Region, Soviet Russia, Europe, on railroad just SW of Velikie Luki and 65 m. N of Vitebsk; near N border of White Russia. Taken by Nazis Aug. 21, 1941 and held until Jan. 1944, for some time a front-line town.

Ne·vers′ (nĕ·vâr′; anc. **No′vi·o·du′num** (nō′vĭ·ō·dū′nŭm). Commune, ❋ of Nièvre dept., cen. France, at confluence of Nièvre and Loire rivers 38 m. ESE of Bourges; pop. 33,699; episcopal see (since 506); 11th-cent. Romanesque church; 13th-cent. cathedral (restored 1879);

15th-cent. courthouse (former ducal palace); medieval gate, 18th-cent. triumphal arch; manufactures cannon, iron cable, chains, porcelain. Capital of former province of Nivernais.

Ne′ves (nã′vĕs). City, Rio de Janeiro state, SE Brazil, on E side of Guanabara Bay just N of Niterói; pop. (1940 est.) 34,603.

Nev′ille′s Cross (nĕv′′lz; -ĭlz). Parish, Durham co., N England, near Durham; pop. 939; site of battle Oct. 17, 1346 in which invading Scots under King David Bruce were defeated, and the king taken prisoner, by forces of Edward III, using novel offensive tactic in which archers and spearmen successfully dislodged and defeated troops in immobile defensive formation.

Nev′in (nĕv′ĭn). Village, SW Caernarvonshire, NW Wales, on N coast of Lleyn Penin.; watering place.

Ne′vis (nē′vĭs; nĕv′ĭs). Island in E West Indies, part of Saint Kitts-Nevis-Anguilla territory of the Leeward Is., British West Indies; area 50 sq. m.; pop. 16,133; sugar raising; chief town Charlestown; birthplace of Alexander Hamilton. Separated from St. Kitts on NW by narrow strait 2 m. wide; a volcanic cone, rising to height of 3596 ft. Discovered by Columbus 1493; colonized by English 1628; taken by French 1782 but restored to the British after the Napoleonic Wars.

Nevis, Ben. See BEN NEVIS.

Nevis, Loch. Inlet of the Sound of Sleat on W coast of Inverness co., NW Scotland; extends inland ab. 14 m.

Nev′ṣe·hir′ (nĕf′shĕ·hēr′) *or* **Nev·shehr′** (nĕf·shĕ′h′r). Town, Niğde vilayet, cen. Turkey in Asia, 40 m. W of Kayseri; pop. 14,135.

New (nū). **1** River ab. 35 m. long, SE North Carolina; rises in N Onslow co., flows S into **New River Inlet** and Atlantic Ocean.
2 River 255 m. long, SW Virginia and S West Virginia; formed by junction of North and South forks in Ashe co., NW North Carolina; flows N across the state of Virginia into West Virginia and joins Gauley river to form Kanawha river in N Fayette co., S cen. West Virginia.
3 Artificial stream 36 m. long, Hertfordshire and Middlesex, SE England; commences near Ware, flows S into reservoirs at Hornsey and Stoke Newington.

New Al′ba·ny (ôl′bȧ·nĭ). **1** City, of Floyd co., S Indiana, on Ohio river across from Louisville, Kentucky; pop. 37,812; plywood and veneer mills; manufactures stoves and boilers, leather products, automobile bodies; strawberries grown in vicinity. Became a city 1839.
2 City, ⊗ of Union co., N Mississippi, 24 m. NW of Tupelo; pop. 5151; in cotton, dairy-farming, and lumbering section.

New Am′ster·dam (ăm′stēr·dăm). **1** The Dutch city on Manhattan I. which became the city of New York; ✳ of New Netherland colony; founded 1625 by Dutch West India Co.; taken by English 1664 and renamed New York. See NEW YORK city and state.
2 Town, ⊗ of Berbice co., NE British Guiana, on E bank of Berbice river near its mouth; 62 m. by rail and ferry SE of Georgetown; pop. (1941 est.) 10,137.
3 Island, Indian Ocean: see AMSTERDAM.

New Archangel. See SITKA.

New′ark (nū′ērk). **1** City, Alameda co., W California, SE of San Francisco; pop. 9884.
2 City, New Castle co., N Delaware, 12 m. WSW of Wilmington; pop. 11,404; settled 1694, chartered 1852 and 1887; in agricultural region; fiber and paper mills; vegetable packing; Univ. of Delaware (founded as Newark Academy 1743; coed.).
3 Manufacturing and industrial city and port of entry, ⊗ of Essex co., NE New Jersey, on Passaic river and Newark Bay 9 m. W of New York City with which it is connected by tunnel ("Tubes"); largest city in the state; pop. 405,220; railroad and transportation center; important airport; insurance center; brewing and distilling, baking, meat packing, printing and publishing; manufactures ink, metal accessories, leather goods, jewelry,

dressed furs, furniture, paint, chemicals, drugs, electrical machines and equipment, aircraft, motor vehicle bodies and parts, cutlery, shoes, clothing, cigars and cigarettes, food preparations; bronze monument of "Wars of America," by Gutzon Borglum. Seat of Newark Colleges (1946; coed.; part of Rutgers Univ.); Newark Coll. of Engineering (1881; coed.).

History: First settled by Puritans 1666; site of Coll. of New Jersey (later Princeton Univ.) 1748–56; Washington's supply base on retreat across state 1776; incorp. as town 1833, as city 1836.
4 Village, Wayne co., W New York, 29 m. ESE of Rochester; pop. 12,868; extensive rose nurseries; manufactures kitchenware, canned and preserved goods, glass.
5 City, ⊗ of Licking co., cen. Ohio, 30 m. E of Columbus; pop. 41,790; settled 1802; manufactures glassware, tires and tubes, stoves, furnaces, lighting fixtures, chemicals, lawn mowers; coal mines, oil wells, sandstone deposits nearby; produces grain, livestock, wool. **Newark Works,** earthworks of prehistoric mound builders in vicinity; cover ab. 4 sq. mi.
6 Municipal borough, Nottinghamshire, N cen. England, 20 m. ENE of Nottingham; pop. 22,909; gypsum and limestone deposits nearby; produces plaster of Paris, farm machinery, iron and brass goods. On the ancient Fosse Way; has castle of 12th–15th cents. which was besieged three times during Civil War.

Newark Bay. A bay in NE New Jersey, SE of Newark; separated from Lower New York Bay on S by Staten I. and connected with Upper New York Bay through Kill van Kull; receives on the N the Passaic and Hackensack rivers.

New Au·gus′ta (ô·gŭs′tȧ). Town, ⊗ of Perry co., SE Mississippi; pop. 275.

Ne·way′go (nē·wā′gō). County in Michigan. See *Table* at MICHIGAN.

New Bal′ti·more (bôl′tĭ·mōr). **1** City, Macomb and St. Clair cos., SE Michigan, on Lake St. Clair 19 m. NE of Detroit; pop. 3159; fishing center and summer resort.
2 Village in New Baltimore town (pop. 1972), Greene co., SE New York, on W bank of Hudson river ab. 14 m. S of Albany; settled 1811; in the days of wooden ships a shipbuilding port.

New Bed′ford (bĕd′fērd). City, a ⊗ of Bristol co., SE Massachusetts, on **New Bedford Harbor** on W side of Buzzards Bay, 50 m. S of Boston; pop. 102,477; manufactures textiles and needles, machinery, tools, brass and iron products; shipping center for fresh fish; has steamer connections with Boston, New York, and Atlantic ports as well as steamer service to Martha's Vineyard and Nantucket. Founded c. 1760 and early became shipping and whaling center; from War of 1812 to c. 1860 leading U.S. whaling port; chartered as city 1847.

New′berg (nū′bûrg). City, Yamhill co., NW Oregon, 21 m. SW of Portland; pop. 4204; founded by Quakers; manufactures wooden utensils, canned fruit; George Fox Coll. (1891; coed.).

New Ber′lin (bûr′lĭn). City, Waukesha co., SE Wisconsin, W of Milwaukee; pop. 15,788.

New′bern (nū′bĕrn). Town, Dyer co., NW Tennessee, 10 m. NE of Dyersburg; pop. 1695; cotton markets.

New Bern (nū′ bĕrn). City and port, ⊗ of Craven co., SE North Carolina, at confluence of Neuse and Trent rivers, 30 m. W of Pamlico Sound; pop. 15,717; fish and livestock market; manufactures lumber, veneer, boxes. Settled by Swiss and Germans 1710; incorporated and made county seat 1723; meeting place of Colonial assembly 1745–61 (except 1752); seat of royal governors 1770–74; chosen provincial capital 1774; fortified port of the Confederacy; captured by Gen. Burnside in Civil War 1862.

New′ber·ry (nū′bĕr′ĭ; -bēr·ĭ). **1** County in South Carolina. See *Table* at SOUTH CAROLINA.
2 Village, ⊗ of Luce co., NE Michigan penin., 58 m. W of Sault Sainte Marie; pop. 2612; lumbering.

3 Town, ⊗ of Newberry co., NW cen. South Carolina, 32 m. ENE of Greenwood; pop. 8208; settled c. 1830; manufactures cotton goods, cottonseed oil and meal, dairy products; cotton growing, lumbering; granite quarries nearby. Newberry Coll. (1856; coed.).

New Beth′le·hem (bĕth′lĕ·ĕm; -hĕm). Borough, Clarion co., W Pennsylvania, 36 m. SE of Oil City; pop. 1599; manufactures brick and tile, furniture.

New·big′gin by the Sea (nû·bĭg′ĭn; nū′bĭg′ĭn). Urban district, Northumberland, N England, on the North Sea 17 m. NNE of Newcastle; pop. 9727.

New Bloom′field (blōōm′fēld). Borough, ⊗ of Perry co., S cen. Pennsylvania; pop. (1950) 1098; planing, hosiery mills; dress factory.

New Bos′ton (bŏs′tйn). City, Scioto co., S Ohio, on Ohio river 4 m. E of Portsmouth; pop. 3984; steel.

New Bran′den·burg (brän′dĕn·bûrg). Anglicized form of NEUBRANDENBURG.

New Braun′fels (broun′fĕlz). Industrial city, ⊗ of Comal co., S cen. Texas, on Guadalupe river 32 m. NE of San Antonio; pop. 15,631; manufactures cotton goods, cottonseed oil, leather, lime; ships wool and mohair; noted for scenic beauty.

Newbridge. See ABERCARN.

New Brigh′ton (brī′t'n). **1** Village, Ramsey co., SE cen. Minnesota, N of Minneapolis; pop. 6448.

2 Residential community, N Staten I., New York City, site of Sailors′ Snug Harbor, a home for retired seamen, founded at bequest of Robert Richard Randall and opened Aug. 1, 1833.

3 Borough, Beaver co., W Pennsylvania, on Beaver river just S of Beaver Falls and 19 m. S of New Castle; pop. 8397; settled 1789; manufactures pottery, clay products, metal products.

4 Ward of Wallasey county borough, Cheshire, NW England, at mouth of the Mersey opp. Liverpool; amusement park, resort.

5 Borough, Canterbury provincial dist., E South I., New Zealand, E suburb of Christchurch on Pacific Ocean; pop. 4810.

New Brit′ain (brĭt′n). **1** Manufacturing city, Hartford co., N Connecticut, 9 m. SW of Hartford; pop. 82,201; produces hardware, cotton and wool knit goods, electrical appliances, rayon undergarments, cutlery; Central Connecticut State College (1849; coed.). Settled 1687; incorporated 1870; consolidated 1905 with the town (incorporated 1850) with which it is coextensive.

2 *formerly* **Neu–Pom′mern** (noi′pôm′ĕrn). Largest island in the Bismarck Archipelago; crescent-shaped with E end ab. 1½ degrees farther N than W tip (Cape Gloucester); ab. 350 m. long, area ab. 13,000 sq. m.; pop. ab. 81,200; chief town and former ✳ Rabaul. Traversed lengthwise by Whiteman Range (highest peak Ulawun, or the Father, 7546 ft.) with several volcanoes, one at E end; sudden violent eruption May 1937 (see Mount VULCAN, MATUPI). Has many good harbors, esp. Blanche Bay, Talasea, Jacquinot Bay, Linden Harbour. Chief islands off coast, belonging to New Britain administrative district, are Lolobau, Vitu Is., Umboi, Long, and Duke of York Is. Rich in tropical vegetation but only coconuts and cocoa of value commercially.

History: First visited and named by William Dampier 1700 but little exploration carried on before end of 19th cent.; made part of German protectorate 1884 (see KOKOPO); after World War I a part of Australian mandate; invaded by Japanese Jan. 1942. Rabaul attacked many times 1943–45 and largely destroyed by American airmen. Landings made Dec. 15, 1943 by U.S. Marines at Arawe and Cape Gloucester and at Talasea Mar. 1944.

3 Administrative district of Territory of New Guinea, including the island of New Britain and adjacent islands; 14,600 sq. m.; pop. (1931) 93,637; ✳ Rabaul.

New Bruns′wick (brŭnz′wĭk). **1** City, ⊗ of Middlesex co., cen. New Jersey, at head of navigation on Raritan river 9 m. W of Perth Amboy; pop. 40,139; railroad, manufacturing, residential, and market center; manufactures pharmaceuticals and surgical supplies, chemicals, motor trucks and automotive parts, needles, musical strings, cigars and cigar boxes, rugs and linoleum, clothing. Rutgers, The State University (1766; coed.); Douglass College (1918); New Brunswick Theological Seminary (1784; separated from Rutgers 1856). Camp Kilmer, military and air base.

History: Settled by English colonists 1681; incorporated as town 1736, as city 1784; alternately headquarters for American and British troops in War for Independence; entered by Washington's defeated army 1776; starting point for Washington's march to final victory at Yorktown 1781.

2 Province, SE Canada, one of the Maritime Provinces (see *Map* at MARITIME PROVINCES); 27,985 sq. m. (including 512 sq. m. of water); pop. 515,697; ✳ Fredericton; divided into the following 15 counties (for pronunciation of their names, see their individual entries):

NAME	LOCA-TION	AREA[1]	POP.[1]	CO. SEAT
Albert	SE	681	9,910	Hopewell Cape
Carleton	W	1,300	22,269	Woodstock
Charlotte	SW	1,243	25,136	St. Andrews
Gloucester	NE	1,854	57,489	Bathurst
Kent	E	1,734	26,767	Richibucto
Kings	S	1,374	22,467	Hampton
Madawaska	NW	1,262	34,329	Edmundston
Northumberland	E	4,671	42,994	Newcastle
Queens	S	1,373	13,206	Gagetown
Restigouche	N	3,242	36,212	Dalhousie
Saint John	S	611	74,497	Saint John
Sunbury	S cen.	1,079	9,322	Burton
Victoria	W	2,074	18,541	Perth
Westmorland	SE	1,430	80,012	Dorchester
York	SW	3,545	42,546	Fredericton

[1] Area = land area in sq. m. Pop. from 1951 Census.

Bounded by Quebec prov. on N, by the Gulf of St. Lawrence and Northumberland Strait (separating it from Prince Edward I.) on E, on S by Bay of Fundy, and on the W by Maine; on SE connected with Nova Scotia by isthmus of Chignecto. Contains one national historic park (Fort Beauséjour). Highest point of land in SE ab. 2000 ft.; larger part lies within basin of St. John river; other rivers the St. Croix (on Maine border), Miramichi, Restigouche, and Nipisiquit. Chief occupations connected with agriculture, forests, fisheries. Chief towns Saint John, Moncton, Fredericton, Edmundston, Campbellton.

History: Down to 1784 was part of French province of Acadia (*q.v.*), then of British province of Nova Scotia. First French settlement (not permanent) made at mouth of St. Croix river 1604 by Sieur de Monts; first English settlement 1762 at Maugerville, after American Revolutionary War received great numbers of Loyalist settlers from U.S.; became separate province 1784; western boundary settled by Ashburton Treaty 1842; joined Nova Scotia, Quebec, and Ontario to form Dominion of Canada 1867 but with considerable opposition and later dissatisfaction.

New′burgh (nū′bûrg). City, Orange co., SE New York, on Hudson river opp. Beacon; 15 m. S of Poughkeepsie; pop. 30,979; shipping point for coal, fruit, and farm and dairy products; shipbuilding, dyeing and bleaching; manufactures artificial leather, felt products (including hats), textiles, carpets and rugs, handbags, lawn mowers, machinery. Stewart Field, U.S. Air Force base.

History: Settled 1708–09; figured prominently in Revolution; Washington's headquarters 1782–83, where he received letter from Lewis Nicola in 1782 urging him to become king, and where the Continental Army was disbanded 1783; *Newburgh Addresses* issued from here 1783 by Gen. John Armstrong.

Newburgh Heights. Village, Cuyahoga co., N Ohio, SE of Cleveland; pop. 3512; suburb of Cleveland.

New′burn (nū′bērn). Urban district, Northumberland,

N England, on the Tyne 5½ m. W of Newcastle; pop. 21,940; in industrial and coal-mining section.

New′bur·y (nū′bĕr·ĭ; nŏŏb′ĕr·ĭ). **1** Town, Essex co., NE corner of Massachusetts, 24 m. ENE of Lowell; pop. 2519; incorp. 1635, one of the oldest towns in the state. **2** Municipal borough, Berkshire, S England, on the Kennet river 53 m. W of London; pop. 17,772; trade center in agricultural section; woolen market; scene of two battles (Sept. 20, 1643 and Oct. 26, 1644) in English Civil War, both to the slight advantage of the Parliamentary armies.

New′bur·y·port′ (-pōrt′). City, a ⊗ of Essex co., NE corner of Massachusetts, at mouth of Merrimack river 25 m. ENE of Lowell; pop. 14,004; settled 1635; formerly shipbuilding and fishing center and port for clipper ships; manufactures silverware, shoes, iron and steel products, textiles, rum. Has many points of historical interest.

New Caesarea. = Nova Caesarea.

New Cal′a·bar (kăl′a·bär). River, S Nigeria, W Africa, a mouth of the Niger river.

New Cal′e·do′nia (kăl′ĕ·dōn′ya̤; -dō′nĭ·a̤). **1** *Fr.* **Nou′-velle′ Ca·lé′do′nie′** (nōō′vĕl′ ka̤·lā′dô′nē′). French territory in SW Pacific Ocean E of Queensland, Australia; includes New Caledonia, Kunie, Loyalty Is., Huon Is., and several other islet groups; 7756 sq. m.; pop. (1942) ab. 55,000; ✱ Nouméa; penal population, formerly large, was less than 100 in 1942. **2** *Fr.* **Nouvelle Calédonie.** Island in SW Pacific Ocean, E of Australia; area with small adjacent islands, 6531 sq. m.; pop. (1936) 53,245; main island of French territory of New Caledonia. It is a long narrow mountainous island 248 m. long by ab. 31 m. wide, extending from ab. 20°S lat. in a southeasterly direction to ab. 22°20′S; higher peaks Mt. Panié in the NE 5413 ft. and Mt. Humboldt in the SE 5361 ft.; good rainfall and many small streams, but except for the coastal plains not particularly fertile; principal crops copra, coffee, cotton; rich in minerals, esp. nickel, iron, and chrome. Reefs border much of its coast line; off its NW point are the Belep Is. and off the S tip the island of Kunie. Natives are Melanesians of the Papuan type. Chief town Nouméa on SW coast, with fine harbor, also Thio, Hienghène, Bourail, and Pam.

History: Its existence made known to Bougainville 1768 and discovered by Capt. Cook 1774; visited by various navigators, explorers, and traders 1792–1840; occupied by France 1853 and set up as a penal colony 1864–94; joined Free French cause July 1940; first American Expeditionary Force arrived Mar. 10, 1942; made an Allied base.

3 Former name of British Columbia (q.v.).

4 See Darien settlement and colony.

New Ca′naan (kā′năn). Residential town and summer resort, SW Fairfield co., SW Connecticut, on New York border; pop. 13,466; settled 1640, incorp. 1801; borough and town consolidated 1935.

New Car·lisle′ (kär·līl′; kär′līl). Village (unincorporated), ⊗ of Bonaventure co., SE Quebec, Canada, on SE coast of Gaspé Penin. on Chaleur Bay; pop. 1617; commercial and railroad center; much frequented by tourists.

New Cas·tile′ (kăs·tēl′); *Span.* **Cas·til′la la Nue′va** (käs·tē′[l]ya̤ lä nwā′vä). Old provincial region, S Castile, Spain; 28,010 sq. m.; bounded on N by Old Castile, NE by Aragon, SE by Valencia and Murcia, S by Andalusia, W by Estremadura; comprises modern provinces of Ciudad Real, Cuenca, Guadalajara, Madrid, and Toledo; ✱ Toledo. For its history, see Castile.

New′cas′tle (nū′kăs′'l). **1** Town, ⊗ of Weston co., NE Wyoming, 75 m. ESE of Gillette; pop. 4345; shipping point for lumber, petroleum, and bentonite; livestock-raising center nearby.

2 *orig.* **King′s Town** (kĭngz′ toun′). Industrial city, E New South Wales, SE Australia, on Pacific Ocean at mouth of Hunter river 100 m. NE of Sydney; pop. 13,663, with 10 suburbs 104,491; founded 1804 as penal colony; has fortified harbor; one of world's important coaling ports; ships iron and steel products, timber, wool, mutton, agricultural products.

3 Town, ⊗ of Northumberland co., E New Brunswick, Canada, on left bank of Miramichi river 14 m. from its mouth; pop. 4248; founded 1785; extensive shipbuilding and lumber trading.

4 *or* **Newcastle upon Tyne** (nū′kăs′'l [*locally* nū-kăs′'l], tĭn; *anciently* **Monk′cñes′ter** (mŭngk′chĕs′-tẽr). City and county borough, Northumberland, N England, on the Tyne 83 m. N of Leeds; pop. 283,156, (1951) 291,723; shipbuilding center; coal and iron, chemicals, refractory wares; cathedral; Royal Free Grammar School (1525); has remains of castle built by Henry II on site of castle of Robert Curt-hose from which town got its modern name; also has remains of bridge, probably built by Hadrian, which gave the name **Pons Ae′li·i** (pŏnz ē′lĭ·ĭ) to the station on the Roman wall; trade in coal began 13th cent., rose to importance 17th cent.

5 *or* **Newcastle under Lyme** (līm). Municipal borough, Staffordshire, W cen. England; pop. 70,028; manufactures cotton, paper, army clothing; no trace of the 12th-cent. castle for which the place is named.

6 Town, W Natal, E Union of South Africa, 150 m. NNW of Durban at foot of Drakensberg Mts.; pop. 4943; produces wood, grain, hemp; center of extensive coal fields; iron and steel works; carbide factory; base of British military operations against Boers in war of 1880–81; treaty of peace signed 1881.

New Cas′tle (nū kăs′'l; nū′ kăs′'l). **1** County in Delaware. See *Table* at Delaware.

2 City, New Castle co., N Delaware, on Delaware river 5 m. S of Wilmington; pop. 4469; good harbor; manufactures steel, rayon, fiber, paint, aircraft. Settled by Swedes before 1651; state capital to 1777; incorporated as city 1875.

3 Industrial city, ⊗ of Henry co., E cen. Indiana, 18 m. S of Muncie; pop. 20,349; founded 1820; manufactures steel products and automobile accessories; nearby farm was birthplace of Wilbur Wright.

4 City, ⊗ of Henry co., N Kentucky, ab. 35 m. NE of Louisville; pop. 699.

5 City, ⊗ of Lawrence co., W Pennsylvania, on the Shenango river 44 m. NNW of Pittsburgh; pop. 44,790; industrial and railroad center; iron ore, coal mines, clay pits; limestone, sandstone quarries; manufactures cement, metal products, tin, chinaware, beer and ale. Incorporated as city 1875.

6 Town, ⊗ of Craig co., western Virginia, ab. 55 m. W of Lynchburg; pop. 200.

New′chwang′ (nū′chwäng′; *Chin.* nĭ·ü′jōō·äng′). **1** City, S Liaoning prov., S Manchuria, on Liao river ab. 30 m. from its mouth. Made a treaty port 1858 by Treaty of Tientsin, but the port actually opened (in 1864) was Yingkow nearer the river's mouth which has replaced the old town in commercial importance.

2 Alternative name of Yingkow (q.v.).

New City. Village, ⊗ of Rockland co., SE New York; pop. (est.) 4000.

New′com′ers·town′ (nū′kŭm′ẽrz·toun′). Village, Tuscarawas co., E Ohio, 30 m. NE of Zanesville; pop. 4273; settled 1815; manufactures brick and tile steel, tin plate; coal and clay deposits nearby.

New Con′cord (kŏn′kôrd). Village, Muskingum co., SE cen. Ohio, 14 m. E of Zanesville; pop. 2127. Muskingum Coll. (1837; coed.).

New Cro′ton Dam *and* **Reservoir** (krō′t'n). See United States, *Dams and Reservoirs.*

New Cum′ber·land (kŭm′bẽr·lănd). **1** Borough, Cumberland co., S Pennsylvania, on Susquehanna river 3 m. S of Harrisburg; pop. 9257; settled 1810; produces hosiery, woolen goods, processed tobacco.

2 City, ⊗ of Hancock co., N tip of West Virginia panhandle, on Ohio river 31 m. NNE of Wheeling; pop. 2076;

shipping point; manufactures brick, pottery, foundry products; clay pits and coal mines nearby.

New Del′hi (dĕl′ĭ). City, Delhi territory, N India, on Jumna river S of Old Delhi; pop. (1941) 93,733; official ✳ of Republic of India. See DELHI. Completed in 1929 when the Viceroy took up residence there; formally opened 1931.

New Dongola. See DONGOLA.

New Dorp (nū′ dôrp′). See RICHMOND borough, New York City.

New Ea′gle (ē′g′l). Borough, Washington co., SW Pennsylvania, on Monongahela river 16 m. S of Pittsburgh; pop. 2670.

New E·cho′ta (ê·kō′tà). Indian town, NW Georgia; site, in Gordon co., NE of Calhoun, marked by a monument; chosen by the Cherokee as their capital 1819; by 1828 had a newspaper; given up by the Cherokee when they signed Dec. 29, 1835 the Treaty of New Echota surrendering all their lands E of the Mississippi river to the United States.

New′ell (nū′ĕl). Town, Hancock co., N tip of panhandle, West Virginia, ab. 38 m. N of Wheeling; pop. 1842; chinaware and pottery manufactures.

New Eng′land (ĭng′glănd). 1 Northeast section of the United States comprising the states of Maine, New Hampshire, Vermont, Massachusetts, Rhode Island, and Connecticut; total area 66,608 sq. m. (land area, 63,159 sq. m.); pop. 10,509,367.

History: Council for New England, incorporated 1620 with Sir Ferdinando Gorges as president, was granted territory from sea to sea bet. 40th and 48th parallels; its jurisdiction ignored by colonies, esp. Massachusetts Bay which was governed by Massachusetts Bay Co. with powers directly from the king; Council surrendered its charter 1635. The New England Confederation (1643–84) was formed by the colonies of Massachusetts Bay, Plymouth, Connecticut, and New Haven for defense against the Indians. The Dominion of New England formed by English government in 1686 made into one province, under rule of Edmund Andros, the colonies of New Hampshire, Massachusetts, Rhode Island, and Connecticut; New York and New Jersey added in 1688 for protection against French; Andros overthrown 1689 and colonies resumed separate existences. For later history see individual states.

2 Mountain range and plateau **(New England Plateau**), ab. 200 m. long by 75 m. broad, NE New South Wales, SE Australia; part of Great Dividing Range; highest Ben Lomond ab. 5000 ft.

New′en·ham. (nū′ĕn·hăm). Cape on SW coast of Alaska bet. Kuskokwim Bay and Bristol Bay, 162°W.

New′fane′ (nū′fān′). Residential village, ⊗ of Windham co., SE corner of Vermont; pop. 146.

New Forest. District in SW Hampshire, S England, bet. the Avon and Southampton water; 145 sq. m., ab. one fourth of which, under private ownership, is cultivated, the remainder, partly bog and heath, administered as a state park; set apart 1079 by William the Conqueror as a hunting ground.

New Found, or **Newfound, Lake.** Lake 6 m. long, ab. 2½ m. wide, cen. New Hampshire, in SE Grafton co.

New′found·land′ (nū′fŭn[d]·lănd′—*the usu. local pron.*; nū′fŭn[d]·lănd, -lănd′; *nonlocally also* nū·foun[d]′lănd). Island in Atlantic Ocean, off E coast of Canada, since 1949 constituting with Labrador a province of the Dominion of Canada; area 42,734 sq. m.; pop. (1951) 353,526; including Labrador area 155,364 sq. m., pop. (1951) 361,416; ✳ St. John's. See LABRADOR. In general a plateau (highest point just above 2000 ft.); triangular in form with Cape Bauld at the N, Cape Race at SE, and Cape Ray at SW; coasts much indented, esp. in the E and S; separated on N from mainland (Labrador) by the Strait of Belle Isle; has many islands along coasts, esp. Belle Isle, Groais, Bell, and Fogo in the N and the French islands of St. Pierre and Miquelon off S

coast; largest rivers the Exploits, Humber, and Gander; chief lakes Grand, Red Indian, and Gander. Chief in-

dustry fishing, esp. for cod (see GRAND BANK); produces lumber and pulpwood for paper; iron ore mines on Bell I. Chief towns St. John's, Corner Brook, Grand Falls, Bonavista, Carbonear.

History: Discovery 1497 by John Cabot resulted at once in visits of fishermen from countries of W Europe; ownership proclaimed formally in 1583 by Sir Humphrey Gilbert who established first colony at St. John's; site of unsuccessful settlements by John Guy 1610 and Sir George Calvert 1621–29 (see FERRYLAND); disputed by France and England; by Treaty of Utrecht 1713 became English, but fishing rights retained by France (see FRENCH SHORE); received first governor 1728; by Treaty of Versailles 1763 was granted coast of Labrador; controversies over fishing rights continued through 19th cent.; received representative government 1832 and responsible government 1855, which was withdrawn 1933; became a colony 1934. In World War II developed great air bases near Botwood, in 1940 granted bases on S and W coasts and near St. John's to U.S. By plebiscite of July 22, 1948, voted in favor of union with the Dominion of Canada; became tenth province of Canada 1949.

New France (frȧns). The possessions of France in North America from the time of the discoveries of Cartier 1534–41, but esp. from 1627 (when the "Company of New France" was founded by Cardinal Richelieu) to 1763, Treaty of Paris, by which France lost to Great Britain and Spain. See QUEBEC province. Strengthened by Colbert's new Company of the West, founded 1664; its boundaries expanded beyond the lower St. Lawrence to cover the Great Lakes and all the Mississippi Valley, the result esp. of the work of the great French missionary explorers Marquette, La Salle, Hennepin, Duluth, Joliet, Nicolet, and others; in 1689 began the long period of rivalry in Europe bet. England and France directly affecting their possessions in the Western Hemisphere through four wars, known in America as King William's War (1689–97), Queen Anne's War (1702–13), King George's War (1744–48), and the French and Indian War (1754–63).

New Geor′gia (jôr′jà; -jyà; -jĭ·à). 1 Group of islands, cen. Solomon Is., including New Georgia I. and Vella Lavella, Ganongga, Kolombangara, Rendova, and Vangunu Is.; administrative center on Gizo I.; part of British Solomon Is. protectorate.

2 Chief island of the group, 40 m. S of Choiseul I., ab. 50

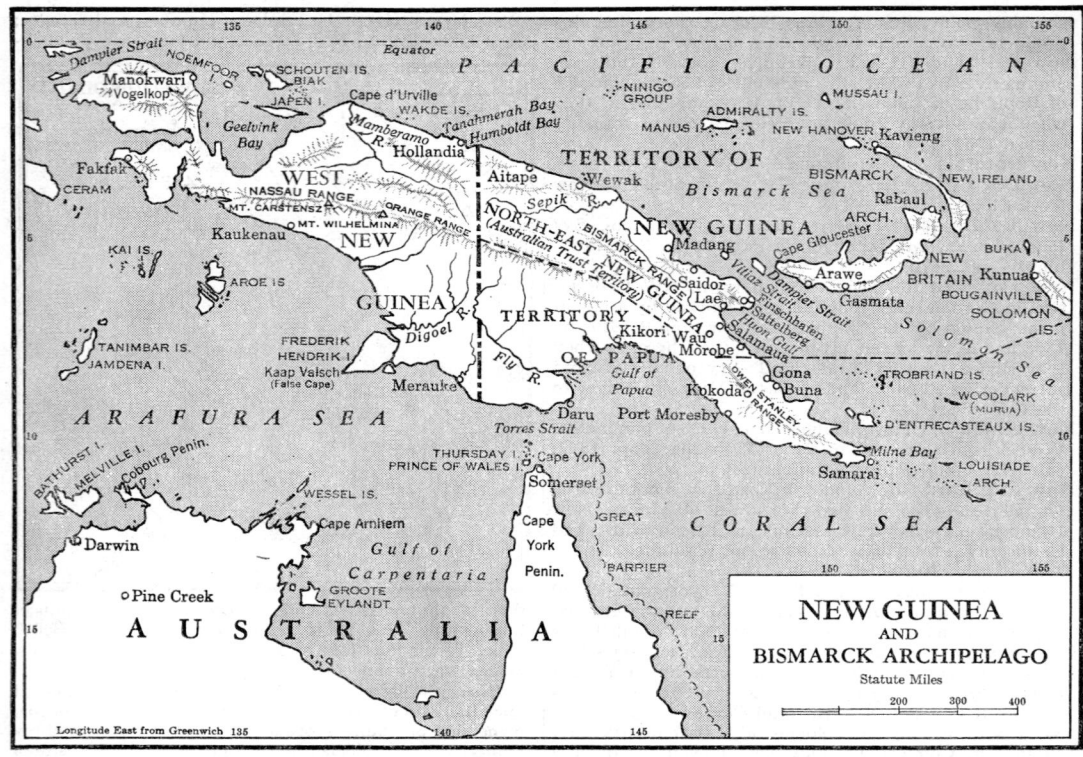

NEW GUINEA
AND
BISMARCK ARCHIPELAGO
Statute Miles

m. long, 10–12 m. wide; highest point 2970 ft.; in SE
enclosed by Vangunu Is. and reefs is Marovo lagoon, one
of largest in world; along W coast E of Munda is the
beautiful Roviana lagoon. Occupied by Japanese 1942
and fortified, esp. at Munda airfield on NW coast; used
as base for attack on Guadalcanal Aug.–Nov. 1942; captured by Americans June–Aug. 1943. See KULA GULF.

New Glasgow. Town, Pictou co., N Nova Scotia, Canada, on East river near Pictou Harbor 37 m. NE of
Truro; pop. 9933; shipbuilding, steelmaking, coal.

New Glouces'ter (glŏs'tẽr; glôs'-). Town, Cumberland
co., SW Maine, 20 m. N of Portland; pop. 3047.

New Goa. See PANGIM.

New Gra·na'da (grȧ·nä'dȧ); *Span.* **Nue'va Gra-
na'da** (nwä'vä grä·nä'thä). **1** Spanish viceroyalty in
NW South America; region conquered and named by
Spaniards 1537–38 under Gonzalo Jiménez de Quesada;
part of viceroyalty of Peru until 1718; as reorganized
1740 included what is now Colombia (and Panama),
Venezuela, and Ecuador; freed from Spanish rule 1819.
See GREAT COLOMBIA.
2 Name of Colombia (with Panama) 1819–30 when it
was part of Great Colombia. See *History* at COLOMBIA.

New·grange' (nū·grānj') The principal tumulus of the
Brugh na Boinne (*q.v.*), co. Meath, NE Eire, on N bank
of the Boyne; the mound, surrounded by remains of a
stone circle, has a domed chamber.

New Guin'ea (gĭn'ĭ) or **Pap'u·a** (păp'ū·ȧ); *Indonesian*
I'ri·an (ē'rē·än). Island of E Malay Archipelago, in W
Pacific Ocean N of Australia; second largest island in the
world; ab. 306,600 sq. m.; pop. ab. 1,167,000; divided
into West New Guinea, North-East New Guinea (part
of Territory of New Guinea), and Territory of Papua
(see these entries).

New Guinea, British. See Territory of PAPUA.

New Guinea, Dutch. See NETHERLANDS NEW
GUINEA.

New Guinea, Territory of. NE section of New Guinea

I. (North-East New Guinea) together with Bougainville,
Buka, and adjacent small islands (Kieta dist.) and the
Bismarck Archipelago; area of mainland territory 69,700
sq. m., pop. ab. 230,500 (recent est. 550,000); including
islands, area 93,000 sq. m., controlled territory 38,860
sq. m.; pop. 400,000 (recent est. 791,000); former ✱
Rabaul, since 1941 Lae; an Australian trust territory.
For description and history see NORTH-EAST NEW
GUINEA and BISMARCK ARCHIPELAGO.

New'gulf' (nū'gŭlf'). Town, Wharton co., SE Texas;
pop. 1419; center of sulfur industry.

New Gulf; *Span.* **Gol'fo Nue'vo** (gôl'fô nwā'vô). Inlet
NE Chubut territory, S Argentina, S of Váldez Penin.

New Hamp'shire (hăm[p]'shẽr; -shĭr). A northeastern
state of U.S.A. an original state of the Union, the 9th to
ratify the Federal Constitution (June 21, 1788); bounded
on N by Canadian province of Quebec, on E by Maine
and (in the extreme SE) the Atlantic Ocean, on S by
Massachusetts, and on W by Vermont; 44th state in
area, 9304 sq. m. (land area 9017 sq. m.); 45th state in
population, 606,921; ✱ Concord. See *Table of States* at
UNITED STATES. Divided into the following 10 counties
(for pronunciation of their names, see their individual
entries):

NAME	LOCATION	AREA[1]	POP.[1]	CO. SEAT
Belknap[2]	cen.	400	28,912	Laconia
Carroll[2]	E	938	15,829	Ossipee
Cheshire	SW corner	717	43,342	Keene
Coos	N	1,822	37,140	Lancaster
Grafton	W	1,716	48,857	Woodsville
Hillsboro	S	890	178,161	Manchester and Nashua
Merrimack	S cen.	929	67,785	Concord
Rockingham	SE[3]	691	99,029	Exeter
Strafford	SE	377	59,799	Dover
Sullivan	SW	537	28,067	Newport

[1] Area = land area in sq. m. Pop. from 1960 Census.
[2] Includes part of Lake Winnipesaukee (larger part in Belknap co.).
[3] Only coastal county in state.

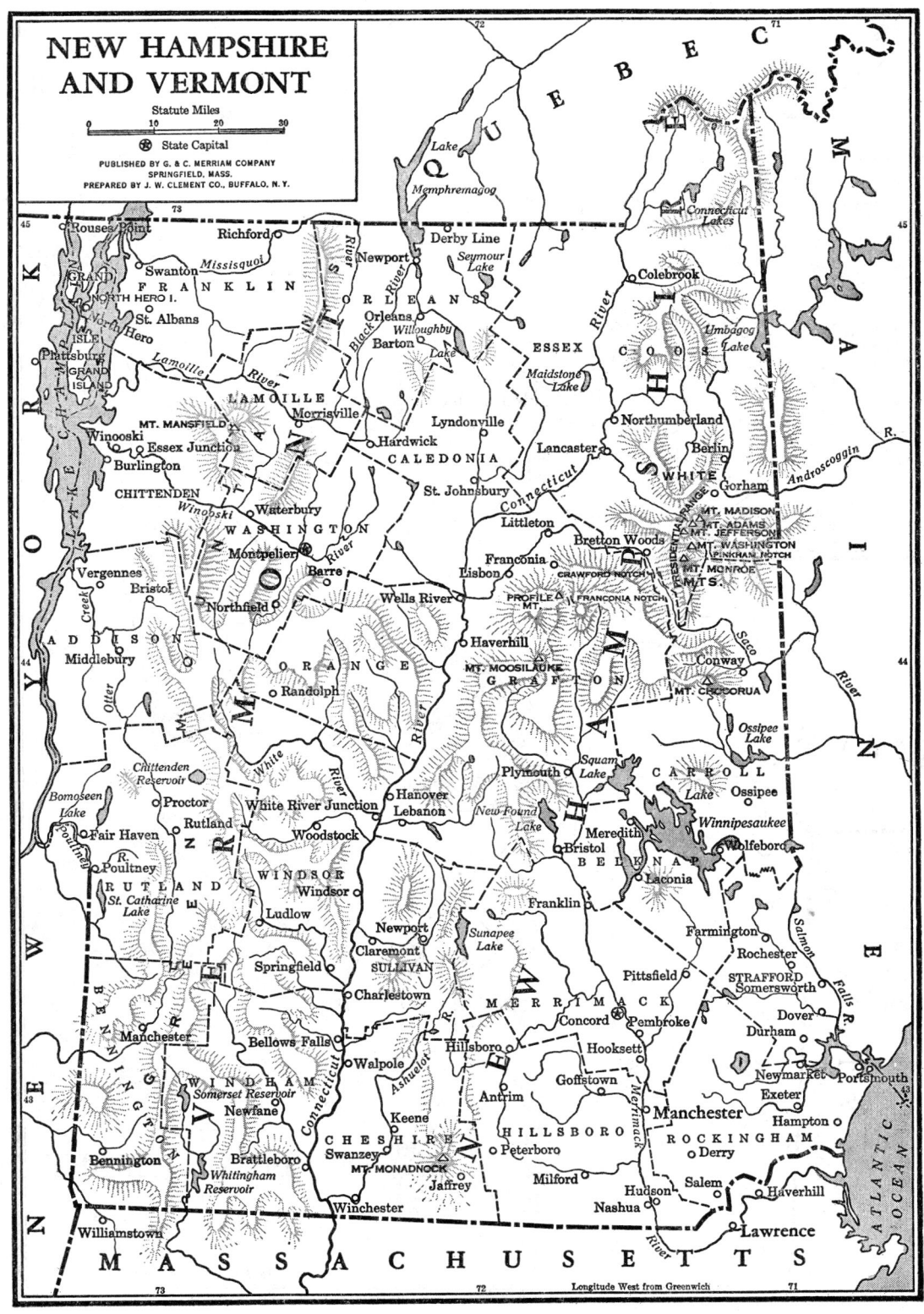

NEW HAMPSHIRE AND VERMONT

Statute Miles

State Capital

PUBLISHED BY G. & C. MERRIAM COMPANY
SPRINGFIELD, MASS.
PREPARED BY J. W. CLEMENT CO., BUFFALO, N. Y.

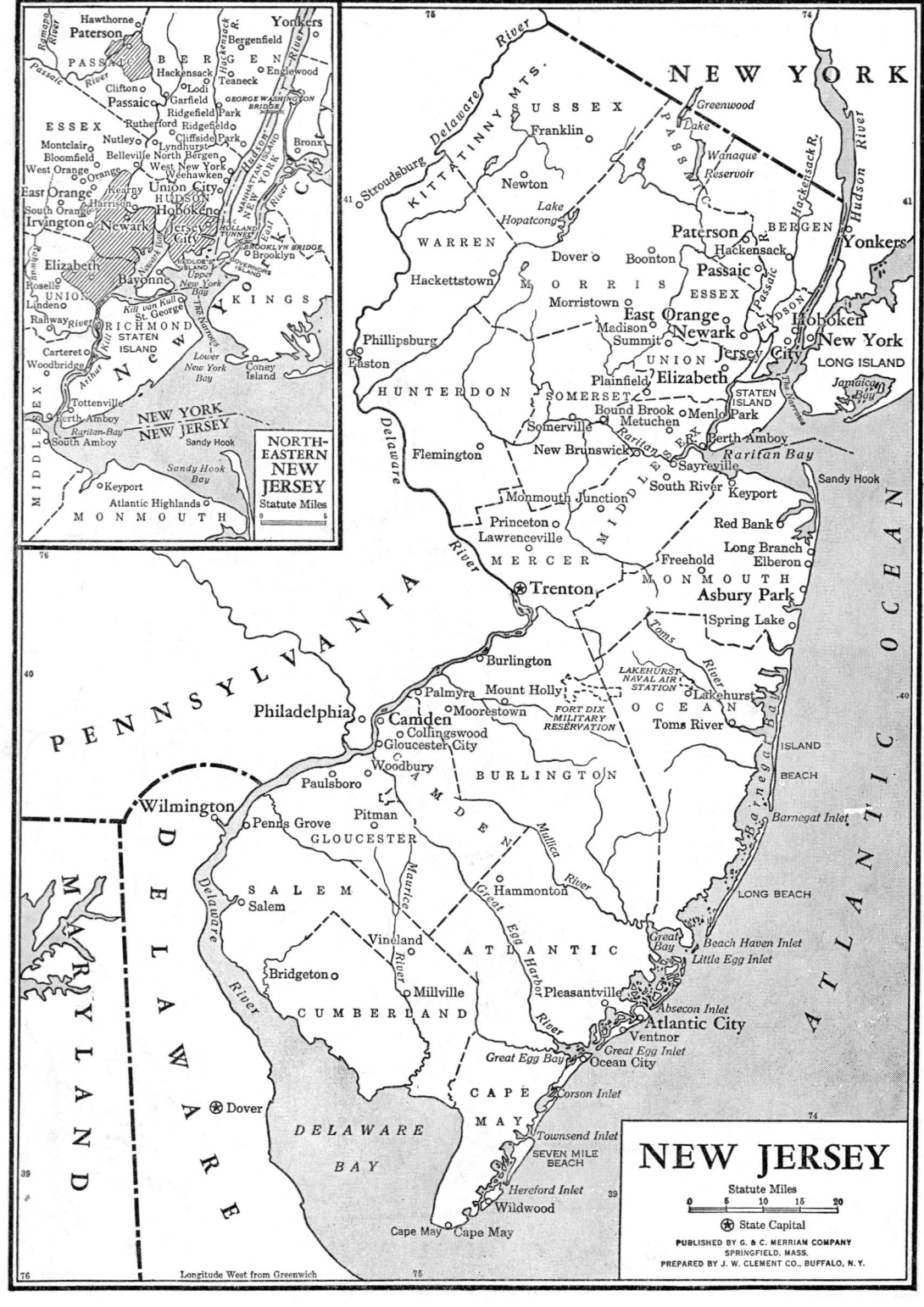

NORTH-EASTERN NEW JERSEY

Statute Miles

NEW JERSEY

Statute Miles

⊛ State Capital

PUBLISHED BY G. & C. MERRIAM COMPANY
SPRINGFIELD, MASS.
PREPARED BY J. W. CLEMENT CO., BUFFALO, N.Y.

Nickname: Granite State. *State flower:* Purple lilac. *Motto:* Live Free or Die. *Chief cities:* Manchester, Nashua, Concord. *Rivers:* Connecticut, forming W boundary; Salmon Falls and Piscataqua, forming SE boundary; Saco, flowing SE across the border into Maine; Merrimack, flowing from S cen. area S across border into Massachusetts. *Mountains:* White Mts. in N cen. part, including highest point in state Mount Washington 6288 ft. in Coos co. *Chief industries:* Manufacturing (cotton and woolen fabrics, boots and shoes, paper), quarrying (granite).

History: Coast explored by Pring 1603; included in grant to Mason and Gorges 1622 and in New Hampshire grant to Mason 1629; first settled by English near Portsmouth 1623; controlled by Massachusetts 1641–43; made a separate royal province 1679 but under same governor as Massachusetts 1699–1741; adopted 1st constitution 1776; relinquished claim to New Connecticut (Vermont) 1782; adopted present constitution 1792 which later was frequently amended; Dartmouth College case decided in U.S. Supreme Court, confirming right of private corporations 1819.

New Hamp′ton (hăm[p]′tŭn). City, ⊗ of Chickasaw co., NE Iowa, 37 m. N of Waterloo; pop. 3456.

New Han′o·ver. 1 County in North Carolina. See *Table* at NORTH CAROLINA.

2 *or* **La·von′gai** (lȧ·vông′gī); *formerly* **Neu–Han·no′-ver** (noi′hä·nō′vẽr; -fẽr). Island in the Bismarck Archipelago, W Pacific Ocean, NW of New Ireland; 460 sq. m.; pop. 4733; chief village Nugima; mountainous, with highest point 2871 ft.; coconut plantations.

New Har′mo·ny (här′mŏ·nĭ). Town, Posey co., SW corner of Indiana, on Wabash river 23 m. WNW of Evansville; pop. 1121; founded (as Harmonie) 1815 by Harmony Society under George Rapp, German religious leader; sold out 1825 to Robert Owen, who renamed it New Harmony and established a Utopian communistic colony; internal dissensions caused breakup of the community 1828.

New Hart′ford (härt′fẽrd). **1** Town, E Litchfield co., NW Connecticut, on Farmington river; pop. 3033; watered by Nepaug river; agriculture; manufactures vacuum cleaners, paper boxes. Settled 1733, incorp. 1740.

2 Village, Oneida co., cen. New York, 5 m. SW of Utica; pop. 2468; manufacturing suburb of Utica.

New·ha′ven (nŭ·hā′vĕn; nŭ′hā′vĕn). Urban district, East Sussex, S England, on seacoast at mouth of the Ouse 55 m. S of London; pop. 7785; popular cross-channel port.

New Ha′ven (nŭ hā′vĕn). **1** County in Connecticut. See *Table* at CONNECTICUT.

2 Industrial and commercial city, a ⊗ of New Haven co., S Connecticut, on New Haven Harbor 36 m. SSW of Hartford; pop. 152,048; 3d largest city in state; port of entry; wholesale distributing center; manufactures munitions, clocks, machines, machine parts and tools, hardware, wire and cable, electrical equipment, rubber goods, clothing, steel goods, paper products, toilet articles; traprock quarries; Connecticut Agricultural Experiment Station; Yale Univ. (founded 1701; at New Haven from 1716); Southern Connecticut State College (1893; coed.); Albertus Magnus Coll. (1925; women).

History: Settled 1638 by Puritans under John Davenport and Theophilus Eaton, the latter civil governor of New Haven Colony 1639–58; at first called Quinnipiac, given present name 1640; with Hartford, joint capital of Connecticut 1701–1875; incorporated 1784; lively maritime trade with West Indies and coastal ports in late 18th cent. and with Orient and Pacific ports in early 19th cent.; became important manufacturing center, a number of its residents, among them Eli Whitney, Charles Goodyear, and Samuel F. B. Morse, making significant contributions to the industrial development of the world. The town (incorporated 1784) and the city were consolidated and made coextensive 1895.

3 Town, Allen co., NE Indiana, 7 m. E of Fort Wayne; pop. 3396.

New Haven Harbor. Inlet of Long Island Sound, on S shore of New Haven co., Connecticut; receives Quinnipiac, Mill, and West rivers.

New Heb′ri·des (hĕb′rĭ-dēz); *Fr.* **Nou′velles′ Hé′-brides′** (nōō′vĕl′-zä′brēd′). Group of islands in SW Pacific Ocean NE of New Caledonia and W of Fiji Is.; 5700 sq. m.; pop. (native; 1938 est.) 50,000; ✳ Vila; under joint British and French administration. Principal islands are Espíritu Santo, Malekula, Efate, Ambrim, Eromanga, Tana, Epi, Aneityum, Maewo, and Pentecost. Larger islands volcanic in origin and quite mountainous; several islands active volcanoes; some of the islands, esp. Efate and Malekula, have good harbors. Natives are Melanesians, strongly mixed with Polynesian strain. Chief products coconuts, cotton, coffee, cocoa, fruits. Discovered 1606 by the Portuguese navigator, Pedro de Queirós; forgotten for 160 years, then visited by Bougainville 1768 and explored by Capt. Cook 1774; visited 1788 by La Pérouse, whose entire expedition was lost on Vanikoro; control of group sought by both French and British who finally signed a convention Oct. 20, 1906 by which a condominium was set up; this superseded by a second protocol 1914, ratified 1922. In World War II American naval base set up (1942) on Espíritu Santo I.

New Hol′land. 1 Borough, Lancaster co., SE Pennsylvania, 15 m. ENE of Lancaster; pop. 3425.

2 Early name of continent of AUSTRALIA.

New Hol′stein (hōl′stīn). City, Calumet co., E Wisconsin, 20 m. NE of Fond du Lac; pop. 2401.

New Hope (hōp). Borough, Bucks co., SE Pennsylvania, on Delaware river 30 m. NNE of Philadelphia; pop. 958; artists' colony (estab. 1900).

New Hun·stan′ton (hŭn·stăn′t'n; -tŭn; hŭn′stŭn). Urban district, Norfolk, E England, on the Wash; pop. (1951) 3414; watering place.

New Hyde Park (hīd). Village, Nassau co., SE New York, on Long Island 17 m. E of New York; pop. 10,808.

New I·be′ri·a (ĭ·bēr′ĭ·ȧ). City, ⊗ of Iberia parish, S Louisiana, 20 m. SSE of Lafayette; pop. 29,062; canneries, rice mills, condiment manufactories; salt and sulfur deposits; muskrat furs.

New′ing·ton (nū′ĭng·tŭn). Suburban residential town, S Hartford co., N Connecticut, SW of Hartford; pop. 17,664; agriculture; settled 1670, incorp. 1871.

New Inlet. Narrow strait leading from Atlantic Ocean through barrier reef off SE coast of Dare co., NE North Carolina.

New Ire′land. 1 Administrative district of the Territory of New Guinea, including the island of New Ireland and adjacent islands; 3340 sq. m.; pop. (1930) 38,416; ✳ Kavieng.

2 *formerly* **Neu–Meck′len·burg** (noi′mĕk′lĕn·bŏŏrĸ; -mä′klĕn-). Island ab. 230 m. long in the Bismarck Archipelago; ab. 2800 sq. m.; pop. 20,516; long and narrow and not volcanic, terrain largely mountainous, with peaks bet. 4000 and 7000 ft.; highest Mt. Lambel 7054 ft.; chief port Kavieng, at NW end, 162 m. NW of Rabaul; harbors also at Namatanai on NE coast, and Muliama on E coast; extensive coconut plantations, esp. on E coast. Most important adjacent island is New Hanover on NW; others are Saint Matthias Group, Tabar Is., Lihir I., Dyaul I., and Tanga I. Visited by Abel Tasman 1642 and by Carteret 1767 but little known of it before 1884 when it became part of German protectorate. In World War II, Kavieng occupied by Japanese Jan. 1942; often bombed, but Japanese forces bypassed.

New Jer′sey (jûr′zĭ). An eastern state of U.S.A., an original state of the Union, the third to ratify the Federal Constitution (Dec. 18, 1787); bounded on N by New York, on E by New York and the Atlantic Ocean, on S by Atlantic Ocean and Delaware Bay, on SW by Delaware Bay and Delaware, and on W by Pennsylvania; 46th state in area, 7836 sq. m. (land area 7522 sq. m.);

8th state in population, 6,066,782; ✻ Trenton. See *Table of States* at UNITED STATES. Divided into the following 21 counties (for pronunciation of their names, see their individual entries):

NAME	LOCATION	AREA[1]	POP.[1]	CO. SEAT
Atlantic	SE; coastal	575	160,880	Mays Landing
Bergen	NE corner	233	780,255	Hackensack
Burlington[2]	S cen.	819	224,499	Mount Holly
Camden	SW	221	392,035	Camden
Cape May	S; coastal	267	48,555	Cape May Court House
Cumberland	SW	503	106,850	Bridgeton
Essex	NE	128	923,545	Newark
Gloucester	SW	329	134,840	Woodbury
Hudson	NE	45	610,734	Jersey City
Hunterdon	NW cen.	435	54,107	Flemington
Mercer	W cen.	228	266,392	Trenton
Middlesex	cen.	312	433,856	New Brunswick
Monmouth	E cen.; coastal	477	334,401	Freehold
Morris	N	468	261,620	Morristown
Ocean[2,3]	E; coastal	639	108,241	Toms River
Passaic	N	194	406,618	Paterson
Salem	SW	350	58,711	Salem
Somerset	N cen.	307	143,913	Somerville
Sussex	N corner	528	49,255	Newton
Union	NE	103	504,255	Elizabeth
Warren	NW	361	63,220	Belvidere

[1] Area = land area in sq. m. Pop. from 1960 Census.
[2] Fort Dix military reservation in NE Burlington co. and NW Ocean co.
[3] Includes Barnegat Bay, extending almost full length of its coast line.

Nickname: Garden State. *State flower:* Violet. *Motto:* Liberty and Prosperity. *Chief cities:* Newark, Jersey City, Paterson, Camden, Trenton, Elizabeth. *Rivers:* Hudson, forming NE boundary; Delaware, forming W boundary. *Highest point:* High Point 1801 ft. in Sussex co. *Chief industries:* Manufacturing (textiles, esp. silk), copper smelting, shipbuilding, machine tools, mining (zinc).

History: Region first settled by Dutch and along Delaware river by Swedes; ceded to English as part of New Netherland 1664 and given the Latin name of Nova Caesarea; its E and N part (East Jersey) became a proprietary colony regranted by duke of York to Berkeley and Carteret and was sold to William Penn and associates 1682; its W and S part (West Jersey), or the lower counties on Delaware river, held by William Penn 1676–1702; became royal province 1702; scene of important battles Trenton, Princeton, and Monmouth of War of American Independence; held first constitutional convention 1776; adopted constitution 1844 (later amended); adopted new constitution 1947.

New Ken′sing·ton (kĕn′zĭng·tŭn). City, Westmoreland co., SW Pennsylvania, on Allegheny river 16 m. ENE of Pittsburgh; pop. 23,485; produces aluminum, cooking utensils, glass, electrical products; coal mines.

New Kent (kĕnt). **1** County in Virginia. See *Table* at VIRGINIA.

2 Village, its ⊗, E Virginia.

New′kirk (nū′kûrk). City, ⊗ of Kay co., N Oklahoma, 14 m. N of Ponca City; pop. 2092; oil wells; wheat, corn.

New Kowloon. See KOWLOON.

New Lamb′ton (lăm[p]′tŭn). Town, E New South Wales, SE Australia; suburb of Newcastle; pop. 6318.

New Lanark. See LANARK.

New′land (nū′lănd). Town and resort, ⊗ of Avery co., W North Carolina; pop. 564.

New Land. See NOVAYA ZEMLYA.

New Lex′ing·ton (lĕk′sĭng·tŭn). Village, ⊗ of Perry co., SE cen. Ohio, 19 m. SSW of Zanesville; pop. 4514; coal mines, gas and oil wells, clay and sand deposits.

New Lis·keard′ (lĭs·kärd′). Industrial town, Timiskaming dist., SE Ontario, Canada, 85 m. N of North Bay, near N end of Lake Timiskaming and N of Cobalt; pop. 4215; foundries, sawmills, brickyards.

New Lon′don (lŭn′dŭn). **1** County in Connecticut. See *Table* at CONNECTICUT.

2 Industrial city, a ⊗ of New London co., SE Connecticut, on Long Island Sound at mouth of Thames river 43

m. E of New Haven; pop. 34,182; port of entry; U.S. naval station and submarine base; shipbuilding center; U.S. Coast Guard Academy (1876; men); U.S. Submarine Officers' School; manufactures machine tools, cotton gins, silk, printing presses, brass and copper tubing, naval equipment, pharmaceuticals; Connecticut Coll. (1911; women). Settled 1646, incorp. 1784; an early whaling and sealing port; burned by the British under Benedict Arnold 1781. Town and city coextensive.

3 City, ⊗ of Ralls co., NE Missouri; pop. 875.

4 Village, Huron co., N Ohio, 23 m. N of Mansfield; pop. 2392; manufactures uniforms, church vestments.

5 City, Outagamie and Waupaca cos., E Wisconsin, 18 m. NW of Appleton; pop. 5288; lumber, brick.

New Mad′rid (măd′rĭd). **1** County in Missouri. See *Table* at MISSOURI.

2 City, its ⊗, SE Missouri, on Mississippi river 28 m. N of Caruthersville; pop. 2867; suffered from severe earthquake 1811–12 which created Reelfoot Lake (*q.v.*) in Tennessee; during the Civil War, occupied by Confederate troops July 28, 1861 to Apr. 8, 1862.

New Margelan. See FERGANA city.

New′mar′ket (nū′mär′kĕt; -kĭt). **1** Town, Rockingham co., SE New Hampshire, 9 m. W of Portsmouth; pop. 3153; manufactures artificial silk, shoes, cotton cloth.

2 Industrial town, York co., SE Ontario, Canada, 30 m. N of Toronto; pop. 5356; leather goods; Friends' Coll.

3 Town, England, on Cambridgeshire-West Suffolk boundary; urban district, West Suffolk, pop. 10,184; rural district, Cambridgeshire, pop. 20,219; horse-racing center.

New′ Mar′ket. Town, S Shenandoah co., N Virginia; pop. 783; victory of Confederates under Breckinridge over Federals under Franz Sigel May 15, 1864.

New Mar′tins·ville (mär′t′nz·vĭl; -tĭnz-). City, ⊗ of Wetzel co., N West Virginia, on Ohio river; pop. 5607.

New Mex′i·co (mĕk′sĭ·kō). A southwestern state of U.S.A., 47th state admitted to Union (1912); bounded on N by Colorado, on E by Oklahoma and Texas, on S by Texas and the Mexican state of Chihuahua, on W by Arizona; 5th state in area, 121,666 sq. m. (land area 121,511 sq. m.); 37th state in population, 951,023; ✻ Santa Fe. See *Table of States* at UNITED STATES. Divided into the following 32 counties (for pronunciation of their names, see their individual entries):

NAME	LOCATION	AREA[1]	POP.[1]	CO. SEAT
Bernalillo	cen.	1,163	262,199	Albuquerque
Catron	W	6,898	2,773	Reserve
Chaves	SE	6,094	57,649	Roswell
Colfax	N	3,765	13,806	Raton
Curry	E	1,403	32,691	Clovis
De Baca	E cen.	2,358	2,991	Fort Sumner
Dona Ana	S	3,804	59,948	Las Cruces
Eddy[2]	SE	4,163	50,783	Carlsbad
Grant	SW	3,970	18,700	Silver City
Guadalupe	E cen.	2,998	5,610	Santa Rosa
Harding	NE	2,136	1,874	Mosquero
Hidalgo	SW corner	3,447	4,961	Lordsburg
Lea	SE corner	4,393	53,429	Lovington
Lincoln	cen.	4,859	7,744	Carrizozo
Los Alamos[3]	N cen.	108	13,037	Los Alamos
Luna	SW	2,957	9,839	Deming
McKinley	NW	5,456	37,209	Gallup
Mora	NE	1,942	6,028	Mora
Otero	S	6,638	36,976	Alamogordo
Quay	E	2,883	12,279	Tucumcari
Rio Arriba	N	5,855	24,193	Tierra Amarilla
Roosevelt	E	2,455	16,198	Portales
Sandoval	NW cen.	3,718	14,201	Bernalillo
San Juan	NW corner[4]	5,515	53,306	Aztec
San Miguel	NE cen.	4,749	23,468	Las Vegas
Santa Fe	N cen.	1,928	44,970	Santa Fe
Sierra	SW	3,034	6,409	Truth or Consequences
Socorro	cen.	7,752	10,168	Socorro
Taos	N	2,256	15,934	Taos
Torrance	cen.	3,340	6,497	Estancia
Union	NE corner	3,817	6,068	Clayton
Valencia	W	5,657	39,085	Los Lunas

[1] Area = land area in sq. m. Pop. from 1960 Census.
[2] Carlsbad Caverns (national park) in SW part of county.
[3] Organized from parts of Sandoval and Santa Fe cos. 1949.
[4] Its NW point the only point in U.S. common to four states (New Mexico, Arizona, Utah, and Colorado).

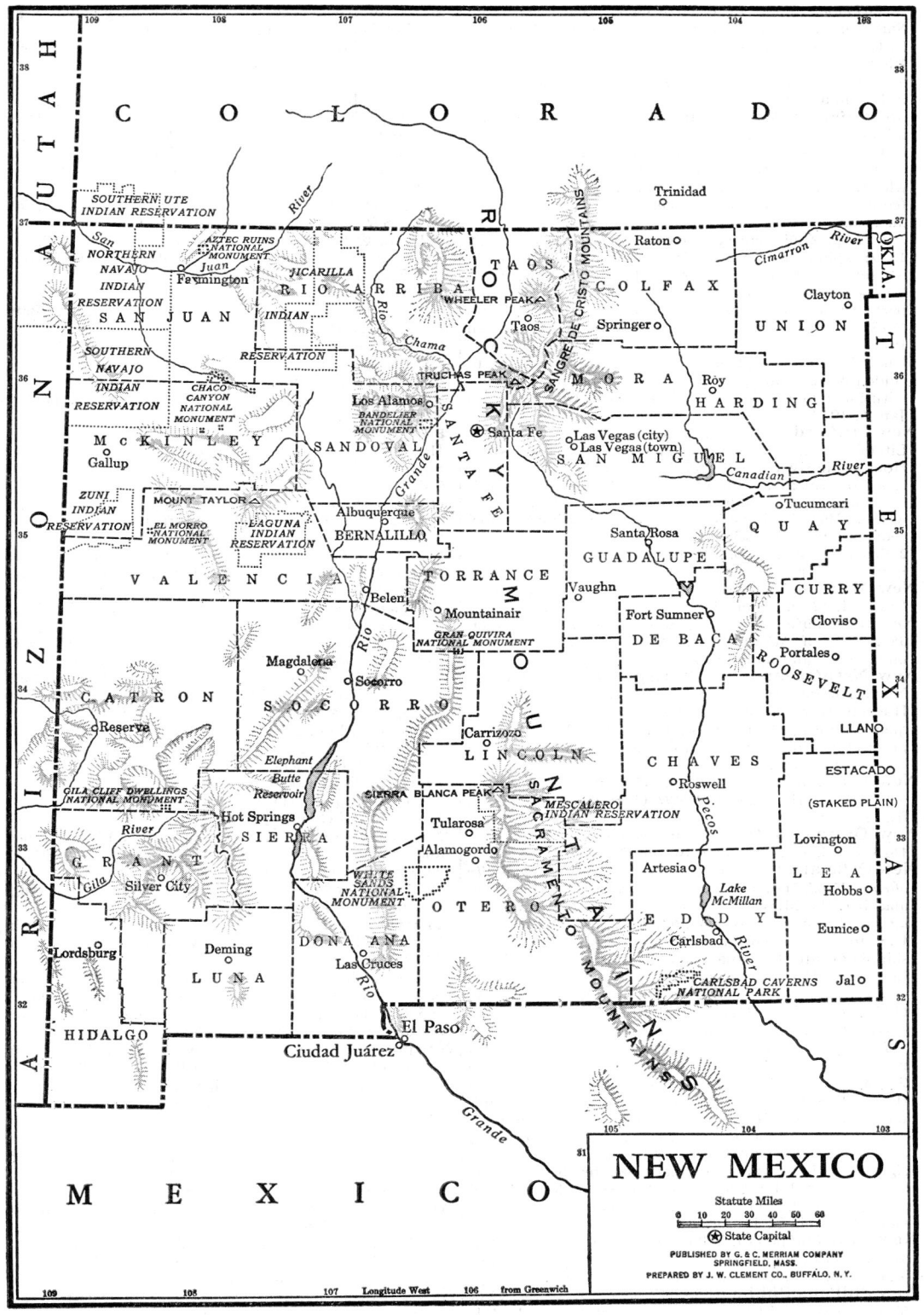

NEW MEXICO

Statute Miles

0 10 20 30 40 50 60

⊛ State Capital

PUBLISHED BY G. & C. MERRIAM COMPANY
SPRINGFIELD, MASS.

PREPARED BY J. W. CLEMENT CO., BUFFALO, N. Y.

Nickname: Land of Enchantment; Sunshine State. *State flower:* Yucca. *Motto:* Crescit Eundo (It Grows as It Goes). *Chief cities:* Albuquerque, Roswell. *Rivers:* Rio Grande, bisecting state from N to S and forming for a few miles a boundary on the S with Texas; Pecos, rising in N cen. area and flowing SE across border into Texas. *Mountains:* In W crossed from N to S by Continental Divide; in S many small isolated ranges: in N the Sangre de Cristo Mts. including Wheeler Peak 13,160 ft., highest point in state. *Chief industries:* Agriculture (cotton, wheat, grain sorghums), sheep and cattle raising, mining (copper, zinc, uranium), petroleum and natural gas production.

History: Zuñi country discovered by Marcos de Niza 1539; explored by Coronado's expedition 1540–42; Spanish settlement begun by Oñate 1598; Santa Fe (*q.v.*) founded in 1609–10; governed by Mexico after 1821; part east of Rio Grande included in annexation of Texas 1845; rest, except for southern strip, included in Gadsden Purchase 1853, ceded to U.S. by Mexico 1848 (Treaty of Guadalupe Hidalgo); organized as territory which included Arizona and part of Colorado 1850; held 1st constitutional convention 1889; admitted to Union as state Jan. 6, 1912.

New Mil′ford (mǐl′fẽrd). **1** Manufacturing town, SW Litchfield co., NW Connecticut; pop. 8318; watered by Housatonic river; settled 1707, incorp. 1712; dairy and tobacco farms; manufactures silver plate, pewter, furniture, uniforms, foundry products; bleaching and dye works. Includes Lake Waramaug. Canterbury School (boys' preparatory school).

2 Borough, Bergen co., NE corner of New Jersey, 8 m. ENE of Paterson; pop. 18,810.

New Mills (mǐlz). Urban district, Derbyshire, N cen. England, 12 m. SE of Manchester; pop. 8473.

New′nan (nū′năn). City, ⊗ of Coweta co., W Georgia, 35 m. SW of Atlanta; pop. 12,169; textile and lumber mills; horse and mule market.

New Neth′er·land (nĕth′ẽr·lănd). Dutch colony in North America 1613–64, occupying lands bordering the Hudson river and later the lower Delaware river; conquered by English 1664 and renamed New York after its proprietor, duke of York; capital New Amsterdam. See NEW YORK state.

New Nor′folk (nôr′fŭk). Town, SE Tasmania, Australia, on Derwent river 20 m. NNW of Hobart; pop. 2126; fruitgrowing.

New Or′ange (ŏr′ĭnj). Name given New York City 1673–74 when reconquered by the Dutch.

New Or′le·ans (ôr′lê·ănz; *locally also* ôr′lănz; *nonlocally often* ôr·lēnz′, ẽr-). City, ⊗ of Orleans parish, SE Louisiana, bet. the Mississippi river and Lake Pontchartrain; largest city in the state; pop. 627,525; greatest market in U.S. for cotton, cottonseed oil, and rice; import and shipping center for bananas and coffee; Tulane Univ. of Louisiana (1834; coed.) and its affiliate H. Sophie Newcomb Memorial Coll. for Women (1886); Loyola Univ. (1849; coed.; Rom. Cath.); Dillard Univ. (1869; coed.); Xavier Univ. (1915; coed.).

History: Founded 1718 by Sieur de Bienville, and made capital of the colony a few years later; ceded to Spain, effective 1764; ceded back to France 1803 and then to U.S. 1803 by Napoleon; incorporated 1805; capital of Louisiana 1812–49; defended Jan. 8, 1815 by Gen. Andrew Jackson against British attack in the battle of New Orleans, fought after treaty of peace had been signed but before news of treaty had reached combatants; captured by Union naval force under Admiral Farragut 1862, and occupied by Union troops under Gen. Benjamin F. Butler.

New Paltz (nū′ pôlts′). Village, Ulster co., SE New York, 10 m. W of Poughkeepsie; pop. 3041; State Univ. of New York Coll. of Education at New Paltz (1828).

New Phil′a·del′phi·a (fĭl′á·dĕl′fĭ·á, -fyá). **1** City, ⊗ of Tuscarawas co., E Ohio, 20 m. S of Canton; pop. 14,241.

2 Borough, Schuylkill co., E cen. Pennsylvania, 5 m. ENE of Pottsville; pop. 1702; coal mining.

New Plym′outh (plĭm′ŭth). **1** Early name (The Colony of New Plymouth) of Plymouth, Massachusetts, 1620–91.

2 Seaport borough, ✻ of Taranaki provincial dist., W North I., New Zealand, on Tasman Sea 160 m. N of Wellington; pop. (1941 est.) 19,400; one of chief dairy centers of New Zealand; founded 1841.

New′port (nū′pōrt). **1** County in Rhode Island. See *Table* at RHODE ISLAND.

2 City, ⊗ of Jackson co., NE Arkansas, on White river 38 m. SW of Jonesboro; pop. 7007; railroad center.

3 Town, ⊗ of Vermillion co., W Indiana; pop. 627.

4 City, a ⊗ of Campbell co., N Kentucky, on Ohio river just E of Covington; pop. 30,070; incorporated as village 1795, as city 1835; manufactures steel.

5 Town, Penobscot co., E cen. Maine, 25 m. W of Bangor; pop. 2322; trading center and fishing resort.

6 Manufacturing town, ⊗ of Sullivan co., SW New Hampshire, 8 m. E of Claremont; pop. 5458; trading center; summer resort.

7 City and seashore resort, Lincoln co., W Oregon, on Pacific Ocean 41 m. W of Corvallis; pop. 5344.

8 Borough, Perry co., S cen. Pennsylvania, 21 m. NW of Harrisburg; pop. 1861; settled 1789; manufactures forged steel, textiles, leather.

9 City, port of entry, and fashionable summer resort, ⊗ of Newport co., SE Rhode Island, on S end of Rhode I. (island) at mouth of Narragansett Bay; pop. 47,049; fisheries; important naval base, including U.S. Torpedo Station (on Goat I.), U.S. Naval Training Station and War College (on Coasters Harbor I.), and U.S. Naval Hospital.

History: Settled 1639 by religious refugees from Massachusetts Bay under William Coddington and John Clarke; united in government with Portsmouth 1640; joined "Incorporation of Providence Plantations" (chartered 1644), separated 1651–54; early shipbuilding, shipping, farming, and fishing center; engaged in slave trade, rum traffic, and privateering; haven for religious refugees (including Quakers and Jews); held by British 1776–79; headquarters of Rochambeau and troops 1780; one of capitals of Rhode Island until 1900.

10 Town, ⊗ of Cocke co., E Tennessee, 18 m. SSE of Morristown; pop. 6448; canned vegetables, lumber.

11 City, ⊗ of Orleans co., N Vermont, on S end of Lake Memphremagog; pop. 5019; first settled 1793; railroad and tourist center; customs port of entry and popular gateway bet. Canada and New England.

12 Town, ⊗ of Pend Oreille co., NE corner of Washington, on Idaho border; pop. 1513.

13 Municipal borough, S England, ⊗ of Isle of Wight in English Channel 10 m. WSW of Portsmouth; pop. 20,426.

14 County borough, ⊗ of Monmouthshire, W England, on the Usk 20 m. WNW of Bristol; pop. 89,203, (1951) 105,285; has extensive docks; exports coal, iron; manufactures metal and rubber goods; Chartist riot 1839.

Newport Beach. City, Orange co., SW California, on Pacific Ocean 18 m. SE of Long Beach; pop. 26,564.

Newport News. Independent city, SE Virginia, at mouth of James river at entrance to Hampton Roads 11 m. NNW of Norfolk; 75 sq. m.; pop. 113,662; with Norfolk and Portsmouth constitutes Port of Hampton Roads. Coal and tobacco port; export and import center; railroad terminus; excellent shipping facilities; large shipbuilding plants and dry docks; manufactures electronic equipment, textiles, mica products, metal fixtures, building accessories, beverages; fisheries. Settled c. 1621; city laid out 1882, incorp. 1896; includes (since 1958) former city of Warwick (until 1952 Warwick co.). See HAMPTON ROADS.

New Prague (prāg). City, Le Sueur and Scott cos., S Minnesota, 22 m. NW of Faribault; pop. 2533.

New Prov′i·dence (prŏv′ĭ·dĕns). **1** Borough, Union co., NE New Jersey, 8 m. SSE of Morristown; pop. 10,243. **2** One of the Bahama Is., in the Atlantic Ocean bet. Andros I. on the W and Eleuthera I. on the E; 58 sq. m.; pop. (1943) 29,391; contains city of Nassau, * of Bahama Is. Site of British air base in World War II.

New′quay′ (nū′kē′). Urban district, Cornwall, SW England, on Atlantic Ocean 42 m. W of Plymouth; pop. 9928; exports kaolin and stone; seaside resort.

New Que·bec′ (kwē·bĕk′; kwĕ-; kĕ-); *Fr.* **Nou′- veau′–Qué′bec′** (nōō′vō′kā′bĕk′). District, N Saguenay co., N and E Quebec, Canada, comprising the region N of Eastmain river and bet. Hudson Bay on the W and Labrador on the E, touching Hudson Strait and Ungava Bay on the N; area about 300,000 sq. m. Organized 1912, constituting in part former region of Ungava (*q.v.*), divided 1927 bet. Quebec prov. and Labrador (Newfoundland). Includes Ungava Penin. in the N.

New Republic; *Du.* **Nieu′we Re′pu·bliek′** (nē′vĕ rä′pü·blēk′). Republic (1884–88) formed by Boers from part of Zululand; capital Vryheid; now in Natal.

New Rich′mond (rĭch′mŭnd). **1** Village, Clermont co., SW Ohio, on Ohio river SE of Cincinnati; pop. 2834. **2** City, St. Croix co., W Wisconsin, 35 m. WNW of Menomonie; pop. 3316.

New River. 1 = ORETI river, South I., New Zealand. **2** Name of several rivers: see NEW, above.

New River Inlet. See NEW river, North Carolina.

New′ Roads′. Town, ⊗ of Pointe Coupee parish, SE cen. Louisiana, on Mississippi river; pop. 3965.

New Ro·chelle′ (rō·shĕl′). City, Westchester co., SE New York, on Long Island Sound; pop. 76,812; purchased 1689 by Huguenots. Coll. of New Rochelle (1904; women). Fort Slocum nearby.

New Rock′ford (rŏk′fērd). City, ⊗ of Eddy co., E cen. North Dakota, SSW of Devils Lake (city); pop. 2177.

New Romney. See ROMNEY.

New Ross (rŏs). Urban district, SW co. Wexford, SE Eire, on Barrow river; pop. 5056; salmon fisheries, brewing, tanning; site of ancient Dominican abbey.

New Russia; *Russ.* **No′vo·ros′si·ya** (nô′vŭ·rôs′syĭ·yȧ). A former region in 18th and 19th cents. of cen. and S Ukraine; ab. 75,000 sq. m., including the territory around modern Dnepropetrovsk, Kherson, and Odessa, and the Crimea; its capital 1765–89 was Kremenchug; its cultural capital Odessa (*q.v.*).

New′ry (nūr′ĭ). **1** Short canalized stream, SE Northern Ireland; flows S bet. cos. Down and Armagh into Carlingford Lough. **2** Urban district, co. Down, SE Northern Ireland, 38 m. SW of Belfast, part extending into co Armagh; pop. 13,264; on the Newry river; has canal connections with Carlingford Lough, Bann river, and Lough Neagh.

New Sa′lem (sā′lĕm). **1** Restored pioneer village, Sangamon co., cen. Illinois, 15 m. NW of Springfield; home of Abraham Lincoln 1831–37; in **New Salem State Park.** **2** Town, Pike co., W Illinois; pop. 172.

New Sarum. See SALISBURY.

New Shore′ham (shōr′ăm). Town coextensive with Block I., Washington co., SE Rhode Island; pop. 486; legal name of Block I., but seldom used.

New Shrews′bur′y (sh[r]ōōz′bĕr′ĭ; -bēr·ĭ). Borough, Monmouth co., E cen. New Jersey; pop. 7313.

New Si·be′ri·an Island (sī·bēr′ĭ·ăn); *Russ.* **No′va·ya Si·bir′** (nô′vȧ·yȧ syĭ·byēr′y′). Large island of New Siberian Is. in E part, 90 m. long by 40 m. wide.

New Siberian Islands; *Russ.* **No′vo Si·bir′ski·e O·stro·va′** (nô′vŭ syĭ·byēr′skĭ·yĕ ŭ·strŭ·vȧ′). Island group in Arctic Ocean bet. Laptev Sea and East Siberian Sea, a part of Yakutsk Republic, Soviet Russia, Asia; Chief islands Kotelny, Faddeevski, and New Siberian I. or Novaya Sibir; the Lyakhov Is. (*q.v.*) are by some included in the group. First visited c. 1773 and since then occasionally by scientific expeditions.

New Smyr′na Beach (smûr′nȧ). City, Volusia co., E Florida, on Atlantic Ocean 15 m. S of Daytona Beach; pop. 8781; bathing, boating, and fishing resort; Spanish mission (1696); before 1930 known as New Smyrna.

New South Wales. State, SE Australia; 309,432 sq. m.; pop. (1933) 2,600,847, (1963 est.) 4,048,598; * Sydney. Southern section of Great Dividing Range (Eastern Highlands) covers E third of state; highest point (at S end) Mt. Kosciusko 7328 ft.; New England Plateau in N and Blue Mts. in cen. part are especially healthful regions; nearly all of state drained by the Darling and its tributaries and the Murray (with Murrumbidgee and Lachlan rivers); Port Jackson, harbor of Sydney, one of finest in world; also good harbors at Newcastle and Jervis Bay. Minerals (lead, tin, copper, coal, gold); exports wool, butter, wheat, fruits, timber, meats. Chief cities Sydney, Newcastle, Wollongong, Cessnock, Broken Hill.

History: Discovered by Capt. Cook 1770; first settled at Botany Bay 1788 by marines and convicts, but soon transferred to Port Jackson (later Sydney); Parramatta and other towns W of Sydney founded before 1798; Newcastle and Maitland soon after. Included all of continent except Western Australia (boundary estab. 1831); interior, esp. Blue Mts. region, opened up 1840–50; South Australia (1836), Victoria (1851), Queensland (1859), and Northern Territory (1863) set up as separate colonies; became part of Commonwealth 1901; ceded 1911 Yass-Canberra (*q.v.*) dist. as site for Federal Capital Territory and in 1917 area on Jervis Bay.

New Spain. Former Spanish viceroyalty in North America, including SW United States, Mexico, Central America N of Panama, West Indies, and also the Philippines in the W Pacific Ocean. Mexico City was the seat of government 1521–1821.

New′stead Abbey (nū′stĕd; -stĭd). Structure in Nottinghamshire, N cen. England, N of Nottingham; family home of Lord Byron; 12th-cent. Augustinian priory, made into a residence 1540.

New Sweden. Swedish colony on the Delaware river; extended from site of Trenton, New Jersey, to mouth of the river, mostly on W side of the river; founded 1638 when Fort Christina (on site of Wilmington) was built; taken by the Dutch 1655.

New Territories. See HONG KONG.

New′ton (nū′t′n). **1** Name of counties in six states of the U.S. See *Tables* at ARKANSAS, GEORGIA, INDIANA, MISSISSIPPI, MISSOURI, TEXAS. **2** City, ⊗ of Baker co., SW Georgia; pop. 529. **3** City, ⊗ of Jasper co., SE cen. Illinois, 20 m. N of Olney; pop. 2901; broom factories, lumber mills. **4** Industrial city, ⊗ of Jasper co., S cen. Iowa, 30 m. E of Des Moines; pop. 15,381; agricultural section. **5** City, ⊗ of Harvey co., SE cen. Kansas, 35 m. E of Hutchinson; pop. 14,877; railroad division point. Bethel Coll. (1887; coed.; Mennonite) in North Newton. **6** Residential city, Middlesex co., NE Massachusetts, 7 m. W of Boston; pop. 92,384; includes 14 villages, among them **Newton Corner, Newton Centre, Newton Highlands, Newton Upper Falls, Newton Lower Falls, West Newton, New′ton·ville** (nū′t′n·vĭl). Andover Newton Theological School (founded 1825) united with Andover Theological Seminary (founded 1807; coed.) is at Newton Centre. **7** City Newton co., E cen. Mississippi, 30 m. W of Meridian; pop. 3178; lumber and cottonseed-oil mills. **8** Town, ⊗ of Sussex co., N corner of New Jersey, 23 m. NW of Morristown; pop. 6563; slate quarries nearby. **9** Town, ⊗ of Catawba co., W cen. North Carolina, 20 m. WSW of Statesville; pop. 6658; textiles, lumber. **10** City, ⊗ of Newton co., E Texas; pop. 1233.

Newton, Mount. Peak 5445 ft. in E West Spitsbergen; highest point on the island and in the group.

Newton Ab′bot (ăb′ŭt). Urban district, Devonshire, SW England, on Teign estuary 15 m. S of Exeter; pop. 16,393; William of Orange proclaimed king here 1688.

Newton Falls. Village, Trumbull co., NE Ohio, on Mahoning river 17 m. WNW of Youngstown; pop. 5038.

Newton Highlands. See NEWTON.

New'ton–le–Wil'lows (nū′t′n-lĕ-wĭl′ōz) *or* **Newton in Ma'ker·field** (mā′kĕr-fēld). Urban district, Lancashire, NW England, 15 m. W of Manchester; pop. 21,862; paper mills, iron foundries, glassworks; coal.

Newton Lower Falls, Newton Upper Falls, Newtonville. See NEWTON.

New To·ron'to (tŭ-rŏn′tŏ). Town, York co., SE Ontario, Canada, on Lake Ontario 7 m. W of Toronto; pop. 11,194.

New'town' (nū′toun′). **1** Town, N cen. Fairfield co., SW Connecticut, on Housatonic river; pop. 11,373; settled 1705, incorp. 1711; manufactures.

2 Former town, Queens co., SE New York, on Long I.; settled 1652; became part of Connecticut 1664, part of New York state 1665; since 1898 part of Queens borough in New York City.

3 See ELMIRA, New York.

4 Borough, Bucks co., SE Pennsylvania, 22 m. NE of Philadelphia; pop. 2323.

5 City, E New South Wales, SE Australia; S suburb of Sydney; pop. 25,293; paint and iron works.

Newtown and Chil'well (chĭl′wĕl). Town, S Victoria, SE Australia; suburb of Geelong; pop. 8556.

Newtown and Llan'llwch·ai'arn (lăn′lōōk-hĭ′ärn; hlăn′hlōōk-). Urban district, Montgomeryshire, E Wales; pop. 5427; comprises parishes of Llanllwchaiarn and Newtown, Newtown being terminus of Montgomery Canal; flannel manufacture, important in early 19th cent., no longer carried on; birthplace of Robert Owen.

New'town·ards' (nū′t′n-ärdz′). Municipal borough, co. Down, SE Northern Ireland, 9 m. E of Belfast at N end of Strangford Lough; pop. 12,237; on site of Dominican priory (1244); NE of the town are ruins of an abbey said to have been founded by St. Finian c. 550.

New'town But'ler (nū′t′n bŭt′lĕr). Village, co. Fermanagh, SW Northern Ireland, 16 m. SE of Enniskillen; site of a battle 1689 in which Enniskillen Protestants defeated Jacobite force.

New Towne (nū′ toun′). See CAMBRIDGE, Mass.

New Ulm (ŭlm′). City, ⊗ of Brown co., S Minnesota, on Minnesota river 24 m. WNW of Mankato; pop. 11,114; flour mills; twice under attack during the Sioux uprising 1862; Dr. Martin Luther Coll. (1884; coed.).

New Urgench. See URGENCH.

New'ville (nū′vĭl). Industrial borough, Cumberland co., S Pennsylvania, 21 m. NE of Chambersburg; pop. 1656.

New Wash'ing·ton (wŏsh′ĭng·tŭn). Municipality, N Capiz prov., Panay, Phil. Is., on coast at base of narrow tongue of land 22 m. W of Capiz; pop. 12,192.

New Wa'ter·ford (wô′tĕr-fĕrd; wŏt′ĕr-). Town, Cape Breton co., E Nova Scotia, Canada, on Atlantic Ocean 8 m. N of Sydney; pop. 10,423; coal-shipping port.

New West'min'ster (wĕs[t]′mĭn′stĕr). City, SW Brit. Columbia, Canada, on Fraser river 12 m. ESE of Vancouver and 16 m. from river's mouth; pop. 28,639; port of call for ocean steamers; fish canneries, lumber mills, ironworks, foundries, and shipyards. Capital of Crown Colonies of British Columbia and Vancouver from 1859 to 1866.

New Whatcom. See BELLINGHAM, Washington.

New Wil'ming·ton (wĭl′mĭng·tŭn). Borough, Lawrence co., W Pennsylvania, 8 m. N of New Castle; pop. 2203. Westminster Coll. (1852; coed.).

New Windsor. See WINDSOR.

New World. The land of the Western Hemisphere; term first used by Peter Martyr, Italian historian, author of *De Rebus Oceanicis et Novo Orbe* (1516) giving first account of discovery of America.

New York (yôrk′). **1** A Middle Atlantic state of U.S.A., an original state of the Union, the 11th to ratify the Federal Constitution (July 26, 1788); bounded on N by Lake Ontario and the Canadian provinces of Ontario and Quebec, on E by Vermont, Massachusetts, and Connecticut, on S by Atlantic Ocean, New Jersey, and Pennsylvania, on W by Pennsylvania, Lake Erie, and the Canadian province of Ontario; 30th state in area, 49,576 sq. m. (land area 47,944 sq. m.); in addition to this area New York has also 4376 sq. m. of water of the Great Lakes; 1st state in population, 16,782,304; ✳ Albany. See *Table of States* at UNITED STATES. Divided into the following 62 counties (for pronunciation of their names, see their individual entries):

NAME	LOCATION	AREA[1]	POP.[1]	CO. SEAT
Albany	E	531	272,926	Albany
Allegany	SW	1,048	43,978	Belmont
Bronx[2]	SE	43	1,424,815	Bronx *or* the Bronx
Broome	S	710	212,661	Binghamton
Cattaraugus	SW	1,335	80,187	Little Valley
Cayuga	cen.	699	73,942	Auburn
Chautauqua	SW corner	1,080	145,377	Mayville
Chemung	S	412	98,706	Elmira
Chenango	S cen.	908	43,243	Norwich
Clinton	NE corner	1,059	72,722	Plattsburg
Columbia	SE	643	47,322	Hudson
Cortland	cen.	502	41,113	Cortland
Delaware	S	1,470	43,540	Delhi
Dutchess	SE	816	176,008	Poughkeepsie
Erie	W[3]	1,054	1,064,688	Buffalo
Essex	NE	1,826	35,300	Elizabethtown
Franklin	NE	1,685	44,742	Malone
Fulton	E	497	51,304	Johnstown
Genesee	W	501	53,994	Batavia
Greene	SE	653	31,372	Catskill
Hamilton	NE cen.	1,747	4,267	Lake Pleasant
Herkimer	NE cen.	1,442	66,370	Herkimer
Jefferson	N	1,293	87,835	Watertown
Kings[2]	SE	76	2,627,319	Brooklyn
Lewis	N cen.	1,293	23,249	Lowville
Livingston	W	638	44,053	Geneseo
Madison	cen.	661	54,635	Wampsville
Monroe	W	673	586,387	Rochester
Montgomery	E	409	57,240	Fonda
Nassau	SE (W Long I.)	300	1,300,171	Mineola
New York[2]	SE	22	1,698,281	New York
Niagara	W[3]	533	242,269	Lockport
Oneida	cen.	1,227	264,401	Rome, Utica
Onondaga	cen.	792	423,028	Syracuse
Ontario[4]	W	649	68,070	Canandaigua
Orange	SE	829	183,734	Goshen
Orleans	W	396	34,159	Albion
Oswego	cen.	968	86,118	Oswego, Pulaski
Otsego[5]	cen.	1,013	51,942	Cooperstown
Putnam	SE	235	31,722	Carmel
Queens[2]	SE	113	1,809,578	Jamaica
Rensselaer	E	665	142,585	Troy
Richmond[2]	SE	60	221,991	Saint George
Rockland	SE	178	136,803	New City
St. Lawrence	N	2,772	111,239	Canton
Saratoga	E	814	89,096	Ballston Spa
Schenectady	E	209	152,896	Schenectady
Schoharie	E	625	22,616	Schoharie
Schuyler[6]	SW cen.	331	15,044	Watkins Glen
Seneca	W cen.	330	31,984	Ovid, Waterloo
Steuben	S	1,408	97,691	Bath
Suffolk	SE[7]	922	666,784	Riverhead
Sullivan	SE	986	45,272	Monticello
Tioga	S	525	37,802	Owego
Tompkins[8]	S cen.	491	66,164	Ithaca
Ulster	SE	1,143	118,804	Kingston
Warren	E[9]	883	44,002	Lake George
Washington	E[9]	837	48,476	Hudson Falls
Wayne	W	607	′67,989	Lyons
Westchester	SE	435	808,891	White Plains
Wyoming	W	598	34,793	Warsaw
Yates	W	344	18,614	Penn Yan

[1] Area = land area in sq. m. Pop. from 1960 Census.
[2] Each of these 5 counties is coextensive with one of the 5 boroughs of New York City and 2 of them are also coextensive with 2 islands, as follows: Bronx co. coextensive with Bronx borough, Kings co. (occupying W corner of Long I.) with Brooklyn borough, New York co. with Manhattan borough and with Manhattan I., Queens co. (on W part of Long I.) with Queens borough, Richmond co. with Richmond borough and with Staten I.
[3] Niagara river (bet. Lakes Ontario and Erie) forms W boundary of Niagara co. and NW boundary of Erie co., with American Fall (Niagara Falls) in former county.
[4] Includes most of Canandaigua Lake (cen.).
[5] Includes Otsego Lake in N cen. part.
[6] Includes lower part of Seneca Lake.
[7] Occupies E part (more than half) of Long I. and includes smaller islands off its coast.
[8] Includes lower part of Cayuga Lake.
[9] Lake George forms NE boundary of Warren co. and NW boundary of Washington co.

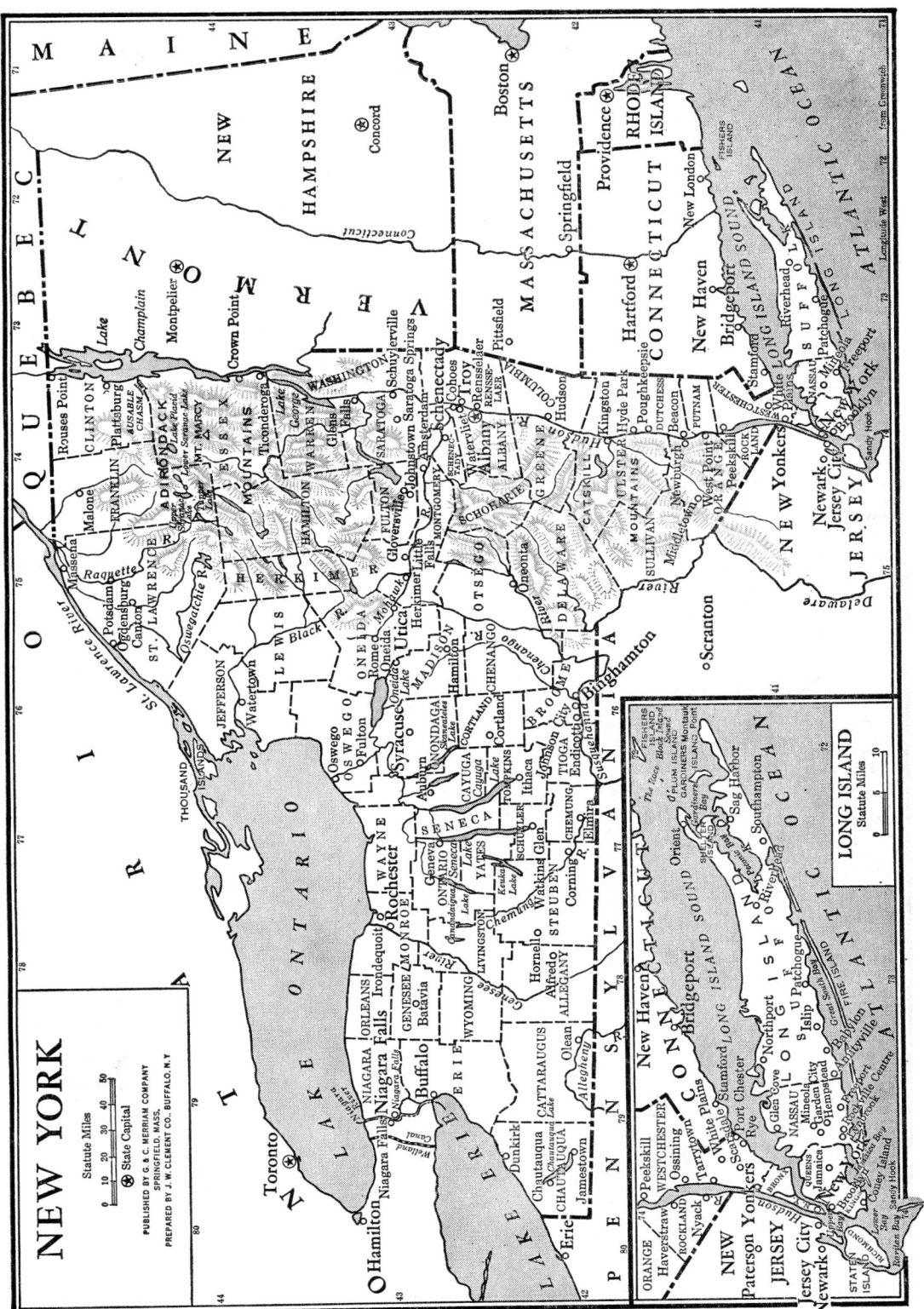

NEW YORK

Statute Miles

PUBLISHED BY G. & C. MERRIAM COMPANY
SPRINGFIELD, MASS.
PREPARED BY J. W. CLEMENT CO., BUFFALO, N.Y.

⊛ State Capital

LONG ISLAND

Statute Miles

Nickname: Empire State, also Excelsior State. *State flower:* Rose. *Motto:* Excelsior (Ever Upward). *Chief cities:* New York City, Buffalo, Rochester, Syracuse, Yonkers, Albany. *Rivers:* Hudson, in E area, flowing into Atlantic Ocean at New York City, and in the S forming boundary bet. New York and New Jersey; St. Lawrence, forming N boundary bet. New York and Canadian province of Ontario; Delaware, forming section of S boundary bet. New York and Pennsylvania; Niagara, forming W boundary bet. New York and the Canadian province of Ontario. *Mountains:* Adirondacks (in NE) and Catskills (in E). Highest point Mount Marcy 5344 ft. in Essex co. in the Adirondacks. *Chief industries:* Manufacturing, shipping, finance, agriculture.

History: Visited by Verrazano 1524; explored by Henry Hudson who sailed up the river now bearing his name 1609; trading posts, founded by Dutch on Manhattan I. and at Fort Nassau 1613, were taken over by Dutch West India Co.; New Amsterdam founded on Manhattan 1625; New Netherland, Dutch colony, conquered by English 1664 and renamed New York after its proprietor, duke of York; became a royal province 1685; held 1st constitutional convention 1776; invaded 1777 by Burgoyne during American Revolution; in 1797 capital was moved to Albany; adopted present constitution 1894.

2 County in New York. See *Table* at NEW YORK state.
3 *or* **New York City;** *sometimes, unofficially,* **Greater New York.** City, SE New York, at mouth of the Hudson river; pop. (of Greater New York) 7,891,957 (in 1950), 7,781,984 (in 1960); largest city in the U.S. and 3d largest in the world; excellent harbor; connected by canal system with Great Lakes region; railroad terminus; shipping point; financial, commercial, and industrial center; comprises 5 boroughs coextensive with 5 counties, Manhattan (New York co.), Bronx (Bronx co.), Brooklyn (Kings co.), Queens (Queens co.), Richmond (Richmong co.); chief industries textiles, clothing, leather goods, paper, machinery, electrical equipment, processed foods. For educational institutions, etc., see the names of the boroughs.

History: Site of a trading post established at S end of Manhattan I. by Henry Hudson 1609 and Adriaen Block 1610; fortified and colonized under name New Amsterdam (*q.v.*) by Dutch West India Co.; island purchased from Indians by Peter Minuit for Dutch West India Co. 1626 for $24 worth of trinkets; Dutch West India Co. sold tracts of land to patroons, who introduced colonists to settle and work their farms; settlements extended to Breuckelen (Brooklyn), New Harlem, Bronx, and Staaten Eylandt (Staten Island); captured by British and named New York 1664 in honor of the king's brother, the duke of York; Richard Nicolls appointed first British governor; Dutch regained control and held it for a short time 1673–74; new city charter granted 1686 which remained in force with minor changes until 1830; scene of Leisler rebellion 1689–91; after the British parliament passed the Stamp Act 1763, Stamp Act Congress met in City Hall and drew up a declaration of rights; boycott of British goods forced repeal of Stamp Act; demonstration against the British government's tax

NEW YORK
METROPOLITAN AREA

Statute Miles
0   5   10

on tea 1773 provincial congress summoned and a state of war recognized by the Continental Congress; on July 4, 1776 George Washington caused the Declaration of Independence to be read to the army assembled on the common; scene of retreat of Washington after the battle of Long Island Aug. 27, 1776; city held by British to the end of the Revolutionary War; capital of state 1784–97, of U.S. 1785–90; George Washington inaugurated first president of the United States in a building (Federal Hall) on the site of the present U.S. subtreasury building on Wall Street; sharp increase in commerce and industry followed the opening of the Erie Canal (1825); suffered disastrous fire 1835; opposed the Civil War at its outbreak 1861, and was scene of serious draft riots 1863; expanded rapidly after Civil War, developing transportation and communication systems; Tweed Ring political scandal exposed 1871; by legislative act of 1896 "Greater New York" was established Jan. 1, 1898. For further details, see the boroughs of MANHATTAN, the BRONX, BROOKLYN, QUEENS, and RICHMOND.

New York Bay. Inlet of Atlantic Ocean at mouth of Hudson river, in SE New York; it consists of **Upper New York Bay** and **Lower New York Bay,** connected by the Narrows; Manhattan I. lies at its NE end.

New York City. See NEW YORK, q.v.

New York Mills. Village, Oneida co., cen. New York, 5 m. E of Utica; pop. 3788.

New York State Barge Canal. Canal system, total length ab. 525 m., connecting Lake Erie at Buffalo, New York, with the Hudson river at a point opp. Troy, near the mouth of the Mohawk river (q.v.); branches connect the main waterway, the Erie Canal (q.v.) with Lake Ontario (see OSWEGO CANAL) and Lake Champlain (see CHAMPLAIN CANAL); natural waterways are used to a large extent, esp. the Oswego, Seneca (see CAYUGA AND SENECA CANAL) and Clyde rivers and Oneida Lake.

New Zea′land (zē′lănd). British self-governing dominion in South Pacific Ocean, comprising (New Zealand proper) two large islands North I. (44,280 sq. m.) and South I. (59,130 sq. m.) and the small islands (constituting counties of South I.) Stewart I. and the Chatham Is.; 103,410 sq. m., with outlying islands (Auckland, Campbell, Kermadec, Cook Is., Niue, Manihiki, etc.) 103,929 sq. m.; pop. of New Zealand proper (1936) 1,491,484, including Maoris 1,573,810, (1941 est.) 1,636,230; ✳ Wellington; administers Tokelau Is. and Ross Dependency for Great Britain, and holds the trusteeship for Territory of Western Samoa. See Map, p. 785; cf. also NAURU. For census purposes, New Zealand proper is divided into the following 9 provincial districts (for pronunciation of their names, see their individual entries):

PROVINCIAL DIST.[1]	LOCATION	AREA[2]	POP.[2]	CAPITAL[1]
Auckland	N North I.	25,400	582,513	Auckland
Canterbury	E South I.	13,940	239,417	Christchurch
Hawke's Bay	E North I.	4,260	79,100	Napier
Marlborough	NE South I.	4,220	20,200	Blenheim
Nelson	N South I.	10,870	58,100	Nelson
Otago:	S South I.			
Otago subdivision		14,050	149,300	Dunedin
Southland subdivision		11,170	72,500	Invercargill
Taranaki	N North I.	3,750	79,600	New Plymouth
Wellington	S North I.	10,870	336,700	Wellington
Westland	W South I.	4,880	18,800	Hokitika

[1] Provincial districts are merely geographical areas with fixed boundaries but without administrative functions. Thus, properly speaking, they have no "capitals."
[2] Area in sq. m. Pop. is official estimate of Apr. 1, 1941 and includes Maoris.

North Island: Mountainous, in cen. part has several ranges with volcanoes Ruapehu 9175 ft., Ngauruhoe 7515 ft., and Tongariro 6458 ft., all in Tongariro National Park; isolated on W coast is Mt. Egmont 8260 ft.; in center is Lake Taupo in midst of remarkable hot springs country; chief rivers Waikato, Rangitaiki,

Wanganui, and Rangitikei; irregular coast line, excellent harbors; chief cities Auckland, Wellington, Wanganui, and Palmerston North.

South Island: Mountainous, with Southern Alps, highest peak Aorangi 12,349 ft., extending almost its entire length and including many glaciers and lakes; largest lakes Wakatipu, Wanaka, Te Anau; chief rivers Wairau, Rangitata, Waitaki, Clutha; coast line irregular; chief cities Christchurch, Dunedin, Invercargill, Timaru, Nelson. Chief exports wool, dairy products, meat, hides and skins, gold. See NORTH ISLAND and SOUTH ISLAND.

History: Discovered by Tasman 1642; visited by Cook 1769 who circumnavigated it; first European settlements made by whalers and missionaries; colonized in 1840 at Port Nicholson by New Zealand Co.; by Treaty of Waitangi 1840 native leaders ceded lands to British who proclaimed New Zealand a crown colony under British sovereignty; in 1843 began series of wars with native Maoris; in new constitution 1852, organized as 6 provinces; transferred capital from Auckland to Wellington 1865; provincial government abolished 1875; annexed Kermadec Is. 1887 and later Niue and other islands; given dominion status 1907; received mandate for Western Samoa 1919; participated in World War I and World War II.

Neyba. See NEIBA.

Ne′zhin (nyā′zhĭn). Town, cen. Chernigov Region, N Ukraine, U.S.S.R., 70 m. NE of Kiev; pop. 37,345; rail junction point on the main Kiev-Moscow line; an old town dating from 12th cent.

Nezib. See NIZIB.

Nez′perce′ (nĕz′pûrs′). Village, ⊗ of Lewis co., W Idaho; pop. 667.

Nez Perce (nĕz′ pûrs′). 1 Mountain 11,900 ft. in cen. Grand Teton National Park, NW Wyoming.
2 County in Idaho. See *Table* at IDAHO.

Nga′mi ('ng-gä′mē). Occasional lake N of Kalahari Desert and S of Okovanggo Basin, NW Bechuanaland Protectorate, South Africa; ab. 20 m. long by 10 m. wide when discovered by David Livingstone in 1849; now just marshland.

Ngan′djoek *or* **Ngan′djuk** ('ng-gän′jōōk). Town, East Java prov., Indonesia, just E of Madiun; pop. 9458.

Nganhui, Nganhwei. Obs. vars. of ANHWEI.

Nganking. See HWAINING.

Ngaoun′dé′ré′ ('ng-goun′dā′rā′). Town, N cen. Cameroun, W Africa; on an airway.

Nga·ru·ro·ro ('ng-gä′rōō-rō′rō). River ab. 70 m. long in E cen. North I., New Zealand; flows S and E into Hawke Bay below Napier.

Nga′tik ('ng-gä′tĭk). Atoll island, Senyavin Is. group, E Caroline Is., W Pacific Ocean, ab. 90 m. SSW of Ponape, 157°32′E long.

Ngau ('ng-gou′). One of the chief islands of Lomai Viti (q.v.).

Ngau′ru·ho′e ('ng-gou′rōō-hō′ā). Volcano 7515 ft. in Tongariro National Park, cen. North I., New Zealand.

Nga′wi ('ng-gä′wē). Town, East Java prov., Indonesia, ab. 17 m. NW of Madun on the Solo river; pop. 10,193.

N′Gela. See FLORIDA ISLAND.

Nge′se·bus (?′ng-gä′să·bōōs). Small island just N of Peleliu, Palau Is., W Pacific Ocean; occupied by U.S. Marines Sept. 28, 1944.

Ngoe′noet ('ng-gōō′nōōt) *or* **Ngu′nut.** Town, East Java prov., Indonesia, on railroad bet. Blitar and Tulungagung; pop. 12,583.

Ngong ('ng-gông′). Town, S Kenya colony, E Africa, just SW of Nairobi; ✳ of Masai extraprovincial dist.

Nha′trang′ (nyä′träng′). Seaport town, SE Annam, Vietnam, on coastal railroad 115 m. S of Binh Dinh; important fisheries; has noted Pasteur Institute for scientific experiments; Cham temple ruins nearby.

Ni·ag′a·ra (nī-ăg′á·rá; -ăg′rá). 1 River ab. 36 m. long, W New York; connects Lake Erie with Lake Ontario and

forms United States-Canada boundary. See NIAGARA FALLS.

2 County in New York. See *Table* at NEW YORK.

3 Village, Marinette co., NE Wisconsin, on Menominee river and Michigan border 52 m. NNW of Marinette; pop. 2098; paper manufactures.

4 See NIAGARA-ON-THE-LAKE, Ontario, Canada.

Niagara Falls. 1 Great falls of the Niagara river, divided by Goat I. into Horseshoe, or Canadian, Fall, 158 ft. high with crest 3010 ft. wide, and American Fall, 167 ft. high and 1060 ft. wide; ab. 6% of water passes over American Fall and 94% over the Horseshoe Fall. Boundary line bet. U.S. and Canada passes through center of Horseshoe Fall, leaving Goat I., now a New York State Reservation, entirely in U.S. Prospect Point on brink of ledge on American side and Queen Victoria Park on Canadian side both afford excellent views of the falls; at foot of American fall is the Cave of the Winds, a rocky chamber 100 ft. by 75 ft., formed by erosion. River below the falls flows bet. high cliffs, at ab. 2 m. forming Whirlpool Rapids; crossed by two bridges bet. the two cities of Niagara Falls.

History: Falls well known to many tribes of Indians before any settlement of Europeans in U.S. or Canada; first visited and described by Father Hennepin 1678, 1683; in center of region of trading posts and frontier forts 18th cent. and in War of 1812 of several engagements (see LUNDY'S LANE, QUEENSTON, CHIPPAWA). In recent years through development of electric energy from water power, has become world's greatest hydroelectrical center.

BUFFALO, NIAGARA FALLS
AND VICINITY
Statute Miles

2 City and tourist resort, Niagara co., W New York, on Niagara river 17 m. NNW of Buffalo; pop. 102,394; extends above and below great falls of the river (Niagara Falls); opp. Niagara Falls, Ontario (bridge connection). In fruit belt; center of electrochemical and electrometallurgical industries; manufactures chemicals, aluminum, special alloys, abrasives, paper products, flour; N.Y. State Niagara Reservation, including Prospect Point, Luna, Goat, and other islands, and Whirlpool and Devil's Hole State Park, Cave of the Winds, and Horseshoe Fall; Niagara Falls power plant (developed from 1890); Niagara Univ. (1856; men and women). Site of a fort until c. 1800; formerly comprised separate villages of Niagara Falls (originally known as Manchester) and

Suspension Bridge (formerly Niagara City), which were consolidated and chartered as one city of Niagara Falls 1892; annexed La Salle 1927.

3 Manufacturing city, Welland co., SE Ontario, Canada, on Niagara river just below the falls; pop. **22,874**. It is opp. Niagara Falls, New York, and connected with it by two bridges; from its Queen Victoria Park is finest view of the falls. Hub of large hydroelectric power development; produces silverware, cereal foods, carborundum, graphite, batteries, automobile accessories. Founded 1850; known as **Clif'ton** (klĭf'tŭn) 1856-60 and as **Sus·pen'sion Bridge** (sŭs·pĕn'shŭn) 1860-81.

Niagara-on-the-Lake *or* **Niagara.** Town, Lincoln co., SE Ontario, Canada, on Lake Ontario at mouth of Niagara river opp. Fort Niagara, New York; pop. 2108; site of Canadian lawn-tennis championship play; founded 1780; first capital of Upper Canada (to 1796); parts of Fort Massassauga still visible; town burned by American general McClure in 1813.

Niagara Peak. Mountain 13,800 ft. in Hinsdale and San Juan cos., SW Colorado.

Nia'mey' (nyä'mā'). Town, ✳ of Niger Republic, West Africa, in W part of the republic on Niger river; pop. ab. 6000.

Ni·an'tic (nĭ·ăn'tĭk). **1** Short stream and wide inlet, SE Connecticut, in W New London co.; flows S into Long Island Sound.

2 Subdivision of town of EAST LYME, Connecticut; scallop fishing; pop. 2788.

Ni·a'ou·sta (nyä'ōō·stä) ; *formerly* **Na'ou·sa** (nä'ōō·sä). City, Thessalonike dept., W cen. Macedonia, N Greece, 45 m. W of Salonika; pop. 10,250.

Ni'as (nē'äs). Island in the Indian Ocean just N of the equator, off W coast of Sumatra, Indonesia; 80 m. long by 30 m. wide; 1569 sq. m.; pop. 187,199; chief village Goenoengsitoli on NE coast; belongs to Tapanoeli residency. Hilly (highest point 2907 ft.) and subject to earthquakes.

Ni·as'sa *or* **Ny·as'sa** (nĭ·ăs'ä; nĭ-). **1** Region in N Mozambique, formerly (1894–1929) administered by Niassa Co.; 1930–41 comprised districts of Cabo Delgado and Niassa; since 1942 constitutes Niassa prov. (see 2, below); chief town Porto Amelia.

2 Province, N Mozambique; comprises former districts of Cabo Delgado (*q.v.*) and Niassa; ✳ Nampula; created 1942 when the Mozambique Company's charter expired and all of Mozambique reverted to the Portuguese government.

3 Former district, NW Mozambique, on Lake Nyasa. See CABO DELGADO.

Ni·bong' Te·bal' (nē·bŏng' tĕ·bäl'). **1** District, S Province Wellesley, Penang settlement, Federation of Malaya; pop. 34,415.

2 Town in district; pop. 3294.

Ni·cae'a (nĭ·sē'á). **1** *Anglicized* **Nice** (nīs). Empire in Asia Minor 1206–61, extending from Black Sea coast E of Sangarius river SW across W Asia Minor to Miletus and the Maeander; ✳ Nicaea on its N border. Bordered on E and SE by sultanate of Rum or Iconium of the Seljuk Turks and on NW by the Latin Empire (1204–61). Its rulers were of the Lascaris family: Theodore I and II, John III (Ducas), John IV, and Michael VIII Palaeologus, who in 1261 restored the Byzantine emperors.

2 *Anglicized* **Nice** (nīs). Ancient city, Asia Minor. See İZNİK.

3 Ancient city, France. See NICE.

Nic'a·ra'gua (nĭk'á·rä'gwá; *Brit. also* -răg'ủ·á). Republic, Central America; bounded on N by Honduras, on E by Caribbean Sea, on S by Costa Rica, and on W by Pacific Ocean; area (including land and water) 57,143 sq. m.; pop. (1943 est.) 1,048,642; ✳ Managua. Traversed along Pacific coast by mountain range, part of the great continental axis, but here in SW, near Brito, W of Lake Nicaragua cut by lowest gap from Alaska to Tierra del Fuego and hence selected as W part of pos-

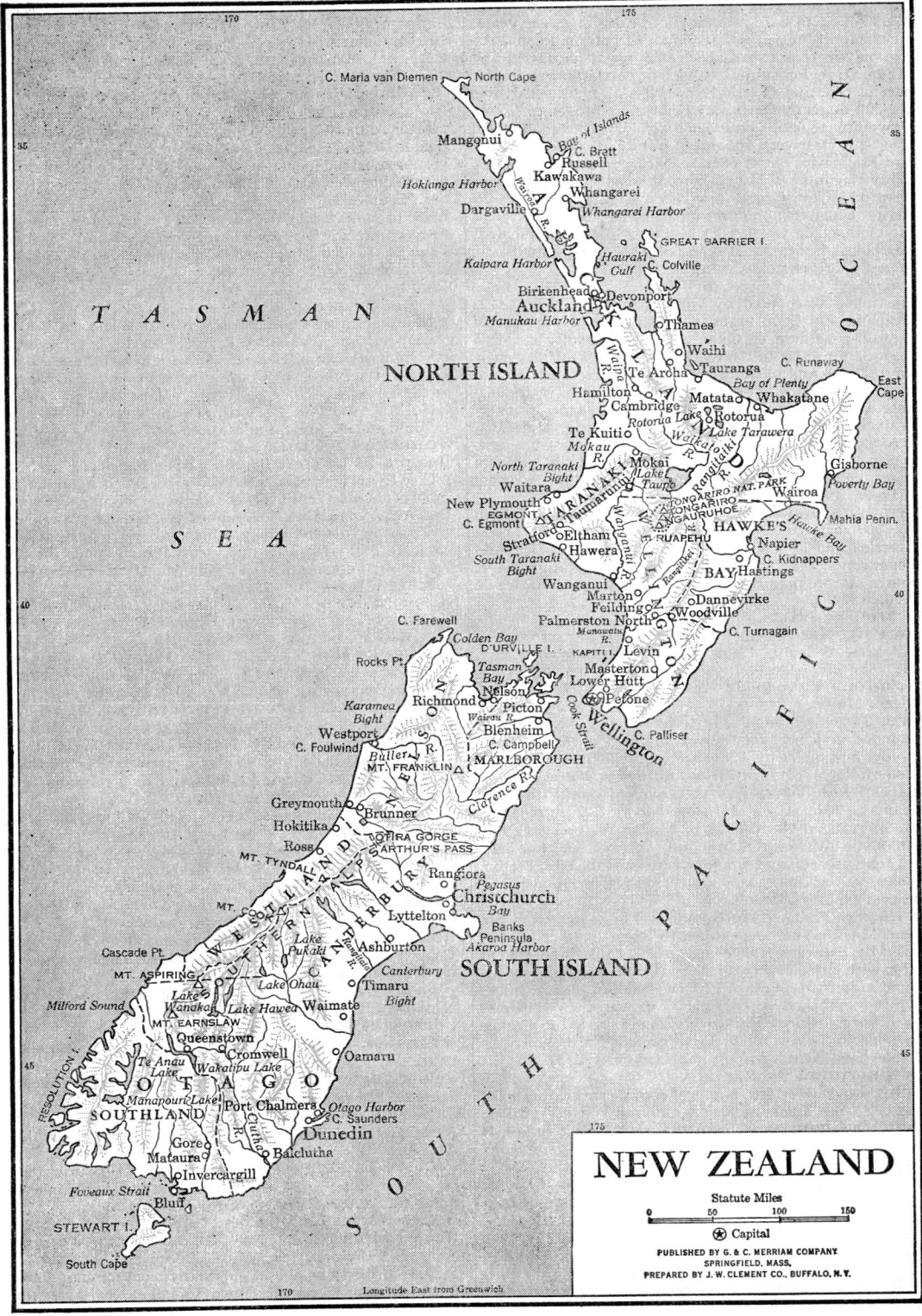

NEW ZEALAND

Statute Miles

0   50   100   150

⊛ Capital

PUBLISHED BY G. & C. MERRIAM COMPANY
SPRINGFIELD, MASS.
PREPARED BY J. W. CLEMENT CO., BUFFALO, N. Y.

sible future canal bet. Atlantic and Pacific Oceans; range is volcanic and has had many eruptions in recent years; most important peaks Cosegüina, Momotombo, and the two on Ometepe I. in Lake Nicaragua (Concepción and Madera); region subject to violent earthquakes; greater part of cen. and N is hilly country. Longer coast line, ab. 300 m., is on Caribbean, known as Mosquito Coast, a swampy region. Boundary with Honduras unsettled (see SEGOVIA river); separated from Costa Rica on S by San Juan river, outlet of Lake Nicaragua; on E coast are many streams 60–210 m. long flowing E to the Caribbean; chief are Grande and Escondido; many cays off coast. Chief economic resources coffee, bananas, forest products, gold. Chief cities Managua, León, Matagalpa, Granada, Jinotega, Masaya, Chinandega, Bluefields; most important port Corinto.

History: Coast discovered by Columbus 1502; Lake Nicaragua discovered by Gil González de Ávila 1522; Granada and León founded by Córdoba 1523; part of captain-generalcy of Guatemala; successfully revolted from Spain 1821; in United Provinces of Central America 1823–38 and in numerous later efforts to unite Central America (*q.v.*); (see SAN JUAN DEL NORTE for dispute with Great Britain); invaded by expeditions of Walker 1855–60; U.S. early began negotiations for canal across Nicaragua (became final in Bryan-Chamorro treaty 1916) and frequently intervened in political crises, notably by maintaining American forces there 1912–25, 1926–33.

Nicaragua, Lake. Large lake in S Nicaragua; length ab. 100 m., area 2972 sq. m.; largest lake in Central America and largest body of fresh water bet. U.S. and Peru; connected with Lake Managua by Tipitapa river; source of San Juan river; discovered by Gil González de Ávila 1522.

Nicaria. = IKARIA.

Ni·ca′stro (nē·käs′trō). Commune, Catanzaro prov., Calabria, S Italy, 17 m. WNW of Catanzaro; pop. 24,998; episcopal see.

Nic′a·tous′ Lake (nĭk′a·tous′). Lake in N Hancock co., E cen. Maine.

Nice. 1 (nēs) Countship, historical region of SE France; bounded anciently on N by Dauphiné, on E and S by Savoy, and on W by Provence; equivalent to E part of modern department of Alpes-Maritimes.

2 (nēs); *Ital.* **Niz′za** (nēt′tsä); *anc.* **Ni·cae′a** (nī·sē′a). Seaport, ✳ of Alpes-Maritimes dept., SE France, on Mediterranean 98 m. ENE of Marseilles; pop. 241,916; famous health resort; cathedral, observatory; fine harbor, extensive quays; manufactures include silk, cotton, paper, leather, oil, soap, liqueurs, dyes, perfumery, essences; exports olive oil.

History: Founded by colony of Phocaeans from ancient Massilia; became subject to Rome in 2d cent. B.C.; ruled by Saracens 10th cent. A.D.; became independent city; with surrounding territory (Countship of Nice) became subject to counts of Provence and, in 1388, to house of Savoy; pillaged by Turks 1543; captured several times by French; held by France 1792–1815; ceded to France by house of Savoy 1860. Birthplace of Garibaldi.

3 (nīs) See NICAEA empire and İZNİK city.

Nicephorium. See RAKKA.

Nich′o·las (nĭk′ō·lăs). Name of counties in two states of the U.S. See *Tables* at KENTUCKY and WEST VIRGINIA.

Nicholas Channel. Channel in the W West Indies, N of W Cuba and S of Cay Sal Bank.

Nicholas II Land. See SEVERNAYA ZEMLYA.

Nich′o·las·ville (nĭk′ō·lăs·vĭl; *Sou. also* -v′l). City, ⊗ of Jessamine co., E cen. Kentucky, 12 m. SSW of Lexington; pop. 4275; trade center in bluegrass section.

Nich′ols Field (nĭk′ŭlz; -′lz). Airport in the Philippine Is. just S of Manila and near Parañaque on E shore of Manila Bay; before 1947 a U.S. base.

Nicholson Viaduct. = *Tunkhannock Viaduct:* see TUNKHANNOCK.

Nick′e·rie (nĭk′ĕ·rē). **1** River ab. 150 m. long in NW Surinam; flows NNW into Atlantic Ocean near border of British Guiana.

2 District, NW Surinam; pop. (1941) 15,650.

3 = NIEUW NICKERIE.

Nic′o·bar Islands (nĭk′ō·bär) *or* **Nic′o·bars** (-bärz). Island group, Bay of Bengal, NW of Sumatra, forming S part of Andaman and Nicobar Islands territory, Indian Union; 635 sq. m.; pop. (1941) 12,452. Comprises 3 groups of islands; chief islands Great Nicobar, Camorta with Nancowry, Car Nicobar, Teressa, and Little Nicobar. See *Map* at BURMA. Occupied by British Government of India 1869; joined to Andaman (*q.v.*) group to form administrative division of Andaman and Nicobar Islands. Held by Japanese in World War II 1942–45.

Nicolaevsk. = NIKOLAEVSK.

Ni′co·let′ (nē′kō′lě′). **1** County, Quebec, Canada. See *Table* at QUEBEC.

2 Manufacturing town, Nicolet co., on S shore of Lake St. Peter 10 m. S of Three Rivers; pop. 4084; cathedral, two monasteries; brickyards, tanneries, foundries.

Nic′ol·let (nĭk′ŭ·lĕt). County in Minnesota. See *Table* at MINNESOTA.

Nic′olls Town (nĭk′ŭlz; -′lz). Town, N coast of Andros I., Bahama Is., West Indies; pop. 399.

Nicomedia. See İZMİT.

Ni·cop′o·lis (nĭ·kŏp′ō·lĭs; nī-). **1** See NIKOPOL.

2 City in ancient Epirus, NW Greece; its ruins are ab. 3 m. N of Preveza on the peninsula bet. the Ionian Sea and the Ambracian Gulf. Founded 31 B.C. by Octavian (Augustus) to commemorate his victory at Actium; became capital of Epirus and Acarnania; famous for its buildings and games (Actian Games). Twice destroyed; rebuilt by Julian and Justinian. See PREVEZA.

Nic′o·si′a (nĭk′ō·sē′a; *Gr.* nyē′kô·sē′ä; *Ital.* nē·kô·zē′ä). **1** District, cen. and W cen. Cyprus, E Mediterranean Sea; 1072 sq. m.; pop. (1931) 110,010.

2 *or* **Lev′ko·si′a** (lěf′kô·sē′ä; *Gr.* läf′kô·sē′ä). City, ✳ of Nicosia dist. and ✳ of Cyprus, W of Famagusta (its port) in cen. part of island; pop. 81,700; many churches and mosques; chief industries tanning and weaving. Formerly a walled city; capital of Cyprus when it was ruled by the Lusignan family 1192–1474; the fine Gothic cathedral and the church of St. Catherine are among the remains of this Crusade period; held by Venetians and besieged and taken by the Turks 1571.

3 Commune, Enna prov., cen. Sicily, 15 m. NNE of Enna; pop. 17,479; episcopal see; 14th-cent. cathedral; medieval castle. Taken by Allies July 29, 1943.

Ni·co′ya (nē·kō′yä). Town on Nicoya Penin., NW Costa Rica; pop. 4215; mother-of-pearl, murex.

Nicoya, Gulf of. Inlet of Pacific Ocean on NW cen. coast of Costa Rica, E of Nicoya Penin.

Nicoya Peninsula. Peninsula extending SE from NW Costa Rica, bet. Gulf of Nicoya and the Pacific Ocean.

Nictheroy. See NITERÓI.

Ni′da (nē′dä). River ab. 75 m. long, S Poland, NE of Kraków; a tributary of the Vistula flowing E and S.

Nidaros. See TRONDHEIM.

Nidwalden. See UNTERWALDEN and *Table* at SWITZERLAND.

Nie′der·bay′ern (nē′děr·bī′ĕrn). Bavarian government district. See *Lower Bavaria*, in *Table* at BAVARIA.

Nie′der·do′nau (nē′děr·dō′nou). Former district of Austria (Ostmark). See *Lower Austria*, in *Table* at AUSTRIA.

Nie′de·re Tau′ern (nē′dě·rě tou′ĕrn). Mountain range in S Austria bet. valleys of the Mur and Enns, highest point ab. 9400 ft.; a range of the Eastern Alps.

Nie′der Herms′dorf (nē′děr hěrms′dôrf); *Pol.* **Ja′sie·ni′ca Dol′na** (yä′shě·nē′tsä dôl′nä). Town, Wrocław dept., SW Poland, just W of Wałbrzych; pop. (1946) 11,706; formerly in Silesia, Germany; coal mining; manufactures explosives. Assigned to Poland by Potsdam Conference 1945.

Niederösterreich. See LOWER AUSTRIA.

Niederrhein. See LOWER RHINE.

Niedersachsen. See LOWER SAXONY.

Nie′der·schle′si·en (nē′dēr-shlā′zē·ĕn). Former province of Prussia. See *Silesia*, in *Table* at PRUSSIA.

Nie′der–Sel′ters (nē′dēr-zĕl′tērs). Commune, in the former Hesse-Nassau province, SW Prussia, Germany; pop. 1525; mineral waters.

Niel (nyĕl). Commune Antwerp prov., N Belgium, on the Rupel just S of Antwerp; pop. 10,275.

Niemen. See NEMAN.

Nien′burg an der We′ser (nēn′bōōrk än dēr vā′zēr). City, in former Hannover prov., Prussia, Germany, on Weser river 28 m. NW of Hannover; pop. 10,406.

Nieśwież. See NESVIZH.

Nieu′we Maas (nē′vĕ màs′). A right branch of the Merwede river after it unites with the Lek river in the Netherlands; empties into North Sea at the Hook of Holland; one of the mouths of the Maas (Meuse) river.

Nieu′wer–Am′stel (nē′vēr-äm′stĕl). Commune, North Holland prov., W Netherlands; SW suburb of Amsterdam; pop. 12,421.

Nieuwe Republiek. See NEW REPUBLIC.

Nieuw Gui·nee′ (nē′ōō gē-nā′). Dutch for NEW GUINEA.

Nieuwkerke. See NEUVE-ÉGLISE.

Nieuw Nick′e·rie (nē′ōō nĭk′ĕ·rē). Coastal town, Nickerie dist., NW Surinam, on Nickerie river near its mouth 122 m. W of Paramaribo; pop. ab. 5000.

Nieuw′poort (nē′ōō·pōrt) *or* **Nieu′port** (nē′ōō·pōrt; *Fr.* nyû′pôr′). Commune West Flanders prov., NW Belgium, on the Yser 10 m. SW of Oostende; pop. 4946; dates from 9th cent.; received present name 1160; scene of several battles or sieges in European wars since 14th cent.: 1488–89, 1600 (when Maurice of Nassau defeated Spaniards under Archduke Albert), and 1749; in World War I scene of almost continuous trench warfare 1914–15 and a center of fighting to end of the war.

Nieuw′veld (nē′ōō-fĕlt). Mountain range in cen. Cape Province, Republic of So. Africa; highest point 6276 ft.

Niè′vre (nyâ′vr′). Department of France. See *Table* at FRANCE.

Niewenstat. See NEUSTADT AN DER HARDT.

Niğ·de′ (nē·y′·dĕ′). **1** Vilayet, cen. Turkey; 5909 sq. m.; pop. 251,858.
2 Town, its ✱, on railroad 75 m. NNW of Adana; pop. 12,307; important town of Seljuk sultanate of Rum 11th–14th cents.; came under Ottoman Turks ab. 1450.

Ni′ger (nī′jēr; *Fr.* nē′zhär′). **1** River ab. 2600 m. long, W Africa; rises in Guinea near Sierra Leone border, flows in a great curve in cen. West Africa, first NE then E and finally SE across border into Nigeria, continues S into Gulf of Guinea; known by many native names, esp. **Jo.′i·ba** (jŏl′i·bà) and **Kwor′ra** (kwŏr′à); estimated area of basin 584,000 sq. m. Above Tombouctou passes through swampy, treeless region with many lakes; its middle course navigable for ab. 1000 m. above Ansongo and in Nigeria but rapids and bars prevent continuous navigation; in Nigeria receives from the E its only large tributary, the Benue (*q.v.*); has very extensive delta (14,000 sq. m.) with unhealthy climate; principal mouths are the Bonny, Brass, New Calabar, Forcados (now the main channel), and Nun; chief products shipped upon it are palm kernels and oil, hence the name **Oil Rivers** for its delta region. First explored by Mungo Park 1796–97 and 1805–06; from 1822 to end of century visited and explored by many British, French, and German travelers.
2 Republic, formerly a French territory (*Fr.* **Ter′ri·toire′ du Ni′ger′** [tĕ′rē′twàr′ dü nē′zhär′]), West Africa, N of Nigeria; 493,822 sq. m.; pop. 2,415,000; ✱ Niamey; largely desert but has a thickly wooded zone in cen. part and along the Niger; chief industries cattle raising and agriculture; orig. (1904) a part of Upper Senegal-Niger colony (see FRENCH SUDAN); made a mili-

tary territory 1912; civil colony formed by decree 1922; included part of Upper Volta territory 1933–47; its status changed to that of a territory 1946; became a republic of the French Community 1958.
3 Province of NIGERIA. See *Table* at NIGERIA.

Ni·ge′ri·a (nī·jēr′ĭ·à). Federation in British Commonwealth, formerly a British colony and protectorate, W Africa, including entire navigable lower course of the Niger river; 356,669 sq. m.; pop. 19,110,859; ✱ Lagos; has 23 provinces divided for administrative purposes into Northern Region, Eastern Region, and Western Region. The Colony (former Lagos colony) is a province of the Western Region. See *Table* below (for pronunciation of the names of provinces, see their individual entries):

PROVINCE[1]	LOCATION IN NIGERIA	AREA (SQ. M.)	POP. (1931)	CAPITAL
WESTERN REGION				
Colony	SW; on coast	1,381	325,020	Lagos
Abeokuta[2]	SW; N of the Colony	4,266	434,526	Abeokuta
Benin[3]	SW; W of Niger	8,627	493,215	Benin
Ijebu	SW	2,456	305,898	Ijebu-Ode
Ondo	SW	8,211	462,560	Akure
Oyo	SW	14,216	1,336,928	Oyo
Warri	S; on coast W part of delta	5,987	444,533	Warri
		45,144	3,802,680	Ibadan
EASTERN REGION[4]				
Calabar	SE; on coast	6,331	899,503	Calabar
Cameroons	SE	16,581	374,872	Buea
Ogoja	SE	7,529	708,538	Ogoja
Onitsha	S cen.; E of Niger	4,937	1,107,745	Onitsha
Owerri	S; E part of delta	10,374	1,599,909	Port Harcourt
		45,752	4,690,567	Enugu
NORTHERN REGION[6]				
Adamawa[7]	E; on upper Benue	35,001	652,361	Yola
Bauchi	NE cen.	25,977	1,025,310	Bauchi
Benue	S cen.; on lower Benue	28,082	987,358	Makurdi
Bornu[8]	NE	45,900	1,118,360	Maiduguri
Ilorin	W; W of Niger	18,095	537,559	Ilorin
Kabba	SW cen.; on both sides of Niger	10,577	462,726	Lokoja
Kano[9]	N	17,602	2,436,844	Kano
Niger[10]	W cen.; E of Niger	25,349	473,067	Minna
Plateau	cen.	10,977	568,738	Jos
Sokoto[11]	NW; NE of Niger	39,940	1,815,178	Sokoto
Zaria	N and cen.	24,278	1,357,423	Zaria
		281,778	11,434,924	Kaduna

[1] As of 1940.
[2] Center of former Egba state.
[3] Former native kingdom (see BENIN).
[4] Includes about half of Cameroons trust territory.
[5] See CAMEROONS.
[6] Includes ab. half of Cameroons trust territory.
[7] Formerly Yola prov.; includes two portions (12,300 sq. m.) of Cameroons trust territory.
[8] Includes N part of Cameroons trust territory; center of former Mohammedan sultanate of Bornu (*q.v.*).
[9] One of the original Hausa states (see SOKOTO).
[10] Formerly Nupe prov.
[11] Seat of former Fulah Empire (see SOKOTO).

Bounded on N by Republic of Niger, on E by Cameroun and Chad, on S by Gulf of Guinea (Bights of Biafra and Benin), and on W by Dahomey and Republic of Niger; forms central part of great area of Sudan; has highland plateau (3000 to 6000 ft.) in cen. and NE region with some mountain ranges; remainder consists of plain, forest, and the extensive unhealthy delta of the Niger. *Chief products:* Palm oil and kernels, cotton, cocoa, groundnuts, animal products; tin, coal, iron. *Chief towns:* Ibadan, Lagos, Ogbomosho, Kano, Ife, Iwo, Abeokuta.

History: For early history, see SONGHAI, BORNU, SOKOTO, BENIN. Region of the Niger (*q.v.*) visited in 18th and 19th cents. by many European explorers; Lagos, first land acquired by Great Britain, ceded by native king 1861; administered by Sierra Leone 1861–74, by

Gold Coast Colony 1874–86; established as Colony and Protectorate of Lagos 1886; Oil Rivers Protectorate (q.v.) established 1890; formed into two "Protectorates of Northern and Southern Nigeria" 1899; became "Colony and Protectorate of Nigeria" 1914; granted administration of mandate of Cameroons (part of German Kamerun) 1922; Southern Provinces redivided into Eastern Provinces and Western Provinces 1939; became a dominion in the British Commonwealth Oct. 1, 1960. By plebiscite 1961 part of the southern section of the former British trust territory of Cameroons voted to join the Republic of Cameroun; the rest and the northern section voted to remain with Nigeria.

Night'in·gale (nīt'n·gāl; -ing·gāl). Most southerly island in Tristan da Cunha group in S Atlantic; 1 m. long.

Ni·gri'ti·a (nī·grĭsh'i·à). A former name of the Sudan.

Nihawand. See NEHAVEND.

Ni·ho'a (nĕ·hō'ä). Islet of Hawaii, one of the Leeward Is. in cen. Pacific Ocean, ab. 125 m. NW of Niihau I.; ½ sq. m.; included in Hawaiian Islands Bird Reservation.

Nihon. See NIPPON.

Ni·i·ga·ta (nē·ē·gä·tä). 1 Prefecture of Japan. See *Table* at JAPAN.

2 City and seaport, its ✳, on NW coast of Honshu 160 m. NNW of Tokyo at mouth of Shinano river; pop. (1945 est.) 174,740; although one of original five open ports of Japan (opened 1859) has not developed as a port because of shallow anchorage and winds.

Ni·i·ha'u (nē·ē·hä'ŏŏ). Island in NW Hawaii, W of Kauai I., from which it is separated by Kaulakahi Channel; 72 sq. m.; pop. 254; with Kauai forms Kauai co.; partly a tableland 1300 ft. high, partly low coral formation; a privately owned sheep ranch; chief village Puuwai.

Ni·i Ji·ma (nē·ē jē·mä). One of the seven islands of Izu Shichito (q.v.).

Ni·i·ta·ka (nē·ē·tä·kä); *Jap.* **Ni·i·ta·ka·ya·ma** (-yä-mä); *also* **Mount Mor'ri·son** (mŏr'ĭ·s'n). Peak 13,599 ft. in S cen. Formosa.

Ní'jar (nē'här). Commune, Almería prov., SE Spain, 18 m. ENE of Almería; pop. 10,107; lead mines.

Nij'kerk (nī'kĕrk). Commune, cen. Netherlands, in Gelderland prov., 5 m. NE of Amersfoort; pop. 9889.

Nij'me'gen (nī'mā'gĕn; *Du.* -кӗ[n]) *or* **Nim'we'gen** (*Ger.* nĭm'vā'gĕn) *or* **Ni'me'guen** (nī'mā'gĕn); *anc.* **No'vi·om'a·gus** (nō'vĭ·ŏm'à·gŭs). Commune, Gelderland prov., E Netherlands, on Waal river 12 m. S of Arnhem; pop. (1939) 95,130; Gothic church of St. Stephen, dating from 1271; stadhouse, built 1554; at one time the residence of the Carlovingian emperors; later a member of the Hanseatic League; a series of six peace treaties signed here 1678–79 (France and Sweden with Holland, Spain, Austria, and Denmark), closing war of France against Holland and her allies and leaving France (under Louis XIV) at height of her power. In center of fighting Sept. 1944.

Nij'ni Novgorod (nīzh'nī; *Russ.* nyēsh'nyĭ). Var. of NIZHNI NOVGOROD.

Nikaria. See IKARIA.

Nik'ki (nĭk'ĭ). Town in NE Dahomey, West Africa; chief town of W Borgu region.

Nik·ko (nĕk·kō; *Angl.* nĭk'ō). City and mountain resort (alt. 2000 ft.), Tochigi prefecture, cen. Honshu, Japan, 7 m. E of Lake Chuzenji (q.v.) and ab. 90 m. N of Tokyo by rail; pop. 33,490. Had Shinto temple from earliest times, and Buddhist temple from c. 767; esp. famous for its beautiful scenery, waterfalls, cryptomeria avenues, sacred bridge, and memorial carved shrines and temples of Iyeyasu (buried here 1617) and Iyemitsu (1651), 1st and 3d shoguns of Tokugawa dynasty.

Nikko Range. Mountain range, N cen. Honshu I., Japan, in which Nikko is situated.

Ni·ko·la'ev (nyĭ·kŭ·lä'yĕf). 1 Region, S Ukraine, U.S.S.R.; borders on Black Sea and contains lower course of Bug river.

2 *also* **Ver'no·le'ninsk** (vĕr'nô·lĕn'ĭnsk; *Russ.* vyĭr·nŭ-lyä'nyĭnsk). City and seaport, its ✳, at confluence of the Bug and Ingul rivers 70 m. NE of Odessa; pop. 167,108; important Black Sea naval station; trades esp. in grain. Founded ab. 1789; captured by Germans Aug. 1941 and base destroyed; retaken by Russians Mar. 13, 1944.

Ni·ko·la'evsk (nyĭ·kŭ·lä'yĕfsk). 1 Seaport town, E Khabarovsk Territory, Soviet Russia, Asia, near mouth of the Amur 400 m. NE of Khabarovsk, with which it is connected by river and rail; pop. 7452; regional center for salmon fishing and canning; harbor closed by ice for six months of the year; nearly destroyed, with much loss of life, at time of Revolution (1917).

2 See NIKOLAEVSKI.

3 See PUGACHEV.

Ni·ko·la'ev·ski (nyĭ·kŭ·lä'yĕf·skĭ), *formerly* **Ni·ko·la'evsk** (nyĭ·kŭ·lä'yĕfsk). Town, NE Stalingrad Region, Soviet Russia, Europe, on left bank of lower Volga 110 m. NNE of Stalingrad, opp. Kamyshin; pop. 19,230.

Nikolainkaupunki *or* **Nikolaistad.** Former names of VAASA, Finland.

Ni'kols·burg (nē'kôls·bŏŏrk); *Czech* **Mi'ku·lov** (mĭ'-kŏŏ·lôf). Commune, S Moravia, Czechoslovakia, ab. 30 m. S of Brno; pop. (1930) 7785; treaty of peace signed here Dec. 31, 1621, bet. Emperor Ferdinand II and Gabriel Bethlen, Prince of Transylvania; truce signed here July 26, 1866 bet. Austria and Prussia.

Ni·kolsk' (nĭ·kôlsk'; *Russ.* nyĭ·kôl'y'sk). Town, SE Vologda Region, N cen. Soviet Russia, Europe, on the Yug river 150 m. WNW of Kirov; pop. ab. 2000.

Ni·kol'sko·e (nĭ·kôl'skŭ·yĕ; *Russ.* nyĭ·kôl'y'·skŭ·yĕ). See KOMANDORSKIE ISLANDS.

Nikolsk–Ussuriiski. See VOROSHILOV.

Ni·ko'pol. 1 (nĭ·kô'pôl) *anc.* **Ni·cop'o·lis** (nĭ·kŏp'ô·lĭs; nĭ-). Commercial town, Pleven dept., N Bulgaria, on Danube river 24 m. NNE of Pleven; pop. (1926) 4963; scene of many battles, esp. 1396 in which Sigismund of Hungary, supported by French, English, and German forces, was defeated by the Turkish sultan Bajazet I; besieged by Ladislas V of Hungary 1444; scene of Turkish defeat 1595 and 1598; captured 1797, 1810, and 1829; burned by Russians 1877. Nearby are remains of fortified stronghold (Nicopolis) built by Roman emperor Trajan.

2 (*pron.* nyĭ·kô'pŭl·y') Town, S Dnepropetrovsk Region, E cen. Ukraine, U.S.S.R., on right bank of Dnieper 55 m. SE of Krivoi Rog; pop. 57,841; important trade center (corn, hemp, wool, and esp. manganese). From early times a strategic crossing point of the Dnieper, scene of many conflicts; once a great camp of the Zaporogian Cossacks; held by Germans Oct. 1941 to Feb. 8, 1944.

Nik'šić (nĭk'shĭch; *Yugoslav* nēk'shĕt·y'). Town, NW Montenegro, S Yugoslavia, 28 m. N of Cetinje; pop. 4164; on N–S trade route; has Byzantine cathedral, given by Russia, and ruins of old Turkish fortress.

Nile (nīl); *Lat.* **Ni'lus** (nī'lŭs); *Arab.*, fr. Greek, **En Nîl** (ăn·nēl'); *modern Egyptian* **El Bahr** (ăl bä'h'r) *or* **Bahr en Nîl.** River in E and NE Africa; the longest river in the world; in the Bible the "great river" (Shihor; *A. V.*, Sihor; *Isaiah* xxiii. 3) of Egypt; 4150 m. from its remotest headstream, the Luvironza, and 3473 m. from Lake Victoria, to Mediterranean; flows generally N from East Africa through Uganda, Republic of Sudan, and Egypt; basin drained estimated at 1,107,227 sq. m. Its headwaters (longest, Kagera, q.v.) drain uplands of N Tanganyika, SW Kenya, and country northeast of Congo basin into Lake Victoria. Nile proper, **Vic·to'ri·a** (vĭk·tōr'ĭ·à) *or* **Som'er·set** (sŭm'ẽr·sĕt; -sĭt), **Nile,** ab. 300 m., leaves N Lake Victoria (alt. ab. 3720 ft.) near Jinja at Ripon Falls (13 ft. high, 1310 ft. across) 30 m. N of equator, flows N to and through Kyoga Lake, then NW over Murchison Falls (118 ft.) into NE corner of Lake Albert (q.v.); leaves N end (alt. c. 2200 ft.) of Lake Albert and flows N through NW Uganda (**Al'bert Nile** [ăl'bẽrt]; crosses into Sudan where it is called

Bahr el Jebel in the swamp (sudd) region; at Lake No (9°29′N) joined by W tributary Bahr el Ghazal, and takes name of **White Nile**, *Arab.* **Bahr el Ab′yad** (ăl ăb′yŏd); flows E to confluence, 1652 m. from Ripon Falls, with Sobat (from highlands of SW Ethiopia), then 520 m. N through Republic of Sudan to Khartoum along W border of Gezira dist.; here joined by **Blue Nile**, *Arab.* **Bahr el Az′raq** (ăz′rŏk), 850 m. long which rises in the mountains of Ethiopia, flows into Lake Tana, then (as the **Ab·bai′** [äb·bï′]) by a wide SE to NW bend enters Republic of Sudan and flows N to join White Nile at Khartoum; thence combined stream flows 200 m. to Atbara, where it is joined by the Atbara, which rises near Lake Tana; thence, without any tributaries to its mouth, in great southwest S-shaped bend crosses into Egypt near Wadi Halfa and flows N about 400 m. to Mediterranean; 12 m. below Cairo enters delta (120 m. wide), which in ancient times had seven branches but now has two principal mouths, each ab. 146 m. long: Rosetta (on W) entering sea just E of Alexandria, and Damietta (on E) just W of Port Said.

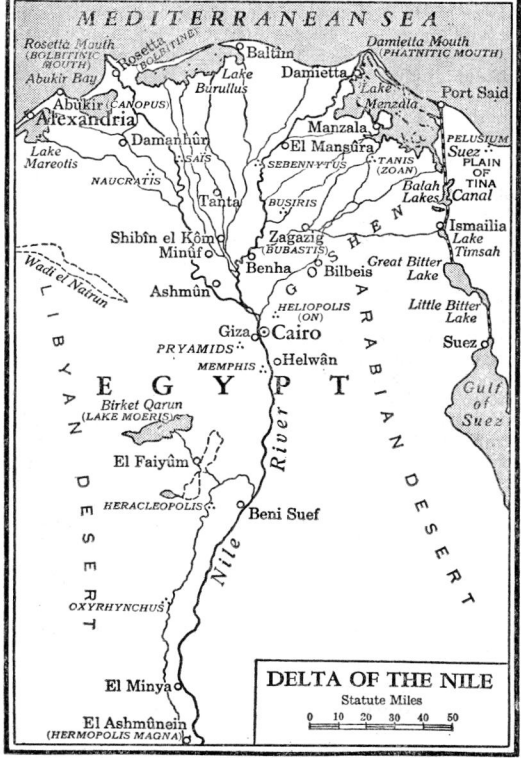

DELTA OF THE NILE
Statute Miles
0 10 20 30 40 50

Generally navigable from sea to Murchison Falls, except in low season along stretch of 900 m. that contains its six so-called cataracts (actually rapids): the 1st just above Aswân (*q.v.*) 24°N, the only one in Egypt proper, where early Mediterranean civilization ended; the 2d in N Republic of Sudan, just above Wadi Halfa ab. 21°50′N, marking roughly the N limits of ancient Cush; the 3d in ancient Nubia ab. 47 m. below Dongola 19°50′N (700 m. by river below Khartoum); the 4th in the great bend of the Nile just above Merowe ab. 18°36′N, obstructed by granite and basalt ridges, the most difficult of all to navigate; the 5th ab. 40 m. below Berber at ab. 18°30′N; the 6th in the desert ab. 55 m. below Khartoum 16°10′N. Three large dams: Aswân, Gebel Aulia (20 m. S of Khartoum) and Makwar (near Sennar on Blue Nile). In Egypt lined with famous struc-

tures and ruins of ancient dynasties, as at Abu Simbel, Luxor and Karnak (site of ancient Thebes), Memphis, Giza. Its source a matter of mystery and legend for centuries, believed to be in "Mountains of the Moon" (probably Mt. Ruwenzori); down to 15th cent. little knowledge gained; upper regions visited by Italian and Portuguese travelers 15th–17th cents. Along its course notable discoveries have been made by European explorers: James Bruce, who discovered source of Blue Nile and traced its course 1768–73; various Egyptian expeditions bet. 1820 and 1842 that explored White Nile as far S as Gondokoro (ab. 5°N); J. H. Speke, who first determined Lake Victoria (*q.v.*) as main reservoir of Nile 1858; Speke and J. A. Grant, who further explored the lake 1860–62 by reaching Nile outlet at Ripon Falls; (Sir) Samuel Baker, who in two journeys 1861–62 and 1863–65 discovered Lake Albert and Murchison Falls. Battle of the Nile fought at Abukir Bay; see Abukir.

Niles (nīlz). **1** Village, Cook co., NE Illinois, 14 m. N of Chicago; pop. 20,393.
2 City, Berrien co., SW Michigan, 48 m. SW of Kalamazoo; pop. 13,842; industrial and trade center.
3 Industrial city, Trumbull co., NE Ohio, on Mahoning river 8 m. NNW of Youngstown; pop. 19,545; iron, sheet steel, fire brick, metal laths; birthplace of William McKinley, 25th president of the U.S.
Niles Center. See Skokie.
Nil·gi·ri (nĭl′gĭ·rĭ). **1** Former Indian state, E Eastern States, Indian Union, near coast of Bay of Bengal; 263 sq. m.; pop. (1941) 73,109.
2 Town, its ✳, now in Orissa, 125 m. SW of Calcutta.
Nilgiri Hills *or* **Nil′gi·ris** (nĭl′gĭ·rĭz). Literally "Blue Mountains," a plateau, average alt. 6500 ft., SW Madras prov., Indian Union; highest point Mt. Dodabetta 8760 ft. Chief aboriginal tribes the Kotas and Todas.
Ni·ló′po·lis (nē·ló′pōō·lēs). City, Rio de Janeiro state, SE Brazil, NW of Rio de Janeiro; pop. (1940 est.) 22,594.
Nilus. See Nile.
Nimburg. See Nymburk.
Nimeguen. See Nijmegen.
Nîmes (nēm), *older* **Nismes** (nēm); *anc.* **Ne·mau′sus** (nē·mô′sŭs). Manufacturing and commercial city, ✳ of Gard dept., S France, 64 m. NW of Marseilles; pop. 93,758; 11th-cent. cathedral (on site of former temple of Apollo); noted esp. for its ancient Roman buildings and monuments, among which are a Corinthian temple (Maison Carrée) restored 1789 and converted into a museum 1823, a magnificent amphitheater (Les Arènes) used as a fortress by Visigoths and Saracens against Franks, remains of an ancient tower (Turris Magna; *Fr.* Tour Magne), two gates, ruins of a nymphaeum, and, nearby, ruins of a famous aqueduct (Pont du Gard). Thought to have been founded by Greek colonists; held by Romans for five centuries; Protestant stronghold in 16th cent.; treaty (Pacification of Nîmes) signed here 1629; scene of uprising 1815.
Nimrud. See Calah.
Ni′mu·le (nē′mōō·lā). Town, Equatoria prov., S Republic of Sudan, on Nile river SSE of Rejaf.
Nimwegen. See Nijmegen.
Nine Point Mesa. Elevation 5551 ft. in cen. Brewster co., W Texas.
Nine′ty–mile Beach (nīn′tĭ·mīl′). Straight stretch of flat coastal land, Gippsland, SE Victoria, SE Australia.
Nin′e·veh (nĭn′ĕ·vĕ); *anc.* **Ni′nus** (nī′nŭs). Ancient capital of Assyria; its ruins on the Tigris river, originally covered by the mound Kuyunjik opp. Mosul, N Iraq. One of the greatest cities of antiquity; excavations, begun by Sir Austen Layard 1845, disclosed many buildings and parts of the walls. Its rise to power began with Sennacherib (705–681 B.C.); contained library and palace of Ashurbanipal; captured and destroyed by Nabopolassar of Babylonia and his allies 612 B.C.
Nin′fas, Cape (nēm′fäs). Cape on NE coast of Chubut territory, S Argentina, at S entrance to New Gulf.

Ning'an' (nĭng'än'); *formerly* **Ning'u'ta'** (nĭng'ōō'tä'). Town, E cen. Kirin prov., E Manchuria, on spur railroad 150 m. ENE of Kirin; pop. ab. 30,000.

Ning'hsien' (nĭng'shĭ-ĕn'); *formerly* **Ning'po'** (nĭng'-pō'). City and treaty port, NE Chekiang prov., E China, ab. 90 m. ESE of Hangchow on S side of Hangchow Bay and on small stream ab. 13 m. from its mouth; pop. (1953) 237,500; exports esp. cotton, salt, fish and fish products, tea. Its present site occupied since 713 A.D.; first visited by Portuguese c. 1520; drove out foreigners 1545; made treaty port by Treaty of Nanking Aug. 1842; has long been a center of learning and religion.

Ning'sia' *or* **Ning'hsia'** (nĭng'shĭ-ä'). **1** Province, W Inner Mongolia, N China; 106,115 sq. m.; pop. (1936 est.) 1,023,143; ✳ Ningsia; bounded on N by Outer Mongolia, on E by Suiyuan prov., on S and W by Kansu prov. Borders desert of Gobi on the N; in the S on the Kansu border is the Ala Shan range (highest point ab. 12,000 ft.); the Hwang Ho follows its SE and E border and at its S end is paralleled by part of the Great Wall. **2** Town, its ✳, on the Hwang Ho 220 m. NNE of Lanchow; pop. ab. 20,000; formerly in Kansu prov.

Ninguta. See NINGAN.

Ningyuan *or* **Ningyüan.** **1** See KULDJA.
2 See SICHANG.

Ni'ni-go Group (nē'nē-gō). See NORTHWESTERN IS-LANDS.

Ni-ni'ni Point (nē-nē'nē). Point on SE coast of Kauai I., Hawaii, just N of Nawiliwili Bay.

Ni'nove' (nē'nôv'). Commune, East Flanders prov., NW cen. Belgium, on the Dender W of Brussels; pop. 10,085.

Ninus. See NINEVEH.

Nio. See IOS.

Ni'o-brar'a (nī'ō-brâr'á). **1** River 431 m. long, flowing from Niobrara co., E Wyoming, E across N Nebraska and into Missouri river in N cen. Knox co., NE Nebraska.
2 County in Wyoming. See *Table* at WYOMING.

Ni.o'ro (nī.ō'rō). Town, W Sudan, West Africa, 200 m. NW of Bamako; pop. ab. 3000; highway center and air-field.

Niort (nyôr). City, ✳ of Deux-Sèvres dept., W France, 83 m. SE of Nantes; pop. 27,830; 15th-cent. Gothic-Renaissance church; celebrated public garden and nurs-ery gardens; manufactures gloves, chamois, leather. De-veloped around castle built by Henry Plantagenet 1155; captured 1224 by Louis VIII; belonged to England 1360–73; became Protestant stronghold; suffered through Revocation of Edict of Nantes 1685.

Ni'pe Bay (nē'pâ). Bay on N coast of Oriente prov., E Cuba.

Nip-hon' (nĭ-pŏn'; nĭp'ŏn). = NIPPON.

Nip'i-gon (nĭp'ĭ-gŏn). Village, W Ontario, Canada, on Nipigon Bay at mouth of Nipigon river; pop. 1773.

Nip'i-gon, Lake (nĭp'ĭ-gŏn); *also* **Nep'i-gon** (nĕp'-). Lake 1730 sq. m. in Thunder Bay dist., SW Ontario, Canada, ab. 35 m. N of Lake Superior; its outlet is **Nipigon River**, ab. 40 m. long, flowing S to **Nipigon Bay** in Lake Superior. Has many wooded islands and steep shores; visited by sportsmen.

Ni-pis'i-guit, *or* **Ne-pis'i-guit Bay** (nĭ-pĭz'ĭ-gwĭt). Southern extension of Chaleur Bay, extending into N Gloucester co., NE New Brunswick, SE Canada; re-ceives the **Nipisiguit River,** ab. 75 m. long, which rises in NW Northumberland co. and flows E and N.

Nip'is-sing (nĭp'ĭ-sĭng). District, Ontario, Canada. See *Table* at ONTARIO.

Nipissing, Lake; *also* **Lake Nep'is-sing** (nĕp'-). Lake 330 sq. m. in Nipissing dist., SE Ontario, Canada, NE of Georgian Bay; its outlet is French river, flowing W to Georgian Bay. Contains many islands; has steamer navigation and is on projected route of canal from Ot-tawa river to Georgian Bay. Part of route of early French explorers to the West (1659–1743).

Nip'ple-top' (nĭp''l-tŏp'). Peak 4620 ft. in the Adiron-dack Mts., Essex co., NE New York.

Nip·pon' (nĭ-pŏn'; nĭp'ŏn; *Jap.* nĕp-pŏn). Properly, Ja-pan; originally, two ideographs, **Ni·hon** (nĕ-hŏn) "ori-gin of light" or "sun origin" (hence, "Land of the Rising Sun"), later conventionalized Nippon, the official Japa-nese name, from the Chinese pronunciation, **Jih'pen'** (rĭr'bŭn'); hence Marco Polo's name **Zi·pan'gu** (zĭ-păng'gōō) [-*gu* from Chinese *kuo*, country] and English (poetical) **Ci·pan'go** (sĭ-păng'gō), and later JAPAN. Also, **Dai Nip·pon** (dī nĕp-pŏn), literally "great Ja-pan."

Nip·pur' (nĭ-pōōr'). Ancient Sumerian and Babylonian city 100 m. SE of Babylon; a religious center, sacred to En-lil. Scene of archaeological excavations, in which many buildings and temple archives were uncovered.

Ni·que'ro (nē-kā'rō). Municipality, Oriente prov., E Cuba, on S shore of Guacanayabo Bay 37 m. SW of Manzanillo; pop. 36,025.

Ni·riz' (nē-rēz'). Town, Fars prov., SW Iran, near SE end of Lake Niriz; pop. ab. 9000; on the old trade route from Kerman to Shiraz.

Niriz *or* **Bakh'ti·gan'** (bȧk'tĕ-gän'). Salt lake 10 m. long, N cen. Fars prov., SW Iran; formerly 60 m. long.

Niš *or* **Nish** (nĭsh; *Yugo.* nēsh); *anc.* **Na·is'sus** *or* **Na-ïs'sus** (nȧ-ĭs'ŭs) *or* **Nis'sa** (nĭs'à). City, E Serbia, former ⊗ of Moravska co., E Yugoslavia, on Nišava river; pop. 35,465; industrial and commercial center; important railroad junction point; cathedral; birthplace of Con-stantine the Great. Held at various periods by Bulgari-ans, Hungarians, and Turks (for ab. 300 years); passed to Serbia 1878 and was capital of Serbia until 1901; taken by Germans 1915 and Apr. 1941; taken by Rus-sians Oct. 13, 1944.

Nisa. See NYSA.

Ni·sae'a (nĭ-sē'à). Plain, ancient Media, just SW of Caspian Sea; famous for its (*Nisaean*) breed of large fine horses used by Persian kings c. 500 B.C.

Ni'ša·va *or* **Ni'sha·va** (nē'shä-vä). River ab. 80 m. long in SE Yugoslavia; flows out of Bulgaria NW into Morava river 8 m. W of Niš.

Ni·sce'mi (nē-shä'mē). Commune, Caltanissetta prov., cen. Sicily, 30 m. SE of Caltanissetta; pop. 20,281.

Nish. See NIŠ.

Ni'sha·pur' (nē'shä-pōōr'). Town, Khurasan prov., NE Iran, ab. 40 m. W of Meshed; pop. ab. 20,000; famous turquoise mines nearby; birthplace and burial place of the Persian poets Omar Khayyám and Farid ud-din Attar. Traditionally founded by Shapur II in 4th cent. A.D.; royal residence until middle of 5th cent.; declined but again flourished under Tahirid and Samanid dy-nasties (c. 820–999); destroyed three times in 13th cent. —twice by earthquakes and once by the Mongols.

Nishava. See NIŠAVA.

Ni·shi·no·mi·ya (nē-shē-nō-mē-yä). City, Hyogo pre-fecture, W Honshu I., Japan, ab. 11 m. E of Kobe on N shore of Osaka Bay; pop. (1945) 90,808; has largest sake breweries in Japan.

Ni·shi No·to·ro, Cape (nē-shē nō-tō-rō). Cape on SW extremity of Karafuto, Sakhalin I., opp. N tip of Hok-kaido I.

Nish'na·bot'na (nĭsh'nȧ-bŏt'nȧ). River 40 m. long, SW Iowa and Missouri; formed by confluence of East Nish-nabotna (ab. 160 m. long) and West Nishnabotna (ab. 160 m. long), flows S across Missouri border and into Missouri river in Atchison co., NW Missouri.

Nisibin, Nisibis. See NUSAYBIN.

Ni'si·da (nē'zē-dä); *anc.* **Ne'sis** (nē'sĭs). Island in the Bay of Naples, S Italy, SE of Pozzuoli.

Nisiro. See NISYROS.

Nismes. See NÎMES.

Nis·qual'ly (nĭs-kwŏl'ĭ) *or* **Nes·qual'ly** (nĕs-). River ab. 70 m. long, W cen. Washington; flows NW from **Nis-qually Glacier** on S slope of Mount Ranier, forming boundary bet. Pierce and Thurston cos., and empties into **Nisqually Reach,** inlet at S end of Puget Sound.

Nissa. See NIŠ.

Nis·san' (nĭ·săn'). Main island of Green Is. group, N Solomon Is., W Pacific Ocean, E of SE New Ireland. Taken by Americans Feb. 1944.

Nis'san (nĭs'ăn). River, S Sweden; flows SW into the Kattegat at Halmstad.

Nistru. See DNIESTER.

Ni'sy·ros (nyē'sĕ·rôs); *Ital.* **Ni'si·ro** (nē'zē·rŏ). An island of the Dodecanese (*q.v.*), S of Kos; 18 sq. m.; pop. (1936) 3391.

Ni'te·rói' (nē'tĕ·roi'); *formerly* **Nic'the·roy'** (nē'tĕ·roi'). City, ✱ of Rio de Janeiro state, SE Brazil; pop. (1940 est.) 125,974; on SE shore of Guanabara Bay opp. Rio de Janeiro, of which it is a residential suburb; noted for its many fine homes in Portuguese style of architecture. First settled 1671; became a city 1836.

Nith (nĭth). River ab. 65 m. long in SW Scotland; rises in Ayrshire, flows SE into Solway Firth 10 m. S of Dumfries.

Ni'tra (nyĭ'trà); *Hung.* **Nyi'tra** (nyĭ'trŏ); *Ger.* **Neu'tra** (noi'trä). **1** River ab. 110 m. long in W Slovakia prov., Czechoslovakia; flows S into Váh river just above Komárno on the Hungarian border.

2 Town, S Slovakia prov., E cen. Czechoslovakia, on Nitra river; pop. (1930) 21,259; traditionally, site of oldest church in Slovakia.

Nit'ri·a (nĭt'rĭ·à) *or* **Nit'ri·ae** (-ē). Desert region of Natron Lakes, Lower Egypt, W of Cairo; in early times seat of famous settlement of anchorites.

Ni'tro (nī'trō). City, SW West Virginia, in Kanawha and Putnam cos. on Kanawha river 13 m. WNW of Charleston; pop. 6894; grew up around powder plant erected by U.S. government 1918; incorp. 1932.

Nit'ta·ny Valley (nĭt''n·ĭ). Fertile valley ab. 30 m. long by 4 m. wide in Centre and Clinton cos., cen. Pennsylvania.

Ni·u'a·fo'o (nē·ōō'à·fô'ō). Island in extreme N part of Tonga Archipelago, SW cen. Pacific Ocean, 400 m. N of Tongatabu; ab. lat. 15°30'S and long. 176°W; area 6 sq. m.; pop. (1937) 1229. Volcanic in origin and has had many eruptions. Because its steep shores make landing on it difficult, it has become known to philatelists as "Tin Can Island," from the practice of delivering mail by sealing it in biscuit tins, lashing them to poles, and towing them ashore.

Ni·u'a·to'bu·ta'bu (nē·ōō'à·tô'bōō·tä'bōō); *formerly* **Kep'pel's Island** (kĕp'ĕlz). Island in N part of Tonga Archipelago, ab. 150 m. N of Vavau group, SW cen. Pacific Ocean; 5 sq. m.; pop. (1937; with Tafahi) 829; ab. lat. 16°S and long. 174°W.

Niuchwang. = NEWCHWANG.

Ni·u'e (nē·ōō'ā), *or* **Sav'age Island** (săv'ĭj). Island in S cen. Pacific Ocean E of Tonga Is. and 350 m. SSE of Samoa, lat. 19°S and long. 170°W; 100 sq. m.; pop. (1940) 4300; chief village and port Alofi, on W coast. A New Zealand dependency, originally part of Cook Is. administration but separate since 1922. Exports copra and bananas, woven hats and baskets. Discovered by Capt. Cook 1774.

Nive (nēv). River ab. 50 m. long, SW France; flows W to the Adour along base of W Pyrenees; several battles on its banks Dec. 1813 resulting in victory of British over French.

Ni'velles (nē'vĕl'). Commune, Brabant prov., cen. Belgium; pop. 12,598; manufactures linens, cotton goods, lace, machinery; convent dating from 7th cent.; 11th-cent. romanesque Church of Saint Gertrude.

Ni'ver'nais' (nē'vĕr'nĕ'). Historical region of cen. France; bounded anciently on N, E, and SE by Burgundy, S and SW by Bourbonnais, W by Berry, NW by Orléanais; ✱ Nevers. Originally inhabited by the Ædui; part of Burgundian kingdom; comprised diocese of Nevers from beginning of 6th cent. A.D.; countship founded at end of 9th cent.; passed successively to Pierre de Courtenay 1184, Robert de Dampierre 1272, to house of Burgundy 1384, to German family of Clèves 1491;

made duchy 1538; passed to Gonzaga family 1565, to Mazarin 1659; French province until Revolution.

Nivernais, Ca'nal' du (kà'nál' dü). Canal 45 m. long, Yonne and Nièvre depts., cen. France; connects Loire river at Decize with the Seine by way of the Seine's tributary, the Yonne river, which it follows above Auxerre.

Nix'on (nĭk's'n). City, Gonzales co., S cen. Texas, 44 m. ESE of San Antonio; pop. 1751; peanuts; poultry.

Ni·zam'a·bad (nĭ·zäm'à·bäd; nĭ·zăm'à·băd). Town, NW Andhra Pradesh, S cen. Indian Union, 100 m. N of Hyderabad.

Nizam's Dominions. See HYDERABAD.

Nizh'ne Kam·chatsk' (nĭzh'nĕ kăm·chätsk'; *Russ.* nyēsh'nyĕ kŭm·chàtsk'). Town, E Kamchatka Penin., in Khabarovsk Territory, Soviet Russia, Asia, on Kamchatka river near its mouth.

Nizh'ne Ko·lymsk' (nĭzh'nĕ kŏ·lĭmsk'; *Russ.* nyēsh'nyĕ kŭ·lĭmsk'). Town, NE Yakutsk A.S.S.R., Soviet Russia, Asia, on left bank of Kolyma river ab. 65 m. above its mouth; Arctic port.

Nizh'ne·u'dinsk (nĭzh'nĕ·ōō'dĭnsk; *Russ.* nyĭsh·nyĕ·ōō'dyĭnsk). Town, W Irkutsk Region, Soviet Russia, Asia, on the upper Uda river; pop. 10,342; a growing industrial city on the Trans-Siberian R.R.

Nizh'ni Nov'go·rod (nĭzh'nĭ nŏv'gŏ·rŏd; *Russ.* nyēsh'nyĭ nôf'gŭ·rŭt). **1** Old government and province of Russia, somewhat larger than the modern Gorki Region.
2 See GORKI.

Nizh'ni Ta·gil' (nĭzh'nĭ tà·gĭl'; *Russ.* nyēsh'nyĭ tŭ·gēl'). City, W Sverdlovsk Region, Soviet Russia, Asia, on E slopes of Ural Mts. 80 m. N of Sverdlovsk; pop. 159,864; blast furnaces; foundries, chemical factories, wagon factories, metallurgical plant; handles products of nearby iron, copper, gold, and platinum mines, the iron coming chiefly from rich mines of Mt. Blagodat to the NE; rail junction; largest railroad-car plant in the Soviet Union. Founded 1725.

Nizhnyaya Tunguska. See *Lower Tunguska* at TUNGUSKA.

Ni·zib' (nĭ·zēb') *or* **Ne·zib'** (nĕ-). Town, N Syria, ab. 22 m. E of Aintab (mod. Gaziantep); scene of battle June 24, 1839, in which army of Ibrahim Pasha of Egypt completely defeated the Turkish forces. Now **Ni·zip'** (nĭ·zēp') in Gaziantep vilayet, S Turkey; pop. 7628.

Niz·wa', Kuh-i- (kōō'hĕ·nĕz·wà'). Mountain 13,501 ft. in E Elburz Mts., N Iran, ab. 55 m. SSE of Babul.

Nizza. See NICE.

Niz'za Mont·fer·ra'to (nēt'tsä mŏnt·fär·rä'tŏ). Commune, Alessandria prov., SE Piedmont, NW Italy, SW of Alessandria; pop. (1931) 9138.

Njommelsaska. See HARSPRÅNG.

Nka'ta ('ng·kä'tà). Town on W cen. shore of Lake Nyasa, Nyasaland protectorate, SE Africa; an administrative center with best anchorage on W side of lake.

Nmai *or* **N'mai Kha** (nà·mī' k'hä'). River (*kha*) ab. 320 m. long in Upper Burma; flows S from SE corner of Tibet to unite with the Mali and form the Irrawaddy river.

No. See THEBES, Egypt.

No, Lake (nō). Lake in S cen. Republic of Sudan, E Africa, where Bahr el Jebel and Bahr el Ghazal join to form the White Nile (see NILE); maximum area 40 sq. m.

Noa. See NOICATTARO.

No·ailles' (nô·ĭ'; *Fr.* nô'ä'y'). **1** Commune, Corrèze dept., cen. France, S of Brive-la-Gaillarde; pop. (1931) 441; castle from which Noailles family is named.
2 Commune, cen. Oise dept., N France, SSE of Beauvais; pop. 1282; belonged to famous Noailles family; adopted name in 17th cent. before which it was known as **Long'-vil'liers'** (lôn'vē'lyä').

No·a·kha'li (nō'äk·hä'lĭ). **1** District, Chittagong division, SE East Bengal, Pakistan; 1658 sq. m.; pop. (1941) 2,217,402.
2 *or* **Su·dha'ram** (sŏŏd·hä'räm). Town, its ✱, 175 m. E of Calcutta, on E side of mouth of Ganges; pop. 13,063.

No′ank (nō′ăngk). Subdivision of town of GROTON, Connecticut; pop. 1116.

No·a′tak (nō·ä′tăk). **1** River ab. 320 m. long, NW Alaska; flows W bet. Brooks Range and Baird Mts., then S to Kotzebue Sound; extensive mineral deposits in its basin. First explored 1885–86.
2 Village and Eskimo mission station in Noatak-Kobuk dist. on right bank of the Noatak near its mouth, ab. 55 m. N of Kotzebue; pop. (est.) 282.

Noatak-Ko·buk′ (-kô·bŏŏk′). District, N Alaska along Arctic coast; pop. (1950) 3604.

No′be·o′ka (nō′bĕ·ō′kä; *Jap.* nô·bĕ·ô·kä). City, Miyazaki prefecture, E coast of Kyushu, Japan; pop. (1945) 56,954.

Nob Hill (nŏb). Hill in SW San Francisco, California; in early days a fashionable residential section.

No′ble (nō′b′l). Name of counties in three states in the U.S. See *Tables* at INDIANA, OHIO, OKLAHOMA.

No′bles (nō′b′lz). County in Minnesota. See *Table* at MINNESOTA.

No′bles·ville (nō′b′lz-vĭl). City, ⊗ of Hamilton co., cen. Indiana, 20 m. NNE of Indianapolis; pop. 7664; in agricultural and horse-breeding section.

Noc, Big Bay de (bā′ dĕ nŏk′). Northern extension of Green Bay on S coast of Delta co., S Michigan penin., just E of **Little Bay de Noc.**

No·ce′ra In·fe·ri·o′re (nō·châ′rä ĕm·fä·rĕ·ō′rå); *anc.* **Nu·ce′ri·a Al′fa·ter′na** (nŭ·sĕr′ĭ·à ăl′fà·tûr′nà). Commune, Salerno prov., Campania, S Italy, 8 m. NW of Salerno; pop. 29,347.

Nocera Su·pe·ri·o′re (sŏŏ·på·rĕ·ō′rå). Commune, Salerno prov., Campania, S Italy, 5 m. NW of Salerno; pop. (1931) 10,528. Taken by Allies Sept. 27, 1943.

No·ce′to (nō·châ′tô). Commune, Parma prov., Emilia, N Italy, 7 m. W by S of Parma; pop. 10,001; castle.

No′ci (nō′chē). Commune, Bari prov., Apulia, SE Italy, 27 m. SE of Bari; pop. (1931) 14,005.

No·co′na (nō·kō′nà). City, Montague co., N Texas, 42 m. E of Wichita Falls; pop. 3127; leather goods center; oil wells.

Nod′a·way (nŏd′à·wā). **1** River 150 m. long, rising in Cass co., SW Iowa, and flowing S into Missouri river in W Andrew co., NW Missouri.
2 County in Missouri. See *Table* at MISSOURI.

No·do·ri (nō·dô·rē). See SHIRANE.

Noehoerowa, Noehoetjoet. See KAI ISLANDS.

Noem′foor (nŏŏm′fōr) *or* **Num′for** (nŏŏm′fôr). Island, W Schouten Is., on W side of entrance to Geelvink Bay, N Neth. New Guinea, 45 m. W of Biak; roughly circular, 14 m. long, 12 m. wide, and generally flat; chief village Namber. Attacked July 1, 1944 by Allied forces who by July 6 gained control of important Japanese airfields at Kamiri and Namber.

Nœux-les-Mines (nû′lä-mēn′). Commune, Pas-de-Calais dept., N France, 14 m. NNW of Arras; pop. (1931) 12,168; coal mines; destroyed in World War I.

No·fil′ia (nō·fĭl′yà), *also* **En Nofilia** (ĕn). Town, N Libya, N Africa, near S cen. coast of the Gulf of Sidra.

Nogaevo. See MAGADAN.

No·gal′es (nō·găl′ĕs; *Span.* nō·gä′lås). **1** City, ⊗ of Santa Cruz co., S Arizona, on Mexican border 60 m. S of Tucson; pop. 7286; port of entry, divided from Mexican town of same name by a single thoroughfare; center of mining and cattle-raising region. Site of old Spanish mission (1687); incorporated 1893; scene of military skirmishes against Pancho Villa 1916.
2 Town, Sonora state, NW Mexico, on the United States frontier adjacent to Nogales, Arizona (see 1, above); pop. 13,866; altitude ab. 4000 ft.
3 Town, Veracruz state, E Mexico; pop. 8479.

No·gal′ Peak (nō·găl′). Mountain 9983 ft. in the Sierra Blanca, S cen. New Mexico.

No′gat (nō′gät). Eastern branch of the lower Vistula, flowing NE out of the main stream into Frisches Haff; ab. 33 m. long. Formerly formed boundary bet. East

Prussia and Free State of Danzig; after World War II entirely in Poland.

No·ga·ta (nō·gä·tä). Town, Fukuoka prefecture, N Kyushu I., Japan; pop. (1945) 43,599; in center of coal-mining region.

No′gent′-le-Ro′trou′ (nô′zhäNl′rô′trōō′). Town, W Eure-et-Loir dept., N cen. France; pop. 6082; the hospital contains tomb of Duc de Sully.

No′gent′-sur-Marne (nô′zhäN′sür·màrn′). Commune, Seine dept., N France, ESE suburb of Paris on Marne river; pop. 21,056; manufactures chemicals, edged tools.

Nogent-sur-Seine (-sân′). Town, NW Aube dept., NE France; pop. 3538; ab. 4 m. SE is a farm on site of the Paraclete (*Fr.* Abbaye du Paraclet) the abbey which Abélard founded for Héloïse 1123.

No·ginsk′ (nō·gĭnsk′; *Russ.* nŭ·gēnsk′); *formerly* **Bo′-go·rodsk′** (bŏg′ô·rôtsk′; *Russ.* bŭ·кŭ·rôtsk′). City, Moscow Region, Soviet Russia, Europe; pop. 81,024; on spur of main railroad line 35 m. E of Moscow.

No·go·yá′ (nō·gô·yä′). Town, Entre Ríos prov., E Argentina, 60 m. SE of Paraná; pop. (est.) 11,880.

Nó′grád és Hont (nō′gräd äsh hônt′). Former Hungarian county.

No·gue′ra Pal′la·re′sa (nō·gä′rä pä′[l]yä·rä′sä). River in NE Spain; flows out of the Pyrenees into Segre river 20 m. NE of Lérida.

Noguera Ri′va·go·ran′zo (rē′vä·gô·rän′thô; -sô). River in NE Spain; flows out of the Pyrenees into Segre river 15 m. N of Lérida.

No·hi′li Point (nō·hē′lē). Point on W coast of Kauai I., Hawaii.

Noi·cat′ta·ro (noi·kät′tä·rô); *before 1863 called* **No′a** (nô′ä) *or* **No′ia** (nô′yä). Commune, Bari prov., Apulia, SE Italy, 8 m. SE of Bari; pop. (1931) 10,674; 13th-cent. Romanesque church.

Noire (nwär). French name of Bo river, Indochina.

Noir′mou′tier′, Île de (ēl′ dĕ nwär′mōō′tyä′). Island in Bay of Biscay off NW coast of Vendée dept., W France; ab. 12 m. long and 1 to 4 m. wide; pop. ab. 7000; belongs to Vendée dept.; site of monastery founded c. 680; chief town **Noirmoutier,** pop. 1812, in NE part of the island.

Noi′sy′-le-Sec (nwä′zēl′sĕk′). Commune, Seine dept., N France, ENE suburb of Paris; pop. 22,359; chemical and metallurgical industry.

No·ji·ma, Cape (nô·jē·mä). Cape, S tip of Chiba prefecture, SE Honshu, Japan, marking SE point of Sagami Sea.

No·ji·ri (nô·jē·rē). Lake on N border of Nagano prefecture, cen. Honshu, Japan, ab. 18 m. S of Takada; ab. 8½ m. in circumference; on a small island in the lake is a temple of Kwannon founded 730.

No′ki·la·la′ki (nō′kĕ·lä·lä′kĕ). Mountain 10,863 ft. in NW cen. Celebes I., Indonesia, SE of Donggala.

No·ko′mis (nō·kō′mĭs). City, Montgomery co., S cen. Illinois, 38 m. SE of Springfield; pop. 2476.

No′ku·hi′va (nō′kŏŏ·hē′và). Var. of NUKU HIVA.

No′la (nō′lä; *Ital.* nô′lä). Commune, Napoli prov., Campania, S Italy, 16 m. ENE of Naples; pop. 18,436; cathedral (remodeled in 14th cent.); seminary; Franciscan convent. Said to have been founded by Etrurians; passed to Rome 313 B.C.; site of battles bet. Marcellus and Hannibal 216 and 215 B.C.

Nolachucky. Var. of NOLICHUCKY.

No′lan (nō′lăn). County in Texas. See *Table* at TEXAS.

Nol′i·chuck′y (nŏl′ĭ·chŭk′ĭ). River ab. 150 m. long, rising in Blue Ridge Mts., W North Carolina, and flowing NW into French Broad river in Tennessee.

No Mans Land (nō′ mănz′ lănd′). Small island in Atlantic Ocean SW of Martha's Vineyard; in Dukes co., SE Massachusetts.

Nom′bre de Dios (nôm′brä thä thyôs′). Spanish port and early settlement on the N coast of Panama, just NE of Portobelo; founded 1510 by Nicuesa; included in Veragua region; abandoned 1597 because it was un-

healthful. Until 1584 was a port of destination for cargo fleets from Spain.

Nome (nōm). City on S side of Seward Penin., W Alaska, 14 m. W of Cape Nome and ab. 100 m. SE of Bering Strait; pop. 2316; commercial center of Seward Penin.; gold and tin mined in region; on N shore of Norton Sound, but has no natural harbor; U.S. Army airport. Began as a mining camp on discovery of gold 1896 in region; in succeeding years scene of phenomenal gold rush.

Nome, Cape. Cape, W Alaska, on S side of Seward Penin., ab. 64°30'N, 165°W.

Nõm'me (nûm'mĕ); *Russ.* **Nym'me** (nĭm'myĕ). City, Harju prov., N Estonia; pop. (1937) 18,644; a SW suburb of Tallin, and only recently separated from it.

No·mo (nō·mō); *Jap.* **Nomo Za·ki** (zä·kē). Cape (Jap. *zaki*) on S side of Nagasaki bay, W Kyushu, Japan.

No'moi Islands (nō'moi). Atoll group in S Caroline Is. in W Pacific Ocean, SE of Truk Is.; 5°30'N lat. and 153°40'E long.

No'mon'han' (nō'mōn'hän'). Town on Khalka river, W Heilungkiang prov., Manchuria, on Outer Mongolia border E of Bor Nor; scene of Russian victory over Japanese 1939.

No·nan'to·la (nō·nän'tō·lä). Commune, Modena prov., Emilia, N Italy, 6 m. NE of Modena; pop. 10,466.

Nondaburi. See NONTHA BURI.

Nong Khai (nông k'hī) or **Nong·ka·ya** (nông·k'hī— *sic*); *also* **Mi Chai** (mē chī). **1** Province, NE Thailand; 2818 sq. m.; pop. 114,927.
2 Town, its *, on right bank of the Mekong 12 m. ESE of Vientiane in Indochina.

Non'ni' (nŭn'nĭ'). River 660 m. long, N Manchuria; rises on E slopes of Great Khingan Mts. in W Heilungkiang prov., flows S and joins Sungari river near Fuyu; waters the fertile N section of Manchurian plain.

No'no·u'ti (nō'nō-ōo'tē). Island (atoll) in cen. part of Gilbert Is., just S of the equator, W Pacific Ocean; 24 m. long by 10 m. wide; pop. (1936) 2084; good anchorage.

Non'such' Island (nŭn'sŭch'). Small island in the Bermuda Is., E of Castle Harbour.

Non·tha Bu·ri (nŭn·bōo·rē—*sic*) or **Non·da·bu·ri** (nŭn·bōo·rē—*sic*). **1** Province, S Thailand; 256 sq. m.; pop. 115,143.
2 Town, its *, on left bank of the lower Chao Phraya, a N suburb of Bangkok.

Noon'mark' (nōon'märk'). Peak 3552 ft. in the Adirondack Mts., Essex co., NE New York.

Noord (nōrt). In the Rhine delta, W Netherlands, a name sometimes given to the Merwede (*q.v.*) bet. Dordrecht and its confluence with the Lek.

Noordbrabant. See NORTH BRABANT.

Noordholland. See NORTH HOLLAND.

Noord'wijk (nōrt'vīk). Commune, South Holland prov., SW Netherlands, on coast 12 m. N of The Hague; pop. 10,130; watering place.

Noot'ka Sound (nōot'ká). Inlet of Pacific Ocean in W Vancouver I., SW British Columbia, Canada, 49°40'N; it forms a good harbor with three arms, one of which is a narrow channel separating **Nootka Island** from Vancouver I. Visited by Capt. Cook 1778; seizure by Spanish 1789 led to breach bet. England and Spain which was settled by Nootka Convention Oct. 28, 1790.

Noph. See MEMPHIS, Egypt.

No·ran'da (nō·răn'dá). Mining town, Timiskaming co., SW Quebec, Canada; pop. 9672; copper and gold.

Norba Caesarea. See ALCÁNTARA.

Nor'cia (nôr'chä). Commune, Perugia prov., Umbria, cen. Italy, 41 m. ESE of Perugia; pop. 8225; 14th-cent. walls; cathedral; 6th-cent. church; birthplace of Saint Benedict.

Nord (nôr). Department of France. See *Table* at FRANCE.

Nordalbingia. See DITHMARSCHEN.

Nor'den (nôr'dĕn). Seaport city, NW Lower Saxony state, W Germany, formerly in Prussia, on North Sea 16 m. N of Emden, E of Ems estuary; pop. 11,025; manufactures iron goods, brandy, dehydrated milk; trades in agricultural products, wine. Oldest town in Ostfriesland.

Nordenskjöld Sea. See LAPTEV SEA.

Nor'den Tunnel (nôr'd'n). Railroad tunnel 10,325 ft. long. Bet. Norden and Eder, Placer and Nevada cos., E California; in the Sierra Nevada Mts.

Nor'der·ney' (nôr'dĕr·nĭ'). Island 9 sq. m. in the North Sea, in cen. part of East Frisian Is. off NW coast of Germany; resort.

Nord Fjord (nōr fyōr'; nōōr' fyōōr'). Inlet of Norwegian Sea on SW cen. coast of Norway.

Nord'hau'sen (nôrt'hou'zĕn). Industrial city, E Germany, in former Saxony province, Prussia, at S foot of Harz Mts. 36 m. NNW of Erfurt; pop. 35,056; important railroad junction; 13th-cent. convent church, 17th-cent. town hall; manufactures tobacco, machinery, cotton goods, brandy, soap. First mentioned 927 A.D.; became city in 12th cent.; free city 1253–1803; to Prussia 1803, kingdom of Westphalia 1807, Prussia 1813; during World War II site of concentration camp.

Nord'kapp' (nōr'käp'; nōōr'-). = NORTH CAPE, Norway.

Nord'kyn', Cape (nōr'kün'; nōōr'-). Cape on NE coast of Norway, 45 m. E of North Cape (*q.v.*); northernmost point of European mainland, 71°8'N.

Nord'land (nōr'län; nōōr'-). See *Table* at NORWAY.

Nörd'ling·en (nûrt'lĭng·ĕn). Commune, Swabia govt. dist., Bavaria, Germany; pop. 8589; scene of two battles in Thirty Years' War: (1) in 1634, in which Swedish army under Duke Bernhard of Saxe-Weimar and Marshal Horn was defeated; (2) in 1645, in which Germans were defeated, Mercy being mortally wounded.

Nor'dre Ber'gen·hus' (nōr'drĕ [nōōr'-] bĕr'gĕn·hōōs'). Former name of *Sogn og Fjordane:* see *Table* at NORWAY.

Nor'dre Trond'hjem (nōr'drĕ [nōōr'-] trôn'yĕm). Former name of *Nord-Tröndelag:* see *Table* at NORWAY.

Nordrhein—Westfalen. See NORTH RHINE-WEST-PHALIA.

Nord Slesvig. See SOUTH JUTLAND.

Nord'strand' (nôrt'shtränt'). One of the Halligen Is. in S part of North Frisian Is. off W coast of Schleswig-Holstein, NW Germany; area 19 sq. m.

Nord—Trön'de·lag (nōr'trûn'dĕ·läg; nōōr'-). County of Norway. See *Table* at NORWAY.

Nord'vik (nôrd'vĭk; *Russ.* nôr'dvyĭk). **1** Bay, a large inlet of Laptev Sea just E of mouth of Khatanga river, NW Yakutsk Republic, Soviet Russia, Asia.
2 Village on E bank of Khatanga river at its mouth S of Nordvik Bay.

Nore (nōr). River 70 m. long in SE Ireland; rises in N co. Tipperary, flows SE through co. Kilkenny into the Barrow river near its mouth.

Nore, the. Sandbank in center of the estuary of the Thames river in SE England, 3 m. NE of Sheerness; at its E end is **Nore Light.** Generally taken as the dividing line bet. the river and its wide estuary; 47¾ m. below London Bridge.

Nor'folk (nôr'fŭk; *in U.S.,* also -fôk). **1** Name of counties in two states of the U.S. See *Tables* at MASSACHUSETTS and VIRGINIA.
2 Residential town, N Litchfield co., NW Connecticut, on Massachusetts border; pop. 1827; incorp. 1758.
3 Town, Norfolk co., E Massachusetts, 21 m. SW of Boston; pop. 3471; trade center in agricultural section.
4 City, Madison co., NE Nebraska, 54 m. NW of Fremont; pop. 13,111; livestock, grain, poultry.
5 Commercial and industrial seaport city and port of entry, SE Virginia, in Norfolk co. but politically independent, on Elizabeth river just S of Hampton Roads; 28 sq. m.; pop. 305,872; with Newport News and Portsmouth, comprises Port of Hampton Roads; ships esp. tobacco, coal, petroleum, grain; excellent natural harbor; extensive shipbuilding yards, automobile assembly plants, packing plants; manufactures fertilizer, cement, foundry

products, peanut and cottonseed oil. U.S. Naval Base and Air Station, U.S. Marine Hospital, and a unit of the U.S. Public Health Service. Settled c. 1688; burned by local patriots to prevent capture by British in Revolution, later rebuilt; incorp. as town 1805, as city 1845; captured and held by Union forces in Civil War. See HAMPTON ROADS.
6 County, Ontario, Canada. See *Table* at ONTARIO.
7 Maritime county, E England; 2055 sq. m.; pop. (1951) 546,550; ⊗ Norwich; other towns are Great Yarmouth, King's Lynn, East Dereham; rivers Ouse, Bure, Yare, Waveney, Nene; fishing, shipping, agriculture.
Norfolk Broads. See the BROADS.
Norfolk Island. Island in S Pacific Ocean, midway bet. New Caledonia and N New Zealand, and 930 m. ENE of Sydney, Australia; 13 sq. m.; pop. ab. 1000; administratively attached to Australia; site of the Pitcairn Islanders' second home. Discovered by Capt. Cook 1774 and used as a British penal colony 1788–1856.
Norge. See NORWAY.
Noric Alps; *Ger.* **Norische Alpen.** See *Table* at ALPS.
Nor′i·cum (nŏr′ĭ·kŭm). Ancient country and Roman province S of Danube river, comprising the modern Lower and Upper Austria, the greater part of Carinthia, Styria, and Salzburg, and a small part of Bavaria; to the N across the Danube was Germania, on the E Pannonia, on the S Pannonia and Italy, and on the W Raetia and Vindelicia. A mountainous country (E Alps) with rich iron mines worked by the Romans. The Celtic inhabitants were conquered by Augustus.
No·ri·ku·ra (nō·rĕ·kŏō·rä). Mountain peak 10,400 ft., Gifu prefecture, W cen. Honshu, Japan.
Nor′mal (nôr′măl). **1** Village, Madison co., N Alabama, 4 m. N of Huntsville; pop. (est.) 1250; Alabama Agricultural and Mechanical College (1873; coed.).
2 Town, McLean co., cen. Illinois, 5 m. N of Bloomington; pop. 13,357; in fruit and nursery garden section. Illinois State Normal University (1857; coed.), oldest state normal institution in the Mississippi valley.
Nor′man (nôr′măn). **1** County in Minnesota. See *Table* at MINNESOTA.
2 City, ⊗ of Cleveland co., cen. Oklahoma, 18 m. S of Oklahoma City; pop. 33,412; agriculture; petroleum, cottonseed oil. University of Oklahoma (1892; coed.).
3 River 190 m. long, N Queensland, Australia; flows NW into Gulf of Carpentaria.
4 See FORT NORMAN.
5 Small island, British Virgin Is., West Indies, S of Tortola I.
Norman, Cape. Cape, N tip of Newfoundland, at NE entrance to the Strait of Belle Isle.
Nor′man·by (nôr′măn·bĭ). One of the D'Entrecasteaux Is. off SE point of Papua, New Guinea, 3 m. SE of Fergusson I.; ab. 43 m. long and bet. 7 and 12 m. wide, 4000 sq. m., on 10°S lat.; separated from East Cape of Papua by Goschen Strait. Has central mountain range (highest point 3500 ft.) and a good harbor.
Norman Coast. See MURMAN COAST.
Nor′man·dy (nôr′măn·dĭ); *Fr.* **Nor′man′die′** (nôr′-män′dē′). Historical region of NW France; bounded anciently on W and N by English Channel, NE by Picardy, E by Île-de-France, S by Maine, SW by Brittany; ✳ Rouen; watered by Seine, Orne, and Eure rivers; includes Cotentin Penin.
History: Under Romans, part of Lugdunensis; part of kingdom of Neustria after Frankish invasion; invaded by Northmen (whence its name) in middle of 9th cent.; region given over to conquerors under Rollo, 1st Duke of Normandy, by Charles III of France 911; united with English kingdom after conquest of England 1066 by William, Duke of Normandy; conquered by French under Philip Augustus 1204, by English 1417, and by French 1450; province of France until Revolution. In World War II scene of "Battle of Normandy," beginning June 12 after Allied landings (June 6–12) on five beaches along a 60-mile stretch from E of Caen W to Montebourg and lasting until Allied breakthrough at St.-Lô and Avranches July 31.
Nor′man Isles (nôr′măn īlz′). = CHANNEL ISLANDS.
Nor′man·ton (nôr′măn·tŭn). **1** Town, N Queensland, Australia, on Norman river 23 m. from Gulf of Carpentaria; pop. ab. 1000; gold fields.
2 Urban district, West Riding, Yorkshire, N England; pop. 19,087; important railroad junction.
Nor′man Wells (nôr′măn). Station on right bank of the Mackenzie 50 m. NW of Fort Norman, W Mackenzie dist., Northwest Territories, Canada; oil wells; opp. starting point of Canol pipeline to Skagway.
No·ro′ton (nō·rō′t′n). Subdivision of town of DARIEN, Connecticut.
Noroton Heights. Subdivision of town of DARIEN, Connecticut.
Norr′bot′ten (nôr′bôt′těn). See *Table* at SWEDEN.
Nör′re·sund′by (nûr′ĕ·sŏon′bü). Town, Aalborg co., NE Jutland, Denmark, opp. Aalborg; pop. (1930) 6909.
Nor′ridge (nôr′ĭj). Village, Cook co., NE Illinois, W suburb of Chicago; pop. 14,087.
Nor′ridge·wock (nôr′ĭj·wŏk). Town, Somerset co., W Maine, on Kennebec river 13 m. NW of Waterville; pop. 1634; near site of an Abnaki Indian village, destroyed by whites Aug. 1724.
Nor′ris, Mount (nôr′ĭs). Peak 9900 ft. in Yellowstone National Park, NW Wyoming.
Norris Lake; *earlier name* **Clinch-Pow′ell Reservoir** (klĭnch′pou′ĕl). Lake formed by **Norris Dam,** one of the dams of the Tennessee Valley Authority (*q.v.*). See CLINCH river.
Nor′ris·town (nôr′ĭs·toun). Manufacturing borough, ⊗ of Montgomery co., SE Pennsylvania, on Schuylkill river 17 m. NW of Philadelphia; pop. 38,925.
Norr′kö′ping (nôr′chû′pĭng). Seaport, Östergötland prov., SE Sweden, SW of Stockholm, at mouth of a river (drains Lake Vättern) at head of a long inlet of **Norrköping Bay;** pop. 75,792; hydroelectric power plant; textiles, paper, carpets, sugar; shipbuilding.
Norr′land (nôr′länd). Northern division of Sweden, comprising Gävleborg, Västernorrland, Jämtland, Västerbotten, and Norrbotten; land area 93,858 sq. m.; pop. 1,147,178.
Norte, Cape Raso do. See Cape RASO.
Nor′te de San′tan·der′ (nôr′tā thä sän′tän·děr′). Department of Colombia. See *Table* at COLOMBIA.
North (nôrth). River, New York. See NORTH RIVER.
North, Cape. Cape at N tip of Cape Breton I., on S side of Cabot Strait at entrance to the Gulf of St. Lawrence, SE Canada.
North Adams. City, Berkshire co., NW Massachusetts; pop. 19,905; paper, textiles, shoes, electrical equipment. Massachusetts State Coll. (1894; coed.).
North Africa. A nonpolitical term often used to include the countries of northern Africa: Morocco, Algeria, Tunisia, Libya (Tripolitania and Cyrenaica); used esp. by Rome of her colonies (see Roman AFRICA), and in modern times in World War II during the campaign Nov. 10, 1942 to May 12, 1943 in which the Allies completely overcame all German and Italian forces.
North Albanian Alps; *Serb.* **Pro·kle′ti·je** (prô·klě′tě·yĕ). Mountain range averaging 6500–8500 ft., running generally W to E in N Albania and S Yugoslavia (Montenegro); highest point 8715 ft.
North·al′ler·ton (nôr·thăl′ẽr·t′n; -tŭn). Urban district, ⊗ of North Riding, Yorkshire, N England; pop. 6087; scene of Battle of the Standard Aug. 22, 1138 in which English forces defeated Scottish supporters of Matilda under King David, her uncle.
Nor′tham. **1** (nôr′thăm) Town, SW Western Australia, on Avon river where it becomes the Swan, 47 m. E of Perth; pop. 4816.
2 (nôr′thăm) Urban district, Devonshire, SW England, on the Torridge 47 m. N of Plymouth; pop. 6470.

North America. Continent (3d in size) in Western Hemisphere; ab. 9,385,000 sq. m.; pop. (1950 est.) ab. 216,300,000; generally considered to include island of Greenland in NE. *Boundaries:* On N, Arctic Ocean (Beaufort Sea on NW); large bodies of water in N Canada: Viscount Melville Sound, Foxe Basin, Hudson Bay and Hudson Strait; on NE, Baffin Bay and Davis Strait; most northerly point (on mainland) tip of Boothia Penin. ab. 72°N, most northerly point on islands Cape Morris Jesup, N Greenland, 83°39′N; many large islands in N, belonging to Canada: Baffin, Ellesmere, Victoria, Banks, Southampton, Parry Is. On E, North Atlantic Ocean (chief inlets: Gulf of St. Lawrence, Bay of Fundy, Chesapeake Bay); most easterly point (continental) SE coast of Labrador ab. 55°42′W; islands: Newfoundland, Anticosti, Prince Edward, Cape Breton, Long, Bermuda Is. On SE, Gulf of Mexico and Caribbean Sea; for islands see WEST INDIES. On S, Pacific Ocean (chief inlets: Gulf of Panama, Gulf of California); most southerly point SE Panama 7°15′N. On W, North Pacific Ocean (chief subdivisions: Gulf of Alaska, Bering Sea); most westerly point (continental) Cape Prince of Wales, Alaska, 168°W; most westerly point on islands Attu I. in Aleutian Is. 173°E; separated from Asia by Bering Strait; most important islands: Vancouver, Queen Charlotte Is., islands of SE Alaska, Aleutian Is., Nunivak, and St. Lawrence. *Mountains, etc.:* Greatest mountain ranges along Pacific coast (esp. Rocky Mts.) extending from Alaska into Mexico and Central America; Great Plains E of Rocky Mts. extending from Arctic Ocean to Gulf of Mexico; lowlands in center around Hudson Bay and in Mississippi Valley; highlands in E (Laurentian Highlands and Appalachian Mts.); low coastal plain along Atlantic; high ice-covered plateau in Greenland; highest point Mt. McKinley, Alaska, 20,320 ft.; lowest Badwater in Death Valley, Calif., 280 ft. below sea level. *Rivers:* Yukon (Canada and Alaska), Mackenzie, Saskatchewan and Nelson (Canada), St. Lawrence and Columbia (Canada and U.S.), Mississippi-Missouri system, Colorado (in SW), Penobscot, Connecticut, Hudson, Delaware, Susquehanna, Potomac, James, Cape Fear, Savannah (Atlantic seaboard, U.S.), Apalachicola, Mobile, Pearl, Sabine, Brazos, Colorado (Texas), to Gulf of Mexico; San Joaquin and Sacramento (W coast), Rio Grande (U.S. and Mexico), Pánuco, Balsas, Grijalva (Mexico). *Lakes:* Great Bear, Great Slave, Winnipeg (Canada); Great Lakes (Superior, Huron, Erie, Ontario—in Canada and U.S.) and Michigan (U.S.), Great Salt Lake (U.S.), Nicaragua. *Political divisions:* Dominion of Canada, United States (including Alaska), Mexico, Central America (q.v.) adjoining South America in extreme S, and West Indies off SE coast enclosing Caribbean Sea. Central America, Mexico, and the West Indies are sometimes known as Middle America.

North·amp'ton (nôr·thăm[p]′tŭn; nôrth·hăm[p]′-). **1** Name of counties in three states in the U.S. See *Tables* at NORTH CAROLINA, PENNSYLVANIA, VIRGINIA. **2** City, ⊗ of Hampshire co., W Massachusetts, on Connecticut river 15 m. N of Springfield; pop. 30,058; manufactures hosiery, cutlery, brushes, caskets; home of Calvin Coolidge. Smith Coll. (1871; women). **3** Borough, Northampton co., E Pennsylvania, on Lehigh river 6 m. N of Allentown; pop. 8866; settled c. 1739; manufactures cement and textiles; brewing, quarrying. **4** County borough, ⊗ of Northamptonshire, cen. England, on the Nene 60 m. NNW of London; pop. 92,341, (1951) 104,429; manufactures boots and shoes; has no remains of the castle which was the meeting place of parliaments from the 12th to the 14th cent.; site of battle 1460 in Wars of the Roses at which Henry VI was defeated and captured by Warwick; Eleanor Cross, one of the three remaining crosses that were erected to mark the stages of the funeral procession of Eleanor (d. 1290), queen of Edward I.

North·amp'ton·shire (-shǐr; -shĕr) *or* **Northampton.** County, cen. England; area 914 sq. m.; pop. (1951) 359,550; ⊗ Northampton; includes the Soke of Peterborough (q.v.) in the NE; other towns Kettering, Wellingborough, Naseby; chief industry agriculture.
North Andaman. One of the Andaman Is. (q.v.).
North Andover. Industrial town, Essex co., NE Massachusetts, 10 m. ENE of Lowell; pop. 10,908; textiles.
North Anna. River, E cen. Virginia; flows SE to unite with South Anna river in E Hanover co. and form Pamunkey river; just above the junction occurred May 23–25, 1864 battle in which the Federals under Grant failed to dislodge Lee's Confederates who were covering Richmond to the S.
North A·pol'lo (à·pŏl′ō). Borough, Armstrong co., W Pennsylvania, 26 m. ENE of Pittsburgh; pop. 1741.
North Arlington. Borough, Bergen co., NE New Jersey, on Passaic river 4 m. N of Newark; pop. 17,477.
North Atlanta. Village, De Kalb co., NW cen. Georgia; N suburb of Atlanta; pop. 12,661.
North Atlantic Ocean. See ATLANTIC OCEAN.
North Attleboro. Town, Bristol co., SE Massachusetts; pop. 14,777; jewelry manufacturing.
North Augusta. City, Aiken co., W South Carolina, on Savannah river across from Augusta, Ga.; pop. 10,348.
North Australia. A territory of Australia 1927–31. See NORTHERN TERRITORY.
North Baltimore. Village, Wood co., NW Ohio, 10 m. N of Findlay; pop. 3011; manufactures brick and tile, foundry and machine shop products.
North Bass Island. See BASS ISLAND.
North Bat'tle·ford (băt′′l·fôrd). City, W Saskatchewan, Canada, on North Saskatchewan river 85 m. WNW of Saskatoon; pop. 7473; railroad and industrial center.
North Bay. City, ⊗ of Nipissing dist., SE Ontario, Canada, on NE shore of Lake Nipissing; pop. 17,944; on transcontinental railroad lines and air lines; mining, lumbering, agriculture; normal school, college; resort.
North Belle·ver'non (bĕl·vûr′nŭn). Borough, Westmoreland co., SW Pennsylvania; pop. 3148.
North Bell'more (bĕl′mōr). Urban community (unincorporated), Nassau co., SE New York, on Long I. E of New York; pop. 19,639.
North Bel'mont (bĕl′mŏnt). Urban area, Gaston co., SW North Carolina; pop. 8328.
North Bend. 1 Village, SW Hamilton co., SW Ohio, WSW of Cincinnati; pop. 622; birthplace of Benjamin Harrison, 23d president of U.S. **2** City, Coos co., SW Oregon, on inlet of Pacific Ocean 4 m. N of Marshfield; pop. 7512; settled 1853; fisheries; manufactures lumber, fish fertilizer, wood pulp.
North Ber'gen (bûr′gĕn). Township, Hudson co., NE New Jersey, 6 m. N of Newark; pop. 42,387.
North Ber'wick (bĕr′ĭk). Royal burgh and parish, East Lothian, SE Scotland, on S shore of Firth of Forth ab. 22 m. E of Edinburgh; pop. (1951) 4580; fashionable watering place, fine beach, golf.
North Borneo *or since 1963* **Sa'bah** (sä′bä). Territory of Federation of Malaysia, formerly a British colony, NE part of Borneo, Malay Archipelago; 29,500 sq. m.; pop. (1931) 270,233, (1960) 454,421; ✳ Jesselton. Almost all mountainous with highest ranges parallel with W coast (highest mountain Kinabulu, 13,455 ft., highest on island of Borneo); cut by open river valleys, esp. the Kinabatangan and Labuk in the E; has coast line of 900 m. bordering on South China Sea, Sulu Sea, and Celebes Sea; much indented by bays, esp. on E coast. Fine timber; chief exports agricultural and jungle products; rubber has increased greatly in importance. Its inhabitants are representatives of many of the Bornean peoples—Malays, Dusuns, Bajaus, Muruts. Chief towns Sandakan, Jesselton, Kudat, Beaufort.
History: English attempts at settlement in 17th and 18th cents. unsuccessful; first concessions in North Borneo granted to Sir James Brooke (see SARAWAK)

1841; new concessions granted by Sultans of Brunei and Sulu to British North Borneo Co., chartered in 1881; territory proclaimed British protectorate 1888 but continued to be administered by company until World War II. Known officially as **British North Borneo** 1886–92. Occupied by Japanese Dec. 17, 1941; recovered in part by British in last months of war. Became a colony of British Empire in 1946 and a territory of Federation of Malaysia in 1963.

North′bor′ough (nôrth′bŭr′ô). Town, Worcester co., cen. Massachusetts, 9 m. ENE of Worcester; pop. 6687.

North Brabant; *Du.* **Noord′bra·bant′** (nōrt′brä·bänt′). Province, S Netherlands; 1965 sq. m.; pop. (1939) 1,033,130; ✳ 's Hertogenbosch; sheep and cattle raising. See BRABANT.

North Brad′dock (brăd′ŭk). Borough, Allegheny co., SW Pennsylvania, 9 m. E of Pittsburgh; pop. 13,204; coal and steel industries.

North Bran′ford Town, New Haven co., S cen. Connecticut; pop. 6771.

North′bridge (nôrth′brĭj). Town, Worcester co., cen. Massachusetts; pop. 10,800; textiles, paper.

North Britain. Scotland—sometimes so called.

North Broms′grove (brŏmz′grōv). Urban district, Worcestershire, W cen. England; pop. 27,924.

North′brook (nôrth′brŏŏk). Village, Cook co., NE Illinois, NW suburb of Chicago; pop. 11,635.

North Brookfield. Town, Worcester co., cen. Massachusetts, 14 m. W of Worcester; pop. 3616.

North Caldwell. Borough, Essex co., NE New Jersey, 6 m. SW of Paterson; pop. 4163.

North Canaan. Town, NW Litchfield co., NW Connecticut, on Massachusetts border; pop. 2836; marble.

North Ca·na′di·an (kȧ·nā′dĭ·ȧn). River 760 m. long, NW and cen. Oklahoma; rises in Union co. NE corner of New Mexico; flows E and SE through Oklahoma City and empties into Canadian river near Eufaula in S McIntosh co., E Oklahoma.

North Can′ton (kăn′t'n; -tŭn). Village, Stark co., NE Ohio, N of Canton; pop. 7727; cheese, suction sweepers.

North Cape. 1 See HORN.

2 Northwest point of New Ireland, Bismarck Archipelago; Kavieng is on it.

3 Cape on N extremity of North I., New Zealand.

4 Cape on N Mageröy I. in Arctic Ocean off N coast of Norway; northernmost point of Europe, lat. 71°10′20″N; Cape Nordkyn, 71°8′N, 45 m. to the E, is northernmost point of European mainland.

North Car′o·li′na (kăr′ô·lī′nȧ). A south Atlantic state of U.S.A., an original state of the Union, the 12th to ratify the Federal Constitution (Nov. 21, 1789); bounded on N by Virginia, on E and SE by the Atlantic Ocean, on S by South Carolina and Georgia, and on W and NW by Tennessee; 28th state in area, 52,712 sq. m. (land area 49,097 sq. m.); 12th state in population, 4,556,155; ✳ Raleigh. See *Table of States* at UNITED STATES. Divided into the following 100 counties (for pronunciation of their names, see their individual entries):

NAME	LOCATION	AREA[1]	POP.[1]	CO. SEAT
Alamance	N cen.	434	85,674	Graham
Alexander	W cen.	255	15,625	Taylorsville
Alleghany	N	230	7,734	Sparta
Anson	S	533	24,962	Wadesboro
Ashe	NW	427	19,768	Jefferson
Avery	W	247	12,009	Newland
Beaufort	E; coastal	831	36,014	Washington
Bertie	NE	693	24,350	Windsor
Bladen	S	879	28,881	Elizabethtown
Brunswick[2]	S; coastal	873	20,278	Southport
Buncombe[3]	W	646	130,074	Asheville
Burke	W	506	52,701	Morganton
Cabarrus	S cen.	360	68,137	Concord
Caldwell	W	476	49,552	Lenoir
Camden	NE	239	5,598	Camden
Carteret[4,5]	SE; coastal	532	30,940	Beaufort
Caswell	N	435	19,912	Yanceyville
Catawba	W cen.	406	73,191	Newton
Chatham	cen.	707	26,785	Pittsboro

NAME	LOCATION	AREA[1]	POP.[1]	CO. SEAT
Cherokee	W tip	454	16,335	Murphy
Chowan	NE	180	11,729	Edenton
Clay	SW	213	5,526	Hayesville
Cleveland	SW	466	66,048	Shelby
Columbus	S	939	48,973	Whiteville
Craven	SE	725	58,773	New Bern
Cumberland	S cen.	661	148,418	Fayetteville
Currituck	NE corner; coastal	273	6,601	Currituck
Dare[5,6]	E; coastal	388	5,935	Manteo
Davidson	cen.	548	79,493	Lexington
Davie	cen.	264	16,728	Mocksville
Duplin	SE	822	40,270	Kenansville
Durham	NE cen.	299	111,995	Durham
Edgecombe	NE	511	54,226	Tarboro
Forsyth	N cen.	424	189,428	Winston-Salem
Franklin	N	494	28,755	Louisburg
Gaston	SW	358	127,074	Gastonia
Gates	NE	343	9,254	Gatesville
Graham	W	289	6,432	Robbinsville
Granville	N	543	33,110	Oxford
Greene	E	269	16,741	Snow Hill
Guilford	N cen.	651	246,520	Greensboro
Halifax	NE	722	58,956	Halifax
Harnett	cen.	606	48,236	Lillington
Haywood[7]	W	543	39,711	Waynesville
Henderson	SW	382	36,163	Hendersonville
Hertford	NE	356	22,718	Winton
Hoke	S	414	16,356	Raeford
Hyde[5]	E; coastal	634	5,765	Swan Quarter
Iredell	cen.	591	62,526	Statesville
Jackson[7]	SW	496	17,780	Sylva
Johnston	E	795	62,936	Smithfield
Jones	SE	467	11,005	Trenton
Lee	cen.	255	26,561	Sanford
Lenoir	E	391	55,276	Kinston
Lincoln	SW cen.	308	28,814	Lincolnton
McDowell	W	442	26,742	Marion
Macon	SW	517	14,935	Franklin
Madison	W	456	17,217	Marshall
Martin	E	481	27,139	Williamston
Mecklenburg	S	542	272,111	Charlotte
Mitchell	W	220	13,906	Bakersville
Montgomery	S cen.	488	18,408	Troy
Moore	cen.	672	36,733	Carthage
Nash	NE	552	61,002	Nashville
New Hanover	SE; coastal	194	71,742	Wilmington
Northampton	NE	540	26,811	Jackson
Onslow	SE; coastal	756	82,706	Jacksonville
Orange	N	398	42,970	Hillsboro
Pamlico	E; coastal	341	9,850	Bayboro
Pasquotank	NE	229	25,630	Elizabeth City
Pender	SE; coastal	857	18,508	Burgaw
Perquimans	NE	261	9,178	Hertford
Person	N	400	26,394	Roxboro
Pitt	E	656	69,942	Greenville
Polk	SW	234	11,395	Columbus
Randolph	cen.	801	61,497	Asheboro
Richmond	S	477	39,202	Rockingham
Robeson	S	944	89,102	Lumberton
Rockingham	N	572	69,629	Wentworth
Rowan	cen.	517	82,817	Salisbury
Rutherford	SW	566	45,091	Rutherfordton
Sampson	SE	963	48,013	Clinton
Scotland	S	317	25,183	Laurinburg
Stanly	S cen.	399	40,873	Albemarle
Stokes	N	459	22,314	Danbury
Surry	N	537	48,205	Dobson
Swain[7]	W	530	8,387	Bryson City
Transylvania	SW	379	16,372	Brevard
Tyrrell	E	399	4,520	Columbia
Union	S	643	44,670	Monroe
Vance	N	269	32,002	Henderson
Wake	E cen.	866	169,082	Raleigh
Warren	N	445	19,652	Warrenton
Washington	E	336	13,488	Plymouth
Watauga	NW	320	17,529	Boone
Wayne	E	555	82,059	Goldsboro
Wilkes	NW cen.	765	45,269	Wilkesboro
Wilson	E	373	57,716	Wilson
Yadkin	NW cen.	335	22,804	Yadkinville
Yancey	W	311	14,008	Burnsville

[1] Area = land area in sq. m. Pop. from 1960 Census.
[2] Includes Cape Fear, on Smith I. off SE corner.
[3] This county name is source of colloquial common noun *buncombe*.
[4] Includes offshore islands from which it is separated by Core Sound (on E) and Bogue Sound (on S).
[5] Cape Hatteras National Seashore Park comprises most of chain of islands (enclosing Pamlico Sound on ocean side) belonging to Dare, Hyde, and Carteret cos., with Cape Hatteras itself on island SE of and belonging to Dare co.
[6] Kitty Hawk (*q.v.*), scene of first airplane flight in U.S. (1903), on sand barrier NE of and belonging to Dare co.
[7] Great Smoky Mountains National Park occupies most of N and E part of Swain co., N section of Jackson co., and NW section of Haywood co. (as well as adjacent section of Tennessee).

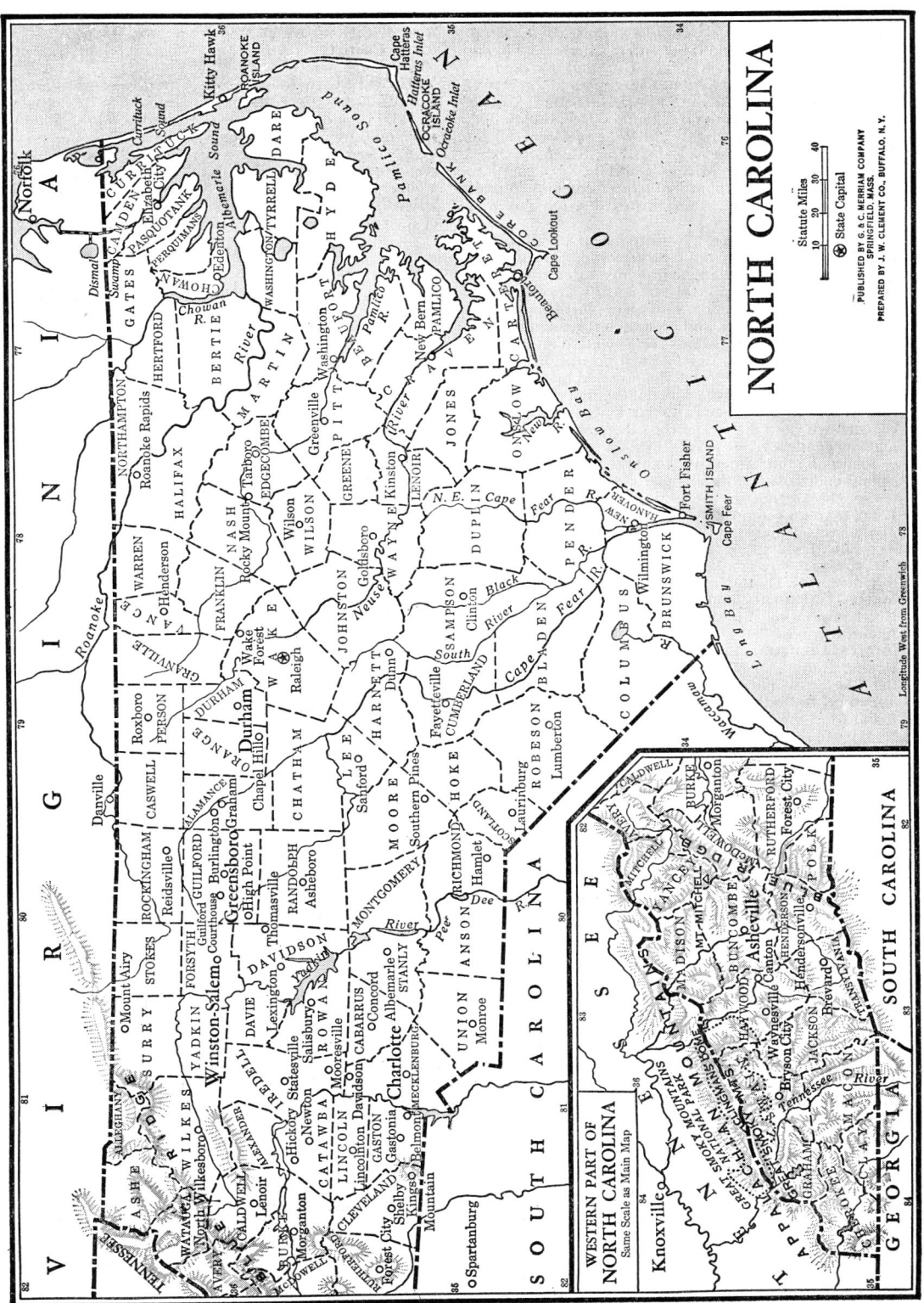

NORTH CAROLINA

Statute Miles

**State Capital

PUBLISHED BY G. & C. MERRIAM COMPANY
SPRINGFIELD, MASS.
PREPARED BY J. W. CLEMENT CO., BUFFALO, N.Y.

WESTERN PART OF
NORTH CAROLINA
Same Scale as Main Map

Nickname: Tarheel State or Old North State, also Turpentine State. *State flower:* Dogwood. *Motto:* To Be Rather Than to Seem. *Chief cities:* Charlotte, Greensboro, Winston-Salem, Raleigh, Durham. *Chief rivers:* Roanoke, entering state from S Virginia and flowing SE across N E corner of state into Albemarle Sound; Yadkin, in cen. area, flowing S to form the Pee Dee. *Mountains:* Ranges of Appalachian Mts. in W. esp. Great Smoky Mts. on Tennessee border, and Blue Ridge to the E. Highest point Mount Mitchell 6684 ft. in Yancey co. *Chief industries:* Agriculture (corn, cotton, tobacco, wheat, peanuts) manufacturing (textiles, tobacco products).

History: Formed a part of Carolina grant given 1663 by King Charles II to eight noblemen of his court (see CAROLINA); became a royal province after the proprietors sold their rights to the crown 1729; at outbreak of American Revolution, a convention of North Carolinians met in Mecklenburg co. and drew up a statement (Mecklenburg Declaration, May 1775) containing phrases closely resembling phrases in the Declaration of Independence (1776); Provincial Congress adopted Apr. 12, 1776 the Halifax resolution that "the delegates for this colony in the Continental Congress be empowered to concur with the delegates of the other colonies in declaring independency"—the first explicit sanction of independence by an American colony; British control of colony ended with Greene's victory at Guilford Courthouse (1781); ratified Federal Constitution Nov. 21, 1789; gave up claim to western lands 1790, now part of Tennessee (cf. State of FRANKLIN); passed ordinance of secession May 20, 1861; secession ordinance declared null and void and slavery abolished Oct. 7, 1865; readmitted to Union July 11, 1868.

North Cat·a·sau′qua (kăt′á·sô′kwȧ). Borough, Northampton co., E Pennsylvania, on Lehigh river N of Allentown, pop. 2805.

North Caucasus. Former extensive region, SE Soviet Russia, Europe, N of the Caucasus Mts. reaching from the Black Sea and Sea of Azov on the W (Krasnodar Territory) to the Astrakhan Region and Dagestan on the E and touching Voronezh and Stalingrad Regions on the N; 110,940 sq. m.; ✻ Rostov; included also 6 autonomous areas on N slopes of the mountains. Its inhabitants comprised many diverse races. Made up largely of earlier Territory of the Don Cossacks, and the Stavropol, Kuban and Terek provs. of Tsarist Russia. Reorganized 1936.

North Central Province. Province, Ceylon; 4009 sq. m.; pop. 97,365; ✻ Anuradhapura; has number of large tanks, or artificial lakes.

North Channel. 1 Strait in NE Lake Huron bet. Manitoulin I. and the Canadian mainland, SE Ontario prov., Canada.

2 Strait of Atlantic Ocean extending bet. NE Ireland and SW Scotland; 14 m. wide at its widest part; connects with Irish Sea on the S.

3 Northern part of entrance to Manila Bay, Phil. Is., bet. Bataan Penin. and Corregidor I.; 3½ m. wide; called Boca Chica by the Spaniards.

North Charleroi. Borough, Washington co., SW Pennsylvania, on Monongahela river 1 m. N of Charleroi; pop. 2259; coal mining.

North Chicago. Industrial city, Lake co., NE corner of Illinois, on Lake Michigan 5 m. S of Waukegan; pop. 20,517; manufactures electrical equipment, chemicals, metal products.

North Chu·sei (chōō·sā); *Jap.* **Chusei Ho·ku** (hô-kōō). Province of Korea. See *Table* at KOREA.

North Clapham. See North and South CLAPHAM.

North College Hill. City, Hamilton co., SW corner of Ohio, 9 m. N of Cincinnati; pop 12,035.

North Conway. Town, Carroll co., E New Hampshire, on Saco river ab. 6 m. N of Conway; pop. 1104; settled 1764; summer and winter resort.

North′cote (nôrth′kŭt; -kōt). City, S Victoria, SE Australia, N suburb of Melbourne; pop. 42,713.

North Country. An occasional name for the northern part of England.

North Da·ko′ta (dȧ·kō′tȧ). A northwestern state of U.S.A., 39th state admitted to Union (1889); bounded on N by Canadian provinces of Saskatchewan and Manitoba, on E by Minnesota, on S by South Dakota, and on W by Montana; 17th state in area, 70,665 sq. m. (land area 70,057 sq. m.); 44th state in population, 632,446; ✻ Bismarck. See *Table of States* at UNITED STATES. Divided into the following 53 counties (for pronunciation of their names, see their individual entries):

NAME	LOCATION	AREA[1]	POP.[1]	CO. SEAT
Adams	SW	990	4,449	Hettinger
Barnes	E	1,486	16,719	Valley City
Benson	N cen.	1,412	9,435	Minnewaukan
Billings	W	1,139	1,513	Medora
Bottineau	N	1,699	11,315	Bottineau
Bowman	SW corner	1,170	4,154	Bowman
Burke	NW	1,121	5,886	Bowbells
Burleigh	S cen.	1,648	34,016	Bismarck
Cass	E	1,749	66,947	Fargo
Cavalier	NE	1,513	10,064	Langdon
Dickey	S	1,144	8,147	Ellendale
Divide	NW corner	1,303	5,566	Crosby
Dunn	W	2,068	6,350	Manning
Eddy	E cen.	643	4,936	New Rockford
Emmons	S	1,546	8,462	Linton
Foster	E cen.	648	5,361	Carrington
Golden Valley	W	1,014	3,100	Beach
Grand Forks	E	1,438	48,677	Grand Forks
Grant	S	1,672	6,248	Carson
Griggs	E	714	5,023	Cooperstown
Hettinger	SW	1,135	6,317	Mott
Kidder	S cen.	1,377	5,386	Steele
La Moure	SE	1,137	8,705	La Moure
Logan	S	1,003	5,369	Napoleon
McHenry	N cen.	1,890	11,099	Towner
McIntosh	S	993	6,702	Ashley
McKenzie	W	2,810	7,296	Watford City
McLean	W cen.	2,287	14,030	Washburn
Mercer	W cen.	1,097	6,805	Stanton
Morton	SW cen.	1,933	20,992	Mandan
Mountrail	NW	1,900	10,077	Stanley
Nelson	E	997	7,034	Lakota
Oliver	W cen.	720	2,610	Center
Pembina	NE corner	1,124	12,946	Cavalier
Pierce	N cen.	1,053	7,394	Rugby
Ramsey	NE	1,214	13,443	Devils Lake
Ransom	SE	863	8,078	Lisbon
Renville	N	901	4,698	Mohall
Richland	SE corner	1,450	18,824	Wahpeton
Rolette	N	913	10,641	Rolla
Sargent	SE	855	6,856	Forman
Sheridan	cen.	995	4,350	McClusky
Sioux	S	1,124	3,662	Fort Yates
Slope	SW	1,226	1,893	Amidon
Stark	SW	1,319	18,451	Dickinson
Steele	E	710	4,719	Finley
Stutsman	SE cen.	2,274	25,137	Jamestown
Towner	N	1,044	5,624	Cando
Traill	E	861	10,583	Hillsboro
Walsh	NE	1,287	17,997	Grafton
Ward	NW cen.	2,048	47,072	Minot
Wells	cen.	1,300	9,237	Fessenden
Williams	NW	2,100	22,051	Williston

[1] Area = land area in sq. m. Pop. from 1960 Census.

Nickname: Flickertail State or Sioux State. *State flower:* Wild prairie rose. *Motto:* Liberty and Union. *Chief cities:* Fargo, Grand Forks, Minot, Bismarck. *Rivers:* Missouri, entering state at upper W border and flowing E, then SE, across S border into South Dakota; Red, forming E boundary. *Highest point:* Black Butte 3468 ft. in Slope co. *Chief industries:* Agriculture (chiefly wheat), cattle raising.

History: See DAKOTA TERRITORY; N part of Dakota Territory (organized 1861); separated from South Dakota 1889; adopted constitution and admitted to Union as state Nov. 2, 1889.

North Devon. = DEVON ISLAND.

North Dome (dōm). **1** Peak 8657 ft. in Sierra Nevada, E Fresno co., C cen. California.

2 Peak 3593 ft. in the Catskill Mts., Greene co., SE New York.

North Downs (dounz). Range of low hills extending

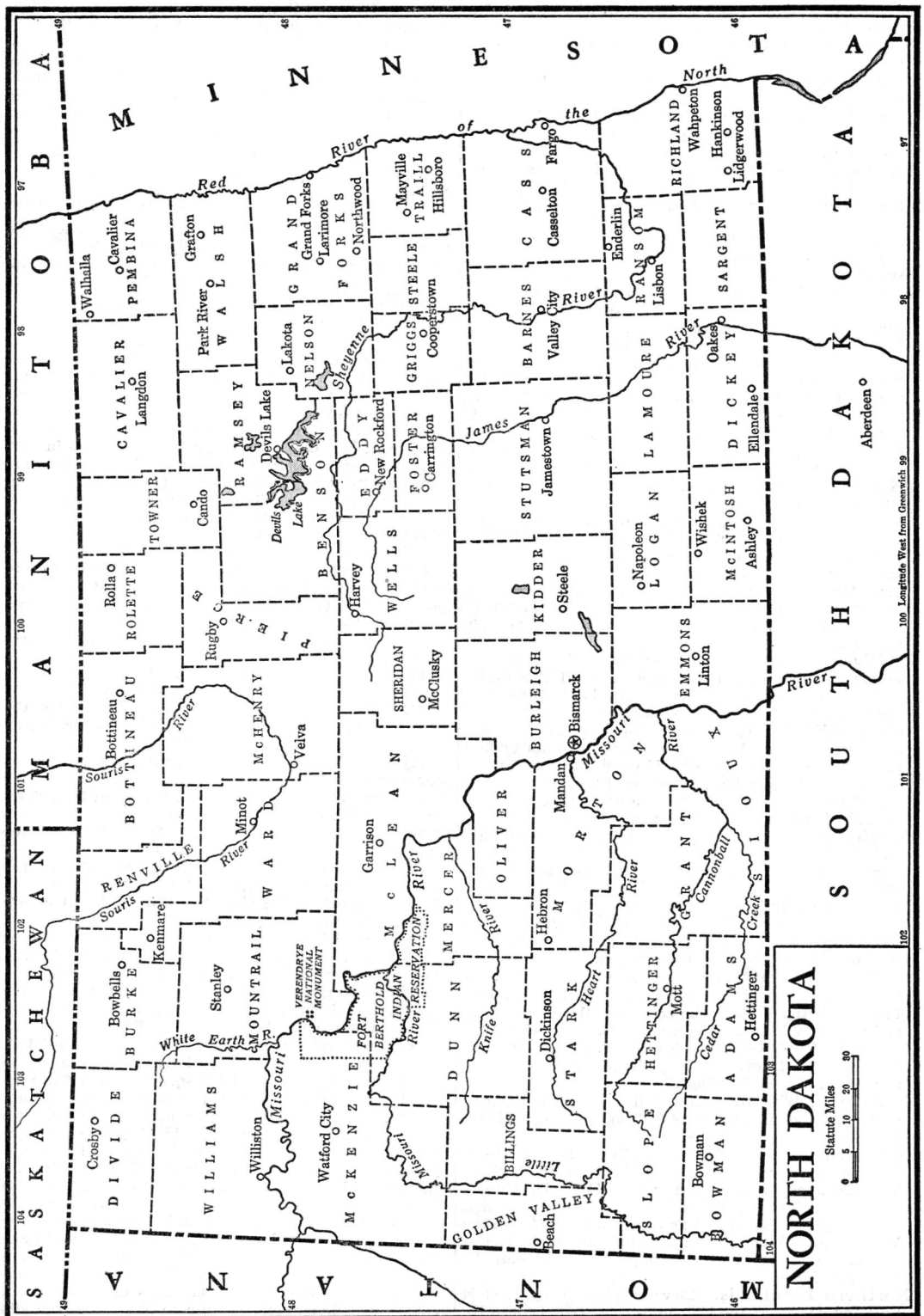

NORTH DAKOTA

Statute Miles

from W to E across S cen. England; highest point Leith Hill 965 ft.

North East. 1 Town, Cecil co., NE Maryland; pop. 1628.

2 Borough, Erie co., NW Pennsylvania, on Lake Erie 16 m. ENE of Erie; pop. 4217; resort.

North East Cape Fear River (fẽr). River ab. 100 m. long, SE North Carolina; rises in Sampson co., flows E and S into Cape Fear river near its mouth.

North–Eastern Provinces. Manchuria—comprising formerly the three NE provinces of China: Heilungkiang, Kirin, and Liaoning; redivided Sept. 1945 into nine provinces.

North East Land; *Norw.* **Nord′ost′ Land′et** (nōr′-ôst′ län′ĕ; nōōr′-). An island of Spitsbergen (*q.v.*), NE of West Spitsbergen, Svalbard; 6400 sq. m.; ice cap.

North–East New Guinea. Northeast part of mainland of New Guinea, constituting the greater part of the Australian trust territory, the Territory of New Guinea (*q.v.*); see also BISMARCK ARCHIPELAGO; 69,700 sq. m.; pop. ab. 230,500 (recent est. 550,000). Bounded on N by Pacific Ocean, on NE by Bismarck Sea, on E by Vitiaz Strait and Solomon Sea, on S by Papua, and on W (141°E long.) by Neth. New Guinea. Comprises four administrative districts: Aitape, Madang, Morobe, and Sepik. Entire cen. region very mountainous with many peaks 9000 to 15,000 ft.; highest 15,400 ft.; much of it unexplored and unknown. Largest river the Sepik in NW; others are the Ramu and Markham. In Bulolo Valley in SE are rich gold fields (see MOROBE). Separated on E from Long I. and Umboi I. and New Britain by Vitiaz Strait and on E coast marked by Huon Penin. and Huon Gulf. Along the coast are several good harbors: Morobe, Salamaua, Saidor, Madang, Wewak, and Aitape; Lae on Huon Gulf is chief town and since 1941 capital of the Territory of New Guinea. See *Map* at NEW GUINEA.

History: First visited in early part of 16th cent. by Portuguese and Spanish navigators and in 17th cent. by Dutch sailors; no part definitely claimed until 1884 when German protectorate was established over NE mainland and islands to NE (Bismarck Archipelago); this possession seized 1914 by Australians and included in mandate granted 1920. In World War II coastal regions and islands seized by Japanese Jan.–Mar. 1942; gradually regained 1943–44 after severe fighting at Buna, Gona, Lae, on Huon Penin., and at Madang and Aitape.

Northeast Passage. A passage by sea bet. the Atlantic and Pacific Oceans along N coast of Europe and Asia; first traversed by Nordenskjöld 1878–79. See ARCTIC REGIONS.

North Emporia. See EMPORIA, Virginia.

Northern. District, N British Honduras; 2180 sq. m.; pop. (1943 est.) 16,118; ✶ Corozal.

Northern Caucasia. = CISCAUCASIA.

Northern Cir·cars′ (sẽr·kärz′; sûr′kärz). A historic name formerly used for the region now in NE Andhra Pradesh, E India, along the coast bet. the Kistna river and Orissa; ✶ Ellore; ceded to Great Britain 1766.

Northern Cook Islands. See MANIHIKI ISLANDS.

Northern District. Former district of N Palestine; now Haifa dist. and Galilee dist.

Northern Division. Former division of N Bombay prov., W Indian Union; 14,068 sq. m.; pop. (1941) 5,276,593.

Northern Dvi·na′ (dvē·nä′); *Russ.* **Se′ver·na·ya Dvi·na′** (syä′vyĭr·nȧ·yȧ dvyĭ·nȧ′). River ab. 1100 m. long including longest tributary, in N Soviet Russia, Europe, chief river of White Sea basin; the river proper, formed by Sukhona and Yug rivers, flows NW into the White Sea at Arkhangelsk; navigable 465 m. to Kotlas 3 m. above confluence with Vychegda; tributaries are the Vaga and Pinega.

Northern Highlands. Elevated plateau region of N Scotland, N part of the Highlands (see SCOTLAND) in In-

verness, Ross and Cromarty, and Sutherland cos.; highest points Ben Dearg 3547 ft. and Ben More 3273 ft.

Northern Ireland. Division of the United Kingdom of Great Britain and Northern Ireland, occupying NE section of the island of Ireland; 5238 sq. m.; pop. (1937) 1,279,745, (1951) 1,370,709; ✶ Belfast; divided into the following six counties (for pronunciation of their names, see their individual entries):

NAME[1]	LOCATION	AREA[2]	POP.[2]	CO. SEAT
Antrim	NE	1,122	674,769[3]	Belfast
Armagh	S	489	114,226	Armagh
Down	SE	952	241,105	Downpatrick
Fermanagh	SW	653	53,040	Enniskillen
Londonderry	NW	804	155,520[4]	Londonderry
Tyrone	W cen.	1,218	132,049	Omagh

[1] In Irish idiom, *county* precedes the name, as in *county Antrim, county Down.*
[2] Area in sq. m. Pop. from 1951 Census.
[3] Includes Belfast county borough (pop. 443,670).
[4] Includes Londonderry county borough (pop. 50,099).

Highland areas are in cos. Londonderry (Sperrin Mts.) and Tyrone; chief rivers Foyle on W boundary and the Upper Bann flowing into Lough Neagh and the Lower Bann, outlet of Lough Neagh (in E cen. part, largest lake in British Isles); other loughs are Foyle (on NW coast), Belfast (including harbor of Belfast) in E, Lough Strangford in E, and Lower and Upper Loughs Erne in SW. Coast borders on North Channel and Irish Sea. See *Map* at IRELAND. Chief industries agriculture, textile manufacturing, and shipbuilding; aircraft, furniture, rope, clothing also manufactured. Chief cities Belfast, Londonderry, Newry, Armagh, Enniskillen.

History: See ULSTER; accepted provisions of Government of Ireland Act 1920 which offered Home Rule to both northern and southern Ireland (see IRELAND); after long dispute, existing boundary with Irish Free State accepted 1925; has consistently opposed union with rest of Ireland and remains part of United Kingdom (see GREAT BRITAIN).

Northern Kingdom. See ISRAEL, 1.

Northern Land. See SEVERNAYA ZEMLYA.

Northern Neck. Region in N colonial Virginia bet. the Rappahannock and Potomac rivers; a part of the Fairfax Proprietary estates 1649–1785.

Northern Nigeria. = NORTHERN REGION, Nigeria.

Northern Penner. See PENNER.

Northern Province. 1 Province, N Sudan; 184,200 sq. m.; pop. 873,059; ✶ Ed Damer.

2 Province, NE Kenya colony, E Africa, including the frontiers of Ethiopia and Somalia; ✶ Isiolo.

3 Province, NE Tanganyika Territory, in E African rift valley; ab. 32,000 sq. m.; pop. 347,761; ✶ Arusha.

4 Former province, NE Uganda, E Africa; 29,121 sq. m.; pop. 533,010; included kingdom of Bunyoro.

5 Province, N Ceylon, on Bay of Bengal and Palk Strait; 3429 sq. m.; pop. 398,874; ✶ Jaffna; includes Jaffna Penin., Mannar I., and other islands off NW coast.

Northern Region. 1 *formerly* **Northern Provinces.** Northern division of Nigeria. See *Table* at NIGERIA.

2 Region, N Ghana. See NORTHERN TERRITORIES.

Northern Rhodesia *or since 1964* **Zam′bi·a** (zăm′bĭ·ȧ). Former British territory, since 1964 an independent republic, S cen. Africa; 290,320 sq. m.; pop. (1940 est.) 1,381,829; ✶ Lusaka. Bounded on N by Congo and Tanganyika, on E by Malawi, on SE by Mozambique, on S by Southern Rhodesia and Caprivi Concession, South-West Africa, and on W by Angola. Divided into nine provinces. Consists of tableland (3000 to 4500 ft.) through which flow three main streams, Zambezi (also forming boundary with S. Rhodesia), Kafue, and Luangwa. Victoria Falls (*q.v.*) is in the Zambezi near Livingstone in SW; Lake Bangweulu is in N and Lake Mweru on Congo boundary in N; S end of Lake Tanganyika touches N boundary. Chief crops maize, tobacco, coffee, wheat; valuable mines of copper, zinc, cobalt, vanadium, gold, and silver. Has extensive radio

and airplane communication systems. Chief towns Lusaka, Broken Hill, Livingstone, Ndola, and Fort Jameson. Part of region (see RHODESIA) claimed by Cecil Rhodes for Great Britain; administered by British South Africa Co. 1889–1923; protectorate proclaimed by British 1900 over Barotseland (*q.v.*); became crown colony 1923; became independent republic of Zambia 1964.

Northern Shan States (shän; shăn). Northern division of Federated Shan States, E cen. Burma; 21,400 sq. m.; pop. 636,107; chief town Lashio in North Hsenwi. Comprises 6 states; most important are North and South Hsenwi, Hsipaw, and Monglon.

Northern Sporades. See SPORADES.

Northern Territories. Former British protectorate N of Ashanti colony, Gold Coast, W Africa; 30,486 sq. m.; pop. 717,275; with N section of Togoland mandate, 41,063 sq. m., pop. 885,417; constitutes (since 1957) the **Northern Region** of Ghana; ✱ Tamale. Plateau region in W part, plain traversed by the Volta in cen. and E parts; chief industries agriculture and raising of livestock. Chief towns Tamale, Wa, Salaga, Bawku. Organized as a protectorate 1897; attached to Gold Coast 1901.

Northern Territory. 1 See TERRITOIRE DU NORD.

2 Territory, N part of Commonwealth of Australia; 523,620 sq. m.; pop. (1933) 4850, (1963 est.) 29,424, including aborigines ab. 48,100; ✱ Darwin. Bounded on S by 26th parallel of S lat., on W and E respectively by 129th and 138th meridians E long., and on N by Timor and Arafura Seas and Gulf of Carpentaria. Greater part of interior is tableland rising gradually to 1700 ft.; excellent grazing land in N but sandy in S; Macdonnell Ranges in S with highest point Mt. Ziel 4955 ft., Arunta Desert in SE, and region of Arnhem Land in N. Chief rivers Victoria, Daly, and Roper. Adjacent islands Bathurst, Melville, and Groote Eylandt. Alice Springs is chief town in S; other localities Birdum, Pine Creek, Katherine, and Daly Waters. Region at first a part of New South Wales; annexed 1863 to South Australia and entered Commonwealth 1901 as part of South Australia; transferred to Commonwealth 1907; divided 1927 into North Australia and Central Australia but by act of 1931 original Northern Territory re-established.

North Esk. 1 River ab. 40 m. long, NE Tasmania, Australia; flows E to join South Esk at Launceston to form the Tamar.

2 Small river in E cen. Scotland, N of the South Esk; flows SE into North Sea near Montrose.

3 See ESK, Midlothian co., SE Scotland.

North'field (nôrth'fēld). **1** Town, Franklin co., NW Massachusetts, on Connecticut river 10 m. NE of Greenfield; pop. 2320; site of Northfield Seminary, a school for girls, estab. 1879 by Dwight L. Moody, a native of the town, who also established 1881 Mount Hermon School, a school for boys, in the neighboring town of Gill.

2 Town, Rice co., S Minnesota, 13 m. N of Faribault; pop. 8707; dairy products, flour; St. Olaf Coll. (1874; coed.; Lutheran); Carleton Coll. (1866; coed.; Congregational).

3 Town, Merrimack co., S cen. New Hampshire, 13 m. N of Concord; pop. 1784. See TILTON.

4 City, Atlantic co., SE New Jersey, 6 m. W of Atlantic City; pop. 5849.

5 Village in Northfield town (pop. 4511), Washington co., N cen. Vermont, 10 m. S of Montpelier; pop. 2159; black-slate and granite works; manufactures flour, lumber, hosiery, woolens; Norwich Univ. (1819; men).

North'fleet (nôrth'flēt). Urban district, Kent, SE England, on the Thames 20 m. E of London; pop. 18,803; docks; makes brick and cement.

North Fond du Lac. Village, Fond du Lac co., E Wisconsin, on Lake Winnebago; pop. 2549.

North Foreland. See FORELAND.

North Fox Island. See FOX ISLANDS, Lake Michigan.

North Fremantle. See FREMANTLE, Australia.

North Frisian Islands. See FRISIAN ISLANDS.

North Gam·bo'a (găm·bō'ȧ; *Span.* găm·bō'ä). Town, Balboa dist., Canal Zone, at SE corner of Gatun Lake; pop. (including Gamboa) 3489.

North Gros've·nor Dale (grōv'nēr). Subdivision of town of THOMPSON, Connecticut; pop. 1874.

North Hale'don (hāl'dŭn). Borough, Passaic co., N New Jersey, 4 m. N of Paterson; pop. 6026.

North Haven. 1 Island in entrance to Penobscot Bay, off S cen. Maine coast.

2 Suburban residential town, cen. New Haven co., S Connecticut, on Quinnipiac river; pop. 15,935.

North Head. 1 Promontory, SW Washington, N side of mouth of Columbia river near Cape Disappointment.

2 Promontory on N side of entrance to Port Jackson, the harbor of Sydney, Australia.

North Hei·an (hā·än); *Jap.* **Heian Ho·ku** (hŏ·kōō). Province of Korea. See *Table* at KOREA.

North He'ro (hēr'ō). Town, ⊗ of Grand Isle co., NW corner of Vermont, on **North Hero Island** in Lake Champlain 10 m. W of St. Albans; pop. 328.

North High'lands (hī'lăndz). Urban area, Sacramento co., N cen. California, NE of Sacramento; pop. 21,271.

North Hilo. District, Hawaii co., Hawaii, NE Hawaii I.; pop. 2493; chief village Laupahoehoe.

North Holland; *Du.* **Noord'hol'land** (nōrt'hôl'änt). Province, W Netherlands; 1163 sq. m.; pop. (1939) 1,690,965; ✱ Haarlem; dairy farming.

North Holland Canal. Canal 46 m. long extending N from Amsterdam, Netherlands, through North Holland prov. to Den Helder; built 1819–25.

North Hsenwi. State in Northern Shan States, Burma; 6422 sq. m.; pop. 243,499; ✱ Hsenwi; chief town Lashio.

North Hsingan. Former province (1932–45), NW Manchukuo; 61,489 sq. m.; ✱ Hulun.

North Illawarra. Town, New South Wales, SE Australia S of Sydney near the coast; pop. (1931) 7782.

North Ingermanland. Northern part of former region of Ingria (*q.v.*); people revolted 1920 against new revolutionary government of Russia and set up short-lived autonomous state, quickly subdued by Soviet forces.

North Island. 1 Island in Atlantic Ocean off Winyah Bay, SE coast of Georgetown co., South Carolina.

2 Northernmost of the three main islands of New Zealand (*q.v.*); 44,280 sq. m.; pop. (1941 est.) 1,077,913. Comprises four provincial districts, Auckland, Hawke's Bay, Taranaki, and Wellington.

North Kanara. See KANARA.

North Kan·kyo (kän·kyō); *Jap.* **Kankyo Ho·ku** (hŏ·kōō). Province of Korea. See *Table* at KOREA.

North Kansas City. Town, Clay co., NW Missouri, N suburb of Kansas City; pop. 5657.

North Karroo. See KARROO.

North Kazakhstan Region. Subdivision of Kazakh S.S.R., Soviet Central Asia, in N part, N of Kokchetav Region and bordering on Kurgan, Tyumen, and Omsk Regions of the R.S.F.S.R.; ✱ Petropavlovsk.

North Kei·sho (kā·shō); *Jap.* **Keisho Ho·ku** (hŏ·kōō). Province of Korea. See *Table* at KOREA.

North Kings'town (kĭngz'toun). Town, Washington co., S Rhode Island, on Narragansett Bay; pop. 18,977; administrative center Wickford village. Formerly part of Kings Towne (Kingstown), incorporated 1674 and divided into North and South Kingstown 1723.

North Kohala. District, Hawaii co., Hawaii, on N point of Hawaii I.; pop. 3386; chief village Kohala.

North Kona. District, Hawaii co., Hawaii, on W side of Hawaii I.; pop. 4451; chief village Kailua.

North Kval'öy' (kväl'ŭ'ü). Island in Arctic Ocean off NW coast of Norway, in Troms co., W of Vannöy I.

North Kyŏngsang. = NORTH KEISHO.

North'lake' (nôrth'lāk'). City, Cook co., NE Illinois, suburb of Chicago; pop. 12,318.

North Land. See SEVERNAYA ZEMLYA.

North Las Vegas. City, Clark co., SE Nevada, N suburb of Las Vegas; pop. 18,422.

North Little Rock; *formerly* **Ar·gen'ta** (är·jĕn'tȧ). Industrial city, Pulaski co., cen. Arkansas, on N bank of Arkansas river opp. Little Rock; pop. 58,032; Shorter Coll. (1884; coed.).

North Loup. River ab. 200 m. long, flowing from cen. Cherry co., N Nebraska, SE to unite with Middle Loup and South Loup rivers and form the Loup river.

North Manchester. Town, Wabash co., N Indiana, 33 m. W of Fort Wayne; pop. 4377; Manchester Coll. (1889; coed.; Church of the Brethren).

North Mankato. City, Nicollet co., S Minnesota, across Minnesota river from Mankato; pop. 5927.

North Ma·roon' Peak (mȧ·rōōn'). Mountain 14,010 ft. in Pitkin co., W cen. Colorado.

North Mer'rick (mĕr'ĭk). Urban area, Nassau co., SE New York, on Long I.; pop. 12,976.

North Miami. City, Dade co., SE Florida; suburb of Miami on Biscayne Bay; pop. 28,708; incorp. 1932.

North Miami Beach. City, Dade co., SE Florida, N of Miami Beach, pop. 21,405.

North Minch (mĭnch). Strait bet. the mainland of NW Scotland and the island of Lewis with Harris in the Outer Hebrides; varies in width bet. 24 and 45 m.

North Muskegon. City, Muskegon co., W Michigan; N suburb of Muskegon; pop. 3855.

North Natoena Islands. See NATOENA ISLANDS.

North Ne·gril' Point (nĕ·grĭl'). Cape on W end of Jamaica, West Indies, N of entrance to Long Bay.

North New Hyde Park. Urban community (unincorporated), Nassau co., SE New York, on Long I. E of New York; pop. 17,929.

North Olm'sted (ŭm'stĕd; -stĭd). City, Cuyahoga co., N Ohio, 13 m. WSW of Cleveland; pop. 16,290; manufactures machine tools.

North Ossetia, *officially* **North Ossetian Autonomous Soviet Socialist Republic.** Autonomous republic, SE Soviet Russia, Europe, on N slopes of cen. Caucasus Mts.; 2393 sq. m.; pop. 328,885, (1941 est.) 345,592; ✻ Dzaudzhikau; a subdivision of the R.S.F.S.R. Bounded on N by Stavropol Territory, on E by Grozny Region, on S by South Ossetia (in Georgia), and on W and NW by Kabardino-Balkarian Republic. Mountainous region watered by unnavigable Terek and tributaries; on its SE border is Mt. Kazbek, one of the highest peaks of the Caucasus; in SW Ossetian Military Road leads over mountains through Mamison Pass to Georgia. One quarter is forest and it has many mineral resources, esp. lead and zinc; chief occupations fruitgrowing, dairying, cattle raising. Only town Dzaudzhikau, but there are several health resorts in the mountains at medicinal springs. Predominant ethnic strain Iranian; chief nationalities Ossetian 84%, Ukrainian 6.8%, Russian 6.6%. Ossets are descended from the Alans, a division of the early Scythian tribes of the region, speak an Indo-Iranian language, and probably have lived in present home since 5th cent. A.D.; converted to Christianity by Queen Tamara in 15th cent.; first came in conflict with Russians 1784 and were conquered 1802. Republic first set up 1924 as part of the Mountain Republic, in 1936 as autonomous republic.

North Pacific Ocean. See PACIFIC OCEAN.

North Pagai. See PAGAI.

North Palisade. See PALISADE, NORTH.

North Park. Elevated tract, Jackson co., N Colorado, bet. Medicine Bow and Park ranges; contains headwaters of the North Platte. See SOUTH PARK.

North Pass. One of the channels at the mouth of the Mississippi river (*q.v.*).

North Pelham. Residential village in Pelham town, Westchester co., SE New York; pop. 5326.

North Plainfield. Borough, Somerset co., N cen. New Jersey, 9 m. N of New Brunswick; pop. 16,993.

North Platte. 1 River 618 m. long in Colorado, Wyoming, Nebraska; rises in Jackson co., N Colorado, flows N across Wyoming border into cen. Wyoming, turns E and SE across Nebraska border through W cen. Nebraska to unite with South Platte river in Lincoln co., SW cen. Nebraska, and form the Platte river.
2 City, ⊗ of Lincoln co., Nebraska, at confluence of North Platte and South Platte rivers; pop. 17,184.

North Point. 1 Point on E coast of Alpena co., NE Michigan, at N entrance to Thunder Bay.
2 Cape at N tip of W end of Prince Edward I., SE Canada, extending into the Gulf of St. Lawrence.

North Polar Regions. See POLAR REGIONS.

North Pole. The N extremity of the earth's axis, at 90°N lat. and the N center from which start all meridians of longitude; the point from which the only direction is S. The area around it (North Polar Regions: see POLAR REGIONS) is entirely water (Arctic Ocean), usually ice-covered. Cf. MAGNETIC POLE.

North'port (nôrth'pōrt). **1** City, Tuscaloosa co., W cen. Alabama, 3 m. N of Tuscaloosa; pop. 5245.
2 Village in town of Huntington, Suffolk co., SE New York, on N coast of Long I.; pop. 5972; center of shipbuilding and allied industries in 19th cent.

North Providence. Town, Providence co., N Rhode Island; NW suburb of Providence; pop. 18,220; administrative center Centerdale village; textiles.

North Read'ing (rĕd'ĭng). Town, Middlesex co., NE Massachusetts, 13 m. ESE of Lowell; pop. 8331.

North Rhine–Westphalia, *Ger.* **Nord'rhein'–West'fa'len** (nôrt'rīn'vĕst'fä'lĕn). State of the German Federal Republic, in W Germany; formed 1946 by union of former Westphalia province, Lippe state, and N part of Rhine province; 13,508 sq. m.; pop. 15,193,000; ✻ Düsseldorf.

North Rich'land Hills (rĭch'lănd). Town, Tarrant co., N Texas, NE of Fort Worth; pop. 8662.

North Ridge'ville (rij'vĭl). Village, Lorain co., N Ohio, ab. 5 m. NE of Elyria; pop. 825.

North Rid'ing (rīd'ĭng). See YORKSHIRE.

North River. Estuary of Hudson river bet. New York and New Jersey; flows into Upper New York Bay; crossed by bridge (George Washington, at 179th St.).

North River Mountain. Peak 3890 ft. in the Adirondack Mts., Essex co., NE New York.

North Riv'er·side' (rĭv'ĕr·sīd'). Village, Cook co., NE Illinois, W suburb of Chicago; pop. 7989.

North Ron'ald·say (rŏn'ld·sā) *or* **North Ron'aldshay** (-shā). Northernmost of the Orkney Is. off N coast of Scotland.

North Roy'al·ton (roi'ăl·tŭn; -t'n). Village, Cuyahoga co., N Ohio, 13 m. S of Cleveland; pop. 9290.

North Sacramento. Suburban residential city, Sacramento co., N cen. California, on American river opp. Sacramento; pop. 12,922; incorp. 1924.

North Saint Paul. Village, Ramsey co., E Minnesota, 7 m. NE of St. Paul; pop. 8520.

North Saskatchewan. See SASKATCHEWAN river.

North Scituate. Village, Providence co., N Rhode Island, NW of Cranston; pop. (est.) 500; administrative center of Scituate.

Norths Coast (nôrths). Section of coast of East Antarctica, 67°S, bet. 125°E and 130°E; part of Wilkes Land and Australian claim.

North Sea *or* **German Ocean;** *anc.* **Ma're Germani·cum** (mā'rē [-rĕ] jĕr·măn'ĭ·kŭm). Arm of the Atlantic Ocean ab. 600 m. long and 350 m. wide extending bet. the European continent on the S and E and Great Britain on the W.

North Sea Canal *or* **Amsterdam Ship Canal.** Canal 17 m. long, Netherlands, from Amsterdam to North Sea at IJmuiden; constructed 1865–76; revived significance of Amsterdam as commercial port.

North Shreveport. Urban area, Caddo parish, NW Louisiana, NW of Shreveport; pop. 7701.

North Smithfield. Town, Providence co., N Rhode Island, near Woonsocket; pop. 7632; seat of government Slatersville village.

North Star Mountain. Peak 13,600 ft. in Park and Summit cos., cen. Colorado.

North Sydney. 1 City, E New South Wales, SE Australia; N suburb of Sydney on N side of Port Jackson; pop. 49,749; connected with municipality of Sydney by great bridge completed Mar. 1932.
2 Town, Cape Breton co., E Nova Scotia; on W side of Sydney Harbor 4 m. SW of entrance; pop. 6836; shipping port for Sydney Mines; shipbuilding, fishing.

North Syracuse. Village, Onondaga co., cen. New York, 8 m. NNE of Syracuse; pop. 7412.

North Taranaki Bight. Gulf N of W bulge on W coast of North I., New Zealand.

North Tarryall Peak. See North TARRYALL PEAK.

North Tarrytown. Residential village, Westchester co., SE New York, on Hudson river 26 m. N of New York and adjoining Tarrytown; pop. 8818; forms one community with Tarrytown, Irvington, and Elmsford; manufactures silk and automobiles. Nearby are Sleepy Hollow, made famous by Washington Irving's *Legend of Sleepy Hollow*, and Sleepy Hollow Cemetery.

North Thompson. See THOMPSON river.

North Tiverton. Village, Newport co., SE Rhode Island, SW of Fall River, Mass.; pop. (est.) 2300.

North Tonawanda. Manufacturing city and port of entry, Niagara co., W New York, 10 m. E of Niagara Falls; pop. 34,757; obtains electric power from Niagara Falls. Tonawanda (*q.v.*) is its sister city.

North Truchas Peak. See TRUCHAS PEAK.

North Tyne. See TYNE.

North U′ist (ū′ĭst; ōō′ĭst). Island of the Outer Hebrides, separated by Little Minch from Skye, off NW coast of Scotland; pop. 2349; administratively part of Inverness co.

North·um′ber·land (nôr·thŭm′bẽr·lănd). 1 Name of counties in two states in the U.S. See *Tables* at PENNSYLVANIA and VIRGINIA.
2 Town, Coos co., N New Hampshire, on Connecticut river 18 m. WNW of Berlin; pop. 2586; textile mills.
3 Industrial borough, Northumberland co., E cen. Pennsylvania, on Susquehanna river 28 m. SSE of Williamsport; pop. 4156. Home of Joseph Priestley 1794–1804.
4 County, New Brunswick, Canada. See *Table* at NEW BRUNSWICK.
5 County, Ontario, Canada. See *Table* at ONTARIO.
6 County, N England, on the border of Scotland; 2019 sq. m.; pop. (1951) 798,175; ⊗ Newcastle (upon Tyne); includes Holy I. or Lindisfarne, the Farne Is., and Coquet Isle; important towns Newcastle, Tynemouth, Berwick upon Tweed, Alnwick, Morpeth, Hexham; coal deposits in SE section; chief rivers Tyne, Tweed, Till, Coquet; Tyne river ports noted for shipbuilding yards and for exports of coal.

Northumberland, Cape. Cape on Indian Ocean, SE corner of South Australia, 38°5′S.

Northumberland Islands. Group of islands off E coast of Queensland, Australia, enclosing Broad Sound, S of Mackay.

Northumberland Strait. Channel ab. 180 m. long and 12–30 m. wide bet. Prince Edward I. and the SE Canadian mainland (E New Brunswick and N Nova Scotia).

North·um′bri·a (nôr·thŭm′brĭ·å). Anglo-Saxon kingdom of Britain, bet. the Humber and the Firth of Forth; formed of Deira and Bernicia (*qq.v.*), traditionally, Anglian kingdoms; during early part of 7th cent. A.D., the leading kingdom of the Heptarchy (*q.v.*); converted to Christianity by marriage connection with Kent (*q.v.*), and again, after subjugation by Mercia (*q.v.*), by Celtic missionaries; its ruler, Oswy, called Synod of Whitby in 664 which determined the adherence to Rome of the English Church; S part ruled by Danes from 9th cent. to 954 when first annexed to Wessex (*q.v.*).

North Umpqua. River ab. 85 m. long, SW Oregon; rises in E Douglas co., flows E uniting with South Ump-

qua river ab. 8 m. NW of Roseburg to form Umpqua river.

North Valley Stream. Urban area, Nassau co., SE New York, in cen. Long I.; pop. 17,239.

North Vancouver. Residential city, S Brit. Columbia, Canada, on Burrard Inlet across from Vancouver; pop 15,687; lumbering, shipbuilding.

North Ver′non (vûr′nŭn). City, Jennings co., SE Indiana, 36 m. S of Shelbyville; pop. 4062; railroad center.

North Versailles. Urban township, Allegheny co., SW Pennsylvania, SE of Pittsburgh; pop. 13,583.

North′ville (nôrth′vĭl). City, Oakland and Wayne cos., SE Michigan, 23 m. WNW of Detroit; pop. 3967.

North Wales. Borough, Montgomery co., SE Pennsylvania, 18 m. N of Philadelphia; pop. 3673.

North War′ren. Residential locality, Warren co., NW Pennsylvania, ab. 3 m. N of Warren; pop. 1458.

North Waziristan. See WAZIRISTAN.

Northwest Angle. The part of Lake of the Woods co., N Minnesota, which is on NW shore of Lake of the Woods N of the 49th parallel; ab. 130 sq. m.; belongs to U.S. instead of Canada because of inadequate survey at time of Treaty of 1783; boundary fixed 1908 and 1925.

North West Cape. Point, W Western Australia, at entrance to Exmouth Gulf, 21°50′S lat.

Northwest Islands. Widely scattered island groups N of New Guinea from 100 to 180 m. W of Manus I. in the Admiralty Is., forming a part of Manus dist. of the Territory of New Guinea; Hermit Is. and Ninigo Group are the most important.

North–Western Province. Province, W Ceylon, on Gulf of Mannar; 3016 sq. m.; pop. 546,966; ✱ Kurunegala. Puttalam is an important coast town.

North–Western Provinces. = *North-West Provinces:* see AGRA presidency.

North–West Frontier Province. Former province in NW Brit. India on Afghanistan frontier (Hazara and five trans-Indus districts); 14,263 sq. m.; pop. 3,038,067; ✱ Peshawar; region now part of Pakistan; former agencies and tribal areas (trans-border area) 24,986 sq. m., pop. (1941) 2,377,599. Trans-border area had five political subdivisions, Malakand (Dir, Swat, and Chitral), Khyber, Kurram, North Waziristan, and South Waziristan. Mountainous area beyond the Indus, the country of the Pathans. On its W border are Sulaiman Mts. in S, Safed Koh, and ranges of Hindu Kush; highest peaks Tirich Mir in NW Chitral 25,263 ft., Himalaya peaks in Hazara dist. 10,000–16,700 ft., Sikaram on Afghanistan border in the Safed Koh 15,619 ft., and Takht-i-Sulaiman in the Sulaiman Mts. 11,100 ft. Rivers are W tributaries of the Indus (Kabul, Kurram, Gomal). Important mountain passes are the Khyber, Gomal, and Malakand (*qq.v.*). Has small area under cultivation; chief crops wheat, maize, barley, rice. Chief towns Peshawar, Kohat, Dera Ismail Khan, Abbottabad, Nowshera, and Bannu. For centuries region has been home of the Pathans, Mohammedans of Indo-Iranian stock, who were partially subjected by Moguls (16th–17th cents.) and later (19th cent.) by Sikhs. At end of Second Sikh War trans-Indus districts annexed by British 1849; province created and separated from Punjab 1901 under present name; hill tribes specially turbulent, causing more than 50 punitive expeditions; most serious rebellion 1919–20. Made autonomous province 1937; became part of Pakistan 1947.

Northwest Passage. A passage by sea bet. the Atlantic and Pacific Oceans along the N coast of America, long sought for by navigators; their searches led to discovery of St. Lawrence river by Jacques Cartier 1534–35, of Frobisher Sound by Martin Frobisher 1576, of Hudson Bay by Henry Hudson 1610; during the 19th cent. explorations were carried on by several British naval officers including Sir John Franklin, John Ross, and Sir Robert McClure who discovered the route during his unsuccessful search (1850–54) for Franklin; the first

(1903–06) to navigate the passage was the Norwegian explorer Roald Amundsen. See ARCTIC REGIONS.

North–West Provinces. Former province of Brit. India. See AGRA presidency.

North West Region. Division of Western Australia in NW part, plateau along coast extending S from Indian Ocean to Murchison river.

Northwest Territories. Division of Canada comprising all Arctic islands N of the mainland, the mainland N of 60° bet. Yukon Territory and Hudson Bay, and islands in Hudson, James, and Ungava Bays; land area 1,253,438 sq. m., area including water, 1,304,903 sq. m.; pop. 16,004; ✱ Yellowknife. Divided into three districts, Mackenzie, Keewatin, and Franklin. Bounded on the S by Hudson Strait, Hudson Bay, and the provinces of Manitoba, Saskatchewan, Alberta, and British Columbia. A vast area including many rivers, lakes, and islands, and the extensive Barren Grounds around Hudson Bay. The Mackenzie Mts. on the Yukon Territory border reach 7000–8500 ft., but most of the region is comparatively low. The Mackenzie river and its tributaries and the great lakes drained by them (esp. Great Bear and Great Slave Lakes) fill nearly two thirds of the mainland area; the Coppermine, Back, Dubawnt, and Kazan are other large streams. Some agriculture in the Mackenzie valley, very little forest land, but considerable mineral wealth as yet largely untouched; hunting and fishing chief occupations of Eskimos and Indians. Territory W of Rupert's Land first created 1820 as **North Western Territory;** leased to Hudson's Bay Co. 1821–69; transferred to the Dominion 1869 by acquisition of territorial rights of Hudson's Bay Co.; as **North West Territory** greatly enlarged 1869–82. Since 1882 its lands E of Hudson Bay and those S of 60°W of the bay have been at various times assigned to other provinces.

Northwest Territory. Region around the Great Lakes and bet. the Ohio and Mississippi rivers, comprising what was earlier known as the *Old Northwest*, a territory of ab. 248,000 sq. m. awarded to U.S. by Treaty of Paris 1783. As the first national territory of the U.S. established by Congress July 13, 1787, officially known as "the Territory Northwest of the River Ohio," it included present States of Ohio, Indiana, Illinois, Michigan, Wisconsin, and part of Minnesota (see these entries). Parts claimed by several seaboard States but relinquished 1781–86 except Western Reserve (*q.v.*); government framework outlined by Ordinance of 1787; first settlement at Marietta 1788. Region divided 1800, forming the Indiana Territory (capital Vincennes, later, in 1813, transferred to Corydon), which included Indiana, Illinois, Wisconsin, much of Michigan and part of Minnesota, and reducing the Northwest Territory (capital Chillicothe) to Ohio and parts of Michigan and Minnesota.

North'wich (nôrth'wĭch). Urban district, Cheshire, NW England, 19 m. SSW of Manchester; pop. 17,480; center of England's salt industry.

North Wildwood. City and seaside resort, Cape May co., S New Jersey, on Atlantic Ocean 32 m. SW of Atlantic City; pop. 3598. See WILDWOOD.

North Wilkes'bor'o (wĭlks'bûr'ō). Town, Wilkes co., NW cen. North Carolina, 30 m. NW of Statesville; pop. 4197; poultry market; tannery, furniture factories.

North'wood (nôrth'wŏŏd). **1** Town, ⊗ of Worth co., N Iowa, 20 m. N of Mason City; pop. 1768.
2 City, Grand Forks co., E North Dakota, 29 m. WSW of Grand Forks; pop. 1195.

North York. Borough, York co., S Pennsylvania, 3 m. N of York; pop. 2290.

North Zen·ra (zĕn·rä); *Jap.* **Zenra Ho·ku** (hō·kōō). Province of Korea. See *Table* at KOREA.

Nor'ton (nôr't'n). **1** County in Kansas. See *Table* at KANSAS.
2 City, ⊗ of Norton co., N Kansas, 120 m. NW of Great Bend; pop. 3345.

3 Town, Bristol co., SE Massachusetts, 11 m. SW of Brockton; pop. 6818; Wheaton Coll. (1834; women).
4 City, SW Virginia, 35 m. NW of Bristol; in Wise co. but politically independent; pop. 5013; coal mining.

Norton Peak. Mountain 10,200 ft. in NW Blaine co., S cen. Idaho.

Norton Sound. Large inlet ab. 200 m. long of NE Bering Sea, in W Alaska, bet. Seward Penin. and mouths of the Yukon.

Nor'um·be'ga (nôr'ŭm·bē'gȧ). Name applied by 16th- and 17th-cent. map makers to undefined region along E coast of North America N of Florida.

Nor·ve'gi·a Cape (nôr·vē'jĭ·ȧ). Cape on Princess Martha Coast, Queen Maud Land, Antarctica; 71°15'S lat., 12°W long.

Nor'velt (nôr'vĕlt). Locality, Westmoreland co., SW Pennsylvania, 6 m. SE of Greensburg; pop. 1211; site of Westmoreland Homesteads, an attempt to combine industrial employment with part-time farming and gardening.

Nor'walk (nôr'wôk). **1** River, SW Connecticut; rises in cen. Fairfield co., flows S into Long Island Sound at South Norwalk.
2 City, Los Angeles co., SW California, SE of Los Angeles; pop. 88,739.
3 Industrial city, SW Fairfield co., SW Connecticut, on Long Island Sound; pop. 67,775; watered by Norwalk river; settled 1650, incorp. 1651; town and city of Norwalk (incorp. 1893) consolidated and made coextensive 1913 and expanded to include surrounding towns and municipalities, among them South Norwalk (*q.v.*); manufactures clothing, silks, cigars, paper, hardware, machinery, shoes, woolens, iron foundings, automobile tires, trucks, engines; oyster culture. Burned by British 1779.
4 Industrial and residential city, ⊗ of Huron co., N Ohio, 15 m. S of Sandusky; pop. 12,900; founded 1816; manufactures furniture; steel and iron works.

Nor'way (nôr'wā). **1** *Norw.* **Nor'ge** (nôr'gĕ). Kingdom, NW Europe, occupying W part of the Scandinavian penin.; length ab. 1100 m. from NE to SW, 260 m. at widest part; bounded on the W by the Atlantic Ocean and the North Sea, on the N by the Arctic Ocean, on the NE by U.S.S.R. and Finland, on the E by Sweden, and on the S by Skagerrak; 119,085 sq. m.; pop. (1960) 3,591,234, (1963 est.) 3,650,000; ✱ Oslo; divided into the following 20 counties (for pronunciation of their names, see their individual entries):

COUNTY	LOCA-TION	AREA[1]	POP.[1]	CO. SEAT
Akershus	SE	1,933	233,747	Oslo[2]
Aust-Agder	S	3,380	77,061	Arendal
Bergen[3]	SW	14	115,689	
Buskerud	S	5,400	168,328	Drammen
Finnmark	N	18,106	71,982	Hammerfest[4]
Hedmark	E	10,141	177,195	Hamar
Hordaland	SW	5,821	225,296	Bergen[5]
Möre og Romsdal	W	5,657	213,027	Kristiansund
Nordland	N	13,953	237,193	Bodö
Nord-Tröndelag	N cen.	8,117	116,635	Levanger
Opland	S cen.	9,152	166,109	Lillehammer
Oslo[6]	SE	6	475,562	
Östfold	SE	1,504	202,641	Moss
Rogaland	SW	3,366	238,662	Stavanger
Sogn og Fjordane	W	6,880	99,844	Florö
Sör-Tröndelag	cen.	6,929	211,648	Trondheim
Telemark	S	5,430	149,848	Skien
Troms	N	9,781	127,549	Tromsö
Vest-Agder	SW	2,642	108,876	Kristiansand
Vestfold	SE	872	174,362	Larvik

[1] Area = land area in sq. m. Pop. from 1960 Census.
[2] Also ✱ of Norway and itself constitutes a county.
[3] Coextensive with the city of Bergen which is also ⊗ of Hordaland co.
[4] Northernmost city in Europe.
[5] Also itself constitutes a county.
[6] Coextensive with the city of Oslo which is also ⊗ of Akershus co.

A mountainous land with Kjölen Mts. forming the N part of the boundary with Sweden (highest point Kebnekaise 6963 ft., in Sweden), the Jotunheimen group in S

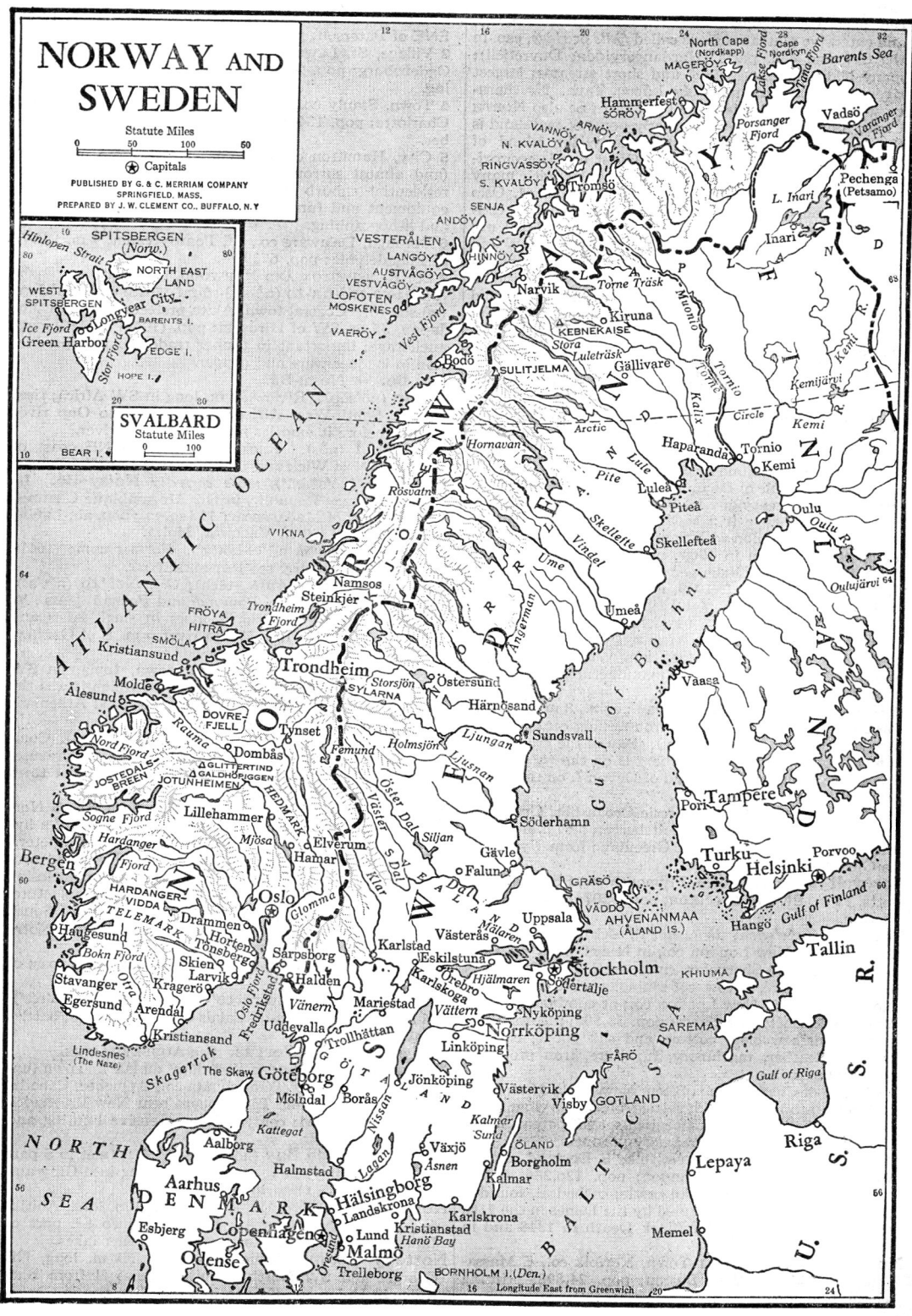

NORWAY AND SWEDEN

Statute Miles
0   50   100   50

⊛ Capitals

PUBLISHED BY G. & C. MERRIAM COMPANY
SPRINGFIELD, MASS.
PREPARED BY J. W. CLEMENT CO., BUFFALO, N.Y.

SPITSBERGEN
(Norw.)

NORTH EAST LAND

WEST SPITSBERGEN

Ice Fjord
Green Harbor
Longyear City

BARENTS I.

EDGE I.

VAERÖY

HOPE I.

BEAR I.

SVALBARD
Statute Miles
0   100

ATLANTIC OCEAN

NORTH CAPE (Nordkapp)
Cape Nordkyn
Barents Sea
MAGERÖY
Hammerfest
SÖRÖY
VANNÖY
ARNÖY
N. KVALÖY
RINGVASSÖY
S. KVALÖY
Tromsö
SENJA
ANDÖY
VESTERÅLEN
LANGÖY
AUSTVÅGÖY
VESTVÅGÖY
LOFOTEN
MOSKENES
Narvik
Torne Träsk
Kiruna
KEBNEKAISE
Stora Luleträsk
Gällivare
SULITJELMA
Bodö
Hornavan
Rosvatn
VIKNA
Namsos
Steinkjer
FRÖYA
Trondheim Fjord
HITRA
SMÖLA
Kristiansund
Molde
Ålesund
DOVRE-FJELL
Dombås
JOSTEDALS BREEN
Sogne Fjord
JOTUNHEIMEN
GLITTERTIND
GALDHÖPIGGEN
Tynset
Femund
Holmsjön
Lillehammer
HEDMARK
Mjösa
Hamar
Elverum
Bergen
Hardanger Fjord
HARDANGER-VIDDA
TELEMARK
Drammen
Haugesund
Bokn Fjord
Horten
Tönsberg
Skien
Larvik
Kragerö
Stavanger
Egersund
Arendal
Kristiansand
Lindesnes (The Naze)
Skagerrak
The Skaw
Oslo
Clomma
Sarpsborg
Halden
Fredrikstad
Oslo Fjord
Drammen
Karlstad
Mariestad
Uddevalla
Trollhättan
Göteborg
Mölndal
Borås
Nissan
Lagan
Kattegat
Aalborg
Halmstad
Hälsingborg
Landskrona
Lund
Malmö
Trelleborg
DENMARK
Aarhus
Esbjerg
Copenhagen
Odense
BORNHOLM I. (Den.)

Arctic Circle
Haparanda
Tornio
Kemi
Kalix
Lule
Pite
Luleå
Piteå
Skellefte
Skellefteå
Oulu
Oulu R.
Oulujärvi
Vindel
Ume
Umeå
Ångerman
Östersund
SYLARNA
Storsjön
Härnösand
Ljungan
Sundsvall
Ljusnan
Öster Dal
Väster Dal
Siljan
Söderhamn
Gävle
Falun
GRÄSÖ
Uppsala
VÄDDÖ
Mälaren
Västerås
Eskilstuna
Örebro
Karlskoga
Hjälmaren
Stockholm
Södertälje
Nyköping
Vänern
Vättern
Norrköping
Linköping
Jönköping
Västervik
Visby
FÅRÖ
GOTLAND
Kalmar Sund
Växjö
Åsnen
Öland
Borgholm
Kalmar
Karlskrona
Kristianstad
Hanö Bay

MAGERÖY
Läkse Fjord
Tana Fjord
Porsanger Fjord
Vadsö
Varanger Fjord
Pechenga (Petsamo)
L. Inari
Inari
Torne Träsk
Muonio
Tornio
Kemijärvi
Kemi
Kemi

Kemijärvi

Kemi
Oulu
Oulujärvi
Pori
Tampere
Vaasa
Turku
Helsinki
Porvoo
GRÄSÖ
AHVENANMAA
(ÅLAND IS.)
Hangö
Gulf of Finland
Tallin
KHIUMA
SAREMA
Gulf of Riga
Riga
Lepaya
Memel

Gulf of Bothnia

BALTIC SEA

NORTH SEA

U. S. S. R.

F I N L A N D

S W E D E N

N O R W A Y

BORNHOLM I. (Den.)
Longitude East from Greenwich

cen. part (Galdhöpiggen 8097 ft., Glittertind 8048 ft.), and extensive plateau regions called *fjells* or *vidde*, esp. in the SW and cen. parts (Hardangervidda, Dovrefjell); many lakes (largest Mjösa) and short streams; largest rivers Glomma, Drammenselv, Lågen, Tana. Northernmost mainland point is Cape Nordkyn (see also NORTH CAPE, Mageröy I.), most southerly point of mainland is the Lindesnes 57°59′N, most westerly the island of Steinsöy 4°30′E off Sogne Fjord. Coast line is approximately 1500 m. long, but is very irregular with many long deep fiords (Sogne Fjord, Hardanger Fjord, Oslo Fjord, Trondheim Fjord) and thousands of islands; estimated shore line of all these would be ab. 12,000 m.; largest island groups Lofoten and Vesterålen off NW and many large individual islands as Senja, North and South Kvalöy, Ringvassöy, Söröy, and Mageröy. Chief industries forestry, mining, fishing, shipbuilding, paper and chemical manufacturing, livestock raising. Chief cities Oslo, Bergen, Trondheim, Stavanger, Drammen, Kristiansand; important ports in far N Tromsö, Hammerfest, Vardö, Kirkenes.

History: In 9th cent. A.D., began Norse expeditions which colonized islands off Scotland, and Ireland, Iceland, and Greenland (*qq.v.*); first converted to Christianity by Olaf Tryggvesson (995–1000); its ruler invaded England 1066; Trondheim capital to 1380; lost war with Hanse Towns and came under German commercial domination; under rule of Denmark (*q.v.*) after Union of Kalmar 1397; by Treaty of Kiel 1814, ceded by Denmark to Sweden which gave it a separate constitution and arranged personal union with Swedish monarchy; dissolved union with Sweden in 1905; neutral in World War I; formally annexed Spitsbergen and Bear I. 1925, Bouvet I. 1928, Jan Mayen I. 1929, and Peter I Island 1931; claimed coast of E Greenland 1931, and Antarctic coast bet. 20°W long. and 45°E long. 1939; occupied by German forces Apr. 9, 1940 to May 8, 1945.

2 Town, Oxford co., W Maine, 18 m. WNW of Lewiston; pop. 3733; summer resort; manufactures snowshoes, skis, sleds, moccasins.

3 City, Dickinson co., S Michigan penin., 8 m. E of Iron Mountain; pop. 3171; former iron-mining center.

Nor·we′gian Bay (nôr·wē′jăn). Bay in the group of islands N of Canada; Axel Heiberg is on the N, S end of Ellesmere I. on the E, NW end of Devon I. on the S, and Amund Ringnes I. on the W.

Norwegian Sea. Part of Arctic Ocean bet. Greenland and Iceland on the W and Spitsbergen and Norway on the E; includes waters off NE Greenland formerly known as Greenland Sea.

Nor′well (nôr′wĕl). Town, Plymouth co., SE Massachusetts, 12 m. ENE of Brockton; pop. 5207; in agricultural section.

Nor′wich (nôr′wĭch; *Brit.* nŏr′ĭj, -ĭch). **1** Industrial town, a ⊗ of New London co., in N cen. part, SE Connecticut, on the Shetucket river; settled 1660, incorp. 1685; agriculture. Now coterminous with the city of Norwich, a ⊗ of New London co.; at confluence of the Yantic and Shetucket rivers; pop. 38,506; incorp. 1784; manufactures woolen, cotton, and silk goods, cutlery, firearms, leather, machinery, furniture, iron products, electrical supplies.

2 City, ⊗ of Chenango co., S cen. New York, 36 m. NNE of Binghamton; pop. 9175; settled 1788; dairying, farming; manufactures pharmaceuticals and patent medicines, farm implements, creamery products.

3 County borough, ⊗ of Norfolk, E England, on the Wensum 97 m. NE of London; pop. 126,236, (1951) 121,226; remains of Norman castle; cathedral, founded 1096; city sacked and occupied by the Danes in the 11th cent. and afflicted by the Black Death in 1348 and in the 17th cent.

Nor′wood (nôr′wŏod). **1** Town, Norfolk co., E Massachusetts, 13 m. SW of Boston; pop. 24,898; printing works, tanneries.

2 Borough, Bergen co., NE corner of New Jersey, 12 m. ENE of Paterson; pop. 2852.

3 Village, St. Lawrence co., N New York, 27 m. E of Ogdensburg; pop. 2200; lumber and paper mills; dairying.

4 Town, Stanly co., S cen. North Carolina, 40 m. E of Charlotte; pop. 1844; manufactures textiles, brick, lumber.

5 City, Hamilton co., SW corner of Ohio, 5 m. NE of (and almost surrounded by) Cincinnati; pop. 34,580; residential suburb of Cincinnati; manufactures office equipment and furniture, laundry machinery; printing and lithographing.

6 Borough, Delaware co., SE Pennsylvania, 9 m. WSW of Philadelphia; pop. 6729.

7 See KENSINGTON AND NORWOOD, Australia.

No·shi·ro·mi·na·to (nō·shē·rō·mē·nä·tō) *or* **No·shi·ro** (nō·shē·rō). Coastal town, Akita prefecture, N Honshu, Japan, 35 m. SW of Hirosaki; pop. (1945) 42,456; good anchorage; important in timber trade; notable production in lacquer ware and copper.

Nosi Be. = NOSSI-Bé.

No′sop (nō′sŏp). River 450 m. long in SW Africa; rises in cen. South-West Africa, flows SSE into Oup river shortly before it empties into the Molopo river.

Noss Head (nŏs). Rocky headland on NE coast of Scotland, N of Wick and S of Sinclair's Bay; lighthouse.

Nos′si-Bé (nŏ′sĕ-bā′), *more correctly* **No′sy-Bé.** Island, Malagasy Republic, in NE Mozambique Channel, off NW coast of Madagascar; 113 sq. m.; pop. ab. 12,000.

Notabile. See CITTÀ VECCHIA, Malta.

Nö′te·borg′ (*Swed.* nû′tĕ·bôr′y′). Former name (1661–1702) of *Shlisselburg:* see PETROKREPOST.

No′teć (nŏ′tĕts·y′; *Angl.* -tĕch); *Ger.* **Net′ze** (nĕt′sĕ). River ab. 275 m. long, Pomorze and Poznań depts., W Poland; formerly in Prussia; rises in small lakes and flows W, emptying into Warta river 6 m. E of Gorzów; navigable for part of its course.

No′ti·um (nō′shĭ·ŭm). Ancient town, Ionia, on SW coast of Asia Minor S of Colophon for which it was the port; Spartan fleet under Lysander defeated Athenians 407 B.C. in nearby waters.

No′to (nō′tō; *Ital.* nô′tô); *anc.* **Ne′tum** (nē′tŭm). Commune, Siracusa prov., SE Sicily, 17 m. SW of Syracuse; pop. 29,992; cathedral; founded 1703 SE of older town destroyed 1693 by earthquake.

Not′od′den (nōt′ôd″n). Town, Telemark co., S Norway; pop. 6192; hydroelectric power plant; site of a hydrogen-fixation plant; iron foundries; exports saltpeter.

No′to Peninsula (nō′tō; *Jap.* nô·tô). Headland projecting N into the Sea of Japan, its E coast enclosing Toyama Bay; the greater part is in Ishikawa prefecture.

No′tre Dame (nō′tĕr dām′). North suburb of South Bend, St. Joseph co., N Indiana; pop. (est.) 6500; Notre Dame Univ. (see SOUTH BEND).

Notre Dame Bay. Inlet of Atlantic Ocean on N coast of Newfoundland.

No′tre–Dame–de–Lo′rette′ (nô′trĕ·dȧm′dĕ·lô′rĕt′). Ridge near Lens, Pas-de-Calais dept., N France; battles May 1915.

Notre Dame des Vertus. See AUBERVILLIERS.

No′tre Dame du Lac (nô′trĕ dȧm′ dü lȧk′). Town (unincorporated), ⊗ of Témiscouata co., S Quebec, Canada, on SW shore of Lake Témiscouata near New Brunswick border; pop. 1364; center of an extensive hunting and fishing region.

Not′ta·wa·sa′ga Bay (nŏt′ȧ·wȧ·sô′gȧ). Inlet in S part of Georgian Bay, Lake Huron, extending into Grey and Simcoe cos., SE Ontario prov., Canada.

Not′ta·way (nŏt′ȧ·wā). River ab. 400 m. long, Abitibi co., SW Quebec, Canada; flows NW into SE part of James Bay; outlet of Mattagami and other lakes.

Notte′ly (nŏt′lĭ). Short stream ab. 50 m. long, NE Georgia and SW North Carolina; flows N from Blue Ridge in Union co., Ga., to join the Hiwassee in Chero-

kee co., N.C.; in its course in Georgia is **Nottely Dam**, one of the dams of the Tennessee Valley Authority (*q.v.*).

Nöt′ter·öy′ (nŭt′ĕr· û′ü). Island in Oslo Fjord, SE Norway; 17 sq. m.; chief town Tönsberg.

Not′ting·ham (nŏt′ĭng·ăm; *in U.S.*, *commonly* -hăm).
1 County in England. See NOTTINGHAMSHIRE.
2 City and county borough, ⊗ of Nottinghamshire, N cen. England, on the Trent 47 m. NE of Birmingham; pop. 268,801, (1951) 306,008; has textile mills; lace manufacture; scene of three parliaments bet. 1330 and 1357; place where Charles I raised his standard 1642 and began the Civil War.

Nottingham Island. Small island at W end of Hudson Strait in SE Franklin District, Northwest Territories, Canada.

Not′ting·ham·shire (-ăm·shĭr; -shĕr) *or* **Nottingham** *or* **Notts** (nŏts). County, N cen. England; area 844 sq. m.; pop. (1951) 841,083; ⊗ Nottingham; other towns Newark, Mansfield, Worksop, East Retford, Southwell; chief river the Trent; agriculture, textiles.

Not′ting Hill (nŏt′ĭng). District, W London, England, partly in Chelsea, chiefly in Kensington.

Not′to·way (nŏt′ō·wā). **1** River 175 m. long, S Virginia; flows from Lunenburg co. SE across North Carolina border to unite with the Blackwater river and form the Chowan river, NE North Carolina.
2 County in Virginia. See *Table* at VIRGINIA.
3 Village, ⊗ of Nottoway co., S cen. Virginia; pop. (1950) 190.

Notts. See NOTTINGHAMSHIRE.

Nouak′chott′ (nwäk′shôt′). Town, ✳ of Islamic Republic of Mauritania, in SW Mauritania near coast.

Nou Island (nōō). See NOUMÉA.

Noulos, Pic. See Monts ALBÈRES.

Nou·mé′a (nōō·mā′à). Town on SW coast of New Caledonia I., SW Pacific Ocean; ✳ of New Caledonia terr.; pop. (1936) 11,108; has large, landlocked harbor, formed partly by Nou I., ab. 4 m. long, with seaplane base, just opp. the town; has modern improvements, a fine market, and steamer connections with Australia, New Zealand, and Indonesia; La Pérouse Coll. Taken over as a major base by Allied forces 1942.

Noun, *or* **Nun, Cape** (nōōn). Cape extending into Atlantic Ocean, NW Africa, in SW Ifni on border of Morocco.

Noup Head (nōōp). Promontory on NW coast of Westray I., Orkney Is., off N coast of Scotland; lighthouse.

Nouveau–Québec. See NEW QUEBEC.

Nouvelle Calédonie. See NEW CALEDONIA.

Nouvelles Hébrides. See NEW HEBRIDES.

No′va Cae′sa·re′a (nō′và sē′zà·rē′à; sĕs′à-; sĕz′à-). Latin name given the colony of New Jersey upon its creation in 1664.

Nova Carthago. = *Carthago Nova:* see CARTAGENA.

Nova Civitas. See NEUSTADT AN DER HARDT.

Novaesium. See NEUSS.

No′va Fri·bur′go (nō′và frē·vōōr′gŏō). City, Rio de Janeiro state, SE Brazil, on railroad 65 m. NE of Rio de Janeiro; pop. (1940 est.) 16,388.

No′va–Gô′a (nō′và·gō′à). = PANGIM.

No′va I·guas·sú′ (nō′và ê·gwà·sōō′). City, Rio de Janeiro state, SE Brazil, NW of Rio de Janeiro; pop. (1940 est.) 20,854.

No′va·li′ches (nō′vä·lē′châs). Town, Bulacan prov., cen. Luzon, Phil. Is., ab. 9 m. NNE of Manila.

No′va Li′ma (nō′và lē′mà). City, Minas Gerais state, E Brazil; S suburb of Belo Horizonte; pop. 16,441.

No′va Lis·bo′a (nō′và lēzh·vō′à); *formerly* **Huam′bo** (wäm′bō). Town in highlands of W cen. Angola, SW Africa; pop. (1934) ab. 2500; alt. 5500 ft.

No·va′ra (nō·vä′rä). **1** Province of Italy. See *Table* at ITALY.
2 *anc.* **No·var′i·a** (nō·vâr′ĭ·à). Commune, its ✳, Piedmont, NW Italy, 28 m. W of Milan; pop. 62,570; 11th-cent. cathedral, 16th-cent. church of San Gaudenzio,

ruins of old castle, episcopal palace; manufactures silks, cottons, linens; important trade in rice and grain. Founded by Celts; in Middle Ages second most important city of duchy of Milan; Swiss victory over French 1513; battle 1821; famous Austrian victory over Piedmontese under Charles Albert of Sardinia Mar. 23, 1849.

No′va Sco′tia (nō′và skō′shà). Province (originally part of Acadia, *q.v.*), SE Canada, one of the Maritime Provinces (see *Map* at MARITIME PROVINCES); 21,068 sq. m. (including 325 sq. m. of water); pop. 642,584; ✳ Halifax; divided into the following 18 counties (for pronunciation of their names, see their individual entries):

NAME	LOCA-TION	AREA[1]	POP.[1]	CO. SEAT
Annapolis	W	1,285	21,747	Bridgetown
Antigonish	N	541	11,971	Antigonish
Cape Breton	E[2]	972	120,306	Sydney
Colchester	cen.	1,451	31,536	Truro
Cumberland	N	1,683	39,655	Amherst
Digby	W	970	19,989	Digby
Guysborough	E	1,611	14,245	Guysborough
Halifax	S	2,063	162,217	Halifax
Hants	cen.	1,229	23,357	Windsor
Inverness	NE[2]	1,409	18,390	Port Hood
Kings	W	842	33,183	Kentville
Lunenburg	S	1,169	33,256	Lunenburg
Pictou	N	1,124	44,002	Pictou
Queens	SW	983	12,544	Liverpool
Richmond	E[2]	489	10,783	Arichat
Shelburne	SW	979	14,392	Shelburne
Victoria	NE[2]	1,105	8,217	Baddeck
Yarmouth	SW	838	22,794	Yarmouth

[1] Area = land area in sq. m. Pop. from 1951 Census.
[2] On Cape Breton I.

Comprises peninsula ab. 375 m. long by 50–100 m. wide, joined to continent by isthmus of Chignecto; includes Cape Breton I. (*q.v.*) on NE, separated from it by Strait (or Gut) of Canso; separated on N from Prince Edward Island by Northumberland Strait, and on W from New Brunswick by Bay of Fundy; contains one national park (Cape Breton Highlands) and six national historic parks; chief cities or towns Halifax, Sydney, Glace Bay, Truro, Dartmouth; chief industries agriculture, coal mining, fishing, steel manufacturing.

History: Coast probably explored by John Cabot 1497–98, Corte-Real 1500–02, and Verrazano 1524; first settlement 1604 by Sieur de Monts, removed 1605 to Port Royal (Annapolis Royal); granted (under name of Nova Scotia) by King James I to Sir William Alexander 1621, but settlement absorbed by French; in colonial wars Port Royal captured by English 1690, restored and again captured 1710; ceded to England by Treaty of Utrecht 1713; French fortress of Louisburg captured 1745 and 1758; Halifax founded 1749; many French Acadians deported 1755—theme of Longfellow's *Evangeline;* settled in 18th cent. by Scottish Highlanders and, after American Revolution, by Loyalists from U.S.; separated from New Brunswick 1784 and set up as a colony with name "Nova Scotia" (*Lat.*, New Scotland); entered Confederation 1867 (see CANADA).

No·va′to (nō·vä′tō). City, Marin co., W California, N of San Francisco; pop. 17,881.

Nová Ves Spišská. = SPIŠSKÁ NOVÁ VES.

No′va·ya La′do·ga (nō′và·yà lä′dŭ·gà). Town, N Leningrad Region, Soviet Russia, Europe, on SE coast of Lake Ladoga at mouth of Volkhov river.

Novaya Sibir. See NEW SIBERIAN ISLAND.

No′va·ya Zem·lya′ (nō′và·yà zyĭm·lyà′). Literally "New Land," two large islands in the Arctic Ocean off NE coast of Soviet Russia, Europe, a part of the Arkhangelsk Region, bet. Barents Sea and Kara Sea; 36,000 sq. m.; islands separated by Matochkin Shar and S island separated from Vaigach I. by Kara Strait; N island permanently ice-covered; has little plant life but many animals, birds, and fish; normally visited in summer by hunters and tourists. Has three small Samoyed villages.

No′va Za·go′ra (nō′vä zä·gô′rä). Town, Stara Zagora dept., cen. Bulgaria, 20 m. E of Stara Zagora; pop. 11,031.

No·vel'da (nŏ·vĕl'dä). Commune, Alicante prov., SE Spain, W of Alicante; pop. (1930) 9508.

No've·le'ta (nō'vȧ·lā'tä). Town, Cavite prov., SW Luzon, Phil. Is., on Manila Bay 4 m. SSW of Cavite.

No·vel·la'ra (nŏ·vȧl·lä'rä). Commune, Reggio nell'Emilia prov., Emilia, N Italy, 10 m. N of Reggio nell'Emilia; pop. 10,637.

Novempopulana. See AQUITANIA TERTIA.

No'vé Zám'ky (nŏ'vâ zäm'kĭ); *Hung.* **Ér'sek·új'vár** (är'shĕk·ōō'y'·vär); *Ger.* **Neu'häu'sel** (noi'hoi'zĕl). Town, S Slovakia prov., E cen. Czechoslovakia, on Nitra river; pop. (1930) 22,141. In early times a Hungarian town; held by Hungary 1938–45.

Nov'go·rod (nŏv'gŏ·rŏd; *Russ.* nôf'gŭ·rŭt). **1** Medieval principality, 11th–15th cent., covering extensive region of all N Russia from Lake Peipus and Lithuania to the Urals. Its history centers in its capital (see **2**, below).
2 City, ✱ of Novgorod Region, NW Soviet Russia, Europe, on both sides of the Volkhov just N of Lake Ilmen; pop. 31,120. One of the oldest cities of Russia and of great importance 11th–15th cent. Originated as a Varangian trading town; conquered by Rurik who became its grand prince c. 862; at first dependent upon Kiev; became capital of principality and was called **Great Novgorod** or **Novgorod the Great**; escaped Mongol invasion 1237–40; ruled by Prince Alexander Nevski 1238–63; developed economically from its favorable location by trade with the Orient and Constantinople and with the Hanse Towns; became rival of Moscow, with many dependent towns in N Russia; its population estimated in 14th cent. at 400,000. Not subject to Tatars and fought successful wars with Germans and Swedes, but overpowered by Ivan III 1471–78 and laid waste by Ivan IV 1570; declined on the rise of St. Petersburg. In World War II held by Germans Aug. 1941–Jan. 20, 1944. Has Kremlin of 11th cent. and several churches, cathedrals, and monasteries dating from period of its supremacy.
3 *or* **Novgorod Se'versk** (nŏv'gŏ·rŏd sā'vērsk; *Russ.* nôf'gŭ·rŭt syä'vyĭrsk). Town, NE Chernigov Region, N Ukraine, U.S.S.R., on right bank of the Desna river 95 m. ENE of Chernigov; pop. 9160; a medieval town, formerly Lithuanian; became Russian in 1654.

Novgorod Region. Region of NW Soviet Russia, Europe, newly created in 1945; bounded on N by Leningrad Region, on NE by Vologda Region, on SE and S by Kalinin Region, on S by Velikie Luki Region, and on W by Pskov Region; ✱ Novgorod; includes Lake Ilmen.

No'vi (nō'vĭ). Village, Oakland co., SE Michigan, NW of Detroit; pop. 6390.

Novibazar. See NOVI PAZAR.

No'vi di Mo'de·na (nŏ'vĕ dĕ mô'dä·nä). Commune, Modena prov., Emilia, N Italy, 17 m. N of Modena; pop. 10,472.

Novi Li'gu·re (lē'gōō·rå). Commune, Alessandria prov., Piedmont, NW Italy, 14 m. SE of Alessandria; pop. 21,157; manufactures silk, woolens; sericulture; scene of Austrian and Russian victory over French 1799.

Noviodunum. 1 See NEVERS, cen. France.
2 See SOISSONS, N France.
3 See NYON, Switzerland.

Noviomagus. 1 See LISIEUX, France.
2 See NIJMEGEN, Netherlands.

No'vi Pa·zar' (nŏ'vĕ pä·zär') *or* **No'vi·ba·zar'** (nŏ'vĕ-bä·zär'). **1** Former Turkish sanjak, divided bet. Serbia and Montenegro in 1913.
2 Town, W Serbia, S Yugoslavia, on a tributary of the Ibar river; pop. 10,364; formerly an important market town. Captured by Turks in 15th cent.; became center of Turkish sanjak which separated Serbia and Montenegro; garrisoned by Austrian troops 1878–1908; evacuated in 1908 as partial compensation to Turkey for Austrian annexation of Bosnia and Herzegovina; occupied by Serbians in First Balkan War 1912; assigned to Serbia 1913; occupied by Germans in 1941.

No'vi Sad (nŏ'vĕ säd'); *Hung.* **Új'vi'dék** (ōō'y'·vĭ'dāk); *Ger.* **Neu'satz** (noi'zäts). City, chief town of Voivodina autonomous prov., NE Yugoslavia, on Danube river; pop. 63,985; commercial and industrial center; shipping point for agricultural products; manufactures chemicals and electrical equipment; founded in 17th cent. as seat of the Serbian patriarch; held by Hungarian troops 1941–45.

Novoaleksandrovsk. See ZARASAI.

No'vo·cher·kassk' (nŏ'vŭ·chĕr·kȧsk'). City, SW Rostov Region, Soviet Russia, Europe, on a delta arm of the Don 25 m. NE of Rostov; pop. 81,286; a commercial city on the main railroad line from Rostov to Voronezh; known especially for its many educational institutions. Founded by Don Cossacks in 1805 and still largely inhabited by them; held by Germans July 1942 to Feb. 1943.

Novogeorgievsk. See MODLIN.

No'vo·gru'dok (nŏ'vŭ·grōō'dŭk); *Pol.* **No'wo·gró'dek** (nŏ'vô·grōō'dĕk). Town, W White Russia, U.S.S.R., S of Neman river and 77 m. SSE of Vilnyus; formerly ✱ of Nowogródek dept., Poland; pop. (1938–39 est.) 11,355; has Mohammedan mosque; manufactures leather; trades in agricultural products. Birthplace of poet Adam Mickiewicz. Variously under Russian, Lithuanian, and Polish rule; in World War II occupied by Germans but recovered by Russians July 1944.

No'vo Ham·bur'go (nŏ'vô ȧNm·bōor'gōō). City, Rio Grande do Sul state, S Brazil, just N of Pôrto Alegre; pop. (1940 est.) 13,029.

No'vo·ka·za'linsk (nŏ'vŭ·kŭ·zȧ'lyĭnsk). Town, S Kazakh S.S.R., Soviet Central Asia, on the lower Syr Darya near its mouth, NE of Lake Aral, and on the Chkalov-Tashkent R.R.

Novokuznetsk. See STALINSK.

Novo Mariinsk. See ANADYR.

No'vo·mos·kovsk' (nŏ'vŭ·mŭs·kôfsk'). Town, cen. Ukraine, U.S.S.R., 16 m. NE of Dnepropetrovsk, on a tributary of the Dnieper; pop. 10,564; was a town of the Zaporogian Cossacks in 17th cent.

Novonikolaevsk. See NOVOSIBIRSK.

Novoradomsk. See RADOMSKO.

No'vo Re·don'do (nŏ'vô rĕ·dŏn'dō). Coastal town, W cen. Angola, SW Africa, 100 m. NNE of Benguela; pop. (1934) ab. 6000.

No'vo·ros·sisk' (nŏ'vŭ·rŭ·syĕsk'). Seaport city, W Krasnodar Territory, Soviet Russia, Europe, on Black Sea coast ab. 65 m. WSW of Krasnodar; pop. 95,280; terminus of branch railroad from Krasnodar, with fair harbor on beautiful bay; has export trade in petroleum, cement, champagne, and tobacco, and formerly in wheat. Formerly a Turkish town, became Russian in 1829; scene of fighting in Civil War when it was held by Denikin 1919–20; in World War II captured by Germans and held for a year, Sept. 11, 1942–Sept. 16, 1943.

Novorossiya. See NEW RUSSIA.

No'vo·si·birsk' (nŏ'vô·si·bīrsk'; *Russ.* nô'vŭ·syĭbyērsk'); *formerly* **No'vo·ni·ko·la'evsk** (nŏ'vŭ·nyĭ·kŭ-lä'yĕfsk). City, ✱ of Novosibirsk Region, in S part, Soviet Russia, Asia, ab. 390 m. E of Omsk; pop. 405,589; on the navigable Ob river and N terminus on the Trans-Siberian R.R. of the Turk-Sib line S to Barnaul, Semipalatinsk, and Central Asia. A great industrial center, sometimes called the "Chicago of Siberia," specializing in the manufacture of agricultural machinery. Trade center for farm products, meat, timber, and varied manufactured articles and near coal and iron mines; also a cultural city with technical college, research institute, libraries and schools. Founded 1896; was capital of West Siberia Region; in World War II received entire industrial plants removed bodily from war areas of W Russia in Europe.

Novo Sibirskie Ostrova. See NEW SIBERIAN ISLANDS.

Novosibirsk Region. Region, SW Soviet Russia, Asia; ✱ Novosibirsk; bounded on N by Tomsk Region, on E

by Kemerovo Region, on S by Altai Territory, on SW by Kazakh S.S.R., and on W by Omsk Region. Lies in basin of middle Ob river with flat steppe and taiga land in N and cen. parts and hilly region in SE; in the SW is Lake Chany. Borders on the Kuznetsk Basin (*q.v.*), one of the great industrial areas of the U.S.S.R. Chief cities Novosibirsk, Kuibyshev, Bolotnoe. For many years the key section of West Siberia Region; crossed by the Trans-Siberian R.R. Organized as new subdivision of R.S.F.S.R. in Asia 1936 and again reorganized and reduced in size 1946.

Novo Urgench. See URGENCH.

No'vo·u'zensk (nŏ'vŏ·ōō'zĕnsk; *Russ.* nô'vŭ·ōō'zyĕnsk). Town, SE Saratov Region, Soviet Russia, Europe, 120 m. SE of Saratov; pop. 10,009; has annual fairs attracting Kirghiz tribes of steppe region.

No'vo·zyb'kov (nŏ'vŭ·zĭp'kŭf). Town, SW Bryansk Region, Soviet Russia, Europe, on railroad ab. 45 m. E of Gomel.

No'vý Ji'čín (nŏ'vē yĭ'chĕn); *Ger.* **Neu'tit'schein** (noi'tĭch'īn). Town, SE Silesia prov., cen. Czechoslovakia, 21 m. SSW of Moravská Ostrava; pop. (1930) 13,785; formerly in NE Moravia.

No'vy Port (nŏ'vĭ pôrt'). Seaport town, Yamalo-Nenets National District, Soviet Russia, Asia, on W shore of Gulf of Ob.

Nowanuggur. See NAVANAGAR.

No'wa Ru'da (nŏ'vä rōō'dä); *Ger.* **Neu·ro'de** (noi-rō'dĕ). Town, SW Wrocław dept., SW Poland, in Sudeten Mts. SE of Wałbrzych; pop. (1946) 10,054; formerly in Silesia, Germany.

No'wa Sól or **No'wa·sól'** (nŏ'vä sōōl'); *Ger.* **Neu'salz' an der O'der** (noi'zälts' än dĕr ō'dĕr). City, N Wrocław dept., SW Poland, on the Odra (Oder) 44 m. NNW of Legnica (Liegnitz); pop. 14,166; formerly in Germany; railroad junction; river port; manufactures textiles, iron goods, enamel work, soap, boarding, leather, glue; dockyards. Taken by Russian army Feb. 15, 1945; assigned to Poland by Potsdam Conference 1945.

No·wa'ta (nŏ·wä'tå). **1** County in Oklahoma. See *Table* at OKLAHOMA.

2 City, its ⊗, NE Oklahoma, 20 m. E of Bartlesville; pop. 4163; oil and gas wells; agriculture; manufactures oil-field equipment.

No'wa·wes' (nŏ'vä·vĕs'; nŏ·vä'vĕs); *now called* **Ba'bels·berg** (bä'bĕls·bĕrκ). City, Potsdam govt. dist., E Germany, on Havel river just E of Potsdam; pop. 26,975; manufactures locomotives, carpets, textiles. Founded 1751 by Frederick the Great.

Now'gong (nou'gŏng). **1** Town, N cen. Assam, NE Indian Union, 56 m. E of Gauhati; pop. 10,400.

2 Town, Chhatarpur state, Central India, 175 m. W of Allahabad; ✱ of former Bundelkhand Agency; pop. 6459.

No'wo·gró'dek (nŏ'vô·grōō'dĕk). **1** Former Polish department (voivodeship) in NE part; 8880 sq. m.; pop. 1,056,780.

2 Town. See NOVOGRUDOK.

Nowo·Mińsk. See MIŃSK MAZOWIECKI.

Now·she'ra (nou·sher'å). Town, West Pakistan, in the former North-West Frontier Province 20 m. E of Peshawar on the Kabul river; pop. 12,829, with cantonment 28,966.

No'wy Dwór Gdań'ski (nŏ'vĭ dvōōr g'dän'y'·skĕ); *Ger.* **Tie'gen·hof** (tē'gĕn·hôf). Town, NE Gdańsk dept., N Poland, ab. 21 m. ESE of Danzig E of the Vistula; pop. (1946) 3639; formerly in Free City of Danzig.

No'wy Sącz (nŏ'vĭ sôNch'); *Ger.* **Neu'san'dez** (noi'-zän'dĕts). Commune, Kraków dept., Poland, on upper Dunajec river in N foothills of Carpathian Mts. 46 m. SE of Kraków; pop. (1938–39 est.) 33,329; manufactures textiles, machinery, chemicals, lumber, leather; on highway leading S through the Carpathians and across Slovakia to Košice.

No'wy Staw (nŏ'vĭ stäf'); *Ger.* **Neu'teich** (noi'tīK). Town, N Gdańsk dept., N Poland, ab. 21 m. SE of Danzig E of the Vistula; pop. (1946) 3766; formerly in the Free City of Danzig.

No'wy Targ (nŏ'vĭ tärk'); *Ger.* **Neu'markt** (noi'-märkt). Commune, Kraków dept., Poland, on upper Dunajec river 45 m. S of Kraków; pop. (1938–39 est.) 11,622; at foot of Tatra Mts.; weaving; trade in wine.

Nox'u·bee (nŏk'shŭ·bē). **1** or **O'ka·nox'u·bee** (ō'kå-). River ab. 130 m. long in E cen. Mississippi and Alabama; rises in Oktibbeha co., NE cen. Mississippi, flows SE across border of Alabama into Tombigbee river, W cen. Alabama, W of Eutaw, Greene co.

2 County in Mississippi. See *Table* at MISSISSIPPI.

No'ya (nŏ'yä). Seaport commune, La Coruña prov., NW Spain, 45 m. SSW of La Coruña; pop. 12,016; agriculture and stock raising; fisheries, fish-salting plants.

Noy'elles'–sous–Lens (nwä'yĕl'sōō·läns'). Commune, Pas-de-Calais dept., N France; pop. (1931) 7634; destroyed during World War I.

Noy'il (noi'ĭl). River ab. 95 m. long, Madras state, S cen. Indian Union; flows E into Cauvery river.

Noy'on' (nwä'yôN'). Manufacturing town, Oise dept., N France; pop. 5891; bishopric from 530; scene of crowning of Pepin the Short 752 and of Charlemagne 768, and of election of Hugh Capet 987; birthplace of John Calvin; often scene of conflict, during Hundred Years' War, in 16th cent., and during World War I when it was ruined 1917–18; of its beautiful cathedral (late 12th cent.) there remained only a tower and the walls of the nave.

Ntukuyu. Var. of TUKUYU.

Nu'ba Mountains (nōō'bå). Group of hills in Republic of Sudan, in S part of Kordofan province.

Nu'bi·a (nū'bĭ·å). Region in Nile valley, NE Africa, N of ab. lat. 16°N, extending northward to include Aswân and the First Cataract, but its boundaries indefinite; now included in Republic of Sudan and Egypt. Mostly desert and includes the Nubian Desert in NE. In ancient times for ab. 1800 years subject to Egypt as a part of Ethiopia; established its independence under Nubian kings and conquered Egypt (XXVth Dynasty, Ethiopian, 712–663 B.C.); capital was at Napata 750 B.C., then at Meroë 500 B.C. Under Romans desert settled by Negro tribe that became united with Hamitic stock and from 6th–14th cents. was a powerful state, with capital Dongola; this kingdom conquered by Arabs in 14th cent. and in 1820–22 by Mehemet Ali of Egypt; under control of the Mahdi 1885–98.

Nu'bi·an Desert (nū'bĭ·ån). Desert area in NE Sudan, E of the Nile river.

Ñu'ble (nyōō'vlå). Province of Chile. See *Table* at CHILE.

Nuceria Alfaterna. See NOCERA INFERIORE.

Nuck'olls (nŭk'ŭlz; -'lz). County in Nebraska. See *Table* at NEBRASKA.

Nu'do Au'san·ga'te (nōō'thŏ ou'säng·gä'tå); *Eng.* **Ausangate Knot.** Mountain 20,013 ft. in Cuzco dept., SE Peru; highest point in the Cordillera de Carabaya.

Nu·e'ces (nŭ·ā'sĕs). **1** River 338 m. long in S Texas; rises near Edwards-Real co. border, flows S and SE into **Nueces Bay**, at head of Corpus Christi Bay.

2 County in Texas. See *Table* at TEXAS.

Nues'tra Se·ño'ra Bay (nwäs'trä så·nyō'rä). Inlet of Pacific Ocean on SW coast of Antofagasta prov., N Chile.

Nuestra Señora de la Asunción. See ASUNCIÓN.

Nueva Caceres. See NAGA.

Nue'va E'ci·ja (nwä'vä ā'sĕ·hä). Province, cen. Luzon, Phil. Is., in central plain; 2120 sq. m.; pop. 416,762; ✱ Cabanatuan. Bounded on N and NE by Nueva Vizcaya, on E by Tayabas, on S by Bulacan, on SW by Pampanga, on W by Tarlac, and on NW by Pangasinan; W two thirds lies in level fertile country watered by the Pampanga and its many tributaries; the SE is hilly and in the NE are the foothills of the Caraballo Mts. Pro-

duces rice, also corn, fruit, sugar cane, and tobacco; some manufacturing industries. Inhabitants are mostly Tagalogs and Ilokanos. Chief towns Cabanatuan, San Jose, Guimba, Cuyapo, Gapan.

Nueva Es·par'ta (ås·pär'tä). State of Venezuela, comprising an island group in the Caribbean Sea, off N coast of Venezuelan mainland; 444 sq. m.; pop. (1941 est.) 69,195; chief island Margarita; ✱ La Asunción.

Nueva Ge·ro'na (hå·rō'nä). Barrio in Isle of Pines municipality, La Habana prov., W Cuba; pop. 2607.

Nueva Granada. See NEW GRANADA.

Nue'va Im'pe·rial' (nwä'vä ēm'på·ryäl'). Town, Cautín prov., S cen. Chile, ab. 380 m. S of Santiago; pop. 6643.

Nueva Pal·mi'ra (päl·mē'rä). River port, Colonia dept., SW Uruguay, on Uruguay river ab. 150 m. NW of Montevideo; shipping point for grain and cattle.

Nueva Paz (päs'). Municipality, E La Habana prov., W Cuba, 47 m. SE of Havana; pop. 14,053.

Nueva Ro·si'ta (rrō·sē'tä). City, Coahuila state, NE Mexico; pop. 25,551.

Nueva San Sal'va·dor' (sän säl'vä·thôr'); *formerly* **San'ta Te'cla** (sän'tä tā'klä). City, ✱ of La Libertad dept., SW El Salvador, 8 m. W of San Salvador; pop. (1942 est.) 23,755; coffee-growing center.

Nueva Se·go'via (så·gō'vyä). Department, NW Nicaragua; 1593 sq. m.; pop. (1943 est.) 29,519; ✱ Ocotal.

Nueva Viz·ca'ya (vēs·kä'yä). Province, N cen. Luzon, Phil. Is.; 2627 sq. m.; pop. 78,505; ✱ Bayombong. Bounded on N by Ifugao subprov. and Isabela prov., on E by Tayabas prov., and on S by Nueva Ecija, on SW by Pangasinan, and on W by Benguet subprov. A hilly and plateau province with much of it above 2000 ft.; in cen. and S parts are the Caraballo Mts. and in the E the foothills of S end of Sierra Madre; in the NE is the upper Cagayan valley and through the W and N sections flows the Magat. Contains much forested region and large areas of fertile land; chief crops rice, sugar, chocolate, tobacco, vegetables; has fine climate. *Chief towns:* Bayombong and Solano.

Nue·vi'tas (nwä·vē'täs). Municipality and town, NE Camagüey prov., E cen. Cuba; pop. (town) 12,029; on a fine harbor, **Nuevitas Bay;** chrome ore mined nearby.

Nuevo, Golfo. See NEW GULF.

Nue'vo La·re'do (nwä'vō lä·rä'thô). City, Tamaulipas state, E Mexico, on the Rio Grande river opp. Laredo, Texas; pop. 28,872; in cotton and cattle district.

Nue'vo Le·ón' (nwä'vō lå·ôn'). State, NE Mexico. See *Table* at MEXICO.

Nu·gi'ma (nōō·gē'må). Chief village of New Hanover I., Bismarck Archipelago, on NW coast.

Nûgs'su·aq (nōōg'sōō·äk). Peninsula on W coast of Greenland in cen. part just N of Disko I.

Nuhurowa. See KAI ISLANDS.

Nuhutjut. See KAI ISLANDS.

Nuits, *in full* **Nuits–Saint–Georges** (nü·ē'săn'zhôrzh'). Town, S Côte-d'Or dept., E France, NNE of Beaune; pop. 3077; noted for wines.

Nukahiva. Var. of NUKU HIVA.

Nu·kha' (nōō·кä'). Town, N Azerbaidzhan, U.S.S.R., at foot of Caucasus Mts. 55 m. NE of Kirovabad; pop. 22,965; chief industry silkworm breeding; has several silk-spinning factories. Once the center of a Tatar khanate, was taken over by Russians in 1819.

Nu Kiang. See SALWEEN.

Nu'ku·a·lo'fa (nōō'kōō·å·lô'få). Seaport on N coast of Tongatabu I., Tonga Is., SW Pacific Ocean; ✱ of Tonga Is.; 2000 m. from Sydney and 1100 m. from Auckland.

Nu'ku·fe·tau' (nōō'kōō·fĕ·tou'). Island (atoll), cen. Ellice Is., W Pacific Ocean, NW of Funafuti I., comprising islets in a reef 24 m. in circuit; pop. (1936) 437.

Nu'ku Hi'va (nōō'kōō hē'vä). Largest of the Marquesas Is., French Polynesia, S Pacific Ocean; 186 sq. m.; pop. 1000; chief village Taiohae; has high ridge (highest point 3888 ft.) and plateau in center; coast line of 70 m.

with several indentations; best harbor is Anaho Bay on N. See TYPEE.

Nu'ku·la'e·la'e (nōō'kōō·lä'å·lä'å). Island (atoll) ab. 6½ m. long at S end of Ellice Is., W Pacific Ocean; pop. (1936) 253.

Nu'ku·nau (nōō'kōō·nou) *or* **By'ron** (bī'rŭn). Island (atoll) 8 m. by 1½ m., SE Gilbert Is., SW Pacific; has several villages. Discovered by Capt. John Byron 1765.

Nu'ku·no'no *or* **Nu'ku No'no** (nōō'kōō nō'nō); *also* **Duke of Clar'ence** (klär'ĕns). Island (atoll) of the Tokelau group, cen. Pacific, N of Samoa.

Nu·kus' (nōō·kōōs'). Town, ✱ of Kara-Kalpak Republic, Uzbek S.S.R., Soviet Central Asia, on right bank of the Amu Darya at head of delta.

Nu·la'to (nōō·lä'tō). Village, W cen. Alaska, on right bank of the Yukon 220 m. E of Nome; pop. (est.) 250.

Null·ar'bor Plain (nŭl·är'bĕr; *now commonly* nŭl'ĕr·bôr). Plain along SW coast of South Australia from E end of Great Australian Bight; extends inland almost to 30°S and W end extends into SE Western Australia; a major rocket research and production center.

Nu·man'ti·a (nû·măn'shi·å). Ancient city of Spain, on the Duero river near modern Soria; involved in war against Rome 143–133 B.C.; it resisted several sieges and was finally taken by Scipio the Younger only after a siege of 15 months.

Nu·ma·zu (nōō·mä·zōō). Town, Shizuoka prefecture, S coast of cen. Honshu, Japan, on NE shore of Suruga Bay across from Shizuoka; pop. (1945) 76,782; noted resort.

Nu·me'a (nōō·mä'å). Var. of NOUMÉA.

Numedalslågen. See LÅGEN.

Numfor. See NOEMFOOR.

Nu·mid'i·a (nû·mĭd'ĭ·å). Ancient country in North Africa; its territory nearly that of modern Algeria. In Second Punic War (218–201 B.C.) its two great tribes divided, one in support of the Romans, the other of the Carthaginians; after 201 Masinissa became its king, followed by his son Micipsa (c. 148–118 B.C.); suffered under civil war and Jugurthine War 111–106 B.C.; became Roman province 46 B.C., later a part of Mauretania; its capital was Cirta and its most important city Hippo, the see of St. Augustine (see BÔNE); flourished until invasion by Vandals 428 A.D.

Nun (nōōn) *or* **Nun Entrance.** One of the mouths of the Niger river, S Nigeria, W Africa.

Nun, Cape. See CAPE NOUN.

Nun·ea'ton (nŭ·nē't'n). Municipal borough, Warwickshire, cen. England, 20 m. E of Birmingham; pop. 54,408; textile mills, ironworks, hat factories; coal mines nearby.

Nu'ni·vak (nōō'nĭ·văk). Second largest island (50 m. long) in Bering Sea, in E part; separated from mainland of SW Alaska and Nelson I. by Etolin Strait; crossed by 167°W; usually fogbound. Inhabited by primitive Eskimos. Has been made a game and bird reservation.

Nun'kiang' (nōōn'ji·äng'). One of the nine new provinces of Manchuria, created Sept. 1945, in N cen. part; 23,912 sq. m.; pop. 2,094,000; ✱ Mergen.

Nuo'ro (nwô'rô). **1** Province of E Sardinia, Italy. See *Table* at ITALY.
2 Commune, its ✱, E Sardinia, 75 m. N by E of Cagliari; pop. 11,459; cathedral.

Nu'pe (nōō'på). = NIGER province.

Nuremberg. See NÜRNBERG.

Nur·hak' Da·ği' (nōōr·häk' dä·ï'). Peak 10,005 ft. in cen. Turkey in Asia, NE of Maraş.

Nuristan. See KAFIRISTAN.

Nur'mes (nōōr'mĕs). Town, SE cen. Finland, in Kuopio dept.; pop. 10,975; at N end of Pielisjärvi ab. 60 m. NE of Kuopio.

Nürn'berg (nürn'bĕrk); *Angl.* **Nu'rem·berg** (nūr'ĕm·bûrg). Commercial and manufacturing city, Middle Franconia govt. dist., Bavaria, Germany, on Pegnitz river 92 m. NNW of Munich; pop. (1939) 430,851; famous for its medieval aspect; 11th-cent. walls (10 gates),

11th-cent. royal palace, town hall, national museum (founded 1852) in 14th-cent. Carthusian monastery, old churches of St. Sebald and St. Lorenz; manufactures toys, machinery, electrical apparatus, clocks and watches, chemicals, dyes, railroad cars, scientific instruments, brass and steel goods, tobacco, beer. Founded in 11th cent.; made free imperial city 1219; became one of greatest and wealthiest of all German free imperial cities; treaty 1532; center of German culture in 16th cent.; to Bavaria 1806; after 1933 made annual meeting place of Hitler's National Socialist party; much of it destroyed in bombings of World War II; taken by Americans Apr. 21, 1945. Birthplace of Hans Sachs and Albrecht Dürer.

Nur'si·a (nûr'shǐ·à; -shà). = NORCIA.

Nus, Cape (nōōs); *Arab.* **Ras Nus** (räs). Cape on S coast of Oman, SE Arabia.

Nu'sa Be·sar' (nōō'sä bå·sär'). Small island off SE coast of Bali, Indonesia, at S end of Lombok Strait (*q.v.*).

Nu·say·bin' (nōō·sǐ·bēn') or **Ni·si·bin'** (nê·sê·bēn'); *anc.* **Nis'i·bis** (nǐs'ǐ·bǐs). Town, Mardin vilayet, SE Turkey in Asia, on railroad on the border of Syria; pop. 1931. A frontier fortress, in early times important on the trade routes; residence of Armenian kings c. 150 B.C. to c. 117 A.D.; a key point for both Romans and Parthians and later a religious center; scene of Egyptian victory over the Turks 1839.

Nus'le (nōōs'lě). Former city, now a part of Prague, Bohemia, Czechoslovakia.

Nut'ley (nŭt'lǐ). Town, Essex co., NE New Jersey, 6 m. N of Newark; pop. 29,513; residential suburb; settled 1680; manufactures paper, silks, woolens, leather goods.

Nut'ter Fort (nŭt'ēr). Industrial town, Harrison co., N West Virginia, 2 m. S of Clarksburg; pop. 2440; manufactures pottery, glassware.

Nu'u·a'nu (nōō'ōō·ä'nōō). Valley, SE Oahu I., Hawaii, including part of Honolulu City.

Nuuanu Pa'li (pä'lě). Cliff and mountain pass, alt. 1207 ft., at head of Nuuanu valley, 6 m. from Honolulu; famous as a scenic spot. Here in 1795 Kamehameha I completed his conquest of the island of Oahu.

Nu'wa·ra E'li·ya (nōō'wà·rà ā'li·yà). Town, Central Province, S cen. Ceylon, on elevated plateau at ab. 6000 ft. alt.; health resort.

Nu'zi (nōō'zē). Archaeological site just SW of Kirkuk, NE Iraq; clay tablet with map of c. 2500 B.C. found here.

Ny'ack (nī'ǎk). Residential village, Rockland co., SE New York, on W shore of Hudson river 25 m. N of New York; pop. 6062; settled 1700; boatbuilding; manufactures sewing machines, boilers.

Nyaktse. See PANGONG.

Nyam'la·gi'ra (nyäm'lä·gǐr'à). Volcano 10,026 ft., E Congo in the Virunga Mts.; erupted 1938.

Ny·an'za (nī·ǎn'zà; nī-). Province, SW Kenya colony, E Africa; ✳ Kisumu.

Ny·as'a or **Ny·as'sa, Lake** (nī·ǎs'à; nī-). Lake in SE Africa, bounded on W and S by Nyasaland on N and NE by Tanganyika Territory, and on E by N Mozambique; ab. 360 m. long, average width 25 m.; ab. 11,000 sq. m.; drains S into Zambezi river.

Ny·as'a·land' (-lǎnd') or since *1964* **Ma·la'wi** (må·lä'-wē). Former British protectorate, since 1964 an independent republic, W and S of Lake Nyasa, SE Africa; land area 37,374 sq. m.; 520 m. long, from 50 to 100 m. wide; pop. (1938) 1,679,977; ✳ Zomba. Consists of elevated plateaus, in several places 5000 to 8000 ft. high (see SHIRE HIGHLANDS); includes part of Lake Nyasa (*q.v.*); lower part crossed by Shire river, outlet of Lake Nyasa. Chief exports tobacco, tea, coffee, cotton. Chief towns Zomba, Blantyre-Limbe, Fort Johnston, Lilongwe. Region visited by Livingstone 1859; Blantyre founded c. 1883; protectorate established 1892; from 1893–1907 called **British Central Africa Protectorate**; federated with Northern and Southern Rhodesia 1953–63.

Nyassa. See NIASSA.

Ny'borg (nü'bôr). Seaport, Svendborg co., Denmark, on Fyn I.; pop. (1945) 9559; shipyards, textile mills, iron foundries, tobacco-processing works; seaside resort.

Nye (nī). County in Nevada. See *Table* at NEVADA.

Nyeman. Var. of NEMAN.

Nyen'chen·tang'lha Range (nyěn'chěn·täng'lä). Mountain range ab. 600 m. long, S Tibet and W Sikang, parallel with the Himalayas and N of the Brahmaputra (Tsangpo) river; peaks 16,590 ft. to highest point 23,250 ft. (**Nyenchentanglha Peak**, 60 m. NW of Lhasa).

Nye'ri (nyä'rê). Town, SW cen. Kenya, N of Nairobi.

Nyezhin. = NEZHIN.

Nyi'ra·gon'go (nyǐr'à·gǒng'gō). Volcano 11,000 ft., E Congo, at N end of Lake Kivu.

Nyí'regy·há'za (nyē'rěd·y'·hä'zǒ). City E of the Tisza in NE Hungary, 30 m. N of Debrecen; pop. (1939) 56,108; in grape-growing region; manufacturing.

Nyi'ri Desert (nyē'rê). Desert area in S Kenya, E Africa, on the border of Tanganyika just NW of Mt. Kilimanjaro.

Nyitra. See NITRA.

Nyitrabánya. See HANDLOVÁ.

Ny'kö'bing (nü'kû'pǐng) or **Ny'kjö'bing** (-kû'-). **1** Seaport, Maribo co., on W coast of Falster I., Denmark; pop. (1945) 16,097; sugar refineries, machine works; manufactures tobacco products, margarine. **2** Town, Thisted co., NW Jutland Penin., Denmark, on E coast of Morsö I.; pop. (1945) 8825; oyster fisheries, iron foundries, tobacco-processing works.

Ny'kö'ping (nü'chû'pǐng). Seaport, ✳ of Södermanland prov., SE Sweden, on the Baltic Sea; pop. 15,680; textile mills, sawmills, furniture factories.

Nyland. See UUSIMAA.

Nym'burk (nǐm'bŏŏrk); *Ger.* **Nim'burg** (nǐm'bŏŏrκ). Town, N cen. Bohemia prov., W Czechoslovakia, on the Labe (Elbe) just E of Prague; pop. (1930) 11,890.

Nymme. See NÕMME.

Nym·phai'on (nǐm·fī'ǒn) or **Nym·phae'um** (nǐm-fē'ŭm), **Cape**; *Gr.* **Ak'ro·tē'ri·on Nymphaion** (ǎk'-rô·tē'rǐ·ǒn). Cape at SE end of Acte Penin., Chalcidice, NE Greece, extending into Aegean Sea; in a storm off this point the fleet of Darius in an expedition against Greece was wrecked 492 B.C.

Nym'phen·burg (nüm'fěn·bŏŏrκ). Former village NW of Munich, Bavaria, Germany, now incorporated in it; secret treaty signed here May 1741, forming an alliance against Austria (War of the Austrian Succession) which finally included France, Bavaria, Spain, Saxony, and Prussia.

Nyon (nyôN); *Ger.* **Neuss** (nois); *anc.* **No'vi·o·du'-num** (nō'vǐ·ô·dū'nŭm). Commune, Vaud canton, W Switzerland, on W shore of Lake of Geneva 13 m. N of Geneva; pop. (1930) 5107; 16th-cent. castle; produces wine; manufactures earthenware; tourist traffic.

Nyong (nyông). River ab. 280 m. long in Cameroun, W Africa; flows W into Bight of Biafra.

Ny'sa (nǐ'sä); *Ger.* **Neis'se** (nǐ'sě). **1** *Ger. also* **Glat'zer Neisse** (glät'sēr). River ab. 120 m. long in SW Poland; rises on the Schneeberg, on Czechoslovak border, and flows NE joining the Odra (Oder) 15 m. NW of Opole. **2** Manufacturing city, W Śląsk dept., S Poland, on the Nysa river 47 m. SSE of Wrocław; pop. 32,604; formerly in Silesia, Germany; churches of 15th and 17th cents., 15th-cent. tower, modern town hall; airport. Founded c. 1220; withstood Hussites 1428; occupied 1621, 1632, and 1642 during Thirty Years' War; to Prussia 1742; occupied by French 1807–08; assigned to Poland by Potsdam Conference 1945.

Nysa Łużycka. See NEISSE river.

Nys'sa (nǐs'à). Town, Malheur co., SE corner of Oregon, on Snake river 12 m. S of its confluence with Malheur river; pop. 2611; dairy products, poultry, sugar beets.

Nystad. See UUSIKAUPUNKI.

Nyu·do, Cape (nyōō·dō). Cape, Akita prefecture, NW coast of Honshu, Japan, 40°N.

O

Oa, Mull of (mŭl, ō). Cape on S tip of Islay I. in the Inner Hebrides, off W coast of Scotland.

O·a'hu (ō·ä'hōō). Island, Hawaii, third in size and most important of the Hawaiian Is.; 589 sq. m.; included in Honolulu co. Geologically once two great volcanoes; erosion has left them as two mountain ranges—the Koolau (highest Konahuanui 3105 ft.) along NE coast parallel with the Waianae (highest Kaala 4030 ft.) along the SW coast with plateau 800–1000 ft. between; Honolulu and Pearl Harbor on S coast. Mountains very rugged (see NUUANU PALI); cen. plateau under wide cultivation. Chief towns besides Honolulu are Waipahu, Ewa, Aiea, Kahuku, Wahiawa, Waialua, Waianae. Early kings of Oahu opposed Kamehameha who finally overcame them 1795; royal residence and influence gradually transferred from Hawaii I. to Oahu in first half of 19th cent.

Oak (ōk). One of the Apostle Is. (*q.v.*).

Oak Bluffs. Town, Dukes co., SE Massachusetts, NE Martha's Vineyard on Nantucket Sound; pop. 1419.

Oak Creek. 1 Town, Routt co., NW Colorado, near Yampa river 35 m. ESE of Craig; pop. 666. **2** City, Milwaukee co., SE Wisconsin, SSE of Milwaukee; pop. 9372.

Oak'dale (ōk'dāl). **1** City, Stanislaus co., cen. California, 23 m. ESE of Stockton; pop. 4980; dairying center; in irrigated district; founded 1871, incorp. 1906. **2** City, Allen parish, SW Louisiana, 37 m. SSW of Alexandria; pop. 6618; in agricultural, lumbering section. **3** Borough, Allegheny co., SW Pennsylvania, 10 m. WSW of Pittsburgh; pop. 1695.

Oak'en·gates' (ōk'ĕn·gāts'). Urban district, Shropshire, W England, 28 m. WNW of Birmingham; pop. 11,659.

Oakes (ōks). City, Dickey co., S North Dakota, 54 m. S of Valley City; pop. 1650; creameries; farming.

Oak'field (ōk'fēld). Village, Genesee co., W New York, 34 m. ENE of Buffalo; pop. 2070; gypsum products.

Oak Grove. Town, ⊗ of West Carroll parish, NE Louisiana, 52 m. ENE of Monroe; pop. 1797; cotton, lumber.

Oak'ham (ōk'ăm). Urban district, ⊗ of Rutlandshire, E cen. England, 19 m. ENE of Leicester; pop. 3537; remains of Norman castle.

Oak Harbor. Village, Ottawa co., N Ohio, 20 m. ESE of Toledo; pop. 2903.

Oak Hill. 1 Village, Jackson co., S Ohio, 25 m. ENE of Portsmouth; pop. 1748. **2** City, Fayette co., S cen. West Virginia, 14 m. N of Beckley; pop. 4711; in farming section.

Oak'land (ōk'lănd). **1** County in Michigan. See *Table* at MICHIGAN. **2** City, ⊗ of Alameda co., W California, on E side of San Francisco Bay nearly opp. the Golden Gate; pop. 367,548; 4th city in size in the state; seaport and industrial center; manufactures iron products, diesel engines, paint, aluminum products; canneries (fruit, vegetables); shipbuilding yards. Connected by Transbay Bridge (completed 1936) with San Francisco (see YERBA BUENA ISLAND). Mills Coll. (1852; women); College of the Holy Names (1868; women; Rom. Cath.); California Coll. of Arts and Crafts (1907; coed.); Chabot Observatory (owned by the city). **3** Town, Kennebec co., SW Maine, 5 m. W of Waterville; pop. 3075. **4** Town, ⊗ of Garrett co., NW corner of Maryland, 52 m. WSW of Cumberland; pop. 1977. **5** Borough, Bergen co., NE New Jersey, NNW of Paterson; pop. 9446.

Oakland City. Residential town, Gibson co., SW Indiana, 28 m. NNE of Evansville; pop. 3016. Oakland City Coll. (1885; coed.; Baptist).

Oakland Park. City, Broward co., SE Florida, N of Fort Lauderdale; pop. 5331.

Oak Lawn. Village, Cook co., NE Illinois, 12 m. SW of Chicago; pop. 27,471.

Oak'leigh (ōk'lī). Town, S Victoria, SE Australia, SE suburb of Melbourne; pop. 11,906.

Oak'ley Dam (ōk'lī) *or* **Goose Creek Dam** (gōōs). Dam completed 1913 across Goose Creek, a S tributary of Snake river, S Cassia co., S Idaho; height 145 ft.; impounds water for irrigation, forming **Goose Creek Reservoir.**

Oak'lyn (ōk'lĭn). Residential borough, Camden co., SW New Jersey, 3 m. SSE of Camden; pop. 4778.

Oak'mont (ōk'mŏnt). Borough, Allegheny co., SW Pennsylvania, on Allegheny river 11 m. ENE of Pittsburgh; pop. 7504; manufactures railroad cars and parts, automobile parts, metal furniture, paints and varnishes.

Oak Park. 1 Residential village, Cook co., NE Illinois, 10 m. W of Chicago; pop. 61,093; settled 1835. **2** City, Oakland co., SE Michigan, NW of Detroit; pop. 36,632.

Oak Ridge. City, Anderson and Roane cos., E Tennessee, 17 m. W of Knoxville; area 59,000 acres; pop. 27,169; Oak Ridge National Laboratory, atomic research and development center (estab. 1943 as Clinton Engineer Works, later called Clinton National Laboratory until 1948) and the Oak Ridge Institute of Nuclear Studies, estab. 1948; produces radioactive isotopes and U-235.

Oak'ville (ōk'vĭl). Town, Halton co., SE Ontario, Canada, on Lake Ontario 22 m. SW of Toronto; pop. 6910; various industries; summer resort.

Oak'wood (ōk'wŏŏd). City, Montgomery co., SW Ohio, 3 m. S of Dayton; pop. 10,493.

Oam'a·ru (ŏm'á·rōō). Borough, Otago provincial dist., E South I., New Zealand, on Pacific Ocean 55 m. NNE of Dunedin; pop. (1941 est.) 7610; has port facilities; limestone quarries.

Oaracta. See QISHM.

O·as' (ō·äs'). Municipality, N cen. Albay prov., Luzon, Phil. Is., 18 m. NW of Legaspi; pop. 23,131; hemp.

O·a'sis Butte (ō·ā'sĭs; ō'á·sĭs). Isolated peak 5685 ft. in W Klamath co., S Oregon, NW of Crater Lake.

O'a'sis' Sa'ha'riennes' (ō'á'zēs' sà'hà'ryĕn'); *Eng.* **Sahar'an O·a'ses** (sà·hâr'ăn [-hâr'ăn] ō·ā'sēz [ō'á·sēz]). Territory of Algeria. See *Table* at ALGERIA.

Oates Coast (ōts). Part of Antarctica W of Victoria Land, 157°–164°E, S of Balleny Is.; partly in Ross Dependency.

Oa·xa'ca (wä·hä'kä). **1** State, SE Mexico. See *Table* at MEXICO. **2** *in full* **Oaxaca de Juá'rez** (thä hwä'râs). City, its ✱; pop. 29,306; altitude ab. 5000 ft.; damaged by earthquake 1931; famous for production of woolen serapes; gold and silver mines nearby; chief crop coffee.

Ob (ōb; *Russ.* ŏp'y'). River ab. 2500 m. long (with the Irtysh, 3200 m.), W Soviet Russia, Asia, flowing NW and N through Novosibirsk and Tomsk Regions and Khanty-Mansi and Yamalo-Nenets National Districts into the Gulf of Ob. Both the main stream and its tributaries are navigable for a total of more than 17,000 m.; its basin exceeds one million sq. m. Its headstreams are the Biya and Katun in Oirot Autonomous Region, rising in the Altai Mts.; its middle course is through extensive swamp land, frozen much of the year; its main tributaries on the right are the Tom, Chulym, Ket, and Vakh, and on the left the Irtysh; chief towns on its banks Novosibirsk, Barnaul, Kolpashevo.

Ob, Gulf of. Inlet of Arctic Ocean, ab. 550 m. long, 50 m. wide, E of Yamal Penin., N Yamalo-Nenets National District, Soviet Russia, Asia.

O'ba (ō'bä) *or* **A·o'ba** (ä·ō'bä). One of the New Hebrides Is., SW Pacific Ocean, ab. 30 m. E of Espíritu Santo; 26 m. long and 9 m. wide; pop. (est.) 6000; coconuts.

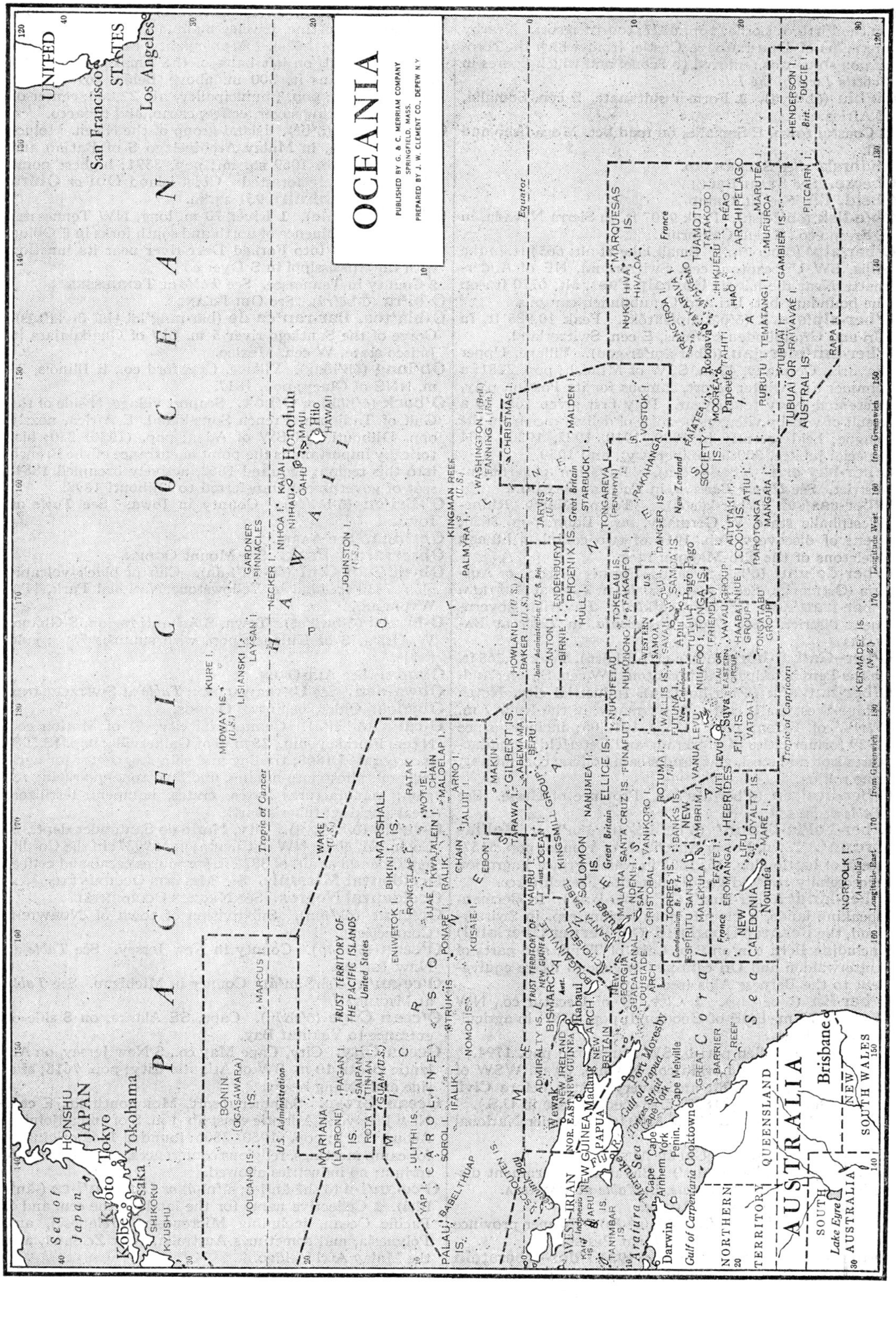

O'ban (ō'băn). Seaport burgh, Argyll co., W Scotland, on the Firth of Lorne; pop. 6227; tourist resort. Nearby are ruins of Dunstaffnage Castle, from which the coronation stone was removed to Scone, and which figures in Scott's *Lord of the Isles.*

Ob'bia (ob'byä). **1** Former sultanate, E cen. Somalia, E Africa.
2 Coastal town, E Somalia, on road bet. Mogadisho and Eil.

Obdorsk. See SALEKHARD.

Óbecse. See STARI BEČEJ.

Obeid, El. See EL OBEID.

Ob'e·lisk (ŏb'ĕ·lĭsk). Peak 9707 ft. in Sierra Nevada, in E Fresno co., S cen. California.

O'ber·alp' (ō'bĕr·älp'). Small lake at alt. 6654 ft. in the Alps, SW Uri canton, cen. Switzerland, NE of Andermatt. Near the lake is **Oberalp Pass,** alt. 6720 ft., on the boundary bet. Uri and Graubünden cantons.

O'ber·alp'stock (ō'bĕr·älp'shtôk). Peak 10,925 ft. in Uri and Graubünden cantons, E cen. Switzerland.

O'ber·am'mer·gau (ō'bĕr·äm'ĕr·gou). Village, Upper Bavaria, Germany, 42 m. SSW of Munich; pop. 2281; a summer and winter resort, famous for its Passion play, presented every tenth year. Play first given 1634 as a result of vow by villagers because of deliverance from the plague; held recently in 1900, 1910, 1922, 1930, 1934 (special jubilee, 300th anniversary), and 1950.

O'ber·bay'ern (ō'bĕr·bī'ĕrn). Bavarian government district. See *Upper Bavaria,* in *Table* at BAVARIA.

O'ber·cas'sel (ō'bĕr·käs'ĕl). Town, North Rhine-Westphalia state, W Germany, near Bonn; pop. 3680; scene of discovery Feb. 1914 of two complete human skeletons of the Cro-Magnon race.

O'ber·do'nau (ō'bĕr·dō'nou). Former district of Austria (Ostmark). See *Upper Austria,* in *Table* at AUSTRIA.

O'ber·fran'ken (ō'bĕr·fräng'kĕn). Bavarian government district. See *Upper Franconia,* in *Table* at BAVARIA.

O'ber–Ga'bel·horn (ō'bĕr·gä'bĕl·hôrn). Peak 13,365 ft. in the Pennine Alps, Valais canton, SW cen. Switzerland.

O'ber·hau'sen (ō'bĕr·hou'zĕn). Industrial city, North Rhine-Westphalia state, W Germany, in the Ruhr 7 m. WNW of Essen; pop. (1939) 191,305; includes since 1929 former cities of Sterkrade and Osterfeld; manufactures iron and steel, glass and steam boilers; coal mining, zinc rolling.

O'ber·hes'sen (ō'bĕr·hĕs'ĕn). Province of Hesse. See *Table* at HESSE.

O'ber·hol'la·brunn' (ō'bĕr·hôl'ä·brŏon') *or* **Hol'la·brunn'.** Town, Lower Austria, N of Vienna; pop. 5157; scene of battle Nov. 16, 1805 in which Prince Bagration successfully resisted greatly superior French force.

O'ber·land' (ō'bĕr·länd'; *Ger.* ō'bĕr·länt'). In German-speaking lands, a mountainous region; esp. in Switzerland, the **Bernese Oberland** (*Ger.* **Berner Oberland**) including Bern canton S of Lake of Thun, and parts of Unterwalden and Uri cantons; in general usage equivalent to the Bernese Alps (see ALPS).

O'ber·lin (ō'bĕr·lĭn). **1** City, ⊗ of Decatur co., NW Kansas, 75 m. ENE of Goodland; pop. 2337; in agricultural section.
2 City, ⊗ of Allen parish, SW Louisiana; pop. 1794.
3 Residential city, Lorain co., N Ohio, 30 m. WSW of Cleveland; pop. 8198; antislavery center before Civil War. Oberlin Coll. (1832; first coed. college in U.S.).

Oberlin Mountain. Peak 8100 ft. in Glacier National Park, NW Montana.

Oberösterreich. See UPPER AUSTRIA.

O'ber·pfalz' (ō'bĕr·pfälts'). Bavarian government district. See *Upper Palatinate,* in *Table* at BAVARIA.

Oberrhein. See UPPER RHINE.

O'ber·schle'si·en (ō'bĕr·shlä'zĕ·ĕn). Former province of Prussia. See *Silesia,* in *Table* at PRUSSIA.

O'ber·stein (ō'bĕr·shtīn); *since* 1933 **I'dar–Oberstein** (ē'där-). City, Birkenfeld, Oldenburg, Germany, in

Nahe river valley 52 m. WNW of Mannheim; pop. 10,713; gem cutting, jewelry manufacture.

Ó'bi·dos (ō'vĕ·thōōs). Municipality and town, Pará state, N Brazil, on left bank of the Amazon where the Trombetas joins it, 500 m. above Belém (690 m. by river steamer); pop. (municipality) ab. 22,000; center of district producing sugar, coffee, cacao, and tobacco.

O'bi Islands (ō'bĕ). Island group of the N cen. Moluccas, Indonesia, in Malay Archipelago S of Batjan and Halmahera; ab. 1069 sq. m.; pop. 3391; highest point 5285 ft.; densely forested. Chief island **Obi** *or* **Obira** (*formerly* **Ombirah**), 951 sq. m.

O·bi'on (ō·bī'ŭn). **1** River 70 m. long, NW Tennessee; formed by confluence of north and south forks in E Obion co., flows SW into Forked Deer river near its junction with the Mississippi in S Dyer co.
2 County in Tennessee. See *Table* at TENNESSEE.

O·bi'ra (ō·bē'rá). See OBI ISLANDS.

O·bla'tos, Bar·ran'ca de (bär·räng'kä thä ō·vlä'tôs). Gorge of the Santiago river 5 m. SW of Guadalajara in Jalisco state, W cen. Mexico.

Ob'long (ŏb'lŏng). Village, Crawford co., E Illinois, 23 m. NNE of Olney; pop. 1817.

O'bock (ō'bŏk) *or* **O'bok.** Seaport village, N side of the Gulf of Tadjoura, French Somaliland, E Africa, nearly opp. Djibouti and SW of Aden; pop. (1936) 250; historically important as the point of entrance of the French into this region; acquired 1862, actively occupied 1884; seat of government transferred to Djibouti 1892.

O'·Bri'en (ō·brī'ĕn). County in Iowa. See *Table* at IOWA.

Obringa. See AARE.

Observatory Peak. See Mount OGDEN.

Ob·sid'i·an Cliff (ŏb·sĭd'ĭ·ăn). Cliff of black volcanic glass 7350 ft. high in Yellowstone National Park, NW Wyoming.

O·bua'si (ō·bwä'sĕ). Town, S Ashanti region, S Ghana, W Africa, S of Kumasi; pop. with suburbs 7598; gold fields.

Óbuda. See ALT-OFEN.

Obwalden. See UNTERWALDEN; *Table* at SWITZERLAND.

Obydos. Older spelling of ÓBIDOS.

O·cal'a (ō·kăl'á). Commercial city, ⊗ of Marion co., N cen. Florida penin., 35 m. S of Gainesville; pop. 13,598; incorporated 1868; trading and shipping center for agricultural, phosphate-mining, and limestone-quarrying region; manufactures boxes, crates, hampers, fertilizer; meat packing; fuller's earth.

O·ca'ña (ō·kä'nyá). City, Norte de Santander dept., N Colombia, 60 m. NW of Cúcuta; pop. 9937; in the Cordillera Oriental at alt. of 3820 ft.; produces cacao and coffee.

Occidental Misamis. See MISAMIS OCCIDENTAL.

Occidental Negros. See NEGROS OCCIDENTAL.

Oc'cum (ŏk'ŭm). Subdivision of town of NORWICH, Connecticut.

O'cean (ō'shăn). County in New Jersey. See *Table* at NEW JERSEY.

O'ce·an'a (ō'shē·ăn'á). County in Michigan. See *Table* at MICHIGAN.

O'cean Cape (ō'shăn). Cape, SE Alaska, on S side of entrance to Yakutat Bay.

Ocean City. City, Cape May co., S New Jersey, on Atlantic Ocean 10 m. SW of Atlantic City; pop. 7618; seaside and fishing resort.

Ocean Grove. Summer resort, Monmouth co., E cen. New Jersey, on Atlantic coast ab. 1 m. S of and adjoining Asbury Park; pop. (1950) 3806; founded 1869 originally for camp meetings, religious conferences, etc.; large auditorium; no industries allowed.

O'ce·an'i·a (ō'shē·ăn'ĭ·á; -ā'nĭ·á) *or* **O'ce·an'i·ca** (-ăn'ĭ·ká). **1** Collective name for the lands of the cen. and S Pacific Ocean, including Micronesia, Melanesia, and Polynesia, and sometimes Australia, New Zealand, and the Malay Archipelago.
2 See FRENCH OCEANIA.

Ocean Island. 1 *or* **Ba·na′ba** (bȧ·nä′bȧ). Island in the W Pacific Ocean, ab. 57 m. (52′) S of the equator bet. the Gilbert Is. and the island of Nauru; 2 sq. m.; pop. (1936) 2791; former ✳ of colony of Gilbert and Ellice Islands. Has large deposits of phosphate rock (estimated at 14 million tons) which are worked conjointly with those on Nauru by British Phosphate Co. Claimed by British 1900 and made part of Gilbert and Ellice Islands Colony 1916; occupied by Japanese 1942.

2 See KURE ISLAND.

Ocean Park. Former name of VENICE, California.

Ocean Pond. See OLUSTEE.

O′cean·port′ (ō′shăn·pōrt′). Borough, Monmouth co., E cen. New Jersey, 6 m. N of Asbury Park; pop. 4937.

O′cean·side′ (ō′shăn·sīd′). Residential city, San Diego co., SW corner of California, on Gulf of Santa Catalina 45 m. N of San Diego; pop. 24,971; beach resort.

Ocean Springs. Town, Jackson co., SE corner of Mississippi, across inlet from Biloxi; pop. 5025; resort.

Oceanus Atlanticus. See ATLANTIC OCEAN.

Oceanus Britannicus. See ENGLISH CHANNEL.

O·ce′a·nus Can·ta′bri·us (ō·sē′ȧ·nŭs kăn·tā′brĭ·ŭs). = *Cantaber Oceanus*: see Bay of BISCAY.

Ocha. See HAGIOS ELIAS.

O·cha′kov (ŭ·chȧ′kŭf). Seaport town, S Ukraine, U.S.S.R., on the Black Sea bet. Odessa and Kherson; pop. ab. 5000.

O·chi·ai (ō·chē·ī). Town, SE Karafuto, Sakhalin I.; pop. (1939 est.) 14,881; on coast 50 m. N of Otomari, with which it is connected by rail; formerly Japanese.

O′chil Hills (ō′κĭl; ōκ′ĭl). Range of hills in Perth co., cen. Scotland; highest peak **Ben Cleuch** (bĕn klōōκ′) 2363 ft.

Och′il·tree (ŏk′′l·trē). County in Texas. See *Table* at TEXAS.

Och·lock′o·nee (ŏk·lŏk′ō·nē). River ab. 135 m. long, S Georgia and NW Florida; rises in Worth co., S Georgia, flows SW across NW Florida into Gulf of Mexico.

O′cho Ri′os (ō′chō rē′ōs). Seaport, N Jamaica, NW of Kingston; resort.

Ochrida. Var. of *Okhrida*: see OHRID.

O·cil′la (ō·sĭl′ȧ). 1 River, Florida. See AUCILLA.

2 City, ⊗ of Irwin co., S Georgia ; pop. 3217.

Oc·mul′gee (ŏk·mŭl′gē). River 255 m. long in cen. Georgia; formed by junction of Yellow and South rivers in Newton co., flows S and SE to join the Oconee in S Montgomery co. and form the Altamaha river.

Ocmulgee National Monument. See UNITED STATES, *National Monuments.*

O·co′a Bay (ō·kō′ä). Bay in S coast of the Dominican Republic, Hispaniola I., West Indies.

O·co′ee (ō·kō′ē). River ab. 70 m. long, NE Georgia and SE Tennessee; rises in S Fannin co., Georgia, flows N and NW to Hiwassee river in Polk co., Tennessee; called **Toc·co′a** (tŏ·kō′ȧ) river in Georgia. In its course in N Georgia is the Blue Ridge Dam and in Tennessee are three dams, **Ocoee No. 1, Ocoee No. 2,** and **Ocoee No. 3,** all in the Tennessee Valley Authority (*q.v.*).

O·co′nee (ō·kō′nē). 1 River ab. 250 m. long in cen. Georgia; rises in Hall co., N Georgia, flows S and SE to join the Ocmulgee and form the Altamaha river in S Montgomery co., SE cen. Georgia.

2 Name of counties in two states in the U.S. See *Tables* at GEORGIA and SOUTH CAROLINA.

O·con′o·mo·woc′ (ŭ·kŏn′ŭ·mŭ·wŏk′). City, Waukesha co., SE Wisconsin, 13 m. ESE of Watertown; pop. 6682; health resort; mineral springs.

O·con′to (ō·kŏn′tō). 1 River ab. 130 m. long in NE Wisconsin; rises in SE Forest co., flows S and E into Green Bay at Oconto.

2 County in Wisconsin. See *Table* at WISCONSIN.

3 City, its ⊗, NE Wisconsin, on Green Bay at mouth of Oconto river 18 m. SSW of Marinette; pop. 4805; manufactures veneers, flooring, leather products.

Oconto Falls. City, Oconto co., NE Wisconsin, 27 m.

N of Green Bay (city); pop. 2331; lumbering, fishing, farming.

O′co·tal′ (ō′kō·täl′). Town, NW Nicaragua, ✳ of Nueva Segovia dept., on upper Segovia river near Honduras border; pop. (1943 est.) 3129.

O·co′te·pe′que (ō·kō′tä·pā′kā). 1 Department, W Honduras; 859 sq. m.; pop. (1945 est.) 45,324.

2 Town, its ✳, on El Salvador border; pop. (1935) 994.

O′co·tlán′ (ō′kō·tlän′). Town, Jalisco state, W cen. Mexico, at NE corner of Lake Chapala; pop. 14,289.

O′cra·coke Island (ō′krȧ·kōk). Island off cen. North Carolina coast, in chain of narrow sandy islands lying bet. Pamlico Sound and Atlantic Ocean; Hatteras Inlet NE of it and **Ocracoke Inlet** SW of it connect the sound with the ocean.

Ocriculum. See OTRICOLI.

October Revolution Island; *Russ.* **O′strov Ok·tya′-br·skoi Re·vo·lyu′tsi** (ō′strŭf ŭk·tyá′bĕr·skoi ryĭ·vŭ-lū′tsi). Central island of the Severnaya Zemlya group, Arctic Ocean, Taimyr National District, Soviet Russia, Asia.

Octodurus. See MARTIGNY-VILLE.

O′cu·ma′re del Tuy (ō′kōō·mä′rā thĕl twē′) *or* **Ocumare.** Town, Miranda state, N Venezuela, 30 m. S of Caracas; pop. (1941 est.) 6496.

Ocussi, Ocussi Ambeno. See OKUSI, OKUSI AMBENO.

O·da·wa·ra (ō·dä·wä·rä). Town, Kanagawa prefecture, SE Honshu, Japan, on Sagami Sea 50 m. SW of Tokyo; pop. ab. 14,000.

O·de·mis′ (ŭ·dĕ·mēsh′). Town, SE İzmir vilayet, W Turkey in Asia, 45 m. ESE of İzmir; pop. 18,720.

Ödenburg. See SOPRON.

O′den·kir′chen (ō′dĕn·kĭr′κĕn). Former city (pop. 20,076), Düsseldorf govt. dist., Rhine Province, Prussia, Germany; part of Gladbach-Rheydt 1929–33, since 1933 part of Rheydt.

O′den·se (ō′thĕn·sĕ). 1 County in Denmark. See *Table* at DENMARK.

2 City, its ⊗, N Fyn I., Denmark; pop. (1945) 92,436; manufactures machinery and textiles; breweries, distilleries, sugar refineries; 14th-cent. Gothic cathedral. Birthplace of Hans Christian Andersen.

O′den·wald′ (ō′dĕn·vält′). Mountainous region ab. 50 m. long in SW Germany in the states of Hesse, Baden-Württemberg, and Bavaria bet. the Neckar and Main rivers; highest point the Katzenbuckel 2057 ft.

O′der (ō′dĕr); *Czech and Polish* **O′dra** (ō′drȧ); *anc.* **Vi-ad′u·a** (vī·ăd′ū·ȧ). River 563 m. long in cen. Europe; rises in the mountains of Silesia, Czechoslovakia; flows N through W Poland (formerly E Germany) to join the Neisse 21 m. SSE of Frankfurt where it forms the boundary bet. Poland and Germany, thence N into the Baltic Sea at Stettiner Haff, passing through Opole (Oppeln), Wrocław (Breslau), Frankfurt, and Stettin (Szczecin) in its course; navigable for most of its length; chief tributaries on the left Nysa (Glatzer Neisse), Kocaba (Katzbach), Bobr, and Lausitzer Neisse; on the right Warta. Internationalized from its confluence with the Oppa at Moravská Ostrava under terms of the Treaty of Versailles 1919. In World War II much fighting along its course in early part of 1945; by Potsdam Conference 1945, its upper course, formerly in Silesia, placed in Poland, and its lower course from confluence with the Neisse made boundary bet. Germany and Poland.

O′der Haff (ō′dĕr häf′). = STETTINER HAFF.

O′der–Neis′se Line (ō′dĕr·nī′sĕ). Boundary line bet. E Germany and W Poland, adopted at the Potsdam Conference 1945 and formed by the Neisse (Lausitzer Neisse) from the Sudeten Mts. to its junction with the Oder S of Frankfurt and the Oder thence N to the Stettiner Haff.

O·der′zo (ō·dĕr′tsō); *anc.* **Op′i·ter′gi·um** (ŏp′ĭ·tûr′jĭ-ŭm). Commune, Treviso prov., Venezia Euganea, NE Italy, 15 m. NE of Treviso; pop. 12,524; 10th-cent. cathedral; Roman museum.

O·des′sa (ô·dĕs′à). **1** City, Lafayette co., W Missouri, 28 m. E of Independence; pop. 2034; trading center in agricultural section.
2 City, ⊗ of Ector co., W Texas, 56 m. WSW of Big Spring; pop. 80,338; oil wells and related industries.
O·des′sa (ô·dĕs′á; *Russ.* ŭ·dyĕs′sá). **1** Region, S Ukraine, U.S.S.R., on NW shore of Black Sea; bordered on SW by lower Dniester.
2 Seaport city, its *, 25 m. NE of the mouth of the Dniester on **Odessa Bay**; pop. 604,223; one of chief ports of the U.S.S.R.; has fine fivefold harbor sheltered by two long breakwaters, blocked by ice usually for less than one month; many manufacturing industries; grain elevators, shipyards; exports grain, lumber, coal, wool, sugar, cattle; town built on terraced hills and noted for its beauty; has Technical University; its cosmopolitan population has encouraged wide use of Esperanto.
History: Region early colonized by Greeks but towns declined; present town founded in 14th cent. by Tatar chief; held later by Lithuanians and Poles; captured by Turks in 16th cent. but finally became Russian in 1789; administrative center of New Russia from 1824; scene of workers' revolution 1905; suffered in civil war 1917–20 and from famine and disease 1921–23; in World War II captured by Axis armies Oct. 16, 1941; recovered by Russians Apr. 10, 1944.
Odessus. See VARNA.
O·diel′ (ô·thyĕl′). River ab. 60 m. long, Huelva prov., SW Spain; flows S and joins the Tinto below Huelva; combined steams flow into the Mediterranean.
O′din (ō′d'n). Village, Marion co., S cen. Illinois, 8 m. NE of Centralia; pop. 1242.
O·dioñg′an (ô·dyông′ăn). Municipality in cen. part of W coast of Tablas I., Romblon prov., Phil. Is., on Tablas Strait 23 m. SW of Romblon; pop. 16,628.
Odomari. See OTOMARI.
O′don′ (ô′dôn″). Short stream of Normandy, NW France, a W tributary of the Orne, entering it at Caen; in World War II severe fighting on its banks in battle of Normandy June–July 1944.
O′·Don′nell, Camp (ô·dŏn′'l). Camp in Pampanga, Luzon, Phil. Is., near San Fernando; used by Japanese in World War II as prison camp for Americans and Filipinos captured in Bataan; taken by Americans Jan. 23, 1945.
O·doorn′ (ô·dōrn′). Commune, Drenthe prov., NE Netherlands, 35 m. SE of Groningen near German border; pop. 12,304.
O·dor·hei′ (ô·dôr·hā′); *Hung.* **Szé′kely·ud′var·hely** (sā′kä·ōōd′vŏr·hā). Town, E Transylvania, Romania, E of Sighişoara; pop. 8592.
Odra. See ODER.
Oea. See TRIPOLI.
Oedanes. See BRAHMAPUTRA.
Oe·le′ë·heu′ë (ōō·lā′ë·hü′ä) *or* **U·le′el·heu′e** (ōō·lā′ĕl - hü′ä). Seaport town, the port of Kutaradja, at N tip of Sumatra, Indonesia, opp. the island of We.
Oels, Oels in Schlesien. See OLEŚNICA.
Oelsnitz. See ÖLSNITZ.
Oel′wein (ōl′wīn). City, Fayette co., NE Iowa, 25 m. ENE of Waterloo; pop. 8282; railroad and industrial center in agricultural section.
O·e′no Island (ô·ā′nō). Uninhabited coral island in S Pacific Ocean, ab. 95 m. NNW of Pitcairn I.; 24°S and 130°41′W; attached to Pitcairn Island colony.
Oe·no′tri·a (ê·nō′trĭ·à). Ancient region, S Italy; comprised Bruttium (modern Calabria) and Lucania; noted for its vineyards; the name (literally "wine land") probably first applied by Greeks.
Oer–Er′ken·schwick (ûr′ĕr′kĕn·shvĭk). Commune, North Rhine-Westphalia state, W Germany, NE suburb of Recklinghausen; pop. 15,036.
Oer′li·kon (ûr′lê·kôn). Commune, Zurich canton, NE cen. Switzerland, N suburb of Zurich; pop. (1930) 12,502; became part of Zurich 1934.

Oesel. See SAREMA.
Oe′ta (ē′tà). Mountain chain in Phthiotis and Phocis dept., cen. Greece; highest point 7080 ft. Forms an E spur of the Pindus Mts. and terminates on the E at Pass of Thermopylae on the Gulf of Lamia; in ancient times was on E border of Aetolia. Scene of the legendary death of Hercules.
Oetztal, Oetztaler. Vars. of ÖTZTAL, ÖTZTALER (Alps).
O′·Fal′lon (ô·făl′ŭn). City, St. Clair co., SW Illinois, 15 m. E of East St. Louis; pop. 4018.
O′fan·to (ô′fän·tô); *anc.* **Au′fi·dus** (ô′fĭ·dŭs). River 103 m. long in SE Italy; flows E through Avellino prov., Campania, into the Adriatic Sea 4 m. NW of Barletta, Apulia.
Of′fa·ly (of′à·lĭ). County, E cen. Eire, in W Leinster prov.; area 771 sq. m.; pop. 51,308; ⊗ Tullamore; rivers Shannon, Brosna, Barrow, Boyne; agriculture, livestock raising.
Of′fa′s Dyke (ôf′áz). Remains of an entrenchment extending from the Wye river to the Dee river in England and Wales, built by Offa (d. 796), king of the Mercians, along W border of Mercia as a fortification against the Welsh.
Of′fen·bach (ôf′ĕn·bäк). Industrial city, Hesse, Germany, on left bank of the Main river just E of Frankfurt am Main; pop. 79,362; manufactures leather, leather goods, machinery, metal goods, chemicals, foodstuffs, paper. Occupied by Allied armies Mar. 29, 1945.
Of′fen·burg (ôf′ĕn·bōōrк). Manufacturing city, SW Baden-Württemberg state, W Germany, at foot of the Black Forest 33 m. N of Freiburg; pop. 16,613; 14th-cent. church; manufactures glass, leather, textiles, tobacco, beer.
Of′fi·da (ôf′fê·dä). Commune, Ascoli Piceno prov., S Marches, cen. Italy; pop. (1931) 7131; ruins of Sabine temple; ancient church.
O′fot·en Fjord (ō′fŏt·'n fyŏr; ōō′fŏŏt·'n fyōōr′) *or* **O′fot·fjord′** (ō′fŏt·fyŏr′; ōō′fŏŏt·fyōōr′). Northeast extension of Vest Fjord on NW coast of Norway; site of port of Narvik.
O′fu (ô′fōō). Westernmost island of the Manua Is. (q.v.) in American Samoa; 3 sq. m.; pop. 605; separated from Olosega (2 sq. m.) on the E by so narrow a channel that the two islands appear to be one. Both islands mountainous; highest point on Ofu 1587 ft., on Olosega 2095 ft.
O·ga′den (ô·gä′dän; *native* wōō·gä·dän). Region, SE Ethiopia, bordering on Somalia; inhabited by Somalis.
O·ga·ki (ō·gä·kê). Town, Gifu prefecture, W cen. Honshu, Japan, just W of Gifu and 20 m. NW of Nagoya; pop. (1945) 50,767; important under the shoguns 16th–19th cent.
O′gal·la′la (ō′gà·lä′là). City, ⊗ of Keith co., W Nebraska, on South Platte river 52 m. W of North Platte; pop. 4250; former cattle-shipping point.
Ogasawara Islands *or* **Ogasawara Gunto.** See BONIN ISLANDS.
Og′bo·mo′sho (ŏg′bô·mō′shō). City, Oyo prov., W Western Region, Nigeria, 50 m. NNE of Ibadan; pop. 86,744.
Og′den (ŏg′dĕn). **1** Town, Boone co., cen. Iowa, 31 m. SSE of Fort Dodge; pop. 1525.
2 Industrial city, ⊗ of Weber co., N Utah, 33 m. N of Salt Lake City; pop. 70,197; railroad center and distributing point; flour mills, meat-packing plants, beet-sugar refineries, canneries; manufactures dresses, aprons, overalls, knit goods; tourist center. U.S. Forest Service regional headquarters; U.S. ordnance and military supply depots; Hill Air Force Base. Settled by the Mormons 1847; incorporated as city 1851.
Ogden, Mount; *formerly* **Observatory Peak.** Mountain 10,102 ft. in Morgan and Weber cos., N Utah, just E of Ogden in Wasatch Range.
Og′dens·burg (ŏg′dĕnz·bûrg). Industrial city, St. Lawrence co., N New York, on St. Lawrence river 55 m. NNE of Watertown; pop. 16,122; port of entry, railroad

terminus and distribution center for coal, grain, lumber; manufactures brass articles, silk, powdered milk, casein. Site purchased in 1792 by Col. Samuel Ogden; incorporated as village 1818; center of American sympathizers in Patriots' War of Canada 1837; chartered as city 1868; at **Heu'vel·ton** (hū'v'l·t'n; -tŭn), just SE of the city, Prime Minister Mackenzie King and President Franklin D. Roosevelt met Aug. 18, 1940 to formulate the "Ogdensburg Agreement" establishing a joint U.S.-Canadian board for studying problems of the defense of the north half of the Western Hemisphere.

O·gee'chee (ô·gē'chĕ). River ab. 250 m. long in E Georgia; rises in Green co., flows SE into Atlantic Ocean on Bryan-Chatham co. border.

O'ge·maw (ō'gĕ·mô). County in Michigan. See *Table* at MICHIGAN.

O'gil·vie Range (ō'g'l·vĭ). Range, cen. Yukon Territory, Canada; average height ab. 4000 ft.; highest point 6600 ft.

O'gle (ō'g'l). County in Illinois. See *Table* at ILLINOIS.

O'gles·by (ō'g'lz·bĭ). Industrial city, La Salle co., N Illinois, 13 m. WSW of Ottawa; pop. 4215; cement works; coal mines.

O'gle·thorpe (ō'g'l·thôrp). **1** County in Georgia. See *Table* at GEORGIA.
2 City, ⊗ of Macon co., SW cen. Georgia; pop. 1169.

Oglethorpe, Mount. Mountain 3290 ft. at S end of Blue Ridge Mts. in N Georgia; S terminus of the Appalachian Trail.

O'glio (ôl'yô); *anc.* **Ol'li·us** (ŏl'ĭ·ŭs). River 175 m. long in N Italy; rises in the Rhaetian Alps, flows SE through Lake Iseo and into Po river 10 m. SW of Mantua.

Og'more and Ga'rw (ŏg'mōr, gä'rōō). Urban district, Glamorganshire, SE Wales; pop. 22,638; coal mining.

O·go'ja (ô·gō'jä). **1** Province of Nigeria. See *Table* at NIGERIA.
2 Town, its ✳, cen. Eastern Region, Nigeria, ab. 120 m. N of Calabar; pop. ab. 1000.

O·go'ki (ô·gō'kĭ). River 300 m. long, a S tributary of the Albany, in cen. Ontario, Canada; rises in chain of lakes and flows NE and E.

O'go·oué' (ō'gô·wä') *or* **O'go·we'**. River ab. 700 m. long, Gabon, W equatorial Africa; flows W into Atlantic Ocean S of Cape Lopez; navigable for ab. 250 m.

O·gu'lin (ô·gōō'lēn). Commune, Croatia federated republic, NW Yugoslavia, 40 m. E of Fiume (Rieka); pop. 7624; ancient castle of Frangipani family.

O·gun'quit (ô·gŭn'kwĭt). Village, York co., SW Maine; fishing village and summer resort; headquarters of a summer theater group.

O'hau, Lake (ō'hou). Lake 23 sq. m. in S cen. South I., New Zealand; from its S end issues the **Ohau River,** one of the headstreams of the Waitaki river.

O'·Hig'gins (ô·hĭg'ĭnz; *Span.* ô·ē'gēns). **1** Peak 9550 ft. in S Chile, W of Lake San Martín.
2 Province of Chile. See *Table* at CHILE.
3 Name given Feb. 1948 to islands in South Shetland Is. claimed by Chile.

O·hi'o (ô·hī'ô). **1** Navigable river 981 m. long in Pennsylvania, Ohio, Indiana, Illinois; formed by confluence of Allegheny and Monongahela rivers at Pittsburgh, SW Pennsylvania, flows W and SW to form Ohio-West Virginia, Ohio-Kentucky, Indiana-Kentucky, and Illinois-Kentucky boundaries; empties into Mississippi river at Cairo, S extremity of Illinois.
2 A north central state of U.S.A., 17th state admitted to Union (1803); bounded on N by Michigan and Lake Erie, on E by Pennsylvania and Ohio river on S by Ohio river, and on W by Indiana; 35th state in area, 41,222 sq. m. (land area 41,000 sq. m.); in addition to this area Ohio has also 3457 sq. m. of water of the Great Lakes; 5th state in population, 9,706,397; ✳ Columbus. See *Table of States* at UNITED STATES. Divided into the following 88 counties (for pronunciation of their names, see their individual entries):

NAME	LOCATION	AREA[1]	POP.[1]	CO. SEAT
Adams	S	588	19,982	West Union
Allen	NW	410	103,691	Lima
Ashland	N cen.	418	38,771	Ashland
Ashtabula	NE corner	706	93,067	Jefferson
Athens	SE	504	46,998	Athens
Auglaize	W	400	36,147	Wapakoneta
Belmont	E	535	83,864	Saint Clairsville
Brown	SW	491	25,178	Georgetown
Butler	SW	471	199,076	Hamilton
Carroll	E	388	20,857	Carrollton
Champaign	W	433	29,714	Urbana
Clark	W	402	131,440	Springfield
Clermont	SW	458	80,530	Batavia
Clinton	SW	412	30,004	Wilmington
Columbiana	E	535	107,004	Lisbon
Coshocton	E cen.	545	32,224	Coshocton
Crawford	N cen.	404	46,775	Bucyrus
Cuyahoga	N	456	1,647,895	Cleveland
Darke	W	605	45,612	Greenville
Defiance	NW	410	31,508	Defiance
Delaware	cen.	459	36,107	Delaware
Erie	N	264	68,000	Sandusky
Fairfield	S cen.	505	63,912	Lancaster
Fayette	SW cen.	406	24,775	Washington Court House
Franklin	cen.	538	682,962	Columbus
Fulton	NW	407	29,301	Wauseon
Gallia	S	471	26,120	Gallipolis
Geauga	NE	407	47,573	Chardon
Greene	SW	416	94,642	Xenia
Guernsey	E	519	38,579	Cambridge
Hamilton	SW corner	414	864,121	Cincinnati
Hancock	NW	532	53,686	Findlay
Hardin	NW cen.	467	29,633	Kenton
Harrison	E	403	17,995	Cadiz
Henry	NW	416	25,392	Napoleon
Highland	S	554	29,716	Hillsboro
Hocking	S cen.	421	20,168	Logan
Holmes	NE cen.	423	21,591	Millersburg
Huron	N	497	47,326	Norwalk
Jackson	S	420	29,372	Jackson
Jefferson	E	411	99,201	Steubenville
Knox	cen.	524	38,808	Mount Vernon
Lake	NE	232	148,700	Painesville
Lawrence	S	456	55,438	Ironton
Licking	cen.	686	90,242	Newark
Logan	W	461	34,803	Bellefontaine
Lorain	N	495	217,500	Elyria
Lucas	NW	343	456,931	Toledo
Madison	SW cen.	464	26,454	London
Mahoning	NE	419	300,480	Youngstown
Marion	cen.	405	60,221	Marion
Medina	N	424	65,315	Medina
Meigs	SE	434	22,159	Pomeroy
Mercer	W	454	32,559	Celina
Miami	W	407	72,901	Troy
Monroe	SE	455	15,268	Woodsfield
Montgomery	SW	465	527,080	Dayton
Morgan	SE	418	12,747	McConnelsville
Morrow	cen.	404	19,405	Mount Gilead
Muskingum	SE cen.	663	79,159	Zanesville
Noble	SE	399	10,982	Caldwell
Ottawa	N	263	35,323	Port Clinton
Paulding	NW	416	16,792	Paulding
Perry	SE cen.	409	27,864	New Lexington
Pickaway	S cen.	507	35,855	Circleville
Pike	S	443	19,380	Waverly
Portage	NE	504	91,798	Ravenna
Preble	SW	428	32,498	Eaton
Putnam	NW	486	28,331	Ottawa
Richland	N cen.	497	117,761	Mansfield
Ross	S	687	61,215	Chillicothe
Sandusky	N	410	56,486	Fremont
Scioto	S	609	84,216	Portsmouth
Seneca	N	551	59,326	Tiffin
Shelby	W	409	33,586	Sidney
Stark	NE	573	340,345	Canton
Summit	NE	413	513,569	Akron
Trumbull	NE	620	208,526	Warren
Tuscarawas	E	551	76,789	New Philadelphia
Union	W cen.	434	22,853	Marysville
Van Wert	NW	409	28,840	Van Wert
Vinton	S	411	10,274	McArthur
Warren	SW	408	65,711	Lebanon
Washington	SE	637	51,689	Marietta
Wayne	NE cen.	551	75,497	Wooster
Williams	NW corner	421	29,968	Bryan
Wood	NW	618	72,596	Bowling Green
Wyandot	NW cen.	406	21,648	Upper Sandusky

[1] Area = land area in sq. m. Pop. from 1960 Census.

Nickname: Buckeye State. *State flower:* Scarlet carnation. *Motto:* (1866–68 only) Imperium in Imperio (a Sovereignty within a Sovereignty). *Chief cities:* Cleveland, Cincinnati, Columbus, Toledo, Akron, Dayton. *Rivers:* Ohio (SE and S boundary) and its tributaries

the Muskingum, Scioto, and Miami; Maumee and Sandusky flowing to Lake Erie. *Highest point:* Campbell Hill in Logan co., 1550 ft. *Chief industries:* Farming and grazing; coal mining; iron and steel, rubber, and pottery.

History: Has many earthwork mounds of prehistoric mound builders; parts claimed by French and by charters of Virginia and Connecticut, and by New York 1609–1786; became part of U.S. by Treaty of Paris 1783; claims to it of other states relinquished 1784–86; included 1787 in Northwest Territory (*q.v.*); 1st settlement at Marietta 1788; W boundary with Indian lands determined by Anthony Wayne's defeat of Indians 1794 at Fallen Timbers and by Treaty of Greenville 1795; Western Reserve (*q.v.*) incorporated 1800; 1st Constitution 1802; admitted to Union Feb. 19, 1803.
3 Name of counties in three states of the U.S. See *Tables* at INDIANA, KENTUCKY, WEST VIRGINIA.

Ohlau. See OŁAWA.

Oh′ligs (ō′lĭks). Former city (pop. 29,804), Düsseldorf govt. dist., Rhine Province, Prussia, Germany; since 1929 part of Solingen (*q.v.*).

O·hoo′pee (ô·hōō′pê). River 125 m. long, Georgia; rises in Washington co., flows SE to Altamaha river in S Tattnall co.

Oh′ra (ō′rä). Commune in former Free City of Danzig territory, Europe; pop. (1924) 12,500; now a S suburb of Danzig, Gdańsk dept., N Poland.

O′hře (ô′h′r-zhĕ); *Ger.* **E′ger** (ä′gēr). River 193 m. long in S Germany and W Czechoslovakia; rises in NE Bavaria, flows ENE across NW Bohemia prov., Czechoslovakia, into the Elbe river at Litoměřice.

O′hrid (ō′krēd). **1** *or* **O·khri′da** (ô·krē′dà); *anc.* **Lych′ni·dus** (lĭk′nĭ·dŭs) *or* **Lych·ni′tis** (lĭk·nĭ′tĭs). Lake 25 m. long in S Yugoslavia and E Albania.
2 *anc.* **Lychnidus.** Town on the lake, W Macedonia republic, SE Yugoslavia; pop. 9776.

Oich, Loch (lŏk oik′). Lake 5 m. long in cen. Inverness co., NW cen. Scotland; part of the chain of lakes incorporated into the Caledonian Canal; drains NE into Loch Ness.

Oil City (oil). Industrial city, Venango co., NW Pennsylvania, on Allegheny river at mouth of Oil Creek, 52 m. SSE of Erie; pop. 17,692; settled 1825; important oil center; oil refineries; manufactures barrels, steel drums, boilers, gas engines, pumping machinery.

Oil Creek. River ab. 50 m. long in NW Pennsylvania; flows S through E Crawford co. and N Venango co., enters Allegheny river at Oil City.

Oil Rivers. The vast delta of the Niger river, S Nigeria, W Africa, of indefinite boundaries. See NIGER river. Protectorate over the region, **Oil Rivers Protectorate,** established by the British in 1890 and administered by the British Royal Niger Company; became Niger Coast Protectorate 1893–99.

Oil′ton (oil′t′n; -tŭn). City, Creek co., E cen. Oklahoma, 30 m. WNW of Sapulpa; pop. 1100; gasoline shipping point.

Oi′me·kon (oi′myĕ·kŭn). Var. of OIMYAKON.

Oi′mya·kon (oi′myà·kŭn). Town, SE Yakutsk Republic, Soviet Russia, Asia, on the upper Indigirka river in mountain range S of the Cherskogo Range; Soviet weather station; a cold pole, one of the coldest places in Siberia; has had temperature of 79° below zero.

Oi′ron′ (wà′rôN′). Commune, Deux-Sèvres dept., W France, ab. 47 m. NNE of Niort; pop. (1931) 778; see SAINT-PORCHAIRE.

Oi′rot Autonomous Region (oi′rŭt**).** Autonomous region of the R.S.F.S.R. occupying E part of Altai Territory, Soviet Russia, Asia; 35,936 sq. m.; pop. 161,431, (1941 est.) 169,631; ✳ Oirot Tura. A mountainous land, comprising the ranges of the NW Altai Mts.; on the S on Kazakh border is Mt. Belukha, 15,157 ft., highest of the Altais; its two main streams are the Katun and Biya which join to form the Ob in SE Altai Territory; chief products cattle, timber, furs. Predominant ethnic strain

Turko-Tatar; the inhabitants Russians 52%, Oirats ab. 37%, and Teleuts 3%. First colonized in 18th cent.; created an autonomous area 1922.

Oirot Tu′ra (tōō′rà); *formerly* **U·la′la** (ōō·lä′lä). Town, ✳ of Oirot Autonomous Region, Soviet Russia, Asia, on Katun river in NW part; pop. ab. 10,000.

Oise (wàz). **1** River 186 m. long in N France; formed by confluence of two streams, one rising near Chimay in Belgium and the other near Rocroi in France; flows SW into Seine river at Conflans-Sainte-Honorine; navigable for ab. 80 m.
2 Department of France. See *Table* at FRANCE.

O·i·ta (ō·ê·tä). **1** Prefecture of Japan. See *Table* at JAPAN.
2 Seaport city, its ✳, NE Kyushu, Japan, 65 m. SE of Moji on Beppu Bay; pop. (1945) 65,781; has steamer connections with Kagoshima and with ports of Inland Sea. In 16th cen. a castle city that controlled nearly all Kyushu; encouraged trade with Portuguese in period before 1600.

O′jai (ō′hī). Residential and resort city, Ventura co., SW California, in Ojai valley of the Sierra Madre Range, 23 m. E of Santa Barbara; pop. 4495; known as Nordhoff until 1916.

O′jo de Lie′bre, La·gu′na (lä·gōō′nä ô′hô thä lyä′vrä). Inlet of Sebastián Vizcaíno Bay on coast of W cen. Lower California.

O′jos del Sa·la′do (ô′hôz thĕl sä·lä′thô). Mountain 22,572 ft. in NW Catamarca prov., NW Argentina, near border of Chile.

O·ka′ (ŭ·kà′). **1** River 530 m. long, cen. Irkutsk Region, Soviet Russia, Asia, flowing N from the Sayan Mts. to the Angara river.
2 River ab. 950 m. long in cen. Soviet Russia, Europe; rises in N part of Kursk Region, flows N and NE with several bends through Orel, Tula, Kaluga, Moscow, and Ryazan Regions to the Volga at Gorki. The largest right (W) tributary of the Volga; navigable for most of its length; important artery for lumber and grain trade; main tributaries the Klyazma, Moksha, and Moskva.

O′ka·han′dja (ō′kà·hän′jà). Town, cen. South-West Africa, 43 m. N of Windhoek; pop. 5417; agriculture, stock farming.

O′ka·lo′a·coo′chee Slough (ō′kà·lō′à·kōō′chê). The northwest section of the Everglades, S Florida, N of Big Cypress Swamp; used as pasture for cattle.

O′ka·loo′sa (ō′kà·lōō′sà). County in Florida. See *Table* at FLORIDA.

O′ka·na′gan Lake (ō′kà·nä′gǎn). Long narrow lake 136 sq. m., ab. 60 m. long, S British Columbia, Canada; its outlet is the Okanagan river, called the Okanogan (*q.v.*) in the U.S.

O′ka·nog′an (ō′kà·nŏg′ǎn). **1** County in Washington. See *Table* at WASHINGTON.
2 Town, its ⊗, N Washington, on Okanogan river; pop. 2001; in farming and lumbering section.
3 *in Canada* **O′ka·na′gan** (-nä′gǎn). River ab. 300 m. long, British Columbia and N Washington; rises in Okanagan Lake, British Columbia, flows S across Washington border and into Columbia river on S boundary of Okanogan co.

Okanoxubee. See NOXUBEE.

Okavango. Var. of OKOVANGGO.

O·ka·ya·ma (ô·kä·yä·mä). **1** Prefecture of Japan. See *Table* at JAPAN.
2 Seaport city, its ✳, W Honshu, Japan, on N side of Inland Sea 75 m. W of Kobe; pop. (1945) 92,862; manufactures esp. cotton products.
3 Town near SW coast of Formosa just N of Takao; in World War II a repair and supply base for Japanese airplanes.

O·ka·za·ki (ô·kä·zä·kê). Town, Aichi prefecture, S Honshu, Japan, 21 m. SE of Nagoya; pop. (1945) 75,666; birthplace of Iyeyasu, founder of the Tokugawa shogunate.

OHIO

Statute Miles

0   10   20   30   40

⊛ State Capital

PUBLISHED BY G. & C. MERRIAM COMPANY
SPRINGFIELD, MASS.
PREPARED BY J. W. CLEMENT CO., BUFFALO, N.Y.

O'kee·cho'bee (ō'kē̇·chō'bē̇). **1** County in Florida. See *Table* at FLORIDA.
2 City, its ⊗, SE cen. Florida penin., 2 m. N of Lake Okeechobee; pop. 2947.

Okeechobee, Lake. Lake in S cen. Florida; largest lake in S United States; ab. 40 m. long by 25 m. wide; greatest depth ab. 20 ft.; elevation 25 ft. above sea level; receives Kissimmee river from N and drains to the sea through the Everglades.

Okeechobee Waterway. See CROSS-FLORIDA WATERWAY.

O'ke·fe·no'kee, *also spelled* **O'ke·fi·no'kee, Swamp** (ō'kē̇·fĭ·nō'kē̇; *local and colloq.*, -fĭ·nŏk'). Swamp, SE Georgia, extending over the state boundary into Columbia and Baker cos., NE Florida; area 660 sq. m.

O·ke'mah (ō̇·kē'mȧ). City, ⊗ of Okfuskee co., E cen. Oklahoma, 25 m. WSW of Okmulgee; pop. 2836.

O·ke'ne (ō̇·kā'nȧ). Town, Kabba prov., Northern Region, Nigeria, 40 m. WSW of Lokoja; pop. 27,592.

O'ker (ō'kĕr). Stream ab. 65 m. long in W cen. Germany; flows N from Harz Mts. to the Aller.

Ok·fus'kee (ŏk·fŭs'kē̇). County in Oklahoma. See *Table* at OKLAHOMA.

O·kha' (ŭ·kȧ'). Town and port on NE coast of N Sakhalin I., Khabarovsk Territory, Soviet Russia, Asia; pop. ab. 17,000; important port open the year round; has railroad connection with oil station on W coast of Sakhalin and for 6 months in winter across the ice of Tatar Strait and by land with Komsomolsk, ab. 200 m.; oil fields nearby.

O'kha·man'dal (ōk'hä·mŭn'd'l). Division, Baroda state, W India, at W end of Kathiawar; 275 sq. m.; pop. 30,334.

O·khotsk' (ō̇·kŏtsk'; *Russ.* ŭ·kôtsk'). Town on NW coast of Sea of Okhotsk, Khabarovsk Territory, Soviet Russia, Asia, 440 m. N of Nikolaevsk; pop. ab. 3500; port closed by ice for more than half the year.

Okhotsk, Sea of. Inlet of Pacific Ocean on coast of Khabarovsk Territory, Soviet Russia, Asia, W of Kamchatka Penin. and the Kuril Is.; 582,000 sq. m.; greatest depth 10,554 ft.; has Sakhalin I. in SW; main traffic outlets Tatar Strait, Soya Strait, and Kuril Strait.

Okhrida. See OHRID lake.

O·ki Archipelago (ō̇·kē̇); *Jap.* **Oki Ret·to** (rĕt·tō). Group of islands in SE Sea of Japan, 44 m. off W coast of island of Honshu; 131 sq. m.; pop. (1945) 39,663; belongs to Shimane prefecture. Largest island Dogo, on SE coast of which is Saigo, the chief port, with fine harbor.

O·ki·e·ra·bu (ō̇·kē̇·ĕ·rä·bōō). Island, S Amami Is., Ryukyu Is., Japan, just N of Okinawa; 37 sq. m.; pop. (1945) 22,987.

O'ki·na'wa (ō'kĭ·nä'wȧ; *Jap.* ō̇·kē̇·nä·wä). **1** Island group in center of chain of Ryukyu Is.; comprises Okinawa and small islands of Ie, Iheya, Kume, and Kerama Is.

2 Only large island in group, bet. East China Sea and Pacific Ocean, 26°30'N, 128°E; ab. 70 m. long; excluding adjacent islands, 794 sq. m.; pop. (1943) 442,497; entirely of coral formation; chief town Naha at S end. Of vital importance in World War II; scene of severe fighting bet. Americans and Japanese Mar.–June 1945; bombed by U.S. carrier planes and bombarded by task force in March; center of island occupied by marines Apr. 1; island soon overrun except for S tip and area around Naha; this part not completely conquered until June 21 (see also YONABARU and SHURI); campaign costly but made possible the establishment of air bases close to Japanese mainland.

3 Prefecture of the Japanese Empire, comprising the S part of the Ryukyu (Nansei) Is. (Okinawa and Sakishima groups); 1482 sq. m.; pop. (1943) 574,579; ✻ Naha. See *Table* at JAPAN.

O·ki no Shi·ma (ō̇·kē̇ nō shē·mä). Small island off SW Shikoku, Japan, on E side of Bungo Strait, 32°43'N; belongs to Kochi prefecture.

O'kla·ho'ma (ō'klȧ·hō'mȧ). **1** A southwestern state of U.S.A., 46th state admitted to Union (1907); bounded on N by Colorado and Kansas, on E by Missouri and Arkansas, on S by Texas, and on W by Texas and New Mexico; 18th state in area, 69,919 sq. m. (land area 69,031 sq. m.); 27th state in population, 2,328,284; ✻ Oklahoma City. See *Table of States* at UNITED STATES. Divided into the following 77 counties (for pronunciation of their names, see their individual entries):

NAME	LOCATION	AREA[1]	POP.[1]	CO. SEAT
Adair	E	569	13,112	Stilwell
Alfalfa	N	867	8,445	Cherokee
Atoka	S	992	10,352	Atoka
Beaver	NW; in pan-handle	1,793	6,965	Beaver
Beckham	W	898	17,782	Sayre
Blaine	W cen.	911	12,077	Watonga
Bryan	S	891	24,252	Durant
Caddo	W cen.	1,275	28,621	Anadarko
Canadian[3]	cen.	885	24,727	El Reno
Carter	S	829	39,044	Ardmore
Cherokee	E	782	17,762	Tahlequah
Choctaw	SE	784	15,637	Hugo
Cimarron	NW[2]	1,832	4,496	Boise City
Cleveland	cen.	547	47,600	Norman
Coal	S	526	5,546	Coalgate
Comanche[3]	SW	1,088	90,803	Lawton
Cotton	SW	629	8,031	Walters
Craig	NE	764	16,303	Vinita
Creek	E cen.	972	40,495	Sapulpa
Custer	W	999	21,040	Arapaho
Delaware	NE	720	13,198	Jay
Dewey	W	977	6,051	Taloga
Ellis	NW	1,222	5,457	Arnett
Garfield	N	1,054	52,975	Enid
Garvin	S cen.	814	28,290	Pauls Valley
Grady	cen.	1,092	29,590	Chickasha
Grant	N	999	8,140	Medford
Greer	SW	637	8,877	Mangum
Harmon	SW	532	5,852	Hollis
Harper	NW	1,034	5,956	Buffalo
Haskell	E	614	9,121	Stigler
Hughes	E cen.	810	15,144	Holdenville
Jackson	SW	780	29,736	Altus
Jefferson	S	755	8,192	Waurika
Johnston	S	636	8,517	Tishomingo
Kay	N	944	51,042	Newkirk
Kingfisher	cen.	894	10,635	Kingfisher
Kiowa	SW	1,032	14,825	Hobart
Latimer	E	737	7,738	Wilburton
Le Flore	E	1,575	29,106	Poteau
Lincoln	cen.	973	18,783	Chandler
Logan	cen.	747	18,662	Guthrie
Love	S	488	5,862	Marietta
McClain	cen.	559	12,740	Purcell
McCurtain	SE corner	1,854	25,851	Idabel
McIntosh	E	715	12,371	Eufaula
Major	NW	945	7,808	Fairview
Marshall	S	360	7,263	Madill
Mayes	NE	676	20,073	Pryor Creek
Murray[4]	S	428	10,622	Sulphur
Muskogee	E	820	61,866	Muskogee
Noble	N	744	10,376	Perry
Nowata	NE	577	10,848	Nowata
Okfuskee	E cen.	638	11,706	Okemah
Oklahoma	cen.	709	439,506	Oklahoma City
Okmulgee	E cen.	700	36,945	Okmulgee
Osage	N	2,293	32,441	Pawhuska
Ottawa	NE corner	461	28,301	Miami
Pawnee	N	591	10,884	Pawnee
Payne	N cen.	692	44,231	Stillwater
Pittsburg	SE	1,359	34,360	McAlester
Pontotoc	S cen.	719	28,089	Ada
Pottawatomie	cen.	797	41,486	Shawnee
Pushmataha	SE	1,423	9,088	Antlers
Roger Mills	W	1,124	5,090	Cheyenne
Rogers	NE	713	20,614	Claremore
Seminole	cen.	629	28,066	Wewoka
Sequoyah	E	703	18,001	Sallisaw
Stephens	S	893	37,990	Duncan
Texas	NW; in pan-handle	2,056	14,162	Guymon
Tillman	SW	861	14,654	Frederick
Tulsa	NE	572	346,038	Tulsa
Wagoner	NE	584	15,673	Wagoner
Washington	NE	425	42,347	Bartlesville
Washita	W	1,009	18,121	Cordell
Woods	NW	1,271	11,932	Alva
Woodward	NW	1,232	13,902	Woodward

[1] Area = land area in sq. m. Pop. from 1960 Census.
[2] W tip of panhandle; only county in U.S. to border four states (Colorado and Kansas on N, New Mexico on W, Texas on S).
[3] Contains military reservations in Canadian co. (Fort Reno, in cen. part) and Comanche co. (Fort Sill) in E cen. part.
[4] Contains Platt National Park in E cen. part.

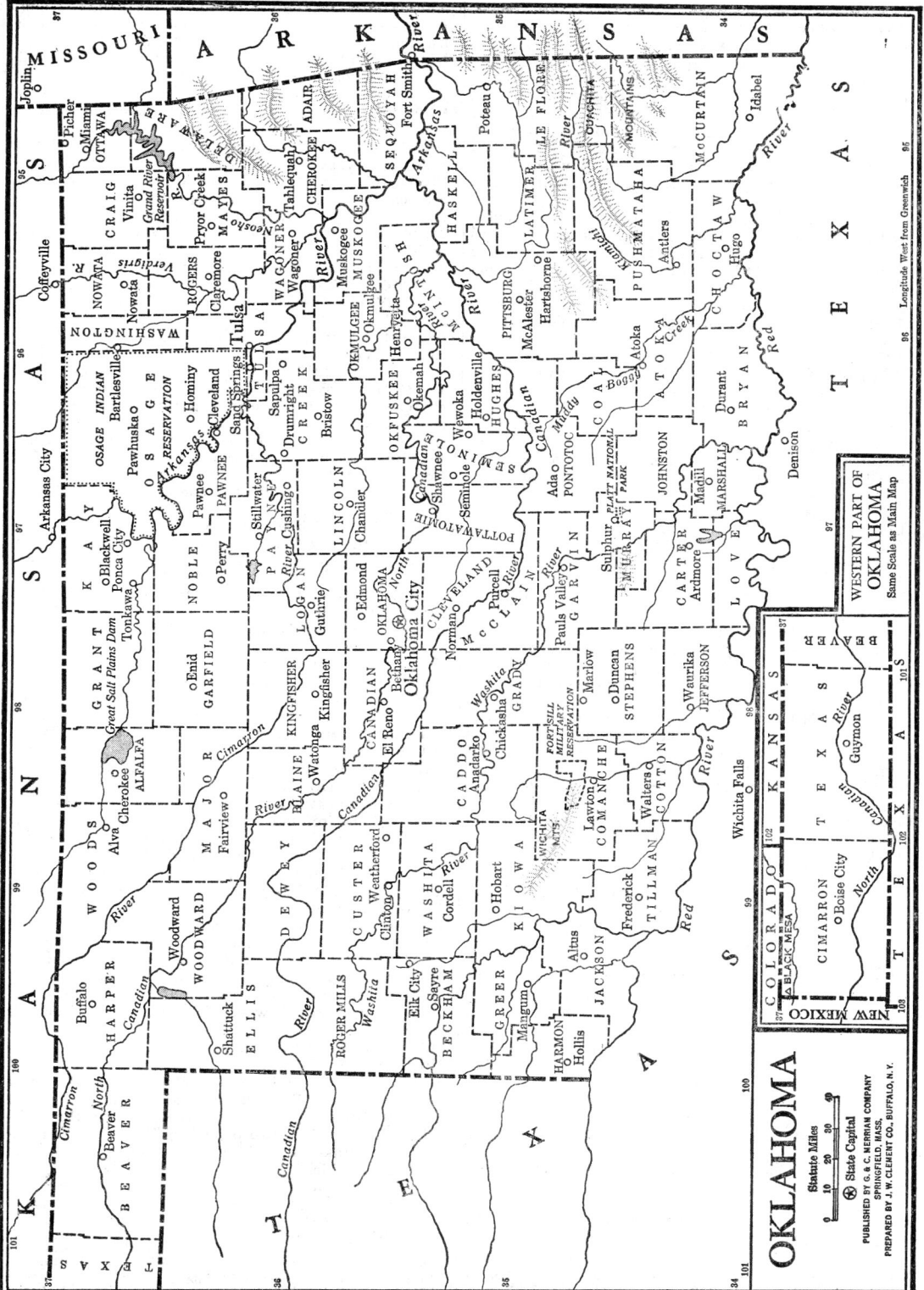

OKLAHOMA

Statute Miles

0   10   20   30   40

⊛ State Capital

PUBLISHED BY G. & C. MERRIAM COMPANY
SPRINGFIELD, MASS.
PREPARED BY J. W. CLEMENT CO., BUFFALO, N.Y.

WESTERN PART OF
OKLAHOMA
Same Scale as Main Map

Nickname: Sooner State.   *State flower:* Mistletoe. *Motto:* Labor Omnia Vincit (Labor Conquers All). *Chief cities:* Oklahoma City, Tulsa, Lawton, Enid. *Rivers:* Red, forming S boundary; Canadian, flowing across central area to empty into the Arkansas near E cen. border; Arkansas, flowing diagonally NW to SE across NE quarter of state. *Mountains:* Highest point Black Mesa 4978 ft. in Cimarron co. in the panhandle; Wichita Mts. in SW; W part of Ouachita Mts in SE. *Chief cities:* Oklahoma City, Tulsa, Lawton, Enid. corn), petroleum production, stock raising, mining (coal and zinc).

History: Except for panhandle, formed part of Louisiana Purchase (*q.v.*) from France 1803; settled by Indians as unorganized Indian Territory 1820–40; part opened to white settlement 1889; W part organized as Oklahoma Territory 1890; rest gradually opened to whites; by Enabling Act of 1906, Indian Territory and Oklahoma Territory were merged and admitted to Union as state Nov. 16, 1907.

2 County in Oklahoma. See *Table* at OKLAHOMA.

Oklahoma City. City, ✳ of Oklahoma and ⊗ of Oklahoma co., cen. Oklahoma, on North Canadian river; largest city in the state; pop. 324,253; leading commercial, financial, industrial, and distributing center of Oklahoma; oil wells; railroad center; agriculture; manufactures iron and steel, furniture, clothing, pottery, electrical equipment, tanks, storage batteries; meat packing, oil refining, automobile assembly plants. Univ. of Oklahoma School of Medicine (1900), Oklahoma City College of Law (1924; coed.), and Oklahoma City Univ. (1911; coed.). Tinker Air Force Base. Opened for white settlement 1889; incorporated 1890; became capital 1910.

Ok′la·wa′ha (ŏk′lȧ·wô′hȧ). River ab. 60 m. long, N cen. Florida penin.; rises in Lake co., flows N and E through Marion and Putnam cos. into St. Johns river; part of its course to be used in proposed canal across Florida.

Ok·mul′gee (ŏk·mŭl′gė). **1** County in Oklahoma. See *Table* at OKLAHOMA.

2 City, ⊗ of Okmulgee co., E cen. Oklahoma, 37 m. S of Tulsa; pop. 15,951; chief industries oil refining, glass making, cotton processing, meat packing, zinc smelting; market for peanuts and pecans; oil and gas wells; coal mines. Capital of the Creek Nation 1868–1907; settled 1872.

O′ko·bo′ji (ō′kȯ·bō′jė). Two lakes, East Okoboji and West Okoboji (ab. 6 m. long, area ab. 6 sq. m.), in cen. Dickinson co., NW Iowa.

O′ko·bo′jo Creek (ō′kȯ·bō′jō). River ab. 75 m. long, cen. South Dakota; rises in Potter co., flows SW into Missouri river in SW Sully co.

O′ko·lo′na (ō′kȯ·lō′nȧ). City, a ⊗ of Chickasaw co., NE Mississippi, 18 m. S of Tupelo; pop. 2622; dairy products.

O′ko·vang′go (ō′kȯ·văng′gō); *Port.* **Cu·ban′go** (kōō-văNng′gōō). River ab. 1000 m. long in SW cen. Africa; rises in cen. Angola; flows S and then E, forming a section of the boundary bet. Angola and South-West Africa; crosses Caprivi Concession and empties into **Okovanggo Basin,** a great marsh N of Lake Ngami in N Bechuanaland Protectorate.

Oks′tin′de·ne (ŏks′tĭn′ĕ·nĕ; ŏōks′-). Peak 6273 ft. in N cen. Norway, S of Svartisen ice field.

Ok·tib′be·ha (ŏk·tĭb′ĕ·hȯ). County in Mississippi. See *Table* at MISSISSIPPI.

O·ku·ji·ri (ō·kŏō·jė·rė) *or* **O·ku·shi·ri** (-shė·rė). Island in the Sea of Japan off SW coast of Hokkaido, Japan; 56 sq. m.; pop. (1945) 6404.

O·ku′si *or* **O·cus′si** (ō·kŏō′sė). Port and military station of the Portuguese on N coast of Timor I., in the exclave of Okusi Ambeno.

Okusi Am·be′no (äm·bā′nō) *or* **Ocussi Ambeno.** A wedge-shaped area ab. 950 sq. m. on N coast of Nether-

lands Timor forming an exclave of Portuguese Timor. Retained by Portugal in treaty of 1859 dividing Timor bet. Portuguese and Dutch; since 1962 part of Indonesia.

O·la′a (ō·lä′ä). Village, Puna dist., Hawaii co., Hawaii, near E coast of Hawaii I. S of Hilo; pop. (est.) 2000; post office for Keaau town.

Ó′lafs·vík′ (ō′läfs·vēk′). Town, W Iceland, on coast on peninsula S of Breidi Fjord.

O·lan′cho (ō·län′chō). Department, E cen. Honduras; 12,986 sq. m.; pop. (1945 est.) 68,133; ✳ Juticalpa.

Ö′land (û′länd). Island in Baltic Sea off SE coast of Sweden, in Kalmar prov. and separated from the mainland by Kalmarsund; 85 m. long; area 519 sq. m.; pop. 26,299; chief town Borgholm, on W coast; alum deposits. Mentioned early (8th cent.) in Scandinavian history; often a battleground in northern wars.

O·la′the (ō·lā′thė). City, ⊗ of Johnson co., E Kansas, 20 m. SW of Kansas City; pop. 10,987; on the old Santa Fe Trail.

O·la′wa (ō·lä′vä); *Ger.* **Oh′lau** (ō′lou). Manufacturing city, E Wrocław dept., SW Poland, on left bank of the Oder (Odra) 18 m. SE of Wrocław; pop. (1946) 13,136; formerly in Silesia, Germany; late 12th-cent. church; 16th-cent. castle (now a school); manufactures zinc white, white lead, electrochemical goods, cigars, tile, stoves; cattle market. Became city 1291; taken Feb. 7, 1945 by Russian troops; assigned to Poland by Potsdam Conference 1945.

Öl′berg (ûl′bĕrĸ). Highest of the hills of the Siebengebirge (*q.v.*), 1509 ft.

Ol′bern·hau (ôl′bĕrn·hou). City, Saxony, East Germany, in the Erz Gebirge 21 m. SE of Chemnitz; pop. 10,004; manufactures furniture, artificial flowers, toys, paper.

Ol′bi·a (ôl′bĭ·ȧ). **1** Ancient name of TERRANOVA PAUSANIA, NE Sardinia.

2 Ancient town on N coast of Black Sea, S Sarmatia, at mouth of the Hypanis.

Olcinium. See ULCINJ.

Old Ba·ha′ma Channel (bȧ·hä′mȧ; *in U.S., also* -hā′-). Channel in W West Indies, N of E cen. Cuba and SE of Santaren Channel.

Old Baldy Peak. Mountain 14,125 ft. in Costilla co., S Colorado.

Old′bur·y (ōld′bĕr·ĭ; -brĭ). Urban district, Worcestershire, W cen. England, 7 m. W of Birmingham; pop. 53,953; manufactures iron and steel products and chemicals; coal and iron mines and limestone quarries nearby.

Old Cas·tile′ (kăs·tēl′); *Span.* **Cas·ti′lla la Vie′ja** (käs·tē′[l]yä lä vyĕ′hä). Old provincial region, N Castile, Spain; 25,490 sq. m.; bounded on N by Bay of Biscay, on NE by Basque Provinces and Navarre, on SE by Aragon, on S by New Castile, on W by León, and on NW by Asturias; comprises modern provinces of Ávila, Burgos, Logroño, Palencia, Santander, Segovia, Soria, and Valladolid; ✳ Burgos. For history, see CASTILE.

Old Clump Hill (klŭmp). Mountain in Delaware co., S New York, in the Catskills near Roxbury (*q.v.*); site of "Woodchuck Lodge" where John Burroughs spent his last years.

Old Deer. See Old DEER.

Old Delhi. See DELHI.

Ol′den·burg (ōl′dĕn·bûrg; *Ger.* ôl′dĕn·bŏōĸĸ). **1** Former German state, NW Germany; 2083 sq. m.; pop. (1939) 582,400; ✳ Oldenburg; formed the following three districts (Landesteile), two of which, Birkenfeld and Lübeck, were taken from it in reorganization of German lands by Nazi leaders 1934:

NAME	LOCATION IN GERMANY	AREA	POP. (1925 CENSUS)	CAPITAL
Birkenfeld	SW[1]	194	55,714	Birkenfeld
Lübeck	N[2]	209	47,617	Eutin
Oldenburg	NW	2,076	442,418	Oldenburg

[1] Exclave N of Saar; now in Rheinland.
[2] Exclave on Baltic; in 1937 incorporated in Schleswig-Holstein.

2 District of Oldenburg. See *Table of Districts*, above. Corresponds approximately to state (*Land*) in Germany in 1939.

3 Manufacturing and commercial city, ✱ of the former state, now in Lower Saxony state, on Hunte river 80 m. W of Bremen; pop. 52,723; 13th-cent. church, 15th-cent. chapel, 17th-cent. Renaissance castle; manufactures glassware, meat products, tobacco, machinery; important horse and cattle markets. First mentioned 1108; made city 1345; surrendered to Canadian forces May 3, 1945 in World War II.

Ol'den·zaal' (ŏl'dĕn·zäl'). Commune, Overijssel prov., E Netherlands, 38 m. ESE of Zwolle near German border; pop. 10,026.

Old Faithful. Geyser in Yellowstone National Park, NW Wyoming; erupts regularly at intervals of ab. 67 minutes.

Old Flet'ton (flĕt'*n). Urban district, Huntingdonshire, E cen. England, S suburb of Peterborough 72 m. N of London; pop. 8955.

Old Forge (fôrj; fōrj). Borough, Lackawanna co., NE Pennsylvania, 6 m. SW of Scranton; pop. 8928; settled c. 1830; center for mining and shipping coal; textile mills.

Old Goa. See GOA.

Old Greenwich. Subdivision of town of GREENWICH, Connecticut.

Old'ham (ŏl'dăm). **1** Name of counties in two states of the U.S. See *Tables* at KENTUCKY and TEXAS.
2 County borough, Lancashire, NW England, on the Medlock 6 m. NE of Manchester; pop. 140,314, (1951) 121,212; cotton-spinning center; manufactures textile machinery; coal deposits nearby.

Old Harbour Bay *or* **Port'land Bight** (pōrt'lănd). Gulf in SE coast of Jamaica, West Indies; fleet anchorage and several areas around the bight leased Sept. 2, 1940 by Great Britain to the United States as naval and air bases.

Old Hick'o·ry (hĭk'ō·rĭ; hĭk'rĭ). Town, Davidson co., N cen. Tennessee, on Cumberland river ab. 10 m. NE of Nashville; pop. (est.) 8500; called Jacksonville until 1923. Built as wartime powder factory community in 1918; bought by E. I. Du Pont de Nemours & Co. 1924; rayon and cellophane manufactures.

Old House Point. Cape on S coast of the island of Jamaica, West Indies, on W side of entrance to Kingston harbor.

Old Ka·saan' National Monument (ká·sän'). See UNITED STATES, *National Monuments*.

Old Lyme (lĭm). Residential town and summer resort, SW New London co., SE Connecticut, at mouth of Connecticut river on left bank; pop. 3068; settled 1665, incorporated 1855; noted for numerous old homes of architectural interest.

Old'man (ōld'măn). River ab. 200 m. long, S Alberta, Canada; rises in Rocky Mts. near the Brit. Columbia border and flows E to unite with the Bow and form the South Saskatchewan river; receives tributaries Belly and St. Mary from the S.

Old Man of Coniston. See CONISTON FELLS.

Old Margelan. See MARGELAN.

Old Northwest. See NORTHWEST TERRITORY.

Old Or'chard Beach (ôr'chĕrd). Town, York co., SW Maine, on Atlantic Ocean 6 m. ENE of Biddeford; pop. 4580; summer resort.

Old Panama, *Span.* **Pa'na·má' Vie'ja** (pä'nä·mä' vyĕ'hä). Old city on S shore of Isthmus of Panama, Pacific port of the Spaniards in 16th and 17th cents.; sacked by the pirate Morgan 1671; now in ruins; present city of Panama a few miles to the SW.

Old Point Com'fort (kŭm'fĕrt). Point, Hampton, SE Virginia, SW of Fort Monroe on N shore of Hampton Roads.

Old Ryazan. See RYAZAN.

Old Sar'um (sâr'ŭm); *anc. Roman* **Sor'bi·o·du'num**

(sôr'bĭ·ō·dū'nŭm). Extinct borough and city in Wiltshire, England, 2 m. N of Salisbury; considerable ruins remain: large mound and traces of the cathedral (an earlier cathedral on the site had burned down four days after its completion 1092) which was razed 1331 to furnish materials for use in Salisbury cathedral; no evidences of the Roman town. Home of kings of Wessex; became seat of bishopric c. 1075 (*Sarum use* formulated by Osmund, bishop 1078–99); see transferred to New Sarum (Salisbury) in 13th cent.; lapsed to the crown, became one of the rotten boroughs (until 1833).

Old Saybrook. See SAYBROOK residential town, Connecticut.

Old Scab Mountain (skăb). Peak 6642 ft. in Yakima co., S Washington.

Old Spanish Trail. See SPANISH TRAIL.

Old' Town'. City, Penobscot co., E cen. Maine, on Penobscot river 11 m. NNE of Bangor; pop. 8626; manufactures canoes, woolens, wood products, paper.

Ol'du·vai' Gorge (ōl'dū·wä'; -vä'). Ravine, N Tanganyika, 150 m. WNW of Mt. Kilimanjaro; site of rich fossil beds where in 1960 an ancient fossil skull of *Zinjanthropus* was found.

Old Westbury. Village, Nassau co., SE New York, on W cen. Long I. SE of Roslyn; pop. 2064.

O'le·an' (ō'lĕ·ăn'; ō'lĕ·ăn'). City, Cattaraugus co., SW New York, on Allegheny river; pop. 21,868; oil refining.

O'·Lea'ry Peak (ō·lêr'ĭ). Mountain 8925 ft. in cen. Coconino co., N cen. Arizona.

O·lek'ma (ŭ·lyĕk'má; ŭ·lyĕk·má'). River ab. 700 m. long, E Soviet Russia, Asia; rises in Yablonoi Mts. in W cen. Chita Region, flows N through S Yakutsk Republic to the Lena river.

O·lek'minsk (ŭ·lyĕk'myĭnsk; ŭ·lyĭk·myēnsk'). Town, S Yakutsk Republic, Soviet Russia, Asia, on N bank of the Lena opp. mouth of the Olekma river; pop. 1300; trading station 335 m. WSW of Yakutsk.

O·le·nek' (ŭ·lyĭ·nyŏk'). River ab. 1325 m. long, NW Yakutsk Republic, Soviet Russia, Asia; rises at W end of Vilyuisk Range, flows generally NE into Laptev Sea W of the Lena.

O'lé'ron', Île d' (ēl' dô'lā'rôN'); *anc.* **U·li'a·rus** (û·lī'-á·rŭs). Island 20 m. long in E Bay of Biscay, off W coast of Charente-Maritime dept., W France; 66 sq. m.; pop. ab. 18,000; chief towns Saint-Pierre, in center of island, and Le Château, port at SE end. In early times a part of Aquitaine; became possession of French king 1370. Noted for its Laws of Oléron, a medieval (12th-cent.) code of maritime laws in use in the island and the judicial decisions connected with them, published by Eleanor, Duchess of Guienne; the code forms the basis of modern maritime law.

O'leś·ni'ca (ô'lĕsh·nē'tsä); *Ger.* **Oels** (ŭls) *or* **Oels in Schle'si·en** (ĭn shlä'zĕ·ĕn). City, E Wrocław dept., SW Poland, 17 m. ENE of Wrocław; pop. (1946) 18,183; formerly in Silesia, Prussia, Germany; late 12th-cent. church, 15th-cent. gate; manufactures shoes, furniture, machinery; granaries, cattle markets. Founded in late 10th cent.; became capital of independent principality 14th cent.; to Prussia 1884; assigned to Poland by Potsdam Conference 1945.

O'le·vu'ga (ō'lä·vōō'gä). Small island off W end of Florida I., SE Solomon Is., W Pacific Ocean.

Ol·ga' (ŏl·gä'; *Russ.* ŭl·y'·gä'). Seaport town on SE coast of Maritime Territory, Soviet Russia, Asia, 175 m. ENE of Vladivostok.

O·lhão' (ōō·lyouN'). Commune, Faro dist., S Portugal, on Atlantic Ocean 5 m. E by N of Faro; pop. 13,934.

Ol'i·fants (ŏl'ĭ·fănts). **1** River ab. 115 m. long in S Cape of Good Hope prov., S Union of South Africa; joins Groote river to form the Gouritz river.
2 River ab. 150 m. long in extreme SW Africa; rises in SW Cape of Good Hope prov., Union of South Africa; flows WNW into Atlantic Ocean ab. lat. 31°38'S.
3 River ab. 350 m. long in SE Africa; rises in S cen.

Transvaal prov., NE Union of South Africa; flows NNE across Mozambique border into Limpopo river.

O'li·mar' (ō'lê·mär'). River ab. 100 m. long in E Uruguay; flows E into Lake Mirim.

O·lím'pi·a (ô·lǐm'pǐ·à; *Port.* ōō·lēᴎm'pyȧ). City, N São Paulo state, SE Brazil, 250 m. NW of São Paulo; pop. 8929.

O·lim'po (ô·lēm'pồ). Department of Paraguay. See *Table* at PARAGUAY.

O·lin'da (ô·lǐn'dȧ; *Port.* ōō·lēᴎn'dȧ). City, Pernambuco state, E Brazil, N suburb of Recife; pop. 38,169.

Olisipo. See LISBON.

Olita. See ALITUS.

O·li'va (ô·lē'vä). **1** See OLIWA.

2 Commune, Valencia prov., E Spain, on Mediterranean Sea 43 m. SSE of Valencia; pop. 18,407; produces corn, wheat, rice, oranges, wine, oil, silk; manufactures sacks and baskets.

Oliva de la Fron·te'ra (thä lä frôn·tā'rä), *formerly* **Oliva de Je·rez'** (hä·rāth'; -rās'). Commune, Badajoz prov., SW Spain, near Portuguese border 38 m. S of Badajoz; pop. 11,330.

O'li·va'res (ō'lê·vä'räs). Peak 20,512 ft. in W San Juan prov., W Argentina, near Chile border.

Olive Bridge Dam. = ASHOKAN DAM.

O'li·ven'za (ō'lê·vän'thä; -sä). Fortified commune, Badajoz prov., SW Spain, near Portuguese border 15 m. SW of Badajoz; pop. 12,492.

Ol'i·ver (ŏl'ĭ·vēr). **1** County in North Dakota. See *Table* at NORTH DAKOTA.

2 Locality, Fayette co., SW Pennsylvania, ab. 2 m. N of Uniontown; pop. 3015.

Ol'ives, Mount of (ŏl'ĭvz); *or* **Ol'i·vet** (ŏl'ĭ·vĕt). **1** Ridge 2½ m. long running N and S on E side of Jerusalem, Palestine (*Acts* i. 12); separated from the city by the valley of the Kidron. At its W foot, outside the city walls, is the Garden of Gethsemane; on its E slope the village of Bethany.

2 A section of this ridge containing its three culminating heights; highest point 2737 ft.

Ol'i·vet'. **1** (ŏl'ĭ·vĕt') City, S Eaton co., S Michigan, 11 mi. SW of Charlotte; pop. 1185; Olivet Coll. (1844; coed.; Congregational).

2 (ō'lĭ·vĕt) Town, ⊗ of Hutchinson co., SE South Dakota; pop. 135.

Ol'i·vette (ŏl'ĭ·vĕt). City, St. Louis co., E cen. Missouri, W of St. Louis; pop. 8257.

O·liv'i·a (ô·lǐv'ǐ·à). Village, ⊗ of Renville co., SW cen. Minnesota, 36 m. ESE of Montevideo; pop. 2355.

O·li'vos (ô·lē'vồs). Town, N suburb of Buenos Aires, Argentina, on SW shore of Río de la Plata.

O·li'wa (ô·lē'vä); *Ger.* **O·li'va** (ô·lē'vä). Former commune of the Free City of Danzig, now a part of Danzig, Gdańsk dept., N Poland, in NW near the coast; pop. ab. 16,000. Founded 1170; several times partially destroyed in wars of 13th to 16th cent.; peace treaty signed here May 3, 1660 by which the war with Sweden (1655–60) was ended, Livonia was ceded to Sweden, and John II Casimir of Poland relinquished claim to Swedish throne.

Ol'kusz (ŏl'kōōsh). Commune, Kraków dept., Poland, 19 m. E of Sosnowiec; pop. (1938–39 est.) 11,046; zinc and lead mining; lead mines famous in Middle Ages.

Ol·la'güe (ô·yä'gwä) *or* **O·ya'hue** (ô·yä'wä). **1** Peak 19,258 ft. in NE Antofagasta prov., N Chile, near the Bolivian border.

2 Town, NE Antofagasta prov., N Chile, at the Bolivian border N of Ollagüe peak; railroad junction; on the highway from Antofagasta to Uyuni, Bolivia.

Ollius. See OGLIO.

Ol'mos Park (ŏl'mŭs). City, Bexar co., S cen. Texas; pop. 2457.

Olm'sted (ŏm'stĕd; ōm'-). County in Minnesota. See *Table* at MINNESOTA.

Ol'mütz (ŏl'mŭts). See OLOMOUC.

Ol'ney. **1** (ŏl'nĭ) City, ⊗ of Richland co., SE Illinois,

54 m. NE of Mount Vernon; pop. 8780; commercial center in agricultural section.

2 (ōl'nĭ) City, Young co., N Texas, 40 m. S of Wichita Falls; pop. 3872; railroad junction; oil wells.

3 (ōl'nĭ; ō'nĭ) Town, N Buckinghamshire, SE cen. England, ab. 59 m. NNW of London; pop. 2438; residence 1767–86 of William Cowper who assisted John Newton, curate, in composition of *Olney Hymns* 1779.

O'lo·mouc (ô'lô·mōts); *Ger.* **Ol'mütz** (ŏl'mŭts). City, cen. Moravia prov., Czechoslovakia, on March (Morava) river; pop. (1930) 66,440; industrial community near the Moravian Gap. Formerly capital of Moravia; fortified by Maria Theresa; besieged for seven weeks 1758 by Frederick the Great; scene of Conference of Olmütz Nov. 20, 1850, in which Prussia was forced to yield to Austrian demands that she abstain from seeking leadership among the German states.

O·lo'nets (ŭ·lô'nyĕts). Town, S Karelia, U.S.S.R., near E shore of Lake Ladoga 112 m. NE of Leningrad; pop. ab. 2000. Peter the Great established ironworks here.

O·lon'ga·po' (ô·lông'gä·pô'). Port, a barrio of Subic municipality, SE Zambales prov., Luzon, Phil. Is., on E coast of Subic Bay and near Bataan border; pop. 8644; has one of best harbors in the Philippines; U.S. naval station and dry dock. Held by Japanese Dec. 1941–Feb. 1, 1945.

Olonos. See ERYMANTHUS.

O'lo'ron'–Sainte–Ma'rie' (ô'lô'rôn'sănt'mȧ'rē'). City, Basses-Pyrénées dept., SW France, 13 m. SW of Pau; pop. 10,300; episcopal see to 1790; ancient city destroyed by Saracens and Normans; rebuilt 1080.

O'lo·se'ga (ô'lô·sā'gȧ). One of the Manua Is. in American Samoa; pop. 429. See OFU.

O·lot' (ô·lôt'). Commune, Gerona prov., NE Spain, 17 m. NW of Gerona; pop. 14,333; college; more than 200 prisoners of war shot here by Carlist leader Savalls.

Öls. Var. of *Oels*: see OLEŚNICA.

Ol'sa (ôl'zä). Small stream, cen. Europe; a tributary of the Oder entering it below Moravská Ostrava; flows NW dividing the Teschen dist. bet. Poland and Czechoslovakia.

Öls'nitz *or* **Oels'nitz** (ûls'nĭts). **1** *in full* **Ölsnitz im Erz Ge·bir'ge** (ĭm ĕrts' gĕ·bĭr'gĕ). Coal-mining city, Saxony, East Germany, 13 m. SW of Chemnitz; pop. 18,266.

2 *in full* **Ölsnitz im Vogt'land** (fōkt'länt). Industrial city, Saxony, East Germany, on the Weisse Elster 25 m. SSW of Zwickau; pop. 17,038; rebuilt after fire 1859; 13th-cent. church; manufactures carpets, cloth, furniture, machinery, beer, leather, tile.

Ol'son Mountain (ōl's'n). Peak 7800 ft. in Glacier National Park, NW Montana.

Olsz'tyn (ôlsh'tĭn). **1** New department of N Poland, when first formed 1945 was called Mazury (*q.v.*).

2 *Ger.* **Al'len·stein** (äl'ĕn·shtīn; *Angl.* äl'ĕn·stīn). Manufacturing city, ✻ of Olsztyn dept., Poland, on Łyna (Alle) river 80 m. SE of Danzig; pop. (1946) 57,189; iron foundries; manufactures machines, stoves, matches, cement; trades in leather, grain, cattle; railroad junction; medieval castle (built 1348). City state 1353; fell to Poland 1466 and to Prussia 1772; occupied by Russians, a maneuver preliminary to the battle of Tannenberg, Aug. 26–30, 1914; awarded to Germany by plebiscite 1920 (see ALLENSTEIN-MARIENWERDER); assigned to Poland by Potsdam Conference 1945.

Olt (ôlt) *or* **A·lu'ta** (ä·lōō'tä); *Ger.* **Alt** (ält). River 308 m. long in S Romania; rises in E Transylvania, flows S, cutting through the Transylvanian Alps at Roşu Pass, then traverses Walachia, and enters the Danube river opp. Nikopol.

Ol'ten (ôl'tĕn). Commune, Solothurn canton, NW Switzerland, on Aare river 7 m. WSW of Aarau; pop. (1941) 15,287; railroad junction; castle; 17th-cent. monastery; manufactures machinery, trucks, shoes, cement, cloth, felt.

Ol·te′ni·a (ŏl·tĕ′nĭ·à; *Romanian* ŏl·tĕ′nyä) *or* **Little Walachia.** Region, S Romania, W division of Walachia; 9294 sq. m.; formerly a province.

Ol′te·ni′ţa (ŏl′tĕ·nē′tsä) *or* **Ol′te·ni′tza** (-tsä); *anc.* **Con′stan·ti·o′la** (kŏn′stăn·tĭ·ō′là). City, S Romania, on Argeş river at its confluence with the Danube; pop. 10,396; battle Nov. 4, 1853 in which Turks under Omer Pasha defeated the Russians.

Oltis. See LOT.

Ol′ton (ōl′t′n; -tŭn). City, ⊗ of Lamb co., NW Texas; pop. 1917.

Oltre Giuba. See JUBALAND.

Ol′tu (ōl′tōō). = OLT river, Romania.

Ol·tu′ (ōl·tōō′) *or* **Ol·ti′** (-tĭ′). Village, NE Erzurum vilayet, NE Turkey in Asia; pop. 1927; fighting bet. Russians and Turks Sept. 1915.

O·lus′tee (ō·lŭs′tē). Village, Baker co., NE Florida, 45 m. SW of Jacksonville; pop. (est.) 400; battle Feb. 20, 1864 in which Confederates under General Joseph Finnegan decisively defeated Federals led by General Truman Seymour; called also battle of **Ocean Pond.**

O′lu·tang′a (ō′lōō·täng′ä). Island in N Moro Gulf, S Zamboanga prov., Mindanao. Phil. Is.; 78 sq. m.; low island covered with mangroves.

Ol·ve′ra (ōl·vā′rä). Commune, Cádiz prov., SW Spain, 62 m. ENE of Cádiz; pop. 10,283; agriculture and stock raising.

Olviopol. See PERVOMAISK.

O·lym′pi·a (ō·lĭm′pĭ·à). **1** City and port of entry, ✳ of Washington and ⊗ of Thurston co., W Washington, at S extremity of Puget Sound; pop. 18,273; manufactures lumber and lumber products, veneer, knit goods; cans fruits and vegetables; oyster industry. Settled 1846; became first port of entry on Puget Sound 1851, capital of newly created Territory of Washington 1853; chartered as town 1859, as city 1890. **2** Plain and sanctuary, ancient Elis. NW Peloponnesus, S Greece, on N bank of the Alpheus river; a center of religious worship of Greece, with notable festival (*Olympian* games) celebrated every fourth year in honor of Zeus. These began 776 B.C., the year that came to be adopted as primary date in Greek chronology (periods known as *Olympiads*); games were chiefly athletic contests. Here in the temple of Zeus was the statue of Olympian Zeus by Phidias; excavation has disclosed ruins of many temples and other buildings.

O·lym′pic Mountains (ō·lĭm′pĭk). Mountain mass, part of the Coast Ranges, in NW Washington in the Olympic Penin. chiefly in Jefferson and Clallam cos.; chief peaks Mount Olympus 7954 ft. and Mount Constance 7777 ft.; part of **Olympic National Park** (see UNITED STATES, *National Parks*).

Olympic Peninsula. Peninsular part of W Washington bounded on W by Pacific Ocean, on N by Juan de Fuca Strait, and on E by Puget Sound.

O·lym′pus (ō·lĭm′pŭs). Mountain range in Thessaly. NE Greece, near coast of Gulf of Salonika; highest peak 9570 ft.; in ancient Greek mythology, the home of the gods. In modern times, in World War II, used by the British as defense post in retreat S through Greece Apr. 1941.

Olympus, Mount. 1 Peak 7954 ft. in Olympic Mts., Jefferson co., NW Washington.
2 See ULU DAĞ.

O·lyn′thus (ō·lĭn′thŭs). Town in ancient Macedonia, NE Greece; its site is on the Chalcidice Penin. at the head of the Toronaic Gulf and bet. Sithonia and Pallene Penins. The most important of the Greek cities on the coast of Macedonia, head of a strong confederacy of Greek towns esp. after 424 B.C. At war with Sparta 382–379 B.C.; finally subdued and held subject 379-375; besieged by Philip of Macedon, and in spite of appeals to Athens and orations of Demosthenes (*Olynthiac* orations), overcome and destroyed by Philip 348 B.C. and its citizens enslaved.

Ol′y·phant (ŏl′ĭ·fănt). Borough, Lackawanna co., NE Pennsylvania, 5 m. NE of Scranton; pop. 5864; settled 1798; coal mines, iron foundries.

Ol·yu·torsk′, Cape (ŭl·yōō·tôrsk′). Point on E coast of Soviet Russia, Asia, at NE base of Kamchatka Penin. extending into Bering Sea; in Koryak National District.

Om (ŏm). River ab. 450 m. long, W Siberia; flows W in Novosibirsk and Omsk Regions to join the Irtysh at Omsk.

O·ma, Cape (ō·mä). Cape on N extremity of Honshu, Japan, projecting into Tsugaru Strait.

O′magh (ō′mä; -mà). Town, ⊗ of co. Tyrone, W cen. Northern Ireland; pop. 6762; linen manufacture; few remains of castle besieged 1509 and destroyed 1641 by Sir Phelim O'Neill.

O′ma·ha (ō′mà·hô; -hä). City, ⊗ of Douglas co., E Nebraska, on the Missouri river 15 m. N of its confluence with Platte river; largest city in the state. pop. 301,598; important railroad center; stockyards, packing houses, grain markets; ore-smelting and manufacturing plants. Offutt Air Force Base. Creighton Univ. (1878; coed.; Rom. Cath.), Municipal Univ. of Omaha (1908 coed.), Duchesne College (1881; women); College of Medicine of Univ. of Nebraska. Site of stockade and trading station 1825; first permanent settlement 1854; capital of Nebraska 1854–67; incorp. as city 1857; outfitting center for overland wagon trains c. 1858–69; site of Trans-Mississippi Exposition June 1–Nov. 1, 1898; visited by disastrous tornado Mar. 23, 1913.

Omaha Beach. West cen. part of Normandy beaches, NW France, NW of Bayeux and NE of Isigny and on either side of the Vire river at the village of Saint-Laurent-sur-Mer; landing place of part of American army in invasion of France June 6–10, 1944.

O′mak (ō′măk). City, Okanogan co., N Washington, on Okanogan river; pop. 4068; lumber.

Omak Lake. Alkaline lake in S Okanogan co., N Washington.

O·man′ (ō·män′). Independent country in SE section of the peninsula of Arabia; ab. 82,000 sq. m.; pop. ab. 500,000; ✳ Masqat; officially known as the sultanate of **Masqat and Oman.** Coastal strip from 150 to 50 m. wide extending from a point 25°N on W coast of Gulf of Oman S of Cape Musandam around Cape Hadd and SW along coast of Arabian Sea past Capes Madraka and Nus to E boundary of Aden Protectorate at ab. 53°30′E long.; to the W borders on the great desert Rub 'al Khali. Has group of high mountains (Jebel Sham 9900 ft.) to the W of Masqat. Some areas are well cultivated; chief export dates, but vegetables and other fruits are raised. Chief towns Masqat and its suburb Matrah, and Sur. Gwadar, a port on the SW coast of Baluchistan, belonged to Oman until 1958, when it was ceded to Pakistan. To the W on the Persian Gulf is Trucial Oman (*q.v.*).
History: Ruled by independent dynasty of emirs under Abbasside caliphate at Baghdad; its capital, Masqat, captured and region controlled by Portuguese 1508–c. 1648; recovered by descendant of Yemen's imam 1741; after decline of its importance in 19th cent., became virtual political and economic dependency of British government of India; as sultanate of Masqat and Oman entered into close ties with Great Britain by treaty of 1939. See PERSIAN GULF RESIDENCY.

Oman, Gulf of. An arm of the Arabian Sea extending bet. N Oman, SE Arabia, and the SE coast of Iran, ab. 340 m. long by 230 m. wide at mouth.

O·ma·na·go (ō·mä·nä·gô). Peak 7546 ft. in the Nikko Range, N cen. Honshu, Japan, N of Lake Chuzenji.

O′ma·ru′ru (ō′mà·rōō′rōō). Town, W cen. South-West Africa, on **Omaruru River** 110 m. NW of Windhoek; pop. 6153; railroad outlet for tin mines; dairying.

Omatako. See OMURAMBA.

O·ma′te (ō·mä′tà) *or* **Huai′na–Pu·ti′na** (wī′nä·pōō·tē′nä). Volcano in the Andes Mts. n Peru, SE of

Arequipa; many great eruptions, esp. bet. 1582 and 1783; most disastrous eruption 1667.

Om·bai' (ôm·bī'). See ALOR.

Ombai Strait. Strait 17 m. wide extending in a curve bet. Alor I. on N and W, Timor on S, and Wetar I. on E; connects Banda Sea with E end of Savu Sea, Lesser Sunda Is., Indonesia.

Om·bi'lin (ôm·bē'lĭn). Village, center of extensive coal mines in Padang Highlands, Sumatra, Indonesia, N of Sawahlunto ab. 40 m. NE of Padang; controlled by government; coal field said to contain 200,000,000 tons of coal of first-class quality.

Om·bi'rah (ôm·bē'rà). See OBI ISLANDS.

Om·bro'ne (ôm·brō'nā); *anc.* **Um'bro** (ŭm'brō). River ab. 100 m. long in NW cen. Italy; flows S and SW through Tuscany and into the N Tyrrhenian Sea 10 m. S of Grosseto.

Om'dur·man' (ŏm'dĕr·măn'; *Arab.* ŏŏm'dĕr·măn'). City, Khartoum prov., NE cen. Republic of Sudan, on left bank of White Nile opp. Khartoum; pop. (1938 est.) 114,457; capital of Mohammed Ahmed 1884; scene of Anglo-Egyptian victory over Mahdi's forces Sept. 2, 1898.

O·me'gna (ô·mān'yä). Commune, Novara prov., Piedmont, NW Italy, at N end of Lake Orta 32 m. NNW of Novara; pop. 11,628; manufactures textiles; has medieval gate and bridge.

O'mei' (ō'mā') *or* **O'mi'** (ō'mē'). Mountain 9957 ft. in SW Szechwan, S cen. China, ab. 30 m. W of Loshan; sacred to Buddhists and visited by many pilgrims. Consists of three peaks, on one of which is a great precipice several thousand feet high; top and pathway to it has many pagodas and temples.

O'me·te'pe (ō'mā·tā'pā). Island in Lake Nicaragua, S Nicaragua; contains the twin volcanoes Concepción and Madera.

O·mi (ō·mē). See BIWA.

O'mi' (ō'mē'). See OMEI.

O'miš (ō'mēsh) *or* **Al·mis'sa** (*Ital.* äl·mēs'sä). Seaport, Bosnia and Herzegovina, W Yugoslavia, SE of Split; pop. (commune) ab. 17,000.

Om'me (ŭm'ĕ). River ab. 45 m. long in W cen. Jutland, Denmark; flows WNW into Ringkøbing Fjord.

O'mo (ō'mō). River ab. 400 m. long in SW Ethiopia, flowing into N end of Lake Rudolf.

O·mo'ka (ô·mō'kà). Chief village on Tongareva I., Manihiki Is., cen. Pacific Ocean.

O·mo·loi' (ŭ·mŭ·loi'). River ab. 380 m. long in N Yakutsk Republic, Soviet Russia, Asia; rises in Verkhoyansk Mts. and flows generally N to Buor Khaya Gulf E of the Lena.

O·mo·lon' (ŭ·mŭ·lôn'). River ab. 600 m. long, NE Khabarovsk Territory, Soviet Russia, Asia, flowing from the Kolyma Range N through Koryak and Chukot National Districts into Kolyma river in NE Yakutsk Republic.

O·mo·no (ô·mô·nô). River ab. 80 m. long, N Honshu, Japan; flows NW into the Sea of Japan near Akita.

Om·pom'pa·noo'suc (ŏm·pŏm'pà·nōō'sŭk). Small river, E Vermont; enters the Connecticut ab. 17 m. N of White River Junction.

Om'ro (ŏm'rō). Town, Winnebago co., E cen. Wisconsin, W of Oshkosh; pop. 1991.

Omsk (ômsk). City, ✳ of Omsk Region, in S part, at confluence of Irtysh and Om rivers 480 m. E of Chelyabinsk, Soviet Russia, Asia; pop. 280,716; on Trans-Siberian R.R.; a center for trade in farm products; has several specialized schools and is important industrially. Founded 1716 as fort; once ✳ of all western Siberia.

Omsk Region. Region, W Soviet Russia, Asia, E of N Ural Mts.; originally 556,033 sq. m., pop. 2,366,603; ✳ Omsk; reduced in 1945 to much smaller area bet. Tyumen and Novosibirsk Regions; N part divided into Khanty-Mansi and Yamalo-Nenets National Districts; on S borders on Kazakh S.S.R. Lies in basin of middle

Irtysh river. Chief occupations agriculture, dairying, stock raising; crossed in cen. part by two trunk railroad lines; chief towns Omsk and Tara. The earlier and larger Omsk Region was the first part of Asia penetrated by Russians (see SIBERIA); its cities and products grew rapidly in latter part of 19th cent ; became part of West Siberia Region; organized as subdivision of R.S.F.S.R. in Asia 1936.

O·mu·ra (ō·mŏŏ·rä). Town, Nagasaki prefecture, NW Kyushu, Japan, on **Omura Bay** (inlet of East China Sea) 12 m. NNE of Nagasaki; pop. (1945) 44,292; because of large aircraft factory grew rapidly in recent years. Bombed by Allies 1944–45.

O'mu·ram'ba (ō'mŭ·räm'bä) *or* **O'ma·ta'ko** (ō'mä·tä'kō). River bed, NE South-West Africa; extends from mountains in N cen. part NE to the Okovanggo river; dry through most of its lower course.

O·mu·ta (ō·mŏŏ·tä). City, NW Kyushu, Japan, in Fukuoka prefecture, on Shimabara Bay 22 m. NW of Kumamoto; pop. (1945) 127,677; extensive coal deposits nearby owned by Mitsui family, who have built large artificial harbor. Has had phenomenal growth in recent years. Bombed frequently by American superfortresses 1944 and 1945.

On. See HELIOPOLIS.

On'a·las'ka (ŏn'à·lăs'kà). City, La Crosse co., W Wisconsin, 5 m. N of La Crosse; pop. 3161.

On'a·wa (ŏn'à·wà; -wô). City, ⊗ of Monona co., W Iowa, 36 m. SSE of Sioux City; pop. 3176; wheat, cattle, hogs, poultry.

On'a·way (ŏn'à·wā). City, Presque Isle co., NE Michigan, 23 m. SSE of Cheboygan; pop. 1388; tourist resort; Onaway State Park to the N.

On'do (ŏn'dō). **1** Province of Nigeria. See *Table* at NIGERIA.
2 Town in W part of Ondo prov., Western Region, SW Nigeria, 105 m. NE of Lagos; pop. 20,859; on automobile road.

O·ne'co (ô·nē'kō). Urban community (unincorporated), Manatee co., Florida, SE of Bradenton; pop. 1530.

O·ne'ga (ô·nĕg'à; *Russ.* ŭ·nyĕ'gà). **1** Bay at SW end of the White Sea extending into the coast of NW Soviet Russia, Europe; bet. Arkhangelsk Region and Karelo-Finnish S.S.R. Receives Onega river.
2 Lake, second in size in Europe, in S Karelo-Finnish S.S.R., Soviet Russia; 3764 sq. m.; 145 m. long by 50 m. wide. Its S shore and the canal along it from the Svir to the Vytegra (see MARIINSK CANAL SYSTEM) lie in Vologda Region. Its outlet is the Svir, flowing from SW corner to Lake Ladoga; main affluents Vodla, Vytegra, and Andoma, on the E; has numerous long arms or inlets and many islands along its N shore; frozen over ab. one half the year; has valuable fisheries and much timber is cut near its shores. Petrozavodsk is only large town on its shores (on W).
3 River ab. 250 m. long in W part of Arkhangelsk Region, Soviet Russia, Europe, flowing from Lakes Vozhe and Lacha to Onega Bay; navigable ab. 100 m.
4 Town at head of the bay and on right bank of Onega river at its mouth, W Arkhangelsk Region, 90 m. S of Arkhangelsk; pop. 5254; chief industry lumber. Settled in 15th cent.

O·ne'glia (ô·nāl'yä). Former commune, now subdivision (pop. 12,234) of commune of IMPERIA, Italy.

O'ne·hung'a (ō'nā·hŏŏng'à). Borough, Auckland provincial dist., N North I., New Zealand, S suburb of Auckland on Manukau Harbor; pop. 11,120.

O·nei'da (ô·nī'dà). **1** River 16 m. long in cen. New York; flows from Oneida Lake, forms section of boundary bet. Onondaga and Oswego cos., joins Seneca river to form Oswego river.
2 Name of counties in three states in the U.S. See *Tables* at IDAHO, NEW YORK, WISCONSIN.
3 City, Madison co., cen. New York, 5 m. SE of Oneida Lake 13 m. WSW of Rome; pop. 11,677; geographic cen-

ter of New York; in farming and dairying region; canneries; manufactures silver-plated ware, furniture, silk. Many of the industries were established by the Oneida Community 2 m. to S, former communistic society of "Perfectionists" established here by John Humphrey Noyes in 1848, reorganized 1881 into a joint-stock company engaged in industrial enterprises.

Oneida Lake. Lake in cen. New York, bounded by Oswego, Oneida, Madison, and Onondaga cos.; ab. 22 m. long and 6 m. wide at its greatest extent; part of N.Y. State Barge Canal system.

O'·Neill' (ȯ-nēl'). City, ⊗ of Holt co., N Nebraska, on Elkhorn river 74 m. WNW of Norfolk; pop. 3181.

O'ne·on'ta (ō'nẽ·ŏn'tȧ). **1** City, ⊗ of Blount co., N cen. Alabama; pop. 4136; in mining region.
2 City, Otsego co., cen. New York, on Susquehanna river 45 m. S of Utica; pop. 13,412; business center of dairying section; railroad terminus; manufactures maple sugar and syrup, gloves, women's silk underwear, automobile trailers; Hartwick Coll. (1928; coed.), State Univ. of New York Coll. of Education at Oneonta (1889; coed.).

O'ne Pu'su (ō'nȧ poō'soō). Settlement on SW cen. coast of Malaita I., SE Solomon Is., W Pacific Ocean.

One Tree Hill. Borough, Auckland provincial dist., N North I., New Zealand, suburb of Auckland; pop. 7920.

O·ni'da (ȯ-nī'dȧ). City, ⊗ of Sully co., cen. South Dakota; pop. 843.

On'ion (ŭn'yŭn). River in Vermont. See WINOOSKI.

O·nit'sha (ȯ-nĭch'ȧ). **1** Province of Nigeria. See *Table* at NIGERIA.
2 Town, its *, S Eastern Region, Nigeria, on Niger river ab. 135 m. from its mouth; pop. 18,084.

On·ne·ko·tan (ŏn-nĕ-kȯ'tän). One of the Kuril Is. (q.v.), at N end, SW of Paramushiro.

Onolzbach. See ANSBACH.

O·no·mi·chi (ō-nȯ-mē-chẽ). Industrial city on the Inland Sea, Hiroshima prefecture, SW Honshu, Japan, 45 m. W of Okayama; pop. (1945) 53,590; has several fine Buddhist temples.

O'non (ō'nŏn). River ab. 610 m. long, NE Outer Mongolia and SW Chita Region, Soviet Russia, Asia, flowing NE to unite with Ingoda river and form the Shilka river.

On'on·da'ga (ŏn'ŭ[n]·dô'gȧ). County in New York. See *Table* at NEW YORK.

Onondaga, Lake. Lake 5 m. long and 1 m. wide in Onondaga co., cen. New York.

Ons'low (ŏnz'lō). County in North Carolina. See *Table* at NORTH CAROLINA.

Onslow Bay. Bay off SE coast of North Carolina bet. Cape Lookout and Cape Fear.

Onst'wed'de (ŏnst'vĕd'ĕ). Commune, Groningen prov., NE Netherlands, 23 m. SE of Groningen near German border; pop. 18,079.

On·ta·ke (ŏn·tä·kĕ). Peak 10,049 ft. on E border of Gifu prefecture, cen. Honshu, Japan; second highest mountain in Japan and second to Fuji only as the most popular sacred peak in Japan; climbed by thousands of pilgrims every summer.

On·tar'i·o (ŏn·târ'ĭ·ō). **1** County in New York. See *Table* at NEW YORK.
2 Residential and commercial city, San Bernardino co., SE California, 20 m. W of San Bernardino; pop. 46,617; founded 1882, incorporated as city 1891; manufactures electrical appliances, metal goods, wine, citrus by-products.
3 Village in Ontario town (pop. 4259), Wayne co., W New York, ab. 17 m. NE of Rochester.
4 City, Malheur co., SE corner of Oregon, on Snake river just S of its confluence with Malheur river; pop. 5101; irrigated farms; produces apples, grain, hogs, dairy products.
5 Province, S and cen. Canada; land area 363,282 sq. m.; pop. 4,597,542; ✱ Toronto; administratively divided into the following 43 counties and 11 districts (for pronunciation of their names, see their individual entries):

NAME	LOCATION	AREA[1]	POP.[1]	CO. SEAT
Algoma Dist.	S	19,320	64,496	Sault Sainte Marie
Brant	SE	421	72,857	Brantford
Bruce	SE	1,650	41,311	Walkerton
Carleton	SE	947	242,247	Ottawa
Cochrane Dist.	E	52,237	83,850	Cochrane
Dufferin	SE	557	14,566	Orangeville
Dundas	SE	384	15,818	Cornwall[2]
Durham	SE	629	30,115	Cobourg[3]
Elgin	SE	720	55,518	Saint Thomas
Essex	SE	707	217,150	Windsor
Frontenac	SE	1,599	66,099	Kingston
Glengarry	SE	478	17,702	Cornwall[2]
Grenville	SE	463	17,045	Brockville[4]
Grey	SE	1,708	58,960	Owen Sound
Haldimand	SE	488	24,138	Cayuga
Haliburton[5]	SE	1,486	7,670	Minden
Halton	SE	363	44,003	Milton
Hastings	SE	2,323	74,298	Belleville
Huron	SE	1,295	49,280	Goderich
Kenora Dist.	W	153,220	39,212	Kenora
Kent	SE	918	79,128	Chatham
Lambton	SE	1,124	74,960	Sarnia
Lanark	SE	1,138	35,601	Perth
Leeds	SE	900	38,831	Brockville
Lennox and Addington	SE	1,170	19,544	Napanee
Lincoln	SE	332	89,366	Saint Catherines
Manitoulin Dist.	S	1,588	11,214	Gore Bay
Middlesex	SE	1,240	162,139	London
Muskoka Dist.	SE	1,585	24,713	Bracebridge
Nipissing Dist.	SE	7,560	50,517	North Bay
Norfolk	SE	634	42,708	Simcoe
Northumberland	SE	734	33,482	Cobourg
Ontario	SE	853	87,088	Whitby
Oxford	SE	765	58,818	Woodstock
Parry Sound Dist.	SE	4,336	27,371	Parry Sound
Peel	SE	469	55,673	Brampton
Perth	SE	840	52,584	Stratford
Peterborough	SE	1,415	60,789	Peterborough
Prescott	SE	494	25,576	L'Orignal
Prince Edward	SE	390	18,559	Picton
Rainy River Dist.	SW corner	7,276	22,132	Fort Frances
Renfrew	SE	3,009	66,717	Pembroke
Russell	SE	407	17,666	L'Orignal[6]
Simcoe	SE	1,663	106,482	Barrie
Stormont	SE	412	48,458	Cornwall
Sudbury Dist.	SE	18,058	109,590	Sudbury
Thunder Bay Dist.	SW	52,471	105,367	Port Arthur
Timiskaming Dist.	SE	5,896	50,016	Haileybury
Victoria	SE	1,348	27,127	Lindsay
Waterloo	SE	516	126,123	Kitchener
Welland	SE	387	123,233	Welland
Wellington	SE	1,019	66,930	Guelph
Wentworth	SE	458	266,083	Hamilton
York	SE	882	1,176,622	Toronto

[1] Area = land area in sq. m. Pop. from 1951 Census.
[2] In Stormont co.
[3] In Northumberland co.
[4] In Leeds co.
[5] A provincial county, annexed to Victoria co. for judicial purposes.
[6] In Prescott co.

Southeast part is large peninsula bet. Ottawa river on NE and St. Lawrence river and Lakes Ontario and Erie on S, Lake Huron and Georgian Bay on W. Remainder of province (ab. 84% of area) is covered with many lakes and rivers and is sparsely settled; bounded on N by Hudson Bay, on E by James Bay and Quebec prov., on SW by Lake Superior and Minnesota, and on W by Manitoba. Contains six provincial parks, three national parks, and two national historic parks. Largely a level country with generally fertile soils; highest point under 2000 ft. Largest lakes of N and W part Lakes Nipigon, Eagle, Seul, St. Joseph, Rainy, and Abitibi; Lake of the Woods belongs in part to U.S.; in SE part Lakes Nipissing, Simcoe, Muskoka, and Kawartha chain are most important. Bordered on SE by Ottawa and St. Lawrence rivers; in populated (SE) part chief rivers the Thames, Grand, Rideau, and Trent, and N of Lakes Huron and Superior are Moose, Albany, Attawapiskat, English, and Severn. In SE also are well-developed canal systems of Rideau, Trent, Welland Ship, and Sault Sainte Marie. Produces esp. fruits, tobacco, sugar beets, dairy products; rich in minerals, gold, copper, and esp. nickel. Chief cities Toronto, Ottawa, Hamilton, Windsor, London, Kitchener, and Kingston.

History: In 17th cent. visited by French explorers

(first by Champlain 1615) and missionaries; scene of many wars bet. French and Iroquois; passed to British 1763; became 1774 part of province of Quebec (*q.v.* for further details); received many loyalist settlers from U.S. during American Revolution; present S boundary established 1783; at division of Quebec prov. 1791 became known as Upper Canada; scene of many battles of War of 1812; scene of unsuccessful uprising 1837; reunited with Lower Canada 1841; as Ontario became one of four provinces of the new Dominion of Canada 1867. 6 County, Ontario, Canada. See *Table* at ONTARIO.

Ontario, Lake; *early Fr. name* **Lac Fron'te·nac'** (lắk' frŏnt'nák'). Lake in U.S. and Canada, easternmost and smallest of the Great Lakes (*q.v.*); bounded on E and S by New York, and on S, W, and N by province of Ontario, Canada, the U.S.-Canada boundary passing through the lake; ab. 193 m. long; area 7540 sq. m.; greatest depth 778 ft.; elevation 246 ft.; connected on SW by Niagara river and Welland Ship Canal with Lake Erie; outlet on NE the St. Lawrence river. See OSWEGO CANAL.

On'te·nien'te (ôn'tá·nyān'tá). Commune, Valencia prov., E Spain, 48 m. SSW of Valencia; pop. 13,564.

On'to·na'gon (ŏn'tô·nô'gŭn; -nä'-). 1 County in Michigan. See *Table* at MICHIGAN.
2 Village, its ⊗, NW Michigan penin., on Lake Superior 50 m. ENE of Ironwood; pop. 2358; lumber, paper.

On'tong Ja'va (ôn'tŏng jä'vá; jäv'á); *formerly* **Lord Howe Islands** (hou). Island group comprising a coral atoll and several islets in the Solomon Is., W Pacific Ocean, 160 m. NE of Santa Isabel, ab. 5°20'S; part of British Solomon Islands protectorate; natives are Polynesians.

Oodeypore. See UDAIPUR.

Ood'na·dat'ta (ōōd'ná·dăt'á). Village and railroad station, N South Australia, 690 m. NNW of Adelaide.

O'o·kiep' (ō·kēp'). Village, NW Cape Province, S Republic of So. Africa, connected by rail with Port Nolloth; center of rich copper mines.

Oo'len (ō'lě[n]). Town, Antwerp prov., N Belgium, near Turnhout; pop. 4367; radium extraction.

Oos'ta·nau'la (ōōs'tá·nô'lá). Navigable river, NW Georgia; formed by confluence of Conasauga and Coosawattee rivers in NW extremity of Georgia, flows S to unite with the Etowah near Rome and form the Coosa river.

Oost·en'de (ōst·ĕn'dĕ); *Fr.* **Os'tende'** (ôs'tänd'); *Eng.* **Ost·end'** (ŏs·tĕnd'; ôs'tĕnd). Commune, seaport, and watering place, West Flanders prov., NW Belgium; pop. (1938 est.) 50,263; fisheries. Seized by the Germans 1914 and used as submarine base; raided by British naval force 1918 which succeeded in partially blocking the harbor by sinking a vessel loaded with concrete across its mouth; in World War II captured by Canadians Sept. 6, 1944.

Oos'ter·hout (ōs'tĕr·hout). Commune, North Brabant prov., S Netherlands, just NE of Breda; pop. 15,109.

Oost'stel'ling·werf' (ōst'stĕl'ĭng·vĕrf'). Commune, Friesland prov., N Netherlands, W of Assen; pop. 14,558.

Oo'ta·ca·mund' (ōō'tá·ká·mŭnd'). Town and hill station, S Madras state, S Indian Union, on plateau (7220 ft. above sea level) 280 m. WSW of Madras; pop. 24,616; beautiful scenery and gardens; hunting and fishing; finest sanatorium in S India; summer residence of governor of Madras.

O'pa-Lock'a (ō'pá·lŏk'á). City, Dade co., SE Florida, NW of Miami; pop. 9810.

Opatija. See ABBAZIA.

O'pa·va (ō'pá·vá); *Ger.* **Trop'pau** (trôp'ou). City, ✳ of Silesia prov., cen. Czechoslovakia, on a tributary of the Oder; pop. (1930) 36,030; manufacturing center; scene of Congress of Troppau Oct. 1820, where the allied powers Russia, Prussia, and Austria, with Great Britain dissenting, adopted the principle of armed intervention to suppress liberal movements in Europe.

O'pe·li'ka (ō'pě·lī'ká). City, ⊗ of Lee co., E Alabama, 57 m. ENE of Montgomery; pop. 15,678; settled c. 1840, incorp. 1854; manufactures textiles, cotton products, brick, fertilizer, flour.

Op'e·lou'sas (ŏp'ĕ·lōō'sás). City, ⊗ of St. Landry parish, S cen. Louisiana, 22 m. N of Lafayette; pop. 17,417; market and shipping point for section yielding cotton, rice, sugar, sweet potatoes, livestock; became capital of the state 1862 for a short time after Union forces occupied Baton Rouge.

O·peq'uon (ō·pĕk'ŭn). Village and creek, Frederick co., N Virginia, just E of Winchester; scene of Union victory Sept. 19, 1864, more often known as the battle of Winchester (*q.v.*).

O'phir (ō'fĕr). 1 Ancient country of unknown location, perhaps in Arabia; rich in gold (*1 Kings* ix. 27, 28).
2 Village, W cen. Alaska, in mountainous region bet. the Yukon and upper Kuskokwim rivers; airport.

Ophir, Mount. 1 *Malay* **Gu'nong Le'dang** (gōō'nông lä'däng). Mountain 4186 ft., NW Johore state, S Malay Penin., near Malacca border; highest in state.
2 Peak 9554 ft. in Barisan Mts., W Sumatra, Indonesia, NW of Bukittinggi.

Ophiusa. See FORMENTERA.

O·pin'a·ka (ō·pĭn'á·kô). River ab. 280 m. long, W and cen. Quebec, Canada, main tributary of the Eastmain river, entering it from the N a few miles above its mouth.

O'pis (ō'pĭs). Ruins of ancient Assyrian city on W bank of the Tigris, E Iraq, ab. 43 m. N of Baghdad; scene of battle 539 B.C. in which Cyrus defeated the Babylonians.

Opitergium. See ODERZO.

Op'la'den (ŏp'lä'dĕn). Manufacturing city, North Rhine-Westphalia state, West Germany, on Wupper river just S of Solingen; pop. 13,225; chemicals, dyestuffs, metal goods.

Op'land' (ŏp'län'; ōōp'-). See *Table* at NORWAY.

O·po'le (ô·pô'lĕ); *Ger.* **Op'peln** (ŏp'ĕln). Manufacturing city, W Śląsk dept., SW Poland, on the Oder (Odra) river 52 m. SE of Wrocław; pop. (1946) 52,992; ✳ of former Oppeln govt. dist., Silesia, Prussia, Germany; railroad junction; 9th-cent. church, 14th-cent. late-Gothic church, 19th-cent. town hall; iron foundries, lumber mills; manufactures cement and cement blocks, cigars, tile; cattle market. Capital to 1532 of independent principality of Oppeln; to Prussia 1742; capital of former province of Upper Silesia. Taken by Russian army Jan. 24, 1945 in World War II; assigned to Poland by Potsdam Conference 1945.

O'pon (ō'pôn). Municipality on NW coast of Mactan I., Cebu prov., on E coast of Cebu I., Phil. Is.; pop. 33,426.

O·por'to (ô·pōr'tô); *Port.* **Pôr'to** (pōr'tōō); *anc.* **Por'tus Ca'le** (pōr'tŭs kā'lĕ). Seaport city, ✳ of Pôrto dist., NW Portugal, on the right bank of the Douro river 2 m. from its mouth and 170 m. N by E of Lisbon; its harbor is at Leixões; pop. (1940) 262,309; ✳ of Douro Litoral prov.; built on steep, terraced slope; has two fine bridges, Gothic medieval cathedral, episcopal palace, and the Torre dos Clérigos; famous since 1698 as shipping point for port wine (so called for the city); also ships fruits, olive and other oils, cork, building materials, onions, salt; manufactures cottons, woolens, silks, linens, lace, pottery, jewelry, leather, glass, preserved foods; sugar refineries, soap works, tobacco factories, foundries. A former capital of N Portugal (to 1174); held by French 1805–09.

Opp (ŏp). City, Covington co., S Alabama, 50 m. W of Dothan; pop. 5535; corn and cotton distributing center; pine lumber.

Op'pa (ŏp'á). River ab. 60 m. long in Silesia prov., Czechoslovakia, flowing into Oder river at Moravská Ostrava.

Op'peln (ŏp'ĕln). 1 Former government district, SE Silesia prov., Prussia, Germany; 3746 sq. m.
2 City. See OPOLE.

Op'pen·heim (ŏp'ĕn·hīm; *Ger.* ôp'-). Town, Hesse, SW Germany, on the Rhine 20 m. S of Mainz; pop. (1933) 4162; wine industry. In World War II American army crossed Rhine here in advance on Frankfort.

Op'pi·do Ma'mer·ti'na (ŏp'pĕ·dô mä'mär·tē'nä). Commune, Reggio di Calabria prov., Calabria, S Italy, 22 m. NE of Reggio di Calabria; pop. (1931) 10,842; episcopal see.

Oppidum Ubiorum. See COLOGNE.

Op'por·tu'ni·ty (ŏp'ŏr·tū'nĭ·tĭ). Urban community (unincorporated), Spokane co., E Washington, E of Spokane; pop. 12,465.

Op'py (ŏ'pē'). Village, Pas-de-Calais dept., N France, 6 m. NE of Albert; scene of fighting 1917–18.

Op'ster·land (ŏp'stēr·länt). Commune, Friesland prov., N Netherlands; pop. 19,431.

O'pus (ō'pŭs). Ancient town, ✻ of Locris Opuntia (Eastern Locris), E cen. Greece, on coast of Euboean Sea.

O·qair' (ô·kīr'; -kär') *or* **U·qair'** (ōō-). Coastal town, al-Hasa prov., E Nejd, Saudi Arabia, NE of Hofuf and opp. Qatar Penin.

O·quaw'ka (ô·kwô'ka). Village, ⊗ of Henderson co., W Illinois, on Mississippi river W of Galesburg; pop. 1090.

O'quirrh Mountains (ō'kwēr). Mountain range in Utah, S of Great Salt Lake.

O·ra'dea (ô·rä'dyä) *or* **Oradea Ma're** (mä'rĕ); *Hung.* **Nagy'vá'rad** (nŏd'y'·vä'rŏd); *Ger.* **Gross'war·dein'** (grōs'vär·dīn'). City of Transylvania, NW Romania, on Körös river near Hungarian border; pop. (1939 est.) 80,872; industrial and commercial center in grape-growing region; Greek Catholic and Roman Catholic cathedrals; also a cultural center. A very old town; its bishopric founded by St. Ladislas in 1080; destroyed by Tatars 1241; passed to Transylvania 1556 for short time, held by Turks 1660–92; after World War I ceded to Romania but again held by Hungary during World War II 1940–45.

O·ra·dell' (ōr'a·dĕl'). Borough, Bergen co., NE corner of New Jersey, 8 m. ENE of Paterson; pop. 7487.

Ö'rae·fa·jö'kull (û'rī'vä·yû'kŭt·l'). Highest peak 6429 ft. in Iceland, near SE coast of the island.

O·rai' (ô·rī'). Town, SW Uttar Pradesh, N Indian Union, 65 m. SW of Cawnpore; pop. 11,349.

O·rai'bi (ô·rī'bĭ). Hopi pueblo, Navajo co., NE Arizona, in Hopi Indian Reservation; pop. (est.) 300; on top of a mesa (alt. 6070 ft.), one of the oldest, and once the largest, of Hopi towns; a Spanish Franciscan mission in 17th cent.

O·ran' (ô·răn'; ô·rän'; *Fr.* ô'räN'). 1 Department of Algeria. See *Table* at ALGERIA.
2 Seaport city, its ✻, NW Algeria, 210 m. WSW of Algiers; pop. (1936) 194,746; strongly fortified by the French, chiefly a modern city; has two harbors. Built by the Moors; taken by the Spaniards 1509; held by Turks (beys of Oran) in 18th cent.; destroyed by earthquake 1791. In World War II most of French squadron in harbor destroyed by British fleet July 3, 1940; taken by Americans Nov. 10, 1942.

Or'ange (ŏr'ĭnj). 1 Counties in eight states in the U.S. See *Tables* at CALIFORNIA, FLORIDA, INDIANA, NEW YORK, NORTH CAROLINA, TEXAS, VERMONT, VIRGINIA.
2 City, Orange co., SW California, 22 m. E of Long Beach; pop. 26,444; in orange-growing region; fruit-packing plants, canneries; poultry raising. Founded 1868 as Richland; given present name 1875.
3 Town, SW New Haven co., S Connecticut, E of the Housatonic river; pop. 8547; agricultural trade center.
4 Town, Franklin co., NW Massachusetts, 14 m. E of Greenfield; pop. 6154; manufactures machinery, tools.
5 City, Essex co., NE New Jersey, 4 m. WNW of and adjoining Newark; pop. 35,789; manufactures calculating machines, pharmaceuticals, electrical supplies, radios, textiles. Settled c. 1666, formerly part of Newark, incorporated as town 1806, as city 1872; separated from East Orange, South Orange, and West Orange 1861–63.

6 Village, Cuyahoga co., N Ohio; pop. 2006; birthplace of James A. Garfield, 20th president of the U.S.
7 City and port of entry, ⊗ of Orange co., E Texas, on Sabine river 22 m. E of Beaumont; pop. 25,605; in rice-growing and truck-farming area; produces oil, gas, timber, sulfur; shipyards; dock facilities; canneries; manufactures lumber, paper, caskets, foundry products. Established as trading post 1800; region once frequented by Jean Laffite's pirates.
8 Town, ⊗ of Orange co., N cen. Virginia, 27 m. NE of Charlottesville; pop. 2955.
9 Town, E New South Wales, SE Australia, in Blue Mts. 130 m. WNW of Sydney; pop. 9632; in fruit-growing district.
10 River ab. 1300 m. long in South Africa; rises in Basutoland, flows W, forming S boundary of Orange Free State; continues W across N cen. and NW Cape of Good Hope prov., in its lower course forming the boundary bet. Republic of South Africa and South-West Africa; empties into Atlantic Ocean at Alexander Bay; numerous dams being constructed along its course to provide hydroelectric power and irrigation for N and E Cape Province.

O'range' (ô'räNzh'; *Angl.* ŏr'ĭnj); *anc.* **A·rau'si·o** (à·rô'zhĭ·ō). City, ✻ of Vaucluse dept., SE France, 13 m. N of Avignon; pop. 12,946; tourist resort; ancient Roman ruins include a triumphal arch, a theater, and an amphitheater; agricultural products. Scene of defeat of Romans under Caepio by Cimbri and Teutons 105 B.C.; episcopal see 3d cent.–1790; capital of former principality; gave name to Dutch princes of Orange; in 1530 became possession of house of Nassau whence it passed to house of princes who were styled princes of Orange-Nassau, and of whom William, afterward William III of England, was one; acquired by Louis XIV 1660; title continued to be held by the cousin of William and his descendants, who are now the royal line of the Netherlands.

Or'ange, Cape (ŏr'ĭnj). Cape on N coast of Brazil, near the French Guiana border.

Orange Bay. Bay on W end of island of Jamaica, West Indies.

Or'ange·burg (ŏr'ĭnj·bûrg). 1 County in South Carolina. See *Table* at SOUTH CAROLINA.
2 City, its ⊗, S cen. South Carolina, 35 m. SSE of Columbia; pop. 13,852; settled in 1730's; manufactures cotton goods, lumber, veneer. Claflin Univ. (1869; coed.), South Carolina State Coll. (1896; coed.).

Or'ange City (ŏr'ĭnj). City, ⊗ of Sioux co., NW Iowa, 38 m. NNE of Sioux City; pop. 2707.

Orange Free State; *S. Afr. Du.* **O·ran'je Vry'staat** (ô·rän'yĕ frē'ĭ·stät). Province, E cen. Republic of So. Africa; 49,647 sq. m.; pop. (1936) 772,060 (ab. 570,000 natives); ✻ Bloemfontein. Bounded on N by Transvaal, on E by Natal, on SE by Basutoland, and on S and W by Cape Province; forms part of inner plateau of South Africa at 4000–5000 ft. above sea level, with higher W slopes of Drakensberg Mts. along E border. Traversed along S border by Orange river, along N by the Vaal and separated for most part from Basutoland by Caledon river; crossed by tributaries of the Vaal river (Modder, Riet, Vet), flowing generally W. Wide plains afford excellent grazing; chief industry stock raising; chief agricultural products grains and fruits. Chief towns Bloemfontein, Kroonstad, Ladybrand, Bethlehem, and Ficksburg.
History: Region N of Orange river first visited by Europeans toward end of 18th cent.; a few settlements made bet 1810–20 but occupancy began 1836 with great trek of Boers; conflicts with Zulus 1837; annexed by British 1848 but sovereignty withdrawn and independence of Boer state recognized 1854; constitution framed by Boers 1854 and country named Orange Free State; strife with Basutos ended 1869 and friendly relations established with Transvaal 1870–99; joined Transvaal in Boer War 1899–1902; overcome by British and annexed

to British dominions as **Orange River Colony** May 28, 1900; granted responsible government 1907; joined Union of South Africa 1910. See HEILBRON.

Orange Lake. Lake ab. 14 m. long in SE corner of Alachua co., N Florida penin.

Orange Range; *Du.* **O·ran'je Ge·berg'te** (ô·rän'yĕ Kĕ·bĕrK'tĕ). Mountain range, E cen. Neth. New Guinea, E of Nassau Range and forming E end of Snow Mts.; highest peak Wilhelmina 15,584 ft.; source of the Digul and many other streams.

Orange River. See 1st ORANGE, 10, above.

Orange Town. Town on Saint Eustatius I. (*q.v.*), West Indies.

Or'ange·ville (ôr'ĭnj·vĭl). Industrial town, ⊗ of Dufferin co., SE Ontario, Canada, 43 m. WNW of Toronto; pop. 3249; trades esp. in grain.

Orange Walk. 1 Former district in British Honduras. See NORTHERN.

2 Town, NW British Honduras, ✳ of former Orange Walk dist.; pop. (1931) 1099.

Orango. See Ilhas dos BIJAGOS.

O·ra'ni·en·baum (ô·rä'nĕ·ĕn·boum; *Russ.* ŭ·rŭ·nyĭn·boum'). Town, NW Leningrad Region, Soviet Russia, Europe, on the Gulf of Finland opp. Kronshtadt; has fine palace which was imperial residence 1727–1914, used by Soviet government as rest home and school.

O·ra'ni·en·burg (ô·rä'nĕ·ĕn·bŏŏrk). City, Brandenburg, E Germany, on Havel river 19 m. NNW of Berlin; pop. 14,710; mentioned in 12th cent. under name of **Böt'zow** (bû'tsō); manufactures chemicals, steel pens; blast furnaces. Concentration camp in World War II.

O·ran'je (ô·rän'yĕ). Peak 2430 ft. in SE Surinam.

Oranje Gebergte. See ORANGE RANGE.

O·ran'je·stad (ô·rän'yĕ·stät). Chief town, Aruba I., Netherlands West Indies, on W coast; oil refineries.

Oranje Vrystaat. See ORANGE FREE STATE.

O·ras' (ô·räs'). Municipality, E Samar, Phil. Is., 45 m. NE of Catbalogan; pop. 20,962; has fair harbor on **Oras Bay**, on Pacific coast.

O'ra·va (ô'rá·và); *Pol.* **O·ra'wa** (ô·rä'vä). District, former county in Hungary (*Hung.* **Ar'va** [är'vŏ]; divided 1920 bet. Poland and Czechoslovakia; now mostly in Slovakia.

O·ra'vi·ţa (ô·rä'vĕ·tsä); *Ger.* **O·ra'wi·tza** (ô·rä'vĕ·tsä). City, SW Romania, near Yugoslav border NE of Belgrade; pop. 9646.

Or'be·tel'lo (ôr'bĕ·tĕl'ō; *Ital.* ôr·bä·tĕl'lô). Commune, Grosseto prov., Tuscany, cen. Italy, on Tyrrhenian Sea 23 m. S of Grosseto; pop. 10,835; Etruscan ruins; cathedral; aviation center.

Or·bi'go (ôr·vē'gŏ). River ab. 90 m. long in NW Spain; rises in N León prov., flows S into Esla river.

Orcadas del Sur. See SOUTH ORKNEY ISLANDS.

Orcades. See ORKNEY ISLANDS.

Or'cas Island (ôr'kăs). See SAN JUAN ISLANDS.

Or'chard Park (ôr'chĕrd). Village and resort, Erie co., W New York, 10 m. SSE of Buffalo; pop. 3278.

Orch'ha (ôrch'hä) *or* **Or'cha** (ôr'chá). Former Indian state, Bundelkhand, Central India, India; 1999 sq. m.; pop. (1941) 363,405; ✳ Tikamgarh; one of the oldest and most progressive of the smaller Indian states.

Or·chil'la (ôr·chē'yä) *or* **Or·chi'la** (-chē'lä). Island ab. 8 m. long belonging to Venezuela in the Caribbean Sea N of N cen. Venezuela, 80 m. NW of La Tortuga.

Or·chom'e·nus (ôr·kŏm'ĕ·nŭs). **1** Ancient town, E Arcadia, cen. Peloponnesus, S Greece, ab. 9 m. NNW of Mantinea.

2 City, now in ruins, in NW Boeotia, ancient Greece; site is 7 m. NE of Lebadea on N bank of the Cephisus. A city of prehistoric period settled by the Minyae; in later historic times generally subject to power of Thebes; opposed to Theban hegemony and sided with Spartans against it 379 B.C.; several times destroyed and rebuilt in 4th cent. B.C.; scene of battle 85 B.C. in which Sulla destroyed an army of Mithridates VI.

Ord (ôrd). **1** City, ⊗ of Valley co., cen. Nebraska, 57 m. NNW of Grand Island; pop. 2413.

2 River ab. 300 m. long, NE Western Australia; flows N to Joseph Bonaparte Gulf near Wyndham.

Ord, Mount. Peak 6750 ft. in N Brewster co., W Texas.

Orde, El. See DONGOLA.

Or'dos (ôr'dŏs). Desert region S of the Hwang Ho, Suiyuan prov., cen. Inner Mongolia, N China; highest point ab. 5000 ft.

Ord Peak (ôrd). Mountain 10,860 ft. in SW Apache co., E Arizona.

Or·du' (ôr·dŏŏ'). **1** Vilayet, N Turkey in Asia; 2309 sq. m.; pop. 283,054.

2 *anc.* **Cot'y·o'ra** (kŏt'ĭ·ôr'à). Town, its ✳, on the Black Sea 80 m. E of Samsun; pop. 9778. Ancient Cotyora was the port in Pontus where the 10,000 Greeks of the Anabasis set sail for home.

Ord'way (ôrd'wā). Town, ⊗ of Crowley co., E Colorado, near Arkansas river; pop. 1254.

Ordzhonikidze. 1 See DZAUDZHIKAU.

2 See YENAKIYEVO.

Ordzhonikidzegrad. See BEZHITSA.

Ordzhonikidze Territory. See STAVROPOL TERRITORY.

Ö're·bro' (û'rĕ·brŏŏ'). **1** Province of Sweden. See *Table* at SWEDEN.

2 City, its ✳, S cen. Sweden, at mouth of Svart river on E shore of Lake Hjälmaren 100 m. W of Stockholm; pop. 58,590; manufactures shoes. Dates back to 11th cent.; scene of many important diets or assemblies, esp. the National Diet of 1810 when Marshal Bernadotte was chosen king of Sweden.

Or'e·gon (ôr'ĕ·gŭn; -gŏn). **1** Earlier name of COLUMBIA river.

2 A northwestern state of U.S.A., 33d state admitted to Union (1859); bounded on N by Washington, on E by Idaho, on S by Nevada and California, and on W by the Pacific Ocean; 10th state in area, 96,981 sq. m. (land area 96,315 sq. m.); 31st state in population, 1,768,687; ✳ Salem. See *Table of States* at UNITED STATES. Divided into the following 36 counties (for pronunciation of their names, see their individual entries):

NAME	LOCATION	AREA[1]	POP.[1]	CO. SEAT
Baker	E	3,084	17,295	Baker
Benton	W	668	39,165	Corvallis
Clackamas	NW	1,890	113,038	Oregon City
Clatsop	NW corner; coastal	820	27,380	Astoria
Columbia	NW	646	22,379	Saint Helens
Coos	SW; coastal	1,611	54,955	Coquille
Crook	cen.	2,980	9,430	Prineville
Curry	SW corner; coastal	1,622	13,983	Gold Beach
Deschutes	cen.	3,027	23,100	Bend
Douglas	SW; coastal[2]	5,062	68,458	Roseburg
Gilliam	N	1,211	3,069	Condon
Grant	E cen.	4,532	7,726	Canyon City
Harney	SE	10,132	6,744	Burns
Hood River	N	529	13,395	Hood River
Jackson	SW	2,817	73,962	Medford
Jefferson	N cen.	1,794	7,130	Madras
Josephine	SW	1,625	29,917	Grants Pass
Klamath[3]	S	5,973	47,475	Klamath Falls
Lake	S	8,270	7,158	Lakeview
Lane	W; coastal	4,573	162,890	Eugene
Lincoln	W; coastal	985	24,635	Toledo
Linn	W	2,294	58,867	Albany
Malheur	SE corner	9,870	22,764	Vale
Marion	NW	1,173	120,888	Salem
Morrow	N	2,059	4,871	Heppner
Multnomah	NW	424	522,813	Portland
Polk	NW	739	26,523	Dallas
Sherman	N	830	2,446	Moro
Tillamook	NW; coastal	1,115	18,955	Tillamook
Umatilla	NE	3,231	44,352	Pendleton
Union	NE	2,032	18,180	La Grande
Wallowa	NE corner	3,178	7,102	Enterprise
Wasco	N	2,387	20,205	The Dalles
Washington	NW	716	92,237	Hillsboro
Wheeler	N cen.	1,707	2,722	Fossil
Yamhill	NW	709	32,478	McMinnville

[1] Area = land area in sq. m. Pop. from 1960 Census.
[2] NW corner borders on Pacific Ocean.
[3] Crater Lake National Park in W part.

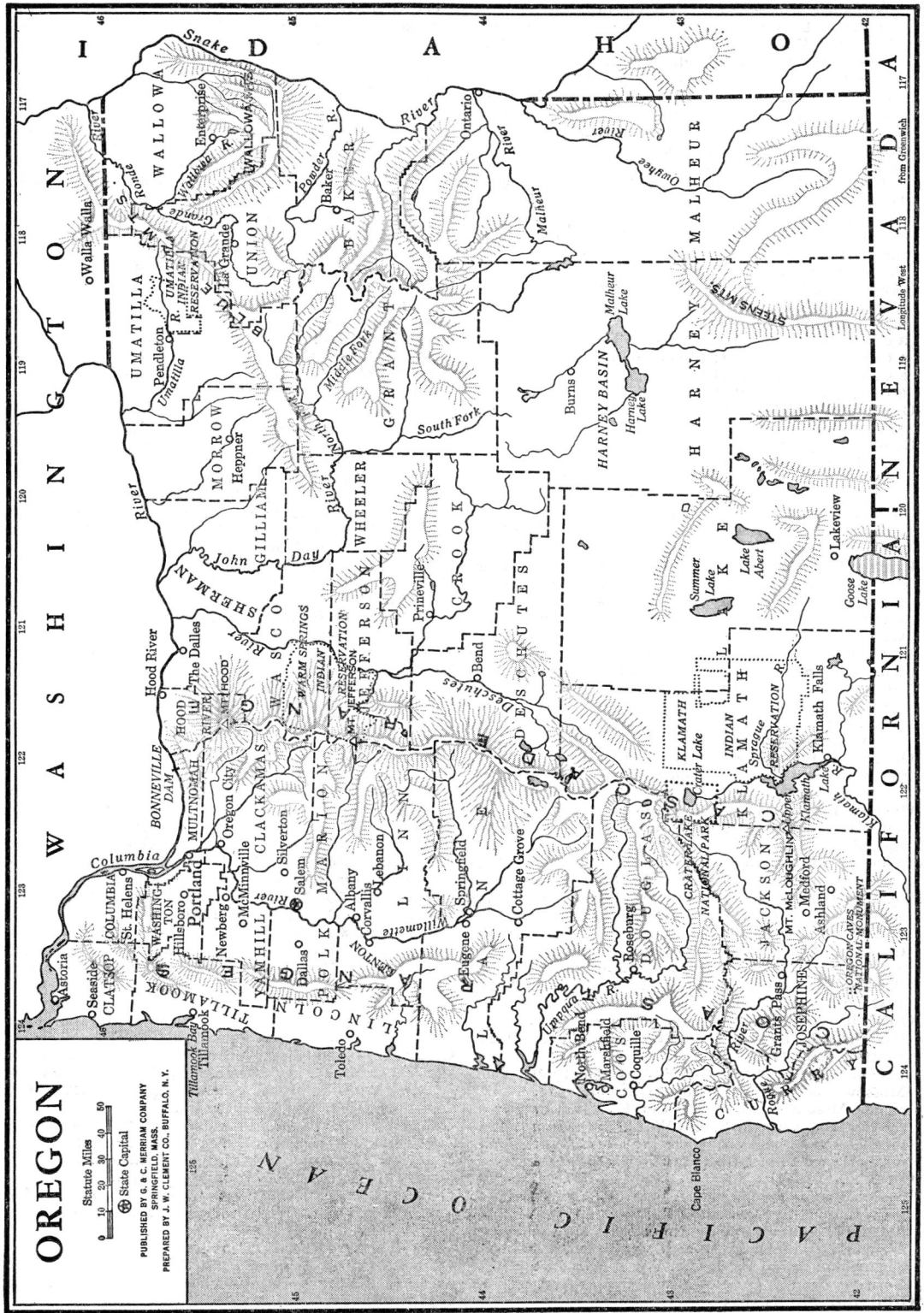

OREGON

Statute Miles
0 10 20 30 40 50

⊕ State Capital

PUBLISHED BY G. & C. MERRIAM COMPANY
OF SPRINGFIELD, MASS.
PREPARED BY J. W. CLEMENT CO., BUFFALO, N.Y.

Nickname: Sunset State; also Valentine State, Webfoot State, Beaver State. *State flower:* Oregon grape. *Motto:* Alis Volat Propriis (She Flies with Her Own Wings). *Chief cities:* Portland, Eugene, Salem, Medford. *Rivers:* Columbia forming most of N boundary; Snake, forming upper E boundary. *Mountains:* Cascade Range, across W cen. part; highest point Mount Hood 11,245 ft.; Blue Mts. and Wallowa Mts. in NE. *Chief industries:* Lumbering, fishing (esp. salmon), sheep raising, agriculture (esp. fruitgrowing).

History: Visited by Ferrelo 1543 and James Cook 1778; Columbia river discovered by Captain Robert Gray of Boston 1792, giving U.S. a claim to the region; explored by Lewis and Clark expedition 1804–06; for a time jointly occupied by England and U.S. (see OREGON COUNTRY); received white settlers with first immigration over Oregon Trail 1842; Great Britain relinquished claim to region 1846; Oregon Territory organized 1848; admitted to Union Feb. 14, 1859.

3 County in Missouri. See *Table* at MISSOURI.
4 City, ⊗ of Ogle co., N Illinois; pop. 3732.
5 City, ⊗ of Holt co., NW Missouri; pop. 887.
6 City, Lucas co., NW Ohio, E of Toledo; pop. 13,319.

Oregon Caves National Monument. See UNITED STATES, *National Monuments.*

Oregon City. City, ⊗ of Clackamas co., NW Oregon, on Willamette river 11 m. S of Portland; pop. 7996; founded 1829 at terminus of old Oregon Trail; water power from falls; tourist and resort business; dairy, poultry, fruit farms. Scene of first meeting of Provisional Legislature 1843; first capital of Oregon Territory 1849–52.

Oregon Country. Region, W North America, between the Pacific coast and the Rocky Mts. extending from the N border of California to Alaska, often so called c. 1818–46; the U.S. portion comprised all of the present states of Washington, Oregon, and Idaho and parts of W Montana and Wyoming; at beginning of the 19th century claimed by Spain, Russia, Great Britain, and the U.S.; given up by Spain 1819 and by Russia 1825; divided at 49th parallel between Great Britain and the U.S. 1846; U.S. portion, scene of mission established by Marcus Whitman 1836, organized as a territory 1848.

Oregon Inlet. Narrow strait leading from Atlantic Ocean through barrier reef off E coast of Dare co., NE North Carolina.

Oregon Trail. An emigrant route to the Oregon Country, ab. 2000 m. long, used esp. bet. 1804 and 1860; started at Independence, W Missouri; crossed Nebraska following Platte and North Platte rivers; crossed Wyoming, traversing the Rocky Mts. through South Pass (*q.v.*) in the Wind River Range; followed Snake river across Idaho to the Columbia river; terminus was Fort Vancouver; part of trail was covered by Lewis and Clark 1805; Capt. Benjamin Bonneville led his exploring party over route 1832–35; despite difficult passage through Blue Mts., wagon travel became very heavy 1842–60.

O·re'kho·vo (ô·ryä'ĸŏ·vŏ). Commune, Vrattsa dept., NW Bulgaria, on S bank of the Danube 40 m. NNE of Vrattsa; pop. (1926) 6076.

O·re'kho·vo–Zu'e·vo (ŭ·ryĕ'ĸŭ·vŭ·zŏŏ'yĭ·vŭ). City, Moscow Region, Soviet Russia, Europe; pop. 99,329; on the Moscow-Gorki R.R. 58 m. E of Moscow and on the Klyazma river. In World War II in the campaign to take Moscow, the point where the German tank forces were planned to meet in the encirclement of the city.

O·rel' (ô·rĕl'; *Russ.* ŭ·ryôl'). City, ✱ of Orel Region, Soviet Russia, Europe, on left bank of Oka river and on main railroad line 205 m. S of Moscow; pop. 110,567; because of its favorable location and its rail connections is a market center for wide area, esp. in grain, livestock, and manufactured goods. In World War II taken by Germans Oct. 1941; retaken by Russians Aug. 5, 1943.

Orellana. See AMAZON.

Orel Region. Region, cen. Soviet Russia, Europe, in the black-earth area N of the Ukraine; 25,669 sq. m.; pop. 3,549,088; ✱ Orel. Bounded on N by Kaluga and Tula Regions, on E by Ryazan and Voronezh Regions, on S by Kursk Region, and on W by the Bryansk Region. Watered by upper course of Oka river and tributaries. Formerly a part of the Central Black Earth Area, a fertile agricultural region. Although there has been some exhaustion of the soil and consequent emigration, agriculture is still the main pursuit; some stock raising and in the urban areas considerable industrial development in recent years. Chief towns Orel, Yelets. Came under Moscow principality in 15th cent. and in 17th cent. was part of Poland; laid waste in civil war 1917–20; W two thirds of province held by German armies 1941–43 in World War II but were retaken Aug.–Sept. 1943.

O'rem (ōr'ĕm). City, Utah co., N cen. Utah, 7 m. NNW of Provo; pop. 18,394; in farming area; canning, steel manufacture.

Ore Mountains (ōr). = ERZ GEBIRGE.

Orenburg. See CHKALOV.

O·ren'se (ô·rän'så). **1** Province of Spain. See *Table* at SPAIN.
2 Commune, its ✱, NW Spain, on Miño river 250 m. NW of Madrid; pop. 28,397; produces wine, corn, flax, fruits; manufactures leather, chocolates, linen, woolens; stock raising; Gothic cathedral (founded 1194); 13th-cent. bridge; under the Visigoths, capital of the Suevi.

O're·sund' (û'rĕ·sŭn'); *Eng.* **the Sound** (sound). Strait bet. Sjælland I., Denmark, and S Sweden, connecting the Kattegat with the Baltic Sea; width at its narrowest section 3½ m.

O·re'ti (ô·rā'tĕ). River ab. 110 m. long in S South I., New Zealand; flows S into Foveaux Strait.

Orfani, Gulf of. See STRYMONIC GULF.

Or'ford, Cape (ôr'fĕrd). Point on S coast of New Britain I., Bismarck Archipelago, near E end, extending into Solomon Sea.

Orford Ness (nĕs'). Headland on SE coast of England, ENE of Ipswich; lighthouse.

Or'gan Mountains (ôr'găn). **1** Range in S Dona Ana co., S New Mexico, extending S across border into Texas. **2** Range in Rio de Janeiro state, SE Brazil. See SERRA DOS ORGÃOS.

Órganos, Sierra de los. See SIERRA DE LOS ÓRGANOS.

Organ Pipe Cactus National Monument. See UNITED STATES, *National Monuments.*

Orgãos, Serra dos. See SERRA DOS ORGÃOS.

Or'ge·ev (ôr'gĕ·yĕf); *Romanian* **Or·hei'** (ôr·hā'). Town, cen. Moldavian S.S.R., U.S.S.R., on tributary of Dniester 23 m. N of Kishinev; pop. 14,805.

Or·hei' (ôr·hā'). **1** Former department, cen. Bessarabia, Romania; 1639 sq. m.; pop. 277,009.
2 Town, its ✱. See ORGEEV.

O'ria (ô'ryä). Commune, Brindisi prov., Apulia, SE Italy, 16 m. SW of Brindisi; pop. 11,516; episcopal see; 13th-cent. castle.

O'ri·ent (ōr'ĭ·ĕnt; -ĕnt). Village and resort, Suffolk co., SE New York, on Long I. near Orient Point; pop. (est.) 300; Orient Beach State Park.

Orient, the. The East; generally, eastern countries. In ancient times, the countries E of the Mediterranean; today the countries of Asia generally, esp. the countries of E Asia; the Far East. See the EAST.

Oriental Province. Province, Republic of Congo (formerly Belgian Congo). See STANLEYVILLE.

Oriental Misamis. See MISAMIS ORIENTAL.

Oriental Negros. See NEGROS ORIENTAL.

O·rien'te (ô·ryän'tå). **1** *formerly* **San·tia'go de Cu'ba** (sän·tyä'gô thä kōō'vä). Province, E Cuba. See *Table* at CUBA.
2 = EASTERN REGION, Ecuador.

O'ri·ent Point (ōr'ĭ·ĕnt; -ĕnt). Point at NE extremity of Long I., New York, at N entrance to Gardiners Bay.

O'ri·hue'la (ô'rĕ·wä'lä). City, Alicante prov., SE Spain,

on Segura river 30 m. SW of Alicante; pop. 43,619; produces and trades in fruit, olives, peppers, grain, cereals, wine; manufactures leather, silk, linen, woolens, hats, oil, flour, dyes; 14th-cent. Gothic cathedral and 18th-cent. episcopal palace; university (founded c. 1560) discontinued 1835. Conquered by Moors 713 and reconquered 1265 by James I of Aragon.

O·ril'lia (ô·rĭl'yȧ). Town, Simcoe co., SE Ontario, Canada, where Lakes Couchiching and Simcoe join 21 m. NE of Barrie; pop. 12,110; summer resort and lake port; wood and enamel products, mining machinery, motorboats. Site of Champlain monument erected 1925.

O·rin'da Village (ô·rĭn'dȧ). Urban community (unincorporated), Contra Costa co., W California, NE of Oakland; pop. 5568.

O'ri·no'co (ōr'ĭ·nō'kō). River ab. 1600 m. long in Venezuela; rises in Serra Parima mountains in S Venezuela, flows W, then N forming a section of the Colombia-Venezuela boundary; turns E in cen. Venezuela and empties through a wide delta into the Atlantic Ocean. In S Venezuela connects with Rio Negro of the Amazon system through the Casiquiare; has many tributaries, esp. the Guaviare, Vichada, and Meta, rising in and flowing E in Colombia, the Apure in W Venezuela, and the Caura and Caroni in SE Venezuela. Navigable in many sections for small vessels but is obstructed by rapids ab. 100 m. from its mouth.

O·rion' (ô·ryôn'). Municipality on E coast of Bataan prov., Luzon, Phil. Is., SSE of Balanga; pop. 10,909.

O·ris'ka·ny (ô·rĭs'kȧ·nĭ). Village, Oneida co., cen. New York, on Mohawk river 7 m. WNW of Utica; pop. 1580. Oriskany Battlefield, scene of Revolutionary battle Aug. 6, 1777, to W of village; an ambush by British and Indians and a defeat for the Americans although they were not driven from the field; losses on both sides severe, Gen. Herkimer killed.

O·ris'sa (ô·rĭs'ȧ). State, E coast of Indian Union, N of Madras prov.; 32,198 sq. m.; pop. 8,728,544; ✻ Bhuvaneshwar. Formerly a division of Bihar and Orissa prov.; constituted separate province 1936, with some additions of districts from Madras and Central Provinces; of very irregular shape, chiefly along coast of the Bay of Bengal; its territory cut into by the Eastern States. An agricultural province, with population almost wholly Hindu. Watered by Mahanadi river. Chief towns Cuttack, Puri, Balasore, Sambalpur. Originally conquered by British 1803; till 1912 a part of Bengal; 1912–36 a subdivision of Bihar and Orissa; its status as autonomous province set aside 1939–41.

Orissa Feudatory States. Indian states formerly in EASTERN STATES Agency; now in E Indian Union.

O·ri·sta'no (ô·rês·tä'nô). Commune, Cagliari prov., S Sardinia, on Gulf of Oristano 54 m. NW of Cagliari; pop. 14,662; 13th-cent. cathedral; Phoenician and Roman necropolis nearby.

Oristano, Gulf of. Inlet of Mediterranean Sea on W cen. coast of Sardinia; 10 m. long; receives Tirso river.

O'ri·ve'si (ô'rĭ·vě'sĭ). Lake, SE Finland in Kuopio dept.

O'ri·za'ba (ōr'ĭ·zä'bȧ; *Span.* ō'rě·sä'vä). 1 See CITLALTEPETL.

2 City, Veracruz state, E Mexico, 65 m. WSW of Veracruz; pop. 47,910; produces cotton, coffee, sugar, tobacco; altitude 3900 ft.; has healthful climate and beautiful scenery; many fine buildings; favorite residence of Maximilian.

Or'khon (ôr'kŏn). River ab. 450 m. long, N Outer Mongolia; flows NE from N edge of the Gobi and joins the Selenga just W of Kiachta at the border; ruins of Karakorum are near its banks.

Ork'ney Islands (ôrk'nĭ) *or* **Ork'neys** (-nĭz); *anc.* **Or'ca·des** (ôr'kȧ·dēz). Archipelago off NE coast of Scotland, comprising **Orkney** co.; 376 sq. m.; pop. (1931) 22,077, (1951) 21,258; ✻ Kirkwall, on Pomona I.; chief islands are Pomona (or Mainland), Hoy, South

Ronaldsay, North Ronaldsay, Sanday, Stronsay, Shapinsay, and Rousay; separated from Caithness co. on the mainland by Pentland Firth; islands are low (highest point 880 ft. on Pomona) and irregular in shape; in S bet. Pomona, Hoy, and South Ronaldsay is Scapa Flow (*q.v.*); chief occupations fishing (esp. herring) and agriculture (fertile soil produces oats, barley, turnips, and fine pasturage for cattle, sheep, and horses). Long a Norse dependency; acquired by Scotland 1472.

Or·lan'do (ôr·lăn'dō). City, ⊗ of Orange co., cen. Florida penin., 78 m. NE of Tampa; pop. 88,135; incorporated 1875; ships citrus fruits; winter resort; U.S. Air Force base.

Or·lan'do, Cape (ôr·lăn'dō; *Ital.* ôr·län'dō). Point on N coast of Sicily, near E end; in World War II landing made just E of cape Aug. 12, 1943 by American forces.

Orlau. See ORLOVÁ.

Or·lé'a'nais (ôr'lā'ȧ'ně'). Historical region of N cen. France; bounded anciently on N by Île-de-France, E by Champagne, Burgundy, and Nivernais, S by Berry, SW by Touraine, W by Maine; ✻ Orléans; watered by Loir, Loire, and Cher rivers; provincial appanage of younger members of ruling house of France.

Or'le·ans (*La.:* ôr'lě·ănz, ôr'lănz; *N.Y.:* ôr'lēnz; *Vt.:* ôr·lēnz'). Name of a parish in Louisiana and of counties in two states of the U.S. See *Tables* at LOUISIANA, NEW YORK, VERMONT.

Or·leans' (ôr·lēnz'). 1 Town, Barnstable co., SE Massachusetts, on inlet of Atlantic Ocean 18 m. ENE of Barnstable; pop. 2342; summer resort.

2 Village, Orleans co., N Vermont, 9 m. S of Newport; pop. 1240.

Or'lé·ans' (ôr'lā'äⁿ'); *anc.* **Au·re'li·a'num** (ô·rē'lĭ·ȧ'nŭm). Commune, ✻ of Loiret dept., N cen. France, on Loire river 70 m. SSW of Paris; pop. 73,155; Gothic cathedral, palace of justice, museum, theater; manufactures cotton goods, sugar, brewery products, hosiery, pottery. Captured by Caesar 52 B.C.; made duchy 1344 by Philip of Valois in favor of his son (the title Duke of Orléans continuing into modern times in French royal family); university instituted here 1312; English siege relieved by Joan of Arc, also called the Maid of Orléans; captured several times in Franco-Prussian War.

Or'lé·ans, Island of (ôr'lě·ănz); *Fr.* **Île d'Or'lé·ans'** (ēl'dôr'lā'äⁿ'). Island in St. Lawrence river 4 m. downstream from the city of Quebec, Quebec prov., E Canada; 21 m. long; 72 sq. m.; pop. 4349; part of Montmorency co.; chief town Sainte Famille.

Or'le·ans, Isle of (ôr'lě·ănz; ôr'lănz); *Fr.* **Île d'Or'lé·ans'** (ēl' dôr'lā'äⁿ'). District around New Orleans, Louisiana, ab. 2800 sq. m., S of Lake Pontchartrain and E of the Mississippi; ceded by France to Spain 1763 at time (Treaty of Paris) when she ceded rest of her Louisiana territory E of the Mississippi to Great Britain.

Or'le·ans, Territory of (ôr'lě·ănz; ôr'lănz). See LOUISIANA.

Or'lé·ans'ville' (ôr'lā'äⁿ'vēl'). Commune, NW Alger dept., N Algeria, on the Chéliff river 105 m. SW of Algiers; pop. 18,487.

Or'lo·vá (ôr'lô·vä); *Pol.* **Or·ło'wa** (ôr·lô'vä); *Ger.* **Or'lau** (ôr'lou). Commune, Silesia prov., Czechoslovakia, just E of Moravská Ostrava in Teschen dist.; pop. (1938–39 est.) 10,040; agricultural center; coal mining. Held by Poland 1938–45.

Or'ly (ôr'lē'). Commune, Seine dept., N France, SSE suburb of Paris; pop. (1931) 5414; airport.

Or·ma'ra (ôr·mä'rä). Headland and town, S coast of Baluchistan, Pakistan, ab. 150 m. W of Karachi.

Or·moc' (ôr·môk') *or* **Mac·Ar'thur** (mȧk·är'thēr). Municipality and port on W coast of Leyte I., Phil. Is., on Ormoc Bay, an inlet of Camotes Sea; pop. 10,629; near delta of Bao river 36 m. SW of Tacloban. In World War II developed by Japanese as strong military base; captured by Americans Dec. 11, 1944 after several weeks of severe fighting.

Or′mond Beach (ôr′mŭnd). City, Volusia co., E Florida, on Atlantic Ocean 7 m. N of Daytona Beach; pop. 8658; motor racing on beach nearby.

Orms′by (ôrmz′bĭ). County in Nevada. See *Table* at NEVADA.

Orms′kirk (ôrmz′kûrk). Urban district, Lancashire, NW England, 11 m. NNE of Liverpool; pop. 20,554; manufactures textile goods and cordage.

Or′muz (ôr′mŭz; *native* ôr·mōōz′, ōor-). See HORMUZ.

Ormuz, Strait of. Strait bet. the N tip of Trucial Oman, SE Arabia, and the S coast of Iran; connects the Persian Gulf with the Gulf of Oman. Island of Qishm is in N part.

Orne (ôrn). **1** River ab. 95 m. long in NW France; flows N in Orne and Calvados depts. past Caen into the English Channel; its bridges seized by Allies on invasion of Normandy June 6, 1944.
2 Department of France. See *Table* at FRANCE.

Ornes (ôrn). Village, Meuse dept., NE France, 8 m. NE of Verdun; in World War I scene of battle Feb. 24, 1916 when it was captured by Germans.

Oro, El. See EL ORO.

O′ro Bay (ōr′ō). Small inlet of Dyke Acland Bay on NE coast of Papua, New Guinea, 20 m. S of Buna; in 1943 site of an Allied base which was often raided by the Japanese, who lost many planes, esp. Apr. and Oct. 1943.

O′ro·co′vis (ō′rȧ·kō′vĕs). Municipality (pop. 20,362) and town (pop. 3005), cen. Puerto Rico; town is 24 m. SW of San Juan.

Oro de Hidalgo, El. See EL ORO DE HIDALGO.

O′ro·fi′no (ōr′ō·fē′nō). City, ⊗ of Clearwater co., NE Idaho, 40 m. E of Lewiston; pop. 2471; lumbering, mining.

O′ro·he′na, Mount (ōr′ō·hā′nȧ). Peak 7339 ft. in center of the island of Tahiti, Society Is., S Pacific Ocean; a double peak, steep and thickly forested.

Orolaunum. See ARLON.

O′ro·no (ōr′ō·nō). **1** Town, Penobscot co., E cen. Maine, on Penobscot river 8 m. NNE of Bangor; pop. 8341; manufactures wood pulp, paper, paddles, oars. Univ. of Maine (1865; coed.).
2 Village, Hennepin co., SE cen. Minnesota, W of Minneapolis; pop. 5643.

O′ron·say (ōr′ŭn·zā; -sā). Small island of the Inner Hebrides near Colonsay, off W coast of Scotland; administratively a part of Argyll co.; ruins of 14th-cent. priory.

O·ron′tes (ō·rŏn′tēz). **1** See ALWAND.
2 *Arab.* **Nahr el ′A′si** (nä′h′r ăl ä′sĭ). Unnavigable river 246 m. long in W Syria; rises in the El Bika valley of Lebanon near Baalbek and flows N to the W of the Anti-Liban Mts. past the cities of Homs and Hama, then turning W and SW through Hatay, S Turkey, past Antioch into the Mediterranean Sea at Süveydiye 40 m. N of Latakia; receives tributary Afrine from the N.

O·ro′pus (ō·rō′pŭs). Ancient town of Boeotia, E cen. Greece, on the coast opp. Eretria; seized by Athenians and became part of Attica.

O′ro·quie′ta (ō′rō·kyä′tä). Municipality, ✳ of Misamis Occidental prov., Mindanao, Phil. Is., on NW shore of Iligan Bay; pop. 21,523; on coastal highway; has good harbor.

O·ro·se′i, Gulf of (ō·rō·zā′ĕ). Widemouthed inlet of Tyrrhenian Sea on E cen. coast of the island of Sardinia.

O′ros·há′za (ō′rōsh·hä′zŏ). Commune 32 m. NE of Szeged, SE Hungary; pop. 25,216; market center for grain, wine, and livestock.

Orotava, La. See LA OROTAVA.

O·ro′te (ō·rō′tä). Peninsula, W coast of Guam, ab. 4 m. long by ½ to 1 m. wide; forms S side of Apra Harbor; site of last stand of Japanese in July 1944.

O′ro·ville (ōr′ō·vĭl). **1** City, ⊗ of Butte co., N California, on Feather river 66 m. N of Sacramento; pop. 6115; in agricultural region; fruit-packing plants, olive canning, gold dredging; manufactures olive oil; founded 1849–50; made ⊗ 1856.

2 Town, Okanogan co., N Washington, on Okanogan river and Osoyoos Lake 5 m. S of Canadian border; pop. 1437; port of entry and customs and immigration station.

Oroya, La. See LA OROYA.

Or′ping·ton (ôr′pĭng·tŭn). Urban district, Kent, SE England, 14 m. SE of London; pop. 63,344; residential suburb of London; gives its name to the Orpington breed of domestic fowls.

Or′re·fors′ (ôr′ĕ·fôrs′; -fôsh′). Town, Kronoberg co., SE Sweden, ab. 26 m. NW of Kalmar; famous crystal glass factory.

Or′rell (ŏr′ĕl). Urban district, Lancashire, NW England, 16 m. NE of Liverpool; pop. 9317.

Or′ring·ton (ŏr′ĭng·tŭn). Town, Penobscot co., E cen. Maine, on Penobscot river 7 m. SSW of Bangor; pop. 2539.

Orrs Island (ôrz). Island in Casco Bay in Cumberland co., off E coast of SW Maine.

Orr′ville (ôr′vĭl). City, Wayne co., NE cen. Ohio, 20 m. SSW of Akron; pop. 6511; railroad division point; manufactures machine castings, drilling machinery, dairy products.

Orsera. See ANDERMATT.

Or′sha (ôr′shȧ). Town, NE White Russia, U.S.S.R., on right bank of the Dnieper 122 m. NE of Minsk; pop. 21,311; on main railroad from Minsk to Moscow and junction for four other lines; has considerable trade in grain and timber, a large electric power station begun in 1928, and large factories in the meat and flax-weaving industries. Dates back to 11th cent.; was long within borders of Poland and several times besieged by Russians who annexed it in 1772. In World War II occupied by Germans July 1941 and retaken by Russians July 1, 1944.

Orsk (ôrsk). Town, E Chkalov Region, Soviet Russia, Europe, on railroad 155 m. E of Chkalov; pop. 65,799; on left bank of Ural river S of Magnitogorsk; has oil refineries and is terminus of pipelines from Gurev and other oil ports at N end of Caspian Sea; also a mining center, with chrome and nickel mines nearby.

Orsona. See OSUNA.

Or′şo·va (ôr′shô·vä). City, SW Romania, in Banat region, on Danube river near the Iron Gate; pop. 8428; port for Danube steamers.

Or′ta, Lake (ôr′tä). See OMEGNA.

Orta No′va (nô′vä). Commune, Foggia prov., Apulia, SE Italy, 11 m. SE of Foggia; pop. 13,033.

Or′te·gal′, Cape (ôr′tä·gäl′). Cape on NW coast of Spain, projecting N coast of La Coruña prov.

Ortelsburg. See SZCZYTNO.

Or′thez′ (ôr′tâz′). Town, N Basses-Pyrénées dept., SW France, on the Gave de Pau ab. 25 m. NW of Pau; pop. 4097; capital of Béarn to 15th cent.; center of Protestantism during 16th cent., site of Calvinist university founded by Jeanne d'Albret and suppressed by Louis XIII; bridge over the river has interesting tower. Wellington defeated Marshal Soult here Feb. 27, 1814.

Or′ti·guei′ra (ôr′tē·gĕ′ĕ·rä; -gā′rä). Seaport commune, La Coruña prov., NW Spain, on inlet of Bay of Biscay 35 m. NE of La Coruña; pop. 22,152; coasting trade; agricultural products; chinaware; linen; fish-salting works.

Ort′ler (ôrt′lēr); *Ital.* **Ort′les** (ôrt′lås). Mountain range of E Alps, bet. Venezia Tridentina and NE Lombardy, N Italy; highest peak the **Ortler** or **Ort′ler-spit′ze** (ôrt′lēr-shpĭt′sĕ), 12,793 ft. high.

Or′ton (ôr′tôn). River ab. 340 m. long of Peru and Bolivia; rises in SE Peru, flows E across N Bolivia into Beni river shortly before it joins the Mamoré river.

Or·to′na (ôr·tō′nä). Commune, Chieti prov., Abruzzi e Molise, cen. Italy, on Adriatic 13 m. E of Chieti; pop. 20,210; early 12th-cent. cathedral, 16th-cent. palace, 15th-cent. castle; small harbor. Suffered from earthquakes 1782 and 1818. In World War II scene of severe fighting; taken by British Dec. 27, 1943.

Or·ton·ville (ôr′t'n·vĭl). City, ⊗ of Big Stone co., W Minnesota, at S end of Big Stone Lake on South Dakota border; pop. 2674; canneries, quarries; in fishing and hunting area.

Or·tyg′i·a (ôr·tĭj′ĭ·à). Name from ancient times of island adjacent to the SE coast of Sicily and separated from the mainland by a narrow canal; a part of the city of Syracuse (q.v.).

Oruba. Var. of ARUBA.

O·ru′ro (ô·rōō′rô). 1 Department of Bolivia. See *Table* at BOLIVIA.
2 City, its ✳, W Bolivia, and formerly a ✳ of Bolivia; pop. (1943 est.) 50,000; alt. 12,119 ft.; 120 m. SSE of La Paz; railroad junction; founded 1604; commercial center of mining district (tin, silver, copper, wolfram, antimony, bismuth).

O′rust (ōō′rŭst). Swedish island in the Kattegat, off SW coast of Sweden SW of Lake Vänern and 28 m. NW of Göteborg; ab. 14 m. long and 10 m. wide; 134 sq. m.

Or·vie′to (ôr·vyâ′tô); *anc.* **Vel·su′na** (vĕl·sū′nà) *or* **Vol·sin′i·i** (vŏl·sĭn′ĭ·ī); *in Middle Ages* **Urbs Ve′tus** (ûrbz vē′tŭs). Commune, Terni prov., Umbria, cen. Italy, 29 m. WNW of Terni; pop. 21,469; episcopal see (from 509); medieval walls; Italian Gothic cathedral (founded 1290) noted esp. for its fine façade (begun 1310) and containing art works; two 11th-cent. churches, 16th-cent. episcopal palace, 10th-cent. papal palace (now a museum of antiquities); Jesuit college; Etruscan necropolis discovered here 1874; medieval mines nearby. One of twelve cities of ancient Etruria.

Or′well (ôr′wĕl; -wĕl). River in Suffolk, E England, extending 10 m. SE from Ipswich to the Stour.

Or′wigs·burg (ôr′wĭgz·bûrg). Borough, Schuylkill co., E cen. Pennsylvania, 7 m. ESE of Pottsville; pop. 2131; founded 1796; cotton, shoe, rayon factories.

Or′yod, Mount (ôr′yôd). Mountain 3838 ft. in SE Bulacan prov., Luzon, Phil. Is.; highest point in province.

Oryokko. See YALU.

Or·zi·nuo′vi (ôr·dzē·nwô′vē). Commune, Brescia prov., Lombardy, N Italy, 17 m. WSW of Brescia; pop. 10,625.

O·sage′ (ô·sāj′; ō′sāj; *attributively, usu.* ō′sāj). 1 River 360 m. long, W Missouri; formed by junction of Marais des Cygnes and Little Osage rivers on border of Bates and Vernon cos., flows E and NE through Lake of the Ozarks formed by Bagnell Dam (see UNITED STATES, *Dams and Reservoirs*), and enters the Missouri river just E of Jefferson City. The Osage is sometimes considered as including the Marais des Cygnes.
2 Name of counties in three states of the U.S. See *Tables* at KANSAS, MISSOURI, OKLAHOMA.
3 City, ⊗ of Mitchell co., N Iowa, 24 m. ENE of Mason City; pop. 3753.

Osage City. City, Osage co., E Kansas, 25 m. NE of Emporia; pop. 2213; in agricultural and dairy section.

O′sa·ka (ō′sä·kä). 1 Prefecture of Japan. See *Table* at JAPAN.
2 Seaport city, its ✳, Honshu, Japan, on NE shore of Osaka Bay; pop. (1938 est.) 3,321,200, (1960) 3,011,563; second city in size in the empire. Situated on both sides of the Yodo river, which has many channels in the city; has many and varied manufactures, esp. as a chemical center and the industrial metropolis of the Orient; large export trade but foreign goods mostly handled at Kobe. Founded at end of 15th cent.; made his capital by Hideyoshi 1583. Its main buildings are the Toyotomi Castle (built 1583–85), mint (estab. 1871), and arsenal; castle and city partially ruined 1868 by Tokugawa party; also suffered great damage by fire 1909. In World War II heavily bombed by American planes on Mar. 14, 1945 and repeatedly in June and July.

Osaka Bay. Inlet of Pacific Ocean on S coast of Honshu, Japan, E of Awaji I. which separates it from the Inland Sea; connected with the ocean by Kitan Strait and Kii Channel; site of ports of Osaka and Kobe.

O·sa′kis (ô·sā′kĭs). Village, Douglas and Todd cos., W cen. Minnesota, 10 m. E of Alexandria; pop. 1396; fishing and summer resort.

O′sa Peninsula (ō′sä). Peninsula on S coast of Costa Rica bet. the Gulf of Dulce and the Pacific Ocean.

O′sa·wat′o·mie (ō′sȧ·wŏt′ô·mĭ; ŏs′ȧ-). City, Miami co., E Kansas, 45 m. SSW of Kansas City; pop. 4622; a station on the Underground Railroad in pre-Civil War days; site of the cabin in which John Brown (known as "Old Brown of Osawatomie") lived (1856) and scene of the bloody fight (Aug. 1856) bet. Brown and his sympathizers and a group of proslavery adherents.

Os′born (ŏz′bẽrn). Former village, Greene co., SW Ohio, 10 m. NE of Dayton. See FAIRBORN.

Os′borne (ŏz′bẽrn). 1 County in Kansas. See *Table* at KANSAS.
2 City, its ⊗, N cen. Kansas, on Solomon river 59 m. W of Concordia; pop. 2049; in wheat and poultry section.

Osca. See HUESCA.

Os′ce·o′la (ō′sė·ō′lȧ; ŏs′ē-). 1 Counties in three states of the U.S. See *Tables* at FLORIDA, IOWA, MICHIGAN.
2 City, a ⊗ of Mississippi co., NE Arkansas, on Mississippi river 16 m. S of Blytheville; pop. 6189; cotton.
3 City, ⊗ of Clarke co., S Iowa, 39 m. SSW of Des Moines; pop. 3350.
4 City, ⊗ of St. Clair co., W Missouri; pop. 1066.
5 City, ⊗ of Polk co., E Nebraska; pop. 951.
6 Borough (P.O. **Osceola Mills**), Clearfield co., W cen. Pennsylvania, 25 m. NNE of Altoona; pop. 1777.

Osceola, Mount. Mountain 4326 ft., N cen. New Hampshire, in N Grafton co.

O′schatz (ōsh′äts; ō′shäts). City, Leipzig district, Saxony, Germany, 31 m. SE of Leipzig; pop. 10,430; manufactures shoes, felt goods, scales, Venetian blinds.

O′schers·le′ben (ōsh′ẽrs-lā′bĕn). Industrial city, Magdeburg dist., East Germany in former Saxony prov., Prussia, 20 m. WSW of Magdeburg; pop. 13,545; machinery, textiles, shoes, cigars, sugar, chemicals, aircraft. Several times destroyed by fire. Bombed by Americans 1944–45.

Os·co′da (ŏs·kō′dȧ). 1 County in Michigan. See *Table* at MICHIGAN.
2 Village, NE Iosco co., NE Michigan, on Lake Huron at mouth of Au Sable river; pop. (township) 4202; resort; Wurtsmith Air Force Base.

Ösel. Var. of *Oesel:* see SAREMA.

O·se′ras (ô·sā′räs). Peak 11,480 ft. in Cordillera Oriental, W cen. Colombia, S of Bogotá.

Osetia. Var. of OSSETIA.

Osh (ôsh). Town, chief town of Osh Region, S Kirgiz S.S.R., Soviet Central Asia, on Uzbek border ab. 30 m. SE of Andizhan; pop. 29,088; at E end of fertile Fergana valley; raises cotton, grain, and fruit, and is site of modern silk factory. The rock Takht-i-Sulaiman, famous in Moslem legends, is just W of the town.

O′sha Peak (ō′shȧ). Mountain 10,223 ft. in W Torrance co., cen. New Mexico.

O′·Shaugh′nes·sy Dam (ô·shô′nĕ·sĭ). See UNITED STATES, *Dams and Reservoirs*.

Osh′a·wa (ŏsh′ȧ·wȧ; -wô; -wä). Industrial city, Ontario co., SE Ontario, Canada, on Lake Ontario 33 m. ENE of Toronto; pop. 41,545; manufactures esp. iron and steel products and automobiles; has port facilities.

Oshima. See AMAMI.

O Shi·ma (ō shē′mä). 1 Group of islands forming an administrative unit of Tokyo prefecture, Japan, comprising N part of islands of Izu Shichito group off SE Honshu; has six main islands, O Shima, To Shima, Nii Jima, Kozu, Miyake, and Mikura; ab. 84 sq. m.; pop. (1945) 16,394. Name sometimes now used geographically to designate the entire Izu Shichito group.
2 Largest island of the group, in N nearest the mainland; ab. 35 sq. m.; pop. (1945) 9517; has active volcano Mihara 2477 ft., subject to frequent eruptions; suffered from earthquake Sept. 1, 1923.

Osh′kosh (ŏsh′kŏsh). **1** City, ⊗ of Garden co., W Nebraska; pop. 1025.

2 City, ⊗ of Winnebago co., E Wisconsin, on W shore of Lake Winnebago; pop. 45,110; settled c. 1836 on site of fur-trading post; developed as lumber center; now business and trading center of farming, dairying, timber area; manufactures lumber products (including sash and doors), dairy and machine-shop products, overalls, beer; transportation center; summer resort. Wisconsin State Coll. (1871; coed.).

O·shog′bo (ô·shŏg′bō). City, Oyo prov., W Western Provinces, Nigeria, on railroad ab. 50 m. NE of Ibadan; pop. 49,599.

Osh Region (ôsh). Region, S Kirgiz S.S.R., Soviet Central Asia, N of the Alai Mts.; chief town Osh.

Osiek, Osjek. Vars. of OSIJEK.

O′si·jek (ô′sĕ·yĕk); *Hung.* **E′szék** (ĕ′sāk); *anc.* **Mur′sa** (mûr′så). City in Slavonia, the E part of Croatia federated republic, N Yugoslavia, on the Drava river; pop. 40,337; commercial and shipping center in agricultural region; textile mills, furniture factories, iron foundries. Settled by Romans early in the Christian era; bishopric in 2d cent. A.D.; scene of battle of Mursa 351 A.D. in which Constantius II defeated Magnentius; under Turkish rule 1526–1687; free city 1809.

O′si·mo (ô′zĕ·mô). Commune, Ancona prov., Marches, cen. Italy, 9 m. S by W of Ancona; pop. 21,182; episcopal see; ancient Roman walls; 8th-cent. cathedral.

O′si·pen′ko (ŏs′ĭ·pĕng′kō; *Ukrain.* ŭ·syĭ·pyĕn′kŭ; *Russ.* ŭ·syĕ′pyĕn·kŭ); *formerly* **Ber·dyansk′** or **Ber·diansk′** (byĭr·dyánsk′). Seaport town, SE Zaporozhe Region, SE Ukraine, U.S.S.R., on N shore of Sea of Azov 45 m. SW of Zhdanov; pop. 51,664; has good harbor and carries on export trade in grains, linseed, wool, skins; large salt lagoons in vicinity. In World War II taken by Germans Oct. 1941; retaken by Russians Sept. 17, 1943.

Os′ka·loo′sa (ŏs′kà·lōō′så). **1** City, ⊗ of Mahaska co., SE cen. Iowa, 55 m. ESE of Des Moines; pop. 11,053; trading center in agricultural and livestock-raising section; coal fields nearby. William Penn Coll. (1873; coed.; Quaker).

2 City, ⊗ of Jefferson co., NE Kansas; pop. 807.

O·skol′ (ŭ·skôl′). River 210 m. long, Soviet Russia, Europe; rises near Stary Oskol in Kursk Region and flows S into Donets river in E Ukraine.

Os′lo (ŏz′lō; ŏs′lō; *Norw.* ôs′lô, ōōs′lōō, ŏsh′lō, ōōsh′lōō). **1** County of Norway. See **2**, below, and *Table* at NORWAY.

2 *formerly* **Chris′ti·an′i·a** or **Kris′ti·an′i·a** (krĭs′chĭ·ăn′ĭ·à; krĭs′tĭ-; *Norw.* krĭs′tĭ·ä′nĭ·à). City, * of Norway and ⊗ of Akershus co., SE Norway, at N end of **Oslo Fjord** (inlet of the Skagerrak extending inland 80 m.) and itself constituting a county (area 6 sq. m.), pop. 253,124, (1938 est. 275,000); largest city in Norway; important commercial, shipping, and manufacturing center; hydroelectric power plants; imports food products, coal, and clothing, and exports wood pulp, cellulose, paper, dairy products, lumber, chemicals. Has university (1811), royal palace, government buildings, national theater, museums, and the 17th-cent. Church of Our Savior. Founded 1048–50 by Harald Haardraade; under Hanseatic League domination in 14th cent.; suffered destructive fire 1624, and was rebuilt by direction of King Christian IV, and named Christiania or Kristiania; captured by Charles XII in 1716; officially named Oslo in 1925. In World War II taken by Germans Apr. 9–10, 1940 and held until end of war.

Os′ma (ŏs′mä). River ab. 100 m. long in N Bulgaria; flows N into Danube river just above Nikopol.

Os·man′a·bad (ŏz·măn′à·băd; *native* ôs·mä′nä·băd). Town, SE Maharashtra state, S cen. India, ab. 35 m. NNE of Sholapur; pop. ab. 10,000.

Os′na·brück′ (ŏs′nä·brük′; *Angl.* ŏz′nà·brŏŏk). **1** Government district, in former Hannover prov., Prussia, Germany; 2395 sq. m.

2 Manufacturing city, its *, 30 m. NE of Münster; pop. 89,079; 12th-cent. late-Romanesque church, 13th-cent. Romanesque cathedral, 15th-cent. Gothic town hall; manufactures textiles, paper, iron and steel, copper and wire goods. Episcopal see founded here 783 by Charlemagne; city named 1078; negotiations leading to Peace of Westphalia (1648) held here 1644; passed to Hannover 1803, to kingdom of Westphalia 1807; reverted to Hannover 1815. In World War II important for its iron and steel mills and as a railroad junction; bombed by Allies 1944–45; captured Apr. 1945.

Os′na·burg (ŏz′nà·bûrg). Eng. corruption of OSNA-BRÜCK.

O′so, Mount (ô′sō). Peak 13,703 ft. in La Plata co., SW Colorado.

O′sor·hei′ (ô′sôr·hā′). = TÂRGU-MUREŞ.

O·sor′no (ô·sôr′nô). **1** Volcanic peak 8727 ft. in E Llanquihue prov., S cen. Chile, on E shore of Lake Llanquihue.

2 Province of Chile. See *Table* at CHILE.

3 City, S cen. Chile, ab. 510 m. S of Santiago; * of Osorno prov.; pop. 25,075; founded 1558; settled largely by Germans.

O·so′wiec (ô·sô′vyĕts); *Russ.* **O·so′vets** (ŭ·sô′vyĕts). Village and fortress, Białystok dept., NE Poland, 32 m. NW of Białystok; for a time 1944–45 taken over by U.S.S.R. but ceded back to Poland.

O·so′yoos Lake (ô·sōō′yŭs). Narrow lake ab. 15 m. long, N Okanogan co., N Washington, extending N across international border into British Columbia.

Os′prey Reef (ŏs′prĭ). Coral reef island in W Coral Sea, 130 m. E of Cape Melville, off NE coast of Queensland, Australia.

Os·ro·e′ne or **Os′rho·e′ne** (ŏz′rô·ē′nĕ). Ancient region, NW Mesopotamia, E of the Euphrates; * Edessa; founded by Seleucus I in 3d cent. B.C.; later, a kingdom, subject for varying periods to Parthia, Armenia, and Rome; kingdom abolished by Caracalla 216 A.D.

Oss (ôs). Commune, North Brabant prov., S Netherlands, S of the Maas and ab. 11 m. ENE of 's Hertogenbosch; pop. 14,618.

Os′sa (ŏs′à; *Mod. Gr.* ô′sä). Peak 6490 ft. in E Thessaly, NE Greece, NE of Larissa near the coast.

Os′sa·baw Island (ŏs′à·bô). Island in Atlantic Ocean off S mainland of Chatham co., SE Georgia.

Os·se′ti·a (ŏ·sē′shĭ·à; -shà). Region of the cen. Caucasus, SE Soviet Russia, Europe; divided into the **North Os·se′tian** (ô·sē′shăn) **Autonomous Soviet Socialist Republic** (a part of the R.S.F.S.R.—see NORTH OSSETIA) and the **South Ossetian Autonomous Region** (a part of the Georgian Republic—see SOUTH OSSETIA).

Os′sett (ŏs′ĕt; -ĭt). Municipal borough, West Riding, Yorkshire, N England, 9 m. S of Leeds; pop. 14,576.

Os′si·ning (ŏs′n·ĭng). Village, Westchester co., SE New York, on E bank of Hudson river overlooking Tappan Zee, 30 m. N of New York; pop. 18,662; residential suburb of New York City; incorporated as village of **Sing Sing** (sĭng′ sĭng′) 1813, as township 1845; manufactures porous plasters, patent medicines, cosmetics, shoes, leather, machinery; marble quarries nearby; Sing Sing state prison (1824) at S end of village.

Os′si·pee (ŏs′ĭ·pē). **1** River, E New Hampshire and SW Maine; flows out of Ossipee Lake E across Maine border into Saco river.

2 Town, ⊗ of Carroll co., E New Hampshire, 21 m. ENE of Laconia; pop. 1409.

Ossipee Lake. Lake ab. 8 m. long in E cen. Carroll co., E New Hampshire; outlet, Ossipee river, flowing E into Saco river.

Os′so·ry (ŏs′ô·rĭ). **1** Ancient kingdom, SW Leinster, Ireland; dissolved 1110.

2 Bishopric, approximately coextensive with ancient kingdom and with modern co. Kilkenny; Protestant diocese includes Ferns and Leighlin.

Os·tash′kov (ŭs·tȧsh′kŭf). Town, W Kalinin Region, Soviet Russia, Europe, on S shore of Lake Seliger at source of the Volga, 100 m. WNW of Kalinin; pop. 15,660. Under German control 1941–42.

O′ste (ō′stĕ). River ab. 80 m. long in NW Germany; flows N in Lower Saxony state to the Elbe river estuary 13 m. SE of Cuxhaven.

Ost′el′bi·en (ôst′ĕl′bē·ĕn). Literally, the region E of the Elbe in Germany, comprising before World War II the state of Mecklenburg and the Prussian provinces of Brandenburg, Pomerania, Silesia, and East Prussia; considered the heart of conservative Germany, the home of the Junker landowners.

Ostende, Ostend. = OOSTENDE.

Ös′ter·dal (ûs′tēr·däl′). The "East Valley" of Norway, parallel to Swedish border and equivalent generally to the course of the Glomma river; traversed by Norway's easternmost railroad from Oslo N through Elverum, Röros, and Stören to Trondheim.

Öster Dal. River in Sweden. See DAL.

O′ster·feld (ō′stēr·fĕlt). Former city (pop. 32,592), Münster govt. dist., Westphalia prov., Prussia, Germany; became part of Oberhausen (q.v.) 1929.

Ös′ter·göt′land (ûs′tēr·yût′länd). Province of Sweden. See Table at SWEDEN.

O′stern·burg (ō′stērn·bōōrκ). Former commune, Oldenburg dist., NW Germany, now S suburb of Oldenburg city.

Ös′ter·ö′ (ûs′tēr·û′). Island of the Faeroes (q.v.), E of Strömö; 111 sq. m.; pop. (1925) 5243.

Osterode, Osterode in Ostpreussen. See OSTRÓDA.

Os′ter·öy′ (ôs′tēr·û′ü; ōōs′-). Island in a fiord N of Bergen on SW coast of Norway; 127 sq. m.; pop. 5670.

Österreich. See AUSTRIA.

Ös′ter·sund′ (ûs′tēr·sŭnd′). City, ✻ of Jämtland prov., W Sweden, on Lake Storsjön; pop. 19,055; manufactures machinery and furniture.

Öst′fold′ (ûst′fôl′). County of Norway. See Table at NORWAY.

Ost′fries′land (ôst′frēs′länt). Region on the coast of the North Sea, NW Germany, bet. NE Netherlands and former Oldenburg prov.; now in Lower Saxony state. Includes the East Frisian Is. (see FRISIAN ISLANDS).

Os′ti·a (ôs′tĭ·ȧ; Ital. ôs′tyä). Village at the mouth of the Tiber river, Latium, Italy, just E of the ancient town of same name, the port of Rome, which according to legend was founded by Ancus Marcius (641–616 B.C.); extensive ruins, dating only from 3d or 4th cent. B.C., include dwellings, baths, temples, and a theater.

Ostia Aterni. See PESCARA seaport.

Ostiago–Vogulsk. = OSTYAGO-VOGULSK.

Ostiak Vogul National District. Var. of Ostyak-Vogul National District; see KHANTY-MANSIS.

Os′ti·an Way (ôs′tĭ·ăn); Lat. **Vi′a Os′ti·en′sis** (vī′ȧ ôs′tĭ·ĕn′sĭs). Ancient road, Italy, from Rome to Ostia following the Tiber; modern road takes nearly the same course, utilizing the ancient bridges.

Ost′land (ôst′länt). Name under Nazi regime for proposed German colony along E border, comprising Estonia, Latvia, Lithuania, and White Russia.

Ost′mark (ôst′märk). Austria under Nazi rule 1938–45, forming an administrative unit (Land) of Germany.

Ostpreussen. See EAST PRUSSIA.

Ostrasia. See AUSTRASIA.

Ostrava, Moravská. See MORAVSKÁ OSTRAVA.

Ostrava, Slezská. See SLEZSKÁ OSTRAVA.

Os·tró′da (ôs·trōō′dä); Ger. **O′ste·ro′de** (ôs′tĕ·rō′dĕ), in full **Osterode in Ost′preus′sen** (in ôst′proi′sĕn). City, SW Olsztyn dept., N Poland, 19 m. W of Olsztyn; pop. 16,482; formerly in East Prussia, Germany; railroad junction; tourist resort; horse and cattle market. Assigned to Poland by Potsdam Conference 1945.

O·strog′ (ŭ·strôk′; Angl. ŏs′trŏg; Pol. **O′stróg** (ôs′-trōōk). Town, W Ukraine, U.S.S.R., 59 m. SE of Lutsk on upper Goryn river; formerly in Wołyń dept., Poland;

pop. 12,955; manufactures textiles, leather. Founded in 9th cent.; first complete Bible in Slavonic printed here 1581.

Os·tro·gozhsk′ (ŭs·trŭ·gôshsk′). Town, W cen. Voronezh Region, Soviet Russia, Europe, 60 m. S of Voronezh; pop. 19,546.

O′stro·łę′ka (ôs′trô·lĕʌng′kä); Russ. **O·stro·len′ka** (ŭ·strŭ·lyĕn′kȧ). Commune, NE Warszawa dept., E cen. Poland, on Narew river 62 m. NNE of Warsaw; pop. (1938–39 est.) 15,000; formerly in Białystok dept. Several battles fought here: Russians defeated by French Feb. 16, 1807; Poles defeated by Russians May 26, 1831; Russians defeated by Germans Aug. 3, 1915.

O′strov (ō′strŭf). Town, Pskov Region, NW Soviet Russia, Europe, ab. 30 m. S of Pskov on the Velikaya river; pop. 10,500; railroad and commercial town on Latvian border.

O′strów or **Ostrów Wiel′ko·pol′ski** (ôs′trōōf vyĕl′kô-pōl′skĕ); Ger. **O·stro′wo** (ôs·trō′vō). Commune, Poznań dept., Poland, 62 m. SE of Poznań; an important railroad junction near former German border; pop. (1938–39 est.) 31,418; manufactures liquors, brick and tile; trades in agricultural products; cattle markets.

O·stro′wiec or **Ostrowiec Świę′to·krzy′ski** (ôs·trô′-vyĕts shvyĕnn′tô·kshĭ′skĕ). Commune, Kielce dept., Poland, on a tributary of the Vistula 33 m. E of Kielce; pop. (1938–39 est.) 29,000; metal goods; iron deposits nearby.

O′strów Ma′zo·wiec′ka (ôs′trōōf mä′zô-vyĕts′kä). Commune, E Warszawa dept., E cen. Poland, 55 m. NE of Warsaw; pop. 17,611; manufactures agricultural machinery, perfume.

Ostrowo. See OSTRÓW.

Ostsee. See BALTIC SEA.

Osttirol. See EAST TIROL.

O·stu′ni (ô·stōō′nē). Commune, Brindisi prov., Apulia, SE Italy, 21 m. WNW of Brindisi; pop. 28,247; 15th-cent. cathedral; medieval towers and remains of walls.

Öst′våg·öy′ (ûst′vôg·û′ü). = AUSTVÅGÖY.

O·stya′go–Vo·gulsk′ (ŭ·styä′gŭ·vŭ·gōōl′y′sk); formerly **Sa·ma′ro·vo** (sŭ·mä′rŭ·vŭ) or **Sa·ma′rovsk** (-rŭ́sk). Town on right bank of the Irtysh just above its junction with the Ob, formerly in Omsk Region, Soviet Russia, Asia, and ✻ of former Ostyak-Vogul National District. Replaced by Khanty-Mansisk just to the N, capital of new Khanty-Mansi National District (q.v.).

Ostyak–Vogul National District. See KHANTY-MANSI.

O·su·mi Islands (ō·sŏ̄ŏ·mē); Jap. **Osumi Gun·to** (gŏ̄ŏn·tō). Group of islands just S of Kyushu I., Japan, part of Kagoshima prefecture; chief islands Tanegashima and Yaku; separated from S tip of Kyushu I. by Osumi, or Van Die′men (văn dē′mĕn), Strait.

O·su′na (ô·sŏ̄ŏ′nä); earlier **O·xu′na** (ô·shōō′nä); anc. **Ur′so** (ûr′sō) or **Or·so′na** (ôr·sō′nȧ). Commune, Sevilla prov., SW Spain, 52 m. ESE of Seville; pop. 24,228; manufactures hats, textiles, soap, iron, esparto goods, pottery; 16th-cent. Gothic church; ducal castle; university (founded 1549) suppressed 1820. Ancient Roman garrison; reconquered from Moors 1240 by Ferdinand III.

Os′wald·twis′tle (ŏz′wȧl[d]·twĭs′'l). Urban district, Lancashire, NW England, on Leeds and Liverpool Canal 19 m. NNE of Manchester; pop. 12,133; manufactures cotton goods, chemicals; coal mining.

Os·we·gatch′ie (ŏs′wē·gäch′ĭ). River ab. 130 m. long in N New York; rises in N Herkimer co., flows NW and NE into St. Lawrence river at Ogdensburg.

Os·we′go (ŏs·wē′gō; ŭ·swē′-; -gŭ). **1** River 24 m. long in cen. New York; formed by junction of Seneca and Oneida rivers, Onondaga co., flows N into Lake Ontario at Oswego, Oswego co.; canalized (the Oswego Canal) and part of the N.Y. State Barge Canal system.
2 County in New York. See Table at NEW YORK.
3 City, ⊗ of Labette co., SE Kansas, 30 m. SW of Pittsburg; pop. 2027; agriculture; livestock.

4 Manufacturing and commercial city, a ⊗ of Oswego co., cen. New York, on Lake Ontario at mouth of Oswego river 33 m. NNW of Syracuse; pop. 22,155; N terminus of Oswego Canal, part of N.Y. State Barge Canal; natural harbor; easternmost Great Lakes port in U.S.; transfer point for rail, canal, and lake shipments (grain, coal, cement, pulp and pulpwood); N.Y. state 1,000,000-bushel grain elevator, hydroelectric power plants, freight warehouses; market center in agricultural region (hay, potatoes, lettuce); manufactures paper and paper products, matches, boilers, oil-well supplies, silk, rayon, and cotton goods; State Univ. of New York Coll. of Education at Oswego (1861; coed.). Site of earliest English trading post on Great Lakes, founded c. 1722 and fortified; Forts Oswego and Ontario erected 1755; captured by Montcalm 1756; retaken by Sir William Johnson 1759; Fort Ontario restored and remained under British control until 1796 (surrendered to U.S. under Jay Treaty); scene of Pontiac's surrender to English 1766; again contested territory in War of 1812; taken by British 1814 and held briefly.
5 City and lake resort, Clackamas co., NW Oregon, on Willamette river 8 m. S of Portland; pop. 8906.
Oswego Canal. Canal connecting Lake Ontario at Oswego, New York, with the Erie Canal at Syracuse, New York; part of the N.Y. State Barge Canal system. See SYRACUSE.
Os′wes·try (ŏz′wĕs·trĭ). Municipal borough, Shropshire, W England, near Welsh border 55 m. WNW of Birmingham; pop. 10,713; center of agricultural section.
Oś·wię′cim (ôsh·vyĕɴɪ′tsēm); *Ger.* **Ausch′witz** (oush′vĭts). Industrial commune, W Kraków dept., S Poland, 33 m. W of Kraków; pop. (1938–39 est.) 13,350; industrial and commercial town. During World War II site of large German concentration camp where many war victims, chiefly Poles and Jews, were killed by torture and "scientific experiments."
O·ta′go (ô·tä′gō). Provincial district and division of district, New Zealand. See *Table* at NEW ZEALAND.
Otago Harbor. Bay, inlet of Pacific Ocean on SE coast of South I., New Zealand, ab. 11 m. long with **Otago Peninsula** on its E side, Dunedin at its head (SW), and Port Chalmers on its W shore.
Otaheite. See TAHITI.
O′ta·hu·hu′ (ô′tä·hōō′; *Maori* ô·tä′hōō·hōō). Borough, Auckland provincial dist., N North I., New Zealand, SE suburb of Auckland; pop. 4980.
O·ta·ru (ô·tä·rōō). City, Hokkaido prefecture, Japan, on W coast of Hokkaido I. ab. 22 m. WNW of Sapporo; pop. (1945) 145,510; has fine harbor on **Otaru Bay** (inlet of Sea of Japan) with shipping connections with Hakodate and with ports of Soviet Russia; trade outlet for agricultural and marine products.
O′ta·va′lo (ô′tä·vä′lô). Town, Imbabura prov., N Ecuador, ab. 42 m. NNE of Quito; pop. (1944 est.) 10,708; manufactures cotton and woolen cloth, ponchos, carpets; settled 1534; destroyed by earthquake 1868.
O·ta′vi (ô·tä′vē). Town, N South-West Africa, W of Grootfontein; in copper-mining region.
Otea. See GREAT BARRIER ISLAND.
O·ter′o (ô·târ′ō). Name of counties in two states of the U.S. See *Tables* at COLORADO and NEW MEXICO.
Othonoí. See FANO.
Oth′rys (ŏth′rĭs; ō′thrĭs; *Mod. Gr.* ô′thrĕs). Mountain range in cen. Greece, extending along the N frontier of Phthiotis and Phocis dept.; highest point ab. 5700 ft.; forms S barrier of Thessalian plain.
O·ti′ra Gorge (ô·tē̱r′á). Narrow cleft in Southern Alps, cen. South I., New Zealand; traversed by highway (Arthur's Pass) and railroad (through **Otira Tunnel**), connecting Christchurch with Greymouth; at W end is the village of Otira.
O′tis Reservoir (ō′tĭs). Reservoir on branch of Farmington river, S of Otis, SE Berkshire co., W Massachusetts.

Ot′ley (ŏt′lĭ). Urban district, West Riding, Yorkshire, N England; pop. 11,568; woolens, leather, machinery manufacture.
O′toe (ō′tō). County in Nebraska. See *Table* at NEBRASKA.
O·to·ma·ri (ō·tô·mä·rê̱) *or* **O·do·ma·ri** (ō·dô-). Seaport, S Karafuto, S Sakhalin I., on Aniwa Bay; pop. (1939 est.) 23,580; former capital of Japanese possession; has steamer service to Otaru on Hokkaido and rail connections with Toyohara and other towns to the N.
O·ton′ (ô·tôn′). Municipality, S Iloilo prov., Panay, Phil. Is., on Iloilo Strait 6 m. W of City of Iloilo; pop. 20,577. Important early settlement of the Spaniards.
O·ton′a·bee (ô·tŏn′á·bê̱). Short stream, a part of Trent river, Peterborough co., SE Ontario, Canada; forms part of Trent Canal system; Peterborough is on it.
Ot′ra (ôt′rä; ōōt′-). River ab. 125 m. long in S Norway; flows S into the Skagerrak at Kristiansand.
O′tran·to (ô′trän·tô; *Angl.* ô·trăn′tō) *anc.* **Hy·drun′tum** (hī·drŭn′tŭm). Town, Lecce prov., SE tip of Apulia, S Italy; pop. (1931) 2953; archiepiscopal see; ancient town of Calabria; destroyed by Turks 1480. During World War II an important supply base.
Otranto, Cape. Cape on SE coast of Italy, on W side of the Strait of Otranto.
Otranto, Strait of. Strait ab. 47 m. wide bet. SE Italy and W Albania, connecting the Adriatic Sea with the Ionian Sea.
O·tri′co·li (ô·trē′kô·lê̱). Commune, Terni prov., S Umbria, cen. Italy, on the Tiber and on the Flaminian Way; pop. (1931) 2153; remains of ancient **O·cric′u·lum** (ô·krĭk′û·lŭm).
Ot·se′go (ŏt·sē′gō). **1** Name of counties in two states of the U.S. See *Tables* at MICHIGAN and NEW YORK.
2 City, Allegan co., SW Michigan, 13 m. N of Kalamazoo; pop. 4142; paper manufacturing.
Otsego Lake. Lake in N cen. Otsego co., cen. New York; ab. 9 m. long and an average of 1 m. wide; elevation 1193 ft.; the city of Cooperstown lies at S end; main source of Susquehanna river. Noted for its association with the novels (Leatherstocking series) of James Fenimore Cooper.
O·tsu (ō·tsōō). City, * of Shiga prefecture, W cen. Honshu, Japan, ab. 10 m. from Kyoto on SW shore of Lake Biwa; pop. (1945) 70,357; imperial residence in 7th cent.; burial place of poet Basho.
Ot·ta·ia′no (ôt·tä·yä′nô). Commune, Napoli prov., Campania, S Italy, 11 m. E of Naples; pop. 11,170.
Ot′ta·wa (ôt′á·wá; -wô; -wä). **1** Name of counties in four states of the U.S. See *Tables* at KANSAS, MICHIGAN, OHIO, OKLAHOMA.
2 City, ⊗ of La Salle co., N Illinois, on Illinois river 40 m. WSW of Joliet; pop. 19,408; manufactures pottery, glass, farm implements; incorporated 1837; scene of first Lincoln-Douglas debate Aug. 21, 1858.
3 City, ⊗ of Franklin co., E Kansas, 37 m. SE of Topeka; pop. 10,673; trade center in agricultural and livestock-raising section; manufactures farm machinery, electric refrigerators, flour. Ottawa Univ. (1865; coed.).
4 Village, ⊗ of Putnam co., NW Ohio, 20 m. N of Lima; pop. 3245; beet-sugar refining; poultry, dairy, and grain farms.
5 River 685 m. long, SE Ontario and S Quebec provs., Canada; forms lower section of boundary bet. Ontario and Quebec provs., and continues E across S Quebec prov. (bet. Two Mountains and Vaudreuil cos.) to empty into the St. Lawrence river (Lake of Two Mountains) at Montreal I. First explored by Champlain 1613; long a transportation route for explorers, missionaries, and traders.
6 City, ⊗ of Carleton co. and * of the Dominion of Canada, SE Ontario, on right bank of Ottawa river and on Rideau Canal 100 m. W of Montreal; pop. 202,045. As seat of Dominion government has many imposing buildings; headquarters of leading scientific and cultural so-

cieties and home of Ottawa Univ. (founded 1848); one of the finest-planned and best-kept cities of Canada. Industries include ironworks, foundries, paper and cement mills; has an active lumber trade. Founded 1827; settled by workers on the Rideau Canal and originally called **By'town** (bī'toun) after Col. By, engineer in charge of the canal surveys; renamed Ottawa in 1854 and selected in 1858 as official capital of Canada by Queen Victoria; original government buildings almost completely destroyed by fire in 1916.

Ottawa Hills. Village, Lucas co., NW Ohio, 4 m. W of Toledo; pop. 3870.

Ottawa Islands. Group of small islands in E Hudson Bay, Keewatin District, E Northwest Territories, Canada, off coast of N Quebec prov.

Ot'ter (ŏt'ẽr). River ab. 40 m. long, SW cen. Virginia; flows S through Bedford co., turns SE and empties into Roanoke river in S Campbell co.

Otter, Peaks of. Two summits in the Blue Ridge, in Bedford and Botetourt cos., W cen. Virginia; height of Southwest Peak 3875 ft., and of Flat Top 4001 ft.

Ot'ter·burn (ŏt'ẽr·bûrn). Parish, N cen. Northumberland, N England; scene of battle 1388 in which English led by Hotspur (Sir Henry Percy) were defeated by the Scots under James Douglas; Douglas was killed and Hotspur captured; celebrated by the English in the ballad *Chevy Chase* and in the old Scottish ballad *The Battle of Otterburn.*

Ot'ter Creek (ŏt'ẽr). **1** River, cen. Utah, flowing N from Piute co. into Sevier river in N Sevier co.
2 River ab. 75 m. long, W Vermont; rises in N Bennington co., flows N into Lake Champlain in NW Addison co.

Otter Creek Reservoir. Reservoir in Otter Creek, SE Piute co., S cen. Utah.

Otter Tail. 1 River ab. 60 m. long, W Minnesota; flows from Otter Tail Lake in cen. Otter Tail co., W cen. Minnesota, W, then S and again W to unite with Bois de Sioux river at Breckenridge, W Minnesota, and form Red River (or Red River of the North).
2 County in Minnesota. See *Table* at MINNESOTA.

Otter Tail Lake. Lake ab. 12 m. long in cen. Otter Tail co., W cen. Minnesota.

Ot'ter·y Saint Mar'y (ŏt'ẽr·ĭ sånt mâr'ĭ). Urban district, Devonshire, SW England; pop. (1951) 4015; manufactures Honiton lace; birthplace of Samuel Taylor Coleridge.

Ot'to·man Empire (ŏt'ō·mǎn) *or* **Turk'ish Empire** (tûr'kĭsh). Former sultanate in Europe, Asia, and Africa, including at greatest extent Syria, Egypt, Iraq, Barbary States, Balkan States, and parts of Russia and Hungary; ✳ Constantinople.
History: Originated in 13th cent. in a group of Turks from cen. Asia who entered Anatolia (already under Seljuks) and established small state, traditionally ruled by Osman I (1288–1326); beginning with Orkhan I (1326–59), an empire was organized on both sides of the Straits (see DARDANELLES); by end of 15th cent., it had liquidated Byzantine Empire (*q.v.*) and included Balkan region, i.e. Rumelia, Macedonia, Thessaly, Morea (Peloponnesus), Serbia, Walachia, Bosnia, Bulgaria, and Albania (*qq.v.*), most of the Aegean Is., rest of Anatolia, and Crimea; overthrew Mamelukes and secured Syria and Egypt; at its height under Suleiman the Magnificent (1520–66) who took Armenia, Azerbaijan, Mesopotamia, and Baghdad, North African coast, and, in Europe, territory from frontier of Holy Roman Empire to shores of Black Sea; although Crete, Cyprus, Arabian coasts, and Caucasus territory were later added to Ottoman holdings, the power of the empire began to decline in late 16th cent.; by series of exhausting wars with Poland, Austria, and Russia in 17th and 18th cents., Turks were expelled from Hungary and northern shores of Black Sea; in 19th cent., because of internal corruption, the steady southward advance of Russia (*q.v.*), and the successful revolts of the Balkans, the weakened Ottoman ruler came to be

known as "Sick Man of Europe"; the problem of preventing too rapid a dissolution of the empire in face of Russian advance became the "Eastern Question" of European diplomacy (caused Crimean War 1854–56); after much negotiation 1888–99 and opposition from other countries, granted Nov. 25, 1899 concessions to Germany for Berlin-Baghdad R.R. (see EGYPT, TUNIS, and TRIPOLI for loss of its African holdings); Macedonia, the last extensive European territory, lost in First Balkan War 1912–13; as one of Central Powers in World War I, was an important area of conflict (see GALLIPOLI PENINSULA, MESOPOTAMIA, etc.); sultan accepted Treaty of Sèvres (1920) by which empire gave up Cyprus, Dodecanese, Smyrna, Mesopotamia, Palestine and Syria, Arabia, Armenia, and control of Straits; meanwhile, the nationalist government at Ankara called congress 1919 and finally proclaimed republic of Turkey (*q.v.*) 1923.

Ot·tum'wa (ŏ·tŭm'wȧ; ŏ-). City, ⊗ of Wapello co., SE Iowa, on Des Moines river 75 m. SE of Des Moines; pop. 33,871; trading and industrial center in agricultural section; ironworks, pork-packing plants, farm-implement factories.

O·tum'ba (ō·tōōm'bä). Town, NE México state, cen. Mexico; pop. ab. 10,000; battle July 7, 1520 fought on plain of Otumba in which Cortes and Spaniards, retreating from Mexico, decisively defeated a large Aztec army.

Ot'way, Cape (ŏt'wä). Cape, S Victoria, SE Australia, 70 m. SW of entrance to Port Phillip Bay.

Otway Water *or* **Bay.** Wide inlet, Magallanes prov., S Chile, bet. Brunswick Penin. on the SE and Riesco I. on the NW, connecting by a narrow passage on the SW with the Strait of Magellan.

Ot'wock (ŏt'vôtsk). Commune, Warszawa dept., E cen. Poland, SE suburb of Warsaw; pop. (1938–39 est.) 19,932; summer resort.

Ötz'ta'ler Alps (ûts'tä'lẽr). Mountain range of the E Alps, in S Tirol-Vorarlberg prov., Austria and N Venezia Tridentina, Italy; highest peak Wildspitze 12,382 ft.; many glaciers. Named from a valley (**Ötz'tal'** [ûts'täl']) and S tributary of the Inn in Tirol, Austria.

Ouach'i·ta *or* **Wash'i·ta** (wŏsh'ĭ·tô). **1** River 605 m. long, SW Arkansas and E Louisiana; navigable 350 m.; rises in Polk co., W Arkansas, flows E and then SE across Louisiana border, and S to the Black river in Catahoula co.
2 Name of a parish in Louisiana and of a county in Arkansas. See *Tables* at ARKANSAS and LOUISIANA.

Ouachita Mountains. Range 1000 to 2800 ft. in W cen. Arkansas and E Oklahoma, a S continuation of Ozark Plateau.

Ouadaï. See WADAI.

Oua'dane' *or* **Oua'dan'** (wȧ'dȧn'); *also* **Wa·dan'** (wă·dȧn'). Oasis, W cen. Mauritania, West Africa. See ADRAR.

Oua'ga·dou'gou (wä'gȧ·dōō'gōō); *also* **Wa'ga·du'gu.** Town, ✳ of Upper Volta, West Africa; pop. 16,595; in a plateau region watered by upper tributaries of the Volta river; terminus of railroad through Bobo-Dioulasso to Abidjan and connected by highways with towns on the Niger in Niger Republic; important trade center; in Ivory Coast 1933–47.

Oua'hi·gou'ya (wä'ē·gōō'yȧ). Town, Upper Volta West Africa, 100 m. NW of Ouagadougou; pop. (1940) 6979.

Oua'kam (wä'käm). Airport of Dakar, Senegal, on Cape Vert Penin. just NNW of the city.

Ouarg'la (wärg'lä) *or* **Warg'la.** Town and oasis, Southern Territories, Algeria, N Africa, SW of Touggourt; pop. 14,565.

Ouar'se'nis' Mas'sif' (wȧr'sā'nēs' mȧ'sēf'). Highland region in NE Oran and NW Alger depts., Algeria.

Oubangui. See UBANGI.

Oubangui–Chari, Oubangui–Chari–Tchad. See UBANGI-SHARI.

Oubon. Var. of UBON.

Ouche (ōōsh). River ab. 60 m. long in Côte-d'Or dept., E France, flowing into Saône river.

Ou'chy' (ōō'shē'). Village, Vaud canton, on the Lake of Geneva in SW Switzerland; the port of Lausanne; treaty 1912.

Ou'de Maas (ou'dĕ mȧs'). Left branch of the Merwede river in Netherlands, flowing into the North Sea just S of the Nieuwe Maas river; it leaves the Merwede near Dordrecht.

Oudenaarde. Flemish form of AUDENARDE.

Ou'de Rijn (ou'dĕ rīn'). Branch of the Lek river in Netherlands; flows N out of the Lek and then W to the North Sea at Katwijk; passes Utrecht and Leiden in its course.

Oudh (oud). A former province of Brit. India, now the NE portion of Uttar Pradesh (earlier United provinces); 24,071 sq. m.; pop. (1941) 14,114,470. Received its name from Ajodhya (q.v.), sacred city of the Hindus and capital of the ancient kingdom of Kosala, which was nearly coextensive with modern Oudh. Overrun by Mohammedan invaders 11th cent. and later; held by British as a fief of the Mogul rulers 1756–1856; annexed to British dominions; with Agra placed under one administrator 1877; made part of United Provinces 1902 under new name.

Oudj'da' or **Ouj'da'** (ōōj'dä'); Arab. **Uj'da** (ōōj'dȧ; -dä). Commercial city, NE Morocco, NW Africa, near the Algerian border; pop. (1936) 34,523.

Oudts'hoorn (ō'ōōts·hōōrn). Town, S Cape Province, S Union of South Africa, near Olifants river 220 m. E of Cape Town; pop. 13,225; in Little Karroo; center of once flourishing ostrich-farming industry, in fertile section watered by irrigation. Cango Caves, noted for exquisite stalactite and stalagmite formations, nearby.

Oued, El. See EL OUED.

Oued Zem (wĕd zĕm). Town, W cen. Morocco, NW Africa, 110 m. E of Mazagan.

Oued–Zé'na'ti' (wĕd'zā'nȧ'tē'). Commune, NE cen. Constantine dept., NE Algeria, just E of Constantine; pop. 14,587.

Ouessant, Île d'. See USHANT.

Ouez'zane' (wĕ'zȧn'); Arab. **Waz·zan'** (wăz·zän'). Sacred city, N Morocco, NW Africa, 60 m. NW of Fez; pop. (1936) 16,442.

Ou'grée (ōō'grā'). Commune, Liège prov., E Belgium, on Meuse river; S suburb of Liège; pop. 20,021.

Oui'dah (wē'dȧ) or **Wi'da** (wē'dȧ); Eng. **Whyd'ah** (hwĭd'ȧ). Seaport town, S Dahomey, West Africa, on lagoon 23 m. W of Cotonou; pop. ab. 11,500; has large orchards of orange and citron trees. Founded as a French trading port in 17th cent.

Oujda. See OUDJDA.

Ou·lad' Naïl Mountains (ōō·lȧd' nīl'; näl'). Range of the Atlas Mts. in N Ghardaïa territory, N cen. Algeria.

Oul'ga'ret' (ōōl'gȧ'rĕ'). Commune, E India, suburb of Pondicherry; pop. (1941), 32,204.

Oul'lins' (ōō'lăn'). Commune, Rhône dept., E cen. France, SSW suburb of Lyons; pop. 16,734; distilleries, oil refineries.

Ou'lu (ou'lōō). **1** Department of Finland. See Table at FINLAND.
2 Swedish **U'le·å·borg'** (ōō'lĕ·ō·bôr'y). Seaport, its *, N cen. Finland, on Gulf of Bothnia and at mouth of Oulu river; pop. (1939 est.) 31,200; shipbuilding yards, sawmills, dairies; exports fish, lumber, tar; tourist resort.

Ou'lu·jär'vi (ou'lōō·yär'vĭ). Lake in cen. Finland; drains NW through **Oulu River** (ab. 80 m. long) into NE Gulf of Bothnia.

Oum er Re·bi'a (ōōm' ŭr rŏ·bē'ȧ; -bē'ȧ). River ab. 250 m. long in cen. Morocco, NW Africa; flows NW into Atlantic Ocean at Mazagan.

Ou'nas (ou'näs). River 175 m. long in NW Finland; flows S into Kemi river.

Oup (ōōp). River bed ab. 300 m. long in SW Africa, extending from S cen. South-West Africa to the Molopo.

Our (ōōr). River 40 m. long forming section of NE boundary bet. Germany and the grand duchy of Luxembourg; flows S into Sauer river E of Diekirch.

Ou·ray' (ū·rā'). **1** County in Colorado. See Table at COLORADO.
2 City, its ⊗, SW Colorado; pop. 785; lead, zinc, silver, and gold mining; hot springs; Ouray State Game Refuge nearby.

Ouray Peak. Mountain 13,955 ft. in Chaffee co., cen. Colorado.

Ourcq (ōōrk). River 49 m. long in Aisne dept., N France; part of the water supply for Paris; battles in Sept. 1914 and in 1918.

Ou·ri'que (ō·rē'kĕ). Commune, Beja dist., S Portugal, 31 m. SSW of Beja; pop. 4565; famous defeat of Moors 1139 resulting in formation of Portuguese kingdom under Alfonso I.

Ou'ro Fi'no (ō'rōō fē'nōō). City, SW Minas Gerais state, E Brazil, 100 m. N of São Paulo; pop. 7323.

Ouro Prê'to (prā'tōō). Town, Minas Gerais state, E Brazil, N of Rio de Janeiro and ab. 35 m. SE of Belo Horizonte; pop. 8751; in mining and agricultural district; famed for its baroque colonial architecture; national monument.

Ourthe (ōōrt). River ab. 100 m. long in SE Belgium; flows N in Luxembourg and Liège provs. into the Meuse.

Ouse (ōōz). **1** or **Great Ouse.** River 160 m. long, cen. and E England; rises in Northamptonshire, flows in a winding course E and NE into the Wash below King's Lynn.
2 River 57 m. long, NE England; formed by confluence of the Swale and Ure rivers in Yorkshire, flows SE to unite with the Trent river and form the Humber; navigable as far as York.
3 River 30 m. long, Sussex, S England.

Ous'sel'tia' (ōō'sĕl'tyȧ'). Town, N cen. Tunisia, 30 m. WNW of Kairouan.

Ou'ta·gam'ie (ou'tȧ·găm'ĭ). County in Wisconsin. See Table at WISCONSIN.

Ou'tardes' (ōō'tärd'). River ab. 200 m. long, S cen. Quebec prov., Canada; rises in Lake Pletipi and flows S to St. Lawrence.

Outer China. See CHINA.
Outer Hebrides. See HEBRIDES.
Outer Island. See APOSTLE ISLANDS.
Outer Mongolia. See MONGOLIAN PEOPLE'S REPUBLIC.
Outer Provinces; Du. **Bui'ten·ge·wes'ten** (boi'tĕ[n]-kĕ·vĕs'tĕ[n]). Those parts of the former Netherlands Indies outside of Java and Madoera; comprised Sumatra, Borneo, Celebes, Moluccas, and Lesser Sunda Is.; 684,064 sq. m.; pop. 19,008,869. See NETHERLANDS INDIES, GREAT EAST.

Outer Rhodes. See APPENZELL.
Outer Ring. See LONDON.
Outer Santa Barbara Channel. Strait bet. Santa Catalina I. and San Clemente I. off NW coast of San Diego co., S California.

O·u'tes (ō·ōō'tās). Commune, La Coruña prov., NW Spain, 44 m. SW of La Coruña; pop. 10,811; agriculture and stock raising; manufactures linen.

Out'jo (ō'ōōt·yō). Town, N cen. South-West Africa, 170 m. NNW of Windhoek; pop. 37,581.

Ou'tre·mont (ōō'trĕ·mŏnt; Fr. ōō'trĕ·môN'). Residential city, a separate municipality of Montreal I., S Quebec, Canada; pop. 30,057; lies N of Mount Royal in cen. part of Montreal I. and is part of Greater Montreal.

Ouya. See OYAK.

O'va·la'u (ō'vä·lä'ōō). One of the Fiji Is., in the Lomai Viti group, SW Pacific Ocean, ab. 12 m. off E coast of Viti Levu, 43 sq. m.; chief town Levuka, ✳ of the colony until 1882. In early days of settlement favored by Europeans for residence.

O·val'le (ō·väl'yä). Town, Coquimbo prov., cen. Chile, 200 m. N of Santiago; pop. 14,807.

Ov·am'bo·land' (ō·văm'bō·lănd'); also **Am'bo·land'**

(ăm′bŏ-). The region in the N part of South-West Africa inhabited by the Ovampo.

O·var′ (ōō·vár′). Commune, Aveiro dist., NW Portugal, near Atlantic Ocean N of Aveiro; pop. 12,729; port.

Overflakkee. See GOEDEREEDE.

O′ver·ijs′sel (ō′vĕr·ī′sĕl). Province, E Netherlands; 1318 sq. m., pop. (1939) 576,723; ✱ Zwolle; livestock raising, dairy farming.

O′ver·land (ō′vĕr·lănd). City, St. Louis co., E Missouri, 10 m. WNW of St. Louis; pop. 22,763.

Overland Park. Urban area, Johnson co., NE Kansas, S of Kansas City; pop. 21,110.

O′ver·lea′ (ō′vĕr·lē′). Urban area, Baltimore co., N Maryland, NE of Baltimore; pop. 10,795.

Overseas Highway. See FLORIDA KEYS.

O′ver·ton (ō′vĕr·t′n; -tŭn). 1 County in Tennessee. See *Table* at TENNESSEE.
2 Town, Clark co., SE Nevada, ab. 48 m. NE of Las Vegas; pop. (est.) 550; houses relics of ancient Indian village of **Lost City** ab. 5 m. S, now covered by Lake Mead.
3 Town, Rusk co., E Texas, ESE of Tyler; pop. 1950.

O′vid (ō′vĭd). Village, a ⊗ of Seneca co., W cen. New York; pop. 789.

O·vie′do (ō·vyā′thō). 1 Province of Spain. See *Table* at SPAIN.
2 *anc.* **As·tu′ri·as** (ăs·t[y]ōōr′ĭ·ăs; *Span.* äs·tōō′ryäs). City, its ✱, NW Spain, 230 m. NNW of Madrid; pop. (1941 est.) 81,948; manufactures ordnance, firearms, explosives, chocolate, textiles, brick and tile, flour; near rich coal fields; 14th-cent. cathedral; 9th-cent. Visigoth churches; city walls; university (founded 1604). Founded c. 750 by Fruela I; capital of Asturias 810–1002; pillaged by Marshal Ney 1809.

Ovilava. See WELS.

Ovoca. See AVOCA.

O′wa (ō′wä). Town, Onitsha prov., S cen. Eastern Provinces, Nigeria, E of the Niger; pop. 22,105.

O·wa·ri Bay (ō·wä·rē). See ISE BAY.

O·was′co Lake (ō·wŏs′kō). Lake ab. 11 m. long and 1 m. wide in Cayuga co., cen. New York; one of the Finger Lakes (*q.v.*); N end outlet flows into Seneca river.

O′wa·ton′na (ō′wȧ·tŏn′ȧ). City, ⊗ of Steele co., S Minnesota, 15 m. S of Faribault; pop. 13,409; mineral springs; in dairy-farming section; known for its butter.

O·we′go (ō·wē′gō). Village, ⊗ of Tioga co., S New York, on Susquehanna river 20 m. W of Binghamton; pop. 5417; in farming section; railroad junction and summer resort, SE gateway to Finger Lakes region; manufactures shoes, chemicals.

O·wei′nat, Jeb′el (jĕb′ĕl ō·wä′năt); *or* **Jebel U·wei′nat** (ōō·wä′-). Mountain 6255 ft. in center of Libyan Desert on NW boundary of Sudan.

Ow′en (ō′ĕn; -ĭn). Name of counties in two states of the U.S. See *Tables* at INDIANA and KENTUCKY.

Owen Falls. Former waterfall in the Victoria Nile in Uganda; 65 ft. high; now submerged by **Owen Falls Dam.**

Owen, Mount. Peak 12,922 ft. in cen. Grand Teton National Park, NW Wyoming.

Ow′ens (ō′ĕnz; -ĭnz). 1 River 125 m. long in E California; rises in W Mono co., flows S, formerly into Owens Lake (*q.v.*); now by way of Los Angeles Aqueduct supplies water to city of Los Angeles.
2 Urban community (unincorporated), Cumberland co., S cen. North Carolina, W of Fayetteville; pop. 5207.

Ow′ens·bor′o (ō′ĕnz·bûr′ō; ō′ĭnz-). City, ⊗ of Daviess co., NW Kentucky, on Ohio river 85 m. WSW of Louisville; pop. 42,471; produces tobacco, grain, dairy products, and livestock; petroleum, gas, and coal fields nearby; transportation center. First settled c. 1800.

Ow′ens Lake (ō′ĕnz; -ĭnz). Dry lake bed in cen. Inyo co., E California; formerly held waters forming body ab. 18 m. long by 10 m. wide and fed by Owens river; water now taken by Los Angeles Aqueduct to Los Angeles.

Ow′en Sound (ō′ĕn; -ĭn). 1 Inlet of SW Georgian Bay, SE Ontario, Canada.
2 Industrial city, ⊗ of Grey co., SE Ontario, Canada, on Owen Sound 105 m. NW of Toronto; pop. 16,423; has excellent harbor and active trade; many manufactures.

Owen Stan′ley Range (stăn′lĭ). Mountain range ab. 600 m. long extending SE and NW on E end of the Territory of Papua, New Guinea; highest peak Mount Victoria 13,240 ft. Crossed by highway through pass in cen. part from Kokoda to Port Moresby.

Ow′en·ton (ō′ĕn·tŭn; ō′ĭn-). City, ⊗ of Owen co., N Kentucky; pop. 1376.

O′wer·ri (ō′wĕr·ĭ). Province of Nigeria. See *Table* at NIGERIA.

Ow′ings·ville (ō′ĭngz·vĭl; *Sou.* also -v′l). City, ⊗ of Bath co., NE Kentucky; pop. 1040.

Owl Creek (oul). Creek in W Butte co., W South Dakota, flowing SE into Belle Fourche river; dammed to form Belle Fourche Reservoir. See BELLE FOURCHE.

Owl Creek Mountains. Range of the Rocky Mts. in NW cen. Wyoming, extending along boundary bet. Hot Springs and Fremont cos.

Owls Head (oulz′ hĕd′). Point of land jutting out from E mainland of Knox co., Maine, into Penobscot Bay, SE of Rockland.

O·wos′so (ō·wŏs′ō). City, Shiawassee co., S cen. Michigan, 26 m. W of Flint; pop. 17,006; center of section growing chiefly sugar beets; furniture, malleable iron.

Ows′ley (ouz′lĭ). County in Kentucky. See *Table* at KENTUCKY.

O·wy′hee (ō·wī′[h]ē). 1 River 250 m. long in SE Oregon; formed by junction of forks in Owyhee co., SW corner of Idaho, flows NW across Oregon boundary, N through Malheur co., and empties into Snake river.
2 County in Idaho. See *Table* at IDAHO.

Owyhee Dam *and* **Reservoir.** See UNITED STATES, *Dams and Reservoirs.*

Ox′ford (ŏks′fẽrd). 1 County in Maine. See *Table* at MAINE.
2 Town, Worcester co., cen. Massachusetts, 10 m. SSW of Worcester; pop. 9282; textiles.
3 Village, Oakland co., SE Michigan, 14 m. N of Pontiac; pop. 2357.
4 City, ⊗ of Lafayette co., N Mississippi, 46 m. WNW of Tupelo; pop. 5283. Univ. of Mississippi (1844; coed.) in nearby suburb.
5 Village, Warren co., NW New Jersey, 13 m. ENE of Phillipsburg; pop. (est.) 1200; iron-mining center.
6 Village, Chenango co., S cen. New York, 28 m. NNE of Binghamton; pop. 1876.
7 Town, ⊗ of Granville co., N North Carolina, 30 m. NNE of Durham; pop. 6978; tobacco and cotton growing; manufactures furniture, lumber products.
8 Village, Butler co., SW Ohio, 12 m. NW of Hamilton; pop. 7828. Miami Univ. (1809; coed.; since 1928 includes Oxford Coll. for women, 1849); Western Coll. (1853; women). Wm. Holmes McGuffey compiled the first of his *Eclectic Readers* here.
9 Borough, Chester co., SE Pennsylvania, 25 m. SE of Lancaster; pop. 3376; founded 1801; in agricultural section; milk center.
10 County, Ontario, Canada. See *Table* at ONTARIO.
11 County in England. See OXFORDSHIRE.
12 *Lat.* **Ox·o′ni·a** (ŏk·sō′nĭ·ȧ). County borough, ⊗ of Oxfordshire, cen. England, on the Thames 52 m. WNW of London; pop. 80,539, (1951) 98,675; Oxford Univ., dating from the 12th cent.; scene of several 13th-cent. parliaments, notably the "Mad Parliament" of 1258 and its resulting Provisions of Oxford; automobile manufacture.

Ox′ford·shire (ŏks′fẽrd·shĭr; -shẽr) *or* **Ox′ford** (ŏks′fẽrd) *or* **Ox′on** (ŏk′sŏn; -s′n). County, cen. England; area 749 sq. m.; pop. (1951) 275,765; ⊗ Oxford; other towns Banbury, Henley on Thames, Woodstock, Cowley; rivers the Thames and its tributaries; agriculture,

manufacturing (farm machinery, automobiles, textiles, paper, leather goods).

Ox'i·a'nus La'cus (ŏk'sĭ·ā'nŭs lā'kŭs). Ancient name of Lake ARAL, Soviet Central Asia.

Ox'kutz·cab' (ôs'kōōts·käv'). Town, Yucatán state, on Yucatán penin., SE Mexico; pop. 5050.

Ox'leys Peak (ŏks'lĭz). Highest mountain 4500 ft. in Liverpool Range, NE New South Wales, SE Australia.

Ox'nard (ŏks'närd). City, Ventura co., SW California, near coast of Santa Barbara Channel 50 m. WNW of Los Angeles; pop. 40,265; founded 1898; sugar refining.

Oxon. See OXFORDSHIRE.

Oxonia. See OXFORD.

Oxuna. See OSUNA.

Oxus. See AMU DARYA.

Ox'y·rhyn'chus (ŏk'sĭ·rĭng'kŭs); *Arab.* **El Bah'na·sa** (ăl bă'h'·nă·sȧ; -să), *also* **Beh'ne·sa** (bă'h'·nă-). Archaeological site on heights above Bahr Yusef, W bank of Nile ab. 54 m. S of El Faiyûm, 28°38′N lat., 30°49′E long. Ancient papyri (*Oxyrhynchus* papyri) discovered here Jan. 1897 and in 1903; fragment contained Jesus' sayings and probably dates from 3d cent. A.D.

O·ya'hue (ō·yä'wå). **1** Volcanic peak 19,226 ft. in SW Bolivia.
2 See OLLAGÜE.

O'yak' (ō'yȧk') *or* **Ou'ya'** (ōō'yȧ'). River ab. 70 m. long in N French Guiana; flows NNE into Atlantic Ocean, separating Cayenne I. from the mainland.

Oyama. See DAISEN.

O'ya'pock' (ō'yȧ'pôk'). **1** *or* **O'ya'pok'**. River ab. 300 m. long in N South America; rises in the Tumuc-Humac Mts. in S French Guiana, flows NE, forming boundary bet. N Brazil and French Guiana, into the Atlantic Ocean through a wide mouth, **Oyapock Bay.**
2 Port, French Guiana, on the Oyapock river N of St. Georges; pop. 1470.

Öy'e·ren (û'ü·ĕrn). Lake in SE Norway, E of Oslo; traversed by the Glomma river.

O'yo (ō'yō). **1** Province of Nigeria. See *Table* at NIGERIA.
2 Town, its ✳, W Western Region, Nigeria, ab. 32 m. N of Ibadan; pop. 48,733.

O·yo·do (ō·yō·dô). River in SE Kyushu, Japan; flows E into Pacific Ocean at Miyazaki.

O'yon'nax' (ô'yô'nȧks'). Commune, Ain dept., E France, 12 m. E of Bourg; pop. 10,166; center of plastics industry.

Oyrat, Oyrot. Vars. of OIROT (Autonomous Region).

Oys'ter Bay (ois'tẽr). **1** Inlet of Long Island Sound, Nassau co., N shore of Long I.
2 Village, Nassau co., SE New York, on Long I., on inlet of Long Island Sound; pop. (est.) 6500; residential suburb of New York City; known as home of Theodore Roosevelt (Sagamore Hill) which is actually in nearby village of **Cove Neck** [kōv] (pop. 299); Roosevelt Memorial Park; Roosevelt's grave in Young's Memorial Cemetery. Oyster Bay is a part of **Oyster Bay** town (pop. 290,055), which also includes the village of **Oyster Bay Cove** (pop. 988).

Oys'ter·mouth' (ois'tẽr·mouth'). Watering place in Glamorganshire, SE Wales, a part of Swansea since 1920.

O'zark (ō'zärk). **1** County in Missouri. See *Table* at MISSOURI.
2 City, ⊗ of Dale co., SE Alabama; pop. 9534; agricultural shipping center.
3 City, a ⊗ of Franklin co., NW Arkansas, on Arkansas river; pop. 1965.
4 City, ⊗ of Christian co., SW Missouri; pop. 1536.

Ozark Plateau; *also* **Ozark Mountains.** Eroded tableland bet. 1500 and 2500 ft. high extending from SW Missouri across NW Arkansas into E Oklahoma; approximately 60,000 sq. m.

O'zarks, Lake of the (ō'zärks). See UNITED STATES, *Dams and Reservoirs* (Bagnell Dam).

O·zau'kee (ō·zô'kē). County in Wisconsin. See *Table* at WISCONSIN.

O·zette', Lake (ō·zĕt'). Lake in W Clallam co., NW Washington.

O·zie'ri (ō·dzyâ'rē). Commune, Sassari prov., NW Sardinia, 25 m. ESE of Sassari; pop. 9893; cathedral; prehistoric burial places nearby.

O·zo'na (ō·zō'nȧ). Town, ⊗ of Crockett co., W Texas, 70 m. SW of San Angelo; pop. 3361; only town in Crockett co.

O·zor'ków (ô·zôr'kōōf); *Russ.* **O·zor·kov'** (ŭ·zŭr·kôf'). Industrial commune, Łódź dept., Poland, on Bzura river 14 m. NNW of Łódź; pop. (1938–39 est.) 16,420; textiles, chemicals.

P

Pa'an' (bä'än'); *formerly* **Ba'tang'** (bä'täng'). Town, cen. Sikang prov., S China, on E bank of Yangtze ab. 180 m. W of Kangting; pop. ab. 6000; beautifully situated at alt. 9000 ft. in a fertile plain just N of that part of the Yangtze that flows through the mountains of S Sikang and NW Yunnan; a trading town on the route bet. Chengtu and India (the Assam-Sikang Road). At formation of Sikang prov. made its capital under the name **Ba'an'fu'** (bä'än'foō'); later replaced by Kangting.

Paar'de·berg (pär'dĕ·bĕrк; -bûrg). Battlefield, W Orange Free State, E cen. Union of South Africa, on the Modder river 23 m. SE of Kimberley; scene of Cronjé's surrender to Lord Roberts Feb. 28, 1900.

Paarl (pärl). Town, SW Cape Province, S Union of South Africa, 30 m. ENE of Cape Town on Great Berg river; pop. 18,580; has extensive fruit gardens and vineyards; produces wine; educational and industrial center. Founded 1690 by Huguenot settlers.

Pab'bay (păb'ā). **1** Island, Scotland, in Outer Hebrides SW of island of Lewis with Harris.
2 Island in Outer Hebrides S of Barra I.

Pa'bia·ni'ce *or* **Pa'bja·ni'ce** (pä'byä·nē'tsĕ). Industrial commune, Łódź dept., Poland, on railroad 10 m. SSW of Łódź; pop. (1938–39 est.) 52,000; textiles, esp. linen. Taken by Germans in 1914 and 1939.

Pab'na (pŭb'nä). **1** District, Rajshahi division, East Bengal, Pakistan; 1836 sq. m.; pop. (1941) 1,705,072.
2 Town, its ✷, on Ganges river 116 m. NNE of Calcutta; pop. 21,904.

Pacaraima, Serra. See SERRA PACARAIMA.

Pac'a·rai'ma Mountains (păk'á·rī'má). Range in W British Guiana; the NE extension of the Serra Pacaraima.

Pa'cas·ma'yo (pä'käz·mä'yô). Seaport, La Libertad dept., NW Peru, ab. 65 m. NW of Salaverry and 360 m. NW of Callao.

Pa·ca'ya (pä·kä'yä). River ab. 100 m. long, a W tributary of the Ucayali river in Loreto dept., NE Peru.

Pa'ce (pä'chå). Town, Messina commune, Sicily, suburb of Messina; pop. (1931) 19,332.

Pa·chá'ca·mac (pä·chä'kä·mäk). Site of a pre-Incan city, ab. 20 m. SE of Lima, Peru; pop. (est.) 1300; famous for remains of the ancient Yuncan civilization with its temple to the god Pachacamac, tombs, and city walls, and for its ruins of the later Incan temple to the sun; sacked by Pizarro 1523; site now occupied by the village of La Mamacoma.

Pa'cha·cha'ca (pä'chä·chä'kä). Short stream, SE Peru, a tributary of the Apurímac near Abancay; in region of its headwaters was probable homeland of Aymara and Quechua Indian tribes.

Pach'aug Pond (păch'ôg). Lake in NE cen. New London co., SE Connecticut; outlet, **Pachaug River,** flowing NW into Quinebaug river.

Pa·chi'no (pä·kē'nô). Coastal commune, Siracusa prov., SE Sicily, near SE tip of Sicily 26 m. SSW of Syracuse; pop. 20,564; tuna fishing.

Pa'chi·te'a (pä'chĕ·tā'ä). River ab. 200 m. long in Peru, flowing from the Andes Mts. into Ucayali river.

Pa·chu'ca, *in full* **Pachuca de So'to** (pä·choō'kä thä sō'tô). City, cen. Mexico, ✷ of Hidalgo state, 50 m. N of Mexico City; pop. 53,354; at alt. ab. 8000 ft.; one of oldest silver-mining centers in Mexico.

Pachynus Promontorium. See Cape PASSERO.

Pa·cif'ic (pá·sĭf'ĭk). **1** County in Washington. See *Table* at WASHINGTON.
2 City, Franklin and St. Louis cos., E Missouri, 33 m. W of St. Louis; pop. 2795; railroad junction; silica deposits nearby.

Pa·cif'i·ca (pá·sĭf'ĭ·kå). City, San Mateo co., W California, on Pacific coast S of San Francisco; pop. 20,995; formed 1957 by consolidation of several communities.

Pacific Grove. Residential and resort city, Monterey co., W California, at S end of Monterey Bay; pop. 12,121; founded 1874.

Pacific Islands. The islands of the Pacific Ocean, divided into Micronesia, Melanesia, and Polynesia (including New Zealand). See OCEANIA.

Pacific Islands, Trust Territory of the. The islands of the Pacific Ocean which after World War I were mandated to Japan and after World War II assigned 1947 to the United States as a trust territory under the United Nations. They comprise the Caroline Is. (with Palau Is.), Marshall Is., and Mariana Is. (except Guam).

Pacific Ocean. Body of water extending from the Arctic circle to the equator (**North Pacific Ocean**) and from the equator to the Antarctic Regions (**South Pacific Ocean**), and from W North America and W South America to Australia, the Malay Archipelago, and E Asia; area ab. 70,000,000 sq. m.; greatest depth (Mindanao Deep) 34,440 ft. off NE Mindanao, Philippine Is.; in at least 8 other places depth exceeds 30,000 ft.

Pa·ci'jan (pä·sē'hän). Island, westernmost of Camotes Is., Cebu prov., Phil. Is.; 34 sq. m.; pop. 16,980; coextensive with San Francisco municipality.

Packhoi. See PAKHOI.

Pa·coi'ma Dam (på·koi'må). See UNITED STATES, *Dams and Reservoirs.*

Pacsan, Mount. See Mount SICAPOO.

Pac·to'lus (păk·tō'lŭs). River in Lydia, Asia Minor, yielding gold-bearing sand; a tributary of the Hermus (mod. Gediz) entering it near Sardis.

Padalung. See PHATTHALUNG.

Pa'dang (pä'däng). **1** Island in Strait of Malacca, off coast of Sumatra ab. 1°N of equator.
2 Seaport city, W Sumatra, Indonesia, 575 m. NW of Djakarta ab. 1° S of equator; pop. 52,054; its port is Telukbajur (formerly Emmahaven) 4 m. to the S; one of most healthful of coastal towns; has rail connections with Bukittinggi and other towns of the Padang Highlands; export center for coal from Ombilin mines; much rubber, tobacco, rice, tea, palm oil produced in vicinity. One of the oldest Dutch settlements in Sumatra, established in 17th cent.; made capital of district on W coast 1664; captured by British 1795 and held until 1819; seized by Japanese Mar. 1942.

Padang Highlands. Elevated region in Barisan Mts., N and NE of Padang, W Sumatra, Indonesia; averages 2000 to 3000 ft., has several peaks above 9000 ft.; chief town Bukittinggi. Noted for beautiful scenery and healthful climate; tourist resort; produces coffee and tea and in SE part are great Ombilin coal mines.

Pa'dang·pan'djang (pä'däng·pän'jäng). Town in Padang Highlands, W Sumatra, Indonesia; pop. 9609; junction point for railroads to Padang, Bukittinggi, and Sawahlunto.

Paddan–Aram. See MESOPOTAMIA.

Pad'ding·ton (păd'ĭng·tŭn). **1** City, E New South Wales, SE Australia, E suburb of Sydney; pop. 24,693.
2 Metropolitan borough of London. See *Table* at LONDON.

Pa'den City (pā'd'n). Town, NW West Virginia, in Tyler and Wetzel cos., on Ohio river 24 m. SSW of Moundsville; pop. 3137; manufactures bottles.

Pa'der·born' (pä'dĕr·bôrn'). Manufacturing and commercial city, in what was formerly Westphalia prov., Prussia, Germany, 50 m. ESE of Münster; pop. 33,719; buildings include 11th-cent. Romanesque cathedral with fine crypt, 11th-cent. chapel; manufactures include Portland cement, leather, tobacco, bakery products (large export trade), beer; publishing houses; cattle markets. Episcopal see founded 777 by Charlemagne; several councils held here under Charlemagne; member of Hanseatic League; university 1614–1819; to Prussia 1802. In

World War II taken by Allied armies Mar. 31–Apr. 2, 1945 and held as pivot point in encirclement of the Ruhr.

Pa·de′ri·a (pá·dā′rĭ·á). Town, S Nepal, near boundary of Uttar Pradesh, N Indian Union, 47 m. N of Gorakhpur. See KAPILAVASTU.

Pad′i·ham (păd′ĭ·ăm). Urban district, Lancashire, NW England, 24 m. N of Manchester; pop. 10,031; cotton goods; coal mining.

Padma. See GANGES DELTA.

Pa′do·va (pä′dô·vä). **1** Province of Italy. See *Table* at ITALY.
2 See PADUA.

Pad′re Island (păd′rĕ). Uninhabited sand reef 100 m. long off the mainland of Kleberg, Kenedy, Willacy, and Cameron cos., S Texas, lying bet. Laguna Madre and the Gulf of Mexico.

Pad′stow (păd′stō). Town near N coast of Cornwall, SW England, NW of Bodmin; pop. (urban district) 2852; formerly important as a port, on an estuary now silted up; bathing resort.

Pad′u·a (păd′ŭ·á); *Ital.* **Pa′do·va** (pä′dô·vä); *anc.* **Pa·ta′vi·um** (pá·tā′vĭ·ŭm). Commune, * of Padova prov., Venezia Euganea, NE Italy, 22 m. W of Venice; pop. 138,709; episcopal see; connected by canal with Adige river; city walled and bastioned, entered by seven gates; buildings include the town hall (Palazzo della Ragione, built 1172–1219, remodeled 1420), 16th-cent. late-Renaissance cathedral (of which Petrarch was a canon), 12th-cent. cathedral baptistery, 15th-cent. episcopal palace, and 13th-cent. church of St. Anthony; famous university (founded in 13th cent.), long noted for its faculties of law and medicine, formerly having among its professors Galileo and Fallopius, and among its students Dante, Petrarch, and Tasso; manufactures include silks, chemicals, machinery, automobiles, leather; trades in oil, grain, wine, cattle. Said to have been founded shortly after destruction of Troy by the Trojan Antenor; under Roman rule; sacked by Alaric, later by Attila; restored by Charlemagne; under Carrara family 1318 ff.; to Venice 1405 whose later history it shared. Birthplace of Livy and the painter Andrea Mantegna. At end of World War II entered by Allies Apr. 28–29, 1945.

Pa·du′cah (pá·dū′ká). **1** City, ⊗ of McCracken co., W Kentucky, on Ohio river just below its confluence with Tennessee river; pop. 34,479; incorp. as village 1830, as city 1856; market and distributing center for section yielding tobacco, grain, fruit, coal, and potter's clay.
2 Town, ⊗ of Cottle co., NW Texas, 87 m. ENE of Lubbock; pop. 2392; cotton gins.

Padus. See PO.

Pae·o′ni·a (pē·ō′nĭ·á; -ōn′yá). Ancient district N of Macedonia in what is now S Yugoslavia; founded according to legend by colonists from Troy; conquered by Philip II of Macedon; chief town Stobi (*q.v.*).

Paes′tum (pĕs′tŭm; pēs′-); *mod.* **Pe′sto** (pĕs′tô). Ancient city, W Lucania, S Italy, on the Gulf of Salerno (anc. Bay of Paestum); founded 6th cent. B.C. by Greek colonists from Sybaris who called it **Pos′ei·do′ni·a** (pŏs′ĭ·dō′nĭ·á; -dōn′yá; pō′sī-); taken by Lucanians 4th cent. B.C. and by Romans 273 B.C.; noted for its roses; destroyed by Saracens 871 A.D.; ruins include portions of three beautiful Doric temples (6th cent. B.C., after 540 B.C., and c. 420 B.C.) and almost the entire walls.

Paestum, Bay of. See Gulf of SALERNO.

Pag (päg); *Ital.* **Pa′go** (pä′gô). **1** Yugoslav island in the Adriatic Sea off N Dalmatian coast; 111 sq. m.; pop. 4349; a part of Croatia, NW Yugoslavia.
2 Town on E coast of the island.

Pa′ga·di′an (pä′gä·dē′än). Municipality, E Zamboanga prov., Mindanao, Phil. Is., on NW shore of Illana Bay; pop. 46,262.

Pa′gai *or* **Pa′gaï** (pä′gī); *also* **Pa′gi** (pä′gī), **Pa′geh** (-gā). Two islands in Indian Ocean, S part of Mentawai Is. off W coast of Sumatra, Indonesia: **North Pa-**

gai, ab. 19 m. long by 18 m. wide, and **South Pagai,** ab. 42 m. long by 13 m. wide; total area 741 sq. m.; pop. 4943.

Pa·gan′ (pá·gän′). **1** Ruined town, Myingyan dist., Upper Burma, on left bank of Irrawaddy 92 m. SW of Mandalay; founded 847 and capital of a powerful dynasty until 1298. Extends 8 m. along the river and many of its original 5000 pagodas and shrines still stand.
2 Island, N cen. Mariana Is., W Pacific Ocean, 8 m. long by 2½ m. wide; ab. 17°30′N.

Pa·ga′ni (pä·gä′nĕ). Commune, Salerno prov., Campania, S Italy, 9 m. NW of Salerno; pop. 19,756.

Pag′a·sae′an Gulf (păg′á·sē′ăn). = Gulf of VOLOS.

Page (pāj). Name of counties of two states in the U.S. See *Tables* at IOWA and VIRGINIA.

Pa·ge′giai (pä·gā′gĕ·ē); *Ger.* **Po·ge′gen** (pŏ·gā′gĕn). **1** Former district of Lithuania (from 1939–45 a part of German Memelgebiet); taken by Russians 1945. See *Table* at LITHUANIA.
2 Town, * of former district, on N bank of the Neman nearly opp. Tilsit.

Pago. See PAG.

Pa·go′da Mountain (pá·gō′dá). Peak 13,491 ft. in Boulder co., N cen. Colorado.

Pagoda Point. Point adjacent to Cape Negrais on SW coast of Burma, on W side of mouth of Bassein river.

Pa′gong (pŭ′gông). = PANGONG.

Pa′go Pa′go (päng′ō päng′ō; pä′gō pä′gō; päng′gō päng′gō); *formerly also* **Pang′o·pang′o.** Village on Tutuila I., Samoa, SW Pacific Ocean, at head of long inlet forming **Pago Pago Harbor,** one of the best harbors in the South Pacific, with important U.S. naval station on its W shore; pop. 1251. Site chosen by Commander Richard W. Meade 1872 and ceded to United States 1878 as a naval and coaling station; made capital of American Samoa 1899.

Pa·go′sa Peak (pá·gō′sá). Mountain 12,674 ft. in Mineral co., S Colorado, in San Juan Mts.

Pagosa Springs. Town, ⊗ of Archuleta co., S Colorado, 50 m. E of Durango; pop. 1374; laid out 1880; health resort; hot mineral springs.

Pag′san·jan′ (päg′säng·hän′). Municipality, E Laguna prov., Luzon, Phil. Is., 3 m. E of Santa Cruz; pop. 8865; on Pagsanjan river and noted for its picturesque gorge and waterfall, also known as **Bo′to·can′** (bō′tô·kän′), ab. 200 ft. drop.

Pa·ha′la (pä·hä′lä). Village, Kau dist., Hawaii co., Hawaii, S part of Hawaii I. near coast; pop. 1392; S gateway to Hawaii National Park.

Pa·hang′ (pá·hŭng′; *Angl.* pá·hăng′). **1** River in Pahang state, Federation of Malaya; 285 m. long, navigable for native ɬ oats for ab. 250 m.; formed in NW part of the state by confluence of the Jelai and Tembeling rivers; flows S and E to South China Sea.
2 A state of the Federation of Malaya, on E coast of Malay Penin.; 13,820 sq. m.; pop. 180,111, (1941 est.) 221,800; * Kuala Lipis; largest state on the peninsula. Bounded on N by Kelantan and Trengganu, on E by South China Sea, on S by Johore, on SW by Negri Sembilan, and on W by Selangor and Perak. Mountainous, with many peaks above 3000 ft.; has the two highest mountains of the peninsula on its border: on the NW, Kerbau 7159 ft. and on the N, Tahan 7185 ft. Most of its area lies within the basin of the Pahang river and tributaries. Kuantan most important port on E coast. Chief industries agriculture and mining. Entered into treaty agreements with British 1887; became member of the Federated Malay States 1895, part of Federation of Malaya 1948.

Pah·le·vi′ (pá·hlá·vē′); *formerly* **En·ze·li′** (ăn·zá·lē′). Seaport city, Gilan prov., NW Iran, on SW coast of Caspian Sea; pop. ab. 37,000; best Iranian harbor on the Caspian; conducts large trade of Resht with Russian ports; connected by highway with Kazvin and Tehran. Held by Russians during World War I.

Pa·ho′a (pä·hō′ä). Village, Puna dist., Hawaii co., Hawaii, E Hawaii I., inland from Cape Kumukahi; pop. 1046.

Pa·ho′kee (pá·hō′kē). Town, Palm Beach co., SE Florida, on SE shore of Lake Okeechobee; pop. 4709; incorp. 1922.

Pah·ran′a·gat Range (pá·răn′á·găt). Range in cen. Lincoln co., E Nevada.

Pah·rock′, or **Pah·roc′, Range** (pá·rŏk′). Small range in N Lincoln co., E Nevada, extending NW into Nye co.

Pahsien. See CHUNGKING.

Pah′ute (pä′ūt), or **Pai′ute** (pī′ūt), **Mesa.** Tableland in cen. Nye co., S Nevada.

Pahute Peak. Mountain 8618 ft. in W Humboldt co., NW Nevada.

Pa·i′a (pä·ē′ä; -ē′á). Town, Makawao dist., Maui co., Hawaii, on N coast of Maui I.; pop. 2149.

Pai′de (pī′dě); *Ger.* **Weis′sen·stein** (vī′sěn·shtīn). City, ✻ of Järva prov., N cen. Estonia, 45 m. SE of Tallin; pop. (1937) 3376; a railroad town on right bank of Parnu river; match factories. Originated as a castle in 13th cent.; several times besieged and captured.

Paign′ton (pān′t′n; -tŭn). Urban district, Devonshire, SW England, on Torbay (inlet of English Channel) 27 m. E of Plymouth; pop. 25,369; seaside resort; remains of old palace of bishops of Exeter, Bishop Miles Coverdale, publisher of the first complete English Bible, being the last occupant (from 1551).

Päi′jän′ne (pä′ī·yän′ně). Lake 90 m. long and 20 m. wide in S Finland; area 608 sq. m.; greatest depth 305 ft.; drains S to Gulf of Finland.

Pai Khoi (pī Koi). Peninsula, E Nenets National District, Soviet Russia, Europe, bet. Kara Sea and Barents Sea; off its NW point is Vaigach I.

Pailingmiao. See POLINGMIAO.

Pa·i·lo′lo (pä·ē·lō′lō). Channel 8 m. wide bet. Maui I. and Molokai I., Hawaii.

Paim′pol′ (păn′pôl′). Village, Côtes-du-Nord dept., NW France, NNW of St-Brieuc on the Gulf of St-Malo; pop. 2649; fishing port; scene of Pierre Loti's *Pêcheurs d'Islande.*

Paine (pān). Peak 8760 ft. in S Chile, E of Hanover I. and S of Stokes peak.

Paines′ville (pānz′vĭl). City, ⊗ of Lake co., NE Ohio, 27 m. NE of Cleveland; pop. 16,116; settled c. 1800; manufactures rayon yarn, alkali, cement; salt wells, nurseries nearby. Lake Erie Coll. (1856; women).

Painted Desert. Region ab. 200 m. long in E Coconino co., N cen. Arizona, E of Colorado and Little Colorado rivers; erosion has worn away much of the sand, exposing many-colored rock surfaces.

Painted Post. Village, Steuben co., S New York, 16 m. W of Elmira; pop. 2570; settled 1789; manufactures machinery, foundry products, gas engines, compressors.

Paint Rock. Village, ⊗ of Concho co., W cen. Texas; pop. (est.) 500.

Paints′ville (pănts′vĭl; *Sou.* also -v′l). City, ⊗ of Johnson co., E Kentucky, 28 m. NNW of Pikeville; pop. 4025.

Pai·sa′no Peak (pī·sä′nō). Mountain 6000 ft. in NW Brewster co., W Texas.

Pais′ley (pāz′lĭ). Burgh, ⊗ of Renfrew co., SW Scotland, 7 m. WSW of Glasgow; pop. (1951) 93,704; the site of J. & P. Coats, Ltd., threadworks, largest in the world; manufactures also paper, textiles, foodstuffs, machinery; formerly known for its shawls (Paisley shawls). Historic abbey, founded 1163 by Walter Fitzalan, ancestor of the Stewarts.

Pa·i′ta (pä·ē′tä). Village on the French island of New Caledonia, SW Pacific Ocean, ab. 10 m. NW of Nouméa; terminus of narrow-gauge railroad from Nouméa (20 m. long).

Pai′ta (pī′tä). Seaport town, Piura dept., NW Peru, ab. 35 m. NW of Piura; pop. (1940 est.) 7177; excellent harbor; shipping point for cotton, hides, and Panama hats.

Pa·ja′res Pass (pä·hä′räs). Mountain pass 4475 ft. through the Cantabrian Mts., N Spain.

Pakaraima Mountains. = PACARAIMA MOUNTAINS.

Pak′chan (päk′chän; pouk′-). Wide river ab. 55 m. long on Isthmus of Kra, extreme S of Burma; flows S into Andaman Sea, forming boundary bet. S Lower Burma and Siam.

Pak′che′ (päk′chě′). See *History* at KOREA.

Pak′hoi′ (bäk′hoi′), *earlier French* **Pack′hoi′.** Treaty port, SW Kwangtung prov., SE China, on Gulf of Tonkin ab. 350 m. W of Hong Kong; pop. (1931 est.) 36,000; has good anchorage and is a natural port of entry for Yunnan, Kwangsi, and Kweichow provs. Made treaty port in 1877 but its trade has declined in recent years.

Pak′i·stan′ (päk′ĭ·stän′; pä′kĭ·stän′)—a Hindustani term meaning "land of the pure." A confederation of regions formerly in the Indian Empire (see INDIA, 2) having a predominantly Moslem population, established Aug. 15, 1947 by Act of Parliament (July 18, 1947) as a self-governing dominion of British Commonwealth of Nations; 365,907 sq. m.; pop. 75,687,000; ✻ (from 1959) Rawalpindi. Comprises two major areas separated from one another by the N cen. part of the Republic of India (about 900 m.): (1) in the W (West Pakistan), Baluchistan, the North-West Frontier Province, Sind, and part of the Punjab (Rawalpindi and Multan divisions and a portion of Lahore division) as well as the princely states of Bahawalpur, Khairpur, Kalat, Kharan, Las Bela, Dir, Swat, and Chitral; (2) in the E (East Pakistan), eastern Bengal, including Dacca and Chittagong divisions and parts of Presidency and Rajshahi divisions, and most of Sylhet dist. of Assam. Pakistan was reorganized 1955 into two provinces (West Pakistan and East Pakistan) and became a republic within the Commonwealth Mar. 2, 1956. See ISLAMABAD.

Paknam. See SAMUT PRAKAN.

Pa·kok′ku (pá·kôk′kōō). **1** District, Magwe division, Upper Burma; 5356 sq. m.; pop. 499,181; ✻ Pakokku. **2** Town, its ✻, on right bank of the Irrawaddy 75 m. SW of Mandalay; pop. 23,115; important trade center.

Pakokku Hill Tracts. Former district in Upper Burma, W of Pakokku dist., now included in Chin Hills.

Paks (pŏksh). Commune, S Hungary, on Danube river 63 m. S of Budapest; pop. 13,442.

Pak′sé′ (pák′sā′). Town, S Laos, Indochina, on E bank of the Mekong.

Pala Bianca. See WEISSKUGEL.

Pa·lach′we (pá·lăch′wē). = PALAPYE.

Pa·la′cios (pá·läsh′ŭz). Town and resort, Matagorda co., SE Texas, on Matagorda Bay 25 m. SW of Bay City; pop. 3676; fishing port; agriculture.

Pa·la′cios, Los (lôs pä·lä′syôs). See LOS PALACIOS.

Palaestina. See PALESTINE.

Pa′la·gru′ža Islands (pä′lä·grōō′zhä) *Ital.* **I′so·le di Pe·la·go′sa** (ē′zō·lä dě pä·lä·gō′sä) ; *Angl.* **Pel′a·go′sa Islands** (pěl′á·gō′sá). Group of islets, cen. Adriatic Sea, SW of Lastovo, Bosnia and Herzegovina, W Yugoslavia; before 1947 belonged to Italy.

Pa·lai′kas·tro (pä·lä′käs·trô). Archaeological site, NE coast of Crete; ruins of town of Middle and Late Minoan periods.

Pa′lam·cot′tah (pä′lăm·kŏt′á). Town, S Madras, S Indian Union, near Tinnevelly; pop. 51,990.

Pa·la′na (pá·lä′ná). Town, ✻ of the Koryak National District, Soviet Russia, Asia, on NW coast of Kamchatka Penin. on Sea of Okhotsk.

Pa·la′nan (pá·lä′nän). Municipality, E Isabela prov., Luzon, Phil. Is., near **Palanan Bay** on Pacific coast; pop. 3109; only important town in E coast of province, near mouth of Palanan river; connected with Ilagan, 37 m. to the W, by rough mountain trails. Place where Gen. Emilio Aguinaldo maintained his headquarters for the Filipino revolutionary government 1900–01 and where he was captured by Gen. Funston Mar. 23, 1901.

Palanga. See POLANGEN.

Pa'lan·pur (pä'lŭn·poŏr). **1** Former Indian state, Western Rajputana States, SW Rajputana, NW Indian Union; 1794 sq. m.; pop. (1941) 315,855; joined Union of Rajasthan June 26, 1947.
2 Town, its ✲, now in Gujerat state, 77 m. N of Ahmadabad; pop. 20,347.

Pa'la·o'a Point (pä'lä·ō'ä). Southernmost point of Lanai I., Hawaii, on Kealaikahiki Channel.

Pa·la'pag (pä·lä'päg). Municipality, NE coast of Samar, Phil. Is., port opp. Batag I.; pop. 19,745.

Pa·lap'ye (pá·lăp'yě). Town, a former ✲ of the Bamangwato tribe, E Bechuanaland Protectorate, cen. South Africa, E of Serowe on a tributary of the Limpopo river and ab. 100 m. S of Francistown.

Pa·lar' (pä·lär'). River 230 m. long in SE India; rises in E Mysore near Kolar, flows ESE into Bay of Bengal.

Pa·la'san (pä·lä'sän). Island 6 sq. m. in Polillo group off E Luzon, Phil. Is., bet. E coast of Polillo I. and Patnanongan I.; in Tayabas prov.

Pa'las de Rey (pä'läz thä rě'ě). Commune, Lugo prov., NW Spain, 19 m. SW of Lugo; pop. 12,156.

Pa·lat'i·nate, The (pá·lăt''n·ăt); *Ger.* **Pfalz** (pfälts).
1 Territory in Germany that was once under the jurisdiction of the counts palatine, who in 14th cent. became electors of the Holy Roman Empire; in two parts: **Lower**, or **Rhine, Palatinate**, on both sides of the Rhine in the area S of the Main river; the **Upper Palatinate** some distance to the east in E Bavaria around Amberg and Regensberg.
2 The Lower, or Rhine, Palatinate.
3 Bavarian government district. See *Table* at BAVARIA.

Pal'a·tine (păl'á·tīn). **1** Village, Cook co., NE Illinois, 28 m. NW of Chicago; pop. 11,504.
2 One of the seven hills of Rome. See SEVEN HILLS.

Pa·lat'ka (pá·lăt'ká). City, ⊗ of Putnam co., NE Florida penin., on St. Johns river 28 m. SW of St. Augustine; pop. 11,028; shipping center; lumber and paper mills; temporarily occupied by Union troops 1864.

Pa·lau' (pä·lou'); *formerly* **Pe·lew'** (pě·loō'). **1** Group of ab. 100 islands and islets of which only 7 are large and inhabited, generally considered a part of the Caroline Is. (Western Carolines), W Pacific Ocean, 1060 m. SE of Manila and ab. the same distance SW of Saipan; 184 sq. m.; pop. (1938 est.) 12,798. Chief island Babelthuap; other islands Urukthapel, Peleliu, Angaur, Eil Malk, and Koror. Under Spanish regime administered as part of the Caroline Is.; sold to Germany 1899; seized by Japan 1914; mandated to Japan 1919 and Koror made administrative headquarters 1921 of all Japanese mandated islands. In World War II taken by Allies Sept. 6–Oct. 13, 1944 (most of fighting on Peleliu; Babelthuap with 30,000 Japanese bypassed); became part of U.S. Trust Territory of the Pacific Islands 1947.
2 See BABELTHUAP.

Pa·lau' (pä·lou'). Town, Coahuila state, NE Mexico; pop. 5116.

Pa·la'ui (pä·lä'wě). Island off NE point of Cagayan prov., Luzon, Phil. Is.; 10 sq. m.; its N tip is Cape Engaño; lighthouse.

Pa·la'uig (pä·lä'wǐg). Municipality, W Zambales prov., Luzon, Phil. Is., on coast at **Palauig Point**, 15°26′N, 10 m. N of Iba; pop. 6026.

Pa·la'wan (pä·lä'wän); *formerly* **Pa·ra'gua** (pä·rä'gwä). Island, SW Phil. Is.; 4550 sq. m.; 278 m. long by 5 to 30 m. wide; with adjacent islands (Calamian, Cuyo, and Cagayan groups and Linapacan I., Dumaran I., Balabac I., and Cagayan Sulu I.) constitutes a province, 5693 sq. m., pop. 93,673; ✲ Puerto Princesa. The province extends from Mindoro Strait SW to Balabac Strait, which separates it from North Borneo, and separates Sulu Sea from South China Sea. The island has a chain of mountains running nearly the entire length; highest Mt. Mantalingajan 6839 ft.; has low land at N end and narrow plain along the coasts; chief products rice, corn, sweet potatoes, coconuts, and fruit. Forests provide valuable woods and island is rich in mineral resources. Chief industry fishing. Inhabitants are Visayans in the N, Moros in the S, and the Bataks and Tagbanuas, primitive tribes, in the interior. There are no large towns; the most important places are Puerto Princesa, Cuyo, Culion, and Coron.

History: Earliest settlements made by Mohammedans; Spanish influence began in the Calamian group and in fort at Taytay in early 18th cent. Several changes in administration made by Spaniards in 19th cent.; for a time divided into three military districts. Civil government established June 1902 under name of Paragua; name changed to Palawan in 1905. In World War II occupied by American forces Mar. 1–2, 1945.

Pa'laz·zo'lo A·cre'i·de (pä'lät·tsô'lô ä·krä'ē·dâ); *anc.* **Ac'rae** (ăk'rē). Commune, Siracusa prov., SE Sicily, 22 m. W of Syracuse; pop. 11,584; ancient Greek theater and necropolis. Founded 664 B.C. by Greeks; suffered from earthquake 1693.

Palazzolo sul·l'O'glio (soōl·lôl'yô). Commune, Brescia prov., Lombardy, N Italy, on Oglio river 19 m. WNW of Brescia; pop. 10,667.

Pal'dis·ki (päl'dĭs·kĭ; *Russ.* pŭl·dyē'skĭ), *formerly* **Bal'tis·ki** (bäl'tĭs·kĭ; *Russ.* bŭl·tyē'skĭ); *Eng.* **Bal'tic Port** (bôl'tĭk). Seaport, NW Estonia, at S of entrance to Gulf of Finland 26 m. W of Tallin; pop. (1937) 662; an icefree port; formerly a Russian naval base.

Pa'lem·bang' (pä'lěm·bäng'). **1** Former residency, SE Sumatra, Neth. Indies; 33,333 sq. m.; pop. 1,098,725; ✲ Palembang; extended nearly across S half of the island to foothills of the Barisan Mts., including the basin of the Musi river. East coast of region faces Bangka I. Oil constitutes three quarters of the value of the exports; other exports rubber, coffee, coal.
2 City and river port, its ✲, on both banks of the Musi river 56 m. from its mouth; pop. 282,900; 2d largest city on Sumatra and its most important trade center, esp. for the oil fields in the S; connected by rail with Telukbetung on Sunda Strait and by highway with Djambi and Bengkulu. In early times capital of a Hindu-Indonesian kingdom; later became a settlement of Arab colonists and was long the chief town of Palembang sultanate, which was responsible for massacre of Dutch in 1811; independent until 1825 when it was conquered by Dutch government; its oil wells destroyed Feb. 1942 before seizure by Japanese parachutists; bombed by Allies Aug. 1944.

Pa·len'ci·a (pá·lěn'shǐ·á; -shá; *Span.* pä·län'thyä, -syä). **1** Province of Spain. See *Table* at SPAIN.
2 *anc.* **Pal·lan'ti·a** (pă·lăn'shǐ·á; -shá). City, its ✲, N Spain, on Carrión river 28 m. N by E of Valladolid; pop. 34,283; manufactures shawls, blankets, fireworks, agricultural machinery, chocolates; episcopal palace, 15th-cent. Dominican church, 14th-cent. Gothic cathedral, bull ring. Ancient capital of the Vaccaei; captured by Romans, Goths, Moors; reconquered by Spaniards in 10th cent.; scene of the Cid's marriage to Ximena 1074; made episcopal see in 11th cent.; residence of Castilian kings 13th–14th cents.; first university in Spain founded here by Alfonso IX in 1208.

Pa·len'que (pä·läng'kâ). Village in N Chiapas state, S Mexico; famous ruins of an ancient city nearby in a forested region.

Pa·ler'mo (pá·lûr'mō; *Ital.* pä·lěr'mō). **1** Province of Italy. See *Table* at ITALY.
2 *anc.* **Pan·or'mus** (pă·nôr'mŭs) or **Pan·hor'mus** (păn·hôr'mŭs). Seaport, its ✲, Sicily, and ✲ of Sicily, on **Bay of Palermo** 265 m. S by E of Rome; pop. 411,879; archiepiscopal see; seaside resort; buildings include 12th-cent. cathedral, royal palace (including esp. the Palatine Chapel of Roger II), archiepiscopal palace, national museum, national library, university (founded 1779), barracks, and arsenal; recently improved harbor; shipbuilding yard and dry dock; active trade, esp. in sulfur, sumach, wine, citrus fruits, and olive oil; important

fisheries; manufactures gloves, marble products, and foundry products.

History: Said to have been founded by Phoenicians; passed to Carthaginians and made capital of their Sicilian possessions; taken by Romans 254 B.C. as a free town, attaining great prosperity; part of Eastern Empire; ruled by Vandals; under Saracens 835–1071; taken 1072 by Roger the Norman and made capital of newly founded Norman kingdom of Sicily; revolted against French and abuses of Charles of Anjou 1282 (the famous Sicilian Vespers), passing to Savoy and later to the Bourbon house of Naples; bombarded during insurrection 1848; seized by Garibaldi 1860 and made part of the kingdom of Italy; captured by Allied forces July 30, 1943.

Pal′es·tine (păl′ĕs-tīn; *in Texas,* -tēn). **1** Village, Crawford co., E Illinois, 32 m. NE of Olney; pop. 1564.

2 City, ⊗ of Anderson co., E Texas, 82 m. E of Waco; pop. 13,974; produces ginned cotton, cottonseed oil, creamery products, manufactures foundry products, boxes; oil and gas wells, also salt, lignite, fuller's earth, and Orangeburg clay deposits in vicinity; Palestine Salt Dome (30,000 ft. in diameter). Site of Fort Houston (1836) nearby.

3 *Lat.* **Pal′aes·ti′na** (păl′ĕs-tī′na̍); *Bib.* **Ca′naan** (kā′nǎn). Country, SW Asia, bordering on the Mediterranean Sea; bounded on the N by Lebanon, on NE by Syria, on E by Jordan, and on SW by Egypt (Sinai Penin.); ab. 270 m. long N to S (from Dan to Beersheba, 150 m.); land area 10,160 sq. m.; pop. 1,035,821, (1944 est.) 1,739,624; ✴ Jerusalem; under British mandate

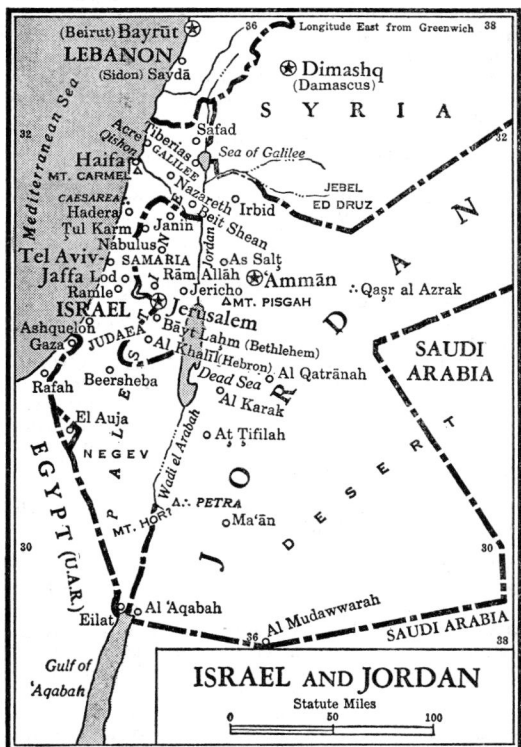

ISRAEL AND JORDAN
Statute Miles
0   50   100

1923–48, divided for administrative purposes into six districts: Galilee, Gaza, Haifa, Jerusalem, Lydda, and Samaria. The Holy Land (*Zech.* ii. 12) of Hebrew and Christian peoples. Ancient Palestine was somewhat larger and included Bashan and Gilead E of the Jordan, the land bet. the Mediterranean and the Jordan gener-

ally being known as Canaan (*q.v.*). Level along the seacoast (including Plain of Sharon) and in the Plain of Esdraelon and the Valley of Jezreel in N cen. part; hilly in N (Galilee); in cen. part (Samaria) has Mt. Ebal 3084 ft. and Mt. Gerizim 2849 ft.; has mountain range 2200 to ab. 3000 ft. in S (Judaea), extending from hill country of Ephraim S to beyond Hebron. Chief river the Jordan (*q.v.*); only other stream of any size the Qishon. Chief industry agriculture, with exports of citrus fruits, olive oil, chocolate, diamonds. Chief towns Jerusalem, Haifa, Tel Aviv, Jaffa, Gaza, and Nablus.

History: From very early times, Palestine influenced by invasion from south (Egypt) and from north and west (Semites and Hittites); conquered by Egypt 1479 B.C. (see MEGIDDO); occupied by Canaanites prior to Hebrew invasion of 15th cent. B.C.; southern coast settled by Philistines probably driven from Crete; for Hebrew kingdoms of Palestine, see ISRAEL, 1, and JUDAH, also JERUSALEM; from 8th cent. B.C., Palestine became successively part of Assyrian, Chaldean, and Persian empires; conquered by Pompey c. 64 B.C.; part of Roman province of Syria during Christ's lifetime c. 4 B.C.–29 A.D.; conquered by Arabs 636 A.D.; except for Crusaders' kingdom of Jerusalem in 12th cent., Palestine was ruled by various Moslem states, including Ottoman Empire 1516–1917; conquered by British under Allenby 1917–18; assigned as British mandate (1920) which became effective 1923; as result of Balfour Declaration 1917, expressing British approval of establishment of national home for Jews in Palestine, received many Jewish immigrants; with reversal of policy by British 1939 and increase in numbers of Jewish immigrants during World War II became scene of increasing conflict bet. Jews and Arabs and opposition of Jews to British control; ceased to be British mandate May 15, 1948. See ISRAEL, 2; TRANSJORDAN.

Pal′es·tri′na (păl′ĕs-trē′na̍; *Ital.* pä′lās-trē′nä); *anc.* **Prae·nes′te** (prē-nĕs′tē). Commune, Roma prov., Latium, cen. Italy, 20 m. ESE of Rome; pop. (1931) 8118; a very ancient city, founded before 8th cent. B.C.; allied itself with Rome 499 B.C., later fought against her; destroyed by Sulla's forces 82 B.C.; rebuilt around a temple of fortune, Praeneste became famous for its oracle and noted as a summer resort for wealthy Romans. Modern town birthplace of Giovanni Pierluigi da Palestrina.

Pa·let′wa (pả-lĕt′wä). Town, ✴ of Arakan Hill Tracts dist. of Arakan division, Lower Burma, on the Kaladan river 85 m. N of Akyab.

Pal′ghat (päl′gät). Town, cen. Kerala state, S Indian Union, on Ponnani river 112 m. WNW of Madura; pop. (1941) 55,160. Fort captured by British in 1768 and used as a base of operations against Tipu Sahib. Seat of Victoria Jubilee Coll.

Pal′grave Point (päl′grāv; pŏl′-). Cape on NW cen. coast of South-West Africa.

Pali. See NUUANU PALI.

Pa′li·nu′ro (pä′lē-nōō′rô); *anc.* **Pal′i·nu′rus** (păl′ĭ-nūr′ŭs). Cape on W coast of Italy, at 40°1′30″N.

Pal′i·sade′, Middle (păl′ĭ-sād′). Peak 14,049 ft. in Sierra Nevada, in E Fresno co., S cen. California.

Palisade, North. Peak 14,254 ft. in Sierra Nevada, in E Fresno co., S cen. California.

Pal′i·sades′ (păl′ĭ-sādz′). A line of high cliffs of traprock ab. 15 m. long on W bank of Hudson river in SE New York and NE New Jersey.

Palisades Interstate Park. A chain of parks extending from Fort Lee, New Jersey, opp. New York City, to Newburgh, New York, and including Bear Mt.; total area ab. 70 sq. m.; river frontage 22 m., including 13 m. of the Palisades.

Palisades Park. Residential borough, Bergen co., NE corner of New Jersey, 9 m. N of Jersey City; pop. 11,943; amusement park.

Pa′li·ta′na (pä′lĭ-tä′na̍). **1** Former Indian state, Western India States, India, in SE Kathiawar Penin.; 300 sq. m.; pop. (1941) 76,432. A Rajput state tributary to both

Baroda and Junagarh; joined a new confederation of Indian states July 7, 1947.

2 Town, its ✳, 70 m. WNW of Surat; pop. 13,343. Nearby is sacred hill of **Sa·trun′ja·ya** (sȧ·trōōn′jȧ·yȧ), covered with Jain temples.

Palk Bay (pŏk; pôlk). Bay on extreme NW coast of the island of Ceylon.

Palk Strait. Channel 40 m. wide bet. N Ceylon and SE India, N of Adam's Bridge.

Pal La·ha′ra (päl lȧ·hä′rȧ). Former Indian state, Eastern States, NE Indian Union, ab. 80 m. NW of Cuttack; 450 sq. m.; pop. (1941) 34,130; ✳ Pal Lahara.

Pallantia. See PALENCIA.

Pal·lan′za (päl·län′zä). Former commune, now subdivision (1931 pop. 8180) of commune of VERBANIA, Italy.

Pal′las (păl′ăs). Hamlet in co. Longford, N cen. Eire, E of Lough Ree; birthplace of Oliver Goldsmith.

Pal·le′ne (pȧ·lē′nė; *Mod. Gr.* pä·lyē′nyė); *also* **Kas·san′dra** (kȧ·săn′drȧ; *Mod. Gr.* kä·sän′drä). Southwest peninsula of Chalcidice, projecting into Aegean Sea on NE coast of Greece, and forming part of E side of the Gulf of Salonika. On narrow isthmus at its base is Potidaea.

Pallice, La. See LA PALLICE.

Pal′li·ser, Cape (păl′ĭ·sėr). Cape on S extremity of North I., New Zealand, at the E entrance to Cook Strait.

Palliser Bay. Bay on S coast of North I., New Zealand, an inlet of Cook Strait W of Cape Palliser.

Palliser Islands. Former name of TUAMOTU ARCHIPELAGO.

Pal′ma or **Palma de Mal·lor′ca** (päl′mä thä mä-[l]yôr′kä). Fortified commune, ✳ of Baleares prov., Spain, and ✳ of Majorca I., on **Bay of Palma**, 162 m. E by N of Valencia; pop. (1941 est.) 115,346; chief port of Balearic Is.; trades in cattle, fruit, and agricultural produce, oil, wine; manufactures alcohol, flour, starch, sugar, leather, pottery, silks and woolens, jewelry; 14th-cent. Gothic cathedral, Moorish palace (the Almudaina), 16th-cent. town hall, palace of Majorcan kings; birthplace and burial place of Raymond Lully; tomb of James II of Aragon. Captured from Moors by James I of Aragon 1229.

Palma, La. See LA PALMA.

Pal′ma di Mon·te·chia′ro (päl′mä dė mōn·tȧ·kyä′rȯ). Commune, Agrigento prov., SW Sicily, near Mediterranean Sea 14 m. SE of Agrigento; pop. 15,615; 17th-cent. cathedral.

Palmas. See MIANGAS.

Pal′mas, Cape (päl′mȧs). Cape extending into Atlantic Ocean on extreme S coast of Liberia, W Africa.

Pal′mas, Gulf of (päl′mȧs). Gulf on SW coast of the island of Sardinia, Italy.

Pal′mas, Las (läs päl′mȧs). **1** Province of Spain, in Canary Is. See *Las Palmas* in *Table* at SPAIN.

2 City of Grand Canary I. See LAS PALMAS.

Pal′mas Al′tas (päl′mäs äl′täs). Cape on N coast of Puerto Rico.

Pal′ma So·ria′no (päl′mä sȯ·ryä′nȯ). Municipality and town, Oriente prov., E Cuba, 18 m. NW of Santiago de Cuba; pop. (town) 15,743.

Palm Beach (päm). **1** County in Florida. See *Table* at FLORIDA.

2 Resort town, Palm Beach co., SE Florida, at N end of island separating Lake Worth (lagoon) from the Atlantic; pop. 6055.

Palm′dale (päm′dāl). Urban area, Los Angeles co., SW California, NE of Los Angeles; pop. 11,522.

Pal′mei·ri′nhas Point (päl′mä·rē′nyȧsh). Cape on NW coast of Angola, W Africa, S of Luanda.

Palm′er (päm′ėr). **1** Town (officially a village), SE Alaska, 6 m. NE of Matanuska in the Matanuska valley; pop. 1181.

2 Town, Hampden co., SW Massachusetts, ENE of Springfield; pop. 10,358; manufactures wire rope.

Palmer Archipelago; *formerly* **Antarctic Archipelago.** Island group bet. South America and Antarctica, 53°W to 78°W, NW of Weddell Sea; includes Anvers I., Brabant I., and other small islands off NW coast of Palmer Penin.; part of Falkland Islands Dependencies.

Palmer Peninsula or *since 1964* **Antarctic Peninsula.** The long narrow tongue of land extending ab. 700 m. from its base in 73°S in Antarctica to ab. 63°S toward the S end of South America, bet. long. 59° and 67°W; separated from South Shetland Is. by Bransfield Strait. Near its base on the W are Alexander I Island and Charcot I. and farther N on the W lies the Palmer Archipelago. Formerly, before full exploration, was thought to be islands (North Graham, South Graham); hence, later, called Graham Land; N part since 1964 called Graham Land, S part Palmer Land. Marks part of W coast of Weddell Sea; covered with shelf ice. At its base is peak of 13,700 ft.

Palm′er·ston (päm′ėr·stŭn). Early name of DARWIN, Northern Territory, Australia.

Palmerston or **A′va·rau′** (ä′vȧ·rou′). Small island (atoll) in cen. Pacific Ocean 270 m. NW of Rarotonga in the Cook Is.; 1 sq. m.; pop. (1936) 90; administered by New Zealand.

Palmerston, Cape. Headland, Queensland, NE Australia, SE of Mackay; 21°33′S.

Palmerston North. City, Wellington provincial dist., S North I., New Zealand, 80 m. NE of Wellington; pop. (1941 est.) 25,500; center of pastoral and dairy region.

Palm′er·ton (päm′ėr·t′n; -tŭn). Industrial borough, Carbon co., E Pennsylvania, on Lehigh river 17 m. NNW of Allentown; pop. 5942; center for refining zinc ore; manufactures zinc oxide, sulfuric acid.

Pal·met′to (păl·mĕt′ō; -ŭ). City, Manatee co., W Florida penin., at lower end of Tampa Bay; pop. 5556; fishing center; fruit and vegetable packeries.

Palmetto Point. Cape on NE coast of the island of Jamaica, West Indies.

Pal′mi (päl′mė). Coastal commune, Reggio di Calabria prov., Calabria, S Italy, 21 m. NNE of Reggio di Calabria; pop. 18,179.

Pal·mil′las, Point (päl·mē′yäs). Cape on SW coast of Las Villas prov., W cen. Cuba, at entrance to Cochinos Bay.

Pal·mi′ra (päl·mē′rä). **1** City, Valle dept., W Colombia, near the Cauca river; pop. 21,235; alt. 3000 ft.; raises coffee, tobacco, cacao.

2 Municipality and town, Las Villas prov., W cen. Cuba, just N of Cienfuegos; pop. (town) 5865.

Pal·mi′to de la Vir′gen (päl·mē′tȯ thä lä vėr′hän). Island in Pacific Ocean off the coast of SW Sinaloa state, Mexico, N of the island of **Palmito del Ver′de** (thĕl vĕr′thä); the two long, narrow islands parallel the coast and appear to be a continuation of a peninsula extending N from coast of Nayarit state.

Palm Springs (päm). Resort city, Riverside co., SE California, 44 m. SE of San Bernardino in Coachella Valley; pop. 13,468; founded 1876.

Pal·my′ra (păl·mī′rȧ). **1** City, ⊗ of Marion co., NE Missouri, 12 m. NW of Hannibal; pop. 2933.

2 Borough, Burlington co., S cen. New Jersey, on Delaware river 7 m. NE of Camden; pop. 7036.

3 Village, Wayne co., W New York, 21 m. E of Rochester; pop. 3476; manufactures esp. steam packings, paper boxes; near Hill Cumorah, glacial drumlin where Joseph Smith claimed to have unearthed gold plates that were source of Book of Mormon (1827).

4 Borough, Lebanon co., SE cen. Pennsylvania, 16 m. E of Harrisburg; pop. 6999; settled 1749; manufactures shoes, textiles; limestone quarries.

5 Village, ⊗ of Fluvanna co., cen. Virginia; pop. (est.) 350.

6 *Bib.* **Tad′mor** (tăd′môr) or **Ta′mar** (tā′mēr). Ruined city 135 m. NE of Damascus, Syria, at an oasis on N edge of Syrian Desert; now a small village. Said to have

been built by Solomon (2 *Chron.* viii. 4) but perhaps confused with Tamar in Palestine (1 *Kings* ix. 18); an ancient Aramaic town; developed at beginning of Christian Era and became prosperous because of its location on trade route from Persian Gulf to Egypt; under Roman suzerainty in 1st cent. A.D.; rose to great prominence 130 to 270 A.D.; devoted to worship of the sun. After death of Odenathus, 266 or 267, rule of kingdom succeeded to his wife Zenobia who declared her country independent. Captured and Zenobia made prisoner 272 by Emperor Aurelian; after people's revolt, city destroyed 273.

Palmyra Island. One of the Line Is. (*q.v.*), at N end of group ab. 960 m. S of Honolulu, in cen. Pacific Ocean; 1 sq. m.; formerly a part of Honolulu co., Hawaiian Is., but excluded from Hawaii when state was organized 1960. Discovered 1802 by Captain Sawle of the American ship *Palmyra;* annexed by kingdom of Hawaii 1862 and by Great Britain 1889; formally taken over by United States 1912, and made a naval airfield 1939.

Pal·my'ras Point (păl·mĭ'răz). Cape, NE coast of India, Orissa state, projecting into the Bay of Bengal N of the Mahanadi river.

Pa'lo (pä'lō). Municipality on E coast of Leyte I., Phil. Is., on San Pedro Bay 7 m. S of Tacloban; pop. 25,471. Taken by American invasion forces Oct. 19, 1944.

Pal'o Al'to. 1 County in Iowa. See *Table* at IOWA.

2 City, Santa Clara co., W California, 17 m. NW of San Jose; pop. 52,287; settled 1891, incorp. 1894; canned fruit, dairy products, insecticides, roentgen-ray tubes. Stanford Univ. (1885; coed.).

3 Borough, Schuylkill co., E cen. Pennsylvania, E suburb of Pottsville; pop. 1445.

4 Battlefield, Cameron co., S Texas, 12 m. NE of Brownsville; scene May 8, 1846 of first battle of Mexican War; Americans under Gen. Zachary Taylor defeated Mexicans under Gen. Mariano Arista.

Pa'lo del Col'le (pä'lō däl kôl'lā). Commune, Bari prov., Apulia, SE Italy, 8 m. SW of Bari; pop. 12,052.

Pal'o Du'ro Canyon (pä'lō dōōr'ō). Canyon of the Red river, NW Texas, in Randall and Armstrong cos. SE of Amarillo; contains a state park.

Pa'lo·ma'ni (pä·lō·mä'nē). Peak 18,924 ft. in W Bolivia, NE of Lake Titicaca.

Pal'o·mar, Mount (păl'ō·mär). Peak 6126 ft. in San Diego co., SW corner of California, 45 m. NNE of San Diego; astronomical observatory, erected by the Rockefeller Foundation for the Carnegie Institution and the California Institute of Technology; location of giant (200-in.) telescope.

Pa·lo'mas Mts. (pä·lō'mäs). Small range in E Yuma co., SW Arizona.

Pa'lom·pon' (pä'lôm·pôn'). Municipality on NW coast of Leyte I., Phil. Is., W of Ormoc and 45 m. WSW of Tacloban; pop. 29,120; scene of last stand of Japanese on Leyte Dec. 1944; finally taken by Americans Dec. 25.

Pal'o Pin'to (păl'ō pĭn'tō; *now less often,* pä'lō). 1 County in Texas. See *Table* at TEXAS.

2 Village, ⊗ of Palo Pinto co., N cen. Texas; pop. (est.) 525; deposits of petrified wood nearby.

Pa·lo'po (pä·lō'pō). Seaport, Celebes govt., Celebes I., Indonesia, on NW shore of Gulf of Bone; pop. 4208.

Pa'los (pä'lōs), *officially* **Pa'los de la Fron·te'ra** (pä'lōz thä lä frôn·tā'rä). Former seaport, Huelva prov., SW Spain, on Río Tinto; pop. (1930) 2201; Columbus sailed from here Aug. 3, 1492; harbor now silted up.

Palos, Cape. Cape on SE coast of Spain, E of Cartagena.

Pa'lo Se'co (pä'lō sā'kō). Leper colony, Canal Zone, on Bay of Panama on W side of canal entrance.

Pa'los Park (pä'lŭs). Village, Cook co., NE Illinois, 10 m. SW of Chicago; pop. 854; Argonne Forest Preserve and National Laboratory (atomic energy experiments).

Pal'os Ver'des Estates (păl'ōs vûr'dēz; păl'ŭs vûr'dĭs). City, Los Angeles co., SW California, S of Los Angeles; pop. 9564.

Pa·louse' (pà·lōōs') *or* **Pe·louse'.** 1 River 220 m. long in NW Idaho and SE Washington; rises in Latah co., NW Idaho, flows W across Washington border, turns S and empties into Snake river on E border of Franklin co.

2 Fertile hilly region, SE Washington and NW Idaho, N of Snake and Clearwater rivers; wheat growing.

Palpana, Cerro. See CERRO PALPANA.

Palti. See YAMDROK TSO.

Pa·lu'an Bay (pä·lōō'än). Inlet of South China Sea in NW coast of Mindoro, Phil. Is.; Americans secured anchorage here and seized town of **Paluan** Jan. 8, 1945.

Pa'lus (pā'lŭs). Latin, "marsh" or "morass," also a shallow sea, as in: (1) **Palus Maeotis.** Sea of AZOV. (2) **Palus Tattaeus.** The Tuz Lake (*q.v.*) in Turkey. (3) **Palus Labeatis.** See Lake SCUTARI. (4) **Palus Tritonis.** See Chott DJERID.

Pal'wal (pŭl'wäl). Town, S East Punjab, NW Indian Union, ab. 35 m. S of Delhi; pop. 10,807; a place of great antiquity, of importance in Aryan traditions, esp. in the Pandava kingdom.

Pam (păm). Town, New Caledonia, SW Pacific Ocean, on E coast of island near NW tip.

Pam'ban Channel (păm'băn). Shallow channel separating Rameswaram I. from the mainland of S India and connecting the Gulf of Mannar with Palk Strait.

Pa'me·ka·san' (pä'mä·kä·sän'). Town, S Madura I., Indonesia, ab. 55 m. E of Surabaja; pop. 13,403.

Pa'miers' (pà·myā'). Commune, Ariège dept., S France, on Ariège river 10 m. N of Foix; pop. 14,035; episcopal see; manufactures flour, paper, metal goods, lumber.

Pa·mir' (pà·mĭr'); *called by natives* **Bam-i-Dun·ya'** (bäm'ē·dōōm·yä'), "Roof of the World." Literally, valley at foot of a mountain peak; such a glacial valley at 12,000 to 14,000 ft. altitude; usually in the plural, **the Pa·mirs'** (pà·mĭrz'), a high altitude region of cen. Asia, mostly in Tadzhik S.S.R., Soviet Central Asia, partly on borders of Sinkiang, Kashmir, and Afghanistan. Many peaks above 20,000 ft.; highest in U.S.S.R. Stalin Peak in Tadzhik S.S.R. 24,590 ft.; highest in China in the Muztagh Ata, Kungur 25,146 ft.; many glaciers. Central mountain knot from which extend great ranges: Tien Shan to N, Kunlun and Karakoram to E, and Hindu Kush to W.

Pam'li·co (păm'lĭ·kō). 1 River bisecting Beaufort co., E North Carolina; actually the estuary of the Tar river (*q.v.*); at its head is Washington, the county seat.

2 County in North Carolina. See *Table* at NORTH CAROLINA.

Pamlico Sound. Sound 80 m. long and 8–30 m. wide, bet. E North Carolina mainland and islands off the coast; receives the Pamlico river on the W, and the Neuse river on the SW.

Pam'pa (păm'pà). Industrial city, ⊗ of Gray co., NW Texas, in the panhandle 52 m. ENE of Amarillo; pop. 24,664; center for agricultural (esp. grain, livestock) area; center of panhandle oil and gas field; oil refineries, carbon-black plants, oil-field supply houses.

Pampa, La. See LA PAMPA.

Pam'pa Aul·la'gas (päm'pä ou·yä'gäs). Town, Oruro dept., SW cen. Bolivia, near SW shore of Lake Poopó.

Pam·pan'ga (päm·päng'gä). 1 *or* **Ri'o Gran'de de Pampanga** (rē'ō grän'dä thä). River 120 m. long in cen. Luzon, Phil. Is.; rises in Caraballo Mts. on N border of Nueva Ecija prov., flows S into Pampanga and enters N Manila Bay in a wide swampy delta in Pampanga and Bulacan provs. Navigable for smaller vessels. Has many tributaries in fertile plain; main branch is the Chico.

2 Province, cen. Luzon, Phil. Is.; 827 sq. m.; pop. 375,281; ✳ San Fernando. Bounded on N by Tarlac, on NE by Nueva Ecija, on E and SE by Bulacan, on S by Manila Bay, on SW by Bataan, and on W by Zambales. Lies in S part of cen. Luzon plain watered by lower Pampanga river and tributaries. Mountains on the W boundary are part of the Zambales range; highest Pinatubo, on the border, 5842 ft.; in the NE is isolated volcanic peak of

Mt. Arayat 3867 ft., but province as a whole is most level of all in the Philippines. Chief occupation agriculture; fishing also important. Entire E part is covered by Candaba swamp and the delta of the Pampanga is an extensive mangrove swamp; many streams afford easy transportation. Great majority of inhabitants are Pampangans. Chief towns San Fernando, Lubao, Angeles, Arayat, and Mexico.

History: In pre-Spanish times home of Pampangans, a brave and progessive tribe, who had many prosperous settlements; overcome by Legaspi 1571–72 after strong resistance. Created 1571 as a province, but of much greater extent than now; its area gradually reduced, esp. in 1754, 1848, and 1860. One of first provinces to join revolution of 1896; relinquished by Americans Dec. 1941, but recovered Jan.–Feb. 1945.

Pampanga Chico. See CHICO.

Pam′pas (păm′păz; *attributively often* -păs; *Span.* päm′-päs). Vast grassy treeless plains of South America extending for nearly 1000 m. from the lower Paraná river to S cen. Argentina, SSW of Buenos Aires.

Pam′pas del Sa′cra·men′to (păm′päz thĕl sä′krä-män′tŏ). Plains in NE Peru, chiefly in S Loreto dept.

Pampeluna. See PAMPLONA.

Pam·phyl′i·a (păm·fĭl′ĭ·à; -fĭl′yà). Ancient district and Roman province in S Asia Minor, a narrow territory on the coast S of Pisidia and bet. Lycia and Cilicia; chief town was Perga. Subject in turn to all the empires that controlled Asia Minor; became Roman 130 B.C. and then included Pisidia. See LYCIA.

Pam·plo′na (päm·plō′nä). **1** City, Norte de Santander dept., N Colombia, on highway NE of Bucaramanga; pop. 13,126.
2 *formerly* **Pam′pe·lu′na** (päm′pà·lōō′nä); *anc.* **Pom·pae′lo** (pŏm·pē′lō). Fortified city, ✳ of Navarra prov., N Spain, 196 m. NNE of Madrid; pop. (1941 est.) 62,650; manufactures flour, soap, leather, liquors, linens, paper, pottery, wax, wines; copper, lead, and iron smelting and casting; 14th-cent. cathedral. Ancient capital of the Vascones; rebuilt by Pompey's sons 68 B.C.; taken by Goths, Franks, Moors; captured from Moors by Charlemagne 778 A.D.; became capital of kingdom of Navarre; on union 1515 of Navarre and Castile, made viceroyalty; fortified by Philip II 1571; captured by French 1808 and by Wellington 1813.

Pa·mun′key (pà·mŭng′kĭ). River ab. 80 m. long in E Virginia; formed by confluence of North Anna and South Anna rivers in E Hanover co., flows SE and unites with Mattaponi river at West Point to form York river.

Pa′na (pā′nà). City, Christian co., cen. Illinois, 30 m. S of Decatur; pop. 6432; coal mines nearby; rose nurseries.

Pa′na·du′ra (pŭn′à·dŏŏr′à). Seaport, W Western Province, Ceylon, on Indian Ocean 16 m. S of Colombo; pop. 12,946.

Pa′na·gyu′ri·shte (pä′nä·gū′rĭ·shtà). Town, N Plovdiv dept., S Bulgaria, in Balkan Mts. 35 m. NW of Plovdiv; pop. (1926) 9575.

Pan′a·ma (păn′à·mô; -mä; păn′à·mô′; -mä′); *Span.* **Pa′na·má′** (pä′nä·mä′). **1** Republic, S Central America, occupying the Isthmus of Panama (*q.v.*); bounded on N by the Caribbean Sea, on E by Colombia, on S by the Pacific Ocean, and on W by Costa Rica; 28,576 sq. m.; pop. (1940) 631,637 (excluding Canal Zone); ✳ Panama. Administratively has seven provinces: Bocas del Toro, Chiriquí, Coclé, Colón, Los Santos, Panama, Veraguas. Has coast line of ab. 760 m. on Pacific side and 470 m. on the Atlantic; traversed by two parallel ranges with valleys and plains in between; highest points are in W near Costa Rica boundary: Chiriquí volcano 11,070 ft., and Mt. Pando 10,371 ft.; in cen. part near the Canal Zone and in the E (Serranía del Darién) average height is ab. 3000 ft. Most important rivers the Chagres, Chepo, Tuira, and only large lake is Gatun in the Canal Zone (*q.v.*). Pacific coast indented by large Gulf of Panama containing several islands (esp. Pearl Is.); on W side

is Azuero Penin., and W of that is island of Coiba; on N coast are Mosquito Gulf and the Gulf of San Blas. Has fertile soil and well-forested mountain slopes; chief economic resources bananas, coffee, cacao, coconuts, and cabinet woods. Chief cities Panama, Colón, David, Penonomé, Santiago.

History: Coast skirted by Columbus 1502; settled at Darien 1510; at Isthmus of Panama, Balboa discovered Pacific Ocean 1513; city of Panama founded 1519; Portobelo the Atlantic port for important Spanish trade across the Isthmus; in viceroyalty of Peru before 18th cent.; in viceroyalty of New Granada, later part of Colombia (*q.v.*); in late 19th cent., projects for a canal across Panama were the subject of negotiations with U.S.; in 1903, Panama revolted from Colombia and was recognized by U.S. to whom it ceded Canal Zone; entered treaties with U.S. 1926, 1936; adopted new constitution 1940.
2 Province, E cen. Panama; 10,446 sq. m.; pop. 188,258; ✳ Panama; includes former Darién prov.
3 *or* **Panama City.** City, ✳ of the province and of the republic of Panama; pop. 111,893; founded 1519.

Panama, Gulf of. Large inlet of Pacific Ocean on S coast of Panama; the inner part (N of the Pearl Is.) on which the city of Panama is located is called the **Bay of Panama.**

Panama, Isthmus of; *formerly* **Isthmus of Dar′i·en′** (dâr′ĭ·ĕn′; dâr′ĭ·ĕn; *Span.* dä·ryän′). The link bet. North America and South America, separating the Atlantic and Pacific Oceans; 420 m. long; forms the Republic of Panama. Sometimes, in a restricted use, the name Isthmus of Panama is reserved for the crossing from Panama to Colón, the course of the Panama Canal, and the name Isthmus of Darien is reserved for the narrow crossing (46 m.) nearest the mainland of South America, and the name Isthmus of San Blas for the narrowest part (31 m.) S of the Gulf of San Blas. Isthmus also crossed by Panama R.R., in general course parallel to the canal, from Colón to Panama City, built 1850–55, and 46½ m. long.

Panama Canal. Ship canal with six pairs of locks built SE across the Isthmus of Panama from Colón on the Caribbean Sea to Balboa on the Bay of Panama, the inner part of the Gulf of Panama, and the Pacific Ocean; length 40.3 m. from shore to shore and 50.7 m. from deep water to deep water; width 100 to 300 ft.; minimum depth 41 ft.; highest elevation above sea level 85 ft. The Atlantic entrance to the Canal is 27 m. W of the Pacific entrance.

Panama Canal Zone. = CANAL ZONE.

Panama City. 1 City, ⊗ of Bay co., NW Florida, on Gulf of Mexico 30 m. ⊗ of Apalachicola river; pop. 33,275; incorp. 1925; paper mills; fisheries; Tyndall Air Force Base (Air Tactical School).
2 See PANAMA CITY.

Panamá Vieja. See OLD PANAMA.

Pan–A·mer′i·can Highway *or* **In′ter–A·mer′i·can Highway.** International highway system extending from Texas to Argentina with branches including all the countries of Central and South America; section bet. Laredo, Texas, and Panama City is 3356 m. long, bet. Panama-Colombia border and Buenos Aires, including alternate routes, was 8097 m. long in 1944; Laredo to Mexico City section completed 1936; during World War II construction work in Central America accelerated through aid of U.S. but only ab. 875 m. of the Central American section are paved and much of the rest, though some of it is dirt road, is impassable, esp. in wet weather; with the Alaska Highway (*q.v.*) and connecting highways in W United States will make a complete highway system from Alaska to Argentina.

Pan′a·mint Mountains (păn′à·mĭnt). Range in Inyo co., E California, W of Death Valley; highest peak Telescope Peak 11,045 ft.

Pa′na·on′ (pä′nä·ôn′). Island SE of Leyte I., Phil. Is., on W side of S end of Surigao Strait; 78 sq. m., 20 m.

long by 6 m. wide; pop. 24,769; chief town Liloan at N end. Occupied by Americans Oct. 21, 1944.

Pa·nar′i·a (pȧ·när′ĭ·ȧ; *Ital.* pä·nä′ryä); *anc.* **Eu·on′y·mus** (û·ŏn′ĭ·mŭs). One of the Lipari Is. (*q.v.*) in the Tyrrhenian Sea N of E Sicily.

Pa·na′ro (pä·nä′rȯ); *anc.* **Scul·ten′na** (skŭl·tĕn′ȧ). River ab. 60 m. long in N Italy; rises on slopes of Monte Cimone; flows N and NE into Po river.

Pa·nay′ (pä·nī′). 1 Island, one of the Visayan Is., cen. Phil. Is.; 4446 sq. m., 6th in size in Phil. Is.; pop. 1,310,174 (not including Guimaras I.); chief town Iloilo. Bounded on N by Sibuyan Sea, on NE by Visayan Sea, on E by Guimaras Strait, on S by Panay Gulf, and on W by Sulu Sea. Comprises three provinces of Antique, Capiz, and Iloilo. In World War II bombed by Allies Sept. 1944; occupied Mar. 18–20, 1945.
2 River ab. 50 m. long, E and cen. Capiz prov., Panay, Phil. Is.; rises in mountains of SW Capiz, flows NE and N to Sibuyan Sea at Capiz. Has four large tributaries; navigable for large native craft for a considerable distance.
3 Municipality, NE Capiz prov., Panay, Phil. Is., 3 m. SE of Capiz; pop. 15,800; old town, first Spanish settlement (1569) on Panay I. and second in the Philippines.

Panay Gulf. Large inlet of NE Sulu Sea, Phil. Is., formed by S Panay I., Guimaras I., and SW Negros I.; ab. 45 m. across from Naso Point to Negros coast; connects by Guimaras Strait with Visayan Sea.

Pan′cake′ Range (păn′kāk′). Range, SE cen. Nevada, in NE Nye co., extending N into White Pine co.

Pan′če·vo (pän′chĕ·vȯ); *Hung.* **Pan′cso·va** (pŏn′chŏ·vȯ). City, Voivodina autonomous prov., NE Yugoslavia, on Danube river opp. Belgrade; pop. 22,113; commercial and shipping center.

Pan·dan′ (pän·dän′). 1 Municipality, N coast of Catanduanes I., Albay prov., Luzon, Phil. Is.; pop. 15,460.
2 Municipality, N Antique prov., Panay, Phil. Is., on bend of coast 66 m. N of San Jose de Buenavista; pop. 19,561.

Pan de A·zú′car (pän dā ä·sōō′kär). 1 Small island in Pacific Ocean off NW coast of Atacama prov., Chile.
2 Peak 15,978 ft. in the cen. Andes Mts., in Venezuela, NE of Mérida.

Panderma. See BANDIRMA.

Pan′dhar·pur (pŭn′dĕr·pŏŏr). Town, SE Maharashtra state, W Indian Union, on Bhima river 185 m. ESE of Bombay; pop. 29,460; favorite place of pilgrimage in the Deccan, with celebrated temple to Vishnu.

Pan′do (pän′dȯ). 1 *formerly called* **Co·lo′ni·al Territories** (kȯ·lō′nĭ·ăl), *Span.* **Co·lo′nias** (kȯ·lō′nyäs). Department of Bolivia. See *Table* at BOLIVIA.
2 Town, Canelones dept., S Uruguay, just NE of Montevideo; pop. ab. 9600.

Pando, Mount. Peak 10,371 ft. in W Panama, in the Cordillera de Talamanca.

Pan·do′si·a (păn·dō′shĭ·ȧ; -shȧ). Ancient town, Lucania, S Italy, W of Heraclea; site of battle 326 B.C. in which Alexander I of Epirus was killed.

Pa·ne′as (pȧ·nē′ăs). = *Baniyas:* see CAESAREA PHILIPPI.

Pa′ne·ve·zhis′ (pä′nĕ·vā·zhēs′); *formerly* **Po·ne·vyezh′** (pŭ·nyĭ·vyĕsh′). 1 District of Lithuania. See *Table* at LITHUANIA.
2 City, its ✳, 55 m. NNE of Kaunas on Daugavpils-Šiauliai railroad; pop. (1938 est.) 26,508; breweries, tobacco and flax factories.

Pan·gae′us, Mount (păn·jē′ŭs); *Mod. Gr.* **Pan·gai′on O′ros** (päng·gyä′ôn ô′rôs). Mountain range, NE Greece, N of Strymonic Gulf; in ancient times noted for gold and silver mines.

Pan·ga′ni (päng·gä′nē). 1 River ab. 330 m. long in NE Tanganyika, E Africa, flowing from Mount Kilimanjaro SE into Indian Ocean opp. the island of Zanzibar. Called **Ru′vu** (rōō′vōō) in its lower course.
2 Coastal town at mouth of Pangani (or Ruvu) river, NE Tanganyika, E Africa; pop. ab. 3000.

Pan′ga·si·nan′ (päng′gä·sĕ·nän′). Province, N cen. Luzon, Phil. Is.; 2021 sq. m.; pop. 742,475; ✳ Lingayen; most populous of all provinces on Luzon. Bounded on N by Lingayen Gulf, La Union prov., and Benguet subprov., on NE by Nueva Vizcaya, on E and SE by Nueva Ecija, on S by Tarlac and Zambales provs., and on W by South China Sea. Central part is broad level plain of the Agno river; in the E has low mountains, the foothills of the Cordillera Central, and in NW on peninsula is somewhat hilly. Chief river the Bued in the N flowing into SE corner of Lingayen Gulf, which is the notable feature of the coast line. On NW shore of the gulf are Cabarruyan I. and Santiago I.; Cape Bolinao is NW point of the peninsula and Dasol Bay is on SW coast. One of richest provinces agriculturally of the Philippines; main products rice, tobacco, and coconuts; important industries salt making and fishing. Inhabitants mainly Pangasinans, Ilokanos, and Sambals. Chief towns Lingayen, San Carlos, Malasiqui, Dagupan, and Urdaneta.
History: Probably a native kingdom in pre-Spanish times; explored 1572 by Spaniards and soon visited by missionaries; created a province 1611; some boundaries changed in 18th cent. Scene of two revolts, 1660 and 1765; experienced rapid economic growth during latter half of 19th cent.; civil government established Feb. 1901. In Dec. 1941 scene of early Japanese landings; in reconquest of Philippines occupied by Americans Jan. 8–31, 1945.

Pang′e·rang′o (päng′ĕ·räng′ō). Extinct volcano 9905 ft. in W Java I., Indonesia, SE of Bogor; twin peak of Mt. Gede.

Panggong. See PANGONG.

Pan·gim′ *or* **Pan·jim′** (păN·zhēn′), *or* **New Go′a** (gō′ȧ). Town and seaport, ✳ of former Portuguese India and of Goa, on Arabian Sea at mouth of Mandavi river; pop. ab. 12,000; comprises the ruins of the old port (Old Goa) and the new town (New Goa) just to the W and nearer the coast; has good harbor and active trade. Became residence of the viceroy 1759.

Pang′kah, Cape (päng′kä). Cape on NE coast of Java I., Indonesia, on W side of entrance to Surabaja Strait.

Pang′ka·lan·bran′dan (päng′kä·län·brän′dän). Town, N Sumatra, Indonesia, near N end on Strait of Malacca 40 m. NNW of Medan; large oil fields.

Pang′kal·pi·nang′ (päng′käl·pĕ·näng′). Town, Indonesia, on NE coast of Bangka I.; pop. 11,970; port; highway center.

Pang′kiang′ (päng′jĭ·äng′) *or* **Man′gan′** (mäng′gän′). Mongol town, W Chahar prov., E Inner Mongolia, N China, on highway from Wanchuan to Urga.

Pang′kor (päng′kôr). Small island, Malaya, in Strait of Malacca, off W coast of S Malay Penin.; formerly belonged to Perak. Ceded to British 1826 and in 1874 became a part of the Dindings, in Penang settlement; retroceded to Perak 1935.

Pan·gla′o (päng·glä′ō). Low flat island off SW Bohol I., Phil. Is., separated from it by a narrow strait; 35 sq. m.; pop. 21,197.

Pang–nga. See PHANGNGA.

Pan′gong (pŭn′gông) *or* **Pang′gong** (pŭng′gông).
1 Long narrow lake in E Kashmir, N India, extending E across Tibetan border; elevation 14,000 ft., ab. 100 m. long; called **Nyak′tse** (nyäk′tsĕ) in Tibet.
2 Mountain range SW and S of Pangong lake; highest peak 22,060 ft.

Pangopango. See PAGO PAGO.

Pan·guil′ Bay (päng·gēl′). Narrow inlet ab. 23 m. long at SW corner of Iligan Bay, N coast of Mindanao, Phil. Is.; lies bet. Misamis Occidental and Lanao provs. Misamis is the port on N side of its entrance.

Pan′guitch (păn′gwĭch). City, ⊗ of Garfield co., S Utah, on Sevier river 34 m. ENE of Cedar City; pop. 1435; livestock raising, mining; sawmills, cheese factory. Situated near Bryce Canyon National Park and Cedar Breaks National Monument.

Pang′u·ta′ran (păng′ōō·tä′rän). **1** Island group, N Sulu Archipelago, Phil. Is., NW of Jolo; ab. 96 sq. m.; co-extensive with Pangutaran municipal dist., pop. 7442. Includes Pangutaran I., Panducan I., and ab. 12 small islands and islets. Heavily wooded; inhabitants mostly engaged in fishing. **2** Largest island of the group; 37 sq. m.; pop. 5437. **3** Town on E side of island.

Pan′han′dle (păn′hăn′d′l). **1** Any arm or projection of land like the handle of a pan; specif.: (a) NW Texas; chief town Amarillo. (b) NW Oklahoma; counties of Beaver, Texas, and Cimarron. (c) N West Virginia; counties along E bank of Ohio: Marshall, Ohio, Brooke, and Hancock; also, NE West Virginia, the "Eastern Panhandle," bet. Maryland and Virginia; hence, nickname "Panhandle State." (d) N Idaho, bet. Washington and Montana; N Shoshone, Kootenai, Bonner, and Boundary cos. (e) SE Alaska. **2** Town, ⊗ of Carson co., NW Texas; pop. 1958.

Panhormus. See PALERMO seaport.

Pa·ni′as (pȧ·nī′ăs). = CAESAREA PHILIPPI.

Pa′nié′, Mount (pȧ′nyä′). Highest peak 5413 ft. on the island of New Caledonia, SW Pacific Ocean, near NE coast.

Pa′ni·pat′ (pä′nē·pŭt′). Town, Punjab state, NW Indian Union, near Jumna river 53 m. N of Delhi; pop. 32,915; of great antiquity, dating back to legendary period; scene of three great battles: Mogul Emperor Baber conquered Ibrahim Lodi of Delhi, Afghan sultan, 1526; Akbar the Great routed army of king of Bengal 1556; Afghan prince Ahmad Shah overcame the Marathas 1761. Came under British rule 1803.

Pa·ni′qui (pä·nē′kê). Municipality, NE Tarlac prov., Luzon, Phil. Is., on a tributary of the Agno and on the Manila-Dagupan railroad 13 m. N of Tarlac; pop. 19,124; an important transportation center; taken Jan. 1945 by Americans in advance on Manila.

Pa·ni′zo (pä·nē′sô). Peak 18,025 ft. in S Potosí dept., SW Bolivia.

Panj. See AB-I-PANDJ.

Panjāb. Var. of PUNJAB.

Panj′deh (pănj′dĕ) or **Penj′deh** (pĕnj′dĕ). Village, Turkmen S.S.R., Soviet Central Asia, on E bank of Kushka river near its junction with the Murghab; scene Mar. 30, 1885 of clash bet. Russian and Afghan forces over a part of boundary in dispute; Afghans defeated and boundary finally settled June 18, 1886, but incident nearly caused war bet. England and Russia.

Panjim. See PANGIM.

Panj·ko′ra (pŭnj·kōr′ȧ). River ab. 90 m. long, N West Pakistan, in former North-West Frontier Province; rises in N Dir state and flows S to join the Swat river N of Peshawar.

Panj·nad′ (pŭnj·näd′). Literally "five rivers," the short course (ab. 50 m.) of the combined Sutlej and Chenab rivers on boundary of SW West Punjab and N Bahawalpur state, Pakistan, which joins the Indus at ab. 29°N. The other three streams are the Beas, Ravi, and Jhelum, rivers of the Punjab region, which join Sutlej and Chenab farther up in their courses.

Pan′kow (päng′kō). Suburban city N of Berlin, Germany; now a part of Greater Berlin.

Pan′na (pŭn′ä). **1** Former Indian state, Bundelkhand, Central India, Indian Union; 2580 sq. m. **2** Town, its ✳, 108 m. N of Jubbulpore; pop. 10,913.

Pan′na·nich or **Pan′na·nich Wells** (păn′ȧ·nĭk). Locality, Aberdeen co., NE Scotland, ab. 2 m. E of Ballater; chalybeate springs.

Pan·no′ni·a (pă·nō′nǐ·ȧ; -nōn′yȧ). Roman province including territory now mostly in Hungary and Yugo-slavia; ✳ Sabaria (Szombathely); W of the Danube, E of Noricum, and N of Dalmatia. Little known before 35 B.C.; conquered by Augustus 9 B.C. and incorporated with Illyria; at beginning of 1st cent. A.D. divided into Pannonia superior (W part) and Pannonia inferior (E part).

Pa·no′la (pȧ·nō′lȧ). Name of counties in two states of the U.S. See *Tables* at MISSISSIPPI and TEXAS.

Panopolis. See AKHMÎM.

Pan·or′mos (pă·nôr′mŏs; *Mod. Gr.* pän′ôr·môs). **1** Small seaport on Mykonos I., Cyclades, Greece; marble. **2** Seaport, Tenos I., Cyclades; pop. ab. 2000.

Panormus. See PALERMO seaport.

Pan·si′pit (pän·sē′pĭt). Stream ab. 8 m. long in Batangas prov., S Luzon, Phil. Is., flowing out of Lake Taal SSW to Balayan Bay. Towns of Taal and Lemery on it.

Pan′ta·nal′ (pănn′tȧ·näl′). Region of swamps and marshland, S Mato Grosso state, SW Brazil, extending ab. 100 m. along E bank of upper Paraguay river; traversed by several tributaries of the Paraguay including the São Lourenço and the Taquarí.

Pan′tar (pän′tär). Island of the Alor group, Lesser Sunda Is., Indonesia, E of Lomblen I., W of Alor I., and 60 m. NW of Timor; 30 m. long by 13 m. wide; pop. ab. 8000. Mountainous, with rugged coast; highest point 4450 ft. Separated on W from Lomblen by Alor Strait and on E from Alor by narrow **Pantar Strait** (ab. 8 m. wide).

Pan·teg′ (păn·tāg′). Former urban district, Monmouth-shire, W England; pop. (1931) 11,499; now in Pontypool.

Pan′tel·le·ri′a (pän′tăl·lȧ·rē′ä); *anc.* **Co·sy′ra** or **Cos·sy′ra** (kô·sī′rȧ). Italian heavily fortified island in the Mediterranean Sea E of NE Tunisia and ab. 70 m. SW of Sicily; 32 sq. m.; pop. (1931) ab. 10,000. In Roman times a place of banishment; in World War II suffered intense air and naval attack by Allies in June 1943 and surrendered June 11.

Pan′ther Mountain (pän′thĕr). **1** Peak 3865 ft. in the Adirondack Mts., Hamilton co., NE cen. New York. **2** Peak 3760 ft. in the Catskill Mts., Ulster co., SE New York.

Panther Peak. 1 Mountain 4448 ft. in the Adirondack Mts., Essex co., NE New York. **2** Mountain 6405 ft. in S Brewster co., W Texas.

Panth Pi·plo′da (pŭnt′h′ pǐ·plō′dȧ). A small administrative unit of former British India, under a chief commissioner; in W part of Central India Agency E of Jaora; 25 sq. m.; pop. (1941) 5267; now in Indian Union.

Panticapaeum. See KERCH.

Pan′ti·co′sa (pän′tê·kō′sä). Village, Huesca prov., NE Spain, in the Pyrenees near French border; medicinal baths and springs.

Pan′tin′ (pän′tăn′). Commune, Seine dept., N France, NE suburb of Paris; pop. 37,716; manufactures cotton thread, tools, foundry products; battle 1814.

Pan·tón′ (pän·tôn′). Commune, Lugo prov., NW Spain, 37 m. S of Lugo; pop. 10,797.

Pan·tu′kan (pän·tōō′kän). Municipality, cen. Davao prov., Mindanao, Phil. Is., on NE shore of Davao Gulf opp. N end of Samal I.; pop. 15,591.

Pá′nu·co (pä′nōō·kô). **1** River ab. 240 m. long of cen. Mexico; rises in Hidalgo state, flows NE into the Gulf of Mexico 7 m. below Tampico. **2** Town, Veracruz state, E Mexico, 25 m. WSW of Tampico; pop. 5942.

Pão de A·çú′car (pouN′ th[ê] ȧ·sōō′kĕr); *Eng.* **Sug′ar-loaf′ Mountain** (shŏŏg′ĕr·lôf′). Rocky peak 1280 ft. in Rio de Janeiro city on W side of entrance to Guanabara Bay, SE Brazil; aerial railroad; fine view of city from its summit.

Pao′ki′ (pou′kē′), *formerly* **Pao′chi′** (-chē′). Town, W Shensi prov., NE cen. China, on Wei river W of Sian.

Paoking. See SHAOYANG.

Pa·o′la (pȧ·ō′lȧ; pǐ-). City, ⊗ of Miami co., E Kansas, 40 m. SSW of Kansas City; pop. 4784; railroad and trade center.

Pa′o·la (pä′ô·lä). Commune, Cosenza prov., Calabria, S Italy, on Tyrrhenian Sea 12 m. WNW of Cosenza; pop. 13,918; 15th-cent. chapel; suffered from earthquake 1887.

Pa·o′li (pä·ō′lǐ; pǐ-). **1** Town, ⊗ of Orange co., S Indiana, 22 m. S of Bedford; pop. 2754.

2 Locality, Chester co., SE Pennsylvania, ab. 8 m. NE of West Chester; pop. (1950) 3029.

Paoning. See LANGCHUNG.

Pao'shan' (bou'shän'); *formerly* **Yung'chang'** (yōong'-chäng'). Town, W Yunnan prov., S China, on Burma Road bet. the Salween and Mekong rivers 70 m. SW of Tali; alt. 5500 ft.; connected by branch highway through Tengchung with the Stilwell Road at Myitkyina in N Burma; 416 m. from Kunming by road. Very old walled town rebuilt 600 years ago.

Paoting. See TSINGYUAN.

Pao'tow' *or* **Pao'tou'** (bou'tō'). Town, cen. Suiyuan prov., cen. Inner Mongolia, N China, on left bank of the Hwang Ho at its great bend; W terminus of Peiping-Suiyuan railroad 90 m. W of Kweisui; has long been a trading town for Mongolian products. Fighting here in Chinese civil war 1945.

Pá'pa (pä'pŏ). City, W Hungary, 80 m. W of Budapest; pop. 20,344.

Pap'a·go Sa·gua'ro (păp'á·gō sá·[g]wä'rō). Former national monument, Maricopa co., SW cen. Arizona; 2050 acres; giant saguaros.

Pa·pa'i·ko'u (pä·pä'ĕ·kō'ōō). Village, South Hilo dist., Hawaii co., Hawaii, on E coast of Hawaii I. N of Hilo; pop. 1591.

Papal States. See STATES OF THE CHURCH.

Pa'pan·da'yan (pä'pän·dä'yän). Volcanic peak 8744 ft., W Java, Indonesia, ab. 12 m. SW of Garut. Frequently climbed by tourists for fine view of Garut plain; great eruption Aug. 1772.

Pa·pan'tla de O·lar'te (pä-pän'tlä thä ō-lär'tä). Town, Veracruz state, E Mexico, NNW of Jalapa; pop. 6644; nearby is an ancient pyramid, 82 ft. square at the base, 60 ft. high, covered with carvings: hieroglyphics, human figures, and reptilian creatures.

Pa'pas (pä'päs); *anc.* **A·rax'os** (á·răk'sŏs) *or* **A·rax'us** (-sŭs). Cape on NW coast of Peloponnesus, S Greece, 20 m. W of Patras.

Pa'pa Stour (pä'pä stōōr'). One of the Shetland Is., NE of N Scotland.

Pa'pa·wa'i Point (pä'pä·wä'ĕ; -vä'ĕ). Point on SW coast of Maui I., Hawaii, NW of Maalaea Bay.

Pa'pe·e'te (pä'pä·ā'tä; *popularly* pá-pē'tĕ). Seaport on NW coast of the island of Tahiti, Society Is., French Oceania, W Pacific Ocean; ✶ of Society Is. and ✶ of French Oceania; pop. (1941) 11,614; commercial town, center for trading schooners and port for steamers to New Zealand, Australia, and San Francisco; has modern buildings, clubs, hotels, and a normal school.

Papendorp. See WOODSTOCK, Union of South Africa.

Paph'la·go'ni·a (păf'lá·gō'nĭ·á). Ancient country and Roman province in N Asia Minor, on the Black Sea, and bounded on the E by Pontus, on the S by Galatia, and on the W by Bithynia. A mountainous country, one of the oldest nations of Asia Minor, but not important historically; subject much of the time to Pontus. Had several Greek colonies, esp. at Sinope.

Pa'phos (pä'fŏs; *Mod. Gr.* pä'fŏs). **1** District, W Cyprus, E Mediterranean Sea; 537 sq. m.; pop. 43,769; ✶ Ktima.

2 Town, SW coast of Cyprus, in Paphos dist., 1 m. S of Ktima; pop. (1942 est.) 4964. The old town of Paphos was probably founded by Phoenicians; its site is ab. 26 m. W of Limassol and 1 m. inland; long famous as the seat of worship of Aphrodite (Cypris) who is said by one legend to have landed here after her birth among the waves near Cythera (see CERIGO); hence, called the Paphian goddess; suffered greatly from earthquakes and several times rebuilt. New Paphos (the present town) was founded c. 1200 B.C., probably by Greeks, on the coast 10 m. WNW of old Paphos and after the Ptolemaic conquest of Cyprus 295 B.C. and Roman occupation 58 B.C. superseded the older town and became important Roman administrative city; its trade in olive oil was esp. flourishing. Visited by St. Paul (*Acts* xiii. 6–13). De-

stroyed by Saracens 960 A.D. and rebuilt in modern times; still has many Roman remains.

Papien. See BO.

Pa·pil'lion (pá-pĭl'yŭn). Village, ✶ of Sarpy co., E Nebraska; pop. 2235.

Pa'pi'neau' (pá'pē'nō'; *Angl.* păp'ĭ·nō). County, Quebec, Canada. See *Table* at QUEBEC.

Pa'pi'neau'ville' (pá'pē'nō'vĭl'; *Angl.* păp'ĭ·nō·vĭl). Village, ✶ of Papineau co., SW Quebec, Canada, on Ottawa river, 35 m. ENE of Ottawa; pop. 1024.

Paps of Ju'ra (păps, jōōr'á). Three mountains on Jura I., in the Inner Hebrides, off W coast of Scotland; highest peak 2571 ft.

Pap'u·a (păp'ŭ·á). See NEW GUINEA.

Papua, Gulf of. Large gulf on S coast of Papua, SE New Guinea, an inlet of the Coral Sea; Port Moresby lies at the E entrance; Kikori river enters at the N and Fly river at SW.

Papua, Territory of; *formerly* **British New Guinea.** The southeastern section of New Guinea I., a territory of Australia; 90,540 sq. m. (mainland 87,786 sq. m.); pop. Europeans (1962 est.) 10,697, Papuans 528,856; ✶ Port Moresby. See *Map* at NEW GUINEA. Includes also the D'Entrecasteaux, Trobriand, and Woodlark Is. and the Louisiade Archipelago off E coast. Bounded on N by North-East New Guinea, on E by Solomon Sea and island groups, on S by Coral Sea, Gulf of Papua, and Torres Strait, and on W by Neth. New Guinea. Has high mountain ranges in NW part and the high Owen Stanley Range in SE; highest point Mt. Victoria NE of Port Moresby 13,240 ft. Coast line indented at S by large Gulf of Papua, with shores low and swampy at deltas of many rivers, esp. the Fly, Kikori, and Purari; on E are several bays: Holnicote, Dyke Acland, Collingwood, Goodenough, and Milne. East Cape marks most easterly point of New Guinea at 151° and Cape Ward Hunt on E coast is near North-East New Guinea boundary. Rich in resources but largely undeveloped; chief exports coconuts, coffee, rubber, and much gold. Natives are divided into Negritos, true Negroid Papuans, and mixed Melanesians. Chief villages, besides Port Moresby, are Samarai, Buna, Daru, and Kikori.

History: South coasts of New Guinea (Papua) visited in 16th and 17th cents. by Portuguese and Spanish navigators and later by French and English. Fly river discovered 1842. Region proclaimed British 1883 and 1884 but not annexed until 1888 (British New Guinea). Australian territory proclaimed Sept. 1906. Invaded July 1942 by Japanese but enemy forces confined to Milne Bay and Buna-Gona areas; all driven out by Jan. 20, 1943.

Pa'pun (pä'pŏŏn). Town, ✶ of Salween dist., Lower Burma, on a tributary of the Salween 120 m. NE of Rangoon; pop. 1422.

Pa'que·tá' (pá'kĕ·tá'). Island in Guanabara Bay NE of the city of Rio de Janeiro, Brazil.

Pa·rá' (pá·rá'). **1** Name given to the navigable E mouth of the Amazon river in Brazil, flowing S and E of Marajó I.; ab. 200 m. long; 40 m. wide at its mouth; receives Tocantins river from the S.

2 State of Brazil. See *Table* at BRAZIL.

3 See BELÉM.

Pa'ra·bia'go (pä'rä·byä'gō). Commune, Milano prov., Lombardy, N Italy, 14 m. NW of Milan; pop. (1931) 11,178.

Pa'ra·ca'le (pä'rä·kä'lā). Municipality on an inlet of the N coast of Camarines Norte, Luzon, Phil. Is., ab. 16 m. NW of Daet; pop. 15,198; has rich mines of gold and coal that were worked by the Spaniards for two centuries.

Pa·ra'cas Peninsula (pä-rä'käs). Peninsula extending from W cen. coast of Peru, S of Lima.

Pa'ra'cel' Islands (pá'rá·sĕl'); *Jap.* **Hi·ra·ta Gun·to** (hĕ·rä·tä gōōn·tō). Group of small islands and reefs in

the South China Sea ab. 250 m. E of cen. Annam, French Indochina, 16°30′N; claimed by France and Japan. Occupied by Japan 1939; returned to China after World War II.

Pa′ra·ćin (pä′rä·tyĕn). Commune, E Serbia, Yugoslavia, ab. 75 m. SE of Belgrade; pop. 7265; glass.

Paraclete. See NOGENT-SUR-SEINE.

Par′a·dise (păr′à·dīs). **1** Urban area, Butte co., N California, N of Sacramento; pop. 8268.
2 Urban area, Stanislaus co., W California, W of San Francisco; pop. 5616.

Paraetonium. See MATRÛH.

Par′a·gould (păr′à·gōōld). City, ⊗ of Greene co., NE Arkansas, 20 m. NE of Jonesboro; pop. 9947; trade center for cotton-growing and truck-gardening region.

Pa·ra′gua (pä·rä′gwä). **1** *or* **Pi·ra′gua** (pĕ-). River ab. 230 m. long in E Bolivia; flows NW into Guaporé river.
2 See PALAWAN.
3 River 435 m. long in E Venezuela; a tributary of the Caroni.

Pa′ra·gua·ná′ Peninsula (pä′rä·gwä·nä′). Peninsula extending from NW coast of Venezuela, enclosing Gulf of Venezuela from the E.

Pa′ra·gua·rí′ (pä′rä·gwä·rē′). **1** Department of Paraguay. See *Table* at PARAGUAY.
2 Town, its ✳, S cen. Paraguay, 35 m. SE of Asunción; pop. ab. 11,775; founded 1775; in wars of independence, scene of victory over Argentine army 1811.

Pa′ra·guas·sú′ (pä′rä·gwä·sōō′). River ab. 320 m. long, Baía state, E Brazil; flows E to All Saints Bay.

Par′a·guay (păr′à·gwī; -gwä; *Span.* pä′rä·gwī′). **1** River ab. 1500 m. long, S cen. South America, navigable for larger vessels to Concepción, for small craft for almost its entire length; rises in Mato Grosso state, SW Brazil, where its upper tributaries form small sections of boundary with Bolivia; flows S to form boundary bet. Brazil and NE Paraguay and, after crossing cen. Paraguay, a section of boundary bet. SW Paraguay and Argentina; empties into the Paraná at SW corner of Paraguay.
2 Republic, cen. South America; bounded on N by Bolivia and Brazil, on E by Brazil and Argentina, on S and W by Argentina; ab. 157,006 sq. m.; pop. (1945 est.) 1,182,877, (later est.) 1,260,424; ✳ Asunción. Divided by the Paraguay river into an E (Oriental) section, 61,693 sq. m., and a W (Occidental) section, 95,313 sq. m., the W section including the part of the Chaco (*q.v.*) which was added to Paraguay 1938. Divided into the following 16 departments (for pronunciation of their names, see their individual entries):

NAME	LOCA-TION	POP.	CAPITAL
	PARAGUAY ORIENTAL		
Alto Paraná	E	3,940	Tacurupucú
Amambay	E	17,861	Pedro Juan Caballero
Caaguazú	E cen.	75,283	Coronel Oviedo
Caazapá	S	72,373	Caazapá
Central	S	333,000	Asunción
Concepción	E	46,823	Concepción
Cordillera	cen.	155,953	Caacupé
Guairá	S cen.	90,528	Villarrica
Itapúa	SE	101,325	Encarnación
Misiones	S	48,531	San Juan Bautista
Neembucú	SW corner	52,787	Pilar
Paraguarí	S	148,768	Paraguarí
San Pedro	cen.	56,441	San Pedro
	PARAGUAY OCCIDENTAL		
Boquerón	NW		Mariscal Estigarribia
Olimpo	NE		Fuerte Olimpo
Presidente Hayes	W cen.		Villa Hayes

Country is mostly low wooded plains, with much swamp land; in E are densely forested low ridges; highest point not much over 2200 ft. *Chief rivers:* Paraguay (see 1, above), the Alto Paraná on E border, and the Pilcomayo which is W tributary of the Paraguay and which forms a section of the boundary with Argentina. *Lakes:* Only large one Lake Ypoa, ab. 100 sq. m., in S near

Paraguay river. *Inhabitants:* Most of inhabitants are of Indian (Guarani) descent. *Chief industries:* Cultivation and preparation of Paraguay tea, agriculture, cattle raising, and timber cutting. *Chief exports:* Quebracho extract, Paraguay tea, meat products, hides, cotton, tobacco, and fruit. *Chief cities:* Asunción, Concepción, Villarrica, Itá, Carapeguá.

History: Asunción, founded 1538, capital of La Plata region; field of Jesuit work among Guarani Indians 1605–1769; a part of viceroyalty of Buenos Aires (*q.v.*), it revolted from Spain 1811; governed by Francia as dictator 1814–40, by his nephew Carlos A. López as president with dictatorial powers 1844–62, and by the latter's son Francisco Solano López 1862–70, who provoked a disastrous war with Brazil, Argentina, and Uruguay 1865–70 by which Paraguay lost 55,000 sq. m. of territory and more than 1,000,000 of its people; after long dispute with Bolivia over the Chaco region, fought Chaco war 1932–35; peace treaty signed July 21, 1938; adopted new constitution 1940 which, however, was set aside on establishment of absolute rule under Higinio Morínigo Nov. 30, 1940; severed diplomatic relations with the Axis powers Jan. 1942; scene of unsuccessful rebellion against the government 1947; ousted Morínigo June 1948; scene of six revolts 1948–49.

Pa′ra·hi′ba *or* **Pa′ra·hy′ba** (pà′rà·ē′và). Older spellings of PARAÍBA.

Parahitinga. See PARAÍBA (DO SUL).

Pa′ra·í′ba (pà′rà·ē′và). **1** Either of two rivers of Brazil: (a) **Paraíba** *or* **Paraíba do Nor′te** (ₜhōō nôr′tĕ), ab. 240 m. long, in Paraíba state; flows NE and E into Atlantic Ocean. (b) **Paraíba** *or* **Paraíba do Sul** (sōōl′), ab. 660 m. long, in E São Paulo and Rio de Janeiro states; flows SW, then turns NE to traverse half the length of Rio de Janeiro state and empty into Atlantic Ocean near Campos; called **Pa′ra·hi·tin′ga** (pà′rà·ē·tēɴɢ′gà) in its upper course.
2 State of Brazil. See *Table* at BRAZIL.
3 See JOÃO PESSOA.

Paraíso, El. See EL PARAÍSO.

Par′a·kou′ (păr′à·kōō′). Town, E cen. Dahomey, West Africa; terminus of railroad from Cotonou.

Par′a·mar′i·bo (păr′à·măr′ĭ·bō). Seaport city, N Surinam, on the Suriname river ab. 13 m. from its mouth; ✳ of Surinam; pop. (1941) 56,233; constitutes Paramaribo dist.; has fine harbor; government house, museum, Roman Catholic cathedral, medical college. Originally an Indian village; became site of French settlement 1640; made capital of colony of Surinam by Lord Willoughby of Parham 1650; partly destroyed by fire 1821 and 1832; before abolition of slavery 1863, estates in vicinity produced much sugar, coffee, and maize.

Pa′ra·mé′ (pà′rà′mā′). Commune, Ille-et-Vilaine dept., NW France, E of St-Malo; pop. 4161; seaside resort.

Par′a·mount (păr′à·mount). City, Los Angeles co., SW California, SE of Los Angeles; pop. 27,249.

Pa·ram′us (pà·răm′ŭs). Borough, Bergen co., NE corner of New Jersey, 6 m. NE of Paterson; pop. 23,238; grows vegetables, esp. celery.

Pa·ra·mu·shi·ro (pä·rä·mōō·shĕ·rŏ) *or* **Pa·ra·mu·shi·ru** (-rōō). Large island at N end of Kuril Is., separated by narrow channel from Shumushu, the northernmost of the chain; highest point 5955 ft.; chief towns Kashiwabara at N end and Masukawa on E coast. Under Japanese strongly fortified naval base, frequently bombed by American planes 1943–44; became Russian 1945 (see KURIL ISLANDS).

Par′a·myth′i·a (păr′à·mĭth′ĭ·à; *Mod. Gr.* pä′rä·mĕthyä′). Town, NW Epirus, Greece, near coast SW of Ioannina.

Pa′ran, Wilderness of (pā′răn; pâr′ăn). Desert region of indefinite location; probably in NE part of Sinai Penin., Egypt, extending into S Palestine; here according to the Biblical account the Israelites sojourned 38 years before entering the Promised Land (*Num.* x. 12).

ARGENTINA, CHILE, PARAGUAY, URUGUAY

Statute Miles

0   100   200   300

⊛ Capitals of Countries

PUBLISHED BY G. & C. MERRIAM COMPANY
SPRINGFIELD, MASS.
PREPARED BY J. W. CLEMENT CO., BUFFALO, N. Y.

Pa·ra·ná' (*Span.* pä'rä·nä'; *Port.* pà'rà·nà'). **1** River 2040 m. long, SE cen. South America; formed by confluence of Rio Grande and Paranaíba river in S cen. Brazil; flows S (sometimes known as **Al'to Paraná** [*Span.* äl'tô; *Port.* -tōō]) and forms SE and S boundary of Paraguay (Guaíra, *q.v.*, cataract located here); continues S through NE Argentina (as **Paraná**) and empties into Río de la Plata; total length, with Rio Grande, 2720 m.; its chief tributaries are: in Brazil (on left bank), Tietê, Paranapanema, Ivaí, Pequerí, Iguassú; (on right bank) Verde, Pardo, Ivinheima; in Argentina, Salado and Gualeguay.
2 River ab. 300 m. long, a headstream of the Tocantins in E Goiaz state, cen. Brazil.
3 State of Brazil. See *Table* at BRAZIL.
4 City, ✱ of Entre Ríos prov., E Argentina, on left bank of Paraná river 80 m. N of Rosario; pop. (est.) 76,600; has large river trade (ocean-going steamers) and railroad trade; founded 1730 by colonists from Santa Fe; capital of the Republic 1852–61.
Pa·ra·na·guá' (pà'rà·nà·gwà'). Town, chief port of Paraná state, S Brazil; pop. (1940 est.) 13,027; chief export Paraguay tea; founded 1560.
Pa·ra·na·í'ba (pà'rà·nà·ē'và), *older spelling* **Pa·ra·na·hi'ba** (-nà·ē'và). One of the headstreams of Paraná river, ab. 530 m. long; rises in W cen. Minas Gerais state, E Brazil; flows W and SW to unite with Rio Grande and form Paraná river.
Pa·ra·na·'pa·ne'ma (pà'rà·nà'pà·nä'má). River ab. 470 m. long, SE Brazil; rises in SE São Paulo state, flows W, forming part of boundary bet. São Paulo and Paraná states, and empties into Paraná river.
Pa·ra·ña'que (pä'rä·nyä'kå). Municipality, SW Rizal prov., Luzon, Phil. Is., on SE shore of Manila Bay ab. 4 m. S of S boundary of Manila; pop. 21,125; produces fine embroidery. Nichols Field just to the E.
Pa'rang (pä'räng). **1** Town (municipal district), SW coast of Jolo I., Sulu prov., Phil. Is., 11 m. SW of Jolo; pop. 22,572.
2 Village, Cotabato prov., SW Mindanao, Phil. Is., on Illana Bay NE of Cotabato; U.S. troops landed here Apr. 19, 1945.
Parapanisus. See PAROPAMISUS.
Pa·ras'nath, Mount (pà·rŭs'nät·h'); *also* **Parasnath Hill.** Eminence 4500 ft. in E Bihar, NE Indian Union, 50 m. E of Hazaribagh; sacred spot and place of pilgrimage of Jains; burial place of their chief saint.
Pa'ray'-le-Mo'nial' (pà'rā'lĕ-mô'nyàl'). Commune, Saône-et-Loire dept., E cen. France, ab. 55 m. NNW of Lyons; pop. 5387; next to Lourdes the most frequently visited pilgrim resort in France; became famous from visions of 17th-cent. nun, Marguerite Marie Alacoque (canonized 1920), origin of the cult of Sacred Heart of Jesus; has notable church (Notre-Dame) and convent of the Visitation.
Par'ba·ti (pär'bà·tï). River 220 m. long, Central India; flows N through W Madhya Pradesh and SE Rajasthan, forming in its course sections of the E Rajasthan boundary, and empties into Chambal river on that boundary.
Par'bha·ni (pŭrb'hà·nï). Town, SE Maharashtra state, Indian Union, 70 m. ESE of Aurangabad; pop. 14,755.
Par'chim (pär'кïm). Commune, Schwerin district, N Germany, 23 m. SE of Schwerin; pop. 11,857. Founded 1210; had prosperous trade in 14th cent. but lost it in Thirty Years' War.
Par'dee Dam *and* **Reservoir** (pär'dĕ; -dē). See UNITED STATES, *Dams and Reservoirs.*
Par'do (pàr'dōō). **1** River ab. 310 m. long in E Brazil; rises in N Minas Gerais state, flows NE and E into Atlantic Ocean.
2 River ab. 290 m. long in S Brazil; rises in SW Minas Gerais state, flows NW to Rio Grande in São Paulo state.
3 River ab. 230 m. long in S Mato Grosso state, SW Brazil; flows SE into Paraná river.
Par'du·bi'ce (pär'dōō·bï'tsĕ). *Ger.* **Par'du·bitz** (pär'-**

dōō·bïts). Industrial town, E Bohemia, Czechoslovakia, on Labe (Elbe) river 60 m. E of Prague; pop. (1930) 28,841; historical town, with remains of walls, a church of the 13th cent., a royal castle; also many fine modern buildings.
Pa're (pä'rā). Town, East Java prov., Indonesia, 50 m. SW of Surabaja; pop. 22,388.
Parecis, Serra dos. See SERRA DOS PARECIS.
Pa're Mountains (pä'rā). Range in NE Tanganyika, British East Africa; N of N end of the range is Mt. Kilimanjaro.
Parenzo. See POREČ.
Pa're·pa're (pä'rà·pä'rà); *also* **Pa're Pa're.** Seaport town, Celebes, Indonesia, on W coast of SW peninsula 80 m. N of Makassar; pop. 6273.
Parganas, Twenty-four. See TWENTY-FOUR PARGANAS.
Par'ham Harbour (pär'ăm). Inlet of **Parham Sound** on N coast of Antigua I., Leeward Is., Brit. W. Indies; site of seaplane base leased to U.S. 1941. See ANTIGUA.
Pa·ri'a (pà·rē'à). River ab. 65 m. long, S Utah; rises in S Garfield co., flows S across Arizona border and into Colorado river at Lees Ferry.
Pa'ria, Gulf of (pä'ryä). Inlet of Atlantic Ocean lying bet. the W coast of the island of Trinidad and the Venezuelan mainland; enclosed on the N by **Paria Peninsula,** extending E from NE coast of Venezuela. See DRAGON'S MOUTHS and SERPENT'S MOUTH.
Pa·ri'a Plateau (pà·rē'à). Tableland 6000 to 7300 ft. in N Coconino co., N Arizona.
Pa·rí'cu·tin (pä·rē'kōō-tēn). Former village, Michoacán state, Mexico, 200 m. W of Mexico City; site of new volcano **Parícutin** 9100 ft. which grew to a height of 1500 ft. above its base in 8 months; started Feb. 20, 1943 in a cornfield.
Pa·ri'da (pä·rē'thà). Island at entrance to Charco Azul Bay on extreme SW Panama.
Parida, La. See Cerro BOLÍVAR.
Pa·ri'ka (pà·rē'kà). Town, N British Guiana, Essequibo co., on E bank of Essequibo river at its mouth, 20 m. W of Georgetown; pop. (1931) 463.
Pa·ri'ma (pä·rē'mà). **1** See Rio BRANCO.
2 Mythical lake indicated on early maps of South America; at first connected with story of El Dorado, but later placed in Guiana.
3 Short headstream ab. 50 m. long, of the Uraricoera river, NW Brazil, rising in the Serra Parima and flowing N; first explored 1924 by hydroplane; also, formerly, name given to main course of Branco and Uraricoera.
Parima, Serra. See SERRA PARIMA.
Pa·ri'ñas, Point (pä·rē'nyäs). Extreme W point of South America, in NW Peru at 81°20'W.
Par'is (pär'ĭs). **1** City, a ⊗ of Logan co., W Arkansas, 42 m. SSE of Fort Smith; pop. 3007; coal mining.
2 City, ⊗ of Bear Lake co., SE Idaho; pop. 746.
3 City, ⊗ of Edgar co., E Illinois, 38 m. S of Danville; pop. 9823; railroad and farm trading center; broom factories.
4 City, ⊗ of Bourbon co., NE Kentucky, 19 m. NE of Lexington; pop. 7791; in bluegrass section.
5 Town, Oxford co., W Maine, 18 m. NW of Lewiston; pop. 3601.
6 City, ⊗ of Monroe co., NE Missouri; pop. 1393.
7 City, ⊗ of Henry co., NW Tennessee, 23 m. W of Tennessee river; pop. 9325; farm trade center, market for cotton, tobacco, livestock; manufactures cosmetics, patent medicines, shirts, cigars, pottery; clay deposits.
8 City, ⊗ of Lamar co., NE Texas, 90 m. NE of Dallas; pop. 20,977; shipping point for agricultural area (esp. cotton, poultry, livestock); manufactures processed foods, cotton and cottonseed products, furniture, boxes; railroad center.
9 Town, Brant co., SE Ontario, Canada, 7 m. WNW of Brantford; pop. 5249; gypsum quarries; manufactures

refrigerators, road machinery, flour, cement, paint, hosiery, and knitted goods.

10 (păr'ĭs; *Fr.* pȧ·rē'); *anc.* **Lu·te'ti·a** (lṳ·tē'shĭ·ȧ; -shȧ) *or* **Lutetia Pa·ris'i·o'rum** (pȧ·rĭz'ĭ·ō·r'ŭm), *later* **Pa·ris'i·i** (pȧ·rĭz'ĭ·ī). City and river port, ✻ of Seine dept. and ✻ of France, on both banks of Seine river 110 m. ESE of Le Havre and 107 m. from the sea; pop. 2,829,746; one of world's greatest population centers, and one of its leading cultural and intellectual centers; financial, commercial, industrial, artistic, and intellectual center of France; served by numerous beautiful boulevards (many built on sites of former city walls), including Boulevard de Sébastopol, Rue Saint-Michel, Rue de Rivoli, Avenue des Champs-Élysées, Avenue de la Grande Armée, Boulevard Saint-Germain, Rue Royal, Rue du Faubourg Saint-Honoré; city centers around Île de la Cité, an island in Seine river; famed Latin quarter, inhabited chiefly by students (whence its name), lies S of Seine; public squares and parks include the Tuileries gardens, Place de la Concorde (containing sculptured fountains and obelisk from Luxor), Place de l'Étoile (with world's largest triumphal arch), Luxembourg gardens, Jardin des Plantes, Places de la République, d'Iéna, de la Bastille, Vendôme, des Innocents (containing a famous fountain), and des États-Unis, and the Champ de Mars (in which is located the famous 984-ft. Eiffel Tower); world-famous buildings include the Hôtel-Dieu (founded 600 A.D.; one of oldest hospitals in Europe), Palais de Justice, 12th-cent. Cathedral of Notre Dame, Louvre (containing richest collection of art in world), Luxembourg palace, Tribunal de Commerce, Sainte-Chapelle, L'Opéra, Palais de l'Élysée (residence of president of France), Bibliothèque Nationale, Panthéon, church of the Madeleine, Hôtel des Invalides, the Tuileries, Bastille, church of Saint-Germain-des-Prés, Halles Centrales, and Bourse; educational institutions include the University of Paris (one of oldest in Europe) of which the Sorbonne is a part, the Institut de France, Collège de France, Institut Pasteur, and the famous Observatoire; noted Père-Lachaise cemetery; enormous commercial and industrial activity; clothing fashion center of world.

History: Pre-Roman settlement on island in Seine; captured 52 B.C. and fortified by Romans; made bishopric in 3d cent. A.D.; came to Clovis, king of the Franks, after victory of 486; seat of a Carolingian count; withstood severe siege by Northmen 885–887; after accession to French throne of Hugh Capet 987, definitely established as capital of France; University of Paris grew up in 12th cent. and was chartered 1200; held by English 1420–36; scene of leading events of French Revolution 1789–92; entered by Allies after Napoleon's defeat 1814; besieged and taken by Germans 1870–71; the following important treaties were signed here: 1763 (concluding Seven Years' War), 1783 (War of American Independence), 1814 and 1815 (Napoleonic Wars), 1856 (Crimean War), 1898 (Spanish-American War); Declaration of Paris signed here 1856; scene of Peace Conference at end of World War I 1919; occupied by Germans June 14, 1940; liberated by Allies Aug. 19–24, 1944. See FRANCE.

Pa·ri'ta, Gulf of (pȧ·rē'tȧ; *Span.* pä·rē'tä). Inlet of the Gulf of Panama on the W, extending into W cen. Panama at the base of Azuero Penin.

Pa'rit Bun'tar (pä'rĭt bŏŏn'tär). Town, NW Perak, on border of Province Wellesley, Federation of Malaya; pop. 2929; station on railroad leading to Prai.

Par'i·um (pâr'ĭ·ŭm) *or* **Par'i·on** (-ŏn) Town in ancient Mysia, Asia Minor, on the SW shore of the Propontis (Sea of Marmara).

Park. Name of counties in three states of the U.S. See *Tables* at COLORADO, MONTANA, WYOMING.

Park City. **1** Former town, Knox co., E Tennessee; now part of Knoxville.

2 City, Summit co., NE Utah, 22 m. ESE of Salt Lake City; pop. 1366; silver, lead, zinc mines in vicinity.

Parke (pärk). County in Indiana. See *Table* at INDIANA.

Parke Peak. Mountain 9100 ft. in Glacier National Park, NW Montana.

Par'ker (pär'kẽr). **1** County in Texas. See *Table* at TEXAS.

2 *officially* **Parker City**. City, Armstrong co., W Pennsylvania, 20 m. NE of Butler; pop. 945.

3 City, ⊗ of Turner co., SE South Dakota; pop. 1142.

Parker Dam. See UNITED STATES, *Dams*.

Parker Peak. **1** Mountain 4848 ft. in Fall River co., SW corner of South Dakota.

2 Mountain 10,200 ft. in Yellowstone National Park, NW Wyoming.

Par'kers·burg (pär'kẽrz·bûrg). City, ⊗ of Wood co., W West Virginia, at confluence of Ohio and Little Kanawha rivers; pop. 44,797; industrial, railroad, and shipping center; river steamer port; clay and coal deposits, gas and petroleum wells, mineral springs; oil-well supplies, iron and steel, rayon, glassware, porcelain.

Parkes (pärks). Town, E cen. New South Wales, SE Australia, 180 m. WNW of Sydney; pop. 5848; mining.

Parkes'burg (pärks'bûrg). Borough, Chester co., SE Pennsylvania, 22 m. E of Lancaster; pop. 2759.

Park Falls. City, Price co., N Wisconsin, 50 m. SSE of Ashland; pop. 2919; lumbering; paper manufacturing.

Park Forest. Village, Cook co., NE Illinois, S of Chicago; pop. 29,993.

Park Hills. City, Kenton co., N Kentucky, 3 m. SW of Covington; pop. 4076.

Park'land (pärk'lănd). Town, Pierce co., W cen. Washington, ab. 6 m. S of Tacoma; pop. (est.) 13,000; Pacific Lutheran Univ. (1890; coed.).

Park Range. A range of the Rocky Mts. in N Colorado; highest peak Mount Lincoln 14,284 ft.

Park Rapids. Village, ⊗ of Hubbard co., N cen. Minnesota, 40 m. S of Bemidji; pop. 3047; lumbering, dairying.

Park Ridge. **1** City, Cook co., NE Illinois, N suburb of Chicago; pop. 32,659.

2 Borough, Bergen co., NE corner of New Jersey, on New York border 12 m. NE of Paterson; pop. 6389.

Park River. City, Walsh co., NE North Dakota, on Park river 46 m. NW of Grand Forks; pop. 1813.

Park'side' (pärk'sīd'). Borough, Delaware co., SE Pennsylvania, SW of Philadelphia; pop. 2426.

Parks'ton (pärks'tŭn). City, Hutchinson co., SE South Dakota, 23 m. S of Mitchell; pop. 1514.

Park'ville (pärk'vĭl). **1** Urban community (unincorporated), Baltimore co., cen. Maryland, NE of Baltimore; pop. (with Carney) 27,236.

2 City, S Platte co., NW Missouri, 9 m. NW of Kansas City; pop. 1229; Park Coll. (1875; coed.).

Par·la'ki·me'di (pẽr·lä'kĭ·mā'dĭ). Town, NE Andhra Pradesh, E Indian Union, on tributary of Vamsadhara river 160 m. SW of Cuttack; pop. 20,072.

Par'ma (pär'mȧ). City, Cuyahoga co., N Ohio, 8 m. S of Cleveland; pop. 82,845.

Par'ma (pär'mȧ; *Ital.* pär'mä). **1** Province of Italy. See *Table* at ITALY.

2 Commune, its ✻, Emilia, N Italy, 75 m. SE of Milan; pop. 71,858; on ancient Roman Aemilian Way; ancient fortifications now form promenade around city; 11th-cent. Romanesque-Gothic cathedral; 13th-cent. red-marble Lombard-Romanesque baptistery; ducal palace; Palazzo della Pilotta, now containing a museum, art gallery, and library; university (founded 1502); manufactures silk, cottons, woolens, felt hats, and dairy products, esp. Parmesan cheese. Birthplace of the painter Parmigiano; residence of Correggio. Traces of prehistoric and Etruscan villages on present site; became Roman colony 183 B.C.; capital of a Lombard duchy and, 1545–1860, of duchy of Parma and Piacenza; became part of kingdom of Italy 1860.

Parma Heights. City, Cuyahoga co., N Ohio, S suburb of Cleveland; pop. 18,000.

Par'mer (pär'mẽr). County in Texas. See *Table* at TEXAS.

Par′na·í′ba (pàr′nȧ·ē′vȧ), *formerly* **Par′na·hy′ba** (-ē′vȧ). **1** River ab. 900 m. long in NE Brazil; flows NE, forming boundary bet. Piauí and Maranhão states, and empties into Atlantic Ocean.
2 Port, N Piauí state, NE Brazil, 11 m. from mouth of the Parnaíba river; pop. (1940 est.) 22,571; chief exports cotton and sugar.
Par·nas′sus (pär·năs′ŭs). **1** Former borough, Westmoreland co., SW Pennsylvania, on Allegheny river ab. 17 m. ENE of Pittsburgh; pop. (1930) 6240; consolidated with New Kensington (*q.v.*) 1931.
2 *modern* **Liá′kou·ra** (lyä′kōō·rä). Mountain 8060 ft. in Phthiotis and Phocis dept., cen. Greece, N of Gulf of Corinth; in ancient times sacred to Apollo and the Muses, esp. the **Cas·ta′lian Spring** (kǎs·tāl′yǎn; -tā′lĭ·ǎn), just above Delphi which lay at its foot to the S. **Co·ry′cian Cave** (kǒ·rǐsh′ǎn; -ǐ·ǎn), a stalactite grotto 350 ft. long and ab. 200 ft. wide, is bet. Delphi and the summit on a plateau.
Par′nes (pär′nēz; *Mod. Gr.* -nyĕs). Mountain 4631 ft. in Attica and Boeotia dept., E cen. Greece, 16 m. N of Athens; an E extension of Mt. Cithaeron.
Par′non (pär′nŏn; *Mod. Gr.* -nôn). Mountain range, E Laconia, SE Peloponnesus, S Greece; highest peak ab. 6000 ft.; shuts in the valley of the Eurotas on the E.
Par′nu (pär′nōō) *or* **Pyar′nu** (pyàr′nōō); *Estonian* **Pär′nu** (pär′nōō); *Russ. formerly* **Per′nov** (pyĕr′nŭf); *Ger.* **Per′nau** (pĕr′nou). **1** Bay on SW coast of Estonia, an inlet of the N part of the Gulf of Riga.
2 River ab. 80 m. long in cen. Estonia, in Järva and Parnu provs.; flows SW into Parnu Bay.
3 Province of Estonia. See *Table* at ESTONIA.
4 Seaport, its ✱, near mouth of Parnu river on Parnu Bay; pop. (1937) 21,186; exports lumber, wood pulp, flax; has ice-free harbor, second most important port in Estonia; resort, noted for its radioactive waters. Founded in 1255; held by Swedes and Poles in 16th cent.; from 1617 to 1710 again under Sweden and 1710 to 1918 Russian.
Par′o·pa·mi′sus (pär′ȯ·pȧ·mī′sŭs; -păm′ĭ·sŭs). **1** Mountain range, NW Afghanistan, at W end of the Hindu Kush, N of Herat and the Hari Rud; highest point 11,772 ft.
2 *or* **Par′a·pa·ni′sus** (pär′ȧ·pȧ·nī′sŭs; -păn′ĭ·sŭs). Ancient name of Hindu Kush range.
Par′os (pâr′ŏs; pä′rŏs; *Mod. Gr.* **Pá′ros** (pä′rôs). **1** Island, cen. Cyclades, in the Aegean Sea 6 m. W of Naxos; in Cyclades dept., Greece; 81 sq. m.; pop. ab. 9000; ✱ Paros; formed by a mountain 2460 ft. high, from which has been obtained a fine white marble, widely used in ancient times by sculptors. Colonized by Ionians from Athens and itself founder of colonies in Thasos, Illyria, etc.; sided with Persians in Greco-Persian Wars; not historically important after 4th cent. B.C.; site of discovery 1627 of a marble tablet, known as the *Parian Chronicle* giving an outline of Greek history from before 1000 B.C. to ab. 354 B.C., one of the Arundel marbles now at Oxford University.
2 *or* **Par′oi·ki′a** (pär′ē·kyē′ä; -ē·kyä′). Town, its ✱, on W coast; pop. 1975.
Par′ot·tee Point (pär′ŭ·tē). Cape on SW coast of the island of Jamaica, West Indies.
Par′o·wan′ (pär′ȯ·wän′; pär′ȯ·wǎn). City, ⊗ of Iron co., SW Utah, 17 m. NE of Cedar City; pop. 1486; center of sheep and cattle area.
Par·ral′ (pär·räl′). **1** Town, Linares prov., S cen. Chile, 197 m. S of Santiago; pop. 10,225.
2 *in full* **Hidalgo del Parral.** City, Chihuahua state, N Mexico, 115 m. S of Chihuahua; pop. 24,231; alt. 6200 ft.; large gold, silver, lead, and zinc mines nearby.
Par′ra·mat′ta (pär′ȧ·mǎt′ȧ). **1** River 18 m. long, actually the tidal estuary of a small creek forming W arm of Port Jackson, E New South Wales, SE Australia.
2 Town on it, suburb 15 m. W of Sydney; pop. 18,075;

first settled 1788; in early years a rival of Sydney and important as an agricultural center; municipality incorp. 1861.
Par′ra·more Island (pär′ȧ·mōr). Island in Atlantic Ocean off SE coast of Accomac co., Virginia.
Par′ras (pär′räs), *in full* **Par′ras de la Fuen′te** (pär′räz thä lä fwän′tä). Town, S Coahuila state, NE Mexico, ab. 120 m. WSW of Monterrey; pop. 15,555; in a wine-producing region.
Par′ret (pär′ĕt; -ĭt). River 35 m. long, Dorsetshire and Somersetshire, SW England; flows NW into Bristol Channel.
Par′ris Island (pär′ĭs). Island of the Sea Is. chain in Beaufort co., S South Carolina, S of Port Royal I.; since 1915 a U.S. Marine Corps training station.
Parrs′bor′o (pärz′bûr′ȯ). Town, Cumberland co., N Nova Scotia, Canada, on N shore of Minas Basin 31 m. S of Amherst; pop. 1906; shipbuilding; exports coal and lumber. In a region rich for geological studies; has footprints of prehistoric animals, plant fossils, etc. (see JOGGINS). Vicinity closely associated with many Micmac Indian legends.
Parrtown. See SAINT JOHN, New Brunswick.
Par′ry, Cape (pär′ĭ). Point extending from N coast of Northwest Territories, Canada, into Amundsen Gulf on E side of Franklin Bay, ab. 70°N, 125°W.
Parry Island. = MAUKE, Cook Is.
Parry Islands. Group of islands in NW Franklin District, Northwest Territories, Canada, N of Viscount Melville Sound; includes Prince Patrick I., Melville I., Bathurst I., Borden I., and Cornwallis I.
Parry Sound. 1 District, Ontario, Canada. See *Table* at ONTARIO.
2 Town, its ⊗, SE Ontario, Canada; port at center of E shore of Georgian Bay; pop. 5183; terminal for lake steamers; lumber; summer resort.
Par·sip′pa·ny-Troy Hills (pär·sĭp′ȧ·nĭ-troi′). Urban township, Morris co., N New Jersey, 6 m. NE of Morristown; pop. 25,557.
Pars′nip (pärs′nĭp). River ab. 145 m. long, E cen. British Columbia, Canada; rises near the bend of the Fraser and flows N to unite with Finlay river and form Peace river.
Par′son Bald (pär′s'n). Peak 4760 ft. in Blount co., E Tennessee.
Par′sons (pär′s'nz). **1** City, Labette co., SE Kansas, 33 m. W of Pittsburg; pop. 13,929; stockyards.
2 City, ⊗ of Tucker co., NE West Virginia, 16 m. NNE of Elkins; pop. 1798.
Parsons Peak. Mountain 12,120 ft. in Sierra Nevada, near E end of boundary bet. Mariposa and Tuolumne cos., cen. California.
Parsonstown. See BIRR.
Par·tab′garh (pär·täb′gär) *or* **Pra·tap′garh** (*native* prä·täp′gŭr·h′). **1** Former Indian state, Southern Rajputana States, S Rajputana, Indian Union; 873 sq. m.; pop. (1941) 91,967; joined Union of Rajasthan June 26, 1947. A Rajput state, inhabited chiefly by Bhils and other aboriginals.
2 Town, its ✱, ab. 78 m. SE of Udaipur.
3 Town, Fyzabad division, SE Uttar Pradesh, N Indian Union, 30 m. N of Allahabad; pop. 3559.
Par·tan′na (pär·tän′nä). Commune, Trapani prov., NW Sicily, 29 m. SE of Trapani; pop. 12,714.
Partenkirchen. See GARMISCH-PARTENKIRCHEN.
Par′the·nay′ (pàr′tĕ·nā′). Town, cen. Deux-Sèvres dept., W France, 27 m. NNE of Niort; pop. 5831; parts of 13th-cent. walls, several churches (11th and 12th cents.).
Par·then′o·pe (pär·thĕn′ȯ·pē). Ancient town, S Italy, on site of Naples (*q.v.*), the place where, according to legend, the Siren Parthenope was cast ashore. The **Par·then′o·pe′an Republic** (-pē′ǎn) was a short-lived republic Jan. 23–June 20, 1799 erected at Naples by Napoleon.

Par′thi·a (pär′thĭ·à). Ancient country in W Asia, nearly coextensive with modern Khurasan prov., NE Iran; a subdivision of Ariana, SE of Hyrcania; formed a province of the Assyrian and Persian Empires and later of the empire of Alexander; on dissolution of Seleucid Empire c. 250 B.C., new Parthian kingdom founded by Arsaces, first of the Arsacidae, a dynasty of ab. 30 kings which ruled until overthrown by Ardashir c. 226 A.D., the first Sassanid ruler of Persia (q.v.). Kingdom at its height, known as Parthian Empire (*Lat.* **Reg′num Par·tho′rum** [rĕg′nŭm pär·thōr′ŭm]) at beginning of 1st cent. B.C., included all regions bet. Euphrates and Indus and bet. Oxus and Indian Ocean; received its first setbacks when checked by Tigranes of Armenia 88–70 B.C. and esp. by the Romans 39–38 B.C. The Parthians were of Scythian race and famous as horsemen and archers. Best known cities were Hecatompylos, Seleucia, and Ctesiphon whose ruins are now in Iraq.

Par′tick (pär′tĭk). Former burgh, Lanark co., S cen. Scotland, now part of Glasgow.

Par·ti·ni′co (pär′tē·nē′kô). Manufacturing and commercial commune, Palermo prov., Sicily, 15 m. WSW of Palermo; pop. 22,960.

Pa·rú′ (pà·rōō′). River 350 m. long in N Brazil; rises in the Tumuc-Humac Mts., flows SE into the Amazon.

Parú (Oes′te [wâsh′tĕ]). River 140 m. long in N Brazil; rises in Tumuc-Humac Mts. W (*Port.* Oeste) of the Parú, flows S to unite with Marapí river and form Erepecurú river.

Pa·rys′ (pà·rīs′). Town, N Orange Free State, E cen. Union of South Africa, on Vaal river 60 m. SW of Johannesburg; pop. 5176; fashionable resort; jam and fruit-preserving factories.

Pas, The. See THE PAS.

Pa′sa·ca′o (pä′sä·kä′ô; -kou′). Municipality, SW Camarines Sur prov., Luzon, Phil. Is., 12 m. SW of Naga and its port on Ragay Gulf; pop. 5594; port of call for steamers.

Pas′a·de′na (păs′à·dē′nà). 1 Suburban residential city, Los Angeles co., SW California, 8 m. NE of Los Angeles; pop. 116,407; founded 1873, incorp. 1886; winter resort; annual New Year's Day Tournament of Roses (flower festival, inaugurated 1890); site of Rose Bowl. California Institute of Technology (founded as Throop Polytechnic Institute 1891; men; reorganized 1921); Pasadena Coll. (1902; coed.).
2 City, Harris co., SE Texas, 10 m. E of Houston; pop. 58,737; in farming section; oil wells; site of Santa Anna's capture (1836) nearby.

Pa·sa′do, Cape (pä·sä′thô). Cape extending into Pacific Ocean on W cen. coast of Ecuador.

Pa·sa·je (pä·sä′hâ). Town, El Oro prov., SW Ecuador, 80 m. S of Guayaquil; pop. (1944 est.) 7409.

Pa·sa′leng Bay (pä·sä′lĕng). Inlet of South China Sea (Babuyan Channel), NE Ilocos Norte prov., Luzon, Phil. Is., E of Mayraira Point; ab. 11 m. wide at mouth.

Pa·sar′ga·dae (pà·sär′gà·dē). Ruined city of ancient Persia, 30 m. NE of later Persepolis; ✳ of Cyrus the Great; said to have been founded by him on the site of his victory over Astyages 549 B.C. Its ruins today are at Mashad-i-Murghab in the plain of Murghab N of Lake Niriz and comprise bases of several large buildings and the Tomb of Cyrus. Surrendered to Alexander 336 B.C.

Pa′say (pä′sī); *now* **Ri·zal′** (rē·säl′; *angl.* rĭ·zäl′). Municipality, SW Rizal prov., Luzon, Phil. Is., on E shore of Manila Bay ab. 1 m. S of S boundary of Manila; pop. 55,161. Nearly destroyed by Japanese Dec. 1941.

Pas′ca·gou′la (păs′kà·gōō′là). 1 Navigable river, SE Mississippi; formed by confluence of Leaf and Chickasawhay rivers in N George co., SE Mississippi, flows S into Mississippi Sound.
2 City, ⊗ of Jackson co., SE corner of Mississippi, on Mississippi Sound 18 m. E of Biloxi; pop. 17,139; coastal resort and fishing center; boatbuilding and shipbuilding.

Pas′co (păs′kō). 1 County in Florida. See *Table* at FLORIDA.
2 City, ⊗ of Franklin co., SE Washington, on the Columbia river; pop. 14,522; developed as supply center during World War II for Richland (q.v.) and Hanford sites of industrial plants of the Manhattan District (q.v.).
3 (päs′kô) Department of Peru. See *Table* at PERU.

Pas′coag (păs′kōg). Village, Providence co., N Rhode Island, ab. 18 m. NW of Providence; pop. 2,983.

Pascua. See EASTER ISLAND.

Pas–de–Ca′lais′ (päd′kä′lĕ′). Department of France. See *Table* at FRANCE.

Pas de Calais. See Strait of DOVER.

Pa′se·walk (pä′zĕ·välk). City, in what was formerly Pomerania prov., Prussia, Germany, 24 m. WNW of Stettin; pop. 11,768; iron foundries, sawmills; manufactures machinery; trades in livestock.

Pashmakli. See SMOLIAN.

Pa′sig (pä′sĭg). 1 Stream ab. 12 m. long, cen. Luzon, Phil. Is.; the outlet of Laguna de Bay flowing NNW in Rizal prov. and City of Manila; navigable for small vessels.
2 Municipality, ✳ of Rizal prov., Luzon, Phil. Is., on N bank of Pasig river near its source and ab. 5 m. from E boundary of City of Manila; pop. 27,541; important market town; partially destroyed at time of Revolution.

Pa′sing (pä′zĭng). Manufacturing city, Upper Bavaria govt. dist., Bavaria, Germany, 4 m. W of Munich; pop. 12,212; paper, paper goods.

Paš′man (päsh′män). Island in Adriatic Sea off coast of Yugoslavia, S of Zadar, bet. Dugi Otok I. and mainland; ab. 34 sq. m.; pop. ab. 4000.

Pas′ni (pŭs′nĭ). Seaport town, Pakistan, on S coast of Kalat, Baluchistan, 75 m. E of Gwadar.

Pa′so (pä′sô). Spanish, literally "pass"; for names of mountain passes beginning with this element see the distinguishing element (e.g., **Paso de Maipú**. See MAIPÚ).

Paso de los To′ros (thä lôs tō′rôs). Town, Tacuarembó dept., N cen. Uruguay; pop. ab. 9000.

Pa′soe·roe·an′ (pä′sōō·rōō·än′) *or* **Pa′su·ru·an′**. Seaport city, East Java prov., Indonesia, at SW corner of Madura Strait; pop. 36,973; on railroad ab. 30 m. S of Surabaja; in former times of much greater commercial importance than now.

Pas′o Ro′bles (păs′ō rō′b'lz); *officially,* **El Paso de Robles** (ĕl). City, San Luis Obispo co., SW California, on the Salinas 24 m. N of San Luis Obispo; pop. 6677; resort; hot springs; almond groves.

Pas′quo·tank (păs′kwô·tăngk). County in North Carolina. See *Table* at NORTH CAROLINA.

Pas′sa·con′a·way (păs′à·kŏn′à·wä). Mountain 4060 ft., S Grafton co., W New Hampshire; highest point in the Sandwich Range, S White Mts.

Pas′sage Island (păs′ĭj). Small island off NE tip of Isle Royale, NW Lake Superior, a part of Keweenaw co., N tip of Michigan penin.

Pas·sa′ic (pă·sā′ĭk). 1 River ab. 100 m. long, NE New Jersey; rises near Morristown, SE Morris co.; flows S, E, and N on the Morris co. line, E across Passaic co., turns S at Paterson, where occur the **Great Falls of the Passaic** 70 ft. high; follows the line of the Essex co. boundary into Newark Bay; navigable 11 m.
2 County in New Jersey. See *Table* at NEW JERSEY.
3 Manufacturing and residential city, Passaic co., N New Jersey, on Passaic river 4 m. S of Paterson; pop. 53,963; textile center; manufactures silks, chemicals, dyes, rubber goods, tin cans, mill machinery, springs, steel cabinets. Site of Dutch settlement c. 1679; incorp. as village 1869, as city 1873; scene of Washington's crossing of Passaic river in his retreat through New Jersey 1776.

Pas′sa·ma·quod′dy Bay (păs′à·mà·kwŏd′ĭ). Inlet of SW Bay of Fundy, SW New Brunswick, Canada, bet. SW New Brunswick and SE Maine, at the mouth of the St. Croix river. Deer I. and Campobello I. in S part of it.

Pas′sa·ro, Cape (päs′sä·rȯ). = Cape PASSERO.

Passarowitz. See POŽAREVAC.

Pas′sau (päs′ou). City, Lower Bavaria and Upper Palatinate govt. dist., Bavaria, Germany, at confluence of Danube, Inn, and Ilz rivers 93 m. ENE of Munich; pop. 24,428; important railroad junction and commercial center; 15th-cent. late-Gothic cathedral, 14th-cent. town hall. Of ancient Celtic origin; treaty signed here 1552 settling religious differences bet. Emperor Charles V and German states. Captured by Allies May 2, 1945.

Pass′chen·dae′le (päs′ĕ[n]·dä′lĕ). Small commune, West Flanders prov., NW Belgium; pop. 3067; stormed by 1st and 2d Canadian brigades Nov. 6, 1917.

Pass Chris′ti·an′ (päs krĭs′chĭ·än′). City, Harrison co., SE Mississippi, on Gulf of Mexico 11 m. W of Gulfport; pop. 3881; coastal resort; oyster fisheries.

Pas′se·ro, Cape (päs′sä·rȯ); *anc.* **Pa·chy′nus Prom′-on·to′ri·um** (på·kī′nŭs prŏm′ŭn·tōr′ĭ·ŭm). Cape projecting into Mediterranean Sea at SE point of the island of Sicily. Naval battle 1718 nearby in which British admiral George Byng destroyed Spanish fleet; in World War II landing place of British forces in invasion of Sicily July 10, 1943.

Passes, the. See MISSISSIPPI river.

Pas′si (pä′sĕ). Municipality, N Iloilo prov., Panay, Phil. Is., on Jalaur river and on railroad 29 m. N of City of Iloilo; pop. 28,060.

Pas′so Fun′do (päs′ȯȯ fōȯNn′dȯȯ). City, N Rio Grande do Sul state, S Brazil, 150 m. NW of Pôrto Alegre; pop. (1940 est.) 17,585.

Pas′sos (pàs′ȯȯs). City, SW Minas Gerais state, E Brazil, 180 m. W of Belo Horizonte; pop. (1940 est.) 12,980.

Pas·sump′sic (pă·sŭm[p]′sĭk). River, NE Vermont; rises in N Caledonia co., flows S into Connecticut river.

Pas·ta′za (päs·tä′sä). River ab. 400 m. long rising in cen. Ecuador and flowing S into Peru to empty into Marañón river, headstream of the Amazon.

Pas′to (päs′tȯ). **1** Volcano 13,990 ft. at S end of Cordillera Occidental in SW Colombia, near Ecuadorian border.
2 City, ✳ of Nariño dept., SW Colombia, on high plateau (8400 ft.) E of Pasto volcano; pop. 27,564; gold mines.

Pas·to′ra Peak (päs·tōr′å). Mountain 9420 ft. in NE Apache co., NE Arizona.

Pas·tra′na (päs·trä′nä). Municipality, N cen. Leyte prov., Phil. Is., 14 m. SW of Tacloban; pop. 8078; severe fighting here in American invasion Oct. 1944.

Pa·su′bio (pä·sȯȯ′byȯ). Peak 7323 ft. in Venezia Tridentina, NE Italy, SE of Rovereto.

Pasuruan. See PASOEROEAN.

Pat′a·go′nia (păt′å·gōn′yå; -gō′nĭ·å). Region in South America S of the Limay and Río Negro rivers, or ab. 40°S, extending to the Strait of Magellan, ab. 1000 m.; ab. 311,000 sq. m.; a barren tableland bet. the Andes and the Atlantic Ocean. Crossed by the Chubut, Deseado, and Chico rivers flowing E to the Atlantic; its Atlantic coast line indented by the Gulfs of San Matías and San Jorge. Practically unexplored before 1869; divided 1881 bet. Chile (Magallanes prov.) and Argentina (territories of Río Negro, Chubut, and Santa Cruz).

Patagonia, Plateau of. Highland area in Patagonia, S Argentina, comprising esp. the W part of Chubut territory.

Pataliputra. See PATNA.

Patalung. See PHATTHALUNG.

Pa′tam·bán′, Cer′ro de (sĕr′rȯ thä pä′täm·bän′). Mountain 12,290 ft., W Michoacán state, SW Mexico, NW of Uruapan.

Pa′tan (pä′tăn). **1** or **Pat′tan** (pä′tăn). Town, Mehsana division, N Baroda, W Indian Union, on Saraswati river 65 m. NNW of Ahmadabad; pop. 29,830; has numerous Jain temples with valuable Jain manuscripts; makes swords, lances, knives, silks, embroidery, and pottery. Occupies site of ancient Gujrati capital, Anhilwara, captured 1024 by Mahmud of Ghazni.

2 See JHALRAPATAN town, Rajasthan, India.
3 Town adjoining Katmandu on the S, E cen. Nepal; pop. 104,928.

Pa·ta·ni (pä·tä·nē). Formerly, a Malay state in the Malay Penin. under Siamese protection, included among the Malay States (*q.v.*); now Pattani prov. in Thailand.

Patan Somnath. See SOMNATH.

Pa·taps′co (på·tăps′kō). River 80 m. long, N cen. Maryland; rises in Carroll co., N Maryland, flows SE into Chesapeake Bay; the city of Baltimore lies on a navigable estuary of this river.

Pat′a·ra (păt′å·rå). One of the chief cities of ancient Lycia, S Asia Minor, on the coast just E of the mouth of the Xanthus.

Patavium. See PADUA.

Pa′tay′ (på′tā′). Town, Loiret dept., N cen. France, NW of Orléans; pop. 1266; scene of defeat of English under Sir John Fastolf and John Talbot, Earl of Shrewsbury, by Joan of Arc June 18, 1429, just after siege of Orléans had been lifted.

Patch′ogue (păch′ŏg). Village and summer resort, Suffolk co., SE New York, on S shore of Long I., on Great South Bay 53 m. E of New York; pop. 8838; Blue Point, famous for blue-point oysters, nearby.

Patera Island. See LAPPA.

Pa′ter·nò′ (pä′târ·nô′). Commune, Catania prov., E Sicily, on SW slope of Mt. Etna 12 m. WNW of Catania; pop. 32,179; 11th-cent. castle. See HYBLA. Taken by British Aug. 1943 in Sicily campaign.

Pat′er·son (păt′ẽr·s'n). Manufacturing city, ⊗ of Passaic co., N New Jersey, on Passaic river 14 m. N of Newark; pop. 143,663; formerly manufactured cotton goods, steam and toy locomotives, revolvers; center of silk industry since c. 1840 (often called the "Silk City" and the "Lyons of America"); silk mills, dyeing and finishing plants; manufactures airplane motors, textile machinery, springs, foundry products, plastics. Land bought from Indians by Dutch settlers 1679; selected in 1791 by tax-free Society for Establishing Useful Manufactures (S.U.M.) as place to work out plan projected by Alexander Hamilton for a Federal industrial city; created township 1831; became ⊗ of newly created Passaic co. 1837; incorp. as city 1851.

Patersonia. Former name of LAUNCESTON, Tasmania.

Path′find′er Dam *and* **Reservoir** (păth′fīn′dẽr). See UNITED STATES, *Dams and Reservoirs.*

Path′ros (păth′rŏs). Upper Egypt, a Biblical name (*Isa.* xi. 11, *Jer.* xliv. 1, 2, 15).

Pa′ti (pä′tĕ). Town, Central Java prov., Indonesia, on railroad 15 m. E of Kudus; pop. 22,444.

Pa·tí′a (pä·tē′å). River ab. 200 m. long in SW Colombia; flows WNW into Pacific Ocean.

Pa′ti·a′la (pŭ′tĭ·ä′lå) or **Put′ti·a′la.** **1** Former Indian state, chief of the three Phulkian states of the Punjab region, NW India; 5942 sq. m.; pop. (1941) 1,936,259; comprises three detached areas now in East Punjab, Indian Union. Founded by a Sikh chieftain c. 1763; came under British control 1809.
2 City, its ✳, now in Punjab state, 130 m. NNW of Delhi; pop. (1941) 69,850.

Pa·til′las (pä·tē′yäs). Municipality (pop. 17,106) and town (pop. 1888), SE Puerto Rico; town near coast just E of Guayama.

Pat′kai Range *or* **Hills** (păt′kī). Hill region extending NE to SW along the border bet. E Assam, NE India, and NW Burma; commonly included with the Naga Hills on the SW. Average height 8000 to 9000 ft. Forms watershed bet. Brahmaputra and Chindwin rivers. See NAGA HILLS.

Pat′mos (păt′mŏs; *Mod. Gr.* pät′mŏs); *Ital.* **Pat′mo** (pät′mȯ). **1** An island of the Dodecanese (*q.v.*), in NW part SSW of Samos; 22 sq. m.; pop. (1936) 3184; scene of Saint John's exile (c. 95 A.D.) where he is supposed to have written the Apocalypse.
2 Town on the island.

Pat′na (pŭt′nȧ). **1** Division, NW Bihar, NE Indian Union; 11,338 sq. m.; pop. (1941) 7,265,950.
2 City, its ✱ and ✱ of Bihar state, on right bank of Ganges river 300 m. NW of Calcutta; pop. (1941) 175,706; formerly a center of the opium trade but now its business is declining. Old city extends 9 m. along river bank; to the W is European suburb of **Ban′ki·pore** (bäng′kĭ·pōr), and to the SW the new capital. Has interesting mosques, a Sikh temple, and other architectural remains. Seat of Univ. of Patna. Founded 5th cent. B.C. as capital, with name **Pa′ta·li·pu′tra** (pä′tȧ·lĭ·poō′trȧ), of Magadha; under Asoka the seat of government of a great empire; continued as important city until 4th and 5th cents. A.D. but described in 7th cent. as a place of ruins; restored to greatness under the Moguls; became capital of Bihar 1541; seized by English agent 1763, recaptured by the Nawab of Bengal in the same year and 200 English prisoners massacred; again captured by the British Nov. 1763.
3 Former Indian state, Eastern States, NE Indian Union, 170 m. W of Cuttack; 2530 sq. m.; pop. (1941) 632,220; ✱ Bolangir (pop. 6473). Now part of Orissa state.
Pat′na·nong′an (pät′nä·nông′än). Island in Polillo group off E Luzon, Phil. Is., E of Polillo; 34 sq. m.; in Tayabas prov.
Pat′nong·on′ (pät′nông·ôn′). Municipality on coast, W Antique prov., Panay, Phil. Is., 12 m. N of San Jose de Buenavista; pop. 20,012.
Pa·to′ka (pȧ·tō′kȧ). River ab. 90 m. long, SW Indiana; rises in Orange co., flows W into Wabash river.
Pa′tos. 1 (pä′tŏos) City, W cen. Minas Gerais state, E Brazil, 190 m. NW of Belo Horizonte; pop. 7143.
2 (pä′tŏs) Island ab. 200 acres, on W side of Dragon's Mouths, strait bet. NW Trinidad and tip of Paria Penin., NE coast of Venezuela; claim to it ceded to Venezuela by Great Britain 1942, ending 150-year long dispute.
Pa′tos, La·go′a dos (lȧ·gō′ȧ thŏŏsh pä′tŏos). Lagoon (lake) 124 m. long and 37 m. wide in E Rio Grande do Sul state, S Brazil; has Pôrto Alegre at its N end and the port of Rio Grande at its S end where it has an outlet to the sea; separated from the Atlantic Ocean by a sandy peninsula ab. 15 m. wide.
Patos, Lago de los. See PORONGOS.
Patos, Los. See LOS PATOS.
Pa·tras′ (pȧ·träs′; pă′rȧs); *Gr.* **Pa′trai** (pä′trä) *anc.* **Pa′trae** (pä′trē). Fortified seaport city, ✱ of Achaea and Elis dept., NW Peloponnesus, Greece, on Gulf of Patras; pop. 61,278; exports olive oil, wine, raisins, currants, sheepskin. Important commercially by 5th cent. B.C.; chief commercial city in the Peloponnesus during Middle Ages; occupied by Turks in 18th and 19th cents. (to 1828); place where Greek War of Independence began 1821.
Patras, Gulf of; *or* Gulf of Cal′y·don (kăl′ĭ·dŏn); *anc.* **Si′nus Cal′y·do′ni·us** (sī′nŭs kăl′ĭ·dō′nĭ·ŭs; -dōn′-yŭs). Inlet of the Ionian Sea on W coast of Greece, joined by narrow strait (Lepanto Strait) to the Gulf of Corinth N of the Peloponnesus.
Pa′tri·a, Lake (pä′trē·ä). Small lake 13 m. NW of Naples, Italy.
Pa·tri′cia (pȧ·trĭsh′ȧ; -ĭ·ȧ). Former district, NW Ontario, Canada, N of Albany river; now N part of Kenora dist. (incorporated in it Apr. 5, 1927).
Pat′rick (păt′rĭk). County in Virginia. See *Table* at VIRGINIA.
Patrick Point. Cape on SE extremity of St. Thomas I., Virgin Is. of the United States, West Indies.
Patrimony of Saint Peter. See Duchy of ROME.
Pattan. See PATAN.
Pat·ta·ni (pät·tä·nē); *also* **Pa·ta·ni** (pä·tä·nē). **1** Province, SW Thailand; 752 sq. m.; pop. 192,178; ✱ Pattani.
2 Town, its ✱, seaport on E coast of Malay Penin. 50 m. SE of Songkhla. Its airport taken by Japanese Dec. 8–9, 1941.
Pat′ten (păt′ʼn). Town, Penobscot co., E cen. Maine, 31

m. WSW of Houlton; pop. 1312; trading and lumbering community; fishing and hunting resort.
Pat′ter·son (păt′ẽr·s′n). Town, St. Mary parish, S Louisiana, 60 m. SE of Lafayette; pop. 2923.
Pat′ti (pät′tē). Commune, Messina prov., NE Sicily, on N coast of Sicily 33 m. W of Messina; pop. 12,350; episcopal see; small harbor.
Pat′ton (păt′ʼn). Borough, Cambria co., SW cen. Pennsylvania, 16 m. WNW of Altoona; pop. 2880; manufactures brick, clay products; coal mining.
Pa·tu′ca (pä·tōō′kä). River ab. 300 m. long, S cen. and E Honduras; rises in several headstreams in mountains of cen. Honduras, flows NE into the Caribbean Sea.
Patuca Point. Cape on NE coast of Honduras, at the mouth of the Patuca river.
Patumdhani. See PRATHUM THANI.
Pâ′tu′rages′ (pä′tü′räzh′). Commune, Hainaut prov., SW Belgium, just SW of Mons; pop. 11,570.
Pa·tux′ent (pȧ·tŭk′s′nt). River ab. 100 m. long, cen. Maryland; rises in NW Howard co., flows S and SE into Chesapeake Bay in E St. Marys co., S Maryland.
Patuxent River. 1 See PATUXENT.
2 U.S. Naval Air Station at Cedar Point, Maryland, on S side of mouth of Patuxent river; Naval Air Test Center; established 1943–44.
Pátz′cua·ro (päts′kwä·rô). Town, N cen. Michoacán state, SW Mexico; pop. 9557; on S shore of **Lake Pátzcuaro**, ab. 30 m. in circumference, alt. 6700 ft.
Pat′zi·cí′a (pät′sē·sē′ä). Town, Chimaltenango dept., S cen. Guatemala; pop. 8270.
Pat·zún′ (pät·sōōn′). Town, Chimaltenango dept., S cen. Guatemala, E of Lake Atitlán; pop. 7525.
Pau (pō). Commune, ✱ of Basses-Pyrénées dept., SW France, on right bank of the Gave de Pau 109 m. S of Bordeaux; pop. 40,451; fine bridge, public squares (Place Royal, Place de la Comédie, etc.), academy, college, etc.; famous castle in which Henry IV was born; winter resort and starting point for tours in Pyrenees; manufactures table linen, paper, leather, rugs, carpets; trades in wine, meats, printed cottons, iron, leather, marble. Birthplace of Bernadotte (Charles XIV of Sweden). Anciently capital of Béarn.
Pau, Gave de (gàv′ dē pō′). River, S France; a mountain stream (*gave*), rises in S Hautes-Pyrénées dept., flows NW into the Adour on boundary bet. Basses-Pyrénées and Landes depts.; Lourdes and Pau are on it. See also GAVARNIE.
Pau′car·tam′bo (pou′kär·täm′bô). Town, E Cuzco dept., SE Peru, on **Paucartambo River** (ab. 180 m. long) which flows NNW into the Urubamba.
Pauil′lac′ (pō′yàk′). Commune, Gironde dept., SW France, on Gironde river ab. 25 m. NW of Bordeaux; pop. (1931) 4836; in the Médoc; noted for its vineyards.
Paul (pôl). Former urban district, Cornwall, SW England, on Mounts Bay; pop. (1931) 5814; now in Penzance.
Paul′ding (pôl′dĭng). **1** Name of counties in two states of the U.S. See *Tables* at GEORGIA and OHIO.
2 Town, a ⊗ of Jasper co., SE cen. Mississippi; pop. (1950) 153.
3 Village, ⊗ of Paulding co., NW Ohio, 37 m. NW of Lima; pop. 2936; beet sugar, brick and tile, flour.
Pau·lis′ta (pou·lēsh′tȧ). City, Pernambuco state, E Brazil; pop. (1940 est.) 12,887.
Pau′lo A·fon′so (pou′lŏo ȧ·fôn′sŏo). Series of three waterfalls in the São Francisco river, Brazil, ab. 190 m. from its mouth bet. Alagoas and Baía states; total height of falls ab. 275 ft.
Pauls′bor′o (pôlz′bûr′ô). Borough, Gloucester co., SW New Jersey, 10 m. SSW of Camden; pop. 8121; manufactures refined oil, fertilizer, paints.
Pauls Valley (pôlz). City, ⊗ of Garvin co., S cen. Oklahoma; pop. 6856; alfalfa, grain, cotton, pecans.
Paumotu Archipelago. See TUAMOTU ARCHIPELAGO.
Paung′de′ (poung′dä′). Town, Prome dist., Lower Burma, SE of Prome; pop. 13,479; on railroad.

Pau'ri (pou'rē). See GARHWAL.

Pau'te (pou'tā). 1 River ab. 110 m. long in SE Ecuador; unites with Zamora river to form Santiago river.
2 Town, Azuay prov., S Ecuador, in Andes Mts. just NE of Cuenca; pop. (1944 est.) 11,490.

Pau'to (pou'tō). River ab. 120 m. long in NE cen. Colombia; flows SE into Meta river.

Pa·vi'a (pä·vē'ä). 1 Province of Italy. See *Table* at ITALY.
2 *anc.* **Ti·ci'num** (tǐ·sī'nŭm). Commune, ✳ of Pavia prov., Lombardy, N Italy, on Ticino river 19 m. S of Milan; pop. 51,741; 15th-cent. cathedral (containing tomb of St. Augustine); 11th-cent. Romanesque church of San Michele; 14th-cent. Visconti castle; several towers (formerly more numerous—whence the epithet "City of a Hundred Towers"); Certosa di Pavia, old Carthusian monastery with fine Gothic church, nearby; university (said to have been founded by Charlemagne 774), three colleges; botanical garden; ancient fortifications replaced 1876 by wide boulevards; manufactures ironfoundry products, chemicals, cement, electrical supplies; trades in wine, rice, oil, silk, cheese, fruit. Important during reign of Augustus; capital of Lombard kings; French defeated by Imperialists 1525 nearby.

Pa·vil'ion Dome (pá·vil'yŭn). Peak 11,355 ft. in Sierra Nevada, E Fresno co., S cen. California.

Pavillons–sous–Bois, Les. See LES PAVILLONS-SOUS-BOIS.

Pav'lo·dar (pǎv'lô·där; *Russ.* pŭ·vlŭ·där'). Town, ✳ of Pavlodar Region, NE Kazakh S.S.R., Soviet Central Asia, on right bank of Irtysh river 180 m. NW of Semipalatinsk; pop. ab. 20,000; in a rich agricultural region and on the railroad ab. halfway bet. Akmolinsk and Barnaul.

Pavlodar Region. Subdivision of Kazakh S.S.R., Soviet Central Asia, in NE part, bounded on N and E by the R.S.F.S.R.; ✳ Pavlodar.

Pav'lof (pǎv'lôf). Volcano 8215 ft. high, SW Alaska Penin., Alaska, 162°W; on W shore of **Pavlof Bay,** inlet ab. 50 m. long on S coast of peninsula.

Pav'lo·grad (pǎv'lô·grǎd; *Russ.* pŭ·vlŭ·grát'). Town ab. 37 m. E of Dnepropetrovsk, E cen. Ukraine, Soviet Russia, Europe; pop. ab. 18,000.

Pa'vlovsk (pá'vlŭfsk). 1 Town, N Altai Territory, Soviet Russia, Asia, on railroad ab. 30 m. W of Barnaul; pop. 20,844.
2 *formerly* **Slutsk** (slōōtsk). Town, Leningrad Region, Soviet Russia, Europe, near Pushkin and just S of Leningrad; pop. 6660; former royal palace and park.

Pa'vlov·ski–Po·sad' (pá'vlŭf·ski·pŭ·sàt'). Town, Moscow Region, cen. Soviet Russia, Europe, on the Klyazma river just E of Moscow; pop. 20,840.

Pa·vul'lo nel Fri·gna'no (pä·vōōl'lô nǎl frē·nyä'nô). Commune, Modena prov., Emilia, N Italy, 21 m. S by W of Modena; pop. 15,990; manufactures glass.

Paw'ca·tuck (pô'ká·tŭk). River, SW Rhode Island; forms S section of Rhode Island-Connecticut boundary.

Paw·hus'ka (pô·hŭs'ká). City, ✳ of Osage co., N Oklahoma, 22 m. W of Bartlesville; pop. 5414; tribal capital of Osage Indians; oil fields; cattle ranches; agriculture.

Paw'ling (pô'lǐng). Residential village, Dutchess co., SE New York, 20 m. SE of Poughkeepsie; pop. 1734; settled by English Quakers c. 1740; dairying, farming; Pawling School for boys (1907).

Paw·nee' (pô·nē'; *attributively also* pô'nē). 1 River ab. 110 m. long, W cen. Kansas; rises in N Gray co., SW Kansas, flows N and E into Arkansas river at Larned, in Pawnee co., cen. Kansas.
2 Name of counties in three states of the U.S. See *Tables* at KANSAS, NEBRASKA, OKLAHOMA.
3 City, ✳ of Pawnee co., N Oklahoma, 30 m. SSE of Ponca City; pop. 2303; site of Pawnee Agency 1876; opened for settlement 1893; agriculture; livestock.

Pawnee City. City, ✳ of Pawnee co., SE Nebraska, 35 m. ESE of Beatrice; pop. 1343.

Paw Paw (pô' pô'). Village, ✳ of Van Buren co., SW Michigan, 17 m. WSW of Kalamazoo; pop. 2970; market center in grape-growing section.

Paw·tuck'et (pô·tŭk'ĕt; -ĭt). Industrial city, Providence co., N Rhode Island, 4 m. NE of Providence on both sides of Blackstone river at **Pawtucket Falls;** pop. 81,001; manufactures thread, textiles and textile machinery; metal goods. Settled 1671; part on E side of river originally belonged to Massachusetts (incorp. as town 1862), part on W side part of North Providence 1765–1874; incorp. as city 1885.

Pawtucket Falls. 1 See LOWELL, Massachusetts.
2 See PAWTUCKET, Rhode Island.

Paw·tux'et (pô·tŭk'sĕt; -sĭt). River ab. 28 m. long in Rhode Island, flowing from Scituate Reservoir E into Providence river.

Pax Augusta. See BADAJOZ.

Pax Julia. See BEJA.

Pax'os (pǎk'sŏs); *Gr.* **Pa·xoi'** (pä·ksē'). One of the Ionian Is., in the Ionian Sea S of Corfu, with which it forms the Corfu dept. of Greece (see *Table* at GREECE); 7 sq. m.; pop. 3037; chief village Gaïon.

Pax'son (pǎk's'n). Village on Richardson Highway, SE Alaska, ab. 165 m. N of Cordova.

Pax'tang (pǎks'tǎng). Borough, Dauphin co., SE cen. Pennsylvania, 4 m. E of Harrisburg; pop. 1916.

Pax'ton (pǎks'tǔn). City, ✳ of Ford co., NE cen. Illinois, 25 m. N of Champaign; pop. 4370; in agricultural region; soybeans; canneries.

Pa·ya·cha'ta (pä·yä·chä'tä). Peak 20,768 ft. in N Tarapacá prov., N Chile.

Payerbach. See REICHENAU.

Pay'erne (pě'yĕrn'); *Ger.* **Pe'ter·ling'en** (pā'tĕr·lǐng'ĕn). Commune, Vaud canton, Switzerland, ab. 10 m. W of Fribourg; pop. (1930) 4951; 10th-cent. abbey founded by Bertha of Burgundy, wife of Robert II of France.

Pay·ette' (pā·ĕt'; *attributively also* pā'ĕt). 1 River, W Idaho; **North Fork** rises in NW corner of Valley co., is one of the two **Payette Lakes;** flows S and in Boise co. is joined by **South Fork** which flows W across Boise co.; combined stream turns W and WNW and empties into Snake river at Payette on Oregon border; total length with North Fork is 110 m., with South Fork is 115 m.
2 County in Idaho. See *Table* at IDAHO.
3 City, ✳ of Payette co., SW Idaho, on Snake river across from Oregon 50 m. NW of Boise; pop. 4451; fruitpacking plants; grain and feed mills; livestock.

Payne (pān). County in Oklahoma. See *Table* at OKLAHOMA.

Payne Lake. Lake 747 sq. m. in the Ungava Penin., Quebec prov., Canada, having outlet (**Payne River**) E into Ungava Bay.

Pay'san·dú' (pī'sän·dōō'). 1 Department of Uruguay. See *Table* at URUGUAY.
2 City and port, its ✳, W Uruguay, on E bank of Uruguay river 210 m. NW of Montevideo; pop. ab. 46,000; founded 1782; center of the meat-packing and frozenmeat industry.

Pays de Waes. See WAES.

Pay'son (pā's'n). City, Utah co., N cen. Utah, 15 m. S of Provo; pop. 4237; farming (esp. onions); manufactures flour, beet sugar.

Pa·yún' (pä·yōōn'). Peak 12,073 ft. in SW Mendoza prov., W Argentina.

Paz, La. See LA PAZ.

Pazardzhik. See TATAR PAZARDZHIK.

Pa'zin (pä'zēn); *Ital.* **Pi·si'no** (pē·zē'nô). Commune, S cen. Istria Penin., NW Yugoslavia, 27 m. N by E of Pulj; pop. 19,094; 13th-cent. cathedral; before 1947 belonged to Italy.

Pea (pē). River ab. 100 m. long, SE Alabama; rises in Bullock co., SE cen. Alabama, flows S and empties into the Choctawhatchee in Geneva co., SE Alabama, near the Florida border.

Pea'bod'y (pē'bŏd'ĭ; -bŭd-ĭ). City, Essex co., NE corner of Massachusetts, 13 m. SE of Lowell; pop. 32,202.

Peabody, Mount. Peak 9200 ft. in Glacier National Park, NW Montana.

Peace (pēs). **1** River ab. 85 m. long, W cen. Florida; rises in Polk co., cen. Florida penin., flows S and SW into Charlotte Harbor, Charlotte co., on SW coast.
2 River 1065 m. long (to head of Finlay), W Canada, formed by confluence of Finlay and Parsnip rivers in E cen. British Columbia, flows E across border of Alberta, turns NE and joins the Slave river just N of its outlet from Lake Athabaska.

Peace Dale. Village, Washington co., S Rhode Island, ab. 2 m. SE of Kingston; pop. (with Wakefield) 5569; manufactures woolens.

Peace River. 1 See PEACE.
2 Town, W Alberta, Canada, on right bank of Peace river where it is joined by the Smoky; pop. 1672. Began as a log fort 1793 built by Alexander Mackenzie; now the center of **Peace River Country,** a prosperous farming region. Connected with Edmonton by railroad and by highway with Dawson Creek in Brit. Columbia where the Alaska Highway begins; also connected by highway with Hay river valley and Hay River post on Great Slave Lake.

Peach (pēch). County in Georgia. See *Table* at GEORGIA.

Peach Tree Creek. Creek in Georgia, flowing into the Chattahoochee river near Atlanta; scene of battle July 20–22, 1864 in which the Confederates failed to drive back Sherman's forces advancing on Atlanta; Gen. Hood's first engagement after replacing Gen. Johnston.

Peak District (pēk). Plateau region in N Derbyshire, N cen. England, at S end of the Pennine Chain; highest point **Kin'der Scout** (kĭn'dĕr skout) or **the Peak** 2088 ft.; region of wild moors, cultivated valleys, and hills with craggy summits.

Peak Ridge. Mountain 4375 ft. in the Adirondack Mts., NE New York.

Peale (pēl) Small island, N part of Wake I. group, bordering the lagoon on the N; airport.

Peale, Mount. Peak 13,089 ft. in N San Juan co., SE Utah; highest in the La Sal group.

Pea Ridge (pē). City in Benton co., NW Arkansas; pop. 380; scene of battle Mar. 7–8, 1862 in which Federal forces under Samuel R. Curtis defeated Confederates under Van Dorn.

Pear'is·burg (pâr'ĭs·bûrg). Town, ⊗ of Giles co., western Virginia; pop. 2268.

Pearl (pûrl). **1** River 490 m. long, cen. and S cen. Mississippi; rises in Neshoba co., flows SW, then S into the Gulf of Mexico, forming in the S section the Louisiana-Mississippi boundary.
2 or **Can·ton'** (kăn·tŏn'; kăn'tŏn); *Chin.* **Chu-kiang** (jōō'jĭ·äng'). River forming a part of the Si delta and flowing from the city of Canton, SE China, to the South China Sea; divided by the Bocca Tigris into the upper and lower Pearl rivers; the lower river constitutes the bay 20 m. wide bet. Hong Kong and Macao; below Canton the upper Pearl is joined by the Tung from the E.
3 Urban community (unincorporated), Rankin co., S cen. Mississippi, S of Jackson; pop. 5081.

Pearl and Her'mes Reef (pûrl, hûr'mēz). Reef in Hawaii consisting of 12 islets, in cen. Pacific Ocean ab. 1000 m. NW of Niihau I.; part of Leeward Is. and included in Hawaiian Islands Bird Reservation.

Pearl Cays or **Islands.** Group of small islands in Caribbean Sea near the coast of SE cen. Nicaragua, outside of Perlas Lagoon.

Pearl City. Village, Ewa dist., Honolulu co., S Oahu I., Hawaii, on Pearl Harbor; pop. (est.) 6000; suffered damage in Japanese attack on Pearl Harbor Dec. 7, 1941.

Pearl Coast. Eastern portion of N coast of Isthmus of Darien (Panama), granted 1508 to Alonso de Ojeda for settlement; earliest successful settlement was Darien (*q.v.*) 1510.

Pearl Harbor. Inlet on S coast of the island of Oahu, Hawaii, 6 m. W of Honolulu, forming a landlocked harbor used by U.S. as a naval base; connected with Pacific Ocean by Pearl Harbor entrance. By treaty of 1887 Hawaii granted U.S. exclusive right to use Pearl Harbor as coaling and repair station; not so used until 1908 when Congress authorized establishment of naval station; dry dock completed 1919; attacked without warning by Japanese air force Sunday morning Dec. 7, 1941.

Pearl Islands. 1 See PEARL CAYS.
2 Group of islands belonging to Panama in the Gulf of Panama; 450 sq. m.; pearl fisheries.

Pearl Lagoon. See PERLAS LAGOON.

Pearl Point. See Punta de PERLAS.

Pearl River. 1 River in Mississippi. See PEARL, 1.
2 County in Mississippi. See *Table* at MISSISSIPPI.
3 Residential village, Rockland co., SE New York, near New Jersey border ab. 12 m. NE of Paterson, New Jersey; pop. (est.) 9000; manufactures machinery.
4 River in China. See PEARL, 2.

Pear'sall (pēr'sôl). City, ⊗ of Frio co., S Texas, 43 m. ESE of Uvalde; pop. 4957; in winter-garden area.

Pear'son (pēr's'n). City, ⊗ of Atkinson co., S Georgia; pop. 1615.

Pea'ry Land' (pēr'ĭ), also **Pea'ry·land'.** Region of N Greenland on Arctic Ocean, forming a mountainous peninsula, 82° to 84°N; does not have the icecap that covers most of Greenland. Its N cape, Morris Jesup, is the most northerly point of land known in the Arctic Regions; penetrated by several fiords; highest point ab. 6500 ft. First visited by Greely and Lockwood 1881–82; explored by Peary 1892 and 1900.

Peb'ble Island (pĕb''l). Island off N coast of West Falkland, Falkland Is.

Peć (pĕch; *Yugoslav* pĕt'y') or **Pech;** *Turk.* **I·pek'** (ĭ·pĕk'). Town, W Kosovo-Metohija autonomous region, S Yugoslavia, ab. 75 m. NW of Skoplje; pop. 13,194; in the Middle Ages, seat of the Patriarchs of the Serbian Orthodox Church.

Pe·chen'ga (pĕ·chĕng'gà; *Russ.* pyĭ·chĕn'gà). **1** Territory. See PETSAMO.
2 *formerly* **Pet'sa·mo** (pĕt'sà·mō; *Finn.* -sà·mô). Village in Murmansk Region, NW Soviet Russia, Europe, in extreme NW part on narrow inlet of Arctic Ocean, 60 m. W of Murmansk; used by Finnish-German forces as a naval and aviation base in World War II. Belonged to Finland 1920–44.

Pechili. See POHAI.

Pe·cho'ra (pĕ·chôr'à; *Russ.* pyĭ·chô'rà). River ab. 1125 m. long in NE Soviet Russia, Europe, chiefly in Komi A.S.S.R.; rises in Middle Ural Mts. in N Molotov Region, flows N, W, and N in great bend into Pechora Bay; its main tributaries the Tsilma and Izhma on the W and the Usa on the E; both the main stream and its tributaries are navigable for most of their courses; has extensive delta; coal fields in its basin.

Pechora Bay. Inlet of Barents Sea ab. 40 m. long on NE coast of Nenets National District, Soviet Russia, Europe; receives Pechora river from the S.

Peck'ville (pĕk'vĭl). Locality, Lackawanna co., NE Pennsylvania, NE of Scranton; post office for borough of Blakely.

Pe·con'ic Bay (pĕ·kŏn'ĭk). Inlet SW of Gardiners Bay at E end of Long I., New York, divided into **Great Peconic Bay** on the W and **Little Peconic Bay** on the E; receives the **Peconic River.**

Pe'cos (pā'kŭs). **1** or **Ri'o Pecos** (rē'ō). River 735 m. long, E New Mexico and W Texas; rises in W Mora co., flows SE through E New Mexico across Texas border and empties into Rio Grande in S Val Verde co., SW Texas.
2 County in Texas. See *Table* at TEXAS.
3 City, ⊗ of Reeves co., W Texas, near Pecos river 40 m. S of New Mexico border; pop. 12,728; in cattle-raising and farming section; oil wells and refining; gypsum, sulfur, silver, copper deposits in vicinity.

Pécs (pāch); *Ger.* **Fünf'kir'chen** (fünf'kir'κĕn). Municipality, S Hungary, W of the Danube; 27 sq. m.; pop. (1939) 70,547; in coal-mining section; 11th-cent. cathedral; occupied by Turks 1543–1686.

Ped'die (pĕd'ĭ). Town, SE Cape Province, S Union of South Africa, 105 m. NE of Port Elizabeth.

Ped'docks Island (pĕd'ŭks). Island in S area of Boston Bay, E Massachusetts, off N tip of Plymouth co.

Pedee. Var. of PEE DEE.

Ped'er·nal' Peak (pĕd'ĕr·năl'). Mountain 7580 ft. in S Rio Arriba co., N New Mexico.

Ped'er·nal'es (pûr'd'n·ăl'ĕs). River ab. 105 m. long, cen. Texas; rises in Gillespie co. and flows E to Colorado river NW of Austin.

Pe·di·as' (pē·thyäs'); *anc.* **Ped'i·ae'us** (pĕd'ĭ·ē'ŭs). River ab. 60 m. long on the island of Cyprus, flowing E to Famagusta Bay at ancient Salamis.

Pe'dras, Point (pā'thräs); *Braz.* **Pun'ta de Pedras** (poōnn'tả thĕ). Cape extending into Atlantic Ocean on SE coast of Paraíba state, E Brazil; most easterly point of South America, 34°55'W.

Pe'dre·gal' (pā'thrả·gäl'). **1** River ab. 50 m. long in SE Mexico; rises in W Chiapas state, flows N to the Tonalá in Tabasco state.
2 Pacific coast port, W Panama; port for David.

Pe'dro Bank (pā'drō; *Span.* pā'thrô). Shoal in NW Caribbean Sea S of Jamaica; includes the Pedro Cays.

Pe'dro Be·tan·court' (pā'thrô vā'täng·koōrt'). Municipality and town, Matanzas prov., W cen. Cuba; town 27 m. SE of Matanzas, pop. (1943) 6030.

Pe'dro Cays (pā'drō; *Span.* pā'thrô). Four small guano islands ab. 45 m. SW of Jamaica; a dependency of Jamaica from 1882.

Pe'dro Juan Ca'bal·le'ro (pā'thrô hwän kä'vä·yä'rô). Town, ✳ of Amambay dept., E Paraguay, on Brazilian border 125 m. ENE of Concepción; pop. ab. 7200.

Pe'dro Mi·guel' (pā'thrô mē·gĕl'; *Angl. locally* pē'tēr mĭ·gil'). Town, Balboa dist., Canal Zone, at the Pedro Miguel Locks in the Panama Canal, just NW of Miraflores; pop. 603.

Pedro Miguel Locks. Double locks in the Panama Canal, Canal Zone, NW of Miraflores Lake and NW of the city of Panama; lower vessels 30½ ft. to level of Miraflores Lake.

Pe'dro Point (pā'drō; *Span.* pā'thrô). Cape on NW tip of the island of Jamaica, West Indies.

Pee'bles (pē'b'lz). **1** *or* **Pee'bles·shire** (-shĭr; -shēr) *or* **Tweed'dale** (twēd'dāl'). County, SE Scotland; 347 sq. m.; pop. (1951) 15,226; ⊗ Peebles; its chief river the Tweed; agriculture, manufacture of woolen goods.
2 Burgh, its ⊗, on the Tweed; pop. 6013; tourist resort; farm trading center; woolen mills.

Pee Dee (pē' dē'). River 233 m. long, North Carolina and South Carolina; formed by junction of Yadkin and Uharie rivers in Montgomery co., S cen. North Carolina, flows SE into South Carolina and into Winyah Bay.

Peek'a·moose' Mountain (pēk'ả·moōs'). Peak 3863 ft. in the Catskill Mts., Ulster co., SE New York.

Peeks'kill (pēks'kĭl). City, Westchester co., SE New York, on Hudson river 39 m. N of New York; pop. 18,737; manufactures yeast and alcohol; dairy farming. In Revolution often sheltered Gen. Washington and other American officers; scene of capture of Edward Palmer, Tory spy (hanged on nearby Gallows Hill); burned by British 1777.

Peel (pēl). **1** River 365 m. long, NW Canada; rises in W Yukon Territory, flows E and then N into Mackenzie river in NW Mackenzie District, Northwest Territories.
2 County, Ontario, Canada. See *Table* at ONTARIO.
3 Town, W Isle of Man, England, on Irish Sea; pop. 2477; fishing center and seaside resort; ancient chapel dedicated to St. Patrick, who is believed to have founded first church in Isle of Man; ruins of castle and cathedral.

Peel (pāl). Marsh area 60 sq. m. in North Brabant and Limburg provs., S Netherlands.

Peel Sound (pēl). Passage bet. Prince of Wales I. and Somerset I. Franklin District, Northwest Territories, Canada.

Pee'ne (pā'nĕ). Navigable river ab. 70 m. long in N Germany; flows E through Pomerania into Stettiner Haff.

Pee'ne·mün'de (pā'nĕ·mün'dĕ). Village on small island at mouth of Peene river, Mecklenburg, eastern Germany, at W end of Usedom I. and NW of Stettiner Haff; developed in World War II with great science laboratories and industrial plants, esp. factories for making robot bombs; severely bombed by Allies Aug. 18, 1943; captured by Russians Apr. 1945 and completely destroyed.

Peg'a·sus Bay (pĕg'ả·sŭs). Inlet of Pacific Ocean on NE cen. coast of South I., New Zealand, N of Banks Penin.; receives the Waimakariri river from the W.

Pe'gli (pĕl'yĕ). Seaport, Genova prov., E cen. Liguria, NW Italy, now part of Genoa; resort.

Peg'nitz (pāg'nĭts). River ab. 60 m. long, Bavaria, S Germany; flows S and W through Nürnberg to unite with the Rednitz at Fürth and form the Regnitz river.

Pe·gu' (pĕ·goō'). **1** River ab. 150 m. long in Pegu dist., Lower Burma; tributary of the Rangoon river.
2 Division of Lower Burma. See *Table* at BURMA.
3 District in Pegu division; 4124 sq. m.; pop. 489,969.
4 Town, ✳ of Pegu dist., 47 m. NE of Rangoon and on railroad from Rangoon to Toungoo and to Martaban; pop. 21,712; has pagodas (most famous, the Shwemaw-daw, 324 ft. high), statues, halls, and traces of ancient walls. Founded in 6th cent. as first capital of Talaings (Mons); flourished later as capital of Toungoo dynasty of Pegu kingdom; when destroyed by Alompra 1757 had pop. of 100,000; site of another kingdom overcome in Second Burmese War by British 1852; seized by Japanese Mar. 8, 1942, recaptured by British May 1944.

Pegu Yo'ma (yō'mả). Mountain range ab. 270 m. long in Lower Burma, extending N and S bet. the Irrawaddy and the Sittang rivers; highest point Mt. Popa 4981 ft. at N end.

Peh (bä) *or* **Pei** (bä). River ab. 220 m. long, cen. Kwangtung prov., SE China; rises in S Hunan and flows S to join the Si delta W of Canton.

Pehanchen. See PEIAN town.

Pehlevi. Var. of PAHLEVI.

Peh'piao', *also* **Pei Pao** (bä'pyou'). Town, E Jehol prov., NE China, on railroad 50 m. NW of Chinhsien; important coal-mining area.

Peh'tai'ho' (bä'dī'hŏ'), *also* **Pei'tai'ho'** (bä'-). Town, NE Hopeh prov., NE China, ab. 15 m. SSW of Chinwangtao; most noted summer resort in N China with fine beach on Gulf of Po Hai; originated 1894–95.

Peh'tang' (bä'täng'), *also* **Pei'tang'** (bä'-). Town, Hopeh prov., NE China, on Gulf of Po Hai, at mouth of Pehtang river 10 m. N of Taku. Treaty signed here 1859; British and French forces landed in operations against Taku forts 1860.

Pei. 1 (bī) *or* **Pei-ho** (bī'hŏ'). Literally "White River," river ab. 350 m. long in Hopeh prov., NE China; rises beyond the Great Wall and flows SE into the Gulf of Po Hai at Taku; navigable for ab. 100 m. See HAI.
2 (bä) See PEH.

Pei'an' (bä'än'). **1** Former province (1932–45), N cen. Manchukuo; 27,596 sq. m.; pop. (1940 est.) 2,318,052.
2 *or* **Peh'an'chen'** (bä'än'jŭn'). Town, its ✳, now in E cen. Heilungkiang prov., N Manchuria, on railroad N to Aigun, ab. 125 m. NE of Lungkiang.

Pei-lin. See SIAN.

Pei'ne (pī'nĕ). City, Lower Saxony state, West Germany, formerly in Hannover prov., Prussia, 17 m. NE of Hildesheim; pop. 17,111; manufactures iron goods, furniture; trades in manufactured goods, wool, grain, mill products. Founded c. 1220.

Pei Pao. See PEHPIAO.

Pei'ping' (bä'pĭng'), *literally* "Northern Peace," *or* **Pe'king'** (pē'kĭng'; *Chin.* bä'jĭng'). City in extensive plain of N Hopeh province, NE China; ✳ of China

and of former Chihli province, pop. (1959 est.) 6,800,000. Not a commercial city but the chief intellectual and literary center of China. Has many modern improvements; consists of Inner or Tatar City (N area), nearly square, and Outer or Chinese City (S area), rectangular, the two together having an area of 25 sq. m. and surrounded by high walls built by the Ming emperor Yung Lo (1403–24), with three gates in the wall bet. the two parts. In the Inner City are the old Imperial city ("Forbidden City") with parks and the Purple Forbidden Palace, former legations, Peking Univ., Lama and Confucian temples, colleges, hospitals, and public buildings; in the Outer City are the Temple of Heaven and Temple of Agriculture.

History: Had various names in ancient times; a frontier town for centuries, known as Ch'i (or Yen, from the district) under Chou dynasty (1122–255 B.C.) and later. Capital of powerful monarchy, 10th to 12th cents. A.D., under the Khitan Mongols and the Kin Tatar dynasty; as Khanbalik became residence of Kublai Khan 1264–67 and capital of China 1267–1368 under Yuan dynasty; known to Europeans as Cambaluc, Marco Polo's name. Under Mings replaced as capital for a short time but in 1421 again chosen as capital and so continued under the Manchus (1644–1912). Scene of severe fighting in Boxer Rebellion 1900–01; in 1928 Nanking made capital and name Peking ("Northern Capital") changed to Peiping. At the Marco Polo Bridge 9 m. SW (see LUKOUCHIAO) on July 7, 1937 fighting broke out bet. Japanese and Chinese troops, the incident that began the Chinese-Japanese War (1937–45); surrendered to Communist forces in 1949 and again made capital.

Pei'pus (pī'pŏŏs); *Estonian* **Peip'si** (pāp'sĭ); *Russ.* **Chud'sko·e O'ze·ro** (chŏŏt'skŭ·yĕ ô'zyĭ·rŭ). Lake, E Estonia and W Pskov Region, Soviet Russia, Europe; 93 m. long; 1357 sq. m. Its outlet is the Narova flowing N to Gulf of Finland; receives from the S the Velikaya and from the W the Ema. Its S extension is sometimes called Lake Pskov (*q.v.*). Russian-Estonian boundary line runs nearly in center except at N end, where entire N shore and Narova river are in Estonia. Center of much fighting in World War II, esp. in Aug. 1941 and Sept. 1944.

Peiraieus, Peiraievs, *or* **Peiraeus.** See PIRAEUS.

Peitaiho. See PEHTAIHO.

Peitang. See PEHTANG.

Pei'war Pass (pā'wär) *or* **Peiwar Ko'tal** (kō'tŭl). Mountain pass at W end of Safed Koh range from NW West Pakistan into Afghanistan, SE of Kabul, in the Kurram valley; scene of defeat of Afghans by Lord Roberts Dec. 1878.

Pe·ka'long'an (pĕ·kä'lông'än). **1** Former residency, NW Middle Java prov., Neth. Indies; 2176 sq. m.; pop. 2,640,124; ✳ Pekalongan. Bounded on N by Java Sea, on E by Semarang residency, on S by Banjumas, and on W by Cheribon residency of West Java prov. Region has considerable area of flat fertile land along the coast with mountain range along S border; chief crop sugar; much rice and some coffee, cocoa, and kapok grown. Chief towns Pekalongan, Tegal, Pemalang, and Batang. **2** City, Indonesia, on N coast and on railroad 55 m. W of Semarang; pop. 65,982; exports sugar.

Pe·kan' (pĕ·kän'). Seaport town on S side of the Pahang river near its mouth, E Pahang state, Federation of Malaysia; pop. 1206; sultan's residence and until 1898 the capital.

Pe'kin (pē'kĭn). City, ⊗ of Tazewell co., cen. Illinois, on Illinois river 10 m. S of Peoria; pop. 28,146; shipping and industrial center in agricultural section; makes cereal products, alcohol, leather and metal products.

Pe'king' (pē'kĭng'; *Chin.* bā'jĭng'). Literally "Northern Capital," capital of China from 1421, under Ming dynasty to 1928. See PEIPING.

Pe·la'gi·an Islands (pĕ·lā'jĭ·ăn; -jăn); *Ital.* **I'so·le Pe·la'gie** (ē'zô·lä pä·lä'jä). Three barren Italian islands, Lampedusa, Linosa, and Lampione (uninhabited),

in the Mediterranean Sea S of Sicily and bet. Malta and Tunisia; pop. (1931) ab. 4000; politically attached to Agrigento prov., Italy. Taken by Allies June 12–13, 1943.

Pelagosa Islands. See PALAGRUŽA ISLANDS.

Pe·lée', Mount (pē·lā'); *Fr.* **Mon'tagne' Pe·lée'** (môN'tàn'y' pē·lā'). Volcano 4428 ft. in N Martinique I., French West Indies; erupted 1902, destroying Saint Pierre and killing more than 30,000 persons, including all the town's inhabitants and many others that had sought refuge there.

Pe'lee, Point (pē'lē). Headland in Essex co., SE Ontario prov., Canada, projecting into Lake Erie; has remarkable beaches and flora; established 1918 as a national park: see CANADA, *National Parks* (Point Pelee).

Pelee Island, 8 m. to the S in Lake Erie, is the most southerly point of the Dominion of Canada, 41°40'N.

Pel'e·liu (pĕl'ē·lū; *popularly* pĕl'ē·lē'ōō). Island ab. 5 m. long by 2 m. wide at S end of Palau Is., W Pacific Ocean, bet. Angaur and Eil Malk; chief village Ngardololok. Many islets and reefs off its N shore. Bombed by American naval and air forces 1944; captured by assault after bitter fighting Sept. 14 to Oct. 13, 1944.

Pe'leng (pä'lĕng). Largest island in the Banggai Archipelago off the E coast of Celebes I., Indonesia, Malay Archipelago; ab. 53 m. long by 32 m. wide; 975 sq. m.

Peleng Strait. Passage bet. E peninsula of Celebes and Peleng I. of the Banggai Archipelago, connecting the Gulf of Tolo with the Molucca Sea.

Pelew. See PALAU.

Pel'ham (pĕl'ăm). **1** City, Mitchell co., SW Georgia, 32 m. S of Albany; pop. 4609; incorporated 1881; peanut-processing plants, cannery, lumber mills, cotton gins; tobacco, peanut, and cottonseed market.

2 Village in Pelham town (pop. 13,404), Westchester co., SE New York, 17 m. NE of New York; pop. 1964; residential suburb of New York City.

Pelham Man'or (măn'ēr). Village in Pelham town (pop. 13,404), Westchester co., SE New York, on Long Island Sound 17 m. NE of New York; pop. 6114; residential suburb of New York City.

Pel'i·can Island (pĕl'ĭ·kăn). Island in Atlantic Ocean, off NE coast of Volusia co., E Florida.

Pelican Point. Cape on W cen. coast of South-West Africa, enclosing Walvis Bay.

Pelican Rapids. Village, Otter Tail co., W cen. Minnesota, 20 m. N of Fergus Falls; pop. 1693; trading and shipping point for livestock and grain.

Pe'li·le'o (pā'lē·lā'ô). Town, Tungurahua prov., cen. Ecuador, just N of Riobamba; pop. (1944 est.) 10,031.

Pe'li·on (pē'lĭ·ŏn); *Mod. Gr.* **Pé'li·on** (pē'lyôn). Peak 5308 ft. in S Larissa dept., E Thessaly, NE Greece, near Volos. In Greek legend figured in the wars of the giants (Aloadae) and was the home of the centaurs, esp. Chiron.

Pe'lje·šac (pĕ'lyĕ·shäts); *Ital.* **Sab'bion·cel'lo** (säb'-byôn·chĕl'lô). Peninsula 43 m. long on coast of Dalmatia, W Yugoslavia, projecting NW into the Adriatic Sea E of Korčula I.

Pel'la (pĕl'à). **1** City, Marion co., S cen. Iowa, 17 m. WNW of Oskaloosa; pop. 5198; settled by Dutch immigrants 1847. Central College (1853; coed.; Dutch Reformed Church of America).

2 (*Mod. Gr.* pâ'lä) Department of Greece. See *Table* at GREECE.

3 Ruins of an ancient city near Genitsa and 24 m. WNW of Salonika, Greece; ancient capital of Macedonia and birthplace of Alexander the Great.

4 Town of ancient Gilead, Palestine, just E of the Jordan.

Pell City (pĕl). Town, ⊗ of St. Clair co., NE cen. Alabama; pop. 4165.

Pel'les·tri'na (pĕl'ĕs·trē'nä; *Ital.* päl·läs·trē'nä). Island 9 m. long in S Lagoon of Venice, Italy; a part of the commune of Venice; pop. (1931) ab. 5000.

Pellew Islands. = SIR EDWARD PELLEW GROUP.

Pell'worm (pĕl'vôrm). One of the Halligen Is., in S part of North Frisian Is. off W coast of Schleswig-Holstein, northwestern Germany, W of Nordstrand; area 15 sq. m.

Pel'ly (pĕl'ĭ). **1** Former city, Harris co., SE Texas, on Galveston Bay; now part of Baytown.
2 River 330 m. long, S cen. Yukon Territory, Canada; rises in Mackenzie Mts. and flows W to unite with Lewes river and form Yukon river.

Pelly, Lake. Lake 331 sq. m. on N part of boundary bet. Mackenzie District and Keewatin District, Northwest Territories, Canada; connects with Lake Garry.

Pelly Bay. Bay, inlet of Gulf of Boothia, in N Keewatin District, Northwest Territories, Canada, W of Simpson Penin.

Pe·lon·cil'lo Mountains (pā'lŭn·sē'yō). Range in extreme SW New Mexico, in SW Hidalgo co. and extending across border into Arizona.

Pel'o·pon·ne'sus (pĕl'ō·pŏ·nē'sŭs) *or* **Pel'o·pon·ne'-sos** (pĕl'ō·pŏ·nē'sŏs; *Mod. Gr.* pä'lô·pô·nyĕ·sôs), *also* **Pel'o·pon·nese'** (pĕl'ō·pŏ·nēs'; -nēz'). **1** Peninsula forming S part of the mainland of Greece; ancient subdivisions: Achaea, Arcadia, Argolis, Corinth, Elis, Laconia, Messenia, and Sicyonia (*qq.v.*); chief cities Corinth and Sparta (*qq.v.*); under the Romans was larger part of the province of Achaea 146 B.C.–c. 4th cent. A.D.; since 12th cent. when it was under the Byzantine Empire often called **Mo·re'a** (mô·rē'ȧ) because of its resemblance in shape to a mulberry leaf (*Lat.* morus).
2 Geographical division of modern Greece, coextensive with the peninsula; 8603 sq. m.; pop. (1938 est.) 1,185,046; forms Greek departments of Achaea and Elis, Arcadia, Argolis and Corinth, Laconia, and Messenia (see *Table* at GREECE).

Pelorus. See Cape FARO.

Pe·lo'tas (pĕ·lō'tȧs). City, SE Rio Grande do Sul state, S Brazil, at S end of Lagoa dos Patos 29 m. NNW of Rio Grande; pop. (1940 est.) 62,674; a center of the dried-meat industry; exports also hides, rice, and grapes.

Pelouse. Var. of PALOUSE.

Pel'to, Lake (pĕl'tō). Inlet of Gulf of Mexico in S Terrebonne parish, SE Louisiana.

Pe·lu'si·ac Branch (pē·lū'shĭ·ăk). Ancient E arm of the Nile river, E of the Phatnitic (Damietta) mouth, now filled up.

Pe·lu'si·um (pē·lū'shĭ·ŭm). Ancient city of Egypt, on Pelusiac Branch of the Nile; ruins are in Plain of Tina E of Suez Canal and ab. 22 m. SE of Port Said, on **Bay of Pelusium,** an inlet of the Mediterranean.

Pel'voux' (pĕl'vōō'). Mountain group in SE France, in the Dauphiné Alps in Hautes-Alpes and Isère depts.; contains Barre des Écrins 13,462 ft., highest peak of the Dauphiné Alps; **Mont Pelvoux** 12,970 ft., just SE of Barre des Écrins, was for a long time considered the highest point.

Pel'zer (pĕl'zēr). Locality, Anderson co., NW South Carolina, on Saluda river ab. 15 m. SSW of Greenville; pop. 4245; textile manufactures.

Pem'a·dum'cook Lake (pĕm'ȧ·dŭm'kōōk). Lake on boundary bet. Penobscot and Piscataquis cos., N cen. Maine; connected with Millinocket Lake on the NE; traversed NW to SE by West Branch of the Penobscot river.

Pe·ma·lang' (pā'mä·läng'). Town, Central Java prov., Indonesia, on railroad near coast bet. Pekalongan and Tegal; pop. 29,249.

Pem'a·quid Point (pĕm'ȧ·kwĭd'). Point, S Lincoln co., S Maine.

Pe·ma'ťang·sian'tar (pĕ·mä'täng·syän'tär). Town, NE Sumatra, Indonesia, 23 m. NE of Lake Toba; pop. 15,328; terminus of branch railroad from Medan.

Pem'ba (pĕm'bȧ). Island in Indian Ocean off NE coast of Tanganyika, E Africa, N of island of Zanzibar; 380 sq. m.; pop. 97,687; ✻ Chake Chake; included with island of Zanzibar in the Zanzibar sultanate.

Pemba Bay. Inlet of Mozambique Channel on NE coast of Mozambique; constitutes harbor for seaport of Porto Amelia.

Pem'bi·na (pĕm'bĭ·nô; -nȧ). **1** County in North Dakota. See *Table* at NORTH DAKOTA.
2 City, Pembina co., NE North Dakota, ab. 22 m. NE of Cavalier; pop. 625; site of earliest trading post (1797–98) and center of white settlement in North Dakota.
3 River ab. 210 m. long in cen. Alberta, Canada; rises near E border of Jasper National Park and flows NE and N into the Athabaska.

Pem'broke (pĕm'brŏk; -brŭk; *in England usually* -brŏŏk). **1** City, ⊗ of Bryan co., SE Georgia, 31 m. W of Savannah; pop. 1450.
2 Town, Plymouth co., SE Massachusetts, 10 m. E of Brockton; pop. 4919; formerly a shipbuilding center.
3 Town, Merrimack co., S cen. New Hampshire, on Merrimack river 6 m. SE of Concord; pop. 3514; settled 1728, incorp. 1759; state game farm.
4 Town in Pembroke township (pop. 5043), Robeson co., S North Carolina, ab. 12 m. NW of Lumberton; pop. 1372. Pembroke State College (1887; coed.).
5 Town, ⊗ of Renfrew co., SE Ontario, Canada, on Allumette Lake across from Allumette I.; pop. 12,704; sawmills, various factories; noted as a trout-fishing center and gateway to Algonquin Provincial Park. Probable site of limit of Champlain's exploration to the West 1613, where he was forced to turn back.
6 County in Wales. See PEMBROKESHIRE.
7 Municipal borough, Pembrokeshire, SW Wales; pop. 12,296; ruins of castle, birthplace of King Henry VII (1457). The large naval dockyard was closed down in 1926.

Pem'broke·shire (pĕm'brŏŏk·shĭr; -brŏk-; -shēr) *or* **Pembroke.** County, SW Wales; area 614 sq. m.; pop. (1951) 90,896; ⊗ Haverfordwest; mining (coal, iron, lead), quarrying (slate), agriculture, cattle raising.

Pem'i·ge·was'set (pĕm'ĭ·jĕ·wŏs'ĕt; -ĭt). River 70 m. long in cen. New Hampshire; rises in N Grafton co., flows S through Franconia Notch, unites with Winnipesaukee river at Franklin to form the Merrimack river; the **Pemigewasset Wilderness** is the region bet. Franconia Notch and Crawford Notch (Saco river) to the E containing many peaks of the White Mts., several over 4000 ft.

Pem'i·scot (pĕm'ĭ·skŏt; -skō). County in Missouri. See *Table* at MISSOURI.

Pen (pĕn). Village, ancient Sussex, S England; probably Penselwood in S Somersetshire, S of Frome; scene of defeat of Canute by Edmund II 1016.

Pen'a·cook (pĕn'ȧ·kŏŏk). Manufacturing village, Merrimack co., S cen. New Hampshire, on the Merrimack river 6 m. N of Concord.

Pe'ña·la'ra, Pi'co de (pē'kŏ thä pā'nyä·lä'rä). Highest peak 7890 ft. in Sierra de Guadarrama, cen. Spain.

Pe·nang' (pĕ·năng'; *native* pē'näng). **1** Island 2½ m. off W coast of the Malay Penin., at N end of Strait of Malacca; ab. 15 m. long by 9 m. wide; 108 sq. m.; pop. 198,871. In early years known as Prince of Wales I.
2 A state of the Federation of Malaya, including Penang I. and Province Wellesley; 388 sq. m.; pop. 340,259, (1941 est.) 419,047; ✻ George Town. Penang I. the first British settlement in Malaya, acquired 1786 by cession to East India Co. from sultan of Kedah; Province Wellesley added 1798. Made separate presidency 1805 and was seat of government for three settlements (Penang, Malacca, Singapore) 1826–36; became part of the crown colony of Straits Settlements 1867; bombed and occupied by Japanese Dec. 1941; became part of Federation of Malaya 1948.
3 Seaport city, ✻ of Penang settlement, officially known as George Town (*q.v.*).

Pen Ar'gyl (pĕn är'jĭl). Borough, Northampton co., E Pennsylvania, 22 m. NE of Allentown; pop. 3693; slate quarries; shoe manufactures.

Pe′ñar·ro′ya–Pue′blo·nue′vo (pā′nyär·rô′yä·pwā′vlô-nwä′vô). Commune, Córdoba prov., S Spain, 40 m. NW of Córdoba; pop. 29,161; iron, lead, and bituminous coal.

Pen·arth′ (pĕn·ärth′). Urban district, and seaport, Glamorganshire, SE Wales; pop. 18,528; watering place, a suburb of Cardiff; ships coal. In World War II a U.S. naval training base.

Pe′ñas, Cape (pā′nyäs); *Span.* **Ca′bo de Peñas** (kä′vô thä). **1** Cape on NW coast of Spain, projecting into Bay of Biscay from Oviedo prov.
2 Cape on E cen. coast of Tierra del Fuego I., off S South America.

Peñas, Gulf of. Inlet of S Pacific Ocean on SW coast of Chile, S of Taitao Penin.

Pen′brook (pĕn′brŏŏk). Borough, Dauphin co., SE cen. Pennsylvania, 3 m. NE of Harrisburg; pop. 3671.

Pen′co (pāng′kŏ). Town, Concepción prov., S cen. Chile, on coast N of Concepción; pop. 6803; coal mines.

Pen·dem′bu (pĕn·dĕm′bŏŏ). Town, SE Sierra Leone protectorate, W Africa, near border of Liberia; terminus of railroad (227 m. long) from Freetown.

Pen′der (pĕn′dēr). **1** County in North Carolina. See *Table* at NORTH CAROLINA.
2 Village, ⊗ of Thurston co., NE Nebraska; pop. 1165.

Pen′dle·ton (pĕn′d'l·tŭn; -t′n). **1** Name of counties in two states of the U.S. See *Tables* at KENTUCKY and WEST VIRGINIA.
2 Residential town, Madison co., cen. Indiana, 26 m. ENE of Indianapolis; pop. 2472.
3 City, ⊗ of Umatilla co., NE Oregon, on Umatilla river ab. 42 m. NW of La Grande; pop. 14,434; produces wheat, livestock; manufactures Indian blankets, robes, flour, saddles, foundry and machine-shop products, leather and woolen goods. Became ⊗ 1865; center for E Oregon cattle country in 1870's and 1880's.

Pend O·reille′ (pŏn′dŭ·rā′). **1** River ab. 100 m. long, N Idaho and NE Washington, outlet of Pend Oreille Lake; flows W and N into Columbia river in Brit. Columbia near Washington boundary.
2 County in Washington. See *Table* at WASHINGTON.

Pend Oreille, Mount. Peak 6785 ft. in Bonner co., N Idaho.

Pend Oreille Lake. Lake ab. 35 m. long and 8 m. wide in cen. Bonner co., N Idaho; an expansion of Clark Fork.

Pe·ne′do (pĕ·nâ′thŏŏ). City, Alagoas state, E Brazil, on the São Francisco near its mouth 70 m. SW of Maceió; pop. (1940 est.) 12,856.

Pēneios. See SALAMBRIA.

Pen′e·tan′gui·shene′ (pĕn′ĕ·tăng′gwĭ·shēn′). Town, Simcoe co., SE Ontario, Canada, on an inlet of Georgian Bay 29 m. NNW of Barrie; pop. 4949; summer resort; prior to disarmament convention with United States, Canada's naval station on the Great Lakes; has memorial church commemorating the establishment of the Jesuits on this site 1634. Visited by Champlain 1615.

Pe·ne′us (pĕ·nē′ŭs). **1** See SALAMBRIA.
2 River ab. 50 m. long, Achaea and Elis dept., NW Peloponnesus, Greece; flows W to Ionian Sea.

Pen′field (pĕn′fēld). Village in Penfield town (pop. 12,601), Monroe co., W New York, ab. 7 m. SE of Rochester; pop. (est.) 3000.

Pen·gan′ga (pĕng·gŭng′gä). River ab. 200 m. long, cen. India; flows E, forming most of the S boundary of Berar region, to the Wardha river.

Penge (pĕnj). Urban district, Kent, SE England, 6 m. S of London; pop. 25,009; part of Greater London.

Peng′hu′ (pŭng′hŏŏ′). **1** See PESCADORES.
2 Island, chief of the Pescadores group.

Peng′lai′ (pŭng′lī′); *formerly* **Teng′chow′** (dŭng′jō′). Town on N coast of Shantung Penin., NE China, on Pohai Strait; pop. ab. 40,000; has good harbor.

Peng′pu′ (pŭng′pŏŏ′). Town, Anhwei prov., E China, on Hwai river 100 m. NW of Nanking; government base during civil war 1946 ff.; evacuated Jan. 19, 1949.

Pen′guin (pĕn′gwĭn; pĕng′-). Municipality and seaport

on N coast of Tasmania, Australia, 10 m. E of Burnie; pop. (municipality) 2832; tourist resort.

Penhsihu. See PENKI.

Pe′nig (pā′nĭk). Industrial town, Saxony, Germany, ab. 30 m. SE of Leipzig; now in Karl-Marx-Stadt dist.; pop. 7410; site of concentration camp during World War II.

Pen′i·kese Island (pĕn′ĭ·kēs). Small island at S end of Buzzards Bay, Massachusetts, N of Cuttyhunk I.; former school of natural history, estab. 1873 by Louis Agassiz, and game sanctuary.

Pen·in′su·la, Point (pĕn·ĭn′sŭ·là). Point, N New York, extending into Lake Ontario NW of Sackets Harbor.

Peninsula, the. **1** A district in SE Virginia, bet. the York and James rivers; Fort Monroe is at its SE tip; Richmond, to the NW, was Federal objective in an unsuccessful campaign Apr. 4–July 1, 1862 during the Civil War; McClellan was opposed by Gen. Johnston and after Fair Oaks (*q.v.*) by Robert E. Lee who took the offensive at Mechanicsville June 26. See also GAINES' MILL and MALVERN HILL.
2 The Iberian Peninsula, including Spain and Portugal; scene of 5th phase of Napoleonic Wars, the Peninsular War 1808–14, in which the British, Portuguese, and Spanish successfully opposed Napoleon's forces and Wellington earned for himself the title of duke; chief battles at La Coruña, Talavera (Talavera de la Reina), and Vitoria (*qq.v.*).

Peninsula Point. Point at S tip of peninsula forming E side of Little Bay de Noc, Delta co., S Michigan penin., jutting into Green Bay.

Peninsular Siam. A name often given to that part of the Malay Penin. within the borders of Siam; it applies esp. to the region S of Prachuap Khiri Khan (ab. 12°N) to the border of the Federation of Malaya.

Pén′ja·mo (pāng′hä·mô). Town, SW Guanajuato state, cen. Mexico, on line S.W. of Guanajuato; pop. 8795.

Penjdeh. See PANJDEH.

Pen′ki′ (bŭn′chē′) *or* **Pen′hsi′hu′** (bŭn′shē′hŏŏ′). Town, S Liaoning prov., S Manchuria, on Antung-Mukden railroad 30 m. E of Liaoyang; pop. (1940 est.) 100,057; large coal mines.

Pen′maen·mawr′ (pĕn′mīn·mour′). Town, Caernarvonshire, NW Wales, on coast near NE entrance to Menai Strait; pop. (urban district) 4218; resort.

Pen′march′ (păn′mär′). Village, Finistère dept., NW France, 18 m. SW of Quimper on a small peninsula which ends in **Point Penmarch**; pop. 823; nearby are remains of the seaport which flourished 14th–16th cents.

Pen′ne (pän′nå); *anc.* **Pin′na** (pĭn′à). Commune, Pescara prov., Abruzzi e Molise, cen. Italy, 15 m. W of Pescara; pop. 12,784; cathedral (10th cent. or earlier).

Pen·nell′, Mount (pĕ·nĕl′). Peak 11,320 ft. in E Garfield co., S Utah.

Pen′ner (pĕn′ēr). Two rivers of SE cen. India: **Northern Penner,** ab. 350 m. long; rises in SE Mysore, flows N and E through S Andhra Pradesh to Bay of Bengal 15 m. below Nellore. **Southern Penner,** 245 m. long; rises in SE Mysore, flows SE across N Madras state into Bay of Bengal S of Cuddalore.

Penn Hills (pĕn). Urban township, Allegheny co., SW Pennsylvania, E suburb of Pittsburgh; pop. 51,512.

Pen′nine Alps (pĕn′īn). See *Table* at ALPS.

Pennine Chain. Mountain range extending S from the Scottish border to Derbyshire and Staffordshire in cen. England; highest peak **Cross Fell** (krôs fĕl) 2930 ft.

Pen′ning·ton (pĕn′ĭng·tŭn). Counties of two states in the U.S. See *Tables* at MINNESOTA and SOUTH DAKOTA.

Pennington Gap. Town, Lee co., SW tip of Virginia, in Cumberland Mts. 51 m. WNW of Bristol; pop. 1799.

Penn·sau′ken (pĕn·sô′kĕn). Town, Camden co., SW New Jersey, just E of Camden; pop. 33,771.

Penns′bor′o (pĕnz′bûr′ô). Town, Ritchie co., NW West Virginia, 36 m. W of Clarksburg; pop. 1660; gas, oil.

Penns′burg (pĕnz′bûrg). Borough, Montgomery co., SE Pennsylvania, 15 m. S of Allentown; pop. 1698.

Penns Grove (pĕnz). Borough, Salem co., SW New Jersey, on Delaware river opp. Wilmington, Delaware, and 24 m. SW of Camden; pop. 6176; dye works, lumber yards.

Penn′syl·va′nia (pĕn′sĭl·vān′yȧ; -vā′nĭ·ȧ). A middle Atlantic state of U.S.A., one of original states of the Union, the 2d to ratify the Federal Constitution (1787); bounded on N by New York, on E by New York and New Jersey, on S by Delaware, Maryland, and West Virginia, and on W by West Virginia and Ohio; 33rd state in area, 45,333 sq. m., not including 735 sq. m. of water of the Great Lakes (land area 45,045 sq. m.); 3d state in population, 11,319,366; ✳ Harrisburg. See *Table of States* at UNITED STATES. Divided into the following 67 counties (for pronunciation of their names, see their individual entries):

NAME	LOCA-TION	AREA[1]	POP.[1]	CO. SEAT
Adams	S	526	51,906	Gettysburg
Allegheny	SW	730	1,628,587	Pittsburgh
Armstrong	W	660	79,524	Kittanning
Beaver	W	441	206,948	Beaver
Bedford	S	1,018	42,451	Bedford
Berks	SE	864	275,414	Reading
Blair	S cen.	531	137,270	Hollidaysburg
Bradford	N	1,147	54,925	Towanda
Bucks	SE	617	308,567	Doylestown
Butler	W	794	114,639	Butler
Cambria	SW cen.	695	203,283	Ebensburg
Cameron	N cen.	401	7,586	Emporium
Carbon	E	405	52,889	Mauch Chunk
Centre	cen.	1,115	78,580	Bellefonte
Chester	SE	760	210,608	West Chester
Clarion	W	599	37,408	Clarion
Clearfield	W cen.	1,144	81,534	Clearfield
Clinton	cen.	902	37,619	Lock Haven
Columbia	E cen.	484	53,489	Bloomsburg
Crawford	NW	1,016	77,956	Meadville
Cumberland	S	555	124,816	Carlisle
Dauphin	SE cen.	520	220,255	Harrisburg
Delaware	SE	185	553,154	Media
Elk	NW cen.	809	37,328	Ridgway
Erie	NW corner	812	250,682	Erie
Fayette	SW	800	169,340	Uniontown
Forest	NW	420	4,485	Tionesta
Franklin	S	754	88,172	Chambersburg
Fulton	S	435	10,597	McConnellsburg
Greene	SW corner	577	39,424	Waynesburg
Huntingdon	S cen.	894	39,457	Huntingdon
Indiana	W cen.	831	75,366	Indiana
Jefferson	W cen.	652	46,792	Brookville
Juniata	S cen.	387	15,874	Mifflintown
Lackawanna	NE	454	234,531	Scranton
Lancaster	SE	945	278,359	Lancaster
Lawrence	W	367	112,965	New Castle
Lebanon	SE cen.	363	90,853	Lebanon
Lehigh	E	347	227,536	Allentown
Luzerne	E	891	346,972	Wilkes-Barre
Lycoming	N cen.	1,215	109,367	Williamsport
McKean	N	997	54,517	Smethport
Mercer	W	681	127,519	Mercer
Mifflin	cen.	431	44,348	Lewistown
Monroe	E	611	39,567	Stroudsburg
Montgomery	SE	492	516,682	Norristown
Montour	E cen.	130	16,730	Danville
Northampton	E	374	201,412	Easton
Northumberland	E cen.	454	104,138	Sunbury
Perry	S cen.	550	26,582	New Bloomfield
Philadelphia[2]	SE	127	2,002,512	Philadelphia
Pike	NE	545	9,158	Milford
Potter	N	1,092	16,483	Coudersport
Schuylkill	E cen.	783	173,027	Pottsville
Snyder	cen.	329	25,922	Middleburg
Somerset	S	1,084	77,450	Somerset
Sullivan	NE cen.	478	6,251	Laporte
Susquehanna	NE	836	33,137	Montrose
Tioga	N	1,150	36,614	Wellsboro
Union	cen.	318	25,646	Lewisburg
Venango	NW	675	65,295	Franklin
Warren	NW	910	45,582	Warren
Washington	SW	857	217,271	Washington
Wayne	NE corner	744	28,237	Honesdale
Westmoreland	SW	1,025	352,629	Greensburg
Wyoming	NE	396	16,813	Tunkhannock
York	S	914	238,336	York

[1] Area = land area in sq. m. Pop. from 1960 Census.
[2] Coextensive with Philadelphia city since annexation by city in 1854 of remaining part of county.

Nickname: Keystone State. *State flower:* Mountain laurel. *Motto:* Virtue, Liberty, and Independence. *Chief*

cities: Philadelphia, Pittsburgh, Erie, Scranton, Allentown. *Rivers:* Delaware, forming E boundary; Susquehanna, flowing N to S through E cen. area; Monongahela in W and SW area, uniting at Pittsburgh with Allegheny river to form the Ohio river; Juniata, in S cen. area, flowing E into the Susquehanna; the Schuylkill in the SE flowing through Philadelphia to the Delaware. *Highest point:* Negro Mt. 3213 ft. in Somerset co. *Chief industries:* Mining (esp. coal), manufacturing (esp. steel and metal products), agriculture.

History: Étienne Brulé first recorded white man to visit this area 1615–16; first settlement made by Swedes on Tinicum I. (*q.v.*) 1643; royal charter granted to William Penn, a Quaker, 1681; settlement encouraged by Penn 1682 ff.; first hospital in America established in Philadelphia 1751; S boundary line determined 1763 and 1767 (see MASON AND DIXON'S LINE); Declaration of Independence pronounced in Philadelphia 1776, and 1st Constitutional Convention chosen; delegation headed by Benjamin Franklin represented Pennsylvania in Federal Constitutional Convention 1787; ratified Federal Constitution Dec. 12, 1787; Johnstown flood disaster May 31, 1889.

Penn Yan (pĕn′ yăn′). Village, ⊗ of Yates co., W New York, at outlet of Lake Keuka 30 m. SW of Auburn; pop. 5770; became ⊗ 1823, incorp. 1833; center for tourist trade of W Finger Lakes; produces grain, grapes, fruit, vegetables; wineries, canneries, flour mills, woodworking and packing plants. Jerusalem colony near here 1790–1819, estab. by Jemima Wilkinson.

Pe·nob′scot (pĕ·nŏb′skŭt; -skŏt). **1** River 101 m. long, cen. Maine; navigable to Bangor (60 m.); flows S into Penobscot Bay; formed by confluence in N cen. Penobscot co. of East Branch, from the N, and West Branch, 112 m. long, which is formed by junction of headstreams in Somerset co., W Maine, and flows generally SE, through three lakes (Seboomook, Chesuncook, and Pemadumcook).

2 County in Maine. See *Table* at MAINE.

Penobscot Bay. Inlet of Atlantic Ocean 30 m. long in SW Hancock co., SE Waldo co., and E Knox co., S Maine, receiving the Penobscot river on the N, and containing a number of islands including Deer I., North Haven I., Vinalhaven I., Isle au Haut.

Pe·ñón′ de Vé′lez de la Go·me′ra (pȧ·nyôn′ dā vā′-lāth [-lāz] thä lä gŏ·mā′rä). Small island off N coast of Morocco, in former Spanish Morocco, ab. 75 m. SE of Ceuta; a presidio of Spain.

Pe′no·no·mé′ (pā′nȯ·nȯ·mā′). Town, cen. Panama, ✳ of Coclé prov.; pop. 2418.

Pe·not′, Mount (pē·nō′). Mountain 2925 ft., cen. Malekula I., New Hebrides, SW Pacific; highest point on the island.

Pen′rhyn (pĕn′rĭn). **1** See TONGAREVA, Manihiki Is.

2 Parish, NE Caernarvonshire, NW Wales, SSE of Bangor; slate quarries, probably largest in the world.

Pen′rith (pĕn′rĭth). Urban district, Cumberland, NW England, on the Eamont 16 m. SSE of Carlisle; pop. 10,490; tourist resort on the edge of the Lake District; trade center in agricultural section.

Pen′sa·co′la (pĕn′sȧ·kō′lȧ). City, ⊗ of Escambia co., NW Florida, on Gulf of Mexico 10 m. E of Alabama border; pop. 56,752; excellent harbor; fisheries; lumber, naval stores; site of U.S. naval air station and air base. Spanish settlement 1559, abandoned 1561; new Spanish settlement 1596; passed to England 1763, and back to Spain 1783; captured by Andrew Jackson 1814, and passed to U.S. 1821; capital of West Florida to 1822; in Civil War, held alternately by Union and Confederate forces.

Pensacola Bay. Inlet of Gulf of Mexico on S coast of Santa Rosa and Escambia cos., NW Florida, receiving the Escambia river on the NW and the Yellow river on the NE; the city of Pensacola is on its W shore.

Pensacola Dam. See GRAND RIVER DAM.

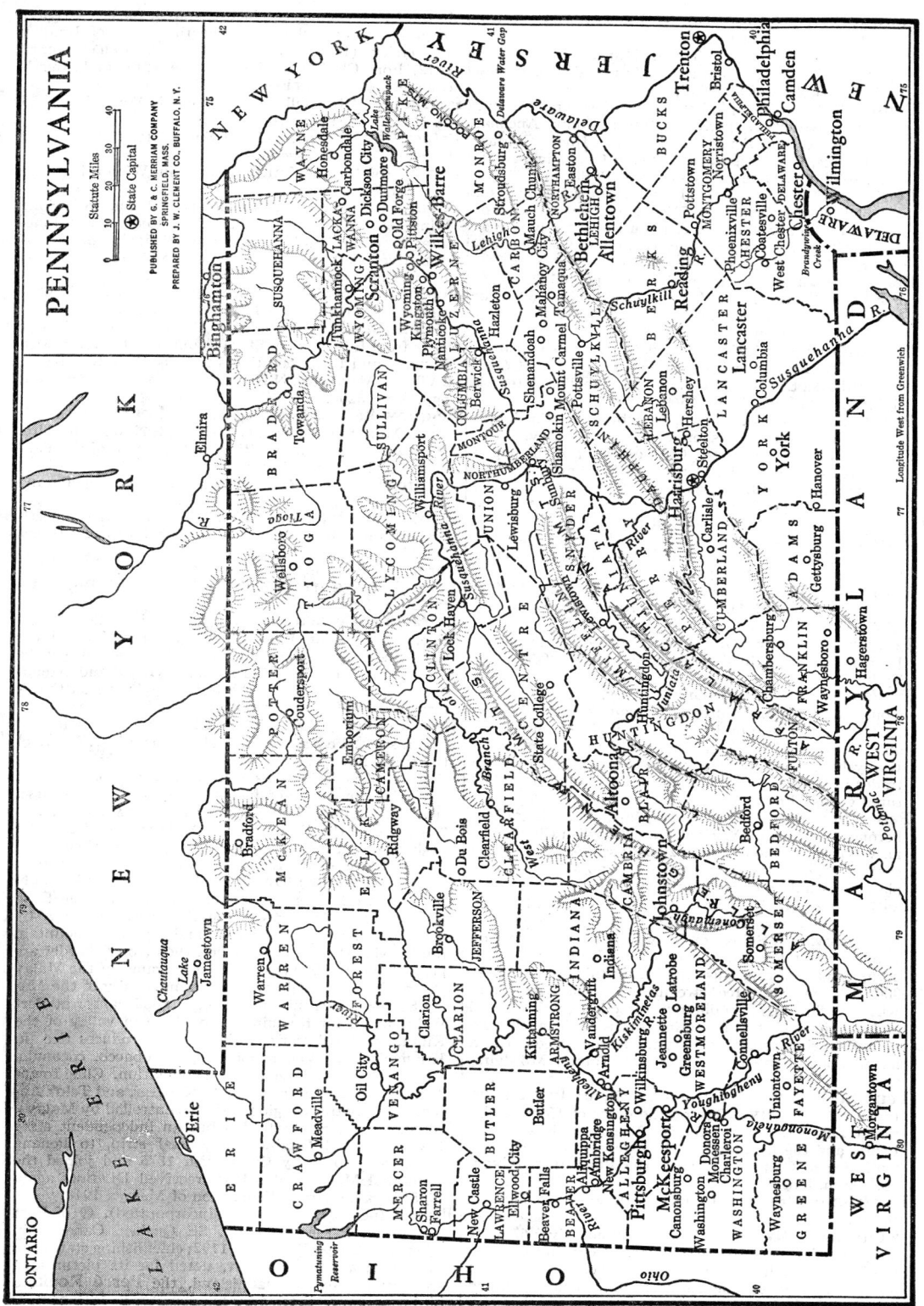

PENNSYLVANIA

Statute Miles

⊛ State Capital

PUBLISHED BY G. & C. MERRIAM COMPANY
SPRINGFIELD, MASS.
PREPARED BY J. W. CLEMENT CO., BUFFALO, N.Y.

Pen·sau′ken (pĕn·sô′kĕn). = PENNSAUKEN town, New Jersey, just E of Camden.

Pens′hurst (pĕnz′hûrst). Town, Kent, SE England, 4½ m. SW of Tonbridge; pop. ab. 1500; mansion of Sidney family, birthplace of Sir Philip Sidney.

Pen·tap′o·lis (pĕn·tăp′ô·lĭs). One of several ancient groups of five cities, specif.: in Italy: Rimini, Ancona, Fano, Pesaro, and Senigallia; in Asia Minor: Cnidus, Cos, Lindus, Camirus, and Ialysus; in Cyrenaica: Apollonia, Arsinoë, Berenice, Cyrene, and Ptolemaïs.

Pen′te·cost (pĕn′tĕ·kôst). Island 28 m. long by 7 m. wide, NE New Hebrides Is., SW Pacific Ocean, 5 m. S of Maewo I. and ab. 60 m. SE of Espíritu Santo; pop. (native; 1938 est.) 7000; productive and well developed, with capable natives of Polynesian descent at N end.

Pen·tel′i·kon (pĕn·tĕl′ĭ·kŏn; Mod. Gr. pân′dâ·lyĕ·kôn′) or **Pen·tel′i·cus** (pĕn·tĕl′ĭ·kŭs). Mountain 3639 ft. in Attica and Boeotia dept., E cen. Greece, 10 m. NE of Athens; yields excellent marble.

Pen·thièvre′ (päN′tyâ′vr′). Ancient countship, Brittany, NW France, within region of present Côtes-du-Nord dept.; ✳ (1134–1420) Lamballe, later ✳ Guingamp; became duchy 1569.

Pen·ti′a (pāᴎN·tē′à). Town, N suburb of Rio de Janeiro, E Brazil, near W shore of Guanabara Bay.

Pen·tic′ton (pĕn·tĭk′tŭn). City, at S end of Okanagan Lake, S Brit. Columbia, Canada, ab. 160 m. E of Vancouver; pop. 10,548; incorporated 1948.

Pent′land Firth (pĕnt′lănd). Channel separating the Orkney Is. from the mainland of Scotland.

Pentland Hills. Range of hills in Midlothian, Lanark, and Peebles cos., SE Scotland; highest peak **Scald Law** (skôld lô) 1898 ft.

Pe·ñue′les (pä·nywä′läs). Municipality (pop. 14,887) and town (pop. 2261), S Puerto Rico; town ab. 8 m. NW of Ponce.

Pen y Fan (pĕn′ ĭ văn′). Highest peak 2907 ft. in Brecon Beacons, S Wales, in Brecknockshire NNW of Merthyr Tydfil.

Pen′za (pĕn′zà; Russ. pyĕn′zá). City, ✳ of Penza Region, Soviet Russia, Europe, on main Tula-Kuibyshev R.R.; pop. 157,145; on left bank of navigable Sura river ab. 140 m. W of the Volga at Syzran and 225 m. W of Kuibyshev; a shipping point by both rail and river; trades in timber, grain, animal products, and manufactured goods. Founded 1666.

Pen·zance′ (pĕn·zăns′; locally pĕn·zäns′). Municipal borough, Cornwall, SW England, on English Channel 65 m. WSW of Plymouth; pop. 20,648; seaport and fishing center; exports tin, copper, kaolin; popular watering place. Birthplace of Sir Humphry Davy.

Penza Region. Region, E cen. Soviet Russia, Europe; 17,563 sq. m.; pop. 1,708,656; ✳ Penza. Bounded on N by Mordovian A.S.S.R., on E by Ulyanovsk Region, on S by Saratov Region, and on W by Tambov Region; occupies part of cen. Russian plateau (highest point ab. 900 ft.) cut by three streams—Moksha, Sura, and Khoper—flowing off in different directions; well wooded and has rich soil; besides agriculture there is much local manufacturing, esp. in wooden and leather goods. Has a mixed population—Great Russians, Tatars, Mordvinians.

Pen′zhin·ska·ya (pyĕn′zhĭn·ská·yà), or **Pen′zhi·na** (pyĕn′zhĭ·ná), **Bay.** Bay on the coast of Koryak National District, Soviet Russia, Asia, bet. Kamchatka Penin. and the mainland, a NE extension of Shelekova Gulf, Sea of Okhotsk; receives the **Penzhina River,** ab. 400 m. long.

Pe·o′ri·a (pê·ōr′ĭ·à). **1** County in Illinois. See Table at ILLINOIS.
2 City, its ⊗, NW cen. Illinois, on Illinois river 67 m. N of Springfield; pop. 103,162; 3d largest city in the state; trading and industrial center in agricultural section; manufactures diesel engines, farm implements, distilled liquors (of which it produces more than any other city in the U.S.), chemicals, glucose, starch, furnaces; center of grain trade; coal deposits nearby. Site of Bradley University (1896; coed.). French settlement until 1812; Fort Clark built on this site 1813, and Americans settled on **Peoria Lake** 1819.

Peoria Heights. Village, Peoria co., NW cen. Illinois, 5 m. N of Peoria; pop. 7064.

Pe′per Bay (pā′pĕr). Inlet of Sunda Strait at W end of island of Java, Indonesia.

Pep′in (pĭp′ĭn; pĕp′ĭn). County in Wisconsin. See Table at WISCONSIN.

Pepin, Lake. Lake ab. 34 m. long and 2–4 m. wide along Minnesota-Wisconsin boundary from Red Wing, Minnesota, to Wabasha, Minnesota; an expansion of Mississippi river as it passes bet. limestone bluffs as much as 400 ft. high, weathered into fantastic shapes.

Pep′per·ell (pĕp′ĕr·ĕl). Town, Middlesex co., NE Massachusetts, 11 m. NE of Fitchburg; pop. 4336.

Pe·quan′nock (pê·kwŏn′ŭk). **1** River, N New Jersey; flows from E Sussex co. SE and unites at Pompton with Ramapo and Ringwood rivers to form Pompton river.
2 Village, Morris co., N New Jersey 7 m. W of Paterson; pop. (est.) 3200.

Pe·quaw′ket (pê·kwô′kĕt; -kĭt) or **Kear′sarge** (kēr′särj). Mountain 3260 ft., Carroll co., E New Hampshire.

Pe′que·ní′ (pā′kä·nē′). River in Panama E of the Panama Canal; flows SW into Madden Reservoir.

Pe′que·rí′ (pā′kĕ·rē′). River ab. 200 m. long, Paraná state, S Brazil, flowing NW into the Paraná.

Pe·quon′nock (pê·kwŏn′ŭk; -ĭk). River, SW Connecticut; rises in cen. Fairfield co., flows S into Long Island Sound at Bridgeport.

Pera. See BEYOGLU.

Per′a·de′ni·ya (pĕr′à·dēn′yà). Village with Royal Botanic Gardens, 3 m. SW of Kandy (q.v.), cen. Ceylon.

Pe·rae′a or **Pe·re′a** (pê·rē′à). Region in ancient Palestine, E of Jordan river ("beyond Jordan," from the Greek, literally, "[the country] on the other side [of the river]"); part of the earlier region of Gilead and extending from the Jabbok on the N to the Arnon on the S; formed part of the Tetrarchy of Herod Antipas.

Pe′rak (pā′räk; pâr′à; pĕr′à). **1** River ab. 200 m. long in Perak state, Federation of Malaya; rises in NE part of the state, flows WSW and S to ab. 4°N where it turns sharply W at Telok Anson into the Strait of Malacca; navigable for small craft for nearly its entire course. Its chief tributary is the Kinta (see KINTA VALLEY).
2 A state of the Federation of Malaya, on W coast of Malay Penin.; includes Dindings; formerly a Federated Malay State of British Malaya; 7980 sq. m.; pop. 785,581, (1941 est.) 992,691; ✳ Taiping. Bounded on N by Province Wellesley, Kedah, and Thailand, on E by Kelantan and Pahang, on S by Selangor, and on W by Strait of Malacca. Has two N and S parallel mountain ranges with the Perak river bet. them; on E border are peaks (6000 to 7000 ft.) of the main range of the Malay Penin. One of most important commercially of the Malay States, has trunk-line railroad, good harbor at Port Weld; noted for tin mines, esp. those in valley of the Kinta, an E tributary of the Perak; produces rice (in Krian dist. in NW), rubber, sugar, tobacco, coconuts, tea, coffee. Has a large Chinese population. Chief towns Taiping, Ipoh, Kampar, Kuala Kangsar, and Telok Anson. In early times region entirely controlled by Malays; conquered by Siamese 1818 but an independent state 1824–74; ceded Dindings, a coastal strip, to Penang 1874; taken over by the British 1875 and joined the Federated Malay States 1895; received Dindings again 1935; became part of Federation of Malaya 1948.

Per′cé′ (pĕr′sā′). Village (unincorporated), ⊗ of East Gaspé co., E Gaspé Penin., SE Quebec, Canada, on coast S of Gaspé Bay; pop. 1192; chief fishing station on the coast; a popular resort, noted for its picturesque scenery; nearby is small island, the **Percé Rock,** a bird sanctuary. Settled by missionaries in 18th cent.

Perche (pĕrsh). Ancient division in N France, now included in departments of Orne, Eure-et-Loir, and Eure; ✳ Mortagne; dairy-farming, stock-raising region, noted esp. for its breed of heavy draft horses (*Percherons*).

Per·di'do (pĕr-dē'dō). River ab. 60 m. long, rising in Escambia co., S Alabama, flowing S and forming boundary bet. SE Alabama and NW Florida; empties into **Perdido Bay**, an inlet of the Gulf of Mexico.

Per·di'do, Mount (pĕr·thē'thô); *Fr.* **Mont Per'du'** (môn' pĕr'dü'). Peak 10,994 ft. in the cen. Pyrenees, NE Spain, on French border S of Luz.

Pe·rei'ra (pā·rē'ĕ·rä; -rā'rä). City, Caldas dept., W cen. Colombia, just S of Manizales; pop. 30,762; cattle center.

Pe're·kop' (pĕr'ĕ·kôp'; *Russ.* pyĭ·ryĕ·kôp'). **1** Isthmus 4 to 14 m. wide connecting the Crimea with Russian mainland. Scene of fighting in World War II; held by Germans Nov. 1941 to Nov. 1943.
2 Village at N end of isthmus, site of early Greek and Tatar settlements and forts. General Wrangel finally defeated here 1920.

Père–La'chaise' (pâr'lȧ'shâz'). Famous cemetery in E section of Paris, France.

Peremyshl. See PRZEMYŚL.

Pe're·slavl' (pĕr'ĕ·slȧv''l; *Russ.* pyĭ·ryĕ·slȧv''ly'). **1** *or* **Plesh·che'e·vo** (plĕsh·chā'ĕ·vō; *Russ.* plyĭsh·chā'-yĭ·vŭ). Small lake in S Yaroslavl Region, Soviet Russia, Europe; on it the first vessels of the Russian navy were built 1691 by Peter the Great.
2 *or* **Pereslavl–Za·les'ki** (-zȧ·lĕs'kĭ; *Russ.* -zŭ·lyä'skĭ). Town on the lake, S Yaroslavl Region, Soviet Russia, Europe; an old town, in early times in the Rostov-Suzdal principality; from c. 1300 in the Moscow principality.

Pe're·ya·slav' (pĕr'ĕ·yȧ·slȧv'; *Russ.* pyĭ·ryĭ·yŭ·slȧf') *or* **Pe're·ya·slavl'** (pĕr'ĕ·yȧ·slȧv''l; *Russ.* pyĭ·ryĭ·yŭ·slȧv'ly'). **1** Medieval principality on the N bank of the Dnieper E of Kiev 11th–13th cents.; chief town Pereyaslav.
2 Town, E Kiev Region, N Ukraine, U.S.S.R., on a small tributary near the left bank of the Dnieper, 50 m. SE of Kiev; pop. 14,975; an agricultural town that has been historically important; founded 993 by Vladimir the Great; chief town of principality from 1054 and a Russian southern outpost for several centuries; plundered by Mongols in 1239; in 17th cent. a key town during Cossack Wars 1648–1712 and headquarters of Bogdan Chmielnicki; treaty signed here 1654; overrun in World War II 1941–44.

Pereyaslavl. 1 = PERESLAVL.
2 See PEREYASLAV.

Pereyaslav–Ryazanski. See RYAZAN city.

Per'ga (pûr'gȧ). Chief town of ancient Pamphylia, Asia Minor; its ruins are at modern **Mur'ta·na'** (mōōr'-tä·nä'); here Paul and Barnabas began their first mission in Asia Minor (*Acts* xiii. 13).

Per'ga·mi'no (pĕr'gä·mē'nō). City, N Buenos Aires prov., E Argentina, 141 m. WNW of Buenos Aires; pop. (est.) 37,956; railroad center.

Per'ga·mum (pûr'gȧ·mŭm), *Gr.* **Per'ga·mon** (-mŏn); *or Lat.* **Per'ga·mus** (-mŭs), *Gr.* **Per'ga·mos** (-mŏs). **1** Ancient Greek kingdom, at its height under Eumenes I and the Attalids, 263–133 B.C., covering most of W Asia Minor; became ally of Rome and on death of Attalus III kingdom bequeathed to Romans; divided bet. Pontus and new province of Asia.
2 *mod.* **Ber'ga·ma'** (bĕr'gä·mä'). Important city in ancient Mysia, Asia Minor, ✳ of the kingdom of Pergamum and for a time of the Roman province of Asia, ab. 18 m. inland from Aeolis coast opp. Lesbos. Flourished for ab. four centuries as a political and cultural capital of the East, rivaling Ephesus and Smyrna in importance. An early seat of Christianity and one of the Seven Churches; remained a center of commercial activity under Byzantines and Ottomans.

Per'gi·ne Val'su·ga'na (pĕr'jĕ·nä väl'sōō·gä'nä). Commune, Trento prov., Venezia Tridentina, NE Italy,

5 m. E of Trento; pop. 11,451; 16th-cent. church; health resort; ferruginous and arsenious spring.

Per'go·la (pĕr'gō·lä). Commune, Pesaro e Urbino prov., Marches, cen. Italy, 25 m. S by W of Pesaro; pop. 11,869; cathedral.

Per·gu'sa (pȧr·gōō'zä), **Lake of.** See ENNA, Sicily.

Per'ham (pûr'ăm). Village, Otter Tail co., W cen. Minnesota, 31 m. NE of Fergus Falls; pop. 2019; summer and fishing resort.

Per'i·bon'ka (pĕr'ĭ·bŏng'kȧ). River 280 m. long, S cen. Quebec prov., Canada; rises in cen. Quebec, flows S into Lake St. John.

Pe·ri'co (pȧ·rē'kō). **1** Municipality and town, Matanzas prov., W cen. Cuba; town is on railroad 20 m. SE of Cárdenas, pop. (1943) 6818.
2 Small fortified island, Bay of Panama, just off SE end of Panama Canal.

Pé'riers' (pā'ryā'). Town, Manche dept., NW France, 14 m. NW of Saint-Lô; taken in battle for Saint-Lô July 16–18, 1944.

Pé'ri·gord' (pā'rē·gôr'). Old division of N Guienne prov., SW France; ✳ Périgueux.

Pé'ri·gueux' (pā'rē·gü'); *anc.* **Ve·su'na** (vĕ·sū'nȧ). Commune, ✳ of Dordogne dept., SW cen. France, 66 m. ENE of Bordeaux; pop. 37,615; 10th-cent. church, prefecture, courthouse, hospital, museum, theater; ancient Roman Tour de Vésonne; manufactures textiles, cutlery, nails, pottery, spirits, leather; Roman ruins (amphitheater, aqueducts, temples, baths) nearby. First inhabited by the Petrocoriani (whence the modern name); Protestant stronghold in 16th cent.

Pe·rim' (pĕ·rĭm'). Island in Bab el Mandeb Strait at the entrance to the Red Sea; 5 sq. m.; pop. 2346; 96 m. W of Aden to which it is administratively attached. Has good harbor with coaling and cable stations and a lighthouse. British since 1857.

Pe'ri·ya·ku·lam (pā'rĭ·yŭ'kōō·lȧm). Town, S Madras state, S Indian Union, 38 m. WNW of Madura; pop. 23,004.

Pe'ri·yar' (pā'rĕ·yär'). River ab. 140 m. long, cen. Kerala, S Indian Union; flows N and W to Arabian Sea N of Cochin; navigable for 60 m.; in Travancore hills has dam 176 ft. high (completed 1895) and tunnel, used for irrigation.

Per'ka·sie (pûr'kȧ·sĭ). Borough, Bucks co., SE Pennsylvania, 18 m. SSE of Allentown; pop. 4650; manufactures cigars, textiles, clothing, photographic supplies.

Per'kins (pûr'kĭnz). Name of counties in two states of the U.S. See *Tables* at NEBRASKA and SOUTH DAKOTA.

Perkins, Mount. Peak 12,557 ft. in Sierra Nevada, E Fresno co., S cen. California.

Per'las, Pun'ta de (pōōn'tä thȧ pĕr'läs); *Angl.* **Pearl Point** (pûrl). Cape projecting S on E cen. coast of Nicaragua, enclosing Perlas Lagoon.

Per'las Archipelago (pĕr'läs). = PEARL ISLANDS, Gulf of Panama.

Perlas Lagoon; *also* **Pearl Lagoon** (pûrl). Inlet of the Caribbean Sea on E cen. coast of Nicaragua.

Per'le·berg (pĕr'lĕ·bĕrк). City, Brandenburg, eastern Germany, on a tributary of the Elbe 69 m. NW of Potsdam; pop. 10,233.

Per'lis (pûr'lĭs). A state of the Federation of Malaya, in NW section of S Malay Penin.; 316 sq. m.; pop. 49,296, (1940 est.) 57,776; ✳ Kangar. Smallest of all the Malay States, located bet. Thailand and NW Kedah; has short coast line on Andaman Sea; has rich alluvial land; raises much rice. Until 1821 subject to Kedah; made separate state by the Thai 1841; came under British protection by treaty of 1909, in which Thailand ceded to Great Britain its rights over the state; became one of the five Unfederated Malay States of British Malaya; part of Federation of Malaya 1948.

Perm. See MOLOTOV.

Për·met' (pĕr·mĕt') *or* **Pre·met'** (prĕ·mĕt'). Town, S Albania, on the Vijosë river NE of Gjinokastër.

Per'nam·bu'co (pûr'năm·bū'kō; -bōō'-; *Port.* pâr'-nănm·bōō'kōō). **1** State of Brazil. See *Table* at BRAZIL. **2** City, its ✳. See RECIFE.

Pernau, Pernov. See PARNU.

Per'nik (pĕr'nĭk). Town, Sofia dept., W Bulgaria, ab. 15 m. SW of Sofia on the Struma; pop. (1926) 12,296.

Pé'ronne' (pā'rôn'). Town, Somme dept., N France, ab. 35 m. NE of Amiens on Somme river; pop. 4087; occupied 1465 by Charles the Bold of Burgundy who was visited here by Louis XI 1468; taken back by Louis XI after Charles's death 1477; in the path of several conflicts: besieged 1536 by Charles V in his third war against Francis I; captured 1815 by Wellington, and Jan. 9, 1871 by Germans who held it again 1914–Mar. 1917 and Mar.–Sept. 1918.

Perouse Bay, La. See LA PEROUSE BAY.

Pérouse Island, La. See VANIKORO.

Pérouse Strait, La. See SOYA STRAIT.

Perovsk. See KZYL-ORDA.

Per·pet'u·a, Cape (pēr·pĕt'ū·á). Cape on SW extremity of Lincoln co., W Oregon.

Per·pi'gnan' (pĕr'pē'nyän'). City, ✳ of Pyrénées-Orientales dept., S France, near Mediterranean 96 m. SE of Toulouse; pop. 72,207; 14th-cent. cathedral; Moorish-style château; 14th-cent. university building; ancient walls; manufactures woolens, silks, chocolate, leather goods, paper; trades in wine, olive oil, honey. Said to have been founded in 10th cent.; capital of Roussillon 12th cent. ff.; chartered 1197; church council met here 1408; united to France 1659.

Per·quim'ans (pēr·kwĭm'ănz). County of North Carolina. See *Table* at NORTH CAROLINA.

Per'ré'gaux' (pĕ'rā'gō'). Commune, Oran dept., NW Algeria, 40 m. ESE of Oran; pop. 17,742.

Perreux–sur–Marne, Le. See LE PERREUX-SUR-MARNE.

Per'rine (pûr'ĭn). Urban community (unincorporated), Dade co., SE Florida, SW of Miami; pop. 6424.

Per'ro, La·gu'na del (lä·gōō'nä dĕl pĕr'ō). Lake in cen. Torrance co., cen. New Mexico.

Perrot, Ile. See ILE PERROT.

Per'ry (pĕr'ĭ). **1** Name of counties in ten states of the U.S. See *Tables* at ALABAMA, ARKANSAS, ILLINOIS, INDIANA, KENTUCKY, MISSISSIPPI, MISSOURI, OHIO, PENNSYLVANIA, TENNESSEE.

2 Industrial city, ⊗ of Taylor co., N Florida, 48 m. ESE of Tallahassee; pop. 8030; sawmills; wood products.

3 City, ⊗ of Houston co., cen. Georgia; pop. 6032.

4 City, Dallas co., S cen. Iowa, 32 m. WNW of Des Moines; pop. 6442; industrial center in agricultural section; canneries; manufactures farm implements.

5 Village, Wyoming co., W New York, 37 m. SSW of Rochester; pop. 4629; manufactures knit goods, septic and gasoline tanks.

6 City, ⊗ of Noble co., N Oklahoma, 36 m. E of Enid; pop. 5210; stock, dairy, poultry, grain farms.

Per'rys·burg (pĕr'ĭz·bûrg). Village, Wood co., NW Ohio, on Maumee river 8 m. SSW of Toledo; pop. 5519; formerly important port and shipbuilding center.

Per'ry's Victory and International Peace Memorial National Monument (pĕr'ĭz). See UNITED STATES, *National Monuments.*

Per'ry·ton (pĕr'ĭ·tйn; -t'n). City, ⊗ of Ochiltree co., NW Texas, in the panhandle near the Oklahoma boundary, 58 m. N of Pampa; pop. 7903; livestock and wheat market; oil-field supply houses.

Per'ry·ville (pĕr'ĭ·vĭl; *Sou.* also -v'l). **1** City, ⊗ of Perry co., cen. Arkansas; pop. 719.

2 City, Boyle co., E cen. Kentucky, 40 m. SW of Lexington; pop. 715; scene of indecisive battle Oct. 8, 1862 bet. Confederates under Bragg and Federals under Buell (Bragg withdrew his forces into Tennessee the next day).

3 City, ⊗ of Perry co., E Missouri, 35 m. NNW of Cape Girardeau; pop. 5117.

Per·sa'no (pär·sä'nō). Village, Salerno prov., S Campania, S Italy, SE of Salerno; fighting Sept. 11–13, 1943.

Per·sep'o·lis (pēr·sĕp'ō·lĭs). Ancient capital of Persia, succeeding Pasargadae, founded by Darius I (521–486 B.C.); its ruins lie ab. 30 m. NE of Shiraz, SW cen. Iran, covering extensive area and comprising palaces of early Persian kings, great staircases, halls, and treasuries. Partially destroyed by Alexander 331 B.C.; place remained of some importance until Arab period. Nearby at Naksh-i-Rustam are remarkable rock tombs of Darius and others. Below ruins excavations have disclosed remains of villages much older, perhaps of c. 4000 B.C.

Per'se·ver'ance Bay (pûr'sĕ·vēr'ăns). Bay in SW coast of St. Thomas I., Virgin Is. of the United States.

Per'shing (pûr'shǐng). County in Nevada. See *Table* at NEVADA.

Per'sia (pûr'zhá; -shá); *Persian* **I·ran'** (ĕ·rän'; *Angl.* ĭ·răn', ĭ-). Kingdom, ancient and modern (see IRAN), SW Asia, varying greatly in its boundaries at different periods; original homeland was *Persis* (modern FARS) inhabited by Persians, an Iranian people; under Cyrus the Great (550–529 B.C.), originally ruler of Anshan (*q.v.*), conquered Media, Lydia, Babylonia (*qq.v.*) and founded Persian Empire which extended from Indus to Mediterranean and from Caucasus to Indian Ocean (later included Egypt); organized by Darius I against whom Greece began Persian Wars; conquered by Alexander the Great 331–327 B.C.; after an interlude of Seleucid, Parthian, and Bactrian rule, Ardashir I, the ruler of Fars, founded Neo-Persian Empire of the Sassanidae (226–641 A.D.); in 7th cent., included Khurasan, Kerman, Mesopotamia, Armenia, Azerbaijan, Fars, Khuzistan, Syria, Egypt, and part of Asia Minor; conquered by Moslem Arabs 633–651; after Mongol conquest in 13th cent., formed separate Mongol dynasty, the Il-khans (1260–1353); modern Persia founded by Safawid rulers (1502–1736), the greatest of whom was Shah Abbas I (1586–1628); held off Turks, but overcome by Afghans 1722 and lost territory to Russia; under Nadir Shah (1736–47) invaded India, captured Bukhara and Khiva; ruled by Kajar dynasty (1794–1925); lost Caucasus (*q.v.*) to Russia in 19th cent.; secured constitution ending absolute rule 1906; Anglo-Russian rivalry over Persia settled in Anglo-Russian Entente 1907; in 1919, rejected agreement giving control to British; League member 1920; recognized as independent by U.S.S.R. 1921; deposed Kajar shahs and proclaimed Riza Shah Pahlavi 1925; officially renamed Iran 1935.

Per'sian Baluchistan (pûr'zhăn; -shăn). Formerly the name of the region in SE part of Kerman prov., Iran, on Baluchistan border; its chief town was Bampur.

Persian Gulf; *anc.* **Si'nus Per'si·cus** (sī'nйs pûr'sĭ-kйs). Arm of the Arabian Sea, bet. the peninsula of Arabia on the W and S, and Iran on the E and N; at N end bordered by short coast lines of Iraq and Kuwait; fully 550 m. long and ab. 200 m. wide at greatest breadth; connected with Gulf of Oman and Arabian Sea through Strait of Ormuz. Bahrein Is. and Qishm I. only islands of importance. Famous for its pearl fisheries.

Persian Gulf States. The areas in and around the Persian Gulf nominally independent but closely dependent upon Great Britain and India for protection and trade: Bahrein Is., Qatar, and the Trucial States. A British political resident acts for all the areas and is represented by political agents at the local centers of Manama, Doha, Dubai, and Abu Dhabi. British interests in the Gulf region began 300 years ago.

Persis. See FARS; PERSIA.

Per'son (pûr's'n). County in North Carolina. See *Table* at NORTH CAROLINA.

Perth (pûrth). **1** City, ✳ of Western Australia, in SW part on Swan river 10 m. from its mouth; pop. 82,294, with suburbs, including Fremantle, 207,464; trade center for extensive wheat, wool, and mining region; seat of Univ. of Western Australia (founded 1911). Founded

1829 by Capt. James Stirling; became a city 1856; developed rapidly after discovery of gold in SW part of state 1891–94.

2 Town (unincorporated), ⊗ of Victoria co., W New Brunswick, Canada, on left bank of St. John river 25 m. S of Grand Falls; pop. 1937.

3 County, Ontario, Canada. See *Table* at ONTARIO.

4 Industrial town, ⊗ of Lanark co., SE Ontario, Canada, 45 m. SW of Ottawa; pop. 5034; manufactures textiles, drugs, shoes, doors, and cosmetics.

5 *or* **Perth'shire** (pûrth'shĭr; -shēr). County, cen. Scotland; area 2493 sq. m.; pop. (1951) 128,072; ⊗ Perth; rivers Forth, Tay; region has some of the finest scenery in Scotland, in the Grampian Mts. and on the shores of its many lochs; chief industries agriculture and livestock grazing; cotton, woolen, and linen goods.

6 Burgh, ⊗ of Perth co., cen. Scotland, on the Tay river 32 m. NW of Edinburgh; pop. (1951) 25,599; once ✸ of Scotland until c. 1452; scene of many parliaments and councils; textile mills. At St. John's church John Knox preached 1559 his noted denunciation of idolatry.

Perth Am'boy (pûrth ăm'boi). City and port of entry, Middlesex co., cen. New Jersey, on Raritan Bay at mouth of Raritan river, 17 m. SSW of Newark; pop. 38,007; good harbor; shipbuilding yards with dry docks; fire-clay deposits in vicinity; lead, copper, and silver smelting and refining plants; manufactures ceramic wares, asphalt, synthetic resin, munitions, pneumatic tools, cables, clothing, cigars. Settled c. 1685 chiefly by Scottish dissenters and by English and Huguenots; made capital of East Jersey 1686 (see BURLINGTON, N.J.); incorporated 1718; railroad terminus 1832; known as summer resort c. 1800–60; tidewater shipping terminus 1876.

Per'tuis (pĕr'tü·ē'; *Angl.* -twē'). Town, Vaucluse dept., SE France, 38 m. SE of Avignon; pop. 4254; ancient clock tower and 14th-cent. church.

Pe·ru' (pĕ·rōō'; pē·rōō'; *Span.* pä·rōō'). Republic, W South America; bounded on N by Ecuador and Colombia, on E by Brazil and Bolivia, on S tip by Chile, and on W by the Pacific Ocean; area (including 1714 sq. m. of Lake Titicaca and 12 sq. m. of insular possessions) 482,257 sq. m.; pop. (1940 est.) 7,023,111; ✸ Lima; divided into the following 23 departments (for pronunciation of their names, see their individual entries):

NAME	LOCA-TION	AREA[1]	POP.[1]	CAPITAL
Amazonas	N	13,947	89,560	Chachapoyas
Ancash	W	14,705	465,135	Huarás
Apurímac	S	8,189	280,213	Abancay
Arequipa	S	21,952	270,996	Arequipa
Ayacucho	S	18,190	414,208	Ayacucho
Cajamarca	N	12,541	568,118	Cajamarca
Callao[2]	W	14	84,438	Callao
Cuzco	SE	55,731	565,458	Cuzco
Huancavelica	S cen.	8,300	265,557	Huancavelica
Huánuco	cen.	15,430	276,833	Huánuco
Ica	SW	9,799	144,547	Ica
Junín[3]	cen.	22,820	500,161	Huancayo
La Libertad	NW	10,209	404,024	Trujillo
Lambayeque	NW	4,615	199,660	Chiclayo
Lima	cen.	15,052	849,171	Lima
Loreto	NE	119,301	321,341	Iquitos
Madre de Dios	SE	58,842	25,212	Puerto Maldonado
Moquegua	S	5,550	35,709	Moquegua
Pasco[3]	cen.			Cerro de Pasco
Piura	NW	15,239	431,487	Piura
Puno[4]	SE	26,140	646,385	Puno
San Martín	N	17,452	120,913	Moyobamba
Tacna	S	4,922	37,512	Tacna
Tumbes	NW	1,591	26,473	Tumbes

[1] Area in sq. m.; includes 1714 sq. m. of Lake Titicaca (in Puno dept.) and 12 sq. m. of insular possessions. Pop. is 1940 est.
[2] Constitutional province with status of a department.
[3] Created out of portion of Junín dept. in 1944; estimated pop. is 90,353.
[4] Includes 1714 sq. m. of Lake Titicaca.

Extends from ab. 0° (equator) on the Putumayo to 18°30′S on coast S of Tacna; widest part ab. 800 m.; greater part covered by Andes: main range, Cordillera Occidental, parallel to coast; Cordillera de Carabaya and Cordillera Oriental in SE, and Cordillera Huayhuash in

cen. part; has many subsidiary ranges, esp. in S. Highest peak Huascarán 22,205 ft. in W; others Nevado Coropuna 21,720 ft., Solimana, Salcantay, Nudo Ausangate, and the volcanoes El Misti and Yucamani in S; many peaks bet. 17,000 and 20,000 ft. Coast line ab. 1400 m. long; coastal belt, 40 to 100 m. wide, bet. Pacific Ocean and coastal ranges; to the E are many valleys and plateaus shut in by the mountains and watered by streams of the Amazon system; in NE is extensive plain (chiefly Loreto dept.). *Rivers, lakes:* Marañón (Amazon) in N, its many tributaries, esp. Napo, Tigre, Pastaza, and

Huallaga; Ucayali in E and its great headstreams Urubamba and Apurímac; sources of Purús and Madre de Dios in SE; in extreme N the Putumayo forms boundary with Colombia; many short streams in coastal belt. Includes NW half of large Lake Titicaca (*q.v.*). *Economic resources:* Cotton, sugar, coffee, coca, cacao, wool, copper, silver, petroleum. *Chief cities:* Lima, Callao, Arequipa, Cuzco, Iquitos, Chiclayo.

History: Seat of Inca empire, established c. 1230 with its capital at Cuzco, which ruled Quito (Ecuador) and parts of modern Bolivia and Chile; reached by Spanish 1522; finally conquered by Pizarro and Almagro 1533; Lima (*q.v.*) founded 1535; scene of strife bet. rival conquistadores 1537–54; in 1542 Spanish erected viceroyalty of Peru which, up to 18th cent., included Panama and all of Spanish South America except Venezuela (see also UPPER PERU); New Granada (see COLOMBIA) 1718 and Buenos Aires (La Plata) 1776 were made separate viceroyalties; Peru declared its independence of Spain under San Martín 1821, but did not achieve final freedom until 1824; fought Spain 1866; defeated in War of the Pacific with Chile 1879–83, and lost Tarapacá and occupation of Tacna and Arica; received Tacna (*q.v.*) 1929 after long dispute with Chile; in dispute with Colombia over Leticia (*q.v.*) 1932–33; adopted new constitution 1933; boundary with Ecuador under dispute for many years; subject of treaties 1860, 1887, and 1890 but not settled until July 1945 when greater part of region E of Andes was assigned to Peru. In World War I broke off relations with Germany 1917 and in World War II with Axis powers in 1941.

Pe·ru′ (pĕ·rōō′; ṗĕ·rōō′; *attributively, also* pē′rōō). **1** City, La Salle co., N Illinois, on Illinois river 15 m. W of Ottawa; pop. 10,460; clock factories, zinc works.
2 City, ⊗ of Miami co., N cen. Indiana, 18 m. N of Kokomo; pop. 14,453; in agricultural section.
3 Village, Nemaha co., SE Nebraska, on Missouri river 58 m. ESE of Lincoln; pop. 1151. Nebraska State Teachers College (1867; coed.).
Pe·ru′gia (pȧ·rōō′jä; *Angl.* pĕ·rōō′jȧ, -jĭ·ȧ). **1** Province of Italy. See *Table* at ITALY.
2 *anc.* **Pe·ru′sia** (pĕ·rōō′zhȧ; -zhĭ·ȧ). Commune, ✳ of Perugia prov., Umbria, cen. Italy, bet. Tiber river and Lake Trasimeno 85 m. N of Rome; pop. 82,407; old wall fortifications and citadel; structures include 15th-cent. Gothic cathedral, 10th-cent. church of San Pietro, 13th-cent. church of San Domenico, 13th-cent. town hall; university (founded 1320); manufactures include velvet, silk, brandy; trades in grain, olive oil, wool, spun silk, cattle.
History: One of 12 principal cities of Etruria; taken by Rome 309 B.C.; captured by the Ostrogoth Totila 547 A.D.; taken by Pepin the Short and ceded to Pope 8th cent.; ravaged by plagues 14th and 15th cents.; became part of Papal States 16th cent.; annexed to kingdom of Italy 1860; in World War II taken by British June 1944.
Perugia, Lake. See Lake TRASIMENO.
Perur. See COIMBATORE commune.
Perusia. See PERUGIA commune.
Pe·ru′vi·an Current (pĕ·rōō′vĭ·ăn; pĕ-; -rōōv′yăn). A cold ocean current formed as a division of the west-wind drift of the South Pacific Ocean, and directed N along the coast of Chile and Peru.
Pé′ru·welz′ (pā′rü′vĕlz′). Manufacturing commune, Hainaut prov., SW Belgium, 16 m. WNW of Mons; pop. 7877.
Per′vo·maisk′ (pĕr′vô·mīsk′; *Russ.* pyïr·vŭ-); *formerly* **Ol′vi·o′pol** (ŏl′vĭ·ô′pôl; *Russ.* ŭl·vyï·ô′pŭl·y′). Town, N Odessa Region, S Ukraine, U.S.S.R., on Bug river 112 m. N of Odessa; pop. 33,794.
Pe′sa·ro (pā′zä·rô); *anc.* **Pi·sau′rum** (pĭ·sô′rŭm; pī-). Seaport, ✳ of Pesaro e Urbino prov., Marches, cen. Italy, on Adriatic 85 m. E by N of Florence; pop. 44,589; old castle and medieval walls; ancient Roman bridge; ducal palace (built 1364) with adjoining Ateneo Pesarese (containing collections of majolica and paintings and library); 15th-cent. Villa Imperiale (built by Sforza family); cathedral of San Francesco; manufactures terra cotta, textiles, machinery, ships; trades in agricultural products. Birthplace of Rossini; residence of Torquato Tasso.
History: Settled by Sicilians; successively ruled by Umbrians, Etruscans, and Senonian Gauls; became Roman colony 184 B.C.; destroyed by Ostrogoths 536 A.D.; given to Pope by Pepin the Short in 8th cent.; under Malatesta 1285 ff., Sforza 1445 ff., and Rovere 1512 ff., families; part of Papal States 1631 ff., of kingdom of Italy 1860 ff.
Pesaro e Ur·bi′no (ȧ̇ ōor·bē′nô). Province of Italy. See *Table* at ITALY.
Pes·ca·do′res (pĕs′kȧ·dōr′ēz; -ēs); *Chin.* **Peng′hu** (pŭng′hōō′); *Jap.* **Hoko Sho·to** (hō·kō shô·tō) *or* **Ho·ko Gun·to** (gōon·tō). Group of ab. 48 islands in Formosa Strait bet. Formosa and the mainland of China, separated from Formosa by **Pescadores Channel** (30 m. wide); 49 sq. m.; pop. 70,000; largest island Penghu, on which is chief town Makung, a great Japanese naval base in World War II. Ceded to Japan by China 1895; retroceded 1946.
Pes·ca·do′res, Point (pĕs′kȧ·dōr′ēz; -ēs; *Span.* pās′kä·thō′rās). Cape extending into Pacific Ocean on the coast of Arequipa dept., S Peru.
Pe·sca′ra (pås·kä′rä). **1** Lower course of the ATERNO river, SE cen. Italy.
2 Province of Italy. See *Table* at ITALY.
3 *anc.* **A·ter′num** (ȧ·tûr′nŭm) *or* **Os′ti·a A·ter′ni** (ŏs′tĭ·ȧ ȧ·tûr′nī). Industrial and commercial seaport, ✳ of Pescara prov., Abruzzi e Molise, cen. Italy, on Adri-

atic at mouth of Pescara river 98 m. ENE of Rome; pop. 51,808; castle; bathing and winter resort. Fortified to 1867; made provincial capital 1927; taken by Allies June 1944.
Pescara Pass. See APENNINES.
Pe·schie′ra del Gar′da (pås·kyâ′rä dȧl gär′dä); *anc.* **A·ril′i·ca** (ȧ·rĭl′ĭ·kȧ), *later* **Pis·car′i·a** (pĭs·kär′ĭ·ȧ). Commune, Verona prov., Venezia Euganea, NE Italy, on SE shore of Lake Garda at source of Mincio river 16 m. W of Verona; pop. 3801; a former frontier fortress, one of Quadrilateral cities (Peschiera, Mantua, Verona, Legnago) important in the Napoleonic Wars.
Pe′schio, Mount (pĕs′kyȯ). Mountain in S range of Alban Hills, W Italy, just N of Velletri; taken by Americans June 1–2, 1944.
Pe′scia (pā′shä). Commune, Pistoia prov., Tuscany, cen. Italy, 14 m. W of Pistoia; pop. 20,898; remains of ancient city walls; 14th-cent. cathedral; sericulture; paper mills.
Pe·sci′na (pȧ·shē′nä). Commune, Aquila prov., Abruzzi e Molise, cen. Italy, 27 m. SE of Aquila; pop. 10,028; 16th-cent. cathedral.
Pe·sha′war (pĕ·shä′wẽr; pĕ·shour′). **1** District of former North-West Frontier Province, Pakistan, W of Indus river; 1547 sq. m.; pop. (1941) 851,833.
2 Tribal areas attached to district; 2299 sq. m.; pop. 305,410.
3 City, ✳ of district and of North-West Frontier Province, on Bara river, tributary of the Kabul, 240 m. NW of Lahore; pop., with cantonment, (1941) 130,967. India's most important strategically located border city, 9 m. from Jamrud, entrance to Khyber Pass, gateway to cen. Asia. Native section of city has active trade, especially with Afghanistan and Central Asia, and large varied bazaars offering horses, woolen stuffs, silks, dyes, goats, fruits, gold thread, precious stones, carpets, sheepskins, etc. Important in 2d cent. A.D. during Indo-Scythian Kushan dynasty under Kanishka; added to Sikh kingdom by Ranjit Singh 1823; during period of British sovereignty (from 1848), a stronghold against the Afghans and an operational base against marauding border tribes. Its cantonment principal military station of North-West Frontier Province.
Peshawur. Var. of PESHAWAR.
Pesh·ko′pi (pĕsh·kô′pē). Town, ✳ of Dibër prefecture, Albania, near Yugoslav border NE of Tiranë.
Pesh′ti·go (pĕsh′tĭ·gō). **1** River ab. 150 m. long, NE Wisconsin; rises in Forest co., flows SE into Green Bay S of Marinette.
2 City, Marinette co., NE Wisconsin, on Peshtigo river 6 m. WSW of Marinette; pop. 2504; manufactures paper, canoes, sailboats, motor launches. Practically destroyed by fire Oct. 8, 1871, same day as great fire in Chicago.
Pes·quei′ra (pĕsh·kā′ē·rȧ). City, E cen. Pernambuco state, E Brazil, on railroad 115 m. W of Recife; pop. 8519.
Pes′sac′ (pĕ′såk′). Commune, Gironde dept., SW France, 4 m. SSW of Bordeaux; pop. 13,004; produces wines.
Pes′si·nus (pĕs′ĭ·nŭs; -nōōs). Ancient city, Galatia, Asia Minor; site of principal shrine of Cybele, the great nature goddess of Anatolia, who was known here as Agdistis or Angdistis, from the rock Agdus on nearby Mount Dindymus, and as Dindymene, from the mountain itself.
Pest. See BUDAPEST.
Pest′er·zsé′bet (pĕsht′tĕr·zhā′bĕt). City, a S suburb of Budapest, cen. Hungary; pop. (1939) 71,150.
Pesto. See PAESTUM.
Pest′szent·lö′rinc (pĕsht′sĕnt·lû′rĭnts). Commune, a SE suburb of Budapest, cen. Hungary; pop. 12,701.
Pe′ta·chal′co Bay (pā′tä·chäl′kȯ). Inlet of the Pacific Ocean on SW coast of Mexico, chiefly in NW Guerrero state.
Pe′tah Tiq′va (pĕ′tä·h′ tĭk′vä). Town, Lydda dist., W

Palestine, 7 m. E of Tel Aviv; pop. (1944 est.) 19,188; modern Jewish settlement.

Pet'al (pĕt'l). Urban area, Forrest co., SE Mississippi, NE of Hattiesburg; pop. 4007.

Pet'a·lu'ma (pĕt'à·lōō'mà). City, Sonoma co., W California, on Petaluma river 16 m. S of Santa Rosa; pop. 14,035; founded by colony of Mexicans 1833; center of poultry-farming region.

Pé'tange' (pā'täNzh'). Commune, grand duchy of Luxembourg, in SW part N of Differdange; pop. (1935) 10,525.

Petch. Var. of PEČ.

Petchabun. See PHETCHABUN.

Petchaburi. See PHET BURI.

Pe·tén' (pā·tān'). **1** or **La·gu'na de Flo'res** (lä·gōō'nä thä flō'räs). Lake ab. 27 m. long, cen. Petén dept., Guatemala.

2 Department, N Guatemala; 13,843 sq. m.; pop. 11,475; ✳ Flores; first center of Mayan civilization.

Peteorde. See PETWORTH.

Pe'ter·bor'o or **Pe'ter·bor'ough** (pē'tĕr·bûr'ō). Manufacturing town, Hillsboro co., S New Hampshire, 16 m. E of Keene; pop. 2963; resort; first permanent settlement 1749; incorporated 1760; has oldest free tax-supported library in U.S. (1833); seat of MacDowell Colony for creative artists (over 600 acres); place where Brigham Young was chosen leader of the Mormon Church.

Pe'ter·bor'ough (pē'tĕr·bûr'ō; *Brit. usu.* -bŭ·rů, -brů). **1** Town, S New Hampshire. See PETERBORO.

2 Town, SE South Australia, 135 m. N of Adelaide; pop. 3057; railroad junction.

3 County, Ontario, Canada. See *Table* at ONTARIO.

4 Industrial city, ⊗ of Peterborough co., SE Ontario, Canada, on Otonabee river and Trent Canal 13 m. N of W end of Rice Lake; pop. 38,272; center of agricultural region; electrical engineering works; important railroad junction. Seat of a provincial normal school. Home of the "Rice Lake" or "Peterborough" birch-bark canoe.

5 Municipal borough, ⊗ of Soke of Peterborough, Northamptonshire, cen. England, on the Nene 75 m. N of London; pop. 53,412; rail and trade center in agricultural section; brickworks; 13th-cent. cathedral, burial place of Catherine of Aragon.

Peterborough, Soke of (sōk). Administrative county in NE section of Northamptonshire, E cen. England; 84 sq. m.; pop. (1951) 63,784; ⊗ Peterborough.

Pe'ter I Island (pē'tĕr thĕ fûrst'). Island 14 m. long off Antarctica in Bellingshausen Sea NE of Thurston Penin.; lat. 69°S and long. 90°35'W; discovered and named by Bellingshausen in expedition of exploration 1819–21; annexed by Norway 1931.

Pe·ter·gof' (pyĭ·tyĕr·gôf'). Var. of *Peterhof:* see PETRODVORETS.

Pe'ter·head' (pē'tĕr·hĕd'; pē'tĕr·hĕd'). Seaport burgh, Aberdeen co., NE Scotland, on a peninsula 30 m. NE of Aberdeen; pop. 12,765; herring fisheries; quarries (red granite). The Old Pretender landed here on Christmas Day 1715.

Peterhof. See PETRODVORETS.

Pe'ter Island (pē'tĕr). One of the British Virgin Is., West Indies, S of Tortola.

Peterlingen. See PAYERNE.

Pe'te·ro'a (pā'tä·rō'ä). Volcanic peak 13,419 ft., E cen. Chile, near border of W Mendoza prov., W Argentina.

Pe'ters·burg (pē'tĕrz·bûrg). **1** Fishing town in Petersburg dist., SE Alaska, ab. 35 m. NNW of Wrangell; pop. 1502.

2 City, ⊗ of Menard co., cen. Illinois, 20 m. NW of Springfield; pop. 2359; coal mines and medicinal springs nearby; canneries, brickyards.

3 City, ⊗ of Pike co., SW Indiana, 18 m. SE of Vincennes; pop. 2939; in agricultural region, near gas and oil wells.

4 Commercial and industrial city, SE Virginia, at head of

navigation of Appomattox river 23 m. S of Richmond; geographically in Dinwiddie co. but politically independent; 6 sq. m.; pop. 36,750; shipping point for tobacco, peanuts, lumber; manufactures cigarettes and other tobacco products, luggage, optical goods, textiles, silk. Site of fort built 1645 at falls of the Appomattox; trading post established 1733; incorporated as town 1784, as city 1850; during latter part of Revolution occupied successively by British and Americans; during Civil War scene of important engagements June 1864 to Apr. 1865 when Grant finally forced Lee's withdrawal from Petersburg and Richmond and his surrender at Appomattox (*q.v.*); nearby is **Petersburg National Military Park:** see UNITED STATES, *National Historical Parks.*

5 Town, ⊗ of Grant co., NE West Virginia, 32 m. S of Keyser; pop. 2079; farm trade center; leather manufactures.

Pe'ters·ham. 1 (pē'tĕrz·hăm) Town, Worcester co., cen. Massachusetts, ab. 25 m. NW of Worcester; pop. 890; site of Harvard Forest, 2100 acres, bird sanctuary (1000 acres) and experiment station for Harvard University's School of Forestry.

2 (pē'tĕr·shăm) City, E New South Wales, SE Australia, SW suburb of Sydney; pop. 26,943.

Peterswald. See PETŘVALD.

Peter the Great Bay (pē'tĕr). Inlet of Sea of Japan at S end of Maritime Territory, Soviet Russia, Asia; its two arms, Amur Bay and Ussuri Bay, are on either side of the peninsula on which Vladivostok is situated.

Pe'ter·war·dein' (pā'tĕr·vär·dīn'); *Serb.* **Pe'tro·va·ra'din** (pĕ'trō·vä·rä'dēn); *Hung.* **Pé'ter·vá'rad** (pā'tĕr·vä'rŏd). Commune, S Voivodina, NE Yugoslavia, on S bank of the Danube opp. Novi Sad; pop. 5101; Peter the Hermit here reviewed First Crusade 1096; scene of battle Aug. 5, 1716 in which Prince Eugene of Savoy defeated the Turks.

Pethah Tiqva. Var. of PETAH TIQVA.

Petit Andely, Le. See LES ANDELYS.

Pet'it Bois Island (pĕt'ĭ bwä'). Island off coast of Alabama-Mississippi boundary, bet. Mississippi Sound and the Gulf of Mexico.

Pe·tit'–Bourg (pē·tē'bōōr'). Town on E coast of Basse-Terre, Guadeloupe, West Indies; pop. (1921) 5650.

Pe·tit'–Ca'nal' (pē·tē'kà'nàl'). Commune, W coast of Grande Terre, Guadeloupe, West Indies; pop. (1921) ab. 7000.

Petit–Charenton. See SAINT-MAURICE.

Pet'it·co'di·ac (pĕt'ĭ·kō'dĭ·ăk). River ab. 60 m. long, SE New Brunswick, Canada; flows NE, E, and then S through wide estuary (20 m. long) to inlet of Chignecto Bay. Moncton is on it.

Pe·tite'–Ros'selle' (pē·tēt'rō'sĕl'); *Ger.* **Klein'ros'-seln** (klīn'rôs'ĕln). Commune, Moselle dept., NE France, near the border of Saarland; pop. (1931) 9745.

Pe·tit' Go'âve' (pē·tē' gô'äv'). Town on N Tiburon Penin., SW Haiti.

Pe·tit'jean' (pē·tē'zhäN'). Town, N Morocco, NW Africa, W of Fez.

Pe·tit' Ma·nan' Point (pē·tĕt' mà·năn'). Southwest point of Washington co., SE Maine.

Petit-Quevilly, Le. See LE PETIT-QUEVILLY.

Pe·tit'–Sa'con'nex' (pē·tē'sà'kô'nĕks'). Former commune in Geneva canton, SW Switzerland; pop. (1920) 15,103; since 1930 part of Geneva.

Petit–Saint–Bernard. Alpine pass. See ALPS.

Pet'it·sik'a·pau Lake (?pĕt'ĭ·sĭk'à·pou). Lake, W Labrador, on border of Quebec prov., Canada, NW in the chain of lakes out of which the Hamilton river flows.

Pe'to (pā'tō). Town, Yucatán state, on Yucatán penin., SE Mexico; pop. 5104; railroad terminus 70 m. SE of Mérida.

Pe·to'ne (pĕ·tō'nĕ). Borough, Wellington provincial dist., S North I., New Zealand, NE suburb of Wellington on Port Nicholson; pop. 10,770.

Pe·tos'key (pĕ·tŏs'kĭ). City, ⊗ of Emmet co., N Michi-

gan, on Lake Michigan 31 m. SW of Cheboygan; pop. 6138; resort center; manufactures lumber and wood products, flour, leather, cement.

Pe'tra (pē'trá; pĕt'rá). Ruined city, SW Jordan, ab. 18 m. NW of Ma'an, lat. 30°15'N and long. 35°35'E, and included in modern **Wa'di Mu'sa** (wä'dĭ mōō'sá; -sä); usually identified with **Se'la** (sē'lá), ancient capital of Edom, from which the Edomites were driven c. 300 B.C. by the Nabataeans whose capital it became until 105 A.D. Remarkable rock city in deep gorge on NE slope of Mt. Hor (*mod.* Jebel Harun); its temples, tombs, dwellings, etc. all carved in rose, crimson, and purple limestone; was a wealthy, commercial city for several centuries with great caravan trade; became chief city of Arabia Petraea. Captured by Moslems in 7th cent. and by Crusaders in 12th cent. Its ruins discovered by Burckhardt in 1812.

Pe·tra·li'a So·pra'na (pâ·trä-lē'ä sô·prä'nä). Commune, Palermo prov., Sicily, 51 m. ESE of Palermo; pop. (1931) 7475.

Petralia Sot·ta'na (sôt·tä'nä). Commune, Palermo prov., Sicily, 49 m. ESE of Palermo; pop. 10,936.

Pe'trich (pĕ'trĭch). Town, extreme SW Bulgaria, in Sofia dept.; pop. (1926) 8380.

Pet'ri·fied Forest National Monument (pĕt'rĭ·fīd). See UNITED STATES, *National Monuments.*

Petrikau. See PIOTRKÓW.

Petroaleksandrovsk. See TURTKUL.

Pet'ro·dvo·rets' (pĕt'rô·dŭ·vŏr·ĕts'; *Russ.* pyĭ·trŭ·dvŭ-ryĕts'); *formerly* **Len'insk** (lĕn'ĭnsk; *Russ.* lyä'nyĭnsk) *and* **Pe'ter·hof** (pē'tĕr·hôf; *Russ.* pyĭ·tyĕr·gôf'). Town on S shore of Kronshtadt Bay, NW Leningrad Region, Soviet Russia, Europe, 12 m. W of Leningrad; pop. 8925; E of Oranienbaum and nearly opp. Kronshtadt; contains former imperial palaces (esp. that of Peter the Great, built 1720) and other palaces, gardens, fountains. Long a center of the gem-cutting industry. Present name adopted 1944.

Petrograd. Capital of Russia 1914–24. See LENINGRAD.

Petrokov. See PIOTRKÓW.

Pe·tro·kre'post (pyĭ·trŭ·kryĕ'pŭst·y'); *formerly* **Shlis'-sel·burg** (shlĭs''l·bûrg; *Russ.* shlyēs·syĭl·y'·bōōrk'), *Ger.* **Schlüs'sel·burg** (shlüs'ĕl·bōōrk). Town, NW Leningrad Region, Soviet Russia, Europe, on exit of Neva river at SW corner of Lake Ladoga; pop. ab. 6000. A Novgorodian town founded 1323; taken and retaken many times in wars bet. Russia and Sweden; captured 1702 by Peter the Great who erected a fortress on an island in the Neva as a key (Ger. *schlüssel*) in his line of defense to the sea; later fortress became imperial prison in which for nearly 200 years many noted prisoners were kept; prison abolished 1917 and made a state museum. In 1941–42 defense line against Germans, again a key point; siege raised 1943.

Pe·tro'le·um (pĕ·trō'lē·ŭm; -trōl'yŭm). County in Montana. See *Table* at MONTANA.

Pe·tro'lia (pē·trō'lyá). **1** Town, Albania, ab. 45 m. NE of Vlona and connected with it by oil pipeline.

2 Oil town, Lambton co., SE Ontario, Canada, 14 m. ESE of Sarnia; pop. 3105; center of petroleum district.

Pe·tro'na Point (pâ·trō'nä). Cape on S coast of Puerto Rico, E of Ponce.

Pet'ro·pav'lovsk (pĕt'rô·päv'lôfsk; *Russ.* pyĭ·trŭ·pá'-vlŭfsk). **1** City, * of North Kazakhstan Region, N edge of Kazakh S.S.R., Soviet Central Asia, on the Trans-Siberian R.R. 170 m. W of Omsk and on the right bank of the Ishim river; pop. 91,678; has rail connection with Akmolinsk and is a market town for caravans coming in from the steppe region to the S; deals in corn, cattle and cattle products, wool and cotton, furs, and tea. Founded 1752.

2 See PETROPAVLOVSK-KAMCHATSKI, Khabarovsk Territory, Soviet Russia, Asia.

Petropavlovsk-Kam·chat'ski (-kăm·chăt'skĭ; *Russ.* -kŭm·chàt'skĭ); *formerly* **Petropavlovsk.** Seaport

town on E coast of S end of Kamchatka Penin., Khabarovsk Territory, Soviet Russia, Asia; pop. ab. 20,000; has good harbor, but icebound half the year; fishing port, has shipyard, and is a center for the fur trade. In 19th cent. a station for the Russian Pacific fleet.

Pe·tró'po·lis (pĕ·trŏp'ô·lĭs; *Port.* pĕ·trô'pŏō·lês). City, Rio de Janeiro state, SE Brazil, 27 m. N of Rio de Janeiro; pop. (1940 est.) 46,829; cool climate (alt. 2634 ft.); summer places of members of diplomatic corps and government. Inter-American Conference for the Maintenance of Continental Peace and Security, Aug. 15 to Sept. 2, 1947, called to implement the Act of Chapultepec (*q.v.*).

Pe·tro·şa'ni (pĕ'trô·shän'; -shä'nĕ); *Hung.* **Pe'tro-zsény'** (pĕ'trô·zhän'y'); *Ger.* **Pe'tro·schen'** (pä'trô-shän'). Town, S Transylvania, Romania, ab. 150 m. NW of Bucharest; pop. 15,380.

Petrovaradin. See PETERWARDEIN.

Pe'trov·grad (pĕ'trôv·gräd); *formerly* **Ve'li·ki Beč-ke'rek** (vĕ'lē·kĕ bĕch·kĕ'rĕk); *Hung.* **Nagy'becs'ke-rek** (nŏd'y'·bĕch'kĕ·rĕk). City, Voivodina autonomous prov., NE Yugoslavia, ab. 30 m. NE of Novi Sad; pop. 32,831; commercial center for grain-producing area; sugar refineries, breweries, distilleries.

Pe·trovsk' (pĕ·trôfsk'; *Russ.* pyĕ-). **1** City, * of Dagestan Republic, SE Soviet Russia, Europe. See MAKHACH-KALA.

2 Town, SW Chita Region, SE Soviet Russia, Asia, on Trans-Siberian R.R. 65 m. SE of Ulan Ude; pop. 19,192; metallurgical center in region of coal, iron, and gold.

3 Town, Saratov Region, SE Soviet Russia, Europe, ab. 50 m. NNW of Saratov; pop. ab. 18,000.

Pet'ro·za·vodsk' (pĕt'rô·zá·vôtsk'; *Russ.* pyĭ·trŭ·zŭ-vôtsk') *or* **Ka·li'ninsk** (kà·lē'nĭnsk; *Russ.* kŭ·lyē'-nyĭnsk). City, * of Karelia, U.S.S.R., in S part on NW shore of Lake Onega, 185 m. NE of Leningrad; pop. 69,728; industrial town on Leningrad-Murmansk R.R.; located near iron mines; has ironworks esp. for manufacture of guns.

Petrozsény. See PETROŞANI.

Pe'tř·vald (pĕ'tĕrzh·vàlt); *Ger.* **Pe'ters·wald** (pä'tĕrs-vält). Town, Silesia prov., cen. Czechoslovakia, just E of Moravská Ostrava; pop. (1930) 10,275.

Pe'tr·žal'ka (pĕ'tĕr·zhàl'ká); *Hung.* **Po'zsony·li'get-fa'lu** (pô'zhŏn·y'·li'gĕt·fô'lōō). Town, SW Slovakia prov., E cen. Czechoslovakia; pop. (1930) 14,196; a suburb of Bratislava.

Pet'sa·mo (pĕt'sá·mō; *Finn.* -sá·mô); *Russ.* **Pe-chen'ga** (pĕ·chĕng'gá; *Russ.* pyĭ·chĕn'gà). **1** Territory, formerly in NE Oulu dept., N Finland, extending nearly to Varanger Fjord, Norway, forming a narrow strip 135 m. long from N to S bordering on W Murmansk Region, Soviet Russia, Europe; 3860 sq. m.; pop. ab. 2000; ceded by Russia to Finland 1920; taken back by Russia 1940 but occupied by Germans 1940–44; now part of Murmansk Region.

2 Chief town of the territory. See PECHENGA.

Pe'tse·ri (pĕ'tsĕ·rĭ). **1** Province of Estonia. See *Table* at ESTONIA.

2 City, its *, near W border of Pskov Region, R.S.F.S.R., 25 m. W of Pskov; pop. (1937) 4728; trade center in flax-growing section.

Pet'tis (pĕt'ĭs). County in Missouri. See *Table* at MISSOURI.

Petuna. See FUYU.

Pet'worth (pĕt'wûrth; -wẽrth; *locally also* pĕt'ẽrth); *medieval* **Peteorde.** Village, West Sussex, England, ab. 42 m. SSW of London; pop. (1921) 2435; Petworth house, formerly owned by Percy family.

Peu'ce (pū'sē; -sĕ). Ancient name of marshy region at mouth of Danube on the Black Sea where two islands are formed by the arms of the river; birthplace of Alaric.

Pev'en·sey (pĕv'ĕn·zĭ; -sĭ). Village, SE Sussex, S England, on coast W of Hastings; site of landing of William the Conqueror 1066; 12th-cent. castle.

Pé·ze·nas' (pāz'nȧs'). Manufacturing town, Hérault dept., S France, 25 m. SW of Montpellier; pop. 6549; residence 1655–56 of Molière, who wrote *Les Précieuses Ridicules* here.

Pfäf'fi·kon (pfĕf'ĕ·kôn). Village, Zurich canton, Switzerland; pop. (1930) 3811; ab. 12 m. E of Zurich at N end of **Lake of Pfäffikon** (*Ger.* **Pfäf'fi·ker See** [-kĕr zā]), a marshy lake noted for many evidences of ancient lake dwellers found on its shores, esp. at Robenhausen at S end, type station for the *Robenhausian epoch*, the stage of neolithic culture immediately preceding the Bronze Age.

Pfalz (pfälts). See PALATINATE, THE and *The Palatinate* in *Table* at BAVARIA.

Pforta. See SCHULPFORTE.

Pforz'heim (pfôrts'hīm). Manufacturing and commercial city, Baden-Württemberg, Germany, on border of the Black Forest 16 m. SE of Karlsruhe; pop. 78,859; 12th-cent. castle church; manufactures costume jewelry, chemicals, machinery, metal goods, leather, paper; trades in lumber, oil, fruit, wine, cattle.

Phais'tos (fīs'tŏs); *Lat.* **Phaes'tus** (fēs'tŭs; fēs'-). Ancient city in S Crete, SW of Knossos, near the shore of Bay of Messara; site of a Minoan palace.

Pha·le'ron (fȧ·lĕr'ŏn; *Mod. Gr.* fä'lyĕ·rôn) *or* **Pha·le'-rum** (fȧ·lĕr'ŭm). Town, an early port of Athens, in Attica, E part of ancient Greece, on **Phaleron Bay**; E of Piraeus, by which it was superseded in 5th cent. B.C. In modern Greece, a seaplane base.

Phal'tan (p'hŭl'tȧn). **1** Former Indian state, Deccan and Kolhapur States, cen. Bombay prov., W Indian Union; 391 sq. m.; pop. (1941) 71,473; joined United Deccan State Aug. 26, 1947.
2 Town, its ✸, ab. 50 m. SE of Poona; pop. 9596.

Phan'a·go'ri·a (făn'ȧ·gōr'ĭ·ȧ). Ancient Greek city on N shore of Pontus Euxinus at entrance to Palus Maeotis (Sea of Azov).

Phang·nga (p'häng·ngä). **1** *or* **Ko Phangnga** (kô). Island (Thai *ko*) in SW Gulf of Siam off E coast of Isthmus of Kra, 8 m. N of Samui I.
2 *or* **Pang-nga** (p'häng·ngä). Province, SW Thailand; 1528 sq. m.; pop. 56,762.
3 *or* **Pang-nga**. Town, its ✸, near W coast of Malay Penin. 40 m. N of Phuket.

Pha·nom Dong Rak (p'hä·nŭm t'hông räk). Mountain range ab. 200 m. long extending E and W along SE boundary of Thailand, separating it from N Cambodia; averages 1200 to 2500 ft. Its W end continues into S Thailand toward Ayudhya, highest point 4167 ft.

Phanos. See FANO.

Phan·rang *or* **Phan Rang** (p'hän·räng). Coastal town, SE Annam, Vietnam, 165 m. ENE of Saigon on river 7 m. from **Phanrang Bay**, an inlet of South China Sea; exports salt; important agricultural center.

Pha'rae (fā'rē; fâr'ē). Ancient town of E Messenia, SW Peloponnesus, S Greece, near modern city of Kalamata.

Pha·ri Dzong (p'hä·rē dzông). Town, S Tibet, in Himalayas near Bhutan border and on highway from Darjeeling to Gyangtse.

Pharnacia. See GİRESUN.

Pha'ros (fā'rŏs; fâr'ŏs). Peninsula in Lower Egypt; in ancient times an island on which was located a famous lighthouse; now part of the site of the city of Alexandria.

Phar'par (fär'pĕr) *or* **Phar'phar** (-fĕr). A river of Damascus (*2 Kings* v. 12); identified by many with the Awaj, a river some distance to the S of the present city, flowing E into swamps.

Pharr (fär). City, Hidalgo co., S Texas, 2 m. E of McAllen; pop. 14,106; packs and ships citrus fruits and farm produce; oil and gas wells nearby.

Phar·sa'lus (fär·sā'lŭs); *Mod. Gr.* **Phár'sa·los** (fär'sä-lôs) *or* **Phar'sa·la** (fär'sä·lä). Town, S Larissa dept., E Thessaly, NE Greece, near the Enipeus river; pop. 3223; scene of Caesar's decisive defeat of Pompey 48 B.C.—called also the battle of **Phar·sa'lia** (fär·sāl'yȧ; -sā'lĭ·ȧ) from the name of the district surrounding the town.

Pharus. See HVAR.

Pha·se'lis (fȧ·sē'lĭs). Coastal town in ancient Lycia, Asia Minor, near border of Pamphylia.

Pha'sis (fā'sĭs). **1** River, W Georgia, U.S.S.R. See RION.
2 Town on Black Sea at mouth of Rion river. See POTI.

Phatnitic. See DAMIETTA mouth of the Nile.

Phat·tha·lung *or* **Pa·ta·lung** (p'hät·t'hä·lŏong); *also* **Pa·da·lung** (p'hät·t'hä·lŏong). **1** Province, SW Thailand; 1704 sq. m.; pop. 117,507.
2 Town, its ✸, on W shore of Lake Thale Luang in Malay Penin. 50 m. NW of Songkhla.

Phazania. See FEZZAN.

Phelps (fĕlps). **1** Name of counties in two states of the U.S. See *Tables* at MISSOURI and NEBRASKA.
2 Village, Ontario co., W New York, 25 m. W of Auburn; pop. 1887.

Phelps Lake. Lake in SE Washington co., E North Carolina, in swamp area bet. Albemarle Sound and Pamlico Sound.

Phenice. See PHOENIX.

Phenice, Phenicia. See PHOENICIA.

Phe'nix City (fē'nĭks). Manufacturing city, a ⊗ of Russell co., E Alabama, on Chattahoochee river across from Columbus, Georgia; pop. 27,630; incorporated 1923; made ⊗ (with branch at Seale *q.v.*) 1935; lumber, brick, cotton textiles, caskets.

Phe'rae (fē'rē). Ancient town in SE Thessaly, NE Greece, ab. 27 m. SE of Larissa. In mythology the home of Admetus; historically, in first half of the 4th cent. B.C., its tyrants controlled Thessaly.

Phet Bu·ri (p'hĕt bŏo·rē); *also* **Pet·cha·bu·ri** *or* **Bej·ra·bu·ri** (p'hĕt·bŏo·rē—sic). **1** Province, SW Thailand; 2436 sq. m.; pop. 155,466.
2 Seaport town, its ✸, on NW shore of Gulf of Siam and on railroad 60 m. SW of Bangkok.

Phet·cha·bun (p'hĕt·chä·bŏon); *also* **Pet·cha·bun** *or* **Bej·ra·bu·ra·na** (p'hĕt·chä·bŏon—sic). **1** Province, cen. Thailand; 4902 sq. m.; pop. 130,807.
2 Town, its ✸, on Sak river 70 m. SE of Phitsanulok; made capital of Thailand by Japanese 1944–45.

Phi·chit (p'hĭ·chĭt); *also* **Pi·chit** *and* **Bi·chit·ra** (p'hĭ·chĭt—sic). **1** Province, W cen. Thailand; 1725 sq. m.; pop. 177,166.
2 Town, its ✸, on Nan river 55 m. N of Nakhon Sawan.

Phi·ga'lia (fĭ·gāl'yȧ; -gā'lĭ·ȧ; fī-). Ancient city in SW Arcadia, cen. Peloponnesus, S Greece, near N border of Messenia; ab. 5 m. to the E is **Bas'sae** (băs'ē), site of a temple of Apollo, still preserved, in which were the beautiful Phigalian marbles or sculptures; these form a frieze ab. 101 ft. long and 2 ft. high, representing in Parian marble in high relief battles bet. Greeks and Amazons and bet. Lapithae and Centaurs; completely preserved, probably the work of Ictinus (c. 430 B.C.); since 1814 in the British Museum.

Phil'a·del'phi·a (fĭl'ȧ·dĕl'fĭ·ȧ; -fyȧ). **1** County in Pennsylvania. See *Table* at PENNSYLVANIA.
2 City, ⊗ of Neshoba co., E cen. Mississippi, 38 m. NNW of Meridian; pop. 5017; peach, apple, and pecan orchards.
3 City, ⊗ of Philadelphia co., SE Pennsylvania, at confluence of Delaware and Schuylkill rivers; coextensive with Philadelphia co. since 1854; pop. 2,002,512. Largest city in the state, and 4th largest in U.S.; commercial, industrial, and financial center; railroad terminus and deepwater port, site of government navy yard; manufactures textiles, petroleum products, carpets and rugs, machinery, chemicals; publishing center, published first newspaper in the Middle Colonies (the *American Weekly Mercury*, 1719), and the first daily newspaper in the U.S. (*Pennsylvania Packet*, 1784); art center, has oldest art institution in the U.S., the Academy of Fine Arts (1805); has first hospital established in U.S., the Pennsylvania Hospital (1751); many institutions of learning: University of Pennsylvania (1740; coed.); Dropsie College for Hebrew and Cognate Learning (1907; coed.); Temple

University (1884; coed.); Drexel Institute of Technology (1891; coed.); La Salle College (1860; men; Roman Catholic); Saint Joseph's College (1851; men; Roman Catho-

lic); Girard College (1848; orphan boys); Divinity School of the Protestant Episcopal Church (1857); Eastern Baptist Theological Seminary (1925; coed.); Lutheran Theological Seminary (1864; men).

History: First settlement on site made by colony of Swedes 1636; English settlement organized by agent of William Penn 1681, and city laid out 1682 and called Philadelphia; chartered 1701; received many immigrants from Scotland and Ireland in early 18th cent.; dominant in shaping policies of the Middle Colonies in 18th cent.; Benjamin Franklin settled in the city 1723. Prominent in opposing British aggression 1763–74; First Continental Congress met in Carpenter's Hall Sept. 5, 1774; Second Continental Congress in the State House May 10, 1775; Declaration of Independence signed in Independence Hall 1776; city held by British Sept. 27, 1777–June 18, 1778; Constitutional Convention met in the city 1787 and adopted Sept. 17, 1787 the Constitution of the United States. Largest and most important city in U.S. in early 19th cent.; capital of Pennsylvania 1683–1799, and capital of U.S. 1790–1800; financial center of U.S. until 1836; leader in antislavery movement; took active part in the Civil War. Held Centennial Exposition 1876 and Sesquicentennial Exposition 1926.

4 See AMMAN, Transjordan.

5 See ALAŞEHIR, Turkey in Asia.

Phi′lae (fī′lē). Island in the Nile river, in Upper Egypt, in lat. 24°N; site of many ancient temples and monuments; now submerged except in July–Oct. when sluices of the Aswân Dam are open.

Phi′li·a·tra′; *Mod. Gr.* **Phi′li·a·trà′** (fē′lyä·trä′). Commune, Messenia dept., SW Peloponnesus, S Greece, on Ionian Sea; pop. 10,036.

Phil′ip (fīl′ĭp). City, ⊗ of Haakon co., W cen. South Dakota; pop. 1114.

Phil′ip·haugh (fīl′ĭp·hô). Village, S Scotland, 2 m. W of Selkirk; scene of battle Sept. 13, 1645 in which earl of Montrose was surprised and defeated by David Leslie.

Phi′lippe·ville′ (fē′lēp′vēl′; *Angl.* fīl′ĭp·vĭl). Commune and seaport city, N Constantine dept., NE Algeria, N of the city of Constantine; pop. of commune (1936) 64,857; iron mines, marble quarries in vicinity; site of a refugee camp during World War II.

Phil′ip·pi (fīl′ĭ·pī). City, ⊗ of Barbour co., N West Virginia, 19 m. ESE of Clarksburg; pop. 2228; scene of battle (called "Philippi Races") in Civil War 1861. Alderson-Broaddus Coll. (1871; coed.).

Phi·lip′pi (fĭ·lĭp′ī; fīl′ĭ·pī). Ruined town in Drama dept., N cen. Macedonia, Greece, ab. 10 m. from the Aegean Sea; developed and fortified by King Philip of Macedon; scene of battle 42 B.C. in which Octavian and Antony defeated Brutus and Cassius; place where St. Paul first preached the gospel in Europe.

Phil′ip·pine Islands (fīl′ĭ·pēn) *or* **Phil′ip·pines** (-pēnz). Group of 7100 islands (2773 being named and 4327 unnamed and unimportant), N Malay Archipelago, SE of Asia; 115,600 sq. m. (land area 114,830 sq. m.); pop. 16,000,303; official ✳ Quezon City, seat of government Manila, summer ✳ Baguio; formerly a dependency of U.S.A., established as a Commonwealth Nov. 15, 1935; now a republic, **Republic of the Philippines**; divided into the following 49 provinces (for pronunciation of their names, see their individual entries):

PROVINCE	LOCATION	AREA[1]	POP.[1]	CAPITAL
Abra	NW Luzon	1,471	87,780	Bangued
Agusan	NE Mindanao	4,120	99,023	Butuan
Albay[2]	SE Luzon	1,548	432,465	Legaspi
Antique	W Panay	1,034	199,414	San Jose de Buenavista
Bataan	W Luzon	517	85,538	Balanga
Batanes[3]	Batan Is.[3]	76	9,512	Basco
Batangas	S Luzon	1,191	442,034	Batangas
Bohol[4]	Bohol	1,575	491,608	Tagbilaran
Bukidnon	N Mindanao	3,104	57,561	Malaybalay
Bulacan	cen. Luzon	1,021	332,807	Malolos
Cagayan	NE Luzon	3,470	292,270	Tuguegarao
Camarines Norte	SE Luzon	829	98,324	Daet
Camarines Sur	SE Luzon	2,060	385,695	Naga
Capiz	N Panay	1,703	405,285	Capiz
Cavite	SW Luzon	498	238,581	Cavite
Cebu[4]	Cebu	1,880	1,068,078	Cebu
Cotabato	SW Mindanao	8,868	298,935	Cotabato
Davao	SE Mindanao	7,529	292,600	Davao
Ilocos Norte	NW Luzon	1,308	237,586	Laoag
Ilocos Sur	NW Luzon	1,037	271,532	Vigan
Iloilo	S and NE Panay	2,048	744,022	Iloilo
Isabela	NE Luzon	4,069	219,864	Ilagan
Laguna	S cen. Luzon	465	279,505	Santa Cruz
Lanao	W cen. Mindanao	2,574	243,437	Dansalan
La Union	NW Luzon	530	207,701	San Fernando
Leyte[4]	Leyte	3,084	915,853	Tacloban
Manila[5]	SW Luzon	14	623,492	
Marinduque[4]	Marinduque	355	81,768	Boac
Masbate	Masbate, Ticao, and Burias Is.	1,571	182,483	Masbate
Mindoro[4]	Mindoro	3,891	131,569	Calapan
Misamis Occidental	N Mindanao	802	210,057	Oroquieta
Misamis Oriental	N Mindanao	1,512	213,812	Cagayan
Mountain Province[6]	N Luzon	5,458	296,874	Bontoc
Negros Occidental	N and W Negros	2,989	824,858	Bacolod
Negros Oriental[7]	E and SE Negros	2,053	394,680	Dumaguete
Nueva Ecija	cen. Luzon	2,120	416,762	Cabanatuan
Nueva Vizcaya	N cen. Luzon	2,627	78,505	Bayombong
Palawan[4]	Palawan	5,693	93,673	Puerto Princesa
Pampanga	cen. Luzon	827	375,281	San Fernando
Pangasinan	N cen. Luzon	2,021	742,475	Lingayen
Rizal	cen. Luzon	791	444,805	Pasig
Romblon[4]	Romblon, Tablas, and Sibuyan Is.	512	99,367	Romblon
Samar[4]	Samar	5,309	546,306	Catbalogan
Sorsogon	SE Luzon	793	247,653	Sorsogon
Sulu[3]	Sulu Archipelago[3]	1,086	247,117	Jolo
Surigao	NE Mindanao	3,079	225,895	Surigao
Tarlac	N cen. Luzon	1,175	264,379	Tarlac
Tayabas	E and S cen. Luzon	4,616	358,553	Lucena
Zambales	W Luzon	1,408	106,945	Iba
Zamboanga	W Mindanao	6,517	355,984	Zamboanga

[1] Area = land area in sq. m. Pop. from 1939 Census.
[2] Includes subprovince of Catanduanes.
[3] Coextensive.
[4] Includes main island and adjacent islands.
[5] Officially, "City of Manila," administratively not in any province.
[6] Includes 5 subprovinces: Apayao, Benguet, Bontoc, Ifugao, Kalinga.
[7] Includes subprovince of Siquijor.

The group comprises the main island of Luzon in the N, Mindanao in the S, Visayan Is. and Mindoro in the center, Palawan and Sulu Archipelago in the SW and other groups; only 462 islands have an area larger than 1

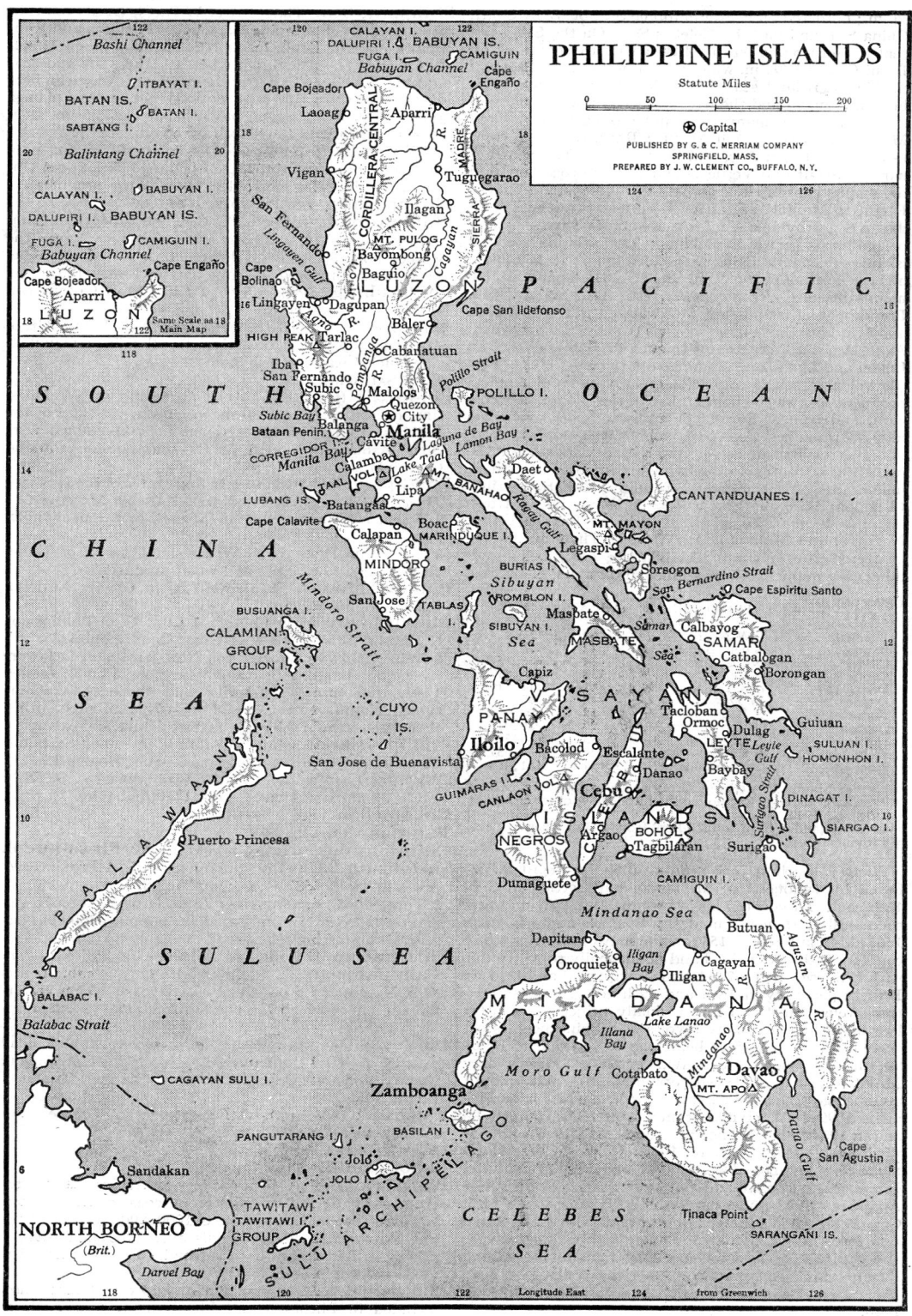

PHILIPPINE ISLANDS

Statute Miles

0 50 100 150 200

⊛ Capital

PUBLISHED BY G. & C. MERRIAM COMPANY
SPRINGFIELD, MASS.
PREPARED BY J. W. CLEMENT CO., BUFFALO, N.Y.

Bashi Channel

ITBAYAT I.
BATAN IS. BATAN I.
SABTANG I.
Balintang Channel

CALAYAN I. BABUYAN I.
DALUPIRI I. BABUYAN IS.
FUGA I. CAMIGUIN I.
Babuyan Channel
Cape Bojeador Cape Engaño
Aparri
LUZON
Same Scale as 18
Main Map

CALAYAN I.
DALUPIRI I. BABUYAN IS.
FUGA I. CAMIGUIN
Babuyan Channel
Cape Bojeador Cape Engaño
Laoag
CORDILLERA CENTRAL
Vigan
Tuguegarao
Ilagan
MT. PULOG
Bayombong
Baguio
Cape Bolinao
Lingayen Dagupan
Cape San Ildefonso
HIGH PEAK Tarlac
Iba Cabanatuan
San Fernando
Subic Malolos POLILLO I.
Quezon City
Subic Bay Manila
Bataan Penin. Balanga
CORREGIDOR Cavite
Manila Bay Calamba
Lake Taal Lamon Bay
LUBANG IS. Lipa Daet
Cape Calavite Batangas CANTANDUANES I.
MT. BANAHAO
Calapan Boac Ragay Gulf
MARINDUQUE I. MT. MAYON
MINDORO Legaspi
BURIAS I. Sorsogon
Sibuyan San Bernardino Strait
San Jose ROMBLON I. Cape Espiritu Santo
TABLAS Masbate
SIBUYAN I. Samar Calbayog
Sibuyan MASBATE SAMAR
Sea Catbalogan
Capiz Borongan
CUYO VISAYAN
IS. Tacloban
PANAY Ormoc Dulag Guiuan
Iloilo LEYTE SULUAN I.
San Jose de Buenavista Bacolod Escalante Leyte HOMONHON I.
Danao Gulf
GUIMARAS I. Baybay
CANLAON VOL. Cebu DINAGAT I.
ISLANDS
NEGROS BOHOL SIARGAO I.
Argao Tagbilaran Surigao
Dumaguete CAMIGUIN I.
Mindanao Sea
Butuan
Dapitan
Oroquieta Iligan Cagayan
Bay Iligan
MINDANAO
Lake Lanao
Illana Davao
Bay Cotabato MT. APO
Moro Gulf Davao
BALABAC I.
Balabac Strait Cape
San Agustin
CAGAYAN SULU I.
Zamboanga
PANGUTARANG I. BASILAN I.
Sandakan Jolo
JOLO I. Tinaca Point
NORTH BORNEO TAWITAWI SARANGANI IS.
(Brit.) TAWITAWI I.
GROUP
Darvel Bay

PACIFIC OCEAN

SOUTH

CHINA

SEA

SULU SEA

CELEBES

SEA

Puerto Princesa

PALAWAN

Mindoro Strait

Longitude East from Greenwich

sq. m.; bordered on E by Philippine Sea, on W by South China Sea, and on S by Celebes Sea. On the SW adjacent to Borneo and on the N Batan Is. are separated by Bashi Channel (92 m. wide) from Formosa. Has several sizable interisland seas—Sulu, Mindanao, Visayan, Sibuyan, Samar—and the irregular coast lines of many of the islands form many bays and fine harbors, such as Manila Bay (see *Map* at MANILA BAY), Lingayen Gulf, Leyte Gulf, Iligan Bay, and Davao Gulf. The San Bernardino Strait and Verde Island Passage together form the main steamship lane across the Archipelago from the Pacific to Manila and farther S Surigao Strait and Mindanao Sea provide a similar route across S part. Archipelago forms part of W Pacific volcanic chain, hence all islands are mountainous with chief ranges in N Luzon; highest peak Apo 9689 ft. in SE Mindanao; ab. 20 mountains are volcanic peaks, esp. Taal and Mayon. Practically all islands are well watered but only Luzon and Mindanao have large streams (Cagayan, Pampanga, Agno, Agusan, Mindanao); Laguna de Bay and Taal on Luzon and Lanao on Mindanao are the chief lakes. Fertile volcanic soil is source of great variety of tropical products, esp. sugar, hemp (abacá), rice, copra, tobacco, corn, and fruits. Forests of hardwoods are extensive, mineral resources (esp. coal, gold, silver, copper, chromite, petroleum) are as yet largely undeveloped, and the industries of fishing and weaving are important. Native inhabitants are composed of many Christian tribes (Tagalog, Visayan, Bikol, Ilokano, etc.), pagan tribes (Igorot, Ifugao, Tinggian, Bukidnon, Bagobo, etc.), Negritos, and Mohammedan Moros. There are twelve chartered cities, including Manila (see *Table*, below); all others are municipalities, municipal districts, or barrios.

CHARTERED CITY[1]	PROVINCE	AREA[2]	POP.[2]
Bacolod[3]	NW Negros	62	57,474
Baguio	S cen. Benguet	22	24,117
Cavite[3]	NE Cavite	4	38,254
Cebu[3]	E Cebu	128	146,817
Dansalan[3]	cen. Lanao	11	11,319
Davao[3]	W Davao	748	95,546
Iloilo[3]	S Iloilo	13	90,480
Quezon	W Rizal	28	39,013
San Pablo	S Laguna	53	46,311
Tagaytay	S Cavite	25	1,657
Zamboanga[3]	SW Zamboanga	1,124	131,455

[1] City of Manila treated separately as a province (see *Table of Provinces*, above). Baguio incorporated 1909; other cities bet. 1918 and 1940.
[2] Area = land area in sq. m. Pop. from 1939 Census.
[3] Provincial capitals.

History: Earliest inhabitants probably Negritos, followed by Indonesians; Mohammedans settled in S in 15th cent. Discovered by Magellan Mar. 1521 and first successful settlements made by Spanish under Legaspi 1565; Manila founded 1571. In first two centuries many conflicts with Moros in S and occasionally some trouble with Chinese. In 1762–63 Manila captured and held by British; generally in 18th and 19th cents. Spanish control strengthened and Moros finally subjected in latter half of 19th cent.; many revolts of Filipino peoples occurred, the most serious being the Revolution of 1896–99; in Spanish-American War battle of Manila Bay May 1, 1898 and treaty with Spain Dec. 10, 1898 brought archipelago under American control; conflict with Filipinos 1899–1901; civil government established 1901–03 and in 1934 independence promised for 1946. Commonwealth established Nov. 15, 1935. In World War II attacked by Japanese Dec. 8, 1941 and Manila captured Jan. 2, 1942; Bataan and Corregidor taken by Japanese Apr.–May 1942 and islands under Japanese rule until Oct. 1944, when MacArthur returned with great invasion force; naval battles of Philippine Sea, Leyte Gulf, and Surigao Strait, and land campaigns on Leyte and Luzon established practical American control by Apr. 1945. Independent government established July 4, 1946.

Philippine Sea. That part of W Pacific Ocean immediately E of the Philippine Is.; touches Formosa and Ryukyu Is. on NW, Bonin Is. on NE, Mariana Is. on E, and W Caroline Is. on S; roughly bet. 10° and 25°N and 125° and 145°E. Named after great victory of American fleet over Japanese in this area, entirely bet. carrier planes, June 19–20, 1944; second naval battle Oct. 25–26, 1944 more often called "Battle of Leyte Gulf" (*q.v.*).

Phi·lip'po·lis (fĭ·lĭp'ô·lĭs). District (1461 sq. m., pop. 5450) and town (pop. 1693), SW Orange Free State, Union of South Africa; the oldest town in the province.

Philippopolis. See PLOVDIV.

Phil'ipps·burg (fĭl'ĭps·bûrg; *Ger.* fē'lĭps·bŏŏrĸ). Commune, Baden-Württemberg state, Germany, near the Rhine; pop. 3050; in 17th and 18th cents. often besieged and plundered; became part of Baden 1803.

Phil'ips·burg (fĭl'ĭps·bûrg). **1** City, ⊗ of Granite co., W Montana; pop. 1107.

2 Borough, Centre co., cen. Pennsylvania, 28 m. NNE of Altoona; pop. 3872; bituminous coal mines; manufactures nickel ware, gunsights.

3 See SAINT MARTIN.

Phi·lis'ti·a (fĭ·lĭs'tĭ·à). Ancient country in SW Palestine, on the coast, ab. 50 m. in length; the land of the Philistines. Its five chief towns (city-kingdoms) were Gaza, Ashkelon, Ashdod, on the coast, and Ekron and Gath inland.

Phil'lips (fĭl'ĭps). Counties in four states of the U.S. See *Tables* at ARKANSAS, COLORADO, KANSAS, MONTANA.

2 Town, Hutchinson co., NW Texas, in the panhandle; pop. 3605.

3 City, ⊗ of Price co., N Wisconsin, 47 m. W of Rhinelander; pop. 1524; fiber and wood products.

Phillips, Mount. Peak 9480 ft. in Glacier National Park, NW Montana.

Phil'lips·burg (fĭl'ĭps·bûrg). **1** City, ⊗ of Phillips co., N Kansas, 102 m. NNW of Great Bend; pop. 3233.

2 Industrial town, Warren co., New Jersey, on Delaware river opp. Easton, Pennsylvania; pop. 18,502; settled 1749; iron mines; foundries and furnaces, machine shops; manufactures sheet iron, cast-iron pipe, drills, chemicals, handbags, bobbins, soft drinks and extracts.

Phillips Island. Island in Atlantic Ocean off SE South Carolina coast, in Beaufort co., S of St. Helena I.

Phil'mont (fĭl'mŏnt). Village, Columbia co., SE New York, 28 m. S of Albany; pop. 1750; dairying.

Philomelion. See AĸSEHIR.

Phintias. See LICATA.

Phit·sa·nu·lok (p'hĭt·sä·nŏŏ·lōk); *also* **Pit·sa·nu·lok** *and* **Bis·nu·lok** (p'hĭt·sä·nŏŏ·lōk—*sic*). **1** Province, W cen. Thailand; 3687 sq. m.; pop. 165,873.

2 Town, its ✱, on Nan river 75 m. N of Nakhon Sawan and on railroad N from Bangkok; pop. ab. 250,000; has several interesting temples.

Phle·grae'an Fields *or* **Plain** (flē·grē'ăn); *Ital.* **Cam'pi Fle·gre'i** (käm'pē flā·grâ'ē). Volcanic region W of Naples and E of Cumae, S Italy; has 13 low craters most recent of which was created 1538; many hot springs and fumaroles.

Phli'us (flī'ŭs). In ancient times chief town of a small district of NE Peloponnesus, Greece, SSW of Sicyon; usually allied with Sparta; home of the poet Timon of Phlius.

Phlo'ri·na (flō'rē·nä). **1** Department of Greece. See *Florina*, in *Table* at GREECE.

2 See FLORINA city.

Phnom Penh. See PNOMPENH.

Pho·cae'a (fô·sē'à). Ancient city on Aegean Sea, northernmost of the Ionian cities on W coast of Asia Minor; an important maritime state c. 1000–600 B.C., one of the first to engage in voyages of discovery; founded Massilia in W Mediterranean; declined under Persian rule. The modern town is Foça (*q.v.*).

Pho'cis (fō'sĭs). Ancient territory in cen. Greece, now included in Phthiotis and Phocis dept. (see *Table* at

GREECE); bounded on N by Eastern Locris, on E by Boeotia, on S by Gulf of Corinth, and on W by Western Locris and Doris. In S cen. part is Mt. Parnassus group and across N half flows Cephisus river. Chief towns Elatea, Delphi, Daulis. Early history obscure but at first controlled oracle at Delphi; after c. 590 B.C. oracle was supervised by Amphictyonic Council; in Grecian wars was changeable; fought against Greeks at Plataea and was usually allied with Sparta; later opposed Thebes, Boeotia, and Thessaly and influence declined; under power of Macedonia and Aetolian League.

Phoe′bus (fē′bŭs). Former town, SE Virginia, in former Elizabeth City co., on Hampton Roads 8 m. E of Newport News; since 1952 part of city of Hampton.

Phoe·ni′ce (fĕ·nī′sĕ). Town of ancient Chaonia, NW Epirus, NW Greece, near the coast.

Phoe·ni′ci·a (fĕ·nĭsh′ĭ·à; -nĭsh′à); *also* **Phe·ni′ci·a** or **Phe·ni′ce** (fĕ·nī′sĕ). Ancient maritime country in W Syria, forming a narrow strip with the Lebanon Mts. as an indefinite E boundary and stretching at its greatest extent ab. 160 m. from Dor (Tantura) just S of Mt. Carmel to Aradus I. (Arwad) at the N. It consisted from early times, c. 1600 B.C., of a group of city-states, as Acre, Tyre, Sidon, etc., which were especially flourishing c. 1200–1000 B.C. Phoenicians were of Semitic race and a branch of the Canaanites; they became the leading traders of ancient world, and founded colonies on N African coast, including Carthage, and in W Mediterranean; introduced alphabet to Europe; under hegemony of Tyre (*q.v.*) 1000–774 B.C.; conquered by Assyrians Chaldeans, Persians, and by Alexander the Great; under Persians federation of three cities formed (see TRIPOLI); ruled by Ptolemies of Egypt 286–197 B.C. and by Seleucid kingdom of Syria 197–82 B.C.; included in Roman province of Syria (*q.v.*).

Phoe′nix (fē′nĭks). **1** City, ✳ of Arizona and ⊗ of Maricopa co., on Salt river in SW cen. part of the state; pop. 439,170; largest city in the state; distributing center for irrigated area producing long-staple cotton, alfalfa, melons, citrus fruits, lettuce, olives, grapes; winter and health resort; machine shops, dairies, cotton gins, breweries, flour mills. U.S. Indian School (1891). Settled 1870; became ⊗ 1871; incorp. as city 1881; became territorial capital 1889 and state capital on Arizona's admission to the Union 1912.
2 Village, Cook co., NE Illinois, 20 m. S of Chicago; pop. 4,203.
3 Village, Oswego co., cen. New York, 14 m. NNW of Syracuse; pop. 2408; dairy products, fruit, tobacco.
4 *or* **Phe′nice** (fē′nĭs). Ancient seaport in Crete, mentioned in *Acts* xxvii. 12; probably modern Loutro (Lutro) on the S coast, ab. long. 24°E.
5 One of the Phoenix Is. in cen. Pacific Ocean, SE of Enderbury I., 3°40′S lat. and 170°40′W long., ab. 3 sq. m.; most fertile of the group, with large coconut groves.

Phoenix Islands. Group of eight small British coral atolls in cen. Pacific Ocean, ESE of Gilbert Is.; lat. 4°S and long. 172°W; 19 sq. m.; pop. ab. 850. Forms part of Gilbert and Ellice Islands colony. Group comprises Canton, Phoenix, Enderbury, Birnie, Sydney, Hull, Gardner, and McKean. Of little commercial value, except for guano deposits, before 1930; after that date, with establishment of transoceanic air routes, suddenly became of great importance because on direct line from Honolulu to New Caledonia and Fiji Is. Canton and Enderbury both American and British 1936–39; dispute settled amicably 1939 and the two islands placed under joint control for 50 years.

Phoe′nix·ville (fē′nĭks·vĭl). Borough, Chester co., SE Pennsylvania, on Schuylkill river 24 m. NW of Philadelphia; pop. 13,797; settled in 1720 by German refugees; manufactures underwear and hosiery, emery wheels, fiber rugs; ironworks.

Phour′noi (fōōr′nyĕ). Small island, N part of Southern Sporades, in Aegean Sea just SW of Samos.

Phrae *or* **Prae** (p′hrä). **1** Province, N Thailand; 2298 sq. m.; pop. 181,732.
2 Town, its ✳, on Yom river 90 m. N of Phitsanulok.

Phra Na·khon (p′hrä nä·k′hôn). Province, S Thailand See BANGKOK.

Phryg′i·a (frĭj′ĭ·à). Ancient country, W cen. Asia Minor. Settled as early as 13th cent. B.C. by race of uncertain origin which occupied extensive lands along Black Sea and Aegean coasts, esp. in Sangarius valley; gradually driven W and S Phrygians made their home in the plateau region bounded on N by Bithynia, on E by Galatia and Lycaonia, on S by Pisidia and Lycia, and on W by Caria, Lydia, and Mysia. Conquered by Lydia 7th cent. B.C.; its art and culture reached its height c. 600 B.C. and had considerable influence on Greece. Overcome by Persia 546 B.C.; divided c. 400 B.C. into **Greater Phrygia**, the inland region, and **Phrygia Mi′nor** (mī′nẽr) along Hellespontus. Passed into power of Alexander who seized its capital Gordium 333 B.C. and soon after 301 became a part of the new kingdom founded by Seleucus; contended for by Pergamum and Syria; fell into Roman hands 133 B.C. and its W part became part of province of Asia; c. 300 A.D. again divided by Diocletian and under Byzantine Empire name disappeared from record.

Phthi′a (thī′à). Ancient name of the district in S Thessaly, NE Greece, later known as Phthiotis, now a part of Phthiotis and Phocis dept. In Homer Phthia was the residence of Achilles.

Phthi·o′tis and Pho′cis (thĭ·ō′tĭs, fō′sĭs). Department of Greece. See *Table* at GREECE.

Phu·ket (p′hoo·kĕt); *also* **Pu·ket** (p′hoo-) *or* **Bhu·ket** (p′hoo-). **1** *formerly* **Sa·lang** (sä·läng) *or* **Junk′sey·lon′** (jŭngk′sĕ·lŏn′). Island, SW Thailand, off W coast of Malay Penin. in Andaman Sea; 294 sq. m.; includes Phuket prov., 206 sq. m., pop. 41,849; large tin mines.
2 Seaport town, ✳ of Phuket prov., at S end of island; pop. ab. 30,000; one of the chief Thailand ports on Indian Ocean.

Phul′kian States (p′hool′kyän). Patiala, Nabha, and Jind, former states of E and SE Punjab, NW Indian Union; 8188 sq. m.; pop. 2,237,770; so called from the Sikh family that established their independence in the 18th cent.

Phu·quoc (p′hoo·kwŏok). Island in SE part of Gulf of Siam, off S shore of Cambodia S of Kampot.

Phy′le (fī′lē; -lĕ). Ruins of an ancient fortress 11 m. NNW of Athens, Attica and Boeotia dept., Greece. Base used by Thrasybulus and his followers in their operations against the Thirty Tyrants 404–403 B.C.

Phyong′an′, North (pyông′än′). Former name of NORTH HEIAN prov., Korea.

Phyongan, South. Former name of SOUTH HEIAN prov., Korea.

Pia·cen′za (pyä·chĕn′tsä). **1** Province of Italy. See *Table* at ITALY.
2 *anc.* **Pla·cen′tia** (plà·sĕn′shà; -shĭ·à). Commune, its ✳, Emilia, N Italy, on Po river 40 m. SE of Milan; pop. 64,210; buildings include ancient church of San Sisto (rebuilt 1499–1511) for which Raphael painted the Sistine Madonna, early 12th-cent. cathedral, 13th-cent. town hall, and 16th-cent. Farnese palace; manufactures silks, cottons, woolens, pottery, machinery, wine, cheese; marble quarries nearby.
History: Founded by Romans 219 B.C.; destroyed by Gauls 200 B.C. and later rebuilt; made W terminus of ancient Roman Aemilian Way; became part of Lombard League 12th cent.; under Visconti family 1337, Sforza family, and popes 1512; given together with Parma to Farnese family by Pope Paul III 1545; part of duchy of Parma and Piacenza 1545–1860; became part of kingdom of Italy 1860.

Piali. See TEGEA.

Pia·no′sa (pyä·nō′sä). **1** *anc.* **Pla·na′si·a** (plà·nā′zhĭ·à; -zhà). Small Italian island in the Mediterranean Sea SW

of the island of Elba; 4 sq. m.; pop. (1931) ab. 1000; highest point 95 ft.; attached to Livorno prov., Italy.
2 Italian islet in cen. Adriatic Sea N of Mount Gargano and 14 m. NE of Tremiti Is.

Pia'pa·yung'an, Mount (pyä'pä·yōōng'än). Mountain 8725 ft., SE Lanao prov., Mindanao, Phil. Is., on Cotabato boundary E of Mt. Ragang.

Piatigorsk. Var. of PYATIGORSK.

Pia'tra–Neamţ (pyä'trä·nyämts'). City, NE Romania, in a densely forested part of Moldavia region, in foothills of the Carpathians and on Bistriţa river, W of Roman; pop. 30,211; manufactures textiles; church founded 1497 by Stephen the Great.

Pi'att (pi'ăt). County in Illinois. See *Table* at ILLINOIS.

Pi·au·í' (pyou·ē'); *formerly spelled* **Pi·au·hy'** (pyou·ē'). State of Brazil. See *Table* at BRAZIL.

Piauí, Serra do. See SERRA DO PIAUÍ.

Pia've (pyä'vå). River 137 m. long in NE Italy; rises in the Carnic Alps S of Lienz, flows S and SE into the Adriatic Sea 22 m. ENE of Venice; scene of battles 1917–18, when it became the line of defense of the Italians after their retreat from Caporetto; the Austrians made several unsuccessful attempts to cross the river.

Piaz'za Ar'me·ri'na (pyät'tsä är'må·rē'nä); *Sicilian* **Chiaz'za** (kyät'tsä). Commune, Enna prov., cen. Sicily, 13 m. SSE of Enna; pop. 24,527; cathedral.

Pi'bor (pē'bôr). River ab. 200 m. long in SE Sudan; flows N and unites with Baro river on border of W Ethiopia to form Sobat river.

Pic (pēk). French term meaning "peak, mountain"; for some entries beginning with *Pic*, see the distinguishing element; as, **Pic de Néthou**, see NÉTHOU.

Pi·ca'ra Point (pǐ·kär'å). Tip of long narrow peninsula on N coast of St. Thomas I., Virgin Is. of the United States, West Indies, which forms E side of Magens Bay.

Pic'ar·dy (pǐk'ēr·dǐ); *Fr.* **Pi'car'die'** (pē'kàr'dē'). Historical region of N France; bounded anciently on N by Strait of Dover, Artois, and Flanders, E by Champagne, S by Île-de-France, SW by Normandy, W by English Channel; ✻ Amiens (to 1790); watered by Somme river.
History: Name first recorded in 13th cent.; military government organized c. 1350 by Valois family; joined to Burgundy 1435; province of France 1477 until Revolution; region scene of heavy fighting in World War I (battle of Picardy Mar. 21, 1918 ff.).

Pic'a·yune' (pǐk'å·yōōn'; pǐk'ǐ·yōōn'). City, Pearl River co., S Mississippi, 35 m. WNW of Gulfport; pop. 7834; tung oil.

Pi·ce'num (pī·sē'nŭm). Ancient Roman province in E Italy, on the Adriatic Sea; chief towns Ancona and Asculum Picenum (Ascoli Piceno), the capital.

Pich'er (pǐch'ēr). City, Ottawa co., NE corner of Oklahoma, on Kansas border 12 m. W of Missouri border; pop. 2553; lead and zinc mines; smelters, foundries.

Pi'chi·lin'que (pē'chē·lēng'kå). United States coaling station on E side of S extremity of Lower California, Mexico; on La Paz Bay adjoining La Paz.

Pi·chin'cha (pē·chēn'chä). **1** Volcano 15,713 ft. in Ecuador, NW of the city of Quito; scene of battle May 24, 1822. See ECUADOR.
2 Province of Ecuador. See *Table* at ECUADOR.

Pichit. See PHICHIT.

Pi'chon' (pē'shôn'). Town, N cen. Tunisia, 23 m. W of Kairouan; captured by Allies Apr. 1943.

Pi·chú'–Pi·chú' (pē·chōō'pē·chōō'). Peak ab. 18,600 ft. in Andes Mts. in Arequipa dept., S Peru, N of city of Arequipa.

Pick'a·way (pǐk'å·wā). County of Ohio. See *Table* at OHIO.

Pick'ens (pǐk'ěnz). **1** Counties in three states of the U.S. See *Tables* at ALABAMA, GEORGIA, SOUTH CAROLINA.
2 Town, ⊗ of Pickens co., NW South Carolina, 19 m. W of Greenville; pop. 2198; pottery, lumber, cotton goods.

Pick'ett (pǐk'ět; -ǐt). County in Tennessee. See *Table* at TENNESSEE.

Pick'wick Landing Dam (pǐk'wǐk). Dam in Tennessee river, Hardin co., SW Tennessee, at village of Pickwick Dam, Tennessee, forming **Pickwick Landing Reservoir** extending along the Alabama-Mississippi boundary and into Lauderdale co., NW Alabama. See *Table* at TENNESSEE VALLEY AUTHORITY.

Pi'co. **1** (*Span.* pē'kô; *Port.* -kōō) Spanish and Portuguese name for "mountain" or "peak"; for names beginning with *Pico*, see the distinguishing element.
2 (pē'kô) See GENERAL PICO, Argentina.
3 (pē'kōō) Island, cen. Azores, in the district of Horta; 175 sq. m.; pop. ab. 22,000; chief town Lajes do Pico; highest point 7460 ft. (see Pico ALTO).

Pi'co Ri·ve'ra (pē'kô rǐ·věr'å). City, Los Angeles co. SW California, SE of Los Angeles; pop. 49,150.

Pic'qui'gny' (pē'kē'nyē'). Commune, Somme dept., N France, 8 m. NW of Amiens; pop. 1079; treaty signed here Aug. 19, 1475 bet. Edward IV of England and Louis XI of France.

Pic'ton (pǐk'tŭn). **1** Town, ⊗ of Prince Edward co., SE Ontario, Canada, on inlet of Lake Ontario 16 m. SE of Belleville; pop. 4287; large canneries.
2 Borough and port on inlet of Cook Strait, Marlborough provincial dist., NE South I., New Zealand; pop. 1285.

Picton Channel. Strait W of Wellington I., off SW coast of Chile, connecting Trinidad Gulf with the Pacific.

Pic'tou (pǐk'tōō). **1** County, Nova Scotia, Canada. See *Table* at NOVA SCOTIA.
2 Town, its ⊗, N Nova Scotia, Canada, on **Pictou Harbor**, an inlet of Northumberland Strait; pop. 4259; outlet for Pictou coal mines and quarries of building stone; has excellent harbor with steamship connections with Prince Edward I. and Halifax, except when icebound during four winter months; center of lobster-fishing industry. Pictou Academy (founded 1818). Founded on site of ancient Indian village in 1763 by colonists from Pennsylvania and Maryland; increased in 1773 by first Scotch immigrants to Nova Scotia who landed here. Present name adopted in 1790.

Pictured Rocks. Cliffs eroded into curious forms on the S shore of Lake Superior, in Alger co., N Michigan penin.

Pi'du·ru'ta·la'ga·la (pǐd'ŭ·rōō'tå·lä'gå·là). Mountain 8294 ft., highest peak in Ceylon, in S Central Province.

Piedad, La. See LA PIEDAD.

Pie·da'de (pyě·thä'thě). Town on N shore of Guanabara Bay, Rio de Janeiro state, E Brazil, ab. 17 m. NNE of Rio de Janeiro.

Pie'de·cues'ta (pyä'thä·kwäs'tä). Town, Santander dept., N cen. Colombia, S of Bucaramanga; pop. 6974.

Pied'mont (pēd'mŏnt). **1** City, Calhoun co., NE Alabama, 20 m. E of Gadsden; pop. 4794; agricultural trading center; cotton and lumber mills; mineral springs.
2 Residential city, Alameda co., W California, suburb of Oakland 5 m. E of San Francisco Bay; pop. 11,117.
3 Village, Anderson and Greenville cos., NW South Carolina, on Saluda river ab. 11 m. SSW of Greenville; pop. 2108; textile manufactures.
4 City, Mineral co., NE West Virginia, on North Branch Potomac river 5 m. NW of Keyser; pop. 2307; produces coal, clay, brick, timber; lumber, paper, and pulp mills.
5 *Ital.* **Pie·mon'te** (pyä·môn'tä). Compartimento of NW Italy (for provincial divisions, area, and pop., see *Table* at ITALY); borders on France and Switzerland; almost entirely surrounded by mountains; slopes to fertile plain producing grains, olives, wine, chestnuts; mineral deposits. Anciently part of Transpadane Gaul; held from 11th cent. by house of Savoy (*q.v.*) one of whose rulers took title of Prince of Piedmont; several areas of it, esp. those around Mont Cenis and the Briga-Tenda region, ceded to France by treaty Feb. 10, 1947.

Piedmont Region *or* **Plateau.** An upland belt, that part of the Atlantic plain of E United States lying E of the Blue Ridge and Appalachian Mts., extending from the Hudson river to cen. Alabama.

Piedras, Las. See LAS PIEDRAS.

Pi·e′dras Blan′cas Point (pē·ä′drås blăng′kås). Point on NW coast of San Luis Obispo co., SW California.

Pie′dras Ne′gras (pyä′thräz nā′gräs). **1** Archaeological site on right bank of the Usumacinta river, NW Guatemala; Maya sculptural art.
2 *formerly* **Ciu·dad′ Por·fi′rio Dí′az** (syōō·thäth′ pôr·fē′ryô the′äs). Town, Coahuila state, NE Mexico; pop. 15,663; on the Rio Grande opp. Eagle Pass, Texas, with which it is connected by an international bridge; N terminus of Mexican International R.R.; port of entry; region has coal mines, cattle raising.

Pie′dras Point (pyä′thräs). Cape on E cen. coast of Argentina, SE of Buenos Aires, extending into the Río de la Plata opp. Brava Point in Uruguay. See BRAVA POINT.

Pie·gan′, Mount (pē·găn′). Peak 9230 ft. in Glacier National Park, NW Montana.

Piek′sä·mä′ki (pyěk′sä·mä′kǐ). Town, S Finland, in Mikkeli dept.; ab. 45 m. N of Mikkeli; pop. 10,567.

Pie′lis·jär′vi (pyě′lǐs·yär′vǐ). **1** Lake, SE Finland, in Kuopio dept., 56 m. long, 422 sq. m.
2 Town, SE Finland, in Kuopio dept., on E shore of the lake; pop. 17,286.

Pie′man (pī′măn). River ab. 70 m. long, NW Tasmania, Australia; rises on W edge of central highlands and flows W to Indian Ocean.

Piemonte. See PIEDMONT, Italy.

Pien–ching. See KAIFENG.

Pierce (pērs). **1** Name of counties in five states of the U.S. See *Tables* at GEORGIA, NEBRASKA, NORTH DAKOTA, WASHINGTON, WISCONSIN.
2 City, ⊗ of Pierce co., NE Nebraska; pop. 1216.

Pi·e′ri·a (pī·ē′rǐ·à). A region of ancient Macedonia, W of the Gulf of Salonika; seat of worship of the Muses; location of the **Pi·e′ri·an Spring** (-ăn), a fountain sacred to the Muses.

Pier′mont (pēr′mŏnt). Residential village, Rockland co., SE New York, on Hudson river 22 m. N of New York; pop. 1906.

Pierre (pēr). City, ✳ of South Dakota and ⊗ of Hughes co., cen. South Dakota, on Missouri river; pop. 10,088; ships livestock; manufactures saddles. Settled 1880; became city 1883, and state capital 1889.

Pierre′fitte′–sur–Seine (pyěr′fēt′sür·sân′). Commune, Seine dept., N France, N suburb of Paris; pop. (1931) 11,645; manufactures electrical equipment.

Pierre′fonds′ (pyěr′fôN′). Town, E Oise dept., N France, SE of Compiègne; mineral springs; château, built 1390–1405, destroyed by Louis XIII, restored by Viollet-le-Duc 1858 ff.

Pi′e·rus (pī′ē·rŭs). Mountain in ancient Pieria, Macedonia, Greece, N of Mt. Olympus.

Pi′es′ka (pē′ěs′kå). Lake in NW Sweden, near Norwegian border; source of the Pite river.

Pieš′t′a·ny (pyěsh′tyà·nǐ); *Hung.* **Pös′tyén** (püsh′-tyän); *Ger.* **Pis′tyan** (pĭs′tyän). Town, SW Slovakia prov., E cen. Czechoslovakia, on the Váh ab. 45 m. NE of Bratislava; pop. (1930) 12,046.

Pie′tar·saa′ri (pyě′tår·sä′rǐ); *Swed.* **Ja′kob·stad′** (yä′-kôp·stä[d]′). Seaport, Vaasa dept., W Finland, on the Baltic Sea; pop. (1939 est.) 6700; trade center; exports lumber; birthplace of the national poet Johan Ludvig Runeberg.

Pietas Julia. See PULJ.

Pie′ter·mar′itz·burg (pē′tēr·mär′ĭts·bûrg); *also* **Mar′-itz·burg.** Town, ✳ of Natal, E Union of South Africa, in S part of Natal 40 m. WNW of Durban (70 m. by rail); pop. with suburbs 9539; grows wattle trees, their bark furnishing mimosa extract for tanning; tanneries, boot and shoe factories, furniture plants. Seat of Natal University College, now a constituent college of the Univ. of South Africa. Founded 1839 and named after two Boer leaders, Pieter Retief and Gert Maritz; incorporated 1854.

Pie′ters·burg (pē′tērz·bûrg). Town, N cen. Transvaal, NE Union of South Africa, 150 m. NNE of Pretoria; pop. 9131; in rich agricultural region; center of a district in which gold, silver, asbestos, apatite, iron, and corundum are found. For a time headquarters of Dutch forces during Boer War.

Pietola. See VIRGILIO.

Pie′tra·per′zia (pyä′trä·pěr′tsyä). Commune, Enna prov., cen. Sicily, 13 m. SW of Enna; pop. 12,753.

Pie′tra·san′ta (pyä′trä·sän′tä). Commune, Lucca prov., Tuscany, cen. Italy, 16 m. NW of Lucca; pop. 21,382; 14th-cent. cathedral; marble works.

Piet Re·tief′ (pēt′ rě·tēf′). Town, SE Transvaal, NE Republic of South Africa, near Swaziland border; pop. 3069.

Pi′geon (pĭj′ŭn). **1** River 40 m. long, extreme NE Minnesota; flows into N Lake Superior, forms section of United States-Canada boundary.
2 River 75 m. long, E Tennessee; rises in W North Carolina, flows NW across Tennessee border and into French Broad river in W Cocke co.

Pigeon Cays. Group of small islands in Caribbean Sea off E coast of Honduras.

Pigeon Cove. Village, Essex co., NE Massachusetts, 33 m. NNE of Boston and ab. 2 m. N of Rockport; pop. 1064; summer resort.

Pigeon Peak. Mountain 13,968 ft. in La Plata co., SW Colorado.

Pig′gott (pĭg′ŭt). City, a ⊗ of Clay co., NE corner of Arkansas, 49 m. NE of Jonesboro; pop. 2776.

Pignerol. See PINEROLO.

Pigs, Bay of. See COCHINOS BAY.

Pihkva. See PSKOV.

Pike (pīk). Name of counties in ten states of the U.S. See *Tables* at ALABAMA, ARKANSAS, GEORGIA, ILLINOIS, INDIANA, KENTUCKY, MISSISSIPPI, MISSOURI, OHIO, PENNSYLVANIA.

Pike o′ Stickle. See LANGDALE PIKES.

Pikes Peak (pīks). Mountain 14,110 ft. in El Paso co., E cen. Colorado, near Colorado Springs; tourist resort, noted for magnificent view from its summit; has mountain railroad and automobile highway to summit. Discovered 1806 by Zebulon M. Pike.

Pikes′ville (pīks′vǐl). Urban community (unincorporated), Baltimore co., cen. Maryland, NW of Baltimore; pop. 18,737.

Pike′ville (pīk′vǐl; *Sou. also* -v′l). **1** City, ⊗ of Pike co., E Kentucky, 42 m. ENE of Hazard; pop. 4754; lumbering and coal-mining section.
2 Town, ⊗ of Bledsoe co., SE cen. Tennessee; pop. 951; mountain resort.

Pi′la (pē′lä); *Ger.* **Schnei′de·mühl** (shnī′dĕ·mül). City, formerly ✳ of Schneidemühl govt. dist., Brandenburg prov., Prussia, Germany, now in NW Poland N of Poznań; pop. 37,518; railroad junction; manufactures machinery, tile, cement, and starch; trades in lumber; cattle and horse markets. In World War II taken by Russians Feb. 14, 1945; assigned to Poland by Potsdam Conference 1945.

Pi·lar′ (pě·lär′). **1** Town, Buenos Aires prov., E Argentina, ab. 28 m. NW of Buenos Aires.
2 *or* **Vil′la del Pi·lar′** (bē′yä thěl pě·lär′). Town and river port, ✳ of Neembucú dept., SW Paraguay, on Paraguay river opp. the mouth of the Bermejo, 120 m. SW of Asunción; pop. ab. 9600; founded 1778 by Pedro Melo de Portugal; seat of a national college.
3 Municipality, NW Sorsogon prov., Luzon, Phil. Is., on inlet W of Sorsogon Bay 22 m. W of Sorsogon; pop. 20,654.
4 Municipality, NE Capiz prov., Panay, Phil. Is., on S shore of Pilar Bay 18 m. ESE of Capiz; pop. 22,301.
5 See PONSON.

Pi·lar′ (pě·lär′), *or* **Pil′lar** (pĭl′ēr), **Cape.** Cape on Desolación I. at W entrance into Strait of Magellan, off S coast of South America.

Pilar Bay. Inlet of SE Sibuyan Sea in NE Capiz prov., Panay, Phil. Is.

Pi'lat' (pē'lä'). Peak 4704 ft. in the Cévennes range, Loire dept., SE cen. France.

Pi·la'tus (pē·lä'tŏŏs). Peak 6995 ft., Unterwalden canton, cen. Switzerland, near border of Lucerne canton; railway.

Pil'co·ma'yo (pēl'kô·mä'yô). River ab. 1000 m. long in S cen. South America; rises in E Andes Mts., W cen. Bolivia, flows SE and forms boundary bet. Argentina and the Chaco region of Paraguay; empties into Paraguay river at Asunción. See CONFUSO river.

Pi'li (pē'lē). **1** Peak 19,849 ft. in E Antofagasta prov., N Chile.

2 Municipality, cen. Camarines Sur prov., Luzon, Phil. Is., on railroad 8 m. SE of Naga; pop. 18,225.

Pi'li·bhit' (pē'lē·bēt'). Town, Rohilkhand division, N Uttar Pradesh, N Indian Union, on a tributary of the Kosi river ab. 50 m. N of Shahjahanpur; pop. 36,892; trades with Nepal.

Pi·li'ca (pē·lē'tsä) or **Pi·li'tsa** (*Russ.* pyĭ·lyē'tsȧ). River ab. 200 m. long in S cen. Poland; rises in SW Poland, flows N and NE into Vistula river above Warsaw.

Pil'lar, Cape (pĭl'ēr). **1** Southeast point of Tasmania, Australia, at S end of Tasman Penin., extending into Tasman Sea.

2 See Cape PILAR.

Pillar Mountain. Peak 2927 ft. in Cumberland co., NW England, in the Lake District.

Pil'la·ro (pē'yä·rô). Town, Tungurahua prov., cen. Ecuador, N of Riobamba; pop. (1944 est.) 8465.

Pil'lars of Her'cu·les (pĭl'ērz, hûr'kŭ·lēz). The two promontories at E end of Strait of Gibraltar: Rock of Gibraltar (anc. Calpe) in Europe, and Jebel Musa (anc. Abila or Abyla) at Ceuta in Africa. Of various explanations for origin of term, most probable is fable that before existence of strait they formed one mountain range which Hercules wrenched apart to join the seas, or that in his travels to find the oxen of Geryon he set them there as a memorial.

Pillau. See BALTIISK.

Pill'nitz (pĭl'nĭts). Royal castle on the Elbe 5 m. SE of Dresden, Saxony, Germany; scene of conference Aug. 1791 at which Emperor Leopold II and Frederick William II, king of Prussia, agreed to unite against France.

Pills'bur'y Sound (pĭlz'bĕr'ĭ; -bēr·ĭ). Body of water off N coast of E end of St. Thomas I., Virgin Is. of the United States, West Indies.

Pi·lo'ña (pē·lō'nyä). Commune, Oviedo prov., NW Spain, 24 m. E of Oviedo; pop. 16,948; mineral baths; marble quarries; mining; stock raising.

Pi'lot Knob (pī'lŭt). **1** Peak 13,750 ft. in San Juan and San Miguel cos., SW Colorado.

2 Peak 7128 ft. in cen. Idaho co., N cen. Idaho.

3 Hill in Iron co., SE Missouri; contains iron ore.

Pilot Peak. 1 Mountain 7508 ft. on S boundary of Plumas co., NE California, in Sierra Nevada Mts.

2 Mountain 8560 ft. in cen. Boise co., W cen. Idaho.

3 Mountain 8061 ft. in N Valley co., W cen. Idaho.

4 Mountain 9207 ft. in S Mineral co., SW Nevada; highest in Excelsior Mts.

5 Mountain 11,740 ft. in NW Park co., in the Absaroka Mts., NW Wyoming.

Pilsen. See PLZEŇ.

Pilt'down' or **Pilt Down** (pĭlt'doun'). Locality in East Sussex, S England, ab. 7 m. N of Lewes; site of discovery 1911-15 of skull and jawbone fragments originally held to derive from a distinctive early Pleistocene hominoid but later shown to be the product of a deliberate hoax.

Pi'ma (pē'mȧ). **1** County in Arizona. See *Table* at ARIZONA.

2 Town, Graham co., SE Arizona, on Gila river; pop. 806.

Pi'men·tel' (pē'mȧn·tĕl'). Seaport, Lambayeque dept.,

NW Peru, 8 m. from Chiclayo; pop. ab. 2000; chief import and export center for Lambayeque dept.

Pim'li·co (pĭm'lĭ·kō). Southwest district of London, England, bet. Westminster and Chelsea; includes Belgravia. In Elizabethan times, a resort famous for its ale.

Pi'ña (pē'nyä). River in Panama and the Canal Zone; flows NW into the Caribbean Sea forming N section of W boundary bet. Panama and the Canal Zone.

Pi·ná'cu·lo (pē·nä'kŏŏ·lô). Peak 7090 ft. in SW Santa Cruz territory, S Argentina, near Chile border.

Pi·nal' (pĭ·nȧl'). County of Arizona. See *Table* at ARIZONA.

Pin'a·le'no Mountains (pĭn'ȧ·lā'nō). Mountain range, including Graham Peak 10,750 ft., in Graham co., SE Arizona.

Pi·nal' Peak (pĭ·nȧl'). Mountain 7850 ft. in SW Gila co., SE cen. Arizona.

Pi'na·ma·la'yan (pē'nä·mä·lä'yän). Municipality in center of E coast of Mindoro I., Phil. Is., on coastal highway 33 m. SE of Calapan; pop. 16,086.

Pi'na·ma·po'an (pē'nä·mä·pō'än). Village on W shore of Carigara Bay, N Leyte I., Phil. Is.; pop. 941; captured by Americans Nov. 5, 1944.

Pi'na·mung·a'jan (pē'nä·mŏŏng·ä'hän). Municipality on W coast of Cebu I., Phil. Is., in cen. part on Tañon Strait 22 m. WSW of City of Cebu; pop. 22,327.

Pi·nar' del Rí'o (pē·när' thĕl rē'ô). **1** Province, W Cuba. See *Table* at CUBA.

2 Municipality and seaport city, its ✱, in S cen. part; pop. (city) 26,241; tobacco.

Pi'ñas (pē'nyäs). Town, El Oro prov., SW Ecuador; pop. (1944 est.) 9710.

Pi'na·tu'bo, Mount (pē'nä·tŏŏ'bô). Mountain on boundary bet. E Zambales and W Pampanga provs., Luzon, Phil. Is.; 5842 ft.

Pin'chot, Mount (pĭn'shō). **1** Peak 13,471 ft. in Sierra Nevada, in E Fresno co., S cen. California.

2 Peak 9375 ft. in Glacier National Park, NW Montana.

Pinciacum. See POISSY.

Pinck'ney·ville (pĭngk'nĭ·vĭl). City, ⊗ of Perry co., SW Illinois, 34 m. SW of Mount Vernon; pop. 3085; in agricultural and coal-mining section.

Pin'da·ré' (pĕn·dä·râ'). River ab. 200 m. long in Maranhão state, NE Brazil; flows NE into Mearim river just before it enters São Marcos Bay.

Pin'dus (pĭn'dŭs). In classic times, a mountain chain in NW Greece, separating Epirus and Thessaly; highest peak ab. 7600 ft.; in modern usage by some extended to include the mountains of SE Albania.

Pine (pīn). **1** County of Minnesota. See *Table* at MINNESOTA.

2 River ab. 125 m. long, E British Columbia, Canada; flows E and N into Peace river near Fort St. John.

Pine, Cape. Cape, SE Newfoundland, W of Cape Race.

Pine' Bluff'. Commercial city, ⊗ of Jefferson co., SE cen. Arkansas, on Arkansas river 43 m. SE of Little Rock; pop. 44,037; wholesale trade center for wide agricultural area; industrial establishments include cotton gins and compresses, cottonseed-oil, lumber, and textile mills, furniture factories, stockyards. Agricultural, Mechanical, and Normal College (1873; coed.; Negro). Settled 1819 as Mount Marie; given present name 1832; incorporated as town 1846, as city 1885; successfully defended against Confederate attack by Colonel Clayton Oct. 25, 1863.

Pine City. Village, ⊗ of Pine co., E Minnesota, 60 m. N of Minneapolis; pop. 1972.

Pine Creek. 1 River ab. 100 m. long, N cen. Pennsylvania; rises in Potter co., N Pennsylvania, flows E and S into West Branch of Susquehanna river in S Lycoming co.

2 Village and station on railroad, N Northern Territory, Australia, 125 m. SSE of Darwin; alluvial gold field.

Pine'dale (pīn'dāl). Town, ⊗ of Sublette co., W Wyoming; pop. 965.

Pine Forest Range. Range in NW Nevada, in Humboldt co.

Pi·ne′ga (pĭ·něg′à; *Russ.* pyĭ·nyĕ′gà). River ab. 400 m. long, Arkhangelsk Region, Soviet Russia, Europe, flowing into the Northern Dvina near its mouth.

Pine Grove. Borough, Schuylkill co., E cen. Pennsylvania, 14 m. WSW of Pottsville; pop. 2267.

Pine Hill. Borough, Camden co., SW New Jersey, 13 m. SSE of Camden; pop. 3939.

Pine′hurst (pīn′hûrst). **1** Winter resort, Moore co., cen. North Carolina, ab. 63 m. SW of Raleigh; pop. 1124; established 1895 by James W. Tufts on the 5000 acres he purchased 1895 from the family of Walter Hines Page; noted esp. for its golf courses and the landscaping of its roads; not an incorporated town.
2 Town, Snohomish co., NW cen. Washington, ab. 5 m. S of Everett; pop. 3989.

Pine Island. Island off W coast of Lee co., SW Florida, S of Charlotte Harbor.

Pine Island Sound. Sound W of Pine I. and E of outer island chain off coast of Lee co., SW Florida.

Pine′land (pīn′lănd). Town, Sabine co., E Texas, ab. 45 m. ESE of Lufkin; pop. 1236; lumber mills.

Pine Lawn. City, St. Louis co., E Missouri, NW suburb of St. Louis; pop. 5943.

Pi·nel′las (pĭ·nĕl′ăs). County in Florida. See *Table* at FLORIDA.

Pinellas Park. City, Pinellas co., W cen. Florida, N of St. Petersburg; pop. 10,848.

Pinellas Peninsula. Peninsula, Pinellas co., W cen. Florida, W of Tampa Bay. St. Petersburg is situated at its S end.

Pine Mountain. **1** Range extending along N section of Kentucky-Virginia boundary.
2 Peak 7700 ft. in Jeff Davis co., W Texas.

Pine Point. **1** Cape on W shore of Dixie co., NW Florida penin., extending into the Gulf of Mexico.
2 Extreme S point, Cumberland co., SW Maine.

Pi·ne·ro′lo (pĕ·nà·rô′lô); *Fr.* **Pi′gne·rol′** (pēn′y′·rôl′). Manufacturing commune, Torino prov., Piedmont, NW Italy, at foot of Alps 22 m. SW of Turin; pop. 21,600; cathedral (begun in 9th cent.), palaces of 15th and 16th cents.; manufactures leather, textiles, paper; trades in agricultural products. Founded around an abbey; important fortress to 1713; belonged to Savoy from 1413, later to kingdom of Sardinia; under French rule 1536–74, 1631–93, and 1801–14.

Pines, Isle of (pīnz). **1** Island in Caribbean Sea. See ISLE OF PINES.
2 French island in the Pacific Ocean. See KUNIE.

Pine View Dam. Dam completed 1937 across Ogden river E of Ogden, Utah; height 103 ft.; impounds water, **Pine View Reservoir,** for irrigation.

Pine′ville (pīn′vĭl; *Sou. also* -v′l). **1** City, ⊗ of Bell co., SE Kentucky; pop. 3181; coal mining.
2 City, Rapides parish, cen. Louisiana, 5 m. NE of Alexandria; pop. 8636; in agricultural section. Louisiana College (1906; coed.; Baptist).
3 Town, ⊗ of McDonald co., SW Missouri; pop. 454.
4 Town, Mecklenburg co., S North Carolina, on South Carolina border 11 m. S of Charlotte; pop. 1514; nearby is birthplace of James Knox Polk, 11th president of U.S.
5 Town, ⊗ of Wyoming co., S West Virginia; pop. 1137.

Ping (pĭng) *or* **Me·ping** (mā·pĭng). River ab. 360 m. long, W Thailand; rises N of Chiang Mai, flows SSE to join with the Nan at Nakhon Sawan to form Chao Phraya.

Ping′e·lap (pĭng′ĕ·lăp). Island group of three small islands halfway bet. Ponape and Kusaie, E Caroline Is., W Pacific; pop. 100.

Pingkiang. See PINKIANG.

Ping′liang′ (pĭng′lĭ·äng′). Town, E Kansu prov., N cen. China, 170 m. E of Lanchow near Shensi border.

Ping′siang′ (pĭng′shĭ·äng′). **1** Town, W Kiangsi prov., SE China, on trib. of Siang river SE of Changsha.
2 Town, SW Kwangsi prov., S China, on Tonkin frontier.

Pin·guen′te (pĕng·gwĕn′tà). Commune, NW Yugoslavia, on Istria Penin. ab. 39 m. NE of Pulj; pop. (1936) 10,222; formerly belonged to Italy.

Pi·nhei′ro (pē·nyā′ē·rōō). City, Pará state, NE Brazil, N suburb of Belém; pop. (1940 est.) 8159.

Pi′ni (pē′nē). See BATOE.

Pink′ham Notch (pĭngk′ăm). Defile E of the Presidential Range, White Mts., N New Hampshire.

Pin′kiang′ (bĭn′jĭ·äng′). **1** Former province (1932–45), E cen. Manchukuo; 24,651 sq. m.; pop. (1940 est.) 4,236,410; ✻ Pinkiang.
2 *or* **Ping′kiang′** (bĭn′jĭ·äng′). City. See HARBIN.

Pink′ie (pĭngk′ĭ). Battlefield near Edinburgh, Scotland; scene of victory of duke of Somerset over the Scots Sept. 10, 1547.

Pinna. See PENNE.

Pin′na·cles National Monument (pĭn′à·k'lz; -ĭ·k'lz). See UNITED STATES, *National Monuments.*

Pi·nole′ (pĭ·nōl′). City, Contra Costa co., W California, N of Oakland; pop. 6064.

Pin·op′o·lis Dam (pĭn·ŏp′ô·lĭs). Dam completed 1941 across Cooper river, cen. Berkeley co., SE South Carolina; height 80 ft.; impounds water, **Lake Moul′trie** (mōl′trĭ) *or* **Pinopolis Reservoir,** for water power.

Pi′nos, Mount (pē′nōs). Peak 8826 ft. in N Ventura co., SW California, in the Coast Ranges (*q.v.*).

Pi′nos–Puen′te (pē′nōs·pwän′tà). Commune, Granada prov., S Spain, 11 m. NW of Granada; pop. 13,186.

Pinsk (pĭnsk; *Russ.* pyēnsk); *Pol.* **Pińsk** (pēn′y′sk). City, S White Russia, U.S.S.R., 103 m. E of Brest on railroad in center of Pinsk Marshes; formerly in Polesie dept., Poland; pop. (1938–39 est.) 36,700; episcopal see; manufactures leather, wooden goods; trades in lumber, fish. Central town of a medieval principality (**Pinsk**) 13th and 14th cents.; in 1569 annexed to Poland, later to Russia 1795 and Poland 1918; in World War II held by Germans 1941–44; retaken by Russians July 14, 1944.

Pinsk Marshes. Vast marshes formerly in Poland, now in W Russia, divided bet. S White Russia and NW Ukraine; drained by the Pripyat river. Now better known as Pripet Marshes (*q.v.*).

Pinsk Region. Subdivision of White Russia, U.S.S.R., in S part; ✻ Pinsk; bounded on S by the Ukraine.

Pin′ta (pēn′tä; *Angl.* pĭn′tà), *or* **Ab′ing·don** (ăb′ĭng·dŭn), **Island.** One of the Galápagos Is. (*q.v.*).

Pintuaria. See TENERIFE.

Pint′wa′ter Range (pĭnt′wô′tēr; -wŏt′ēr). Small range in N Clark co., SE Nevada, extending N into Lincoln co.

Pin′yon Peak (pĭn′yŭn). Mountain 9945 ft. in NW Custer co., cen. Idaho.

Pi·oche′ (pē·ōch′). Village, ⊗ of Lincoln co., E Nevada; pop. (est.) 1500.

Piom·bi′no (pyŏm·bē′nô). Commune, Livorno prov., Tuscany, cen. Italy, on Ligurian Sea 43 m. S of Leghorn; pop. 27,672; early 15th-cent. citadel, 14th-cent. church; iron and steel works. Under Pisan rule in Middle Ages; as a principality, under the Visconti family 1399 ff.; to Spain 1603; bought by Ludovisi family 1634, passing to Buoncompagni family 1700; to French 1801, Tuscany 1815.

Pio′tr·ków (pyô′tēr·kōōf); *Russ.* **Pe·tro·kov′** (pyĭ·trŭ·kôf′; *Angl.* pĕt′rŏ·kôf); *Ger.* **Pe′tri·kau** (pā′trē·kou). Commune, Łódź dept., Poland, 28 m. SSE of Łódź; pop. (1938–39 est.) 52,875; manufactures textiles. Under Polish kings seat of most important court of assizes— hence sometimes called **Piotrków Try′bu·nal′ski** (trĭ′bōō·näl′skē).

Pio′ve di Sac′co (pyô′vă dĕ säk′kô). Commune, Padova prov., Venezia Euganea, NE Italy, 12 m. SE of Padua; pop. 15,272.

Pi′per Peak (pī′pēr). Mountain 9500 ft. in W Esmeralda co., SW Nevada.

Pipe Spring National Monument (pīp). See UNITED STATES, *National Monuments.*

Pipe′stone′ (pīp′stōn′). **1** County in Minnesota. See *Table* at MINNESOTA.
2 City, its ⊗, SW Minnesota, 40 m. SW of Marshall; pop. 5324; just to the N is **Pipestone National Monument:** see UNITED STATES, *National Monuments.*
Piq′ua (pĭk′wä; -wȧ). City, Miami co., W Ohio, 27 m. N of Dayton; pop. 19,219; formerly important canal port; manufactures knitwear, woolen blankets and felts, farm implements, wood products, furniture; grain elevators; meat packing; limestone quarries nearby. Settled 1797; scene of fighting in French and Indian War, and supply base in War of 1812.
Pi′ra·ci·ca′ba (pē′rȧ·sē·kä′vȧ). City, SE cen. São Paulo state, SE Brazil, 42 m. WNW of Campinas; pop. (1940 est.) 32,483; trades in coffee, cotton, and sugar.
Pi·rae′us (pī·rē′ŭs); *Gr.* **Pei′rai·eus′** (pē′râ·âfs′); *also transliterated* **Pei′rai·evs′** (pē′râ·âfs′) *and* **Pei·rae′us** (pī·rē′ŭs). Seaport city, Attica and Boeotia dept., E Central Greece and Euboea, Greece, on the Saronic Gulf 5 m. SW of Athens; pop. 251,328; seaport for Athens; one of leading Greek ports. Planned by Themistocles c. 490 B.C. and built during the time of Pericles, replacing port of Phaleron to the E; connected with Athens by walls; arsenal built here 347–323 B.C., destroyed by Sulla 86 B.C. The hill **Mu·nych′i·a** (mŭ·nĭk′ĭ·ȧ) in its E part was its citadel. Began modern development after Greek War of Independence. In World War II badly damaged by German planes Apr. 1941.
Piragua. Var. of PARAGUA.
Pi·ra·juí′ (pē·rȧ·zhwē′). City, SW São Paulo state, SE Brazil, 175 m. WNW of São Paulo; pop. 5292.
Pi·rá′mi·de (pē·rä′mĕ·thä). Peak 11,090 ft. in S Chile, W of Lake San Martín.
Pi·ra′nhas (pē·rä′nyȧs). River ab. 250 m. long in NE Brazil; flows N through Rio Grande do Norte state into Atlantic Ocean.
Pi·ra′no (pē·rä′nō). Seaport, Free Territory of Trieste, on SW coast of Gulf of Trieste 14 m. SW of Trieste; pop. (1936) 15,117; 14th-cent. cathedral; scene of victory of Venetian fleet over fleet of Frederick Barbarossa and the Genoese 1177.
Pi·ra·po′ra (pē·rȧ·pō′rȧ). City, Minas Gerais state, E Brazil, on the São Francisco 190 m. NNW of Belo Horizonte; pop. 7513.
Pi′ras·su·nun′ga (pē′rȧ·sōō-nōōnng′gȧ). City, São Paulo state, SE Brazil, 60 m. N of Campinas; pop. (1940 est.) 10,137; railroad junction town.
Pirate Coast. See TRUCIAL OMAN.
Pi·ray′ (pē·rä′ê; -rī′). River 150 m. long in cen. Bolivia; flows N into the Río Grande.
Pi·ra·yú′ (pē′rä·yōō′). Town, Paraguarí dept., S cen. Paraguay; pop. ab. 9260.
Pi·riá′ (pē·ryä′). Island in Atlantic Ocean, off NW coast of Maranhão state, Brazil, at mouth of Gurupí river.
Pi·riá′po·lis (pē·ryä′pō·lĕs). Town, Maldonado dept., S Uruguay; pop. ab. 8600; coastal town 50 m. E of Montevideo; one of chief bathing resorts of Uruguay.
Pi′ri·be·buy′ (pē′rē·vȧ·vwē′). Town, S Cordillera dept., cen. Paraguay; pop. ab. 14,590.
Pir′ma·sens (pĭr′mä·zĕns). Manufacturing city, S Rhineland-Palatinate state, West Germany, 40 m. WNW of Karlsruhe; pop. 42,996; manufactures leather goods. French defeated nearby by duke of Brunswick Sept. 14, 1793; taken by Americans Mar. 22, 1945.
Pir′na (pĭr′nä). Manufacturing city, Dresden district, East Germany, on Elbe river 11 m. SE of Dresden; pop. 30,460; rayon, cellulose, paper, iron, glass.
Pi′roe *or* **Pi′ru** (pē′rōō). Village, most important locality at W end of Ceram I., Indonesia, at head of **Piru Bay,** an inlet of Ceram Sea nearly closed by Amboina I.
Pi′rot (pē′rŏt). Town, SE Serbia, E Yugoslavia, on the Nišava river ab. 33 m. ESE of Niš; pop. 11,238; manufactures jewelry and carpets. Became part of Serbia 1878; occupied by Bulgarians 1885 and 1941.

Pir Pan·jal′ (pēr′ pŭn·jäl′). Mountain range, SW Kashmir, N India; highest ab. 15,000 ft.
Pir Panjal Pass. Mountain pass, altitude 11,398 ft., in the Pir Panjal range, ab. 50 m. S of Srinagar.
Pi′sa (pē′zȧ; *Ital.* pē′sä). **1** Province of Italy. See *Table* at ITALY.
2 *anc.* **Pi′sae** (pī′sē). Commune, its *, Tuscany, cen. Italy, on Arno river 43 m. W by S of Florence; pop. 72,468; winter resort; buildings include the Gothic church of Santa Maria della Spina, 11th-cent. Romanesque cathedral, 12th-cent. baptistery, leaning tower (campanile of cathedral; built 1174–1350; deviates 16½ ft. from the perpendicular), university (founded 1338; museum of Tuscan natural history), Campo Santo, 11th-cent. Palazzo Medici, 16th-cent. Palazzo Lanfreducci, Museo Civico (containing 12th-cent. documents), and numerous fine churches; manufactures include cottons, machinery, glass, hats, alabaster.
  History: One of 12 cities in Etruscan confederation; made Roman colony 180 B.C.; rose to prominence in Italy in 9th and 10th cents. A.D.; conquered Sardinia and Corsica 1052; defeated Saracens near Palermo 1063; pop. in 1100 estimated to have been ab. 150,000; sided with Ghibellines; defeated in long struggle with Genoa at Leghorn 1284; lost Sardinia, Corsica, and Balearic Is. 1300; subjugated by Aragon 1325; sold to Florence 1406; Council of Pisa held 1409 (Pope Gregory XII and antipope Benedict XIII deposed and Pope Alexander V elected); rebelled against Florentine rule 1494–1509; as part of grand duchy of Tuscany, became part of kingdom of Italy 1860; in World War II anchor point of German defense line and center of long conflict July 31 to Sept. 2, 1944. Birthplace of Galileo.
Pi·sa′gua (pē·sä′gwä). Seaport, Tarapacá prov., N Chile, ab. 40 m. N of Iquique; pop. (commune) 2199; in war with Peru and Bolivia (the "Nitrate War"), scene of a battle in which Chilean forces won 1879; northernmost nitrate port of the republic.
Pisaurum. See PESARO.
Piscaria. See PESCHIERA DEL GARDA.
Pis·cat′a·qua (pĭs·kăt′ȧ·kwô). River ab. 12 m. long, Maine and New Hampshire; formed by junction of Cocheco and Salmon Falls rivers 3 m. E of Dover, New Hampshire, flows SE forming S section of Maine-New Hampshire boundary. The tidal harbor from Portsmouth to the sea (3 m.) one of best in United States.
Pis·cat′a·quis (pĭs·kăt′ȧ·kwĭs). County in Maine. See *Table* at MAINE.
Pis·cat′a·way (pĭs·kăt′ȧ·wā). Village, part of Piscataway township (pop. 19,890), Middlesex co., cen. New Jersey, N of Raritan river and E of New Brunswick.
Pis′co (pēs′kō). Seaport on Pisco Bay, Ica dept., SW Peru, 130 m. S of Callao; pop. (1940 est.) 14,609; chief port bet. Callao and Mollendo.
Piscopi. See TELOS.
Pi·se′co Lake *or* **Inlet** (pĭ·sē′kō). Lake ab. 5 m. long in S Hamilton co., NE cen. New York; drains S through Sacandaga river into Sacandaga Reservoir.
Pi′sek (pē′sĕk). Industrial town, Bohemia prov., W Czechoslovakia, 55 m. SW of Prague on Otava river; pop. (1930) 16,973; in cattle and grain region.
Pis′gah, Mount (pĭz′gȧ). **1** Mountain 10,084 ft., Clear Creek and Gilpin cos., cen. Colorado, in the Front Range of the Rocky Mts.
2 Peak 3365 ft. in the Catskill Mts., Delaware co., S New York.
3 Ridge of Abarim Mts. in ancient Palestine, E of N end of the Dead Sea; highest point 2644 ft.; now in Transjordan; **Ne′bo** (nē′bō) was an alternative name for it or for its top (*Deut.* xxxiv. 1).
Pi·shin′ (pī·shēn′). District, N Baluchistan, N of Quetta, a plateau region on the frontier, ceded to British by Afghanistan 1879; administratively in the Quetta-Pishin dist.
Pishin Lo′ra (lō′rȧ). River ab. 300 m. long in N and

NW Baluchistan; flows SW into Hamun-i-Lora; part of course is in SE Afghanistan.

Pishpek. See FRUNZE.

Pi·sid′i·a (pĭ·sĭd′ĭ·á; pī-). Ancient country, S Asia Minor, cut off from the Mediterranean by Pamphylia; bounded on NW by Phrygia, on NE by Lycaonia, on SE by Cilicia, and on SW by Lycia. A mountainous region; its inhabitants never entirely subdued by Persians, Macedonians, or Romans; until time of Constantine was generally considered a part of Pamphylia.

Pisino. See PAZIN.

Pis′ki (pĭsh′kĭ). Village on Mureş river, S Transylvania, Romania, SW of Alba Iulia; scene of victory of Hungarians under Bem over Austrians Feb. 1849.

Pisse′vache′ (pēs′vȧsh′). Beautiful waterfall 215 ft. high in Valais canton, SW cen. Switzerland.

Pi·stic′ci (pês·têt′chê). Commune, Matera prov., Lucania, S Italy, 20 m. S by W of Matera; pop. 11,560.

Pi·sto′ia (pês·tō′yä). **1** Province of Italy. See *Table* at ITALY.

2 *anc.* **Pis·to′ri·a** (pĭs·tōr′ĭ·á) *or* **Pis·to′ri·ae** (-ĭ·ē). Commune, its ✱, Tuscany, cen. Italy, 17 m. NW of Florence; pop. 72,212; buildings include 12th-cent. cathedral, 14th-cent. baptistery, three 12th-cent. churches, 13th-cent. convent of San Franceso al Prato, 14th-cent. Ospedale del Ceppo; manufactures cutlery, needles, musical instruments, glass, paper, firearms, textiles.

History: Catiline defeated and killed here 62 B.C.; part of medieval margraviate of Tuscany; became free city 1115; important European banking center c. 1200; under Florentine rule 1306–25; became part of Tuscany 1530 and of kingdom of Italy 1860.

Pi·sto′ja (pês·tō′yä). Var. of PISTOIA.

Pistyan. See PIEŠT′ANY.

Pi·suer′ga (pê·swêr′gä). River ab. 140 m. long in N Spain; rises in the Cantabrian Mts., flows SSW into Duero river 9 m. below Valladolid.

Pit (pĭt). River ab. 280 m. long, N California; has source in N Modoc co., NE California, and flows S and W into the Sacramento in W cen. Shasta co.

Pit′cairn (pĭt′kârn). Borough, Allegheny co., SW Pennsylvania, 13 m. E of Pittsburgh; pop. 5383; coal mining; manufactures bricks, electrical goods.

Pitcairn Island. 1 British colony, annexed 1839, comprising Pitcairn I., with the islands of Henderson, Ducie, and Oeno, annexed in 1902.

2 Isolated island in S Pacific Ocean, lat. 25°S and long. 130°W, ab. 100 m. SSE of nearest island of the Tuamotus and equidistant bet. Tahiti and Easter I.; 2¼ m. long, area 2 sq. m.; only village Adamstown, on N side. Of volcanic origin, highest point 1000 ft.; has fertile soil. Discovered 1767 by Philip Carteret; uninhabited until 1790 when a colony was founded by the mutineers from the English ship *Bounty;* their existence unknown until 1808. Descendants of these colonists still live there; pop. (1936) ab. 220. In 1856 inhabitants removed to Norfolk I. but later many returned. Brought under High Commissioner for the Western Pacific 1898.

Pitch Lake (pĭch). Deposit of natural asphalt in SW Trinidad, West Indies; extends over 114 acres.

Pi′te (pē′tĕ). River ab. 200 m. long, N Sweden; rises in Pieska Lake near Norwegian border, flows SE into the head of the Gulf of Bothnia.

Pi′te·å′ (pē′tĕ·ō′). Seaport town, S Norrbotten prov., N Sweden, at mouth of the Pite river on the Gulf of Bothnia; pop. 4744.

Pi·teş′ti (pê·têsht′; -têsh′tê). City, S cen. Romania, in Muntenia region on Argeş river NW of Bucharest; pop. 19,630; petroleum center.

Pi′thi′viers′ (pē′tê′vyä′). Town, Loiret dept., N cen. France, 25 m. NE of Orléans; pop. 5540.

Pi′thom (pī′thŏm). Ancient city of Egypt, ab. 12 m. W by S of Ismailia in E Goshen, identical with or near Succoth; one of the treasure cities built for Pharaoh by the Hebrews (*Exod.* i. 11).

Pi′ti (pē′tĕ). Town and port of entry on Apra Harbor, W Guam; pop. 1467.

Pit′kin (pĭt′kĭn). County in Colorado. See *Table* at COLORADO.

Pit′man (pĭt′mǎn). Residential borough, Gloucester co., SW New Jersey, 15 m. S of Camden; pop. 8644; in farm and orchard area.

Pi′ton′ (pē′tôN′). French word for "mountain peak," used esp. in the French West Indies and the Mascarene Is.; for names beginning with *Piton,* see the distinguishing element. The **Pi′tons′** (pē′tôN′) of Saint Lucia I. are two conical mountains (2619 ft. and 2461 ft.) forming prominent landmarks.

Pi′truf·quén′ (pē′trōōf·kän′). Town, Cautín prov., S cen. Chile, S of Temuco; pop. 5193.

Pitsanulok. See PHITSANULOK.

Pitt (pĭt). County in North Carolina. See *Table* at NORTH CAROLINA.

Pitt, Mount. Former name of Mount McLOUGHLIN, Oregon.

Pitt Island. 1 See CHATHAM ISLANDS.

2 Island off W coast of British Columbia, Canada, bet. Banks I. and the mainland S of mouth of Skeena river.

Pitt Lake. Lake in SW British Columbia, Canada, formed by a widening of the **Pitt River** near its junction with the Fraser river E of Vancouver.

Pitts′bor′o (pĭts′bûr′ō). **1** Village, ⊗ of Calhoun co., N cen. Mississippi; pop. 205.

2 Town ⊗ of Chatham co., cen. North Carolina; pop. 1215.

Pitts′burg (pĭts′bûrg). **1** County in Oklahoma. See *Table* at OKLAHOMA.

2 Industrial city, Contra Costa co., W California, near mouth of Sacramento river at its confluence with the San Joaquin; pop. 19,062; founded 1835, incorporated 1911; coal discovered here 1863; manufactures steel, chemical products, rubber goods, lumber, asbestos products; salmon and fruit canneries.

3 Industrial and mining city, Crawford co., SE Kansas, 30 m. S of Fort Scott; pop. 18,678; coal deposits; ironworks. Kansas State College (1903; coed.).

4 City, ⊗ of Camp co., NE Texas, 42 m. NW of Marshall; pop. 3796; in farming, forest, and mining area; ships sweet potatoes.

Pitts′burgh (pĭts′bûrg). Industrial city and river port, ⊗ of Allegheny co., SW Pennsylvania, at confluence of Allegheny and Monongahela rivers where they form the Ohio; pop. 604,332; 16th largest city in the U.S.; former boatbuilding center and original center of petroleum

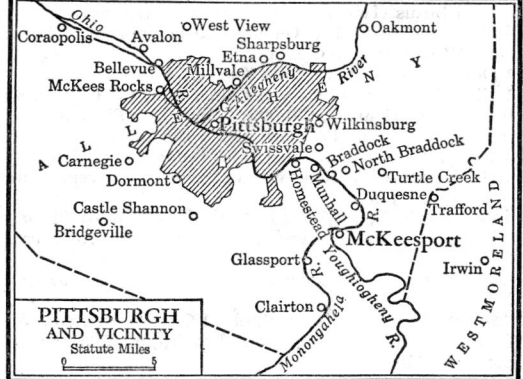

PITTSBURGH AND VICINITY
Statute Miles

industry; steel and iron works, glass factories, oil refineries; manufactures coke and by-products, clay products, electrical devices, air brakes, vanadium and radium products, aluminum, rolling-mill machinery, cork, white lead, chemicals, explosives; printing and publishing; soft coal mines, gas and oil wells, clay pits; home of

world's first commercial radio broadcasting station. Buhl Planetarium (1939); Mellon Institute (1913); U.S. Bureau of Mines experiment station; Carnegie Institute and Library (1895); Duquesne Univ. (1878; coed.); Mount Mercy College (1929; women); Pennsylvania College for Women (1869); Carnegie Institute of Technology (1900; includes Margaret Morrison Carnegie College for Women); Univ. of Pittsburgh (1787; coed.); Pittsburgh Theological Seminary (1794; coed.). Settled around Fort Pitt (earlier Fort Duquesne, under the French) after 1758; incorporated as city 1816; birthplace of precursor of American Federation of Labor (1881). Birthplace of Stephen Collins Foster.

Pittsburg Landing. Hamlet, Hardin co., SW Tennessee, on W bank of Tennessee river; scene of battle, usually called battle of Shiloh from the name of the nearby church, Apr. 6–7, 1862 in which Confederates under Gen. Albert Sidney Johnston made successful surprise attack on Grant's Union forces who, however, with fresh reinforcements finally compelled Confederate withdrawal (Johnston was killed Apr. 6 and command taken over by Gen. Beauregard). See UNITED STATES, *National Historical Parks* (Shiloh National Military Park).

Pitts′field (pĭts′fēld). **1** City, ⊗ of Pike co., W Illinois, 40 m. ESE of Quincy; pop. 4089; trade center.
2 Town, Somerset co., W Maine, 20 m. NNE of Waterville; pop. 4010; trading center for agricultural section; textile mills.
3 City, ⊗ of Berkshire co., W Massachusetts, on Housatonic river 40 m. WNW of Springfield; pop. 57,879; industrial center; manufactures textiles, paper, plastics, electrical machinery; summer and winter resort. Cultural center, esp. for music and drama. First settled 1743 but abandoned after Indian attack; again settled 1752; incorporated as city 1891.
4 Town, Merrimack co., S cen. New Hampshire, on Suncook river 12 m. NE of Concord; pop. 2419; manufactures shoes, sports clothes; corn cannery.

Pitts′ford (pĭts′fērd). Village, Monroe co., W New York, 7 m. ESE of Rochester; pop. 1749; residential suburb of Rochester.

Pitts′ton (pĭts′tŭn). City, Luzerne co., E Pennsylvania, on Susquehanna river 8 m. NE of Wilkes-Barre; pop. 12,407; settled c. 1762; railroad and industrial center; coal mining; manufactures stoves, silk, paper, machinery; fire-clay deposits.

Pitt′syl·va′nia (pĭt′sĭl·vān′yȧ; -vā′nĭ·ȧ). County in Virginia. See *Table* at VIRGINIA.

Pit′y·u′sae (pĭt′ĭ·ū′sē). Ancient name (*Eng.* Pine Islands) of W group of Balearic Is. comprising the two islands Ebusus (Iviza) and Ophiusa (Formentera).

Piu′ra (pyōō′rä). **1** River ab. 200 m. long in N Peru; flows W into Pacific Ocean.
2 Department of Peru. See *Table* at PERU.
3 City, its ✳, on Piura river ab. 35 m. SE of its port Paita; pop. (1940 est.) 20,093; founded by Pizarro 1532; trading center for NW Peru and S Ecuador.

Pi′ute (pī′ūt). County in Utah. See *Table* at UTAH.

Piute Reservoir. Reservoir in Sevier river, cen. Piute co., S cen. Utah.

Piz′zo (pĕt′tsô), *in full* **Pizzo di Ca·la′bri·a** (dē kä-lä′brĕ·ä). Seaport commune, Catanzaro prov., cen. Calabria, S Italy, on Tyrrhenian Sea; pop. (1931) 7622; scene of trial and execution Oct. 13, 1815 of Joachim Murat.

Pla·cen′tia (plȧ·sĕn′shȧ; -shĭ·ȧ). **1** City, Orange co., SW California, 20 m. ENE of Long Beach; pop. 5861; incorporated 1926.
2 Commune, Italy. See PIACENZA.
3 Town, SE Newfoundland, on E shore of Placentia Bay 62 m. WSW of St. John's; pop. (1942 est.) 1200; summer resort. Founded 1660 by the French, who fortified it and held it until Treaty of Utrecht 1713.

Placentia Bay. Wide inlet of Atlantic Ocean ab. 75 m. long, SE Newfoundland, W of St. John's; Argentia and

Placentia are on its E shore. Here on the British battleship *Prince of Wales* the Atlantic Charter was signed Aug. 14, 1941 by President Roosevelt and Winston Churchill.

Plac′er (plăs′ẽr). County in California. See *Table* at CALIFORNIA.

Plac′er Mountain (plăs′ẽr; plä′sẽr). Peak 8827 ft. in cen. Santa Fe co., N cen. New Mexico.

Plac′er·ville (plăs′ẽr·vĭl). City, ⊗ of El Dorado co., E California, 36 m. ENE of Sacramento; pop. 4439; gold mining; slate quarries; dairying.

Pla·ce′tas (plä·sā′täs). Municipality and town, Las Villas prov., W cen. Cuba; pop. of town (1943) 20,375; town is railroad junction point 20 m. SE of Santa Clara.

Plac′id, Lake (plăs′ĭd). Lake ab. 5 m. long and 1½ m. wide at its greatest extent, N Essex co., NE New York; elevation 1860 ft. See LAKE PLACID resort village.

Plad′da (plăd′ȧ). Low rocky island in Firth of Clyde, S of Arran I., off SW coast of Scotland; lighthouse.

Plain′edge (plān′ĕj′). Urban area, Nassau co., SE New York, in cen. Long I.; pop. 21,973.

Plain′field (plān′fēld). **1** Town, SE Windham co., NE Connecticut, on Quinebaug river; pop. 8884; settled 1689, incorp. 1699; cotton thread, woolen goods; agriculture.
2 Town, Hendricks co., cen. Indiana, 14 m. W of Indianapolis; pop. 5460.
3 City, Union co., NE New Jersey, 11 m. WSW of Elizabeth; pop. 45,330; residential suburb of New York City; manufactures printing presses, machinery, motor trucks and engines, electric motors, radio condensers, chemicals, tools, hosiery. Settled by Quakers and Scotch Presbyterians c. 1685; incorporated as city 1869.

Plain′pa′lais′ (plăn′pȧ′lĕ′). Former commune in Geneva canton, SW Switzerland; pop. (1920) 35,320; since 1930 part of Geneva.

Plains (plānz). Town, ⊗ of Yoakum co., NW Texas; pop. 1195.

Plains of A′bra·ham (ā′brȧ·hăm). Plateau W of old city of Quebec, Canada; battlefield Sept. 13, 1759 where the British under Gen. Wolfe defeated the French under Gen. Montcalm, decisive battle of Seven Years' War; now National Battlefields Park within the city limits.

Plain′view (plān′vū). **1** Village, Wabasha co., SE Minnesota, 20 m. ENE of Rochester; pop. 1833; canneries.
2 Urban area, Nassau co., SE New York, on Long I. E of New York; pop. 27,710.
3 City, ⊗ of Hale co., NW Texas, 42 m. N of Lubbock; pop. 18,735; produces cotton, wheat, alfalfa. Wayland Baptist Coll. (1909; coed.).

Plain′ville (plān′vĭl). Manufacturing town, SW Hartford co., N Connecticut, W of New Britain; pop. 13,149; electrical supplies, steel bearings, brass goods.

Plain′well (plān′wĕl; -wĕl). City, Allegan co., SW Michigan, 11 m. N of Kalamazoo; pop. 3125; paper mills, canneries.

Plai·sance′ (plĕ·zäns′). Coastal town, N British Guiana, in Demerara co., E of Georgetown; pop. (1931) 1896.

Pla′ka (plä′kä). Chief town of island of Melos, Cyclades dept., Greece; pop. 788.

Planasia. See PIANOSA.

Planches, Les. See LES PLANCHES.

Plan′et Deep (plăn′ĕt; -ĭt). Ocean depth 30,865 ft., SW Pacific Ocean, NW of Solomon Is.

Pla′nitz (plä′nĭts). City, Karl-Marx-Stadt dist., East Germany, SW suburb of Zwickau; pop. 24,004; manufactures cigars, brushes, knitted goods, linens.

Plan′ka, Cape (pläng′kä). Cape on Dalmatian coast, W Yugoslavia; long. 16°E, W of Split.

Plan′kin·ton (plăng′kĭn·tŭn). City, ⊗ of Aurora co., SE cen. South Dakota; pop. 644.

Pla′no (plā′nō). **1** City, Kendall co., NE Illinois, 26 m. WNW of Joliet; pop. 3343; farm machinery.
2 City, Collin co., NE Texas, 15 m. N of Dallas; pop. 3695; in agricultural section.

Plant City (plănt). City, Hillsborough co., W cen. Florida penin., 20 m. E of Tampa; pop. 15,711; shipping center for vegetables and fruit, esp. strawberries.

Plants'ville (plănts'vĭl). Subdivision (pop. 2793) of town of SOUTHINGTON, Connecticut; manufactures nuts and bolts.

Plaque'mine (plăk'mĭn; plăk'ĕ·mĭn). Town, ⊗ of Iberville parish, S Louisiana, on Mississippi river 13 m. SSW of Baton Rouge; pop. 7689; incorporated 1838; site of Plaquemine Locks, with a lift of 55 ft., built 1909 to connect **Bayou Plaquemine** and the Intracoastal Canal with the Mississippi river.

Plaque'mines (plăk'mĭnz; plăk'ĕ·mĭnz). Parish in Louisiana. See *Table* at LOUISIANA.

Pla'ri·del' (plä'rĕ·dĕl'). Municipality, Misamis Occidental prov., Mindanao, Phil. Is., on S shore of Mindanao Sea NW of Iligan Bay; pop. 21,905.

Pla·sen'cia (plä·sĕn'shä; -shǐ·ä; *Span.* plä-sān'thyä, -syä). Commune, Cáceres prov., W Spain, 43 m. NNE of Cáceres; pop. 16,255; agricultural products, wine; manufactures leather, chinaware, cork; 15th-cent. cathedral.

Plas'sey (plăs'ĭ). Village, NW Nadia dist., West Bengal, NE Indian Union, on E bank of Bhagirathi river ab. 80 m. N of Calcutta; site of Clive's victory June 23, 1757 with small force of ab. 3000 over army of 68,000 of Siraj-ud-daula; historically the beginning of the British Empire in the East.

Pla'ta (plä'tà). Short form of LA PLATA, used in English for the viceroyalty of La Plata.

Plata, La. See LA PLATA.

Pla'ta, Rí'o de la (rē'ō thä lä plä'tä); *Brit.* **River Plate** (plāt'). Estuary 225 m. long of Paraná and Uruguay rivers, bet. Uruguay and Argentina; at mouth extreme width is ab. 138 m., at Montevideo ab. 60 m., opp. Buenos Aires and above, 25 to 28 m. Discovered by Solís 1516; explored by Sebastian Cabot 1526–30; first permanent settlement in La Plata region was at Asunción 1538.

Pla·tae'a (plà·tē'à) or **Pla·tae'ae** (-tē'ē). Ancient city in SE Boeotia, E cen. Greece, 9 m. S of Thebes and near Attica border. Its independence protected by Athens; sent 1000 men to aid Athenians at Marathon 490 B.C.; destroyed by Persians 480 B.C. but scene the next year 479 B.C. of the defeat of Mardonius and the Persians by Pausanias and the Greeks that assured the independence of Greece; later attacked by Thebes 431 B.C., besieged for two years 429–427 and destroyed; rebuilt but destroyed a third time by Thebans 373 B.C.; existed as an obscure town until Middle Ages.

Plá'ta·no, Rí'o del (rē'ō thĕl plä'tä·nô). River ab. 325 m. long, Chiapas state, Mexico; rises in W Guatemala, flows NW and N across Chiapas state and empties into the Bay of Campeche.

Plate, River. See Río de la PLATA.

Pla·teau' (plă·tō'; plăt'ō). Province of Nigeria. See *Table* at NIGERIA.

Plateau Mountain. Peak 3855 ft. in the Catskill Mts., Greene co., SE New York.

Pla'to (plä'tô). Town, Magdalena dept., N Colombia, on the Magdalena ab. 65 m. SE of Cartagena; pop. 5814.

Platte (plăt). **1** River ab. 300 m. long, S Iowa and NW Missouri; rises in Union co., S Iowa, enters Missouri river in Platte co., NW Missouri, ab. 15 m. NW of Kansas City, Kansas.
2 River 310 m. long (with North Platte ab. 900 m.), cen. Nebraska; formed by confluence of North Platte and South Platte in Lincoln co., SW cen. Nebraska, flows E into Missouri river below Omaha.
3 Name of counties in three states of the U.S. See *Tables* at MISSOURI, NEBRASKA, WYOMING.
4 City, Charles Mix co., S South Dakota, 50 m. WSW of Mitchell; pop. 1167; railroad terminus; flour and feed mills; creamery.

Platte City. City, ⊗ of Platte co., NW Missouri; pop. 1188.

Plattensee. See BALATON.

Platte'ville (plăt'vĭl). City, Grant co., SW corner of Wisconsin, 60 m. WSW of Madison; pop. 6957; founded 1827; center of section noted for lead and zinc mines; dairying. Wisconsin State Coll. (1866; coed.).

Platt National Park (plăt). See UNITED STATES, *National Parks*.

Platts'burg (plăts'bûrg). **1** City, ⊗ of Clinton co., NW Missouri, 33 m. N of Kansas City; pop. 1663.
2 See PLATTSBURGH.

Platts'burgh or **Platts'burg** (plăts'bûrg). City, ⊗ of Clinton co., NE corner of New York, on W shore of Lake Champlain 20 m. S of Canadian border; pop. 20,172; manufactures wood-pulp and paper products, razor blades, concrete blocks. Settled c. 1784; scene of naval battle off nearby Valcour I. 1776; siege and battle (land engagements in and near village and naval battle on Lake Champlain) 1814; made site of U.S. military reservation 1814. Reservation held annual citizens' military training camp 1916–39; turned over to N.Y. State 1946, became site of Champlain College (coed.); reverted to federal government 1952 and made site of Air Force base, activated 1956. State U. of New York College of Education (1889; coed.).

Platts'mouth (plăts'mŭth). City, ⊗ of Cass co., E Nebraska, on Missouri river 17 m. S of Omaha; pop. 6244; railroad and trade center; ceramic clay deposits.

Plau'en (plou'ĕn), *also* **Plauen im Vogt'land** (im fōkt'länt). Manufacturing city, Karl-Marx-Stadt dist., E Germany, on Weisse Elster 29 m. SW of Zwickau; pop. (1939) 110,342; one of most important cotton-manufacturing centers in Germany. Probably founded by Slavs in 12th cent.; came under Bohemia 1327; to Saxony 1466. A former capital of Vogtland.

Pla'ya, Point (plä'yä). Cape extending into Atlantic Ocean from E Venezuela coast, near British Guiana boundary.

Pla'za Huin·cul' (plä'sä wĕng·kōol'). Town, cen. Neuquén territory, W Argentina, 50 m. E of Zapala.

Pleas'ant, Lake (plĕz'nt). **1** See LAKE PLEASANT DAM, Arizona.
2 Lake in S cen. Hamilton co., NE cen. New York.

Pleasant, Mount. Peak 4775 ft. in S Coos co., N New Hampshire, SW of Mt. Washington.

Pleasant Bay. **1** Inlet of Atlantic Ocean on S coast of Washington co., SE Maine.
2 Inlet of Atlantic Ocean on SE coast of Cape Cod, SE Massachusetts.

Pleasant Grove. City, Utah co., N cen. Utah, 10 m. NNW of Provo; pop. 4772; grows fruit and berries.

Pleasant Hill. **1** Urban area, Contra Costa co., W California, NE of Oakland; pop. 23,844.
2 Town, Sabine parish, W Louisiana, 60 m. S of Shreveport; pop. 907; battle Apr. 9, 1864 when the Confederates under Richard Taylor made a partially successful attack on Federals under Nathaniel Banks.
3 City, Cass co., W Missouri; pop. 2689.

Pleasant Hills. Borough, Allegheny co., SW Pennsylvania, S suburb of Pittsburgh; pop. 8573.

Pleasant Island. See NAURU.

Pleas'an·ton (plĕz'n·tŭn). **1** City, Alameda co., W California, 15 m. E of San Francisco Bay; pop. 4203.
2 City, Atascosa co., S Texas, 33 m. S of San Antonio; pop. 3467; agriculture, livestock; oil, gas, clay deposits.

Pleasant Ridge. City, Oakland co., SE Michigan; pop. 3807; residential suburb of Detroit.

Pleas'ants (plĕz'nts). County in West Virginia. See *Table* at WEST VIRGINIA.

Pleas'ant·ville (plĕz'nt·vĭl). **1** City, Atlantic co., SE New Jersey, 5 m. WNW of Atlantic City; pop. 15,172.
2 Residential village, Westchester co., SE New York, 30 m. NNE of New York; pop. 5877; publishing industry.

Pleasure Ridge Park. Urban area, Jefferson co., N cen. Kentucky, S of Louisville; pop. 10,612.

Pleis'se (plī'sĕ). River ab. 60 m. long in **Saxony and**

Thuringia, cen. Germany; flows N to the Weisse Elster at Leipzig.

Plen′ty, Bay of (plĕn′tĭ). Large inlet of Pacific Ocean on NE coast of North I., New Zealand.

Plen′ty·coos Peak (plĕn′tĭ·kōōs). Mountain 10,938 ft. in W Park co., on boundary of Yellowstone National Park, NW Wyoming.

Plen′ty·wood′ (plĕn′tĭ·wŏŏd′). City, ⊗ of Sheridan co., NE corner of Montana; pop. 2121; trade center in grain-producing section.

Ple′red (plä′rĕt). Town, West Java prov., Indonesia, just W of Cheribon; pop. 13,335.

Pleshcheevo. See PERESLAVL.

Pless. See PSZCZYNA.

Ples′sis·ville (plĕs′ĭ·vĭl; *Fr.* plĕ′sē′vĭl′). Village, Megantic co., S Quebec, Canada, 24 m. WNW of Thetford Mines; pop. 5094; lumber.

Plet′i·pi Lake (plĕt′ĭ·pĭ). Lake 138 sq. m. in S cen. Quebec prov., Canada, with outlets S through Peribonka and Outardes rivers.

Ple′ven (plĕ′vĕn). **1** Department, N Bulgaria; 5960 sq. m.; pop. (1934) 996,686.

2 *or* **Plev′na** (plĕv′nä). City, its *; pop. (1934) 31,520; trade center for cattle, wine, and attar of roses; captured from the Turks by the Russians Dec. 10, 1877, after a siege of 143 days.

Pley′ben′ (plā′bă̈n′). Town, Finistère dept., NW France, ab. 16 m. N of Quimper; pop. 1295; 16th-cent. church with interesting wood carvings.

Plinlimmon. See PLYNLIMMON.

Płock (plôtsk); *Ger.* **Plozk** (plôtsk). Commune, Warszawa dept., Poland, on Vistula river 55 m. WNW of Warsaw; pop. (1938–39 est.) 35,200; has 12th-cent. cathedral (contains tombs of Polish dukes and kings of 11th and 12th cents.) and remains of old ducal castle; manufactures liquors, tile. Under Prussia 1793–1806 and Russia 1815–1918; battle 1915; overrun by Germans 1939 but retaken 1945.

Plöck′en (plŏk′ĕn); *Ital.* **Mon′te Cro′ce** (mŏn′tä krō′chä). Pass over the Carnic Alps bet. S Carinthia, Austria, and Venetia, Italy; altitude 4467 ft.; connects upper valley of the Drau (Drava) with Udine, Italy. Was important in 1917 campaign of World War I.

Ploeg′steert (plōōĸ′stärt). Commune, West Flanders prov., NW Belgium, 9 m. S of Ieper on French border; pop. 5098; captured by Germans Apr. 10, 1918.

Ploen. See PLÖN.

Plo′ër′mel′ (plô′ĕr′mĕl′). Town, Morbihan dept., NW France, ab. 25 m. NNE of Vannes; pop. 2513; 16th-cent. church of St. Armel, named for the hermit who lived in the district in 6th cent. and after whom the town is named.

Plo·eş′ti (plô-yĕsht′; -yĕsh′tĕ). City, SE cen. Romania, 35 m. N of Bucharest; pop. (1939 est.) 77,376; commercial and industrial center in E foothills of Transylvanian Alps in important petroleum-producing area; oil fields bombed by Allied airplanes Aug. 1943 and often thereafter; captured by Russians Aug. 31, 1944.

Plomb du Can′tal′ (plôn′ dü kän′täl′). Peak 6093 ft. in the Auvergne Mts., cen. France.

Plom′bières′-les–Bains (plôn′byâr′lā·bă̈n′). Commune, Vosges dept., NE France; pop. 1565; ab. 15 m. S of Épinal; hot springs.

Plo′mo (plō′mô). Mountain 22,300 ft. in S cen. Chile, E of Valparaíso near border of Argentina.

Plön *or* **Ploen** (plün). Commune, E Schleswig-Holstein, N Germany, SE of Kiel on **Lake Plön** (*Ger.* **Plö′ner See** [plü′nẽr zā′]); pop. 3973.

Płońsk (plôn′y′sk). Commune, Warszawa dept., Poland, 36 m. NW of Warsaw; pop. 10,393.

Plott Balsam Mountain (plŏt). Peak 6200 ft. in Haywood co., W North Carolina.

Plou′gas′tel′-Da′ou′las′ (plōō′gàs′tĕl′dà′ōō′läs′). Commune, W Finistère dept., NW France, on a bay which separates it from Brest to the W; pop. (1931) 6914.

Plov′div (plôv′dĭf). **1** Department, S Bulgaria; 6115 sq. m.; pop. (1934) 801,755.

2 *Gr.* **Phil′ip·pop′o·lis** (fĭl′ĭ·pŏp′ô·lĭs); *anc.* **Eu·mol′pi·as** (û·mŏl′pĭ·ăs). City, its *, on the Maritsa N of the Rhodope Mts.; pop. 162,518; commercial center in region producing attar of roses; also trades in wheat, silk, tobacco, and manufactured goods. Ancient Eumolpias, a Thracian town, taken by Philip II of Macedonia 342 B.C. and renamed after him; made capital of Thracia by the Romans; captured by the Goths c. 251 A.D. with great slaughter; prospered in time of Crusades but practically destroyed under Bulgarian tsar 1207; later under Greeks and Turks; scene of the rout of the Turkish army under Suleiman Pasha Jan. 17, 1878 by the Russians. See EASTERN RUMELIA.

Plozk. See PŁOCK.

Plum (plŭm). Borough, Allegheny co., SW Pennsylvania, E suburb of Pittsburgh; pop. 10,241.

Plu·ma′jes Point (plōō·mä′häs). Cape on W coast of Cuba, S of Guadiana Bay.

Plu′mas (plōō′mäs). County in California. See *Table* at CALIFORNIA.

Plum Island (plŭm). **1** Island 8½ m. long in Atlantic Ocean off NE coast of Essex co., NE Massachusetts, just S of mouth of the Merrimack.

2 Island 3 m. long at E end of Long Island Sound, off NE extremity of Long I., New York.

Plum′stead (plŭm′stĕd; -stĭd). Parish, Woolwich metropolitan borough, London, England; pop. ab. 76,000; E suburb of Woolwich.

Plu·vi′gner′ (plü·vē′nyä′). Town, Morbihan dept., NW France, 15 m. NW of Vannes; pop. 1680.

Plym′outh (plĭm′ŭth). **1** Name of counties of two states in the U.S. See *Tables* at IOWA and MASSACHUSETTS.

2 Town, SE Litchfield co., NW Connecticut, N of Waterbury; pop. 8981; settled 1728, incorp. 1795; lumber mills, granite quarries; foundry; manufactures locks; first clock factory in America set up here 1807.

3 City, ⊗ of Marshall co., N Indiana, 23 m. S of South Bend; pop. 7558; in agricultural section.

4 Town, ⊗ of Plymouth co., SE Massachusetts, on Plymouth Bay 18 m. SE of Brockton; pop. 14,445; site of first permanent white settlement in New England; oldest town in New England; manufactures textiles and cordage. The **Colony of New Plymouth,** founded by the Pilgrims 1620, was governed under the Mayflower Compact, since the Pilgrims had no charter, until 1691 when it became part of Massachusetts Bay Colony.

5 City, Wayne co., SE Michigan, 22 m. W of Detroit; pop. 8766; manufactures air rifles.

6 Village, Hennepin co., SE Minnesota, NW suburb of Minneapolis; pop. 9576.

7 Manufacturing town, Grafton co., W New Hampshire. on Pemigewasset river 20 m. NW of Laconia; pop. 3210; resort. Plymouth Teachers College (1870; coed.).

8 Town, ⊗ of Washington co., E North Carolina, 10 m. S of W end of Albemarle Sound; pop. 4666; scene of several naval battles during Civil War; canneries, fisheries, lumber mills.

9 Borough, Luzerne co., E Pennsylvania, on Susquehanna river 4 m. W of Wilkes-Barre; pop. 10,401; settled 1768; coal mining and shipping.

10 Village, Windsor co., E Vermont, ab. 14 m. SE of Rutland; pop. 308; birthplace and grave of Calvin Coolidge, 30th president of the U.S.

11 City, Sheboygan co., E Wisconsin, 13 m. W of Sheboygan; pop. 5128; manufactures cheese, furniture.

12 Seaport on SW coast of Montserrat I., Leeward Is., West Indies Federation; * of Montserrat territory, Leeward Islands; pop. 2500.

13 City and county borough, Devonshire, SW England, on Plymouth Sound bet. Plym and Tamar estuaries 190 m. WSW of London; pop. 208,182, (1951) 208,985; is a British seaport and naval base, with a naval engineering college, naval barracks, hospital, etc.; trade center for

tin, copper, lead, granite, kaolin; manufactures chemicals and china; first town to declare for William of Orange as king of England 1688; last port touched by the ship *Mayflower* before its voyage across the Atlantic 1620. In World War II repeatedly bombed by Germans in spring of 1941 and much damaged; served as largest U.S. naval amphibious and operating base in England.

Plymouth Bay. Inlet of Atlantic Ocean on E coast of Plymouth co., SE Massachusetts.

Plymouth Colony. See PLYMOUTH, Massachusetts.

Plymouth Sound. Inlet of the English Channel on SW coast of England, on the boundary bet. Devonshire and Cornwall; site of the city of Plymouth.

Plyn·lim′mon or **Plin·lim′mon** (plĭn·lĭm′ŭn). Mountain 2468 ft. in cen. Wales, on boundary bet. Cardiganshire and Montgomeryshire; center of a mountain group containing the source of several rivers, including the Severn, Wye, and Ystwyth.

Pl′zeň (pŭl′zĕn·y′); *Ger.* **Pil′sen** (pĭl′zĕn). City, province of Bohemia, Czechoslovakia, 52 m. WSW of Prague; pop. (1930) 114,704; breweries; manufactures munitions, locomotives, airplanes, electric motors; 14th-cent. cathedral, 16th-cent. town hall, museum.

Pnom′penh′ or **Pnom–Penh** (p'nôm′pĕn′); or **Phnom Penh** (p'nôm′-). City, * of Cambodia, Indochina, in SE Cambodia at junction of Tonle Sap river with the Mekong 130 m. WNW of Saigon; pop. 102,678; market center for products of Cambodia, Laos, and E Siam; contains large palace of Cambodian kings and Buddhist temple on a hill (Thai *pnom* or *phnom*). Important town when Khmer kingdom flourished 9th to 12th cents.; became Cambodian capital 1860 and French seat of government 1886.

Po (pō; *Ital.* pô); *anc.* **Pa′dus** (pā′dŭs) and, *in mythology*, **E·rid′a·nus** (ė·rĭd′'n·ŭs). River 418 m. long in N Italy; rises on the slopes of Viso, flows NE to Turin and then E across Piedmont and Lombardy into the Adriatic Sea through several mouths; navigable to beyond Turin. Its chief tributaries in the W are the Dora Baltea, Dora Riparia, and Tanaro; others, from the N, serving as outlets of the Alpine lakes, are the Ticino, Adda, Oglio, and Mincio. Important industrial cities in its valley (Milan, Turin, Padua, Verona, Brescia).

Po′as (pō′äs). Volcano 8600 ft. in Costa Rica, ab. 19 m. NW of the city of San José.

Po·be′da Peak (pŭ·byĕ′dä); *Russ.* **Pik Po·be′dy** (pyĕk pŭ byĕ′dĭ). Mountain 24,406 ft., highest in Tien Shan range, Central Asia, on the border between Kirgiz S.S.R. and Sinkiang, China.

Po′ca·hon′tas (pō′kȧ·hŏn′tȧs). **1** Name of counties of two states in the U.S. See *Tables* at IOWA and WEST VIRGINIA.
2 City, ⊗ of Randolph co., NE Arkansas, on Black river 33 m. NNW of Jonesboro; pop. 3665.
3 Town, ⊗ of Pocahontas co., NW cen. Iowa, 30 m. NW of Fort Dodge; pop. 2011.
4 Town, Tazewell co., SW Virginia, on West Virginia border 37 m. WNW of Pulaski; pop. 1313; coal mining.

Po′ca·tel′lo (pō′kȧ·tĕl′ō; -tĕl′ŭ). City, ⊗ of Bannock co., SE Idaho, 60 m. N of Utah border and 70 m. W of Wyoming border; pop. 28,534; incorporated as village 1889, as city 1893; railroad center; livestock, cheese, potatoes. Idaho State Univ. (1901; coed.).

Pochow. See POHSIEN.

Pock′ling·ton Reef (pŏk′lĭng·tŭn). Reef in S Solomon Sea, off SW Solomon Is., W Pacific Ocean.

Po′co·moke (pō′kō·mōk). River ab. 55 m. long, SE Maryland; rises in S Delaware, flows S across Maryland border and into Pocomoke Sound in SE Somerset co.

Pocomoke City. Town, Worcester co., SE Maryland, 22 m. S of Salisbury; pop. 3329; shipping center for agricultural section.

Pocomoke Sound. Inlet of Chesapeake Bay on S coast of Somerset co., Maryland, and NW coast of Accomac co., Virginia, receiving Pocomoke river on NE.

Po′co·no Mountains (pō′kō·nō); *often* **Po′co·nos** (-nōz). Ridge ab. 1600 ft. high in E Pennsylvania, chiefly in Pike, Monroe, and Carbon cos., extending parallel with and ab. 15 m. NW of, the Kittatinny Mountains.

Po′ços de Cal′das (pō′sōōzh thĕ käl′däs). Watering place, Minas Gerais state, E Brazil; pop. (1940 est.) 13,819; altitude ab. 4000 ft.; sulfur baths.

Po′co·to·paug′ Lake (pō′kō·tô·pôg′). Lake in NE Middlesex co., S Connecticut; outlet is stream flowing S into Salmon river.

Pod′go·ri·ca or **Pod′go·ri′tsa** (pôd′gô·rē′tsä); *since 1946 officially* **Ti′to·grad** (tē′tô·gräd). Town, * of Montenegro, S Yugoslavia; pop. 10,651.

Pod·gó′rze (pôd·gōō′zhĕ). Former town in Kraków dept., S Poland; since 1919 part of Kraków.

Po di Pri·ma′ro (pô′ dĕ prē·mä′rô). Name applied to the lower course of the Reno river, Italy.

Podium Anicensis. See LE PUY.

Podkamennaya Tunguska. See *Stony Tunguska* at TUNGUSKA.

Podkarpatská Rus. See CARPATHIAN RUTHENIA.

Pod′mo·kly (pôd′mô·klĭ); *Ger.* **Bo′den·bach** (bō′dĕn·bäĸ). City, N Bohemia prov., W Czechoslovakia, on the German border ab. 50 m. NNW of Prague; pop. (1930) 22,648; on Labe (Elbe) river; manufactures textiles, porcelain, chemicals.

Po·do′lia (pô·dōl′yȧ; -dō′lĭ·ȧ); *Russ.* **Po·dolsk′** (pô·dōlsk′; *Russ.* pŭ·dôl′y′sk). Former region on left bank of middle Dniester; incorporated in medieval kingdom of Poland 1431; held by Turks 1672–99; became Russian 1793 and was later a province of Russia; now in W Ukraine, nearly coextensive with Kamenets Podolsk Region; chief town Kamenets Podolski.

Po·dolsk′ (pô·dōlsk′; *Russ.* pŭ·dôl′y′sk). **1** See PODOLIA.
2 Industrial town, Moscow Region, Soviet Russia, Europe; pop. 72,422; on railroad 25 m. S of Moscow; cement and lime factories, railroad repair shops.

Po′dor (pō′dôr). Town on the Senegal river, N Senegal, West Africa; pop. ab. 81,000.

Po′dunk (pō′dŭngk). A name often used by newsmen to designate any very small and insignificant place, as typical of lack of contact with the progress of the world; it is of Indian origin, the hamlet of Podunk, Massachusetts, near Worcester, dating back to 1666; there is also a Podunk in Connecticut, but there is no post office of that name.

Poelau. See PULAU.

Poel′ca·pel′le (pōōl′kȧ·pĕl′ĕ). Small commune, West Flanders prov., NW Belgium, NNE of Ieper (Ypres); pop. 2011; stormed by British Oct. 4, 1917; marked the limit of British advance in the third battle of Ypres; scene of death in action Sept. 11, 1917 of the French military aviation ace Capt. Guynemer.

Poer′ba·ling′ga (pōōr′bä·lĭng′gä) or **Pur′ba·ling′ga.** Town, Central Java prov., Indonesia, NNE of Banjumas; pop. 16,435.

Poer′wa·kar′ta (pōōr′wä·kär′tä) or **Pur′wa·kar′ta.** Town, West Java prov., Indonesia, ab. 60 m. SE of Batavia; pop. 15,141.

Poer′wo·da′di (pōōr′wô·dä′dĕ) or **Pur′wo·da′di.** Town, Central Java prov., Indonesia; pop. 10,840; railroad junction point 35 m. E of Semarang.

Poer′wo·ker′to (pōōr′wô·kĕr′tō) or **Pur′wo·ker′to.** Town, Central Java prov., Indonesia, just NW of Banjumas; pop. 33,266.

Poer′wo·red′jo (pōōr′wô·rĕj′ō) or **Pur′wo·re′jo.** Town, Central Java prov., Indonesia, ab. 25 m. SW of Magelang; pop. 24,645.

Poe′ting or **Pu′ting** (pōō′tĭng); *Du.* **Tan′djoeng Poeting** (tän′jōōng). Cape on SW coast of Borneo, Indonesia, projecting into Java Sea, 111°46′E.

Poge, Cape (pōg). Northeast point of Chappaquiddick I., E Martha's Vineyard, Massachusetts.

Pogegen. See PAGEGIAI.

Pog'gi·bon'si (pôd'jĕ·bôn'sĕ). Commune, Siena prov., Tuscany, cen. Italy, 16 m. NW of Siena; pop. 13,866; 13th-cent. church and convent.

Pog'gio·re·a'le (pôd'jō·rå·ä'lå). Town, Naples commune, S Italy, suburb of Naples; pop. (1931) 29,897.

Pogranichnaya. See SUIFENHO, Manchuria.

Po'hai' (bŏ'hī'); *formerly* **Pe'chi'li'** (bā'jĭr'lĭ'). Strait ab. 70 m. wide, NE China, bet. Liaotung Penin., S Manchuria, and N Shantung; connects Po Hai with the Yellow Sea.

Po Hai (bŏ' hī') *or* **Gulf of Chih'li'** (jĭr'lĭ'). The NW arm of the Yellow Sea enclosed by S Manchuria and Hopei and Shantung provs. of China; its NE extension is the Gulf of Liaotung.

Po'hsien' (bŏ'shĭ·ĕn'); *formerly* **Po'chow'** (bŏ'jō'). Commercial city, NW Anhwei prov., E China; pop. ab. 100,000.

Poictiers. See POITIERS.

Poin'sett (poin'sĕt; -sĭt). County in Arkansas. See *Table* at ARKANSAS.

Poinsett, Lake. Lake in S Hamlin co., E South Dakota.

Point de Galle. See GALLE.

Pointe à Ga'ti'neau' (pwăn'-tȧ gȧ'tē'nō'). Village, Hull co., SW Quebec, Canada, at confluence of Gatineau and Ottawa rivers opp. Hull and Ottawa; pop. 3874.

Pointe a la Hache (point' ăl'ȧ häsh'). Village, ⊗ of Plaquemines parish, SE Louisiana; pop. (est.) 600.

Pointe-à-Pi'tre (pwăn'-tȧ-pē'tr'). Seaport, SW Grande Terre I., E Guadeloupe, West Indies; largest town in Guadeloupe; pop. (1936) 43,551.

Pointe Aux Barques (point' ō bärk'). North tip of the Thumb, E Michigan. See the THUMB.

Pointe aux Trem'bles (pwăn'-tō trän'bl'). Town on NE shore of Montreal I., S Quebec, Canada, on St. Lawrence river 10 m. N of Montreal; pop. 8241.

Pointe Claire (point klâr'; *Fr.* pwănt' klâr'). City, ⊗ of Jacques Cartier co., on Montreal I., S Quebec, Canada, on St. Lawrence river 15 m. WSW of Montreal; pop. 8753.

Pointe Cou·pee' (point' kōō·pē'; *Fr.* pwănt' kōō'pā'). Parish in Louisiana. See *Table* at LOUISIANA.

Pointe Levi. See LEVIS.

Pointe–Noire (pwănt'nwâr'). City and port, SW Congo Republic, on the Atlantic SE of Loango; formerly ✳ of Middle Congo; pop. 56,865.

Point Grey (point grā'). Former city, British Columbia, Canada, now part of Vancouver.

Point Mar'i·on (măr'ĭ·ŭn; mâr'-). Borough, Fayette co., SW Pennsylvania, on Monongahela river at West Virginia border; pop. 1853; platted 1842; glassworks; sand and gravel pits.

Point Mountain. Peak 8300 ft. in Glacier National Park, NW Montana.

Point Pe'lee National Park (pē'lĕ). See CANADA, *National Parks.*

Point Pleas'ant (plĕz''nt). **1** Borough and shore resort, Ocean co., E New Jersey, on Atlantic Ocean 10 m. S of Asbury Park; pop. 10,182.
2 Village, S Clermont co., SW Ohio, on the Ohio river; birthplace of Ulysses S. Grant, 18th president of the United States.
3 City, ⊗ of Mason co., W West Virginia, on Ohio river 35 m. NNE of Huntington; pop. 5785; shipyards, ironworks; coal mines. Named by George Washington in 1770; American victory over Shawnee Indians 1774; incorporated as town 1833.

Point Pleasant Beach. Borough and seaside resort, Ocean co., E New Jersey, near Point Pleasant; pop. 3873.

Point Rob'erts (rŏb'ĕrts). Village, Whatcom co., NW Washington; pop. (1950) 310; on **Point Roberts,** the tip of a peninsula extending S into Strait of Georgia from British Columbia; separated from mainland of Whatcom co. by Boundary Bay.

Pois'sy' (pwȧ'sē'); *anc.* **Pin·ci'a·cum** (pĭn·sī'ȧ·kŭm). Commune, Seine-et-Oise dept., N France, on Seine river 11 m. WNW of Paris; pop. 12,502; distillery; fine church (in which Saint Louis was baptized 1215).

Poi'tiers' (pwȧ'tyā'); *formerly spelled* **Poic'tiers'** (pwȧ'-); *anc.* **Li·mo'num** (lĭ·mō'nŭm; lī-). City, ✳ of Vienne dept., W cen. France, 100 m. ESE of Nantes; pop. 44,235; 12th-cent. Romanesque-Gothic cathedral; university; Roman and Gallic remains; palace of former counts of Poitou (*q.v.*).

Poi'tou' (pwȧ'tōō'). Historical region of W cen. France, bounded anciently on NW by Brittany, on N by Anjou and Saumurois, on NE by Touraine, by E Marche, SE by Limousin, S by Angoumois and Aunis, W by Atlantic Ocean; ✳ Poitiers; watered by Sèvre-Nantaise and Sèvre-Niortaise rivers.

History: Inhabited by ancient Pictones or Pictavi; conquered by Romans and made part of Aquitania; conquered by Visigoths 418 A.D.; Visigoths under Alaric II defeated near Poitiers by Franks under Clovis 507 A.D.; Saracens defeated by Charles Martel 732 on a site bet. Poitiers and Tours; made countship by Charlemagne 778; part of duchy of Aquitaine 990; passed to Louis VII of France 1137 and later to Henry II of England; confiscated by Philip Augustus 1203; occupied 1356–69 by English after defeat of John the Good by Edward, the Black Prince, Sept. 19, 1356 at Maupertuis, 7 m. SE of Poitiers; appanage of Jean de Berry 1369–1416; reunited with French crown 1416; province of France until Revolution, when territory was divided into three departments, most westerly the Vendée (see VENDÉE and *Table* at FRANCE) famous for the series of peasant insurrections against the Revolutionary government (Wars of the Vendée 1793–96).

Pokrovsk. See ENGELS.

Po'la (pō'lȧ; *Ital.* pô'lä). **1** Former name of Istria prov.: see *Table* at ITALY.
2 City. See PULJ.

Po'land (pō'lănd). **1** Medieval kingdom in E Europe, extending at its greatest extent (including the Grand Principality of Lithuania) from the Gulf of Riga to the lower Dnieper river and including modern Poland, Lithuania (except Memel), White Russia, ¾ of the Ukraine, etc. Its chief capital was Kraków.

History: Slavic duchy under Piast dynasty emerged in late 10th cent. in region bet. Oder and Warta rivers; under Boleslav I (992–1025), it conquered territory including Slavs W to the Oder, Moravia, and Kraków, and was recognized as Polish kingdom; invaded by Mongols 1241; its personal union with Lithuania (*q.v.*) by marriage 1386 established Jagellon dynasty; after long struggle with Teutonic Knights, obtained West Prussia and East Prussia (*q.v.*) 1466; after 1572, Polish crown became elective, and the nobility stronger than the monarch; in 17th cent. several disastrous wars led to loss of much territory. New wars and political weakness led to three partitions: 1772, 1793, and 1795, in which Poland was completely dismembered and divided among Russia, Prussia, and Austria. Part erected by Napoleon, 1807–15, as Grand Duchy of Warsaw. See kingdom and republic of POLAND, below.
2 A kingdom in E Europe under the Russian crown, established by the Congress of Vienna 1815 from part of the Grand Duchy of Warsaw; called also **Congress Poland** or **Russian Poland**; ab. 49,000 sq. m.; ✳ Warsaw. Organized as autonomous kingdom of Poland in personal union with Russia 1815–30; lost autonomy after Polish Revolt 1830–31; after unsuccessful rising of Jan. 1863, became merely a Russian province; invaded by Germans and Austrians in World War I 1914–18; proclaimed independent republic 1918. See republic of POLAND, below.
3 *Pol.* **Pol'ska** (pôl'skä). Republic, cen. Europe, Baltic Sea to Carpathian Mts.; 150,459 sq. m.; pop. (1939 est.) 34,775,000; ✳ Warsaw. Bounded (1946) on N by the

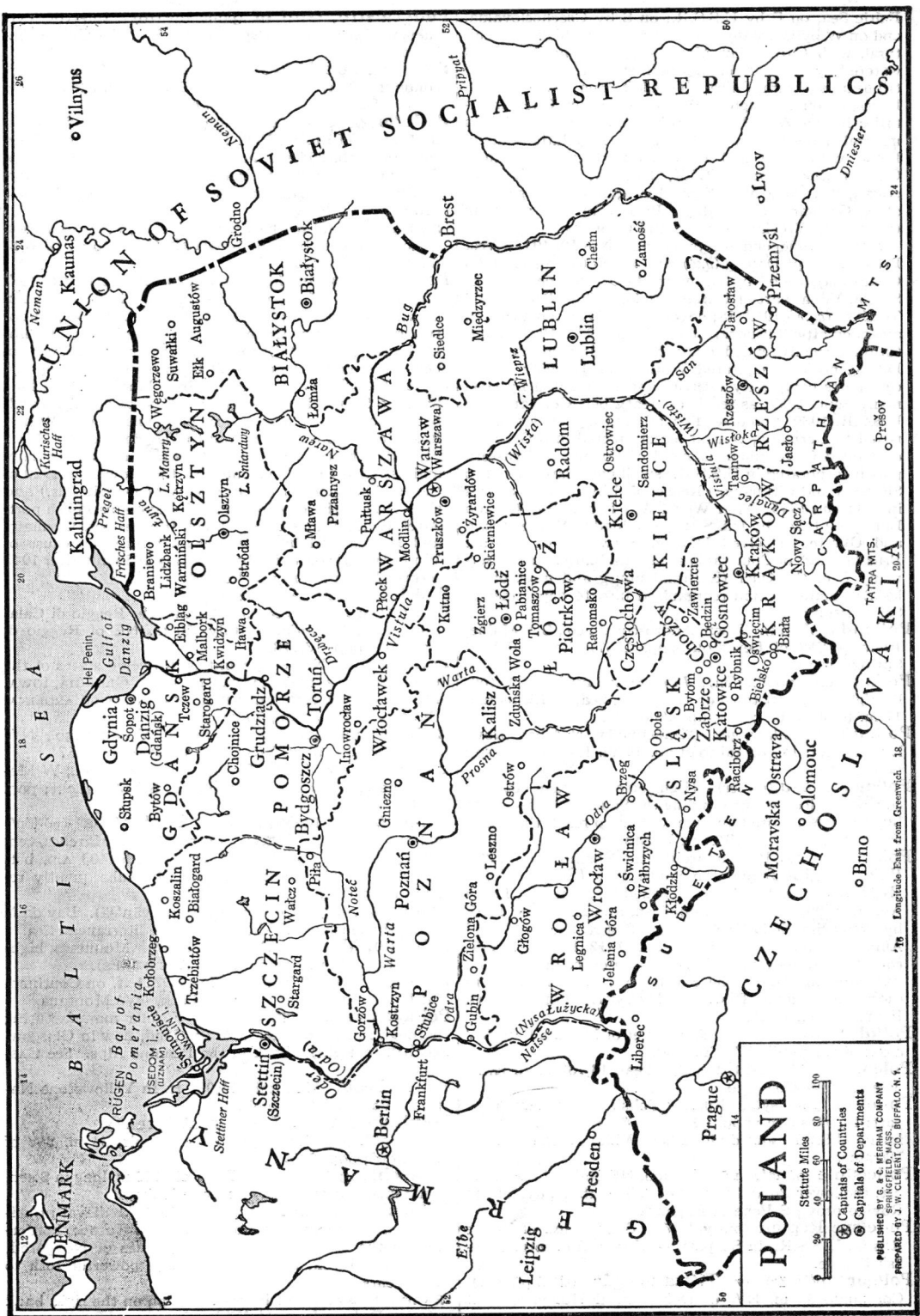

POLAND

Statute Miles

⊛ Capitals of Countries
⊚ Capitals of Departments

PUBLISHED BY G. & C. MERRIAM COMPANY
SPRINGFIELD, MASS.
PREPARED BY J. W. CLEMENT CO., BUFFALO, N. Y.

Baltic Sea, on E by U.S.S.R., on S by Czechoslovakia, and on W by Germany. A level country, chiefly agricultural, with Carpathian Mts. along its S border. Well watered by the Vistula (its main stream) and its many tributaries (Bzura, Pilica, on the left; Bug, San, Wisłoka. Dunajec, on the right), Warta and other Oder tributaries in the W. Has extensive forests and is rich in mineral deposits, esp. coal and oil. Population chiefly Poles, with Jews and Germans next in importance. Chief towns Warsaw, Łódź, Kraków, Poznań, Bydgoszcz, Katowice, and Częstochowa; and the large cities of E Germany assigned to Poland in 1945: Stettin (Szczecin), Wrocław, Zabrze, and Chorzów.

History: Independence proclaimed Nov. 9, 1918; West Prussia, except Danzig (*q.v.*), and Posen (see also POLISH CORRIDOR), ceded by Germany 1919; obtained part of Silesia, Vilna, part of Ukraine and of White Russia, and Teschen (*qq.v.*) 1919–38; governed by 1921 constitution, amended after Pilsudski's coup d'état 1926; 1935 constitution formally ended democratic parliamentary rule; Danzig crisis precipitated World War II 1939; E and cen. parts completely overrun and subjugated by Germany Sept. 1939; as result of treaty bet. Germany and U.S.S.R. 1939, Pomorze, Poznań, and Upper Silesia annexed to Germany, central sector erected into German-controlled Government-General of Poland, and eastern part incorporated in U.S.S.R.; small parts later ceded to Slovakia and Lithuania. Reoccupied by Russian armies in 1944 and 1945. After World War II part E of Curzon Line (*q.v.*) taken by U.S.S.R. and added to White Russia and Ukraine; received Danzig, S two thirds of East Prussia, most of Pomerania along the Baltic, and E Germany E of the Oder (E Brandenburg and most of Silesia); administration reorganized into 14 departments. See NEISSE river.

Po′land (pō′lănd). Town, Androscoggin co., SW Maine, 10 m. WSW of Lewiston; pop. 1537; site of Poland Spring; resort.

Po·lang′en (pō·läng′ĕn); *Lithuanian* **Pa·lan′ga** (pä-läng′gä). Seaport town on the Baltic Sea, W Lithuania, 17 m. N of Memel; pop. ab. 4000.

Po·lan′gui (pō·läng′gē). Municipality, N Albay prov., Luzon, Phil. Is., on railroad ab. 19 m. NW of Legaspi; pop. 21,086.

Po′lar Plateau (pō′lẽr). High region, average 6000 ft., covered by icecap, surrounding the South Pole; ascended by Roald Amundsen and party, first to reach the South Pole, Dec. 1911. See POLAR REGIONS.

Polar Regions. Regions around the North Pole (**North Polar Regions**) and the South Pole (**South Polar Regions**); North Pole first reached by Robert E. Peary Apr. 6, 1909, by Byrd, Amundsen, and Ellsworth 1926, by Otto Schmidt 1937; South Pole first reached by Roald Amundsen Dec. 14, 1911, by Scott 1912, by Byrd 1929; conditions of extreme cold and fields of ice are of much wider extent around the South Pole. See ARCTIC REGIONS, ANTARCTIC REGIONS, MAGNETIC POLE, SOUTH POLE, NORTH POLE.

Pol′dhu Cove (pŏl′dū). Small inlet of Mounts Bay, SW coast of Cornwall, SW England.

Pole Creek Mountain (pōl). Peak 13,737 ft. in Hinsdale co., SW Colorado.

Po·le′sie (pō·lĕ′syĕ). Former Polish department, in E part; 14,169 sq. m.; pop. 1,131,359; ✷ Brest Litovsk; now in the U.S.S.R. and divided bet. White Russia and the Ukraine.

Po·le′si·ne (pō·lä′zĕ·nä). Region, NE Italy, the lowland bet. the lower Po and the lower Adige, ab. equivalent to Rovigo prov., S Venezia Euganea.

Po·le′sye Region (pŭ·lyä′syĕ). Subdivision of White Russia, U.S.S.R., in SE part, ✷ Mozyr; E of former Polish Polesie.

Pol′gár (pŏl′gär) *or* **Ti′sza·pol′gár** (tǐ′sŏ·pŏl′gär). Commune 35 m. NW of Debrecen, E Hungary, E of Tisza river; pop. 14,097.

Po·li·ca′stro, Gulf of (pō·lē·käs′trō). Inlet of Tyrrhenian Sea in SW coast of Italy, S of the Gulf of Salerno.

Po·li·gna′no a Ma′re (pō·lē·nyä′nō ä mä′rå). Seaport commune, Bari prov., Apulia, SE Italy, on the Adriatic 21 m. ESE of Bari; pop. 16,677; fisheries.

Po·lil′lo (pō·lē′yō). **1** Group of islands in Pacific Ocean off E coast of Luzon, Phil. Is., on N side of Lamon Bay; total area ab. 297 sq. m.; pop. 8084; comprises Polillo, Jomalig, Patnanongan, Palasan, and ab. 17 islets; formerly a part of Infanta dist., now a part of Tayabas prov.
2 Largest island of the group, 14°45′N, separated from Luzon mainland by **Polillo Strait** (36 m. long, 12 to 18 m. wide); 234 sq. m.

Po′ling′miao′ (bō′lǐng′myou′) *or* **Pai′ling′miao′** (bī′-lǐng′myou′). Mongol trading town, N cen. Suiyuan prov., cen. Inner Mongolia, N China; separation point of two great western trade routes, one WNW to Dzhibkhalantu (Uliassutai) and Dzhirgalantu (Kobdo) in Outer Mongolia, the other W to towns of Sinkiang.

Polish Corridor. A narrow strip of land ab. 90 m. long by 25 to 55 m. wide in N part of Pomorze dept., Poland, bet. former German provinces of Pomerania on W and East Prussia on E, extending to Danzig and the Baltic Sea. By Treaty of Versailles 1919 taken from Germany and assigned to Poland but with the provisions 1920 of the establishment of the Free City of Danzig (*q.v.*) and after 1921 of the development of Gdynia as Polish port. After World War I caused much friction bet. Germany and Poland and in 1939 was an immediate cause of World War II; occupied by Germany 1939 but after 1945 returned with Danzig to Poland.

Polish Silesia. See SILESIA.

Po·li′ste·na (pō·lês′tä·nä). Commune, Reggio di Calabria prov., Calabria, S Italy, 30 m. NE of Reggio di Calabria; pop. 13,118.

Polk (pōk). **1** Name of counties in twelve states of the U.S. See *Tables* at ARKANSAS, FLORIDA, GEORGIA, IOWA, MINNESOTA, MISSOURI, NEBRASKA, NORTH CAROLINA, OREGON, TENNESSEE, TEXAS, WISCONSIN.
2 Residential borough and resort, Venango co., NW Pennsylvania, 13 m. WSW of Oil City; pop. 3574.

Pol·la′chi (pō·lä′chǐ). Town, Coimbatore dist., W Madras state, S Indian Union, 90 m. SE of Calicut; pop. 22,112.

Pol·len′za (pōl·lĕn′tsä); *anc.* **Pol·len′ti·a** (pō·lĕn′-shǐ·å). Commune, Macerata prov., S cen. Marches, cen. Italy; pop. (1931) 5142; scene of battle 403 A.D. bet. Stilicho and Goths under Alaric who subsequently retired from Italy.

Pol·len′za, Bay of (pō·lyän′thä; pō·yän′sä). Bay on N coast of the island of Majorca, W Mediterranean Sea.

Pol·li′no, Mon′te (mŏn′tå pōl·lē′nō). Mountain, highest in Lucanian Apennines (see APENNINES).

Pol′lock, Mount (pŏl′ŭk). Peak 9211 ft. on Continental Divide in Glacier National Park, NW Montana.

Pol′lok·shaws′ (pŏl′ŭk·shôz′). Former manufacturing borough in Renfrew co., SW Scotland, now in Glasgow.

Pol′lux (pŏl′ŭks). Peak in the Pennine Alps. See CASTOR.

Pollux Peak. Mountain 11,081 ft. in Yellowstone National Park, NW Wyoming.

Polnisch–Ostrau. See SLEZSKÁ OSTRAVA.

Po′lo (pō′lō). City, Ogle co., N Illinois, 34 m. SW of Rockford; pop. 2551.

Po·lo·chic′ (pō′lō·chēk′). River ab. 180 m. long in S cen. Guatemala; flows ESE into Lake Izabal.

Po′lotsk (pō′lŏtsk; *Russ.* pŏ′lŭtsk). **1** Medieval principality in the region S of Lake Peipus, N Europe, bordering on the other medieval principalities of Novgorod, Smolensk, Pinsk, and Volhynia; esp. powerful 10th to 12th cents.
2 City, its ✷ and ✷ of Polotsk Region, on the right bank of the Dvina river, N White Russia, U.S.S.R.; pop.

24,816. One of the oldest cities of Russia, granted 862 by Rurik to his followers; as capital of the principality a city of 100,000 population and a great trade center. Has had long and varied history; came under Lithuanians 1320; in 16th cent. besieged five times by Russians and captured by Ivan the Terrible 1563; became Polish 1579 and its influence reduced by plague and fires; annexed by Russia 1772 and partly destroyed by French 1812; in World War II taken by Germans Aug. 21, 1941; retaken by Russians July 4, 1944.

Polotsk Region. Region, N White Russia, U.S.S.R.; borders on Latvia on NW and on Velikie Luki Region of R.S.F.S.R. on NE; * Polotsk.

Polska. See POLAND republic.

Pol′son (pŏl′s'n). City, ⊗ of Lake co., NW Montana, on S end of Flathead Lake; pop. 2314; trade center in agricultural section.

Pol·ta′va (pŭl·tä′vȧ). 1 Region, E cen. Ukraine, U.S.S.R., crossed by the Psel and Vorskla tributaries of the Dnieper.
2 City, its *, on right bank of Vorskla river 85 m. WSW of Kharkov; pop. 130,305; center of an agricultural district in black-earth region; raises grains, sugar beets, tobacco, fruits, and serves as a grain-collection point; specializes in leather manufactures. In origin dates back to 12th cent.; given to Tatar prince in 1430 by Lithuania and was later a Cossack stronghold under Chmielnicki; scene of victory July 8, 1709 of the Russians under Peter the Great over the Swedes under Charles XII; battle marked the beginning of Russian influence in Europe; in World War II held by Germans from Sept. 1941 to Sept. 23, 1943.

Poltoratsk. See ASHKHABAD.

Po·lyar′ny (pŭ·lyȧr′nĭ); *formerly* **A·le·ksan′drovsk** (ŭ·lyĭ·ksȧn′drŭĭsk). Small ice-free port at mouth of Tuloma river, NW Murmansk Region, Soviet Russia, Europe; now largely replaced as a port by Murmansk.

Po·lyg′y·ros (pȯ·lĭj′ĭ·rȯs); *Mod. Gr.* **Po·lý′gy·ros** (pô-lyē′yĕ·rôs). Town, * of Chalcidice dept., S Macedonia, NE Greece; pop. 2477; in center of peninsula ab. 30 m. SE of Salonika.

Pol′y·ne′sia (pŏl′ĭ·nē′zhȧ; -zhĭ·ȧ; -shȧ; -shĭ·ȧ). Islands of the cen. Pacific Ocean, bet. 30°N and 47°S lat.; a subdivision of Oceania. They include the large islands of New Zealand and the groups of the Hawaiian Is., Samoa, Line Is., French Polynesia, Cook Is., Phoenix Is., Ellice Is., Tonga, and Easter I. See *Map* at OCEANIA. The islands are mostly small; many are coral atolls, others are of volcanic origin. The greater part of the inhabitants are Polynesians, a brown race, perhaps related to the Malay, but many are of mixed origin. Their languages belong to a subfamily of the Austronesian languages. Foremost representatives are the Hawaiians, Maoris, Marquesans, Samoans, Tongans, and Tahitians.

Pom′er·a′nia (pŏm′ēr·ān′yȧ; -ā′nĭ·ȧ); *Ger.* **Pom′mern** (pôm′ērn). 1 Historical region on Baltic Sea, at its greatest extent comprising the territory bet. Stralsund and the Vistula and including Rügen I. Occupied by Slavic and other peoples, entire area bet. Oder and Vistula conquered by Boleslav III of Poland 1119–23; in 12th cent. western part steadily penetrated by Germans who erected duchy of Pomerania (included territory on both banks of the lower Oder); eastern part (see POMERELIA) came to be held by Teutonic Knights and was ceded to Poland 1466 as part of West Prussia. Duchy came under suzerainty of Brandenburg which divided it with Sweden 1648, keeping the part E of the Oder, **Farther Pomerania** (*Ger.* **Hin′ter·pom′mern** [hĭn′tēr·pôm′ērn]), and giving to Sweden **Hither Pomerania** (*Ger.* **Vor′pom′mern** [fōr′pôm′ērn]), including both banks of the Oder as well as territory to the W, with Rügen I. and Usedom I.; Sweden ceded S part of Hither Pomerania to Prussia 1720, keeping N part, **Swedish Pomerania** (the island of Rügen and the adjoining territory on the mainland N of the Peene river),

until 1815 when she ceded it also to Prussia. Invaded and conquered by Russians Mar.–Apr. 1945; the section E of the Oder (but including Stettin, mainly on left bank) assigned to Poland by the Potsdam Conference 1945.
2 *Ger.* **Pom′me·rel′len** (pôm′ĕ·rĕl′ĕn). Department of Poland. See POMORZE.
3 Former province of Prussia. See *Table* at PRUSSIA.

Pomerania, Bay of; *Ger.* **Pom′mer·sche Bucht** (pôm′ēr·shĕ bŏŏkt). Widemouthed inlet of Baltic Sea bet. NE Germany and NW Poland, N of Stettin.

Pom′er·e′lia (pŏm′ēr·ēl′yȧ; -ē′lĭ·ȧ); *Ger.* **Pom′me·rel′len** (pôm′ĕ·rĕl′ĕn). Ancient region on the Baltic Sea W of the Vistula; originally part of Pomerania (*q.v.*) but gradually became separated from it and was distinct from it when the duchy of Pomerania was created in 12th cent.; came under Teutonic Knights; ceded to Poland 1466; at partitions of Poland in 18th cent. went to Prussia; to Poland again 1918 and included in Pomorze (*q.v.*) dept.

Pom′er·oy (pŏm′ēr·oi; pŏm′′roi). 1 Village, ⊗ of Meigs co., SE Ohio, on Ohio river 38 m. SW of Marietta; pop. 3345; settled 1816; coal mines, salt wells; manufactures metal and wooden articles, oil-well supplies, chemicals.
2 City, ⊗ of Garfield co., SE Washington, 27 m. SW of Pullman; pop. 1677; grain (wheat), dairy, stock farms, fruit.

Pom′fret (pŭm′frĕt; -frĭt). Residential town and summer resort, N cen. Windham co., NE Connecticut, WSW of Putnam; pop. 2136; incorporated 1713; Pomfret School (1894; boys preparatory school).

Po·mi·glia′no d'Ar′co (pȯ·mē·lyä′nȯ där′kȯ). Commune, Napoli prov., Campania, S Italy, at N foot of Vesuvius 8 m. NE of Naples; pop. 13,907.

Pom′mel Peak (pŭm′ĕl; pŏm′-). Mountain 6630 ft. in S Brewster co., W Texas.

Pommerellen. 1 See POMERELIA.
2 See POMORZE.

Pommern. See POMERANIA.

Pommersche Bucht. See Bay of POMERANIA.

Pom′mer·sche Haff (pôm′ēr·shĕ häf). = STETTINER HAFF.

Po·mo′na (pȯ·mō′nȧ). 1 City, Los Angeles co., SW California, 25 m. E of Los Angeles; pop. 67,157; commercial and shipping center; citrus fruit canneries; oil refineries; manufactures pumps, paint, tile; residential city and health resort. Founded 1875, incorp. 1887.
2 or **Main′land′** (mān′lănd′; -lănd). Largest of the Orkney Is., off N coast of Scotland; 190 sq. m.; pop. 13,352; chief towns Kirkwall and Stromness.

Po·mo′rze (pȯ·mô′zhĕ); *Eng.* **Pom′er·a′nia** (pŏm′ēr·ān′yȧ; -ā′nĭ·ȧ); *Ger.* **Pom′me·rel′len** (pôm′ĕ·rĕl′ĕn). Polish department, in N part; 9920 sq. m.; pop. 1,086,259; * Toruń; formed 1918 from E part of Prussian province of Pomerania; as reorganized after World War II increased in size, in N cen. part on both sides of lower Vistula, S of Gdańsk dept. and NE of Poznań, * Bydgoszcz. See POMERELIA.

Pomorze Za·chod′nie (zä·кȯd′nyĕ). Department, NW Poland, before World War II in Pomerania prov., Prussia, Germany; now called Szczecin (*q.v.*).

Pompaelo. See PAMPLONA.

Pom′pa·no Beach, *formerly* **Pom′pa·no** (pŏm′pȧ·nō). City, Broward co., SE Florida, near Atlantic Ocean 32 m. N of Miami; pop. 15,992; incorporated 1927; truck gardening; fishing. Moved inland from the coast after suffering damage in hurricane 1928.

Pom·pe′i (pŏm′pā′ē; *Angl.* pŏm·pā′ē, -pā′); *before 1928* **Val′le di Pom·pe′i** (väl′lā dĕ pŏm·pā′ē). Commune, Napoli prov., Campania, S Italy, 14 m. ESE of Naples; pop. 11,792; much-visited pilgrimage church (Santuario della Madonna del Rosario); geophysical observatory; mineral springs; near ancient Pompeii (*q.v.*).

Pom·pe′ii (pŏm·pā′ē; -pā′; -pē′[y]ĭ). Ancient city, Campania, S Italy, 15 m. SE of Naples near the foot of

Mt. Vesuvius and near Herculaneum (*q.v.*); founded late 6th cent. or early 5th cent. B.C. by Oscans (though the Greeks considered its founder to be Hercules); completely under Rome by 80 B.C.; became site of many villas belonging to Roman nobility and when it was destroyed by the eruption of Vesuvius 79 A.D. Pliny the Elder was one of the victims; more than half of the city has been excavated, revealing its regular plan, the forum, temples, baths, theaters, and many dwellings.

Pomp′ton (pŏm[p]′tŭn). River, N New Jersey; formed at Pompton just S of Pompton Lakes by confluence of Pequannock, Ramapo, and Ringwood rivers, flows S into Passaic river.

Pompton Lakes. Borough, Passaic co., N New Jersey, 9 m. NW of Paterson; pop. 9445; settled by Dutch 1682; formerly had iron furnaces; truck farming; manufactures electric blasting batteries and metallic caps, textiles; site of Washington's headquarters.

Po′na·pe (pō′nȧ·pā); formerly **As·cen′sion** (ă·sĕn′shŭn). Island of the Senyavin Is. group in E part of the Caroline Is., W Pacific Ocean, 410 m. E of Truk I.; 134 sq. m.; pop. (1938 est.) 11,467. One of the largest islands of the cen. Pacific, very fertile and hilly; surrounded by a barrier reef enclosing many small islands. Has settlements all around the coast, but practically uninhabited in the interior. Notable for its many ruins of an earlier race. In World War II its garrison of 10,000 Japanese bypassed by Allies 1944.

Pon′ca (pŏng′kȧ). City, ⊗ of Dixon co., NE Nebraska; pop. 924.

Ponca City. City, Kay co., N Oklahoma, on Arkansas river 52 m. ENE of Enid; pop. 24,411; oil refining, farming, stock raising, flour milling; oil and gas wells, grain elevators; meat-packing plants.

Pon′ce (pŏn′sȧ). Municipality (pop. 145,586) and seaport city (pop. 114,286), S Puerto Rico; 3d largest city in Puerto Rico; excellent harbor; considerable import and export trade; ships sugar, tobacco, fruit, and lace goods; manufactures cotton goods and tobacco products.

Ponce de Le′on Bay (pŏns′ dĕ lē′ŭn). Inlet of Gulf of Mexico on SW coast of Florida, from Cape Sable to Cape Romano.

Pon′cha·tou′la (pŏn′chȧ·tōō′lȧ). Town, Tangipahoa parish, SE Louisiana, 41 m. NNW of New Orleans; pop. 4727; shipping point for area producing vegetables and berries, esp. strawberries.

Pon′der·a′ (pŏn′dĕr·ā′). County in Montana. See *Table* at MONTANA.

Pon′di·cher′ry (pŏn′dĭ·chĕr′ĭ; -shĕr′ĭ); *Fr.* **Pon′di′-ché′ry′** (pôN′dē′shā′rē′). 1 Chief settlement of former French India, on Coromandel Coast 90 m. S of Madras completely surrounded by South Arcot dist.; 112 sq. m.; pop. (1941) 204,653. Under the French ruled by a governor, with privy council and general council, and represented in French National Assembly; to India 1954. 2 Seaport and chief town of settlement, ✳ of French India; pop. (1941) 53,101; an open roadstead but with good trade; has textile industry. Site acquired 1674 but first permanent settlement made 1683 by François Martin; held by Dutch 1693–97; several times taken by British 1761, 1778, 1793, 1803 but each time restored; finally 1816 permanently restored.

Pon′do (pŏn′dō). Village on N coast of New Britain I. at E end 45 m. SW of Rabaul, Bismarck Archipelago, W Pacific Ocean; center for drying copra.

Pon′do·land (pŏn′dō·lănd′). One of the Transkeian Territories, E Cape Province, S Union of South Africa, on coast of Indian Ocean bet. Umtata river and Natal border (Umtamvuna river); 3906 sq. m.; pop. 331,374; ✳ Port St. Johns. Inhabited by Pondos, a Bantu race akin to the Zulus. Annexed to Cape Colony 1894.

Ponente, Riviera di. See RIVIERA.

Ponevyezh. See PANEVEZHIS.

Pon′fer·ra′da (pōm′fĕr·rä′thä). Commune, León prov.,

NW Spain, 50 m. W by S of León; pop. 13,008.

Pon′go de Man′se·ri′che (pông′gŏ thä män′sȧ·rē′chä). Canyon ab. 2000 ft. deep through which the Marañón river flows after its big curve around to the E in N Peru; flow is very rapid and the gorge narrows to as little as 100-ft. width in places (*pongo* = narrows).

Pon·go′la (pŏng·gō′lȧ). River ab. 120 m. long flowing bet. SE Transvaal and N Natal, Union of South Africa; unites with Usutu river to form Maputo river in Mozambique.

Pon·na′ni (pô·nä′nĭ). 1 River 120 m. long, W Madras and cen. Kerala states, S Indian Union; flows W to Arabian Sea at Ponnani; part of its course forms N boundary of Cochin. 2 Seaport town at mouth of river, 38 m. S of Calicut; pop. 16,210; here Tipu Sahib was repulsed by British Nov. 1782.

Po′no·ro′go (pō′nô·rō′gō). Market town, East Java prov., Indonesia, 20 m. S of Madiun; pop. 21,680.

Pons Aelii. See NEWCASTLE UPON TYNE.

Pon·son′ (pôn·sôn′). Island, easternmost of Camotes Is., Cebu prov., Phil. Is.; 13 sq. m.; pop. 8142; coextensive with municipality of Pilar.

Pons Vetus. See PONTEVEDRA.

Pon′ta Del·ga′da (pōNN′tȧ thäl·gȧ′thȧ). 1 District of Portugal. See *Table* at PORTUGAL. 2 Fortified seaport commune, its ✳, in Azores on SW coast of São Miguel I.; chief town of Azores; pop. (1940) 21,048; winter resort; trades, esp. with Britain, in tea, earthenware, hats, spirits, wheat, corn, oranges.

Pon′ta Gros′sa (pōNN′tȧ grô′sȧ). City, Paraná state, S Brazil, 60 m. WNW of Curitiba; pop. (1940 est.) 29,864.

Pont-à-Mous′son′ (pôN′-tȧ·mōō′sôN′). Industrial commune, Meurthe-et-Moselle dept., NE France, on Moselle river 12 m. NNW of Nancy; pop. 11,343; manufactures hardware. Founded in 13th cent.; university founded here 1572 (transferred to Nancy 1768); taken by Louis XIII 1632; a front-line position in World War I, held by the French from Sept. 1914; starting point of Americans in battle of St-Mihiel Sept. 12, 1918.

Pon′tar′lier′ (pôN′tȧr′lyā′). Manufacturing commune, Doubs dept., E France, on Doubs river near Swiss border 29 m. SSE of Besançon; pop. 12,840; manufactures distilled liquors, clocks; trades in dairy products.

Pon′tas·sie′ve (pôn′täs·syä′vȧ). Commune, Firenze prov., Tuscany, cen. Italy, on the Arno 10 m. E of Florence; pop. 15,000.

Pont–Au′de·mer′ (pôN′-tōd′mâr′). Commune, Eure dept., N France, ab. 39 m. NW of Évreux; pop. 5636; a river port on the Risle, a tributary of the Seine.

Pont–A′ven′ (pôN′-tȧ′vĕn′). Village at head of estuary on coast of Bay of Biscay, Finistère dept., Brittany, NW France, ab. 18 m. WNW of Lorient; pop. of commune 1678; artist colony.

Pont′char·train′, Lake (pŏn′chĕr·trān′). Lake in SE Louisiana; ab. 40 m. long, 600 sq. m.; connected through Lake Borgne with Gulf of Mexico, and by canal with Mississippi river. The city of New Orleans lies bet. it and the Mississippi river.

Pont du Fahs (pôN′ dü fäs′). Town, N Tunisia, N Africa, ab. 12 m. W of Zaghouan; battles Apr.–May 1943.

Pon′te·cor′vo (pôn′tä·kôr′vô). Commune, Frosinone prov., Latium, cen. Italy, 21 m. SE of Frosinone; pop. 14,437; a former principality; largely destroyed in World War II.

Pon′te·de′ra (pôn′tä·dā′rä). Commune, Pisa prov., Tuscany, cen. Italy, on the Arno 13 m. ESE of Pisa; pop. 17,890.

Pon′te·fract (pŏn′tĕ·frăkt; *locally also* pŭm′frĕt, -frĭt, pŏm′-). Municipal borough, West Riding, Yorkshire, N England, near confluence of Aire and Calder rivers 13 m. SE of Leeds; pop. 23,173; site of ancient castle, scene of the death of King Richard II 1400; noted for Pomfret cakes (licorice).

Pon′te No′va (pōNn′tĕ nô′và). City, SE cen. Minas Gerais state, E Brazil; pop. (1940 est.) 11,950; railroad junction point 65 m. SE of Belo Horizonte.

Pon′te·ve′dra (pôn′tå-vä′thrä). 1 Municipality, W Negros Occidental, Negros, Phil. Is., on Guimaras Strait 20 m. S of City of Bacolod; pop. 20,495.
2 Municipality, NE Capiz prov., Panay, Phil. Is., just W of head of Pilar Bay 13 m. SE of Capiz; pop. 23,241.
3 Province of Spain. See *Table* at SPAIN.
4 anc. **Pons Ve′tus** (pŏnz vē′tŭs). Commune, ✳ of Pontevedra prov., NW Spain, on inlet of Atlantic Ocean 65 m. SW of Lugo; pop. 36,968; sardines, hats, leather, pottery, nitric acid; cattle shipping; Gothic church.

Pon′thier′ville′ (pôN′tyä′vēl′). Town, S Stanleyville prov., NE Congo, on the Congo river; river navigation terminus above Stanley Falls.

Pon′thieu′ (pôN′tyû′). Ancient region in N France, in Picardy; ✳ Abbeville; became countship at end of 9th cent.; passed to Castile 1251; held by England (acquired through marriage of Eleanor of Castile to Edward I) 1272–1336, 1360–69; finally to French crown 1690.

Pon′ti·ac (pŏn′tĭ-ăk). 1 City, ⊗ of Livingston co., NE cen. Illinois, 35 m. NNE of Bloomington; pop. 8435; creameries, incubators, farm-implement works; state penitentiary. Settled c. 1830; platted 1837, incorp. as village 1856, as city 1872.
2 City, ⊗ of Oakland co., SE Michigan, 25 m. NNW of Detroit; pop. 82,233; manufactures automobiles, rubber goods, automobile accessories, machinery, varnish; trade center for summer resort region. Settled 1818; chartered as city 1861.
3 County, Quebec, Canada. See *Table* at QUEBEC.

Pontiae. See PONTINE ISLANDS.

Pon′ti·a′nak (pŏn′tē-ä′näk). City, W Borneo, Indonesia, at mouth of small stream on N edge of Kapuas delta; pop. 45,196; large trading port and distributing center for West Borneo region; exports coconuts, rubber, sago, and forest products, also gold; has large Chinese population; located almost exactly on the equator (2′S). Formerly seat of a sultanate and as early as 13th cent. had relations with China; occupied by Japanese Feb. 2, 1942.

Pon′ti·cel′li (pŏn′tē-chĕl′lĕ). Former commune in Napoli prov., Campania, S Italy, now part of Naples; pop. (1931) 15,846.

Pon′tine (pŏn′tēn; -tīn), or **Pon·zia′ne** (pôn·tsyä′nå), **Islands**; anc. **Pon′ti·ae** (pŏn′shĭ-ē). Island group in Tyrrhenian Sea W of Naples; administratively a part of Napoli prov., Campania, Italy; pop. (1931) 6827; chief islands **Pon′za** (pŏn′tsä) and **Pon·ti′ne** (pŏn·tē′nå); used as a place of banishment in ancient times and again under Mussolini.

Pon′tine Marshes (pŏn′tēn; -tīn). District, SW Latium, cen. Italy; bounded on N by the Lepini Mts., separated from sea by low sand hills which prevent natural drainage; for many centuries an unhealthful region of malarial swamps; traversed by the Appian Way, built 312 B.C. when first attempts at drainage were made; most recent reclamation projects begun 1926 under Mussolini; region now comprises the new province of Littoria (see *Table* at ITALY) and has several cities, esp. Littoria (*q.v.*) and **Pon·ti′nia** (pŏn·tē′nyä). In SE part on a promontory which in ancient times seems to have been an island is Monte Circeo (*q.v.*); possibly the region was once all under water.

Pon′ti·vy′ (pôn′tē′vē′). Town, Morbihan dept., NW France, ab. 30 m. NNW of Vannes; pop. 6375; made military headquarters of Brittany by Napoleon who constructed a new town which was known as Napoléonville and which in layout remains quite distinct from the old town.

Pont–l′Ab′bé′ (pôn′lå′bā′). Town, Finistère dept., NW France, ab. 12 m. SW of Quimper; pop. 5309; Bretons of the region are called the Bigouden from the name of the distinctive headdress of the women.

Pont l′É′vêque′ (pôn′ lä′vâk′). Town, Calvados dept., NW France, 25 m. NE of Caen; pop. 2317; noted for its cheese.

Pon′toise′ (pôn′twàz′); anc. **Bri′va Is′a·rae** (brī′và ĭs′à-rē) and **Pon·tis′a·rae** (pŏn·tĭs′à-rē). Commune, Seine-et-Oise dept., N France, on Oise river 18 m. NNW of Paris; pop. 12,183; trades in grain and flour. Owes origin to Celtic bridge built here; joined to crown 1082; made commune 1188; numerous sieges in 14th, 15th, and 16th cents.; States-General met here 1561; seat of parliament 1652, 1720, 1753.

Pon′tor′son′ (pôn′tôr′sôn′). Town, SW Manche dept., Normandy, NW France, ab. 12 m. SW of Avranches; pop. 2266; starting point for excursions to Mont-Saint-Michel; taken by Americans Aug. 1, 1944.

Pon′to·toc (pŏn′tō-tŏk). 1 Name of counties in two states of the U.S. See *Tables* at MISSISSIPPI and OKLAHOMA.
2 City, ⊗ of Pontotoc co., N Mississippi, 17 m. W of Tupelo; pop. 2108; in agricultural section.

Pon·tre′mo·li (pŏn·trâ′mô-lê). Commune, Apuania prov., Tuscany, cen. Italy, 28 m. NNW of Apuania; pop. 14,537; 17th-cent. cathedral.

Pont Rouge (pôn′ rōōzh′). Village, Portneuf co., S Quebec, Canada, on Jacques Cartier river and on railroad 25 m. W of Quebec; pop. 2413.

Pont–Saint–Es′prit′ (pôn′săn′-tĕs′prē′). Town, Gard dept., S France; pop. 3290; on the Rhone which is here crossed by a 13th–14th cent. bridge 1000 yards long, built by friars, widened in 1860.

Pon′tus (pŏn′tŭs). 1 Ancient country in NE Asia Minor, originally that part of Cappadocia along the shore of Pontus Euxinus (Black Sea) E of Halys river; ancient ✳ Amasia. As kingdom, bounded on E and SE by Armenia, on S by Cappadocia, and on W by Galatia and Paphlagonia. Mountainous, watered by Iris river. Kingdom established 4th cent. B.C. by Ariobarzanes II and continued with expanding borders until 66 B.C. when its last king, Mithridates the Great, was overcome by Pompey; annexed as province of Roman Empire 62 B.C. Christianity introduced in first century A.D. Chief cities Trapezus (see TRABZON), Amasia, Cerasus, and Cotyora.
2 or **Pontus Euxinus.** See BLACK SEA.

Pon′ty·pool′ (pŏn′tĭ-pōōl′). Urban district, Monmouthshire, W England, on the Afon Llwydd 25 m. NW of Bristol; pop. 42,683; in a coal-mining, ironworking, and tinplate-manufacturing section.

Pon′ty·pridd′ (pŏn′tĭ-prĕth′; -prĭd′). Urban district, Glamorganshire, SE Wales; pop. 38,622; coal mines, iron foundries, chain works.

Ponza, Ponziane Islands. See PONTINE ISLANDS.

Poole (pōōl). Municipal borough, Dorsetshire, S England, on English Channel 40 m. W of Portsmouth; pop. 57,211; (1951 pop.) 82,958; fishing and yachting center; manufactures pottery.

Poo′na (pōō′nå). 1 Former district, Central Division, Bombay prov., W Indian Union; 5347 sq. m.; pop. (1941) 1,359,408.
2 City, its ✳, on tributary of Bhima river 80 m. ESE of Bombay; pop., with cantonments and suburbs, (1941) 258,197; has rice and sugar refineries, ironworks, tanneries, and cotton and paper mills; radio station and airport. Residence of governor of Bombay during rainy season. Possesses numerous old palaces and temples, especially the temple of Parvati, and modern government buildings; headquarters of southern command with cantonment and arms and ammunition factory at suburb of Kirkee (4 m. NW); seat of various professional schools and educational institutions, including the government Deccan College. Given as fief in 1604 by sultan of Ahmadnagar to a Maratha chief, under whom it became capital of the Marathas; became British in 1818.

Poonch or **Punch** (pōōnch). Town, NW Jammu prov., Jammu and Kashmir state, N India, 45 m. SW of Srinagar; pop. 8152.

Po'o·pó', Lake (pō'ō·pō'). Lake 80 m. long in W cen. Bolivia; altitude ab. 12,000 ft., 505 ft. lower than Lake Titicaca; receives Desaguadero river from Lake Titicaca to the N.

Pootoo. See PUTO SHAN.

Pootung. See SHANGHAI.

Po'pa, Mount (pō'på). Extinct volcano 4981 ft. in cen. Burma, at N end of Pegu Yoma; highest point in the range.

Po'pa·yán' (pō'på·yän'). City, ✻ of Cauca dept., SW Colombia, S of Cali at foot of Mt. Puracé, in mining region; pop. 18,292; bet. the Cordillera Occidental and Cordillera Central ranges of the Andes at alt. 5700 ft.; a leading cultural center of Colombia. Founded 1536.

Pope (pōp). Name of counties in three states of the U.S. See *Tables* at ARKANSAS, ILLINOIS, MINNESOTA.

Po'pe·ring'e (pō'pĕ·rĭng'ĕ). Commune, West Flanders prov., NW Belgium, 7 m. W by N of Ieper (Ypres); pop. 11,605; in section producing hop and hemp; just behind British front line during World War I. Toc H, British association for Christian social service, founded here Dec. 1915.

Popes Creek (pōps). Small stream in Westmoreland co., Virginia, flowing into the Potomac; Wakefield, George Washington's birthplace, is on its left bank.

Pop'lar (pŏp'lẽr). **1** City, Roosevelt co., NE Montana, on Missouri river 70 m. E of Glasgow; pop. 1565.
2 Metropolitan borough of London. See *Table* at LONDON.

Poplar Bluff. City, ⊗ of Butler co., SE Missouri, 63 m. WSW of Cape Girardeau; pop. 15,926; trade center in agricultural section; woodworking plants; iron-ore and ceramic-clay deposits nearby.

Pop'lar·ville (pŏp'lẽr·vĭl; *Sou.* also -v'l). Town, ⊗ of Pearl River co., S Mississippi, 37 m. SSW of Hattiesburg; pop. 2136; tung oil, naval stores.

Popo, Grand. See GRAND POPO.

Po·po' Agie (pō·pō'zĭ·ĕ—*sic*). River, W cen. Wyoming; rises in Wind River Mts., SW Fremont co., flows NE and unites with Wind river to form Big Horn river.

Po·po'ca·te'petl (pō·pō'kä·tā'pĕt·'l; *Angl.* pō'pō·kăt'ĕ-pĕt''l). Volcano 17,887 ft. Puebla state, SE cen. Mexico, 30 m. W of Puebla; contains crater over ½ m. in circumference and 250 ft. deep.

Po'po·ma·na'siu, Mount (?pō'pō·má·nä'syŏō). Highest peak 8005 ft. in Kavo Mts. near S coast, Guadalcanal I., SE Solomon Is., W Pacific Ocean.

Pop'pels·dorf (pŏp'ĕls·dôrf). Former village, Rhine Province, Prussia, Germany, now part of Bonn.

Pöp'pen·dorf (pûp'ĕn·dôrf). Village, NW Germany, just NE of Lübeck, near the coast; refugee camp in British Zone 1947, chiefly for Jews.

Pop'pi (pŏp'pĕ; *Angl.* pŏp'ĕ). Commune, Arezzo prov., E Tuscany, cen. Italy, on Arno river; pop. (1931) 8911; birthplace of the sculptor Mino da Fiesole; castle.

Pop'u·lo'ni·um (pŏp'ū·lō'nĭ·ŭm; -lōn'yŭm); *mod.* **Pop'u·lo'ni·a** (-lō'nĭ·å; -lōn'yå). Ancient town of Etruria, Italy, on coast of Ligurian Sea N of Piombino; had metal manufactures (iron from Elba, tin, and copper); large part of walls remain, also tombs and a water reservoir; site of a medieval castle; besieged by Sulla 82 B.C.

Po'quis (pō'kĕs). Peak 18,832 ft. in E Antofagasta prov., N Chile, near Argentina boundary.

Porali. See PURALI.

Po'ra Po'ra (pōr'å pōr'å). = BORA BORA.

Por·ban'dar (pôr·bŭn'dẽr). **1** Former Indian state, SW Kathiawar, Western India States, India, on Arabian Sea; 642 sq. m.; pop. (1941) 146,648. Joined a new confederation of Indian states July 7, 1947 within the Indian Union.
2 Town, its ✻, on Arabian Sea 275 m. NW of Bombay; pop. 33,383; port with extensive trade coastwise and with East Africa and Iran. Birthplace of Mahatma Gandhi.

Por'cher Island (pôr'chẽr). Island off W British Columbia, Canada, N of Pitt I. and near mouth of Skeena river.

Por·cu'na (pôr·kōō'nä). Commune, Jaén prov., S Spain, 25 m. WNW of Jaén; pop. 13,493.

Por'cu·pine (pôr'kû·pīn). River ab. 400 m. long, N Yukon Territory, Canada, and NE Alaska; flows N then W to Yukon river at Fort Yukon, Alaska.

Porcupine Mountains *or* **Range.** Range in Gogebic and Ontonagon cos., NW extremity of upper Michigan penin.; highest point **Porcupine Mountain** 2023 ft., in Ontonagon co., also highest point in the state.

Por'de·no'ne (pôr'dā·nō'nä); *Ger.* **Por'te·nau** (pôr'tĕ-nou). Commune, Friuli prov., Venezia Euganea, NE Italy, 37 m. W by S of Udine; pop. 22,174; 15th-cent. cathedral, 13th-cent. Gothic town hall.

Po'reč (pō'rĕch); *Ital.* **Pa·ren'zo** (pä·rĕn'tsō). Commune in NW Yugoslavia, on coast of Istria Penin. 30 m. NNW of Pulj; pop. (1936) 12,036; 6th-cent. basilica; before 1947 belonged to Italy.

Porfirio Díaz. = *Ciudad Porfirio Díaz:* see PIEDRAS NEGRAS.

Po'ri (pō'rĭ); *Swed.* **Björ'ne·borg'** (byûr'nĕ·bôr'y'). Seaport, a ✻ of Turku-Pori dept., SW Finland; pop. (1939 est.) 20,700; shipping center; manufactures machinery, textiles, paper, matches, cellulose. See TURKU.

Pork'ka·la Peninsula (pôrk'kä·lä). Small tongue of land, S Finland, projecting into the Gulf of Finland ab. 19 m. W of Helsinki; ceded by Finland to Russia in exchange for Hangö 1944; returned to Finland 1956.

Por'la·mar' (pôr'lä·mär'). Port, Nueva Esparta state, Venezuela, chief town of Margarita I., in Caribbean Sea off N coast of Venezuela; pop. ab. 25,000.

Po'ro (pō'rō). Island, central island of Camotes group, Cebu prov., Phil. Is.; 39 sq. m.; pop. 18,223; coextensive with municipalities of Poro and Tudela.

Po·ron'gos (pō·rông'gōs). Salt swamp region in NE Córdoba prov., N cen. Argentina, N of Mar Chiquita; no outlet. Includes **La'go de los Pa'tos** (lä'gō thä lōs pä'tōs).

Po'ros (pō'rōs); *Mod. Gr.* **Pó'ros** (pō'rôs); *anc.* **Ca·lau'ri·a** (kå·lô'rĭ·å). Greek island in Saronic Gulf 7 m. S of Aegina near coast of Argolis; attached to Attica and Boeotia dept., Greece; 8 sq. m.; pop. 6449.

Por'que·rolles' (pôr'kĕ·rôl'). One of the Hyères Is. (*q.v.*).

Por'ren'truy' (pô'rän'trü·ē'). Commune, N Bern canton, Switzerland, ab. 27 m. SW of Basel; pop. (1930) 5805; watch manufacturing; customs station.

Pors'ang'er Fjord (pôrs'äng'ẽr). Inlet of Arctic Ocean on N coast of Norway; extends S inland 249 m.

Pors'grunn (pôrs'grōōn'). Seaport, Telemark co., S Norway, near coast NW of Larvik; pop. 8899; noted for its manufacture of porcelain; lumber, wood products.

Por·suk' (pôr·sōōk') *or* **Pur·sak'** (pōōr·säk'). River ab. 200 m. long in W Turkey in Asia; rises near Murat Daği and flows N and E into Sakarya river.

Port Ad'e·laide (ăd''l·ād). City, SE South Australia, on Gulf of St. Vincent at mouth of Torrens river; pop. 29,847; seaport of Adelaide.

Port'a·down' (pōrt'å·doun'). Municipal borough, co. Armagh, S Northern Ireland; pop. 17,202; linen and cotton goods; agricultural center.

Portae Syriae. = *Syriae Portae* (Eng. *Syrian Gates*). see BAILAN.

Por'tage (pōr'tĭj). **1** Name of counties of two states in the U.S. See *Tables* at OHIO and WISCONSIN.
2 Town, Porter co., NW Indiana, NW of Valparaiso; pop. 11,822.
3 Borough, Cambria co., SW cen. Pennsylvania, 15 m. ENE of Johnstown; pop. 3933; coal mining.
4 City, ⊗ of Columbia co., S cen. Wisconsin, on Wisconsin river 34 m. N of Madison; pop. 7822; farm trade center; manufactures hosiery, shoes, beer, granite products; settled 1835 on site of Fort Winnebago (1828); site early used as a portage bet. Fox and Wisconsin rivers which

are ab. 1½ m. apart at this point and now connected by a canal owned by the Federal government.

Portage Falls. Waterfall 110 ft. high in the Genesee river, W New York, 45 m. SSW of Rochester.

Portage Lake. 1 Lake in N cen. Aroostook co., N Maine; drains S into Aroostook river.
2 Lake in Houghton co., NW Michigan penin., an inlet of Keweenaw Bay; Keweenaw Waterway (q.v.) passes through it.

Portage la Prai'rie (lä prâr'ĭ). City, S Manitoba, Canada, on Assiniboine river 54 m. W of Winnipeg; pop. 8511; important rail center and grain market; maintains flour mills, grain elevators, and various manufacturing plants. Founded 1853 on the site of Fort La Reine (erected in 1738).

Por'tage·ville (pôr'tĭj·vĭl). City, New Madrid co., SE Missouri, 18 m. N of Caruthersville; pop. 2505; cotton gins.

Port Al·ber'ni (ăl·bûr'nĭ). Resort city, E cen. Vancouver I., Brit. Columbia, Canada, at head of Alberni Canal 75 m. W of Vancouver; pop. 7845; trading and distributing point for surrounding territory; has fine landlocked harbor; connected by rail with Victoria.

Por'ta·le'gre (pôr'tá·lä'grĕ). **1** District of Portugal. See *Table* at PORTUGAL.
2 Fortified commune, its ✳, E cen. Portugal, near Spanish frontier 100 m. ENE of Lisbon; pop. 11,050; 16th-cent. cathedral; manufactures woolens; trades in cork.

Por·tal'es (pôr·tăl'ĕs). City, ⊗ & E New Mexico, 18 m. SW of Clovis; pop. 9695; in irrigated farm country; produces esp. tomatoes, peanuts, sweet potatoes; dairying. Eastern New Mexico University (1934; coed.)

Port Al'fred (ăl'frĕd; -frĭd). **1** Town, Chicoutimi co., S Quebec, Canada, on Ha! Ha! Bay, S bank of Saguenay river 9 m. ESE of Chicoutimi; pop. 3937.
2 Resort town, SE Cape Province, S Republic of So. Africa, at mouth of Kowie river 80 m. ENE of Port Elizabeth; pop. 4251; founded 1825; formerly a seaport, harbor now silted up.

Port Al'le·ga'ny (ăl'ĕ·gā'nĭ; ăl'ĕ·gā'nĭ). Borough, McKean co., N Pennsylvania, on Allegheny river 22 m. ESE of Bradford; pop. 2742; manufactures glass, silk.

Port Al'len (ăl'ĕn; -ĭn). **1** Town, ⊗ of West Baton Rouge parish, SE cen. Louisiana, on Mississippi river across from Baton Rouge; pop. 5026.
2 Airport station on Hanapepe Bay near Hanapepe village, S Kauai I., Hawaii; U.S. coast and geodetic survey station.

Port Amelia. See PORTO AMELIA.

Port An'ge·les (ăn'jĕ·lĕs). City and port of entry, ⊗ of Clallam co., NW Washington, on Juan de Fuca Strait opp. Victoria, Brit. Columbia, and 65 m. WNW of Seattle; pop. 12,653; lumber, pulp and paper mills; fisheries.

Port An·to'ni·o (ăn·tō'nĭ·ō). Seaport, NE Jamaica I., British West Indies, 26 m. NE of Kingston (75 m. by coastal railroad) on a bay divided in two parts by a promontory; pop. (1943 est.) 5412; important port in banana industry.

Port Apra. See APRA HARBOR.

Port Aransas. See ARANSAS PASS, Texas.

Port Ar'thur (är'thẽr). **1** City and port of entry, Jefferson co., SE Texas, on Sabine Lake 18 m. S of Beaumont; pop. 66,676; connected with Gulf of Mexico by inland ship canal and deepwater channels; shipping center of oil-refining district; rice and cotton growing, stock raising; large import and export trade; seaplane base; hunting and fishing resort.
2 Settlement, Tasmania, Australia. See TASMAN PENINSULA.
3 City, ⊗ of Thunder Bay dist., SW Ontario, Canada, on NW shore of Lake Superior 3 m. N of Fort William (q.v.), ab. 200 m. NE of Duluth; pop. 31,161; important transshipment port; has transcontinental railroad con-

nections, 16 large grain elevators, docks, and one of the largest shipbuilding yards in Canada; also has pulp and paper mills; tourist center. Founded 1866, became a city 1907.
4 *Jap.* **Ryo·jun** (ryō·jŏŏn); *Chin.* **Lü'shun'kow'** (lü'shŏŏn'kō'). Seaport town at S end of Liaotung Penin., Kwantung, Manchuria, SW of Dairen; pop. 142,184; on Strait of Pohai opp. N coast of Shantung; surrounded by hills on three sides, its harbor divided into two ports connected by a narrow channel; town divided into New Town and Old Town; terminus of South Manchuria Railway running N to Dairen, Mukden, and Changchun; has a few industries. Harbor used in T'ang dynasty (618–907); made a naval station by Emperor K'ang-hsi. First visited by British 1860; made chief naval base by Chinese; taken by Japanese in 1894 but returned to China; included in lease to Russia 1898, who built strong defenses around it; scene of naval engagements and protracted land siege from June 1904; captured by Japanese Jan. 2, 1905; included in Kwantung Leased Territory 1905, 1915; after 1945 by treaty made a Sino-Russian naval base.

Port Au·gus'ta (ô·gŭs'tá). Seaport, S South Australia, at head of Spencer Gulf 175 m. NNW of Adelaide; pop. 3270; trading center and shipping point for wheat-growing region and cattle and sheep raising.

Port-au-Prince (pôrt'ō·prĭns'; *Fr.* pôr'tō'prăɴs'). Chief seaport and ✳ of the Republic of Haiti, Hispaniola I., West Indies; pop. (1936 est.) 115,000; has excellent harbor on SE shore of Gulf of Gonaïves, protected by Gonave I.; center of railroad and communication lines. Univ. of Haiti. Laid out 1749; has suffered from earthquakes and fires.

Port-aux-Basques (pôrt'ō·băsk'). Town on Cabot Strait at SW tip of Newfoundland; pop. 808; active, year-round harbor and terminus of transinsular railroad.

Port'bail' (pôr'bá'y'). Town near W coast of Cotentin Penin., Normandy, Manche dept., NW France, ab. 20 m. W of Carentan; pop. (1931) 456; its capture by Allies June 18, 1944 opened up corridor across the peninsula.

Port Baltic. = *Baltic Port:* see PALDISKI, Estonia.

Port Blair (pôrt blâr). Seaport town on SE coast of South Andaman I.; ✳ of Andaman and Nicobar Islands ter., India, on one of the best harbors of S Asia, 11°42′N. First occupied by Lieut. Blair, R.N., 1789; abandoned 1796–1856; made a penal colony 1858; seized by Japanese Mar. 23, 1942 and held as naval and air base until 1945; resumed civil administration Oct. 1945 and abolished penal colony.

Port Bou (pôrt vō'ŏŏ). Town, Gerona prov., NE Spain, on coast and on French border; pop. (1930) 3976; customs station.

Port Bou·et' (pôr' bwĕ'). Seaport, Ivory Coast, West Africa, port of Abidjan on S side of lagoon opp. the capital.

Port Bur'well (pôrt bûr'wĕl; -wĕl). Harbor on SW coast of Killinek I., NE Quebec, Canada, just off N tip of Labrador.

Port Car'bon (kär'bŭn). Borough, Schuylkill co., E cen. Pennsylvania, 3 m. ENE of Pottsville; pop. 2775; suburb of Pottsville.

Port Castries. See CASTRIES.

Port Chal'mers (chä'mẽrz). Borough, Otago provincial dist., SE South I., New Zealand, on Otago Harbor 10 m. NE of Dunedin; pop. 2575.

Port' Ches'ter (pôrt' chĕs'tẽr). Village, Westchester co., in town of Rye (q.v.), SE New York, on Long Island Sound 25 m. NE of New York, near Connecticut boundary; pop. 24,960; residential suburb of New York.

Port Clar'ence (klăr'ĕns). Inlet at W end of Seward Penin., NW of Nome, W Alaska.

Port Clin'ton (klĭn't'n; -tŭn). City, ⊗ of Ottawa co., N Ohio, on Lake Erie 30 m. ESE of Toledo; pop. 6870; fruit handling, fishing, canning, boatbuilding; limestone and gypsum deposits nearby.

Port Col′borne (kŏl′bẽrn). Town, Welland co., SE Ontario, Canada, on NE shore of Lake Erie at S end of Welland Ship Canal; pop. 8275; has grain elevator, flour mills, blast furnace, nickel refinery; port of call for lake steamers.

Port Con′way (kŏn′wā). Hamlet, S King George co., NE Virginia, on the Rappahannock; birthplace of James Madison, 4th president of the U.S.

Port Cooper. See LYTTELTON.

Port Co·quit′lam (kô·kwĭt′lăm). City, SW British Columbia, Canada, just N of the Fraser river 15 m. E of Vancouver; pop. 3232; on Canadian Pacific Ry., has railroad yards.

Port Corn·wal′lis (kôrn·wŏl′ĭs). Village and fine harbor, E coast of North Andaman I., Andaman Is., Indian Union; first settled 1792.

Port Cred′it (krĕd′ĭt). Village, Peel co., SE Ontario, Canada, on Lake Ontario 13 m. WSW of Toronto; pop. 3643.

Port Cros (pôr′ krō′). One of the Hyères Is. (*q.v.*).

Port Cyg′net (sĭg′nĕt; -nĭt). Town, S Tasmania, Australia, on coast near mouth of Huon river 25 m. S of Hobart; pop. 839; good harbor; fine fruit orchards.

Port Dal·hou′sie (dăl·hōō′zĭ). Resort village, Lincoln co., SE Ontario, Canada, at Lake Ontario end of old Welland Canal; pop. 2616.

Port Dal′rym′ple (dăl′rĭm′p′l). Port at mouth of Tamar river, N Tasmania, Australia; one of the earliest settlements (Oct. 1804) on the island; military post until 1846.

Port Dar′win (där′wĭn). 1 See DARWIN.
2 Inlet of Clarence Strait, N Northern Territory, Australia, on which Darwin is situated.

Port-de-Paix (pôr′dĕ-pĕ′). Seaport, NW Haiti, 35 m. N of Gonaïves and opp. Tortue I.; pop. (1936 est.) 5000.

Port De·pos′it (pôrt dĕ·pŏz′ĭt). Town, Cecil co., NE corner of Maryland; pop. 953; on the Susquehanna at a place where the river banks are 200-ft. cliffs; site of Jacob Tome Institute, founded by Jacob Tome (1810–98) businessman and philanthropist; granite quarries.

Port-des-Ga′lets′ (pôr′dā′gá′lĕ′). Seaport on NW coast of the French island of Réunion in the Indian Ocean E of Madagascar; best harbor on Réunion; railroad terminus.

Port Di′a·mond (dī′á·mŭnd). Port on NE cen. coast of Malaita I., SE Solomon Is., W Pacific Ocean.

Port Dick′in·son (dĭk′ĭn·s′n). Village, Broome co., S New York, 2 m. N of Binghamton; pop. 2295.

Port Dick′son (dĭk′s′n). Seaport, SW coast of Negri Sembilan state, Federation of Malaya; pop. 2667; terminus of railroad branch line from Seremban; only good shipping point in the state; health resort.

Port d′I·lhe′o Bay (pôrt dĕ-lyâ′ōō). Inlet of Atlantic Ocean on W cen. coast of South-West Africa, S of Walvis Bay.

Port Do′ver (dō′vẽr). Village, Norfolk co., SE Ontario, Canada, on Long Point Bay, inlet of Lake Erie, 25 m. S of Brantford; pop. 2440.

Port Durnford. See BIRCAO.

Port Eads (ēdz). Station, Plaquemines parish, SE Louisiana, at mouth of middle course of Mississippi river in the delta; lighthouse, pilot's station, government engineers' quarters.

Port E·liz′a·beth (ê-lĭz′á·bĕth). Town, SE Cape Province, S Union of South Africa, on W side of Algoa Bay ab. 410 m. E of Cape Town; pop. with suburbs 109,841; second city of the province in importance and one of dominion's chief ports; open harbor with breakwater and jetties; foundries, mills, tanneries, shoe factories, fruit canneries, and two large American automobile assembling plants; resort; has campanile commemorating arrival of original settlers and maintains world-famous Snake Park with some 2000 reptiles. Site of a British military station, Fort Frederick, built 1799; town founded in 1820 by British immigrants.

Port El′len (ĕl′ĕn; -ĭn). Seaport village, S coast of Islay I., Inner Hebrides, Argyll co., W Scotland.

Portenau. See PORDENONE.

Port-en-Bes′sin′ (pôr′äⁿ·bĕ′săⁿ′). Fishing village, Calvados dept., Normandy, NW France, ab. 5 m. N of Bayeux on shore of Bay of the Seine; pop. (1931) 1408; marked approximately the division point bet. British and American landing beaches during invasion June 1944.

Por′ter (pōr′tẽr). County in Indiana. See *Table* at INDIANA.

Por′ter·dale (pōr′tẽr·dāl). Town, Newton co., N cen. Georgia, 30 m. ESE of Atlanta; pop. 2365; textile mills.

Porter Mountain. Peak 4070 ft. in the Adirondack Mts., Essex co., NE New York.

Por′ter·ville (pōr′tẽr·vĭl). City, Tulare co., S cen. California, 45 m. N of Bakersfield; pop. 7991; founded 1856; trade center for fruit, cotton, vegetables; cattle and poultry raising; tungsten mining.

Port Es′sing·ton (ĕs′ĭng·tŭn). Inlet of Arafura Sea, N coast of Coburg Penin., Northern Territory, Australia.

Port-É′tienne′ (pôr′-tā′tyĕn′). Seaport town at Cape Blanc, NW Mauritania, West Africa.

Port Ev′er·glades (pōrt ĕv′ẽr·glādz). Seaport, Broward co., SE Florida, just S of Fort Lauderdale.

Port Flor′ence (flŏr′ĕns). Former name of KISUMU, Kenya.

Port Fos′ter (fŏs′tẽr). See SOUTH SHETLAND ISLANDS.

Port Franc′qui′ (pôr′ frän′kē′) or **I·le′bo** (ê·lā′bō). Town, Lusambo prov., S cen. Congo, cen. Africa, bet. the Kasai and the Sankuru rivers at their junction; terminus of railroad from Bukama, ab. 1400 m. to SE.

Port Fu·ad′ (pōrt fōō·äd′). Seaport, NE Egypt, at N end of Suez Canal opp. Port Said.

Port Gen′til′ (pôr′ zhäⁿ′tē′). Seaport, W Gabon, W equatorial Africa, 100 m. SW of Libreville.

Port Ger·mein′ (pōrt jẽr·mān′). Town, South Australia, on NE coast of Spencer Gulf; pop. ab. 5000.

Port Gib′son (gĭb′s′n). ⊗ of Claiborne co., SW Mississippi, 28 m. S of Vicksburg; pop. 2861; in cotton-growing section; scene of battle Apr. 30–May 1, 1863 in Grant's Vicksburg campaign.

Port Glas′gow (glăs′gō; -gō; glăz′gō; *Brit. also* glăs′-, glăz′-). Burgh, Renfrew co., SW Scotland, on the Clyde; pop. 21,612; a seaport, with shipbuilding yards, iron and brass foundries, cordage works; adjoins Greenock.

Port Hack′ing (hăk′ĭng). Inlet of South Pacific Ocean, New South Wales, SE Australia, just S of Botany Bay.

Port Hamilton. See KYOMON.

Port Har′court (här′kẽrt; -kōrt). Seaport near the mouth of the Bonny river, ✻ of Owerri prov., S Eastern Region, Nigeria; pop. 15,201; port second in importance in Nigeria; established 1914 to handle coal shipments, but also trades in palm oil.

Port Har′ri·son (hăr′ĭ·s′n). Station in cen. E coast of Hudson Bay, Quebec prov., Canada.

Port Hawkes′bur′y (hôks′bĕr′ĭ; -bẽr·ĭ; -brĭ). Coastal town, Inverness co., NE Nova Scotia, Canada, on Strait of Canso; pop. 1034.

Porth·cawl′ (pôrth·kôl′). Urban district, Glamorganshire, SE Wales; pop. 9529; watering place.

Port Hen′ry (hĕn′rĭ). Village and resort, Essex co., NE New York, on Lake Champlain 45 m. S of Plattsburg; pop. 1767; iron mines and iron smelter.

Port Her′ald (hĕr′ăld). Trading port in extreme S Nyasaland protectorate, SE Africa, on Shire river on border of Mozambique.

Port Hood (hŏŏd). Town, ⊗ of Inverness co., NE Nova Scotia, Canada, port on W coast of Cape Breton I.; pop. 647.

Port Hope (hōp). Town, Durham co., SE Ontario, Canada, port on Lake Ontario 62 m. ENE of Toronto; pop. 6548; has considerable lake trade, a refinery for radium ore, and various other industries; summer resort area. Settled 1778.

Port Hud′son (hŭd′s'n). Village, East Baton Rouge parish, Louisiana, on Mississippi river; besieged by Federals under Nathaniel P. Banks for six weeks 1863, surrendered July 9, after fall of Vicksburg.

Port Hue·ne′me or **Hueneme** (wī·nē′mĕ). Seaport city, Ventura co., S California, on Santa Barbara Channel ab. 40 m. W of Los Angeles, near **Point Hueneme;** made a naval base in World War II, esp. as training center for Seabees; pop. 11,067.

Port Hu′ron (hūr′ŭn). City, ⊗ of St. Clair co., SE Michigan, at Lake Huron end of St. Clair river; pop. 36,084; lake port and railroad center; supply point for beach resorts; manufactures paper, farm implements, automobile parts, cement, textiles; early home of Thomas A. Edison.

Por′ti·ci (pôr′tē·chĕ). Commune, Napoli prov., Campania, S Italy, on Bay of Naples 4 m. ESE of Naples; pop. 26,049; sea bathing.

Por′tile de Fier. See IRON GATE.

Port Is′a·bel (ĭz′á·bĕl). City and fishing resort, Cameron co., S Texas, on Gulf of Mexico 20 m. ENE of Brownsville; pop. 3575.

Port Jack′son (jăk′s'n). Inlet of South Pacific Ocean, New South Wales, SE Australia, forming one of the finest natural harbors in the world; city of Sydney is on its S shore and N suburbs of Sydney on its N shore; has width of about 1½ m. at its mouth; ab. 8 m. long to the point where it merges with the mouth of the Parramatta river. Its shores are irregular, broken by steep points that enclose bays that form smaller harbors. Great bridge across the harbor opened Mar. 19, 1932.

Port Jef′fer·son (jĕf′ẽr·s'n). Village, Suffolk co., SE New York, on Long I., on Long Island Sound ab. 13 m. N of Patchogue; pop. 2336; former shipbuilding center, now builds cruisers, sloops, pleasure craft.

Port Jer′vis (jûr′vĭs). City and summer resort, Orange co., SE New York, on Delaware river 38 m. W of Newburgh; pop. 9268; manufactures glassware, silverplated ware, silk, rayon, and cotton fabrics, concrete blocks. Settled by Dutch and Huguenot farmers c. 1698; destroyed by Indians 1779; incorporated as city 1907.

Port Ken′ne·dy (kĕn′ē·dĭ). See THURSDAY ISLAND.

Port′land (pōrt′lănd). 1 Agricultural town, N Middlesex co., S Connecticut, on Connecticut river NE of Middletown; pop. 7496; settled 1690, incorporated 1841; former sandstone-quarrying center.

2 City, ⊗ of Jay co., E Indiana, 26 m. NE of Muncie; pop. 6999; trading center for agricultural section; manufactures overalls, jackets, and shirts; birthplace of Elwood Haynes (1857–1925), inventor.

3 Seaport city, ⊗ of Cumberland co., SW Maine, on Casco Bay; pop. 72,566; largest city in the state; shipping point for lard, meat, wheat, and flour; receiving port for wood pulp, oil, clay, coal; was capital of Maine 1820–32; birthplace of Henry Wadsworth Longfellow; site of founding 1881 of Young People's Society of Christian Endeavor by Rev. Francis E. Clark.

4 Village, Ionia co., S cen. Michigan, 21 m. NW of Lansing; pop. 3330; shipping point for agricultural section; flour mills.

5 Industrial city and river port, ⊗ of Multnomah co., NW Oregon, on Willamette river 10 m. SE of its confluence with Columbia river; pop. 372,676; largest city in the state; excellent fresh-water harbor; terminus for over 50 steamship lines; manufacturing, transportation, and distributing center for agricultural and lumbering region; manufactures lumber, pulp and paper, flour and cereals, woolen goods, canned goods, butter and cheese, packed meats. Lewis and Clark College (1867; coed.); Univ. of Oregon Medical School (1887); Univ. of Portland (1901; coed.); Reed College (1911; coed.). Settled c. 1842, incorp. 1851; annexed East Portland and Albina 1891.

6 Town, SW Victoria, SE Australia, on **Portland Bay** 185 m. WSW of Melbourne; pop. 2518; port of call for coastal and transoceanic vessels. Portland College.

7 Urban district, Dorsetshire, S England, 4 m. S of Weymouth; pop. 11,324; limestone quarries; naval safe anchorage; on the **Isle of Portland,** a limestone peninsula, its connection with the mainland being a stretch of shingle 200 yds. wide; its tip is the **Portland Bill;** lighthouse; in nearby waters Dutch were defeated by Admiral Blake Feb. 18, 1653.

Portland, Cape. Cape on NE coast of Tasmania, Australia, on Banks Strait.

Portland Bight. See OLD HARBOUR BAY.

Portland Canal. Narrow inlet ab. 80 m. long bet. SE Alaska and W Brit. Columbia, 55°N, 130°W; inlet is very deep with steep sides and in some places mountains 5000 to 6000 ft. on both sides.

Portland Point. Cape projecting into the Caribbean Sea from S coast of Jamaica, on SW side of Portland Bight.

Port Laoighise. See MARYBOROUGH.

Port La·vac′a (lá·văk′á). City, ⊗ of Calhoun co., S Texas, 25 m. SE of Victoria; pop. 8864; fisheries (esp. oysters and shrimp); oil wells.

Port Limón (pōrt). = PUERTO LIMÓN, Costa Rica.

Port Lin′coln (lĭng′kŭn). Town, S South Australia, near mouth of Spencer Gulf on W side, 175 m. W of Adelaide; pop. 3006; fine harbor.

Port Lloyd (loid). Anchorage at Chichi Jima in the Bonin Is., Japan; coaling station proposed here in 1853 by Commodore Perry.

Port Lo′ko (lō′kō). Town, NW Sierra Leone, W Africa, on a branch of Rokel river 35 m. NE of Freetown.

Port Lou′is (lōo′ĭ[s]). 1 Seaport city, ✳ of the island of Mauritius, Indian Ocean, E of Madagascar; pop., with suburbs, (1941) 57,028; on NW coast; has good harbor; chief port of island; British coaling station.

2 (Fr. pôr′ lwē′) Seaport town, NW Grande Terre I., E part of island of Guadeloupe, West Indies; pop. (1931 est.) 7292.

Port Lyau′tey′ (pôr′ lyō′tā′; Angl. pōrt lē′ō·tā′) or **Ké′ni′tra′** (kā′nē′trā′). River port 10 m. from the Atlantic Ocean and ab. 30 m. NE of Rabat, NW Morocco, NW Africa; pop. (1936) 17,601; landing here by American forces Nov. 1942.

Port Lyt′tel·ton (pōrt lĭt′l·tŭn). Inlet of South Pacific on E coast of South I., New Zealand, ab. 9 m. long, forming harbor of Lyttelton, the shipping port of Christchurch to the N.

Port Mac·quar′ie (má·kwôr′ĭ). Town, E New South Wales, SE Australia, on Pacific Ocean at mouth of Hastings river 200 m. NNW of Sydney; pop. 1726; has active dock and is shipping port for dairying and agricultural region.

Port·mad′oc (pōrt·măd′ŭk). Town, S Caernarvonshire, NW Wales, on NE coast of Cardigan Bay; pop. 4060; shipping point for slate.

Port Madryn. = PUERTO MADRYN.

Port Mahon. See MAHON.

Port Ma·ri′a (má·rī′á). Seaport, N Jamaica I., British West Indies, 28 m. NNW of Kingston; pop. (1943 est.) 3167.

Port Mel′bourne (mĕl′bẽrn). Town, S Victoria, SE Australia, SW suburb of Melbourne on Port Phillip Bay; pop. 12,903; port for Melbourne.

Port Mol′ler (mŏl′ẽr). Inlet and harbor, N coast of Alaska Penin., SW Alaska; an inlet of Bering Sea.

Port Moo′dy (mōo′dĭ). City, SW British Columbia, Canada, at head of Burrard Inlet 12 m. E of Vancouver; pop. 2246; deals extensively in lumber and operates an oil refinery.

Port Mores′by (mōrz′bĭ). Seaport on S coast of Territory of Papua, New Guinea, on SE coast of Gulf of Papua, ab. 350 m. ENE of Cape York, Australia; ✳ of Papua; pop. (1938) 2628; has deep landlocked harbor inside coral reef. Discovered Feb. 1873 by Capt. John Moresby; occupied by British from Thursday I. Apr. 4, 1883; chief settlement of newly annexed territory 1888;

raided by Japanese planes Feb. 1942 and goal of unsuccessful land attack over Owen Stanley Range Dec. 1942–Jan. 1943.

Port Nech′es (nĕch′ĕz; -ĭz). City, Jefferson co., SE Texas, near mouth of Neches river 13 m. ESE of Beaumont; pop. 8696; oil refineries; synthetic rubber plant.

Port Nel′son (nĕl′s'n). Trading post on N bank of **Port Nelson** (the mouth of Nelson river), NE Manitoba, Canada, opp. York Factory; first post in Manitoba, established 1670 by Hudson's Bay Company.

Port′neuf′ (pôr′nûf′). County, Quebec, Canada. See *Table* at QUEBEC.

Port Nich′ol·son (pōrt nĭk′ŭl·s'n; -'l·s'n); *called also* **Wel′ling·ton Harbour** (wĕl′ĭng·tŭn). Harbor on SW extremity of North I., New Zealand, an inlet of Cook Strait; the city of Wellington is located on this harbor.

Port Nol′loth (nŏl′ŭth). Seaport town, NW Cape Province, S Republic of So. Africa, on Atlantic Ocean 50 m. SSE of mouth of Orange river; pop. 1572; in barren country; diamonds found in vicinity.

Port Nor′ris (nŏr′ĭs). Village, Cumberland co., SW New Jersey, 11 m. S of Millville; pop. 1789; oysters.

Pôr′to (pōr′tōō). 1 District of Portugal. See *Table* at PORTUGAL.

2 City, its ✳. See OPORTO.

Pôr′to A·le′gre (pōr′tōō à·lä′grĕ). Seaport city, ✳ of Rio Grande do Sul state, S Brazil, on inlet at N end of Lagoa dos Patos opp. mouth of Jacuí river; pop. (1940 est.) 262,678; most important Brazilian commercial center S of São Paulo, a modern, well-built city trading chiefly in cattle, meat products, hides, tobacco, rice, beans, and wool; also has varied industries; two airports and three broadcasting stations. Large foreign (German and Italian) population. Founded 1743.

Pôr′to A·me′lia (pōr′tōō à·mà′lyà) *or* **Port A·me′lia** (pōrt à·mēl′yà; -mē′lĭ·à). Seaport town on Pemba Bay, Niassa prov., NE Mozambique; pop. (1935 est.) 1959; ✳ of former Cabo Delgado dist.

Porto Bardia. See BARDIA.

Pôr′to·bel′lo (pōr′tō·bĕl′ō). Seaport, Scotland, now part of Edinburgh; seaside resort; birthplace of Sir Harry Lauder.

Pôr′to·be′lo (pōr′tō·vā′lō); *also* **Pôr′to Bel′lo** (pōr′tō bĕl′ō) *and* **Puer′to Bel′lo** (pwĕr′tō bĕl′ō). Seaport village on the Caribbean coast of Panama 20 m. NE of Colón; in banana-growing area. Just W of Columbus's earlier colony of Nombre de Dios; after 1584 one of the two American ports yearly receiving and sending out the royal Spanish fleets; the great emporium of South American trade in 16th and 17th cents.; terminus at N end of Spanish causeway across isthmus. Sir Francis Drake died aboard ship off the town and was buried at sea (1596).

Porto d'Anzio. See ANZIO.

Porto Edda. See SANTI QUARANTA.

Pôr′to Em·pe′do·cle (pōr′tō ăm·pā′dō·klå). Seaport commune, Agrigento prov., SW Sicily, on Mediterranean 4 m. SW of Agrigento; pop. 14,764; a point of attack in Allied invasion of Sicily July 1943.

Pôr′to Fa·ri′na (pōr′tō fä·rē′nä). Town, Tunisia, N Africa, ab. 20 m. E of Bizerte on a lagoon; bombarded by Admiral Blake 1655; ruins of ancient Utica (*q.v.*) 10 m. to the SE.

Pôr′to·fer·ra′io (pōr′tō·fär·rä′yō). Seaport commune, Livorno prov., Tuscany, Italy, on N coast of Elba I. 48 m. S of Leghorn; pop. 11,650; chief port of Elba I. Napoleon lived here in exile 1814–15.

Pôr′to·fi′no (pōr′tō·fē′nō). Commune, Genova prov., Liguria, NW Italy, on coast SSW of Rapallo; tourist resort; pop. 1053.

Port of Spain *or* **Port-of-Spain.** Seaport, NW Trinidad, on Gulf of Paria; ✳ of Trinidad and Tobago; pop. 93,954; has sheltered harbor; exports petroleum, asphalt, cocoa, coffee, fruit, rum.

Pôr′to Gran′de (pōr′tōō grăNN′dĕ) *or* **Min·del′lo**

(mēNN·då′lōō). Seaport town on NW São Vicente I., Cape Verde Is.; excellent harbor; coaling station.

Pôr′to·gru·a′ro (pôr′tō·grōō·à′rō). Commune, Venezia prov., Venezia Euganea, NE Italy, 34 m. NE of Venice; pop. 18,425; 14th-cent. Gothic palace.

Pôr′to·mag·gio′re (pôr′tō·mäd·jō′rä). Commune, Ferrara prov., Emilia, N Italy, 14 m. SE of Ferrara; pop. 25,008.

Pôr′to Mau·ri′zio (pôr′tō mou·rē′tsyō). 1 Former name of Imperia prov.: see *Table* at ITALY.

2 Former commune; now subdivision (pop. 9921) of commune of IMPERIA, Italy.

Pôr′to–No′vo (pôr′tō·nō′vō). Seaport town, ✳ of Dahomey, West Africa, in SE part on coastal lagoon; pop. (1938 est.) 27,500; terminus of railroads inland and along coast to Cotonou. In 19th cent. was seat of native kingdom.

Pôr′to No′vo (pōr′tō nō′vō). Seaport town, South Arcot dist., Madras state, SE Indian Union, 35 m. S of Pondicherry; pop. 13,762. Site of Sir Eyre Coote's victory July 1781 over Haidar Ali, important to British in saving Madras presidency.

Port Or′chard (pōrt ôr′chĕrd). Town, ⊗ of Kitsap co., W Washington, on Puget Sound 15 m. WSW of Seattle; pop. 2778.

Porto Rico. See PUERTO RICO.

Pôr′to San′to (pōr′tōō sănN′tōō). One of the Madeira Is., 26 m. NE of the island of Madeira; 7 m. long; 17 sq. m.; pop. 2238; first island of the group to be sighted by Zarco 1418; visited by Columbus c. 1479; airport.

Pôr′to Tol′le (pôr′tō tōl′lä). Commune, Rovigo prov., Venezia Euganea, NE Italy, on Po river 30 m. ESE of Rovigo; pop. (1931) 13,918; sugar.

Pôr′to Tor′res (pōr′tō tôr′räs); *anc.* **Tur′ris Lib′i·so′nis** (tûr′ĭs lĭb′ĭ·sō′nĭs). Seaport, Sassari prov., NW Sardinia; pop. (1931) 6576; basilica, ruins of a temple and of a Roman aqueduct.

Pôr′to·Vec′chio (pōr′tō·vĕk′kyō). Seaport, SE Corsica, on a very shallow inlet of the Tyrrhenian Sea; pop. 2009; cork-oak forests and salt deposits nearby.

Pôrto Velho. See VELHO.

Pôr′to·vie′jo (pōr′tō·vyĕ′hō). Town, ✳ of Manabí prov., W Ecuador, on E bank of Portoviejo river 90 m. NW of Guayaquil; pop. (1944 est.) 9138; founded 1534; manufactures Panama hats and baskets.

Pôr′to Vi′ro (pōr′tō vē′rō); *formerly* **Ta′glio di Porto Viro** (täl′yō dĕ). Commune, Rovigo prov., Venezia Euganea, NE Italy, on Po river 21 m. E by S of Rovigo; pop. 23,652.

Port·pat′rick (pōrt·păt′rĭk). Decayed seaport, Wigtown co., SW Scotland; pop. ab. 1000; nearest port of Great Britain to Ireland; summer resort.

Port Pat′te·son (păt′ĕ·s'n). See VANUA LAVA.

Port Phil′lip Bay (fĭl′ĭp); *also, often, in short form,* **Port Phillip.** Harbor of Melbourne, S Victoria, SE Australia; 31 m. long by 20 m. wide; 800 sq. m. First entered and explored 1835.

Port Pir′ie (pĭr′ĭ). Seaport, S South Australia, on E side of Spencer Gulf at its N end, 125 m. NNW of Adelaide; pop. 11,680; in wheat-growing region; has poor harbor but is principal outlet for Broken Hill mines; has extensive ore smelters.

Port Ra′da·ma′ Bay (*Fr.* pôr′ rà·då′mà′). Inlet of Mozambique Channel on NW coast of Madagascar.

Port Ra′di·um (pōrt rä′dĭ·ŭm). Mining village on E shore of Great Bear Lake, Mackenzie District, NW Territories, Canada, just S of Arctic Circle; pop. 225; site of formerly important pitchblende mine.

Port·ree′ (pōrt·rē′). Village on E coast of Skye I., Inner Hebrides, Inverness co., NW Scotland; fishing and cloth weaving; tourist center.

Port Re·pub′lic (rĕ·pŭb′lĭk). Village, Rockingham co., NW Virginia, in Shenandoah Valley; battle June 9, 1862 in which Stonewall Jackson defeated two brigades of Federals.

Port Resolution. See TANA.

Port Rex. See EAST LONDON.

Port Rich'mond (rĭch'mŭnd). Community on N shore of Staten I. (Richmond borough), New York City; a business center for the island; residence of Aaron Burr when he died 1836.

Port Roy'al (roi'ăl). **1** Town on **Port Royal Island,** one of the Sea Is., in Beaufort co., S South Carolina; pop. 686; colony of French Huguenots founded here by Jean Ribaut 1562.
2 Fortified town at entrance to Kingston harbor, SE Jamaica, West Indies Federation; pop. ab. 1000; early capital of Jamaica colony; haunt of buccaneers; destroyed by earthquakes 1692 and 1907; formerly used as a British naval station; use of dockyard leased to U.S. Sept. 2, 1940.
3 See ANNAPOLIS ROYAL.

Port Royal National Historic Park. See CANADA, *National Historic Parks.*

Port Royal Sound. Inlet of Atlantic Ocean bet. islands St. Helena and Hiltonhead off SE coast of South Carolina at entrance to Broad river.

Port·rush' (pōrt·rŭsh'). Urban district, N coast of co. Antrim, NE Northern Ireland; pop. 4166; watering place and seaport; nearby is Giant's Causeway (*q.v.*).

Port Said (sīd'; säd'). Seaport city, Canal governorate, NE Egypt, on the Mediterranean Sea at the N end of Suez Canal on narrow sand strip bed. Mediterranean and Lake Manzala; pop. (1937) 124,749. Founded 1859, became largest coaling station in the world; has lighthouse 174 ft. high and a huge statue of Ferdinand de Lesseps.

Port Saint Joe (sănt jō'). Town, Gulf co., NW Florida, 75 m. SW of Tallahassee on St. Joseph Bay; pop. 4217; paper mills; fisheries; lumber.

Port Saint Johns (sănt jŏnz'). Seaport town, ✳ of Pondoland, NE Cape Province, S Union of South Africa, at mouth of Umzimvubu river 153 m. SW of Durban; pop. 734; enclosed by sheer cliffs; in region producing cotton and sugar; exports marble.

Port Sand'wich (săn[d]'wĭch; *Brit. also* -wĭj). See MALEKULA.

Port'sea (pōrt'sĭ). **1** Island 4 m. long and 3 m. wide off S coast of Hampshire, S England, site of the city of Portsmouth.
2 Ward of Portsmouth, Hampshire, S England; Portsmouth dockyards and naval station.

Port Shep'stone (shĕp'stŭn). Town at mouth of Umzimkulu river, S Natal, E Union of South Africa, 72 m. SSW of Durban; pop. 1705; center of a fertile farming district, but its harbor not developed.

Port Simp'son (sĭm[p]'s'n). Indian village, W Brit. Columbia, Canada, on coast 25 m. N of Prince Rupert and on S side of entrance to Portland Canal.

Ports'lade by Sea (pōrts'lād). Urban district, East Sussex, S England, near Brighton; pop. 13,572; manufacturing and shipping center; Roman and Anglo-Saxon remains nearby.

Ports'mouth (pōrts'mŭth). **1** Seaport city and port of entry, Rockingham co., SE New Hampshire, on Atlantic Ocean at mouth of Piscataqua river; pop. 25,833; former shipping center; summer resort; manufactures buttons, shoes, tools, paper, matches; Portsmouth navy yard on nearby Seavey's I. (part of Kittery, Maine), builds submarines and repairs battleships; naval hospital and naval prison; Isles of Shoals 10 m. from harbor. Settled 1623; incorporated as town by Massachusetts under present name 1653; capital of provincial government for nearly 100 years before Revolution; incorporated as city 1849; Russo-Japanese treaty signed here 1905.
2 Industrial city, ⊗ of Scioto co., S Ohio, on Ohio river at mouth of Scioto river; pop. 33,637; founded 1803; railroad center, shipping and distributing point; manufactures iron and steel, clay products (esp. fire brick), wire, shoes; clay and sandstone deposits. Indian mounds and prehistoric earthworks nearby.

3 Town, Newport co., SE Rhode Island, on N end of Rhode Island (island) and on the Sakonnet river 8 m. NNE of Newport; pop. 8251; farming, shipbuilding, fishing; site for summer homes and residences; old coal mines nearby. Settled in 1638 by colonists from Massachusetts Bay Colony led by John Clarke and William Coddington, followed by Anne Hutchinson; joined "Incorporation of Providence Plantations" (chartered 1644); scene of battle of Rhode Island 1778.
4 Commercial and industrial seaport city, ⊗ of Norfolk co., SE Virginia, but politically independent, on Elizabeth river across from Norfolk; 6 sq. m.; pop. 114,773; with Norfolk and Newport News, comprises Port of Hampton Roads; railroad and steamship center, shipyards, commercial fisheries and seafood-packing houses; ships cotton, tobacco, lumber, produce; manufactures cottonseed oil, paint, fertilizer, foundry products, lumber, hosiery, chemicals. Site of U.S. navy yard (1752; burned by Confederates 1862). Platted 1750; established as town 1752, as city 1858; refused to harbor Tory refugees from Norfolk in Revolution; subsequently invaded by British; burned 1821, and rebuilt. See HAMPTON ROADS.
5 Seaport on NW coast of Dominica I., Windward Is., West Indies Federation.
6 Village, Frontenac co., SE Ontario, Canada, on Lake Ontario 4 m. W of Kingston; pop. 3411.
7 Seaport and county borough, Hampshire, S England, on island of Portsea in English Channel 65 m. SW of London; pop. (1931) 249,283; (1951) 233,464; a leading British naval base. Birthplace of Charles Dickens and George Meredith. Its suburb Southsea is a popular watering place. Severely bombed Nov. 1940.

Portsmouth Island. Island off cen. North Carolina coast, bet. S Pamlico Sound and Atlantic Ocean.

Port Stan'ley (stăn'lĭ). **1** Village, Elgin co., SE Ontario, Canada, on Lake Erie 8 m. S of St. Thomas; pop. 1491; serves as port for St. Thomas and London (Ontario); has fine sandy beach and is popular summer resort.
2 See STANLEY, Falkland Islands.
3 See MALEKULA, New Hebrides.

Port Ste'phens (stē'vĕnz). Fine harbor on E coast of New South Wales, SE Australia, NE of Sydney; lighthouse.

Port Sual. See SUAL.

Port Su·dan' (sōō·dăn'). Seaport and railroad terminus on Red Sea, E Kassala prov., NE Sudan; pop. (1938 est.) 21,773; forms with Suakin a special administration, pop. ab. 29,000; exports gum arabic, cotton, salt. Founded 1905.

Port Sul'phur (sŭl'fẽr). Industrial settlement, Plaquemines parish, SE Louisiana, on Mississippi river 20 m. SE of New Orleans; pop. 2868; established 1933 near some sulfur deposits.

Port Sun'light' (sŭn'lĭt'). Model industrial town, Cheshire, England, on S bank of the Mersey near Liverpool; pop. ab. 5000; founded by Viscount Leverhulme, chairman of Lever Bros., Ltd., soap manufacturers.

Port Su'san (sū'z'n). Inlet in upper Puget Sound bet. Camano I. and Snohomish co., NW Washington.

Port Swet'ten·ham (swĕt'n-ăm; swĕt'năm). Seaport town 27 m. SW of Kuala Lumpur, W Selangor state, Federation of Malaya; pop. 9535; chief port of the federation; terminus of branch railroad line from Kuala Lumpur.

Port Tal'bot (pōrt tôl'bŭt). Urban district and seaport, W Glamorganshire, SE Wales; pop. 44,024; shipping point for coal.

Port Tau·fiq' (pōrt tou·fēk'); *formerly* **Port Tew'fik** (tū'fĭk). Town, port of Suez, Egypt, at S end of Suez Canal at head of Gulf of Suez; railroad terminus.

Port Town'send (toun'zĕnd). City and port of entry, ⊗ of Jefferson co., W Washington, on W side of entrance to Puget Sound 30 m. WNW of Everett; pop. 5074; settled 1851; chartered as city 1860; good harbor; manufac-

tures paper, lumber; ships farm and dairy products; tourist center.

Por'tu·gal (pôr'tụ̆·găl; pôr'-; _Port._ pōͅr·tōō·gäl'); _anc._ **Lu'si·ta'nia** (lū'sĭ·tän'yȧ; -tā'nĭ·ȧ). Republic, formerly a kingdom, occupying W section of the Iberian Penin.; bounded on N and E by Spain, on S and W by Atlantic Ocean; 34,240 sq. m.; pop. (1940) 7,185,143; including the Azores and Madeira Is., 35,430 sq. m., pop. 7,722,152; ✳ Lisbon; including colonial possessions, 839,325 sq. m., pop. 18,552,996. Continental Portugal is divided into 11 provinces and 18 districts (see _Tables_, below); for pronunciation of their names, see their individual entries:

PROVINCES OF CONTINENTAL PORTUGAL[1]

NAME	LOCA-TION	AREA (SQ. M.)	POP. (1940)	CAPITAL	DISTRICTS
Algarve	S	1,958	317,628	Faro	Faro
Alto Alentejo	SE cen.	5,220	394,325	Évora	Évora, Portalegre
Baixo Alentejo	S	3,969	275,441	Beja	Beja
Beira Alta	NE cen.	4,055	759,729	Viseu	Viseu, Guarda
Beira Baixa	E cen.	2,588	299,670	Castelo Branco	Castelo Branco
Beira Litoral	W cen.	3,924	1,195,222	Coimbra	Aveiro, Coimbra, Leiria
Douro Litoral	NW	881	938,288	Oporto	Pôrto
Estremadura	SW	3,032	1,338,987	Lisbon	Lisboa, Setúbal
Minho	NW	1,868	741,510	Braga	Braga, Viana do Castelo
Ribatejo	W cen.	2,583	421,996	Santarém	Santarém
Trás-os-Montes e Alto Douro	NE	4,162	502,347	Vila Real	Bragança, Vila Real

[1] Extra-continental Portugal includes Azores (_q.v._) and Madeira (_q.v._) Is.

DISTRICTS, INCLUDING THOSE IN THE AZORES AND MADEIRA

NAME[1]	LOCATION BY PROVINCES	AREA (SQ. M.)	POP. (1940)
Angra do Heroísmo[2]		268	70,502[2]
Aveiro	N Beira Litoral	1,070	429,870
Beja	coextensive with Baixo Alentejo	3,969	275,441
Braga	S Minho	1,054	482,914
Bragança	E Trás-os-Montes e Alto Douro	2,526	213,233
Castelo Branco	coextensive with Beira Baixa	2,588	299,670
Coimbra	cen. Beira Litoral	1,527	411,677
Évora	S Alto Alentejo	2,853	207,952
Faro	coextensive with Algarve	1,958	317,628
Funchal[3]		302	250,124
Guarda	E Beira Alta	2,122	294,166
Horta[4]		294	49,216[4]
Leiria	S Beira Litoral	1,326	353,675
Lisboa	N Estremadura	1,061	1,070,103
Ponta Delgada[5]		326	134,217[5]
Portalegre	N Alto Alentejo	2,368	186,373
Pôrto	coextensive with Douro Litoral	881	938,288
Santarém	coextensive with Ribatejo	2,583	421,996
Setúbal	S Estremadura	1,971	268,884
Viana do Castelo	N Minho	814	258,596
Vila Real	W Trás-os-Montes e Alto Douro	1,636	289,114
Viseu	W Beira Alta	1,933	465,563

[1] The capital city has the same name.
[2] In Azores; consists of Terceira, São Jorge, and Graciosa Is. Pop. 1930 Census; total for Azores (1940) 484,278.
[3] Coextensive with Madeira Is.
[4] In Azores; consists of Pico, Fayal, Flores, and Corvo Is. Pop. 1930 Census.
[5] In Azores; consists of São Miguel and Santa Maria Is. Pop. 1930 Census.

Its 500-m. coast line affords good harbors only at the mouths of the principal rivers: the Tejo (Tagus) in cen. part, the Guadiana in S flowing into Gulf of Cádiz, the Douro and the Minho in the N; each of these rises in Spain, forms in part of its course a portion of the Portu-guese-Spanish boundary, and flows through narrow gorges and restricted valleys; there are no inland lakes but there are lagoons at Aveiro and at Lisbon at the mouth of the Tagus. Mountains are parts of the E–W ranges of the Iberian Penin.: the highest, the Serra da Estrella 6532 ft., the W extension of the Sierra de Guadarrama; the mountains in the N, a SW extension of the Cantabrian Mts.; and those in the S, a SW extension of the Guadalupe Mts. Chief exports wines, sardines, cork, olive oil, resin, wolfram, tin; agriculture and fishing are important industries. Chief cities Lisbon, Oporto, Funchal (Madeira Is.), Setúbal, Braga, Évora.

History: Inhabited in ancient times by Lusitanians who were subjugated by Rome from 2d cent. B.C.; conquered by Visigoths in 5th cent. A.D. and, later, by Moors; territory bet. Minho and Douro rivers reconquered in 11th cent. by ruler of León and Castile; granted to Henry of Burgundy as county of Portugal 1095; became independent kingdom under Alfonso I (1139–85); carried on war with Castile and expanded its territory southward, expelling Moors from Algarve in 13th cent.; after 1385, ruled by Aviz dynasty under whom it came to flourish as maritime and colonial power; in 15th and 16th cents., Portuguese opened African coast, found Cape route to Indies, colonized Brazil, and secured trade monopoly in India and East Indies; Lisbon (_q.v._) became European trading center; Spanish dependency 1580–1640; lost much of empire to Dutch (see NETHERLANDS INDIES) and to English (see BRITISH INDIA); for chief remaining colonies, see esp. ANGOLA, MOZAMBIQUE, PORTUGUESE INDIA, MACAO, PORTUGUESE TIMOR; in late 17th cent., became dependent ally of Great Britain; occupied by French 1807–14; its revolt 1820 inaugurated unsettled period during which it lost Brazil; proclaimed republic 1910; in war against Germany 1916–18; adopted new constitution, making it an authoritarian corporative state; neutral in World War II but friendly to Allies.

Por'tu·ga·le'te (pôr'tōō·gä·lā'tå). Commune, Vizcaya prov., N Spain, on Bay of Biscay 5 m. NW of Bilbao; pop. 10,612.

Por'tu·gue'sa (pôr'tōō·gā'sä). **1** River ab. 250 m. long in W Venezuela; flows SE to join the Apure river 5 m. above San Fernando.
2 State of Venezuela. See _Table_ at VENEZUELA.

Portuguese Congo. The Cabinda (_q.v._) exclave of Angola, N of the mouth of the Congo.

Portuguese East Africa. Area formerly including most of the E coast of Africa now limited to Mozambique. See MOZAMBIQUE.

Portuguese Guinea. Portuguese colony in W Africa, extending inland from the coast bet. republics of Senegal and Guinea, West Africa; area 13,944 sq. m.; pop. (1938) 415,220, (1940) 351,089; ✳ Bissau. Includes Bijagos Archipelago; traversed in cen. part by Geba river. Discovered by Portuguese 1446; in 17th and 18th cents. was active in supplying slave trade; claims of British relinquished 1870 and boundaries established by convention with France 1886.

Portuguese India. Former Portuguese possessions on W coast of India, comprising the territory of Goa and the districts of Damão and Diu; 1537 sq. m.; ✳Pangim, in Goa; annexed 1962 by India.

Portuguese Nyasaland. Northern part of Mozambique, comprising Niassa prov. (_q.v._).

Portuguese Timor. Portuguese colony comprising the eastern half of the island of Timor, Lesser Sunda Is., and an exclave (Okusi Ambeno) on the N coast of Indonesian Timor; 7330 sq. m.; pop. 463,796; ✳ Dili. Has mountain range lengthwise through the center; highest points Kablac 9580 ft. at W end and Mata Bia 7710 ft. at E end; marshlands along some parts of the coast and no long rivers. Produces fine coffee, sandalwood, copra, rubber, wax.

History: Known to Portuguese in 16th cent.; scene of

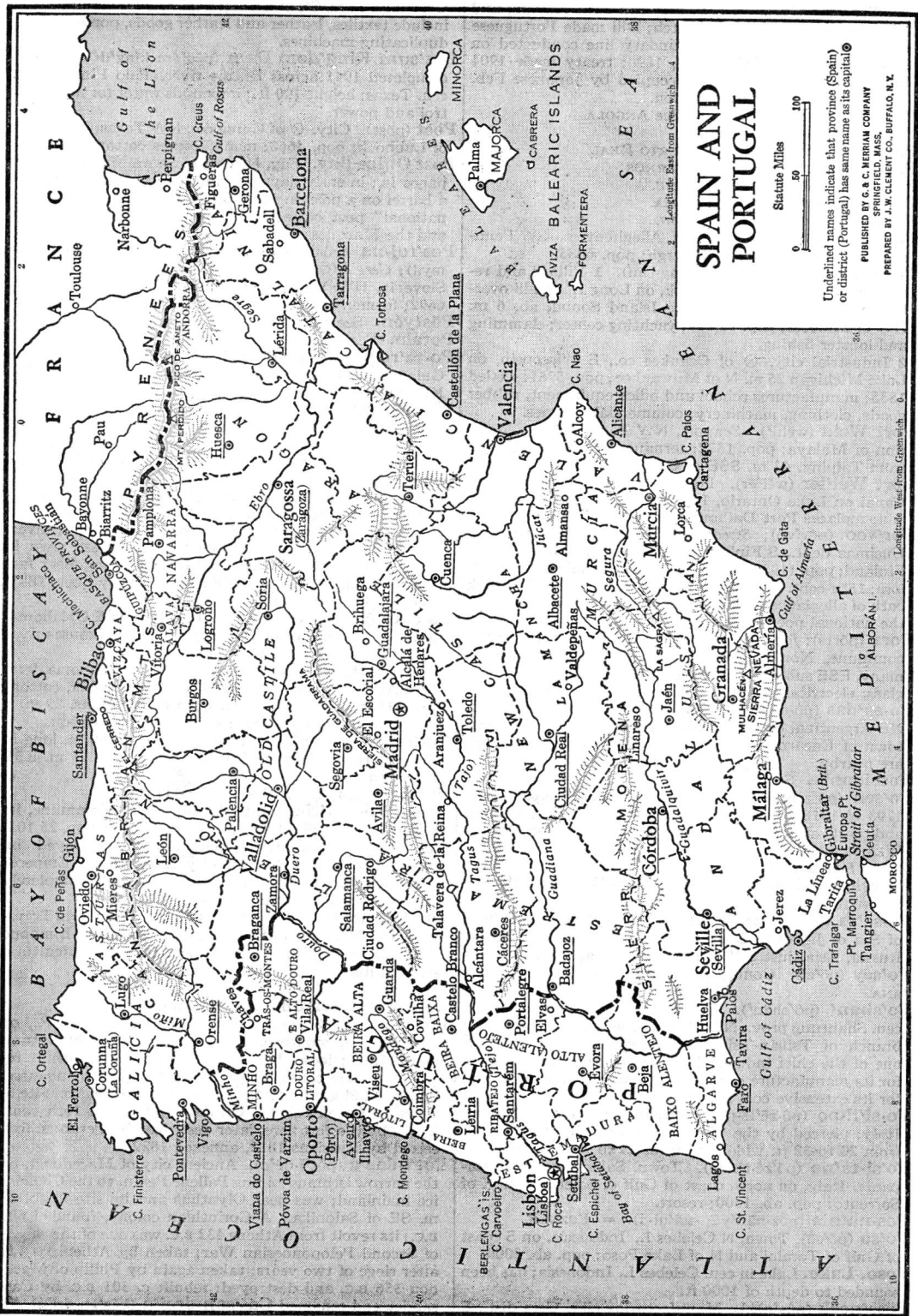

SPAIN AND PORTUGAL

Statute Miles

0   50   100

PUBLISHED BY G. & C. MERRIAM COMPANY
SPRINGFIELD, MASS.
PREPARED BY J. W. CLEMENT CO., BUFFALO, N.Y.

Underlined names indicate that province (Spain)
or district (Portugal) has same name as its capital ⊙

conflict with Dutch in 17th cent.; in 1618 Kupang and W end of island seized by Dutch; Dili made Portuguese capital; negotiations over boundary line conducted on several occasions: 1859, 1893, 1898; treaty made 1904 but not ratified until 1914; occupied by Japanese Feb. 1942. See NETHERLANDS TIMOR.

Portuguese West Africa. See ANGOLA.

Portus Cale. See OPORTO.

Portus Gaditanus. See PUERTO REAL.

Portus Iulius. See Lake AVERNUS.

Portus Lemanis. See LYMPNE.

Portus Magnus. See ALMERÍA.

Portus Magonis. See MAHÓN.

Port Vue (pôrt vū'). Borough, Allegheny co., SW Pennsylvania, 10 m. SE of Pittsburgh; pop. 6635.

Port Wash'ing·ton (wŏsh'ĭng·tŭn). **1** Village and resort, Nassau co., SE New York, on Long I., on hill overlooking Manhasset Bay, Long Island Sound, ab. 6 m. NW of Mineola; pop. 15,657; yachting center; clamming and lobster fishing.
2 Industrial city, ⊗ of Ozaukee co., E Wisconsin, on Lake Michigan 25 m. N of Milwaukee; pop. 5984; settled 1835; manufactures school and office equipment, rubber goods, clothing, machinery; commercial fisheries.

Port Weld (wĕld'). Seaport, NW Perak state, Federation of Malaya; pop. 1572; terminus of branch railroad from Taiping, 44 m. SSE of George Town (Penang).

Port Wel'ler (wĕl'ēr). Port at N end of Welland Ship Canal on Lake Ontario, Lincoln co., SE Ontario, Canada; replaces Port Dalhousie as canal terminus.

Por'voo (pôr'vō); *Swed.* **Bor'gå** (bôr'gō). Seaport, Uusimaa dept., S Finland, E of Helsinki on the Gulf of Finland; pop. (1939 est.) 7100; exports lumber and cellulose; 15th-cent. cathedral; place where Finnish Diet took oath of allegiance 1809 to Alexander I of Russia; home of the national poet Runeberg.

Porz (pôrts); *formerly* **Heu'mar** (hoi'mär). Industrial commune, North Rhine-Westphalia state, West Germany, ESE suburb of Cologne on the Rhine; pop. 12,060; glass, electrical goods, cable, agricultural machinery.

Po·sa'das (pō·sä'thäs). Town, * of Misiones territory, NE Argentina, on the Paraná river opp. the Paraguayan town of Encarnación; pop. (est.) 38,516; Iguassu Falls are nearby.

Poseidonia. See PAESTUM.

Po'sen (pō'zĕn). **1** Former province of Prussia (from 1793 to 1918); now forms POZNAŃ, province of Poland, and part of former province of GRENZMARK POSEN-WESTPREUSSEN.
2 See POZNAŃ city, Poland.

Posesiones Españolas del Sáhara Occidental. See SPANISH WESTERN SAHARA.

Po·se'ta (pŭ·syĕ'tȧ), *or* **Po·set'** (pŭ·syĕt'), **Bay.** Inlet of Sea of Japan at S tip of Maritime Territory, Soviet Russia, Asia, just SW of Peter the Great Bay.

Po'sey (pō'zĭ). County in Indiana. See *Table* at INDIANA.

Po'shan' (pō'shän'). Town, in mountainous district, cen. Shantung prov., NE China, 55 m. ESE of Tsinan on branch of Tsinan-Tsingtao railroad; pop. ab. 50,000; one of the chief industrial centers of Shantung, known for its manufacture of pottery, glass, and dyestuffs, and for its extensive coal mines.

Po·si'li·po (pō·zē'lē·pō). Promontory SW of Naples, Italy; pierced by the "Grotto," a tunnel 2264 ft. long, from 20 to 32 ft. wide, and from 23 to 71 ft. high.

Po'si·ta'no (pō'zē·tä'nō). Town, Salerno prov., Campania, Italy, on north coast of Gulf of Salerno 6 m. E of Sorrento; pop. ab. 1500; resort.

Pos·na'nia (pŏz·nän'yȧ; -nä'nĭ·ȧ). = POZNAŃ.

Po'so (pō'sō). Town, N Celebes I., Indonesia, on S coast of Gulf of Tomini and N of Lake Poso; pop. ab. 3000.

Poso, Lake. Lake in cen. Celebes I., Indonesia; has been sounded to depth of 1000 ft.

Pöss'neck (pûs'nĕk). Manufacturing city, Gera dist., E

Germany, 33 m. SE of Erfurt; pop. 14,625; manufactures include textiles, leather and leather goods, porcelain, and duplicating machines.

Pos'sum King'dom Dam (pŏs'ŭm kĭng'dŭm). Dam completed 1941 across Brazos river, Palo Pinto co., N cen. Texas; height 190 ft.; impounds water for flood control and power.

Post (pōst). City, ⊗ of Garza co., NW Texas, 40 m. SSE of Lubbock; pop. 4663; manufactures cotton textiles.

Post Office Bay. Bay, N coast of Santa María I., Galápagos Is.; in early days of sailing vessels on the Pacific, a barrel on a pole on shore of the bay formed an "international" post office for voyagers bet. South America and the Marquesas.

Pos'toj·na (pōs'toi·nä); *Ital.* **Pos·tu'mia** (pōs·tōō'myä); *Ger.* **A'dels·berg** (ä'dĕls·bĕrk). Commune, W Slovenia, NW Yugoslavia, ENE of Trieste; pop. (1931) 6692; formerly in NE Italy; stalactite caves nearby.

Pöstyén. See PIEŠT'ANY.

Potala. See LHASA.

Po·ta'ro (pō·tä'rō). River ab. 100 m. long of cen. British Guiana; flows E into Essequibo river; gold deposits. See KAIETEUR FALLS.

Po·ta'to Knob (pō·tä'tō). Peak 6419 ft. in Yancey and Buncombe cos., W North Carolina.

Potch'ef·stroom' (pôch'ĕf·strōōm'). Town, S Transvaal, NE Republic of So. Africa, 75 m. SW of Johannesburg; pop. 19,099; center of farm district and largest cattle-raising section in South Africa. Seat of a normal college, a theological college, school of agriculture, and Potchefstroom University College, a part of the University of South Africa. Founded 1838, oldest town in Transvaal; scene of a civil war bet. opposing Boer factions 1862 and of capture of British force by Boers 1881; occupied by British during Boer War 1900.

Po'teau (pō'tō). **1** River ab. 90 m. long in E Oklahoma; flows N in Le Flore co. and empties into Arkansas river on the Arkansas border.
2 City on the river, ⊗ of Le Flore co., E Oklahoma, 9 m. W of Arkansas border; pop. 4428; glass, lumber, cotton.

Po·teet' (pō·tēt'). City, Atascosa co., S Texas, 29 m. S of San Antonio; pop. 2811; in agricultural section.

Po·ten'za (pō·tĕn'tsä). **1** Small river ab. 60 m. long in NE cen. Italy; flows ENE into Adriatic Sea 2½ m. ESE of Loreto.
2 Province of Italy. See *Table* at ITALY.
3 *anc.* **Po·ten'ti·a** (pō·tĕn'shĭ·ȧ; -shȧ). Commune, its *, Lucania, S Italy, 84 m. E by S of Naples; pop. 25,103; cathedral; 13th-cent. church; almost destroyed by earthquake 1857. Ancient city captured by Emperor Frederick II, later by Charles of Anjou, and completely destroyed in 13th cent.

Pot'gie'ters·rust' (pôt'ĸē'tĕrs·rûst'). Town, cen. Transvaal, NE Republic of So. Africa, on branch of Limpopo river 125 m. NNE of Pretoria; pop. 3414; in agricultural section; lime and tin found in vicinity.

Pothea. See KALYMNOS town.

Potholes Reservoir. See MOSES LAKE.

Po'ti (pō'tĭ). Seaport town, W Georgia, U.S.S.R., on Black Sea at mouth of Rion river, 40 m. N of Batum; pop. 14,671; located in a marshy and unhealthful region, but has considerable export trade in manganese, lumber, and grain; connected by rail with Tiflis. Site of an early Greek colony, **Pha'sis** (fā'sĭs); in 16th cent. Turks built a fort here, later destroyed by Persians; first seized by Russians 1812, annexed 1829.

Pot'i·dae'a (pŏt'ĭ·dē'ȧ). Ancient city of Macedonia, on the narrow isthmus joining Pallene Penin. to the Chalcidice mainland; was near Olynthus and its site is ab. 38 m. SE of Salonika. A Corinthian colony, founded 609 B.C.; its revolt from Athens 432 B.C. was one of the causes of Second Peloponnesian War; taken by Athenians 429 after siege of two years; taken again by Philip of Macedon 356 B.C. and destroyed; rebuilt c. 301 B.C. by Cassander and renamed **Cas'san·drei'a** (kăs'ăn·drī'ȧ).

Pot Mountain (pŏt). Peak 6990 ft. in E Clearwater co., NE Idaho.

Po·to'mac (pŏ·tō'mĭk). River ab. 500 m. long (including South Branch), West Virginia, Virginia, and Maryland; formed by confluence of **North Branch** (ab. 110 m. long, flows NE from Tucker co., West Virginia, forms West Virginia-Maryland boundary) and **South Branch** (ab. 140 m. long, rises in Pendleton co., West Virginia) on N boundary of Hampshire co., NE West Virginia; flows E and SE 287 m. to form West Virginia-Maryland and Virginia-Maryland boundaries and empties into Chesapeake Bay; navigable for large vessels to Washington, D.C.; above Washington are the Great Falls (*q.v.*).

Po·to'si (pŏ·tō'sĭ). City, ⊗ of Washington co., E Missouri, 58 m. SW of St. Louis; pop. 2805; lead and barite deposits nearby.

Po·to·sí' (pō'tō·sē'). **1** Department of Bolivia. See *Table* at BOLIVIA.
2 City, its ✳; pop. (1943 est.) 40,000; altitude 13,600 ft., one of highest cities in world; situated at base of the famous silver-producing Cerro Rico de Potosí (15,380 ft.) ab. 50 m. S of Sucre; also produces tin, copper, and lead. Mines opened 1545; city, founded 1547, by 1650 had become the largest city (pop. 160,000) in the Western Hemisphere.

Po'to·si Mountain (pō'tō·sē). Peak 8500 ft. in SW Clark co., SE Nevada.

Po·to'si Peak (pō·tō'sĭ; pō'tō·sē). Mountain 13,768 ft. in Ouray co., SW Colorado.

Po·to'tan (pō·tō'tän). Municipality, E cen. Iloilo prov., Panay, Phil. Is., near right bank of Jalaur river and on railroad 17 m. N of City of Iloilo; pop. 33,020.

Po'tre·ril'los (pō'trä·rē'yōs). Subdivision (pop. 11,735) of Chañaral commune, N cen. Chile; copper mines.

Po'tro (pō'trō). Peak 19,127 ft. in NW La Rioja prov., NW Argentina, on border of Chile.

Pots'dam (pŏts'dăm). **1** Village, St. Lawrence co., N New York, 27 m. E of Ogdensburg; pop. 7765; dairy farms, paper plant; seat of Clarkson College of Technology (1895; men), State Univ. of New York College of Education (1816; coed.). Settled by co-operative community formed 1803–04, disbanded 1810; incorp. 1831.
2 (*Ger.* pôts'däm) Former government district, W Brandenburg prov., Prussia, Germany; 7658 sq. m.
3 (*Ger.* pôts'däm) Manufacturing city, its ✳ and ✳ of Brandenburg prov., former Prussia, on Havel river 17 m. SW of Berlin; pop. (1939) 136,165; manufactures include optical and surgical instruments. Founded c. 1300; first attained prominence as residence of Frederick William, the Great Elector; embellished by numerous German rulers and particularly by Frederick the Great (who built Sans Souci palace in which Voltaire sojourned); Peace of Potsdam, ratifying alliance bet. Russia and Prussia against France, signed here 1805; after World War II site of conference of American, British, and Russian leaders July 17–Aug. 2, 1945 at which preliminary details of administration of Germany were determined and at which lands of E Germany (E of Oder and Neisse rivers) were assigned to Poland.

Pot'ta·wat'o·mie (pŏt'á·wŏt'ō·mĭ). Name of counties in two states of the U.S. See *Tables* at KANSAS and OKLAHOMA.

Pot'ta·wat'ta·mie (pŏt'á·wŏt'á·mĭ). County in Iowa. See *Table* at IOWA.

Pot'ter (pŏt'ẽr). Counties in three states of the U.S. See *Tables* at PENNSYLVANIA, SOUTH DAKOTA, TEXAS.

Pot'ter·ies, the (pŏt'ẽr·ĭz). District in Staffordshire, W cen. England, noted for its production of china and earthenware; the Five Towns (actually six: Stoke on Trent, Burslem, Fenton, Hanley, Longton, Tunstall) combined 1910 to form Stoke on Trent county borough; setting of Arnold Bennett's trilogy of novels *Clayhanger* (1910), *Hilda Lessways* (1911), and *These Twain* (1916).

Potts'town (pŏts'toun). Industrial borough, Montgomery co., SE Pennsylvania, on Schuylkill river 17 m. ESE of Reading; pop. 26,144; manufactures iron and steel products, hosiery and other knit goods, silk, iron, aluminum, and brass castings, agricultural implements; iron and limestone deposits.

Potts'ville (pŏts'vĭl). City, ⊗ of Schuylkill co., E cen. Pennsylvania, on Schuylkill river 28 m. NNW of Reading; pop. 21,659; manufacturing center of anthracite mining region. Settled c. 1780; became ⊗ 1851; involved in uprising of the Molly Maguires in 1860's and 1870's.

Pough·keep'sie (pō·kĭp'sĭ). City and river port, ⊗ of Dutchess co., SE New York, on E bank of Hudson river 65 m. N of New York; pop. 38,330; cantilever railroad bridge and suspension highway bridge (Mid-Hudson Bridge) across Hudson; lumber-distribution center; manufactures cough drops and other confections, ball and roller bearings, farm implements, oil clarifiers, automobile parts, clothing. Vassar College (1861; women). Settled by Dutch c. 1698; became state capital 1778 and meeting place of Colonial legislature 1778, 1780, 1781, 1782, 1788, 1795; incorporated as village 1799, chartered as city 1854.

Poulo Condore. See Poulo CONDORE.

Poult'ney (pōlt'nĭ). **1** River ab. 35 m. long, W Vermont; rises in N Rutland co., flows NW, W, and SW into S end of Lake Champlain, forming for a few miles the New York-Vermont state boundary.
2 Village on river in Poultney town (pop. 3009), Rutland co., W Vermont, 15 m. WSW of Rutland; pop. 1810; slate quarries.

Pour'ri', **Mont** (môN' pōō'rē'). Peak 12,428 ft. in the Graian Alps, E France.

Pour'ta'let', **Col de** (kôl' dē pōōr'tà'lĕ'). Mountain pass 5468 ft. in W Pyrenees on boundary bet. Huesca prov., Spain, and Basses-Pyrénées dept., SW France, just E of Col de Somport (*q.v.*).

Pou'so A·le'gre (pō'zōō á·lä'grĕ). City, S Minas Gerais state, E Brazil, 180 m. WNW of Rio de Janeiro; pop. (1940 est.) 11,741.

Pov'er·ty Bay (pŏv'ẽr·tĭ). Inlet of Pacific Ocean on E coast of North I., New Zealand; Gisborne is on it.

Pó'voa de Var·zim' (pō'vwá thĕ vẽr·zēN'). Commune, Pôrto dist., NW Portugal, on Atlantic Ocean 20 m. NNW of Oporto; pop. (1920) 12,360; bathing resort; fishing port. Birthplace of the novelist José Maria Eça de Queiroz (1843–1900).

Pow'der (pou'dẽr). **1** River 150 m. long, E Oregon; rises in S Baker co., flows N and then curves SE into Snake river on E cen. boundary of Baker co.
2 River 375 m. long, N Wyoming and SE Montana; formed by confluence of forks in Johnson co., N Wyoming, flows N across Montana border into Yellowstone river in Prairie co., E Montana.

Powder River. 1 See POWDER.
2 County in Montana. See *Table* at MONTANA.

Pow'ell (pou'ĕl). **1** River ab. 150 m. long, NE Tennessee; rises in Wise co., SW Virginia, flows SW across Tennessee border and into Clinch river at Norris Dam.
2 Name of counties in two states of the U.S. See *Tables* at KENTUCKY and MONTANA.
3 Town, Park co., NW Wyoming, 22 m. NNE of Cody; pop. 4740; in farming and petroleum-producing section.

Powell, Mount. Peak 13,534 ft. in Summit co., cen. Colorado.

Powell River. 1 River in Tennessee. See POWELL.
2 Town, S Brit. Columbia, Canada, on Strait of Georgia 80 m. NW of Vancouver; produces pulp and newsprint.

Pow'er (pou'ẽr). County in Idaho. See *Table* at IDAHO.

Pow'e·shiek (pou'ĕ·shēk). County in Iowa. See *Table* at IOWA.

Pow·ha·tan' (pou'á·tăn'). **1** County in Virginia. See *Table* at VIRGINIA.
2 Town, a ⊗ of Lawrence co., NE Arkansas, on Black river; pop. 136.
3 Village, ⊗ of Powhatan co., E cen. Virginia; pop. (est.) 300.

Pow·hat'an Point (pou·hǎt''n; pou'á·tăn'). Village, Belmont co., E Ohio, on Ohio river; pop. 2147; coal.

Po'yang' Hu (pō'yäng' hōō'). Lake (*hu*), N Kiangsi prov., SE China; 90 m. long and 20 m. wide, 2d largest lake in China; receives the Kan (the largest) and practically all other rivers of Kiangsi; its outlet is the Kan.

Poy'gan, Lake (poi'găn). Lake ab. 10 m. long and 3 m. wide in W Winnebago co., E Wisconsin, and extending W into Waushara co.; an expansion of Wolf river.

Po'ža·re·vac (pō'zhä·rĕ·väts); *Ger.* **Pas·sa'ro·witz** (pä·sä'rô·vĭts). Town, Serbia, E Yugoslavia, 35 m. SE of Belgrade, near the Morava river and 8 m. from its port on the Danube; pop. 14,055; market town; scene of signing of treaty July 21, 1718 bet. Turkey, Austria, and Venice; taken by Serbs 1804; occupied by Germans 1941.

Po'že·ga (pō'zhĕ·gä); *Hung.* **Po'zse·ga** (pō'zhĕ·gŏ). Town, Slavonia, E part of Croatia, N Yugoslavia, N of the Sava ab. 140 m. WNW of Belgrade; pop. 7110.

Po'zières' (pō'zyâr'). Village, Somme dept., N France, NE of Albert near Bapaume; captured by British July 1916.

Poz'naṅ (pôz'nän·y'); *Ger.* **Po'sen** (pō'zĕn). **1** Polish department, in W cen. part; 10,849 sq. m.; pop. 2,113,783; as reorganized in 1946 increased in size by addition on W of part of Brandenburg.

2 City, its ✳, on both banks of Warta river 167 m. W of Warsaw; pop. (1938–39 est.) 272,000; archiepiscopal see (primacy of Poland); Roman Catholic cathedral, archiepiscopal palace, town hall, libraries, and museums; university; a leading intellectual center in Poland; important commercial and railroad center; manufactures machinery, vehicles, fertilizer, beer, liquors. One of oldest towns in Poland; member of Hanseatic League; during century (1815–1914) of German occupation preceding World War I, center of Polish life in Germany; a Russian objective in campaign of 1914–15; to Poland after World War I; seized by Germany 1939 but retaken by Russians Feb. 1945 and returned to Poland.

Po'zo·blan'co (pō'thô·vläng'kô; pō'sô-). Commune, Córdoba prov., S Spain, 34 m. N of Córdoba; pop. 16,702; silver-bearing galena mines.

Pozsony. See BRATISLAVA.

Pozsonyligetfalu. See PETRŽALKA.

Poz·zal'lo (pôt·tsäl'lô). Commune, Ragusa prov., SE Sicily, 15 m. SSE of Ragusa; pop. 10,090.

Poz·zuo'li (pôt·tswô'lè); *anc.* **Pu·te'o·li** (pů·tē'ô·lī). Commune, Napoli prov., Campania, S Italy, on **Bay of Pozzuoli** 6 m. W of Naples; pop. 29,690; fishing port; cathedral; ancient Roman ruins, including an amphitheater, temples, and the Serapeum (perhaps a temple, the columns of which show evidence of having once been in contact with sea water); mineral baths; ordnance factory. Founded by Greek exiles from Samos and named by them Dicaearchia; became Roman colony 194 B.C.; in ancient times one of greatest ports in Italy and important winter and health resort; suffered numerous volcanic convulsions during Middle Ages. Nearby is Lake Avernus, the legendary mouth of hell.

Pra·chin Bu·ri *or* **Pra·chin·bu·ri** (prä·chǐn·bŏŏ·rē). **1** Province, S Thailand; 4622 sq. m.; pop. 185,746.

2 Town, its ✳, on railroad 65 m. ENE of Bangkok.

Pra·chu·ap Khi·ri Khan *or* **Pra·chu·ab Gi·ri·khand** (prä·chŏŏ·äp k'hǐ·rē·k'hän). **1** Province, SW Thailand; 2422 sq. m.; pop. 59,474.

2 Town, its ✳, seaport on W coast of Gulf of Siam, E upper Malay Penin. 140 m. SSW of Bangkok.

Prác'ti·cos, Point (präk'tē·kôs). Cape on NE coast of Camagüey prov., E cen. Cuba.

Prades (prȧd). Commune, Pyrénées-Orientales dept., S France, 25 m. SW of Perpignan; scene of series of annual music festivals founded 1950 by Pablo Casals; pop. 5393.

Pra·du'ro e Sas'so (prä·dōō'rô å säs'sô). Commune, Bologna prov., Emilia, N Italy, 9 m. SW of Bologna; pop. (1931) 11,750.

Prae. See PHRAE.

Praeneste. See PALESTRINA.

Prae'nes·ti'na, Vi'a (vī'ȧ prē'nĕs·tī'nȧ). Ancient road ab. 23 m. long, Italy, from Rome to Praeneste.

Præst'ö' (prĕst'û'). **1** County in Denmark. See *Table* at DENMARK.

2 Town, its ⊗, SE Sjælland I., on **Præstö Bight**; pop. (1930) 1435.

Pra'ga (prä'gä). Town on right bank of the Vistula river across from Warsaw, Poland.

Prague (präg; prāg); *Czech* **Pra'ha** (prä'há); *Ger.* **Prag** (präк). City, ✳ of Czechoslovakia and of province of Bohemia, Czechoslovakia, on both sides of the Vltava (Moldau) river 160 m. NNW of Vienna; pop. (1965) 1,025,240; commercial, industrial center; manufactures textiles, chemicals, paper, glass, machinery; 15th-cent. cathedral, 14th-cent. palace; scene of the Defenestration of Prague 1419, when Hussites hurled the burgomaster and others from the windows of the town hall; scene of a 2d Defenestration 1618, when certain deputies hurled two royal commissioners and a secretary from the windows of the palace; scene of the signing of a treaty 1635 by the German states, and of the signing of a peace 1866 bet. Austria and Prussia ending the Seven Weeks' War; scene of battle May 6, 1757 in which Frederick the Great defeated the Austrians; scene of Congress of Prague July 5–Oct. 11, 1813, when the Allied Powers failed to come to an agreement with Napoleon. Became capital of new Czechoslovak state Oct. 1918; taken over by Nazi Germany Mar. 1939 but restored 1945.

Pra'hoe (prä'hŏŏ) *or* **Pra'u** (prä'ŏŏ). Mountain 10,285 ft., cen. Java, Indonesia, SW of Semarang. See DIENG PLATEAU.

Prah·ran' (prä·rän'). City, S Victoria, SE Australia, SE suburb of Melbourne; pop. 51,647.

Prai (prī). Seaport on coast of Province Wellesley, Penang settlement, Federation of Malaya, S of Butterworth; pop. 2682; railroad terminus opp. George Town on Penang I.; exports tin and rubber.

Prai'a (prī'ȧ). Town on São Tiago I., Cape Verde Is.; ✳ of Cape Verde Is.; pop. ab. 6000.

Praia de Copacabana. See COPACABANA BEACH.

Prai'rie (prâr'ĭ). Name of counties in two states of the U.S. See *Tables* at ARKANSAS and MONTANA.

Prai'rie du Chien (prâr'ĭ dů shēn'). City, ⊗ of Crawford co., SW Wisconsin, on Mississippi river near its confluence with Wisconsin river 53 m. S of La Crosse; pop. 5649; trade and distribution center of agricultural section; manufactures pearl buttons, barrels, veneer, woolens. Settled by French c. 1781; surrendered by British to U.S. 1786; scene of battle in War of 1812; again held by British 1814–16; site of American Fur Co. post (1835).

Prairie Grove. City, Washington co., NW Arkansas, 10 m. S of Fayetteville; pop. 1056; scene of battle Dec. 7, 1862 in which Federal troops under Francis J. Herron defeated Confederate forces of Thomas C. Hindman.

Prairie Provinces. The Canadian provinces of Manitoba, Saskatchewan, and Alberta—popularly so called.

Prai'ries', Ri·vière' des (rē'vyâr' dā prē'rē'). River ab. 28 m. long, part of the course of the St. Lawrence river N of Montreal I., separating it from Jesus I., S Quebec, Canada; flows NE.

Prairie Village. City, Johnson co., NE Kansas, S of Kansas City; pop. 25,356.

Prall's Island (prôlz). Island in Arthur Kill off NW shore of Staten I., N.Y.; part of Richmond borough.

Pram·ba'nan (präm·bä'nän); *also* **Bram·ba'nan** (bräm-). Town, S cen. Java, Indonesia, on Jogjakarta border and on railroad ab. 12 m. ENE of Jogjakarta; on plain nearby are ruins of many Hindu (Brahmanic) temples, ab. 1100 years old.

Pran'hi·ta (prän'hǐ·tä). River ab. 80 m. long in E Maharashtra state, cen. Indian Union; formed by confluence of Wainganga and Wardha rivers, flows S,

forming part of boundary between Maharashtra and Andhra Pradesh, to Godavari river.

Pras'lin' (prä'lăn'). See SEYCHELLES.

Pra'so·ne'si (prä'sô·nyē'sĕ), or **Pras'so** (präs'sô), **Cape.** Cape at S extremity of the island of Rhodes.

Pratapgarh. See PARTABGARH.

Pra'tas (prä'täs). Cluster of reefs and islets in South China Sea bet. Hong Kong and Luzon, ab. 200 m. SE of Hong Kong; belongs to China.

Pra'ter, Mount (prä'tĕr). Peak 13,501 ft. in Sierra Nevada, E Fresno co., S cen. California.

Pra·thum Tha·ni or **Pa·tum·dha·ni** (prä·t'hŏŏm·t'hä·nē). 1 Province, S Thailand; 605 sq. m.; pop. 123,337.

2 Town, its ✳, on the Chao Phraya a few miles N of Bangkok.

Prä'ti·gau (prâ'tĕ·gou) or **Prät'ti·gau** (prĕt'ĕ·gou). Highland valley in N Graubünden canton, E Switzerland, NE of Chur.

Pra'to in To·sca'na (prä'tô ĕn tôs·kä'nä). Commune, Firenze prov., Tuscany, cen. Italy, 11 m. NW of Florence; pop. 70,206; 13th-cent. cathedral, 14th-cent. palaces, 13th-cent. castle, art gallery; manufactures textiles.

Pra'to·la Pe·li'gna (prä'tô·lä pâ·lēn'yä). Commune, Aquila prov., Abruzzi e Molise, cen. Italy, 31 m. SE of Aquila; pop. 10,444.

Pratt (prăt). 1 County in Kansas. See *Table* at KANSAS.

2 City, its ⊗, S cen. Kansas, 54 m. WSW of Hutchinson; pop. 8156; trade center in wheat and dairy section.

Pratt'ville (prăt'vĭl; *Sou. also* -v'l). City, ⊗ of Autauga co., cen. Alabama, 12 m. NW of Montgomery; pop. 6616; settled 1816; manufactures cotton gins.

Praust. See PRUSZCZ GDAŃSKI.

Prav'dinsk (präv'dēnsk); *Ger.* **Fried'land** (frēt'länt). Commune, formerly in Königsberg govt. dist., East Prussia prov., Germany; since 1945 in Poland; pop. (1925) 3233; battle June 14, 1807 in which the Russians under Gen. Bennigsen were defeated by French under Napoleon who proceeded to occupy Königsberg, 27 m. NW.

Pra'via (prä'vyä). Commune, Oviedo prov., NW Spain, 19 m. NW of Oviedo; pop. 11,208.

Pre·ang'er (prâ·äng'ēr); *in full* **Preanger Regencies.** Former Dutch residency in Java, Indonesia; was divided in 1925 into **West Preanger, Middle Preanger,** and **East Preanger;** East and Middle Preanger were united in 1932 to form Priangan residency, and West Preanger was attached to Buitenzorg residency. Extensive mountainous region of ab. 8400 sq. m. Formerly part of Mataram; first came under Dutch influence 1677; acquired by cession 1705; for more than two centuries the region specially devoted to coffee culture under a rigid system of government administration.

Prebeza. See PREVEZA.

Pre'ble (prĕb''l). County in Ohio. See *Table* at OHIO.

Prê'cheur' (prĕ'shûr'). Former coast town, NW Martinique I., French West Indies, at foot of Mont Pelée whose eruption 1902 destroyed the town.

Pre·dap'pio Nuo'va (prâ·däp'pyô nwô'vä). Village, Forlì prov., SE Emilia, N Italy, ab. 10 m. SSW of Forlì; pop. 2292 (commune, 8251); birthplace of Benito Mussolini.

Pre·daz'zo (prâ·dät'tsô). Commune, Trento prov., S Venezia Tridentina, NE Italy; pop. (1931) 3100; resort; in Dolomites on a tributary of the Adige SE of Bolzano.

Pre·deal' Pass (prĕ·dyäl'); *Hung.* **Tö'mös Pass** (tû'mûsh). Chief pass, altitude 3445 ft., in the Transylvanian Alps, Romania, 10 m. S of Brașov.

Před'most (pēr·zhĕd'môst). Village near Přerov, cen. Moravia, Czechoslovakia; site of important and extensive paleolithic remains; excavations since 1800 have uncovered human burials, flint implements, ivory and bone carvings, mammoth remains.

Pre'gel (prā'gĕl). Navigable river 80 m. long, formerly in province of East Prussia, Germany; flows W through

Kaliningradsk Region, R.S.F.S.R., into Frisches Haff. After World War II by decision of the Potsdam Conference July 17–Aug. 2, 1945, its main course and part of the Angerapp assigned to U.S.S.R.

Prei'gnac' (prĕ'nyâk'). Commune, Gironde dept., SW France; pop. (1931) 2293; produces fine white wine (see SAUTERNES).

Premet. See PËRMET.

Pré'mon'tré', Abbey of (prā'môN'trā'). Abbey near Laon, Aisne dept., N France; founded 1119 by St. Norbert, founder of the Premonstratensians, a very strict order of regular canons.

Pren'tiss (prĕn'tĭs). 1 County in Mississippi. See *Table* at MISSISSIPPI.

2 Town, ⊗ of Jefferson Davis co., S Mississippi; pop. 1321.

Prenz'lau (prĕnts'lou). City, Neubrandenburg dist., East Germany, formerly in Potsdam govt. dist., Brandenburg, 28 m. WSW of Stettin; pop. 21,622; manufactures iron goods, machinery, cigars, margarine, dairy products, sugar. Became city 1234; to Brandenburg 1250; scene of Prussian surrender to French 1806.

Prep'a·ris Channels (prĕp'à·rĭs). Passage 140 m. wide in E Bay of Bengal, bet. Cape Negrais, Burma, and the mouths of the Irrawaddy on the N and Great and Little Coco Is. of the Andamans on the S; the channel is divided in the center by the **Preparis Isles** into **Preparis North Channel** and **Preparis South Channel.**

Pře'rov (pēr·zhě'rôf); *Ger.* **Pre'rau** (prā'rou). Town, cen. Moravia prov., Czechoslovakia, 65 m. NE of Brno; pop. (1930) 22,362; textile mills.

Pré–Saint–Gervais, Le. See LE PRÉ-SAINT-GERVAIS.

Pres'cot (prĕs'kŭt). Urban district, Lancashire, NW England, 7 m. E of Liverpool; pop. 12,474; manufactures watches and clocks, electrical equipment, and cables.

Pres'cott (prĕs'kŭt). 1 City, ⊗ of Yavapai co., cen. Arizona, 78 m. NNW of Phoenix; pop. 12,861; located on 5347-ft. plateau; center for copper, gold, silver, lead, and zinc mining; military post; annual "Frontier Days" rodeo 1889 ff.; territorial capital 1863–67, 1877–89.

2 Commercial city, ⊗ of Nevada co., SW Arkansas, 48 m. NE of Texarkana; pop. 3533.

3 County, Ontario, Canada. See *Table* at ONTARIO.

4 *before 1860* **Johns'town** (jŏnz'toun). Town, Grenville co., SE Ontario, Canada, on St. Lawrence river 50 m. S of Ottawa; pop. 3518; formerly a steamer transfer point; center of dairy district; grain elevators. Founded 1797.

Pres'i·den·cy (prĕz'ĭ·dĕn·sĭ). Former division in S Bengal prov., NE Brit. India; 16,402 sq. m.; pop. (1941) 12,817,087; ✳ Calcutta; in 1947 divided with ⅖ of area assigned to West Bengal, Indian Union, and ⅗ assigned to East Bengal, Pakistan.

Pres'i·den'te Hayes (prä'sĕ·thän'tâ ĭs'; hāz'). Department of Paraguay. See *Table* at PARAGUAY.

Pres'i·den·te Pru·den'te (prä'zĕ·thänn'tĕ prŏŏ-thänn'tĕ). City, SW São Paulo state, SE Brazil, on railroad near Paraná river; pop. (1940 est.) 12,764.

Presidente Vargas. See ITABIRA.

Pres'i·den'tial Range (prĕz'ĭ·dĕn'shăl). Range of the White Mts., chiefly in S Coos co., N New Hampshire, bet. Pinkham Notch on E and Crawford Notch on W; highest peak Mount Washington 6288 ft.

Pre·sid'i·o (prĕ·sĭd'ĭ·ō). County in Texas. See *Table* at TEXAS.

Pre'šov (prĕ'shôf); *Hung.* **E'per·jes'** (ĕ'pĕr·yĕsh'). Town, E Slovakia prov., E cen. Czechoslovakia, 20 m. N of Košice; pop. (1930) 21,870; important railroad junction.

Pres'pa, Lake (prĕs'pà); *Serbo-Croat.* **Pres'pan·sko Je'ze·ro** (prĕs'pän·skô yĕ'zĕ·rô). Lake 14 m. long and 8 m. wide on the boundary bet. SW Yugoslavia, SE Albania, and N Greece, 15 m. SW of Bitolj; drains NW into Lake Ohrid through a subterranean channel. Near it is the smaller **Lake Ma'la Pres'pa** (mä'lä prĕs'pä).

Presque Isle. 1 (prĕsk'ĭl'; ēl') Peninsula, NW Pennsylvania, in Lake Erie, forming Presque Isle Bay, harbor of Erie; state park.
2 (prĕsk' ēl') County in Michigan. See *Table* at MICHIGAN.
3 (prĕsk' ĭl') City, Aroostook co., N Maine, 40 m. N of Houlton; pop. 12,886; in section yielding potatoes, oats, hay.
Pressburg. See BRATISLAVA.
Pres·tat'yn (prĕs·tăt'ĭn). Urban district, Flintshire, NE Wales; pop. 8809; resort.
Pres·teign' (prĕs·tēn'). Urban district, Radnorshire, E Wales; pop. 1257; most easterly spot in Wales.
Pres'ton (prĕs'tŭn). **1** County in West Virginia. See *Table* at WEST VIRGINIA.
2 Town, N cen. New London co., SE Connecticut, SE of Norwich; pop. 4992; named 1687; agriculture; manufactures rayon.
3 Town, ⊗ of Webster co., W Georgia; pop. 232.
4 City, ⊗ of Franklin co., SE Idaho, 65 m. SSE of Pocatello; pop. 3640; flour mill, creamery, grain elevators.
5 Village, ⊗ of Fillmore co., SE Minnesota, 30 m. SE of Rochester; pop. 1491.
6 City, S Victoria, SE Australia, N suburb of Melbourne; pop. 33,447.
7 Industrial town, Waterloo co., SE Ontario, Canada, on Grand river 8 m. ESE of Kitchener; pop. 7619; much visited for its mineral springs; manufactures woolens, furnaces, brushes, flour, agricultural implements, shoes.
8 County borough, ⊗ of Lancashire, England, on the Ribble 30 m. NNE of Liverpool; pop. (1931) 119,001, (1951) 119,243; seaport, with shipbuilding yards; textile mills; manufactures iron and brass goods. Birthplace of Sir Richard Arkwright.
Pres'ton·pans' (prĕs'tŭn·pănz'). Burgh, East Lothian co., SE Scotland, 8 m. E of Edinburgh; pop. 2907; coal mining, breweries; watering place; scene of a rout of troops under Sir John Cope by Prince Charles Edward and his Highlanders Sept. 21, 1745.
Pres'tons·burg (prĕs'tŭnz·bûrg). City, ⊗ of Floyd co., E Kentucky, 20 m. NW of Pikeville; pop. 3133; coal mining.
Prest'wich (prĕst'wĭch). Urban district, Lancashire, NW England, 5 m. NNW of Manchester; pop. 34,387; cotton-manufacturing center.
Prest'wick (prĕst'wĭk). Burgh, Ayr co., SW Scotland, ab. 3 m. N of Ayr; pop. 11,386; tourist resort; noted golf course; international airport, built during World War II.
Pre·to'ri·a (prē·tōr'ĭ·à). City, S cen. Transvaal, ✳ of Transvaal and administrative ✳ of Union of South Africa, on small tributary of Limpopo river ab. 34 m. N of Johannesburg; pop. with suburbs 128,621. Founded 1855 by Marthinus W. Pretorius, first president of South African Republic, and named after his father, Andries Pretorius, Boer Voortrekker leader. Chosen 1860 as capital of new Boer confederation but not actually used as seat of government until 1864; in Boer War surrendered to Lord Roberts May 1900; articles of peace ending war signed here May 31, 1902; first meeting of Parliament of Transvaal 1907; made administrative seat of Union government 1910. Univ. of Pretoria chartered 1930. Home and burial place of S. J. Paulus Kruger, president of South African Republic 1883–1900.
Pret'ty·boy' Dam (prĭt'ĭ·boi'). Dam completed 1933 across Gunpowder river, N Baltimore co., NE Maryland; height 167 ft.; forms **Prettyboy Reservoir,** chief reserve for water supply of Baltimore.
Preussen. See PRUSSIA.
Preussisch Eylau. See BAGRATIONOVSK; EYLAU.
Preussisch–Stargard. See STAROGARD.
Pre've·za or **Pre'be·za** (prā'vâ·zä). **1** Department of Greece. See *Table* at GREECE.
2 Seaport town, its ✳, at entrance to Ambracian Gulf; pop. 8659. In Middle Ages superseded Nicopolis, the Roman town just to N of it; taken from Venetians by

French 1797; taken from French by Ali Pasha 1798; recovered from Turks by Greeks 1912.
Pri·a·mur' (pryĭ·ŭ·moor'). Former province in E Far Eastern Region, Soviet Russia, Asia; ✳ Khabarovsk; later a part of Maritime Territory and Khabarovsk Territory.
Pri·ang'an (prē·äng'än). Former residency, SE West Java prov., Neth. Indies; 5271 sq. m.; pop. 3,448,797; ✳ Bandung; included former East Preanger and Middle Preanger (see PREANGER). Region mountainous, esp. in E part; includes volcanic peaks of Papandayan, Tjikuraj, Guntur, and Galunggung. Principal crop coffee. Chief towns Bandung, Tasikmalaja, Garut, and Tjimahi.
Pri·bai·kal' (pryĭ·bī·kál'). Former Russian province, now in Buryat-Mongol A.S.S.R., Soviet Russia, Asia.
Prib'i·lof Islands (prĭb'ĭ·lŏf); *also* **Fur Seal Islands.** Group of islands in SE Bering Sea, Alaska, ab. 180 m. N of Unalaska; pop. 482; comprise St. Paul and St. George, and two smaller islands, Walrus and Otter. Islands are hilly with no harbors; noted as fur-seal grounds and habitat of blue and white foxes and breeding place of enormous numbers of birds. Visited annually by 80% of fur seals of world (at present ab. 2,330,000); commercial killing operations now directly controlled by U.S. government. First sighted 1767; visited 1786 by Russian explorer G. Pribilof; leased to commercial companies 1870 to 1910 whose methods nearly exterminated the seals; taken over by U.S. 1910.
Přì'bram (pĕr·zhĭ'bràm). Town, W cen. Bohemia prov., W Czechoslovakia, in mountainous region 33 m. SW of Prague; pop. 9062; ancient silver and lead mines.
Price (prīs). **1** River, E cen. Utah; flows through cen. Carbon and NE Emery cos. into Green river; in Carbon co., flows through a steep-walled canyon.
2 County in Wisconsin. See *Table* at WISCONSIN.
3 City, ⊗ of Carbon co., E cen. Utah, on Price river 62 m. SE of Provo; pop. 6802; coal and asphalt mines.
Price Peak. Mountain 10,603 ft. in Sierra Nevada, E Tuolumne co., cen. California.
Price'ville (prīs'vĭl). Village, Matane co., on Gaspé Penin., SE Quebec, Canada, 29 m. WSW of Matane; pop. 2810; on the St. Lawrence river.
Prich'ard (prĭch'ĕrd). Industrial city, Mobile co., SW corner of Alabama, 3 m. NW of Mobile; pop. 47,371; incorporated 1925; cotton mills, chemicals.
Pri·e'go de Cór'do·ba (prē·ā'gŏ thä kôr'thô·vä). Commune, Córdoba prov., S Spain, 48 m. SE of Córdoba; pop. 25,181; agricultural products; manufactures liquors, leather, pottery, cotton textiles; ancient castle; medieval church; fortified by Moors.
Pri·e'ne (prī·ē'nĕ). Ancient Greek city in W Asia Minor, near the mouth of the Maeander river (modern Menderes); scene of archaeological excavations. One of the 12 Ionian Cities, active in Ionian revolt; prosperous under Romans and Byzantine dominion; seized by Ottomans late in 13th cent.
Pries'ka (prēs'kà). Town, N cen. Cape Province, S Union of South Africa, on Orange river 150 m. WSW of Kimberley; pop. 3090; farm land devoted chiefly to merino sheep; blue asbestos, diamonds, copper, galena, and saltpeter found in vicinity.
Priest Lake (prēst). Lake 24 m. long, 14 m. wide, N Bonner co., N Idaho.
Priest'ly Lake (prēst'lĭ). Lake in N Piscataquis co., N cen. Maine; headwaters of Allagash river.
Pri'lep (prē'lĕp). City, S Macedonia, SE Yugoslavia, ab. 47 m. S of Skoplje; pop. 21,405; ✳ of Serbian empire in medieval period; 14th-cent. monastery; birthplace of Marko Kraljević; occupied by Bulgaria 1941.
Pri·lu'ki (prī·loo'kĭ; *Russ.* pryĭ·loo'kĭ). Town, S Chernigov Region, N Ukraine, U.S.S.R., on a tributary of the Sula ab. 85 m. E of Kiev; pop. 28,754; railroad town, chiefly agricultural; dates from 12th cent.
Pri·me'ro (prē·mā'rô). River ab. 130 m. long, Córdoba prov., N cen. Argentina; flows NE into Mar Chiquita.

Prim′ghar (prĭm′gär). Town, ⊗ of O'Brien co., NW Iowa; pop. 1131.

Pri′mor·je′ (prē′môr-yĕ′) *or* **Pri′mor·ska′** (-skä′). Former county, W Yugoslavia; 7476 sq. m.; pop. 882,920; ⊗ Split; now chiefly in Croatia and Herzegovina.

Primorski Krai. See MARITIME TERRITORY.

Prince (prĭns). County, Prince Edward I., Canada. See *Table* at PRINCE EDWARD ISLAND.

Prince Al′bert (ăl′bērt). City, S cen. Saskatchewan, Canada, on North Saskatchewan river 83 m. NNE of Saskatoon; pop. 17,149; founded 1866; has large trade in furs, lumber, and lumber products; packing plants.

Prince Albert National Park. See CANADA, *National Parks.*

Prince Albert Peninsula. Northwest section of Victoria I., W Franklin District, Northwest Territories, Canada.

Prince Albert Sound. Inlet, W Victoria I., W Franklin District, Northwest Territories, Canada.

Prince Charles Fore′land (chärlz fōr′lănd). Island 60 m. long W of West Spitsbergen, from which it is separated by **Foreland Sound**; has high mountain peaks; area 241 sq. m.

Prince Charles Island. Island of Canadian Arctic Archipelago, E Franklin dist., Northwest Territories, in Foxe Basin; discovered 1948; 3500 sq. m.

Prince Ed′ward (ĕd′wērd). 1 County in Virginia. See *Table* at VIRGINIA.
2 County, Ontario, Canada. See *Table* at ONTARIO.

Prince Edward Island. Island in the Gulf of St. Lawrence, SE Canada, constituting a province (one of the Maritime Provinces: see *Map* at MARITIME PROVINCES) of the Dominion of Canada; 2184 sq. m.; pop. 98,429; ✳ Charlottetown; divided into the following three counties:

NAME	LOCA-TION	AREA¹	POP.¹	CO. SEAT
Kings	E	641	17,943	Georgetown
Prince	W	778	37,735	Summerside
Queens	cen.	765	42,751	Charlottetown

¹ Area = land area in sq. m. Pop. from 1951 Census.

Separated from New Brunswick and Nova Scotia by Northumberland Strait; very irregular in shape with many deep inlets. Highest point ab. 500 ft. Agriculture, fisheries, forestry, and fox farming are chief industries; summer resort business also extensive. Has one national park. Chief towns Charlottetown and Summerside.

History: Discovered by Jacques Cartier 1534; called **Île–St–Jean** [ēl′săN′zhäN′] (*Eng.* **Isle St. John** [īl sănt jŏn′]) by Champlain; renamed 1798 after Edward, Duke of Kent; colonized by French; ceded to British 1763 and became separate province 1769; resettled by Scotch immigrants at beginning of 19th cent.; entered Confederation 1873.

Prince Edward Island National Park. See CANADA, *National Parks.*

Prince Edward Islands. Two islands in the S Indian Ocean, 1500 m. SE of Cape Town, S Africa, 46°35′S, 38°20′W; belong to Union of South Africa.

Prince Fred′er·ick (frĕd′ēr-ĭk; frĕd′rĭk). Town, ⊗ of Calvert co., S Maryland; pop. (est.) 500.

Prince George (jôrj′). 1 County in Virginia. See *Table* at VIRGINIA.
2 Village, its ⊗, SE Virginia; pop. (1950) 75.
3 City, cen. Brit. Columbia, Canada, at confluence of Fraser and Nechako rivers; pop. 4703; railroad division point; important center for lumbering and fur trading.

Prince Georg′es (jôr′jĕz; -jĭz). County in Maryland. See *Table* at MARYLAND.

Prince Har′ald Coast (här′ăld). Section of coast, East Antarctica, on Indian Ocean, ab. 69°S lat., 34° to 39°E long.; in Norwegian claim, part of Queen Maud Land.

Prince Island. See PRINCIPE ISLAND.

Prince of Wales, Cape (wālz). Cape on Bering Strait at W tip of Seward Penin., Alaska; most westerly point of mainland of North America, 168°W.

Prince of Wales Island. 1 Largest island of Alexander Archipelago, in S part, SE Alaska; ab. 135 m. long by 40 m. wide; 1500 sq. m.; has valuable mineral deposits, forests, salmon fisheries. Chief towns Hydaburg and Craig.
2 Island in Torres Strait W of Cape York, Queensland, Australia, just S of Thursday I.
3 Island 14,000 sq. m., cen. Franklin District, Northwest Territories, Canada, bet. Victoria I. and Somerset I.
4 See PENANG island.

Prince of Wales Strait. Narrow channel ab. 170 m. long bet. Banks I. and NW Victoria I., in W Franklin District, Northwest Territories, Canada.

Prince O′lav Coast (ō′lăv; *Norw.* -läv, -läf). Section of coast of Antarctica, on Indian Ocean, ab. 68°S lat., bet. 39° and 49°30′E long.; a part of Queen Maud Land; discovered 1930; within Norwegian claims.

Prince Pat′rick Island (păt′rĭk). Island 7100 sq. m., one of the Parry Is., NW Franklin District, Northwest Territories, Canada.

Prince Re′gent Inlet (rē′jĕnt). Channel ab. 60 m. wide bet. E Somerset I. and NW Baffin I., off N Canada mainland; connects with Gulf of Boothia on the S and Lancaster Sound on the N.

Prince Ru′pert (rōō′pērt). City, W British Columbia, Canada, on Pacific Ocean at head of Dixon Entrance 10 m. N of mouth of Skeena river; pop. 8546; has fine sheltered harbor with large government dry dock and extensive wharfage; W terminus of transcontinental railroad (Canadian National), completed 1914; headquarters of important halibut and other fisheries; has cold-storage plants, sawmills, shipbuilding plants, lumber mills.

Prince Rupert's Land. Historical region, northern and Western Canada, comprising drainage basin of Hudson Bay; granted 1670 by King Charles II to Hudson's Bay Company, purchased from it 1869 by the Dominion.

Princ′es Islands (prĭn′sĕz; -sĭz); *Turk.* **Kı·zıl′ A·da·lar′** (kĭ·zĭl′ ä·dä·lär′); *anc.* **De′mo·ne′si In′su·lae** (dē′mŏ·nē′sĭ ĭn′sȯ·lē). Nine small islands in E part of the Sea of Marmara, near Asia Minor coast S of İstanbul; pop. 16,807. In Byzantine history served as places of banishment; many monasteries, convents, tombs, etc.

Prin′cess Anne (prĭn′sĕs [-sĭs] ăn′). 1 County in Virginia. See *Table* at VIRGINIA.
2 Town, ⊗ of Somerset co., SE Maryland; pop. 1351. Maryland State Coll. (1886; coed.).
3 Village, ⊗ of Princess Anne co., SE Virginia; pop. (est.) 250.

Princess As′trid Coast (ăs′trĭd). Section of coast of East Antarctica, on South Atlantic Ocean, ab. 70°S lat., bet. 5° and 20°30′E long.; in Norwegian claim, part of Queen Maud Land.

Princess Char′lotte Bay (shär′lŏt). Inlet of Coral Sea on NE coast of Queensland, Australia, W of Cape Melville.

Princess E·liz′a·beth Land (ê·lĭz′à·bĕth). Coast region of Antarctica formerly located bet. Enderby Land on W and Wilkes Land on E ab. 70°E to 85°E; in British claim of 1908 and Australian claim of 1933. Its coast bordered on Lars Christensen Coast on the W; not shown on recent maps.

Princess Mar′i·an′na (mär′ĭ·ăn′à; măr′-), *or* **Dour′ga** (dŏŏr′gà), **Strait.** Channel bet. S New Guinea and Frederik Hendrik I.

Princess Mar′tha Coast (mär′thà); *formerly* **Crown Princess Martha Land.** Section of coast of Antarctica E of Coats Land and of Weddell Sea; ab. long. 5°E to 16°30′W; largely ice-covered; a part of Queen Maud Land, claimed by Norwegian government 1939.

Princess Ragn′hild Coast (räng′n·hĭl). Section of coast of Antarctica, a part of Queen Maud Land, bet. 20°30′ and 34°E long.; claimed by Norwegian government 1939.

Princess Roy'al Harbour (roi'ăl). Arm of King George Sound, S coast of Western Australia; harbor of Albany.

Princess Royal Island. Island off the coast of British Columbia, Canada, lat. 53°N; borders on Caamaño Sound on the W.

Prince'ton (prĭns'tŭn). **1** City, ⊗ of Bureau co., N Illinois, 33 m. W of Ottawa; pop. 6250; in agricultural section; farm and dairy products, nursery gardens, fruit.
2 Residential city, ⊗ of Gibson co., SW Indiana, 27 m. N of Evansville; pop. 7906.
3 City, ⊗ of Caldwell co., W Kentucky, 42 m. E of Paducah; pop. 5618; tobacco and livestock market; flour mills, textile mills, quarries, machine shops.
4 Village, Mille Lacs co., E cen. Minnesota, 28 m. E of St. Cloud; pop. 2353; in dairy-farming section; shipping point for large quantities of butter.
5 City, ⊗ of Mercer co., N Missouri, 42 m. N of Chillicothe; pop. 1443; trade center in livestock-raising and dairy-farming section.
6 Borough, Mercer co., W cen. New Jersey, 11 m. NNE of Trenton; pop. 11,890; residential and educational center; printing and publishing. Princeton Univ. (chartered 1746; opened as College of New Jersey at Elizabethtown, now Elizabeth, 1747; removed to Princeton 1756; renamed 1896); Princeton Theological Seminary (estab. 1812); Rockefeller Institute for Medical Research. Settled by Quakers 1696; scene of battle of Princeton in the Revolution Jan. 2–3, 1777 (ending at Nassau Hall on Princeton Univ. campus); seat of Continental Congress June–Nov. 1783.
7 City, ⊗ of Mercer co., S West Virginia, 11 m. NE of Bluefield; pop. 8393; in lumbering, coal-mining, and farming section; manufactures flour, textiles. Settled 1826; scene of engagements in Civil War May 16, 1862; burned by retreating Confederates.

Princeton, Mount. Peak 14,177 ft. in Sawatch Range, Chaffee co., cen. Colorado.

Prince Wil'liam (wĭl'yăm). County in Virginia. See *Table* at VIRGINIA.

Prince William Sound. Inlet of Gulf of Alaska, S Alaska, E of Kenai Penin., 90 to 100 m. across; Montague I. and Hinchinbrook I. lie across its entrance.

Prin'ci·pe (prēn'sĕ·på). District on E coast of Luzon, Phil. Is.; in Spanish times a dependency of Nueva Ecija, annexed to Tayabas prov. June 12, 1902; its capital was Baler.

Prin'ci·pe (prĭn'sĭ·pē; *Port.* prēn'sĕ·pĕ), *or* **Prince** (prĭns), **Island.** Portuguese island in the Gulf of Guinea, N of São Tomé; 58 sq. m.; pop. (1936) ab. 7000; with São Tomé (*q.v.*) forms a Portuguese colony.

Prine'ville (prīn'vĭl). City, ⊗ of Crook co., cen. Oregon, 30 m. NE of Bend; pop. 3263; founded 1868; poultry, dairy, and stock farms; agriculture.

Prin'gle (prĭng'g'l). Borough, Luzerne co., E Pennsylvania, 2 m. N of Wilkes-Barre; pop. 1418.

Prin'ki·po' (prĭng'kĕ·pō'). One of the Princes Is. in the E part of the Sea of Marmara; place of exile for Byzantine empresses.

Prin'sen (prĭn's'n). Island 47 sq. m. at S end of Sunda Strait off the SW tip of Java, Indonesia.

Prin'sen·ha'ge (prĭn's'n·hȧ'kĕ). Commune, North Brabant prov., S Netherlands, a SW suburb of Breda; pop. 11,114.

Prin'za·pol'ca (prēn'sä·pôl'kä). **1** River ab. 120 m. long, E cen. Nicaragua; flows E into the Caribbean Sea at the town of Prinzapolca; gold deposits.
2 Seaport on E coast of Nicaragua, at mouth of river; shipping point for nearby mines.

Pri'pet (prĭp'ĕt). Anglicized form of Russian PRIPYAT.

Pripet, *or* **Pri'pyat** (pryē'pyȧt·y'), **Marshes;** *also* **Pinsk Marshes** (pĭnsk; *Russ.* pyēnsk). Extensive marshlands, S White Russia and NW Ukraine in U.S.S.R., ab. 300 m. E and W and 140 m. N and S, chiefly on both sides of the Pripyat (Pripet) river (*q.v.*);

formerly in Polesie prov., E Poland. Densely wooded and nearly uninhabited, mostly impassable except in winter when frozen; formerly marked a natural boundary bet. Poland and U.S.S.R. and for centuries have greatly affected the strategy of military invasions or mass movements of peoples. In World War I scene of campaigns 1914 and 1915; in World War II bypassed by German armies 1941 and by Russians 1943–44.

Pri'pyat (pryē'pyȧt·y'); *Pol.* **Pry'peć** (prĭ'pĕch); *Angl.* **Pri'pet** (prĭp'ĕt). River ab. 500 m. long, NW Ukraine and S White Russia; rises W of Kovel (formerly in Wołyń dept., Poland), and flows E through the Pripet Marshes (*q.v.*) to the Dnieper in NW Ukraine, joining it near White Russian border 50 m. N of Kiev. Navigable for 300 m. and connected by canals with the Bug (tributary of the Vistula) and Neman rivers. Has many tributaries flowing through the marshes.

Pripyat Marshes. See PRIPET MARSHES.

Prishib. See LENINSK.

Priš'ti·na (prēsh'tĕ·nä). Town, Kosovo-Metohija autonomous prov., S Yugoslavia, ab. 48 m. NNW of Skoplje; pop. 16,948; trading center in mining region; in medieval period a capital of Serbian empire; 14th-cent. monastery nearby.

Pri'vas' (prē'vä'). Commune, ✳ of Ardèche dept., SE France, W of Rhone river 107 m. NNW of Marseilles; pop. 3805; a Protestant stronghold in 16th cent.

Pri·ver'no (prē·vĕr'nô). Commune, Littoria prov., Latium, cen. Italy, 16 m. E by N of Littoria; pop. 13,631.

Priz'ren (prēz'rĕn). Town, Kosovo-Metohija autonomous prov., S Yugoslavia, ab. 40 m. WNW of Skoplje; pop. 18,952; archiepiscopal see (Roman Catholic), episcopal see (Greek); burial place of Serbian king Dushan (d. 1355); many mosques. Taken by Serbs 1912; headquarters of Serbian government during World War I; occupied by Italy during World War II.

Priz'zi (prēt'tsĕ). Commune, Palermo prov., Sicily, 28 m. S by E of Palermo; pop. 10,042.

Pro'bo·ling'go (prō'bô·lĭng'gō). Seaport city on N coast of East Java prov., Indonesia; pop. 37,009; on Madura Strait 45 m. SE of Surabaja.

Pro'ci·da (prô'chē·dä); *anc.* **Proch'y·ta** (prŏk'ĭ·tȧ). Island 2 m. long in the Bay of Naples, Campania compartimento, Italy; pop. (1931) ab. 10,000; highest point 250 ft.; made up of two volcanic craters; small town of **Procida** on NE coast has a castle used as a prison.

Proconnesus. See MARMARA.

Proc'tor (prŏk'tēr). **1** Village, St. Louis co., NE Minnesota, 7 m. SW of Duluth; pop. 2963; before 1939 called **Proc'tor·knott'** (-nŏt').
2 Village in Proctor town (pop. 2102), Rutland co., W Vermont, 5 m. NNW of Rutland; pop. 1978; center of marble industry.

Prod'da·tur (prŏd'ȧ·tŏŏr). Town, S Andhra Pradesh, S Indian Union, on Northern Penner river 160 m. NW of Madras; pop. 20,124.

Profile Mountain. See CANNON MOUNTAIN, New Hampshire.

Pro·gre'so (prô·grā'sô). **1** Seaport town on San Cristóbal I., Galápagos Is.
2 Seaport, Yucatán state, on Yucatán penin., SE Mexico; pop. 11,990; port for Mérida; chief exports sisal, chicle, hides.

Progreso, El. See EL PROGRESO.

Pro Ho·gar' (prō' ô·gär'). Town, Federal District, cen. Mexico; pop. 7163.

Prokletije. See NORTH ALBANIAN ALPS.

Pro·ko'pevsk (prŭ·kô'pyĕfsk). City, S end of Kuznetsk Basin, adjacent to Stalinsk, on Kemerovo Region, Soviet Russia, Asia; pop. 107,227; mining center.

Prome (prōm). **1** District, Pegu division, Lower Burma; 2938 sq. m.; pop. 410,651.
2 Town, its ✳, on left bank of Irrawaddy 150 m. N of Rangoon; pop. 28,295; commercial town and river port; one of the oldest towns in Burma. Has several fine pago-

das and was once capital of flourishing kingdom; later subject to Pegu; taken twice by British in Burmese Wars 1825 and 1852; taken by Japanese Apr. 1942.

Promised Land *or* **Land of Promise.** Canaan; so called because promised to Abraham (*Gen.* xv. 18; xvii. 8).

Promontore, Cape. See Cape KAMENJAK.

Promontorium Sacrum. See Cape SAINT VINCENT.

Prom′on·to′ry Point (prŏm′ŭn·tō′rĭ; *esp. Brit.*, -tĕr·ĭ, -trĭ). Point forming S end of elevated peninsula extending into N part of Great Salt Lake, Box Elder co., NW corner of Utah; its coast line traversed by Lucin Cutoff of Southern Pacific R.R. To the N ab. 30 m. is **Promontory,** locality 30 m. W of Brigham where on May 10, 1869 last spike was driven completing first transcontinental railroad in U.S.; commemorated by Golden Spike Monument.

Proph′ets·town (prŏf′ĕts·toun; -ĭts-). Shawnee Indian village at the confluence of the Tippecanoe and Wabash rivers, W Indiana, ab. 7 m. NNE of Lafayette; destroyed in battle of Tippecanoe Nov. 7, 1811.

Propontis. See Sea of MARMARA.

Pro·pri·á′ (prŏō·prĕ·à′). City, Sergipe state, E Brazil, on the São Francisco 55 m. NNE of Aracajú; pop. (1940 est.) 10,414.

Pro·sku′rov (prŭ·skŏō′rŭf). Town, ✳ of Kamenets Podolski Region, W Ukraine, U.S.S.R., on upper course of the Bug river 55 m. N of Kamenets Podolsk; pop. 26,350; on the main railroad line from W Ukraine to SE Poland and junction for other lines. Dates from 15th cent. in Podolia; in World War II occupied by the Germans 1941–44.

Pros′na (prŏs′nä). River ab. 100 m. long, W Poland; flows N, forming a section of the boundary bet. Łódź and Poznań depts., and empties into Warta river 38 m. SE of Poznań.

Pros′pec·tors Mountain (prŏs′pĕk·tĕrz). Peak 11,231 ft. in S Grand Teton National Park, NW Wyoming.

Pros′pect Park (prŏs′pĕkt). **1** Residential borough, Passaic co., N New Jersey, 2 m. N of Paterson; pop. 5201. **2** Borough, Delaware co., SE Pennsylvania, 10 m. SW of Philadelphia; pop. 6596.

Prospect Point. See NIAGARA FALLS.

Prospect Reservoir. Large reservoir, New South Wales, SE Australia, ab. 12 m. W of Sydney.

Pros′ser (prŏs′ẽr). City, ⊗ of Benton co., S Washington, on Yakima river 48 m. SE of Yakima; pop. 2763; ships cattle and sheep.

Pro′stĕ·jov (prô′styĕ·yôf); *Ger.* **Pross′nitz** (prŏs′nĭts). City, cen. Moravia prov., Czechoslovakia, ab. 25 m. NE of Brno; pop. (1930) 33,481; textile mills; trade center for grain.

Pro·vence′ (prô·väns′); *Lat.* **Pro·vin′ci·a** (prô·vĭn′shĭ·à; -shà). Historical region of SE France; bounded anciently on N by Dauphiné, E by countship of Nice, S by Mediterranean, W by Languedoc, NW by Comtat Venaissin; ✳ Aix; watered by Durance and Rhone rivers; diverse topography, including plateaus in W, Alpine chains in E, ancient massifs along sea, and vast plains; one of great provincial governments of ancien régime; its language, Provençal, important in medieval literature and, since 19th-cent. revival, significant in modern literature.

History: Part of Roman Gallia Narbonensis (see GAUL); invaded by Visigoths, Burgundians, Ostrogoths, and Franks; became part of realm of Lothair I by Treaty of Verdun 843 A.D.; kingdom of Provence ruled by Charles, son of Lothair, 855–865; under Charles the Bald 865–879; second kingdom of Provence (Cisjurane Burgundy) 879–933; with Transjurane Burgundy became kingdom of Arles (*q.v.*) 933; made countship 1113; passed as dowry to Charles of Anjou 1246; under Angevin rule to 1481; passed to Louis XI of France 1481; invaded 1524 by Constable of France and 1536 by

Charles V; suffered in Wars of Religion; invaded 1704 by troops of Prince Eugene and 1746 by duke of Savoy; province of France until Revolution.

Prov′i·dence (prŏv′ĭ·dĕns). **1** Navigable river, a N arm of Narragansett Bay, formed by the confluence of two small rivers in the city of Providence, Rhode Island. **2** County in Rhode Island. See *Table* at RHODE ISLAND. **3** City, Webster co., W Kentucky, 33 m. WSW of Henderson; pop. 3771. **4** Original name of ANNAPOLIS, Maryland. **5** Industrial city and port of entry, ✳ of Rhode Island and ⊗ of Providence co., N Rhode Island, at head of Providence river; largest city in the state; pop. 207,498; excellent harbor; called southern gateway of New England; manufactures jewelry, silverware, and allied products, cotton and worsted goods, tools, machinery, soap; printing and publishing. Brown Univ. (1764) and its affiliate Pembroke Coll. for women (1892); Providence Coll. (1917), Rhode Island School of Design (1877); Rhode Island College (1854). Founded by Roger Williams 1636; joined "Incorporation of Providence Plantations" (chartered 1644); figured in King Philip's War and, later, in Revolution (schooner *Gaspee* destroyed here 1772); engaged in profitable rum, slave, and molasses trade, privateering, and shipping 1680 ff.; incorporated as city 1831. **6** See FORT PROVIDENCE, Canada. **7** Small British island in the Indian Ocean NNE of Madagascar, lat. 9°S and long. 51°E; dependency of Seychelles.

Providence Bay; *Russ.* **Pro·vi·de′ni·ya** (prŭ·vyĭ·dyä′nyĭ·yà). Inlet of Bering Sea, SE Chukotski Penin., NE Soviet Russia, Asia, NW of St. Lawrence I.

Providence Channel, North West *and* **North East.** Channels in the Bahama Is., West Indies, bet. Atlantic Ocean and the Straits of Florida, S of Grand Bahama I. and Abaco I. and N of Bimini, Berry Is., and Eleuthera.

Providence Plantations. See RHODE ISLAND.

Pro·vi·den′cia, Is′la de (ēz′lä thä prô′vĕ·thän′syä). Small island in W Caribbean Sea off E coast of Nicaragua; belongs to Colombia and with San Andrés I. constitutes the intendancy of San Andrés y Providencia (see *Table* at COLOMBIA).

Prov′i·den′ci·a′les (prŏv′ĭ·dĕn′sĭ·ä′lĕs). One of the Caicos Is. See TURKS AND CAICOS ISLANDS.

Provideniya. See PROVIDENCE BAY.

Provinces, the. The Dominion of Canada.

Prov′ince·town′ (prŏv′ĭns·toun′). Town, Barnstable co., SE Massachusetts, on N tip of Cape Cod; pop. 3389; fishing and summer resort; art center, seat of Cape Cod School of Art (founded 1901 by Charles W. Hawthorne); seat of a little theater group, the Provincetown Players, organized (1915) and directed until 1922 by George Cram Cook. First landing place of Pilgrims Nov. 11 [O.S.], 1620; Mayflower Compact drawn up in harbor Nov. 21, 1620; incorporated 1727.

Prov′ince Welles′ley (prŏv′ĭns wĕlz′lĭ). A division of Penang settlement, Federation of Malaya, located on the mainland of Malay Penin. opp. Penang I.; 280 sq. m.; pop. 141,388, (1941 est.) 171,587. State railroad from Singapore crosses it to Prai, opp. George Town. Chief town Butterworth. Ceded to Great Britain by Kedah 1798; part of Federation of Malaya 1948.

Provincia. See PROVENCE.

Provincias Vascongadas. See BASQUE PROVINCES.

Pro′vins′ (prô′văN′). Town, E Seine-et-Marne dept., N France, ab. 25 m. E of Melun; pop. 7354; noted for its roses; manufactures bricks, porcelain, gas engines; has three interesting churches. Flourished 9th–13th cents.; suffered from plague 14th cent., Hundred Years' War 14th–15th cents., and the religious wars of the 16th cent. during which it was besieged and taken by Henry IV 1592.

Pro′vo (prō′vō). **1** River ab. 40 m. long, N cen. Utah; rises in W end of Uinta Mts., flows SW into Utah Lake;

site of dam for irrigation and for Provo and Salt Lake City water supply.

2 Commercial and industrial city, ⊗ of Utah co., N cen. Utah, on Provo river 3 m. from Utah Lake 38 m. SSE of Salt Lake City; pop. 36,047; packing plants, brickyards, blast furnaces and foundries, flour mills; summer resort and tourist center. Brigham Young Univ. (1875; coed.). Settled by Mormons 1849; chartered as city 1851.

Provo Peak. Mountain 11,054 ft. in Utah co., N cen. Utah, E of the city of Provo in the Wasatch Range.

Prow′ers (prō′ērz). County in Colorado. See *Table* at COLORADO.

Proy′art′ (prwà′yàr′). Village, Somme dept., N France, 12 m. SW of Péronne; battle Mar. 27–28, 1918.

Pru′dence Island (prōō′d′ns). Island in Narragansett Bay, NW of Rhode I. (island), a part of Newport co., Rhode Island.

Prud′hoe (prŭd′ō; prŭd′hō). Urban district, Northumberland, N England, on the Tyne 11 m. W of Newcastle; pop. 9571.

Prud′nik (prōōd′nēk); *Ger.* **Neu′stadt** *or* **Neustadt in O′ber·schle′si·en** (noi′shtät ĭn ō′bēr·shlä′zĕ·ĕn). City, SW Śląsk dept., S Poland, W of Zabrze near Czechoslovakian border; pop. 17,371; formerly in Silesia, Germany; manufactures linen, damask, shoes, leather. Scene of battles bet. Prussians and Austrians 1745, 1760, 1779, in Silesian Wars and in War of the Bavarian Succession. Assigned to Poland by Potsdam Conference 1945.

Prüm (prüm). Town, W Germany, in Rhineland-Palatinate state 35 m. N of Trier near Belgian border; pop. 2843; scene of severe fighting in World War II Feb.–Mar. 1945.

Prusa. See BURSA.

Prus′sia (prŭsh′à); *Ger.* **Preus′sen** (proi′sĕn). Former German state, N and cen. Germany; 113,545 sq. m.; pop. 38,175,989, (1939) 41,762,040; ✳ Berlin; other important cities included Cologne, Breslau, Königsberg, Magdeburg, Hannover, Stettin, Kassel, Koblenz, Münster, Schleswig, Düsseldorf; chiefly a plain, watered by Rhine, Oder, Elbe, and Weser rivers among others; important coal mines, metal deposits, agriculture, heavy industry. Divided into the following 12 provinces, which were formerly subdivided into government districts [Regierungsbezirke] (for pronunciation of their names, see their individual entries):

ENGLISH NAME	GERMAN NAME	LOCATION IN PRUSSIA	AREA	POP. (1939 CENSUS)	CAPITAL
Berlin	Stadt Berlin	E	341	4,332,242	Berlin
Brandenburg[1]	Brandenburg	NE cen.	14,778	3,023,443	Potsdam
East Prussia	Ostpreussen	NE	15,382	2,649,017	Königsberg
Hanover	Hannover	NW	14,944	3,537,390	Hannover
Hesse-Nassau[2]	Hessen-Nassau	SW	6,504	2,688,922	Kassel
Hohenzollern	Hohenzollern	[3]	441	74,151	Sigmaringen
Pomerania	Pommern	N	14,826	2,405,021	Stettin
Rhine Province[4]	Rheinprovinz[5]	SW	9,450	7,931,942	Koblenz
Saxony	Sachsen	S	9,856	3,622,546	Magdeburg
Schleswig-Holstein	Schleswig-Holstein	NW	6,055	1,598,328	Kiel
Silesia[6]	Schlesien	SE	14,290	4,846,333	Breslau
Westphalia	Westfalen	W	7,805	5,205,705	Münster

[1] Includes former province of Grenzmark Posen-Westpreussen.
[2] Annexed Waldeck Apr. 1, 1929.
[3] Exclave in S Württemberg.
[4] Called also Rhenish Prussia.
[5] Called also Rheinland.
[6] Formerly formed two provinces, Oppeln *or* Upper Silesia, *Ger.* Oberschlesien (capital Oppeln) and Lower Silesia, *Ger.* Niederschlesien (capital Breslau). By plebiscite in 1919 part of Upper Silesia assigned to Poland; annexed to Germany 1939; nearly all of Silesia became part of Poland 1945.

History: Early Prussians a people of Baltic stock dwelling along shore east of the Vistula; finally conquered, converted to Christianity, and colonized by Teutonic Knights 13th cent. (see EAST PRUSSIA); in 1466, western Prussia ceded by Teutonic Knights to Poland, while East Prussia became Polish fief; secularized and erected as duchy under Polish suzerainty 1525; in 17th cent., its ruler, Elector of Brandenburg, secured duchy's independence of Poland; kingdom of Prussia erected from all holdings of Brandenburg (*q.v.*) 1701; as strong military state, especially under Frederick II 1740–86, Prussia expanded to include territories on Rhine, E Pomerania 1720, Silesia 1742–63, and western part of Poland (*q.v.*) 1772–95; received Rhine Province and part of Saxony 1815; provinces of West and East Prussia united 1824–78; strong German customs union (*Ger.* Zollverein) formed under Prussian leadership 1819–44; until 1918 ruled according to 1850 constitution; secured Lauenburg and administration of Schleswig (*q.v.*) 1865; after war against Austria 1866, annexed electoral Hesse, Nassau, Frankfurt, Hannover, Holstein, Austrian Silesia, and some South German territory; led North German Confederation 1867–71; German Empire (see GERMANY), of which Prussian king became Emperor William I, founded under Prussian leadership 1871; became republic 1918; annexed Waldeck 1929; after World War II by decision of Potsdam Conference 1945 lost the entire E part, portions of Silesia, Brandenburg, Pomerania, and East Prussia going to Poland and the N part of East Prussia to the U.S.S.R.; dissolved as an administrative unit 1947.

Prussia, East *and* **West.** See EAST PRUSSIA and WEST PRUSSIA.

Pruszcz Gdań′ski (prōōshch g′dän′y·skĕ); *Ger.* **Praust** (proust). Commune, E cen. Gdańsk dept., N Poland, S of city of Danzig, formerly in Free City of Danzig territory; pop. ab. 4000.

Prusz′ków (prōōsh′kōōf). Commune, ✳ of Warszawa dept., Poland, 7 m. WSW of Warsaw; pop. (1938–39 est.) 27,120; electric plant.

Prut (prōōt); *Ger.* **Pruth** (prōōt). River ab. 500 m. long, E boundary of Romania; rises in SW Ukraine (formerly Poland) in the Carpathian Mts. and flows SSE into the Danube river at Reni, below Galaţi, 75 m. from the Black Sea. Formerly almost entirely within Romania, separating Moldavia from Bessarabia (now part of Moldavian S.S.R.). Treaty of the Pruth (July 21, 1711) signed on its banks near Iaşi by which Tsar Peter of Russia was compelled by the Turks to return Azov.

Pry′or Creek (prī′ēr). City (post office, **Pryor**), ⊗ of Mayes co., NE Oklahoma, 41 m. ENE of Tulsa; pop. 6476; U.S. Dept. of Agriculture experiment station.

Prypeć. See PRIPYAT.

Przas′nysz (pshäs′nĭsh). Commune, Warszawa dept., Poland, 53 m. N of Warsaw; pop. 7838; scene of battles World War I bet. Germans and Russians Feb. and July 1915; Germans ultimately successful.

Prze′myśl (pshĕ′mĭsh); *Russ.* **Pe′re·myshl′** (pĕr′ĕ·mĭsh′′l; *Russ.* pyĭ·ryĕ·mĭsh′ly′). Fortified city, E Rzeszów dept., SE Poland, on San river near Ukraine border 54 m. W of Lvov, formerly in Lwów dept., Poland; pop. (1938–39 est.) 58,500; Roman and Greek Catholic episcopal sees. Seat of Ukrainian princes 11th–13th cents.; Austrian fortress in World War I; besieged by Russians 1914–15; in the first siege, Sept. 24, 1914 to Oct. 11, Russians were unsuccessful; in the second, Nov. 6, 1914 to Mar. 22, 1915, was taken by Russians but soon (in June) had to be given up; was only land fortress in the war to withstand prolonged siege.

Pr.he·valsk′ (pĕr·zhĕ·väl′y′sk); *formerly* **Ka′ra·kol′** (kä′rä·kûl′). Town, NE Kirgiz S.S.R., Soviet Russia, Asia, at E end of Issyk Kul; center of agricultural region and of trade routes E and N; port for steamer traffic on the lake. Name changed in honor of the Russian explorer Nikolai M. Przhevalski, who died here 1888.

Psa·ra′ (psä·rä′) *or* **I′psa·ra′** (ē′psä·rä′); *Mod. Gr.* **Psa·rà′** (psä·rä′); *anc.* **Psy′ra** (sī′rà). One of the Ae-

gean Is. W of Chios; 35 sq. m.; pop. ab. 4000; captured by Turkey 1824; after Balkan War annexed to Greece 1914.

Psel *or* **Psiol** (psyôl). River ab. 420 m. long, Soviet Russia, Europe, mostly in Ukraine; rises in Kursk Region and flows S to the Dnieper near Kremenchug; has winding course through fertile region.

Psiloriti. See IDA.

Pskov (pskôf). **1** *Estonian* **Pih'kva** (pē'kvà). Southern arm of Lake Peipus, bet. Estonia and W Pskov Region, Soviet Russia, Europe; ab. 400 sq. m.; receives Velikaya river.

2 City, ✱ of Pskov Region, Soviet Russia, Europe, on Velikaya river near SE shore of Lake Pskov (Lake Peipus), 155 m. SW of Leningrad; pop. 59,898; 9 m. from mouth of navigable Velikaya in a region famous for its fine flax; has a linen factory and is a thriving commercial city, exporting grains, flax, timber, fish, skins; important railroad center. An old city, known in the 9th cent.; its growth and history paralleled that of Novgorod; until 1348 a dependency of Novgorod but having free institutions; in 11th and 12th cents. its possession frequently disputed bet. Russians and Germans and Lithuanians; captured 1510 by Basil Ivanovich, prince of Moscow, and incorporated into Muscovy; scene of later conflicts or sieges 1502, 1581, 1615; held by Germans in World War II 1941–44; recaptured by Russians July 22, 1944.

Pskov Region. Region, NW Soviet Russia, Europe; bounded on N by Leningrad Region, on E by Novgorod Region, on S by Velikie Luki Region, and on W by Latvian and Estonian Republics; ✱ Pskov; formed 1945 out of Leningrad Region; includes part of Lake Peipus.

Psyra. See PSARA.

Pszczy'na (pshchi'nä); *Ger.* **Pless** (plĕs). Town, SE Śląsk dept., SW Poland, 15 m. SE of Rybnik; pop. ab. 7660; formerly in Prussia.

Ptar'mi·gan Peak (tär'mĭ·găn). Mountain 13,736 ft. in Park and Lake cos., cen. Colorado.

Pte'ri·a (tē̱r'ĭ·à). A place in ancient Cappadocia, Asia Minor, described by Herodotus; probably the ruined capital of the Hittite nation, modern Bogazköy (*q.v.*).

Ptol'e·ma'ïs (tŏl'ĕ·mā'ĭs). **1** Ancient town on left bank of Nile, Egypt, halfway bet. Hermopolis Magna and Thebae.

2 See TOLMETA, Cyrenaica, Libya.

3 See ACRE, Palestine.

Pu·call'pa (pōō·kï'pä). Town, S Loreto dept., NE Peru, on the lower Ucayali river; terminus of newly completed (1945) highway from Lima.

Pu'cio Point (pōō'syô). Northwestern point of Panay I. and of Antique prov., Phil. Is.; marks boundary with Capiz.

Puck (pōōtsk). Town, N Poland, on NW coast of Gulf of Danzig, N of Gdynia; on W shore of **Puck'ka Bay** (pōōts'kä), inlet of NW Gulf of Danzig formed by Hel Penin.

Puck'a·way, Lake (pŭk'à·wä). Lake in W Green Lake co., cen. Wisconsin.

Puck'le·church' (pŭk''l·chûrch'); *Old English* **Pu'clan Cyr'can** (pōō'klän kür'kän). Ancient locality, Gloucestershire, SW England, ab. 10 m. NE of Bristol; Edmund I, king of the English, killed here 946.

Pud'sey (pŭd'zĭ, -sĭ). Municipal borough, West Riding, Yorkshire, N England, 6 m. W of Leeds; pop. 30,276; manufactures woolens; dyeing.

Pu'duk·kot'tai (pōō'dŏŏk·kŏt'tī). **1** Former Indian state, Madras States, in S Madras, S India, bet. Tanjore and Madura; 1185 sq. m.; pop. (1941) 438,348.

2 Town, its ✱, 38 m. SSW of Tanjore; pop. 28,776.

Pue'bla (pwā'vlä; *Angl.* pŭ·ĕb'là). **1** State, SE cen. Mexico. See *Table* at MEXICO.

2 *in full* **Pue'bla de Za'ra·go'za** (pwā'vlä thä sä'rä·gō'sä). City, its ✱; pop. 138,491; altitude 7150 ft.; one of the oldest and most famous cities in Mexico; cathedral

with paintings ascribed to Murillo and Velázquez; textile mills, pottery manufacturing. See CHOLULA.

Pu·eb'lo (pŭ·ĕb'lō). **1** County in Colorado. See *Table* at COLORADO.

2 Manufacturing and commercial city, its ⊗, SE cen. Colorado, on Arkansas river 40 m. SSE of Colorado Springs; pop. 91,181; trade center for irrigated agricultural region; gold, silver, and copper smelters; iron and steel foundries, machine shops, glass factories, tileworks, meat-packing plants; limestone quarries, ore deposits, and coal and oil fields nearby; hunting and fishing resort. Platted 1859–60; incorporated as town 1870, absorbing Fountain City; incorporated as city 1873.

Pue'blo Bo·ni'to (pwā'vlō vô·nē'tô). Literally "beautiful village," largest of prehistoric pueblo ruins, Chaco Canyon National Monument, New Mexico; covers 3 acres; town flourished 10th–12th cents.

Pu·eb'lo Gran'de (pŭ·ĕb'lō grän'dĕ). Prehistoric ruin 5 m. E of Phoenix, Maricopa co., SW cen. Arizona; partly excavated mound is 30 ft. high, 300 ft. long, 150 ft. wide, surrounded on three sides by a wall containing a remarkable amount of stone for a pueblo ruin.

Pueblonuevo. See PEÑARROYA-PUEBLONUEVO.

Pue'blo Nue'vo del Mar (pwā'vlō nwä'vô thĕl märˈ). Former commune, Valencia, Spain, now part of Valencia city; seaside resort.

Pue'blo Vie'jo, La·gu'na del (lä·gōō'nä thĕl pwā'vlō vyē'hô). Inlet of Gulf of Mexico in E cen. Mexican coast, S of the mouth of the Pánuco river.

Puen'te Al'to (pwän'tä äl'tô). Town, Santiago prov., cen. Chile, just S of Santiago; pop. 10,145.

Puen'te·a·re'as (pwän'tä·ä·rā'äs). Commune, Pontevedra prov., NW Spain, 18 m. SSE of Pontevedra; pop. 14,634.

Puen'te del In'ca (pwän'tä thĕl ēng'kä). Natural bridge in the Andes Mts., W Argentina, W of city of Mendoza; height 65 ft. over the Cuevas river; length of span 70 ft.; width 90 ft.

Puen'te–Ge·nil' (pwän'tä–hä·nēl'). Commune, Córdoba prov., S Spain, 35 m. S of Córdoba; pop. 27,552; agricultural products; stone and lime quarries; manufactures soap, leather, flour, pottery.

Pu·e'o Point (pōō·ā'ô). Cape on E cen. coast of Niihau I., Hawaii.

Puer'co (pwĕr'kō). River ab. 120 m. long, NW New Mexico and E Arizona; rises in McKinley co., NW New Mexico, flows SW across Arizona border and joins the Little Colorado river in E cen. Arizona, in Navajo co.

Puer'ta, Point (pwĕr'tä). Cape on E coast of Puerto Rico.

Puer'ta·ci'tas (pwĕr'tà·sē'tàs). Mountains (literally "little doors") 6000 ft. in S Jeff Davis co., W Texas.

Puer'to Ar·muel'les (pwĕr'tô är·mwä'yäs). Pacific coast port, extreme W Panama, on Charco Azul Bay; pop. 3328.

Puerto Arrecife. See ARRECIFE.

Puer'to A'ya·cu'cho (pwĕr'tô ä'yä·kōō'chô). Town, ✱ of Amazonas territory, S Venezuela, on the Orinoco and on Colombia border; pop. (1941 est.) 878.

Puerto Bar'rios (vär'ryôs). Atlantic seaport, E Guatemala, on the Gulf of Honduras, ✱ of Izabal dept.; pop. 15,784.

Puerto Bello. See PORTOBELO.

Puerto Ber'rio (vĕr'ryô). River port, Antioquia dept. NW Colombia, on Magdalena river ab. 320 m. S of Barranquilla; pop. 5487.

Puerto Bo·lí'var (vô·lē'vär). Port on SW coast of Ecuador, 75 m. S of Guayaquil; the port of Machala (*q.v.*).

Puerto Ca·bel'lo (kä·vä'yô). Seaport, Carabobo state, N Venezuela, 70 m. W of Caracas; pop. (1941 est.) 16,772; the port of Valencia.

Puerto Ca·be'zas (kä·vä'säs). Seaport on NE coast of Nicaragua; pop. (1940) 1500; shipping point for bananas and timber.

Puerto Can·sa′do (kän·sä′thỏ). Coastal town, S Morocco, NW Africa, NNE of Cape Yubi.

Puerto Car·re′ño (kär·rě′nyỏ). Town, * of Vichada commissary, E Colombia, at the junction of the Meta with the Orinoco.

Puerto Ca·sa′do (kä·sä′thỏ). Town, Boquerón dept., NW Paraguay, on W bank of Paraguay river near Brazil border and 200 m. N of Asunción; pop. ab. 6300; railroad terminus and river port for Chaco region.

Puerto Cas·til′la (käs·tē′yä). Seaport on N coast of Honduras, across a bay just N of Trujillo; built and developed by the United Fruit Co.; pop. ab. 1700; exports bananas; founded 1525 by an agent sent by Cortes.

Puerto Co·lom′bia (kỏ·lôm′byä). Seaport, Atlántico dept., N Colombia, 12 m. NW of Barranquilla, and formerly its port; now a bathing resort.

Puerto Cor·tés′ (kôr·tās′). Seaport, Cortés dept., NW Honduras, on the Gulf of Honduras; pop. (1940) 7019; founded c. 1525; largest Atlantic port in Honduras; exports bananas.

Puerto de Ca′bras (thä kä′vräs). Chief port of Fuerteventura I., Canary Is., Spain; pop. (1930) 3441.

Puerto de San′ta Ma·rí′a (sän′tä mä·rē′ä); *generally called* **El Puer′to** (ĕl pwĕr′tỏ). Commune, Cádiz prov., SW Spain, on Bay of Cádiz at mouth of Guadalete river 8 m. NE of Cádiz; pop. 29,197; manufactures leather, soap, hats, wines, brandies, glass, starch, flour; fisheries; exports sherry from Jerez; Gothic church.

Puerto De·se·a′do (dā′sä·ả′thỏ). Town and bay on E coast of Santa Cruz territory, S Argentina, at the mouth of Deseado river; pop. of town ab. 2000.

Puerto Gallegos. See GALLEGOS river port.

Puerto Ibañeta. See RONCESVALLES.

Puerto La Cruz (lä krōōs′). City and port, Anzoátegui state, N Venezuela, NE of Barcelona; oil refineries; pop. 28,385.

Puer′to Li·món′ *or* **Limón** (pwĕr′tỏ lē·môn′). Seaport, * of Limón prov., E cen. Costa Rica; pop. (1943 est.) 9760; chief port of Costa Rica; center of the banana trade; exporting port for coffee shipments.

Puer′tol·la′no (pwĕr′tỏ·[l]yä′nỏ). Commune, Ciudad Real prov., S cen. Spain, 24 m. SSW of Ciudad Real; pop. 24,676; mineral baths; agricultural products; coal, iron, lead, manganese mines.

Puer′to Ma′dryn (pwĕr′tỏ mä′thrĕn). Seaport on NE coast of Chubut territory, S Argentina, on New Gulf; pop. ab. 2300; finest port in Patagonia.

Puerto Mal′do·na′do (mäl′dỏ·nä′thỏ). Town, * of Madre de Dios dept., SE Peru, at junction of the Tambopata and Madre de Dios rivers ab. 525 m. E of Lima; pop. ab. 1000.

Puerto México. See COATZACOALCOS.

Puer′to Montt (pwĕr′tỏ mônt′). Seaport on Gulf of Ancud, S cen. Chile, 12 m. S of Lake Llanquihue and ab. 570 m. S of Santiago; * of Llanquihue prov.; pop. 21,360; terminus of the southern railroad; settled largely by German immigrants.

Puerto Mu′tis (mōō′tēs). Pacific coast port, SW cen. Panama, at the head of the Gulf of Montijo.

Puerto Na·ta′les (nä·tä′lås). Town, Magallanes prov., S Chile, N of the Strait of Magellan near Argentina border; pop. 6475.

Puerto Orotava. See LA OROTAVA.

Puer′to Pa′dre (pwĕr′tỏ pä′thrả). Municipality and town, Oriente prov., E Cuba; town on inlet on N coast 30 m. NW of Holguín; pop. (1943) 8187.

Puerto Pi·nas′co (pē·näs′kỏ). Town, Boquerón dept., NW Paraguay, on W bank of Paraguay river ab. 178 m. N of Asunción; pop. ab. 7000; makes quebracho products.

Puerto Pla′ta (plä′tä). **1** Province, N Dominican Republic. See *Table* at DOMINICAN REPUBLIC.

2 *formerly* **San Fe·li′pe de Puerto Plata** (säm fä·lē′pả thä). Commune and seaport city, its *; pop. of commune (1941) 58,190, of city (1944 est.) 15,366; exports tobacco, sugar, hides, coffee, cacao, hardwoods.

Puer′to Prin·ce′sa (pwĕr′tỏ prĕn·sä′sä). Municipality, * of Palawan, on sheltered harbor in cen. part of E coast, Phil. Is.; pop. 10,887; has most of the trade of the island. In Spanish times a penal colony; succeeded Cuyo as capital ab. 1903; occupied by American forces Feb. 28, 1945.

Puerto Prín′ci·pe (prēn′sē·pả). Former name of CAMAGÜEY province and city, Cuba.

Puer′to Re·al′ (pwĕr′tỏ rrē·äl′); *anc.* **Por′tus Gad′i·ta′nus** (pôr′tŭs găd′ĭ·tä′nŭs). Seaport, Cádiz prov., SW Spain, on Bay of Cádiz 7 m. E of Cádiz; pop. 14,854; rebuilt 1488 by Ferdinand and Isabella.

Puer′to Ri′co (pwĕr′tŭ rē′kō) *formerly* **Por′to Rico** (pôr′tŭ). Island of the West Indies, in the Atlantic Ocean 70 m. E of Hispaniola; 3435 sq. m. (land area 3423 sq. m.); pop. 2,349,544; * San Juan; belongs to U.S.A. At E end of Greater Antilles; has coastal plain, narrow in S, mountain ranges in interior, highest point Cerro de Punta 4398 ft.; rivers not useful for navigation but they supply water power and irrigation; the few lakes are very small and are located in the coastal plain; chief products for export are sugar, tobacco, coffee and fruits (grapefruit and pineapples); chief cities San Juan, Ponce, and Mayagüez.

History: Discovered by Columbus Nov. 19, 1493; no colonization attempted until 1508 when Ponce de León set out to explore the island; Caparra founded 1509 but abandoned 1511; de León made governor 1510; after gold supply depleted, island neglected by Spain until

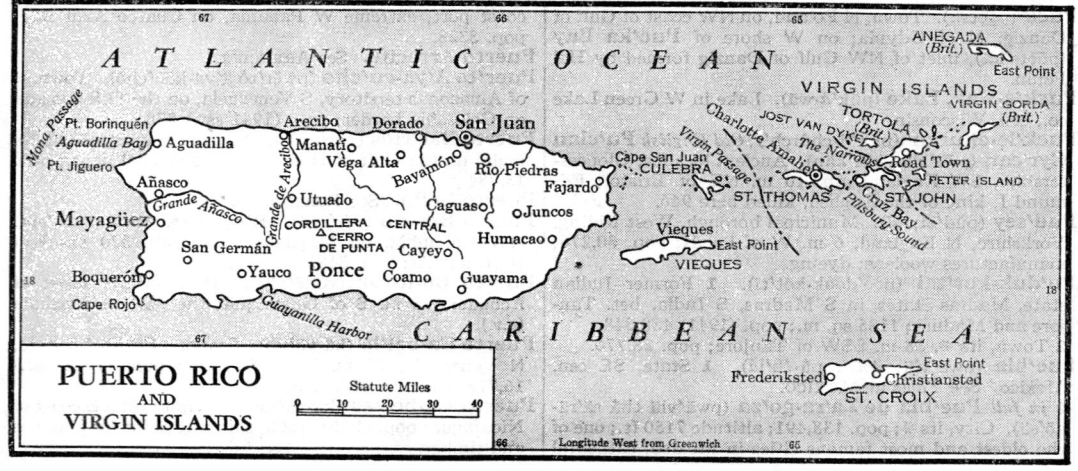

1533 when fortifications around San Juan were begun; first American troops landed on S coast July 25, 1898 during Spanish-American War; American occupation began Oct. 18, 1898, treaty ceding the island signed Dec. 10, 1898; name changed officially to Puerto Rico 1932; on adoption of constitution 1952 became a commonwealth with autonomy in internal affairs.

Puer'to Sas'tre (pwĕr'tô säs'trä). Town, Boquerón dept., NW Paraguay, on Paraguay river opp. point where border of Brazil meets the Paraguay river.

Puerto Sauce. See SAUCE.

Puer'to Suá'rez (pwĕr'tô swä'räs). River port, Santa Cruz dept., E Bolivia, near Paraguay river, NE Chaco region; 11 m. W of Corumbá, Brazil; by difficult overland route 391 m. SE of Santa Cruz; customs post and export center for rubber and coffee.

Puerto Te·ja'da (tĕ·hä'thä). Town, Cauca dept., SW Colombia, just S of Cali; pop. 5566.

Puerto Va'ras (vä'räs). Town on Lake Llanquihue, Llanquihue prov., S cen. Chile, ab. 12 m. N of Puerto Montt; pop. 5273; settled mostly by Germans.

Puer'to·vie'jo (pwĕr'tô·vyĕ'hô). = PORTOVIEJO.

Puer'to Wil'ches (pwĕr'tô wēl'chäs). River port, Santander dept., N cen. Colombia, on Magdalena river N of Barrancabermeja.

Pu·ga·chev' (pŏŏ·gŭ·chôf'); *formerly* **Ni·ko·la'evsk** (nyĭ·kŭ·lä'yĕfsk) *and* **Pu·ga·chevsk'** (pŏŏ·gŭ·chôfsk'). Town, E Saratov Region, Soviet Russia, Europe, 120 m. ENE of Saratov on the navigable Irgiz river; pop. 17,460; a trading town, esp. in grain and farm products; terminus of a branch of the Saratov-Uralsk railroad. Founded 1762 by Raskolniks.

Pu'get Sound (pū'jĕt; -jĭt). Arm of Pacific Ocean extending S in W Washington from E end of Juan de Fuca Strait through Admiralty Inlet, having many branches;

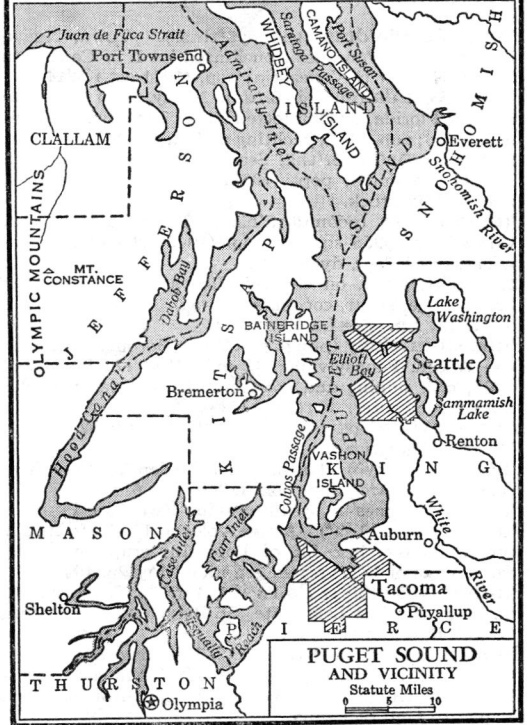

PUGET SOUND
AND VICINITY
Statute Miles
0 5 10

ab. 80 m. long at its greatest extent; important U.S. navy yard at Bremerton is on its W shore opp. Seattle. Explored by George Vancouver 1792.

Pugh, Mount (pū). Peak 7150 ft. in Snohomish co., NW cen. Washington.

Puglia; Puglie, Le. See APULIA.

Puig'cer·dá' (pwĕg'thĕr·thä'; -sĕr·thä'). Fortified frontier commune, Gerona prov., NE Spain, 80 m. NNW of Barcelona; pop. (1930) 2842. See BOURG-MADAME.

Pu'ji·lí' (pŏŏ'hĕ·lē'). Town, Cotopaxi prov., cen. Ecuador, ab. 50 m. S of Quito; pop. (1944 est.) 9138.

Pu·ka'ki, Lake (pŏŏ·kä'kē). Lake, S cen. South I., New Zealand, near foot of Aorangi.

Pu'ka·pu'ka (pŏŏ'kä·pŏŏ'kä). Chief island of the Danger Is., in Manihiki Is. group, cen. Pacific Ocean, N of Cook Is.; ab. 2 sq. m.

Puket. See PHUKET.

Pu'kow' (pŏŏ'kō'). Port on N bank of the Yangtze, W Kiangsu prov., E China, opp. Nanking; railroad terminus of Tientsin-Pukow line (628 m. from Tientsin); has frequent railroad ferry service and some local trade by junks.

Pu'la·ca'yo (pŏŏ'lä·kä'yô). Town, Potosí dept., SW Bolivia, 12 m. E of Uyuni; alt. 13,600 ft.; pop. ab. 8000; large silver mine.

Pu·lang'i (pŏŏ·läng'ĕ). See MINDANAO river.

Pu·lar' (pŏŏ·lär'). Peak 20,340 ft. in E Antofagasta prov., N Chile, near Argentina border.

Pu·las'ki (pŭ·läs'kĭ; pŭ-; *Pulaski, N.Y., is* -kĭ). **1** Name of counties in seven states of the U.S. See *Tables* at ARKANSAS, GEORGIA, ILLINOIS, INDIANA, KENTUCKY, MISSOURI, VIRGINIA.

2 Village, a ⊗ of Oswego co., cen. New York, near Lake Ontario 30 m. SSW of Watertown; pop. 2256.

3 Town, ⊗ of Giles co., S Tennessee, 28 m. S of Columbia; pop. 6616; trading center for region producing grains, cotton, tobacco, cattle; tomato canning; birthplace of first Ku-Klux shortly after Civil War.

4 Industrial town, ⊗ of Pulaski co., SW Virginia, in Allegheny Mts. 52 m. WSW of Roanoke; pop. 10,469; produces grain, iron, zinc, lumber, coal; textile and lumber mills.

Pu'lau (pŏŏ'lou); *also* **Poe'lau** (pŏŏ'lou) *and* **Pu'lo** (pŏŏ'lō). Malay term meaning "island," often used with names of islands in the Malay Archipelago, as **Pulau Langkawi** (see Pulau LANGKAWI).

Pu·ła'wy (pŏŏ·lä'vĭ). Industrial commune, Lublin dept., E Poland, on E bank of Vistula river; pop. (1938–39 est.) 14,000; agricultural college; formerly seat of Czartoryski family.

Pul'i·cat (pŭl'ĭ·kát). **1** Town, Madras, S Indian Union, at S end of Pulicat Lagoon; pop. 4164; Dutch built fort here 1610; long their chief settlement on Coromandel Coast; several times captured, became British 1825.

2 Var. of PALGHAT.

Pulicat Lagoon. Shallow lagoon in Andhra Pradesh and Madras states, India, ab. 37 m. along coast W of Sriharikota I.

Pulj (pŏŏl'y'); *Ital.* **Po'la** (pō'lä; *Ital.* pô'lä); *anc.* **Pi'e·tas Ju'lia** (pī'ĕ·tăs jŏŏl'yá; jŏŏ'lĭ·á). Fortified seaport at S tip of Istrian Penin., Croatia federative republic, NW Yugoslavia, 53 m. S of Trieste; pop. 46,259; formerly in Venezia Giulia, NE Italy; commercial port and naval base; marine arsenal, shipbuilding works; 8th-cent. cathedral, castle, 14th-cent. church; Roman remains include an amphitheater, temples, a triumphal arch, and city gates.

History: Established as Roman military and naval base 178 B.C.; destroyed 39 B.C. in war against Illyrians and Dalmatians and rebuilt 35 B.C.; mere fishing village during Middle Ages; taken by Venetians 1148; scene of Genoese victory over Venetians 1379 and practically destroyed; to Austria by Peace of Campoformio 1797 and Congress of Vienna 1815; became chief Austro-Hungarian naval station; to Italy by Treaty of St-Germain 1919; in disputed area after World War II; assigned to Yugoslavia by treaty of 1947.

Pul'ko·vo (pŏŏl'kŭ·vŭ). Village, cen. Leningrad Region,

Soviet Russia, Europe, 10 m. S of Leningrad; seat of national observatory 30°19′40″E, 59°46′19″N; founded 1839. Frequently used in U.S.S.R. as base for measurements instead of Greenwich. Its regular work interrupted during years after Russian Revolution 1919–21 and during World War II.

Pul′liam Bluff (pŏŏl′yăm). Peak 6921 ft. in S Brewster co., W Texas.

Pull′man (pŏŏl′măn). **1** Former manufacturing suburb of Chicago, Illinois, now a part of Chicago. **2** City, Whitman co., SE Washington, 65 m. S of Spokane; pop. 12,957; commercial center of wheat-growing area. Washington State Univ. (1890; coed.).

Pulo. See PULAU.

Pu′log, Mount (pŏŏ′lôg). Highest peak 9606 ft. in N Luzon, Phil. Is., in S end of Cordillera Central at point where Benguet, Ifugao, and Nueva Vizcaya provs. meet.

Pulte′ney·town (pŭlt′nĭ·toun; pōlt′-). Former burgh, now part of Wick, Caithness, Scotland; built 1808 by British Fisheries Association; now business center for Wick.

Pul·to′va, Pul·to′wa (pŏŏl·tō′vȧ). Vars. of POLTAVA.

Pul′tusk (pŏŏl′tōōsk). Industrial commune, Warszawa dept., Poland, on Narew river 32 m. N of Warsaw; pop. (1938–39 est.) 17,401. Scene of Saxon defeat by Charles XII of Sweden Apr. 21, 1703; Russians defeated by French under Napoleon 1806; taken by Germans 1915 and 1939.

Pu′lu·wat′ (pŏŏ′lōō·wät′). Atoll, cen. Caroline Is., W Pacific Ocean, 180 m. W of Truk, 149°E long.

Pu′na (pŏŏ′nä; *Angl.* -nȧ). District, Hawaii co., Hawaii, SE Hawaii I.; pop. (1950) 6747; chief town Keaau.

Pu·ná′ (pŏŏ·nä′). Island 29 m. long in the Gulf of Guayaquil, SW Ecuador.

Puna de Atacama. See Puna de ATACAMA.

Pu′na·kha (pŏŏn′ȧk·hȧ). Town on Machu river, W cen. Bhutan.

Punch. See POONCH.

Pun′gwe (pŏŏng′gwĕ); *Port.* **Pun′gue** (pŏŏNng′gwĕ). River ab. 200 m. long, S cen. Mozambique; flows SE into Indian Ocean at Beira.

Pun·jab′ (pŭn·jäb′; pŭn′jäb; -jäb[′]); *Hind.* **Pan·jāb′** (pŭn·jäb′). **1** Former province, NW Brit. India; 99,089 sq. m.; pop. (1941) 28,418,819; included 34 Indian states under Punjab government, 38,146 sq. m., pop. (1941) 5,503,554; total area 137,235 sq. m., pop. (1941) 33,922,373; ✻ Lahore, summer ✻ Simla. Divided Aug. 1947 into East Punjab (*q.v.*), Indian Union, with ab. ⅓ the area and ½ the population of the original region, and West Punjab (*q.v.*), Pakistan. Greater part occupied the valleys of the Indus and the five great tributaries (hence its name, Hind. *panj* five and *āb* waters) of the Indus: Jhelum, Chenab, Ravi, Beas, and Sutlej; these rivers now chiefly in West Punjab, the Sutlej forming part of the boundary. NE part (Kangra dist. in East Punjab) is wholly in the Himalayas. Agriculture is main industry, but cotton factories, weaving industry, and other varied manufacturing lines are increasing. Chief cities were Lahore, Amritsar, Multan, Rawalpindi, and Sialkot. Has many evidences of prehistoric culture; was influenced by Alexander's Greek settlers 4th cent. B.C.; part of Asoka's empire 3d cent. B.C.; in succeeding centuries tributary to various rulers; from time of Mahmud of Ghazni (997–1030) to 18th cent. overrun by invading hosts (cf. PANIPAT); under the Sikhs 1799–1849; annexed to Brit. India 1846 and 1849; North-West Frontier Province set apart from it 1901 and Delhi prov. in 1912; constituted autonomous province 1937. See PAKISTAN. **2** Former state, India. See EAST PUNJAB. **3** *or* **Pun·jab′i Su′ba** (pŭn·jäb′ĭ sōō′bä; -jäb′-). State, NE India, formed 1966 from NW districts of former Punjab state; 29,205 sq. m.; pop. 11,806,812; ✻ Chandigarh.

Punjab States. Group of Indian states under former Punjab government; ✻ Lahore.

Punjab States Agency. Former group of 45 Indian states and estates in the Punjab in political relations with the crown representative through the resident at Lahore. The 14 most important of these (including Patiala, Bahawalpur, Khairpur, Chamba, Jind, and others) had an area of 38,146 sq. m. and a population (1941) of 5,503,554. A second group, known as **Punjab Hill States** (most important Tehri Garhwal and Sirmur), have an area of 11,375 sq. m. and pop. (1941) of 1,090,644.

Pu′no (pŏŏ′nô). **1** Department of Peru. See *Table* at PERU. **2** Town, its ✻, on W shore of Lake Titicaca 218 m. by rail E of Arequipa; pop. (1940 est.) 15,999; altitude 12,641 ft.

Pun Run, Lake (pŏŏn rōōn′). Lake in Junín dept., cen. Peru; altitude ab. 14,200 ft.

Punt (pŏŏnt). Ancient Egyptian name for a part of Africa not certainly identified, but probably the Somali coast. Visited by Queen Hatshepsut of the XVIIIth dynasty (reigned in 15th cent. B.C.), her voyage being depicted in reliefs in the Deir el-Bahri temple near Thebes; after this visit established trade with Egypt and for many years exported much myrrh, gold, ebony, incense, also animals and fruits.

Punta, Cerro de. See CERRO DE PUNTA.

Pun′ta A·re′nas (pŏŏn′tä ä-rā′näs); *called also* **Ma′gal·la′nes** (mä′gä-yä′näs). Seaport city, ✻ of Magallanes prov., S Chile, on Brunswick Penin. ab. midway of the Strait of Magellan and 1429 naut. m. from Valparaíso; pop. 29,883; southernmost city in Chile (53°10′S). Exports mutton, wool, fur, skins, and timber. Originally a penal colony 1843; town founded 1849.

Punta Argentera. See Punta ARGENTERA.

Punta del Es′te (thĕl ās′tā). Town, Maldonado dept., S Uruguay, 70 m. E of Montevideo; pop. ab. 6500; seaside resort.

Punta de Pie′dras (thä pyä′thräs). Town, Nueva Esparta state, Venezuela, on Margarita I. in Caribbean Sea off N coast of Venezuela; pop. (1941 est.) 5214.

Pun′ta Gor′da (pŭn′tȧ gôr′dȧ). **1** City, ⊗ of Charlotte co., SW Florida, on Charlotte Harbor 20 m. in from Gulf of Mexico; pop. 3157; yachting and tarpon-fishing resort. **2** (*Span.* pōōn′tä gôr′thä) Seaport, ✻ of Toledo dist., S British Honduras; pop. (1931) 1119; sugar, bananas, rice, and livestock.

Pun′ta·re′nas (pŏŏn′tä-rā′näs). **1** Province, W cen. Costa Rica; 3955 sq. m.; pop. (1943 est.) 45,727; bananas, pearl shell, dyewoods. **2** Seaport, its ✻, on Gulf of Nicoya; pop. (1943 est.) 8265; cattle, sugar, coconuts.

Puntilla, La. See LA PUNTILLA.

Punx′su·taw′ney (pŭngk′sŭ·tô′nĭ). Borough, Jefferson co., W cen. Pennsylvania, 17 m. SW of Du Bois; pop. 8805; coal mining and coke industries; meat packing; farm trade center. Settled 1772.

Pu′pa·yax′ (pŏŏ′pä·yäк′). Peak 19,080 ft. in W Bolivia, NE of Lake Titicaca.

Pu′quio (pŏŏ′kyô). Town, Ayacucho dept., S Peru, near coast NW of Arequipa; pop. (1940 est.) 6183.

Pur-. For names in Java beginning **Pur-**, see POER-.

Pu′ra·cé′ (pŏŏ′rä·sä′). Active volcano 15,420 ft. in SW cen. Colombia, just SE of Popayán; eruption during earthquake of 1827; recent eruption May 26, 1949.

Pu·ra′li (pŏŏ·rä′lĭ) *or* **Po·ra′li** (pô·rä′lĭ). River ab. 310 m. long, cen. Las Bela state, SE Baluchistan, Pakistan; flows S into Sonmiani Bay.

Pu·ra′ri (pŏŏ·rä′rĭ). River ab. 280 m. long, E cen. New Guinea I.; rises on N slope of mountains in cen. North-East New Guinea, flows generally SSE through E cen. Papua to Gulf of Papua.

Pur′beck, Isle of (pûr′bĕk). Peninsula district 12 m. long in Dorsetshire, S England; extends E into English Channel; harbor of Poole is on N; of geological interest; source of Purbeck marble.

Pur·cell' (pẽr·sĕl'). City, ⊗ of McClain co., cen. Oklahoma, on Canadian river 34 m. S of Oklahoma City; pop. 3729; cotton gins, cottonseed-oil mills.

Purcell Range. Subsidiary mountain range in SE British Columbia, Canada, bet. the Selkirk Mts. and the main range of the Rocky Mts.; highest Mt. Farnham 11,342 ft.

Pur'dy, Lake (pûr'dĭ). Reservoir formed by dam across Cahaba river, ab. 13 m. SE of Birmingham, Alabama; built 1910, enlarged 1928; provides water power.

Pu·ré'pe·ro de E·chaiz' (pōō·rā'pā·rŏ thả å·chīs'). Town, Michoacán state, SW Mexico, ESE of Zamora; pop. 7132.

Pur'fleet (pûr'flēt). Former urban district, Essex, SE England, on the Thames; pop. (1931) 8511.

Pur'ga·toire' (pûr'gả·twär'; pĭk'ĕt·wīr'). River 190 m. long, S and SE Colorado; rises in W Las Animas co., flows NE into Arkansas river in Bent co.

Pur'ga·to'ry Peak (pûr'gả·tōr'ĭ). Mountain 13,719 ft. in Costilla and Las Animas co., S Colorado, in the Sangre de Cristo Mts.

Pu'ri (pōōr'ē) or **Ja'gan·nath** (jŭ'găn·nät'h') or **Jug'ger·naut** (jŭg'ẽr·nôt). Seaport town, E Orissa state, E Indian Union, on Bay of Bengal 260 m. SSW of Calcutta; pop. 37,568. One of India's most renowned places of pilgrimage for Hindus. Main temple constructed in 12th cent. and sacred to Krishna under the name Jagannath. Scene of many festivals; at the Rathayatra, one of the principal festivals, often attended by 100,000 pilgrims, the image of Jagannath is carried through the streets on a great car with gigantic wheels.

Puriramya. See BURIRAM.

Pur'me·rend' (pûr'mĕ·rĕnt'). Commune, North Holland prov., W Netherlands, 8 m. NNE of Amsterdam; pop. 6057.

Pur'na (pōōr'nä). River nearly 200 m. long, cen. India; flows SE in NW Hyderabad to the upper Godavari river.

Pur'ne·a (pûr'nĕ·ả). Town, Bhagalpur division, NE Bihar, NE Indian Union, N of the Ganges ab. 50 m. NE of Bhagalpur; pop. 15,474.

Pursak. See PORSUK.

Pur'sat' (pōōr'sät'). Town, cen. Cambodia, Indochina, S of the Tonle Sap and on railroad 100 m. NW of Pnompenh.

Pu·ruán'di·ro, officially **Puruándiro de Cal'de·rón'** (pōō·rwän'dĕ·rŏ thả käl'dả·rôn'). Town, Michoacán state, SW Mexico, just W of Lake Cuitzeo; pop. 8643.

Pu·ru'li·a (pōō·rōō'lĭ·ả). Town, SE Bihar, NE Indian Union, 140 m. WNW of Calcutta; pop. 25,974.

Pu·rus' (pōō·rōōs'). Navigable river ab. 2000 m. long in NW cen. South America; rises in Andes Mts. in SE Peru, flows NE across Amazonas state, Brazil, and into Amazon river above Manaus.

Pur'vis (pûr'vĭs). Town, ⊗ of Lamar co., S Mississippi; pop. 1614.

Pusan. See FUSAN.

Push'kar (pŏŏsh'kẽr). Lake 7 m. W of Ajmer, in E cen. Rajasthan, NW cen. Indian Union; one of India's most sacred waters, it is scene of annual pilgrim fair and site of only temple in India dedicated to Brahma.

Push'kin (pŏŏsh'kĭn; Russ. pōōsh'-); formerly **Tsar'sko·e Se·lo'** (tsàr'skŭ·yĕ syĕ·lô') and **Det'sko·e Selo** (dyĕt'skŭ·yĕ). Town, NW Leningrad Region, Soviet Russia, Europe, on railroad 15 m. S of Leningrad; pop. 19,284. Originally a Finnish village taken 1708 by Peter the Great and presented to his wife Catherine as a summer residence, Tsarskoe Selo ("The Tsar's Village"). Imperial palace erected 1728 and for nearly two centuries used as court residence; has beautiful parks with other palaces; now a health resort with buildings converted to museums, schools, hospitals, etc. Imperial palace was first building on European continent to be lighted by electricity 1887. After Revolution 1917 name changed to Detskoe Selo ("Children's Village") and later to Pushkin in honor of Russia's great poet.

Push'ma·ta'ha (pŏŏsh'mả·tä'hä; -tô'hô). County in Oklahoma. See Table at OKLAHOMA.

Pusht-i-Kuh (pŏŏsht'ē·kōō'h'). Mountain range in W Iran, extending NW to SE along the boundary with Iraq; source of a headstream of the Karkheh river; highest point 5092 ft.

Püs'pök·la'dány (püsh'pŭk·lŏ'dän·y'). Commune 30 m. SW of Debrecen, E Hungary; pop. 15,233.

Pu'ster·thal' (pōōs'tẽr·täl') or **Val Pu'ste·ri'a** (väl pōōs'tả·rē'ä). Valley N of the Carnic Alps in NE Venezia Tridentina, Italy, and W Carinthia prov., Austria.

Putao. Native name of FORT HERTZ.

Pu'teaux' (pü'tō'). Industrial commune, Seine dept., N France, NW suburb of Paris on Seine river; pop. 43,829.

Puteoli. See POZZUOLI.

Pu'ti·gna'no (pōō'tē·nyä'nŏ). Commune, Bari prov., Apulia, SE Italy, 23 m. SE of Bari; pop. 16,677.

Put-in-Bay (pŏŏt'ĭn'). **1** Bay in South Bass I., Lake Erie, in Ottawa co., Ohio; scene of Commodore Perry's victory over the British fleet Sept. 10, 1813.
2 Village, Ottawa co., N Ohio, on Put-in-Bay; pop. 357; vineyards; summer resort.

Puting. See POETING.

Put'na (pōōt'nä). River 81 m. long, Moldavia, NE Romania; flows N, E, and SE into Siret river.

Put'nam (pŭt'năm). **1** Name of counties in nine states of the U.S. See Tables at FLORIDA, GEORGIA, ILLINOIS, INDIANA, MISSOURI, NEW YORK, OHIO, TENNESSEE, WEST VIRGINIA.
2 Manufacturing city, a ⊗ of Windham co., NE Connecticut, on Quinebaug river at mouth of Mill river 21 m. NE of Willimantic; pop. 6952; organized as municipality 1855, incorp. 1895; in agricultural region; manufactures silk and cotton thread, woolen goods, rayon, hats, footwear, steam heaters, castings, and other products; Cargill Falls near center of city. Part of town of Putnam (pop. 8412; incorp. 1855).

Put'ney (pŭt'nĭ). Ward of Wandsworth metropolitan borough, London, England; pop. 34,718.

Pu'to' Shan (pōō'tō' shän') or **Pu'to'** (pōō'tō'); also **Poo'too'** (pōō'tōō'). Small island 3 m. long in Chu Shan archipelago, Chekiang prov., E China, just SE of Chu Shan I.; one of the three sacred spots of Chinese Buddhism; has large monastery and is covered with temples, monuments, etc.; famous for its natural beauty and its sacredness as a pilgrimage center.

Putrid Sea. See SIVASH.

Put'ta·lam (pŭt'ả·lảm). Seaport town, North-Western Province, Ceylon, 80 m. N of Colombo; pop. 6709.

Puttiala. See PATIALA.

Pu'tu·ma'yo (pōō'tōō·mä'yŏ). **1** River ab. 980 m. long, NW South America; rises in SW Colombia, flows SE, forming large section of Peru-Colombia boundary, crosses border into Brazil, where it is known as the **I·çá'** (ē·sá'), and empties into Amazon river; flows through rubber-producing region.
2 Commissary of Colombia. See Table at COLOMBIA.

Pu'u Ku·ku'i (pōō'ŏŏ kōō·kōō'ē). Mountain 5790 ft. on Maui I., at W end, Hawaii.

Puu'la·ve'si (pōō'lả·vĕ'sĭ). Lake, Mikkeli dept., S Finland.

Pu'u·ne'ne (pōō'ŏŏ·nā'nå). Town, Wailuku dist., Maui co., Hawaii, on N Maui I. near coast just E of Wailuku; pop. 3054.

Pu'u Po'a Point (pōō'ŏŏ pō'ä). Cape on N coast of Kauai I., Hawaii; pop. (est.) 200.

Pu'u·wa'i (pōō'ŏŏ·wä'ē). Village, W coast of Niihau I., Kauai co., Hawaii.

Puy or **Puy-en-Velay, Le.** See LE PUY.

Puy·al'lup (pū·ăl'ŭp). **1** River ab. 50 m. long, W cen. Washington; flows NW into Puget Sound at Tacoma.
2 City, Pierce co., W cen. Washington, on Puyallup river 8 m. ESE of Tacoma; pop. 12,063; farming, fruit and berry growing, lumbering, dairying; canneries and fruit-packing plants, sawmills, box factories.

Puy–de–Dôme (pü·ēd'dōm'). Department of France. See *Table* at FRANCE.

Puy de Dôme. Mountain. See Puy de DÔME.

Puy de Sancy. See Puy de SANCY.

Pu·ye'hue, La'go (lä'gŏ pōō·yä'wä). Lake in Osorno prov., S cen. Chile, N of Puerto Montt.

Puy'mo'rens', Col de (kôl' dē pü·ē'mô'räNs'). Mountain pass 6286 ft., Pyrénées-Orientales dept., S France, in the Pyrenees just NE of Andorra.

Pwll·he'li (pōōl·hĕl'ĭ). Town, Caernarvonshire, NW Wales, on S coast of Lleyn Penin. on Cardigan Bay; pop. (1951) 3861; watering place, fine beach.

Pyandzh. Var. of *Panj*: see AB-I-PANDJ.

Pya'pon' (pyä'pōn'). 1 District, Irrawaddy division, Lower Burma; 2076 sq. m.; pop. 334,158.

2 Town, its ✽, in Irrawaddy delta 45 m. SW of Rangoon; pop. 12,338.

Pyarnu. See PARNU.

Pya'si·na (pyä'sĭ·nȧ; *Russ.* pyȧ'syĭ·nȧ). River ab. 350 m. long, N Taimyr National District, Soviet Russia, Asia; in W part of Taimyr Penin., flows N into the Arctic Ocean (Kara Sea).

Pya'ti·gorsk' (pyȧt'ĭ·gôrsk'; pyä'tĭ-; *Russ.* pyĭ·tyĭ-). Town, S Stavropol Territory, Soviet Russia, Europe, on a tributary of the Kuma river 140 m. WNW of Grozny; pop. 62,875; health resort, with sulfur springs and mud baths, on a plateau on the N slopes of the Caucasus and on spur track of Rostov-Baku R.R.; has some industries and several scientific institutions.

Pyaw'bwe (pyou'bwä). Town, cen. Burma, S of Mandalay and just N of Yamethin; taken by British Apr. 11, 1945.

Pyd'na (pĭd'nȧ). Ancient town in Macedonia, N Greece; ruins on W shore of Gulf of Salonika. Scene of battle 168 B.C. in which the Romans under Aemilius Paulus defeated the Macedonians under their last king, Perseus, thus bringing to an end the empire of Alexander.

Pyeng·yang (pyûng·yäng). = HEIJO.

Py'hä·kos'ki (pü'hȧ·kôs'kĭ). Rapids in Oulu river near its mouth SE of Oulu, W Finland; known to Finns as the "Holy Rapids."

Pyin'ma·na' (pyĭn'mȧ·nä'). Town on the Sittang river in Yamethin dist., Upper Burma; pop. 17,656; on railroad 150 m. S of Mandalay.

Py'los (pī'lŏs; *Mod. Gr.* pē'lôs). 1 Fortified seaport, SW Messenia dept., SW Peloponnesus, S Greece; pop. 2315; its harbor (one of the best in all Greece) is protected by a small island; held by Athenians against Spartans in Peloponnesian War. In modern times called Navarino (*q.v.*).

2 Town, N cen. ancient Elis, NW Peloponnesus, Greece, on the Peneus river.

3 Town near coast in Triphylia dist., S ancient Elis.

Py'ma·tu'ning Reservoir (pī'mȧ·tū'nĭng). Reservoir in Crawford co., NW Pennsylvania, and Ashtabula co., NE Ohio; formed by **Pymatuning Dam,** impounding waters of Beaver and Shenango rivers.

Pyongyang. See HEIJO.

Py'ote (pī'ōt). City, Ward co., W Texas, ab. 200 m. ESE of El Paso; pop. ab. 420; U.S. Air Force base (aircraft storage).

Pyr'a·mid Lake (pĭr'ȧ·mĭd). Lake ab. 30 m. long and from 4 to 13 m. wide in S Washoe co., NW Nevada.

Pyramid Mountain. 1 Peak 8100 ft. in Glacier National Park, NW Montana.

2 Peak 8240 ft. in Chelan co., cen. Washington.

Pyramid Peak. 1 Mountain 10,020 ft. in Sierra Nevada, in E cen. Eldorado co., E California.

2 Mountain 14,000 ft. in Pitkin co., W cen. Colorado.

3 Mountain 9594 ft. in NE Lemhi co., E cen. Idaho.

4 Mountain 7800 ft., N Cascade Range, NW Washington.

5 Mountain 10,300 ft. in E Yellowstone National Park, NW Wyoming.

Pyr'a·mids (pĭr'ȧ·mĭdz). Ancient monuments 5 m. W of Giza, near Cairo, Egypt, W of the Nile—the true pyramids, 3 in number: largest, Pyramid of Khufu (or Cheops), built by Khufu, 1st king of IVth dynasty, reigned c. 2900–2877 B.C.; second in size and age, Pyramid of Khafre (or Chephren), built by Khafre, 3d king of IVth dynasty, reigned c. 2850 B.C.; smallest and most perfect of the three, Pyramid of Menkure, built by Menkure, a king of the IVth dynasty, reigned c. 2800 B.C. Largest pyramid was originally ab. 482 ft. in height and had a base covering nearly 13 acres; built of huge limestone blocks and had inner sepulchral chambers, sloping passages, etc. Other pyramids built in Egypt, esp. the Step Pyramid of Zoser at Saqqara (*q.v.*); also those (not true pyramids) erected by Assyrians and Mayas (see CHICHÉN ITZÁ, CHOLULA). The Battle of the Pyramids occurred July 21, 1798 across the Nile from Cairo and N of the Pyramids; it resulted in a victory for Napoleon over the Mamelukes and gave him control over Egypt; the victory neutralized by defeat of the French fleet Aug. 1–2, 1798 by Nelson in Battle of the Nile (see ABUKIR).

Pyramus. See CEYHAN.

Pyr'e·nees (pĭr'ē·nēz; *Fr.* **Py'ré'nées'** (pē'rā'nā'); *Span.* **Pi'ri·ne'os** (pē'rē·nā'ôs); *anc.* **Pyr'e·nae'i Mon'tes** (pĭr'ĕ·nē'ī mŏn'tēz). Mountain range extending ab. 270 m. along the French-Spanish border from the Bay of Biscay to the SW coast of the Gulf of Lions; highest peak Pico de Aneto 11,169 ft. in the Maladettas in cen. part; an effective barrier bet. the two countries, has principal highways only at ends near coasts; traversed by few passes, notably Somport, Pourtalet, and Puymorens, all over 5000 ft., and the pass at Roncesvalles 3648 ft. made famous by the *Chanson de Roland* and often used by armies; mountains noted for many streams (*gaves*) and waterfalls and for distinctive formations called *cirques*, deep, steep-walled, amphitheatric recesses at upper ends of valleys.

Py'ré'nées' (pē'rā'nā'). **1** See PYRENEES.

2 Departments of France: **Basses–Pyrénées** (bäs'-), **Hautes–Pyrénées** (ōt'-), and **Py'ré'nées'–O'rien'tales'** (pē'rā'nā'-zô'ryäN'tȧl'). See *Table* at FRANCE.

Pyrgos. See LETRINOI.

Py·rox'ene Peak (pī·rŏk'sēn; pī-). Peak 9000 ft., Madison co., SW Montana.

Pytho. See DELPHI.

Pyu (pyōō). Town, Toungoo dist., cen. Lower Burma, on railroad and highway W of the Sittang 30 m. S of Toungoo; pop. 7807.

Q

Q. For many names beginning with Q-, especially those of Arabic or Turkish origin, see the more usual forms in English beginning with K-; as, for **Qandahar, Qara Bogaz Gol,** see KANDAHAR, KARA BOGAZ GOL.

Qa'bes (kä'bĕs). Var. of GABÈS.

Qādisīyah, al-. See KADISIYA.

Qâhirah, al-. See CAIRO city.

Qa·in' (kä·ēn'). Town, E Iran, on the north-to-south highway 175 m. S of Meshed; pop. ab. 10,000. Situated in a broad valley at 4500 ft. altitude; raises saffron as a special product and has an active industry in carpets and felts. A very old town near the Afghan border; has often changed overlords.

Qairwan. See KAIROUAN.

Qais or **Kais** (kīs). Island in SE cen. Persian Gulf, ab. 10 m. off S coast of Iran, W of Lingeh; pop. ab. 2000. In Middle Ages an important trade center; under Arab rule it controlled Oman and provided a market where goods of the Middle East were exchanged; declined after 14th cent.

Qal'at el 'Aqaba. See 'AQABA.

Qal'at el Mafraq. See MAFRAK.

Qal'′at el Mu·dau'wa·ra (kŏl'ăt ăl mōō·dou'wŭ·rŏ). Village, SW Jordan, on Saudi Arabia border ESE of 'Aqaba.

Qal'′at Sam·an' or **Kal'aat Sam·an'** (kŏl'ăt săm·än'). Town, NW Syria, NW of Alep; monastery; home of Simeon Stylites who lived 30 years on top of a pillar.

Qalunya. See EMMAUS.

Qal·yub' (kŏl·yōōb'). Town, Qalyubîya prov., Lower Egypt, 10 m. N of Cairo, at head of Nile delta.

Qal'yu·bî'ya (kŏl'yōō·bê'yȧ; -yȧ). Province, Lower Egypt. See *Table* at EGYPT.

Qamaran. See KAMARAN.

Qamr Bay (kŏm'ēr); *formerly* **Ka'mar Bay** (kŏm'ēr). Inlet of the Arabian Sea on S coast of Arabia, E Hadhramaut, E of Cape Fartak.

Qantara, El. See EL QANTARA.

Qara, El. See EL QARA.

Qa'ra Dagh (kä'rä dä'). **1** Mountain range, N Azerbaijan, NW Iran, S of Araks river; highest point 9545 ft. **2** Mountain range, NE Iraq, on Iran border SE end of mountains of Kurdistan; highest point 5923 ft.

Qara Kul. See KARA KUL.

Qara–Qalpaq. = KARA-KALPAK.

Qa'ra Qash or **Ka'ra·kash'** (kä'rä·käsh'). River, SW Sinkiang, W China; rises in Karakoram range on Kashmir border, flows N and NE through E end of Kunlun Mts. to join the Khotan below Khotan city.

Qaraqorum. Var. of KARAKORUM.

Qara Qum. See KARA KUM.

Qa'ra Shahr or **Ka'ra·shahr'** (kä'rä·shä'h'r); *Chin.* **Yen'ki** (yĕn'jē'). Town, cen. Sinkiang, W China, on N shore of Bagrach Kol ab. 120 m. SSW of Urumchi; trade center on main caravan and motor highway across Sinkiang on N border of Takla Makan Desert.

Qa'ra Su (kä'rä sōō') or **Ka'ra** (kä'rä). River ab. 160 m. long, Azerbaijan, NW Iran; flows N into Araks river on the U.S.S.R. border.

Qar'gha·liq' or **Kar'gha·lik'** (kär'gä·lĭk'); *Chin.* **Yeh'cheng'** (yĕ'chŭng'). Town, S of Yarkand, SW Sinkiang, W China, on caravan and motor highway; pop. ab. 10,000.

Qarqar. See KARKAR.

Qars. = KARS.

Qârûn, Birket. See BIRKET QÂRÛN.

Qa·sim' (kŏ·sēm'). Province, N cen. Nejd, Saudi Arabia; pop. ab. 75,000; chief towns Buraida and Anaiza.

Qasimiye, Nahr el. See LITANI.

Qasr, El. See EL QASR.

Qasr el Az'raq (kŏs'ēr ăl ăz'rŏk). Town and oasis, N Jordan, 55 m. E of Amman.

Qa'tar or **Ka'tar** (kŏ'tŏr). Peninsula ab. 120 m. long and sheikdom, E Arabia, E of al-Hasa and NW of Trucial Oman, projecting into SW Persian Gulf; 8500 sq. m.; pop. ab. 25,000; ✻ Doha; consists chiefly of low hills and sandy areas. Sheikdom, since 19th cent. dependent upon protection of Great Britain; like Trucial Oman (*q.v.*) entered series of agreements ending piracy and promising not to deal with foreign powers other than Great Britain; status determined by treaty of 1916.

Qa·ti'a or **Ka·ti'a** (kŏ·tē'yȧ; -yä). Village, Egypt, near Mediterranean Sea, 25 m. E of the Suez Canal; battles bet. British and Turks Apr. and Aug. 1916.

Qa·tif' (kŏ·tēf'). Seaport of al-Hasa, E Nejd, Saudi Arabia, on Persian Gulf 37 m. NW of Bahrein I.; has old Karmathian fort. Taken by Wahabis from Turks 1914.

Qatrani, El. See EL QATRANI.

Qat·ta'ra Depression (kŏt·tä'rŏ). Low area in N Egypt, 130 m. W of Cairo and 40 m. S of the seacoast; ab. 7000 sq. m.; deepest point 440 ft. below sea level; because it was impassable to armies and vehicles, it formed the anchor at S end of British defense line at El Alamein in NW Egypt July 1942, stopping Rommel's invasion; followed by Allied success, Oct. 19 to Nov. 3, 1942, at El Alamein (*q.v.*).

Qazaq. = *Kazakh:* see KAZAKH SOVIET SOCIALIST REPUBLIC.

Qazvin. See KAZVIN.

Qe'na (kē'nȧ; kä'-). **1** Province, Upper Egypt. See *Table* at EGYPT.
2 *anc.* **Cae'ne** (sē'nē), **Cae·nep'o·lis** (sē·nĕp'ô·lĭs). City, ✻ of Qena prov., Upper Egypt, on right bank of the Nile at the bend below Luxor and 280 m. SSE of Cairo; pop. (1937) 34,431; a trade center, noted for its manufacture of water jars and bottles.

Qena, Wa'di (wä'dĭ). Watercourse in E cen. Egypt, extending S to the Nile river at Qena.

Qift (kĭft); *anc.* **Cop'tos** (kŏp'tŏs). Village in Qena prov., Egypt, on right bank of the Nile, an ancient city N of Thebes; Coptos was starting point of 5-day caravan route from the Nile to the Red Sea.

Qirghiz. See KIRGHIZ.

Qisarya. See CAESAREA.

Qishm (kĭsh'm) *also* **Kishm. 1** *anc.* **O'a·rac'ta** (ō'ȧ·răk'tȧ). Island 68 m. long at SE end of Persian Gulf in Strait of Ormuz; 516 sq. m.; pop. ab. 15,000; chief town Qishm. Belongs to Laristan prov., S Iran; separated from mainland by Clarence Strait. Town of Basidu is at W end. Island is generally rocky and barren but has some fertile areas.
2 Chief town of Qishm I. at its E tip; pop. ab. 3000.

Qishn (kĭsh'n). Chief town of Mahra sultanate, E Hadhramaut, E Aden Protectorate, S Arabia, 200 m. ENE of Mukalla; sultanate includes Socotra I. and is under British protection.

Qi'shon or **Ki'shon** (kī'shŏn; kĭsh'ŏn). Small river ab. 50 m. long, N Palestine; rises near Mt. Gilboa and flows NW through the Plain of Esdraelon to the Mediterranean just N of Haifa. On its banks Sisera was defeated by the Israelites (*Judges* v. 21) and the prophets of Baal slain by Elijah (*1 Kings* xviii. 40).

Qizil Orda. Var. of KZYL-ORDA.

Qizil Qum. See KYZYL KUM.

Qi'zil U·zun' (kĭ'zĭl ōō·zōōn') or **Ki'zil U·zen'** (kĭ'zĭl ü·zĕn'). River ab. 450 m. long in NW Iran; rises in mountains SE of Lake Urmia and flows N then SE, then turns NE through the Elburz Mts. to Caspian Sea E of Resht; called Sefid Rud in its lower course.

Qo·mul' (kŏ·mōōl'); *formerly* **Ha'mi'** (hä'mē'). Town and oasis, E Sinkiang, W China, on caravan and motor highway N of the Takla Makan desert from Kansu to Kashgar; also W terminus of highway from Kweisui; pop. ab. 6000. Ancient frontier trading town.

Qoseir, El. See EL QUSEIR.

Qsar el Kbir, El. See ALCÁZARQUIVIR.

Quab′bin Dam *and* **Reservoir** (kwŏb′ĭn). See UNITED STATES, *Dams and Reservoirs.*

Qua′boag (kwā′bŏg). River, cen. Massachusetts; rises in **Quaboag Pond** in S cen. Worcester co., flows W and joins Swift river in N Hampden co., to form Chicopee river.

Quad′rant Mountain (kwŏd′rănt). Peak 10,200 ft. in Yellowstone National Park, NW Wyoming.

Quak′er·town′ (kwāk′ẽr-toun′). Borough, Bucks co., SE Pennsylvania, 13 m. S of Allentown; pop. 6305; founded by Quakers 1715; manufactures hosiery, clothing, luggage.

Qua′nah (kwä′nà). City, ⊗ of Hardeman co., N Texas, 24 m. WNW of Vernon; pop. 4564; manufactures cottonseed oil, plaster; gypsum deposits.

Quan′da·ry Peak (kwŏn′dá·rĭ; -drĭ). Mountain 14,256 ft. in Summit co., cen. Colorado.

Quang′ngai′ (kwäng′ngī′). Coastal town, Annam, Vietnam, ab. 130 m. SE of Hue.

Quang′tri′ *or* **Quang–tri** (kwäng′trē′). Town, N cen. Annam, Vietnam, on coastal railroad 30 m. NW of Hue; pop. ab. 3000; important agricultural center.

Quan′ti·co (kwŏn′tĭ·kō). Town, Prince William co., NE Virginia, on Potomac river 18 m. NNE of Fredericksburg; pop. 1015; U.S. Marine Corps base, first established as a naval base in Revolutionary War; made Marine Corps camp in 1917 and a permanent base 1918; can accommodate 400 officers and 3000 enlisted men.

Quan′tock Hills (kwŏn′tŭk). Range of hills 8 m. long in NW Somersetshire, SW England; highest point 1262 ft.

Qu'Ap′pelle′ (kà′pěl′). **1** River ab. 270 m. long, S Saskatchewan, Canada; flows E across Manitoba border and into the Assiniboine river; Moose Jaw is near its source. **2** Town, SE Saskatchewan, on railroad 30 m. E of Regina; pop. 492.

Qua′ra·í′ (kwä′rá·ē′). River ab. 130 m. long forming W section of Uruguay-Brazil boundary; flows W into Uruguay river.

Qua′re′gnon′ (kà′rẽ′nyôN′). Commune, Hainaut prov., SW Belgium, just W of Mons; pop. 18,331; industrial town.

Quarnero. See VELIKI KVARNER.

Quarnerolo. See MALI KVARNER.

Quar′ry Bank (kwŏr′ĭ). Former urban district, Staffordshire, W cen. England; pop. (1931) 8100.

Quar′tu Sant′·E′le·na (kwär′tōō sän·tä′lā·nä). Commune, Cagliari prov., S Sardinia, 4 m. E of Cagliari; pop. 12,201.

Quathlamba. See DRAKENSBERG MOUNTAINS.

Qua′tre Bornes (kà′trē bôrn′). Residential town bet. Port Louis and Curepipe, NW Mauritius; pop. (1931) 9275.

Qua′tre Bras (kà′trē brà′). Village, Brabant prov., cen. Belgium, ab. 20 m. SSE of Brussels; battlefield where Wellington defeated the French under Ney June 16, 1815, just before the battle of Waterloo.

Quay (kwā). County in New Mexico. See *Table* at NEW MEXICO.

Qu·chan′ *or* **Ku·chan′** (kōō-chän′). Town, N Khurasan prov., NE Iran, on highway 80 m. NW of Meshed; pop. ab. 12,000; center of a fertile and populous district; chief product grain. Suffered severely in 19th cent. from several earthquakes; in 1893 practically destroyed with great loss of life, but rebuilt.

Quds esh Sherif, El. See JERUSALEM.

Que, Isle of. See SELINSGROVE, Pennsylvania.

Quean·bey′an (kwēn·bē′ăn). Town, SE New South Wales, SE Australia, pop. 4019; SE suburb of Canberra, outside Australian Capital Territory.

Qué′ant′ (kā′äN′). Village, Pas-de-Calais dept., N France, 11 m. W of Cambrai; fortress on the Hindenburg Line during World War I. See DROCOURT.

Que·bec′ (kwĕ·běk′; kwĕ-; kĕ-; kĕ-); *Fr.* **Qué′bec′** (kā′bĕk′). **1** Province, E Canada; land area 523,860 sq. m.; pop. 4,055,681; ✻ Quebec; divided into the following 66 counties, some of which are subdivided (for pronunciation of their names, see their individual entries):

NAME	LOCA-TION	AREA[1]	POP.[1]	CO. SEAT
Abitibi	SW	76,725	86,356	Amos
Argenteuil	SW	783	25,872	Lachute
Arthabaska	S	666	36,957	Arthabaska
Bagot	S	346	19,224	Saint Liboire
Beauce	S	1,128	54,973	Beauceville East
Beauharnois	S	147	38,742	Beauharnois
Bellechasse	S	653	25,332	Saint Raphaël
Berthier	S	1,816	24,717	Berthier
Bonaventure	on Gaspé Penin.	3,464	41,121	New Carlisle
Brome	S	488	13,393	Knowlton
Chambly	S	138	77,931	Longueuil
Champlain	S	8,586	85,745	Sainte Geneviève de Batiscan
Charlevoix	S	2,215	28,259	La Malbaie and Baie Saint Paul
Châteauguay	S	265	17,857	Sainte Martine
Chicoutimi	S	17,800	115,904	Chicoutimi
Compton	S	933	23,856	Cookshire
Dorchester	S	842	33,313	Sainte Hénédine
Drummond	S	532	53,426	Drummondville
Frontenac	S	1,370	30,733	Megantic
Gaspé	on Gaspé Penin.	4,648	62,530	Percé and Sainte Anne des Monts
Hull	SW	2,571	92,582	Maniwaki and Hull
Huntingdon	S	361	13,457	Huntingdon
Iberville	S	198	13,507	Iberville
Joliette	S	2,506	37,251	Joliette
Kamouraska	S	1,038	26,672	Saint Pascal
Labelle	SW	2,392	27,197	Mont Laurier
Lake Saint John		23,723	82,006	Saint Joseph d'Alma and Roberval
Laprairie	S	170	18,639	Laprairie
L'Assomption	S	247	23,205	L'Assomption
Levis	S	272	43,625	Saint Romuald
L'Islet		773	22,996	Saint Jean Port Joli
Lotbinière	S	726	27,985	Sainte Croix
Maskinongé	S	2,378	19,478	Louiseville
Matane	on Gaspé Penin.	3,382	64,182	Matane and Amqui
Megantic	S	780	45,325	Inverness
Missisquoi	S	375	24,689	Bedford
Montcalm	S	3,894	17,520	Sainte Julienne
Montmagny	S	630	24,514	Montmagny
Montmorency	S	2,198	21,389	Château Richer and Sainte Famille
Montreal and Jesus Islands	S	294	1,358,075	Montreal, Pointe Claire, and Sainte Rose
Napierville	S	149	9,203	Napierville
Nicolet	S	626	30,335	Bécancour
Papineau	SW	1,581	29,381	Papineauville
Pontiac	SW	9,560	20,696	Campbell's Bay
Portneuf	S	1,440	43,453	Cap Santé
Quebec	S	2,745	252,890	Loretteville
Richelieu	S	221	30,801	Sorel
Richmond	S	544	34,102	Richmond
Rimouski	S	2,089	53,220	Rimouski
Rouville	S	243	19,506	Marieville
Saguenay	SE	315,176	42,664	Tadoussac
Saint Hyacinthe		278	38,101	Saint Hyacinthe
Saint Johns	S	205	28,702	Saint Johns
Saint Maurice	S	1,820	93,855	Yamachiche
Shefford	S	567	43,722	Waterloo
Sherbrooke	S	238	62,166	Sherbrooke
Soulanges	S	136	9,233	Coteau Landing
Stanstead	S	432	34,642	Ayer's Cliff
Témiscouata	S	1,874	65,550	Rivière du Loup and Notre Dame du Lac
Terrebonne	S	782	67,437	Saint Jérôme
Timiskaming	SW	8,977	55,102	Ville Marie
Two Mountains	S	279	21,048	Sainte Scholastique
Vaudreuil	S	201	17,378	Vaudreuil
Verchères	S	199	17,729	Verchères
Wolfe	S	680	18,153	Ham Sud
Yamaska	S	365	16,071	Saint François du Lac

[1] Area = land area in sq. m. Pop. from 1951 Census.

Three fifths of its area is the N part of Saguenay co. (New Quebec dist.), very sparsely inhabited. Bounded

on N by Hudson Strait, on E by Labrador and Gulf of St. Lawrence, on SE by New Brunswick, on S by United States and Ottawa river, and on W by Ontario prov., James Bay, and Hudson Bay. Its general elevation is low but the Laurentian Highlands N of Quebec city average ab. 2000 ft.; the mountains of the Gaspé Penin. are the highest in the province (Mt. Jacques Cartier 4350 ft.). Contains two national historic parks and four large provincial parks. Has many large lakes and rivers; in the S is the great artery of the St. Lawrence in the populous part, with its many tributaries. The height of land running generally NE and SW forms the watershed for many rivers flowing W and NW into Hudson Bay and NE into Ungava Bay. Lake St. John and its outlet the Saguenay river in the S part are best known; this region and the two provincial parks are favorite resort regions. The population is 81% of French origin. Chief industry agriculture, but mining, the fisheries, and forest products, esp. pulpwood, also important. Chief cities Montreal (largest city in the Dominion), Quebec, Three Rivers, Sherbrooke, Hull, Shawinigan Falls, and St. Johns.

History: From 1627 to 1763 this region formed the most important part of New France, claimed as result of discoveries and explorations of Jacques Cartier 1534–41 and of Samuel de Champlain 1603 and 1608–15; lower St. Lawrence site of many new settlements 1615–1763; lost to British in French and Indian War 1754–63 (see QUEBEC city, below). As first set up under the British, comprised the valleys of the Ottawa and lower St. Lawrence rivers; as established by the Quebec Act 1774 the province of Quebec included additional territory W of the Ottawa river and S to the Ohio (as far W as the Mississippi); as result of American Revolution, received many loyalist settlers in region W of the Ottawa and lost to the U.S. 1783 lands now included in Minnesota, Wisconsin, Michigan, Ohio, Indiana, and Illinois (see NORTHWEST TERRITORY), the remaining territory being divided 1791 into Upper Canada (chiefly English) and Lower Canada (chiefly French); on recommendation of Durham report 1839, the two parts reunited 1841; united 1867 with New Brunswick and Nova Scotia to form the Dominion of Canada, Upper Canada then becoming the present province of Ontario (*q.v.*) and Lower Canada the present province of Quebec; boundary with Labrador determined 1825 but changed 1927 to grant more territory to Newfoundland (Labrador); gained Ungava Penin. from Northwest Territories 1912.

2 County, Quebec, Canada. See *Table* above.

3 City, ✳ of Quebec prov., Canada, on N bank of St. Lawrence river above Island of Orleans and 180 m. below Montreal; pop. 164,016. Port of entry for Atlantic steamers with excellent harbor 300 m. from Gulf of St. Lawrence. Strikingly located upon a rocky promontory which rises from the edge of the St. Lawrence and St. Charles rivers in sheer cliffs; consists of old Lower Town, with narrow streets and ancient houses along the shore, and Upper Town, surrounded by massive wall, part of early fortifications. Exports cattle, timber, grain, and manufactures various articles of leather, wood, etc. Important railroad center with fine bridge across the St. Lawrence; receives its light and power from Montmorency and Shawinigan Falls. Notable for its provincial government buildings, cathedrals, old Church of Notre Dame des Victoires, and the Chateau Frontenac; also seat of Laval Univ. (founded 1852) and many schools and cultural institutions. Its population is predominantly French Canadian (ab. 92%).

History: Located on site of old Indian town of **Stad′-a·co′na** (stăd′á·kō′ná), visited by Jacques Cartier in 1535 and 1541; first settlement made by Champlain as a trading post 1608. Captured by the British 1629 but returned to the French by Treaty of St-Germain 1632. Capital of New France 1663 to 1763. In 1690 and 1711 unsuccessfully attacked by British fleets; taken by British under Gen. Wolfe in historic battle of the Plains of

Abraham 1759 in which both Wolfe and the French leader, Montcalm, met death. Besieged by French force 1760 and stormed with disastrous defeat by American troops under Benedict Arnold and Richard Montgomery 1775. Became capital of united Canada 1851–55 and 1859–65. Allied Conference held here Aug. 11–24, 1943, during World War II.

Quebec West; *Fr.* **Qué′bec′–Ouest** (kā′bĕk′wĕst′). Town, Quebec co., S Quebec, Canada, W suburb of Quebec; pop. 7295.

Que′bra·dil′las (kā′vrä·thē′yäs). Municipality (pop. 13,075) and town (pop. 2131), NW Puerto Rico; town on N coast ab. 14 m. ENE of Aguadilla.

Qued′lin·burg (kvād′lēn·boŏrк). City, in what was formerly Saxony prov., Prussia, Germany, 33 m. SSW of Magdeburg; pop. 27,014; 10th-cent. castle, 11th-cent. church, 14th-cent. town hall; known esp. for flower and seed growing.

Queen Adelaide Archipelago. See Archipelago of REINA ADELAIDA.

Queen Al′ex·an′dra Range (ăl′ĕg·zăn′drá; ăl′ĭg-; *Brit. also* -zän′-). Mountain range in Victoria Land, Ross Dependency, Antarctica; lat. 84°S and long. 169°E; highest peak Mt. Kirkpatrick ab. 14,600 ft.

Queen Annes (ănz). County in Maryland. See *Table* at MARYLAND.

Queen Car′o·la Harbour (kăr′ō·lá; ká·rō′lá). Anchorage on W coast of Buka I., NW Solomon Is., W Pacific Ocean.

Queen Channel. Inlet of Joseph Bonaparte Gulf, NW Northern Territory, Australia; receives Victoria river.

Queen Char′lotte Islands (shär′lŏt). Group of islands off W British Columbia, Canada, separated from mainland by Hecate Strait and from islands of S Alaska on the N by Dixon Entrance; 3970 sq. m.; pop. 2389. Main islands are Graham, Moresby, Louise, Lyell, Kunghit, and several smaller. Chief villages are Masset, Skidegate and Rose Harbour. Inhabitants are mainly Haida Indians. Rich in natural resources, as coal and other minerals, forests, and fisheries, largely undeveloped.

Queen Charlotte Sound. Body of water off W British Columbia coast, W Canada, bet. N end of Vancouver I. and S Queen Charlotte Is.

Queen Charlotte Strait. Channel bet. N Vancouver I. and the mainland of Canada, connecting Queen Charlotte Sound with Johnstone Strait.

Queen E·liz′a·beth Islands (ê·lĭz′á·bĕth). The islands of N Canada N of the water passage extending from M'Clure Strait to Lancaster Sound; includes the Parry Islands, Sverdrup Islands, Devon, and Ellesmere.

Queen Mar′y Coast (mâr′ĭ). Region of Antarctica extending E from Cape Filchner, 91°52′E, to ab. 102°E at the Antarctic Circle W of Wilkes Land; claimed by the British.

Queen Maud Gulf (môd). Gulf in NW Keewatin District and NE Mackenzie District, Northwest Territories, Canada, bet. SE Victoria I. and the mainland.

Queen Maud Land. Section of Antarctica W of Enderby Land long. 16°30′W–49°30′E and extending S to Polar Plateau and to Coats Land on the W; claimed by Norwegian government 1939. Prince Olav Coast forms a part of its coast.

Queen Maud Range. Mountain range in S Ross Dependency, Antarctic Continent, S of Ross Shelf Ice; extends 500 m. SE from lat. 84°S and from long. 175°E to 145°W, on edge of Polar Plateau.

Queen′s. See LAOIGHIS.

Queens (kwēnz). **1** County in New York. See *Table* at NEW YORK.

2 Borough of New York City, on W end of Long I., coextensive with Queens county (see *Table* at NEW YORK); 108 sq. m.; pop. 1,809,578; largest in area of the five boroughs of New York City; extends from Brooklyn to Long Island Sound, Newtown Creek, and East River; connected with mainland by Hell Gate Bridge bet. the

Bronx and Astoria, and with Manhattan by Queensboro Bridge and electric railroad tunnels beneath East river; has ab. 200 m. of waterfront; manufactures bakery products, clothing, hosiery, pianos, paint, silk; governed as part of New York City (*q.v.*) by a mayor and city council; has a borough president, with local and county functions conducted independently of central municipal government. Settled c. 1635; chartered as borough 1898; includes former Long Island City (*q.v.*) and former towns of Newtown, Flushing, and Jamaica (*qq.v.*), together with a section formerly included in town of Hempstead, etc.; La Guardia Airport; Kennedy (formerly Idlewild) International Airport. St. John's University (1870) in Jamaica.
3 County, New Brunswick, Canada. See *Table* at NEW BRUNSWICK.
4 County, Nova Scotia, Canada. See *Table* at NOVA SCOTIA.
5 County, Prince Edward I., Canada. See *Table* at PRINCE EDWARD ISLAND.
Queens·bur·y and Shelf (kwēnz′bẽr·ĭ, -brĭ; shelf′). Urban district, West Riding Yorkshire, N England; pop. 9067.
Queens′cliff (kwēnz′klĭf). Seaport, S Victoria, SE Australia, at mouth of Port Phillip Bay 40 m. SSW of Melbourne; pop. 1969; popular watering place.
Queens′land (kwēnz′lănd; -lănd). State, NE Australia; 670,500 sq. m.; pop. (1933) 947,534, (1963 est.) 1,566,218; * Brisbane. E half contains parallel N and S ranges of Great Dividing Range (Eastern Highlands) with highest part in the Atherton Plateau in the N. Low coastlands along W side of Cape York Penin.; cen. and S parts slope gradually to W (Artesian Basin) where upper tributaries of Darling and Barcoo rivers rise. Several streams (including Mitchell, Gilbert, Flinders) flow W or NW to Gulf of Carpentaria; others (Burdekin, Brisbane, Fitzroy) enter S Pacific. Along NE coast for ab. 1250 m. extends Great Barrier Reef (*q.v.*). N point is Cape York, separated by Torres Strait from S New Guinea. Northern two thirds in Torrid Zone. Largest island is Fraser, off SE coast. *Chief towns:* Brisbane, Rockhampton, Townsville, Toowoomba, Ipswich, and Cairns. *Chief exports:* Meat, hides, skin, wool, dairy products, sugar.
History: Coast first visited by Capt. Cook 1770; 1st settlement (penal) on Moreton Bay 1824; opened to free settlers 1842, when Brisbane was founded. Part of New South Wales until 1859; became one of states of Australian Commonwealth 1901.
Queens–Mid′town′ Tunnel (kwēnz′mĭd′toun′). Vehicular tunnel under the East river bet. Manhattan I., New York City and Queens borough on W end of Long I.; opened 1940.
Queens′ton (kwēnz′tŭn). Village, Lincoln co., Ontario, Canada, on Niagara river; scene of attempt Oct. 13, 1812 by American forces under Maj. Gen. Stephen Van Rensselaer to invade Canada; British commander Maj. Gen. Isaac Brock was killed, but American force that had gained the heights above the village was captured by Maj. Gen. Sheaffe; usually called battle of Queenston Heights.
Queens′town (kwēnz′toun). **1** See COBH.
2 Town, W Tasmania, Australia, 12 m. NW of N end of Macquarie Harbour; pop. 3808; center of mining and timber region; operates large copper smelters and produces gold, silver, and copper; known as "Copper City."
3 Borough, Otago provincial dist., S South I., New Zealand, on Wakatipu Lake 110 m. WNW of Dunedin; pop. 860; popular lake and mountain resort.
4 Town, E Cape Province, S Republic of So. Africa, in upper valley of Great Kei river 160 m. NE of Port Elizabeth; pop. 18,254; founded 1853; in district producing mainly wool and wheat. Queen's Coll. for Boys.
Queen Victoria Park. See NIAGARA FALLS.
Quel′i·ma′ne (kĕl′ĭ·mä′nĕ) *or* **Quil′i·ma′ne** (kĭl′-).
1 River, Mozambique, SE Africa, N of the Zambesi.

2 Former district, E cen. Mozambique, N of Zambesi river; 39,800 sq. m.; pop. 877,000; now constitutes Zambezia prov.
3 Seaport town, on Quelimane river ab. 14 m. inland from its mouth; * of former Quelimane dist., now chief town of Zambezia prov.; pop. (1935 est.) 9702.
Quelpart. See SAISHU.
Que·ma′do de Güi′nes (kâ·mä′thō thâ gwē′nâs). Municipality and town, Las Villas prov., W cen. Cuba; town 32 m. NW of Santa Clara, pop. (1943) 8414.
Que·moy′ (k[w]ē·moi′). Island, SE China, in Formosa Strait E of Amoy; with **Little Quemoy,** island to the W, and several islets, comprises the Quemoy Is. group.
Que′na·ma′ri Knot (kā′nä·mä′rē). Mountain 19,193 ft. in Puno dept., SE Peru, NW of Lake Titicaca.
Que′pos, Point (kā′pōs). Cape on W cen. coast of Costa Rica, projecting into the Pacific Ocean.
Quer′cy′ (kĕr′sē′). Ancient county, S France; in region now occupied by departments of Lot and Tarn-et-Garonne; lower part, * Montauban, ceded to Henry III of England 1259; whole region held by English 1360 until they were driven out 1440; suffered severely during religious wars of 16th cent. when it was a center of Protestantism.
Que·ré′ta·ro (kâ·rā′tä·rō). **1** State, cen. Mexico. See *Table* at MEXICO.
2 City, cen. Mexico, * of Querétaro state, 160 m. NW of Mexico City; pop. 33,629; altitude 5900 ft.; site of a pre-Aztec settlement; scene of execution of Emperor Maximilian 1867; 16th-cent. cathedral; opal mines.
Quer′furt (kvär′fŏŏrt). Commune, Saxony, Germany, SW of Halle; pop. 5022; home of Bruno of Querfurt (Saint Bonifacius).
Que·sa′da (kâ·sä′thä). Commune, Jaén prov., S Spain, 39 m. E of Jaén; pop. 11,309; several times taken and sacked by Moors; reconquered definitively 1309.
Ques·nel′ (kwĕ·nĕl′; *Fr.* kĕ′nĕl′). River ab. 75 m. long, S cen. British Columbia, Canada; flows NW out of **Quesnel Lake** (147 sq. m.) into Fraser river.
Quesnoy, Le. See LE QUESNOY.
Quet′i·co Provincial Park (kwĕt′ĭ·kō). Canadian provincial park, SW Ontario, in lake region just N of United States (Minnesota) boundary; 1720 sq. m.; a wilderness area set aside for camping and fishing.
Quet′ta (kwĕt′ä). Town, Pakistan, in Baluchistan, 450 m. WSW of Lahore; pop. 34,881, with cantonment 60,272; important rail junction, carries on lucrative trade with Iran, W Afghanistan, and Central Asia; located on a plain enclosed by high mountains; controls Bolan and Khojak Passes and routes heading into S Afghanistan. Seat of Indian staff college (founded 1907). Occupied by British during First Afghan War 1839–42, and annexed in 1876; developed into a strong fortress; British headquarters of western command; practically destroyed in severe earthquake June 1935, but rebuilt.
Quetta–Pi·shin′ (-pĭ·shēn′). District, cen. Baluchistan; 5310 sq. m.; pop. (1941) 156,289; * Quetta.
Quet·zal′co·al′co (kĕt·säl′kō·äl′kō). = COATZACOALCOS.
Que·zal′te·nan′go (kâ·säl′tâ·näng′gō). **1** Department, SW Guatemala; 753 sq. m.; pop. 233,655; * Quezaltenango.
2 City, its * and 2d largest city in Guatemala; pop. 33,538; altitude 7800 ft.; in grain-growing region.
Que·zal′te·pe′que (kâ·säl′tâ·pā′kā). Town, La Libertad dept., SW El Salvador; pop. (1942 est.) 6382.
Que′zon City (kā′sôn). City, W Rizal prov., Luzon, Phil. Is., official * of the Republic of the Philippines; adjoining Manila on the NE; 28 sq. m.; pop. 107,977; created in 1940; extends E to Marikina river; consists of 11 barrios set apart from Caloocan, Marikina, Pasig, and San Juan del Monte.
Quiaca, La. See LA QUIACA.
Quiangan. See KIANGAN.
Quib·dó′ (kēv·thō′). City, * of Chocó intendancy, W

Colombia, on the Atrato river 80 m. WNW of Manizales; pop. 5278.

Qui'be·ron' (kē'brôN'). Town, Morbihan dept., NW France; pop. 1764; at tip of **Quiberon Peninsula,** a narrow, sandy peninsula, 6 m. long, forming W side of **Quiberon Bay,** site of naval battle, Nov. 20, 1759 during Seven Years' War, in which English fleets under Boscawen and Hawke defeated the French. Scene July 20–21, 1795, of defeat of French royalists who landed at base of peninsula but were driven back by forces of Gen. Hoche.

Qui·ché' (kē·chā'). 1 Department, W cen. Guatemala; 3235 sq. m.; pop. 158,662; ✳ Santa Cruz Quiché.
2 See SANTA CRUZ QUICHÉ.

Quid'i Vid'i (kĭd'ĭ vĭd'ĭ; kwĭ'dȧ vĭ'dȧ). Locality, N of Quidi Vidi Lake, suburb of St. John's, Newfoundland; leased to U.S. 1940 as Army base, used as a post for a defensive force. Renamed **Fort Pep'per·rell** (pĕp'-ĕr-ĕl).

Quie'pe (kyā'pĕ). Island in Atlantic Ocean off SE coast of Baía state, Brazil, 70 m. SSW of Salvador (Bahia).

Quié'vrain' (kyā'vrăN'). Commune, Hainaut prov., Belgium; pop. 5219; customs station, on the French frontier bet. Mons and Valenciennes.

Quiin·dy' or **Quiyn·dy'** (kēn·dē'). Town, Paraguarí dept., S Paraguay, 55 m. SE of Asunción; pop. ab. 14,500; formerly capital of a department of same name.

Quilimane. See QUELIMANE.

Quill Lakes (kwĭl). Two connected lakes, 163 sq. m., in SE cen. Saskatchewan prov., Canada.

Quil·lo'ta (kē·yō'tä). Town, Valparaíso prov., cen. Chile, 30 m. NE of Valparaíso; pop. 17,232.

Quil'mes (kēl'mȧs). City, Buenos Aires prov., E Argentina, 8 m. SE of Buenos Aires; pop. 115,113; industrial center and summer resort.

Qui·lon' (kē·lôn') or **Kol'lam** (kŏl'ăm). Town, SE Kerala state, S India, formerly in Travancore state, on Malabar Coast 130 m. SW of Madura; pop. 33,739. Seaport with extensive trade, exporting timber, coconuts, oil, pepper, tea, and coffee.

Quil'pie (kwĭl'pĭ). Inland town, S cen. Queensland, Australia; pop. of district 1969; terminus of railroad from Brisbane.

Quil·pué' (kēl·pwä'). Town, Valparaíso prov., cen. Chile, 12 m. by rail from Valparaíso; pop. 9167.

Quim'per' (kăN'pâr'). Manufacturing and commercial commune, ✳ of Finistère dept., NW France, near Bay of Biscay 112 m. W of Rennes; pop. 18,814; 13th–15th-cent. Gothic cathedral; sardine fisheries; manufactures pottery (called Quimper or Brittany ware), paper, leather, brewery products. Capital of old countship of Carnouailles.

Quim'per'lé' (kăN'pĕr'lā'). Commercial town, Finistère dept., NW France, ab. 13 m. NW of Lorient; pop. 5815; restoration of an 11th-cent. Romanesque abbey church of Ste-Croix.

Quim'sa·cha'ta (kēm'sä·chä'tä). Peak 19,882 ft. in N Chile, W of Lake Poopó.

Quim'sa·cruz' (kēm'sä·krōōs'). Peak 19,357 ft. in W Bolivia, SE of Lake Titicaca.

Qui·na·la·sag' (kē'nä·lä·säg'). Island in Pacific off N coast of Caramoan Penin., NE Camarines Sur prov., Luzon, Phil. Is.; 13 sq. m.; pop. 652.

Qui·na'ta (kē·nä'tä). Peak 7415 ft. in S Venezuela, N of the Orinoco.

Qui'na·uan' Point (kē'nä·wän'). Point, SW coast of Bataan Penin., Luzon, Phil. Is.; extends into South China Sea WNW of Mariveles, 14°30'N.

Qui·nault' Lake (kwē·nŭlt'). Lake in N Grays Harbor co., W Washington, on W slope of Coast Range; traversed by **Quinault River** which rises to the NE in Jefferson co. and flows SW to the Pacific Ocean.

Quin'cy (kwĭn'sĭ; *Quincy in Mass. is* -zĭ). 1 Village, ⊗ of Plumas co., NE California; pop. (with East Quincy) 2723; winter sports.

2 City, ⊗ of Gadsden co., N Florida, 20 m. WNW of Tallahassee; pop. 8874; tobacco mart; deposits of fuller's earth in the vicinity.
3 City, ⊗ of Adams co., W Illinois, on Mississippi river across from Missouri; pop. 43,793; settled ab. 1822; commercial, industrial, and distributing center in agricultural and livestock-raising section; flour mills, foundries, brick kilns. Quincy Coll. (1860; coed.).
4 City, Norfolk co., E Massachusetts, 8 m. S of Boston; pop. 87,409; shipyards, granite quarries; birthplace of John Adams, 2d president of the U.S. and of John Quincy Adams, 6th president of the U.S.; site of settlement of Merrymount or Mt. Wollaston where Thomas Morton established his trading post c. 1625.

Quin·dí'o Pass (kēn·dē'ô). Mountain pass, altitude 11,435 ft. in the Cordillera Central, in Colombia, lat. 4°36'N.

Quin·e·baug (kwĭn'ė·bôg). River ab. 100 m. long in S Massachusetts and E Connecticut; rises in E Hampden co., SW Massachusetts, flows SE across Connecticut border, then S across E Connecticut into the Shetucket N of Norwich.

Qui'né'ville' (kē'nā'vēl'). Commune, Manche dept., Normandy, NW France, on E coast of Cotentin Penin. ab. 17 m. SE of Cherbourg; pop. (1931) 335; at N end of Utah Beach in World War II.

Qui'nhon' (kwē'nyôn'). Town on coast of SE Annam, S Vietnam, port of Binh Dinh; pop. ab. 5000; has shallow harbor. A capital of the Chams in early times.

Quinn Canyon Mountains (kwĭn). Small range in W Lincoln co. and E cen. Nye co., SE cen. Nevada.

Quin'ni·pi·ac' (kwĭn'ĭ·pĭ·ăk'; kwĭn'ĭ·pĭ·ăk'). River, cen. Connecticut; rises in SW Hartford co., flows S through cen. New Haven co. and empties into New Haven Harbor.

Quin·sig'a·mond, Lake (kwĭn·sĭg'a·mŭnd). Lake in cen. Worcester co., cen. Massachusetts, on E border of city of Worcester.

Quin·ta'na Ro'o (kēn·tä'nä rrô'ô). Territory in E Yucatán penin., SE Mexico; 19,438 sq. m.; pop. 18,485; ✳ Chetumal; divided Dec. 1931 bet. Yucatán and Campeche states and re-established Jan. 1935.

Quin'te, Bay of (kwĭn'tĕ). Inlet of Lake Ontario extending N of Prince Edward co., SE Ontario, Canada; extends from Trenton E to Napanee, with many inlets and islands. Favorite resort of vacationists; connected with Georgian Bay by Trent Canal (q.v.).

Quin'to (kēn'tô). River ab. 250 m. long in Córdoba prov., N cen. Argentina; rises in San Luis prov.; flows ESE into a marsh.

Qui·quió' (kē·kyō'), **Qui·quy'o** (kē·kē'ô). = QUYQUYO.

Qui·raing' (kwĭ·răng'). Mountain 1779 ft. in N Skye I., off NW coast of Scotland; remarkable rock formations.

Qui·ri·guá' (kē'rē·gwä'). Ancient Mayan city in E Guatemala, in the Motagua valley; ruins of temple and carved monoliths.

Quir'i·nal (kwĭr'ĭ·n'l; kwĭ·rī'n'l). One of the seven hills of Rome. See SEVEN HILLS.

Qui·ro'ga, Point (kē·rō'gä). Cape, NE Chubut territory, S Argentina, W of entrance to Gulf of San José opp. Point Buenos Aires (q.v.).

Qui'ros (kē'rôs). = SWAINS ISLAND.

Quis'ling Cove (kwĭz'lĭng). Inlet on NW coast of Kiska I. in the Aleutians, Alaska; Americans landed here Aug. 15, 1943.

Quis·que'ya (kĭs·kā'yä). Indian name for HISPANIOLA.

Quis·tel'lo (kwēs·tĕl'lô). Commune, Mantova prov., SE Lombardy, N Italy, 14 m. SE of Mantua; pop. (1931) 9464.

Qui'ta Sue'ño Bank (kē'tä swä'nyô). Shoal in W Caribbean Sea off NE coast of Nicaragua; controlled by U.S.A. and Colombia.

Quit'man (kwĭt'mȧn). 1 Name of counties in two states of the U.S. See *Tables* at GEORGIA and MISSISSIPPI.
2 City, ⊗ of Brooks co., S Georgia, 17 m. W of Valdosta;

pop. 5071; shipping point for hams, sausages, vegetables, melons.

3 Town, ⊗ of Clarke co., E Mississippi; pop. 2030.

4 City, ⊗ of Wood co., NE Texas; pop. 1237; nurseries, watermelon raising; oil wells, refinery.

Qui′to (kē′tô). **1** Former Spanish presidency, now Ecuador (*q.v.*); won independence and incorporated with Great Colombia under presidency of Simón Bolívar 1822; union disrupted by constitutional assembly which proclaimed the constitution of the republic of Ecuador 1830.

2 City, N Ecuador, on fertile plateau, ab. 114 m. from the Pacific coast and 170 m. NE of Guayaquil; lies almost on the equator just SE of the volcano Pichincha and at an altitude of ab. 9300 ft.; ✱ of Pichincha prov. and ✱ of Ecuador; pop. (1944 est.) 165,924. A pre-Columbian town, captured by the Incas 1470; taken by the Spanish under Sebastián de Belalcázar 1533; audiencia established 1563; town destroyed by eruption of Pichincha 1660; Spanish governor deposed by revolutionary junta 1809; acquired independence by victory of Gen. Sucre over the Spanish in battle of Pichincha May 24, 1822; during Spanish rule, capital of presidency of Quito; has suffered repeatedly from earthquakes, esp. in 1797, 1844, 1859, 1868, 1887. Has a wireless station and an airport; national palace, municipal building, observatory, national library, central university (founded 1787), military school, normal institutes, national conservatory of music, polytechnics school, colonial churches.

Qui′vi·cán′ (kē′vē·kän′). Municipality, La Habana prov., W Cuba, 20 m. S of Havana; pop. 6042.

Qui·vi′ra (kǐ·vēr′á; *Span.* kē·vē′rä). Mythical town of fabulous wealth sought 1541 by Coronado, generally located near Great Bend, Barton co., cen. Kansas; a site in cen. New Mexico was mistakenly identified with it and has been set aside as the Gran Quivira National Monument (see UNITED STATES, *National Monuments*).

Quiyndy. See QUIINDY.

Qum (kŏŏm) *or* **Kum. 1** Former province of Iran.
2 Its chief city, NW cen. Iran, 75 m. SSW of Tehran; pop. ab. 30,000; center of grain and cotton region and important junction for several highways; on railroad connecting Tehran with head of the Persian Gulf; has numerous mosques and, being site of shrine of Fatima, sister of Imam Riza, is a place for Shiite pilgrimages.

Qumran. = KHIRBAT QUMRAN.

Quneitra, El. See EL KUNEITRA.

Qun′fi·dha, al– (ăl·kŏŏn′fŏŏ·dá; -zá). Port on the Red Sea, NW Asir, W Arabia.

Qungur. See KUNGUR.

Quoich, Loch (lŏκ koiκ′). Lake in W Inverness co., NW Scotland.

Qurna, Al. See AL QURNA.

Quseir, El. See EL QUSEIR.

Qusur, El. See LUXOR.

Qutr el Masri, El. See EGYPT.

Quy′quy·ó′ (kē′kē·ô′). Town, Paraguarí dept., S Paraguay; pop. ab. 6590; manganese and copper.

R

Raab. 1 See Rába river.
2 See Győr city.
Raa'he (rä′hĕ). Town, Oulu dept., W Finland, on Gulf of Bothnia 35 m. SW of Oulu; pop. 4700.
Raal'te (räl′tĕ). Commune, Overijssel prov., E Netherlands, 12 m. SE of Zwolle; pop. 9641.
Raamses. See Ramses.
Raa'say, Sound of (rä′zā). Channel bet. E Skye I. and Raasay I. in the Inner Hebrides, off NW coast of Scotland.
Raasay Island. One of the Inner Hebrides NE of Skye I., off NW coast of Scotland; 12 m. long; administratively a part of Inverness co.
Rab (räb); *Ital.* **Ar'be** (är′bä). **1** Yugoslav island E of the Mali Kvarner at the head of the Adriatic Sea off coast of Croatia; 74 sq. m.; pop. 6354; marble quarries, silk industry; resort.
2 Town on W coast of the island.
Ra'ba (rä′bä). Town on Bima Bay, NE coast of Sumbawa I., Lesser Sunda Is., Indonesia; pop. 6781; chief town on Sumbawa.
Rá′ba (rä′bŏ); *Ger.* **Raab** (räp). Navigable river ab. 160 m. long in SE Austria and W Hungary; rises in province of Styria, Austria, flows E and NE across Hungarian border and into the Danube river.
Ra·bat' (rä·bät′). City, NW coast of Morocco, NW Africa, ✳ of Morocco; pop. 156,209; situated at the mouth of the Bou Regreg opposite Salé (*q.v.*); modern French quarter quite separate from the native town; beautiful minaret, the Hassan tower, is S of the town and the palace of the sultan SW; on site of a camp established 12th cent. by Abd-al-Mumin, founder of Almohade dynasty; important only since beginning of French protectorate 1912. An objective in Allied invasion of North Africa Nov. 1942.
Ra·baul' (rä·boul′). Town and port on NE New Britain I., Bismarck Archipelago, W Pacific Ocean; ✳ of New Britain dist. and until 1941 ✳ of the Territory of New Guinea; pop. (1939 est.) ab. 9700; on Simpson Harbour, the inner, landlocked part of Blanche Bay and almost surrounded by active and extinct volcanoes. Well laid out and established as capital of German New Guinea 1910; chief town of Australian mandate 1920–41; nearly destroyed by volcanic eruption of Matupi and Vulcan May 29–30, 1937; seat of government removed to Lae 1941; seized by Japanese Jan. 23, 1942 and made naval and air base; many times bombed by Allied air forces 1943–45; its value neutralized by Allied landings at Arawe, Cape Gloucester, and Talasea Dec. 1943–Mar. 1944.
Rabbah, *or* **Rabbath, Ammon.** See Amman.
Rabbit Ears Pass. Mountain highway pass 9680 ft., Jackson, Routt, and Grand cos., N Colorado, in Park Range of Rocky Mts., in a small range called the **Rabbit Ears Range** named for peculiar formation on summit of **Rabbit Ears Peak** 10,719 ft.
Ra'bun (rä′bŭn). County in Georgia. See *Table* at Georgia.
Ra'cal·mu'to (rä′käl·mōō′tŏ). Commercial commune, Agrigento prov., SW Sicily, 11 m. NE of Agrigento; pop. 13,061; sulfur and salt mining.
Rac'co·ni'gi (räk′kŏ·nē′jĕ). Town, Cuneo prov., SW Piedmont, NW Italy, 24 m. S of Turin, pop (commune) 8643; château, summer residence of kings of Italy from 1900.
Rac·coon' (rä·kōōn′; *attributively, also* räk′ōōn). River 190 m. long, W cen. Iowa; rises in Buena Vista co., NW Iowa, flows SE into Des Moines river at Des Moines.
Raccoon Island. Island in Atlantic Ocean, in NE Charleston co., South Carolina, NE of Charleston.
Raccoon Mountains. Ridge, alt. ab. 2000 ft., in NE Alabama, chiefly in DeKalb and Jackson cos., running

from NE to SW parallel with course of Tennessee river in that area.
Raccoon Point. Point at W tip of Isles Dernieres, off S coast of Terrebonne parish, SE Louisiana.
Race, Cape (rās). Southeast point of Newfoundland, extending into the Atlantic Ocean, 46°37′N.
Race, the. Strait S of SE Connecticut, bet. Fishers I. and islands off NE Long I., connecting Long Island Sound with Block Island Sound and the Atlantic Ocean.
Race of Al'der·ney (ôl′dẽr·nĭ). Dangerous channel bet. the island of Alderney and the coast of France.
Race Point. Small peninsula at tip of Cape Cod, SE Massachusetts, N of Provincetown; lighthouse.
Ra·ci'bórz (rä·tsē′bōōsh); *Ger.* **Ra'ti·bor** (rät′ĭ·bôr; *Ger.* rä′tĕ·bôr, -bōr). City, S Śląsk dept., SW Poland, 42 m. SSE of Opole on Odra (Oder) river near Czechoslovakia border; pop. (1946) 52,000; formerly in Silesia prov., Germany; 15th-cent. Gothic church; manufactures electrical supplies, hats, machinery, ironware; shipbuilding. Capital of duchy 1288–1532; principality created 1821; in World War II taken by Russians Feb. 4, 1945; assigned to Poland by the Potsdam Conference July–Aug. 1945.
Ra·cine' (rä·sēn′; rå-). **1** County in Wisconsin. See *Table* at Wisconsin.
2 City, its ⊗, SE Wisconsin, on Lake Michigan 23 m. S of Milwaukee; pop. 89,144; 3d largest city in the state; port of entry; has excellent harbor; shipping point and industrial center; manufactures automobile accessories, farm machinery, knitted products, food products, shoes. Incorporated as village 1841, as city 1848.
Radak. See Ratak.
Ră·dă·u'ți *or* **Ra·da·u'tsi** (rä·dä·ōōts′; -ōō′tsĕ); *Ger.* **Ra'dautz** (rä′douts). Town, N Romania, in S Bucovina region ab. 35 m. WNW of Botoşani; pop. 16,808; now on Ukraine border; cathedral, containing tombs of Moldavian princes.
Rad'cliffe (răd′klĭf). Urban district, Lancashire, NW England, on the Irwell 8 m. NNW of Manchester; pop. 27,551; cotton mills, chemical factories, coal mines.
Ra'de·berg (rä′dĕ·bĕrk). Industrial city, Dresden dist., East Germany, 8 m. NE of Dresden; pop. 15,651; 16th-cent. castle; manufactures glass, metal goods, radios, enamelware, refrigerators, beer; mineral bath nearby.
Ra'de·beul (rä′dĕ·boil). City, Dresden dist., East Germany, NW suburb of Dresden on Elbe river; pop. 12,428; manufactures chemicals, pharmaceutical goods, perfume, dyes, rubber, asbestos, metal goods, shoes.
Ra'de·vorm·wald' (rä′dĕ·fôrm·vält′). Industrial city, North Rhine-Westphalia state, West Germany, 25 m. E of Düsseldorf; pop. 11,823; manufactures bicycles, files, skates, textiles, electrical goods.
Rad'ford (răd′fẽrd). City, Montgomery co., western Virginia, but politically independent, 14 m. ENE of Pulaski; 5 sq. m.; pop. 9371; manufactures foundry products, lumber. Radford Coll. (founded 1910 as State Teachers Coll.; became 1944 the Woman's Division of Virginia Polytechnic Institute).
Ra'dhan·pur (räd′hän·pōōr). **1** Former Indian state, NW Gujarat, Western India States, India; 1150 sq. m.
2 Town, its ✳, ab. 85 m. NW of Ahmadabad; pop. 11,225.
Rad'nor (răd′nẽr). Urban township, Delaware co., SE Pennsylvania, W of Philadelphia; pop. 21,697.
Rad'nor·shire (răd′nẽr·shĭr; -shẽr) *or* **Rad'nor** (răd′-nẽr) County, E Wales; area 471 sq. m.; pop. (1951) 19,998. ⊗ Llandrindod Wells; hilly area; industries, livestock raising, quarrying (limestone, sandstone).
Ra'dom (rä′dôm) Industrial commune, Kielce dept., Poland, 37 m. NE of Kielce; pop. (1938–39 est.) 77,900; railroad junction; 16th-cent. Gothic church; manufactures leather, metal, lumber, pottery, textiles, tobacco. Prominent in Polish history esp. 13th to 16th cents.;

came under Austria 1795–1815 and Russia 1815–1918; taken by Central Powers 1915.

Ra·dom′sko (rä-dôm′skô); *Russ.* **No′vo·ra′domsk** (nô′vŭ-rä′dŭmsk). Commune, Łódź dept., Poland, 48 m. S of Łódź; pop. (1938–39 est.) 26,350; manufactures metal goods, wooden goods.

Ra·do·mysl′ (rȧ-dŭ-mĭs′ly′). Town, E Zhitomir Region, W Ukraine, U.S.S.R., on left bank of Teterev river 55 m. W of Kiev; pop. 12,930.

Rad·vi′lish·kis (räd-vĭ′lĭsh-kĭs). Town, Shaulyai dist., N Lithuania, on main railroad line 15 m. SE of Shaulyai; pop. (1938 est.) 6745.

Ra′e Ba·re′li (rä′ĕ bȧ-rä′lĕ). Town, S cen. Uttar Pradesh, N Indian Union, 45 m. SSE of Lucknow; pop. 18,180; has several ancient buildings, among them a fort, palace, and several fine mosques.

Rae′ford (rā′fērd). Town, ⊗ of Hoke co., S North Carolina, 20 m. WSW of Fayetteville; pop. 3058; cotton mills.

Rae Strait (rā). Channel bet. E King William I. and N Canada mainland, N Keewatin District.

Rae′ti·a (rē′shĭ·ȧ; -shȧ) *or* **Rhae′ti·a.** Ancient Roman province S of the Danube river; included most of what is now Tirol-Vorarlberg prov. in Austria and Graubünden canton in E Switzerland. Bounded on N by Vindelicia, on E by Noricum, on S by Italy, and on W by Gaul. Added to Roman Empire in reign of Augustus.

Raetian Alps. = *Rhaetian Alps:* see *Table* at ALPS.

Raetia Secunda. See VINDELICIA.

Ra′fa (rä′fȧ); *anc.* **Ra·phi′a** (rȧ-fī′ȧ). Village on the frontier bet. Egypt and Southern District, Palestine, on the Mediterranean Sea coast; actually two villages: Palestine village (pop. ab. 1000), scene of battle 720 B.C. when Sargon II of Assyria defeated the Philistines and Egyptians, and in 217 B.C. scene of the defeat of Antiochus the Great by Ptolemy IV Philopator of Egypt; the Egyptian village (also called **Er Rafa** [är]), scene Jan. 9, 1917 of British victory over the Turks.

Ra′fa·e′la (rä′fä·ā′lä). City, Santa Fe prov., E cen. Argentina, just NW of Santa Fe; pop. (est.) 25,931; important communications center.

Raf·fa′da·li (räf-fä′dä-lē). Commune, Agrigento prov., SW Sicily, 7 m. NNW of Agrigento; pop. 11,207.

Ra·gang′, Mount (rä-gäng′). Active volcano 9236 ft. in SE Lanao prov., Mindanao, Phil. Is., on Cotabato boundary.

Ra·gay′ Gulf (rä-gī′). An inland water of cen. Philippine Is., a N arm of the Sibuyan Sea in SE Luzon, bet. Tayabas prov. on the W and Camarines Sur on the E; ab. 60 m. long and 32 m. wide at its mouth or S end; Burias I. is S of its mouth.

Ra′gaz (rä′gäts) *or* **Ra′gatz.** Town, E Saint Gallen canton, NE Switzerland, on the Rhine at entrance to a gorge; pop. (1930) 2166; thermal waters.

Rages. See RHAGES.

Rag′ged Island (răg′ĕd; -ĭd). One of the Bahama Is., in Atlantic Ocean N of E end of Cuba and W of Acklins I.; with adjacent cays, 5 sq. m.; pop. (1943) 417.

Ragged Top, Mount. Peak 6207 ft. in Lawrence co., W South Dakota.

Rag′lan (răg′lǎn). Town, Monmouthshire, W England, 6½ m. SW of Monmouth; site of castle begun c. 1465, besieged 10 weeks 1646; gave title to Field Marshal Lord Raglan (d. 1855).

Ra·gu·sa (rä-gōō′zä). **1** Province of Italy. See *Table* at ITALY.

2 *anc.* **Hy′bla He·rae′a** (hī′blä hē-rē′ȧ). Commune, ✳ of Ragusa prov., SE Sicily, 113 m. SE of Palermo; pop. 49,530; cathedral. In World War II junction point of Americans and Canadians in occupation of Sicily July 1943.

3 Seaport of Dalmatia, Yugoslavia. See DUBROVNIK.

Ra·ha′, Har′rat ar (hŭr′rŏt ŭr rŏ·hä′). Elevated tract, N Hejaz, NW Arabia; highest point 7000 ft.

Ra′had (rä′hǎd). River ab. 270 m. long in E Africa; rises in NW Ethiopia near Lake Tana, flows NW across border into Republic of Sudan and empties into the Blue Nile (Bahr el Azraq).

Ra·haeng (rä-häng). **1** Province, W Thailand; 5268 sq. m.; pop. 93,247.

2 Town, its ✳, on left bank of Ping river opp. Tak 40 m. from Burma border and 70 m. W of Phitsanulok.

Rahiroa. See RANGIROA.

Rah′way (rô′wā). **1** Short stream, NE New Jersey; rises in Essex co., flows S through Union co., enters Arthur Kill 5 m. S of Elizabeth.

2 City, Union co., NE New Jersey, on Rahway river 5 m. SSW of Elizabeth; pop. 27,699; founded c. 1720; produces fruit and vegetables; printing houses, cooperage works; manufactures drugs and chemicals, cereal products, steel cabinets.

Rai. See RHAGES.

Ra′ia·té′a (rä′yä·tā′ä). One of the Leeward Is. group of the Society Is., French Polynesia, S Pacific Ocean, 130 m. WNW of Tahiti and just S of Tahaa; 75 sq. m.; pop. (with Tahaa) ab. 4000. In its center is Mount Temehani 3389 ft.

Rai′chur (rī′chōor). Town, W Mysore state, S cen. Indian Union, 110 m. SW of Hyderabad in the doab bet. the Kistna and Tungabhadra rivers; pop. 27,910; contains an old fort and a palace.

Rai·des′tos (rī-dĕs′tŏs). Greek form of *Rhaedestus:* see TEKIRDAĞ.

Rai′dhak (rĭd′häk). River, W Bhutan; flows S across Indian border to the Brahmaputra.

Rai′garh (rī′gär; *native* -gŭr·h′). **1** Former Indian state, Eastern States Agency, NE Indian Union; 1444 sq. m.; pop. (1941) 312,643.

2 Town, its ✳, 185 m. NW of Cuttack; pop. ab. 13,000; makes tussah silk.

Rain (rīn). Village in Swabia, Bavaria, on the Lech river near its confluence with the Danube 22 m. N of Augsburg; pop. ab. 2000. In battle here Apr. 15, 1632 Count Tilly was defeated by Gustavus Adolphus and mortally wounded.

Rain′bow′ Bridge National Monument (rän′bō′). See UNITED STATES, *National Monuments.*

Rainbow City. See SILVER CITY, Canal Zone.

Rainbow Peak. 1 Mountain 9329 ft. in N Valley co., W cen. Idaho.

2 Mountain 9860 ft. in Glacier National Park, NW Montana.

Raincy, Le. See LE RAINCY.

Rai′nelle (rä′nĕl). Town, Greenbrier co., SE West Virginia; pop. 649; lumber and lumber products.

Rai·nier′, Mount (rȧ-nēr′; rä-nēr′; rän′yēr). Peak 14,410 ft. in Pierce co., W cen. Washington; highest point in Cascade Range and in the state; sometimes called **Ta·co′ma** (tȧ-kō′mȧ), the Indian name; in Mount Rainier National Park (see UNITED STATES, *National Parks*).

Rains (rānz). County in Texas. See *Table* at TEXAS.

Rain′y Lake (rān′ĭ). Lake ab. 50 m. long on N boundary of Minnesota, bet. Minnesota and Canadian province of Ontario; area 324 sq. m.; outlet Rainy river.

Rainy River. 1 River ab. 80 m. long flowing from Rainy Lake to Lake of the Woods, forming part of the Canada-U.S. boundary, bet. SW Ontario prov. and N Minnesota; leaves Rainy Lake at Koochiching Falls.

2 District, Ontario, Canada. See *Table* at ONTARIO.

3 Town, Rainy River dist., SW Ontario, Canada, on Rainy river 55 m. W of Fort Frances; pop. 1348; railroad divisional point and river port.

Rai′pur (rī′pŏor). Town, SE Madhya Pradesh, Indian Union, 162 m. E of Nagpur; pop. (1941) 63,465; seat of Rajkumar College; has ruins of large ancient fort.

Rai′ra·khol (rī′rȧk·hōl). Former Indian state, Eastern States, NE Indian Union, N of the Mahanadi river; area now in NE Orissa state; 857 sq. m.; pop. (1941) 38,185; ✳ Rairakhol.

Rai'sin (rā'z'n). River 150 m. long, SE Michigan; rises in Hillsdale co., flows NE, curves SE, and turns E into Lake Erie at Monroe, in Monroe co. See MONROE, Michigan.

Raismes (râm). Industrial commune, Nord dept., N France, 3 m. NNW of Valenciennes; pop. (1931) 12,866; coal mines; manufactures railroad equipment, ship's anchors and chains.

Raï'va·va'é (rī'va·vä'ā). See TUBUAÏ ISLANDS.

Ra'ja (rä'yä). Peak 7474 ft. in Schwaner Mts., W cen. Borneo, Indonesia.

Rajaburi. See RAT BURI.

Ra'ja·gri'ha (rä'jà·grē'hà). Ancient city, S Bihar, NE Indian Union, in the hills SSW of Bihar; its greatness indicated by extensive ruins; as capital of kingdom of Magadha under Bimbisara (d. 554? B.C.), home for many years of Gautama Buddha. Now site of modern village of **Raj'gir** (räj'gir), a place of pilgrimage.

Ra'jah·mun'dry (rä'jà·mōon'drē). City, NE Andhra Pradesh, E Indian Union, on left bank of Godavari river 295 m. NNE of Madras; pop. (1941) 74,564; lively timber trade. Seized from princes of Orissa by Mohammedans 1470; to Hindus early 16th cent., and again taken by Mohammedans 1572; taken by French 1753 and from latter by British 1758.

Ra'jang (rä'jäng) or **Re'jang** (rā'jäng). Chief river of cen. Sarawak, Borneo, ab. 300 m. long; flows SW and W into South China Sea; chief town on its course Sibu; navigable for over 100 m.; has wide delta.

Ra'ja·sthan (rä'jà·stän). 1 See RAJPUTANA.
2 State, NW Indian Union; a union of former states, ✱ Jaipur; 132,077 sq. m.; pop. 15,972,000; orig. organized 1947 as **Union of Rajasthan**; reorganized 1956 with addition of Ajmer and other areas.

Rajbari. See GOALANDA.

Raj'garh (räj'gär; native -gŭr·h'). 1 Former state, Bhopal, Central India; now in Madhya Pradesh; 926 sq. m.
2 Town, its ✱, 80 m. NE of Ujjain; pop. 6759.

Rajgir. See RAJAGRIHA.

Raj'kot (räj'kōt). 1 Former state, N cen. Kathiawar, Western India States, W Indian Union; 282 sq. m.
2 Town, its ✱ and formerly ✱ of Western India States Agency, 125 m. WSW of Ahmadabad; pop. (1941) 52,178; important rail center and main educational center of Kathiawar with Rajkumar College for sons of native princes. Civil and military station.

Raj'ma·hal Hills (räj'mà·häl). Low range of hills, E Bihar state, NE Indian Union, S and W of the Ganges river; highest ab. 2000 ft.

Raj·nand'gaon (räj·nänd'goun). Town, S Madhya Pradesh, E cen. India, formerly ✱ of Nandgaon state, Eastern States, 125 m. E of Nagpur; pop. 15,977.

Raj·pi'pla (räj·pē'plä); formerly **Raj·pee'pla.** 1 Former Indian state, Gujarat States, W Indian Union, S of the Narbada river; 1515 sq. m.; pop. (1941) 249,032; formerly in Rewa Kantha Agency; on July 7, 1947 joined new confederation of Indian states. A Rajput state with fertile soil and teak forests.
2 Town, its ✱, NE of Surat; pop. 13,302.

Raj'pu·ta'na (räj'pōō·tä'nà) or **Ra'ja·sthan** (rä'jà·stän). Literally "the country of the Rajputs," region of NW Indian Union, formerly including the Rajputana Agency (q.v.) and Ajmer-Merwara prov. (q.v.). Bounded on the N by Bahawalpur (Pakistan) and East Punjab (Indian Union), on the E by S East Punjab and the United Provinces, on the SE and S by the Central India and the Gujarat States, and on the W by Sind (Pakistan). The Aravalli Range crosses the S part of the region from NE to SW; the NW part is largely desert (Thar, or Indian, Desert) but to the SE the country is generally quite fertile. Chief rivers Luni, Chambal, and Banas. The bulk of the population is Hindu, but the Rajputs are in a minority. Before the coming of the Mohammedans, several powerful dynasties ruled the region, but by the 11th cent. A.D. these were largely overcome; in

the centuries following there was much disruption under the Moguls and later under the Marathas; after 1817 the Rajput states came by treaties under British protection; in 1947 became part of Indian Union.

Rajputana Agency. Formerly the official name of a group of 21 Indian states in the Rajputana region; 132,559 sq. m.; pop. (1941) 13,670,208. The Resident for the Crown resided at Abu; he dealt directly with Bikaner and under him were four agencies: Jaipur Residency, Western Rajputana States, Eastern Rajputana States, and the Mewar and Southern Rajputana States (qq.v.).

Raj·sha'hi (räj·shä'hī). 1 Former division, N Bengal, NE Brit. India; 19,642 sq. m.; pop. (1941) 12,040,465; divided Aug. 15, 1947 with ab. ⅔ of area and population in East Bengal, Pakistan, and ⅓ in West Bengal, Indian Union. See EAST BENGAL, WEST BENGAL.
2 District in division; 2526 sq. m.; pop. (1941) 1,571,750; now in East Bengal, Pakistan.
3 formerly **Ram'pur Bo·a'li·a** (räm'pōōr bō·ä'lī·à). Town, ✱ of district and of former division, now in East Bengal, Pakistan, on Ganges river 125 m. N of Calcutta; pop. 27,064; seat of a government college.

Ra·ka·hang'a (rä'kà·häng'à). Atoll 3 m. in diameter in the Manihiki group, cen. Pacific Ocean, N of the Cook Is. ab. 25 m. NW of Manihiki; pop. (1936) 290; produces coconuts; administered by New Zealand with the Cook Is.

Ra·ka'ia (rà·kā'yà). River 85 m. long in E cen. South I., New Zealand; flows SE into Pacific Ocean.

Ra'ka·po'shi (rü'ka·pō'shi) or **Ra'ka·pu'shi** (-pōōsh'ī). Peak ab. 25,560 ft. in the Karakoram Range, Kashmir, N India, NNE of Gilgit.

Rakata. See KRAKATAU.

Rak'ka (rŏk'kŏ); Arab. **al-Raq'qah** (äl·rŏk'kŏ); anc. **Ni'ce·pho'ri·um** (nī'sē·fōr'ĭ·ŭm). Town, N cen. Syria, on the left bank of the Euphrates river 105 m. E of Alep; pop. ab. 8000; near the confluence of the Balikh with the Euphrates. Prominent under the Abbassides; a favorite residence of Harun al-Rashid and the home of the Arab astronomer al-Battani.

Ra'kos·pa'lo·ta (rä'kŏsh·pŏ'lō·tŏ). City, cen. Hungary; pop. 36,923; NE suburb of Budapest.

Ra'kov·nik (rà'kŏv·nyĭk); Ger. **Ra'ko·nitz** (rä'kō·nǐts). Town, W cen. Bohemia, W Czechoslovakia, 33 m. W of Prague; pop. (1930) 11,073.

Ra'ków (rä'kōof). Village, Kielce dept., Poland, on a tributary of the Vistula 23 m. SE of Kielce; in 16th and 17th cents. home of the Racovians, a group of Polish Socinians.

Ra·ku·to (rä·kōo·tō). River ab. 270 m. long in S Korea; flows S into Korea Strait at Pusan; navigable for ab. 125 m.

Rak've·re (råk'vě·rě); Ger. **We'sen·berg** (vā'zěn·běrк). Town, ✱ of Viru prov., NE Estonia, 58 m. E of Tallin; pop. (1937) 9951; on main railroad line bet. Narva and Tallin.

Ra'leigh (rô'lĭ). 1 County in West Virginia. See Table at WEST VIRGINIA.
2 Town, ⊗ of Smith co., S cen. Mississippi, ab. 45 m. SE of Jackson; pop. 614.
3 City, ✱ of North Carolina and ⊗ of Wake co., E cen. North Carolina, 50 m. S of Virginia border; pop. 93,931; trade and distribution center for cotton and tobacco; manufactures cotton yarns and textiles, cottonseed oil, furniture, building supplies, automobile bodies; printing and publishing houses. Meredith Coll. (1891, women), Shaw Univ. (1865; coed.), St. Augustine's Coll. (1867; coed.; Episcopal), North Carolina State University at Raleigh (1889; coed.). Site chosen for capital 1788; laid out 1792, incorp. 1795; occupied by Gen. Sherman 1865; birthplace of Andrew Johnson, 17th president of the U.S.

Raleigh Bay. Bay off E coast of North Carolina bet. Cape Hatteras and Cape Lookout.

Ra'lik (rä'lĭk). Western chain of islands in the Marshall Is., W Pacific Ocean; includes ab. 14 atolls in long chain of ab. 750 m. More important atolls Jaluit, Kwajalein, Wotho, and Eniwetok.

Ralls (rôlz). **1** County in Missouri. See *Table* at MISSOURI.
2 Town. Crosby co., NW Texas, 27 m. E of Lubbock; pop. 2229; cotton, grain, livestock market.

Ra·mac'ca (rä·mäk'kä). Commune, Catania prov., E Sicily, 23 m. WSW of Catania; pop. (1931) 12,521.

Ra·ma'di (rŏ·mä'dē). Town, cen. Iraq, on right bank of Euphrates river 60 m. W of Baghdad; starting point of highway across the desert to Mediterranean towns. In World War I scene of battle Sept. 28–29, 1917 in which British under Maude defeated the Turks.

Ra'mah (rä'mȧ). See ARIMATHEA.

Ram'al·lah' (räm'ăl·lä'h'). **1** Subdistrict, Jerusalem dist., cen. Palestine; 264 sq. m.; pop. 39,062, (1938 est.) 43,485.
2 Town, its ✳, in the hill country 9 m. N of Jerusalem; pop. 4286.

Ram'a·po (răm'ȧ·pō). River, S New York and N New Jersey; rises in New York N of the Ramapo Mts., flows SE traversing the range, then S and SW just S of the range to unite at Pompton (just S of Pompton Lakes) with the Pequannock and Ringwood rivers to form the Pompton river.

Ramapo Deep. Ocean depth 34,626 ft., W Pacific Ocean, SE of Honshu, Japan, 142°28'E long., 30°43'N lat., in Japan Trough.

Ramapo Mountains. Range of the Appalachian Mts. extending NE–SW in S New York (Rockland and Orange cos.) and N New Jersey (Bergen co.); in N Y. section are the villages of Suffern, Sloatsburg, and Tuxedo Park; highest point about 1200 ft.

Ram'ber·vil'lers' (räN'bĕr'vē'lä'). Town, Vosges dept., NE France, 15 m. NE of Épinal; pop. 4806; noted for the time when it was defended by a force of 200 National Guardsmen against 2000 Prussians Oct. 9, 1870.

Ram'bouil'let' (räN'bōō'yĕ'). Town, Seine-et-Oise dept., N France, 28 m. SW of Paris; pop. 4857; château, now the summer residence of the presidents of France, built 14th cent. (only one tower of original structure remains) by d'Angennes family which owned the land for 300 years; Mme. de Rambouillet's husband was the first marquis 1612 (Charles d'Angennes); Forest of Rambouillet nearby.

Ram·bu'tyo (räm·bōō'tyō). Island 10 m. long by 8 m. wide in Admiralty Is., 35 m. ESE of Manus I., Bismarck Archipelago, W Pacific Ocean; highest point 700 ft.

Ram'durg (räm'dōōrg). Former Indian state, S Bombay prov., Indian Union, E of Belgaum; 166 sq. m.; pop. (1931) 35,454; ✳ Ramdurg; one of the seven states which united to form the United Deccan State Aug. 26, 1947.

Rame Head (rām). Headland on the coast of Cornwall, SW England, on the W side of Plymouth Sound.

Ra·mes'wa·ram (rä·měs'wȧ·rȧm). **1** Island, S Madras state, S Indian Union, bet. Palk Strait and the Gulf of Mannar, at the W end of Adam's Bridge.
2 Village on the island; pop. 8423; has fine temple of Dravidian architecture and one of the oldest of Hindu Shrines; visited annually by thousands of pilgrims.

Ram·gan'ga (räm·gŭng'gä). River ab. 370 m. long, Uttar Pradesh, N Indian Union; rises in Tehri dist. in the Himalayas, flows S into the Ganges near Kanauj; navigable for short distance only.

Ram'garh (räm'gär; *native* -gŭr·h'). Town, Madhya Pradesh, cen. India, ab. 65 m. SE of Jubbulpore; coal.

Ra'mil'lies (rä'mē'yē'; *Angl.* răm'ĭ·lĭz, -lēz). Village, Brabant prov., cen. Belgium, 13 m. NE of Namur; scene of battle in which Marlborough defeated the French under Villeroi May 12–23, 1706.

Ramle, Er. See ER RAMLE.

Ram'leh (räm'lĕ). City, NE suburb and seaside resort of Alexandria, Egypt; pop. (1927) 51,500.

Ram·mac'ca (räm·mäk'kä). Var. of RAMACCA.

Ram'nad (räm'näd). Town, S Madras, S Indian Union, on base of peninsula on Palk Strait 63 m. SE of Madura; pop. 16,817.

Ram'na·gar (räm'nȧ·gĕr). **1** Town, formerly ✳ of Benares state, SE Uttar Pradesh, N Indian Union, on S bank of Ganges opp. Benares; pop. 12,493.
2 Village, Gujranwala dist., N West Punjab, Pakistan, 55 m. NNW of Lahore; pop. 4768; here Nov. 22, 1848 Gen. Hugh Gough won victory in Second Sikh War.

Râm'ni·cul–Să·rat' (rĭm'nē·kōōl·sȧ·rät'). Town, E Romania, in NE Muntenia region ab. 78 m. NE of Bucharest; pop. 15,013; commercial center; has often been a battlefield: Moldavians against Wallachians, Turks against Wallachians, Austrians, and Russians; rebuilt since destructive fire 1854.

Râmnicul–Vâl'cea (-vĭl'chä). City, S cen. Romania, in Oltenia region on Olt river ab. 98 m. NW of Bucharest; pop. 15,162; has cathedral and episcopal palace; in vicinity are four famous monasteries, thermal springs, and salt mines.

Ra'moth Gil'e·ad (rä'mŏth [-mŭth] gĭl'ē·ăd [-ăd]). Ancient town of Gilead, E of the Jordan and N of the Jabbok, Palestine, a city of refuge (*Deut.* iv. 43); a place contended for in wars bet. Israel and Syria. Its location not certainly identified.

Ram'page Mountain (răm'pāj). Peak 6840 ft. in Glacier National Park, NW Montana.

Ram'part (răm'pärt; -pērt). Village, E cen. Alaska, S of the Yukon river WNW of Fairbanks.

Ram'pur (räm'pōōr). **1** Former Indian state, N Uttar Pradesh, N Indian Union; 894 sq. m.; pop. (1941) 477,042; level and fertile country E of the Ganges, watered by the Kosi and Ramganga rivers. State founded in 18th cent.; ruled over by a nawab, a Rohilla Pathan of the family descended from the founder.
2 City, its ✳, on Kosi river 115 m. E of Delhi; pop. (1941) 89,322; produces sugar, sword blades, pottery, and damask. Seat of popular Arabic college.

Rampur Boalia. See RAJSHAHI.

Ram'ree (räm'rē). **1** Island ab. 50 m. long in Bay of Bengal off W coast of Burma, in Kyaukpyu dist.; the town of Kyaukpyu, capital of the district, is at its N end. Occupied by Indian troops Jan. 21–Feb. 17, 1945, after withdrawal of Japanese.
2 Village on E coast of island.

Rams'bot'tom (rămz'bŏt'ŭm). Urban district, Lancashire, NW England, on the Irwell 12 m. N of Manchester; pop. 14,587; manufactures articles of iron and brass, cotton goods, machinery.

Ram'ses (răm'sēz); *also* **Ra·am'ses** (rä·ăm'sēz). Ancient city of Egypt, in Goshen probably near Tanis; one of the treasure cities built for Pharaoh (Ramses II) by the Hebrews (*Exod.* i. 11).

Ram'sey (răm'zĭ). **1** Name of counties in two states of the U.S. See *Tables* at MINNESOTA and NORTH DAKOTA.
2 Residential borough, Bergen co., NE corner of New Jersey, 9 m. N of Paterson; pop. 9527; shipping center for surrounding dairy farms.
3 Urban district, Huntingdonshire, E cen. England, 65 m. N of London; pop. 5772; agricultural center. Few remains of the 10th-cent. Benedictine abbey.
4 Town on NE coast of Isle of Man, England; pop. 4198; seaside resort.
5 Island ab. 2 m. long in St. George's Channel off SW coast of Wales, ab. 3 m. W of St. David's Head, N of entrance to St. Brides Bay.

Rams'gate (rămz'gāt; *Brit.* -gĭt). Municipal borough, Kent, SE England, on North Sea 17 m. N of Dover; pop. 35,748; yachting and fishing port and resort; Hengist and Horsa and St. Augustine are believed to have landed hereabouts.

Ram'tek (răm'tăk). Town, NE Maharashtra state, India, 24 m. NNE of Nagpur; pop. 8939; long a sacred spot for Hindus; has many old temples.

Ra′mu (rä′mōō). River ab. 300 m. long in Madang dist., N cen. North-East New Guinea, flowing NW and N. Its valley held by Japanese 1942–43 but retaken by Americans and Australians in latter part of 1943.

Ra′na (rä′nä). River in cen. Norway; flows SW into Ranen Fjord.

Ra·nan (rä·nän). Coastal town, ✳ of North Kankyo prov., NE Korea, WSW of port of Seishin, pop. 17,839; a new town, laid out since Russo-Japanese War (1904–05); military and administrative headquarters.

Ra′nau (rä′nou). Lake in S end of Barisan Mts., S Sumatra, Indonesia.

Ran·ca′gua (räng·kä′gwä). City, cen. Chile, 48 m. S of Santiago; ✳ of O'Higgins prov.; pop. 31,018; El Teniente copper mines in the vicinity; scene of a battle Oct. 1 and 2, 1814 in which Chilean revolutionists under José Carrera and Bernardo O'Higgins were overcome by the Spaniards.

Rance (räns). River ab. 60 m. long in Brittany, NW France; flows N into the English Channel at Saint-Malo.

Ran′chi (rän′chē). **1** District, Chota Nagpur division, S Bihar, NE India; 7159 sq. m.; pop. 1,675,413.

2 Town, its ✳ and summer ✳ of Bihar, 210 m. WNW of Calcutta; pop. (1941) 54,178; has radium institute and two large mental hospitals.

Ran′cho Cor′do·va (rän′chō kôr′dȯ·vȧ). Urban area, Sacramento co., N cen. California; pop. 7429.

Ran′cho Ve·loz′ (rän′chō vȧ·lōs′). Municipality, Las Villas prov., W cen. Cuba, 20 m. W of Sagua la Grande; pop. 8470.

Ran·chue′lo (rän·chwä′lō). Municipality, Las Villas prov., W cen. Cuba, 14 m. WSW of Santa Clara; pop. 8154.

Ran′co (räng′kȯ). Lake, S cen. Chile, SE of Valdivia; resort.

Rand, the. = WITWATERSRAND.

Ran′dall (răn′d'l). County in Texas. See *Table* at TEXAS.

Ran′dall's Island (răn′d'lz). Island in East river, New York, part of Manhattan borough; 194 acres; formerly site of a children's hospital and an institution for juvenile delinquents; now site of parks, playgrounds, a municipal stadium; meeting place of three arms of the Triborough Bridge.

Ran·daz′zo (rän·dät′tsȯ). Commune, Catania prov., E Sicily, on N slope of Mt. Etna 23 m. NNW of Catania; pop. 13,684; archaeological museum. In World War II key point in German retreat from Sicily; captured by Americans Aug. 13, 1943.

Ran′ders (rän′ērs). **1** County of Denmark. See *Table* at DENMARK.

2 Seaport, its ⊗, E Jutland Penin., Denmark, on the Guden river where it enters Randers Fjord 15 m. from the Kattegat; pop. (1945) 36,434; commercial center in a dairy-farming section; exports fish and dairy products.

Randers Fjord. Inlet of the Kattegat on NE cen. coast of Jutland Penin., Denmark; receives the Guden river.

Rand′fon·tein (ränt′fôn·tān′). City, S Transvaal, NE Union of South Africa, 28 m. W of Johannesburg; pop. 28,775; at W end of Witwatersrand gold fields; the Randfontein gold mine is one of largest in the world. See KRUGERSDORP.

Ran′dle·man (răn′d'l·mȧn). Town, Randolph co., cen. North Carolina, 16 m. S of Greensboro; pop. 2232; center for textile and hosiery manufactures.

Ran′dolph (răn′dŏlf; -d'lf). **1** Name of counties in eight states of the U.S. See *Tables* at ALABAMA, ARKANSAS, GEORGIA, ILLINOIS, INDIANA, MISSOURI, NORTH CAROLINA, WEST VIRGINIA.

2 Residential town, Kennebec co., SW Maine, on Kennebec river 7 m. S of Augusta; pop. 1724.

3 Town, Norfolk co., E Massachusetts, 6 m. N of Brockton; pop. 18,900; former shoe-manufacturing center; home of Mary Wilkins Freeman.

4 Town, ⊗ of Rich co., N Utah; pop. 537.

5 Village in Randolph town (pop. 3414), Orange co., E Vermont, 20 m. SSW of Barre; pop. 2122; manufactures farm implements, rubber stamps, furniture, sheet gelatin; creameries. **Randolph Center,** to the E, is the seat of Vermont Agricultural and Technical Institute (coed., 1957).

Randolph, Fort. See FORT RANDOLPH.

Randolph Field. United States Air Force base and military reservation, Bexar co., S cen. Texas, ab. 18 m. NE of San Antonio.

Rand′wick (rănd′wĭk). City, E New South Wales, SE Australia, SE suburb of Sydney on Pacific Ocean and Botany Bay; pop. 78,962.

Ran′en·burg (răn′ĕn·bŏȯrg; *Russ.* rȧ·nyĕn·bŏȯrk′). Town, S Ryazan Region, Soviet Russia, Europe, WNW of Michurinsk; pop. 9570.

Ra′nen Fjord (rä′nĕn) or **Ran′fjord′** (rän′fyȯr′; -fyōȯr′). Inlet of Norwegian Sea on W coast of Norway opp. Dönna I.; receives Rana river from the E.

Ran·ga′ma·ti (rŭng·gä′mä·tĭ). See CHITTAGONG HILL TRACTS.

Rangasa, Tandjung. See MANDAR, GULF OF.

Rang′au·nu′ Bay (räng′ou·nŏȯ′). Inlet of Pacific Ocean on NE coast of N extension of North I., New Zealand.

Range′ley (rānj′lĭ). Town, Franklin co., W Maine, on Rangeley Lake 56 m. WNW of Waterville; pop. 1087; trading center for the Rangeley Lakes region.

Rangeley Lakes. Chain of lakes in W Maine, in Franklin and Oxford cos., including Rangeley, Mooselookmeguntic, Upper Richardson, Lower Richardson, and Umbagog lakes, extending over 50 m. in length and covering an area of 80 sq. m.; elevation bet. 1200 and 1500 ft.; resort for fishermen and sportsmen.

Rang′er (rān′jēr). City, Eastland co., N cen. Texas, 40 m. E of Abilene; pop. 3313; oil wells and refineries.

Ranger Peak. Mountain 8810 ft. in NE Idaho co., N cen. Idaho.

Rang′i·o′ra (räng′ē·ôr′ȧ). Borough, Canterbury provincial dist., E South I., New Zealand, on inlet of Pegasus Bay 17 m. N of Christchurch; pop. 2165; wheat.

Rang′i·ro′a (räng′ē·rō′ȧ) or **Ra′hi·ro′a** (rä′hē·rō′ȧ). Atoll, with a lagoon 45 m. long and 15 m. wide, largest in the Tuamotu Archipelago, French Oceania, in S Pacific Ocean, 200 m. NNE of Tahiti; has good harbor within the lagoon.

Rang′i·tai′ki (räng′ē·tī′kē). River ab. 100 m. long in cen. and N cen. North I., New Zealand; flows NE and N into Bay of Plenty.

Rang′i·ta′ta (räng′ē·tä′tȧ). River 74 m. long in E cen. South I., New Zealand; flows SE into Canterbury Bight.

Rang′i·tik′ei (räng′ē·tĭk′ē). River 115 m. long in SW North I., New Zealand; flows S and SW into Cook Strait.

Rang′i·to′to (räng′ē·tō′tō). Island on E coast of North I., New Zealand, in outer harbor of Auckland; a lava cone 859 ft. high.

Ran·goon′ (răng·gŏȯn′; răng′gŏȯn). **1** *also* **Hlaing** (hling). River ab. 185 m. long in Lower Burma; E outlet of the Irrawaddy in the Irrawaddy delta.

2 Seaport city on Rangoon river 21 m. from its mouth, S Burma; ✳ of Pegu division, Lower Burma, and ✳ of Burma; constitutes Rangoon Town dist. in Pegu division; pop. 400,415; before World War II one of the most important commercial cities of S Asia, esp. in its trade in rice; well laid out with notable public buildings, parks, gardens, a university, and the great gilt-covered Shwe Dagon pagoda; had fine river port; cosmopolitan population. Founded in 6th cent., but at first not prominent; part of Pegu kingdom; rebuilt by Alompra 1753 and site of English factory 1790; captured by British 1824, restored, and again taken in Second Burmese War 1852; destroyed by fire 1850, badly damaged by earthquake and tidal wave 1930 and largely destroyed by Japanese Jan. and Feb. 1942 (occupied Mar. 8); bombed by Allies 1943–45 and retaken May 2–4, 1945.

Rangoon Town. District of Pegu division, Lower Burma, coextensive with the city of Rangoon; 77 sq. m.

Rang'pur (rŭng'pŏor). **1** District, Rajshahi division, formerly in N Bengal, NE Brit. India, now in East Bengal, Pakistan; 3606 sq. m.; pop. (1941) 2,877,847.
2 Town, its ✻, on tributary of Jamuna river 230 m. NNE of Calcutta; pop. 20,749.

Ra'ni·ganj (rä'nĕ·gŭnj'). Town, Burdwan dist., West Bengal, NE Indian Union, on N bank of Damodar river ab. 105 m. NW of Calcutta; pop. 16,373; coal mines.

Ra'ni·khet (rä'nĕ·kĕt'). Hill station and military sanitarium, NE Uttar Pradesh, N Indian Union, 75 m. NE of Moradabad; pop. 3772; alt. 6000 ft.

Ran'kin (răng'kĭn). **1** County in Mississippi. See *Table* at MISSISSIPPI.
2 Borough, Allegheny co., SW Pennsylvania, on Monongahela river 7 m. E of Pittsburgh; pop. 5164; steel.
3 City, ⊗ of Upton co., W Texas; pop. 1214.

Ran'noch, Loch (lŏk răn'ŭk). Lake 9 m. long in Perth co., cen. Scotland.

Rann of Cutch. See Rann of CUTCH.

Ra·nong (rä·nông). **1** Province, SW Thailand; 1359 sq. m.; pop. 21,350.
2 Town, its ✻, port on W coast of Malay Penin. at mouth of the Pakchan river ab. 8 m. E of Victoria Point in Burma.

Ran'pur (rän'pŏor). Former Indian state, SE Eastern States, NE Indian Union; 204 sq. m.; pop. (1941) 51,366; ✻ Ranpur; near coast 45 m. SW of Cuttack.

Ran'sart' (räN'sàr'). Commune, Hainaut prov., SW Belgium, just N of Charleroi; pop. 10,223.

Ran'som (răn'sŭm). County in North Dakota. See *Table* at NORTH DAKOTA.

Ran'te·ma'ri·o (rän'tä·mä'rē·ō). Mountain 11,286 ft. near Palopo in N cen. part of the SW peninsula of Celebes I., Indonesia; highest point of Celebes.

Ran·toul' (răn·tōol'). Village, Champaign co., E cen. Illinois, 15 m. N of Champaign; pop. 22,116; site of Chanute Field which has a U.S. Air Force Technical School.

Ra·oeng' or **Ra·ung'** (rä·ōong'). Mountain 10,932 ft., the highest point of the Idjen volcanic plateau, E Java, Indonesia.

Ra·oul' (rä·ōol'), or **Sun'day** (sŭn'dĭ), **Island.** Largest island of the Kermadec Is. (*q.v.*).

Raoul, Cape (roul). Southern point of Tasman Penin., Tasmania, Australia, W of Cape Pillar and at E entrance to Storm Bay; extends into Tasman Sea.

Ra'pa (rä'pä). Island at SE end of chain of Tubuaï Is., S Pacific Ocean, 27°36′S lat. and 144°17′W long., ab. 20 m. in circumference; mountainous (highest 2077 ft.) and well-wooded; has fine harbor. Home of a primitive Polynesian stock, formerly numerous; pop. (1936) 267. In early 19th cent. much visited by whalers; first missionaries arrived 1817.

Ra·pal'lo (rä·päl'lō). Commercial seaport commune, Genova prov., Liguria, NW Italy, on **Gulf of Rapallo,** an inlet of Ligurian Sea, 16 m. ESE of Genoa; pop. 13,947; health resort; two treaties signed here after World War I: (1) Nov. 12, 1920 bet. Italy and Yugoslavia which made Fiume an independent city; (2) Apr. 16, 1922 bet. Russia and Germany in which both renounced claims to war indemnities.

Rapa Nui. See EASTER ISLAND.

Ra·pel' (rä·pĕl'). River, Chile; flows NW, enters Pacific Ocean SW of Santiago.

Raphia. See RAFA.

Rap'i·dan' (răp'ĭ·dăn'; răp'ĭ·dăn'). River ab. 70 m. long, N Virginia; rises in Blue Ridge Mts., flows E into Rappahannock river on boundary bet. Culpeper and Spotsylvania cos.

Rap'id City (răp'ĭd). City, ⊗ of Pennington co., SW South Dakota, in E part of Black Hills 45 m. E of Wyoming border; pop. 42,399; trading and distributing center for mining, lumbering, and farming area; tourist resort; manufactures cement, flour, concrete; meat packeries, creameries; granite quarries. U.S. Air Force base. South Dakota School of Mines and Technology (1885; coed.).

Ra·pides' (rȧ·pēd'). Parish in Louisiana. See *Table* at LOUISIANA.

Ra'pi·do (rä'pĕ·dô). Short river, SE Latium compartimento, cen. Italy, flows SW past Cassino to the Liri; in World War II in campaign in Italy formed German defense line; held against unsuccessful attempt of Americans to cross Jan. 20–23, 1944; finally crossed by Americans May 1944.

Rap'pa·han'nock (răp'ȧ·hăn'ŭk). **1** River 185 m. long, NE Virginia; navigable to Fredericksburg; rises in Blue Ridge Mts., Rappahannock co., N Virginia, flows SE forming a long estuary emptying into Chesapeake Bay; scene of Civil War campaign Nov. 1863.
2 County in Virginia. See *Table* at VIRGINIA.

Rappoltsweiler. See RIBEAUVILLÉ.

Rap'ti (răp'tē). River ab. 400 m. long, N India; flows NW in Nepal and then SE in Uttar Pradesh to the Gogra river; navigable in its lower course.

Ra'pu Ra'pu (rä'pōo rä'pōo). Island, Albay prov., Luzon, Phil. Is., farthest E in chain of islands off E coast; 25 sq. m.; its chief town Rapu Rapu on S coast (pop. of municipality 12,011) also chief town of the island group; has coal mines. Occupied by Americans Apr. 13, 1945.

Raqqah, al–. See RAKKA.

Raq'uette (răk'ĕt; -ĭt). River ab. 140 m. long in N New York; rises in Hamilton co., flows N through St. Lawrence co. into St. Lawrence river near Massena.

Raquette Lake. Lake ab. 10 m. long in N Hamilton co., NE cen. New York; elevation 1775 ft.; drains through stream flowing NE into Long Lake; summer resort.

Rar'i·tan (răr'ĭ·tăn; -t'n). **1** River ab. 75 m. long in N cen. New Jersey; formed by confluence of branches in W Somerset co., flows E into Raritan Bay.
2 Urban township, Monmouth co., E cen. New Jersey, E of Keyport; pop. 15,334.
3 Borough, Somerset co., N cen. New Jersey, 11 m. WNW of New Brunswick; pop. 6137.

Raritan Bay. Inlet of Atlantic Ocean in Middlesex co., cen. New Jersey; receives the Raritan river and Arthur Kill on the NW; city of Perth Amboy is on NW shore.

Rar'o·ton'ga (rär'ô·tŏng'gȧ). Chief island of the Cook Is., in SW part of group, S Pacific Ocean; lat. 21°S and long. 169°45′W; 26 sq. m.; pop. (1936) 5054; chief village Avarua on N coast, ✻ of Cook Is.; exports copra, oranges, bananas, tomatoes. Highest point 2110 ft. One of the most healthful and attractive of all Polynesian islands. Discovered 1820; claimed by Germany bet. 1880 and 1889, but formally annexed by Great Britain 1889; transferred to New Zealand 1901.

Ras (räs). Arabic word meaning "cape"; for many names beginning with it, see the distinguishing element.

Ras at Tan·nu'ra (räs' ăt tăn·nōo'rȧ). Peninsula and cape (*ras*) just E of Qatif on W coast of Persian Gulf, al-Hasa, Saudi Arabia, ab. 35 m. NW of Bahrein; oil pipelines and refineries.

Ras Da·shan' (räs' dä·shän'). Peak 15,160 ft. in the Simyen Mts., N Ethiopia, NE of Gondar and Lake Tana; highest peak in Ethiopia.

Ra·sei'nyai (rä·sā'nyĭ). **1** District of Lithuania. See *Table* at LITHUANIA.
2 Town, its ✻, ab. 50 m. NW of Kaunas; pop. (1938 est.) 6181; capital of Samogitia (as **Ros·sie'ny** [rŭs·sē'nĭ] in 14th–15th cents.

Ras el Ge·nei'na (räs' ăl gĕ·nä'nȧ; -nä'nȧ). Mountain 5328 ft., S cen. Sinai Penin., NE Egypt; highest point of Egma Plateau.

Rashid. See ROSETTA.

Ra·shin (rä·shĕn). Seaport, North Kankyo prov., extreme NE Korea; pop. 28,775; one of the best ports on entire E coast of Korea; terminus of recently built railroad to Manchuria; this railroad just N of Rashin was scene of part of Changkufeng clash bet. Japan and

Soviet Russia in 1938. Bombed by Americans Aug. 2, 1945; taken by Russians Aug. 12, 1945.

Ra·sho·wa (rä·shŏ·wä). Small island in cen. part of Kuril chain, Soviet Russia, Asia, NE of Shimushiru, ab. 47°45′N, 153°E.

Rasht (räsht). Var. of RESHT.

Ras Muari. Cape on Arabian Sea, W Pakistan. See Ras MUARI.

Ra′so, Cape (rä′zōō). Cape extending into Atlantic Ocean on coast of Amapá state, N Brazil, N of the mouth of the Amazon.

Ras Sham′ra (räs shăm′rŏ). Site of ancient city of Ugarit (q.v.), near coast just N of Latakia, Syria; its archaeological objects, discovered 1929, have been of very great value; they include clay tablets of second millennium B.C. bearing texts in a cuneiform alphabet (Ugaritic), objects of art and daily use of Late Bronze Age, etc.

Ras·ska′zo·vo (rŭs·skä′zŭ·vŭ). Town, cen. Tambov Region, Soviet Russia, Europe, a few miles E of Tambov; pop. 25,168.

Ra′statt (räsh′tät; räs′tät), *less commonly* **Ra′stadt** (-tät). City, Baden-Württemberg, W Germany, 13 m. SW of Karlsruhe; pop. 14,003; manufactures machinery, metal goods, furniture, shoes. Became city 1705; Treaty of Rastatt signed here 1714 bet. Austria and France supplementing Treaty of Utrecht (War of the Spanish Succession); insurrection 1849.

Rastenburg. See KĘTRZYN.

Ra′tak (rä′täk) *or* **Ra′dak** (-däk). Eastern chain of islands in the Marshall Is., in W Pacific Ocean; includes 18 atolls in long chain of ab. 700 m. More important atolls are Mili, Majuro, Maloelap, Wotje, Likiep, and at extreme NW, Bikini.

Rat Bu·ri *or* **Ra·ja·bu·ri** (rät·bōō·rē—*sic*). **1** Province, SW Thailand; 2030 sq. m.; pop. 271,156.
2 Town, its ✳, on Klong river 50 m. WSW of Bangkok; on railroad.

Rat′cliff (răt′klĭf). Town, Houston co., E Texas, ab. 35 m. SW of Nacogdoches; pop. (1950) 2200.

Ra′the·daung (rä′thĕ·doun). Village, Akyab dist., W Upper Burma, on Mayu river 25 m. NNW of Akyab; fighting here in 1943 and 1944.

Ra′the·now (rä′tĕ·nō). City, Potsdam dist., East Germany, on Havel river 33 m. NW of Potsdam; pop. 27,588; manufactures optical instruments, precision tools, machinery, and lumber. Became city 1295; suffered during Thirty Years′ War, esp. 1631–41; occupied by the Swedes for a short time in June 1675.

Rath′lin (răth′lĭn). Island in the North Channel off the NE coast of Northern Ireland; administratively in co. Antrim.

Rath′mines′ and Rath′gar′ (răth′mīnz′, răth′gär′). South suburb of Dublin, Eire; pop. 45,629; has limestone quarries.

Ratibor. See RACIBÓRZ.

Ra′ting·en (răt′ĭng·ĕn; *Ger.* rä′tĭng-). City, W North Rhine-Westphalia state, W Germany, 6 m. N of Düsseldorf; pop. 15,288; late 11th-cent. church; 16th-cent. town hall; manufactures iron goods, textiles, glass, ceramic goods, paper, chemicals, tile, meat products.

Ratisbon *or* **Ratisbona.** See REGENSBURG.

Rätische Alpen. = *Rhaetian Alps*: see *Table* at ALPS.

Rat Island (răt). Small island in center of Rat Is., Alaska, 178°19′E, E of Kiska and NW of Amchitka.

Rat Islands. Group of islands, W Aleutian Is., SW Alaska, extending from 175°45′E to 179°40′E; comprises Kiska (q.v.), Amchitka, Semisopochnoi, Rat, and a number of islets.

Rat·lam′ *or* **Rut·lam′** (rŭt·läm′). **1** Former Indian state, Malwa, W Central India; 687 sq. m.; pop. (1941) 126,117; became member June 1947 of Union of Rajasthan.
2 Town, its ✳, 60 m. NW of Indore; pop. 37,675; seat of maharaja′s palace and a college.

Rat·na′gi·ri (rŭt·nä′gĭ·rĭ). Town, SW Maharashtra state, W Indian Union, on Arabian Sea 136 m. S of Bombay; pop. 23,906; port of call for coastal steamers.

Rat′na·pu′ra (rŭt′nà·pōōr′à). Town, ✳ of Sabaragamuwa prov., SW cen. Ceylon, near Kala Ganga river 42 m. ESE of Colombo; pop. 8497; center of precious-stone industry. Nearby is Maha Saman Dewale, wealthy Buddhist temple.

Ra·ton′ (rà·tōn′). City, ⊗ of Colfax co., N New Mexico, 115 m. NE of Santa Fe near Colorado border; pop. 8146; alt. 6400 ft.; railroad and tourist center, gateway to Raton Range; formerly stage station on Santa Fe Trail; coal mining, farming, stock raising.

Raton Pass. Mountain pass 8560 ft., Las Animas co., SE Colorado, on Colorado-New Mexico boundary just N of Raton, New Mexico; highway and railroad; formerly traversed by a branch of the Santa Fe Trail; used by military expeditions 1720 and 1806 and by Gen. Stephen Watts Kearny′s army 1846.

Raton Range. Range in SE Colorado, extending S across border into Colfax co., N New Mexico.

Rat Portage. See KENORA.

Rat′tray Head (răt′rā). Cape on NE cen. coast of Scotland, S of Kinnairds Head; lighthouse.

Rat′ze·burg (rät′sĕ·bōōrк). **1** Former bishopric, N Germany, just E of Lübeck; established 1154 by Henry the Lion; its small territory administered by Mecklenburg 1554–1610; made part of Mecklenburg 1648.
2 Town, its ✳, ab. 11 m. S of Lübeck; pop. 4508.

Raucoux. See ROCOURT.

Rau′far·höf′n (rû′ĭ·vär·hûp′n). Village and port on NE coast of Iceland near Cape Rifstangi.

Rau′ka·wa (rou′kà·wà). = COOK STRAIT.

Rau·ku′ma·ra Range (rou·kōō′mà·rà). Mountain range in NE North I., New Zealand.

Rau′ma (rou′mà). **1** Seaport, Turku-Pori dept., SW Finland, on the Gulf of Bothnia 25 m. S of Pori; pop. (1939 est.) 9300; exports lumber and cellulose; paper mills.
2 River, cen. Norway; flows NW into Romsdalsfjord SE of Molde; has several waterfalls; its valley is called Romsdal (q.v.).

Raung. See RAOENG.

Rauxel. See CASTROP-RAUXEL.

Ra·val′li (rà·văl′ĭ). County in Montana. See *Table* at MONTANA.

Ra′va·nu′sa (rä′vä·nōō′zä). Commune, Agrigento prov., SW Sicily, 23 m. E by S of Agrigento; pop. 14,555; trades in sulfur.

Ra′va Rus′ska·ya (rä′và rōōs′skà·yà); *Pol.* **Ra′wa Ru′ska** (rä′vä rōō′skä). Town, W Ukraine, U.S.S.R., 32 m. NNW of Lvov; formerly in Lwów dept., Poland; pop. (1938–39 est.) 12,000; stone quarries; oil factory. Battles in World War I; taken by Russians Sept. 1914; retaken by Austro-German army June 1915.

Ra·vel′lo (rä·vĕl′lō). Village, Salerno prov., S Campania, S Italy; 1227 ft. above the sea, beautiful view; palace, 11th cent., restored 19th cent.; cathedral, 11th and 18th cents.; 12th-cent. church.

Ra·ve′na (rà·vē′nà). Village, Albany co., E New York, on Hudson river 11 m. S of Albany; pop. 2410.

Ra·ven′na. **1** (rà·vĕn′à; *locally often* rĭ·văn′à) City, ⊗ of Portage co., NE Ohio, 15 m. ENE of Akron; pop. 10,918; settled 1799; manufactures excavating machinery, iron castings, rubber goods.
2 (rà·vĕn′à; *Ital.* rä·văn′nä) Province of Italy. See *Table* at ITALY.
3 (rà·vĕn′à; *Ital.* rä·vän′nä) Commune, ✳ of Ravenna prov., Emilia, N Italy, 61 m. NE of Florence; pop. 81,086; formerly a seaport and ancient Roman naval base; now connected with Adriatic by canal; episcopal see; rich in Roman and Byzantine architectural art, esp. of 5th–8th cents., represented chiefly by churches, such as San Giovanni Evangelista (425), San Appolinare Nuovo (526), San Vitale (530), Santa Agata (435); 4th-cent.

cathedral destroyed 1773 and rebuilt; historical monuments include tomb of Theodoric, tomb of Dante (died here 1321), Lord Byron's house; remains of ancient harbor nearby; manufactures lace, wine, textiles, glass, leather, bricks, agricultural implements.

History: Said to have been founded by Sabines; made part of Roman Gallia Cisalpina 191 B.C.; important naval station under Augustus; residence of numerous emperors and of Odoacer, who was conquered by the Ostrogoth Theodoric; stronghold of the Ostrogoths 493 A.D. ff.; conquered 540 by Belisarius and made capital of Byzantine Empire in Italy (exarchate of Ravenna); passed to Lombards 752 and Franks; became independent republic in 13th cent.; under Polenta family, Venetians, and popes; part of papal dominions 1509–1859; became part of kingdom of Italy 1860. In World War II taken by Allies Dec. 5, 1944.

Ra'vens·burg (rä'věnz·bûrg; *Ger.* rä'věns·bŏŏrk). Manufacturing city, Baden-Württemberg state, Germany, 47 m. SSW of Ulm; pop. 17,012; 14th-cent. church; 15th-cent. town hall; manufactures machinery, textiles, dyes; fine vineyards. Founded in 11th cent.; free imperial city 1276–1803; member of Swabian League in 14th cent.; to Bavaria 1803.

Ra'ven·spur' (rä'věn·spûr'). Former seaport town, East Riding, Yorkshire, NE England, at mouth of Humber near Spurn Head; landing place of Edward IV 1471 in Wars of Roses; swept away by sea soon after.

Ra'vi (rä'vē); *anc.* **Hy'dra·o'tes** (hī'drȧ·ō'tēz; hĭd'rá-). River ab. 450 m. long in N India; one of the "Five Rivers" of the Punjab; rises in the Himalayas, flows SW diagonally across West Punjab, Pakistan, to the Chenab; NE of Lahore forms part of boundary bet. East Punjab and West Punjab.

Ra'wa Harbour (rä'wä). Fine anchorage on E coast of Bougainville I., NW Solomon Is., W Pacific Ocean; Kieta is situated on it.

Ra'wal·pin'di (rä'vȧl·pĭn'dē; *Angl.* rôl·pĭn'dĭ). **1** Division, N West Pakistan.
2 District in division; 2022 sq. m.; pop. (1941) 785,231.
3 City, ✳ of division and district, 90 m. ESE of Peshawar, temporary ✳ of Pakistan from 1959 pending construction of new capital city nearby; pop. (1951) 237,219; locomotive works, iron foundry, other industries. Strategically located, controlling routes to Kashmir; before 1947 had India's largest military station and was headquarters of northern army. Treaty signed here Aug. 8, 1919 by which Great Britain recognized complete independence of Afghanistan. See ISLAMABAD.

Rawa Ruska. See RAVA RUSSKAYA.

Raw'hide' (rô'hīd'). Mining camp, Mineral co., SW Nevada, ab. 35 m. NNE of Hawthorne; scene of spectacular gold rush (led by Tex Rickard and others) inspired by Goldfield boom and financial slump of 1907.

Ra'wicz (rä'vēch); *Ger.* **Ra'witsch** (rä'vĭch). Industrial commune, Poznań dept., W cen. Poland, 50 m. S of Poznań; pop. (1938–39 est.) 10,912.

Rawitsch. See RAWICZ.

Raw'ka (räf'kä). River ab. 50 m. long in W Poland, a tributary of the Bzura; constituted Russian defense line Dec. 1914 to July 1915.

Raw'lins (rô'lĭnz). **1** County in Kansas. See *Table* at KANSAS.
2 City, ✳ of Carbon co., S Wyoming, 28 m. SW of confluence of Medicine Bow and North Platte rivers; pop. 8968; railroad division point; trade and supply center for petroleum fields, sheep and cattle ranches, coal mines.

Raw'marsh' (rô'märsh'). Urban district, West Riding, Yorkshire, N England, near Rotherham; pop. 18,793; ironworks, potteries, coal mines.

Raw'son (rô's'n; *Span.* rou'sôn). Seaport, ✳ of Chubut territory, S Argentina, near the mouth of Chubut river; pop. (est.) 2500.

Raw'ten·stall (rô't'n·stôl). Municipal borough, Lancashire, NW England, on the upper Irwell 17 m. N of Man-

chester; pop. 25,426; manufactures cotton, wool, and leather goods.

Ray (rā). County in Missouri. See *Table* at MISSOURI.

Ray, Cape. Southwest point of Newfoundland, on Cabot Strait opp. N tip of Cape Breton I.

Rayak. See RIYAQ.

Ray'leigh (rā'lĭ). Urban district, Essex, SE England, 32 m. ENE of London; pop. 9388.

Ray'mond (rā'mŭnd). **1** Town, a ⊗ of Hinds co., SW cen. Mississippi, ab. 28 m. ESE of Vicksburg; pop. 1381; in Civil War scene of battle May 12, 1863, a victory for Grant's forces.
2 City, Pacific co., SW corner of Washington, on Willapa Bay 21 m. S of Aberdeen; pop. 3301; ships fruits, farm produce, lumber products; oyster culture.
3 Market town, S Alberta, Canada, 16 m. SSE of Lethbridge; pop. 2279; has beet-sugar refineries; seat of an agricultural school.

Raymond Peak. Mountain 10,075 ft. in Sierra Nevada in E Alpine co., E California.

Ray'mond·ville (rā'mŭn[d]·vĭl; *Sou.* also -v'l). City, ⊗ of Willacy co., S Texas, 42 m. N of Brownsville; pop. 9385; shipping point for citrus fruits and farm produce.

Rayne (rān). City, Acadia parish, S Louisiana, 16 m. W of Lafayette; pop. 8634; center of Louisiana frog industry; rice mills.

Rayn'ham (rān'hăm). Town, Bristol co., SE Massachusetts, 10 m. SSW of Brockton; pop. 4150; trade center.

Ra·yong (rä·yông). **1** Province, S Thailand; 1452 sq. m.; pop. 67,929.
2 Town, its ✳, port on NE coast of Gulf of Siam 80 m. SE of Bangkok.

Raystown. See BEDFORD borough, Pennsylvania.

Ray'town (rā'toun). City, Jackson co., W Missouri, SE suburb of Kansas City; pop. 17,083.

Ray'ville (rā'vĭl; *Sou.* also -v'l). Town, ⊗ of Richland parish, NE Louisiana, 22 m. E of Monroe; pop. 4052.

Raz, Pointe du (pwănt' dü rä'). Headland 240 ft. above the sea, W Finistère dept., NW France, S of Brest.

Ra·zelm', Lake (rä·zĕlm'). Coastal lake or lagoon, N Dobruja, Romania, just S of mouth of the Danube; yields much fish.

Raz'grad (räz'grät). Town, Shumen dept., NE Bulgaria, ab. 25 m. NW of Shumen; pop. (1926) 15,421.

Ré, Île de (ēl' dē rā'). Island 16 m. long in E Bay of Biscay, off W coast of Charente-Maritime dept., W France, opp. La Rochelle; 28 sq. m.; pop. ab. 9000; chief town St-Martin on NE coast.

Rea, Lough. See LOUGHREA.

Read'ing (rĕd'ĭng). **1** Residential town, Middlesex co., NE Massachusetts, 11 m. N of Boston; pop. 19,259.
2 City, Hamilton co., SW corner of Ohio, 9 m. N of Cincinnati; pop. 12,832; laid out 1798; manufactures lithographs, fireworks, matches, chemicals.
3 Commercial and industrial city, ⊗ of Berks co., SE Pennsylvania, on Schuylkill river 50 m. WNW of Philadelphia; pop. 98,177; manufactures iron and steel, iron pipe, textiles, hosiery and hosiery machinery, optical goods, hardware, automobile frames, pretzels; anthracite and bituminous coal mines nearby. Albright College (1856; coed.). Settled 1733; became ⊗ 1752; base for forts in French and Indian Wars, and Hessian prison camp in Revolution; produced cannon for Revolutionary and Civil Wars.
4 County borough, ⊗ of Berkshire, S England, on the Kennet at its confluence with the Thames 39 m. W of London; pop. 97,149, (1951 pop.) 114,176; manufactures paper, farm implements; especially known for biscuits, and seed nurseries; seat of a university, and of a grammar school dating from the 15th cent.

Rea'gan (rā'găn). County in Texas. See *Table* at TEXAS.

Reagan Dam. See UNITED STATES, *Dams and Reservoirs.*

Re·al (rē′ôl). County in Texas. See *Table* at Texas.

Re·al′ del Mon′te (rrě·äl′ děl môn′tā); *formerly* **Mi′-ne·ral′ del Monte** (mě′nä·räl′). Town, Hidalgo state, cen. Mexico, just ENE of Pachuca; pop. 13,536.

Ré·a′o (rä·ä′ō) *or* **Cler′mont′–Ton′nerre** (klěr′môn′-tô′něr′). Island 10 m. long by 1½ m. wide in E part of the Tuamotu Archipelago, French Polynesia, S Pacific Ocean; lat. 18°32′S and long. 136°21′W.

Rear′guard′, Mount (rẽr′gärd′). Peak 12,350 ft. in S Carbon co., S Montana.

Reate. See Rieti.

Re·bun (rě·bōōn). Small island in N Sea of Japan, off NW coast of island of Hokkaido, Japan.

Re·ca·na′ti (rä·kä·nä′tē). Commune, Macerata prov., Marches, cen. Italy, 9 m. NNE of Macerata; pop. 16,823; 14th-cent. Gothic cathedral; home of the poet Leopardi.

Re·cherche′ Archipelago (rě·shěrsh′). Group of small islands in Indian Ocean off S coast of Western Australia, at W end of Great Australian Bight.

Re·chi′tsa (rě·chĭt′sả; *Russ.* ryĭ·chē′tsả). Town, Gomel Region, SE White Russia, U.S.S.R., W of Gomel; in World War II battle Nov. 22–25, 1943 in which Germans were defeated.

Re·ci′fe (rě·sē′fě); *formerly* **Per′nam·bu′co** (pûr′năm-bū′kō; -bōō′-; *Port.* pâr′nănm·bōō′kōō). Coastal city, E Pernambuco state, E Brazil; ✻ of Pernambuco state; pop. (1940 est.) 327,753; one of most important ports of Brazil; built partly on the mainland, partly on a peninsula and on an island in a lagoon formed by two rivers; near Point Pedras, the most easterly point of South America; naval base; exports sugar, cotton, hides and skins; peninsula first settled by Portuguese 1535; held 1630–54 by Dutch who extended the settlement on the island; portion on the mainland is most modern part. In World War II an American air base.

Re·ci′fe, Cape (rě·sē′fě). Cape on SE coast of Cape Province, Union of South Africa, on W side of Algoa Bay 6 m. SW of Port Elizabeth.

Recița. See Reșița.

Reck′ling·hau′sen (rěk′lĭng·hou′zěn). Mining, manufacturing, and commercial city, North Rhine-Westphalia state, West Germany, 30 m. SW of Münster; pop. 84,518; ironworks; coal mines; manufactures beer, chemicals, liquors, textiles, lumber. Founded in 12th cent.; made city 1236; member of Hanseatic League; passed to Prussia 1815. Taken by Allies Apr. 3, 1945 at end of World War II.

Re·co·a′ro (rä·kō·ä′rō). Commune, NW Vicenza prov., SW cen. Venezia Euganea, NE Italy; pop. (1931) 7027; mineral springs.

Rec′tor (rěk′tēr). City, Clay co., NE corner of Arkansas; pop. 1757.

Re·cu′let (rě·kü′lě). Peak 5642 ft. in Ain dept., E France; highest peak in the Jura Mts.

Red (rěd). Name of three rivers of the U.S. (one partly in Canada) and one in the Federation of Indochina. See Red River.

Re·dan′ (rě·dăn′). Fortification, S part of Sevastopol, Crimea, Soviet Russia, Europe; stormed unsuccessfully June and Sept. 1855 during Crimean War by the English; evacuated Sept. 10 by Russians.

Redang. See Great Redang.

Red′ Bank′. 1 Residential borough and resort, Monmouth co., E cen. New Jersey, on Navesink river ab. 6 m. inland from Atlantic Ocean, 15 m. SE of Perth Amboy; pop. 12,482; settled before Revolution by Dutch and English colonists; summer boating and yachting events, winter iceboat races; fishing and crabbing; clay and gravel deposits; produces esp. potatoes, asparagus, apples; manufactures uniforms, marine railways, washing machines, cosmetics, medicines.
2 Town, Hamilton co., SE Tennessee, near Chattanooga; pop. (with White Oak) 10,777.

Red Basin. See Szechwan.

Red Bay. City, Franklin co., NW Alabama, on Mississippi border 30 m. S of Tennessee river; pop. 1954.

Red Bluff. City, ⊗ of Tehama co., N California, on Sacramento river 38 m. NW of Chico; pop. 7202; trading center.

Red′boy′ (rěd′boi′). Mountain 6021 ft. in Grant co., E cen. Oregon.

Red′car′ (rěd′kär′). Municipal borough, North Riding, Yorkshire, N England, on the North Sea 33 m. SSE of Newcastle and 8 m. NE of Middlesbrough; pop. 27,512; seaside resort; racecourse.

Red Cedar. River 70 m. long, W Wisconsin; flows from Barron co. S into Chippewa river in S Dunn co.

Red Cloud. City, ⊗ of Webster co., S Nebraska, on Republican river 35 m. S of Hastings; pop. 1525; in grain-growing section.

Red′cloud′ Peak (rěd′kloud′). Mountain 14,050 ft. in Hinsdale co., SW Colorado.

Red Cone. Mountain 7372 ft. in W Klamath co., S Oregon, N of Crater Lake.

Red Deer. 1 River ab. 385 m. long, S Alberta, Canada; rises in Banff National Park, SW Alberta, flows SE and E into the South Saskatchewan river near the Alberta boundary.
2 River ab. 140 m. long in S cen. Canada; rises in E cen. Saskatchewan, flows E across border of Manitoba prov., through **Red Deer Lake** (97 sq. m.), into Lake Winnipegosis.
3 City, S Alberta, Canada, on Red Deer river 85 m. N of Calgary; pop. 7575; railroad divisional point; in prosperous dairy section.

Red′ding (rěd′ĭng). 1 City, ⊗ of Shasta co., N California, on Sacramento river 67 m. NNW of Chico; pop. 12,773; shipping point for lumbering, mining, and farming region; tourist center and supply point; made ⊗ 1887.
2 Town, cen. Fairfield co., SW Connecticut; pop. 3359; incorp. 1767; agriculture; wire drawing, weaving.

Red′ditch (rěd′ĭch). Urban district, Worcestershire, W cen. England, near Birmingham; pop. 22,207; manufactures needles, fishhooks.

Red Eagle Mountain. Peak 8800 ft. in Glacier National Park, NW Montana.

Red′fern′ (rěd′fûrn′). Town, E New South Wales, SE Australia, S suburb of Sydney; pop. 18,837; ironworks, railroad shops, factories.

Red′field′ (rěd′fēld′). City, ⊗ of Spink co., NE cen. South Dakota, 41 m. S of Aberdeen; pop. 2952; in agricultural section.

Redfield Mountain. Peak 4606 ft. in the Adirondack Mts., Essex co., NE New York.

Red′fish′ Lake (rěd′fĭsh′). Lake in W Custer co., cen. Idaho.

Red Indian Lake. Lake 64 sq. m. and 37 m. long in cen. Newfoundland; traversed by Exploits river.

Red′key′ (rěd′kē′). Town, Jay co., E Indiana, 17 m. NE of Muncie; pop. 1764.

Red Lake. 1 Lake 38 m. long in Beltrami co., N Minnesota, divided into **Upper Red Lake** and **Lower Red Lake**; the Red Lake river flows through the two lakes.
2 River 135 m. long, NW Minnesota; flows W out of Lower Red Lake, turns SW to empty into Red River of the North opp. Grand Forks, North Dakota.
3 County in Minnesota. See *Table* at Minnesota.

Red Lake Falls. City, ⊗ of Red Lake co., NW Minnesota, 17 m. S of Thief River Falls; pop. 1520.

Red′lands (rěd′lăndz). Residential city, San Bernardino co., SE California, 8 m. ESE of San Bernardino; pop. 26,829; canning, dairy, and shipping center for citrus fruits. Univ. of Redlands (1907; coed.).

Red Lick Mountain. Peak 3533 ft. in Pocahontas co., E cen. West Virginia.

Red Li′on (lī′ŭn). Borough, York co., S Pennsylvania, 8 m. SE of York; pop. 5594.

Red Lodge. City, ⊗ of Carbon co., S Montana, 57 m. SW of Billings; pop. 2278; in coal-mining section.

Red'mond (rĕd'mŭnd). City and resort, Deschutes co., cen. Oregon, 18 m. NNE of Bend; pop. 7996; potato culture, dairying, turkey raising; alfalfa.

Red Mountain. 1 Peak 11,933 ft. in Sierra Nevada, in E Fresno co., S cen. California.

2 Peak 13,500 ft. in Chaffee and Pitkin cos., W cen. Colorado.

3 Peak 9300 ft. in Glacier National Park, NW Montana.

4 Peak 8802 ft. in S Lewis and Clark co., W cen. Montana.

5 Peak 8304 ft. in Baker co., E Oregon.

6 Peak 7784 ft. in N Whatcom co., NW Washington.

Red'nitz (rād'nĭts). River ab. 50 m. long in Bavaria, S Germany; flows N to unite with the Pegnitz river at Fürth and form the Regnitz river.

Red Oak. City, ⊗ of Montgomery co., SW Iowa, 37 m. SE of Council Bluffs; pop. 6421; manufactures calendars, iron products, cement; canneries.

Re-don' (rĕ-dôn'). Town, SW Ille-et-Vilaine dept., NW France, on the Vilaine ab. 38 m. SSW of Rennes; pop. 5201; on site of monastery founded 9th cent.

Re-don'da (rĕ-dŏn'då). Small uninhabited island ab. 1 sq. m. in the Leeward Is., British West Indies; a part of Antigua territory; rocky, highest point 1000 ft.; source of phosphate.

Re'don-de-'la (rrĕ'thôn-dā'lä). Commune, Pontevedra prov., NW Spain, 15 m. S of Pontevedra; pop. 16,927; manufactures linen, china.

Re-don'do Beach (rĕ-dŏn'dō). Residential and resort city, Los Angeles co., SW California, on Pacific Ocean 17 m. SE of center of Los Angeles; pop. 46,986; founded 1888.

Red Peak. 1 Mountain 11,700 ft. in Sierra Nevada, in E Mariposa co., cen. California.

2 Mountain 13,600 ft. in Costilla and Las Animas cos., S Colorado.

Red Point. Cape on SW coast of St. Thomas I., Virgin Is. of the U.S., West Indies.

Redriff. See ROTHERHITHE.

Red River. 1 Navigable river 1018 m. long, in S cen. United States; rises in high plains in E New Mexico; flows E, crossing Texas panhandle and then becoming boundary bet. Texas and Oklahoma and for a short distance boundary bet. Texas and Arkansas; turns S in SW Arkansas and crosses border into Louisiana, flows SE across Louisiana and into the Mississippi river.

2 River, N Tennessee; rises in Sumner co., flows NW across border of Kentucky, re-enters Tennessee and flows SW into Cumberland river at Clarksville.

3 *or* **Red River of the North.** River ab. 310 m. long, or with longest tributary ab. 700 m., in N cen. U.S. and S cen. Canada; formed by junction at Breckenridge, W Minnesota, of the Otter Tail river from the E and Bois de Sioux river from Lake Traverse to the S; flows N forming Minnesota-North Dakota boundary, crosses Canadian border and continues N to S Lake Winnipeg, S Manitoba, Canada. Chief tributaries the Sheyenne and Red Lake rivers in U.S. and the Assiniboine in Canada; drains rich wheat lands. In Canada first settled as Scottish colony known as Red River Settlement (*q.v.*).

4 Parish in Louisiana and county in Texas. See *Tables* at LOUISIANA and TEXAS.

5 River in Indochina. See COI.

Red River Settlement. Colony established 1811–16 by Scottish leader, earl of Selkirk, in valley of Red River of the North, now in Manitoba. Destroyed 1816 in conflict with North-West Fur Co., but village of Kildonan (now part of Winnipeg) restored 1817. Two forts built 1821 and 1835; purchase of territorial rights 1869 by Dominion government caused rebellion led by Louis Riel.

Red Russia. 1 In 18th cent. a region of S Poland bet. Volhynia and the Carpathian Mts. in the area around the upper Dniester; now a part of W Ukraine and SE Poland.

2 Colloquially, the Soviet Union.

Red'ruth (rĕd'rōōth; rĕd-rōōth'). Former urban district, Cornwall, SW England, 49 m. WSW of Plymouth; now part of Camborne-Redruth urban district.

Red'scar' Bay (rĕd'skär'). Small bay on S coast of Papua, New Guinea I., N of Port Moresby.

Red Sea. 1 *anc.* **Si'nus A·rab'i·cus** (sī'nŭs å·rǎb'ĭ-kŭs). Inland sea bet. Arabia and NE Africa; ab. 1450 m. long; area ab. 178,000 sq. m.; greatest depth 7254 ft., near Port Sudan; on the N connects with Mediterranean Sea through the Gulf of Suez and the Suez Canal; on the S connects with Arabian Sea through the strait of Bab el Mandeb; in the Great Rift Valley (*q.v.*).

2 See ERYTHRAEAN SEA.

3 Former province, Anglo-Egyptian Sudan, now E part of Kassala prov., Sudan.

4 Coastal district on the Red Sea, E Egypt. See *Table* at EGYPT.

Red Springs. Town, Robeson co., S North Carolina, 25 m. SW of Fayetteville; pop. 2767; medicinal sulfur spring; silk, rayon, and lumber mills. Flora Macdonald Coll. (1896; women).

Red Tank. Town, Balboa dist., Canal Zone, on the Panama Canal near the Pedro Miguel Locks; pop. (1950) 1949.

Red Volta. See Red VOLTA.

Red Willow. County in Nebraska. See *Table* at NEBRASKA.

Red Wing. City, ⊗ of Goodhue co., SE Minnesota, on Mississippi river 40 m. SE of St. Paul; pop. 10,528; trading and distributing center; manufactures marine motors, pottery and clay pipe, plate glass.

Red'wood' (rĕd'wŏŏd). **1** River 90 m. long, SW Minnesota; flows NE and in Lyon and Redwood cos. into Minnesota river.

2 County in Minnesota. See *Table* at MINNESOTA.

Redwood City. City, ⊗ of San Mateo co., W California, 5 m. W of San Francisco Bay and ab. 18 m. SE of San Francisco; pop. 46,290; incorp. 1867; formerly known for shipbuilding industries, canneries, saltworks, redwood shipping.

Redwood Falls. City, ⊗ of Redwood co., SW Minnesota, on the Redwood river 33 m. ENE of Marshall; pop. 4285.

Ree, Lough (lŏk rē'). Lake 16 m. long and 1 to 7 m. wide in cen. Ireland, E of Roscommon; the river Shannon flows S through the lake.

Reed City (rēd). City, ⊗ of Osceola co., cen. Michigan, 26 m. SSW of Cadillac; pop. 2184; in lake fishing region; flour mill; woolen mill.

Reed'ley (rēd'lĭ). City, Fresno co., S cen. California, 20 m. ESE of Fresno; pop. 5850; founded 1889.

Reeds'burg (rēdz'bûrg). City, Sauk co., S cen. Wisconsin, 26 m. W of Portage; pop. 4371; in agricultural and dairy-farming section.

Reef Point (rēf). Cape on NW coast of N extension of North I., New Zealand, forming S side of Ahipara Bay.

Reel'foot' Lake (rēl'fŏŏt'). Shallow lake ab. 18 m. long on boundary bet. Lake and Obion cos., NW Tennessee; formed as result of the earthquake at New Madrid (*q.v.*) 1811–12.

Reeves (rēvz). County in Texas. See *Table* at TEXAS.

Re-fu'gio (rĕ-fū'rĭ-ō—*sic*). **1** County in Texas. See *Table* at TEXAS.

2 Town, its ⊗, S Texas, 38 m. N of Corpus Christi; pop. 4944; oil wells and refineries. Founded 1790, the year a mission was built on site; municipality established and pueblo of Refugio founded 1834; chartered 1842.

Re-gal-bu'to (rā-gäl-bōō'tô). Commune, Enna prov., cen. Sicily, 21 m. ENE of Enna; pop. 11,218.

Re'gen (rā'gĕn). River 68 m. long in Bavaria, S Germany; flows W out of Bohemian Forest, then S into the Danube river at Regensburg.

Re'gens·burg (rā'gĕnz·bûrg; *Ger.* rā'gĕns·bŏŏʀk); *formerly in Eng.* **Rat'is·bon** (rǎt'ĭs·bŏn; -ĭz-); *medieval* **Rat'is·bo'na** (rǎt'ĭs·bō'nå; -ĭz-); *anc.* **Re·gi'num** (rē-jī'nŭm) *or* **Cas'tra Re·gi'na** (kǎs'trå rē-jī'nå). City

of Lower Bavaria and Upper Palatinate govt. dist., Bavaria, Germany, on Danube river 65 m. NNE of Munich; pop. 76,948; 13th-cent. Gothic cathedral, 14th-cent. town hall, 12th-cent. bridge, old gate (Porta Praetoria); active trade center; manufactures machinery, chemicals, boats, foodstuffs, stained glass.

History: Of Celtic origin (c. 500 B.C.); settled by Romans 179 A.D.; made episcopal see 739; made free imperial city 1245; ineffectual Catholic League to enforce edict of Worms against Luther formed here 1524; seven diets held here 1531–1613; seat of imperial diet 1663–1803; truce 1684; stormed by French under Napoleon 1809 (subject of a poem by Robert Browning); to Bavaria 1810; became free port 1853. Fighter-plane factories developed in World War II; often bombed by Allies 1942–44; taken by Allied armies Apr. 27, 1945.

Reg′ga·ne (rĕg′gă·nĕ). Town, E Aïn-Sefra territory, W Algeria, on the route of the projected trans-Saharan railroad; on Greenwich meridian in 26°30′N lat.

Reg·gel′lo (rǎd·jĕl′lỏ). Commune, Firenze prov., Tuscany, cen. Italy, 11 m. SE of Florence; pop. 14,389.

Reg′gio di Ca·la′bri·a (rǎd′jỏ dĕ kä·lä′brĕ·ä); *often shortened to* **Reggio** *or* **Reggio Calabria**. **1** Province of Italy. See *Table* at ITALY.

2 *anc. Gr.* **Rhe′gi·on** (rē′jĭ·ŏn); *Lat.* **Rhe′gi·um** *or* **Re′gi·um** (rē′jĭ·ŭm). Seaport and manufacturing commune, * of Reggio di Calabria prov., Calabria, S Italy, on Strait of Messina 202 m. SSE of Naples; pop. 119,804; archiepiscopal see; cathedral; manufactures olive oil, essential oils, silk.

History: Founded by Greek colonists at end of 8th cent. B.C. as sister city to Zancle; destroyed by Dionysius (the Elder) of Syracuse 386 B.C.; allied with Rome 270 B.C.; conquered by Alaric 410 A.D., Totila 549, Saracens 918, Pisans 1005, Guiscard 1060, and the Aragonese 1282; devastated by earthquake 1783 and 1908. In World War II occupied by British Sept. 3, 1943 after Sicilian campaign.

Reggio nel′l′E·mi′lia (nǎl′lä·mē′lyä); *often shortened to* **Reggio** *or* **Reggio Emilia**. **1** Province of Italy. See *Table* at ITALY.

2 *anc.* **Re′gi·um Lep′i·dum** (rē′jĭ·ŭm lĕp′ĭ·dŭm). Commercial and manufacturing commune, its *, Emilia, N Italy, 71 m. NNW of Florence; pop. 93,913; 9th-cent. cathedral; 10th-cent. Basilica di San Prospero; 15th-cent. town hall; ancient walls and ramparts; manufactures locomotives; export trade in agricultural products. Birthplace of Ariosto. Lombard duchy in early Middle Ages; under Este family of Modena 1527 ff.; became part of kingdom of Italy 1859.

Re·gil′lus, Lake (rė·jĭl′ŭs). Ancient name of a small unidentified lake near Rome, Italy; scene of battle c. 496 B.C. in which Latins were defeated by the Romans.

Re·gi′na (rė·ji′nȧ). City, * of Saskatchewan prov., Canada, in S part of province 357 m. W of Winnipeg; pop. 71,319; on transcontinental rail and air lines; important trade and distribution center in wheat and cattle country; has grain elevators, flour mills, oil refinery, assembly plants for automobiles and farm machinery, and various manufactures. Has many educational and cultural institutions. Founded 1882; from 1883 to 1905 capital of Northwest Territories of Canada and made capital of new Saskatchewan prov. in 1905; headquarters of the Royal Canadian Mounted Police before 1920.

Reginum. See REGENSBURG.

Región Oriental. See EASTERN REGION.

Regio Syrtica. See TRIPOLI region.

Re′gi·stan′ (rā′gė·stän′). Extensive desert region, S Afghanistan.

Regium. See REGGIO DI CALABRIA seaport.

Regium Lepidum. See REGGIO NELL'EMILIA.

Re′gla (rrĕ′glä). Municipality and town, La Habana prov., W Cuba; pop. (1943; town) 23,037; an E suburb of Havana.

Reg′nitz (rāg′nĭts). River in Bavaria, S Germany; formed by confluence of Pegnitz and Rednitz rivers at Fürth, flows N into the Main river 3 m. NW of Bamberg.

Regnum Parthorum. See PARTHIA.

Reg′u·la′tion Peak (rĕg′ū·lā′shŭn). **1** Mountain 10,500 ft. in Sierra Nevada, in E Tuolumne co., cen. California.

2 Mountain 10,000 ft. in E Yellowstone National Park, NW Wyoming.

Re·ho′both (rė·hō′bŭth; -bōth). **1** *or* **Rehoboth Beach.** City, Sussex co., S Delaware, on Atlantic Ocean just S of Delaware Bay; pop. 1507; summer beach resort; dairies, cannery.

2 Town, Bristol co., SE Massachusetts, 10 m. NNW of Fall River; pop. 4953.

3 Town, cen. South-West Africa, on railroad 50 m. S of Windhoek; pop. 9727; seat of administration of Griquas, particularly of the branch known as Bastards.

Rehoboth Bay. Inlet of Atlantic Ocean S of Rehoboth, on E coast of Sussex co., Delaware.

Re·ho′vot *or* **Re·ho′voth** (rė·hō′vōt). Town, Lydda dist., W Palestine, ab. 4 m. SW of Er Ramle; one of principal modern Jewish settlements.

Reich (rīk). Literally "empire"; (1) originally, the Holy Roman Empire (the **First Reich**) from its founding in the 9th cent. to 1806; (2) the empire established by Bismarck (the **Second Reich**) 1871 to 1919; (3) following the dissolution of the Second Reich and the succeeding German Republic (1919 to 1933), the state (the **Third Reich**) created by Hitler and Nazis in 1933 and lasting to 1945.

Rei′che·nau (rī′kĕ·nou). **1** Island 4½ m. long in W arm of Lake Constance, Baden-Württemberg, Germany, just W of Konstanz. Site of Benedictine Abbey, founded 724, independent until 1540.

2 Village, Lower Austria, ab. 20 m. SW of Wiener Neustadt; pop. (1923) 5065; forms with adjacent **Pay′erbach** [pī′ĕr·bäk] (pop. 3610) a favorite summer and health resort.

Rei′chen·bach (rī′kĕn·bäk). **1** *also* **Reichenbach im Vogt′land** (ĭm fōkt′länt). City, Karl-Marx-Stadt dist., Germany, 10 m. SW of Zwickau; pop. 30,862; manufactures textiles, machinery, sugar. Founded 1140; made city 1271.

2 See DZIERŻONIÓW, Poland.

3 River in Bern canton, Switzerland; rises in Great Scheidegg, flows NNE into Aare river; has five cascades, one over 200 ft. high.

Reichenberg. See LIBEREC.

Rei′chen·hall′ *or* **Bad Reichenhall** (bät rī′kĕn·häl′). Town, Upper Bavaria, Germany, 10 m. SW of Salzburg; pop. (1939) 13,156; salt mines; baths, health resort since 19th cent.

Reichs′land (rīks′länt). **1** Formerly, 1806–71, all German crownlands.

2 From 1871 to 1918 ALSACE-LORRAINE.

Reich′stadt (rīk′shtät). Village, N Bohemia, Czechoslovakia, just E of Česká Lípa; pop. ab. 2000; ducal castle; dukedom given to Napoleon II 1818; scene of signing of secret agreement bet. Austria-Hungary and Russia July 1876.

Reids′ville (rēdz′vĭl; *Sou. also* -v′l). **1** City, ⊗ of Tattnall co., SE cen. Georgia; pop. 1229.

2 Industrial city, Rockingham co., N North Carolina, 20 m. NNE of Greensboro; pop. 14,267; tobacco market and port of entry; manufactures cigarettes, cotton, silk and rayon textiles, shoe polishes, food products.

Rei′gate (rī′gāt; *Brit.* -gĭt). Municipal borough, Surrey, S England, 18 m. S of London; pop. 42,234; residential suburb of London; remnants of pre-Norman castle; burial place of (2d) Baron Howard, commander of English fleet that defeated Spanish Armada.

Reikjavik. Var. of REYKJAVÍK.

Reims (rēmz; *Fr.* răNs); *older* **Rheims** (rēmz; *Fr.* răNs); *anc.* **Du′ro·cor·to′rum** (dūr′ỏ·kôr·tōr′ŭm); *later* **Re′mi** (rē′mī). Manufacturing and commercial city, Marne dept., NE France, on Vesle river 83 m. ENE

of Paris; pop. 116,687; famous 13th-cent. Gothic cathedral, one of the most magnificent in France (see below); noted for production of wines (esp. champagne), textiles (esp. merino and woolen goods), brewery and distillery products; ancient Roman triumphal arch; numerous other Gallo-Roman remains nearby; ancient city gates.

History: Ancient capital of the Remi; made episcopal see 4th cent. A.D.; sacked by Vandals 406; Clovis and his officers baptized in ancient cathedral 496; old cathedral scene of numerous historical rites; made archiepiscopal see 8th cent.; Philip Augustus crowned in cathedral 1179, the cathedrals of Reims subsequently becoming the place of coronation (until 1830) of a long line of French kings; first cathedral destroyed by fire at beginning of 13th cent.; present magnificent cathedral begun 1211 and completed in following century, has famous western façade and four rose windows of 13th-cent. glass; a Roman-Catholic English translation of New Testament published here 1582; cathedral seriously damaged by German bombardment in World War I, repaired and reconstructed 1927 by John D. Rockefeller at cost of $1,000,000; town hall and famous abbey of St. Remy (converted into a hospital before war) laid waste by German bombardment and city devastated by fire, World War I. In World War II reached by American forces by end of Aug. 1944; scene of surrender May 7, 1945 of all land, sea, and air forces of the Third Reich.

Rei'na A'de·lai'da, Archipelago of (rrĕ'ĕ·nä ä'thä-lä'ĕ·thä). Group of islands in S Pacific Ocean, off SW coast of Chile, N of W end of the Strait of Magellan.

Rein'beck (rīn'bĕk). Town, Grundy co., NE cen. Iowa, 20 m. SW of Waterloo; pop. 1621; cannery; seed growing; corn, hogs, cattle.

Rein'deer' Island (rān'dēr'). Island in cen. Lake Winnipeg, SE Manitoba prov., Canada.

Reindeer Lake. Lake 2436 sq. m. in cen. Canada, lying on the N section of the Saskatchewan-Manitoba boundary; its outlet is the **Reindeer River**, ab. 60 m. long, flowing S to the Churchill.

Rei·no'sa (rā·nō'så; *Span.* rrĕ·ĕ·nō'sä). Town, Santander prov., N Spain; on the Ebro ab. 4 m. from its source, in the Cantabrian Mts. at 2790 ft.; pop. ab. 4000; resort.

Rein'stein, Mount (rīn'stīn). Peak 12,595 ft. in Sierra Nevada, in E Fresno co., S cen. California.

Re·jaf' (rĕ·jăf'). Town, Equatoria prov., S Sudan, on Bahr el Jebel river S of Juba.

Rejang. See RAJANG.

Re·ka'ta Bay (rå·kä'tå). Bay on NW coast of Santa Isabel I. in the NE Solomon Is., W Pacific Ocean; used as a base by the Japanese 1942–43.

Re·li'zane' (rĕ·lē'zän'). Commune, NE Oran dept., NW Algeria, on railroad 75 m. E of Oran; pop. 15,380; in irrigated agricultural area.

Re'ma'gen (rā'mä'gĕn). Town, N Rhineland-Palatinate state, West Germany, on left bank of the Rhine 20 m. NW of Koblenz; pop. 4775. Founded as early as 11th cent.; site of the Ludendorff bridge (built 1916–18) across the Rhine, which was the only one undestroyed before Allied advance into Germany in Mar. 1945; bridge seized Mar. 8 and Rhine crossed; bridgehead on E bank opposite enlarged Mar. 8–19; bridge collapsed Mar. 17.

Rem'bang (rĕm'bäng). **1** District, Central Java prov., Indonesia.
2 Seaport town, Central Java prov., Indonesia, on coast 45 m. ENE of Semarang; pop. 13,791.

Re·me'dios (rrĕ·mā'thyōs). Town and municipality (*in full* **San Juan de los Remedios** [säng hwän' thä lôr]), Las Villas prov., W cen. Cuba; town near coast, 23 m. E of Santa Clara, near coast; pop. (1943) 10,485.

Remi. See REIMS.

Re·mi're·mont' (rĕ·mēr'môN'). Commune, Vosges dept., NE France, on Moselle river 12 m. SSE of Épinal;

pop. 10,462; textiles; built around famous old abbey (founded 620).

Re·mou'champs' (rĕ·mōō'shäN'). Village in Liège prov., E Belgium, on the Amblève river; location of a remarkable double cavern.

Rem'pang (rĕm'päng). Island, Riouw Archipelago, Indonesia, SSE of Batam; selected by British command Oct. 1945 as internment area for Japanese prisoners.

Rems (rĕms). River ab. 40 m. long in Württemberg, Germany, flowing into the Neckar river just N of Stuttgart.

Rem'scheid (rĕm'shīt). Manufacturing city, North Rhine-Westphalia state, West Germany, near the Wupper river 25 m. ESE of Düsseldorf; pop. (1939) 103,437; since 1929 includes former cities of Lennep and Lüttringhausen; principal seat of German toolmaking industry and cutlery manufacture.

Renaix. See RONSE.

Ren'dez·vous Peak (rän'dĕ·vōō; rĕn'-). Mountain 10,924 ft. in Teton National Forest, S of Grand Teton National Park, NW Wyoming.

Rendina, Gulf of. See STRYMONIC GULF.

Ren·do'va (rĕn·dō'vå). Island off SW cen. coast of New Georgia I., cen. Solomon Is., W Pacific Ocean; separated from New Georgia by Blanche Channel. Part of British Solomon Islands protectorate. Seized by Americans June 30–July 2, 1943 and used as base in operations against Munda.

Rends'burg (rĕnts'bŏŏrк). City, Schleswig govt. dist., Schleswig-Holstein, northern Germany, on the Kiel Canal 13 m. S of Schleswig; pop. 17,145; 13th-cent. church; 16th-cent. town hall; shipping center; manufactures iron goods, leather. Founded before 1199; to Holstein 1252; became city 1339, fortified 1539; stronghold of Schleswig-Holstein army during German-Danish war 1848–50.

Reneia. See DELOS.

Ren'frew (rĕn'frōō). **1** County, Ontario, Canada. See *Table* at ONTARIO.
2 Manufacturing town, Renfrew co., SE Ontario, Canada, on Bonnechère river 32 m. SE of Pembroke; pop. 7360; important railroad junction point; makes flour, brick, tile, woolens, and machinery; near graphite and molybdenite mines.
3 *or* **Ren'frew·shire** (-shīr; -shēr). County, SW Scotland; area 227 sq. m.; pop. (1951) 324,652; ⊗ Paisley; other towns Greenock, Port Glasgow, Johnstone; rivers Clyde, Gryfe; agriculture, livestock raising, dairying, coal and iron mining, shipbuilding, distilling, manufacturing (textiles, chemicals).
4 Burgh, Renfrew co., SW Scotland, near S bank of the Clyde ab. 7 m. W of Glasgow; pop. 17,093; a small section of the burgh is in Lanark co.; shipbuilding yards, engineering works.

Ren'gat (rĕng'gät). Town, Inderagiri dist., E cen. Sumatra, Indonesia, on right bank of the Inderagiri river; pop. 1949.

Ren'go (rrĕng'gô). Town, O'Higgins prov., cen. Chile, 65 m. S of Santiago; pop. 6730.

Re'ni (rĕn; rĕ'nĕ). Town at mouth of Prut river on the Danube, above the delta and E of Galaţi; formerly in Bessarabia; now in Izmail Region, SW Ukraine.

Ren'kum (rĕng'kŭm). Commune, Gelderland prov., E Netherlands, on the Neder Rijn just W of Arnhem; pop. (1939) 21,033.

Ren'nell (rĕn'l). Raised atoll of coral limestone, an island in NE Coral Sea, 120 m. SW of San Cristobal I., S Solomon Is., W Pacific Ocean, in lat. 11°30'S and long. 160°W; ab. 50 m. long and 12 m. wide; pop. ab. 1000.

Rennes (rĕn); *anc.* **Con·da'te** (kŏn·dā'tĕ); *Breton* **Roazon.** Manufacturing and commercial city, ✳ of Ille-et-Vilaine dept., NW France, at junction of Ille and Vilaine rivers 193 m. WSW of Paris; pop. 98,538; manufactures agricultural implements, paper, shoes, hats, gloves, leather; trades in wax, honey, dairy products,

lace, cotton and linen yarns, pottery; university (founded 1735); cathedral, archiepiscopal palace, old parliament house, town hall, museum, palace of justice. Former capital of Brittany; partly destroyed by fire 1720. In World War II seized by Americans Aug. 2–3, 1944.

Re′no (rē′nō). **1** County in Kansas. See *Table* at KANSAS.

2 City, ⊗ of Washoe co., NW corner of Nevada, on Truckee river 20 m. N of Lake Tahoe; 2d largest city in the state; pop. 51,470; settled 1859; became ⊗ 1871; incorp. as town 1879, as city 1901; legal center of state (easy divorce laws); commercial center and market of cattle-raising area, including part of California; meat packing, flour and lumber milling, dairy and poultry products; manufactures rock products, bricks, stoves, soap; distribution center for mines of Nevada; legal gambling since 1931. Univ. of Nevada (at Elko 1874–85; moved and reopened at Reno 1886; coed.), including Mackay School of Mines (1907); Experiment Station of U.S. Bureau of Mines.

Re′no (rā′nō); *anc.* **Re′nus** (rē′nŭs). River 137 m. long, N Italy; rises in the Apennines, flows N and E into the Adriatic Sea N of Ravenna.

Re·no′vo (rē·nō′vō). Borough, Clinton co., cen. Pennsylvania, on Susquehanna river 41 m. W of Williamsport; pop. 3316; railroad repair shops, tanneries; deposits of soft coal and clay nearby.

Rens′se·laer′ (rĕn′sĕ·lĕr′; rĕns·lĕr′; rĕn′sĕ·lēr; rĕns′lēr). **1** County in New York. See *Table* at NEW YORK.

2 City, ⊗ of Jasper co., NW Indiana, 40 m. NNW of Lafayette; pop. 4740; trading center for agricultural section. Saint Joseph's Coll. (1889; coed.) in Collegeville, S suburb.

3 City, Rensselaer co., E New York, across Hudson river from Albany; pop. 10,506; industrial suburb of Albany; manufactures dyes and chemicals, felts, woolen goods, concrete blocks; railroad shops.

Ren′ton (rĕn′t′n; -tŭn). City, King co., W cen. Washington, 12 m. SSE of Seattle; pop. 18,453; coal mines, clay pits; lumber mills, foundries.

Ren′ville (rĕn′vĭl). Name of counties in two states of the U.S. See *Tables* at MINNESOTA and NORTH DAKOTA.

Re′pe·len–Baerl (rā′pĕ·lĕn·bärl′), *occasionally* **Re′peln–Baerl** (rā′pĕln-). Commune, North Rhine-Westphalia, Germany, NW of Duisberg; pop. 14,087; coal.

Reph′a·im (rĕf′ā·ĭm; rē·fā′ĭm). Valley in S Palestine, extending SW from Jerusalem; reputed home of the Rephaim, a Neolithic tribe of giants (*Gen.* xiv. 5; *2 Sam.* v. 18); scene of conflicts bet. David and the Philistines.

Re·pub′lic (rē·pŭb′lĭk). **1** County in Kansas. See *Table* at KANSAS.

2 City, ⊗ of Ferry co., NE Washington; pop. 1064; gold mines.

Re·pú′bli·ca de Pa′na·má′ (rrĕ·poō′vlĕ·kä thä pä′nä·mä′). Spanish for republic of PANAMA.

República Dominicana. See DOMINICAN REPUBLIC.

Re·pub′li·can (rē·pŭb′lĭ·kăn). River 445 m. long, Nebraska and Kansas; rises in E Colorado, flows NE and E through S Nebraska, then SE through NE cen. Kansas to unite with the Smoky Hill river at Junction City in Geary co. and form the Kansas river.

República Oriental del Uruguay. See URUGUAY.

Republic of South Africa. See UNION OF SOUTH AFRICA.

République libanaise. See LEBANON republic.

Re·pulse′ Bay (rē·pŭls′; rē′pŭls). **1** Inlet of Pacific Ocean, E Queensland, Australia, bet. Mackay and Bowen, 20°45′S.

2 Small inlet at N end of Roes Welcome, N Hudson Bay, in S part of isthmus connecting Melville Penin. with mainland; divided bet. Keewatin and Franklin Districts, Northwest Territories, Canada.

3 Trading station and port on SW coast of Melville Penin., Franklin District, Northwest Territories, Canada, on Repulse Bay at head of Roes Welcome.

Re·que′na (rrĕ·kā′nä). Commune, Valencia prov., E Spain, 36 m. W of Valencia; pop. 19,422; mineral baths; produces silk, wine, oil, saffron, grain, fruit; conquered by the Cid, taken by Moors, reconquered by Alfonso VIII 1219.

Re·sac′a (rĕ·săk′ä). Town, N Gordon co., NW Georgia; pop. (est.) 325; called Dublin until renamed by veterans of the battle of Resaca de la Palma; scene of Civil War battle May 15, 1864.

Re·sa′ca de la Pal′ma (rrĕ·sä′kä thä lä päl′mä). Battlefield in Cameron co., S Texas, ab. 4 m. N of Brownsville; scene of victory May 9, 1846 of Americans under Zachary Taylor over Mexicans under Mariano Arista; second encounter of the Mexican War, Mexicans driven across the Rio Grande.

Res′er·va′tion Peak (rĕz′ẽr·vā′shŭn). Mountain 10,618 ft. on E boundary of Yellowstone National Park, NW Wyoming.

Re·serve′ (rē·zûrv′). **1** Urban area, St. John the Baptist parish, SE Louisiana; pop. 5297.

2 Village, ⊗ of Catron co., W New Mexico, 70 m. NNW of Silver City; pop. (est.) 300.

Resht (rĕsht; *Iranian* räsht). Industrial city, NW Iran, near the shore of the Caspian Sea, ✻ of Gilan prov.; pop. ab. 122,000; silk-manufacturing center; has large trade, partly through its port of Pahlevi; connected by motor transport road with Kazvin and Tehran to the SE. Suffered considerably from fighting in World War I.

Resiczabánya. See REŞIŢA.

Re·si′na (rā·zē′nä). Commune, Napoli prov., Campania, S Italy, on Bay of Naples 5 m. ESE of Naples; pop. 30,707; starting point for ascent of Mt. Vesuvius; built over ruins of ancient Herculaneum (*q.v.*).

Re·sis·ten′cia (rrĕ·sēs·tān′syä). City, ✻ of Chaco territory, N Argentina, on the bank of the Paraná river facing Corrientes; pop. (est.) 25,150.

Re′şi·ţa (rĕ′shĕ·tsä) *or* **Re′ci·ţa** (rĕ′chĕ-); *Hung.* **Re′si·cza·bá′nya** (rĕ′shĭ·tsŏ·bän′yŏ). Commune, SW Romania, 65 m. SE of Arad; pop. ab. 20,000; center of iron-producing region.

Res′o·lu′tion (rĕz′ŏ·lū′shŭn). See FORT RESOLUTION.

Resolution Island. 1 Island 975 sq. m. off SE tip of Baffin I. and on N side of entrance to Hudson Strait, SE Franklin District, Northwest Territories, Canada.

2 Island off SW coast of South I., New Zealand.

Res′ti·gouche (rĕs′tĭ·goōsh; rĕs′tĭ·goōsh′). **1** River 125 m. long in New Brunswick, Canada; rises in NW New Brunswick, flows NW, then E in a wide estuary into Chaleur Bay; famous salmon stream.

2 County, New Brunswick, Canada. See *Table* at NEW BRUNSWICK.

Res′ur·rec′tion Bay (rĕz′ŭ·rĕk′shŭn). Inlet of Gulf of Alaska, SE Kenai Penin., S Alaska; Seward at its head.

Re′szel (rĕ′shĕl); *Ger.* **Rös′sel** (rûs′ĕl). City, cen. Olsztyn dept., N Poland, ab. 10 m. W of Kętrzyn; pop. 4180; formerly belonged to East Prussia, Germany.

Re′tal·hu·leu′ (rrĕ′tä·loō·lā′oō). **1** Department, SW Guatemala; 726 sq. m.; pop. 69,974.

2 Town, its ✻; pop. 6549; in coffee-growing area near the coast ab. 22 m. SSW of Quezaltenango.

Re·thel′ (rē·tĕl′). Commune, Ardennes dept., NE France, on the Aisne 20 m. SW of Mézières; pop. 5586; seat of countship 10th cent. to 16th cent., made a duchy 1581, acquired by Mazarin 1663; occupied by Germans 1914–18 during World War I.

Re·thondes′ (rē·tônd′). Village near Compiègne, N France, in the Forêt de Laigue; place where armistice of World War I was signed Nov. 11, 1918.

Re·thým′nē (rā·thĕm′nyĕ). **1** Department of Greece. See *Table* at GREECE.

2 Seaport, its ✻. See RETHYMNON.

Re′thym·non (rā′thĕm·nôn); *also* **Re·thým′nē** (rā·thĕm′nyĕ) and **Re′ti·mo** (*Ital.* râ′tĕ·mō). Seaport town, ✻ of Rethýmnē dept., on N coast of island of Crete, ab. 38 m. W of Candia; pop. 8632.

Ré'u'nion' (rā'ü'nyôN'; *Angl.* rĕ-ūn'yŭn); *formerly* **Bour'bon** (boor'bŭn; *Fr.* boor'bôN'). Island of the Mascarene Is., in the Indian Ocean ab. 400 m. E of Madagascar; of oval shape, ab. 39 m. long by 28 m. wide; 970 sq. m.; pop. (1936) 208,858; ✻ Saint-Denis, on N coast; formerly a French colony, since Jan. 1, 1947 an overseas department of France; very mountainous, highest point Piton des Neiges 10,068 ft. in cen. part; coast has few indentations, chief harbor at Port-des-Galets at NW corner; other towns St-Paul, St-Louis, and St-Pierre; produces sugar and vanilla. Annexed to France 1643 and named Bourbon; official name Réunion since 1848; first systematic colonization 1664; held by British July 8, 1810 to Apr. 1815.

Reus (rrĕ'ōōs). Commune, Tarragona prov., NE Spain, 6 m. NW of Tarragona; pop. 32,285; trades in wine, grain, fruit; manufactures machinery, cotton, silk, linen, dynamite, soap, candy, leather; Gothic church. Began rise to commercial importance after establishment c. 1750 of English colony here.

Reuss (rois). **1** River 80 m. long in cen. Switzerland; rises in S Uri canton, flows N through Bay of Uri and Lake of Lucerne into Aare river near its junction with the Rhine river.
2 Name of two former principalities in Thuringia: **Reuss-Greiz** (rois'grīts'), ✻ Greiz, and **Reuss-Schleiz-Ge'ra** (rois'shlīts'gā'rä), ✻ Gera. Both became part of Thuringia 1918.

Reu'ter Peak (roo'tēr). Peak 8700 ft. in Glacier National Park, NW Montana.

Reut'ling·en (roit'ling·ĕn). City, Baden-Württemberg state, Germany, 19 m. S of Stuttgart; pop. 30,501; manufactures textiles, leather, machinery. Founded before 1090; free imperial city 1240–1802; scene of victory of Swabian League over Ulrich von Württemberg 1377; to Württemberg 1802.

Revakantha. See REWA KANTHA.

Reval, Revel. See TALLIN.

Rev'eille Range (rĕv'ĕl). Range in cen. Nye co., S Nevada; highest point **Reveille Peak** 8910 ft.

Rev'el·stoke (rĕv'l·stōk). City, SE British Columbia, Canada, on left bank of Columbia river just S of Mount Revelstoke National Park; pop. 2917; railroad divisional point in valley bet. Monashee and Selkirk ranges; conducts large trade in mining supplies and operates a large smelter and various small industries; center for hunting and fishing excursions.

Revelstoke, Mount. Mountain over 7000 ft., SE British Columbia, SW Canada, just W of Selkirk Mts.; comprises Mount Revelstoke National Park (see CANADA, *National Parks*).

Re·vere' (rĕ·vēr'). City, Suffolk co., E Massachusetts, 5 m. NE of Boston; pop. 40,080; seaside resort, known esp. for its three-mile-long expanse of fine sandy beach.

Re·ver'mont' (rĕ·vĕr'môN'). Western ridge of the Jura Mts., E Ain and E Jura depts., E France; highest point 2529 ft.

Reversing, *or* **Reversible, Falls.** See SAINT JOHN river, New Brunswick.

Re·vil'la Gi·ge'do (rrĕ·vē'yä hĕ·hā'thô). Group of islands in the Pacific Ocean ab. 420 m. W of and under administrative control of the state of Colima, Mexico, 19°N, 111°W; total area 320 sq. m. The largest of the group is Socorro, a rocky mountainous island 24 m. long and 9 m. wide. The westernmost of the group is Roca Partida.

Re·vil'la·gi·ge'do Island (rĕ·vil'ȧ·gi·gē'dō). Large island 50 m. long by 25 m. broad, SE Alaska, off mainland E of Prince of Wales I.; in SE Alexander Archipelago. Ketchikan is on its SW coast.

Re'wa (rā'wä). Largest river on Viti Levu I., in the Fiji Is., SW Pacific Ocean; flows SE across E side of the island and empties into the Pacific Ocean; navigable for ab. 40 m.

Re'wa (rē'wȧ). **1** Former Indian state, Baghelkhand, E Central India; 12,830 sq. m.; pop. (1941) 1,820,445.
2 Town, its ✻ and former ✻ of Baghelkhand Agency, 110 m. SSW of Allahabad; pop. 25,206. Founded 1618.

Re'wa Kan'tha *or* **Re'va·kan'tha** (rā'wä känt'hȧ). Former British agency, Gujarat States, W India, chiefly on banks of lower Narbada river; 978 sq. m.; pop. 117,342; comprised 15 of states formerly in Bombay prov., and also the Dangs; joined new confederation of Indian states July 7, 1947.

Re·wa'ri (rȧ·wä'rī). Town, Gurgaon dist., S Punjab state, NW Indian Union, 50 m. SW of Delhi; pop. 26,269; produces brassware.

Rex'burg (rĕks'bûrg). City, ⊗ of Madison co., E Idaho, 25 m. NE of Idaho Falls; pop. 4767; laid out by Mormon settlers 1883; made ⊗ 1913; commercial center for farming and stock-raising section; creameries; sugar beets.

Rey, Is'la del (ēz'lä thĕl rĕ'ĕ; rä'). Island 15 m. long, largest of the Pearl Is., in Gulf of Panama; chief town San Miguel.

Reyes, Los. See LOS REYES.

Reyes, Point. Point at S extremity of peninsula jutting out on W coast of Marin co., California, ab. 30 m. NW of Golden Gate; reputed to be windiest and foggiest place on W coast of United States S of Bering Sea, averaging 137 days of fog a year; area included in Point Reyes National Seashore (established 1962).

Rey'kja·nes', Cape (rā'kyä·nâs'). Cape on SW extremity of Iceland.

Rey'kja·vík' (rā'kyä·vēk'). City, ✻ of Iceland, seaport on SW coast, 64°10'N, 21°58'W; pop. (1944) 44,281; university, publishing houses. British and American base during World War II.

Reyn'olds (rĕn'ldz). County in Missouri. See *Table* at MISSOURI.

Reynolds, Mount. Peak 9147 ft. in Glacier National Park, NW Montana.

Reyn'olds·burg (rĕn'ldz·bûrg). Village, Franklin co., cen. Ohio, W of Columbus; pop. 7793.

Reyn'olds·ville (rĕn'ldz·vïl). Borough, Jefferson co., W cen. Pennsylvania, 8 m. WSW of Du Bois; pop. 3158; bituminous coal mining; brick, glass, textiles, caskets.

Rey·no'sa (rrĕ·ĕ·nō'sä). City, Tamaulipas state, E Mexico, on the Rio Grande; pop. (1959 est.) 108,540.

Rezaieh. See RIZAIYEH.

Re·zé' (rĕ·zā'). Industrial commune, Loire-Atlantique dept., NW France, on Loire river opp. Nantes; pop. (1931) 12,325; foundries; hats, furniture, shoes, rugs.

Re'zegh (rĕ'zĕg). Village, NE Cyrenaica, Libya, ab. 18 m. SSE of Tobruk; battle Nov. 1941.

Re'zek·ne (rā'zĕk·nĕ); *Russ., formerly* **Rye'zhi·tsa** (ryä'zhi·tsȧ). **1** Administrative district, cen. Latgale prov., E Latvia; 1642 sq. m.
2 *Ger.* **Ro·sit'ten** (rô·zīt'ĕn). Town, its ✻, 55 m. NE of Daugavpils; pop. (1935) 13,139; railroad junction on trunk line from Daugavpils to Pskov; trade center near border of Russia. Founded 1285 by Teutonic Knights; under Lithuanian and Polish rule most of period 1560–1772; under Russian rule 1772 ff.; scene of battles in World War I; seized 1918–19 by Bolshevik forces which were expelled 1920 by Latvian-Polish army. In World War II seized by German armies 1941; recovered 1945.

Re·zon'ville' (rĕ·zôN'vēl'). Commune, Moselle dept., NE France, just W of Metz; pop. 306; scene of part of the battle of Mars-la-Tour Aug. 16, 1870.

Rha. See VOLGA.

Rha·da'mes (rȧ·dăm'ĕs; -dä'mĕs). Var. of *Ghadames:* see GADÀMES.

Rhaedestus. See TEKIRDAĞ.

Rhaetia. See RAETIA.

Rhaetian Alps. See *Table* at ALPS.

Rhaetia Secunda. Var. of *Raetia Secunda:* see VINDELICIA.

Rha'ges (rā'jĕz; -jĭz); *anc.* **Rha'gae** (rā'jē); *Bib.* **Ra'ges** (rā'jĕz; -jĭz) [*Apocrypha, Tobit* i. 14]; *Pers.* **Rai** (rī); *Gr.* **Eu·ro'pus** (û·rō'pŭs). City of ancient Media; its ruins are ab. 5 m. SE of Tehran, N Iran. According to

tradition founded 3000 B.C.; excavations disclose extensive fortifications, towers, and buildings. Reckoned with Nineveh and Ecbatana (mod. Hamadan) as one of the great cities of antiquity. Made capital of Median Empire; flourished until Middle Ages but suffered from earthquakes and finally destroyed by Tatars in 12th cent. A.D. Under the Sassanids (226–641 A.D.) was seat of Zoroastrianism. Reputed birthplace of Harun al-Rashid.

Rham′nus (răm′nŭs). Locality on coast of Attica, Greece, N of Marathon and ab. 24 m. NE of Athens; ancient Temple of Nemesis, now in ruins.

Rhea (rā). County in Tennessee. See *Table* at TENNESSEE.

Rhe′den (rā′dĕ[n]). Commune, Gelderland prov., E Netherlands, on IJssel just E of Arnhem; pop. 27,377.

Rhegion *or* **Rhegium.** See REGGIO DI CALABRIA seaport.

Rhei′dol (rī′dŏl). River, cen. Wales; rises NW of Plynlimmon, flows SW and S, makes sharp turn W (site of Devil's Bridge, *q.v.*) and enters Cardigan Bay at Aberystwyth.

Rheims. See REIMS.

Rhein. See RHINE.

Rhei′ne (rī′nĕ), *also* **Rheine in West′fa′len** (ĭn vĕst′fä′lĕn). City, North Rhine-Westphalia state, West Germany, on Ems river 25 m. NNW of Münster; pop. 17,732; 15th-cent. church; 15th-cent. castle.

Rheinfall. See SCHAFFHAUSEN FALLS.

Rhein′fel′den (rīn′fĕl′dĕn) *or* **Rhein′feld** (rīn′fĕld). Commune, NW Aargau canton, N Switzerland, on the Rhine; pop. (1930) 3927; scene of battle Feb. 28, 1638 during Thirty Years' War in which the Huguenot leader duc de Rohan was mortally wounded.

Rhein′gau (rīn′gou). Small district, SW Hesse-Nassau prov., former Prussia, Germany; produces wine.

Rhein′hau′sen (rīn′hou′zĕn). Industrial commune, North Rhine-Westphalia state, West Germany, SW suburb of Duisburg on the Rhine; pop. 32,446; river port; ironworks, coal mining.

Rhein′hes′sen (rīn′hĕs′ĕn). Province of Hesse. See *Table* at HESSE.

Rhein′land (rīn′länt). 1 Province of former Prussia. See *Rhine Province* in *Table* at PRUSSIA.
2 See RHINELAND.

Rheinland–Pfalz. See RHINELAND-PALATINATE.

Rhein′pfalz′ (rīn′pfälts′). = *Rhine Palatinate:* see The PALATINATE.

Rhein′pro·vinz′ (rīn′prŏ·vĭnts′). Province of former Prussia. See *Rhine Province* in *Table* at PRUSSIA.

Rhein′wald·horn′ (rīn′vält·hôrn′). Highest peak 11,145 ft. in the Adula range, Lepontine Alps, SE Switzerland.

Rhe·ne′a (rĕ·nē′à; *Mod. Gr.* rĕ·nyē′ä). Small island, N Cyclades, S Aegean Sea, W of Mykonos; bet. it and Mykonos is the island of Delos.

Rhe′nen (rā′nĕ[n]). Commune, Utrecht prov., cen. Netherlands, on Neder Rijn SE of Utrecht; pop. 7689.

Rhen′ish Prussia (rĕn′ĭsh). Province of former Prussia. See *Rhine Province* in *Table* at PRUSSIA.

Rhenus. See RHINE.

Rhetian Alps. Var. of *Rhaetian Alps:* see *Table* at ALPS.

Rheydt (rīt). City, North Rhine-Westphalia, W Germany, S of München-Gladbach; pop. 88,700. See GLADBACH-RHEYDT.

Rhin (răN). 1 See RHINE.
2 Departments of France: **Bas–Rhin** (bä′răN′) and **Haut–Rhin** (ō′-). See *Table* at FRANCE.

Rhine (rīn); *Ger.* **Rhein** (rīn); *Fr.* **Rhin** (răN); *Du.* **Rijn** (rīn); *anc.* **Rhe′nus** (rē′nŭs). River 820 m. long in W Europe; formed by confluence of Hinter Rhein and Vorder Rhein in SE Switzerland; flows through Lake Constance W, N, and NW to the North Sea, forming in its course W boundary of Liechtenstein and Austria, and

SW boundary of Germany; navigable to Basel. The Upper Rhine (*Ger.* Oberrhein) extends from Basel to Mainz; the Lower Rhine (*Ger.* Niederrhein) begins at Bonn and leaves Germany near Cleve; in Netherlands it curves W and divides into two branches, the Neder Rijn to the N and the Waal to the S. One branch (IJssel) of the Neder Rijn flows N into IJsselmeer; the main course of the Neder Rijn is W, where it becomes known as the Lek, which unites with the Merwede and continues to the North Sea as the Nieuwe Maas. The Waal unites with the Maas (Meuse) and in its S arm flows into the Hollandsch Diep; its N arm, known as the Merwede, divides into the Oude Maas and Nieuwe Maas (see MAAS), both entering the North Sea close together just S of the Hook of Holland. In this wide delta are various islands of South Holland and Zeeland provs. of Netherlands. In all its course are many canals connecting with other streams in Netherlands and with the Rhone, Marne, and Danube systems in Germany and France. Its river trade is very extensive and both in German legend and history it has borne a prominent part. Its main tributaries on the right the Neckar, Main, Lahn, Sieg, Ruhr, and Lippe; on the left the Aare, Ill, Nahe, Moselle, and Erft. Chief cities on its banks Konstanz, Schaffhausen, Basel, Karlsruhe, Mannheim, Ludwigshafen, Mainz, Wiesbaden, Koblenz, Bonn, Cologne, Düsseldorf, Duisburg-Hamborn, and Rotterdam. In World War II its course was a major line of defense Feb.–Mar. 1945; first crossed by Allies by bridge at Remagen (*q.v.*). For *Falls of the Rhine,* see SCHAFFHAUSEN FALLS.

Rhine′beck (rīn′bĕk). Residential village, Dutchess co., SE New York, on Hudson river 16 m. N of Poughkeepsie; pop. 2093; connected by ferry with **Rhine′cliff** (rīn′klĭf) [1950 pop. 614] with Kingston; settled by Dutch before 1690, later by Palatines.

Rhine′land′ (rīn′länd′; -lănd); *English form of Ger.* **Rhein′land** (rīn′länt). 1 Recently and popularly, the part of W Germany W of the Rhine river (left bank of the Rhine); ab. 9000 sq. m.; pop. ab. 5,440,000; chief city Cologne.
2 Officially same as *Rhine Province:* see *Table* at PRUSSIA.

Rhine′land′er (rīn′lăn′dēr). City, ⊗ of Oneida co., N Wisconsin, 37 m. NNW of Antigo; pop. 8790; former lumbering center; now trading and supply center for fishermen, hunters, and canoeists in the north woods and lakes region of the state; manufactures paper.

Rhine′land′–Pa·lat′i·nate; *Ger.* Rhein′land–Pfalz′ (rīn′länt·pfälts′). A state of the Federal Republic of Germany, chiefly W of the Rhine; 7654 sq. m.; pop. 3,313,800; ✻ Mainz.

Rhine Palatinate. See The PALATINATE.

Rhine Province. Province of former Prussia. See *Table* at PRUSSIA.

Rhin–et–Mo′selle′ (răN′-nā-mô′zĕl′). Department of France 1801–15; ✻ Koblenz; comprised region on W bank of the Rhine which was given to France by Treaty of Lunéville 1801; to Prussia by the Congress of Vienna.

Rhinns *or* **Rinns, the** (rĭnz). 1 Peninsula extending into Atlantic Ocean on W coast of island of Islay, Inner Hebrides, off W coast of Scotland; terminates in **Rhinns,** *or* **Rinns, Point;** lighthouse.
2 *also* the **Rhinns of Galloway.** Peninsula on extreme SW coast of Scotland, in Wigtown co., W of Loch Ryan and Luce Bay and terminating on the N in Corsewall Point and on the S in the Mull of Galloway.

Rhinocolura. See EL 'ARISH.

Rhio. See RIOUW.

Rho (rô). Commune, Milano prov., Lombardy, N Italy, 8 m. NW of Milan; pop. 19,823; 16th-cent. sanctuary.

Rhoda. See RODA.

Rhodanus. See RHONE.

Rhode Is′land (rōd ī′lănd; rō·dī′lănd). 1 *or* **A·quid′neck Island** (à·kwĭd′nĕk). Island 15 m. long in Narragansett Bay, SE Rhode Island; the city of Newport is on its SW coast. Purchased by Anne Hutchinson,

William Coddington, and others, and settled at Portsmouth 1638; name changed to Rhode Island 1644.

2 *officially* **Rhode Island and Providence Plantations.** Northeastern seaboard state of U.S.A., an original state of the Union; bounded on N and E by Massachusetts, on S by the Atlantic Ocean, and on W by Connecticut; 50th state in area, 1214 sq. m. (land area 1058 sq. m.); 39th state in population, 859,488; ✴ Providence. See *Table of States* at UNITED STATES. Divided into the following five counties (for pronunciation of their names, see their individual entries):

NAME	LOCATION	AREA¹	POP.¹	CO. SEAT
Bristol	E	25	37,146	Bristol
Kent	cen.	172	112,619	East Greenwich
Newport	SE	115	81,891	Newport
Providence	N	422	568,778	Providence
Washington	S	324	59,054	West Kingston

¹ Area = land area in sq. m. Pop. from 1960 Census.

Nickname: Little Rhody. *State flower:* Violet. *Motto:* Hope. *Chief cities:* Providence, Pawtucket, Warwick, Cranston. *Rivers:* Pawtuxet, Blackstone, and the Pawcatuck, forming lower SW boundary. *Highest point:* Jerimoth Hill 812 ft., in W. *Chief industries:* Textile manufacturing, foundry and machine work; jewelry making.

History: Settled by religious exiles, chiefly from Massachusetts, including Roger Williams, who settled at Providence 1636, and Anne Hutchinson, who settled at Portsmouth on Aquidneck I. 1638; scattered settlements united when charter granted by Charles II to Roger Williams 1663; charter provisions continued in effect until Dorr's Rebellion 1842, when new constitution was framed, adopted, and finally declared in effect May 3, 1843; last state to ratify Federal Constitution May 29, 1790.

Rhodes (rōdz); *Ital.* **Ro'di** (rô'dē); *Latin* **Rho'dus** (rō'dŭs); *Gr.* **Ro'dos, Rho'dos** (rō'dŏs; *Mod. Gr.* rô'thôs). **1** Island in the Southern Sporades (see SPORADES), SE Aegean Sea, off SW coast of Turkey in Asia, in the Dodecanese group; 45 m. long by 22 m. at greatest width; area 545 sq. m.; pop. (1936) 61,886. Chief island of Italian Aegean Islands 1912–45; returned to Greece 1945. Has mountain range extending length of island, highest point Mt. Attairo 3986 ft.; fine climate and fertile soil; exports fruit, vegetables, and wine.

2 City, its ✴, ✴ of Italian Aegean Islands, and ✴ of the group under Greece after 1945, at NE point of island; pop. (1936) 27,466; administrative center of Dodecanese; modern city, with two harbors, built mostly by Knights of St. John of Jerusalem (also known as Knights of Rhodes), has medieval appearance with fortifications and buildings generally unaltered. Probably settled in historic times by Dorians; established many colonies in Mediterranean area; city founded 408 B.C.; constant political struggles of citizens placed city for various periods under Sparta, Athens, and Caria; held briefly by Alexander; besieged 305–304 B.C. by Demetrius Poliorcetes; for several centuries an ally of Rome. Had varied medieval history but chief event was its conquest 1310 by Knights of St. John of Jerusalem; held against Turks but finally evacuated 1522. Occupied by Italy 1912 and finally ceded to Italy by Turkey 1923; returned to Greece 1945.

Rhodes, Outer *and* **Inner.** See APPENZELL.

Rho·de'sia (rô·dē̃'zhà; -zhĭ·à). **1** Region, cen. South Africa, S of Belgian Congo, formerly administered by British South Africa Company; now forms the state of ZAMBIA and colony of SOUTHERN RHODESIA. Named after Cecil J. Rhodes. There are evidences that man has inhabited the region since earliest times: (1) human skulls and paleolithic hand axes; (2) many Bushman rock paintings; (3) great ruined stone buildings (see ZIMBABWE); (4) gold fields by some supposed to be source of gold of Ophir of King Solomon's times.

2 = SOUTHERN RHODESIA.

Rhodes Peak (rōdz). Mountain 7940 ft. in E Clearwater co., NE Idaho.

Rhodes Point. Point, Maryland, on Smith I. in lower Chesapeake Bay.

Rhod'o·pe (rŏd'ô·pē; *Mod. Gr.* rô·thô'pē); *Turk.* **Dospad' Dagh** (dŏs·pät' dä'); *Bulg.* **Des'po·to Pla'ni·na'** (dĕs'pô·tô plä'nĭ·nä'). **1** Mountain range in Balkan Penin., SE Europe; runs SE from SW Bulgaria along border bet. Bulgaria and Macedonia, Greece; highest point Musala 9595 ft.; lies bet. Balkan Mts. and Aegean Sea; in Roman Empire marked boundary bet. Thrace and Macedonia.

2 Department of Greece. See *Table* at GREECE.

Rhodos, Rhodus. See RHODES.

Rhön (rûn). Mountain range in cen. Germany, in NW Bavaria, W Thuringia, and E Hesse; highest peak Wasserkuppe 3116 ft.

Rhon'dda (rŏn'dà; *Welsh* r'hŏn'thà); *formerly* **Ys'trad·y·fod'wg** (ŭs'tràd·ĭ·vŏd'ŏog). Urban district, Glamorganshire, SE Wales; pop. 141,346, (1951) 111,357; in a valley region ab. 12 m. long, 4 m. wide, formed mainly by two rivers, the **Rhondda Fawr** (vour) and the **Rhondda Fach** (vàk) separated by ridge 600–1690 ft. high; produces coal.

Rhone (rōn); *Fr.* **Rhône** (rōn); *anc.* **Rhod'a·nus** (rŏd''n·ŭs). River 504 m. long in Switzerland and France; rises in the Alps and flows SW to Martigny where it turns NW and flows into E end of Lake Geneva; issues from SW end of Lake Geneva, crosses French border through an opening in the Jura Mts., and continues S through Lyons, Avignon, and Tarascon to Arles; empties into the Gulf of Lions, S France, through several branches; navigable for ab. 300 m.

Rhône (rōn). Department of France. See *Table* at FRANCE.

Rhudd'lan (rĭth'làn; -lăn; *Welsh* r'hĭth'-). Civil parish of St. Asaph, Flintshire, N Wales; pop. 1519; site of Norman castle (demolished by Cromwell's troops 1646) at which Edward I enacted 1284 the statute for the government of Wales.

Rhu More (rōō' môr'; môr'). Headland on NW coast of Scotland, N of Loch Broom; encloses Enard Bay on SW.

Rhyl (rĭl; *Welsh* r'hĭl). Urban district and seaport at mouth of the Clwyd, NW Flintshire, NE Wales; pop. 18,745; watering place.

Rhym'ney (rŭm'nĭ; *Welsh* r'hŭm'-). **1** Urban district, Monmouthshire, W England, on the Rhymney 38 m. NW of Bristol; pop. 9134; iron deposits.

2 River 30 m. long on border bet. England (Monmouthshire) and Wales (Glamorganshire); flows SE into Bristol Channel E of Cardiff.

Rhyndacus. See ATRANOS.

Rhy'o·lite (rī'ô·līt). Town, S Nye co., cen. and S Nevada; boom mining city (pop. 8000 from 1905–08) following Goldfield stampede; Death Valley nearby.

Ria'chos (ryä'chôs). Small island in Atlantic Ocean off SE coast of Buenos Aires prov., Argentina.

Riad. Var. of RIYADH.

Ri·al'to. **1** (rĭ·ăl'tō) Residential city, San Bernardino co., SE California, 4 m. W of San Bernardino; pop. 18,567; orange-packing houses.

2 (rĭ·ăl'tō; *Ital.* rĕ·äl'tô) Island and district on the Grand Canal, Venice, Italy; site of the exchange and the center of commercial activity; connected with San Marco I. by the **Rialto Bridge**, built ab. 1590, which has a double row of shops with a broad footway between.

Riazan. See RYAZAN.

Ribachi Peninsula. Var. of RYBACHI PENINSULA.

Ri·ba·te'jo (rē·và·tâ'zhōō). Province of Portugal. See *Table* at PORTUGAL; ESTREMADURA.

Rib'ble (rĭb''l). River in NW England; rises in W Yorkshire, flows S and W through Lancashire into the Irish Sea through an estuary extending past Preston.

Rib'bon Falls (rĭb'ŭn). Waterfall 1612 ft. in Yosemite National Park, E cen. California.

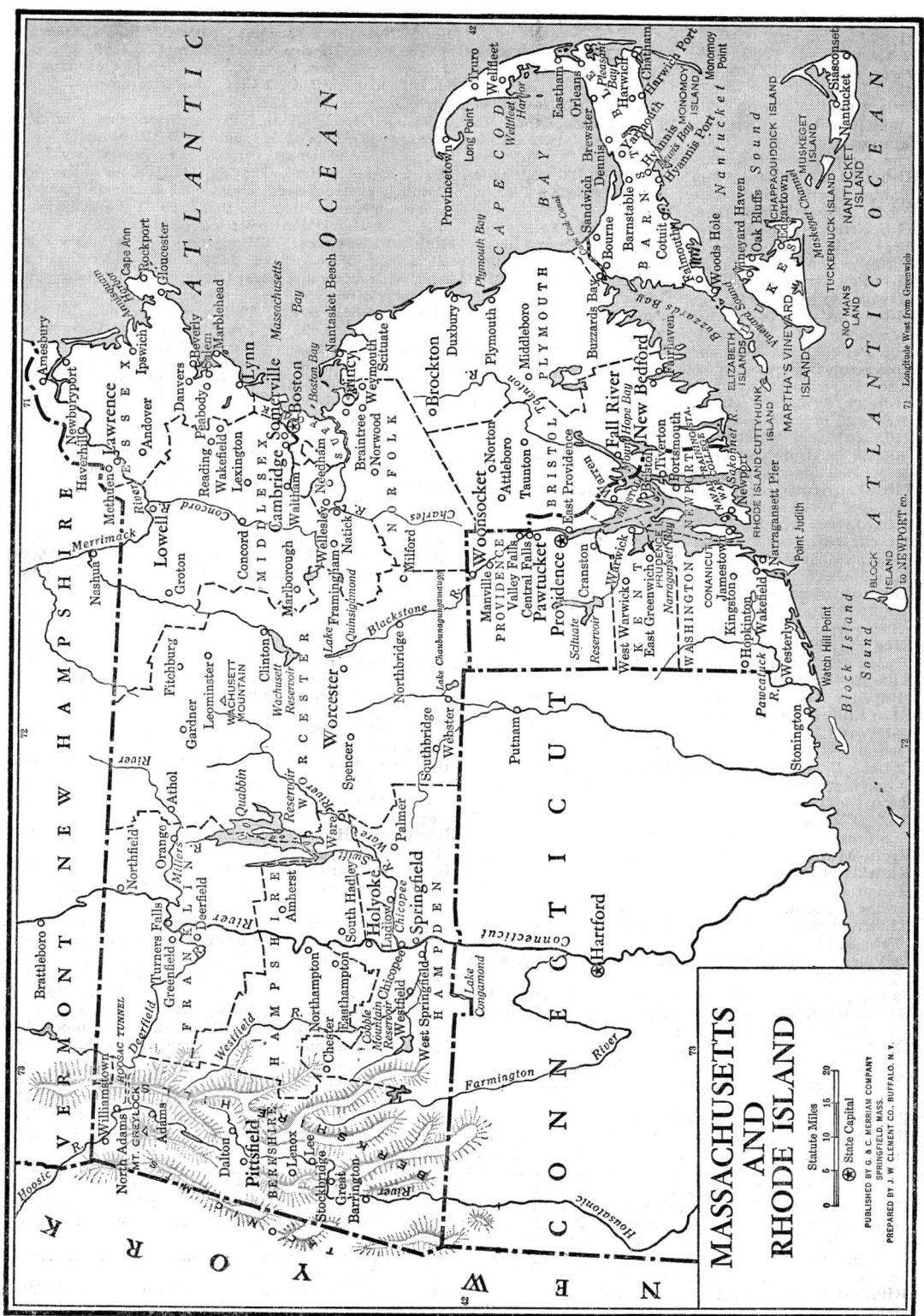

MASSACHUSETTS
AND
RHODE ISLAND

Statute Miles

PUBLISHED BY G. & C. MERRIAM COMPANY
SPRINGFIELD, MASS.
PREPARED BY J. W. CLEMENT CO., BUFFALO, N. Y.

⊕ State Capital

Ri'be (rē'bĕ). **1** County of Denmark. See *Table* at DEN-MARK.

2 Town, its ⊗, SW Jutland Penin., Denmark, on Ribe river; pop. (1945) 6770; Our Lady Church, dating from the 12th cent.

Ri'beau'vil'lé' (rē'bō'vē'lä'); Ger. **Rap'polts·wei'ler** (räp'ōlts·vī'lēr). Commune, N Haut-Rhin dept., NE France; pop. (1931) 5000; saline springs, two Gothic churches; ruins of three castles.

Ri·bei'ra (rē·vā'ĕ·rȧ; -vä'rȧ). River ab. 200 m. long in Paraná and São Paulo states, S Brazil, flowing SW and SE into the Atlantic Ocean.

Ri·bei'ra (rē·vĕ'ĕ·rä; -vä'rä). Commune, La Coruña prov., NW Spain, 38 m. SW of La Coruña and across the bay from Villagarcía de Arosa; pop. 18,760.

Ri·bei'ra Gran'de (rē·vä'ĕ·rȧ [-vä'rȧ] grän'dĕ). See SANTO ANTÃO.

Ri·bei·rão' Pre'to (rē·vä·rouN' prā'tōō). City, N cen. São Paulo state, SE Brazil, on railroad 180 m. NNW of São Paulo; pop. (1940 est.) 47,891; in center of rich coffee-growing region; also produces cereals, cotton, alfalfa, and sugar; distributing point for wide area.

Ri·be'ra (rē·bā'rä). Commune, Agrigento prov., SW Sicily, 20 m. NW of Agrigento; pop. 14,607.

Ri'be·ral'ta (rē'vä·räl'tä). Town, in El Beni dept., N Bolivia, on Beni river at its confluence with the Madre de Dios; Bolivian customhouse; rubber and nuts.

Rib Mountain (rĭb). Elevation 1940 ft. in Marathon co., cen. Wisconsin; highest point in the state.

Ricamarie, La. See LA RICAMARIE.

Ric'car·ton (rĭk'ẽr·t'n; -tŭn). Borough, Canterbury provincial dist., E South I., New Zealand, suburb of Christchurch; pop. 5085.

Ric·cio'ne (rēt·chō'nȧ). Commune, Forlì prov., SE Emilia, N Italy, SE of Rimini on the Adriatic coast; pop. (1931) 7313; resort.

Rice (rīs). Name of counties in two states of the U.S. See *Tables* at KANSAS and MINNESOTA.

Rice Bowl. Name given to the provinces of Hunan and Hupeh in E cen. China where much rice is raised.

Rice Lake. **1** City, Barron co., NW Wisconsin, 45 m. NNW of Chippewa Falls; pop. 7303; trading and supply center, esp. for vacationists.

2 Lake 27 sq. m. in N Northumberland co., SE Ontario, Canada; forms part of Trent Canal system; fishing.

Rich (rĭch). County in Utah. See *Table* at UTAH.

Rich, Cape. Cape, SE Ontario prov., Canada, extending from N Grey co. into Georgian Bay.

Rich, Mount. Peak 4081 ft. in Gilmer co., N Georgia.

Rich'ards Island (rĭch'ẽrdz). Large island in Beaufort Sea at mouth of Mackenzie river, NW Northwest Territories, Canada.

Rich'ard·son (rĭch'ẽrd·s'n). **1** County in Nebraska. See *Table* at NEBRASKA.

2 Village on Tanana river and Alaska Highway, 45 m. SE of Fairbanks, E Alaska.

3 City, Dallas co., NE Texas, N of Dallas; pop. 16,810.

Richardson Highway. Old highway N from Valdez, S Alaska, to Fairbanks, 371 m.; now merges with Alaska Highway at Big Delta; from it a new cutoff runs from Gulkana NE to Alaska Highway at Tanacross; joined at Copper Center by Glenn Highway from Anchorage on the W.

Richardson Lakes. See RANGELEY LAKES.

Richardson Mountains. Range in N Yukon Territory, Canada; average height ab. 4000 ft.; separates Porcupine river from lower Mackenzie river; forms an E extension of the Brooks Range of Alaska.

Rich'bor·ough (rĭch'bŭ·rȧ; -brȧ). Port, Kent, SE England, on the estuary of the Stour river SW of Ramsgate; on the site of ancient **Ru·tu'pi·ae** (rōō·tū'pĭ·ē), an important Roman port; beginning of Watling St.; ruins of castle; modern port established during World War I.

Rich'e·lieu (rĭsh'ĕ·lōō; Fr. rē'shē·lyû'). **1** River 210 m. long, S Quebec, Canada; flows N from Lake Champlain to the head of Lake St. Peter in the St. Lawrence at Sorel. Noted for its scenery; in early times an important travel route. Discovered by Champlain 1609.

2 County, Quebec, Canada. See *Table* at QUEBEC.

Rich'field (rĭch'fēld). **1** City, ⊗ of Morton co., SW corner of Kansas; pop. 122.

2 Village, Hennepin co., SE cen. Minnesota, 7 m. S of Minneapolis; pop. 42.523; suburb of Minneapolis.

3 City, ⊗ of Sevier co., cen. Utah, on Sevier river 55 m. E of S end of Sevier Lake; pop. 4412; center of dairying, farming, livestock area; cheese and flour manufactures; mountain-lion hunting. Settled c. 1863; abandoned during Black Hawk War; resettled in early 1870's.

Richfield Springs. Village, Otsego co., cen. New York, 21 m. SSE of Utica; pop. 1630; health and summer resort, with mineral springs; Great White Sulphur Spring in center of village.

Rich'ford (rĭch'fẽrd). Village and port of entry in Richford town (pop. 2316), Franklin co., NW Vermont, in Green Mts. on Missisquoi river 24 m. NE of St. Albans; pop. 1663; manufactures veneers, furniture, plywood.

Rich Hill (rĭch). City, Bates co., W Missouri, 18 m. N of Nevada; pop. 1820; coal, zinc, and lead deposits; hardwood timber.

Rich'i·buc'to (rĭsh'ĭ·bŭk'tō). Town (unincorporated), ⊗ of Kent co., E New Brunswick, Canada, on inlet of Northumberland Strait; pop. 3580. Founded 1787.

Rich'land (rĭch'lănd). **1** River 40 m. long, S Tennessee; rises in SW Marshall co., flows S into Elk river near Alabama border.

2 Name of a parish in Louisiana and of counties in six states of the U.S. See *Tables* at ILLINOIS, LOUISIANA, MONTANA, NORTH DAKOTA, OHIO, SOUTH CAROLINA, WISCONSIN.

3 City, Benton co., SE Washington, on the Columbia river WNW of Pasco; pop. 23,548. Originally a farming community, it was developed 1943–45 as a residential community for employees of Hanford Engineer Works for the separation of plutonium (on U.S. Atomic Energy Commission reservation, to NW). See HANFORD, Washington.

Richland Bal'sam (bôl'săm). Peak 6540 ft. in Haywood co., W North Carolina.

Richland Center. City, ⊗ of Richland co., SW Wisconsin, 53 m. WNW of Madison; pop. 4746; trade center in agricultural and dairy-farming section; shipping point for livestock.

Richland Hills. Town, Tarrant co., NE Texas, NE of Fort Worth; pop. 7804.

Rich'lands (rĭch'lăndz). Town, Tazewell co., SW Virginia, 42 m. NNE of Bristol; pop. 4963; coal mining, brickmaking.

Rich'mond (rĭch'mŭnd). **1** Name of counties in four states of the U.S. See *Tables* at GEORGIA, NEW YORK, NORTH CAROLINA, VIRGINIA.

2 Industrial city, Contra Costa co., W California, on E shore of San Francisco Bay 9 m. NNW of Oakland; pop. 71,854; founded 1899, incorp. 1905; commercial port; ferries to San Francisco; oil refining, food processing, automobile assembly plant; manufactures china, radiators, chemicals, porcelain products, tile.

3 Industrial city, ⊗ of Wayne co., E Indiana, 35 m. SE of Muncie; pop. 44,149; founded 1805, incorp. 1818; manufactures farm equipment, engines and boilers, flour, clothing. Earlham College (1847; coed.; Society of Friends).

4 City, ⊗ of Madison co., E cen. Kentucky, 24 m. SSE of Lexington; pop. 12,168; in bluegrass region; tobacco and livestock market; frequently a battlefield during the Civil War. Site of Eastern Kentucky State College (1906; coed.).

5 Town, Sagadahoc co., S Maine, on Kennebec river 16 m. S of Augusta; pop. 2185.

6 Village, Macomb co., SE Michigan, 19 m. WSW of Port Huron; pop. 2667.

7 City, ⊗ of Ray co., NW Missouri, 38 m. ENE of Kansas City; pop. 4604; trade center in agricultural, livestock-raising, and coal-mining section.

8 Borough, Richmond co., SE New York, coextensive with Staten I. and Richmond co., SW part of New York City; 57 sq. m.; pop. 221,991; includes Shooters' I., Prall's I., Meadow I., part of Buckwheat I., a few small islands to W and N, and Hoffman I. and Swinburne I. in Lower New York Bay; SW of Brooklyn, and separated from Long I. by the Narrows and from the mainland of New Jersey by Kill van Kull on N (spanned by Bayonne Bridge) and Arthur Kill on W (crossed by Goethals Bridge to Elizabeth and by Outerbridge to Perth Amboy); municipal ferry connections with Manhattan and Brooklyn. Has a free port, with large piers, and a 35-mile water front; beach resorts on Atlantic coast; residential sections and trade centers, including Saint George (⊗ of Richmond co.), Port Richmond, West New Brighton, Tompkinsville, Stapleton, New Dorp, Tottenville (scene 1776 of unsuccessful peace conference bet. British and Americans after battle of Long Island); shipbuilding yards, lumber mills, printing and publishing plants, oil storage tanks and refineries; manufactures soap and oil, fertilizer. Wagner Memorial Lutheran Coll. (1886; brought here from Rochester 1918); Sailors' Snug Harbor for retired sailors at New Brighton (*q.v.*). Governed as part of New York City by a mayor and city council; has a borough president, with local and county functions conducted independently of central municipal government. See also NEW YORK city.

History: Staten I. granted to Pauw by the Dutch West India Co. 1630, regranted to de Vries; passed to British 1664 and became part of the province of New Jersey; won for New York by Capt. Christopher Billopp 1668; merged as a borough of New York City 1898.

9 Town, Washington co., S Rhode Island; pop. 1986.

10 Town, ⊗ of Fort Bend co., SE Texas, 28 m. WSW of Houston; pop. 3668; in farming section.

11 City and port of entry, ✳ of Virginia and ⊗ of Henrico co., E cen. Virginia, but politically independent, on James river; largest city in the state; 21 sq. m.; pop. 219,958; tobacco market; wholesale and retail trade center; printing and publishing plants; manufactures tobacco products, paper, machinery, fertilizer, flour. Univ. of Richmond (1832; coed.); Medical Coll. of Virginia (1838; coed.); Union Theological Seminary (1812); Virginia Union Univ. (1865; coed.); Richmond Professional Institute (1917; coed.). Early home of Edgar Allan Poe.

History: Developed as trading center around Fort Charles, built at falls 1645; founded 1733; laid out as town 1737 (subsequently occupied seven hills); incorp. 1742; became ⊗ 1759; scene of 2d and 3d Virginia Conventions in 1775 (at time of Patrick Henry's plea for liberty or death); made capital of Virginia 1779; figured prominently in Revolution; plundered and burned by British under Benedict Arnold 1781; incorp. as town (but called city) 1782; scene of Virginia Convention 1788 for ratification of new Federal Constitution and of Aaron Burr's trial for treason 1807; became the Confederate capital July 1861 at beginning of Civil War and remained the major objective of the Union army until its capture 1865; evacuated and burned by own people 1865, subsequently rebuilt.

12 City, S Victoria, SE Australia, E suburb of Melbourne; pop. 39,616; manufacturing community.

13 County, Nova Scotia, Canada. See *Table* at NOVA SCOTIA.

14 County, Quebec, Canada. See *Table* at QUEBEC.

15 Town, ⊗ of Richmond co., S Quebec, Canada, on St. Francis river 20 m. NNW of Sherbrooke; pop. 3471; founded 1798; railroad divisional point and seat of Coll. of St. Francis.

16 Municipal borough, Surrey, S England, on the Thames 10 m. WSW of London; pop. 41,945; part of

Greater London, a residential suburb and holiday resort; site of the royal Palace of Sheen, used as residence by Edward III, Richard II, Henry V, Henry VII, and Elizabeth I.

17 Borough, Nelson provincial dist., N South I., New Zealand, at head of Tasman Bay; pop. 1125.

Richmond Bay. See MALPEQUE BAY.

Richmond Gulf *or* **Lake.** Lake near SE coast of Hudson Bay, Canada, opp. Belcher Is., bet. Clearwater Lake and the bay.

Richmond Heights. 1 City, St. Louis co., E Missouri, 7 m. W of St. Louis; pop. 15,622.

2 Village, Cuyahoga co., N Ohio, NE of Cleveland; pop. 5068.

Richmond Hill. Peak 6057 ft. in Lawrence co., W South Dakota.

Rich Mountain (rĭch). **1** *formerly* **Blue Mountain.** Peak 2750 ft. in Ouachita Mts., Polk and Scott cos., W Arkansas; second highest point in state. See MAGAZINE MOUNTAIN.

2 Locality, Randolph co., West Virginia; scene of battle July 11, 1861 in which Federals under Rosecrans defeated the Confederates under Col. Pegram.

Rich′rath–Reus′rath (rĭk′rät·rois′rät). Industrial commune, North Rhine-Westphalia, W Germany, SW of Solingen; pop. 14,148; textiles, iron goods.

Rich′wood (rĭch′wŏŏd). **1** Village, Union co., W cen. Ohio, 13 m. SSW of Marion; pop. 2137.

2 City, Nicholas co., cen. West Virginia, 63 m. E of Charleston; pop. 4110; lumber and paper mills.

Rick′en Tunnel (rĭk′ĕn). Railroad tunnel 5.33 m. long, W St. Gallen canton, NE Switzerland, E of Lake of Zurich.

Rick′mans·worth (rĭk′mănz·wûrth). Urban district, Hertfordshire, SE England, at confluence of Chess and Colne rivers 20 m. WNW of London; pop. 24,518.

Ri′co (rē′kō). Mining town, ⊗ of Dolores co., SW Colorado; pop. 353.

Ricomagus. See RIOM.

Rid′der·kerk (rĭd′ēr·kĕrk). Commune, South Holland prov., SW Netherlands, on a delta island of the Rhine just E of Rotterdam; pop. 14,797.

Ri·deau′ (rĭ·dō′). Lake ab. 126 sq. m. on S border of Lanark co., SE Ontario, Canada. Its outlet is **Rideau River** which flows from S Frontenac co. NE through Rideau Lake to the Ottawa river at Ottawa. The lake and river, with constructed section from Rideau Lake to Lake Ontario, form the **Rideau Canal,** 126¼ m. long with 47 locks, connecting Kingston on Lake Ontario with the Ottawa river below Chaudière Falls. The canal divides Ottawa city; it was built 1826 by British government for military purposes at suggestion of duke of Wellington. Now used commercially only; has branch 6½ m. long from Rideau Lake to Perth.

Ridge′crest′ (rĭj′krĕst′). Urban area, Kern co., S California, NE of Bakersfield; pop. 5099.

Ridge′field (rĭj′fēld). **1** Suburban residential town, W Fairfield co., SW Connecticut, on New York border; pop. 8165; incorp. 1709; battle Apr. 27, 1776.

2 Borough, Bergen co., NE corner of New Jersey, 8 m. N of Jersey City; pop. 10,788.

Ridgefield Park. Village, Bergen co., NE New Jersey, 8 m. ESE of Paterson; pop. 12,701; residential suburb.

Ridge′land (rĭj′lănd). Town, ⊗ of Jasper co., S South Carolina; pop. 1192.

Ridge′ley (rĭj′lĭ). Residential town, Mineral co., NE West Virginia, on North Branch of Potomac river opp. Cumberland, Maryland; pop. 1229.

Ridge′town (rĭj′toun). Town, Kent co., SE Ontario, Canada, 17 m. E of Chatham; pop. 2365; in rich agricultural region; has a few small factories.

Ridge′wood (rĭj′wŏŏd). Residential village, Bergen co., NE corner of New Jersey, 5 m. NNE of Paterson; pop. (est.) 22,200; scene of American and British encampments in Revolution; fighting in locality 1780.

Ridg'way (rĭj'wā). Borough, ⊗ of Elk co., NW cen. Pennsylvania, 20 m. N of Du Bois; pop. 6387; settled 1817; manufactures electrical machinery, snow plows, lumber; tanneries.

Riding, East, North, *and* **West.** See YORKSHIRE.

Rid'ing Mountain National Park (rīd'ĭng). See CANADA, *National Parks.*

Riding Mountains. Plateau ab. 2200 ft. in SW cen. Manitoba prov., Canada, W of Lake Manitoba; forms main part of Riding Mountain National Park.

Rid'ley (rĭd'lĭ). Urban township, Delaware co., SE Pennsylvania, SW of Philadelphia; pop. 35,738.

Rid'ley Park (rĭd'lĭ). Residential borough, Delaware co., SE Pennsylvania, 10 m. WSW of Philadelphia; pop. 7387.

Riduna. See ALDERNEY.

Ried (rēt). Town, Upper Austria, Austria, W of Linz; pop. 6520; treaty of alliance bet. Emperor Joseph of Germany and Bavaria signed here 1813.

Riège, La. See ARIÈGE.

Rie'ka (ryĕ'kä) *or* **Ri·je'ka** (rĕ·yĕ'kä); *Ital.* **Fiu'me** (fyōō'mâ); *Ger.* **Sankt Veit am Flaum** (zängkt fīt' äm floum'). Seaport, ⊗ of former Carnaro prov., Venezia Giulia e Zara, NE Italy, on NE coast of the Veliki Kvarner, inlet of Adriatic Sea, 105 m. E by S of Venice; since 1947 seaport of Croatia, NW Yugoslavia; pop. 53,896; episcopal see; summer resort; cathedral (founded 1377); naval academy; town hall; Roman triumphal arch said to have been erected by Claudius II Gothicus; trades in flour, sugar, lumber, wine, rice, tobacco, jute; manufactures ships, torpedoes, machines, olive oil, lumber, tobacco.

History: In Byzantine Empire; ruled by own dukes in 9th cent.; has been held by Austria, Croatia, France, and Hungary; occupied by Italy in 1918; its disposal became an issue which caused Italy to leave Peace Conference 1919; occupied by irregular troops under D'Annunzio 1919; by Treaty of Rapallo bet. Italy and Yugoslavia 1920, set up as independent free city; taken over by Fascists and order restored by Italian troops 1922; formally annexed to Italy 1924; transferred to Yugoslavia by Italian peace treaty 1947.

Rie'sa (rē'zä). City, Dresden dist., E Germany, on Elbe river 39 m. E of Leipzig; pop. 24,218; river port; 16th-cent. town hall; steel, cotton, marble goods.

Ries'co (ryäs'kŏ). Island, Magallanes prov., S Chile, N of the W end of Strait of Magellan; separated from Brunswick Penin. by Otway Water.

Rie'sen Ge·bir'ge *or* **Rie'sen·ge·bir'ge** (rē'zĕn·gĕ·bîr'gĕ). Mountain range extending along boundary between SW Poland (in region formerly included in Silesia prov., Prussia, Germany) and N Czechoslovakia; part of Sudeten Mts.; highest Schneekoppe 5266 ft.

Rie'si (ryâ'sĕ). Commune, Caltanissetta prov., cen. Sicily, 19 m. S by E of Caltanissetta; pop. 19,709; sulfur.

Riet (rēt). River ab. 200 m. long, SW Orange Free State, Union of South Africa; flows W into the Vaal.

Rie'ti (ryâ'tē). **1** Province of Italy. See *Table* at ITALY.
2 *anc.* **Re·a'te** (rē·ä'tē). Commune, its ⊛, Latium, cen. Italy, 42 m. NNW of Rome; pop. 34,769; has a 12th-cent. cathedral, 1st-cent. (A.D.) Roman bridge, and remains of medieval walls; radioactive mineral spring nearby; vicinity produces cattle, horses, swine, grain, sugar beets. Anciently a capital of the Sabines; became Roman municipium; birthplace of Marcus Terentius Varro 116 B.C.; Guelph free city 1154–98 A.D.; became part of States of the Church 1354.

Rie'vaulx (rē'vō). Abbey, Yorkshire, England, 20 m. N of York; Saint Ethelred abbot here 1146–66.

Rif, Riff. See ER RIF.

Rifs'tan'gi, Cape (rĭfs'toung'gĭ). Cape, NE Iceland, W of Raufarhöfn.

Rift Valley. = GREAT RIFT VALLEY.

Rift Valley Province (rĭft). Province, W Kenya colony, E Africa; ⊛ Nakuru.

Ri'ga (rē'gȧ); *Lettish* **Rī'ga** (rē'gä); *Russ.* **Ri'ga** (ryē'-gȧ). **1** Administrative district, SW Vidzeme prov., N Latvia; 2493 sq. m.; exclusive of Riga City.
2 Manufacturing city and commercial seaport, ⊛ of Latvia and of Vidzeme prov., Latvia, at S extremity of the Gulf of Riga on the Dvina river 8 m. above its mouth; 81 sq. m.; pop. (1938 est.) 385,864; manufactures paper, wood products, paints, machinery, textiles, shoes, cement, and rubber goods; exports flax, skins and hides, dairy produce, timber, and meats. Old town has some Hanseatic warehouses, several churches, a castle, and the Livonian Ritterhaus, remaining from the medieval period. Has national university established 1919, formerly the Riga Polytechnic Institute, and modern suburbs on both sides of the river. Formerly chief Russian Baltic port; Daugavgriva (*q.v.*) at Dvina mouth serves as its port for large vessels.

History: Founded 1158; established as a trading settlement 1201 by Bishop of Livonia and joined Hanseatic League 1282; fought over by Poles and Russians and burned 1558 in Livonian War (see LIVONIA); fell under Polish domination 1581; taken over by Gustavus Adolphus of Sweden 1621 and granted self-government; ceded to Peter the Great of Russia 1710 after the defeat at Poltava of Charles XII of Sweden; port closed 1915 in World War I; evacuated by Russians 1915; occupied by Germans 1917; independence of Latvia proclaimed at Riga Nov. 1918; independence recognized by Russia in treaty signed here Aug. 11, 1920; in World War II taken by Germans June 29, 1941 and retaken by Russian armies Oct. 13, 1944.

Riga, Gulf of. Inlet of NE Baltic Sea extending S into N coast of Latvia, ab. 100 m. long by 60 m. wide; receives the Dvina river.

Ri'gas Jūr'ma·la (rē'gäs yōōr'mä·lä); *Ger.* **Ri'ga-Strand** (rē'gä-shtränt'). Town, SW Vidzeme prov., Latvia, a W suburb of Riga; pop. (1935) 7863; seaside resort.

Rig'by (rĭg'bĭ). City, ⊗ of Jefferson co., E Idaho, 15 m. NE of Idaho Falls; pop. 2281; settled by Mormons 1884; incorp. as village 1903, as city 1915; made ⊗ 1914; center of irrigated farming and dairy section; sugar beets, potatoes.

Ri'gi (rē'gē) *or* **Ri'ghi** (rē'gē). Mountain mass in cen. Switzerland, bet. Lake of Lucerne and Lake of Zug; highest peaks the **Ri'gi-Kulm'** (-kŏŏlm') 5905 ft. in NW, and **Ri'gi-Schei'degg** (-shī'dĕk) 5462 ft. in SE.

Rig'o·let' (rĭg'ō·lĕt'). Trader post and village at head of Hamilton Inlet on narrows leading to Lake Melville, SE Labrador.

Ri·i·shi·ri (rĕ·ē·shē·rē). Island in N Sea of Japan, off NW coast of island of Hokkaido, Japan.

Rijeka. See RIEKA.

Rijn. See RHINE.

Rijs'wijk (rīs'vīk); *Eng.* **Rys'wick** (rĭz'wĭk; rīz'-). Commune, South Holland prov., SW Netherlands, suburb of The Hague; pop. 15,934. The Treaty of Ryswick, signed here Sept. 20, 1697 by France with Netherlands, England, and Spain, ended War of the Palatinate bet. England and France, acknowledged William III as king of England and Anne as his successor, mutually restored conquests of England and France in America, and allowed France to retain Alsace; separate treaty signed Oct. 30, 1697 by France and the Empire.

Ri'ker's Island (rī'kērz). Island in the East river off S coast of the Bronx, New York City, New York; attached to Bronx borough; large modern penitentiary.

Ri·ku·chu (rĕ·kŏŏ·chōō). Old province, N Honshu, Japan, now Iwate prefecture.

Ri·ku·zen (rĕ·kŏŏ·zĕn). Old province, N Honshu, Japan, now part of Miyagi prefecture.

Ri'la Dagh (rē'lä dä'). Range of mountains in SW Bulgaria, at W end of the Rhodope Mts.; highest point Musala 9595 ft.; contains sources of Isker, Maritsa, and Mesta rivers.

Ri′ley (rī′lĭ). County in Kansas. See *Table* at KANSAS.

Ri·mac′ (rĕ·mäk′). River, a short mountain stream of Peru, flowing through the city of Lima into the Pacific Ocean.

Ri′ma·ta′ra (rē′mä·tä′rä). See TUBUAÏ ISLANDS.

Ri′mav·ská So′bo·ta (rĭ′máf·skä sô′bô·tȧ); *Hung.* **Ri′ma·szom′bat** (rĭ′mŏ·sŏm′bŏt). Commune, S Slovakia, Czechoslovakia, 42 m. NW of Miskolc; pop. 8026; in Hungary 1938–45.

Ri′mi·ni (rĭm′ĭ·nĭ; *Ital.* rē′mē·nė); *anc.* **A·rim′i·num** (ȧ·rĭm′ĭ·nŭm). Seaport, Forlì prov., Emilia, N Italy, on Adriatic 27 m. ESE of Forlì; pop. 64,738; 13th-cent. cathedral; 15th-cent. castle of the Malatestas; ancient Roman bridge, triumphal arch (27 B.C.), and amphitheater; mineral springs; commercial fisheries. Founded by Umbrians; under Celtic rule; became Roman colony 268 B.C.; made terminus of Flaminian Way 220 B.C.; important militarily in Second Punic War and later against Gothic invasions; under Malatesta family in Middle Ages; passed to Venetians 1503, to Papal States 1528, and to kingdom of Italy 1860. In World War II German anchor at E end of Gothic Line; taken by Allies Sept. 21, 1944.

Ri·mous′ki (rĭ·mōōs′kĭ). **1** County, Quebec, Canada. See *Table* at QUEBEC.

2 Town, its ⊗, on S bank of St. Lawrence river; pop. 11,565; port of call for ocean steamers; carries on extensive lumber trade; resort of anglers, hunters, and summer vacationists.

Rimp′fisch·horn′ (rĭmp′fĭsh·hôrn′). Peak 13,790 ft. in the Pennine Alps, in Switzerland N of Monte Rosa.

Rin·cón′ (rĕng·kôn′). **1** Peak 18,353 ft. in E Antofagasta prov., N Chile, on Argentina boundary.

2 Municipality (pop. 8706) and town (pop. 1094, W Puerto Rico; town is on coast ab. 9 m. SW of Aguadilla.

Rincón Bay. Bay in S coast of Puerto Rico.

Rin′con Peak (rĭng′kŏn). Mountain 8465 ft. in E Pima co., S Arizona.

Rin·dja′ni, Gu′nung (gōō′nŏŏng rĭn·jä′nė). Volcanic peak 12,224 ft. in N part of Lombok I., Indonesia; one of highest peaks of Malay Archipelago.

Rin′e·an′na (rĭn′ė·ăn′ȧ). Village, co. Clare, SW Eire, ab. 14 m. W of Limerick on N bank of the Shannon; site of Shannon airport, superseding that at Foynes.

Ring′gold (rĭng′gōld). **1** County in Iowa. See *Table* at IOWA.

2 City, ⊗ of Catoosa co., NW Georgia; pop. 1311.

Ring′kö′bing (rĭng′kü′bĭng). **1** County of Denmark. See *Table* at DENMARK.

2 Town, its ⊗, W Jutland Penin., Denmark, at N end of Ringköbing Fjord; pop. 4049.

Ringköbing Fjord. Lagoon on W cen. coast of Jutland, Denmark; receives Omme and Skjerne rivers.

Ring′nes′ Islands (rĭng′nās′). The Ellef Ringnes and Amund Ringnes islands of the Sverdrup Is., N Franklin District, Northwest Territories, Canada, W of Axel Heiberg I.

Ring′vass·öy′ (rĭng′väs·ú′ü). Island in Arctic Ocean off NW coast of Norway, SW of Vannöy I., in Troms co.; pop. 1371.

Ring′wood (rĭng′wŏŏd). River, N New Jersey; rises in Orange co., SE New York, flows S through Passaic co., New Jersey, and unites with Pequannock and Ramapo rivers to form Pompton river.

Rinns, the. See the RHINNS.

Rin′tja (rĭn′chä). Small island off W end of Flores I., Netherlands Indies, ESE of Komodo I.

Ri′o (rē′ō; *Span.* rē′ō; *Port.* rē′ōō). For most names of rivers beginning with Rio (Span. *Río*, Port. *Rio*, "river"), see the distinguishing element.

Ri′o (rē′ō; *Port.* rē′ōō). See RIO DE JANEIRO.

Ri′o Al′to Peak (rē′ō äl′tō). Mountain 13,573 ft. in Custer and Saguache cos., S cen. Colorado.

Ri′o Ar·ri′ba (rē′ō ȧ·rē′bȧ). County in New Mexico. See *Table* at NEW MEXICO.

Ri′o·bam′ba (rē′ō·väm′bä). City, ⁕ of Chimborazo prov., cen. Ecuador, 110 m. S of Quito and ab. 20 m. SE of Chimborazo volcano; pop. (1944 est.) 27,459; original town a few miles distant destroyed by earthquake 1797; first constitution of republic of Ecuador proclaimed here Aug. 14, 1830; seat of a superior court.

Ri′o Blan′co (rē′ō blăng′kō). County in Colorado. See *Table* at COLORADO.

Ri′o Bran′co (rē′ōō vrănng′kōō). **1** River in Brazil. See BRANCO, RIO.

2 Territory of Brazil. See *Table* at BRAZIL.

3 City, ⁕ of Acre territory, W Brazil, on Acre river; rubber, timber.

Ri′o Bra′vo (rē′ō vrä′vō) or **Río Bravo del Nor′te** (thĕl nôr′tä). Mexican name of the Rio Grande, bet. U.S. and Mexico. See RIO GRANDE.

Río Ca·ri′be (kä·rē′vä). Town, Sucre state, N Venezuela, E suburb of Carúpano; pop. (1941 est.) 6110.

Ri′o Cha′ma (rē′ō chä′má). River ab. 100 m. long, N New Mexico; rises in Conejos co., S Colorado, flows S across state border and empties into the Rio Grande in SE Rio Arriba co., N New Mexico.

Rí′o Cla′ro (rē′ō klä′rō). City, São Paulo state, SE Brazil, 90 m. NW of São Paulo; pop. 34,618.

Rí′o Cuar′to (rē′ō kwär′tō). Town, Córdoba prov., N cen. Argentina, ab. 125 m. S of Córdoba; pop. (est.) 37,786; transportation and agricultural center.

Ri′o de Ja·nei′ro (rē′ō dĕ jȧ·nā′rō; zhȧ-; -nâr′ō; -nĭr′ō; *Port.* rē′ōō t̶h̶ĕ̶ zhȧ·nā′ė·rōō). **1** State of Brazil. See *Table* at BRAZIL.

2 *colloq.* **Ri′o** (rē′ō; *Port.* rē′ōō). Commercial seaport, SE Brazil; former ⁕ of Brazil and (since 1960) of new Guanabara state; pop. 3,307,163; on SW shore of Guanabara Bay, has one of largest and most beautiful harbors in the world; built on an alluvial plain, the mountains come down to the shore of the bay in places, notably in Sugarloaf Mt. (*Port.* Pão de Açúcar) 1280

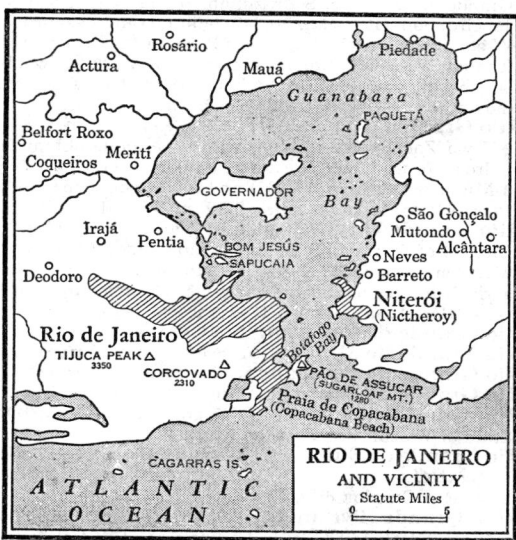

RIO DE JANEIRO
AND VICINITY
Statute Miles
0 5

ft. at the entrance to the bay and just W of it the Corcovado (*q.v.*) 2310 ft., a very sharp rocky peak; fine streets, esp. the Avenida Beira-Mar which is built along the shore; government buildings, Guanabara Palace (former residence of the president of the republic), national library, national museum, historical museum, National School of Art, botanical gardens, zoological gardens, Santos Dumont airport.

History: Guanabara Bay discovered by Portuguese in early 16th cent. (not possible to prove accuracy of traditional date, 1502); first settled by French under Villega-

gnon 1555; French settlement attacked by Portuguese 1560, French driven out 1567; settlement attacked by French 1710, 1711; became wealthy only after discovery of gold and diamonds in Minas Gerais made it natural outlet for mineral export; made capital of colonial Brazil 1763 (see SALVADOR), of empire 1822, and of republic of Brazil 1889; scene of Pan-American congress 1906.

Rio de Janeiro Bay. = GUANABARA BAY.

Ri′o Dell (rē′ō dĕl′). Urban community (unincorporated), Humboldt co., NW California, SE of Eureka; pop. 3222.

Ri′o del Rey (rē′ō dĕl rā′). Seaport and estuary on the coast of British Cameroons, W Africa, E of Cross river.

Ri′o de O′ro (rē′ō thå ō′rō). **1** Narrow bay on the coast of Río de Oro zone of Spanish Sahara, NW Africa; harbor of Villa Cisneros. **2** Southern zone of Spanish Sahara, NW Africa. See SPANISH SAHARA. **3** Name often applied to region in NW Africa now including Spanish Sahara and the former Southern Protectorate of Morocco.

Río Gallegos. See GALLEGOS.

Río Grande (rē′ō grănd′; grän′dĕ; rĭ′ō grănd′). **1** *Mex.* **Río Bra′vo** (vrä′vō) or **Río Bravo del Nor′te** (thĕl nôr′tā). River 1800 m. long, SW Colorado, cen. New Mexico, and SW and S Texas; rises in San Juan Mts. near E boundary of San Juan co., SW Colorado, flows SE, then S through San Luis Park and across cen. New Mexico, forms W and SW boundary of Texas and the Texas-Mexico boundary; the section in S part of Brewster co., Texas, includes canyons of the Big Bend National Park; empties into the Gulf of Mexico. **2** County in Colorado. See *Table* at COLORADO.

Río Gran′de (rē′ōō grănn′dĕ). **1** Name of a river in Africa and two rivers in Brazil. See RIO GRANDE. **2** or **São Pe′dro do Ri′o Gran′de do Sul** (souNm pā′thrōō thōō rē′ōō grănn′dĕ thōō sōōl′). City, SE Rio Grande do Sul state, S Brazil, ab. 780 m. SW of Rio de Janeiro; pop. (1940 est.) 50,340; built on sandy peninsula W of entrance to the Lagoa dos Patos at its S end; ab. 5 ft. above sea level; exports preserved meat, hides, woolens, beans, onions. Fort built nearby 1737; settlement moved to present site 1745; became a city 1807.

Ri′o Gran′de (rē′ō grän′då). **1** See RÍO GRANDE. **2** Town, Zacatecas state, cen. Mexico, terminus of branch railroad 70 m. NNW of Zacatecas; pop. 5111. **3** Municipality (pop. 17,233) and town (pop. 2763), NE Puerto Rico; town on railroad 19 m. ESE of San Juan.

Río Grande City (rē′ō grănd′; grän′dĕ; rĭ′ō grănd′). City, ⊗ of Starr co., S Texas, on Rio Grande 38 m. W of McAllen; pop. 5835; shipping and distribution point in agricultural region; oil and gas wells. Occupied by Spanish settlers 1753; founded 1847; incorp. 1926.

Rio Grande de Cagayan. See CAGAYAN.

Rio Grande de Mindanao. See MINDANAO river.

Rio Grande de Pampanga. See PAMPANGA river.

Río Grande de Santiago. See SANTIAGO.

Ri′o Gran′de do Nor′te (rē′ōō grănn′dĕ thōō nôr′tĕ). State of Brazil. See *Table* at BRAZIL.

Rio Grande do Sul (sōōl′). **1** State of Brazil. See *Table* at BRAZIL. **2** = RIO GRANDE city, Brazil.

Ri′o Grande Pyramid (rē′ō grănd′; grăn′dĕ; rĭ′ō grănd′). Peak 13,827 ft. in Hinsdale co., SW Colorado.

Rio Grande Reservoir. Reservoir in upper course of Rio Grande river, cen. Hinsdale co., SW Colorado.

Ri′o·ha′cha or **Rí′o Ha′cha** (rē′ō ä′chä). Seaport, W Magdalena dept., NE Colombia; pop. 5650; on W side of base of Guajira Penin. ab. 90 m. E of Santa Marta; has active trade with Curaçao. One of the oldest towns in Colombia.

Rioja, La. See LA RIOJA.

Rio Jemez. = JEMEZ RIVER.

Riom (ryôN); *anc.* **Ri·com′a·gus** (rĭ·kŏm′å·gŭs). Commune, Puy-de-Dôme dept., S cen. France, 8 m. N of

Clermont-Ferrand; pop. 11,425; ancient capital of duchy of Auvergne; site of ducal palace occupied by law courts; scene of trial Feb. 19–Apr. 2, 1942 of Édouard Daladier, Léon Blum, Maurice G. Gamelin, Pierre Jacomet, and others by the Vichy government which had set up the Supreme Court of Justice July 30, 1940 to investigate charges against leaders of the Third Republic.

Rí′o Mu′ni (rē′ō mōō′nĕ). The mainland part of Spanish Guinea, W Africa, bet. Cameroun and the Muni river; 10,040 sq. m.; pop. 138,797; chief town Bata.

Ri·on′ (ryĭ·ôn′); *anc.* **Pha′sis** (fā′sĭs). River ab. 180 m. long, W Georgia, U.S.S.R.; rises in the Caucasus Mts., flows SW and W to the Black Sea at Poti. Navigable for nearly half its course; has hydroelectric station at Kutais. The ancient Phasis famous in Greek legends concerning Colchis, the Golden Fleece, and the Argonauts; for a time held to be boundary bet. Europe and Asia.

Rí′o Ne′gro (rē′ō nā′grō). **1** River. See NEGRO, RÍO. **2** Territory of Argentina. See *Table* at ARGENTINA. **3** Department of Uruguay. See *Table* at URUGUAY.

Ri·o·ne′ro in Vul′tu·re (rē·ō·nā′rō ĕm vōōl′tōō·rå). Commune, Potenza prov., Lucania, S Italy, 21 m. N by W of Potenza; pop. 13,075.

Rí′o Pie′dras (rē′ō pyā′thräs). Former municipality (1950 pop. 143,989) and city (1950 pop. 132,438), NE Puerto Rico; annexed to San Juan 1951, forming a SE section of that city; seat of Univ. of Puerto Rico (founded 1903).

Rí′o Prê′to (rē′ōō prā′tōō). City, NW cen. São Paulo state, SE Brazil, 260 m. NW of São Paulo; pop. (1940 est.) 24,335.

Ríos, Los. See LOS RÍOS.

Rí′o·su′cio (rē′ō·sōō′syō). Town, Caldas dept., W cen. Colombia, just NW of Manizales; pop. 5801.

Rí′o Tin′to (rē′ōō tĕNN′tōō). City, Paraíba state, E Brazil; pop. (1940 est.) 14,467.

Ríotinto, Minas de. See MINAS DE RÍOTINTO.

Ri′ouw or **Ri′au** (rē′ou) or **Rhi′o** (rē′ō). **1** Another name for BINTAN island, Indonesia. **2** *officially* **Riouw and Dependencies.** Former residency in the Netherlands Indies, comprising Riouw, Lingga, and other islands, and the district of Inderagiri on the E cen. coast of Sumatra; 12,232 sq. m.

Riouw Archipelago. Group of islands in Indonesia, off SE end of the Malay Penin., separated from Singapore by Singapore Strait; 2279 sq. m.; pop. 77,149. Comprises the islands of Bintan, Batam, Rempang, the Karimun group, and smaller islands; all, including Singapore I. (*q.v.*), were once part of Johore sultanate. Occupied by Japanese 1942.

Rí′o Ver′de or **Rí′o·ver′de** (rē′ō·vĕr′thå). Town, San Luis Potosí state, cen. Mexico, 65 m. E of San Luis Potosí; pop. 8503.

Ri′o Vis′ta (rē′ō vĭs′tå). Town, Solano co., cen. California, on Sacramento river 32 m. SSW of Sacramento; pop. 2616; founded 1857; pipes natural gas.

Rip′ley (rĭp′lĭ). **1** Name of counties in two states of the U.S. See *Tables* at INDIANA and MISSOURI. **2** City, ⊗ of Tippah co., N Mississippi, 28 m. SW of Corinth; pop. 2668. **3** Village, Chautauqua co., SW corner of New York, on Lake Erie near Pennsylvania border ab. 27 m. NW of Jamestown; pop. 1247; formerly the Gretna Green of New York state. **4** Village, Brown co., SW Ohio, on Ohio river 42 m. SE of Cincinnati; pop. 2174; station on Underground Railroad; tobacco warehouses and factories, shoe factories. **5** Town, ⊗ of Lauderdale co., W Tennessee, 23 m. S of Dyersburg; pop. 3782; manufactures veneer, lumber, cottonseed products. **6** Town, ⊗ of Jackson co., W West Virginia; pop. 2756. **7** Urban district, Derbyshire, N cen. England, 10 m. NNE of Derby; pop. 18,194.

Rip′on (rĭp′ŭn). **1** City, Fond du Lac co., E Wisconsin, 20 m. W of Fond du Lac; pop. 6163; site of a Fourieristic

communistic community 1844–50; reputed birthplace of the Republican party, in a meeting Mar. 20, 1854, of Whigs, anti-Nebraska Democrats, and Free Soilers. Ripon Coll. (1851; coed.; Congregational).

2 Municipal borough, West Riding, Yorkshire, N England, on the Ure 23 m. N of Leeds; pop. 9464; trade center in agricultural section; watering place; 12th-cent. Norman cathedral with 7th-cent. Saxon remnants. Fountains Abbey ruins are at Studley Royal nearby.

Ripon Falls. Former waterfall in the Victoria Nile near where it issues from Lake Victoria, Uganda, SE cen. Africa; now submerged by Owen Falls Dam.

Ri·po′sto (rē-pôs′tō). Seaport, Catania prov., E Sicily, on E coast of Sicily 18 m. NNE of Catania; pop. 11,594.

Rip′pold·sau′ (rĭp′ôlt·zou′). Village, Baden-Württemberg, Germany, in Black Forest ab. 22 m. S of Baden-Baden; watering place.

Rip′shin′ Ridge (rĭp′shĭn′). Elevation 4500 ft. in Carter co., NE Tennessee.

Ris′ca (rĭs′kȧ). Urban district, Monmouthshire, W England, on the Ebbw river 26 m. WNW of Bristol; pop. 15,131.

Ris′don (rĭz′dŭn). Suburb of Hobart, Tasmania, Australia, ab. 4 m. above it on the left bank of the Derwent. First settled 1803 by English navy lieutenant, John Bowen, but settlement moved across the river 1804 and name changed to Hobart.

Rish′ra (rĭsh′rȧ). Town, Hooghly dist., West Bengal, Indian Union, on right bank of Hooghly river 12 m. N of Calcutta; site of first power mill for spinning jute yarns set up in India 1855.

Rishra Kon′na·gar (kŏn′ȧ·gēr). Town, West Bengal, NE Indian Union, 52 m. W of Calcutta; pop. 26,868.

Rish′ton (rĭsh′tŭn). Urban district, Lancashire, NW England, 22 m. NNW of Manchester; pop. 5794; paper mills.

Ris′ing Sun (rīz′ĭng). City, ⊗ of Ohio co., SE Indiana, on Ohio river 60 m. SE of Shelbyville; pop. 2230.

Rising Wolf Mountain. Peak 9505 ft. in Glacier National Park, NW Montana.

Ri′son (rī′z′n). Commercial city, ⊗ of Cleveland co., S Arkansas; pop. 889.

Rist′na, Cape (rĭst′nȧ); _Russ._ **Rist′na** (ryēst′nȧ). Western point of Hiiumaa I., W of Estonia.

Ritch′ie (rĭch′ĭ). County in West Virginia. See _Table_ at WEST VIRGINIA.

Ritch′ie's Archipelago (rĭch′ĭz). Island group in Andaman Is., Indian Union, E of South Andaman I.; largest islands Havelock, Henry Lawrence, and Neill.

Ri′to Al′to Peak (rē′tō ăl′tō). Mountain 13,573 ft. bet. Saguache and Custer cos.. Colorado, in the Sangre de Cristo Mts.

Rit′ter, Mount (rĭt′ēr). Peak 13,156 ft. in Sierra Nevada, in NE Madera co., cen. California.

Ritt′man (rĭt′măn). Village, Wayne co., NE cen. Ohio, 15 m. SW of Akron; pop. 5410.

Ritz′ville (rĭts′vĭl). City, ⊗ of Adams co., E Washington, 60 m. SW of Spokane; pop. 2173; milling and shipping center of wheat country.

Riukiu. Var. of RYUKYU.

Ri′va (rē′vä). Commune, Trento prov., Venezia Tridentina, NE Italy, at N end of Lake Garda 19 m. SW of Trent; pop. 10,426; palaces of 14th and 15th cents.; sericulture; fisheries; tourist resort.

Ri′va·da′via (rē′vä·thä′vyä). **1** See COMODORO RIVADAVIA.

2 Town, Mendoza prov., W Argentina, just SE of Mendoza; pop. 6375.

Ri·van′na (rĭ·văn′ȧ). River ab. 65 m. long, cen. Virginia; rises in Blue Ridge Mts., flows E and SE into James river on SE boundary of Fluvanna co.

Ri·va·ro′lo Li′gu·re (rē·vä·rô′lō lē′gōō·rȧ). Former commune in NW Italy, now a NW suburb of Genoa.

Ri′vas (rē′väs). **1** Department, SW Nicaragua; 849 sq. m.; pop. (1943 est.) 54,265.

2 Town, its ✳, on W shore of Lake Nicaragua; pop. (1943 est.) 6935.

Rive-de-Gier (rēv′dē·zhyā′). Industrial commune, Loire dept., SE cen. France, 13 m. NE of Saint-Étienne; pop. 14,483; coal mines.

Ri·ve′ra (rē·vä′rä) **1** Department of Uruguay. See _Table_ at URUGUAY.

2 Town, its ✳, N Uruguay, on Brazil border opp. Livramento, ab. 270 m. N of Montevideo; pop. ab. 17,000.

Riv′er Cess (rĭv′ēr sĕs′). Coastal town, SW Liberia, W Africa, in cen. part of coast SE of Grand Bassa.

Riv′er·dale′ (rĭv′ēr·dāl′). **1** Village, Cook co., NE Illinois, 14 m. S of Chicago; pop. 12,008.

2 Town, Prince Georges co., S cen. Maryland, 8 m. NE of Washington; pop. 4389.

River Edge. Borough, Bergen co., NE corner of New Jersey, 4 m. N of Hackensack; pop. 13,264.

River Falls. City, Pierce and St. Croix cos., W Wisconsin, 12 m. NE of confluence of Mississippi and St. Croix rivers; pop. 4857. Wisconsin State Coll. (1874; coed.).

River Forest. Residential village, Cook co., NE Illinois, 16 m. W of Chicago; pop. 12,695. Rosary Coll. (1848; women); Concordia Teachers Coll. (1864; coed.).

River Grove. Village, Cook co., NE Illinois, 10 m. NW of Chicago; pop. 8464.

Riv′er·head′ (rĭv′ēr·hĕd′). Locality, ⊗ of Suffolk co., SE New York, at E end of Long I. on the Peconic river; pop. 5830; in agricultural (potatoes, cauliflower) and duck-raising country; important radio receiving station. Settled 1690; near scene of skirmish bet. British and Americans in War of 1812; became ⊗ 1929.

Riv′er·i′na (rĭv′ēr·ī′nȧ). District, S New South Wales, SE Australia; 26,600 sq. m.; bounded on N by Murrumbidgee river and on S by Murray river; chief towns Albury and Wagga Wagga; flat fertile land, important for agriculture since development of irrigation; sheep and wheat in W portion.

River Junction. Former name of town of CHATTAHOOCHEE, Florida; named changed 1941.

River Oaks. City, Tarrant co., NE Texas, NW suburb of Fort Worth; pop. 8444.

River of Doubt. = Rio ROOSEVELT.

River Point. Village, Kent co., cen. Rhode Island, ab. 7 m. SW of Cranston; governmental center of West Warwick town; textile, soap manufactures.

River Rouge (rōōzh′). Industrial city, Wayne co., SE Michigan, on Detroit river 6 m. SW of Detroit; pop. 18,147; automobiles, marine engines; shipbuilding.

Riv′ers·dale′ (rĭv′ērz·dāl′). Town, S Cape Province, S Union of South Africa, 165 m. E of Cape Town; pop. 4160; in farm country.

Riv′er·side′ (rĭv′ēr·sīd′). **1** County in California. See _Table_ at CALIFORNIA.

2 Residential, resort, and commercial city, ⊗ of Riverside co., SE California, 10 m. SSW of San Bernardino; pop. 84,332; in irrigated region producing citrus and deciduous fruits; manufactures fruit-packing, canning, and spraying equipment. U.S. Air Force base (March Field); Subtropical Agricultural Station of Univ. of California. Founded 1870, incorp. 1886. See Mount RUBIDOUX.

3 Subdivision of town of GREENWICH, Connecticut.

4 Residential village, Cook co., NE Illinois, 8 m. W of Chicago; pop. 9750.

5 Resort town, Burlington co., S cen. New Jersey, on Delaware river 10 m. NE of Camden; pop. (1950) 7199.

6 Village, Providence co., N Rhode Island, ab. 5 m. SE of Providence in town of East Providence; pop. (est.) 12,000.

7 Town, Essex co.. SE Ontario Canada, on Detroit river opp. Detroit; pop. 9214.

Riv′er·ton (rĭv′ēr·t′n; -tŭn). **1** Village, Sangamon co.. cen. Illinois, 8 m. ENE of Springfield; pop. 1536.

2 Borough, Burlington co., S cen. New Jersey, on Delaware river 8 m. NE of Camden; pop. 3324.

3 City, Fremont co., cen. Wyoming, 25 m. NE of Lan-

der; pop. 6845; in irrigated section producing sugar beets, grain, alfalfa, honey.

Riv·er·view′ (rĭv′ẽr-vū′). City, Wayne co., SE Michigan, S suburb of Detroit; pop. 7237.

Rives′altes′ (rēv′zȧlt′). Town, Pyrénées-Orientales dept., S France, 5 m. N of Perpignan; pop. 4917.

Rives′ville (rēvz′vĭl; rēz′-). Town, Marion co., N West Virginia, 4 m. N of Fairmont; pop. 1191; coal mining.

Ri·vier′a Beach (rĭ·vẽr′ȧ). Town, Palm Beach co., SE Florida, just N of West Palm Beach; pop. 13,046.

Ri·vie′ra (rĭ·vyâ′rä; Angl. rĭv′ĭ·ȧr′ȧ). Beautiful region bordering on Mediterranean Sea in SE France and NW Italy, esp. the coast extending from Cannes to La Spezia. The Italian Riviera is divided into **Riviera di Po·nen′te** (dĕ pō·nĕn′tä) W of Genoa, and **Riviera di Le·van′te** (lā·vän′tä) E of Genoa; the French Riviera is also called **Côte d'A′zur′** (kōt′ dȧ′zür′). See CORNICHE.

Ri·vière′ du Loup (rē′vyâr′ dü lōō′). 1 County, part of Témiscouata co., S Quebec, Canada. See TÉMISCOUATA. 2 City, its ⊗, on Rivière du Loup just above its confluence with St. Lawrence river; pop. 9425; important railroad center and popular summer resort.

Rivière du Mou′lin′ (dü mōō′lăɴ′). Village, Chicoutimi co., S Quebec, Canada, on Saguenay river just E of Chicoutimi; pop. 2580.

Ri·vière′ Noire, Pi′ton′ de la (pē′tôɴd′ lä rē·vyâr′ nwâr′). Highest mountain in Mauritius, in SW part; 2730 ft.

Ri·vière′ Sa′lée′ (rē′vyâr′ sȧ·lā′). Strait 4 m. long extending bet. Basse-Terre and Grande Terre, Guadeloupe, West Indies.

Rivières du Sud. See FRENCH GUINEA.

Ri′vo·li (rē′vō·lĕ; Angl. rĭv′ō-). Commune, Torino prov., Piedmont, NW Italy, 8 m. W of Turin; pop. 10,939.

Rivoli Ve·ro·ne′se (vā·rō·nā′sä). Commune, Verona prov., Venezia Euganea, NE Italy, on Adige river 14 m. NW of Verona; pop. 1586; scene of victory of Napoleon over Austrians Jan. 15, 1797.

Rix′höft, Cape (rĭks′höft). Cape projecting into the Baltic Sea on coast of Poland, opp. Brüster Ort at entrance to Bay of Danzig; just W of base of Hel Penin.

Ri·yadh′ (rĭ·yäd′). City, ✳ of Nejd and a ✳ of Saudi Arabia, in E cen. part ab. 235 m. from Persian Gulf; pop. 150,000; at an oasis; enclosed by walls; on the pilgrimage road bet. Mecca and Iran; contains royal palace, great mosque, and many smaller mosques.

Ri·yaq′ (rĭ·yäk′); formerly **Ra·yak′** (rȯ·yäk′). Town, E Lebanon Republic, on railroad just E of Zahle.

Riyeka. Var. of RIEKA.

Ri·za′i·yeh′ (rē·zä′ē·yȧ′) or **Re·za′i·eh′** (rȧ·zä′ē·yȧ′); formerly **Ur′mi·a** (ŏŏr′mĭ·ȧ; Pers. ŏŏr′mē·yȧ′). City, NW Iran, in Azerbaijan prov. W of Lake Urmia; pop. (est.) 50,000; in fertile region, raising esp. fruits and tobacco; has ancient Nestorian church and American Mission college. Reputed birthplace of Zoroaster.

Ri·zal′ (rĭ·säl′; Angl. rĭ·zäl′). 1 Province, cen. Luzon, Phil. Is.; 791 sq. m.; pop. 444,805; ✳ Pasig; includes geographically but not administratively the cities of Manila and Quezon. Bounded on the N by Bulacan, on E by Tayabas and Laguna, on S by Laguna de Bay, on SW by Cavite, and on W by Manila Bay. Along Manila Bay and the Pasig land is low and flat; in the E part are hills and low mountain ranges. The main stream of the province is the Pasig, flowing NNW from the Laguna de Bay across SW part and through the City of Manila to Manila Bay; other streams flow S or SW to the Laguna de Bay or to the Pasig, the most important being the Marikina (and Montalban). On the S marked by two large arms of Laguna de Bay separated by peninsula ending in Tipao Point and by Talim I. Has fertile soil and raises many different products. Poultry and livestock raising is important, also fishing. Inhabitants are Tagalogs. Chief towns Pasig, Pasay, Quezon City, Caloocan, Makati.

History: Created June 1901 out of the former Spanish military district of Morong and several towns of the for-

mer province of Manila. These regions contained some of the oldest towns in the Philippines that were prosperous settlements before the arrival of the Spaniards; their history closely connected with that of Manila. Caloocan, Pasig, and other places were scenes of first outbreaks of Revolution of 1896. See MANILA.
2 Municipality, NE Nueva Ecija prov., Luzon, Phil. Is., on upper Pampanga river 18 m. NE of Cabanatuan; pop. 15,936.
3 Municipality, Rizal prov., Luzon, Phil. Is. See PASAY.

Ri·ze′ (rē·zĕ′) or **Ço·ruh′** (chō·rōōk′). Seaport, ✳ of Çoruh vilayet, NE Turkey in Asia, on the Black Sea ab. 40 m. E of Trabzon; pop. 13,861.

Riz·zu′to, Cape (rĭ·zōō′tō; Ital. rĕt·tsōō′tō). Cape on E coast of Calabria compartimento, S Italy, projecting into Ionian Sea N of Gulf of Squillace.

Rju′kan (ryōō′kän). 1 Waterfall 780 ft. high in Telemark co., S Norway.
2 Town, Telemark co., S Norway, 75 m. W of Oslo; pop. 7881; industrial center; its nitrate and hydroelectric plants destroyed 1943 during World War II; has postwar plant for making heavy water.

Road′ Town′. Town on Tortola I. in the British Virgin Is., Leeward Is., Brit. West Indies; ✳ of Virgin Is.; pop. (1941 est.) 700.

Roag, Loch (lŏk rōg′). Inlet of Atlantic Ocean on W coast of island of Lewis with Harris, in the Outer Hebrides, off NW coast of Scotland.

Roane (rōn). Name of counties in two states of the U.S. See *Tables* at TENNESSEE and WEST VIRGINIA.

Roan High Knob (rōn). Peak 6285 ft. in Mitchell co., W North Carolina, on the Tennessee border.

Ro′anne′ (rō′ȧn′); anc. **Ro·dum′na** (rō·dŭm′nȧ). Manufacturing commune, Loire dept., SE cen. France, on Loire river 45 m. NNW of Saint-Étienne; pop. 41,460; coal mining; foundries, potteries, textile mills.

Ro′a·noke (rō′ȧ·nōk). 1 River 380 m. long in S Virginia and NE North Carolina; navigable for 200 m.; formed by confluence of forks in Montgomery co., western Virginia, flows E and SE across North Carolina border in NE Warren co., and continues SE into Albemarle Sound.
2 County in Virginia. See *Table* at VIRGINIA.
3 City, Randolph co., E Alabama, 5 m. W of Georgia border and 35 m. NE of Martin Lake; pop. 5288; cotton products; overalls.
4 City, Roanoke co., W cen. Virginia, but politically independent, 148 m. W of Richmond; 11 sq. m.; pop. 97,110; in bowl bet. Blue Ridge Mts. and Allegheny Mts.; railroad center; tourist resort; manufactures rayon and textiles, iron and foundry products, canned foods, structural steel, chemicals, furniture. Laid out 1834; incorp. as town 1874, as city 1884.

Roanoke Island. Island 12 m. long near S entrance to Albemarle Sound, Dare co., North Carolina; Manteo, ⊗ of Dare co., is on it; at N end is Fort Raleigh, site of first English settlement in North America 1585, established by Sir Walter Raleigh, remained only ten months; site of a second colony July 1587 with Capt. John White appointed governor by Raleigh; by 1591 all the colonists had vanished; during the Civil War island captured Feb. 8, 1862 by the Federals under Gen. Burnside. See CROATAN.

Roanoke Rapids. Industrial city, Halifax co., NE North Carolina, 35 m. NNE of Rocky Mount; pop. 13,320; knitting, damask, and paper mills.

Roanoke Sound. Inlet of Atlantic Ocean bet. Roanoke I. and Bodie I. off NE coast of North Carolina.

Roar′ing Spring (rōr′ĭng). Borough, Blair co., S cen. Pennsylvania, 13 m. S of Altoona; pop. 2937.

Ro·a·tán′ (rō·ä·tän′). 1 Island 30 m. long, largest of the Bay Is., in the Caribbean Sea N of N cen. Honduras.
2 or **Cox′in's Hole** (kŏk′s′nz). Town on Roatán I.; ✳ of Islas de la Bahía dept., Honduras; pop. (1935) 904; exports coconuts and bananas.

Roazon. See RENNES.

Rob′bins (rŏb′ĭnz). Village, Cook co., NE Illinois, S suburb of Chicago; pop. 7511.

Rob′bins·dale (rŏb′ĭnz·dāl). City, Hennepin co., SE cen. Minnesota, 5 m. NW of Minneapolis; pop. 16,381.

Rob′bins·ville (rŏb′ĭnz·vĭl; *Sou.* also -v′l). Town and mountain resort, ⊗ of Graham co., W North Carolina; pop. 587.

Robenhausen. See PFÄFFIKON.

Rob′ert Lee (rŏb′ẽrt lē′). City, ⊗ of Coke co., W cen. Texas; pop. 990.

Rob′erts (rŏb′ẽrts). Name of counties in two states of the U.S. See *Tables* at SOUTH DAKOTA and TEXAS.

Roberts, Point. See POINT ROBERTS.

Rob′erts·dale′ (rŏb′ẽrts·dāl′). Locality, Huntingdon co., S cen. Pennsylvania, ab. 27 m. SE of Altoona; pop. (est.) 800.

Rob′ert·son (rŏb′ẽrt·s′n). **1** Name of counties in three states in the U.S. See *Tables* at KENTUCKY, TENNESSEE, TEXAS.
2 Town, SW Cape Province, S Union of South Africa, in the Breede river valley in Little Karroo 85 m. E of Cape Town; pop. 4945.

Rob′erts·port′ (rŏb′ẽrts·pôrt′). Seaport, NW Liberia, W Africa, NW of Monrovia and SE of mouth of Mano river.

Ro′ber·val′ (rô′bẽr′vàl′). Town, ⊗ of West Lake St. John co., Quebec, Canada, on W shore of Lake St. John; pop. 4897; center for vacationists and sportsmen.

Rob′e·son (rŏb′ē̇·s′n). County in North Carolina. See *Table* at NORTH CAROLINA.

Robe′son Channel (rōb′s′n). North section of passage bet. Ellesmere I. and Greenland, extending NE to Lincoln Sea.

Rob′e·so′nia (rŏb′ē̇·sōn′yȧ). Borough, Berks co., SE Pennsylvania, W of Reading; pop. 1579; textile mills.

Rob′in·son (rŏb′ĭn·s′n). City, ⊗ of Crawford co., E Illinois, 28 m. NE of Olney; pop. 7226.

Robinson, Camp Joseph T. Military reservation, Pulaski co., cen. Arkansas, N of Little Rock; during World War I known as Camp Pike.

Rob′ins Point (rŏb′ĭnz). Point at S tip of Harford co., NE Maryland, extending into upper Chesapeake Bay.

Rob′son, Mount (rŏb′s′n). Peak 12,972 ft. in Mount Robson Park, E British Columbia, Canada; highest of the Rocky Mts. in Canada.

Robs′town (rŏbz′toun). City, Nueces co., S Texas, 15 m. W of Corpus Christi; pop. 10,266; in agricultural section.

Ro′by (rō′bĭ). City, ⊗ of Fisher co., NW cen. Texas; pop. 913.

Ro′ca, Cape (rō′kȧ); *Port.* **Ca′bo da Roca** (kä′vōō thä). Cape on SW cen. coast of Portugal, long. 9°30′W; westernmost point in continental Europe.

Ro′ca·fuer′te (rrō′kä·fwẽr′tä). Town, Manabí prov., W Ecuador, near coast 100 m. NW of Guayaquil; pop. (1944 est.) 14,125.

Ro′ca Par·ti′da (rrō′kä pär·tē′thä). Westernmost island of the Revilla Gigedo group (*q.v.*) in the Pacific Ocean off cen. Mexico.

Ro′cas (rō′käs). Island in the Atlantic Ocean 125 m. NE of Cape São Roque, NE Brazil, 33°45′W, 3°55′S; belongs to Brazil.

Roc′ca·bru′na (rôk′kä·brōō′nä). Italian form of ROQUEBRUNE.

Roc′ca·stra′da (rôk′kä·strä′dä). Commune, Grosseto prov., Tuscany, cen. Italy, 17 m. N by E of Grosseto; pop. 11,431.

Roch (rŏch). River 12 m. long, Lancashire, NW England; rises near Yorkshire border, flows SW into the Irwell S of Bury.

Ro′cha (rrō′chä). **1** Department of Uruguay. See *Table* at URUGUAY.
2 City, its ✳, SE Uruguay, 100 m. E of Montevideo; pop. ab. 25,000.

Roch′dale (rŏch′dāl). County borough, Lancashire, NW England, on the Roch 10 m. NNE of Manchester; pop.

87,734; manufactures cotton and woolen goods; scene of an experiment in co-operative marketing 1844 embodying what have become known as the Rochdale principles.

Roche′fort′ (rôsh′fôr′). **1** Town, Namur prov., SE Belgium, 15 m. SE of Dinant; pop. 3436; in World War II taken by Germans in their sudden advance of Dec. 1944; retaken by Allies Dec. 30.
2 *unofficially* **Rochefort–sur–Mer** (-sür·mâr′). Fortified city, Charente-Maritime dept., W France, on Charente river 19 m. SSE of La Rochelle; pop. 29,482; near Bay of Biscay; naval station since 1666; military and commercial harbors; large arsenal; shipyards, metal foundries; tile, beer, candles, sailors′ clothing.

Roche–la–Mo′lière′ (rôsh′lä·mô′lyâr′). Commune, Loire dept., SE cen. France, ab. 2 m. from St-Étienne; pop. (1931) 9658; coal mines.

Ro·chelle′ (rô·shĕl′). City, Ogle co., N Illinois, 25 m. S of Rockford; pop. 7008.

Rochelle, La. See LA ROCHELLE, France.

Ro·chelle′ Park (rô·shĕl′). Urban township, Bergen co., NE corner of New Jersey, E of Paterson; pop. 6119.

Rochers du Calvados. See CALVADOS REEF.

Roch′es·ter (rŏch′ĕs′tẽr; -ĭs·tẽr). **1** City, ⊗ of Fulton co., N Indiana, 40 m. S of South Bend; pop. 4883; founded 1831; resort center on Lake Manitou.
2 Residential village, Oakland co., SE Michigan, 9 m. E of Pontiac; pop. 5431.
3 City, ⊗ of Olmsted co., SE Minnesota, 70 m. SSE of St. Paul; pop. 40,663; in agricultural section; seat of the Mayo clinic, established 1889 by Dr. William James Mayo and his brother Dr. Charles Horace Mayo, one of the most widely known medical centers in the world.
4 Manufacturing city, Strafford co., SE New Hampshire, 9 m. NNW of Dover; pop. 15,927; incorp. as town 1722, as city 1891; woolen goods, shoes, fiberboard, brick.
5 Manufacturing city and port of entry, ⊗ of Monroe co., W New York, 70 m. ENE of Buffalo; pop. 318,611; on New York State Barge Canal; bisected by Genesee river; coal-shipping port, freight terminal, and point of call for passenger steamers; formerly important flour-milling center, later known for extensive nurseries and seed houses; manufactures cameras and photographic supplies, shoes, fiberboard, canned foods, optical goods, thermometers, glass-lined steel tanks, carbon paper and typewriter ribbon, check protectors, dental equipment, telephone apparatus and radios. Rochester Institute of Technology (1829; coed.), Univ. of Rochester (1850; coed.) and its Eastman School of Music and Eastman Theater (founded 1918; opened 1922), Colgate-Rochester Divinity School (merger 1928 of Colgate Theological Seminary, Hamilton, 1817, and Rochester Theological Seminary, 1850), Nazareth Coll. (1924; women).
History: First permanent white settlement 1812; incorp. as village 1817, as city 1834; cradle of modern spiritualism 1848 ("Rochester knockings" of Fox sisters); center of abolition movement and station on Underground Railroad.
6 Residential borough, Beaver co., W Pennsylvania, on Ohio river 23 m. NW of Pittsburgh; pop. 5952.
7 *anc.* **Du′ro·bri′vae** (dūr′ô·brī′vē). City and municipal borough, Kent, SE England, on the Medway 28 m. ESE of London; pop. 43,899; cathedral. Nearby is Gadshill (*q.v.*), the home of Charles Dickens.

Roche–sur–Yon, La. See LA ROCHE-SUR-YON.

Rock (rŏk). **1** River 300 m. long, S Wisconsin and N Illinois; rises in Washington co., SE Wisconsin, flows S and SW across NW corner of Illinois, and empties into the Mississippi in W Rock Island co., NW Illinois.
2 Name of counties in three states of the U.S. See *Tables* at MINNESOTA, NEBRASKA, WISCONSIN.

Rock, the. 1 = Rock of GIBRALTAR.
2 = CORREGIDOR—a colloquial name frequently used during World War II.

Rock′all (rŏk′ôl). Tiny rock island in North Atlantic Ocean, ab. 250 m. NW of Ireland, in 57°36′N, 13°41′W.

Rock′a·way′ (rŏk′á·wā′). Borough, Morris co., N New Jersey, 8 m. N of Morristown; pop. 5413; formerly center of iron-mining district; bleaching, printing, and dye works, rolling mills, tanneries.

Rockaway Beach. Beach on S shore of Long I., in the borough of Queens, New York City, New York; on the narrow peninsula which shelters Jamaica Bay from the Atlantic.

Rockaway Inlet. Channel on S shore at W end of Long I., New York, connecting Jamaica Bay with the Atlantic; crossed by the Marine Parkway Bridge (540-foot lift span), joining Brooklyn with Rockaway Beach.

Rock′bridge′ (rŏk′brĭj′). County in Virginia. See *Table* at VIRGINIA.

Rock′cas′tle (rŏk′kås″l). County in Kentucky. See *Table* at KENTUCKY.

Rock′chuck′, Mount (rŏk′chŭk′). Peak 11,150 ft. in cen. Grand Teton National Park, NW Wyoming.

Rock Creek Butte. Peak 9097 ft. highest in Blue Mts., NE Oregon, in Baker co.

Rock′dale (rŏk′dāl). **1** County in Georgia. See *Table* at GEORGIA.
2 Village, Will co., NE Illinois, suburb WSW of Joliet; pop. 1272.
3 City, Milam co., cen. Texas, 33 m. W of Bryan; pop. 4481; oil refining, cottonseed processing; ships lignite.
4 City, E New South Wales, SE Australia, S suburb of Sydney on W shore of Botany Bay; pop. 39,123.

Rock′e·fel′ler Plateau (rŏk′ĕ·fĕl′ẽr; rŏk′fĕl′ẽr). Elevated region at ab. 80°S lat., 135°W long., in Marie Byrd Land, E of Ross Dependency, Antarctica; averages 2500 ft. to 4500 ft. Discovered 1934.

Rock Falls. City Whiteside co., NW Illinois, 50 m. SW of Rockford; pop. 10,261.

Rock′ford (rŏk′fẽrd). **1** Town, ⊗ of Coosa co., E cen. Alabama; pop. 328; Indian relics.
2 City, ⊗ of Winnebago co., N Illinois, 65 m. W of Waukegan; pop. 126,706; settled 1834, incorp. as town 1839, as city 1853; manufactures farm implements, machine tools, cement, artificial stone, furniture. Rockford Coll. (coed.; founded as seminary 1847, chartered as college 1892).
3 City, Kent co., W Michigan, 13 m. NNE of Grand Rapids; pop. 2074; tanneries, shoe factories.

Rock·hamp′ton (rŏk·hăm[p]′tŭn). City, E Queensland, Australia, on Fitzroy river 325 m. NNW of Brisbane; pop. 29,373; distribution and shipping point for extensive dairying and farming region and mining district; has port facilities for smaller steamers.

Rock Hill **1** City, St. Louis co., E Missouri, 9 m. W of St. Louis; pop. 6523.
2 City, York co., N South Carolina, 64 m. N of Columbia; pop. 29,404; manufactures cotton textiles, cottonseed oil, automobile bodies, hosiery. Winthrop Coll., state college for women (1886 in Columbia; transferred 1895).

Rockies. See ROCKY MOUNTAINS.

Rock′ing·ham (rŏk′ĭng·hăm). **1** Name of counties in three states of the U.S. See *Tables* at NEW HAMPSHIRE, NORTH CAROLINA, VIRGINIA.
2 Town, ⊗ of Richmond co., S North Carolina, 52 m. W of Fayetteville; pop. 5512; produces esp. cotton and peaches; manufactures cotton, lumber, paper specialties.
3 Village in Rockingham town (pop. 5704), Windham co., SE corner of Vermont.

Rock Is′land (rŏk′ ī′lănd). **1** County in Illinois. See *Table* at ILLINOIS.
2 City, its ⊗, NW Illinois, on the Mississippi river 78 m. NW of Peoria; pop. 51,863; commercial and industrial city, railroad center, and river port; settled 1826, incorp. as city 1849; manufactures farm machinery, hardware, electrical equipment, oil burners, furnaces, stoves; United States arsenal (estab. 1862). Augustana Coll. and Theological Seminary (1860; coed.; Lutheran).
3 Village, Stanstead co., S Quebec, Canada, on Vermont

border 34 m. SSW of Sherbrooke; pop. 1646; forms single community with Stanstead village and Derby Line, Vt.

Rock′land (rŏk′lănd). **1** County in New York. See *Table* at NEW YORK.
2 City, ⊗ of Knox co., S Maine, on W shore of Penobscot Bay 37 m. ESE of Augusta; pop. 8769; center of Penobscot Bay resort area; yachting, motorboating, deep-sea fishing; granite quarries nearby.
3 Industrial town, Plymouth co., SE Massachusetts, 6 m. ENE of Brockton; pop. 13,119; shoe factories.
4 Town, Russell co., SE Ontario, Canada, on Ottawa river 20 m. ENE of Ottawa; pop. 2348; produces lumber.

Rock′ledge (rŏk′lĕj). Borough, Montgomery co., SE Pennsylvania, 10 m. NNE of Philadelphia; pop. 2587.

Rock′mart (rŏk′märt). City, Polk co., NW Georgia, 18 m. SSE of Rome; pop. 3938.

Rock′port (rŏk′pōrt). **1** City, ⊗ of Spencer co., SW Indiana, on Ohio river 28 m. E of Evansville; pop. 2474.
2 Town, Knox co., S Maine, on W shore of Penobscot Bay 37 m. E of Augusta; pop. 1893.
3 Town, Essex co., NE corner of Massachusetts, on Atlantic Ocean 30 m. NE of Boston; pop. 4616; summer resort, artist colony, fishing center; granite quarries.
4 City, ⊗ of Atchison co., NW corner of Missouri; pop. 1310.
5 City and resort, ⊗ of Aransas co., S Texas, on Aransas Bay 28 m. NE of Corpus Christi; pop. 2989; fish, shrimp, oyster industry; tourist trade; boatbuilding.

Rock Rapids. City, ⊗ of Lyon co., NW corner of Iowa, 63 m. N of Sioux City; pop. 2780; in an agricultural and dairy section.

Rock River. See ROCK.

Rocks Point (rŏks). Cape on NW coast of South I., New Zealand, at N end of Karamea Bight.

Rock′springs′ (rŏk′sprĭngz′). Town, ⊗ of Edwards co., SW cen. Texas; pop. 1182.

Rock Springs. City, Sweetwater co., SW Wyoming, 40 m. N of Utah border; pop. 10,371; coal mines; supply point for hunting and fishing parties in nearby mountains.

Rock′stand Knob (rŏk′stănd). Peak 6002 ft. in W North Carolina.

Rock′stone (rŏk′stōn). Town, N British Guiana, in Essequibo co. on E bank of the Essequibo river 58 m. S of Georgetown.

Rock Valley. Town, Sioux co., NW Iowa, 48 m. N of Sioux City; pop. 1693.

Rock′ville (rŏk′vĭl). **1** Manufacturing city (pop. 9478) in town of VERNON, Connecticut; settled 1716, incorp. 1889; manufactures envelopes, wool fabrics, silk fishlines; has exceptional water power.
2 Town, ⊗ of Parke co., W Indiana, 23 m. NNE of Terre Haute; pop. 2756.
3 City, ⊗ of Montgomery co., cen. Maryland, 15 m. NNW of Washington; pop. 26,090.

Rockville Centre. Village, Nassau co., SE New York, on Long I. 19 m. ESE of New York; pop. 26,355; residential suburb of New York City.

Rock′wall (rŏk′wôl). **1** County in Texas. See *Table* at TEXAS.
2 City, its ⊗, NE Texas; pop. 2166.

Rock′well, Mount (rŏk′wĕl; -wĕl). Peak 9250 ft. in Glacier National Park, NW Montana.

Rockwell City. City, ⊗ of Calhoun co., NW cen. Iowa, 25 m. WSW of Fort Dodge; pop. 2313; center of Iowa corn belt.

Rock′wood (rŏk′wŏŏd). City, Roane co., E Tennessee, 6 m. SE of Harriman; pop. 5345; manufactures stoves, silk, hosiery; coal and iron deposits nearby; section grows fruit, corn, and tobacco; Indian mounds in vicinity.

Rock′y (rŏk′ĭ). River, N Ohio; rises in Medina co., flows N and NE into Lake Erie on W boundary of the city of Cleveland.

Rocky Face. Peak 6031 ft. in W North Carolina.

Rocky Ford. Melon-shipping city, Otero co., SE Colorado, on Arkansas river 12 m. WNW of La Junta; pop.

4087; trade center for irrigated region producing sugar beets, onions, and muskmelons; beet-sugar factory, vegetable cannery; gave name to type of muskmelon grown here and elsewhere.

Rocky Hill. 1 Town, S Hartford co., N Connecticut, on W bank of Connecticut river; pop. 7404; settled c. 1650, incorp. 1843; iron founding, manufacture of rayon, quarrying.

2 Borough, Somerset co., N cen. New Jersey, ab. 4 m. NNE of Princeton; pop. 528. Washington wrote his farewell address to the army here.

Rocky Knob. Peak 4164 ft. in Towns co., N Georgia.

Rocky Mount. 1 City, Edgecombe and Nash cos., NE North Carolina, 52 m. E of Raleigh; pop. 32,147; settled 1818; incorp. as town 1867, as city 1907; market for leaf tobacco; industrial center and railroad division point; grows tobacco, cotton, corn, peanuts; manufactures cotton yarns, pile fabrics, broad silks, cottonseed oil and meal, cordage, lumber and dairy products.

2 Industrial town, ⊗ of Franklin co., SW cen. Virginia; pop. 1412.

Rocky Mountain. Peak 4586 ft. in Union and Towns cos., N Georgia.

Rocky Mountain National Park. See UNITED STATES, *National Parks.*

Rocky Mountains *or* **Rock′ies** (rŏk′ĭz). Mountain system in W North America, extending from the Mexican frontier to the Arctic, through Arizona, New Mexico, Colorado, Utah, Nevada, Wyoming, Idaho, and Montana, the Canadian provinces of Alberta and British Columbia, and Yukon Territory; highest peak in U.S. section of this range is Mount Elbert 14,431 ft. in Colorado; highest in Canadian section Mt. Robson 12,972 ft. in British Columbia.

Rocky Mountains National Park. = *Banff National Park:* see CANADA, *National Parks.*

Rocky Point. 1 Point on SW coast of Los Angeles co., SW California, W of Long Beach, extending into Pacific Ocean.

2 Village, Suffolk co., SE New York, on Long I. ab. 14 m. W of Riverhead; pop. 2261; site of one of most powerful radio transmitting stations in the world.

Rocky River. City, Cuyahoga co., N Ohio, on Lake Erie 8 m. W of Cleveland; pop. 18,097; residential suburb of Cleveland.

Rocky Trail Peak. Peak 6488 ft. in W North Carolina.

Ro′court′ (rŏ′kōōr′) *or* **Rau′coux′** (rō′kōō′). Commune, Liège prov., E Belgium, just N of Liège; pop. 2345; scene of battle Oct. 11, 1746 in which Austrian allies under Prince Charles of Lorraine were defeated by the French under Marshal Saxe.

Ro′croi′ *or* **Ro′croy′** (rŏ′krwä′). Town, Ardennes dept., NE France, near Belgian frontier; pop. 968; scene of battle May 19, 1643 in which the French under the duc d'Enghien (the Great Condé) defeated the Spanish.

Ro′da *or* **Rho′da** (rō′då). Island in the Nile river near Cairo; has an ancient Nilometer.

Roda, La. See LA RODA.

Ro′das (rrō′tḥäs). Municipality, Las Villas prov., W cen. Cuba, 15 m. NNW of Cienfuegos; pop. 21,288.

Ro′de·wisch (rō′dĕ·vĭsh). Industrial city, Karl-Marx-Stadt dist., East Germany, 14 m. SSW of Zwickau; pop. 10,572.

Ro′dez′ (rŏ′dâz′); *anc.* **Seg′o·du′num** (sĕg′ō·dū′nŭm). Manufacturing and commercial commune, ✱ of Aveyron dept., S France, on Aveyron river 78 m. NE of Toulouse; pop. 18,450; episcopal see (created in 4th cent.); Gothic cathedral (13th–16th cents.); manufactures textiles; agricultural trade center. Ancient capital of the Rutheni (whence its present name); capital of Rouergue until 1789; center of Catholicism during religious wars of 16th cent.

Rodg′ers Peak (rŏj′ērz). Mountain 13,056 ft. high in Yosemite National Park, California, on E border of the park near Mt. Lyell.

Rodi. See RHODES.

Ro′ding (rō′dĭng). River 30 m. long, Essex co., SE England; flows S and SW into the Thames 2 m. SE of East Ham.

Ro·do′ni, Cape (rō·dō′nē). Cape extending into Adriatic Sea, NW coast of Albania, N of Durrës.

Ro·do′pi (rô·thô′pē). Var. of RHODOPE.

Rodos. See RHODES.

Rodosto. See TEKIRDAĞ.

Ro·dri′gues *or* **Ro·dri′guez** (rō·drē′gĕs). British island of the Mascarene Is., in the Indian Ocean ab. 500 m. E of Madagascar; 40 sq. m.; pop. (1962) 18,674; a dependency of Mauritius; highest point 1300 ft.; many limestone caves in W part; chief town Port Mathurin. Discovered by Portuguese 1645; colonized by French from Mauritius; taken by English 1809–10.

Rodumna. See ROANNE.

Roeb′ling (rōb′lĭng). Town, Burlington co., S cen. New Jersey, on Delaware river ab. 7 m. S of Trenton; pop. (with Florence) 3272; estab. by J. A. Roebling, founder of steel-cable factory which built Brooklyn Bridge and supplied cables for other well-known bridges.

Roe′bourne (rō′bẽrn). Town, W Western Australia, on Indian Ocean 200 m. ENE of Exmouth Gulf; pop. 487; in rich mineral district.

Roe′buck′ Bay (rō′bŭk′). Inlet of Indian Ocean, NW Western Australia, just SW of Dampier Land, 18°5′S.

Roe′land Park (rō′lănd). City, Johnson co., E Kansas, S suburb of Kansas City; pop. 8949.

Roe′pat *or* **Ru′pat** (rōō′pät). Island of Indonesia, in the Strait of Malacca off E coast of Sumatra.

Roer. See RUR.

Roer·mond′ (rōōr·mônt′). Commune, Limburg prov., SE Netherlands, near German border at confluence of the Rur and the Maas; pop. 16,677; 13th-cent. Romanesque church; manufactures textiles, paper. In medieval times the chief town of Upper Gelderland (see GELDERLAND). In World War II in area of active fighting Jan.–Feb. 1945; abandoned by Germans Mar. 1–2.

Roe′se·la′re (rōō′sĕ·lä′rĕ) *or* **Rou′se·la′re** (rou′-); *Fr.* **Rou′lers′** (rōō′lâr[s]′). Commune, West Flanders prov., NW Belgium; pop. (1938 est.) 30,334; manufactures linen; in chicory-growing section; scene of battle 1794 in which French under Pichegru and Macdonald defeated the Austrians; captured by the Germans Oct. 18, 1914 and held by them until recaptured by the French Oct. 14, 1918.

Roes Wel′come (rōz wĕl′kŭm). Strait 50 to 115 m. wide and 170 m. long in N Keewatin District, E Northwest Territories, Canada, bet. W Southampton I. and the mainland; a part of N Hudson Bay.

Rofreit. See ROVERETO.

Ro·ga′chev′ (rŭ·gŭ·chôf′). Town, E White Russia, U.S.S.R., on right bank of Dnieper river at its junction with the Drut, ab. 60 m. NNW of Gomel; pop. 9300.

Ro′ga·land′ (rō′gä·län′; rōō′-). County of Norway. See *Table* at NORWAY.

Ro′gans Hill (rō′gănz). Town, New South Wales, Australia, ab. 13 m. NW of Sydney.

Rog′er Mills (rŏj′ēr mĭlz′). County in Oklahoma. See *Table* at OKLAHOMA.

Rog′ers (rŏj′ērz). 1 County in Oklahoma. See *Table* at OKLAHOMA.

2 Commercial city, Benton co., NW corner of Arkansas, 20 m. N of Fayetteville; pop. 5700; mountain resort; in region growing fruit and vegetables.

Rogers, Mount. Peak 5929 ft. in Grayson and Smyth cos., SW Virginia; highest point in Virginia.

Rogers City. City, ⊗ of Presque Isle co., NE Michigan, on Lake Huron 30 m. NW of Alpena; pop. 4722; limestone quarries nearby.

Rogers Lake. = MUROC DRY LAKE.

Rogers Pass. Pass 4302 ft. in Selkirk Mts., SE Brit. Columbia, Canada, NE of Revelstoke, through which passes the Canadian Pacific Ry.; discovered 1883.

Rogers Peak. Mountain 7300 ft. in Glacier National Park, NW Montana.

Rog'ers·ville (rŏj'ērz·vĭl; *Sou. also* -v'l). Town, ⊗ of Hawkins co., NE Tennessee; pop. 3121; tobacco.

Rog'ge·veld (rŏg'ĕ·fĕlt). Mountain range in W Cape Province, Union of South Africa, W of Nieuwveld; highest point 5249 ft.

Ro·glia'no (rô·lyä'nô). Commune, Cosenza prov., Calabria, S Italy, 7 m. SSE of Cosenza; pop. (1931) 12,706.

Ro'go·a·gua'do, Lake (rrô'gô·ä·gwä'thô). Lake in N Bolivia, draining S and E into Mamoré river.

Rogoźnica. See GROSS ROSEN.

Rogue (rōg). River 220 m. long, SW Oregon, rises in Crater Lake National Park, flows S and SW into Pacific Ocean in W Curry co.

Ro·ha'tyn (rŭ·há'tĭn). Commune, W Ukraine, U.S.S.R., 35 m. SE of Stanislav; pop. (1921) 5810; formerly in Poland; mineral springs.

Ro'hil·khand' (rō'hĭl·kŭnd') *or* **Ba·reil'ly** (bá·rā'lĭ). Division of N Uttar Pradesh, N Indian Union; area 10,865 sq. m.; pop. (1941) 6,195,996; ✻ Bareilly. Practically coextensive with region of N India occupied since early part of 18th cent. by the Rohilla tribe of Afghans. An early ruler was made Nawab by the Delhi emperor; the region was divided in 1749 and power of Rohillas overcome 1774 by united forces of British and Nawab of Oudh. See RAMPUR.

Roh'tak (rō'tŭk). **1** District, Ambala division, S Punjab state, NW Indian Union; 2246 sq. m.; pop. (1941) 956,399.
2 Town, its ✻, 44 m. WNW of Delhi; pop. 35,235; trade center with textile industry.

Roi (roi). Islet of Kwajalein (*q.v.*) atoll, Marshall Is.; taken by Americans Feb. 1–3, 1944.

Roi Et *or* **Roi Ed** (roi ĕt). **1** Province, E Thailand; 1996 sq. m.; pop. 430,640.
2 Town, its ✻, near the Si river and 70 m. SE of Khon Kaen.

Ro'jo, Cape (rrô'hô). **1** Cape on coast of N Veracruz state, Mexico, extending into Gulf of Mexico.
2 Cape at SW end of Puerto Rico, on SE side of Mona Passage.

Ro'kan (rō'kän). River ab. 225 m. long in N cen. Sumatra, Indonesia; flows NE into the Strait of Malacca.

Ro·kel' *or* **Ro·kelle'** (rô·kĕl') *or* **Se'li** (sā'lĕ). River ab. 300 m. long in Sierra Leone, W Africa; flows S and W into Atlantic Ocean at Freetown; called the Sierra Leone at its estuary.

Ro'kish·kis (rō'kĭsh·kĭs). **1** District of Lithuania. See *Table* at LITHUANIA.
2 Town, its ✻, NE Lithuania, 35 m. W of Daugavpils; pop. 4325.

Ro·ku·go, Cape (rô·kōō·gō). Cape on W coast of Honshu I., Japan, NW of Toyama Bay at end of Noto Penin.

Ro·lette' (rô·lĕt'). County in North Dakota. See *Table* at NORTH DAKOTA.

Rol'la (rŏl'á). **1** City, ⊗ of Phelps co., S cen. Missouri; pop. 11,132. Missouri School of Mines (1870; coed.), a college of the Univ. of Missouri.
2 City, ⊗ of Rolette co., N North Dakota; pop. 1398.

Roll'ing Fork (rōl'ĭng). Town, ⊗ of Sharkey co., W Mississippi; pop. 1619.

Rolling Meadows. City, Cook co., NE Illinois, NW suburb of Chicago; pop. 10,879.

Rolling Mountain. Peak 13,694 ft. in San Juan co., SW Colorado.

Rolling Thunder. Peak 10,902 ft. in N Grand Teton National Park, NW Wyoming.

Rol'lins Pass (rŏl'ĭnz). Mountain pass 11,680 ft. in Boulder and Grand cos., N Colorado, in Front Range of Rocky Mts.; railroad.

Röm. See RÖMÖ.

Ro'ma (rō'má). Town, SE Queensland, Australia, N of Condamine river 275 m. WNW of Brisbane; pop. 3369.

Ro'ma (rō'mä). **1** Province of Italy. See *Table* at ITALY.
2 See ROME.

Ro'ma (rō'má) *or* **Ro'mang** (rō'mäng). Island, S Moluccas, Indonesia, E of Wetar I. and NE of Timor; ab. 15 m. long by 10 m. wide; pop. 1289.

Ro·ma'gna (rô·män'yä); *anc.* **Ro·ma'nia** (rô·män'yá; -mä'nĭ·à). From about the 8th cent. a province of the States of the Church; ✻ Ravenna; under nominal papal control until ab. 1500; seized by Cesare Borgia 1501 and held by the pope until 1796; as part of Emilia incorporated 1796–1814 in Italian Republic and Napoleon's kingdom of Italy; restored to papacy 1815; revolt of 1831 put down by Austrian forces; joined Piedmont 1860. Now forms Italian provinces of Bologna, Ferrara, Ravenna, and Forlì.

Ro'magne'–sous–Mont'fau'con' (rô'mȧn'y'·sōō-môn'fō'kôn'). Village, Meuse dept., NE France, near Montfaucon; site of largest American military cemetery in France, contains graves of over 14,200 soldiers.

Ro·main', Cape (rô·mān'). Cape on island off mainland in Charleston co., South Carolina, extending into Atlantic Ocean.

Ro·maine' (rô·mān'; *Fr.* rô'mĕn'). River ab. 225 m. long, Saguenay co., SE Quebec, Canada; rises in SW Labrador, flows S across Quebec into the Gulf of St. Lawrence opp. W end of Anticosti I.

Ro'main'ville (rô'măn'vēl'). Commune, Seine dept., N France, NE suburb of Paris; pop. 18,422; battle 1814.

Ro'man (rô'män). City, NE Romania, in cen. Moldavia region, on Moldova river on railroad 28 m. N of Bacău; pop. 28,948; commercial center; seat of a bishopric.

Romana, La. See LA ROMANA.

Ro'man Africa (rō'măn). See Roman AFRICA.

Roman Apennines. See APENNINES.

Roman Campagna. See CAMPAGNA DI ROMA.

Roman Empire. The empire of ancient Rome, beginning with the imperial rule of Augustus 27 B.C.; at its greatest extent (c. 117 A.D.) included all S Europe, Britannia, N Africa, Egypt, Asia Minor, N coast of Pontus Euxinus (Black Sea), Armenia and regions S of the Caucasus, Mesopotamia and adjoining regions, Syria, Palestine, and NW corner of Arabia. See *Color Plate* II.

History: Founded by Octavian who gained control of Italy and the west 43–35 B.C. and of east 31 B.C.; as Augustus 27 B.C.–14 A.D., Octavian annexed Egypt 30 B.C. and advanced Roman frontiers to Rhine and Danube; held Germany to Elbe 6 B.C.–13 A.D.; later major additions to territory were Dacia, Mesopotamia, and Assyria; from 3d cent. suffered decline caused, in part, by external factors, such as pressure of Persia and of barbarian tribes from across Danube and Germany; divided for administration by line running from the Danube to Adriatic Sea S of Dalmatia; for eastern empire after 395, see BYZANTINE EMPIRE; invaded during 5th cent. by successive waves of Visigoths, Huns, Vandals, Ostrogoths, and others; end of western empire conventionally dated 476 (defeat and death of Romulus Augustulus, last Emperor of the West); for medieval "revival" of Rome's imperial authority in west, see HOLY ROMAN EMPIRE.

Romang. See ROMA island.

Romani. See RUMANI.

Ro·ma'nia (rô·män'yá; -mä'nĭ·à); *also frequently* **Rou·ma'nia** (rōō-) *and* **Ru·ma'nia** (rōō-). Country, E Europe, one of the Balkan States; 91,671 sq. m.; pop. (1945) 16,409,367; ✻ Bucharest; bounded on N and NE by U.S.S.R. (Moldavian S.S.R. on NE), on E by Black Sea, on S by Bulgaria, on SW by Yugoslavia, and on W and NW by Hungary; on the S has the Danube which marks part of boundary with Yugoslavia and Bulgaria; on NE separated from the U.S.S.R by Prut river. Before World War II divided into nine provinces: Oltenia, Muntenia, Dobruja, Moldavia, Bessarabia, Bucovina, Banat, Transylvania, and Crişana-Maramureş, most of which still form semipolitical subdivisions. In the N pene-

ROMANIA
Statute Miles
0 10 20 30 40 50 60

trated by the SE end of the Carpathian Mts., uniting in the center of the country with the E end of the Transylvanian Alps (highest point Negoi 8346 ft.). For the greater part consists of rolling and well-watered plains with remarkably fertile soil. Besides the Prut, other important tributaries of the Danube are Siret, Ialomiţa, Argeş (with its tributary the Dambovita), Olt, Jiu, and Timiş (which enters the Danube in Yugoslavia); the Transylvanian plains are watered by the Mureş and Someş, tributaries of the Tisza. Marshlands occur along the lower Danube and in its delta; its shore line from Sulina at the mouth of the Danube extends ab. 125 m. to a point N of Cape Caliacra. Natural resources comprise esp. petroleum (largest fields in Europe, centering about Ploeşti), agricultural crops (wheat, corn, barley), vineyards, forests, iron and salt mines. Chief cities Bucharest, Cluj, Iaşi, Timişoara, Ploeşti, Brăila, and Galaţi; chief port Constanţa.

History: For earlier history, see DACIA, MOLDAVIA, WALACHIA, and DANUBIAN PRINCIPALITIES; autonomous Danubian Principalities united and took name of Romania 1861; invaded by Russia in Russo-Turkish War 1877–78; lost Bessarabia to Russia 1878; gained Dobruja; complete independence from Turkey recognized by powers 1878; became kingdom 1881; forced Bulgaria to cede southern Dobruja 1913; entered World War I on side of Allies 1916; disastrously defeated; territory enlarged by addition of Bessarabia, Transylvania, Banat, Bucovina (*qq.v.*) 1918–20; signed treaty with Czechoslovakia, thus joining the Little Entente, Apr. 23, 1921; possession of Bessarabia tacitly recognized by Russia in Soviet-Romanian nonaggression pact 1933; entered Balkan Pact 1934 (see BALKAN STATES); in 1940 forced to cede Bessarabia and northern Bucovina (total 21,000 sq. m.) to Russia, part of northern Transylvania (17,400 sq. m.) to Hungary, and southern Dobruja (2880 sq. m.) to Bulgaria; N Transylvania returned by treaty with

Allies 1947. In World War II under authoritarian regime of Ion Antonescu forced to fight on side of Germany; overrun by Russia in 1944 and withdrew from the conflict Aug. 23, 1944; proclaimed people's republic Dec. 1947.

Ro·ma′nia (rṓ·măn′yà; -mä′nĭ·à). **1** The Roman Empire, esp. the Byzantine Empire—so called by its neighbors.

2 The Latin Empire (*q.v.*), set up by the Crusaders 1204–61.

3 See ROMAGNA.

4 See RUMELIA.

Ro·ma′nia, Cape (rṓ·măn′yà; -mä′nĭ·à). Cape on SE extremity of the Malay Penin., in Johore state at E end of Singapore Strait.

Ro·ma′no, Cape (rṓ·mä′nṓ; -mä′nṓ). Cape on island in Gulf of Mexico, off W coast of Collier co., SW Florida.

Ro·ma′no Cay (rrṓ·mä′nṓ). Island off N coast of Camagüey prov., E cen. Cuba, in the Camagüey Archipelago.

Ro′mans·horn′ (rō′mäns·hôrn′). Commune, Thurgau canton, NE Switzerland; pop. (1930) 6095; on S shore of Lake Constance, gateway to Switzerland from S Germany.

Ro′mans′-sur-I′sère′ (rô′män′sür·ē′zâr′). Commune, Drôme dept., SE France, on Isère river 11 m. NE of Valence; pop. 19,489; 13th-cent. Gothic-Romanesque church; manufactures hats, shoes, clothing, silk, leather. Founded by St. Barnard 862; most important city in the Dauphiné during Middle Ages.

Roman States. = *Papal States:* see STATES OF THE CHURCH.

Ro·man′zof, Cape (rṓ·măn′zŏf). Cape on W coast of Alaska; extends into Bering sea in 61°47′N, 166°W.

Rom·blon′ (rŏm·blŏn′). **1** Province, cen. Phil. Is., island group of the Visayan Is. in Sibuyan Sea SE of Mindoro and S of Luzon; comprises three large islands—Tablas, Sibuyan, and Romblon—and ab. 30 small and

dependent islands; 512 sq. m.; pop. 99,367; ✳ Romblon. Islands generally low except Sibuyan, which has peak 6750 ft. high. Soil is fertile; chief crops abacá and copra. Rich in minerals, esp. gold on Sibuyan and marble on Romblon. Chief towns Romblon on Romblon I., and Odiongan and Looc on Tablas.

History: Islands known to Spaniards from early times, visited at least as early as 1582; received first Recollect missionaries 1635; in 17th and 18th cents. often ravaged by Moros; organized into a comandancia 1853; civil government established Mar. 1901; after World War II occupied by Americans Mar. 11, 1945.

2 Smallest of the three important islands of Romblon group, E of N Tablas I. and W of Sibuyan; 32 sq. m.; pop. 13,106.

3 Municipality, ✳ of Romblon prov.; comprises the island of Romblon and three small adjacent islands; pop. 14,309; on NW coast of Romblon I. is excellent harbor; active trading port on interisland passage from San Bernardino Strait to Verde Island Passage.

Rom′bo (rōΝm′bōō). One of the Cape Verde Is.

Rome (rōm). **1** City, ⊗ of Floyd co., NW Georgia, 55 m. NW of Atlanta; pop. 32,226; cotton market; textile, lumber, and cottonseed-oil mills; Shorter Coll. (1873; women). Founded 1834 and made ⊗ 1835; occupied by some of Sherman's forces 1864.

2 Manufacturing city, a ⊗ of Oneida co., cen. New York, on Mohawk river 15 m. WNW of Utica; pop. 51,646; railroad and industrial center in farming and dairying country; brass and copper mills, foundries, knitting mills, canneries, brick and lumber yards. U.S. government radar research and electronics center; Griffiss Air Force Base. First settled 1760 on site of Fort Stanwix (erected 1758, called Fort Schuyler 1776); storm center in French and Indian War and in Revolution; place where Stars and Stripes are said to have been unfurled for first time; resettled 1786; incorp. as village 1819, as city 1870.

Rome (rōm); *Ital.* **Ro′ma** (rō′mä); *anc.* **Ro′ma** (rō′mà). City, ✳ of Roma prov., Latium, cen. Italy, on both sides of Tiber river 16 m. from its mouth and 117 m. NW of Naples; pop. (1936) 1,155,722; (1961) 2,160,773; ✳ of the republic of Italy; ✳ of Roman Empire and later ✳ of the States of the Church; often called the "Eternal City," "City of the Seven Hills," and the "Holy City"; early city built on seven hills (see SEVEN HILLS) enclosed by Servian Wall, now extends for several miles along both banks of Tiber river and includes Vatican City, autonomous administrative center of the Roman Catholic Church (for account of papal properties in Rome, see VATICAN CITY); imperial Rome divided into 14 Augustan Regions and enclosed by the Aurelian Wall; modern city has fine public squares (Piazza del Popolo, di Venezia, di San Pietro, etc.), thoroughfares (Corso Umberto Primo, Via Venti Settembre, etc.), and city gates (Porta Pinciana, Porta Pia, Porta Maggiore, etc.); notable churches include Santa Pudenziana, Santa Maria in Trastevere, San Paolo fuori le mura, and Il Gesù; educational institutions include the university, Accademia di San Luca, American College, American School of Classical Studies; numerous fine libraries; noted for its palaces, as the Barberini, Colonna, Corsini, Rospigliosi, and Farnese palaces; remains of ancient city include the Colosseum, catacombs, temples, baths (esp. the Baths of Caracalla), aqueducts, arches, Forum, etc.

History: During 8th cent. B.C., early settlements on hills united to form one city (traditional date of founding of Rome 753 B.C.); predominantly Latin in population, but ruled as Etruscan city-kingdom to 6th cent. B.C.; according to tradition, republic founded 509 B.C.; by 275 B.C. Rome, having defeated Etruscan towns, Latin League, Samnites, and Greek cities in south, was supreme in Italy; began overseas expansion in Punic Wars 264–241, 218–201, 149–146 B.C. (see CARTHAGE); conquered Sicily, Sardinia, Cisalpine Gaul, Spain, and

former Carthaginian islands in Mediterranean; by defeat of Macedonia (*q.v.*) 197 B.C., attained hegemony in Greece; established provinces of Illyricum, Macedonia, Africa, Achaia, and Asia; gradually acquired Balearic Is., southern Gaul, Cilicia, Bithynia, Cyrene, and Crete; Syria conquered by Pompey who captured Jerusalem 63 B.C. and reorganized eastern provinces; Gaul annexed by Caesar (58–51 B.C.) who first attempted to invade Britain 55 B.C.; after battle of Actium 31 B.C., all of Roman lands controlled by Octavian, the first Roman emperor, 27 B.C. (for later history of Roman rule, see ROMAN EMPIRE); city of Rome the capital of Roman Empire until Constantine dedicated Constantinople 330 A.D. (see ISTANBUL); sacked by Alaric and Visigoths 410; after Ravenna (*q.v.*) became political capital of Italy, bishop of Rome, the chief defender of city, gradually obtained temporal authority and began to claim primacy among western bishops; Duchy of Rome, a Byzantine fief, 6th–8th cents.; for its theoretical position as capital of revived Roman empire, see HOLY ROMAN EMPIRE; seat of Papacy and (except 1309–77) of temporal rule of States of the Church (*q.v.*); sacked by Spanish 1527; occupied by French who erected Roman Republic 1798; annexed to French Empire 1809, but later restored to Pope; scene of republican rising 1849; taken over as capital of kingdom of Italy 1870 (see VATICAN CITY for part belonging to Papacy). In World War II captured by Allies June 4, 1944.

Rome, Duchy of; *anc.* **Du·ca′tus Ro′mae** (dṻ·kā′t𝑢s rō′mē). A division of the Byzantine Empire 6th cent. to 8th cent., comprising most of modern Latium, cen. Italy; later, a province of the States of the Church, called the **Patrimony of Saint Pe′ter** (sånt pē′tĕr).

Ro′me·o (rō′mē·ō). Village, Macomb co., SE Michigan, 19 m. NE of Pontiac; pop. 3327; in fruitgrowing section.

Ro·me′ro (rrô·mā′rô). Town, Buenos Aires prov., E Argentina, 32 m. SE of Buenos Aires.

Rom′ford (rŭm′fĕrd; rŏm′-). Urban district, Essex, SE England, 13 m. ENE of London; pop. 35,918, (1951 pop.) 87,991; iron foundries, breweries.

Ro′mil′ly–sur–Seine (rô′mē′yē′sür-sân′). Commune, Aube dept., NE France, 23 m. NW of Troyes; pop. 13,977. General headquarters of French 5th Army in 1914.

Rom′ney. 1 (rŏm′nĭ) City, ⊗ of Hampshire co., NE West Virginia, in E panhandle on South Branch Potomac river 15 m. ESE of Keyser; pop. 2203; manufactures barrels, flour, lumber; marble and granite works; hunting and fishing resort. Served as military headquarters for both armies during Civil War.

2 (rŏm′nĭ; rŭm′-) Seaport town, Kent, SE England; one of the Cinque Ports; now **New Romney,** a municipal borough in Romney Marsh district; pop. 2356.

Rom′ney Marsh (rŏm′nĭ; rŭm′nĭ). Coastal pasture tract in Kent, SE England, NE of Rye; 39 sq. m.; before end of 13th cent. the Rother river flowed through it to the sea.

Rom′ny (rôm′nĭ). Town, W Sumy Region, NE Ukraine, U.S.S.R., on upper Sula river 58 m. W of Sumy; pop. 25,174; has tobacco factories and flour mills.

Röm′ö′ (rûm′ṳ′) *or* **Röm** (rûm). One of the North Frisian Is. in the North Sea off W coast of S Jutland Penin.; 39 sq. m.; pop. (1925) 766; belongs to Denmark.

Ro′mo·ran′tin′ (rô′mô′rän′tăn′). Manufacturing town, Loir-et-Cher dept., N cen. France, ab. 24 m. SE of Blois; pop. 6941; 15th-cent. castle where Francis II signed edict that prevented establishment of the Inquisition in France 1560.

Roms′dal (rôms′däl). Valley of the Rauma (*q.v.*), Norway; steep mountains on either side, esp. Vengetinder 5960 ft., **Roms′dals·horn′** (rôms′däls·hôrn′) 5105 ft., and Troldtinder 6010 ft.

Roms′dals·fjord′ (rôms′däls·fyôr′; -fyōōr′). Fiord, long inlet of Norwegian Sea, W cen. Norway, E of Ålesund; Åndalsnes at head of it; receives Rauma river.

Rom′sey (rŭm′zĭ). Town and municipal borough, Hampshire, S England, ab. 7 m. NW of Southampton; pop. 6281; site of a Norman abbey church of 12th cent. with remains of an earlier Saxon church beneath it.

Ro·nan′ (rō·nän′). City, Lake co., NW Montana, 45 m. N of Missoula; pop. 1334.

Ron·ca′de (rōng·kä′dä). Commune, Treviso prov., Venezia Euganea, NE Italy, 7 m. SE of Treviso; pop. (1931) 11,206.

Roncador, Serra do. See SERRA DO RONCADOR.

Ron′ca·dor′ Cay (rōng′kä·thôr′). Small island in W Caribbean Sea, off E coast of Nicaragua; controlled by U.S.A. and Colombia.

Ron′ca·dor Reef (rōng′kä·dôr). Reef, Solomon Is., S of Ontong Java and N of Santa Isabel, ab. 6°10′S.

Ron·ca′glia (rōng·käl′yä). Former village, Piacenza prov., Emilia, N Italy; now part of commune of Piacenza (*q.v.*); diets held here (1155 et al.) by Holy Roman Emperors, esp. Frederick I.

Ron′ces·val′les (rōn′thäz·vä′lyäs; rōn′säz·vä′yäs); *Fr.* **Ron′ce·vaux′** (rôns′vō′). Hamlet and commune in Navarra prov., N Spain; pop. ab. 1000; in the Pyrenees ab. 5 m. from the French boundary; mountains here crossed by the **Puer′to I′ba·ñe′ta** (pwĕr′tō ē′vä·nyä′tä), *often called* **Pass of Roncesvalles,** a celebrated mountain pass 3648 ft. where Roland met his death 778. See FUENTERRABIA.

Ron′ce·verte (rŏn′sĕ·vĕrt). City, Greenbrier co., SE West Virginia, on Greenbrier river 26 m. E of Hinton; pop. 1882; trading and railroad center of farming and stock-raising area.

Ron′co, *in full* **Ron′co Scri′via** (rōng′kō skrē′vyä). Commune, Genova prov., E cen. Liguria, NW Italy, N of Genoa; pop. (1931) 4422; railroad tunnel 5.16 m. long.

Ron′co·fer·ra′ro (rōng′kō·fär·rä′rō). Commune, Mantova prov., Lombardy, N Italy; pop. (1931) 10,953.

Ron′co·le *or* **Le Ron′co·le** (lā rōng′kō·lä). Village, Parma prov., NW cen. Emilia, N Italy, near Busseto (*q.v.*) S of Cremona; pop. 1734; birthplace of Giuseppe Verdi.

Ron′da (rrôn′dä). Commune, Málaga prov., S Spain, 40 m. W of Málaga; pop. 26,170; produces grain, wine, oil; manufactures flour, brandies, leather, hats, soap, chocolates; Roman and Moorish remains; reconquered by Ferdinand the Catholic 1485; Moorish uprising 1501.

Ron′deau Provincial Park (rŏn′dō). Canadian provincial park, Kent co., SE Ontario; 8 sq. m.; comprises point of land in Lake Erie 18 m. SE of Chatham; game preserve, with fine forests and camping facilities.

Ron′de·bosch (rôn′dĕ·bôs). Town, Cape Province, S Union of South Africa, ab. 6 m. SE of Cape Town; pop. (white) ab. 3500; founded 1657 by free burghers, servants of Dutch East India Co., who had obtained their freedom; beautiful residential city—site of Cecil Rhodes's home Groote Schuur, now official residence of dominion's premier and location of Univ. of Cape Town.

Ron′dorf (rôn′dôrf). Industrial commune, North Rhine-Westphalia state, West Germany, just S of Cologne; pop. 12,520.

Ron′dout (rŏn′dout). **1** Creek in Ulster co., SE New York; flows NE to join Walkill river ab. 6 m. below Kingston, where the combined stream empties into Hudson river. See MERRIMAN DAM.
2 Former village in Ulster co., New York, on the Hudson river; now part of Kingston.

Rong′buk (rŏng′bōok). Valley in S Tibet, Outer China, and three glaciers on the N slope of Mt. Everest.

Ronge, Lac la (läk′ lä rôNzh′). Lake 344 sq. m. in N Saskatchewan, Canada; its outlet flows N into Churchill river.

Rong′e·lap (rông′ĕ·läp). Atoll, Marshall Is., W cen. Pacific Ocean, at NW end of Ratak Chain ab. 80 m. E of Bikini atoll.

Rong′e·rik (rông′ĕ·rĭk). Atoll, Marshall Is., W cen. Pacific Ocean, near NW end of Ratak Chain E of Bikini and

Rongelap; place to which population of Bikini was removed at time of atomic-bomb tests 1946.

Ro′ni·u, Mount (rō′nē·ōō). Peak 4341 ft. on the SE peninsula (Tahiti-iti) of the island of Tahiti, Society Is., S Pacific Ocean.

Rön′ne (rûn′ĕ). Seaport, ⊗ of Bornholm co., on the W coast of Bornholm I., Denmark; pop. (1945) 11,497; manufactures terra cotta and faïence; stone quarries.

Rons′dorf (rôns′dôrf). Former city (pop. 15,174), Düsseldorf govt. dist., Rhine Province, Prussia, Germany; since 1929 a manufacturing section of Wuppertal.

Ron′se (rôn′sĕ); *Fr.* **Re·naix′** (rē·nĕ′). Manufacturing and commercial commune, East Flanders prov., NW cen. Belgium; pop. (1938 est.) 25,261.

Roo′de·poort′ (rōō′dĕ·pōōrt′). City, S Transvaal, NE Union of South Africa, 12 m. W of Johannesburg; pop. 41,572; residential and gold-mining community.

Rood′house′ (rōōd′hous′; rōd′-). City, Greene co., W Illinois, 45 m. WSW of Springfield; pop. 2352.

Roof Butte (rōōf; rŏof). Butte 9575 ft. in NE Apache co., NE Arizona.

Rooke. See UMBOI.

Rooks (rōoks). County in Kansas. See *Table* at KANSAS.

Roor′kee *or* **Rur′ki** (rōōr′kē). Town, N Uttar Pradesh, N Indian Union, 19 m. E of Saharanpur; pop. 17,476; headquarters of workers and shops for Ganges canal; Thomason Civil Engineering Coll. (1848).

Roo′se·be′ke (rō′sĕ·bā′kĕ). Village in East Flanders, Belgium, just E of Roeselare; scene of battle Nov. 27, 1382 in which Charles VI of France defeated the Flemish insurgents who had revolted because of taxes imposed by the regent Louis, Duke of Anjou.

Roo′sen·daal en Nis′pen (rō′sĕn·däl ĕ nĭs′pĕ[n]). Commune, North Brabant prov., S Netherlands; pop. (1939) 26,148.

Roo′se·velt (rō′zĕ·vĕlt; -vĕlt). **1** Counties in two states of the U.S. See *Tables* at MONTANA and NEW MEXICO.
2 Settlement, Gila co., cen. Arizona, near Roosevelt Dam and Lake; pop. (est.) 1628.
3 Urban community (unincorporated) Nassau co., SE New York, on Long Island SW of Hempstead; pop. 12,883.

Roosevelt, Mount. Peak 5676 ft. in Lawrence co., W South Dakota.

Roosevelt, Ri′o (rē′ōō); *formerly* Rio da Dú′vi·da (thä thōō′vĕ·thä)—"River of Doubt." River ab. 200 m. long, W cen. Brazil; rises in W Mato Grosso state, flows N into SE Amazonas state where it joins the Aripuanã river; explored by Theodore Roosevelt 1914; lower course of the Aripuanã sometimes called Rio Roosevelt.

Roosevelt Dam. See UNITED STATES, *Dams and Reservoirs.*

Roosevelt Island. **1** = THEODORE ROOSEVELT ISLAND.
2 Ice-covered island ab. 90 m. long in E Ross Shelf Ice, Ross Dependency, Antarctica, S of the Bay of Whales.

Roosevelt Lake. 1 See FRANKLIN D. ROOSEVELT LAKE.
2 See UNITED STATES, *Dams and Reservoirs* (Roosevelt Dam).

Ro′per (rō′pēr). River ab. 325 m. long, navigable for ab. 90 m., NE Northern Territory, Australia; flows N and E to Limmen Bight on W side of Gulf of Carpentaria.

Ro′que·brune′, *in full* **Roquebrune–Cap–Mar′tin′** (rô′kē·brün′käp′mär′tăn′). Commune, Alpes-Maritimes dept., SE France, near coast bet. Monaco and Menton; pop. (1931) 6888; formerly under princes of Monaco from whom it (with Menton) revolted 1848; independent 1848–60 when it became part of France.

Roque′fort (rōk′fērt; *Fr.* rôk′fôr′). Commune, Landes dept., SW France, ab. 12 m. NE of Mont-de-Marsan; pop. (1931) 1009.

Roque′fort′–sur–Soul′zon′ (rôk′fôr′sür·sōol′zôN′). Town, SE Aveyron dept., S France; pop. 1245; town built against limestone cliffs in which are caves where Roquefort cheeses are ripened.

Ro'que Gon·zá'lez de San'ta Cruz (rrô'kå gôn·sä'låz thä sän'tä krōōs'). Town, Paraguarí dept., S Paraguay; pop. ab. 9800.

Roques, Los. See Los Roques.

Ro·rai'ma (rrô·rī'mä; *Port.* rōō·rī'må). Flat-topped mountain 9 m. long and 3 m. wide in Serra Pacaraima, near junction of boundaries of Brazil, Venezuela, and British Guiana; highest point 8620 ft.; steep slopes, many waterfalls (one almost 2000 ft.), source of many rivers of Guiana, of the Amazon system to the S, and of Orinoco system to the W.

Rorke's Drift (rôrks). Locality on a tributary of the Tugela river, N Natal, E Union of South Africa, 21 m. SE of Dundee; scene of successful British defense against Zulus 1879.

Rör'os' (rû'rōs'; -rōōs'). Commune, SE Sör-Tröndelag prov., cen. Norway 35 m. by road from Swedish frontier; pop. 2302; copper mines.

Ror'schach (rôr'shäk). Commune, Saint Gallen canton, NE Switzerland, on S shore of Lake Constance 6 m. NE of Saint Gallen; pop. (1941) 10,591; bathing and health resort; tourist center.

Ro'sa, Mon'te (môn'tä rô'zä). Mountain of the Pennine Alps, on the Swiss-Italian border; a mountain mass, has ten summits, the highest the Dufourspitze 15,217 ft., highest point in the Pennine Alps. At altitude of 11,500 ft. is Italian laboratory for nuclear research.

Ro·sa'les (rrô·sä'lås). Municipality, SE Pangasinan prov., Luzon, Phil. Is., on left bank of the Agno 27 m. ESE of Lingayen; pop. 15,837; railroad terminus; has airfield, captured by Americans Jan. 1945.

Ro'sa·lie Peak (rō'zà·lē). Mountain 13,574 ft. in Park co., cen. Colorado.

Ros'a·lind Bank (rŏz'à·lĭnd; rō'zà-). Shoal in Caribbean Sea halfway bet. W Jamaica and E Honduras.

Ro·sa'rio (rrô·sä'ryô). 1 Commercial city, Santa Fe prov., E cen. Argentina, on the Paraná river 190 m. by rail NW of Buenos Aires; pop. (est.) 521,210; river port, shipping point for N Argentina; sugar refinery, meatpacking plant, flour mills. Founded 1730, growth began only in latter part of 19th cent.

2 Town, Sinaloa state, W Mexico, on railroad just SE of Mazatlán; pop. 8323.

3 Town, San Pedro dept., cen. Paraguay, on the left bank of Paraguay river 70 m. N of Asunción; pop. ab. 6000.

4 Municipality, SE cen. Batangas prov., Luzon, Phil. Is., 13 m. NE of Batangas; pop. 34,130.

5 Municipality, S La Union prov., Luzon, Phil. Is., near E shore of Lingayen Gulf; pop. 6806; key point of fighting in N cen. Luzon Feb. to May 1945.

6 Town, Colonia dept., SW Uruguay, ab. 10 m. N of its port Sauce and 80 m. NW of Montevideo; pop. ab. 8500.

Ro·sá'rio (rōō·zá'ryōō). Town, Rio de Janeiro state, E Brazil, ab. 16 m. N of Rio de Janeiro.

Rosario, Sierra del. See Sierra del Rosario.

Ro·sa'rio Cay (rrô·sä'ryô). Island in N Caribbean Sea, E of Isle of Pines and S of W Cuba.

Ro·sa'rio de la Fron·te'ra (rrô·sä'ryô thä lä frôntä'rä). Town, Salta prov., N Argentina; altitude 3200 ft.; medicinal hot springs.

Ro·sar'i·o Strait (rô·zär'ĭ·ô). Strait, NW Washington, lying bet. San Juan Is. on the W and Skagit co. on the E.

Ro·sa'rio Ta'la (rrô·sä'ryô tä'lä). Town, Entre Ríos prov., E Argentina; pop. (est.) 10,568.

Ro·sar'no (rô·zär'nô). Commune, Reggio di Calabria prov., Calabria, S Italy, 32 m. NNE of Reggio di Calabria; pop. (1931) 11,282.

Ro'sas, Gulf of (rō'zás; *Span.* rrô'säs). Inlet of Mediterranean Sea on NE coast of Spain, S of Cape Creus.

Roscianum. See Rossano.

Ros'coff' (rôs'kôf'). Seaport town, N Finistère dept., NW France; pop. 2206; exports vegetables.

Ros·com'mon (rŏs·kŏm'*ŭ*n). **1** County in Michigan. See *Table* at Michigan.

2 Village, its ⊗, N cen. Michigan; pop. 867.

3 County, N cen. Eire, in Connacht prov.; 951 sq. m.; pop. 77,566; ⊗ Roscommon; sheep grazing, coal mining.

4 Town, ⊗ of co. Roscommon, N cen. Eire; pop. 2040; giant 13th-cent. castle; Dominican priory.

Ros·crea' (rŏs·krā'). Town, NE co. Tipperary, S Eire; pop. 3060; ruins of Augustinian priory founded in 7th cent.; remnants of 13th-cent. castle.

Rose (rōz). Small uninhabited island in American Samoa, in SW cen. Pacific Ocean, ab. 70 m. E of Tau.

Rose, Mount. Peak 10,800 ft. in S Washoe co., NW Nevada, in Carson Range; winter sports area.

Ro·seau' (rô·zō'). **1** County in Minnesota. See *Table* at Minnesota.

2 Village, its ⊗, NW Minnesota, 20 m. WSW of Lake of the Woods; pop. 2146; trading center of farming section.

3 Seaport, Dominica I., Windward Is., Brit. West Indies; ✳ of Dominica colony; pop. ab. 9000.

Rose'bank' (rōz'băngk'). Town, E suburb of Cape Town, S Union of South Africa; pop. (white) ab. 7000.

Rose'bud' (rōz'bŭd'). **1** Creek ab. 100 m. long, SE Montana; rises in E Big Horn co., flows NE into Yellowstone river in Rosebud co.

2 County in Montana. See *Table* at Montana.

3 Village and agency in Rosebud Indian Reservation, Todd co., S South Dakota, ab. 45 m. NE of Martin; pop. (est.) 600.

4 City, Falls co., cen. Texas, 20 m. E of Temple; pop. 1644; in farming and ranching section.

Rose'burg (rōz'bûrg'). City, ⊗ of Douglas co., SW Oregon, 45 m. E of Coos Bay; pop. 11,467; produces fruit, turkeys, Douglas fir timber; extensive rose culture; canneries, sawmills, woodworking plants.

Rose'dale (rōz'dāl). **1** Former city, Wyandotte co., Kansas; annexed to Kansas City 1922.

2 City, a ⊗ of Bolivar co., NW Mississippi, on Mississippi river 31 m. N of Greenville; pop. 2339; cotton.

3 Urban community (unincorporated) Richland co., N cen. Ohio, SW of Akron; pop. 8204.

Ro·seg', Piz (pēts' rô·zäj'). Mountain 12,936 ft. in the Rhaetian Alps, Switzerland, W of Piz Bernina.

Rose Hill (rōz). Residential town, NW Mauritius, bet. Port Louis and Curepipe; pop., with adjacent Beau Bassin, (1931) 20,418.

Rose'land (rōz'lånd; -länd'). Borough, Essex co., NE New Jersey, 10 m. NW of Newark; pop. 2804.

Ro·selle' (rô·zěl'). Residential borough, Union co., NE New Jersey, 2 m. W of Elizabeth and adjoining Roselle Park; pop. 21,032; first community in world to have streets lighted by incandescent bulbs; housed laboratory of Thomas A. Edison in which he installed first electric lighting plant in world.

Roselle Park. Residential borough, Union co., NE New Jersey, 3 m. W of Elizabeth and adjoining Roselle; pop. 12,546; produces American Oriental rugs, iron, cement.

Rose'mead (rōz'mēd). City, Los Angeles co., SW California, E of Alhambra; pop. 15,476.

Rose'mont (rōz'mŏnt). Locality, Montgomery co., SE Pennsylvania, ab. 6 m. S of Norristown; pop. (est.) 5000; Rosemont Coll. (1921; women).

Ro'sen·berg. **1** (rō'z'n·bûrg) City, Fort Bend co., SE Texas, 31 m. WSW of Houston; pop. 9698; railroad center; in farming section.

2 (rō'zěn·běrk) See Ružomberok.

Ro'sen·daël' (rô'zän'däl'). Commune, Nord dept., N France, E suburb of Dunkerque; pop. (1931) 15,808; seaside resort; shipbuilding; jute weaving; breweries.

Rose·neath' (rōz'nēth'). Parish, Dunbarton co., W cen. Scotland, on Gare Loch ab. 23 m. NW of Glasgow; pop. 1923; U.S. naval and amphibious base in World War II.

Ro'sen·heim (rō'zěn·hīm). Industrial city, Bavaria, Germany, at foot of Alps on Inn river 34 m. SE of Munich; pop. 17,998; machinery, lumber; salt.

Rose Peak (rōz). Mountain 8787 ft. in N Greenlee co., E Arizona.

Rose Point *or* **Spit.** Cape, NE Graham I., N Queen Charlotte Is., off W Brit. Columbia, Canada.

Ro·se'to (rô·zē'tō). Borough, Northampton co., E Pennsylvania, 24 m. NE of Allentown; pop. 1630.

Ro·se'to de'gli A·bruz'zi (rô·zā'tô dâl'yĕ ä·brōōt'tsĕ). Commune, Teramo prov., Abruzzi e Molise, cen. Italy, on Adriatic Sea 17 m. E of Teramo; pop. 10,985.

Rose'ton (rōz'tŭn). Village, Orange co., SE New York, on Hudson river 4 m. N of Newburgh.

Ro·set'ta (rô·zĕt'à); *Arab.* **Ra·shid'** (rŏ·shēd'); *anc.* **Bol'bi·ti'ne** (bŏl'bĭ·tī'nĕ). **1** In the delta of the Nile river, N Egypt, the W branch of the river; ab. 146 m. long; now the wider channel of the Nile. Its mouth is the **Rosetta Mouth** (*anc.* **Bol'bi·tin'ic Mouth** [bŏl'bĭ·tĭn'ĭk]).
2 City on left bank of the Rosetta mouth of the Nile river, Beheira prov., Lower Egypt; pop. (1937) 25,684. The Rosetta stone, a piece of black basalt, was found near here 1799; it bore a trilingual inscription (in hieroglyphics, demotic characters, and Greek) and furnished the clue to Jean F. Champollion, French Egyptologist, toward deciphering Egyptian hieroglyphics.

Rose'ville (rōz'vĭl). **1** City, Placer co., E California, 18 m. NE of Sacramento; pop. 13,421; fruit shipping; wines.
2 Residential city, Macomb co., SE Michigan, 13 m. NE of Detroit; pop. 50,195.
3 Village, Ramsey co., E Minnesota, N suburb of St. Paul; pop. 23,997.

Ro'si·clare (rō'zĭ·klâr). City, Hardin co., SE Illinois, on Ohio river across from Kentucky; pop. 1700; fluorite quarries nearby.

Ro·si·gna'no Ma·rit'ti·mo (rô·zē·nyä'nô mä·rēt'tē·mô). Commune, Livorno prov., Tuscany, cen. Italy, near Ligurian Sea 10 m. ESE of Leghorn; pop. 17,601.

Ros'ig·nol' (rŏs'ĭg·nŏl'). Town, NE British Guiana, in Berbice co.; situated on W bank of Berbice river opp. New Amsterdam, 61 m. by rail SE of Georgetown.

Ro·sil'los Mountains (rô·sē'yōs). Range 5420 ft. in S Brewster co., W Texas.

Ro·şio'rii-de-Ve'de (rô·shyô'rē·dĕ·vĕ'dĕ). Commune, Walachia, S Romania, ab. 58 m. SW of Bucharest; pop. 11,443.

Rositten. See REZEKNE.

Ros'kil·de (rŭs'kĭl'ĕ). City at head of Roskilde Fjord, NE Sjælland, Denmark, W of Copenhagen; ⊗ of Copenhagen co.; pop. (1945) 23,497; capital of Denmark from 10th cent. to 1443; cathedral, dating from 11th cent.; scene of the signing of the Peace of Roskilde 1658 bet. Denmark and Sweden.

Roskilde Fjord. Eastern extension of Ise Fjord on N coast of Sjælland, Denmark; extends S inland for ab. 25 m.

Ro·slavl' (rŭ·slâv'l'y'). Town, S Smolensk Region, Soviet Russia, Europe; pop. 28,974; railroad junction town 65 m. SE of Smolensk serving as collection and trading point of an agricultural district. In World War II taken by German armies in Aug. 1941 and not recaptured by Russians until Sept. 25, 1943.

Ros'lyn (rŏz'lĭn). **1** Residential village, Nassau co., SE New York, on Long I. ab. 4 m. N of Mineola; pop. 2681; home and burial place of William Cullen Bryant. Adjacent villages are **Roslyn Harbor** and **Roslyn Estates**, of which **Roslyn Heights** is the post office.
2 Locality, Montgomery co., SE Pennsylvania, ab. 11 m. E of Norristown; pop. (est.) 5000.
3 City, Kittitas co., cen. Washington, 37 m. WSW of Wenatchee; pop. 1283; coal mining.
4 Suburb of Dunedin, New Zealand.

Ros'ny'-sous-Bois (rō'nē'sōō·bwä'). Commune, Seine dept., N France, E suburb of Paris; pop. 14,691.

Ro·so·li'ni (rô·zô·lē'nē). Commune, Siracusa prov., SE Sicily, 25 m. SW of Syracuse; pop. 14,052.

Ross (rŏs). **1** County in Ohio. See *Table* at OHIO.
2 Residential town, Marin co., W California, 14 m. NW of San Francisco; pop. 2551.

3 Urban township, Allegheny co., SW Pennsylvania N of Pittsburgh; pop. 25,952.
4 Borough, Westland provincial dist., W South I., New Zealand, on coast 13 m. SW of Hokitika; pop. 480.

Ross, Mount. 1 Peak 7300 ft., N Cascade range, NW Washington.
2 Peak 6120 ft. on Kerguelen I., in the Indian Ocean; highest point on the island.

Ross and Crom'ar·ty (rŏs, krŏm'ēr·tĭ). County, N Scotland, including Lewis I. in the Outer Hebrides; 3089 sq. m.; pop. (1951) 60,503; ⊗ Dingwall; a mountainous region with many lochs; sheep raising, fishing.

Ros·sa'no (rŏs·sä'nô); *anc.* **Ros'ci·a'num** (rŏs'ĭ·ā'nŭm). Commune, Cosenza prov., Calabria, S Italy, near Gulf of Taranto 29 m. NE of Cosenza; pop. 15,393; archiepiscopal see; valuable 6th-cent. manuscript of gospels.

Ross'bach (rôs'bäκ). Village, Saxony prov., S Prussia, Germany, 8 m. SW of Merseburg; scene of battle Nov. 5, 1757, during Seven Years' War, in which Frederick the Great defeated the French and Austrians.

Ross Barrier. See Ross SHELF ICE.

Ross'berg (rôs'bĕrκ). Former commune (pop. 23,420), Oppeln govt. dist., Silesia prov., Prussia, Germany; since 1927 part of Beuthen, now Bytom (in Poland).

Rossbodenhorn. See FLETSCHHORN.

Ross Dependency (rŏs). Section of Antarctica lying S of 60°S lat. and bet. 160°E and 150°W long.; includes Balleny Is., Coulman I., Ross I., Scott I., and the shores of Ross Sea (Edward VII Penin. and part of Victoria Land, *qq.v.*), also Little America and Roosevelt I. in the Ross Shelf Ice; proclaimed British July 30, 1923; administered for Great Britain by New Zealand.

Ros·seau' Lake (rŏ·sō'; rŏs'ō). One of the Muskoka lakes in Muskoka dist., SE Ontario, Canada; connected with lakes Joseph and Muskoka (*q.v.*).

Ros'sel (rŏs'l). Island ab. 18 m. long and 7 m. wide, easternmost of the Louisiade Archipelago, Territory of Papua, in Solomon Sea 22 m. NE of Tagula I.

Rössel. See RESZEL.

Ross'ford (rôs'fērd). Village, Wood co., NW Ohio, 3 m. S of Toledo; pop. 4406; glass manufactures.

Rossieny. See RASEINYAI.

Ros'sig·nol, Lake (rŏs'ĭg·nŭl). Lake in Queens co., SW Nova Scotia prov., Canada.

Ross Island (rŏs). **1** *formerly* **James Ross Island.** Island 39 m. long by 31 m. wide in Weddell Sea, Antarctica, Falkland Is. Dependencies; off E coast of Palmer Penin. in 64°10'S, 57°40'W.
2 Island in Ross Sea, W Ross Dependency, Antarctica, at W end of Ross Shelf Ice; separated from Victoria Land by McMurdo Sound; highest point Mount Erebus 13,200 ft.; has also Mt. Terror 10,750 ft.
3 Island in N Mergui Archipelago (*q.v.*), Burma.
4 See Lakes of KILLARNEY.

Ros'si·ter (rŏs'ĭ·tēr). Locality, Indiana co., W cen. Pennsylvania, 22 m. NE of Indiana; pop. (est.) 1078.

Rossiya. See RUSSIA.

Ross'land (rŏs'lănd; -länd'). Residential city, SE Brit. Columbia, Canada, near U.S. border 5 m. W of Trail; pop. 4604; center of mining district and headquarters for winter sports.

Ross·lare' (rŏs·lâr'). Town, co. Wexford, SE Eire; pop. 189; port of call for England-to-Ireland passenger steamers.

Ross'lau (rôs'lou). Manufacturing city, Halle dist., E Germany, on Elbe river N of Dessau; pop. 12,520.

Ross of Mull. See Ross of MULL.

Ross Quadrant (rŏs). Formerly, the quarter section of Antarctica (*q.v.*) bet. 90°W and 180°W; now chiefly E part of Ross Dependency, Marie Byrd Land, and W part of Ellsworth Highland.

Ross Sea. Arm of S Pacific Ocean bet. Victoria Land and Edward VII Penin., extending into Antarctica to ab. 85°S; borders on S on extensive area of Ross Shelf Ice. Discovered 1841 by Capt. James Ross.

Ross Shelf Ice; *also* **Ross Barrier.** Ice wall 50 to 200 ft. high and 400 m. long, and the ice shelf back of it, bordering on S part of Ross Sea and extending from Ross I. to Edward VII Penin., Antarctica; its S edge lies along foot of Queen Maud and Queen Alexandra Ranges. Discovered 1841 by Capt. James Ross; crossed 1903–04 by Capt. Scott to 82°17′S; S end passed 1908 by Shackleton's expedition.

Ross-shire (rŏs'shĭr; -shēr; rŏsh′-). = Ross and Cromarty county, Scotland.

Ross'ville (rŏs'vĭl; *Sou.* also -v'l). City, Walker co., NW Georgia, on Tennessee border 23 m. WNW of Dalton; pop. 4665; industrial suburb of Chattanooga, Tenn.

Ros'tock (rŏs'tŏk; *Ger.* rôs'tôk) *or* **Ro·stock–War'ne·mün'de** (rôs'tôk·vär'nĕ·mün'dĕ). Seaport and manufacturing city, ✳ of Rostock dist., East Germany, on the Warnow river 8 m. from the Baltic and 41 m. WSW of Stralsund; pop. (1939) 122,399; university (founded 1419); airport; trades in agricultural produce, salt; important fisheries; manufactures machinery, chemicals. An old town, commercially important from early times; a Hanse Town from 13th cent. and especially prosperous in latter half of 15th cent. Site of large Heinkel aircraft factory; frequently bombed in World War II Apr. 1942 and later.

Ros'tov (rŏs'tŏv; *Russ.* rŭ·stôf′). **1** Principality, cen. Russia, c. 9th cent. to 13th cent.; united with Suzdal (*q.v.*) as Rostov-Suzdal (*q.v.*) principality; superseded by Vladimir and Moscow.

2 *also, frequently,* **Rostov–on–Don** (-ŏn·dŏn′). City, ✳ of Rostov Region, SE Soviet Russia, Europe, in SW part on N bank of the Don ab. 28 m. from its mouth on the Gulf of Taganrog (Sea of Azov); pop. 510,253; once more prosperous as a trade center but declined on silting up of the Don; has regained some by construction of canal to Sea of Azov; does large distribution and transfer business of grain, machinery, manufactured goods, etc., to the Caucasus; a large industrial and cultural center; has important rail connections in all directions, and has an airport on main air lines. Founded 1761 above Azov (*q.v.*); suffered great damage in civil war of 1919–20. In World War II seized Nov. 21, 1941 by German army, retaken by Russians a week later, occupied by Germans again July 25, 1942 and recaptured Feb. 1943 in Russian winter campaign.

3 *or* **Ro·stov′ Ve·li′ki** (rŭ·stôf′ vyĭ·lyē′kĭ). Town, S Yaroslavl Region, Soviet Russia, Europe, on small lake 35 m. SW of Yaroslavl; pop. 23,305; on the Moscow-Yaroslavl railroad; a commercial town with metal foundries, flour mills, and local industries of drying vegetables and medicinal herbs. Founded by Slavs c. 862; exerted great influence on early Russian history as capital of Rostov-Suzdal principality 10th to 14th cents. Has fine 12th-cent. cathedral, interesting Kremlin (citadel) and other old structures. Declined in power after seizure by Mongols 1239–42; came under Moscow 1474; frequently plundered by Tatars, Lithuanians, and Poles, 15th to 17th cents.

Rostov Region. Region, SE Soviet Russia, Europe, on the lower Don; 36,130 sq. m.; pop. 2,894,038; ✳ Rostov. Bounded on N by Voronezh Region, on E by Stalingrad Region, on SE by Astrakhan Region, on S by Stavropol Territory, on SW by Krasnodar Territory, and on W by the Stalino and Voroshilovgrad Regions of the Ukraine. Consists mostly of fertile plains along the Don and its tributaries and agriculture is essential occupation; also considerable fishing and some cattle raising. Wheat is an important export. Chief towns Rostov, Taganrog, Novocherkassk, Shakhty, Kamensk Shakhtinski. Region of the lower Don held by Golden Horde (Tatars) c. 1237–1480; most of area came under Russians ab. the middle of 16th cent. except S part which remained Turkish (part of Khanate of the Crimea) c. 1481–1784; long inhabited by Don Cossacks; in World War II overrun by German armies 1942.

Ro·stov′–Suz′dal (rŭ·stôf′sŏŏz′dăl·y′). Medieval Russian principality, in cen. part of Russia, NE of modern Moscow; ✳ Rostov; chief towns Rostov, Suzdal, Vladimir (*q.v.*), Tver, and Moscow; absorbed early in 14th cent. by rapidly growing Moscow principality.

Ro′şu (rô′shŏŏ) *or* **Tur′nu Roşu** (tŏŏr′nŏŏ); *Ger.* **Ro′ter·turm′** (rō′tēr·tŏŏrm′). Mountain pass in the Transylvanian Alps, cen. Romania, S of Sibiu; traversed by Olt river; battle Sept. 26–29, 1916.

Rös'vatn′ (rûs′vät″n). Lake, S Nordland co., N Norway.

Ros'well (rŏz′wĕl; -wĕl). **1** Residential city, Fulton co., NW cen. Georgia, 18 m. N of Atlanta; pop. 2983; incorp. 1854.

2 City, ⊗ of Chaves co., SE New Mexico, 95 m. N of Texas border; pop. 39,593; in cattle, sheep, and farming country; oil refinery, cottonseed-oil mill, creameries; meat-packing house; potash mines. Walker Air Force Base; New Mexico Military Institute.

Ro'syth′ (rō′sīth′). Village, Fife, E Scotland, on N shore of Firth of Forth; planned as big naval base, work begun 1909, secondary to Scapa Flow during World War I; since 1925 used for care and maintenance.

Ro'ta (rō′tä). Island, S end of Mariana Is., W Pacific, midway bet. Guam and Tinian; ab. 35 sq. m.; highest point 1612 ft.; Japanese base used in attack on Guam Dec. 11, 1941; severely bombed by Americans during latter half of 1944 but not occupied until end of the war.

Ro·tan′ (rō·tăn′). City, Fisher co., NW cen. Texas, 28 m. N of Sweetwater; pop. 2788; gypsum manufactures; railroad terminus.

Roterturm. See Roşu.

Ro'then·burg ob der Tau'ber (rō′tĕn·bŏŏrĸ ôp dēr tou′bēr). Commune, Bavaria, Germany, on Tauber river 31 m. SSE of Würzburg; pop. (1939) 9332; became free imperial city 1172; at height of its prosperity at end of 14th cent.; interesting medieval walls, towers, and gates remain.

Roth'er (rŏth′ēr). **1** River 21 m. long, Derbyshire and West Riding, Yorkshire, N England; flows into the Don at Rotherham.

2 Either of two small streams in Sussex, S England: (1) In Hampshire and W Sussex. (2) In E Sussex, partly on boundary of Kent (see Romney Marsh); flows into English Channel.

Roth'er·ham (rŏth′ēr·ăm). County borough, West Riding, Yorkshire, N England, at confluence of Rother and Don rivers 6 m. NE of Sheffield; pop. 69,691, (1951 pop.) 82,334; in an iron and coal section; manufactures iron and steel goods, chemicals, glass, pottery.

Roth'er·hithe (rŏth′ēr·hīth) *or* **Red'riff** (rĕd′rĭf). Parish in Southwark metropolitan borough, London, England; terminus of Grand Surrey Canal; commercial dockyards.

Rothe'say (rŏth′sī; -sā). Manufacturing burgh, ⊗ of Bute co., on the island of Bute off SW coast of Scotland; pop. 10,145; resort; ruins of 11th-cent. castle.

Roth'well (rŏth′wĕl; -wĕl; *locally also* rō′ĕl). Urban district, West Riding, Yorkshire, N England; pop. 24,283; manufactures rope and twine.

Ro'ti (rō′tē) *or* **Rot'ti** (rō′tē). Island, Indonesia, SW of Timor; 50 m. long by 10 or 12 m. wide; ab. 466 sq. m.; pop. 59,221; chief village Baä.

Roti Strait. Channel bet. SW end of Timor I. and the island of Roti, Indonesia; connects Savu Sea with Timor Sea.

Ro·to·a'va (rō′tō·ä′vä). Chief village of Fakarava atoll, lat. 16°S and long. 146°W, Tuamotu Archipelago, S Pacific Ocean; pop. ab. 100; former headquarters of French administrator.

Rotomagus. See Rouen.

Ro·to·ma'ha·na (rō′tō·mä′hȧ·nä; -mȧ·hä′nä). Lake in N cen. North I., New Zealand, in the Rotorua dist. S of Lake Tarawera; famous for its sinter terraces ("pink" and "white" terraces) which were destroyed by an eruption of Mount Tarawera June 10, 1886.

Ro·ton'do, Mon'te (môn'tā rō·tôn'dō). Peak 8610 ft. in cen. part of the island of Corsica.

Ro·ton'do, Piz'zo (pêt'tsō rō·tôn'dō). Peak 10,490 ft., highest in the Saint Gotthard range of the Lepontine Alps, S cen. Switzerland.

Ro·to·ru'a (rō'tŏ·rōō'à). Borough, Auckland provincial dist., N cen. North I., New Zealand, at SW end of **Rotorua Lake** 120 m. SE of Auckland; pop. (1941 est.) 6540; in volcanic region, with thermal springs, healing waters, vapor and mud baths, beautiful scenery and excellent hunting and fishing; seat of government-owned sanatorium.

Rot'ter·dam (rŏt'ĕr·dăm; *Du.* rôt'ĕr·däm'). 1 Manufacturing and commercial city and seaport, ✳ of South Holland prov., W Netherlands, on both sides of the Nieuwe Maas ab. 15 m. from the North Sea; pop. (1939) 619,686; has system of canals connecting with the Rhine river and all parts of the Netherlands; chief industries shipbuilding, manufacture of cigars, chemicals, spirits, leather, refining of sugar; birthplace of Erasmus; 15th-cent. Gothic Church of St. Lawrence, Boyman's Museum; zoological and botanical gardens. Central part of city destroyed by German bombings May 14, 1940.
2 Urban community (unincorporated), Schenectady co., E New York, NW of Schenectady; pop. 16,871.

Rott'hau'sen (rôt'hou'zĕn). Former commune in Rhine Province, Prussia, Germany, now part of Gelsenkirchen.

Rotti. See ROTI.

Rot'tum·er·oog' (rôt'ŏŏ·mĕr·ōĸ'). Island in the North Sea 4 m. SW of Borkum; easternmost of the Dutch West Frisian Is.

Rott'weil (rôt'vīl). City, Baden-Württemberg state, Germany, on Neckar river 49 m. SSW of Stuttgart; pop. 10,556; silk, powder. Founded by Romans.

Ro·tu'ma (rō·tōō'mà). Chief island and small group of eight islands in SW Pacific Ocean, lat. 12°30'S and long. 177°7'E, 220 m. NNW of Fiji Is.; ab. 8 m. long, area 14 sq. m.; pop. (1940) 3075; joined with the Fiji Is. 1881 in forming the British colony of Fiji. Chief village Motusa. Beautiful and healthful, remains unexploited. Original Rotumans were pure Polynesians. Discovered 1791; in years following became resort for escaped convicts.

Rouad, Île. See ARWAD.

Rou'baix' (rōō'bĕ'). Manufacturing and commercial city, Nord dept., N France, 7 m. NE of Lille; pop. 107,105; manufactures textiles (esp. woolens and linens), carpets, leather. Rose to industrial prosperity in 19th cent.; suffered under German occupation 1914–18.

Rou·en' (rōō·än'; rōō·äN'; *Fr.* rwäN); *anc.* **Ro·tom'a·gus** (rō·tŏm'à·gŭs). Commercial and manufacturing city, ✳ of Seine-Maritime dept., N France, on right bank of Seine river 71 m. NW of Paris; pop. 122,832; famous 13th-cent. Gothic cathedral, 14th-cent. abbey of Saint Ouen (in which Joan of Arc was sentenced to death 1431), 15th-cent. church of St. Maclou, the Tour de la Grosse Horloge, 15th-cent. palace of justice, archiepiscopal palace, 15th-cent. Hôtel de Bourgthéroulde, and the ancient Halles or market buildings; professional and technical schools, museum of antiquities, etc.; noted esp. for cotton manufactures; manufactures also woolen goods, machinery, chemicals, and has refineries and smelting works; trades in cotton, coal, petroleum, corn, flour, brandy, wine, manufactured goods, agricultural produce.
History: Built in pre-Roman times; captured and sacked by Normans 9th cent. A.D.; medieval capital of Normandy; held by English 1418–49; Joan of Arc burned here 1431 (in the Place de la Pucelle, named for her); taken by Huguenots 1562; occupied by Germans 1870; in World War II often bombed, esp. its railroad yards 1942–44; taken by Allies Aug. 31, 1944.

Rou·ergue' (rwĕrg). Ancient province (until 1789) of S France, in region now comprising Aveyron dept. and a

small part of Tarn-et-Garonne; ✳ Rodez; medieval countship came eventually to Armagnac family; passed to crown 1472.

Rouffaer. See TARIKOE.

Rouge (rōōzh). 1 River ab. 120 m. long in SW Quebec prov., Canada; flows S and empties into the Ottawa river in SW Argenteuil co.
2 French name of the COI river of Tonkin, Indochina.

Roulers. See ROESELARE.

Roum. See RUM.

Roumania. See ROMANIA.

Roumelia. = RUMELIA.

Round'house' Rock (round'hous'). Peak 4255 ft. in Cheyenne co., W Nebraska.

Round Lake Beach. Village, Lake co., NE Illinois, W of Waukegan; pop. 5011.

Round'top' (round'tŏp'). 1 Mountain 4419 ft. in Scotts Bluff co., W Nebraska.
2 Elevation 2030 ft. in Tioga co., N Pennsylvania.

Round Top. Elevation comprising Little Round Top and Big Round Top, forming a granite spur at S end of Cemetery Ridge (*q.v.*), Gettysburg, Pennsylvania; vantage point held by Union forces in third day of battle of Gettysburg.

Round'up' (round'ŭp'). City, ⊗ of Musselshell co., cen. Montana, 45 m. N of Billings; pop. 2842; in coal-mining section.

Round'way' Down (round'wā'). Hill near Devizes, Wiltshire, SW England; Parliamentary forces under Sir William Waller defeated here by Royalists 1643.

Rouphia. See ALPHEUS.

Rou'say (rou'zĭ). One of the Orkney Is., off N coast of Scotland; ab. 4 m. long and 3 m. wide.

Rouselare. See ROESELARE.

Rous'es Point (rous'ĭz). Village and port of entry, Clinton co., NE corner of New York, at upper end of Lake Champlain at Canadian border 21 m. N of Plattsburg; pop. 2160; in farming country; manufactures chemical products, skis; U.S. customhouse, immigration station.

Rous·sil'lon' (rōō'sē'yôn'). Historical region of S cen. France; bounded anciently on N by Languedoc, on S by the Pyrenees, on W by Andorra, on NW by Countship of FOIX; ✳ Perpignan (12th cent. ff.). Inhabited originally by Iberians; made part of Roman Gallia Narbonensis (see GAUL); began separate existence at beginning of 10th cent.; united to Aragon 1172; acquired by Louis XIV 1659 (Treaty of the Pyrenees); province of France under ancien régime.

Routt (rout). County in Colorado. See *Table* at COLORADO.

Rou'ville' (rōō'vĭl'). County, Quebec, Canada. See *Table* at QUEBEC.

Rou'vroy' (rōō'vrwä'). Commune, Pas-de-Calais dept., N France, 9 m. NE of Arras; pop. (1931) 10,224; coal mines.

Roux (rōō). Commune, Hainaut prov., SW Belgium, NW suburb of Charleroi; pop. 10,683.

Rou·yn' (rwän; *Angl.* rōō'in). Mining town, Timiskaming co., SW Quebec, Canada, 240 m. NW of Ottawa and on railroad N of Lake Timiskaming; pop. 14,633; center of great copper-mining and gold-mining district.

Ro·va'to (rō·vä'tō). Commune, Brescia prov., Lombardy, N Italy, 12 m. WNW of Brescia; pop. 10,207.

Ro·ve·re'to (rō·vâ·rā'tō); *Ger.* **Ro'freit** (rō'frīt). Commune, Trento prov., Venezia Tridentina, NE Italy, on Adige river 13 m. SSW of Trent; pop. 20,758; 14th-cent. castle; 15th-cent. church; art and historical collections; World War (I) museum. Scene of Napoleon's victory over the Austrians Aug. 15, 1796; scene of Austrian and Italian operations in World War I.

Rove Tunnel (rōv; *Fr.* rôv). Tunnel 4½ m. long, 59 ft. wide, and 50 ft. high in Bouches-du-Rhône dept., SE France, in the hills NW of Marseilles, providing a sea-level passageway for the Marseilles-Rhone canal.

Ro'vi·a'na (rō'vê·ä'nà). Lagoon. See NEW GEORGIA.

Ro·vi′go (rō·vē′gō). **1** Commune, Alger dept., N Algeria, in foothills just S of Algiers; pop. 12,088.
2 Province of Italy. See *Table* at ITALY.
3 Commune, ✳ of Rovigo prov., Venezia Euganea, NE Italy, 36 m. SW of Venice; pop. 39,954; 17th-cent. cathedral; 9th-cent. church; old city walls; manufactures leather, candles. First mentioned in 9th cent.; under counts of Este from 1194; to Venice 1395 ff.
Ro′vinj (rō′vĕn·y'); *Ital.* **Ro·vi′gno** or **Rovigno d'I′-stri·a** (rō·vĕn′yō dĕs′trĕ·ä). Manufacturing seaport commune, Istria Penin., Croatia, NW Yugoslavia, on Adriatic Sea 17 m. NNW of Pulj; pop. 10,028; formerly in Italy. Institute for marine biology.
Rov′no (rôv′nŭ); *Pol.* **Rów′ne** (rōōv′nĕ). **1** Region, W Ukraine, U.S.S.R., formerly in SE Poland.
2 *Ger.* **Row′no** (rôv′nō). Industrial commune, W Ukraine, U.S.S.R., 42 m. ESE of Lutsk; formerly in Wołyń dept., Poland; pop. (1938–39 est.) 46,680; important railroad junction; manufactures textiles, agricultural machinery, oil, soap, matches. Dates from 12th cent.; battle 1915; occupied by Germans Feb. 1918 and by Russians 1939, again by Germans 1941 and by Russians 1944.
Rovuma. See RUVUMA.
Row′an (*Ky.*, rou′ăn; *N.C.*, rō·ăn′). Name of counties in two states of the U.S. See *Tables* at KENTUCKY and NORTH CAROLINA.
Ro·way′ton (rō·wā′t'n). Subdivision of town and city of NORWALK, Connecticut.
Row′ley (rou′lĭ). Town, Essex co., NE corner of Massachusetts, 22 m. ENE of Lowell; pop. 2783; settled 1638, incorp. 1639; said to be site of first fulling mill in America; now in agricultural section.
Row′ley Re′gis (rou′lĭ rē′jĭs; rō′lĭs). Urban district, Staffordshire, W cen. England, 7 m. W of Birmingham; pop. 49,409; iron foundries, potteries, coal mines nearby.
Równe, Rowno. See ROVNO.
Row′ter, Mount (rou′tēr). Peak 13,750 ft. in Gunnison co., W cen. Colorado.
Rox′bor′o (rŏks′bûr′ō). City, ⊗ of Person co., N North Carolina, 27 m. N of Durham; pop. 5147.
Rox′burgh (rŏks′bûr′ō; -bŭ·rŭ; -brŭ) or **Rox′burgh-shire** (-shĭr; -shēr). County, SE Scotland; 666 sq. m.; pop. (1951) 45,562; ⊗ Jedburgh; the rivers Teviot, Tweed; mountainous region; chief industry sheep raising; manufactures tweed cloth, woolen hosiery.
Rox′bur′y (rŏks′bĕr′ĭ; -bēr·ĭ; -brĭ). **1** Residential district, S Boston, Massachusetts; formerly a city, became part of Boston 1868; founded 1630.
2 Town, Delaware co., S New York, 18 m. E of Delhi; pop. (est.) 2238; birthplace of John Burroughs and Jay Gould.
Rox′en, Lake (rôk′s'n). Lake ab. 16 m. long, SE Sweden, bet. Lake Vättern and the Baltic Sea; Linköping is near its S shore.
Ro′xo, Cape (rō′shōō). Point on W coast of Africa, at S end of coast of Senegal 12°19′N.
Roy (roi). **1** Village, Harding co., NE New Mexico, 58 m. NNW of Tucumcari; pop. 633.
2 City, Weber co., NE Utah, SW of Ogden; pop. 9239.
Roy′al, Mount (roi′ăl); *Fr.* **Mont Roy′al′** (môn′ rwä′yàl′). A height 763 ft. in center of Montreal city, Quebec, Canada.
Roy′ale′ (rwä′yàl′). One of the Safety Is. (*q.v.*).
Royale, Isle. See ISLE ROYALE.
Roy′al Gorge (roi′ăl gôrj′). Scenic gorge 4.5 m. long in the Grand Canyon of the Arkansas river just W of Canon City, S cen. Colorado; its red granite walls rise sheerly more than 1000 ft. Railroad runs through bottom of gorge, suspended by Hanging Bridge at narrowest part; above crossed by Royal Gorge Suspension Bridge 1053 ft. above the Arkansas river; said to be highest bridge in the world, completed 1929.
Royal Leamington Spa. See LEAMINGTON, England.
Royal Oak. City, Oakland co., SE Michigan, 12 m. N of

Detroit; pop. 80,612; residential suburb of Detroit.
Roy′al·ton (roi′ăl·tŭn; -t'n). Village, Franklin co., S Illinois, 35 m. SSW of Mount Vernon; pop. 1225.
Roy′an′ (rwä′yäN′). Commune, Charente-Maritime dept., W France, on Atlantic Ocean at mouth of the Gironde; pop. 12,192; popular beach resort; formerly important sardine fisheries. In World War II largely destroyed by bombing 1945.
Roye (rwä). Town, Somme dept., N France, 18 m. N of Compiègne; pop. 5106; battles Mar. 1917 and Aug. 27, 1918.
Roy′ers·ford (roi′ērz·fērd). Borough, Montgomery co., SE Pennsylvania, on Schuylkill river 27 m. NW of Philadelphia; pop. 3969; tools, stoves, steel forgings, bottles.
Roys′ton (rois′tŭn). **1** City, Franklin, Hart, and Madison cos., NE Georgia, NE of Athens; pop. 2333.
2 Urban district, West Riding, Yorkshire, N England; pop. 8137.
Roys′ville (roiz′vĭl). Town, W Liberia, W Africa, just NW of Monrovia on the coast.
Roy′ton (roi′t'n). Urban district, Lancashire, NW England, 9 m. NE of Manchester; pop. 14,772.
Rózsahegy. See RUŽOMBEROK.
Ruad. = *Rouad:* see ARWAD.
Ru·a′ha (rōō·ä′hä). River. ab. 300 m. long in cen. Tanganyika, E Africa; flows E into Rufiji river.
Ru·an′da; *now* **Rwan·da** (rōō·än′dà). Republic, cen. Africa, N of Burundi; area 10,166 sq. m.; pop. ab. 3,000,000; ✳ Kigali; until 1962 part of Ruanda-Urundi.
Ruanda–U·run′di (-ōō·rōōn′dĕ). Former Belgian trust territory, SE cen. Africa; 21,234 sq. m.; pop. (1938 est.) 3,752,742; ✳ Usumbura; bounded on N by Uganda, E and S by Tanganyika, and W by Republic of Congo; NE shore of Lake Tanganyika formed its SW boundary, Lake Kivu on border between it and the Congo; comprised two districts, Ruanda in N, Urundi in S; rich cattle country. Formerly part of German East Africa; ceded to Belgium 1919 as mandatary of the League of Nations; united administratively with Belgian Congo (*q.v.*) 1925–60; made a trust territory Dec. 1946; divided 1962 into two independent countries, Rwanda and Burundi. See RUANDA, URUNDI.
Ru·a·pe′hu (rōō′ä·pā′hōō). Volcano 9175 ft. in S cen. North I., New Zealand, in Tongariro National Park.
Ru·a·pu′ke (rōō′ä·pōō′kà). Small island at E end of Foveaux Strait off S coast of South I., New Zealand.
Rub′ al Kha′li (rōōb′ al kä′lē) or **Ar Ri·mal′** (ŭr ri·mäl′); *Eng.* **Great Sand′y Desert** (săn′dĭ). Desert region in S Arabia, extending S from Nejd to Hadhramaut, and from Yemen to Oman; ab. 300,000 sq. m.; practically unexplored and unknown. By some geographers also called **Dah′na** (dä′h'·nà) or **Da′ha·na** (dä′-hä·nà), a name which is more correctly restricted to the area of red sand in NE Nejd which sends a narrow tongue down into the S desert.
Rubi. See RUVO DI PUGLIA.
Ru′bi·con (rōō′bĭ·kŏn); *mod.* **Fiu′mi·ci′no** (fyōō′mē-chē′nō). Small river in N cen. Italy; flows E into Adriatic Sea in lat. 44°10′N just N of Rimini; with the Apennines, formed boundary bet. Italy and Cisalpine Gaul in the time of the ancient Roman republic. Its crossing in 49 B.C. by Julius Caesar with his army began a civil war between Pompey and the senate.
Ru′bi·doux′, Mount (rōō′bĭ·dōō′). Rocky height, Riverside, Riverside co., SE California; has on its top a cross dedicated to memory of Junípero Serra. Spanish missionary to the Indians; Easter sunrise services.
Ru′by (rōō′bĭ). Village on S bank of the Yukon, W cen. Alaska, ab. 240 m. W of Fairbanks; pop. (est.) 170; river port and gold mines.
Ruby Lake. Lake in S Elko co. and N White Pine co., NE Nevada.
Ru′by Mines (rōō′bĭ mīnz′). South section of Katha dist., along Irrawaddy river S of Katha, Upper Burma; formerly itself a district.

Ruby Range. Range chiefly in S Elko co., NE Nevada, extending S into White Pine co.

Ru′da. 1 (rōō′dȧ) Former name of RODA.
2 (rōō′dä) Mining commune, E Śląsk dept., SW Poland, just E of Zabrze; pop. (1929) 23,560.

Ru′da Pa′bja·nic′ka (rōō′dä pä′byä·nĕts′kä). Industrial commune, Łódź dept., Poland, 5 m. S of Łódź; pop. (1938–39 est.) 20,034; textiles.

Rü′des·heim (rü′dĕs·hīm) or **Rüdesheim am Rhein** (äm rīn′). Commune, Hesse state, West Germany, on the Rhine 19 m. WSW of Wiesbaden; pop. (1933) 4740; vineyards, in the Rheingau.

Rud′kö′bing (rōō′kû′bing). Town on W coast of Langeland I., Denmark; pop. 4111.

Rud′nik Mountains (rōō′dnĕk). Low mountain range in N Serbia, NE Yugoslavia; scene of battle in which Serbians defeated Austrians in the "Battle of the Ridges" Dec. 1914.

Ru′dolf (rōō′dōlf). Former province in NE Uganda, now in Turkana extraprovincial dist., NW Kenya colony.

Rudolf, Lake. Lake in N Kenya, E Africa; 170 m. long and 30 m. wide; area ab. 3475 sq. m.; N tip is bet. Ethiopia and SE Sudan.

Ru′dolph (rōō′dōlf). Island, northernmost of Franz Josef Land, in Arctic Ocean; Russian base and meteorological station.

Ru′dol·stadt′ (rōō′dōl·shtät′). Manufacturing city, Karl-Marx-Stadt, East Germany, on Saale river 49 m. W of Zwickau; pop. (1939) 19,471; airport; manufactures porcelain, chemicals, X-ray materials.

Ru·eil′–Mal′mai′son′ (rü·ā′y′·mȧl′mā′zôN′). Industrial commune, Seine-et-Oise dept., N France, on Seine river 8 m. W of Paris; pop. 26,796; manufactures automobiles, chemical products, photographic supplies, foundry products; tombs of Empress Josephine and Queen Hortense.

Ru·fi′ji (rōō·fē′jĕ). Navigable river ab. 250 m. long in E Africa; rises in S cen. Tanganyika; flows NE and E into Indian Ocean opp. island of Mafia.

Ru′fisque′ (rü′fēsk′). Commune in W Senegal, West Africa, near Dakar and 10 m. E of Cape Vert; pop. (1936) ab. 20,000.

Rug′by (rŭg′bĭ). **1** City, ⊗ of Pierce co., N cen. North Dakota, 65 m. E of Minot; pop. 2972; grain, stock, dairy, poultry farms. Determined by the Geological Survey to be the geographic center of North America.
2 Urban district, Warwickshire, cen. England, on the Avon 28 m. ESE of Birmingham; pop. 45,418; railroad junction; site of Rugby School, opened 1574 and chartered 1777.

Ruge′ley (rōōj′lĭ). Urban district, Staffordshire, W cen. England, 9 m. SE of Stafford; pop. 8525; iron founding, coal mining.

Rü′gen (rü′gĕn). Island of very irregular shape in the Baltic Sea off NW coast of the province of Pomerania, Prussia; largest island of Germany; 374 sq. m.; pop. 53,900; chief town Bergen. Separated by the narrow Strelasund from the mainland and connected by ferry with Stralsund. Chief industry fishing. Seized by the Danes 1168; united with Pomerania 1325 and with Sweden 1648; became part of Prussia 1815.

Ruh′la (rōō′lä). Commune, Erfurt dist., East Germany, just S of Eisenach; pop. (1933) 8212; summer resort; mineral springs.

Ruhr (rōōr; Ger. rōōr). River 144 m. long in W Germany; flows NW and W in Westphalia prov. and joins the Rhine at Ruhrort (a part of Duisburg-Hamborn); navigable to Witten, ab. 30 m. The **Ruhr′ge·biet′** (rōōr′gĕ·bēt′), the valley of the Ruhr, is a mining region and includes many great industrial cities, as Essen, Bochum, Duisburg-Hamborn, Gelsenkirchen, Dortmund, Oberhausen, etc. See *Map* at GERMANY. In World War I the district was of great military importance; at end of war occupied Jan. 1923 to July 1925 by France and Belgium because of Germany's default in

reparations. In World War II bombed severely and continuously 1942–45; in Allied advance into Germany 1945 surrounded and cut off Mar.–Apr.; occupied and cleared by Apr. 18.

Ruhr′ort′ (-ôrt′). Former town in Rhine Province, Prussia, Germany, now part of Duisburg.

Ru–i–Khaf (rōō′yĕ·kȧf′) or **Khaf.** Town, Khurasan prov., NE Iran, ab. 40 m. from the border of Afghanistan and 120 m. S of Meshed.

Ruis′lip North′wood (rīs′lĭp nôrth′wōŏd). Urban district, Middlesex, SE England, 16 m. WNW of London; pop. 68,274; part of Greater London; residential.

Rui′vo, Pi′co (pē′kōō rwē′vōō). Volcanic peak 6056 ft. on the island of Madeira; highest point in the Madeira Is.

Ruiz (rwēs). Peak 17,390 ft. in the Andes Mts., in Caldas dept., W cen. Colombia.

Rukhlovo. See SKOVORODINO.

Ru′ki (rōō′kĕ). River ab. 250 m. long, NW Congo, S cen. Africa; flows W into the Congo river at Coquilhatville at the equator; has several long tributaries, esp. the Busira.

Ruk′wa, Lake (rŭk′wȧ). Shallow lake ab. 20 m. long in SW Tanganyika, E Africa.

Rum (rōōm) or **Roum** (rōōm); also **I·co′ni·um** (ī·kō′nĭ·ŭm). Arabic name used indefinitely by Moslems for the people of the Byzantine Empire—from *Rōmaivi*, Romans, the name the Byzantine Greeks applied to themselves; hence: (1) That part of the Byzantine Empire in Asia Minor. (2) Later, the Seljuk sultanate ab. 1200, occupying most of Asia Minor. Its capital was Iconium.

Rum, Isle of (rŭm). Island of the Inner Hebrides, off W coast of Scotland; 8 sq. m.; administratively a part of Inverness co.; chiefly a deer preserve.

Rum, Sound of (rŭm). Channel bet. Rum I. and Eigg I. in the Inner Hebrides, off W coast of Scotland.

Ru′ma (rōō′mä). Commune, Voivodina, NE Yugoslavia, 35 m. NW of Belgrade; pop. ab. 12,000.

Ru·ma·di′ya (rōō·mä·dē′yȧ; -yä). = RAMADI.

Ru·ma′ni (rōō·mä′nĭ), formerly **Ro·ma′ni** (rô-). Village near Qatia, E of Suez Canal, Egypt; severe fighting Apr. and Aug. 4–5, 1916 bet. British and Turks.

Rumania. See ROMANIA.

Rum′burk (rōōm′bōōrk); Ger. **Rum′burg** (rōōm′-bōōrk). Town, N Bohemia prov., W Czechoslovakia, E of Labe (Elbe) river and N of Česká Lípa; pop. (1930) 10,466.

Rum Cay (rŭm). One of the Bahama Is., in the Atlantic Ocean SSW of San Salvador (Watlings I.); 29 sq. m.; pop. (1943) 219.

Ru′me·lange′ (rüm′länzh′); Ger. **Rü′me·ling′en** (rü′-mĕ·ling′ĕn). Commune, Luxembourg, Europe, in extreme S on French border S of Esch; pop. (1930) 5260.

Ru·me′lia (rōō·mēl′yȧ; -mē′lĭ·ȧ). European division (*Turk.* Rumeli, the land of the Romans or Byzantines, sometimes called **Ro·ma′nia** [rô·mān′yȧ; -mā′nĭ·ȧ]) of the old Turkish empire; included Albania, Macedonia, and Thrace. See EASTERN RUMELIA.

Ru′me·li′ Hi′sa·ri′ (rōō′mĕ·lē′ hi′sä·rĭ′). Village, Turkey in Europe, on W bank of the Bosporus 7 m. NE of İstanbul of which it is a suburb; has fortifications with great tower, built by Mohammed II 1452. Site of Robert College.

Rum′ford (rŭm′fērd). Town, Oxford co., W Maine, 35 m. NNW of Lewiston; pop. 10,005; paper mills.

Rummel. See Wadi el KEBIR.

Ru·moi (rōō·moi). Seaport, Hokkaido prefecture, W coast of Hokkaido I., Japan, 65 m. N of Sapporo; pop. 25,748; on branch railroad line; has grown from small fishing village to considerable export town.

Rum′son (rŭm′s′n). Borough and summer resort, Monmouth co., E cen. New Jersey, 16 m. SE of Perth Amboy; pop. 6405; scene of motorboat and sailboat racing in summer, and skating contests and iceboat regattas in winter.

Run′a·way′, Cape (rŭn′à·wā′). Cape on NE coast of North I., New Zealand, at E side of entrance to the Bay of Plenty.

Run′corn (rŭng′kĕrn). Urban district, Cheshire, NW England, on the Mersey 10 m. ESE of Liverpool; pop. 23,933; terminus of the Bridgewater Canal; boatbuilding, chemical manufacture; ironworks.

Rung′we (rŏong′wā). Volcanic peak 10,416 ft. in SW Tanganyika, E Africa, N of Lake Nyasa.

Run′nels (rŭn′lz). County in Texas. See *Table* at TEXAS.

Run′ne·mede (rŭn′ĕ·mēd). Residential borough, Camden co., SW New Jersey, 7 m. S of Camden; pop. 8396; settled by Quakers 1683.

Run′ny·mede (rŭn′ĭ·mēd). Meadow on S bank of the Thames in Surrey, S England, near Egham, W of Staines; Magna Charta signed here by King John June 15, 1215 A.D.; in the river off the meadow is Magna Charta I., popularly considered to be site of the signing.

Ru·pan′co, La′go (lä′gō rōō·päng′kō). Lake in Osorno prov., S cen. Chile, N of Puerto Montt.

Ru′pel′ (rü′pĕl′). Stream ab. 7 m. long in N cen. Belgium; formed by confluence of the Dyle and Nethe rivers, flows NW into the Schelde 8 m. SW of Antwerp.

Rupella. See LA ROCHELLE, France.

Ru′pel Pass (rōō′pĕl). Mountain pass, valley of Strymon river, Macedonia, NE Greece; used by Germans in invasion of Greece Apr. 1941.

Ru′pert (rōō′pĕrt). **1** City, ⊗ of Minidoka co., S Idaho, on Snake river 40 m. E of Twin Falls; pop. 4153; laid out by government engineers as model city 1905; incorp. as village 1906, as city 1917; agricultural center; potatoes, sugar beets, dairy products, livestock.
2 River 380 m. long, W Quebec prov., Canada; flows out of Lake Mistassini W into James Bay at Rupert House.

Rupert House. Village and trading post at mouth of Rupert river, W Quebec, Canada, on S bank.

Ru′pert's Land (rōō′pĕrts). The territory of the Hudson's Bay Company 1670–1869, N Canada, forming the drainage basin of Hudson Bay. In 1869 it became a part of North West Territory (see NORTHWEST TERRITORIES).

Ruphia. = *Rouphia:* see ALPHEUS.

Rup′pert Coast (rōō′pĕrt). Section of Antarctica on coast of Marie Byrd Land E of Edward VII Penin. in ab. 140°30′ to 147°W long.

Ru′pu·nu′ni (rōō′pŭ·nōō′nĭ). River ab. 250 m. long in British Guiana; rises in SW and flows N and E into Essequibo river.

Rur (rōōr; *Ger.* rōōr) *or* **Roer** (rōōr; *Du.* rōōr). River ab. 130 m. long in the Rhineland, western Germany; rises in hills W of Rhine and flows NNW to the Maas at Roermond in Netherlands; fighting along its banks in World War II, esp. near Düren and Jülich; dam near source blown up Feb. 1945, delaying Allied advance.

Rurki. See ROORKEE.

Ru·ru′tu (rōō·rōō′tōō). See TUBUAÏ ISLANDS.

Rusaddir. See MELILLA.

Ru′se (rōō′sä); *Turk.* **Rus·chuk′** (rōōs·chōōk′). City, Shumen dept., NE Bulgaria, on Danube river 40 m. S of Bucharest; pop. (1934) 49,447; commercial and industrial center. An old town, fortified in Roman times, destroyed by barbarians in 7th cent.; important in Russo-Turkish Wars of 19th cent.

Rusein, Piz. See TÖDI.

Rusellae. See GROSSETO.

Rush (rŭsh). Name of counties in two states of the U.S. See *Tables* at INDIANA and KANSAS.

Rush′den (rŭsh′dĕn). Urban district, Northamptonshire, cen. England, 14 m. ENE of Northampton; pop. 16,321; boot and shoe factories.

Rush′more, Mount (rŭsh′mōr). Peak 6040 ft. in Black Hills, W South Dakota, NE of Harney Peak; faces of Washington, Lincoln, Jefferson, and Theodore Roosevelt, carved 1927–41 by Gutzon Borglum, are a national memorial.

Rush′ville (rŭsh′vĭl). **1** City, ⊗ of Schuyler co., W Illinois, 45 m. ENE of Quincy; pop. 2819.
2 City, ⊗ of Rush co., E cen. Indiana, 40 m. ESE of Indianapolis; pop. 7264; shipping point for corn and hogs.
3 City, ⊗ of Sheridan co., NW Nebraska; pop. 1228.

Rusk (rŭsk). **1** Name of counties in two states of the U.S. See *Tables* at TEXAS and WISCONSIN.
2 Town, ⊗ of Cherokee co., E Texas, 28 m. E of Palestine; pop. 4900; fuller's earth, lignite, oil, gas deposits.

Rusk, Mount. Peak 3680 ft. in the Catskill Mts., Greene co., SE New York.

Ruspina. See MONASTIR, Tunisia.

Russ. See NEMAN.

Rus′sell (rŭs′l). **1** Name of counties in four states of the U.S. See *Tables* at ALABAMA, KANSAS, KENTUCKY, VIRGINIA.
2 City, ⊗ of Russell co., cen. Kansas, 37 m. N of Great Bend; pop. 6113; trade center in agricultural and grazing section, near petroleum and natural-gas deposits.
3 City, Greenup co., NE Kentucky, on Ohio river 5 m. NNW of Ashland; pop. 1458.
4 County, Ontario, Canada. See *Table* at ONTARIO.
5 Borough, Auckland provincial dist., N North I., New Zealand, on Bay of Islands 115 m. NNW of Auckland; old whaling port; has oldest buildings in New Zealand; site first chosen 1840 as future capital of colony but soon relinquished for Auckland.

Russell, Mount. Peak 14,190 ft. in Sierra Nevada in W Inyo co., E California.

Russell Cave. Limestone cavern, Jackson co., NE corner of Alabama, W of Bridgeport; remains of early pre-Columbian man. Made a national monument 1961.

Russell Islands. Group of small islands 30 m. NW of Guadalcanal I., SE cen. Solomon Is., W Pacific Ocean; part of British Solomon Is. protectorate; occupied by Americans Feb. 21, 1943.

Russell Springs. City, ⊗ of Logan co., W Kansas; pop. 93.

Rus′sell·ville (rŭs′l·vĭl; *Sou. also* -v′l). **1** City, ⊗ of Franklin co., NW Alabama, 20 m. S of Wilson Dam and Tennessee river; pop. 6628; surrounding area produces brown iron ore, asphalt, limestone; agricultural trading center.
2 City, ⊗ of Pope co., NW cen. Arkansas, near Arkansas river 64 m. NW of Little Rock; pop. 8921; coal mining.
3 City, ⊗ of Logan co., S Kentucky, 35 m. E of Hopkinsville; pop. 5861; stronghold of Confederate sympathizers during the Civil War.

Rus′sia (rŭsh′à); *Russ.* **Ros·si′ya** (rŭ·syē′yà). **1** Former empire, E Europe and N and W Asia; ✻ St. Petersburg (Petrograd); its territories (except for Finland and Kars) are now comprised in the Union of Soviet Socialist Republics (U.S.S.R.). For geographical description and maps, see UNION OF SOVIET SOCIALIST REPUBLICS.
History: Region settled by eastern Slavs 5th–8th cents. A.D.; entered from north in 9th cent. by Varangians (Scandinavians) who established Novgorod and Kiev (*qq.v.*) and traded from Baltic to Black Sea; Kiev lost supremacy to independent principalities, such as Suzdal and Vladimir; invaded 1224 and conquered 1237–40 by Mongols; Tatar Khanate of the Golden Horde, capital at Sarai, levied tribute on all Russia; in 14th–15th cents. princes of Moscow (*q.v.*) rose to lead and began defeat of Tatars and subjugation of rival principalities; under Ivan IV 1533–84, first tsar, Russia conquered Astrakhan and Kazan and pushed into Siberia; under Romanov dynasty 1613–1917; in war with Poland 1654–67 wrested part of Ukraine to middle Dnieper; in Great Northern War 1700–21, Peter I (the Great) secured "window" on Baltic (see BALTIC PROVINCES); annexed Lithuania and rest of Ukraine as share of partitions of Poland 1772–95; spread to northern coast of Black Sea bet. Dnieper and Dniester 1774 and 1792; acquired Finland 1809; acquired Bessarabia 1812; invaded by French 1812; annexed Georgia, Dagestan, and

other territory in Caucasus 1813; received most of Grand Duchy of Warsaw 1815; Russian southward advance against Ottoman Empire of key importance to Europe (see CRIMEA); Chinese cession of left bank of Amur and of Ussuri, 1858 and 1860, marked active policy in Far East; sold Alaska (*q.v.*) to U.S. 1867; in Central Asia advanced to borders of Afghanistan (*q.v.*); secured Sakhalin 1875, rights in Liaotung Penin. 1895 and Kwantung 1898; defeated in war with Japan 1904–05, Russia lost hold in Manchuria; unsuccessful revolution 1905; Russian foreign policy, dictated by its vital interest in Balkans and the Straits, brought her into World War I on side of Allies 1914–17; overthrew tsarist regime Mar. 1917; set up government of soviets Nov. 1917 after Bolshevist revolution. For history after 1917, see UNION OF SOVIET SOCIALIST REPUBLICS.
2 Popularly, the Union of Soviet Socialist Republics.

Rus′sian (rŭsh′ăn). River ab. 100 m. long, NW California; rises in cen. Mendocino co. and flows S into Sonoma co. and then W into the Pacific Ocean.

Russian America. See ALASKA.

Russian Island. See RUSSKI island.

Russian Poland. See POLAND, kingdom 1815–1918.

Russian So′vi·et Federated Socialist Republic (sō′vĭ·ĕt; sō′vĭ·ĕt′; sô·vyĕt′; sŏv′ĭ·ĕt); *commonly shortened to* **Soviet Russia.** Republic, E Europe and N and W Asia, the largest constituent republic (ab. 72% of the total area) of Union of Soviet Socialist Republics (*q.v.*, for map); 6,310,594 sq. m.; pop. (1939) 109,165,436; (area in Europe 1,370,887 sq. m., pop. 85,191,803; in Asia 4,939,707 sq. m., pop. 23,973,633); ✳ Moscow; comprises various administrative subdivisions: 6 territories, 45 regions, 12 autonomous soviet socialist republics, 6 autonomous regions, and 10 national districts. Its mountains include the entire Ural range and the various ranges of E Siberia, and its highest peaks are in Kamchatka; in Europe it contains the great plain of the Volga and Northern Dvina, in Asia the valleys of the Ob, Yenisei, Lena, and Amur; in the N in both continents is the belt of tundra, farther S extensive forests, steppes, and fertile areas. Has great mineral resources, esp in the Ural Mts. and Kuznetsk Basin. Chief cities Moscow, Leningrad, Gorki, Rostov (on Don), Stalingrad.

History: As the main part of old tsarist empire was first to come under control of Soviets Nov. 7, 1917; its first constitution adopted July 10, 1918; joined other soviet republics 1922 to form Union of Soviet Socialist Republics (*q.v.*). See also RUSSIA; cf. SOVIET RUSSIA IN ASIA and SIBERIA.

Russian Turkistan. See TURKISTAN.

Rus′ski (rōōs′kĭ). **1** Cape on NE coast of Arkhangelsk Region, Soviet Russia, Europe, 69°N, 55°E; on E shore of Barents Sea N of Pechora delta.
2 *Eng.* **Rus′sian Island** (rŭsh′ăn). Island bet. Amur Bay and Ussuri Bay, just S of Vladivostok, Maritime Territory, S Soviet Russia, Asia.

Rust′burg (rŭst′bûrg). Village, ⊗ of Campbell co., S cen. Virginia; pop. (est.) 350.

Rus·tchuk′. Var. of *Ruschuk:* see RUSE.

Rus′ten·burg (rŭs′tĕn·bûrg). Town, SW cen. Transvaal, NE Union of South Africa, on branch of Limpopo river ab. 70 m. W of Pretoria; pop. 6104; grows fruit, tobacco, and cotton.

Rus′ton (rŭs′tŭn). City, ⊗ of Lincoln parish, N Louisiana, 33 m. W of Monroe; pop. 13,991; trading center in agricultural section; cotton, vegetables, dairy products; natural-gas deposits nearby. Louisiana Polytechnic Institute (1894; coed.).

Rü′string·en (rüs′trĭng·ĕn). Manufacturing and commercial city, Lower Saxony state, W Germany, W suburb of Wilhelmshaven; pop. 48,969; bathing resort; shipbuilding and repair works; manufactures machinery, precision tools; trades in oil, fish.

Rut′ba (rōōt′bà; -bä), *also* **Rutba Wells.** Town and watering place, W Iraq, on Wadi Hauran in the Syrian

Desert; a junction of highways from the Euphrates to the Mediterranean coast; police and radio station.

Ru′te (rōō′tâ). Commune, Córdoba prov., S Spain, 45 m. SSE of Córdoba; pop. 18,903; marble and jasper quarries.

Ruth (rōōth). Town, White Pine co., E Nevada, ab. 3 m. W of Ely; pop. (1950) 1244; copper mining.

Ru·the′ni·a (rōō·thē′nĭ·à; -thēn′yà). Former autonomous region, later a province of Czechoslovakia. See CARPATHIAN RUTHENIA.

Ruth′er·ford (rŭth′ẽr·fẽrd; *in N.J., usu.* rŭth-).
1 Name of counties in two states of the U.S. See *Tables* at NORTH CAROLINA and TENNESSEE.
2 Borough, Bergen co., NE corner of New Jersey, 7 m. SSE of Paterson; pop. 20,473; residential suburb of New York City.

Ruth′er·ford·ton (rŭth′ẽr·fẽrd·tŭn). Town, ⊗ of Rutherford co., SW North Carolina, in Blue Ridge Mts. on edge of piedmont plateau 25 m. W of Shelby; pop. 3392; gold-mining center 1790–1840; textile mills, lumber plants; grows grain, cotton, sweet potatoes.

Ruth′er·glen (rŭth′ẽr·glĕn). Burgh, Lanark co., S cen. Scotland, on the Clyde 3 m. SE of Glasgow; pop. 24,225; became royal burgh 1126; shipbuilding, dyeworks, chemical factories; coal deposits nearby.

Ruth′in (rĭth′ĭn). Municipal borough, ⊗ of Denbighshire, N Wales; pop. 3599; site of castle attacked by Owen Glendower 1400; 14th-cent. church of St. Peter.

Ruth Mountain (rōōth). Peak 6800 ft. in cen. Whatcom co., NW Washington.

Ruth Siple, Mount. See Mount SIPLE.

Ruthven. See KINGUSSIE.

Ruth′well (rŭth′wĕl; -wĕl). Village, S Dumfries co., S Scotland, on Solway Firth; site of Ruthwell Cross, 18 ft. high, having runic inscriptions.

Ru′ti·glia′no (rōō′tē·lyä′nô). Commune, Bari prov., Apulia, SE Italy, 11 m. SE of Bari; pop. (1931) 10,907; Norman church.

Rutlam. See RATLAM.

Rut′land (rŭt′lănd). **1** County in Vermont. See *Table* at VERMONT.
2 Town, Worcester co., cen. Massachusetts, 12 m. NW of Worcester; pop. 3253.
3 Industrial city, ⊗ of Rutland co., W Vermont, 22 m. E of Poultney river entrance on Lake Champlain; pop. 18,325; railroad center and center of marble industry; manufactures scales, boilers, dairy and maple-sugar equipment; fishing and hunting resort. Chartered by New Hampshire 1761; settled 1770; Fort Rutland estab. 1775; became a northern outpost of Vermont in Revolution; made ⊗ 1784; scene of sessions of legislature 1784–1804; organized as city 1892; disastrous flood June 3, 1947.
4 Small island off S point of South Andaman I., Andaman Is., Bay of Bengal; separated from Little Andaman I. by Duncan Passage.
5 County in England. See RUTLANDSHIRE.

Rut′land·shire (rŭt′lănd·shĭr; -shẽr) *or* **Rutland.** County, E cen. England; 152 sq. m.; pop. (1938 est.) 17,860; ⊗ Oakham; Welland river flows along SE border; agriculture and livestock raising.

Rut′ledge (rŭt′lĭj). Town, ⊗ of Grainger co., NE Tennessee; pop. 793.

Rüt′li (rüt′lē) *or* **Grüt′li** (grüt′lē). Meadow in Uri canton, cen. Switzerland, where the first League of the Three Forest Cantons (Uri, Schwyz, and Unterwalden) was formed 1291.

Rutupiae. See RICHBOROUGH.

Ru′vo di Pu′glia (rōō′vô dĕ pōōl′yä); *anc.* **Ru′bi** (rōō′bĭ). Commune, Bari prov., Apulia, SE Italy, 9 m. W of Bari; pop. 25,452; 13th-cent. cathedral; ancient town noted for its ceramic art 5th–2d cents. B.C.

Ru′vu (rōō′vōō). River in Tanganyika Territory, E Africa, the lower course of the Pangani (*q.v.*).

Ru·vu′ma (rōō·vōō′mà); *Port.* **Ro·vu′ma** (rōō-).

River 400 m. long, SE Africa; rises in S Tanganyika; flows E, forming boundary bet. Tanganyika and Mozambique; has important headstreams in both Tanganyika and Mozambique; empties into Indian Ocean N of Cape Delgado.

Ru·wan′diz (rōō·wăn′dĭz). Town in mountains of Kurdistan, NE Iraq, 80 m. E by N of Mosul; pop. ab. 9000; on the highway from the Tigris to Tabriz.

Ru′wen·zo′ri, Mount (rōō′[w]ĕn·zōr′ē). Mountain group in cen. Africa, bet. Lake Albert and Lake Edward and on the boundary bet. Uganda and the Congo; central peak Mount Stanley, with two summits, Mt. Margherita 16,791 ft. and Mt. Alexandra 16,750 ft.; discovered by Stanley 1889; identified with Ptolemy's "Mountains of the Moon."

Ru′wer (rōō′vĕr). Short stream ab. 25 m. long, W Rhineland-Palatinate state, W Germany; flows into the Mosel below Trier; in wine-producing region.

Ru′žom·be′rok (rōō′zhŏm·bĕ′rŏk); *Hung.* **Ró′zsa·hegy** (rō′zhŏ·hĕd′y′); *Ger.* **Ro′sen·berg** (rō′zĕn·bĕʀk). Town, N Slovakia prov., E cen. Czechoslovakia, on the Váh 118 m. NE of Bratislava; pop. (1930) 15,668.

Rwanda. See RUANDA.

Ry′an, Loch (lŏk rī′ăn). Inlet on SW coast of Scotland, in Wigtown co., Galloway; extends S inland ab. 9 m. with the town of Stranraer at its head; fine harbor.

Ry′an Peak (rī′ăn). Mountain 11,900 ft. in S Custer co., cen. Idaho.

Rya·zan′ (rē′á·zăn′; *Russ.* ryĕ·zàn′y′); *also* **Ria·zan′.**
1 Medieval principality, cen. Russia, SE of Moscow; ✳ Old Ryazan; included Murom to the NE and Kolomna on the Moskva. A border state of warlike inhabitants, forced to continuous conflict; became subject to Moscow in 14th cent.
2 City, ✳ of Ryazan Region, cen. Soviet Russia, Europe, on right bank of Oka river 120 m. SE of Moscow; pop. 95,358; on the main railroad from Moscow to Kuibyshev; an industrial town with factories for farm machines, textiles, leather, wooden goods. The old town, as capital of the principality known as **Old Ryazan,** on the Oka some 30 m. SE, dated back to 11th cent. Captured by Mongols 1237 and several times suffered damage from the Tatars; now only ruins of old fort remain. Replaced in 13th cent. by **Pe′re·ya·slav′-Rya·zan′ski** (pĕr′ĕ·yà·slăv′rē′á·zăn′skĭ; *Russ.* pyĭ·ryĭ·yŭ·slăf′ryĕ·zàn′y′·skĭ) as residence of Ryazan princes. Name changed to Ryazan 1778.

Ryazan Region. Region, cen. Soviet Russia, Europe, crossed by Oka river; 18,567 sq. m.; pop. 2,265,873; ✳ Ryazan. Bounded on N by Vladimir Region, on NE by Gorki Region, on E by Mordovian A.S.S.R., on S by Tambov and Voronezh Regions, and on W by Tula and Moscow Regions. Level, well-watered area, with many lakes and large forests; chiefly agricultural with rye, oats, millet, potatoes, and fruit the main crops. Has many peasant industries, esp. in textiles, leather, and wooden products. Only large town is Ryazan. Region organized 1936. See RYAZAN principality.

Ry·bach′e (rĭ·bàch′yĕ). Town, N Kirgiz S.S.R., Soviet Central Asia, at W end of Issyk Kul.

Ry·ba′chi Peninsula (rĭ·bà′chĭ). Irregular land projection ab. 17 m. wide, extending into Barents Sea on NW coast of Murmansk Region, Soviet Russia, Europe, N of Kola Bay and Murmansk and NE of Pechenga; its base touches the former Finnish boundary line.

Ry′bá·ře (rĭ′bär·zhĕ); *Ger.* **Fi′schern** (fĭsh′ĕrn). Town, W Bohemia prov., W Czechoslovakia, opp. Karlovy Vary; pop. (1930) 11,810.

Ry′binsk (rĭ′byĭnsk). See SHCHERBAKOV.

Rybinsk Reservoir; *also called* **Sea of Rybinsk.** Large lake, N cen. Soviet Russia, Europe, for the greater part in NW Yaroslavl Region; formed (completed in 1941) by damming waters of upper Volga; on N receives the Suda and Sheksna rivers.

Ryb′nik (rĭb′nĕk). Coal-mining and manufacturing

commune, SE Śląsk dept., SW Poland, 20 m. SW of Katowice; pop. (1938–39 est.) 28,498; manufactures machinery, furniture, beer.

Ry′dal (rī′d′l). Village, Westmorland, NW England, on **Rydal Water,** a small lake just E of Grasmere; site of Rydal Mount, home of Wordsworth from 1813 to 1850; 2 m. NW of the village are the **Rydal Falls.**

Ryde (rīd). **1** City, E New South Wales, SE Australia, NW suburb of Sydney on N shore of Parramatta river; pop. 27,860.
2 Municipal borough on Isle of Wight, S England, in English Channel 6 m. SW of Portsmouth; pop. 20,084; popular watering place.

Rye (rī). **1** Town, Rockingham co., SE New Hampshire, on Atlantic Ocean 4 m. S of Portsmouth; pop. 3244; includes summer resort of **Rye Beach.**
2 Residential city in town of Rye (pop. 38,147), Westchester co., SE New York, on Long Island Sound 24 m. NE of New York; pop. 14,225; founded 1660; organized as town of Connecticut before settlement of border line in 1700. **Rye Beach** nearby; home of John Jay.
3 Municipal borough, East Sussex, S England; pop. 4511; one of the Cinque Ports (*q.v.*).

Rye′gate′ (rī′gāt). Town, ⊗ of Golden Valley co., cen. Montana; pop. 314.

Rye House (rī). Village, Hertfordshire, SE England, 2 m. from Ware; site of remains of the manor house (Rye House) at which a conspiracy to kill Charles II and James, Duke of York, is alleged to have been made. Lord William Russell and Algernon Sidney were implicated and executed.

Ryezhitsa. See REZEKNE.

Ry·ma′nów (rĭ·mä′nōōf). Commune, W Ukraine, U.S.S.R., 100 m. WSW of Lvov; formerly in Lwów dept., Poland; pop. 3617; Greek Catholic episcopal see; important spa and summer resort in foothills of Carpathian Mts.; produces petroleum.

Ryojun. See PORT ARTHUR, Manchuria.

Ryssel. See LILLE.

Ryswick. See RIJSWIJK.

Ry′ton (rī′t′n). Urban district, Durham, N England, on the Tyne 6 m. W of Newcastle; pop. 13,779.

Ryu′kyu Islands (rĭ·ōō′kū) *or* **Nan·sei Islands** (nän·sā); *Jap.* **Ryu·kyu Ret·to** (rū·kū rĕt·tō); *also* **Lu′chu′,** *or* **Loo′choo′, Islands** (lōō′chōō′). Island chain, W Pacific Ocean, extending in a 600-mile-long arc between Formosa and Kyushu I., Japan; includes Sakishima, Okinawa, and Amami island groups; chief town Naha on Okinawa I.; area ab. 847.9 sq. m.; pop. (1950) 914,937; highest point in N, a volcano 3215 ft. on Nakano Shima in Tokara Is. (part of Amami group). Came under political influence of China 1372; became tributary to Japan as well as China 1451 and Japanese protectorate 1609; integral part of Japan by 1879; under the Japanese the Amami group belonged to Kagoshima pref. and the Okinawa and Sakishima groups constituted Okinawa pref.; after World War II placed under U.S. military government 1945; received native civil government 1951 but remained under U.S. occupation except for the Amami group, which was returned to Japan Dec. 1953.

Rze′szów (zhĕ′shōōf). **1** Department, SE Poland; comprises W part of former Lwów dept. and E Kraków dept.
2 Manufacturing commune, its ✳, 45 m. E of Tarnów on main east-to-west highway through Galicia; pop. (1938–39 est.) 37,116; founded in 14th cent. by Casimir III; in peace times a prosperous town but overrun in both World War I and II.

Rzhev (rzhĕf). City, S Kalinin Region, Soviet Russia, Europe, on both banks of upper Volga 125 m. WNW of Moscow; pop. 54,081; commercial and industrial city at junction of four railroads; dates from 11th cent.; border town during era of medieval principalities; in World War II held by Germans Oct. 1941–Mar. 1943; base for attacks on Moscow; retaken by Russians Jan.–Mar. 1943.

S

Sa·ad′a·bad′ (så·äd′å·bäd′). Suburb of Tehran, Iran, containing palace of king; nonaggression pact signed here July 9, 1937 by Turkey, Iran, Iraq, and Afghanistan.

Saadani. See SADANI.

Saa′le (zä′lĕ). River 226 m. long in cen. Germany; rises in the Fichtel Gebirge range, NE Bavaria, flows N into the Elbe river in Saxony, 18 m. SE of Magdeburg; navigable as far as Halle.

Saale, Frän′ki·sche (frĕng′kĭ·shĕ). River ab. 70 m. long in Bavaria, S cen. Germany; rises in the Rhon Mts., flows SW into Main river NW of Würzburg.

Saal′feld (zäl′fĕlt; *also* **Saalfeld an der Saa′le** (än dĕr zä′lĕ). Manufacturing city in Gera dist., E Germany, on Saale river 29 m. SSE of Erfurt; pop. 17,960; 13th-cent. church, 16th-cent. town hall, 17th-cent. castle; manufactures chocolates, paper, machinery, dyes, wire. Founded c. 1200.

Saa′ne (zä′nĕ); *Fr.* **Sa′rine** (så′rēn′). River 78 m. long in SW Switzerland; rises in Bernese Alps, flows N through Fribourg canton and into Aare river 10 m. WNW of Bern.

Saar (zär); *Fr.* **Sarre** (sår). **1** River 84 m. long, Moselle dept., France, and Saarland and Rhineland-Palatinate, Germany; flows N and NNW across German border to the Mosel (Moselle) just above Trier. In World War II severe fighting on its banks Dec. 1944–Jan. 1945.

2 See SAARLAND.

Saar′brück′en (zär′brük′ĕn); *Fr.* **Sar′re·bruck′** (så′-rĕ·brük′). Industrial city, ✳ (since 1935) of Saarland, Germany, on Saar river on Franco-German frontier ab. 39 m. SE of Trier; pop. (1939) 135,080; important coal mines; seat of iron, steel, and engineering works; manufactures include glass, chemicals, pottery, soap, paper cement, brandy, cigarets, aluminum, leather, confections; many fine buildings, among them an 18th-cent. castle, the Ludwigskirche, and an industrial and natural history museum; fine schools, charitable institutions, and seat of numerous public offices.

History: Seat of Nassau-Saarbrücken family 1381–1797; occupied by French 1793–1815; first battle of Franco-Prussian War fought nearby (at Spicheren) Aug. 6, 1870; enlarged 1909 to include industrial suburbs of Sankt Johann and Malstatt-Burbach; after World War I, capital of government of the Saar established by League of Nations; returned by plebiscite to Germany Mar. 1, 1935; in World War II severe fighting in vicinity; taken by Allies Feb.–Mar. 1945.

Saar′burg (zär′bŏoʀk). German form of SARREBOURG.

Saa′re (sä′rĕ). **1** Province of Estonia. See *Table* at ESTONIA.

2 *or* **Saaremaa.** = SAREMA.

Saar′ge·münd′ (zär′gĕ·münt′). Former name of SARRE-GUEMINES.

Saar′land′ (zär′länt′; *Angl.* -lǎnd′) *or* **Saar′ge·biet′** (zär′gĕ·bēt′), *also* **Saar** (zär); *Fr.* **Sarre** (sår). Region in W Europe between France and Germany, since 1957 a state of the Federal Republic of Germany, in the valley of the Saar river N of Lorraine, W of Rhineland-Palatinate, and SE of Luxembourg; since Jan. 1, 1957 in Germany; area before World War II 743 sq. m., expanded after the war to 991 sq. m.; pop. 987,650; ✳ Saarbrücken. A hilly region, fertile and thickly forested, noted for its rich coal mines and its industrial development especially in iron and steel and the manufacture of glass, ceramics, and pottery. Chief towns besides the capital Neunkirchen, Dudweiler, and Sulzbach.

History: Became part of France 1766 but by Treaty of Paris 1815 divided between Prussia and Bavaria; by Treaty of Versailles 1919 coal mines assigned to France and territory placed under administration of the League of Nations; returned to Germany by plebiscite 1935;

after World War II assigned to French occupation zone, became united economically to France; subject of treaty signed Oct. 27, 1956 by France and West Germany turning the region over to West Germany; returned to Germany Jan. 1, 1957 by plebiscite.

Saar′lau′tern (zär′lou′tĕrn) *or* **Saar′lou′is** (zär′lōō′ĕ; *Fr.* sår′lwē′). Fortified manufacturing commune, Saarland, Germany, on left bank of the Saar 11 m. WNW of Saarbrücken; pop. (1939) 33,356; founded 1681 by Louis XIV; birthplace of Marshal Ney; much bombed during World War II.

Saaz. See ŽATEC.

Sa′ba (sä′bå). Island, NE West Indies, in Leeward Is. 16 m. NW of St. Eustatius; 5 sq. m.; pop. (1942) 1238; ✳ the Bottom; belongs to the Dutch territory of Curaçao; an extinct volcano, its coasts are sheer cliffs ab. 2800 ft. high; the capital built on a crater floor 800 ft. high is reached by steps in the rock ("the Ladder"). First occupied by Dutch 1632.

Saba, Saba′. See SHEBA.

Ša′bac (shä′bäts). Town, NW Serbia, Yugoslavia, 40 m W of Belgrade on Sava river; pop. 12,563; trade center and river port; founded in 15th cent.

Sa′ba·dell′ (sä′vä·thĕl′). Manufacturing commune, Barcelona prov., NE Spain, 8 m. N by W of Barcelona; pop. (1941 est.) 48,256; produces agricultural products, wine, oil; manufactures cotton, wool, and silk textiles, iron, paper, leather, china, arms, brandies.

Sabah. See NORTH BORNEO.

Sa·ba′ki (så·bä′kĕ). River ab. 120 m. long in SE Kenya colony, E Africa; formed by confluence of Athi and Tsavo rivers, flows E into Indian Ocean.

Sa·ba′na Archipelago-(så·vä′nä). Group of islands off N coast of Las Villas prov., W cen. Cuba.

Sabana Gran′de (grän′då). **1** Municipality (pop. 15,910) and town (pop. 3318), SW Puerto Rico; town is 24 m. WNW of Ponce.

2 Town in Federal District, N Venezuela; pop. (1941 est.) 13,959.

Sa·ba′na·lar′ga (så·vä′nä·lär′gä). Town, Atlántico dept., N Colombia, 30 m. S of Barranquilla; pop. 11,432.

Sa′ba·ne′ta (sä′vä·nā′tä). Commune, Montecristi prov., Dominican Republic, SE of Montecristi.

Sa′bang (sä′bäng). Seaport on the island of We off N Sumatra, Indonesia; pop. 6855; has healthful climate and fine harbor, with considerable trade; first port of call from Indian and western ports on routes to Singapore and E Asia. Held by Japanese 1942–45 but frequently bombed by Allies 1944–45.

Sa′ba·nil′la (sä′vä·nē′yä), *in full* **Sabanilla del En′co·men′da·dor′** (thĕl äng′kō·mān′dä·thôr′). Municipality, Matanzas prov., W cen. Cuba, 12 m. S of Matanzas; pop. 7665.

Sa′ba·ra·ga′mu·wa (?sŭ′bä·rå·gŭ′mōō·wä). Province, SW cen. Ceylon; 1893 sq. m.; pop. 578,368; ✳ Ratnapura. Terrain mainly composed of mountains and mountain plains; highest peak Adam's Peak 7365 ft.; arable land devoted largely to rubber cultivation.

Sa′ba·ri (sŭ′bå·rē). River ab. 130 m. long, E cen. India; rises in S Orissa and flows SW along SE boundary of Madhya Pradesh into Godavari river in N Andhra Pradesh.

Sabaria. See SZOMBATHELY.

Sa′bar Kan′tha (sŭ′bĕr kŭnt′hå). Formerly a political agency of the Western India States Agency; 5408 sq. m.; pop. (1941) 457,813; was in N Gujarat and comprised the states of the former Banas Kantha and Mahi Kantha Agencies.

Sa′bar·ma′ti (sä′bĕr·mŭ′tē). River ab. 200 m. long, W India; rises in the Aravalli Range in Rajputana, flows S into the head of Gulf of Cambay, W of the mouth of Mahi river.

Sa·bas'tya (sȧ·bŏs'tĭ·yȧ; -yă). = *Sebastye:* see SA-MARIA.
Sabatinus. See Lake BRACCIANO.
Sa·bau'dia (sȧ·bou'dyä). Town, Littoria prov., SW Latium, cen. Italy, on the coast N of Monte Circeo; pop. 4890; recently built on reclaimed land in Pontine Marshes.
Sabbioncello. See PELJEŠAC.
Sa·be'ta Peak (sȧ·bē'tȧ). Mountain 13,600 ft. in Chaffee co., cen. Colorado.
Sa·beth'a (sȧ·bĕth'ȧ). City, Nemaha co., NE Kansas, 43 m. NW of Atchison; pop. 2318.
Sa'bi (sä'bĭ). 1 *also* **Sa'bie.** River 125 m. long in Transvaal and Mozambique, SE Africa; flows E into Komati river.
2 See SAVE river, Southern Rhodesia and Mozambique.
Sabi Game Preserve. = KRUGER NATIONAL PARK.
Sa·bi'na (sȧ·bī'nȧ). Village, Clinton co., SW Ohio, 35 m. ESE of Dayton; pop. 2313; in corn-growing section.
Sab'i·nal' (săb'ĭ·năl'). City, Uvalde co., SW Texas, 20 m. ENE of Uvalde; pop. 1747; in ranching and farming section; wool, mohair.
Sa'bi·nal' Cay (sä'vĕ·näl'). Island off NE coast of Camagüey prov., E cen. Cuba, in the Camagüey Archipelago.
Sa·bi'nas (sä·vē'näs). 1 See SALADO river, NE Mexico.
2 Town, Coahuila state, NE Mexico, on Sabinas river 70 m. SW of Piedras Negras; pop. 6825.
Sabinas Hi·dal'go (ê·thäl'gô). Town, Nuevo León state, NE Mexico, 55 m. N of Monterrey; pop. 6912.
Sa·bine' (sȧ·bēn'). 1 Navigable river 380 m. long, E Texas and W Louisiana; formed by confluence of forks in Hunt co., NE Texas, flows S to Louisiana border, forming S section of Texas-Louisiana boundary, and empties through Sabine Lake and Sabine Pass into the Gulf of Mexico.
2 Parish in Louisiana and county in Texas. See *Tables* at LOUISIANA and TEXAS.
Sabine, Cape. Point on E coast of Ellesmere I., N Canada, extending into Smith Sound, ab. 79°N; here part of Greely's expedition perished 1884.
Sabine, Mount. Peak 9859 ft. in Admiralty Range, Victoria Land, Antarctica; lat. 72°5'S and long. 169°10'E.
Sabine Crossroads. Hamlet in DeSoto parish, Louisiana, ab. 40 m. S of Shreveport; battle Apr. 8, 1864 in which Federal forces under Gen. Banks were defeated.
Sabine Lake. Lake bet. Louisiana and Texas, 5 m. from the Gulf of Mexico, formed by expansion of Sabine river, which flows through it and Sabine Pass to the Gulf of Mexico.
Sabine–Nech'es Waterway (-nĕch'ĕz; -ĭz). System of waterways at Port Arthur, Texas; includes the ship canal at Port Arthur, Sabine Pass, and the **Sabine–Neches Canal** which comprises the Neches river as far as Beaumont and the Sabine river as far as Orange.
Sabine Pass. Outlet for Sabine river extending from Sabine Lake to Gulf of Mexico on boundary bet. Louisiana and Texas.
Sabiya'. See As SABYA.
Sa'ble, Cape (sä'b'l). 1 Cape at SW tip of Florida penin. in Monroe co., enclosing Whitewater Bay; southernmost point of the U.S., ab. 25°7'N lat.
2 Southern point of Cape Sable I., SW Nova Scotia, Canada, 43°40'N, 65°45'W.
Sable Island. Low, sandy island, Nova Scotia, Canada, in North Atlantic Ocean 95 m. SE of Cape Canso, 43°55'N, 60°W; ab. 20 m. long and 1 m. wide, the exposed part of a sand bar along W edge of Gulf Stream. Dangerous to navigation and the scene of more than 200 recorded wrecks; called the "graveyard of the Atlantic." In recent years has been equipped with two lighthouses (one of which had to be dismantled 1948), life-saving station, and radio.
Sables–d'Olonne, Les. See LES SABLES-D'OLONNE.

Sa'blé'–sur–Sarthe (sȧ'blä'sür·sȧrt'). Commune, SW Sarthe dept., NW France, on the Sarthe; pop. (1931) 5810; 14th–16th cent. castle, restored.
Sab'ra·ta *or* **Sab'ra·tha** (săb'rȧ·tȧ) *or* **A·brot'o·num** (ȧ·brŏt'n·ŭm). Ancient town, Roman Africa, on coast 48 m. W of Tripoli; founded 7th–6th cents. B.C. by Phoenician settlers from Tyre; one of three chief cities of Tripolis (see TRIPOLI region); remains include Roman and Byzantine fortifications, temples, forum, theater, two Christian basilicas.
Sa'bra·ton (sä'brȧ·tŭn). Former industrial town, Monongalia co., West Virginia; pop. (1940) 1810; annexed to Morgantown 1949; site of Thomas Decker's settlement (founded 1758, destroyed by Mingo Indians 1759).
Sa·bri'na (sȧ·brī'nȧ). See SEVERN.
Sa·bri'na Coast (sȧ·brī'nȧ; -brē'nȧ). Section of coast of Wilkes Land, Antarctica, on Indian Ocean bet. ab. 115° and 117°E; probably first seen 1839 by British navigator John Balleny.
Sab·tang' (săb·täng'). Island, most southerly of Batan Is., N Phil. Is.; 13 sq. m.; pop. 1844.
Sa'by·a, As (ăs sä'bĭ·yȧ); *or* **Sa'bi·ya'** (sä'bĭ·yȧ). City, * of Asir principate, SW Arabia; pop. ab. 20,000; at foot of mountain range ab. 40 m. inland from Red Sea.
Sab'za·war' (säb'zȧ·vär'; -wär'). 1 Town, W Afghanistan, on highway 75 m. S of Herat.
2 Town, Khurasan prov., NE Iran, 110 m. W of Meshed; pop. ab. 15,000; on the highway to Tehran.
Sac (sôk). County in Iowa. See *Table* at IOWA.
Sac'an·da'ga (săk'ăn·dô'gȧ). River ab. 50 m. long, E New York; rises in Piseco Lake and flows SE through Sacandaga Reservoir into the Hudson river in N Saratoga co.
Sacandaga Reservoir. Reservoir in Sacandaga river, E Fulton and W Saratoga cos., E New York; 42 sq. m. and 27 m. long; completed 1930; regulates flow of upper Hudson. Now a summer resort.
Sa'ca·te·pé'quez (sä'kä·tä·pā'kås). Department, S cen. Guatemala; 180 sq. m.; pop. 83,024; * Antigua.
Sac'ca·rel'lo (säk'kä·rĕl'lô). Mountain 7216 ft., NW Italy, on boundary bet. Liguria and Piedmont; highest point in the Ligurian Alps.
Sac City (sôk). City, ⊗ of Sac co., W Iowa, 43 m. W of Fort Dodge; pop. 3354; in agricultural, dairy, and livestock-raising section; corn canneries.
Sac'co (säk'kô). River, cen. Italy; flows SE, joins the Liri S of Frosinone.
Sach'seln (zäk'sĕln). Commune, Unterwalden canton, cen. Switzerland, near Sarnen; pop. 2016; nearby is birthplace of Nicholas of Flüe.
Sach'sen (zäk'sĕn). 1 See SAXONY, former state of Germany.
2 Province of Prussia. See *Saxony*, in *Table* at PRUSSIA.
Sachsen–Coburg und Gotha. See SAXE-COBURG-GOTHA.
Sach'sen·hau'sen (zäk'sĕn·hou'zĕn). Town, Brandenburg, East Germany, on the Havel river N of Berlin; Nazi concentration camp.
Sachsenland. See SAXONLAND.
Sächsische Schweiz. See SAXON SWITZERLAND.
Sa·ci'le (sä·chē'lå). Commune, Friuli prov., Venezia Euganea, NE Italy, 23 m. NE of Udine; pop. 10,616; 15th-cent. cathedral.
Sack'ets Harbor (săk'ĕts; -ĭts). Village and summer resort, Jefferson co., N New York, on Lake Ontario 11 m. WSW of Watertown; pop. 1279; settled 1801; during War of 1812, when it served as U.S. naval station, scene of several engagements.
Säck'ing·en (zĕk'ĭng·ĕn). Town, SW Baden-Württemberg, Germany, on the Rhine E of Basel; pop. 5002; site of monastery founded by Saint Fridolin in 6th cent.; scene of Scheffel's poem *Der Trompeter von Säckingen* (1853).
Sack'ville (săk'vĭl). Industrial town, Westmorland co., SE New Brunswick, Canada, 25 m. SE of Moncton and

near the Nova Scotia boundary; pop. 2873. Founded 1761. Has various small industries; ships fruit, cattle, potatoes. Mt. Allison Univ. (1858).

Sa'co. 1 (sô'kō; sä'kō; săk'ō) River 104 m. long, E cen. New Hampshire and SW Maine; rises in White Mts. W of Mt. Washington, NE cen. New Hampshire, flows S and SE across Maine border and SE into Atlantic Ocean 6 m. below Saco, York co., SW Maine.
2 (sô'kō; sä'kō) Residential city, York co., SW Maine, on Saco river just N of Biddeford; pop. 10,515; founded c. 1622.

Sacralias. See ZALLAKA.

Sac'ra·men'to (săk'rȧ·měn'tō). **1** River 382 m. long, NW California; rises near Mt. Shasta in Siskiyou co., N California, and flows S into Suisun Bay, E extension of San Francisco Bay, W cen. California; navigable for 180 m.
2 County in California. See *Table* at CALIFORNIA.
3 City, ✳ of California and ⊗ of Sacramento co., N cen. California, on Sacramento river at the head of navigation 72 m. NE of San Francisco; pop. 191,667; industrial and distributing center for agricultural and mining section; canneries, packing houses, flour, lumber, and feed mills, printing and publishing houses; manufactures metal products. Crocker Art Gallery contains notable collection of paintings. McClellan Air Force Base and Mather Air Force Base (with U.S. Air Force Bomb School). Part of a grant to John Sutter 1841; incorporated as city 1850; made capital of California 1854.

Sacramento Mountains. Range in S New Mexico, in Otero co. and extending N into Lincoln co. and E into Chaves and Eddy cos.; in center of region between the Pecos river and the Rio Grande; name sometimes includes range to the S known as Guadalupe Mts.

Sa'cri·fi'cios (sä'krē·fē'syôs). Small island in the Gulf of Mexico, 3 m. S of the city of Veracruz, Mexico; a place of sacrifice under the Aztecs; contains remains of ancient temples.

Sacrum Promontorium. See Cape CORSE.

Sac'sa·hua·man' (säk'sä·wä·män'). Ancient fortress of early Inca construction on a hill just N of Cuzco, Peru.

Sada, Cape. See Cape ASHIZURI.

Sá da Ban·dei'ra (sä' thȧ văNn·dā'ē·rȧ). Inland town, SW Angola, SW Africa, E of Mossâmedes.

Sa·da'ni *or* **Saa·da'ni** (sä·dä'nē). Seaport, Tanganyika, Africa, opp. Zanzibar I.; pop. ab. 2000.

Sad'dle (săd'l) *or* **Va·lu'a** (vä·lōō'ȧ). Island, one of the Banks Is. in the New Hebrides, W Pacific Ocean, NE of Vanua Lava.

Sad'dle·back' (săd'l·băk') *or* **Blen·cath'a·ra** (blĕn·kăth'ȧ·rȧ). Mountain 2847 ft., Cumberland, NW England, in the Lake District 4¼ m. NE of Keswick.

Saddleback Mountain. 1 Peak ab. 4000 ft. in Franklin co., W Maine, near Rangeley Lakes.
2 Peak 4530 ft. in the Adirondack Mts., Essex co., NE New York.

Sad'dle Brook (săd'l). Urban township, Bergen co., NE New Jersey, E of Paterson; pop. 13,834.

Sad'dle Mountain (săd'l). **1** Peak 8225 ft. on E boundary of Idaho co., N cen. Idaho.
2 Peak 3266 ft. in Clatsop co., NW corner of Oregon.
3 Peak 6976 ft. in S cen. Klamath co., S Oregon.
4 Peak 10,678 ft. in Yellowstone National Park, NW Wyoming.

Saddle Mountains. Range in S Kittitas and S Grant cos., cen. Washington.

Sad'dle·worth (săd'l·wûrth). Urban district, West Riding, Yorkshire, N England; pop. 16,762.

Sa'di·ya (sŭ'dĭ·yä). **1** Frontier tract, NE Assam prov., NE Indian Union; 3309 sq. m.; pop. (1941) 60,118.
2 Town, its ✳, on the Luhit tributary near its junction with the Brahmaputra, ab. 575 m. NE of Calcutta. In World War II after the loss of the Burma Road (1942) it became the supply base for road building and the starting point for two new transportation routes to China: (1)

across N tip of Burma, via Fort Hertz, and S Sikang to Sichang, where it turned N to meet (2), the N route via Paan and Kangting to Chengtu in Szechwan prov.

Sa·do (sä·dô). Mountainous island in E Sea of Japan, off NW coast of island of Honshu, Japan; 331 sq. m.; pop. (1945) 119,086. Chief town Aikawa (pop. 8621); in early times, a place of exile. Gold and silver mines.

Sa'do (sä'thōō). River ab. 70 m. long, S Portugal; flows NW into Atlantic Ocean at Setúbal; wide estuary.

Sa·do'wa (zä·dô'vä; zä'dô·vä). Village, NE Bohemia, Czechoslovakia. See KÖNIGGRÄTZ.

Saena Julia. See SIENA.

Sa'fad *or* **Sa'fed** (sô'făd). **1** Subdistrict, Galilee dist., N Palestine; 269 sq. m.; pop. 39,713, (1938 est.) 44,123.
2 Town, its ✳, on highway E from Acre and 7 m. NNW of the Sea of Galilee; pop. 9441; a fortified place in time of the Crusaders. Formerly seat of a Hebrew school of mysticism.

Sa·fed' Koh (sȧ·făd' kō'h'). **1** Mountain (*koh*) range, NW Afghanistan, E of Herat and N of the Hari Rud; highest ab. 11,000 ft.
2 Mountain range, E Afghanistan, SE of Kabul on Pakistan border, an offshoot of the Hindu Kush; its remarkable evenness of height presents appearance of towering wall; highest peak Mt. Sikaram 15,619 ft. Peiwar Pass is at W end.

Safe'ty Harbor (sāf'tĭ). City, Pinellas co., W cen. Florida peninsula, N of St. Petersburg; pop. 1787.

Safe'ty Islands (sāf'tĭ); *Fr.* **Îles du Sa'lut'** (ēl' dü sȧ'lü'). French group of three islands, Royale, Joseph, and Devil's I., in the Atlantic Ocean 7 m. off the N coast of French Guiana; for many years used by France for a penal settlement.

Saffi. See SAFI.

Saf'ford (săf'ērd). City, ⊗ of Graham co., SE Arizona, on Gila river; pop. 4648; founded 1872; farming.

Saf'fron Hill (săf'rŭn). District, London, England, N of Holborn, formerly a haunt of ballad singers.

Saffron Wal'den (wôl'dĕn). Municipal borough, Essex, SE England, 40 m. NNE of London; pop. 6825; saffron cultivation was an important occupation from 14th to 18th cents.

Saffurye. See SEPPHORIS.

Sa'fi (sä'fī) *or* **Saf'fi.** Fortified seaport, W cen. Morocco, NW Africa, SW of Casablanca; pop. (1936) 25,159; as nearest port to Marrakesh has considerable trade; old Portuguese citadel. Allies landed here Nov. 8, 1942.

Safid Rud. Var. of SEFID RUD.

Sa·ga (sä·gä). **1** Prefecture of Japan. See *Table* at JAPAN.
2 City, its ✳, NW Kyushu, near coast of Shimabara Bay 43 m. NE of Nagasaki; pop. (1945) 52,940; a fishing and coal-mining center.

Sag'a·da·hoc' (săg'ȧ·dȧ·hŏk'). **1** Early name for the KENNEBEC river, Maine.
2 County in Maine. See *Table* at MAINE.

Sa·gaing' (sȧ·gīng'). **1** Division, NW Upper Burma (see BURMA); 50,086 sq. m.; pop. 1,918,058; including certain of the Northern Shan States and area not administered; 73,230 sq. m.; ✳ Sagaing.
2 District, S Sagaing division, Upper Burma; 1878 sq. m.; pop. 335,965; ✳ Sagaing.
3 Town, ✳ of division and of district, on right bank of the Irrawaddy opp. Ava 10 m. W of Mandalay; pop. 14,127; formerly a capital of Burma; terminus of railroad to Myitkyina and port of call for river steamers.

Sa·gal'lo (sȧ·gäl'ō). Seaport on the Gulf of Tadjoura, French Somaliland, SW of the town of Tadjoura.

Sa·ga·mi Sea (sä·gä·mē). Widemouthed bay on SE coast of Honshu, Japan, in Kanagawa prefecture SSW of Tokyo; scene of American naval attack July 1945.

Sagan. See ŻAGAŃ.

Sa'gar (sä'gēr). **1** Island at the mouth of the Hooghly river, S West Bengal, NE Indian Union.
2 See SAUGOR.

Sagauli. See SEGAULI.
Sa·gay′ (sä·gī′). Municipality, NE Negros Occidental, Negros, Phil. Is., on Visayan Sea 37 m. NE of City of Bacolod; pop. 53,767.
Saghalien. See SAKHALIN.
Sag Harbor (săg). Village, Suffolk co., SE New York, at E end of Long I., S of Shelter I., on Gardiners Bay 25 m. W of Montauk Point; pop. 2346; formerly important whaling port (esp. 1840–60); shore resort; yachting facilities; in farming country.
Sag′i·naw (săg′ĭ·nô). **1** Navigable river 20 m. long, cen. Michigan; formed by confluence of the Flint and Shiawassee rivers, flows N into Saginaw Bay.
2 County in Michigan. See *Table* at MICHIGAN.
3 City, its ⊗, cen. Michigan, on Saginaw river 32 m. NNW of Flint; pop. 98,265; port of entry and railroad center; in agricultural section yielding esp. sugar beets and beans; near coal, oil, graphite, and salt deposits; manufactures automobiles and automobile parts, machinery, furniture, school supplies, beet sugar.
Saginaw Bay. Inlet of Lake Huron on coast of E cen. Michigan, E of Arenac co., E of Bay co., NW of Tuscola co., and W of Huron co.
Sa·go′ne, Gulf of (sä·gō′nȧ); *Fr.* **Golfe de Sa′gone′** (gôlf′ dē sȧ·gôn′). Inlet on W coast of Corsica, N of Ajaccio.
Sagra, La. See LA SAGRA.
Sagres. See Cape SAINT VINCENT.
Sagrus. See SANGRO.
Sa·guache′ (sȧ·wŏch′). **1** County in Colorado. See *Table* at COLORADO.
2 Town, its ⊗, S Colorado; pop. 722.
Saguache Range. See SAWATCH RANGE.
Sa′gua de Tá′na·mo (sä′gwä thä tä′nä·mô). Municipality, Oriente prov., E Cuba, near N coast 33 m. N of Guantánamo; pop. 28,694.
Sagua la Gran′de (lä grän′dä). **1** River in N Las Villas prov., W cen. Cuba; flows N.
2 Municipality and town, Las Villas prov., W cen. Cuba; town is railroad center 30 m. NNW of Santa Clara, pop. (1943) 15,539.
Sa·gua′ro Lake (sȧ·gwä′rō; sȧ·wä′-). See STEWART MOUNTAIN DAM, Arizona.
Saguaro National Monument. See UNITED STATES, *National Monuments.*
Sag′ue·nay′ (săg′ĕ·nā′; săg′ĕ·nā). **1** River 125 m. long, S Quebec prov., Canada; flows from Lake St. John E into St. Lawrence river at Tadoussac; including the Peribonka river, ab. 405 m. long. Navigable for large vessels 50 m. to Ha! Ha! Bay and for smaller to Chicoutimi. Leaves Lake St. John by two channels, Big Discharge and Little Discharge, which enclose the island of Alma (*q.v.*). Its fall 314 ft. is a source of hydroelectric power and its shores are in many places high cliffs 1000 to 1800 ft. Noted for its scenery, its boating and fishing, and as a summer resort region.
2 County, Quebec, Canada. See NEW QUEBEC and *Table* at QUEBEC.
Sa·gui′et el Ham′ra (sȧ·gē′ĕt ăl hăm′rȧ); *also* **Se·ki′a el Hamra** (sĕ·kē′ȧ). **1** River, Spanish Sahara, NW Africa.
2 Northern zone of Spanish Sahara, NW Africa. See SPANISH SAHARA.
Sa·gun′to (sä·gōōn′tô); *formerly* **Mur·vie′dro** (mōōr·vyä′thrô); *anc.* **Sa·gun′tum** (sȧ·gŭn′tŭm). Fortified commune, Valencia prov., E Spain, near Mediterranean 15 m. NNE of Valencia; pop. 20,253; agricultural products, oil, wine; manufactures linen, brandies; exports iron ore; garrisoned castle; ancient Roman theater and other Roman and Greek remains. Settled by Greeks 3d cent. B.C.; allied with Rome; made famous heroic resistance to siege by Carthaginian forces under Hannibal 219–218 B.C.; made Roman municipium; captured by Moors 713 A.D.; reconquered by James of Aragon 1238; captured by French under Suchet 1808; end of republic

proclaimed here 1874 and Bourbons, in person of Alfonso XII, restored to throne; medieval name (Murviedro) discarded in favor of earlier name (Sagunto) 1877.
Sa′ha·gún′ (sä′ä·gōōn′). Commune, León prov., Spain; pop. ab. 3000; ruins of Benedictine monastery; scene of start of Sir John Moore's retreat before Napoleon Dec. 1808.
Sahama. Var. of SAJAMA.
Sa·hand′, Kuh–i– (kōō′hĕ·sȧ·hȧnd′). Mountain 12,105 ft. in NW Iran, E of Lake Urmia and just S of Tabriz.
Sa·har′a (sȧ·hâr′ȧ; sȧ·hȧr′ȧ); *Arab.* **Sah′ra** (sŏ′hrä). Vast region of deserts and oases in N Africa, of varied surface and irregular relief, ranging from 100 ft. below sea level to 11,201 ft. above (in Tibesti region); ab. 3,500,000 sq. m. Extends from Atlas Mts. and Atlantic coast of Spanish Sahara E to Red Sea; bordered on S by the Sudan region.
Saharan Atlas. See ATLAS MOUNTAINS.
Saharan Oases. See OASIS SAHARIENNES.
Sa·ha′ran·pur (sȧ·hä′rȧn·pōōr). City, Meerut division, NW Uttar Pradesh, N Indian Union, 100 m. N of Delhi; pop. (1941) 108,263; railroad junction.
Sahra. See SAHARA.
Sa·hua′yo, *in full* **Sahuayo de Por·fi′rio Dí′az** (sä·wä′yô thä pôr·fē′ryô thē′äs). Town, Michoacán state, SW Mexico, SE of Lake Chapala; pop. 10,465.
Sai′bai (sī′bī). Island off SW coast of the Territory of Papua, SE New Guinea, W of Daru and on N side of Torres Strait.
Sa′ï′da′ (*Fr.* sä′ē′dä′; *Arab.* sī′dȧ, -dä). **1** Commune, cen. Oran dept., NW Algeria, 75 m. SE of Oran; pop. 13,809.
2 *or* **Saida.** See SIDON, Lebanon Republic.
Sa·id′a·bad′ (sä·ēd′ȧ·bäd′). Town, E Fars prov., SW Iran, ab. 200 m. E of Shiraz and on highway SW of Kerman; pop. ab. 8000.
Sa′ï′da′ Mountains (sä′ē′dä′; *Arab.* sī′dȧ, -dä). Branch range of the Atlas Mts., in Maritime Atlas, cen. Oran dept., Algeria; highest ab. 3870 ft.
Sai′da·pet (sī′dȧ·pĕt). Town, E Madras state, S Indian Union, SSW suburb of Madras; pop. 33,037.
Sai′dor (sī′dôr). Coast town, on NE coast of North-East New Guinea, on Vitiaz Strait ab. 55 m. ESE of Madang; has good harbor; occupied by Allied troops Jan. 2, 1944.
Sai·go (sī·gō). See OKI ARCHIPELAGO.
Sai·gon′ (sī·gŏn′; sī′gŏn); *Fr.* **Sa′ï′gon′** (sä′ē′gôn′). Commercial city, Vietnam, ✳ of South Vietnam, in Cochin China, on the **Saigon River,** a branch of the Donnai; pop. (with Cholon) 1,800,000; river port 34 m. from the sea, but one of the finest in the Far East and the most important in Indochina; well-built modern city with fine government and commercial buildings; handled much of export business of S areas of French dependency. Captured by French 1859 and ceded by Annamese 1862; taken by Japanese Sept. 1940 and made an air base.
Saigon–Cho′lon′ (-shô′lôn′). Special administrative division, Cochin China, South Vietnam.
Saihun. See SYR DARYA.
Sai·la′na (sī·lä′nȧ). Former Indian state, W cen. India; 300 sq. m.; pop. (1941) 40,228; joined Union of Rajasthan June 26, 1947.
Sail′ly′–Sail′li·sel′ (sä′yē′sä′yē′zĕl′). Village, Somme dept., N France, 6 m. N of Péronne; severe fighting throughout 1916 to 1918, esp. during battle of the Somme July to Nov. 1916.
Sai′maa, Lake (sī′mä). Large lake 680 sq. m. in SE Finland, in Viipuri and Mikkeli depts.; drains E through Vuoksi river into Lake Ladoga; connected with Vyborg by Saimaa Canal.
Sain′don (sän′dŭn). Village, Matane co., on Gaspé Penin., SE Quebec, Canada; pop. 2220.
Saint. The following are foreign equivalents for the word "saint" often occurring in place names: *Fr.*, Saint or Sainte; *Ital. and Span.*, San, Santa, Santo; *Port.*, São;

Ger. and *Scandinavian,* Sankt; *Romanian,* Sfânta, Sfântul; *Du.,* Sint; *Slovak,* Svätý; *Serb.,* Sveti; *Bulg.,* Svetiya; *Russ.,* Svyatoi; *Hung.,* Szent; *Gr.,* Hagios, Hagion.

Saint Abb's Head (sånt ăbz′). Cape on SE coast of Scotland, near English border, projecting into North Sea; lighthouse.

Saint–A'cheul' (săɴ′-tȧ·shûl′). Hamlet and gravel pit near Amiens, Somme dept., N France; paleolithic remains discovered here; type station of the *Acheulean* or third Paleolithic period.

Saint–Af'frique' (săɴ′-tȧ′frēk′). Manufacturing town, Aveyron dept., S France, ab. 27 m. SSE of Rodez; pop. 4096.

Saint Ag'a·tha (sånt ăg′ȧ·thȧ). Town, Aroostook co., N Maine, 14 m. E of Fort Kent; pop. 1137; headquarters for fishing and camping parties.

Saint Ag'nes Head (ăg′něs; -nĭs). Promontory on W coast of Cornwall, SW England, WNW of Truro.

Saint Aignan. See MISIMA.

Saint Al'bans (sånt ôl′bănz). 1 City, ⊗ of Franklin co., NW Vermont, near Lake Champlain 25 m. N of Burlington; pop. 8806; trading and shipping center in agricultural and dairying area; railroad center; manufactures maple products and maple sugar-making equipment, poultry and stock feeds, canned goods, lime, creamery products; summer resort. Incorporated as town 1788, as city 1897; scene of bank raid by Confederates 1864.
2 City, Kanawha co., W cen. West Virginia, on Kanawha river 12 m. W of Charleston; pop. 15,103.
3 *anc.* **Ver'u·la·mi·um** (vĕr′ũ·lā′mĭ·ŭm; vĕr′ŏŏ-). City and municipal borough, Hertfordshire, SE England, on the Ver 20 m. NNW of London; pop. 44,106; ancient Roman settlement burned by Boadicea 61 A.D.; site of a noted Benedictine abbey, now a very large cathedral, founded in 793 and home of famous chroniclers, including Roger of Wendover, Matthew Paris, and Thomas Walsingham.

Saint Al'ban's Head (ôl′bănz). Headland on the coast of Dorsetshire, S England.

Saint A'lex'is' de la Grande Baie (săɴ′-tȧ′lĕk′sēd′ lȧ gräɴd′ bā′); *more commonly* **Grande Baie.** Village, Chicoutimi co., S Quebec, Canada, at head of Ha! Ha! Bay, S bank of Saguenay river 12 m. ESE of Chicoutimi; pop. 2974; extensive lumber trade.

Saint–A'mand' (săɴ′-tȧ′män′), *sometimes* **Saint–Amand–les–Eaux** (-lä-zō′). Manufacturing city, Nord dept., N France, 22 m. SE of Lille; pop. 14,762; manufactures machinery, hardware, ceramic ware, textiles, foundry products; thermal mineral springs; built around abbey founded 647 by Saint Amand; important center for production of faïence in 18th cent.

Saint–Amand–Mont–Rond (-môɴ′rôɴ′). Town, Cher dept., cen. France, ab. 23 m. SSE of Bourges; pop. 8413.

Saint An'dré', Cape (săɴ′-täɴ′drā′). Cape extending into Mozambique Channel on NW cen. coast of the island of Madagascar.

Saint An'drews (sånt ăn′drōōz). 1 Town, ⊗ of Charlotte co., SW New Brunswick, Canada, on Passamaquoddy Bay at mouth of St. Croix river; pop. 1458. Founded 1783. Summer resort; good harbor.
2 Seaport burgh, Fife co., E Scotland, on **Saint Andrews Bay**; pop. 9459; seat of St. Andrews Univ. (1411, oldest university in Scotland); site of famous golf links.

Saint An'drew Sound (sånt ăn′drōō). Inlet of Atlantic Ocean on NE coast of Camden co., SE Georgia, receiving the Satilla river on the W.

Saint Ann (sånt ăn′). City, St. Louis co., E Missouri, NW suburb of St. Louis; pop. 12,155.

Saint Ann Bay (sånt ăn′). Inlet of Atlantic Ocean in NE Cape Breton I., Nova Scotia, Canada.

Saint Anne (sånt ăn′). Town, ✳ of Alderney I., Channel Is.

Saint Anne's on the Sea (ănz′). Former urban district, Lancashire, W England, on the coast S of Black-

pool; pop. ab. 15,000; now part of Lytham St. Anne's municipal borough (since 1924).

Saint Ann's Bay (ănz′). Town and bay on N coast of island of Jamaica, West Indies; pop. of town 3500.

Saint Ann's Head. Cape on SW extremity of Wales, N of entrance to Milford Haven; lighthouse.

Saint An'tho·ny (ăn′thô·nĭ). 1 City, ⊗ of Fremont co., E Idaho, 40 m. NE of Idaho Falls; pop. 2700; grain, potatoes, sugar beets, seed peas.
2 Village, Hennepin and Ramsey cos., Minnesota, N suburb of Minneapolis; pop. 5084.
3 Seaport, NE Newfoundland, on Atlantic Ocean 20 m. S of Cape Bauld; pop. 842. Grenfell Mission center, has hospital, estab. c. 1900, and children's home.

Saint Anthony, Falls of. Waterfall 50 ft. high in the Mississippi river in the center of the city of Minneapolis, Minnesota; total fall including rapids above and below is ab. 85 ft.; furnishes extensive industrial power. Discovered 1680 by Hennepin; center of first settlement in area 1837.

Saint As'aph (sånt ăs′ăf). Town, Flintshire, NE Wales; cathedral, one of smallest in Great Britain.

Saint Au'gus·tine (sånt ô′gŭs·tēn). City, ⊗ of St. Johns co., NE Florida, on Atlantic Ocean 35 m. SE of Jacksonville; pop. 14,734; port of entry; winter and summer resort. Florida Memorial College (1892; coed.). Oldest permanent existing European settlement on continent of North America; founded by Pedro Menéndez de Avilés 1565; burned by Sir Francis Drake 1586; great stone fort of San Marcos (Fort Marion 1825–1942, renamed Castillo de San Marcos 1942) begun 1672, completed 1756; attacked by British in 18th-cent. wars; a refuge of Tories during American War of Independence (see FLORIDA).

Saint Augustine Inlet. Narrow strait leading from Atlantic Ocean through barrier reef opp. cen. St. Johns co., NE Florida.

Saint Aus'tell (ôs′t'l; *locally* ô′s'l). Urban district, Cornwall, SW England, on **Saint Austell Bay** 28 m. W of Plymouth; pop. 23,634; center of kaolin production in England; pleasure resort.

Saint–A'vold' (săɴ′-tȧ′vôl′). Town, Moselle dept., NE France, 23 m. E of Metz; pop. 4281; United States military cemetery.

Saint Bar'thé'le·my *or* **Saint–Bar'thé'le·my** (săɴ′bȧr′tāl′mē′). Island in Guadeloupe dept., French West Indies, in Leeward Is.; 9 sq. m.; pop. (1938 est.) 2479.

Saint Bath'ans, Mount (sånt băth′ănz). Peak 6837 ft. in S cen. South I., New Zealand.

Saint Bees Head (bēz′). Cape on NW coast of England, projecting into Irish Sea S of entrance to Solway Firth; lighthouse.

Saint–Be·noît' (săɴ′bĕ·nwä′). Town on E coast of the French island of Réunion in the Indian Ocean E of Madagascar; pop. ab. 12,000; E terminus of coastal railroad (80 m. long) from Saint-Pierre.

Saint Benoît Jo'seph' La'bre (zhō′zĕf′ lȧ′br′). Village, Matane co., on Gaspé Penin., SE Quebec, Canada; pop. 2599.

Saint Ber·nard' (sånt bĕr·närd′). 1 Parish in Louisiana. See *Table* at LOUISIANA.
2 Village, its ⊗, SE Louisiana; pop. (est.) 350.
3 City, Hamilton co., SW corner of Ohio, 5 m. N of Cincinnati; pop. 6778; suburb of Cincinnati.
4 (*Fr.* săɴ′ bĕr′när′) Two Alpine passes, Great Saint Bernard and Little Saint Bernard. See ALPS.

Saint Bonaventure. See ALLEGANY, New York.

Saint Bon'i·face (sånt bŏn′ĭ·fās). City, S Manitoba, Canada, on Red river across from Winnipeg; pop. 26,342; part of Greater Winnipeg. Largely French Canadian in its population; Roman Catholic headquarters for northwest Canada. Has fine large cathedral. Important for its packing plants, grain elevators, and flour mills. Seat of Manitoba Agricultural Coll. and of St. Boniface Coll., an associate of Univ. of Manitoba.

Saint Botolph's Town. See BOSTON.

Saint Bride's Bay (sănt brīdz′). Inlet of St. George's Channel on the SW extremity of Wales.

Saint–Bri′euc′ (săN′brē′ü′). Manufacturing and commercial city, ✳ of Côtes-du-Nord dept., NW France, on English Channel 70 m. NE of Quimper; pop. 31,640; 13th-cent. cathedral (restored), episcopal palace, town hall; manufactures iron, steel, lumber, brushes, woolens, and agricultural implements; coasting trade in fish and agricultural products.

Saint Cath′a·rine, or **Cath′er·ine, Lake** (sănt kăth′-ēr·ĭn; kăth′rĭn). Lake in SW Rutland co., W Vermont.

Saint Cath′a·rines (kăth′ēr·ĭnz; kăth′rĭnz). Industrial city, ⊗ of Lincoln co., SE Ontario, Canada, on Welland Ship Canal just S of Lake Ontario; pop. 37,984; shipbuilding; manufactures rubber and paper products; center of fruit-growing district; mineral springs, noted health resort. Founded 1796.

Saint Cath′er·ine, Mount (kăth′ēr·ĭn; kăth′rĭn). Mountain, N Grenada I., Windward Is., West Indies Federation; 2749 ft., highest point on the island.

Saint Catherine Point. Cape on N extremity of Bermuda I., in the Bermuda Is.

Saint Cath′er·ines Island (kăth′ēr·ĭnz; kăth′rĭnz). Island in Atlantic Ocean, off E mainland of Liberty co., SE Georgia.

Saint Cath′er·ine's Point (kăth′ēr·ĭnz; kăth′rĭnz). Cape on S tip of Isle of Wight, off S coast of England; lighthouse.

Saint Catherines Sound. Inlet of Atlantic Ocean on E coast of Liberty co., SE Georgia.

Saint–Cha′mond′ (săN′shà′môN′). Manufacturing commune, Loire dept., SE cen. France, 7 m. NE of Saint-Étienne; pop. 14,711; coal mines; forges, steel mills, bronze and copper foundries; manufactures railroad equipment, fieldpieces, silk products.

Saint Charles (sănt chärlz′). **1** Name of a parish in Louisiana and of a county in Missouri. See *Tables* at LOUISIANA and MISSOURI.

2 City, Kane co., NE Illinois, 37 m. W of Chicago; pop. 9269; trading center in agricultural section.

3 City, Winona co., SE Minnesota, 21 m. E of Rochester; pop. 1882.

4 City, ⊗ of St. Charles co., E Missouri, on Missouri river 20 m. NW of St. Louis; pop. 21,189; trade center for surrounding agricultural section. Lindenwood College for Women (1827; Presbyterian). Originally a fur-trading post; incorporated as village 1809, as city 1849; capital of Missouri Territory, and first capital of Missouri state 1821–26.

Saint Christopher. See SAINT KITTS.

Saint Clair (sănt klâr′). **1** Navigable river ab. 40 m. long, SE Michigan; connects Lake Huron with Lake St. Clair; forms United States-Canada boundary.

2 Name of counties in four states of the U.S. See *Tables* at ALABAMA, ILLINOIS, MICHIGAN, MISSOURI.

3 City, St. Clair co., SE Michigan, on St. Clair river 10 m. S of Port Huron; pop. 4538; salt deposits.

4 Borough, Schuylkill co., E cen. Pennsylvania, 4 m. WNW of Pottsville; pop. 5159; founded 1831; coal mining and shipping.

Saint Clair, Lake. 1 Lake bet. Michigan and Canadian province of Ontario; the U.S.-Canada boundary passes through it; ab. 30 m. long; area ab. 460 sq. m.; maximum depth 26 ft.; connects with Lake Huron by St. Clair river, and with Lake Erie by Detroit river.

2 Lake, E cen. Tasmania, Australia, source of Derwent river; 9 m. long; ab. 16 sq. m.; noted for its scenery and fishing.

Saint Clair Shores. City, Macomb co., SE Michigan, on Lake St. Clair 13 m. NE of Detroit; pop. 76,657.

Saint Clairs′ville (klârz′vĭl). Village, ⊗ of Belmont co., E Ohio, 24 m. SSW of Steubenville; pop. 3865; manufactures hardwood, dairy products; coal mines in vicinity.

Saint–Claude′ (săN′klōd′); *anc.* **Con·da′te** (kŏn-dä′tĕ). Manufacturing commune, Jura dept., E France, 25 m. SE of Lons-le-Saunier; pop. 11,381; 15th-cent. cathedral; manufactures wood objects; cutting of precious stones. Founded in pre-Roman times.

Saint Clem′ent Bay (sănt klĕm′ĕnt). Inlet of Potomac river on SW shore of St. Marys co., S Maryland.

Saint–Cloud (săN′klōō′). Commune, Seine-et-Oise dept., N France, WSW suburb of Paris near Seine river; pop. 16,597; new national porcelain manufactory (formerly located at Sèvres); Parisian resort; formerly residence of French monarchs; scene of murder of Henry III 1589; royal castle built by Louis XIV 1658; scene of Napoleon's coup of the 18th Brumaire; Blücher's headquarters 1815; Napoleon III signed declaration of war against Prussia here 1870.

Saint Cloud (sănt kloud′). **1** City, Osceola co., cen. Florida penin., 23 m. S of Orlando; pop. 4353.

2 City, Benton, Sherburne, and Stearns cos., ⊗ of Stearns co., cen. Minnesota, on Mississippi river 58 m. NW of Minneapolis; pop. 33,815; trade center for agricultural section; granite quarries. St. Cloud State College (1866; coed.).

Saint Croix (sănt kroi′). **1** River ab. 75 m. long, forming S section of boundary bet. Maine and the Canadian province of New Brunswick; flows S from Chiputnetticook Lakes into Passamaquoddy Bay.

2 River 164 m. long, NW Wisconsin and E Minnesota; rises in Douglas co., NW Wisconsin, flows SW and forms part of Wisconsin-Minnesota boundary until it empties into the Mississippi below St. Paul; navigable ab. 54 m. to the Dalles (dălz) in Interstate Park where a deep gorge has been cut.

3 County in Wisconsin. See *Table* at WISCONSIN.

4 or **San′ta Cruz** (săn′tà krōōz′). Largest and most populous of the Virgin Is. of the United States, in the West Indies, ab. 37 m. S of St. Thomas; 82 sq. m.; pop. 14,973; chief town Christiansted; only other town is Frederiksted, at W end; produces sugar cane. Discovered 1493 by Columbus; in turn became possession of Dutch, English, Spanish, and French; purchased by Denmark 1753.

Saint–Cyr–l'É′cole′ (săN′sēr′là′kôl′). Commune, Seine-et-Oise dept., N France, 3 m. W of Versailles; pop. (1931) 8277; site of military school, established 1808.

Saint David. See MAPIA.

Saint Da′vid Island (sănt dā′vĭd). Island, NE Bermuda Is., N of Castle Harbour.

Saint Da′vid's (dā′vĭdz); *anc.* **Me·ne′via** (mĕ·nēv′yà; -nē′vĭ·à). Parish, Pembrokeshire, SW Wales; pop. 1644; cathedral of 12th–14th cents.; according to tradition, see of Menevia founded in 6th cent. by Saint David, patron saint of Wales.

Saint David's Head. 1 Cape at E end of Saint David I., NE Bermuda Is.; easternmost point of the islands, ab. 64°39′W.

2 Cape, Pembrokeshire, SW coast of Wales, extending into St. George's Channel; cliffs ab. 100 ft. high; most western point of Wales, 5°20′W.

Saint–De·nis′ (săNd′nē′; *Angl.* sănt dĕn′ĭs). **1** Manufacturing commune, Seine dept., N France, 7 m. NNE of Paris; pop. 78,401; metallurgical and chemical works; manufactures soap, candles, glue, gelatin, dyes, varnishes, leather, liquors; famous 12th-cent. Gothic abbatial church containing tombs of French monarchs, among them Louis XII, Henry II, Catherine de Médicis, Louis of Orléans, Francis I, Claude of France, Louis XVI, Marie Antoinette, Louis XIII; celebrated abbey of Saint Denis founded here 626 by the Merovingian king Dagobert I; Abelard resided here as monk in 12th cent.; the banner of Saint Denis, the oriflamme, served as royal standard until reign of Charles III; called **Fran′ciade′** (frän′syàd′) during the Revolution.

2 City, ✳ of French island of Réunion in the Indian Ocean, on N coast; pop. (1936) 30,762.

Saint–Denis–du–Sig (-dü·sēg′). Commune, Oran dept., NW Algeria, just SE of Oran; pop. 10,608.

Saint–Denis–le–Gast (-lē·gȧst′). Commune, Manche dept., Normandy, NW France, 12 m. N of Avranches; pop. 851; scene of breakthrough of American armored forces July 30, 1944.

Saint–Dié (săn′dyā′). Manufacturing commune, Vosges dept., NE France, on Meurthe river 25 m. ENE of Épinal; pop. 20,315; 12th-cent. cathedral and church, 17th-cent. episcopal palace; manufactures cotton goods, metal goods, machinery, and distilled liquors. Built around a monastery founded by Saint Deodatus in the 7th cent.

Saint–Di′zier′ (săn′dē′zyā′); *anc.* **Des′i·de′ri·i Fa′- num** (dĕs′ĭ·dĕr′ĭ·ī fā′nŭm). Manufacturing commune, Haute-Marne dept., NE France, on Marne river 39 m. N of Chaumont; pop. 19,149; iron, steel, copper, and bronze foundries. Besieged and taken 1544; battle nearby 1814.

Saint Do′mingue′ (săn′ dô′măng′). French form of Santo Domingo, early name of Dominican Republic, sometimes applied to entire island (see Hispaniola).

Sainte–A′dresse′ (săn′-tȧ′drĕs′). Commune, Seine-Inférieure dept., N France, near Le Havre; pop. (1931) 4668; seat of Belgian government Oct. 13, 1914 to Dec. 1918 during World War I.

Sainte A′gathe′ des Monts (săn′-tȧ′gȧt′ dā môn′). Resort town, Terrebonne co., S Quebec, Canada, 52 m. NW of Montreal; pop. 5169; sportsmen's headquarters.

Sainte–Anne (săn′-tän′). Commune and village, S coast of Grande Terre, Guadeloupe, French West Indies; pop. (commune) ab. 14,000, town (1921) 10,033.

Sainte Anne (sånt ăn′; *Fr.* săn′-tän′). **1** See Fort Sainte Anne, Vermont.
2 River ab. 50 m. long in Charlevoix and Montmorency cos., S Quebec, Canada; flows S into the St. Lawrence at Sainte Anne de Beaupré.
3 Village, S Quebec, Canada. See Sainte Anne de Chicoutimi.

Sainte Anne de Beau′pré′ (sånt ăn′ dē bō′prā′; *Fr.* săn′-tän′). Village, Montmorency co., S Quebec, Canada, on St. Lawrence river 21 m. NE of Quebec; pop. 1827. Site of famous shrine (estab. 1620) and church to Saint Anne (the original building, dedicated 1658, destroyed by fire in 1922 and replaced by a large and beautiful structure).

Sainte Anne de Belle′vue′ (sånt ăn′ dē bĕl′vū; *Fr.* săn′-tän′ dē bĕl′vü′). Unincorporated town at SW end of Montreal I., S Quebec, Canada, on Lake St. Louis 21 m. WSW of Montreal; pop. 3342; summer resort; Macdonald Coll. of Agriculture.

Sainte Anne de Chi′cou′ti·mi (sånt ăn′ dē shĭ·kōō′-tĭ·mĭ; *Fr.* săn′-tän′ dē shē′kōō′tē′mē′); *often,* **Sainte Anne.** Village, Chicoutimi co., S Quebec, Canada, on N bank of Saguenay river 3 m. NW of Chicoutimi; pop. 3966.

Sainte Anne des Monts (sånt ăn′ dā môn′; *Fr.* săn′-tän′). Town (unincorporated), ⊗ of West Gaspé co., on Gaspé Penin., SE Quebec, Canada, on St. Lawrence river at its mouth; pop. 2762; important agricultural parish on Gaspé Penin. highway; has steamer connections with Quebec; a resort and sportsmen's center and principal entrance to Gaspé Park.

Sainte Anne's Point. See Fredericton.

Sainte–Baume (sănt′bōm′). Mountain chain in Bouches-du-Rhône and Var depts., SE France; highest point 3785 ft.; site of grotto (La Grotte de Sainte Madeleine) where Mary Magdalene is supposed to have spent the end of her life, popular place of pilgrimage.

Sainte–Croix (săn′tē·krwä′). Commune, Vaud canton, W Switzerland; pop. (1930) 6340; at 3500 ft., in the Jura Mts.

Sainte Croix (sånt kroi′; *Fr.* săn′tē krwä′). Village, ⊗ of Lotbinière co., S Quebec, Canada, on S bank of the St. Lawrence river 28 m. SW of Quebec; pop. 1080. Parish is

chiefly agricultural but has a few manufacturing plants. One of the oldest in Canada, its church dating back to 1694.

Sainte Fa′mille′ (sănt′ fȧ′mē′y′). Village (unincorporated), a ⊗ of Montmorency co., S Quebec, Canada, on N shore of Orleans I., 28 m. NE of Quebec; pop. 772; chief village on the island.

Sainte Gen′e·vieve (sånt jĕn′ĕ·vēv). **1** County in Missouri. See *Table* at Missouri.
2 City, its ⊗, E Missouri, on Mississippi river 46 m. S of St. Louis; pop. 4443; trading center for agricultural section; lime kilns; marble quarries; site of first settlement, by the French, in Missouri c. 1735.

Sainte Ge·ne·viève′ de Ba′tis′can′ (sănt′ zhĕn·vyâv′ dē bȧ′tēs′kȧn′). Village (unincorporated), ⊗ of Champlain co., S Quebec, Canada, on Batiscan river near its mouth, 18 m. NE of Three Rivers; pop. 1467.

Sainte Hé′né′dine′ (săn′-tā′nā′dēn′). Village (unincorporated), ⊗ of Dorchester co., S Quebec, Canada, 21 m. SSE of Quebec; pop. 1162.

Sainte Ju′lienne′ (sănt′ zhü′lyĕn′). Village (unincorporated), ⊗ of Montcalm co., S Quebec, Canada, 32 m. N of Montreal; pop. 1274; agricultural center for general farming, tobacco growing, and dairying.

Saint E·li′as, Cape (sånt ē·lī′ȧs). Point, S end of Kayak I. off SE coast of Alaska.

Saint Elias, Mount. 1 Peak 18,008 ft. in the Saint Elias Range, on the boundary bet. SW Yukon Territory, Canada, and E Alaska.
2 = Mount Hagios Elias.

Saint Elias Range. Mountain range ab. 250 m. long in SW Yukon Territory, Canada, and E Alaska, near the Pacific Ocean; highest peak Mt. Logan 19,850 ft. On its S slopes are the great Malaspina and Guyot glaciers in Alaska.

Saint El′mo (sånt ĕl′mō). City, Fayette co., S cen. Illinois, 40 m. NNE of Centralia; pop. 1503.

Saint–Éloi. See Sint-Eloois-Vijve.

Saint–É′loy′–les–Mines (săn′-tā′lwä′lā–mēn′). Mining commune, Puy-de-Dôme dept., S cen. France, NNW of Clermont-Ferrand; pop. (1931) 7008.

Sainte–Marguerite. See Îles de Lérins.

Sainte–Ma·rie′ (sånt·mȧ·rē′; *Fr.* săn′mȧ′rē′). Commune, NE coast of Martinique, French West Indies; pop. ab. 13,000.

Sainte–Ma·rie′ *or* **Sainte–Marie–de–Mad′a·gas′- car, Île** (ēl′ sånt·mȧ·rē′[dē·măd′ȧ·găs′kẽr]; *Fr.* ēl′ sănt′-mȧ′rē′[dē·mȧ′dȧ′gȧs′kȧr′]). French island in the Indian Ocean off NE cen. coast of Madagascar; 64 sq. m.; pop. ab. 8000.

Sainte Ma·rie′ (sånt mȧ·rē′; *Fr.* sănt′ mȧ′rē′). Village, Beauce co., S Quebec, Canada, on Chaudière river 28 m. SSE of Quebec; pop. 2431.

Sainte–Marie, Cape. Extreme S tip of the island of Madagascar.

Sainte–Ma·rie′–aux–Mines (sånt·mȧ·rē′ō·mēn′; *Fr.* sănt′mȧ′rē′); *Ger.* **Mar′kirch** (mär′kĭrk). Commune, Haut-Rhin dept., NE France; pop. (1931) 9011; silver, copper, and lead mines in the vicinity, worked 9th-19th cents.; weaving industry.

Sainte Mar·tine′ (sånt mär·tēn′; *Fr.* sănt′ mär′tēn′). Village (unincorporated), ⊗ of Châteauguay co., S Quebec, Canada, 21 m. SSW of Montreal; pop. 843.

Sainte–Me·ne·hould′ (sănt′mē·nōō′). Commune, NE Marne dept., NE France, on the Aisne; pop. (1931) 4234; on W border of the Argonne Forest; occupied by Germans Sept. 1914 but regained by French and became their headquarters for the Argonne sector.

Sainte–Mère–É′glise (sănt′mâr′ā′glēz′). Commune, Manche dept., NW France, ab. 20 m. SE of Cherbourg; pop. (1931) 1173; taken June 6–10, 1944 by American air-borne division in invasion of Normandy.

Sainte Rose (sånt rōz′; *Fr.* sănt′ rōz′). Town, ⊗ of Jesus I., S Quebec, Canada, on Rivière des Mille Îles 14 m. NW of Montreal; pop. 3660; summer resort.

Saintes (sănt); *anc.* **Me′di·o·la′num** (mē′dĭ·ō·lā′-nŭm; mĕd′ĭ-). Manufacturing city, Charente-Maritime dept., W France, on Charente river 40 m. SE of La Rochelle; pop. 21,160; Roman remains, including esp. a fine amphitheater; 11th-cent. cathedral, 6th-cent. church (restored in 16th cent.), palace of justice; manufactures iron, copper, textiles, pottery, leather; trades in wheat, corn, timber, brandy. Ancient capital of Santones; formerly capital of province of Saintonge; scene of defeat of Henry III by Louis IX 1242.

Saintes, Les. See LES SAINTES.

Sainte–Sa′vine′ (sănt′să′vēn′). Commune, Aube dept., NE France, suburb of Troyes; pop. 10,406.

Sainte Scho′las′tique′ (sănt′ skō′lás′tĭk′). Village, ⊗ of Two Mountains co., S Quebec, Canada, 27 m. WNW of Montreal; pop. 836; center of farming and dairying district, on railroad line. Founded 1855.

Saint–Es′tèphe′ (săN′-tĕs′tĕf′). Commune, Gironde dept., SW France, on the Gironde ab. 25 m. NNW of Bordeaux; pop. (1931) 2426; in the Médoc; celebrated red wines from the Châteaux Cos d'Estournel and Montrose.

Sainte Thé′rèse′ (sănt′ tā′râz′). 1 Island ab. 3 m. long in the St. Lawrence at the foot of Montreal I., S Quebec, Canada.

2 Town, Terrebonne co., S Quebec, Canada, 18 m. NW of Montreal; pop. 7038; railroad junction; has furniture and piano factory.

Saint–É′tienne′ (săN′-tā′tyĕn′). Manufacturing city, ✻ of Loire dept., SE cen. France, 32 m. SW of Lyons; pop. 190,236; rich coal fields; metallurgical establishments producing one third of France's output of steel; manufactures metal goods, machinery, ornaments, ribbons, laces, hemp cables, pottery, silks; school of mines; town hall, art gallery.

Saint–Étienne–du–Rou′vray′ (-dü-rōō′vrā′). Commune, Seine-Inférieure dept., N France, 3 m. S of Rouen; pop. (1931) 10,741; Renaissance church; textiles.

Saint Eu′gène′ (săN′-tû′zhän′; -tü′zhân′). Suburb of city of Algiers, N Algeria; pop. 9410.

Saint Eus′tache′ (săN′-tûs′tásh′; -tüs′tásh′). Village, Two Mountains co., S Quebec, Canada, on Rivière des Mille Îles across from Jesus I.; pop. 2615.

Saint Eu·sta′ti·us (sănt û·stā′shĭ·ŭs; -shŭs). Small island of the Leeward Is., West Indies, NW of St. Kitts; 7 sq. m.; pop. (1942) 1119; belongs to the Netherlands; administratively a part of Curaçao territory; its town, Orange Town, exports yams and sweet potatoes.

Saint Fé′li′cien′ (săN′ fā′lē′syăN′). Village, Lake St. John co., S Quebec, Canada, on Ashuapmuchuan river near its mouth, W of Lake St. John; pop. 2656; industrial center, esp. for agricultural products and lumber.

Saint–Flo′rent′, Gulf of (săN′flô′räN′). Inlet, NW coast of Corsica; the town of **Saint-Florent** is on it.

Saint–Flour (săN′flōōr′). Manufacturing commune, E Cantal dept., S cen. France; pop. 5384; built on a steep rock; cathedral of 14th–15th cents.

Saint–Fons (săN′fôn′). Industrial commune, Rhône dept., E cen. France, near Rhone river 4 m. SSE of Lyons; pop. (1931) 10,660.

Saint Fran′cis (sănt frăn′sĭs). 1 River, N Maine; with Lake St. Francis (actually an expansion of the river) forms a section of the extreme N boundary of Maine, and flows into St. John river.

2 River 425 m. long, SE Missouri and E Arkansas; rises in Iron co., SE Missouri, flows S and forms section of boundary bet. SE Missouri and NE Arkansas, continues S through E Arkansas into Mississippi river; navigable 125 m.

3 County in Arkansas. See *Table* at ARKANSAS.

4 City, ⊗ of Cheyenne co., NW corner of Kansas; pop. 1594.

5 City, Milwaukee co., SE Wisconsin, SW of Milwaukee; pop. 10,065.

6 *Fr.* **Saint–Fran′çois′** (săN′frăN′swá′). River 165 m.

long, S Quebec prov., Canada; flows SW out of Lake Saint Francis in Frontenac co., then NW into Lake St. Peter in the St. Lawrence river below Sorel.

Saint Francis, Cape. 1 See Cape FRANCIS, Newfoundland.

2 Cape on SE coast of Cape Province, South Africa, W of St. Francis Bay.

Saint Francis, Lake. 1 Lake in N Maine. See SAINT FRANCIS river.

2 Lake 83 sq. m., S Quebec and SE Ontario provs., Canada, 35 m. SW of the city of Montreal, formed by a widening of the St. Lawrence river.

3 Lake, Frontenac co., S Quebec, Canada. See SAINT FRANCIS river, Canada.

Saint Francis Bay. Bay on SE coast of Cape Province, South Africa, E of Cape St. Francis.

Saint Fran′cis·ville (sănt frăn′sĭs·vĭl; *Sou. also* -v′l). Town, ⊗ of West Feliciana parish, E cen. Louisiana; pop. 1661.

Saint–Fran′çois′ (săN′frän′swá′). 1 River in Canada. See SAINT FRANCIS.

2 Commune, SE coast of Grande Terre, Guadeloupe, French West Indies; pop. ab. 7000.

Saint Fran′cois (sănt frăn′sĭs). County in Missouri. See *Table* at MISSOURI.

Saint Fran′çois′ du Lac (săN′ frän′swá′ dü lâk′). Village, ⊗ of Yamaska co., S Quebec, Canada, S of Lake St. Peter and ab. 25 m. SE of Three Rivers; pop. 763; one of oldest parishes in Quebec, established 1714.

Saint Ga′bri′el′ de Bran′don′ (săN′ gá′brē′ĕl′ dĕ bräN′dôN′). Village, Berthier co., S Quebec, Canada, 42 m. W of Three Rivers on S shore of Lake Maskinongé; pop. 2661; trading center for large area; has important lumber industry; summer resort.

Saint Gall (sănt gôl′); *Ger.* **Sankt Gal′len** (zängkt gäl′ĕn); *Fr.* **Saint–Gall** (săN′gál′; *Angl.* sănt·gôl′, -gál′, -gäl′). 1 Swiss canton, in Alps; includes Lake Wallen and part of Lake Constance; stone quarries; pastures; lumber; textile manufacturing. See *Table* at SWITZERLAND.

2 Commune, its ✻, NE Switzerland, 39 m. E of Zurich; pop. (1941) 62,530; 17th and 18th-cent. abbey buildings (now seat of public offices), cathedral, town hall, museums, library, etc.; trade center; manufactures fine laces, embroidery. Developed around Benedictine abbey founded in early 7th cent. by Saint Gall, an Irish missionary; became free imperial city 1304; joined Swiss Confederation 1454; abbey famous seat of learning in Middle Ages.

Saint–Gau′dens′ (săN′gō′dăns′). Town, Haute-Garonne dept., S France, ab. 50 m. SSW of Toulouse; pop. 4238; church of 11th–12th cents.; important in medieval times.

Saint George (sănt jôrj′). 1 Town, Knox co., S Maine, on Atlantic Ocean inlet 36 m. ESE of Augusta; pop. 1588; on the site of Fort St. George, built 1719–20, attacked by Indians 1722–24, 1744, 1747, 1755, rebuilt 1809, captured by English in War of 1812.

2 Post Office station, ⊗ of Richmond co., SE New York, N Staten I. on Upper New York Bay. See RICHMOND borough, New York City.

3 Town, ⊗ of Dorchester co., SE South Carolina, 28 m. SSE of Orangeburg; pop. 1833; agriculture, lumbering, cattle raising.

4 City, ⊗ of Washington co., SW corner of Utah, 50 m. SSW of Cedar City; pop. 5130; founded 1861; winter headquarters of Brigham Young.

5 Town on S coast of St. George's I., N Bermuda Is.; pop. (1939) 1281; founded 1612, first settlement in Bermuda, was capital until 1815.

Saint George, Cape. 1 Cape at S extremity of Flag I., in Gulf of Mexico, off S coast of Franklin co., NW Florida.

2 Peninsula, SE New South Wales, SE Australia, S of Beecroft Head and with it encloses Jervis Bay.

3 Cape and peninsula N of St. Georges Bay, SW Newfoundland.

4 Cape, S point of New Ireland, Bismarck Archipelago; ab. 5°S at N end of Solomon Sea.

Saint George, Point. Point on W coast of Del Norte co., NW California.

Saint George, or **Saint George's, Channel** (jôrj, jôr′jĭz). Passage ab. 20 m. wide bet. S end of New Ireland on E and NE New Britain on W, Bismarck Archipelago; connects Bismarck Sea with Solomon Sea.

Saint George Island. 1 Island off coast of Franklin co., NW Florida, bet. Gulf of Mexico on the S and St. George Sound and Apalachicola Bay on the N.

2 Island in Potomac river near its mouth, in St. Marys co., S Maryland.

3 Island, most southerly of Pribilof Is. (*q.v.*) in Bering Sea, Alaska; 10 m. long by ab. 4 m. wide; 27 sq. m.; pop. 183.

4 Island in the Azores. See SÃO JORGE.

5 Island in Danube delta. See SFÂNTU GHEORGHE.

Saint Georges (săN′ zhôrzh′). Town, E French Guiana, ab. 90 m. SE of Cayenne on Oyapock river; pop. ab. 1000.

Saint George's (sånt jôr′jĭz). **1** Town on Grenada I., Windward Is., West Indies Federation; * of Grenada territory, and administrative * of the Windward Is.; pop. (1939 est.) 6500; excellent harbor.

2 Seaport, SW Newfoundland, at E end of St. Georges Bay; pop. 1133; located in a timber, mining, and fertile farm district.

Saint Georges Bay (jôr′jĭz). Inlet of Gulf of St. Lawrence in SW Newfoundland.

Saint George's Cay. Small island in Caribbean Sea off NE coast of British Honduras; resort; scene of defeat of Spaniards by British settlers Sept. 10, 1798.

Saint George's Channel. 1 See SAINT GEORGE CHANNEL.

2 Strait bet. Wales on the E and Ireland on the W; joins Atlantic Ocean and Irish Sea.

Saint Georges East (sånt jôr′jĭz ēst′); *Fr.* **Saint-Georges Est** (săN′zhôrzh′ ĕst′). Village, Beauce co., S Quebec, Canada, on E bank of Chaudière river 30 m. E of Thetford Mines; pop. 2657; center of farming and lumbering region. Settled c. 1736.

Saint George's Island. An island in N Bermuda Is., on W side of Castle Harbour; first of the islands to be colonized by English 1612, settlement at St. George on S coast.

Saint George Sound. Inlet of Gulf of Mexico in S coast of Franklin co., NW Florida.

Saint–Ger·main′ (sånt-jĕr-māN′; *Fr.* săN′zhĕr′măN′), *in full* **Saint–Ger′main′–en–Laye** (săN′zhĕr′măN′-năN-lā′). Commune, Seine-et-Oise dept., N France, on Seine river 11 m. WNW of Paris; pop. 22,539; summer resort; Parisian residential suburb; noted for vast forest and park; terrace of St. Germain one of finest promenades in Europe; 14th-cent. castle (birthplace of Charles IX, Margaret of Valois, Henry II, Louis XIV, now a museum); treaties signed here 1570, 1632, 1679, and, bet. Allied Powers and Austria, 1919.

Saint–Gilles (săN′zhēl′). **1** *Flemish* **Sint–Gil′lis** (sĭnt-kĭl′ĭs). Commune, Brabant prov., cen. Belgium, a suburb of Brussels; pop. (1938 est.) 61,341.

2 Town, Gard dept., S France, ab. 12 m. SSE of Nîmes; pop. 4402; medieval countship held by counts of Toulouse; site of first priory in Europe founded by the Knights of St. John of Jerusalem; of the 12th-cent. church only the beautiful west front and the crypt remain, the rest being 17th-cent. Gothic.

Saint–Go′bain′ (săN′-gô′băN′). Town, Aisne dept., N France, ab. 7 m. NW of Laon; pop. 1549; in the **Fo′rêt′ de Saint–Gobain** (fô′rĕd′ săN′); site of glass manufactures established 1685; during World War I, held by Germans until Oct. 1918 as a strongly fortified point on the Hindenburg Line.

Saint Gott′hard (sånt gŏt′ĕrd; *Ger.* [zängkt] gôt′härt) or **Saint Got′hard** (sånt gŏt′ĕrd; gŏth′ĕrd; *Fr.* săN′ gô′tàr′). **1** Mountain range of the Lepontine Alps, mostly bet. Uri and Ticino cantons, SE cen. Switzerland; highest peak Pizzo Rotondo 10,490 ft.

2 Alpine pass and tunnel. See ALPS.

Saint Gotthard. See SZENTGOTTHÁRD.

Saint Gow′an's Head (sånt gou′ănz). Cape on SW corner of Wales, S of Pembroke.

Saint He·le′na (sånt′l-ē′nà; sånt′ hĕ·lē′nà). **1** Parish in Louisiana. See *Table* at LOUISIANA.

2 City, Napa co., W cen. California, 22 m. N of San Pablo Bay; pop. 2722; founded 1853, incorp. 1876 and 1889; in agricultural region producing esp. grapes and prunes; manufactures wines, olive oil.

3 British island in South Atlantic Ocean, ab. 1200 m. from W coast of Africa, lat. 15°57′S and long. 5°42′W; 47 sq. m.; pop. (1931) 3995, (1938 est.) 4474; * Jamestown; with Ascension I. (since 1922) and the Tristan da Cunha Is. (since 1938) constitutes a British crown colony. The crater rim of a volcano long extinct; highest point 2704 ft.; marked by gorges and valleys, many springs, and plains in the NE. Discovered May 21, 1502 by a Portuguese navigator; first visited by English 1588; taken over by British East India Co. 1651; Napoleon's place of exile 1815–1821; detention camp for Boer prisoners during Boer War 1899–1902.

Saint Helena Bay. Bay on W coast of Cape Province, Union of South Africa.

Saint Hel′e·na Island (hĕl′ĕ·nà). Island ab. 13 m. long in Beaufort co., S South Carolina.

Saint Helena Sound. Inlet on N coast of Saint Helena I., South Carolina.

Saint Hel′ens (sånt hĕl′ĕnz; -ĭnz). **1** City and river port, ⊗ of Columbia co., NW Oregon, on Columbia river 25 m. N of Portland; pop. 5022; fishing and shipping center; manufactures insulating board, paper and pulp, lumber, dairy products; stone quarries nearby.

2 Former urban district, E coast of Isle of Wight, S England, 7 m. SSW of Portsmouth; since 1932 in Ryde.

3 County borough, Lancashire, NW England, 10 m. ENE of Liverpool; pop. 106,789, (1951 pop.) 110,276; chief center of glass manufacture in England; also produces chemicals, patent medicines, and pottery; deposits of coal and fire clay nearby.

Saint Helens, Mount. Peak 9671 ft. in NW Skamania co., S Washington.

Saint Hel′ier (sånt hĕl′yēr). Commercial town and civil parish on the island of Jersey, Channel Is., **in the** English Channel 122 m. SSW of Southampton; * of Jersey bailiwick; pop. 25,824; residential community and watering place; residence of Victor Hugo 1852–55. Victoria College (1852).

Saint–Honorat. See Îles de LÉRINS.

Saint Hu′bert (sånt hū′bĕrt; *Fr.* săN′-tü′bâr′). Post office and village (unincorporated), Chambly co., Quebec prov., E Canada, just E of Montreal.

Saint Hy′a·cinthe (sånt hī′à·sĭnth; *Fr.* săN′-tyà′săNt′). **1** County, Quebec, Canada. See *Table* at QUEBEC.

2 Industrial city, its ⊗, on Yamaska river 34 m. ENE of Montreal; pop. 20,236; produces shoes, leather and woolen goods, machinery, organs. Seat of a Roman Catholic cathedral, a Dominican college, and many other religious institutions. Settled 1760.

Saint Ig′nace (sånt ĭg′nàs). City, ⊗ of Mackinac co., SE Michigan penin., on Straits of Mackinac; pop. 3334; fisheries.

Saint Ignace Island. Island in N Lake Superior, off S shore of Thunder Bay dist., SW Ontario, Canada.

Saint–I′mier (săN′-tē′myā′). Manufacturing commune, Bern canton, Switzerland, ab. 12 m. W of Biel; pop. (1930) 6504; manufactures watches; resort.

Saint Ives (sånt īvz′). Municipal borough on NW coast of Cornwall, SW England, on **Saint Ives Bay** 60 m. W of Plymouth; pop. 9037; fishing town and watering place.

Saint Jacques (săn' zhäk'). Village, Montcalm co., S Quebec, Canada, 28 m. N of Montreal; pop. 1729; tobacco-growing center. Founded 1772.

Saint Jacques, Cape. Point on E coast of Cochin China, Vietnam, N of entrance to Saigon, ab. 10°20′N.

Saint James (sânt jāmz'). **1** Parish in Louisiana. See *Table* at LOUISIANA.

2 City, ⊗ of Watonwan co., S Minnesota, 33 m. WSW of Mankato; pop. 4174.

3 City, Phelps co., S cen. Missouri, 10 m. E of Rolla; pop. 2384; ships vegetables, berries, and dairy products.

Saint James, Cape. Cape, S tip of Kunghit I., S Queen Charlotte Is., off W British Columbia, Canada.

Saint-Jean (săn'zhän'). County and city, S Quebec, Canada. See SAINT JOHNS.

Saint-Jean, Île-. See PRINCE EDWARD ISLAND.

Saint Jean, Lac. See Lake SAINT JOHN.

Saint-Jean-Cap-Fer'rat' (săn'zhän'kàp'fě'rà'). Commune, Alpes-Maritimes dept., SE France, E of Nice; fishing port, resort; pop. 1573.

Saint-Jean-d'Acre. See ACRE city, Palestine.

Saint-Jean-d'An'gé'ly (săn'zhän'dän'zhā'lē'). Town, Charente-Maritime dept., W France, ab. 35 m. SE of La Rochelle; pop. 5702; suffered much during religious wars of 16th cent. when it was a strong Protestant center; finally taken by Louis XIII 1621.

Saint-Jean-de-Luz (săn'zhänd'lüz'). Coast town, Basses-Pyrénées dept., SW France, on the Bay of Biscay SW of Biarritz near Spanish border; pop. 5775; a Basque town; important fishing and trading port 14th–17th cents.; now mainly a resort.

Saint-Jean-de-Mau'rienne' (săn'zhänd'mô'ryĕn'). Town, Savoie dept., E France, SE of Chambéry; pop. 2359; ecclesiastical town dating from 6th cent.; cathedral mainly 15th cent. Allied conference Apr. 19, 1917.

Saint Jean Port Jo'li' (săn' zhän' pôr' zhō'lē'). Town (unincorporated), ⊗ of L'Islet co., S Quebec, Canada, on S bank of St. Lawrence river 55 m. NE of Quebec; pop. 2180; agricultural center. Parish founded 1721.

Saint Jé'rôme' (săn' zhā'rōm'). Industrial town, ⊗ of Terrebonne co., SW Quebec, Canada, 28 m. NW of Montreal; pop. 17,685; sawmills, pulp, paper, rubber, and knitting mills, foundries. Seat of a normal school. Founded 1852. Has annual Passion play.

Saint Joe Mountains (sânt jō'). Range 6148 ft. in Shoshone co., NE Idaho.

Saint John (sânt jŏn'). **1** See also SAINT JEAN, SAINT JOHNS, SAINT JOHN'S.

2 City, ⊗ of Stafford co., cen. Kansas, 47 m. W of Hutchinson; pop. 1753; trade center in agricultural section; originally settled 1879 by Mormons.

3 Village, St. Louis co., E Missouri, W suburb of St. Louis; pop. 7342.

4 River 450 m. long in NE United States and SE Canada; rises in NW Maine (Somerset co.), flows NE and for 70 m. forms a part of the boundary bet. Maine and New Brunswick, turns SE through W New Brunswick, then E and S to Bay of Fundy at St. John. Navigable to Fredericton (86 m.) for large vessels, Fredericton to Grand Falls, and for ab. 65 m. above Grand Falls for smaller boats. At Grand Falls, ab. 220 m. from its mouth, is great cataract ab. 75 ft. high; at its mouth in St. John harbor narrowed to gorge 450 ft. wide with sides ab. 100 ft. high; here are famous falls (**Re·vers'ing** [rĕ·vûr'sĭng], *or* **Re·vers'i·ble** [rĕ·vûr'sĭ·b'l], **Falls**) which are named from the reversal of the river's flow at high tide, the water being forced upstream from the Bay of Fundy. Chief tributaries Allagash and Aroostook in Maine, Madawaska in Quebec and New Brunswick, Tobique and Nashwaak.

5 County in New Brunswick, Canada. See *Table* at NEW BRUNSWICK.

6 Seaport city, ⊗ of St. John co., S New Brunswick, Canada, on Bay of Fundy at mouth of St. John river; pop. 50,779; has deep and capacious harbor, always ice-free; terminus for coastal and transatlantic shipping; its chief exports are agricultural products, lumber, and fish; manufactures machinery, tools, shoes, cotton goods. Founded 1783 on site of old Indian village and later French posts; mouth of the St. John river scene of several naval engagements bet. French and English from 1690 to 1758, when the post was captured by force of English and American colonists and named Fort Frederick. Fort Frederick destroyed by American privateers 1775; actual establishment of present community made in 1783 by group of 10,000 Loyalists; settlement first called **Parr'-town** (pär'toun) in honor of Nova Scotia's governor. Oldest incorporated town in Canada, charter dating from 1785; seat of provincial government 1784–86. Large part of city destroyed by conflagration in 1877.

7 River ab. 175 m. long, cen. Liberia; rises on NE boundary, flows SW to Atlantic Ocean near Grand Bassa.

Saint John, Cape. Cape on N coast of Newfoundland, NW point of entrance to Notre Dame Bay.

Saint John, Isle. See PRINCE EDWARD ISLAND.

Saint John, Lake; *Fr.* **Lac Saint-Jean** (làk' săn'-zhän'). Lake 350 sq. m., Lake St. John co., S Quebec prov., Canada; receives the Ashuapmuchuan, Mistassini, and Peribonka rivers on the N; its outlet is the Saguenay (*q.v.*) river to the E, leaving by two channels. Much frequented by sportsmen and fishermen.

Saint John, Mount. Peak 11,412 ft. in cen. Grand Teton National Park, NW Wyoming.

Saint John Island. **1** One of the Virgin Is. of the United States in the West Indies 4 m. E of St. Thomas; 19 sq. m.; pop. 925; highest point 1270 ft.; produces bay leaves for bay rum industry of St. Thomas. See VIRGIN ISLANDS.

2 Island off Kwangtung prov., SE China. See CHANG-CHUEN.

Saint John River. See SAINT JOHN.

Saint Johns (sânt jŏnz'). **1** Navigable river 276 m. long, E Florida; rises in Brevard co., E cen. Florida, flows N into Atlantic Ocean NE of Jacksonville.

2 County in Florida. See *Table* at FLORIDA.

3 City, ⊗ of Apache co., E Arizona; pop. 1310.

4 City, ⊗ of Clinton co., S cen. Michigan, 20 m. N of Lansing; pop. 5629; trade center in agricultural section.

5 Town on the island of Antigua, Leeward Is., West Indies Federation; administrative ✳ of the Leeward Islands and of Antigua territory in this group; pop. (1942 est.) 10,000.

6 *Fr.* **Saint-Jean** (săn'zhän'). County, Quebec, Canada. See *Table* at QUEBEC.

7 *Fr.* **Saint-Jean.** City, ⊗ of St. Johns co., S Quebec, Canada, on Richelieu river 21 m. SE of Montreal; pop. 19,305; active trading center in grain, produce, and lumber; has numerous factories; railroad junction point and head of Chambly Canal. Founded 1666; in its early history, important fortified position (Fort St. John) blocking Champlain valley approach; rebuilt 1749; a chief base of supplies for Burgoyne and Carleton in 1776–77. Picturesque community with its colonial houses and abandoned fortifications.

Saint John's (jŏnz'). City, ✳ of Newfoundland, on Atlantic Ocean on the SE coast; pop. (1951) 52,873; possesses splendid landlocked harbor accessible to the largest ships; port of call for transatlantic and coastwise steamers and terminus of railroad across the island; distribution, trade, and export center of province; maintains dry dock capable of taking the biggest vessels and is headquarters of fisheries and fishing fleets, which, with whale and sea-oil refineries, constitute its main industries; operates iron foundries, machine shops, woolen mills, tanneries, tobacco factories, and ropewalks; codfish, paper, pulp, fish and animal oils, and sealskins constitute its principal exports. Since discovery of Newfoundland by John Cabot in 1497 has probably been an inhabited site; became a British colony 1583, established by Sir Humphrey Gilbert; twice captured and destroyed

by the French and their Indian allies; last retaken by the British in 1762.

Saint Johns'bur'y (sånt jŏnz'bĕr'ĭ; -bĕr·ĭ). Village in St. Johnsbury town (pop. 8869), ⊗ of Caledonia co., NE Vermont, 30 m. ENE of Montpelier; pop. 6809; settled 1786; business, industrial, and shipping center of agricultural area; maple sugar industry; manufactures scales, granite memorials, lumber products.

Saint John's Point (jŏnz'). Cape on NE coast of Ireland, S of Strangford Lough and at N side of entrance to Dundrum Bay; lighthouse.

Saint Johns'ville (jŏnz'vĭl). Village, Montgomery co., E New York, on Mohawk river 30 m. E of Utica; pop. 2196; farm shipping and trading center; manufactures felt shoes, underwear, dresses, gloves.

Saint John the Bap'tist (sånt jŏn', băp'tĭst). Parish in Louisiana. See *Table* at LOUISIANA.

Saint Jo'seph (jō'zĕf; -zĭf). **1** River 210 m. long, S Michigan and NW Indiana; rises in Hillsdale co., S Michigan, flows W along S Michigan, curves S and W in NW Indiana, then NW into Lake Michigan at St. Joseph, W Berrien co., SW Michigan; navigable for a short distance. **2** River ab. 110 m. long, NW Ohio and NE Indiana; rises in S Michigan, flows SW across NW corner of Ohio and unites with St. Marys river at Fort Wayne in Allen co., NE Indiana, to form the Maumee river. **3** Name of counties in two states of the U.S. See *Tables* at INDIANA and MICHIGAN. **4** Town, ⊗ of Tensas parish, NE Louisiana; pop. 1653. **5** City, ⊗ of Berrien co., SW corner of Michigan, on Lake Michigan at mouth of St. Joseph river 49 m. WSW of Kalamazoo; pop. 11,755; distributing point for fruit-growing section; market for nearby health resorts; lumber and paper mills, machine shops, rubber-goods factories. **6** Village, Stearns co., cen. Minnesota, 7 m. W of St. Cloud; pop. 1487. College of Saint Benedict (1913; women). **7** City, ⊗ of Buchanan co., NW Missouri, on Missouri river 46 m. NNW of Kansas City; pop. 79,673; railroad, industrial, and distributing center; stockyards, packing plants, flour mills, grain elevators, paper factories; has large livestock market.

Saint Jo'seph (sånt jō'zĕf; -zĭf; *Fr.* săN' zhō'zĕf'). **1** Village, Beauce co., S Quebec, Canada, on Chaudière river 40 m. SSE of Quebec; pop. 2417; agricultural community; one of oldest parishes in the county, established 1736. **2** Village, New Brunswick, Canada, ab. 15 m. SE of Moncton; Saint Joseph's Univ. (1864; men). **3** Village, Richelieu co., S Quebec, Canada, on S bank of St. Lawrence river adjoining Sorel; pop. 3349.

Saint Jo'seph, Lake (sånt jō'zĕf; -zĭf). Lake 245 sq. m. in SW Ontario prov., Canada; a source of the Albany river flowing into James Bay.

Saint Joseph Bay. Inlet of Gulf of Mexico on SW coast of Gulf co., NW Florida.

Saint Jo'seph' d'Al'ma' (săN' zhō'zĕf' dàl'mà'). Town, ⊗ of East Lake St. John co., S Quebec, Canada, on S bank of Saguenay river 5 m. E of Lake St. John; pop. 7975; formerly an agricultural center; now important industrially with sawmills, pulp and paper mills, and other factories, and nearby (**Isle Ma'ligne'** [ēl' mà'lēn'y']) a great hydroelectric station on the Saguenay.

Saint Jo'seph de Grant'ham (sånt jō'zĕf [-zĭf] dě grăn'tăm; -thăm). Town, Drummond co., S Quebec, Canada; pop. 6576.

Saint Joseph Island. 1 Island, Aransas co., S Texas, bet. Aransas Bay and Gulf of Mexico. **2** Island ab. 19 m. long at N end of Lake Huron, just E of Chippewa co., Michigan; belongs to Ontario, Canada.

Saint Joseph Point. Point at N end of narrow peninsula extending from SW coast of Gulf co., NW Florida, into Gulf of Mexico.

Saint Joseph River. See SAINT JOSEPH.

Saint–Josse–ten–Noode (săN'zhôs'tăN·nōd'); *Flemish* **Sint–Joost–ten–Noo'de** (sĭnt·yōst'tĕ·nō'dĕ). Commune, Brabant prov., cen. Belgium, a suburb of Brussels; pop. 30,917.

Saint–Ju'lien' (săN'zhü'lyăN'). Commune, Gironde dept., SW France, on the Gironde estuary near Pauillac; pop. (1931) 1217; produces notable red wine.

Saint–Ju'nien' (săN'zhü'nyăN'). Industrial commune, Haute-Vienne dept., W cen. France, 18 m. WNW of Limoges; pop. 10,375; hydroelectric power plant; produces paper, gloves, leather, woolens, machinery.

Saint Just *or* **Saint Just in Pen·with'** (sånt jŭst', pĕn·wĭth'). Urban district, Cornwall, SW England, ab. 4 m. N of Land's End; pop. (1951) 4122; tin mines nearby; amphitheater where miracle plays were produced in medieval times.

Saint Kil'da (sånt kĭl'dà). **1** City, S Victoria, SE Australia, SE suburb of Melbourne on Port Phillip Bay; pop. 46,582; residential community and watering place. **2** Borough, Otago provincial dist., SE South I., New Zealand, S suburb of Dunedin on Pacific coast; pop. 8160. **3** An island of Scotland, westernmost of the Outer Hebrides, in the Atlantic Ocean W of the Sound of Harris, at 8°36′W.

Saint Kitts (kĭts') *or* **Saint Chris'to·pher** (krĭs'tŏ·fēr). Island of E West Indies, a part of Saint Kitts-Nevis state, Leeward Is., British West Indies; 68 sq. m.; pop. 29,818; ✻ Basseterre. Has long narrow point of land extending to SE, its tip separated by strait 2 m. wide from island of Nevis. Mountainous, of volcanic origin; fertile and well watered; highest point at NW end 4314 ft.; Mt. Misery 3771 ft. in center; has good macadamized road around the island. Besides Basseterre only other town is Old Road. Discovered by Columbus 1493; settled by British 1625, the first of the Leeward Is. to be colonized by British; sent colonies to Antigua and Montserrat 1632; held jointly by French and English 1628 to 1713, but returned to Great Britain by Treaty of Utrecht 1713; held by French 1782–83.

Saint Kitts–Ne'vis (kĭts'nē'vĭs; nĕv'ĭs). Former territory of the Leeward Is., West Indies Federation; comprises islands of St. Kitts, Nevis, Anguilla, and Sombrero; 152 sq. m.; pop. (1958) 58,579; ✻ Basseterre; became an associated state of British Commonwealth 1967.

Saint Lam'bert (sånt lăm'bĕrt; *Fr.* săN' läN'bâr'). Residential city, Chambly co., S Quebec, Canada, on St. Lawrence river across from Montreal; pop. 8615; connected with it by Victoria Bridge; center for pleasure boats; part of Greater Montreal.

Saint Lan'dry (sånt lăn'drĭ). Parish in Louisiana. See *Table* at LOUISIANA.

Saint Lau'rent' (săN' lô'räN'). **1** Town, Montreal I., S Quebec, Canada, 6 m. W of Montreal; pop. 20,426; parts have recently been annexed to Montreal city; manufactures chemicals and foundry products. **2** *or* **Saint Laurent du Ma'ro'ni'** (dü mà'rô'nē'). Seaport, N French Guiana, on the Maroni near its mouth; pop. 1877.

Saint–Lau'rent'–sur–Mer (săN'lô'räN'sür·mâr'). Commune, Calvados dept., NW France, on the coast of the Bay of the Seine 8 m. NW of Bayeux; pop. 215; small resort with fine beach. In invasion of Normandy in World War II an American beachhead June 6, 1944; great artificial harbor destroyed off this beach by gale June 19–22, 1944.

Saint Law'rence (sånt lô'rĕns; lŏr'ĕns). **1** County in New York. See *Table* at NEW YORK. **2** Navigable river ab. 760 m. long, S Quebec and SE Ontario provs., Canada; flows NE out of Lake Ontario into the Gulf of St. Lawrence; including the waterway provided by the Great Lakes, ab. 2100 m. long. Leaving Lake Ontario the St. Lawrence proper passes through the Thousand Is. (*q.v.*) and for ab. 120 m. forms the bound-

ary bet. New York state and Ontario; on entering Quebec prov. it widens into Lake St. Francis, then passes through Lake St. Louis and the Lachine Rapids past Montreal I.; at Sorel passes through another expansion, Lake St. Peter, and below Quebec around Orleans I. into a wide stream fully 90 m. wide at its mouth in the Gulf of St. Lawrence. Navigable for ocean-going vessels to Montreal and for smaller craft (via Lachine Canal) to Kingston; a source of water power. Its chief tributaries are the Ottawa, St. Maurice, and Saguenay on the N, and the Richelieu, Yamaska, St. Francis, and Chaudière on the S. Chief cities on it are Ogdensburg (New York), Kingston and Cornwall (Ontario), and Montreal, Sorel, Three Rivers, and Quebec (Quebec). The headstream of the greater St. Lawrence is the St. Louis river in Minnesota, U.S.; thence the waterway passes through Lake Superior, the St. Marys river (by the Sault Sainte Marie Canals, *q.v.*), Lake Huron, St. Clair river, Lake St. Clair, Detroit river, Lake Erie, Niagara river (by the Welland Ship Canal, *q.v.*), and Lake Ontario into the St. Lawrence proper. See SAINT LAWRENCE SEAWAY.

Saint Lawrence, Cape. Point, N coast of Cape Breton I., Gulf of St. Lawrence, W of Cape North.

Saint Lawrence, Gulf of. Deep gulf of the Atlantic Ocean off E coast of Canada, bet. Newfoundland and the Canadian mainland (Quebec, New Brunswick, and Nova Scotia provs.); receives the St. Lawrence river in the NW; connected with the Atlantic Ocean through the Strait of Belle Isle on the NE (N of Newfoundland), Cabot Strait on the E (bet. Newfoundland and Cape Breton I.), and Strait of Canso on SE (bet. Nova Scotia mainland and Cape Breton I.). Has many islands, Anticosti, Prince Edward I. (province), Magdalen Is., and islands along the shores.

Saint Lawrence Island. Island, W Alaska, in the Bering Sea 150 m. S of Bering Strait and 118 m. from nearest Alaskan mainland; 95 m. long by ab. 10 to 35 m. wide; highest point ab. 2000 ft. Chief settlements Gambell at NW point and Savoonga on N cen. coast; inhabited by Eskimos; discovered 1728. Extensive archaeological excavations conducted here by the University of Alaska, tracing development of Eskimo culture for 2000 years.

Saint Lawrence Islands National Park. See CANADA, *National Parks.*

Saint Lawrence Seaway. Waterway, Canada and U. S., along upper St. Lawrence river bet. Montreal and Lake Ontario, in Ontario, Quebec, and New York; affords deep-draft navigation bet. Atlantic Ocean and Great Lakes; includes a system of canals, locks, and dams; hydroelectric project; constructed 1955–59.

Saint Laz′a·rus, Islands of (sånt lăz′ȧ·rŭs). Magellan's name for Philippine Islands.

Saint–Lé′o′nard′–de–No′blat′ (săɴ′lā′ȯ′nàr′dē·nȯ′blȧ′). Town, Haute-Vienne dept., W cen. France, ab. 12 m. E of Limoges; pop. 3230; 11th–12th cent. church.

Saint Leon′ards (sånt lĕn′ẽrdz). Town, Sussex, S England, W suburb of Hastings; resort.

Saint Li′boire′ (săɴ′ lē′bwär′). Village, ⊗ of Bagot co., S Quebec, Canada, 12 m. E of St. Hyacinthe; pop. 534.

Saint–Lô (sånt·lō′; *Fr.* săɴ′lō′); *anc.* **Bri′o·ve′ra** (brī′ȯ·vẽr′ȧ), *later* **Lau′dus** (lô′dŭs). Commune, ✳ of Manche dept., NW France, 34 m. W of Caen; pop. 11,814; manufactures textiles (cotton, duck) and clothing; horse breeding. Fortified by Charlemagne; pillaged by Normans 889, Geoffrey Plantagenet 1141, Edward III of England 1346, and Protestants 1567 and 1574. In battle of Normandy in World War II an important German defense base; attacked by Allies July 7, 1944; its capture July 18 after severe fighting resulted in unhinging entire W end of German line and was followed by Allied break-through.

Saint–Lou·is′ (săɴ′lwē′). **1** Commune, Haut-Rhin dept., NE France, on the Swiss frontier; pop. 6375.
2 City, Senegal, West Africa; on **Saint–Louis Island**

at mouth of the Senegal river; pop. (1942) 40,338; founded 1658; capital of Senegal until 1958 and of French West Africa 1895–1902.
3 Town on the SW coast of the island of Réunion in the Indian Ocean; pop. (1936) 19,195.

Saint Lou′is (sånt loo′ĭs). **1** River ab. 220 m. long, NE Minnesota; rises near E border of St. Louis co., NE Minnesota, flows SW, then turns SE to empty into Lake Superior at Duluth; sometimes considered the ultimate source of the St. Lawrence river.
2 Name of counties in two states of the U.S. See *Tables* at MINNESOTA and MISSOURI.
3 City, Gratiot co., cen. Michigan, 17 m. SSE of Mt. Pleasant; pop. 3808; near petroleum and natural gas fields; mineral springs.
4 City, Missouri, on Mississippi river ab. 10 m. below its confluence with the Missouri (see *Map* at MISSOURI); independent of Saint Louis co.; pop. 750,026; largest city in the state and 10th largest city in U.S.; world's largest raw-fur market; manufactures stoves, sugar-mill machinery, woodenware, terra cotta and brick, shoes. Saint Louis University (1818; Roman Catholic); Washington University (1853; coed.). Founded 1764 by Pierre Laclède; ceded by France to U.S. 1803; chartered as city 1822; Unionist in sympathy during Civil War; scene of Louisiana Purchase Exposition 1904.

Saint Lou′is, Lake (sånt loo′ĭs; *Fr.* săɴ′ lwē′). Lake in S Quebec prov., Canada, SW of Montreal and below Ile Perrot, formed by a widening of St. Lawrence river.

Saint Lou′is Park (sånt loo′ĭs). City, Hennepin co., SE cen. Minnesota, 6 m. WSW of Minneapolis; pop. 43,310; suburb of Minneapolis.

Saint Louis River. See SAINT LOUIS.

Saint Lu′cia (sånt lū′shȧ; lū·sē′ȧ). Largest of the Windward Is. in E West Indies, S of Martinique and N of St. Vincent; 233 sq. m.; pop. 92,089; ✳ Castries; a territory of West Indies Federation. High mountainous volcanic mass, Canaries Mountain 3145 ft., near the S and the Pitons (2619 ft. and 2461 ft.) on SW coast; has rich soil, exports sugar, cocoa, logwood, spices, and coconuts. Probably discovered by Columbus 1502; first settlement by English 1605; contended for by French and English in 17th cent., regarded by both as neutral in 1748 but changed hands many times in wars of late 19th cent. and in Napoleonic Wars; finally became British 1814; in World War II naval base on Gros Islet Bay, N of Castries, leased by Great Britain to U.S. Sept. 3, 1940.

Saint Lucia, Cape. Cape extending into Indian Ocean on E cen. coast of Natal, South Africa.

Saint Lucia Bay. 1 Inlet of Celebes Sea, on extreme NE coast of Indonesian part of island of Borneo, Malay Archipelago; N of Tarakan I.
2 *also* **Lake Saint Lucia.** Inlet of Indian Ocean, on E coast of Natal, South Africa, N of Cape Saint Lucia.

Saint Lucia Channel. Channel bet. the islands of Martinique and Saint Lucia in the West Indies.

Saint Lu′cie (lū′sĭ). County in Florida. See *Table* at FLORIDA.

Saint Lucie Canal. Canal linking the Atlantic coast at Stuart, Florida, with Lake Okeechobee; part of the Cross-Florida Waterway (*q.v.*).

Saint Lucie Inlet. Narrow strait leading from Atlantic Ocean through barrier reef off NE coast of Martin co., SE Florida; E terminus of St. Lucie Canal.

Saint–Maix′ent′–l′É′cole′ (săɴ′mĕk′săɴ′lā′kôl′). Town, Deux-Sèvres dept., W France, 15 m. NE of Niort by rail; pop. 4095; abbey church, built 12th–15th cent., destroyed by Protestants 1568, rebuilt 17th cent.

Saint–Ma′lo (săɴ′mȧ′lō′). Fortified commercial seaport, Ille-et-Vilaine dept., NW France, on rocky island in Atlantic Ocean at mouth of Rance river 40 m. NNW of Rennes; pop. 13,836; manufactures hosiery, sailcloth, nets, cordage; shipbuilding; trades in agricultural products, wine; bathing resort; school of hydrography; 15th-cent. Gothic-Renaissance cathedral, ancient castle, town

hall, customhouse. Site of a monastery in 6th cent.; became episcopal see in 12th cent.; headquarters of many privateers 17th and 18th cents.; episcopal see suppressed 1790. Birthplace of Jacques Cartier. In World War II surrendered to Allies Aug. 17, 1944.

Saint–Malo, Gulf of. Inlet of English Channel, NW coast of France, bet. peninsulas of Normandy and Brittany.

Saint–Man'dé' (săN'mäN'dā'). Commune, Seine dept., N France, ESE suburb of Paris near the Bois de Vincennes; pop. 22,253; manufactures furniture, chemical products.

Saint Marc (sănt märk'; *Fr.* săN' märk'). **1** See SAINT MARC DES CARRIÈRES, Canada.

2 Town, W Haiti, 44 m. NW of Port-au-Prince; pop. ab. 3000.

Saint Marc des Car'rières' (săN' märk' dā kȧ'ryâr'), *often* **Saint Marc** (*Eng.* sănt märk'; *Fr.* săN' märk'). Village, Portneuf co., S Quebec, Canada, 40 m. W of Quebec; pop. 2351.

Saint Mar'ga·ret Bay (sănt mär'gȧ·rĕt; -rĭt; mär'grĕt; -grĭt). Inlet of Atlantic Ocean, in S Nova Scotia, Canada, SW of Halifax.

Saint Mar'ies (mâr'ĭz). City, ⊗ of Benewah co., NW Idaho, 30 m. SSE of Coeur d'Alene; pop. 2220; lumbering.

Saint Mark (sănt märk'). The island of San Marco, E part of Venice; used in name of Republic of Saint Mark formed by Manin 1848–49. See *History* at VENICE.

Saint Mar'tin (sănt mär'tĭn; -t'n). Parish in Louisiana. See *Table* at LOUISIANA.

Saint Mar'tin (sănt mär'tĭn; -t'n; *Fr.* săN' mȧr'tăN'); *Du.* **Sint Maar'ten** (sĭnt mȧr'tĕ[n]). Island of E West Indies in Leeward Is. group E of Brit. Virgin Is. and ab. 43 m. NNW of St. Kitts; 38 sq. m.; pop. ab. 8000; N section is a dependency of the French department of Guadeloupe and has area 20 sq. m. and population (1938 est.) 6450, with ✳ Marigot (1938 est. pop. 2420); S section is administratively a part of Curaçao, Neth. West Indies, and has area 17 sq. m. and population (1942) 1928, with ✳ Philipsburg. Produces salt and exports cotton and livestock. Occupied by French and Spanish bet. 1640 and 1648; divided 1648 bet. French and Dutch.

Saint Mar'tin, Lake (sănt mär'tĭn; -t'n). Lake 125 sq. m. in S cen. Manitoba, Canada, E of N Lake Manitoba; Dauphin river, connecting Lakes Manitoba and Winnipeg, passes through it.

Saint–Mar'tin'–Bou'logne' (săN'mȧr'tăN'bōō'lôn'y'). Commune, Pas-de-Calais dept., N France, suburb of Boulogne; pop. (1931) 7530.

Saint Mar'tin·ville (sănt mär'tĭn·vĭl; mär't'n-; *Sou. also* -v'l). Town, ⊗ of St. Martin parish, S Louisiana, 13 m. ESE of Lafayette; pop. 6468; place to which a number of Acadians were sent from Nova Scotia 1755 and later; the Evangeline Oak marks the reputed landing place of the Acadians, and the meeting place of Emmeline Labiche and Louis Arcenaux—the Evangeline and Gabriel of Longfellow's poem *Evangeline.*

Saint Mar'y (mâr'ĭ). **1** Parish in Louisiana. See *Table* at LOUISIANA.

2 River ab. 75 m. long, SW Alberta, Canada, and NW Montana, U.S.A.; rises in two lakes (**Upper Saint Mary,** in Glacier National Park, and **Lower Saint Mary**) and flows NNE to the Oldman near Lethbridge.

Saint Mary, Cape. Point of land projecting W along W coast of Nova Scotia, SE Canada, on S side of entrance to **Saint Mary Bay,** a narrow inlet of the Atlantic ab. 40 m. long, in Digby co.

Saint Mary, Island of; *or* **Saint Mary's Island.** Island in the Gambia river near its mouth, Gambia crown colony, W Africa; site of the town of Bathurst, ✳ of Gambia; forms principal part of colony, from which the protectorate is administered.

Saint Marylebone. Metropolitan borough of London. See *Table* at LONDON.

Saint Mary Peak. Highest peak 3900 ft. in Flinders Range, E South Australia, NNE of Port Augusta.

Saint Mar'ys (mâr'ĭz). **1** River 175 m. long, SE Georgia and NE Florida; rises in Okefenokee Swamp, SE Georgia, forms a section of E Georgia-Florida boundary, and empties into Cumberland Sound N of Amelia I. and NNE of Jacksonville.

2 River ab. 63 m. long, E Michigan penin.; forms boundary bet. U.S. and Canada; flows from Whitefish Bay on Lake Superior, descending ab. 20 ft. in a mile at **Saint Marys Falls** where canals have been built (see SAULT SAINTE MARIE CANALS), then flows around Sugar I. and Neebish I., W of Saint Joseph I. (Canada) and through Detour Passage into N end of Lake Huron.

3 River ab. 110 m. long, NW Ohio and NE Indiana; rises in SW Auglaize co., NW Ohio, flows N and NW to unite with St. Joseph river at Fort Wayne, Allen co., NE Indiana, and form the Maumee river.

4 County in Maryland. See *Table* at MARYLAND.

5 City, Pottawatomie co., NE Kansas, on Kansas river 24 m. WNW of Topeka; pop. 1509; one of the oldest towns in Kansas, site of a Roman Catholic mission to the Potawatomi Indians 1847–48.

6 See SAINT MARYS CITY, Maryland.

7 City, Auglaize co., W Ohio, on Lake St. Marys 20 m. SW of Lima; pop. 7737; settled 1795; manufactures woolens, furniture, paper, foundry products.

8 Industrial borough, Elk co., NW cen. Pennsylvania, 24 m. NNE of Du Bois; pop. 8065; manufactures carbon and clay products, electrical supplies, beer, lumber, leather.

9 City, ⊗ of Pleasants co., NW West Virginia, on Ohio river; pop. 2443; gas and oil wells, oil refinery; glass.

10 Town, Perth co., SE Ontario, Canada, on Thames river 10 m. SW of Stratford; pop. 3995; produces cement, flour, dairy supplies, lumber, textiles.

Saint Marys, Lake; *also* **Grand Lake** *or* **Reservoir.** Lake 9 m. long and 3 m. wide in Auglaize and Mercer cos., W Ohio, formed by damming Wabash river.

Saint Mar'y's Bay (mâr'ĭz). Inlet of Atlantic Ocean, SE Newfoundland, ab. 40 m. long.

Saint Marys City, *formerly* **Saint Marys.** Village, Saint Marys co., S Maryland; first settlement in Maryland made here Mar. 1634 by Leonard Calvert, arriving in the ships *Ark* and *Dove;* site purchased from the Indians; prospered as capital of Maryland until 1694; later declined rapidly until few traces of town remained; revived 1934 at Tercentenary Celebration and site now maintained by state of Maryland.

Saint Mary's Island. See Island of SAINT MARY.

Saint Mar'y's Loch (mâr'ĭz lŏĸ'). Lake 3 m. long in Selkirk co., SE Scotland.

Saint Marys River. Name of three rivers in the U.S.: see SAINT MARYS above.

Saint–Ma'thieu', Pointe de (pwăNt' dē săN'mȧ'tyû'). Cape on the NW coast of France, near Brest.

Saint Mat'thew Island (sănt măth'ū). **1** Island, cen. Bering Sea, Alaska; 60°20′N, 172°30′W, ab. 135 m. W of Nunivak I.; includes Hall islet off NW; uninhabited.

2 Island in Mergui Archipelago (*q.v.*), Burma.

Saint Mat'thews (măth'ūz). **1** City, Jefferson co., N cen. Kentucky, E suburb of Louisville; pop. 8738.

2 Town, ⊗ of Calhoun co., cen. South Carolina, 13 m. NNE of Orangeburg; pop. 2433; produces cotton, pecans, cattle, hogs, pine timber.

Saint Mat·thi'as Group (sănt mǎ·thī'ǎs). Group of small islands in N Bismarck Archipelago, W Pacific Ocean, NNW of island of New Hanover; largest is Mussau; Emirau I. in S part of group occupied by U.S. Marines Mar. 19, 1944.

Saint–Maur–des–Fos'sés' (săN'môr'dā·fô'sā'). Industrial commune, Seine dept., N France, SE suburb of Paris on Marne river; pop. 56,740; treaty signed here 1465.

Saint'–Mau'rice' (săN'mô'rēs'); *formerly* **Pe·tit'–Cha'ren'ton'** (pē·tē'shä'räN'tôN'). Commune, Seine

dept., N France, SE suburb of Paris; pop. 11,324; Protestant stronghold 1606–85.

Saint Mau′rice (sȧnt mô′rĭs; môr′ĭs; *Fr.* săN′ mô′rēs′). **1** River 325 m. long, S Quebec prov., Canada; flows S from Gouin Reservoir into the St. Lawrence river at Three Rivers; chief tributary the Mattawin from the W. See SHAWINIGAN FALLS.

2 County, Quebec, Canada. See *Table* at QUEBEC.

Saint–Maur–sur–Loire (săN′môr′sür′lwȧr′). Hamlet, Maine-et-Loire dept., W France, on Loire river near Saumur; site of Benedictine monastery founded by St. Maurus in 6th cent.

Saint Mi′chael (sȧnt mī′kĕl; -k′l). **1** Village, W Alaska, on S coast of Norton Sound and SW of Unalakleet; pop. (est.) 211.

2 Island of the Azores. See SÃO MIGUEL.

Saint Mi′chaels (mī′kĕlz; -k′lz). Town, Talbot co., Maryland, on E shore of Chesapeake Bay W of Easton; pop. 1484.

Saint Michaels Bay. Bay, E coast of Labrador, 52°44′N.

Saint Mi′chael′s Mount (mī′kĕlz; -k′lz). Lofty rock in Mounts Bay, Cornwall, SW England; seat of an ancient castle.

Saint Mi′chel′ de La′val′ (săN′ mē′shĕl′ dē là′vàl′). Town, Montreal I., S Quebec, Canada, N of Montreal city; pop. 10,539.

Saint–Mi′hiel′ (săN′mē′yĕl′). Commune, Meuse dept., NE France; pop. 4366; battle Sept. 12–14, 1918, one of the great battles at the close of World War I; Germans driven from salient held since 1914 in first great American offensive under Gen. Pershing.

Saint–Mo·ritz′ (sȧnt·mô·rĭts′; *Fr.* săN′mô′rēts′); *Ger.* **Sankt Mo·ritz′** (zängkt mô·rĭts′; *often in Switzerland,* säm′mô·rĭts′; *by non-Swiss German speakers, often* zängkt mō′rĭts); *Romansh* **San Mu·rez′zan** (sän′ mōo-rĕt′sän). Commune, Graubünden canton, E Switzerland, on Inn river in upper Engadine 28 m. SSE of Chur; pop. (1930) 3968; bathing, health, and winter resort.

Saint–Na′zaire′ (săN′nȧ′zâr′). Seaport and manufacturing commune, Loire-Atlantique dept., NW France, at mouth of Loire river 33 m. WNW of Nantes; pop. 43,281; iron and steel manufactories; shipbuilding yards; ancient granite dolmen nearby. Thought to occupy site of ancient **Car′bi·lo** (kär′bĭ·lō) where a Roman fleet was built 56 B.C.; port of debarkation and supply base for American Expeditionary Force 1917–18; in World War II German U-boat base after 1940; surrounded by Allies Aug. 1944; surrendered May 1945.

Saint–Nec′taire′ (săN′nĕk′târ′). Village, Puy-de-Dôme dept., S cen. France; pop. ab. 1000; mineral springs; beautiful Romanesque church.

Saint Neots (sȧnt nēts′). Urban district, Huntingdonshire, England, ab. 50 m. N of London; pop. (1951) 4697; 15th-cent. church and stone bridge.

Saint Nich′o·las (nĭk′ô·lăs). See SÃO NICOLÃO.

Saint Nicholas, Mount. Peak 9380 ft. in Glacier National Park, NW Montana.

Saint Nicholas Point; *Du.* **Sint Ni′co·laas Punt** (sĭnt nē′kō·làs pŭnt). Cape at NW end of the island of Java, Indonesia, on Sunda Strait where the strait opens into Java Sea. Naval battle off this point Feb. 28, 1942 in which U.S.S. *Houston* and other Allied vessels were destroyed by Japanese.

Saint–Ni′co·las′ (săN′nē′kô′lä′). **1** = SINT-NIKLAAS.

2 Commune, Liège prov., E Belgium, W suburb of Liège; pop. 8818.

3 *or* **Saint Nicolas du Port** (dü pôr′). Commune, Meurthe-et-Moselle dept., NE France, ab. 8 m. SE of Nancy; pop. (1931) 5554; Gothic church of 15th–16th cents.; noted for its fairs in 16th and 17th cents.

Saint–O′mer′ (săN′-tô′mâr′). Fortified commune, Pas-de-Calais dept., N France, 40 m. NW of Arras; pop. 18,373; 13th-cent. Gothic cathedral; old episcopal palace (now courthouse), town hall, arsenal; manufactures

hosiery, textiles, tobacco, pipes; trades in flour, sugar, paper, liquors. General headquarters for British army in France for a time in World War I.

Sain′tonge′ (săN′tônzh′). Ancient province of France, on the Bay of Biscay N of the Gironde; comprised most of present department of Charente-Maritime and small part of Charente; ✳ Saintes; country of the Santones; ceded to England 1360, retaken by DuGuesclin 1371; passed to crown 1375.

Saint–Ou·en′ (săN′-twăN′). Manufacturing and commercial commune, Seine dept., N France, N suburb of Paris on Seine river; pop. 51,106; manufactures metal goods, railroad equipment, tools, chemicals, pharmaceutical products, soap, industrial oils, rubber products.

Saint Pancras. Metropolitan borough of London. See *Table* at LONDON.

Saint Pas′cal′ (săN′ pàs′kàl′). Village, ⊗ of Kamouraska co., S Quebec, Canada, 85 m. ENE of Quebec; pop. 1736; near right bank of St. Lawrence river and on highway to Gaspé Penin.

Saint–Paul (sȧnt·pôl′; *Fr.* săN′pôl′). Town on NW coast of Réunion I., S of Port-des-Galets; pop. (1936) 21,485.

Saint Paul (sȧnt pôl′). **1** City, ✳ of Minnesota and ⊗ of Ramsey co., E Minnesota, on Mississippi river 10 m. E of Minneapolis (see *Map* at MINNESOTA); pop. 313,411; 2d largest city in Minnesota; twin city with Minneapolis; railroad, commercial, and distributing center; trading center for livestock; manufactures machinery, meat products, paints and varnishes. Hamline University (1854; coed.; Methodist); Macalester College (1885; coed.; Presbyterian); College of St. Catherine (1911; women; Roman Catholic); College of St. Thomas (1885; men; Roman Catholic). Made capital of Minnesota Territory 1849; chartered as city 1854; became capital of the state 1858.

2 City, ⊗ of Howard co., E cen. Nebraska, 21 m. N of Grand Island; pop. 1714; trading and shipping center in agricultural section.

3 River ab. 280 m. long in Liberia, W Africa, flowing into the Atlantic Ocean near Monrovia.

4 (*Fr.* săN′ pôl′) Uninhabited French island 3 sq. m. in S Indian Ocean, 38°43′S, 77°32′E, just S of Amsterdam I.; a dependency of Madagascar.

Saint Paul, Cape (sȧnt pôl′). Cape extending into the Bight of Benin on SE coast of Ghana, W Africa, E of the mouth of the Volta river.

Saint Paul de Lo·an′da (sȧnt pôl′ dĕ lô·ȧn′dȧ). = *São Paulo de Loanda:* see LUANDA.

Saint Paul Island (sȧnt pôl′). **1** Island most northerly of Pribilof Is. (*q.v.*) in Bering Sea, Alaska; 35 sq. m.; 13 m. long by ab. 6 m. wide; pop. 299.

2 Island in Cabot Strait, ab. 14 m. off Cape North, N Cape Breton I., at entrance to Gulf of St. Lawrence, E Canada; lighthouse.

Saint Pauls (sȧnt pôlz′). Town, Robeson co., S North Carolina, 19 m. S of Fayetteville; pop. 2249; cotton mills.

Saint Paul′s Bay (sȧnt pôlz′). = BAIE SAINT PAUL.

Saint Paul′s Rocks; *Port.* **Ro·che′dos São Pau′lo** (rō̄-shâ′t͟hōos soun pou′lōo). Group of volcanic rocks in the Atlantic Ocean, 1°N, 29°15′W, ab. 600 m. NE of Natal, Brazil.

Saint Pe′ter (sȧnt pē′tẽr). City, ⊗ of Nicollet co., S Minnesota, on Minnesota river 12 m. N of Mankato; pop. 8484; shipping point for livestock; woolen mill, creameries. Gustavus Adolphus College (1862; coed.; Lutheran).

Saint Peter, Lake. Lake ab. 130 sq. m. in S Quebec prov., Canada, 60 m. NE of the city of Montreal; formed by a widening of St. Lawrence river.

Saint Peter Port. Town and civil parish, Guernsey, Channel Is.; pop. 16,720; ✳ of Guernsey bailiwick; house of Victor Hugo is preserved as he left it (his residence 1855–70).

Saint Pe'ters (sănt pē'tẽrz). **1** Town, E New South Wales, SE Australia, S suburb of Sydney; pop. 12,552.
2 Town, SE South Australia, NE suburb of Adelaide; pop. 11,601.

Saint Peter's (pē'tẽrz). See BROADSTAIRS AND SAINT PETER'S.

Saint Pe'ters·burg (sănt pē'tẽrz·bûrg). **1** Resort city, Pinellas co., W cen. Florida penin., on W shore of Tampa Bay; pop. 181,298; ships fish, fruit, and vegetables; attracts many tourists in the winter season.
2 Capital of Russia 1712–1914. See LENINGRAD.

Saint Phil'ip and Saint James Bay (fĭl'ĭp, jāmz'). Large inlet on N coast of Espíritu Santo I., New Hebrides Is., SW Pacific, bet. two peninsulas.

Saint-Pierre (săN'pyâr'; *Angl.* sănt-pẽr'). Town on SW coast of the island of Réunion, Indian Ocean; pop. (1936) 17,924.

Saint Pierre (sănt pẽr'). **1** (*Fr.* săN' pyâr') Town, Montreal I., S Quebec, Canada, on N bank of Lachine Canal bet. Montreal and Lachine; pop. 4976; manufactures railroad cars and glass.
2 *Fr.* **Saint-Pierre** (săN'pyâr'). Town, Martinique I., French West Indies; had pop. of 26,000 before its destruction by volcanic eruption of Mount Pelée 1902.
3 *Fr.* **Saint-Pierre** (săN'pyâr'). Small island off S coast of Newfoundland, in Atlantic Ocean; part of French territory of Saint Pierre and Miquelon; 10 sq. m.; pop. (1936) 4195; chief town Saint Pierre. High and rocky and of very irregular shape.
4 *Fr.* **Saint-Pierre** (săN'pyâr'). Town on Saint Pierre I. off Newfoundland; pop. (1936) 3396; seat of government of territory of Saint Pierre and Miquelon; its fine harbor is port for fishing fleet.
5 Small island in the Indian Ocean 240 m. NNE of Madagascar; belongs to British colony of Seychelles.
6 (*Fr.* săN' pyâr') Island in Lake of Biel, W Switzerland; home of Rousseau 1765.

Saint Pierre and Miq'ue·lon (sănt pẽr', mĭk'ẽ·lŏn); *Fr.* **Saint-Pierre et Mi'que·lon'** (săN'pyâr' ā mē'klôN'). French territory consisting of two small islands, Saint Pierre and Miquelon, in the Atlantic Ocean just S of Newfoundland; 93 sq. m.; pop. (1936) 4715; ✻ Saint Pierre. Chief occupation cod fishing, which for years made the colony prosperous, but which has recently declined considerably. Visited by French fishermen 16th and 17th cents., esp. Bretons and Basques; settlement increased by French expelled from Newfoundland 1713 and from Acadia 1763. For the next 100 years and more fishing rights of French on the islands and on the French Shore (*q.v.*) a source of serious trouble; differences finally settled 1904. Classified as a territory 1946 by French Constitution of Fourth Republic.

Saint-Pierre-de-Chartreuse. See La Grande CHARTREUSE.

Saint-Pierre-Quil'bi'gnon' (săN'pyâr'kēl'bē'nyôN'). Commune, Finistère dept., NW France, WSW suburb of Brest; pop. (1931) 11,947; beach resort; manufactures flour, furniture.

Saint-Pierre-Saint-Paul (săN'pyâr'săN'pôl'). Commune, Alger dept., N Algeria; pop. 10,366.

Saint-Pol-de-Lé'on' (săN'pôl'dē·lä'ôN'). Town, Finistère dept., NW France, ab. 30 m. NE of Brest and ab. 1 m. from the coast; pop. 3689; 13th–14th cent. cathedral.

Saint-Pol-sur-Mer (săN'pôl'sür·mâr'). Commune, Nord dept., N France, WSW suburb of Dunkerque; pop. (1931) 12,422; beach resort.

Saint-Por'chaire' (săN'pôr'shâr'). Town, Deux-Sèvres dept., W France, near Bressuire 38 m. N of Niort; pop. 523; site of manufacture in 16th cent. of *Saint-Porchaire faïence*, also called *faïence d'Oiron* because once thought to have been made in Oiron.

Saint-Priest (săN'prēst'). Commune, NW Isère dept., SE France; pop. (1931) 5957; castle of the ancient countship.

Saint-Pri'vat' (săN'prē'vä'). Village, Moselle dept., NE France, 7 m. NW of Metz; pop. 1019; scene of critical phase of battle of Gravelotte Aug. 18, 1870.

Saint-Quen'tin' (săN'kän'tăN'; *Angl.* sănt-kwĕn't'n, -tĭn). Manufacturing commune, Aisne dept., N France, on Somme river 25 m. NW of Laon; pop. 49,028; 12th-cent. Gothic church, 16th-cent. town hall; manufactures linen (important center since 16th cent.), cottons, woolens, tulle, embroidery, lace, foundry products, machinery, brick and tile. Once important center of literature and art; battles 1557, 1870, 1918; almost completely destroyed by Germans in World War I and later restored.

Saint-Ra'pha·ël (săN'rä'fä'ĕl'). Town, Var dept., SE France, on the Riviera ab. 18 m. SW of Cannes; pop. 5627. Severe fighting at time of Allied invasion Aug. 1944.

Saint Ra'pha·ël (săN' rà'fä'ĕl'). Village, ⊗ of Bellechasse co., S Quebec, Canada, 24 m. E of Quebec; pop. 955; farming community; has electric power plant.

Saint Ray'mond (sănt rā'mŭnd; *Fr.* săN' rā'môN'). Village, Portneuf co., S Quebec, Canada, on Ste. Anne river 28 m. W of Quebec; pop. 3139.

Saint Re'gis Falls (sănt rē'jĭs). Village, Franklin co., NE New York, 17 m. SW of Malone; pop. (est.) 800; lumber and paper mills.

Saint Regis Indian Reservation. Settlement ab. 9 m. long and 3 m. wide, partly in Franklin co., NE New York, and partly in Huntingdon co., Quebec, Canada, on right bank of St. Lawrence river ab. 20 m. NW of Malone, New York; pop. (U.S.) 1774; farming, basketmaking, etc.; inhabited chiefly by descendants of Saint Regis tribe of Iroquois Indians; home of Eleazar Williams 1850–58.

Saint Ré'mi' (săN' rä'mē'). Village, Napierville co., S Quebec, Canada, 17 m. S of Montreal; pop. 1845.

Saint-Ré'my' (săN'rä'mē'). Town, Bouches-du-Rhône dept., SE France, ab. 15 m. NE of Arles; pop. 3253.

Saint-Ri'quier' (săN'rē'kyä'). Town, Somme dept., N France, ab. 8 m. NE of Abbeville; pop. 963; abbey founded 7th cent.

Saint Ro'mu·ald' *or* **Saint Romuald d'Etch'e·min'** (săN' rô'mü·âl' dĕch'măN'). Town (unincorporated), ⊗ of Levis co., S Quebec, Canada, ab. 6 m. SW of Levis; pop. 4027; an industrial parish and formerly a shipping center.

Saint-Sauveur. See LUZ.

Saint-Sau'veur'-le-Vi'comte' (săN'sō'vûr'lẽ·vē'kôNt'). Commune, Manche dept., NW France, 18 m. S of Cherbourg; pop. (1931) 2092. An old Norman town, once a possession of Sir John Chandos; in World War II taken by Americans June 18, 1944.

Saint Sé·bas'tien, Cape (sănt sẽ·băs'chăn; *Fr.* săN'sä'bàs'tyăN'). Cape projecting into N Mozambique Channel on extreme NW coast of the island of Madagascar.

Saint-Ser'van'–sur-Mer (săN'sĕr'väN'sür·mâr'). Seaport, Ille-et-Vilaine dept., NW France, at mouth of the Rance 2 m. S of Saint-Malo; pop. 10,546; sea bathing; manufactures furniture.

Saint Si'mon Island (sănt sī'mŭn). Island in Atlantic Ocean S of entrance to Altamaha Sound, E coast of Glynn co., SE Georgia.

Saint So·phi'a Ridge (sô·fī'à). Peak 13,100 ft. in Ouray and San Miguel cos., SW Colorado.

Saint Ste'phen (stē'vĕn). Town, Charlotte co., SW New Brunswick, Canada, on St. Croix river 15 m. NW of its mouth and at head of navigation; pop. 3769; exports lumber; has several industrial plants.

Saint Tam'ma·ny (tăm'à·nĭ). Parish in Louisiana. See *Table* at LOUISIANA.

Saint Thom'as (sănt tŏm'ăs). **1** One of the Virgin Is. of the United States, in the West Indies, ab. 40 m. E of Puerto Rico; separated from Culebra I. on W by Virgin Passage; 32 sq. m.; pop. 16,201; ✻ Charlotte Amalie on S coast; second in size and most important commercially

of the group; of volcanic origin, with range of hills traversing island E to W (highest point 1550 ft.). Coast line much indented, with **Saint Thomas Harbor**, the harbor of Charlotte Amalie, one of the best anchorages in West Indies. Produces bay oil and bay rum. Discovered and named by Columbus 1493; first settlement by Dutch 1657, who soon abandoned it; occupied by Danes 1666 and 1672; in 19th cent. twice held temporarily by English. See VIRGIN ISLANDS, WEST INDIES.

2 See CHARLOTTE AMALIE.

3 City, ⊗ of Elgin co., SE Ontario, Canada, near Lake Erie 15 m. S of London; pop. 18,173; founded 1810. Important railroad junction and divisional point; connected with Port Stanley, its port on Lake Erie; has large agricultural trade. Seat of Alma Coll. (founded 1877).

4 Portuguese island in Gulf of Guinea. See SÃo TOMÉ.

Saint Thom'as's Mount (sånt tŏm'ås·ĭz). Town, Madras state, S Indian Union, **7** m. SW of Madras; pop. 9293. On the "Mount" (220 ft.) in the town stands old Portuguese church, a place of pilgrimage for Indian Roman Catholics (the "Christians of Saint Thomas") said originally to have been converted by the apostle St. Thomas. Treaty with Haidar Ali signed here 1769.

Saint Tho·mé (sånt tô·mā'); *Port.* **São To·mé** (souɴ' tōō·mâ'). Originally Portuguese fort 1615–69 on Coromandel Coast, India; now part of the city of Madras (*q.v.*). Occupied by English 1749; battle bet. French and English 1759.

Saint Tite (săɴ' tēt'). Town, Champlain co., S Quebec, Canada, 27 m. N of Three Rivers; pop. 2856.

Saint–Trond. = SINT-TRUIDEN.

Saint–Tro'pez' (săɴ'trô'pě'). Commune, Var dept., SE France, on Bay of St. Tropez, SSW of Fréjus; fishing port, resort; pop. 4161. Nearby is the famous beach Plage de Pampelonne.

Saint Ubes. See SETÚBAL.

Saint–Va'lé'ry'–sur–Somme (săɴ'và'lā'rē'sür·sôm'). Town, Somme dept., NE France, on S side of mouth of the Somme just NW of Abbeville; pop. 2827; point of departure of William the Conqueror 1066 on his second and successful attempt to cross the English Channel for invasion of England. Cf. DIVES.

Saint–Ve·nant' (săɴv'näɴ'). Commune, Pas-de-Calais dept., N France, on the Lys river N of Béthune; pop. 3840; as fortified place important in latter part of Thirty Years' War and in War of the Spanish Succession.

Saint Vin'cent (sånt vĭn's'nt). **1** Island off SW coast of Franklin co., NW Florida, bet. Apalachicola Bay on E and Gulf of Mexico on W.

2 Territory, West Indies Federation, in the Windward Is.; comprises St. Vincent I. and the northern Grenadines (including Union and Bequia); 150 sq. m.; pop. 47,961; ✳ Kingstown, on SW coast of St. Vincent I.

3 Principal island of the colony, S of Saint Lucia and W of Barbados; ab. 18 m. long by 11 m. wide; area ab. 133 sq. m.; pop. 44,278; ✳ Kingstown; volcanic, with many hills and valleys; highest point La Soufrière volcano 4048 ft.; noted for its fine sea-island cotton; also produces arrowroot, copra, cocoa, sugar, molasses, spices; has fine botanical garden, established 1768. One of the original homes of the Carib Indians; island supposed to have been sighted by Columbus 1498; granted 1627 by Charles I for English settlement and several times later by English sovereigns, but possession by English not confirmed until Treaty of Paris 1763; held by French 1779–83. Has suffered much from hurricanes (esp. 1898) and volcanic eruptions (Soufrière May 1902).

4 See SÃo VICENTE.

Saint Vincent, Cape. **1** *Port.* **Ca'bo de São Vi·cen'te** (ká'vōō thě souɴ' vě·sāɴn'tě). Roman name **Pro'mon·to'ri·um Sa'crum** (prŏm'ŏn·tōr'ĭ·ŭm sā'krŭm)—"Sacred Promontory." Cape, SW point of Portugal, ab. 118 m. S of Lisbon. Regarded by ancient geographers Marinus and Ptolemy as westernmost point of Europe. On the cape or nearby at **Sa'gres** [så'grĕsh]

(3 m. E) Prince Henry the Navigator established c. 1418 his school of navigation and observatory; lighthouse now on site of ruins. In great naval battle fought 25 to 30 m. SW of cape English admiral Sir John Jervis (later Earl of St. Vincent) decisively defeated Spanish fleet under Don José de Córdoba Feb. 14, 1797; other naval battles off the cape were: defeat of English and Dutch 1693 by French Admiral Tourville; defeat of Spanish 1780 by English Admiral Rodney; and defeat 1833 of fleet of Portuguese usurper Dom Miguel by fleet of Dom Pedro I.

2 Cape on W coast of the island of Madagascar; lat. 22°S.

Saint Vincent, Gulf of. Gulf, South Australia, E of Yorke Penin., ab. 100 m. long, in 138°E long.; connected with Indian Ocean by Investigator Strait on SW and Backstairs Passage on S; Kangaroo I. across its entrance. Adelaide and Port Adelaide, its seaport, are on its E shore.

Saint Vi'tal, Point (vī't'l). Point in SE Chippewa co., E Michigan penin., extending into Lake Huron.

Saint–Vith (săɴ'vēt'). Town, Liège prov., E Belgium, near Luxembourg border 35 m. SE of Liège; pop. 2524; formerly German. In World War II in the Battle of the Bulge (E Belgium), taken by Germans Dec. 1944 and retaken by Americans after severe fighting Jan. 23, 1945.

Saint–Y'ri·eix'–la–Perche (săɴ'-tē'ryě'là·pěrsh'). Town, S Haute-Vienne dept., W cen. France; pop. 3299; china-clay deposits.

Saint Yves. See SETÚBAL.

Sai·pan' (sī·pän'; *Angl.* sī·păn', sī'păn). **1** Island, S cen. Mariana Is., W Pacific Ocean; 14 m. long and 2 to 5 m. wide; area 70 sq. m.; pop. (1940 est.) ab. 45,000; former ✳ Garapan, new ✳ Chalan Kanoa. Hilly with highest point 1554 ft.; at N end, Marpi Point, are high cliffs. On SE coast is wide inlet, Magicienne Bay; best anchorage is Tanapag Harbor on W coast just N of Garapan. Spanish possession 1565–1899; German 1899–1914; included in Japanese mandate 1919, and developed as naval base with several airfields; captured by Americans after severe fighting June 15 to July 9, 1944; developed into great American air base, used Nov. 1944 to end of war.

2 Village, W coast of Angaur I., S Palau Is.

Sai'ram Nor (sī'räm nōr') *or* **Zai'ram Nor** (zī'räm). Lake (*nor*) 290 sq. m., NW Sinkiang, W China, S of the Dzungarian Ala Tau.

Sa·irt' (sä·yĭrt'). = SIIRT.

Sair'us·su' (sīr'ŏŏ·sŏŏ'). Mongol village and trading center, SE Mongolian People's Republic, on N edge of the Gobi; caravan and motor route from Kweisui in Suiyuan divides here into highways N to Urga and NW to Dzhibkhalantu (Uliassutai).

Sa'is (sā'ĭs). Important city in ancient Egypt, ancient capital of Lower Egypt, in the Nile delta on the Canopic branch of the river; lat. 30°57′N and long. 30°48′E.

Sai·shu (sī·shŏŏ); *Jap.* **Saishu To** (tō); *Korean* **Che'ju'** (chû'ĭ·jŏŏ'); *formerly* **Quel'part** (kwĕl'pärt). Island 60 m. off S tip of Korea, N East China Sea; 44 m. long; 710 sq. m.; pop. ab. 200,000; chief town Saishu, on N coast (pop. 36,138). Belongs to Korea. Highest point Kanra, an extinct volcano, ab. 6500 ft. Chief industries fishing, cattle and pony raising, and the manufacture of hats for Korean trade.

Sai·ta·ma (sī·tä·mä). Prefecture of Japan. See *Table* at JAPAN.

Sa·ja'ma (sä·hä'mä); *also* **Sa·ha'ma** (sä·ä'mä). Peak 21,390 ft. in W Bolivia, near Chilean boundary.

Sa'jó (sŏ'yō). River ab. 100 m. long in Czechoslovakia and Hungary; rises in Slovakia, flows S and SE to the Tisza; Miskolc, Hungary, is on it.

Sa·ka·e·ha·ma (sä·kä·ě·hä·mä). Town on E coast, Karafuto, S Sakhalin I., on railroad 50 m. N of Otomari; formerly Japanese.

Sa·kai (sä·kī). City, Osaka prefecture, W cen. Honshu, Japan, 6 m. S of Osaka on Osaka Bay; pop. (1945)

168,348. In 15th and 16th cents. developed important trade with Chinese and Portuguese; declined after 1635 and in recent years with silting up of harbor has lost its standing as a seaport; weaving (silk, silk gauze, woolen fabrics, cotton rugs, etc.).

Sa·ka′ka (să·kä′kȧ; -kä). Town, N Nejd, Saudi Arabia, ab. 35 m. ENE of Jauf; pop. ab. 10,000.

Sakartvelo. See GEORGIA.

Sa·kar′ya (sä·kär′yä); *anc.* **San·gar′i·us** (săng·gâr′- ĭ·ŭs). River ab. 300 m. long in NW Turkey in Asia; rises in mountains N of Afyon Karahisar and flows in double curve E, W, and N into the Black Sea 80 m. E of the Bosporus. The Porsuk and Ankara are its chief tributaries; Adapazari is chief town on its banks.

Sa·ka·ta (sä·kä·tä). Seaport city, Yamagata prefecture, N Honshu, Japan, 85 m. N of Niigata; pop. (1945) 44,619; chief industry distribution of rice; has imposing Shinto shrine.

Sa′kha·lin (săk′ȧ·lēn; -lĭn; *Russ.* sȧ·kŭ·lyēn′); *formerly* **Sa′ghal·ien′** (sä′gäl·yĕn′); *Jap.* **Ka·ra·fu·to** (kä·rä- fōō·tô). 1 Island N of Japan in W part of Sea of Okhotsk; 24,560 sq. m.; ab. 600 m. long, 16 to 100 m. wide; pop. 343,943, (1938 est.) ab. 420,000; separated from Russian mainland on W by Gulf of Tatary and narrow Tatar Strait and from Hokkaido, Japan, on S by Soya Strait; in SE are two large inlets Taraika Bay and Aniwa Bay. Has cold, bleak, foggy climate; covered with forests; in S mountainous, highest point 4360 ft.; abundance of fish in its short streams and along its shores; coal deposits, oil fields.

History: In early times Chinese; first visited by Japanese c. 1630; explored by them ab. end of 18th cent.; disputed bet. Japan and Russia 1853–75; first settled by Russians 1857, came entirely under Russian control 1875 when Japan gave it up in exchange for Kuril Is.; occupied by Japanese 1905; S part below 50°N granted to Japan by Treaty of Portsmouth 1905, returned to Russia 1946 after defeat of Japan by Allies in World War II.

2 District, part of Khabarovsk Territory, Soviet Russia, Asia, N half of Sakhalin I. N of 50°; 10,625 sq. m.; pop. ab. 80,000; chief town Aleksandrovsk; Okha important port on E side. Tatar Strait frozen over much of the winter allowing transportation across the ice from island to Nikolaevsk and Komsomolsk. See 1, above.

Sakhalin, Gulf of. Inlet of Sea of Okhotsk bet. N end of Sakhalin I. and mainland of Khabarovsk Territory, Soviet Russia, Asia; on S connects with Tatar Strait.

Sakhar. See SUKKUR.

Sakhara. = SAQQARA.

Šakiai. See SHAKYAI.

Sakis–Adasi. See CHIOS.

Sa·ki·shi·ma Islands (sä·kĕ·shē·mä). Group of ab. 20 small islands in S section of Ryukyu Is., Okinawa prefecture, Japan, in W Pacific Ocean off E coast of N Formosa; all formed of coral reefs; 343 sq. m.; pop. (1945) 98,813. Largest are Miyako, Ishigaki, and Iriomote. Had airfields, frequently bombed by British and U.S. carrier planes Apr. to June 1945.

Sakkara. = SAQQARA.

Sak·ma′ra (sŭk·mȧ′rȧ). River ab. 300 m. long, E Soviet Russia, Europe; rises in S Ural Mts. in Bashkir Republic and flows S and W to the Ural river at Chkalov.

Sa·kon Na·khon *or* **Sa·kol Na·korn** (sä·kŭn nä· k'hôn). 1 Province, NE Thailand; 3833 sq. m.; pop. 212,627.

2 Town, its ✱, on a small lake with outlet to the Mekong, 50 m. W of Nakhon Phanom.

Sa·kon′net River (sȧ·kŏn′ĕt; -ĭt). Inlet of Atlantic Ocean extending into Newport co., SE Rhode Island, E of Rhode I. (island).

Sa·ko′ta (sȧ·kō′tȧ). Town, Amhara, NW Ethiopia, ab. 100 m. NE of Lake Tana.

Sak′ti (sŭk′tĕ). Former Indian state, Eastern States, NE Indian Union, 45 m. E of Bilaspur; 137 sq. m.; pop. (1941) 54,517; ✱ Sakti (pop. ab. 3000).

Sa·ku·ra·ji·ma (sä·kōō·rä·jĕ·mä). Volcano 3752 ft. on a peninsula (formerly an island) ab. 6½ m. long by 5 m. wide in Kagoshima Bay, S Kyushu, Japan; had destructive eruption in 1914.

Sal (säl). One of the Cape Verde Is., N of Boa Vista; 87 sq. m.; pop. ab. 750; manufactures salt.

Sal, Cay (kē′ săl′). Lighthouse in W Bahama Is. See CAY SAL BANK.

Sal, La. See LA SAL.

Sala. See IJSSEL.

Salaberry de Valleyfield. See VALLEYFIELD.

Sa·la′da Bay (sä·lä′thä). Inlet of Pacific Ocean on W coast of Atacama prov., N cen. Chile.

Sa·la·dil′lo (sä′lä·thē′yô; *usu. in Argentina,* -thē′zhô). Name of several rivers in Argentina, esp.: (1) The upper course of the Dulce (*q.v.*). (2) River in N cen. part, in Córdoba prov., flowing E, joining Tercero river to form the Carcaraña, a tributary of the Paraná.

Sa·la′do (sä·lä′thô). 1 River 60 m. long in W cen. Oriente prov., E Cuba; flows W into Cauto river.

2 River ab. 250 m. long in Coahuila and Nuevo León states, NE Mexico; flows SE into the Rio Grande river; in upper course known as the **Sa·bi′nas** (sä·vē′näs).

Salado, Río′ (rē′ô). 1 Three rivers in Argentina: (1) River ab. 1120 m. long, in N part; rises in Andes Mts. and is known in its upper course as the **Río del Ju′ra·men′to** (thĕl hōō′rä·män′tô); flows SE into the Paraná river at Santa Fe. (2) River ab. 850 m. long, in W part; flows S forming boundary bet. Mendoza and San Luis provs., turns SE and empties into Colorado river; known as **Des′a·gua·de′ro** (dās′ä·gwä·thä′rô) in its upper course, and as **Cha′di·le′o** (chä′thē·lä′ô) in its course through La Pampa territory. (3) River ab. 415 m. long, in E part, in Buenos Aires prov.; flows W into Río de la Plata.

2 Small river, Cádiz prov., S Spain, near Tarifa; battle on its bank Oct. 30, 1340 in which Alfonso XI of Castile as ally of Alfonso IV of Portugal defeated the Moors.

Sa′la·ga (sä′lȧ·gȧ). Town, N Northern Region, Ghana, W Africa, E of the Volta and ab. 60 m. SSE of Tamale; pop. 4826.

Salahiyeh. See DURA-EUROPOS.

Sa·la′jar *or* **Sa·la′yar** (sä·lä′yär). Long narrow island in Flores Sea, 11 m. off S coast of SW peninsula of Celebes I. at entrance to the Gulf of Bone, Malay Archipelago; 51 m. long; 256 sq. m.; pop. 76,107. Chief town Benteng, in cen. part of W coast. Inhabitants mainly Macassarese, who are excellent boatmen and boatbuilders. Chief crops copra, cotton, tobacco, and hemp.

Salajar Strait. Channel bet. Salajar I. and Celebes I. in the Malay Archipelago.

Sa′lak (sä′läk). Volcano 7254 ft., W Java, Indonesia, SW of Bogor; tea and coffee plantations on its slopes. Severe eruptions 1669 and 1699.

Sa·la·má′ (sä′lä·mä′). Town, cen. Guatemala; ✱ of Baja Verapaz dept.; pop. 8000.

Sal′a·man′ca (săl′ȧ·măng′kȧ). City, Cattaraugus co., SW New York, on Allegheny river 13 m. WNW of Olean; pop. 8480; within Allegany Indian Reservation, from whom ground is leased; resort; in dairying and farming region.

Sal′a·man′ca (săl′ȧ·măng′kȧ; *Span.* sä′lä·mäng′kä). 1 Town, Guanajuato state, cen. Mexico, 17 m. S of Guanajuato; pop. 11,985.

2 Province of Spain. See *Table* at SPAIN.

3 *anc.* **Sal·man′ti·ca** (săl·măn′tĭ·kȧ) *or* **Hel·man′ti·ca** (hĕl-). Manufacturing commune, ✱ of Salamanca prov., W Spain, on Tormes river 107 m. WNW of Madrid; pop. (1941 est.) 73,120; manufactures leather, hats, pottery; celebrated medieval university (founded c. 1220 by Alfonso IX), leading center of Arabic learning in Europe; 12th-cent. Romanesque and 16th-cent. Gothic cathedrals; notable colonnaded square, the Plaza Mayor, lined with Renaissance and other picturesque structures; Roman bridge; theater, bull ring. Important

city of the Vettones; conquered by Hannibal 222 B.C.; became Roman military station on the road from Augusta Emerita (Mérida) to Asturica Augusta (Astorga); captured by Goths and later by Moors; reconquered from Moors 1095; occupied by French during Peninsular War; French defeated by English under Wellington 1812.

Sal·a·mau′a (săl′à·mou′à). Coastal town, E North-East New Guinea, on W shore of Huon Gulf ab. 19 m. S of Lae; pop. (1939 est.) 2068; has good harbor; supply town and port for the Morobe gold fields; air route to Wau ab. 32 m. Seized by Japanese Mar. 8, 1942; made a military base; scene of much fighting bet. Apr. 1942 and Sept. 1943; finally captured by Allied forces Sept. 11.

Sa·lam′bri·a (sà·lăm′brî·à; *Ital.* sä·läm′brĕ·ä); *Mod. Gr.* **Pē′nei·os′** (pē′nyĕ·ôs′); *anc.* **Pe·ne′us** (pê·nē′ŭs). River ab. 125 m. long, Thessaly, N cen. Greece; rises in Pindus Mts., flows SE and ENE through plain of Thessaly and Vale of Tempe into the Gulf of Salonika.

Sa′la·mi′na (sä′lä·mē′nä). Town, Caldas dept., W cen. Colombia, NNW of Manizales; pop. 6183.

Sal′a·mis (săl′à·mĭs; *Mod. Gr.* sä′lä·mēs′). **1** Chief city of Cyprus in ancient times, on E coast; its site 3 m. N of Famagusta. Had good harbor with active trade with Phoenicia, Egypt, and Cilicia. According to tradition founded by Teucer, a hero of the Trojan War, c. 1180 B.C.; was a strong Hellenic center during struggle bet. Greece and Persia; scene of naval victory 449 B.C. for Greeks and again 306 B.C. when Demetrius I defeated Ptolemy I. Suffered often from earthquakes. Visited by Paul and Barnabas (*Acts* xiii. 4, 5). Under the Eastern Roman Empire known as **Con·stan′ti·a** (kŏn·stăn′-shǐ·à; -shà), after Constantius II who rebuilt it 337–361.

2 *or* **Kou·lou′ri** (kōō·lōō′rē). Island in the Saronic Gulf, Attica and Boeotia dept., Greece, near Piraeus; 36 sq. m.; pop. ab. 15,000; forms an irregular semicircle with large inlet on the W and is S boundary of Bay of Eleusis. Famous naval battle fought 480 B.C. in narrow strait off NE coast, in which allied Greeks under Themistocles defeated Persians under Xerxes. See CYNOSURA.

3 *also called* **Koulouri**. Commune on NE Salamis I. W of Piraeus; pop. 12,564.

Sal·a·mo′nie (săl′à·mō′nĭ). River ab. 100 m. long, Indiana; flows NW from SE Jay co. to Wabash river in E Wabash co.

Salang. Malay name of PHUKET I.

Sa·lar′ de U·yu′ni (sä·lär′ thä ōō·yōō′nĕ). Extensive salt marsh in SW Bolivia, near border of Chile.

Sa·lar′i·an Way (sà·lâr′ĭ·ăn); *Lat.* **Vi′a Sa·lar′i·a** (vī′à sà·lâr′ĭ·à). Ancient Roman road ab. 150 m. long, from Rome NE through Reate (Rieti) and Asculum Picenum (Ascoli Piceno) to Adriatic coast; route by which the Sabines got their salt from the sea.

Sa′las (sä′läs). Commune, Oviedo prov., NW Spain, 24 m. WNW of Oviedo; pop. 13,851.

Sa′la·ti′ga (sä′là·tē′gà). Town, Central Java prov., Indonesia, ab. 25 m. S of Semarang; pop. 24,274; health resort.

Sa′la·ver′ry (sä′lä·vĕr′rĕ). Seaport and the port of Trujillo 9 m. N, La Libertad dept., NW Peru.

Sa′la·wa′ti (sä′lä·wä′tĕ). Island off W Vogelkop Penin., NW Neth. New Guinea, roughly circular in shape with greatest diameter ab. 30 m.; pop., with smaller adjacent island of Batanta, 4663. Separated by narrow channel from mainland of New Guinea; administered as part of Sorong subdivision of Ternate division.

Salayar. See SALAJAR.

Sa′la-y-Go′mez (sä′lä-ê-gō′mås). Uninhabitable rocky island in S Pacific Ocean, 210 m. ENE of Easter I.; lat. 26°28′S and long. 105°W; belongs to Chile.

Sal′can·tay′ (säl′kän·tī′). Peak 20,550 ft. in Cordillera Oriental, Peru, NW of Cuzco.

Sal·chak′et (?săl·chăk′ĕt; -ĭt). Village on Tanana river and on Alaska Highway, 36 m. SE of Fairbanks, E Alaska; airport nearby.

Sal′combe (sôl′kŭm). Coast town, Devonshire, SW England, on English Channel; pop. 2576; resort; U.S. naval training base in World War II.

Saldae. See BOUGIE.

Sal·da′nha Bay (săl·dăn′yà). Bay on SW coast of Cape Province, South Africa, at ab. lat. 33°S.

Salduba. See SARAGOSSA.

Sale (sāl). **1** Town, SE Victoria, SE Australia, 120 m. ESE of Melbourne; pop. 4264; chief town of Gippsland in a fertile agricultural district.

2 Urban district, Cheshire, NW England, on the Mersey 5 m. SW of Manchester; pop. 43,167; residential suburb of Manchester.

Sa′lé′ (sä′lā′); *Arab.* **Sla** (slä). Seaport, NW Morocco, NW Africa, at the mouth of the Bou Regreg opp. Rabat of which it is a suburb; pop. (1936) 31,823; important esp. in Middle Ages; in 17th cent. an independent republic and a center of the Barbary pirates (sometimes called *Sallee rovers* or *salleemen*).

Sa′le·ba′boe *or* **Salebabu** (sä′lä·bä′bōō). One of the Talaud Is. (*q.v.*), Indonesia.

Sa′leh Bay (sä′lĕ). Large inlet of Flores Sea on N coast of Sumbawa I., Lesser Sunda Is., Indonesia, ab. 45 m. long by 22 m. wide. Nearly cuts the island into two parts; its entrance nearly closed by Mojo I.

Sa·lei′er (sä·lī′ĕr). = SALAJAR.

Sa·le·khard′ (sŭ·lyĕ·kȧrt′); *formerly* **Ob·dorsk′** (ŭb·dôrsk′). Town on Ob river near its mouth, ✳ of Yamalo-Nenets National District, Soviet Russia, Asia.

Sa′lem (sä′lĕm). **1** County in New Jersey. See *Table* at NEW JERSEY.

2 City, ⊗ of Fulton co., N Arkansas; pop. 713.

3 City, ⊗ of Marion co., S cen. Illinois, 13 m. ENE of Centralia; pop. 6165; in agricultural and coal-mining section; fruit-packing and shipping center; oil; birthplace of William Jennings Bryan.

4 City, ⊗ of Washington co., S Indiana, 28 m. NW of New Albany; pop. 4546; birthplace of John Hay.

5 City, a ⊗ of Essex co., NE corner of Massachusetts, on Atlantic Ocean 14 m. NE of Boston; pop. 39,211; seaport, port of entry, and seaside resort; founded 1626 by Roger Conant and emigrants from Cape Ann; became prominent for fishing, shipping, and shipbuilding activities; center of the "witch" craze in the late 17th cent., 19 "witches" were executed here in 1692; birthplace of Nathaniel Hawthorne; now manufactures textiles, shoes, radio tubes. Massachusetts State College (1854; coed.).

6 City, ⊗ of Dent co., SE cen. Missouri, 26 m. SSE of Rolla; pop. 3870; iron mines nearby.

7 Town, Rockingham co., SE New Hampshire, 12 m. E of Nashua; pop. 9210; manufactures shoes; horse racing at Rockingham Park in nearby **Salem Depot** (pop. 2523). Part of Haverhill, Massachusetts until 1741; incorporated 1750.

8 City, ⊗ of Salem co., SW New Jersey, on navigable Salem creek near its confluence with Delaware river 16 m. WNW of Bridgeton; pop. 8941; in farming region; fur market for muskrat pelts; produces canned goods, linoleums, glassware, chemicals. Settled 1641; successively under Swedish, Dutch, and English rule; founded by English Quakers 1675; became port of entry for vessels 1682; incorporated as village 1695, as city 1858; scene of fighting and plundering in Revolutionary War.

9 Former city, Forsyth co., North Carolina; now part of Winston-Salem (*q.v.*).

10 City, Columbiana co., E Ohio, 17 m. SW of Youngstown; pop. 13,854; manufactures china, lumber, furnaces, automobile bodies, machinery, metal products, flour, dairy products. Founded by Quakers 1801; station on Underground Railroad.

11 City, ✳ of Oregon and ⊗ of Marion co., NW Oregon, on Willamette river 44 m. SSW of Portland; pop. 49,142; marketing and distributing center of agricultural area (esp. fruits and vegetables, hops, flax, livestock); canneries, paper, linen, and woolen mills, packing houses,

sawmills. Willamette Univ. (1842; coed.). Founded 1840; territorial capital 1851, continued as capital of state of Oregon 1859.

12 City, ⊗ of McCook co., SE South Dakota; pop. 1188.

13 Town, ⊗ of Roanoke co., W cen. Virginia, 8 m. W of Roanoke; pop. 16,058; manufactures cigarette machinery, bricks, elevators; summer resort; mineral springs. Roanoke Coll. (1853; coed.).

14 City, Harrison co., N West Virginia, 13 m. W of Clarksburg; pop. 2366; settled in 1790 by Seventh Day Baptists; glass; gas, oil wells. Salem Coll. (1888; coed.).

15 City, cen. Madras state, S Indian Union, 175 m. SW of Madras; pop. (1941) 129,702; picturesquely situated; has active trade and is seat of a municipal college.

16 Ancient name of JERUSALEM; a shortened form associated with the Hebrew word for "peaceful."

Salem Heights. Urban area, Marion co., NW Oregon, SW suburb of Salem; pop. 10,770.

Sa·le′mi (sä-lâ′mē). Commune, Trapani prov., NW Sicily, 22 m. SE of Trapani; pop. 17,308. Garibaldi declared himself dictator of Sicily here May 14, 1860.

Sal′en·tine Peninsula (săl′ĕn·tĭn). The peninsula forming the "heel" of Italy, from the ancient name, Sallentinum Promontorium, of Cape Santa Maria di Leuca at its tip. Cf. IAPYGIA.

Sa·ler′no (sä-lĕr′nō; *Angl.* sȧ-lûr′nō). **1** Province of Italy. See *Table* at ITALY.

2 *anc.* **Sa·ler′num** (sȧ-lûr′nŭm). Seaport, its ⁎, Campania, S Italy, on Gulf of Salerno 29 m. ESE of Naples; pop. 67,009; ruins of ancient Paestum nearby; 11th-cent. Gothic cathedral; tombs of Margaret of Anjou, Gregory VII, St. Matthew; manufactures include textiles, glass, paper, ceramics, iron goods, leather, thread. Founded by Greeks; became Roman colony 194 B.C.; in Middle Ages passed to Goths, Lombards, Normans, and kingdom of Naples; famous in medieval period for its school of medicine founded by Robert Guiscard in 11th cent.; became part of kingdom of Italy in 19th cent.; in World War II landing place of American army Sept. 9, 1943; established as base by Sept. 18 after severe fighting.

Salerno, Gulf of; *anc.* **Bay of Paes′tum** (pĕs′tŭm; pēs′-). Inlet of Tyrrhenian Sea on SW coast of Italy, S of the Bay of Naples.

Sal′ford (sôl′fẽrd). County borough, Lancashire, NW England, on the Irwell adjacent to Manchester; pop. 223,438, (1951 pop.) 178,036; engineering and electrical goods, cotton, iron, chemicals, ready-made clothing; large docks on Manchester Ship Canal.

Sal′gó·tar′ján (shŏl′gō-tŏr′yän). City, N Hungary, 52 m. NE of Budapest; pop. 16,951.

Sal·hu′tu or **Sal·hoe′toe, Mount** (säl·hōō′tōō). Peak 4020 ft., highest point on Amboina I., Moluccas, Indonesia.

Sal′i (săl′ē). = SALÉ.

Sa·li′da (sȧ-lī′dȧ). City, ⊗ of Chaffee co., cen. Colorado, on Arkansas river 65 m. WSW of Colorado Springs; pop. 4560; founded by railroad 1880; center for region producing gold, silver, lead, granite; medicinal springs.

Sa′lies′ (sȧ-lēs′). Town, Basses-Pyrénées dept., SW France, ab. 27 m. E of Bayonne; pop. 2630; mineral springs.

Sa·li′na (sȧ-lī′nȧ). **1** City, ⊗ of Saline co., cen. Kansas, on Smoky Hill river 58 m. NNE of Hutchinson; pop. 43,202; trading and shipping center in grain and livestock-raising section; elevators; flour mills, farm implement manufactories. Schilling Air Force Base; Camp Phillips. Kansas Wesleyan University (1886; Methodist); Marymount College (1922; women).

2 City, Sevier co., cen. Utah, on Sevier river 18 m. NNE of Richfield; pop. 1618; shipping center for livestock, coal, salt, farm produce; mountain-lion hunting center. First settled c. 1866; abandoned during Indian troubles; resettled 1871.

Sa·li′na (sä-lē′nä); *anc.* **Did′y·me** (dĭd′ĭ·mē; -mē). One of the Lipari Is. (*q.v.*); 5 m. long; chief town Malfa.

Sa·li′na Cruz (sä-lē′nä krōōs′). Seaport, Oaxaca state, Mexico, on the Gulf of Tehuantepec; pop. 5393; terminus of Tehuantepec National Railway.

Sa·li′nas (sȧ-lē′nȧs). **1** River 150 m. long, W California; rises in S cen. San Luis Obispo co. and flows NW into Monterey Bay on NW coast of Monterey co.

2 City, ⊗ of Monterey co., W California, 10 m. E of Monterey Bay and 47 m. SSE of San Jose; pop. 28,957; founded 1856; market center for dairy farms and truck gardens.

3 (*Span.* sä-lē′näs) Seaport town and resort on Santa Elena Penin., W Guayas prov., W Ecuador, ab. 70 m. W of Guayaquil; pop. (1944 est.) 6589; in district producing salt, petroleum, sulfur, and pitch; has cable station and naval school.

4 (*Span.* sä-lē′näs) Municipality (pop. 23,133) and town (pop. 3666), S Puerto Rico; town on coast 20 m. E of Ponce.

Sa·li′nas, Cape (sȧ-lē′nȧs; *Span.* sä-lē′näs). Cape on S tip of the island of Majorca, W Mediterranean Sea.

Salinas, Point. Cape on NE coast of Puerto Rico, W of entrance to San Juan harbor.

Salinas Bay. **1** Inlet of Pacific Ocean on extreme NW coast of Costa Rica.

2 Inlet of Pacific Ocean, on coast of Peru, N of Salinas Promontory.

Salinas Promontory. Headland extending into Pacific Ocean from the Peruvian coast ab. 70 m. NNW of Lima.

Sa·line′ (sȧ-lēn′). **1** River ab. 175 m. long, S cen. Arkansas; navigable 100 m.; rises in Saline co., flows S into the Ouachita near the Louisiana boundary.

2 River ab. 200 m. long, W and N cen. Kansas; rises in W Thomas co., NW Kansas, flows E into Smoky Hill river near Salina, Saline co., cen. Kansas.

3 Name of counties in five states of the U.S. See *Tables* at ARKANSAS, ILLINOIS, KANSAS, MISSOURI, NEBRASKA.

Saline di Barletta. See MARGHERITA DI SAVOIA.

Sa·line′ Lake (sȧ-lēn′). Lake in N cen. Louisiana, on boundary bet. Winn and Natchitoches parishes.

Sa·line′ville (sȧ-lēn′vĭl). Village, Columbiana co., E Ohio, 20 m. NNW of Steubenville; pop. 1898; former salt-mining center; coal deposits nearby.

Sa′lins′ (sȧ-lăn′). Fortified town, N Jura dept., E France; pop. 3965; watering place.

Salis′bur′y (sôlz′bĕr′ĭ, -bẽr·ĭ; -brĭ). **1** Resort town, NW Litchfield co., NW Connecticut, on New York and Massachusetts borders; pop. 3309; settled 1719; incorporated 1741; winter sports, summer music festivals; former iron-mining center; small manufactures.

2 City, ⊗ of Wicomico co., SE Maryland, 50 m. ENE of mouth of Potomac river; pop. 16,302; 2d largest port in Maryland; woodworking factories, packing houses, canneries, iron and steel products; shipping point for fruits and vegetables. Maryland State Teachers College (1925; coed.).

3 Town, Essex co., NE corner of Massachusetts, 27 m. ENE of Lowell; pop. 3154.

4 City, Chariton co., N cen. Missouri, 15 m. W of Moberly; pop. 1787.

5 Industrial city, ⊗ of Rowan co., cen. North Carolina, in piedmont section 37 m. NNE of Charlotte; pop. 21,297; founded 1753; incorporated as village 1755, as city 1770; manufactures textiles, lumber, refrigerator supplies, medicines; granite quarries; cotton, grain, farm products. Catawba College (1851; brought to Salisbury 1924; coed.), Livingstone College (incorp. 1879; coed.).

6 Town, ⁎ of Southern Rhodesia and of Mashonaland prov., NE Southern Rhodesia, 240 m. NE of Bulawayo; pop. (1962 est.) 314,200; founded 1890; in gold-mining district and in region suitable to agriculture, stock raising, and fruit growing.

7 or **New Sar′um** (sâr′ŭm). Municipal borough, Wiltshire, S England, on the Avon 22 m. NW of Southamp-

ton; pop. 32,910; cathedral; near site of Old Sarum (*q.v.*) which was seat of bishopric before building of New Sarum in 13th cent.

Salisbury Beach. Village and summer resort, Essex co., NE corner of Massachusetts, on Atlantic Ocean E of Salisbury.

Salisbury Island. Small island at W end of Hudson Strait, SE Franklin District, Northwest Territories, Canada, S of Foxe Penin.

Salisbury Plain. Undulating tract in Wiltshire, S England, near the city of Salisbury; average elevation 400 ft.; highest point **West′bur′y Down** (wĕst′bĕr′ĭ; -bĕr·ĭ; -brĭ) 775 ft.; contains Stonehenge (*q.v.*).

Salisbury Sound. Channel bet. S Chichagof I. and N Baranof I., SE Alaska.

Sal′ke·hatch′ie (sôl′kĕ·hăch′ĭ). River 60 m. long, S South Carolina; rises in W Barnwell co., flows SE to unite with Little Salkehatchie river and form Combahee river.

Sal′khad (săl′ᴋŏd). Town, S cen. Jebel ed Druz territory, Syria, ab. 16 m. SSE of Es Suweida.

Sal′la (säl′lä). Region, Oulu dept., N Finland, E of Kemijärvi; in part ceded to U.S.S.R. by treaties of 1940 and 1944.

Sal′lau′mines′ (sȧ′lō′mēn′). Commune, Pas-de-Calais dept., N France, 10 m. NNE of Arras; pop. (1931) 14,749; coal mines.

Sal′lee (săl′ē). Var. of SALÉ.

Sallentinum Promontorium. See SANTA MARIA DI LEUCA.

Sal′li·saw (săl′ĭ·sô). City, ⊗ of Sequoyah co., E Oklahoma, 39 m. SE of Muskogee; pop. 3351; farming; manufactures lumber, cottonseed oil; home of Sequoyah nearby.

Salmantica. See SALAMANCA.

Salm′on (săm′ŭn). **1** River, cen. Connecticut; rises in S Tolland co., flows SW into Connecticut river.

2 River 420 m. long, cen. Idaho; rises in S Custer co., cen. Idaho, flows N, then W across Idaho, and again N to empty into Snake river at S extremity of Nez Perce co., W Idaho.

3 City, ⊗ of Lemhi co., E cen. Idaho, at confluence of Salmon and Lemhi rivers; pop. 2944; distributing point for agricultural, stock-raising, and mining section.

Sal·mo′ne, Cape (săl·mō′nē). Cape at E end of island of Crete, S of Cape Sidero; mentioned in St. Paul's account of his fourth journey (*Acts* xxvii. 7).

Salmon Falls (săm′ŭn). River ab. 40 m. long, Maine and New Hampshire; rises in Great East Pond, SE Carroll co., E New Hampshire, flows S forming a section of Maine-New Hampshire boundary and joins Cocheco river 3 m. E of Dover to form the Piscataqua river.

Salmon Falls Dam. Dam completed 1912 across Salmon Falls Creek, a S tributary of Snake river, Twin Falls co., SW Idaho; height 220 ft.; impounds water for irrigation. Dam also known as **Salmon River Dam;** reservoir variously known as **Salmon Falls, Salmon Creek,** *or* **Salmon River, Reservoir.** Cf. CEDAR CREEK DAM.

Salmon River Mountains. Group of mountain ranges in cen. Idaho, chiefly in Valley, Custer and Lemhi cos.; includes many peaks above 9000 ft., highest 10,328 ft.; source of Salmon and Boise rivers and other tributaries of the Snake. See SAWTOOTH MOUNTAINS.

Sa′lo·ma′gue Harbor (sä′lō·mä′gä). Inlet and sheltered anchorage on N coast of Ilocos Sur prov., Luzon, Phil. Is., 15 m. N of Vigan.

Sa′lo·mon′, Cape (sä′lô·môn′). = Cape SALMONE.

Sa·lo′na (sȧ·lō′nä). **1** Roman colony on coast of Dalmatia; founded 78 B.C.; residence 305–313 A.D. of Diocletian (born 245 at Dioclea, a nearby village) who built palace and other buildings on site of Spalatum (see SPLIT) 3 m. S; captured several times by Goths and Huns and destroyed by Avars 639.

2 (*Mod. Gr.* sä·lô′nä) See AMPHISSA.

Sa′lon′–de–Pro′vence′ (sȧ′lôn′dĕ·prô′väns′). Commune, Bouches-du-Rhône dept., SE France, 28 m. NNW of Marseilles; pop. 13,482; manufactures soap, olive oil.

Sal′o·ni′ka (săl′ō·nē′kȧ; sȧ·lŏn′ĭ·kȧ; săl′ô·nī′kȧ); *officially* **Thes′sa·lo·ni′kē** (thä′sä·lô·nyē′kyē). *Also* **Sal′o·ni′ki** (săl′ō·nē′kĭ; *Mod. Gr.* sä′lô-nyē′kyē); *before* 315 B.C. called **Ther′ma** (thûr′mȧ), *afterwards* **Thes′-sa·lo·ni′ca** (thĕs′ȧ·lô·nī′kȧ; -lŏn′ĭ·kȧ). Seaport city, ✱ of Thessalonike dept., W cen. Macedonia, NE Greece, at head of Gulf of Salonika; pop. 236,524; excellent harbor; exports include grain, silk, cocoons, manganese, chrome, opium, tobacco; has customs-free zone used by Yugoslavia.

History: Paul's epistles to the Thessalonians addressed to converts here; massacre of insurrectionists by Theodosius 390 A.D.; taken by Saracens 904 and by Normans 1185; capital of 13th-cent. kingdom created 1204 out of remains of Byzantine Empire by Baldwin I for his rival Boniface III, Count of Montferrat; occupied by Turks 1430–1912; swept by great fires 1890, 1917; headquarters of Young Turks 1908; seat of Greek provisional government 1916; important base for Allied operations in World War I; large marshland reclamation project begun 1935. Taken by Germans in World War II Apr. 8–9, 1941; retaken by Greeks Oct. 30, 1944.

Salonika, Gulf of; *or* **Ther·ma′ic Gulf** (thûr·mā′ĭk); *anc.* **Ther·ma′i·cus Si′nus** (thûr·mā′ĭ·kŭs sī′nŭs). Arm of the NW Aegean Sea, extending into NE coast of Greece, E of Thessaly and W of Chalcidice and Pallene Penins.

Sa′lon·ta (sȧ′lôn·tä); *Hung.* **Nagy′sza′lon·ta** (nŏd′y′sŏ′lôn·tŏ). City, W Romania, in Transylvania near Hungarian border, 25 m. SSE of Oradea; pop. 15,176; transferred to Hungary 1940–45.

Salop. 1 See SHROPSHIRE.

2 See SHREWSBURY.

Saloum. See SALUM.

Sal′pi, Lake (säl′pē). Lake 8½ m. long near the coast in Foggia prov., Apulia, SE Italy.

Sal·sette′ (săl·sĕt′). Island 18 m. long, N of Bombay I., Indian Union; 250 sq. m.; pop. 146,933; chief town Thana.

Salsk (sälsk; *Russ.* säl′y′sk). Town, S Rostov Region, Soviet Russia, Europe; pop. (1926) 6900; railroad junction point S of the Manych; taken by Germans in Caucasus drive July 31, 1942; retaken by Russians early in 1943.

Sal′so (säl′sô). River 89 m. long on the island of Sicily, flowing from Madonie Mts. into the Mediterranean Sea.

Sal′so·mag·gio′re (säl′sô·mäd·jō′rä). Commune, Parma prov., Emilia, N Italy, 18 m. W of Parma; pop. 15,259; mineral baths.

Salt (sôlt). **1** River ab. 200 m. long in E and cen. Arizona; rises in Apache co., E Arizona, flows W into Gila river in Maricopa co. W of Phoenix; water utilized for irrigation and water power through a system of dams forming a 60-mile chain of lakes including Roosevelt Dam and Lake, Horse Mesa Dam and Apache Lake, Mormon Flat Dam and Canyon Lake, and Stewart Mountain Dam and Saguaro Lake.

2 River ab. 100 m. long, N cen. Kentucky; rises in Boyle co., cen. Kentucky, flows N, then W into Ohio river below Louisville.

3 River 200 m. long, NE Missouri; rises in Schuyler co., N Missouri, flows SE into Mississippi river in E Pike co., E Missouri.

Sal′ta (säl′tä). **1** Province of Argentina. See *Table* at ARGENTINA.

2 City, its ✱, N Argentina, 140 m. N by W of Tucumán; pop. (est.) 42,931.

Salt Block Mountain (sôlt). Peak 2768 ft. in Garrett co., NW corner of Maryland.

Salt Cay. One of Turks Is. See TURKS AND CAICOS ISLANDS.

Salt′coats′ (sôlt′kōts′). Seaport burgh, Ayr co., SW

Scotland, on the Firth of Clyde 30 m. SW of Glasgow; pop. 13,108; formerly known for its salt mines and for shipbuilding.

Sal'tee Islands (săl'tĭ). Two small islands in St. George's Channel, off SE coast of Ireland, E of Waterford.

Salt Fjord (sôlt; *Norw.* sält). Inlet of Norwegian Sea on NW coast of Norway, extending E from SE entrance to Vest Fjord, in Nordland co.

Salt Fork (sôlt). River, NW Texas; unites with Double Mountain Fork in Stonewall co. to form the Brazos river.

Salt'holm (sält'hŭlm). Danish island in the Öresund, opp. Copenhagen, in the Sjælland group; 4½ m. long; 6 sq. m.

Sal·til'lo (säl·tē'yô). City, NE Mexico, ✻ of Coahuila state; pop. (1960) 92,327; altitude ab. 5000 ft.; center of mining and agricultural area.

Salt Island (sôlt). One of the British Virgin Is., West Indies.

Salt Lake. 1 County in Utah. See *Table* at UTAH.
2 Name of two lakes in Western Australia: (1) Lagoon on W coast N of Shark Bay. (2) Lake in SW cen. part, N of Lake Barlee.

Salt Lake City. City, ✻ of Utah and ⊗ of Salt Lake co., N Utah, on Jordan river 13 m. E of Great Salt Lake; pop. 189,454; largest city in the state; commercial and industrial center in agricultural and mining (silver, gold, lead, copper, coal, iron) area; livestock market; oil refining, smelting, printing and publishing, meat packing, grain milling, canning; manufactures beet sugar, iron, steel, and clay products, radios, textiles. Notable buildings include Mormon Temple and Tabernacle (in Temple Square), state capitol, state cathedral. Coll. of St. Mary-of-the-Wasatch (1926–1960); Univ. of Utah (1850; coed.); Westminster Coll. (1875; coed.). Headquarters of Mormon Church since 1847. Settled by Mormons under leadership of Brigham Young 1847; outfitting point on route to California during gold rush of 1849; chartered 1851; served successively as capital of Provisional State of Deseret (*q.v.*), Territory of Utah, and (except 1851–56, 1858) state of Utah; figured in "Utah War" of 1857–58 and as center of dispute bet. U.S. government and Mormon Church after 1865.

Salt Lake Region. Extensive region in SW cen. Western Australia; contains many salt lakes; rich mining region, especially in gold.

Sal'to (säl'tô). 1 Town, Buenos Aires prov., E Argentina, 107 m. from Buenos Aires; fossil remains discovered nearby.
2 Department of Uruguay. See *Table* at URUGUAY.
3 City and port, ✻ of Salto dept., NW Uruguay, at head of navigation on E bank of Uruguay river opp. Concordia, Argentina, 260 m. NW of Montevideo; pop. ab. 46,000; commercial and shipping center; chief industry salting and canning of meats.

Salto, El. See EL SALTO.

Sal'ton Sink (sôl't'n; -tŭn). Depression 280 ft. below sea level in Riverside and Imperial cos., SE California; became a lake 1891 but later dried up; lake began to form again 1893; waters from Colorado river diverted into it 1905 and it has since become known as **Salton Sea**, 235 ft. below sea level; break in river closed July 1907.

Salt'pond' (sôlt'pŏnd'). Seaport town, S Ghana, West Africa, just E of Cape Coast; pop. 6369.

Salt Range (sôlt). Mountain range in India, bet. the Indus and Jhelum rivers, NW West Punjab, Pakistan; highest peak ab. 5000 ft.; salt beds.

Salt River. Name of three rivers in the U.S.: see SALT.

Salt River Range. Range in N Lincoln co., W Wyoming along Idaho border, extending to Snake river on N.

Salt Sea. An occasional Biblical name for the Dead Sea (*Num.* xxxiv. 3; *Josh.* xv. 2).

Salt Springs Dam. See UNITED STATES, *Dams and Reservoirs.*

Salt'ville (sôlt'vĭl; *Sou.* also -v'l). Town, Smyth and Washington cos., SW Virginia, 32 m. NE of Bristol; pop. 2844; scene of engagement during Civil War 1864; salt wells.

Sa·lu·a·fa'ta (säl'wȧ·fä'tȧ). Harbor on N coast of Upolu I., Western Samoa, SW cen. Pacific Ocean; formerly (1879–99) a German coaling station.

Saluces, Saluciae. See SALUZZO.

Salud, La. See LA SALUD.

Sa·lu'da (sȧ·lōō'dȧ). 1 River 200 m. long, W cen. South Carolina; rises in Blue Ridge Mts., NW South Carolina, flows SE through Lake Murray and unites near Columbia with Broad river to form Congaree river.
2 County in South Carolina. See *Table* at SOUTH CAROLINA.
3 Town, ⊗ of Saluda co., W South Carolina, 27 m. ESE of Greenwood; pop. 2089.
4 Village, ⊗ of Middlesex co., E Virginia; pop. (est.) 300.

Saluda Dam. See UNITED STATES, *Dams and Reservoirs.*

Sa·lum' (sȧ·lōōm'); *Fr.* **Sa'loum'** (sȧ·lōōm'). River 100 m. long, Senegal, West Africa; flows into Atlantic Ocean just N of Gambia; navigable for 60 m.; has wide mouth containing many islands; Kaolack is on it.

Sa·lûm' (sȧ·lōōm') or **Sol·lum'** (sŏ·lōōm'); *also* **El Sol·lum'** (*Arab.* ăs säl·lōōm'); *anc.* **Cat'a·bath'mus Mag'na** (kăt'ȧ·băth'mŭs măg'nȧ). Village, extreme NW Egypt, on the **Gulf of Sa·lûm'** (sȧ·lōōm'), an inlet of the Mediterranean Sea, ab. 275 m. W of Alexandria. Several times taken in North African campaigns of World War II: by Italians Sept. 1940; by British Dec. 16, 1940; by Germans Apr. 1941; and finally by British Jan. 13, 1942.

Sa·luz'zo (sä·lōōt'tsō); *Fr.* **Sa'luces'** (sȧ'lüs'); *anc.* **Sa·lu'ci·ae** (sȧ·lū'shĭ·ē; -sĭ·ē). Commune, Cuneo prov., Piedmont, NW Italy, 18 m. N by W of Cuneo; pop. 15,938; early 16th-cent. cathedral; castle; manufactures textiles, ironware. Formed medieval margraviate from 11th cent.; to France 1548, Piedmont 1601.

Sal'va·dor (săl'vȧ·dôr; *Port.* säl'vȧ·thôr'); *formerly* **São Sal'va·dor'** (soun säl'vȧ·thôr') or **Ba·hi'a** (bȧ·ē'ȧ). Commercial seaport, E coast of Baía state, E Brazil; ✻ of Baía state on All Saints Bay; pop. (1940 est.) 293,278; fourth city in size in Brazil; on a peninsula with modern part of city on heights back of the harbor; has extensive trade, exporting esp. sugar, cotton, cacao, tobacco, tropical woods; has cathedral dating from 1572, and has many churches and other buildings built in 16th and 17th cents.
History: Town (in early times usually called Bahia) and royal captaincy founded by Thomé de Sousa who had been sent by John III of Portugal 1549; seat of bishopric after 1552; town captured and sacked by Dutch 1624, but recaptured by Portuguese 1625; successfully defended against attempt of Dutch to take it 1637; as capital of Portuguese colonies in Brazil 1549–1763, center of colonization and trade; after removal of Brazilian capital to Rio de Janeiro, capital of district and later of state of Baía.

Salvador, El. See EL SALVADOR.

Sal'va·dor, Lake (säl'vȧ·dôr). Lake in St. Charles, Jefferson, and Lafourche parishes, SE Louisiana.

Sal·va'ges (säl·vä'zhĕs) or **Sel·va'gens** (sĕl·vȧ'zhä-ĕnsh). Group of small uninhabited islands of the Madeiras, ab. 180 m. SSE of Madeira.

Sal'va·tier'ra (säl'vȧ·tyĕr'rä). Town, Guanajuato state, cen. Mexico; pop. 8341; on railroad near Lake Cuitzeo ab. 125 m. NW of Mexico City.

Sal'ween or **Sal'win** (säl'wēn); *Chin.* **Lu Kiang** (lōō'jĭ·äng') or **Nu Kiang** (nōō'). 1 River ab. 1750 m. long in SE Asia; rises in Tanglha Mts., E Tibet, flows E through Sikang, then S through W Yunnan prov. of SW China; continues S through Shan States, Burma, and on into

Lower Burma, in its lower course forming a section of Siam-Burma boundary; empties into Gulf of Martaban at Moulmein. Its upper course in Tibet and China wild and picturesque, in places in China flows through gorges and bet. hills 3000 to 6000 ft. Navigable for native boats in several long sections. Crossed by Burma Road at the Huiting bridge (at alt. 2785 ft.) bet. Lungling and Paoshan in Yunnan. Has few tributaries. Its lower course scene of fighting in early 1942; its middle course in N Burma scene of fighting in 1944, esp. in May.

2 District, Tenasserim division, Lower Burma; 2582 sq. m.; pop. 53,186; ✳ Papun.

Sal·ya'ny or **Sal·ya'ni** (sŭl·yà'nĭ). Town, SE Azerbaidzhan, U.S.S.R., on the Kura in its delta 72 m. SW of Baku; pop. 12,589.

Sal'yers·ville (săl'yērz·vĭl; *Sou.* also -v'l). Town, ⊗ of Magoffin co., E Kentucky; pop. 1173.

Sal'zach (zäl'tsäk). River ab. 130 m. long in W Austria; rises in N slopes of Hohe Tauern, flows E and N through Salzburg prov. past Salzburg to the German border; continues N, forming the boundary bet. Bavaria, Germany, and Upper Austria; empties into Inn river ab. 30 m. N of Salzburg. See GOLLINGER.

Salz'burg (zälts'bŏŏrk; *Angl.* sôlz'bûrg). **1** Province of Austria. See *Table* at AUSTRIA.

2 *anc.* **Ju·va'vum** (jōō·vā'vŭm). Manufacturing city, its ✳, on Salzach river 71 m. ESE of Munich; pop. (1939) 77,523; summer resort; 17th-cent. Renaissance cathedral; two archiepiscopal palaces; university (founded 1622; reestablished 1964); manufactures include musical instruments, marble ornaments, iron goods, cement, artificial wool; birthplace of Mozart. Of ancient Celtic origin; ruled for more than ten centuries by prince-archbishops.

Salz'git'ter; *formerly* **Wa'ten·stedt–Salzgitter** (vä'tĕn·shtĕt·zälts'gĭt'ēr). City, SE Lower Saxony, W Germany, SW of Brunswick; steel mills; pop. 105,433.

Salz'kam'mer·gut' (zälts'käm'ēr·gōōt'). District in Styria and Upper Austria provs. of Austria; contains great salt deposits, used from prehistoric times. Now a tourist resort with picturesque lakes, mountains (Dachstein) in S part, and several small towns, esp. Hallstatt (*q.v.*), noted for its early cultural remains.

Salz'we'del (zälts'vä'dĕl). City, Magdeburg dist., East Germany, 55 m. NNW of Magdeburg; pop. 14,916; manufactures chemicals, calico, beet sugar, straw rope, beer, bakery products. Probably founded in 8th cent.; became city 1223; a Hanse Town.

Sa'ma (sä'mä). **1** See LANGREO.

2 River ab. 250 m. long, Tacna dept., S Peru; flows into Pacific Ocean.

Samakov. = SAMOKOV.

Sa'mal (sä'mäl). Island ab. 17 m. long, N end of Davao Gulf, Davao prov., Mindanao, Phil. Is.; 96 sq. m.; pop. 7473; coextensive with municipality of Samal (village of Samal on W coast). Forms shelter for Davao harbor to the W. Occupied by Americans May 8, 1945.

Sa·ma'les (sä·mä'lås). Group of islands, E Sulu Archipelago, Phil. Is., E of Jolo and SW of Basilan; ab. 45 sq. m.; comprises ab. 20 small islands; largest, Tongquil I. (19 sq. m.) and most important, Balanguingui I. Chief town Tungkil, pop. (municipal district) 2893.

Samana. See ATWOOD CAY.

Sa'ma·ná (sä'mä·nä'). **1** Province, NE Dominican Republic. See *Table* at DOMINICAN REPUBLIC.

2 *formerly* **San'ta Bár'ba·ra de Samaná** (sän'tä vär'vä·rä thä). Commune, its ✳, NE Dominican Republic; pop. 15,723; cacao, coconuts, honey, wax.

Samaná, Bay of. Inlet 40 m. long on NE coast of Dominican Republic; extends E and W, protected on N by **Cape Samaná** which extends E from coast.

Samanala. See ADAM'S PEAK.

Samannud. See SEBENNYTUS.

Sa'man·ti' (sä'män·tĭ'). River ab. 100 m. long, the W headstream of the Seyhan river in E cen. Turkey in Asia;

rises at N end of Anti-Taurus Mts. and flows S into the Seyhan at ab. 37°30'N.

Sa'mar (sä'mär). Island, one of the Visayan Is., E Phil. Is.; 5124 sq. m.; constitutes with adjacent islands a province, 5309 sq. m., pop. 546,306, ✳ Catbalogan. Of irregular shape, having many inlets and offshore islands, 150 m. long from NW to SE and ab. 75 m. at widest point and third in size of the Philippines group. Touches San Bernardino Strait on NW, Pacific Ocean on N and E, Leyte Gulf on S, and Samar Sea on W; on SW separated from Leyte by very narrow San Juanico Strait. Has very rugged surface so that density of population is not large; mountains low, highest point 2789 ft. in N cen. part. Well watered, with many short navigable rivers on both coasts. Its climate healthful but because of its frontage on the Pacific is at times exposed to violent typhoons. Agriculture not extensively pursued; rice, coconuts, cacao, and abacá are raised. Inhabitants are mainly Visayans, with some Bikols and Tagalogs. Chief towns Catbalogan, Basey, Calbayog, Guiuan, and Borongan.

History: First island of archipelago discovered 1521 by Spaniards (first landing on Homonhon, *q.v.*); in early times under jurisdiction of Cebu; united with Leyte in separate province 1735 but after 1768 constituted a province by itself; until beginning of 19th cent. often attacked by Moro pirates; granted civil government June 1902; came under Japanese control 1942; retaken by Americans Oct. 1944.

Sa·ma'ra (sŭ·mà'rà; *Angl.* sà·mâr'à). **1** River ab. 360 m. long in Chkalov and Kuibyshev Regions, SE Soviet Russia, Europe, flowing W into the Volga river at Kuibyshev. Buzuluk is on it.

2 Region and city. See KUIBYSHEV.

Sa'ma·rai' (sä'mä·rī'). Village and port of entry on small island off SE tip of the Territory of Papua, New Guinea, just SE of Milne Bay; important as commercial and shipping center. Nearly destroyed by Japanese Jan. 1942.

Samarang. See SEMARANG.

Sa·mar'i·a (sà·mâr'ĭ·à). **1** = ISRAEL, or Northern Kingdom; the territory occupied by the Ten Tribes (*1 Kings* xxi. 1; *2 Kings* xvii. 24).

2 District of ancient Palestine, in cen. part, extending from the Mediterranean to the Jordan and lying S of Galilee and N of Judaea. In 6 A.D. made by Augustus a division of the province of Judaea.

3 District of modern Palestine, in N cen. part, formerly a part of the Haifa-Samaria dist.; includes the subdistricts Jenin, Nablus, Tulkarm; 1263 sq. m.; pop. 156,445, (1942 est.) 222,734; ✳ Nablus; parts included in new state of Israel 1948.

4 *modern* **Se·bas'tye** (sä·bŏs'tĭ·yà; -yä). City, ✳ of ancient Samaria, in Palestine, and of the kingdom of Israel; the Holy City of the Samaritans. On N and S highway ab. midway bet. the Mediterranean and the Jordan and 35 m. N of Jerusalem. Built on a hill 887 B.C. by Omri; strengthened by Ahab and its idolatry and corruption led to complete overthrow by Shalmaneser V and Sargon II 724–721 B.C. (*2 Kings* xvii. 3–6); inhabitants transported into captivity; taken by Alexander and in 107 B.C. by John Hyrcanus, who destroyed it.

Sam'a·rin'da (săm'à·rĭn'dà). Coastal town, E Borneo, Indonesia, on lower course of Mahakam river ab. 30 m. from its mouth; pop. 11,086; important trading town for products of the river region, also for nearby coal and oil fields. Town and airport occupied by Japanese Jan. 1942.

Sam'ar·kand (săm'ēr·kănd; săm'ēr·kănd'); *Turki* **Sa'mar·qand'** (sä'mär·känd'). **1** Former province, Russian Turkistan; ab. 26,620 sq. m.; now incorporated in Uzbek S.S.R.

2 Region, N Uzbek S.S.R., Soviet Central Asia.

3 City, cen. Uzbek S.S.R., Soviet Central Asia, in fertile valley of the Zeravshan 180 m. SW of Tashkent; pop.

134,346; has beautiful and healthful location on W spurs of Alai Mts., alt. 2358 ft. Citadel separates native part from new Russian city which has modern industrial developments and railroad connections with Chkalov and the S Caspian. Has several notable Moslem colleges, palace and tomb of Tamerlane, minarets, shrines, etc. One of the oldest cities in the Soviet Union; as **Mar'a-can'da** (mär'á-kăn'dá), capital of Sogdiana, destroyed by Alexander the Great 329 B.C.; Clitus slain here by Alexander 328 B.C.; again became important 7th cent. A.D.; on the "Silk Route" from China to Europe; conquered by Arabs 710–712 A.D.; under Samanids (874–999) and successors a famous seat of Arab culture; besieged and destroyed by Genghis Khan 1221 but later (1370) made the capital of Tamerlane's empire. By 1700 almost uninhabited; came in time under the Chinese, the emir of Bukhara, and the Russians, who took it under Gen. Kaufmann 1868 after a bitter struggle; in 1924 included in the Uzbek S.S.R. and until 1930 was its capital.

Samarobriva. See AMIENS.

Samarovo or **Samarovsk.** See OSTYAGO-VOGULSK.

Samarqand. See SAMARKAND.

Sa·mar'ra (să-mŭr'rä). Town, N cen. Iraq, 65 m. NNW of Baghdad, on the E bank of the Tigris river; pop. ab. 8000; head of navigation for small steamers. In 9th cent. residence of Abbasside rulers. Sacred to Shiite Moslems. Occupied by British Apr. 23, 1917.

Sa'mar Sea (sä'mär). Interisland body of water, E Phil. Is., bounded by Luzon on N, Samar on E, Leyte on S, and Masbate on W; connects by San Bernardino Strait with the Pacific on N and joins Visayan Sea on SW.

Sa·mas'si (să-mäs'sĕ) or **Sa·mas'su** (-sōō). River ab. 50 m. long in S Sardinia; flows S into Gulf of Cagliari at Cagliari.

Sa·ma'wa (să-mä'wá; -wä). Town, SE cen. Iraq, on the right bank of the Euphrates river near the lower junction of the Hindiya with the main stream; pop. ab. 10,000; an important trade and agricultural center on the Baghdad-Basra railroad and on caravan routes from Basra to Hilla and An Najaf.

Sam'bal·pur (sŭm'bál-pŏŏr). Town, N Orissa state, E Indian Union, on N bank of Mahanadi river 140 m. NW of Cuttack; pop. 15,017; * of former Orissa Feudatory States.

Sam'bas (säm'bäs). **1** River ab. 90 m. long in NW West Borneo, Indonesia, Malay Archipelago; flows W and SW into South China Sea.
2 Former native state in NW part of West Borneo residency, W Borneo, Neth. Indies; 4756 sq. m.; pop. 184,407. Large Chinese population; rich gold mines.
3 Town on Sambas river ab. 30 m. from its mouth; pop. ab. 12,000.

Sam'bhal (sŭm'bál). Town, Rohilkhand division, NW cen. Uttar Pradesh, N Indian Union, 80 m. E of Delhi; pop. (1941) 53,887.

Sam·bia'se (säm-byä'zå). Commune, Catanzaro prov., Calabria, S Italy, 19 m. WNW of Catanzaro; pop. (1931) 15,093; hot sulfur springs; health resort.

Sam·bo'dja (säm-bō'jä). Oil field near Balikpapan, E coast of Borneo, Indonesia; captured by Australians July 18, 1945.

Sam'bor (säm'bôr). Manufacturing commune, W Ukraine, U.S.S.R., on Dniester river 50 m. WSW of Lvov; formerly in Lwów dept., Poland; pop. (1938–39 est.) 23,500; a railroad junction town.

Sam'bo·rom·bón' Bay (säm'bŏ-rôm-bôn'). Inlet of Atlantic Ocean S of the mouth of Río de la Plata on E coast of Buenos Aires prov., E Argentina.

Sam'bre (sän'br'). River ab. 100 m. long in N France and S cen. Belgium; rises in Aisne dept., N France, flows ENE across the Belgian border and into the Meuse river at Namur; scene of British victory Nov. 1918.

Sam·mam'ish Lake (să-măm'ĭsh). Lake 9 m. long in King co., W cen. Washington.

Sam·nan' (săm·năn'). Town, * of Samnan-Damghan prov., N cen. Iran, S of Elburz Mts.; pop. ab. 16,000; on Tehran-Meshed highway 110 m. E of Tehran (145 m. by the highway). A place of great age.

Samnan–Dam·ghan' (-däm·gän'). Province, N cen. Iran; 36,270 sq. m.; * Samnan.

Sam'ni·um (săm'nĭ-ŭm). Country in ancient cen. Italy, the modern Abruzzi e Molise compartimento and part of Campania compartimento. Its inhabitants, the Samnites, were enemies of the Romans until conquered c. 290 B.C.; they spoke Oscan.

Sa·mo'a (să-mō'á) or **Samoa Islands.** **1** formerly **Nav'i·ga'tors Islands** (năv'ĭ-gā'tẽrz). Group of islands in SW cen. Pacific Ocean N of Tonga Is. and NE of Fiji Is.; ab. 4200 m. SW of San Francisco; bet. 13°25′ and 14°30′S lat. and 168° and 173°W long.; 1209 sq. m.; pop. ab. 78,000. Formerly a kingdom; now divided (see below) into **American Samoa**, islands E of 171°W long., 76 sq. m., pop. (1941) 13,273, and **Territory of Western Samoa**, islands W of 171°W long., trust territory of New Zealand, 1133 sq. m., pop. (1943) 64,671. Islands are volcanic, with soil generally fertile; copra is chief commercial product. Natives are of pure Polynesian race; the island group was probably for centuries the cradle of Polynesian settlement.

History: Discovered 1722 by Jacob Roggeveen, a Dutchman; visited 1768 and named (Navigators Islands) by Louis de Bougainville; visited by U.S. naval officers Charles Wilkes 1839 and Richard Meade 1872, the latter visit ultimately resulting in securing Pago Pago (*q.v.*) as U.S. naval base; under native rulers until c. 1860; U.S., British, and German interest in islands produced period of international friction and internal dissension culminating in civil war and German intervention 1887; tense situation eased by destruction of U.S. and German naval forces (3 warships each; the single British warship escaped) in harbor of Apia by terrific hurricane of Mar. 15–16, 1889; neutrality and independence of islands under three-power supervision established by tripartite agreement 1889; difficulties in administration led to agreement of 1899 by which, Britain having ceded her interests to Germany in exchange for territory elsewhere, the islands were divided bet. U.S. and Germany (see above); German Samoa mandated to New Zealand 1919. See also AMERICAN SAMOA and Territory of WESTERN SAMOA.
2 Former German colony, comprising the islands in the Samoa group W of long. 171°W; now a trust territory of New Zealand as Territory of Western Samoa (*q.v.*).
3 Short for AMERICAN SAMOA.

Sam'o·gi'ti·a (săm'ŏ-jĭsh'ĭ-á; -jĭsh'á). Baltic region, coextensive with most of modern Lithuania, a lowland country N of the Neman; * Rossieny. In 14th cent. held by Teutonic Knights; surrendered to Poland by Treaty of Thorn (Toruń) 1411.

Sa'mo·kov (sä'mō-kôf). Town, Sofia dept., W Bulgaria, 30 m. SSE of Sofia; pop. (1926) 10,432.

Sa'mos (sä'mŏs; *Mod. Gr.* sä'mŏs). **1** *Turk.* **Su·sam'-A·da·si'** (sōō-säm'ä-dä-sĭ'). Island in Aegean Sea off W coast of Turkey in Asia; 181 sq. m.; pop. 58,584; with Ikaria I. forms a department of Greece (see *Table* at GREECE). By some considered an island of the Southern Sporades (see SPORADES). Mountainous with highest point 4725 ft. at W end; has very fertile soil and exports wine, tobacco, raisins, and olive oil. Settled by Ionians at early period; became great commercial center with trade throughout ancient world. Under the tyrant Polycrates (c. 535–522 B.C.) also a cultural center, esp. in sculpture; great Temple of Hera built. Birthplace of Pythagoras ("Samian Sage"). Conquered by Persia but freed after battle of Mycale 479 B.C.; member of Delian League and later subject for varying periods to Athens or Sparta, then to Rome, Byzantium, and Turks; passed to Greece 1912; under Axis control in World War II but retaken by British and Greek troops Oct. 6, 1944.

2 Ancient town on SE coast of Samos I., one of the 12 Ionian Cities; now in ruins.

Sa·mos'a·ta (sȧ·mŏs'ȧ·tȧ); *mod.* **Sam·sat'** (säm·sät'). Ruined city of ancient Syria on right bank of Euphrates river ab. 30 m. NNW of Edessa (mod. Urfa); Kurdish village of Samsat, SE Turkey in Asia, on its site. In ancient times an important crossing of the river; long a frontier fort, linked with Edessa, and a caravan station. Capital of Hellenistic kingdom of Commagene under Seleucids 3d cent. B.C., and later, 72 A.D., of a Roman province.

Sa'mo·sir', Pu'lau (pōō'lou sä'mô·sēr'). Island 30 m. long by ab. 10 m. wide in Lake Toba, N cen. Sumatra I., Indonesia.

Sam'o·thrace (săm'ô·thrās); *Gr.* **Sa·mo·thrá'kē** (sä'-mô·thrä'kyĕ); *anc.* **Sam'o·thra'ce** (săm'ô·thrā'sē) *or* **Sam'o·thra'cia** (-thrā'shȧ; -shĭ·ȧ). **1** Greek island in NE Aegean Sea 14 m. NNW of Turkish island of İmroz; belongs to Evros dept., Western Thrace, Greece; 68 sq. m.; pop. 3866. Has prominent peak 5905 ft., the highest point on any of the Aegean Is.; has no good harbor. Was not important politically in ancient times but here Demetrius Poliorcetes erected the famous sculpture known as the Nike of Samothrace (now in the Louvre, Paris) to commemorate a naval victory at Cyprus over the Egyptians 306 B.C. See AEGEAN ISLANDS.
2 Town on the island; pop. 2055.

Sam·pa'loc Point (säm·pä'lôk). Point at SW side of entrance to Subic Bay, S Zambales prov., Luzon, Phil. Is.

Sam'pang (säm'päng). Town near S coast of Madura I., East Java prov., Indonesia; pop. 12,673.

Sam'pan·man'gio, Cape (säm'pän·män'jō). North point of island of Borneo, Brit. North Borneo; in 7°N.

Sam'pier·da·re'na (säm'pyär·dä·rä'nä). Former commune, Genova prov., E cen. Liguria, NW Italy, now part of Genoa; pop. (1931) 53,176.

Samp'son (săm[p]'s'n). County in North Carolina. See *Table* at NORTH CAROLINA.

Samsat. See SAMOSATA.

Sam'shui' (säm'shwā'). Walled town and treaty port, cen. Kwangtung prov., SE China, on N bank of Si river at its junction with the Peh ab. 27 m. W of Canton; pop. (1931 est.) 9160; has large distribution trade by river junks and steamers; opened as treaty port 1897.

Sams'ö' (säms'û'). Island in Sjælland group, forming a part of Denmark, lying bet. W tip of the island of Sjælland and the E coast of Jutland Penin.; 15 m. long; 44 sq. m.; pop. (1925) 7295.

Sam'son (săm[p]'s'n). City, Geneva co., SE Alabama, 8 m. N of Florida border and 40 m. WSW of Dothan; pop. 1932.

Sam's Point (sămz). Peak 2255 ft. in Ulster co., SE New York; highest peak in the Shawangunk Mts.

Sam·sun' (säm·sōōn'). **1** Vilayet, N Turkey in Asia; 3555 sq. m.; pop. 337,817.
2 *anc.* **A·mi'sus** (ȧ·mī'sŭs). Seaport city, its ✳, on **Samsun Bay,** an inlet of the Black Sea, ab. 200 m. NE of Ankara; pop. (1940) 36,917; located bet. the deltas of the Kızıl Irmak and the Yeşil Irmak; has fair harbor and a thriving trade, serving as outlet for inland towns of N Turkey; exports esp. tobacco, also cereals and wool. Ancient Amisus was important Greek settlement on the Euxine and later a rich trading town of Pontus.

Sam'thar (sŭm'tēr). **1** Former Indian state, Bundelkhand, N Central India; area 189 sq. m.; pop. (1941) 38,279.
2 Town, its ✳, 55 m. SE of Gwalior; pop. 6966.

Sa'mui' *or* **Ko Samui** (kô sä'mŏō'ĭ). Island (Siamese *ko*) in SW Gulf of Siam off E coast of Isthmus of Kra 65 m. N of Nakhon Si Thammarat.

Sa·mut Pra·kan (sä·mŏŏt prä·kän), *or* **Pak·nam** (päknäm). **1** Province, S Thailand; 351 sq. m.; pop. 132,479.
2 Town, its ✳, lower port of Bangkok at the mouth of the Chao Phraya 12 m. SSE of the capital.

Samut Sa·khon (sä·k'hôn) *or* **Tha Chin** (t'hä chĕn);

also **Ma·ha Chai** (mä·hä chī). **1** Province, S Thailand; 293 sq. m.; pop. 84,200.
2 Town, its ✳, at mouth of Tha Chin river on left bank, ab. 21 m. SW of Bangkok.

Samut Song·khram (sŭng·k'hräm); *formerly* **Me·klong** (mä·klông). Seaport, W Thailand, at mouth of Klong river 40 m. SW of Bangkok.

San. See SAINT.

San (sän). River ab. 280 m. long in Rzeszów dept., SE Poland; flows out of the Carpathian Mts. NNW into Vistula river 4 m. NE of Sandomierz; formerly formed part of boundary bet. W Ukraine and Poland; battle line in several battles May 1915.

San·'a' *or* **San·aa'** (sŏn·ä'). Walled commercial city, cen. Yemen, SW Arabia; ✳ of Yemen; pop. ab. 25,000; in the mountains at an elevation of 7250 ft., connected by a highway with its port Hodeida ab. 40 m. distant. An old walled city, probably a center of the Himyarite kingdom; in Middle Ages held by Abyssinian rulers; later by Moslems and Turks as a holy Moslem city with 48 mosques. Has interesting ruins. See SHEBA and *History* at ADEN.

Sanafiri. Island in Red Sea. See TIRAN.

Sa'na·ga (sä'nȧ·gȧ). River ab. 430 m. long in Cameroun, W Africa; flows WSW into the Bight of Biafra opp. the island of Fernando Poo.

San A'gus·tin', Cape (sän ä'gōōs·tēn'). South extremity of long peninsula marking E side of Davao Gulf, SE Davao prov., Mindanao, Phil. Is., 6°17'N.

San Am·bro'sio (sän' äm·brō'zhō; *Span.* sän' äm·brō'syô). Island in Pacific Ocean ab. 550 m. off W cen. coast of Chile, close to San Félix I.; belongs to Chile.

Sa·na'na (sä·nä'nä). **1** *also, formerly,* **Su'la Be·si'** (sōō'lä bĕ·sē') *or* **Besi.** Island, smallest but most important of the three islands of the Sula Is., E of Celebes, Malay Archipelago.
2 Chief village of Sula Is. at N end of Sanana I.; residence of Dutch commissioner.

San'a·nan'da (sän'ȧ·nän'dȧ). Settlement on S coast of Holnicote Bay, N coast of E Papua, New Guinea I. Scene of final fighting in Buna-Gona campaign; Japanese army destroyed here Jan. 20–23, 1943.

Sanandaj. See SINNEH.

Sa'nan·di'ta (sä·nän·dē'tä). Town, S Bolivia, near the Argentine border; oil wells.

San An·dre'as (sän' ăn·drā'ăs; sän' ăn-). Village, ⊗ of Calaveras co., cen. California; pop. 1416.

San Andreas Rift. The zone of faults which extends along the coast of N California, through the San Francisco Penin., and SE toward the head of the Gulf of California; it was movement along a part of this zone that caused the San Francisco earthquake of 1906.

San An·drés' (sän' än·dräs'). **1** Small island in Caribbean Sea off E coast of Nicaragua; belongs to Colombia.
2 Town on island, ✳ of San Andrés y Providencia intendancy.

San Andrés It·za'pa (ĕt·sä'pä). Town, Chimaltenango dept., S cen. Guatemala; pop. 4608.

San An·dres' Mountains (sän' än·dräs'; sän' ăn-). Range in S cen. New Mexico, chiefly in S Socorro and N Dona Ana cos., E of the Rio Grande.

San An·drés' Tux'tla (sän' än·dräs' tōōs'tlä); *also* **Tuxtla.** Town, Veracruz state, E Mexico, 80 m. SE of Veracruz; pop. 10,154; center of research of joint expedition of National Geographic Society and Smithsonian Institution, where carved objects of early Maya civilization were found.

San Andrés y Pro'vi·den'cia (ê prō'vê·thän'syä). Intendancy of Colombia. See *Table* at COLOMBIA.

San Ánʹgel (sän äng'hĕl). Town, Federal District, cen. Mexico, SSW of Mexico City; pop. 9121; fruitgrowing.

San An'ge·lo (sän ăn'jĕ·lō). City and health resort, ⊗ of Tom Green co., W cen. Texas, 77 m. SSW of Abilene; pop. 58,815; distributing center for stock-raising, wool-growing, agricultural, and oil-field area; cattle, wool, and

mohair market; manufactures cottonseed oil, dairy and petroleum products, foundry and machine-shop products. Goodfellow Air Force Base, with U.S. Air Force Pilot School.

San An·sel'mo (săn' ăn·sĕl'mō; săn' ăn-). Residential town, Marin co., W California, 14 m. NW of San Francisco; pop. 11,584. San Francisco Theological Seminary (1871; coed.; Presbyterian).

San An·to'ni·o (săn' ăn·tō'nĭ·ō; săn' ăn-; *Span.* sän' än·tō'nyō; *the Texas river and city are in Texas colloquially sometimes* săn' ăn·tōn'). **1** River ab. 200 m. long, S Texas; rises in city of San Antonio, receives waters of Medina river in Bexar co., flows SE through Wilson, Karnes, and Goliad cos., forms boundary line bet. Refugio and Victoria cos., and empties into San Antonio Bay.

2 Commercial and industrial city and port of entry, ⊗ of Bexar co., S cen. Texas, on San Antonio river 74 m. SW of Austin; pop. 587,718; gateway to Mexico; connections with ports of Houston and Corpus Christi; distributing center, shipping point, and market for agricultural products, livestock, wool; produces, refines, and ships oil; meat packing, pecan shelling, brewing; manufactures iron and steel products, soap, condiments, flour, food, clothing; oil and gas fields nearby; winter and health resort; mineral springs. Military and aviation center; headquarters of Fort Sam Houston (1865); Kelly, Lackland, Brooks, and Randolph Air Force Bases, Camp Normoyle, and other military posts nearby. Incarnate Word Coll. (1881; women); Our Lady of the Lake Coll. (1896; women); St. Mary's Univ. of San Antonio (1852; coed.); Trinity University, moved from Waxahachie 1942 (1869; coed.).

History: Franciscan mission San Antonio de Valero (later the Alamo) and presidio and villa of San Antonio de Bexar (originally spelled Bejar) established 1718; villa of San Fernando, first regular civil municipality, established by Canary Islanders 1731; fort, villa, and settlement consolidated into San Antonio de Bexar (later called San Antonio) 1793–94; became city 1809. Figured in Franco-Spanish struggles, Mexican and Indian incursions, Mexican-Spanish War, Texas Revolution; served as military station and administrative center of Province of Texas; besieged and captured in battle of San Antonio 1835–36 and historic siege of the Alamo 1836 (recaptured following Texan victory at San Jacinto 1836).

3 Seaport and resort, Santiago prov., cen. Chile, 58 m. from Santiago; pop. 11,859.

4 Town, Central dept., cen. Paraguay, on Paraguay river SE of Asunción; pop. ab. 5500.

5 Municipality, SW Nueva Ecija prov., Luzon, Phil. Is., near right bank of Pampanga river W of San Isidro and 14 m. SSW of Cabanatuan; pop. 18,084.

6 Municipality, SW Zambales prov., Luzon, Phil. Is., near coast 10 m. NW of Subic; pop. 5164; Americans landed on coast bet. here and San Narciso Jan. 29, 1945.

San Antonio, Cape. 1 Cape extending into Atlantic Ocean on E coast of Buenos Aires prov., E Argentina, S of Samborombón Bay.

2 Cape at W extremity of Cuba, projecting into Yucatán Channel.

3 Cape on N coast of Alicante prov., SE Spain.

San Antonio Bay. Inlet of Gulf of Mexico, S Calhoun co., S Texas, receiving San Antonio river on N.

San An·to'nio de Ca·be'zas (săn' än·tō'nyō thä kä·vä'säs). Municipality, Matanzas prov., W cen. Cuba; pop. 9593.

San Antonio de las Ve'gas (läz vä'gäs). Municipality, La Habana prov., W Cuba, just S of Havana; pop. 8921.

San Antonio de las Vuel'tas (vwĕl'täs). Municipality, Las Villas prov., W cen. Cuba, 16 m. ENE of Santa Clara; pop. 28,209.

San Antonio de los Ba'ños (lōz vä'nyōs). Municipality and town, La Habana prov., W Cuba; town 20 m. SW of Havana, pop. (1943) 14,456.

San Antonio de los Co'bres (lōs kō'vräs). Town, ⁕ of former Los Andes territory, NW Argentina, now in Salta prov., 75 m. NW of Salta; pop. ab. 1000.

San An·to'ni·o Peak (săn' ăn·tō'nĭ·ō; săn' ăn-). **1** Mountain 10,080 ft. in Los Angeles co., S California, highest in San Gabriel Mountains.

2 Mountain 10,833 ft. in NE Rio Arriba co., N New Mexico.

San Au'gus·tine (săn ô'gŭs·tēn). **1** County in Texas. See *Table* at TEXAS.

2 Town, its ⊗, E Texas, 37 m. ENE of Lufkin; pop. 2584; in lumbering, farming, and livestock-raising section.

San Bar'to·lo·me'o in Gal'do (säm bär'tō·lō·mâ'ō ĕng gäl'dō). Commune, Benevento prov., Campania, S Italy, 24 m. NE of Benevento; pop. 10,434.

San Be·ne·det'to del Tron'to (säm bâ·nä·dĕt'tō dâl trōn'tō). Seaport, Ascoli Piceno prov., Marches, cen. Italy, on Adriatic 16 m. ENE of Ascoli Piceno; pop. 17,461.

San Benedetto Po (pō). Commune, Mantova prov., Lombardy, N Italy, 10 m. SE of Mantua; pop. 13,573.

San Be·ni'to (săn' bĕ·nē'tō). **1** County in California. See *Table* at CALIFORNIA.

2 City, Cameron co., S Texas, 18 m. N of Brownsville; pop. 16,422; agricultural and recreational center; ships citrus fruits and vegetables; canneries.

San Ber·nar·di'no (*Eng.* săn bûr'nēr·dē'nō; *Span.* säm bĕr'när·thē'nō; *Ital.* säm bär·när·dē'nō). **1** County in California. See *Table* at CALIFORNIA.

2 City, its ⊗, SE California, 55 m. E of Los Angeles; pop. 91,922; site named 1810, settled 1851, laid out 1853; incorporated as town 1868, as city 1886; in agricultural and mining region; health resort. U.S. Air Force base.

3 See SAN BERNARDINO STRAIT.

4 Mountain pass in Lepontine Alps, alt. 6767 ft., Graubünden canton, SE Switzerland, on highway SW of Splügen.

San Bernardino Mountain. Peak 10,630 ft. in San Bernardino Mts., S California.

San Bernardino Mountains. Mountain range in SW San Bernardino co., extending SE into cen. Riverside co., S California; one of the series of ranges bordering the Mojave Desert on the SW; between the San Gabriel Mts. and the San Jacinto Mts.; highest point San Gorgonio Mt., 11,485 ft., located at SE end.

San Bernardino Strait. Strait bet. S Sorsogon prov., SE Luzon, and N end of Samar I., Phil. Is., ab. 27 m. long by 5 m. wide at narrowest point; by some extended to include Ticao Pass (*q.v.*). The main entrance to the Philippine Is. from the E forming with the Sibuyan Sea and Verde Island Passage the main channel for ships from U.S. and the Pacific to Manila and the South China Sea. In Pacific at E end is **San Bernardino** rock, an islet 7 m. off Bulusan, on which is one of most important lighthouses in the archipelago. Scene of great naval battle Oct. 24–25, 1944 in which one part of Japanese fleet was decisively defeated. Islands in it seized by U.S. forces Jan.–Mar. 1945.

San Ber·nar'do (săn' bĕr·när'dō; *Span.* säm' bĕr·när'thō). **1** City, Santiago prov., cen. Chile, 10 m. S of Santiago; pop. 20,673.

2 Group of small islands in the Caribbean Sea off NW coast of Colombia, at entrance to Gulf of Morrosquillo.

San Blas, Cape (săn bläs'). Low point of land projecting into Gulf of Mexico from SW coast of Gulf co., NW Florida.

San Blas, Cor'dil·le'ra de (kôr'thĕ·yä'rä thä säm bläs'). Range in NE Panama, S of the Gulf of San Blas.

San Blas, Gulf of (săn bläs'; *Span.* säm bläs'). Inlet of the Caribbean Sea on the N coast of Panama, E of the Panama Canal.

San Blas, Isthmus of. Narrowest section of the Isthmus of Panama (*q.v.*), bet. the Gulf of San Blas on the N and the Bay of Panama on the S; ab. 31 m. wide.

San Blas, Point. Cape on N coast of Panama, N of the Gulf of San Blas.

San'born (săn'bĕrn). County in South Dakota. See *Table* at SOUTH DAKOTA.

San Bru'no (săn brōō'nō). City, San Mateo co., W California, S of San Francisco; pop. 29,063.

San Buenaventura. See VENTURA seaport, California.

San Car'los (săn kär'lŭs). **1** River ab. 40 m. long, SE Arizona; forms part of NW boundary of Graham co.; flows in curve W to S and into San Carlos Reservoir formed by the Coolidge Dam (see UNITED STATES, *Dams and Reservoirs*).
2 Residential city, San Mateo co., W California, 17 m. SE of San Francisco; pop. 21,370; incorporated 1925.

San Car'los (*Span.* säng kär'lōs). **1** Town, Ñuble prov., S cen. Chile, 15 m. N of Chillán; pop. 9411.
2 River 75 m. long in Costa Rica; flows NE into the San Juan river.
3 Municipality, cen. Pangasinan prov., Luzon, Phil. Is., on Manila-Dagupan R.R. 10 m. SE of Lingayen; pop. 47,334; largest town in the province; on border of Agno delta.
4 Municipality, NE Negros Occidental, Negros, Phil. Is., near N end of Tañon Strait 33 m. ESE of City of Bacolod; pop. 69,990; largest town in the province.
5 Town, Maldonado dept., S Uruguay, ab. 9 m. N of Maldonado and 65 m. E of Montevideo; pop. ab. 10,700.
6 Town, ✳ of Cojedes state, NW cen. Venezuela, ab. 130 m. SW of Caracas; pop. (1941 est.) 3650.

San Carlos de Bariloche. See BARILOCHE.

San Car'los Reservoir (săn kär'lŭs). See UNITED STATES, *Dams and Reservoirs* (Coolidge Dam).

San Ca·scia'no in Val di Pe'sa (säng' kä·shä'nō ĕm väl' dĕ pā'zä). Commune, Firenze prov., Tuscany, cen. Italy, 10 m. S by W of Florence; pop. 14,216.

San Ca·tal'do (säng' kä·täl'dō). Commune, Caltanissetta prov., cen. Sicily, 4 m. W of Caltanissetta; pop. 17,138; sulfur mining.

Sán'chez (sän'châs). Seaport commune, Samaná prov., NE Dominican Republic, 24 m. from Samaná; pop. (1941) 7846; produces cacao, coffee, rice, coconuts.

San'chi (sän'chĭ). Village, W Madhya Pradesh, N cen. Indian Union, ab. 23 m. NE of Bhopal. Site of several Buddhist topes or stupas, the oldest buildings now standing in India; erected either in the time of or before King Asoka c. 250 B.C. The Great Stupa (or Tope) is a memorial shrine in the shape of a solid dome of stone and brick, ab. 103 ft. in diameter and 42 ft. high.

San Ci'pri·a'no Bay (sän thē'prē·ä'nō; sän sē'-). Bay on SW coast of Spanish Sahara, NW Africa.

San Cle·men'te (säng' klĕ·mĕn'tĕ). **1** City, Orange co., SW California, SE of Los Angeles; pop. 8527.

San Cle·men'te (säng' klä·mān'tä). Peak 13,314 ft. in S Argentina, near Lake Buenos Aires and the Chilean border.

San Cle·men'te Island (săn' klĕ·mĕn'tĕ). Island in SW part of Santa Barbara group in Pacific Ocean, S of Santa Catalina I.; part of Los Angeles co., SW California; U.S. naval base.

San·co' Point (säng·kō'). Point, E coast of Mindanao, Phil. Is., at S end of Surigao prov., 8°15′N.

San Cris·to'bal (sän' krĭs·tō'b'l; *Span.* säng' krĕs·tō'väl). **1** Mountain ab. 4900 ft. on SE border of Laguna prov., Luzon, Phil. Is., partly in Tayabas prov.; an extinct volcano with beautiful fresh-water lake in its crater.
2 *or* **Ma·ki'ra** (mä·kē'rä); *also* **San Cris·to'val** (sän' krĭs·tō'v'l; *Span.* säng' krĕs·tō'väl). Island in S Solomon Is., W Pacific Ocean, 38 m. SE of Guadalcanal; 80 m. long and 22 m. wide at greatest width. Somewhat mountainous; most of its settlements, including Kira Kira, location of the government station, and Star Harbour, are along the N shore.

San Cris·tó'bal (sän' krĭs·tō'b'l; *Span.* säng' krĕs·tō'väl). **1** Municipality, Pinar del Río prov., W Cuba, on railroad 45 m. ENE of Pinar del Río; pop. 19,695.

2 Commune (1941 pop. 83,374) and town (1944 est. pop. 7923), ✳ of Trujillo prov., S Dominican Republic.

3 *or* **Pro·gre'so** (prō·grä'sō). Seaport town, ✳ of Colón territory (Galápagos Is.), Ecuador, on San Cristóbal I.
4 *also known as* **Chat'ham Island** (chăt'ăm). One of the Galápagos Is. (*q.v.*); ab. 24 m. long, 8 m. wide; produces sugar cane, coffee; only town is San Cristóbal or Progreso, administrative center of the islands.
5 Lake in the Valley of Mexico, cen. Mexico, 12 m. NNE of the city of Mexico.
6 *in full* **San Cris·tó'bal de las Ca'sas** (säng' krĕs·tō'väl thä läs kä'säs). City, Chiapas state, SE Mexico, ab. 40 m. E of Tuxtla; pop. 11,768.
7 City, ✳ of Táchira state, W Venezuela; pop. (1941 est.) 31,344; in mountains at SW end of Cordillera Mérida and S of Lake Maracaibo, near Colombia border.

Sanc'ti Spí'ri·tus (sängk'tē spē'rĕ·tōōs). Municipality and town, E Las Villas prov., W cen. Cuba, 45 m. SE of Santa Clara; pop. (1943; town) 14,164; trading center for sugar and cattle.

San Cui·cuil'co (säng' kwĕ·kwēl'kō) *or* **Cuicuilco.** Hill ab. 12 m. S of Mexico City, Mexico; artificial mound, 412 ft. in diameter, 52 ft. high; probably an ancient temple.

San'cy', Puy de (pü·ēt' sän'sē'). Peak 6185 ft. in Puy-de-Dôme dept., S cen. France; highest peak of the Monts Dore in the Auvergne Mts.

San·da'kan (sän·dä'kän). Seaport town, NE Brit. North Borneo, on Sandakan Harbour, an inlet of the Sulu Sea having a length of 15 m. and an entrance 1¼ m. wide; pop. (1951) 14,499; a residency ✳, formerly ✳ of North Borneo, largest town in the colony; suffered much destruction during Japanese occupation 1942–45; capital transferred to Jesselton 1947.

Sandalwood Island. See SOEMBA.

San'day (sän'dā). Island 12 m. long in NE part of the Orkney Is. off N coast of Scotland; pop. 1160.

Sand'bach (sän[d]'băch). Urban district, Cheshire, NW England, 24 m. S of Manchester; pop. 9250.

San'de·fjord' (sän'ĕ·fyōr'; -fyōōr'). Seaport, Vestfold co., SE Norway, SSW of Oslo near the mouth of Oslo Fjord; pop. 5930; base for whaling fleets operating in Arctic waters; shipbuilding yards, whale-oil refineries, chemical works.

San'ders (sän'dērz). County in Montana. See *Table* at MONTANA.

San'der·son (sän'dēr·s'n). Town, ⊗ of Terrell co., W Texas, 55 m. SSE of Fort Stockton; pop. 2189; ships sheep, cattle, wool, mohair.

San'ders·ville (sän'dērz·vĭl; *Sou. also* -v'l). City, ⊗ of Washington co., cen. Georgia, 58 m. SW of Augusta; pop. 5425; established 1796; incorporated 1812; cotton trade and manufacturing center.

Sand'gate (sän[d]'gät; -gĭt). Seaport town, SE Queensland, Australia, suburb of Brisbane; pop. 8200.

Sand'ham'mar, Cape (sänd'häm'ēr; *Swed.* sänd'häm'mär). Cape on S extremity of Sweden, projecting into Baltic Sea at S side of Hanö Bay.

Sand'hurst (sänd'hûrst). **1** See BENDIGO, Australia.
2 Civil parish in Berkshire, S England; pop. 5244. Site of Royal Military Academy, founded 1799 as Royal Military College, merged 1946 with Royal Military Academy at Woolwich.

San·di'a Peak (sän·dē'ä). Mountain 10,609 ft. in SE Sandoval co., cen. New Mexico.

San Di·e'go (sän' dĭ·ā'gō). **1** County in California. See *Table* at CALIFORNIA.
2 Seaport and resort city, and port of entry, its ⊗, SW corner of California, on San Diego Bay ab. 12 m. N of Mexican border; pop. 573,224; excellent harbor; trade, distributing, and shipping center for fruit-raising section. Discovered 1542 by Don Juan Rodríguez Cabrillo, first white man to reach the W coast; site of San Diego de Alcala Mission 1769; pueblo organized 1835, thus making San Diego the oldest municipality in California; cap-

tured by Commodore Stockton 1846; site of World's Fair 1935. U.S. naval and marine base. San Diego State College (1897; coed.). See also UNITED STATES, *National Monuments* (Cabrillo National Monument), LA JOLLA.
3 City, ⊗ of Duval co., S Texas, 50 m. W of Corpus Christi; pop. 4351; livestock; oil and gas wells.
San Di·e′go, Cape (săn′ dĭ·ā′gō; *Span.* sän dyä′gŏ). Cape on E end of Tierra del Fuego I., S Argentina.
San Di·e′go Bay (săn′ dĭ·ā′gō). Inlet of Pacific Ocean in San Diego co., SW corner of California; 12 m. long, 1–3 m. wide; 22 sq. m.; landlocked; forms harbor for the city of San Diego.
San Die′go del Val′le (sän dyä′gŏ thĕl vä′yä). Municipality, Las Villas prov., W cen. Cuba, 12 m. NW of Santa Clara; pop. 14,421.
Sand Island (sănd). **1** See APOSTLE ISLANDS.
2 See MIDWAY.
Sandju. See SANJU.
Sand′ö′ (sän′û′). Island in S part of the Faeroes (*q.v.*); 43 sq. m.; pop. (1925) 1347.
San·do′mierz (sän·dô′myĕsh); *Russ.* **San′do·mir** (săn′dŏ·mĭr; *Russ.* săn·dŭ·myēr′). Commune, Kielce dept., Poland, on Vistula river 52 m. ESE of Kielce; pop. (1938–39 est.) 10,115; Gothic cathedral, Renaissance town hall. Dates from 11th cent.; important in Lithuanian history; frequently damaged in border wars; in World War II taken by Russians Aug. 16, 1944.
San Do·min′go (săn′ dŏ·mĭng′gō). = SANTO DOMINGO, early name of Dominican Republic and name of earliest settlement on Hispaniola.
San Domino. See TREMITI ISLANDS.
San Do·nà′ di Pia′ve (sän′ dŏ·nä′ dĕ pyä′vĕ). Commune, Venezia prov., Venezia Euganea, NE Italy, on Piave river 19 m. NE of Venice; pop. 22,849.
San·do′val (săn·dō′v'l). **1** County in New Mexico. See *Table* at NEW MEXICO.
2 Village, Marion co., S cen. Illinois, 7 m. N of Centralia; pop. 1356.
San′do·way (săn′dŏ·wā). **1** District, Arakan division, Lower Burma; 4157 sq. m.; pop. 129,245.
2 Town, its ✳, near coast of Bay of Bengal 63 m. WSW of Prome; pop. 4070.
San′down–Shank′lin (săn′doun·shăngk′lĭn). Urban district, E Isle of Wight, S England, on English Channel; pop. 12,693.
Sandown Park. Fashionable racecourse near Esher, Surrey, S England.
Sand′point′ (săn[d]′point′). City, ⊗ of Bonner co., N Idaho, on Pend Oreille Lake; 45 m. N of Coeur d'Alene; pop. 4355; lumbering.
San′dray (săn′drā). See BARRA.
San′dring·ham (săn′drĭng·ăm). **1** Town, S Victoria, SE Australia, SE suburb of Melbourne on Port Phillip Bay; pop. 18,079.
2 Village, Norfolk, E England, near E shore of the Wash; Sandringham House, royal residence.
Sand Springs. Industrial city, Tulsa co., NE Oklahoma, on Arkansas river 8 m. W of Tulsa; pop. 7754.
Sand′stone′ (sănd[d]′stōn′). Village, Pine co., E Minnesota, 58 m. SW of Duluth; pop. 1552; in agricultural and dairy-farming section.
San·dur′ (săn·door′). **1** Former Indian state, NW Madras States, S India, N of Mysore; 158 sq. m.; pop. (1941) 15,814.
2 Town, its ✳, ab. 25 m. W of Bellary; pop. 4226.
San·dus′ky (săn·dŭs′kĭ; săn-). **1** River ab. 150 m. long, N Ohio; rises in W Richland co., N cen. Ohio, flows W, then N into Sandusky Bay.
2 County in Ohio. See *Table* at OHIO.
3 City, ⊗ of Sanilac co., E Michigan, 38 m. NNW of Port Huron; pop. 2066; in cattle-raising section; dairy products.
4 Industrial city and port of entry, ⊗ of Erie co., N Ohio, on Lake Erie 50 m. W of Cleveland; pop. 31,989; excellent harbor; shipping point for coal, lumber, iron

ore, grain, fish; commercial fisheries; wineries, meat-packing and fruit-canning plants; manufactures clay products, crayons and artists' materials, paper boxes, foundry products; gypsum mines, gravel, sand, and clay deposits nearby. Settled 1816; became ⊗ 1838; incorporated 1845.
Sandusky Bay. Inlet of Lake Erie on N coasts of Sandusky and Erie cos., N Ohio; the city of Sandusky lies S of the entrance to the bay.
Sand′vi′ken (sänd′vē′kĕn). Town, Gävleborg prov., E Sweden, WSW of Gävle; pop. 17,182.
Sand′wich (săn[d]′wĭch; *Brit. also* -wĭj). **1** City, De Kalb co., N Illinois, 30 m. WNW of Joliet; pop. 3842.
2 Town, Barnstable co., SE Massachusetts, just S of Cape Cod end of Cape Cod Canal; pop. 2082; famous for glass made here c. 1827–88. Cape's oldest settlement, founded 1637.
3 Former town, Essex co., SE Ontario, Canada; annexed to Windsor 1935.
4 Municipal borough, Kent, SE England; pop. 4142; one of the Cinque Ports; famous golf links.
Sandwich Island. = EFATE.
Sandwich Islands. See HAWAII.
Sandwich Mountain. Mountain 3993 ft., Carroll and Grafton cos., New Hampshire, at W end of Sandwich Range.
Sandwich Range. Southern range of the White Mts., New Hampshire; highest point Passaconaway 4060 ft.; includes Mt. Chocorua 3475 ft.
San′dwip (sŭn′dwēp). Island at the E mouth, Ganges-Brahmaputra delta, East Bengal, Pakistan; 126 sq. m.; pop. 139,351.
Sand′y (săn′dĭ). **1** River 55 m. long, W Maine; rises in W Franklin co., flows SE and E into Kennebec river in S Somerset co.
2 = BIG SANDY river, Kentucky and West Virginia.
Sandy Cape. Cape, N point of Fraser I. off SE coast of Queensland, Australia, 24°30′S.
Sandy Hook. 1 Peninsula 6 m. long in NE Monmouth co., E cen. New Jersey, ab. 15 m. S of S tip of Manhattan I.; encloses **Sandy Hook Bay** (inlet of Raritan Bay) on W; lighthouse.
2 Subdivision (est. pop. 1500) of town of NEWTOWN, Connecticut.
3 City, ⊗ of Elliott co., NE Kentucky; pop. 195.
San Es′ta·nis·la′o (sän äs′tä·nēz·lä′ŏ). Town, San Pedro dept., cen. Paraguay, 90 m. NE of Asunción; pop. ab. 9690.
San Eugenio; *also* **San Eugenio del Cuareim.** See ARTIGAS.
San Fa·bian′ (säm′ fä·vyän′; *Angl.* săn fā′bĭ·ăn). Municipality, N Pangasinan prov., Luzon, Phil. Is., on SE shore of Lingayen Gulf 13 m. ENE of Lingayen; pop. 19,362; important coast town, scene of severe fighting on landing of American forces Jan. 1945.
San Fe·li′ce sul Pa·na′ro (säm′ fä·lē′chä sool pä-nä′rŏ). Commune, Modena prov., Emilia, N Italy, 17 m. NE of Modena; pop. 11,396.
San Fe·li′pe (säm′ fä·lē′pä). **1** Town, cen. Chile, ab. 48 m. N of Santiago; ⊗ of Aconcagua prov.; pop. 13,168.
2 Mountain 10,207 ft., cen. Oaxaca state, SE Mexico, N of Oaxaca near the Pan-American Highway.
3 City, ✳ of Yaracuy state, NW Venezuela, 125 m. W of Caracas; pop. (1941 est.) 10,133.
San Felipe de Puerto Plata. See PUERTO PLATA commune.
San Fe·li′u de Gui·xols′ (säm′ fä·lē′ōō thä gē·hōls′). Seaport, Gerona prov., Catalonia, NE Spain; pop. (1930) 9082.
San Fé′lix (säm fā′lĕks). Island in Pacific Ocean ab. 550 m. off W cen. coast of Chile, close to San Ambrosio I.; belongs to Chile.
San Fer·di·nan′do di Pu′glia (säm fär·dĕ·nän′dŏ dĕ pōol′yä). Commune, Foggia prov., Apulia, SE Italy, 29 m. SE of Foggia; pop. (1931) 11,256.

San Fer·nan'do (săn' fĕr·năn'dō). **1** City, Los Angeles co., SW California, enclave of Los Angeles; pop. 16,993; San Fernando Rey de España mission nearby.
2 Seaport, SW Trinidad, West Indies; pop. 14,353.
San Fer·nan·do (săn' fĕr·năn'dō; *Span.* säm' fĕr-nän'dô). **1** Seaport, Buenos Aires prov., E Argentina, on the Río de la Plata just N of Buenos Aires; pop. (est.) 46,950.
2 Town, cen. Chile, 80 m. S of Santiago; * of Colchagua prov.; pop. 14,419; founded by José Manso de Velasco 1742.
3 River ab. 170 m. long in N Tamaulipas state, Mexico; rises in mountains S of Monterrey and flows E into Laguna Madre.
4 Municipality on E coast of Cebu I., Phil. Is., on Bohol Strait 17 m. SW of City of Cebu; pop. 17,562.
5 Municipality, * of La Union prov., NW Luzon, Phil. Is., on the coast 45 m. N of Dagupan; pop. 23,366; has an excellent harbor sheltered by San Fernando Point and much coastal trade with Manila and other ports; on main W coast highway and terminus of railroad to Manila. Fishing is an important industry. Taken by Japanese Dec. 1941; fighting in American invasion Jan. 1945.
6 Municipality, * of Pampanga prov., cen. Luzon, Phil. Is., 35 m. NNW of Manila on tributary of the Pampanga river and on Manila-Dagupan R.R.; pop. 35,662; center of sugar industry and of a large area of rice cultivation. In reconquest of Philippines captured by Americans Jan. 29–30, 1945.
7 *formerly* **Is'la de Le·ón'** (ēz'lä thã lã·ôn'). Seaport, Cádiz prov., SW Spain, 7 m. SE of Cádiz; pop. 38,581; fortified town; naval academy, arsenal, southernmost observatory in Europe, Roman bridge.
8 *in full* **San Fer·nan'do de A·pu're** (säm' fĕr·nän'dô thã ä·pōō'rã). Town on Apure river, * of Apure state, W Venezuela, 185 m. S of Caracas; pop. (1941 est.) 8751.
San Fer·nan'do de A'ta·ba'po (säm' fĕr·nän'dô thã ä'tä·vä'pô). Town, former * of Amazonas territory, S Venezuela, on the Atabapo and Orinoco rivers.
San Fernando de Ca'ma·ro'nes (thã kä'mä·rô'näs). Municipality, Las Villas prov., W cen. Cuba, 25 m. WSW of Santa Clara; pop. 10,641.
San Fernando de Monte Cristi. See MONTECRISTI commune.
San Fer·nan'do Point (săn' fĕr·năn'dō; *Span.* säm' fĕr·nän'dô). Point on coast of NW Luzon, Phil. Is., La Union prov., 16°38'N, just W of San Fernando and marking northeasternmost point of Lingayen Gulf.
San Fer·nan'do Valley (săn' fĕr·năn'dō). Valley, Los Angeles co., S California, NW of cen. Los Angeles; partly included in city of Los Angeles; farming area, many suburban residential communities.
San'ford (săn'fĕrd). **1** City, ⊗ of Seminole co., cen. Florida penin., 20 m. NNE of Orlando; pop. 19,175; center of Florida's celery belt.
2 Industrial town, York co., SW Maine, 15 m. W of Biddeford; pop. 14,962; mohair-plush fabrics, blankets. Nasson Coll. at Springvale (1912; coed.).
3 City, ⊗ of Lee co., cen. North Carolina, 31 m. NNW of Fayetteville; pop. 12,253; in cotton, tobacco region.
Sanford, Mount. Mountain 16,208 ft. at W end of Wrangell Mts., S Alaska.
San Fran·cis'co (săn' frăn·sĭs'kō). **1** River 105 m. long, W New Mexico and E Arizona; rises in Catron co., W New Mexico, flows W across Arizona border and into the Gila river in Greenlee co., SE Arizona.
2 County in California. See *Table* at CALIFORNIA.
3 Seaport city, its ⊗, W California, on W side of San Francisco Bay and on Pacific Ocean and Golden Gate; pop. 742,855; magnificent harbor; connected with Marin co. to the N by Golden Gate bridge and with Yerba Buena I. (*q.v.*) and Oakland to the E by the Transbay bridge; financial, commercial, and industrial center, railroad terminus, and W coast shipping and distributing point; exports consist mainly of cereals, flour, fruit (esp.

canned and dried fruit), gold, silver, petroleum and petroleum products, and cotton; imports consist mainly of coffee, tea, silk, rubber, wool, sugar; industries include meat packing, sugar refining, coffee roasting and spice

SAN FRANCISCO AND VICINITY

grinding, printing and publishing, and machine shops. Univ. of San Francisco (1855; coed.); San Francisco Coll. for Women (1930); San Francisco State Coll. (1899; coed.); Univ. of California, Medical Center.
History: San Francisco Bay entered 1769 by Don Gaspar de Portolá, Spanish governor of Lower California; Spanish mission and presidio established on site 1776 by Juan Bautista de Anza; pueblo called Yerba Buena established 1777 by Padre Junípero Serra; passed from Spanish to Mexican control 1821 after Mexico's successful revolution against Spain; occupied by U.S. naval base under Capt. J. B. Montgomery July 9, 1846; name changed to San Francisco 1847; growth stimulated by gold discoveries in nearby areas 1848; incorp. as city 1850, and lawlessness curbed by vigilance committees; made terminus of Pony Express 1860, and of first transcontinental railroad 1869; suffered serious damage from an earthquake and subsequent fire Apr. 18, 1906 (see SAN ANDREAS RIFT). Site of organization meeting of United Nations Apr.–June 1945.
4 = SÃO FRANCISCO.
San Fran·cis'co (săn' frăn·sĭs'kō; *Span.* säm' frän-sēs'kô). **1** Town, Córdoba prov., N cen. Argentina; pop. (est.) 19,651; midway bet. Córdoba and Santa Fe.
2 Town, NE El Salvador, * of Morazán dept.; pop. 9514.
3 Municipality on SE coast of Pacijan I., Camotes Is., Cebu prov., Phil. Is., ab. 41 m. NE of City of Cebu; pop. 16,980; largest town of the Camotes.
San Fran·cis'co, Pa'so de (pä'sô thã säm' frän-sēs'kô). Andean mountain pass on Argentina-Chile border, bet. NW Catamarca prov., NW Argentina, and E cen. Atacama prov., N cen. Chile; altitude 15,505 ft.
San Fran·cis'co Bay (săn' frăn·sĭs'kō). Inlet of Pacific Ocean ab. 60 m. long (N-S, including San Pablo Bay) and 3 to 12 m. wide, W cen. California, connecting with the Pacific through the Golden Gate (*q.v.*); the city of San Francisco is S of its Pacific entrance and the city of Oakland is on its E shore. See SAN PABLO BAY and SUISUN BAY.
San Fran·cis'co de la Sel'va (säm' frän-sēs'kô thã lä sĕl'vä). = COPIAPÓ.
San Francisco de Li·ma'che (thã lē·mä'chã). Town, Valparaíso prov., cen. Chile; pop. 6322.
San Francisco del O'ro (thĕl ō'rô). Town, Chihuahua state, N Mexico; pop. 10,809.
San Francisco del Rin·cón' (rĕng·kôn'). Town, Guanajuato state, cen. Mexico, 35 m. W of Guanajuato; pop. 12,015.

San Francisco de Ma′co·rís′ (thä mä′kô·rēs′). Commune (1941 pop. 61,712) and city (1944 est. pop. 15,418), N cen. Dominican Republic, * of Duarte prov.; produces sugar, molasses, wax, timber.

San Francisco de Pau′la, Cape (thä pou′lä). Cape extending into Atlantic Ocean on E coast of Santa Cruz territory, S Argentina.

San Fran·cis′co Peaks (săn′ frăn·sĭs′kō); *also* **San Francisco Mountain**. Three peaks in S cen. Coconino co., N Arizona: Humphreys, or **San Francisco Mountain**, 12,611 ft., highest point in Arizona; Agassiz 12,340 ft.; and Fremont 11,940 ft.

San Francisco Range. Range in W Catron co., W New Mexico, extending across border into Arizona.

San Fra·tel′lo (säm′ frä·tĕl′lô). Commune, Messina prov., NE Sicily, 54 m. WSW of Messina; pop. 10,737; ruined 1754 and 1922 by landslides. Founded by Lombards.

San Fructuoso. See TACUAREMBÓ.

San′ga (săng′gà). River ab. 400 m. long in the Congo Republic, E equatorial Africa; flows S into the Congo river.

San Ga′bri·el (săn gā′brĭ·ĕl; *Span.* säng gä′vrĕ·ĕl′). **1** River ab. 60 m. long, SW California; rises in San Gabriel Mts., flows SW across Los Angeles co. into Pacific Ocean near Long Beach.
2 Residential city, Los Angeles co., SW California, 8 m. ENE of Los Angeles; pop. 22,561; San Gabriel Arcángel mission nearby; starting point for colonizers of Los Angeles 1781.
3 Town, Carchi prov., N Ecuador, ab. 80 m. NNE of Quito, in Andes Mts.; pop. (1944 est.) 7847.
4 Cape on E cen. Lower California projecting into the Gulf of California.

San Ga′bri·el′ Chi·lac′ (säng gä′vrĕ·ĕl′ chĕ·läk′). Town, Puebla state, SE cen. Mexico, 60 m. SE of Puebla; pop. 6091.

San Ga′bri·el Dams (săn gā′brĭ·ĕl). See UNITED STATES, *Dams and Reservoirs.*

San Ga′bri·e′le, Mount (säng gä′brĕ·â′lä). Peak 2119 ft., Slovenia, NW Yugoslavia, NE of Gorizia, Italy.

San Ga′bri·el Mountains (săn gā′brĭ·ĕl). Mountain range in SW California, SW of Mojave Desert, between it and coastal plain in which Los Angeles is situated; chiefly in Los Angeles co.; highest point San Antonio Peak 10,080 ft.

San Gal·lán′ (säng′ gä·yän′). Island in Pacific Ocean off W cen. coast of Peru.

San′ga·mon (săng′gà·mŭn). **1** River 225 m. long, cen. Illinois; rises in S McLean co., flows SW and W into Illinois river at NW extremity of Cass co.
2 County in Illinois. See *Table* at ILLINOIS.

San·gan′, Koh-i- (kō′hē·säng·gän′). Peak 12,872 ft. in cen. Afghanistan, SW of Herat.

Sangarius. See SAKARYA.

Sang·a′ Sang·a′ (säng·ä′ säng·ä′). Island, SW Sulu Archipelago, SW Phil. Is., separated by narrow strait from W Tawitawi I.; 18 sq. m.; pop. 1485; forms part of Bonggaw municipality. Airfield seized by American forces Apr. 2, 1945.

San·gay′ (säng·gī′). Volcano 17,749 ft. high in cen. Ecuador.

Sang′er (săng′ēr). City, Fresno co., S cen. California, 14 m. ESE of Fresno; pop. 8072; fruit growing and packing, truck farming; lumber, boxes, cement pipe; raisins, wine.

Sang′er·hau′sen (zäng′ēr·hou′zĕn). City, Halle dist., E Germany, 37 m. NNE of Erfurt; pop. 11,951; vast municipal rose gardens; manufactures machinery, foodstuffs, wooden goods. First mentioned 991 A.D.

San Ger·mán′ (säng′ hĕr·män′). Municipality (pop. 27,667) and town (pop. 7790), SW Puerto Rico; first settled early in the 16th cent.; church built 1538 by Dominican friars. Inter American Univ. of Puerto Rico (1912; coed.).

San Germano. See CASSINO.

Sang′er·ville (săng′ēr·vĭl). Town, Piscataquis co., N cen. Maine, 8 m. W of Dover-Foxcroft; pop. 1157; birthplace of Sir Hiram Maxim.

Sang′i·he (säng′ĭr), *or* **Sang′i** (säng′ē), **Islands.** Group of volcanic islands, Indonesia, bet. NE end of Celebes I. and S end of Mindanao I. and SW of the Talaud group; 314 sq. m.; pop. 134,904; main islands are Sangihe, Siau, Tahulandang, and Biaro. Largest of the group at N end, **Sangihe,** *formerly* **Great Sang′ir** (säng′ĭr), ab. 30 m. long by 8 to 17 m. wide, suffered from destructive eruptions of volcano Gunung Awu (6102 ft.) in 1856 and 1892; has very fertile soil; raises much copra and some hemp and nutmegs; chief town Tahuna. First came under Dutch 1677.

San Gil (säng hēl′). Town, Santander dept., N cen. Colombia, S of Bucaramanga; pop. 7811.

San Gi·mi·gna′no (sän′ jĕ·mē·nyä′nô). Commune, Siena prov., Tuscany, cen. Italy, 19 m. NW of Siena; pop. 11,270; numerous medieval towers (some destroyed in World War II), walls, gates, and several 13th-cent. and 14th-cent. palaces, 12th-cent. cathedral, and 13th-cent. church of St. Augustine.

San Gior′gio a Cre·ma′no (sän jôr′jô [jôr′jō] ä krä-mä′nô). Commune, Napoli prov., Campania, S Italy, on Bay of Naples 3 m. E by S of Naples; pop. (1931) 12,026.

San Giorgio Mag·gio′re (mäd·jō′rä). Island in the Lagoon of Venice, NE Italy.

San Gio·van′ni in Fio′re (sän′ jô·vän′nē ēm fyō′rä). Commune, Cosenza prov., Calabria, S Italy, 23 m. E by S of Cosenza; pop. 14,556; 12th-cent. convent.

San Giovanni in Per·si·ce′to (ēm pär·sĕ·chä′tô). Commune, Bologna prov., Emilia, N Italy, 13 m. NNW of Bologna; pop. 20,859.

San Giovanni Ro·ton′do (rô·tôn′dô). Commune, Foggia prov., Apulia, SE Italy, 19 m. NNE of Foggia; pop. 13,093.

San Giovanni Val·dar′no (väl·där′nô). Commune, Arezzo prov., Tuscany, cen. Italy, 20 m. WNW of Arezzo; pop. 10,631; lignite mining.

Sangir. Var. of *Sangi:* see SANGIHE ISLANDS.

San Giu·sep′pe Ve·su·via′no (sän′ jōō·zĕp′pā vä-zōō·vyä′nô). Commune, Napoli prov., Campania, S Italy, 12 m. E of Naples; pop. (1931) 12,330.

San·gley′ Point (säng·glē′ē; -glä′). Point at NE tip of Cavite Penin., NE Cavite prov., Luzon, Phil. Is., on N side of entrance to Cañacao Bay; part of Cavite naval base.

San′gli (säng′glĭ). **1** Former Indian state, Deccan and Kolhapur States, in S Bombay prov., Indian Union, just NE of Goa; 1146 sq. m.; pop. (1941) 293,381; a Southern Maratha state; joined new United Deccan State Aug. 26, 1947.
2 Town, its *, on Kistna river 190 m. SE of Bombay; pop. 29,818.

San′gol·quí′ (säng′gôl·kē′). Town, Pichincha prov., N cen. Ecuador; pop. (1944 est.) 8029.

San Gor·go′ni·o Mountain (săn′ gôr·gō′nĭ·ō). Peak 11,485 ft. in San Bernardino co., S California; highest of San Bernardino Mts.

San Gorgonio Pass. Mountain pass 2560 ft. at SE end of San Bernardino Mts., San Bernardino co., S California; a gateway bet. San Gorgonio Mt. and San Jacinto Peak and connecting the San Bernardino Valley with the Coachella Valley.

San′gre de Cris′to Mountains (săng′grĕ dĕ krĭs′tō). A range of the Rocky Mts., extending from Chaffee co., cen. Colorado, to Santa Fe co., N cen. New Mexico; highest peak Blanca Peak 14,390 ft.

Sangre de Cristo Pass. Mountain pass 9459 ft., Costilla co., S Colorado, in the Sangre de Cristo Mts. of the Rocky Mts.; used before 1800; abandoned road.

San′gre Gran′de (săng′grĕ grän′dĕ). Town near E coast of Trinidad, West Indies Federation, SE of Port of Spain; pop. 2448.

San′gro (säng′grô); *anc.* **Sa′grus** (sā′grŭs). River ab. 65 m. long in SE cen. Italy; flows out of the Apennines NE into the Adriatic Sea 12 m. SE of Ortona.

San′grur (sŭng′grŏor). Town, former ✳ of Jind state, cen. Punjab state, NW Indian Union, in N part of state 58 m. W of Ambala; pop. 13,901.

Sanhsing. See I-LAN.

San′i·bel Island (săn′ĭ-bĕl). Island in Gulf of Mexico, off SW coast of Lee co., SW Florida.

San Ig·na′cio (sän′ ĕg·nä′syô). Town, cen. Misiones dept., S Paraguay; pop. ab. 7930.

San′i·lac (săn′l·ăk). County in Michigan. See *Table* at MICHIGAN.

San Il′de·fon′so (săn ĭl′dĕ·fôn′sō; *Span.* sän ĕl′dä-fôn′sô). **1** Municipality, NW Bulacan prov., Luzon, Phil. Is., on E side of Candaba swamp near Pampanga border; pop. 16,395.

2 *or* **La Gran′ja** (lä gräng′hä). Commune, Segovia prov., cen. Spain, 7 m. SE of Segovia; pop. (1930) ab. 4000; founded 1450 by Henry IV; seat of former summer palace of kings of Spain; scene of two treaties bet. Spain and France: Aug. 19, 1796, by which Spain joined France against England; and Oct. 1, 1800, by which France (Napoleon) secured Louisiana in exchange for Parma in Italy.

San Ildefonso, Cape. Point on E coast of Luzon, Tayabas prov., Phil. Is., SE of entrance to Casiguran Sound, 16°N.

San I·si′dro (săn′ ê·sē′thrô). **1** Town, Buenos Aires prov., E Argentina, a suburb of Buenos Aires (city); pop. (est.) 61,581.

2 Municipality on NW coast of Leyte I., Phil. Is., 45 m. WNW of Tacloban; pop. 30,063. Battle in **San Isidro Bay** Dec. 7, 1944 in which an entire Japanese convoy was sunk by American planes.

3 Municipality, S Nueva Ecija prov., Luzon, Phil. Is., 13 m. S of Cabanatuan; pop. 12,078; on left bank of Pampanga river and on main highways; capital of the province 1852–1912.

Sanitary and Ship Canal. See ILLINOIS WATERWAY.

San Ja·cin′to (săn′ ja·sĭn′tô). **1** River ab. 100 m. long in SE Texas, flowing from Walker co. into Galveston Bay; battle near its mouth Apr. 21, 1836 in which Americans under Gen. Sam Houston decisively defeated Mexicans under Santa Anna.

2 County in Texas. See *Table* at TEXAS.

San Ja·cin′to (*Span.* säng′ hä-sēn′tô). **1** Town, Bolívar dept., N Colombia, 48 m. SE of Cartagena; pop. 5891.

2 Municipality, E coast of Ticao I., Masbate prov., Phil. Is., port on Ticao Pass 15 m. NE of Masbate; pop. 15,134.

San Ja·cin′to Mountains (săn ja·sĭn′tô). Range in SW California, chiefly in Riverside co., extending SE toward Salton Sea; generally considered as one of the Coast Ranges; highest peak **San Jacinto Peak** 10,805 ft.

San Ja·vier′ (säng′ hä·vyĕr′); *sometimes called* **San Javier de Lon′co·mil′la** (thä lông′kô·mē′yä). Town, Linares prov., S cen. Chile, 160 m. S of Santiago; pop. 5183.

San Jerónimo Ixtepec. See CIUDAD IXTEPEC.

San Joa·quin′ (săn′ wô·kēn′). **1** River 350 m. long in cen. California; formed by junction of forks in SE Madera co., flows W then NW into Sacramento river near its mouth; navigable 88 miles for ocean-going vessels.

Flor′ence Lake Dam [flôr′ĕns] (completed 1926; 166 ft. high) at upper end of its S fork in NE Fresno co. forms **Florence Lake,** from which water is diverted to **Hun′ting·ton Lake** (hŭn′tĭng·tŭn) 14 m. SW, where **Huntington Lake Dam** (completed 1917; 186 ft. high) across Big Creek tributary impounds it for hydro-electric power; ab. 8 m. SSW of Huntington Lake is **Sha′ver Lake** (shä′vĕr), another reservoir for water power, formed by **Shaver Lake Dam** (completed 1927; 183 ft. high) across Stevenson Creek tributary; lower in

course bet. Fresno and Madera cos. is Friant Dam, forming Millerton Lake (see UNITED STATES, *Dams and Reservoirs*).

2 County in California. See *Table* at CALIFORNIA.

3 (*Span.* säng′ hwä·kēn′) Municipality, SW Iloilo prov., Panay, Phil. Is., at W end of Iloilo Strait on Panay Gulf 31 m. WSW of City of Iloilo; pop. 23,779.

San Joa·quín′ (săn′ wŏ·kēn′; *Span.* säng′ hwä·kēn′). Town, Caaguazú dept., E Paraguay; pop. ab. 5000.

San Joaquin Ridge. Mountain 13,500 ft. in San Miguel co., SW Colorado.

San Jor′ge (säng hôr′hä). **1** River ab. 250 m. long in N Colombia, flowing NE into Cauca river; lower course through marshy region.

2 Lake port on W cen. shore of Lake Nicaragua, Rivas dept., SW Nicaragua; connected by rail with Rivas and the Pacific port of San Juan del Sur.

3 Small island in E cen. Solomon Is. in W Pacific Ocean, off SE coast of Santa Isabel I., with which it forms Thousand Ships Bay. Part of British Solomon Islands protectorate.

San Jorge, Gulf of. 1 Widemouthed inlet of Atlantic Ocean on E coast of Chubut and Santa Cruz territories, S Argentina.

2 Inlet of Mediterranean Sea on E coast of Spain, S of Tarragona and N of Cape Tortosa.

San Jorge Bay. Inlet of NE Gulf of California on NW coast of the state of Sonora, Mexico.

San Jo·se′ (săn′ ê·sē′thrô). **1** Commercial and manufacturing city, ⊗ of Santa Clara co. W California, on Coyote and Guadalupe rivers, SE of San Francisco Bay and ab. 40 m. SE of San Francisco; pop. 204,196; fruit-packing center; distributing point for fresh fruit and vegetables; meat-packing houses, lumber mills, flour mills, boatbuilding yards, pottery works, machine shops. San Jose State College (1857; coed.). Founded 1777; first state capital Dec. 1849–Feb. 1851; incorporated 1850.

2 (*Span.* säng′ hô·sä′) Municipality, N cen. Nueva Ecija prov., Luzon, Phil. Is., ab. 21 m. N of Cabanatuan; pop. 28,666; in foothills near source of Chico river.

3 (*Span.* säng′ hô·sä′) Municipality on Mangarin Bay, SW coast of Mindoro I., Phil. Is.; pop. 11,788; has good harbor; taken by Americans Dec. 15, 1944 and new airfield built nearby in short time.

San Jo·sé′ (săn′ [h]ô·zā′; *Span.* säng′ hô·sä′). **1** Province, cen. Costa Rica; 1729 sq. m.; pop. (1943 est.) 229,504; coffee, sugar, corn.

2 City, ✳ of San José prov. and of Costa Rica; pop. (1943 est.) 74,872; altitude 3816 ft.; trades in coffee. Founded 1738; became capital 1823.

3 Town, Bolívar prov., cen. Ecuador; pop. (1944 est.) 5428.

4 Seaport, Escuintla dept., S Guatemala; chief exports coffee, honey, sugar, hides, forest products.

5 Island 20 m. long off SE coast of Lower California, in the Gulf of California.

6 Town, Caaguazú dept., cen. Paraguay; pop. ab. 11,150.

7 One of Pearl Is., Gulf of Panama; ab. 25 sq. m.

8 Department of Uruguay. See *Table* at URUGUAY.

9 City on San José river, S Uruguay, 55 m. NW of Montevideo; ⊗ of San José dept.; pop. ab. 30,000.

San Jo·sé′, Gulf of (*Span.* säng′ hô·sä′). Inlet of Gulf of San Matías on NE coast of Chubut territory, S Argentina; enclosed by Váldez Penin.

San Jo·se′ de Bue′na·vis′ta (săn′ [h]ô·zā′ dĕ bwä′nä-vĭs′tä; *Span.* säng′ hô·sä′ thä vwä′nä·vēs′tä). Municipality, ✳ of Antique prov., in S part, Panay, Phil. Is.; port on coast of Sulu Sea; pop. 29,140; has a poor harbor but nevertheless an active coastal trade.

San Jo·sé′ de Cú′cu·ta (säng′ hô·sä′ thä kōō′kōō·tä). = CÚCUTA.

San Jo·sé′ de las La′jas (säng′ hô·sä′ thä läz lä′häs). Municipality and town, La Habana prov., W Cuba; town is railroad junction point 18 m. SE of Havana, pop. 7949.

San Jo·sé' de los Ra'mos (säng' hŏ·sä' thä̱ lôr rä'mŏs). Municipality, Matanzas prov., W cen. Cuba, 33 m. ESE of Cárdenas; pop. 8506.

San'ju' *or* **San'dju'** (sän'jōō'). Town, SW Sinkiang, W China, in 37°13'N, 78°27'E; pop. ab. 35,000; on N slope of Kunlun Shan 80 m. W of Khotan, ab. 30 m. N of **Sanju Pass** (16,530 ft.).

San Juan (săn wŏn'). **1** River 360 m. long, Colorado, New Mexico, and Utah; rises in Archuleta co., S Colorado, flows SW across New Mexico border, bends W then NW across SW Colorado into Utah, and empties into Colorado river in SW San Juan co., SE Utah.
2 Name of counties in four states of the U.S. See *Tables* at COLORADO, NEW MEXICO, UTAH, WASHINGTON.
3 City, Hidalgo co., S Texas, 6 m. E of McAllen; pop. 4371; ships citrus fruits, vegetables.

San Juan (*Span.* säng hwän'). **1** River ab. 160 m. long in W Argentina; main course N in San Juan prov., forming a headstream of the Desaguadero (Río Salado).
2 Province of Argentina. See *Table* at ARGENTINA.
3 City, ✻ of San Juan prov., W Argentina, 83 m. N of Mendoza; pop. (est.) 80,000; has wine trade; birthplace of Domingo Faustino Sarmiento, president of Argentina 1868–74.
4 River ab. 160 m. long in W Colombia; flows S and W into the Pacific Ocean; the Calima is a tributary.
5 Peak 3792 ft. in S Las Villas prov., W cen. Cuba.
6 River ab. 150 m. long in states of Nuevo León and Tamaulipas, NE Mexico; flows NE into Rio Grande.
7 River ab. 100 m. long in S Nicaragua; flows E out of Lake Nicaragua into the Caribbean Sea; forms E section of Nicaragua-Costa Rica boundary. See SAN JUAN DEL NORTE seaport.
8 *formerly called* **Bol·bok'** (bôl·bôk'). Municipality, SE Batangas prov., Luzon, Phil. Is., near Tayabas border and ab. 4 m. inland from Tayabas Bay; pop. 24,837.
9 Municipality and seaport city, NE cen. coast of Puerto Rico; ✻ of Puerto Rico; pop. (municipality) 451,658, (city) 432,377; built on an island in a large bay which has a narrow entrance, connected with mainland by a causeway and bridges; exports (chiefly to U.S.) sugar, tobacco, fruit, cacao; manufactures clothing, sugar, cigars and cigarettes. School of Tropical Medicine of the University of Puerto Rico.
History: Site first visited (1508) by Ponce de León who made a settlement 1509 on the mainland (see CAPARRA); in 1511 Caparra abandoned and present site on island settled; fortifications begun 1533, El Morro castle built 1539–84; attacked by Drake and Hawkins 1595; held by the British under Lord Clifford for a short time 1598; sacked by the Dutch 1625; attacked again unsuccessfully by British 1797; occupied by Americans 1898.
10 *in full* **San Juan de los Mor'ros** (säng hwän' dä lôz môr'rôs). Town, ✻ of Guárico state, N cen. Venezuela, 50 m. SW of Caracas; pop. (1941 est.) 6150.

San Juan, Cape. 1 Cape extending into the Gulf of Guinea on the SW coast of Río Muni, W Africa, at N side of entrance to Corisco Bay.
2 Cape at NE tip of Puerto Rico; lighthouse.
3 Cape on E tip of Staten I., in South Atlantic Ocean off E point of Tierra del Fuego I.

San Juan, Point. Cape on S coast of Camagüey prov. E cen. Cuba, at N entrance to Guacanayabo Bay.

San Juan Bau·tis'ta (säng hwäm' bou·tēs'tä). **1** See VILLAHERMOSA, Mexico.
2 Town, ✻ of Misiones dept., S Paraguay, 240 m. SE of Asunción; pop. ab. 8130.

San Juan Cap'is·tra'no (săn wŏn' kăp'ĭs·trä'nō). Village, Orange co., SW California, SE of Los Angeles; pop. 1120; site of Spanish mission founded 1776.

San Juan·ci'to (säng hwän·sē'tō). Town, S cen. Honduras, 20 m. from Tegucigalpa; site of the Rosario mine (silver, gold); pop. ab. 1000.

San Juan de la Ma·gua'na (säng hwän' dä lä mä-gwä'nä). Commune (1941 pop. 47,556) and town (1944

est. pop. 5809), ✻ of Benefactor prov., W cen. Dominican Republic.

San Juan del Mon'te (dĕl mŏn'tä). Municipality, W Rizal prov., Luzon, Phil. Is., N of the Pasig; pop. 18,870; borders on Manila to the W and on Quezon City to the N.

San Juan del Nor'te (dĕl nôr'tä). **1** District (comarca), SE Nicaragua; pop. (1940) 1678; ✻ San Juan del Norte. Politically included in Zelaya dept.
2 *or* **Grey'town** (grā'toun). Seaport, its ✻, extreme SE coast of Nicaragua, at mouth of San Juan river; pop. (1940) 440. The port (formerly called Greytown by the English) and region (Mosquito Coast) along the Caribbean coast N of the mouth of the San Juan, claimed by Great Britain 1841–48, port occupied 1848; river under consideration 1849–50 by U.S. for ship canal to Pacific via Lake Nicaragua; dispute settled by Clayton-Bulwer Treaty Apr. 19, 1850 whereby the two countries agreed to neutralization of any proposed interoceanic canal; control of coastal region finally given up by Great Britain by 1860.

San Juan de los La'gos (dä lôz lä'gôs). Town, Jalisco state, W cen. Mexico, 80 m. NE of Guadalajara; pop. 5792.

San Juan de los Remedios. = REMEDIOS.

San Juan de los Ye'ras (dä lôz yä'räs). Municipality, Las Villas prov., W cen. Cuba; pop. 11,283.

San Juan del Rí'o (dĕl rē'ŏ). Town, Querétaro state, cen. Mexico, 25 m. SE of Querétaro; pop. 6678.

San Juan del Sur (sŏŏr'). Seaport on SW coast of Rivas dept., SW Nicaragua; pop. ab. 1500; outlet for products of S and SW Nicaragua, esp. cacao, coffee, sugar, and woods.

San Juan de Sal'va·men'to (dä säl'vä·män'tŏ). See STATEN ISLAND.

San Juan de U·lú'a (ōō·lōō'ä), *often* **San Juan de Ul·lo'a** (ōō·yō'ä). A small island off Veracruz, Mexico, containing a fort defending the harbor. See VERACRUZ.

San Juan Hill (săn wŏn'; *Span.* säng hwän'). Elevation near Santiago de Cuba, E Cuba; captured by American troops in Spanish-American War July 1, 1898. See EL CANEY.

San Jua·ni'co Strait (säng' hwä·nē'kŏ). Narrow passage 25 m. long and from ⅛ to 3 m. wide, extending E and S bet. SW Samar and NE Leyte, Phil. Is., from Samar Sea to San Pedro Bay. Noted for its scenery and navigable to vessels of fair size, but dangerous because of swift current and numerous islands. Has many pueblos on its banks; Tacloban at its S end. In occupation of Leyte secured on both sides by Americans Oct. 30, 1944.

San Juan Islands (săn wŏn'). Group of islands lying bet. Haro and Rosario Straits, off NW Washington, including Orcas I., San Juan I., and Lopez I., and constituting as a group San Juan co., Washington.

San Jua·ni'to (säng' hwä·nē'tŏ). Small island of the Tres Marías group (*q.v.*) in the Pacific Ocean off W cen. Mexico.

San Juan Ji'qui·pil'co (säng hwäng' hē'kē·pēl'kŏ). Town, México state, cen. Mexico; pop. 5241.

San Juan Mountains (săn wŏn'). A range of the Rocky Mts., in SW Colorado, extending NW and SE through several counties and containing rugged and well-forested peaks, several above 14,000 ft.; highest are Uncompahgre Peak 14,306 ft., Mt. Wilson 14,250 ft., and Mt. Sneffels 14,143 ft.

San Juan Ne'po·mu·ce'no (säng hwäng' nä'pŏ·mōō-sā'nŏ). Town, Caazapá dept., S Paraguay; pop. ab. 14,340.

San Juan No·nual'co (säng hwän' nŏ·nwäl'kŏ). Town, La Paz dept., S El Salvador; pop. (1942 est.) 5611.

San Juan Teotihuacán. See TEOTIHUACÁN.

San Juan y Mar·tí'nez (säng hwän' ĕ mär·tē'näs). Municipality, Pinar del Río prov., W Cuba; pop. 22,830; on railroad 15 m. SW of Pinar del Río.

San Ju·lián' (säng' hōō·lyän'). Seaport on S Atlantic, Santa Cruz territory, S Argentina, ab. 200 m. N of E entrance to Strait of Magellan; here Magellan wintered Mar. 1519–Aug. 1520 on his circumnavigation voyage.

San Jus'to (säng hōōs'tō). Town, Buenos Aires prov., E Argentina, W suburb of Buenos Aires.

San·khe'da Me·was' (sŭngk·hä'dá má·wäs'). One of two groups of former Indian districts and estates, formerly in the Rewa Kantha Agency, now a part of Gujarat States, E Gujarat, Indian Union; 104 sq. m.; pop. 24,662.

San'kiang' (sän'jĭ·äng'). Former province (1932–45), E Manchukuo; 34,761 sq. m.; pop. (1940 est.) 1,417,888; ✱ Kiamusze.

Sankt. See SAINT.

Sankt Andrä. See SZENTENDRE.

Sankt An'ton am Arl'berg (zängkt än'tōn äm ärl'bĕrk). Village resort and sports center, Tirol, W Austria, at E end of Arlberg tunnel, alt. 4221 ft.; pop. (1923) 1260; skiing.

Sankt Beatenberg. See BEATENBERG.

Sankt Go·ar' (zängkt' gō·är'). Town, W Germany, on the Rhine river 24 m. WNW of Wiesbaden; pop. ab. 1000; Lorelei (*q.v.*) nearby.

Sankt Gott'hard (zängkt gôt'härt). German for SAINT GOTTHARD.

Sankt Ing'bert (ĭng'bĕrt). Commune, Saarland, Germany, ab. 7 m. NE of Saarbrücken; pop. (1927) 20,790.

Sankt Joachimsthal. See JÁCHYMOV.

Sankt Michel. See MIKKELI city.

Sankt Pöl'ten (zängkt pŭl'tĕn). City, Lower Austria prov., Austria, 35 m. W of Vienna; pop. (1939) 44,451; 11th-cent. cathedral; textiles, machinery, metal goods.

Sankt Veit am Flaum. See RIEKA.

San·ku'ru (säng·kōō'rōō). River ab. 340 m. long in the Congo basin; flows WNW in S cen. Congo and empties into Kasai river at 4°23'S; upper course called the Lubilash (*q.v.*).

San Lá'za·ro, Cape (sän lä'sä·rô). Point on SW coast of Lower California, extending into the Pacific Ocean W of Magdalena Bay.

San Laz'za·ro (sän läd'dzä·rô). Small island in the Lagoon of Venice, NE Italy; seat of an Armenian monastery.

San Lazzaro Par·men'se (pär·mĕn'så). Commune, Parma prov., Emilia, N Italy, 2 m. SE of Parma; pop. 10,325.

San Le·an'dro (săn' lē·än'drō). City, Alameda co., W California, 15 m. SE of Oakland; pop. 65,962; in dairy-farming region.

San Lo·ren'zo (săn'lō·rĕn'zō). Urban area, Alameda co., W California, SE of Oakland; pop. 23,773.

San Lo·ren'zo (săn' lō·rĕn'zō; *Span.* sän' lō·rän'sô, *in Spain also* -thō). 1 Peak ab. 12,000 ft. in NW Santa Cruz territory, S Argentina, on border of Chile.
2 Town, Valle dept., S Honduras, on an inlet of the Gulf of Fonseca 80 m. by road S of Tegucigalpa; pop. 2701.
3 Municipality (pop. 27,950) and town (pop. 5551), E Puerto Rico; town on railroad 20 m. SE of San Juan.
4 Commune, Las Palmas prov. (E Canary Is.), Spain, in NE Grand Canary I., 2 m. W of Las Palmas; pop. (1930) 13,929; agricultural products.

San Lorenzo, Cape. Cape extending into Pacific Ocean on W cen. coast of Ecuador.

San Lo·ren'zo de la Fron·te'ra (sän' lō·rän'sô thä lä frôn·tä'rä). Town, a suburb of Asunción, Central dept., S cen. Paraguay; pop. ab. 11,130.

San Lo·ren'zo Island (sän' lō·rĕn'zō; *Span.* sän' lō·rän'sô). Island ab. 5 m. long in Pacific Ocean off the city of Callao, Peru.

San·lú'car de Bar'ra·me'da (sän·lōō'kär thä vär'rä·mä'thä). Fortified seaport, Cádiz prov., SW Spain, at mouth of Guadalquivir river 18 m. N by W of Cádiz; pop. 32,848; resort; manufactures explosives, wine, flour, salt; trades in sherry, salt, tropical fruits, and agricul-

tural produce; fisheries; 14th-cent. church, ruins of Moorish castle, Montpensier ducal castle, Roman ruins; port for embarkation for Columbus's 3d voyage 1498, and Magellan's voyage 1519.

San Lu'cas, Cape (săn lōō'kăs; *Span.* sän lōō'käs). South extremity of Lower California, extending into the Pacific Ocean.

San Lu'is (săn lōō'ĭ[s]). Town, ⊗ of Costilla co., S Colorado; pop. (1950) 1239.

San Luis (sän lwēs'). 1 Province of Argentina. See *Table* at ARGENTINA.
2 City, its ✱, cen. Argentina, 140 m. E by S of Mendoza; pop. (est.) 30,021.
3 Municipality and town, Oriente prov., E Cuba; town is on railroad just N of Santiago de Cuba, pop. 10,819.
4 Municipality and town, Pinar del Río prov., W Cuba; town is near S coast 11 m. S of Pinar del Río, pop. 7389.

San Luis d'Apra. See APRA HARBOR.

San Luis Ji'lo·te·pe'que (hē'lō·tá·pā'kä). Town, Jalapa dept., SE Guatemala, 30 m. E of Guatemala; pop. 7458.

San Lu'is O·bis'po (săn lōō'ĭs ō·bĭs'pō). 1 County in California. See *Table* at CALIFORNIA.
2 City, its ⊗, SW California, 12 m. from Pacific Ocean and ab. 80 m. NW of Santa Barbara; pop. 20,437; founded 1772, became pueblo 1844, incorporated as city 1856; in agricultural region; dairy farming; oil refining. California State Polytechnic Coll. (1901; coed.). San Luis Obispo de Tolosa mission.

San Lu'is Park *or* **Valley** (săn lōō'ĭ[s]). An area of irrigated land ab. 120 m. long and 60 m. wide bet. mountain ranges chiefly in Costilla co., S Colorado; southernmost of a chain of high, grassy areas enclosed by snow-capped peaks (see NORTH PARK).

San Lu'is Peak (săn lōō'ĭ[s]). Mountain 14,149 ft. in Saguache co., S Colorado.

San Luis Po'to·sí' (sän lwēs' pō'tô·sē'). 1 State, cen. Mexico. See *Table* at MEXICO.
2 City, its ✱, cen. Mexico, NE of Léon; pop. 77,161; altitude 6300 ft.; center of rich agricultural and silver-mining district; has many smelters, refining plants, factories, mills.

San Mar·cel'lo Pi·sto·ie'se (sän' mär·chĕl'lō pĕs·tô·yä'så). Commune, Pistoia prov., Tuscany, cen. Italy, 13 m. NW of Pistoia; pop. 10,559.

San Mar'co (sän mär'kô). One of the two large islands of Venice, Italy; in English often known as Saint Mark (*q.v.*).

San Mar'co in La'mis (sän mär'kô ĕn lä'mēs). Commune, Foggia prov., Apulia, SE Italy, 17 m. N by E of Foggia; pop. 19,608.

San Mar'cos (sän mär'kŭs). City and pleasure resort, ⊗ of Hays co., S cen. Texas, 30 m. S of Austin; pop. 12,713; in cotton-growing section; cottonseed oil and grist mills, cotton gins and compresses; subterranean and hot springs. Southwest Texas State Coll. (1899; coed.).

San Mar'cos (sän mär'kŭs; *Span.* sän mär'kôs). 1 Department, W Guatemala; 1464 sq. m.; pop. 204,208.
2 Town, its ✱; pop. (1938 est.) 7436; coffee trade.

San Ma·ri'no (săn' má·rē'nō). Suburban residential city, Los Angeles co., SW California, 11 m. NE of Los Angeles and E of Pasadena; pop. 13,658; founded 1913; nearby is the Huntington Library and Art Gallery.

San Ma·ri'no (*Ital.* sän' mä·rē'nō). 1 Republic, S Europe, cen. Italian penin. 11 m. SSW of Rimini (Italy); 24 sq. m.; pop. (1939) 14,545; on Mount Titano near Adriatic; smallest republic in the world and claims to be oldest state in Europe; eminently democratic form of government: legislative powers vested in grand council of 60 members elected by popular vote; executive powers vested in two regents appointed by grand council every six months; judicial powers vested in magistrates of Italian citizenship. No public debt; has extradition treaties with England, Belgium, Netherlands, and U.S.; treaty of friendship with Italy June 28, 1897 (latest re-

newal Mar. 31, 1939); exports wine, cattle, and building stone quarried on Mount Titano; agriculture. Traditionally founded in 4th cent. by St. Marinus of Dalmatia; except for a few short periods has preserved its independence; protected by Montefeltro family of Urbino; its independence recognized by Papacy 1631. Entered by German troops Aug. 10, 1944; occupied by British Sept. 23, 1944.

2 City, its *; pop. ab. 4000; manufactures silk; built around hermitage dating from 441 A.D.; entered by one road; city walls, governor's palace, six churches, town hall and other public buildings.

San Mar·tín' (sän' mär·tēn'). **1** See GENERAL SAN MARTÍN town, Buenos Aires prov., E Argentina.

2 Town, Mendoza prov., W Argentina, just E of Mendoza; pop. (est.) 8000.

3 Department of Peru. See *Table* at PERU.

San Martín, Lake. Lake in S Chile and S Argentina, on border bet. S Aysén prov. in Chile and SW Santa Cruz territory in Argentina.

San Martín del Rey Au·re'lio (děl rě'ě [rā'] ou·rā'lyō). Commune, Oviedo prov., NW Spain, 7 m. SE of Oviedo; pop. 18,151; agriculture and stock raising; coal mines; tomb of Aurelio, king of Oviedo.

San Martín Tex'me·lu·cán' (tās'mä·lōō·kän'). Town, Puebla state, SE cen. Mexico, NW of Puebla; pop. 7572.

San Ma·te'o (săn' má·tā'ō). **1** County in California. See *Table* at CALIFORNIA.

2 Residential city, San Mateo co., W California, on SW shore of San Francisco Bay; pop. 69,870; town site platted 1863.

San Ma·tí'as, Gulf of (sän' mä·tē'äs). Inlet of Atlantic Ocean in SE Río Negro territory, S cen. Argentina, enclosed on S by Váldez Penin. in Chubut territory.

San'men' Bay (sän'mŭn'). Bay on E coast of Chekiang prov., E China, S of Ninghsien.

San Mi·che'le, Mon'te (mŏn'tā sän' mĕ·kâ'lā). Mountain bet. Gradisca and Gorizia, Venezia Giulia, NE Italy, E of the Isonzo, dominating Gorizia to the NE and the Carso to the SE; scene of fighting Aug. 1916.

San Mi·guel (săn' mĭ·gĭl'). **1** River ab. 85 m. long, SW Colorado; rises in San Juan Mts. in SE San Miguel co. and flows NW into the Dolores river in W Montrose co.

2 Name of counties in two states of the U.S. See *Tables* at COLORADO and NEW MEXICO.

San Mi·guel' (săn' mĕ·gěl'). **1** River ab. 475 m. long of E Bolivia, sometimes known as the **I'to·na'ma** (ē'tō·nä'mä) in its lower course; flows NNW into Guaporé river on the Brazil-Bolivia boundary.

2 Town, Bolívar prov., W Ecuador, near Riobamba; pop. (1944 est.) 8215.

3 Town, Cotopaxi prov., cen. Ecuador, in Andes Mts. 60 m. S of Quito; pop. (1944 est.) 8085.

4 Department, E El Salvador; 1344 sq. m.; pop. (1942 est.) 172,266; * San Miguel.

5 City, E El Salvador, * of San Miguel dept., 65 m. E of San Salvador at foot of San Miguel volcano 7120 ft.; pop. (1942 est.) 18,930; chief products coffee, sisal, cattle.

6 *in full* **San Miguel de Al·len'de** (dä ä·yān'dä). Town, Guanajuato state, cen. Mexico, 35 m. E of Guanajuato; pop. 9030.

7 Town, N Misiones dept., S Paraguay; pop. ab. 5790.

8 Seaport town, N Isla del Rey, Pearl Is., Gulf of Panama.

9 Island, Albay prov., Luzon, Phil. Is., smallest of group off E coast of Luzon bet. Lagonoy Gulf and Tabaco Bay NW of Cagraray I.; 8 sq. m.; forms part of Tabaco municipality. Has important fisheries.

10 Municipality, NW Bulacan prov., Luzon, Phil. Is., on E edge of Candaba Swamp 23 m. NNE of Malolos; pop. 26,759; produces much rice; has iron mines and mineral springs nearby.

San Miguel, Gulf of. Inlet of the Gulf of Panama, extending E into SE Panama.

San Miguel Bay. Large inlet of Pacific Ocean on N coast of SE Luzon, Phil. Is., ab. 25 m. long by 12 to 17 m. wide; lies bet. Camarines Norte prov. on NW and Camarines Sur on S and E. Has capacious and safe anchorage.

San Miguel de I·bar'ra (dä ē·vär'rä). = IBARRA.

San Miguel de la Palma. See LA PALMA.

San Miguel el Al'to (ěl äl'tō). Town, Jalisco state, W cen. Mexico, 70 m. NE of Guadalajara; pop. 5442.

San Mi·guel' Island (săn' mĭ·gĭl'). Island at NW end of Santa Barbara group in Pacific Ocean; part of Santa Barbara co., SW California, and separated from mainland by Santa Barbara Channel.

San Miguel Passage. Strait bet. Santa Rosa I. and San Miguel I., off S Santa Barbara co., SW California.

San Miguel Peak. Mountain 13,700 ft. in Dolores and San Miguel cos., SW Colorado.

San Mi·nia'to (săn' mě·nyä'tō). Commune, Pisa prov., Tuscany, cen. Italy, 23 m. E by S of Pisa; pop. 21,463; 10th-cent. cathedral.

San Murezzan. See SAINT-MORITZ.

San Nar·ci'so (sän' när·sē'sō). Municipality, SW Zambales prov., Luzon, Phil. Is., on coast road 24 m. S of Iba; pop. 9723. Founded 1849. Americans landed near here Jan. 29, 1945.

San'ni·can'dro Gar·ga'ni·co (sän'nĕ·kän'drō gär·gä'nĕ·kō). Commune, Foggia prov., Apulia, SE Italy, 25 m. N of Foggia; pop. 14,366.

San Ni·co·las' (sän nē'kō·läs'). Municipality, NE Pangasinan prov., Luzon, Phil. Is., on E tributary of the Agno 35 m. E of Lingayen; pop. 16,088.

San Ni·co·lás' (sän nē'kō·läs'). **1** Town, Buenos Aires prov., E Argentina, on Paraná river; pop. 28,729.

2 Municipality, La Habana prov., W Cuba, 35 m. SE of Havana; pop. 16,509.

San Nic'o·las Island (săn nĭk'ō·lăs). Island in cen. Santa Barbara group in Pacific Ocean; part of Ventura co., SW California.

Sân·ni·co·la'ul–Ma're (sĭn·nē'kō·lä'ool·mä'rě); *Hung.* **Nagy'szent·mi'klós** (nŏd'y'·sěnt·mē'klōsh). Commune, SW Romania, on the Mureş river 25 m. SE of Szeged; pop. (1920) 9230; site of discovery in 1799 of remarkable gold ornamented utensils, probably of 10th-cent. Turkish origin.

San'nois' (sá'nwä'). Commune, Seine-et-Oise dept., N France, NNW suburb of Paris; pop. (1931) 11,757.

Sa'nok (sä'nôk). Commune, Rzeszów dept., SE Poland, on San river 35 m. S of Rzeszów and near Ukraine border; pop. (1938–39 est.) 17,863; manufactures vehicles; oil well; on highway leading S over Lupków Pass in the East Beskids to Slovakia.

San Pab'lo (săn păb'lō). City, Contra Costa co., W California, N of Berkeley; pop. 19,687.

San Pa'blo (säm pä'vlō). City, S Laguna prov., Luzon, Phil. Is., 17 m. SW of Santa Cruz; 53 sq. m.; pop. 46,311; largest town in the province, an important rail and highway center in a valley near several small crater lakes. Created a city May 7, 1940; occupied by American forces Apr. 1, 1945.

San Pablo Au·to'pan (ou·tō'pän). Town, México state, cen. Mexico, NW of Mexico City; pop. 5533.

San Pab'lo Bay (săn păb'lō). North extension of San Francisco Bay (*q.v.*), W cen. California.

San Pa'blo del Mon'te (säm pä'vlō thĕl môn'tā). Town, Tlaxcala state, cen. Mexico; pop. 7652.

San Pas·qual' *or* **San Pas·cual'** (săn' păs·kwôl'). Locality, San Diego co., SW California, ab. 40 m. NE of San Diego; site of battle Dec. 6, 1846 in which U.S. troops under Gen. Stephen W. Kearny suffered greater losses but were not prevented by Spanish-Californian troops from reaching San Diego.

San Pa·tri'ci·o (săn' pá·trĭsh'ĭ·ō). County in Texas. See *Table* at TEXAS.

San Pe'dro (săn pē'drō). **1** River ab. 100 m. long, SE Arizona; flows NW into the Gila river in Pinal co.

2 Formerly a city, Los Angeles co., SW California; an-

nexed to Los Angeles 1909; pop. (est.) 54,383; has fine harbor; port of entry; U.S. military and naval base.
3 Urban community (unincorporated), Nueces co., S Texas, W of Corpus Christi; pop. 7634.
San Pe'dro (säm pā'thrŏ). **1** Town, Buenos Aires prov., E Argentina, port on the Paraná river 90 m. NW of Buenos Aires; pop. ab. 15,000.
2 River ab. 60 m. long in S cen. Camagüey prov., E cen. Cuba; flows SW and W into Caribbean Sea; the city of Camagüey is situated on its upper course.
3 River ab. 200 m. long, Durango and Nayarit states, W Mexico; flows S and W past Tuxpan to the Pacific.
4 *in full* **San Pedro de las Co·lo'nias** (thä läs kô·lō'nyäs). Town, Coahuila state, NE Mexico, 165 m. W of Monterrey; pop. 15,713.
5 Department of Paraguay. See *Table* at PARAGUAY.
6 Town, ✳ of San Pedro dept., cen. Paraguay, on Jejuy river ab. 90 m. N of Asunción; pop. ab. 14,790.
San Pe'dro, Point. 1 (săn pē'drō) Point on NW coast of San Mateo co., W California.
2 (säm pā'thrŏ) Cape on coast of SW Antofagasta prov., N Chile, S of Nuestra Señora Bay.
San Pe'dro Bay. 1 (săn pē'drō) Inlet of San Pedro Channel, S Los Angeles co., California; Long Beach is on it, San Pedro to the SW.
2 (säm pā'thrŏ) Inlet of Pacific Ocean on SW cen. coast of Chile, NW of Puerto Montt.
3 (säm pā'thrŏ) Inlet of Leyte Gulf, E Phil. Is., bet. SW Samar and NE Leyte; connects by San Juanico Strait with Samar Sea. Tacloban is at its NW corner.
San Pe'dro Channel (săn pē'drō). Strait bet. S California mainland and Santa Catalina I., off W coast of Orange co., SW California.
San Pedro de las Colonias. See SAN PEDRO town, Mexico.
San Pedro del Durazno. See DURAZNO.
San Pe'dro de Lloc (säm pā'thrŏ thä yôk'). Town, La Libertad dept., NW Peru, N of Trujillo; pop. 5286.
San Pedro de los Pi'nos (thä lôs pē'nŏs). Town, Federal District, cen. Mexico, SE of Mexico City; pop. 13,188.
San Pedro del Pa'ra·ná' (thĕl pä'rä·nä'). City, Itapúa dept., SE Paraguay; pop. ab. 14,670.
San Pedro de Ma'co·rís' (thä mä'kô·rēs'). **1** Province, SE Dominican Republic. See *Table* at DOMINICAN REPUBLIC.
2 Commune (1941 pop. 40,988) and city (1944 est. pop. 22,513), its ✳; exports sugar and molasses.
San Pe'dro Mountain (săn pē'drō). Peak 10,624 ft. in SW Sandoval co., NW cen. New Mexico.
San Pe'dro Sa'ca·te·pé'quez (säm pā'thrŏ sä'kä·tå·pā'kås). Town, San Marcos dept., W Guatemala, W of Quezaltenango; pop. 5469.
San Pedro Su'la (sōō'lä). Town, NW Honduras, ✳ of Cortés dept.; pop. (1940) 20,392; bananas, sugar.
San'pete (săn'pēt). County in Utah. See *Table* at UTAH.
San Pier d'A·re'na (säm' pyår dä·rā'nä). = SAMPIERDARENA.
San Pie'tro (säm pyâ'trŏ). Island in Mediterranean Sea off SW coast of the island of Sardinia; 20 sq. m.; pop. (1931) ab. 8000; attached to Cagliari prov., Italy; chief town Carloforte, site of International Latitude Observatory on 39°8'N lat., one of five such observatories in the world: see GAITHERSBURG, Maryland; KITAB, Uzbek S.S.R.; MIZUSAWA, Japan; UKIAH, California.
San Pitch (săn pĭch'). River ab. 60 m. long, cen. Utah; flows SW through Sanpete co. into Sevier river.
San'quhar (săng'kĕr). Burg, Dumfries, Scotland, 26 m. NW of Dumfries by rail; pop. (1951) 2381; scene of publication by Richard Cameron 1680 and James Renwick 1685 of the Covenanters' declarations renouncing allegiance to Charles II and James VII; ruined castle.
San Ra·fael' (săn' rȧ·fĕl'). **1** River ab. 90 m. long, E cen. Utah; flows SE through Emery co. into Green river.

2 Suburban residential city, ⊗ of Marin co., W California, 13 m. NW of San Francisco; pop. 20,460; processes dairy products; manufactures leather products. Hamilton Air Force Base. Dominican College of San Rafael (1850; women).
San Ra'fa·el' (sän rä'fä·ĕl'). **1** Town, Mendoza prov., W Argentina, 120 m. S of Mendoza; pop. (est.) 20,822; in important agricultural and fruit-raising district.
2 Province, W Dominican Republic. See *Table* at DoMINICAN REPUBLIC.
3 Town, México state, cen. Mexico, just W of Mexico City; pop. 5150.
San Ra·món' (sän' rä·môn'). Town, Canelones dept., S Uruguay, 45 m. N of Montevideo; pop. ab. 6000.
San Re·mi'gio (sän' rrĕ·mē'hyô). Municipality on NW coast of Cebu I., Phil. Is., at N end of Tañon Strait 56 m. N of City of Cebu; pop. 21,232.
San Re'mo (săn rē'mō). Urban community (unincorporated), Suffolk co., SE New York, on Long Island E of New York; pop. 11,996.
San Re'mo (săn rä'mō; rē'mō; *Ital.* sän râ'mô). Seaport, Imperia prov., Liguria, NW Italy, on Ligurian Sea 12 m. WSW of Imperia; pop. 31,769; famous health, tourist, and winter resort; flower market; 12th-cent. Romanesque cathedral. Site of international conference Apr. 19–26, 1920 of representatives of countries in World War I.
San Ro·mán', Cape (săn' rrô·män'). Cape extending into Caribbean Sea on N extremity of Paraguaná Penin., NW Venezuela.
San Ro'que (săn rrô'kå). Commune, Cádiz prov., SW Spain, 54 m. SE of Cádiz; pop. 12,371.
San Roque, Cape. See Cape SÃO ROQUE.
San Sa'ba (săn sä'bȧ; săb'ȧ). **1** River ab. 150 m. long, Texas; flows ENE from Schleicher co. to Colorado river on E boundary of San Saba co.
2 County in Texas. See *Table* at TEXAS.
3 Town, its ⊗, cen. Texas, on San Saba river; pop. 2728; market for wool, mohair, grain, pecans, livestock.
San Sal'va·dor (săn săl'vȧ·dôr; *Span.* sän säl'vä·thôr').
1 One of the Bahama Is., ESE of Cat I. (*q.v.*) at 24°N lat.; known also, esp. formerly, as **Wat'lings Island** *or* **Wat'lings** (wŏt'lĭngz); 60 sq. m.; pop. (1943) 693; now generally identified, in preference to Cat I. which was formerly so identified, with the first landfall (Oct. 12, 1492) of Columbus in the New World, an island which Columbus says was called **Gua'na·ha'ni** (gwä'nä-hä'nē) by the native Lucayans before he renamed it San Salvador. Has lighthouse near NE end (estab. 1887).
2 Peak 6000 ft. in El Salvador.
3 Department, SW cen. El Salvador; pop. 230,951.
4 City, ✳ of El Salvador and of San Salvador dept., 23 m. from the port of La Libertad; pop. (1942 est.) 105,193; altitude over 2000 ft.; chief commercial and cultural center of the republic, with many modern features.
5 = SÃO SALVADOR, Angola, Africa.
6 *also known as* **James Island** (jāmz). One of the Galápagos Is. (*q.v.*).
San'sa·por' (sän'så·pôr'). Village on NW coast of Vogelkop Penin., NW Neth. New Guinea, opp. Waigeo I. and NE of Sorong. In World War II in advance of Allies toward the Philippines, seized in surprise landing by American forces July 30, 1944; this led a little later to occupation of Morotai.
San Se'bas·tián' (sän sā'väs·tyän'; *Angl.* săn' sĕ·băs'chǎn). **1** Settlement on E side of Gulf of Urabá, NW Colombia, made 1509 by Ojeda; unsuccessful and later removed to Darien (*q.v.*).
2 Municipality (pop. 33,451) and town (pop. 4019), NW Puerto Rico; town is 12 m. SE of Aguadilla.
3 Chief town and port, Gomera I., Canary Is., Spain; pop. 6652.
4 Commercial fortified seaport, ✳ of Guipúzcoa prov., N Spain, on Bay of Biscay 48 m. E of Bilbao; pop. (1941 est.) 104,237; trades in wool, flour, wine, cutlery, copper,

lead, firearms; fisheries, sawmills, flour mills, breweries; manufactures soap, candles, glass, paper, preserves; schools of navigation, commerce; watering place; formerly summer residence of Spanish royal family and court; strategically located near French frontier, several times besieged, notably in 1813 by Wellington.

San Sebastián, Cape. Cape on NE coast of Tierra del Fuego I., Argentina, off S South America.

San Sebastián Bay. Bay on NE coast of Tierra del Fuego I., Argentina.

Sansego. See SUŠAK.

San·se·pol'cro (sän'sȧ-pōl'krō). Commune, Arezzo prov., Tuscany, cen. Italy, on Tiber river 15 m. ENE of Arezzo; pop. 11,111; 11th-cent. cathedral.

San Ser'vo·lo (sän sĕr'vō·lō). Island in the Lagoon of Venice, NE Italy.

San Se·ve·ri'no Mar'che (sän' sȧ·vȧ·rē'nō mär'kā). Commune, Macerata prov., Marches, cen. Italy, near Potenza river 16 m. W by S of Macerata; pop. 16,101; episcopal see.

San Severino Ro'ta (rō'tä). Commune, Salerno prov. Campania, S Italy, 7 m. N of Salerno; pop. 13,404.

San Se·ve'ro (sän' sȧ·vȧ'rō). Commune, Foggia prov., Apulia, SE Italy, 20 m. NNW of Foggia; pop. 37,702; episcopal see.

Sansing. = *Sanhsing:* see I-LAN.

San Ste'fa·no (sän stĕf'ȧ·nō; *Ital.* sän stä'fä·nō, stä'-); *Turk.* **Ye'şil·köy'** (yĕ'shĕl·kû'ĕ). Village, İstanbul vilayet, Turkey in Europe, on the Sea of Marmara ab. 7 m. W of İstanbul; pop. ab. 2000. Treaty signed here Mar. 3, 1878 ending the Russo-Turkish War; its terms were: Romania, Serbia, and Montenegro recognized as independent; Bulgaria made a principality; part of Armenia ceded to Russia by the Porte, an indemnity paid, and reforms promised; modified by Treaty of Berlin July 13, 1878.

Sant (sŭnt) *or* **Santh** (sŭnt'h'). Former Indian state, Gujarat States, W India; 390 sq. m.; pop. (1941) 94,257.

Santa. See SAINT.

San'ta (sän'tä). River ab. 185 m. long in N cen. Peru; empties into Pacific Ocean at Chimbote ab. 75 m. SE of Trujillo. Large hydroelectric plant on its banks.

San'ta A'na (sän'tä än'ȧ). Residential and commercial city, ⊗ of Orange co., SW California, 20 m. E of Long Beach; pop. 100,350; founded 1869, incorporated 1886; manufactures agricultural tools, glassware, woolens.

San'ta A'na (*Span.* sän'tä ä'nä). 1 Municipality, Matanzas prov., W cen. Cuba, S of Matanzas; pop. 5540.
2 Town, Manabí prov., W Ecuador, ab. 80 m. NW of Guayaquil; pop. (1944 est.) 11,470.
3 Volcanic peak 8300 ft. in El Salvador. See IZALCO.
4 Department, NW El Salvador; 1374 sq. m.; pop. (1942 est.) 195,271.
5 City, NW El Salvador, ✱ of Santa Ana dept.; pop. (1942 est.) 46,343; commercial center, esp. for coffee; trade and business metropolis of W part of the republic.
6 Peak 2625 ft. on Paraguaná Penin., NW Venezuela.

San'ta An'a Bay (sän'tä än'ȧ; *Span.* sän'tä ä'nä). Bay on SW coast of Spanish Sahara, NW Africa.

Santa Ana de Coro. See CORO.

San'ta An'a Mountains (sǎn'tȧ ǎn'ȧ). Range of mountains, S California, along border between Orange and Riverside cos.; highest point 5696 ft.

San'ta An'na (sǎn'tȧ ǎn'ȧ). Town, Coleman co., cen. Texas, 20 m. W of Brownwood; pop. 1320; glass factory.

San'ta Bar'ba·ra (sǎn'tȧ bär'bȧ·rȧ). 1 County in California. See *Table* at CALIFORNIA.
2 Residential and seaside resort city, its ⊗, SW California, on Santa Barbara Channel ab. 80 m. NW of Los Angeles; pop. 58,768; trading center; oil wells nearby. Univ. of California, Santa Barbara campus (1909; coed.; moved to new campus at Goleta [to the W] 1954). Founded as Spanish presidio 1782; mission established 1786; incorporated as city 1850.
3 (*Span.* sän'tä vär'vä·rä) Municipality, cen. Pan-

gasinan prov., Luzon, Phil. Is., near Calasiao and 12 m. E of Lingayen; pop. 15,125.
4 (*Span.* sän'tä vär'vä·rä) Municipality, S cen. Iloilo prov., Panay, Phil. Is., on Jaro river and on railroad 12 m. NNW of City of Iloilo; pop. 35,406.

San'ta Bár'ba·ra (sän'tä bär'bȧ·rȧ; bär'brä; *Span.* sän'tä vär'vä·rä). 1 Department, W Honduras; 2864 sq. m.; pop. (1945 est.) 88,629.
2 Town, its ✱; pop. (1935) 2540.
3 Mining town, Chihuahua state, near Parral, NE Mexico; pop. 13,902.

San'ta Bar'ba·ra Channel (sǎn'tȧ bär'bȧ·rȧ; bär'brä). Strait bet. S California mainland and the island chain of Santa Barbara Is., off coast of Santa Barbara and Ventura cos., SW California.

Santa Bárbara de Samaná. See SAMANÁ commune.

San'ta Bar'ba·ra Island (sǎn'tȧ bär'bȧ·rȧ; bär'brä). Island, cen. Santa Barbara group in Pacific Ocean; part of Santa Barbara co., SW California; part of island included in Channel Islands National Monument (see UNITED STATES, *National Monuments*).

Santa Barbara Islands. Chain of islands ab. 160 m. long off S California coast, separated from mainland by Santa Barbara and San Pedro Channels, in Santa Barbara, Ventura, and Los Angeles cos.; includes islands of San Miguel, Santa Rosa, Santa Cruz, Anacapa, Santa Barbara, San Nicolas, Santa Catalina, and San Clemente.

San'ta Cat'a·li'na (sǎn'tȧ kǎt″l·ē'nȧ). 1 *or* **Catalina.** Island in SW Santa Barbara group in Pacific Ocean; 70 sq. m.; part of Los Angeles co., SW California; tourist resort.
2 Small island in lower Gulf of California, off SE coast of Lower California.

Santa Catalina, Gulf of. Inlet of Pacific Ocean on W coast of Orange and San Diego cos., SW California.

Santa Catalina Mountains. Small range in NE corner of Pima co., S Arizona; highest point Mount Lemmon 9180 ft.

San'ta Cat'a·ri'na (sǎn'tȧ kǎt'ȧ·rē'nȧ; *Port.* săNn'tȧ kä'tȧ·rē'nȧ). 1 Island in Atlantic Ocean off the E cen. coast of Santa Catarina state, S Brazil.
2 State of Brazil. See *Table* at BRAZIL.

San'ta Clar'a (sǎn'tȧ klär'ȧ). 1 River ab. 75 m. long, S California; rises in Los Angeles co. and flows W through Ventura co. to Santa Barbara Channel near Ventura.
2 County in California. See *Table* at CALIFORNIA.
3 City, Santa Clara co., W California, 5 m. NW of San Jose; pop. 58,880; fruit-packing houses, canneries. University of Santa Clara (1851; men; Rom. Cath.). Santa Clara mission. Settled 1777, became town 1852, rechartered 1867, incorporated 1926.

San'ta Cla'ra (*Span.* sän'tä klä'rä). 1 Former name of Las Villas prov., Cuba. See *Table* at CUBA.
2 Municipality, city, cen. Las Villas prov., W cen. Cuba; ✱ of Las Villas prov.; pop. (city) 27,925; railroad city, and important sugar and tobacco center; its port is Cienfuegos.
3 An island of the Juan Fernández group. See JUAN FERNÁNDEZ.

Santa Clara Bay. Bay in N coast of Matanzas prov., W cen. Cuba, E of Cárdenas Bay.

San'ta Co·lo'ma de Gra'ma·net' (sän'tä kō·lō'mä thä grä'mä·nĕt'). Commune, Barcelona prov., NE Spain, N suburb of Barcelona; pop. 10,310.

San'ta Cruz (sǎn'tȧ krōōz'). 1 Island at NW end of Santa Barbara group in Pacific Ocean; part of Santa Barbara co., SW California; separated from mainland by Santa Barbara Channel.
2 River ab. 150 m. long, S Arizona; rises in E Pima co. S of Tucson, flows NW into Gila river in NW Pinal co.
3 Name of counties in two states of the U.S. See *Tables* at ARIZONA and CALIFORNIA.
4 City, ⊗ of Santa Cruz co., W California, at N end of Monterey Bay; pop. 25,596; beach resort; in orchard,

vineyard, and farm region; founded 1769; mission founded 1791; incorporated as city 1866.

5 See SAINT CROIX island, Virgin Is. of the U.S.

San'ta Cruz (săn'tȧ krōōz'; *Span.* sän'tä krōōs').
1 River ab. 250 m. long in S Argentina; flows E out of Lake Argentino in W Santa Cruz territory and empties into Atlantic Ocean at Santa Cruz.
2 Territory of Argentina. See *Table* at ARGENTINA.
3 Port, E Santa Cruz territory, S Argentina, at mouth of Santa Cruz river; one of the best of the natural ports of Patagonia.
4 Department of Bolivia. See *Table* at BOLIVIA.
5 City, ✳ of Santa Cruz dept., E Bolivia; pop. (1943 est.) 32,800; in fertile region producing esp. sugar, coffee, and petroleum; founded in 16th cent.
6 *also known as* In'de·fat'i·ga·ble Island (ĭn'dė·făt'ȧ·gȧ·b'l). One of the Galápagos Is. (*q.v.*).
7 Municipality, S Ilocos Sur prov., Luzon, Phil. Is., on coast highway 34 m. S of Vigan; pop. 12,948.
8 Municipality, ✳ of Laguna prov., Luzon, Phil. Is., on SE shore of Laguna de Bay 34 m. SE of Manila; pop. 17,649; connected by highway, railroad, and boat with Manila and carries on important trade, esp. in rice and sugar. Made capital of province 1858.
9 Municipality, NW Zambales prov., Luzon, Phil. Is., on coast 30 m. N of Iba; pop. 11,194.
10 Municipality, NE coast of Marinduque I., Phil. Is., 18 m. E of Boac; pop. 24,537; a port of entry.
11 Municipality, W Davao prov., Mindanao, Phil. Is., on W shore of Davao Gulf 21 m. SW of City of Davao; pop. 33,808.
12 Chief island of Santa Cruz Is., SW Pacific Ocean. See NDENI.

Santa Cruz Bay. Inlet of Atlantic Ocean on E cen. coast of Santa Cruz territory, S Argentina; receives the Santa Cruz and Chico rivers from the W and NW.

Santa Cruz Channel. Strait bet. Santa Cruz I. and Santa Rosa I., off S coast of Santa Barbara co., SW California.

San'ta Cruz da Gra·ci·o'sa (sänn'tȧ krōōzh' thȧ grȧ·sē·ô'zȧ). Chief town of Graciosa I., cen. Azores.

San'ta Cruz de Bra'vo (sän'tä krōōz' thȧ vrä'vô). See FELIPE CARRILLO BRAVO.

Santa Cruz de Ga'le·a'na (gä'lä·ä'nä). Town, Guanajuato state, cen. Mexico; pop. 6904.

Santa Cruz de la Pal'ma (krōōth' [krōōz'] thȧ lä päl'mä). Chief town, La Palma I., Canary Is., Spain; pop. 11,605.

Santa Cruz del Nor'te (krōōz' thĕl nôr'tä). Municipality and town, La Habana prov., W Cuba; town is on N coast 27 m. E of Havana; pop. (1943) 6265.

Santa Cruz del Seibo *or* **Seybo.** See SEIBO commune.

San'ta Cruz del Sur (sän'tä krōōz' thĕl sŏŏr'). Municipality, Camagüey prov., E cen. Cuba; pop. 31,099; on S coast 50 m. S of Camagüey.

Santa Cruz de Te'ne·ri'fe (krōōth' [krōōz'] thȧ tā'nä·rē'fä). **1** Province of Spain. See *Table* at SPAIN.
2 Commercial and seaport city, its ✳, W Canary Is., Spain, chief city on Tenerife I., on NE coast 57 m. NW of Las Palmas; pop. (1941 est.) 73,299; agricultural products; manufactures wine, brandy, pottery, lime, matches, chocolates; metal founding; military fortifications; gubernatorial palace; 16th-cent. church.

San'ta Cruz do Sul (sän'tȧ krōōz' thŏŏ sŏŏl'; *Port.* sănn'tȧ krōōs'). City, E cen. Rio Grande do Sul state, S Brazil, 80 m. WNW of Pôrto Alegre; pop. (1940 est.) 9602.

San'ta Cruz Islands (săn'tȧ krōōz'). Island group in SW Pacific Ocean N of the New Hebrides and 240 m. E of S part of the Solomon Is.; 380 sq. m.; pop. (1931) 5080; chief island Ndeni; administratively attached to the British protectorate of Solomon Is. Other islands are Vanikoro, Utupua, and a number of islets, including Tinakula, an active volcano. Rarely visited and has unimportant trade in copra. Discovered 1595 by Men-

daña. In World War II site of naval engagement Oct. 26, 1942 in which American vessels and carrier planes defeated the Japanese but suffered loss of the *Hornet*.

San'ta Cruz Qui·ché' (sän'tä krōōs' kė·chä') *or* Quiché. Town, W cen. Guatemala; ✳ of Quiché dept.; pop. (1938 est.) 4332.

San'ta E·le'na (sän'tä ȧ·lā'nä). **1** Peninsula in W Guayas prov., W Ecuador, on N side of the Gulf of Guayaquil; its tip is La Puntilla and on its N side is Santa Elena Bay; site of most of Ecuador's oil fields.
2 Town on Santa Elena Penin., Guayas prov., W Ecuador, ab. 65 m. W of Guayaquil; pop. (1944 est.) 12,731; oil fields.
3 Town, Usulután dept., SE El Salvador; pop. (1942 est.) 5100.
4 Town, Cordillera dept., cen. Paraguay; pop. ab. 5900.

Santa Elena, Cape. Cape on NW coast of Costa Rica, extending into the Pacific Ocean.

Santa Elena Bay. See SANTA ELENA peninsula.

Santa Eugenia, Point. See Point EUGENIA.

Santa Eulalia. Former name of AQUILES SERDÁN.

San'ta Fe (sän'tȧ fā'). **1** River ab. 70 m. long, N Florida penin.; flows from E Alachua co., N Florida penin., W into the Suwannee river.
2 County in New Mexico. See *Table* at NEW MEXICO.
3 City, ✳ of New Mexico and ⊗ of Santa Fe co., ab. 40 m. W of Las Vegas, N cen. New Mexico, bet. the Pecos and Rio Grande; pop. 34,676; tourist center and health resort, surrounded by mountains; art center, with blended cultures of three races; known for Mexican and Indian curios, blankets and rugs, and Indian jewelry; shipping center for piñon nuts, fruit, livestock, copper, gold, iron, silver, turquoise. Has notable buildings and monuments, including Palace of the Governors (c. 1609; used for state museum since 1909, also as headquarters for state Historical Society, etc.), San Miguel Church (c. 1636), Cathedral of St. Francis (1869), Old Fort Marcy (1846); Laboratory of Anthropology (1923). Indian pueblos and Bandelier National Monument in vicinity.

History: Founded by Spaniards 1609–10, oldest capital city in U.S.; center of explorations and missions to the Indians in Spanish times; in hands of Indians 1680–92; retaken by the Spanish 1692; trading center for Spanish and Indians; opened trade with U.S. following Mexican independence from Spain in 1821; W terminus of Santa Fe Trail; occupied by Gen. Stephen W. Kearny 1846; made territorial capital 1851; alternately occupied by Confederate and Federal forces 1862.

San'ta Fe (*Span.* sän'tä fä'). **1** Province of Argentina. See *Table* at ARGENTINA.
2 City, its ✳, E cen. Argentina, on E bank of Salado river 90 m. N of Rosario; pop. (est.) 149,926; river port.
3 *also* **Santa Fe de Bogotá.** See BOGOTÁ, Colombia.
4 Village, Nueva Vizcaya prov., Luzon, Phil. Is., N of Balete Pass and SSW of Bayombong; in World War II scene of severe fighting in American conquest of Luzon; taken May 27, 1945; opened route to Cagayan valley.

San'ta Fe (săn'tȧ fā'; *Span.* sän'tä). Barrio in Isle of Pines municipality, La Habana prov., Cuba; pop. 1810.

San'ta Fe de An·tio'quia, de Gua'na·jua'to (sän'tä fä' thȧ än·tyô'kyä, gwä'nä·hwä'tô). = ANTIOQUIA, GUANAJUATO.

San'ta Fe Peak (săn'tȧ fā'). Mountain 13,146 ft. in Summit and Clear Creek cos., cen. Colorado.

Santa Fe Springs. City, Los Angeles co., SW California, N of Long Beach; pop. 16,342.

Santa Fe Trail. Commercial route to the West, used esp. 1821–80; started in W Missouri (first at Franklin, now nonexistent, then at Independence, and later at Westport, now Kansas City); proceeded along the prairie divide bet. the tributaries of the Kansas and Arkansas rivers to the great bend of the Arkansas, followed the Arkansas almost to the mountains, then turned south to Santa Fe, here giving a choice of three routes: the west-

ernmost branch, the Taos Trail, crossed the Sangre de Cristo Range at La Veta Pass, the middle branch went through Raton Pass (*q.v.*), and the shortest route, from present site of Cimarron, Kansas, went SW across Cimarron valley; trail first traced by William Becknell 1821; wagons used on his second trip 1822 and thereafter by many traders until 1880 when completion of railroad to Santa Fe reduced importance of the wagon road. See NATIONAL OLD TRAILS ROAD.

Sant'·A′ga·ta de′ Go′ti (sän·tä′gä·tä dä gô′tĕ). Commune, Benevento prov., Campania, S Italy, 15 m. WSW of Benevento; pop. 10,936; episcopal see.

Sant'Agata di Mi·li·tel′lo (dĕ mē·lē·tĕl′lô). Commune, Messina prov., NE Sicily, on Tyrrhenian Sea 52 m. WSW of Messina; pop. (1931) 14,791.

San′ta Ge′no·ve′va (sän′tä hā′nô·vā′vä). Mountain 7894 ft. in S Lower California, Mexico.

San′ta I·nés′ (sän′tä ē·nās′). Chilean island in Tierra del Fuego Archipelago (*q.v.*); separated from Brunswick Penin. on E by Strait of Magellan.

Santa Inés Za′ca·tel′co (sä′kä·tĕl′kô). Town, Tlaxcala state, cen. Mexico; pop. 7029.

San′ta Is′a·bel (sän′tȧ ĭz′ȧ·bĕl; *Span.* sän′tä ē′sä·vĕl′).
1 Chief town on the island of Fernando Poo, off Spanish Guinea, W Africa; ✳ of Spanish Guinea; pop. of district 15,064.
2 Municipality (pop. 14,542) and town (pop. 4712), S Puerto Rico; town is on coast ab. 13 m. E of Ponce.
3 *or* **Isabel.** Island in E cen. Solomon Is., W Pacific Ocean, ab. 40 m. E of SE Choiseul I. and separated from it by Manning Strait; ab. 140 m. long; 1500 sq. m. Part of British Solomon Islands protectorate. Has mountain chain the length of the island; highest Mt. Marescot 3900 ft. Has many coconut plantations; chief villages are Kia at N end and Tunnibuli at S end. Under German control from 1886 to 1899. Rekata Bay on its NW coast was used as a Japanese base in 1942–43.

San′ta I′sa·bel′ de las La′jas (sän′tä ē′sä·vĕl′ dä läz lä′häs). Municipality, Las Villas prov., W cen. Cuba, 22 m. W of Santa Clara; pop. 14,607.

San′tal Par′ga·nas (sŭn′täl pŭr′gȧ·näz). District, Bhagalpur division, E Bihar state, NE Indian Union; 5480 sq. m.; pop. (1941) 2,234,497; ✳ Dumka.

San′ta Lu·cí′a (sän′tä lōō·sē′ä). **1** River ab. 100 m. long in Uruguay, flowing into Río de la Plata 7 m. NW of Montevideo.
2 City, Canelones dept., S Uruguay, just N of Montevideo; pop. ab. 27,000.

San′ta Lu·ci′a Range (sän′tȧ lōō·sē′ȧ). Mountain range in Monterey and San Luis Obispo cos., SW California; one of the Coast Ranges.

San′ta Lu·zi′a (sänn′tȧ lōō·zē′ä). One of the Cape Verde Is.; 18 sq. m.; highest point 885 ft.

San′ta Mar′ga·ri′ta (sän′tȧ mär′gȧ·rē′tȧ; *Span.* sän′tä mär′gä·rē′tä). Island in Pacific Ocean off SW coast of Lower California, at the entrance to Magdalena Bay.

San′ta Mar′ghe·ri′ta Li′gu·re (sän′tä mär′gä·rē′tä lē′gōō·rä). Commune, Genova prov., Liguria, NW Italy, on Ligurian Sea 16 m. ESE of Genoa; pop. (1931) 9383; lacemaking; coral fisheries; winter health resort.

San′ta Ma·ri′a (sän′tȧ mȧ·rē′ȧ). **1** River ab. 45 m. long, W Arizona; rises in Yavapai co., flows W to join Big Sandy river and form Williams river.
2 City, Santa Barbara co., SW California, 52 m. NW of Santa Barbara; pop. 20,027; founded 1871; in region producing grain, beans, flower seeds.
3 *or* **Gau′a** (gou′ä). One of the Banks Is., N New Hebrides Is., SW Pacific Ocean, ab. 12 m. long by 10 m. wide; has central peak 2300 ft.

San′ta Ma·ri′a (*Port.* sänn′tȧ mȧ·rē′ȧ). **1** Cape on SW cen. coast of Angola, SW Africa, N of Cape Santa Marta.
2 Island, SE Azores, in Ponta Delgada dist.; 42 sq. m.; pop. ab. 6000; used by Allies in latter part of World War II as military and naval base.
3 City, cen. Rio Grande do Sul state, S Brazil; pop. (1940

est.) 39,492; connected by rail with Pôrto Alegre; center of prosperous agricultural region producing alfalfa, timber, rice, yerba, maté; has considerable manufacturing industry.

San′ta Ma·ri′a (*Span.* sän′tä mä·rē′ä). Municipality, S Bulacan prov., Luzon, Phil. Is., 10 m. E of Malolos; pop. 14,987; center of a rich rice and fruit region; has active market because of its nearness to Manila. Suffered much during Philippine rebellion 1899.

San′ta Ma·rí′a (*Span.* sän′tä mä·rē′ä). **1** Volcanic peak 6200 ft. in SW Mendoza prov., W Argentina.
2 Island in Pacific Ocean off W cen. coast of Chile, at entrance to Gulf of Arauco.
3 *also known as* **Charles Island** (chärlz). One of the Galápagos Is. (*q.v.*). See also POST OFFICE BAY.
4 Volcano 12,300 ft. in Guatemala, in Sierra Madre range near Quetzaltenango; frequent eruptions bet. 1900 and 1930.

Santa Maria, Cape. Cape on island off coast of Algarve prov., S Portugal.

Santa María, Cape. Cape projecting from SE coast of Uruguay.

San′ta Ma·rí′a A′sun·ción′ Tla·xia′co (sän′tä mä·rē′ä ä′sōōn·syôn′ tlä·syä′kô). Town, Oaxaca state, SE Mexico; pop. 6604.

San′ta Ma·ri′a Bay (sän′tȧ mȧ·rē′ȧ). Bay in NW coast of St. Thomas I., Virgin Is. of the U.S., West Indies.

San′ta Ma·ri′a Ca′pua Ve′te·re (sän′tä mä·rē′ä kä′pwä vâ′tā·rä). Commune, Napoli prov., Campania, S Italy, 16 m. N of Naples; pop. 38,173; 5th-cent. cathedral; Roman ruins.

San′ta Ma·rí′a Cay (*Span.* sän′tä mä·rē′ä). Island off NE coast of Las Villas prov., W cen. Cuba.

San′ta Ma·rí′a de Je·sús′ (sän′tä mä·rē′ä thä hā·sōōs′). Town, Sacatepéquez dept., S cen. Guatemala; pop. 6049.

Santa María del Buen Ai′re (thĕl vwän ī′rä). See BUENOS AIRES.

Santa María del Ro·sa′rio (thĕl rrô·sä′ryô). Municipality, La Habana prov., W Cuba, 8 m. ESE of Havana; pop. 6597.

San′ta Ma·rí′a di Le′u·ca, Cape (sän′tä mä·rē′ä dĕ lä′ōō·kä); *anc.* **Sal′len·ti′num Pro′mon·to′ri·um** (săl′ĕn·tī′nŭm prŏm′ŭn·tôr′ĭ·ŭm). Cape on SE coast of Apulia compartimento, SE Italy, at the tip of the "heel," on SE side of entrance to the Gulf of Taranto. See SALENTINE PENINSULA.

Santa María la Antigua del Darién. See DARIEN settlement and colony.

San′ta Mar′ta (sän′tȧ mär′tȧ; *Span.* sän′tä mär′tä). Seaport on N coast of Colombia, ✳ of Magdalena dept., 50 m. E of Barranquilla; pop. 25,113; historic town, founded 1525; important in Spanish era; in modern times port with fine harbor for rich banana district.

San′ta Mar′ta, Cape (sän′tȧ mär′tȧ). Cape on SW cen. coast of Angola, SW Africa.

Santa Marta, Sierra Nevada de. See SIERRA NEVADA DE SANTA MARTA.

San′ta Mar′ta Gran′de, Cape (sän′tȧ mär′tȧ grän′dĕ; *Port.* sănn′tȧ mär′tȧ grănn′dĕ). Cape on E coast of Santa Catarina state, S Brazil.

Santa Maura. See LEUKAS.

San′ta Mon′i·ca (sän′tȧ mŏn′ĭ·kȧ). Suburban residential and resort city, Los Angeles co., SW California, on **Santa Monica Bay** 15 m. W of center of Los Angeles; pop. 83,249; founded 1875; incorporated 1886; has airport and aircraft factories.

Sant'·A′na·sta′sia (sän·tä′näs·tä′zyä). Commune, Napoli prov., Campania, S Italy, near Mt. Vesuvius 7 m. E of Naples; pop. 12,146.

San′tan·der′ (sän′tän·dĕr′). **1** Department of Colombia. See *Table* at COLOMBIA.
2 Province of Spain. See *Table* at SPAIN.
3 Manufacturing and commercial seaport, ✳ of Santan-

der prov., N Spain, on Bay of Biscay 212 m. N of Madrid; pop. (1941 est.) 101,909; summer resort; fisheries, fish-salting works, shipyards, paper factories, foundries, breweries, sugar refineries; manufactures also textiles, chemicals, soap, candles, glass, perfumes, hats, noodles; Gothic cathedral; caves of Altamira and Castillo nearby; sacked by French under Soult 1808.

Santander Nor'te (nôr'tȧ). = NORTE DE SANTANDER.

Sant'·An'ge·lo (sän·tän'jȧ·lȯ). Village on Garigliano river, Latium, S Italy, near Cassino; assaulted unsuccessfully by Allied forces Jan. 20–23, 1944.

Sant'Angelo Lo·di·gia'no (lȯ·dē·jä'nȯ). Commune, Milano prov., Lombardy, N Italy, 20 m. SE of Milan; pop. 9428.

Sant'Anna do Livramento. See LIVRAMENTO.

San'ta·no'ni Peak (sän'tȧ·nȯ'nĭ). Mountain 4621 ft. in the Adirondack Mts., Essex co., NE New York.

Sant'·An'ti·mo (sän·tän'tē·mȯ). Commune, Napoli prov., Campania, S Italy, 6 m. N of Naples; pop. (1931) 11,220.

Sant'An·ti'o·co (sän'-tän·tē'ȯ·kȯ). 1 Island in Mediterranean Sea off SW coast of the island of Sardinia; 41 sq. m.; pop. (1931) ab. 9000; attached to Cagliari prov., Italy; connected with Sardinia by a causeway.
2 *anc.* **Sul'ci** (sŭl'sī). Town on the island; pop. of commune (1931) 6593; founded by Carthaginians; antiquities include remains of ancient walls, tombs both Punic and Roman, and catacombs.

San'ta Pau'la (sän'tȧ pô'lȧ). City, Ventura co., SW California, 33 m. E of Santa Barbara; pop. 13,279; founded 1875; oil refining; lemons.

Sant'·Ar·can'ge·lo di Ro·ma'gna (sän'tär·kän'jä·lȯ dē rȯ·män'yä). Commune, Forlì prov., Emilia, N Italy, 23 m. ESE of Forlì; pop. 11,668.

San'ta·rém' (sän'tȧ·rĕm'; *Port.* sănn'tȧ·räēn', -răēn'). 1 City on right bank of Amazon river where the Tapajoz joins it, W Pará state, N Brazil; pop. (1940 est.) 7666; port of call for river steamers; has extensive trade in rubber, cacao, Brazil nuts, tobacco, and sugar; also trades in fish. Founded 1661 by a Jesuit missionary.
2 District of Portugal. See *Table* at PORTUGAL.
3 Commune, ✳ of Santarém dist. and of Ribatejo prov., W cen. Portugal, on right bank of Tagus river 43 m. NE of Lisbon; pop. 12,106; river port; trades in olive oil, wine, fruit, grain; fisheries.

San'ta·ren' Channel (sän'tȧ·rĕn'); *also* **San'ta·rem' Channel** (-rĕm'). Channel in W Bahama Is., British West Indies, bet. Great Bahama Bank on E and Cay Sal Bank on W, and N of cen. part of Cuba.

San'ta Ri'ta. 1 (sän'tȧ rē'tȧ) Village, Grant co., SW New Mexico, ab. 12 m. NNE of Silver City; pop. 1772; open-pit copper mines.
2 (*Port.* sänn'tȧ rē'tȧ) City, Paraíba state, E Brazil; pop. (1940 est.) 10,867; a SW suburb of João Pessóa.

San'ta Ro'sa (sän'tȧ rȯ'zȧ). 1 County in Florida. See *Table* at FLORIDA.
2 City, ⊗ of Sonoma co., W California, 50 m. NNW of San Francisco; pop. 31,027; founded 1868; in agricultural region; stock raising, dairy farming; manufactures shoes, macaroni, chemical products; geysers, petrified forest, Redwoods State Park nearby. Home and experimental gardens of Luther Burbank.
3 Town, ⊗ of Guadalupe co., E cen. New Mexico on Pecos river ab. 38 m. NE of Vaughn; pop. 2220; ranching, agriculture, copper mining; ships livestock, wool.

San'ta Ro'sa (*Span.* sän'tä rrȯ'sä). 1 Town, ✳ of La Pampa territory, S cen. Argentina, ab. 310 m. SW of Buenos Aires; pop. (est.) 13,305.
2 Town, El Oro prov., SW Ecuador, near SE shore of Gulf of Guayaquil; pop. (1944 est.) 7184.
3 Mining town, E El Salvador, NE of San Miguel; pop. 12,131; gold and silver mines.
4 Department, S Guatemala; 1141 sq. m.; pop. 169,774; ✳ Cuilapa.
5 *in full* **San'ta Ro'sa de Co·pán'** (sän'tä rrȯ'sä thä

kȯ·pän'). Town, W Honduras, ✳ of Copán dept.; pop. (1940) 6018; a center of mining and cattle-raising area; 35 m. to the W is ruined city of Copán, southernmost point of the Old Empire of the Mayas, now largely buried under tropical vegetation and alluvial deposits; consists of courtyards, ball courts, stone columns, etc.
6 Town, Misiones dept., S Paraguay; pop. ab. 5200.
7 Municipality on W shore of Laguna de Bay, Laguna prov., Luzon, Phil. Is; pop. 15,069.

San'ta Ro'sa de Ca·bal' (sän'tä rrȯ'sä thä kä·väl'). Town, Caldas dept., W cen. Colombia, on E slope of Cordillera Occidental 30 m. SW of Manizales; pop. 9329.

San'ta Ro'sa Island (sän'tȧ rȯ'zȧ). 1 Island at NW end of Santa Barbara group in Pacific Ocean; part of Santa Barbara co., SW California; separated from mainland by Santa Barbara Channel.
2 Narrow island in Gulf of Mexico, lying along S coast of Santa Rosa and Okaloosa cos., NW Florida; belongs to Escambia co.

San'ta Ro·sa·lí'a (sän'tȧ rȯ'zȧ·lē'ȧ; *Span.* sän'tä rrȯ'sä·lē'ä). Town, South District of Lower California territory, NW Mexico, on W coast of Gulf of California; pop. 5451; copper mines; gypsum deposits.

San'ta Ro'sa Mountains (sän'tȧ rȯ'zȧ). Small range in N Nevada, in Humboldt co.; highest peak 9600 ft.

Santa Rosa Necoxtla. See CAMERINO MENDOZA.

Santa Tecla. See NUEVA SAN SALVADOR.

San'ta Te·re'sa di Ri'va (sän'tä tâ·râ'zä dē rē'vä). Commune, Messina prov., NE Sicily, on Strait of Messina 20 m. SSW of Messina; pop. 11,386.

San·tee' (sän·tē'; *attributively, also* sän'tē'). River 143 m. long, SE cen. South Carolina; formed by confluence of Congaree and Wateree rivers, flows SE into Atlantic Ocean.

Santee Dam. Dam 45 ft. high across Santee river, bet. Clarendon and Berkeley cos., SE cen. South Carolina; completed 1941; provides power from water impounded in **Lake Mar'i·on** (măr'ĭ·ŭn; mâr'-) *or* **Santee Reservoir,** a broad lake 40 m. long extending back to junction of Congaree and Wateree rivers.

San·teet'iah, Lake (sän·tēt'lȧ). Lake ab. 5 sq. m. in Graham co., W North Carolina, in resort area of Great Smoky Mts. SW of the national park.

Santeetlah Dam. See *Table* at TENNESSEE VALLEY AUTHORITY.

Sant'el·pi'dio a Ma're (sän'tâl·pē'dyȯ ä mä'rā). Commune, Ascoli Piceno prov., Marches, cen. Italy, near Adriatic coast 22 m. NNE of Ascoli Piceno; pop. 14,658; earthquake 1915.

Sant·e'ra·mo in Col'le (sän·tâ'rä·mȯ ēng kȯl'lä). Commune, Bari prov., Apulia, SE Italy, 23 m. S by W of Bari; pop. 17,069.

Sant'·Eu·fe'mia, Gulf of (sän'tȧ·ōō·fâ'myä); *anc.* **Gulf of Hip·po'ni·a'tes** (hĭ·pȯ'nĭ·ā'tēz) *or* **Gulf of Vi'bo** (vē'bō). Inlet of Tyrrhenian Sea on W coast of Calabria, S Italy.

Santh. See SANT.

San'ti·a'go (sän'tĭ·ä'gȯ; *Span.* sän·tyä'gȯ; *Port.* sănn-tyȧ'gōō). 1 *in full* **San·tia'go do Bo'quei·rão'** (sänn-tyä'gōō thōō vō'kä·rouⁿ'). City, W Rio Grande do Sul state, S Brazil, 90 m. WNW of Santa Maria; pop. 8372.
2 One of the Cape Verde Is. See SÃO TIAGO.
3 Province of Chile. See *Table* at CHILE.
4 *or* **San·tia'go de Chi'le** (sän·tyä'gȯ thä chē'lȧ). City in cen. Chile, ✳ of Santiago prov. and of Chile, 116 m. ESE of Valparaíso on the Mapocho river; 4th largest city in South America; pop. 952,075; built on plain, altitude 1706 ft., in view of high Andean peaks to the E; archbishop's see; contains many fine public buildings, including cathedral (destroyed 1647, rebuilt 1748), president's palace, national legislature, national museum, national library, Univ. of Chile (founded 1842). Founded in 1541 by the Spanish conqueror Pedro de Valdivia; has suffered much from earthquakes and revolutionary outbreaks; occupied by Gen. San Martín's forces 1817; site

of fifth session of Pan-American Congress Mar. 25 to May 3, 1923.

5 = SANTIAGO DE CUBA.

6 Province, N cen. Dominican Republic. See *Table* at DOMINICAN REPUBLIC.

7 *or* **San·tia'go de los Ca'bal·le'ros** (sän-tyä'gŏ thä lōs kä'vä-yä'rōs). Commune (1941 pop. 140,208) and city (1944 est. pop. 52,943), N cen. Dominican Republic, ✱ of Santiago prov.; produces tobacco, coffee, cacao.

8 River ab. 130 m. long in SE Ecuador and NW Peru; formed by confluence of Paute and Zamora rivers in SE Ecuador, flows E across border of Peru, and S into Marañón river.

9 = SAN SALVADOR, Galápagos Is.

10 *also* **Rí'o Gran'de de San·tia'go** (rē'ŏ grän'dä thä sän'tyä'gŏ). River of SW Mexico; rises ab. 18 m. W of the city of Mexico, flows through Lake Chapala W into the Pacific Ocean; length below Lake Chapala 340 m.; known as **Ler'ma** (lĕr'mä) river above Lake Chapala. See JUANACATLÁN.

11 Mountain 9272 ft., W Panama; highest in Sierra de Tabasara.

12 Town, SW cen. Panama, ✱ of Veraguas prov.; pop. 4253.

13 Town, Misiones dept., S Paraguay; pop. ab. 8600.

14 Island marking NW corner of Lingayen Gulf, Pangasinan prov., Luzon, Phil. Is., opp. Bolinao municipality; 8 sq. m.; pop. 3922.

15 Municipality, SW Isabela prov. Luzon, Phil. Is., junction point on main highway N from cen. Philippines to Cagayan valley; pop. 34,154. In World War II taken by Americans June 15, 1945.

16 *or* **San·tia'go de Com'pos·te'la** (sän-tyä'gŏ thä kôm'pŏs-tā'lä). Commune, La Coruña prov., NW Spain, 32 m. S by W of La Coruña; pop. 49,191; manufactures linen, silverware, liquors, soap, chocolates, crystal, paper; agricultural products; 11th-cent. cathedral, said to have been built on site of grave of the apostle St. James and to contain his remains; probably most visited place of pilgrimage in western Europe— whence the epithet "Mecca of Spain"; university (founded 1532); 16th-cent. hospice for pilgrims, built by Ferdinand and Isabella; mineral springs; formerly capital of Galicia.

Santiago, Cape. Point on SW coast of Batangas prov., Luzon, Phil. Is., in Verde Island Passage on SW side of entrance to Balayan Bay.

San·tia'go A'ti·tlán' (sän-tyä'gŏ ä'tē-tlän'); *formerly* **Atitlán.** Town, Sololá dept., S Guatemala, on S shore of Lake Atitlán; pop. 6742.

Santiago Bay. Bay on S coast of Oriente prov., E Cuba.

Santiago de Chile. See SANTIAGO city, Chile.

Santiago de Compostela. See SANTIAGO commune, Spain.

San·tia'go de Cu'ba (sän-tyä'gŏ thä kōō'vä). **1** Former name of Oriente prov., Cuba. See *Table* at CUBA.

2 Seaport on S coast of Cuba; ✱ of Oriente prov.; pop. 120,577; on a landlocked bay 6 m. long, 3 m. wide, connected with Caribbean by long narrow channel beneath battlements of Morro Castle (alt. 200 ft.); iron, copper, manganese mines in the mountains of the vicinity. Founded 1514, capital of the island until 1589; endured several severe earthquakes; during Spanish-American War center of military action (see EL CANEY and SAN JUAN HILL) and scene of destruction of the Spanish fleet under Cervera July 3, 1898 virtually ending the war.

Santiago de Guayaquil. See GUAYAQUIL.

San·tia'go de las Ve'gas (sän-tyä'gŏ thä läz vā'gäs). Municipality and town, La Habana prov., W Cuba, 10 m. S of Havana; pop. (town) 9385.

Santiago del Es·te'ro (thĕl äs·tā'rŏ). **1** Province of Argentina. See *Table* at ARGENTINA.

2 City, its ✱, N Argentina, on the Dulce river ab. 88 m. SE of Tucumán; pop. (est.) 58,925; on edge of marsh

region of N cen. Argentina; has rail connection with Buenos Aires. Founded 1553; fine old church and convent date from c. 1590.

Santiago de los Caballeros. See SANTIAGO commune, Dominican Republic.

Santiago de Ma·rí'a (thä mä-rē'ä). Town, Usulután dept., SE El Salvador; pop. (1942 est.) 5988.

Santiago do Boqueirão. See SANTIAGO city, Brazil.

Santiago Island. See SANTIAGO.

San·tia'go Ix·cuin'tla (sän-tyä'gŏ ēs-kwēn'tlä). Town, Nayarit state, W Mexico, on the Santiago river ab. 20 m. from its mouth; pop. 7322. Founded 1531.

San'ti·a'go Mountains (sän'tĭ·ä'gŏ). Range in W cen. Brewster co., W Texas, extending S to the Rio Grande river; across the river in Mexico the range is called Del Carmen Mts.

Santiago Peak. Mountain 6521 ft. in W cen. Brewster co., W Texas.

San·tia'go Tux'tla (sän-tyä'gŏ tōōs'tlä). Town, Veracruz state, E Mexico; pop. 5392.

San·tia'go–Za·mo'ra (sän-tyä'gŏ·sä·mō'rä). Province, E Ecuador; ✱ Macas; formed 1925; with Napo-Pastaza prov. (*q.v.*) constitutes the Eastern Region (*Span.* Región Oriental) of Ecuador. Represents part of former larger province of same name; boundaries settled 1942.

San'ti·am' (sän'tĭ·ăm'). River, NW Oregon; formed by confluence of branches (North Santiam and South Santiam) on SW boundary of Marion co., flows W into Willamette river; length with longest branch ab. 75 m.

San'ti·pur (sän'tĭ·pōōr). Town, Nadia dist., West Bengal, NE Indian Union, on left bank of Hooghly river 45 m. N of Calcutta; pop. 24,992.

San'ti Qua·ran'ta (sän'tē kwä·rän'tä) *or* **Por'to Ed'da** (pôr'tŏ ĕd'dä). Adriatic seaport, S Albania, NE of island of Corfu; pop. ab. 5000; developed as commercial port under Italian influence and officially known as Porto Edda 1940–45. Captured by Greeks Dec. 6, 1940 and held until Germans invaded the Balkans Apr. 1941.

Sän'tis *or* **Sen'tis** (zĕn'tĭs). Peak 8216 ft. in Appenzell canton, NE Switzerland; highest point in the canton.

Santo. See SAINT.

San'to (sän'tŏ). See ESPÍRITU SANTO island, New Hebrides.

Santo, Mount. 1 Mountain 2237 ft. on S end of Bainsizza plateau, formerly in compartimento of Venezia Giulia e Zara, NE Italy; E of the Isonzo and N of Gorizia; severe fighting May and Aug. 1917; since treaty of 1947 in NW Yugoslavia near boundary line.

2 Mountain 6195 ft. on W coast of Espíritu Santo I., New Hebrides Is., SW Pacific; highest point on the island.

San'to A'gos·ti'nho, Cape (sănn'tōō ä'gōōsh·tē'-nyōō). Cape extending into Atlantic Ocean on E coast of Pernambuco state, E Brazil, S of Recife (Pernambuco).

Santo A·ma'ro (ä·mä'rōō). City, E Baía state, E Brazil, NW of Salvador; pop. (1940 est.) 11,051.

Santo An·dré' (ănn·drä'). City, São Paulo state, SE Brazil; pop. (1940 est.) 62,978.

Santo An·tão' (ănn·toun'). Island in extreme NW of the Cape Verde Is.; 266 sq. m.; pop. 34,000; ✱ Ribeira Grande (pop. ab. 5000); highest point 7300 ft.; mineral springs; produces coffee, sugar, and fruit.

San'to Do·min'go (sän'tŏ dŏ·mĭng'gŏ; *Span.* sän'tŏ thŏ·mĕng'gŏ). **1** Town on Osa Penin. in SW Costa Rica, on Gulf of Dulce.

2 Municipality, Las Villas prov., W cen. Cuba, 20 m. NW of Santa Clara; pop. 25,730; railroad junction and shipping point in sugar-raising district.

3 Early name of the island of HISPANIOLA.

4 Former name of DOMINICAN REPUBLIC.

5 City founded by Spanish in 1496 (oldest continuous European settlement in Americas), on S coast of W

Hispaniola (*q.v.*); called Ciudad Trujillo (*q.v.*) between 1936 and 1961.

6 *officially* **District of Santo Domingo;** *Span.* **Distri'to de San'to Do·min'go** (děs·trē'tô thä sän'tô thô·mēng'gô). District, S Dominican Republic. See *Table* at DOMINICAN REPUBLIC.

Santo Domingo, Point. Cape on SW coast of Pinar del Río prov., W Cuba, on N side of Cortés Bay.

Santo Domingo de Basco. See BASCO.

San'to Do·min'go Te·huan'te·pec' (sän'tô thô·mēng'gô tä·wän'tä·pěk'). Town, Oaxaca state, SE Mexico; pop. 6731.

San'to·rin' (sän'tô·rēn'); *Gr.* **Thē'ra** (thē'rä); *anc.* **The'ra** (thĕr'å). Volcanic island, S Cyclades, in the Aegean Sea on N side of Sea of Candia; in Cyclades dept., Greece; 30 sq. m.; pop. ab. 17,000; ✱ Thēra. Its surface has much tufa which is exported as a cement. Has had numerous volcanic eruptions; earliest recorded 196 B.C., latest 1866. Has prehistoric remains, and is thought to have been settled early by Phoenicians and Spartans; c. 630 B.C. sent colonists to found Cyrene in Libya.

San'tos (săn'tŭs; *Port.* săNN'tŏŏs). Seaport, SE São Paulo state, SE Brazil, 45 m. SSE of São Paulo and ab. 200 m. WSW of Rio de Janeiro; pop. (1940 est.) 158,774; located on an island in a tidal inlet (sometimes called the Santos river) in low, marshy region; has fine port and dock facilities; greatest coffee-exporting port in the world; also exports bananas, citrus fruits, sugar, rice, and meat products. Its residential and resort section, Guarujá, has one of the finest beaches in South America. Settled 1543–46, a few years after the settlement of São Vicente (*q.v.*); captured by Thomas Cavendish 1591.

Santos, Los. See LOS SANTOS.

San'tos Du·mont' (săNN'tŏŏzh dŏŏ·mōNNt'; *Angl.* săn'tŭs dŏŏ·mŏnt'). City, Minas Gerais state, E Brazil; pop. (1940 est.) 11,583.

Santo Stefano. = SAN STEFANO.

San'to Sti'no di Li·ven'za (sän'tô stē'nô dě lē·věn'tsä). Commune, Venezia prov., Venezia Euganea, NE Italy, 22 m. NE of Venice; pop. 10,968.

San'to To·mas' (sän'tô tô·mäs'). **1** Municipality, NE Batangas prov., Luzon, P'hil. Is., on railroad and highway NE of Lake Taal; pop. 16,544; at W base of Mt. Maquiling and ab. 10 m. S of Laguna de Bay.
2 University buildings and campus in N part of the City of Manila, Phil. Is., used by Japanese in World War II as a prison camp for Americans.

Santo Tomas, Mount. Mountain 7406 ft., S Benguet subprov., Mountain Province, Luzon, Phil. Is., S of Baguio.

San'to To·mé' de Gua·ya'na (sän'tô tô·mā' thä gwä·yä'nä) *or* **San To·mé' de Gua·ya'na** (sän' tó·mā') *or* **Ciu·dad' Guayana** (syŏŏ·thäth'). City, NE Bolívar state, E Venezuela, at confluence of Orinoco and Caroní rivers; pop. (est. 1964) 65,000; founded 1961.

San'tu·ao' (sän'dŏŏ'ou'). Treaty port, N coast of Fukien prov., SE China, on Santu I. in Santuao Bay, ab. 48 m. N of Minhow (70 m. by sea); pop. (1931 est.) 9000; has exceptionally fine harbor; opened by imperial decree to foreign trade 1899; formerly had large tea trade.

San Va'len·tín' (säm bä'län·tēn'). Peak 13,313 ft. in S Chile, W of Lake Buenos Aires.

San Va·len·ti'no in A·bruz'zo Ci·te·rio're (säm' vä·län·tē'nô ēn ä·brŏŏt'tsô chě·tä·ryō'rä). Commune, Pescara prov., Abruzzi e Molise, cen. Italy, 20 m. SW of Pescara; pop. 10,464.

San'vic' (sän'věk'). Industrial commune, Seine-Maritime dept., N France, ENE suburb of Le Havre; pop. (1931) 15,327; distilleries; produces lubricating oil; site of fort defending Le Havre.

San Vi·cen'te (säm' bě·sän'tä). **1** Peak 7246 ft. in El Salvador.
2 Department of El Salvador; 883 sq. m.; pop. (1942 est.) 100,978.

3 City, its ✱, cen. El Salvador; pop. (1942 est.) 13,158; industrial and commercial center; trades in corn, tobacco, indigo, coffee, sugar cane; damaged by earthquake 1937.

San Vi·cen'te de Al·cán'ta·ra (säm' bě·thän'tä [běsän'-] thä äl·kän'tä·rä). Commune, Badajoz prov., SW Spain, 35 m. NNW of Badajoz; pop. 10,269.

San Vi'to (säm vē'tô). Cape on SW coast of Sicily.

San Vito al Ta'glia·men'to (äl täl'yä·mān'tô). Commune, Friuli prov., Venezia Euganea, NE Italy, 22 m. WSW of Udine; pop. 11,583.

San Vito de'i Nor·man'ni (dā'ē nôr·män'nē). Commune, Brindisi prov., Apulia, SE Ita.y, 13 m. WNW of Brindisi; pop. 14,558; airport.

San·ya'ti (sän·yä'tē). River ab. 260 m. long, N cen. Southern Rhodesia; flows NW into Zambezi river.

São (souN). See SAINT.

São Bor'ja (souN vôr'zhå). City, W Rio Grande do Sul state, S Brazil, on W bank of Uruguay river on Argentina border; pop. (1940 est.) 8774.

São Brás de Al'por·tel' (vräzh' thē äl'pŏŏr·tâl'). Commune, Faro dist., S Portugal, 10 m. N of Faro; pop. 10,942.

São Car'los (souNng kár'lŏŏs). City, E cen. São Paulo state, SE Brazil, on railroad 130 m. NW of São Paulo; pop. (1940 est.) 24,763.

São Fran·cis'co (souN' frän·sēsh'kŏŏ). **1** Island 20 m. long in Atlantic Ocean off NE coast of Santa Catarina state, Brazil.
2 River ab. 1800 m. long in E Brazil; rises in S cen. Minas Gerais state, flows N, NE, and E into Atlantic Ocean S of Maceió.
3 *formerly* **São Francisco do Sul** (thŏŏ sŏŏl'). Seaport town, Santa Catarina state, S Brazil, on São Francisco I. 90 m. N of Florianópolis; pop. (1940 est.) 10,280.

São Ga'bri·el' (souNng gà'vrē·âl'). City, Rio Grande do Sul state, S Brazil, 60 m. SSW of Santa Maria; pop. (1940 est.) 12,461.

São Gon·ça'lo (souNng' gŏN·så'lŏŏ). City, Rio de Janeiro state, SE Brazil, on E side of Guanabara Bay opp. Rio de Janeiro; pop. (1940 est.) 8612.

São João (souN zhwouN'). Island off N coast of Maranhão state, Brazil, at entrance to Turiassú Bay.

São João da Bo'a Vis'ta (thä võ'å vēsh'tä). City, E São Paulo state, SE Brazil, 110 m. N of São Paulo; pop. (1940 est.) 12,190.

São João del Rei (thĕl rā'ē). City, S Minas Gerais state, E Brazil, 82 m. S of Belo Horizonte; pop. (1940 est.) 22,912.

São Jor'ge (souN zhôr'zhě); *Eng.* **Saint George** (sånt jôrj'). Island, cen. Azores, W of Terceira, in the district of Angra do Heroísmo; 40 sq. m.; pop. ab. 16,000.

São Jo·sé' Bay (souN' zhŏŏ·zâ'). Bay on NE coast of Brazil, in Maranhão state, SE of Maranhão I.

São José do Ri'o Par'do (thŏŏ rē'ŏŏ pár'dŏŏ). City, E São Paulo state, SE Brazil, 135 m. N of São Paulo; pop. (1940 est.) 8641.

São José dos Cam'pos (thŏŏsh känm'pŏŏs). City, São Paulo state, SE Brazil, near São Paulo; pop. (1940 est.) 13,584; site of large aviation center.

São Le'o·pol'do (souN lā'ŏŏ·pôl'dŏŏ). City, Rio Grande do Sul state, S Brazil; pop. (1940 est.) 14,003; N suburb of Pôrto Alegre.

São Lou·ren'ço (souN' lō·rän'sŏŏ). **1** River ab. 340 m. long in Mato Grosso state, SW Brazil; flows SW through large marsh area (Pantanal de São Lourenço) into Paraguay river near Bolivian border; the Cuiabá is a tributary on the N.
2 Watering place, S Minas Gerais state, E Brazil, ab. equidistant from Rio de Janeiro and São Paulo; pop. (1940 est.) 7443; altitude ab. 2800 ft. on N slopes of Serra da Mantiqueira; mineral waters and baths.

São Luiz (souN lwēs'). **1** *or* **São Luiz do Ma'ra·nhão** (lwēzh' thŏŏ mà'rà·nyouN'). See MARANHÃO island.
2 *unofficially called* **São Luiz do Maranhão.** Seaport

city, ✳ of Maranhão state, NE Brazil, on the island of Maranhão; pop. (1940 est.) 59,476; manufactures cotton and sugar. Founded 1612 by a Frenchman; taken by Portuguese 1615, by Dutch 1641, retaken by Portuguese 1644.

São Luiz Gon·za′ga (SOUN lwēzh′ gōN·zȧ′gȧ). City, NW Rio Grande do Sul state, S Brazil, 95 m. NNW of Santa Maria; pop. 6162.

São Ma·nuel′ (SOUN′ mȧ·nwâl′). River nearly 600 m. long in cen. Brazil; flows NW out of Mato Grosso state, forming part of boundary bet. Mato Grosso and Pará states; joins with Juruena (q.v.) to form the Tapajoz river.

São Mar′cos Bay (SOUN mȧr′kōos). Inlet of Atlantic Ocean on NE coast of Brazil, in Maranhão state, W of Maranhão I.

São Mi·guel′ (SOUN′ mê·gâl′); *Eng.* **Saint Mi′chael** (sånt mĭ′kĕl; -k′l). Island, E Azores, in the district of Ponta Delgada; 297 sq. m.; pop. ab. 117,000; chief town Ponta Delgada; largest island of the group.

Sa·o′na Island (sä·ō′nä). Small island 13 m. long of the West Indies, in the N cen. Caribbean Sea off SE coast of Hispaniola.

Saône (sōn); *anc.* **A′rar** (ā′rär). River ab. 300 m. long in E France; rises in Vosges dept., NE France, flows SSW into Rhone river at Lyons; receives the Doubs from the E; navigable for over 200 m.

Saône, Haute– (ōt′sōn′). Department of France. See *Haute-Saône* in *Table* at FRANCE.

Saône–et–Loire (sōn′ā·lwár′). Department of France. See *Table* at FRANCE.

São Ni·co·lá′o (SOUN′ nê·kōō·lä′ōō); *Eng.* **Saint Nich′-o·las** (sånt nĭk′ō·lȧs). One of the Cape Verde Is.; 30 m. long; 135 sq. m.; pop. ab. 12,000; highest point 4280 ft. One of first of the group to be colonized; at height of its prosperity in middle of 18th cent.

São Pau′lo (SOUNM pou′lōō). **1** State of Brazil. See *Table* at BRAZIL.

2 City, its ✳, SE Brazil, on the Tietê river 45 m. NNW of Santos, its port; pop. (1965 est.) 5,251,000; second largest city in Brazil and third in size in South America; altitude ab. 3000 ft.; one of the most rapidly growing cities in the world; great railroad center; manufactures cotton, hosiery, glass, furniture, flour; has several large suburbs; modern and healthful, with many parks, fine public buildings, large public market, stadium, art gallery, Ypiranga Museum (on site where independence of Brazil was declared Sept. 7, 1822); also Polytechnic School, Normal School, School of Agriculture. Founded by Jesuit priests 1554 on site of Indian village Piratininga; name changed later to São Paulo; became administrative center of surrounding region 1681.

São Paulo de Loanda. See LUANDA.

São Pedro do Rio Grande do Sul. See RIO GRANDE.

São Ro′que (SOUN rô′kĕ), *or* **San Ro′que** (sän rrô′kä), **Cape.** Cape, E coast of Rio Grande do Norte, NE Brazil, N of Natal.

Saorstat Eireann, Saorstát Éireann. See EIRE.

São Sal′va·dor′ (SOUN säl′vȧ·thôr′). **1** Town, N Angola, Africa; pop. ab. 4000; ancient capital of kingdom of Congo 16th to 18th cents.

2 Seaport, E Brazil. See SALVADOR.

São Se′bas·tião′ (sä′vȧsh·tyouN′). Island in Atlantic Ocean off NE coast of São Paulo state, Brazil; belongs to Brazil

São Sebastião, Cape. Cape extending into Mozambique Channel on SE coast of Mozambique, SE Africa, N of Inhambane.

São Tia′go (SOUN tyä′gōō); *also* **San′ti·a·go** (săn′tǐ-ä′gō). Largest of the Cape Verde Is.; 359 sq. m.; pop. ab. 59,000; chief town Praia, ✳ of the group; highest point 4500 ft.; mountainous, many ravines and streams; grows coffee, oranges, sugar cane.

São To·mé′. 1 *or* **São Tho·mé′** (SOUNN′ tōō·mâ′); *Eng.* **Saint Thom′as** (sånt tŏm′ȧs). Portuguese island

in the Gulf of Guinea, on the equator, W Africa; 319 sq. m.; pop. (1936) ab. 52,000; with Principe I. (q.v.), forms the Portuguese province **São Tomé e Prin′ci·pe** (ê prēN′sĕ·pĕ), ab. 377 sq. m., pop. (1940) 60,490; exports cacao, coffee, coconuts, copra, palm oil, cinchona.

2 Part of Madras city, India, originally a Portuguese port. See SAINT THOMÉ.

São Tomé, Cape. Cape extending into Atlantic Ocean on NE coast of Rio de Janeiro state, SE Brazil.

São Vi·cen′te (SOUN′ vê·sāNn′tĕ); *Eng.* **Saint Vin′-cent** (sånt vĭn′s'nt). **1** City, São Paulo state, SE Brazil, on same island with Santos, SSE of São Paulo; pop. (1940 est.) 13,130. First settlement 1532 on São Paulo coast; not successful at first and burned by Cavendish 1591.

2 One of the Cape Verde Is.; 75 sq. m.; pop. ab. 8000; chief town Porto Grande; highest point 2400 ft.; coaling station.

São Vicente, Cabo de. See Cape SAINT VINCENT.

Sa·pe′le (sä·pā′lĕ). Port in Niger delta, N Warri prov., S Nigeria; pop. ab. 4000; on the Benin river at the junction of its headstreams.

Sap′e·lo Island (săp′ĕ·lō). Island in Atlantic Ocean, off E mainland of McIntosh co., SE Georgia; to the NW is Sapelo Sound.

Sa′pe Strait (sä′pä). Channel ab. 13 m. wide, bet. E end of Sumbawa I. and Komodo I. (part of Flores group), Lesser Sunda Is., Indonesia; connects Flores Sea with Indian Ocean.

Sa·poe′di *or* **Sa·pu′di** (sä·pōō′dĕ). Island, Malay Archipelago, E of Madura I., in East Java prov., Indonesia; area with adjacent small islands, 94 sq. m., pop. 63,534.

Sap′pa (săp′ȧ). River ab. 150 m. long, NW Kansas and SW Nebraska; rises in Sherman co., NW Kansas, flows NE into Nebraska and joins Beaver creek 10 m. before emptying into Republican river in Harlan co.

Sap′phire Mountains (săf′ĭr). A range of the Rocky Mts. in W Montana, extending along the boundary bet. Granite and Ravalli cos.

Sap·po·ro (säp·pô·rô). City on W Hokkaido I., near head of Otaru Bay, Japan; ✳ of Hokkaido prefecture; pop. (1938 est.) 210,300; varied manufactures; breweries; imperial university (agricultural college). Laid out 1869 by the government as a colonizing center for the development of the island.

Sa′pu·cai′a (sä′pōō·kī′ȧ). Small island in Guanabara Bay, N of the city of Rio de Janeiro, Brazil, and S of Bom Jesús I.

Sa′pu·cay′ (sä′pōō·kī′). Town, Misiones dept., S cen. Paraguay; pop. ab. 6280.

Sa·pul′pa (sȧ·pŭl′pȧ). City, ⊗ of Creek co., E cen. Oklahoma, 13 m. SSW of Tulsa; pop. 14,282; oil and gas wells; cattle shipping, cotton marketing, food packing; manufactures glass, brick and tile, pottery.

Saq·qa′ra (sŭk·kä′rȯ; săg·gä′rȯ). Modern village in Lower Egypt just SW of ruins of Memphis; site of the necropolis of ancient Memphis; Step Pyramid, the oldest Egyptian pyramid, built by Zoser, first king of the IIId dynasty; also pyramids of the Vth and VIth dynasties and many mastabas.

Sa′ra (sä′rä). Municipality, NE Iloilo prov., Panay, Phil. Is., 48 m. NE of City of Iloilo; pop. 22,419.

Sarabat. See GEDIZ.

Sa·ra Bu·ri *or* **Sa·ra·bu·ri** (sä·rä·bōō·rē). **1** Province, S Thailand; 2309 sq. m.; pop. 182,749.

2 Town, its ✳, on right bank of the Sak river and on the railroad 20 m. NE of Ayudhya and ab. 65 m. NE of Bangkok.

Sarafand. See ZAREPHATH.

Sar′a·gos′sa (săr′ȧ·gŏs′ȧ); *Span.* **Za·ra·go′za** (thä′rä-gō′thä; sä′rä·gō′sä). **1** Province, NE Spain. See *Zaragoza*, in *Table* at SPAIN.

2 *anc.* **Sal·du′ba** (săl·dū′bȧ); *later* **Cae′sar·au·gus′ta** (sē′zēr·ȯ·gŭs′tȧ). City, ✳ of Zaragoza prov., NE Spain,

on Ebro river 170 m. NE of Madrid; pop. (1941 est.) 239,851; manufacturing and railroad center; active trade, esp. in wheat and flour; university; two cathedrals, La Seo (12th-cent. Gothic) and El Pilar (17th cent.); 13th-cent. church, former royal palace, the exchange (the Lonja; 1551), Moorish citadel, palace of counts of Luna.

History: Celt-Iberian settlement of Salduba; taken by Romans 25 B.C.; made Roman military station and trade center; captured by Visigoths and 712 by Moors; reconquered 1118 by Alfonso I of Aragon; made capital of Aragon to 15th cent.; French defeat by English nearby 1710; underwent two famous sieges by French 1808–09, known to many readers through Byron's commemoration of the "Maid of Saragossa" in *Childe Harold.*

Sa·ra·gu'ro (sä'rä·gōō'rō). Town, Loja prov., SW Ecuador; pop. 7890; in Andes Mts. 60 m. S of Cuenca.

Sa·rai' (sä·ri'). City, ancient ✱ of the Khanate of the Golden Horde, near modern Leninsk (*q.v.*), SE Russia, Europe, E of the lower Volga. Founded by Batu Khan 1241; for 200 years the Tatar (Kipchak) seat of government to which Russians paid tribute; seized by a vassal of Tamerlane 1382; declined after 1480 when Ivan III threw off Tatar yoke.

Sa·rai'ke·la (sä·ri'kä·lä). Former Indian state, NE Eastern States, NE Indian Union, on boundary of S Bihar; 446 sq. m.; pop. (1941) 154,844; ✱ Saraikela; geographically in Orissa.

Sa·ra·je·vo (sä'rä·yĕ·vô) *or* **Se·ra·je·vo** (sĕ'-). City, ✱ of Bosnia and Herzegovina, cen. Yugoslavia, ab. 157 m. SW of Belgrade; pop. 78,173; in valley of upper Bosna river at alt. 1800 ft.; has many fine mosques; industrial center; manufactures carpets and tobacco products. Founded in early 15th cent.; under Turkish rule 1440–1878; passed to Austria-Hungary 1878 and was made capital of Bosnia and Herzegovina; scene of assassination of Archduke Francis Ferdinand June 28, 1914, precipitating World War I; became part of newly organized Kingdom of the Serbs, Croats, and Slovenes 1918; held by Germans Apr. 1941 until recapture Apr. 1945.

Sa·rakhs' (sà·ràks'). Fortified town, Khurasan prov., NE Iran; pop. ab. 10,000; on Hari Rud river at Turkmen S.S.R. border 90 m. ENE of Meshed.

Sa·ra·mac'ca (sä'rä·mäk'ä). **1** River ab. 250 m. long in cen. and N cen. Surinam; flows N into Atlantic Ocean. **2** District of Surinam; pop. (1941) 9866.

Sa·ra'na (sà·rä'nà). Valley and pass in mountains of NE Attu I., W Aleutians, Alaska, leading from **Sarana Bay** on S to Chichagof Harbor to the N; severe fighting May 1942.

Sar'a·nac (săr'à·năk). River ab. 100 m. long, NE New York; outlet of Saranac Lakes in Franklin co., flows NE into Lake Champlain at Plattsburg.

Saranac Lake. Village, Essex and Franklin cos., NE New York, near Lower Saranac Lake 36 m. S of Malone; pop. 6421; in Adirondack region; alt. 1540 ft.; settled 1819; health resort, originally esp. for the tubercular; summer and winter sports; Dr. Edward L. Trudeau's outdoor sanatorium (1884) and laboratory; Will Rogers Memorial Sanatorium (1930) in vicinity; home of Robert Louis Stevenson 1887–88.

Saranac Lakes. Three lakes in S Franklin co., NE New York, **Upper Saranac Lake** ab. 8 m. long, **Middle Saranac Lake** ab. 2½ m. wide, and **Lower Saranac Lake** ab. 5 m. long; elevation 1540 ft.

Sa·ra·nap (săr'à·năp). Urban area, Contra Costa co., W California; S of Walnut Creek; pop. 6450.

Sarandë. See SANTI QUARANTA.

Sa·ran·dí' del Yi (sä'rän·dē' thĕl yē'). Town, Durazno dept., cen. Uruguay; pop. ab. 5600.

Sarandí Gran'de (grän'då). Town, Florida dept., S cen. Uruguay; pop. ab. 5000.

Sa·ran·ga'ni Bay (sä'räng·gä'nĕ). Inlet of Celebes Sea, S Mindanao, in SE part of Cotabato rov., Phil. Is.; 19 m. long by 9 m. wide. Town of Buayan at its head.

Sarangani Islands. Island group, SW Davao prov.,

Mindanao, Phil. Is., 8 m. off Tinaca Point SW of entrance to Davao Gulf; 36 sq. m.; pop. 2226. Comprises two islands, Balut and **Sarangani** (smaller and easternmost of the two, ab. 14 sq. m.), and an islet.

Sarangani Strait. Passage bet. Sarangani Is. and S tip of Mindanao, Phil. Is.

Sa'ran·garh (sä'ràn·gär; *native* -gŭr'h'). **1** Former Indian state, Eastern States, NE Indian Union; 541 sq. m.; pop. (1941) 140,785. **2** Town, its ✱, 60 m. W of Sambalpur; now in E Madhya Pradesh; pop. ab. 7000.

Sa·ransk' (sù·ränsk'). Town, ✱ of Mordovian Republic, Soviet Russia, Europe; pop. 21,458; in cen. part on branch of Moscow-Kuibyshev R.R. W of Ulyanovsk.

Sa·ra·pi·quí' (sä'rä·pē·kē'). River of Costa Rica; flows N into the San Juan river; link in waterway from cen. Costa Rica to the Caribbean Sea.

Sa·ra'pul (sù·rä'pōōl). Town on Kama river, SE Udmurt Republic, Soviet Russia, Europe, 35 m. SE of Izhevsk; pop. 32,400; center of an agricultural area.

Sa·ra·sa'ra (sä'rä·sä'rä). Peak ab. 19,500 ft. in Cordillera Occidental, Peru.

Sar'a·so'ta (sàr'à·sō'tà). **1** County in Florida. See *Table* at FLORIDA. **2** City, its ⊗, W cen. Florida penin., on Gulf of Mexico 15 m. S of mouth of Tampa Bay; pop. 34,083; winter resort; citrus fruits and celery; fishing; John and Mable Ringling Museum of Art.

Sarasota Bay. Inlet of Gulf of Mexico on coast of NW Sarasota and SW Manatee cos., W Florida penin.

Sa'ras·wa'ti (sù'ràs·wŭ'tē) *or* **Sa'ras·va'ti** (-vŭ'tē). **1** A sacred river of Punjab state, NW Indian Union, frequently mentioned in the Vedas and identified by Hindus with the goddess Sarasvati. In early times held to be the Indus, later one of its tributaries; its modern equivalent, known as the **Sar'su·ti** (sŭr'sōō·tē), loses itself in the sands of Rajputana. **2** River ab. 120 m. long of S Rajputana and Baroda; rises in Mt. Abu and flows SW to Little Rann of Cutch.

Sar'a·to'ga (sàr'à·tō'gà). **1** County in New York. See *Table* at NEW YORK. **2** City, Santa Clara co., W California, SW of San Jose; pop. 14,861. **3** Village, now Schuylerville (*q.v.*), on W bank of Hudson river, Saratoga co., E New York, ab. 10 m. E of Saratoga Springs; has given its name to two battles fought just to the S, near Stillwater, Sept. 19, 1777 and Oct. 7, 1777, that resulted in Gen. Burgoyne's surrender of British forces at Saratoga Oct. 17, 1777 to Americans under Gen. Gates; marked the turning point of the Revolutionary War in favor of the Americans. Actual fighting of the two battles occurred at Freeman's Farm and Bemis Heights (Gen. Gates's headquarters) ab. 3 m. N of Stillwater; site set apart June 22, 1948 as **Saratoga National Historical Park:** see UNITED STATES, *National Historical Parks.*

Saratoga Lake. Lake ab. 7 m. long by 2 m. wide in Saratoga co., E New York, SE of Saratoga Springs; drains into Hudson river; summer resort.

Saratoga Passage. Strait bet. Camano I. and Whidbey I. in upper Puget Sound, Washington.

Saratoga Springs. City, Saratoga co., E New York, W of Hudson river in Adirondack foothills, 33 m. N of Albany; pop. 16,630; land ceded to Dutch by Indians 1684; mineral springs said to have been visited for health by Sir William Johnson 1767; grew as health resort following discovery of curative powers of waters (in systematic use since 1774; bottled and shipped since 1826) and became social and sporting center of country esp. following establishment of Saratoga race track and facilities for outdoor sports; over 150 springs and wells and surrounding lands purchased by state from 1910 and made state reservation. Skidmore Coll. (1911; women).

Sa·ra'tov (sù·rä'tŭf). City, ✱ of Saratov Region, SE Soviet Russia, Europe, on W bank of the Volga 220 m. N of

Volgograd; pop. 644,000; industrial, farming, and trading center; prevented by shoals in the Volga from being a river port of first rank; has iron foundries, sawmills, railroad shops, and various factories; natural-gas fields nearby; has a university, museums, institutes and technical schools; birthplace of the writer and revolutionist Chernyshevski. Founded 1605.

Saratov Region. Region, SE Soviet Russia, Europe, on both sides of the lower Volga; 31,806 sq. m.; pop. 1,798,805; ✷ Saratov. Bounded on N by Penza, Ulyanovsk, and Kuibyshev Regions, on E by Kazakh S.S.R. of Soviet Central Asia, on S by Stalingrad Region, and on W by Voronezh and Tambov Regions. Formerly surrounded on three sides the German Volga A.S.S.R., abolished 1941. Occupies E part of great cen. plateau; E of Volga is steppe region. Well watered by Volga, which here has elevation of not more than 20 ft., and its tributaries. Has practically no forests; soil and climatic conditions not favorable to agriculture. Chief crops grains. Chief towns Saratov, Balashov, Volsk.

History: Area has evidence (bronze articles in kurgans) that it was inhabited in prehistoric times; followed in ancient European history by Scythians, later by the Mordvinians and various Slavic peoples; came under the Khazars in 8th and 9th cents. and under the Russians in 18th cent.; under Soviet Russia included in the Lower Volga Area 1928; later (1936) reorganized as a separate region.

Sa·ra'via (sä·rä'vyä). Municipality, NW Negros Occidental, Negros, Phil. Is., near coast 15 m. N of City of Bacolod; pop. 21,289.

Sa·ra'wak (så·rä'wä[k]). **1** Ter. of Fed. of Malaysia in W part of Borneo; ab. 50,000 sq. m.; pop. estimated at 490,000; ✷ Kuching, on the **Sarawak River** (short stream in SW part). Touches Brunei and Brit. North Borneo on NE and Indonesian Borneo on E and S; coast line of 450 m. extends along South China Sea on W and NW. A rich tropical land, well watered by navigable rivers (Rajang, Baram, Limbang, and Batang Lupar), and generally mountainous, esp. along E and S borders. Various tropical products raised and exported are sago, coconuts, pepper, rubber, rattans; also rich in petroleum, first produced in 1910. Inhabitants are mainly Mohammedan Malays, pagan Dyaks and Muruts, and many Chinese. Chief towns Kuching, Sibu, and Miri.

History: Brunei (*q.v.*) visited in 1839 and 1840 by Sir James Brooke who sought to quell piracy; S part of Brunei (originally ab. 7000 sq. m.) ceded 1841 to Brooke by sultan and became independent state of Sarawak; additional territory received 1861, 1882, 1884; by agreement of 1888 became a British protectorate and for three generations was governed by the Brooke family; occupied by Japanese 1941–45; became British crown colony 1946; joined Fed. of Malaysia 1963.

2 Town, its ✷. See KUCHING.

Sar'da (sär'då; *native* sŭr'dä). River ab. 220 m. long, N India; rises in N Uttar Pradesh, flows S (as Kali river) along border of W Nepal, then SE through Uttar Pradesh into Gogra river NE of Lucknow.

Sardica. See SOFIA.

Sar·din'i·a (sär·dĭn'ĭ·å; -dĭn'yå); *Ital.* **Sar·de'gna** (sär·dân'yä). Island 164 m. long and 61 m. wide in the Mediterranean Sea W of S Italian penin.; politically, together with some smaller islands, constitutes a compartimento of Italy (see *Table* at ITALY); mountainous, highest point 4468 ft. in NE; chief rivers Tirso in center, Samassi in S, and Flumendosa in SE; separated on N from Corsica by Strait of Bonifacio; more important inlets on its coast are Gulf of Asinara on NW, Oristana on W, and Cagliari on S. Chief towns Cagliari, Sassari, and Iglesias. Site of International Latitude Observatory on 39°8'N lat. is at Carloforte, on San Pietro I. off SW coast. See *Map* at ITALY.

History: Settled by Phoenicians and Greeks before it came under control of Carthage during 6th cent. B.C.;

taken by Romans 238 B.C.; in Vandal kingdom 5th cent. A.D.; reconquered by Byzantine Empire 533; from 8th cent., raided by Moslems whose hold was broken by Pisa 1052; object of rivalry bet. Genoese and Pisans who were driven out by Aragonese 14th–15th cents.; held by Austria 1713–20; ceded to Savoy 1720 in exchange for Sicily, after which ruler of Savoy and Piedmont took title King of Sardinia (see SAVOY); during World War II used as air base by Germans until Italian surrender; Germans evacuated the island Sept. 1943.

Sar'dis (sär'dĭs). **1** Town, a ⊗ of Panola co., NW Mississippi, 40 m. ENE of Clarksdale; pop. 2098; site of a dam and reservoir designed to control flood waters in the Tallahatchie river basin.

2 *or* **Sar'des** (sär'dēz). Ancient city in Asia Minor, in a strategic position in the Hermus valley ab. 50 m. E of Smyrna; chief city and capital of ancient kingdom of Lydia, and an important city in Roman and Byzantine times; captured by both Persians and Athenians in 6th cent. B.C. and by Antiochus the Great after a two-year siege in 213 B.C.; one of the Seven Churches of Asia Minor (*Rev.* i–iii); suffered much from attacks of Seljuk Turks who took possession of it early in 14th cent.; surrendered to Ottoman power c. 1390 and destroyed 1402 by Tamerlane. Site has many ruins, esp. of a great Ionic temple; earliest known coins (700 B.C.) found here.

Sardis Dam *and* **Reservoir.** See UNITED STATES, *Dams and Reservoirs.*

Sa'rek·tjåk'ko (sä'rĕk·chôk'kŏ). Peak 6855 ft. in N Sweden, in Kjölen Mts.; near source of Lule river.

Sa're·ma (så'ryĭ·må); *Estonian* **Saa're·maa** (sä'rĕ·mä); *Ger.* **Oe'sel** (û'zĕl). Island in E Baltic Sea off W coast of Estonia and N of Gulf of Riga; 1010 sq. m.; attached to Saare prov. of Estonia. Conquered by Teutonic Knights of the Sword 1227, governed by its own bishops till 1561; for nearly a hundred years it was held by the Danes but passed to Sweden 1645; as part of Livonia was united to Russia 1721 and became part of Estonia 1918. In World War II seized by Germans 1941 but recovered in 1944.

Sa·rep'ta (så·rĕp'tå). = ZAREPHATH.

Sar·gas'so Sea (sär·gǎs'ō). The large tract of comparatively still water in the North Atlantic Ocean—so named from the floating seaweed there; may be considered to lie bet. the parallels 25°–30°N and the meridians 30°–70°W.

Sar'gent (sär'jĕnt). County in North Dakota. See *Table* at NORTH DAKOTA.

Sar·go'dha (sẽr·gōd'hå). Town, ✷ of Shahpur dist., West Punjab, Pakistan, 106 m. WNW of Lahore; pop. 26,761.

Sa·ri' (sä·rē'). Town, ✷ of Mazanderan prov., N Iran, 17 m. E of Babul; pop. 8000.

Sa·ria'ya (sä·ryä'yä). Municipality, S Tayabas prov., Luzon, Phil. Is., 7 m. WNW of Lucena; pop. 25,736.

Sa'ri Ba·ir' (sä'rĭ bä·yĭr'); *Turk.* **Sa'rı Ba·yır'.** Rugged hills in cen. Gallipoli Penin., Turkey in Europe; scene of unsuccessful attack of Anzac forces on Turkish position Aug. 6–10, 1915.

Sa·ri·gan' (sä'rĕ·gän') *or* **Sa·ri·guan'** (-gwän'). Small island, cen. Mariana Is., 100 m. N of Saipan, 16°42'N; highest point 1801 ft.

Sa·rı·ka·mış' *or* **Sa·ri·ka·mish'** (sä'rĭ·kä·mĭsh'). Town, SW Kars vilayet, NE Turkey in Asia, ab. 30 m. SW of Kars; pop. 6791; formerly included in Russian Armenia. Scene of battle Dec. 1914 in World War I in which Turks were decisively defeated by Russians.

Sarine. See SAANE.

Sar–i–Pul *or* **Sar'i·pul'** (sår'ê·pōōl'). **1** Town, N Afghanistan, 75 m. SW of Mazar-i-Sharif; pop. ab. 18,000; chief town of a former khanate of the same name.

2 *anc.* **Hol·wan'** (hôl·wän'). City, W Iran, W of modern Kermanshah, in mountains near Iraq border.

Sa·ri'ta (så·rē'tå). Village, ⊗ of Kenedy co., S Texas; pop. (est.) 500.

Sar′ju (sär′jōō). River ab. 150 m. long in W Nepal and Uttar Pradesh, N India; flows NW and S into the Gogra river.

Sark (särk). **1** *Fr.* **Sercq** (sĕrk). One of the Channel Is., in the English Channel; 2 sq. m.; comprises **Great Sark** (pop. 536) and **Little Sark** (pop. 35) connected by an isthmus; included in Guernsey bailiwick; chief landing place Creux.
2 Small stream of Dumfries, Scotland. See ESK river, S Scotland.

Sar′kad (shŏr′kŏd). Commune, SE Hungary, 60 m. S of Debrecen, near Romanian border; pop. 12,212.

Sar′lat′ (sår·lä′). Mining and commercial town, Dordogne dept., SW cen. France, ab. 32 m. SE of Périgueux; pop. 3726; 11th–12th cent. church, numerous old houses (14th–16th cents.).

Sar·ma′tia (sär·mā′shȧ; -shĭ·ȧ). **1** In 4th cent. B.C. land of Sarmatians, a people NE of Black Sea. Later, in time of Roman Empire, the region, without definite boundaries, bet. the Vistula and Volga, corresponding to S Russia in Europe and Poland and bordering on Germania and Dacia; divided by ancient Tanais (mod. Don) river. Its peoples were probably ancestors of the Slavs.
2 Poetic for POLAND.

Sar′mi (sär′mē). Village, N coast of Neth. New Guinea, 125 m. W of Hollandia; taken by Allies May 17, 1944.

Sar·mien′to (sär·myān′tō). **1** Peak ab. 7200 ft., Chile, in SW Tierra del Fuego I.
2 See GENERAL SARMIENTO town, Argentina.

Sar′mi·zeg′e·tu′sa (sär′mĭ·zĕj′ĕ·tū′sȧ). Ancient town, SW cen. Dacia, ESE of modern Lugoj in W Romania; capital of Dacia; occupied by Trajan 102 A.D.

Sar·nath′ (sär·nät′h′). Archaeological site 3½ m. N of Benares, Uttar Pradesh, N Indian Union; here was the Deer Park in which Gautama Buddha first taught. Ruins consist of the court of the monastery, a great stupa of Asoka 130 ft. high, and remains of Asoka's memorial pillar.

Sar′nen (zär′nĕn). Commune, * of Obwalden demicanton and of Unterwalden canton, cen. Switzerland, 37 m. E of Bern; pop. (1930) 5282; health resort; manufactures straw hats.

Sarnen, Lake of; *Ger.* **Sar′ner See** (zär′nĕr zā). Lake ab. 4 m. long and 1 m. wide in cen. Switzerland, in Unterwalden canton.

Sarner–Aa. See AA.

Sar′ni·a (sär·nĭ·ȧ). City, ⊗ of Lambton co., SE Ontario, Canada, on St. Clair river at S end of Lake Huron; pop. 34,697; opp. Port Huron, Michigan, with which it is connected by bridge and tunnel (2¼ m. long); industries include saltworks, lumber mills, oil refinery, grain elevator; has active port. Settled 1833.

Sar′no (sär′nō). Manufacturing and commercial commune, Salerno prov., Campania, S Italy, 12 m. NW of Salerno; pop. 21,998; episcopal see; iron, iodine, and sulfur springs; mineral baths.

Sar′ny (sär′nĭ). Town, W Ukraine, U.S.S.R., ab. 85 m. E of Kovel; formerly in Poland; railroad junction, held by Germans from June 1941 until retaken by Russians Jan. 12, 1944.

Sar′on, Plain of (sâr′ŭn). = Plain of SHARON.

Sa·ron′ic Gulf (sȧ·rŏn′ĭk) *or* **Gulf of Ae·gi′na** (ē·jī′nȧ); *anc.* **Si′nus Sa·ron′i·cus** (sī′nŭs sȧ·rŏn′ĭ·kŭs). Inlet of Aegean Sea on SE coast of Greece, S of Attica and Boeotia dept.

Sa·ron′no (sä·rŏn′nō). Manufacturing commune, Varese prov., Lombardy, N Italy, 18 m. SE of Varese; pop. 29,017; pilgrimage church (13th–17th cents.).

Sa′ros Gulf (sä′rŏs; sâr′ŏs). Inlet of NE Aegean Sea extending E into SW coast of Turkey in Europe, at the base of Gallipoli Penin.

Sá′ros·pa′tak (shä′rōsh·pŏ′tŏk). Commune, NE Hungary, 40 m. NE of Miskolc; pop. 12,522.

Sarps′borg (särps′bôr). City, Östfold co., SE Norway, on W bank of Glomma river; pop. 12,392; hydroelectric power plant; chemical works, textile and paper mills, zinc smelters, electrical equipment factories. City rebuilt 1838 on site of a ruined medieval town.

Sarps′foss (särps′fôs). Waterfall 60 ft. high and 164 ft. wide in the Glomma river near its mouth in SE Norway.

Sar′py (sär′pī). County in Nebraska. See *Table* at NEBRASKA.

Sarre. 1 See SAAR river.
2 See SAARLAND.

Sarre, La. See LA SARRE.

Sarre′bourg′ (sår′bōōr′). Commune, Moselle dept., NE France, 44 m. NW of Strasbourg; pop. 9561.

Sarrebruck. See SAARBRÜCKEN.

Sarre′gue·mines′ (sår′gē·mēn′). Town, Moselle dept., NE France, on Sarre river at German border 42 m. E of Metz; pop. 16,001; iron and copper foundries; manufactures faïence (since 1785).

Sar′ria (sär′ryä). Commune, Lugo prov., NW Spain, 19 m. SSE of Lugo; pop. 15,167; agricultural products; manufactures leather, dairy products; stock raising.

Sars, Le. See LE SARS.

Sar′si·na (sär′sĭ·nȧ). Ancient town in mountains of N Umbria, cen. Italy, birthplace of Plautus c. 254 B.C.

Sars·toon′ *or* **Sars·tún′** (särs·tōōn′). River ab. 70 m. long, E cen. Guatemala; flows E into the Gulf of Amatique; forms S boundary of British Honduras.

Sarsuti. See SARASWATI.

Sar′tène′ (sår·tân′). Town, S Corsica, France, 23 m. SSE of Ajaccio; pop. 4275.

Sarthe (sårt). **1** River ab. 175 m. long, NW France; rises in Orne dept., flows S to unite with Mayenne river near Angers and form Maine river.
2 Department of France. See *Table* at FRANCE.

Sar′trou′ville′ (sår′trōō′vēl′). Commune, Seine-et-Oise dept., N France, NW suburb of Paris on Seine river; pop. (1931) 17,354.

Sarum, New. See SALISBURY, England.

Sarum, Old. See OLD SARUM.

Sarus. See SEYHAN.

Sa′ry Su (sä′rĭ sōō′). River ab. 520 m. long, cen. Kazakh S.S.R., Soviet Central Asia, flowing S into the desert, not quite reaching the Syr Darya.

Sar·za′na (sär·dzä′nä). Commune, La Spezia prov., Liguria, NW Italy, 7 m. E of La Spezia; pop. 13,492; 13th-cent. cathedral; airport.

Sa′sa·la·guan′, Mount (sä′sä·lä·gwän′). Mountain 1120 ft. at S end of Guam, Mariana Is.

Sa′sa·ram (sŭ′sȧ·räm). Town, Shahabad dist., W Bihar state, NE Indian Union, 90 m. WSW of Patna; pop. 25,175. Contains tomb of Emperor Sher Shah (1540–45), India's finest example of Pathan architecture, and tombs of Sher Shah's father and son.

Sasau. See SÁZAVA.

Sa·se·bo (sä·sĕ·bô). Seaport city on large inlet of outer Omura Bay, NW Kyushu I., Japan, in Nagasaki prefecture; pop. (1938 est.) 213,400; one of the larger naval bases of Japan, established 1886, with naval dockyard, arsenal, etc. Bombed by Americans June–July 1944.

Sa·se′no (sä·zā′nō); *anc.* **Sa′son** (sä′sŏn). Small island in N Strait of Otranto at the entrance to the harbor of Vlona (Valona), Albania, opp. the heel of Italy; ab. 4 m. long; area 2 sq. m. Seized by Italy Oct. 31, 1914 and held as a naval base until its return by treaty Feb. 1947.

Sas·katch′e·wan (săs·kăch′ē·wăn; săs-; -wŏn). **1** River of SW and S cen. Canada, flowing from the Rocky Mts. E into N Lake Winnipeg; upper part divided into 2 branches, **North Saskatchewan** (760 m.) and **South Saskatchewan** (865 m.); length of river after confluence of its branches, E of Prince Albert, 340 m. The South Saskatchewan and its tributary the Bow constitute the longest headstream of the Nelson river with a total length of 1205 m.; including the Nelson 1660 m. The main tributaries of the North Saskatchewan are the Battle, Brazeau, and Clearwater; of the South Saskatchewan the Red Deer, Bow, and Oldman.

2 Province, W Canada, cen. province of the Prairie Provinces; land area 237,975 sq. m.; pop. 831,728; ✳ Regina; has no counties but is subdivided into 18 census divisions. Bounded on N by Mackenzie District, on E by Manitoba, on S by U.S.A. (North Dakota and Montana), and on W by Alberta. Entirely a plains region with prairie in S and wooded country containing many lakes and swamps in N. Highest point in SW corner 4243 ft.; average elevation 1000 to 2000 ft. Watered in N by headstreams of the Mackenzie flowing into Lake Athabaska, in cen. part by the Churchill, in S cen. and SW by the Saskatchewan and branches, and in the SE by Assiniboine and tributaries. Its large lakes include Athabaska (E half), Reindeer, Wollaston, Churchill, Rouge, etc. It has one large national park, the Prince Albert, in cen. part and seven provincial parks. The chief agricultural province of Canada (81%); wheat the main crop; other products oats, cattle, lumber, fish, and in minerals, gold, copper, zinc, and potash. Chief cities Regina, Saskatoon, Moose Jaw, Prince Albert.

History: For two centuries 1670–1869 region controlled by Hudson's Bay Co.; S part explored by the La Vérendryes c. 1743–49; part of Northwest Territory to 1869 with few settlements before that date; S half set up 1882 as districts of Saskatchewan and Assiniboia and N half made a part of district of Athabaska; established as a province 1905.

3 Former district, cen. Canada, formed 1882 out of Northwest Territories bet. Athabaska on N and Assiniboia on S, bet. 55°N and 52°; 101,000 sq. m.; ✳ Battleford. Most of it included in Saskatchewan prov. 1905.

Sas′ka·toon′ (săs′kȧ·tōon′). City, S cen. Saskatchewan, Canada, on South Saskatchewan river 150 m. NW of Regina; pop. 53,268; in fertile farm country devoted principally to wheat; supply and trade center for large area; grain elevators, flour mills; foundries, creameries, tanneries, and machine shops. Seat of University of Saskatchewan (1907; coed.), of a provincial normal school and provincial agricultural school; also has church and collegiate schools.

Saskatoon Mountain Reserve. Canadian provincial park, W Alberta, 3000 acres; lookout point in hills near Grande Prairie.

Sason. See SASENO.

Sas′sa·fras (săs′ȧ·frăs). River 20 m. long, NE Maryland; rises in NW Delaware, flows W into upper Chesapeake Bay.

Sassafras Mountain. Peak 3548 ft. in Pickens co., NW South Carolina; highest point in the state.

Sas·san′dra (să·săn′drȧ). **1** River ab. 300 m. long, W Ivory Coast Republic, West Africa; flows S into the Atlantic Ocean.

2 Seaport at mouth of the river, SW Ivory Coast Republic, 145 m. W of Abidjan.

Sas′sa·ri (säs′sä·rē). **1** Province of Italy. See *Table* at ITALY.

2 Commune, its ✳, Sardinia, Italy, 110 m. NNW of Cagliari; pop. 55,373; 18th-cent. cathedral, 18th-cent. town hall; university (founded 1565); manufactures tobacco; trades in grain, oil, fruits, cheese. In early Middle Ages called Thatari; became free city 1223 under protection of Pisa and later of Genoa; conquered by Aragonese 1323; became part of Piedmont (kingdom of Sardinia) 1720 and, with it, of kingdom of Italy 1860.

Sas·se′no (sä·zā′nō). = SASENO.

Sas′so·fer·ra′to (säs′sō·fär·rä′tō); *anc.* **Sen·ti′num** (sĕn·tī′nŭm). Commune, Ancona prov., Marches, cen. Italy, 37 m. WSW of Ancona; pop. 12,996. Near ancient town Romans defeated allied Etruscan, Samnite, and Gaulish forces 295 B.C., thus establishing themselves in cen. Italy.

Sass′town (săs′toun). Coastal town, SE Liberia, W Africa, 53 m. NW of Cape Palmas.

Sas·suo′lo (säs·swô′lō). Commune, Modena prov., Emilia, N Italy, 11 m. SW of Modena; pop. 12,958.

Sa·ta·no, Cape (sä·tä·nō). Cape, S extremity of Kyushu I., Japan.

Sa·ta′ra (sä·tä′rä). Town, S Maharashtra state, W India, near Kistna river 120 m. SE of Bombay; pop. 26,379; one of the chief cities of the Maharashtra region; has interesting fort dating from 12th cent.; new palace contains famous jewels of Satara family.

Satara Ja·girs′ (jä·gērz′). Five former Indian states— Akalkot, Aundh, Bhor, Jath, and Phaltan—once tributary to Satara, later in the Kolhapur and Deccan States Agency; area now in S Maharashtra state.

Sa·til′la (sȧ·tĭl′ȧ). River ab. 220 m. long, S and SE Georgia; navigable at its mouth; rises in Irwin co., flows E, S, and again E into St. Andrew Sound.

Săt·mar′ (sȧt·mär′). = SATU-MARE.

Satna. See SUTNA.

Sá′tor·al′ja·új′hely (shä′tŏr·ŏl′yŏ·ōō′y′·hä). City, NE Hungary, on a tributary of the Bodrog near Czechoslovakian border; pop. 21,617; in grape-growing section.

Sat′pu·ra Range (sät′pōō·rȧ). Range of hills in W cen. India, bet. the Narbada and Tapti rivers; average elevation ab. 3000 ft.

Satrunjaya. See PALITANA.

Sa·tsu·ma (sä·tsōō·mä; *Angl.* săt·sōō′mȧ). Old province in S Kyushu I., Japan, now in Kagoshima prefecture; famous for its pottery, dating from close of 16th cent., and the hard-glazed ware, a later production. Home of a powerful clan, at first much opposed to foreign influence 1858–68, but after Restoration (in 1869) offered their lands to the emperor as an aid to terminate feudalism.

Sat′tel·berg (sät′′l·bûrg). Village and mission station on Huon Penin., just W of Finschhafen, SE North-East New Guinea; severe fighting Sept.–Nov. 1943.

Sat·ti′ma (sȧ·tē′mȧ). Peak 13,214 ft. in cen. Kenya, E Africa, N of Nairobi.

Sa·tu-Ma′re (sä·tōō·mä′rĕ); *Hung.* **Szat′már-Né′me·ti** (sŏt′mär-nä′mĕ·tĭ). City, NW Romania, near Hungarian border on Someş river; pop. (1939 est.) 51,708; commercial center; cathedral; with N Transylvania was part of Hungary 1940–45.

Sa·tun *or* **Sa·tul** *or* **Se·tul** (sä·tōōn). **1** Province, SW Thailand; 1192 sq. m.; pop. 42,944.

2 Town, its ✳, near W coast of Malay Penin., just NNW of Perlis state in Federation of Malaya.

Sa·tur′ni·an (sȧ·tûr′nĭ·ȧn). Original name of the Capitoline Hill. See SEVEN HILLS.

Sau. See SAVA.

Sau′ce *or* **Puer′to Sau′ce** (pwĕr′tō sou′sä). Small port on La Plata estuary, Colonia dept., SW Uruguay, 78 m. WNW of Montevideo. pop. 8000; port for Rosario.

Sa·u′di Arabia (sä·ōō′dĭ; sou′-). Country, SW Asia, occupying most of Arabian penin.; a kingdom; ✳✳ Riyadh and Mecca; 870,000 sq. m.; pop. 6,630,000. Bounded on N by Transjordan (now Jordan), Iraq, and Kuwait, on E by Persian Gulf, Qatar, Trucial Oman, and Oman, on S by Oman, Aden Protectorate, and Yemen, on W by Red Sea. A plateau region, average elevation 2500 ft., with band of highlands having elevations of 7000 to 10,000 ft. in W near Red Sea coast in Hejaz. Includes great deserts of An Nafud (in the N) and Rub 'al Khali (in the S). Has productive oil fields on Persian Gulf coast. Chief towns Riyadh, Hofuf, Mubarraz, Buraida, Anaiza, and Hail in Nejd, Mecca, Medina, and Jidda in Hejaz, and As Sabya in Asir.

History: A dual kingdom formed 1926 by ibn-Saud as king of Nejd and Hejaz (*qq.v.*) and as a single kingdom renamed Saudi Arabia 1932; fought successful war against Yemen (*q.v.*) but independence of latter guaranteed by Great Britain 1934; absorbed Asir 1933; entered treaty of nonaggression and brotherhood with Iraq 1936; formed agreement with Egypt 1937 by which recognition was obtained of its annexation of Hejaz; has participated in negotiations for Arab federation since exploitation of its oil by American interests 1940. Neutral in World War II.

Sau'er (zou'ĕr). River ab. 100 m. long in Belgium, Luxembourg, and W Germany; rises in Belgian province of Luxembourg, flows E across the duchy of Luxembourg into the Moselle river 7 m. SW of Trier in Rhine Province, Prussia; navigable for ab. 40 m. Scene of severe fighting in World War II in the Battle of the Bulge Dec. 1944–Jan. 1945.

Sau'ga·tuck (sô'gà·tŭk). River ab. 20 m. long, SW Connecticut; rises in cen. Fairfield co., flows S into Long Island Sound at the old shipping port of Saugatuck.

Sau'geen Peninsula (sô'gēn). = BRUCE PENINSULA.

Sau'ger·ties (sô'gēr·tĭz). Village, Ulster co., SE New York, on W side of Hudson river 11 m. N of Kingston; pop. 4286; settled in early 1700's; in agricultural country; formerly shipping point for bluestone and limestone from nearby quarries, and port of call for river boats; manufactures paper, leather, canvas, women's dresses.

Sau'gor (sô'gĕr) or **Sa'gar** (sä'gĕr). Town, Jubbulpore Division, N Madhya Pradesh, Indian Union, 180 m. N of Nagpur; pop. (1941) 50,733; beautifully situated at 1700 ft. elevation in Vindhya Mts. Has old Maratha fort in which Europeans were besieged during Sepoy Mutiny.

Sau'gus (sô'gŭs). 1 Residential town, Essex co., NE corner of Massachusetts, 8 m. NNE of Boston; pop. 20,666.

2 See LYNN city, Massachusetts.

Sa·uj'bu·lagh' (sä·ōōj'bŏŏ·läg') or **Mah'a·bad'** (mà'hä·bäd'). Town, Azerbaijan prov., NW Iran, 20 m. S of Lake Urmia; pop. ab. 7000; center of Kurdish independence movement.

Sauk (sôk). 1 River 120 m. long, cen. Minnesota; flows from Osakis Lake, SW Todd co., to Mississippi river above St. Cloud.

2 County in Wisconsin. See *Table* at WISCONSIN.

Sauk Centre. City, Stearns co., cen. Minnesota, on the Sauk river 39 m. WNW of St. Cloud; pop. 3573; railroad and trade center in agricultural section; boyhood home of Sinclair Lewis and setting for several of his novels.

Sauk Rapids. Village, Benton co., cen. Minnesota, on Mississippi river 3 m. N of St. Cloud; pop. 4038; flour mills; near granite deposits.

Sault Sainte Ma·rie' (sōō' sànt mà·rē'). 1 City, ⊗ of Chippewa co., E Michigan penin., at the falls on the Saint Marys river (*q.v.*) bet. Lakes Huron and Superior; pop. 18,722; connected by bridge and ferry with Canadian city of same name across the river; a port of entry on the Sault Sainte Marie Canals, an important rail and water shipping point for agricultural products of the region and for the city's manufactures which include paper, nickel steel, machinery, leather, clothing, lumber; center of a summer recreation region. Site early used as a river crossing by Indians; reached by Étienne Brulé c. 1618 and by Jean Nicolet 1634; first settled by Marquette 1668; incorporated 1887.

2 Industrial city, ⊗ of Algoma dist., S Ontario, Canada, at the falls on St. Marys river (*q.v.*) across from Sault Sainte Marie, Michigan; pop. 32,452; processes iron and steel, has shipbuilding concerns, pulp and paper mills; a railroad city and port of entry on the Sault Sainte Marie Canal; handles products of a large agricultural and mining region; noted as a summer resort. Early crossing for Indians and explorers; founded 1887 on site of trading post established by Marquette in 1668.

Sault Sainte Marie Canals or **Soo Canals** (sōō). Two U.S. ship canals and a Canadian ship canal at Saint Marys Falls on the Saint Marys river (*q.v.*); first U.S. canal begun 1853, completed 1855; since then replaced and enlarged; today is divided: the N canal (U.S.), completed 1919, is 1.61 m. long, 80 ft. wide and 24.5 ft. deep; the S canal (U.S.), completed 1896, is 1.56 m. long, 100 ft. wide and 18 ft. deep; the Canadian canal, completed 1895, is 1.38 m. long, 150 ft. wide and 22 ft. deep; there are five locks (one on the Canadian canal), one of the two largest, the Davis lock, being 1350 ft. long bet. the gates, 80 ft. wide and having a lift of 20.5 ft.

Sau'mur' (sō'mür'). Manufacturing commune, Maine-et-Loire dept., W France, on Loire river 28 m. SE of Angers; pop. 17,158; manufactures sparkling white wines, jewelry, machinery, foods; 11th-cent. and 12th-cent. churches, 13th-cent. castle (now arsenal); site of Armored Corps School. Site inhabited by Gallo-Romans; strong center of Protestantism in 16th cent., declining commercially after revocation of Edict of Nantes; Vendeans defeated Republicans in neighborhood 1793.

Sau'mu'rois' (sō'mü'rwà'). Historical region of NW France; bounded anciently on N by Anjou, E by Touraine, S and W by Poitou; now included in Maine-et-Loire and Vienne depts.; ✳ Saumur.

Saun'ders (sôn'dĕrz; sän'-). County in Nebraska. See *Table* at NEBRASKA.

Saunders, Cape. Cape on SE coast of South I., New Zealand, S of entrance to Otago Harbor.

Sau·rash'tra (sou·räsh'trà). Former state (1948–56) of Indian Union, in Kathiawar penin.; became 1956 part of Bombay state; since 1960 in Gujerat state.

Saur'baer' (sû'ir·bîr'). Town, NW Iceland, on NW shore of Breidi Fjord.

Sau'sa·li'to (sô'sà·lē'tō). Suburban residential city, Marin co., W California, on San Francisco Bay 3 m. NW of San Francisco; pop. 5331; fishing and yachting resort. Forts Barry and Baker.

Sau'ternes' (sō'tĕrn'). Commune, Gironde dept., SW France, on tributary of the Garonne ab. 20 m. SSE of Bordeaux; pop. 689; center of a district including Barsac, Bommes, Preignac, and Fargues, noted for production of excellent white wine; the finest *sauterne* is from the vineyards of the Château Yquem.

Sa'va (sä'vä). 1 Commune, Ionio prov., Apulia, SE Italy, 17 m. ESE of Taranto; pop. 12,331.

2 *Fr.* **Save** (sàv); *Ger.* **Sau** (zou); *Hung.* **Szá'va** (sä'vŏ); *anc.* **Sa'vus** (sä'vŭs). River ab. 450 m. long, N Yugoslavia; rises on Italian-Yugoslav border, flows E into Danube river at Belgrade; navigable for ab. 360 m.

3 Former county, N Yugoslavia; 14,324 sq. m.; pop. 2,603,633; ⊗ Zagreb; later Savska co.; now ab. equivalent to Croatia federated republic.

Savage Island. See NIUE.

Sav'age.'s Station (săv'ĭj·ĭz). Battlefield near Richmond, Virginia, where Confederates under Magruder made unsuccessful attack on Federals under Sumner June 29, 1862, in the Seven Days' Battles.

Sa·vai'i (sä·vī'ē). Largest island in Samoa, in SW cen. Pacific Ocean; 703 sq. m.; included in Territory of Western Samoa, a New Zealand trust territory. Has many rocky mountains, several of them semiactive volcanoes; highest point Mt. Mauga Sili 6094 ft.

Sa'va·lan', Kuh-i- (kōō'hē·sà'và·län'). Peak 15,784 ft. in Azerbaijan, NW Iran, ab. 85 m. E of Tabriz and near Ardebil.

Sa·van'na (sà·văn'à). City, Carroll co., NW Illinois, on Mississippi river 55 m. WSW of Rockford; pop. 4950.

Sa·van'nah (sà·văn'à). 1 Navigable river 314 m. long, E Georgia; formed by confluence of Tugaloo and Seneca rivers in W Anderson co., NW South Carolina, flows SE forming Georgia-South Carolina boundary, and empties into Atlantic Ocean at Savannah.

2 Seaport city, ⊗ of Chatham co., SE Georgia, at mouth of Savannah river; pop. 149,245; oldest and 2d largest city in the state; 2d cotton port of United States; shipping point also for naval stores and tobacco; many fine old colonial houses; Chatham Air Force Base. Savannah State College (1890; coed.) is located at Industrial College, a suburb. Founded by Oglethorpe 1733; seat of colonial government 1754; capital of Georgia 1777–78 and 1782; held by British 1778–82 in American Revolution; held by Union army 1864. Site of joint meeting of International Bank and International Monetary Fund Boards of Governors Mar. 1946.

3 City, ⊗ of Andrew co., NW Missouri, 14 m. N of St. Joseph; pop. 2455; livestock, poultry, and grain growing.

4 Town, ⊗ of Hardin co., SW Tennessee, on Tennessee river 45 m. ESE of Jackson; pop. 4315; center of activity during construction 1935–38 of Pickwick Landing Dam (*q.v.*); marble quarries.

Sa·van′na–la–Mar (sȧ·văn′ȧ·lȧ·mär′). Seaport on S coast at W end of Jamaica I., West Indies Fed.; pop. (1943 est.) 4046; shipping point for district producing sugar, coffee, ginger, and logwood; destroyed by earthquake 1740 and rebuilt.

Sa′vant·va′di (sä′vȧnt·vä′dĭ) *or* **Sa′want·wa′di** (sä′wȧnt·wä′dĭ). **1** Former Indian state, Deccan and Kolhapur States, S Bombay prov., W Indian Union; 937 sq. m.; pop. (1941) 252,050. A Maratha state with history dating back to 6th cent.; suffered much from rivalry of Portuguese at Goa in 16th and 17th cents. **2** Town, its ✳, near coast 63 m. SSW of Kolhapur.

Savaria. See SZOMBATHELY.

Sa′ve (sä′vĕ); *Eng.* **Sa′bi** (sä′bĭ). River ab. 400 m. long, SE Africa; rises in cen. Southern Rhodesia, flows ESE across border into Mozambique, continues E across S Mozambique into Mozambique Channel; its large tributary in Southern Rhodesia is the **Lun′di** (lŭn′dĭ) river.

Save (sȧv). **1** River ab. 90 m. long in S France; rises on the slopes of the Pyrenees, flows NE into Garonne river 15 m. NNW of Toulouse. **2** See SAVA.

Sa′vent·hem (sä′vĕn·tĕm). Commune, Brabant prov., cen. Belgium; pop. 6970; NE suburb of Brussels.

Sa′verne (sȧ′vĕrn′) *or* **Za′bern** (tsä′bĕrn). Commune, Bas-Rhin dept., NE France, ab. 20 m. NW of Strasbourg; pop. (1931) 8436; important in Roman times when it was called **Tres Ta·ber′nae** (trēz tȧ·bûr′nē); held by bishops of Metz under the Carolingians and by the bishops of Strasbourg 13th–18th cents.; several ruined castles in vicinity; scene of incident (Zabern affair) Nov. 1913 when a German officer insulted Alsatian civilians.

Sa′vi·glia′no (sä′vē·lyä′nŏ). Commune, Cuneo prov., Piedmont, NW Italy, 18 m. N by E of Cuneo; pop. 17,511; Benedictine abbey; manufactures textiles; trades in cattle.

Sa′vi′gny′–sur–Orge (sȧ′vē′nyē′sür·ôrzh′). Commune, Seine-et-Oise dept., N France, 9 m. S of Paris; pop. (1931) 11,582; manufactures shoes and gloves; famous old castle.

Sa′vi·ña′o (sä′vē·nyä′ŏ). Commune, Lugo prov., NW Spain, 30 m. SSW of Lugo; pop. 12,595.

Sa′vo (sä′vō). Small island of volcanic origin in SE Solomon Is., W Pacific Ocean, ab. 8 m. N of W end of Guadalcanal I. (Cape Esperance) and 18 m. W of Florida I.; highest point 1600 ft. Part of British Solomon Islands protectorate. Notable for naval and air battles in Guadalcanal campaign, esp. the night of Aug. 8–9, 1942 when Allied forces lost four cruisers, and Nov. 12–13, 1942 resulting in defeat of Japanese.

Savoe, Savoe Sea. See SAWOE, SAWOE SEA.

Savoia. See SAVOY.

Sa′voie′ (sȧ′vwȧ′). **1** Departments of France: **Haute-Savoie** (ōt′-) and **Savoie.** See *Table* at FRANCE. **2** See SAVOY.

Sa·vo′na (sä·vō′nä). **1** Province of Italy. See *Table* at ITALY. **2** Seaport, its ✳, Liguria, NW Italy, on Gulf of Genoa 23 m. WSW of Genoa; pop. 64,199; fortified harbor; early 17th-cent. cathedral, 16th-cent. castle of Saint George; Sansoni palace (in which Pius VII was held prisoner 1809–12); industrial center producing iron, glass, chemicals, pottery, leather, and bricks; trades in raw silk and southern fruits. Destroyed 641 B.C. by the Lombards; made countship by Charlemagne; under Genoese rule 1528 ff.

Sa′von·lin′na (sä′vôn·lĭn′nä). City, Mikkeli dept., S Finland, built on a large island in the Lake Saimaa region; pop. (1939 est.) 7900; summer resort.

Sa·voon′ga (sȧ·vōōng′gȧ). Eskimo village on N coast of St. Lawrence I., Bering Sea, Alaska; pop. (1950) 249.

Sa·voy′ (sȧ·voi′); *Fr.* **Sa′voie′** (sä′vwȧ′); *Ital.* **Sa·vo′ia** (sä·vō′yä). Historical region of SE France and NW Italy, of varying limits, now chiefly in French departments of Haute-Savoie and Savoie; chief city Chambéry.

History: From 11th cent., counts of Savoy ruled area in western Alp region as part of kingdom of Arles (*q.v.*); became virtually independent and expanded its territory to encircle Lake Geneva and to include plain of Piedmont in Italy; raised to duchy 1416 by Emperor Sigismund; territory scene of many conflicts, at times allied with France, at times with Italy; involved in wars bet. France and Spain with alternating allegiances; under Charles Emmanuel I lost territories beyond the Rhone; joined Grand Alliance 1704; by Treaty of Utrecht 1713 received island of Sicily and held it until 1720 when it was exchanged for the island of Sardinia and the kingdom of Sardinia was formed (included Piedmont, Savoy, and island of Sardinia), the dukes of Savoy becoming kings of Sardinia. Kingdom of Sardinia sided with Royalists in French Revolution and as result lost territory of Savoy 1792 and Piedmont 1796; restored to Victor Emmanuel I by Congress of Vienna 1815 and Genoa added; in 1860 Sardinia, Genoa, and Piedmont joined other states of Italy to form kingdom of Italy with house of Savoy ruling, while territory of Savoy, with Nice (*q.v.*), was ceded to France.

Savoy Alps. See *Table* at ALPS.

Sav′ska (säv′skä). Former county (1929–45), N and NW Yugoslavia kingdom; 14,324 sq. m.; pop. 2,603,633; ✳ Zagreb; now (since 1945) approximately coextensive with Croatia federated republic of Yugoslavia.

Savu, Savu Sea. See SAWOE, SAWOE SEA.

Savus. See SAVA river, Yugoslavia.

Sa′vu·sa′vu Bay (sä′vōō·sä′vōō). Inlet of Pacific Ocean on S coast of Vanua Levu I., Fiji Is.

Sa′wah·loen′to *or* **Sa′wah·lun′to** (sä′wä·lōōn′tô). Town, Padang Highlands, W cen. Sumatra, Indonesia, ab. 45 m. ENE of Padang; pop. 15,146; outlet for Ombilin coal mines.

Sa·wan·kha·lok (sä·wän·k′hä·lōk) *or* **Swan·ka·lok** (swän·kä·lōk); *also* **Wang Mai Khon** (wäng mī k′hôn). **1** Province, W Thailand; 2709 sq. m.; pop. 151,417. **2** Village, its ✳, on left bank of Yom river, 40 m. NW of Phitsanulok; has one of three temples celebrated in Thailand for architecture.

Sawantwadi. See SAVANTVADI.

Sa·watch′, *or* **Sa·guache′, Range** (sȧ·wŏch′). A range of the Rocky Mts. in cen. Colorado; highest peak Mount Elbert 14,431 ft.

Saw Grass Lake (sô). Lake in S Brevard co., E cen. Florida; outlet St. Johns river flowing N.

Sa′woe *or* **Sa′wu** *or* **Sa′vu** (sä′vōō). Island of the Lesser Sunda Is., Indonesia, WSW of Timor and SE of Sumba; 23 m. long by 10 m. wide; with nearby islands 200 sq. m., pop. 33,632. Only port Seba on NW coast.

Sawoe, *or* **Savu,** *or* **Sawu, Sea.** Part of Indian Ocean in Indonesia, lying S of Flores, Lomblen, and Pantar Is., W of Timor, N of Sawu I., and E of Sumba I.; connected with Timor Sea by Roti Strait.

Saw′teeth (sô′tēth′). Mountain 4138 ft. in the Adirondack Mts., Essex co., NE New York.

Saw′tooth′ Mountain (sô′tōōth′). Peak 7748 ft. in Jeff Davis co., W Texas.

Sawtooth Mountains. Large group of mountain ranges and masses in S cen. Idaho, in Custer, Blaine, and Camas cos.; form S part of Salmon River Mts. and contain a number of peaks above 9000 ft., many alpine lakes, and the sources of Boise and Big Wood rivers; resort area and game reserves.

Sawtooth Range. Mountain range along border bet. Custer and Boise cos., S cen. Idaho; a range in W part of the Sawtooth Mts. (*q.v.*), with many peaks 7000 ft. to nearly 11,000 ft.

Sawtooth Ridge. Ridge in N cen. Washington, extend-

ing along the NE shore of Lake Chelan and along boundary bet. Okanogan and Chelan cos.

Saw'yer (sô'yẽr). County in Wisconsin. See *Table* at WISCONSIN.

Sax'a Ru'bra (săk'så rōō'brȧ). Town of ancient Etruria, Italy, on Flaminian Way ab. 9 m. N of Rome, just W of the Tiber; scene 312 A.D. of Constantine's victory over Maxentius who, in trying to escape to Rome over the Tiber, was drowned in crossing the **Mil'vi·an Bridge** [mǐl'vǐ·ăn] (*Lat.* **Pons Mul'vi·us** [pŏnz mŭl'vǐ·ŭs]; *mod.* **Pon'te Mol'le** [pŏn'tå môl'lå]) just N of Rome; the battle, usually called the "battle of Milvian Bridge," is associated with the legend of the flaming cross and the words, *in hoc signo vinces* ("by this sign thou shalt conquer"), which appeared in the heavens and led Constantine to accept Christianity.

Saxe (săks). French name of SAXONY used in English chiefly in names of former duchies in Thuringia which from 1485 to 1547 was in the electorate of Saxony; in the 19th cent. these were **Saxe–Al'ten·burg** (săks'äl'tĕn-bŏŏrk) in the E, **Saxe–Wei'mar–Ei'se·nach** (-vī'mär·ī'zĕ·näk) in the N and W and SE (grand duchy after 1815), **Saxe–Mei'ning·en** (-mī'nǐng·ĕn) in the SW, and **Saxe–Go'tha** (-gō'thå; -tȧ) in the NW, all now (since 1920) in Thuringia, and **Saxe–Co'burg** (-kō'bûrg) in the S, now (since 1920) in Bavaria.

Saxe–Co'burg–Go'tha (săks'kō'bûrg·gō'thå; -gō'tå); *Ger.* **Sach'sen–Co'burg und Go'tha** (zäk'sĕn·kō'bŏŏrk ŏŏnt gō'tä). Name of Saxe-Coburg after it acquired Gotha 1826.

Sax'on·land' (săk's'n·lǎnd'); *Ger.* **Sach'sen·land'** (zäk'sĕn·länt'). Region in S part of Transylvania, Romania; chief town Braşov.

Sax'on Switzerland (săk's'n); *Ger.* **Säch'si·sche Schweiz** (zĕk'sǐ·shĕ shvīts'). Mountainous region SE of Dresden, Saxony, Germany, in E end of the Erz Gebirge.

Sax'o·ny (săk's'n·ǐ); *Ger.* **Sach'sen** (zäk'sĕn). 1 Former German state, cen. Germany; 5788 sq. m.; pop. 4,994,281, (1939) 5,206,861; ✱ Dresden; contains Erz Gebirge and Elbe basin; extensive deposits of coal, iron, copper, silver, lead, tin; manufactures textiles, machinery, porcelain, books, tobacco; agricultural and stock-raising interests; important cities include Leipzig, Chemnitz, Plauen, Zwickau. Divided into the following five circles [Kreishauptmannschaft] (for pronunciation of their names, see their individual entries):

NAME[1]	LOCATION IN SAXONY	AREA IN SQ. M.	POP. (1925 CENSUS)
Bautzen[2]	NE	954	461,155
Chemnitz	W	800	980,838
Dresden[2]	E	1,674	1,393,026
Leipzig	NW	1,377	1,307,256
Zwickau	SW	983	852,006

[1] The circle and its capital city have the same name.
[2] Dresden and Bautzen circles combined 1932 to form Dresden-Bautzen circle; capital Dresden.

History: Occupied by the Saxons who controlled much of N Germany west of the Elbe until finally subdued by Charlemagne 772–804 A.D.; as duchy of East Frankish kingdom, repulsed Wends and incorporated Thuringia; its duke elected German emperor (Henry I, first of Saxon line 919); extended east of the Elbe by Henry the Lion from whom Frederick Barbarossa took duchy, splitting it up 1180; march of Meissen on lower Elbe the nucleus of new duchy of Saxony which became an electorate; in 15th cent., electoral and ducal Saxony (which broke into separate small duchies) belonged to two lines of rulers; elector an active participant, usually on the Austrian side, in 18th-cent. wars; became kingdom 1806; received rule of grand duchy of Warsaw 1807; lost northern part of territory to Prussia (became Prussian province of Saxony) 1815; rest of kingdom free state in German Empire 1871–1918; republic 1918; lost status as free state 1933–35.

2 Province of former Prussia. See *Table* at PRUSSIA.

Say (sā). Town, W Niger Republic, West Africa, on Niger river SE of Niamey; pop. ab. 8000 (district pop. 69,000); marked the boundary bet. British and French territory 1890–98; district ceded to France 1898.

Sa·yan' Mountains (sä·yän'). Mountain range extending E and W bet. Tuva Autonomous Region (former Tannu Tuva) and the Krasnoyarsk Territory and Irkutsk Region of Soviet Russia, Asia; highest peak Munko Sardik 11,453 ft.; average height 7000 to 9000 ft. Siberian side is steep; at ab. 92°E pierced by the upper Yenisei.

Say'brook (sā'brŏŏk). 1 *officially* **Old Saybrook.** Residential town, SE Middlesex co., S Connecticut, on Long Island Sound on W bank of mouth of Connecticut river opp. Old Lyme; pop. 5274; agriculture, fishing, small manufactures. First occupied by Dutch 1623; founded as fort 1635 by Gov. Winthrop of Massachusetts Bay Colony; center of Pequot War; acquired by purchase by Connecticut Colony; former site of the Collegiate School (1701) which became nucleus of Yale College; incorporated 1854.

2 Subdivision of town of Old Saybrook (see 1, above), Connecticut.

3 Town, S cen. Middlesex co., S Connecticut, on Connecticut river; pop. 2968; agriculture; manufacturing (piano actions, organ supplies, electrical goods). Settled by colonists from Old Saybrook 1635; united with Connecticut 1644; includes village of **Deep River,** by which name the town itself was long known locally and is now, since 1947, designated officially.

Sayles'ville (sālz'vǐl). Village, Providence co., N Rhode Island, ab. 2 m. NW of Central Falls.

Sayre (sâr). 1 City, ⊗ of Beckham co., W Oklahoma, 43 m. WSW of Clinton; pop. 2913; gas fields nearby; market for broomcorn, livestock, farm products; manufactures carbon black, butter, gasoline.

2 Borough, Bradford co., N Pennsylvania, on Susquehanna river at New York border; pop. 7917; railroad center; railroad shops; manufactures silk, knit goods, foundry products.

Sayre'ville (sâr'vǐl). Borough, Middlesex co., cen. New Jersey, on Raritan Bay inlet 5 m. ESE of New Brunswick; pop. 22,553.

Says Law (sāz). Mountain 1749 ft., East Lothian co., SE Scotland; highest peak of the Lammermuir Hills.

Sa·yu'la (sä·yōō'lä). Town, Jalisco state, W cen. Mexico, on **Lake Sayula,** SW of Lake Chapala; pop. 9340.

Say'ville (sā'vǐl). Village, Suffolk co., SE New York, on Long I. and Great South Bay, ab. 5 m. SW of Patchogue; pop. (est.) 6500; yachting center; packing and shipping point for blue point oysters.

Sá'za·va (sä'zȧ·vȧ); *Ger.* **Sa'sau** (zä'zou). River ab. 100 m. long, cen. Czechoslovakia; flows W into Moldau river 12 m. S of Prague.

Sbeit'la (sbīt'lä; -lȧ; sbät'-); *anc.* **Su·fet'u·la** (sṳ·fĕt'ṳ·lȧ). Town, N cen. Tunisia, N Africa, ab. 100 m. WNW of the port of Sfax and on railroad leading NE to Sousse; ancient town flourished during time of Antoninus and Marcus Aurelius; ruins include the Forum, temples, baths. In World War II taken by Germans Feb. 17–18, 1943; retaken by Americans Mar. 1.

Sca·fa'ti (skä·fä'tē). Manufacturing commune, Salerno prov., **Campania,** S Italy, 14 m. WNW of Salerno; pop. 16,037.

Sca'fell' (skô'fĕl'). Mountain 3162 ft. in Cumberland, NW England, in the Lake District 11 m. SW of Keswick; second highest peak in England.

Sca'fell' Pike (skô'fĕl'). Peak 3210 ft. in Cumberland, NW England, in Cumbrian Mts. 1 m. NE of Scafell; highest peak in England.

Sca'la Nuo'va, Gulf of (skä'lä nwô'vä). Italian name of KUŞADASI Gulf.

Scaldis. See SCHELDE.

Scald Law. See PENTLAND HILLS.

Scale Force (skāl' fōrs'). Waterfall ab. 120 ft. high in

the Lake District, NW England, in Cumberland near Keswick.

Scalp Level (skălp). Borough, Cambria co., SW cen. Pennsylvania, 7 m. SE of Johnstown; pop. 1445.

Scamander. See MENDERES.

Scamp'ton (skăm[p]'tŭn). Parish, Lincolnshire, E England, 6 m. NNW of Lincoln; large airfield, developed during and since World War II.

Scan'di·a (skăn'dĭ·à). Ancient name of S Scandinavian peninsula.

Scan·dia'no (skän·dyä'nô). Commune, Reggio nell'Emilia prov., Emilia, N Italy, 8 m. S by E of Reggio nell'Emilia; pop. 13,080.

Scan·dic'ci (skän·dēt'chē). Commune, Firenze prov., Tuscany, cen. Italy, SW of Florence; pop. 12,955.

Scan'di·na'vi·a (skăn'dĭ·nā'vĭ·à; -nāv'yà). 1 Ancient name of the country of the Norsemen.
2 Sweden, Norway, Denmark, and Iceland; the lands where Old Norse was spoken or where any of the Scandinavian languages are spoken today.
3 In a restricted sense, the peninsula occupied by Norway and Sweden.

Scania. See SKÅNE.

Scan'tic (skăn'tĭk). River, N cen. Connecticut; rises in Hampden co., S Massachusetts, flows SW into Hartford co., N Connecticut, and into Connecticut river N of Windsor.

Scap'a Flow (skăp'à flō'). Sea basin 15 m. long and 8 m. wide in Orkney Is., off N coast of Scotland; chief British naval base in World War I; in it Germans scuttled their fleet after the war June 21, 1919.

Scar'ba (skär'bà). Island in the Inner Hebrides, N of Jura, off W coast of Scotland; 9 sq. m.; height 1470 ft.

Scar'bor'o or **Scar'bor'ough** (skär'bûr'ō; esp. Brit., -bŭ·rŭ, -brŭ). Town, Cumberland co., SW Maine, 7 m. S of Portland; pop. 6418.

Scar'bor'ough (skär'bûr'ō; esp. Brit., -bŭ·rŭ, -brŭ).
1 See SCARBORO, Maine.
2 Municipal borough, North Riding, Yorkshire, N England, on North Sea 37 m. N of Hull; pop. 43,983; seaport and seaside resort; site of Bronze Age village and of ancient Roman watchtower.
3 See TOBAGO.

Scardona. See SKRADIN.

Scarp (skärp). Small island 3 m. long of the Outer Hebrides, W of the island of Lewis with Harris, off NW coast of Scotland; pop. 95; administratively a part of Inverness co.

Scarpanto, Scarpanto Strait. See KARPATHOS, KARPATHOS STRAIT.

Scarpe (skärp; Fr. skárp). River 62 m. long in Pas-de-Calais dept., N France; flows into Schelde river.

Scars'dale (skärz'dāl). Residential town, Westchester co., SE New York, 20 m. NNE of New York City; pop. 17,968.

Scat'ter·y Island (skăt'ẽr·ĭ). See KILRUSH.

Sceaux (sō). Town, Seine dept., N France, S of Paris; pop. 6413; site of castle, destroyed at the Revolution, which was scene during 17th cent. of literary court of the duchesse du Maine; present castle built 19th cent.

Scebeli, Uebi. See Webbe SHIBELI.

Schaer'beek (skär'bāk). Commune, Brabant prov., cen. Belgium, a NE suburb of Brussels; pop. (1938 est.) 123,468.

Scha'fer (shä'fẽr). Village, former ⊗ of McKenzie co., W North Dakota; pop. (1950) 100; near **Schafer Springs.**

Schaff·hau'sen (shäf·hou'zĕn). 1 Swiss canton. See Table at SWITZERLAND.
2 Commune, its ✳, N cen. Switzerland, on Rhine river 23 m. N of Zurich; pop. (1941) 22,498; 11th-cent. minster, town hall, gates and towers, castle; railroad junction; owes industrial development to power derived from Schaffhausen Falls in Rhine river; manufactures include textiles, machinery, tools, and clocks and watches.

Schaffhausen Falls or **Falls of the Rhine**; Ger. **Rhein'fall** (rīn'fäl). Waterfall in Rhine river near Schaffhausen, Switzerland; 370 ft. wide, has two principal falls, 50 and 60 ft. high.

Schar'hörn (shär'hŭrn). Small island in Heligoland Bight, NW Germany, at mouth of Elbe river.

Schässburg. See SIGHIŞOARA.

Schaulen. See SHAULYAI.

Schaum'burg–Lip'pe (shoum'boŏrK·lĭp'ĕ). Former German state, NW Germany; 131 sq. m.; pop. (1939) 54,162; ✳ Bückeburg; fertile region; lumber and textile industries. Former principality founded 1613; divided 1640 into Brunswick-Lüneburg, Hesse-Cassel, Lippe; became republic 1918; lost sovereignty to Germany 1933-35.

Scheggia Pass. See APENNINES.

Schei'degg (shī'dĕk). Village, Bern canton, cen. Switzerland, E of Lauterbrunnen in the Bernese Alps, alt. 6770 ft.; resort and starting point of Jungfrau railway; lies on **Little Scheidegg** (Ger. **Klei'ne Scheidegg** [klī'nĕ]), pass N of the Jungfrau and leading from Lauterbrunnen to Grindelwald; noted for magnificent view; to NE is **Great Scheidegg** (Ger. **Gros'se Scheidegg** [grō'sĕ]), pass at 6434 ft. leading from Grindelwald to the valley of the Aare; just NW of the Wetterhorn.

Schel'de (sKĕl'dĕ) or **Scheldt** (skĕlt); Fr. **Es'caut'** (ĕs'kō'); anc. **Scal'dis** (skăl'dĭs). Navigable river 270 m. long in W Europe; rises in Aisne dept., N France, flows N and NE through W Belgium to the city of Antwerp, turns NW and empties into the North Sea through two estuaries, East Schelde and West Schelde, in Netherlands.

Schemnitz. See BANSKÁ ŠTIAVNICA.

Sche·nec'ta·dy (skĕ·nĕk'tà·dĭ). 1 County in New York. See Table at NEW YORK.
2 City, its ⊗, E New York, on Mohawk river 13 m. NW of Albany; pop. 81,682; commercial and industrial center in agricultural region; large electric plant and laboratories (producing electric generating machinery, radio transmitting apparatus, induction motors, and refrigerators); locomotive works; printing, bookbinding, and lithographing establishments. Union College (1795; associated with Union Univ.). On site of former Indian village; land purchased by Dutch and settled c. 1662; seized by English 1664; scene of massacre by French and Indians 1690; chartered as city 1798; important river port in early days; became railroad center 1831.

Sche've·ning'en (sKā'vĕ·nĭng'ĕ[n]). Seaside resort, South Holland prov., SW Netherlands, included in The Hague commune; pop. 44,211; scene of British naval victory 1653 over the Dutch under Admiral Tromp.

Schie·dam' (skĕ·däm'). Commune, South Holland prov., SW Netherlands, 3 m. W of Rotterdam near the Maas; pop. (1939) 62,685; distilleries (gin).

Schie·hal'lion (shĕ·hăl'yŭn). Peak 3547 ft. in Perth co., cen. Scotland.

Schier'mon'nik·oog' (sKēr'môn'ĭk·ōK'). Island 8 m. long, Netherlands, easternmost of the West Frisian Is., 10 m. E of Ameland I.; lighthouse; administratively a part of Friesland prov.

Schif'fer·stadt (shĭf'ẽr·shtät). Agricultural commune, SE Rhineland-Palatinate, West Germany, in Rhine valley 7 m. SSW of Ludwigshafen; pop. 10,284; prehistoric artifact (called the "Golden Hat") found nearby 1835.

Schild'pad (sKĭlt'pät), or **Schil'pad** (skĭl'-), **Islands**; also **Tur'tle Islands** (tûr't'l). Group of islands in E part of the Gulf of Tomini, off NE coast of Celebes I., Indonesia; extend nearly 80 m. E and W; chief islands Batudaka (largest), Talata Koh, and Togian.

Schil'ler Park (shĭl'ẽr). Village, Cook co., NE Illinois, NW suburb of Chicago; pop. 5687.

Schil'tig·heim (Ger. shĭl'tĭk·hīm; Fr. shēl'tē'gĕm'). Industrial commune, Bas-Rhin dept., NE France, NW suburb of Strasbourg; pop. 22,074; sparkling wines.

Schimitz. See ŽIDENICE.

Schi'o (skē'ō). Manufacturing commune, Vicenza prov., Venezia Euganea, NE Italy, near Monti Lessini 16 m. NW of Vicenza; pop. 21,739; cathedral.

Schlei (shlī); *Dan.* **Sli** (slē). Inlet of the Baltic Sea in E Schleswig-Holstein, Germany.

Schlei'cher (shlī'kēr). County in Texas. See *Table* at TEXAS.

Schle'si·en (shlä'zĕ·ĕn). Province of Prussia. See SILESIA.

Schles'wig (shlĕs'wĭg; *Ger.* shläs'vĭk, shlĕs'-); *Dan.* **Sle'svig** (slĭ'svĕ). **1** Historical region, NW Germany; a former duchy of the Danish crown, now largely in Schleswig-Holstein, Germany.

History: German mark of Schleswig attached to Holy Roman Empire 934–1027; in 1027 ceded to Denmark; in 14th cent., as Danish fief, came to be ruled by Holstein (*q.v.*), a part of German Empire; from 1460, in personal union with Holstein, ruled by Danish royal house of Oldenburg; its status as part of Schleswig-Holstein (*q.v.*) caused trouble bet. Germany and Denmark and later bet. Prussia and Austria; by agreement, administered by Prussia 1865–66; northern Schleswig (*Dan.* Nord Slesvig) awarded to Denmark by plebiscite 1920 (see SOUTH JUTLAND).

2 Government district, Schleswig-Holstein, former Prussia, Germany; 5814 sq. m.

3 Seaport city, ✱ of Schleswig govt. dist., at W end of Schlei inlet 70 m. NNW of Hamburg; pop. 18,451; 13th-cent. Romanesque cathedral (remodeled in Gothic style 14th and 15th cents.); zoological garden; manufactures woolens, lace, sugar, leather, earthenware. First mentioned in 9th cent.; became city at end of 12th cent.; capital of Danish rule in Schleswig-Holstein; occupied by Austrians 1864; to Prussia 1865; capital of Prussian province of Schleswig-Holstein 1879–1917.

Schles'wig–Hol'stein (shlĕs'wĭg·hōl'stīn; *Ger.* shläs'-[shlĕs']vĭk·hōl'shtīn). **1** Province, former Prussia, Germany. See *Table* at PRUSSIA.

2 State of the Federal Republic of Germany; area 6052 sq. m.; pop. (1957 est.) 2,264,300); ✱ Kiel.

History: See HOLSTEIN and SCHLESWIG which were duchies held by king of Denmark, although Holstein was also a German state; in 1848–50 became issue of war bet. Germanic Confederation and Denmark because of Danish nationalist desire to incorporate Schleswig; in 1863 Danish annexation of Schleswig, contrary to previous agreement involving complicated problem of succession to Danish throne, brought war bet. Denmark and Austria and Prussia 1864; under joint administration of Austria and Prussia 1865 whose rivalry for domination of Germany (*q.v.*) was brought to head by Schleswig-Holstein issue in war of 1866; annexed to Prussia as province of Schleswig-Holstein 1866.

Schlettstadt. See SÉLESTAT.

Schley (slī). County in Georgia. See *Table* at GEORGIA.

Schlüsselburg. Var. of *Shlisselburg:* see PETROKRE-POST.

Schmal'kal'den (shmäl'käl'dĕn); *Eng.* **Smal'kald** or **Smal'cald** (smôl'kôld). Manufacturing city, E Germany, former Hesse-Nassau prov. of Prussia, 30 m. SW of Erfurt; pop. 10,440; 15th-cent. town hall, 16th-cent. castle; manufactures iron goods, salt. Mentioned 874 A.D.; became city 1227; League of Schmalkalden formed here 1531.

Schmölln (shmŭln). Industrial city, Thuringia, E Germany, 13 m. NNW of Zwickau; pop. 13,467.

Schnee'berg (shnā'bĕrk). **1** Highest peak 3447 ft. in the Fichtel Gebirge, NE Bavaria, S cen. Germany, NE of Bayreuth.

2 Peak 4665 ft. in S Sudeten Mts., on border bet. Silesia in Czechoslovakia and Wrocław dept., SW Poland; source of Nysa river.

Schnee'kop'pe (shnā'kŏp'ĕ). Highest peak 5266 ft. in the Riesen Gebirge range bet. Czechoslovakia and Wrocław dept., SW Poland.

Schnei'de·mühl (shnī'dĕ·mül). **1** Former government district, Brandenburg prov., Prussia, Germany; 2971 sq. m.

2 City. See PIŁA.

Scho'field (skō'fēld). City, Marathon co., cen. Wisconsin, on Wisconsin river 4 m. S of Wausau; pop. 3038; paper mills.

Schofield Barracks. United States army post, Wahiawa dist., cen. Oahu I., Hawaii. First buildings erected 1909; later, c. 1918, barracks greatly developed; at beginning of World War II was one of the largest military posts in U.S.

Scho·har'ie (skō·hăr'ĭ). **1** County in New York. See *Table* at NEW YORK.

2 Village, its ⊗, E New York; pop. 1168.

Schön·brunn' (shün·broon'). Imperial palace in Vienna, Austria; peace treaty signed here Oct. 14, 1809, ending the fifth phase of the Napoleonic Wars.

Schö'ne·beck–Bad Salz·el'men (shü'nĕ·bĕk bät' zälts·ĕl'mĕn). City, E Germany, in what was formerly Saxony prov., Prussia, on left bank of Elbe river 10 m. SSE of Magdeburg; pop. 33,440; manufactures chemicals, metal goods; salt pits. Formed 1932 from former cities of Schönebeck and Salzelmen and former commune of Frohse an der Elbe.

Schön·hau'sen (shün·hou'zĕn). Village, E Germany, on the Elbe ab. 35 m. NNE of Magdeburg; pop. 2140; Bismarck's birthplace.

Schon'ne·beck (shôn'ĕ·bĕk). Coal-mining commune, North Rhine-Westphalia state, West Germany, NE suburb of Essen; pop. 11,488.

Schoo'dic Lake (skoo'dĭk). Lake, cen. Maine, in SE Piscataquis co.

Schoodic Point. Point, SE Hancock co., SE Maine.

School'craft (skool'kráft). County in Michigan. See *Table* at MICHIGAN.

Schoo'ne·veldt (sкō'nĕ·vĕlt). Locality on S shore of the mouth of the Schelde river, Zeeland, SW Netherlands; naval battle off here 1673 bet. the Dutch fleet under de Ruyter and the combined English and French fleets.

Schoo'ten or **Scho'ten** (sкō'tĕ[n]). Commune, Antwerp prov., N Belgium, just NE of Antwerp; pop. 13,236.

Scho'ter·land (sкō'tĕr·länt). Commune, Friesland prov., N Netherlands, 18 m. SSE of Leeuwarden; pop. 17,379.

Schou'ten Islands (sкou'tĕ[n]). **1** or **Mi·so're Islands** (mĕ·sô'rä). Island group in the Pacific Ocean across the entrance to Geelvink Bay, off N coast of Neth. New Guinea; 1230 sq. m.; pop. 25,487; chief islands Biak, Supiori, and Numfoor; chief settlement Bosnek on SE coast of Biak. Biak occupied by Americans May 27, 1944; Numfoor on July 6.

2 Group of small islands off N coast of North-East New Guinea.

Schou'wen (sкou'vĕ[n]). Island in Zeeland prov., SW Netherlands, in estuary of Schelde river; 83 sq. m.; pop. ab. 24,000; chief town Zierikzee. See DUIVELAND.

Schram'berg (shräm'bĕrк). City, Baden-Württemberg, Germany 30 m. NE of Freiburg; pop. 12,113; clock-making center.

Schreck'horn, Gross (grōs shrĕk'hôrn). Peak 13,386 ft. in the Bernese Alps, SW cen. Switzerland, N of the Finsteraarhorn and S of the Wetterhorn.

Schroon (skroon). River ab. 50 m. long, NE New York; rises in cen. Essex co., flows S through Schroon Lake into Hudson river in cen. Warren co.

Schroon Lake. **1** Lake 10 m. long by 1½ m. wide in Essex co., NE New York; the Schroon river flows through it.

2 Village and resort in Schroon town (pop. 1220), Essex co., NE New York, in Adirondack Mts. and near head of Schroon Lake, 17 m. W of Ticonderoga; pop. (est.) 800.

Schroon Mountain. Peak 3200 ft. in Adirondack Mts., Essex co., NE New York.

Schu'len·burg (shōō'lĕn·bûrg). City, Fayette co., SE cen. Texas, 46 m. SW of Brenham; pop. 2207; in farming section; flour mills.

Schul'pfor'te (shōōl'pfôr'tĕ) *or* **Schul'pfor'ta** (-tä) *or* **Pfor'ta.** Village, N Hesse state, West Germany, 2 m. SW of Naumburg on the Saale; site of school (founded 1543 by Maurice, Duke of Saxony) which occupies a former Cistercian monastery founded 1140.

Schurz, Mount (shŏŏrts). Peak 11,141 ft. in W Park co., NW Wyoming.

Schütt, Great *and* **Little.** See GREAT SCHÜTT; LITTLE SCHÜTT.

Schuy'ler (skī'lĕr). **1** Counties in three states of the U.S. See *Tables* at ILLINOIS, MISSOURI, NEW YORK. **2** City, ⊗ of Colfax co., E Nebraska, on Platte river 30 m. W of Fremont; pop. 3096; trade center in agricultural and livestock-raising section.

Schuy'ler·ville (skī'lĕr·vĭl). Village and tourist resort, Saratoga co., E New York, on W bank of Hudson river 32 m. N of Albany; pop. 1361; settled 1689 and called **Saratoga;** burned in Indian raid 1745; restored and incorporated as village of Schuylerville 1831; scene of Burgoyne's surrender to Gates Oct. 17, 1777, after the battles fought near Stillwater. See SARATOGA.

Schuyl'kill (skool'kĭl; *locally usu.* skōō'k'l). **1** River 131 m. long, SE Pennsylvania; rises in Schuylkill co., E cen. Pennsylvania, flows SE into Delaware river at Philadelphia. **2** County in Pennsylvania. See *Table* at PENNSYLVANIA.

Schuylkill Haven. Borough, Schuylkill co., E cen. Pennsylvania, on Schuylkill river 5 m. S of Pottsville; pop. 6470; settled 1748; manufactures shoes, textiles.

Schwa'bach (shvä'bäк). City, N Bavaria, Germany, 8 m. SSW of Nürnberg; pop. 11,782.

Schwaben. See SWABIA.

Schwäbisch–Gmünd. See GMÜND.

Schwäbisch–Hall. See HALL.

Schwa'ner Mountains (sкvä'nĕr). Range in SW cen. Borneo, Malay Archipelago, S of the Kapuas river; highest peak Raja 7474 ft.

Schwang'au (shväng'ou). Village, SW Bavaria, W Germany, NE of Füssen; resort; two famous castles (Hohenschwangau and Neuschwanstein).

Schwarz'burg (shvärts'booрк). Village ab. 9 m. SW of Rudolstadt, Thuringia, Germany; pop. ab. 1000; gives its name to two former principalities, **Schwarzburg–Ru'dol·stadt** (-rōō'dōl·shtät) and **Schwarzburg–Son'ders·hau'sen** (-zôn'dĕrs·hou'zĕn), now in Thuringia.

Schwarze Elster. See ELSTER.

Schwar'zen·berg (shvär'tsĕn·bĕrk). City, Karl-Marx-Stadt dist., East Germany, in the Erz Gebirge 20 m. SE of Zwickau; pop. 11,465; makes household furnishings.

Schwarz'wald' (shvärts'vält'). **1** See BLACK FOREST. **2** Circle of Württemberg. See *Table* at WÜRTTEMBERG.

Schwe'chat (shvä'кät). Town, Lower Austria prov., NE Austria, on the Leitha, SE suburb of Vienna; pop. 8570; scene of defeat 1848 of Hungarians by Prince Windisch-Graetz.

Schweidnitz. See ŚWIDNICA.

Schwein'furt (shvīn'foort). City, Lower Franconia govt. dist., Bavaria, Germany, on Main river 66 m. E of Frankfurt am Main; pop. 36,336; 15th-cent. church, 16th-cent. town hall; manufactures ball bearings, chemical products, dyes, soap; river port; agricultural trade. First mentioned 791; made imperial city 1282. In World War II center of German ball-bearing production; heavily bombed by Allied planes 1942–45; taken by American forces Apr. 12, 1945.

Schweiz. See SWITZERLAND.

Schwelm (shvĕlm). Manufacturing city, North Rhine-Westphalia state, West Germany, E of Wuppertal; pop. 21,692; manufactures metal goods, rubber goods, paper, linen, damask. Mentioned before 650 A.D.; became city 1496.

Schwen'ning·en (shvĕn'ing·ĕn). Clock-manufacturing city, Baden-Württemberg state, West Germany, 34 m. E of Freiburg; pop. 18,978.

Schwe·rin' (shvä·rēn'). City, formerly ✳ of Mecklenburg, Germany, on SW shore of Lake Schwerin 60 m. E of Hamburg; pop. 48,157; railroad junction; Renaissance grand ducal castle, 13th-cent. Gothic cathedral, arsenal; manufactures machinery, cloth, tobacco, beer, and lacquered goods. Mentioned 1018. See MECKLENBURG.

Schwerin, Lake. Lake 14 m. in length and 3 m. average width in Mecklenburg, N Germany, 8 m. S of Wismar; drains into Elbe river.

Schwer'te (shvĕr'tĕ). Industrial city, North Rhine-Westphalia state, West Germany, on Ruhr river 7 m. SSE of Dortmund; pop. 16,465; manufactures iron and nickel ware.

Schwiebus. See ŚWIEBODZIN.

Schwientochlowitz. See ŚWIĘTOCHŁOWICE.

Schwyz (shvēts); *also* **Schwiz** (shvēts). **1** Swiss canton. See *History* and *Table* at SWITZERLAND. **2** Commune, its ✳, E cen. Switzerland, 22 m. E of Lucerne; pop. (1930) 8256; tourist center.

Schyl. See JIU.

Sciac'ca (shäk'kä). Seaport, Agrigento prov., SW Sicily, on Mediterranean 30 m. NW of Agrigento; pop. 22,713; hot sulfur and ferruginous springs nearby.

Sci'cli (shē'klē). Commune, Ragusa prov., SE Sicily, 9 m. S of Ragusa; pop. 21,827.

Scil'la (shĭl'à; *Ital.* shēl'lä); *anc.* **Scyl'la** (sĭl'à). Headland projecting into the Strait of Messina from the coast of Reggio di Calabria prov., S Italy. See CHARYBDIS.

Scil'li·um (sĭl'ĭ·ŭm) *or* **Scil'la** (sĭl'à). Ancient town, Byzacium, Roman province of Africa, near modern Sbeitla in Tunisia; gives its name to the *Scillitan martyrs,* twelve Christians, seven men and five women, executed in Carthage July 17, 180 A.D., whose martyrdom is the earliest on record for the Roman province of Africa.

Scil'ly Isles *or* **Islands** (sĭl'ĭ). **1** Group of 140 small islands off Lands End, SW England; 5½ sq. m.; pop. 1732; ✳ Hugh Town; administratively a part of Cornwall; market gardening and flower growing; anciently a haunt of pirates, and later of smugglers. **2** *Fr.* **Îles Scil'ly'** (ēl' sē·lē'). Group of islets forming atoll, W Society Is., S Pacific Ocean, ab. 150 m. W of Bora Bora.

Scinde (sĭnd). ⇒ SIND.

Scio. See CHIOS.

Sci·o'to (sī·ō'tō; -tŭ). **1** River 237 m. long, cen. and S Ohio; rises in Auglaize co., W Ohio, flows E, then S through Columbus and Chillicothe to empty into Ohio river at Portsmouth, S Scioto co., S Ohio. **2** County in Ohio. See *Table* at OHIO.

Scit'u·ate (sĭt'ṳ·āt). **1** Town, Plymouth co., SE Massachusetts, on Atlantic Ocean 16 m. ENE of Brockton; pop. 11,214; summer resort; now known for the gathering and preparation of Irish moss. **2** Town, Providence co., N Rhode Island, W of Cranston; pop. 5210; administrative center North Scituate village; settled 1710; textile mills, ironworks.

Scituate Dam. Dam completed 1928 across Pawtuxet river, N cen. Rhode Island; height 180 ft.; impounds water, **Scituate Reservoir,** for water supply of Providence.

Sco'bey (skō'bĭ). City ⊗ of Daniels co., NE Montana; pop. 1726.

Scodra. See SHKODËR.

Sco'field Reservoir (skō'fēld). Reservoir in NW Carbon co., E cen. Utah.

Sco·glit'ti (skŏ·lyĕt'tē). Town on S coast of Sicily, SE of Gela; in World War II a beachhead in Allied invasion of Sicily, secured by American forces July 11, 1943.

Scone (skōōn). Parish, Perth co., Scotland, just NE of Perth; pop. 3013; New Scone is a modern village, Old Scone site of abbey founded 1115, destroyed 1559, where Scottish kings were crowned until 1651; the *Stone of*

Scone or *Stone of Destiny* upon which early Scottish kings sat at coronation is said to have been brought to Scone by Kenneth MacAlpine (d. ?858 A.D.) from a castle on Loch Etive; it was taken to England by Edward I 1296 and is now in Westminster Abbey beneath the coronation chair.

Sconset. See SIASCONSET.

Sco'pus, Mount (skō'pŭs). Mountain, N extension of Mount of Olives, E of Jerusalem, Palestine; site of Hebrew Univ., inaugurated Apr. 1925.

Scor·di'a (skôr·dē'ä). Commune, Catania prov., E Sicily, 19 m. SW of Catania; pop. 11,672.

Scores'by Sound (skōrz'bĭ). Large inlet of Norwegian Sea on E coast of Greenland, in cen. part just N of 70°N; has many fiords and two large islands; length of NW fiord 280 m. On N side of entrance is Eskimo and Danish settlement of **Scores'by·sund'** (-sŏŏn'), established 1925; German meteorological station set up here 1930–31; radio and seismological station.

Scotch Plains (skŏch). Urban township, Union co., NE New Jersey, 10 m. W of Elizabeth; pop. 18,491.

Sco'tia (skō'shà). **1** Village, Schenectady co., E New York, on Mohawk river 15 m. NW of Albany; pop. 7625; residential suburb.
2 Medieval Latin name of Scotland, still sometimes used poetically and in the modern names Nova Scotia and Scotia Sea.

Scotia Sea. Part of South Atlantic SE of Falkland Is. and South America; lies within the Falkland Islands Dependencies and is bordered by South Sandwich Is., South Georgia I., and South Orkney Is.

Scot'land (skŏt'lănd). North part of the island of Great Britain, a part of the United Kingdom of Great Britain and Northern Ireland; 29,794 sq. m.; pop. (1931) 4,842,980, (1951 pop.) 5,095,969; ✳ Edinburgh; lies bet. 54°38'N (Mull of Galloway) and 60°51'N (N point of Shetland Is.); bounded on N by Atlantic Ocean, on E by North Sea, on S by England and Irish Sea, on W by Atlantic Ocean; greatest length of mainland 274 m., Mull of Galloway to Cape Wrath (see also DUNNET HEAD, JOHN O'GROAT'S HOUSE); greatest width 154 m.; divided into the following 33 counties (for pronunciation of their names, see their individual entries):

NAME	LOCATION	AREA[1]	POP.[1]	CO. SEAT
Aberdeen	NE	1,971	308,055	Aberdeen
Angus	E	874	274,870	Forfar
Argyll	W	3,110	63,270	Lochgilphead
Ayr	SW	1,132	321,184	Ayr
Banff	NE	630	50,135	Banff
Berwick	SE	457	25,060	Duns
Bute	SW	218	19,285	Rothesay
Caithness	N	686	22,705	Wick
Clackmannan	cen.	55	37,528	Clackmannan
Dumfries	S	1,073	85,656	Dumfries
Dunbarton	W cen.	244	164,263	Dumbarton
East Lothian	SE	267	52,240	Haddington
Fife	E	505	306,855	Cupar
Inverness	NW	4,211	84,924	Inverness
Kincardine	E	382	47,341	Stonehaven
Kinross	E cen.	82	7,418	Kinross
Kirkcudbright	S	899	30,742	Kirkcudbright
Lanark	S cen.	892	1,614,125	Lanark
Midlothian	SE	366	565,746	Edinburgh
Moray	NE	476	48,211	Elgin
Nairn	NE	163	8,719	Nairn
Orkney	NE	376	21,258	Kirkwall
Peebles	SE	347	15,226	Peebles
Perth	cen.	2,493	128,072	Perth
Renfrew	SW	227	324,652	Paisley
Ross and Cromarty	N	3,089	60,503	Dingwall
Roxburgh	SE	666	45,562	Jedburgh
Selkirk	SE	267	21,724	Selkirk
Stirling	cen.	451	187,432	Stirling
Sutherland	N	2,028	13,664	Dornoch
West Lothian	SE	120	88,576	Linlithgow
Wigtown	SW	487	31,625	Wigtown
Zetland	N	550	19,343	Lerwick

[1] Area in sq. m. Pop. is 1951 Census.

Divided physically into three regions: **(1)** Highlands (see NORTHERN HIGHLANDS), nearly two thirds of N part

of country, comprising the Grampians and many smaller ranges; highest Ben Nevis 4406 ft.; noted for scenery; **(2)** Central Lowlands, valleys of the Clyde, Tay, and Forth; **(3)** Southern Uplands, in S, with ranges of hills in which highest points are 2600–2700 ft.; Cheviot Hills and Tweed river on English border. Includes three large island groups: Shetland Is. in N, Orkney Is., separated from mainland by Pentland Firth, and Hebrides (*qq.v.*); and many islands off W coast (largest Mull, Islay, Jura, Arran, Bute, Rum, etc.); has many deep inlets (firths): Forth, Clyde, Moray, Solway, Lorne. Too mountainous for extensive agriculture; sheep raising and fishing important; one of chief manufacturing and shipbuilding countries of Europe. Chief cities Edinburgh, Glasgow, Dundee, Aberdeen, Paisley, Greenock.

History: Occupied by Picts when invaded by Romans after 80 A.D.; area south of rampart from Forth to Clyde held briefly by Romans (see GREAT BRITAIN); in 5th cent., included four kingdoms: of the Picts in highlands north of Forth, of Scots (of Irish extraction) in western highlands, of Strathclyde in south, and a part in southeast belonging to Anglo-Saxon kingdom of Northumbria; Picts converted to Christianity by St. Columba c. 565; in 685 Picts broke Anglo-Saxon power on border; invaded by Norse from late 8th cent.; Picts conquered Scots in 9th cent. and Lothian and Strathclyde were added by Malcolm II (1005–34) to unite Scottish kingdom; from 11th cent., came under Anglicizing influence; its ruler was forced to do homage to English crown 1174, the source of frequent future disputes; in war with England, defeated in 1304, but in 1314 won independence under Robert Bruce at Bannockburn; ruled by house of Stuart 1371–1688; acquired Orkneys and Shetlands 1472; in frequent intermittent conflict with England until accession of King James VI of Scotland as James I of England brought about personal union of two kingdoms 1603; united with England by Parliamentary act 1707 (see GREAT BRITAIN).

Scot'land (skŏt'lănd). **1** Counties in two states of the U.S. See *Tables* at MISSOURI and NORTH CAROLINA.
2 City, Bon Homme co., SE South Dakota, 26 m. NW of Yankton; pop. 1077.

Scotland Neck. Town, Halifax co., NE North Carolina, 25 m. ENE of Rocky Mount; pop. 2974.

Scot'land·ville (skŏt'lănd·vĭl; *Sou.* also -v'l). Town, East Baton Rouge parish, Louisiana, 5 m. N of Baton Rouge; pop. (est.) 6000; Southern University and Agricultural and Mechanical College (1880; coed.).

Scott (skŏt). **1** Name of counties in eleven states of the U.S. See *Tables* at ARKANSAS, ILLINOIS, INDIANA, IOWA, KANSAS, KENTUCKY, MINNESOTA, MISSISSIPPI, MISSOURI, TENNESSEE, VIRGINIA.
2 Urban township, Allegheny co., SW Pennsylvania, SW of Pittsburgh; pop. 19,094.

Scott, Cape. Cape, NW tip of Vancouver I., off W British Columbia, Canada.

Scott, Mount. 1 Peak 7850 ft. on S cen. boundary of Siskiyou co., N California.
2 Peak 2400 ft. in N Comanche co., SW Oklahoma.
3 Peak 8938 ft. in W Klamath co., near E shore of Crater Lake, S Oregon.

Scott City. City, ⊗ of Scott co., W Kansas, 72 m. NW of Dodge City; pop. 3555.

Scott'dale (skŏt'dāl). Borough, Westmoreland co., SW Pennsylvania, 17 m. NNE of Uniontown; pop. 6244; iron alloys, sheet metal, mining supplies; coal mines.

Scott Field. United States Air Force base, 6 m. E of Belleville, St. Clair co., Illinois; U.S. Air Force Technical School, established 1917.

Scott Island. Small island N of Ross Sea in Ross Dependency, Antarctica, ab. 315 m. NE of Cape Adare; ab. lat. 67°24'S and long. 179°55'W.

Scott Islands. Group of small islands in Pacific Ocean off extreme NW tip of Vancouver I., Brit. Columbia, Canada; meteorological station.

SHETLAND
ISLANDS
Same Scale as
Main Map

SCOTLAND

Statute Miles

0   25   50   75   100

PUBLISHED BY G. & C. MERRIAM COMPANY
SPRINGFIELD, MASS.
PREPARED BY J. W. CLEMENT CO., BUFFALO, N. Y.

Scotts′bluff′ (skŏts′blŭf′). City, Scotts Bluff co., W Nebraska, on North Platte river 20 m. E of Wyoming border; pop. 13,377; trade center in irrigated agricultural section producing sugar beets, potatoes, beans, and alfalfa.

Scotts′ Bluff′. 1 Butte 4662 ft. in Scotts Bluff co., W Nebraska; site of **Scotts Bluff National Monument** (see UNITED STATES, *National Monuments*). **2** County in Nebraska. See *Table* at NEBRASKA.

Scotts′bor′o (skŏts′bûr′ō). City, ⊗ of Jackson co., NE Alabama; pop. 6449; agricultural trading center.

Scotts′burg (skŏts′bûrg). Town, ⊗ of Scott co., SE Indiana, 27 m. N of New Albany; pop. 3810.

Scotts′dale (skŏts′dāl). **1** City, Maricopa co., SW cen. Arizona, E suburb of Phoenix; pop. 10,026. **2** Town, NE Tasmania, Australia, 28 m. NE of Launceston; pop. 1042; in fruit-orchard and poultry district; tin and gold mined nearby.

Scotts′ville (skŏts′vĭl; *Sou. also* -v′l). Town, ⊗ of Allen co., S Kentucky, 23 m. SE of Bowling Green; pop. 3324.

Scran′ton (skrăn′t′n; -tŭn). Commercial and industrial city, ⊗ of Lackawanna co., NE Pennsylvania, 20 m. W of Lake Wallenpaupack; pop. 111,443; settled c. 1788; anthracite coal-mining center; manufactures textiles (esp. silk), laces, shoes, mattresses, furniture, mining machinery. Univ. of Scranton (1888; coed.); International Correspondence Schools (1891); Marywood College (opened 1915; women).

Screv′en (skrĭv′ĕn). County in Georgia. See *Table* at GEORGIA.

Scroo′by (skrōō′bĭ). Village, Nottinghamshire, cen. England, ab. 18 m. S of Sheffield; home of William Brewster and other Pilgrims who later founded Plymouth colony in New England.

Scru′ton Peak (skrōō′t′n). Mountain 5950 ft. in Pennington co., SW South Dakota.

Scu′gog, Lake (skū′gŏg). Lake 39 sq. m. at junction of Ontario, Durham, and Victoria cos., SE Ontario, Canada; connects with Trent Canal by Scugog river.

Scultenna. See PANARO.

Scun′thorpe and Frod′ing·ham (skŭn′thôrp, frŏd′-ing·ăm). Urban district, the Parts of Lindsey, Lincolnshire, E England, 18 m. WSW of Hull; pop. 54,245; iron smelters.

Scupi. See SKOPLJE.

Scur′dy Ness (skûr′dĭ nĕs). Headland on E coast of Scotland, S of Montrose; lighthouse.

Scur′ry (skûr′ĭ). County in Texas. See *Table* at TEXAS.

Scu′ta·ri (skōō′tȧ·rĭ; *Ital.* -tä·rē). **1** See ÜSKÜDAR. **2** See SHKODËR.

Scutari, Lake; *anc.* **Pa′lus La′be·a′tis** (pā′lŭs lā′-bē·ā′tĭs). Lake on boundary bet. Montenegro, SW Yugoslavia, and NW Albania; ab. 130 sq. m.; receives Morača river on the N and drains into Bojana river in Albania; Shkodër is at its SE end.

Scylla. See SCILLA.

Scyros. See SKYROS.

Scyth′i·a (sĭth′ĭ·ȧ; sĭth′-). Ancient name of sections of Europe and Asia now included in Russia; the country had undefined boundaries, but the Scythians, a nomadic and savage race, dwelt chiefly in the steppes N and NE of the Black Sea and in the region E of Aral Sea. They are mentioned as early as the 7th cent. B.C. when they were driven out of Media; in 2d cent. B.C. they were conquered by the Sarmatians and a little later practically disappeared.

Scythopolis. See BEISAN.

Sea Bright (sē′ brīt′). Borough, Monmouth co., New Jersey, on Atlantic Ocean; pop. 1138; summer resort.

Sea′brook (sē′brŏŏk). Town, Rockingham co., SE New Hampshire, on Atlantic Ocean 13 m. S of Portsmouth; pop. 2209.

Sea Cliff. Residential village, Nassau co., SE New York, on Long I., on Long Island Sound 21 m. ENE of New York; pop. 5669; orig. planned as summer resort.

Sea′ford. 1 (sē′fērd) City, Sussex co., ⊕ Delaware, on Nanticoke river 15 m. W of Georgetown; pop. 4430; platted 1799; shipping point for sweet potatoes, oysters, lumber; canning, oyster packing. **2** (sē′fērd) Urban community (unincorporated), Nassau co., SE New York, on Long Island E of New York; pop. 14,718. **3** (sē′fērd; sē′fôrd′) Urban district, East Sussex, S England, pop. 9023; seaside resort; fisheries.

Sea′forth (sē′fōrth). Town, Huron co., SE Ontario, Canada, 22 m. SE of Goderich; pop. 2118.

Seaforth, Loch (lŏk). Inlet of the Minch on E coast of island of Lewis with Harris in the Outer Hebrides, off NW coast of Scotland.

Sea Gardens. Eastern part of harbor of Nassau, New Providence I., Bahama Is.; beautiful growth of submarine life can be seen through glass-bottomed boats.

Sea Girt (sē′ gûrt′). Borough, Monmouth co., E cen. New Jersey, on Atlantic coast ab. 7 m. S of Asbury Park; pop. 1798; near state military encampment.

Sea′graves (sē′grāvz). City, Gaines co., NW Texas, 60 m. SW of Lubbock; pop. 2307.

Sea′ham Harbour (sē′ăm). Urban district, Durham, N England, 16 m. SE of Newcastle; pop. 26,138.

Sea Islands. Chain of islands in Atlantic Ocean off coasts of South Carolina, Georgia, and Florida, bet. the Santee and St. Johns rivers; famous for the production of sea-island cotton.

Seal (sēl). River ab. 240 m. long in N Manitoba, Canada; flows E through a chain of lakes into Hudson Bay.

Seal, Cape. Cape on S cen. coast of Cape Province, Union of South Africa.

Sea′lark′ Channel (sē′lärk′). Channel ab. 3 m. wide bet. Guadalcanal and Florida Is., SE Solomon Is., W Pacific Ocean. See FLORIDA ISLAND.

Seal Beach. Resort city, Orange co., SW California, on Pacific Ocean 8 m. below Long Beach; pop. 6994.

Seale (sēl). Town, a ⊗ (see PHENIX CITY) of Russell co., E Alabama; pop. (1950) 343.

Seal Islands. See LOBOS ISLANDS.

Seal Rock. Island in Pacific Ocean, in Lincoln co., W Oregon.

Sea′ly (sē′lĭ). City, Austin co., SE cen. Texas, ab. 48 m. W of Houston; pop. 2328; in agricultural section.

Sea of Rybinsk. See RYBINSK RESERVOIR.

Sea Point. Town, suburb (including Green Point) 4 m. W of Cape Town on Table Bay, Cape Province, S Union of South Africa; pop. (white) ab. 8000.

Sear′cy (sûr′sĭ). **1** County in Arkansas. See *Table* at ARKANSAS. **2** City, ⊗ of White co., NE cen. Arkansas, 48 m. NE of Little Rock; pop. 7272; Harding College (1924; coed.).

Searles Lake (sûrlz). Lake, N San Bernardino co., SE California; extends a little way into Inyo co.; important source of potash and borates.

Sea′side′ (sē′sīd′). **1** City, Monterey co., W California, N of Monterey; pop. 19,353. **2** City, and seaside resort, Clatsop co., NW corner of Oregon, on Pacific Ocean 15 m. S of Astoria; pop. 3877; clam and crab fisheries; timber.

Sea′ton Del′a·val (sē′t′n dĕl′ȧ·văl). Former urban district, Northumberland, N England, NE of Newcastle; now in **Seaton Valley** urban dist., pop. 26,435.

Seat Pleas′ant (sēt plĕz′nt). Town, Prince Georges co., S cen. Maryland, 6 m. E of Washington; pop. 5365.

Se·at′tle (sė·ăt′l). Commercial and industrial seaport city, ⊗ of King co., W cen. Washington, bet. Elliott Bay of Puget Sound and Lake Washington (*q.v.*); largest city in the state; pop. 557,087; export and import trade center; railroad terminus, shipping center; headquarters of several steamship lines and for fishing boats and pleasure craft; Pacific terminus of Yellowstone Trail; lumber, fish (esp. salmon, halibut), shipbuilding, paper, flour industries, etc.; processed agricultural products; aircraft manufactures; tourist resort. U.S. naval air station

(on Lake Washington); municipal airport at Boeing Field; Fort Lawton (1897) in vicinity. Univ. of Washington (1861; coed.); Seattle Univ. (1892; coed.); Seattle Pacific Coll. (1891; coed.). Settled 1851, incorp. as city 1869; grew rapidly as outfitting center for gold fields of Alaska 1897 ff., and following development of transportation and opening of Panama Canal 1914; scene of Alaska-Yukon-Pacific Exposition 1909.

Seaturo, Mount. See WEST PEAK.

Se·ba′go Lake (sē·bā′gō). Lake ab. 13 m. long and 10 m. wide in SW Maine, in cen. Cumberland co.; resort.

Sebaste *or* **Sebastia.** See SIVAS.

Se·bas′tian (sē·băs′chăn). County in Arkansas. See *Table* at ARKANSAS.

Sebastian, Cape. Cape on W coast of Curry co., SW corner of Oregon.

Se′bas·tián′ Viz′ca·í′no Bay (sā′väs·tyän′ vēs′kä-ē′nō). Large inlet of Pacific Ocean on W coast of Lower California.

Se·bas′ti·cook Lake (sē·băs′tǐ·ko͝ok). Lake, S cen. Maine, near SW boundary of Penobscot co.

Se·bas′to·pol. 1 (sē·băs′tō·pōl) City, Sonoma co., W California, 7 m. SW of Santa Rosa; pop. 2694.
2 (sē·băs′tō·pōl; sĕb′ăs·tō′p'l) See SEVASTOPOL.

Sebastye. See SAMARIA.

Seb′cha di Tau·or′ga (sĕb′chä dē tou·ôr′gä). Salt marsh, N Tripolitania, Libya, N Africa, extending along W shore of the Gulf of Sidra.

Sebenico. See ŠIBENIK.

Se·ben′ny·tus (sē·bĕn′ǐ·tŭs); *mod.* **Sa′man·nud′** (sä′măn·no͞od′). Ancient city in Nile delta, Egypt, on W bank of Damietta mouth; ruins are SW of El Mansûra.

Se′be·waing (sē′bē·wǐng). Village, Huron co., E Michigan, on Saginaw Bay 25 m. ENE of Bay City; pop. 2026; in grape-growing section; beet-sugar refinery; fisheries.

Seb′ha (sĕb′hà). Oasis, N Fezzan, SW Libya, N Africa; chief town Sebha, on the highway from the Sudan to Tripoli, ✱ of the Fezzan.

Şebinkarahisar. See KARAHISSAR.

Seb′kret el Kour′zi·a (sĕb′krĕt ĕl ko͝or′zǐ·à). Saline lake, N cen. Tunisia, W of Zaghouan; scene of fighting Apr. and May 1943.

Seb′nitz (zāp′nǐts). City, Dresden dist., East Germany, 24 m. ESE of Dresden; pop. 11,849; manufactures artificial flowers, textiles, paper, buttons.

Se·boe′is Lake (sē·bō′ǐs). Lake, cen. Maine, in SE Piscataquis co.

Se·boe′koe (sà·bo͞o′ko͞o) *or* **Se·bu′ku.** Small island in SW Makassar Strait, E of Laut I., SE of Borneo, Indonesia.

Se·boo′mook Lake (sē·bo͞o′mo͝ok). Lake ab. 12 m. long, cen. Somerset co., W Maine, an expansion of the West Branch of the Penobscot river just E of junction of its headstreams.

Se·bou′ *or* **Se·bu′** (sē·bo͞o′). River ab. 180 m. long in NW Morocco; flows N, then W into Atlantic Ocean N of Rabat; navigable up as far as Fès.

Sebra, Bay of. See BIZERTE.

Se′bring (sē′brǐng). 1 City, ⊗ of Highlands co., cen. Florida penin., 50 m. SE of Lakeland; pop. 6939.
2 Village, Mahoning co., NE Ohio, 21 m. SW of Youngstown; pop. 4439; manufactures dinnerware, enamelware; near coal mines.

Seb′se·war′, Seb′ze·war′ (sĕb′zĕ·wär′). = SABZAWAR, Iran.

Sebuku. See SEBOEKOE.

Se·cau′cus (sē·kô′kŭs). Town, Hudson co., NE New Jersey, 5 m. NNW of Jersey City; pop. 12,154; in stock-farm region; rendering plants, silk and wire mills.

Sec′chia (sĕk′kyä). River 98 m. long in N Italy; rises in the Apennines, flows N into Po river 12 m. SE of Mantua.

Seccondee. = SEKONDI.

Se·chu′ra Bay (sà·cho͞o′rä). Inlet of Pacific Ocean on NW coast of Peru.

Se·con·di·glia′no (sā·kôn·dē·lyä′nō). Town, Naples commune, Italy, suburb of Naples; pop. (1931) 24,362.

Secretary Island. Island off SW coast of South I., New Zealand.

Se·cun′der·a·bad′ *or* **Si·kan′dar·a·bad′** (sē·kŭn′dĕr-ä·bäd′). Town and former British cantonment, N Andhra Pradesh, S cen. India, 6 m. NE of Hyderabad; pop. 120,801 (includes Bolarum, cavalry brigade headquarters, 17 sq. m.). Formerly one of the largest of the British military stations in India, with infantry and cavalry brigades.

Se·da′lia (sē·dāl′yà). City, ⊗ of Pettis co., W cen. Missouri, 58 m. W of Jefferson City; pop. 23,874; shipping point in agricultural section; dairies, packing plants, flour mills.

Se·dan′ (sē·dăn′). 1 City, ⊗ of Chautauqua co., SE Kansas, 28 m. WSW of Independence; pop. 1677; in agricultural section near petroleum deposits.
2 (*Fr.* sē·dän′) Manufacturing city, Ardennes dept., NE France, on Meuse river 11 m. ESE of Mézières; pop. 18,559; manufactures cloth. Scene of famous battle of Franco-Prussian War, resulting in French defeat and surrender of Napoleon III with 100,000 men Sept. 2, 1870; occupied by Germany during World War I; taken by Germans in World War II May 1940 and held until retaken by Americans Aug. 31, 1944.

Sedd el Bahr (sĕd′-dăl bä′h'r); *Turk.* **Sedd′ül·ba·hir′** (sĕd′dül·bä·hîr′). Village with adjacent forts on the S end of Gallipoli Penin., Turkey in Europe, just E of Cape Helles; one of the landing places of British forces Apr. 1915.

Sedge′moor (sĕj′mo͝or). Tract of moorland in Somersetshire, SW England; scene of duke of Monmouth's defeat July 6, 1685 by Feversham and Churchill.

Sedg′ley (sĕj′lĭ). Urban district, Staffordshire, W cen. England, near Wolverhampton; pop. 23,104.

Sedg′wick (sĕj′wĭk). Name of counties in two states of the U.S. See *Tables* at COLORADO and KANSAS.

Sed′l·ča·ny (sĕd′′l·chä′nĭ); *Ger.* **Seid′litz** (zĭd′lĭts; *Angl.* sĕd′-). Village, cen. Bohemia, Czechoslovakia, 25 m. S of Prague; pop. (1930) 2430.

Sedlez. See SIEDLCE.

Sed′li·ce (sĕd′lĭ·tsĕ); *Ger.* **Sed′litz** (zĕd′lĭts; *Angl.* sĕd′-). Town, SW Bohemia, Czechoslovakia, SSW of Prague and 11 m. NW of Písek; pop. (1921) 1370; mineral springs; gave name to Seidlitz powders.

Se′dro Wool′ley (sē′drō wo͝ol′ĭ). City, Skagit co., NW Washington, on Skagit river 20 m. SSE of Bellingham; pop. 3705; in agricultural and timber section.

Sedunum. See SION.

See′heim (sē′hām). Town, S South-West Africa, on Great Fish river, at 2300 ft. elevation; railroad junction point.

See′konk (sē′kŏngk). 1 Navigable river ab. 5 m. long, NE Rhode Island; formed by the widened Blackstone river at Pawtucket; the most northerly point of Narragansett Bay tidewater, flows S into Providence river at Providence.
2 Town, Bristol co., SE Massachusetts, 10 m. NW of Fall River; pop. 8399.

See′land (*Ger.* zā′länt). = SJÆLLAND.

See′lis·berg (zā′lĭs·bĕʀк). Village and resort, Uri canton, Switzerland, on Bay of Uri; pop. (1930) 660.

Seeonee. Var. of SEONI.

Se·fid′ Rud (sē·fēd′ ro͞od′). The Qizil Uzun (*q.v.*) river in its lower course.

Se·frou′ (sē·fro͞o′). Town, N cen. Morocco, NW Africa, E of Meknes; pop. (1931) 9890.

Sef′ton (sĕf′tŭn). Mountain range 10,390 ft., W cen. South I., New Zealand.

Seg *or* **Seg O′ze·ro** (syĕk ô′zyĭ·rŭ). Lake (*ozero*) 481 sq. m. in cen. Karelia, NW U.S.S.R., Europe; outlet is Vyg Lake and river to the White Sea.

Se·gau′li *or* **Sa·gau′li** (sà·gou′lĭ). Town, NW Bihar state, NE Indian Union, 85 m. N of Patna; former Brit-

ish military station. Treaty signed here Mar. 3, 1816 that defined the English relations with Nepal.

Se·ge·din, Se'ghe·din (sĕ'gĕ·dēn). = SZEGED.

Se·ges'ta (sĕ·jĕs'tá) or **Se·ges'te** (-tĕ). Ancient city in NW Sicily; its ruins, near modern Alcamo, are scanty but include a well-preserved theater. Often in disputes with Selinus; besieged by Dionysius; 10,000 of its men massacred 307 B.C. by Agathocles, tyrant of Syracuse; besieged by Carthaginians during First Punic War.

Segesvár. See SIGHIȘOARA.

Segodunum. See RODEZ.

Segontia. See SIGÜENZA.

Sé'gou' (sā'gōō'). Town on Niger river, S Mali (formerly French Sudan), West Africa, 120 m. ENE of Bamako; pop. 22,000.

Se·go'via (sĕ·gō'vyä; Angl. sĕ·gō'vĭ·á). 1 also called **Co'co** (kō'kō) or **Wanks** (wăngks). River ab. 450 m. long in N Nicaragua; flows NE into the Caribbean Sea; greater part of its course has formed for many years boundary bet. Nicaragua and Honduras; Mosquitia, coastal region to the N of it, now claimed by Nicaragua; if new boundary is upper Patuca and a line W of lower Patuca, the Segovia will be wholly in Nicaragua. 2 Province of Spain. See Table at SPAIN.
3 Commune, its ✳, cen. Spain, 40 m. NNW of Madrid; pop. 24,977; walled town, defended by turreted alcazar; manufactures linen, glass, paper; 16th-cent. Gothic cathedral; ancient Roman aqueduct (built by Trajan) still in use; a former residence of kings of Castile and León; sacked by French 1808.

Seg Ozero. See SEG.

Se'gre (sā'grä). River ab. 160 m. long in Catalonia, NE Spain; rises in the Pyrenees, flows SW past Lérida into Ebro river.

Se·gu' (sȧ·gōō'). = SÉGOU.

Se·guam' (?sȧ·gwäm'). Island of the Andreanof group in the Aleutians, SW Alaska, separated on the E from Amukta I. by Amukta Pass and on the W from Amlia I. by **Seguam Pass.**

Se·guin' (sĕ·gēn'). City, ⊗ of Guadalupe co., S cen. Texas, 33 m. ENE of San Antonio; pop. 14,299; flour mills, cottonseed-oil mills; pecans, livestock, poultry; oil wells. Texas Lutheran Coll. (1891; coed.).

Se·gun'do (sȧ·gōōn'dō). River ab. 130 m. long in Córdoba prov., N cen. Argentina; flows ENE into Mar Chiquita.

Se·gu'ra (sȧ·gōō'rä). 1 Mountain range in SE Spain, mostly in Jaén and Albacete provs.; highest peak Yelmo 5927 ft. 2 River 155 m. long in SE Spain; rises in the Segura Mts., flows E and SE into the Mediterranean Sea.

Se·hore' (sĕ·hōr'). Town, W Madhya Pradesh, cen. India, 20 m. W of Bhopal; pop. 13,860.

Sei'bo or **Sey'bo** (sĕ'ĕ·vō; sā'vō). 1 Province, E Dominican Republic. See Table at DOMINICAN REPUBLIC. 2 formerly **San'ta Cruz del Seibo** or **Seybo** (sän'tä krōōz' thĕl). Commune, its ✳; pop. 46,670; produces cacao, coffee, wax, sugar.

Seibus. See SEYBOUSE.

Seiche'prey' (sĕsh'prā'). Village, Meuse dept., NE France, E of St-Mihiel; battle Apr. 20, 1918 during American advance in St-Mihiel sector.

Seidlitz. See SEDLČANY.

Sei'er·ö' (sī'ĕr·û'). Small island of Denmark off NW coast of Sjælland I., in Seierö Bight; pop. (1925) 894.

Seierö Bight. Bay on NW coast of Sjælland I., Denmark.

Seihun. See SEYHAN.

Sei·ko·shin (sā·kō·shĕn). Seaport, S South Kankyo prov., Korea; pop. ab. 2000; port of Kanko ab. 10 m. SE of it.

Sei'lan (sĕ'ĕ·län). Early Italian form (used by Marco Polo) of CEYLON.

Sei'land (sĕ'ĕ·län). Island in Arctic Ocean off NW coast of Norway, in Finnmark co.; 229 sq. m.; pop. 862.

Seille (sâ'y'). River 80 m. long, Lorraine, NE France; flows W and NW to the Moselle at Metz; forms part of S boundary of Moselle dept.

Seilun. See SHILOH.

Seim (sām; Russ. syä'ĭm); also **Seym.** River ab. 435 m. long in SW cen. Soviet Russia, Europe, flowing W through Kursk Region of R.S.F.S.R. and Sumy Region of the Ukraine to the Desna river E of Chernigov.

Sei'nai (sā'nĭ). 1 District of Lithuania. See Table at LITHUANIA.
2 Town, formerly in S Lithuania, E of Suwałki; later Sejny (q.v.) in Poland, in the Suwałki dist. assigned to Germany 1939; in White Russia, Grodno Region, 1944–45, but ceded back to Poland Aug. 1945.

Sei'nä·jo·ki (sā'nä·yŏ'kĭ). Town, SW cen. Finland, in Vaasa dept.; pop. 7098; railroad junction point 35 m. SE of Vaasa.

Seine (sān; Fr. sân). 1 anc. **Seq'ua·na** (sĕk'wȧ·nȧ). River 480 m. long in N France; rises in Côte-d'Or dept., E France; flows NW through Paris and on into the English Channel near Le Havre; navigable for ab. 350 m. 2 Department of France. See Table at FRANCE.

Seine, Bay of the; Fr. **Baie de la Seine** (bād' lä sân'). Inlet of the English Channel, N coast of Normandy, NW France; along its curving coast line, from Cotentin Penin. on W to mouth of the Seine on E, are many popular watering places.

Seine–et–Marne (sän'ā·märn'; Fr. sân'ā·màrn'). Department of France. See Table at FRANCE.

Seine–et–Oise (sân'ā·wàz'). Department of France. See Table at FRANCE.

Seine–Ma'ri'time (sân'mȧ'rē'tēm'); formerly **Seine–In'fé'rieure'** (sân'än'fā'ryûr'). Department of France. See Table at FRANCE.

Se'ir (sē'ēr). 1 Country. See EDOM. 2 Mountain range of ancient Edom, along E side of Wadi el 'Araba; highest point Mt. Hor 4430 ft.

Seis de Sep·tiem'bre (sĕ'ĭz thä sĕ·tyäm'brä) or **Mo·rón'** (mō·rôn'). City, Buenos Aires prov., E Argentina, a W suburb of Buenos Aires; pop. (est.) 110,344.

Sei·shin (sā·shĕn) or **Chong·jin** (chông·jĭn). Seaport, North Kankyo prov., NE Korea, just E of Ranan; pop. (1938 est.) 72,353; once a mere fishing village, has grown rapidly since it was made open port 1908.

Sei·shu (sā·shōō). City, ✳ of North Chusei prov., S cen. Korea, 70 m. SSE of Keijo; pop. 20,243.

Seis·tan' (sās·tän'). Former province, E Iran; ✳ Nasratabad (now Shahr-i-Zabul); as modern district now divided politically bet. Iran and Afghanistan. Actually a depression with much marshland including Lake Helmand; corresponds nearly with ancient Drangiana. Under the Safawids (1502–1736) played important part in Persian history; in 19th cent. was center of dispute bet. Persia and Afghanistan.

Sej'ny (sā'nĭ); formerly **Sei'nai** (sā'nĭ) in Lithuania. Town, NE Białystok dept., NE Poland, E of Suwałki; pop. ab. 3000; ceded to Poland by Soviet Russia 1945.

Sekia el Hamra. See SAGUIET EL HAMRA.

Se·ki·ga·ha·ra (sĕ·kĕ·gä·hä·rä). Town, SW Gifu prefecture, cen. Honshu, Japan, WSW of Gifu; pop. 5823; site of great battle in 1600 in which the shogun Iyeyasu gained complete control of the government.

Sek'on·di' (sĕk'ŭn·dē'). Seaport and commercial town, SW Ghana, West Africa, 110 m. WSW of Accra and just E of Takoradi; pop. 21,614; connected by rail with Takoradi and inland with Kumasi. Site of Dutch and English forts built in the 17th cent.; became chief port of Gold Coast; now replaced by Takoradi with more modern harbor.

Se'la (sē'lȧ). City, ✳ of ancient Edom. See PETRA.

Se·lang'or (sĕ·läng'ēr). One of the states of the Federation of Malaya, on the W coast of S Malay Penin.; 3160 sq. m.; pop. 533,197, (1941 est.) 701,552; ✳ Kuala Lumpur. Bounded on N by Perak, on E by Pahang and Negri Sembilan, on S and W by Strait of Malacca. Gen-

erally level with mountain range along E boundary; not as well watered as other Malay States. Has extensive tin mines; mining of tin and production of rubber are two chief industries. Has large Chinese population. Crossed by the main railroad line along W coast of peninsula and by the branch from Kuala Lumpur to Port Swettenham, the chief port of the federation. Its capital, Kuala Lumpur, is also capital of the federation; other towns Klang, Kuala Kubu, and Kajang. Overrun by the Dutch 1783–84; made commercial treaty with British 1818 who took control of the state 1874; became part of the Federated Malay States 1895 and of the Federation of Malaya 1948.

Se′la·nik (sĕ′lä·nĭk′). Turkish name of SALONIKA.

Se·la′roe (sä·lä′rōō) *or* **Se·la′ru**. Island ab. 32 m. long by 4 to 8 m. wide of the Tanimbar group, in S Moluccas, Indonesia, E Malay Archipelago, off S end of Jamdena I.; pop. 5591.

Se·la′tan (sä·lä′tän); *Du* **Tan′djoeng Selatan** (tän′-jōōng). Cape on S coast of Borneo, Indonesia, projecting into Java Sea, 4°10′S lat., 114°38′E long.; southernmost point of the island of Borneo.

Selat Tebrau. See JOHORE STRAIT.

Selb (zĕlp). City, Upper Franconia govt. dist., Bavaria, Germany, 40 m. SSW of Zwickau; pop. 13,366; manufactures porcelain and earthenware.

Sel′by (sĕl′bĭ). **1** City, ⊗ of Walworth co., N South Dakota; pop. 979.
2 Urban district, West Riding, Yorkshire, N England, on the Ouse river S of York; pop. 10,217; traditional birthplace of King Henry I.

Sel·do′vi·a (sĕl·dō′vĭ·á). Village near S tip of Kenai Penin., S Alaska, on Cook Inlet; pop. 460.

Se′le (sā′lā). Short stream ab. 20 m. long, Campania, S Italy; flows W to Gulf of Salerno ab. 8 m. S of Salerno; divided the American and British beaches in Allied landing at Salerno Sept. 9–10, 1943.

Se′lem·dzha′ (sĕl′ĕm·jä′; *Russ.* syĭ·lyĕm·jä′). River ab. 330 m. long, main tributary of the Zeya in S Khabarovsk Territory, Soviet Russia, Asia; rises in SE spurs of Stanovoi Mts. and flows SW to the Zeya ab. 120 m. NE of Blagoveshchensk.

Se′len·ga′ (sĕ′lĕng·gä′). River 750 m. long, N cen. Asia; rises near Dzhibkhalantu in W Outer Mongolia and flows E; joined by the Orkhon near U.S.S.R. border which it crosses just W of Kyakhta, flows N through Buryat Mongol A.S.S.R., turns W at Ulan-Ude to enter Lake Baikal on SE.

Sé′les′tat′ (sā′lĕs′tà′); *Ger.* **Schlett′stadt** (shlĕt′shtät). Commune, Bas-Rhin dept., NE France, near Ill river 34 m. SW of Strasbourg; pop. 11,363; manufactures cottons and paper. Became free city under the Hohenstaufens; taken by Swedes 1632; taken by French 1634 and French rule confirmed by Peace of Westphalia; bombarded and besieged 1815; taken by Germans 1870; reverted to French rule after World War I.

Se·leu′ci·a (sĕ·lū′shĭ·á; -shá). Name of several cities in ancient Syria and Asia Minor, esp.: (1) *or* **Seleucia Tra′che·o′tis** (trä′kē·ō′tĭs). Ancient city, Cilicia, SE Asia Minor, SW of Tarsus, on the Calycadnus (mod. Göksu) near its mouth; site of modern Silifke. (2) City, now in ruins, on W bank of Tigris, cen. Iraq, opp. Ctesiphon and ab. 20 m. SSE of Baghdad. Founded by Seleucus Nicator 312 B.C. to become chief city of Seleucid Empire; developed extensive trade and at one time was said to have 600,000 inhabitants; superseded by Ctesiphon under the Persians; sacked by Romans c. 162 A.D. See PARTHIA. (3) *or* **Seleucia Pi·e′ri·a** (pī·ēr′ĭ·á). Ancient port of Antioch, now seaport town, SW Hatay, S Turkey in Asia. See SÜVEYDIYE.

Sel′fridge Field (sĕl′frĭj). United States Air Force base at Mount Clemens, Macomb co., SE Michigan; built during World War I, much enlarged and improved 1934 and later; 650 acres; annual Mitchell Trophy Air Race.

Seli. See ROKEL.

Se′li·ger (sĕl′ĭ·gēr; *Russ.* syä′lyĭ·gēr). Lake, N Kalinin Region, Soviet Russia, Europe; 57 m. long; 100 sq. m.; discharges into headwaters of the Volga river.

Sel′ig·man (sĕl′ĭg·măn). Town, Yavapai co., cen. Arizona; pop. (est.) 900; trading center.

Se′lins·grove′ (sē′lĭnz·grōv′). Borough, Snyder co., cen. Pennsylvania, on Susquehanna river (which here contains an island, the **Isle of Que** [kū]) 36 m. N of Harrisburg; pop. 3948; manufactures textiles, paper boxes. Susquehanna Univ. (1858; coed.).

Se·li′nus (sē·lī′nŭs). Greek city, S coast of ancient Sicily; its ruins are near Castelvetrano; founded 7th cent. B.C.; destroyed by Carthaginians 409 B.C.; partly rebuilt by Hermocrates 408 B.C.; inhabitants transferred to Lilybaeum 250 B.C.

Sel′kirk (sĕl′kûrk). **1** See FORT SELKIRK.
2 Resort town, SE Manitoba, Canada, on Red river 23 m. NNE of Winnipeg, near S end of Lake Winnipeg; pop. 6218; has iron and steel rolling mills, shipyards, coldstorage warehouses, and a government fish hatchery. Port of call for Lake Winnipeg steamers. Established near the Red River Settlement of the earl of Selkirk.
3 *or* **Sel′kirk·shire** (-shĭr; -shēr). County, SE Scotland; area 267 sq. m.; pop. (1951) 21,724; ⊗ Selkirk; hilly region; chief industry sheep raising. Sir Walter Scott was sheriff depute of Selkirk for 33 years.
4 Burgh, ⊗ of Selkirk co., SE Scotland, on Ettrick river 30 m. SE of Edinburgh; pop. 5853; agricultural center; woolen manufactures.

Selkirk Mountains *or* **Sel′kirks** (sĕl′kûrks). Range of the Rocky Mts. ab. 200 m. long, SE British Columbia, Canada, within the big bend of the Columbia river; highest peak Mt. Sir Sanford 11,590 ft. Crossed by the Canadian Pacific Railways at Rogers Pass near the Illecillewaet Glacier (*q.v.*), contains part of Glacier National Park and Mount Revelstoke National Park (see CANADA, *National Parks*).

Sel·la′sia (sĕ·lā′zhá; -zhĭ·á). Town in ancient Laconia, SE Peloponnesus, S Greece, ab. 5 m. N of Sparta; scene of battle 222 or 221 B.C. in which Antigonus Doson, king of Macedonia, defeated the Spartans under Cleomenes III.

Selle (sĕl). Small river in Nord dept., N France, flowing into Schelde river; scene of fighting Oct. 1918.

Sel′lers·ville (sĕl′ērz·vĭl). Borough, Bucks co., SE Pennsylvania, 19 m. SSE of Allentown; pop. 2497; founded 1738.

Selling Tso. See ZILLING TSO.

Sel·lore′ Island (sĕ·lōr′). Island in Mergui Archipelago (*q.v.*), Burma.

Selm (zĕlm). Industrial commune, North Rhine-Westphalia state, West Germany, 20 m. S of Münster; pop. 10,842.

Sel′ma (sĕl′má). **1** Manufacturing city, ⊗ of Dallas co., SW cen. Alabama, on Alabama river 40 m. W of Montgomery; pop. 28,385; agricultural distributing center; river port; industries include cotton and cottonseed-oil mills, ironworks, lumber mills, cheese factories. Craig Air Force Base with U.S. Air Force Special Staff School. Settled 1817; during Civil War, site of Confederate supply depot; captured by Federal troops 1865.
2 City, Fresno co., S cen. California, 15 m. SE of Fresno; pop. 6934; packs muscat grapes.
3 Industrial town, Johnston co., E North Carolina, 27 m. SE of Raleigh; pop. 3102; manufactures textiles, lumber, cottonseed oil.

Selmeczbánya. See BANSKÁ ŠTIAVNICA.

Sel′mer (sĕl′mēr). Town, ⊗ of McNairy co., SW Tennessee; pop. 1897.

Sel′sey Bill (sĕl′sĭ bĭl′). Headland on S coast of England, E of Portsmouth.

Se·luk′we (sĕ·lŭk′wĕ). Town, NE Matabeleland, Southern Rhodesia, S Africa, near Gwelo and ab. 100 m. ENE of Bulawayo; pop. (1930) 714; center of mining, ranching, and agricultural district.

Selvagens. See SALVAGES.

Sel′vas (sĕl′vȧz; *Port.* sâl′vȧs; *Span.* sĕl′väs). Extensive forested region of the upper Amazon river basin in N cen. South America.

Sel·zae′te (sĕl·zȧ′tĕ). Commune, East Flanders prov., NW cen. Belgium, ab. 27 m. W of Antwerp near the Netherlands boundary; pop. 8783.

Se·mang′ka Bay (sȧ·mäng′kä). Bay on S end of Sumatra, Indonesia, W of Lampong Bay; opens on Sunda Strait.

Se·ma′rang or **Sa·ma′rang** (sȧ·mä′räng). **1** Former residency, N Middle Java prov., Neth. Indies; 2088 sq. m.; pop. 2,011,616; ✻ Semarang. Important coastal region on Java Sea, bounded on NE and E by Djapara-Rembang residency, on S by Soerakarta govt. and Kedoe residency, and on W by Pekalongan residency. Region is mostly level but borders on high mountains in SW; has many short streams and is specially suitable for raising sugar and kapok; also produces coffee. Part of early sultanate of Mataram. Chief towns Semarang, Salatiga, Ambarawa, and Kendal.
2 Seaport city, its ✻, now ✻ of Central Java prov., Indonesia; pop. 217,796; third city in size in Java and one of its important ports; on N coast railroad ab. 255 m. E of Batavia and 165 m. W of Surabaja; also connected by rail with Jogjakarta and Madiun; has good harbor although unsafe in northwest monsoon; headquarters of many steamship companies and mercantile houses; has large proportion of Europeans and Chinese in its population. Under Dutch control from c. 1748.

Semendria. See SMEDEREVO.

Se′me·ni (sĕm′ĕ·nė). River 120 m. long, cen. Albania, formed by confluence of two headstreams N of Berati; flows W to Adriatic.

Se·me′nov (syĭ·myô′nŭf). Highest peak 15,350 ft. of Kirgiz Range, N Kirgiz S.S.R., Soviet Central Asia.

Se·me′roe (sĕ·mĕ′rōō) or **Se·me′ru.** Active volcano 12,060 ft. in E Java I., Indonesia, SE of Malang; highest mountain in Java; joins with Tengger Mts. to the N.

Sem′gal′len (zĕm′gäl′ĕn). German name of ZEMGALE.

Se·mi′chi Islands (sĕ·mē′chī). Small island group at W end of Aleutian Is., SW Alaska, in the Near Is. ESE of Attu; includes Shemya (*q.v.*).

Se·mi′di Islands (sĕ·mē′dī). Group of eight islands off the S coast of Alaska, in lat. 56°10′N.

Semien Mountains. See SIMYEN MOUNTAINS.

Se·mi·na′ra (sȧ·mė·nä′rä). Commune, Calabria, S Italy, on W coast N of Reggio di Calabria; pop. 5920; scene of several battles, esp. that of 1503 in which the French were defeated by the Spanish under García de Paredes.

Sem′ing·ton (sĕm′ĭng·tŭn). Parish, Wiltshire, S England, 3 m. NE of Trowbridge; pop. 449; terminus of Wilts and Berks Canal.

Sem′i·noe Dam (sĕm′ĭ·nō). Dam completed 1939 across North Platte river, N Carbon co., S cen. Wyoming; height 296 ft.; impounds water, **Seminoe Reservoir,** for flood control, irrigation, and power.

Sem′i·nole (sĕm′ĭ·nōl). **1** Name of counties in three states of the U.S. See *Tables* at FLORIDA, GEORGIA, OKLAHOMA.
2 City, Seminole co., cen. Oklahoma, 13 m. ESE of Shawnee; pop. 11,464; oil production (since 1926); oil refineries, cotton gins; manufactures carbon black.
3 City, ⊗ of Gaines co., NW Texas, 62 m. N of Odessa; pop. 5737.

Se·mi·pa·la′tinsk (sĕm′ĭ·pȧ·lät′ĭnsk; *Russ.* syĭ·myĭ-pŭ·lȧ′tyĭnsk). City, ✻ of Semipalatinsk Region, NE Kazakh S.S.R., Soviet Central Asia, on right bank of Irtysh river 445 m. SE of Omsk, on Turkistan-Siberian R.R.; pop. 109,779; has extensive trade in livestock and cattle products, wool, and grain.

Semipalatinsk Region. Subdivision of Kazakh S.S.R., Soviet Central Asia, in NE part; bounded on N by Altai Territory of R.S.F.S.R., on NE by East Ka-

zakhstan, on SE by China (Sinkiang), on S by Taldy-Kurgan Region, on W by Karaganda Region, and on NW by Pavlodar Region; ✻ Semipalatinsk.

Se′mi·ra′ra Islands (sä′mĕ·rä′rä). Island group bet. SE Mindoro I. and NW Panay I., cen. Phil. Is.; ab. 50 sq. m.; pop. 3947; marks S end of Tablas Strait; comprises three large islands, Semirara, Sibay, and Caluya, and several smaller ones. Chief town Caluya. Forms part of Antique prov.

Sem′i·so·poch′noi (sĕm′ĭ·sô·pŏch′noi). Small island in N part of Rat Is. group, Aleutians, SW Alaska, E of Kiska; sea-lion rookery.

Sem′li·ki (sĕm′lĭ·kĭ). River ab. 110 m. long in E cen. Africa connecting Lake Edward and Lake Albert.

Semlin. See ZEMUN.

Sem′me·ring Pass (zĕm′ĕ·rĭng). Mountain pass, alt. 3215 ft., in E Alps, Austria, 23 m. SW of Wiener Neustadt, bet. Lower Austria and Styria; railroad tunnel.

Semnan. Var. of SAMNAN.

Se·mois′ (sĕ·mwä′). River ab. 120 m. long in SE Belgium and NE France; flows NW in Luxembourg prov., crosses French border and empties into Meuse 9 m. N of Mézières.

Sem′pach (zĕm′päk). Commune, Lucerne canton, cen. Switzerland, on Lake of Sempach 8 m. NW of Lucerne; pop. (1930) 1248. Scene of victory of Swiss confederates over Austrian army July 9, 1386; traditional scene of heroic death of Arnold von Winkelried.

Sempach, Lake of. Lake 4 m. long and 1 m. wide in N cen. Switzerland, in Lucerne canton NW of Lake of Lucerne; outlet to the N into Aare river.

Sempione. = *Simplon:* see ALPS.

Sem′pre·vi′sta (sĕm′prȧ·vẽs′tä). Highest peak 5040 ft. in the Lepini Mts., SE Roma prov., cen. Italy.

Se′na (sā′nȧ). Town, E Tete dist., Mozambique, SE Africa, 2 m. from Zambezi river on S side; nearby is bridge across the Zambezi; 18th-cent. fort.

Sena Gallica. See SENIGALLIA.

Sen′a·to′bi·a (sĕn′ȧ·tō′bǐ·ȧ). Town, ⊗ of Tate co., NW Mississippi, 45 m. NE of Clarksdale; pop. 3259.

Sen·dai (sĕn·dī). City, ✻ of Miyagi prefecture, N Honshu, Japan, near E coast 180 m. N of Tokyo; pop. (1938 est.) 234,200; largest city of N Japan; only moderately important industrially but is a cultural center with Tohoku Imperial University (founded 1907) and several technical schools. Its castle now in ruins but has fine memorial to Date Masamune, a famous feudal lord (1567–1636) of the time of Hideyoshi; the daimiate founded by him controlled the region for 270 years.

Sen′e·ca (sĕn′ė·kȧ). **1** River ab. 76 m. long, W cen. New York; flows from Seneca Lake at N end to Cayuga Lake (canalized, part of N.Y. State Barge Canal system) then N and E joining the Oneida river to form the Oswego river.
2 River, NW South Carolina; rises among Blue Ridge Mts. in W North Carolina, flows S across South Carolina border and unites with Tugaloo river W of Anderson to form the Savannah river; in its upper course called the Ke′o·wee (kē′ô·wē).
3 Name of counties in two states of the U.S. See *Tables* at NEW YORK and OHIO.
4 City, ⊗ of Nemaha co., NE Kansas, 50 m. NE of Manhattan; pop. 2072; in agricultural section.
5 Town, Oconee co., NW South Carolina, 22 m. WNW of Anderson; pop. 5227; trading center for surrounding farms and nearby cotton mills.

Seneca Falls. Manufacturing village, Seneca co., W cen. New York, on Seneca river 11 m. W of Auburn; pop. 7439; settled in last part of 18th cent.; in farming and orchard region; coal and tobacco market; manufactures pumps, machine tools, precision tools, flour; scene of first women's rights convention in U.S. 1848.

Seneca Lake. Lake in W New York, chiefly in Yates and Seneca cos.; one of the Finger Lakes (*q.v.*); ab. 35 m. long and from 1 to 3 m. wide; ab. 600 ft. deep at its

deepest point; connected at N end with Cayuga Lake by canalized Seneca river, part of the N.Y. State Barge Canal system.

Se′ned (sĕ′nĕd). Town, cen. Tunisia, bet. Gafsa and Maknassy; fighting near here Feb. 1943.

Sen·e·gal′ (sĕn′ĕ·gôl′; sĕn′ĕ·gôl); *Fr.* **Sé′né′gal′** (sā′nā′-gȧl′). 1 River ab. 1050 m. long in W Africa; rises in the Fouta Djallon highlands of Guinea near the border of Sierra Leone, flows N and NW, forming the N boundary of the Republic of Senegal, empties into Atlantic Ocean at Saint-Louis; in its upper course, above its union at Bafoulabé with the Bakoy, known as **Ba′fing′** (bȧ′-fēn′y′; -făng′) river; its chief tributary on the S is the Falémé, in E Senegal; navigable to the Bafing at high water.

2 Republic, W Africa, S of Senegal river; 74,112 sq. m.; pop. 2,300,000; ✻ Dakar; includes former (1924–46) circumscription of Dakar (with Gorée and Rufisque) and territory Casamance, bet. Gambia and Portuguese Guinea, ✻ Ziguinchor. Bounded on N and NE by Mauritania, on E by Sudan, on S by Guinea and Portuguese Guinea, and on W by the Atlantic; in its S part narrow British colony of Gambia extends as exclave ab. 200 m. on both sides of Gambia river separating Casamance from main part of territory. Mostly low on coast and only slightly elevated in cen. part, with mountain region in SE; lower Senegal river and its chief tributary the Falémé form N and E boundary; other streams are the upper Gambia, the Casamance, and the wide estuary of the Salum. Coast line extends ab. 120 m. S from mouth of Senegal river to Cape Vert (its W point) and Dakar, thence S for 190 m. (not including Gambia coast) to a point just SE of Cape Roxo. Only good port Dakar. Chief exports ground nuts and oil, hides and skins, gums. Other towns besides Dakar are Saint-Louis (former capital), Thiès, Kaolack, and Ziquinchor.

History: First settlements were Portuguese (15th cent.); first French settlement at Saint-Louis (founded 1658); coastal region object of much rivalry and conflict in 18th and 19th cents. bet. French and Portuguese; French possession recognized 1814; after beginning of administration of Gen. Faidherbe 1854 great improvement in organization and development and hinterland explored; revolt 1899–1900 put down. In World War II Dakar became important as naval and air base; colony reclassified as a territory 1946; a republic within French Community, member of the Mali Federation (see MALI) 1959–60.

Sen·e·gam′bi·a (sĕn′ĕ·găm′bĭ·ȧ). Region of the Senegal and Gambia rivers, W Africa, now (since 1904) mostly in Senegal and W Mali.

Sen′e·kal (?sĕn′ĕ·kăl). Town, Orange Free State, Union of South Africa, ab. 100 m. NE of Bloemfontein; pop. 3802.

Senf′ten·berg (zĕnf′tĕn·bĕrʀ). City, Cottbus dist., E Germany, formerly in Brandenburg prov., Prussia; on the Schwarze Elster 25 m. NNW of Bautzen; pop. 17,472; lignite mining; briquettes, tile, glass, iron.

Senglea. See COSPICUA.

Seniavin Islands. = SENYAVIN ISLANDS.

Se·ni·gal′lia (sâ·nē·gäl′lyä); *anc.* **Se′na Gal′li·ca** (sē′nȧ gäl′ĭ·kȧ). Seaport, Ancona prov., Marches, cen. Italy, on Adriatic coast 18 m. NW of Ancona; pop. 28,327; 15th-cent. castle, 18th-cent. cathedral. An ancient capital of the Senones; captured by Romans 283 B.C.; became Roman military colony; Hasdrubal defeated by Romans nearby.

Se′nio (sâ′nyȯ). River ab. 55 m. long, Emilia, N Italy; rises in Apennines and flows NE to the Adriatic S of Comacchio; fighting on its banks Apr. 1945.

Senj (sĕn′y′); *Hung.* **Zengg** (zĕng). Seaport, Croatia, N Yugoslavia, on Morlacca channel; pop. 3072; occupied by Italy during World War II.

Sen′ja (sĕn′yä). Island in Arctic Ocean off NW coast of Norway, in Troms co.; 604 sq. m.; pop. 8577.

Sen′lac (sĕn′lăk). Hill in Sussex, S England, near Hastings; battle 1066 (generally called "Battle of Hastings").

Sen′lis′ (säɴ′lēs′). Town, Oise dept., N France, ab. 28 m. NNE of Paris; pop. 5607; ancient town, has remains of Gallo-Roman walls; early Gothic cathedral; by treaty signed here bet. Charles VIII and Emperor Maximilian I, May 23, 1493, Charles gave up Franche-Comté.

Sen·nar′ *or* **Sen·naar′** (sän·när′). 1 Region and ancient kingdom in E Sudan, chiefly bet. the White Nile and Blue Nile.

2 Town, Blue Nile prov., E Sudan, on the Blue Nile river S of Wad Medani; pop. (1938 est.) 8000; capital of the ancient kingdom of Sennar; railroad terminus. Dam built at village of Makwar just above Sennar, opened 1926 as Makwar Dam; name changed later to **Sennar Dam.**

Senne (sĕn). River 64 m. long, W cen. Belgium; flows N out of Hainaut prov. through Brussels and into the Rupel river, a tributary of the Schelde.

Senones. See SENS.

Sens (säɴs); *anc.* **A·gen′di·cum** (ȧ·jĕn′dĭ·kŭm), *later* **Sen′o·nes** (sĕn′ȯ·nēz). City, Yonne dept., NE cen. France, on Yonne river 32 m. NNW of Auxerre; pop. 17,783; 12th-cent. Gothic cathedral; remains of ancient Roman fortifications; manufactures agricultural implements, cloth, glue; trades in hemp, flax, corn, wine.

Sen′sun·te·pe′que (sän′sōōn·tā·pā′kä). Town, N cen. El Salvador, ✻ of Cabañas dept.; former center of indigo-growing area.

Sen′ta (sĕn′tä); *Hung.* **Zen′ta** (zĕn′tŏ). City, Voivodina autonomous prov., NE Yugoslavia, on right bank of the Tisza ab. 80 m. NNW of Belgrade; pop. 31,960; trade center in agricultural region; scene of battle Sept. 11, 1697 in which Prince Eugene of Savoy defeated the Turks.

Sen·ta′ni, Lake (sĕn·tä′nē). Small lake, NE Neth. New Guinea, ab. 10 m. SW of Hollandia and Humboldt Bay; site of Japanese airfields captured by forces of Allied Nations Apr. 26, 1944.

Sen′ti·nel, the (sĕn′tĭ·nĕl; -n'l). Mountain 8100 ft. in Glacier National Park, NW Montana.

Sentinel Dome. Peak 9127 ft. in the Sierra Nevada, E Fresno co., S cen. California.

Sentinel Mountains. Group of high mountains, Ellsworth Highland, Antarctica, bet. 77° and 78°S and bet. 86° and 92°30′W; highest peak estimated at ab. 12,500 ft. Discovered Nov. 1935 by Lincoln Ellsworth.

Sentinel Peak. Mountain 3858 ft. in the Adirondack Mts., Essex co., NE New York.

Sentinum. See SASSOFERRATO.

Sentis. See SÄNTIS.

Sen·ya′vin Islands (sĕn·yä′vĭn). Island group in E part of the Caroline Is., 158°E, W Pacific Ocean; chief island Ponape.

Seo de Urgel. See Seo de URGEL.

Se′o·nath′ (sā′ȯ·nät′h′). River ab. 200 m. long, E India; flows N and E in E Madhya Pradesh to Mahanadi river.

Se·o′ni (sâ·ō′nē). 1 Former district, now in S cen. Madhya Pradesh, E cen. India.

2 Town in district 70 m. NNE of Nagpur; pop. 16,081.

Seoul. See KEIJO.

Sep′a·ra′tion Point *or* **Head** (sĕp′ȧ·rā′shŭn). Cape on N coast of South I., New Zealand, forming SE side of Golden Bay and NW point of Tasman Bay.

Se′pi (sā′pē). Village at SE tip of Santa Isabel I., Solomon Is.

Se′pik (sā′pĭk). 1 River ab. 600 m. long in NW part of North-East New Guinea, in the Sepik dist. of the Territory of New Guinea; rises in mountains on W and SW boundaries, flows E into Pacific Ocean; navigable for ab. 300 m. One of its headstreams is in Neth. New Guinea.

2 Administrative district in W part of North-East New Guinea, Territory of New Guinea, S of Aitape dist.; 22,700 sq. m.; pop. (1930) 22,073; ✻ Ambunti.

Sep'pho·ris (sĕf'ŏ·rĭs); *mod.* **Saf·fur'ye** (să·fŏŏr'yĕ). Ruined town and ancient capital of Galilee, N Palestine; in early centuries of Christian Era a rival of Tiberias; a seat of learning, with rabbinical schools.

Sepsiszentgyörgy. See SFÂNTUL-GHEORGHE.

Sept–Îles (sĕ'tēl'). Group of islands off the coast of Côtes-du-Nord dept., Brittany, NW France.

Sep'ti·ma'ni·a (sĕp'tĭ·mā'nĭ·à). Ancient territory in S France, from mouth of the Rhone to the Pyrenees on the S, and extending NW to the Cévennes Mts.

Sep'ti·mer Pass (zĕp'tĕ·mĕr; *Angl.* sĕp'tĭ-). Mountain pass, altitude 7582 ft., in the Rhaetian Alps, SE Switzerland, above Upper Engadine valley.

Sequana. See SEINE.

Se·quatch'ie (sė·kwăch'ĭ). **1** River, SE cen. Tennessee; rises in S Cumberland co., flows SW into Tennessee river in S Marion co.
2 County in Tennessee. See *Table* at TENNESSEE.

Se·quoi'a–Kings Canyon National Park (sė·kwoi'à–kĭngz'). Sequoia National Park and Kings Canyon National Park (see these names at UNITED STATES, *National Parks*) considered as one administrative unit.

Se·quoy'ah (sė·kwoi'à). County in Oklahoma. See *Table* at OKLAHOMA.

Se·ra'bit el Kha'dim (sė·rä'bĭt ăl kä'dĭm). Mountain, SW Sinai Penin., NE Egypt; site of discovery of alphabetic inscriptions dating from c. 1900 B.C.

Se'ra·fi·mo'vich (sĕr'à·fĭ·mō'vĭch; *Russ.* syĭ·rŭ·fyĭ·mô'vyĭch). Town, Stalingrad Region, SE Soviet Russia, Europe, on the Don NW of Stalingrad; first attack of Russian forces in envelopment of Stalingrad Nov. 1942.

Se·raing' (sė·răn'). Mining and manufacturing commune, Liège prov., E Belgium, on Meuse river SSW of Liège; pop. (1938 est.) 42,981; manufactures steel, locomotives, and heavy-metal products.

Serajevo. See SARAJEVO.

Se'ram (sā'răm). = CERAM.

Ser'am·pore (sĕr'ăm·pōr). Town, West Bengal, NE Indian Union, on right bank of Hooghly river 13 m. N of Calcutta; pop. (1941) 55,339. Occupied by Danes from 1755 to 1845, when it was known as **Fred'er·iks·na'gar** (frĕd'ĕr·ĭks·nŭ'gĕr; frĕd'rĭks-).

Se'rang (sā'räng). **1** = CERAM.
2 Town, West Java prov., Indonesia; pop. 11,163; inland town on railroad to Batavia and 5 m. S of old port of Bantam.

Se·ran'tes (sā·rän'tås). Commune, La Coruña prov., NW Spain, 4 m. E of La Coruña on inlet of Atlantic Ocean; pop. (1930) 11,648; stock raising.

Se·ra·vez'za (sā·rä·vāt'tsä). Commune, Lucca prov., Tuscany, cen. Italy, 17 m. NW of Lucca; pop. 12,655; early 15th-cent. cathedral; marble quarries, mercury and tin mines.

Ser'a·wat'ti (sĕr'à·wät'ė), *or* **Ser·wat'ti** (sĕr·wät'ė), **Islands.** Former name of island group in S Banda Sea, S Moluccas, E Malay Archipelago, NE of Timor I.; includes the islands of the Damar and Leti groups, Roma, etc.

Ser'bi·a (sûr'bĭ·à); *formerly* **Ser'vi·a** (sûr'vĭ·à); *Serb.* **Sr'bi·ja** (sûr'bė·yä). Former Balkan kingdom; 36,937 sq. m.; * Belgrade; now one of the six federated republics of Yugoslavia. Mountainous country with short ranges and spurs, running in various directions, highest on Bulgarian border; bordered on N by the Danube and traversed in E cen. part by the Morava and in cen. by its tributaries the Western Morava and Ibar. Chief cities Belgrade, Niš, Kragujevac, Novi Pazar.
  History: Settled by Serbs, a south Slavic people, who were pushed across Danube into Moesia (*q.v.*) by Avars in 7th cent. A.D.; nominally under Byzantine suzerainty, by 10th cent. were united and converted to eastern Christianity; became independent in 12th cent. but soon broken by dynastic struggles and loss of territory to Hungary and Bulgaria; became leading Slav kingdom under Stephen Dushan (1331–55) who ruled Serbs,

Greeks, Bulgars, and Albanians; seat of Patriarchate of Serbs 1346–1766; defeated by Turks at battle of Kosovo (*q.v.*) 1389; after alternately resisting and cooperating with Turks, became part of Ottoman Empire 1459; northern Serbia held by Austria 1718–39; revolted against Turkey under leadership of Karageorge 1804–13, and again in 1815–17, led by Miloš Obrenović; guaranteed autonomy 1829 and ruled by hereditary prince 1830; secured withdrawal of Turkish garrisons 1867; made completely independent of Turkey 1878, but deprived of Bosnia and Herzegovina (*q.v.*); defeated by Bulgaria (*q.v.*) 1885; after 1903 and especially after "annexation crisis" of 1908–09 (see AUSTRIA-HUNGARY), pushed by extreme nationalists into anti-Austrian policy; disappointed at formation of Albania (*q.v.*) at end of First Balkan War; received territory in Macedonia after Second Balkan War 1913; blamed by Austria for assassination of Archduke Francis Ferdinand (1914) which Austria used as excuse for ultimatum and declaration of war on Serbia, ultimately precipitating World War I; utterly defeated by Central Powers; at collapse of Austro-Hungarian monarchy, proclaimed united Kingdom of Serbs, Croats, and Slovenes 1918 (see YUGOSLAVIA); at reorganization of Yugoslavia 1929 region divided to form the counties of Vardarska and Moravska and parts of Zetska, Dvinska, and Dunavska cos.; reunited 1945 to form a republic in the Federal People's Republic of Yugoslavia.

Ser·bo'nis, Lake (sĕr·bō'nĭs). Former lake and marsh, now dry, Lower Egypt, near coast E of the Suez Canal; described by Herodotus as place in which whole armies were engulfed; called **Ser·bo'ni·an Bog** (-bō'nĭ·ăn; -bōn'yăn) by Milton (*Paradise Lost*).

Serbs, Cro'ats, and Slo'venes, Kingdom of the (sûrbz', krō'ăts, slō'vēnz); *Serb.* **Kra'lje·vi'na Sr'ba, Hr'va·ta i Slo've·na'ca** (krä'lyĕ·vē'nä sûr'bä, hûr'vä·tä ê slō'vĕ·nä'tsä). Former name of YUGOSLAVIA.

Ser'chio (sĕr'kyô). River ab. 60 m. long, Tuscany, NW Italy; flows SE, SW, and W into the Ligurian Sea.

Sercq. See SARK.

Serdica. See SOFIA.

Ser'do·bol' (sĕr'dô·bôl'; *Russ.* syĭr·dŭ·bôl'y'); *Finn.* **Sor'ta·va'la** (sôr'tä·vä'lä). Town, S Karelia, U.S.S.R., on N shore of Lake Ladoga 120 m. N of Leningrad; pop. 4600; has rail connections and trade by steamer on the lake; its industrial plants handle wood, granite, and marble. In early times a Russian town, later Swedish; became Finnish in 1917, but was returned to U.S.S.R. by treaty 1940.

Se·re'gno (sā·rān'yô). Commune, Milano prov., Lombardy, N Italy, 13 m. N of Milan; pop. (1931) 17,833.

Se·rem'ban (sė·rĕm'băn). Town, * of Negri Sembilan state, Federation of Malaya, in W part; pop. 21,453, (1937 est.) 27,839; on coastal railroad ab. 42 m. NW of Malacca; connected with Port Dickson and Malacca by branch railroads.

Serena. = LA SERENA, Chile.

Se·ren·dib' (*Arab.* sŭ·rŏn·dēb'); *also* **Ser'en·dip** (sĕr'ĕn·dĭp). Arabic name (*Sarandīb*, probably from the Sanskrit) of Ceylon, long used by mariners of the Persian Gulf, and the form occurring in the *Arabian Nights*.

Seres. See SERRAI city, Greece.

Se'ret (sĕr'ĕt; *Russ.* syä'ryĭt). River ab. 150 m. long in W Ukraine; flows S and SE into Dniester river at Khotin; formerly in SE Galicia, Poland.

Sereth. See SIRET.

Sergiev. See ZAGORSK.

Sergiopol. See AYAGUZ.

Ser·gi'pe (sĕr·zhē'pĕ). State of Brazil. See *Table* at BRAZIL.

Sergo. See KADIYEVKA.

Ser'gy' (sĕr'zhē'). Village, Aisne dept., N France, 3 m. SE of Fère-en-Tardenois; fighting July 28–29, 1918.

Ser'i·ca (sĕr'ĭ·kà). Name applied by ancient Greeks and Romans to a region of E Asia ab. equivalent to mod-

ern China; its people, the Seres, were said to have culti-
vated silkworms and made silken fabrics.
Se·ri'na'gar (sĕ·rē'nŭg'ẽr). Var. of SRINAGAR.
Ser·in'di·a (sẽr·ĭn'dĭ·à). Section of Asia bet. the Pamirs
and the Pacific watershed, including Sinkiang prov., W
China.
Se·rin'ga·pa·tam' (sĕ·rĭng'gà·pà·tăm'). Town, My-
sore state, S India, ab. 8 m. N of Mysore; pop. 6300.
Former capital of Mysore under Tipu Sahib whose fort
and palace were here on an island in Cauvery river;
treaty signed here with the British 1792; in Fourth
Mysore War 1799 besieged and captured by the British
and Tipu killed; contains his mausoleum and that of his
son, Haidar Ali.
Seringes–et–Nesles. See FÈRE-EN-TARDENOIS.
Se·ri'phos (sĕ·rī'fŏs; *Mod. Gr.* sâ'rē·fôs). Island in W
Cyclades, Aegean Sea, S of Kythnos; in Cyclades dept.,
Greece; ab. 25 sq. m.; pop. ab. 4000. Colonized by
Ionians from Athens.
Ser·ma'ta (sĕr·mä'tà). Island, Indonesia, in the South
West Is. NE of Timor.
Ser'mi·de (sĕr'mĕ·dà). Commune, Mantova prov.,
Lombardy, N Italy, on Po river 26 m. ESE of Mantua;
pop. 10,572.
Ser·mio'ne (sâr·myō'nà) or **Sir·mio'ne** (sĕr·myō'nà);
anc. **Sir'mi·o** (sûr'mĭ·ō). Peninsula and village in
Brescia prov., Lombardy, N Italy, on S shore of Lake
Garda.
Ser·mo·ne'ta (sâr·mô·nā'tä). Town, Littoria prov.,
Latium, cen. Italy, on edge of Pontine Marshes NW of
Littoria; pop. 3123.
Se'rov (sĕr'ôf; *Russ.* syĕ'rŭf); *formerly* **Na·dezh'dinsk**
(nà·dĕzh'dĭnsk; *Russ.* nŭ·dyäzh'dyĭnsk). City, Sverd-
lovsk Region, Soviet Russia, Asia, E of Ural Mts. on
railroad ab. 200 m. N of Sverdlovsk; pop. 64,719.
Se·row'e (sà·rō'à). Town, E Bechuanaland Protector-
ate, South Africa, 250 m. N of Mafeking; capital of
Bamangwato tribe; pop. 15,935.
Ser'pa (sâr'pà). Commune, Beja dist., S Portugal, near
Guadiana river 17 m. ESE of Beja; pop. 10,662.
Serpent Mound. = GREAT SERPENT MOUND.
Ser'pent's Mouth (sûr'pĕnts). Strait ab. 10 m. wide
bet. NE Venezuela and the S coast of the island of Trini-
dad; connects Gulf of Paria with the Atlantic Ocean. Cf.
DRAGON'S MOUTHS.
Ser·pu'khov (sĕr·pōō'kôf; *Russ.* syĕr·pōō'kŭf). City,
Moscow Region, Soviet Russia, Europe; pop. 90,766;
on railroad and on navigable Oka 56 m. S of Moscow;
textile and dyeing industries; trades esp. in grain and
timber. An old town of Moscow principality with
fortress and cathedral dating back to 14th cent.; served
as a defense of Moscow against Tatars and Mongols.
Ser'ra A'ca·ra·hy' or **Ser'ra A'ca·ra·í'** (sâr'rà à'kà-
rà·ē'). Mountain range forming boundary bet. S British
Guiana and Brazil; highest peak ab. 2500 ft.
Serra Cu'ru·pi·rá' (kōō'rōō·pê·rà'). Mountain range in
N South America, extending along a section of boundary
bet. Venezuela and Brazil.
Serra da Es·trel'la (thà êsh·trâ'là). Mountain range 75
m. long in Beira prov., Portugal; highest point 6532 ft.,
highest point in Portugal.
Serra da Man'ti·quei'ra (mănn'tê·kä'ê·rà). Mountain range, SE Brazil, on border of São Paulo, Minas
Gerais, and Rio de Janeiro states; highest peak Itatiaía
9255 ft.
Serra das Di·vi·sões' (thàzh thê·vê·zōêNs'). Mountain
range in S cen. Brazil.
Serra de A'mam·ba·hy' (thê à'mănm·bà·ē'); *in Paraguay* **Cor'dil·le'ra de A'mam·bay'** (kôr'thê·yā'rà
thà à'màm·bī'). Mountain range in S Mato Grosso
state, SW Brazil, extending along a section of Brazil-
Paraguay boundary.
Ser'ra·di·fal'co (sĕr'rä·dê·fäl'kô). Commune, Caltanissetta prov., cen. Sicily, WSW of Caltanissetta; pop.
(1931) 9302.

Ser'ra do Es·tron'do (sâr'rà thōō êsh·trōNn'dōō).
Mountain range in NE cen. Brazil, in N Goiaz state bet.
the Araguaia and Tocantins rivers.
Serra do Mar (màr'). Coastal mountain range in S
Brazil, chiefly in Santa Catarina, Paraná, and São Paulo
states; highest point 7323 ft. in the Serra dos Orgãos.
Serra do Mon·chi'que (mōN·shē'kĕ). Mountain range,
S Portugal; highest point 2960 ft.
Serra do Piau·í' (pyou·ē'). Mountain range in NE
Brazil, extending along boundary bet. Baía and Piauí
states.
Serra do Ron'ca·dor (rōNng'kà·thôr'). Mountain
range in cen. Brazil, in NE Mato Grosso state.
Serra dos Ai'mo·rés' (thōōz ī'mōō·râs'). Area, E Brazil, in dispute bet. Minas Gerais and Espírito Santo
states; 3435 sq. m.; pop. (1940 est.) 67,103.
Serra dos Or'gãos (ôr'gouNs); *Eng.* **Or'gan Moun-
tains** (ôr'găn). Mountain range in Rio de Janeiro
state, SE Brazil, ab. 30 m. from Rio de Janeiro; highest
peak 7323 ft.; part of the Serra do Mar.
Serra dos Pa're·cis' (thōōsh pà'rê·sēs'). Range of
mountains in Mato Grosso state, SW Brazil, E of, and
parallel with, the NE border of Bolivia.
Serra do Tom'ba·dor' (thōō tōNm'bà·thôr'). Range
of mountains in N cen. Mato Grosso state, SW Brazil.
Serra Ge·ral' (zhĕ·räl'). Mountain range in E Santa
Catarina state, S Brazil.
Ser'rai (sâ'rā); *Mod. Gr.* **Sér'rai** (sâ'rà). 1 Department
of Greece. See *Table* at GREECE.
2 *also* **Ser'res** or **Ser'es** (sĕr'ĕs; *Bulg.* sĕ'răs or -rĕs);
anc. **Si'ris** (sī'rĭs). City, its ✷, near N end of Lake
Akhinou and ab. 42 m. NE of Salonika; pop. 29,640; cen-
ter of agricultural industry. Capital of Serbian emperor
14th cent.; long under Turkish occupation; occupied by
Bulgarians 1916–18 in World War I; center of revolt
1935; again occupied by Bulgarians 1941–44 in World
War II.
Ser·ra'na Bank (sĕr·rä'nä). Shoal in W Caribbean Sea
off NE coast of Nicaragua; controlled by U.S.A. and
Colombia.
Ser'ra·ní'a de Cuen'ca (sĕr'rä·nē'ä thà kwäng'kä).
Mountain range in E cen. Spain, in Cuenca and Guada-
lajara provs.
Ser·ra'no (sĕr·rä'nô). Island in Pacific Ocean off SW
coast of Chile, N of Wellington I.
Ser'ra Pa'ca·rai'ma (sĕr'à păk'à·rī'mä; *Port.* sâr'rà
pà'kà·rī'mà). Mountain range in N South America, ex-
tending W to E along section of Brazil-Venezuela bound-
ary; highest peak Roraima 8620 ft.
Serra Pa·ri'ma (pà·rē'mà). Mountain range in N South
America, extending W and S along a section of the
Venezuela-Brazil boundary; highest peak ab. 8000 ft.;
source of the Orinoco river.
Ser'ra·ri'a (sâr'rà·rē'à). Island in the mouth of the
Amazon river, N of NW Marajó I., off NE coast of Pará
state, Brazil.
Ser·rat', Cape (sĕr·rät'). Cape on N coast of Tunisia,
W of Bizerte.
Ser'ra Vas·sa'ry (sĕr'à và·sä'rĭ). Mountain range
forming part of boundary bet. S British Guiana and
Brazil, a W extension of Serra Acarahy; source of Esse-
quibo river and of several rivers of Brazil.
Serre (sâr). Village 7 m. N of Albert, Somme dept., N
France; battle Aug. 14, 1918.
Serres. See SERRAI city.
Sert. See SIIRT.
Servia. See SERBIA.
Serwatti Islands. See SERAWATTI ISLANDS.
Se·sa'jap (sĕ·sä'yäp). River ab. 200 m. long in NE part
of island of Borneo; rises in NE Sarawak and flows E in
Indonesian Borneo (Kalimantan) to the Celebes Sea.
Has large delta with many islands. See TARAKAN.
Se'sen·heim (zā'zĕn·hīm). Village, N Alsace, France,
ab. 18 m. NNE of Strasbourg near the Rhine; noted as
home from 1760 of Frederike Brion, friend of Goethe.

Se′sia (sâ′zyä). River 86 m. long in N Italy; rises on slopes of Monte Rosa, flows S into Po river 5 m. E of Casale Monferrato.

Ses′sa Au·run′ca (sĕs′sä ou·rōong′kä); *anc.* **Sues′sa Au·run′ca** (swĕs′à ô·rŭng′kà). Commune, Napoli prov., Campania, S Italy, 33 m. NNW of Naples; pop. 25,387; early 12th-cent. cathedral; Roman ruins; sulfur springs.

Ses′ser (sĕs′ẽr). City, Franklin co., S Illinois, 20 m. SSW of Mount Vernon; pop. 1764.

Ses·ta′o (sâs·tä′ō). Commune, Vizcaya prov., N Spain, 5 m. NW of Bilbao; pop. 18,625; iron foundries.

Se′sto Fio·ren·ti′no (sĕs′tō fyō·rän·tē′nō). Commune, Firenze prov., Tuscany, cen. Italy, 5 m. NW of Florence; pop. 17,535.

Ses′tos (sĕs′tŏs). Ruined town on the Dardanelles (Hellespont), Turkey in Europe; at narrowest point of the strait opp. Abydos; N terminus of bridge of boats built 481 B.C. by Xerxes for the crossing of his armies for invasion. Scene of legend of Hero and Leander.

Se′sto San Gio·van′ni (sĕs′tō sän′ jō·vän′nē). Industrial commune, Milano prov., Lombardy, N Italy, NE suburb of Milan; pop. (1931) 30,568.

Se′stri Le·van′te (sĕs′trē lâ·vän′tā). Commune, Genova prov., Liguria, NW Italy, on Ligurian Sea 21 m. ESE of Genoa; pop. 16,237; winter and seaside resort.

Sestri Po·nen′te (pō·nĕn′tā). Industrial subdivision (pop. 24,522) of commune of Genoa (*q.v.*), Italy; shipbuilding yards, machine works, tobacco factories.

Setabis. See JÁTIVA.

Sète (sĕt); *formerly* **Cette** (sĕt). Fortified commercial and manufacturing seaport, Hérault dept., S France, 18 m. SSW of Montpellier on a strip of land which separates the Étang de Thau from the Mediterranean; pop. 37,324; bathing resort; after Marseilles, leading seaport of southern France; school of hydrography; trades in wine, salt, fish, dried fruits, brandy, dyes, perfumes; shipbuilding, metallurgy, petroleum refining.

Se′te La·go′as (sâ′tĕ lá·gō′ás). City, Minas Gerais state, E Brazil, just N of Belo Horizonte; pop. (1940 est.) 10,388.

Sete Pon′tes (pōn′tĕs). City, Rio de Janeiro state, SE Brazil; pop. (1940 est.) 24,290.

Sete Quedas. See GUAÍRA.

Se′ti (sâ′tē). River ab. 120 m. long, W Nepal; flows S into the Karnali river.

Setia. See SEZZE.

Sé′tif (sâ′tēf). Commune, NW cen. Constantine dept., NE Algeria, on railroad 60 m. W of Constantine; pop. (1936) 36,041.

Se·tit′, Bahr (bä′h′r sĕ·tēt′). River 350 m. long, E Africa; headstream of the Atbara; rises in N cen. Ethiopia where it is called the **Tak·ka·ze** (tû·kû·zä), flows N and then W, forming a section of the Ethiopia-Eritrea boundary, and crosses into Anglo-Egyptian Sudan.

Seto Naikai. See INLAND SEA.

Seto no Uchi. See INLAND SEA.

Set′te Co·mu′ni, Al′ti·pia′no de′i (äl′tĕ·pyä′nō dä′ē sĕt′tä kô·mōō′nē). Literally "Plateau of the Seven Communes"; highland region in N Vicenza prov., Venezia Euganea, NE Italy; pop. (1931) ab. 30,000; chief town Asiago; battle June 15–16, 1918.

Se·tú′bal (sĕ·tōō′b′l; *Port.* -väl). **1** District of Portugal. See *Table* at PORTUGAL.

2 *formerly called in English* **Saint Ubes** (sänt ūbz′) *or* **Saint Yves** (īvz′). Seaport, its ✱, SW Portugal, on **Bay of Setúbal** (receives the Sado river) 19 m. SE of Lisbon; pop. (1940) 35,071; one of finest harbors in Portugal; manufactures and trades in muscatel wine, corks, laces, salt; shipbuilding; royal residence in time of John II.

Se·tul (sä·tōōn). Formerly, a Malay state in the Malay Penin. under Siamese protection, included among the Malay States (*q.v.*); now Satun prov. in Thailand.

Seul. Var. of *Seoul*: see KEIJO.

Seul, Lake (sūl); *Fr.* **Lac Seul** (làk′ sūl′). Lake 392 sq. m. in W Ontario prov., Canada; outlet is English river (a headstream of the Winnipeg).

Seul Choix Point (sē shwä′). Point on SE coast of Schoolcraft co., S Michigan penin., in Lake Michigan.

Se·van′ (sĕ·vän′) *or* **Se·vang′** (sĕ·väng′). **1** Lava island in NW Lake Sevan, Armenian S.S.R., Soviet Union.

2 *Turk.* **Gök′cha** (gŭk′chä); *anc.* **Lych·ni′tis** (lĭk·nī′tĭs). Lake 540 sq. m. in N Armenian S.S.R., Soviet Union; altitude 6345 ft.; shut in by high mountains in NE part of Armenian plateau; largest lake in Transcaucasia. Its outlet is the Zanga, a tributary of the Araks. Has abundance and great variety of fish.

Se·vas′to·pol (sĕ·väs′tō·pŏl; sĕv′ås·tô′p′l; *Russ.* syĭvŭs·tô′pŭl·y′); *formerly* **Se·bas′to·pol** (sĕ·bäs′tō·pôl; sĕb′ås·tô′p′l). Seaport city and naval base, SW Crimea, Soviet Russia, Europe, forming a peninsula 40 m. SW of Simferopol; pop. 111,946; on inlet of the Black Sea (**Sevastopol Bay**), which forms large deep harbor, one of the best in Europe, and receives the Chernaya river at its E end; cultural center and metropolis for the health resorts of the Crimea.

History: Dates back to very early period; site of Greek colony founded in 5th cent. B.C., which in 2d cent. became part of the kingdom of the Cimmerian Bosporus; see CRIMEA for succeeding changes in sovereignty; Tatar settlement founded here in 16th cent. under the name **Akh·tiar′** (ŭk·tyàr′); after its acquisition by Russia made the chief naval base in the Black Sea 1783; strongly fortified 1826. Famous for its two sieges: (1) in Crimean War, taken by allied nations after 322 days Oct. 1854 to Sept. 11, 1855 (see REDAN and MALAKHOV); (2) in World War II taken by Germans, with tremendous losses, after 250 days Oct. 1941 to July 2, 1942; recaptured by Russians May 10, 1944. In civil war 1918–21 was headquarters of Wrangel's army.

Seven Devils Mountains. Mountain range ab. 40 m. long, W Idaho, E of Snake river in Adams and Idaho cos.; highest point ab. 7900 ft.

Seven Hills. Village, Cuyahoga co., N Ohio, S of Cleveland; pop. 5708.

Seven Hills. The seven hills upon and about which was built the city of Rome (*q.v.*). According to tradition, the original city of Romulus was built upon the *Palatine* hill (later the site of the palaces of the Caesars), though later he united with his settlement those upon the *Capitoline* and *Quirinal*. The *Caelian* was said to have been added by Tullus Hostilius; the *Aventine*, by Ancus Marcius; the *Esquiline* and *Viminal*, by Servius Tullius, who built a wall (the *Servian Wall*) around the whole group. The Capitoline hill (originally called the *Saturnian*) anciently comprised two peaks, the *Capitolium*, which was earlier known as the *Tarpeian Rock*, and the Arx. In early times the hills, which are of volcanic origin, were very abrupt.

Seven Hunters, the. See FLANNAN ISLANDS.

Seven Mile Beach. Island off E cen. Cape May co., S New Jersey.

Sev′en·oaks′ (sĕv′ĕn·ōks′; sĕv′nōks′). Urban district, Kent, SE England, 20 m. SSE of London; pop. 14,834.

Seven Pines. See FAIR OAKS.

Seven Sisters Falls. Waterfall in a small stream emptying into Stor Fjord on W coast of Norway.

Seven Troughs Peak. Mountain, 7497 ft. in W Pershing co., NW Nevada.

Sev′ern (sĕv′ẽrn). **1** Navigable inlet of Chesapeake Bay ab. 10 m. long, E Anne Arundel co., cen. Maryland; Annapolis is located 2 m. from its mouth.

2 River ab. 420 m. long, NW Ontario, Canada; has source in several large lakes in W Ontario, flows NE into Hudson Bay.

3 River, SE Ontario, Canada. See Lake SIMCOE.

4 *anc.* **Sa·bri′na** (sá·brī′ná). River 210 m. long in E Wales and W England; rises in E cen. Wales, flows in a great curve NE, E, and S, crossing English border near

Shrewsbury and continuing S into Bristol Channel; navigable for ab. 180 m.; the "Shakespeare" Avon is one of its chief tributaries.

Severnaya Dvina. See NORTHERN DVINA.

Se′ver·na·ya Zem·lya′ (syä′vyĭr·nȧ·yȧ̇ zyĭm·lyä′); *Eng.* **Northern,** or **North, Land;** *formerly known as* **Nich′o·las II Land** (nĭk′ō·lȧs). Island group in Arctic Ocean, dividing Laptev Sea from Kara Sea, N of Taimyr Penin., Krasnoyarsk Territory, Soviet Russia, Asia; comprises three large islands, Bolshevik, Komsomolets, and October Revolution, and a number of smaller islands; separated from mainland by Vilkitski Strait. Discovered 1913.

Severodvinsk. See MOLOTOVSK.

Se·vier′ (sĕ·vēr′). **1** River 279 m. long, SW cen. Utah; formed by confluence of forks in W Garfield co., S Utah, flows N, then turns SW in E Juab co., empties into Sevier Lake in cen. Millard co., W Utah.
2 Name of counties in three states of the U.S. See *Tables* at ARKANSAS, TENNESSEE, UTAH.

Sevier Lake. Lake ab. 25 m. long in Millard co., W Utah; waters strongly saline; receives Sevier river from N; no outlet.

Se·vier′ville (sĕ·vēr′vĭl; *Sou.* also -v′l). Town, ⊗ of Sevier co., E Tennessee; pop. 2890.

Se·vil′la. **1** (sä·vē′yä) Town, Valle dept., W Colombia; pop. 10,450.
2 (sä·vē′[l]yä) Province of Spain. See *Table* at SPAIN.

Se·ville′ (sĕ·vĭl′; *esp. Brit.*, sĕv′′l, -ĭl); *Span.* **Se·vil′la** (sä·vē′[l]yä); *anc.* **His′pa·lis** (hĭs′pȧ·lĭs). City, ✻ of Sevilla prov., SW Spain, on Guadalquivir river 62 m. NNE of Cádiz; pop. (1941 est.) 312,874. Famous for its walks (*paseos*), picturesque suburbs, and many fine buildings, esp.: cathedral (1402–1511), the Giralda (tower of the Almohades) considered finest structure in Spain, Alcazar (Moorish palace of 12th cent.) and its garden; university (founded 1502). Birthplace of Velázquez and Murillo.

History: Iberian settlement at early period; prosperous under Romans, chief city of Baetica; chief town of southern Spain under Vandals and Goths 5th–8th cents.; captured 712 A.D. by Moors under Musa; an important city in Moorish Western Caliphate 712–1248; captured 1248 by Ferdinand III of León and Castile; after 1492, center of Spanish colonial trade (Casa de Contratación, begun 1598); in 17th cent. declined in rivalry with Cádiz; occupied 1808–12 by French under Soult; site of Spanish-American Exhibition 1929.

Se·vli′e·vo (sȧ·vlē′yȧ·vô). Town, Pleven dept., N cen. Bulgaria, N of the Balkan Mts. and ab. 35 m. SE of Pleven; pop. (1926) 9325.

Se·vran′ (sĕ·vräN′). Commune, Seine-et-Oise dept., N France, ENE suburb of Paris; pop. (1931) 10,071; powder works; manufactures brakes.

Sè′vre–Nan′taise′ (sâ′vrē·näN′tâz′). River ab. 80 m. long in W France; rises in Deux-Sèvres dept., flows NW into Loire river opp. Nantes.

Sè′vre–Nior′taise′ (sâ′vrē·nyôr′tâz′). River ab. 95 m. long in W France; rises in Deux-Sèvres dept., flows W into Bay of Biscay.

Sè′vres (sâ′vr′). Commune, Seine-et-Oise dept., N France, on Seine river 6 m. SW of Paris; pop. 15,501; normal school; famous national manufactory of porcelain (transferred here from Vincennes 1756) and museum of ceramics; glassworks, distilleries and breweries, nursery gardens; treaty signed here 1920 bet. Allies and Turkey.

Sèvres, Deux–. See *Deux-Sèvres*, department of France, in *Table* at FRANCE.

Se·wa′nee (sĕ·wô′nĕ; -wŏn′ĕ). Village and summer resort, Franklin co., S Tennessee, ab. 38 m. NW of Chattanooga; pop. 1464; sandstone quarries nearby. Univ. of the South (1857; men).

Sew′ard (sū′ẽrd). **1** Name of counties in two states of the U.S. See *Tables* at KANSAS and NEBRASKA.
2 Town, S Alaska, on Resurrection Bay, an inlet of Gulf of Alaska, on SE shore of Kenai Penin.; pop. 1891; important port, open all the year, and S terminal of government-owned Alaska railroad running N to Fairbanks. For many years an army post.
3 City, ⊗ of Seward co., SE Nebraska, 22 m. WNW of Lincoln; pop. 4208. Concordia Teachers College (1894; coed.; German Lutheran).

Seward, Mount. **1** Peak 8879 ft. in Glacier National Park, NW Montana.
2 Peak 4404 ft. in the Adirondack Mts., Franklin co., NE New York.

Seward Peninsula. Peninsula, W Alaska, ab. 180 m. long, 130 m. broad, bet. Kotzebue Sound on N and Norton Sound on S; its W tip, Cape Prince of Wales on Bering Strait, is most westerly point of continent of North America. Nome is on its S coast. Has rich gold deposits.

Sew′ell (sū′ĕl). Town, Colchagua prov., cen. Chile; railroad terminus E of Rancagua and mining center at 8000 ft. for El Teniente copper mines at 10,000 ft.

Se·wick′ley (sĕ·wĭk′lĭ). Residential borough, Allegheny co., SW Pennsylvania, on Ohio river 12 m. WNW of Pittsburgh; pop. 6157.

Sexi. See ALMUÑÉCAR.

Seybo. See SEIBO.

Sey′bouse′ (sā′bōōz′) or **Sei′bus** (sā′bōos). Unnavigable river ab. 140 m. long in NE Algeria, N Africa; flows N into the Mediterranean at Bône.

Sey·chelles′ (sā·shĕl′; -shĕlz′). British group of islands in the Indian Ocean E of NE Tanganyika, ab. lat. 4°S and long. 56°E; chief islands Mahé (55 sq. m., pop. ab. 22,000), Praslin (15 sq. m., pop. ab. 2000), and La Digue (4 sq. m., pop. ab. 1000); together with outlying islands S and SE of Seychelles and N of 11°S, constitutes a British crown colony with an area of 156 sq. m., pop. (1931) 27,444, (1940 est. 32,150), ✻ Victoria on Mahé. Chief products coconuts, cinnamon, and essential oils. First claimed by French 1744; taken by English 1794 and made a dependency of Mauritius 1810; by expansion of powers of administrative officers became a crown colony 1897 and 1903.

Sey′dis·fjör′dur (sā′thĭs·fyûr′thür). Town on NE coast of Iceland; pop. (1942) 850.

Sey·han′ (sā·hän′) or **Sei·hun′** (sā·hoon′). **1** *anc.* **Sar′us** (sâr′ŭs). River ab. 780 m. long in S cen. Turkey in Asia; rises in NE Anti-Taurus Mts., flows SSW into the Mediterranean Sea E of Mersin. Adana is on left bank of its lower course; the Samanti is its chief tributary.
2 Vilayet, S Turkey in Asia; 7986 sq. m.; pop. 358,557; ✻ Adana.
3 City. See ADANA.

Se·yi′di·e (sĕ·yĭd′ĭ·yĕ). Former province in S Kenya colony, E Africa; ✻ Mombasa.

Seym. See SEIM.

Sey′mour (sē′mōr). **1** Manufacturing town, W New Haven co., S Connecticut, on Housatonic river N of Ansonia; pop. 10,100; watered by Naugatuck river; settled 1680, incorporated 1850; manufactures woolen goods, mohair plush, hardware, fountain pens, paper, wire, cables, rubber and brass products; site of first successful woolen mill in U.S. (1806).
2 Industrial city, Jackson co., S Indiana, 38 m. ESE of Bloomington; pop. 11,629; railroad junction; manufactures wood products, pottery, stoves, textiles.
3 Town, Wayne co., S Iowa, 45 m. WSW of Ottumwa; pop. 1117.
4 City, ⊗ of Baylor co., N Texas, 48 m. WSW of Wichita Falls; pop. 3789; cotton compress and gins.

Seymour, Mount. Peak 4120 ft. in Franklin co., NE New York.

Seymour Island. Small island of Galápagos Is.; during World War II U.S. air base Dec. 1941 until evacuated by U.S. forces July 1, 1946.

Seymour Lake. Lake in E Orleans co., N Vermont.

Seyne–sur–Mer, La. See LA SEYNE-SUR-MER.

Sé'zanne' (sā'zàn'). Town, SW Marne dept., NE France; pop. 4911; vicinity was scene of Foch's victory in the first battle of the Marne Sept. 9, 1914 when his forces drove the Germans under von Bülow into the marshes of St-Gond to the NE.

Sez'ze (sāt'tsä); *anc.* **Se'ti·a** (sē'shĭ·à; -shà). Commune, Littoria prov., Latium, cen. Italy, 9 m. ENE of Littoria; pop. 16,432; episcopal see; ancient Roman amphitheater and temple of Saturn.

Sfânta, Sfântul. See SAINT.

Sfân'tu Gheor'ghe (sfĭn'tŏō gyôr'gĕ); *Eng.* **Saint George** (sānt jôrj'). Large island in cen. part of Danube delta, E Romania.

Sfân'tul–Gheor'ghe (sfĭn'tŏōl·gyôr'gĕ); *Hung.* **Sep'-si·szent'györgy** (shĕp'shĭ·sĕnt'dyûrd'y'). City, cen. Romania, in Transylvanian Alps on the upper Olt NNE of Braşov; pop. 10,942.

Sfax (sfäks). Seaport city, E Tunisia, N Africa, 78 m. S of Sousse on N shore of Gulf of Gabès; pop. (1936) 43,333; second largest city in Tunisia; exports olive oil, phosphates, sponges; famous for its olive trees. Settled by Phoenicians and later by Romans; a few remains of ancient Roman settlement on site; bombarded by French 1881; occupied by Axis troops Nov. 1942; captured by the British Apr. 10, 1943.

's Gravenhage. See THE HAGUE.

Sgurr–nan–Gil·lean' (?sgûr'nàn·gĭ·lēn'). Mountain 3167 ft., N Cuillin Hills, S Skye I., Inner Hebrides Is.

Sha·ba'ni (shä·bä'nĕ). Town, S cen. Southern Rhodesia, S Africa, 90 m. SW of Salisbury; pop. 11,000; asbestos mines.

Sha'ba·rakh U'su (shä'bä·räk ōō'sŏō). Literally "Place of the Muddy Waters," an archaeological site, ab. 103°40'E, 44°N, in S Outer Mongolia, ab. 600 m. NW of Wanchuan (Kalgan); dinosaur eggs discovered at Flaming Cliffs near here in 1925.

Shack'el·ford (shăk''l·fẽrd). County in Texas. See *Table* at TEXAS.

Shack'le·ton Inlet (shăk''l·tŭn; -t'n). Inlet ab. 10 m. wide in W side of Ross Shelf Ice, Ross Dependency, Antarctica; in ab. 82°22'S, 163°E; occupied by glacier.

Shackleton Shelf Ice. Large field of shelf ice ab. 165 m. long on the Queen Mary Coast, Antarctica; extends E from ab. 94°40'E to beyond 102°E and out into Indian Ocean for more than 130 m.

Sha'drinsk (shăd'rĭnsk; *Russ.* shà'dryĭnsk). Town, NW Kurgan Region, Soviet Russia, Asia; on a tributary of Tobol river; on Sverdlovsk-Kurgan railroad.

Shad'well (shăd'wĕl, -wĕl). Former estate, Virginia, site ab. 5 m. E of Charlottesville, Albemarle co.; birthplace of Thomas Jefferson, 3d president of the U.S.

Sha'dy·side (shā'dĭ·sīd'). Village, Belmont co., E Ohio, on Ohio river 27 m. S of Steubenville; pop. 5028; casket making.

Sha'fer Butte (shā'fẽr). Mountain 7591 ft. in S Boise co., W cen. Idaho.

Shafer Lake. Lake, NW Indiana, N of Freeman Lake (*q.v.*), formed in Tippecanoe river by Norway Dam (built 1923).

Shah'a·bad (shä'hä·bäd). **1** District, Patna division, W Bihar, NE Indian Union; 4408 sq. m.; pop. (1941) 2,328,581; ✻ Arrah. **2** Town, S Punjab state, NW Indian Union, 16 m. S of Ambala; pop. 12,293. **3** Town, cen. Uttar Pradesh, N Indian Union, 80 m. NW of Lucknow; pop. 21,101.

Shah'da·ra (shä'dà·rà). Suburb of Lahore, West Punjab, Pakistan, ab. 5 m. NW across the Ravi river; pop. 8262; contains tomb of the Mogul emperor Jahangir.

Shah Fu'la·di' (shä fŏō'lä·dē'). Highest peak 16,872 ft. in the Koh-i-Baba range, E cen. Afghanistan.

Sha·hi' (shä·hē'). **1** See Lake URMIA. **2** Island, N cen. part of Lake Urmia, NW Iran; highest point 7161 ft.

Shahjahanabad. = *Old Delhi:* see DELHI.

Shah'ja·han'pur (shä'jà·hän'pŏōr). City, Rohilkhand division, cen. Uttar Pradesh, N Indian Union, on affluent of Ramganga river 100 m. NW of Lucknow; pop. (1941) 110,163. Founded 1647 by Nawab Bahadur Khan, a Pathan leader, during the reign of Shah Jahan. Has military cantonment.

Sha'ho' (shä'hō'; *Chin.* -hŭ'). Small river, a tributary of the Liao, and town, 15 m. S of Mukden, Manchuria; battle Oct. 1904, in which the Russians were defeated by the Japanese.

Shah·pur' (shä·pŏōr'). Ancient city in Fars prov., SW Iran, W of Shiraz and N of Kazerun; famous ruins.

Shah'pur (shä'pŏōr). **1** District, Rawalpindi division, N West Punjab, Pakistan; 4770 sq. m.; pop. (1941) 998,921; ✻ Sargodha. **2** Town in district near Jhelum river; pop. 8545.

Shah'pu·ra (shä'pŏō·rà). **1** Former Indian state, SE Rajputana, NW India; 405 sq. m.; pop. (1941) 61,173. **2** Town, its ✻, 60 m. SE of Ajmer; now in Rajasthan; pop. 9298.

Shah'ri·za' (shä'rĭ·zä'). Town, Isfahan prov., cen. Iran, 50 m. S of Isfahan; pop. ab. 15,000.

Shahr–i–Za·bul' (shä'h'r·ĕ·zä·bŏōl'); *formerly* **Nas·rat'a·bad'** (nàs·rät'ä·bäd'). Town, E Iran, 275 m. ENE of Kerman, ✻ of Seistan dist. in cen. part of Lake Helmand depression.

Shah Rud (shä' rŏōd'). River ab. 100 m. long in N Iran; flows W parallel with and S of the Elburz Mts. and empties into the Sefid Rud 40 m. S of Resht.

Shaikh 'Othman. = SHEIKH 'OTHMAN.

Shaikh Sa'id. Var. of CHEIK-SAÏD.

Shak'er Heights (shāk'ẽr). Residential city, Cuyahoga co., N Ohio, 8 m. E of Cleveland; pop. 36,460.

Sha·khri·syabz' (shŭ·kryĭ·syàps'). City, SE Uzbek S.S.R., Soviet Central Asia, 40 m. S of Samarkand. See KITAB.

Shakh'ty (shäk'tĭ); *formerly* **A·le·ksan'drovsk Gru·shev'ski** (ŭ·lyĭ·ksàn'drŭfsk grŏō·shĕf'skĭ). City, SW Rostov Region, Soviet Russia, Europe, on railroad ab. 35 m. NE of Rostov; pop. 155,081; mining town in E part of Donets coal region.

Shak'o·pee (shăk'ō·pē). City, ⊗ of Scott co., SE Minnesota, on Minnesota river 18 m. SW of Minneapolis; pop. 5201; manufactures stoves, ironware, lime.

Sha·kyai' (shä·kā'); *formerly* **Ša·kiai'** (shä·kā'). **1** District of Lithuania. See *Table* at LITHUANIA. **2** Town, its ✻, 32 m. W of Kaunas; pop. 2044.

Sha'la, Lake (shä'lä). Lake in cen. Ethiopia, in area S of Addis Ababa.

Sha'la·mar, *or* **Sha'li·mar, Gardens** (shäl'à·mär; *native* shä'lä-, -lĭ-). Beautiful oriental gardens laid out in 1637 by the Mogul emperor Shah Jahan, 6 m. E of Lahore, West Pakistan, India.

Sha'ler (shä'lẽr). Urban township, Allegheny co., SW Pennsylvania, N of Pittsburgh; pop. 24,939.

Sham, Jeb'el (jĕb'ĕl shäm'). Highest peak in Oman, SE Arabia, 9900 ft.; in the Jebel Akdar.

Sham'be (shäm'bĕ). Town, Upper Nile prov., SE Sudan, on Bahr el Jebel (Nile) NNW of Mongalla.

Sha'meen' (shä'mĭn'; -mĭ·ĕn'). Low, sandy island in Pearl river at Canton, China, in SW part of city; ab. ½ of a sq. m.; pop. ab. 2000. Set apart 1859 as foreign settlement quarter; improved and built up by British and French.

Sha'mo' (shä'mō'). Literally "Sandy Waste," Chinese name of the GOBI desert, and sometimes of MONGOLIA.

Sha·mo'kin (shà·mō'kĭn). City, Northumberland co., E cen. Pennsylvania, 21 m. WNW of Pottsville; pop. 13,674; industrial, commercial, and mining center of anthracite coal region. Incorporated as borough 1864.

Sham'rock (shăm'rŏk). City, Wheeler co., NW Texas, in the panhandle 44 m. ESE of Pampa; pop. 3113; railroad junction and shipping point; gas and oil wells; carbon black and gasoline extraction plants; livestock.

Sha·na (shä·nä). See ETOROFU.

Shan·da'ken Tunnel (shăn·dä'kĕn). Tunnel, Greene co., SE New York; 18.1 m. long, built 1917–24; part of New York City's water-supply system.

Shan·ga'ni (shäng·gä'nĕ). River in W cen. Southern Rhodesia, S Africa; flows WNW into Zambezi river near Victoria Falls.

Shang'hai' (shäng'hī'; (*Chin.* shäng'hī'). Commercial city and treaty port, SE Kiangsu prov., E China, on Hwang Pu (Whangpoo) river 13 m. from its mouth in the Yangtze delta and 150 m. SE of Nanking. **Greater Shang'hai'** pop. (1957 est.) 7,100,000, comprises: (1) the City, or the Old City (Chin. **Hu–tsên** [kōō'-chŭng']), dating from the 11th cent., on the left bank of the Hwang Pu surrounded by walls 3 m. in circumference; (2) the International settlement, N of the City, 9

SHANGHAI AND YANGTZE RIVER MOUTH

sq. m., pop. (1936 est.) 1,450,685; estab. 1854 and 1863; has extensive waterfront on the Hwang Pu; (3) the French concession, W of the City and SW of the International settlement, 4 sq. m., pop. (1934 est.) 498,193; created 1849, enlarged 1863; (4) **Nan'tou'** or **Nan'tao'** (nän'tō'), Chinese suburb in S; (5) **Cha'pei'** (jä'bā'), Chinese suburb in N separated from International settlement by Soochow creek; (6) **Poo'tung'** (pōō'dōōng'), Chinese suburb across the Hwang Pu on right bank, district of factories, godowns, and commercial buildings; and (7) **Woo'sung'** (wōō'sōōng'), treaty port and N suburb at mouth of Hwang Pu. Other sections: **Hong'-kew'** (hŏng'kū'; *Chin.* hōōng'kō'), district in NE part; so-called American concession, in part absorbed by International settlement; **Hung'jao'** (hōōng'chĭ-ou'), government airdrome just outside western limits. Foreign concessions have been separately administered. Largest city in China and its industrial center; transacts transoceanic business and handles vast amount of trade, esp. of N and cen. China; its Bund, embankment along International settlement riverfront is commercial center with fine modern business buildings and several notable monuments; banking, missionary, and educational center; St. John's Univ.

History: Of small importance before 1840; opened 1842 as one of first five treaty ports; developed rapidly with increase of concession areas; attacked Jan.–Mar. 1932 by Japanese who withdrew in May; scene of severe fighting in Japanese-Chinese War Aug.–Nov. 1937; its foreign settlements occupied by Japanese 1941 and entire city under complete Japanese control after Dec. 7; restored to China Aug. 1945; taken by Communists May 1949.

Shanhaikwan. See LINYU.

Shank'lin (shăngk'lĭn). Former urban district, SE Isle of Wight, S England, on English Channel 13 m. SSW of Portsmouth. See SANDOWN-SHANKLIN.

Shan'non (shăn'ŭn). **1** Counties in two states of the U.S. See *Tables* at MISSOURI and SOUTH DAKOTA. **2** Navigable river ab. 240 m. long in N, cen., and SW Eire; chief river in Ireland and longest in British Isles; rises in N co. Cavan in N Eire, flows S through a number of lakes (including Lough Ree and Lough Derg) to Limerick, where it turns W and empties into Atlantic Ocean through a long deep estuary. **3** Large airfield at Rineanna, Eire, on N bank of estuary of the Shannon.

Shannon Dam. Dam completed 1926 across Baker river, tributary of Skagit river, NW Washington; height 263 ft.; impounds water for power, forming **Lake Shannon** in Skagit and Whatcom cos.

Shan'non·town' (shăn'ŭn-toun'). Urban area, Sumter co., E cen. South Carolina, SE of Sumter; pop. 7064.

Shan'si' (shän'sē'). Province, NE China; 60,491 sq. m.; pop. (1936 est.) 11,601,026; ✳ Yangku; bounded on N by Suiyuan and on NE by Chahar, provinces of Inner Mongolia, on E by Hopeh and Honan, on S by Honan, and on W by Shensi. One of the Five Northern Provinces. A plateau forming an intermediate region bet. arid Mongolia and the fertile plain of N China; its W and S boundaries are the Hwang Ho; a tributary, the Fen, traverses most of the province from NE to SW. Its N border is marked by a section of the Great Wall and further S is crossed by another section. Covered by great loess deposits, it was the home of early Chinese agriculture; also has enormous beds of coal (ab. 52% of China's total) and was once notable for its iron industry. Chief exports cereals; also produces wool and opium. Chief towns Yangku, Tatung, Fenyang. In its NE part is the sacred mountain Wu Tai Shan (ab. 10,000 ft.), visited by many pilgrims.

History: For centuries has been an integral part of the various northern kingdoms of China; after the Revolution (1911) was a "model province" (1912–28) under its governor Yen Hsi-shan; in Chinese-Japanese War (1937–45) was in part occupied by Japanese forces and was the scene of much guerrilla warfare.

Shan State. See FEDERATED SHAN STATES.

Shan·tar'ski·e Islands (shŭn·tär' skĭ·yĕ). Island group near coast of W Sea of Okhotsk, Khabarovsk Territory, Soviet Russia, Asia; crossed by 55°N.

Shan'tung' (shăn'tŭng'; -tōōng'; *Chin.* shän'dōōng'). Province, NE China; 69,198 sq. m.; pop. (1936 est.) 38,029,294; ✳ Tsinan; one of the Five Northern Provinces; bounded on NW and W by Hopeh prov. and on S by Honan and Kiangsu; its E part is a peninsula separating Gulf of Po Hai from the Yellow Sea. Bet. 1852 and 1938 and since 1947 traversed by lower course of the Hwang Ho; in the W crossed by the Grand Canal. Has two elevated regions: one in cen. part (highest point the sacred mountain of Tai 5048 ft.) and the other in E end of peninsula S of Chefoo (highest point above 5000 ft.). Has highest density population of all provinces of China. Its lowlands and valleys are fertile, producing varied agricultural crops; silk industry important; also rich in coal and iron deposits. Has several good harbors, esp. Tsingtao, Chefoo, Weihaiwei, and Penglai; other towns Tsinan, Lini, Weihsien, Tsining, and Taian.

History: Probably occupied by Chinese cultivators from very early times; became influential in Chinese history because it was the birthplace of Confucius (c. 551–479 B.C.) and of Mencius, and because of Tai (*q.v.*); made a province under the Ming dynasty (1368–1644); its chief port, Chefoo, opened 1863 as a treaty port; Weihaiwei leased (1898; returned 1930) to Great Britain and Kiaochow dist. to Germany 1898. In World War I Tsingtao captured by Japanese army 1914 (returned 1922); was in part concerned in the secret demands on China by Japan in 1915; occupied 1937 by Japanese; restored to China 1945; in Chinese civil war came under control of the Communist forces with their capture of Tsinan Sept. 1948.

Shantung Peninsula. East section of Shantung prov., NE China, bet. the Gulf of Po Hai and the Yellow Sea.

Shao'hing' (shou'shing') *or* **Shao'hsing'** (-shǐng'). City, N Chekiang prov., E China, ab. 40 m. ESE of Hangchow on rich delta plain; pop. (1953) 130,600; center for trade in silk, cotton, rice, and a liquor of special flavor. An old town, seat of government of a powerful king of Yüeh in 5th cent. B.C.

Shao'yang' (shou'yäng'); *formerly* **Pao'king'** (bou'-chǐng'). Town, cen. Hunan prov., SE cen. China, on right bank of upper Tzu river ab. 120 m. SW of Changsha; Japanese base 1944–45.

Shap'in·say (shǎp'in·sā). One of the Orkney Is. off N coast of Scotland; ab. 5 m. long; pop. 487; ancestral home of Washington Irving.

Shaq·ra' (shŭk·rä'). Town, cen. Nejd, Saudi Arabia, ab. 100 m. WNW of Riyadh; pop. ab. 20,000.

Sha'ra' (shä'rä'). River, N cen. Jehol, NE China; flows E and unites with other streams to form the Liao river.

Sha·rak'pur (shá·rŭk'pŏŏr). See SHEIKHUPURA.

Sha·ra'va·ti (shá·rä'vá·tē). Stream ab. 60 m. long, W India. See Falls of GERSOPPA.

Shar'ba·tat', Cape (shär'bá·tăt'); *Arab.* **Ras ash Shar'ba·tat'** (räs' ăsh shŭr'bă·tăt'). Cape on SE coast of Oman, SE Arabia, extending into the Arabian Sea, NE of Cape Nus.

Shari. See CHARI.

Sha·rif'kha·neh' (shá·rēf'kä·nä'). Town, Azerbaijan prov., NW Iran, on N shore of Lake Urmia (*q.v.*).

Shar'jah (shär'já; -jä). Town, Trucial Oman, SE Arabia, on SE coast of the Persian Gulf.

Shark (shärk), *or* **Sharks** (shärks), **Bay.** Large bay, inlet of Indian Ocean, W Western Australia, in 25°S; pearl fishing.

Shar'key (shär'kǐ). County in Mississippi. See *Table* at MISSISSIPPI.

Sharks Point (shärks). Cape on S side of estuary of Congo river, Africa.

Shar'on (shăr'ŭn). **1** Residential and resort town, W Litchfield co., NW Connecticut, S of Salisbury on New York border; pop. 2141; incorporated 1739; in Litchfield hills.
2 Residential town, Norfolk co., E Massachusetts, 9 m. WNW of Brockton; pop. 10,070.
3 Industrial city, Mercer co., W Pennsylvania, on Ohio border 18 m. NNW of New Castle; pop. 25,267; in iron-ore and coal region; coal mining and shipping, steel milling; manufactures electrical transformers, steel products.

Sharon, Plain of. Coastal plain ab. 50 m. long by 10 m. wide, W Palestine, extending from Mt. Carmel to Jaffa; very fertile.

Sharon Hill. Borough, Delaware co., SE Pennsylvania, 7 m. WSW of Philadelphia; pop. 7123.

Sharon Springs. 1 City, ⊗ of Wallace co., W Kansas, pop. 966.
2 Village and health resort, Schoharie co., E New York, ab. 34 m. W of Schenectady; pop. 351; White Sulphur Springs in center of village.

Sharp (shärp). County in Arkansas. See *Table* at ARKANSAS.

Sharp Mountain. Ridge in Schuylkill co., E cen. Pennsylvania, forming the S boundary of the Pottsville coal basin.

Sharps'burg (shärps'bûrg). **1** Town, Washington co., N Maryland, on W side of Antietam Creek; pop. 861; nearby is Antietam Battlefield Site, commemorating battle (Sept. 16–17, 1862) of Antietam (sometimes called battle of Sharpsburg) when Federals under McClellan met Lee's first invasion of the north in the Civil War, causing Lee's withdrawal from Maryland into Virginia.
2 Industrial borough, Allegheny co., SW Pennsylvania, on Allegheny river 6 m. NE of Pittsburgh; pop. 6096; coal mining and shipping; manufactures blowtorches, hardware, foundry and machine-shop products, welding equipment.

Sharps'ville (shärps'vǐl). Industrial borough, Mercer co., W Pennsylvania, 19 m. NNW of New Castle; pop. 6061; manufactures metal products.

Shar·qat' (shŭr·kät'). Village, N Iraq, on right bank of Tigris river 60 m. S of Mosul at site of ancient Sumerian settlement of Ashur; scene of final battle of Mesopotamian campaign Oct. 1918 resulting in overthrow of Turkish forces.

Sharq el Urdunn. See TRANSJORDAN.

Sharqi, Jebel esh. See ANTI-LIBAN.

Shar·qi'ya (shŭr·kē'yá). Province, Lower Egypt. See *Table* at EGYPT.

Sha'si' (shä'sē'; *Chin.* -shǐr'). Treaty port, S Hupei prov., E cen. China, on N bank of Yangtze 120 m. by air W of Hankow, 304 m. by river above Hankow and 83 m. below Ichang; pop. (1931 est.) 113,526; adjoins older city of Kingchow (see KIANGLING). Prosperous town since T'ang dynasty (618–907 A.D.) and chief river port of region during Taiping Rebellion.

Shas'ta (shăs'tá). County in California. See *Table* at CALIFORNIA.

Shasta, Mount. Peak, cone of an extinct volcano, 14,162 ft. high, in Cascade Range, Siskiyou co., N California; 6th in height of California's mountains but because of its isolation most impressive; covered with glaciers. Discovered 1827, first climbed 1854.

Shasta Dam *and* **Lake.** See UNITED STATES, *Dams and Reservoirs.*

Shasta Springs. Village and summer resort, Siskiyou co., N California, near Mt. Shasta.

Sha·su·ko·tan (shä·sŏŏ·kô·tän). One of the Kuril Is. in N part of chain, S of Onnekotan; highest point 3097 ft.

Shat–el–Arab. Var. of SHATT-AL-ARAB.

Shat Melrir. = CHOTT MELRIR.

Sha'to Plateau (shä'tō). Tableland on N boundary bet. Coconino and Navajo cos., N Arizona.

Shatt–al–Ar'ab (shät'ăl·är'ăb; *Arabic* shŏt'ĭl·ŭ'rŏb). The river, ab. 120 m. long, formed by the confluence of the Tigris and Euphrates rivers, SE Iraq, flowing SE into Persian Gulf; it is generally considered to begin at Al Qurna, flowing past Iraqi port of Basra, past Khorram-shahr and Abadan in Iran, and entering the gulf near the port of Fao in Iraq; forms in part the boundary bet. Iran and Iraq. Navigation above Abadan is difficult because of bar at Fao and silt in the delta region. On E shore is Abadan I. at N end of which it receives the Karun river. For the most part formed since ancient times because formerly Bassorah (Basra) was much nearer the sea.

Shatt Dijla. See TIGRIS.

Shatt el Hodna. See Chott el HODNA.

Shatt el Jerid. = Chott DJERID.

Shatt el Melghir. See Chott MELRIR.

Shatt el Shergui. See Chott ech CHERGUI.

Shat'tuck (shăt'ŭk). Town, Ellis co., NW Oklahoma, 31 m. WSW of Woodward; pop. 1625.

Shau'ki'wan' (shou'jē'wän'). Town, NE Hong Kong I., Hong Kong colony, China; pop. (1931) 19,946; E suburb of Victoria.

Shau·lyai' (shou-lä'); *formerly* **Shav'li** (shäv'lyǐ). **1** District of Lithuania. See *Table* at LITHUANIA.
2 *Ger.* **Schau'len** (shou'lĕn). City, its ✱, N Lithuania, 75 m. NNW of Kaunas; pop. (1938 est.) 31,299; railroad and commercial center in agricultural and lumbering region; manufactures machinery and leather. Battlefield Nov. 1919 where a combined force of Lithuanians and Letts defeated Germans; in World War II held by Germans 1941–44.

Shau'na·von (shô'ná·vŭn). Town, SW Saskatchewan, Canada, 50 m. SW of Swift Current; pop. 1625; on Canadian Pacific Railway.

Sha·va'no Peak (shá·vä'nō). Mountain 14,179 ft. in Chaffee co., cen. Colorado.

Shaver Lake *and* **Shaver Lake Dam.** See SAN JOAQUIN river, California.

Sha′vers Mountain (shā′vĕrz). Ridge extending along boundary bet. Randolph and Pocahontas cos., E cen. West Virginia.

Shavli. See SHAULYAI.

Shaw (shô). Town, Bolivar co., NW Mississippi, 20 m. NE of Greenville; pop. 2062; trade center; cotton.

Shaw′an·gunk Mountains (shŏng′gŭm). Range in SE New York, part of the Kittatinny Mt. (q.v.), chiefly in Orange, Sullivan, and Ulster cos.; highest peak Sam's Point 2255 ft., in Ulster co.

Sha′wa·no (shô′nō). **1** County in Wisconsin. See *Table* at WISCONSIN.
2 City, its ⊗, E cen. Wisconsin, 34 m. WNW of Green Bay (city); pop. 6103; agriculture; dairy farming.

Shawano Lake. Lake ab. 6 m. long and 3 m. wide in Shawano co., E cen. Wisconsin; drains into Wolf river.

Sha·win′i·gan Falls (shȧ·wĭn′ĭ·gǎn), *also formerly* **Sha·wen′e·gan Falls** (-wĕn′ė·gǎn). Manufacturing city, St. Maurice co., S Quebec, Canada, on St. Maurice river 18 m. NNW of Three Rivers; pop. 26,903; a large industrial center; makes aluminum, pulp and paper, carbide, cellophane. **Shawinigan Falls** (165 ft. high) furnishes power for local plants and light and power for Montreal 70 m. distant.

Shaw·nee′ (shô·nē′; shô′nē). **1** County in Kansas. See *Table* at KANSAS.
2 City, Johnson co., E Kansas, S suburb of Kansas City; pop. 9072.
3 City, ⊗ of Pottawatomie co., cen. Oklahoma, on North Canadian river 38 m. ESE of Oklahoma City; pop. 24,326; oil wells; oil refineries, cotton gins, cottonseed-oil, flour, and feed mills; dairy products. Oklahoma Baptist Univ. (1906; coed.).

Shaw′nee·town (shô′nė·toun; shŏn′ė-). City, ⊗ of Gallatin co., SE Illinois, near Ohio river 10 m. below its confluence with Wabash river; pop. 1280; former river port in agricultural and mining area; mines yield coal, lead, fluorite; prehistoric Indian mounds nearby. Disastrous flood of 1937 caused removal of town four miles to the hills back of the river.

Shcha′ra (shchȧ′rȧ); *Pol.* **Szcza′ra** (shchä′rä). River ab. 100 m. long, W White Russia, U.S.S.R.; flows NNW from Pripet Marshes to Neman river.

Shcher·ba·kov′ (shchĭr·bŭ·kôf′); *formerly* **Ry′binsk** (rĭ′bynsk). City, W Yaroslavl Region, Soviet Russia, Europe, on right bank of Volga; pop. 139,011; important port on the Volga, at SE end of Rybinsk Reservoir and terminal of the Leningrad-Volga waterway (see MARIINSK CANAL SYSTEM); transshipment point for goods brought from the Baltic area. Lumber, petroleum, grain, building materials; shipyards.

She′ba (shē′bȧ); *more correctly* **Sa′ba** (sä′bȧ); *Arab.* **Sa′ba′** (sä′bä′). Ancient country in S Arabia, probably included Yemen and Hadhramaut—the Biblical name. Its inhabitants were Sabaeans, a Semitic race of very ancient culture; its language was closely related to Ethiopic and its people were early colonizers of Ethiopia. Wealthy and commercially strong because of its position on the India-Africa trade route (cf. story of Queen of Sheba's visit to Solomon, *1 Kings* x). Its chief cities were San'a and Marib.

Shebeli. Var. of SHIBELI.

Shebin Karahisar. = *Sebinkarahisar*: see KARAHISAR.

She·boy′gan (shė·boi′gǎn). **1** County in Wisconsin. See *Table* at WISCONSIN.
2 City, its ⊗, E Wisconsin, on Lake Michigan 51 m. N of Milwaukee; pop. 45,747; large cheese-shipping center; manufactures enamelware and plumbing fixtures. Lakeland Coll. (1862; coed.).

Sheboygan Falls. City, Sheboygan co., E Wisconsin, 3 m. W of Sheboygan; pop. 4061; farm machinery.

Shechem. See NABLUS.

Shed′i·ac (shĕd′ĭ·ăk). Resort town, Westmorland co., SE New Brunswick, Canada, on Northumberland Strait 15 m. ENE of Moncton; pop. 2010; has excellent sandy beach; known for its oysters and splendid fishing; transatlantic airport on New York-Shediac-Botwood-Shannon air route. Founded 1750.

Shee′lin, Lough (lŏk shē′lĭn). Lake ab. 5 m. long in NE cen. Ireland, in S co. Cavan, ENE of Longford; drains SW through Inny river into Loch Ree.

Sheep Haven. Inlet of Atlantic Ocean on N coast of co. Donegal, N Eire, W of Lough Swilly.

Sheep Mountain. 1 Peak 4507 ft. in Banner co., W Nebraska.
2 Peak 6120 ft. in Snohomish co., NW cen. Washington.
3 Peak 11,190 ft. in Uinta co., SW Wyoming.

Sheep Rock. Peak 6017 ft. in Baker co., E Oregon.

Sheer′ness′ (shēr′nĕs′). Urban district, Kent, SE England, on Isle of Sheppey 38 m. E of London; pop. 15,727; seaport and British government dockyard; resort.

Shef′field (shĕf′ēld). **1** Industrial city, Colbert co., NW Alabama, on Tennessee river near Wilson Dam; pop. 13,491; iron products, fertilizers, coal products.
2 Town, Berkshire co., W Massachusetts, on Housatonic river 24 m. S of Pittsfield; pop. 2138; summer resort.
3 Locality in Sheffield township (pop. 2621), Warren co., NW Pennsylvania, ab. 12 m. SSE of Warren; pop. 1971; former tannery center.
4 City and county borough, West Riding, Yorkshire, N England, on the Don 68 m. NNE of Birmingham; pop. 511,757, (1951 pop.) 512,834; center of the cutlery industry; also manufactures armor plate, various other products of steel, silver-plated and electroplated goods; site of Norman castle (destroyed 1644) where Mary, Queen of Scots was prisoner most of the time 1570–84. Sheffield Univ. (begun as Firth College 1879; univ. 1905).

Sheffield Lake. Village, Lorain co., N Ohio, on Lake Erie W of Cleveland; pop. 6884.

Shef′ford (shĕf′ērd). County, Quebec, Canada. See *Table* at QUEBEC.

Sheikh, Jebel esh. See Mount HERMON.

Sheikh ′Oth·man′ (shĭk [shāk] ŏth·mǎn′). Town, Aden colony, SW Arabia, ab. 6 m. N of the city of Aden; pop. (1931) 12,167.

Sheikh Sa′id. See CHEIK-SAÏD.

Sheikh′u·pu·ra′ (shāk′hŏō·pŏō·rä′). District, Lahore division, West Punjab, Pakistan; 2303 sq. m.; pop. (1941) 852,508; ✻ Sharakpur (pop. 5056).

She′kar Dzong (shē′kär dzông′). Village, S Tibet, Outer China, N of Mt. Everest and ab. 160 m. W of Gyangtse.

Shek′lung′ (shĕk′lŏong′). Town, Kwangtung, SE China, on the Tung river 40 m. E of Canton.

Shek·sna′ (shĕk·snä′). Navigable river ab. 280 m. long in Vologda and Yaroslavl Regions, Soviet Russia, Europe; rises in Lake Beloe and flows S; near Cherepovets enters Rybinsk Reservoir (q.v.); before 1940 entered the Volga river just W of Shcherbakov. Forms important part of the Mariinsk Canal System (q.v.); through canal to Lake Kubenskoe connects with the Northern Dvina.

She·lag′ski, Cape (shė·làk′skĭ). Point on N coast of Chukot National District, Soviet Russia, Asia, on East Siberian Sea, ab. 170°30′E.

Shel·bi′na (shĕl·bī′nȧ). City, Shelby co., NE Missouri, 28 m. NE of Moberly; pop. 2067; trading and shipping point in agricultural section.

Shel′burn (shĕl′bērn). Town, Sullivan co., SW Indiana, 20 m. S of Terre Haute; pop. 1299; coal mining.

Shel′burne (shĕl′bērn). **1** Town, Franklin co., NW Massachusetts, 4 m. W of Greenfield; pop. 1739; manufactures cutlery.
2 County, Nova Scotia, Canada. See *Table* at NOVA SCOTIA.
3 Seaport town, ⊗ of Shelburne co., SW Nova Scotia, Canada, on inlet of Atlantic Ocean 43 m. E of Yarmouth; pop. 2040; has fine harbor and is noted shipbuilding center. Founded 1783 on site of old French village; largely inhabited in early years by Loyalists from U.S.

Shelburne Falls. Town, Franklin co., NW Massachusetts, ab. 4 m. from Shelburne; partly in Shelburne township and partly in Buckland township; pop. 2097.

Shel'by (shĕl'bĭ). **1** Name of counties in nine states of the U.S. See *Tables* at ALABAMA, ILLINOIS, INDIANA, IOWA, KENTUCKY, MISSOURI, OHIO, TENNESSEE, TEXAS. **2** City, Bolivar co., NW Mississippi, 20 m. SSW of Clarksdale; pop. 2384; in cotton-growing section. **3** City, ⊗ of Toole co., N Montana, 75 m. NNW of Great Falls; pop. 4017; near petroleum and natural-gas deposits. **4** City, ⊗ of Cleveland co., SW North Carolina, 21 m. W of Gastonia; pop. 17,698; manufactures textiles, cottonseed products, processed foods; foundry and machine shops. **5** City, Richland co., N cen. Ohio, 11 m. NW of Mansfield; pop. 9106; trade and industrial center in agricultural section.

Shel'by·ville (shĕl'bĭ·vĭl; *Sou.* also -v'l). **1** City, ⊗ of Shelby co., cen. Illinois, 32 m. SSE of Decatur; pop. 4821; trade center in agricultural section. **2** City, ⊗ of Shelby co., cen. Indiana, 27 m. SE of Indianapolis; pop. 14,317; trading center in the corn belt; manufactures furniture. **3** City, ⊗ of Shelby co., N cen. Kentucky, 20 m. W of Frankfort; pop. 4525; in bluegrass section; agricultural trade center and tobacco market. **4** City, ⊗ of Shelby co., NE Missouri; pop. 657. **5** Town, ⊗ of Bedford co., S cen. Tennessee, 25 m. S of Murfreesboro; pop. 10,466; manufactures rubber goods, pencils, graphite, knit goods.

Shel'don (shĕl'dŭn). City, O'Brien co., NW Iowa, 32 m. NW of Cherokee; pop. 4251.

She'le·ko'va Gulf (shĕl'ĕ·kŏ'vȧ; *Russ.* shā'lyĭ·kŭ·vȧ). Large inlet ab. 200 m. wide in NE part of Sea of Okhotsk, Khabarovsk Territory, Soviet Russia, Asia; Penzhinskaya Bay is an extension on the NE. Its E shore is the NW part of Kamchatka Penin.

Shelia, Jebel. See Djebel CHÉLIA.

Sheliff. See CHÉLIFF.

Shel'i·kof Strait (shĕl'ĭ·kŏf). Strait ab. 150 m. long and 25 to 30 m. wide bet. mainland (Alaska Penin.) on W and Kodiak and Afognak Is. on E; connects with Cook Inlet at N end.

Shell Creek Range (shĕl). Range in E White Pine co., E Nevada.

Shel'ley (shĕl'ĭ). City, Bingham co., SE Idaho, 8 m. SW of Idaho Falls; pop. 2612; center of potato region.

Shell Lake (shĕl). Village, ⊗ of Washburn co., NW Wisconsin; pop. 1016.

Shel'ter Island (shĕl'tẽr). Island 6 m. long in Gardiners Bay, E Long I., New York; summer resort.

Shelter Island Heights. Village and summer resort, Suffolk co., SE New York, on Shelter I. at E end of Long Island between Peconic and Gardiners Bays. **Shelter Island,** village and resort in Shelter Island town (pop. 1312) is ab. 2 m. E on Shelter I.; refuge of Quakers 1652.

Shel'ton (shĕl't'n; -tŭn). **1** Manufacturing city, Fairfield co., SW Connecticut, on Housatonic river opp. Derby 8 m. N of Long Island Sound; pop. 18,190; incorporated 1915; manufactures textiles, tacks, pins, wire, hardware. The town (settled 1697, incorporated 1789) is coextensive with the city. **2** City, ⊗ of Mason co., W Washington, on inlet of Puget Sound 17 m. NW of Olympia; pop. 5651; manufactures pulp, lumber; oyster culture.

She'ma·kha' (shĕ'mä·kä'). Town, E Azerbaidzhan, U.S.S.R., 65 m. WNW of Baku in S slopes of E Caucasus Mts.; pop. 4807; an old trading town known to Ptolemy as Kamachia; silk manufacturing has been its chief industry. Former capital of Shirvan khanate, subject to Persia; taken and destroyed 1742 by Nadir Shah as punishment for their religion; rebuilt but seized by Russians 1795 and permanently annexed 1805. Has suffered much from violent earthquakes, esp. in 1902,

and from fighting during civil war period after 1917. Has declined from a town of ab. 20,000 population.

Shem'ya (shĕm'yȧ). Small island in the Semichi Is. at W end of Aleutian Is., SW Alaska, E of Attu; location of a U.S. Air Force base.

Shen'an·do'ah (shĕn'ăn·dō'ȧ). **1** River 55 m. long, N Virginia; formed by junction of north and south forks in Warren co., flows NE across NE tip of West Virginia and empties into Potomac river at Harpers Ferry. **2** County in Virginia. See *Table* at VIRGINIA. **3** City, Page co., SW Iowa, 44 m. SE of Council Bluffs; pop. 6567; seed and nursery shipping center; manufactures cement blocks, chemicals, pharmaceuticals. **4** Borough, Schuylkill co., E cen. Pennsylvania, 11 m. N of Pottsville; pop. 11,073; settled 1835; anthracite coal mining; manufactures textiles, packed meats. **5** Town, Page co., N Virginia, 15 m. E of Harrisonburg; pop. 1839.

Shenandoah National Park. See UNITED STATES, *National Parks.*

Shenandoah Valley. Valley drained by the Shenandoah river bet. the Allegheny and Blue Ridge Mts., ab. 110 m. long and 25 m. wide, extending SW from Harpers Ferry; scene of important operations during Civil War, esp. at Cedar Creek, Harpers Ferry, Martinsburg, and Winchester, including Sheridan's famous ride from Winchester to Cedar Creek where his arrival turned a defeat into victory.

She·nan'go (shĕ·năng'gō). River ab. 100 m. long, W Pennsylvania; rises in Crawford co., flows S and joins Mahoning river 4 m. SW of New Castle, Lawrence co., to form Beaver river.

Shen'di (shĕn'dĭ). Town, Northern prov., NE Sudan, on right bank of Nile river 100 m. NNE of Khartoum; pop. (1938 est.) 14,237; manufactures leather and iron, grows coffee.

Shengking. See LIAONING.

She·nip'sit Lake (snĭp'sĭk). Small lake in NW cen. Tolland co., N Connecticut, W of Tolland.

Shen·kursk' (shĕn·kōōrsk'). Town on right bank of Vaga river, S Arkhangelsk Region, Soviet Russia, Europe, 185 m. S of Arkhangelsk; pop. ab. 2000.

Shen'si' (shĕn'sē'; *Chin.* shän'shē'). Province, NE cen. China; 72,334 sq. m.; pop. (1936 est.) 9,717,881; ✻ Sian; bounded on NW and N by Suiyuan prov. of Inner Mongolia, on E by Shansi, Honan, and Hupeh, on S by Szechwan, and on W by Kansu; separated from Shansi by the Hwang Ho. Crossed in cen. part by the Wei, King, and Lo rivers and in the S by the Han; bordered on N by the Great Wall; divided climatically N and S by the Chin Ling Shan (highest point ab. 11,000 ft.) and bordered on S, separating it from Szechwan prov., by the Ho Pa Shan and Ta Pa Shan (highest ab. 9843 ft.). Covered extensively by the loess, which makes it agriculturally rich; most important crops wheat, maize, barley and other cereals, fruits, and cotton; is very rich in coal deposits (ab. ⅓ of China's entire resources).

History: For centuries a region in which Chinese civilization has developed, its capital Sian, under various names, being chief city of the empire for long periods down to 12th cent. A.D.; suffered greatly during the Mohammedan rebellion 1861–76 and also from a severe famine early in 20th cent. Since beginning of Chinese-Japanese War 1937 has been headquarters (at Yenan) of the Eighth Route (Communist) Army against the Japanese and later Communist headquarters in civil war with National forces.

Shenyang. See MUKDEN.

She·paug' (shĕ·pôg'). River ab. 35 m. long, W Connecticut; rises in N cen. Litchfield co., flows S into Housatonic river.

She'pe·tov'ka (shĕp'ĕ·tôf'kȧ; *Russ.* shĭ·pyĕ·tôf'kȧ). Town, N Kamenets Podolski Region, W Ukraine, U.S.S.R., 70 m. W of Berdichev; pop. 14,690; important railroad junction on main line to Kovel.

Shep′herds·town (shĕp′ẽrdz·toun). Town, Jefferson co., NE West Virginia, in E panhandle on Potomac river, ab. 15 m. SW of Hagerstown, Maryland; pop. 1328. Shepherd Coll. (1871; coed.).

Shep′herds·ville (shĕp′ẽrdz·vĭl; *Sou.* also -v′l). City, ⊗ of Bullitt co., cen. Kentucky; pop. 1525.

Shep′par·ton (shĕp′ẽr·t′n; -tŭn). Town, N Victoria, SE Australia, on Goulburn river 102 m. NNE of Melbourne; pop. 5699.

Shep′pey, Isle of (shĕp′ĭ). Island 9 m. long in the mouth of the Thames, SE England; bridge connections with Kentish mainland.

Shep′shed (shĕp′shĕd). Urban district, Leicestershire, cen. England, 12 m. NW of Leicester; pop. 6235.

Shep′ton Mal′let (shĕp′tŭn măl′ĕt). Urban district, Somersetshire, SW England, 22 m. SW of Bath; pop. (1951) 5131; church has oak roof of 13th cent. with 350 panels each of different design; market cross 50 ft. high (1500).

She·qua′ga Falls (shĕ·kwô′gà). Waterfall 156 ft. high, in Montour Falls, New York.

Sher′borne (shûr′bẽrn). Urban district, Dorsetshire, S England, 50 m. W of Southampton; pop. 5987; trade center in agricultural section.

Sher′bro (shûr′brō). Estuary of four small rivers on SW coast of Sierra Leone, W Africa, opp. Sherbro I.

Sherbro Island. Island off SW coast of Sierra Leone, W Africa; town of Bonthe is on its E coast. With Turner's Penin. and several small mainland areas and islands comprises Bonthe dist. of Sierra Leone.

Sher′brooke (shûr′brŏŏk). **1** County, Quebec, Canada. See *Table* at QUEBEC.
2 Industrial city, its ⊗, at confluence of Magog and St. Francis rivers 85 m. E of Montreal; pop. 50,543; has abundant power from falls in river; varied manufactures; machine shops, cotton and woolen mills; large lumber trade; important railroad and agricultural center near asbestos mines.

Sher′burne (shûr′bẽrn). **1** County in Minnesota. See *Table* at MINNESOTA.
2 Village, Chenango co., S cen. New York, 32 m. SSW of Utica; pop. 1647; textile and dairying center; boyhood home of Brigham Young 1804 ff.

Sherburne Peak. Mountain 8500 ft. in Glacier National Park, NW Montana.

Shergui, Shatt el. See Chott ech CHERGUI.

Sher′i·dan (shĕr′ĭ·d′n). **1** Name of counties in five states of the U.S. See *Tables* at KANSAS, MONTANA, NEBRASKA, NORTH DAKOTA, WYOMING.
2 City, ⊗ of Grant co., S cen. Arkansas; pop. 1938; cotton ginning.
3 Town, Hamilton co., cen. Indiana, 25 m. N of Indianapolis; pop. 2165.
4 City, ⊗ of Sheridan co., N Wyoming, 13 m. S of Montana border; pop. 11,651; railroad division point; coal deposits nearby; manufactures flour, livestock feeds, cereal products, sugar (from sugar beets), brick and tiles, dairy products.

Sheridan, Mount. 1 Peak 13,700 ft. in Lake and Park cos., cen. Colorado.
2 Peak 10,250 ft. in Yellowstone National Park, NW Wyoming.

Sher′iff Knob (shĕr′ĭf). Peak 3400 ft. in Union co., N Georgia.

Sher′iff·muir (shĕr′ĭf·mŭr; shĕr′ĭ·mŭr). Battlefield, S Perth co., cen. Scotland, just W of the Ochil Hills; scene of battle Nov. 13, 1715 bet. Jacobites under John Erskine, Earl of Mar, and Royalists under Archibald Campbell in which the advance of the Jacobites was checked; battle gave its name to the whole rebellion (*Sherramoor* or *Sherrymoor*).

Sher′man (shûr′mán). **1** Name of counties in four states of the U.S. See *Tables* at KANSAS, NEBRASKA, OREGON, TEXAS.
2 Industrial city, ⊗ of Grayson co., NE Texas, 60 m. N

of Dallas; pop. 24,988; transportation and marketing center for agricultural (esp. onions) and stock-raising area; textile and flour mills; machine shops; ironworks; manufactures harnesses, mattresses, condensed milk, paper boxes; Perrin Air Force Base with U.S. Air Force Pilot School. Austin Coll. (1849, Huntsville; to Sherman 1876; coed.).

Sherman, Fort. See FORT SHERMAN.

Sherman, Mount. Peak 14,037 ft. in Park and Lake cos., cen. Colorado.

Sher′rill (shĕr′ĭl). City, Oneida co., cen. New York, 19 m. W of Utica; pop. 2922; manufactures silverware.

Shershel. See CHERCHEL.

's Her′to′gen·bosch' (sĕr′tō′кĕn·bôs′); *Fr.* **Bois–le–Duc** (bwä′lẽ·dük′). Commune, ✳ of North Brabant prov., S Netherlands, at the confluence of Aa and Dommel rivers; pop. (1939) 48,782; cathedral of St. John; stadhouse, with carillon; museum.

Sher′wood (shûr′wŏŏd). Village, former ⊗ of Irion co., W cen. Texas; pop. ab. 200.

Sherwood Forest. Ancient royal forest, chiefly in Nottinghamshire, cen. England; remains near Mansfield, Rotherham, and vicinity.

Shet′land (shĕt′lănd). **1** or **Zet′land** (zĕt′lănd); or **Shetland Islands.** Archipelago off N Scotland, 50 m. NE of Orkney Is.; includes islands of Unst, Fetlar, Whalsay, Mainland, Foula, Papa Stour, Yell; total area 550 sq. m.; pop. (1931) 21,421, (1940 est.) 19,700; constitutes Zetland co.; northernmost British territory in Europe; fisheries, sheep and cattle raising, native horses (Shetland ponies). Long a Norse dependency; acquired by Scotland 1472.
2 County of Scotland. See ZETLAND.

She·tuck′et (shĕ·tŭk′ĕt; -ĭt). River ab. 20 m. long, E Connecticut; formed by confluence of Willimantic and Natchaug rivers at Willimantic, flows SE to unite with the Yantic and form the Thames.

Shey·enne′ (shī·ĕn′; -ăn′). River ab. 325 m. long, cen. and SE North Dakota; rises in Sheridan co., cen. North Dakota, flows E, then S and again E into Red River of the North above Fargo.

Shi′a·was′see (shī′à·wôs′ē). **1** River ab. 100 m. long, SE Michigan; flows from Oakland co. N to unite with Flint river to form Saginaw river in Saginaw co.
2 County in Michigan. See *Table* at MICHIGAN.

Shi′bar Pass (shē′bär). Mountain pass, alt. 9800 ft., E Afghanistan, NW of Kabul, on highway to N Afghanistan.

Shi·be′li, Web′be (wĕb′ā shĭ·bā′lĭ; *native* wûb·bā shē·bā·lē); *Ital.* **Ue′bi Sce·be′li** (wâ′bĕ shä·bā′lĕ). River ab. 700 m. long, E Africa; rises in cen. Ethiopia, flows SE across border of Somalia, approaches the coast near Mogadiscio, then turns SW and flows ab. 200 m. parallel with the coast 20 m. inland to be lost in a swamp just N of Juba river.

Shibenik. Var. of ŠIBENIK.

Shi·bîn′ el Kôm (shĭ·bēn′ ăl kōm′). Town, ✳ of Minufîya prov., Lower Egypt, in Nile delta 40 m. NNW of Cairo; pop. (1937) 32,712.

Shick′shin′ny (shĭk′shĭn′ĭ). Borough, Luzerne co., E Pennsylvania, on Susquehanna river 17 m. WSW of Wilkes-Barre; pop. 1843.

Shick′shock Mountains (shĭk′shŏk). Mountains in N Gaspé Penin., Quebec prov., Canada; highest point ab. 4000 ft.

Shiel, Loch (lŏк shēl′). Lake 16 m. long and 1 m. wide in W Scotland, along the border bet. Argyll and Inverness cos., 16 m. W of Fort William.

Shif′nal or **Shiff′nal** (shĭf′n'l). Parish, Shropshire, W England, 17 m. E of Shrewsbury; church of St. Andrew; Tong (*q.v.*) is 3 m. to the E.

Shi·ga (shē·gä). Prefecture of Japan. See *Table* at JAPAN.

Shi·ga′tse (shē·gä′tsĕ). Town, second to Lhasa in importance, SE Tibet, Outer China, on S bank of Tsangpo

(Brahmaputra) river ab. 140 m. W of Lhasa; pop. ab. 9000; has extensive trade because of its location on western caravan route from Gyangtse to Ladakh. About 1 m. SW is the famous walled and fortified monastery (**Te′shi Lum′po** [tĕ′shĕ lŏŏm′pō] *or* **Ta′shi·lum′po** [tä′shĕ·lŏŏm′pō]) of the Teshu Lama, second in authority in Tibet to the Dalai Lama; ab. 3500 priests live in the monastery.

Shih′kia′chwang′ (shǐr′jǐ·ä′jwäng′). Town, W Hopeh prov., NE China, ab. 75 m. SW of Tsingyuan; railroad junction point connecting with Peiping, Hankow, and Yangku.

Shihor. See NILE.

Shi·kar′pur (shǐ·kär′pŏŏr). City, N Sind, W Pakistan, near right bank of Indus river 240 m. NNE of Karachi; pop. (1941) 62,746; trades in silks and precious stones, dealing largely with Central Asia; exports indigo, metals, henna, spices, opium, and grains.

Shi·ko′ku (shǐ·kō′kŏŏ; *Jap.* shĕ·kō·kŏŏ). The smallest of the four principal islands of Japan, S of Honshu and E of Kyushu; 7246 sq. m.; pop. (1945 est.) 3,836,378; chief town Tokushima. Bordered on N by Inland Sea; separated from Honshu on E by Kii Channel and from Kyushu on W by Bungo Strait. Divided into 4 prefectures, Ehime, Kagawa, Kochi, and Tokushima; and 4 old provinces. Has no good harbors; crossed by range of high mountains with many branches; highest Ishizuchiyama 6500 ft. Chief products tea, camphor, rice, fruit, tobacco; also copper and antimony. From early times held in turn by feudal families until subjugated (c. 1590) by Hideyoshi; subdivided by him; daimiate of Tosa (old province in S part) powerful until Restoration 1868.

Shi·ko·tan (shĕ·kō·tän). One of the Kuril Is. (*q.v.*) just E of Hokkaido.

Shi·ku·ka (shĕ·kŏŏ·kä). Town, N Karafuto, Sakhalin I., on N shore of Taraika Bay; pop. (1939 est.) 23,864; formerly Japanese; railroad terminus.

Shil′don (shǐl′dŭn). Urban district, Durham, N England, 25 m. S of Newcastle; pop. 14,513; railroad locomotive works.

Shil′ka (shǐl′kà). **1** River ab. 300 m. long, SW cen. Chita Region, Soviet Russia, Asia; formed by confluence of Ingoda and Onon rivers, flows NE to unite with the Argun to form the Amur river.
2 Town on N bank of the river ab. 110 m. E of Chita, on Trans-Siberian R.R.

Shil′la (shǐl′à). **1** Peak 23,050 ft. in SE Kashmir, N India.
2 See SILLA.

Shil·le′lagh (shǐ·lā′lĕ). Town, SW co. Wicklow, Eire; famous for its oaks, whence comes the name for a cudgel originally applied only to cudgels made of oak or blackthorn saplings.

Shil′ling·ton (shǐl′ǐng·tŭn). Borough, Berks co., SE Pennsylvania, 5 m. SSW of Reading; pop. 5639; manufactures building blocks, textiles, lumber.

Shil·long′ (shǐl·lông′). Town, W cen. Assam, NE Indian Union, 310 m. NE of Calcutta; pop. 26,536; ✱ of Assam state and of Khasi and Jaintia Hills dist. Entirely destroyed by earthquake in 1897 but rebuilt. Favorite health and vacation resort; has military cantonment.

Shi′loh (shī′lō; *mod.* **Sei·lun′** (sī·lŏŏn′; sā-). Village in cen. ancient Palestine, 15 m. W of Jordan river on E slope of Mt. Ephraim; meeting place and sanctuary of Israelites, where a tabernacle was set up (*Josh.* xviii. 1) and where the ark of the covenant was kept until captured by the Philistines.

Shiloh National Military Park. See UNITED STATES, *National Historical Parks.*

Shi·ma·ba·ra (shĕ·mä·bä·rä). Peninsula, W Kyushu, Japan, E of Nagasaki; site of early establishment of Christianity, its inhabitants and those on nearby island of Amakusa suffered persecution; they rebelled 1637–38 and ab. 37,000 of them were massacred 1638 in old castle by order of Iyemitsu.

Shimabara Bay. Inlet of East China Sea on W coast of Kyushu, Japan, NE of Nagasaki.

Shi·ma·ne (shĕ·mä·nĕ). Prefecture of Japan. See *Table* at JAPAN.

Shi·ma·nov′ski (shǐ·mŭ·nôf′skǐ). Town, S Khabarovsk Territory, Soviet Russia, Asia, on Trans-Siberian R.R., 115 m. N of Blagoveshchensk.

Shim′bu Line (shǐm′bŏŏ). Japanese defense line on Luzon, Phil. Is., E of Manila; taken by Americans May 18, 1945 after more than a month of fighting.

Shi·mi·zu (shĕ·mē·zŏŏ). Seaport, Shizuoka prefecture, on S coast of cen. Honshu, Japan, on Suruga Bay; pop. (1945) 60,268; the port of Shizuoka; exports much tea. Shelled by American destroyer fleet July 31, 1945.

Shi·mo·da (shĕ·mō·dä). Seaport, Shizuoka prefecture, S Honshu, Japan, on SE coast of Izu Penin.; pop. ab. 5000; visited by Commodore Perry and opened to American commerce 1854; place where Townsend Harris, first U.S. consul general to Japan, established his office 1857; closed 1859 to foreign trade and Yokohama opened instead. Suffered from severe earthquake 1856.

Shi·mo′ga (shĕ·mō′gà). Town, cen. Mysore state, S India, on Tunga river (upper tributary of the Tungabhadra) 150 m. WNW of Bangalore; pop. 20,661; has cotton mills and iron and steel works.

Shi′mo·no·se′ki (shǐm′ō·nō·sĕk′ĭ; *Jap.* shĕ·mô·nô·sĕ·kĕ), *formerly* **A·ka·ma·ga·se·ki** (ä·kä·mä·gä·sĕ·kĕ); *popularly called* **Ba·kan** (bä·kän). Seaport city, Yamaguchi prefecture, SW extremity of Honshu, Japan, on Shimonoseki Strait opp. Moji (1½ m.) and connected with it by tunnel under the strait; pop. (1945) 155,623; has extensive harbor with docks, shipyards, etc., and steamer connections with ports of Soviet Russia, Korea, and China; key to W gateway of Inland Sea.

History: Famous for naval battle 1185 at Dan no Ura (E end of town) in which the Minamoto clan under Yoshitsune decisively defeated the Taira Clan. Bombarded Sept. 5–8, 1864 by joint fleet of four nations (England, France, Holland, and the U.S.) in action against Choshu daimio for continued firing on foreign ships; for damages shogun paid indemnity (American portion refunded 1883). Increased rapidly in prosperity after Restoration 1868. Treaty of peace for Chinese-Japanese War signed here Apr. 17, 1895, important in Far Eastern affairs. Bombed by Americans 1945.

Shimonoseki Strait. Narrow strait separating extreme SW Honshu I. and extreme N Kyushu I., Japan; only ¼ m. wide at its narrowest point; W outlet of Inland Sea, with strong tidal movements. Shimonoseki and Moji are on opposite sides (1½ m. apart) but connected by tunnel under the strait.

Shi·mu·shi·ru (shĕ·mŏŏ·shĕ·rŏŏ). One of the Kuril Is. (*q.v.*), in cen. part of chain.

Shin, Loch (lŏκ shǐn′). Lake 17 m. long in Sutherland co., N Scotland.

Shi·na′fi′ya (shǐ·nä′fē′yà; -yä). Lake and marsh region in S cen. Iraq, traversed by Hindiya river.

Shi·na·no (shĕ·nä·nō). River ab. 225 m. long, W cen. Honshu, Japan; rises in Nagano prefecture, flows N into the Sea of Japan at Niigata.

Shi′nar (shī′nẽr; -när). A country known to the early Hebrews as a plain in Babylonia (*Gen.* xi. 2 & xiv. 1); probably equivalent to Sumer (*q.v.*).

Shin′bwi·yang′ (shǐn′bwē·yäng′). Town, N Burma, on the upper Chindwin at foot of Hukawng valley and on the Stilwell Road.

Shin·chi·ku (shĕn·chĕ·kŏŏ). Seaport city, NW coast of Formosa I., 37 m. SW of Taihoku; pop. (1935) 52,107. Japanese airfield, bombed by Americans Jan. 1945.

Shi′ner (shī′nẽr). Town, Lavaca co., SE cen. Texas, 46 m. N of Victoria; pop. 1945; farming, dairying.

Shin·gi·shu (shĕn·gĕ·shŏō). City near the mouth of the Yalu river, ✱ of North Heian prov., Korea; pop. (1938 est.) 52,384; railroad terminus; connected with Antung, Manchuria, by long iron bridge over the Yalu; has large

lumber trade; manufactures paper, exports rice, soybeans, fish, timber, and furs. A new town founded after Russo-Japanese War.

Shin·gu (shĕn·gōō). Town, Wakayama prefecture, on S coast of W Honshu, Japan, 55 m. SE of Wakayama; pop. (1945) 29,070; place of pilgrimage; has ruins of famous Shinto temple.

Shinn′ston (shĭn′stŭn). City, Harrison co., N West Virginia, 8 m. N of Clarksburg; pop. 2724; settled by Quakers c. 1779; coal mines; manufactures flour, lumber.

Shinshu. See CHINJU.

Shi·o, Cape (shē·ō). Cape on S extremity of Honshu I., Japan, in Wakayama prefecture.

Ship Island (shĭp). Island, a low sandy bar ab. 7 m. long, in Gulf of Mexico, off SE coast of Harrison co., SE Mississippi. In early part of 18th cent. harbor and base for French exploration of Gulf coast region; British naval base in War of 1812. Reserved for military purposes 1847 by U.S. government; point of contention in Civil War and in latter part a Confederate prison camp. Quarantine station established 1878 and lighthouse 1879.

Ship′ka, or **Šip′ka, Pass** (shĭp′kä; *Angl.* -kà). Mountain pass, alt. 4376 ft., in the Balkan Mts., cen. Bulgaria, bet. Gabrovo on N and Kazanlik on S; scene of fierce battles 1877 during the Russo-Turkish War.

Ship′ley (shĭp′lĭ). Urban district, West Riding, Yorkshire, N England, on the Aire 10 m. WNW of Leeds; pop. 32,585.

Ship′pan Point (shĭp′ăn). Point on SW coast, Fairfield co., Connecticut, S of Stamford.

Ship′pens·burg (shĭp′ĕnz·bûrg). Borough, Cumberland and Franklin cos., S Pennsylvania, 10 m. NE of Chambersburg; pop. 6138; founded 1730; manufactures furniture, clothing, paper novelties, flour. Shippensburg State College (1873; coed.).

Ship′pi·gan Island (shĭp′ĭ·găn). Low, wooded island off NE tip of New Brunswick, SE Canada, S of Miscou I.

Ship′shaw (shĭp′shô). River ab. 90 m. long, S Quebec prov., Canada, a N tributary of the Saguenay flowing into it below Lake St. John; large hydroelectric plant for aluminum production.

Shi·rai·to·no·ta·ki (shē·rī·tō·nô·tä·kĕ). Waterfall in S Honshu, Japan, near Fuji; 87 ft. high and 420 ft. wide.

Shi·ra·ka·mi (shē·rä·kä·mē). Cape at S extremity of Hokkaido I., Japan.

Shi·ra·ka·wa (shē·rä·kä·wä). River in W cen. Kyushu I., Japan; flows W through Kumamoto into Shimabara Bay.

Shi′ra·ki (shē′rä·kē). Steppe region, a semidesert plain in E Georgia, U.S.S.R., bet. two N tributaries of the Kura SE of Tiflis; extensive oil fields.

Shi·ra·ku·mo·no·ta·ki (shē·rä·kōō·mô·nô·tä·kĕ). Waterfall ab. 300 ft. high in cen. Honshu, Japan, W of Nikko, E of Lake Chuzenji, and near the waterfall Kegon-no-taki.

Shi·ra·ne (shē·rä·nĕ). Name of 3 mountain groups in Japan: (1) Mountain, S cen. Honshu, W of Kofu, with 3 summits, Nodori 9970 ft., Ainotake 10,200 ft., and Kaigane 10,472 ft. (2) Mountain 7657 ft., Nagano prefecture, on border E of Nagano. (3) Mountain 8458 ft. with 2 summits, in Nikko Range W of Nikko, Gumma prefecture.

Shi·raz′ (shē·räz′; *Angl.* -răz′). Industrial and commercial city, SW cen. Iran; ✻ of Fars prov., and was ✻ of Karim Khan (from 1760); pop. ab. 129,000; on the great highway and trade route from Tehran to port of Bushire; produces a fine wine, also brocades, rugs, silk floss, and mosaics. Although ruins are in its vicinity, it is not an ancient city, its importance dating from Mohammedan conquest. Has many fine mosques, including the largest in Iran. Burial place with tomb of Persian poet Hafiz, and birthplace of the poet Saadi and the Bab (Mirza Ali Mohammed of Shiraz). Has often been much damaged by earthquakes. Ruins of ancient Persepolis (*q.v.*) lie ab. 30 m. to the NE.

Shi′re (shē′rà) or **Shi′ré**; *Port.* **Chi′re** (shē′rĕ). River ab. 370 m. long in S Nyasaland and cen. Mozambique, SE Africa; flows from Lake Nyasa S into Zambezi river; in Nyasaland has several cataracts, esp. Murchison Falls.

Shire, or **Shiré, Highlands.** Hill country along E bank of Shire river, S Nyasaland; altitude 3000 ft.; healthful climate; residential section for Europeans; includes Blantyre, Limbe, and Zomba.

Shi·re·to·ko, Cape (shē·rĕ·tô·kô). Cape on NE extremity of Hokkaido I., Japan.

Shi·ri·ya, Cape (shē·rĕ·yä). Cape on NE extremity of Honshu I., Japan.

Shir′ley (shûr′lĭ). Town, Middlesex co., NE Massachusetts, 7 m. SE of Fitchburg; pop. 5202.

Shirpurla. See LAGASH.

Shir·van′ (shēr·vän′). Medieval khanate on W shore of Caspian Sea S of the E end of the Caucasus Mts.; ✻ Shemakha. Subject to Persia 15th–19th cents.; conquered by Russia 1805–06 and annexed 1813; now forms a part of NE Azerbaidzhan S.S.R.

Shir′wa, Lake (shir′wä). = Lake CHILWA.

Shi·shal′din (shĭ·shăl′dĭn). Volcano 9978 ft., S Unimak I., SW Alaska; has had several eruptions in recent years; locally known as "Smoking Moses."

Shish′ma·ref (?shĭsh′må·rĕf). Village on Shishmaref Inlet, NW coast of Seward Penin., W Alaska; pop. (1950) 194.

Shit′tim (shĭt′ĭm). **1** Place of encampment of Israelites in ancient Moab E of the Jordan and opp. Jericho (*Num.* xxv. 1).

2 Valley, usually dry, on W side of lower Jordan N of Dead Sea, Palestine.

Shiuchow. See KUKONG.

Shi·ve·luch′, Sop′ka (sôp′kà shĭ·vyĕ·lōōch′). Volcano (*sopka*) 10,942 ft. at N end of Eastern Range, Kamchatka Penin., Khabarovsk Ter., Soviet Russia, Asia.

Shive′ly (shīv′lĭ). City, Jefferson co., N cen. Kentucky, S suburb of Louisville; pop. 15,155.

Shiv′wits Plateau (shĭv′wĭts). Tableland 5800 to 6200 ft. in N Mohave co., NW Arizona.

Shi·zu·o·ka (shē·zōō·ō·kä). **1** Prefecture of Japan. See *Table* at JAPAN.

2 City, in ✻, 55 m. SW of Tokyo, near W shore of Suruga Bay; pop. (1945) 161,720; industrial city, with varied manufactures; its port is Shimizu. Residence of Iyeyasu, founder of the Tokugawa shogunate, from 1607.

Shka′ra Tau (shkä′rä tou′). Mountain (*tau*) 17,040 ft. in a N spur of the Caucasus Mts. SE of Elborus, in S Kabardino-Balkarian Republic, Soviet Russia, Europe.

Shko′dër (shkô′dĕr) or **Shko′dra** (shkô′drä); *Ital.* **Scu·ta·ri** (skōō′tá·rĭ; *Ital.* -tä·rĕ). **1** Prefecture, NW Albania; 1880 sq. m.; pop. 132,336.

2 *anc.* **Sco′dra** (skō′drà). Fortified town, Shkodër prefecture, bet. Drin river and Lake Scutari; pop. 29,209; trading center, esp. for tobacco, grain, wool, leather, and timber; cathedral. Former capital of Albania; stronghold of Scanderbeg in 15th cent.; under Turkish rule 1479–1913; battlefield in World War I.

Shkum′bi (shkōōm′bē). River ab. 50 m. long in cen. Albania, flowing into Adriatic Sea; approximately the ethnological division line bet. the Ghegs of the N and the Tosks of the S.

Shlisselburg. See PETROKREPOST.

Sho′a (shō′à). Province, cen. Ethiopia; former kingdom; ✻ Addis Ababa; a government (province) 1936–41 of Italian East Africa, 25,283 sq. m., pop. (1939 est.) 1,850,000.

Shoals (shōlz). Town, ⊗ of Martin co., SW Indiana, 40 m. E of Vincennes; pop. 1022.

Shoal′wa′ter, Cape (shōl′wô′tĕr; -wŏt′ĕr). Cape on NW coast of Pacific co., SW Washington, at N entrance to Willapa Bay.

Sho·do (shō·dō); *Jap.* **Sho·do·shi·ma** (shō·dō·shē·mä). Island on W side of Harima Sea, Japan, bet. the S coast of Honshu and the NE coast of Shikoku, W of Awaji I.

Shoe′bur·y·ness′ (shōō′bẽr·ĭ·nĕs′; shōō′brĭ-). **1** Cape on the coast of Essex co., SE England.
2 Town, Essex, SE England, at mouth of Thames estuary in Southend-on-Sea county borough; resort.
Sho·ji (shō·jĕ). Lake in S Honshu, Japan, near Fuji.
Sho·ka (shō·kä). City, cen. part of W coast of Formosa I., SW of Taichu; pop. (1935) 51,236.
Sho′la·pur (shō′lä·pŏŏr). City, SE Maharashtra, W Indian Union, 170 m. W of Hyderabad; pop. (1941) 212,620; trade center; produces cotton goods, blankets, and silks. Has old fort prominent in Deccan wars. Scene of British victory 1818 over the Marathas.
Sho·nan (shō·nän). Literally "Light of the South"— Japanese name of Singapore after its capture Feb. 1942.
Shoot′ers′ Island (shōōt′ẽrz). Island in Newark Bay close to N coast of Staten I., New York; part of Richmond borough; shipbuilding.
Shoreditch. Metropolitan borough of London. See *Table at* LONDON.
Shore′ham by Sea (shōr′ăm). Urban district, West Sussex, S England; pop. 13,052.
Shore′view′ (shōr′vū′). Village, Ramsey co., E Minnesota, N suburb of St. Paul; pop. 7157.
Shore′wood (shōr′wŏŏd). Village, Milwaukee co., SE Wisconsin, 4 m. N of Milwaukee; pop. 15,990.
Short Heath (shôrt hĕth). Former urban district, Staffordshire, W cen. England; pop. (1931) 5047.
Short′land Islands (shôrt′lănd). Group of islands, comprising **Shortland Island**, Fauro I., and other small islands in Bougainville Strait off S end of Bougainville, NW Solomon Is., W Pacific Ocean; part of British Solomon Islands protectorate. Chief town Faisi, on Shortland I. Japanese base in World War II.
Sho·sho′ne (shō·shō′nĕ). **1** River, NW Wyoming; rises in Park co., flows NE into Bighorn river in N Big Horn co.; formed by uniting of two headstreams, North Fork and South Fork, in Buffalo Bill Reservoir near Cody; length with longest headstream ab. 120 m.
2 County in Idaho. See *Table* at IDAHO.
3 City, ⊗ of Lincoln co., S Idaho; pop. 1416; shipping point for wool.
Shoshone Cavern National Monument. See UNITED STATES, *National Monuments.*
Shoshone Dam. See UNITED STATES, *Dams.*
Shoshone Falls. Waterfall 210 ft. in the Snake river, near Twin Falls, S Idaho.
Shoshone Lake. Lake ab. 12 m. long and 8 m. wide in Yellowstone National Park, NW Wyoming, W of Yellowstone Lake; alt. 7800 ft.; a source of Snake river.
Shott el Jerid. = *Shatt el Jerid:* see Chott DJERID.
Shot′ter·y (shŏt′ẽr·ĭ). Village 1 m. W of Stratford on Avon, Warwickshire, cen. England; birthplace of Anne Hathaway.
Shott Melghir, Shott Melrir. Vars. of Chott MELRIR.
Shqipni, Shqipri. See ALBANIA.
Shreve′port (shrēv′pōrt). City, ⊗ of Caddo parish, NW corner of Louisiana, on Red river 18 m. E of Texas border; pop. 164,372; settled ab. 1835; commercial, industrial, and financial center for section yielding cotton, lumber, petroleum, and natural gas; Barksdale Air Force Base with pilot school. Centenary College (1825, moved from Jackson to Shreveport 1907; coed.; Methodist).
Shrews′bur′y (sh[r]ōōz′bẽr′ĭ; -bẽr·ĭ; *in England, also* shrōz′-). **1** Town, Worcester co., cen. Massachusetts, 5 m. ENE of Worcester; pop. 16,622; trade center.
2 City, St. Louis co., E Missouri, W suburb of St. Louis; pop. 4730.
3 *or* **Sal′op** (săl′ŭp). Municipal borough, ⊗ of Shropshire, W England, on the Severn (which surrounds it on three sides) 40 m. WNW of Birmingham; pop. 44,926; railroad center; brewing, tanning; grammar school. Important town on Welsh border; founded 5th cent., became part of Mercia at end of 8th cent. and named Scrobesbyrig (mod. Shrewsbury) or Sloppesbury (mod. Salop); became seat of one of oldest English earldoms,

first granted 1071 to Roger de Montgomery who 1083 established an abbey; scene of many conflicts with Welsh; plain N of the town scene of battle 1403 in which Sir Henry Percy (Hotspur) was defeated and killed by forces of Henry IV.
Shrewsbury River. See NAVESINK RIVER.
Shrivijaya. See SRIVIJAYA.
Shrop′shire (shrŏp′shĭr; -shẽr) *or* **Sal′op** (săl′ŭp). County, W England, on border of Wales; 1347 sq. m.; pop. (1951) 289,844; ⊗ Shrewsbury; other towns are Wenlock, Bridgnorth; chief river Severn; agriculture, grazing, coal mining; manufactures chinaware, bricks.
Shtip. See ŠTIP.
Shu (shōō). One of the three kingdoms formed at the breakup of the Chinese Empire on the fall of the Eastern Han dynasty 220 A.D.; comprised Szechwan and most of Kweichow and Yunnan and lasted until 264 A.D.
Shufu. See KASHGAR.
Shuk′san, Mount (shŭk′săn). Peak 9038 ft. in cen. Whatcom co., NW Washington.
Shumadia *or* **Shumadiya.** See ŠUMADIJA.
Shu′ma·gin (shōō′má·gĕn). Island group off SE coast of Alaska Penin., SW Alaska, in Pacific Ocean; chief island and village is Unga.
Shum′chun′ (shōōm′chōōn′). City, S Kwangtung prov., SE China, ab. 23 m. N of Kowloon and just outside British territory; trade and customs town.
Shu′men (shōō′mĕn). **1** Department, NE Bulgaria; 5690 sq. m.; pop. (1934) 1,020,499.
2 City, its ✳, ab. 50 m. W of Varna; pop. (1934) 25,486; has important trade in grain and wine; strategically important stronghold and often besieged in wars with Turks; surrendered to Russians June 22, 1878; in 1950 re-named **Ko·la′rov·grad** (kŭ·lär′ŭf·grăd).
Shu·mu·shu (shōō·mōō·shōō). Small island of the Kurils (*q.v.*) off N point of Paramushiro.
Shu′nem (shōō′nĕm). Town of Canaan, later of Galilee, Palestine, N of Mt. Gilboa on the edge of the Valley of Jezreel; its inhabitants were Shunammites (*1 Kings* i. 3).
Shung′nak (shŭng′năk). Village on N bank of upper Kobuk river, NW Alaska; pop. 141.
Shun·sen (shōōn·sĕn). Town, ✳ of Kogen prov., E Korea, 50 m. ENE of Keijo; pop. ab. 3500.
Shur, Wilderness of (shûr). Desert region, N Sinai Penin., NE Egypt, near the Mediterranean Sea; traversed for three days by the Israelites (*Exod.* xv. 22).
Shu·ri (shōō·rĕ). City at S end of Okinawa I., Ryukyu Is., Japan, ab. 3 m. ENE of Naha; pop. (1945) 17,537; former capital of Okinawa prefecture. Has strongly fortified castle on hill ab. halfway bet. Naha and Yonabaru; under attack from Americans Apr. and May 1945; taken by marines May 30.
Shu·rup′pak (shōō·rōōp′ăk). Ancient city of Sumer, now the village of **Fa′ra** (fǔ′rŏ) in lower Mesopotamia, SE Iraq, ab. 55 m. NW of An Nasiriya; was probably subject to Lagash; disappeared from the records c. 2300 B.C.; its excavations have brought to light much information.
Shush, Shushan. See SUSA.
Shu·sha′ (shōō·shä′). Town, SW Azerbaidzhan, U.S.S.R., just S of Stepanakert; pop. ab. 5000.
Shush·tar′ (shōōsh·tär′). Town, Khuzistan prov., S Iran, N of Ahwaz, SW Iran, on the Karun river at head of navigation; pop. ab. 20,000. Has ruins of a large citadel and remains of an elaborate canal system; its commerce consists chiefly of carpets, woolen cloth, canvas, earthenware, and metalwork. Has been a stronghold of the Kharijites and of the Shiites.
Shu′swap Lake (shōō′swŏp). An irregularly shaped lake 124 sq. m., 42 m. long, SE British Columbia, Canada, ab. 35 m. W of Revelstoke; outlet is the Thompson river.
Shu′tar·gar·dan′ (shōō′tàr·gàr·dän′). Mountain pass at the W end of Safed Koh, E Afghanistan; altitude 10,800 ft.; important in SE approach to Kabul.

Shu′ya (shōō′yȧ). Town, cen. Ivanovo Region, Soviet Russia, Europe, ab. 20 m. SE of Ivanovo; pop. 57,950; has large textile factories.

Shwe′bo (shwā′bō). **1** District, Sagaing division, Upper Burma; 5749 sq. m.; pop. 446,790.
2 Town, its ✳, 50 m. NNW of Mandalay; pop. 11,286; center of rice-growing region. Birthplace and capital of Alompra, founder of last Burmese dynasty. In World War II captured by British Jan. 9, 1945.

Shwe′daung (shwā′doung). Town, Prome dist., Lower Burma, on Irrawaddy river just S of Prome; pop. 8408.

Shwe′li (shwā′lē). River ab. 350 m. long in E Upper Burma; flows SW out of Yunnan prov. in SW China, crossing Burma-China boundary at Namhkam, continues SW in Northern Shan States, turns N and empties into Irrawaddy river below Katha. For many miles runs parallel with Burma Road which crosses it near Namhkam.

Shy·ok′ (shē̇·ōk′). River, E and cen. Kashmir, N India; rises on the S slopes of the Karakoram Range, S of Karakoram Pass, curves SE, S, and NW and flows into the Indus in Baltistan E of Skardu.

Si (shē) or **Si-kiang** (shē′ji·äng′); _Eng._ **West River.** Large river (_kiang_), more than 1000 m. long, the great commercial highway of SE China, known in its upper course as the Hungshui (_q.v._); the Si proper begins in E Kwangsi at Kweiping where the Hungshui unites with the Siang, then flows E ab. 300 m. through Kwangtung prov. into China Sea near Macao and W of the island of Hong Kong; the city of Canton is in its delta (see PEARL RIVER). Navigable for large vessels to Tsangwu and for smaller vessels beyond. Receives the tributaries Kwei and Peh from the N.

Si (sē). River nearly 300 m. long, E Thailand; N and chief tributary of the Mun river, joining it at 50 m. above its mouth.

Sia′han Range (sī·ä′hän). Mountain range extending SW and NE in W cen. Baluchistan; separates Kharan from Baluchistan proper; highest point 6775 ft.

Sia′kwan′ (syä′kwän′). Town, Yunnan, S China, on Burma Road near S end of Erh Hai (Tali Lake); market town and junction for branch road to Tali 10 m. N.

Si·al′kot (sī·äl′kōt). **1** District, Lahore division, West Punjab, Pakistan; 1576 sq. m.; pop. (1941) 1,190,497.
2 City, its ✳, near left bank of Chenab river 70 m. N of Lahore; pop. (1941) 138,348. Site of ancient fort and mausoleum of Sikh apostle Nanak (d. 1538). A military cantonment.

Si·am′ (sī·ăm′; sī′ăm); _official name 1939–45 and since 1949_ **Thai′land** (tī′lănd); _Siamese_ **Mu′ang–Thai** (mōō′äng·t′hī′). Independent country in SE Asia, consisting of Siam proper and Peninsular Siam; area (1937) 198,247 sq. m.; pop. 14,464,489; ✳ Bangkok. Siam proper is bounded on the W and NW by Burma, on NE, E, and SE by French Indochina, and on S by the Gulf of Siam; Peninsular Siam is a long narrow strip extending S to and occupying the cen. section of the Malay Penin., and is bounded on E by the Gulf of Siam, on S by the Federation of Malaya, and on W by the Bay of Bengal (Andaman Sea). Mountainous in the NW with the highest point Doi Inthanon 8468 ft., near Burma border; farther S along Burma border are Dawna Range and Bilauktaung Range and on the SE along the Cambodia border is the Phanom Dong Rak. Large cen. area is a plain lying in the basins of the Chao Phraya and its tributaries and in the E the tributaries of the Mekong. See _Map_ at BURMA. Primarily an agricultural country, chief crop rice; produces also coconuts, tobacco, rubber, cotton, and forest products (esp. teak); extensive mineral resources. Has several good harbors and numerous islands along its 1700-mile coast line. Inhabitants are chiefly Thai (Siamese) with many, possibly 1,000,000 Chinese; other Mongolian peoples represented are Laos, Burmese, Cambodians, Malayans, and Annamese. Only

large city Bangkok; other important towns Chiang Mai, Chiang Rai, Ayudhya, Ubon, Rahaeng, and Phitsanulok; in Peninsular Siam, Songkhla, Nakhon Si Thammarat, Ranong, and Phuket.
History: In ancient times part of the Mon-Khmer kingdom; had no history of its own until c. 12th cent. A.D.; separate state formed by Thai people 1350 with Ayuthia (Ayudhya) as capital; frequently overrun by Burmese in 15th and 16th cents. and Ayuthia destroyed 1767; lost Tenasserim to Burma. Visited by Europeans (Portuguese and Dutch) 16th and 17th cents. and later (in 18th cent.) by British and French who seized parts of Siamese territory. Renounced claim to Cambodia 1863 and ceded territory E of Mekong to French 1893. In early 20th cent. signed many treaties and conventions with European and Asiatic countries; yielded to British its rights over four Unfederated Malay States 1909. Became constitutional monarchy 1932; came under influence of Japan 1936–40; attacked Indochina 1940; seized by Japan Dec. 1941 and declared war on Great Britain and U.S.A. Jan. 25, 1942. By Japanese action received two Shan States from Burma and four of the Unfederated Malay States (Kedah, Kelantan, Perlis, and Trengganu) July 5, 1943; after defeat of Japan 1945 restored these states.

Siam, Gulf of; _also_ **Gulf of Thailand.** Large inlet of South China Sea mostly in Thailand, but its SE shore formed by Cambodia and Cochin China (SW part of Vietnam); ab. 385 m. from NW to SE and 385 m. wide at its widest part (in S). Chao Phraya and Tha Chin rivers enter at NW point.

Si′an′ (shē′än′). **1** or **Chang′an′** (chäng′än′); _also_ **Si′king′** (shē′jǐng′), **Si′ngan′** (shē′än′), **Si-gnan** (shē′än′). City, ✳ of Shensi prov., NE cen. China, in S cen. part of province on S bank of Wei, ab. 80 m. above its junction with the Hwang Ho; pop. ab. 1,000,000; strategically located on a broad loess terrace on overland trade routes, esp. that from E China up the Wei valley through Kansu and Sinkiang to the west (the old "Silk Road"), for centuries a point of exchange of goods of S and E China with those of the west. One of the most interesting historically of all Chinese cities; built square in plan with extensive walls (30 ft. high, 10 m. in circuit) and towers; contains fine temples and public buildings, old fortifications and many tombs and historical remains, esp. in **Pei-lin** (bā′lǐn′), S of the city, a collection of more than 1000 historical stone tablets or monuments; among them was found 1625 the notable Nestorian tablet giving in its inscription an account of a Christian Chinese colony in the city in the 7th and 8th cents. A.D. Under the name **Hsien-yang** (shǐ·ĕn′-yäng′) was capital of the first universal emperor, Shih Huang Ti (247–210 B.C.); under later dynasties generally the capital of the empire (under Han dynasty as **Chang-an**—also its modern official name; under T'ang dynasty as **Siking**). Visited by Marco Polo in 13th cent. (known to him as **Ken–zan–fu** [kĕn′zän′fōō′]). The starting point of various religious influences in China: Buddhist, Jewish, Mohammedan, Nestorian. Successfully withstood siege 1868–70 during Mohammedan rebellion; was refuge of Empress Dowager and Emperor Kuang Hsü after Boxer rebellion 1900–02; scene of communist kidnaping of Generalissimo Chiang Kai-shek in Dec. 1936.
2 Town, N Liaoning prov., S Manchuria, 70 m. S of Changchun; pop. 32,475; in coal-mining area.

Siang (shǐ·äng′); _also_ **Hsiang** (shǐ·äng′). **1** Navigable river ab. 350 m. long, cen. Hunan prov., SE cen. China; rises in NE Kwangsi and flows N into Tungting Hu (lake); Changsha is on it. Its valley highly developed agriculturally and for centuries has been a north-south trade route; also has important mineral resources in coal, antimony, and lead.
2 or **Si·yang′** (shǐ·yäng′); _formerly_ **Yu** (yü). River ab. 400 m. long, S China, a S tributary of the Si (_q.v._); rises

in SE Yunnan and flows generally E in Kwangsi prov. to unite at Kweiping with the Hungshui to form the Si proper; near Yungning receives the Li from the S.

Siang'shan' (shǐ·äng'shän'). Town, Chekiang prov., E China, 120 m. S of Shanghai on S shore of **Siangshan Bay,** long narrow inlet of East China Sea S of Ninghsien; Japanese naval supply base in latter part of Chino-Japanese War 1943–45.

Siang'tan' (shǐ·äng'tän'). City, E Hunan prov., SE cen. China, on Siang river 17 m. S of Changsha; pop. ab. 300,000; at head of steam navigation; important trading center for routes to the S; in center of region that grows some of the finest tea of China.

Siang'yang' (shǐ·äng'yäng'). Town, N Hupeh prov., E cen. China, on right bank of the Han 170 m. NW of Hankow; pop. ab. 40,000.

Siang'yun' (shǐ·äng'yün'). Town, cen. Yunnan prov., S China, on Burma Road 30 m. SE of Tali; junction point.

Siaoe or **Siau** (syou). See SANGIHE ISLANDS.

Sia'pa (syä'pä). River ab. 200 m. long in S Venezuela; flows W into Casiquiare river.

Siar·ga'o (syär·gä'ō). Island, part of Surigao prov., off NE coast of Mindanao, Phil. Is.; 169 sq. m.; pop. ab. 22,000; chief municipality Dapa. Separated from Dinagat I. on the W by Dinagat Sound.

Si'a·scon'set (sī'à·skŏn'sĕt; -sĭt); *locally* **Scon'set** (skŏn'sĕt; -sĭt). Summer resort, originally a fishing hamlet, on Nantucket I., Massachusetts; first wireless station in U.S., built 1901, dismantled 1918.

Sia'si (syä'sē). **1** Chief island of Tapul group, cen. Sulu Archipelago, Phil. Is.; 30 sq. m.; pop. (municipal dist.) 29,259.

2 Town, on W shore of Siasi I.

Šiauliai. = SHAULYAI.

Si'ba·lom' (sē'vä·lôn'). Municipality, S Antique prov., Panay, Phil. Is., interior town ab. 10 m. NE of San Jose de Buenavista; pop. 22,178.

Ši·be'nik (shē·bĕ'nĕk); *Ital.* **Se·be·ni'co** (sā·bā·nē'kô). Seaport city, Croatia federal republic, Yugoslavia, 30 m. NW of Split; pop. 37,284; good harbor; hydroelectric power works; exports bauxite; 15th-cent. cathedral, 16th-cent. town hall.

Si·be'ri·a (sī·bēr'ǐ·à). **1** Popularly the whole of N Asia, not marked by definite limits on S and W—so called from the Cossack name (**Si·bir'** [syǐ·byēr'y']) of the first Tatar fort in the region conquered by Cossacks 1581. See ISKER.

2 That part of N Asia bet. the Ural Mts. and the Pacific Ocean; comprises the greater part of Soviet Russia in Asia (*q.v.*). Formerly divided into West Siberia Region, East Siberia Region, and the viceroyalty of the Far East; now comprises 17 subdivisions of the R.S.F.S.R.: Sverdlovsk, Chelyabinsk, Omsk, Novosibirsk, Irkutsk, Chita, Tomsk, Kurgan, Tyumen, and Kemerovo Regions; Maritime, Khabarovsk (includes the Jewish Autonomous Region), Krasnoyarsk (includes Khakass Autonomous Region), and Altai (includes Oirot Autonomous Region) Territories; the Tuva Autonomous Region, and the Yakutsk and Buryat-Mongol Autonomous Soviet Socialist Republics. Molotov Region, now in Soviet Russia in Asia, is W of the Urals and the territory it comprises was not formerly considered a part of Siberia but of Russia in Europe. Between 1930 and 1937 eight national districts were established within the geographical limits of the above subdivisions.

An immense region (4,887,223 sq. m., pop. [1939] 21,891,467) with natural resources only partially developed. The N belt along the Arctic Ocean consists of open, frozen tundra, rich in fur-bearing animals; in the W are low plains, some with extensive marshland; in the S and cen. parts are several plateaus; in the E and SE numerous mountain ranges: Eastern Range on Kamchatka, containing highest peak in Siberia (Klyuchevskaya Sopka 15,666 ft.); Anadyr, Cherskogo, Kolyma, and Verkhoyansk Ranges, Stanovoi and Yablonoi Mts.,

and the Sikhote Alin along the coast of the Sea of Japan; Sayan Mts. on the S border and Ural Mts. on the W. Its great rivers, the Ob, Yenisei, and Lena, flow N to the Arctic Ocean, and the Amur on its SE border E to Tatar Strait; other rivers are the Khatanga, Yana, Indigirka, Kolyma, and Anadyr. In the S, in the Buryat-Mongol A.S.S.R., is the large Lake Baikal. At Verkhoyansk (*q.v.*) is one of the poles of cold.

Bordered by Kara, Laptev, and East Siberian Seas on N (parts of the Arctic Ocean) and by Bering Sea, Sea of Okhotsk, and Sea of Japan on E (parts of the Pacific). Has 3 large peninsulas, Taimyr, Chukotski, and Kamchatka; principal islands off its coasts are Severnaya Zemlya group, New Siberian Is., Wrangel, Komandorskie Is., and Sakhalin. Has many large cities, some of which have had very rapid growth in recent years; the 7 largest are Sverdlovsk, Omsk, Chelyabinsk, Irkutsk, Vladivostok, Khabarovsk, and Krasnoyarsk. Two areas, Ural Industrial Area and Kuznetsk Basin (*qq.v.*), with large resources in coal, iron, copper, manganese, etc., have had phenomenal development since 1920.

History: Tatar Khanate of Siberia conquered for Russia by Cossacks under Ermak Timofeev 1581; region of Amur river (*q.v.*) reached by Russians in 1644 and partly abandoned by Treaty of Nerchinsk 1689; Maritime Province was ceded to Russia by China 1860; connected with Russia by Trans-Siberian R.R., built 1891–1906. Eastern Siberia the scene of activities of anti-Bolshevist Admiral Kolchak and of Allied intervention 1918–19; reconquered by Bolshevists and made part of R.S.F.S.R. In World War II its W part, esp. the industrial and mining areas, served successfully as basis for Russia's war effort; in E part large army along the Amur and Manchukuo border kept Siberia neutral in war of United Nations against Japan.

Si'be·roet' or **Si'be·rut'** (sē'bĕ·rōōt'). Largest island ab. 54 m. long by 27 m. wide of Mentawai Is. off W coast of Sumatra opp. Padang, Indonesia; pop. 9314.

Siberoet, or **Siberut, Strait.** Channel ab. 27 m. wide bet. Siberut I. on S and Batu Is. on N, off W coast of Sumatra.

Si'bi (sē'bē). **1** District, NE Baluchistan, Pakistan; 11,457 sq. m.; pop. (1941) 164,899; includes tribal areas.

2 Town on railroad at S end of Bolan Pass, 73 m. SE of Quetta; pop. 9532.

Si·bil·li'ni Mountains (sē·bēl·lē'nē). Range of the Roman Apennines, SW Marches, cen. Italy; includes Monte Vettare 8128 ft., highest point in the Roman Apennines.

Sibir. 1 See SIBERIA.

2 See ISKER ancient town, W Siberia.

Si·biu' (sē·byōō'); *Hung.* **Nagy'sze'ben** (nŏd'y'·sĕ'-bĕn); *Ger.* **Her'mann·stadt'** (hĕr'män·shtät'). City, W cen. Romania, N of the Transylvanian Alps; pop. (1939 est.) 50,247; cathedral, 14th-cent. Gothic church, museum, art gallery. An early Roman colony refounded in 12th cent. by Saxon colonists from Nürnberg.

Sib'ley (sĭb'lǐ). **1** County in Minnesota. See *Table* at MINNESOTA.

2 City, ⊗ of Osceola co., NW Iowa, 46 m. NNW of Cherokee; pop. 2852; in agricultural and livestock-raising section; creameries, brick kilns.

Si·bol'ga (sē·bôl'gä). Coastal town, NW Sumatra, Indonesia, on Tapanuli Bay; pop. 10,765; has highway connections with Lake Toba region to the N and with Padang Highlands to the S.

Si·bo·ney' (sē'bô·nā'; *Span.* sē'vô·nĕ'ĕ). Town on S coast of Cuba, just E of Santiago de Cuba; with Daiquirí to the E was landing place of U.S. forces June 20, 1898.

Si·bong'a (sē·bông'ä). Municipality on E coast of Cebu I., Phil. Is., 28 m. SW of City of Cebu; pop. 21,803; has good anchorage on Bohol Strait.

Sib·sa'gar (sĭb·sä'gĕr). Town, NE Assam, NE Indian Union, near left bank of Brahmaputra 85 m. SW of Sadiya; pop. 6669; center of tea cultivation.

Si'bu (sē'bōō). Commercial town 60 m. upstream at head of delta of Rajang river, W Sarawak, Borneo, 115 m. NE of Kuching.

Si'bu·guey' Bay (sē'vōō·gě'ĕ; -gā'). Large inlet of Moro Gulf in SE coast of Zamboanga prov., Mindanao, Phil. Is.; its mouth is ab. 35 m. wide from Olutanga I. on the E to SW peninsula on the W.

Si·bu'tu (sē·vōō'tōō). Low, wooded island, westernmost of the Sulu Archipelago, Phil. Is.; 39 sq. m.; pop. ab. 3100; SW of Tawitawi and separated from it by Sibutu Passage; ab. 25 m. SE of the NE point of British North Borneo. After conclusion of treaty with Spain Dec. 10, 1898, by which Philippine possessions were ceded to U.S., it was discovered that this island was omitted; by a supplementary convention concluded Nov. 7, 1900 and proclaimed Mar. 23, 1901 $100,000 was granted Spain for correction of the oversight.

Sibutu Passage. Channel ab. 12 m. wide in SW Sulu Archipelago, Phil. Is., separating Sibutu I. on the SW from Tawitawi I.; one of the main channels of navigation connecting Sulu Sea and Celebes Sea.

Si·bu·yan' (sē'vōō·yän'). Island, E part of Romblon prov., cen. Phil. Is., in Sibuyan Sea; 173 sq. m.; pop. 19,764, chief municipality Cajidiocan. Mountainous with **Mount Sibuyan** in center 6750 ft., highest point in province.

Sibuyan Sea. Body of interisland water, cen. Phil. Is., NW of Visayan Sea; bordering it are Marinduque I. and S coast of Luzon on the N and enclosing it on other sides are the Visayan islands of Burias, Masbate, Panay, and Tablas. Sibuyan I. and Romblon I. are within it. From this sea in Oct. 1944 part of the Japanese fleet emerged through San Bernadino Strait to engage American fleet off Leyte.

Si'ca·poo' (sē'kä·pō') or **Pac·san'** (päk·sän'), **Mount.** Mountain in Cordillera Central of NW Luzon, Phil. Is.; highest point 7743 ft. in Ilocos Norte prov. on Apayao border.

Sicca Veneria. See LE KEF.

Si'chang' (shē'chäng'); *formerly* **Ning'yuan'** (nĭng'-yü·än'). Town, SE Sikang prov., S China, on a tributary of the Yangtze 285 m. SW of Chungking; junction point for Assam-Sikang road E from Sadiya and for highway N from Burma Road to Chengtu.

Sic'i·lies, the Two (sĭs'ĭ·lĭz). Former kingdom consisting of S Italy and the island of Sicily (*q.v.*).

Sic'i·ly (sĭs'ĭ·lĭ); *Ital. and anc.* **Si·ci'lia** (*Ital.* sē·chēl'yä; *anc.* sĭ·sĭl'yä, -sĭl'ĭ·à); *anc. also* **Tri·nac'ri·a** (trĭ·năk'-rĭ·à; trī-). Largest island in the Mediterranean Sea, W of extreme S point of the Italian penin.; 9926 sq. m.; pop. 4,000,078; ✳ Palermo; politically, a compartimento of Italy (see *Table* at ITALY); separated from Italy by narrow Strait of Messina and from Africa (NE Tunisia) by a narrow part of the Mediterranean (ab. 90 m.). Volcano

of Etna 10,741 ft. dominates its E end; entire island is mountainous with most of it a plateau having highest

range along N coast (highest point 6467 ft.); rivers numerous but small, largest the Simeto. Coast line regular with several wide inlets, esp. Gulf of Castellammare on NW and Gulf of Catania on E; Cape Passero is SE point and chief islands are Lipari Is. off NE coast, Egadi Is. at W end, and Ustica I. farther out to NW in Tyrrhenian Sea. Chief products fruits, olives and olive oil, wines, vegetables; sulfur is most important mineral. Chief cities Palermo, Catania, Messina, Trapani, Syracuse (Siracusa), Caltanissetta.

History: Originally inhabited by Sicani; from 8th cent. B.C. colonized by Greeks who drove to west coast the earlier Phoenician settlements; Syracuse (*q.v.*) became leading city of ancient Sicily and, for a time, successfully resisted cities under Carthage; former Carthaginian territory in Sicily, conquered by Rome in 3d cent. B.C., became first Roman province; part of Vandal and Ostrogothic kingdoms and of Byzantine Empire; overrun by Moslems 9th cent. A.D.; Sicily and Naples conquered by Normans 1072–91 who founded kingdom of **the Two Sicilies,** consisting of S Italy and Sicily; became Hohenstaufen territory by marriage of its heiress to future Emperor Henry VI; under Emperor Frederick II (d. 1250), despite struggle with Papacy, kingdom of Two Sicilies eclipsed other European states in cultural brilliance and administration; conquered 1266 by Charles of Anjou whose harsh rule caused uprising and massacre (Sicilian Vespers) 1282, his expulsion from Sicily, and the introduction of the rule of the house of Aragon (finally established after war lasting until 1302); Naples (*q.v.*) remained Angevin; Sicily under separate Aragonese dynasty 1295–1409; reunited with Naples from 1442; under Spanish rule to 1713; held by Savoy 1713–20, by Austria 1720–35; see NAPLES for later years of its history in connection with Italy. In World War II invaded by Americans July 9–10, 1943 and by British July 10; Allied conquest of island completed by Aug. 16 (38 days).

Si·cua'ni (sē·kwä'nē). Town, Cuzco dept., SE Peru; highway and railroad junction point on the Urubamba river 70 m. SE of Cuzco; pop. (1940 est.) 7036; alt. 11,650 ft.

Siculum Fretum. See Strait of MESSINA.

Si'cy·on (sĭsh'ĭ·ŏn; sĭs'ĭ-); *Gr.* **Sik'y·on** (sĭk'ĭ·ŏn). Ancient city in NE Peloponnesus, S Greece, ab. 10 m. NW of Corinth and near the S shore of the Gulf of Corinth; chief town of the district of Sicyonia. Influential in Greek history, esp. when it assumed leadership of Ionians under the tyrant Cleisthenes at beginning of 6th cent. B.C.; famous for its artists and art schools. After 500 B.C. generally followed Sparta or Corinth, but in 3d cent. B.C. was prominent under Aratus as a leader in the Achaean League; declined after 146 B.C.

Si'cy·o'ni·a (sĭsh'ĭ·ō'nĭ·à; sĭs'ĭ-). Small district of ancient Greece, in NE Peloponnesus, comprising the territory immediately around the city of Sicyon; touched upon Corinth, Argolis, Arcadia, and Achaea.

Si·da·mo (sē·dä·mō). Region, S Ethiopia, S of Addis Ababa and the chain of lakes in the Great Rift Valley.

Sid'cup (sĭd'kŭp). Former urban district, Kent, SE England, on the Cray 10½ m. ESE of London; now in Chislehurst and Sidcup urban district.

Side'ling Hill (sīd'lĭng). Ridge in S Pennsylvania, extending SW in Huntingdon and Bedford cos. to the Maryland border; highest point 2195 ft.

Si·der'no (sē·děr'nō). Commune, Reggio di Calabria prov., Calabria, S Italy, 33 m. ENE of Reggio di Calabria; pop. (1931) 13,488.

Si'de·ro, Cape (sē'thâ·rō). Point, NE tip of Crete, projecting into Caso Strait.

Si'de·ro'ka·stron (sē'thĕ·rō'kä·stron); *Turk.* **De'mir His·sár'** or **De'mir Hi·sar'** (dĕ'mĭr hĭ·sär'). Commune, Serrai dept., cen. Macedonia, Greece, on Struma river near Bulgarian frontier NNW of Serrai; pop. 9689.

Sidh'pur or **Siddh'pur** (sĭd'pŏŏr; *native* sĭd'h'·pŏŏr). City, Mehsana division, E Gujarat state, W India,

on Saraswati river 63 m. N of Ahmadabad; pop. 20,468; very old town with ruins of ancient temple of Rudra Mala; place of pilgrimage.

Si'di Abd'al·lah' (sē'dĭ ăb'dŏol·lä'h'). See BIZERTE.

Sidi Ah'med (ä'mĕd). Town, N Tunisia, N Africa, on N shore of Lake Bizerte ab. 6 m. SW of the city of Bizerte.

Sidi Bar·râ'ni (bă·rä'nĭ). Coastal village, NW Egypt, E of Buqbuq and W of Matrûh. In World War II scene of much fighting in North Africa campaign; captured by Italians Sept. 1940, by British Dec. 11, 1940; taken by Rommel's army 1941 but recaptured Nov. 10–11, 1942 in Rommel's retreat.

Si'di–bel–Ab·bès' (sē'dĭ·bĕl·ȧ·bĕs'). Commune, N cen. Oran dept., NW Algeria, 40 m. S of Oran; pop. (1936) 51,094; alt. 1552 ft.; an old walled town used by French as military base.

Sidi–bou–Zid (-bōō·zēd'). Town, cen. Tunisia, 10 m. WSW of Faïd Pass; pop. ab. 300.

Sidi–el–Ha'ni (-ĕl·hä'nĭ). Lake, NE Tunisia, near coast SSW of Sousse; dry at times.

Sidi–Nsir (-nȧ·sĭr'). Village, N Tunisia, near Mateur; fighting Apr. 26–27, 1943.

Sidi–O'mar (-ō'mär; -mēr). Village, NE Cyrenaica, Libya, N Africa, SW of Capuzzo; battles nearby 1941 and 1942.

Sidi–Re·zegh' (-rĕ·zĕg'). Locality, Cyrenaica, NE Libya, S of Tobruk; taken by British Nov. 26, 1941; evacuated June 19, 1942.

Sid'law Hills (sĭd'lô). Range of hills in Perth and Angus cos., cen. Scotland; highest point **Auch'ter·house' Hill** (ŏκ'tẽr·hous') 1399 ft.

Sid'ley, Mount (sĭd'lĭ). Peak ab. 12,000 ft., Marie Byrd Land, Antarctica, in 77°25′S and 129°W; discovered 1934.

Sid'mouth (sĭd'mŭth). Urban district, Devonshire, SW England, on English Channel at mouth of the Sid 13 m. ESE of Exeter; pop. 10,403; seaside resort. There is a tradition that an old town lies buried under the sea near here, Roman relics having been washed up from time to time.

Sid'ney (sĭd'nĭ). 1 Town, ⊗ of Fremont co., SW corner of Iowa; pop. 1057.

2 City, ⊗ of Richland co., E Montana, on Yellowstone river 50 m. NE of Glendive; pop. 4564; trade center in irrigated section producing esp. sugar beets and wheat.

3 City, ⊗ of Cheyenne co., W Nebraska, 61 m. SE of Scottsbluff; pop. 8004; railroad junction point.

4 Village, Delaware co., S New York, on Susquehanna river 30 m. ENE of Binghamton; pop. 5157; manufactures magnetos for airplane motors and motor trucks, tractors, and stationary, portable, and marine engines.

5 Manufacturing city, ⊗ of Shelby co., W Ohio, 30 m. NW of Springfield; pop. 14,663; produces engine lathes, road scrapers, washing machines, aluminum ware.

Si'do·ar'djo or **Si'do·ar'jo** (sē'dō·är'jō). Town, East Java prov., Indonesia, near coast ab. 15 m. S of Surabaja; pop. 12,082.

Si'don (sī'd'n) or **Zi'don** (zī'-); Fr. **Sa'ï'da'** (sȧ'ē'dȧ'); Arab. **Sai'da** (sī'dä; -dȧ). Seaport, SW Lebanon Republic, 22 m. N of Tyre; pop. ab. 10,000; a powerful citystate and in early times a chief city of ancient Phoenicia. Modern town surrounded by fruit orchards; formerly had good harbor (now half silted up). Ancient city was older than Tyre and noted for its wealth and trade and skilled workmen in manufacture of glass and purple dyes; captured by many of the powers and peoples of antiquity—Philistines, Assyria, Babylonia, Egypt (7th cent. B.C.), Alexander, Seleucids, and Romans; beautified by Herod the Great. During the Crusades, bet. 1107 and 1291, taken and retaken many times. Its commerce restored in 18th cent. but bombarded 1840 by allied fleets and occupied by British in Oct. 1918.

Sid'ra, Gulf of (sĭd'rȧ); anc. **Syr'tis Ma'jor** (sûr'tĭs mā'jẽr). Inlet of Mediterranean Sea on NE coast of Tripolitania and NW coast of Cyrenaica, Libya, N Africa.

Sie'ben·bür'gen (zē'bĕn·būr'gĕn). German name of TRANSYLVANIA.

Sie'ben·ge·bir'ge (zē'bĕn·gĕ·bĭr'gĕ). Literally "seven hills"; hills in the Westerwald, western Germany, on right bank of the Rhine 6 m. SSE of Bonn, including Drachenfels 1053 ft., Löwenburg 1506 ft., and Ölberg 1509 ft.

Siedl'ce (shĕd'̓l·tsĕ); Ger. **Sed'lez** (zĕd'lĕts). Industrial commune, Lublin dept., E Poland, 66 m. NNW of Lublin; pop. (1938–39 est.) 40,962; episcopal see; important railroad junction; manufactures include leather, pottery. Seat of Russian administrative division 1867–1915. Taken by German armies Sept. 17, 1939; retaken by Russians in latter part of 1944.

Sieg (zēκ). River ab. 80 m. long in W Germany; flows W into the Rhine 2 m. N of Bonn.

Sieg'burg (zēκ'bŏorκ). City, North Rhine-Westphalia state, West Germany, on Sieg river 14 m. SE of Cologne; pop. 19,405; 12th-cent. church; manufactures chemicals, clay goods, iron goods; once a cloth-making and leatherworking town. Made city 1182.

Sie'gen (zē'gĕn). Industrial city, North Rhine-Westphalia state, West Germany, on Sieg river 49 m. E of Cologne; pop. 31,205; two 13th-cent. churches; manufactures steel, iron goods, etc. Birthplace of the painter Rubens.

Siegfried Line. See WESTWALL.

Sieg'mar (zēκ'mär). Industrial commune, Karl-Marx-Stadt dist., East Germany, W suburb of Chemnitz; pop. 10,019.

Sie'men·stadt (zē'mĕn·shtät). Town, NW suburb of Berlin, Germany; had great industrial plants, esp. Siemens Electrical Works; severely damaged in bombings during World War II.

Sie·mia'no·wi'ce Ślą'skie (shĕ·myä'nô·vē'tsĕ shlôN'-skyĕ); formerly **Siemianowice–Hu'ta Lau'ra** (-hōō'tä lou'rä). Industrial city, Śląsk dept., just E of Katowice, S Poland; pop. (1938–39 est.) 38,701; coal mining; ironworks; manufactures machinery, screws, etc.

Si'em·ré'ap (sē'ĕm·rĭ'ȧp); also **Si'em Re'ap.** Town, NW Cambodia, Indochina, on highway just N of NW end of Tonle Sap; pop. ab. 1000. Official station for visitors to ruins of Angkor (q.v.) and in recent years has become increasingly important.

Sie'na (syâ'nä; Angl. sĭ·ĕn'ȧ). 1 Province of Italy. See Table at ITALY.

2 anc. **Sae'na Ju'lia** (sē'nȧ jōōl'yȧ; jōō'lĭ·ȧ). Commune, its ✳, Tuscany, cen. Italy, 33 m. S of Florence; pop. 48,664; surrounded by Etruscan or medieval walls; buildings include a 13th-cent. Gothic-Romanesque cathedral, church of San Giovanni (under the cathedral; formerly a baptistery), the Palazzo Pubblico with fine campanile, Palazzo Piccolimini (containing government archives), Loggia dei Nobili (in imitation of the Florentine Loggia dei Lanzi), Palazzo Buonsignori, Accademia di Belle Arti, Accademia dei Fisiocritici (natural history museum), and 13th-cent. university; Fontebranda (immortalized by Dante); manufactures cloth, hats, sugar, spirits, and bakery products.

History: Founded by Etruscans, passing later to Romans and Lombards; at time of Frankish invasions, formed countship; became independent in 12th cent.; seat of Ghibelline faction and rival of Florence; conquered by Charles of Anjou 1270 and forced to join Guelph confederation; became seat of Sienese school of art, second in importance only to Florence and Rome, producing such artists as Duccio and Jacopo della Quercia; era of artistic splendor ended by Black Death 1348; under Visconti of Milan for short time; under Pandolfo Petrucci 1487 ff.; taken by Spaniards 1531, French, and later (1557) by Florence whose subsequent history it shared. In World War II occupied by Allies July 3, 1944.

Sie'radz (shĕ'räts). Commune, Łódź dept., Poland, on Warta river 35 m. WSW of Łódź; pop. (1938–39 est.)

11,359; manufactures leather, lumber, yeast. Seat of independent medieval principality, later residence of voivode and meeting place of Polish national assembly.

Sie′ro (syä′rô). Commune, Oviedo prov., NW Spain, 9 m. ENE of Oviedo; pop. 30,931; coal mines; manufactures leather, soap, linen.

Sierpc (shĕrpts). Industrial commune, Warszawa dept., E Poland, 70 m. NW of Warsaw; pop. 10,051.

Si·er′ra (sĭ·ĕr′à). Name of counties in two states of the U.S. See *Tables* at CALIFORNIA and NEW MEXICO.

Si·er′ra An′cha (sĭ·ĕr′à än′chà). Ridge in cen. Gila co., cen. Arizona, NE of Roosevelt Lake.

Si·er′ra Blan′ca (sĭ·ĕr′à bläng′kà). 1 Range in S cen. New Mexico, chiefly in N Otero and S Lincoln cos.

2 Village, ⊗ of Hudspeth co., W Texas; pop. (est.) 1000.

Sierra Blanca Peak or **White Mountain.** Mountain 12,003 ft. in N Otero co., S New Mexico.

Sier′ra de Al′ca·raz′ (syĕr′rä thä äl′kä·räth′; äl′kä-räs′). Mountain range in SW cen. Spain, mostly in Albacete prov.

Sierra de Co·al′co·mán′ (kô·äl′kô·män′). Range of SW Mexico, a part of the Sierra Madre Occidental; extends NW to SE near the coast in Michoacán state.

Sierra de Fa′ma·ti′na (fä′mä·tē′nä). Mountain range in the Andes Mts., in La Rioja prov., NW Argentina; highest peak **Ne·va′do de Famatina** (nä·vä′thô thä), *also called* **Ne′gro O·ve′ro** (nä′grô ô·vä′rô), 19,751 ft.

Sierra de Ga′ta (gä′tä). Mountain range in W Spain and E Portugal, separating the basins of the Tagus and Douro rivers; highest peak 5690 ft.

Sierra de Gre′dos (grä′thôs). Mountain range in W cen. Spain, W of Madrid; highest peak Plaza de Almanzor 8692 ft.

Sierra de Guadalupe. See GUADALUPE MOUNTAINS.

Sier′ra de Gua′dar·ra′ma (syĕr′rä thä gwä′thär-rä′mä). Mountain range in cen. Spain; highest peak Pico de Peñalara 7890 ft.

Sierra de I′ma·ta′ca (ē′mä·tä′kä). Mountain range in E Venezuela, S of Orinoco delta.

Sierra de Juá′rez (hwä′räs). Range in N Lower California, Mexico.

Sierra de la Gi·gan′ta (lä hē·gän′tä). Range along SE coast of Lower California, Mexico.

Sierra de la Ven·ta′na (vän·tä′nä). Mountain range in S Buenos Aires prov., E Argentina.

Sierra de la Vic·to′ria (vĕk·tō′ryä). Range at S end of Lower California, Mexico; highest peak 7894 ft.

Si·er′ra del Ca·bal′lo Muer′to (sĭ·ĕr′à dĕl kà·bä′yō mwĕr′tō). Range of the Santiago Mts. extending to the Mexican border in S Brewster co., W Texas; locally called Dead Horse Mountains (translation).

Sier′ra del Du·raz′no (syĕr′rä thĕl dōō·räs′nô). Range in SW Chihuahua state, Mexico; a part of the Sierra Madre Occidental.

Sier′ra de los Ór′ga·nos (syĕr′rä thä lôs ôr′gä·nôs). Mountain range in W Pinar del Río prov., W Cuba; highest ab. 2500 ft.

Sier′ra del Ro·sa′rio (syĕr′rä thĕl rrô·sä′ryô). Mountain range in N Pinar del Río prov., W Cuba.

Sierra del Tan·dil′ (tän·dēl′). Mountain range in S Buenos Aires prov., E Argentina.

Sierra de Me′ren·dón′ (thä mä′rän·dôn′). Range extending SW to NE along Guatemala-Honduras boundary, Central America.

Sierra de Mérida. = CORDILLERA MÉRIDA.

Sier′ra de Mi·sio′nes (syĕr′rä thä mē·syō′nás). Mountain range in NE Argentina, chiefly in Misiones territory, and extending NE into S Brazil.

Sierra de Na′ya·rit′ (nä′yä·rēt′). Range in W cen. Mexico, part of Sierra Madre Occidental; extends N to S in Durango and Nayarit states.

Sierra de Oa·xa′ca (wä·hä′kä). Range in S Mexico, a part of the Sierra Madre del Sur; extends W to E in S Oaxaca state.

Sierra de Ta′ba·sa′ra (tä′vä·sä′rä). Range in W Panama; highest point Mt. Santiago 9272 ft.

Si·er′ra Gal·li′nas (sĭ·ĕr′à gà·yē′nás). Range in cen. New Mexico, chiefly in Torrance and Lincoln cos.

Si·er′ra Le·one′ (sĭ·ĕr′à lē·ōn′; sĭr′à). 1 River in Sierra Leone, W Africa, the estuary of the Rokel river; flows into the Atlantic Ocean at Freetown.

2 Former British colony and protectorate, since 1961 a dominion of the British Commonwealth, in W Africa; 27,940 sq. m.; pop. 1,768,480; ✻ Freetown; bounded on N and E by Guinea, on SE by Liberia, on SW and W by the Atlantic. The *colony* comprised Sierra Leone Penin., Turner's Penin., two small districts on mainland, Sherbro I. and several small islands—all along the coast, 271 sq. m., pop. 96,422, (1940 est. 121,100); also certain sections of the mainland administered as a protectorate totaling ab. 2250 sq. m. The *protectorate* (including regions so administered) 27,669 sq. m., pop. 1,672,058. A plateau region with many hills; along N border has mountains exceeding 3000 ft. Has numerous streams, all flowing SW; most important the Rokel (called Sierra Leone at its estuary); the Mano, and its tributary the Morro, separating it from Liberia, has thickly forested valley. Coast line is 400 m. with excellent harbor at Freetown (*q.v.*). Leading products are palm oil and kernels, piassava, ginger, kola nuts, cocoa, coffee, rice. Gold, iron, chrome ore deposits; diamonds. Inhabitants are various Negro tribes: Mendi, Temne, Bullom, and others. Chief towns Freetown, Bonthe, Waterloo, Port Loko.

History: Coast region first visited by Portuguese 1462; followed by English slave traders; settlements on coast proposed c. 1787 by English philanthropists for runaway and freed slaves and other Negroes. Freetown first established 1788 on land purchased from Temne chief; colony failed but re-established 1794 and in 1807 transferred its rights to British crown. In early years colony had many administrative changes and a reputation for being unhealthy. Hinterland gradually penetrated; after collision with French 1893 region acquired by treaty 1895 and proclaimed a protectorate 1896; became an independent member of British Commonwealth 1961.

Sierra Leone Peninsula. Peninsula ab. 28 m. long and 9 m. wide extending into Atlantic Ocean on W coast of Sierra Leone.

Si·er′ra Mad′re (sĭ·ĕr′à mäd′rĕ; mä′drä; *Span.* syĕr′rä mä′thrä). 1 Range in S Wyoming, extending S into N Colorado; part of the Continental Divide.

2 City, Los Angeles co., SW California, 13 m. NE of Los Angeles; pop. 9732; in orange-growing region.

3 Range in SE Mexico, extending SE into N Guatemala; chiefly in S Chiapas state, Mexico.

4 Main mountain range of NE Luzon, Phil. Is., extending ab. 215 m. along coast of Pacific Ocean, turning SW at its S end to join the Cordillera Central in N Nueva Vizcaya; averages 3500 to 5000 ft. with highest point 6188 ft. By some applied also to continuation of range S into Bicol Penin.

Sier′ra Ma′dre del Sur (syĕr′rä mä′thrä thĕl sōōr′). Coastal range in S Mexico, along SW and S coasts of Guerrero and Oaxaca states.

Sierra Madre Oc′ci·den·tal′ (ôk′sē·thän·täl′). Range of mountains in Mexico running parallel to Pacific Ocean coast and bordering cen. Mexican plateau on the W.

Sierra Madre O′rien·tal′ (ō′ryän·täl′). Range of mountains in Mexico running parallel to Gulf of Mexico coast and bordering cen. Mexican plateau on the E.

Sier′ra Ma·es′tra (syĕr′rä mä·äs′trä). Mountain range in Oriente prov., E Cuba, extending W and E along the S coast; highest peak Pico Turquino 6560 ft.

Sier′ra Mo·re′na (syĕr′rä mô·rä′nä). Mountain range in SW Spain, bet. the Guadiana and Guadalquivir rivers; highest peak Estrella, 4274 ft.

Si·er′ra Ne·vad′a (sĭ·ĕr′à nĕ·väd′à; -vä′dà; *Span.* syĕr′rä nä·vä′thä). 1 Mountain range extending for ab. 430 m. N to S in E California, parallel to the Coast

Ranges; highest peak Mount Whitney 14,495 ft. See CASCADE RANGE.

2 Mountain range in S Spain, mostly in Granada and Almería provs.; highest peak Mulhacén 11,420 ft.

Sier′ra Ne·va′da de Co·cuy′ (syĕr′rä nä·vä′thä thä kô·kwē′). Mountain range of the Cordillera Oriental, E Andes, in Colombia; highest peak Nevada de Chita 18,022 ft.

Sierra Nevada de Mérida. See CORDILLERA MÉRIDA.

Sierra Nevada de San′ta Mar′ta (sän′tä mär′tä). Mountain range in N Colombia, on the Caribbean coast; highest peak 19,030 ft.

Sier′ra San Pe′dro Már′tir (syĕr′rä säm pā′thrô mär′tēr). Range in N Lower California, Mexico.

Sier′ras de Cór′do·ba (syĕr′räz thä kôr′thô·vä). Mountain range in cen. Argentina, in San Luis and W Córdoba provs.; highest peak Champaquí 9350 ft.

Sier′ra Ta′ra·hu·ma′re (syĕr′rä tä′rä·ōō·mä′rä). Range in W and S cen. Chihuahua state, Mexico; a part of the Sierra Madre Occidental.

Sierre (syâr). Commune, cen. Valois canton, Switzerland, on the Rhone; pop. (1930) 4956; resort.

Sie′vers·hau′sen (zē′fērs·hou′zĕn; zē′vērs-). Village, Lower Saxony state, W Germany, ab. 15 m. E of Hannover; Maurice of Saxony defeated Albert Alcibiades here July 9, 1553 but was mortally wounded.

Sigeum. See YENIŞEHIR.

Si′ghet′ (sĕ·gĕt′); *Hung.* **Má′ra·ma′ros·szi′get** (mä′rŏ·mŏ′rôsh·sĭ′gĕt). City, N Romania, 45 m. E of Satu-Mare near the Russian border; pop. 27,684; in Hungary 1940–45.

Si′ghi·şoa′ra (sē′gĕ·shwä′rä); *Hung.* **Se′ges·vár′** (shĕ′gĕsh·vär′); *Ger.* **Schäss′burg** (shĕs′bōōrĸ). City, cen. Romania, in Transylvania region 45 m. NE of Sibiu; pop. 13,096; an old city built around a castle on a hill; founded by German colonists 1280; battlefield 1849 where Russians defeated Hungarian insurrectionists.

Si·gir′i·ya (sĭ·gĭr′ĭ·yȧ) *or* **Si·gir′i** (sĭ·gĭr′ĭ). Fortress rock, N cen. Ceylon, N of Kandy; ruined ancient capital of Ceylon serving as refuge for King Kasyapa in 5th cent. A.D.

Si′gli (sē′glĕ). Town on N coast of Sumatra, Indonesia, just E of Kutaradja; pop. 3327.

Sig′lu·fjör′dur (sĭk′lü·fyûr′thür). Town, N Iceland, in cen. part of N coast; pop. (1942) 2790.

Sig′ma·ring′en (zēĸ′mä·rĭng′ĕn). **1** Former government district, coextensive with province of Hohenzollern, Prussia, Germany; 441 sq. m.

2 Agricultural city, its ✱ and ✻ of former Hohenzollern prov., now in Baden-Württemberg, on Danube river 30 m. S of Reutlingen; pop. 5299; site of a castle, the ancestral home of the Hohenzollerns; chartered in 13th cent.; became property of the Hohenzollerns 1535.

Sig·nakh′ (sĭg·näĸ′). Town, Georgian S.S.R., Russia in Europe, 68 m. E of Tiflis near the Alasan river; pop. ab. 4000; in oil region.

Sig′nal Butte (sĭg′nȧl; -n′l). Height 4583 ft. in Scotts Bluff co., W Nebraska.

Signal Hill. 1 Peak 6500 ft. in Custer co., SW South Dakota.

2 City, Los Angeles co., SW California, 18 m. SSE of Los Angeles and E of Long Beach; pop. 4627; oil wells.

3 Elevation 1504 ft. in cen. Saint Thomas I., Virgin Is., West Indies.

Signal Hill National Historic Park. See CANADA, *National Historic Parks.*

Si-gnan. See SIAN.

Sig′our·ney (sĭg′ēr·nĭ). City, ⊗ of Keokuk co., SE cen. Iowa, 25 m. E of Oskaloosa; pop. 2387.

Sigs′bee Deep (sĭgz′bē′). Deepest point 12,425 ft. in Gulf of Mexico, in SW cen. part.

Sig·sig′ (sēg·sēg′). Town, Azuay prov., S Ecuador, just SE of Cuenca; pop. (1944 est.) 10,321.

Si′gua·ne′a Bay (sē′gwä·nā′ä). Bay on W coast of Isle of Pines, West Indies.

Si·güen′za (sĕ·gwän′thä; -sä); *anc.* **Se·gon′ti·a** (sĕ·gŏn′shĭ·ȧ). Town, Guadalajara prov., cen. Spain, ab. 70 m. NE of Madrid; pop. 4850.

Sihor. See NILE.

Si′hsien′ (shē′shyĕn′); *formerly* **Hwei′chow′** (hwā′jō′). City, SE Anhwei, E China; a commercial city noted for its bankers.

Si Hu (shē′ hōō′) *or* **Si-wu** (sē′wōō′). Literally "Western lake"; the lake W of the city of Hangchow, Chekiang prov., E China; noted for its scenic beauty and the many pagodas, temples, and literary and historic shrines on its shores.

Si·hun′ (sĭ·hōōn′). = SEYHAN.

Si·irt′ (sĕ·yĭrt′) *or* **Sert** (sĕrt). **1** Vilayet, SE Turkey in Asia; 5522 sq. m.; pop. 131,198.

2 *anc.* **Ti·gra′no·cer′ta** (tĭ·grä′nŏ·sûr′tȧ). Town, its ✱, on a tributary of the Tigris 85 m. E of Diyarbekir; pop. 15,849. Tigranocerta was fortified capital of Armenia; here 69 B.C. Lucullus defeated Tigranes and in 59 A.D. it was captured by Roman general Corbulo.

Si·kan′dar·a·bad′ (sĭ·kŭn′dēr·ȧ·bäd′). **1** Town, Meerut division, W Uttar Pradesh, N Indian Union; pop. 18,974.

2 See SECUNDERABAD.

Si·kan′dra (sĭ·kŭn′drȧ). Village 6 m. NW of Agra, Uttar Pradesh, N Indian Union; site of Tomb of Akbar, fine mausoleum of red sandstone.

Si′kang′ (shē′käng′). Province, S China, now a province of China Proper but formerly considered an outer dependency; 143,437 sq. m.; pop. (1936 est.) 968,187, (1940 est.) 1,755,542; ✱ Kangting; bounded on N by Tsinghai prov., on E by Szechwan, on S by Yunnan and India, and on W by Tibet; area much increased 1944 by relocation of W boundary at ab. 93°E long., thus taking a large section of E Tibet; no new area figures available. Forms E part of Tibetan plateau with nearly all of it above 10,000 ft.; bordered on the S by the E end of the Himalayas with peaks as high as 25,000 ft.; E edge cut by the great gorges of three streams—Salween, Mekong, and Yangtze—all of which have their upper courses in the province. In E part near Szechwan border is Mt. Minya Konka, highest mountain in China, 24,900 ft. Formed 1908 out of E Tibet and W mountainous part of Szechwan; made a province c. 1928. Chief towns Kangting (Tatsienlu), Paan (Batang), Yaan, Hweili, Chamdo, Sichang.

Si′kar (sĭ′kēr). Town, NE Rajasthan, formerly in Jaipur state, NW Indian Union, NW of Jaipur; pop. 26,297.

Si·ka·ram′, Mount (sĭ′kȧ·rȧm′). Highest peak 15,619 ft. in Safed Koh range, E Afghanistan, SE of Kabul on Indian border.

Si·kas′so (sĕ·käs′ō). Town, S Mali, West Africa, ab. 190 m. SE of Bamako near Ivory Coast boundary; pop. (1940) 11,859.

Sikes′ton (sīks′tŭn). City, Scott co., SE Missouri, 30 m. S of Cape Girardeau; pop. 13,765; cotton compresses, cotton gins, cottonseed-oil mill.

Si′kho·te A·lin′ (sē′ĸô·tä ä·lēn′). Mountain range extending 650 m. along the E coast of Maritime Territory, Soviet Russia, Asia; average height 4000 to 5000 ft.; highest point 6083 ft., at S end. Rich in minerals (coal, iron, graphite, manganese, gold, tin, lead, zinc, and silver).

Si′ki·a′na (sē′kĕ·ä′nȧ). Chief island of the Stewart Is., E Solomon Is., 110 m. E of Malaita; has no entrance to its lagoon; inhabited by small group of Polynesians.

Si-kiang. See SI.

Siking. See SIAN—its name under T'ang dynasty and also used in modern times.

Sik′i·nos (sĭk′ĭ·nŏs; *Mod. Gr.* sē′kyĕ·nôs). Island ab. 17 sq. m., S Cyclades, S Aegean Sea, E of Melos and W of Ios.

Sik′kim (sĭk′ĭm). Territory, NE Indian subcontinent; a protectorate of Republic of India; 2745 sq. m.; pop. (1941) 121,520; ✱ Gangtok. Bounded on N and NE

by Tibet, on SE by Bhutan, on S by Darjeeling dist. of West Bengal, and on W by Nepal, extending ab. 70 m. from N to S. Located on S slope of the Himalayas, alt. of ranges from ab. 1000 ft. to Mt. Kanchenjunga 28,146 ft., third highest mountain in the world, on W border; chief river the Tista. Main British trade route with Tibet passes from Kalimpong in N Bengal across SE Sikkim over the Jelep-la (*q.v.*) to the Chumbi valley. Inhabitants chiefly Nepalese, with Bhutias and Lepchas. Buddhism is the state religion. Relations with British began in 1816; site of Darjeeling ceded to them in 1839; in 1890 British protectorate recognized by China. Ruler is a maharaja, assisted by a council.

Siktivkar. Var. of SYKTYVKAR.

Sikyon. See SICYON.

Sil (sēl). River ab. 100 m. long, NW Spain; rises in NW León prov., flows SSW into Miño river.

Silagian Mountains; *Ital.* **La Sila.** See *Calabrian Apennines* at APENNINES.

Si·lang' (sĕ·läng'). Municipality, SE cen. Cavite prov., Luzon, Phil. Is., 19 m. S of City of Cavite; pop. 18,909; center of agricultural region.

Si·la'o (sĕ·lä'ô). Town, Guanajuato state, cen. Mexico, just WSW of Guanajuato; pop. 13,880.

Si·lay' (sĕ·lī'). Municipality, NW Negros Occidental, Negros, Phil. Is., on Guimaras Strait 10 m. N of City of Bacolod; pop. 39,483; has good coastwise trade.

Silay, Mount. Mountain 5035 ft., N Negros Occidental, Negros, Phil. Is.

Sil·char' (sĭl·chär'). Town, S cen. Assam, NE Indian Union, on highway to Manipur; British supply base in Burma campaign in World War II.

Sil'ches·ter (sĭl'chĕs·tẽr; -chĭs·tẽr). Village, N Hampshire, S England; site of ancient Roman town **Cal·le'va A·treb'a·tum** (kă·lē'vá á·trĕb'á·tŭm), excavated 1889–1909; walls, earth banks of a Roman amphitheater, and ruins of forum, baths, etc., uncovered.

Şi·le' (shĕ·lĕ'). Town, Kocaeli vilayet, NW Turkey in Asia, on Black Sea coast E of the Bosporus.

Si'ler City (sī'lẽr). Town, Chatham co., cen. North Carolina, 28 m. SE of Greensboro; pop. 4455; flour, cotton, grist mills; livestock, poultry.

Si'ler's Bald (sī'lẽrz bôld). Peak 5620 ft. in Sevier co., E Tennessee, in Great Smoky Mountain National Park; a peak of the Great Smoky Mts. near the North Carolina border.

Si·le'sia (sī·lē'zhá; -zhĭ·á; -shá; -shĭ·á; sĭ-). Region in E Europe, comprising: (1) Former Prussian province (**Schle'si·en** [shlā'zĕ·ĕn]), 14,290 sq. m., pop. (1939) 4,846,333; formerly divided into two provinces (see *Table* at PRUSSIA): Lower Silesia, ✱ Breslau, and Oppeln (or Upper Silesia), ✱ Oppeln. Comprises wide valley of the upper Oder (almost wholly navigable), bordered on SW by the Sudeten range, with highest point 5266 ft. in the Riesen Gebirge at N end; generally fertile and for centuries essentially agricultural; in modern times important also for sheep raising and textile industry and its extensive coal and iron mines; also has railroads and many industrial towns (known formerly under their German names: Breslau, Hindenburg, Beuthen, Liegnitz, Gleiwitz). For centuries a part of Poland and at one time divided into many principalities; passed to Bohemia in 14th cent., to Holy Roman Empire 1478; suffered greatly in Thirty Years' War. Seized by Prussia from Austria 1742; Maria Theresa's attempt to recover brought about Second Silesian War. After much unrest SE part with Polish population majority assigned to Poland in 1921. In World War II invaded by Russian armies Jan.-Apr. 1945; greater part assigned to Poland by Potsdam Conference July 17-Aug. 2, 1945 (see 3, below). (2) Austrian Silesia, region S of Prussian Silesia in S Sudeten range; originally part of Moravia, containing sources of Oder and March rivers; in 1849 made separate crownland. Greater part, **Slez'sko** (slĕs'kô), 1719 sq. m., pop. ab. 670,000 passed to Czechoslovakia by Treaty

of Versailles 1919; became part of the province of Moravia and Silesia; chief towns Opava, Krnov, Slezská Ostrava; E strip of this (Teschen, *q.v.*) divided 1920 with Poland; seized by Germany 1938; recovered 1945. (3) Polish Silesia, region (**Śląsk** [shlônsk]), 1600 sq. m., pop. ab. 1,130,000, at SE end of Prussian Silesia, with great wealth of coal and iron. Because of predominant Polish-speaking population assigned 1921 to Poland; included many large mining and industrial communities, as Katowice, Chorzów, Sosnowiec, Będzin. Disputes over coal exports adjusted 1926 in favor of Germany. Occupied by Germans 1939; recovered for Poland 1945 and incorporated in an enlarged Polish Silesia, comprising in addition former German Silesia and divided into two new provinces, Śląsk (Upper Silesia) and Wrocław (Lower Silesia).

Silesia Peak. Mountain 13,599 ft. in Custer and Saguache cos., S cen. Colorado.

Si'lex, Mount (sī'lĕks). Peak 13,634 ft. in San Juan co., SW Colorado.

Sil'hou·ette' (sĭl'ŏo·ĕt'). One of the Seychelles (*q.v.*); 8 sq. m.

Si·lif·ke' (sĕ·lĕf·kĕ'). See SELEUCIA, Cilicia, Asia Minor.

Si·li'gu·ri (sĭ·lē'gōō·rê). Town, Darjeeling dist., West Bengal, Indian Union; pop. 6067; by direct line ab. 30 m. SSE of Darjeeling and connected with it by picturesque narrow-gauge (2 ft.) railroad of 50 m., ascending from 400 ft. to ab. 7000 ft. (average elevation of Darjeeling).

Si·lis'tra (sĭ·lĭs'trá; *Romanian* sĕ·lē'strä), *also* **Si·lis'tri·a** (sĭ·lĭs'trĭ·á; *Bulg.* sĭ·lĭs'trĭ·yä); *anc.* **Du·ros'to·rum** (dŭ·rŏs'tô·rŭm). City, NE Bulgaria, in Dobruja region, on Danube river; pop. 17,415; trade center in grain, fish, wool, and wines; under Bulgarian rule 1878–1913; to Romania 1913–40.

Si·li·vri' (sĕ·lĕ·vrē'). Port on the Sea of Marmara, İstanbul vilayet, Turkey in Europe, ab. 35 m. W of İstanbul; pop. 3318.

Sil'jan (sĭl'yàn). Lake 137 sq. m. in cen. Kopparberg prov., cen. Sweden; drains into Dal river.

Sil'ke·borg (sĭl'kĕ·bôrk). City, Aarhus co., E Jutland Penin., Denmark, 27 m. W of Aarhus; pop. (1945) 20,955; health resort in lake region.

Silk Road *or* **Route.** Route from E China up the Wei valley through Kansu and Sinkiang to the west; at Tunhwang, oasis town in extreme W Kansu just WSW of Ansi, divided into two ancient caravan routes that led westward: "South Road" (Chin. *Nan Lu*), along N Astin Tagh and Kunlun mountain ranges S of the Takla Makan to Khotan and Yarkand, thence W and S through high passes of Pamirs and Hindu Kush to the Oxus and India; "North Road" (Chin. *Pei Lu*), along N edge of the Takla Makan through Kurla, Kucha, and Aqsu to Kashgar, thence by way of Fergana to the Jaxartes and towns of Turkistan; this "North Road" later became the "Middle Road" and was superseded by the true "North Road" from Ansi via Qomul, Turfan, Qara, Shahr to its junction at Kurla; routes were used for shipments of silk to western markets and for travel by ambassadors, pilgrims, and early missionaries, and for centuries was of great importance to China.

Sill, Mount (sĭl). Peak 14,254 ft. in Sierra Nevada, Fresno co., S cen. California.

Sil'la (sĭl'á); *also* **Shil'la** (shĭl'á). Early Korean kingdom established, probably in 3d cent. A.D., after the elimination of Chinese influence, in SE part of peninsula; adopted Buddhism 528, drove out Japanese, and from 670 to 935 dominated all Korea.

Sil'laj·huay' (sĕ'yäk·wī') *or* **Sil'laj·guay'** (sĕ'yäk-gwī'). Peak 19,669 ft. in W Bolivia, on the Chilean boundary NW of Salar de Uyuni.

Sil·le'da (sĕ·[l]yä'thä). Commune, Pontevedra prov., NW Spain, 28 m. NE of Pontevedra; pop. 12,201.

Sillein. See ŽILINA.

Sil'ler·y (sĭl'ẽr·ĭ; *Fr.* sē'y'·rē'). Village, Marne dept., NE France, just SE of Reims; famous for champagne.

Sil′li·man, Mount (sĭl′ĭ·măn). Peak 11,188 ft. in Sierra Nevada, N Tulare co., S cen. California.

Si·lo′am (sĭ·lō′ăm; sī-). Pool within the walls, SE part of Jerusalem, Palestine (*John* ix. 7); its outlet flowed into the Kidron Valley.

Si′loam Springs (sī′lōm). Commercial city, Benton co., NW corner of Arkansas, in Ozarks 23 m. NW of Fayetteville; pop. 3953; founded 1880; health resort; iron and sulfur springs. John Brown Univ. (1919; coed.).

Sil′pi·a (sĭl′pĭ·à). Ancient town, Baetica, S Hispania, N of the Baetis (Guadalquivir); scene of defeat of Carthaginian general Mago 206 B.C. by Scipio Africanus.

Sils, Lake of (zĭls); *Ger.* **Sil′ser See** (zĭl′zĕr zā′). Small lake 3 m. long and 1 m. wide in Graubünden canton, E Switzerland, in SW part of Upper Engadine.

Sils′bee (sĭlz′bē). City, Hardin co., E Texas, 19 m. N of Beaumont; pop. 6277; lumber and oil industries.

Si·lu′te (shĭ·loo′tā). **1** District of Lithuania (1939–45 a part of Memelgebiet). See *Table* at LITHUANIA.
2 *Ger.* **Hey′de·krug** (hī′dĕ·krook). Its chief town, W Lithuania, near mouth of Neman river SSE of Memel; pop. 4350.

Sil′ver Bank (sĭl′vēr). Bank in Atlantic Ocean off N coast of Hispaniola in the West Indies.

Silver Bank Passage. Channel in N cen. West Indies, SE of Mouchoir Bank and NW of Silver Bank.

Silver Bow (bō′). County in Montana. See *Table* at MONTANA.

Silver City. 1 Ghost town, Owyhee co., SW corner of Idaho; important in 1889 (pop. ab. 2000) for production of silver.
2 Town, ⊗ of Grant co., SW New Mexico, ab. 45 m. NW of Deming; pop. 6972; shipping point in mining (esp. gold, iron, silver) and stock-raising region; health resort. New Mexico State Teachers College (1893; coed.); Gila Cliff Dwellings National Monument to NE. Founded 1870 as Spanish settlement; became ⊗ 1874; incorporated 1876.
3 *now* **Rainbow City.** Town, Cristobal dist., Canal Zone, adjoining Cristobal; pop. 3688.

Silver Creek. 1 Village, Chautauqua co., SW corner of New York, on Lake Erie 28 m. S of Buffalo; pop. 3310; in grape and fruit region; ships grapes and manufactures wines and unfermented grape juice.
2 New Philadelphia, Pennsylvania—formerly its post office name.

Sil′ver·heels′, Mount (sĭl′vēr·hēlz′). Peak 13,835 ft. in Park co., cen. Colorado.

Silver Peak Mountains. Small range in W Esmeralda co., SW Nevada.

Silver Plume Mountain. Peak 13,500 ft. in Clear Creek co., N cen. Colorado.

Silver Run Peak. Mountain 12,610 ft. in Carbon co., S Montana; second highest in state.

Silver Spring. Urban community (unincorporated), Montgomery co., cen. Maryland, N suburb of Washington; pop. 66,348.

Silver Springs. Village, Marion co., N Florida; near Ocala; site of 150 springs which form a pond ab. 35 ft. deep, source of **Silver River,** tributary of the Oklawaha to the E.

Sil′ver·tip′ Peak (sĭl′vēr·tĭp′). Mountain 10,400 ft. in Park co., NW Wyoming.

Sil′ver·ton (sĭl′vēr·t′n; -tŭn). **1** Town, ⊗ of San Juan co., SW Colorado; pop. 822.
2 Residential village, Hamilton co., SW corner of Ohio, 8 m. NE of Cincinnati; pop. 6682.
3 City, Marion co., Oregon, ENE of Salem; pop. 3081.
4 City, ⊗ of Briscoe co., NW Texas; pop. 1098.

Sil′ver·town (sĭl′vēr·toun). City, Upson co., W cen. Georgia, 40 m. W of Macon; pop. (1950) 3387; textile mills, manufacturing esp. tire cord.

Sil′ves (sĭl′vĕsh). Town, S coast of Portugal, 18 m. NNW of Faro; pop. ab. 9600; formerly capital of Algarve prov.; sacked by Ferdinand I of Castile; destroyed in earth-

quake 1755; small Gothic cathedral; Moorish castle.

Sil′vies (sĭl′vēs). River 75 m. long, E cen. Oregon; rises in S Grant co., flows S into Malheur Lake, Harney co.

Sil′vis (sĭl′vĭs). City, Rock Island co., NW Illinois, 9 m. E of Rock Island; pop. 3973.

Sil·vret′ta (sĭl·vrĕt′à; *Ger.* zĭl·vrĕt′ä). Mountain group along border bet. E Switzerland and SW Tirol, Austria, heights **Piz Li·nard′** (pēts′ lĕ·närt′) 11,198 ft., **Flucht′horn′** (flooKt′hôrn′) 11,162 ft.

Sim, Cape (sĭm). Cape on SW coast of Morocco, NW Africa, 31°10′N.

Simalur. See SIMEULOEE.

Si·man′cas (sĕ·mäng′käs). Commune, Valladolid prov., N cen. Spain, 8 m. SW of Valladolid; pop. (1930) 1195; national archives are kept in the castle; very ancient city; scene of victory of Ramiro II over Caliph Abder-Rahman 934.

Si·mang′gang (sĕ·mäng′gäng). Town, S Sarawak, NW Borneo, on Batang Lupar river 80 m. ESE of Kuching.

Si·ma′ra (sĕ·mä′rä). Island in Romblon group, Phil. Is., N of Tablas I.; 8 sq. m.; pop. 4000.

Si·mav′ (sĕ·mäv′). **1** River in NW Turkey in Asia; the main headstream of the Susigirlik; flows W and N.
2 Town on upper Simav river, Kütahya vilayet, 60 m. E of Akhisar; pop. 5853.

Simbirsk. See ULYANOVSK.

Sim′coe (sĭm′kō). **1** County, Ontario, Canada. See *Table* at ONTARIO.
2 Town, ⊗ of Norfolk co., SE Ontario, Canada, 20 m. S of Brantford and ab. 8 m. from the shore of Lake Erie; pop. 7269; fruit canneries textile industries.

Simcoe, Lake. Lake 271 sq. m., SE Ontario, Canada, ab. 40 m. N of Toronto; 30 m. long by 20 m. wide; outlet is Severn river flowing N and W into Georgian Bay, ab. 45 m. Much patronized by vacationists; has many summer colonies on its shores. Barrie and Orillia are chief towns on it.

Si·me′to (sĕ·mä′tō). River, E Sicily; rises W of Mt. Etna, flows E, S, and SE into Mediterranean S of Catania.

Si′meu·loe′ë or **Si′meu·lu′e** (sē′mû·loo′ĕ) or **Si·ma′-lur** (sĕ·mä′loor). Island of Indonesia, in the Indian Ocean off NW coast of Sumatra; ab. 54 m. long by 14 m. wide; 683 sq. m., with adjacent islands 712 sq. m.; pop. 19,302; chief settlement Sinabang, on SE coast. Attached to Atjeh govt. Forest-covered with central ridge; highest point 1860 ft.; surrounded by reefs.

Sim′fer·o′pol (sĭm′fĕr·ô′p′l; *Russ.* syĭm·fyĕ·rô′pŭl·y′). City, ✳ of Crimea Region, S Soviet Russia, Europe, in S part, on Sevastopol-Kharkov R.R.; pop. 142,678; has industrial plants, but chief importance lies in surrounding orchards and vineyards and its fruit and vegetable canneries. In first cent. B.C. a small Scythian town and fortress; settled by Tatars as **Ak Me·chet′** (äk′ mĕ·chĕt′) in 16th cent.; seized and partially destroyed by Russians 1736; became permanently Russian 1784 under its modern name; in World War II held by Germans from Nov. 1941 to Apr. 1944; retaken by Russians Apr. 13, 1944.

Simi. See SYMĒ.

Sim′la (sĭm′là). Town and hill resort, NW India, ✳ of Himachal Pradesh, situated in a small outlying area of Punjab state within Himachal Pradesh, 53 m. NE of Ambala; pop. (including Jutogh cantonment) 18,614; summer ✳ of former British Government of India and ✳ of the former provincial government of Punjab. Connected by railroad with Kalka and Ambala (68 m.); beautifully situated on ridge of Himalayas, at elevations varying from 6600 to 8000 ft. (highest point Mt. Jakko). Has several sanatoria and schools. First English house built in 1819.

Simla Hill States. Formerly a group of Indian states in NE Punjab, NW India, around Simla; 4960 sq. m.; pop. 331,000. Chief states were Bashahr, Jubbal, Keonthal, and Nalagarh.

Sim′me (zĭm′ĕ). River ab. 35 m. long, SW cen. Switzerland; rises in S Bern canton, flows N and NE into Lake of Thun.

Sim′o·ïs (sĭm′ō·ĭs); *mod.* **Dom·brek′** (dûm·brĕk′). Small river near ancient Troy, Asia Minor; tributary of Scamander (mod. Menderes).

Si′mons·town′ (sī′mŭnz·toun′). Town, SW Cape Province, S Republic of So. Africa, on W shore of False Bay 20 m. S of Cape Town; pop. 4748. Founded 1741 by Dutch as naval and military depot; since 1898 under jurisdiction of British admiralty; now headquarters of South African Naval Squadron; a tidal basin, with dockyards, arsenal, naval hospital; strongly fortified, known as "Gibraltar of the South"; British force that captured Cape Town in 1795 disembarked here.

Simplon. Alpine pass and tunnel. See ALPS.

Simp′son (sĭm[p]′s′n). **1** Name of counties in two states of the U.S. See *Tables* at KENTUCKY and MISSISSIPPI.
2 Village, Lackawanna co., Pennsylvania, ab. 18 m. NE of Scranton.
3 See FORT SIMPSON, Canada.
4 Island in Chonos Archipelago, in Pacific Ocean off SW coast of Chile.

Simpson Harbour. Inner, landlocked part of Blanche Bay on NE coast of New Britain I., Bismarck Archipelago, W Pacific Ocean, forming the harbor of Rabaul.

Simpson Peninsula. Part of mainland of NE Keewatin District, Northwest Territories, Canada, ab. 40 m. wide, projecting into Gulf of Boothia; bet. Pelly Bay on W and Committee Bay on E.

Sims′bur′y (sĭmz′bĕr′ĭ; -bēr·ĭ). Town, NW cen. Hartford co., N Connecticut, S of Granby; pop. 10,138; watered by Farmington river; safety-fuse factory; incorporated 1670; first colonial copper coins (Higley coppers) minted here 1737 and 1739; copper obtained from mines at East Granby, then part of Simsbury.

Si·myen′, *or* **Se·mien′, Mountains** (sĭ·myän′). Mountains in N Ethiopia, E Africa; highest Ras Dashan 15,160 ft.

Sin, Wilderness of (sĭn). Arid region along SW coast of Sinai Penin., NE Egypt, on E side of Gulf of Suez; traversed by the Israelites during the Exodus (*Ex.* xvi. 1; xvii. 1).

Si′na (sē′nȧ). River ab. 170 m. long, S cen. India, in SE Maharashtra; flows SE and empties into Bhima river.

Si′nai (sī′nī; sī′nā·ī); *Arab.* **Si′na** (sē′nȧ; -nä). **1** Peninsula ab. 140 m. long, politically in NE Egypt, geographically part of Asia, bet. Gulf of Suez on W and Gulf of 'Aqaba on E at N end of Red Sea; very mountainous, contains plateaus of El Tih and Egma, and at S end Gebel Musa group.
2 Province (frontier administrative division) of Egypt, Sinai Penin. (settled area); inhabited by nomad Arabs; has a few small towns, El 'Arish, El Qantara, and Tor. See *Table* at EGYPT.

Sinai, Mount. Probably a mountain of the Gebel Musa group in S Sinai Penin., but not certainly identified; supposed to be the same as Biblical Mt. Horeb (*Ex.* iii. 1). See Gebel MUSA.

Si·na′ia (sĕ·nä′yä). Town, SE Transylvania, Romania, 21 m. S of Brașov; pop. 3906; castle, former royal residence; monastery founded 1695, all there was to the town until ab. 1850.

Si′na·lo′a (sē′nä·lō′ä). State, W Mexico. See *Table* at MEXICO.

Si′na·lun′ga (sē′nä·lōōng′gä); *formerly* **A·si′na·lun′ga** (ä·sē′nä·lōōng′gä). Commune, Siena prov., Tuscany, cen. Italy, 23 m. ESE of Siena; pop. 10,411.

Sin·cé′ (sĕn·sā′). Town, Bolívar dept., N Colombia; pop. 8287.

Sin′ce·le′jo (sēn′sä·lĕ′hō). Town, Bolívar dept., N Colombia, 80 m. S of Cartagena; pop. 11,014.

Sin′clair's Bay (sĭng′klârz; sĭn′-; sĭn·klârz′). Inlet of North Sea on extreme NE coast of Scotland, N of town of Wick.

Sind (sĭnd). **1** *or* **Sindh** (sĭnd). River 240 m. long, cen. India; rises in Tonk state, flows NE through Gwalior into the Jumna E of Gwalior.
2 Former province of W Pakistan and earlier of Brit. India; 48,136 sq. m.; pop. (1941) 4,535,008; ✱ Karachi; in 1947 became part of Pakistan. Bounded on N by Baluchistan and West Punjab, on E by Rajputana, on S by the Rann of Cutch, on SW by Arabian Sea, and on W by Baluchistan. Khairpur state formed large indentation in NE. Region is generally flat, lying along both banks of the Indus; chief occupation agriculture and rice is chief crop; other exports wheat, cotton, barley, oilseeds. A large area under cultivation is irrigated by Sukkur (*q.v.*) barrage. Chief cities Karachi, great seaport and airport in SW, Hyderabad in S cen. part, and Shikarpur and Sukkur in the N.
History: Important evidences of prehistoric culture in the region; invaded by Alexander 325 B.C.; later part of Ganges empire of Chandragupta. Since beginning of Christian era has often been crossed by invaders, but long remained semi-independent under local dynasties; under Akbar made part of the Delhi empire; conquered by Sir Charles Napier 1842–43 and annexed to British India as N part of Bombay presidency; transferred 1936 and constituted an autonomous province Apr. 1, 1937; became part of Pakistan Aug. 1947.

Sin·dang′an (sĕn·däng′än). Municipality, N Zamboanga prov., Mindanao, Phil. Is., on E shore of **Sindangan Bay** (inlet of Sulu Sea ab. 100 m. NNE of Zamboanga); pop. 33,069.

Sin′dan·gla′ya (sĭn′dän·glä′yä). Village and mountain health resort, W Java, Indonesia, on slope of Mt. Gede at 3500 ft. elevation, SE of Bogor.

Sin′der (sĭn′dĕr). Var. of ZINDER.

Sin′e·pux′ent Inlet (sĭn′ĕ·pŭk′s'nt). Narrow strait leading from Atlantic Ocean through barrier reefs, E Worcester co., SE Maryland.

Si′nes (sē′nĕsh). Town, Estremadura prov., SW Portugal, on coast S of Setúbal; pop. 5610; birthplace of Vasco da Gama.

Sin′feng′ (shĭn′fŭng′). Town, S Kiangsi prov., SE China, ab. 33 m. S of Kanhsien; an American airfield in World War II, taken by the Japanese but recovered July 1945.

Sin′ga (sĭn′gȧ; -gä). Town, cen. Blue Nile prov., E Sudan, on the Blue Nile river.

Sin·ga′lang–Tan·di′kat (sĭng·gä′läng–tän·dē′kät). Volcanic peak 9439 ft. in the Padang Highlands, W Sumatra, Indonesia, just S of Bukittinggi.

Singan. See SIAN.

Sin′ga·pore (sĭng′gȧ·pōr; sĭng′ȧ-; -pōr′). **1** Island off S end of Malay Penin., SE Asia; 27 m. long by 14 m. wide; 217 sq. m.; pop. 557,745, (1941 est.) 769,216; comprises the main part of Singapore state. Separated from the Malay Peninsula by narrow Johore Strait ab. ¾ of a mile wide and from Batam and other islands of the Riouw Archipelago on the S by Singapore Strait; 77 m. N of the equator. Hilly (highest point 520 ft.), well cultivated, and has many villages; crossed by railroad connecting the causeway over Johore Strait with Johore Bahru and towns of Federation of Malaya.
2 Republic in British Commonwealth, S of Malay Penin.; former British crown colony; from 1963 to 1965 a state of Federation of Malaysia, comprising Singapore I. and a few adjacent islets. 225 sq. m.; pop. (1966 est.) 1,864,900; ✱ Singapore. Established as part of the colony of Straits Settlements 1826. Colony formerly included island of Labuan off Borneo (1907–46) and Christmas I. (1900–58) and Cocos Is. (1903–55) in the Indian Ocean.
3 Seaport city on S coast of island, on Singapore Strait, ✱ of Singapore state and chief city of former British Malaya; pop. of municipality 445,719, (1937 est.) 520,164; has excellent harbor (36 sq. m.), fine government and commercial buildings, some factories, and a botanical

garden; carries on extensive trade, esp. in rubber and tin, with all parts of the world.

History: A Malay city of importance (named in Malay from Sanskrit *Singhapura*, "Lion City") in 13th cent.; destroyed by Javanese 1365 and remained a ruin until refounded by Sir Thomas Raffles Jan. 29, 1819; attached to British settlement of Benkoelen until 1823; became property of East India Co. 1824, a part of the new colony of Straits Settlements 1826, and capital of the colony 1836. Developed as a great port and trade center (often called "Crossroads of the Far East") and later as naval base, with docks, powerhouses, repair shops, etc. In World War II violently attacked by Japanese Dec. 1941 and Jan. 1942; captured Feb. 15, 1942 and renamed Shonan; bombed by Allied planes 1944 and 1945; incorporated 1946 in British Crown Colony of Singapore.

Singapore, Strait of. Channel ab. 50 m. long by 10 m. wide bet. Singapore I. on the N and Batam, Bintan, and other islands of the Riouw Archipelago on the S; connects South China Sea with Strait of Malacca.

Sin·ga·ra′dja (sĭng′gä·rä′jä). **1** Division of former Bali and Lombok residency, N part of Bali I., Neth. Indies; 834 sq. m.; pop. 217,899.

2 Town on N Bali I., ✳ of Bali, Indonesia, and chief town on Bali; pop. 12,345; well laid-out town with important market facilities; its harbor is Buleleng.

Sing Bu·ri *or* **Sin·gha·bu·ri** (sĭng·bŏŏ·rē—*sic*). **1** Province, SW cen. Thailand; 314 sq. m.; pop. 98,540.

2 Town, its ✳, on the Chao Phraya and on railroad 40 m. N of Ayudhya.

Sing′en (zĭng′ĕn). Industrial city, Baden-Württemberg, W Germany, 15 m. WNW of Konstanz; pop. 11,470; foodstuffs, iron, steel, aluminum ware.

Sing′ha·sa·ri (sĕng′ä·sä′rĕ) *or* **Sing′o·sa·ri** (sĕng′ô-). A powerful Malay kingdom of E Java in the 13th cent. (1222–92) with capital at Singhasari, now a village just N of Malang; its story is the source of many Javanese legends.

Singh′bhum′ (sĭng′bŏŏm′). District, Chota Nagpur division, S Bihar state, NE Indian Union; 3905 sq. m.; pop. (1941) 1,144,717; ✳ Chaibasa.

Singidunum. See BELGRADE.

Sin·git′ic Gulf (sĭn·jĭt′ĭk) *or* **Gulf of Ha′gi·on O′ros** (ä′yôn ô′rôs). Inlet of Aegean Sea on NE coast of Greece, S of Chalcidice and bet. the peninsulas of Acte and Sithonia.

Sing′ka·rak′ (sĭng′kä·räk′). Mountain lake ab. 12 m. long by 5 m. wide in Padang Highlands, W Sumatra, Indonesia, NE of Padang.

Sing·ka′wang (sĭng·kä′wäng). Town, West Borneo prov., Borneo, Indonesia, on South China Sea coast 70 m. N of Pontianak; pop. 7127.

Sing′kep (sĭng′kĕp). Island, SW Lingga Archipelago, Indonesia; 320 sq. m.; pop. 9376; SW of Lingga I. and separated from E coast of Sumatra by Berhala Strait; tin mines.

Sin′gle·shot′ Mountain (sĭng′g'l·shŏt′). Peak 7700 ft. in Glacier National Park, NW Montana.

Sin′gle·ton (sĭng′g'l·tŭn; -t′n). Town, E New South Wales, SE Australia, on Hunter river 90 m. N of Sydney; pop. 3669; center of fruitgrowing, farming, dairying, and timbering region; known for its dairy products and coal mines. Oldest town of Hunter river valley.

Singora. See SONGKHLA.

Sing Peak (sĭng). Mountain 10,544 ft. in Sierra Nevada, E Madera co., cen. California.

Sing Sing. See OSSINING.

Sin′gu′ (sĭn′gŏŏ′). Town, Myingyan dist., Lower Burma, on left bank of the Irrawaddy N of Yenangyaung; oil fields second to Yenangyaung in importance.

Si′ning′ (shē′nĭng′) *or* **Hsi′ning′** (shē′-). City, ✳ of Tsinghai prov., W cen. China, in E part of province on Sining river 125 m. WNW of Lanchow; pop. ab. 40,000; important trade station on route to Sikang and Lhasa; formerly in Kansu prov.

Sin′kiang′ (shĭn′jĭ·äng′). Province, formerly an outer dependency, W China, in cen. Asia, WNW of the original 18 provinces (see CHINA); 705,769 sq. m.; pop. (1936 est.) 4,360,020 (other estimates vary from 2,500,000 to 3,700,000); ✳ Urumchi; bounded on NE by Outer Mongolia, on E by Kansu prov., on SE by Tsinghai, on S by Tibet, on SW by India, and on W and NW by U.S.S.R. Tableland above 2000 ft. surrounded on three sides by high mountain ranges: on S by Kunlun Mts. (Astin Tagh), on SW by Pamirs, on W by Tien Shan (which extend E as N boundary of Takla Makan desert), on NW by the Ala Tau, and on the N and NE by the Altai Mts.; cen. part is extensive Takla Makan desert, which includes the Tarim basin (in places less than 1000 ft. alt.), watered seasonally by the Tarim river and its branches, the Yarkand, Khotan, etc.; in the S are other desert streams, the Keriya, Cherchen, etc.; in the N the headstreams of the Irtysh. Has many salt lakes, esp. Turfan depression (below sea level) and Bagrach Kol in center, Lop Nor in SE, and Ebi Nor in NW. Inhabitants include various peoples speaking the Turkic languages and mostly Mohammedan in religion. Some agriculture practiced along the rivers; wool, cotton, and silk raised and some jade and gold mined. Politically W and cen. parts correspond to Chinese, or Eastern, Turkistan; Dzungaria and Chuguchak are regions in N. Chief towns Urumchi (Tihwa), Yarkand, Kashgar, Khotan, Kuldja, Aqsu, and Qomul. See *Map* at CHINA.

History: Possibly the earliest home of the human race; inhabited since earliest times by nomad tribes. Important in Chinese history as the region traversed by the "Silk Road" by which China traded with the West. Controlled by Uigurs for centuries; later entered by Mongolians who fought for it against Chinese, Tibetans, and Mohammedans; conquered by Genghis Khan in 13th cent. and under his successor became E half of khanate of Jagatai. Came under Chinese control (vaguely 16th cent., definitely 1872); after 1917 under Russian influence; established as a Chinese province 1942; revolt and civil war 1944–45; granted autonomy 1946.

Sink′ing Spring (sĭngk′ĭng). Borough, Berks co., SE Pennsylvania, 6 m. W of Reading; pop. 2244; founded 1793; manufactures textiles, foundry products.

Sin-le-No′ble (săⁿl′nô′bl′). Commune, Nord dept., N France, 2 m. ESE of Rouen; pop. (1931) 12,133; coal mines; iron foundries; sugar refineries; textile mills.

Sin′min′ (shĭn′mĭn′) *or* **Hsin′min′** (shĭn′-). Town, SW Liaoning prov., S Manchuria, 35 m. W of Mukden; pop. 32,995; treaty port W of the Liao on the Mukden-Tientsin railroad.

Sin′nai (sēn′nī). Commune, Cagliari prov., S Sardinia, 7 m. NNE of Cagliari; pop. 10,412.

Sin′na·ma′ry *or* **Sin′na·ma′rie** (sē′nä′mä′rē′). **1** River ab. 100 m. long, N French Guiana; flows N into Atlantic Ocean 70 m. NW of Cayenne.

2 Coastal town, N French Guiana; pop. 1451.

Sin·neh′ (sĭn·nä′) *or* **Sa′nan·daj′** (sä′nän·däj′). Town, NW Iran, on highway to Mosul 100 m. NNW of Hamadan; ✳ of former province of Ardelan; pop. ab. 32,000; on border of Iranian Kurdistan.

Sin′ni (sēn′nē) *or* **Sin′no** (sēn′nô); *anc.* **Si′ris** (sī′rĭs). River ab. 60 m. long, S Italy; flows E into Gulf of Taranto 19 m. SW of the mouth of Bradano river.

Sin·nu′ris (sĭn·nŏŏ′rĭs). Town, Faiyûm prov., Upper Egypt, SE of Birket Qârûn; pop. ab. 19,000.

Si′no (sē′nô) *or* **Green′ville** (grēn′vĭl). Coastal town, SE Liberia, W Africa, 105 m. NW of Cape Palmas.

Si·no′bong, Mount (sĭ·nô′bông); *or* **Mount Lo′ser** (lô′sĕr). Mountain 11,092 ft. at NW end of Sumatra, Indonesia, near coast.

Si·nop′ (sē·nôp′). **1** Vilayet, N Turkey in Asia; 2221 sq. m.; pop. 185,613.

2 *anc.* **Si·no′pe** (sĭ·nō′pē). Seaport, its ✳, on narrow part of a peninsula extending into the Black Sea; pop.

4896; best harbor on Turkish coast bet. Bosporus and Batum. Has some trade and contains relics of the ancient Sinope, said to have been founded early in the 8th cent. B.C.; destroyed by Cimmerians, it was restored by colonists from Miletus; became leading Greek settlement on the Euxine; captured by Pharnaces I 183 B.C. and made capital of Pontic kingdom; in Mithridatic Wars captured 70 B.C. by Lucullus; in Middle Ages part of empire of Trebizond and was taken by Turks in 1461. Birthplace of Diogenes and of Mithridates the Great.

Sin′o·pah Mountain (sĭn′ō·pä). Peak 8435 ft. in Glacier National Park, NW Montana.

Sinope. See SINOP.

Sin′qu (sĭng′kōō). River, Basutoland, S Africa; a headstream of the Orange river.

Sint. See SAINT.

Sint A′mands·berg (sĭnt á′mänts·bĕrK); *formerly* **Mont–Saint–A′mand′** (môN′săN′-tá′män′). Commune, East Flanders prov., NW cen. Belgium; pop. 18,976; NE suburb of Gent.

Sin′tang (sĭn′täng). Town, West Borneo prov., W Borneo, Indonesia, on left bank of Kapuas river 200 m. up from Pontianak; pop. 4474.

Sint–E·loo′is–Vij′ve (sĭnt-á·lō′ĭs-vĭ′vĕ); *Fr.* **Vive–Saint–É′loi′** (vēv′săN′-tá′!wà′); *also* **Saint–Éloi.** Village 3 m. S of Ieper (Ypres), West Flanders prov., NW Belgium; in World War I scene of heavy engagements 1915, 1916, 1918.

Sint–Gillis. = SAINT-GILLES.

Sint–Joost–Ten–Noode. = SAINT-JOSSE-TEN-NOODE.

Sint–Ka′te·lij′ne–Wa′ver (sĭnt-kà′tĕ-lĭ′nĕ-và′vĕr); *Fr.* **Wa′vre–Sainte–Ca′the·rine′** (và′vrĕ-săNt′kà′trēn′). Commune, Antwerp prov., Belgium; pop. 8543.

Sint–Lambrechts–Woluwe. See WOLUWE-SAINT-LAMBERT.

Sint Maarten. See SAINT MARTIN.

Sint Ni′co·laas (sĭnt nē′kŏ·làs). Village, SE coast of Aruba I., Neth. West Indies; near one of largest oil refineries in the world.

Sint Nicolaas Punt. See SAINT NICHOLAS POINT.

Sint–Ni′klaas (sĭnt·nē′klàs); *Fr.* **Saint–Ni′co′las′** (săN′nē′kŏ′lä′). Commercial and manufacturing commune, East Flanders prov., NW cen. Belgium, 14 m. ENE of Gent; pop. (1938 est.) 41,933.

Sin′ton (sĭn′t'n; -tŭn). Town, ⊗ of San Patricio co., S Texas, 20 m. N of Corpus Christi; pop. 6008; in farming and stock-raising section; cotton gins; gas and oil wells.

Sin′tra (sēN′trà); *older* **Cin′tra** (sēN′trà). Commune, Lisboa dist., W Portugal, 12 m. NW of Lisbon; pop. 7979; wealthy resort; Moorish castle, royal palace, convent; marble quarries; convention signed here 1808 by French, English, and Portuguese military leaders.

Sint–Trui′den (sĭnt-troi′dĕ[n]); *Fr.* **Saint–Trond** (săN′trôN′). Manufacturing commune, Limburg prov., NE Belgium, 20 m. NW of Liège; pop. 16,480; captured by the Germans 1914.

Si′nus (sī′nŭs). Latin for "gulf, bay"; in classical names, as Sinus Saronicus, Sinus Thermaicus, see the second element of its Anglicized form.

Sinus Aelaniticus. See Gulf of 'AQABA.

Sinus Arabicus. See RED SEA.

Sinus Cantabricus. See Bay of BISCAY.

Sinus Gallicus. See Gulf of LIONS.

Sinus Ligusticus. See LIGURIAN SEA.

Sinus Pagasaeus. See Gulf of VOLOS.

Sin′yang′ (shĭn′yäng′). Town, S Honan, E cen. China, S of Hwai river on Peiping-Hankow R.R.; center of fighting in Chinese-Japanese War, esp. in Jan. 1943.

Si′o (sē′ō). Village, E North-East New Guinea, on N coast of Huon Penin.; taken by Allies Feb. 13, 1944.

Sion. See ZION.

Sion (syôN); *Ger.* **Sit′ten** (zĭt′ĕn); *anc.* **Se·du′num** (sĕ·dū′nŭm). Commune, ✻ of Valais canton, SW cen. Switzerland, 50 m. S of Bern; pop. (1930) 7944; tourist resort; produces fruit and wine; trades in cattle; pil-

grimage church of 9th-13th cents., Gothic cathedral (with 9th-cent. clock tower), 17th-cent. town hall. Made episcopal see in 6th cent.

Sioux (sōō). Name of counties in three states of the U.S. See *Tables* at IOWA, NEBRASKA, NORTH DAKOTA.

Sioux Center. Town, Sioux co., NW Iowa, 40 m. N of Sioux City; pop. 2275.

Sioux City. City, ⊗ of Woodbury co., W Iowa, on Missouri river at confluence of Big Sioux and Floyd rivers; pop. 89,159; railroad center and river port; trade and industrial center in agricultural section; manufactures farm implements and machinery, dairy products, and flour; packing plants, sandstone quarries. Morningside Coll. (1894; coed.); Briar Cliff Coll. (1930; women).

Sioux Falls. City, ⊗ of Minnehaha co., SE South Dakota, on Big Sioux river; pop. 65,466; largest city in the state; commercial and industrial center for agricultural and stock-raising territory, and distributing point for farm machinery, trucks, automobiles; meat-packing and food-processing plants; manufactures biscuits and crackers, flour, brooms, millwork; quartzite quarries. Augustana Coll. (1860; coed.); Sioux Falls Coll. (1883; coed.). Indian mounds nearby. First settled 1856; became military post 1865; incorp. as village 1877, as city 1883.

Sioux Lookout. Town, Kenora dist., W Ontario, Canada, 120 m. E of Kenora; pop. 2364; railroad divisional point and gateway for prospectors to an extensive mining region to the N and NW; center of lake region and an air patrol base.

Si·par′i·a (sĭ·pär′ĭ·à). Town, SW Trinidad, West Indies Federation, SE of Pitch Lake.

Siph′nos (sĭf′nŏs); *Mod. Gr.* **Síph′nos** (sēf′nŏs). **1** Greek island in W Cyclades, Aegean Sea, SE of Seriphos and NE of Melos; in Cyclades dept., Greece; 29 sq. m.; pop. ab. 4000; chief town Artemon (pop. 1308). Noted for its gold and silver mines.
2 Town on E coast of island; pop. ab. 1000.

Šipka Pass. See SHIPKA PASS.

Si′ple, Mount (sī′p'l); *formerly* **Mount Ruth Siple** (rōōth). Mountain ab. 15,000 ft. on coast of Marie Byrd Land, Antarctica, extending into the South Pacific at ab. 73°15′S and 123°W bet. Wrigley Gulf and Amundsen Sea; discovered 1940.

Si·po′ra (sē·pō′rà). Central island ab. 27 m. long by 12 m. wide of Mentawai Is. off W coast of Sumatra, Indonesia; pop. 3892.

Sip·par′ (sĭ·pär′). City of ancient Babylonia on the right bank of the Euphrates river ab. 16 m. SSW of Baghdad. In the early period a center of the worship of the Sumerian sun-god, Shamash. Excavations, begun in 1882, have uncovered remains of a great temple and many thousands of religious and historic clay tablets. Sargon's capital in 8th cent. B.C.

Sip′sey (sĭp′sĭ). Navigable river ab. 150 m. long, NW Alabama; rises in NW Alabama, flows S into the Tombigbee river in S Pickens co., W cen. Alabama.

Si′quia (sē′kyä). River 95 m. long, S cen. Nicaragua, flowing E into the Escondido river.

Si′qui·jor′ (sē′kē·hôr′). **1** Island, one of the Visayan Is. and a subprovince of Negros Oriental, Phil. Is.; 130 sq. m.; pop. 59,507; chief municipality Siquijor. In NW part of Mindanao Sea, SE of Negros, S of Cebu, and SW of Bohol; ab. 12 m. from N to S and 17 m. E to W. Hilly (highest point 1394 ft.), fertile, and most densely populated island of the archipelago. Has several good harbors. Chief products copra, rice, corn, abacá, and tobacco. Chief towns Siquijor, Lazi, and Maria. Until 1854 formed with Bohol a dependency of Cebu; from that time until after American occupation a subprovince of Bohol; later transferred to Negros Oriental.
2 Municipality, NW coast of Siquijor I., 16 m. SE of Dumaguete; pop. 15,200; chief town of the island.

Si′ra (sē′rä). Peak 10,500 ft. in Huánuco dept., cen. Peru.

Si·ra·cu′sa (sē·rä·kōō′zä). **1** Province of Italy, in SE Sicily. See *Table* at ITALY.
2 See SYRACUSE city, Sicily.

Si·raj′ganj (sĭ·räj′gŭnj). Town, Pabna dist., East Bengal, Pakistan, on Jamuna river 155 m. NNE of Calcutta; pop. 32,467; river port, with large trade, especially in gunny or jute cloth. Founded early in 19th cent.

Sir Darya. See SYR DARYA.

Sir Don′ald, Mount (sûr dŏn″ld). Peak 10,808 ft. in Selkirk Mts., SE Brit. Columbia, Canada.

Sir Edward Pel·lew′ Group (pĕ·lū′; pĕl′ū). Island group in SW part of Gulf of Carpentaria, Australia; belongs to Northern Territory.

Si·ret′ (sē·rĕt′); *Ger.* **Se′reth** (zā′rĕt). **1** River ab. 270 m. long, NE Romania; rises in the Carpathian Mts. in Bucovina, flows SSE into Danube river above Galaţi; chief tributary the Bistriţa.
2 Town, N Romania, in Bucovina region; pop. 10,025.

Sirguja. See SURGUJA.

Sir·han′, Wa′di (wä′dĭ sĭr·hän′). Region, NW Saudi Arabia; extends NW to SE just E of Jordan in Syrian Desert; altitude ab. 1850 ft.; contains many pools of brackish water.

Si′rik, Cape (sē′rĭk); *Malay* **Tan′jong Si′rik** (tän′-jŏng sē′rĭk). Cape on SW coast of Sarawak, Borneo, on an island in delta of Rajang river, projecting into South China Sea.

Siris. 1 See SERRAI city, Greece.
2 See SINNI river, Italy.

Sirmio, Sirmione. See SERMIONE.

Sir′mi·um (sûr′mĭ·ŭm). Important city in ancient Pannonia; its site is on the Sava river near modern Mitrovica (Sremska Mitrovica), NE Yugoslavia.

Sir·mur′ or **Sir·moor′** (sĭr·mōōr′); *also* **Na′han** (nä′-hȧn). Former Indian state, E Punjab States, East Punjab, NW Indian Union; 1091 sq. m.; ✳ Nahan.

Si·ro′hi (sĭ·rō′hĭ). **1** Former Indian state, Western Rajputana States, SW Rajputana, NW Indian Union; 1988 sq. m.; pop. (1941) 233,879; region contains Mount Abu (*q.v.*); hilly and covered with dense jungle.
2 Town, its ✳, 53 m. NW of Udaipur; pop. 7463.

Sir Sanford or **Sir Sandford** (sēr săn′fērd), **Mount.** Peak 11,590 ft., highest in Selkirk Mts., SE Brit. Columbia, Canada; ab. 50 m. N of Revelstoke.

Sirs el Lai·ya′na (sĭrs′ ăl lī·yä′nȧ; -nä). Town, Minûfîya prov., Lower Egypt; pop. ab. 17,000.

Sir′te (sēr′tä). Town on coastal road, N Libya, N Africa, SE of Misurata on S shore of the Gulf of Sidra; very poor harbor; starting point of many caravan routes. In World War II taken by British Dec. 26, 1942.

Si′sak (sē′säk) or **Si′sek** (-sĕk); *Hung.* **Szi′szek** (sĭ′sĕk); *anc.* **Si′sci·a** (sĭsh′ĭ·ȧ). Town, N Yugoslavia, on the Sava river 30 m. SE of Zagreb; pop. 10,910; ancient town important in the Roman Empire; during 3d cent. had chief mint and treasury; Turks defeated here 1593 and 1641; part of Austria-Hungary 1641–1918.

Sisapon. See ALMADÉN.

Sis′ki·you (sĭs′kĭ·yōō). County in California. See *Table* at CALIFORNIA.

Siskiyou Peak. Mountain 7147 ft. in S Jackson co., SW Oregon, in **Siskiyou Mountains**, range in SW Oregon and N California, highest point Mt. Ashland 7530 ft. in S Jackson co., Oregon. See KLAMATH MOUNTAINS.

Sis′op·hon (sĭs′ŭp·hŏn). Town, W Cambodia, SW Indochina, N of Battambang and near Siamese border; in last few centuries has been several times transferred bet. Siam and Cambodia.

Sis′sek (zĭs′ĕk). German form of SISAK.

Sis′se·ton (sĭs′ĕ·t'n; -tŭn). City, ⊗ of Roberts co., NE corner of South Dakota, 53 m. N of Watertown; pop. 3218; agricultural trading center.

Sis′sonne′ (sē·sôn′). Town, Aisne dept., N France; pop. 1409; military camps; German outpost during World War I until retaken Oct. 1918.

Sis·tan′ (sēs·tän′). = SEISTAN.

Sis′ters·ville (sĭs′tērz·vĭl; *Sou. also* -v′l). City, Tyler co., NW West Virginia, on Ohio river 28 m. SSW of Moundsville; pop. 2331; oil wells and refineries.

Sistova. See SVIŠTOV.

Si′ta·bal′di (sē′tä·bŭl′dē). Fort and suburb, city of Nagpur, Indian Union.

Si·ta′mau (sē·tä′mou). Former Indian state, Malwa, NW Central India, India; 191 sq. m.; pop. (1941) 33,461.

Si′ta·pur′ (sē′tä·pōōr′). Town, Lucknow division, cen. Uttar Pradesh, N Indian Union, 50 m. NNW of Lucknow; pop. 27,820; has good grain trade; site of former military cantonment.

Si·tho′nia (sĭ·thōn′yȧ; -thō′nĭ·ȧ); *Mod. Gr.* **Lon′gos** (lông′gôs). Middle peninsula of Chalcidice, Macedonia, NE Greece, ab. 31 m. long, bet. Singitic Gulf on E and Toronaic Gulf on W; highest point ab. 2200 ft. In early times inhabited by Thracians.

Sit′ka (sĭt′kȧ). Town on W coast of Baranof I., SE Alaska, 932 statute m. N of Seattle, Washington; pop. 3237. Formerly chief commercial center on Pacific coast of North America; founded as New Archangel by Aleksandr Baranov in 1799–1800; chief town of Russian America and continued as capital under American flag 1867–1906. Now has island trade, a coaling station, several schools, and U.S. naval base.

Sitka National Monument. See UNITED STATES, *National Monuments.*

Si′toe·bon′do (sē′tōō·bȯn′dō) or **Si′tu·bon′do.** Town, East Java prov., Indonesia, on railroad near coast of SE Madura Strait; pop. 15,238.

Si′tra (sĭ′trō). Small island, Bahrein Is., Persian Gulf, off NW coast of Bahrein I.

Sitsang. See TIBET.

Sit′tang (sĭt′täng). River 350 m. long, E cen. Burma; flows S into the head of the Gulf of Martaban. Toungoo and Pyinmana are on its banks. Scene of severe fighting in early part of 1942 and in May 1945.

Sit′tard (sĭt′ärt). Commune, Limburg prov., SE Netherlands, 13 m. NNE of Maastricht on German border; pop. 14,566.

Sit′taung (sĭt′toung). Town, Upper Chindwin dist., W Upper Burma, on right bank of Chindwin river near Manipur border.

Sitten. See SION.

Sit′ting·bourne and Mil′ton (sĭt′ĭng·bȯrn, -bȯrn; mĭl′t'n, -tŭn). Urban district, Kent, SE England, on Milton Creek 39 m. ESE of London; pop. 21,904; situated on the old route followed by pilgrims on their way to Canterbury; brick and cement works.

Si·u′slaw (sī·ū′slô). River ab. 60 m. long, W Oregon; rises in cen. Lane co., flows W into Pacific Ocean, W Lane co.; navigable 10 to 30 m.

Si·ut′ (sĭ·ōōt′). Var. of ASYÛT.

Si·vas′ (sĭ·väs′). **1** Vilayet, E cen. Turkey in Asia; 10,322 sq. m.; pop. 432,996.
2 *anc.* **Se·bas′te** (sē·băs′tē) or **Se·bas′ti·a** (sē·băs′-chĭ·ȧ; -tĭ·ȧ) or **Ca·bi′ra** (kȧ·bī′rȧ). City, its ✳, on right bank of upper Kızıl Irmak 225 m. E of Ankara; pop. (1940) 41,247. Has some manufactories and important trade. Under Diocletian and Byzantine emperors Sebastia was one of chief cities of Asia Minor; came under the Seljuks 1071 and captured by Tamerlane 1400; later restored as Ottoman town.

Si′va·sa·mu′dram (sē′vȧ·sȧ·mōō′drȧm). See CAUVERY.

Si·vash′ (sĭ·väsh′; *Russ.* syĭ·vȧsh′), or **Pu′trid Sea** (pū′trĭd). Salt lagoons and marshes in N and NE Crimea Penin., S Soviet Russia, Europe; enclosed by the Arabat Penin. Contains valuable mineral salts.

Si′ve·rek (sē′vĕ·rĕk′). Town, Urfa vilayet, SE Turkey in Asia, ab. 50 m. NE of Urfa; pop. 14,942.

Siv′ri·hi·sar′ (sēv′rĭ·hĭ·sär′). Town, Eskişehir vilayet, W cen. Turkey in Asia, 58 m. ESE of Eskişehir; pop. 6121; important as fortress town on Byzantine military road to the east.

Si'wa (sē'wȧ; -wä); *anc.* **Am·mo'ni·um** (ȧ·mō'nĭ·ŭm).
1 Oasis in NW Egypt, Western Desert prov., N of Libyan Desert; ancient seat of the oracle of Jupiter Ammon; pop. ab. 5000.
2 Town, in S part of the oasis.
Si·wa'lik Range *or* **Hills** (sĭ·wä'lĭk). Range of foothills 2000 to 3500 ft. in N India, parallel with the main Himalayan system and extending SE from N East Punjab into the United Provinces, Indian Union; remarkable for its geological formation, containing a wealth of paleontological remains.
Si–wu. See SĪ HŪ.
Six Counties. The six counties (Antrim, Armagh, Down, Fermanagh, Londonderry, and Tyrone) of the former Irish province of Ulster, now Northern Ireland.
Siyang. See SIANG tributary of the Si, S China.
Si'yeh, Mount (sī'yě). Peak 10,004 ft. in Glacier National Park, NW Montana.
Sjæl'land (shěl'làn); *Eng.* **Zea'land** (zē'lănd).
1 Group of islands in E Denmark territorial waters; 2901 sq. m.; pop. (1925) 1,340,061; includes Sjælland, Möen, Samsö, Amager, Saltholm, and smaller islands.
2 Largest of the islands of Denmark, and site of the capital and chief city, Copenhagen; bounded on the N and NW by the Kattegat, on the W by the Great Belt, on the S by narrow channels separating it from smaller islands, and on the E by the Baltic Sea and Öresund; 2709 sq. m.; pop. (1925) 1,203,713.
Ska'dar (skä'där). Serbian for SCUTARI.
Ska'ga Fjord (skä'gä). Inlet of the Arctic Ocean on N coast of Iceland.
Ska'gen (skå'gěn). Town, Hjörring co., NE Jutland Penin., Denmark, at the N extremity of Jutland on the Skaw; pop. (1945) 6446.
Skagen, Cape. See the SKAW.
Skag'er·rak *or* **Skag'e·rak** (skăg'ēr·ăk; skäg'ě·räk). Broad arm of the E cen. North Sea, extending bet. Norway on the N and Denmark on the S, and connecting with the Kattegat on the E; ab. 150 m. long and 80 m. wide.
Skag'it (skăj'ĭt). **1** River ab. 200 m. long, NW Washington; rises in Brit. Columbia, flows S across Washington border and W into Skagit Bay, SW Skagit co.
2 County in Washington. See *Table* at WASHINGTON.
Skagit Bay. Inlet on boundary bet. Skagit and Snohomish cos., NW Washington.
Skag'way (skăg'wā). City, SE Alaska, at head of Lynn Canal, 80 m. N of Juneau; pop. 659; terminal of railroad N to Whitehorse in Yukon Territory, Canada. Founded 1897 and a boom town in the Klondike gold rush 1897–98 as starting point over White Pass to the Yukon gold fields.
Ska·ma'nia (skȧ·măn'yȧ; -mä'nĭ·ȧ). County in Washington. See *Table* at WASHINGTON.
Skå'ne (skō'ně) *or* **Sca'nia** (skän'yȧ; skä'nĭ·ȧ). S section of Sweden, comprising provinces of Kristianstad and Malmöhus; land area 4210 sq. m.; pop. 797,743.
Skan'e·at'e·les (skăn'ē·ăt'lĕs; *locally usu.* skĭn'ē-). Village and resort, Onondaga co., cen. New York, at N end of Skaneateles Lake 8 m. E of Auburn; pop. 2921; on site of Indian village; settled by whites c. 1792; headquarters for abolitionist activities and station on Underground Railroad before Civil War.
Skaneateles Lake. Lake in cen. New York, chiefly in Onondaga and Cayuga cos.; one of the Finger Lakes (*q.v.*); ab. 16 m. long and 1½ m. wide; outlet from N end flows into Seneca river.
Skap'tar (skăp'tär; *Icelandic* -tä). Volcanic mountain in SE Iceland, N of Öraefajökull; violent eruption in 1783.
Ska'ra·borg' (skä'rä·bôr'y'). Province of Sweden. See *Table* at SWEDEN.
Skar'du (skär'dōō; *native* skŭr'-) *or* **Skar'do** (skär'dō). Town with strong fort, on left bank of the Indus above the great gorge, N cen. Kashmir state, N India, 95 m. NNE of Srinagar; pop. ab. 2000; in the Himalayas at

elevation of ab. 7500 ft.; chief town of Baltistan.
Skaw, the (skô); *or* **Cape Ska'gen** (skå'gěn). Cape on N extremity of Jutland Penin., Denmark; extends into the Skagerrak.
Skee'na (skē'nȧ). River 335 m. long, W Brit. Columbia, Canada; rises in N cen. Brit. Columbia, flows S and then W into Hecate Strait; in its lower course forms a wide inlet.
Skeg'ness' (skěg'něs'). Urban district, Parts of Lindsey, Lincolnshire, E England, on North Sea 48 m. SSE of Hull; pop. 12,554; popular resort.
Skel·lef'te (shě·lěf'tě). River 324 m. long in Västerbotten and Norrbotten provs., N Sweden; flows SE into the Gulf of Bothnia.
Skel·lef'te·å' (shě·lěf'tě·ō'). Coastal town, Västerbotten prov., N Sweden, at the mouth of Skellefte river; pop. 11,492.
Skel'ligs (skěl'ĭgz). Three small islands off Bolus Head, co. Kerry, SW coast of Ireland: Great Skellig, Little Skellig, and Lemon Rock. Great Skellig has 2 lighthouses and the ruins of a monastery, said to be founded by St. Finan, once a place of pilgrimage.
Skel'mers·dale (skěl'měrz·dāl). Urban district, Lancashire, NW England, 13 m. NE of Liverpool; pop. 6211.
Skel'ton and Brot'ton (skěl't'n [-tŭn], brŏt'n). Urban district, North Riding, Yorkshire, N England; pop. 13,655; ironstone quarries.
Sker'ries (skěr'ĭz). Group of islets in S Irish Sea, off NW extremity of the island of Anglesey, Wales; lighthouse.
Sker'row, Loch (lŏk skěr'ō). Lake in Kirkcudbright co., S Scotland; noted for beautiful scenery.
Ski·a·thos (skī'ȧ·thŏs); *Mod. Gr.* **Ski'a·thos** (skyē'ȧ·thôs). An island in the Northern Sporades (see SPORADES); 16 sq. m.; pop. 3213; in W end of the group, nearest the mainland; belongs to Euboea dept., Greece.
Ski'a·took' (skī'(ȧ·)tōōk'; -tōōk'). Town, Tulsa and Osage cos., NE Oklahoma, N of Tulsa; pop. 2503.
Skid'daw (skĭd'ô; skĭ·dô'). Mountain 3054 ft. in cen. Cumberland, NW England, in the Lake District E of Bassenthwaite Lake.
Skid'e·gate Inlet (skĭd'ě·gĭt; -gāt). Channel separating Graham I. from Moresby I. in the Queen Charlotte Is., off W Brit. Columbia, Canada.
Ski'en (shä'ěn; shē'ěn). City, ⊗ of Telemark co., S Norway; pop. 15,596; trade center in iron and copper mining section; exports ores, lumber, and paper.
Ski'ens·elv' (shä'ěns·ělv'; shē'-). River ab. 150 m. long in S Norway; flows S into Skagerrak.
Skier'nie·wi'ce (skyěr'nyě·vē'tsě). Industrial commune, Łódź dept., cen. Poland, 42 m. SW of Warsaw; pop. (1938–39 est.) 21,214; railroad junction point. Scene of meeting bet. emperors of Germany, Austria, and Russia 1844.
Ski'hist, Mount (?skē'hĭst). Peak 9660 ft. in S Brit. Columbia, Canada, W of Fraser river.
Skip'ton (skĭp'tŭn). Urban district, West Riding, Yorkshire, N England; pop. 13,210; woolen and cotton manufacture; quarrying.
Ski've (skē'vě). Town, Viborg co., N cen. Jutland Penin., Denmark, on inlet of Lim Fjord 16 m. WNW of Vyborg; pop. (1945) 12,369.
Skjál'fan'da (skyoul'vän'dä). River in NE cen. Iceland; flows N into Arctic Ocean W of Húsavík.
Skjeg'ge·dals·foss' (shěg'ě·däls·fôs'). Waterfall 525 ft. in a small stream E of Hardanger Fjord, Hordaland co., SW Norway.
Skjer'ne (skyǎr'ně). River in W cen. Jutland Penin., Denmark; flows W into Ringköbing Fjord.
Skobelev. See FERGANA city.
Sko'kie (skō'kǐ); *formerly* **Niles Center** (nīlz). Village, Cook co., NE Illinois, 15 m. N of Chicago; pop. 59,364.
Sko·ko'mish (skō·kō'mĭsh). River ab. 35 m. long, W Washington, rises in Mason co., flows SW through Lake Cushman into Hood Canal. See CUSHMAN DAM.
Sko'mer (skō'měr) *or* **Skok'holm** (skŏk'hŏm). Islands

in St. George's Channel off SW coast of Wales, S of entrance to St. Bride's Bay.

Skop'e·los (skŏp'ĕ·lŏs); *Mod. Gr.* **Skó'pe·los** (skŏ'pâ-lŏs). **1** An island in the Northern Sporades (see SPORADES); 47 sq. m.; pop. 6124; second largest island in the group; belongs to Euboea dept., Greece. **2** Town on E coast of Skopelos I.; pop. 4075.

Skop'lje (skŏp'lyĕ) *or* **Skop'je** (skŏp'yĕ); *Turk.* **Üs·küb'** (üs·küb'); *anc.* **Scu'pi** (skū'pī). City, Macedonia, S Yugoslavia, on Vardar river 200 m. SSE of Belgrade; pop. 171,893; commercial and industrial center; cathedral; university; museum; an ancient capital of Serbia and since 1945 chief town of new federated republic of Macedonia. In World War II taken by Germans in Apr. 1941 and made a military base.

Sköv'de (shûv'dĕ). Town, Skaraborg prov., S Sweden, bet. lakes Vättern and Vänern; pop. 15,736; military post.

Sko·vo·ro'di·no (skŭ·vŭ·rô'dyĭ·nŭ); *formerly* **Rukh'lo·vo** (rōōk'lŭ·vŭ). Town, E Chita Region, Soviet Russia, Asia, on Trans-Siberian R.R.; railroad and highway junction point, connects with Amur river, 35 m. S.

Skow·he'gan (skou·hē'găn). Town, ⊗ of Somerset co., W Maine, on Kennebec river 15 m. NNW of Waterville; pop. 7661; textiles, paper, wooden products.

Skra'din (skrä'dēn); *Ital.* **Scar·do'na** (skär·dō'nä). Commune, Croatia federated republic, Yugoslavia, 35 m. NW of Split; pop. 13,219; town is small port several miles from the Adriatic on the Kerka (*q.v.*).

Skunk (skŭngk). River 264 m. long, SE Iowa; rises in Hamilton co., N cen. Iowa, flows SE into the Mississippi below Burlington, Des Moines co., SE Iowa.

Skutari. Var. of SCUTARI.

Skye (skī). Island of the Inner Hebrides off NW coast of Scotland; 48½ m. long; pop. 8265; administratively a part of Inverness co.; sheep and (West Highland) cattle raising; fisheries; marble quarrying, whisky distilling; noted for wild, mountainous scenery.

Sky'kje·fos' (shü'kĕ·fôs'). Waterfall 650 ft., Hordaland, SW Norway, near inner Hardanger Fjord.

Sky·ko'mish (skī·kō'mĭsh). River, NW cen. Washington; rises in Cascade Mts., flows W through S Snohomish co. and joins Snoqualmie river to form the Snohomish river.

Sky'light' Mountain (skī'līt'). Peak 4920 ft. in the Adirondack Mts., Essex co., NE New York.

Sky'ring Water (skī'rĭng'). Large salt-water lake on the South American mainland in extreme S Chile, NW of Otway Water.

Sky'ros (skī'rŏs), *also sp.* **Ský'ros** (skyē'rôs), *and* **Scy'ros** (sī'rŏs). **1** An island in the Northern Sporades (see SPORADES), in N cen. Aegean Sea E of Euboea; 79 sq. m.; pop. 3179; largest island in the group; belongs to Euboea dept., Greece. Important in the legends of Greece, esp. those connected with Theseus. Occupied by Athenians 469 B.C. Here the English poet, Rupert Brooke, died and was buried (1915). **2** Town on Skyros I., on NE coast; pop. 2878.

Sla. See SALÉ.

Sla'gel·se (slâ'[g]ĕl·sĕ). Town, Sorö co., SW Sjælland, Denmark; pop. (1945) 18,073.

Slaith'waite (slāth'wāt; slāth'-; *locally also* slŏ'ĭt, slou'ĭt). Former urban district, West Riding, Yorkshire, N England; pop. (1931) 5183.

Sla'met (slä'mĕt). Peak 11,247 ft. in W cen. Java I., Indonesia.

Sla'ney (slā'nĭ). River ab. 60 m. long in SE Ireland; rises in co. Wicklow, flows S through co. Wexford into Wexford Harbour; navigable as far as Enniscorthy.

Slan·ka'men (släng·kä'mĕn); *Hung.* **Sza'lán·ke'mén** (sŏ'läng·kă'mān). Commune, Voivodina autonomous prov., NE Yugoslavia, on the Danube opp. the mouth of the Tisza; pop. (1921) 4389; scene of battle Aug. 19, 1691 in which Louis William I, Margrave of Baden-Baden, defeated the Turks.

Śląsk (shlônsk). **1** *Eng.* **Silesia.** Former Polish department, in SW part; 1969 sq. m.; pop. 1,298,352; ✱ Katowice; in reorganization after 1945 enlarged and divided into two departments, now called Śląsk and Wrocław. **2** New department, SW Poland, W of Kraków dept.; ✱ Katowice; borders on Czechoslovakia; formed after 1945 (*at first called* **Śląsk Dą·brow'ski** [shlônsk dônm·brôf'-skĕ]) from former Polish Silesia and former German Upper Silesia. **3** See SILESIA.

Śląsk Dolny. See WROCŁAW dept.

Slate Mountain (slāt). Peak 8209 ft. in cen. Coconino co., N cen. Arizona.

Sla'ter (slā'tēr). City, Saline co., W cen. Missouri, 36 m. N of Sedalia; pop. 2767.

Sla'ters·ville (slā'tērz·vĭl). Village, Providence co., N Rhode Island, ab. 4 m. W of Woonsocket; pop. (est.) 1000; seat of government for North Smithfield; manufactures cotton textiles.

Sla'ti·na (slä'tĕ·nä). City, Muntenia region, S Romania, on Olt river; pop. 11,010; on railroad 30 m. E of Craiova.

Slat'ing·ton (slāt'ĭng·tŭn) Borough, Lehigh co., E Pennsylvania, on Lehigh river 13 m. NNW of Allentown; pop. 4316; settled 1737; slate quarries.

Sla'ton (slā't'n). City, Lubbock co., NW Texas, 18 m. SE of Lubbock; pop. 6568; railroad division point; in stock-raising section; cotton gins and compresses.

Slave, *also* **Great Slave** (slāv). River ab. 265 m. long bet. Lake Athabaska and Great Slave Lake, W cen. Canada; receives Peace river just below its outlet from Lake Athabaska and enters Great Slave Lake at Fort Resolution.

Slave Coast (slāv). The coast of Upper Guinea, W Africa, along the Bight of Benin and bet. the Benin and Volta rivers, approximately from 1° to 5°E long.; along coasts of Nigeria, Dahomey, and Togo. From this region most of the slaves were taken during the three centuries bet. 1500 and 1800.

Slav'go·rod (slăv'gŏ·rŏd; *Russ.* slăf'gŭ·rŭt). Agricultural town, W Altai Territory, SW Soviet Russia, Asia, on branch railroad 210 m. W of Barnaul; pop. ab. 16,100.

Slavkov. See AUSTERLITZ.

Sla·vo'ni·a (slă·vō'nĭ·à; -vōn'yà); *Serb.* **Sla·vo'ni·ja** (slä·vō'nĕ·yä). Region in SE Europe bet. the Sava river on the S and the Drava and Danube rivers on N and E in N Yugoslavia; the E part of former Croatia and Slavonia crownland; since 1945 has formed part of new federated republic of Croatia, Yugoslavia. Region from early times a part of kingdom of Croatia (*q.v.*) with history of which it is closely connected.

Sla·vyansk' (slă·vyánsk'). Town, N Stalino Region, E Ukraine, U.S.S.R., on tributary of the Donets 55 m. N of Stalino; pop. 75,542; railroad town in Donbas with industrial plants producing graphite, glass, and china; has also large saltworks and nearby are mineral waters and mud baths.

Sla'wi (slä'wĕ). Town, Central Java prov., Indonesia, a few miles S of Tegal; pop. 17,115.

Slay'ton (slā't'n). Village, ⊗ of Murray co., SW Minnesota, 27 m. NNW of Worthington; pop. 2487; dairy products.

Slea'ford (slē'fērd). Urban district, ⊗ of Parts of Kesteven, Lincolnshire, E England, on the Slea 32 m. of Nottingham; pop. 7282; site of Roman and Saxon settlements; Norman castle.

Slea Head (slā). Cape on SW coast of Ireland, on N side of entrance to Dingle Bay.

Sleat, Point of (slāt). Cape on S tip of Skye I. in the Inner Hebrides, off NW coast of Scotland.

Sleat, Sound of. Body of water off W coast of Scotland, bet. SE side of the island of Skye and the Scottish mainland.

Sleeping Bear Point. Point on W coast of Leelanau co., NW Michigan, extending into Lake Michigan.

Sleeping Deer Mountain. Peak 9885 ft. in W cen. Lemhi co., E cen. Idaho.

Sleepy Eye. City, Brown co., S Minnesota, 37 m. WNW of Mankato; pop. 3492.

Sleepy Hollow. Valley near Tarrytown, New York, made famous by Washington Irving's *Legend of Sleepy Hollow;* Washington Irving buried here.

Slesvig. See SCHLESWIG.

Sles'wick (slĕs'wĭk; slĕz'-). Var. of SCHLESWIG.

Slez'ská O'stra·va (slĕs'kä ô'strå·và); *formerly Ger.* **Pol'nisch–O'strau** (pôl'nĭsh·ôs'trou). City, Silesia prov., cen. Czechoslovakia, opp. Moravská Ostrava; pop. (1930) 22,239; coal mining.

Slezsko. See SILESIA.

Sli. See SCHLEI.

Sli·dell' (slī·dĕl'). Town, St. Tammany parish, SE Louisiana, 30 m. NE of New Orleans; pop. 6356; clay products.

Slide Mountain (slīd). **1** Peak 11,092 ft. in Sierra Nevada, E Tuolumne co., cen. California. **2** Peak 10,200 ft. in N Clark co., E Idaho, on the Montana boundary. **3** Highest peak 4204 ft. in the Catskill Mts., Ulster co., SE New York.

Slie'drecht (slē'drĕkt). Commune, South Holland prov., SW Netherlands, on the lower Waal SE of Rotterdam; pop. 13,146.

Slie'ma and Gzi'ra (slē'mä, g'zē'rä). Town, E Malta, across bay NW of Valletta; pop. (1931) 19,730.

Slieve Bin'gian (slēv bĭn'yǎn). Mountain 2449 ft. in Mourne Mts., SE co. Down, SE Northern Ireland.

Slieve Car (kär'). Mountain 2369 ft. in NW co. Mayo, NW Eire.

Slieve Com'me·dagh (kŏm'ĕ·dä) Mountain 2512 ft. in Mourne Mts., SE co. Down, SE Northern Ireland.

Slieve Don'ard (dŏn'ĕrd). Highest peak 2796 ft. in the Mourne Mts., co. Down, SE Northern Ireland.

Slieve Mish (mĭsh'). Mountain range 14 m. long in cen. co. Kerry, SW Eire; highest peak 2796 ft.

Slieve Mis'kish (mĭs'kĭsh). Mountain range in SW co. Cork, S Eire, bet. Bantry Bay and Kenmare river; highest peak 2251 ft.

Slieve'more' (slēv'mōr'). Mountain 2204 ft. on N coast of Achill I. off W coast of co. Mayo, W Eire.

Slieve'na·man' (slēv'nå·män'). Mountain 2364 ft. in SE co. Tipperary, S Eire, NE of Clonmel.

Slieve Snaght (slēv snäкt'). Mountain 2240 ft. in co. Donegal, N Eire.

Sli'go (slī'gō). **1** County, N Eire, in Connacht prov.; 694 sq. m.; pop. 67,447; ⊗ Sligo; livestock raising, dairy farming, fishing, agriculture. **2** Municipal borough and seaport, ⊗ of co. Sligo, N Eire, on **Sligo Bay** (inlet of Atlantic Ocean); pop. 12,565; butter; brewing, grain milling; exports hogs and cattle. Ruins of 13th-cent. Dominican abbey; site of 13th-cent. castle. Nearby are megalithic remains and the traditional burial place of Queen Mab (identified with an early queen of Connacht).

Slippery Rock. Borough, Butler co., W Pennsylvania, 17 m. ENE of New Castle; pop. 2563. Slippery Rock State Coll. (1889; coed.).

Sli'ven (slī'vĕn) *or* **Sliv'no** (slēv'nô). City, Burgas dept., E Bulgaria, on railroad 60 m. W of Burgas; pop. (1934) 30,571; produces textiles, wine, and attar of roses. Has often been a center of conflict: in medieval times bet. Bulgaria and Constantinople, and in 19th cent. bet. Russians and Turks.

Sliv'ni·ca (slĭv'nĭ·tsä) *or* **Sliv'ni·tza** (-tsä). Commune, Sofia dept., W Bulgaria, 19 m. NW of Sofia; pop. 3622; scene of battle Nov. 17–19, 1885 in which the Bulgarians defeated the Serbs.

Sloan (slōn). Village, Erie co., W New York, 5 m. E of Buffalo; pop. 5803.

Sloan Peak. Mountain 7790 ft. in Snohomish co., NW cen. Washington.

Sloats'burg (slōts'bûrg). Village, Rockland co., SE New York, near New Jersey state line 31 m. NNW of New York; pop. 2565.

Sloch'te·ren (slôк'tĕ·rĕ[n]). Commune, Groningen prov., NE Netherlands, 8 m. E of Groningen; pop. 13,456.

Slo'ka (slwô'kä). Town, SW Vidzeme prov., N Latvia, on S shore of Gulf of Riga just W of Riga; pop. (1935) 5285.

Slo'nim (slô'nyĭm); *Pol.* **Slo'nim** (slô'nēm). Town, W White Russia, U.S.S.R., on Szczara river 43 m. SSW of Novogrudok; formerly in Nowogródek dept., Poland; pop. 16,284; scene of battle Sept. 13–18, 1915 in which Russians were defeated by Germans.

Slope (slōp). County in North Dakota. See *Table* at NORTH DAKOTA.

Slot, the (slŏt). Long open-water passage in cen. Solomon Is., W Pacific, running NW and SE ab. 300 m. from the Shortland Is. to Florida I. and Savo I.—so called in World War II by Americans because it was the regular course followed by Japanese planes and vessels in their attempts to save Guadalcanal Aug. to Nov. 1942.

Slough (slou). Municipal borough, Buckinghamshire, SE cen. England, 20 m. W of London; pop. 66,439; manufactures motors.

Slo·va'ki·a (slô·vä'kĭ·à; -vǎk'ĭ·à); *Czech* **Slo'ven·sko** (slô'vĕn·skô). Province, E cen. Czechoslovakia, bet. Poland on the N and Hungary on the S; area (1935) 18,921 sq. m.; pop. (1930) 3,329,793; ✳ Bratislava; rivers Váh and Hron; livestock raising, agriculture, mining.

History: Settled in 6th and 7th cents. A.D. by Slovaks, a Slavic people; part of Great Moravia in 9th cent.; conquered by Magyars in 906, it remained in kingdom of Hungary (*q.v.*) until 1918; Slovak National Council joined Czechs in forming Czechoslovakia (*q.v.*) 1918; Slovakian autonomy, long the goal of Slovaks, granted in 1938 after dismemberment of Czechoslovak state; region along S border assigned to Hungary 1938–45; declared itself independent Mar. 14, 1939 but on Mar. 16 taken under the protection of the German Reich; an ally of the Axis powers during World War II; liberated bet. Oct. 1944 and May 1945 and ceased to be independent Slovak state Apr. 1945.

Slo·ve'ni·a (slô·vē'nĭ·à; -vēn'yà); *Serb.* **Slo·ve'ni·ja** (slô·vĕ'nĕ·yä). Federated republic, NW Yugoslavia; area 7817 sq. m.; pop. (1961) 1,591,523; ✳ Ljubljana; bounded on N by Austria, on E and S by Croatia federated republic, and on W by Italy.

History: Region settled by Slovenes in 6th cent. A.D.; except for 1809–13 when it was part of Slavic Illyrian Provinces (*q.v.*) erected by Napoleon, most of territory inhabited by Slovenes belonged to Austria; when Dual Monarchy was established 1867, all Slovenes (including those in Hungary) were grouped under Austria where they remained, largely in provinces of Carniola and Styria, until 1918; becoming independent 1918, joined other south Slavs in proclaiming Kingdom of Serbs, Croats, and Slovenes 1918 (see YUGOSLAVIA); constituted approximately Dravska co. 1929–45; made a federated republic 1945 on formation of the Federal People's Republic of Yugoslavia.

Sloy, Loch (lŏк sloi'). Small loch ab. 1 m. long, Dunbarton co., W Scotland, at NW end of Loch Lomond; its outlet flows SE to Loch Lomond; site of huge hydroelectric project 1948.

Słu·bi'ce (slōō·bē'tsĕ). City, W Poznań dept., W Poland, on E bank of the Oder opp. Frankfurt an der Oder, Brandenburg, Germany; pop. (1946) 76,990; before boundary revisions of 1945 part of Frankfurt.

Sluis *or* **Sluys** (slois); *Fr.* **É'cluse'** (ā'klüz'). Commune, Zeeland prov., SW Netherlands; pop. 2788; on the Belgian border on an inlet which was formerly large enough to accommodate many ships; scene of naval battle June 24, 1340 in which Edward III of England almost completely destroyed the French fleet.

Sluis′kin (slōōs′kĭn). Waterfall 300 ft. on S side of Mt. Rainier, Pierce co., W cen. Washington.

Słupsk (slōōpsk); *Ger.* **Stolp** (shtôlp). City, W Gdańsk dept., N Poland, 39 m. ENE of Koszalin; pop. (1946) 48,060; formerly in Pomerania, Germany; railroad junction; manufactures furniture, agricultural implements, machinery, dairy products. First mentioned 1180; became city 1310; member of Hanseatic League; captured by Russian armies Mar. 9, 1945; assigned to Poland by Potsdam Conference 1945.

Slutsk (slōōtsk). **1** Town, S cen. White Russia, U.S.S.R., 60 m. S of Minsk; pop. 14,299; railroad terminus with sawmills and flour mills. Annexed to Russia 1795.
2 See PAVLOVSK town, Leningrad Region, Soviet Russia, Europe.

Sluys. See SLUIS.

Slyne Head (slīn). Cape on W coast of Ireland, in W co. Galway, projecting into Atlantic Ocean; lighthouse.

Smaa′le·ne·nes′ (smô′lĕ·nĕ·nās′). Former name of *Östfold*: see *Table* at NORWAY.

Smack′o′ver (smăk′ō′vĕr). City, Union co., S Arkansas, 12 m. N of El Dorado; pop. 2434; incorp. 1922; oil wells.

Små′land′ (smô′länd′). Former district, SE Sweden, nearly coextensive with the modern provinces of Kalmar, Kronoberg, and Jönköping.

Småland Highlands. Plateau region in S Sweden, S of Lake Vättern.

Smalcald *or* **Smalkald.** See SCHMALKALDEN.

Şma·li′ A·na·do·lu′ Da·ğla·rı′ (shmä·lē′ ä·nä·dô·lōō′ dä·lä·rī′). Mountain range (*dağları*) ab. 520 m. long in N Turkey in Asia, along Black Sea coast from ab. 33°E long. to the Georgian border at 42°E; has many peaks 9000 to 12,000 ft.

Smal′ling·er·land′ (smäl′ĭng·ĕr·länt′). Commune, Friesland prov., N Netherlands, on canal 12 m. NE of Heerenveen; pop. 15,346.

Small Point. Point, SW Sagadahoc co., S Maine.

Small′thorne (smôl′thôrn). Former urban district in Staffordshire, W cen. England, now part of Stoke on Trent.

Sma′ra (smä′rä). Settlement on Saguiet el Hamra river, Saguiet el Hamra zone, N Spanish Sahara, NW Africa; administrative post.

Sme′de·re·vo (smĕ′dĕ·rĕ·vô); *Ger.* **Se·men′dri·a** (zä·mĕn′drē·ä). Town, Serbia, E Yugoslavia, 25 m. ESE of Belgrade on Danube river; pop. 10,489; trade center in grape-growing region; shipbuilding yards; 15th-cent. castle with 19 square towers; capital of Serbia 1430–59 when Belgrade was held by the Turks; occupied by Germans during World War II.

Sme′la (smĕl′à; *Russ.* smyĕ′là). Town, SE Kiev Region, N cen. Ukraine, U.S.S.R., ab. 16 m. SW of Cherkassy; pop. 23,320; key communications point.

Smeroe. Var. of SEMEROE.

Smeth′port (smĕth′pōrt). Borough, ⊗ of McKean co., N Pennsylvania, 15 m. SE of Bradford; pop. 1725; oil and gas wells.

Smeth′wick (smĕth′ĭk). County borough, Staffordshire, W cen. England, W suburb of Birmingham; pop. 84,406, (1951 pop.) 76,397; engineering works; glass and chemical factories.

Smí′chov (smē′кôf); *Ger.* **Smi′chow** (smĭk′ō). City, SW suburb of Prague, Bohemia, Czechoslovakia, on left bank of Vltava; pop. (1921) 56,250.

Smi′ley Mountain (smī′lĭ). Peak 11,506 ft. in S Custer co., cen. Idaho.

Smith (smĭth). Name of counties in four states of the U.S. See *Tables* at KANSAS, MISSISSIPPI, TENNESSEE, TEXAS.

Smith Center. City, ⊗ of Smith co., N Kansas, 65 m. WNW of Concordia; pop. 2379; in corn-growing and dairy section.

Smith′ers (smĭth′ērz). City, Fayette co., S cen. West Virginia; pop. 1696.

Smith′field (smĭth′fēld). **1** Town, ⊗ of Johnston co., E North Carolina, 26 m. SE of Raleigh; pop. 6117; manufactures art pottery, cotton, lumber, bricks.
2 Town, Providence co., N Rhode Island, 10 m. NW of Providence; pop. 9442; government center Georgiaville; incorp. as town 1731; farming; textile and scythe manufactures.
3 City, Cache co., N Utah, 8 m. N of Logan; pop. 2512; farming (peas, sugar beets), dairying, stock raising; pea cannery; manufactures flour, brick, and tile.
4 Town, Isle of Wight co., SE Virginia, on James river 13 m. W of Newport News; pop. 917; ham-packing plants; peanuts.
5 *or* **West Smithfield.** Region in London, England; originally a scene of tournaments, later a trading center and place of executions; scene 1133–1840 of Bartholomew Fair, a great annual fair beginning on St. Bartholomew's Day, later, 1840–55, held at Islington; now site of chief London meat market.
6 Town, S Orange Free State, E cen. Union of South Africa, near Caledon river 80 m. S of Bloemfontein; pop. 2384; in fertile farm country.

Smith Island (smĭth). **1** Marshy island in lower Chesapeake Bay, SW Somerset co., SE Maryland, its southern tip extending into Virginia.
2 Island in Atlantic Ocean at SE extremity of North Carolina; Cape Fear constitutes its S tip.
3 Island in Atlantic Ocean, S extremity of Northampton co., Virginia.

Smith′land (smĭth′lănd). City, ⊗ of Livingston co., W Kentucky; pop. 541.

Smith Peak. Mountain 7750 ft. in E Tuolumne co., cen. California.

Smiths Falls (smĭths). Factory town, Lanark co., SE Ontario, Canada, on Rideau river 41 m. SSW of Ottawa; pop. 8441; railroad divisional point and junction.

Smith Sound. Channel ab. 50 m. long and 35 m. wide separating NW Greenland from coast of SE Ellesmere I.; connects Kane Basin with Baffin Bay.

Smith′ville (smĭth′vĭl; *Sou.* also -v′l). **1** Town, ⊗ of De Kalb co., cen. Tennessee; pop. 2348.
2 City, Bastrop co., S cen. Texas, on Colorado river 38 m. ESE of Austin; pop. 2933; cottonseed-oil mills.

Smoke′stack′ Rock (smōk′stăk′). Peak 4326 ft. in Banner co., W Nebraska.

Smok′ies (smōk′ĭz). = GREAT SMOKY MOUNTAINS.

Smok′y (smōk′ĭ). River ab. 245 m. long, W Alberta, Canada; rises in Rocky Mts. near Brit. Columbia border and flows N into Peace river at Peace River town.

Smoky Cape. Cape on N New South Wales coast, SE Australia, 165 m. NE of Newcastle.

Smoky Hill. River 540 m. long, cen. Kansas; rises in Cheyenne co., E Colorado, flows E through cen. Kansas to unite with the Republican river at Junction City in Geary co. and form the Kansas river.

Smoky Hill Buttes. Buttes 1580 ft. in McPherson co., cen. Kansas.

Smoky Mountains. = GREAT SMOKY MOUNTAINS.

Smö′la (smû′lä). Island in Norwegian Sea off W coast of Norway, WSW of Hitra I.

Smo·lensk′ (smô·lĕnsk′; *Russ.* smŭ·lyĕnsk′). **1** Medieval principality, 12th–14th cents., in W Russia S of Novgorod and W of Rostov-Suzdal; ✱ Smolensk; at first covered wide area. Allied with princes of Kiev; overcome 1408 by Lithuanians.
2 City, ✱ of Smolensk Region, Soviet Russia, Europe, on left bank of upper Dnieper; pop. 156,677; a trade and distribution center for a large area, favorably located for river transport and, in modern times, an important railroad junction; manufactures machinery and has smelting furnaces, sawmills, factories for making bricks and pottery, and a large textile industry; a cultural center with a cathedral, libraries and museums, and educational institutions. One of the oldest cities of Russia, dating from the 9th cent.; in early times enjoyed a large trade

with Constantinople; capital of Smolensk principality 12th to 14th cents.; annexed to Lithuania 1408; declined in influence in wars bet. Lithuania and Russia but finally became Russian 1667; practically destroyed in Napoleonic campaign Aug. 17–18, 1812 when Russians were defeated; regained prosperity in modern times until World War II when it was taken by Germans after great battle July 20–Aug. 9, 1941; recaptured by Russians after bitter fighting Sept. 25, 1943.

Smolensk Region. Region, W Soviet Russia, Europe; 28,911 sq. m.; pop. 2,690,779; ✱ Smolensk. Bounded on N by Velikie Luki and Kalinin Regions, on E by Moscow and Kaluga Regions, on S by Bryansk Region, and on W by White Russia. Occupies part of W plateau of Russia, containing source of the Dnieper river and of several headstreams of the Volga and Dvina; largely agricultural although it has many forests, esp. in the N. Chief crops grains, flax, potatoes; its animal and dairy industries have increased rapidly under Soviet administration. Smolensk and Roslavl are only large towns. In early times was territory contested by Lithuania, Russia, and Poland; became permanently Russian 1654; suffered much during Napoleon's campaign 1812 and was scene of some fighting in civil war of 1918–20; in World War II held by Germans from July 1941 to Sept. 1943.

Smo·lian′ (smô·lyän′); *before 1934* **Pash′ma·kli** (päsh′mä·klĭ). Town, Plovdiv dept., S Bulgaria, S of the city of Plovdiv in Rhodope Mts. near Greek border; pop. (1926) 3003.

Smooth′face′ Mountain (smōōth′fās′). Mountain with two peaks, south 10,417 ft. and north 10,500 ft., in Yellowstone National Park, NW Wyoming.

Smor·go′nie (smôr·gô′nyĕ). Locality formerly in Wilno prov., Poland, 45 m. ESE of Wilno; pop. ab. 4000; severe fighting Oct. 1915 and July 1917 in World War I; now in Molodechno Region, White Russia.

Smyr′na (smûr′nȧ). 1 Short stream, N cen. Delaware; forms section of boundary bet. New Castle and Kent cos.; empties into Delaware river.

2 Town, Kent co., cen. Delaware, 10 m. N of Dover; pop. 3241; in region growing fruit and grain.

3 See IZMIR.

Smyrna, Gulf of. See Gulf of İZMIR.

Smyrnaeus, Sinus. See Gulf of İZMIR.

Smyth (smĭth). County in Virginia. See *Table* at VIRGINIA.

Snae′fell′ (snā′fĕl′). Highest peak 2034 ft. on the Isle of Man, in the Irish Sea off NW coast of England.

Snae′fells·jö′kull (snī′fĕls·yû′küt·l′). Mountain 4710 ft. and glacier, W Iceland, NW of Reykjavík on peninsula on N side of Faxa Bay.

Snaght, Slieve. See SLIEVE SNAGHT.

Snake. 1 River 1038 m. long in NW United States; rises in Yellowstone National Park, NW Wyoming, flows S, then SW, W, and N across Idaho in a big arc; turns N and forms parts of Idaho-Oregon and Idaho-Washington boundaries; turns W at Lewiston, cuts across SE Washington and empties into the Columbia river in S Franklin co., SE Washington; on the Idaho-Oregon boundary has created a canyon more than 40 m. long and more than 7000 ft. deep at one point; has numerous remarkable springs; in section in S Idaho N of Twin Falls has several cascades, esp. Twin Falls and Shoshone Falls (qq.v.) and is used to irrigate the desert region to the S (see also *American Falls Dam and Reservoir* at UNITED STATES, *Dams and Reservoirs*).

2 River 135 m. long, Minnesota; rises in S Aitkin co. E of Mille Lacs, flows S and E into St. Croix river in Pine co.

Snake Creek. 1 Creek 80 m. long, N Nebraska; rises in Sheridan co., flows E into Niobrara river in Cherry co.

2 River ab. 60 m. long, NE cen. South Dakota; rises in W Faulk co., flows E into Dakota (James) river in W Spink co.

Snake Mountain. Peak 3365 ft. in Rabun co., NE Georgia.

Snake Range. Range in E White Pine co., E Nevada; highest point Wheeler Peak 13,058 ft.; Lehman Caves National Monument in it.

Snares Islands *or* **the Snares** (snârz). Group of uninhabited islets SW of New Zealand, in S Pacific Ocean at 48°S and 168°E.

Sneed′ville (snēd′vĭl; *Sou. also* -v'l). Village, ⊗ of Hancock co., NE Tennessee; pop. 799.

Sneek (snāk). Commune, Friesland prov., N Netherlands, 14 m. SSW of Leeuwarden; pop. 14,854; transportation center (canal and railroad) and market town.

Sneeuw′berg (snē′ōō·bĕrк). Mountain range and peak 8208 ft., cen. Cape Province, S Union of South Africa.

Sneeuw Gebergte. See SNOW MOUNTAINS.

Snef′fels, Mount (snĕf′ĕlz). Peak 14,143 ft. in the San Juan Mts., Ouray co., SW Colorado.

Śniar′dwy (shnyär′dvĭ); *Ger.* **Spir′ding** (shpĭr′dĭng). Lake 10 m. long and ab. 47 sq. m. in SE Olsztyn dept., N Poland; formerly in East Prussia, Germany; connected by canals with Lake Mamry and other smaller lakes. In section assigned to Poland by Potsdam Conference 1945.

Śniatyn. See SNYATIN.

Sni′zort, Loch (lŏк snē′zôrt). Inlet of the Little Minch on N Skye I. in the Inner Hebrides, NW of Scotland.

Snö′het′ta (snû′hĕt′ä). Snow-capped peak 7500 ft. in cen. Norway, in the Dovrefjell plateau.

Sno·ho′mish (snô·hō′mĭsh). 1 River 65 m. long, NW cen. Washington; formed by junction of Skykomish and Snoqualmie rivers in SW Snohomish co., flows NW into Puget Sound.

2 County in Washington. See *Table* at WASHINGTON.

3 City, Snohomish co., NW cen. Washington, 8 m. SE of Everett; pop. 3894; trade center in agricultural section.

Sno·qual′mie (snô·kwŏl′mĭ). River ab. 70 m. long, W cen. Washington; flows W and N in King co., crosses into Snohomish co. and joins Skykomish river to form Snohomish river.

Snoqualmie Falls. Waterfall 268 ft. in the Snoqualmie river, King co., W cen. Washington.

Snow′don (snō′d'n). Massif in Caernarvonshire, NW Wales; has five peaks, the highest 3560 ft. being the highest mountain in Wales; region often called **Snow·do′nia** (snō·dōn′yȧ; -dō′nĭ·ȧ).

Snow Hill (snō). 1 Town, ⊗ of Worcester co., SE Maryland, 18 m. SSE of Salisbury; pop. 2311.

2 Town, ⊗ of Greene co., E North Carolina; pop. 1043.

Snow′mass′ Mountain (snō′mȧs′). Peak 14,077 ft. in Pitkin and Gunnison cos., W cen. Colorado.

Snow Mountains (snō); *Du.* **Sneeuw Ge·berg′te** (snā′ōō кĕ·bĕrк′tĕ). Range of high mountains in cen. Neth. New Guinea running E and W from boundary of Brit. New Guinea (141°E) to the narrow isthmus S of Geelvink Bay, ab. 425 m. long; comprises the subordinate ranges of Nassau and Orange (qq.v.). Highest point is Carstensz Toppen 16,404 ft. in Nassau Range; has many peaks above 13,000 ft. Not known or explored until 20th cent.

Snow Peak. Mountain 10,933 ft. in Sierra Nevada, in E Tuolumne co., cen. California.

Snow′slip′ Mountain (snō′slĭp′). Peak 7290 ft. in Glacier National Park, NW Montana.

Snow Water Lake. Lake, E cen. Elko co., NE Nevada.

Snow′y (snō′ĭ). River ab. 240 m. long in SE New South Wales and E Victoria, SE Australia; flows S through Gippsland from Australian Alps to South Pacific Ocean; hydroelectric project.

Snowy Mountain. Peak 3903 ft. in the Adirondack Mts., Hamilton co., NE cen. New York.

Snug Harbor (snŭg). Village on W side of Cook Inlet, S Alaska.

Snya′tin (snyȧ′tyĭn); *Pol.* **Śnia′tyn** (shnyä′tĭn). Town, SW Ukraine, U.S.S.R., on Prut river 50 m. SE of Stanislav; formerly in Stanisławów dept., Poland; pop. 10,915.

Sny′der (snī′dẽr). 1 County in Pennsylvania. See *Table* at PENNSYLVANIA.

2 City, ⊗ of Scurry co., NW cen. Texas, 33 m. NW of Sweetwater; pop. 13,850; in livestock-raising section; manufactures ginned cotton, cottonseed products.

Soan. See SOHAN.

Soap Lake (sōp). City, Grant co., cen. Washington, at S end of the Grand Coulee; pop. 1591; on **Soap Lake**, containing minerals and salts; health resort.

Soar (sōr). River in Leicestershire, cen. England, flowing N into the Trent 12 m. ESE of Derby.

So′a Salt Pan (sō′á). = MAKALAKARI.

So′bat (sō′băt). River in E cen. Africa; formed by confluence of Pibor and Baro rivers on extreme W border of Ethiopia; flows W into White Nile river; length from source of the Baro 460 m.

So·bie′cin (sô-byĕNN′chēn); *Ger.* **Herms′dorf** (hĕrms′-dôrf). Town, SW Wrocław dept., SW Poland, W of Wałbrzych; pop. (1946) 11,233; formerly in Silesia, Prussia, Germany.

So·bo *or* **So·bo·san** (sô-bô[·sän]). Peak 5766 ft. in E cen. Kyushu I., Japan, E of Mt. Aso.

Sobota Rimavská. = RIMAVSKÁ SOBOTA.

So·bral′ (sōō-vräl′). City, NW Ceará state, NE Brazil, 125 m. W of Fortaleza on railroad; pop. (1940 est.) 13,625.

So·braon′ (sô-broun′). Village, Lahore dist., Punjab state, NW Indian Union, 45 m. SE of Lahore on right bank of the Sutlej; on opp. bank was site of battle Feb. 16, 1846 in which British under Sir Hugh Gough were victors over the Sikhs, ending First Sikh War.

So·cha′czew (sô-kä′chĕf). Commune, Warszawa dept., Poland, 32 m. W of Warsaw; pop. 10,822.

Soche. See YARKAND town.

So′chi (sō′chĭ). Seaport town, S Krasnodar Territory, Soviet Russia, Europe, on Black Sea near Georgia border 110 m. SSE of Krasnodar; pop. 10,376; health resort; fine beaches; large sanatorium for Red Army.

Social Circle. City, Walton co., N cen. Georgia, 38 m. ESE of Atlanta; pop. 1780.

So·ci′e·ty Islands (sô-sī′ĕ·tĭ); *Fr.* **Îles de la So·cié′té′** (ēl′ dē là sô′syä′tā′). Island group in W part of French Oceania, S Pacific Ocean; area ab. 650 sq. m.; pop. (1941) 37,303; chief island Tahiti, ✳ Papeete. Comprises two groups: Windward Is. (Tahiti, Mooréa, and a few islets); and the Leeward Is. (*q.v.*). Volcanic in origin and quite mountainous with several high peaks; produce copra, pearl shell, vanilla, phosphate rock. First discovered 1607 by Portuguese navigator Pedro Fernandes de Queirós; rediscovered 1767 and claimed for Great Britain by Samuel Wallis; claimed for France 1768 by French commander Louis de Bougainville who, however, did not at that time push the claim; visited by the scientific expedition sent out by British Royal Society 1768 on ship *Endeavour* commanded by Lieut. James Cook, later known as the famous Pacific Ocean explorer Captain Cook; taken over by the French as a protectorate 1843.

Soc′na (sŏk′ná). Town, Giofra oasis, NW cen. Libya.

So·com′pa (sô-kôm′pä). Volcanic peak 19,786 ft. in E Antofagasta prov., N Chile, near Argentina border.

So′co·nus′co (sō′kô-nōōs′kô). Volcanic peak 7872 ft. in SW Chiapas state, Mexico, ab. 26 m. SE of Tuxtla Gutiérrez.

So·cor′ro (sô-kôr′ō; *Span.* sô-kôr′rô). **1** County in New Mexico. See *Table* at NEW MEXICO.

2 City, ⊗ of Socorro co., cen. New Mexico, on the Rio Grande 70 m. S of Albuquerque; pop. 5271; settled by Spaniards 1817; developed following discovery of silver nearby in 1867. New Mexico School of Mines (1889; coed.).

3 Town, El Paso co., W tip of Texas, on the Rio Grande ab. 15 m. SE of El Paso; pop. (est.) 1500.

4 See HUAMBLÍN island off Chile.

5 See TRES MORROS peak, Colombia.

6 Town, Santander dept., N cen. Colombia; pop. 7891.

7 An island of the Revilla Gigedo group (*q.v.*) in the Pacific Ocean off cen. Mexico.

So·co′tra *or* **So·ko′tra** (sô-kō′trá). Island in Indian Ocean, S of Arabia and ab. 130 m. E of Cape Guardafui; 1400 sq. m.; pop. ab. 12,000; ✳ Tamridah; in physical geography an island of Africa; belongs to Sultan of Qishn on coast of Aden Protectorate. On direct route from Suez to India; has no harbors but several good anchorages. Mountains in center; highest 4686 ft. Chief products dates, aloes, dragon's blood, ghee. Known to the ancients; in Middle Ages a haunt of pirates and corsairs; except for a short occupancy by the Portuguese (1507–11) has been a dependency of Arabia; subject of a treaty made by British with sultan 1876; came under British protection 1886.

So′da Lake (sō′dá). **1** Large dry sink, at times a lake, in Mojave Desert, NE cen. Bernardino co., California.

2 Lake in Caddo parish, NW Louisiana, E of and connected with Caddo Lake.

So′dan·ky′lä (sō′dán-kü′lä). Town, N Finland, in Oulu dept., on tributary of Kemi river 55 m. NNW of Kemijärvi; pop. 5928.

So′da Springs (sō′dá). City, ⊗ of Caribou co., SE Idaho, 45 m. ESE of Pocatello; pop. 2424; medicinal springs; creameries, cheese factories, sawmills.

Sö′der·hamn′ (sû′dĕr·hám′′n). Seaport, Gävleborg prov., E Sweden, on an inlet of the Gulf of Bothnia; pop. 9683; shipping point for timber, wood pulp, iron ore, and fish; burned by the Russians 1621.

Sö′der·man·land′ (sû′dĕr·mán·länd′). Province of Sweden. See *Table* at SWEDEN.

Sö′der·täl′je (sû′dĕr·tĕl′yĕ). Town, Stockholm prov., SE Sweden, a suburb of Stockholm; pop. 18,909; textile mills, distilleries, match factories.

Sod′om (sŏd′ŭm). City in the plain of the Jordan, Palestine, notorious for its wickedness; destroyed, together with Gomorrah (*Gen.* x. 19; xviii. 20; xix. 24–28); sites of both cities unknown, possibly now beneath waters of Dead Sea.

So′dor (sō′dĕr). Medieval diocese comprising the "Southern islands" (*Norse* **Suthr·ey′jar** [sŭth·rā′-yär]), modern Hebrides and the Isle of Man; now, as Sodor and Man, includes only the Isle of Man.

So′dus (sō′dŭs). Village, N Wayne co., W New York, in Sodus town (pop. 6587) near Lake Ontario 29 m. E of Rochester; pop. 1645; in fruit country. The village resort of **Sodus Point** is about 3 m. to the NE on **Sodus Bay**, inlet of Lake Ontario.

Soe′bang (sōō′bäng) *or* **Su′bang.** Town, E Batavia residency, West Java prov., Indonesia, ab. 25 m. NNE of Bandung; pop. 10,539.

Soe·ka·boe′mi (sōō′kä·bōō′mĕ) *or* **Su′ka·bu′mi.** City, West Java prov., Indonesia, on railroad 28 m. SSE of Bogor; pop. 34,191; former capital of West Preanger (see PREANGER). Health resort with sanatorium at S foot of Mt. Salak; noted for its fine climate and scenery.

Soe·ka·ra′dja (sōō′kä·rä′jä) *or* **Su′ka·ra′dja.** Town, Central Java prov., Indonesia, just N of Banjumas; pop. 16,632.

Soe′la (sōō′lá), *or* **Su′la, Islands;** *also, formerly,* **Xul′la Islands** (shōō′lá). Island group, Indonesia, S of Molucca Sea and bet. Celebes I. on the W and the Ceram Sea on the E; 1872 sq. m.; pop. 20,137; chief town Sanana on Sanana I. Comprises islands of Taliabu, Mangole, and Sanana, and several small islands. Mountainous, little known and but slightly developed. Inhabitants are primitive stock.

Soem′ba (sōōm′bá) *or* **Sum′ba;** *Eng.* **San′dal·wood Island** (săn′d'l·wŏŏd′). Island of the Lesser Sunda Is., Indonesia, S of Flores and SE of Sumbawa, 140 m. long by 50 m. at widest; 4305 sq. m.; pop. 182,326; chief town Waingapu. Separated from Timor on the E by Sawu Sea. Mainly a plateau of ab. 2000 ft. with highest point at 4019 ft.; has good harbors on N coast, esp. at Waingapu. Famous in early times for its sandalwood trees, now found only in interior regions; not much developed; grows rice, maize, tobacco and exports horses.

Traces of very early inhabitants left in megalithic structures. Formerly tributary to Sumbawa; its chieftains made treaty with Dutch 1756, renewed and revised several times in 19th cent.; uprising in 1914; occupied by Japanese 1942.

Soem·ba'wa (sŏm·bä'wä) or **Sum·ba'wa.** Island of the Lesser Sunda Is., Indonesia, E of Lombok I. and W of Flores I.; 175 m. long by 55 m. at widest; 5693 sq. m.; pop. 314,843; chief town Raba. Separated on W from Lombok by Alas Strait and on E from Komodo I. (a dependency of Flores) by Sape Strait; has very irregular coast line with deep indentation (Saleh Bay) in center of N coast. On NE coast is Bima Bay, one of best harbors in Indonesia. Mountainous throughout with highest point, the volcano Mt. Tambora, at tip of peninsula on N coast, 9354 ft. Not extensively developed but has fertile soil and tropical products of many kinds can be raised; horse- and cattle-raising industries important. Originally divided into six native states whose condition of allegiance has often changed during last two centuries; relations with Dutch first began early in 18th cent.; final treaty of 1905 settled arrangements with various chieftains; occupied by Japanese 1942.

Soem'bing (sŏm'bĭng) or **Sum'bing.** Volcanic peak 11,060 ft. in Central Java prov., Indonesia; overlooks Magelang plain from the W.

Soe'me·dang (sŏo'mĕ·däng) or **Su'me·dang.** Town, West Java prov., Indonesia, ab. 20 m. E of Bandung; pop. 12,448.

Soe'me·nep (sŏo'mĕ·nĕp) or **Su'me·nep.** Inland town, E end of Madura I., East Java prov., Indonesia, pop. 17,824.

Soen'da Deep (sŏon'dä). Deepest known part of the Indian Ocean 24,452 ft., off S coast of Java, Indonesia near Wharton Deep (see JAVA TROUGH).

Soenda Isles. See SUNDA ISLES.

Soen'da (sŏon'dä), or **Sun'da** (sŏon'dä; sŭn'dä), **Strait.** Channel bet. the islands of Sumatra and Java, connecting the Java Sea with the Indian Ocean; 16 m. wide at its narrowest part. In its center is volcanic island of Krakatau (q.v.); on S side of entrance is Prinsen I. On N side two large bays of S Sumatra—Lampong and Semangka—open into it. Naval battle Mar. 1, 1942 in which American vessels were lost after battle of Java Sea.

Soe'pi·o'ri (sŏo'pē·ō'rē) or **Su'pi·o'ri.** Island ab. 17 m. long by 6 m. wide, just W of Biak in the Schouten Is., N of Geelvink Bay, N Neth. New Guinea; very rugged surface with highest point 3392 ft.; occupied by Allies Sept. 7, 1944.

Soe'ra·ba'ja (sŏor'ä·bä'yä) or **Su'ra·ba'ja** or **Su'ra·ba'ya. 1** Former residency, cen. East Java prov., Indonesia; 1362 sq. m.; pop. 1,904,674; ✻ Surabaja. Bounded on N by Bodjonegoro residency, on E by Madoera Strait, on S by Malang, and on SW and W by Kediri. Chiefly a fertile plain watered by the Solo and Brantas rivers; most important crop is sugar but tobacco, maize, coffee, cassava, and rice are also raised. Crossed by several railroads. Chief towns Soerabaja, Modjokerto, Djombang, and Sidoardjo. Before 17th cent. a small commercial kingdom, overcome 1625 by Mataram; came under Dutch control 1743; overrun by Japanese 1942.

2 Seaport city, its ✻ and ✻ of East Java prov., at mouth of Kali Mas river on Surabaja Strait, near W end of Madura Strait; pop. 935,700; second largest city of Indonesia; chief port of Java and one of the most important trade centers of the Far East; its roadstead sheltered by Madura I.; connected by river transportation with inland districts; chief export sugar. To the S along the Kali Mas are fine residential suburbs, esp. Wonokromo. Before World War II the principal Dutch naval base in the East Indies, with naval station, extensive piers and docks, and steamer connections with ports of Australia and E Asia; much of its docks and water-

front destroyed by Japanese bombing raids in Feb. 1942; one of the last Dutch defenses in Java; taken by Japanese Mar. 8.

Soerabaja Strait. Narrow passage ab. 24 m. long bet. NE Java and Madura I., Indonesia; connects Java Sea with W end of Madura Strait. Forms right-angle turn at S end where the Kali Mas enters it.

Soe'ra·kar'ta (sŏor'ä·kär'tä) or **Su'ra·kar'ta. 1** Former protected native (Mohammedan) principality, S cen. Java, Indonesia; 2331 sq. m.; pop. 2,564,848; ✻ Surakarta. Constitutes a government geographically within Central Java prov., E of Jogjakarta; has short coast line on Indian Ocean. Area quite mountainous with high peaks of Merbabu and Merapi in the NW and Lawu on its E border. Agriculturally rich, esp. in the valley of the Solo; chief crop sugar. Founded 1755 at the breakup of Mataram sultanate; its prince (Susuhunan) was under advice of Dutch resident from 1830; occupied by Japanese 1942.

2 also **So'lo** (sō'lō). City, its ✻, on Solo river in S cen. Java, 50 m. SE of Semarang; pop. 369,800; contains the palaces and extensive grounds of the native ruler; produces sugar, textiles (batiks).

Soest (zōst). City, North Rhine-Westphalia state, West Germany, 33 m. SE of Münster; pop. 20,995; railroad junction on E border of the Ruhrgebiet; manufactures iron goods, incandescent lamps, shoes, sport goods; trade center for grain, cattle.

Soest (sŏost). Commune, Utrecht prov., cen. Netherlands, 11 m. NE of Utrecht; pop. 13,893.

So·fa'la (sō·fä'lä). **1** Former district, SE Mozambique, SE Africa; now part of Manica and Sofala prov. (q.v.).

2 Seaport village, Manica and Sofala prov., SE Mozambique, S of Beira; ancient Arab and early Portuguese port; pop. (1935 est.) ab. 2000.

So·feg'gin (sō·fĕj'ĭn). Short river, dry at certain seasons, in N Tripolitania, N Africa; flows NE into W Gulf of Sidra.

So'fi·a (sō'fĭ·ȧ; sō·fē'ȧ); Bulgarian **So'fi·ya** (sō'fĭ·yä). **1** Department, W Bulgaria; 6502 sq. m.; pop. (1934) 1,152,053; ✻ Sofia.

2 formerly **Sre'dets** (srĕ'dĕts); anc. **Ser'di·ca** (sûr'dĭ·kȧ) or **Sar'di·ca** (sär'-). City, its ✻ and ✻ of Bulgaria; pop. (1956) 725,756, (1959) 671,192; the most important transportation center in the Balkans, connecting directly with İstanbul and Belgrade; near sources of four rivers which cut through surrounding mountains. Has healthful climate and varied manufactures; modern part built after independence of Bulgaria established; has two universities, royal palace, cathedral, opera house, museum, and government buildings. Founded as Serdica by Trajan in 2d cent. A.D.; a favorite residence of Constantine the Great; burned by Huns 447; established as Bulgarian town 809 but came under Byzantine rule in 11th cent.; captured by Turks 1382; for ab. five centuries had prevailing Turkish population, with many mosques; occupied by Russians 1829 and 1878; became Bulgarian capital 1879 replacing Trnovo (q.v.).

So'ga·mo'so (sō'gä·mō'sō). **1** River ab. 200 m. long of N cen. Colombia; flows N and NW into the Magdalena river.

2 City, Boyacá dept., cen. Colombia, in the Cordillera Oriental 110 m. NE of Bogotá; pop. 5216.

Sog'di·a'na (sŏg'dĭ·ä'nȧ; -ăn'ȧ). Province of Persian Empire, 525 B.C., in NE part, conquered by Cyrus the Great; Maracanda (mod. Samarkand) was its capital; invaded by Alexander of Macedon 329–327 B.C.; conquered by Diodotus, satrap of Bactria (q.v.), later by the Parthians and Persians. For the later history, see BUKHARA.

Sog'ne Fjord (sông'nĕ fyōr'; fyŏŏr'). Inlet of Norwegian Sea on W coast of Norway, ab. lat. 61°N; extends E inland 115 m.

Sogn og Fjord'a·ne (sông''n ô fyō'rä·nĕ; fyŏŏ'-). County of Norway. See Table at NORWAY.

So'god (sō'gôd). Municipality at head of Sogod Bay, S Leyte, Phil. Is., ab. 60 m. S of Tacloban; pop. 28,222.

Sogod Bay. Inlet of Mindanao Sea in S Leyte, ab. 35 m. long and 4 to 8 m. wide. Panaon I. forms part of its E shore and Limasawa I. is at its mouth.

So·hâg' (sô·hǎg'). Important city in Girga prov., Upper Egypt; pop. (1937) 31,889; on left bank of the Nile ab. 50 m. SE of Asyût.

So·han' (sô·hän') or **So·an'** (sô·än'). River ab. 130 m. long, NW Punjab, NW India, flowing from the Himalayas SW into the Indus river.

So·har' (sōō·här'). Seaport town, Oman, SE Arabia, on Gulf of Oman 140 m. NW of Masqat; pop. ab. 6000.

So·ho' (sô·hō'). A district in London, England, south of Oxford Street, since 1685 chiefly a foreign quarter (French, Italian, and Swiss); famous for its narrow streets and, in modern times, for its restaurants; in it is **Soho Square**, once a fashionable residential section.

Soi'gnies' (swà'nyē'). Commune, Hainaut prov., SW Belgium, 23 m. SSW of Brussels; pop. 10,625; blue-limestone quarries.

Soi'roc·co'cha (soi'rô·kô'chä). Peak ab. 18,600 ft. in Cordillera Oriental, Peru.

Sois'sons' (swà'sôN'); *anc.* **No'vi·o·du'num** (nō'vĭ·ô·dū'nŭm), *later* **Au·gus'ta Sues'si·o'num** (ô·gŭs'tà swĕs'ĭ·ō'nŭm). Commune, Aisne dept., N France, on Aisne river 18 m. SW of Laon; pop. 20,090; 12th-cent. Gothic cathedral (ruined during World War I; restored 1931); 11th-cent. abbey in which Thomas à Becket lived during part of his exile; 12th-cent. Romanesque church; ancient Roman remains include large amphitheater; iron and copper metallurgy; foundries, forges, glassworks, sugar mills.

  History: Anciently chief town of Belgian Gaul; occupied by the Suessiones; here Clovis defeated Syagrius 486, Charles Martel defeated the Neustrians 716–717, and Robert I was defeated and killed by Charles the Simple 923; captured by Germans 1870, 1914, 1918; reduced to almost complete ruin by German bombardments in World War I; in World War II taken by Allies Aug. 27–28, 1944.

So'kal (sô'kál). Town, W Ukraine, U.S.S.R., on Bug river 45 m. NNE of Lvov; formerly in Lwów dept., Poland; pop. (1938–39 est.) 12,135; place of pilgrimage.

Sö·ke' (sû·kĕ'). Town, Aydın vilayet, SW Turkey in Asia, near coast at mouth of Menderes; pop. 10,778.

So·khon'do (sǔ·ᴋôn'dǔ). Highest peak 8228 ft. in the Yablonoi Mts., SW Chita Region, Soviet Russia, Asia, near Mongolia border.

So'ko·to (sō'kô·tō). 1 Province of Nigeria; S part is fertile and is largely given up to cattle raising and agriculture; N part merges into desert area of Sudan. See *Table* at NIGERIA.

  2 Sultanate in Sokoto prov., NW Nigeria; ab. 25,000 sq. m.; pop. 1,324,000. With its dependencies, it once formed the Fulah Empire, pop. 8,000,000, with estimated area of 100,000 sq. m. Region was inhabited by Hausas and developed under Berber and Arab influences 12th to 18th cents.; had many small kingdoms under Mohammedan rulers; these subdued 1801–04 by Fulah tribes who established new sultanate of Sokoto; after decline in power its ruler made treaty 1885 with British who took over control 1903; religious uprising put down 1906.

  3 Town, ✳ of Sokoto prov., on Kebbi river ab. 250 m. WNW of Kano; pop. 20,358; ✳ of former Fulah Empire.

Sokotra. See SOCOTRA.

So·lai' (sô·lī'). Town, W cen. Kenya colony, E Africa, N of Nakuru; terminus of railroad branch line.

Solana, La. See LA SOLANA.

So·la'no (sô·lä'nô). 1 County in California. See *Table* at CALIFORNIA.

  2 Municipality, NW Nueva Vizcaya prov., Luzon, Phil. Is., on Magat river just NE of Bayombong; pop. 17,878; largest town in province.

Sol'dier Mountain (sōl'jẽr). Peak 7460 ft. in Glacier National Park, NW Montana.

Sole Bay. See SOUTHWOLD BAY.

So'le·dad' (sō'lä·thä[th]'). Town, Atlántico dept., N Colombia, S suburb of Barranquilla; pop. 11,500.

Solenhofen. See SOLNHOFEN.

So'lent, the (sō'lĕnt). Channel extending bet. the Isle of Wight and the mainland of S England; varies in width bet. 2 and 5 m.

So'lesmes' (sô'lâm'). 1 Town, Nord dept., N France, E of Cambrai on Selle river; pop. 5184; scene of fighting during British retreat from Mons 1914.

  2 Village, Sarthe dept., NW France, on Sarthe river ab. 23 m. SW of Le Mans; pop. 451; Benedictine abbey noted for studies in plain chant.

Sol'fe·ri'no (sôl'fĕ·rē'nô). Village, Mantova prov., SE Lombardy, N Italy, 5 m. W of the Mincio river; scene of indecisive battle June 24, 1859 bet. French and Sardinian troops under Napoleon III and Austrians under Emperor Francis Joseph.

So'li (sō'lĭ) or **So'loi** (-loi). Ancient town, Cilicia, Asia Minor, on coast SW of Tarsus; founded by colonists from Argos and Rhodes; in Mithridatic War destroyed by Tigranes, rebuilt by Pompey. Source of the English word *solecism*, because of the bad Greek spoken there.

So·lie'ra (sô·lyä'rä). Commune, Modena prov., Emilia, N Italy; pop. (1931) 10,999.

So'li·gny'–la–Trappe (sô'lē'nyē'lá·tràp'). Commune, Orne dept., NW France, NE of Alençon; pop. (1931) 711; site of La Trappe, monastery (founded c. 1140) of the Trappist Order founded 1664 by Armand de Rancé.

So'li·ma'na (sô'lē·mä'nä). Peak ab. 20,735 ft. in Cordillera Occidental, Arequipa dept., S Peru.

So·li·mões' (sōō·lē·mōĕns'). Brazilian name of upper Amazon from Peruvian border to mouth of the Rio Negro.

So'ling·en (zō'lĭng·ĕn). Industrial city, North Rhine-Westphalia state, West Germany, in the Ruhr valley 14 m. ESE of Düsseldorf; pop. (1939) 138,587; since 1929 includes former cities of Gräfrath, Höhscheid, Ohligs, and Wald; manufactures include iron and steel goods, cutlery, surgical instruments, leather boxes, parts for motor vehicles.

Sol'i·tar'i·o, El (ĕl sôl'ĭ·târ'ĭ·ō). Peak 5131 ft. in W Brewster co., W Texas.

Sól'ler (sō'[l]yẽr). Town, NW Majorca, Balearic Is.; pop. (1930) 8830; tourist resort.

Sollum. See SALÛM.

Sol'na (sôl'nà). City, N suburb of Stockholm, Sweden; pop. 31,743.

Soln'ho'fen (zôln'hō'fĕn) or **So'len·ho'fen** (zō'lĕn·hō'fĕn). Village, Middle Franconia dist., Bavaria, Germany; remains of archaeopteryx discovered here 1739.

So'lo (sō'lō). 1 River 335 m. long in cen. and NE cen. Java, Indonesia; rises in mountains near S coast, flows N then ENE into Java Sea opp. the W end of the island of Madura just N of Grissee; largest river in Java. Navigable for small craft in its upper course. Called **Beng·a'wan** (bĕng·ä'wän) in its lower course.

  2 See SOERAKARTA.

So'logne' (sô'lôn'y'). Plateau region ab. 1800 sq. m. in cen. France, in departments Cher, Loire-et-Cher, and Loiret; a marshy district, now largely reclaimed and used for agriculture.

Soloi. See SOLI.

So'lo·lá' (sō'lô·lä'). 1 Department, SW Guatemala; 410 sq. m.; pop. 86,625.

  2 Town, its ✳; pop. (1938 est.) 5294; altitude ab. 7000 ft.; overlooks Lake Atitlán.

Sol'o·mon (sôl'ô·mŭn). 1 River ab. 120 m. long, N cen. Kansas; formed by confluence of North Fork and South Fork in W Mitchell co., flows SE into Smoky Hill river in W Dickinson co.

  2 Village on N shore of Norton Sound, W Alaska, ab. 30 m. E of Nome; pop. (est.) 400.

Solomon Islands. Group of islands in W Pacific Ocean E of the island of New Guinea; 16,120 sq. m.; pop. ab. 157,000; Bougainville, Buka, and Green Is. form the Kieta dist. of the Territory of New Guinea, 3720 sq. m., pop. (1930) 56,087; remaining islands, including Guadalcanal, Malaita, New Georgia, Choiseul, Santa Isabel, Florida, Savo, Gizo, San Jorge, Rendova, Russell Is., and many small islands, together with the Santa Cruz Is., form British Solomon Islands protectorate, 12,780 sq. m., pop. (1931) ab. 100,000, ✳ Honiara, on Guadalcanal.

History: First discovered by Álvaro de Mendaña 1567 and later explored by Mendaña and Pedro de Queirós; not seen by Europeans for 200 years; visited by Bougainville 1768, by D'Urville 1837–40, and by missionaries and traders 1845–93; in agreement of 1886 divided bet. Great Britain and Germany, the latter receiving the northern islands (Bougainville, Choiseul, Santa Isabel); islands in SW part came under British dominion 1893. Kieta dist. (Bougainville and Buka) retained by Germany 1899; German group taken by Australian forces 1914 and became Australian mandate, as part of Territory of New Guinea (*q.v.*) 1920. In World War II occupied (except for Malaita and San Cristobal) 1942 by Japanese who developed harbors and established airfields, esp. around Buin, Munda, and Tulagi; invaded by Americans who landed on Guadalcanal Aug. 7, 1942, completely occupied it by Feb. 1943, made landings on New Georgia and Bougainville (*qq.v.*) 1943, but with development of campaign on New Guinea bypassed ab. 120,000 Japanese in the islands. For other facts about World War II in the islands, see Savo, Coral Sea, the Slot.

Sol′o·mons (sŏl′ō·mŭnz). Town, Calvert co., Maryland, on an island at N side of Patuxent river mouth; pop. 183; during World War II base for training men in use of amphibious craft.

Solomon Sea. Northern part of Coral Sea; enclosed on the W by New Guinea, on NW by New Britain, and on E by the Solomon Is.

So′lon (sō′lŭn). Village, Cuyahoga co., N Ohio, 13 m. ESE of Cleveland; pop. 6333.

So·lor′ (sō·lôr′). Small mountainous island of the Lesser Sunda Is., Indonesia, in Savu Sea, off E tip of Flores I. and W of Lomblen I.; 25 m. long by 3 or 4 m. wide; 114 sq. m.; copra, fishing. The islands of Solor, Adonara, and Lomblen are sometimes known as the **Solor Islands.**

So·lo·thurn (zō′lō·tŏŏrn). **1** Swiss canton. See *Table* at Switzerland.

2 Commune, ✳ of Solothurn canton, NW Switzerland, on Aare river 19 m. N of Bern; pop. (1941) 15,414; 18th-cent. cathedral, town hall, clock tower of 5th or 6th cent.; manufactures clocks and watches; stone quarries; tourist center.

So·lo·vets′ki Islands (sŏl′ŭ·vĕts′kĭ; *Russ.* sŭ·lŭ·vyāts′-kĭ). Island group in SW White Sea, Arkhangelsk Region, Soviet Russia, Europe, 30 m. E of Kem; pop. ab. 3000. **So·lo·vetsk′** (sŏl′ŭ·vĕtsk′; *Russ.* sŭ·lŭ·vyĕtsk′), the largest, 180 sq. m., is site of a former monastery, built in 1429; in 16th and 17th cents. used as a fortress against Swedes; in recent times buildings made into a social center for development of local resources; in 1917 became a political prison and place of exile.

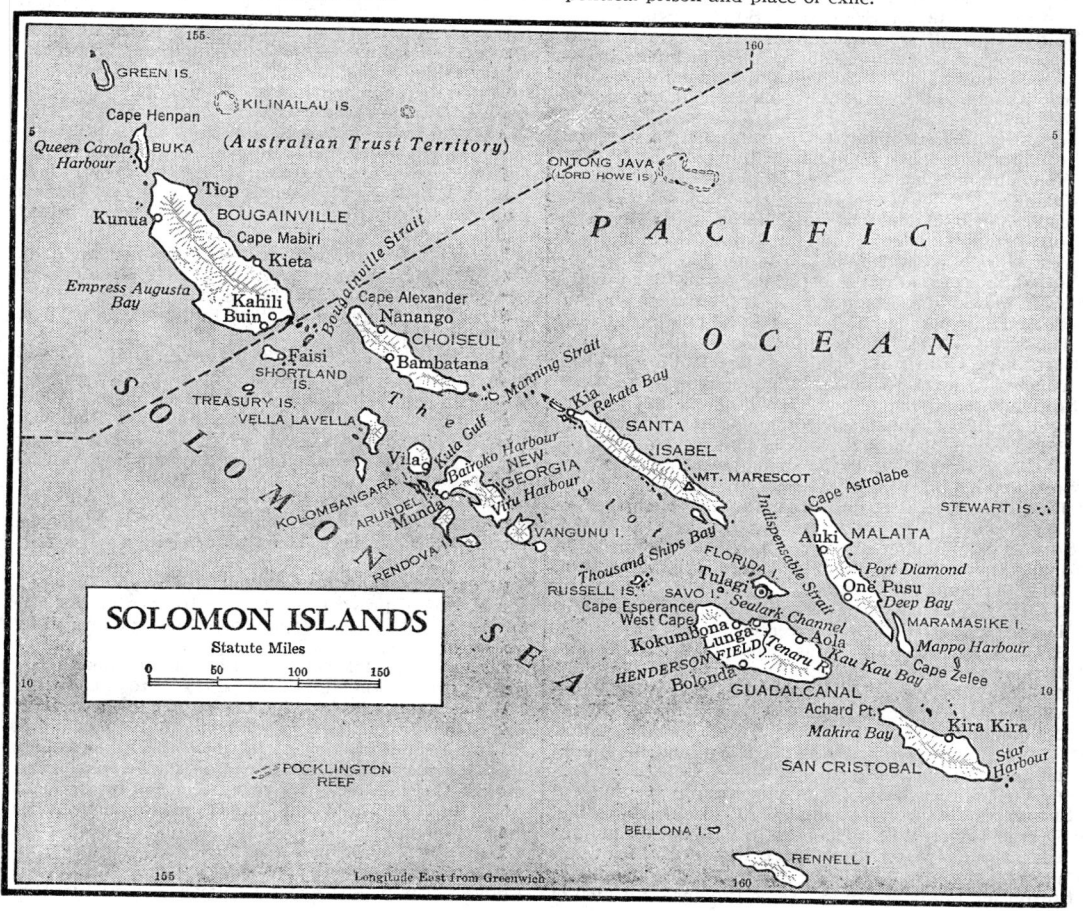

SOLOMON ISLANDS

Statute Miles

0   50   100   150

Solt (shŏlt). Commune, Hungary, on the Danube opp. Dunaföldvár; ab. 50 m. S of Budapest; pop. 7430.

Sol'ta (shŏl'tä); *Ital.* **Sol'ta** (sŏl'tä). Yugoslav island 14 m. long in the Adriatic Sea opp. Split, Dalmatia, Yugoslavia; 21 sq. m.; pop. ab. 4000.

So·luch' (sȯ·lōōk'). Town, W Cyrenaica, NE Libya, S of Bengasi with which it is connected by railroad.

So'lu'tré', *in full* **Solutré–Pouil'ly'** (sȯ'lü'trā'pōō'-yē'). Village, Saône-et-Loire dept., E cen. France, near Mâcon; site of rock shelter where prehistoric human remains have been found; type station of the Solutrean epoch of paleolithic culture, distinguished by beautifully chipped stone implements.

Sol'vay (sŏl'vā). Village, Onondaga co., cen. New York, 5 m. W of Syracuse; pop. 8732; manufactures soda ash, chemicals, ammonia, dyes, oven coke; limestone and gypsum quarries nearby.

Sol'way Firth (sŏl'wā). Inlet of Irish Sea on the boundary bet. England and Scotland; extends inland 38 m.

Solway Moss (mŏs). District in Cumberland, NW England, NW of Esk river near Scottish border; scene of battle Nov. 25, 1542 in which the English defeated the Scots under James V.

So·ma' (sȯ·mä'). Town, Manisa vilayet, W Turkey in Asia, on railroad 20 m. NNW of Akhisar; pop. 3820.

So'main' (sô'măN'). Industrial commune, Nord dept., N France, 20 m. E of Arras; pop. 10,511; coal mines.

So·ma'li·a (sȯ·mä'lē à). Republic, E Africa; a union of former British Somaliland and Italian Somaliland, formed 1960; (est.) 262,000 sq. m.; pop. (1960 est.) 1,900,000; ✳ Mogadishu.

Somalia Italiana. See ITALIAN SOMALILAND.

So·ma'li·land' (sȯ·mä'lē·lănd'). Region in E Africa bet. the equator and the Gulf of Aden, including Italian Somaliland and British Somaliland (now united forming the Republic of Somalia), French Somaliland, and SE Ethiopia; area ab. 300,000 sq. m.

Somaliland Protectorate. See BRITISH SOMALILAND.

Som'bor (sŏm'bôr); *Hung.* **Zom'bor** (zŏm'bôr). City, Voivodina autonomous prov., NE Yugoslavia, near the Danube ab. 95 m. NW of Belgrade; pop. 32,334; commercial center in agricultural and livestock-raising area.

Som'bre·re'te (sŏm'brā·rā'tĕ). Town, Zacatecas state, cen. Mexico, 83 m. NW of Zacatecas; pop. 5628.

Som·bre'ro (sŏm·brâr'ō; -brĕr'ō). Small island of the West Indies, in Anegada Passage bet. Anegada and Anguilla Is.; a part of Saint Kitts-Nevis territory, in the Leeward Is., West Indies Federation.

Sombrero Channel. Strait bet. Katchall I. and Little Nicobar I. in the Nicobar Is., Bay of Bengal.

Som'ers (sŭm'ērz). Town, NW Tolland co., N Connecticut, E of Enfield on Massachusetts border; pop. 3702; incorp. as town by Massachusetts 1734; annexed to Connecticut 1749; dairy farming; woolen mill.

Som'ers·by (sŭm'ērz·bĭ). Parish, the Parts of Lindsey, Lincolnshire, E England, near Louth; birthplace of Tennyson.

Som'er·set (sŭm'ēr·sĕt; -sĭt). **1** Name of counties in four states of the U.S. See *Tables* at MAINE, MARYLAND, NEW JERSEY, PENNSYLVANIA.
2 City, ⊗ of Pulaski co., SE cen. Kentucky, 40 m. S of Danville; pop. 7112; trading center.
3 Town, Bristol co., SE Massachusetts, 4 m. N of Fall River; pop. 12,196.
4 Village, Perry co., SE cen. Ohio, 18 m. SW of Zanesville; pop. 1361; boyhood home of Gen. Philip Sheridan.
5 Borough, ⊗ of Somerset co., S Pennsylvania, 25 m. SSW of Johnstown; pop. 6347; farming, lumbering, mining; produces maple sugar.
6 County in England. See SOMERSETSHIRE.

Somerset Dam. Dam completed 1913 across branch of Deerfield river, W Windham co., S Vermont; height 106 ft.; impounds water, **Somerset Reservoir,** for water power.

Somerset East. Town, SE Cape Province, S Union of South Africa, 83 m. N of Port Elizabeth; pop. 6034; at E end of Great Karroo; center for raising sheep and angora goats. Founded 1825.

Somerset Island. Island 9000 sq. m. in cen. Franklin District, Northwest Territories, Canada, at E of Prince of Wales I. and N of Boothia Penin. Acording to former calculations (1946) included location, in cen. part ab. 73°35′N, 92°20′W, of North Magnetic Pole (see MAGNETIC POLE).

Somerset Nile. = *Victoria Nile:* see NILE.

Som'er·set·shire (-shǐr; -shēr) *or* **Somerset.** County, SW England; area 1620 sq. m.; pop. (1951) 551,188; ⊗ Taunton; other towns Bath, Wells, Bridgwater, Weston super Mare, Yeovil, Frome, Glastonbury; rivers Avon, Parrett, Axe, Exe; cattle raising, dairying (Cheddar cheese), fruitgrowing. Called the *Cider county.*

Somerset West. Town, SW Cape Province, S Union of South Africa, 30 m. ESE of Cape Town near NE shore of False Bay; pop. 3929; in agricultural district; produces excellent wine; manufactures chemicals and explosives. Copper, tin, and bismuth nearby. See STRAND.

Som'ers Islands (sŭm'ērz). See BERMUDA ISLANDS.

Somers Point. City, Atlantic co., SE New Jersey, on Great Egg Bay 10 m. WSW of Atlantic City; pop. 4504; known as Egg Harbor in Revolutionary days.

Som'ers·ville (sŭm'ērz·vĭl). Subdivision of town of SOMERS, Connecticut; woolens.

Som'ers·worth (sŭm'ērz·wûrth). City, Strafford co., SE New Hampshire, on Salmon Falls river 5 m. N of Dover; pop. 8529; incorp. as town 1754, as city 1893; cotton and woolen mills.

Som'er·ton (sŭm'ēr·t'n; -tŭn). City, Yuma co., SW corner of Arizona, 10 m. S of Yuma; pop. 1613.

Som'er·vell (sŭm'ēr·vĕl). County in Texas. See *Table* at TEXAS.

Som'er·ville (sŭm'ēr·vĭl; *Sou.* also -v'l). **1** City, Middlesex co., NE Massachusetts, 3 m. NW of Boston; pop. 94,697; has packing houses, foundries, machine shops, automobile assembly plants, coffee processing works. Originally part of Charlestown, settled 1630; place where first ship built in Massachusetts was launched 1631; magazine for American forces 1775; incorp. as town 1842 and chartered as city 1871.
2 Borough, ⊗ of Somerset co., N cen. New Jersey, 10 m. WNW of New Brunswick; pop. 12,458; Washington's headquarters 1778–79; became ⊗ c. 1784.
3 Town, ⊗ of Fayette co., SW Tennessee, 43 m. E of Memphis; pop. 1820.
4 City, Burleson co., E cen. Texas, 15 m. NNW of Brenham; pop. 1177; railroad, lumber, and farming center.

So·meş' (sô·mĕsh'); *Hung.* **Sza'mos** (sŏ'mŏsh). River ab. 200 m. long in NE Hungary and NW Romania; formed by junction of Great Someş (from Carpathians) and Little Someş (rises in Bihorului Mts.); flows NW into Tisza river.

Somma, Monte. See VESUVIUS.

Som·ma·ti'no (sŏm·mä·tē'nŏ). Commune, Caltanissetta prov., cen. Sicily, 11 m. SE of Caltanissetta; pop. 10,924.

Som'ma Ve·su·via'na (sŏm'mä vȧ·zōō·vyä'nä). Commune, Napoli prov., Campania, S Italy, near Mt. Vesuvius 9 m. E by N of Naples; pop. 13,487; damaged by volcanic eruption 1794.

Somme (sôm). **1** River 147 m. long in N France; rises near St-Quentin in Aisne dept., flows W to Amiens and NW past Abbeville into the English Channel; scene of one of the great battles, July 1–Nov. 18, 1916, of World War I, a series of conflicts in which the Allies, chiefly British under Haig and Rawlinson, made some gains against German lines. Its valley occupied by Germans May–June 1940 in World War II; recovered by Allies Aug. 1944.
2 Department of France. See *Table* at FRANCE.

Somme'py' (sôm'pē'). Village, Marne dept., NE France, 23 m. E of Reims; American memorial to U.S.

and French soldiers who fought in the region during World War I.

Som′mer·feld (zôm′ĕr·fĕlt); *also* **Sommerfeld in der Nie′der·lau′sitz** (ĭn dĕr nē′dĕr·lou′zĭts). See LUBSKO.

Som·nath′ *or* **Pa′tan Somnath** (pŭ′tăn sŏm·nät′h′). Port on S coast of Kathiawar, W Indian Union, near the modern Veraval; famous in Hindu legends as the spot where Krishna was shot by the Bhils. Has several ancient temples; one was looted by Mahmud of Ghazni in 1024 when the "Gates of Somnath" were carried off to his capital; in 1842 Lord Ellenborough brought back to Agra what was said to be these gates.

So′mo·sier′ra Pass (sō′mŏ·syĕr′rä). Mountain pass 4757 ft. in the Sierra de Guadarrama, cen. Spain.

So·mo′to (sŏ·mō′tŏ). Town in NW Nicaragua, ✻ of Madriz dept., near Honduras border; pop. (1943 est.) 2362.

Som′port′, Col de (kôl′ dĕ sôn′pôr′); *anc.* **Sum′mus Por′tus** (sŭm′ŭs pôr′tŭs; pôr′-). Mountain pass 5380 ft. in W Pyrenees N of Jaca, on boundary bet. Huesca dept., Spain, and Basses-Pyrénées dept., France; used by Saracens under Abd-er-Rahman 732.

Son (sōn) *or* **So′ne** (sō′nä). River 487 m. long, NE cen. India; rises in N Bilaspur dist., E Madhya Pradesh, flows NW, then E and NE to the Ganges river near Dinapur; source of irrigation system for Bihar.

Sön′der·borg (sŭn′ĕr·bôrɢ). 1 Former county of Denmark, comprising Als I. and part of SE Jutland Penin.; under German rule 1864–1919; now forms part of Aabenraa-Sönderborg co. See *Table* at DENMARK.
2 Town, Aabenraa-Sönderborg co., SW Als I. off SE coast of Jutland, Denmark, 17 m. NE of Flensburg; pop. (1945) 14,125; bathing resort; trade center of Als I.

Son′ders·hau′sen (zôn′dĕrs·hou′zĕn). Commune, N Thuringia, East Germany, N of Erfurt; pop. (1933) 10,677; former ✻ of Schwarzburg-Sondershausen; castle.

Sön′dre Ber′gen·hus′ (sŭn′rĕ băr′gĕn·hōōs′). Former name of *Hordaland:* see *Table* at NORWAY.

Söndre Trond′hjem (trôn′yĕm). Former name of *Sör-Tröndelag:* see *Table* at NORWAY.

Son′dri·o (sôn′drē·ō). 1 Province of Italy. See *Table* at ITALY.
2 Commune, its ✻, Lombardy, N Italy, on the Adda river 62 m. NE of Milan; pop. 11,672; near Bernina Pass; produces wines and silk.

Sone. See SON.

So′ne·que′ra (sō′nä·kā′rä). Peak 18,652 ft. in S Potosí dept., SW Bolivia.

Song–Bo. See BO.

Songdo. See KAIJO.

Son·ge′a (sông·gā′ä). Town, S Mahenge prov., S Tanganyika, E Africa, E of Lake Nyasa; communications center.

Song′hai, *or* **Song′hay, Empire** (sông′hī). A Negro medieval empire in Africa 10th–16th cents., in the region of the bend of the Niger in W cen. Sudan; chief town Tombouctou; under Mohammedan influence; besides Sudanese, included many Moors and Fulah; destroyed by Spanish and Portuguese force 1591.

Songjin. See JOSHIN.

Song·khla *or* **Song·kla** (sŭng·k′hlä); *Malay* **Sin·go′ra** (sĭng·gôr′ä). 1 Province, SW Thailand; 2510 sq. m.; pop. 301,382.
2 Seaport, its ✻, on E coast of Malay Penin. 50 m. NW of Pattani; airfield taken by Japanese Dec. 8–9, 1941.

Songkoi. See COI.

Song′we (sông′wä). River ab. 100 m. long in Tanganyika, E Africa, flowing into N end of Lake Nyasa; forms N boundary of Nyasaland.

Son′hat (sōn′hät). See KOREA state, India.

Son′mi·a′ni Bay (sŏn′mĭ·ä′nĭ). Inlet of Arabian Sea on SE coast of Baluchistan, off coast of Las Bela.

Son′ne·berg (zôn′ĕ·bĕrɢ). City, S Thuringia, E Germany, 44 m. S of Erfurt; pop. 19,157; a center of German toy-manufacturing industry.

So·no′ma (sŏ·nō′má). County in California. See *Table* at CALIFORNIA.

So·no′ra (sŏ·nōr′á; *Span.* -nō′rä). 1 City, ⊗ of Tuolumne co., cen. California, 45 m. E of Stockton; pop. 2725; in Mother Lode region; mining, lumbering, and agricultural industries.
2 City, ⊗ of Sutton co., SW cen. Texas, 65 m. S of San Angelo; pop. 2619; railroad terminus; market for wool and mohair; goat and sheep raising.
3 River ab. 300 m. long in Sonora state, NW Mexico; flows SW and W into upper Gulf of California near Tiburón I.
4 State, NW Mexico. See *Table* at MEXICO.

Sonora Pass. Mountain pass 9623 ft. in Mono, Alpine, and Tuolumne cos., E California; one of important passes through the Sierra Nevada Mts. used by early emigrants and explorers.

Sonora Peak. Mountain 11,429 ft. on boundary bet. Mono and Alpine cos., E cen. California.

Son′pur (sōn′pŏŏr). 1 Former Indian state, Eastern States, NE Indian Union; 948 sq. m.; pop. (1941) 248,873; geographically in Orissa.
2 Town, its ✻, on right bank of Mahanadi river 140 m. W of Cuttack; pop. 8502.

Son′so·na′te (sôn′sŏ·nä′tä). 1 Department, SW El Salvador; 866 sq. m.; pop. (1942 est.) 123,967.
2 City, its ✻; pop. (1942 est.) 17,232; center of rich agricultural district.

Son′tay′ (sôn′tī′). Town, cen. Tonkin, N Vietnam, on highway 25 m. WNW of Hanoi; on right bank of Coi river just S of its junction with the Bo.

Sont′ho·fen (zônt′hō′fĕn). Town, S Bavaria, Germany, on upper Iller river in mountains 25 m. E of Bregenz; pop. 4619; selected by Hitler and Nazi leaders as site for military training school and as future stronghold of the Reich.

Sontius. See ISONZO.

Son′yea (sôn′yä; sŏn′-). Village, Livingston co., W New York, ab. 26 m. NW of Hornell; pop. ab. 500.

Soo Canals. See SAULT SAINTE MARIE CANALS.

Soochow. See WUHSIEN.

So′per·ton (sō′pēr·t′n; -tŭn). City, ⊗ of Treutlen co., E cen. Georgia, 90 m. WNW of Savannah; pop. 2317.

So·phe′ne (sŏ·fē′nē). District in SW ancient Armenia, E of the Euphrates, bordering on Mesopotamia on the S and on Cappadocia on the W; became Roman under Pompey ab. 63 B.C.

Sophia. Var. of SOFIA.

So·poe′tan *or* **So·pu′tan** (sŏ·pōō′tän). Peak 5994 ft. in NE Celebes I., Indonesia, just S of Manado.

So′pot (sō′pôt); *Ger.* **Zop′pot** (tsôp′ôt). Commune, ✻ of Gdańsk dept., N Poland, in former Free City of Danzig territory, a seaside resort on the Gulf of Danzig ab. 8 m. NNW of Danzig; pop. (1929) 30,835.

Sop′ron (shôp′rôn); *Ger.* **Ö′den·burg** (û′dĕn·bŏŏrɢ). Autonomous city, W Hungary, near Austrian boundary; 50 sq. m.; pop. (1939) 35,957; strategically situated on an important road through a gap in the mountains, site of a Roman colony; has three churches, 13th, 15th, and 17th cents.; the only part of Burgenland (*q.v.*) which remained in Hungary when rest of province was transfered to Austria Feb. 1922.

So′ra (sô′rä). Commune, Frosinone prov., Latium, cen. Italy, on Liri river 14 m. ENE of Frosinone; pop. 20,841; 12th-cent. cathedral; damaged by earthquake 1349, 1634, 1915.

So·rac′te (sŏ·răk′tē); *Ital.* **So·rat′te** (sŏ·rät′tä). Mountain 2267 ft. high in Italy, near the Tiber river 24 m. NE of Rome.

So·ra′pis (zŏ·rä′pĭs). Peak 10,795 ft. in the Dolomites, NE Italy, bet. Venezia Euganea and Venezia Tridentina.

So·ra′ta (sŏ·rä′tä). 1 Mountain in Bolivia, E of Lake Titicaca, consisting of the peaks Ancohuma and Illampu (*qq.v.*).
2 Village, La Paz dept., W Bolivia, E of **Lake Titicaca**

and at foot of Mt. Illampu; health resort; scene of Indian massacre in revolt of 1781.

Sorath. See SORUTH.

Soratte. See SORACTE.

Sorau, Sorau in der Niederlausitz. See ŻARY.

Sorbiodunum. See OLD SARUM.

So'rel' (sô'rĕl'). Industrial city, ⊗ of Richelieu co., S Quebec, Canada, on S bank of St. Lawrence river at mouth of Richelieu river 35 m. SW of Three Rivers; pop. 14,961; river port; shipbuilding yards; varied manufactures; trades in farm produce and grain; has regular ferry across river to Berthier. Founded 1672 on site of earlier Fort Richelieu (erected 1665).

So-rell' (sô-rĕl'). Town, SE Tasmania, Australia, on Pitt Water at mouth of Sorell river 15 m. ENE of Hobart; pop. (municipality) 2218; in district devoted to dairying and general farming.

Sorell, Cape. Point on W coast of Tasmania at entrance to Macquarie Harbour.

Sorell, Lake. Lake 19 sq. m., E cen. Tasmania; source of Clyde river, a tributary of the Derwent. Situated in picturesque mountain scenery; a part of its W shore, known as Diamond Beach, abounds in quartz, carnelian, and agate pebbles.

So-re-si'na (sô-rā-zē'nä). Commune, Cremona prov., Lombardy, N Italy, 12 m. NW of Cremona; pop. 11,314.

So'ria (sō'ryä). 1 Province of Spain. See *Table* at SPAIN. 2 Commune, its ✱, N cen. Spain, on Duero river 113 m. NE of Madrid; pop. 13,054.

So-ria'no (sô-ryä'nô). 1 Department of Uruguay. See *Table* at URUGUAY.
2 Town, Soriano dept., SW Uruguay, at mouth of the Río Negro 162 m. NW of Montevideo; settled 1624, said to be oldest settlement in Uruguay; transshipping point for Mercedes.

Sor'mo-vo (sôr'mŭ-vŭ). Former city, now NW suburb of Gorki, Gorki Region, Soviet Russia, Europe.

Sor'ö' (sō'rû'). 1 County of Denmark. See *Table* at DENMARK.
2 Town, its ⊗, SW Sjælland, Denmark; pop. 2852.

So-ro'ca (sô-rô'kä). 1 Former department, NE Bessarabia, Romania, on the middle Dniester; 1672 sq. m.; pop. 315,774.
2 Town, its ✱. See SOROKI.

So'ro-ca'ba (sō'rōō-kà'vå). City, SE São Paulo state, SE Brazil, 68 m. W of São Paulo; pop. (1940 est.) 48,594; center of rich cotton-growing region; active industrial and trading city.

Soroka. See BELOMORSK.

So-ro'ki (sŭ-rô'kĭ); *Romanian* **So-ro'ca** (sô-rô'kä). Town, NE Moldavian S.S.R., U.S.S.R., on right bank of Dniester 30 m. SE of Mogilev Podolski; pop. 14,661; raises fruit, corn, tobacco, and wool for export. Originally a Genoese colony; here in 15th cent. Stephen the Great of Moldavia erected fortress and castle; often changed hands bet. Poles, Russians, and Turks; held by Axis powers 1941-44 in World War II.

So'rok-sár (shō'rōk-shär). Commune, 20 m. SE of Budapest, cen. Hungary; pop. 18,052.

So-rol' (sô-rôl'). Atoll island, W Caroline Is., W Pacific Ocean, SE of Yap in 8°N, 140°E.

So'ron (sō'rôn). Town, Agra division, W Uttar Pradesh, N Indian Union, 107 m. SE of Delhi near right bank of Ganges; pop. 12,200; an ancient town with fine temples; place of pilgrimages.

So'rong (sô'rông). 1 Subdivision of former Ternate division, Moluccas residency of Neth. Indies; comprised narrow strip of NW coast of Vogelkop Penin., NW Neth. New Guinea, and the adjacent islands of Salawati, Batanta, Waigeo, Misoöl, and other smaller islands E of Djailolo Passage; 4367 sq. m.; pop. 18,952; administered from Tidore.
2 Port, its chief settlement, on Dampier Strait, coast of NW Neth. New Guinea, opp. N end of Salawati I.; was Japanese base 1942-44.

Sör'öy' (sûr'û'ü). Island in Arctic Ocean off NW coast of Norway, in Finnmark co.; 315 sq. m.; pop. 2187.

Sor-ren'to (sôr-rĕn'tô); *anc.* **Sur-ren'tum** (sŭ-rĕn'tŭm). Seaport, Napoli prov., Campania, S Italy, on **Sorrento,** or **Sur-ren'tine** (sŭ-rĕn'tīn; sûr'ĕn-tīn), **Peninsula,** on S side of Bay of Naples 17 m. S by E of Naples; pop. 27,286; cathedral; palaces of 15th and 16th cents.; ancient ruins; in picturesque and fertile region abounding in orange, lemon, olive, and mulberry groves; famous summer resort. Birthplace of Torquato Tasso. Seized by Allied forces Sept. 1943, as part of battle of Salerno.

Sor'so-gon' (sôr'sô-gôn'). 1 Province, SE Luzon, Phil. Is.; 793 sq. m.; pop. 247,653; ✱ Sorsogon; comprises SE tip of Luzon and formerly included islands of Masbate, Burias, and Ticao as Masbate subprov. Coast line irregular, its W coast being deeply indented by Sorsogon Bay. Mountainous, with Bulusan volcano its most noted peak; ranges are covered with excellent timber. Streams are short, but soil, of volcanic origin, is fertile. Hemp (abacá) is the main crop, but coconuts, corn, sugar cane, and pili nuts are also grown. Inhabitants are Bikols. Chief towns Sorsogon, Bulan, Gubat, Pilar, and Bacon.
History: Under Spanish government a part of Albay prov.; early in 17th cent. visited by Spaniards who established mission at Casiguran; many of the galleons used in the Manila-Acapulco trade built here; civil government established Apr. 1901.
2 Municipality, its ✱, at head of Sorsogon Bay in N cen. part of province; pop. 22,097; fine harbor; port of call for vessels from Manila; has large export trade in hemp.

Sorsogon Bay *or* **Gulf.** Deep, landlocked body of water, cen. Sorsogon prov., Luzon, Phil. Is., 19 m. long and from 3 to 8 m. wide; opens onto Ticao Pass, NW of San Bernardino Strait.

Sortavala. See SERDOBOL.

Sor-ti'no (sôr-tē'nô). Commune, Siracusa prov., SE Sicily, 16 m. WNW of Syracuse; pop. 10,058.

Sör–Trön'de-lag (sûr'trûn'dĕ'läg). County of Norway. See *Table* at NORWAY.

So'ruth (sō'rōōt-h') *or* **So'rath** (sō'rát-h'); *anc.* **Su-rash'tra** (sōō-räsh'trá). Southern division of Kathiawar penin., Gujarat state, W Indian Union; chief state Junagarh.

Sör've-maa' (sûr'vĕ-mä'); *Ger.* **Swor'be** (svôr'bĕ). Peninsula, S Sarema I., Estonia.

Sos (sōs), *in full* **Sos del Rey Ca-tó'li-co** (sōz thĕl rrĕ'ĕ kä-tō'lĕ-kô). Commune, Zaragoza prov., N Spain, 60 m. NNW of Saragossa; pop. 3393; birthplace of Ferdinand V of Aragon.

Sos-na' (sŭs-nà'). River ab. 150 m. long, Orel Region, S Soviet Russia, Europe; flows E to join the Don E of Yelets.

Sos-no'wiec (sôs-nô'vyĕts); *also, unofficially,* **Sos'no-wi'ce** (sôs'nô-vē'tsĕ). Industrial city, E Śląsk dept., SW Poland, 4 m. NE of Katowice; pop. (1938-39 est.) 130,000; railroad junction; important coal-producing center; iron foundries, rolling mills, metalworks, blast furnaces, wire mills, machinery factories. Began its development from a small village to a large industrial city 1880.

So'sua (sō'swä). Refugee settlement on N coast of Dominican Republic, E Hispaniola I., on high fertile land 16 m. E of Puerto Plata; founded Jan. 1940 with aid of government as an agricultural project; covers ab. 26,000 acres.

Sos'va (sôs'vá). River ab. 350 m. long, chiefly in N Khanty-Mansi National District, Soviet Russia, Asia; flows S and E to the Ob in its lower course near the town of Berezovo.

So-ta'ra (sô-tä'rä). Volcanic peak 14,550 ft. in SW Colombia, in the Cordillera Central S of Popayán.

So'to la Ma-ri'na (sō'tô lä mä-rē'nä). River ab. 160 m. long in cen. Tamaulipas state, Mexico; flows E into Gulf of Mexico.

Sot'ra (sōt'rä; sōōt'rä). Island off SW coast of Norway, near Bergen; 67 sq. m.; pop. 5249.

Sot·te·ville'-lès-Rou·en' (sôt'vēl'lĕ-rwäⁿ'). Industrial commune, Seine-Inférieure dept., N France, S suburb of Rouen on left bank of Seine; pop. 26,657; cotton textiles.

Sou'chez' (sōō'shā'). Village, 4 m. SW of Lens, Pas-de-Calais dept., N France; pop. (1931) 1033; battle Sept. 25, 1915 in which it was captured by the French.

Souda Bay. = SUDA BAY.

Soudan. See SUDAN.

Soudan français. See FRENCH SUDAN.

Soúdas, Kólpos. See SUDA BAY.

Sou'der·ton (sou'dēr-t'n; -tŭn). Borough, Montgomery co., SE Pennsylvania, 26 m. N of Philadelphia; pop. 5381; manufactures textiles, furniture, shoes.

Soueida. See ES SUWEIDA.

Soueidié. See SÜVEYDIYE.

Sou'fri'ère' (sōō'frē'âr'). **1** Volcanic peak 3002 ft., S Montserrat, Leeward Is., West Indies; highest point on island.
2 See LA SOUFRIÈRE volcano, on St. Vincent I.
3 Town on W coast, St. Lucia I., Windward Is., Brit. West Indies, near Canaries Mt.

Soufrière, Grande. See GRANDE SOUFRIÈRE.

Soufrière, La. See LA SOUFRIÈRE.

Souil'lac' (sōō'yäk'). Small town on S coast of the island of Mauritius, in Indian Ocean E of Madagascar.

Souk–Ah'ras (sōōk'ä'hrôs); anc. **Ta·gas'te** (tȧ·gǎs'tĕ). Commune, Constantine dept., NE Algeria, S of Bône; pop. 14,370.

Söul. Var. of Seoul: see KEIJO.

Sou'langes' (sōō'läⁿzh'). County, Quebec, Canada. See Table at QUEBEC.

Sound, the. See ÖRESUND.

Sounds National Park. See FIORDLAND NATIONAL PARK.

Sou'ni·on, Cape (sōō'nĭ·ŏn; Mod. Gr. sōō'nyôn). = Cape COLONNA.

Sou·phli' (sōō·flē'); Mod. Gr. **Sou·phli'** (sōō·flyē'). Town on Maritsa river, Evros dept., Western Thrace, NE Greece, ab. 32 m. NE of Alexandroúpolis; pop. 7307.

Sour. See TYRE.

Sou'ris (sōōr'ĭs; Fr. sōō'rē'). **1** River 500 m. long, S Canada; rises in S Saskatchewan, flows in big curve SE, N, and NE through Saskatchewan, North Dakota, and Manitoba to the Assiniboine SE of Brandon. In North Dakota also called the **Mouse** river.
2 Town, SW Manitoba, Canada, on Souris river 20 m. SW of Brandon; pop. 1584; railroad divisional point and center of wheat region; has flour mills and grain elevators. Seat of a provincial demonstration farm.

Sou'ris (sōōr'ĭ). Town, Kings co., E Prince Edward I., Canada, on Gulf of St. Lawrence 15 m. W of E end of island; pop. 1183.

Sour Lake (sour). City, Hardin co., E Texas, 19 m. WNW of Beaumont; pop. 1602; former health resort (medicinal springs).

Sousse (sōōs) or **Su'sa** (sōō'sȧ; -sǎ); anc. **Had'ru·me'-tum** (hǎd'rōō·mē'tŭm). Coastal town, NE Tunisia, N Africa, on S shore of the Gulf of Hammamet; pop. (1936) 28,465; older than Carthage, ancient city important under Carthaginians and under Romans; medieval walls, a citadel, many catacombs; exports phosphates, oils. Important German base in World War II, taken by British Apr. 1943.

South (south). River ab. 70 m. long, SE North Carolina; rises in E cen. North Carolina, flows S into Black river in E Bladen co.

South Africa. Geographically that part of Africa south of the middle course of the Zambezi; generally, in modern usage, equivalent to UNION (now REPUBLIC) OF SOUTH AFRICA.

South African Republic; Dutch **Zuid A'fri·kaans'-che Re'pub·liek'** (zoit ȧ'frē·kän'sĕ rā'püb·lēk'). The Dutch (Boer) republic 1856–77 and 1881–1902, corresponding to the region also known as the Transvaal (q.v.).

South'all Nor'wood (south'ôl nôr'wŏŏd). Urban district, Middlesex, SE England, 9 m. W of London; pop. 38,940, (1951 pop.) 55,900; part of Greater London.

South Am'boy (ǎm'boi). City, Middlesex co., cen. New Jersey, on Raritan Bay across from Perth Amboy; pop. 8422; transfer point for shipping coal; clay pits, terracotta works; manufactures uniforms, underwear, cigars.

South America. Continent (4th in size) in Western Hemisphere; ab. 7,035,357 sq. m.; pop. (1938 est.) 91,368,605; comprises greater part of Latin America; ab. 4600 m. N to S and 3200 m. at greatest width. *Political divisions:* Republics of Colombia, Venezuela, Brazil, Ecuador, Peru, Bolivia, Paraguay, Uruguay, Chile, and Argentina; European possessions of British Guiana, Surinam (Netherlands), and French Guiana. The Falkland Is. are a British crown colony and Curaçao, Bonaire, and Aruba form part of the Curaçao overseas territory of the Netherlands.

Boundaries: On N, Caribbean Sea; chief inlets: Gulf of Darien (Colombia), Gulf of Venezuela and Lake Maracaibo, Gulf of Paria (Venezuela); most northerly point, Point Gallinas in Colombia, 12°15'N; chief islands: Curaçao, Bonaire, and Aruba of Neth. West Indies, Margarita (Venezuela), and Trinidad and Tobago (British West Indies). On NE and E, Atlantic Ocean; chief inlets: mouth of Amazon, estuary of Río de la Plata, and in Argentina, Bahía Blanca, and Gulfs of San Matías and San Jorge; most easterly point, Point Pedras, just N of Recife, Brazil, 34°55'W; off Brazil E of Cape São Roque is Fernando de Noronha I. and E of S extremity of Argentina lie the Falkland Is. On S, Drake Passage; Strait of Magellan borders on extreme S of mainland; to the S is large island of Tierra del Fuego and many adjacent smaller islands, including Horn I. on which is Cape Horn, generally considered the most southerly point of South America, 55°59'S; most southerly point of mainland is Cape Froward, S point of Brunswick Penin., Chile, in 53°53'43"S. On W, Pacific Ocean; chief inlets: Corcovado Gulf (Chile) and Gulf of Guayaquil (Ecuador); most westerly point, Point Pariñas, Peru, 81°20'W; islands: Galápagos Is., 600 m. off Ecuador coast. On NW, Panama, republic and isthmus, connecting with Central America.

Mountains: On W side bordering the Pacific for entire length of continent are the Andes (q.v.); highest point Aconcagua 23,081 ft. Other ranges: in N, chiefly in Venezuela and on border bet. Venezuela and the Guianas (on N) and Brazil (on S), the Serras Curupirá, Parima, and Acarahy, and the Tumuc-Humac Mts.; in E, the highland of Brazil (Goiaz, Minas Gerais, Baía, São Paulo, and Paraná states) and the plateau of Mato Grosso; and in S the mountains in Córdoba prov., Argentina. Lowland regions are known as the llanos in the N, the selvas of the Amazon, and the pampas of the Paraná basin; the Chaco is the swamp region of the S cen. part. *Rivers:* Amazon in N Brazil with headstreams in Colombia, Peru, and Bolivia and many large tributaries; Orinoco in the N (Venezuela and Colombia), connecting with Rio Negro of the Amazon system through the Casiquiare; Magdalena in Colombia, Essequibo in British Guiana; in E, Paranaíba and São Francisco in E Brazil; in S, Uruguay (bet. Uruguay, Argentina, and Brazil), the Paraná system, with its two large headstreams the Alto Paraná and the Paraguay, and many tributaries, and in cen. and S Argentina the Salado, Negro, and Chubut; in W, in the Andes many short streams. *Lakes:* Lake Titicaca (Peru and Bolivia), one of the highest large lakes in the world (alt. 12,500 ft.); Poopó in Bolivia, Lagôa dos Patos in S Brazil, Mirim in Uruguay and Brazil, Mar Chiquita in cen. Argentina; many resort lakes in S Andes, esp. Nahuel Huapí, Todos los Santos, Llanquihue.

South·amp′ton (sou·thăm[p]′t*ŭ*n; south·hăm[p]′-).
1 County in Virginia. See *Table* at VIRGINIA.
2 Village and seaside resort, Suffolk co., SE New York, on S shore of Long I. 33 m. W of Montauk Point; pop. 4582; settled 1640; truck-garden center; near Shinnecock Indian Reservation.
3 Town, Bruce co., SE Ontario, Canada, port on Lake Huron 23 m. WSW of Owen Sound; pop. 1700.
4 Administrative county, S England: = HAMPSHIRE.
5 County borough, Hampshire, S England, at head of Southampton Water 70 m. WSW of London; pop. 176,007, (1951) 178,326; seaport, major transatlantic passenger port, with dockyards; shipbuilding yards; yachting center; point of embarkation for the Pilgrim Fathers 1620. U.S. naval training base in World War II.
Southampton Island. Island 19,100 sq. m., N Hudson Bay, Keewatin District, Northwest Territories, Canada.
Southampton Water. Estuary of the Test river which flows SW and S in Hampshire, S England.
South Andaman. One of the Andaman Is. (*q.v.*).
South and East Borneo. See South and East BORNEO.
South An′na (ăn′*à*). River ab. 75 m. long, E cen. Virginia; flows SE to unite with North Anna river in E Hanover co. and form Pamunkey river.
South Arabia, Federation of. See SOUTH YEMEN.
South Ar′gen·tine Peak (är′jĕn·tēn). Mountain 13,600 ft. in Clear Creek and Summit cos., cen. Colorado.
South Atlantic Ocean. See ATLANTIC OCEAN.
South Australia. State, Australia, in cen. part S of 26°S; 380,070 sq. m.; pop. (1933) 580,949 (excluding ab. 2700 full-blooded aboriginals), (1963 est.) 1,008,994; ✳ Adelaide. It has relatively little land above 2000 ft.; in NW is extension of western plateau; in NE is large section (including Lake Eyre) of Artesian Basin with many mud and marsh depressions; in S varied physiographical region with Mullarbor Plain in W, salt lakes and Flinders Range in E, Eyre and Yorke Penins. and Kangaroo I.; in SE an extension of Murray river lowland. Shore line generally low but several good harbors on Spencer Gulf and Gulf of St. Vincent, inlets of Indian Ocean. Chief river is lower course of Murray (ab. 500 m. in South Australia). Much pastoral land; around Adelaide good mining region (esp. copper, iron, gypsum, and opals).
History: Shore probably first visited by F. Thyssen 1627; discoveries by Flinders 1802 and Capt. Sturt 1830 opened up S part; formed into a British province 1836; first Constitution 1856; included Northern Territory (*q.v.*) 1863–1901; franchise extended to women 1894 who first voted in election of 1896; joined federation 1900.
South Ba′li (bä′lê); *Du.* **Zuid–Ba′li** (zoit′bä′lê). Division of Bali and Lombok residency, Lesser Sunda Is., Indonesia; 532 sq. m.; pop. 883,494; chief town Denpasar.
South Bass Island. See BASS ISLAND.
South Beloit. City, Winnebago co., N Illinois, on Wisconsin border 16 m. N of Rockford; pop. 3781.
South Bend (bĕnd′). **1** City, ⊗ of St. Joseph co., N Indiana, 68 m. NW of Fort Wayne; pop. 132,445; manufactures wagons, farm equipment and machinery, aircraft, sewing machines. Univ. of Notre Dame (1842; men; Roman Catholic) and Saint Mary's Coll. (1844; women) at Notre Dame, suburb 2 m. N. Originally site of an Indian village, then of a French mission and trading post; American trading post established here by John Jacob Astor 1823.
2 City, ⊗ of Pacific co., SW Washington, on Willapa Bay; pop. 1671; lumber port; fisheries (oysters, crabs).
South Ber′wick (bûr′wĭk). Town, York co., SW Maine, on New Hampshire border 24 m. SW of Biddeford; pop. 3112; birthplace of Sarah Orne Jewett.
South Beveland. See BEVELAND.
South′bor′o (south′bûr′ō). Town, Worcester co., cen. Massachusetts, 14 m. E of Worcester; pop. 3996.
South′bor·ough (south′bŭ·r*ŭ*; -br*ŭ*). Urban district, Kent, SE England, 27 m. SSE of London; pop. 8823.
South Boston. Town, S Virginia, 28 m. ENE of Dan-

ville, in Halifax co. but politically independent; pop. 5974; tobacco market.
South Bound′ Brook′. Industrial borough, Somerset co., N cen. New Jersey; pop. 3626.
South′bridge (south′brĭj). Industrial town, Worcester co., cen. Massachusetts, 17 m. SW of Worcester; pop. 16,523; textiles and optical goods; has good water power. Incorporated 1816.
South Brisbane. Former municipality, Queensland, Australia, suburb of Brisbane; pop. ab. 37,000.
South Bulgaria. = EASTERN RUMELIA.
South Burlington. Town, Chittenden co., NW Vermont; pop. 6903.
South Bur′ro Mountain (bûr′ō). Peak 12,746 ft. in E Summit co., NE Utah.
South′bur′y (south′bĕr′ĭ; -bĕr·ĭ). Town, NW New Haven co., S Connecticut, on Housatonic river; pop. 5186; settled 1673, incorp. 1787.
South Can′on (kăn′*ŭ*n). Locality, Fremont co., S cen. Colorado, on Arkansas river S of Canon City; includes Lincoln Park (unincorp.) and Brookside and Prospect Heights (towns); total pop. 2689.
South Cape. 1 See KA LAE.
2 Cape on S end of Stewart I., New Zealand.
South Car′o·li′na (kăr′ō·lī′n*à*). Southeastern seaboard state of U.S.A., an original state of the Union, the 8th to ratify the Federal Constitution (May 23, 1788); bounded on N by North Carolina, on E and SE by the Atlantic Ocean, on S, SW, and W by Georgia; 40th state in area, 31,055 sq. m. (land area 30,305 sq. m.); 26th state in population, 2,382,594; ✳ Columbia. See *Table of States* at UNITED STATES. Divided into the following 46 counties (for pronunciation of their names, see their individual entries):

NAME	LOCATION	AREA[1]	POP.[1]	CO. SEAT
Abbeville	W	507	21,417	Abbeville
Aiken	W	1,097	81,038	Aiken
Allendale	SW	418	11,362	Allendale
Anderson	NW	775	98,478	Anderson
Bamberg	SW	395	16,274	Bamberg
Barnwell	SW	553	17,659	Barnwell
Beaufort	S; coastal[2]	672	44,187	Beaufort
Berkeley	SE	1,100	38,196	Moncks Corner
Calhoun	cen.	377	12,256	Saint Matthews
Charleston	SE; coastal[2]	945	216,382	Charleston
Cherokee	N	394	35,205	Gaffney
Chester	N	585	30,888	Chester
Chesterfield	NE	793	33,717	Chesterfield
Clarendon	E cen.	598	29,490	Manning
Colleton	S; coastal[2]	1,048	27,816	Walterboro
Darlington	NE	545	52,928	Darlington
Dillon	NE	407	30,584	Dillon
Dorchester	SE	569	24,383	St. George
Edgefield	W	481	15,735	Edgefield
Fairfield	N cen.	699	20,713	Winnsboro
Florence	E	805	84,438	Florence
Georgetown	E; coastal	813	34,798	Georgetown
Greenville	NW	789	209,776	Greenville
Greenwood	W	447	44,346	Greenwood
Hampton	SW	562	17,425	Hampton
Horry	E; coastal	1,152	68,247	Conway
Jasper	S	578	12,237	Ridgeland
Kershaw	N cen.	786	33,585	Camden
Lancaster	N	504	39,352	Lancaster
Laurens	NW	701	47,609	Laurens
Lee	NE cen.	409	21,832	Bishopville
Lexington	cen.	716	60,726	Lexington
McCormick	W	403	8,629	McCormick
Marion	E	480	32,014	Marion
Marlboro	NE	482	28,529	Bennettsville
Newberry	NW cen.	628	29,416	Newberry
Oconee	NW	670	40,204	Walhalla
Orangeburg	S cen.	1,105	68,559	Orangeburg
Pickens	NW	501	46,030	Pickens
Richland	W cen.	748	200,102	Columbia
Saluda	W	442	14,554	Saluda
Spartanburg	NW	830	156,830	Spartanburg
Sumter	E cen.	665	74,941	Sumter
Union	NW	515	30,015	Union
Williamsburg	E	931	40,932	Kingstree
York	N	685	78,760	York

[1] Area = land area in sq. m. Pop. from 1960 Census.
[2] Includes islands of the Sea Is. chain.

Nickname: Palmetto State. *State flower:* Yellow jasmine (Carolina jessamine). *Motto:* Dum Spiro, Spero

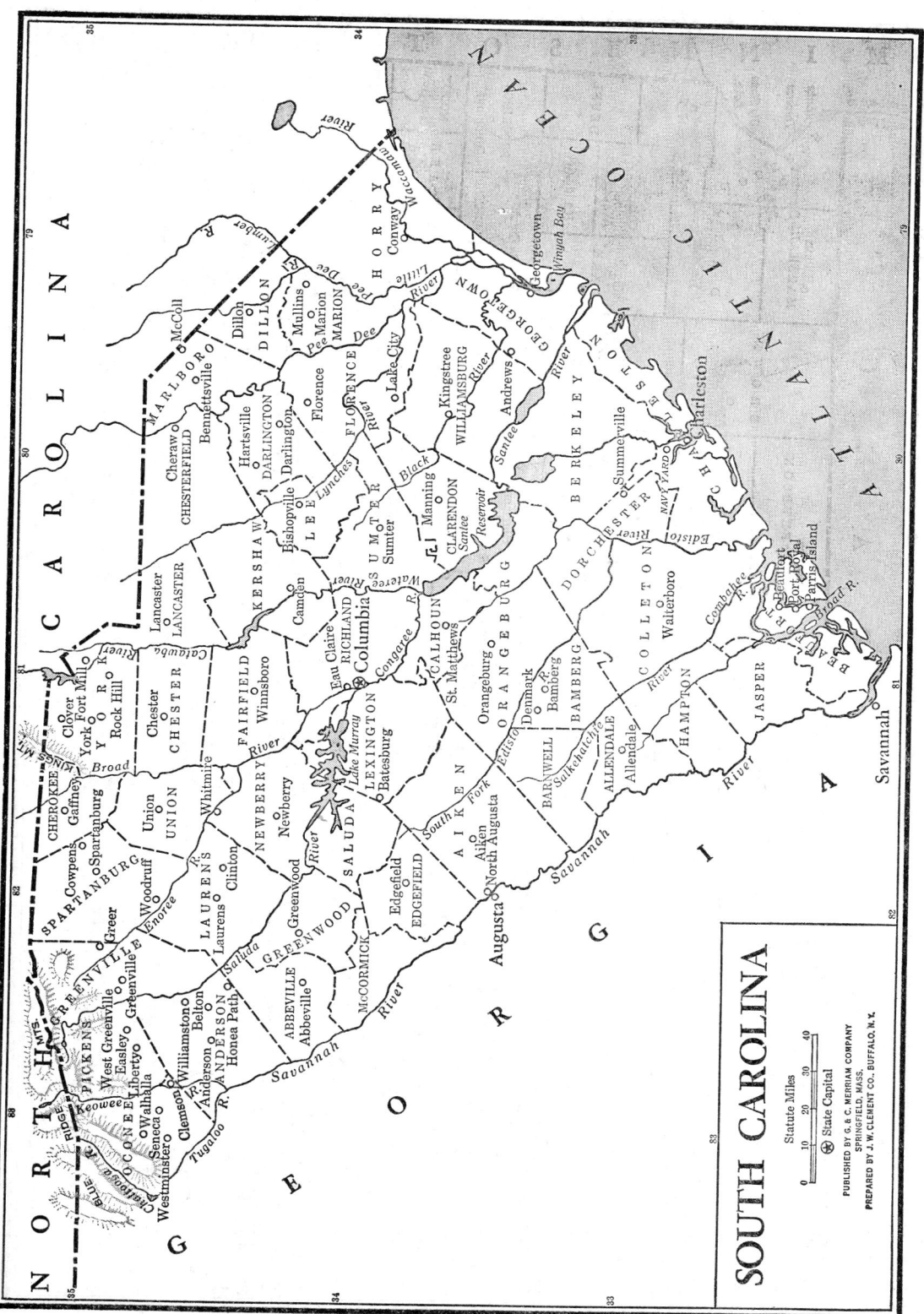

SOUTH CAROLINA

Statute Miles

0 10 20 30 40

⊕ State Capital

PUBLISHED BY G. & C. MERRIAM COMPANY
SPRINGFIELD, MASS.

PREPARED BY J. W. CLEMENT CO. BUFFALO, N.Y.

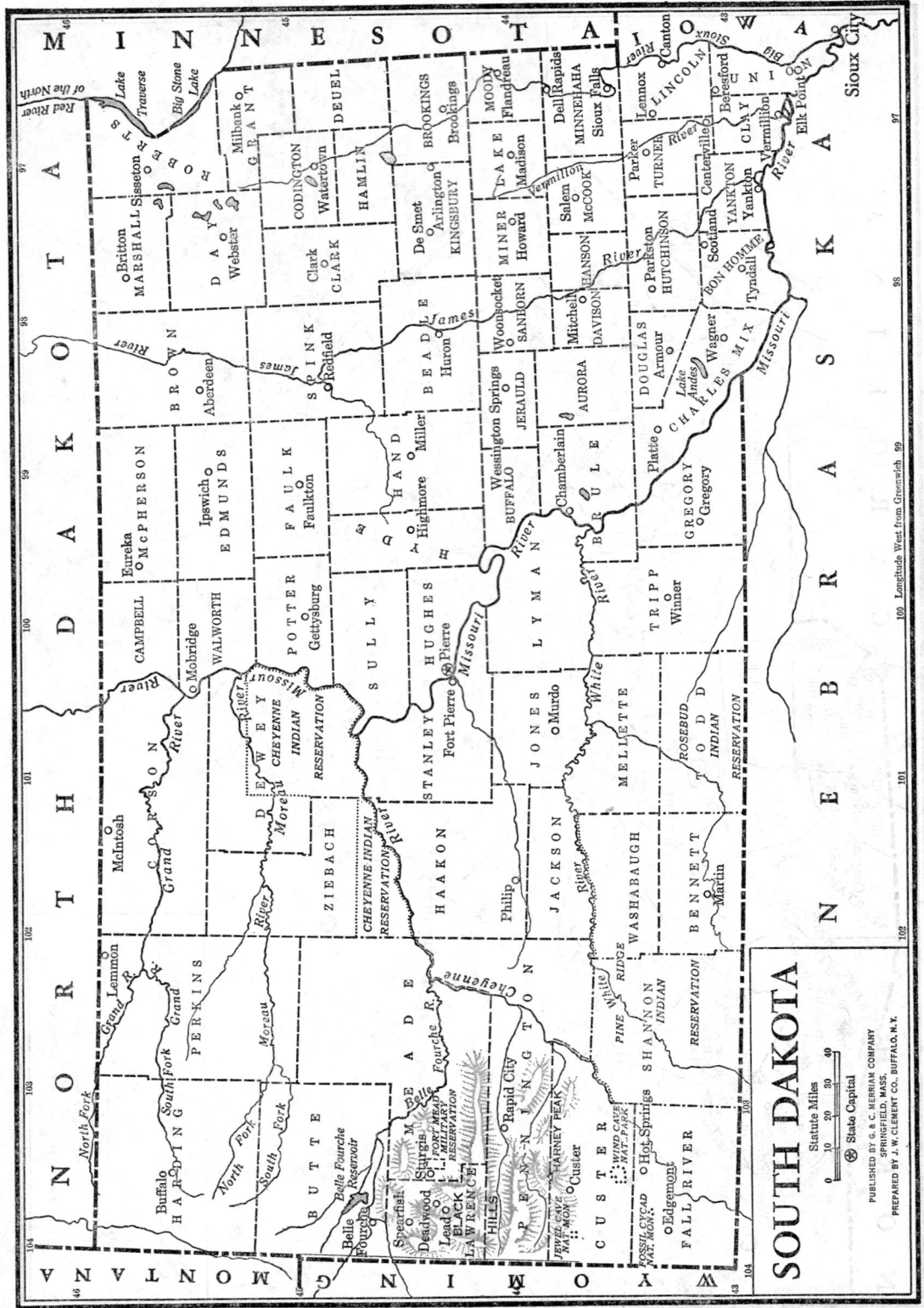

SOUTH DAKOTA

Statute Miles

0   10   20   30   40

⊕ State Capital

PUBLISHED BY G. & C. MERRIAM COMPANY
SPRINGFIELD, MASS.

PREPARED BY J. W. CLEMENT CO. BUFFALO, N.Y.

(While I Breathe, I Hope). *Chief cities:* Columbia, Greenville, Charleston, Spartanburg. *Rivers:* Pee Dee, crossing border from S North Carolina and flowing SE into Winyah Bay; Wateree and Congaree uniting in cen. area to form the Santee flowing SE into the Atlantic; Edisto, in S area flowing SE into the Atlantic; Tugalos and Savannah, forming NW, W, and SW boundary. *Lakes:* No large natural lakes, but several artificial ones, esp. Lake Murray in cen. part, formed by Saluda Dam (see UNITED STATES, *Dams and Reservoirs*), Lake Marion or Santee Reservoir (see SANTEE DAM), Lake Moultrie (see PINOPOLIS DAM) and Wateree Pond, formed by a dam in the Wateree river. *Highest point:* Sassafras Mt. 3548 ft. on NW boundary in the Blue Ridge. *Islands:* Has a number of islands off SE coast including Edisto, Hiltonhead, and Parris I. and constituting the N part of the Sea Is. chain. *Chief industries:* Agriculture (cotton, corn, tobacco, rice), lumbering.

History: Reached by Spanish 1521; settled by French Huguenots at Port Royal 1562; region included in Carolina grant given 1663 by Charles II to eight noblemen of his court (see CAROLINA); Charleston (*q.v.*) founded 1680; became Royal Province 1729; scene of several engagements during American Revolution, notably Kings Mountain, Cowpens, Eutaw Springs, and Camden, and brought under American control by Gen. Greene's defeat of British under Cornwallis at battle of Guilford Courthouse 1781; ceded western lands to U.S. 1787; ratified Federal Constitution May 23, 1788; first state to secede from Union, passing ordinance of secession Dec. 20, 1860; Confederate forces attacked Fort Sumter Apr. 12, 1861, in the initial action of the Civil War; ordinance of secession repealed and slavery abolished 1865; readmitted to the Union June 25, 1868; adopted its present constitution 1895.

South Carpathians. Name sometimes given to the Transylvanian Alps, which are an extension of the Carpathian Mts. bending to the W in Transylvania, Romania; connected on E with N part of the range by the Moldavian Carpathian Mts. which extend NW–SE along the border bet. Moldavia and Transylvania.

South Carter. Mountain 4645 ft. in Coos co., N New Hampshire, NE of Mt. Washington.

South Channel. Southern part of entrance to Manila Bay, Luzon, Phil. Is., bet. mainland of Cavite prov. and Corregidor I., 6½ m. wide; called Boca Grande by the Spaniards.

South Charleston. City, Kanawha co., W cen. West Virginia, on Kanawha river 4 m. W of Charleston; pop. 19,180; center for manufacture of chemicals; U.S. naval ordnance plant.

South Chicago Heights. Village, Cook co., NE Illinois, 28 m. S of Chicago; pop. 4043; residential suburb of Chicago Heights.

South China Sea. Part of the Pacific Ocean enclosed by SE China, Federation of Indochina, Malay Penin., the island of Borneo, the Philippine Is., and the island of Formosa. See CHINA SEA.

South Chu·sei (chōō·sā); *Jap.* **Chu·sei Nan** (chōō·sā nän). Province of Korea. See *Table* at KOREA.

South Clapham. A ward of Wandsworth metropolitan borough, London, England (see *Table* at LONDON).

South Coates′ville (kōts′vĭl). Borough, Chester co., SE Pennsylvania, W of Philadelphia; pop. 2032.

South Con′nells·ville (kŏn′lz·vĭl). Borough, Fayette co., SW Pennsylvania, on Youghiogheny river 11 m. NE of Uniontown; pop. 2434.

South Coventry. Subdivision (pop. 3568) of town of COVENTRY, Connecticut.

South Da·ko′ta (dȧ·kō′tȧ). Northwestern state of U.S.A., 40th state admitted to Union (1889); bounded on N by North Dakota, on E by Minnesota and Iowa, on S by Nebraska, and on W by Wyoming and Montana; 16th state in area, 77,047 sq. m. (land area 76,536 sq. m.); 40th state in population, 680,514; ✱ Pierre. See

Table of States at UNITED STATES. Divided into the following 67 counties (for pronunciation of their names, see their individual entries):

NAME	LOCATION	AREA[1]	POP.[1]	CO. SEAT
Aurora	SE cen.	711	4,749	Plankinton
Beadle	E cen.	1,261	21,682	Huron
Bennett	S	1,187	3,053	Martin
Bon Homme	SE	580	9,229	Tyndall
Brookings	E	801	20,046	Brookings
Brown	NE	1,677	34,106	Aberdeen
Brule	S	829	6,319	Chamberlain
Buffalo	S cen.	494	1,547	Gannvalley
Butte	W	2,251	8,592	Belle Fourche
Campbell	N	763	3,531	Mound City
Charles Mix	S	1,131	11,785	Lake Andes
Clark	NE	976	7,134	Clark
Clay	SE	403	10,810	Vermillion
Codington	NE	691	20,220	Watertown
Corson	N	2,525	5,798	McIntosh
Custer[3]	SW	1,552	4,906	Custer
Davison	SE	432	16,681	Mitchell
Day	NE	1,060	10,516	Webster
Deuel	E	636	6,782	Clear Lake
Dewey	N cen.	1,893	5,257	Timber Lake
Douglas	S	435	5,113	Armour
Edmunds	N	1,153	6,079	Ipswich
Fall River	SW corner	1,748	10,688	Hot Springs
Faulk	N cen.	997	4,397	Faulkton
Grant	NE	684	9,913	Milbank
Gregory	S	1,023	7,399	Burke
Haakon	W cen.	1,815	3,303	Philip
Hamlin	E	520	6,303	Hayti
Hand	E cen.	1,436	6,712	Miller
Hanson	SE	431	4,584	Alexandria
Harding	NW corner	2,683	2,371	Buffalo
Hughes	cen.	762	12,725	Pierre
Hutchinson	SE	814	11,085	Olivet
Hyde	cen.	869	2,602	Highmore
Jackson	SW cen.	809	1,985	Kadoka
Jerauld	SE cen.	528	4,048	Wessington Springs
Jones	S cen.	973	2,066	Murdo
Kingsbury	E	819	9,227	De Smet
Lake	E	571	11,764	Madison
Lawrence	W	800	17,075	Deadwood
Lincoln	SE	576	12,371	Canton
Lyman	S cen.	1,685	4,428	Kennebec
McCook	SE	577	8,268	Salem
McPherson	N	1,151	5,821	Leola
Marshall	NE	875	6,663	Britton
Meade	W	3,466	12,044	Sturgis
Mellette	S	1,306	2,664	White River
Miner	E	571	5,398	Howard
Minnehaha	SE	815	86,575	Sioux Falls
Moody	E	523	8,810	Flandreau
Pennington	SW	2,776	58,195	Rapid City
Perkins	NW	2,866	5,977	Bison
Potter	N cen.	887	4,926	Gettysburg
Roberts	NE corner	1,111	13,190	Sisseton
Sanborn	SE cen.	571	4,641	Woonsocket
Shannon[2]	SW	2,100	6,000	
Spink	NE cen.	1,506	11,706	Redfield
Stanley	cen.	1,495	4,085	Fort Pierre
Sully	cen.	1,061	2,607	Onida
Todd[2]	S	1,388	4,661	
Tripp	S	1,620	8,761	Winner
Turner	SE	611	11,159	Parker
Union	SE corner	454	10,197	Elk Point
Walworth	N	737	8,097	Selby
Washabaugh[2]	SW	1,061	1,042	
Yankton	SE	524	17,551	Yankton
Ziebach	NW cen.	1,982	2,495	Dupree

[1] Area = land area in sq. m. Pop. from 1960 Census.
[2] Three counties (occupied by Indian reservations) remain unorganized, being attached for judicial purposes to adjacent counties, as follows: Shannon (attached to Fall River), Todd (to Tripp), Washabaugh (to Jackson). Washington county added to Shannon co., in 1943, Armstrong county to Dewey co. 1954.
[3] Contains (in S cen. part) Wind Cave National Park.

Nickname: Sunshine State. *State flower:* Pasqueflower. *Motto:* Under God the People Rule. *Chief cities:* Sioux Falls, Rapid City, Aberdeen. *Rivers:* Missouri, bisecting state from N to S and receiving from the W the waters of the Moreau in the N cen. area, the Cheyenne in the cen. area, and the White in the S area. *Lakes:* Numerous small lakes in E and on NE boundary are Big Stone Lake and Lake Traverse; in W in Butte co. is the Belle Fourche Reservoir formed by Belle Fourche Dam. *Highest point:* Harney Peak 7242 ft. in the Black Hills in SW. *Chief industries:* Agriculture, cattle grazing, flour milling, mining (gold, silver, tin).

History: See DAKOTA TERRITORY. First settlement established within present state was at Fort Pierre 1817; constituted S part of Dakota Territory, organized 1861; gold discovered in the Black Hills area 1874; admitted to Union Nov. 2, 1889.

South Downs (dounz′). Range of low hills extending W to E from W Dorsetshire to E Sussex in S England; highest point **Bus′ter Hill** (bŭs′tẽr) 889 ft.

Southeast Cape. Southeast point of Tasmania on the South Pacific Ocean.

Southeast Island. = *Sud-Est* island: see TAGULA.

South East Islands. Group of islands of Indonesia, in SE part; includes Tanimbar, Kai, and Aru Is.

South Emporia. See EMPORIA, Virginia.

South′end′ on Sea (south′ĕnd′). County borough, Essex, SE England, at mouth of the Thames estuary 36 m. E of London; pop. 120,115, (1951 pop.) 151,830; popular seaside resort.

Southern Alps. Mountain range in W cen. South I., New Zealand, extending almost the entire length of the island; highest peak Aorangi 12,349 ft.; many peaks from 8000 to 11,000 ft.; its mountains, lakes, glaciers, etc. afford magnificent scenery; crossed in only one place by railroad and highway through Otira Gorge and Arthur's Pass, Christchurch to Greymouth.

Southern Bug. See BUG river, SW Ukraine.

Southern Central India States. Former agency, group of Indian states, SW Central India; 5101 sq. m.; pop. (1941) 720,957; chief state Dhar.

Southern Cook Islands. = COOK ISLANDS.

Southern Deccan; *sometimes called* **Deccan Proper.** The southern and southeastern parts of the plateau region of S India, in Mysore, Andhra Pradesh, and Madras; drained by the Kistna and Northern Penner rivers; on S separated by a deep valley from the Nilgiri Hills in W Madras prov. See DECCAN.

Southern Desert. Province, S Egypt. See *Table* at EGYPT.

Southern District. Former district in S Palestine, now divided into Gaza and Lydda dists.

Southern Dvina. See DVINA.

Southern Highlands of Indochina. The interior highland region of S Annam from ab. 14°N to 11°N lat.; created 1946 as an autonomous region within the Federation of Indochina (see FRENCH INDOCHINA).

Southern Indian Lake. Lake 1060 sq. m., NW Manitoba, Canada; Churchill river flows through it.

Southern Karroo. See KARROO.

Southern Ma·ra′tha States (má·rä′tá). Former agency, S Bombay prov., W India; later in Deccan and Kolhapur States (*q.v.*).

Southern Morava. Branch of Morava river, Yugoslavia. See MORAVA.

Southern Nigeria. = SOUTHERN PROVINCES.

Southern Ocean. The regions of the Atlantic, Indian, and Pacific oceans surrounding Antarctica, esp. extending S from Cape Horn, the Cape of Good Hope, and the S coast of Australia. Also called Antarctic Ocean (see ANTARCTIC REGIONS).

Southern Penner. See PENNER.

Southern Pines. Town and winter resort, Moore co., cen. North Carolina, 30 m. W of Fayetteville; pop. 5198; writers' colony.

Southern Protectorate of Morocco. The southern zone of the former Spanish possessions in Morocco; 10,039 sq. m.; pop. 12,000; a coastal region extending from Cape Yubi NE to Cape Noun at the mouth of the Wad Dra and inland to ab. 8°40′W.

Southern Province. Province, S Ceylon, on Indian Ocean; 2146 sq. m.; pop. 771,204; ✱ Galle. Has deposits of precious stones, anthracite, and plumbago.

Southern Provinces. Former division of Nigeria, now divided into the Western Provinces and Eastern Provinces. See *Table* at NIGERIA.

Southern Rajputana States Agency. Formerly a group of Indian states in Mewar and Southern Rajputana.

Southern Rhodesia *or now often* **Rhodesia.** British self-governing colony, SE Africa; 150,333 sq. m.; pop. (1961 est.) 3,849,000; ✱ Salisbury; bounded on N by Zambia, on E by Mozambique, on S by Transvaal, on SW and W by Bechuanaland Protectorate; comprises two main divisions, Mashonaland and Matabeleland, subdivided into ab. 32 districts; administered by a governor and legislative council. Forms part of great South African plateau sloping from SW to NE; cen. part at average elevation of 4000 to 5000 ft. is broad watershed bet. Zambezi (boundary with Zambia) and Limpopo and Sabi systems on SE. These large streams have many tributaries, esp. Sanyati flowing to Zambezi in NW and Lundi to Sabi in SE. In NW is Victoria Falls (*q.v.*) in the Zambezi. Chief crops maize and tobacco; ranching is important. Has extensive gold fields; asbestos, coal, and chrome also mined. *Chief towns:* Salisbury, Bulawayo, Umtali, Gwelo, and Hartley. See *Map* at UNION OF SOUTH AFRICA.

History: Region under administration of British South Africa Company 1889–1923; Europeans voted in a referendum to accept responsible government 1922; colonial government set up Sept. 1, 1923; federated with Northern Rhodesia and Nyasaland 1953–63.

Southern Shan States. Southern division of Federated Shan States, E cen. Burma; 36,416 sq. m.; pop. 870,230; chief town Taunggyi. Comprises 36 states, some very small; largest is Kengtung, others are Mongnai, Mongpan, and Lawksawk. Crossed by railroad to Taunggyi and by good highways.

Southern Sporades. See SPORADES.

Southern Territories; *Fr.* **Ter′ri′toires′ du Sud** (tĕ′rē′twàr′ dü süd′). The southern part of Algeria, in the Sahara, a former French colony formed of territories of Aïn-Sefra, Ghardaia, Touggourt, and Oasis Sahariennes; 770,158 sq. m.; pop. (1936) 642,651. Saharan Atlas range in N, rest of region comprises desert and plateau of Sahara extending S as far as 19°10′N; chief towns Colomb-Béchar, Ghardaia, Touggourt, and Ouargla; the division organized by decree of Aug. 14, 1905. See *Table* at ALGERIA.

Southern Urals. See URAL MOUNTAINS.

South Esk. 1 River in E cen. Scotland; rises in the E slopes of the Grampian Mts., flows SE into North Sea at Montrose.

2 See ESK river, Midlothian co., SE Scotland.

3 River ab. 110 m. long, NE Tasmania; flows generally W then N to join North Esk at Launceston to form the Tamar.

South Euclid. City, Cuyahoga co., N Ohio, 10 m. E of Cleveland; pop. 27,569; suburb of Cleveland.

South Farmingdale. Urban community (unincorporated), Nassau co., SE New York, on Long Island E of New York; pop. 16,318.

South′field (south′fēld). City, Oakland co., SE Michigan, S of Pontiac; pop. 31,501.

South Foreland. See FORELAND.

South Fork. Borough, Cambria co., SW cen. Pennsylvania, 7 m. ENE of Johnstown; pop. 2053.

South Fork Edisto. See EDISTO.

South Fort Mitch′ell (mĭch′ĕl). City, Kenton co., N Kentucky, 4 m. S of Covington; pop. 4086.

South Fox Island. See FOX ISLANDS, Lake Michigan.

South Fulton. City, Obion co., NW Tennessee, on Kentucky border 35 m. WNW of Paris; pop. 2512.

South′gate. 1 City, Wayne co., SE Michigan, S of Detroit; pop. 29,404.

2 (south′gĭt; -gāt). Urban district, Middlesex, SE England, N suburb of London; pop. 55,577, (1951 pop.) 73,376; part of Greater London.

South Gate (south′ gāt). Suburban industrial city, Los Angeles co., SW California, 7 m. SSE of Los Angeles; pop. 53,831; incorp. 1923; manufactures furniture, cork

products, building materials, machinery, chemicals, paper products.

South Georgia. Island in S Atlantic Ocean on N border of Scotia Sea, ab. 1100 m. E of Tierra del Fuego, 54°S, 37°W; one of the Falkland Islands Dependencies (*q.v.*); 1450 sq. m.; permanent pop. ab. 750; chief town Grytviken Harbour, on Cumberland Bay. Highest point 9200 ft. Annexed to Great Britain by Capt. James Cook in his circumnavigation of Antarctic Continent 1772–75.

South Glastonbury. Subdivision of town of GLASTONBURY, Connecticut.

South Glens Falls. Village, Saratoga co., New York, on Hudson river opposite Glens Falls and 17 m. NE of Saratoga Springs; pop. 4129.

South Greensburg. Borough, Westmoreland co., SW Pennsylvania, 26 m. ESE of Pittsburgh; pop. 3058.

South Had'ley (hăd'lĭ). Town, Hampshire co., W Massachusetts, N of Springfield; pop. 14,956. Mount Holyoke Coll for women, founded by Mary Lyon 1837.

South Ha'ven (hā'věn). City, Van Buren co., SW Michigan, on Lake Michigan 37 m. WNW of Kalamazoo; pop. 6149; lakeside resort; port of entry; fruit-shipping center.

South Hei·an (hā·än); *Jap.* **Hei·an Nan** (hā·än nän). Province of Korea. See *Table* at KOREA.

South Hill. Town, Mecklenburg co., S Virginia, 45 m. E of South Boston; pop. 2569; tobacco, cotton market.

South Holland. Village, Cook co., NE Illinois, 17 m. S of Chicago; pop. 10,412.

South Holland; *Du.* Zuid'hol'land (zoit'hôl'änt). Province, SW Netherlands; 1212 sq. m.; pop. (1939) 2,167,299; ✳ Rotterdam; other cities The Hague, Schiedam, Leiden; agriculture; dairy farming.

South Hol'ston Dam (hôl'stŭn). See *Table* at TENNESSEE VALLEY AUTHORITY.

South Houston. Town, Harris co., SE Texas, SW of Houston; pop. 7523.

South Hsenwi. State of Northern Shan States, Burma; 2351 sq. m.; pop. 82,672; ✳ Mongyai.

South Hsingan. Former province (1932–45), W Manchukuo; 30,502 sq. m.; pop. (1940 est.) 1,026,235; ✳ Wangyehmiao.

South Huntington. Urban community (unincorporated). Suffolk co., SE New York on W cen. Long I.; pop. 7084.

South'ing·ton (sŭth'ĭng·tŭn). Town, SW Hartford co., N Connecticut, W of Berlin; pop. 22,797; incorp. 1779; agriculture; manufactures hardware, tools, plumbing supplies, brass products, paper boxes, automobile forgings, bolts, screws.

South Island. 1 Island in Atlantic Ocean, S of entrance to Winyah Bay, SE coast of Georgetown co., South Carolina.
2 Central and largest island of New Zealand, 525 m. long; 59,130 sq. m.; pop. (1941 est.) 558,317. Comprises 5 provincial districts: Marlborough, Nelson, Westland, Canterbury, and Otago, and subdivisions Otago and Southland, of Otago provincial dist. Chief cities Christchurch, Dunedin, Invercargill, and Timaru. Chatham Is. and Stewart Is. constitute counties of South I. See NEW ZEALAND.

South Jacksonville. Former city, Duval co., Florida; since 1932 part of Jacksonville.

South Jutland; *Dan.* Syd'li·ge Jyl'land (sŭth'lĭ·gĕ yül'än). Southern section of Jutland, the mainland part of Denmark, forming Danish counties of Haderslev, Aabenraa-Sönderborg, and Tönder; constitutes the Danish part of Schleswig (*q.v.*), known as **Nord Sle'svig** (nôr slī'svĕ).

South Kalimantan. See BORNEO, South and East.

South Kanara. Former district of W Madras prov., S Indian Union; 4045 sq. m.; pop. 1,523,516; ✳ Mangalore.

South Kan·kyo (kän·kyō); *Jap.* **Kan·kyo Nan** (kän-kyō nän). Province of Korea. See *Table* at KOREA.

South Kazakhstan Region. Subdivision of Kazakh S.S.R., Soviet Central Asia, in SE part, bordering on Kzyl-Orda, Karaganda, and Dzhambul Regions of the Kazakh S.S.R. on the W and N and on the Kirgiz and Uzbek Republics on the SE, S, and SW; ✳ Chimkent.

South Kei·sho (kā·shō); *Jap.* **Kei·sho Nan** (kā·shō nän). Province of Korea. See *Table* at KOREA.

South Kensington. See KENSINGTON.

South Kings'town (kĭngz'toun). Town, SE Washington co., S Rhode Island; pop. 11,942; administrative center Wakefield. Former stronghold of Narraganset Indians; once part of Kings Towne (Kingstown), incorp. in 1674 and divided into North and South Kingstown in 1723; textile manufactures; includes villages of Kingston, West Kingston, and Wakefield.

South Kohala. District, Hawaii co., Hawaii, on N Hawaii I.; pop. 1538; chief village Waimea.

South Kona. District, Hawaii co., Hawaii, SW part of Hawaii I.; pop. 4292; chief village Kealakekua.

South Kvalöy. Island in Arctic Ocean off NW coast of Norway, in Troms co., S of Ringvassöy I.

South'land (south'lănd; -länd). Subdivision of Otago provincial dist. of New Zealand. See *Table* at NEW ZEALAND.

South Lookout Peak. Mountain 13,500 ft. in San Juan and San Miguel cos., SW Colorado.

South Loup. River 150 m. long, cen. Nebraska; rises in Logan co., flows E and SE to union with North Loup and Middle Loup and form the Loup river.

South Magnetic Pole. See MAGNETIC POLE.

South Manchester. Subdivision of town of MANCHESTER, Connecticut.

South Marsh Island. Island bet. Tangier Sound and Chesapeake Bay in NW Somerset co., SE Maryland.

South Melbourne. City, S Victoria, SE Australia, S suburb of Melbourne on Port Phillip Bay; pop. 42,951.

South Miami. City, Dade co., SE Florida, 7 m. SW of Miami; pop. 9846; shipping point for citrus fruits and tomatoes.

South Milwaukee. City, Milwaukee co., SE Wisconsin, on Lake Michigan 9 m. S of Milwaukee; pop. 20,307.

South Modesto. Urban community (unincorporated), Stanislaus co., cen. California; pop. 5465.

South'mont (south'mŏnt). Borough, Cambria co., SW cen. Pennsylvania; pop. 2857.

South Mountain. Ridge in S Pennsylvania and W Maryland; battle Sept. 14, 1862 (called Boonsboro by the Confederates) in which McClellan defeated Lee's army on its first invasion of the North, preliminary to the battle of Antietam.

South Na·han'ni (na·hăn'ĭ). River 350 m. long, SW Mackenzie District, Northwest Territories, Canada; a N tributary of the Liard flowing SE from the Mackenzie Mts.; reputed rich deposits of gold in upper valley.

South Natoena Islands. See NATOENA ISLANDS.

South Na·varre' Peak (na·vär'). Mountain 7800 ft. in Chelan co., cen. Washington.

South Ne·gril' Point (ne·grĭl'). Cape at W end of Jamaica, West Indies, at S entrance to Long Bay.

South New Guinea; *Dutch* Zuid–Nieuw–Gui·nee' (zoit'nē'oō·gĕ·nā'). Province of S Neth. New Guinea, including Frederik Hendrik I. and the swampy coast region from ab. 5°S lat. to the Papua boundary; 40,072 sq. m.; pop. 16,346; chief town Merauke.

South Norfolk. Former city, SE Virginia, on Elizabeth river 3 m. S of Norfolk; merged 1963 with Norfolk county in new city of Chesapeake (*q.v.*).

South Norwalk. Former city (incorp. 1870), now a subdivision of town and city of NORWALK, Connecticut; manufacturing center of city.

South Nyack. Village, Rockland co., SE New York, on Hudson river near Nyack and 24 m. N of New York; pop. 3113.

South Ock'en·don (ŏk'ĕn·dŭn). Town, Essex, SE England, 12 m. E of London; pop. 1355.

South Ogden. City, Weber co., N Utah pop. 7405.

South′old (south′ōld). Village and summer resort in Southold town (pop. 13,295), Suffolk co., SE New York, on N extension of Long I. ab. 18 m. NE of Riverhead; pop. (est.) 1500.

South Orange. Village, Essex co., NE New Jersey, 5 m. W of Newark; pop. 16,175; together with Orange, East Orange, West Orange, and Maplewood, forms residential suburban community for New York City; manufactures toilet preparations, plastic articles, bituminous products, cement blocks. Seton Hall Univ. (1856; coed.).

South Orkney Islands or **South Orkneys.** Group of islands in S Atlantic Ocean S of Scotia Sea, ab. 850 m. NE of Palmer Penin., and SE of S extremity of South America, 61°S, 45°W; one of the Falkland Islands Dependencies (q.v.). Largest island is Coronation I. Used as a base for whalers; discovered 1821 by British and American sealers; still claimed by Argentina (*Span*.

South Os·se′ti·a (ŏ·sĕ′shĭ·à; -shà), *officially* **South Os·se′tian Autonomous Region** (ŏ·sĕ′shăn). Autonomous region, N Georgia, U.S.S.R.; 1428 sq. m.; pop. (1941 est.) 111,501; ✳ Stalinir. Bounded on N by North Ossetia, and on other three sides by Georgia. High plateau region on S slopes of Caucasus; inhabitants mostly occupied with grazing sheep and goats; has some peasant industries. Predominant ethnic strain is Iranian; chief nationalities Ossetian 69%, Georgian 27%. For early history and some account of Ossets, see NORTH OSSETIA. Suffered much in confusion after Revolution 1917; created an autonomous area in 1922.

South Pacific Ocean. See PACIFIC OCEAN.

South Pagai. See PAGAI.

South Par′is (păr′ĭs). Town, ⊗ of Oxford co., W Maine, 17 m. WNW of Lewiston; pop. 2063; manufactures wooden toys.

South Park. Tableland in Park co., cen. Colorado; contains source of the South Platte; with North Park, Middle Park, and San Luis Park (qq.v.) forms a N–S chain of grassy plateaus enclosed by snow-capped mountains.

South Pasadena. Residential city, Los Angeles co., SW California, 4 m. NE of Los Angeles; pop. 19,706; orchards; lion, alligator, and ostrich farms.

South Pass. 1 One of the channels at the mouth of the Mississippi river (q.v.).
2 Wide, level pass 7550 ft., Fremont co., SW cen. Wyoming, at S end of Wind River Range; discovered 1824, used first for wagons 1832 by Capt. Benjamin Bonneville's exploring party. See OREGON TRAIL.

South Pitts′burg (pĭts′bûrg). City, Marion co., S Tennessee, on Tennessee river 24 m. W of Chattanooga; pop. 4130; manufactures hosiery, lumber, stoves, cast-iron goods, cement.

South Plainfield. Borough, Middlesex co., cen. New Jersey, 6 m. NNE of New Brunswick; pop. 17,879.

South Platte. River 424 m. long, Colorado and W Nebraska; rises in NW Park co., cen. Colorado, flows SE then NE across Nebraska boundary to join the North Platte river in Lincoln co., SW cen. Nebraska, and form the Platte river.

South Point. 1 See KA LAE.
2 Point at SE tip of Marsh I., off S coast of Louisiana.
3 Point on SE coast of Alpena co., NE Michigan, at S entrance to Thunder Bay.

South Pole. The S extremity of the earth's axis, at 90°S lat. and the S center from which start all meridians of longitude; the point from which the only direction is N. The area around it (**South Polar Regions:** see POLAR REGIONS) is a lofty plateau (Polar Plateau) in W cen. part of Antarctica (q.v.). Cf. MAGNETIC POLE.

South′port (south′pōrt). **1** Subdivision of town of FAIRFIELD, Connecticut.
2 City, and resort, ⊗ of Brunswick co., S North Carolina, at mouth of Cape Fear river 22 m. S of Wilmington; pop. 2034.
3 Town, SE Queensland, Australia, on Pacific Ocean opp.

S end of Stradbroke I. 45 m. SSE of Brisbane; pop. 4216; watering place.
4 County borough, Lancashire, NW England, on Irish Sea 17 m. N of Liverpool; pop. 84,057; seaside resort.

South Portland. Residential city, Cumberland co., SW Maine, SE suburb of Portland; pop. 22,788.

South River. 1 River in North Carolina. See SOUTH.
2 Borough, Middlesex co., cen. New Jersey, 6 m. SE of New Brunswick; pop. 13,397; sand and clay deposits; manufactures brick, tile.

South Ron′ald·say (rŏn′′ld·sā). One of the Orkney Is., off N coast of Scotland.

South Sacramento. Urban community (unincorporated), Sacramento co., N California; pop. (with Fruitridge) 16,443.

South Saint Paul. City, Dakota co., SE Minnesota, on Mississippi river 4 m. SSE of St. Paul; pop. 22,032; stockyards, packing houses, tanneries.

South Salt Lake. City, Salt Lake co., N Utah, ab. 4 m. S of Salt Lake City; pop. 9520.

South Sandwich Deep. Ocean depth 27,106 ft., S Atlantic Ocean, near South Sandwich Is.

South Sandwich Islands. Group of small volcanic islands in S Atlantic Ocean at E end of Scotia Sea ab. 1350 m. ESE of Cape Horn, South America; one of the Falkland Islands Dependencies (q.v.); lat. 56° to ab. 59°S, long. 26°15′W. Discovered 1775.

South San Francisco. Suburban industrial city, San Mateo co., W California, 9 m. S of San Francisco; pop. 39,418; steel mills, machine shops, stockyards, refineries, packing plants; manufactures pipe, castings, paint, ink, wire; aviation center.

South San Gabriel. Urban community (unincorporated), Los Angeles co., SW California; pop. 26,213.

South Saskatchewan. See SASKATCHEWAN river.

South′sea′ (south′sē). Residential district and watering place in S part of Portsmouth, England, within the city limits on the Spithead; navy memorials.

South Sea; *Span.* **El Mar del Sur** (ĕl mär′ thĕl sŏŏr′). The Pacific Ocean—so named by Balboa on his discovery of it 1513. In the plural, **South Seas,** the waters of the Southern Hemisphere, esp. the South Pacific Ocean.

South Sea Islands. Islands of the South Pacific Ocean —equivalent in general usage to Oceania.

South Sea Mandated Territories. Collective name of the Caroline, Marshall, and Mariana (excluding Guam) Is. (qq.v.), in W Pacific Ocean N of the equator, while they were under Japanese mandate 1919–45.

South Shetland Islands or **South Shetlands.** Group of islands N of the Palmer Penin. and separated from its N tip by Bransfield Strait; in Falkland Islands Dependencies (q.v.), S of Drake Passage and ab. 550 m. SE of Cape Horn, bet. 61° and 63°S lat. and bet. 54° and 63°W long. Chief islands Livingston, King George (the largest, with harbor at Admiralty Bay), Deception (with harbor at Port Foster and with a submerged volcano), Elephant, Clarence, and Greenwich. Rocky and mountainous, has several fine summer harbors with whaling and fishing activities. Discovered 1819 by English navigator William Smith. In recent years, esp. 1946–48, their ownership an issue of dispute bet. Great Britain and the republics of Argentina and Chile.

South Shields (shēldz). County borough, Durham, N England, on North Sea at mouth of the Tyne on its S bank 10 m. E of Newcastle; pop. 113,455, (1951 pop.) 106,605; extensive docks; shipping point for coal; manufactures glass, chemicals, paints; fisheries.

South Sioux City. City, Dakota co., NE Nebraska, across Missouri river from Sioux City, Iowa; pop. 7200.

South Stillwater. = BAYPORT.

South Suburban Municipality. Municipality, Twenty-four Parganas dist., West Bengal, NE Indian Union, S suburb of Calcutta; pop. (1941) 63,479.

South Ta′ra·na′ki Bight (tä′rà·nä′kĕ). Gulf S of the bulge on W coast of North I., New Zealand.

South Te′ton (tē′tŏn). Peak 12,505 ft. in cen. Grand Teton National Park, NW Wyoming.

South Thompson. See THOMPSON river.

South Tirol. See TIROL.

South Tucson. City, Pima co., S Arizona; pop. 7004.

South Tyne. See TYNE.

South U′ist (ū′ist; ōō′ist). Island of the Outer Hebrides, separated by Little Minch from Skye, off NW coast of Scotland; pop. 2810; administratively part of Inverness co.

South Umpqua. River 85 m. long, SW Oregon; rises in E Douglas co., flows E and then N uniting with North Umpqua river ab. 8 m. NW of Roseburg to form the Umpqua river.

South Victoria Land. See VICTORIA LAND.

Southwark. Metropolitan borough of London. See *Table* at LONDON.

South Waziristan. See WAZIRISTAN.

South′well (south′wĕl; -wĕl; *locally* sŭth′′l). Parish, Nottinghamshire, N cen. England; pop. 2991; cathedral; near place where Charles I surrendered himself to the Scots 1646.

South-West Africa; *S. Afr. Dutch* **Suid′wes′-A′fri·ka** (soit′vĕs′ä′frĭ·kä). Territory, SW Africa, a mandate of the Union of South Africa; 317,725 sq. m. (including Walvis Bay 318,099 sq. m.); pop. (1936) 283,784 (including Walvis Bay 314,194); ✳ Windhoek. Walvis Bay with its fine harbor (374 sq. m., pop. 30,410) is actually part of Cape Province. Bounded on N by Angola, on E by Bechuanaland and Cape Province, on S by Cape Province, and on W by Atlantic Ocean; includes Caprivi Concession (*q.v.*) in NE. Divided into three (nonpolitical) regions Amboland in N, Damaraland in center, Great Namaqualand in S. Greater part is plateau 3000 to 4000 ft.; highest point 7942 ft. near Windhoek. Namib Desert extends along the coast; in N is extensive depression with salt pans, esp. Etosha Pan. The Cunene and Okovanggo rivers form part of boundary on N with Angola and the Orange river forms boundary with Cape Province. Chief industries farming and cattle raising; copper and diamonds are exported. Chief towns Windhoek, Keetmanshoop, Lüderitz, and Walvis Bay. See *Map* at UNION OF SOUTH AFRICA.

History: Bartholomeu Dias landed at the harbor on which Lüderitz is situated 1486; region not much visited before middle of 19th cent.; annexed by Germany 1885 and administration taken over 1892; officially known as German Southwest Africa (*Ger.* **Deutsch-Süd·west′-a′fri·ka** [doich′züt·vĕst′ä′frĕ·kä]); after the Hottentot races were defeated by the Herreros, the latter were conquered 1904–08 by the Germans; captured in World War I by forces from Union of South Africa, which received it as mandate 1919 from League of Nations.

South Westbury. Urban community (incorporated), Nassau co., SE New York, on Long Island E of New York; pop. 11,977.

Southwest, *or* **South West, Cape.** Southwest point of Tasmania on the South Pacific Ocean.

Southwest Fargo. See FARGO, North Dakota.

Southwest Greensburg. Borough, Westmoreland co., SW Pennsylvania, 26 m. ESE of Pittsburgh; pop. 3264.

South West Islands. Group of islands in SE part of Indonesia, on S edge of Banda Sea and NE of Timor; includes Wetar I., Kisar I., Damar Is., Moa, Sermata.

South West Miramichi. See MIRAMICHI BAY.

Southwest Pass. 1 One of the channels at the mouth of the Mississippi river (*q.v.*).

2 Narrow strait leading from Gulf of Mexico into Vermilion Bay, bet. mainland of SE Vermilion parish and Marsh I., S Louisiana.

Southwest Peak. See Peaks of OTTER.

South′wick (south′wĭk). **1** Town, Hampden co., SW Massachusetts, 9 m. WSW of Springfield; pop. 5139.

2 Urban district, West Sussex, S England; pop. 10,718.

Southwick on Wear (wēr). Former urban district,

Durham, N England, now part of Sunderland.

South Williamsport. Borough, Lycoming co., N cen. Pennsylvania, S suburb of Williamsport; pop. 6972.

South Windsor. Town, E Hartford co., N Connecticut, NE of Hartford; pop. 9460; incorp. 1845; tobacco.

South′wold (south′wōld). Municipal borough, Suffolk, E England; pop. 2473; seaside resort; 15th-cent. church; on **Southwold,** *or* **Sole** (sōl), **Bay,** scene of naval battle in which the Dutch under De Ruyter were defeated by the English under James, Duke of York, May 28, 1672.

South Yemen. Republic, S coast of Arabian peninsula, SW Asia, W of Muscat and Oman; 61,900 sq. m.; pop. ab. 900,000; ✳ Al Ittihad; formerly the Federation of South Arabia, a British protectorate consisting of numerous Arab states and the British crown colony of Aden; became an independent republic including the islands of Kamaran, Socotra, and Perim Nov. 30, 1967.

South Zen·ra (zĕn·rä); *Jap.* **Zenra Nan** (nän). Province of Korea. See *Table* at KOREA.

So′vetsk (sô′vĕtsk); *Ger.* **Til′sit** (til′zĭt; *in English, also* -sĭt). Manufacturing and commercial city, Kaliningradsk Region, Soviet Russia, Europe, on left bank of Neman river 37 m. NNW of Gusev; pop. 50,834; formerly in Gumbinnen govt. dist., East Prussia prov., Germany; airport; 18th-cent. baroque town hall; churches of 16th and 18th cents.; weather observation station; manufactures include lumber, wooden goods, iron, machinery, cheese, beer, brandy, yeast, leather; trades in lumber, grain, eggs, butter, cheese, cattle.

History: Built 1408; became city 1552; treaty bet. France, Russia, and Prussia signed here 1807; in World War I occupied by Russians Sept. 9, 1914; in World War II occupied by Russian troops 1944; assigned to U.S.S.R. by Potsdam Conference 1945.

So·vet′ska·ya Ga′van (sŭ·vyĕt′skä·yȧ gȧ′vȧn·y′). Literally "Soviet Harbor"; town and port on the Gulf of Tatary, N coast of Maritime Territory, Soviet Russia, Asia, 190 m. SE of Komsomolsk; connected by rail with Komsomolsk; has 5000-ton floating dock.

Soviet Central Asia. See Soviet CENTRAL ASIA.

So′vi·et Russia (sō′vĭ·ĕt; sō′vĭ·ĕt′; sŏ·vyĕt′; sŏv′ĭ·ĕt). The Russian Soviet Federated Socialist Republic (*q.v.*). See also RUSSIA and UNION OF SOVIET SOCIALIST REPUBLICS.

Soviet Russia in Asia. The Asiatic part of the U.S.S.R. comprising Siberia (*q.v.*) and Molotov Region (W of the Ural Mts., formerly considered a part of Russia in Europe) of the R.S.F.S.R. and Soviet Central Asia (see Soviet CENTRAL ASIA).

Soviet Union. The Union of Soviet Socialist Republics (*q.v.*).

Sow′er·by (sou′ẽr·bĭ). Urban district, West Riding, Yorkshire, N England; pop. 18,770.

So·ya, Cape (sō·yä). Cape on N extremity of Hokkaido I., Japan.

Soya Strait; *also* **La Pé·rouse′ Strait** (lä′ pē·rōōz′; *Fr.* là pä rōōz′). Channel ab. 25 m. wide bet. NW Hokkaido I., Japan, and S tip of Sakhalin I.

Sozh (sôsh). Navigable river ab. 250 m. long, an E tributary of the Dnieper in W Russia; rises near Smolensk and flows S in Smolensk Region and White Russia to join the Dnieper below Gomel.

Sozopol. See APOLLONIA town, NE Thrace.

Spa (spà; *Angl.* spä, spô). Commune, Liège prov., E Belgium; pop. 8193; medicinal mineral springs.

Spac′ca·for′no (späk′kä·fôr′nô). Commune, Ragusa prov., SE Sicily, 16 m. SE of Ragusa; pop. (1931) 12,099.

Spain (spān); *Span.* **Es·pa′ña** (ȧs·pä′nyä); *anc.* **His·pa′ni·a** (hĭs·pä′nĭ·ȧ; -pän′yȧ). A state, formerly a kingdom, in SW extremity of Europe, occupying greater part of Iberian Penin. and including the Balearic and Canary Is.; area of mainland territory 193,144 sq. m., pop. (1941 est.) 25,284,212; area of Balearic and Canary Is. 3463 sq. m., pop. (1941 est.) 776,568; total area

196,607 sq. m., pop. (1941 est.) 26,060,780, (1948 est.) 27,761,487; ✴ Madrid. Mainland territory is bounded on N by the Bay of Biscay and France, on E and S by Mediterranean Sea, and on W by Portugal and the Atlantic Ocean. See *Tables* below, for the modern provinces and former divisions of Spain (for pronunciation of their names, see their individual entries):

PROVINCES OF MODERN SPAIN, INCLUDING THE BALEARIC AND CANARY ISLANDS

PROVINCE[1]	LOCATION IN FORMER DIVISIONS OF SPAIN	AREA IN SQ. M.	POP. (1941 EST.)
Álava[2]	S Basque Provinces	1,175	114,795
Albacete	N Murcia	5,737	376,326
Alicante	S Valencia; on Mediterranean	2,185	611,277
Almería	E Andalusia; on Mediterranean	3,360	359,730
Ávila	SW Old Castile	3,042	236,044
Badajoz	S Estremadura; on Portuguese border	8,451	737,613
Baleares[3]		1,935	410,060
Barcelona	cen. Catalonia; on Mediterranean	2,968	1,943,355
Burgos	E Old Castile	5,480[4]	383,023
Cáceres	N Estremadura; on Portuguese border	7,667	513,402
Cádiz	SW Andalusia; on Mediterranean and Atlantic	2,834	603,452
Castellón de la Plana	N Valencia; on Mediterranean	2,495	312,475
Ciudad Real	S New Castile; in La Mancha	7,620	535,981
Córdoba	N cen. Andalusia	5,299	764,552
Cuenca	E New Castile	6,636	335,548
Gerona	NE Catalonia; on French border	2,264	323,493
Granada	E Andalusia; S coast	4,928	745,860
Guadalajara	NE New Castile	4,676	204,861
Guipúzcoa[5]	NE Basque Provinces	728	334,352
Huelva	W Andalusia; on Portuguese border	3,913	365,888
Huesca	N Aragon; on French border	5,848	232,962
Jaén	NE Andalusia	5,203	759,727
La Coruña	NW Galicia; on Atlantic	3,051	893,434
Las Palmas[6]		1,279	330,474
León	N León	5,936	497,756
Lérida	NW Catalonia	4,690	300,086
Logroño	NE Old Castile	1,946	223,608
Lugo	NE Galicia	3,814	514,786
Madrid	NW New Castile	3,084	1,600,081
Málaga	S cen. Andalusia; on Mediterranean	2,812	682,184
Murcia	S Murcia; on Mediterranean	4,453	726,300
Navarra[7]	S Navarre; borders on Pyrenees	4,055	371,497
Orense	S Galicia; on N Portuguese border	2,694	460,085
Oviedo	Asturias; on Bay of Biscay	4,205	839,580
Palencia	NW Old Castile	3,256	218,734
Pontevedra	SW Galicia; on Atlantic	1,695	644,819
Salamanca	S León; on Portuguese border	4,829	392,915
Santa Cruz de Tenerife[8]		1,528	366,508
Santander	N Old Castile; on Bay of Biscay	2,108	398,412
Segovia	SE Old Castile	2,635	189,942
Sevilla	W Andalusia	5,428	969,105
Soria	E Old Castile	3,983	159,890
Tarragona	S Catalonia; on Mediterranean	2,505	342,779
Teruel	S Aragon	5,720	233,790
Toledo	W New Castile	5,919	484,765
Valencia	cen. Valencia; on Mediterranean	4,150	1,269,620
Valladolid	W Old Castile	2,922	335,969
Vizcaya (*Also* Biscaya; *Eng.* Biscay)[9]	NW Basque Provinces	836	510,716
Zamora	cen. León; on NE Portuguese border	4,097	301,227
Zaragoza	W and cen. Aragon	6,726	596,942

[1] Unless otherwise noted, its capital city has the same name.
[2] Capital Vitoria.
[3] Island group in W Mediterranean, comprising Majorca, Minorca, Iviza, Formentera, and several smaller islands. (See BALEARIC ISLANDS.) Capital Palma.
[4] Including an exclave (Treviño) in Álava prov.
[5] Capital San Sebastián.
[6] E province of Canary Is. (*q.v.*), consisting principally of islands of Grand Canary, Lanzarote, and Fuerteventura.
[7] Capital Pamplona.
[8] W province of Canary Is. (*q.v.*), consisting of islands of Tenerife, La Palma, Gomera, and Hierro.
[9] Capital Bilbao.

FORMER DIVISIONS OF SPAIN[1]

NAME	DESCRIPTION	LOCATION IN SPAIN	MODERN PROVINCES
Andalusia (*Span.* Andalucía)	region	S	Almería, Cádiz, Córdoba, Granada, Huelva, Jaén, Málaga, Sevilla
Aragon (*Span.* Aragón)	region and anc. kingdom	NE	Huesca, Teruel, Zaragoza
Asturias	region and anc. kingdom	NW	Oviedo
Basque Provinces (*Span.* Provincias Vascongadas)	region	N	Álava, Guipúzcoa, Vizcaya
Catalonia (*Span.* Cataluña)	region and former auton. republic	NE	Barcelona, Gerona, Lérida, Tarragona
Estremadura *or* Extremadura	region	W cen.	Badajoz, Cáceres
Galicia	region and anc. kingdom	NW	La Coruña, Lugo, Orense, Pontevedra
León	region and anc. kingdom	NW	León, Salamanca, Zamora
Murcia	region and anc. kingdom	SE	Albacete, Murcia
Navarre[2] (*Span.* Navarra)	anc. kingdom	N	Navarra
New Castile (*Span.* Castilla la Nueva)	region	cen.	Ciudad Real, Cuenca, Guadalajara, Madrid, Toledo
Old Castile (*Span.* Castilla la Vieja)	region	N cen.	Ávila, Burgos, Logroño, Palencia, Santander, Segovia, Soria, Valladolid
Valencia	region and anc. kingdom	E	Alicante, Castellón de la Plana, Valencia

[1] For additional information, see the individual entries.
[2] Ancient kingdom now comprises Spanish province of Navarra and W part of French department of Basses-Pyrénées.

Mountains: On NE, separating Spain from France, the Pyrenees (highest Pico de Aneto 11,169 ft.); greater part of peninsula is plateau (*meseta*), averaging 2000 ft. alt. and rising in the N in the Cantabrian Mts., in the cen. part in the Sierra de Gredos and Sierra de Guadarrama (N of Madrid), and in the SW the Sierra Morena; near the SE coast along the Mediterranean is the range of the Sierra Nevada, containing the peak Mulhacén 11,420 ft., the highest point in Spain. *Rivers and lakes:* Only lowlands besides the narrow strips along the E coast of the Mediterranean are the valleys of the Ebro, Tagus, and Guadiana, and esp. that of the Guadalquivir; other notable rivers are the Miño, Duero, Segura, and Jucár; no large lakes. *Coast line:* Has few indentions and consequently few good harbors; on the Mediterranean are the Gulfs of Rosas and Almería and the harbors of Alicante and Málaga; at Strait of Gibraltar (separating Spain from Africa) is Bay of Algeciras; and on Atlantic the Gulf of Cádiz in S and harbors of La Coruña and Santander in N; prominent capes are Creus (NE), Nao (E), Gata (SE), Point Marroquí and Cape Trafalgar (S), Capes Finisterre and Ortegal (NW); its southernmost point, Point Marroquí, in 36°2′N, is southernmost point of Europe. *Economic resources:* Chiefly agricultural (grains, oranges, wines, hides, and cork) and mineral (coal, iron, lead, potash, mercury, and zinc). *Chief cities:* Madrid, Barcelona, Valencia, Seville, Saragossa, Málaga.

History: Southern and eastern coasts colonized by Phoenicians and Greeks; Mediterranean coastal region ruled by Carthage which ceded it to Rome 201 B.C.; Tarraconensis (Hither Spain), Boetica (Farther Spain), and Lusitania were provinces of Roman Empire; invaded by Vandals 409 A.D.; Toledo the seat of Visigothic kingdom 534–712; conquered by Moslems from North Africa 711–719; most of Spain ruled by Ommiad dynasty of Córdoba (*q.v.*) 756–1031, except in north where there

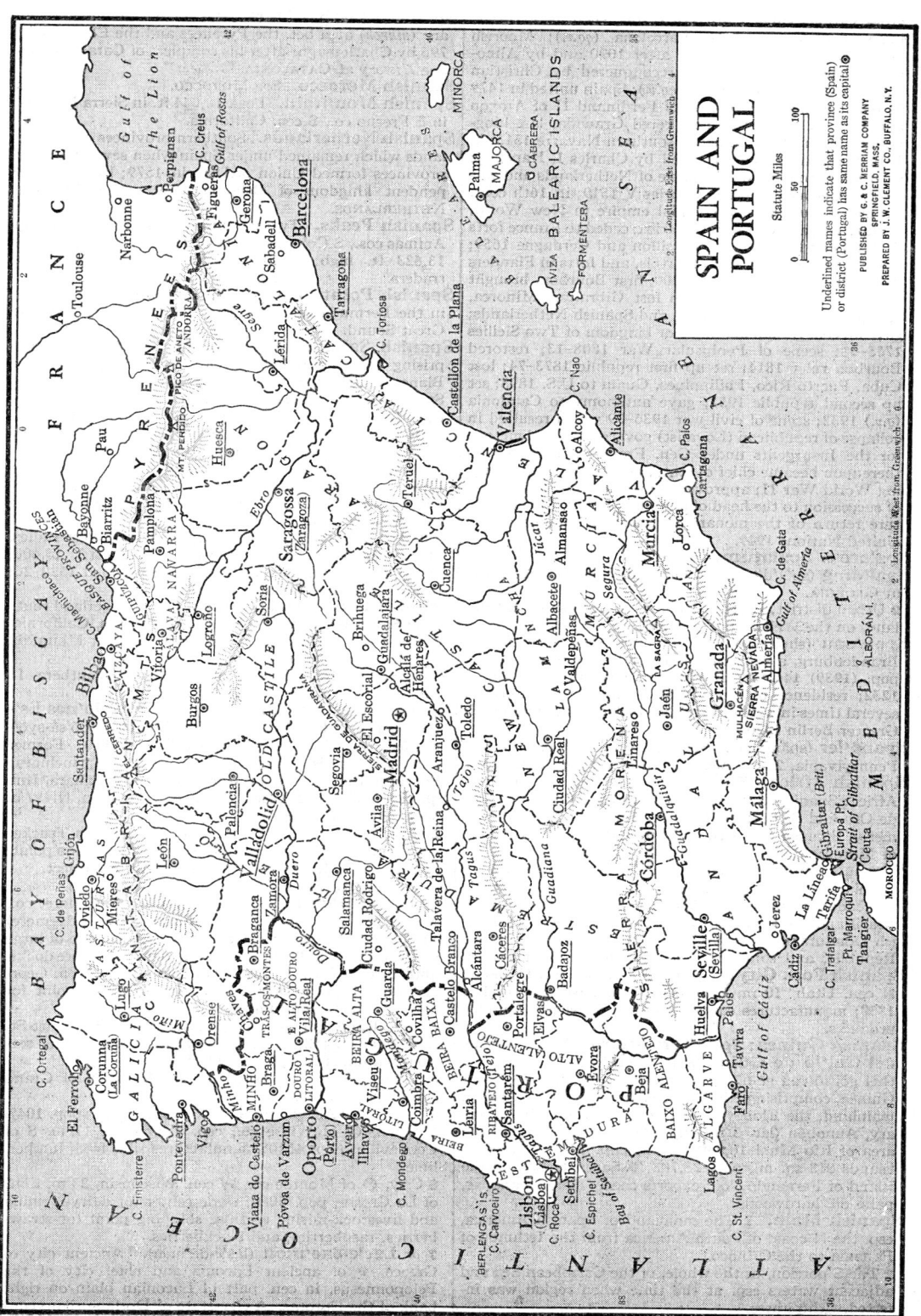

SPAIN AND
PORTUGAL

Statute Miles

Underlined names indicate that province (Spain)
or district (Portugal) has same name as its capital ⊙

PUBLISHED BY G. & C. MERRIAM COMPANY
SPRINGFIELD, MASS.
PREPARED BY J. W. CLEMENT CO., BUFFALO, N.Y.

arose various small Christian states, such as Asturias, León, Galicia, Navarre, Barcelona (*qq.v.*); Moorish Spain, ruled by Almoravides after 1090 and by Almohades after 1147, gradually reconquered by Christian states of Castile and Aragon (*qq.v.*); Spain united in 1479 as result of marriage (1469) of Ferdinand II of Aragon and Isabella of Castile; conquered Granada, last kingdom of Moors 1492; annexed southern Navarre 1515; in 1516 Spanish throne ascended by Charles I, Hapsburg ruler who brought to Spain rule of Netherlands and was elected German emperor Charles V 1519; in 16th cent. Spanish acquired huge colonial empire in New World, Philippines, and in northern Africa; ceded to France forts in Artois and Flanders, Roussillon and Cerdagne 1659; lost Franche-Comté, rest of Artois, and forts in Flanders 1678; accession of Philip V 1700, first Bourbon, brought on war through which Spain lost Gibraltar, Minorca, Sardinia, Sicily, Luxembourg, and Spanish Netherlands; gave up here Italian holdings for kingdom of Two Sicilies 1735–38; scene of Peninsular War 1808–13; restored Bourbon ruler 1814; set up first republic 1873–74; lost Cuba, Puerto Rico, Philippines, Guam to U.S. 1898; set up second republic 1931; gave autonomy to Catalonia (*q.v.*) 1932; scene of civil war 1936–39 which resulted in collapse of republican (Loyalist) government and victory for the Insurgents under Gen. Francisco Franco who thereupon became chief of state; nominally neutral during World War II; approved by referendum 1947 a law of succession to the head of state making possible the future return of the monarchy; remained outside of the United Nations 1949.

Spalato *or* **Spalatum.** See SPLIT.

Spal′ding (spôl′dĭng). **1** County in Georgia. See *Table* at GEORGIA.

2 Urban district, Parts of Holland, Lincolnshire, E England, on the Welland; pop. 11,031.

Span′dau (shpän′dou). Commune, East Germany, in Brandenburg, a western suburb of Berlin on the Spree; pop. (1939) 146,408; an old city, receiving civic rights 1232; residence of electors of Brandenburg; captured several times in wars of 17th and 19th cents.; united with Greater Berlin 1920.

Spang′ler (spăng′lẽr). Borough, Cambria co., SW cen. Pennsylvania, 22 m. WNW of Altoona; pop. 2658; coal.

Spanish Africa. The colonial possessions of Spain in Africa: Spanish Guinea, Spanish Sahara (including Río de Oro and Saguiet el Hamra), Ifni territory, and, formerly, Spanish Morocco and the Southern Protectorate of Morocco.

Spanish America. Those parts of America settled by Spaniards and now governed or occupied chiefly by their descendants; includes all of South America (except Brazil and the Guianas), Central America (except British Honduras), Mexico, Cuba, Puerto Rico, Dominican Republic, and some small islands in the West Indies.

Spanish Fork City *or* **Spanish Fork.** City, Utah co., N cen. Utah, 10 m. S of Provo; pop. 6472; settled c. 1850; manufactures canned goods, beet sugar, foundry products.

Spanish Guinea; *Span.* **Ter′ri·to′rios Es′pa·ño′les del Gol′fo de Gui·ne′a** (tĕr′rē·tō′ryôs ās′pä·nyō′lâz thĕl gôl′fō thä gē·nā′ä). Spanish colony in the Gulf of Guinea, comprising Río Muni territory on the W African mainland, the Elobeys and Corisco in Muni river estuary, Annobón (lat. 2°S; long. 5°E), and Fernando Poo; area of Río Muni 10,040 sq. m., pop. 138,797; area of islands 813 sq. m., pop. 28,708; ✳ Santa Isabel, on the island of Fernando Poo; exports cacao, coffee, bananas, palm oil, hardwoods.

Spanish Main. 1 The mainland of Spanish America, esp. the N coast of South America from the Isthmus of Panama to the Orinoco.

2 The S portion, or the whole, of the Caribbean Sea and adjacent waters esp. at the time when region was infested with pirates.

Spanish March *or* **Mark.** Region, NE Spain, a boundary (*march*) area bet. the Pyrenees and the Ebro, set up 795 by Charlemagne after his conquest of Catalonia 778. See *History* at CATALONIA.

Spanish Morocco. See MOROCCO.

Spanish Mountain. Peak 10,044 ft. in Sierra Nevada, in E Fresno co., S cen. California.

Spanish Netherlands. Southern provinces of Netherlands which remained under Spain when seven northern provinces formed Union of Utrecht 1579; became independent kingdom of Belgium 1830. See BELGIUM, NETHERLANDS.

Spanish Peaks. Two mountains in Huerfano and Las Animas cos., S Colorado; E peak 12,708 ft. high, W peak 13,623 ft. high; landmarks for early explorers and traders.

Spanish Point. Cape on W cen. coast of Bermuda I., in the Bermuda Is., extending W bet. Grassy Bay and Great Sound.

Spanish Sahara. Spanish colony, NW Africa, comprising two zones: Río de Oro, extending from Cape Blanc N to Cape Bojador, area 73,362 sq. m., and Saguiet el Hamra, extending from Cape Bojador to latitude 27°40′N, area 32,047 sq. m.; the colony is bounded on N by Morocco, on E and S by Mauritania, on W by the Atlantic Ocean; total area 105,409 sq. m., pop. ab. 25,000; ✳ Villa Cisneros; formerly administered from Cabo Yubi, Spanish town on SW coast of Morocco. Chief towns Villa Cisneros in Río de Oro and Smara in Saguiet el Hamra.

Spanish Town. Town, SE cen. Jamaica I., West Indies, ab. 20 m. W of Kingston; pop. (1943 est.) 13,600; originally called St. Iago de la Vega; founded 1520–26; former capital of Jamaica (until 1870).

Spanish Trail *or* **Old Spanish Trail.** Overland route from Santa Fe, New Mexico, to Los Angeles, California, dating from 1775; used first by the Spanish; Mountain Meadows (*q.v.*) is on it.

Spanish Wells. Island off N tip of Eleuthera I., Bahama Is.; 1 sq. m.; pop. (1943) 665.

Spanish Western Sahara; *Span.* **Po′se·sio′nes Es′-pa·ño′las del Sá′ha·ra Oc′ci·den·tal′** (pō′sä·syō′nâs äs′pä·nyō′läz thĕl sä′ä·rä ōk′sĕ·thän·täl′). Former name of Spanish possessions in W Africa, including Southern Protectorate of Morocco, Spanish Sahara, Ifni.

Sparks (spärks). **1** Town, Cook co., S Georgia, NNW of Valdosta; pop. 1158.

2 City, Washoe co., NW corner of Nevada, on Truckee river 3 m. E of Reno; pop. 16,618; railroad division point; near site of U.S. Spanish Springs irrigation project.

Sparnacum. See ÉPERNAY.

Spar′rows Point (spăr′ōz). Town, Baltimore co., Maryland; pop. (with Fort Howard and Edgemere) 11,775; on Patapsco river SE of Baltimore; site of large tidewater steel mill, shipyards, and deep-water ore docks.

Spar′ta (spär′tȧ). **1** City, ⊗ of Hancock co., cen. Georgia; pop. 1921; incorp. as ⊗ 1805; shipping point for dairy products and lumber.

2 City, Randolph co., SW Illinois, 45 m. SE of East St. Louis; pop. 3452; in agricultural and coal-mining section; manufactures plows and rayon.

3 Village, Kent co., W Michigan, 13 m. N of Grand Rapids; pop. 2749.

4 Town, ⊗ of Alleghany co., N North Carolina; pop. 1047.

5 Town, ⊗ of White co., cen. Tennessee, 17 m. S of Cookeville; pop. 4510; manufactures silk, feed, lumber, lime.

6 City, ⊗ of Monroe co., W cen. Wisconsin, 23 m. ENE of La Crosse; pop. 6080; trade center for dairy-farming and livestock-raising section; shipping point for strawberries, raspberries, and blackberries.

7 *or* **Lac′e·dae′mon** (lăs′ē·dē′mŏn). Ancient city of Greece, ✳ of ancient Laconia and chief city of the Peloponnesus, in cen. part of Laconian plain on right bank of the Eurotas. A city-state of Dorian origin; con-

quered Messenia 736–716 B.C.; became leading state in Peloponnesus and founder of Peloponnesian League; after long contest with Athens (*q.v.*), known as Peloponnesian Wars 460–404 B.C., Sparta attained hegemony in Greece; Spartan power broken by Thebes at battle of Leuctra 371 B.C.; lost independence when it joined Achaean League 192 B.C.; made part of Roman province of Achaea (*q.v.*) 146 B.C.

8 *Gr.* **Spar′të** (spär′tĕ). Town, ✻ of Laconia dept., SE Peloponnesus, S Greece; pop. (1963 est.) 20,000; S of the remains of ancient city.

Spar′tan·burg (spär′t'n·bûrg). **1** County in South Carolina. See *Table* at SOUTH CAROLINA.
2 Commercial and industrial city, ⊗ of Spartanburg co., NW South Carolina, at foot of Blue Ridge Mts. 30 m. ENE of Greenville; pop. 44,352; diversified farming; manufactures textiles, bags, fertilizer, lumber, paper boxes, flour and feed, iron and steel products; marble and granite works. Wofford Coll. (1851; coed.); Converse Coll. (1889; coed.). Cowpens and Kings Mt. battlefields in environs. Settled c. 1785.

Spar·tel′, Cape (spär·tĕl′). Cape on NW coast of Morocco, NW Africa, at the Strait of Gibraltar.

Spar·ti·ven′to (spär·tĕ·vĕn′tô). **1** Cape on S extremity of Italy, the SE point of Reggio di Calabria prov.
2 Cape on S extremity of the island of Sardinia, in the Mediterranean Sea W of Italy.

Spassk (späsk). Town, SW Maritime Territory Soviet Russia, Asia, on Trans-Siberian R.R. 120 m. N of Vladivostok; pop. ab. 11,000; SE of Lake Khanka.

Spa′tha, Cape (spä′thä). Point at tip of peninsula on NW coast of Crete, NW of Canea.

Spav′i·naw Creek (spăv′ĭ·nô). Stream, NE cen. Oklahoma, dammed to form **Lake Spavinaw**, 6 m. long, impounding 20,000,000,000 gallons of water used as supply for the city of Tulsa.

Spear′fish′ (spēr′ĭsh′). City, Lawrence co., W South Dakota, 12 m. NNW of Lead; pop. 3682; tourist center. Black Hills Teachers Coll. (1883; coed.).

Spearfish Peak. Mountain 5976 ft. in Lawrence co., W South Dakota.

Spear′man (spēr′măn). Town, ⊗ of Hansford co., NW Texas, in the panhandle; pop. 3555.

Spec′ta·cle Island (spĕk′tȧ·k'l; -tĭ·k'l). Island in S area of the harbor of Boston, Massachusetts.

Speed′way′ (spēd′wā′). Town, Marion co., cen. Indiana, 5 m. W of Indianapolis; pop. 9624; site of the Indianapolis Motor Speedway, where the annual 500-mile International Sweepstakes races are held.

Spei′chern (shpī′kẽrn). Var. of SPICHERN.

Speights′town (spīts′toun; *locally also* spīks′-). Town, NW Barbados I., Lesser Antilles, Brit. West Indies; pop. (1938 est.) 1500.

Spe·nard′ (spĕ·närd′). Urban community (unincorporated), S cen. Alaska, S of Anchorage; pop. 9074.

Spen′bor·ough (spĕn′bŭ·rŭ; -brŭ). Urban district, West Riding, Yorkshire, N England, 7 m. S of Leeds; pop. 36,977.

Spen′cer (spĕn′sẽr). **1** Name of counties in two states of the U.S. See *Tables* at INDIANA and KENTUCKY.
2 Town, ⊗ of Owen co., SW cen. Indiana, 14 m. NW of Bloomington; pop. 2557; birthplace of William Vaughn Moody (1869–1910), poet and playwright.
3 City, ⊗ of Clay co., NW Iowa; pop. 8864.
4 Industrial town, Worcester co., cen. Massachusetts, 10 m. W of Worcester; pop. 7838; shoe factories.
5 City, Rowan co., cen. North Carolina, NE suburb of Salisbury; pop. 2904; railroad division point.
6 Town, ⊗ of Van Buren co., cen. Tennessee; pop. 870.
7 City, ⊗ of Roane co., W cen. West Virginia, 35 m. NNE of Charleston; pop. 2660; gas wells.

Spencer, Cape. 1 Point on mainland, SE Alaska, on N side of entrance to Cross Sound.
2 South tip of Yorke Penin., SE South Australia, on E side of entrance to Spencer Gulf.

Spencer, Mount. Peak 3135 ft. in cen. Piscataquis co., N cen. Maine.

Spencer Gulf, *also* **Spen′cer's Gulf** (spĕn′sẽrz). Large inlet, South Australia, bet. Yorke and Eyre Penins.; 175 m. long and ab. 90 m. at its widest part; its entrance bet. Capes Catastrophe and Spencer partly shut off by Thistle I. and Gambier Is. Its chief ports are Port Lincoln, Port Pirie, and Port Augusta.

Spen′cer·ville (spĕn′sẽr·vĭl). Village, Allen co., NW Ohio, 13 m. W of Lima; pop. 2061.

Spen′ny·moor (spĕn′ĭ·mo͝or). Urban district, Durham, N England, 21 m. S of Newcastle; pop. 19,784.

Sper·mun′de Archipelago (spẽr·mŭn′dĕ). Group of small low islands surrounded by coral reefs in SE Makassar Strait, off SW coast of Celebes Is., Malay Archipelago.

Sper′rin Mountains (spĕr′ĭn). Mountain range, cos. Londonderry and Tyrone, Northern Ireland; highest peak 2240 ft.

Spe·su′ti·e Island (spĕ·so͞o′shĭ·ĕ). Island in upper Chesapeake Bay, easternmost point of Harford co., NE Maryland.

Spe′tsai (spâ′tsä); *Mod. Gr.* **Spé′tsai;** *Ital.* **Spez′zia** (spĕt′tsyä). Island in the Gulf of Argolis, in Argolis and Corinth dept., Greece; 7 sq. m.; pop. ab. 4000.

Spey (spā). River ab. 110 m. long in Inverness, Banff, and Moray cos., NE Scotland; flows NE into Moray Firth; noted for salmon fishing.

Spey′er (shpī′ẽr); *Anglicized* **Spires** (spīrz); *anc.* **Civ′itas Ne·me′tum** (sĭv′ĭ·tăs nĕ·mē′tŭm; nĕm′ĕ·tŭm), *later* **Spi′ra** (spī′rä). City, ✻ of Palatinate govt. dist., Bavaria, Germany, on the Rhine 22 m. N of Karlsruhe; pop. 25,609; famous 11th-cent. Romanesque cathedral (rebuilt in 18th and 19th cents.) containing remains of numerous German sovereigns; manufactures include airplanes, tobacco, cigars, leather, shoes, cotton goods, beer, tile, wine, machinery, iron goods. First cathedral built by Frankish king Dagobert (628–639); became free imperial city 1111; famous Diet of Spires convened here 1592; destroyed by the French 1689 and 1794; part of the French department of Donnersberg 1801–14; passed to Bavaria 1814.

Spe′zia, Gulf of (spâ′tsyä). Small bay, inlet of Gulf of Genoa, on E coast of Genova prov., NW Italy; excellent harbor.

Spezia, La. See LA SPEZIA.

Spezzia. See SPETSAI.

Spha·ki·a′ (sfä·kyä′). Small coastal town, SW Crete, S of Canea.

Sphinx, Mount (sfĭngks). Peak 10,860 ft. in SE cen. Madison co., SW Montana.

Spice Islands. See MOLUCCAS.

Spi′cer Islands (spī′sẽr). Two small islands in center of Foxe Basin, Northern Territories, Canada, ab. 68°N, 79°10′W. Discovered 1879; all trace of existence of islands lost until rediscovered Aug. 28, 1946.

Spi′che·ren′ *or* **Spick′e·ren′** (spē′krĕn′); *Ger.* **Spi′chern** (shpĭk′ẽrn). Village and heights in Moselle dept., France, E of Forbach and near Saarbrücken in the Saar; battle Aug. 6, 1870 in which Germans under Steinmetz defeated French under Frossard.

Spie′ker·oog (shpē′kẽr·ōк). Island ab. 6 sq. m., East Frisian Is., off NW coast of Germany bet. Langeoog and Wangerooge.

Spi·naz·zo′la (spē·nät·tsō′lä). Commune, Bari prov., Apulia, SE Italy, 41 m. WSW of Bari; pop. 12,020.

Spin′dale (spĭn′dāl). Town, Rutherford co., SW North Carolina, 23 m. W of Shelby; pop. 4082.

Spink (spĭngk). County in South Dakota. See *Table* at SOUTH DAKOTA.

Spi·on′ Kop (spē·ôn′ kôp′; *Angl.* spī′ŭn kŏp′). Hill in Natal, Republic of So. Africa, 24 m. WSW of Ladysmith; scene of battle Jan. 24, 1900 in which the Boers defeated the British under Sir Redvers Buller.

Spira. See SPEYER.

Spirding. See ŚNIARDWY.

Spire Point (spīr). Peak 8220 ft. in N cen. Washington, on boundary bet. Skagit and Chelan cos.

Spires. See SPEYER.

Spir'it Lake (spĭr'ĭt). **1** Lake ab. 10 m. long on N boundary of Dickinson co., NW Iowa.

2 City, ⊗ of Dickinson co., NW Iowa, 51 m. NNE of Cherokee; pop. 2685; in lake region.

Spiš. See SZEPES.

Spiš'ská No'vá Ves (spĭsh'skä nô'vä vĕs'); _Hung._ **I'gló** (ĭ'glō); _Ger._ **Zip'fer Neu'dorf** (tsĭp'fēr noi'dôrf). Town, E Slovakia prov., E cen. Czechoslovakia, on headstream of the Tisza; pop. (1930) 12,889.

Spisz (spĭsh), **Spits** (spĭch). Vars. of _Spiš:_ see SZEPES.

Spit'al·fields' (spĭt'l·fēldz'). Two wards of Stepney borough, E London, England; pop. 5711; former center of silk weaving.

Spit'head' (spĭt'hĕd'; -hĕd'). Roadstead on S coast of England, off Portsmouth harbor bet. Portsea I. and the NE coast of the Isle of Wight; connects with the Solent on the W; frequent rendezvous of British fleet.

Spits'ber'gen (spĭts'bûr'gĕn). Norwegian archipelago forming part of Svalbard Archipelago in the Arctic Ocean 360 m. N of Norway; 24,225 sq. m., pop. ab. 2000; chief settlement Green Harbor; has extensive coal deposits; chief islands West Spitsbergen, North East Land, Edge I., Barents I.; highest point Mt. Newton 5445 ft., on West Spitsbergen. Probably known to Vikings but discovered in modern times by William Barents in June 1596; became officially a part of Norway Aug. 14, 1925. See ARCTIC REGIONS.

Spiż. See SZEPES.

Split (splĭt; _Yugo._ splēt) _or_ **Spljet** (splyĕt); _Ital._ **Spa'la·to** (spä'lä·tô); _anc._ **Spal'a·tum** (spăl'á·tŭm). Seaport on the Adriatic, in Croatia federated republic, Yugoslavia; pop. 35,332; excellent harbor; industrial, shipping, and commercial center; seaside resort; cathedral, amphitheater, museum, art gallery. Nearby colony of Salona (_q.v._) founded 78 B.C.; on its destruction by the Avars 639 A.D. its inhabitants founded new town of Spalatum; seat of the metropolitan of Dalmatia until 12th cent.; passed to Hungary in 12th cent., to Venice 1327; recovered by Hungary and held for a time by Bosnia, it passed again to Venice 1420; secured by Austria 1813; became part of Kingdom of the Serbs, Croats, and Slovenes 1918; county seat of Primorje co. in reorganized Yugoslavia 1929–45.

Split Mountain (splĭt). Peak 14,051 ft. in Sierra Nevada, in Fresno and Inyo cos., SE cen. California.

Splügen; _Ital._ **Spluga.** Alpine pass. See ALPS.

Spo·kane' (spō·kăn'). **1** River ab. 120 m. long, E Washington; rises in Coeur d'Alene Lake, Kootenai co., N Idaho, flows W across Washington border and into Columbia river in N Lincoln co.

2 County in Washington. See _Table_ at WASHINGTON.

3 City, ⊗ of Spokane co., E Washington, on falls of Spokane river 18 m. W of Idaho border; pop. 181,608; commercial, financial, and industrial center of Inland Empire; extensive farming, lumbering, mining interests; diversified manufactures; grain elevators, railroad shops. Gateway to recreation area and national parks; seat of Fort George Wright, U.S. military post (1894); Spokane Air Force Base. Gonzaga Univ. (1887; men), Whitworth Coll. (1890; coed.), Holy Names Coll. (1907; women). Settled 1872; incorp. as Spokane Falls 1881; reincorporated as Spokane 1890, as city 1891.

Spo·le'to (spō·lā'tô); _anc._ **Spo·le'ti·um** (spō·lē'shĭ·ŭm). Commune, Perugia prov., Umbria, cen. Italy, 30 m. SE of Perugia; pop. 32,341; 11th-cent. cathedral; 13th-cent. town hall; numerous old churches (5th–14th cents.). Founded by Etruscans; became Roman 240 B.C.; one of leading cities of ancient Umbria; became center of a Lombard duchy which covered most of E cen. Italy 570 A.D.; after fall of Carolingians, Guy of Spoleto (Duke Guido) proclaimed himself king of Italy 889 and

was crowned emperor of the West 891; fell to States of the Church 1198; became part of kingdom of Italy 1860.

Spoon'er (spōōn'ēr). City, Washburn co., NW Wisconsin, 25 m. N of Rice Lake (city); pop. 2398; trade and supply center in resort region of woods and lakes.

Spor'a·des (spŏr'á·dēz; _Mod. Gr._ spô·rä'thâs). Two groups of islands in the Aegean Sea, the **Northern Sporades** (_Gr._ Vo·rei'ai Spo·ra'des [vô·rē'â spô·rä'thâs]) and the **Southern Sporades.** Chief islands of the Northern Sporades, off the mainland coast of Magnesia (Thessaly) and the island Euboea, are Skyros, Skopelos, Skiathos, and Alonēsos; administratively attached to Euboea dept., Greece. Chief islands of the Southern Sporades are Rhodes and the Dodecanese, which belonged to Italy 1912–47; also included in the Southern Sporades by some geographers are the islands of Samos, Ikaria, Chios, and Lesbos.

Spot Mountain (spŏt). Peak 7800 ft. in Glacier National Park, NW Montana.

Spots'wood (spŏts'wŏŏd). Borough, Middlesex co., cen. New Jersey, SE of New Brunswick; pop. 5788.

Spot·syl·va'nia (spŏt'sĭl·văn'yá; -vā'nĭ·á). **1** County in Virginia. See _Table_ at VIRGINIA.

2 Village, its ⊗, NE Virginia, 11 m. SW of Fredericksburg; battles of **Spotsylvania Court House** May 8–21, 1864, result indecisive, bet. Federals under Grant and Confederates under Lee included battle at the Bloody Angle May 12.

Spot'ted Range (spŏt'ĕd; -ĭd). Small range in S Nevada, in Clark, Lincoln, and S Nye cos.

Sprague (sprăg). **1** River, S Oregon; rises in SW Lake co., flows W across Klamath co., into the Williamson river near Upper Klamath Lake.

2 Town, N New London co., SE Connecticut, N of Norwich; pop. 2509; watered by Shetucket river; in fruitgrowing region; manufactures cottons and woolens, paper boxes, hospital supplies.

Sprat'ly Islands (sprăt'lĭ). Group of small islands, actually reefs, in cen. part of South China Sea, ab. 280 m. SE of Camranh Bay and 775 m. NE of Singapore; seized by Japan June 1940 and made submarine base.

Spray (sprā). Town, North Carolina. See LEAKSVILLE.

Spreck'els·ville (sprĕk'lz·vĭl). Town, Wailuku dist., Maui co., Hawaii, on N coast of Maui I.; pop. (est.) 1000; sugar plantations.

Spree (shprā). River 220 m. long in E cen. Germany; rises in mountains of Saxony near Czech border, flows N out of Saxony past Bautzen and Cottbus and through Berlin, where it joins the Havel river at Spandau; navigable for vessels of light draught.

Spree'wald' (shprā'vält'). Woody and marshy district in the Spree valley, NW of Cottbus, Brandenburg, in E Germany.

Sprem'berg (shprĕm'bĕrĸ). City, Brandenburg, E Germany, on Spree river 14 m. S of Cottbus and 77 m. SE of Berlin; pop. 12,726; manufactures textiles, machinery, and paper.

Spring (sprĭng). River ab. 60 m. long, NE Arkansas; rises in S Missouri, crosses Arkansas border in Fulton co., flows SE into Black river.

Spring'bok (sprĭng'bŏk) _or_ **Spring'bok·fon·tein'** (sprĭng'bôk·fŏn·tān'). Village, NW Cape Province, S Republic of So. Africa; ✱ of Little Namaqualand; pop. 1706; in copper district near O'okiep.

Spring City (sprĭng). **1** Borough, Chester co., SE Pennsylvania, on Schuylkill river 28 m. NW of Philadelphia; pop. 3162; knit goods, textiles, stoves, machine tools, steel.

2 Town, Rhea co., E cen. Tennessee, 25 m. SSW of Harriman; pop. 1800.

Spring'dale (sprĭng'dāl). **1** City, Washington co., NW Arkansas, 12 m. N of Fayetteville; pop. 10,076; markets grapes, grape juice, apples, strawberries; fruit and vegetable canneries.

2 Subdivision of town of STAMFORD, Connecticut.

3 Borough, Allegheny co., SW Pennsylvania, on Allegheny river 14 m. NE of Pittsburgh; pop. 5602.

Spring'er (sprĭng'ẽr). Town, Colfax co., N New Mexico, on Cimarron river 38 m. S of Raton; pop. 1564; was county seat 1882–97; in cattle and sheep country.

Springer, Mount. Peak 3820 ft. in Dawson co., N Georgia.

Spring'field (sprĭng'fēld). **1** Town, ⊗ of Baca co., SE corner of Colorado; pop. 1791.

2 City, ⊗ of Effingham co., E Georgia; pop. 858.

3 City, ⊗ of Sangamon co., cen. Illinois, and ✻ of Illinois, on Sangamon river 190 m. SW of Chicago; pop. 83,271; in agricultural section near coal fields; diversified manufacturing; home and burial place of Abraham Lincoln; Lincoln tomb and monument, designed and executed by Larkin G. Meade, in Oak Ridge cemetery. Concordia Theological Seminary (1846; men; Lutheran); Lincoln Coll. of Law (1911; coed.). Settled 1818; incorp. as town 1832, as city 1840; made capital of Illinois 1837.

4 City, ⊗ of Washington co., cen. Kentucky, 25 m. W of Danville; pop. 2382; among records in the county courthouse are the marriage bond of Thomas Lincoln, father of Abraham Lincoln, and the certificate of marriage of Thomas Lincoln and Nancy Hanks. See HARRODSBURG, Kentucky.

5 City, ⊗ of Hampden co., SW Massachusetts, on Connecticut river 5 m. N of Connecticut border; pop. 174,463; manufactures arms, tools, electric equipment, gasoline pumps, oil burners, package machinery, magnetos, air-conditioning equipment, plastics; home of Merriam-Webster *Dictionaries*. Springfield Coll., International Y.M.C.A. Coll. (1885); American International Coll. (1885; coed.); Western New England Coll. (1919; coed.). Founded 1636; burned during King Philip's War 1675; scene of Shays' Rebellion 1786–87; site of United States Armory 1794–1968.

6 City, Brown co., S Minnesota; pop. 2701.

7 City, ⊗ of Greene co., SW Missouri; pop. 95,865; trade and industrial center in agricultural and mining section; stone quarries and lead and zinc mines nearby. Drury Coll. (1873; coed.; Congregational); Southwest Missouri State Coll. (1905; coed.).

8 Residential suburban township, Union co., NE New Jersey, ab. 6 m. NW of Elizabeth; pop. 14,467; scene of battle in Revolution June 23, 1780 in which Gen. Greene repulsed the British; old Revolutionary cemetery.

9 Industrial city, ⊗ of Clark co., W Ohio, 23 m. NE of Dayton; pop. 82,723; transportation and trading center in agricultural section (hogs, corn); manufactures agricultural machinery, motor trucks, engines, automobile parts, electrical equipment, metal caskets, incubators. Wittenberg Univ. (1842; coed.). Settled 1799; became ⊗ 1818; incorp. as town 1827, as city 1850.

10 City, Lane co., W Oregon, 5 m. E of Eugene; pop. 19,616; lumbering center; manufactures flax products.

11 Urban township, Delaware co., SE Pennsylvania, ab. 5 m. NE of Chester; pop. 26,733.

12 Urban township, Montgomery co., SE Pennsylvania, SW suburb of Philadelphia; pop. 20,652.

13 City, Bon Homme co., SE South Dakota, on Missouri river ab. 28 m. W of Yankton; pop. 1194. Southern State Teachers Coll. (estab. 1881; opened 1897; coed.).

14 City, ⊗ of Robertson co., N Tennessee, 23 m. N of Nashville; pop. 9221; loose-leaf tobacco market; woolens (esp. blankets), flour, lumber.

15 Industrial village in Springfield town (pop. 9934), Windsor co., E Vermont, on Black river 33 m. SE of Rutland; pop. 6600; machinery and machine tools.

16 Urban area, Fairfax co., NE Virginia; pop. 10,783.

Springfield, Lake. Artificial lake completed 1935 in Sangamon co., cen. Illinois; 15 m. long; shore line 45 m.; source of water supply for Springfield.

Springfield Place. Urban community (unincorporated), Calhoun co., S Michigan, W of Battle Creek; pop. 5136.

Spring'fon·tein' (sprĭng'fôn·tān'). Town, S Orange Free State, E cen. Union of South Africa, on Cape Town railroad line 85 m. SSW of Bloemfontein; pop. 2054.

Spring Garden. Urban township, York co., S Pennsylvania, S of York; pop. 11,387.

Spring'hill (sprĭng'hĭl). **1** City, Webster parish, NW Louisiana, 38 m. NNE of Shreveport; pop. 6437.

2 Coal-mining town, Cumberland co., N Nova Scotia, Canada, 15 m. SE of Amherst; pop. 7138.

Spring Hill. Residential suburb of Mobile, Alabama; Spring Hill Coll. (1830; coed.; Roman Catholic).

Spring Lake. Borough, Monmouth co., E cen. New Jersey, on Atlantic Ocean 6 m. S of Asbury Park; pop. 2922; summer resort.

Spring'lands (sprĭng'lăndz; -lăndz'). Town, NE British Guiana, in Berbice co. on W bank of Courantyne river near its mouth, 95 m. SE of Georgetown.

Spring Mountain Range. Mountain range in W cen. Clark co., SE Nevada.

Springs (sprĭngz). City, S Transvaal, NE Union of South Africa, 29 m. E of Johannesburg; pop. 86,874; one of oldest settlements in the Rand; center of rich gold and coal region and also trade center for eastern Transvaal agricultural districts.

Spring Valley. 1 City, Bureau co., N Illinois, on Illinois river 18 m. W of Ottawa; pop. 5371; coal mining.

2 Village, Fillmore co., SE Minnesota; pop. 2628.

3 Village, Rockland co., SE New York; pop. 6538.

Spring'view' (sprĭng'vū'). Village, ⊗ of Keya Paha co., N Nebraska; pop. 281.

Spring'ville (sprĭng'vĭl; *Sou.* also -v'l). **1** Village, Erie co., W New York, 27 m. SSE of Buffalo; pop. 3852.

2 City, Utah co., N cen. Utah, 5 m. S of Provo; pop. 7913; art center; flour, feed, canned goods, beet sugar.

Sprottau. See SZPROTAWA.

Spruce Hill. Peak 2588 ft. in Berkshire co., W Massachusetts. See HOOSAC MOUNTAINS.

Spruce Knob. Peak 4860 ft. in Pendleton co., E West Virginia; highest point in the state.

Spruce Mountain. Peak 11,041 ft. in SE cen. Elko co., NE Nevada.

Spruce Pine. Town, Mitchell co., W North Carolina, in Blue Ridge Mts. 36 m. NE of Asheville; pop. 2504; mining and refining of feldspar, kaolin, mica, cyanite.

Spruce Ridge Top. Peak 6076 ft. in W North Carolina.

Spruce'top' (sprōōs'tŏp'). Peak 3620 ft. in the Catskill Mts., Greene co., SE New York.

Spur (spûr). City, Dickens co., NW Texas, 53 m. E of Lubbock; pop. 2170; stock raising; farming.

Spurn Head (spûrn). Cape on E coast of England, in Yorkshire, at NE entrance to mouth of the Humber river; lighthouse.

Spurr, Mount (spûr). Mountain peak 11,050 ft. W of head of Cook Inlet, SW Alaska.

Spuy'ten Duy'vil (spī't'n dī'v'l). District of N New York City, formerly a village, on Hudson river just N of Spuyten Duyvil Creek.

Spuyten Duyvil Creek. Narrow channel N of Manhattan I., New York, separating the island from the mainland and connecting Hudson and Harlem rivers.

Spy (*Fr.* spē; *Flemish* spī). Commune, Namur prov., S Belgium, 6 m. W of Namur; pop. 3383; cave where two skeletons were found 1886 representing a type of paleolithic man.

Squam Lake (skwŏm). Lake ab. 6 m. long and 4 m. wide in cen. New Hampshire, on boundary bet. Grafton, Belknap, and Carroll cos.; resort.

Squa'pan Lake (skwô'păn). Lake in E cen. Aroostook co., N Maine.

Squaw Peak (skwô). **1** Mountain 8960 ft. in E California, in Sierra Nevada W of Lake Tahoe.

2 Mountain 8660 ft. in SE Idaho co., N cen. Idaho.

Squaw Valley. Valley, E California, in the Sierra Nevada on E slopes of Squaw Peak; ski resort.

Squil·la′ce, Gulf of (skwĕl·lä′chä). Inlet of Ionian Sea on SE coast of Calabria compartimento, S Italy.

Squin·za′no (skwĕn·tsä′nō). Commune, Lecce prov., Apulia, SE Italy, 9 m. NW of Lecce; pop. (1931) 10,366.

Sra′gen (srä′gĕn). Town, NE Surakarta govt., cen. Java, Indonesia, on railroad ab. 17 m. NE of Surakarta; pop. 15,382.

Srbija. See SERBIA.

Sredets. See SOFIA.

Sredinny Khrebet. See CENTRAL RANGE.

Sred′ne Ko·lymsk′ (sryäd′nyĭ kŭ·lĭmsk′). Town, NE Yakutsk A.S.S.R., Soviet Russia, Asia, on left bank of middle (Russ. *sredne*) course of Kolyma river.

Srem. See SYRMIA.

Sremska Mitrovica. See MITROVICA.

Sremski Karlovci. See KARLOWITZ.

Sre′tensk (sryā′tyĭnsk). Town, S Chita Region, Soviet Russia, Asia, on S bank of Shilka river 180 m. E of Chita; terminus of spur of Trans-Siberian R.R.

Sriem, Srijem, Srjem. Vars. of *Srem:* see SYRMIA.

Sri′ha·ri·ko′ta Island (srē′hȧ·rĭ·kō′tȧ). Jungle-covered island 30 m. long off SE coast of India, N of Madras and E of Pulicat Lagoon.

Sri·na′gar (srĕ·nŭg′ẽr). **1** District, Kashmir state, N India. See KASHMIR SOUTH.

2 City, ✱ of Kashmir division and district and ✱ of Kashmir state, SW Kashmir, N India, on Jhelum river 180 m. N of Lahore at an altitude of 5250 ft.; pop. (1941) 207,787; operates carpet mills, now replacing former shawl-weaving industry, and does copper, silver, leather, and wood work. A picturesque city with splendid mountain scenery; has palaces, mosques, fortress, museum, and archaeology institute. To the NE lies Dal Lake with its renowned floating gardens. Scene of Thomas Moore's *Lalla Rookh*.

Sri·ran′gam (srĕ·rŭng′gȧm). Town, SE Madras state, S Indian Union, on island in Cauvery river 2 m. N of Trichinopoly and 30 m. W of Tanjore; pop. 24,663; place of pilgrimage to great temple, dedicated to Vishnu.

Sri·vi·ja′ya (srĕ·wĭ·jô′yȧ) *or* **Shri′vi·ja′ya** (shrē′vĭ-jä′yȧ). Hindu-Malayan empire of wide extent in SE Asia, 12th cent. A.D. See MALAY ARCHIPELAGO.

Sri′vil·li·put·tur′ (srē′vĭ·lĭ·pŏŏ·tŏŏr′). City, S Madras, S Indian Union, 40 m. SW of Madura; pop. 32,385.

Ssupingchieh. See SZEPINGKAI.

Staal′bjerg·huk′, Cape (stäl′byärk·hōōk′). Cape, W Iceland, N of Breidi Fjord.

Stabiae. See CASTELLAMMARE DI STABIA.

Stablo. See STAVELOT.

Stadacona. See QUEBEC city.

Sta′de (shtä′dĕ). **1** Government district, former Hannover prov., Prussia, Germany, 2620 sq. m.

2 Manufacturing city, its ✱, 22 m. W of Hamburg; pop. 11,985; manufactures leather, salt, tile, hemp, lumber, oil, rubber goods; trades in lumber. First mentioned 988; member of Hanseatic League.

Stad–Hardenberg. See HARDENBERG.

Städ′jan (städ′yàn). Peak 3710 ft. in SW cen. Sweden, near the Norwegian border.

Stadt Ber·lin′ (shtät′ bĕr·lēn′). Province of former Prussia. See *Berlin* in *Table* at PRUSSIA.

Stadt′lohn (shtät′lōn). Commune, North Rhine-Westphalia state, NW Germany, W of Münster near Netherlands border; pop. 6548; scene of victory Aug. 6, 1623 of Catholic League under Count of Tilly over Imperial forces under Christian of Brunswick.

Staf′fa (stăf′ȧ). Small island of the Inner Hebrides, Scotland, 7 m. W of Mull; location of **Fin′gal's Cave** (fĭng′gȧlz), 227 ft. long, 117 ft. high.

Staf′ford (stăf′ẽrd). **1** Name of counties in two states of the U.S. See *Tables* at KANSAS and VIRGINIA.

2 Town, N Tolland co., N Connecticut, on Massachusetts border E of Somers; pop. 7476; watered by Willimantic river; settled and incorp. 1719; agriculture, manufacturing; includes borough of Stafford Springs (*q.v.*).

3 City, Stafford co., cen. Kansas, 38 m. W of Hutchinson; pop. 1862.

4 Village, ⊗ of Stafford co., NE Virginia; pop. (est.) 500.

5 County in England. See STAFFORDSHIRE.

6 Municipal borough, ⊗ of Staffordshire, W cen. England, on the Sow 25 m. NNW of Birmingham; pop. 40,275; shoe manufacturing. Birthplace of Izaak Walton.

Staf′ford·shire (-shĭr; -shẽr) *or* **Stafford** *or* **Staffs** (stăfs). County, W cen. England; 1153 sq. m.; pop. (1951) 1,621,013; ⊗ Stafford; other towns are Burton upon Trent, Stoke on Trent, Willenhall, Wednesbury, West Bromwich; rivers the Trent and its tributaries; coal mining, manufacturing (iron and steel products, pottery, glass, textiles, chemicals), brewing. Its regions contain much of the Black Country (*q.v.*).

Stafford Springs. Industrial borough (pop. 3322) in town of STAFFORD, Connecticut; incorp. 1873; mineral springs; formerly a health resort; market center; manufactures woolen and cotton goods, worsteds, yarns.

Stag Dome (stăg). Peak 7707 ft. in Sierra Nevada, in E Fresno co., S cen. California.

Sta·gi′ra (stȧ·jī′rȧ) *or* **Sta·gi′ros** (-rŏs). Town in ancient Macedonia, NE Greece, on E Chalcidice Penin., on Strymonic Gulf. Birthplace of Aristotle ("the Stagirite").

Stai′er·dorf–A′ni·na (shtī′ẽr·dôrf·ä′nĕ·nä); *Ger.* **Stei′-er·dorf–A′ni·na** (shtī′ẽr·dôrf·ä′nĕ·nä). Commune, SW Romania, ab. 55 m. SE of Timişoara; pop. 10,269.

Staines (stānz). Urban district, Middlesex, SE England, on the Thames 19 m. WSW of London; pop. 39,983; part of Greater London.

Stains (stăN). Commune, Seine dept., N France, NNE suburb of Paris; pop. (1931) 14,539.

Staked Plain. See LLANO ESTACADO.

Stalin. See BRAŞOV; STALINO; VARNA.

Sta′lin·a·bad′ (stä′lĭn·ȧ·bäd′); *earlier, and since 1961,* **Dyu·sham′be** (dŭ·shäm′bĕ). City, ✱ of Tadzhik S.S.R., Soviet Central Asia, in W part of Stalinabad Region; pop. 82,540; manufactures cotton and silk; railroad terminus, connecting via Termez with Bukhara.

Stalinabad Region; *now* **Dyushambe Region.** Subdivision of Tadzhik S.S.R., Soviet Central Asia, in W part; ✱ Dyushambe.

Sta′lin·grad (stä′lĭn·grăd; stäl′ĭn-; *Russ.* stŭ·lyĭn·grȧt′) *or earlier* **Tsa·ri′tsyn** (tsŭ·ryē′tsĭn); *since 1961,* **Vol′-go·grad** (vŏl′gô·grăd; *Russ.* vŏl·gŭ·grȧt′). City, ✱ of Volgograd Region, Soviet Russia, Europe, in S part of region on the Volga ab. 280 m. from its mouth; pop. 445,476; the only industrial city of an agricultural area; has tractor factory, sawmills, factories for metal goods, machinery, chemicals, naphtha refining; important as a river port and because of its direct rail connection with Moscow, Krasnodar, and the Donbas, also as E terminal of Volga-Don canal.

History: Originated as a Russian fort 1589 as defense against Kalmuck, Cossack, and other raiders; captured by Stenka Razin 1670; importance increased rapidly with building of railroads; held by Bolsheviki 1917; a point of conflict during civil war 1919–20, for a time held by Denikin; name changed 1925 in honor of Josef Stalin and again in 1961. Suffered terrible destruction in World War II when it was the scene of some of the most violent fighting of the war: attack begun Aug. 20, 1942; entered, but not completely occupied, by German army during siege of 66 days Sept. 14 to Nov. 19, 1942; German forces threatened by Russian counteroffensive begun in Nov.; finally recaptured, together with large German force, on surrender of Gen. Paulus Feb. 2, 1943.

Stalingrad Region; *now* **Volgograd Region.** Region, SE Soviet Russia, Europe, on the lower Volga; 52,264 sq. m.; pop. 2,289,049; ✱ Volgograd. On the SE a long arm of the region extends along the Volga to the Caspian Sea; on the NE a part of the former German Volga Republic has been (1941) incorporated in it. Flat steppe land E of the Volga, fairly good brown soil bet.

Volga and Don rivers, and rich black earth W of the Don. In good years when rainfall is adequate crops of wheat, rye, millet, fruits, and vegetables are grown. Besides the two main streams, region is crossed by Don tributaries—Khoper and Medveditsa; also contains the Volga-Don canal. In E are Elton and other lakes which are productive sources of salt. In addition to agriculture many peasant industries are pursued, as fishing, tanning, flour milling, textile making.

History: Region in 5th cent. occupied by Bulgars, in 10th by Khazars; after Mongol invasion of Europe, Batu Khan fixed upon lands of the lower Volga as home of the Golden Horde and established Sarai (*q.v.*) as his capital; conquest of this Tatar territory begun in 15th cent. by Russians, who established Astrakhan 1557 and Tsaritsyn 1589 and in 17th and 18th cents. were in continual conflict with Nogai, Kirghiz and Kalmuck tribesmen; in latter part of 18th cent. scene of Pugachev's rebellion; after Revolution of 1917 there was much disorder for several years. Suffered great famine 1921; became part of Lower Volga Area 1928; made a subdivision of R.S.F.S.R. 1936; in World War II its S part reached in farthest eastern advance of German armies 1942 (see STALINGRAD).

Sta·li·nir′ (stŭ·lyĭ·nyēr′); *formerly, and since 1961,* **Tskhin′va·li** (tskĭn′vä·lĭ). Town, ✷ of South Ossetia, Georgia, U.S.S.R., 60 m. NW of Tiflis.

Sta′lin Line (stä′lĭn; -lēn; stăl′ĭn; stăl′ēn; *Russ.* stä′lyĭn). In early part of World War II a Russian fortified line extending S from Leningrad to a point W of Kiev chiefly along W bank of Dnieper, to serve as protection to Moscow; penetrated by Germans in 1941 and completely overcome in great battle of Smolensk July 20–Aug. 9, 1941.

Stal′i·no (stä′lyĭ·nŭ) *or* **Sta′lin** (stä′lĭn; -lēn; stăl′ĭn; stăl′ēn; *Russ.* stä′lyĭn); *now* **Do·netsk′** (dŭ·nyĕtsk′). **1** Region, E Ukraine, U.S.S.R.; cen. part of Donbas, touches on N shore of Sea of Azov.

2 *formerly also* **Yu′zov·ka** (yōō′zŭf·kȧ). City, its ✷, on Kalmius river 100 m. NW of Rostov; pop. 462,395; one of the great industrial centers of the Donbas; has foundries, chemical works, smelteries, mills, and factories. Founded 1870 by a British subject named Hughes (hence **Hughes′ov·ka** [hūz′ŭf·kȧ], or in Russia **Yu′zov·ka** [yōō′zŭf·kȧ]); developed rapidly up to World War I and then again after 1924. In World War II held by Germans Oct. 22, 1941–Sept. 9, 1943.

Sta·li′no·gorsk (stă·lē′nŏ·gôrsk; *Russ.* stŭ·lyĭ·nŭ·gôrsk′) *or* **Bob′ri·ki** (bŏb′rĭ·kĭ; *Russ.* bôb′ryĭ·kĭ). Industrial city, S Moscow Region, Soviet Russia, Europe, ab. 35 m. ESE of Tula; pop. 76,207.

Sta′lin Peak (stä′lĭn; -lēn; stăl′ĭn; stăl′ēn; *Russ.* stä′lyĭn) *or* **Gar·mo′ Peak** (gär·mō′); *now* **Mount Communism.** Highest peak ab. 24,590 ft. in the Russian Pamirs, SE Tadzhik S.S.R., Soviet Central Asia; highest peak in the Soviet Union. See also GERLSDORFER SPITZE.

Sta′linsk (stä′lyĭnsk); *formerly, and since 1961,* **No′vo·kuz·netsk′** (nō′vŏ·kōōz·nĕtsk′; *Russ.* nô′vŭ·kōōz·nyĕtsk′). City, S Kemerovo Region, Soviet Russia, Asia, at head of navigation of Tom river 190 m. SE of Novosibirsk; pop. 169,538; at S end of Kuznetsk Basin; has rail connections with Magnitogorsk through Barnaul and Akmolinsk and with other cities of the Molotov Region through Novosibirsk and Omsk. Chief industrial center of the newly developed coal-mining district. First settled 1617 and until recently a small town.

Stal′lu·pö′nen (shtäl′ōō·pŭ′nĕn). Commune, in former East Prussia prov., Germany, just E of Gumbinnen (Gusev); pop. 6296; battle Aug. 17, 1914 in which Germans fought a successful delaying action. Now in Kaliningradsk Region, Soviet Russia, Europe.

Sta′ly·bridge (stä′lĭ·brĭj). Municipal borough Cheshire, NW England, on the Tame 10 m. E of Manchester; pop. 22,544.

Stam′baugh (stăm′bô; -bô). City, Iron co., SW Michi-

gan penin., 32 m. WNW of Iron Mountain; pop. 1876; iron mining.

Stam·boul′ *or* **Stam·bul′** (stăm·bōōl′). Turkish name of old part of Constantinople (now İstanbul, *q.v.*), S of the Golden Horn; the site of ancient Byzantium. Sometimes by extension used as name for the entire city.

Stam′ford (stăm′fẽrd). **1** City (formerly town), Fairfield co., SW Connecticut, on Long Island Sound and New York border; pop. 92,713; settled 1641, annexed to Connecticut 1662, incorp. 1893. Includes manufacturing center (formerly city of Stamford, town and city governments consolidated 1949), 20 m. WSW of Bridgeport, incorp. 1893; manufactures locks, hardware, typewriters, ball and roller bearings, tools, machinery, cloth, clothing, furniture, electrical fixtures, diesel engines, boats, chemicals, cosmetics, rubber products, oil burners.

2 City, Jones co., NW cen. Texas, 35 m. N of Abilene; pop. 5259; agricultural and ranching center; manufactures dairy products, brick and tile; flour, cottonseed oil.

3 Municipal borough, Parts of Kesteven, Lincolnshire, E England, on the Welland 35 m. SE of Nottingham; pop. 10,899; site of Saxon, Danish, and Norman fortified settlements.

Stamford Bridge. Village in East Riding, Yorkshire, N England, 8 m. ENE of York; scene of battle Sept. 25, 1066 in which King Harold II defeated his brother Tostig and Harold Haardraade, King of Norway, Tostig's ally, just before Battle of Hastings.

Stampalia. See ASTYPALAIA.

Stam′pede Tunnel (stăm′pēd). Railroad tunnel 9850 ft. long, King and Kittitas cos., W cen. Washington, in Cascade Range.

Stamps (stămps). City, Lafayette co., SW Arkansas, 34 m. E of Texarkana; pop. 2591; watermelons; oil.

Stan′ards·ville (stăn′ẽrdz·vĭl; *Sou. also* -v'l). Town, ⊗ of Greene co., N cen. Virginia; pop. 283.

Stan′ber′ry (stăn′bĕr′ĭ; -bẽr·ĭ). City, Gentry co., NW Missouri, 37 m. NNE of St. Joseph; pop. 1409.

Stan′der·ton (stăn′dẽr·t'n; -tŭn). Town, SE Transvaal, NE Republic of So. Africa, on Vaal river 90 m. ESE of Johannesburg; pop. 5596; in farm district yielding teff, oats, potatoes, and corn and also important in breeding and raising of sheep, cattle, and horses. Scene of much action in first Boer War 1880–81.

Standing Indian. Mountain 5500 ft. in Clay co., SW North Carolina.

Stan′dish (stăn′dĭsh). City, ⊗ of Arenac co., E Michigan; pop. 1214.

Standish with Lang′tree (lăng′trē). Urban district, Lancashire, NW England, NE of Liverpool; pop. 8991.

Stand′ley Lake Dam (stănd′lĭ). Dam completed 1911 across branch of South Platte river, Jefferson co., cen. Colorado; height 113 ft.; impounds water for irrigation, forming **Standley Lake.**

Stan′ford (stăn′fẽrd). **1** Post office of Stanford University in W Palo Alto, Santa Clara co., W California.

2 Residential city, ⊗ of Lincoln co., E cen. Kentucky, 10 m. SE of Danville; pop. 2019.

3 Town, ⊗ of Judith Basin co., cen. Montana; pop. 615.

Stang′er (stăng′ẽr). Town, E Natal, E Republic of So. Africa, near coast 40 m. NNE of Durban; pop. 2877; farm center, esp. for raising sugar. Burial place of Chaka, Zulu warrior and chieftain.

Stanimaka. See ASENOVGRAD.

Stanislau. See STANISLAV.

Stan′is·laus (stăn′ĭs·lô; -lôs). **1** River 95 m. long in N cen. California; rises in Alpine co. near Nevada border, flows SW into San Joaquin river bet. San Joaquin and Stanislaus cos. See MELONES DAM.

2 County in California. See *Table* at CALIFORNIA.

Stanislaus Peak. Mountain 11,202 ft. in S Alpine co., E cen. California, in the Sierra Nevada.

Sta·ni·slav′ (stä·nyĭ·slȧf′); *Pol.* **Sta′ni·sła′wów** (stä′-nĕ·slä′vōof); *Ger.* **Sta′nis·lau** (shtä′nĭs·lou; stä′-). Commercial and industrial city, SW Ukraine, U.S.S.R.,

69 m. SSE of Lvov; * of former Stanisławów dept., Poland; now * of Stanislav Region in W Ukraine; pop. (1938–39 est.) 71,218; railroad junction; Greek Catholic episcopal see; oil refineries, textile mills, machine shops, tanneries. Capital of a Russian principality seized 1340 by Casimir III of Poland; in World War I scene of much fighting in 1915 and 1916 when it changed hands several times bet. Russians and Austrians; in July 1917 taken by Central Powers; occupied in World War II by Russians 1939, by Germans 1941, and again by Russians 1944.

Stanislav Region. Subdivision, W Ukraine, U.S.S.R., * Stanislav; corresponds approximately with former Polish department of Stanisławów.

Sta·ni·sla'wów (stä'ně·slä'võõf). **1** Former Polish department, in SE part; 6520 sq. m.; pop. 1,476,538. See STANISLAV REGION.

2 City, its *. See STANISLAV.

Stan'ley (stăn'lĭ). **1** County in South Dakota. See *Table* at SOUTH DAKOTA.

2 City, ⊗ of Mountrail co., NW North Dakota; pop. 1795; grain, stock, dairy, poultry farms.

3 City, Chippewa co., W Wisconsin, 20 m. E of Chippewa Falls; pop. 2014; trade center in agricultural section.

4 *formerly* **Circular Head.** Town, NW Tasmania, Australia, on peninsula on Bass Strait 37 m. WNW of Burnie; pop. (municipality) 6597; Tasmanian port nearest to Melbourne; a popular seaside resort at the foot of the headland Circular Head (*q.v.*).

5 Urban district, Durham, N England, 18 m. SSW of Newcastle; pop. 48,123.

6 Urban district, West Riding, Yorkshire, N England; pop. 16,672.

7 *or* **Port Stanley.** Town, * of Falkland Is., South Atlantic Ocean, on E coast of East Falkland; pop. (1940) 1246; has good harbor.

Stanley, Mount. See Mount RUWENZORI.

Stanley Falls. Seven cataracts of the upper Congo river, in Congo, S cen. Africa, on the equator, above Stanleyville, extending ab. 60 m.

Stanley Pool. Expansion of Congo river bet. Congo Republic and Republic of Congo, ab. lat. 4°S; Léopoldville, capital of Republic of Congo, is situated on its SW shore, and Brazzaville, capital of Congo Republic, on its NW shore.

Stanley Range. See BARRIER RANGE.

Stan'ley·ville (stăn'lĭ·vĭl). **1** *now called* **Eastern Province** *or* **Oriental Province.** Province, NE Republic of Congo (formerly Belgian Congo), S cen. Africa; 196,968 sq. m.; native pop. (1938) 2,382,217.

2 *now called* **Ki'san·ga'ni** (kē'sän·gä'ně). City, its *, on the Congo river; pop. (1964) ab. 100,000.

Stan'ly (stăn'lĭ). County in North Carolina. See *Table* at NORTH CAROLINA.

Stann Creek (stăn). **1** District, cen. Brit. Honduras; 840 sq. m.; pop. (1943 est.) 6872.

2 Coastal town, its *, E cen. coast of British Honduras; pop. (1943 est.) 6300.

Stan'o·voi Range (stăn'ô·voi); *Russ.* **Sta·no·voi' Khre·bet'** (stä·nŭ·voi' krĭĭ·byĕt'). Mountain range in E Soviet Russia, Asia, mostly bet. Yakutsk Republic and Khabarovsk Territory; highest peak at E end 8143 ft.; watershed bet. Arctic and Pacific Ocean streams.

Stans (shtäns). Commune, * of Nidwalden demicanton, Unterwalden canton, cen. Switzerland, 7 m. SSE of Lucerne; pop. (1930) 2916; 17th-cent. parish church with 12th-cent. Romanesque tower, town hall, convents; tourist center. Captured by French 1798.

Stans'bur'y Island (stănz'bĕr'ĭ; -bĕr·ĭ). Peninsula, formerly an island, in SW Great Salt Lake, Utah; 11½ m. long and 5½ m. wide.

Stan'stead (stăn'stĕd; -stĭd). **1** County, Quebec, Canada. See *Table* at QUEBEC.

2 Village, on S border of county, E of Lake Memphremagog near the U.S. boundary at Derby Line, Vermont;

pop. 856; Stanstead Wesleyan Coll., a preparatory school (1872; coed.).

Stan'thorpe (stăn'thôrp). Town, SE Queensland, Australia, 100 m. SW of Brisbane on New South Wales border at N end of New England Plateau; pop. 6934; tin mines and uranium deposits.

Stan'ton (stăn't'n; -tŭn). **1** Name of counties in two states of the U.S. See *Tables* at KANSAS and NEBRASKA.

2 City, Orange co., SW California, SW of Anaheim; pop. 11,163.

3 City, ⊗ of Powell co., E Kentucky; pop. 753.

4 City, ⊗ of Montcalm co., cen. Michigan; pop. 1139.

5 City, ⊗ of Stanton co., NE Nebraska, 12 m. ESE of Norfolk; pop. 1317.

6 City, ⊗ of Mercer co., W cen. North Dakota; pop. 409.

7 City, ⊗ of Martin co., NW Texas; pop. 2228.

Stanton Peak. Mountain 11,666 ft. in Sierra Nevada, E Tuolumne co., cen. California.

Sta'ples (stā'p'lz). City, Todd co., cen. Minnesota, 26 m. W of Brainerd; pop. 2706; railroad division point; in agricultural and dairy-farming section; creameries, cheese factories.

Staples, the. = FARNE ISLANDS.

Sta'ple·ton (stā'p'l·t'n; -tŭn). **1** Village, ⊗ of Logan co., cen. Nebraska; pop. 359.

2 See RICHMOND borough, New York City.

Sta'ra Ka'nji·ža (stä'rä kä'nyĕ·zhä); *Hung.* **Ma'gyar·ka'ni·zsa** (mŏ'dyôr·kŏ'nĭ·zhŏ). Town, N Voivodina autonomous prov., NE Yugoslavia, 90 m. NNW of Belgrade on Tisza river; pop. 19,094.

Stara Planina. See BALKAN MOUNTAINS.

Starav, Ben. See BEN STARAV.

Sta'ra·ya Rus'sa (stä'rä·yà rōōs'sà). Town, cen. Novgorod Region, NW Soviet Russia, Europe, 15 m. S of Lake Ilmen; pop. 26,700; trades in grain and flax; resort, with mineral springs, salt lakes, sanatoriums, parks. An old town under Novgorod, dating back at least to 12th cent.; suffered much in medieval wars; later belonged to Moscow. A strong point in German defense line 1941–44; after much bitter fighting retaken 1944 by Russians.

Sta'ra Za·go'ra (stä'rä zä·gô'rä). **1** Department, S and cen. Bulgaria; 6002 sq. m.; pop. (1934) 812,633.

2 City, its *, on S slope of Balkan Mts. 50 m. ENE of Plovdiv; pop. (1934) 29,825; trade center in rose-growing section, producing attar of roses; scene of Turkish victory 1877 over the Russians.

Star'buck (stär'bŭk). Small island of the Line Is. in cen. Pacific Ocean, in 5°35'S lat. and 155°W long. and 110 m. SSW of Malden I.; formerly yielded guano; now uninhabited. Discovered 1823; in area claimed by both Great Britain and United States.

Star City (stär). City, ⊗ of Lincoln co., SE Arkansas; pop. 1573.

Star'gard (*Pol.* stär'gärt; *Ger.* shtär'gärt); *Ger. also* **Stargard in Pom'mern** (ĭn pôm'ĕrn). City, W cen. Szczecin dept., NW Poland, ESE of Stettin; pop. (1946) 19,200; formerly in Pomerania, Germany; well-preserved city walls and fine medieval gates; 13th-cent. church, 16th-cent. town hall; manufactures agricultural implements, beer, liqueurs, tobacco. An early Hanse town; destroyed 1633 in Thirty Years' War; in World War II taken by Russians Mar. 5, 1945; assigned to Poland by Potsdam Conference 1945.

Star Harbour. Inlet and trading station on N coast at SE end of San Cristobal I., SE Solomon Is., W Pacific Ocean.

Sta'ri Be'čej (stä'rĕ bĕ'chä); *Hung.* **Ó'be'cse** (ô'bĕ·chĕ). Town, N Voivodina autonomous prov., NE Yugoslavia, 60 m. NNW of Belgrade on Tisza river; pop. (1921) 19,658.

Stari Grad (gräd'); *Ital.* **Cit·ta·vec'chia** (chĕt·tä·vĕk'kyä). Seaport on NW coast of Hvar I., Bosnia and Herzegovina, W Yugoslavia; pop. (1921) 3764.

Stark (stärk). Name of counties in three states of the U.S. See *Tables* at ILLINOIS, NORTH DAKOTA, OHIO.

Starke (stärk). **1** County in Indiana. See *Table* at INDIANA.

2 City, ⊗ of Bradford co., NE Florida; pop. 4806.

Star'ken·burg (shtär'kĕn·bŏŏrK). Province of Hesse. See *Table* at HESSE.

Stark'ville (stärk'vil; *Sou. also* -v'l). City, ⊗ of Oktibbeha co., NE cen. Mississippi, 23 m. W of Columbus; pop. 9041; dairy-farming and livestock-raising center; shipping point for cattle. Mississippi State Coll. (1878; coed.) at suburb State College.

Starn'berg (shtärn'bĕrK). Village, S Bavaria, Germany, at N end of Würm Lake ab. 10 m. SSW of Munich; pop. (1933) 4879; health resort; in area guarded by Nazis for their last retreat.

Starnberger See. See WÜRM.

Sta·ro·dub' (stȧ·rŭ·dōōp'). Town, W Bryansk Region, Soviet Russia, Europe, 80 m. SW of Bryansk; pop. 10,919. An old town, important in Russian medieval history; was destroyed by Mongols in 13th cent., fought over by Russians, Lithuanians, and Poles down to 1686 when it became permanently Russian; in World War II behind German lines 1941-43.

Sta·ro'gard (stä·rô'gärt); *Ger.* **Preus'sisch–Star'-gard** (proi'sĭsh-shtär'gärt). Commune, Gdańsk dept., N Poland, 64 m. N of Toruń; pop. (1938–39 est.) 15,356; manufactures chemicals, brandy, shoes, tobacco, furniture; suffered much destruction in World War II.

Sta'ro·kon·stan·ti'nov (stä'rŭ·kŭn·stŭn·tyē'nŭf). Town, W Ukraine, U.S.S.R., 160 m. SSW of Kiev; pop. ab. 15,000.

Star Peak (stär). **1** Mountain 13,562 ft. in Gunnison and Pitkin cos., W cen. Colorado.

2 Mountain 8400 ft. in Chelan co., cen. Washington.

Starr (stär). County in Texas. See *Table* at TEXAS.

Start Point (stärt). **1** Cape on S coast of Devonshire, SW England; lighthouse; at S end of **Start Bay**, wide inlet of English Channel on Devonshire coast S of Dartmouth.

2 Cape on NE tip of Sanday I., Orkney Is., off N coast of Scotland; lighthouse.

Starved Rock. Locality on S bank of Illinois river, near Ottawa, La Salle co., N Illinois, 90 m. SW of Chicago; narrow strip of high bluff above river, highest point 140 ft., steep on all sides with flat top (½ acre); now part of **Starved Rock State Park**, oldest (opened 1912) of Illinois state parks, 900 acres; contains also springs, trails, bluffs, caves. Of historical interest; visited by Jolliet and Marquette 1673 on return from exploration of the Mississippi and by Marquette 1675 just before his death, also by La Salle and Tonti 1679; Fort St. Louis erected here on summit 1682, abandoned 1702, burned by Indians 1721. Story of Illinois Indians starving on Rock (c. 1770) is purely legendary.

Sta'ry O·skol' (stä'rĭ ŭ·skôl'). Town, E Kursk Region, Soviet Russia, Europe, 80 m. SE of Kursk.

Stass'furt (shtäs'fŏŏrt). Salt-mining city, E Germany, in what was formerly Saxony prov., Prussia, 21 m. S of Magdeburg; pop. 16,144.

State College. 1 Post office for Mississippi State Univ., SE suburb of Starkville (*q.v.*), NE cen. Mississippi.

2 Suburb of Las Cruces (*q.v.*), New Mexico; site of New Mexico State Univ. of Agriculture, Engineering, and Science; pop. (with Mesilla Park) 4387.

3 Suburb of FARGO (*q.v.*), North Dakota; site of State Agricultural College.

4 Borough, Centre co., cen. Pennsylvania, 22 m. NW of Lewistown; pop. 22,409. Pennsylvania State Univ. (1855; coed.).

Stat'en Island (stăt''n). **1** Island in New York Bay 5 m. S of Manhattan; 60 sq. m.; ab. 15½ m. long by 7 m. wide; separated on E from Long I. by the Narrows and on W from New Jersey by narrow Arthur Kill connecting Newark Bay on N with Raritan Bay on S. Forms Richmond Borough, New York City, and Richmond co., New York state. Part of island granted by Dutch West

India Company to David Pietersen de Vries 1636; first settlement 1641. See RICHMOND borough, New York City.

2 *Span.* **Is'la de los Es·ta'dos** (ēz'lä thä lôs ȧs·tä'thôs). Argentine island ab. 45 m. long in S Atlantic Ocean off E tip of Tierra del Fuego; chief town San Juan de Salvamento, at E end. See TIERRA DEL FUEGO territory.

Sta'ten·ville (stä't'n·vil; *Sou. also* -v'l). Town, ⊗ of Echols co., S Georgia, 20 m. ESE of Valdosta.

State of Vatican City. Full name of VATICAN CITY.

States'bor'o (stāts'bûr'ō). City, ⊗ of Bulloch co., E Georgia, 47 m. WNW of Savannah; pop. 8356; cotton; lumber. Georgia Southern College (1908; coed.) at nearby Collegeboro.

States of the Church *or* **Papal States;** *Ital.* **Lo Sta'to del'la Chie'sa** (lô stä'tô däl'lä kyä'zä). Temporal domain of the pope in cen. Italy 755–1870; area 16,000 sq. m.; ✱ Rome, during periods when actually under control of papacy.

History: Temporal power of medieval papacy based upon Donation of Pepin 755 A.D., by which king of Franks promised to pope lands in cen. Italy, conquered from Lombards but formerly Byzantine; acquired duchy of Benevento 1052; strengthened and expanded by Innocent III (d. 1216) who controlled Ravenna, Romagna, Spoleto, the Pentapolis, and for a time, much of Tuscany; from 1274 to 1791 included Comtat Venaissin in S France; during residence of pope at Avignon (*q.v.*) 1309–77, completely under rule of virtually independent lords; boundaries to 19th cent. were re-established by Julius II (1503–13) who regained Romagna; annexed Ferrara by reversion 1598; invaded by French 1796; territorial status altered during Napoleonic Wars; established as Roman Republic 1798–99; annexed to France 1809; restored to papacy 1815; in 1860, Romagna, Marches, and Umbria joined Piedmont; Rome (*q.v.*) annexed to kingdom of Italy 1870; temporal authority in Vatican City (*q.v.*) granted to pope 1929.

States'ville (stāts'vil; *Sou. also* -v'l). City, ⊗ of Iredell co., cen. North Carolina, 37 m. N of Charlotte; pop. 19,844; founded 1789; manufactures textiles, lumber products, veneer, processed tobacco, machinery. Mitchell Coll. (1853; coed.). Following the organization of the Statesville Audubon Club in 1930, the entire city by ordinance became a bird sanctuary.

Sta'thar (stä'thär). Town, N Iceland, at head of Húna Bay.

Sta'ti·a (stä'shĭ·ȧ; -shȧ). ꞊ SAINT EUSTATIUS.

Stato della Chiesa, Lo. See STATES OF THE CHURCH.

Sta'to del'la Cit·tà' del Va'ti·ca'no (stä'tô däl'lä chĕt·tä' däl vä'tē·kä'nô). Full Italian name of VATICAN CITY.

Statue of Liberty National Monument. See UNITED STATES, *National Monuments.*

Staub'bach Falls (shtoup'bäK). Waterfall ab. 1000 ft. high near Lauterbrunnen, Switzerland; slight flow.

Staun'ton (stôn't'n; -tŭn; stän'-). City, Macoupin co., SW cen. Illinois, 32 m. NE of East St. Louis; pop. 4228; in coal-mining and agriculture section.

Staun'ton (stän't'n; -tŭn). **1** Old name for the upper Roanoke river above its junction with Dan river in S Virginia.

2 City, ⊗ of Augusta co., N cen. Virginia, but politically independent, 35 m. WNW of Charlottesville; 2 sq. m.; pop. 22,232; in Shenandoah Valley bet. Blue Ridge and Allegheny Mts.; commercial center of agricultural area; manufactures furniture, clothing, woolens, flour, dairy products. Mary Baldwin Coll. (1842; women). Birthplace of Woodrow Wilson, 28th president of the U.S. Established 1738; briefly capital of Virginia 1781; chartered as town 1801; as city 1871; served as base of supplies during Civil War; originated city-manager form of municipal government 1908.

Sta·vang'er (stä·väng'ēr). **1** Former name of *Rogaland* co., SW Norway: see *Table* at NORWAY.

2 Seaport, ⊗ of Rogaland co., SW Norway, on **Stavanger Fjord,** a S branch of Bokn Fjord, 190 m. WSW of Oslo; pop. 46,780; shipping center; shipbuilding yards, fish canneries (herring, sardines); cathedral of St. Swithin, dating from 11th cent.; museum. Founded in 8th cent.; in World War II seized by Germans Apr. 9, 1940.

Sta've·lot′ (stå′vlō′); *Flemish* **Sta′blo** (stå′blō). Commune, Liège prov., Belgium, on the Amblève river 21 m. SE of Liège; pop. 4878; Romanesque tower of ancient Benedictine abbey founded 651. In World War II in the Battle of the Bulge Dec. 1944–Jan. 1945, reached by Germans Dec. 18 but held by Allies against further advance on Liège.

Stav′ro·pol (stăv′rŏ·pôl; *Russ.* stàv′rŭ·pŭl·y′, stŭv·rô′-pŭl·y′); *bet. 1940 and 1944 called* **Vo′ro·shi′lovsk** (vōr′ŏ·shē′lŏfsk; *Russ.* vŭ·rŭ·shi′lŭfsk) *in honor of Gen. Kliment E. Voroshilov.* City, ✷ of Stavropol Territory, Soviet Russia, Europe, on tributary of upper Kalaus in W part; pop. 85,100; manufacturing city, esp. of textiles and agricultural machinery; in a plateau region (alt. 2030 ft.) with healthful climate; has rail connections with Rostov. In World War II held by Germans for a few months 1942–43 at their farthest advance into the Caucasus.

Stavropol Territory; *formerly* **Or′dzho·ni·kid′ze Territory** (ôr′jŏn·ĭ·kĭd′zĕ; *Russ.* ŭr·jŭ·nyĭ·kēd′zĕ). Territory, SE Soviet Russia, Europe; 34,078 sq. m.; pop. 1,706,881; ✷ Stavropol; a subdivision of the R.S.F.S.R. Contains high land in W part and plain in the E, watered by Kuma and Terek rivers, the latter mostly on S border. Agriculture is leading occupation; also some stock raising and fishing along the Caspian. Chief towns Stavropol, Pyatigorsk, Georgievsk. In medieval times a part of the khanate of the Golden Horde; became Russian in 16th cent.; E part home of the Terek Cossacks and in modern times whole region formed E half of North Caucasus region; Ordzhonikidze Territory created 1936; reorganized and renamed 1944.

Stav·ros′ (stăv·rôs′); *Mod. Gr.* **Stav·ròs′.** Town, Chalcidice dept., S Macedonia, NE Greece, on NE coast of the Chalcidice Penin., on S shore of the Strymonic Gulf E of Salonika.

Staw′ell (stô′ĕl). Town, W Victoria, SE Australia, 130 m. WNW of Melbourne; pop. 4751; mining town in center of gold district.

Steamboat Springs. Town, ⊗ of Routt co., NW Colorado, on Yampa river 38 m. E of Craig; pop. 1843; recreational center; medicinal mineral springs.

Stearns (stûrnz). County in Minnesota. See *Table* at MINNESOTA.

Stębark. See TANNENBERG.

Steele (stēl). **1** Name of counties in two states of the U.S. See *Tables* at MINNESOTA and NORTH DAKOTA.
2 City, Pemiscot co., SE corner of Missouri, 12 m. WSW of Caruthersville; pop. 2301.
3 City, ⊗ of Kidder co., S cen. North Dakota; pop. 847.

Stee′le (shtā′lĕ). Former city (pop. 33,823), Düsseldorf govt. dist., Rhine Province, Prussia, Germany; since 1929 part of Essen (*q.v.*).

Steele, Mount (stēl). Peak 16,644 ft. in St. Elias Range in SW Yukon Territory, Canada, near Alaska border.

Steel Mountain (stēl). Peak 9752 ft. in N Elmore co., SW cen. Idaho.

Steel′ton (stēl′t'n; -tŭn). Borough, Dauphin co., SE cen. Pennsylvania, on Susquehanna river just S of Harrisburg; pop. 11,266; steelworks.

Steel′ville (stēl′vĭl). City, ⊗ of Crawford co., SE cen. Missouri; pop. 1127.

Steen′ker′ke (stān′kĕr′kĕ) *or* **Steen′kerque′** (stĕn′-kĕrk′; stăn′-). Village in Hainaut prov., SW Belgium; scene of battle July 23–Aug. 3, 1692 in which the French under the duc de Luxembourg defeated the English under William III.

Steens Mountain (stēnz). Mountain mass, SE Harney co., SE Oregon; highest point 9354 ft.

Steen′wijk (stān′vīk). Commune, Overijssel prov., E Netherlands, NNW of Meppel; pop. 7224.

Stee′ple (stē′p'l). Mountain with two peaks, 2746 ft. and 2687 ft., in Cumberland, NW England, in the Lake District.

Steep Point (stēp). Extreme W point of mainland of Australia, in 113°8′E, S of Shark Bay.

Stef′a·nie, Lake (stĕf′á·nĭ). Shallow saline lake ab. 37 m. long in SW Ethiopia, E of N end of Lake Rudolf; elevation ab. 1900 ft.

Ste′fans·son Strait (stĕf′′n·s'n). Strait 40 m. long in Antarctica bet. E Palmer Penin. and Hearst I. to S; 3 m. wide at narrowest point; filled with shelf ice.

Stef′fen (stĕf′′n). Peak 7218 ft. in W Chubut territory, S Argentina, on Chile border.

Stef′fis·burg (shtĕf′ĭs·bŏŏrk). Commune, Bern canton, Switzerland, N of Thun; pop. (1930) 6755.

Ste′ge (stā′gĕ). Town on W coast of Möen I., Denmark; pop. 2459.

Ste′ger (stā′gẽr). Village, Cook and Will cos., NE Illinois, 28 m. S of Chicago; pop. 6432.

Steier. See STEYR.

Steierdorf–Anina. See ȘTAIERDORF-ANINA.

Stei′er·mark (shtī′ẽr·märk). Province of Austria. See *Styria* in *Table* at AUSTRIA.

Steinamanger. See SZOMBATHELY.

Stein′kirk (stēn′kûrk). = STEENKERKE.

Stein′kjer′ (stān′kẽr′). Town, Nord-Tröndelag co., N cen. Norway, N of Levanger and at the head of Trondheim Fjord; pop. 2749; lumber port and railroad station; scene of fighting bet. Germans and British Apr. 1940.

Steinschönau. See KAMENICKÝ ŠENOV.

Steins′öy′ (stān′sŭ′ü). Small Norwegian island off Sogne Fjord; the most westerly point of Norway, in 4°30′E long., 61°5′N lat.

Stel′la·land′ (stĕl′á·länd′). Boer republic in S Africa 1882–85; ab. 5000 sq. m.; ✷ Vryburg; established in W Transvaal as part of westward expansion of Boers (see GOSHEN, South Africa), now part of Bechuanaland in Cape Province, Union of South Africa.

Stel′lar·ton (stĕl′ẽr·t'n; -tŭn). Town, Pictou co., N Nova Scotia, Canada, 7 m. S of New Glasgow; pop. 5575; in coal-mining and industrial region.

Stel′len·bosch (stĕl′ĕn·bŏs′; *Angl.* -bŏŏsh′). Residential town, SW Cape Province, S Union of South Africa, 25 m. E of Cape Town; pop. 8782; center of fertile farm district yielding fruits, tobacco, wheat, and vegetables, beautifully laid out like an old Dutch town; educational center; seat of Stellenbosch Univ. and a Dutch theological seminary. Founded by Gov. Simon van der Stel in 1681; next to Cape Town the oldest town in South Africa.

Stel′ler, Mount (stĕl′ẽr). Mountain ab. 10,000 ft. in Chugach Mts., S Alaska. Bering Glacier is on it.

Stel′vio Pass (stĕl′vyŏ). Mountain pass 9049 ft. in the Ortler Mts., bet. Italy and Switzerland.

Ste·nay′ (stĕ·nā′). Town, N Meuse dept., NE France, on Meuse river 26 m. NNW of Verdun; pop. 2260; an old town, residence of the kings of Austrasia; held by Spanish in middle of 17th cent.; taken by siege by Marshall Fabert for Louis XIV in 1654; last town taken by Americans in World War I, on morning of Armistice Day Nov. 11, 1918.

Sten′dal (shtĕn′däl). Manufacturing city, E Germany, in the former Saxony province of Prussia, 32 m. NNE of Magdeburg; pop. 29,701; 12th-cent. Gothic cathedral; old city gates; manufactures include metal goods, chemicals. Founded in 12th cent.

Ste·pa·na·kert′ (stĕ·pä·nä·kĕrt′). Town, ✷ of Nagorno-Karabakh Autonomous Region, Azerbaidzhan, U.S.S.R., in mountains at edge of Armenian plateau; 62 m. SSE of Kirovabad; pop. 3118.

Ste′phens (stē′vĕnz). Name of counties in three states of the U.S. See *Tables* at GEORGIA, OKLAHOMA, TEXAS.

Ste′phen·son (stē′vĕn·s'n). County in Illinois. See *Table* at ILLINOIS.

Ste′phen·ville (stē′vĕn·vĭl; *Sou. U.S.* also -v′l). 1 City, ⊗ of Erath co., N cen. Texas, 60 m. SW of Fort Worth; pop. 7359; cotton, grain, livestock; coal mines; gas wells. 2 Town on SW coast of Newfoundland, near head of St. Georges Bay; pop. (1942 est.) 1050. U.S. Air Force landing field.

Stepney. Metropolitan borough of London. See *Table* at LONDON.

Step·noi′ (stĕp·noi′; *Russ.* styĕp-); *formerly* **E·lis′ta** (ĕ·lĭs′tà; *Russ.* ĕ·lyē′stà). Town, * of former Kalmyk Republic, Soviet Russia, Europe, now in W part of Astrakhan Region; pop. 8500; in the steppe region 220 m. ESE of Rostov. In World War II occupied by German force Aug. 1942 but retaken by Russians before the end of the year; renamed Stepnoi 1943 during World War II.

Steppes, the (stĕps). Region, W cen. Asia. See KIRGIZ STEPPE.

Sterk′ra′de (shtĕrk′rä′dĕ). Former city (pop. 50,757), Düsseldorf govt. dist., Rhine Province, Prussia, Germany; became part of Oberhausen (*q.v.*) 1929.

Ster′ling (stûr′lĭng). 1 County in Texas. See *Table* at TEXAS. 2 City, ⊗ of Logan co., NE Colorado, on South Platte river 40 m. NE of Fort Morgan; pop. 10,751; beet-sugar refining. 3 Industrial city, Whiteside co., NW Illinois, 48 m. SW of Rockford; pop. 15,688; manufactures builders' hardware, farm implements, gas engines, wire products. 4 City, Rice co., cen. Kansas, on Arkansas river 20 m. NW of Hutchinson; pop. 2303. Sterling Coll. (1887; coed.; Presbyterian). 5 Town, Worcester co., cen. Massachusetts, 10 m. S of Fitchburg; pop. 3193; in fruitgrowing section. 6 *or* **Sterling City.** City, ⊗ of Sterling co., W cen. Texas; pop. 854.

Sterling, Mount. Peak 5835 ft. in E Great Smoky Mts., Haywood co., W North Carolina.

Sterling Peak. Mountain 7377 ft. in S Jackson co., SW Oregon.

Ster·li·ta·mak′ (styĭr·lyĭ·tŭ·màk′). Town, S cen. Bashkir Republic, Soviet Russia, Europe, on left bank of Belaya river 75 m. S of Ufa; pop. 25,155; has brick factories, sawmills, and flour mills. Formerly capital of republic 1919–22.

Šter′berk (shtĕrn′bĕrk); *Ger.* **Stern′berg** (shtĕrn′bĕrk). Town, N cen. Moravia prov., Czechoslovakia, 10 m. N of Olomouc; pop. (1930) 12,767.

Stern Park Gardens. See LIDICE, Illinois.

Sterzing. See VIPITENO.

Stet·tin′ (shtĕ·tēn′). 1 Former government district, W Pomerania prov., Prussia, Germany; 6216 sq. m.; since 1932 includes former government district of Stralsund; ab. one half now in Poland. 2 *Pol.* **Szcze·cin′** (shchĕ·tsĕn′). Seaport and manufacturing and commercial city, formerly * of Stettin govt. dist. and * of Pomerania prov., Prussia, Germany, near mouth of Oder river on left bank and S of Stettiner Haff, 78 m. NE of Berlin; pop. (1939) 268,915; under Germans was principal port for Berlin; now * of Szczecin dept. in NW Poland. Has 14th-cent. royal palace; important shipbuilding center; manufactures iron goods, machinery, clothing, chemicals, cement, oil, paper, sugar, foodstuffs, brewery and distillery products; trades in iron, coal, soda, coffee, cotton, grain, fish, timber. Largest city in Pomerania 1124; joined Hanseatic League 1360; ducal residence 12th–17th cents.; peace of Stettin 1570 closed Northern Seven Years' War bet. Denmark and Sweden; to Sweden 1648 by Treaty of Westphalia; to Brandenburg 1678, Prussia 1720. In World War II frequently bombed 1944–45; taken Apr. 26, 1945 by Rus-

sian armies after long siege and battle. By Potsdam Conference 1945 city and E part of government district assigned to Poland.

Stet·ti′ner Haff (shtĕ·tē′nĕr häf′). Large lagoon on coast bet. Pomerania, N Germany, and Szczecin dept., NW Poland, opening into the Bay of Pomerania bet. the islands of Usedom (*Pol.* Uznam) and Wolin, which shut it off from the Baltic Sea; receives the Oder river.

Steu·ben′ (stū·bĕn′). Name of counties in two states of the U.S. See *Tables* at INDIANA and NEW YORK.

Steu′ben·ville (stū′bĕn·vĭl). Industrial city, ⊗ of Jefferson co., E Ohio, on Ohio river 50 m. S of Youngstown; pop. 32,495; settled 1765 on site of old Fort Steuben (1787); chief industry steel; manufactures iron, glass, tin, pottery, dinnerware; coal mines nearby.

Ste′ven·age (stē′vĕn·ĭj). Urban district, Hertfordshire, SE England, 28 m. N of London; pop. 6627.

Ste′vens (stē′vĕnz). Counties in three states of the U.S. See *Tables* at KANSAS, MINNESOTA, WASHINGTON.

Stevens Dam. See UNITED STATES, *Dams and Reservoirs.*

Ste′ven·son (stē′vĕn·s'n). Town, ⊗ of Skamania co., S Washington; pop. 927.

Stevenson, Mount. Peak 10,300 ft. in Yellowstone National Park, NW Wyoming.

Stevens Point. City, ⊗ of Portage co., cen. Wisconsin, 30 m. S of Wausau; pop. 17,837; manufactures paper, lumber products, farm implements, fishing tackle. Wisconsin State Coll. (1894; coed.).

Stew′art (stū′ẽrt). 1 Name of counties in two states of the U.S. See *Tables* at GEORGIA and TENNESSEE. 2 River 320 m. long in cen. Yukon Territory, Canada; flows W in S Klondike region to Yukon river.

Stewart Island. Island in Pacific Ocean S of South I., New Zealand; forms a county of South I.; 670 sq. m.; pop. (1936) 617; mountainous, forested.

Stewart Islands. Atoll group 110 m. E of N end of Malaita I., SE cen. Solomon Is., W Pacific Ocean; chief island Sikiana. Inhabitants are Polynesians; no harbor but there is some trade in copra. U.S. naval victory Oct. 30, 1942.

Stewart Manor. Village, Nassau co., SE New York, on Long I. 17 m. E of New York; pop. 2422.

Stewart Mountain Dam. Dam completed 1930 across Salt river below Mormon Flat Dam, E Maricopa co., S cen. Arizona; height 207 ft.; impounds water for power, forming **Sa·gua′ro Lake** (sà·gwä′rō; sà·wä′-) 10 m. long.

Stewart Peak. Mountain 14,032 ft. in Saguache co., S Colorado.

Steyns′burg (stānz′bûrg). Town, E cen. Cape Province, Union of South Africa, 170 m. N of Port Elizabeth; pop. 2866; sheep-raising center.

Steyr (shtīr); *also* **Stei′er** (shtī′ĕr). Iron-manufacturing city, Upper Austria prov., Austria, on Steyr river at its confluence with the Enns 16 m. SSE of Linz; pop. (1939) 31,165; manufactures cutlery, files, nails, scythes, small arms, bicycles, trucks, automobiles, tractors, and ball bearings.

Stick′ney (stĭk′nĭ). Village, Cook co., NE Illinois, W suburb of Chicago; pop. 6239.

Stig′ler (stĭg′lẽr). City, ⊗ of Haskell co., E Oklahoma, 38 m. SSE of Muskogee; pop. 1923; coal mines; timber; agriculture.

Sti·kine′ (stĭ·kēn′). River 335 m. long in NW Brit. Columbia, Canada, and S Alaska; rises in Stikine Mts. and flows W and SW through the Coast Mts. and across S Alaska to the Pacific Ocean.

Stikine Mountains. Range ab. 400 m. long, S Yukon and N Brit. Columbia, Canada; a range of the Rocky Mts.; highest Mt. Cushing 8676 ft. in N Brit. Columbia.

Sti′kle·stad′ (stī′klĕ·stä′). Village, Nord-Tröndelag co., N cen. Norway, on Trondheim Fjord NE of Trondheim; scene of battle in which King Olaf II of Norway was killed 1030.

Still′wa′ter (stĭl′wô′tẽr; -wŏt′ẽr). **1** County in Montana. See *Table* at MONTANA.
2 City, ⊗ of Washington co., E Minnesota, on St. Croix river 15 m. ENE of St. Paul; pop. 8310; former lumbering center.
3 Village, Saratoga co., New York, on W bank of Hudson river ab. 21 m. N of Albany; pop. 1398. Battle fought ab. 3 m. N in Revolutionary War generally known as the battle of Saratoga (*q.v.*).
4 City, ⊗ of Payne co., N cen. Oklahoma, 42 m. S of Ponca City; pop. 23,965; farming, milling, food processing; cotton gins, grain elevators, hatcheries, creameries; gas and oil fields nearby. Founded 1889. Oklahoma State University (1891; coed.).

Stillwater Mountains. Range in cen. Churchill co., W Nevada.

Stil′ton (stĭl′t′n; -tŭn). Parish in Huntingdonshire, E cen. England; gives name to cheese originally and still made in Leicestershire.

Stil′well (stĭl′wĕl; -wẽl). City, ⊗ of Adair co., E Oklahoma, 44 m. E of Muskogee; pop. 1916; farming, fruit-growing, lumbering.

Stilwell Road. Military highway 1044 m. long connecting NE India with Kunming, Yunnan prov., China; named by Chiang Kai-shek in honor of American general Joseph W. Stilwell on completion Jan. 1945 of the Ledo Road (*q.v.*) linking NE India with the Burma Road (*q.v.*); comprises the Ledo Road and the Chinese portion of the Burma Road; officially abandoned Oct. 1945.

Stim′son, Mount (stĭm′s′n). Peak 10,155 ft. in Glacier National Park, NW Montana.

Stin·nett′ (stĭ·nĕt′). Town, ⊗ of Hutchinson co., NW Texas; pop. 2695.

Štip *or* **Shtip** (shtēp); *Turk.* **Ish·tib′** (ĕsh·tēb′; -tēp′). Town, Macedonia federated republic, SE Yugoslavia, 40 m. SE of Skoplje; pop. 12,080; an old town, in early times belonging to the Byzantines, later to the Serbs, and Turkish from 1389 to 1913.

Sti′ring′–Wen′del′ (stē′rĕn′y′[-răng′]văn′dĕl′); *Ger.* **Stie′ring·en-Wen′del** (shtē′rĭng·ĕn·vĕn′dĕl). Commune, Moselle dept., NE France, 34 m. ENE of Metz; pop. (1931) 11,128; coal mines.

Stir′ling (stûr′lĭng). **1** *or* **Stir′ling·shire** (-shĭr; -shẽr). County, cen. Scotland; area 451 sq. m.; pop. (1951) 187,432; ⊗ Stirling; other towns Falkirk, Kilsyth, Grangemouth; rivers Forth, Avon, Endrick, Carron; coal mining, manufacturing (textiles and iron products), farming.
2 Burgh, its ⊗, on the Forth river 36 m. NW of Edinburgh; pop. 26,960; woolens, iron founding. Ancient castle, birthplace of James II of Scotland; scene of the coronation of infant Mary, Queen of Scots, and James VI of Scotland; battle (also known as Stirling Bridge) Sept. 11, 1297 in which Wallace defeated English under earl of Surrey.
3 Island, one of the Treasury group off S end of Bougainville, Solomon Is., W Pacific Ocean. Landing of Americans Oct. 26–27, 1943.

Stirling Range. Mountain range in SE Territory of Papua, New Guinea, forming the SE extension of the Owen Stanley Range to the shores of Milne Bay.

Stjern′öy′ (styärn′ŭ′ü). Island in Arctic Ocean off NW coast of Norway, in Finnmark co. S of Söröy I.; at mouth of Alta Fjord; pop. 250.

Sto′bi (stō′bī). Ancient town of Paeonia (in Macedonia after 336 B.C.) dating probably from the 6th cent. B.C.; esp. prominent in Roman times when it was capital of Roman province of Macedonia; destroyed by earthquake 518 A.D. Its ruins not far from Bitolj in Macedonia, Yugoslavia.

Stochód. See STOKHOD.

Stock′ach (shtŏk′äk). Commune, S Baden-Württemberg state, W Germany, NW of Konstanz; pop. (1933) 3007; scene of two battles: Mar. 25, 1799 in which Charles Louis, Archduke of Austria, defeated French

under General Jourdan, and May 3, 1800 in which General Moreau defeated the Austrians.

Stock′bridge (stŏk′brĭj). Town, Berkshire co., W Massachusetts, 12 m. S of Pittsfield; pop. 2161; summer resort in the Berkshire Hills. Stockbridge Mission House, built 1739 by Rev. John Sergeant, first missionary to Stockbridge Indians.

Stock′e·rau (shtôk′ĕ·rou). City, Lower Austria prov., Austria, NNW of Vienna on arm of Danube river; pop. 11,148; manufactures machinery, chemicals.

Stock′holm (stŏk′hōm; *Swed.* stôk′hôlm′). **1** Province, Sweden. See *Table* at SWEDEN.
2 Seaport city, ✱ of Sweden, geographically within and ✱ of Stockholm prov., but itself administered as a separate province (area 55 sq. m.), SE Sweden, on the Baltic Sea; pop. 654,864; largest city in Sweden; shipbuilding yards, food and tobacco processing plants, textile and paper mills, rubber and chemical works, tanneries, breweries. Notable buildings include the city hall, the stadium built 1912 for the Olympic games, the Riddarkyrka, burial place of the kings and notable men of Sweden, Nobel Institute, and the national museum.
History: According to tradition, founded by Birger of Bjälbo in 13th cent. on an island in outlet of Lake Mälaren; in 14th cent. attracted a large German population and became an important commercial city, often siding with but not belonging to the Hanseatic League.

Stock′port (stŏk′pōrt). County borough, Cheshire, NW England, on the Mersey 6 m. S of Manchester; pop. 125,490, (1951 pop.) 141,660; manufactures cotton goods, iron and brass wares, and machinery.

Stocks′bridge (stŏks′brĭj). Urban district, West Riding, Yorkshire, N England; pop. 10,277.

Stock′ton (stŏk′tŭn). **1** Commercial and manufacturing city, ⊗ of San Joaquin co., cen. California, on Stockton Channel and San Joaquin river 53 m. E of Oakland; pop. 86,321; port; chief distributing point for agricultural products of San Joaquin Valley; manufactures agricultural and other machinery, flour, feeds, paper products, leather goods, trucks, paper boxboard, canned goods. Univ. of the Pacific (founded 1851; moved here 1924; coed.). Site purchased 1842; settled 1847 as outfitting center for gold miners; made ⊗ 1850.
2 City, ⊗ of Rooks co., N Kansas; pop. 2073.
3 City, ⊗ of Cedar co., W Missouri; pop. 838.
4 Town, E New South Wales, SE Australia, suburb of Newcastle; pop. 5700; shipbuilding yards; has coal industries.
5 *or* **Stockton on Tees** (tēz). Municipal borough, Durham, N England, 4 m. from mouth of the Tees in North Sea and 33 m. SSE of Newcastle; pop. 74,024; shipbuilding yards.

Stockton Islands See APOSTLE ISLANDS.

Stock′ville (stŏk′vĭl). Village, ⊗ of Frontier co., S Nebraska; pop. 91.

Stod′dard (stŏd′ẽrd). County in Missouri. See *Table* at MISSOURI.

Sto′er, Point of (stō′ẽr). Cape on NW coast of Scotland, at S entrance to Eddrachillis Bay; lighthouse.

Stoke, East (stōk). *also* **Stoke.** Village, Nottinghamshire, cen. England, near Newark; scene of battle June 16, 1487 in which Lambert Simnel the pretender was defeated by Henry VII.

Stoke Newington. Metropolitan borough of London. See *Table* at LONDON.

Stoke on Trent (trĕnt). City and county borough, Staffordshire, W cen. England, 38 m. N of Birmingham; pop. 276,639, (1951 pop.) 275,095; center of the Staffordshire pottery-making industry; also, coal mines and brick kilns; home of leaders in pottery, including Josiah Wedgwood (see BURSLEM), Josiah Spode, Herbert Minton. See the POTTERIES.

Stoke Po′ges (pō′jĭs; -jĭz). Parish in Eton rural district, Buckinghamshire, SE cen. England; pop. 2110; generally considered the scene of Gray's "Elegy."

Stokes (stōks). **1** County in North Carolina. See *Table* at NORTH CAROLINA.

2 Peak 7020 ft. in Andes Mts., S Chile, near Argentina border and E of Hanover I.

Sto'khod (stô′ĸŭt); *Pol.* **Sto'chód** (stô′ĸŏŏt). River ab. 90 m. long in NW Ukraine, U.S.S.R., formerly in E Poland; flows into Pripyat river from the S; battles on its banks in 1916.

Stol'berg (shtôl′bĕrĸ), *also* **Stolberg im Rhein'land** (ĭm rīn′länt) *or* **bei Aa'chen** (bī ä′ĸĕn). City, North Rhine-Westphalia, West Germany, on Belgian border 7 m. E of Aachen; pop. 17,111; lead and zinc works; manufactures cutlery, glass, soap, glycerine. In World War II taken by Allied forces in latter part of 1945.

Stol·bo'va (stŭl·bô′vä). Village, Leningrad Region, NW Soviet Russia, Europe, near S end of Lake Ladoga; by terms of treaty signed here June 1617, ending war bet. Russia and Sweden, Russia cut off from Baltic Sea.

Stolb'tsy (stôlp′tsĭ); *Pol.* **Stołp'ce** (stôlp′tsĕ). Town, W cen. White Russia, U.S.S.R., on Neman river 40 m. ESE of Novogrudok; formerly in Nowogródek dept., Poland; pop. 6278; former frontier railroad junction.

Stoll'berg (shtôl′bĕrĸ), *also* **Stollberg im Erz'ge·bir'ge** (ĭm ĕrts′gĕ·bĭr′gĕ; ärts′-). City, Karl-Marx-Stadt dist., East Germany, 10 m. SW of Karl-Marx-Stadt; pop. 10,502.

Stolp. See SŁUPSK.

Stol'pe (shtôl′pĕ). River ab. 90 m. long in Poland and formerly in the province of Pomerania, Prussia, Germany, flowing NW into the Baltic Sea.

Stone (stōn). **1** River in Tennessee. See STONE RIVER.

2 Name of counties in three states of the U.S. See *Tables* at ARKANSAS, MISSISSIPPI, MISSOURI.

3 Urban district, Staffordshire, W cen. England; pop. 8299.

Stone'ham (stōn′ăm). Residential town, Middlesex co., NE Massachusetts, 9 m. N of Boston; pop. 17,821.

Stone'ha·ven (stōn′hā′vĕn; stōn′hā′vĕn). Seaport burgh, ⊗ of Kincardine co., E Scotland; pop. 4438.

Stone'henge (stōn′hĕnj; stōn′hĕnj′). An assemblage of upright stones on the Salisbury Plain 7 m. N of Salisbury, England, originally in two concentric circles enclosing two rows of smaller stones. Much uncertainty exists as to its origin and purpose; probably dates back to the Bronze Age in Britain.

Stone'leigh (stōn′lē). Urban community (unincorporated), Baltimore co., N Maryland, N of Baltimore; pop. (with Rodgers Forge) 15,645.

Stone Mountain. 1 Massive monadnock of gray granite in De Kalb co., NW cen. Georgia, near Atlanta; 1686 ft. high; selected as site of a Confederate memorial, to be carved on the NE wall of the mountain; work begun 1917 and continued 1923–25 by Gutzon Borglum; after Borglum's dismissal work taken up by Augustus Lukeman 1925; only a small section completed.

2 Peak 3500 ft. in Carter co., NE Tennessee.

Stones River (stōnz). River 60 m. long, Tennessee; formed by confluence of East Fork and West Fork in N Rutherford co., flows N into Cumberland river E of Nashville; on West Fork near Murfreesboro occurred battle (also known as battle of Murfreesboro, *q.v.*) Dec. 31, 1862–Jan. 2, 1863, a drawn contest but strategical victory for Union forces; site of battle has been set aside as **Stones River National Military Park** (see UNITED STATES, *National Historical Parks*).

Stone'wall (stōn′wôl). **1** County in Texas. See *Table* at TEXAS.

2 Village, Gillespie co., cen. Texas, on Pedernales river; birthplace of Lyndon B. Johnson, 36th president of the U.S., nearby.

Ston'ey Creek (stōn′ĭ). Village, Wentworth co., SE Ontario, Canada, at W end of Lake Ontario; scene of battle June 6, 1813 in which the British under General Vincent defeated the Americans under Generals Chandler and Winder.

Ston'ing·ton (stŏn′ĭng·tŭn). Town, SE New London co., SE Connecticut, on Long Island Sound E of Groton; pop. 13,969; settled 1649, incorp. 1801; agriculture; manufactures machinery, printing presses, woolens, velvets, rayon, thread. Includes (1) borough of Stonington; pop. 1622; incorp. 1801 (first such incorporation in Connecticut); important in early times as shipbuilding, shipping, and fishing center; under attack by British 1775 and 1812; and (2) Mystic (*q.v.*).

Ston'y Creek (stōn′ĭ). River, S Pennsylvania, flowing N from Somerset co. to unite with the Little Conemaugh river at Johnstown and form the Conemaugh.

Stony Man Mountain. Peak 4010 ft. in the Blue Ridge Mts., Page co., N Virginia.

Stony Mountain. Peak 3844 ft. in the Catskill Mts., SE New York.

Stony Point. 1 Point on W cen. coast of Jefferson co., N New York, extending into Lake Ontario SW of Sackets Harbor.

2 Village in Rockland co., SE New York; pop. 3330; named from a rocky promontory on the Hudson; in Revolutionary War an American blockhouse 1776–79; taken by British May 31, 1779 and converted into a strong fort; taken by Gen. Anthony Wayne July 15–16, 1779; evacuated as untenable July 18.

Stony Tunguska. See TUNGUSKA.

Stop'pen·berg (shtôp′ĕn·bĕrĸ). Former commune (pop. 13,794), Düsseldorf govt. dist., Rhine Province, Prussia, Germany; since 1929 part of Essen (*q.v.*).

Stor (stōr). River ab. 55 m. long in NW cen. Jutland Penin., Denmark; flows W into North Sea.

Sto'ra' Lu'le·träsk' (stŏŏ′rä′ lŏŏ′lĕ·trĕsk′). Lake in NW Sweden; source of the Lule river.

Stora Sjö'fall'et (shû′fäl′ĕt). Waterfall 121 ft. in upper Lule river, N Sweden.

Stor'a'van (stŏŏr′ä′vän). Lake 66 sq. m. in Västerbotten prov., N Sweden; drained by Skellefte river.

Stord (stōrd; stŏŏrd). Island off SW coast of Norway, ab. 30 m. S of Bergen, in Hordaland co.; 92 sq. m.

Stö'ren (stû′rĕn). Town, Sör-Tröndelag co., cen. Norway, ab. 40 m. S of Trondheim; pop. 2468.

Sto're Sot'ra (stō′rĕ sŏt′rä; stō′rĕ sŏŏt′rä). = SOTRA.

Sto'rey (stōr′ĭ). County in Nevada. See *Table* at NEVADA.

Stor' Fjord' (stōr′ fyŏr′; stŏŏr′ fyŏŏr′). **1** Fiord separating the main island of Spitsbergen from Barents I. and Edge I.

2 Inlet of the Norwegian Sea on W coast of Norway; extends inland over 70 m., E of Ålesund.

Stor'foss' (stōr′fŏs′; stŏŏr′-). Rapids in the Tana river, NE Norway, ab. 45 m. from its mouth.

Storm Bay (stôrm). Large inlet of South Pacific Ocean, SE Tasmania, Australia, bet. Tasman Penin. and Bruni I.; receives Derwent river.

Storm'berg (stôrm′bûrg). **1** Mountain range in NE Cape Province, Republic of So. Africa.

2 Village, N Cape Province, Republic of So. Africa, S of Burghersdorp; scene of battle Dec. 10, 1899 in which the Boers defeated the English.

Storm King (stôrm). Mountain 1340 ft. in Highlands of the Hudson, SE New York, overlooking Hudson river on W bank N of West Point.

Storm King Peak. Mountain 13,749 ft. in San Juan co., SW Colorado.

Storm Lake. 1 Lake in S Buena Vista co., NW Iowa.

2 City, ⊗ of Buena Vista co., NW Iowa, 20 m. ESE of Cherokee; pop. 7728. Buena Vista Coll. (1891; coed.; Presbyterian).

Stor'mont (stôr′mŏnt). County, SE Ontario, Canada, separated from New York on the S by the St. Lawrence river. See *Table* at ONTARIO.

Storms, Cape of. See Cape of GOOD HOPE.

Storm'y Mountain (stôr′mĭ). Peak 7219 ft. in Chelan co., cen. Washington.

Stor'no·way (stôr′nô·wā). Seaport burgh, Ross and

Cromarty co., N Scotland, on Lewis I.; pop. 4954; chief town of Lewis with Harris; fisheries.

Storrs (stôrz). Subdivision (pop. 6054) of town of MANSFIELD, Connecticut; Univ. of Connecticut (1881; coed.).

Stor'sjön' (stōōr'shûn'). Lake 176 sq. m. in Jämtland prov., W Sweden; Östersund is on its E shore.

Stort (stôrt). River 22 m. long, Essex and Hertfordshire, SE England; flows S and SW to the Lea at Hoddesdon.

Stor'u'man (stōōr'ōō'màn). Lake 63 sq. m. in Väster-botten prov., N Sweden; drained by Ume river.

Sto'ry (stōr'ĭ). County in Iowa. See *Table* at IOWA.

Stough'ton (stō't'n). 1 Town, Norfolk co., E Massa-chusetts, 5 m. NW of Brockton; pop. 16,328; shoes. 2 City, Dane co., S Wisconsin, 14 m. SSE of Madison; pop. 5555; farm trade center; manufactures trailers.

Stour (stour; stōr). 1 River 60 m. long in SE England; flows bet. Essex and Suffolk cos. and into North Sea at Harwich. 2 River 55 m. long in S England; flows across Dor-setshire from NW to SE, enters Hampshire, and empties into the Avon at Christchurch. 3 River 40 m. long in Kent, SE England; flows NE past Canterbury and empties into North Sea through two arms which cut off the island of Thanet; navigable as far as Canterbury. 4 River 20 m. long, cen. England; rises in Oxfordshire and flows NW to the Avon 1½ m. SW of Stratford on Avon, Warwickshire. 5 River 20 m. long in W cen. England; flows S in Staf-fordshire and Worcestershire past Kidderminster and into the Severn at Stourport.

Stour'bridge (stour'brĭj; stōōr'-; stûr'-; stōr'-). Munic-ipal borough, Worcestershire, W cen. England, on the Stour 11 m. W of Birmingham; pop. 37,247; glassmaking.

Stour'port (stour'pôrt; stōōr'-). Urban district, Worces-tershire, W cen. England; pop. 10,140.

Stow (stō). Village, Summit co., NE Ohio, NE of Akron; pop. 12,194.

Stowe (stō). 1 Urban area, Montgomery co., SE Penn-sylvania, NW of Philadelphia; pop. 11,730. 2 Town, Lamoille co., N Vermont, SE of Mt. Mansfield ski area; pop. 1901.

Stowey, Nether. See NETHER STOWEY.

Stra·bane' (strá·băn'). Urban district, N co. Tyrone, W cen. Northern Ireland, on Mourne and Finn rivers; pop. 6620; linen manufacture.

Strad'broke (străd'brōk). Island ab. 64 m. long off SE coast of Queensland, Australia; encloses part of Moreton Bay.

Straf'ford (străf'ĕrd). County in New Hampshire. See *Table* at NEW HAMPSHIRE.

Stra'han (strŏ'ăn). Town, W Tasmania, Australia, at N end of Macquarie Harbour; pop. (municipality) 722; center of mineral and timber section.

Strahl'horn (shträl'hôrn). Peak 13,750 ft. in the Pen-nine Alps, Switzerland, N of Monte Rosa.

Straits, the (stráts). 1 Name formerly used specifically to designate the Strait of Gibraltar; later, the Strait of Malacca. 2 The link bet. the Mediterranean and Black Seas, in-cluding the Bosporus and Dardanelles (*qq.v.*), to which the name came to be applied when with Russian expan-sion to Black Sea the "Straits Question," the issue of fortification by Ottoman Empire and of terms of passage bet. Black Sea and Mediterranean, became a problem in European diplomacy; opened to passage of Russian ves-sels 1774; by Straits Convention (1841), basic settlement of 19th cent., the five great powers agreed to principle of closing Straits to foreign war vessels; after closure to merchant vessels in World War I 1914, became object of Allies to reopen Straits in Dardanelles campaign 1915; occupied by Allies 1918 (see ZONE OF THE STRAITS); by terms of Treaty of Lausanne 1923, demilitarized and placed under supervision of international commission,

actually controlled by Turkey; remilitarized by Turkey as provided by Convention of Montreux 1936; special rights in control demanded by Russia 1946–47. 3 Short for STRAITS SETTLEMENTS.

Straits Settlements. Former British crown colony on the Strait of Malacca, comprising Singapore, Penang, and Malacca settlements on the S and W coast of the Malay Penin., SE Asia, and adjacent islands; 1242 sq. m.; pop. 1,104,307; including outlying parts of Singapore settlement (Cocos Is. and Christmas I.) and Labuan, 1338 sq. m. and pop. 1,094,423, (1941 est.) 1,435,895; ✳ Singapore. United 1826 under one government as a presidency of India with capital at Penang; incorporated under Bengal 1830; capital removed to Singapore 1836; taken from control of Indian government 1867 and transferred to British Secretary of State for the Colonies; after 1886 Cocos Is., Christmas I., and Labuan brought under control of Governor of Straits Settlements and later incorporated in the Colony, although Labuan was constituted a separate settlement 1912; in World War II overrun and seized by Japanese 1941–42; held by Japa-nese until 1945. Broken up 1946 when Singapore settle-ment was made a separate crown colony, Malacca and Penang made part of Union of Malaya, and Labuan be-came attached to North Borneo.

Stral'sund (shträl'zŏŏnt; shträl·zŏŏnt'). 1 Former gov-ernment district, Pomerania prov., Prussia, Germany; from 1932 part of Stettin govt. dist.; since 1945 com-prises the larger part of Pomerania remaining to Ger-many. 2 Manufacturing seaport city, Rostock dist., E Germany, on the Strelasund opp. Rügen I. in the Baltic 88 m. NW of Stettin; pop. 39,469; 13th-cent. church of St. Nicho-las, 13th-cent. church of St. Mary, 13th-cent. town hall; beer, brandy, beet sugar; shipbuilding. *History:* Became city 1234; member of Hanseatic League; peace treaty signed here 1370 (see HANSE TOWNS); famous siege by Wallenstein 1628; to Sweden by Peace of Westphalia 1648; changed hands repeatedly (1678, 1715, 1720, 1807, 1814) until it passed to Prussia 1815; capital until 1932 of Stralsund govt. dist.

Strand (stränd). Town, SW Cape Province, S Union of South Africa, on NE shore of False Bay adjoining Somerset West; pop. 5927; seaside resort.

Strang'ford Lough (străng'fĕrd lŏĸ). Inlet of Irish Sea on E coast of Northern Ireland; extends N inland ab. 19 m. in co. Down.

Stran·raer' (străn·rär'). Seaport burgh, Wigtown co., SW Scotland, at head of Loch Ryan; pop. 8622; fisheries.

Stras'bourg (sträs'bûrg; sträz'-; *Fr.* sträz'bŏŏr'); *Ger.* **Strass'burg** (sträs'bûrg; sträz'-; *Ger.* shträs'bŏŏrĸ); *anc.* **Ar·gen'to·ra'tum** (är·jĕn'tō·rā'tŭm). Manufac-turing and commercial city, ✳ of Bas-Rhin dept., NE France, on the Ill river ab. 2 m. W of its confluence with the Rhine, 83 m. SE of Metz; pop. 193,119; fortified; in center of rich coal fields; episcopal see (since 3d or 4th cent.); famous Gothic cathedral of 10th to 14th cents. contains noted 14th-cent. astronomical clock; university (founded 1567), one of best equipped in Europe; other structures include the chamber of commerce, governor's palace, town hall, museums, old episcopal palace; sometimes called the City of Bells—in allusion to the many bells in its cathedral and churches. Commercial trade center, handling much of the traffic bet. France, Germany, and Switzerland; manufactures include pâtés de foie gras (in which it has a large trade), machinery, leather goods, clothing, furniture, carpets, surgical in-struments, tobacco, gloves, liquor, and musical instru-ments; foundries, locomotive works, chemical works, tanneries. *History:* Important in Celtic times; passed to Romans; destroyed by Attila; captured and rebuilt by Clovis; fa-mous Oath of Strasbourg taken here 842; became prin-cipal town in domain of Lothair I (later called Lorraine); people achieved independence from bishops 14th cent.;

Gutenberg completed invention of printing from movable type here 15th cent.; seized by Louis XIV 1681; captured by Germans 1870 and ceded to Germany after Franco-Prussian War; reverted to France 1919; center of fighting Nov. 1944–Apr. 1945.

Stras'burg (strŏz'bûrg). Town, Shenandoah co., N Virginia, 18 m. SSW of Winchester; pop. 2428; manufactures lumber, dairy products, flour, silk.

Strassburg. See STRASBOURG city, France.

Strassburg. See AIUD town, Romania.

Strat'a Flor'i·da (străt'ȧ flŏr'ĭ·dȧ); _Welsh_ **Ys'trad Fflur** (ûs'trȧd flïr'). Ruins of Cistercian abbey, Cardiganshire, W Wales, SE of Aberystwyth near the Teifi river; flourished 12th cent., destroyed by fire at end of 13th cent.; not many ruins.

Strat'ford (străt'fẽrd). **1** Suburban residential town, SE Fairfield co., SW Connecticut, on Long Island Sound at mouth of Housatonic river E of Bridgeport; pop. 45,012; settled 1639; resort and fishing port; manufactures planes, wheels, springs.

2 Town, ⊗ of Sherman co., NW Texas; pop. 1380.

3 Estate, Westmoreland co., E Virginia, on Potomac river near George Washington Birthplace National Monument; birthplace of Robert E. Lee.

4 City, ⊗ of Perth co., SE Ontario, Canada, 28 m. W of Kitchener; pop. 18,785; railroad center and divisional point with railroad repair shops; varied manufactures. Seat of a collegiate institute and a provincial normal school. Founded 1832.

5 District in county borough of West Ham, Essex, SE England, on Lea river; pop. 68,138; part of Greater London; railroad equipment.

6 Borough, Taranaki provincial dist., W North I., New Zealand; pop. ab. 3000.

Stratford le Bow. See BOW.

Stratford on A'von (ā'vŭn; ăv'ŭn). Municipal borough, Warwickshire, cen. England, 21 m. SSE of Birmingham; pop. 14,980; birthplace and burial place of William Shakespeare.

Stratford Point. Point on E coast, Fairfield co., Connecticut, on W side of mouth of Housatonic river.

Strath'aird' Point (străth'ârd'). Cape on S coast of Skye I. in the Inner Hebrides, off NW coast of Scotland, projecting into Cuillin Sound.

Strath·clyde' (străth·klīd'). Medieval Celtic kingdom of Scotland, S of the Clyde river; ✳ Dumbarton; established c. 7th cent.; threatened and ravaged by Picts and Norsemen 8th and 9th cents.; suffered defeat by English at Brunanburh 937 and also in 945–946; added to Scottish kingdom by Malcolm II (king 1005–34); S part known as Cumbria (_q.v._).

Strath·co'na (străth·kō'nȧ). See EDMONTON.

Strathcona Park. Canadian provincial park, cen. Vancouver I.; 828 sq. m.; alpine area with fine scenery; a game sanctuary and fishing resort.

Strath'field (străth'fēld). Former town, now suburban area in W part of Greater Sydney, New South Wales, Australia.

Strath·more' (străth·mōr'). Great valley of cen. Scotland, S of the Grampian Mts., remarkable for beauty, fertility, and populousness.

Strath·roy' (străth·roi'). Town, Middlesex co., SE Ontario, Canada, 22 m. W of London; pop. 3708; manufactures iron castings, stoves, furniture.

Strath Spey (străth spā'). District and valley in Inverness, Banff, and Moray cos., NE Scotland.

Strat'ton and Bude (străt''n, būd'). Urban district, Cornwall, SW England; pop. 2568; Stratton scene of battle May 16, 1643 in which Royalists under Sir Ralph Hopton defeated Parliamentarians under the earl of Stamford.

Stratton Mountain. Peak 3859 ft. in W Windham co., SE Vermont.

Stra'tus (strā'tŭs). Chief town of ancient Acarnania, W Greece, on W bank of the Achelous river.

Strau'bing (shtrou'bĭng). Manufacturing city, Lower Bavaria and Upper Palatinate govt. dist., Bavaria, Germany, on Danube river 23 m. ESE of Regensburg; pop. 23,593; buildings include a 12th-cent. church, 14th-cent. Gothic church, 14th-cent. town hall, late 15th-cent. ducal palace; manufactures ceramic ware, beer.

Straw'ber'ry (strô'bĕr'ĭ, -bẽr·ĭ). River ab. 60 m. long, N cen. Utah; rises in Wasatch co., flows E into Duchesne river in cen. Duchesne co.

Strawberry Mountains. Range in cen. Grant co., E cen. Oregon.

Strawberry Point. Northeast point of Plymouth co., E Massachusetts, E of Hingham; marks the S limit of Massachusetts Bay.

Strawberry Reservoir. Reservoir in Strawberry river, S Wasatch co., N cen. Utah.

Strea'tor (strē'tẽr). City, La Salle co., N Illinois, 50 m. NE of Peoria; pop. 16,868; incorp. 1882; glass and bottles, drain and sewer pipes, farm implements; coal.

Street Mountain (strēt). Peak 4216 ft. in the Adirondack Mts., Essex co., NE New York.

Strehlen. See STRZELIN.

Stre'la·sund (shtrā'lä·zŏŏnt). Strait ab. 1½ m. wide and 15 to 20 m. long bet. Rügen I. and the mainland, Mecklenburg, Germany; Stralsund is on its W shore.

Stre'sa (strā'zä). Town in commune of **Stresa Borro·me'o** [bŏr·rō·mā'ō] (pop. [1931] 4539) on W shore of Lake Maggiore, Novara prov., NE Piedmont, NW Italy; pop. (1931) 2584; resort; scene of conference bet. representatives of 15 nations Sept. 5–20, 1932 during which recommendations for economic collaboration of European countries were decided upon and submitted to the Commission of Inquiry for European Union; scene of conference bet. representatives of France, Great Britain, and Italy Apr. 11–14, 1935 in effort to show united opposition to the rearmament of Germany.

Stret'ford (strĕt'fẽrd). Urban district, Lancashire, NW England, 4 m. SW of Manchester; pop. 56,791, (1951) 61,532; industrial community.

Strick'land (strĭk'lănd). River ab. 225 m. long, main tributary of the Fly river, W Papua, New Guinea I.; rises in mountains of cen. part of the island and flows S and SW through large swamp area to join the Fly on E ab. in the middle of its course.

Striegau. See STRZEGOM.

Strip'ed Mountain (strīp'ĕd; -ĭd; strīpt). Peak 13,160 ft. in Sierra Nevada, E Fresno co., S cen. California.

Strom'bo·li (strŏm'bō·lĭ; _Ital._ strŏm'bō·lē); _anc._ **Stron'gy·le** (strŏn'jĭ·lē). One of the Lipari Is. (_q.v._); contains the active volcano Stromboli, height 3040 ft.

Strom'lo, Mount. (strŏm'lō). Elevation, Australian Capital Territory, SE Australia, 7 m. W of Canberra; astronomical observatory (74-inch telescope) of Australian National Univ.

Strom'ness' (strŏm'nĕs'). Burgh, SW coast of Pomona I., Orkney Is., NE Scotland; pop. 1503; fine harbor.

Ström'ö' (strûm'û'). Largest island of the Faeroes (_q.v._); 28 m. long; 144 sq. m.; pop. 5791; chief town Thorshavn.

Strongs'ville (strôngz'vĭl). Village, Cuyahoga co., N Ohio, 14 m. SSW of Cleveland; pop. 8504.

Strongyle. See STROMBOLI.

Stron'say (strŏn'sā). One of the Orkney Is. off N coast of Scotland; 7¼ m. long; pop. 650; site of a well whose water was once believed to cure leprosy.

Stroph'a·des (strŏf'ȧ·dēz; _Mod. Gr._ strŏ·fä'thäs). Island group (two small islands) in Ionian Sea S of Zante and ab. 30 m. W of Peloponnesus, Greece.

Stroud (stroud). **1** City, Lincoln co., cen. Oklahoma, 34 m. NNE of Shawnee; pop. 2456; manufactures cottonseed oil and cake, asphalt products, gasoline, dairy feed. **2** Urban district, Gloucestershire, SW cen. England, on Thames and Severn canal 8 m. S of Gloucester; pop. 15,977; woolen cloth manufacture; dyeworks.

Strouds'burg (stroudz'bûrg). Borough, ⊗ of Monroe co., E Pennsylvania, 30 m. NNE of Allentown; pop.

6070; in Blue Mts. region near the Delaware Water Gap and the Pocono foothills; site of Fort Penn (1776).

Struma. See STRYMON.

Strum'ble Head (strŭm'b'l). Cape on N side of SW projection of Wales, NE of St. David's Head; lighthouse.

Stru'mi·ca (strōō'mē·tsä) or **Stru'mi·tsa.** **1** River ab. 50 m. long in SE Yugoslavia, flowing E into the Struma (Strymon) river.

2 District in valley of Strumica river, E Macedonia, SE Yugoslavia; formerly in Bulgaria. Valley forms **Strumica Gap,** connecting Struma and Vardar rivers; taken by Germans Apr. 1941.

3 Town, E Macedonia, SE Yugoslavia, on Strumica river; pop. 9586; passed from Turkish rule to Bulgarian 1913, and to newly organized Yugoslavia 1919; site of a castle of the Serbian hero Marko Kraljević; battlefield in the Balkan Wars and in World War I.

Strum'ni·tza (strōōm'nē·tsä). = STRUMICA.

Struth'ers (strŭth'ĕrz). City, Mahoning co., NE Ohio, on Mahoning river 5 m. SE of Youngstown; pop. 15,631; industrial suburb of Youngstown; manufactures steel, iron, metal products.

Stry (strē); *Pol.* **Stryj** (strē). **1** River 110 m. long in W Ukraine, U.S.S.R., formerly in S Poland; flows from the Carpathian Mts. NE to the Dniester river S of Lvov.

2 City, SW Ukraine, U.S.S.R., on Stry river 44 m. NW of Stanislav; formerly in Stanisławów dept., Poland; pop. (1938–39 est.) 34,000; center of lumber industry. In World War I Russians driven back by Germans May–June 1915.

Stry'mon (strī'mŏn; *Mod. Gr.* strē·môn'); *Bulg.* **Stru'ma** (strōō'må; *Bulg.* -mä). River ab. 225 m. long in SW Bulgaria and N Greece; rises SW of Sofia, flows S and SE through Lake Akhinou into the Strymonic Gulf (Aegean Sea).

Stry·mon'ic Gulf (strī·mŏn'ĭk) or **Gulf of Ren·di'na** (rän·dē'nä) or **Or·fa'ni** (ôr·fä'nyĕ). Inlet of Aegean Sea on the NE coast of Greece, NE of Chalcidice Penin., Greece; receives the Strymon river.

Stry'pa (strī'pä). River ab. 60 m. long in SW Ukraine, U.S.S.R., a tributary of the Dniester river bet. Ternopol and Stanislav; battle along its course July 1917. Formerly in SE Poland.

Strze'gom (s'chĕ'gôm); *Ger.* **Strie'gau** (shtrē'gou). City, cen. Wrocław dept., SW Poland, 31 m. WSW of Wrocław; pop. (1946) 15,918; formerly in Silesia, Germany; granite quarrying; manufactures paper. Assigned to Poland by Potsdam Conference 1945.

Strzel'ce O·pol'skie (s'chĕl'tsĕ ô·pôl'skyĕ); *Ger.* **Gross Streh'litz** (grōs shtrā'lĭts). Town, cen. Śląsk dept., SW Poland, SE of Opole; pop. (1946) 11,523; formerly in Silesia, Germany.

Strze'lin (s'chĕ'lēn); *Ger.* **Streh'len** (shtrā'lĕn). City, SE Wrocław dept., SW Poland, 22 m. S of Wrocław; pop. (1946) 12,337; formerly in Silesia, Germany. Assigned to Poland by Potsdam Conference 1945.

Stu'art (stū'ĕrt). **1** City, ⊗ of Martin co., SE Florida, on S end of Indian river 37 m. N of West Palm Beach; pop. 4791; yachting and fishing resort (sharks).

2 City, Adair and Guthrie cos., SW cen. Iowa, 40 m. W of Des Moines; pop. 1486.

3 Town, ⊗ of Patrick co., S Virginia; pop. 974.

4 See ALICE SPRINGS, Australia.

5 River ab. 220 m. long in Brit. Columbia, Canada; flows from Stuart Lake SE into Nechako river.

Stuart, Mount. Peak 9470 ft. in SW Chelan co., cen. Washington.

Stuart Lake. Lake 221 sq. m. in cen. Brit. Columbia, Canada; drains SE through Stuart river.

Stu'arts (stū'ĕrts), or **Stu'art** (stū'ĕrt), **Range.** Range of hills, N cen. South Australia, W of Lake Eyre and NW of Lake Torrens.

Stuhlweissenburg. See SZÉKESFEHÉRVÁR.

Stump'y Point (stŭm'pĭ). Cape on NW St. Thomas I., Virgin Is. of the U.S., at W entrance to Santa Maria Bay.

Stu'ra (stōō'rä). River 44 m. long in NW Italy, in Cuneo prov., Piedmont; flows E and NE into Tanaro river.

Stur'bridge (stûr'brĭj). Industrial town, Worcester co., cen. Massachusetts, 18 m. SW of Worcester; pop. 3604; tanneries, shoe factories, cotton mill.

Stur'geon (stûr'jŭn). **1** Locality, Allegheny co., SW Pennsylvania, 13 m. SW of Pittsburgh; pop. (with Noblestown) 1709.

2 River 106 m. long, SE Ontario, Canada; rises in E Ontario, flows SSE into Lake Nipissing.

Sturgeon Bay. City, ⊗ of Door co., NE Wisconsin, on Sturgeon Bay, an inlet of Green Bay, 38 m. NE of Green Bay (city); pop. 7353; canal connects Green Bay with Lake Michigan; vacation resort; quarries, shipbuilding plants; grows cherries.

Sturgeon Falls. Town, Nipissing dist., SE Ontario, Canada, on N shore of Lake Nipissing 25 m. W of North Bay; pop. 4962; manufactures wood pulp and paper; on transcontinental railroad.

Stur'gis (stûr'jĭs). **1** City, Union co., W Kentucky, 32 m. SW of Henderson; pop. 2209; coal mining.

2 City, St. Joseph co., S Michigan, 35 m. S of Kalamazoo; pop. 8915; manufactures furniture.

3 City, ⊗ of Meade co., W South Dakota, in Black Hills 8 m. ENE of Lead; pop. 4639; near Fort Meade (*q.v.*).

Stuts'man (stŭts'măn). County in North Dakota. See *Table* at NORTH DAKOTA.

Stutt'gart. **1** (stŭt'gärt) City, a ⊗ of Arkansas co., E Arkansas, 33 m. NE of Pine Bluff; pop. 9661; incorp. as city 1887; railroad center.

2 (shtŏŏt'gärt) Manufacturing city, ✳ of Baden-Württemberg, West Germany, on Neckar river 38 m. ESE of Karlsruhe; pop. (1939) 459,538, (1958 est.) 619,907; 12th-cent. church; one of most important publishing centers in the world; manufactures textiles, chemicals, machinery, leather, furniture, vehicles, paper, cigars, dyes; active trade center. Residence of Hegel. First mentioned 1229; made city c. 1270; residence of rulers of Württemberg 1482 ff.; seat of Reichstag and National Assembly at time of Kapp Putsch 1920; bombed often in World War II; entered by French troops Apr. 22, 1945.

Stym·pha'lis (stĭm·fā'lĭs); *Mod. Gr.* **Stym'fa·li'as** (stēm'fä·lyē'äs) or **Za'ra·ka'** (zä'rä·kä'). Lake in NE ancient Arcadia (in modern Argolis and Corinth dept.), NE Peloponnesus, S Greece. In Greek mythology the scene of the slaying by Hercules of the man-eating (Stymphalian) birds.

Styr (stîr). River ab. 300 m. long in NW Ukraine, U.S.S.R.; flows N into Pripyat river in the Pripet Marshes, W of the Goryn; battle line in World War I; formerly in E Poland.

Styr'i·a (stĭr'ĭ·à); *Ger.* **Stei'er·mark** (shtī'ĕr·märk). Province of Austria (see *Table* at AUSTRIA). Mountainous part of cen. and SE Austria watered by the Mur, Mürz, and Enns rivers; has much fertile soil under cultivation; noted for its iron mines, esp. at Erzberg (*q.v.*), worked since Roman times. Chief towns Graz, Leoben, and Bruck. In 9th cent. a part of Carinthia under Charlemagne; became separate as a mark 1085; became a duchy 1180; came under the Hapsburgs 1246.

Styx (stĭks). Short stream, Achaea and Elis dept., NW Peloponnesus, Greece; flows N to Gulf of Corinth; associated to some extent in Greek geography with the mythological Styx of the underworld.

Su·a'di (sōō·ä'dĭ). See GANGPUR.

Sua'kin (swä'kĭn; *Arab.* swä'kĭn, sǎ·wä'-); *also* **Sua'-kim** (swä'kĭm). Seaport on Red Sea, E Kassala prov., NE Sudan, S of Port Sudan; pop. ab. 15,000. See PORT SUDAN.

Sual or **Port Sual** (swäl). Municipality, NW Pangasinan prov., Luzon, Phil. Is., port on small harbor at SW corner of Lingayen Gulf ab. 11 m. W of Lingayen; pop. 6396; at W end of American landings Jan. 14, 1945.

Suan'hwa' (sü·än'hwä'). Town, S Chahar prov., Inner

Mongolia, NE China, 18 m. SE of Wanchuan (Kalgan); on highway NW of Peiping and S of the Great Wall.

Sua′ra (swä′rȧ). = ZUARA.

Suárez. See CORONEL SUÁREZ.

Subang. See SOEBANG.

Su·bar′na·re′kha (sŏŏ·bŭr′nȧ·räk′hȧ). River ab. 240 m. long, Bihar and Bengal, NE India; flows SE into Bay of Bengal SW of the mouth of the Hooghly river and NE of Balasore.

Su·ba′sio, Mon′te (mȯn′tȧ sŏŏ·bä′zyȯ). Mountain 4231 ft. in cen. Apennines, Umbria, cen. Italy; town of Assisi is located on S slope of a W spur.

Sub·han′ Dağ′la·ri′ (sŏŏp·hän′ dä′lä·rḯ′). Mountain range in E Turkey in Asia, N of Lake Van; highest point 14,040 ft.

Su′bi·a′co (sŏŏ′bḯ·ä′kō). Municipality, SW Western Australia, W suburb of Perth; pop. 16,813.

Su·bia′co (sŏŏ·byä′kȯ). Commune, Roma prov., W Latium, cen. Italy, 50 m. E of Rome; pop. (1931) 8804; site of first monastery founded by St. Benedict c. 505; first printing press in Italy set up here 1464.

Su′bic (sŏŏ′bĭk) or **Su′bĭg** (-bĭg). Municipality, S Zambales prov., Luzon, Phil. Is., at head of Subic Bay (*q.v.*) 35 m. SSE of Iba; pop. 14,923; one of the two fine harbors (see OLONGAPO) on Subic Bay.

Subic, or Subĭg, Bay. Inlet of South China Sea ab. 7 m. long in S Zambales prov., Luzon, Phil. Is.; affords protected anchorage 35 m. N of entrance to Manila Bay. Its SE shore is part of Bataan prov.; mouth divided by small Grande I. In early times haunted by pirates. American naval base established here 1901; seized by Japanese Jan. 1942; retaken by Americans Jan. 29, 1945.

Sub·lette′ (sŭb·lĕt′). 1 County in Wyoming. See *Table* at WYOMING.

2 City, ⊗ of Haskell co., SW Kansas; pop. 1077.

Su′bo·ti·ca (sŏŏ′bȯ·tē·tsä) or **Su′bo·ti·tsa**; *Hung.* **Sza′bad·ka′** (sȯ′bȯd·kȯ′); *Ger.* **Ma·ri′a-The·re′si·o′pel** (mä·rē′ȧ·tä·rä′zē·ō′pĕl). City, N Voivodina autonomous prov., NE Yugoslavia, near Hungarian frontier; pop. 100,058; industrial and commercial center in grain-growing area; manufactures iron products; university; occupied by Hungary 1941–45.

Succession States. The Central European states of Czechoslovakia, Yugoslavia, Romania, Poland, Austria, and Hungary, which now as a whole or in part occupy the lands of the former monarchy of Austria-Hungary—often so called after World War I.

Suc′coth (sŭk′ŏth; -ōth). 1 Locality in Goshen, ancient Egypt, E of the Nile delta, probably the same as Pithom; first encampment of the Israelites in the Exodus (*Exod.* xii. 37; xiii. 20).

2 Town of ancient Palestine, E of the Jordan and near the N bank of the Jabbok (*Gen.* xxxiii. 17).

Su·cea′va (sŏŏ·chä′vä). 1 River ab. 110 m. long, N Romania, in Bucovina region, flowing into Siret river.

2 Town, N Romania, in SE Bucovina region on the Suceava river; pop. ab. 17,000; capital of Moldavia 1401–1565; 14th-cent. church; early 17th-cent. monastery nearby.

Su·chan′ (sŏŏ·chän′). Town, S Maritime Territory, Soviet Russia, Asia, near coast 60 m. E of Vladivostok; coal mines.

Su·chia′te (sŏŏ·chyä′tå). 1 River in W Guatemala; flows S and SW into Pacific Ocean; forms section of Guatemala-Mexico boundary.

2 Town, S Chiapas state, SE Mexico, port on the Suchiate river opp. Ayutla in Guatemala; railroad terminus.

Su·chi′te·pé′quez (sŏŏ·chē′tå·pā′kås). Department, SW Guatemala; 960 sq. m.; pop. 182,162; ✳ Mazatenango.

Su·chi·to′to (sŏŏ′chē·tō′tȯ). Town, Cuscatlán dept., cen. El Salvador; pop. (1942 est.) 10,350.

Suchow. 1 Town, NW Kansu prov., N cen. China. See KIUCHUAN.

2 Town, NW Kiangsu prov., E China. See TUNGSHAN.

3 City, SW Szechwan prov., S cen. China. See IPIN.

Süch′teln (zük′tĕln). City, North Rhine-Westphalia, Germany, 20 m. WNW of Düsseldorf; pop. 10,323; manufactures velvet, silk, paper, iron goods.

Su′cia Bay (sŏŏ′syä). Bay on S shore of Puerto Rico at its W end, enclosed by Cape Rojo on the W.

Suck (sŭk). River ab. 50 m. long in W cen. Ireland; flows SSE in Connacht prov. into the Shannon river N of Lough Derg.

Su′cre (sŏŏ′krå). 1 *formerly* **Chu′qui·sa′ca** (chŏŏ′kē-sä′kä). City, ✳ of Chuquisaca dept., and constitutional ✳ of Bolivia; pop. (1943 est.) 30,000; altitude 9331 ft.; 318 m. by road SE of La Paz; seat of the national Supreme Court, the Univ. of San Francisco Xavier (1624), and the Archbishopric of La Plata; cathedral (1553). Founded as Chuquisaca 1538; scene of start of revolt against Spain May 1809; name changed 1840 to Sucre in honor of first president of Bolivia.

2 State of Venezuela. See *Table* at VENEZUELA.

Sucro. See ALCIRA.

Su·cza′wa (sŏŏ·chä′vä). = SUCEAVA.

Su′da (sŏŏ′dȧ). River ab. 130 m. long, W Vologda Region, N cen. Soviet Russia, Europe; flows SE and near Cherepovets enters the Rybinsk Reservoir (*q.v.*); formerly united with the Sheksna.

Su′da Bay (sŏŏ′dȧ; *Gr.* sŏŏ′thä); *Gr.* **Kól′pos Soú′das** (kȯl′pȯs sŏŏ′thäs). Inlet on N coast of Crete, near W end, shut in on NW by Akroteri Penin.; just E of Canea, only good harbor on N coast; in World War II site of a British base which was captured by German airborne troops May 26–27 1941.

Su·dan′ (sŏŏ·dän′); *Fr.* **Sou′dan′** (sŏŏ′däN); *Arab.* **Bi·lâd′-es–Su·dan′** (bĭ·läd′ås-sŏŏ·dän′), literally "country of the blacks." 1 Region, N cen. Africa, S of the Sahara and Libyan Deserts—not a political unit; extends across the African continent from W coast 4000 m. to mountains of Ethiopia, with widest part nearly 1000 m.; total approximate area 2,000,000 sq. m.; pop. ab. 40,000,000. Includes major parts of republics of Senegal, Guinea, Mali, Niger, Chad, and Sudan, Gambia, Upper Volta, and the N sections of the countries bordering on the Atlantic from Portuguese Guinea to Cameroun; occupies the basin of the Senegal and cen. parts of the Niger and Nile basins, and the Lake Chad region. Consists of desert, grassy steppes, and extensive plains; ethnologically that part of Africa N of the equator inhabited by Negro peoples under Mohammedan influence and in medieval times site of the Negro empires of Bornu, Songhai, Fulah.

2 Republic, NE Africa: see ANGLO-EGYPTIAN SUDAN.

3 *or* **Su′da·nese′ Republic.** Republic, W Africa, now called **Ma′li** (mä′lē): see FRENCH SUDAN.

Sud′bur′y (sŭd′bĕr′ĭ; -bẽr·ĭ; -brĭ). 1 Town, Middlesex co., NE Massachusetts, 18 m. W of Boston; pop. 7447. Settled 1638; important town at time of Revolutionary War. Wayside Inn (first building 1686 known as Howe Tavern) subject of Longfellow's *Tales of a Wayside Inn.*

2 District, Ontario, Canada. See *Table* at ONTARIO.

3 Mining city, ⊗ of Sudbury dist., SE Ontario, Canada, 38 m. N of Georgian Bay and 165 m. E of Sault Ste. Marie; pop. 42,410; center of world's richest nickel mines; also produces copper, platinum, and palladium ore smelting; lumbering and making of wood pulp. Seat of a government school of mines and a Jesuit college.

4 Municipal borough, West Suffolk, E England, on the Stour 52 m. NE of London; pop. 6614; manufactures silk goods. Birthplace of Thomas Gainsborough.

Sud′die (sŭd′ĭ). Town, N British Guiana, in Essequibo co., on W bank of Essequibo river at its mouth 35 m. NW of Georgetown; nearby is site of U.S. base in World War II.

Su′der·ö′ (sŏŏ′thẽr·û′). Southernmost island of the Faeroes (*q.v.*); 64 sq. m.; pop. (1925) 5141.

Sud–Est. See TAGULA.

Su·de'ten (sōō·dā't'n; *Ger.* zōō-). **1** *also* **Su·de'tes** (sōō·dē'tēz) *or* **Su·det'ic Mountains** (sōō·dĕt'ĭk). Mountain ranges in the provinces of Bohemia (on NE) and Silesia, N Czechoslovakia, WNW of the Carpathians, and extending along the SW boundary of the former province of Silesia, Germany (now in Poland), and continuing W along the boundary of S Saxony. They consist of several smaller mountain groups or ranges: Riesen Gebirge, Lausitzer Gebirge, Eulen Gebirge; highest Schneekoppe 5266 ft. in the Riesen Gebirge, and Schneeberg 4665 ft. at S end.
2 *or* **Su·de'ten·land'** (-lănd'; *Ger.* -länt'). Originally the mountainous region comprising the Sudeten on N borders of Bohemia and Silesia in Czechoslovakia; after the crisis of 1938–39 applied also to all the borderlands of Bohemia and Moravia inhabited by German-speaking people; 8719 sq. m.; pop. (1939) 2,945,261. These irregularly shaped border areas seized by Germans Sept. 1938 (cession officially approved Nov. 21, 1938) and later (Mar. 1939) absorbed into the German Reich; restored to Czechoslovakia 1945.

Sudharam. See NOAKHALI.

Sue'ca (swā'kä). Commune, Valencia prov., E Spain, 22 m. S of Valencia; pop. 19,890; produces rice.

Sue Peaks (sū). Mountains 5835 ft. and 5857 ft. in S Brewster co., W Texas.

Suessa Aurunca. See SESSA AURUNCA.

Sues'su·la (swĕs'ū·lȧ). Ancient Samnite town N of modern Caserta, Campania compartimento, S Italy, near the Caudine Forks; battle 343 B.C. in the first Samnite War.

Su·ez' (sōō·ĕz'; sōō'ĕz; *esp. Brit.*, sōō'ĭz). **1** Governorate, Lower Egypt. See **2**, below, and *Table* at EGYPT.
2 Seaport city at the N end of the Gulf of Suez and at the S terminus of Suez Canal; pop. (1937) 49,686; constitutes the governorate of Suez. In 7th cent. was terminal point of canal connecting Red Sea with the Nile; under Ottoman Empire (16th cent.) became naval and trading station; later, port of departure for Jidda and India.

Suez, Gulf of. Northwest arm of the Red Sea; joined to the Mediterranean Sea by the Suez Canal.

Suez, Isthmus of. Isthmus 72 m. wide connecting NE Africa with Asia; Gulf of Suez and the Red Sea on the S, and the E Mediterranean Sea on the N.

Suez Canal. Ship canal across Isthmus of Suez, NE Africa; connects Red Sea with E Mediterranean; ab. 100 m. long from Suez to Port Said; 197 ft. wide, 42.5 ft. deep; built 1859–69; engineer for its construction was Ferdinand de Lesseps. Passes along E edge of Lake Manzala and through Lake Timsah and the Bitter Lakes; Ismailia is large town on its banks in cen. part; opened Nov. 16, 1869; ownership formerly rested with a French company in which British government held control, under a concession that was due to expire Nov. 1968; nationalized by Egypt 1956.

Sufetula. See SBEITLA.

Suf'fern (sŭf'ērn). Village, Rockland co., SE New York, 28 m. NNW of New York; pop. 5094; residential suburb in summer-resort region; summer theater.

Suf'field (sŭf'ēld). Agricultural town, N Hartford co., N Connecticut, on Massachusetts border; pop. 6779; settled 1670; incorp. 1674 by Massachusetts; annexed to Connecticut 1749; tobacco; Suffield Academy.

Suf'folk (sŭf'ŭk; *in U.S., also* -ôk). **1** Name of counties in two states of the U.S. See *Tables* at MASSACHUSETTS and NEW YORK.
2 City, SE Virginia, ⊗ of Nansemond co., but politically independent, on Nansemond river 18 m. WSW of Portsmouth; 2 sq. m.; pop. 12,609; commercial center and railroad junction; peanut market; manufactures peanut-packing machines, processed peanuts, veneers, caskets. Established 1742; incorp. as town 1808; burned by British in Revolution 1779 and occupied by Federal forces in Civil War 1862; became independent city 1910.
3 County, E England; area 1482 sq. m.; pop. (1951)

442,439; divided into the administrative counties **East Suffolk** (871 sq. m.; pop. 321,849; ⊗ Ipswich) and **West Suffolk** (611 sq. m.; pop. 120,590; ⊗ Bury St. Edmunds); other towns Beccles, Newmarket, Sudbury, Lowestoft, Felixstowe; rivers Waveney, Stour, Deben, Orwell, Alde; fisheries, livestock raising.

Suffolk Broads. See the BROADS.

Sufli. = SOUPHLI.

Su·ga'na (sōō·gä'nä). Valley in Venezia Tridentina compartimento, NE Italy, NE of Rovereto.

Sug'ar Creek (shŏŏg'ēr). City, Jackson co., W Missouri, 9 m. E of Kansas City; pop. 2663.

Sugar Grove. Locality, Pendleton co., E West Virginia, ab. 10 m. S of Franklin.

Sugar Hill. See LISBON town, New Hampshire.

Sugar Island. Island in Chippewa co., E and NE Michigan penin., in Saint Marys river N of Neebish I.

Sugar Loaf Hill. Height in S Okinawa, Ryukyu Is., Japan, dominating approach to Shuri; scene of fierce fighting in May 1945, recaptured by Americans five times.

Sug'ar·loaf' Key (shŏŏg'ēr·lōf'). See FLORIDA KEYS.

Sugarloaf Mountain. **1** Peak 6164 ft. in SE Elko co., NE Nevada.
2 Peak 3647 ft. in Catskill Mts., Greene co., New York.
3 See PÃO DE AÇÚCAR.

Sugar Loaf Mountains. Ridge 2600 ft. in Le Flore co., E Oklahoma.

Sugar Notch. Borough, Luzerne co., E Pennsylvania, 5 m. SW of Wilkes-Barre; pop. 1524.

Sugbu. See CEBU.

Sug'la, Lake (sōō'lȧ); *Turk.* **Sug'la Gö·lü'** (sōō'lä gú·lü'). Lake (*gölü*) in SW Turkey in Asia, N of the Gulf of Antalya and SE of Lake Beyşehir.

Suhl (zōōl). Manufacturing city, Erfurt dist., E Germany, 30 m. SSW of Erfurt; pop. 15,579; 15th-cent. church; metal goods, porcelain, toys.

Sui'chwan' (swā'chwän'). Town, W Kiangsi prov., China, 50 m. NW of Kanhsien; in World War II an American airfield, captured by Japanese 1944 and recaptured 1945.

Suid–A'fri·ka (soit'ä'frĭ·kä). The South African Dutch name for (the Union of) South Africa.

Suidwes–Afrika. See SOUTH-WEST AFRICA.

Sui'fen'ho' (swā'fŭn'hŭ'); *formerly (Russian)* **Po·gra·nich'na·ya** (pŭ·grŭ·nyĕch'nȧ·yȧ). Town, E Kirin prov., E Manchuria, 90 m. NNW of Vladivostok; on former Chinese Eastern Ry. at U.S.S.R. border.

Suifu. See IPIN.

Suir (shŏŏr). River 100 m. long in SE Ireland; rises in N co. Tipperary, flows S and E into Waterford Harbour.

Suisse. See SWITZERLAND.

Sui·sun' Bay (sŭ·sōōn'). Inlet of San Francisco Bay, cen. California, lying on boundary bet. Contra Costa and Solano cos., W cen. California; connected with San Pablo Bay by Carquinez Strait. Crossed by Martinez Bridge, a vertical lift bridge with clearance of 291.5 ft.

Suit'land (sūt'lănd). Urban community (unincorp.), Prince Georges co., Maryland, E of Washington, D.C.; pop. (with Silver Hills) 10,300.

Sui'yuan' (swā'yü·än'). **1** Province, cen. Inner Mongolia, N China; 112,493 sq. m.; pop. (1936 est.) 2,083,693; ✻ Kweisui; bounded on N by Outer Mongolia, on NE and E by Chahar prov., on S by Shansi and Shensi provs. of China, and on W by Ningsia prov. One of the Five Northern Provinces. Borders desert of the Gobi on the N; mountainous in S and W. Crossed in cen. part by the big bend of the Hwang Ho; its S part, region S of the Hwang Ho, known as the Ordos; also crossed by caravan highways from Wanchuan through Kweisui to Urga and Sinkiang. Chief towns Kweisui, Paotow, Polingmiao. See MONGOLIA, MÊNG CHIANG.
2 See KWEISUI.

Suk–. For names in Java beginning **Suk–,** see SOEK–.

Suk–Ahras. = SOUK-AHRAS.

Su′ket (sŏō′kăt). Former Indian state, E Punjab States, E Punjab, NW India; 392 sq. m.; pop. (1941) 71,092; ✳ Suket (35 m. NNW of Simla).

Su·khan′–Dar·ya′ (sŏō-ᴋän′där·yä′). Subdivision of the Uzbek S.S.R., Soviet Central Asia, in SE part bet. Turkmen S.S.R. on W and Tadzhik S.S.R. on E and on the S bordering on Afghanistan; ✳ Termez.

Su·kho′na (sŏō·ᴋô′nà). River ab. 350 m. long, chiefly in Vologda Region, N cen. Soviet Russia, Europe; rises in Lake Kubenskoe and flows E to unite with the Yug river near Veliki Ustyug in NE part of the region and form the Northern Dvina river.

Su·kho·thai, also **Su·ko·tai** (sŏō·k'hō·t'hī). Village on Yom river, W Thailand, 30 m. NW of Phitsanulok; has one of the three temples of Thailand celebrated for architecture. Important formerly as the capital of a Tai-Khmer state of the same name that flourished 1256 to 1350.

Su′khu·mi (sŏō′ᴋŏō·mĭ); anc. **Di′os·cu′ri·as** (dī′ŏs-kūr′ĭ·ăs); also **Su·khum′** (sŏō·ᴋŏōm′). Seaport town, ✳ of Abkhazia, Georgia, U.S.S.R., on Black Sea 100 m. NW of Kutaisi; pop. 28,136; has poor harbor but its healthful situation sheltered by foothills of W Caucasus make it one of the finest of Black Sea resorts; trades in tobacco, hardwoods, and fruit; botanic gardens.

Suk′ker·top′pen (sŏōk′ĕr·tôp′ĕn). Headland and Danish settlement on an island on SW coast of Greenland, 65°22′N, N of Godthaab; pop. 1397; chief occupations of Eskimos are reindeer raising, seal hunting, and whaling.

Suk′kur (sŏōk′kŏōr) or **Sa′khar** (sŭk′hĕr). **1** District, N Sind, Pakistan; area 5550 sq. m.; pop. (1941) 692,556. **2** Town, its ✳, on right bank of Indus river 240 m. NE of Karachi; pop. (1941) 66,466; center of great irrigation system, known as the Lloyd or Sukkur barrage, built 1928–32. Height of dam 190 ft.; cost ab. $75,000,000.

Sukotai. See SUKHOTHAI.

Su′la (sŏō′là). River ab. 240 m. long, N cen. Ukraine, U.S.S.R.; rises near Konotop and flows S to the Dnieper above Kremenchug.

Sula Besi. See SANANA island.

Su′lai·ma·ni′ya (sŏō′lä·mă·nē′yà; -yă; sŏō′lĭ-). **1** Province (liwa), NE Iraq; pop. (1935 est.) 184,204. **2** Town, Sulaimaniya prov., NE Iraq, in mountains 60 m. E of Kirkuk near Iranian border; pop. (1935 est.) 30,000.

Su·lai·man′ Range (sŏō·lĭ·män′). Mountain range N cen. W Pakistan, W of Indus river; highest, twin peaks at N end, Takht-i-Sulaiman ("throne of Solomon") 11,100 ft.

Sula Islands. See SOELA ISLANDS.

Sulawesi. See CELEBES.

Sulci. See SANT' ANTIOCO town.

Sul do Sa′ve (sŏōl dŏō sà′vĕ). Province, S Mozambique, SE Africa; includes territory S of Save river; comprises districts of Lourenço Marques and Inhambane; ✳ Lourenço Marques.

Su′let (sŏō′lĕt). = ŠOLTA.

Sul′grave (sŭl′grāv). Village, SW Northamptonshire, England, 7 m. NE of Banbury; site of Sulgrave Manor, an ancestral home of George Washington, now a museum.

Su′li (sŏō′lyĕ). Mountain stronghold formerly in S Albania, now in Epirus, NW Greece, S of Ioannina. Home of the Suliotes, a mixed Greek and Albanian people, who long resisted the Turks.

Sulimov. See CHERKESSK.

Su·li′na (sŏō-lē′nä). Port, E Romania, on the Black Sea at the cen. mouth of the Danube (called the Sulina branch); pop. 5924.

Su′li·tjel′ma (sŏō′lĭ·tyĕl′mä). Peak 6158 ft. in the Kjölen Mts., N Norway, on the Swedish border.

Sul·la′na (sŏō·yä′nä). City, Piura dept., NW Peru, 32 m. NE of Paita; pop. (1940 est.) 22,344; cinchona bark.

Sul′li·van (sŭl′ĭ·văn). **1** Name of counties in six states of the U.S. See Tables at INDIANA, MISSOURI, NEW HAMPSHIRE, NEW YORK, PENNSYLVANIA, TENNESSEE.

2 City, ⊗ of Moultrie co., cen. Illinois, 25 m. SE of Decatur; pop. 3946. **3** City, ⊗ of Sullivan co., SW Indiana, 25 m. S of Terre Haute; pop. 4979; coal-mining center. **4** City, Crawford and Franklin cos., SE cen. Missouri, 63 m. SW of St. Louis; pop. 4098.

Sullivan Island. Island, S cen. Mergui Archipelago (q.v.), Burma.

Sul′ly (sŭl′ĭ). County in South Dakota. See Table at SOUTH DAKOTA.

Sul′lys Hill (sŭl′ĭz). National game preserve, Benson co., NE North Dakota, just S of Devils Lake; 1½ sq. m.; estab. 1914; has esp. buffaloes, elk, deer.

Sul·mo′na (sŏōl·mō′nä); anc. **Sul′mo** (sŭl′mō). Industrial commune, Aquila prov., Abruzzi e Molise, cen. Italy, 35 m. SE of Aquila; pop. 21,289; cathedral; medieval remains.

Sul′phur (sŭl′fĕr). **1** or **Sulphur Fork of Red River.** River ab. 200 m. long, NE Texas; rises in Fannin co., flows E across Arkansas border and into Red river in SW Arkansas. **2** City, Calcasieu parish, SW Louisiana, 10 m. W of Lake Charles; pop. 11,429; sulfur deposits. **3** City, ⊗ of Murray co., S Oklahoma, 24 m. NNE of Ardmore; pop. 4737; health resort; mineral water.

Sulphur Island. = Iwo JIMA, Volcano Is., Japan.

Sulphur Springs. City, ⊗ of Hopkins co., NE Texas, 27 m. E of Greenville; pop. 9160; railroad and industrial center; manufactures condensed milk, cheese, cottonseed oil, brick; coal mines.

Sultanabad. See IRAQ city, Iran.

Sul·tan′ Dağ′la·rı (sŏōl·tän′ dä′lä·rĭ′). Mountain range extending NW and SE in W cen. Turkey in Asia, N of Lake Beyşehir; highest point 6330 ft.

Sul·tan′pur (sŏōl·tän′pŏōr). **1** Town, Fyzabad division, SE cen. Uttar Pradesh, N Indian Union, on right bank of Gumti river 60 m. N of Allahabad; pop. 11,334. **2** Town. See KULU.

Su′lu (sŏō′lŏō). **1** Province, SW Phil. Is., coextensive with the Sulu Archipelago; 1086 sq. m.; pop. 247,117; ✳ Jolo. Chain of islands extending 180 m. SW from Basilan I. to Borneo and separating the Sulu Sea from the Celebes Sea; comprises five groups: Samales, Pangutaran, Jolo and adjacent islands, Tapul, Tawitawi and adjacent islands, all together 369 named islands, and more than 500 nameless small islands. Many coral reefs around the island groups. Soil is rich, forests luxuriant, and islands have a great variety of products, but fishing is most important industry. Thickly inhabited, chiefly by Mohammedan Malays (Moros)—the Samal Laut and Sulus. Only municipality is Jolo.

History: Visited by foreign traders long before Legaspi colonized Cebu. Inhabitants converted to Mohammedanism ab. the end of 14th cent.; revolted against Spaniards 1578–1600 and did not come under Spanish control until 19th cent.; were ruled by Moro sultans; during these years, esp. in 17th and 18th cents., Moros conducted many destructive piratical raids against Spaniards and Filipinos of Visayan Is. and Luzon. The archipelago finally became Spanish protectorate in latter half of 19th cent.; suffered from civil war 1884–94; came under Americans 1899 and made part of Moro Province 1903; civil government established 1914; sultanate terminated by treaty of Apr. 1940, in which ownership of Sulu Archipelago transferred to Commonwealth of Philippines. **2** See JOLO.

Su·lu′an (sŏō·lŏō′än). Small island ab. 2 sq. m. in Phil. Is., 10 m. E of Homonhon I. and ab. 13 m. S of S point of Samar, Phil. Is. Landmark for ships approaching cen. Philippines (Leyte Gulf or Surigao Strait) from the Pacific. First land of the Archipelago sighted by Magellan Mar. 16, 1521; first landing (simultaneously with Homonhon) of American forces on their return to the Philippines Oct. 19, 1944 in World War II.

Su′lu Archipelago (sōō′lōō). Chain of islands, SW Phil. Is., extending from Basilan I. to Borneo and constituting Sulu prov. (*q.v.*).

Sulu Sea. Large interisland sea of the Phil. Is. in SW part; extends N and S ab. 350 m. bet. 5° and 10°N lat. and ab. 425 m. E and W from entrance to Mindanao Sea to Balabac Strait. Bordered on N by Cuyo Is., on E by islands of Panay, Negros, and W Mindanao, on SE by Sulu Archipelago, on SW by North Borneo, and on W and NW by Palawan I. Open sea except for three small clusters of islands.

Sul′za (zōōl′tsä); *also* **Bad–Sul′za** (bät-). Town, Thuringia, E Germany, NE of Weimar; pop. (1933) 3958; Nazi concentration camp.

Sulz′bach (zōōlts′bäk). Town, Saarland, SW Germany, ab. 6 m. NNW of Saarbrücken; pop. (1927) 24,950; coal mining; manufactures dyes.

Sulz′ber′ger Bay (sülz′bûr′gēr). Large inlet ab. 100 m. wide of Ross Sea, NW Marie Byrd Land, Antarctica, E of Edward VII Penin. and Little America, 77°S, 151°W; discovered 1929.

Sulzer Belchen. See Ballon de GUEBWILLER.

Sum-. For names in Java beginning **Sum-**, see SOEM-.

Šu·ma′di·ja (shōō·mä′dĕ·yä); *Eng.* **Shu·ma′di·a** (shōō·mä′dĭ·*a*) *or* **Shu·ma′di·ya** (-dĭ·yä). Region, N Serbia, E Yugoslavia, bet. the Danube and Western Morava and W of the Morava; chief town Kragujevac; forest-covered hills.

Su·ma′tra (sōō·mä′tra). Large island in W part of Indonesia, S of the Malay Penin., SE Asia; 166,789 sq. m.; pop. 7,601,706; including islands along its W coast, 172,152 sq. m., pop. 7,841,175. Formerly divided administratively into two governments (Atjeh and Sumatra East Coast), six residencies (Benkoelen, Djambi, Lampong Districts, Palembang, Sumatra West Coast, and Tapanoeli), and the district of Inderagiri (part of Riouw residency). The large island groups along SE coast bet. Singapore and Java Sea formed two more residencies—Riouw and Bangka—which were parts of Sumatra as a division of the Neth. Indies; total area with these, 182,812 sq. m., pop. 8,254,843. Separated on NE from Malay Penin. by Strait of Malacca and at S end from Java by Sunda Strait. Divided into two almost equal parts by the equator; 1060 m. long by 248 m. at greatest width. Along its W coast extends for the length of the island the Barisan Mts. containing many peaks 6000 ft. to 12,000 ft.; highest Kerintji 12,467 ft.; many of volcanic origin, some active today. Its E and SE parts are jungle lowlands with numerous rivers having many tributaries—chief are Hari, Inderagiri, Kampar, and Asahan; Lake Toba in the N is only large lake. Chief agricultural products rubber and tobacco; raises also coconuts, coffee, cotton, spices, and maize; has large production of coal and tin. Its peoples are Malayan (the majority Mohammedan) with many subdivisions, including Indonesian races such as the Battaks and Lampongs. Chief cities Palembang, Medan, Padang, Telukbetung, and Djambi.

History: Visited by Hindu emigrants, who established a kingdom in 7th cent.; invaded by Arabs in the 13th cent.; first known to Europeans in early part of 16th cent.; W coast settlements established by Dutch 1663–64, and elsewhere on island settlements also made by Portuguese and English; parts acquired from native sultans by treaty; was object of great rivalry with English, who held it for short periods bet. 1796 and 1814; last remaining British possession (Benkulen) given up 1824; Achin (*q.v.*) in N not overcome until into 20th cent.; has been developed agriculturally since c. 1850; occupied by Japanese 1942–45.

Sumatra East Coast. Former government along E coast of Sumatra, Neth. Indies, from N of Medan to S end of Strait of Malacca; 36,509 sq. m.; pop. 1,693,200, ✳ Medan. Region includes mountainous area to N and E of Lake Toba and low marshy region, with numerous

islands, along the cen. part of the E coast. Has many rivers, all flowing N or NE; most important the Kampar, Rokan, and Asahan. Medan and its port Belawan are chief commercial centers, esp. for nearby large plantations of rubber and tobacco. Northern coastal area, formerly known as the Deli region, was part of Achin (*q.v.*); southern part undeveloped jungle. Tobacco cultivation introduced by Dutch c. 1864. Occupied by Japanese 1942.

Sumatra West Coast. Former residency in W Sumatra, Neth. Indies, along coast from just N of equator to ab. 2°30′S; 19,214 sq. m.; pop. 1,910,298; ✳ Padang. Included cen. part of Barisan Mts. and Padang Highlands (*q.v.*) region and also the Mentawai Is., an especially healthful and well-developed and populous area. Region produces coffee, tea, rice, spices, coconuts, and has large coal deposits at Ombilin. Chief towns Padang, Bukittinggi, and Sawahlunto. Parts of W coast region, esp. Indrapura and Padang, came under Dutch 1663–64. Occupied by Japanese Mar. 1942.

Su·may′ (sōō·mī′). Seaport town, W Guam, W Pacific Ocean, on the Orote Peninsula on S side of Apra Harbor.

Sumba. See SOEMBA.

Sumbawa. See SOEMBAWA.

Sum′burgh Head (sŭm′bŭ·rŭ; -brŭ). Cape on S tip of Mainland I., Shetland Is., NNE of Scotland; lighthouse.

Su′mer (sōō′mēr). The southern division of ancient Babylonia; from ab. the 4th millennium B.C. a kingdom of non-Semitic people. Little is known about it but Sumerians supposed to have invented cuneiform system of writing. About 2600–2400 B.C., esp. under Sargon I (c. 2637–2582 B.C.), united gradually with Akkadians; combined empire overcome c. 1950 B.C. by the Semitic Babylonian kingdom. Gudea (fl. c. 2350 B.C.) was one of its great rulers; its chief cities were Nippur, Lagash, Larsa, Erech, and Ur—all near the lower Euphrates. Probably the same as the Biblical **Shi′nar** [shī′nēr; -när] (*Gen.* x. 10).

Su·mi·da (sōō·mĕ·dä). River ab. 180 m. long, SE Honshu, Japan; flows S through the city of Tokyo into Tokyo Bay.

Sum′mer Island (sŭm′ēr). Island in N Lake Michigan, at N entrance to Green Bay; belongs to Delta co., S Michigan penin.

Summer Lake. Lake ab. 15 m. long in cen. Lake co., S Oregon.

Sum′mers (sŭm′ērz). County in West Virginia. See *Table* at WEST VIRGINIA.

Sum′mer·side (sŭm′ēr·sīd). Town, ⊗ of Prince co., W Prince Edward I., Canada, on Northumberland Strait 35 m. W of Charlottetown; pop. 6547; exports farm produce and oysters; summer resort. Founded 1780 by Daniel Green, Quaker Loyalist from Pennsylvania.

Sum′mers·ville (sŭm′ērz·vĭl). Town, ⊗ of Nicholas co., cen. West Virginia; pop. 2008.

Sum′mer·ville (sŭm′ēr·vĭl; *Sou. also* -v′l). **1** City, ⊗ of Chattooga co., NW Georgia; pop. 4706; incorp. 1839; textile mills.

2 Town and resort, Dorchester co., SE South Carolina, 22 m. NW of Charleston; pop. 3623; manufactures rayon fabrics, lumber.

Sum′mit (sŭm′ĭt). **1** Elevation 2130 ft. in McKean co., N Pennsylvania.

2 Name of counties in three states of the U.S. See *Tables* at COLORADO, OHIO, UTAH.

3 Village, Cook co., NE Illinois, 12 m. WSW of Chicago; pop. 10,374.

4 Residential city, Union co., NE New Jersey, 10 m. W of Newark; pop. 23,677; site used as sentry point in Revolutionary days; grows roses, fruit; manufactures silk goods, chemicals.

5 Town, Canal Zone, E of the Panama Canal and NW of Miraflores Lake; pop. (1950) 66; on the railroad.

Summit Hill. Borough, Carbon co., E Pennsylvania, 28 m. S of Wilkes-Barre; pop. 4386; coal mining.

Summit Mountain. Peak 8775 ft. in Glacier National Park, NW Montana.

Summus Portus. See Col de SOMPORT.

Sum'ner (sŭm'nẽr). **1** Name of counties in two states of the U.S. See *Tables* at KANSAS and TENNESSEE.
2 Town, Bremer co., NE Iowa, 27 m. NE of Waterloo; pop. 2170.
3 Town, a ⊗ of Tallahatchie co., NW Mississippi; pop. 551.
4 City, Pierce co., W cen. Washington, 11 m. E of Tacoma; pop. 5874; industrial and trading center; manufactures lumber and lumber products, yeast, vinegar; canneries, dairies.

Su·mo·to (soō·mō·tô). Chief town of Awaji I. (*q.v.*), Japan; pop. (1945) 33,926.

Sum·pan'go (soōm·päng'gô). Town, Sacatepéquez dept., S cen. Guatemala; pop. 7299.

Sum'perk (shoōm'pĕrk); *Ger.* **Mäh'risch–Schön'-berg** (mâ'rĭsh·shŭn'bĕrk). Town, NW Moravia prov., cen. Czechoslovakia, on March (Morava) river 28 m. NNW of Olomouc; pop. (1930) 15,707.

Sum·pra·bum' (soōm'prä·boōm'). Town in N Burma, on highway N of Myitkyina SE of Chaukan Pass.

Sum'ter (sŭm'tẽr). **1** Name of counties in four states of the U.S. See *Tables* at ALABAMA, FLORIDA, GEORGIA, SOUTH CAROLINA.
2 Industrial city, ⊗ of Sumter co., E cen. South Carolina, 42 m. E of Columbia; pop. 23,062; manufactures furniture, barrels, lumber, textiles, chemicals, foundry and machine-shop products; tourist center; Shaw Air Force Base. Morris Coll. (1908; coed.).

Su'my (soō'mĭ). Town, ✳ of Sumy Region, Ukraine, U.S.S.R., near the Psel river 95 m. NW of Kharkov; pop. 63,883; manufactures agricultural machinery, clothing, leather goods; has mills and sugar refineries.

Sumy Region. Region, subdivision of Ukraine, U.S.S.R., in N part; ✳ Sumy; on N and E borders on Bryansk and Kursk Regions of the R.S.F.S.R.; fertile black-earth region, crossed by the Seim, Psel, and Vorskla rivers.

Sun (sŭn). River ab. 100 m. long, NW cen. Montana; rises in W Teton co., flows S and E into Missouri river at Great Falls, Cascade co., cen. Montana.

Sun'a·pee (sŭn'à·pê). Manufacturing and resort town, Sullivan co., SW New Hampshire, on Sunapee Lake 12 m. E of Claremont; pop. 1164.

Sunapee Lake. Lake on boundary bet. Sullivan and Merrimack cos., SW cen. New Hampshire; ab. 9 m. long and from 1 to 3 m. wide; summer resort.

Su'nart, Loch (lŏк soō'nẽrt). Inlet of the Atlantic Ocean in Argyll co., W Scotland, S of Loch Shiel and N of Loch Linnhe.

Sun'bur'y (sŭn'bĕr'ĭ; -bẽr·ĭ; -brĭ). **1** Commercial and industrial city, ⊗ of Northumberland co., E cen. Pennsylvania, on Susquehanna river 30 m. SSE of Williamsport; pop. 13,687; ships coal; manufactures textiles, processed foods, machine parts; site of Fort Augusta (1756) nearby. Laid out 1772; in 1883 Thomas A. Edison set up and operated an incandescent electric lighting plant here.
2 County, New Brunswick, Canada. See *Table* at NEW BRUNSWICK.

Sunbury on Thames. Urban district, Middlesex, SE England, 15 m. WSW of London; pop. 23,396; part of Greater London.

Sunchow. See KWEIPING.

Sun'cook (sŭn'kŏŏk). **1** River, S cen. New Hampshire; rises in **Suncook Ponds**, SE Belknap co., flows S into Merrimack river in SE Merrimack co., S cen. New Hampshire.
2 Industrial village, Merrimack co., S cen. New Hampshire in town of Pembroke, SE of Concord; pop. 2318; cotton mills.

Sun'da (sŭn'dà), *or* **Soen'da** (soōn'dä), **Isles.** Islands of the Malay Archipelago, divided into two groups:

Greater Sunda Islands, comprising Java, Sumatra, Borneo, and Celebes (*qq.v.*) and adjacent islands, 514,953 sq. m., pop. 52,043,898; and **Lesser Sunda Islands,** comprising chain of islands E from Bali to and including Alor and Timor, but not Wetar, 28,421 sq. m., pop. 3,460,059.

Sun'dance' (sŭn'dăns'). Town, ⊗ of Crook co., NE corner of Wyoming; pop. 908. Devils Tower National Monument is 20 m. to NW.

Sundarbans. See GANGES DELTA.

Sunda Strait. See SOENDA STRAIT.

Sun'day (sŭn'dĭ) *or* **Sun'days** (-dĭz). River ab. 200 m. long in Cape Province, Union of South Africa, flowing into Algoa Bay.

Sunday Island. = RAOUL ISLAND.

Sunday Strait. Channel, the entrance to King Sound E of Cape Leveque, N Western Australia.

Sund'by·berg' (sŭnd'bü·bẽr'y'). City, Stockholm prov., SE Sweden, a NW suburb of Stockholm; pop. 13,708; manufactures cables.

Sun'der·bunds (soōn'dẽr·bŭndz). = SUNDARBANS.

Sun'der·land (sŭn'dẽr·lănd). County borough, Durham, N England, on North Sea on S side of mouth of the Wear 12 m. SE of Newcastle; pop. 185,824, (1951 pop.) 181,515; shipbuilding center; shipping point, esp. for coal; fisheries, coal mines; manufactures paper, chemicals, pottery. A very old town, frequently called **Wear'-mouth** (wẽr'mŭth; -mouth) in Saxon times. Monkwearmouth on N side of the mouth of the Wear was birthplace of Bede and contained the abbey where he was educated. **Bishop's Wearmouth,** an early settlement of the church on the S side of the river, is now within the borough of Sunderland but was long used as the name of the port.

Sund'gau (zoōnt'gou). Region in S Alsace, now chiefly in Haut-Rhin dept., NE France.

Sunds'vall (sŭnts'vàl). Seaport, Västernorrland prov., E Sweden, on the Gulf of Bothnia; pop. 20,074; trade center; exports lumber, wood pulp, cellulose.

Sun'flow'er (sŭn'flou'ẽr). **1** River 200 m. long, NW Mississippi; flows S from Coahoma co. to Yazoo river on border bet. Yazoo and Sharkey cos.
2 County in Mississippi. See *Table* at MISSISSIPPI.

Sung *or* **Sung Shan** (soōng' shän'). Mountain (*shan*) 9200 ft., N Honan prov., E cen. China, ab. 35 m. ESE of Loyang; one of the Five Sacred Mountains of China.

Sun'ga·ri' (soōn'gä'rĭ'). Chief river of Manchuria and chief tributary of the Amur, ab. 800 m. long; rises in Chang Pai Shan on N border of Korea, flows NW past Yungki to join the Nonni near Fuyu, then turns sharply E and NE through a fertile plain to join the Amur at Tungkiang; navigable to Yungki.

Sungaria. See DZUNGARIA.

Sung'ei Pa·ta'ni (soōng'ĭ pà·tä'nĕ). Town, SW Kedah state, Federation of Malaya, near coast ab. 15 m. N of Butterworth; pop. 7703; on W coast railroad running N to Alor Star and Thailand.

Sungei U'jong (oō'jông). Former state, W Malay Penin.; became a part of Negri Sembilan state (*q.v.*) 1895; its chief town was Seremban.

Sung'kiang' (soōng'jĭ·äng'). **1** New province of Manchuria in cen. part; 30,703 sq. m.; pop. 4,923,000; ✳ Harbin (Pinkiang); created 1945.
2 Town, S Kiangsu, E China, 25 m. SW of Shanghai on the Hwang Pu river; pop. ab. 50,000; burial place of Gen. Frederick T. Ward, leader of "Ever-Victorious Army" at time of Taiping Rebellion; also has temple erected by Chinese in his honor.

Sung'koi' (soōng'koi'). Var. of *Songkoi:* see COI.

Sung Shan. See SUNG.

Sung'tze' (soōng'dzü'). **1** River ab. 50 m. long, Hupeh and Hunan provs., E cen. China; flows N from NW corner of the lake Tungting Hu to the Yangtze river at Kiangling. In World War II scene of much fighting 1943–44.

2 Town, S Hunan prov., E cen. China, on S bank of the Yangtze W of Kiangling and above mouth of Sungtze river.

Sunium Promontorium. See Cape COLONNA.

Su'ni·ya, Hor (hôr sōō'nĭ·yå; -yă). Large lake or marshland area, ab. 80 m. long by 10 m. wide, along W bank of lower Tigris, SE Iraq.

Sunk Island (sŭngk). Parish 7334 acres in the estuary of the Humber, East Riding, Yorkshire, England; formerly an islet.

Sunlight Peak. 1 Mountain 14,060 ft. in La Plata co., SW Colorado.

2 Mountain 11,977 ft. in W Park co., NW Wyoming.

Sun'ny·side' (sŭn'ĭ·sīd'). City, Yakima co., S Washington, 33 m. SE of Yakima; pop. 6208; farming, dairying.

Sun'ny·vale' (sŭn'ĭ·vāl'). City, Santa Clara co., W California, 8 m. WNW of San Jose; pop. 52,898; settled 1849, incorp. 1924; trade center.

Sun Prairie. City, Dane co., S Wisconsin, 11 m. NE of Madison; pop. 4008.

Sun'ray' (sŭn'rā'). Town, Moore co., NW Texas, in the panhandle ab. 55 m. N of Amarillo; pop. 1967.

Sun River. River in Montana. See SUN.

Sunset Crater. Volcanic crater, area 5 sq. m., in cen. Coconino co., N cen. Arizona, E of San Francisco Peaks and ab. 15 m. NE of Flagstaff; central feature of **Sunset Crater National Monument:** see UNITED STATES, *National Monuments.*

Sunshine Peak. Mountain 14,018 ft. in Hinsdale co., SW Colorado.

Sün'tel (zün'tĕl) *or* **Sün'tel·berg** (-bĕrK). Elevation 1433 ft., S Lower Saxony, W Germany, on N bank of Weser; here Wittekind destroyed Frankish army 782.

Sun Valley. Resort center, Sawtooth Mts., Blaine co., cen. Idaho, just N of Ketchum; Sun Valley Lodge, built by Union Pacific R.R., opened Sept. 1936; during World War II became site of a naval convalescent hospital.

Sun·ya'ni (sōōn·yä'nē). Town, W cen. Ashanti, Ghana, W Africa, on Kumasi-Pamu motor road 80 m. NW of Kumasi.

Suojärvi. See SUOYARVI.

Suo'men·lin'na (swô'mĕn·lĭn'nå); *Swedish* **Sve'a·borg'** (svä'å·bôr'y'). Fortress in the harbor of Helsinki, S Finland; built by the Swedes 1749; captured by Russians 1808; bombarded by French-British fleet 1855 in Crimean War.

Suomen Tasavalta. See FINLAND.

Suomi. See FINLAND.

Suo'mus·sal'mi (swô'mŏŏs·säl'mĭ). Town, E Finland, in Oulu dept., near Karelian border 105 m. E of Oulu; pop. 8959.

Suo Sea. See SUWO SEA.

Su·o·yar'vi (sōō·ŭ·yär'vyĭ); *Finnish* **Suo'jär·vi** (swô'-yär·vĭ). Town, SW Karelia, U.S.S.R., N of Lake Ladoga and on railroad 65 m. WNW of Petrozavodsk; pop. 11,747; in 1940 taken by Russia from Finland.

Supanburi. See SUPHAN BURI.

Su·pe'ri·or (sů·pēr'ĭ·ĕr; sů-). **1** Town (unincorporated), Pinal co., S Arizona; pop. 4875; formerly silver mines, now copper.

2 Town, ⊗ of Mineral co., W Montana; pop. 1242.

3 City, Nuckolls co., S Nebraska, on Kansas border 43 m. SSE of Hastings; pop. 2935; trade and distribution center in agricultural section.

4 City, ⊗ of Douglas co., NW corner of Wisconsin, at extreme W end of Lake Superior opposite Duluth, Minnesota; pop. 33,563; port of entry; railroad center, and lake transportation terminus; grain center and shipping point for iron and copper ore; manufactures flour, lumber products, engines. Wisconsin State College (1896; coed.).

5 Town, Sweetwater co., SW Wyoming, 20 m. NE of Rock Springs; pop. 241; coal mining.

Superior, Lake. Lake in U.S. and Canada, largest and northernmost and westernmost of the 5 Great Lakes (*q.v.*) and largest body of fresh water in the world; bounded on N and E by province of Ontario, Canada, on S by Michigan and Wisconsin, on W by Minnesota, the U.S.-Canada boundary passing through it; ab. 350 m. long; area 31,820 sq. m.; greatest depth 1290 ft.; elevation 602 ft.; at SE end connected by St. Marys river with Lake Huron.

Su·phan Bu·ri *or* **Su·pan·bu·ri** (sōō·p'hän·bōō·rē). **1** Province, SW Thailand, 2015 sq. m.; pop. 287,126.

2 Town, its ✻, on left bank of the Tha Chin 30 m. WNW of Ayudhya.

Supiori. See SOEPIORI.

Suq ash Shu·yukh' (sōōk' ŏsh shŏŏ·yōōK'). Town, SE Iraq, on right bank of Euphrates river 15 m. SE of An Nasiriya; pop. ab. 12,000.

Su·qreir', Nahr (nä'h'r sōō·krär'). River, S Palestine; flows NW into the Mediterranean.

Sur-. For names in Java beginning **Sur-**, see SOER-.

Sur (sōōr). **1** Seaport town, E Oman, SE Arabia, on the Gulf of Oman 70 m. SE of Masqat and near Cape Hadd; pop. ab. 10,000.

2 = *Es Sur:* see TYRE.

Sur, Point (sûr). Point on NW coast of Monterey co., W California.

Su'ra (sōōr'å; sōō'rå). Ancient city of Babylonia, on the Euphrates just W of Thapsacus; in Roman times a border stronghold; site of famous Talmudic school 609 to 1038.

Su·ra' (sōō·rå'). River ab. 525 m. long in E cen. Russia in Europe; rises in E Penza Region and flows N through or on the border of Ulyanovsk Region and Chuvash A.S.S.R. to the Volga below Gorki; navigable to Penza.

Surabaja, Surabaya. See SOERABAJA.

Surakarta. See SOERAKARTA.

Su·ra·kha·ny' (sōō·rå·Kŭ·nĭ'). Town, E Azerbaidzhan S.S.R., U.S.S.R., on the peninsula 7 m. E of Baku; rich oil fields.

Su'ram Mountains (sōō'räm). Mountain range 5000 to 6000 ft. in cen. Georgian S.S.R., U.S.S.R., WNW of Tiflis; separates the Rion and Kura river basins and forms a connecting link bet. the Caucasus Mts. on N and highlands of Armenia on S; lowest point is **Suram Pass** (3500 ft.) near town of **Suram;** crossed by railroad (tunnel 2½ m. long) from Baku to Black Sea.

Surashtra. See SURUTH.

Su·rat' (sōō·răt'; *native* sōō'răt). City, SE Gujarat, W Indian Union, on Tapti river near its mouth 150 m. N of Bombay; pop. (1941) 171,443; trade and distribution headquarters; has cotton, rice, and paper mills, and soap works; makes a specialty of production of silk brocade, gold and silver wire, carpets, and inlaid work. Chief seaport and commercial city of India under Akbar Jahangir and Shah Jahan; destroyed by Portuguese 1520, 1530, and 1531; conquered by Akbar 1573. English factory founded 1612, the first in India and beginning of British Empire in India; seat of British Indian government till 1687; began to decline at beginning of 19th cent.; population at one time reputed to have been 800,000.

Surat Agency. Formerly an agency in N Bombay prov., W India, comprising three small Indian states Bansda, Dharampur, and Sachin; later part of Gujarat States Agency; the states joined the Indian Union 1947.

Su·rat Tha·ni *or* **Su·rat·dha·ni** (sōō·rät·t'hä·nē). **1** Province, SW Thailand; 5235 sq. m.; pop. 175,851.

2 Railroad town and port, its ✻, on Gulf of Siam on E side of Malay Penin. 70 m. NW of Nakhon Si Thammarat.

Sur'bi·ton (sûr'bĭ·t'n). Municipal borough, Surrey, S England, 10 m. WSW of London; pop. 60,675; part of Greater London.

Su'resnes' (sü'rân'). Manufacturing commune, Seine dept., N France, W suburb of Paris on Seine river; pop. 32,018; machinery, automobiles, chemicals, perfumes, printed cloth goods; American military cemetery.

Sur·gu′ja (sŏor·gōo′já) *or* **Sir·gu′ja** (sĭr-). Former Indian state, Eastern States, NE Indian Union; 6067 sq. m.; pop. (1941) 551,752. Ceded to British in 1818.

Sur·gut′ (sŏor·gōot′). Town, S Khanty-Mansi National District, Soviet Russia, Asia, on right bank of Ob river in swamp region 270 m. NE of Tobolsk.

Su′ri (sōo′rĭ). Town, West Bengal, NE Indian Union, ab. 105 m. NNW of Calcutta; pop. 10,908.

Su′ri·ba′chi, Mount (sōo′rĭ·bä′chĭ). Active volcano 556 ft. high, S tip of Iwo Jima, in Volcano Is.; overlooked S Japanese (Motoyama) airfield on the island. Taken by U.S. Marines Feb. 23, 1945 and flag raising on its summit provided one of the finest photographs to come out of World War II. Top of mountain leveled off by U.S. engineers after island established as base.

Su′ri·ga′o (sōo′rĕ·gä′ō). 1 Province, NE Mindanao, Phil. Is.; 3079 sq. m.; pop. 225,895; ✳ Surigao. A narrow coastal province along the Pacific, bordering on W end of Mindanao Sea at the NW, bounded by Agusan prov. on the W, and touching NE Davao prov. for a few miles on the S; includes off the N coast the large islands of Dinagat, Siargao, and Bucas Grande, and many small islands. Coast is irregular with many indentations, largest being Lanuza and Lianga Bays. Much of it occupies E slopes of Diuata Mts. Rivers are short; N two thirds of Lake Mainit is in NW part. Most important agricultural crops hemp (abacá), copra, and corn; much fine timber; mining is well developed. Inhabitants mainly Visayans although some Negritos are found in the mountains. Chief towns Surigao, Cantilan, Lianga, Tago, and Hinatuan.

History: Coast explored in middle of 16th cent. and missions established as early as 1597; settlement difficult because of Moro raids, esp. the destructive attack of 1752; made part of a province 1849 and given military government 1860; civil government set up by Americans May 1901 and its present boundaries determined 1911.

2 Municipality, ✳ of Surigao prov., at N tip of mainland on narrow strait opp. Dinagat I.; pop. 34,339; one of oldest Spanish towns in the Philippines.

Surigao Strait. Channel ab. 90 m. long and 10 to 25 m. wide in SE Phil. Is. bet. Leyte I. on W and Dinagat I. on E and touching NE point of Mindanao on SE; connects Pacific Ocean with Mindanao Sea. In World War II on Oct. 23–25, 1944 S division of Japanese fleet defeated here by American fleet.

Su·rin (sōo·rĭn′). 1 Province, SE Thailand; 3551 sq. m.; pop. 338,994.

2 Town, its ✳, on railroad 95 m. E of Nakhon Ratchasima.

Su′ri·nam (sōo′rĭ·năm); *Du.* **Su′ri·na′me** (sü′rĕ·nä′mĕ); *often called* **Netherlands**, *or* **Dutch, Guiana.** 1 Country in northern South America, constituting a territory of the kingdom of the Netherlands; bounded on N by the Atlantic Ocean, on E by French Guiana, on S by Brazil, and on W by British Guiana; 55,143 sq. m.; pop. (1941) 183,730 (inclusive of Negroes and Indians living in the forests); ✳ Paramaribo. Divided into the following districts: Commewijne, Coronie, Marowijne, Nickerie, Paramaribo, Saramacca, Surinam. Greater part (in cen. and S) is forested plateau region and extensive savannahs; mountain ranges in cen. part and S have peaks 3300 and 4200 ft. (Wilhelmina Mts.) and the Tumuc-Humac Mts. on Brazilian border reach 2700–3000 ft.; entire S part almost completely unexplored. Has many rivers, esp. the Courantyne (or Corantijn) on British Guiana border, the Maroni (or Marowijne) and its headstream, the Itany, on French Guiana border, and the Suriname, Saramacca, Cop-

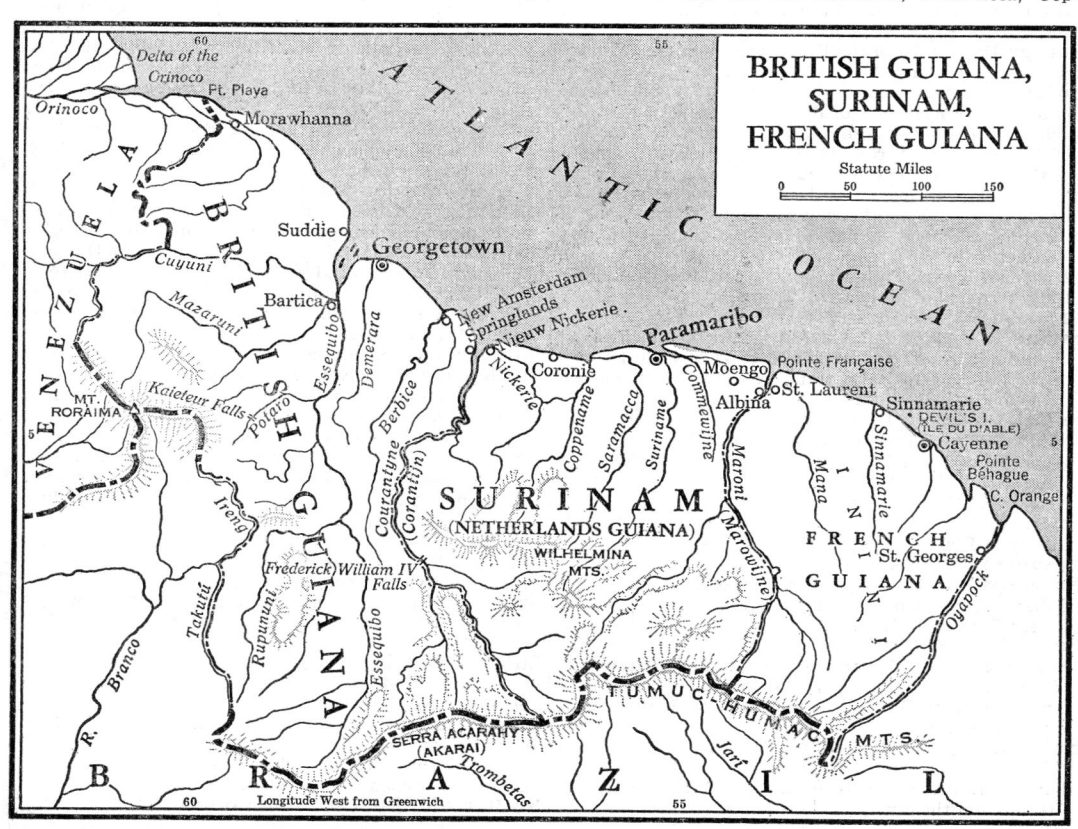

BRITISH GUIANA, SURINAM, FRENCH GUIANA

Statute Miles
0   50   100   150

pename, and Commewijne flowing N through cen. part. Agricultural areas along the coast and river courses; chief products sugar, citrus fruits, coffee, rice, bananas, and timber; mineral resources chiefly bauxite and gold. Chief cities Paramaribo, Nieuw Nickerie.

History: First settled by the English; first permanent settlement sent by Lord Willoughby of Parham 1650; capitulated to the Dutch and was ceded to them by Treaty of Breda 1667; held by the English 1799–1802 and 1804–16; given autonomy 1949.
2 District of Surinam; pop. (1941) 46,377.

Su·ri·na′me (sū′rḗ·nȧ′mḗ). River ab. 400 m. long in N Surinam; flows N into Atlantic Ocean at Paramaribo.

Surkh·ab′ (sŏŏr·kȧb′). River ab. 400 m. long, a N tributary of the Amu Darya, in N and cen. Tadzhik S.S.R., Soviet Central Asia; flows W and SW.

Sur′ma (sŏŏr′mä). River ab. 560 m. long, NE India; rises in Manipur state (where it is called the Barak, *q.v.*), flows W in Assam past Sylhet; divides into two branches, the southern called the Kusiyara (*q.v.*); these reunite forming the Meghna (*q.v.*) in East Bengal.

Surma Valley and Hill Division. Southern division of Assam, NE Indian Union; 24,124 sq. m.; pop. (1941) 4,218,875; ✳ Shillong.

Surrentine Peninsula, Surrentum. See SORRENTO.

Sur′rey (sûr′ĭ; sŭr′ĭ). County, S England; area 722 sq. m.; pop. (1951) 1,601,555; ⊗ Kingston on Thames; other towns Guildford, Croydon, Richmond, Reigate, Godalming, Wimbledon, Dorking, Epsom; rivers Wey, Mole, both tributaries of the Thames; largely residential; chief occupations market gardening, dairy farming, sheep grazing.

Sur′ry (sûr′ĭ; sŭr′ĭ). **1** Name of counties in two states of the U.S. See *Tables* at NORTH CAROLINA and VIRGINIA.
2 Town, ⊗ of Surry co., SE Virginia; pop. 288.

Su·ru·ga (sŏŏ·rŏŏ·gä). Old province, S Honshu, Japan, now part of Shizuoka prefecture.

Suruga Bay. Inlet of the Pacific Ocean on the SE coast of Honshu, Japan, SW of Tokyo.

Su′sa. **1** (sū′zȧ; -sȧ); *Biblical* **Shu′shan** (shōō′shăn; -shăn). Ancient city, ✳ of Elam (*q.v.*), now ruins at the village of **Shush** (shōōsh) on the railroad ab. 15 m. S of Dizful, SW Iran. Settled in very early times, it came to be the winter residence of Achaemenian kings (7th cent. to 331 B.C.); its palace and treasure house were in a strong citadel. Made Persian capital by Cyrus; scene of the story of Esther, the Jewish queen of the Persian king Ahasuerus.
2 (sōō′zä) Town, Torino prov., W cen. Piedmont, NW Italy; terminal of Mont Cenis Pass.
3 (sōō′sȧ, -sä) See SOUSSE.

Su′šac (sōō′shäts); *Ital.* **Caz′za** (kät′tsä). Small island in Adriatic Sea off Dalmatian coast W of Lastovo; formerly belonged to Italy; transferred to Yugoslavia by treaty of 1947.

Su′šak (sōō′shäk). **1** *Ital.* **San′se·go** (sän′sȧ·gồ). Small island SW of Lošinj I., Croatia, NW Yugoslavia, in group SE of Istria Penin.; formerly in Venezia Giulia e Zara, NE Italy; 1½ sq. m.; pop. (1931) ab. 1000; by treaty of 1947 assigned to Yugoslavia.
2 Seaport, W Croatia, NW Yugoslavia; pop. 16,104; suburb of Fiume; commercial and shipping center.

Susam–Adasi. See SAMOS.

Su′san·ville (sū′z'n·vĭl). City, ⊗ of Lassen co., NE California, at head of Honey Lake Valley 40 m. E of Lassen Peak; pop. 5598.

Su′si·a·na (sū′zĭ·ā′nȧ; -ăn′ȧ). In ancient times used occasionally as equivalent to ELAM; later, as a province of the Persian Empire, nearly coextensive with the modern province of Khuzistan; named from Susa, ancient Elamitic capital.

Su′sı·gır·lık′ (sōō′sĭ·gĭr·lĭk′). River ab. 100 m. long, NW Turkey in Asia; flows N to Sea of Marmara E of Bandırma; receives two tributaries from the E, the Atranos and the Simav.

Su·sit′na (sŏŏ·sĭt′nȧ). **1** River 280 m. long, S Alaska; flows W and S from E end of Alaska Range to Cook Inlet.
2 Village near mouth of Susitna river.

Suspension Bridge. Former name (1860–81) of NIAGARA FALLS city, Welland co., SE Ontario, Canada.

Sus′que·han′na (sŭs′kwĕ·hăn′ȧ). **1** River 444 m. long, cen. New York, Pennsylvania, and Maryland; rises in Otsego Lake, Otsego co., cen. New York, flows S across Pennsylvania border and across E Pennsylvania and NE corner of Maryland to empty into N Chesapeake Bay. By the use of canals it has been made navigable for a short distance from its mouth. The **West Branch of Susquehanna River,** ab. 200 m. long, rises in SW cen. Pennsylvania and flows NE and E across cen. Pennsylvania to unite with the Susquehanna near Sunbury, Northumberland co.
2 County in Pennsylvania. See *Table* at PENNSYLVANIA.
3 *or* **Susquehanna Depot.** Borough, Susquehanna co., NE Pennsylvania, 36 m. N of Scranton; pop. 2591; in farming and cattle-raising section.

Sus′sex (sŭs′ĕks; -ĭks). **1** Name of counties in three states of the U.S. See *Tables* at DELAWARE, NEW JERSEY, VIRGINIA.
2 Village, ⊗ of Sussex co., SE Virginia, S of Petersburg.
3 Town, Kings co., S New Brunswick, Canada, 43 m. NE of St. John; pop. 3224; industrial and agricultural town on St. John-Moncton railroad.
4 Anglo-Saxon kingdom, S England. Traditionally founded 477 but little known about its early history; subject at times in 6th and 7th cents. to Kent and Mercia; in conflict with Wessex in 8th cent. and in 825 became part of it. See the HEPTARCHY.
5 County, S England, on the English Channel; 1457 sq. m.; pop. (1938 est.) 831,580; divided into two administrative counties, **East Sussex** (829 sq. m.; pop. 618,083; ⊗ Lewes) and **West Sussex** (628 sq. m.; pop. 318,661; ⊗ Chichester); other towns Brighton, Eastbourne, Bexhill, Worthing, Hastings, Arundel, Rye, Horsham; rivers Arun, Ouse, Rother, Adur; sheep raising (Southdown sheep), farming, fisheries.

Suth′er·land (sŭth′ẽr·lȧnd). **1** Town, E New South Wales, SE Australia, ab. 10 m. S of the center of Sydney, SW of Botany Bay.
2 *or* **Suth′er·land·shire** (-shĭr; -shẽr). County, N Scotland; area 2028 sq. m.; pop. (1951) 13,664; ⊗ Dornoch; mountainous region; deer-hunting resort; fisheries.

Sutherland Falls. Waterfall 1904 ft. high in N Southland division, South I., New Zealand, near W coast 16 m. S of the head of Milford Sound. One of the world's highest waterfalls, plunges down in three sections of 815, 751, and 338 ft.

Suthreyjar. See SODOR.

Sut′lej (sŭt′lĕj). River 900 m. long, N India, one of the "Five Rivers" of the Punjab; rises in SW Tibet near Lake Manasarowar, flows W through the Himalayas across Himachal Pradesh and Punjab state, India, then SW across West Punjab region of Pakistan, to join the Chenab and form the Panjnad (*q.v.*). In its middle course its waters furnish irrigation for a large area in E part of West Punjab.

Sut′na *or* **Sat′na** (sŭt′nä; -nȧ). Town, NE Madhya Pradesh, NE India, 90 m. SW of Allahabad; a former ✳ of Baghelkhand Agency; pop. 11,176.

Su′tri (sōō′trḗ). Town, Viterbo prov., N Latium, cen. Italy, ab. 30 m. NNW of Rome; pop. (1931) 3007; church synod 1046.

Su′tro Tunnel (sōō′trō). Drainage tunnel 4½ m. long, built (completed 1878) to drain the Comstock mine, near present site of Virginia City, Nevada.

Sut′ter (sŭt′ẽr). County in California. See *Table* at CALIFORNIA.

Sutter Creek. City, Amador co., cen. California, 36 m. ESE of Sacramento; pop. 1219; gold mines.

Sut′ter's Mill (sŭt′ẽrz). See COLOMA.

Sut'ton (sŭt″n). **1** County in Texas. See *Table* at TEXAS.

2 Town, Worcester co., cen. Massachusetts, 8 m. SSE of Worcester; pop. 3638.

3 Town, ⊗ of Braxton co., cen. West Virginia; pop. 967.

Sutton and Cheam (chēm). Urban district, Surrey, S England, 12 m. S of London; pop. 46,500, (1951 pop.) 80,664; part of Greater London.

Sutton Cold'field (kōld'fēld). Municipal borough, Warwickshire, cen. England, 8 m. NE of Birmingham; pop. 29,928; residential suburb of Birmingham; holiday resort.

Sutton in Ash'field (ăsh'fēld). Urban district, Nottinghamshire, N cen. England, 13 m. N of Nottingham; pop. 40,521; manufactures hosiery; coal mines, lime works.

Sutton-on-the-Forest; *also* **Sutton-in-the-Forest.** Village, North Riding, Yorkshire, England, 8 m. N of York; pop. 451; residence for 22 years (1738–59) of Lawrence Sterne.

Suursaari. See HOGLAND.

Su'va (sōō'và). Seaport town on SE coast of Viti Levu I., Fiji Is., SW Pacific Ocean; ✳ of Fiji colony; pop. 8394, including suburbs 15,522; attractive, well-built town; on Kandavu Passage, has one of finest harbors in South Pacific; an excellent medical school.

Suvalkai, Suvalki. See SUWAŁKI.

Sü·vey'di·ye' (sü-vī'dĕ-yĕ'); *Fr.* **Souei'dié'** (swä'dyā'). Seaport town, SW Hatay, S Turkey in Asia, just N of mouth of the Orontes river ab. 35 m. S of İskenderon; pop. 5500; formerly an important town in Alexandretta sanjak. Just to the N is site of ancient **Se·leu'ci·a** (sĕ-lū'shĭ-à; -shà) *or* **Seleucia Pi·e'ri·a** (pī·ēr'ĭ·à), which was founded by Seleucus Nicator 300 B.C.; strongly fortified, it became a great city and seaport, the port of Antioch; held by Egyptians 246 to 219 B.C but recovered by Antiochus the Great; became independent c. 108 B.C. and its freedom confirmed by Pompey; disappeared c. 6th cent. A.D.

Su'vla Bay (sōō'vlä). Small bay on W coast of Gallipoli Penin., Turkey in Europe, just S of **Suvla Cape;** landing of Anzacs and battle Aug. 6, 1915.

Su·vo'rov (sōō-vô'rŭf) *or* **Su·war'row** (sōō-wŏr'ō). Island 2 sq. m. in S cen. Pacific Ocean, NNW of Cook Is. and E of Samoa, 13°S and 163°W; has good anchorage but is uninhabited; administered by New Zealand.

Su'vo Ru'diš·te (sōō'vô rōō'dĕsh·tĕ). Highest peak 7020 ft. in Kopaonik range, Serbia, S cen. Yugoslavia.

Su·wa (sōō·wä). Lake in W cen. Honshu, Japan, within sight of Fuji; ab. 10 m. in circumference; altitude 2600 ft.

Su·wal'ki (sōō·väl'kĕ); *Russ.* **Su·val'ki** (sōō·vál'kĭ); *Lith.* **Su·val'kai** (sōō·väl'kī). **1** District just E of Masurian Lakes, formerly in W Soviet Russia, Europe; scene of several battles in World War I in Feb. to July 1915, esp. Feb. 7–14. After 1919 divided, N part to Lithuania (see SEINAI), S part to Poland, incorp. in Białystok dept. Assigned to Germany 1939 and after outbreak of war with Russia held until retaken by Russia 1944; temporarily part of White Russia 1944–45 but ceded back to Poland Aug. 1945 by the Soviet Union (see BIAŁYSTOK).

2 Chief city of Suwałki dist., NE Poland, 68 m. N of Białystok; pop. (1938–39 est.) 23,066; textiles. Center of conflict 1915 in World War I.

Su·wan'nee (sōō·wô'nĕ; -wŏn'ĕ). **1** River ab. 240 m. long, SE Georgia and N Florida penin.; rises in Ware co., SE Georgia, flows SW across Florida into Gulf of Mexico at Suwannee Sound.

2 County in Florida. See *Table* at FLORIDA.

Suwannee Sound. Inlet of Gulf of Mexico on W coast of Levy co., NW Florida penin., receiving Suwannee river on N.

Suwarrow. See SUVOROV.

Suweida, Es. See ES SUWEIDA.

Su·wo (sōō·wō). Old province in SW Honshu, Japan, now part of Yamaguchi prefecture.

Su·wo, *or* **Su·o** (sōō·wō), **Sea.** The western part of the Inland Sea, Japan, bet. SW Honshu and NE Kyushu; connects with Sea of Japan by Shimonoseki Strait.

Suz'dal (sōōz'dál·y'). **1** Principality, cen. Russia, c. 9th cent. to 13th cent.; united with Rostov (Rostov-Suzdal principality); later, c. 1150, with Vladimir (*q.v.*); ultimately absorbed by it and by Moscow.

2 Town, SW Ivanovo Region, Soviet Russia, Europe, 22 m. N of Vladimir; pop. 6600; once capital of Suzdal principality; has old monasteries and churches.

Suz·za'ra (sōōd·dzä'rä). Commune, Mantova prov., Lombardy, N Italy 11 m. S by W of Mantua; pop. 15,450.

Sval'bard (sväl'bär). Norwegian possessions in the Arctic Ocean, including Spitsbergen (*q.v.*) group and Bear I. (*q.v.*); 24,294 sq. m.; pop. ab. 2000. See *Map* at NORWAY.

Sva·ne'ti·a (svä·nē'shĭ·à; -shà). District, N Georgia, U.S.S.R., in Caucasus Mts. above the sources of the Ingur and Rion. In medieval times a small semi-independent state, separated from Georgia but dominated by Persians or Turks. Svans, an ancient Caucasian race, now number ab. 13,000.

Svart (svärt). **1** Short river, S cen. Sweden; flows E into W end of Lake Hjälmaren at Örebro.

2 Short river, E Sweden; flows S into Lake Mälaren at Västerås.

Svart'i'sen (svärt'ē'sĕn). Ice field ab. 230 sq. m. in N Norway, on the Arctic Circle; source of glaciers descending almost to sea level.

Svä'tý (svä'tē). See SAINT.

Svätý Mikuláš, Liptovský. = LIPTOVSKÝ SVÄTÝ MIKULÁŠ.

Sveaborg. See SUOMENLINNA.

Sve'a·land' (svä'à·länd'). Middle division of Sweden, land area 31,022 sq. m.; pop. 2,247,820; comprises Stockholm (city and province), and provinces of Uppsala, Södermanland, Värmland, Örebro, Västmanland, and Kopparberg.

Svend'borg (svĕn'bôr). **1** County, Denmark. See *Table* at DENMARK.

2 Seaport, its ⊗, SE Fyn I., Denmark; pop. (1945) 21,356; industrial and trading center in fruitgrowing section; shipbuilding yards, textile mills, cement works, breweries.

Svensk'sund (svĕnsk'sŭnd). Section in N part of Gulf of Finland off Kotka, S Finland, where in 1790 Count Karl August Ehrensvärd in command of the Swedish fleet won a decisive victory over the Russian fleet.

Sverd·lovsk' (svŭrd·lôfsk'; *Russ.* svyĕrd-); *before 1924* **E·ka'te·rin·burg'** (ĕ·kăt'ĕr·ĭn·bûrg'; *Russ.* yĭ·kà·tyĭ·ryĭn·bōōrk'). City, ✳ of Sverdlovsk Region, Soviet Russia, Asia, in S part; pop. 425,544; largest city of the R.S.F.S.R. in Asia; on E slopes of Ural Mts. in the center of the great Ural Industrial Area, and its leading economical and cultural city; has long been a mining center with furnaces and factories processing the iron, copper, gold, and platinum from mines in the Ural Mts. in the vicinity; has workshops for cutting, polishing, and engraving precious stones, and also many mills and factories, a mint, hospital, meteorological observatory, and the Ural State Univ.; railroad junction city and a W terminus of the Trans-Siberian R.R.

History: Founded 1721 by Peter the Great and named after his wife, (the Empress) Catherine I (Russ. *Ekaterina*); place where the Czar Nicholas II and his family were held as prisoners by the Bolsheviks after the Revolution 1917 and all killed July 16, 1918; renamed 1924 after a Communist leader.

Sverdlovsk Region. Region, W Soviet Russia, Asia; 85,229 sq. m.; pop. 2,512,175; ✳ Sverdlovsk. Crossed from N to S by Ural Mts. (*q.v.*) where rise tributaries of both the Tobol and Kama; for the most part lies on the

E slopes of the mountains and has rich soil. Agriculture and cattle raising have been carried on here by Russians for two centuries; forests also are valuable assets. In comparatively recent years its mineral wealth has transformed it into an industrial region. Long a part of the Ural Area and now forms the center of the great Ural Industrial Area (*q.v.*). Chief cities Sverdlovsk, Nizhni Tagil, and Krasnouralsk. Organized as a subdivision of the R.S.F.S.R. in Asia 1936.

Sver′drup Islands (svĕr′drŏŏp). Group W of Ellesmere I. in Arctic Archipelago, Franklin District, Northwest Territories, Canada; chief islands Axel Heiberg, Ellef Ringnes, Amund Ringnes, and Isachsen.

Sverige. See SWEDEN.

Sveti. See SAINT.

Svetiya. See SAINT.

Svi′len·grad (svĕ′lĕn·grät). Town, SE Bulgaria, on Maritsa river near border of Turkey, pop. (1926) 8423.

Svir (svĭr; *Russ.* svyēr). Navigable river ab. 140 m. long in NE Leningrad Region, NW Soviet Russia, Europe, flowing from Lake Onega to Lake Ladoga; has large hydroelectric power station on its banks. Its course forms part of the Mariinsk Canal System (*q.v.*). Formed battle line bet. Finns and Russians 1941 and bet. Germans and Russians 1944.

Svi·štov′ (svĭ·shtôf′) or **Svi·shtov′;** *Anglicized* **Sis′to·va** (sĭs′tŏ·và). Town, Pleven dept., N Bulgaria, on the Danube 38 m. ENE of Pleven; pop. (1926) 12,046. Treaty of Sistova signed here Aug. 4, 1791 determining the boundary bet. Austria and Turkey.

Svi′ta·vy (svĭ′tà·vĭ); *Ger.* **Zwit′tau** (tsvĭt′ou). Town, NW Moravia prov., cen. Czechoslovakia, 38 m. N of Brno near Bohemia border; pop. (1930) 10,441.

Svi·ya′ga (svĭ·yä′gà; *Russ.* svyĭ·yà′gà). River ab. 250 m. long in E Soviet Russia, Europe; rises in S Ulyanovsk Region, flows N into Volga river just W of Kazan; near Ulyanovsk it approaches within 4 m. of the Volga.

Svizzera. See SWITZERLAND.

Svo·bod′ny (svŭ·bôd′nĭ). Town, SW Khabarovsk Territory, Soviet Russia, Asia, on Zeya river and on Trans-Siberian R.R.; pop. ab. 10,000; electric power station and cold-storage plants.

Svolder. See SWOLD.

Svyatoi. See SAINT.

Swa′bi·a (swä′bĭ·à); *Ger.* **Schwa′ben** (shvä′běn). **1** Duchy in medieval Germany, nearly coextensive with modern Württemberg, Hesse, W Bavaria, and part of Baden. Original inhabitants were Suevi (whence its name) and Alamanni; conquered by Franks in 5th cent. A.D. Duchy from 10th cent., a fief of Emperor Henry IV and ruled by Hohenstaufen kings and emperors 1105–1254; divided in 1268. Leagues of Swabian cities formed esp. 1331 and 1488–1534. Chief cities of duchy Augsburg, Ulm, Freiburg, Konstanz.
2 Bavarian government district. See *Table* at BAVARIA.

Swad′lin·cote District (swŏd′lĭn·kōt). Urban district, Derbyshire, N cen. England, 26 m. NE of Birmingham; pop. 20,909.

Swain (swān). County in North Carolina. See *Table* at NORTH CAROLINA.

Swain Reefs. Coral reefs at S end of Great Barrier Reef, Queensland, Australia, 22°S.

Swains (swānz). Small island in American Samoa, in SW cen. Pacific Ocean, 200 m. NW of the island of Tutuila; lat. 11°S and long. 171°W; 1 sq. m.; pop. (1940) 147. Formerly a part of the Tokelau Is. under the jurisdiction of Gilbert and Ellice Islands Colony; transferred to U.S. 1926.

Swains′bor′o (swānz′bûr′ŏ; -bŭ·rŭ). City, ⊗ of Emanuel co., E cen. Georgia, 33 m. WNW of Statesboro; pop. 5943; cotton gins, turpentine stills, machine shops; exports hogs and poultry.

Swa′kop (svä′kŏp). River ab. 225 m. long in South-West Africa, flowing into Atlantic Ocean N of Walvis Bay.

Swa′kop·mund′ (svä′kôp·mûnt′). Town, W South-West Africa, on Atlantic Ocean 175 m. W of Windhoek; pop. (1936) 1978; formerly chief port of German Southwest Africa but now closed to shipping; favorite vacation resort.

Swale (swāl). River ab. 75 m. long in Yorkshire, N England; flows S to unite with the Ure river and form the Ouse.

Swamp′scott (swŏmp′skŭt). Town, Essex co., NE corner of Massachusetts, on Massachusetts Bay 11 m. NE of Boston; pop. 13,294; summer resort.

Swan (swŏn). **1** River ab. 150 m. long, SW Western Australia; flows W to Indian Ocean; called Avon in upper course. Perth situated on it near its mouth. Discovered and named 1697 by Willem de Vlamingh, Dutch navigator.
2 River ab. 110 m. long, E Saskatchewan and W Manitoba, Canada; flows NE into Swan Lake.

Swan′age (swŏn′ĭj). Urban district, Dorsetshire, S England, on English Channel 33 m. SW of Southampton; pop. 6853; seaside resort; stone quarrying.

Swan Islands (swŏn). Two small islands in W Caribbean Sea, N of Honduras; lat. 17°30′N and long. 84°W; owned by United States.

Swankalok. See SAWANKHALOK.

Swan Lake. **1** Lake in Nicollet co., S Minnesota.
2 Lake 121 sq. m., W Manitoba, Canada; receives Swan river from SW and drains N into Lake Winnipegosis.

Swan′land (swŏn′lănd; -lănd). Region, SW Western Australia—the plateau to the E of the upper Swan (Avon) river.

Swan Point. Point on SW shore of Kent co., NE Maryland, extending into upper Chesapeake Bay.

Swan Quarter. Town, ⊗ of Hyde co., E North Carolina; pop. (est.) 265.

Swan Range. A range of the Rocky Mts. in W Montana, chiefly in Flathead and Powell cos.

Swan River. **1** River in Canada. See SWAN.
2 Town, W Manitoba, Canada, on Swan river 30 m. SW of Swan Lake; pop. 2290; on Canadian National Rys. W of Lake Winnepegosis.

Swans′combe (swŏnz′kŭm). Urban district, Kent, SE England, on the Thames 10 m. E of London; pop. 8295.

Swan′sea. **1** (swŏn′sē; -zē) Town, Bristol co., SE Massachusetts, 3 m. NW of Fall River; pop. 9916; settled 1632, incorp. 1668; scene of first bloodshed in King Philip's War 1675; now trade center in agricultural section.
2 (swŏn′sē; -zē) Village, York co., SE Ontario, Canada, on Lake Ontario 6 m. W of Toronto; pop. 8072.
3 (swŏn′zē; -sē) County borough and seaport, Glamorganshire, SE Wales; pop. 164,797, (1951 pop.) 160,832; smelters; center of tin-plate industry; shipbuilding yards.

Swans Island (swŏnz). Island in Atlantic Ocean off S coast of SE Maine; belongs to Hancock co.

Swan′son Mountains (swŏn′s'n). Mountain range ab. 3000 ft. high forming a subsidiary range of the Edsel Ford Ranges, Marie Byrd Land, Antarctica, in ab. 77°S, 145°W; discovered 1934.

Swan′ton (swŏn′t'n; -tŭn). **1** Manufacturing village, Fulton co., NW Ohio, 19 m. W of Toledo; pop. 2306.
2 Town, Franklin co., NW Vermont, on Missisquoi river 8 m. N of St. Albans; pop. 3946.

Swan′zey (swŏn′zĭ). Town, Cheshire co., SW corner of New Hampshire, 4 m. S of Keene; pop. 3626; Yale Demonstration and Research Forest nearby.

Swarth′more (swôrth′mōr; *locally usu.* swôth′-). Borough, Delaware co., SE Pennsylvania, 11 m. W of Philadelphia; pop. 5753; residential suburb of Philadelphia. Swarthmore Coll. (1864; coed.).

Swat (swät). **1** River ab. 400 m. long in North-West Frontier Province, Pakistan; rises in N Swat state, flows SW and SE into Kabul river in the province N of Peshawar.
2 One of three former states, at one time in Malakand

Agency, North-West Frontier Agencies, NW India, in the valley of the Swat river, NNE of Peshawar. The inhabitants, Swatis, are Afghans and Sunni Mohammedans. Since 1947 a part of Pakistan.

Swa'tow' (swä'tou'). Commercial town and treaty port, E Kwangtung prov., SE China, at mouth of Han river on S side ab. 170 m. NW of Hong Kong; pop. (1931 est.) 178,636; has excellent harbor; outlet for Chaoan; exports tea, sugar, oranges, tobacco, grass cloth, paper; an important emigration port. Has grown from small fishing village in latter half of 19th cent.; opened to foreign trade 1858; in early years scene of many kidnappings and hostility to foreigners. In World War II held by Japanese until 1945.

Swa'zi·land' (swä'zĕ·lănd'). Former British protectorate in SE Africa, enclosed on N, W, and S by Transvaal and on E by Mozambique and Natal; 6705 sq. m.; pop. 389,492, chiefly Swazi of Bantu race; ✻ Mbabane. High veld in cen. and W parts (average 4000 ft.), drained by Komati, Umbeluzi, and Usutu rivers. Has varied agricultural products, considerable livestock, and is rich in minerals (asbestos, gold, coal). Formerly administered by Resident Commissioner responsible to High Commissioner for Basutoland, Bechuanaland Protectorate, and Swaziland. The Swazi part of Zulu nation until 1843; friendly with Boers who recognized their independence 1881 and 1884; administered by Transvaal 1895; sided with British in Boer War 1899–1902; placed under authority of Transvaal 1903; authority over protectorate granted 1906 to British High Commissioner; an independent constitutional monarchy since Sept. 6, 1968.

Swe'den (swē'd'n); *Swedish* **Sve'ri·ge** (svär'yĕ). Kingdom, NW Europe, occupying the E and larger section of the Scandinavian penin.; 970 m. long and 250 m. at widest point; bounded on the W by Norway, on the NE by Finland, on the E by the Gulf of Bothnia, on the E and S by the Baltic Sea, and on the SW by the Kattegat; 173,349 sq. m. (land area 158,395 sq. m.); pop. 6,597,348; ✻ Stockholm. See *Map*, p. 1100. For administrative purposes divided into the City of Stockholm and the following 24 provinces (for pronunciation of their names, see their individual entries):

PROVINCE	LOCA-TION	AREA[1]	POP.[1]	CAPITAL
Alvsborg	SW	4,917	336,406	Vänersborg
Blekinge	S	1,173	147,256	Karlskrona
Gävleborg	E	7,607	274,125	Gävle
Göteborg and Bohus	SW	1,988	502,445	Göteborg
Gotland[2]	off SE coast	1,225	59,609	Visby
Halland	SW	1,900	153,752	Halmstad
Jämtland	W	19,961	143,347	Östersund
Jönköping	S	4,447	249,714	Jönköping
Kalmar	SE	4,455	229,978	Kalmar
Kopparberg	cen.	11,645	253,060	Falun
Kristianstad	S	2,484	251,518	Kristianstad
Kronoberg	S	3,825	152,926	Växjö
Malmöhus	SW	1,871	546,225	Malmö
Norrbotten	N	40,740	228,109	Luleå
Örebro	S cen.	3,559	233,835	Örebro
Östergötland	SE	4,265	329,206	Linköping
Skaraborg	S	3,268	244,024	Mariestad
Södermanland	SE	2,633	198,494	Nyköping
Stockholm	SE	2,985	310,043	Stockholm[3]
Uppsala	E	2,055	143,841	Uppsala
Värmland	SW	7,425	271,423	Karlstad
Västerbotten	N	22,831	226,798	Umeå
Västernorrland	E	9,921	276,649	Härnösand
Västmanland	E	2,610	179,701	Västerås

[1] Area = land and inland water area in sq. m. (not including 3504 sq. m. for Lakes Vänern, Vättern, Mälaren, and Hjälmaren). Pop. from 1944 Census.
[2] Comprises the islands of Gotland, Fårö, Karlsö, etc.
[3] Administered as a separate province (55 sq. m.; pop. 654,864).

The N part of the boundary with Norway is marked by the Kjölen Mts. which include Sweden's highest peak, Kebnekaise 6963 ft. and which are source of many rivers in Norrland flowing SE to Gulf of Bothnia, esp. Ljusnan, Indal, Ångerman, Lule, and the Torne (Tornio) on the

Finnish border; abundant water power, and many waterfalls and lakes. In S third of country (Svealand and Götaland) is lowland, including Dal river and several large lakes, the largest being Vänern, Vättern, Mälaren, and Hjälmaren, with total area of 3504 sq. m. Separated from Sjælland I., Denmark, on S by narrow strait of the Öresund and from Jutland Penin., Denmark, by the Kattegat; has two large islands Gotland and Öland off SE in Baltic. Extreme N forms part of Lapland. Primarily an agricultural country (grains, vegetables, sugar beets, dairy products) but has many important industries, esp. manufactures of iron and steel, electrical machinery, porcelain, glass, and forest products. *Chief cities:* Stockholm, Göteborg, Malmö, Norrköping, Hälsingborg, and Örebro.

History: Inhabitants of Sweden among Scandinavian (Viking) raiders of 9th cent. A.D.; united and converted to Christianity by 11th cent.; conquered Finns in 12th cent., united with Denmark and Norway 1397; broke away under house of Vasa (1523–1654) under which Swedes began territorial expansion; took Reval and Estonia 1561, eastern Karelia and Ingria 1617, and Livonia 1629; acquired Jämtland and Herjedalen and islands of Gotland and Sarema 1645; through participation in Thirty Years' War (Swedish phase 1630–35) won territory on German mainland, Hither Pomerania and Rügen, part of Farther Pomerania, Wismar, bishoprics of Bremen and Verden; leading Baltic power in 17th cent.; Danish territories in southern Scandinavia were ceded to Sweden 1660; greatly weakened by defeat in Great Northern War 1700–21, as result of which Sweden lost most of German territories and Livonia, Estonia, Ingria, and Karelia; Finland (*q.v.*) and Åland Is. were gradually lost to Russia 1743–1809; received constitution 1809; gave up Swedish Pomerania in return for Norway which entered personal union with Sweden 1814; acknowledged independence of Norway 1905; neutral in both World War I and II.

Swedes'bor'o (swēdz'bûr'ŏ; -bŭ·rŭ). Borough, Gloucester co., SW New Jersey, 17 m. SSW of Camden; pop. 2449; settled by Swedes c. 1642; shipping station for farm produce.

Swedish Pomerania. See POMERANIA.

Sweet' Bri'ar (swēt' brī'ẽr). Village, Amherst co., cen. Virginia, ab. 12 m. N of Lynchburg. Sweet Briar Coll. (1901; women).

Sweet Grass. County in Montana. See *Table* at MONTANA.

Sweet'wa·ter (swēt'wô'tẽr; -wŏt'ẽr). **1** River ab. 175 m. long in cen. Wyoming; rises in SW Fremont co., flows E to Pathfinder Reservoir, which was formed by damming up the North Platte river.
2 County in Wyoming. See *Table* at WYOMING.
3 City, Monroe co., SE Tennessee, 41 m. SW of Knoxville; pop. 4145.
4 Commercial and industrial city, ⊗ of Nolan co., NW Texas, 40 m. W of Abilene; pop. 13,914; manufactures gypsum products, feeds, cottonseed oil, dairy products; ships livestock, cotton, oats, wheat; oil refineries.

Sweetwater, or **Fresh'wa'ter** (frĕsh'-), **Lake.** Lake in Ramsey co., NE North Dakota.

Swel'len·dam (swĕl'ĕn·dăm). Town, SW Cape Province, S Union of South Africa, 115 m. E of Cape Town in Breede river valley; pop. 3784; in rich agricultural district. One of the oldest towns in South Africa, founded 1745; in 1795 rebelled against Dutch East India Company but surrendered to English in same year.

Swett Peninsula (swĕt). Peninsula extending W from SW coast of Chile, SSE of the Gulf of Peñas.

Świd·ni·ca (shvĕd·nē'tsä); *Ger.* **Schweid'nitz** (shvīt'-nĭts). City, S cen. Wrocław dept., SW Poland, 33 m. SW of Wrocław; pop. (1946) 34,182; formerly in Silesia, Germany; 14th-cent. church; 13th-cent. town hall; manufactures electric clocks, radio parts, linens, cottons, machinery. Founded at beginning of 13th cent.; suffered

NORWAY AND SWEDEN

Statute Miles

50   100   50

⊛ Capitals

PUBLISHED BY G. & C. MERRIAM COMPANY
SPRINGFIELD, MASS.
PREPARED BY J. W. CLEMENT CO., BUFFALO, N.Y

SPITSBERGEN
(Norw.)

NORTH EAST
LAND

WEST
SPITSBERGEN

Hinlopen Strait

Longyear City

BARENT I.

Ice Fjord
Green Harbor

EDGE I.

HOPE I.

BEAR I.

SVALBARD
Statute Miles
0   100

ATLANTIC OCEAN

North Cape
(Nordkapp)

MAGERÖY

Cape
Nordkyn

Barents Sea

Hammerfest

SÖRÖY

Porsanger
Fjord

Vadsö

Varanger
Fjord

VANNÖY

ARNÖY

N. KVALÖY

Pechenga
(Petsamo)

RINGVASSÖY

S. KVALÖY

Tromsö

L. Inari

Inari

SENJA

ANDÖY

VESTERÅLEN

LANGÖY

HINNÖY

AUSTVÅGÖY

Narvik

Torne Träsk

VESTVÅGÖY

LOFOTEN

Kiruna

MOSKENES

KEBNEKAISE

VAERÖY

Stora
Luleträsk

Gällivare

Bodö

SULITJELMA

Arctic

Circle

Kemijärvi

Kemi

Hornavan

Haparanda

Tornio

VIKNA

Rösvatn

Pite

Lule

Luleå

Kemi

Oulu

Oulu R.

Piteå

Skellefte

Skellefteå

Ume

Vindel

Oulujärvi

Namsos

Steinkjer

Trondheim
Fjord

FRÖYA

HITRA

Umeå

Ångerman

SMÖLA

Kristiansund

Trondheim

Storsjön

Östersund

SYLARNA

Vaasa

Molde

Tynset

Härnösand

Ålesund

Nord Fjord

DOVRE-
FJELL

Dombås

Ljungan

Sundsvall

JOSTEDALS-
BREEN

Rauma

GLITTERTIND

GALDHÖPIGGEN

JOTUNHEIMEN

Femund

Holmsjön

HEDMARK

Ljusnan

Pori

Tampere

Sogne Fjord

Lillehammer

Siljan

Söderhamn

Hardanger

Mjösa

Elverum

Gävle

Turku

Porvoo

Bergen

Fjord

Hamar

Falun

Helsinki

HARDANGER-
VIDDA

Oslo

Glomma

GRÄSÖ

VÄDDÖ

AHVENANMAA
(ÅLAND IS.)

Hangö

Gulf of Finland

TELEMARK

Drammen

Horten

Uppsala

Haugesund

Tönsberg

Västerås

Tallin

Bokn Fjord

Skien

Karlstad

Mälaren

Stavanger

Larvik

Kragerö

Sarpsborg

Eskilstuna

Hjälmaren

Stockholm

KHIUMA

Egersund

Arendal

Halden

Örebro

Södertälje

Karlskoga

SAREMA

Kristiansand

Uddevalla

Vänern

Mariestad

Vättern

Nyköping

Lindesnes
(The Naze)

Trollhättan

Norrköping

FÅRÖ

Skagerrak

The Skaw

Göteborg

Linköping

Gulf of Riga

Jönköping

Västervik

Visby

GOTLAND

Riga

Mölndal

Borås

NORTH

Nissan

Lagan

Kalmar
Sund

Lepaya

Aalborg

Växjö

ÖLAND

Kattegat

Åsnen

Borgholm

SEA

Halmstad

Kalmar

Aarhus

Hälsingborg

Memel

DENMARK

Landskrona

Karlskrona

Esbjerg

Copenhagen

Lund

Kristianstad

Malmö

Hanö Bay

Odense

Trelleborg

BORNHOLM I. (Den.)

Longitude East from Greenwich

much in Hussite wars 15th cent., Thirty Years' War, and in Silesian Wars, esp. when besieged 1757–59 and 1761–62; assigned to Poland by Potsdam Conference 1945.

Świe·bo′dzin (shvyĕ·bô′jēn); *Ger.* **Schwie′bus** (shvē′- boͦos). Town, W cen. Poznań dept., W Poland, SW of Poznań; pop. (1946) 10,432; formerly in Brandenburg, Germany.

Świę′to·chło·wi′ce (shvyĕNn′tô·kłô·vē′tsĕ); *Ger.* **Schwien·toch′lo·witz** (shvēn·tôk′lô·vĭts). Commune in Polish Silesia (Śląsk dept.); suburb of Chorzów; pop. ab. 23,000.

Swift (swĭft). **1** River, cen. Massachusetts; rises in Franklin co., flows S through Quabbin Reservoir to Three Rivers (village) 16 m. ENE of Springfield, where it is joined by Quaboag river to form Chicopee river. **2** County in Minnesota. See *Table* at MINNESOTA.

Swift′ Cur′rent. City, SW Saskatchewan, Canada, 105 m. W of Moose Jaw; pop. 7458; railroad divisional point and trading center for large wheat district.

Swift′cur′rent Mountain. Peak 8300 ft. on Continental Divide in Glacier National Park, NW Montana.

Swil′ly, Lough (lŏk swĭl′ĭ). Inlet of Atlantic Ocean on N coast of Ireland in N co. Donegal, Eire; extends inland 24 m.

Swin′burne Island (swĭn′bĕrn). Island off E coast of Staten I., New York, in Lower New York Bay; part of Richmond borough.

Swin′don (swĭn′dŭn). Municipal borough, Wiltshire, S England, 70 m. W of London; pop. 62,401, (1951 pop.) 68,932; locomotives and rolling stock.

Swi′ne (svē′nĕ). Stream ab. 10 m. long forming main outlet of Stettiner Haff bet. islands of Uznam and Wolin; actually the mouth of the Oder; Świnioujście (Swinemünde) is on W side of mouth.

Świ′no·ujś′cie (shvē′nô·oͦo′ĕsh·chĕ); *Ger.* **Swi′ne·mün′de** (svē′nĕ·mün′dĕ). Seaport city, NW Szczecin dept., NW Poland, on Baltic Sea on N coast of Uznam I. at mouth of the Swine river 37 m. NNW of Stettin (Szczecin); pop. (1946) 26,593; port of Stettin; resort; manufactures lumber, furniture; shipbuilding. Formerly in Prussia, Germany; bombed in World War II; its harbor place where German battleship *Lützow* was sunk Apr. 1945; captured by Russians May 5, 1945; assigned to Poland by Potsdam Conference 1945.

Swin′ton (swĭn′t′n; -tŭn). Urban district, West Riding, Yorkshire, N England, 10 m. NE of Sheffield; pop. 11,922; potteries (formerly noted for Rockingham ware), iron foundries, glassworks.

Swinton and Pen′dle·bur′y (pĕn′d′l·bĕr′ĭ; -bĕr·ĭ; -brĭ). Urban district, Lancashire, NW England, 4 m. NW of Manchester; pop. 41,294; cotton; coal mining.

Swish′er (swĭsh′ẽr). County in Texas. See *Table* at TEXAS.

Swiss′vale (swĭs′vāl). Industrial borough, Allegheny co., SW Pennsylvania, 7 m. E of Pittsburgh; pop. 15,089; manufactures switches and signals, glass products.

Swit′zer·land (swĭt′sẽr·lănd); *Fr.* **Suisse** (sü·ēs′); *Ger.* **Schweiz** (shvīts); *Ital.* **Sviz′ze·ra** (zvēt′tsä·rä); *Latin* **Hel·ve′ti·a** (hĕl·vē′shï·á; -shá). Federal republic (also known as the **Swiss Confederation**) in cen. Europe; bounded on N by Germany, on E by Austria and Liechtenstein, on SE and S by Italy, and on W by France; 15,940 sq. m.; pop. (1941) 4,265,703; * Bern. A region of many mountains, lakes, and rivers, divided politically into 22 cantons (districts) whose people differ in language (German, French, Italian, and Romansh are spoken) and ethnology. See *Table*, below, and *Map*, p. 1103.

Mountains: Jura Mts. in the W and the Swiss Alps in S and E including the Bernese, Lepontine, Pennine, and the Rhaetian Alps (see ALPS); highest peak Monte Rosa 15,217 ft. *Chief rivers:* In S part the Rhone, which has its source in E Valais canton; in E and N, forming part of the N boundary, the Rhine; in cen. and NW part the Aare, the largest river completely within Switzerland. *Lakes:* In SW the Lake of Geneva on French border, in W Lake of Neuchâtel, on the N boundary Lake Constance, and in cen. part Lakes of Lucerne, Zurich, Wallen, Brienz, and Thun. *Chief products:* (In agriculture) cereals, vegetables, sugar beets; cheese and condensed milk, wines; (in manufacturing) watches and clocks, chemical products, machines, instruments, embroideries. *Chief cities:* Zurich, Basel, Bern, Geneva, Lausanne, St. Gall.

History: Occupied by Helvetians who were conquered by Romans; southwest invaded by Burgundians, northeast by Alamanni; made part of Frankish empire; part in kingdom of Arles (*q.v.*, see also BURGUNDY); region without political unity under Holy Roman Empire; in 1291 the Forest Cantons, Uri, Schwyz, and Unterwalden,

CANTONS OF SWITZERLAND

NAME[1]	LOCATION	AREA[2]	POP.[2]	CAPITAL	ENTRANCE DATE[3]	LANGUAGE[4]
Aargau	N cen.	542	270,463	Aarau	1803	Ger.
Appenzell Inner Rhodes[5]	N E	61	13,383	Appenzell	1513	Ger.
Appenzell Outer Rhodes[5]	N E	101	44,756	Herisau	1513	Ger.
Basel-Land[6]	N W	164	94,459	Liestal	1501	Ger.
Basel-Stadt[6]	N W	14	169,961	Basel	1501	Ger.
Bern, *Fr.* Berne	N W, W cen.	2,658	728,916	Bern	1353	Fr.; Ger.
Fribourg, *Ger.* Freiburg	W cen.	647	152,053	Fribourg	1481	Fr.; Ger.
Geneva, *Fr.* Genève	SW	107	174,855	Geneva	1815	Fr.
Glarus	E cen.	267	34,771	Glarus	1352	Ger.
Graubünden, *Fr.* Grisons	E	2,774	128,247	Chur	1803	Ger.; Rom.
Lucerne, *Ger.* Luzern	cen.	579	206,608	Lucerne	1332	Ger.
Neuchâtel	W	312	117,900	Neuchâtel	1815	Fr.
Nidwalden[7]	cen.	112	17,348	Stans	1291	Ger.
Obwalden[7]	cen.	183	20,340	Sarnen	1291	Ger.
Saint Gall[8]	N E	800	286,201	Saint Gall	1803	Ger.
Schaffhausen	N cen.	114	53,772	Schaffhausen	1501	Ger.
Schwyz	E cen.	351	66,555	Schwyz	1291	Ger.
Solothurn	N W	306	154,944	Solothurn	1481	Ger.
Thurgau	N E	397	138,122	Frauenfeld	1803	Ger.
Ticino	SE cen.	1,088	161,882	Bellinzona	1803	Ital.
Uri	cen.	415	27,302	Altdorf	1291	Ger.
Valais, *Ger.* Wallis	SW cen.	2,026	148,319	Sion	1815	Fr.; Ger.
Vaud	W	1,256	343,398	Lausanne	1803	Fr.
Zug	N cen.	92	36,643	Zug	1352	Ger.
Zurich, *Ger.* Zürich	N E cen.	665	674,505	Zurich	1351	Ger.

[1] For pronunciations, see their individual entries.
[2] Area in sq. m. Pop. from 1941 Census.
[3] Date of entrance into Swiss Confederation.
[4] The *predominant* language or languages in the canton.
[5] Appenzell Inner Rhodes (*Ger.* Appenzell Inner Rhoden) and Appenzell Outer Rhodes (*Ger.* Appenzell Ausser Rhoden) are demi- cantons which together constitute the canton of Appenzell (*q.v.*); completely encircled by St. Gallen canton.
[6] Basel-Land (rural Basel) and Basel-Stadt (urban Basel) are demicantons which together constitute the canton of Basel (*Fr.* Bâle).
[7] Nidwalden and Obwalden are demicantons which together constitute Unterwalden canton.
[8] *Ger.* Sankt Gallen, *Fr.* Saint-Gall.

formed anti-Hapsburg league which became nucleus of Swiss Confederation; added Lucerne, Zurich, Glarus, Bern, and Zug by 1353. Solothurn and Fribourg joined confederation 1481 and later, Basel and Appenzell; various cantons expanded their territories and won virtual independence in 15th cent. (not recognized until 1648); center of Protestant Reformation (see ZURICH and GENEVA) which divided cantons and inaugurated a period of political and religious rivalry; organized by French as Helvetic Republic 1798–1803; with new cantons added 1803 and 1815, restored as independent confederation of 22 cantons 1815; after war of Sonderbund (seven Roman Catholic cantons, Lucerne, Uri, Schwyz, Unterwalden, Zug, Fribourg, and Valais, against the Protestants) adopted new constitution 1848, present constitution 1874; perpetual neutrality guaranteed by international agreement 1815 (Congress of Vienna) and 1919 (Treaty of Versailles); remained neutral in World Wars I and II.

Swit′zer·land (swĭt′sẽr·lănd). County in Indiana. See *Table* at INDIANA.

Swold (swōld); *Ger.* **Svol′der** (svôl′dẽr). Small island, not identified, in Baltic Sea off N coast of Germany near Rügen I.; scene 1000 A.D. of semilegendary naval battle of the Norsemen in which Olaf I of Norway was killed and his fleet destroyed by a coalition of Swedish and Danish kings.

Sworbe. See SÕRVEMAA.

Swoy′ers·ville (swoi′ẽrz·vĭl). Borough, Luzerne co., E Pennsylvania, 4 m. N of Wilkes-Barre; pop. 6751; manufactures ornamental iron and steel, textiles; anthracite coal mines.

Syas (syás′y′). River ab. 150 m. long, E Leningrad Region, Soviet Russia, Europe; flows NW to S end of Lake Ladoga, just E of the Volkhov river. With its tributary, the Tikhvinka, forms part of a canal system connecting the lake with the Volga through the Mologa to Shcherbakov (Rybinsk).

Syb′a·ris (sĭb′à·rĭs). Ancient city in S Italy, on N side of mouth of Crathis river on the Gulf of Tarentum, site near modern **Ter′ra·no′va di Si′ba·ri** (tĕr′rä·nô′vä dē sē′bä·rē), Cosenza prov., N Calabria, pop. (1931) 3421. Founded c. 720 B.C. by Achaeans, the oldest city of Magna Graecia; became noted for its luxury; defeated in war with Crotona and was destroyed 510 B.C.

Sycaminum. See HAIFA.

Syc′a·more (sĭk′à·môr). City, ⊗ of De Kalb co., N Illinois, 30 m. ESE of Elgin; pop. 6961; founded 1836; commercial and industrial center; canneries, wire factories, brassworks.

Syd′en·ham (sĭd′′n·ăm; sĭd′năm). 1 Town, S suburb of Sydney, New South Wales, SE Australia. 2 Two wards of Lewisham metropolitan borough, London, England; pop. ab. 30,000; site of the Crystal Palace, an immense structure of glass and iron, designed by Sir Joseph Paxton, which constituted the principal building of the first International Exposition 1851 and was removed here 1854 and destroyed by fire 1936. 3 Former borough, South I., New Zealand, now part of Christchurch.

Sydlige Jylland. See SOUTH JUTLAND.

Syd′ney (sĭd′nĭ). 1 City, ✳ of New South Wales, Australia, in E part on Port Jackson (q.v.) on Pacific Ocean; pop. with suburbs (1966) 2,444,735, largest city in Australia; has one of world's finest harbors, capable of accommodating the largest vessels; most active port in Australia; distributing and trading center for large pastoral and mining region; maintains numerous important industries (manufacture of clothing and machinery, preparation of food products and beverages); has Anglican cathedral, Roman Catholic cathedral; many fine parks; botanic gardens, zoological gardens; University of Sydney; connected with North Sydney (q.v.) by bridge across Port Jackson. First British settlement in Australia; founded 1788 by British officials in

charge of group of convicts (penal settlement had been established on Botany Bay, q.v.).

SYDNEY AND VICINITY
Statute Miles

2 Industrial and commercial city, ⊗ of Cape Breton co., E Nova Scotia, Canada, on **Sydney Harbor,** an inlet of Atlantic Ocean; pop. 31,317; steel and coal center with many mills, foundries, and furnaces; a natural harbor, commodious and sheltered; has steamship connections with Montreal, Halifax, and Newfoundland. First English settlement 1784; capital of Cape Breton I. 1784–1820. 3 One of the smaller islands of the Phoenix Is. (q.v.), in SE part of group, S Pacific Ocean, S of Enderbury I.

Sydney Mines (mīnz). Town, Cape Breton co., E Nova Scotia, Canada, on Atlantic Ocean 10 m. N of Sydney; pop. 8410; in coal-mining region; has large steel plant; foundries.

Syed′lets (syĕd′lyĭts). Var. of SIEDLCE.

Syene. See ASWÂN.

Sykes′ville (sīks′vĭl). Borough, Jefferson co., W cen. Pennsylvania, 8 m. SSW of Du Bois; pop. 1479; coal mining, lumbering; manufactures textiles.

Syk·tyv·kar′ (sĭk·tĭf·kär′); *formerly* **Ust Sy·solsk′** (ōōst′ sĭ·sôlsk′; *Russ.* ōōst′y′ sĭ·sôl′y′sk). Town, ✳ of Komi Republic, Soviet Russia, Europe, on the Sysola river just above its junction with the Vychegda, 220 m. N of Kirov.

Syl′a·cau′ga (sĭl′à·kô′gà). City, Talladega co., E cen. Alabama, 42 m. SE of Birmingham; pop. 12,857; marble quarries; textiles, cottonseed oil.

Syl′lar·na′ (sü′lär·nä′). Peak 5781 ft. in W cen. Sweden, on the Norwegian border.

Syl·het′ (sĭl·hĕt′). 1 Former district, Surma Valley and Hill division, SW Assam, NE Brit. India; pop. (1941) 3,116,602. Divided 1947 with ab. ⅚ of area transferred to East Bengal, Pakistan, the other sixth (E part) remaining in Assam, Indian Union. 2 Town, ✳ of district in East Bengal, now in Pakistan, on Surma river 280 m. NE of Calcutta; pop. 21,435; exports rice and tea. Seat of Murarichand Coll. and Sanskrit Coll.

Sylt (sĭlt; *Ger.* zĭlt). Island 22 m. long in the North Sea, off W coast of Schleswig-Holstein, West Germany; chief island of North Frisian Is.; connected with mainland by causeway; popular summer resort. Chief town Keitum.

Syl′va (sĭl′và). Town, ⊗ of Jackson co., SW North Carolina, 40 m. WSW of Asheville; pop. 1564; tannery, paperboard plant.

Syl·va′ni·a (sĭl·vā′nĭ·à; -vän′yà). 1 City, ⊗ of Screven co., E Georgia, 55 m. NW of Savannah; pop. 3469; lumber, cotton.

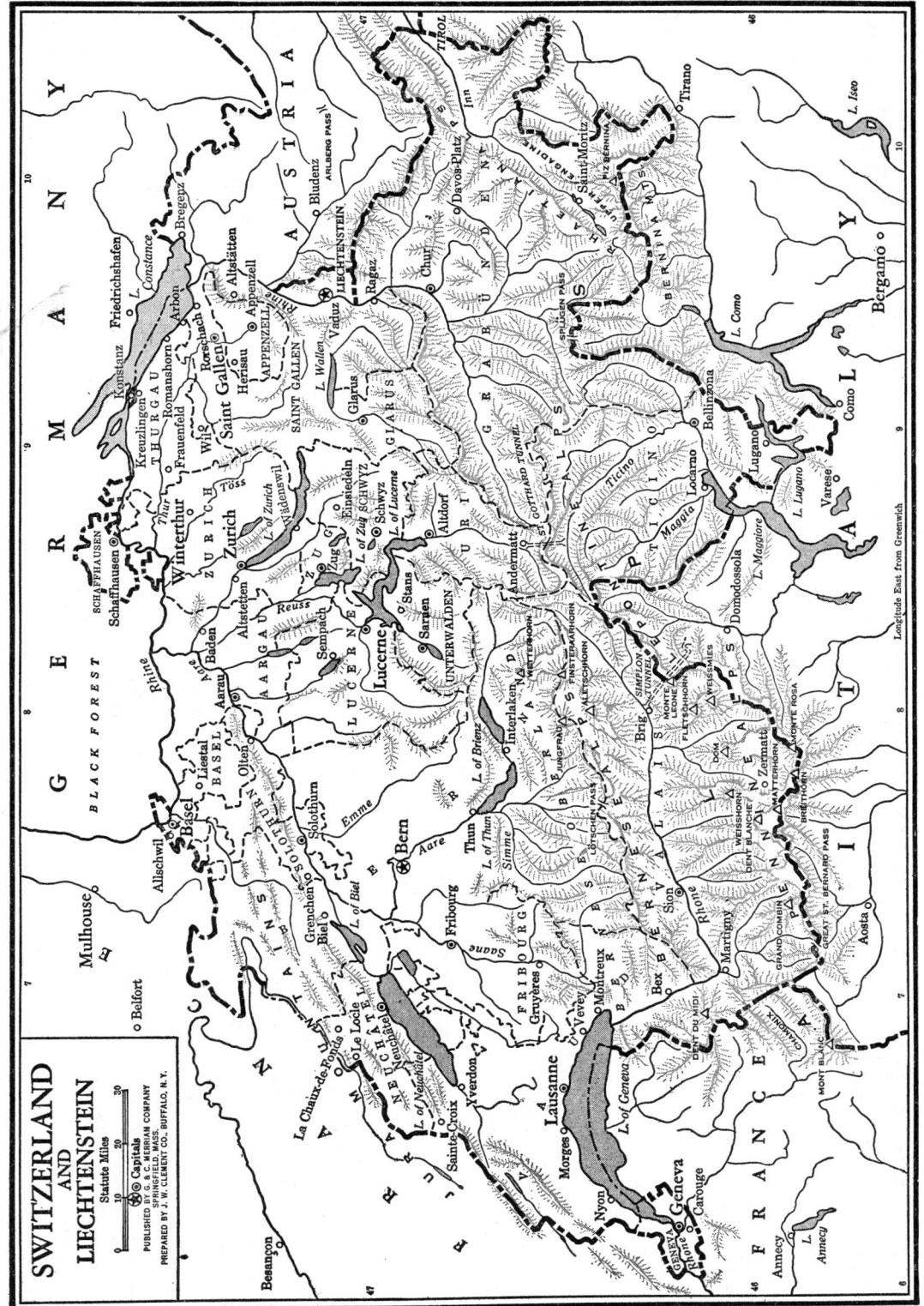

SWITZERLAND
AND
LIECHTENSTEIN

Statute Miles

⊛◉ Capitals

PUBLISHED BY G. & C. MERRIAM COMPANY
SPRINGFIELD, MASS.
PREPARED BY J. W. CLEMENT CO., BUFFALO, N.Y.

2 Village, Lucas co., NW Ohio, on Michigan border 10 m. WNW of Toledo; pop. 5187; manufactures cement and cement blocks.

Syl·ves'ter (sĭl-vĕs'tẽr). City, ⊗ of Worth co., S Georgia, 20 m. E of Albany; pop. 3610.

Sylvia, Mount. See TSUGITAKA.

Sy'mē (sī'mē; *Mod. Gr.* sē'mĕ); *Ital.* **Si'mi** (sē'mē).
1 Island of the Dodecanese (*q.v.*), NW of Rhodes; 25 sq. m.; pop. (1936) 6195.
2 Town on the island.

Symi. Var. of *Simi*: see SYMĒ.

Sym'me·try Spire (sĭm'ĕ·trĭ). Peak 10,546 ft. in cen. Grand Teton National Park, NW Wyoming.

Syra. See SYROS.

Syr'a·cuse (sĭr'à·kūs; *for the place in Sicily, also* sĭr'à·kūz *and, esp. Brit.*, sī'rà·kūz). **1** City, ⊗ of Hamilton co., W Kansas; pop. 1888.
2 Commercial and manufacturing city, ⊗ of Onondaga co., cen. New York, 12 m. S of W end of Oneida Lake; pop. 216,038; trade center in agricultural region; important railroad point; served by barge terminal with facilities for handling oil, soda products, potash, pig iron, fertilizer; manufactures motor vehicle bodies and parts, tool steels, soda ash and by-products, air-conditioning equipment, chinaware, cans, typewriters, electrical machines and appliances, plated silverware, agricultural implements (including chilled plows), foundry and machine-shop products; printing and publishing industry; limestone quarries in vicinity. Syracuse Univ. (continuation of Genesee Coll., estab. at Lima, N.Y., 1849; chartered 1870; moved to Syracuse 1871; coed.) and its affiliated New York State Coll. of Forestry (1911; Experimental Station 1912), U.S. Government Weather Observation Bureau (1902); Le Moyne Coll. (1946; coed.; Roman Catholic).
History: Territory visited by French 1620, subsequently by English; salt springs discovered 1654; trading post set up by whites c. 1786; saltworks established c. 1789 and flourished until after Civil War; salt settlements sprang up, including Salina (also called Salt Point, now N section of Syracuse) and site of present Syracuse, latter became important port on Erie Canal at junction with Oswego Canal (opened 1838); Salina incorporated as village 1824, Syracuse 1825; became ⊗ 1827; Syracuse and Salina, together with Lodi first incorporated as city of Syracuse 1848.
3 Province of Italy: = *Siracusa:* see *Table* at ITALY.
4 *Ital.* **Si·ra·cu'sa** (sē·rä·kōō'zä); *anc.* **Syr'a·cu'sae** (sĭr'à·kū'sē; -zē). Seaport, ✻ of Siracusa prov., SE Sicily, on Ionian Sea 130 m. SE of Palermo; partly on Ortygia I. (separated from mainland by narrow canal); pop. 53,166; cathedral; castle; 14th-cent. palaces; salt-water fountain (Fonte Aretusa); airport; famous ruins include 5th-cent. (B.C.) Greek temple and theater, parts of city walls and fortifications, aqueducts of the period of Hiero II, Roman amphitheater, and numerous catacombs; exports olive oil, citrus fruits.
History: Founded 734 B.C. by Corinthian colonists; became largest and most important city in Sicily extending its influence throughout Sicily and S Italy; seized by tyrant of Gela 485 B.C.; ruled by despotic Hiero I 478–466; democratic government established 465; Athenians defeated by Syracusans in land and sea engagements 413; under Dionysius the Elder 405–367 and Dionysius the Younger 367–356 and 347–344; democracy re-established 337; under Agathocles the Tyrant 316–289; Carthaginians repulsed by Pyrrhus 278; Hiero II made king 270; allied with Rome in First Punic War; fell to Romans 212 after three years of resistance; conquered by Byzantines 535 A.D. and made capital of Sicily; residence 663–668 of Emperor Constans II; conquered by Arabs 878 and by Normans 1085, becoming part of the kingdom of the Two Sicilies. Birthplace of Theocritus and Archimedes. Not important in medieval times. In World War II taken by British July 12, 1943.

Syr Dar·ya' (sǐr' där·yä'; *Angl.* där'yä); *Turki* **Sir Darya** (sēr') *or* **Sai·hun'** (sī·hōōn'); *anc.* **Jax·ar'tes** (jǎk·sär'tēz). River ab. 1500 m. long, in Kirgiz, Uzbek, and Kazakh Republics, Soviet Central Asia; formed by two headstreams in Kazakh S.S.R. rising in the Tien Shan; flows W and NW into Lake Aral at its NE corner; flows through the fertile Fergana valley; its lower course on E edge of Kyzyl Kum Desert; part of its course in ancient times separated the Scythian tribes from Sogdiana. In recent times has often changed its course.

Syr'i·a (sĭr'ĭ·à); *Heb.* **A'ram** (*Angl.* ā'rǎm; âr'ǎm); *Arab.* **Esh Shâm** (ăsh shăm'). **1** Ancient country in Asia, at E end of Mediterranean Sea, covering modern Syria, Lebanon, Palestine, and Jordan, and, according to some, N Arabia.
History: Conquered by Egypt c. 1471 B.C.; part of Babylonian, Assyrian, and Persian empires; conquered by Alexander the Great; ruled by the Seleucidae who carried on war against Egypt in 3d cent. B.C.; made a Roman province by Pompey 64 B.C.; invaded on several occasions by Persians before Khosrau II conquered it 611 A.D.; overrun by Moslem Arabs 635–636; seat of Ommiad dynasty with capital at Damascus (*q.v.*) 661–750; in hands of Seljuks and later, of Fatimids, during early Crusades; came under Ottoman Turks 1516; invaded by French 1798–99; occupied by Mehemet Ali, revolting governor of Egypt, 1831–33 and 1839–40; scene of insurrection 1860–61; saw end of Turkish rule 1917.
2 *Fr.* **Sy'rie'** *or* **La Syrie** (là sē'rē'). Former French mandate at E end of the Mediterranean Sea, roughly co-

SYRIA (Western Part)
AND LEBANON
with boundaries of former territories
LATAKIA and JEBEL ED DRUZ
Statute Miles
0   50   100

extensive with the northern or main part of ancient Syria; bounded on N by Turkey, on E and SE by Iraq,

on S by Transjordan and Palestine, and on W by the Mediterranean. Known as the **Le·vant′ States** (lĕ-vănt′) it comprised the republics of Syria and Lebanon, and the territories of Latakia and Jebel ed Druz; 76,030 sq. m.; pop. (1935) 2,897,956, (1938 est.) 3,630,000; administrative ✳ Beirut, legislative ✳ Damascus; formerly six vilayets of SE Turkey. In the SE is N part of the Syrian Desert; in center a plateau region (elevation 1500–4500 ft.); in NE the upper part of the plain of Mesopotamia; along the coast on the W the Lebanon and Anti-Liban mountain ranges (highest 10,135 ft.) and their N extension; in SW is Jebel Druze 5791 ft. In E cen. part is the Euphrates, flowing from NW to SE and receiving on the left the tributaries Balikh and Khabur; rivers near the Mediterranean are the Litani in Lebanon and the Orontes in Lebanon and Syria with outlet in Turkey; both valleys are part of Fertile Crescent. Chief exports textiles, fruit, vegetables. Chief cities Damascus, Beirut, Alep, Homs, Hama, Tripoli, Latakia.

History: Became French mandate 1920; in 1925 Damascus and Alep were united to form state of Syria which became republic 1930 (see 3, below); Lebanese Republic formed 1926; Sanjak of Alexandretta (*q.v.*), previously autonomous, was ceded to Turkey 1939; under control of Vichy forces 1940–41; taken over by British and Free French June–July 1941; ceased to be French mandate Sept. 27, 1941.

3 Republic, cen. and E part of former French mandate; pop. (1935) 1,696,638, (1938 est.) 2,487,000; ✳ Damascus. Independence proclaimed Sept. 27, 1941; incorporated Latakia and Jebel ed Druz 1942; complete independence established Jan. 1, 1944 but British and French troops not all withdrawn until 1946; merged with Egypt in the United Arab Republic Feb. 1, 1958; withdrew Sept. 29, 1961.

Syriae Portae. See BAILAN.

Syr′i·am (sĭr′ĭ·ăm). Town, Hanthawaddy dist., Lower Burma, on Rangoon river opp. Rangoon; pop. 15,070; seaport; oil refineries.

Syr′i·an Desert (sĭr′ĭ·ăn). Extensive desert region in N Arabia, SE Syria, W Iraq, and NE Transjordan, bet. lat. 30° and 34°N and long. 36° and 44°E; its W part known as **El Ha·mad′** (ăl hă·măd′), a name applied by some to the entire desert; crossed by pipelines connecting the oil fields of Kirkuk with Haifa and Tripoli.

Syrian Gates. See BAILAN.

Syrie *or* **La Syrie.** See SYRIA former French mandate.

Syr′mi·a (sûr′mĭ·à); *Serb.* **Srem** (srĕm); *Hung.* **Sze′-rém** (sĕ′rām). Region in N Yugoslavia, formerly the E division of Slavonia, later that part of Dunavska and Drinska cos. bet. the Danube and Sava rivers; since 1945 corresponds to E part of Croatia federated republic.

Sy′ros (sī′rŏs; *Mod. Gr.* sē′rôs) *or* **Sy′ra** (sī′rà; *Mod. Gr.* sē′rä). **1** Island, cen. Cyclades, in Aegean Sea; 31 sq. m.; pop. ab. 28,000; chief town Hermoupolis, which is also capital of Cyclades dept., Greece. Haven of many Greek refugees during War of Independence; in 19th cent. of considerable commercial importance.

2 Town. See HERMOUPOLIS.

Syrtica, Regio. See TRIPOLI region.

Syrtis Major. See Gulf of SIDRA.

Syrtis Minor. See Gulf of GABÈS.

Syz′ran (sĭz′rán; *Russ.* sĭs′rán·y′). City, SW Kuibyshev Region, Soviet Russia, Europe, on right bank of the Volga 80 m. W of Kuibyshev; pop. 77,679; on railroad from Moscow to Kuibyshev and Chelyabinsk which crosses the Volga here on long bridge; handles grain.

Szabadka. See SUBOTICA.

Sza′bolcs (sŏ′bŏlch). Former Hungarian county.

Szalankamen. See SLANKAMEN.

Szamos. See SOMEŞ.

Szar′vas (sŏr′vŏsh). Commune, SE Hungary, on the Körös ab. 83 m. SE of Budapest; pop. 27,167; livestock market, esp. for horses.

Szat′már (sŏt′mär). Former Hungarian county.

Szatmár–Németi. See SATU-MARE.

Száva. See SAVA.

Szczara. See SHCHARA.

Szczeb·rze′szyn (shchĕb·zhĕ′shĭn). Town, Lublin prov., Poland, ab. 47 m. SSE of Lublin; pop. 7496.

Szcze′cin (shchĕ′tsēn). **1** *when first formed after World War II called* **Po·mo′rze Za·chod′nie** (pô·mô′zhĕ zä·kôd′nyĕ). Department, NW Poland, formerly in Pomerania prov., Prussia, Germany; ✳ Stettin (Szczecin).

2 Seaport. See STETTIN.

Szcze·ci′nek (shchĕ·tsĕ′nĕk); *Ger.* **Neu′stet·tin′** (noi′-shtĕ·tēn′). City, E Szczecin dept., NW Poland, 41 m. SE of Koszalin; pop. (1946) 18,689; railroad junction; summer resort. Founded 1310 by duke of Pomerania; occupied by Russian army Jan. 1945; assigned to Poland by Potsdam Conference 1945.

Szczyt′no (shchĭt′nô); *Ger.* **Or′tels·burg** (ôr′t'lz·bûrg; *Ger.* ôr′tĕls·bŏork). City, S cen. Olsztyn dept., N Poland, 27 m. SE of Olsztyn; pop. (1946) 14,312; formerly in East Prussia, Germany; lumber, tile, beer, sandstone, dairy products; cattle and horse market. Founded 13th cent.; became city 1616; occupied and burned by Russians 1914; in World War II taken by Russians Jan. 1945; assigned to Poland by Potsdam Conference 1945.

Sze′chwan′ *or* **Sze′chuan′** (sŭ′chwän′; *Angl.* sĕ′-). Province, S cen. China; 166,485 sq. m.; pop. (1936 est.) 52,963,269; ✳ Chengtu; bounded on N by Kansu and Shensi provs., on E by Hupeh, on S by Kweichow and Yunnan, and on W by Sikang; touches Tsinghai on the NW and Hunan on the SE. Largest of the provinces of China Proper and the most populous; well-watered plateau province, heart of which is known as the Red Basin; crossed in S section by the Yangtze and in the cen. part by three of its tributaries, Min, To, and Kialing, flowing N to S. On NE bordered by Ta Pa Shan range and on W by mountains rising steeply to border of Tibetan plateau (edge of which is 10,000 to 20,000 ft.). In mountains in SE the Yangtze flows through the Yangtze Gorges (*q.v.*); rivers in the Red Basin are navigable and there is much junk traffic. Produces winter cereals as well as tropical crops (rice, tea, sugar, hemp, etc.); exports silk, hides, musk, white wax; mineral resources extensive but not developed. Chief cities Chungking, Chengtu, Wanhsien, Ipin, Loshan.

History: In early years of Chinese history its population entirely non-Chinese; incorporated (c. 3d cent. A.D.) in empire under Chin dynasty; although long isolated by its mountain barriers, now definitely Chinese. Wanhsien on the Yangtze opened 1917 to foreign trade. After outbreak 1937 of war with Japan, government removed from coast to Chungking establishing that city as capital of China; also its population and influence increased by migration of industries, government bureaus, schools, etc.; headquarters of military forces; bombed frequently by Japanese 1938–45.

Sze′chwan·ese Alps (sŭ′chwän·ēz; -ēs; sĕ′-). The high ranges of mountains on the NW, W, and SW borders of Szechwan prov., S cen. China, the E scarp of the Tibetan plateau, from 10,000 to 24,900 ft. (Minya Konka, highest, in Sikang).

Sze′ged (sĕ′gĕd); *Ger.* **Sze′ge·din** (sā′gä·dēn). Autonomous city, S Hungary, on the Yugoslav border; 315 sq. m.; pop. (1939) 131,893; important port on Tisza river; industrial and commercial center; university. Old town ruined by flood 1879; taken by Russians Oct. 6, 1944.

Székelyudvarhely. See ODORHEI.

Szé′kes·fe′hér·vár′ (sā′kĕsh·fĕ′hār·vär′); *Ger.* **Stuhl′-weis′sen·burg** (shtōōl′vīs′ĕn·bŏork). Autonomous city, W cen. Hungary; 46 sq. m.; pop. (1939) 42,438; market center for wine and fruit; scene of crowning of kings of Hungary 1027–1527; many of its buildings destroyed 1686 at end of Turkish occupation.

Szek′szárd (sĕk′särd); *formerly also* **Szeg′szárd** (sĕg′-). City, S Hungary, 85 m. S of Budapest; pop. 13,264.

Sze′mao′ (sŭ′mou′). Town and treaty port, S cen. Yunnan prov., S China, E of the Mekong and 165 m. WSW of Mengtsz; pop. (1931 est.) 20,000; opened for trade 1895; customs outpost for Shans and other native peoples in vicinity and across the line in Burma.

Szeming. See AMOY.

Szent. See SAINT.

Szent′en·dre′ (sĕnt′ĕn·drĕ′); *Ger.* **Sankt An′drä** (zängkt än′drâ). City, N Hungary, on a branch of the Danube ab. 12 m. N of Budapest; pop. 7214; metal industries.

Szent′es (sĕnt′ĕsh). City, SE Hungary, 30 m. N of Szeged; pop. 33,691.

Szent′gott·hárd′ (sĕnt′gôt·härd′); *Eng.* **Saint Gott′-hard** (sânt gŏt′ērd). Commune, W Hungary, on Rába river, on Austrian boundary; scene of battle Aug. 1, 1664 in which imperial forces under General Montecuccoli defeated the Turks. See VASVÁR.

Sze′pes (sĕ′pĕsh); *Ger.* **Zips** (tsĭps); *Czech* **Spiš** (spĭsh); *Pol.* **Spiž** (shpĕsh). Former county in N Hungary, now largely in Slovakia, Czechoslovakia (small part in Poland).

Sze′ping′kai′ (sŏō′pĭng′gī′) *or* **Ssu′ping′chieh′** (sŏō′-pĭng′chĭ·ĕ′). Town, formerly in E Liaoning prov., S Manchuria, 70 m. SSW of Changchun; since 1945 ✳ of the new province of Liaopeh; pop. ab. 8000; junction point on South Manchuria Ry. for Liaoyuan and Taonan; fighting during civil war 1947–48.

Szerém. See SYRMIA.

Szigetköz. See LITTLE SCHÜTT.

Szi′get·vár′ (sĭ′gĕt·vär′). Commune, S Hungary, W of Pécs; pop. 5960; object of siege Aug. 5–Sept. 7, 1566 in which Miklós Zrinyi with ab. 3000 men heroically defended the city against Suleiman I.

Sziszek. See SISAK.

Szol′nok (sŏl′nŏk). City, E cen. Hungary, ab. 55 m. SE of Budapest; pop. 35,514; industrial and commercial center; Franciscan convent.

Szom′bat·hely′ (sŏm′bŏt·hā′); *Ger.* **Stein′am-ang′er** (shtīn′äm·äng′ēr); *anc.* **Sa·bar′i·a** (så·băr′ĭ·å) *or* **Sa·var′i·a** (-vär′-). City, W Hungary, near Austrian frontier; pop. 37,616; commercial center in rich wine-producing region; cathedral; episcopal palace; museum. Ancient Sabaria was the Roman capital of Pannonia; in World War II taken by Russians Mar. 29, 1945.

Szpro·ta′wa (shprô·tä′vä); *Ger.* **Sprot′tau** (shprôt′ou). Industrial town, NW Wrocław dept., SW Poland, on Bobr river 37 m. NW of Legnica; pop. (1946) 12,578; formerly in Silesia, Germany; iron goods, textiles, wax goods. Assigned to Poland by Potsdam Conference 1945.

Szy·dło′wiec (shĭ·dlô′vyĕts). Commune, Kielce dept., Poland, 22 m. NNE of Kielce; pop. 10,590.

T

Ta·al′ (tä·äl′). **1** Volcano 984 ft. on Volcano I. (14 m. in circumference, 6 sq. m.) in center of Lake Taal, cen. Batangas prov., Luzon, Phil. Is.; its crater is $1\frac{1}{4}$ to $1\frac{1}{3}$ m. in diameter. Has had 9 recorded eruptions since 1709, those of 1754 and 1911 especially severe.
2 Municipality, Batangas prov., Luzon, Phil. Is., on Pansipit river near its mouth, SW of Lake Taal and near the NE coast of Balayan Bay; pop. 23,004; named after older town destroyed by the eruption of Mt. Taal in 1754.

Taal, Lake; *formerly* **Lake Bom·bon′** (bôm·bôn′). Lake, cen. Batangas prov., Luzon, Phil. Is., ab. 40 m. S of Manila; 17 m. long by 12 m. wide; 94 sq. m.; its outlet is the Pansipit river flowing S to Balayan Bay.

Ta′a·nach (tä′à·năk). Ancient city of Canaan, on S side of Plain of Esdraelon ab. 5 m. SE of Megiddo. Near here Sisera was defeated by Barak and Deborah (*Judges* v. 19); important during Solomon's reign.

Taa′sing′e (tô′sĭng′ĕ). Island of Denmark, in the Baltic Sea S of Fyn I.; 27 sq. m.; pop. (1925) 4277.

Tab. See ZUHREH.

Ta·ba′co (tä·bä′kō). Municipality on E coast of Albay prov., Luzon, Phil. Is., on Tabaco Bay; pop. 29,957; has best harbor in the province; N of Mt. Mayon and ab. 15 m. N of Legaspi.

Tabaco Bay. Inlet of Lagonoy Gulf on E coast of Albay prov., Luzon, Phil. Is.; ab. 12 m. long; San Miguel I. and Cagraray I. enclose it on the E; it affords sheltered harbors for Tabaco and Bacacay.

Ta′ba·cun′do (tä′vä·kōōn′dô). Town, Pichincha prov., N cen. Ecuador, just NE of Quito; pop. (1944 est.) 6988.

Ta·ba′py (tä·vä′pĕ). Town, Paraguarí dept., S cen. Paraguay, ab. 40 m. SE of Asunción.

Ta·bar′ca (tä·bär′kà; *Arab.* tŏ·bŭr′kŏ·h′). Town, NW Tunisia, N Africa, near Algerian border ab. 80 m. WSW of Bizerte.

Ta·bar′ Islands (tä·bär′). Group of small islands in NE part of the Bismarck Archipelago, W Pacific Ocean, off NE coast of island of New Ireland; comprise the three islands of Tabar, Tatau, and Simberi. Practically unexplored until 1910.

Tabariya. See TIBERIAS.

Tabariya, Bahr. See Sea of GALILEE.

Ta·bas′ (tä·bäs′). **1** Town, S Khurasan, NE Iran, at N border of the Dasht-i-Lut 180 m. NE of Yezd; pop. ab. 5000.
2 Town, E Iran, E of Birjand near Afghan border.

Tabasara, Sierra de. See SIERRA DE TABASARA.

Ta·bas′co (tä·bäs′kō; *Span.* tä·väs′kŏ). **1** State, SE Mexico. See *Table* at MEXICO.
2 = GRIJALVA river.

Ta′ba·tin′ga (tä′vä·tēng′gà). Town, Amazonas state, W Brazil, on the Amazon at Peruvian and Colombian frontier; adjoins Leticia, Colombia.

Ta·ber′nes de Vall·dig′na (tä·vĕr′năz thä vä[l]·y′·dēg′nä). Commune, Valencia prov., E Spain, 29 m. SSE of Valencia; pop. 11,411.

Ta′bi·te′u·e′a (tä′bĕ·tä′ōō·ā′ä). Island (atoll) ab. 50 m. long near S end of Gilbert Is., ab. 80 m. S of the equator, W Pacific Ocean; has five villages and largest population (3856 in 1936) of any island in the group.

Ta′blas (tä′vläs). Largest island of Romblon group, Romblon prov., cen. Phil. Is., in W part marking part of W border of Sibuyan Sea; 265 sq. m.; pop. 52,241; chief municipality Odiongan. Long narrow island (ab. 40 m. long), separated by Tablas Strait, 31 to 35 m. wide, from E Mindoro, and at its N end by a channel 8 m. wide, from Romblon I. Has low mountain range through its center. Looc on SW coast has fairly good harbor.

Tablas, Las. See LAS TABLAS.

Tablas Strait. Wide passage (ab. 35 m.) bet. Mindoro on the W and Tablas, Simara, and Banton Is. on the E,

Phil. Is.; connects E end of Verde Island Passage with Sulu Sea.

Ta′ble Bay (tä′b′l). Inlet 6 m. wide forming the harbor of Cape Town, SW Cape Province, Union of South Africa.

Table Cape. 1 Cape on E cen. coast of North I., New Zealand, at the base of Mahia Penin.
2 Cape, NW Tasmania, Australia, N of Wynyard.
3 Town, Tasmania. See WYNYARD.

Table Mountain. 1 Peak 8283 ft. in cen. Churchill co., W Nevada.
2 Peak 3856 ft. in the Catskill Mts., Ulster co., SE New York.
3 Peak 6243 ft. in Kittitas co., cen. Washington.
4 Peak 11,101 ft. in Teton Range, W Teton co., NW Wyoming.
5 Peak 10,600 ft. in Yellowstone National Park, NW Wyoming.
6 Mountain 3550 ft. in Cape Province, Union of South Africa, S of Cape Town.

Table Rock. Peak 4319 ft. in Scotts Bluff co., W Nebraska.

Ta′ble·top′ Mountain (tä′b′l·tŏp′). Peak 4440 ft. in the Adirondack Mts., Essex co., NE New York.

Ta·bo′ga (tä·bō′gä; *Span.* tä·vō′gä). Small island belonging to Panama, in the Gulf of Panama 10 m. S of the city of Panama.

Ta′bo·gon′ (tä′bō·gôn′). Municipality on NE coast of Cebu I., Phil. Is., 47 m. N of City of Cebu; pop. 20,201.

Tá′bor (tä′bôr). Town, S cen. Bohemia prov., W Czechoslovakia, on Lužnice river 47 m. S of Prague; pop. (1930) 14,251; manufactures textiles and tobacco products; founded 1420 by Jan Žižka, a Hussite; remained Protestant stronghold (of Taborites) during Hussite Wars; 15th-cent. church.

Ta′bor, Mount (tä′bôr). Mountain 1929 ft., SE Galilee, N Palestine, 6 m. E by S of Nazareth; notable in Biblical (*Ps.* lxxxix. 12) and Roman times.

Ta·bo′ra (tä·bōr′à). **1** Former province, now part of Western Province, of Tanganyika, E Africa.
2 Town, W cen. Tanganyika, on railroad 430 m. WNW of Dar es Salaam; ✻ of Western Province; pop. ab. 25,000; trade and strategic center; modern town founded by Arabs 1820; taken by Belgian force Sept. 19, 1916 in World War I and turned over to British.

Ta′bor City (tä′bẽr). City, Columbus co., S North Carolina, on South Carolina border 55 m. W of Wilmington; pop. 2338; market for tobacco, beans.

Ta·bou′ or **Ta·bu′** (tä·bōō′). Seaport, SW Ivory Coast Republic, West Africa, a few miles E of Cape Palmas and the Liberian border.

Ta·briz′ (tä·brēz′); *anc.* **Tau′ris** (tô′rĭs). Commercial city, NW Iran; ✻ of Azerbaijan prov.; pop. ab. 214,000; second in size in Iran. In a valley (alt. 4400 ft.) ab. 38 m. E of N end of Lake Urmia and of Kuh-i-Sahand; on the main trade route from Iran to Turkish Armenia and Russian Armenia; has rail connection (80 m. long) with Dzhulfa on the Araks in Azerbaidzhan S.S.R. Probably dates back to period before the Christian Era and has for centuries been an important commercial city; has many mosques and bazaars but few remains of architectural interest; exports rugs and dried fruit. Has often suffered from severe earthquakes and was partially destroyed by invaders—Arabs, Turks, and Mongols—and esp. by Tamerlane 1392, but always rebuilt; became Persian under Shah Abbas I 1618; held briefly by Turks 1721–30 and by Russians 1827–28; object of conflict bet. Turks and Russians in World War I and of international dispute in 1946.

Ta′ca·ná′ (tä′kä·nä′). **1** Volcano 13,333 ft. in SW Guatemala, on the Guatemala-Mexico boundary in the Sierra Madre range.

2 Town, SW Guatemala, NE of the volcano; pop. ab. 12,000.

Tacape. See GABÈS.

Tacarigua. See VALENCIA.

Ta·chi·ka·wa (tä-chē-kä-wä). Industrial town, Tokyo prefecture, SE Honshu, Japan, 19 m. W of Tokyo; pop. (1945) 34,586; bombed Apr. 4, 1945.

Ta'chin' Shan (dä'chin' shän'). Mountain range in SE China, along the border bet. Fukien and Kiangsi provs.; highest ab. 3500 ft.

Tá'chi·ra (tä'chē-rä). State of Venezuela. See *Table* at VENEZUELA.

Ta·clo'ban (tä-klō'bän). Municipality, NE coast of Leyte I., * of Leyte prov., Phil. Is., at S end of San Juanico Strait and on NW shore of San Pedro Bay; pop. 31,233; has good harbor with coastwise trade. Made capital by Spanish in 19th cent. and as port opened to foreign trade 1874; seized by Japanese 1942 and retaken with its airport by American forces Oct. 21, 1944; made temporary capital of Phil. Is. by Americans Oct. 22.

Tac'na (täk'nä; *Span.* täk'nä). **1** Department, extreme S Peru; 4922 sq. m.; pop. (1940 est.) 37,512; * Tacna; mostly an arid desert region enclosed on E by foothills of the Andes. Part of **Tacna–A·ri'ca** (-ȧ-rē'kȧ; *Span.* -ä-rē'kä) region, which was occupied by Chile from 1884 (see ANCÓN for Treaty of Ancón 1883) to 1930 when region was divided bet. Peru (Tacna dept.) and Chile (Arica dept. in Tarapaca prov.). See ARICA.

2 Town, its *, ab. 40 m. by rail N of Arica, Chile; pop. (1940 est.) 11,378. Peruvian and Bolivian forces defeated near here by Chileans 1880.

Ta·co'ma (tȧ-kō'mȧ). Seaport city, * of Pierce co., W cen. Washington, on Puget Sound 26 m. S of Seattle; pop. 147,979; lumber center; railroad terminus; deep-sea harbor; smelting and electrochemical plants, fisheries; manufactures gas, lumber and timber products, processed foods, bakery products; resort (gateway to Mt. Rainier National Park). University of Puget Sound (1888; coed.). Fort Lewis and McChord Field (U.S. Air Force base) in environs. First settled 1852; became ⊗ 1880, city 1883.

Tacoma, Mount. See Mount RAINIER.

Ta·con'ic Mountains (tȧ-kŏn'ĭk). Ridge extending along Massachusetts-New York boundary and into Vermont; highest peak Equinox Mt. 3816 ft. in Bennington co., SW Vermont.

Ta·co'ra (tȧ-kŏr'ȧ; *Span.* tä-kō'rä). Peak 19,522 ft. in Tacna dept., S Peru.

Ta'cua·rem·bó' (tä'kwä-räm-bō'). **1** Department of Uruguay. See *Table* at URUGUAY.

2 *or* **San Fruc·tuo'so** (säm' frōōk-twō'sō). City, its *, N cen. Uruguay, 215 m. N of Montevideo; pop. ab. 24,000; trade center for wool, hides, and skins.

Ta'cua·rí' (tä'kwä-rē'). River ab. 90 m. long, E Uruguay; flows E into Lake Mirim.

Ta·cu'ba (tȧ-kōō'bȧ; *Span.* tä-kōō'vä). City, Federal District, cen. Mexico, W of Mexico City.

Ta'cu·ba'ya (tä'kōō-vä'yä). City, Federal District, cen. Mexico; pop. 105,783; picturesque and fashionable suburb SW of Mexico City; site of National Astronomical Observatory. Site of old Aztec settlement, founded c. 1270; important Spanish center in 17th and 18th cents.; became residence of archbishop 1737.

Ta'cu·ru'pu·cú' (tä'kōō-rōō'pōō-kōō') *or* **Her'nan·da'rias** (ěr'nän-dä'ryäs). Town, * of Alto Paraná dept., E Paraguay, on the Paraná river.

Tacutú. See TAKUTÚ.

Tadjik. Var. of TADZHIK.

Ta·djou'ra *or* **Ta·ju'ra** (tȧ-jōōr'ȧ). Seaport on N side of the Gulf of Tadjoura, French Somaliland, E Africa, SW of Obock; pop. (1936) 673.

Tadjoura *or* **Tajura, Gulf of.** Inlet of the Gulf of Aden on E coast of French Somaliland, NE Africa.

Tadmor. See PALMYRA.

Tad'ous·sac (tăd'ŭ-săk; *Fr.* tȧ'dōō'sȧk'). Village, ⊗ of

Saguenay co., SE Quebec, Canada, on N bank of St. Lawrence river at mouth of the Saguenay on its left bank, 117 m. NE of Quebec; pop. 1064; popular summer resort. An Indian village in time of Jacques Cartier 1534–42; trading station for furs and fish; settlement made 1600, oldest in Canada.

Ta·dzhik' Soviet Socialist Republic (tä-jĭk'; -jēk') *or* **Ta·dzhik'i·stan'** (tä-jĭk'ĭ-stän'; -stän'; tä-jē'kĭ-); *also* **Ta·jik' S.S.R.** *or* **Ta·jik'i·stan'.** Constituent republic of the Union of Soviet Socialist Republics, Central Asia; 55,545 sq. m.; pop. 1,485,091, (1941 est.) 1,560,540; * Stalinabad. Bounded on N by Uzbek and Kirgiz S.S. Republics, on E by Sinkiang, on S by Afghanistan, and on W by Uzbek S.S.R. Very mountainous region, its E part (coextensive with Gorno-Badakhshan Autonomous Region) containing the Pamirs (*q.v.*) and Trans Alai mountain systems; highest point Stalin (formerly Garmo) Peak 24,590 ft., highest point in the U.S.S.R.; W part also mountainous, marked by several valleys of N tributaries of the Amu Darya, which forms the S boundary with Afghanistan. Has no railroad except E end of that from Bukhara to Stalinabad; has great mineral wealth, as yet undeveloped. Predominant ethnic strain Iranian; chief nationalities Tadzhik 78%, Uzbek 18%; illiteracy high. Chief occupations farming, stock raising; exports grain, wool, fruit; has some local industry. Chief towns Stalinabad, Khorog, Leninabad, Garm. Acquired as part of Russian Turkistan 1895; made part of the R.S.F.S.R. 1924 and became a constituent republic 1929.

Taedong. River, Korea: see DAIDO.

Taegu. See TAIKYU.

Taejon. See TAIDEN.

Taenarum. See Cape MATAPAN.

Ta·eng'a (tä-ĕng'ä). Island in E cen. part of Tuamotu Archipelago, French Polynesia, S Pacific Ocean.

Ta·fa'hi (tä-fä'hē); *formerly* **Bos·caw'en** (bŏs-kô'ĕn; -kô'ĭn). Island 7 sq. m. in the N part of Tonga Is., SW cen. Pacific Ocean, ab. 125 m. E of Niuafoo and 6 m. from Niuatobutabu (*q.v.*).

Ta'fel·berg (tä'fĕl-bĕrK). **1** Name of two hills on Curaçao I., Neth. West Indies: (1) in NW part of the island, 754 ft.; (2) in SE part, 636 ft., a source of calcium phosphate.

2 Plateau 3300 ft., N Surinam; 65 sq. m.

Taff (tăf). River ab. 40 m. long, SE Wales; flows SE through Glamorganshire into Bristol Channel at Cardiff.

Ta'fi·lelt' (tä'fē-lĕlt') *or* **Ta'fi·lalt'** (-lält') *or* **Ta'fi·let'** (tä fē-lĕt'). Oasis in SE Morocco; ab. 533 sq. m.; pop. ab. 100,000; chief town Bou-Am (Abuam); celebrated for its dates.

Taf'na (täf'nȧ). Unnavigable river in NW Algeria, N Africa, flowing N into Mediterranean Sea.

Taft (tăft). **1** City, Kern co., S California, 28 m. SW of Bakersfield; pop. 3822; oil fields.

2 City, San Patricio co., S Texas, 15 m. N of Corpus Christi; pop. 3463; in agricultural section.

3 (*native* täft) Town, Yezd prov., cen. Iran, 15 m. SW of Yezd; pop. ab. 7000.

Taf·tan', Kuh–i– (kōō'hē-täf-tän'). Volcano 13,261 ft. near Baluchistan border, SE Iran, 65 m. S of Zahidan.

Taft'ville (tăft'vĭl). Subdivision (est. pop. 3598) of town of NORWICH, Connecticut.

Ta·fu'a, Mount (tȧ-fōō'ȧ). Peak 2194 ft. of volcanic origin on W Upolu I., Western Samoa, SW cen. Pacific.

Ta'gan·rog (täg'ȧn-rŏg; *Russ.* tȧ-gȧn-rôk'). City, SW Rostov Region, Soviet Russia, Europe, on N shore of Gulf of Taganrog 45 m. W of Rostov; pop. 188,808; has only a fair harbor but has been large grain export center; still exports and imports many items and excels especially in metal manufacture (instruments, machinery, etc.); on railroad bet. Rostov and E Ukraine; has large fishing interests. Pisan colony founded on its site by 13th cent. but destroyed by Mongols; settled later by Turks; annexed to Russia 1769; bombarded 1855 by Allies in

Crimean War; in World War II held through most of 1941–43 by Germans, but recaptured by Russians Aug. 30, 1943.

Taganrog, Gulf of. Northeast arm of the Sea of Azov, S Soviet Russia, Europe; receives the Don river.

Tagaste. See SOUK-AHRAS.

Ta′gay·tay′, City of (tä′gī·tī′). Chartered city on S border of Cavite prov., Luzon, Phil. Is.; 25 sq. m.; pop. 1657; comprises **Tagaytay Ridge,** a mountain range, highest ab. 2000 ft., running E and W along N Batangas boundary NW of Lake Taal.

Tag′bi·la′ran (täg′bĕ·lä′rän). Town, * of Bohol prov. Phil. Is., in SW part on narrow strait opp. Panglao I.; pop. 15,617; has shallow harbor.

Ta·gi′nae (tȧ·jī′nē). Ancient village in the Apennines, cen. Italy, near modern Gubbio; Totila, Gothic king, defeated and killed here 552 by the Byzantine general Narses.

Tag′ish Lake (tăg′ĭsh). Lake 139 sq. m. across boundary of S Yukon Territory and N Brit. Columbia, Canada, W of Atlin Lake; discharges into Lewes river.

Ta·giu′ra (tä·jōō′rä). Seaport oasis in NW Libya, N Africa, E of Tripoli.

Ta′glia·coz′zo (täl′yä·kôt′tsô). Commune, Aquila prov., Abruzzi e Molise, cen. Italy, 21 m. SSW of Aquila; pop. 10,327; 13th-cent. Gothic church, 14th-cent. castle; scene of battle Aug. 1268 in which Conradin was defeated by Charles I of Anjou.

Ta′glia·men′to (täl′yä·mān′tô). River 106 m. long in N Italy; flows S from the Carnic Alps into the head of the Gulf of Venice.

Taglio di Porto Viro. See PORTO VIRO.

Ta·go′ (tä·gō′). Municipality in cen. part of Pacific coast of Surigao prov., Mindanao, Phil. Is., ab. 70 m. SE of Surigao; pop. 15,271.

Ta·go′lo Point (tä·gō′lô). North point of Zamboanga prov., Mindanao, Phil. Is., just NW of Dapitan; extends into W end of Mindanao Sea.

Ta′gu·bud′, Mount (tä′gōō·bōōd′). Mountain 7615 ft. in SE Davao prov., Mindanao, Phil. Is., ab. 45 m. ENE of City of Davao; just to the S is source of Agusan river.

Ta′gu·din′ (tä′gōō·dēn′). Municipality, S Ilocos Sur prov., Luzon, Phil. Is., on coast highway 43 m. S of Vigan and on N bank of Amburayan river; pop. 13,115. Formerly in Amburayan subprov. of Mountain Province and its capital; relocated in Ilocos Sur in 1920.

Ta′gu·la (tä′gōō·lä) or **Sud–Est** (sü′-dĕst′). Island ab. 50 m. long and 6 to 15 m. wide in S Louisiade Archipelago, Territory of Papua, off SE point of New Guinea, 50 m. SE of Misima I.; highest point 2645 ft.; very rich in gold-bearing soil.

Ta′gum (tä′gōōm). Town (municipal district), cen. Davao prov., Mindanao, Phil. Is., at head of Davao Gulf 27 m. NE of City of Davao; pop. 19,808.

Ta′gus (tä′gŭs); *Span.* **Ta′jo** (tä′hô); *Port.* **Te′jo** (tā′-zhō). River 566 m. long in Spain and Portugal, longest river in Iberian Penin.; rises in E cen. Spain ab. 80 m. E of Madrid, flows W across cen. Spain to Portuguese border; continues W forming a section (ab. 25 m.) of Spanish-Portuguese boundary, then turns SW and empties into Atlantic Ocean at Lisbon; ab. 10 m. above Lisbon expands into a lagoon ab. 7 m. wide which narrows at Lisbon to a channel ab. 2 m. wide and 8 m. long, partly blocked by a sand bar; navigable ab. 100 m. (as far as Abrantes).

Ta·ha′a (tä·hä′ä) or **Ta·ha′o** (-ō). One of the Leeward Is. group of the Society Is., French Polynesia, S Pacific Ocean, just N of Raiatéa; pop. (with Raiatéa) ab. 4000.

Ta′han, Gu′nong (gōō′nông tä′hän). Mountain (*gunong*) 7185 ft. in N Pahang state on Kelantan boundary, Federation of Malaya, S Malay Penin.; highest peak in the peninsula.

Tah′cheng′ (tä′chŭng′); *formerly* **Chu′gu′chak′** (chōō′gōō′chäk′). Town, * of Chuguchak dist., N

Sinkiang, W China; on W frontier on border of Kazakh S.S.R., Soviet Central Asia, and on caravan and motor highway from Urumchi NW to Ayaguz.

Ta′hei′ho′ (dä′hä′hŭ′); *Jap. official name* **Hei′ho′** (hä′hŭ′). Town, NE Heilungkiang prov., N Manchuria, on the Amur river below Blagoveshchensk and 12 m. N of Aigun; pop. 11,791; * of former Heiho prov., N Manchukuo. Captured by Russians Aug. 10, 1945 at the end of World War II.

Tahent, Djebel. See HILL 609.

Ta·hi′ti (tȧ·hē′tē); *formerly* **O′ta·hei′te** (ō′tȧ·hē′tĕ; -hä′-); *Fr.* **Ta·ï′ti′** (tȧ′ē′tē′). Island of E group (Windward Is.) of the Society Is., French Polynesia, S Pacific Ocean; lat. 17°30′S, long. 149°30′W; 402 sq. m.; pop. (1941) 23,133; * Papeete. The largest and most important of the French islands of the S Pacific; the main part (Tahiti-nui) is nearly circular and very mountainous with several high peaks (highest Orohena, in the center, 7339 ft.) and fertile but narrow coastal strip; to the SE connected by narrow isthmus with broad peninsula (Tahiti-iti). All villages are on the coast. Political as well as commercial center of French Polynesia; in 1940 joined the Free French movement.

Tahlab. See TALAB.

Tah′le·quah (täl′ĕ·kwô). City, ⊗ of Cherokee co., E Oklahoma, 26 m. ENE of Muskogee; pop. 5840; became permanent capital of Cherokee Nation 1839; machine shops; cotton ginning, food canning, agriculture. Northeastern State College (founded 1846 as Cherokee National Female Seminary; now coed.).

Ta′hoe, Lake (tä′hō). Lake about 22 m. long by 10 m. wide on N cen. California-Nevada boundary; elevation 6225 ft.; greatest depth over 1500 ft.; outlet Truckee river; tourist resort.

Ta′hoe·lan′dang or **Ta·hu·lan′dang** (tä′hōō·län′-däng). One of the main islands of the Sangihe Is. (*q.v.*).

Ta·hoe′na or **Ta·hu′na** (tȧ·hōō′nȧ). Chief town on Sangihe I. (see SANGIHE ISLANDS).

Ta·ho′ka (tȧ·hō′kȧ). City, ⊗ of Lynn co., NW Texas, 32 m. S of Lubbock; pop. 3012; ships cotton, cattle, grain.

Tahpanhes. See DAPHNAE.

Tah′ta (tä′tȧ; *Arab.* tä′h′·tô). Town, Girga prov., cen. Upper Egypt, on the Nile river SSE of Asyût; pop. ab. 21,000.

Ta′hua (tä′wä). Peak 17,457 ft. in W Bolivia, S of Lake Poopó.

Ta·hua′ta (tȧ·wä′tȧ), *also* **Ta·ua′ta.** One of the Marquesas Is., French Polynesia, S Pacific Ocean, ab. 3 m. S of Hiva Oa.

Tahura. See KAULA.

Ta′hure′ (tȧ·ür′). Village and hill in Marne dept., NE France, 30 m. ESE of Reims; battles Oct. 7, 1915, when taken by the Germans, and Sept. 25, 1918 when retaken by Allies.

Tai (tī) or **Tai′ Shan′** (tī′ shän′). A sacred mountain of China, 5048 ft. high, in W Shantung prov., 32 m. S of Tsinan (45 m. by way of Taian, the usual point of approach); from Taian to top 15 m., final ascent by 6300 stone steps. Many temples on the road and on the top, from which can be seen one of the finest views in China. Visited annually by many pilgrims, sometimes ascended by as many as 10,000 in one day; has been considered as sacred for several thousand years.

Tai′an′ (tī′än′). Town, W cen. Shantung prov., NE China, on railroad 37 m. S of Tsinan; pop. ab. 90,000; famous as starting point of ascent of Tai mountain; a very old place dating back traditionally to an emperor of the 23d cent. B.C. Has several large and interesting temples, visited by throngs of Tai pilgrims.

Tai·chung (tī·chōōng); *Jap.* **Tai·chu** (tī·chōō); *formerly* **Tai·wan** (tī·wän). City, W cen. Formosa, on railroad along W coast; pop. 207,000.

Tai·den (tī·dĕn); *now* **Tae·jon** (tă·jôn). City, * of South Chusei prov., W Korea, on railroad 70 m. NW of

Taegu; pop. 36,379; trades chiefly in fish, petroleum and cereals; has grown rapidly in recent years.

Tai'erh'chwang' (tī'ûr'jwäng'). Village, S Shantung prov., NE China, on Grand Canal S of Lini; Chinese victory over Japanese Mar.–Apr. 1938.

Tai'e·ri (tī'ě·rē). River 125 m. long, SE South I., New Zealand; flows SE into Pacific Ocean near Dunedin.

Ta'if (tä'ïf). Town, S Hejaz, W Arabia, ab. 40 m. SE of Mecca; pop. ab. 8000; summer ✻ of Hejaz and resort of Mecca citizens; in mountains at 6000 ft. altitude; produces great variety of fruits; famous for its roses. Important town in time of Mohammed; resisted him 630 but finally capitulated; taken by Arabs from the Turks 1916 and captured by ibn-Saud 1924.

Tai·ha·ku (tī·hä·kōō). Peak 8111 ft., South Kankyo prov., N Korea.

Tai'heng' Shan (tī'hěng' shän'). Mountain range on boundary bet. N Honan prov. and SE Shansi prov., NE China, N of the Hwang Ho.

Tai·ho·ku (tī·hŏ·kōō); *now* **Tai'pei'** *or* **Tai'peh'** (tī'bā'). Inland city, ✻ of Formosa (Taiwan), at N end of island; pop. 759,200; formed by amalgamation of three independent cities; established as capital by Japanese and built up as a modern city with fine administration buildings and parks; a center of tea, camphor, tobacco, and lumber industries.

Taih'pa Ga (tī'pä gä'). Village on the Chindwin river, in Hukawng valley, N Burma, on the Stilwell Road; taken by Americans Feb. 1, 1944.

Tai Hu (tī' hōō'). Literally "Great lake," a lake (*hu*) 44 m. long in Kiangsu and Chekiang provs., E China; Hwang Pu is one of its outlets. Large city of Wuhsien is near its E shore.

Tai·kyu (tī·kyōō); *now* **Tae·gu** (tä·gōō). Walled city, ✻ of North Keisho prov., SE Korea, 60 m. N of Fusan; pop. (1960) 698,277; chief city of the two Keisho provs.; commercial center with modern conveniences; market for silk industry. Important historically as far back as 8th cent. A.D.

Tai'ma (tī'má; -mǎ; tä'-); *Bib.* **Te'ma** (tē'má). Oasis and ancient commercial town in NW Nejd, Arabia.

Tai·myr' National District (tī·mïr'; tī'mïr). A national district in N cen. Siberia, Soviet Russia, Asia, approximately coextensive with the Taimyr Penin.; 286,643 sq. m.; pop. (1926) 8000; ✻ Dudinka; geographically in Krasnoyarsk Territory. Entirely within the Arctic Circle; has rich mineral deposits, esp. nickel, copper, platinum, and gold. Inhabitants are Mongol tribes.

Tai·myr', *or* **Tai·mir', Peninsula** (tī·mïr'; tī'mïr). Large peninsula, NW Siberia, Soviet Russia, Asia, wholly within the Taimyr National District bet. the Yenisei and Khatanga rivers; includes Cape Chelyuskin, the northernmost point of Asia, 77°35'N, 105°E; crossed in cen. part by **Taimyr River** 400 m. long, flowing E and N through the large, irregular-shaped **Taimyr Lake** to **Taimyr Bay**, in 100°E. To the W of the bay is **Taimyr Island**.

Tai·nan (tī·nän). City on SW coast of Formosa I.; pop. (1957) 229,000; former treaty port, with Ampin as its port. One of oldest cities in the island, long a political and cultural center, but with establishment of Taihoku as capital, its supremacy is now commercial only. Occupied by Dutch in 17th cent.; ruins of their old fort remain.

Taínaron. See Cape MATAPAN.

Ta'i·o·ha'e *or* **Ta'i–o–ha'e** (tä'ē·ô·hä'å; tī'ô·hī'). Chief village on S shore of Nuku Hiva I., Marquesas Is., S Pacific Ocean; huge prehistoric stone platforms of unknown origin nearby.

Tai'pa (tī'pá). See MACAO colony.

Taipeh, Taipei. See TAIHOKU.

Taipi. See TYPEE.

Tai'ping' (tī'pïng'). 1 *in Burma called* **Tay'ing'** (tī'-ïng'). River ab. 170 m. long in China and Upper Burma;

flows SW out of Yunnan prov., crosses Burmese border and empties into Irrawaddy river at Bhamo.

2 City, ✻ of Perak state, Federation of Malaya, in NW part on railroad 50 m. SE of George Town (Penang); pop. 30,070, (1937 est.) 38,719.

Tai'po' (tī'pō'). Town, ✻ of Northern District of New Territories, Hong Kong colony, China, at head of inlet of Mirs Bay on railroad to Canton.

Tai·ra (tī·rä). Town and river port, Fukushima prefecture, Honshu, Japan, 75 m. NE of Nikko, near Pacific coast; pop. 28,474.

Tai Shan. See TAI.

Tai·shet' (tī·shět'). Town, W Irkutsk Region, Soviet Russia, Asia, near Krasnoyarsk Territory boundary; on Trans-Siberian R.R., starting point of railroad (the Baikal-Amur-Magistral R.R.), now under construction, to the N of Lake Baikal through Kirensk, Bodaibo, and Ust Nyukzha to Komsomolsk (*q.v.*).

Tai·ta'o, Cape (tī·tä'ô). Cape extending into Pacific Ocean on NW tip of Taitao Penin., SW Chile.

Taitao Peninsula. Peninsula extending into Pacific Ocean from the SW coast of Chile, S of Chonos Archipelago and N of the Gulf of Peñas.

Taïti. See TAHITI.

Tai·to (tī·tō); *now* **Tai·tung** (-tōōng). Coastal town, SE Formosa.

Tai'vu Point (tī'vōō). Cape on NE coast of Guadalcanal I. in the Solomon Is. in the W Pacific Ocean; ab. 40 m. E of Cape Esperance; marks E limit of American invasion coast 1942.

Taiwan. 1 Island. See FORMOSA.

2 City on Formosa. See TAICHU.

Taiwan Strait. See FORMOSA STRAIT.

Tai'ya Inlet (tī'yá). Upper arm, ab. 15 m. long, of Chilkoot Inlet, SE Alaska. See LYNN CANAL.

Taiyuan. See YANGKU.

Ta·'izz' (tä·ïz'). Town in highlands of S Yemen, SW Arabia, 32 m. E of Mocha; pop. ab. 4000; formerly a large city and center of fertile district.

Tajik, Tajikistan. See TADZHIK, TADZHIKISTAN.

Tajo. See TAGUS.

Ta'ju·mul'co (tä'hōō·mōōl'kô) *or* **Ta'ja·mul'co** (tä'-hä-). Volcanic mountain 13,816 ft. in W Guatemala; highest point in Central America.

Ta·ju'na (tä·hōō'nä). River ab. 100 m. long, cen. Spain; flows SW through Guadalajara prov. and on into Jarama river ab. 7 m. NE of Aranjuez.

Tajura; Tajura, Gulf of. See TADJOURA and Gulf of TADJOURA.

Tak (täk). Town, NW Thailand, on Ping river opp. Rahaeng; administrative center.

Ta·ka·chi·ho·da·ke (tä·kä·chě·hŏ·dä·kě). See KIRISHIMA.

Ta·ka·da (tä·kä·dä) *or* **Ta·ka·ta** (tä·kä·tä). City, Niigata prefecture, NW Honshu, Japan, 65 m. ENE of Toyama; pop. (1945) 36,108.

Ta·ka·ha·ma (tä·kä·hä·mä). Town, Ehime prefecture, on NW coast of Shikoku I., Japan; port of Matsuyama.

Ta·ka·ma·tsu (tä·kä·mä·tsōō). City, ✻ of Kagawa prefecture, NE Shikoku I., Japan; pop. (1945) 72,656; has fine harbor and is one of most important ports of call on Inland Sea; noted for its beautiful gardens.

Ta·ka·na·be (tä·kä·nä·bě). Town, Miyazaki prefecture, SE coast of Kyushu I., Japan; pop. (1945) 16,566.

Ta·ka·o (tä·kä·ô) *or* **Ta'kow** (tä'kou); *now* **Kao'-hsiung'** (gou'shï·ōŏng'). City, SW coast of Formosa; pop. 275,000; treaty port and rail center; exports rice and sugar.

Ta·ka·o·ka (tä·kä·ô·kä). City, Toyama prefecture, Honshu, Japan, 15 m. W of Toyama; pop. (1945) 121,574; center of rice trade; produces lacquer ware and for more than two centuries has been a leader in the bronze-ware industry, producing sword fittings, pipes, and Buddhist paraphernalia, excelling esp. in metal inlaying.

Ta'ka·pu'na (tä'kȧ·pōō'nȧ). Borough, Auckland provincial dist., N North I., New Zealand, N suburb of Auckland; pop. 6910.

Ta·ka·sa·ki (tä·kä·sä·kĕ). Industrial city, Gumma prefecture, cen. Honshu, Japan, 10 m. SW of Maebashi; pop. (1945) 79,712; important market in the silk trade.

Takata. See TAKADA.

Ta·kaw' (tȧ·kô'). Town, Kengtung state, E cen. Southern Shan States, Burma, on right bank of Salween; highway from towns of cen. Burma to Kengtung and Thailand crosses Salween here.

Ta Khingan Shan. = *Great Khingan Mountains:* see KHINGAN.

Ta'khi·no', Lake (tä'kĕ·nô'). = Lake AKHINOU.

Takht–i–Su·lai·man' (täkt'ē·sōō·lĭ·män')—literally "throne of Solomon." **1** Twin peaks at N end of the Sulaiman Range, cen. West Pakistan; the higher peak, sometimes known as **Kai'sar·garh'** (kī'sēr·gär'), 11,289 ft.

2 See OSH, Kirgiz S.S.R., Soviet Central Asia.

Tak'ka·kaw (tăk'ȧ·kô). Waterfall 1200 ft., Yoho National Park, SE Brit. Columbia, Canada; source is glacier in Rocky Mts.; its waters flow into Yoho river.

Tak·ka·ze (tû·kû·zā). The upper course of the Bahr Setit in Ethiopia; headstream of the Atbara.

Ta'kla Ma·kan' (tä'klä mä·kän'). Desert, forming greater part of Tarim basin, depression in cen. Sinkiang, W China, bet. Tien Shan on N and Kunlun Mts. on S; ab. 38° to 41'N and 78° to 88°E, ab. 600 m. across; desert marked by shifting sand dunes; soil is fertile, with irrigation capable of producing fine crops.

Ta·ko'ma Park (tȧ·kō'mȧ). City, Montgomery and Prince Georges cos., cen. Maryland, 6 m. N of Washington; pop. 16,799; Columbia Union College (1904; coed.; Seventh-Day Adventist).

Ta·ko·ra'di (tä'kŏ·rä'dĕ). Seaport, SW Ghana, W Africa, ab. 113 m. WSW of Accra; pop. ab. 5000; railroad terminus of line via Sekondi (3 m. to E) to Kumasi; has fine harbor.

Takow. See TAKAO.

Ta'ku' (tä'kōō'; *Chin.* dä'gōō'). Town, E Hopei prov., NE China, on right bank of mouth of Hai river 37 m. E of Tientsin; pop. ab. 7000; formerly site of forts guarding approach to Tientsin which were several times attacked by foreign forces, esp. in 1860 and in 1900 in the Boxer Rebellion, and finally demolished by terms of treaty of 1902. See TANGKU.

Ta'ku·tú' (tä'kōō·tōō'); *Port.* **Ta'cu·tú'** (tȧ'kōō·tōō'). River 220 m. long, British Guiana and N Brazil; flows N, forming a section of the boundary bet. SW British Guiana and Brazil, curves W into N Brazil and S to unite with the Uraricoera river and form the Rio Branco. Cf. IRENG.

Ta'la (tä'lä). Town, Jalisco state, W cen. Mexico, W of Guadalajara; pop. 5460.

Ta·lab' *or* **Tah·lab'** (tȧ·läb'). River ab. 175 m. long, SE Iran; rises near Zahidan and flows SE to the border, then along the Iran-Pakistan boundary to Hamun-i-Mashkel.

Talabriga. 1 See AVEIRO seaport, Portugal.

2 See TALAVERA DE LA REINA commune, Spain.

Ta'la·gan'te (tä'lä·gän'tȧ). Town, Santiago prov., cen. Chile, SW of Santiago; pop. 5105.

Ta·la'kag (tä·lä'käg). Municipality, NW Bukidnon prov., Mindanao, Phil. Is.; pop. 8126.

Talamanca, Cordillera de. See CORDILLERA DE TALAMANCA.

Ta·la'na Hill (tȧ·lä'nȧ). See DUNDEE town, Natal, E Republic of South Africa.

Ta'lang (tä'läng). Volcanic peak 8520 ft. in Barisan Mts., W Sumatra, Indonesia; in the Padang Highlands just E of Padang.

Ta·la'ra (tä·lä'rä). Seaport, Piura dept., NW Peru, ab. 40 m. N of Paita and 610 m. NW of Lima; oil refinery; export center for petroleum industry.

Ta'la·se'a (tä'lä·sā'ä). Settlement on E side of Willaumez Penin. on N coast of New Britain, Bismarck Archipelago, W Pacific Ocean; has fine harbor and active trade in copra. Occupied by U.S. Marines Mar. 6, 1944.

Ta·lass' (tŭ·làs'). Subdivision of Kirgiz S.S.R., Soviet Central Asia, in NW part NE of Tashkent.

Talat. See MAHA SARAKHAM.

Ta·la'ta Koh (tä·lä'tȧ kō'). See SCHILDPAD ISLANDS.

Ta'laud (tä'lout), *or* **Ta'laur** (tä'lour), **Islands.** Island group belonging to Indonesia, in the Pacific Ocean NE of Celebes I. and SE of the island of Mindanao, Phil. Is., in 4°15'N; 494 sq. m.; pop. 23,825; chief town Beo. Comprises the main large island of Karakelong, two small islands S of it (Salebabu and Kaburuang), and the group of islets to the NE, Nenusa Is. Undeveloped; copra is only important product. First came under Dutch 1677.

Ta'la·ve'ra (tä'lä·vä'rä). Municipality, cen. Nueva Ecija prov., Luzon, Phil. Is., 8 m. N of Cabanatuan; pop. 20,442.

Talavera de la Rei'na (tħä lä rrĕ'ĕ·nä); *anc.* **Tal'a·bri'ga** (tăl'ȧ·brī'gȧ). Commune, Toledo prov., cen. Spain, on Tagus river 41 m. WNW of Toledo; pop. 18,631; manufactures textiles, leather, pottery, jewelry, brandies, chocolates, flour, corks, brick and tile, candles, soap; 15th-cent. bridge. Captured by Romans under Quintus Fulvius Flaccus; conquered by Arabs under Tariq; reconquered by Alfonso VI 1082; scene of famous defeat of French under Joseph Bonaparte by Wellington and Cuesta 1809.

Ta·la'yan (tä·lä'yän). Municipal district and village, Cotabato prov., Mindanao, Phil. Is., 25 m. SE of Cotabato.

Tal'bot (tôl'bŭt; tôl'-). Name of counties in two states of the U.S. See *Tables* at GEORGIA and MARYLAND.

Talbot, Cape. Point on N coast of Western Australia, a few miles W of Cape Londonderry.

Tal'bot Island (tăl'bŭt). Island in Atlantic Ocean off coast of Duval co., NE Florida, N of mouth of St. Johns river.

Tal'bot·ton (tôl'bŭt·'n; tôl'-). City, ⊗ of Talbot co., W Georgia; pop. 1163.

Tal'ca (täl'kä). **1** Province of Chile. See *Table* at CHILE.

2 City, its *, cen. Chile, 155 m. S of Santiago on the Claro river; pop. 50,464; an important trade and communications center, and an old town (founded 1692) with cultural achievement; one of the largest manufacturing cities in Chile.

Tal'ca·hua'no (täl'kä·wä'nŏ). Port in Concepción prov., S cen. Chile, 9 m. NW of Concepción; pop. 35,774; good anchorage; naval base.

Tal'cher (täl'chĕr). Former Indian state, E Eastern States, NE India; 388 sq. m.; pop. (1941) 86,432; * Talcher (55 m. NW of Cuttack); area now in Orissa state.

Tal'dy–Kur·gan' (täl'dĭ·kŏŏr·gȧn'). Town, * of Taldy-Kurgan Region, E Kazakh S.S.R., SE of Lake Balkhash and ab. 140 m. NE of Alma Ata.

Taldy–Kurgan Region. Subdivision of Kazakh S.S.R., Soviet Central Asia, bet. Semipalatinsk Region on N and Alma Ata Region on S and bordering on E on Sinkiang, China.

Ta'lence' (tȧ'läns'). Commune, Gironde dept., SW France, SW suburb of Bordeaux; pop. (1931) 18,944; produces wine.

Tale Sap. See THALE LUANG.

Ta'li' (dä'lē'). **1** *formerly* **Tung'chow'** (tōōng'jō'). Town, E Shensi prov., NE cen. China, 60 m. ENE of Sian; pop. ab. 50,000.

2 Commercial city, W cen. Yunnan prov., S China, on W shore of Erh Hai (Tali Lake) 180 m. W of Kunming; pop. ab. 26,000; market for Chinese, Mongols, and Tibetans, picturesquely located at 6900 ft. above sea level bet. lake and high mountains; on branch of Burma Road 10 m. N of it and most important point bet. Lashio

and Kunming; junction point for routes N to Likiang and Paan. An old city famous for its marble.

Ta′li·a′boe (tä′lĕ·ä′bōō) *or* **Ta′li·a′bu.** Largest of the Sula Is., W Moluccas, E of Celebes I., Indonesia; ab. 68 m. long by 26 m. at its greatest width; highest point 4331 ft.; pop. 3606.

Tal′ia·ferro (tŏl′ĭ·vēr). County in Georgia. See *Table* at GEORGIA.

Ta′li·bon′ (tä′lĕ·bôn′). Municipality on N coast of Bohol I., Phil. Is., 48 m. NE of Tagbilaran; pop. 26,077.

Talien, Talienwan. See DAIREN.

Tal′i·hi′na (tăl′ĭ·hē′nȧ). Town, Le Flore co., E Oklahoma, 34 m. SW of Poteau; pop. 1048; health and sports resort.

Ta′li·ko′ta (tä′lĭ·kō′tȧ) *or* **Ta′li·kot** (tä′lĭ·kōt). Town ab. 40 m. SE of Bijapur, N Mysore state, W Indian Union. Scene in 1565 of great battle in which Mohammedan chieftains of the Deccan united in overthrowing the Hindu kingdom of Vijayanagar.

Tali Lake. See ERH HAI.

Ta·lim′ Island (tä·lēm′). Island in N cen. Laguna de Bay, cen. Luzon, Phil. Is.; 10 m. long, ab. 11 sq. m.; belongs to Rizal prov.; has valuable stone quarries. Its S point is **Talim Point,** 14°18′N.

Ta·li′say (tä·lē′sī). **1** Municipality on E coast of Cebu I., Phil. Is., at N end of Bohol Strait 6 m. SW of City of Cebu; pop. 20,077.
2 Municipality, NW Negros Occidental, Negros, Phil. Is., on Guimaras Strait 5 m. N of City of Bacolod; pop. 40,547.

Ta′li·sa′yan (tä′lĕ·sä′yän). Municipality, Misamis Oriental prov., Mindanao, Phil. Is., on S shore of Mindanao Sea nearly opp. Camiguin I.; pop. 17,476; on W side of entrance to Gingoog Bay.

Tal′la·de′ga (tăl′ȧ·dē′gȧ). **1** County in Alabama. See *Table* at ALABAMA.
2 City, its ⊗, E cen. Alabama, 44 m. E of Birmingham; pop. 17,742; trade center, esp. for dairy products, cotton, grain; manufactures cotton textiles, cottonseed oil, pipe fittings; iron mines, marble and limestone quarries. Talladega Coll. (founded 1867, chartered 1869; coed.). Battle of Talledega Nov. 9, 1813 in which Andrew Jackson defeated band of Creek Indians.

Tal′la·has′see (tăl′ȧ·hăs′ē). City, ⊗ of Leon co., N Florida, and ✳ of Florida, 25 m. N of Apalachee Bay; pop. 48,174; lumber mills and tobacco-packing plants; old colonial mansions and fine modern government buildings. Florida State University (1857; coed.); Florida Agricultural and Mechanical University (1887; coed.). Made capital of Florida territory 1823; scene of adoption of the ordinance of secession 1861.

Tal′la·hatch′ie (tăl′ȧ·hăch′ē). **1** River 301 m. long, N Mississippi; rises in Tippah co., flows SW to unite with Yalobusha river in Leflore co. and form the Yazoo river; navigable for ab. 100 m.
2 County in Mississippi. See *Table* at MISSISSIPPI.

Tal′la·poo′sa (tăl′ȧ·pōō′sȧ). **1** Navigable river 268 m. long, Alabama; rises in Paulding co., NW Georgia, flows SW across Alabama border E of Heflin, S and then W to join the Coosa river in cen. Alabama and form the Alabama river.
2 County in Alabama. See *Table* at ALABAMA.
3 City, Haralson co., W Georgia, 35 m. S of Rome; pop. 2744; incorporated 1860; gold, silver, and copper deposits nearby; lithia spring.

Tal′ley Mountain (tăl′ĭ). Elevation 3800 ft. in S Brewster co., W Texas.

Tal′lin *or* **Tal′linn** (tăl′ĭn; *Estonian* täl′lĭn); *Russ.* **Tal′lin** (täl′yĭn), *formerly* **Re′vel** (rā′vĕl; *Russ.* ryä′-vyĭl·y′); *Ger.* **Re′val** (rā′väl). Seaport city, ✳ of Estonia and of Harju prov., N Estonia, on the Gulf of Finland opp. Helsinki and ab. 200 m. W of Leningrad; pop. (1937) 145,755; has good harbor, large shipbuilding yards, and airport; manufactures paper, furniture, cellulose, textiles, dairy products; a picturesque city with many medieval structures—a citadel, two cathedrals, an old town hall, and many churches; also has many modern buildings. First visited by Danes 1093 and in 1219 town founded by them; held temporarily 1228–37 by Livonian Knights; member of Hanseatic League 1284. Sold by Danes to Teutonic Order 1346; under Swedish domination 1561, and granted a measure of autonomy 1675; captured by Peter the Great of Russia 1710 who made it a port for his Baltic fleet. Occupied by German army 1918, by Russians in 1940, and again by Germans in Aug. 1941 in World War II; retaken by Russians Sept. 22, 1944.

Tall′madge (tăl′mĭj). City, Summit co., NE Ohio, 4 m. E of Akron; pop. 10,246.

Tal·lu′lah (tȧ·lōō′lȧ). Village, ⊗ of Madison parish, NE Louisiana, 57 m. E of Monroe; pop. 9413; in cotton-growing section; cottonseed-oil mills.

Ta·lo′ga (tȧ·lō′gȧ). Town, ⊗ of Dewey co., W Oklahoma; pop. 322.

Tal′si (täl′sĭ). Administrative district, NE Kurzeme dist., W Latvia; 840 sq. m.

Tal·tal′ (täl·täl′). Seaport, Antofagasta prov., N Chile; pop. 5659; exports nitrates and ores.

Taluti Bay. See TELOETI BAY.

Ta′ma (tä′mȧ). **1** County in Iowa. See *Table* at IOWA.
2 City, Tama co., E cen. Iowa; pop. 2925.

Ta′ma (tä′mä). Peak 13,126 ft. in N Colombia, 20 m. ESE of Cúcuta.

Ta·ma′le (tȧ·mä′lĕ). Town, ✳ of Northern Region, N Ghana, W Africa, formerly ✳ of Northern Territories protectorate of the Gold Coast, 270 m. N of Accra; pop. 12,941, (1937 est.) 18,591; in plain E of the Volta, connected by highway with Kumasi and with towns in N and W of the Northern Region; trade center for large region.

Tamalipta. See TAMLUK.

Tam′al·pa′is, Mount (tăm′ăl·pī′ăs). Peak 2606 ft. in Marin co., W California, NW of San Francisco and overlooking the Pacific Ocean and San Francisco Bay; scenic resort.

Ta·man′ (tŭ·män′). Peninsula (ab. 25 m. long) and cape, E side of Kerch Strait, W Krasnodar Territory, Soviet Russia, Europe; has oil wells. **Taman Lake,** ab. 4 m. wide, extends eastward ab. 20 m. in middle of peninsula.

Tam′an·ras′set (tăm′ăn·răs′ĕt). Wadi, S Algeria, N of the Adrar des Iforas.

Ta·ma′qua (tȧ·mä′kwȧ). Borough, Schuylkill co., E cen. Pennsylvania, 15 m. ENE of Pottsville; pop. 10,173; settled 1799; coal mining; manufactures flour, foundry and machine-shop products, explosives.

Ta′mar (tä′mēr). **1** River 60 m. long, SW England; rises in NW Devonshire, flows SSE, forming boundary bet. Devon and Cornwall, empties into the English Channel through Plymouth Sound.
2 Wide, navigable river ab. 40 m. long, N Tasmania, Australia, formed by confluence at Launceston of the North and South Esk rivers; flows N to Bass Strait at Port Dalrymple.
3 Ancient city. See PALMYRA.

Ta·ma′ra (tȧ·mä′rȧ). Largest island of the Los Is. (*q.v.*).

Tam′a·ri′da (tăm′ȧ·rē′dȧ). = TAMRIDAH.

Ta·ma·shi·ma (tä·mä·shĕ·mä). Port, SW Okayama prov., W Honshu, Japan, on N shore of Inland Sea; pop. (1945) 28,039.

Ta′ma·tave′ (tä′mä·täv′). Port, E coast of Madagascar; pop. (1936) 21,421; chief seaport of Madagascar; terminus of railroad from Tananarive.

Ta′mau·li′pas (tä′mou·lē′päs). State, E Mexico. See *Table* at MEXICO.

Ta·ma·zu′la de Gor·dia′no (tä′mä·sōō′lä thä gôr-thyä′nō). Town, Jalisco state, W cen. Mexico, S of Lake Chapala; pop. 5228.

Tam·bai·chi (täm·bī·chē). Town, Nara prefecture, W cen. Honshu, Japan, ab. 6 m. S of Nara; pop. (1945)

19,371; headquarters of a Shinto sect; scene of pilgrimages.

Tam′be·lan′ Islands (tăm′bȧ·län′). Group of 17 small islands of Indonesia, in the South China Sea bet. the S tip of Malay Penin. and W coast of Borneo; administratively a part of Riouw prov.

Tam′bo (täm′bō). 1 River ab. 150 m. long, S Peru; flows SW into Pacific Ocean SE of Mollendo.
2 See APURÍMAC river.

Tam′bo·pa′ta (täm′bō·pä′tä). River ab. 160 m. long, SE Peru; flows N into the Madre de Dios at Puerto Maldonado.

Tam′bo·ra (täm′bō·rä). Volcano 9354 ft. on the N coast of Sumbawa, Indonesia; had disastrous eruption in 1815 when it lost much of its top; was formerly ab. 13,000 ft. high.

Tam·bov′ (tŭm·bôf′). City, * of Tambov Region, in cen. part, cen. Soviet Russia, Europe, on unnavigable Tsna 260 m. SE of Moscow; pop. 121,285; railroad junction point; grain center, with elevator and flour mills; also has railroad shops, ironworks, distilleries, brickworks. Founded 1636 as a fort in defense of Moscow from Tatar and Kalmuck raids; became a central provincial town 1796.

Tambov Region. Region, cen. Soviet Russia, Europe; 12,468 sq. m.; pop. 1,882,139; * Tambov. A level blackearth region, with hills 450 to 800 ft. and valleys of the upper Tsna (a tributary of the Moksha) and in the S of the upper courses of Don tributaries. Its population, mainly Great Russian, are engaged esp. in grain production. Groups of Mordvinians make up part of the inhabitants. Chief towns Tambov, Michurinsk, Morshansk, and Kirsanov. Was a part of Moscow principality from an early date, but conflicts with Tatars kept colonization down until Russian authority was enforced under tsars toward end of 17th cent.; suffered 1917–20 during the time of the civil war; organized 1928 as a district of the Central Black Earth Area; in 1936 made a separate subdivision of the R.S.F.S.R. In World War II its W border approached, but not reached, by furthest advance of German armies 1941.

Tame (tām). 1 Small river in cen. England, flowing past the city of Birmingham into the Trent in Staffordshire.
2 River 18 m. long, Yorkshire, Lancashire, and Cheshire, NW England, flows SW to the Mersey at Stockport.

Tamesis or **Tamesa.** See THAMES.

Ta′met (tä′mĕt). Short river, dry at certain seasons, in N Tripolitania, W Libya, N Africa; flows N into Gulf of Sidra.

Tam′gué′ (tän′gā′). See FOUTA DJALLON.

Ta·mia′hua, Lake of (tä·myä′wä). Coastal lagoon ab. 60 m. long in N Veracruz state, Mexico; at S end has outlet to Gulf of Mexico.

Ta′mines′ (tȧ′mēn′). Commune, Namur prov., S Belgium; pop. 6285; manufactures glass, mirrors, etc.

Ta′mise′ (tȧ′mēz′). Manufacturing commune, East Flanders prov., NW cen. Belgium, on Schelde river; pop. 13,418.

Tam·luk′ (tȧm·lōōk′). Town, Burdwan division, West Bengal, NE Indian Union, ab. 30 m. SW of Calcutta. In ancient times, as **Ta′ma·lip′ta** (tä′mȧ·lĭp′tȧ), a seaport at the mouth of the Ganges from which the Chinese Buddhist pilgrims embarked; it is now 60 m. from the sea with fine temple; but most of its ancient remains are buried in the silt of the Hooghly.

Tam′ma·ny, Mount (tăm′ȧ·nĭ). Peak ab. 1480 ft. forming the New Jersey (E) side of Delaware Water Gap.

Tammerfors. See TAMPERE.

Tam′pa (tăm′pȧ). City, ⊗ of Hillsborough co., W cen. Florida penin., on NE end of Tampa Bay; pop. 274,970; tourist resort and fishing center; chief industry cigar making; exports fruit, lumber, and phosphate rock; MacDill Air Force Base. University of Tampa (1931). Site of Indian village visited by Narváez 1528 and by De Soto 1539; later a resort for pirates; American settle-

ment begun 1823 with establishment of Fort Brooke by U.S. government; incorporated 1855.

Tampa Bay. Inlet of Gulf of Mexico on W coast of Hillsborough co., W Florida penin.; the city of Tampa is at its NE end and St. Petersburg on W shore.

Tam′pe·re (täm′pĕ·rĕ); Swed. **Tam′mer·fors′** (tăm′ĕr·fôrs′; -fôsh′). City, * of Häme dept., SW Finland, on Lake Näsijärvi; pop. (1939 est.) 75,800; 2d largest city in Finland; hydroelectric power plant; textile and paper mills, iron foundries, locomotive works, shoe factories.

Tam·pi′co (täm·pē′kō; Span. täm·pē′kŏ). Seaport, S Tamaulipas state, E Mexico; pop. 81,312; chief commercial center in NE Mexico; located on the Pánuco river 7 m. from its mouth; petroleum refineries and storage tanks.

Tampico, Lake of. Lake ab. 200 sq. m. in N Veracruz state, Mexico, just S of Pánuco river and N of Lake Tamiahua.

Tam′pin (tăm′pĭn). Town, S Negri Sembilan state, Federation of Malaya, on border of Malacca; pop. 1744; railroad junction on main west coast line.

Tam·ri′dah (tăm·rē′dȧ); formerly **Ha′di·bu** (hä′dĭ·bōō). Chief town of Socotra I., Indian Ocean, S of Arabia; on NE coast.

Tamsui. See TANSUI.

Tam′worth (tăm′wûrth; -wẽrth). 1 Town, E New South Wales, SE Australia, 190 m. N of Sydney; pop. 9918; trade center of farming section; gold and diamonds found nearby.
2 Municipal borough, Staffordshire, W cen. England, at confluence of Tame and Anker rivers 15 m. NE of Birmingham; pop. 12,889; coal, fireclay; Tamworth swine originally bred here.

Ta′na (tä′nȧ). 1 River ab. 500 m. long, E Africa; rises in S cen. Kenya, flows in a curve NE, E, and S into Indian Ocean at Formosa Bay.
2 or **Tan′na** (tä′nȧ). Island 22 m. long by 12 m. wide, S New Hebrides, SW Pacific Ocean, ab. 25 m. S of Eromanga; pop. (native; 1938 est.) 6500; one of the most fertile and beautiful islands of the S Pacific. Chief white settlement Port Resolution on E coast; highest point 3200 ft. About 3 m. inland from Port Resolution is a low volcano, almost continually active. Main agricultural products coconuts, sugar, taro, yams.

Ta′na (tä′nä); Finn. **Te′no** (tĕ′nô). River ab. 200 m. long, NE Norway; flows N and NE, forming a section of boundary bet. Norway and Finland, and empties into Tana Fjord.

Ta′na (tä′nä) or **Tsa′na** (tsä′-), **Lake.** Lake in N Ethiopia, E Africa; 47 m. long and 44 m. wide; ab. 1100 sq. m.; source of the Blue Nile.

Tan′a·cross (tăn′ȧ·krôs), earlier **Tan′a·na Crossing** (tăn′ȧ·nô). Station on Alaska Highway and on Tanana river ab. 150 m. SE of Fairbanks, Alaska; junction with new cutoff from Richardson Highway; airport.

Ta′na Fjord (tä′nä). Inlet of Arctic Ocean on NE coast of Norway; receives the Tana river from the S.

Ta·na′ga (tȧ·nä′gȧ). Island, W Andreanof Is., Aleutians, SW Alaska, 178°W; has active volcano. **Tanaga Bay** is on W coast; **Tanaga Pass** separates it from small islands on W.

Tan′a·gra (tăn′ȧ·grȧ; tȧ·năg′rȧ). Ancient town in E Boeotia, E cen. Greece, ab. 14 m. E of Thebes; scene of battle 457 B.C. in which the Spartans defeated the Athenians. Figurines (terra-cotta statuettes) were made here and exported to many Mediterranean countries; they are now valuable museum works of art.

Ta′nah·ba′la (tä′nä·bä′lä). See BATOE.

Ta′nah·be·sar′ (tä′nä·bĕ·sär′). Large island of the Aru Is. (q.v.), Indonesia; actually, five closely packed islands.

Ta′nah·ma′sa (tä′nä·mä′sä). See BATOE.

Ta′nah·me′rah Bay (tä′nä·mā′rä). Inlet of Pacific Ocean on NE coast of Neth. New Guinea, ab. 40 m. W of Hollandia. Landings made here by Allied forces at same time as at Hollandia Apr. 22, 1944.

Tan'a·is (tăn'å·ĭs). **1** The Don river—ancient Greek name.
2 Greek colony at the mouth of the Tanais near the modern Azov.

Ta'nam·bo'go (tä'näm·bō'gō). Small island, E of Tulagi off S shore of Florida I., SE Solomon Is., W Pacific Ocean; attached to Gavutu I. by causeway and part of Japanese base; taken by U.S. Marines Aug. 7–8, 1942.

Tan'a·na (tăn'å·nô). **1** River ab. 475 m. long, chief S tributary of the Yukon, E and cen. Alaska; rises in glaciers of NE Wrangell Mts., flows NW to the Yukon at Tanana, 152°W; navigable for ab. 225 m. and for smaller vessels nearly to its source. Fairbanks is on it and Alaska Highway follows it for nearly its entire course.
2 Village, cen. Alaska, at junction of Tanana with Yukon; pop. (est.) 220.

Tanana Crossing. See TANACROSS.

Ta'na'na'rive' (Fr. tá'ná'nä'rēv'); Malagasy **Ta-na'na·ri'vo** (tä·nä'nä·rē'vō); Eng. **An'ta·nan'a·ri'vo** (ăn'tá·nän'á·rē'vō). City, ✳ of Malagasy Republic (Madagascar), in E cen. part; built on a basaltic ridge at elevation of 4060 ft.; pop. (1936) 126,515; library, experimental garden, observatory.

Ta·na'o Pass (tä·nä'ô). Channel ab. 10 m. wide extending along N coast of Camarines Norte prov., Luzon, Phil. Is., separating it from the Calagua Is.

Ta'na·pag' Harbor (tä'nä·päg'). Anchorage on W coast of Saipan, Mariana Is., just N of Garapan; best harbor of the island.

Tana River. See TANA.

Ta'na·ro (tä'nä·rô); anc. **Tan'a·rus** (tăn'á·rŭs). River 171 m. long, N Italy; rises in the Maritime Alps; flows N and NE into Po river 10 m. NE of Alessandria.

Ta·na'uan (tä·nä'wän). **1** Municipality on E coast of Leyte I., Phil. Is., on San Pedro Bay 9 m. S of Tacloban; pop. 21,934. Taken by American forces Oct. 25, 1944.
2 Municipality, NE Batangas prov., Luzon, Phil. Is., on railroad and highway from Batangas to Calamba; pop. 26,186; NE of Lake Taal and ab. 24 m. N of Batangas; in center of fine sugar, tobacco, and fruit region. Taken by Americans Mar. 27, 1945.

Tan'chuk' (dän'jōōk'). Town, SE Kwangsi, SE China, on right bank of the Si river below Kweiping and ab. 60 m. W of Tsangwu; in World War II site of American air base which was abandoned to Japanese Nov. 1, 1944 and retaken by Chinese July 9, 1945.

Tan'ci·ta'ro (tän'sĕ·tä'rô). Mountain 12,664 ft. in Michoacán state, SW Mexico, just W of Uruapan.

Tan'da (tän'dä). Town, Fyzabad dist., E Uttar Pradesh, N Indian Union, on Gogra river 85 m. N of Benares; pop. 21,177.

Tan·dil' (tän·dēl'). City, Buenos Aires prov., E Argentina, 190 m. S of Buenos Aires; pop. (est.) 31,115; center of rich agricultural district; health and pleasure resort.

Tandil, Sierra del. See SIERRA DEL TANDIL.

Tan'djoeng (tän'jōōng). Malay word (Dutch transliteration) meaning cape or point.

Tan'djoeng·pan·dan' or **Tan'djung·pan·dan'** (tän'jōōng·pän·dän'). Town, NW coast of Billiton I., Indonesia; pop. 15,708; has large Chinese population.

Tan'djoeng·pi·nang' or **Tan'djung·pi·nang'** (tän'-jōōng·pĭ·näng'). Town, Indonesia, on SW coast of Bintan I. E of Sumatra and ESE of Singapore; pop. 5789.

Tan'djoeng·pri'ok or **Tan'djung·pri'ok** (tän'jōōng·prē'ŏk). Port of Djakarta, Java, Indonesia, 6 m. E of the old city on Batavia Bay; pop. 25,781; has large harbor facilities, first constructed 1877–86. See BATAVIA.

Tandjung Rangasa. See MANDAR, GULF OF.

Ta·ne·ga·shi·ma (tä·nĕ·gä·shĕ·mä). Largest of the Osumi Is. (q.v.), off S end of Kyushu I., S Japan; ab. 25 m. long; ab. 176 sq. m.; pop. (1945) 44,839.

Ta'ney (tä'nĭ). County in Missouri. See Table at MISSOURI.

Ta'ney·town (tô'nĭ·toun). City, Carroll co., N Maryland, 32 m. E of Hagerstown; pop. 1519.

Tan'ez·rouft' (tăn'ĕz·rōōft'). Desert region, SW Algeria and N Sudan, an exceptionally barren part of the Sahara, called by the natives a "desert within a desert."

Tan'field (tăn'fēld). Former urban district, Durham, N England, on affluent of the Tyne 7 m. SW of Newcastle; (1931) pop. 9236; now in Stanley.

Tan'ga (tăng'gä). **1** Province, NE Tanganyika, E Africa; 16,102 sq. m.; pop. 363,372.
2 Seaport, its ✳; pop. ab. 11,000.

Tan'ga Islands (tăng'gä). Island group, E Bismarck Archipelago, W Pacific Ocean, ab. 55 m. off the E coast of New Ireland; comprises four islands, largest Malendok and Boang.

Tan'gan·yi'ka (tăn'găn·yē'kä; tăng'găn-). **1** Province, NE Northern Rhodesia; 24,020 sq. m.; pop. 106,449; ✳ Abercorn.
2 Former republic of the British Commonwealth, E Africa, formerly the greater part of German East Africa, since 1964 united with Zanzibar as independent republic of **Tan'za·ni'a** (tăn'zä·nē'á); area ab. 360,000 sq. m. (including ab. 20,000 sq. m. of water) pop. ab. 5,300,000; ✳ Dar es Salaam. Bounded on N by Uganda and Kenya, on E by Indian Ocean, on S by Mozambique, Nyasaland, and Northern Rhodesia, on W by Lake Tanganyika and Republic of the Congo, and on NW by Rwanda and Burundi. Greater part is high plateau with average alt. 3000 to 4000 ft.; has many heights 7000 to 10,400 ft., esp. in S cen. part and around N end of Lake Nyasa; in NE on the Kenya border are the Kilimanjaro peaks, the highest in Africa, 19,317 ft. Chief rivers are Rufiji (in S cen. part, flowing E to Indian Ocean), Ruvuma (on S border), Pangani (in NE), and the lower course of the Kagera (in NW). In W are a number of lakes and marshy regions (largest Lake Rukwa, in SW) and within its borders it includes S half of Lake Victoria, ab. ⅓ of Lake Tanganyika, and a section of NE Lake Nyasa. Coast line is ab. 450 m. with narrow coastal strip; Mafia is large island opp. mouth of Rufiji river and off NE coast are the islands of Zanzibar protectorate. Inhabitants are chiefly Bantu tribes. Occupations mainly agricultural; products are sisal hemp (world's largest producer), cotton, coffee, hides; forest products are important. Chief towns Dar es Salaam, Tanga, and Kilwa on coast; Arusha, Tabora, Dodoma in interior; Kigoma on Lake Tanganyika, and Mwanza on Lake Victoria.

History: Coast dominated in turn by Arabs, Portuguese, and rulers of Oman and Zanzibar (q.v.); under Karl Peters, Germans made treaties with natives 1884–85; German East Africa Co. received charter and Germany declared East Africa a protectorate 1885; its boundaries with British East Africa (see KENYA) determined by agreements of 1886, 1890; put down native risings 1888, 1891–93, 1905; captured by British 1914–16; name changed to Tanganyika when (except Ruanda and Urundi) it became a British mandate 1920; granted a legislative council 1926; made 1946 a trust territory under the United Nations; became a Brit. dominion 1961 and a Commonwealth republic Dec. 9, 1962; federated with Zanzibar Apr. 25, 1964.

Tanganyika, Lake. Lake in SE Africa, on boundary bet. W Tanganyika and E Congo; ab. 400 m. long and bet. 30 and 45 m. wide; 12,355 sq. m.; greatest depth 4700 ft.

Tang'er·mün'de (täng'ĕr·mün'dĕ). City, Magdeburg dist., East Germany, on Elbe river 62 m. W of Berlin; pop. 13,173; 12th-cent. church, 15th-cent. town hall.

Tan·gier' (tăn·jēr'; esp. attributively, tăn'jēr); also sometimes **Tan·giers'** (tăn·jērz'; tăn'jērz); Fr. and Ger. **Tan'ger'** (Fr. tän'zhä'; Ger. tän'jĕr, täng'ĕr); Span. **Tán'ger** (täng'hĕr); anc. **Tin'gis** (tĭn'jĭs). Seaport, summer ✳ of Morocco, at W end of the Strait of Gibraltar; with surrounding territory constituted until 1956

Tangier Zone or **International Zone** (225 sq. m.); pop. 180,000. A Roman city (Tingis), later taken successively by Vandals, Byzantines, and Arabs; taken 1471 by Portuguese who lost it to Spain 1580 and regained it 1656; on marriage 1662 of Catherine of Braganza to Charles II came into possession of English who gave it up to Moors 1684. Zone established Dec. 18, 1923 and Feb. 7, 1924 by the Tangier Convention (revised 1928) bet. England, France, and Spain providing for permanent neutralization of the area and government by an international commission. During World War II controlled by Spain; international administration restored Oct. 11, 1945; international status abolished Oct. 29, 1956. See MOROCCO.

Tangier, Bay of. Inlet of the Strait of Gibraltar on N coast of Africa; Tangier is on its W side.

Tangier Island. Island in lower Chesapeake Bay, belonging to Accomac co., E Virginia.

Tangier Sound. Inlet of Chesapeake Bay on W shore of Somerset co., SE Maryland.

Tan·gi·pa·hoa (tăn′jĭ·pá·hō′; tănch′pá·hō′). Parish in Louisiana. See *Table* at LOUISIANA.

Tang·koe′ban·pra′hoe or **Tang·ku′ban·pra′hu** (täng·kōō′bän·prä′hōō). Mountain 6809 ft., E Java, Indonesia, N of Bandung.

Tang′ku′ (täng′gōō′). Town, E Hopeh prov., NE China, ab. 27 m. E of Tientsin; part of the port of Taku, forming its chief landing place for passengers and cargo. Destroyed by fire 1900 but soon rebuilt. In Chinese civil war taken over by Communist forces Jan. 1949.

Tang–la (däng′lä′); *also* **Dang′la′** or **Dang–la** (däng′-lä′). Pass in Himalayas, S Tibet, E of Sikkim; alt. ab. 15,200 ft.; leads N out of Chumbi valley.

Tang′lha′ (däng′lä′); *also* **Dang′la′** or **Dang–la.** Mountain range 20,000 ft., E Tibet, Outer China, lat. 33°N and long. 88°–94°E; its E extension forms border bet. NW Sikang and S Tsinghai and separates headstreams of Mekong and Salween rivers. See TANG PASS.

Tang Pass (däng). Pass in Tanglha Mts. on border bet. SW Tsinghai and NE Tibet, Outer China; alt. 16,760 ft.; on highway N from Lhasa to Tsinghai and Kansu.

Tang′ra Tso (däng′rä tsō′); *also* **Dang′ra Yum** (däng′rä yŏŏm′). Lake 45 m. long, cen. Tibet, Outer China, lat. 31°N, long. 86°30′E.

Tang′shan′ (täng′shän′). 1 Town, NE Hopeh prov., NE China, ab. 68 m. NE of Tientsin; center of rich coal fields, products of which are exported through Chinwangtao.
2 Spa and hot-spring resort, N Hopeh prov., ab. 18 m. N of Peiping.

Tang·ub′ (täng·ōōb′). Municipality, S Misamis Occidental prov., Mindanao, Phil. Is., on N shore of Panguil Bay 29 m. S of Oroquieta; pop. 44,743.

Tan′gut′ (tän′gōōt′). Ancient region of varying limits, NW China, ab. equivalent to parts of modern Kansu and Ningsia; mentioned by Marco Polo; name now applied, esp. by the Mongols, to the Tibetans.

Ta·nim′bar (tá·nĭm′bär; tän′ĭm·bär′), or **Ti′mor·laut′** (tē′môr·lout′), **Islands;** *also* **Te·nim′bar Islands** (tĕ·nĭm′bär; tĕn′ĭm·bär′). Island group of ab. 66 islands, SE Moluccas, Indonesia, Malay Archipelago, E by N of Timor I.; area 2096 sq. m.; pop. 31,847; now attached to Ambon division of Maluku province. Comprises the large island of Jamdena, the islands of Larat and Selaru, and many small islands. Mostly of coralline formation, but partly volcanic; has extensive swamps and few harbors. Maize, rice, coconut and sago palms, fruits are grown. No high elevations. First visited 1839 by a British sea captain; opened up by Dutch c. 1878 but never much developed.

Ta′nis (tā′nĭs); *Bib.* **Zo′an** (zō′ăn). Ruined city in the Nile delta, Lower Egypt, near **Tanis Lake** (now Manzala) and the modern village of San.

Tan·jay′ (täng·hī′). Municipality, E Negros Oriental, Negros, Phil. Is., near S end of Tañon Strait 17 m. NNW of Cumaguete; pop. 30,979.

Tan′jong (tän′jông). Malay word meaning cape or point.

Tan·jore′ (tăn·jōr′). 1 District, cen. Madras state, S Indian Union; 3738 sq. m.; pop. (1941) 2,563,375.
2 City, its ✳, on right bank of Cauvery river 190 m. SSE of Madras; pop. (1941) 68,702; produces jewelry, carpets, and embroidery; has 11th-cent. temple to Siva, with great tower (208 ft.), palace of the raja within the fort, and pagodas. Capital from time to time since 10th cent. of Chola dynasty; independent state established here in 16th cent. by a governor of Vijayanagar; under Madura sovereignty in 1662; conquered by Marathas 1674 who held it to 1799; came into British possession 1855. Scene of activities of earliest Protestant missionaries in India.

Tanna. See TANA.

Tan′nen·berg (tän′ĕn·bûrg; *Ger.* tän′ĕn·bĕrκ); *Pol.* **Ste̜′bark** (stĕNm′bärk). Village, Olsztyn dept., NE Poland, 15 m. SE of Ostróda (Osterode); site of two battles: (1) 1410, in which Teutonic Knights were completely defeated by the Poles and Lithuanians; (2) Aug. 26–30, 1914, in which Germans under Hindenburg severely defeated Russians under Rennenkampf. Before 1945 in East Prussia, Germany.

Tann·fors′en (tän·fôr′sĕn; -fôsh′ĕn). Waterfall 121 ft., W cen. Sweden, near Åreskutan Mt.

Tannou Touva. = *Tannu Tuva:* see TUVA.

Tan′nu O′la (tän′ōō ō′lä; *native* täng′nōō ō·lä′). Mountain range running E and W bet. NW Outer Mongolia and S Tuva Autonomous Region.

Tannura, Ras at. See RAS AT TANNURA.

Tannu Tuva. See TUVA.

Ta·ñon′ Strait (tä·nyôn′). Passage bet. Cebu I. and Negros I., cen. Phil. Is., ab. 100 m. long and varying in width from 3 to 27 m.

Tan·qui′jo Reef (täng·kē′hō). Reef in Gulf of Mexico, N of Tuxpan Reef, off coast of N Veracruz state, Mexico.

Tan′sui′ (tän′sōō′ĕ) or **Tam′sui′** (täm′sōō′ĕ). 1 Short stream ab. 50 m. long, N Formosa I.; rises in mountains of NE Formosa and flows NNW past Taihoku and Tansui to Formosa Strait.
2 Seaport, N Formosa I., 20 m. NW of Taihoku; pop. ab. 23,000; treaty port, one of the two ports of Taihoku; has steamer connections with Hong Kong.

Tan′ta (tŏn′tŏ). City, ✳ of Gharbîya prov., N Lower Egypt; pop. (1937) 95,260; communications point in center of Nile delta 55 m. N of Cairo; noted for its Moslem festivals and fairs.

Tan·tu′ra (tŏn·tōō′rŏ); *anc.* **Dor** (dôr) or **Do′ra** (dōr′á). Modern town, W Palestine, on site of ancient Canaanitish town on Mediterranean coast ab. 14 m. S of Mt. Carmel; Dor marked S limit of Phoenician rule at height of its power. A kingdom in the time of the judges of Israel c. 1200–1000 B.C. (*Josh.* xi. 2; *Judges* i. 27), but excavations show that it was a very old settlement. Of some importance during the Crusades.

Tanzania. See TANGANYIKA.

Tao′nan′ (tou′nän′). Town, N Liaoning prov., S Manchuria, on a tributary of the Nonni river 125 m. NNW of Liaoyuan; pop. 47,888. Before 1902 a small village; as a result of an agreement bet. Chinese government and Mongolian tribes became a prosperous town; has government offices, trading stores, and is distribution point for wide territory; handles much kaoliang and cereals.

Ta′or·mi′na (tä′ôr·mē′nä); *anc.* **Tau′ro·me′ni·um** (tô′rŏ·mē′nĭ·ŭm). Commune on E coast of Sicily in Messina prov.; pop. 7580; on a hill, has beautiful views; church built into a 3d-cent. temple; theater reconstructed from a Greek original; Roman remains; medieval castle. Occupied in 8th cent. B.C.; refounded by Carthaginians 397 B.C.; after death of Hiero II (215 B.C.) became allied to Rome; burned by the Saracens 902 A.D.

Taos (tous). 1 County in New Mexico. See *Table* at NEW MEXICO.
2 Town and resort, its ⊗, N New Mexico, 55 m. NNE

of Santa Fe; pop. 2163; legal name Don Fernando de Taos; important commercial center in days of Santa Fe Trail; seat of art colony. Community (total pop. 7179) includes also Taos Pueblo (to NE) and Ranchos de Taos (to SE).

Taos Trail. See SANTA FE TRAIL.

Taou'den'ni' (tou'dĕ'nē'). Oasis, Mali Republic, West Africa, 425 m. NNW of Tombouctou in NE El Djouf; saltworks.

Ta'pa (tä'pȧ). Town, Järva prov., N cen. Estonia; pop. (1937) 3834; railroad junction 45 m. E of Tallin.

Ta'pa·chu'la (tä'pä·chōō'lä). Town, Chiapas state, SE Mexico, on railroad near Guatemalan border; pop. 15,187; chief product coffee.

Ta'pa·joz' (tä'pȧ·zhôs'). River ab. 500 m. long, N Brazil; formed by junction of Juruena (total length with Juruena ab. 1100 m.) and São Manoel rivers on S end of the border bet. Amazonas and Pará states, flows NE into the Amazon river at Santarém; important rubber plantations along its banks, esp. Fordlandia and Belterra (qq.v.).

Ta'pa·noe'li (tä'pä·nōō'lê) or **Ta'pa·nu'li.** Former residency of Neth. Indies, on NW coast of island of Sumatra; 15,084 sq. m.; pop. 1,042,583; * Sibolga, lying bet. Atjeh govt. on the N and Sumatra West Coast residency on the S and including Nias I. Region very mountainous with many peaks above 6000 ft. In the NE is Lake Toba, the largest of the mountain lakes of Sumatra, and the surrounding region known as Batakland. Various tropical products are raised, esp. by the Battaks who make up most of the population and who are skilled in native industries. Chief towns Sibolga and Padangsidimpuan. Region did not come under Dutch control until the 19th cent.

Tapanoeli, or **Tapanuli, Bay.** Inlet of the Indian Ocean on the NW coast of Sumatra, Indonesia, opp. Nias I.; Sibolga is on its NE shore.

Ta'pan'shang' (dä'bän'shäng'). Town, N cen. Jehol, NE China (* of former West Hsingan prov., W Manchukuo); in mountainous region 125 m. N of Chengteh.

Ta Pa Shan (dä' bä' shän'). Mountain range on border bet. S Shensi and NE Szechwan provs., cen. China; highest ab. 9843 ft.; its E end forms W edge of Hupeh basin and on S it is cut by the Yangtze Gorges (q.v.).

Ta'po·tchau' (tä'pŏ·chō'); also **Ta'po·cho'.** Mountain ridge, cen. Saipan I., Mariana Is., W Pacific; highest point 1554 ft.; severe fighting during American conquest of island June 1944.

Tap'pa·han'nock (tăp'ȧ·hăn'ŭk). Town, ⊗ of Essex co., E Virginia; pop. 1086.

Tap'pan (tăp'ăn). Village in Rockland co., SE New York, near Haverstraw; pop. (est.) 2100; scene of Major André's execution 1780.

Tap'pan Zee (tăp'ăn zē'). Expansion 12 m. long of the Hudson river bet. Westchester and Rockland cos., SE New York; 2–3 m. wide.

Ta·prob'a·ne (tȧ·prŏb'ȧ·nē). Ancient and medieval name of Ceylon, being the Latin form from the Greek Taprobanē, from Sanskrit Tamraparni, originally the name of district on NW coast, literally "pool covered with red lotus."

Tap'ti (täp'tē). Unnavigable river 436 m. long, W cen. India; flows W from mountains of SW Madhya Pradesh to Gulf of Cambay near Surat in Maharashtra state.

Ta'pu·a·e·nu'ku, Mount (tä'pōō·ä·ä·nōō'kōō). Highest peak 9465 ft. in Kaikoura Range, Marlborough provincial dist., NE South I., New Zealand.

Ta·pul' (tä·pōōl'). 1 Island group, cen. Sulu Archipelago, Phil. Is., bet. Jolo I. and Tawitawi I.; ab. 100 sq. m.; pop. 47,755; largest is Siasi. Includes also islands of Tapul, Lapac, and Lugus and ab. 70 other small islands and islets. See SULU province.
2 Island in Tapul group, N of Siasi I. and S of Jolo; 11 sq. m.; pop. 8278; forms part of Tapul municipal district (pop. 18,496).

Ta'qua·rí' (tä'kwȧ·rē'). River ab. 450 m. long, S cen. Brazil; rises in S cen. Mato Grosso state, flows WSW into Paraguay river near Bolivian border; lower part traverses the Pantanal (marshes).

Ta'qua·ri·tin'ga (tä'kwȧ·rê·tēnng'gȧ). City, São Paulo state, SE Brazil, ab. 185 m. NW of São Paulo; pop. 8247.

Tar (tär). River, NE North Carolina; rises in Granville co., N North Carolina, flows SE into a wide estuary known as Pamlico river, Beaufort co., E North Carolina; 215 m. long, including Pamlico river.

Tar'a (tär'ȧ). Parish in co. Meath, E Eire, 22 m. NW of Dublin; ancient capital (Hill of Tara) of Irish monarchs, abandoned c. 560. Pre-Christian religious center.

Ta'ra (tä'rȧ). Town, NE Omsk Region, Soviet Russia, Asia, on the Irtysh 135 m. N of Omsk.

Tarabulus el Gharb. See TRIPOLI city, Libya.

Tarabulus esh Sham. See TRIPOLI town and seaport, Lebanon.

Ta·rai·ka Bay (tä·rī·kä). Large inlet on E coast of S Sakhalin I.

Ta'ra·kan' (tä'rä·kän'). 1 Island, Indonesia, in E Celebes Sea, off NE coast of Borneo; 117 sq. m.; pop. 11,700; in delta of Sesajap river. Has exceptionally rich oil fields; taken by Japanese after battle Jan. 10–12, 1942 and after destruction of wells by Dutch; retaken by Australians May 1–19, 1945.
2 Town on W side of island.

Ta'ra·na'ki (tä'rȧ·nä'kê). 1 Provincial district of New Zealand. See Table at NEW ZEALAND.
2 See EGMONT, New Zealand.

Tar'an·say (tär'ăn·sā). Island ab. 4½ m. long of the Outer Hebrides, SW of island of Lewis with Harris, off NW coast of Scotland.

Ta'ran·to (tä'rän·tō; Angl. tăr'ăn·tō, tȧ·răn'tō). 1 Former name of Ionia prov.: see Table at ITALY.
2 anc. **Ta·ren'tum** (tȧ·rĕn'tŭm). Seaport and naval base, * of Ionia prov., Apulia, SE Italy, on Gulf of Taranto 156 m. E by S of Naples; pop. 117,722; cathedral (founded 4th cent.; rebuilt 11th cent.), 10th-cent. castle, naval arsenal; fisheries. Gave name to tarantula and tarantella. Founded by Greeks 8th cent. B.C., became most important city of Magna Graecia; taken by Rome 272 B.C. and made Roman colony 123 B.C.; taken by Ostrogoths 494 A.D., Byzantines 540, Lombards 675, Arabs 856, Saracens 929, and Normans 1063 becoming part of kingdom of Naples; became naval base after joining kingdom of Italy 1861. In World War II naval base raided by British planes Nov. 11–12, 1940; port taken by British Sept. 9, 1943.

Taranto, or **Tarentum, Gulf of.** Inlet 70 m. long of Ionian Sea on SE coast of Italy.

Ta'ra·pa·cá' (tä'rä·pä·kä'). 1 Province, N Chile; 21,346 sq. m.; pop. (1943 est.) 99,724; * Iquique. See History at ANCÓN and ARICA.
2 Town, SE corner of Colombia, on S bank of Putumayo river at Brazil frontier, N of Leticia.

Ta'ra·po'to (tä'rä·pō'tō). Town, San Martín dept., N Peru, on a tributary of the Huallaga river 90 m. E of Chachapoyas; pop. (1940 est.) 9249.

Ta'rare' (tȧ·rȧr'). Manufacturing commune, Rhône dept., E cen. France, 22 m. NW of Lyons; pop. 10,395; textiles.

Ta'ra·ru'a Range (tä'rȧ·rōō'ȧ). Mountain range in SW North I., New Zealand.

Ta'ras'con' (tä'räs'kôn'). Town, Bouches-du-Rhône dept., SE France, on left bank of the Rhone N of Arles; pop. 5058.

Ta·rasp' (tä·räsp'). Village, Graubünden canton, Switzerland, in the Lower Engadine; medieval castle; mineral baths.

Ta·ra'wa (tȧ·rä'wȧ; tär'ȧ·wȧ; native tä'rä·wä'). Island (atoll), N cen. Gilbert Is., ab. 90 m. N of the equator; comprises chain of islets in reef around lagoon ab. 18 m. long by 13 m. at widest point; pop. (1936) 2640. Chief islet and village is Betio at S end; before World War II

had government hospital, leper station, and school. Occupied by Japanese 1942; seized by U.S. Marines after bitter and costly four-day battle Nov. 21–24, 1943; made ✳ of Gilbert and Ellice Is. after the war.

Ta·ra·we'ra (tä'rȧ·wä'rȧ). River ab. 45 m. long, N cen. North I., New Zealand; flows N out of Lake **Tarawera** (SE of Rotorua and at foot of Mt. Tarawera) into Bay of Plenty.

Tarawera, Mount. Volcanic peak 3770 ft., N cen. North I., New Zealand, ab. 90 m. NNW of Napier; an eruption June 10, 1886 destroyed the sinter ("pink" and "white") terraces of Rotomahana.

Tar'bat Ness (tär'bȧt nĕs'). Headland on NE coast of Scotland, S of Dornoch Firth; lighthouse.

Tar'bert, Loch (lŏk tär'bērt). Sea inlet ab. 6 m. long in cen. Jura I., Inner Hebrides, off W Scotland; nearly cuts the island in two.

Tarbert, West Loch *and* **East Loch.** **1** Two sea inlets, one from the SW and one from the E, which nearly meet at the base of Kintyre Penin. on SW coast of Scotland, and thus nearly cut the peninsula off from the mainland.
2 Two sea inlets, one from the W and one from the E, which nearly meet across the S section of Lewis with Harris I. in the Outer Hebrides, Scotland.

Tarbes (tärb); *anc.* **Bi·gor'ra** (bĭ·gŏr'ȧ). City, ✳ of Hautes-Pyrénées dept., SW France, on Adour river 23 m. ESE of Pau; pop. 34,749; 12th-cent. Romanesque-Transition cathedral; old episcopal palace (now prefecture); manufactures leather, paper; trades in agricultural products, cattle, iron. Capital of old countship of Bigorre; scene of English victory over French 1814.

Tar'bor'o (tär'bûr'ŏ; -bŭ·rȧ). Industrial town, ⊗ of Edgecombe co., NE North Carolina, 14 m. E of Rocky Mount; pop. 8411; meeting place of North Carolina legislature 1787. Manufactures cotton cloth, cottonseed products, veneers; cotton, tobacco, peanut, and corn crops.

Tar·cen'to (tär·chĕn'tŏ). Commune, Friuli prov., Venezia Euganea, NE Italy, 12 m. N of Udine; pop. 10,435.

Ta·ren'tum (tȧ·rĕn'tŭm). **1** Borough, Allegheny co., SW Pennsylvania, on Allegheny river 17 m. NE of Pittsburgh; pop. 8232; manufactures wrapping paper, metal and wooden products, glass; coal mining.
2 See TARANTO seaport.

Târ'go·viş'te (tĭr'gô·vĕsh'tĕ). City, S cen. Romania, in cen. Walachia region, on Ialomiţa river 45 m. NW of Bucharest; pop. 22,482; commercial center; has one of finest churches in Romania, built in 16th cent. Capital of Walachia 1383–1698; defended against Turks in 1597.

Târ'gu–Jiu (tĭr'gōō·zhyōō'). Town, SW Romania, in Oltenia region, on Jiu river ab. 50 m. NNW of Craiova; pop. 12,944; former garrison town on lower slopes of Transylvanian Alps; trade center, esp. in lumber and petroleum.

Târgu–Mu'reş (-mōō'rĕsh); *Hung.* **Ma'ros–Vá'sár·hely'** (mŏ'rŏsh·vä'shär·hā'). City, N cen. Romania, in NE Transylvania region on Mureş river; pop. 38,116; 15th-cent. Gothic church; palace, museum, library; in modern times a trade center, esp. in lumber, petroleum, grain, wine, tobacco. Chief town of the Szeklers. In region ceded by Hungary to Romania 1918 but again, with the rest of northern Transylvania, was part of Hungary 1940–45.

Târgu–Neam'ţu (-nyăm'tsōō) *or* **Târ'gul–Neamţ** (tĭr'gōōl·nyämts'). Commercial town, NE Romania, in N Moldavia region 60 m. WNW of Iaşi; pop. 9127; founded 13th cent. by Teutonic Order; fortress and ancient monastery town.

Târgu–Oc'na (-ôk'nä). Town, E Romania, in Moldavia region, in E Transylvanian Alps 45 m. W of Bârlad; pop. 12,592; salt mines.

Ta·ri'fa (tä·rē'fä); *anc.* **Ju'lia Jo'za** (jōōl'yȧ jō'zȧ; jōō'lĭ·ȧ) *or* **Julia Tra·duc'ta** (trȧ·dŭk'tȧ). Seaport, Cádiz prov., SW Spain, on Point Marroquí 51 m. SE of Cádiz; pop. 14,815; manufactures lime, brick, tile, cork, leather; fisheries and fish-salting works. Roman settlement; taken and fortified by Moors; reconquered by Sancho IV 1292; besieged by French 1812.

Tar'iff·ville (tär'ĭf·vĭl). Subdivision (est. pop. 650) of town of SIMSBURY, Connecticut; tobacco sorting and packing.

Ta·ri'ja (tä·rē'hä). **1** Department of Bolivia. See *Table* at BOLIVIA.
2 City, its ✳; pop. (1943 est.) 17,000; altitude 6398 ft.; 85 m. by road from La Quiaca, Argentina; commercial center of S Bolivia.

Tarikaikea. See MAMBERAMO.

Ta·ri'koe (tä·rē'kōō); *Du.* **Rouf'faer** (rou'fär). Western upper tributary ab. 150 m. long of the Mamberamo river in Neth. New Guinea; joins the Taritatoe near 3°10'S to form the Mamberamo; its sources are in W Snow Mts.

Ta'rim' (dä'rēm'). Chief river 1250 m. long of Sinkiang prov., W China; formed by union of Yarkand and Khotan rivers, W Sinkiang, flows E along N edge of Takla Makan (*q.v.*), then SE into the area of Lop Nor; gives its name to the entire basin ab. 350,000 sq. m. enclosed by the Tien Shan, the Pamirs, and the Kunlun Mts. and including Lop Nor and the Turfan depressions in the E.

Ta·ri·ta'toe (tä·rē·tä'tōō); *Du.* **I'den·burg** (ē'd'n·bûrg; *Du.* ē'dĕn·bûrK). River ab. 225 m. long in NE cen. Neth. New Guinea, chief tributary of the Mamberamo river; flows generally W, uniting with the Tarikoe in 138°30'E, 3°10'S; its sources are in the N slopes of Snow Mts. and in mountains of NE Neth. New Guinea.

Tar'ka·stad (tär'kä·stät). Town, SE Cape Province, S Union of South Africa, 120 m. NW of East London; pop. 2791; center of agricultural and sheep-raising district.

Tar'khan·kut', Cape (tär'kăn·kōōt'; *Russ.* tĕr·kŭn·kōōt'). Extreme W point of the Crimea, S Soviet Russia, Europe, projecting into the Black Sea.

Tar'ki·o (tär'kĭ·ō). **1** River 125 m. long, SW Iowa and NW Missouri; East, Middle, and West Forks rise in Montgomery co., Iowa, flow S, unite at Tarkio, Missouri, flow into the Missouri river.
2 City, Atchison co., NW corner of Missouri, 56 m. NW of St. Joseph; pop. 2160; trade center in corn-growing section. Tarkio College (1883; coed.; Presbyterian).

Tar·kwa' (tär·kwä'; *native* tä·kwä'). Town, W Gold Coast Colony, Gold Coast, W Africa, on Ankobra river and on railroad ab. 40 m. NW of Sekondi; pop. ab. 3000; gold fields.

Tar'lac (tär'läk). **1** Province, N cen. Luzon, Phil. Is., in cen. plain; 1175 sq. m.; pop. 264,379; ✳ Tarlac. Western half is mountainous, comprising E slopes of Zambales Mts.; E part watered by tributaries of the Agno and Pampanga Chico. Chief occupation agriculture; produces rice, sugar, tobacco, vegetables, pineapples. Inhabitants Tagalogs, Ilokanos, Pangasinans, and Pampangans. Chief towns Tarlac, Concepcion, Camiling, and Gerona.
History: Through most of Spanish rule a part of Pampanga; part created as a military comandancia 1860 and extended 1873; joined revolt of 1896; civil government established Feb. 1901; came under control of Japanese Dec. 1941; recovered by Americans Jan. 1945.
2 Municipality, its ✳, in E cen. part on a tributary of the Agno and on the Manila-Dagupan R.R. 65 m. N of Manila; pop. 55,682; chief trade center of the province. Founded 1686; in World War II partly destroyed by Japanese before capture by Americans Jan. 20, 1945.

Tar'ma (tär'mä). Town, Junín dept., cen. Peru, 95 m. NE of Lima; pop. (1940 est.) 7876; alt. 10,000 ft.

Tarn (tärn). **1** River 233 m. long, S France; rises in Lozère dept. on the slopes of Lozère Mts., flows W and SW into Garonne river.
2 Department of France. See *Table* at FRANCE.

Tarn–et–Ga′ronne′ (tär′-nä-gȧ′rôn′). Department of France. See *Table* at FRANCE.

Tar·no′pol (tär-nô′pôl). **1** Former Polish department, in SE part; 6370 sq. m.; pop. 1,603,313.

2 City. See TERNOPOL.

Tar′nów (tär′nŏŏf). Industrial and commercial city, Kraków dept., Poland, on Biała river 45 m. E of Kraków; pop. (1938–39 est.) 54,997; episcopal see; Gothic town hall; cathedral; manufactures machinery, iron goods, lumber, knitted goods; oil refineries. An old town and a religious and cultural center in 15th and 16th cents.; occupied by Germans in World War I and II.

Tar·now′skie Gó′ry (tär-nôf′skyĕ gŏŏ′rĭ); *also*, *unofficially*, **Tar′no·wi′ce** (tär′nŏ-vē′tsĕ); *Ger.* **Tar′no·witz** (tär′nŏ-vĭts). Mining commune, E cen. Śląsk dept., SW Poland, 16 m. NNW of Katowice; pop. (1938–39 est.) 17,549; coal deposits nearby; manufactures metal goods, lumber, cement, beer. Formerly in Silesia, Germany.

Ta′ro (tä′rŏ). River ab. 90 m. long, N Italy; flows NE from the Apennines into Po river.

Ta′rou′dant′ (*Fr.* tȧ′rŏŏ′dän′). Oasis in W Morocco, E of Agadir, NW Africa; pop. ab. 10,000.

Tar·pe′ian Rock (tär-pē′[y]ăn). See SEVEN HILLS.

Tar′pon Springs (tär′pŭn). Resort city, Pinellas co., W cen. Florida penin., on Gulf of Mexico 28 m. N of St. Petersburg; pop. 6768; sponge fisheries.

Tar·qui′nia (tär-kwē′nyȧ); *anc.* **Tar·quin′i·i** (tär-kwĭn′ĭ-ī); *in medieval times called* **Cor·ne′to** (kôr-nā′tô). Town, Viterbo prov., N Latium, cen. Italy, ab. 60 m. NW of Viterbo; pop. (1936) 6368; medieval fortifications (25 towers and a castle); government museum containing Etruscan antiquities in the Palazzo Vitelleschi; necropolis of great archaeological interest. Chief of the 12 Etruscan cities; date of its coming under Roman domination not certain.

Tarracina. See TERRACINA.

Tarraco. See TARRAGONA commune.

Tar′ra·co·nen′sis, *also* **His·pa′ni·a Tarraconensis** (hĭs-pā′nĭ-ȧ [-pān′yȧ] tär′ȧ-kŏ-nĕn′sĭs). Roman province comprising the greater part (N, cen., and SE) of ancient Spain (Hispania); ✳ Tarraco; other two provinces were Lusitania and Baetica.

Tar′ra·go′na (tär′ȧ-gō′nȧ; *Span.* tär′rä-gō′nä). **1** Province of Spain. See *Table* at SPAIN.

2 *anc.* **Tar′ra·co** (tär′ȧ-kō). Commune, its ✳, NE Spain, on Mediterranean 54 m. W of Barcelona; pop. 35,648; manufactures silk, paper, flour, tobacco; Roman walls and aqueduct; 12th-cent. cathedral; archiepiscopal palace; center of Carthusian wine industry since 1903. Captured by Romans 218 B.C.; capital of Roman province of Tarraconensis; made capital of Catalonia; taken by Visigoths 475 A.D.; under Moors 713–1089; captured by British 1705; sacked by French under Suchet 1811.

Tar′rant (tär′ănt). County in Texas. See *Table* at TEXAS.

Tarrant City. City, Jefferson co., cen. Alabama, 10 m. NNE of Birmingham; pop. 7810.

Tar·ra′sa (tär-rä′sä). Manufacturing commune, Barcelona prov., NE Spain, 14 m. NNW of Barcelona; pop. 45,081; produces leather, iron beds, machinery, flour, soap, chinaware, textiles (esp. cottons and woolens).

Tar River. See TAR.

Tar′ry·all′ Peak, North (tär′ĭ-ôl′). Peak 11,400 ft. in the Rocky Mts., Park co., cen. Colorado.

Tar′ry·town (tär′ĭ-toun). Residential village, Westchester co., SE New York, on Hudson river 24 m. N of New York; pop. 11,109; forms one community with North Tarrytown, Elmsford, and Irvington; on site of former Indian village; developed as trading post; part of grant of Philipse Manor 1680; important center during Revolution; scene of André's capture 1780; home of Washington Irving (described in his *Sketch Book*) to S near Irvington (Sunnyside) and burial place (Sleepy Hollow) to N of village. Marymount College for Women (1907).

Tar′shish (tär′shĭsh). Ancient maritime country, a land distant from Palestine; by some located in S Spain and identified with Tartessus (*q.v.*); often mentioned in the Old Testament, as in *Isa.* xxiii. 1, *Jer.* x. 9, *Ezek.* xxvii. 12.

Tar′so *or* **Tarso Tie·ro′ko** (tär′sō tyĕ·rō′kō). Mountain peak 10,430 ft., one of the highest in the Tibesti Mts., NW Chad Republic, N cen. Africa.

Tar′sus (tär′sŭs). Town, Içel vilayet, S Turkey in Asia, on railroad 23 m. W of Adana; pop. 24,848; has considerable trade but is not very healthful. Ruins of ancient city are quite extensive; it was on the Cydnus river and mentioned in very early times c. 850 B.C.; later probably an Ionian colony; successively under Persia, Syria, Rome; chief city of Cilicia and important because of nearness to Cilician Gates; captured by Arabs in 7th cent. and in turn held by Crusaders and rulers of Lesser Armenia; became Turkish in 16th cent. Birthplace of Saint Paul.

Tar′tar Republic (tär′tēr). = TATAR REPUBLIC.

Tartary. See TATARY.

Tar·tes′sus *or* **Tar·tes′sos** (tär-tĕs′ŭs). Ancient kingdom and its chief port on SW coast of Hispania (Spain) near the mouth of the Guadalquivir in modern Andalusia; founded c. 1200 B.C.; prospered in trade of silver and tin and by some identified with the Biblical Tarshish (*q.v.*). Later developed by Phoenicians and Greeks; destroyed by Carthaginians 480 B.C.

Tar′tu (tär′tŏŏ; *Estonian* tär′tŏŏ). **1** Province of Estonia. See *Table* at ESTONIA.

2 *Ger.* **Dor′pat** (dôr′pät); *Russ.*, *formerly*, **Yur′ev** (yŏŏr′yĕf). City, its ✳, E Estonia, on Ema river W of Lake Peipus; pop. (1937) 60,046; manufactures iron, wood, and leather products. Site of Tartu Univ. (founded 1632 by Gustavus Adolphus as Univ. of Dorpat). Founded as a castle built 1030 by Yaroslav, grand prince of Kiev; captured by Teutonic Knights 1224; member of Hanseatic League; successively under Russian, Polish, and Swedish (1600) domination; became Russian 1704. Occupied by Germans Feb.–Dec. 1918, and by Bolshevik forces Dec. 1918–Jan. 1919; Bolsheviks expelled by Estonian army Jan. 14, 1919; peace signed here Feb. 2, 1920 bet. Soviet Russia and Estonia; another treaty, signed here Oct. 14, 1920, established peace bet. Finland and Russia. Held by Germans in World War II from 1941 to 1944.

Tar·tus′ (tȯr·tŏŏs′); *anc.* **Tor·to′sa** (tôr-tō′sȧ). Coastal town, W Syria, N of Tripoli and ab. 42 m. S of Latakia; fishing port.

Tarudant. = TAROUDANT.

Ta·ru·mai (tä·rŏŏ·mī). Active volcano 2969 ft., S Hokkaido I., Japan, S of Sapporo.

Ta·ru·tao, Pu·lo (pŏŏ·lō tä·rŏŏ·tou). Island (*pulo*), SW Thailand, off W coast of Malay Penin. at N end of Strait of Malacca, just N of Langkawi I.

Tar·vi′sio (tär·vē′zyŏ). Frontier commune, NE Friuli prov., E Venezia Euganea, NE Italy, at N end of Julian Alps; pop. (1931) 6724; formerly in Carinthia.

Tarvisium. See TREVISO commune.

Täsch′horn (tĕsh′hôrn). Peak 14,758 ft. in SW Switzerland, in the Pennine Alps.

Tas·co′sa (tăs-kō′sȧ). Former town, Oldham co., N Texas, ab. 30 m. NW of Amarillo; noted in the 1870's and 1880's as a tough frontier town.

Ta·shauz′ (tä·shouz′). **1** Subdivision of Turkmen S.S.R., Soviet Central Asia, in N part bordering on the Uzbek S.S.R.

2 Town, its ✳, on the Kara-Kalpak border 35 m. NW of Khiva.

Ta′shi Chho Dzong (tä′shĕ chō dzŏng′). Town, W Bhutan, just SW of Punakha; former summer ✳ of Bhutan; has fortress; near ✳, Thimbu, built here 1962.

Ta′shih′kiao (dä′shĭr′chĭ·ou′). Town, S Liaoning prov., S Manchuria, ab. 95 m. SSW of Mukden; railroad junction point for Yingkow, 14 m. distant.

Tashilumpo. See Shigatse.

Tash·kent' (tăsh·kĕnt'; *native* täsh-). **1** Subdivision, Uzbek S.S.R., Soviet Central Asia, in NE part; a narrow area bet. SE Kazakh S.S.R. and N Tadzhik S.S.R.; Tashkent is its chief town.

2 *or* **Tash·kend'** (tăsh·kĕnt'; *native* täsh-). City, ✻ of Uzbek S.S.R., Soviet Central Asia, in NE part of the republic, to the E of the Syr Darya on a small tributary; pop. 585,005; situated in an oasis; with irrigation cultivation, raises much fruit and agricultural produce; has a number of important manufacturing industries. Town founded probably as early as 7th cent. A.D.; captured by Russians 1865 and new city built nearby.

Tash'kur·ghan' (tăsh'kōōr·gän'); *anc.* **A·or'nos** (à·ôr'nŏs). Town, Afghan Turkistan, 30 m. E of Mazar-i-Sharif; founded c. 1750 and became important trade mart bet. India and Bukhara; 3 m. to the N are ruins of the ancient town of Khulm. Ancient Aornos in Bactria was on the line of march of Alexander the Great 330–329 B.C.

Ta'sik·ma·la'ja (tä'sĭk·mä·lä'yä) *or* **Ta'sik·ma·la'ya.** Town, West Java prov., Indonesia, on railroad 50 m. SE of Bandung; pop. 25,605; in fertile plain surrounded by high mountains.

Ta'sim·bo'ko (tä'sĭm·bō'kō). Village on N coast of Guadalcanal I., SE Solomon Is., W Pacific. bet. Koli Point and Taivu Point; Japanese base attacked by U.S. Marines Sept. 8, 1942.

Ta'si·us'saq *or* **Ta'si·us'sak** (tä'sĕ·ōō'săk). Town on an island in Baffin Bay, W coast of Greenland, 73°22'N.

Tas'man, Mount (tăz'măn). Peak 11,467 ft. in Southern Alps range, W cen. South I., New Zealand, NE of Aorangi; 2d highest mountain in New Zealand; in Mount Cook National Park.

Tasman Bay. Inlet of Tasman Sea, W of Cook Strait, on N coast of South I., New Zealand; the city of Nelson is situated on its SE shore.

Tasman Head. Southern point of Bruni I., SE Tasmania, Australia, extending into South Pacific Ocean.

Tas·ma'ni·a (tăz·mā'nĭ·à; -mān'yà); *formerly* **Van Die'men's Land** (văn dē'mĕnz). Island, South Pacific Ocean, S of Australia; 26,304 sq. m., ab. 180 m. N to S and 190 m. E to W; pop. (1933) 227,599, (1963 est.) 361,320; ✻ Hobart; a state of the Commonwealth of Australia. It includes Macquarie I. (89 sq. m.) to the SE in lat. 54°45'S, King I. 50 m. to the NW, Hunters Is. off the NW point, the Furneaux Group off the NE point, and Bruni I. off the SE coast. Central part a highland including the Great Western Range and several mountains above 4000 ft. (highest Ben Lomond 5160 ft.). Chief rivers Tamar in N, to which is joined the Esk and Macquarie river systems; Derwent in cen. and SE part; Gordon and Pieman rivers in W; and Arthur river in NW. Lakes are grouped in the center: Great Lake, Lake St. Clair, Lake Echo, and Lake Sorell. More important features of the coast line: on NE, Cape Portland; on E, Freycinet Penin.; on SE, Tasman Penin., Cape Pillar, Storm Bay, Southeast Cape; on SW, Southwest Cape; on W, Cape Sorell, Macquarie Harbour; on NW Cape Grim, and Circular Head on N coast. Chief cities Hobart, Launceston, Burnie, Stanley, and Devonport.

History: Discovered and named Van Diemen's Land 1642 by Abel Tasman, Dutch navigator; renamed Tasmania 1853; taken over by Great Britain 1803 and for a time used as an auxiliary penal settlement; colony granted responsible government 1856; federated as state of Australian Commonwealth 1901. Aboriginal Tasmanians became extinct 1876.

Tas'man Peninsula (tăz'măn). Peninsula ab. 20 m. wide by 26 m. long on SE coast of Tasmania, Australia, E of Storm Bay and Hobart. Capes Raoul and Pillar are at its S extremity. Port Arthur on its S coast near Cape Raoul was a penal settlement from 1833 to 1870.

Tasman Sea. The part of South Pacific Ocean bet. SE Australia and W New Zealand, ab. 1200 m. across.

Tas'sa·fa·ron'ga (tăs'à·fà·rông'gà). Village on NW coast of Guadalcanal I., SE Solomon Is., W Pacific, W of Kokumbona; held by Japanese for five months during battle for Guadalcanal 1942.

Tas'so Island (tăs'ō). Small island in Sierra Leone river, ENE of Freetown, Sierra Leone, W Africa. The village of Tasso is on its NW coast.

Ta'ta·ko'to (tä'tà·kō'tō). Island in E part of the Tuamotu Archipelago, S Pacific Ocean, ab. 17°S and 138°W.

Tatar Pass. See Jablonica Pass.

Ta·tar' Pa'zar·dzhik' (tä·tär' pä'zär·jĭk'); *formerly* **Pazardzhik.** City, Plovdiv dept., S Bulgaria, on the N bank of the Maritsa river 22 m. W of Plovdiv; pop. (1934) 23,228.

Ta'tar Republic (tä'tēr); *officially* **Tatar Autonomous Soviet Socialist Republic;** *also* **Ta'tar·stan'** (tä'tēr·stän'). Autonomous republic, E Soviet Russia, Europe, at bend of Middle Volga; pop. 2,919,423, (1941 est.) 3,067,740; ✻ Kazan; a subdivision of the R.S.F.S.R. Bounded on N by Kirov Region and Udmurt Republic, on E by Bashkir Republic, on S by Chkalov, Kuibyshev, and Ulyanovsk Regions, on W by Chuvash Republic, and on NW by Mari Republic. In level country on both sides of Volga and includes lower course of Kama; both streams and their tributaries important for transportation and irrigation. Chief occupation agriculture; raising of wheat, oats, rye, and flax, and livestock, with some dairying and beekeeping. Forests extensive. Peasant industries well developed, esp. in leather work. Crossed by two main rail lines from Moscow to Soviet Asia. Chief towns Kazan, Yelabuga, Chistopol, and Bugulma. Predominant ethnic strain Turko-Tatar; chief nationalities Tatar 50.4%, Russian 41.8%. Area, formerly backward culturally, has been greatly advanced since the Revolution; has university at Kazan and a number of specialized schools and institutions.

History: In early times (5th cent. A.D.) colonized by Bulgars who developed a powerful state; conquered by Mongols in 13th cent.; in 15th cent. became Tatar khanate, which was overcome by rulers of Moscow principality 1552; created autonomous republic 1920.

Tatar Strait. See Gulf of Tatary.

Ta'ta·ry (tä'tà·rĭ) *or*, *less correctly*, **Tar'ta·ry** (tär'tà·rĭ). Historically, an indefinite region in Asia and Europe, extending from the Sea of Japan to the Dnieper river. The Tatars were tribes, mostly of Turkic origin, whose descendants today inhabit certain areas of Europe and Asia, as the Tatar A.S.S.R. (*q.v.*), the Crimea, the region of the Caucasus Mts., and several areas in Siberia; originally the Mongols were called Tatars; historically, in Russia, the name is applied generally to any invading Asiatic horde and esp. to the Golden Horde and their descendants who from the steppe region E of the lower Volga ruled the Russians from 1237 to 1480 as the Kipchak khanate.

Tatary, Gulf of. Wide strait 175 to 70 m. wide forming the N end of the Sea of Japan bet. E coast of Maritime Territory, Soviet Russia, Asia, and W coast of Sakhalin I. Its narrower N end, 70 to 10 m. wide, 51°N to 54°N, bet. Khabarovsk Territory and Sakhalin I., is known as **Ta'tar Strait** [tä'tēr] (*Russ.* **Ta·tar'ski Pro·liv'** [tŭ·tär'skĭ prŭ·lyĕf']).

Tate (tāt). County in Mississippi. See *Table* at Mississippi.

Ta·te·ya·ma (tä·tĕ·yä·mä). Volcanic peak 9892 ft., W cen. Honshu, Japan, SE of Toyama.

Ta'ti (tä'tĕ). Town, NE Bechuanaland Protectorate, S Africa, on border of Southern Rhodesia SE of Francistown; chief town of a district important for its gold (discovered 1864).

Ta·to'i (tä·toi'); *Mod. Gr.* **Ta·tó'ï** (tä·toi'). Town, E Attica and Boeotia dept., Greece, ab. 16 m. N of Athens; summer residence of former royal family; airport.

Ta·toosh′ Island (tȧ·tōōsh′). Small island off Cape Flattery, NW Washington; lighthouse; meteorological station.

Ta′tra Mountains (tä′trȧ) *or* **High Tatra** (*Czech* **Vy′so·ké Ta′try** [vĭ′sȯ·kȧ tȧ′trĭ]) **Mountains.** Chief mountain group of the cen. Carpathian Mts., N Slovakia, Czechoslovakia; highest peak Gerlsdorfer Spitze 8737 ft.; many small lakes; famous resort region.

Tatsienlu. See KANGTING.

Tattaeus, Palus. See TUZ LAKE.

Tatt′nall (tăt′n′l). County in Georgia. See *Table* at GEORGIA.

Ta–tu (dä′dōō′). Chinese name of Khanbalik (*q.v.*).

Ta·tuí′ (tȧ·twē′). City, São Paulo state, SE Brazil, 75 m. W of São Paulo; pop. (1940 est.) 10,514.

Ta′tung′ (dä′tŏŏng′). City, N Shansi prov., NE China, 180 m. W of Peiping; pop. ab. 50,000; has rail connections with Wanchuan (Kalgan) and Kweisui and has a good trade in livestock, coal, and furs; a very old town, its fortress dating back to the Ch′in and Han dynasties B.C. Nearby, ab. 10 m. distant, are the remarkable cave temples of Yunkang with stone Buddha images. Scene of fighting 1946 in Chinese civil war.

Tau (tou). Largest of the Manua Is. (*q.v.*) in American Samoa, in E part of group; 17 sq. m.

Tauata. See TAHUATA.

Tau′ba·té′ (tou′vȧ·tā′). City, São Paulo state, SE Brazil, 75 m. ENE of São Paulo on the Paraíba river; pop. (1940 est.) 28,070.

Tau′ber (tou′bēr). River 75 m. long in Bavaria, Germany; rises W of Ansbach, flows NW to the Main at Wertheim, N Baden.

Tau′ern (tou′ērn). Tunnel for railroad through the Hohe Tauern range of the Alps, 5.31 m. long, alt. 4021 ft., connecting the valley of the Gasteiner Ache in Salzburg, Austria, with NW Carinthia.

Tauern, Hohe. See *Table* at ALPS.

Tauern, Niedere. See NIEDERE TAUERN.

Tau·ghan′nock Falls (tŭ·găn′ŭk). Waterfall 215 ft. in a small stream in Tompkins co., New York, 1 m. from Cayuga Lake and 10 m. NW of Ithaca.

Tau·hu′nu (tou·hōō′nōō). Village, W coast of island of Manihiki, Manihiki Is., cen. Pacific Ocean.

Tau′ma·ru·nu′i (tou′mȧ·rōō·nōō′ē). Borough, Wellington provincial dist., W North I., New Zealand, on Wanganui river 170 m. N of Wellington; pop. 2480; resort and starting point for tourists to Tongariro National Park.

Taum Sauk Mountain (tôm′ sôk′). Peak 1772 ft. in Iron co., SE Missouri; highest point in the state.

Taung′gyi′ (toun′jē′). Town in Yawnghwe state, Southern Shan States, Burma, 95 m. SE of Mandalay; ✳ of Federated Shan States and chief town of Southern Shan States; pop. 8652.

Taung′myo′ Range (toun′myō′). Mountain range along the coast in Amherst dist., Lower Burma, extending S from Moulmein.

Taungs (toungz). Town, N Cape Province, S Union of South Africa, on an affluent of Vaal river 80 m. N of Kimberley; important tribal center. Taungs skull, a fossil skull of previously unknown race of anthropoid apes, found here.

Taun′ton (tän′t′n; tôn′-; tän′-). **1** River, SE Massachusetts; rises in N cen. Plymouth co., flows S into Mount Hope Bay at Fall River; navigable as far as Taunton.
2 Industrial city, a ⊗ of Bristol co., SE Massachusetts, on Taunton river at head of navigation 13 m. N of Fall River; pop. 41,132; manufactures textiles and textile machinery, marine engines, stoves, britannia ware, machine tools, silverware. Founded 1638; its industrial development began with establishment of an ironworking factory in 1656.
3 Municipal borough, ⊗ of Somersetshire, SW England, on the Tone 38 m. SW of Bristol; pop. 33,613; trade center for agricultural section.

Tau′nus (tou′nŏŏs). Mountain range in Hesse state, W Germany, E of the Rhine river and N of the lower Main; highest peak Grosser Feldberg 2886 ft.

Tau′po, Lake (tou′pō). Lake 238 sq. m. in cen. North I., New Zealand.

Tau·ra·ge′ (tou′rä·gä′). **1** District of Lithuania. See *Table* at LITHUANIA.
2 *Ger.* **Tau′rog′gen** (tou′rôg′ĕn). Town, its ✳, 65 m. WNW of Kaunas and NE of Tilsit; pop. (1938 est.) 10,465. Meeting place of a convention 1812 to consider neutrality bet. Russia and neighboring states.

Tau·rang′a (tou·räng′ȧ). Borough, Auckland provincial dist., N North I., New Zealand, on **Tauranga Harbor** (inlet of Bay of Plenty) 95 m. SE of Auckland; pop. 2790.

Taurasia. See TURIN.

Tau′reau′ Reservoir (tô′rō′). Reservoir in SW Quebec prov., Canada; outlet E through Mattawin river into St. Maurice river.

Tau′ria·no′va (tou′ryä·nô′vä). Commune, Reggio di Calabria prov., Calabria, S Italy, 28 m. NE of Reggio di Calabria; pop. (1931) 19,206.

Tau′ric Cher′so·nese (tô′rĭk kûr′sȯ·nēz; -nēs). The Crimea peninsula, part of the kingdom of the Cimmerian Bosporus; acquired by Rome 47 B.C.

Tau′ri·da (tô′rĭ·dȧ); *Russ.* **Ta·vri′da** (tŭ·vryē′dȧ). Former Russian government, now included in Crimea and S Ukraine.

Tauris. See TABRIZ.

Tauroggen. See TAURAGE.

Tauromenium. See TAORMINA.

Tau′rus Mountains (tô′rŭs); *Turk.* **To·ros′ Dağ′la·rı′** (tô·rôs′ dä′lä·rî′). Mountain chain in S Turkey in Asia, running parallel to the Mediterranean coast; has many high peaks, three above 11,000 ft.; crossed N of Tarsus by famous pass of Cilician Gates. To the NE the extension of the range is the Anti-Taurus (*q.v.*).

Ta·var′es (tȧ·vâr′ĕz). City, ⊗ of Lake co., cen. Florida penin., 28 m. NW of Orlando; pop. 2724; resort; citrus fruit growing.

Ta·vas′te·hus (tȧ·vȧs′tĕ·hōōs). **1** Swedish name of Häme dept., Finland: see *Table* at FINLAND.
2 See HÄMEENLINNA.

Tav·da′ (tŭf·dä′). **1** River ab. 650 m. long, W Siberia, chiefly in NE Sverdlovsk Region, Soviet Russia, Asia; flows SE from Ural Mts. to Tobol river SW of Tobolsk.
2 Town, E Sverdlovsk Region, on lower Tavda river ab. 125 m. W of Tobolsk.

Ta′ver′ny′ (tȧ′vĕr′nē′). Commune, Seine-et-Oise dept., France, just NNW of Paris; pop. (1931) 5303; church of 12th and 13th cents.

Ta′ve·u′ni (tä′vȧ·ōō′nĕ). One of the Fiji Is., in SW Pacific Ocean, 2 m. SE of Vanua Levu; 28 m. long; 166 sq. m.; chief village Waiyevo. Highest point 4070 ft. Grows coffee, sugar, cinchona, and tropical fruits and vegetables.

Ta′vi·gna′no (tä′vē·nyä′nȯ). River, cen. Corsica, flowing ESE to Tyrrhenian Sea.

Ta·vi′ra (tȧ·vē′rȧ). Commercial city, Faro dist., S Portugal, on Atlantic Ocean 18 m. NE of Faro; pop. 12,762; trades in white wines, mineral waters; tuna and sardine fisheries.

Tav′is·tock (tăv′ĭs·tŏk). Urban district, Devonshire, SW England, 17 m. N of Plymouth; pop. 5889.

Ta′vo·la′ra (tä′vȯ·lä′rä). Small island ab. 2½ sq. m. off NE coast of Sardinia, E of Terranova Pausania; pop. ab. 100; its settlement dates back to Roman times; since 1886 has considered itself independent.

Ta·voy′ (tȧ·voi′). **1** River ab. 90 m. long in Tavoy dist., Lower Burma; flows S into Andaman Sea E of Tavoy Penin. Its lower course for 30 m. forms a wide estuary.
2 District, Tenasserim division, Lower Burma; 5390 sq. m.; pop. 179,964.
3 Town, its ✳, on left bank of Tavoy river ab. 30 m. from its mouth; pop. 29,018.

Tavoy Island. Island in Andaman Sea off W coast of Lower Burma, S of Tavoy Point; northernmost of the Mergui Archipelago.

Tavoy Point. Cape extending into Andaman Sea at S end of **Tavoy Peninsula,** on W coast of Lower Burma at the mouth of Tavoy river, 13°30′N.

Tavrida. See TAURIDA.

Taw (tô). River ab. 50 m. long, Devonshire, SW England; flows NW into Barnstaple Bay through an estuary at Barnstaple.

Ta′was City (tô′wăs). City, ⊗ of Iosco co., NE Michigan; pop. 1810.

Ta′wau (tä′wou). **1** Residency, SE Brit. North Borneo; 7170 sq. m.; pop. 26,785.

2 Town, its ✳, port on coast of Celebes Sea.

Ta′wi (tŭ′wē). River ab. 95 m. long, Jammu, N India; flows SW in S Kashmir to Chenab river on the N Punjab border.

Ta′wi·ta′wi (tä′wē·tä′wē). **1** Island group, SW Sulu Archipelago, Phil. Is., comprising Tawitawi I., Sanga Sanga I., Simunul I., several smaller islands, and a number of clusters of small islands, totaling ab. 100; 360 sq. m.; pop. 24,054. See SULU province.

2 Large island of the group ab. 34 m. long by 6 to 14 m. wide; 229 sq. m.; pop. ab. 3280; of volcanic origin, with rich soil and covered with tropical vegetation. Highest point 1751 ft. Chief village (municipal district) Balimbing. Occupied by Americans Apr. 5, 1945.

Tawnggyi. Var. of TAUNGGYI.

Tawng′peng′ (tông′pĕng′). State of the Northern Shan States, Burma; 938 sq. m.; pop. 58,398; ✳ Namtu.

Tax′co, *in full* **Taxco de A′lar·cón′** (täs′kō thä ä′lärkôn′). Town, Guerrero state, S Mexico, ab. 45 m. S of Mexico City; pop. 4963; gold and silver mines; artists′ and tourists′ resort; silverware manufacture.

Tax′i·la (tăk′sĭ·là). Ruins of ancient town, just E of Indus river SW of Rawalpindi, West Punjab, Pakistan; of archaeological interest; the town was in the Persian Empire, visited by Alexander the Great 326 B.C., and later an important Buddhist center.

Tay (tā). Largest river in Scotland, ab. 120 m. long; rises near W border of Perth co., flows NE through **Loch Tay** (15 m. long) and then SE into the Firth of Tay.

Tay, Firth of. Estuary of the Tay river in E Scotland, N of the Firth of Forth; extends inland 25 m.; empties into North Sea.

Ta·ya′bas (tä·yä′bäs). **1** Province, E and S cen. Luzon, Phil. Is.; 4616 sq. m.; pop. 358,553; ✳ Lucena. Forms a long strip of territory of very irregular shape along the Pacific or E coast of Luzon; extends from SE Isabela prov. 16°35′N to Bondoc Point on Sibuyan Sea 13°10′N, an air-line distance of 240 m. Mountainous, with S end of Sierra Madre in the N and continuation of range, sometimes known as the Caraballo Sur, to the S; coast line includes many indentations, esp.: Baler Bay, Lamon Bay, and on S coast Ragay Gulf, Tayabas Bay, and Mompog Pass separating it from the island of Marinduque. Includes islands of Polillo group and Alabat on Pacific coast. Tagalogs live in the S; Ilokanos, Negritos, and primitive tribes are found in the N. Chief towns Lucena, Tiaong, Sariaya, Infanta, and Lopez.

History: Explored by Spaniards soon after settlement of Manila; original province, of small area, created 1591; much of the present province was during Spanish rule under jurisdiction of other provinces; suffered from revolt of 1841 and often from depredations of Moro pirates; boundaries increased in 1902 and 1920.

2 Municipality, SW Tayabas prov., 8 m. N of Lucena; pop. 18,172; largest town in province. Formerly the capital; a road and commercial center.

Tayabas Bay. Inlet in SW coast of Tayabas prov., S Luzon, Phil. Is.; W side borders on Batangas prov.; on SE connects with Mompog Pass. Lucena is on it.

Ta′yeh′ (dä′yě′). Town, Hupeh prov., E cen. China, 60 m. SE of Hanyang near Yangtze river; iron mines.

Ta·yg′e·tus (tä·ĭj′ĕ·tŭs). Mountain range in S Peloponnesus, Greece, forming border bet. Laconia and Messenia depts., and extending S in W Laconia along coast of Gulf of Messenia; highest point Hagios Elias 7904 ft.

Taying. See TAIPING.

Tay′lor (tā′lẽr). **1** Name of counties in seven states of the U.S. See *Tables* at FLORIDA, GEORGIA, IOWA, KENTUCKY, TEXAS, WEST VIRGINIA, WISCONSIN.

2 Village, ⊗ of Loup co., cen. Nebraska; pop. 280.

3 Borough, Lackawanna co., NE Pennsylvania, 3 m. WSW of Scranton; pop. 6148; coal mining.

4 City, Williamson co., cen. Texas, 28 m. NE of Austin; pop. 9434; trading and shipping center of cotton, dairying, and poultry-raising region; manufactures cotton products, mattresses, packed meats and other foods; oil refineries.

Taylor, Mount. Peak 11,380 ft. in NE Valencia co., W New Mexico.

Taylor Mountain. **1** Peak 13,600 ft. in Chaffee co., cen. Colorado.

2 Peak 9968 ft. in W cen. Lemhi co., E cen. Idaho.

Taylor Park Dam. Dam completed 1937 across **Taylor River,** tributary of Gunnison river, E Gunnison co., W cen. Colorado; height 204 ft.; impounds water for irrigation, forming **Taylor Park Reservoir.**

Tay′lors·ville (tā′lẽrz·vĭl; *sou. also* -v′l). **1** City, ⊗ of Spencer co., cen. Kentucky; pop. 937.

2 Town, ⊗ of Alexander co., W cen. North Carolina, in Blue Ridge Mt. foothills 18 m. WNW of Statesville; pop. 1470.

Tay′lor·ville (tā′lẽr·vĭl). City, ⊗ of Christian co., cen. Illinois, 25 m. SE of Springfield; pop. 8801; industrial, commercial, and coal-mining center.

Tay·tay′ (tī·tī′). Town on coast at N end of Palawan I., Phil. Is.; pop. 4173; established as a fort by Spaniards in early part of 18th cent.; held against Moro attacks and became capital of province of N end of island ab. 1818; replaced as capital by Cuyo, which was later replaced by Puerto Princesa.

Ta Yu Ling. See MEILING.

Taz (täz). River ab. 600 m. long, NW Siberia, Soviet Russia, Asia; rises in W Krasnoyarsk Territory, flows N and NW through E Yamalo-Nenets National District into **Taz Bay,** E arm of Gulf of Ob, 230 m. long, 35 m. at its widest part.

Ta′za (tä′zä). Town, N Morocco, NW Africa, E of Fez; pop. (1936) 14,973.

Taze′well (tăz′wĕl; -wěl). **1** Name of counties in two states of the U.S. See *Tables* at ILLINOIS and VIRGINIA.

2 Town, ⊗ of Claiborne co., NE Tennessee; pop. 1264.

3 Town, ⊗ of Tazewell co., SW Virginia; pop. 3000.

Tbilisi. See TIFLIS.

Tch-. For many names beginning thus, see CH-.

Tche Kam (chä′ kàm′). See KWANGCHOWAN.

Tchongking. = CHUNGKING.

Tczew (chěf); *Ger.* **Dir′schau** (dĭr′shou). Commune, E cen. Gdańsk dept., N Poland, on left bank of Vistula river 20 m. SSE of Danzig and just S of S border of Free City of Danzig territory; pop. (1938–39 est.) 25,398; important railroad junction connecting Baltic ports (Gdynia and Danzig) with Warsaw and W Poland; two fine bridges; manufactures sugar, paper, agricultural machinery. At beginning of World War II scene of fighting in early part of Sept. 1939.

Teague (tēg). City, Freestone co., E cen. Texas, 45 m. E of Waco; pop. 2728; in cotton and grain belt; cotton industries; livestock.

Te A′nau Lake (tā ä′nou). Lake in SW South I., New Zealand; 40 m. long; 132 sq. m.; a source of the Waiau river.

Tea′neck (tē′něk). Township, Bergen co., NE corner of New Jersey, 8 m. E of Paterson; pop. 42,085; residential suburb of New York metropolitan district.

Te·a′no (tā·ä′nō); *anc.* **Te·a′num Sid′i·ci′num** (tē·ä′nŭm sĭd′i·sī′nŭm). Commune, Napoli prov., Cam-

pania, S Italy, 29 m. N by W of Naples; pop. 13,684; early 12th-cent. cathedral, 8th-cent. church of San Benedetto, 10th-cent. church of Santa Maria de Foris; mineral springs.

Tea'pot' Dome (tē'pŏt'). United States naval oil reservation in Natrona co., cen. Wyoming; leased 1922 to private interests by Secretary of the Interior Albert B. Fall; later returned to government when Congressional investigation revealed irregularities in the transaction. See ELK HILLS.

Te A'ro·ha (tā ä'rō·à). Borough, Auckland provincial dist., N North I., New Zealand, on Thames river 70 m. SE of Auckland; pop. 2430; popular health resort with hot medicinal springs.

Teate. See CHIETI.

Teb, El. See EL TEB.

Te·bes'sa (tē·bĕs'à); anc. **The·ves'te** (thē·vĕs'tē). Commune, E Constantine dept., NE Algeria, near Tunisia border; pop. 11,550; as Theveste strategic town of Roman Africa, founded 1st cent. A.D.; site of extensive ruins. In World War II American base; threatened by German raid Feb.–Mar. 1943.

Te'bi·cua·ry' (tā'vē·kwä·rē'). River ab. 250 m. long, S Paraguay; flows W into Paraguay river.

Te·bing'ting'gi (tē·bǐng'tǐng'gē). 1 Town, NE Sumatra, Indonesia; pop. 14,026; on railroad just SE of Medan; center of tobacco cultivation.

2 Town, SE Sumatra, on S branch of Musi river ab. 60 m. E of Benkulen.

Tebing Tinggi. Island in Strait of Malacca off E coast of Sumatra, Indonesia, W of Singapore.

Té·bour'ba (*Angl.* tå·bōōr'bà). Town, N Tunisia, N Africa, ab. 32 m. W of the city of Tunis; battle May 4–8, 1943 in which British drove out the Germans.

Tecalutla. See NECAXA.

Teche, Bay'ou (bī'ōō [bī'ô, bī'ŭ] tĕsh'). Navigable stream ab. 175 m. long in Louisiana, flowing into Atchafalaya river; in Longfellow's "Evangeline Country."

Tec·pán' Gua'te·ma'la (tĕk·pän' gwä'tå·mä'lä). Town, Chimaltenango dept., S cen. Guatemala; pop. 5671.

Te·cua'la (tå·kwä'lä). Town, Nayarit state, W Mexico; pop. 6456.

Te·cu'ci (tē·kōōch'; -kōō'chĕ). City, S Moldavia region, E Romania, on a tributary of the Siret ab. 30 m. SSW of Bârlad; pop. 17,259.

Te·cum'seh (tē·kŭm'sĕ; -sĕ). 1 City, Lenawee co., S Michigan, 22 m. SSW of Ann Arbor; pop. 7045; trade center for agricultural section yielding esp. celery.

2 City, ⊗ of Johnson co., SE Nebraska, 31 m. E of Beatrice; pop. 1887; petroleum deposits nearby.

3 City, Pottawatomie co., cen. Oklahoma, 5 m. S of Shawnee; pop. 2630.

4 Town, Essex co., SE Ontario, Canada, on Lake St. Clair 10 m. E of Windsor; pop. 3543.

Ted'ding·ton (tĕd'ǐng·tŭn). Town, Middlesex, SE England, on the Thames in Twickenham municipal borough; Bushey Park; National Physical Laboratory.

Te·dzhen' (tĕ·jĕn'); formerly **Te·jend'** (tĕ·jĕnd'). The lower course of the Hari Rud (*q.v.*) in S Turkmen S.S.R., Soviet Central Asia; also the oasis near which the stream loses itself in sands of Kara Kum Desert.

Tees (tēz). River 70 m. long, N England; flows E along boundary bet. Yorkshire and Durham, empties into North Sea at Middlesbrough; navigable up to Stockton on Tees.

Tee'wi·not, Mount (tē'wĭ·nŏt). Peak 12,317 ft. in cen. Grand Teton National Park, NW Wyoming.

Tef·fé' (tå·fâ'). River ab. 500 m. long, Amazonas state, W Brazil; flows NE into Solimões river.

Te·gal' (tå·gäl'). Seaport, Central Java prov., Indonesia, on N coast railroad 50 m. W of Pekalongan; pop. 43,015; exports sugar; has numerous sugar mills.

Te'ge·a (tē'jē·à). Ancient city in SE Arcadia, cen. Peloponnesus, S Greece; the modern **Pi·a·li'** (pyä·lyē'),

in the department of Arcadia. Tegeans fought bravely at Plataea and supported Sparta in Peloponnesian Wars; fought against Sparta at Leuctra. Had famous temple of Athena Alea with work by the sculptor Scopas. See ARCADIA.

Te'ge·len (tā'ẖĕ·lĕ[n]). Commune, Limburg prov., SE Netherlands, just S of Venlo on German border; pop. 10,559.

Te'gern·see' (tā'gĕrn·zā'). 1 Lake 4 m. long in Bavaria, S Germany, 30 m. SSE of Munich, in foothills of Alps at 2382 ft. elevation; much frequented resort.

2 Village on lake; 15th-cent. church; castle.

Teg'na·pa'tam (tĕg'nà·pŭt'ăm). See FORT SAINT DAVID.

Te·gu'ci·gal'pa (tē·gōō'sĭ·gäl'pà; *Span.* tå·gōō'sĕ·gäl'pä). 1 See FRANCISCO MORAZÁN.

2 City, ✱ of Francisco Morazán dept., Honduras, and ✱ of Honduras; pop. (1940) 47,223; founded in 16th cent.; altitude ab. 3300 ft.; silver and gold mines nearby.

Te·hach'a·pi (tē·hăch'à·pī). City, Kern co., SW California, ESE of Bakersfield; pop. 3161.

Tehachapi Mountains. Range in S cen. California, running E-W bet. S end of the Sierra Nevada and the Coast Ranges; highest point 7950 ft.; at E end is **Tehachapi Pass,** 3793 ft., leading from Mojave Desert into the San Joaquin valley.

Te·ha'ma (tē·hä'mà). County in California. See *Table* at CALIFORNIA.

Te·ha'ma (tĭ·hä'mà; -mä). See TIHAMA.

Te·hip'i·te Dome (tē·hĭp'ĭ·tē). Peak 7713 ft. in Sierra Nevada in E Fresno co., S cen. California.

Te·hran' (tē·hrän') or **Te'he·ran'** (tĕ'ē·răn'; -rän'; tā'ĕ-; tē'ĕ-). 1 Province, N Iran; 13,717 sq. m.

2 City, its ✱ and ✱ of Iran, ab. 65 m. S of the Caspian Sea at foot of S slope of Elburz Mts.; pop. (1956) 1,512,082; altitude 3810 ft.; connected by highways and trade routes in all directions with chief towns of Iran and by rail with Bandar Shahpur in the SW and Bandar Shah to the NE. Old city has palace, museum, 12 gates but generally narrow streets; fine modern residential city has grown up recently in W part with Mohammedan colleges, American Mission, hospitals, and schools. Founded in 12th cent.; made capital c. 1788 by Agha Mohammed Khan. Site of conference Nov. 26–Dec. 2, 1943 bet. Churchill, Stalin, and Roosevelt.

Teh'ri (tā'rē). 1 or **Tehri Garh·wal'** (gŭr·wäl'). Former Indian state, NW Uttar Pradesh, N India; 4516 sq. m.; pop. (1941) 397,369; ✱ Tehri. Area lies entirely in the Himalayas with ranges 20,000 to 23,000 ft.; contains also the sources of both the Ganges and the Jumna and hence has many places of pilgrimage. State was established 1815 by the British after war with Nepal and administered formerly with Punjab States.

2 Town, its ✱, in the Himalayas on the Bhagirathi river 145 m. NE of Delhi; pop. 3387.

3 See TIKAMGARH.

Te'hsien' (dŭ'shĭ·ĕn'). Town, NW Shantung prov., NE China, on Grand Canal near Hopeh border 65 m. NW of Tsinan.

Te·hua (dŭ'hwä'). Town, S cen. Fukien prov., SE China, 45 m. NW of Tsinkiang; noted for its white porcelain (*blanc de chine*).

Te'hua·cán' (tā'wä·kän'). Town, Puebla state, SE cen. Mexico, 65 m. SE of Puebla; pop. 16,278; mineral springs.

Te·huan'te·pec (tĕ·wän'tĕ·pĕk; *Span.* tå·wän'tå·pĕk'). Town, Oaxaca state, S Mexico, on the Tehuantepec river; pop. 6734; hot springs; fruits, sugar, and vegetables.

Tehuantepec, Gulf of. Widemouthed inlet of the Pacific Ocean in SE Mexico, bounded by states of Oaxaca and Chiapas.

Tehuantepec, Isthmus of. Isthmus 130 m. wide in S Mexico, bet. the Bay of Campeche on the N and the Gulf of Tehuantepec on the S.

Teide, Pico de. See Pico de TEYDE.

Tei′fi (tī′vĭ). River 60 m. long, W Wales; flows SW and W into S Cardigan Bay.

Teign (tĭn; tēn). River, Devonshire, SW England; rises in Dartmoor and flows SE into the English Channel at Teignmouth.

Teign′mouth (tĭn′mŭth; tēn′-). Urban district, Devonshire, SW England, at mouth of the Teign 12 m. S of Exeter; pop. 10,589; seaport and watering place; yachting center; fisheries.

Teil, Le. See LE TEIL.

Teima. = TAIMA.

Tejend. See TEDZHEN.

Tejo. See TAGUS.

Te·ka′mah (tĕ·kä′mȧ). City, ⊗ of Burt co., E Nebraska, 28 m. NE of Fremont; pop. 1788; trade center in agricultural section.

Te·ka′po (tā·kä′pō). River in cen. South I., New Zealand; flows from S end of **Lake Tekapo** (32 sq. m.); one of the headstreams of the Waitaki river.

Te·kax′ (tā·käs′), *in full* **Te·kax′ de Ál′va·ro O′bre·gón′** (tā·käz′ thä äl′vä·rō ō′vrä·gôn′). Town, Yucatán state, on Yucatán penin., SE Mexico, on railroad ab. 60 m. S of Mérida; pop. 6061; Maya ruins.

Te·kir′dağ′ (tĕ·kēr′dä′). 1 Vilayet, S Turkey in Europe; 2297 sq. m.; pop. 194,252.

2 *Ital.* **Ro·do′sto** (rō·dôs′tō); *anc.* **Bi·san′the** (bĭ·săn′thē) *or* **Rhae·des′tus** (rē·dĕs′tŭs). Commercial port, its ✱, on the Sea of Marmara 78 m. W of İstanbul; pop. ab. 19,724; was long the trading port for region around Edirne, but railroad to Dede Agach (Alexandroúpolis) deprived it of its importance. Ancient Bisanthe was a Thracian town on the Propontis.

Tek·ke′ (tĕk·kĕ′). District of Ottoman Empire, SW coast of Asia Minor, nearly equivalent to modern Antalya vilayet, Turkey in Asia.

Te·ko′a (tē·kō′ȧ). **1** City, Whitman co., SE Washington, on Idaho border 35 m. SSE of Spokane; pop. 911; railroad shops.

2 Ancient village, Palestine, 5 m. S of Bethlehem; home of the prophet Amos (*Amos* i. 1).

Tekrit. See TIKRIT.

Te Ku·i′ti (tā koō·ē′tē). Borough, Auckland provincial dist., NW North I., New Zealand, on Waipa river 105 m. S of Auckland; pop. 2475. Station for Waitomo Caves (*q.v.*).

Te′la (tā′lä). Seaport, NW coast of Honduras, in Atlántida dept., halfway bet. Puerto Cortés and La Ceiba; pop. (1940) 8969; a center of the banana trade.

Te′la·vi (tĕ′lä·vĕ). Town, E Georgian S.S.R., U.S.S.R., 40 m. NE of Tiflis; pop. 8766.

Tel A·viv′ (tĕl′ ȧ·vēv′; ä·vēv′). Jewish city, W Palestine, NW of Jerusalem, in Lydda subdistrict; pop. 46,101, (1944 est.) 155,277; a well-built modern city serving as supply center for Jewish agricultural colonies in Palestine. Founded 1909 by colonists from Jaffa; has grown phenomenally with the immigration of Jews from Europe and other lands and financial aid given by Zionist organizations; capital of the new state of Israel 1948 to 1950.

Tel′de (tĕl′dā). Commune, Las Palmas prov. (E Canary Is.), Spain, on E Grand Canary I. 6 m. S of Las Palmas; pop. 22,298.

Tel Defenneh. See DAPHNAE.

Tel′e·graph Plateau (tĕl′ē·gráf). The bottom of the Atlantic Ocean bet. Newfoundland and Ireland where the ocean is shallow and many cables have been laid.

Tel el Amarna. = TELL EL ′AMARNA.

Tel el Kebir. = TELL EL-KEBIR.

Tel′e·mark (tĕl′ē·märk; *Norw.* tā′lĕ-). **1** Mountain and lake region in S Norway, in Telemark co.; highest peak Gausta over 6000 ft.

2 County in Norway. See *Table* at NORWAY.

Tel′e·scope Peak (tĕl′ē·skōp). Mountain 11,045 ft. in Panamint Mts., SE Inyo co., E California.

Tel′fair (tĕl′fâr). County in Georgia. See *Table* at GEORGIA.

Tel′ford (tĕl′fĕrd). Borough, Bucks and Montgomery cos., SE Pennsylvania, 21 m. S of Allentown; pop. 2763.

Te·lin·ga′na (tā′lĭng·gä′nȧ). Eastern division of Hyderabad state, S cen. India; 41,502 sq. m.; pop. 7,554,598; inhabited chiefly by the Telugu, a Dravidian people.

Tel·ka′lakh (tĕl·kȧ′lŭk). Town, S Latakia, Syria, on Lebanon border and on railroad from Tripoli to Homs.

Tell (tĕl). Hilly maritime region from 50 to 100 m. wide in NE Algeria and N Tunisia, N Africa.

Tell Ar·pa′chi·ya (tĕl är·pä′chĭ·yä). Ancient Assyrian city, part of Nineveh; its site is just N of Mosul, N Iraq, bet. the sites of Nineveh and Dur Sharrukin (see KHORSABAD).

Tell As′mar (tĕl ăs′mēr); *anc.* **Esh·nun′na** (ĕsh·nŭn′ȧ). Locality, E Iraq, 33 m. ENE of Baghdad; archaeological site where numerous stone statuettes and copper objects of the Sumerians have been found, dating c. 3000 to 2700 B.C.

Tell At′las (tĕl ăt′lȧs). = *Maritime Atlas:* see ATLAS MOUNTAINS.

Tell Basta. See BUBASTIS.

Tell City (tĕl). City, Perry co., S Indiana, on Ohio river 40 m. E of Evansville; pop. 6609; furniture factory; distillery.

Tell ed·Du·weir′ (tĕl′ ĕd′doō·wār′). The mound marking the site of ancient Lachish (*q.v.*), Judaea, S Palestine.

Tell el ′A·mar′na (tĕl′ ĕl′ ȧ·mär′nȧ). A station on the Nile river in ancient times, midway bet. Thebes and Memphis, site of the capital of Amenhotep IV; in the ruins important documents (Tell el ′Amarna tablets and Tell el ′Amarna letters) were found 1887, providing an important source of our knowledge of the period (Amarna Age) c. 1375–1360 B.C.

Tell el Far′rah (tĕl′ ĕl fär′ä). See TIRZAH.

Tell el-Ke·bir′ (tĕl′ ĕl′kĕ·bĭr′). Village, Sharqîya prov., N Egypt, near Zagazig; scene of victory of British over Egyptians Sept. 13, 1882.

Tell el Kha·li′fa (tĕl′ ĕl′ kȧ·lē′fä; kȧ-). Village, SW Jordan, the site of ancient Ezion-geber; archaeological excavations.

Tell el-O·beid′ (tĕl′ ĕl′ō·bād′; -bīd′). Locality, S Iraq, near right bank of lower Euphrates, SW of An Nasiriya and near site of Ur of the Chaldees; archaeological objects found here, esp. clay tablets of Sumerian kings of Ur.

Tel′ler (tĕl′ēr). **1** County in Colorado. See *Table* at COLORADO.

2 Village on Port Clarence Inlet, W Seward Penin., W Alaska, ab. 60 m. NNW of Nome; pop. (est.) 181.

Tel′li·cher′ry (tĕl′ĭ·chĕr′ĭ). Town, NW Kerala state, S Indian Union, on the Malabar Coast 168 m. WSW of Bangalore; pop. 30,349; commercial seaport and distribution point; exports sandalwood, coffee, spices, cardamons, cocoa, and coconuts. Has interesting old fort. Factory established here by British East India Co. 1683. Withstood two years′ siege 1780–82. Seat of Brennan College (founded 1862).

Tell Je·zar′ (tĕl′ jĕ·zär′). Site of ancient GEZER.

Tel·loh′ (tĕ·lō′). Village, SE Iraq, bet. lower Euphrates and Tigris rivers ab. 120 m. NW of Basra; site of ancient city of Lagash (*q.v.*).

Tel′lu·ride (tĕl′ū·rīd). City, ⊗ of San Miguel co., SW Colorado, 40 m. S of Montrose; pop. 677; founded as gold-mining camp 1875; gold, silver, lead mines; timber; stock raising; tourist resort.

Te·loek′be·toeng′ *or* **Te·luk′be·tung′** (tĕ·loōk′bĕ·toōng′). Seaport town, S Sumatra, Indonesia; pop. 25,170; at head of Lampong Bay on Sunda Strait; export town for pepper and coffee; connected with Palembang by rail and highway.

Te·loe′ti, *or* **Ta·lu′ti**, **Bay** (tĕ·loō′tē). Inlet of Banda Sea on S coast of Ceram I., Maluku prov., Indonesia.

Te'lok An'son (tĕ'lō ăn's'n). Town on the Perak river, a commercial port near its mouth, S Perak state, Federation of Malaya; pop. 14,671.

Te·lo'lo·a·pán' (tā·lō'lō·ä·pän'). Town, Guerrero state, S Mexico, 28 m. W of Iguala; pop. 5140.

Telo Martius. See TOULON.

Te'los (tē'lŏs); *Ital.* **Pi'sco·pi** (pēs'kō·pē). An island of the Dodecanese (*q.v.*), bet. Nisyros and Khalkē and NW of Rhodes; 25 sq. m.; pop. (1936) 1215.

Tel'pos-iz' *or* **Tel'pos Iz** (tĕl'pôs ĭz'). Peak 5558 ft. in the N Ural Mts., Soviet Russia, on the boundary bet. Europe and Asia, lat. 64°N.

Tel'shai (tĕl'shä); *Lith.* **Tel'šiai** (tĕl'shä). **1** District of Lithuania. See *Table* at LITHUANIA. **2** *Russ. formerly* **Tel'shi** (tyäl'y'·shĭ). Town, its *, 40 m. W of Shaulyai; pop. (1938 est.) 5812.

Tel'town (tĕl'toun). Village, co. Meath, Eire, 35 m. NW of Dublin; in early times scene of the great annual festival said to be instituted by the god Lug in honor of his foster mother Tailte and revived 1924 at Dublin as the Tailtean Games.

Telukbajur. See EMMAHAVEN.

Telukbetung. See TELOEKBETOENG.

Te'ma (tā'mȧ). Seaport city, SE Ghana, 20 m. ENE of Accra; pop. 27,000; new harbor, completed 1961.

Tema. See TAIMA.

Temagami, Lake. See Lake TIMAGAMI.

Te·mang'goeng (tĕ·mäng'gōong) *or* **Te·mang'-gung.** Town, Middle Java prov., Indonesia, ab. 17 m. N of Mageland; pop. 12,676.

Te'ma·tang'i (tā'mä·täng'ē). Outlying atoll of the Tuamotu Archipelago, in SW part 640 m. SE of Papeete.

Tem'be·ling (?tĕm'bĕ·lǐng). River, a headstream of the Pahang river, NE Pahang state, Federation of Malaya; joins with the Jelai to form the Pahang at ab. 4°N.

Témbi. See Vale of TEMPE.

Tem'bo, Mount (tĕm'bō). Mountain 3936 ft., N Gabon W equatorial Africa; highest point in the territory.

Tem'bu·land' (tĕm'bōō·lănd'). One of the Transkeian Territories, E Cape Province, Union of South Africa, bet. upper Great Kei river and the Umtata; 3339 sq. m.; pop. (1936) 282,116; * Umtata; includes Bomvanaland along the coast. Pastoral country, inhabited by Tembus, a Kaffir tribe.

Teme (tēm). River ab. 60 m. long, E Wales and W England; rises in E Wales near the English border, flows S and E across the border, and curves S to join the Severn near Worcester.

Te'me·ha'ni, Mount (tā'mě·hä'nē). Peak 3389 ft. on island of Raiatéa, Society Is., S Pacific Ocean.

Tem'er·loh (tĕm'ẽr·lō). Village, SW Pahang state, Federation of Malaya; pop. 1109; on cen. peninsula railroad and on left bank of Pahang river. In fighting area during Japanese invasion of peninsula Dec. 1941–Jan. 1942.

Temeš. See TIMIŞ.

Temesvár. See TIMIŞOARA.

Te'me·ti'u, Mount (tā'mȧ·tē'ōō). Peak 4134 ft., highest on Hiva Oa I., Marquesas Is., S Pacific Ocean.

Temir–Khan–Shura. See BUINAKSK.

Te'mir Tau (tā'mĭr tou'). Town in mountains at S end of Kuznetsk Basin, Kemerovo Region, Soviet Russia, Asia, ab. 50 m. S of Stalinsk; important because of recent discovery of high-grade iron ore.

Témiscamingue. See TIMISKAMING.

Té'mis·coua'ta (tĕm'ĭs·kwăt'ȧ; *Fr.* tā'mēs'kwä'tä'). **1** Lake 24 m. long, 29 sq. m., Témiscouata co., S Quebec prov., Canada; its outlet a tributary of St. John river. **2** County, Quebec, Canada; divided into **Ri'vière' du Loup** (rē'vyâr' dü lōō') co., 723 sq. m., pop. 37,375, ⊗ Rivière du Loup, and **Témiscouata** co., 1151 sq. m., pop. 28,175, ⊗ Notre Dame du Lac. See *Table* at QUEBEC.

Temiskaming. See TIMISKAMING.

Tem'pe (tĕm'pē). City, Maricopa co., SW cen. Arizona, on Salt river 9 m. E of Phoenix; pop. 24,897; in farming, dairying, and stock-raising region; Arizona State Univ. (1885; coed.).

Tem'pe, Vale of (tĕm'pē); *Mod. Gr.* **Tém'bi** (tâm'bē). Beautiful valley ab. 5 m. long in NE Thessaly, Greece; traversed by the Salambria (ancient Peneus) river in its lower course; lies bet. Mts. Olympus and Ossa.

Tem'peh (tĕm'pě). Town, East Java prov., Indonesia, near S coast SE of Malang; pop. 10,965.

Tem'per·ley' (tĕm'pẽr·lě'ē; -lā'). Town, Buenos Aires prov., E Argentina, a suburb of Buenos Aires (city).

Tem'pio, in full Tempio Pau·sa'nia (tĕm'pyō pou·zä'nyä). Commune, Sassari prov., NW Sardinia, 30 m. ENE of Sassari; pop. 15,752; episcopal see.

Tem'ple (tĕm'p'l). Commercial and industrial city, Bell co., cen. Texas, 34 m. S of Waco; pop. 30,419; railroad center and health resort; manufactures cottonseed oil, foundry and lumber products; in agricultural and stock-raising section.

Temple, Mount. Mountain 11,636 ft. in Banff National Park, Alberta, Canada, near Canadian Pacific Railway and near Brit. Columbia border.

Temple City. Urban community (unincorporated), Los Angeles co., SW California, E suburb of Los Angeles; pop. 31,838.

Tem'ple·ton (tĕm'p'l·t'n; -tŭn). Industrial town, Worcester co., cen. Massachusetts, 14 m. W of Fitchburg; pop. 5371.

Tem·ryuk' (tĕm'rĭ·ōōk'; *Russ.* tyĭm·rŭk'). Town, W Krasnodar Territory, Soviet Russia, Europe, on SE shore of Sea of Azov 75 m. W of Krasnodar; pop. 15,000; has fair harbor and considerable activity in fisheries.

Te·mu'co (tā·mōō'kō). City, * of Cautín prov., S cen. Chile, 80 m. NNE of Valdivia on the Cautín river; pop. 42,035; trade center, esp. in grains, fruit, and timber.

Te'na (tā'nä). Town, E cen. Ecuador, 70 m. SE of Quito; * of Napo-Pastaza prov. (*q.v.*).

Ten'a·fly (tĕn'ȧ·flī). Residential borough, Bergen co., NE corner of New Jersey, 11 m. E of Paterson; pop. 14,264; settled by Dutch and French Huguenots.

Ten'a·kee Inlet (tĕn'ȧ·kē). Inlet opening into Chatham Strait on E coast of Chichagof I., SE Alaska.

Te·na'li (tā·nä'lī). City, cen. Andhra Pradesh, E Indian Union, near Kistna river 160 m. ESE of Hyderabad; pop. 34,580.

Te'nan·cin'go, in full Tenancingo de De'gol·la'do (tā'nän·sēng'gō thä thā'gō·yä'thō). Town, México state, cen. Mexico, 40 m. SW of Mexico City E of Nevada de Toluca; pop. 6644.

Te·nan'go, in full Tenango de A·ris'ta (tā·näng'gō thä ä·rēs'tä). Town, México state, cen. Mexico, SW of Mexico City; pop. 5480.

Tenango de Rí'o Blan'co (thä rē'ō vläng'kō). Town, Veracruz state, E Mexico; pop. 9466.

Te·na'ru (tā·nä'rōō). Small river, N coast of Guadalcanal I., SE Solomon Is., W Pacific Ocean; empties into strait bet. Guadalcanal I. and Florida I. just E of Henderson Field. Battle Aug. 21, 1942.

Te·nas'ser·im (tĕ·năs'ẽr·ĭm). **1** River ab. 250 m. long, Tavoy and Mergui dists., Lower Burma; flows S and empties into Andaman Sea at Tenasserim. **2** Ancient region, later a province, along W coast of Indochina Penin. See YANDABU. **3** Division in S Lower Burma: see *Table* at BURMA. **4** Town, Mergui dist., Lower Burma, at mouth of Tenasserim river.

Ten'by (tĕn'bĭ). Municipal borough and seaport, Pembrokeshire, SW Wales, on Carmarthen Bay; pop. 4597; seaside resort and fishing center.

Tenda. See BRIGA-TENDA.

Ten Degree Channel. Passage in Bay of Bengal 90 m. wide, bet. Little Andaman I., southernmost island of the Andaman Is., and Car Nicobar, N island of the Nicobar Is., India; extends E and W along lat. 10°N.

Ten'dra (tĕn'drȧ; *Russ.* tyĕn'drȧ). Island 33 m. long in

the Black Sea 40 m. E of Odessa, Ukraine, U.S.S.R.; part of Nikolaev Region.

Tène, La. See LA TÈNE.

Tenedos. See BOZCAADA.

Ten′er·ife (tĕn′ẽr·ĭf; -ēf; *Span.* tā′nȧ·rē′fȧ; *older* **Ten′er·iffe** (tĕn′ẽr·ĭf; -ēf; *anc.* **Pin′tu·ar′i·a** (pĭn′-tṳ·âr′ĭ·ȧ). Largest of the Canary Is. (*q.v.*), Santa Cruz de Tenerife prov., Spain, in Atlantic Ocean 40 m. WNW of Grand Canary I.; 782 sq. m.; pop. (1930) 218,877; precipitous coast; its highest point, the volcanic Pico de Teyde (called also Peak of Tenerife) reaches 12,192 ft.; fertile soil, producing palms, dates, grapes, cotton, sugar, grain, and fruits; disastrous earthquake 1704; chief city Santa Cruz de Tenerife.

Tenerife, Pico de; Peak of Tenerife. See Pico de TEYDE.

Teneriffe. See TENERIFE.

Teng. See NAM TENG.

Tengchow. See PENGLAI.

Teng′chung′ (tŭng′chōŏng′); *formerly* **Teng′yueh′** (tŭng′yü·ĕ′) *or* **Mo′mein′** (mō′mān′). Treaty port town, W Yunnan prov., S China, 105 m. SW of Tali; pop. (1931 est.) 19,000. Opened for trade 1886, esp. with Bhamo in Burma; also connected by routes with Tali and with Myitkyina in Burma; W of Salween river, connected with Burma Road at Lungling. Taken by Chinese Sept. 1944 after being held by Japanese for two years.

Ten′ge (tĕng′gȧ); *also* **Ten′ke** (-kȧ). Town, Elisabethville prov., S Congo, 65 m. NW of Elisabethville; railroad junction point.

Teng′ger Mountains (tĕng′gẽr). Mountain group, E Java, Indonesia, S of Pasuruan; highest 9088 ft. Contains the Bromo, and on N slope is health resort of Tosari; on S joined with Semeru (*q.v.*).

Ten·giz′ (tĕng·gēz′), *or* **Ten·iz′** (tĕng·ēz′), **Lake.** Lake in steppe region of S Akmolinsk Region, Kazakh S.S.R., Soviet Central Asia, SW of Akmolinsk; has no outlet.

Teng′ri Khan (tĕng′rĕ kän′); *also* **Khan Tengri.** Mountain 23,620 ft. in the cen. Tien Shan range, Central Asia, on the border bet. Kirgiz S.S.R. and Sinkiang, W China.

Tengri Nor. See NAM TSO.

Tengyueh. See TENGCHUNG.

Tenimbar Islands. See TANIMBAR ISLANDS.

Ten·ka′si (tĕng·kä′sĭ). Town, S Madras, S Indian Union, ab. 90 m. SW of Madura; pop. 27,338.

Tenke. See TENGE.

Ten′ley·town (tĕn′lĭ·toun). Locality, NW suburb of Washington, D.C.; highest point 420 ft., in District of Columbia.

Ten′nes·see′ (tĕn′ĕ·sē′; tĕn′ĕ·sē). **1** Navigable river 652 m. long, E Tennessee, N Alabama, W Tennessee, and W Kentucky; formed by confluence of Holston and French Broad rivers near Knoxville, flows SW into N Alabama, W across N Alabama, then N across W Tennessee and W Kentucky and empties into Ohio river. Steady flow of water and sharp descent in certain areas have made river valuable for water-power project and creation of storage reservoirs. Muscle Shoals, a series of rapids ab. 37 m. long on S border of Lauderdale co., NW Alabama, was by 1890 known to have great potential water power; Wilson Dam at its W end near Florence, Alabama, was begun during World War I and Wheeler Dam, at its E end, much later; both became 1933 part of the Tennessee Valley Authority (*q.v.*).

2 Southeast central state of U.S.A., 16th state admitted to Union (1796); bounded on N by Kentucky and Virginia, on E by North Carolina, on S by Georgia, Alabama, and Mississippi, and on W by Arkansas and Missouri; 34th state in area, 42,244 sq. m. (land area 41,797 sq. m.); 17th state in population, 3,567,089; ✱ Nashville. See *Table of States* at UNITED STATES. Divided into the following 95 counties (for pronunciation of their names, see their individual entries):

NAME	LOCATION	AREA[1]	POP.[1]	CO. SEAT
Anderson	E	338	60,032	Clinton
Bedford	S cen.	482	23,150	Shelbyville
Benton	W	430	10,662	Camden
Bledsoe	SE cen.	404	7,811	Pikeville
Blount[2]	E	579	57,525	Maryville
Bradley	SE	338	38,324	Cleveland
Campbell	N	447	27,936	Jacksboro
Cannon	cen.	271	8,537	Woodbury
Carroll	W	596	23,476	Huntingdon
Carter	NE	355	41,578	Elizabethton
Cheatham	NW cen.	305	9,428	Ashland City
Chester	W	285	9,569	Henderson
Claiborne	NE	446	19,067	Tazewell
Clay	N	235	7,289	Celina
Cocke[2]	E	434	23,390	Newport
Coffee	S cen.	435	28,603	Manchester
Crockett	W	269	14,594	Alamo
Cumberland	E cen.	679	19,135	Crossville
Davidson	N cen.	533	399,743	Nashville
Decatur	W	346	8,324	Decaturville
De Kalb	cen.	276	10,774	Smithville
Dickson	NW cen.	486	18,839	Charlotte
Dyer	NW	527	29,537	Dyersburg
Fayette	SW	704	24,577	Somerville
Fentress	N	498	13,288	Jamestown
Franklin	S	560	25,528	Winchester
Gibson	NW	607	44,699	Trenton
Giles	S	619	22,410	Pulaski
Grainger	NE	310	12,506	Rutledge
Greene	NE	617	42,163	Greeneville
Grundy	S cen.	358	11,512	Altamont
Hamblen	NE	174	33,092	Morristown
Hamilton	SE	576	237,905	Chattanooga
Hancock	NE	230	7,757	Sneedville
Hardeman	SW	655	21,517	Bolivar
Hardin[3]	SW	587	17,397	Savannah
Hawkins	NE	494	30,468	Rogersville
Haywood	W	519	23,393	Brownsville
Henderson	W	515	16,115	Lexington
Henry	NW	599	22,275	Paris
Hickman	W cen.	613	11,862	Centerville
Houston	NW	207	4,794	Erin
Humphreys	W	555	11,511	Waverly
Jackson	N	327	9,233	Gainesboro
Jefferson	E	318	21,493	Dandridge
Johnson	NE corner	299	10,765	Mountain City
Knox	E	511	250,523	Knoxville
Lake	NW corner	164	9,572	Tiptonville
Lauderdale	W	485	21,844	Ripley
Lawrence	S	634	28,049	Lawrenceburg
Lewis	SW cen.	285	6,269	Hohenwald
Lincoln	S	580	23,829	Fayetteville
Loudon	E	240	23,757	Loudon
McMinn	SE	435	33,662	Athens
McNairy	SW	569	18,085	Selmer
Macon	N	304	12,197	Lafayette
Madison	N	561	60,655	Jackson
Marion	S	507	21,036	Jasper
Marshall	S cen.	377	16,859	Lewisburg
Maury	W cen.	614	41,699	Columbia
Meigs	SE	206	5,160	Decatur
Monroe	SE	662	23,316	Madisonville
Montgomery	NW	543	55,645	Clarksville
Moore	S	124	3,454	Lynchburg
Morgan	NE cen.	539	14,304	Wartburg
Obion	NW	550	26,957	Union City
Overton	N	439	14,661	Livingston
Perry	W	419	5,273	Linden
Pickett	N	157	4,431	Byrdstown
Polk	SE corner	436	12,160	Benton
Putnam	N cen.	406	29,236	Cookeville
Rhea	E cen.	323	15,863	Dayton
Roane	E	354	39,133	Kingston
Robertson	N	476	27,335	Springfield
Rutherford	cen.	630	52,368	Murfreesboro
Scott	N	549	15,413	Huntsville
Sequatchie	SE cen.	273	5,915	Dunlap
Sevier[2]	E	603	24,251	Sevierville
Shelby	SW corner	751	627,019	Memphis
Smith	N cen.	325	12,059	Carthage
Stewart	NW	484	7,851	Dover
Sullivan	NE	428	114,139	Blountville
Sumner	N	549	36,217	Gallatin
Tipton	W	458	28,564	Covington
Trousdale	N	116	4,914	Hartsville
Unicoi	NE	185	15,082	Erwin
Union	NE	212	8,498	Maynardville
Van Buren	cen.	255	3,671	Spencer
Warren	cen.	442	23,102	McMinnville
Washington	NE	327	64,832	Jonesboro
Wayne	S	741	11,908	Waynesboro
Weakley	NW	576	24,227	Dresden
White	cen.	383	15,577	Sparta
Williamson	cen.	593	25,267	Franklin
Wilson	N cen.	580	27,668	Lebanon

[1] Area = land area in sq. m. Pop. from 1960 Census.
[2] Includes part of Great Smoky Mountains National Park.
[3] Shiloh National Military Park in SW part of county.

KENTUCKY
AND
TENNESSEE

Statute Miles

0 10 20 30 40

★ State Capital

PUBLISHED BY G. & C. MERRIAM COMPANY
SPRINGFIELD, MASS.
PREPARED BY J. W. CLEMENT CO., BUFFALO, N. Y.

Nickname: Volunteer State. *State flower:* Iris. *Motto:* Agriculture, Commerce. *Chief cities:* Memphis, Nashville, Chattanooga, Knoxville. *Rivers:* Mississippi, forming W boundary; Tennessee (see 1, above). *High point:* Clingmans Dome 6642 ft., on Tennessee-North Carolina border. *Chief industries:* Agriculture (cotton, corn), lumbering, mining (esp. coal).

History: Originally a part of the French Louisiana claim; included in charter of Carolina 1663; claim to region ceded by France to Great Britain 1763; region explored by Daniel Boone 1769; acknowledged by Great Britain as a part of United States 1783; temporary state of Franklin (*q.v.*) formed 1784; North Carolina relinquished claims 1790; Territory South of the Ohio, coterminous with Tennessee, organized 1790; admitted to Union June 1, 1796; passed ordinance of secession May 6, 1861; scene of battles in Civil War, notably Shiloh, Chattanooga, Stone River, Nashville; slavery abolished and ordinance of secession declared null and void 1865; first of seceding states to be reorganized and readmitted to Union (July 24, 1866).

Tennessee Pass. Mountain pass 10,424 ft., Lake and Eagle cos., NW cen. Colorado, in the Front Range of the Rocky Mts.; used since c. 1873; railroad.

Tennessee Valley Authority. *Abbr.* **TVA** (tē′vē′ā′) A United States Government Administrative Agency created by Congressional Act May 18, 1933 and later amendments, to develop the Tennessee river system in the interests of transportation, flood control, and national defense and to generate and sell surplus electricity to avoid waste of water power. The region of the system (40,910 sq. m.; pop. ab. 3,000,000) includes a large part of E and W Tennessee, a large area in N Alabama, and smaller areas in W Kentucky, NE Mississippi, N Georgia, W North Carolina, and SW Virginia, and extends from Paducah, Kentucky, to the sources of tributaries of the Tennessee river in Virginia, North Carolina, and Georgia. Elevations range from 300 ft. above sea level at Paducah to more than 6000 ft. in mountains of E Tennessee. This multiple-purpose water-control project includes (1948) 24 major dams and several smaller dams (see *Table,* p. 1129), a 627-mile navigation channel of 9-ft. draft, and many hydroelectric power stations, aluminum and nitrate plants, and dehydrators. Hydroelectric power generated for private and industrial use by 1948 was 2,570,902 kilowatts. First dam completed as early as 1912 (and with others subsequently purchased by the TVA) but most have been constructed since 1936.

Ten′nille (těn′′l). City, Washington co., cen. Georgia, 60 m. SW of Augusta; pop. 1837.

Teno. See TANA.

Te·noch′ti·tlán′ (tâ·nŏch′tē·tlän′). Ancient name of Mexico City, which with Texcoco and Tlacopán formed the Aztec confederacy and became the capital of the Aztec empire. Founded 1325 in the marshes of Lake Texcoco and by the time of the arrival of the Spaniards was a large and powerful city; occupied by Cortes Nov. 8, 1519 but evacuated with heavy losses July 7, 1520; destroyed by Spaniards 1521.

Te·nom′ (tě·nŏōm′). Town, W cen. Sabah, 60 m. S of Jesselton.

Te′nos (tē′nŏs); *Mod. Gr.* **Tē′nos** *or* **Ti′nos** (tē′nŏs). **1** Island, NE Cyclades, part of Cyclades dept., Greece; 79 sq. m.; pop. ab. 12,000; fertile, produces much wine. **2** Chief town of island, on S coast; pop. 2485.

Ten·ryu (těn·rū). River 134 m. long, S cen. Honshu, Japan; rises in Nagano prefecture, flows S into Pacific Ocean W of Suruga Bay.

Ten′sas (těn′sô). **1** River in Alabama. See TENSAW. **2** Parish in Louisiana. See *Table* at LOUISIANA.

Tensas River *or* **Bayou;** *called also* **Ten′saw River** (těn′sô). River 250 m. long, NE Louisiana; flows from East Carroll parish S into Ouachita river.

Ten′saw *or* **Ten′sas** (těn′sô). Navigable river ab. 40 m. long, SW Alabama; formed (with the Mobile river) by

confluence of Tombigbee and Alabama rivers, flows S into Mobile Bay at Mobile.

Ten·sift′ (těn·sĭft′). River ab. 124 m. long, W Morocco, NW Africa; flows W through city of Marrakesh into Atlantic Ocean.

Ten Thousand Islands. Group of many small islands in Gulf of Mexico, off SW Collier co., SW Florida.

Ten Thousand Smokes, Valley of. See VALLEY OF TEN THOUSAND SMOKES.

Tentyra. See DENDERA.

Te′o·cal′co (tā′ô·käl′kô). Town, S Hidalgo state, cen. Mexico, on railroad W of Pachuca.

Te′o·cal·ti′che (tā′ô·käl·tē′chä). Town, Jalisco state, W cen. Mexico, 70 m. NE of Guadalajara; pop. 7915.

Te′o·do′ro (tā′ô·thô′rōō). = Rio ROOSEVELT.

Te·ó′fi·lo O·to′ni (tā·ô′fē·lōō ô·tō′nĕ). City, E cen. Minas Gerais state, E Brazil, 230 m. NE of Belo Horizonte; pop. (1940 est.) 12,254.

Te′os (tē′ŏs). Ancient city on the coast of Asia Minor, on S shore of peninsula of Smyrna; one of the 12 Ionian Cities; birthplace of Anacreon.

Te′o·ti′hua·cán′ *or* **San Juan Teotihuacán** (säng hwän′ tā′ô·tē′wä·kän′). Town, México state, cen. Mexico, 30 m. NE of Mexico City; site of famous Toltec ruins, including the Pyramid of the Sun (216 ft. high) with terraced sides and stairs leading to the summit, the Pyramid of the Moon (ab. 150 ft. high), the Temple of Tlaloc (rain-god) and of Quetzalcoatl (lord of the air and wind). Cf. CHOLULA.

Te·pa′ti·tlán′, *in full* **Tepatitlán de Mo·re′los** (tâ·pä′tē·tlän′ dä mô·rā′lôs). Town, Jalisco state, W cen. Mexico, 43 m. ENE of Guadalajara; pop. 8894.

Te′pe Gaw·ra′ (tĕ′pĕ gou·rä′). Ancient Assyrian city, just NNE of Nineveh; site a few miles E of Khorsabad, N Iraq.

Te·pe′ji del Rí′o (tâ·pĕ′hĕ thĕl rē′ô). Town, Hidalgo state, cen. Mexico; pop. 5815.

Te′pe·le′nĕ (tā′pä·lā′nĕ) *or* **Te′pe·le′ni** (-nĕ). Town, S Albania, on Vijosë river SE of Vlona; fighting in neighborhood 1940–41.

Te′pex·pán′ (tā′pâs·pän′). Village near Texcoco, NE México state, cen. Mexico; site of discovery 1947 of 10,000-year-old skeleton ("Tepexpán man"), probably the oldest human remains found in Western Hemisphere.

Te·pic′ (tâ·pēk′). Town, W Mexico, ✳ of Nayarit state, near W coast 110 m. NW of Guadalajara; pop. 17,547.

Te′pli·ce–Ša′nov (tĕ′plĭ·tsĕ·shä′nôf); *Ger.* **Tep′litz–Schö′nau** (tĕp′lĭts·shû′nou). City, N Bohemia prov., W Czechoslovakia, in the Erz Gebirge near German border; pop. (1930) 30,911; watering place, with warm mineral springs; scene of formation (Treaty of Teplitz Sept. 9, 1813) of 6th coalition against Napoleon, including Prussia, Russia, Sweden, Great Britain, Austria.

Te′quen·da′ma Falls (tā′kän·dä′mä). Waterfall 475 ft. high in the Funza river (a tributary of the Magdalena) 10 m. S of the city of Bogotá, Colombia.

Teques, Los. See LOS TEQUES.

Te·rai′ (tě·rī′). A swampy lowland belt in India, N of the Ganges and at the foot of the Himalayas.

Te·ra·mo (tâ′rä·mô). **1** Province of Italy. See *Table* at ITALY.

2 *anc.* **In′ter·am′na** (ĭn′tĕr·ăm′nả) *or* **In′ter·am′ni·a** (-nĭ·ả). Commune, its ✳, Abruzzi e Molise, cen. Italy, 82 m. NE of Rome; pop. 33,796; astronomical observatory; 12th-cent. cathedral; remains of ancient Roman theater. Under Byzantine rule in Middle Ages; conquered by Normans 1156 and absorbed by kingdom of Naples.

Ter·cei′ra (tĕr·sā′ê·rả). Island, cen. Azores, in the district of Angra do Heroísmo; 233 sq. m.; pop. ab. 48,000; ✳ Angra do Heroísmo. Site of Lagens Field, U.S. Air Force base.

Ter·ce′ro (tĕr·sā′rô). River in Córdoba prov., cen. Argentina; unites with Saladillo river to form Carcarañá river.

Name[1]	Location		Year of First Use	Max. Height (in Feet)	Length of Crest (in Feet)	Useful Controlled Storage (in Acre-Feet)	Area of Reservoir at Gate-top Level (in Acres)
	State	River and Distance from Mouth					
DAMS ON TENNESSEE RIVER[2]							
Kentucky	Ky.	22.4 m.	1944	206	8,422	4,010,800	158,300
Pickwick Landing	Tenn.	206.7 m.	1938	113	7,715	418,400	42,800
Wilson	Ala.	259.4 m.	1925	137	4,862	52,500	15,800
Wheeler	Ala.	274.9 m.	1936	72	6,342	347,500	67,100
Guntersville	Ala.	349 m.	1939	94	3,979	162,900	69,100
Hales Bar	Tenn.	431.1 m.	1913	112	2,315	13,100	6,750
Chickamauga	Tenn.	471 m.	1940	129	5,800	329,400	34,500
Watts Bar	Tenn.	529.9 m.	1942	112	2,960	377,600	38,600
Fort Loudoun	Tenn.	602.3 m.	1943	122	4,190	109,300	14,500
DAMS ON TRIBUTARIES OF TENNESSEE RIVER[3]							
Apalachia	N.C.	Hiwassee riv., 66.1 m.	1943	150	1,308	35,730	1,123
Blue Ridge	Ga.	Toccoa riv., 16 m.	1931	167	1,000	183,000	3,290
Calderwood	Tenn.	Little Tennessee riv., 43.6 m.	1930	230	897	4,090	538
Chatuge	N.C. and Ga.	Hiwassee riv. above Hiwassee, 120.9 m.	1942[4]	144	2,850	229,300	7,150[5]
Cheoah	N.C.	Little Tennessee riv., 51.4 m.	1919	230	770	7,260	640
Cherokee	Tenn.	Holston riv., 52.2 m.	1942	175	6,760	1,473,100	30,200
Douglas	Tenn.	French Broad riv., 32.2 m.	1943	202	1,705	1,419,700	30,600
Fontana[6]	N.C.	Little Tennessee riv., 61 m.	1945	480	2,365	1,157,300	10,670
Glenville	N.C.	W. Fork Tuckaseigee riv., 9.7 m.	1941	150	900	66,670	1,462
Great Falls	Tenn.	Caney Fork, trib. of Cumberland riv.	1916	92	800	49,400	2,270
Hiwassee	N.C.	Hiwassee riv., 75.8 m.	1940	307	1,287	364,700	6,240
Nantahala	N.C.	Nantahala riv., 22.8 m.	1942	250	1,042	124,900	1,605
Nolichucky	Tenn.	Nolichucky riv., 46 m.	1913	7	[8]	8,050	930
Norris	Tenn.	Clinch riv., 79.8 m.	1936	265	1,860	2,281,000	34,200
Nottely	Ga.	Nottely riv., 21 m.	1942[4]	184	2,300	184,000	4,290
Ocoee No. 1	Tenn.	Ocoee riv., 11.9 m.	1912	135	840	33,100	1,900
Ocoee No. 2	Tenn.	Ocoee riv., 24 m.	1913	30	450	none	small[8]
Ocoee No. 3	Tenn.	Ocoee riv., 29.2 m. above Ocoee No. 2	1943	110	612	9,370	606
Santeetlah	N.C.	Cheoah riv., 9.3 m.	1928	200	1,150	131,000	2,850
South Holston[9]	Tenn.	S. Fork Holston riv., 49.8 m.		290	1,550	660,000	8,000
Watauga[9]	Tenn.	Watauga riv., 35.5 m.		318	900	627,000	6,400
Wilbur	Tenn.	Watauga riv., 38 m.	1912	[10]	363	427	61

[1] The same name often applies to the reservoir or lake.   [2] Listed in the order of their location from the mouth of the Tennessee to its source near Knoxville.   [3] Listed in alphabetical order.   [4] Date of closure. Power-generating facilities not yet provided.   [5] Reservoir straddles state line.   [6] Highest dam east of the Rocky Mts.   [7] Average full head 67.5 ft.   [8] No definite figure available.   [9] Under construction.   [10] Average full head 58 ft.

Te′rek (tā′rĕk; *Russ.* tyä′ryĭk). **1** River ab. 380 m. long, Soviet Russia, Europe, N of Caucasus Mts.; rises in Georgia at the base of Mt. Kazbek and flows N through Daryal Pass, turning E near Nalchik through steppe region to a wide delta on NW shore of Caspian Sea; some of its delta streams are dry during part of the year. **2** Former Russian government N of Caucasus Mts. now largely included in Kabardino-Balkarian, North Ossetian, and Dagestan Autonomous Republics, and Grozny Region, SE Soviet Russia, Europe.

Terek Pass. Mountain pass, alt. 12,730 ft., in W Tien Shan range, Central Asia, 40 m. N of Kashgar, E of Turugart Pass; much traveled route from W Sinkiang to Kirgiz S.S.R. and the fertile Fergana valley.

Te′re·si′na (tā′rĕ·zē′nȧ). City, ✻ of Piauí state, NE Brazil, on Parnaíba river 270 m. from Parnaíba; pop. (1940 est.) 35,254.

Te′re·só′po·lis (tā′rĕ·zô′pōō·lês). City, Rio de Janeiro state, SE Brazil, a mountain resort (3000 ft.) near Petrópolis, N of Rio de Janeiro; pop. 9877.

Te·res′sa (tĕ·rĕs′ȧ). One of the Nicobar Is. (*q.v.*).

Tergeste. See TRIESTE seaport.

Terglou. See TRIGLAV.

Te′ri·o·ki (tĕ′rĭ·yô′kĭ); *Finnish* **Te′ri·jo′ki** (tĕ′rĭ·yô′kĭ). Town, NW Leningrad Region, U.S.S.R., N shore of Gulf of Finland ab. 30 m. WNW of Leningrad; pop. 8278; formerly in Viipuri dept., Finland; taken by Russians Dec. 1939; here a short-lived puppet government formed Dec. 1939 by Finnish Communists, known as Terijoki "People's Government."

Ter·liz′zi (tär·lēt′tsē). Commune, Bari prov., Apulia, SE Italy, 16 m. W of Bari; pop. 21,612.

Ter·mez′ (tĕr·mĕz′). Town on N bank of the Amu Darya, SE Uzbek S.S.R., Soviet Central Asia, on Afghan border 160 m. S of Samarkand; pop. 5025; ✻ of the Sukhan-Darya region; on railroad; has an airport.

Ter′mi·ni I·me·re′se (tĕr′mē·nē ē·mā·rā′sā); *anc.* **Ther′mae Him′er·en′ses** (thûr′mē hĭm′ēr·ĕn′sēz). Seaport, Palermo prov., Sicily, on N coast 22 m. ESE of Palermo; pop. 20,845; remains of ancient Roman theater; 17th-cent. cathedral; convent; museum; mineral springs. Near ancient Himera (*q.v.*).

Tér′mi·nos, La·gu′na de (lä·gōō′nä thä tĕr′mē·nôs). Inlet, SE Bay of Campeche, on shore of state of Campeche, SE Mexico; enclosed by Carmen I.

Ter′mo·li (tĕr′mô·lē). Port, Campobasso prov., S Abruzzi e Molise, cen. Italy, on the Adriatic Sea; pop. 8755; 13th-cent. cathedral, castle.

Ter′monde′ (tĕr′mônd′). Commune, East Flanders prov., NW cen. Belgium, at the confluence of the Schelde and Dender rivers SW of Antwerp; pop. 9835; captured and pillaged by the Germans Sept. 1914.

Ter·na′te (tĕr·nä′tȧ). **1** Northern division of former Moluccas residency, E Netherlands Indies; 115,831 sq. m.; pop. 492,758; ✻ Ternate. Comprised large island of Halmahera, Batjan and Obi groups, and the small islands of Ternate and Tidore—all in the Moluccas proper; also four regions of N part of Neth. New Guinea and the islands off their shores Waigeo and Misoöl to the NW and Schouten Is., Japen I., and others to the N. **2** Small island, but one of most important of the Moluccas, in Indonesia, off the W coast of Halmahera I.; ab. 25 sq. m.; pop. 19,533. Consists mainly of a conical volcano ab. 5600 ft. high, with three peaks; has suffered many eruptions in the last four centuries, the severest in 1763 and 1840; thickly forested; has remarkably fertile soil. Long famous for its spices, esp. cloves. In 16th cent. a sultanate; settled by Portuguese 1521 who were expelled 1581; alliance bet. sultan and the Dutch 1607; sultan extended his territory by conquests in the Moluccas and Celebes, but conflicts with Dutch began 1635; finally completely subjected to Dutch 1683; seized by Japanese 1942. See AMBOINA. **3** Town, on S side of island at foot of volcano; pop. 7126; port of call for steamers.

4 Municipality, on NW coast of Cavite prov., Luzon, Phil. Is., 15 m. SW of City of Cavite; pop. 4082; terminus of coastal road. Founded 1660 by Jesuits with exiles from the Moluccas brought by the Spanish government when those islands were abandoned.

Terneuzen. See NEUZEN.

Ter′ni (tĕr′nē). **1** Province of Italy. See *Table* at ITALY. **2** *anc.* **In′ter·am′na Na′hars** (ĭn′tĕr·ăm′nȧ nä′härz). Commune, its ✻, Umbria, cen. Italy, on Nera river 49 m. N by E of Rome; pop. 68,890; 17th-cent. cathedral; Roman remains; waterfalls (Cascata delle Marmore 650 ft.) nearby furnish industrial power; manufactures steel, iron, calcium carbide, armaments, linen. Destroyed by Totila 546 A.D., Narses 553, Lombards 755, and Archbishop Christian of Mainz 1174; joined Papal States 1420.

Ter·no′pol (tĕr·nô′pŭl; *Russ.* tyĕr·nô′pŭl·y′); *Pol.* **Tar·no′pol** (tär·nô′pôl). **1** Subdivision of the Ukraine, U.S.S.R., in W part, approximately the former Tarnopol dept. of Poland. **2** City, its ✻, 70 m. ESE of Lvov; pop. (1938–39 est.) 40,000; ✻ of former Tarnopol dept., Poland; manufactures machinery, alcohol, candy, chalk, soap; famous horse market; important railroad junction. Founded 1540; a prominent town under the Polish kings; occupied by Russians at beginning of World War I, held from 1915 to July 1917, when it was taken by armies of Central Powers; taken by Germans 1941, and retaken by Russians Mar. 1944.

Ter′ra Al′ta (tĕr′ȧ äl′tȧ). Town, Preston co., N West Virginia, 27 m. SE of Morgantown; pop. 1504; resort.

Ter·ra·ci′na (tĕr′rä·chē′nä); *anc.* **Anx′ur** (ăngk′sĕr); *later* **Tar′ra·ci′na** (tär′ȧ·sī′nȧ). Seaport, Littoria prov., Latium, cen. Italy, just SE of Pontine Marshes and W of Gaeta; pop. 23,559; ruins of ancient temple of Jupiter; cathedral; ancient town on Appian Way. In World War II was W end of German defense line (Hitler Line) across Italy 1944.

Ter·ral′ba (tĕr·räl′bä). Commune, Cagliari prov., S Sardinia, 44 m. NW of Cagliari; pop. 11,767.

Ter′ra·no′va Bracciolini (tĕr′rä·nô′vä). Var. of TERRANUOVA BRACCIOLINI.

Terranova di Sibari. See SYBARIS.

Terranova di Sicilia. See GELA.

Terranova Pau·sa′nia (pou·zä′nyä); *anc.* **Ol′bi·a** (ôl′bĭ·ȧ). Commune, Sassari prov., Sardinia, on NE coast of Sardinia 50 m. E by N of Sassari; pop. 10,157; harbor; 11th-cent. church; airport.

Ter′ra·nuo′va Brac′cio·li′ni (tĕr′rä·nwô′vä brät′chô·lē′nē). Commune, Arezzo prov., Tuscany, cen. Italy, 16 m. WNW of Arezzo; pop. (1931) 11,561.

Terre′bonne′ (tĕr′bŏn′; -bôn′). **1** Bayou in Terrebonne parish, SE Louisiana; flows S into Terrebonne Bay. **2** Parish in Louisiana. See *Table* at LOUISIANA. **3** County, Quebec, Canada. See *Table* at QUEBEC. **4** Town, Terrebonne co., on left bank of the Rivière des Mille Îles 14 m. N of Montreal; pop. 3200. In early days headquarters for fur traders; founded 1727.

Terrebonne Bay. Inlet of Gulf of Mexico on SE coast of Terrebonne parish, SE Louisiana.

Ter′re Haute (tĕr′ĕ hōt′). City, ⊗ of Vigo co., W Indiana, on Wabash river 67 m. WSW of Indianapolis; pop. 72,500; coal mining; manufactures brick and tile, steel products, boilers, pasteboard containers. Rose Polytechnic Institute (1874; men); Indiana State Teachers Coll. (1865; coed.); nearby is Saint Mary-of-the-Woods Coll. (1840; women; Rom. Cath.).

Ter′rel, Mount (tĕr′ĕl). Peak 11,560 ft. in Sevier co., cen. Utah.

Ter′rell (tĕr′ĕl). **1** Name of counties in two states of the U.S. See *Tables* at GEORGIA and TEXAS. **2** Industrial city, Kaufman co., NE Texas, 27 m. E of Dallas; pop. 13,803; cottonseed, lumber, wheat, dairy products, and feed crops.

Terrell Hills. City, Bexar co., S cen. Texas, NE of San Antonio; pop. 5572.

Terre'noire' (tĕr'nwår'). Town, Loire dept., SE cen. France, just E of Saint-Étienne; pop. 3256; steelworks.

Terres Mauvaises. See BAD LANDS.

Ter'ri'toire' du Nord (tĕ'rē'twår' dü nôr'); *Eng.* **Northern Territory.** Occasional name for N part of Algeria; politically part of France, comprises Alger, Oran, and Constantine depts.; 80,919 sq. m.; pop. (1936) 6,592,033; ✻ Algiers. See *Table* at ALGERIA.

Territoires du Sud. See SOUTHERN TERRITORIES.

Territorios Españoles del Golfo de Guinea. See SPANISH GUINEA.

Ter'ror, Mount (tĕr'ẽr). 1 Peak 8360 ft. in Skagit co., NW Washington.

2 Extinct volcano 10,750 ft. on Ross I. in Ross Sea, Antarctica, in 77°30'S lat., 168°40'E long.

Ter'ry (tĕr'ĭ). 1 County in Texas. See *Table* at TEXAS.

2 City, ⊗ of Prairie co., E Montana; pop. 1140.

Terry Peak. Mountain 7071 ft. in Lawrence co., W South Dakota.

Ter'ry·ville (tĕr'ĭ·vĭl). Subdivision (pop. 5231) of town of PLYMOUTH, Connecticut; manufacturing.

Ter·schel'ling (tĕr·sкĕl'ĭng). Island of Netherlands in the West Frisian Is., bet. Vlieland I. and Ameland I. off NW Friesland prov.; 16 m. long; 41 sq. m.; pop. ab. 3000; administratively part of North Holland prov.

Ter'try' (tĕr'trē); *formerly* **Tes'try'** (tĕs'trē'). Village, Somme dept., N France; pop. (1931) 209; battle 687 by which Pepin of Herstal (Pepin II) became ruler of all the Franks.

Te·ruel' (tã·rwĕl'). 1 Province of Spain. See *Table* at SPAIN.

2 Commune, its ✻, E Spain, 138 m. E of Madrid; pop. 16,172; manufactures brandies, leather, soap, chinaware, flour, woolens; 15th-cent. Gothic cathedral, 16th-cent. aqueduct. Conquered by Romans 196 B.C.; under Moorish rule; reconquered by Alfonso II of Aragon 1171; became city 1347; attacked by Carlists 1874.

Ter'vue'ren' (tĕr'vü'rĕn'). Commune, Brabant prov., cen. Belgium, 10 m. E of Brussels; pop. 6303; royal park, 506 acres; Musée du Congo Belge.

Te'schen (tĕsh'ĕn). 1 Former duchy, E Austrian Silesia; ab. 2820 sq. m.; founded 1290.

2 Region, part of former duchy; ab. 850 sq. m.; in dispute after World War I bet. Poland and Czechoslovakia; divided July 1920 ab. equally bet. the two. Larger part including the E part of the city became Polish (see CIESZYN); smaller part on W bank of Olsa river (Tĕšín Český) remained in Czechoslovakia. During Czech crisis of 1938 S part demanded by Poland and occupied Oct. 2, adding 419 sq. m. and pop. of 241,698 to Poland. Overrun by German army Sept. 1939. Czech district and town restored after end of World War II.

3 Town, ✻ of former duchy, divided by Olsa river into (Czech) Tĕšín Český, and (Polish) Cieszyn towns (*qq.v.*).

Teshi Lumpo. See SHIGATSE.

Te·shi·o (tĕ·shē·ō). River 192 m. long, N Hokkaido, Japan; flows NW into the Sea of Japan.

Tĕšín. See CIESZYN.

Tĕ'šín Čes'ký (tyĕ'shĕn chĕs'kē). 1 Small region in Silesia prov., cen. Czechoslovakia, the part of Teschen that remained in Czechoslovakia in partition of 1920. See TESCHEN.

2 Town in the region, Silesia prov., Czechoslovakia, on Osla river opp. Cieszyn (*q.v.*); pop. (1930) 10,536.

Tes'lin (tĕz'lĭn). Village on E shore of Teslin Lake, S Yukon, Canada, near British Columbia boundary; a station on the Alaska Highway; airport.

Teslin Lake. Long, narrow lake 245 sq. m., NW Canada, lying across the Yukon-British Columbia border; regarded as a source of the Yukon river. Its outlet is **Teslin River,** ab. 100 m. long, a tributary of the Lewes.

Tes'sin' (*Fr.* tĕ'săn'; *Ger.* tĕ·sēn'). = *Ticino*, Swiss canton: see *Table* at SWITZERLAND.

Test (tĕst). River, Hampshire, S England. See SOUTHAMPTON WATER.

Testa del Gargano. See Mount GARGANO.

Teste, La. See LA TESTE.

Testigos, Los. See LOS TESTIGOS.

Testry. See TERTRY.

Te'te (tā'tĕ). 1 District, W Mozambique, SE Africa, bet. Nyasaland and Southern Rhodesia, in the Zambesi valley; 46,600 sq. m.; pop. ab. 367,000; now belongs to Manica and Sofala prov.

2 Town, its ✻, on Zambesi river; pop. (1935 est.) 3235.

Te'te·rev (tĕt'ĕ·rĕf; *Russ.* tyă'tyĭ·ryĕf). River ab. 170 m. long, W Ukraine, U.S.S.R.; rises W of Berdichev and flows NE to the Dnieper N of Kiev.

Te'ti·pa'ri (tā'tĕ·pä·rē). Small island of the New Georgia Is., cen. Solomon Is., W Pacific, SE of Rendova.

Tet'nuld (tĕt'nŭld; *Russ.* tyĕt'nōōl·y't). Mountain 15,920 ft. in W cen. Caucasus range, on the border of Georgia, U.S.S.R., near the source of the Ingur river.

Te'ton (tē'tŏn). 1 River ab. 160 m. long, NW cen. Montana; rises in W Teton co., flows E into Missouri river.

2 Name of counties in three states of the U.S. See *Tables* at IDAHO, MONTANA, WYOMING.

Teton Range. Range in Teton co., NW Wyoming, extending N into Yellowstone National Park; S portion, which includes Grand Teton, highest peak (13,766 ft.) in the range, is in Grand Teton National Park.

Te'to·vo (tĕ'tô·vô); *Turk.* **Kal'kan·de·len'** (käl'kän·dĕ·lĕn'). City, Kosovo-Metohija autonomous prov., S Yugoslavia, ab. 25 m. W of Skoplje; pop. 16,372.

Te'trarch·y (tē'trär·kĭ; tĕt'rär-). Literally "the fourth part of a province"; the district or jurisdiction of a tetrarch; in the Roman Empire esp.: (1) **Tetrarchy of Her'od An'ti·pas** [hĕr'ŭd ăn'tĭ·păs] (4 B.C.–40 A.D.), Galilee and Peraea, (2) **Tetrarchy of Phil'ip** [fĭl'ĭp] (4 B.C.–34 A.D.), Ituraea, Trachonitis, Batanaea, etc.; these two tetrarchies reunited 41–44 A.D. under Herod Agrippa, (3) **Tetrarchy of Ly·sa'ni·as** [lĭ·sā'nĭ·ăs] (c. 29 A.D.), Abilene in SW Syria (*Luke* iii. 1).

Tetschen. See DĔČIN.

Tet'ten·hall (tĕt'n·hôl; -'n·ôl). Urban district, Staffordshire, W cen. England; pop. 7742.

Te·tuán' (tã·twän'). City, N Morocco, N Africa, 25 m. S of Ceuta; pop. 78,427; was capital of former Spanish Morocco; has port on the Mediterranean.

Tetulia. See GANGES DELTA.

Te·tyu'khe (tyĭ·tū'kĕ). Seaport town on SE coast of Maritime Territory, Soviet Russia, Asia, 215 m. NE of Vladivostok.

Teu'co (tā'ōō·kô). River 300 to 400 m. long, N Argentina, the middle course of the Bermejo; flows SE forming part of boundary bet. Formosa and Chaco territories.

Teu'to·burg Forest (tū'tô·bûrg); *Ger.* **Teu'to·bur'ger Wald** (toi'tô·bōōr'gĕr vält'). Range of hills in Lower Saxony and North Rhine-Westphalia states, W Germany, S of Osnabrück; highest point ab. 1530 ft. Scene of great battle 9 A.D. in which Varus and Roman legions were utterly defeated by Arminius and German tribes.

Tevere. See TIBER.

Te·ve·ro'ne (tã·vã·rō'nã). = ANIENE.

Te'vi·ot (tē'vĭ·ŭt; tĕv'ĭ-). River ab. 40 m. long, Roxburgh co., SE Scotland, flowing NE into the Tweed; its valley is called **Te'vi·ot·dale'** (-dāl').

Te·wae'wae Bay (tā·wī'wī). Bay on S coast of South I., New Zealand; receives Waiau river.

Tewkes'bur·y (tūks'bĕr·ĭ; -brĭ). Municipal borough, Gloucestershire, SW cen. England, at confluence of the Avon and the Severn; pop. 5292; scene of battle May 3, 1471, during the Wars of the Roses, in which Edward IV's Yorkists defeated the Lancastrian forces of Queen Margaret.

Tewks'bur·y (tōōks'bĕr·ĭ). Town, Middlesex county, NE Massachusetts, 5 m. SE of Lowell; pop. 15,902.

Tex·ad'a Island (tĕk·săd'á). Island 30 m. long in cen. Strait of Georgia, bet. Vancouver I. and the British Columbia mainland, SW Canada; has copper mines.

Tex'ar·kan'a (tĕk'sär·kăn'á; tĕk'sēr-). Twin cities on

Arkansas-Texas border: (1) City, ⊗ of Miller co., SW corner of Arkansas, ab. 137 m. SW of Little Rock; pop. 19,788. (2) City, Bowie co., NE Texas, 30 m. SE of Oklahoma border; pop. 30,218. Separated from each other by an imaginary line bisecting the combined business district, and forming a unit socially, commercially, and industrially, but each having separate municipal, county, and state governments; name formed from *Tex*as, *Ark*ansas, and Louisi*ana;* official post-office designation Texarkana, Arkansas-Texas. Railroad and industrial center; manufactures lumber, cotton and cottonseed-oil products, textiles, galvanized iron, baskets and boxes, refined sulfur, processed foods. Founded 1873 on site of Caddo village.

Tex'as (tĕk′săs). **1** A southwestern state of U.S.A., 28th state admitted to Union (1845); bounded on N by Oklahoma, on E by Arkansas and Louisiana, on SE and S by Gulf of Mexico and Mexican state of Tamaulipas, on SW and W by Mexican states of Coahuila and Chihuahua and by New Mexico; 2d largest in area, 267,339 sq. m. (land area 263,513 sq. m.); 6th state in population, 9,579,677; ✳ Austin. See *Table of States* at UNITED STATES, and *Map*, pp. 1134–1135. Divided into the following 254 counties (for pronunciation of their names, see their individual entries):

NAME	LOCATION	AREA[1]	POP.[1]	CO. SEAT
Anderson	E	1,068	28,162	Palestine
Andrews	NW	1,504	13,450	Andrews
Angelina	E	857	39,814	Lufkin
Aransas	S; coastal	276	7,006	Rockport
Archer	N	917	6,110	Archer City
Armstrong	NW	909	1,966	Claude
Atascosa	S	1,206	18,828	Jourdanton
Austin	SE cen.	662	13,777	Bellville
Bailey	NW	832	9,090	Muleshoe
Bandera	SW cen.	765	3,892	Bandera
Bastrop	S cen.	885	16,925	Bastrop
Baylor	N	857	5,893	Seymour
Bee	S	842	23,755	Beeville
Bell	cen.	1,079	94,097	Belton
Bexar	S cen.	1,247	687,151	San Antonio
Blanco	cen.	719	3,657	Johnson City
Borden	NW	914	1,076	Gail
Bosque	cen.	1,003	10,809	Meridian
Bowie	NE	921	59,971	Boston
Brazoria	SE; coastal	1,441	76,204	Angleton
Brazos	E cen.	583	44,895	Bryan
Brewster[2]	W	6,208	6,434	Alpine
Briscoe	NW	887	3,577	Silverton
Brooks	S	904	8,609	Falfurrias
Brown	cen.	949	24,728	Brownwood
Burleson	E cen.	679	11,177	Caldwell
Burnet	cen.	1,003	9,265	Burnet
Caldwell	S cen.	544	17,222	Lockhart
Calhoun	S; coastal	537	16,592	Port Lavaca
Callahan	N cen.	857	7,929	Baird
Cameron	S; coastal	883	151,098	Brownsville
Camp	NE	190	7,849	Pittsburg
Carson	NW	899	7,781	Panhandle
Cass	NE	965	23,496	Linden
Castro	NW	876	8,923	Dimmitt
Chambers	SE; on Galveston Bay	618	10,379	Anahuac
Cherokee	E	1,054	33,120	Rusk
Childress	NW	701	8,421	Childress
Clay	N	1,101	8,351	Henrietta
Cochran	NW	782	6,417	Morton
Coke	W cen.	915	3,589	Robert Lee
Coleman	cen.	1,282	12,458	Coleman
Collin	NE	886	41,247	McKinney
Collingsworth	NW	899	6,276	Wellington
Colorado	SE cen.	950	18,463	Columbus
Comal	S cen.	567	19,844	New Braunfels
Comanche	cen.	972	11,865	Comanche
Concho	W cen.	1,004	3,672	Paint Rock
Cooke	N	902	22,560	Gainesville
Coryell	cen.	1,043	23,961	Gatesville
Cottle	NW	901	4,207	Paducah
Crane	W	796	4,699	Crane
Crockett	W	2,794	4,209	Ozona
Crosby	NW	911	10,347	Crosbyton
Culberson	W	3,848	2,794	Van Horn
Dallam	NW corner	1,494	6,302	Dalhart
Dallas	NE	893	951,527	Dallas
Dawson	NW	899	19,185	Lamesa
Deaf Smith	NW	1,507	13,187	Hereford
Delta	NE	276	5,860	Cooper
Denton	N	942	47,432	Denton

NAME	LOCATION	AREA[1]	POP.[1]	CO. SEAT
De Witt	S	910	20,683	Cuero
Dickens	NW	930	4,963	Dickens
Dimmit	S	1,341	10,095	Carrizo Springs
Donley	NW	909	4,449	Clarendon
Duval	S	1,814	13,398	San Diego
Eastland	N cen.	955	19,526	Eastland
Ector	W	907	90,995	Odessa
Edwards	SW cen.	2,075	2,317	Rocksprings
Ellis	NE cen.	953	43,395	Waxahachie
El Paso	W tip	1,054	314,070	El Paso
Erath	N cen.	1,085	16,236	Stephenville
Falls	cen.	761	21,263	Marlin
Fannin	NE	906	23,880	Bonham
Fayette	SE cen.	936	20,384	La Grange
Fisher	NW cen.	906	7,865	Roby
Floyd	NW	993	12,369	Floydada
Foard	N	676	3,125	Crowell
Fort Bend	SE	862	40,527	Richmond
Franklin	NE	293	5,101	Mount Vernon
Freestone	E cen.	862	12,525	Fairfield
Frio	S	1,116	10,112	Pearsall
Gaines	NW	1,479	12,267	Seminole
Galveston	SE; coastal	430	140,364	Galveston
Garza	NW	914	6,611	Post
Gillespie	cen.	1,055	10,048	Fredericksburg
Glasscock	W	864	1,118	Garden City
Goliad	S	871	5,429	Goliad
Gonzales	S cen.	1,058	17,845	Gonzales
Gray	NW	937	31,535	Pampa
Grayson	NE	927	73,043	Sherman
Gregg	NE	284	69,436	Longview
Grimes	E cen.	801	12,709	Anderson
Guadalupe	S cen.	715	29,017	Seguin
Hale	NW	979	36,798	Plainview
Hall	NW	896	7,322	Memphis
Hamilton	cen.	844	8,488	Hamilton
Hansford	NW	907	6,208	Spearman
Hardeman	N	685	8,275	Quanah
Hardin	E	895	24,629	Kountze
Harris	SE	1,730	1,243,158	Houston
Harrison	NE	892	45,594	Marshall
Hartley	NW	1,489	2,171	Channing
Haskell	N	888	11,174	Haskell
Hays	S cen.	670	19,934	San Marcos
Hemphill	NW	909	3,185	Canadian
Henderson	NE	940	21,786	Athens
Hidalgo	S	1,541	180,904	Edinburg
Hill	NE cen.	1,028	23,650	Hillsboro
Hockley	NW	903	22,340	Levelland
Hood	N cen.	426	5,443	Granbury
Hopkins	NE	793	18,594	Sulphur Springs
Houston	E	1,232	19,376	Crockett
Howard	NW	912	40,139	Big Spring
Hudspeth	W	4,533	3,343	Sierra Blanca
Hunt	NE	910	39,399	Greenville
Hutchinson	NW	884	34,419	Stinnett
Irion	W cen.	1,073	1,183	Mertzon
Jack	N	944	7,418	Jacksboro
Jackson	SE	854	14,040	Edna
Jasper	E	969	22,100	Jasper
Jeff Davis	W	2,258	1,582	Fort Davis
Jefferson	SE; coastal	945	245,659	Beaumont
Jim Hogg	S	1,143	5,022	Hebbronville
Jim Wells	S	846	34,548	Alice
Johnson	N cen.	740	34,720	Cleburne
Jones	NW cen.	956	19,299	Anson
Karnes	S	758	14,995	Karnes City
Kaufman	NE	816	29,931	Kaufman
Kendall	S cen.	670	5,889	Boerne
Kenedy	S; coastal	1,407	884	Sarita
Kent	NW	901	1,727	Clairemont
Kerr	SW cen.	1,101	16,800	Kerrville
Kimble	W cen.	1,274	3,943	Junction
King	NW	944	640	Guthrie
Kinney	SW	1,391	2,452	Brackettville
Kleberg	S; coastal	851	30,052	Kingsville
Knox	N	854	7,857	Benjamin
Lamar	NE	906	34,234	Paris
Lamb	NW	1,022	21,896	Olton
Lampasas	cen.	726	9,418	Lampasas
La Salle	S	1,501	5,972	Cotulla
Lavaca	SE cen.	975	20,174	Hallettsville
Lee	cen.	644	8,949	Giddings
Leon	E cen.	1,099	9,951	Centerville
Liberty	E	1,173	31,595	Liberty
Limestone	E cen.	932	20,413	Groesbeck
Lipscomb	NW	934	3,406	Lipscomb
Live Oak	S	1,072	7,846	George West
Llano	cen.	947	5,240	Llano
Loving	W	647	226	Mentone
Lubbock	NW	892	156,271	Lubbock
Lynn	NW	915	10,914	Tahoka
McCulloch	cen.	1,066	8,815	Brady
McLennan	cen.	1,035	150,091	Waco
McMullen	S	1,159	1,116	Tilden
Madison	E cen.	478	6,749	Madisonville
Marion	NE	400	8,049	Jefferson
Martin	NW	911	5,068	Stanton

NAME	LOCATION	AREA[1]	POP.[1]	CO. SEAT
Mason	cen.	935	3,780	Mason
Matagorda	SE; coastal	1,141	25,744	Bay City
Maverick	SW	1,279	14,508	Eagle Pass
Medina	S cen.	1,353	18,904	Hondo
Menard	W cen.	914	2,964	Menard
Midland	W	938	67,717	Midland
Milam	cen.	1,027	22,263	Cameron
Mills	cen.	734	4,467	Goldthwaite
Mitchell	NW cen.	922	11,255	Colorado
Montague	N	937	14,893	Montague
Montgomery	E	1,090	26,839	Conroe
Moore	NW	912	14,773	Dumas
Morris	NE	261	12,576	Daingerfield
Motley	NW	1,011	2,870	Matador
Nacogdoches	E	963	28,046	Nacogdoches
Navarro	NE cen.	1,084	34,423	Corsicana
Newton	E	941	10,372	Newton
Nolan	NW	921	18,963	Sweetwater
Nueces	S; coastal	838	221,573	Corpus Christi
Ochiltree	NW	905	9,380	Perryton
Oldham	NW	1,466	1,928	Vega
Orange	E	356	60,357	Orange
Palo Pinto	N cen.	959	20,516	Palo Pinto
Panola	E	880	16,870	Carthage
Parker	N cen.	904	22,880	Weatherford
Parmer	NW	859	9,583	Farwell
Pecos	W	4,736	11,957	Fort Stockton
Polk	E	1,094	13,861	Livingston
Potter	NW	901	115,580	Amarillo
Presidio	W	3,877	5,460	Marfa
Rains	NE	235	2,993	Emory
Randall	NW	911	33,913	Canyon
Reagan	W	1,133	3,782	Big Lake
Real	SW cen.	625	2,079	Leakey
Red River	NE	1,033	15,682	Clarksville
Reeves	W	2,600	17,644	Pecos
Refugio	S; coastal	771	10,975	Refugio
Roberts	NW	892	1,075	Miami
Robertson	E cen.	874	16,157	Franklin
Rockwall	NE	147	5,878	Rockwall
Runnels	W cen.	1,060	15,016	Ballinger
Rusk	E	944	36,421	Henderson
Sabine	E	564	7,302	Hemphill
San Augustine	E	612	7,722	San Augustine
San Jacinto	E	619	6,153	Coldspring
San Patricio	S; coastal	689	45,021	Sinton
San Saba	cen.	1,122	6,381	San Saba
Schleicher	W cen.	1,331	2,791	Eldorado
Scurry	NW cen.	909	20,369	Snyder
Shackelford	N cen.	887	3,990	Albany
Shelby	E	819	20,479	Center
Sherman	NW	914	2,605	Stratford
Smith	NE	939	86,350	Tyler
Somervell	N cen.	197	2,577	Glen Rose
Starr	S	1,207	17,137	Rio Grande City
Stephens	N cen.	926	8,885	Breckenridge
Sterling	W cen.	914	1,177	Sterling City
Stonewall	NW	927	3,017	Aspermont
Sutton	SW cen.	1,493	3,738	Sonora
Swisher	NW	888	10,607	Tulia
Tarrant	N	877	538,495	Fort Worth
Taylor	NW cen.	913	101,078	Abilene
Terrell	W	2,388	2,600	Sanderson
Terry	NW	898	16,286	Brownfield
Throckmorton	N	913	2,767	Throckmorton
Titus	NE	418	16,785	Mount Pleasant
Tom Green	W cen.	1,543	64,630	San Angelo
Travis	cen.	1,015	212,136	Austin
Trinity	E	704	7,539	Groveton
Tyler	E	927	10,666	Woodville
Upshur	NE	589	19,793	Gilmer
Upton	W	1,312	6,239	Rankin
Uvalde	SW	1,588	16,814	Uvalde
Val Verde	SW	3,242	24,461	Del Rio
Van Zandt	NE	855	19,091	Canton
Victoria	S	893	46,475	Victoria
Walker	E	786	21,475	Huntsville
Waller	SE	507	12,071	Hempstead
Ward	W	827	14,917	Monahans
Washington	SE cen.	611	19,145	Brenham
Webb	S	3,295	64,791	Laredo
Wharton	SE	1,079	38,152	Wharton
Wheeler	NW	916	7,947	Wheeler
Wichita	N	612	123,528	Wichita Falls
Wilbarger	N	954	17,748	Vernon
Willacy	S; coastal	595	20,084	Raymondville
Williamson	cen.	1,126	35,044	Georgetown
Wilson	S cen.	802	13,267	Floresville
Winkler	W	887	13,652	Kermit
Wise	N	909	17,012	Decatur
Wood	NE	723	17,653	Quitman
Yoakum	NW	830	8,032	Plains
Young	N	888	17,254	Graham
Zapata	S	1,080	4,393	Zapata
Zavala	S	1,292	12,696	Crystal City

[1] Area = land area in sq. m. Pop. from 1960 Census.
[2] Big Bend National Park on the Rio Grande (*q.v.*) in S part.

Nickname: Lone Star State. *State flower:* Bluebonnet. *Motto:* Friendship. *Chief cities:* Houston, Dallas, San Antonio, Fort Worth, El Paso. *Rivers:* Red, forming N and NE boundary (with Oklahoma) and a boundary with Arkansas for a few miles; Trinity, in E area, flowing SE into Galveston Bay; Brazos, cen. area, flowing SE into Gulf of Mexico; Colorado, cen. area, flowing SE into Matagorda Bay; Rio Grande, forming S and SW boundaries. *Highest point:* Guadalupe Peak 8751 ft., in W area. *Chief industries:* Agriculture (cotton, corn, wheat, oats, rice), cattle and sheep raising, petroleum production, mining (coal, mercury, sulfur).

History: Period of discovery and exploration by Spaniards 1519–1684; La Salle attempted French settlement at Matagorda Bay 1685, laying basis for French claim to region as part of Louisiana; effective Spanish occupation began 1715; United States acquired French claim in Louisiana Purchase 1803; United States claim to Texas relinquished by treaty with Spain 1819; Texas a province of Mexico; Declaration of Independence from Mexico Mar. 2, 1836; army under Sam Houston won decisive battle of San Jacinto 1836, gaining independence for the Republic of Texas; sought annexation to United States, and was admitted to Union Dec. 29, 1845; boundary with Mexico along the Rio Grande river fixed after Mexican War by Treaty of Guadalupe Hidalgo 1848; passed ordinance of secession Feb. 1, 1861; ordinance of secession declared null and void 1866; readmitted to Union Mar. 30, 1870.

[2] Name of counties in two states of the U.S. See *Tables* at MISSOURI and OKLAHOMA.

Texas City. City and resort, Galveston co., SE Texas, on Galveston Bay 9 m. NW of Galveston; pop. 32,065; ships oil, cotton, sulfur; oil and sugar refineries; fisheries. On Apr. 16, 1947 ravaged by severe explosions of ammonium nitrate on freighter in harbor and by succeeding blasts and fires in the city; more than 400 lives lost, with great property damage.

Tex·co'co, *in full* **Texcoco de Mo'ra** (tās·kō'kō thä mō'rä); *also* **Tez·cu'co** (tās·kōō'kō). Town, México state, cen. Mexico, on E side of Lake Texcoco; pop. 5437. In Aztec times an important town and seat of the Tezcucan kings; one of the three pueblos forming the Aztec confederation (see TENOCHTITLÁN); used by Cortes as base for operations against Mexico City.

Texcoco or **Tezcuco, Lake.** Shallow lake 12 m. long in México state, cen. Mexico, just E of Mexico City; maximum depth 7 ft.; surface elevation above sea level 7340 ft.; was much larger in Aztec period; in its W part Tenochtitlán, Aztec stronghold and capital, was built.

Tex'el (tĕk'sĕl; tĕs'ĕl). Island of Netherlands, one of the West Frisian Is. in the North Sea off the N coast of North Holland prov.; 13 m. long; 71 sq. m.; comprises a commune of North Holland prov.; pop. 7610.

Tex·o'ma, Lake (tĕk·sō'má). See UNITED STATES, *Dams and Reservoirs* (Denison Dam).

Tey'de or **Tei'de** or **Te'ne·ri'fe, Pi'co de** (pē'kŏ thä tĕ'ĕ·thä [tä'thä], tä'nä·rē'fä); *Eng.* **Peak of Ten'er·ife** (tĕn'ẽr·ĭf; -ēf). Volcanic mountain 12,192 ft. on the island of Tenerife in the Canary Is. (*q.v.*).

Tezcuco. See TEXCOCO.

Te'ziu·tlán' (tā'syōō·tlän'). Town, Puebla state, SE cen. Mexico, 90 m. NW of Veracruz; pop. 8386; an old town near border of Veracruz state; copper mines.

Te·zon'te·pec' de Al·da'ma (tā·sōn'tä·pĕk' thä äl·dä'mä). Town, Hidalgo state, cen. Mexico; pop. 5207.

Tez'pur (tĕz'pŏŏr). Town, N Assam, NE Indian Union, on Brahmaputra river 90 m. NE of Shillong; pop. 5047.

Tha'ba·nchu' or **Tha'ba N'chu** (tä'bän·chōō'). District (1312 sq. m., pop. 24,355) and town (pop. 711), cen. Orange Free State, Union of South Africa.

Tha'bor', Mont (môn' tá'bôr'). Mountain 10,437 ft. on border bet. France and Italy, SW of Modane and W of Col de Fréjus; small area to S transferred from Italy to France 1947.

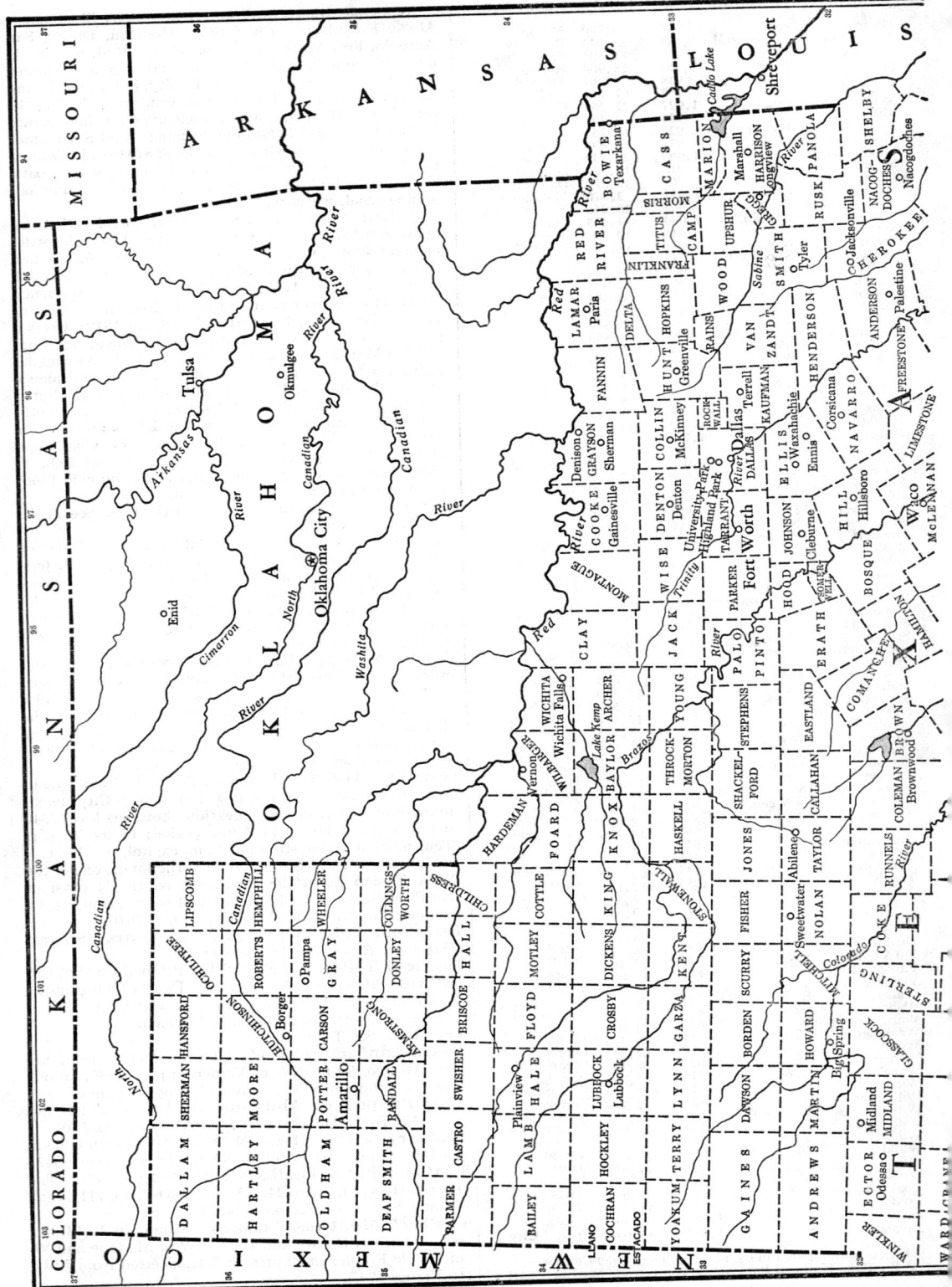

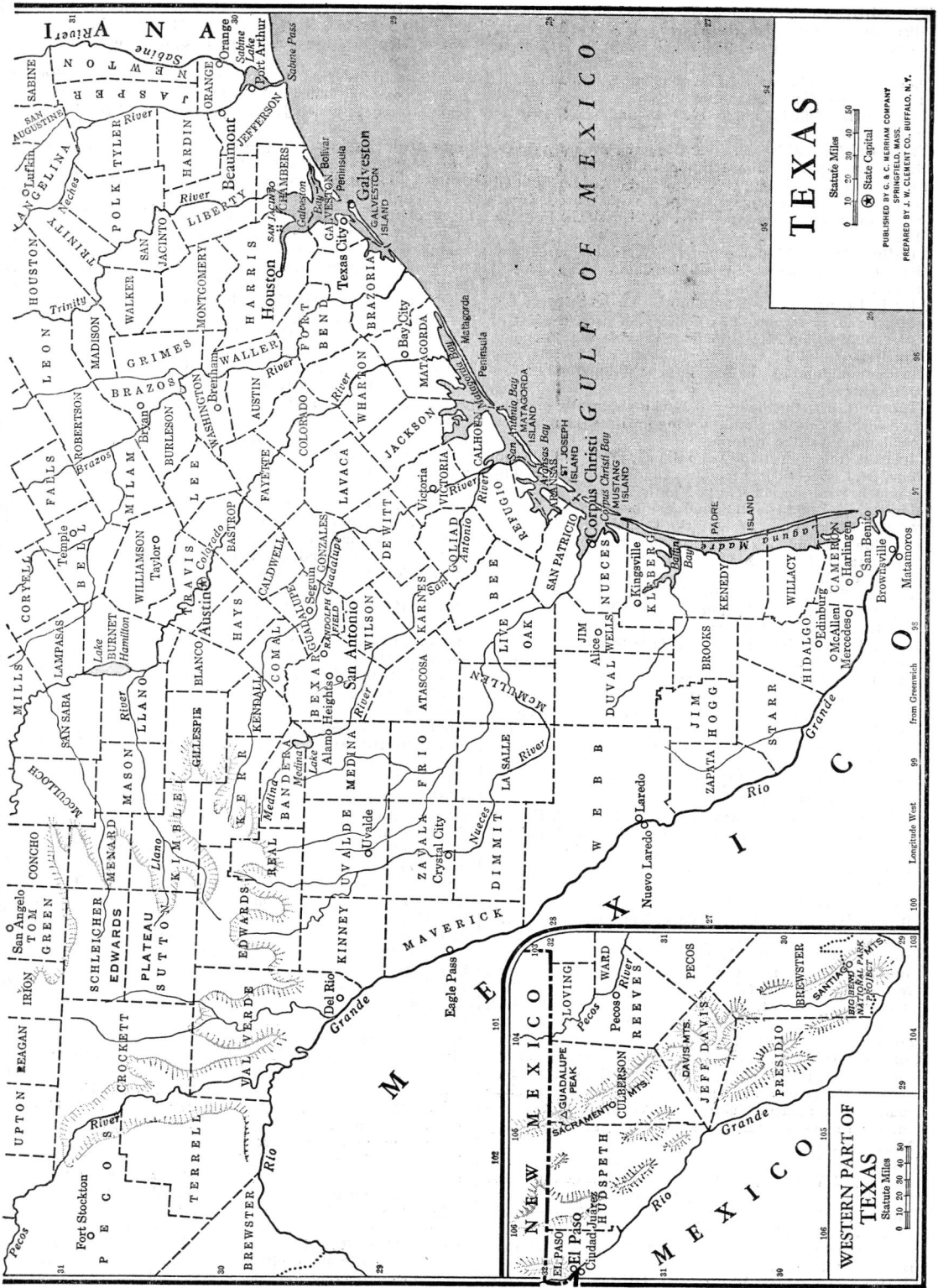

TEXAS

Statute Miles

⊛ State Capital

0 10 20 30 40 50

PUBLISHED BY G. & C. MERRIAM COMPANY
SPRINGFIELD, MASS.
PREPARED BY J. W. CLEMENT CO., BUFFALO, N.Y.

GULF OF MEXICO

WESTERN PART OF TEXAS

Statute Miles

0 10 20 30 40 50

Tha Chin (t'hä chēn). **1** River ab. 135 m. long, the W distributary of the main river system of W cen. Thailand, of which the Chao Phraya is E stream; flows S from Uthai Thani, where it leaves the Chao Phraya, to the Gulf of Siam at Samut Sakhon ab. 21 m. SW of Bangkok. **2** Town. See SAMUT SAKHON.

Thailand. Official name 1939–45 and since 1949 of Siam (*q.v.*).

Thak′hek′ (t'häk′hĕk′). Town on the Mekong, Laos, Indochina, opp. Nakhon Phanom in Thailand.

Tha′la (tä′lä). Village, NW Tunisia, NW of Sbeitla and W of Kasserine Pass, gateway to Algerian plateau country; Rommel's raid stopped here by Americans Feb. 22, 1943.

Tha′le (tä′lĕ). Manufacturing city, Magdeburg dist., East Germany, 38 m. SW of Magdeburg; pop. 13,545; resort; mineral baths.

Tha·le Lu·ang (t'hä·lä lōō·äng) *or* **Ta·le Sap** (t'hä·lä säp). Lake, or lagoon, near Gulf of Siam on E coast of SW Thailand, on Malay Penin. Songkhla is at S end.

Thal′wil (täl′vēl). Commune, Zurich canton, NE cen. Switzerland, on Lake of Zurich; pop. (1930) 7943; industrial center.

Thame (tām). Small river in Buckinghamshire and Oxfordshire, S cen. England, flowing into the Thames bet. Abingdon and Wallingford.

Thames (tĕmz). **1** (*locally also* thämz, tāmz) River 15 m. long, SE Connecticut; actually a tidal estuary formed by confluence of Shetucket and Yantic rivers at Norwich, flows S into Long Island Sound 3 m. below New London. **2** River 135 m. long, SE Ontario, Canada; rises in Perth co., flows S and SW past London, St. Thomas, and Chatham to Lake St. Clair. In War of 1812 battle (battle of the Thames) fought on its banks just E of Thamesville Oct. 5, 1813, in which the Americans under Gen. William H. Harrison defeated the British and Indians; Indian leader, Tecumseh, killed. **3** *anc.* **Tam′e·sis** (tăm′ĕ·sĭs) *or* **Tam′e·sa** (-sà). River 209 m. long, S England; its headstreams, the Churn and Isis (Thames), rise on the slopes of the Cotswold Hills in Gloucestershire; flows E across S cen. England into a great estuary, through which it empties into the North Sea; London is situated on both its sides 47¾ m. (by actual course—not air line) from London Bridge to the Nore (*q.v.*); navigable as far as London. **4** River ab. 80 m. long, N North I., New Zealand; flows N into the Firth of Thames. **5** Borough, Auckland provincial dist., N North I., New Zealand, on Firth of Thames 50 m. ESE of Auckland; pop. 4735; trading center of gold-mining region.

Thames, Firth of. Southern extension of Hauraki Gulf on N coast of North I., New Zealand; receives the Thames river from the S.

Thames′ville (tĕmz′vĭl). Village, Kent co., SE Ontario, Canada, on Thames river; pop. 968. See THAMES, 2.

Thamugadi, Thamugadis. See TIMGAD.

Tha′na (tä′nä; *native* t'hä′-). Town, W Maharashtra, W Indian Union, on NE shore of Salsette I. 21 m. NNE of Bombay; pop. 21,816. In time of Marco Polo (13th cent.) a leading port of India; an early settlement of the Portuguese, who were driven out 1737 by the Marathas.

Than′et, Isle of (thăn′ĕt; -ĭt). Area, 42 sq. m., at NE end of Kent, SE England, cut off from the mainland by arms of the river Stour, one of which roughly parallels course of an ancient channel, the Wantsum, once wide enough to make Thanet a true island; scene of many Norse invasions.

Thanh′hoa′ (t'hän′y'·hwä′). Town near coast, N Annam, N Vietnam, on Haiphong-Saigon railroad just S of Tonkin border; pop. ab. 16,000.

Thann (tän). Town, Haut-Rhin dept., NE France, ab. 16 m. NW of Mulhouse; pop. 6376; manufactures chemical products, machinery, textiles; 14th-cent. church; ruins of castle nearby.

Thap′sa·cus (thăp′sà·kŭs); *mod.* **Dib′se** (dĭb′sĕ); *Bib.*

Tiph′sah [tĭf′sà] (*I Kings* iv. 24). Ancient city on the S bank of the middle Euphrates river, N Syria, ab. 60 m. ESE of Alep; location of a famous ford, much used in ancient times.

Thap′sus (thăp′sŭs). Ancient town in N Africa; its site is on E coast of Tunisia SE of modern town of Sousse; battle 46 B.C. in which Julius Caesar defeated the Pompeians.

Thar and Par′kar (tär [*native* t'hŭr], pär′kĕr). District, SE Sind, West Pakistan; 13,649 sq. m.; pop. (1941) 581,004; ❋ Mirpur Khas; E portion forms part of Thar, or Indian, Desert.

Thar, *or* **Indian, Desert.** Region of sandy desert, NW India, between Aravalli Range on E and Indus river on W, Sutlej river on N and Arabian Sea on S; 500 m. long, more than 100,000 sq. m.; average alt. 250 ft. to 750 ft., highest ab. 1000 ft. on W slope of Aravalli Range. Annual rainfall less than 15 in.; has continuous high temperatures. Politically covers Bahawalpur state of Pakistan, E Sind, and the Rajputana states of Bikaner, Jaisalmer, Jodhpur, and part of Jaipur in Indian Union.

Thar′ra·wad′dy (thär′à·wŏd′ĭ). **1** District, Pegu division, Lower Burma; 2815 sq. m.; pop. 508,319. **2** Town, its ❋, 65 m. N of Rangoon; pop. 7131.

Tha′sos (thä′sŏs); *Mod. Gr.* **Thá′sos** (thä′sŏs). **1** Greek island in N Aegean Sea, opp. the mouth of the Nestos; 152 sq. m.; pop. ab. 12,000; politically a part of Kavalla dept., NE Macedonia, Greece; mountainous, highest point 3428 ft. Early colonized by Phoenicians, later (in 8th cent. B.C.) by Parians; seized by Persians under Mardonius; later came under Athens, but revolted twice in 5th cent. B.C. **2** Chief town of island, on N coast; now in ruins.

Thatch′er (thăch′ĕr). Town, Graham co., SE Arizona, ab. 80 m. NE of Tucson; pop. 1581; settled 1881.

Tha·ton′ (thä·tōn′). **1** Coastal district of Tenasserim division, Lower Burma; 4870 sq. m.; pop. 532,628. **2** Town, its ❋, near NE coast of Gulf of Martaban 35 m. NNW of Moulmein; pop. 16,851.

Thau, É′tang′ de (ā′tän′ dē tō′). Salt lagoon ab. 40 sq. m., S France, on coast of Hérault dept.; separated from the Mediterranean (Gulf of Lions) by a narrow strip of sand on which Sète is located.

Thaun′gyin′ (thoun′jĭn′). River 150 m. long, Lower Burma; flows NW into Salween river on the Burma-Thailand boundary, and in its own course forms a section of that boundary E of the Dawna Range.

Thayer (thâr). **1** County in Nebraska. See *Table* at NEBRASKA. **2** City, Oregon co., S Missouri, 22 m. SE of West Plains; pop. 1713; ships timber and dairy products.

Tha·yet′myo′ (thä·yĕt′myō′; *Angl.* thăt′myō′). **1** District, Magwe division, Upper Burma; 4642 sq. m.; pop. 274,177. **2** Town, its ❋, on the Irrawaddy river opp. Allanmyo, 40 m. N of Prome; pop. 9279; large oil field.

Thebae. See THEBES.

The·ba′id (thē·bā′ĭd; thē′bà·ĭd). The district about Thebes (either in Egypt or in Boeotia).

The·ba′is (thē·bā′ĭs; thē′bà·ĭs). Roman province of Upper Egypt.

Theb′ar·ton (thĕb′ër·t'n; -tŭn). Town, SE South Australia, W suburb of Adelaide; pop. 14,644.

Thebes (thēbz). **1** *classical* **The′bae** (thē′bē); *later* **Di·os′po·lis** (dī·ŏs′pō·lĭs). Ancient ruined city in Upper Egypt, on the left bank of the Nile S of modern Qena, but in early times included also Karnak and Luxor (*qq.v.*) on the right bank. Town of great antiquity preserving its importance because of the temple of Karnak and, on decline of Memphis and after the brief rule of the Heracleopolitan dynasties, became capital of Upper Egypt giving its name to the XIth (2160–2000 B.C.), XIIth (2000–1788 B.C.), and XIIIth dynasties of the Middle Kingdom, although the Theban rulers continued to make their residence at Memphis until c. 1580

B.C. Obscured for two centuries under the Xoite dynasty and the Hyksos kings, rose again under the XVIIIth dynasty of the New Kingdom; its rulers (the Diospolite dynasties, XVIIIth to XXth, see DIOSPOLIS) from c. 1580 B.C. to 1090 B.C. represent the great period of Egyptian power and achievement. Known as No in Biblical history (as in *Jer.* xlvi. 25, *Nahum* iii. 8) and to the Greeks through Homer's *Iliad* as the "hundred-gated" city; center of worship of Amen (or Amon) and famous for its vast temples, gateways, statues, sphinxes, tombs, obelisks, etc. Center of Egyptian civilization but declined after 10th cent. B.C. Sacked by Assyrians 671 B.C., later by Persians, and esp. by Romans 30–29 B.C. under Cornelius Gallus. Here in Valley of Kings near Luxor in 1922 tomb of Tutankhamen, ruler of the XVIIIth (Diospolite) dynasty, c. 1358 B.C., was discovered containing mummies and great wealth of jewels, objects of art, etc., in superb condition.

2 *Gr.* **Thē′vai** (thē′vâ). Commune, Attica and Boeotia dept., E Central Greece and Euboea division, Greece, 33 m. NNW of Athens; pop. 7648; in low hilly country.

History: An old city, traditionally founded by Cadmus; closely identified with many of the early legends of Greece (as Dirce, Epigonus, Oedipus, the Sphinx, etc.). Historically, settled before 1000 B.C. by Boeotians; began struggles against Athens at end of the 6th cent. B.C.; headed Boeotian League c. 600–550 B.C. Sided with Persians against Greeks and was punished after defeat of Persians. Under Athenian rule 457–447 B.C.; joined Sparta against Athens in Peloponnesian War; left Sparta and joined Argos, Athens, and Corinth in the Corinthian War 395–387 B.C. Under Spartan rule 382–379 B.C.; regained freedom 379, destroyed Spartan supremacy at Leuctra 371 B.C. (the period of Theban leadership 379–362 B.C.); joined Athens against Philip of Macedon and shared defeat at Chaeronea 338 B.C.; almost totally destroyed by Alexander 336 B.C. Home of Pindar and produced the great generals Epaminondas and Pelopidas.

The Dalles (dălz) or **Dalles City.** City, ⊗ of Wasco co., N Oregon, on Columbia river 13 m. W of its confluence with Deschutes river ab. 72 m. E of Portland; pop. 10,493; E terminus of 200-mile waterway from the sea, opened by completion of Bonneville Dam and lock; trading, fishing, and manufacturing center; salmon-packing plants, flour and lumber mills, canneries; ships fruit, grain, meat, wool. Indian mart found here by Lewis and Clark 1805; first settled by whites 1838; chartered 1857.

Thed′ford (thĕd′fẽrd). Village, ⊗ of Thomas co., cen. Nebraska; pop. 303.

The Hague. See THE HAGUE.

Theiss. See TISZA.

The′o·dore Roo′se·velt Island (thē′ȏ·dȯr rō′zĕ·vĕlt; -vĕlt; rōō′-); *formerly* **An′a·los′tan Island** (ăn′′l·ȏs′tăn). Island in the Potomac river, in the District of Columbia; 90 acres; site of a memorial to President Theodore Roosevelt.

Theodosia. See FEODOSIYA.

Théodule Pass. See MATTERJOCH.

Theophilo Ottoni. = TEÓFILO OTONI.

The′ot·mal′li (tā′ȏt·mäl′ē). See DETMOLD.

The Pas (thē pä′). Town, W Manitoba, Canada, on S bank of Saskatchewan river 100 m. W of N end of Lake Winnipeg; pop. 3376; in big timber country on site of an old Hudson's Bay Co. trading post; active lumbering and market town; starting point of new railroad to Churchill.

Thera, Thēra. See SANTORIN.

The·ra′sia (thĕ·rā′zhâ; -zhĭ·â); *Mod. Gr.* **Thē′ra·sí′a** (thē′rä·sē′ä). Small island off W coast of Santorin I., S Cyclades, S Aegean Sea; probably part of the rim of a volcano crater, connected with W Santorin (*q.v.*).

Therezina. = TERESINA.

Therma. See SALONIKA.

Thermae Himerenses. See TERMINI IMERESE.

Thermaic Gulf. See Gulf of SALONIKA.

Thermia. See KYTHNOS.

Ther·mop′o·lis (thẽr·mŏp′ȏ·lĭs). Town, ⊗ of Hot Springs co., NW cen. Wyoming; pop. 3955; medicinal hot springs; coal and petroleum deposits; sugar beets.

Ther·mop′y·lae, Pass of (thẽr·mŏp′ĭ·lē). Locality, E Greece, bet. Mt. Oeta and S shore of Gulf of Lamia 9 m. SSE of town of Lamia; in ancient times a narrow pass along the coast, now a rocky plain ab. 6 m. from the sea. Here the Greeks, Spartans, and Thespians under Leonidas checked the Persian invaders in battle 480 B.C. Other battles here: (1) in 279 B.C. Brennus and Gauls checked for several months by the Greeks; (2) in 191 B.C. Antiochus III of Syria defeated by Romans; (3) Apr. 20-25, 1941 German army held in rearguard action by Anzacs.

Thé′rou·anne′ (tā′rwàn′). Village, Pas-de-Calais dept., N France, S of St-Omer; formerly a fortress; taken by the English in 1380 and 1513, and destroyed by the Emperor Charles V in 1553.

Thes′pi·ae (thĕs′pĭ·ē; thĕs·pī′ē). Ancient town in S cen. Boeotia, E cen. Greece, E of Mt. Helicon and ab. 10 m. WSW of Thebes. Worshiped Eros and the Muses and possessed a famous statue of Eros made by Praxiteles. Several hundred of its inhabitants fought and died with Leonidas at Thermopylae and others were at Plataea 479 B.C.; town destroyed by Xerxes; friendly to Athens and suffered much in its opposition to Thebes.

Thes·pro′ti·a (thĕs·prō′shĭ·â; -shâ). A district of ancient Epirus, NW Greece, on W coast extending S from Thyamis river to Ambracian Gulf. The Thesprotians were the earliest inhabitants of Epirus; their oracle at Dodona was the great center of Pelasgic worship.

Thessalonica. See SALONIKA.

Thes′sa·lo·ni′ke (thĕs′â·lȏ·nī′kĕ); *Mod. Gr.* **Thes′sa·lo·ní′kē** (thä′sä·lȏ·nyē′kyĕ). **1** Department of Greece. See *Table* at GREECE. **2** City. See SALONIKA.

Thes′sa·ly (thĕs′â·lĭ); *Gr.* **Thes′sa·li′a** (*Mod. Gr.* thā′sä·lyē′ä). Geographical division of modern Greece; includes E cen. portion of Greek penin.; 5148 sq. m.; pop. (1938 est.) 562,020; forms Greek departments of Larissa and Trikkala (see *Table* at GREECE). Ancient Thessaly corresponds generally to modern division: an extensive plain region almost completely hemmed in by mountains—Pindus range on W, Cambunian Mts. on N, Othrys Mts. along the S border, and Mts. Olympus, Ossa, and Pelion along the coast. Drained by Salambria river (ancient Peneus) with many confluents, entering Aegean Sea through Vale of Tempe. Land of many early migrations and cultures, esp. the Aeolic; figured prominently in many Greek legends (Argonauts, centaurs, Achilles); early inhabitants were not enough united to have much historical influence. Subject to Macedonia 4th to 2d cent. B.C.; scene of several great battles of ancient history; in Middle Ages had many Rumanian inhabitants; ceded to modern Greek kingdom 1881; in World War II was a main area of conflict bet. Germans and forces of British and Greeks.

Thet′ford (thĕt′fẽrd). **1** Town, Orange co., E Vermont; pop. 1049; comprises several villages along the Connecticut river N of White River Junction. **2** Municipal borough, Norfolk, E England, 27 m. SW of Norwich; pop. 4445; trade center in agricultural section.

Thetford Mines (mīnz′). City, Megantic co., S Quebec, Canada, 52 m. S of Quebec; pop. 15,095; mines and processes asbestos, being center of region producing 85% of world's supply. Founded 1802 but grew slowly until 1876 when asbestos was discovered.

Theux (tû). Commune, Liège prov., E Belgium, 12 m. SE of Liège; pop. 5221; formerly capital of a marquisate.

Thēvai. See THEBES, Greece.

Theveste. See TEBESSA.

The Vil′lage (thē vĭl′ĭj). City, Oklahoma co., cen. Oklahoma, NW suburb of Oklahoma City; pop. 12,118.

Thiais (tyē′). Commune, Seine dept., N France, S of Paris; pop. (1931) 7034.

Thian Shan. = TIEN SHAN.

Thiau'court' (tyō'kōōr'). Village, Meurthe-et-Moselle dept., NE France, ab. 16 m. ENE of St-Mihiel; taken by Americans Sept. 12, 1918; St-Mihiel American military cemetery.

Thi·bet' (tĭ·bĕt'). Var. of TIBET.

Thib'o·daux' (tĭb'ō·dō'). City, ⊗ of Lafourche parish, SE Louisiana, on Bayou Lafourche 49 m. WSW of New Orleans; pop. 13,403; commercial and distributing center for agricultural section; petroleum deposits nearby.

Thick'a·net'ley Bald (thĭk'á·nĕt'lĭ bôld). Peak 4054 ft. in Gilmer co., N Georgia.

Thief (thēf). River 30 m. long, NW Minnesota; flows S out of **Thief Lake** in NE Marshall co. and empties into Red Lake river in N Pennington co.

Thief River Falls. City, ⊗ of Pennington co., NW Minnesota, 50 m. W of Upper Red Lake; pop. 7151; trading and distributing point for agricultural section; ships large quantities of hay and forage.

Thiel'sen, Mount (tēl's'n; thēl'-). Peak 9178 ft., N of Crater Lake, on boundary bet. Douglas and Klamath cos., S Oregon.

Thielt (tēlt). Commune, West Flanders prov., NW Belgium, 15 m. SE of Brugge (Bruges); pop. 11,538; market town; captured by the Germans 1914 and used for a long time as German headquarters on the Flanders front.

Thie'ne (tyâ'nå). Manufacturing commune, Vicenza prov., Venezia Euganea, NE Italy, 12 m. NNW of Vicenza; pop. 10,954.

Thienen. See TIENEN.

Thiep'val' (tyĕp'vàl'). Village, Somme dept., N France, just N of Albert; frequent fighting, esp. Sept. 1916 and Aug. 1918.

Thiers (tyâr). Manufacturing commune, Puy-de-Dôme dept., S cen. France, 23 m. ENE of Clermont-Ferrand; pop. 16,181; manufactures cutlery, toys, paper, etc. Made barony 1569.

Thi·ès' (tyĕs). Town, Senegal, West Africa, 40 m. E of Cape Vert; pop. (1942) 32,769, on railroad leading through Kayes to Bamako in Mali Republic.

Thim'ble Islands (thĭm'b'l). Group of islands in Long Island Sound off the S coast of New Haven co., Connecticut.

Thim·bu (thĭm'bōō). Town, W Bhutan; ✳ of Bhutan.

Thing'ey'ri (thĕng'gyä'rĭ). Town, NW Iceland, W of Glamujökull.

Thing'val'la Water (thĕng'g'·vät'lä). Lake, SW Iceland, E of Reykjavík.

Thing'vel'lir (thĕng'g'·vĕt'lĭr). Level plain with lava floor near Thingvalla Water, SW Iceland, ab. 25 m. E of Reykjavík; meeting place from 930 A.D. to recent years of the Althing, parliament of Iceland.

Thinis. See THIS.

Thi'o (tē'ō). Town on E coast of New Caledonia, SW Pacific Ocean, ab. 48 m. NNW of Nouméa.

Thion'ville' (tyôN'vēl'); *Ger.* **Die'den·ho'fen** (dē'-dĕn·hō'fĕn). Industrial commune, Moselle dept., N France, on Moselle river 16 m. N of Metz; pop. 18,934; railroad center; center of iron-mining district; trades in agricultural products, lumber, wine. Taken by Germans after disastrous siege 1870; reverted to France 1919.

Thirl'mere (thûrl'mēr). Lake ab. 4 m. long in the Lake District, Cumberland, NW England; provides part of Manchester water supply.

This (thĭs) *or* **Thi'nis** (thī'nĭs). Ancient city of Egypt near the great bend of the Nile NW of Abydos and near the modern Girga; native city of Menes and capital of the Ist and IId dynasties, to which it gave its name (Thinite).

Thi'sted (tē'stĕth). **1** County in Denmark. See *Table* at DENMARK.
2 Town, its ⊗, NW Jutland Penin.; pop. (1946) 9425.

This'til Fjord (thĭs'tĭl). Bay, inlet of Arctic Ocean, NE Iceland, bet. Capes Rifstangi and Langanes.

Thi'vai (thē'vâ). = THEBES, Greece.

Thjórs'á (thyōrs'ou). River ab. 150 m. long, S cen. Iceland; flows SW into Atlantic Ocean.

Thok Ja'lung (tôk jä'lōōng). Gold field in the Aling Kangri Mts., W Tibet, Outer China; altitude 12,325 ft.

Tho'len (tō'lĕ[n]). Island of SW Netherlands, in Zeeland prov.; 46 sq. m.; pop. ab. 15,000.

Thom'as (tŏm'ås). Name of counties in three states of the U.S. See *Tables* at GEORGIA, KANSAS, NEBRASKA.

Thomas Cole Mountain (kōl). Peak 3935 ft. in the Catskill Mts., Greene co., SE New York.

Thomas Peak. See BALDY PEAK.

Thomas Range. Range in W Utah, at S end of Great Salt Lake Desert.

Thom'as·ton (tŏm'ås·tŭn). **1** Industrial town, SE Litchfield co., NW Connecticut, on Naugatuck river; pop. 5850; incorporated 1875; manufactures clocks, watches, glass, automatic machine parts, rolled brass.
2 City, ⊗ of Upson co., W cen. Georgia, 38 m. W of Macon; pop. 9336; founded 1825; textile mills; center of peach-growing area.
3 Town, Knox co., S Maine, on inlet of Atlantic Ocean 35 m. ESE of Augusta; pop. 2780; manufactures Portland cement.

Thom'as·ville (tŏm'ås·vĭl; *Sou.* also -v'l). **1** Town, Clarke co., SW Alabama, 80 m. NNE of Mobile Bay; pop. 3182; lumber and agricultural trade center.
2 City, ⊗ of Thomas co., S Georgia, 40 m. W of Valdosta; pop. 18,246; incorporated 1826; naval stores, tobacco; cotton; winter health resort; hunting and fishing.
3 City, Davidson co., cen. North Carolina, 7 m. SSW of High Point; pop. 15,190; chair factories; cotton, rayon, and silk mills; section grows tobacco, corn, wheat.

Tho'mond (tōō'mŭnd). Medieval principality in N part of Munster prov., S Eire.

Thomp'son (tŏm[p]'s'n). **1** Manufacturing town, NE Windham co., NE Connecticut, on Massachusetts and Rhode Island borders N of Putnam; pop. 6217; watered by French and Quinepaug rivers; incorporated 1785; in agricultural region; cotton and woolen mills.
2 River, S British Columbia, Canada, main tributary of the Fraser river; total length 270 m.; rises among the Rocky Mts. near E boundary of British Columbia, flows S (as **North Thompson River**, 185 m. long) and turns W and SW to the Fraser river. Joined at Kamloops by a branch (120 m. long) from Shuswap Lake usually known as the **South Thompson River.**

Thompson Falls. Town, ⊗ of Sanders co., NW Montana; pop. 1274.

Thompson Island. 1 Island in S area of the harbor of Boston, Massachusetts.
2 Island in South Atlantic Ocean charted by British Admiralty in 54°S and 4°E, near Bouvet I.; probably volcanic, has now disappeared.

Thompson Peak. Mountain 10,546 ft. in N Santa Fe co., N cen. New Mexico.

Thomp'son·ville (tŏm[p]'s'n·vĭl). Subdivision (est. pop. 11,000) of town of ENFIELD, Connecticut; manufactures rugs and carpets, paper, hardware; tobacco growing, truck farming.

Thom'son (tŏm's'n). **1** City, ⊗ of McDuffie co., E Georgia, 30 m. W of Augusta; pop. 4522; textile mills.
2 River ab. 300 m. long, upper tributary of Barcoo river, cen. Queensland, Australia; flows SW; dry bed part of the year.

Thong'wa' (thŏn'wä'). Town, Hanthawaddy dist., S Lower Burma, near W coast of Gulf of Martaban 23 m. E of Rangoon; pop. 10,546.

Tho'non'–les–Bains (tō'nôN'lä·bănʹ). Commune, Haute-Savoie dept., E France, on Lake Geneva 37 m. NNE of Annecy; pop. 12,183; summer resort; mineral baths; manufactures alimentary pastes, cigarette paper, lumber.

Thorn. See TORUŃ.

Thor'na·by on Tees (thôr'ná·bĭ, tēz'). Municipal borough, North Riding, Yorkshire, N England, 31 m.

SSE of Newcastle; pop. 23,413; shipyards; iron foundries; pottery.

Thorn'ap'ple (thôrn'ăp''l). River ab. 100 m. long, S Michigan, flowing from Eaton co. to Grand river.

Thorn'ton (thôrn't'n; -tŭn). 1 Village, Adams co., NE cen. Colorado, N of Denver; pop. 11,353.
2 Village, Providence co., N Rhode Island, ab. 4 m. SW of Providence; administrative center of Johnston.

Thornton Cleve'leys (klēv'līz). Urban district, Lancashire, NW England, on Irish Sea 33 m. N of Liverpool; pop. 15,437.

Thor'o·fare' Buttes (thûr'ŏ·fâr'). Mountain 11,417 ft., SW Park co., NW Wyoming.

Thor'old (thûr'ŭld). Industrial town, Welland co., SE Ontario, Canada, on Welland Ship Canal 3 m. SE of St. Catharines; pop. 6397; foundries, flour, paper, and knitting mills; printing and publishing concerns.

Thors·havn' (tōrs·houn'). Town, chief town of the Faeroes and ⊗ of Færö co., Denmark, located on Strömö I.; pop. 2496; temporarily occupied 1942–45 by the British as a measure of defense.

Thôrs'höfn' (thōrs'hûp'n'). Town, NE Iceland, on Thistil Fjord.

Thor'vald Nil'sen Mountains (tōr'väl [tōōr'-] nĭl'-s'n). Mountain group in Queen Maud Range, Ross Dependency, Antarctica, ab. lat. 86°S, 158°W; highest peaks 13,000 ft. Discovered by Amundsen 1911.

Thospitis. See VAN lake.

Thou·ars' (twär); *anc.* **To·ar'ci·um** (tŏ·är'shĭ·ŭm). Commune, Deux-Sèvres dept., W France, 49 m. N of Niort; pop. 10,077; agricultural trade center; manufactures textiles, distillery products. Taken by Pepin the Short 754 A.D.; made viscountship in 11th cent.; to France 1476; made duchy 1563; Protestant stronghold in wars of religion in 16th cent.

Thou'rout' (tōō'rōō'). Manufacturing commune, West Flanders prov., NW Belgium; pop. 10,840.

Thou'sand Islands (thou'z'nd). 1 Group of ab. 1500 islands in a widening of the upper St. Lawrence river, New York state, and Ontario, Canada, just below Kingston. Summer resort, with many hotels and villas. Some of the islands belong to Canada (see *Saint Lawrence Islands* at CANADA, *National Parks*) and some to the United States. The Thousand Islands International Bridge (five spans, bet. islands; total length 8½ m.; opened Aug. 18, 1938) connects Collins Landing, New York, ab. 3 m. SW of Alexandria Bay, with Ivy Lea, Ontario, below Gananoque.
2 Group of small islands (actually ab. 100) in SW Java Sea and off coast of Java NW of Batavia, Indonesia; base for fishermen.

Thousand Lake Mountain. Peak 11,250 ft. in W Wayne co., S cen. Utah.

Thousand Ships Bay. Bay at extreme SE end of Santa Isabel I., E cen. Solomon Is., W Pacific Ocean; formed partly by San Jorge I. on the W.

Thrace (thrās). Region of E Balkan Penin., SE Europe, varying in limits at different periods: (1) Ancient **Thra'ce** (thrā'sē) *or* **Thra'ci·a** (thrā'shĭ·à·-shà) bordered on Euxine (Black Sea) S of the Ister (Danube), on the Propontis (Sea of Marmara), on the N Aegean except for narrow strip of Greek settlements, and on the W on Macedonia. Drained by Hebrus (mod. Maritsa) and included Rhodope Mts. Early Thracians a mixed race, akin to Illyrians. Country reduced to Roman province in time of Vespasian (69–79 A.D.); Lower Moesia formed out of its N part. Corresponded generally to cen. and S Bulgaria, Turkey in Europe, and NE Greece. Overrun by Goths, Huns, and other barbarian invaders; part of Eastern Roman Empire but part fell to Turks 1361 and all of it became Turkish after 1453; in 1878 N part separated as Eastern Rumelia. (2) Modern Thrace is S part of ancient region, now divided by the Maritsa river into Western Thrace and Eastern Thrace. **Western Thrace**, *Gr.* **Dy'ti·kē' Thra'kē** (thē'tē·kyē' thrä'-

kyē), constitutes a geographical division of Greece, occupying the extreme NE corner of the country and including the departments of Evros and Rhodope (see *Table* at GREECE), 3362 sq. m., pop. (1938 est.) 354,889; chief towns Alexandroúpolis, Komotinē, and Xanthe; **Eastern Thrace** constitutes Turkey in Europe (see TURKEY). A theater of the First Balkan War in which great battle of Lüleburgaz was fought; after Second Balkan War part assigned to Bulgaria, but by treaties of 1919 and 1920 boundaries changed and nearly all Thrace became Greek 1920–23.

Thra'cian Sea (thrā'shăn). The NW part of the Aegean Sea; bordered on N by the peninsulas of Chalcidice, on S by the Northern Sporades, and on W by the mainland of Thessaly; its NW arm is the Gulf of Salonika.

Three Brothers. Mountain 7370 ft. in Chelan co., cen. Washington.

Three Fingers. Mountain 6845 ft. in Snohomish co., NW cen. Washington.

Three Forks. Town, Gallatin co., SW Montana, on Jefferson river ab. 4 m. SW of locality where it joins Madison and Gallatin rivers to form the Missouri; pop. 1161.

Three Kings Islands. Group of three small islands in S Pacific Ocean NNW of N extremity of North I., New Zealand; 34°5′S; 3 sq. m.

Three Oaks. Manufacturing village, Berrien co., SW corner of Michigan; pop. 1763; featherbone.

Three Pagodas Pass. Mountain pass at S end of Dawna Range, bet. SE Burma and W Thailand, at 15°20′N and ab. 100 m. SSE of Moulmein; for centuries used as connecting highway bet. Burma and the plains of the lower Chao Phraya in Thailand.

Three Points, Cape. Cape extending into the Gulf of Guinea on SW coast of Gold Coast Colony, W Africa, 2°W long.; 4°42′N lat.; "the land nearest nowhere"; i.e., the land nearest 0° lat. and 0° long. (also zero alt.), where Greenwich meridian and equator cross 360 m. off coast of W Africa in Gulf of Guinea; nearest town is Accra.

Three Rivers. 1 City, St. Joseph co., S Michigan, 24 m. S of Kalamazoo; pop. 7092.
2 *Fr.* **Trois–Ri·vières'** (trwä'rē'vyâr'). Industrial city, St. Maurice co., S Quebec, Canada, on N bank of St. Lawrence river at mouth of the St. Maurice river, 75 m. NE of Montreal; pop. 46,074; on Lake St. Peter; produces paper and pulp, stoves, iron pipes. Seminaire Saint-Joseph. Founded 1634 by Champlain.

Three Sisters. Adjacent peaks 10,354 ft., 10,094 ft., 10,053 ft., in Lane co., W Oregon.

Throck'mor'ton (thrŏk'môr't'n). 1 County in Texas. See *Table* at TEXAS.
2 Town, its ⊗, N Texas; pop. 1299.

Throgs Neck (thrŏgz). Cape projecting into Long Island Sound from the coast of Bronx co., SE New York.

Throop (trōōp). Borough, Lackawanna co., NE Pennsylvania, 4 m. NE of Scranton; pop. 4732; coal mining.

Throtmannia. See DORTMUND.

Thu·bur'bo Ma'jus (thŭ·bûr'bō mā'jŭs). Ancient city, Roman Africa, site SW of modern Tunis; founded by Octavian; ruins have been excavated.

Thug'ga (thŭg'à); *mod.* **Doug'ga** (dōō'gà). Ancient city, N Africa, SW of Carthage; ruins 68 m. SW of Tunis, Tunisia; important Punic city; most of ruins are of buildings constructed under the Romans, including a temple of Jupiter, Juno, and Minerva built by Marcus Aurelius (d. 180), the temple of Caelestis, forum, etc.

Thuile, La. See LA THUILE.

Thu·in' (tü·ăn'). Commune, Hainaut prov., SW Belgium, just SW of Charleroi; pop. 6705.

Thu'le. 1 (thū'lē) The northernmost part of the habitable world—so called by the ancients; according to some it was Norway, to others, Iceland, or more probably Mainland, the largest of the Shetland Is., hence the Latin phrase *ultima Thule*.
2 (tōō'lē) Eskimo settlement NW Greenland, on

coast of Hayes Penin. N of Cape York; Danish trading post (founded 1910). Its name has been given to a form of Eskimo culture found here but extending over all Arctic Regions where Eskimos dwell. U.S. Air Force base.

Thumb, the (thŭm). **1** Peak 13,885 ft. in Sierra Nevada, E Fresno co., S cen. California.
2 Peninsula of E Michigan, bet. Lake Huron and Saginaw Bay; the "thumb" of mitten-shaped lower Michigan; chiefly Huron co.; its tip is Pointe Aux Barques.

Thun (tōōn). Commune, Bern canton, Switzerland, at head of Lake of Thun on Aare river 15 m. SSE of Bern; pop. (1941) 20,239; 18th-cent. church, town hall, 15th-cent. castle; largest Swiss armory; railroad junction; manufactures metal goods, pottery; tourist resort.

Thun, Lake of; *Ger.* **Thu′ner·see′** (tōō′nĕr·zā′). Lake 10 m. long in cen. Switzerland, formed by an expansion of the Aare river.

Thunder Bay. 1 Inlet of Lake Huron 12 m. long on E coast of Alpena co., NE Michigan.
2 River ab. 50 m. long, NE Michigan; flows into Thunder Bay at Alpena.
3 Inlet of NW Lake Superior, Ontario prov., Canada.
4 District, Ontario, Canada. See *Table* at ONTARIO.

Thunder Cape. Bold headland SE of Thunder Bay, Ontario prov., Canada, projecting into Lake Superior.

Thunderer. Peak 10,600 ft. in Yellowstone National Park, NW Wyoming.

Thunder Mountain. Peak 13,578 ft. in Sierra Nevada, N Tulare co., S cen. California.

Thunersee. See Lake of THUN.

Thur (tōōr; *Angl.* tōōr). River 80 m. long, NE Switzerland; rises in cen. Saint Gallen canton, flows N to Thurgau canton (named for this river) and turns W; joins the Rhine in N Zurich canton.

Thur′gau (tōōr′gou; *Angl.* tōōr′-). Swiss canton. See *Table* at SWITZERLAND.

Thur′go′vie′ (tür′gō′vē′). = THURGAU, Swiss canton.

Thu′ri·i (thūr′ĭ·ī). Ancient Greek city in Lucania, S Italy, near site of Sybaris; founded 443 B.C. by Greek colonists, among them Herodotus and Lysias. Prosperous and powerful until plundered by Hannibal 204 B.C.

Thu·rin′gi·a (thū·rĭn′jĭ·à); *Ger.* **Thü′ring·en** (tü′rĭng·ĕn). Former German state; the land around the Thuringian Forest, approximately bet. Werra river on W and Weisse Elster on E, and crossed by the Saale; comprised former Thuringian States (see REUSS, SAXE, SCHWARZBURG), 4540 sq. m., pop. (1939) 1,760,595, ✻ Weimar. Region is rich agriculturally; its forested hills contain many health centers and resorts; esp. noted for its cities Weimar, Gera, Jena, Gotha, Eisenach, Altenburg.
History: Region conquered by Franks in 6th cent. and generally under Frankish rule from 634 to 804 when Charlemagne founded the Thuringian Mark. In medieval period had many changes in rulers and political status; from 1485 to 1918 identified with duchy and kingdom of Saxony. States combined under Weimar republic 1919–33 but after 1934 under the Reich included in Saxony.

Thu·rin′gi·an Forest (thū·rĭn′jĭ·ăn); *Ger.* **Thü′ring·er Wald** (tü′rĭng·ĕr vält′). Wooded mountain range in Thuringia, cen. Germany; highest point ab. 3225 ft.

Thur′les (thûr′lĕs). Urban district, cen. co. Tipperary, S Eire; pop. 5648; fox-hunting, fishing, and horse-racing center; remains of 12th-cent. castle.

Thurn′scoe (thûrn′skō). Former urban district, West Riding, Yorkshire, N England; pop. (1931) 10,548.

Thurs′day Island (thûrz′dĭ). Small island, N Queensland, Australia, in Torres Strait 30 m. NW of Cape York; pop. 1047; center of pearl-fishing industry; has excellent harbor (Port Kennedy).

Thur′so (thûr′sō). Burgh, Caithness co., N Scotland, at mouth of Thurso river; pop. 3203.

Thurs′ton (thûrs′tŭn). Counties in two states of the

U.S. See *Tables* at NEBRASKA and WASHINGTON.

Thurston, Mount. Peak 3134 ft. in E Vanua Levu I., Fiji Is., SW Pacific Ocean; highest point on the island.

Thurston Peninsula *or* **Thurston Island.** Island of Antarctica bet. Bellinghausen and Amundsen Seas; before 1961 thought to be a peninsula of Marie Byrd Land.

Thu′sis (tōō′zĭs). Village, Graubünden canton, E Switzerland; pop. (1930) 1292; resort; ruins of castle nearby.

Thyamis. See KALAMAS.

Thyatira. See AKHISAR.

Thyland. See VENDSYSSEL-THY.

Thym′bra (thĭm′brà). Battlefield site, Asia Minor, SE of ancient Troy; scene of battle 546 B.C. in which Cyrus the Great defeated Croesus, king of Lydia; as described by Xenophon in the *Cyropaedia* has served as a model for tactics from Scipio to Napoleon.

Thys′ville′ (tēs′vēl′). Town, W Léopoldville prov., W Congo, SW of Léopoldville; pop. (1938) 3124.

Tia′hua·na′co (tyä′wä·nä′kŏ) *or* **Tia′hua·na′cu** (-kōō). Site of prehistoric ruins adjacent to mountain village of **Tiahuanaco,** near SE end of Lake Titicaca, W Bolivia, on railroad 38 m. W of La Paz. Ruins consist of statues, monoliths, pillars, carvings, remains of great Temple of the Sun, etc., and are of great antiquity, preceding the Aymara and Inca civilizations.

Ti′a Jua′na (tē′à wä′nà). Village, San Diego co., California; part of San Ysidro; opp. Tijuana, Mexico.

Tía Juana. See TIJUANA.

Tian Shan. See TIEN SHAN.

Tia·ong′ (tyä·ông′). Municipality, SW Tayabas prov., Luzon, Phil. Is., 19 m. W of Lucena; pop. 27,179.

Tia′ret′ (tyà′rĕ′). Commune, E Oran dept., NW Algeria, ab. 110 m. E of Oran; pop. 20,894; on an important pass (alt. 3550 ft.) in N Atlas Mts. Its site occupied in Roman times; seat of a Mohammedan dynasty in medieval times; became possession of Turks in 16th cent., taken by French 1843.

Ti′ber (tī′bĕr); *Ital.* **Te′ve·re** (tā′vå·rå); *anc.* **Ti′ber·is** (tĭ′bĕr·ĭs). River 244 m. long in cen. Italy; rises in the Tuscan Apennines, flows S through Umbria and Latium; in Latium turns SW, flows through Rome which is 16 m. from its mouth at Ostia on the Tyrrhenian Sea; navigable at certain seasons to ab. 30 m. N of Rome.

Ti·be′ri·as (tĭ·bēr′ĭ·ăs). **1** Subdistrict, Galilee dist., N Palestine; 175 sq. m.; pop. 26,975, (1938 est.) 31,720.
2 *modern* **Ta′ba·ri′ya** (tŏ′bŭ·rē′yà; -yä). Ancient town, its ✻ and Roman ✻ of Galilee, on the W shore of the Sea of Galilee; pop. (1944 est.) 12,104. Built by Herod Antipas 21 A.D. and named after the emperor Tiberius. A center of Jewish learning from 2d to 6th cent. and seat of Sanhedrin and of rabbinical schools; the Talmud edited here.

Tiberias, Sea of. See Sea of GALILEE.

Ti·bes′ti Mountains (tĭ·bĕs′tĭ). Mountain group, NW Chad, N cen. Africa, in cen. Sahara region; highest peak Emi Koussi 11,201 ft.

Ti·bet′ (tĭ·bĕt′); *Chin.* **Si′tsang′** (shē′tsäng′). Country of cen. Asia, nominally an outer dependency of China; 469,294 sq. m.; pop. (1936 est.) 3,722,011; ✻ Lhasa; bounded on N by Sinkiang, on NE by Tsinghai, on E by Sikang, on S by Bhutan, Nepal, and India, and on W by India. In 1944 reduced in area by ab. one third and considerably in population, by relocation of W boundaries of Sikang and Tsinghai; no new figures available. A plateau, the highest country in the world, averaging ab. 16,000 ft.; its lowland regions and valleys are bet. 12,000 and 15,000 ft., its mountain ranges rise to 20,000 and 24,000 ft., even the mountain passes are generally 14,000 to 18,000 ft. Bordered on N by the Kunlun Mts.; the S part, comprising valley or plain of Tsangpo (upper Brahmaputra) is separated from Nepal, India, and Bhutan by the Himalayas (containing highest peaks in the world); subsidiary ranges are the Kailas Range and Aling Kangri. Its N region (**Chang Tang** [jäng′

däng′]) has a terrain much broken up by mountain ranges, valleys, and lakes. The Salween river has its source in Tanglha Range in E part and flows generally SE in a great gorge through Sikang; the Indus and its tributary the Sutlej rise in the SW. Many lakes are scattered over all the plateau; the largest are Nam Tso, Zilling Tso, and Kyaring Tso. Tibetans are an ancient race of Mongolian type and their ruler is the Dalai Lama; practically all are Lamaists (Buddhists). Agriculture carried on only in a few favored regions; principal industry cattle raising. Chief towns Lhasa, Gyangtse, Shigatse, Gartok. See *Map* at CHINA.

History: Buddhism introduced in 7th cent. A.D. First came under Chinese control during Manchu dynasty in 1720; generally closed to foreigners until late in 19th cent. when (1890, 1893) by Sikkim Convention boundaries and commercial relations bet. Tibet and India were determined; Anglo-Tibetan Convention signed 1904; invaded by Communist Chinese 1950; made an autonomous region within Communist China 1965.

Tibet, Little. See BALTISTAN.

Tibet, Nearer. An earlier name for E Tibet, now forming W Tsinghai and Sikang provs. of China.

Tibiscus. See TIMIŞ.

Tibur. See TIVOLI.

Tib′u·ron (tĭb′ŭ·rŏn). Peninsula N of San Francisco, California, extending into San Francisco Bay.

Ti′bu′ron′ (tē′bü′rôn′). 1 Peninsula in SW Haiti; ab. 140 m. long, 18 to 36 m. wide; mountainous, contains the Massif de la Hotte.

2 Cape, the SW point of Tiburon Penin., Haiti.

Ti′bu·rón′ (tē′vōō·rôn′). Island 34 m. long off W cen. coast of Sonora state, Mexico, in Gulf of California.

Ti′bu·rón′, Cape (tē′vōō·rôn′). Cape on W coast of Colombia at the entrance to the Gulf of Darien.

Ti·ca′o (tē·kä′ô). Narrow, hilly island, Masbate prov., Phil. Is., off NE coast of Masbate I. and separated from Luzon (Sorsogon prov.) by Ticao Pass; 129 sq. m.; pop. 29,797; coextensive with 2 municipalities of San Jacinto and San Fernando, both with population centers on E coast. Occupied by American forces Mar. 1945.

Ticao Pass. Strait bet. SW Sorsogon prov., SE Luzon, Phil. Is., and Ticao I.; ab. 37 m. long by 10 or 12 m. wide; sometimes considered as W part of San Bernardino Strait.

Tice (tīs). Urban community (unincorporated), Lee co., SW Florida, NE of Fort Myers; pop. 4377.

Ti·ci′no (tē·chē′nô). 1 *anc.* **Ti·ci′nus** (tĭ·sī′nŭs). River 154 m. long, Switzerland and Italy; rises on the slopes of Saint Gotthard, flows SE and then SW in Ticino canton, traverses Lago Maggiore and continues S into Po river 3½ m. SSE of Pavia; navigable below Lake Maggiore; Hannibal defeated Romans on the banks of this river 218 B.C.

2 Swiss canton in Lepontine Alps, watered by Ticino river; crossed by St. Gotthard railroad. Formed 1803 by union of former cantons of Lugano and Bellinzona. See *Table* at SWITZERLAND.

Ticinum. See PAVIA commune.

Ti′con·der·o′ga (tī′kŏn·dēr·ō′gȧ; tī·kŏn′-). Village, Essex co., NE New York, on N outlet of Lake George and near Lake Champlain; pop. 3568; tourist center in resort region. Old Fort Carillon (restored as museum 1909) built at head of Lake Champlain by French 1755 and garrisoned by force under Montcalm 1758; defended from Abercrombie's attack 1758; taken by Gen. Amherst 1759, and became Fort Ticonderoga; captured by Ethan Allen 1775, retaken by Burgoyne 1777; kept by British until Burgoyne's surrender. Incorporated 1889.

Ti·cul′ (tē·kōōl′). Town, Yucatán state, on Yucatán penin., SE Mexico, 40 m. S of Mérida; pop. 9034.

Tid′dim (tĭd′ĭm). Town, Chin Hills dist., W Upper Burma, just E of Manipur river and S of Manipur border; a headquarters town of Japanese forces in campaign against India 1943–45.

Ti·do′re (tē·dô′rā). 1 Former division of the Moluccas, E Neth. Indies, later a subdivision of Ternate division, including for administrative purposes the island of Tidore, the E and S parts of Halmahera, and the four subdivisions of Sorong, Manokwari, West New Guinea, and Hollandia, and their adjacent islands, of W and N Neth. New Guinea.

2 Small island of the Moluccas in Indonesia, off W coast of Halmahera I. ab. 1 m. S of Ternate I.; 30 sq. m.; pop. 19,126. Has several volcanic peaks, highest ab. 5700 ft.; fertile soil; raises tobacco, coffee, and fruits; formerly produced much spice. Former seat of an ancient and powerful sultanate, long a rival of Ternate; occupied 1521 by Portuguese, who built a fort 1571; deserted by Portuguese 1605 and occupied by Spanish 1606; conquered by Dutch 1654; reduced to a dependency but with a ruling sultan; seized by Japanese 1942.

3 Town and port on E side of island; a walled town dating back to years before the coming of the Portuguese.

Tid′worth (tĭd′wûrth). Town, Wiltshire, S England, on the border of Hampshire; military camp; large technical school established during World War II.

Tiegenhof. See NOWY DWÓR GDAŃSKI.

Tieh′ling′ (tĭ·ĕ′lĭng′). Town, cen. Liaoning prov., S Manchuria, on left bank of Liao river and on South Manchuria Ry. 40 m. NE of Mukden; pop. 52,835; an old town, formerly had considerable river trade.

Tiel (tēl). Commune, Gelderland prov., E Netherlands, on the Waal 20 m. SE of Utrecht; pop. 12,341.

Tien Chih (tĭ·ĕn′ chĭr′). Lake, cen. Yunnan prov., S China, just S of Kunming.

Tie′nen *or* **Thie′nen** (tē′nĕ[n]); *Fr.* **Tir′le·mont′** (tēr′lē·môn′). Commercial and manufacturing commune, Brabant prov., cen. Belgium; pop. 20,935; breweries; captured by the Germans 1914. Has fine church begun in 12th cent.

Tien Shan (tĭ·ĕn′ shän′) *or* **Tian Shan** (tĭ·än′). Lofty mountain chain (*shan*) in Central Asia, in Kirgiz Republic of Soviet Central Asia and in Sinkiang prov., W China; highest point Pobeda Peak 24,406 ft.

Tien′shui′ (tĭ·ĕn′shwä′) *formerly* **Tsin′chow′** (tsĭn′-jō′). Market city on Wei river, 190 m. W of Sian, SE Kansu prov., N cen. China; pop. ab. 150,000.

Tien′tsin′ (tĭn′tsĭn′; *Chin.* tĭ·ĕn′jĭn′). City and treaty port, ✳ of Hopei prov., NE China, at junction of the Pei and Grand Canal where they form the Hai river, ab. 80 m. SE of Peiping; pop. (1936 est.) 1,292,025; connected by Grand Canal with the Yangtze; for centuries an important commercial and military city; today an educational center; has temple memorial to Li Hungchang. Foreign concessions granted to many countries (first to British in 1860). Treaty signed here 1858 opened 11 ports to foreign trade; occupied by British and French 1858 and again in 1860, when its port was first actually opened to trade; two other treaties signed here (1871, 1885); scene of siege and severe fighting in Boxer uprising 1900; governed by international commission 1900–07 which razed its walls; in civil war that followed World War II taken by Communist forces Jan. 1949.

Ti·er′ra Am′a·ril′la (tĭ·ĕr′ȧ äm′ȧ·rĭl′ȧ). Village, ⊗ of Rio Arriba co., N New Mexico; pop. (est.) 500.

Ti·er′ra Blan′ca (tĭ·ĕr′ȧ bläng′kȧ; *Span.* tyĕr′rä vläng′kä). Town, Veracruz state, E Mexico; railroad junction point ab. 50 m. S of Veracruz; pop. 7255; coffee raising.

Ti·er′ra Bom′ba (tĭ·ĕr′ȧ bŏm′bȧ; *Span.* tyĕr′rä vôm′bä). Small island in the Caribbean Sea off NW coast of Colombia, near city of Cartagena.

Ti·er′ra del Fu·e′go (tĭ·ĕr′ȧ dĕl′ fōō·ā′gō, fū-; *Span.* tyĕr′rä thĕl fwä′gō). 1 Archipelago off S South America comprising all islands W of Strait of Magellan; 27,600 sq. m.; separated from Antarctic Archipelago on S by Drake Passage. Its main island, Tierra del Fuego, is divided bet. Chile (W half) and Argentina (E half); of its groups of smaller islands the eastern (including Staten I.) belongs

to Argentina, and the southern (including Hoste I., Navarino I., Wollaston Is., and Diego Ramírez Is.) and western (including Desolación, Santa Inés, Clarence, and Dawson) belong to Chile.

2 Chief island of Tierra del Fuego archipelago; 18,530 sq. m.; W half belongs to Magallanes prov., Chile; E half and nearby Staten I. constitute **Tierra del Fuego Territory** of Argentina (see *Table* at ARGENTINA).

Tie·tê' (tyĕ·tä'). River ab. 500 m. long in São Paulo state, SE Brazil; rises in mountains near Atlantic coast, flows W through cen. São Paulo state and empties into Paraná river; São Paulo is on it.

Tiet·jerk'ste·ra·deel' (tēt·yĕrk'stĕ·rà·dāl'). Commune, Friesland prov., N Netherlands; pop. 16,316.

Ti'e·ton (tī'ĕ·t'n). River ab. 25 m. long, S Washington; rises in W Yakima co., flows NE into Naches river.

Tieton Dam. Dam completed 1925 across **Tieton River,** tributary of Naches river, W Yakima co., S Washington; height 222 ft.; impounds water, **Tieton Reservoir,** for irrigation.

Tieton Peak. Mountain 7775 ft. in Yakima co., S Washington.

Tif'fa·ny Mountain (tĭf'à·nĭ). Peak 8275 ft., Okanogan co., N Washington.

Tif'fin (tĭf'ĭn). Industrial city, ⊗ of Seneca co., N Ohio, 25 m. ENE of Findlay; pop. 21,478; settled 1817; manufactures glass tableware, sanitary pottery, abrasives, transmission machinery; clay and glass-sand deposits nearby. Heidelberg Coll. (1850; coed.).

Tif'lis (tĭf'lĭs; *Russ.* tyĭ·flyēs'); *officially, Georgian* **Tpi'li·si** *or* **Tbi'li·si** (t'pĭ'lĭ·sĭ), *literally* "Warm Springs." City, ✻ of Georgia, in SE part, and formerly ✻ of Transcaucasian Federation, U.S.S.R., on both banks of Kura river 280 m. WNW of Baku; pop. 519,175; in hill country at elevation of 1350 ft.; varied manufactures; has hydroelectric station. Has for centuries been on the great trade highway bet. Europe and Asia, an active center for exchange of Persian, Russian, and Turkish goods; S terminus of modern Georgian Military Road over Daryal Pass to Dzaudzhikau; on oil pipeline. Founded as early as 4th cent. A.D., with its Zion Cathedral dating from ab. that time; made a place of residence 570 for Persian rulers; 7th to 9th cent. suffered much in attacks by Greeks, Arabs, and Khazars; plundered by Tamerlane c. 1386 and fought over by Persians and Russians, the latter acquiring permanent possession 1799; rebelled against Tsarist government 1905 and was selected as seat of new administration 1917; became capital of new Transcaucasian Federation in 1921 and of Georgian A.S.S.R. 1936.

Tift (tĭft). County in Georgia. See *Table* at GEORGIA.

Tif'ton (tĭf'tŭn). City, ⊗ of Tift co., S Georgia, 40 m. ESE of Albany; pop. 9903; incorp. 1891; tobacco market; cotton, tomatoes.

Tigara. See Point HOPE.

Tig·ba'uan (tĕg·bä'wän). Municipality, S Iloilo prov., Panay, Phil. Is., on Iloilo Strait 15 m. W of City of Iloilo; pop. 17,092. One of the oldest towns on Panay.

Ti'ger (tī'gēr). River 100 m. long, South Carolina; rises in NW in Greenville co., flows SE into the Broad river forming for several miles the boundary bet. Union and Newberry cos.

Ti'ger Bay (tī'gēr); *Port.* **Ba·i'a dos Ti'gres** (bà·ē'à thōōsh tē'grĕsh). Inlet of Atlantic Ocean on SW coast of Angola, SW Africa.

Tiger Hill. See DARJEELING.

Ti·ghi'na (tĕ·gē'nä). **1** Former department, SE Bessarabia, Romania; 2445 sq. m.; pop. 307,629.

2 Town, its ✻. See BENDERY.

Tigranocerta. See SIIRT.

Ti'gre (tē'grä). **1** Seaside resort, Buenos Aires prov., E Argentina, 20 m. N of Buenos Aires.

2 River ab. 350 m. long in Ecuador and Peru; rises in cen. Ecuador, flows SE across border into Peru and empties into Marañón river, headstream of Amazon river.

Ti·gre' (tĭ·grā'; tĭg'rā). Former kingdom and province, N Ethiopia (Abyssinia), E Africa; ✻ Aduwa.

Ti'gre Island (tē'grä). Island in the Gulf of Fonseca, Honduras; chief town Amapala.

Tigres, Baia dos. See Bay of TIGERS.

Ti'gris (tī'grĭs); *Arab.* **Shatt Dij'la** (shŏt dĭj'là; -lä); *Bib.* (*Gen.* ii. 14; *Dan.* x. 4) **Hid'de·kel** (hĭd'ĕ·kĕl). River ab. 1150 m. long in SE Turkey in Asia and Iraq; rises in a lake in the mountains of Kurdistan, S of Elâziz, Turkey; flows SSE past Diyarbekir in Turkey and Mosul and Baghdad in Iraq, and unites in SE Iraq at Al Qurna with the Euphrates river to form the Shatt-al-Arab. Has many tributaries on left bank, esp. the Great Zab, Little Zab, and Diyala in Iraq. Navigable for small steamers bet. Baghdad and a point just above Al Qurna; usually above Baghdad by rafts only. Since ancient times connected with Euphrates in their lower courses by irrigation canals; probably in Sumerian times its lower course was much more to the W. Sites of ruins of many ancient cities are on its banks, as Nineveh, Calah, Ashur, Ctesiphon, and Seleucia.

Tih, El. See EL TIH.

Ti·ha'ma *or* **Te·ha'ma** (tĭ·hä'mà; -mä). Low coastal plain, SW Arabia, along the Red Sea, from S Hejaz to Bab el Mandeb strait.

Tihwa. See URUMCHI.

Ti·jua'na (tĕ·hwä'nä) *or* **Tí'a Jua'na** (tē'à wä'nà; *Span.* tē'ä hwä'nä). Town, North District of Lower California territory, NW Mexico; pop. 16,486.

Ti·ju'ca Peak (tĕ·zhōō'kà). Mountain 3350 ft. on SW side of the city of Rio de Janeiro, SE Brazil.

Ti·ju'cas Bay (tĕ·zhōō'kàs). Inlet of Atlantic Ocean on E coast of Santa Catarina state, S Brazil, N of Florianópolis.

Ti·kal' (tĕ·käl'). Ancient Mayan city in N Guatemala, NE of Lake Petén; ruins.

Ti·kam'garh (tĕ·kŭm'gär; *native* -gŭr·h') *or* **Teh'ri** (tā'rĕ; *native* tä'hrĕ). Town, ✻ of Orchha state, India, ab. 100 m. SSE of Gwalior; pop. 14,366.

Ti'kho·retsk (tĭk'ŏ·rĕtsk'; *Russ.* tyĭ·kŭ·ryĕtsk'). Town, Krasnodar Territory, SE Russia in Europe, ab. 100 m. S of Rostov; key railroad junction point and scene of fighting Jan. and Feb. 1943.

Tikh'vin (tĭk'vĭn; *Russ.* tyēk'vyĭn). Town, E Leningrad Region, Soviet Russia, Europe, 110 m. ESE of Leningrad; pop. 11,500; on S bank of the **Tikh'vin·ka** (tyēk'vyĭn·kà), tributary of the Syas, which forms part of canal system connecting Lake Ladoga with the Volga at Shcherbakov (Rybinsk) via the Mologa river and Rybinsk Reservoir.

Ti·krit' *or* **Te·krit'** (tĭ·krēt'). Town, N cen. Iraq, on the W bank of the Tigris river ab. 100 m. NNW of Baghdad; pop. ab. 5000; birthplace of Saladin (1138). Battle Nov. 6, 1917 in World War I in which it was captured from the Turks.

Til'burg (tĭl'bûrg; *Dutch.* -bûrk). Commune, North Brabant prov., S Netherlands, 34 m. SE of Rotterdam; pop. (1939) 97,338; has grown in recent years into one of the most important of Dutch industrial centers.

Til'bur'y (tĭl'bĕr'ĭ; -bēr·ĭ). **1** Town, Kent and Essex cos., SE Ontario, Canada, 17 m. SW of Chatham, near mouth of Thames river; total pop. 2682.

2 Former urban district, Essex, SE England, on the Thames 22 m. E of London; pop. (1931) 16,825; extensive docks, now included in the Port of London.

Til'den (tĭl'dĕn). Village, ⊗ of McMullen co., S Texas; pop. ab. 600.

Till (tĭl). Small river in extreme N England, flowing N into the Tweed on the border of Scotland.

Til'la·mook (tĭl'à·mŏok). **1** County in Oregon. See *Table* at OREGON.

2 City, its ⊗, NW Oregon, on S end of **Tillamook Bay** (inlet of Pacific Ocean) 50 m. S of Astoria; pop. 4244; co-operative cheese factories; manufactures butter, lumber; fisheries; logging.

Til′leur′ (tē′yûr′). Commune, Liège prov., E Belgium; pop. 6664; W suburb of Liège; blast furnaces, coke ovens, smelters.

Till′man (tĭl′măn). County in Oklahoma. See *Table* at OKLAHOMA.

Till·son·burg (tĭl′s′n·bûrg). Town, Oxford co., SE Ontario, Canada, 28 m. ESE of London; pop. 5330.

Til′ly (tē′yē′), *officially* **Tilly–sur–Seulles** (-sür·sûl′). Village, Calvados dept., NW France, 7 m. SSE of Bayeux; pop. (1931) 498; in World War II taken by Allies June 7–11, 1944.

Ti′los (tē′lôs). = TELOS.

Tilsit. See SOVETSK.

Til′till Mountain (tĭl′tĭl). Peak 8951 ft. in Sierra Nevada, in E Tuolumne co., cen. California.

Til′ton (tĭl′t′n; -tŭn). Town, Belknap co., cen. New Hampshire, 7 m. SW of Laconia; pop. 2137; united industrially, commercially, and residentially with Northfield, to the S, across Winnipesaukee river; manufactures hosiery and woolen goods.

Til′tons·ville (tĭl′t′nz·vĭl; tĭl′tŭnz-). Village, Jefferson co., E Ohio, on Ohio river 13 m. S of Steubenville; pop. 2454.

Ti·ma′ga·mi *or* **Te·ma′ga·mi, Lake** (tĭ·mä′gȧ·mĭ). Lake 90 sq. m. in Ontario prov., Canada, N of Lake Nipissing and SW of Lake Timiskaming; in forest reserve; noted for its excellent fishing.

Ti·man′ (tĭ·măn′; *Russ.* tyĭ·màn′). Height of land, NW Komi Republic, Soviet Russia, Europe, with N end in W Nenets National District; not over 1000 ft.

Tim′a·ru (tĭm′ȧ·rōō). Seaport, Canterbury provincial dist., E South I., New Zealand, on Pacific Ocean 95 m. SW of Christchurch; pop. (1941 est.) 19,200; exports flour, wool, and frozen meat; opals found in vicinity.

Tim′ba·lier′ Bay (tăm′bȧl·yā′). Inlet of Gulf of Mexico on SW coast of Lafourche parish, S Louisiana.

Timbalier Island. Island off SE Louisiana, in Lafourche parish, bet. Timbalier Bay and the Gulf of Mexico.

Tim′ba·ú′ba (tēNm′bȧ·ōō′vȧ). City, Pernambuco state, E Brazil, near the coast just NW of Recife; pop. 8662.

Tim′ber Crater (tĭm′bēr). Peak 7360 ft. in W Klamath co., S Oregon, N of Crater Lake.

Timber Lake. City, ⊗ of Dewey co., N cen. South Dakota; pop. 624.

Timber Mountain. Peak 10,280 ft. in S Nye co., S Nevada.

Tim′ber·wolf′, Mount (tĭm′bēr·wo͝olf′). Peak 6435 ft. in Yakima co., S Washington.

Tim′bo (tĭm′bō). Town, Guinea, West Africa, in the Fouta Djallon region 140 m. NE of Conakry; pop. ab. 3000; terminus of highway.

Timbuctoo. Var. of *Timbuktu:* see TOMBOUCTOU.

Timbuktu. See TOMBOUCTOU.

Tim·gad′ (tĭm·găd′); *anc.* **Tham′u·ga′di** (thăm′ū·gä′dĭ) *or* **Tham′u·ga′dis** (-dĭs). Ruined city in Constantine dept., NE Algeria, ESE of Batna; extensive ruins include the capitol, forum, theater (auditorium, almost complete, has capacity of 4000 people), baths (well-preserved mosaic floors), and an arch of Trajan. Founded 100 A.D. by Trajan, declined after 5th cent.; revived for a time in 7th cent.; not mentioned in history since 647.

Tim′miș (tē′mĕsh); *Serb.* **Te′meš** (tĕ′mĕsh); *anc.* **Tibis′cus** (tĭ·bĭs′kŭs). River ab. 270 m. long in W Romania, flowing W and S to the Danube in Yugoslavia just below Belgrade.

Ti·mis′ka·ming *or* **Te·mis′ka·ming** (tĭ·mĭs′kȧ·mĭng); *Fr.* **Té′mis′ca′mingue′** (tā′mĭs′ka′măng′). **1** Lake 117 sq. m. in SW Quebec and SE Ontario provs., Canada; discharges SE into the Ottawa river. **2** District, Ontario, Canada. See *Table* at ONTARIO. **3** County, Quebec, Canada. See *Table* at QUEBEC. **4** Town, Timiskaming co., on left bank of Timiskaming

river, 100 m. S of Rouyn (138 m. by highway) and ab. 40 m. NNE of North Bay, Ontario; pop. 2787.

Ti′mi·șoa′ra (tē′mĕ·shwä′rä); *Hung.* **Te′mes·vár′** (tĕ′mĕsh·vär′). City, SW Romania, near the Timiş river and near the Yugoslav border 75 m. NE of Belgrade; pop. (1939 est.) 89,872; industrial, commercial, and railroad center; Roman Catholic and Greek Catholic cathedrals; museum; municipal theater. Under Turkish rule 1552–1716; captured by Eugene of Savoy 1716; passed to Austria, who held it until the end of World War I; passed to Romania 1919.

Tim′mins (tĭm′ĭnz). Mining town, Cochrane dist., E Ontario, Canada, on Mattagami river 135 m. N of Sudbury; pop. 27,743; center of Canada's richest goldmining region; has meat-packing plant; manufactures paper, mining machinery, washing machines, and tools.

Tim′mons·ville (tĭm′ŭnz·vĭl; *Sou. also* -v′l). Town, Florence co., E South Carolina; pop. 2178.

Ti′mok (tē′mŏk). River ab. 100 m. long in E Yugoslavia; flows NE into Danube river 18 m. NNW of Vidin; in part forms boundary bet. Yugoslavia and Romania.

Ti·mo′ni·um (tĭ·mō′nĭ·ŭm). Urban community (unincorporated), Baltimore co., N Maryland, N of Baltimore; pop. (with Lutherville) 12,265.

Ti′mor (tē′mŏr; tē·môr′). **1** Island in S Malay Archipelago, easternmost of the Lesser Sunda Is., bet. Savu Sea on the W and Timor Sea on the E; ab. 400 m. NW of Australia; ab. 300 m. long by 10 to 65 m. wide; 13,094 sq. m.; pop. 813,860; formerly divided bet. the Dutch and the Portuguese; see NETHERLANDS TIMOR, PORTUGUESE TIMOR. **2** Division of the residency of Timor and dependencies, including Netherlands Timor, Roti and Sawu Is.; 6430 sq. m.; pop. 442,907. **3** *or* **Timor and Dependencies;** *also* **Timor Archipelago.** Former residency, forming with Bali and Lombok residency the Lesser Sunda Is. of Neth. Indies; comprised four divisions: islands of Sumbawa, Sumba, and Flores and W half of Timor I., with adjacent smaller islands; 24,449 sq. m.; pop. 1,657,376; ✱ Kupang.

Ti′mor·laoet′, or Ti′mor·laut′, Islands (tē′môr·lout′). The Tanimbar Is. (*q.v.*); but more correctly and in native usage applied only to the two large islands of Jamdena and Selaru.

Timor Sea. Arm of the Indian Ocean ab. 300 m. wide bet. Timor I. and the NW coast of Australia.

Ti·mo·ta·kem′ (tē·mō·tȧ·kāĕm′). Peak in Tumuc-Humac Mts. in S French Guiana on Brazil border.

Tim′pah·ute′ Range (tĭm′pȧ·ūt′). Small range in W Lincoln co., SE Nevada.

Tim′pa·no′gos, Mount (tĭm′pȧ·nō′gŭs). Peak 12,008 ft. in N cen. Utah; highest peak in Wasatch Range.

Timpanogos Cave National Monument. See UNITED STATES, *National Monuments.*

Tim·sah′ (tĭm·sä′h′). Lake in NE Egypt, at mid-point of Suez Canal; connected with the Nile river by the Ismailia Canal.

Tin, Cape (tĭn). Cape on N coast of Cyrenaica, NE Libya, N Africa, W of entrance to Gulf of Bomba.

Ti′na, Mon′te (mŏn′tä tē′nä). Mountain in the Dominican Republic. See TRUJILLO, MONTE.

Ti′na, Plain of (tē′nä). Plain, NW Sinai Penin., NE Egypt, E of Suez Canal and near the Mediterranean; in it are ruins of Pelusium.

Ti·na′ca Point (tē·nä′kä). Most southerly point of Mindanao, 5°35′N, Phil. Is., in SW Davao prov.

Ti′na·ga′ (tē′nä·gä′). Largest island of the Calagua group off N coast of Camarines Norte, SE Luzon, Phil. Is., 14 m. NE of Paracale; 5 sq. m.

Ti′na·ku′la (tē′nä·kōō′lä), *or* **Vol·ca′no** (vŏl·kä′nō), **Island.** Small island, one of the Santa Cruz Is., SW Pacific Ocean, ab. 18 m. N of Ndeni I.; an active volcano 2200 ft. high.

Tin Can Island (tĭn′ kăn′). See NIUAFOO.

Tin′che·bray′ (tăNsh′brā′). Town, NW Orne dept.,

NW France; pop. 2074; scene Sept. 28, 1106 of victory of Henry Beauclerc over his brother Robert Curt-hose (Robert II of Normandy).

Ti·ne′o (tē·nā′ṓ). Commune, Oviedo prov., NW Spain, 32 m. W of Oviedo; pop. 21,338; agriculture, stock raising; lime; dairy products.

Tingchow. See CHANGTING.

Ting′gi (tǐng′gē). Small island in South China Sea off E coast of Johore, S Malay Penin.

Ting′hai′ (dǐng′hī′). Commercial seaport, ✳ of Chu Shan archipelago, on S shore of Chu Shan I., Chekiang prov., E China.

Tingis. See TANGIER.

Tin′gi·ta′na (tǐn′jǐ·tā′nȧ; -tăn′ȧ; -tä′nȧ). Region, NW Africa; in Roman times, the W part of Mauretania; corresponds in part to modern Morocco.

Tin′gui·ri·ri′ca (tēng′gē·rē·rē′kä). Volcano 14,107 ft. in W Argentina, S of Santiago, Chile.

Ti·nha′re (tē·nyȧ′rĕ). Island in Atlantic Ocean off E coast of Baía state, Brazil.

Ti′ni·an′ (tē′nē·än′; *Angl.* tǐn′ĭ·ăn′). Island, S Mariana Is., W Pacific Ocean, 3 m. SSW of Saipan; 10 m. long by ab. 5 m. wide; area 20 sq. m.; chief town Tinian on SW coast. Contains ruins of colossal columned tombs; in early times, Spanish, then German (see MARIANA ISLANDS), included in Japanese mandate 1919; occupied by American forces July 23–Aug. 1, 1944.

Tin′i·cum (tǐn′ĭ·kŭm). Small island in Delaware river just below Philadelphia; first settlement within Pennsylvania, made 1643 by Gov. Johan Printz of Swedish colony. Cf. CHESTER, Pennsylvania.

Tin′ley Park (tǐn′lǐ). Village, Cook co., NE Illinois, SW suburb of Chicago; pop. 6392.

Tin′ne·vel′ly (tǐn′ĕ·vĕl′ĭ; tǐ·nĕv′ĕ·lǐ). Town, S Madras prov., S Indian Union, 88 m. SSW of Madura; pop. (1941) 60,676; has notable temple of Siva; scene of early labors of St. Francis Xavier; Christian missionary headquarters for southern India. Came under British rule 1801.

Tinos. See TENOS.

Tin·tag′el Head (tǐn·tăj′ĕl). Cape on W coast of Cornwall, SW England; site of ruins of Tintagel Castle, reputed birthplace of King Arthur.

Tin′tern Abbey (tǐn′tĕrn). Famous ruins in Monmouthsire, W England, 4½ m. N of Chepstow, on the river Wye. Founded 1131 by Walter de Clare for Cistercian monks; building in ruins dates from 13th cent.

Tin′to (tǐn′tō; *Span.* tēn′tō). River 70 m. long in Huelva prov., SW Spain, flowing into the Odiel river below Huelva; combined streams flow into the Mediterranean.

Ti·o′ga (tĭ·ō′gȧ). **1** River ab. 40 m. long, SW New York; rises in N Pennsylvania near W boundary of Bradford co., flows N across New York border to unite with Cohocton river near Corning and form the Chemung river. **2** Name of counties in two states of the U.S. See *Tables* at NEW YORK and PENNSYLVANIA.

Tio′man (tyō′män). Island in South China Sea off SE Pahang, S Malay Penin.

Ti′o·nes′ta (tĭ′ō·nĕs′tȧ). Borough, ⊗ of Forest co., NW Pennsylvania; pop. 778.

Ti′op (tē′ŏp). Settlement on N coast of Bougainville I., NW Solomon Is., W Pacific Ocean.

Ti·o′ro Strait (tē·ō′rō). Channel bet. SE Celebes I. and the island of Muna, Indonesia.

Ti·pa′o Point (tē·pä′ō). Point at S tip of peninsula extending into Laguna de Bay, S Rizal prov., Phil. Is.; is close to N end of Talim I.

Tiphsah. See THAPSACUS.

Ti′pi·ta′pa (tē′pē·tä′pä). River in W Nicaragua; flows out of Lake Managua SE into Lake Nicaragua.

Tip′pah (tǐp′ȧ). County in Mississippi. See *Table* at MISSISSIPPI.

Tipp City (tǐp); *formerly* **Tippecanoe City.** Village, Miami co., W Ohio, 14 m. N of Dayton; pop. 4267.

Tip′pe·ca·noe′ (tǐp′ē·kȧ·nōō′). **1** River ab. 200 m. long, N Indiana; rises in **Tippecanoe Lake** in NE cen. Kosciusko co., N Indiana, flows W and then S into Wabash river in W cen. Indiana. See FREEMAN LAKE, SHAFER LAKE. At the junction of the Tippecanoe with the Wabash near the Indian village of Prophetstown, Gen. William H. Harrison defeated Nov. 7, 1811 the Indians under Tecumseh. **2** County in Indiana. See *Table* at INDIANA.

Tip′pe·ra (tǐp′ĕ·rä). District, SE East Bengal, Pakistan; 2531 sq. m.; pop. (1941) 3,860,139; ✳ Comilla.

Tip′pe·rar′y (tǐp′ĕ·râr′ĭ). **1** County, S Eire, in Munster prov.; 1643 sq. m.; pop. 137,835; ⊗ Clonmel; divided into North Riding and South Riding; agriculture, livestock raising, lead mining, slate quarrying. **2** Urban district, SW co. Tipperary, S Eire, 24 m. SE of Limerick; pop. 5384; processes dairy produce, esp. butter; site of 13th-cent. friary and castle.

Tip′per·muir (tǐp′ĕr·mūr). Battlefield near Perth, Scotland; scene Sept. 1, 1644 of victory of Montrose over Covenanters under earl of Wemyss.

Tip′ton (tǐp′tŭn). **1** Name of counties in two states of the U.S. See *Tables* at INDIANA and TENNESSEE. **2** City, ⊗ of Tipton co., cen. Indiana, 15 m. S of Kokomo; pop. 5604. **3** City, ⊗ of Cedar co., E Iowa, 23 m. ENE of Iowa City; pop. 2862; in agricultural section. **4** Urban district, Staffordshire, W cen. England, 8 m. NW of Birmingham; pop. 39,382; in coal-mining section; anchors and steel cables.

Tipton, Mount. Peak 7364 ft. in cen. Mohave co., NW Arizona.

Tip′ton·ville (tǐp′tŭn·vĭl; *Sou. also* -v′l). Town and resort, ⊗ of Lake co., NW Tennessee, 3 m. E of Mississippi river at SW end of Reelfoot Lake; pop. 2068.

Ti·ra′ (tē·rä′). Var. of TIRE.

Ti′rah (tē′rä; *native* -rä·h′). Mountainous region in former Khyber Agency, North-West Frontier Province, India, WSW of Khyber Pass and Peshawar; scene of campaign 1897–98 in which British forces put down an uprising of Afridi and Orakzai tribes. Now in Pakistan.

Ti·ran′ (tē·rän′). Island at N end of Red Sea; with Sanafiri I. lies across entrance to Gulf of ‘Aqaba; both belong to Saudi Arabia. Tiran I. separated by **Strait of Tiran** from SE coast of Sinai Penin.

Ti·ra′në (tē·rä′nĕ) *or* **Ti·ra′na** (-nä). **1** Prefecture, cen. Albania; 328 sq. m.; pop. 57,808. **2** Town, Tiranë prefecture, cen. Albania, 18 m. E of Durrës; ✳ of Albania; pop. 30,806; college; national library; government buildings. Greater part of population is Moslem. Founded in 17th cent. by a Turkish general.

Ti·ra′no (tē·rä′nō). Commune, Sondrio prov., N Lombardy, N Italy, near the Swiss border; pop. 6772; scene of massacre of Protestants July 11, 1620; church of Madonna di Tirano, object of many pilgrimages.

Ti·ras′pol (tǐ·räs′pŭl; *Russ.* tyǐ·räs′pŭl·y′). City, ✳ (1930–40) of Moldavian A.S.S.R., Soviet Union, on the Dniester 55 m. NW of Odessa; pop. 25,748; an industrial center now in SE part of Moldavian S.S.R.

Tiravalur. See TIRUVARUR.

Tir′co·naill′ (tǐr′kŭ·näl′). County Donegal, Eire.

Ti·re′ (tē·rĕ′); *anc.* **Tyr′rha** (tǐr′ȧ). Town, İzmir vilayet, W Turkey in Asia, on branch railroad 38 m. SE of İzmir; pop. 20,315.

Ti·ree′ *or* **Ty·ree′** (tǐ·rē′). **1** Island of the Inner Hebrides, off W coast of Scotland; 30 sq. m.; pop. 1448; administratively a part of Argyll co.; horse breeding, marble quarrying. **2** Strait bet. the islands of Tiree and Mull in the Inner Hebrides, off W coast of Scotland.

Tîrgoviște. Var. of TÂRGOVIȘTE.

Tirgu–Jiu. Var. of TÂRGU-JIU.

Tir′hut (tǐr′hōōt). Division, N Bihar state, NE Indian Union; 12,594 sq. m.; pop. (1941) 11,959,827; ✳ Muzaffarpur.

Ti′rich Mir (tē′rĭch mēr′). Highest peak 25,263 ft. in the Hindu Kush range, N West Pakistan, N of Chitral, on border of Afghanistan.

Tir′le·mont′ (tēr′lĕ·môN′); *Flem.* **Thie′nen** (tē′nĕ[n]). Commercial and manufacturing commune, Brabant prov., cen. Belgium, 11 m. SE of Louvain; pop. 20,935; 12th–15th cent. church still unfinished.

Tirnovo. See TRNOVO.

Ti·rol′ *or* **Ty·rol′** (tĭ·rōl′; tĭr′ŏl; tĭ′rōl; tĭr′ŏl; tĭr′ŭl; *Ger.* tĕ·rōl′); *Ital.* **Ti·ro′lo** (tĕ·rô′lô). A province in west Austria, bet. the Vorarlberg on the W and the province of Salzburg on the E; see *Table* at AUSTRIA. A very mountainous region with Bavarian Alps along N border and Ötztaler Alps in S cen. part (since 1919 when South Tirol was ceded to Italy, have marked S border). See *Brenner Pass*, at ALPS. Traversed W to E by the Inn and in the NW by the Lech; before 1919 by the Adige in the S. Agriculture and mining are chief industries, but there is considerable manufacturing. Chief town Innsbruck.

History: Inhabited in early times by Celtic race; became part of Raetia in 1st cent. A.D.; under various counts and bishops until 14th cent.; passed to Hapsburgs 1363. Tirolese have been strongly independent people; their land scene of peasant uprising 1525 during Reformation, and after its cession to Napoleon 1805 by Treaty of Pressburg they carried on vigorous but unsuccessful revolt against French and Bavarians 1809–10; reunited with Austria 1814. Its S part (called Upper Adige by Italians) transferred to Italy by Treaty of St-Germain 1919.

Ti·rol′–Vor′arl′berg (*Ger.* tĕ·rōl′fōr′ärl′bĕrk). Former province of Austria. See *Table* at AUSTRIA.

Ti′rou·bou′va·né (tĭr′ŏŏ·bŏŏ′vȧ·nā). Commune, Pondicherry settlement, in former French India; pop. (1941) 21,348.

Tirreno, Mare. See TYRRHENIAN SEA.

Tir′schen·reuth (tĭr′shĕn·roit). Town, Upper Palatinate, Bavaria, Germany, in mountains near Czech border; pop. 5346; reached by Amer. army Apr. 23, 1945.

Tir′so (tēr′sô). River ab. 90 m. long, cen. Sardinia, flowing SW into Gulf of Oristano.

Tiruchirapalli. See TRICHINOPOLY.

Ti′ru·van·na′ma·lai (tĭr′ŏŏ·vȧ·nä′mȧ·lī). Town, E Madras state, S Indian Union, 110 m. SW of Madras; pop. 27,769; fine temple.

Ti′ru·va′rur (tĭr′ŏŏ·vä′rŏŏr) *or* **Ti′ra·va′lur** (tĭr′ȧ·vä′lŏŏr). Town, E Madras state, S Indian Union, 38 m. E of Tanjore; pop. 20,371.

Ti′ryns (tī′rĭnz). Prehistoric citadel N of Nauplia, in Argolis, E Peloponnesus, S Greece. In legends connected with Perseus and Hercules; historically, a Dorian city, founded as early as 2000 B.C. under Cretan influence; declined, with Mycenae, as Argos grew in power; destroyed by Argives c. 469 B.C. Ruins of massive walls, palace, hall, etc., have been uncovered and give valuable information of pre-Homeric life in Greece.

Tir′zah (tûr′zȧ). Ancient Canaanite town, cen. Palestine; its site supposed to be Tell el Farrah, just NE of Nablus; for a time (c. 911–887 B.C.) capital of the Northern Kingdom of Israel (*1 Kings* xv. 21, 33).

Tisa. See TISZA.

Tis′bur′y (tĭz′bĕr′ĭ; -bĕr·ĭ). Town, Dukes co., SE Massachusetts, on Martha's Vineyard; pop. 2169; summer resort, including Vineyard Haven.

Tish′o·min′go (tĭsh′ô·mĭng′gō). **1** County in Mississippi. See *Table* at MISSISSIPPI.
2 City, ⊗ of Johnston co., S Oklahoma, 28 m. E of Ardmore; pop. 2381; ✳ of Chickasaw Nation 1856–1907.

Tisia. See TISZA.

Tissus. See TISZA.

Tis′ta (tĭs′tä). River ab. 300 m. long, NE India; rises on edge of Tibetan plateau, flows S through Sikkim and across both West Bengal, India, and East Pakistan into the Brahmaputra at ab. 25°10′N, which from the point of confluence becomes known as Jamuna river.

Tis′te·dals·elv′ (tĭs′tĕ·däls·ĕlv′). River in S Norway; flows S through several long shallow lakes connected by rapids and empties into Oslo Fjord.

Ti′sza (tĭ′sŏ); *Ger.* **Theiss** (tīs); *Serb.* **Ti′sa** (tē′sä); *anc.* **Tis′sus** (tĭs′ŭs) *or* **Ti′si·a** (tĭzh′ĭ·ȧ). River ab. 800 m. long in W Ukraine, E Hungary, and NE Yugoslavia; rises in the Carpathian Mts. in W Ukraine (former Carpathian Ruthenia); flows W, forming a section of Russian-Romanian boundary; continues SW across Hungary and into NE Yugoslavia; empties into Danube river ab. 28 m. N of Belgrade; its largest tributaries are the Someş and the Mureş from Transylvania on the E; navigable for light-draught boats for ab. 450 m.

Tiszapolgár. See POLGÁR.

Ti·ta′garh (tĭ·tä′gĕr; *native* -gŭr·h′). Town, Twenty-four Parganas dist., S West Bengal, Indian Union, on Hooghly river 13 m. N of Calcutta; pop. (1941) 57,416.

Ti·ta′no, Mount (tĕ·tä′nô). Mountain 2437 ft. on which the city of San Marino is built, San Marino republic, Italy; notable for its three peaks.

Ti′ti·ca′ca, Lake (tĭt′ĭ·kä′kȧ; *Span.* tē′tē·kä′kä). Lake ab. 110 m. long and 45 m. wide on Peru-Bolivia boundary; area ab. 3500 sq. m.; altitude 12,500 ft.; highest large navigable lake in the world; drains S through Desaguadero river into Lake Poopó. Traversed by steamboats bet. Puno in Peru and Guaqui in Bolivia. The Cordillera Real of the Andes is on its E shore. Was in center of early South American civilizations (see TIAHUANACO).

Titograd. See PODGORICA.

Titius. See KERKA.

Tit′ta·ba·was′see (tĭt′ȧ·bȧ·wôs′ē). River ab. 65 m. long, E Michigan; flows from Ogemaw co. S into the Saginaw river in Saginaw co.

Titterstone Clee Hill. See CLEE HILLS.

Ti′tus (tī′tŭs). County in Texas. See *Table* at TEXAS.

Ti′tus·ville (tī′tŭs·vĭl; *Sou. also* -v′l). **1** City, ⊗ of Brevard co., E Florida, on Indian river 35 m. E of Orlando; pop. 6410; fruit-packing plants.
2 City, Crawford co., NW Pennsylvania, on Oil Creek 14 m. N of Oil City; pop. 8356; oil and gas wells; manufactures petroleum and its by-products, oil-well machinery and supplies, machines and tools, metal products, cutlery, canoes, building supplies. Settled 1796; first oil well in U.S. drilled here 1859 ("Drake's Folly").

Tium′pan Head (tūm′păn). Cape on NE coast of island of Lewis with Harris, Outer Hebrides, off NW coast of Scotland; lighthouse.

Tiv′er·ton (tĭv′ẽr·t′n; -tŭn). **1** Town and summer resort, Newport co., SE Rhode Island, on Sakonnet river 8 m. NE of Newport; pop. 9461; oyster and fishing industries, textile manufactures. Incorp. as Massachusetts town 1692; annexed to Rhode Island 1746; figured in Revolutionary War as asylum for Americans fleeing from Rhode I. (island) and as mustering point for Colonial forces.
2 Municipal borough, Devonshire, SW England, at confluence of Exe and Lowman rivers 48 m. NE of Plymouth; pop. 10,869; lacemaking center; nearby is Blundell's school, founded 1604.

Ti′vo·li (tĭv′ô·lĭ; *Ital.* tē′vô·lē); *anc.* **Ti′bur** (tī′bẽr). Commune, Roma prov., Latium, cen. Italy, 16 m. ENE of Rome; pop. 20,875; cathedral with 12th-cent. campanile; Villa d'Este; remains of ancient temples and villas, esp. of Hadrian's villa; manufactures paper, copper products. Powerful Roman city before its defeat by Praeneste 338 B.C.; well known as residential suburb of Rome 1st cent. B.C.

Tix′tla, *in full* **Tixtla de Guer·re′ro** (tēs′tlä thä gĕr·rĕ′rô). Town, Guerrero state, S Mexico, just N of Chilpancingo; pop. 6130.

Ti′za·pán′ (tē′sä·pän′). Town, Federal District, cen. Mexico, ab. 14 m. SSW of Mexico City; pop. 8428.

Ti′zi·mín′ (tē′sĕ·mēn′). Town, Yucatán state, on Yucatán penin., SE Mexico; pop. 6697; railroad terminus ab. 65 m. E of Mérida.

Ti′zi–n–Tam·jurt′ (tĭ′zĭn·tăm·jŏŏrt′). Mountain peak, Grand Atlas Mts., Morocco; claimed to be 14,764 ft. but height not confirmed. See TOUBKAL.

Ti′zi′–Ou′zou′ (tē′zē′ōō′zōō′). Commune, NE Alger dept., N Algeria, ab. 65 m. E of Algiers; pop. (1936) 40,526.

Tiz·za′na (tĕt·tsä′nä). Commercial commune, Pistoia prov., Tuscany, cen. Italy, 7 m. from Pistoia; pop. (1931) 13,427; mineral springs.

Tja·re′me (chä·rä′mä). Volcano 10,098 ft., West Java prov., Indonesia, SSW of Cheribon.

Tje·poe′ (chĕ·pōō) or **Tje·pu′** Town, Central Java prov., Indonesia, ab. 35 m. SE of Rembang; pop. 21,861.

Tji·a′mis (chĕ·ä′mĭs) or **Chi·a′mis.** Town, West Java prov., Indonesia, just E of Tasikmalaja ab. 60 m. SE of Bandung; pop. 13,864.

Tji·an′djoer (chĕ·än′jŏŏr) or **Tji·an′djur** or **Chi·an′jur.** Town, West Java prov., Indonesia, on railroad 35 m. SE of Bogor; pop. 20,812; in plateau region E of Mt. Gede.

Tji·koe′raj (chĕ·kōō′rä) or **Tji·ku′raj** or **Chi·ku′raj.** Mountain 9255 ft. in West Java prov., Indonesia, SSW of Garut; highest extinct volcano in the mountain groups around Garut.

Tji·la′tjap (chĕ·lä′chäp) or **Chi·la′chap.** Seaport on SW coast of Central Java prov., Indonesia; pop. 28,309; only harbor on S coast of Java. In World War II used as last port of Allied defense in Java; refuge of U.S.S. *Marblehead* and *Houston* after battles of Java Sea Feb. 1942.

Tji′le·doeg (chĕ′lĕ·dōōk) or **Tji′le·dug** or **Chi′le·dug.** Town, West Java prov., Indonesia, near coast just SE of Cheribon; pop. 20,002.

Tji′li·wong (chĕ′lĕ·wông) or **Chi′li·wong.** River ab. 50 m. long, W Java, Indonesia; rises on N slopes of Mt. Pangerango and flows N to Djakarta Bay at Djakarta.

Tji·ma′hi (chĕ·mä′hĕ) or **Chi·ma′hi.** Town, West Java prov., Indonesia, on railroad just NW of Bandung; pop. 21,994.

Tjirebon. See CHERIBON.

Tla′co·lu′la de Ma′ta·mo′ros (tlä′kŏ·lōō′lä thä mä′tä·mō′rŏs). Town, Oaxaca state, SE Mexico; pop. 5297; E suburb of Oaxaca.

Tla′co·pán′ (tlä′kŏ·pän′). = TENOCHTITLÁN.

Tlal·pán′ or **Tlal·pam′** (tläl·pän′). Town, Federal District, cen. Mexico, S of Mexico City; pop. 10,439; picturesque suburban and resort town. Founded by Spaniards soon after the Conquest; has church begun in 1532. Residence of some of early Spanish viceroys.

Tlal′pu·ja′hua de Ra·yón′ (tläl′pōō·hä′wä thä rä·yôn′). Town, Michoacán state, SW Mexico, E of Lake Cuitzeo and 70 m. NW of Mexico City; pop. 5385.

Tlal·til′co (tläl·tēl′kŏ). Town, Federal District, cen. Mexico; pop. 5481.

Tla′que·pa′que (tlä′kä·pä′kä). Town, Jalisco state, W cen. Mexico; pop. 11,486.

Tlax·ca′la (tläs·kä′lä). **1** State, cen. Mexico. See *Table* at MEXICO.
2 *in full* **Tlaxcala de Xi′coh·tén′catl** (thä hē′kŏ·tǎng′kät·′l); *also* **Tlas·ca′la.** Town, cen. Mexico, ✲ of Tlaxcala state; pop. 3261; in mountainous region bet. Veracruz and Mexico City, alt. 7500 ft.; surrounded by hills and in view of high peaks (Malinche, Popocatepetl, Iztaccihuatl); has oldest church—Church of San Fernando—in North America, founded 1521. Home of a Nahua people, the Tlascalans, akin to Aztecs and Toltecs, who came here from the plains E of Lake Texcoco; they were enemies of the Aztecs in Tenochtitlán (Mexico City) and opposed Cortes on his march inland but were defeated 1519 and became his ally, aiding in his conquest of Montezuma. City (then with pop. ab. 30,000) was refuge for Spaniards when driven out of Mexico City June 1520.

Tlem·cen′ or **Tlem·sen′** (tlĕm·sĕn′). Commercial city, W Oran dept., 75 m. SW of Oran near the Morocco bor-der, NW Algeria; pop. (1936) 51,530; alt. 2500 ft.; Arab city with many mosques, also towers, walls, minarets of earlier time. Capital of an Arab sultanate after 1282 and a flourishing town (pop. perhaps of 125,000); under Turkish rule in 16th cent.; Abd-el-Kader's capital 1837–42; French after 1842.

Tlemcen Mountains. Range of Little Atlas Mts., in W Oran dept., NW Algeria.

Tmolus, Mount. See BOZ DAĞ.

To (tō); *formerly* **Lu** (lōō). River ab. 200 m. long, tributary of the Yangtze in Szechwan prov., S cen. China; flows SSE bet. the Min and the Kialing.

To′a Al′ta (tō′ä äl′tä). Municipality (pop. 15,711) and town (pop. 1284), NE cen. Puerto Rico, 10 m. SW of San Juan.

Toa Ba′ja (bä′hä). Municipality (pop. 19,698) and town (pop. 1084), NE Puerto Rico, W of San Juan.

To′a·no Range (tō′á·nō). Small range in NE Nevada, in Elko co.; crossed by a pass at 6940 ft.

Toarcium. See THOUARS.

To′ba, Lake (tō′bà). Lake in the Barisan Mts. in N cen. Sumatra I., Indonesia; 45 m. long, 502 sq. m., and elevation 2370 ft.; probably occupies the crater of an extinct volcano. Drains E through the Asahan river into the Strait of Malacca; contains the large island of Samosir. In center of Batakland (*q.v.*) and administratively in NE Tapanoeli residency.

To·ba′go (tō·bā′gō). Island of the West Indies, administratively a part of the British dominion of Trinidad and Tobago; lies in the Atlantic Ocean off NE coast of Venezuela and ab. 20 m. NE of Trinidad; ab. 26 m. long, area 116 sq. m.; pop. 33,333; ✲ Scarborough. Chief products cacao, coconuts, and rubber. Discovered by Columbus 1498; first settled by English 1616; has changed hands more often than any other island of the West Indies, having been at various times held by English, Dutch, and French; remained English after 1814. United with Trinidad by Order of Council 1898 and became part of the colony of Trinidad and Tobago Jan. 1, 1899.

To·bar′ra (tō·vär′rä). Commune, Albacete prov., SE Spain, 30 m. SSE of Albacete; pop. 13,110; watering place, with sulfur springs; iron peroxide seams nearby; center of agricultural section.

To·ba·ta (tō·bä·tä). Former coastal town, Fukuoka prefecture, N Kyushu I., Japan, ab. 10 m. WSW of Moji, opp. Wakamatsu; pop. (1945) 56,585; exports coal; has polytechnic institute. See KITA-KYUSHU.

To′ba·tí′ (tō′vä·tē′). Town, Cordillera dept., cen. Paraguay, E of Asunción; pop. ab. 8370.

To·bol′ (tō·bôl′; *Russ.* tŭ·bôl′y′). River ab. 800 m. long in U.S.S.R.; rises in SE foothills of Ural Mts. in N Kazakh S.S.R. and flows NNE through E Chelyabinsk, Kurgan, and Tyumen Regions to the Irtysh river at Tobolsk; navigable to Kurgan.

To·bolsk′ (tō·bôlsk′; *Russ.* tŭ·bôl′y′sk). City, N Tyumen Region, Soviet Russia, Asia, on Irtysh river where it is joined by the Tobol, 300 m. NW of Omsk; pop. 23,500; formerly a center of trade in fish and furs but lost much to Omsk because of no rail connections; has a Kremlin built by Swedish prisoners as a model of the structure in Moscow. Founded 1587 by Cossacks; long a place for exiles. See ISKER.

To′bruk′ (tō′brŏŏk); *Ital.* **To′bruch** (tō′brŏŏk); *anc.* **An′ti·pyr′gos** (ăn′tĭ·pûr′gŏs). Port on coastal road, NE Cyrenaica, Libya, N Africa; pop. before World War II ab. 4200; military post developed by Italians. Scene of much fighting in World War II; taken by British Dec. 1940; besieged by Germans for 8 months Mar.–Nov. 1941; surrendered to Rommel June 21, 1942; retaken by British Nov. 30, 1942.

To′can·tins′ (tō′kǎnn·tēNs′). River ab. 1700 m. long in E cen. and NE Brazil; rises in S cen. Goiaz state, flows N into Pará river.

Toc·co′a (tŏ·kō′á). **1** River, NE Georgia: see OCOEE.
2 City, ⊗ of Stephens co., NE Georgia, 33 m. NE of

Gainesville; pop. 7303; trading center for farm and orchard section; textile mills.

To'chi (tō'chǐ). **1** River ab. 180 m. long, Afghanistan and Pakistan; flows through North Waziristan and Bannu dist. to unite with the Kurram as tributary of the Indus river.
2 Agency, India. See WAZIRISTAN.

To·chi·gi (tō·chě·gē). **1** Prefecture of Japan. See *Table* at JAPAN.
2 Town, S Tochigi prefecture, Japan, 50 m. N of Tokyo; pop. (1945) 41,711; silk weaving and lumbering.

To·cón' Point (tō·kôn'). Cape on SW coast of Puerto Rico, E of Cape Rojo.

To'co·pil'la (tō'kō·pē'yä). Seaport, Antofagasta prov., N Chile, 100 m. N of Antofagasta; pop. 15,516; ships nitrates, sulfate, iodine, and copper ore.

To'cor·pu'ri, Cer'ros de (sĕr'rōz thä tō'kôr·pōō'rē). Mountain 22,162 ft. in SW Bolivia, near Chilean border.

To·cu'yo (tō·kōō'yō). River ab. 200 m. long in NW Venezuela, flowing NE into Caribbean Sea.

Tocuyo, El. See EL TOCUYO.

Todd (tŏd). Counties in three states of the U.S. See *Tables* at KENTUCKY, MINNESOTA, SOUTH DAKOTA.

To'di (tō'dě); *anc.* **Tu'der** (tū'dēr). Commune, Perugia prov., Umbria, cen. Italy, on Tiber river 24 m. S of Perugia; pop. 20,459; ancient and medieval walls; ancient Roman amphitheater; 11th-cent. cathedral; 16th-cent. church of Santa Maria della Consolazione.

Tö'di (tû'dě) *or* **Piz Ru·sein'** (pēts' rōō·zīn'). Highest peak 11,887 ft. of the N Swiss Alps, in Glarus canton, E cen. Switzerland.

Tod'mor'den (tŏd'môr'd'n; tŏd'mēr·d'n). Municipal borough, West Riding, Yorkshire, N England, on the Calder 20 m. NNE of Manchester; pop. 19,072.

To'dos los San'tos (tō'thōz lōs sän'tōs). Lake in Llanquihue prov., S cen. Chile, N of Puerto Montt; one of the beautiful Chilean resort lakes.

Todos os Santos, Baía de. See ALL SAINTS BAY.

Toe'ban (tōō'bän) *or* **Tu'ban.** Seaport, N Java coast, East Java prov., Indonesia, 55 m. NW of Surabaja; pop. 23,285.

Toe Head (tō). Cape extending NW into Atlantic Ocean from S part of island of Lewis with Harris in the Outer Hebrides, off NW coast of Scotland.

Toe'kang·be'si, *or* **Tu'kang·be'si, Islands** (tōō'-käng·bā'sě). Group of ab. 16 islands in W Banda Sea SE of Butung Is., SE Celebes govt., Celebes, Indonesia; administratively part of Butung; largest island Wangi-wangi.

Toe'loeng·a'goeng (tōō'lōōng·ä'gōōng) *or* **Tu'lung-a'gung.** City, East Java prov., Indonesia, 20 m. S of Malang; pop. 31,767.

Tofo, El. See EL TOFO.

To·fu'a (tō·fōō'ä). Volcanic island in W part of Haabai group, Tonga Is., SW cen. Pacific Ocean; 5 m. long by 4 m. wide; 21 sq. m.; uninhabited. Large lake in crater.

To'ga (tŏng'gä; *native* tông'ä). = *Tonga*, transliteration of native name of TONGA ISLANDS used on postage stamps.

Togara Islands. See TOKARA ISLANDS.

Tog'gen·burg (tŏg'ĕn·bōŏrk). District, St. Gallen canton, NE Switzerland, in upper valley of the Thur; a rich pastoral region and resort area; chief town Wattwil. Scene of almost continuous religious strife from 15th to 18th cent.; Toggenburg war ended 1712 in defeat of Catholic cantons by Protestants.

To'gi·an (tō'gě·än). See SCHILDPAD ISLANDS.

To'go (tō'gō). **1** Former German protectorate in W Africa lying bet. Gold Coast and Dahomey; divided 1919 into French and British mandates; 34,934 sq. m.; pop. at end of World War I slightly more than 1,000,000. Its coast land a part of the Slave Coast (*q.v.*); region acquired by Germany 1884; hinterland and frontier boundaries not fixed until 1899; captured by Anglo-French forces Aug. 1914 (see 2, below, and TOGOLAND).

2 *formerly* **French Togo.** Republic, W Africa, consisting of E Togo (former German protectorate); 21,893 sq. m.; pop. 1,090,000; ✳ Lomé; a trust territory under the United Nations 1946–58. Narrow strip of territory extending ab. 340 m. inland, touching French territory of Niger on the N; bounded on E by Dahomey, on S by Bight of Benin, and on W by British trust territory of Togoland. Interior is hilly, with many streams, extensive forests, and some fertile areas; trades chiefly in palm oil and kernels, cocoa, rubber, and copra. Part of region taken by Anglo-French forces Aug. 26, 1914 from Germans; control assumed by French 1914, 1916, and 1920, by agreements with Great Britain; mandate assignment to France approved July 20, 1922; became trust territory Dec. 1946; trusteeship abolished Nov. 14, 1958, became an autonomous republic within French Community; became independent Apr. 27, 1960.

3 British trust territory. See TOGOLAND.

To'go·land' (tō'gŏ·lǎnd'). Region, E Ghana, W Africa; former British trust territory consisting of W Togo (former German protectorate); 13,041 sq. m.; pop. 392,000; for administrative purposes included until 1957 in the Gold Coast, the S section, 2464 sq. m., ✳ Ho, being attached to Gold Coast Colony and the N section, 10,577 sq. m., to Northern Territories protectorate; now comprises **Trans–Vol'ta Togoland** (trăns·vŏl'tä) region of Ghana. Has no coast line; S boundary terminates near Lomé. Became British mandate July 20, 1922; after World War II became a trust territory (agreement approved Dec. 13, 1946) remaining under administration of Great Britain; became part of Ghana Mar. 6, 1957.

To·gu·chi (tō·gōō·chě). Town on coast of NW Okinawa, Ryukyu Is., Japan, near Motobu; pop. 20,000.

Tohopeka. See HORSESHOE BEND.

To·hope'ka·li'ga Lake (tō·hōp'kà·lǐ'gà). Lake in NW Osceola co., cen. Florida penin.

Toi·ya'be Mountains (toi·yä'bě). Range in cen. Nevada, extending N and S in Lander and Nye cos.

To·ka·chi (tō·kä·chě). **1** Peak, Japan. See HOKKAIDO.
2 River 120 m. long, cen. Hokkaido, Japan.; flows SE into Pacific Ocean at Otsu.

To·kai·do (tō·kī·dō). Old division of Honshu, Japan.

To'kaj (tō'koi); *Eng.* **To·kay'** (tō·kā'; tō'kā). Town, N Hungary, on Tisza river near where the Bodrog flows into it; pop. 5844; center of vine-growing region.

To·ka·ra Islands (tō·kä·rä); *also* **To·ga·ra Islands** (tō·gä·rä). Group of small islands S of Kyushu, Japan, and in northernmost part of Ryukyu chain; in Kagoshima prefecture. See RYUKYU ISLANDS.

To·ka·shi·ki (tō·kä·shě·kě). Largest of Kerama Is., Japan; 10 sq. m.; pop. 1377.

To·kat' (tō·kät'). **1** Vilayet, N cen. Turkey in Asia; 4020 sq. m.; pop. 309,863.
2 Town, its ✳, 50 m. NW of SIVAS; pop. 22,166.

To'ke·lau' (tō'kě·lou') *or* **Un'ion** (ūn'yŭn). Island group in cen. Pacific Ocean ab. 275 m. N of island of Savaii, Samoa; 4 sq. m.; pop. (1942 est.) 1364. Chief islands Fakaofo, Atafu, and Nukonono. Formerly part of the Gilbert and Ellice Islands Colony but transferred 1926 to New Zealand.

To'ke·wan'na Peak (tō'kě·wŏn'à). Mountain 13,173 ft. in E Summit co., NE Utah.

Tokio. See TOKYO.

Tok·mak' (tôk·mäk'). Town, N Kirgiz S.S.R., Soviet Central Asia, just E of Frunze on the Chu river.

To·ku·no Shi·ma (tō·kōō·nō shě·mä). Island, cen. Amami Is., Ryukyu Is., Japan.

To·ku·shi·ma (tō·kōō·shě·mä). **1** Prefecture of Japan. See *Table* at JAPAN.
2 Seaport city, its ✳, on E coast of Shikoku I. on Kii Channel, chief city on Shikoku I.; pop. (1945) 80,681; has close connection by water with Osaka and Hyogo.

To·ku·ya·ma (tō·kōō·yä·mä). Town, E Yamaguchi prefecture, SW Honshu, Japan, 50 m. E of Shimonoseki; pop. (1945) 71,021; port at W end of Inland Sea.

To'ky·o (tō'kĭ-ō; *Jap.* tō-kyō); *also* **To'ki·o**. **1** Prefecture of Japan. See *Table* at JAPAN.
2 *formerly* **E·do** (ĕ-dō) *or* **Ye·do** (yĕ-dō). City, its ✲ and ✲ of Japanese Empire, on NW shore of Tokyo Bay, SE Honshu; pop. (1945) 2,675,203, (1955, with suburbs) 8,033,529; has many canals; Sumida river flows through it; its port is Yokohama to the S; before World War II had developed manufacture of electrical equipment, airplane parts, and machine tools; site of Imperial palace, Imperial Univ. (oldest of all educational centers of Japan, founded 1877), many schools, hospitals, temples, and shrines. Founded 1457; under the name Yedo was capital of Tokugawa Shogunate from 1603, and after the Restoration 1868 replaced Kyoto as Imperial capital; its name then changed to Tokyo. Practically destroyed Sept. 1, 1923 by earthquake and its succeeding tidal wave and fire (150,000 lives lost, estimated property damage ab. 4½ billion dollars); rebuilt on modern lines; reconstruction completed 1930. Bombed by American airplanes Apr. 18, 1942, and later, 1944 and 1945, frequently; by Aug. 1945 nearly all destroyed.
Tokyo Bay. Inlet of W Pacific Ocean on SE coast of Honshu, Japan, ab. 30 m. long by 23 m. wide, providing a spacious harbor for Tokyo, Yokohama, and Yokosuka. Connects with the Pacific by Uraga Strait.
Tol (tŏl). Largest island in Truk (*q.v.*), in W part.
To·la'go Bay (tŏ·lä'gō). Inlet of Pacific Ocean on E coast of North I., New Zealand, ab. midway bet. East Cape and Poverty Bay.
To·la'ni Lakes (tŏ·lä'nē). Small lakes near E boundary of Coconino co., N cen. Arizona.
Tolbiacum. See ZÜLPICH.
Tolbukhin. See BAZARGIC.
To·le'do (tŏ·lē'dō). **1** Village, ⊗ of Cumberland co., SE cen. Illinois; pop. 998.
2 City, ⊗ of Tama co., E cen. Iowa, 17 m. E of Marshalltown; pop. 2850.
3 Industrial city and port of entry, ⊗ of Lucas co., NW Ohio, on Maumee river at SW corner of Lake Erie; pop. 318,003. Land and water shipping center (esp. coal, oil, corn, automobiles); manufactures glass, steel and iron products, automobiles, oil-well supplies, petroleum and clay products, machinery and tools, scales, presses, enamel and porcelain ware, steel ships. Seat of the University of Toledo (1872; coed.) and Mary Manse College (1873; women). On site of Fort Industry, built in 1794 by Anthony Wayne; settled c. 1820; figured in "Toledo War" of 1835-36, a dispute bet. Ohio and Michigan over location of their common boundary; incorp. 1837.
4 City, ⊗ of Lincoln co., W Oregon, 35 m. W of Corvallis; pop. 3053; shipping point for lumber, fruit, livestock; salmon fisheries.
To·le'do (tŏ·lē'dō; *Span.* tō-lā'thō). **1** District, S British Honduras; 2215 sq. m.; pop. (1943 est.) 6649; ✲ Punta Gorda.
2 Municipality on W coast of Cebu I., Phil. Is., in cen. part 19 m. W of City of Cebu; pop. 34,413.
3 Province of Spain. See *Table* at SPAIN.
4 *anc.* **To·le'tum** (tŏ·lē'tŭm). Commune, ✲ of Toledo prov., cen. Spain, on Tagus river 40 m. SSW of Madrid; pop. 34,592; manufactures small arms, textiles, and, esp., the famous Toledo sword blades; archbishopric, see of primate of Spain; 13th-cent. Gothic cathedral, metropolitan church of Spain; Moorish bridge, alcazar, city walls, 15th-cent. Franciscan convent, 13th-cent. synagogue (made church in 15th cent., barracks in 18th cent.); Roman remains, including esp. an aqueduct. Home of Lope de Vega.
History: Stronghold of the Carpetani; conquered by Rome 193 B.C.; became Roman colony and capital of Roman Spain; Visigothic capital in Spain 534-712; center of conflict bet. Arianism and Roman Catholic orthodoxy; site of numerous church councils A.D. 396, 400, 589, etc.; conquered by Moors under Musa 712; a pro-

vincial capital in the caliphate of Córdoba 712-1031; became independent Moorish state 1035; under Moors, grew commercially and industrially, becoming famous for the manufacture of swords; center of Arabic and Hebrew culture; reconquered from Moors 1085 by the Cid and Alfonso VI of León and Castile; capital of New Castile and of the united kingdoms of León and Castile 1087-1560; noted for its tolerance of Jews and Arabs in 11th-15th cents.; several times occupied by French during Peninsular War 1808-14.
To·le'do, Mon'tes de (mōn'tāz thä tō-lā'thō). Mountain range in cen. Spain, WSW of Toledo.
To'len·ti'no (tōl'ĕn-tē'nō; *Ital.* tō-län-tē'nō); *anc.* **Tol'en·ti'num** (tōl'ĕn-tī'nŭm). Commune, Macerata prov., Marches, cen. Italy, 12 m. WSW of Macerata; pop. 14,356; cathedral of 8th and 9th cents.; 15th-cent. church of San Nicola. Treaty bet. Napoleon and Pope Pius VI signed here 1797; Murat defeated by Austrians here 1815.
Toletum. See TOLEDO.
Tol'fa (tōl'fä). Town, Roma prov., W Latium, cen. Italy, bet. Civitavecchia and Lake Bracciano; pop. 4671; alum mining.
Toliganj. See TOLLYGUNGE.
To·li'ma (tō·lē'mä; *Span.* -mä). **1** Volcano 18,438 ft. in the Cordillera Central of the Andes, W cen. Colombia.
2 Department of Colombia. See *Table* at COLOMBIA.
Tol'land (tōl'ănd). **1** County in Connecticut. See *Table* at CONNECTICUT.
2 Agricultural town, its ⊗, N Connecticut, in N cen. Tolland co. on Willimantic river; pop. 2950; named 1715; dairying.
Tol'le·son (tōl'ĕ·s'n). Town, Maricopa co., SW cen. Arizona, 10 m. W of Phoenix; pop. 3886.
Tol'ly·gunge *or* **Tol'i·ganj** (tōl'ĭ·gŭnj). Town, Twenty-four Parganas dist., S West Bengal, Indian Union; SE suburb of Calcutta; pop. (1941) 58,594.
Tol·me'ta (tōl·mā'tä); *anc.* **Ptol'e·ma'ïs** (tōl'ĕ·mā'ĭs). Town on coast of Cyrenaica, NE Libya, 60 m. NE of Bengasi; ancient Ptolemaïs, port of Barca which it superseded during the time of the Ptolemies, was one of the cities of the Pentapolis.
Tol·mi'no (tōl·mē'nō); *Ger.* **Tol'mein** (tōl'mīn). Commune, NW Yugoslavia, on Isonzo river in region that belonged to Italy before 1947; pop. (1931) 6799; starting point of a German-Austrian assault Oct. 24, 1917.
Tol'na (tōl'nŏ); *Ger.* **Tol'nau** (tōl'nou). Commune, S Hungary, on the Danube 80 m. S of Budapest; pop. 8017; castle.
To'lo, Gulf of (tō'lō). Inlet of Banda Sea on E cen. coast of Celebes I., Malay Archipelago; smallest of the three great gulfs of Celebes. Bordered on NE by the Banggai Archipelago and connected by Peleng Strait with the Molucca Sea.
To·lo'sa. **1** (tō·lō'sà) City, France. See TOULOUSE.
2 (tō·lō'sä) Manufacturing commune, Guipúzcoa prov., N Spain, 11 m. SW of San Sebastián; pop. 13,583; iron and copper founding; manufactures paper, metal products; occupied by French 1808-13.
To·lu'ca (tō·lōō'kä; *Span.* -kä). **1** Subdivision of the plateau of Anáhuac (*q.v.*) in cen. Mexico; mean elevation 8570 ft.
2 *in full* **To·lu'ca de Ler'do** (tō·lōō'kä thä lĕr'thō). City, cen. Mexico, ✲ of México state; pop. 43,429; altitude 8700 ft.; summer resort; government meteorological station.
To·lu'ca, Ne·va'do de (nä·vä'thō thä tō·lōō'kä). Volcanic peak 15,026 ft. in México state, Mexico, near Toluca; crater partly filled with a lake formed by melting snow.
To'lun (dō'lōōn) *or* **To'lun·no·erh'** (dō'lōōn·nŏ·ûr'); *formerly* **Do'lon** (dō'lōn). Mongol town near right bank of upper Lwan river, SE Chahar prov., E Inner Mongolia, N China, ab. 120 m. NW of Chengteh; pop. ab. 30,000; treaty mart, formerly in Chihli prov., China, on

highway from Peiping through Wanchuan to Chengteh; has large local bell-manufacturing industry.

Tom (tŏm; *Russ.* tôm). River ab. 450 m. long, SE Tomsk and cen. Kemerovo Regions, Soviet Russia, Asia; rises in NW Altai Mts. and flows NNW into the Ob river near Tomsk; flows through the Kuznetsk Basin (*q.v.*).

Tom, Mount (tŏm). Peak 1214 ft. in Connecticut River valley near Holyoke, Hampden and Hampshire cos., W Massachusetts.

To'mah (tō'má). City, Monroe co., W cen. Wisconsin, 15 m. E of Sparta; pop. 5321.

Tom'a·hawk (tŏm'á·hôk). City, Lincoln co., N Wisconsin, 20 m. N of Merrill; pop. 3348; paper and pulp mills; supply point for vacationists in forest and lake region.

To·ma'hu, Mount (tō·mä'hōō). Mountain 7969 ft. in NW Buru I., Indonesia; highest point on island.

To·ma'les Bay (tō·mä'lĕs). Inlet of Pacific Ocean on NW coast of Marin co., W California.

Tomanivi, Mount. See Mount VICTORIA.

To·ma·ri·o·ru (tō·mä·rĕ·ō·rōō). Town on cen. part of W coast of Karafuto, Sakhalin I.; pop. (1939 est.) 10,456; formerly Japanese; a government coal-mining experiment station.

To·mar'us, Mount (tō·mâr'ŭs). Mountain ab. 6100 ft. high, S cen. Epirus, NW Greece; was in ancient district of Thesprotia; oracle of Dodona (*q.v.*) was on its E slope.

Tom'a·sak'i, Mount (tŏm'á·sä'kĭ). Peak 12,271 ft. in S Grand co., E Utah.

Tomaschow. 1 See TOMASZÓW.

2 See TOMASZÓW LUBELSKI.

To·ma'szów or **Tomaszów Ma'zo·wiec'ki** (tō·mä'-shōōf mä'zō·vyĕts'kĕ); *Ger.* **To·ma'schow** (tō·mä'shō). Industrial commune, Łódź dept., cen. Poland, 30 m. SE of Łódź; pop. (1938–39 est.) 45,204; textiles, machinery, brick and tile.

Tomaszów Lu·bel'ski (lōō·bĕl'skĕ); *Ger.* **To·ma'schow** (tō·mä'shō). Commune, Lublin dept., E Poland, 67 m. SSE of Lublin on border of W Ukraine, U.S.S.R.; pop. 10,433.

Tombador, Serra do. See SERRA DO TOMBADOR.

Tom·big'bee (tŏm·bĭg'bē). River 409 m. long in Alabama; navigable for 350 m.; formed by junction of E fork and W fork near Amory, Mississippi, crosses Alabama border W of Carrollton, flows S into the Alabama river to form the Mobile and Tensaw rivers flowing into Mobile Bay at Mobile.

Tom'bo Island (tŏm'bō). Small island off the coast of Guinea, West Africa; Conakry, ✳ of the territory, is on it and is joined to the mainland by an iron bridge.

Tom'bouc'tou' (tôN'bōōk'tōō') or **Tim·buk'tu** (tĭm·bŭk'tōō; tĭm'bŭk·tōō'). Town, Mali (formerly French Sudan), West Africa, E of Lake Faguibine and near Niger river; pop. (1940) 6432; known as "the port of the Sudan in the Sahara"; a crossroads of camel caravan trade routes across the Sahara; has extensive ruins, as it was formerly much larger than now; has great mosque. Settled in 11th cent. by the Tuaregs; by 15th cent. was one of the great cities of the Negro Songhai Empire; captured by Moors 1591; in 17th cent. declined rapidly; several times captured and plundered in 19th cent.; became French 1893.

Tomb'stone' (tōōm'stōn'). City, SW cen. Cochise co., SE corner of Arizona, 20 m. NNW of Bisbee; pop. 1283; formerly (c. 1879–87) a mining center widely known for its rich mines and its lawlessness and crime.

To·mé' (tō·mā'). Town, Concepción prov., S cen. Chile, 20 m. by rail N of Concepción; pop. 10,722; port for Concepción.

To'mel·lo'so (tō'mä·[l]yō'sō). Commune, Ciudad Real prov., S cen. Spain, 51 m. ENE of Ciudad Real; pop. 28,982; wine, cereals, vegetables; stock raising; manufactures leather, cloth.

Tom Green (tŏm grēn). County in Texas. See *Table* at TEXAS.

Tomi, Tomis. See CONSTANȚA.

To·mi'ni (tō·mē'nĕ) or **Go'ron·ta'lo** (gōr'ŏn·tä'lō), **Gulf of.** Large inlet of Molucca Sea extending deep into the coast of N Celebes I., Malay Archipelago; ab. 240 m. long; contains the Schildpad Is.

To·mi'ño (tō·mē'nyō). Commune, Pontevedra prov., NW Spain, 31 m. SSW of Pontevedra; pop. 10,281.

To'mo (tō'mō). River ab. 260 m. long in E Colombia; flows E into Orinoco on Venezuelan border.

Tömös Pass. See PREDEAL.

Tomp'kins (tŏm[p]'kĭnz). County in New York. See *Table* at NEW YORK.

Tomp'kins·ville (tŏm[p]'kĭnz·vĭl; *Sou.* also -v'l). 1 See RICHMOND borough, New York City.

2 City, ⊗ of Monroe co., S Kentucky; pop. 2091.

Toms (tŏmz). River ab. 25 m. long, E New Jersey; rises in SW Monmouth co., flows SE into Barnegat Bay.

Tomsk (tŏmsk; *Russ.* tômsk). City, ✳ of Tomsk Region, in SE part, Soviet Russia, Asia, on right bank of Tom river near its junction with the Ob; pop. 141,215; has rail connections with the main line of the Trans-Siberian R.R.; an educational center with a university and large technological institute (founded 1900), libraries, and headquarters of various scientific societies. One of the oldest towns of W Siberia, founded 1604 as a fort; became important after 1824, when gold was discovered in the district. See KUZNETSK BASIN.

Tomsk Region. Region, W Soviet Russia, Asia; ✳ Tomsk.

Toms River (tŏmz). 1 River. See TOMS.

2 Town and summer resort, ⊗ of Ocean co., E New Jersey, on inlet of Barnegat Bay 22 m. SSW of Asbury Park; pop. 6062; fisheries, boatbuilding, clay pits. Discovered 1673; settled before 1727; center for guerrilla fighting in Revolution; burned by British 1782; became ⊗ when town was rebuilt.

To'na·lá' (tō'nä·lä'). 1 River ab. 90 m. long, E Veracruz prov., E Mexico; flows NNW to Gulf of Mexico and in lower course forms boundary with Tabasco prov.; receives the Pedregal.

2 Town, E Veracruz state, SE Mexico, at mouth of Tonalá river; pop. 6379.

To·na'le Pass (tō·nä'lā). Mountain pass, altitude 6182 ft., in the Lombard Alps, NW of Trent, bet. Lombardy and Venezia Tridentina, NE Italy.

Ton'a·wan'da (tŏn'á·wŏn'dà). 1 Manufacturing city, Erie co., W New York, 9 m. N of Buffalo; pop. 21,561; railroad and transportation center in agricultural region; manufactures steel, lumber, shingles, fiberboard, paper, motorboats. **North Tonawanda** (*q.v.*), its sister city, is on opp. side of Tonawanda creek.

2 Urban community (unincorporated), Erie co., W New York, S of city of Tonawanda; pop. 83,771.

Ton'bridge (tŭn'brij). Urban district, Kent, SE England, on the Medway 25 m. SSE of London; pop. 19,239; manufactures wooden articles.

Ton·da'no (tŏn·dä'nō). Town at extreme NE tip of Celebes I., Indonesia; pop. 15,007; resort town in plateau region just S of Manado.

Tön'der (tŭn'ĕr). 1 County, Denmark. See *Table* at DENMARK.

2 Town, its ⊗, SW Jutland Penin., Denmark, near German border; pop. (1945) 6778.

To·ne (tō·nĕ). River 200 m. long, E Honshu, Japan; flows SE and E into Pacific Ocean E of Tokyo.

Tong (tŏng). 1 Village, Kent, SE England, 2 m. E of Sittingbourne and Milton; site of Tong Castle, now a high mound encircled by a moat, a Saxon fortress.

2 Village, Shropshire, W England, 20 m. E of Shrewsbury; site of castle, originally medieval, rebuilt 18th cent.; nearby is Boscobel House where Charles II hid 1651 after the battle of Worcester.

Ton'ga (tŏng'gá; *native* tŏng'ä), or **Friend'ly** (frĕnd'lĭ) **Islands.** Archipelago ab. 200 m. long in SW cen. Pacific Ocean E of Fiji Is., containing ab. 150 islands and islets,

divided into 3 groups, Tongatabu, Vavau, and Haabai, together with Niuafoo and Niuatobutabu further to the N; area 250 sq. m.; pop. (1939) 34,130; ✳ Nukualofa. In the N the Vavau group, and Tofua of the Haabai group, are high and mountainous, of volcanic origin; the other islands are low-lying, of coral formation. Main exports are copra and bananas. The Tongans are a branch of the Polynesian race and among its finest representatives; tradition says Tongan kings have ruled for a thousand years. Islands discovered 1606 by two Dutch navigators; visited by Tasman 1643 and by Capt. Cook 1773 and 1777; modern kingdom estab. 1845; declared a neutral region in 1886; became British protectorate 1900.

Ton'ga·land' (tŏng'gȧ·lănd') or **Am'a·ton'ga·land'** (ăm'ȧ-). Region on coast S of Mozambique, SE Africa; ab. 600 sq. m.; pop. ab. 13,500; formerly British protectorate, ruled by Zulu hereditary dynasty. Incorp. 1898 with Ingwavuma dist., N Zululand, as part of Natal.

Ton'ga·re'va (tŏng'gȧ·rĕv'ȧ; native tông'ä·rä'vä) or **Pen'rhyn** (pĕn'rĭn). Island (atoll) of the Manihiki Is., cen. Pacific Ocean, N of Cook Is.; land area 3 sq. m., with lagoon area of 108 sq. m.; pop. (1936) 467; chief village Omoka; administered with Cook Is.

Tong'a·ri'ro (tŏng'[g]ȧ·rē'rō). Volcano 6458 ft. in cen. North I., New Zealand, in **Tongariro National Park** (235 sq. m.) which includes also Ruapehu and Ngauruhoe volcanoes.

Tong'a·ta'bu (tŏng'[g]ȧ·tä'bōō). **1** Island group in S Tonga Is., SW cen. Pacific Ocean, including islands of Tongatabu and Eua; ab. 133 sq. m.; pop. (1939) 15,754. **2** Island, largest in Tonga Is., in S part, SW cen. Pacific Ocean; ab. 100 sq. m.; pop. (1937) 15,274; chief town Nukualofa, ✳ of the protectorate. A large, flat coral island, well provided with roads.

Tong'e·ren (tŏng'ĕ·rĕ[n]); Fr. **Ton'gres** (tôN'gr'). Manufacturing and commercial commune, Limburg prov., NE Belgium, 12 m. NW of Liége; pop. 11,607.

Tongking. See TONKIN.

Tong·quil' (tŏng·kēl'). Island 19 sq. m. in Samales group, Sulu Archipelago, Phil. Is. See SAMALES.

Tongue (tŭng). River 246 m. long, SE Montana; rises in Sheridan co., N Wyoming, flows N across Montana border into Yellowstone river in Custer co., SE Montana.

Tongue of the Ocean. Strait in the Bahama Is., West Indies, bet. Andros I. on the W and New Providence I. and Exuma Is. on the E; very deep water.

Tonk (tôngk). **1** Former Indian state, Jaipur, NW Indian Union; consisted of 6 areas separated from one another, mostly in SE Rajputana but part in Central India; 2543 sq. m.; pop. (1941) 353,687. Ruler was a Mohammedan of Afghan descent. **2** Town, its ✳, E Rajputana, near right bank of Banas river 60 m. S of Jaipur; pop. 35,798.

Ton'ka·wa (tŏng'kȧ·wô). City, Kay co., N Oklahoma, 13 m. W of Ponca City; pop. 3415; oil wells; agriculture, ranching, oil refining.

Ton'kin' (tŏn[g]'kĭn') or **Tong'king'** (tŏng'kĭng'). Former French protectorate, N French Indochina, in 19th cent. a department of Annam; 44,660 sq. m.; pop. 8,700,000; ✳ Hanoi; since 1946 the N part of the Republic of Vietnam. Bounded on N by China (provinces of Yunnan and Kwangsi), on E by Gulf of Tonkin, on S by Northern Annam, and on S and SW by Laos. Mountains on N border and in W; highest point 10,310 ft. near Laokay. Chief river the Coi (or Songkoi) river and its tributaries which form channels of trade with China; delta of Coi is rich fertile agricultural region. Produces rice (chief crop), also cotton, sugar, tobacco, coffee, jute. Inhabitants mainly Annamese. Chief towns Hanoi, Haiphong, Namdinh, and frontier trading stations of Laokay and Langson.

History: Formed part of China in early times; recently, after 1801, united to Annam; first visited by French expedition 1866; Hanoi attacked 1873 and finally seized 1882; joined with other areas controlled by French to form French Indochina 1887; occupied by Japanese 1940–45; formed part of new state of Vietnam set up 1945–46.

Tonkin, Gulf of. Arm of the South China Sea ab. 300 m. long, E of Tonkin and N and W of Hainan I., S China.

Ton'le Sap (tŏn'lä săp'). **1** Literally "Great Lake"; Fr. **Grand Lac** (grän' lȧk'). Lake ab. 87 m. long in W Cambodia, SW Indochina; receives flood waters of the Mekong river; area varies from 1000 to 9500 sq. m. according to season. Has great abundance of fish. Just N of its NW shore lies the great ruins of Angkor (q.v.). **2** River ab. 75 m. long, its outlet in cen. Cambodia, flowing SE to the Mekong river at Pnompenh.

Ton'neins' (tô'năNs'). Commune, Lot-et-Garonne dept., SW France, on Garonne river 53 m. SE of Bordeaux; pop. 4585.

To'no·lai Harbour (tō'nô·lī). Large anchorage on Bougainville Strait at S end of Bougainville I., NW Solomon Is., W Pacific; Buin and Kahili are on it.

To'no·pah (tō'nô·pä). Village, ⊗ of Nye co., cen. and S Nevada, 78 m. ESE of S end of Walker Lake; pop. 1679; formerly mining (gold and silver) center (gold discovered 1900); distributing center for gasoline, machinery, blasting powder, whiskey, and foodstuffs.

Tonquin. Var. of TONKIN.

Töns'berg (tûns'bĕr). Seaport, Vestfold co., SE Norway, located on N end of Nötteröy I.; pop. 11,997; oldest city in Norway; home port for whaling fleets; manufactures machinery, paper, wood products, dairy products; ships fish and lumber.

Ton'to (tŏn'tō; Span. tôn'tō). River 135 m. long, SE cen. Mexico; flows E and NE across SE Veracruz state into the Bay of Campeche.

Tonto Basin. Region in N Gila co., cen. Arizona, alt. above 2000 ft.; shut in by Mogollon Mesa on the N and by mountain ranges on E and W; traversed by **Tonto Creek,** 60 m. long, which flows S to the Salt river at Roosevelt Lake; fine forests and grazing land; just S of Roosevelt Lake is **Tonto National Monument:** see UNITED STATES, *National Monuments.*

Too·el'e (tōō·ĕl'ĕ; twĕl'ĕ). **1** County in Utah. See *Table* at UTAH. **2** City, its ⊗, NW Utah, 25 m. SW of Salt Lake City; pop. 9133; settled 1849; mining (silver, lead, copper) and smelting center.

Toole (tōōl). County in Montana. See *Table* at MONTANA.

Toombs (tōōmz). County in Georgia. See *Table* at GEORGIA.

Too·wong' (tōō·wŏng'). Former town in Queensland, Australia; now part of Brisbane.

Too·woom'ba (tŭ·wōōm'bȧ). City, SE Queensland, Australia, 65 m. W of Brisbane; pop. 26,430; trade center for extensive agricultural, timber, fruit, and pastoral hinterland; alt. 1920 ft.; summer resort.

Top (tŏp; Russ. tôp). Large lake, N Karelia, U.S.S.R.; its outlet is Pongoma river flowing E to White Sea N of Kem.

To·pe'ka (tô·pē'kȧ). City, ✳ of Kansas and ⊗ of Shawnee co., NE Kansas, on Kansas river 55 m. W of Kansas City; pop. 119,484; railroad construction shops; flour mills, packing houses, brass and bronze foundries; zinc, lead, and coal mines in vicinity; U.S. Air Force base. Washburn Municipal Univ. of Topeka (1865; coed.). Town on the old Oregon Trail; settled 1854 by anti-slavery colonists from Lawrence; prominent during the political struggles bet. the pro-slavery and anti-slavery factions before the Civil War; made capital of Kansas when the state was admitted into the Union 1861.

To'po Chi'co (tō'pô chē'kô). Hot springs 4 m. NW of Monterrey, Nuevo León state, NE Mexico; resort.

To·po'la (tô·pō'lä); Hung. **To'po·lya** (tō'pô·yŏ). Commune, Voivodina autonomous prov., NE Yugoslavia, S of Subotica; pop. ab. 14,000.

Topolia. See COPAIS.

To·po'lo·bam'po (tō̄-pō'lō̄-väm'pō̄). Village and port on coast of NW Sinaloa state, W Mexico, on Gulf of California; has good harbor.

Topolya. See TOPOLA.

Top'pe·nish (tŏp'ĕ-nĭsh). City, Yakima co., S Washington, 17 m. SSE of Yakima; pop. 5667; agriculture (potatoes, sugar beets, wheat, fruit).

Tops'ham (tŏp'săm). Town, Sagadahoc co., S Maine, at mouth of Androscoggin river; pop. 3818.

Top'ton (tŏp'tŭn). Borough, Berks co., SE Pennsylvania, 18 m. NE of Reading; pop. 1684.

To·qui'ma Range (tō̄-kē'mȧ). Range in N Nye co., cen. Nevada.

Tor (tôr). Town on Sinai Penin., NE Egypt, on E coast of Gulf of Suez; pop. 1045.

Tor'bay' (tôr'bā'). **1** or **Tor Bay.** Inlet of the English Channel on the coast of Devonshire, SW England, near Torquay.
2 Town, SE Newfoundland, on Atlantic Ocean 8 m. N of St. John's; pop. (1942 est.) 1700; summer resort; has airport.

Tor·cel'lo (tôr-chĕl'lō̄). Island in the Lagoon of Venice, 6 m. NW of the city, NE Italy; contains ruins of a cathedral.

Torda. See TURDA.

Tor·de·sil'las (tôr'thȧ-sē'[l]yäs). Village, cen. Valladolid prov., N Spain, on the Duero; pop. (1930) 4071; church, convent; residence of Juana la Loca (Joanna the Mad) 1509–55. Treaty signed here June 7, 1494 bet. Spain and Portugal by which the line of demarcation bet. their respective discoveries in the New World (estab. 1493) was moved 270 leagues further west (to ab. 46°W), thus granting to Portugal the E part of Brazil.

Tor'gau (tôr'gou). Manufacturing city, Leipzig dist., E Germany, in former Saxony prov. of Prussia on Elbe river SE of Dessau; pop. 12,647; 15th-cent. late-Gothic church; Renaissance castle of 16th and 17th cents.; manufactures glass, ceramic ware, mineral oil, agricultural implements, envelopes. Grew up around castle first mentioned 973 A.D.; city first mentioned 1288; Austrians defeated by Frederick the Great nearby 1760. In World War II front patrols of 1st Ukrainian Army of U.S.S.R. and U.S. 1st Army met here Apr. 27, 1945 thus cutting Germany in two and bringing together Russian and Allied troops in their campaign against Germany.

Torg'hat'ten (tôrg'hät''n). Peak on a small island off W cen. coast of Norway; at a height of ab. 400 ft. from its base it is penetrated by a natural tunnel 553 ft. long, 200 to 250 ft. high, and 35 to 56 ft. wide.

To·ri'no (tō̄-rē'nō̄). **1** Province of Italy. See *Table* at ITALY.
2 See TURIN.

Tor·ko'ro, Cape (tôr-kōr'ō̄). Point on N coast of New Britain I., Bismarck Archipelago, W Pacific Ocean, near its E end; extends into Bismarck Sea.

Tor'men·tine, Cape (tôr'mĕn-tīn). Point, SE New Brunswick, Canada, extending into Northumberland Strait; most easterly point of New Brunswick.

Tormentoso, Cabo. See Cape of GOOD HOPE.

Tor'mes (tôr'mâs). River 176 m. long in W Spain; flows N and NW into Douro river on Portuguese border.

Tor·na'do Mountain (tôr-nā'dō̄). Peak 10,169 ft. in Rocky Mts., SW Canada, on border bet. SE Brit. Columbia and Alberta.

Tor'ne (tōr'nĕ); *Finnish* **Tor'ni·o** (tôr'nĭ-ō̄). River ab. 250 m. long in N and NE Sweden; issues from Torne Träsk in NW Sweden; flows SE and S, forming in its lower course a section of the Swedish-Finnish boundary, and empties into the head of the Gulf of Bothnia.

Torne Träsk (trĕsk'). Lake (*träsk*) 124 sq. m. in NW Sweden; source of the Torne river.

Torn'gat Mountains (tôrn'găt). Mountain range, extreme N tip of Labrador; extends N to Cape Chidley; highest point Cirque Mt. 5500 ft., at S end.

Tor'ni·o (tôr'nĭ-ō̄). **1** *Swed.* **Tor'ne·å'** (tôr'nĕ-ō̄'). Seaport, Oulu dept., W Finland, built on an island in the Tornio river at its mouth, opp. the Swedish town of Haparanda; pop. 2285; manufactures leather.
2 River in N Sweden. See TORNE.

To'ro. **1** (tō̄'rō̄) District, formerly a native kingdom, Western Province, Republic of Uganda, E Africa, near Mt. Ruwenzori.
2 (tō̄'rō̄) Peak 20,930 ft. in cen. Chile, near border of Argentina.
3 (tō̄'rō̄) Town, Zamora prov., NW cen. Spain, on right bank of the Duero 35 m. W of Valladolid; pop. (1930) 7700; an old town with fine bridge and 12th-cent. cathedral. Seat of Spanish Cortes 1371, 1442, and 1505; battle here in 1476 in which Ferdinand of Aragon defeated the Portuguese.

To'ro·ki'na, Cape (tōr'ō̄-kē'nȧ). Point on W coast of Bougainville I., N Solomon Is., on N side of Empress Augusta Bay. Landing place of American forces Nov. 1, 1943; Allied air base developed here.

Tö'rök·szent'mi·klós' (tû'rûk-sĕnt'mĭ-klôsh'). Commune, 65 m. SE of Budapest, E Hungary; pop. 30,426.

Tor'o·na'ic Gulf (tôr'ō̄-nā'ĭk); *Gr.* **To'ro·nai'os Kol'-pos** (tō̄'rô̄-nā'ôs kôl'pôs); *also* **Gulf of Kas·san'dra** (kȧ-sän'drȧ; *Gr.* kä-sän'drä). Inlet of N Aegean Sea bet. the Sithonia and Pallene Penins. of Chalcidice, NE Greece. Ruins of ancient Olynthus are at its head.

To·ron'to (tṵ-rŏn'tō̄). **1** City, Jefferson co., E Ohio, on Ohio river 7 m. N of Steubenville; pop. 7780; manufactures clay products, sheet steel, tinplate, dairy and foundry products; coal mines and clay pits nearby.
2 Commercial city, ⊗ of York co. and ✳ of Ontario prov., Canada, in SE part at W end of Lake Ontario; pop. (1951) 675,754, metropolitan area 1,117,470; extensive harbor facilities; exports principally timber, woolens, bacon, grains, horses, manufactured articles; manufactures esp. farm machinery; active publishing trade; has several large packing houses and a municipal abattoir. Buildings include parliament buildings, Superior Court of Ontario building, etc. Known as "a city of churches"; also, as "a city of homes." In Exhibition Park holds annually the important Canadian National Exhibition. Seat of Toronto University (founded 1827; coed.) and affiliates, as Victoria University (1836; coed.; federated with University of Toronto 1890); Ontario College of Art (1912; coed.).
History: Occupies the site of old French trading post, Fort Rouillé (founded c. 1749); city founded as **York** by British Loyalists 1793; succeeded Niagara-on-the-Lake as capital of Upper Canada 1796; twice sacked by American troops during the War of 1812; received city charter 1834 and changed name to Toronto; had as first mayor William Lyon Mackenzie, leader of abortive uprising of 1837; capital of Canada 1849–51 and 1855–59; lower part of city destroyed by fire 1904.

Toronto, Lake. Lake in SE cen. Chihuahua state, N Mexico, produced by damming of the Conchos river; site of an airport.

Toronto Mountain. Peak 5350 ft. in Jeff Davis co., W Texas.

Toros Dağları. See TAURUS MOUNTAINS.

Tor·quay' (tôr-kē'). Municipal borough, Devonshire, SW England, 30 m. ENE of Plymouth; pop. 46,165, (1951 pop.) 53,216; seaside resort; yachting center; manufactures terra cotta and pottery; situated on Torbay (an inlet of the English Channel), from which William of Orange landed in 1688.

Tor·rá' (tôr-rä'). Peak 11,660 ft. in the Cordillera Occidental of the Andes, W Colombia.

Tor'rance (tôr'ăns). **1** County in New Mexico. See *Table* at NEW MEXICO.
2 Industrial and residential city, Los Angeles co., SW California, 15 m. SSW of Los Angeles; pop. 100,991; founded 1911, incorp. 1921; oil fields, machine and tool shops, steel plant, airplanes.

Tor're An'nun·zia'ta (tŏr'râ än'nōon·tsyä'tä). Commune, Napoli prov., Campania, S Italy, on Bay of Naples 12 m. SE of Naples; pop. 72,935; seaside resort; harbor; ferruginous warm springs.

Torre del Gre'co (dâl grä'kŏ). Commune, Napoli prov., Campania, S Italy, on Bay of Naples 7 m. SE of Naples; pop. 51,401; seaside resort; damaged several times by earthquakes and volcanic eruptions.

Tor're·don'ji·me'no (tŏr'rĕ·thông'hĕ·mä'nŏ). Commune, Jaén prov., S Spain, 12 m. W of Jaén; pop. 16,069; agriculture, stock raising; oil, liquors, soap.

Tor're·la·ve'ga (tŏr'rĕ·lä·vä'gä). Commune, Santander prov., N Spain, 14 m. SW of Santander; pop. 19,315; leather, flour, chocolates; salting works.

Tor're·mag·gio're (tŏr'râ·mäd·jō'râ). Commune, Foggia prov., Apulia, SE Italy, 21 m. NW of Foggia; pop. 15,198; castle.

Tor'rens (tŏr'ĕnz). **1** Shallow salt lake 130 m. long, E South Australia, N of Spencer Gulf, 25 ft. below sea level.
2 River 50 m. long, South Australia; flows W to Gulf of St. Vincent; Adelaide on it.

Tor·ren'te (tôr·rän'tâ). Commune, Valencia prov., E Spain, 8 m. SW of Valencia; pop. 13,586.

Tor're·ón' (tŏr'rĕ·ôn'). City, Coahuila state, NE Mexico; pop. 75,796; altitude 3800 ft.; textile mills, flour mills, smelters; in cotton-growing district; mines nearby.

Tor'res Islands (tŏr'ĕs). Group of 4 small islands, not of volcanic origin, at N end of the New Hebrides, SW Pacific Ocean, 50 m. NW of Vanua Lava; largest is Hiu I.

Torres Strait. Strait ab. 80 m. wide bet. the island of New Guinea and the N tip of Cape York Penin. on the mainland of Australia; connects Arafura Sea and Coral Sea; Australian boundary is ab. 3 m. from New Guinea shore. Has many reefs, shoals, and islands (**Torres Strait Islands**), and is dangerous to navigation; larger islands inhabited by ab. 4000 natives. Strait discovered by the Spanish navigator Torres in 1606; traversed by Cook in 1770.

Tor'res Ve'dras (tŏr'rĕzh vâ'thrásh). Commune, Lisboa dist., W Portugal, 26 m. N of Lisbon; pop. 8413; noted particularly for its 28-mile stretch of fortifications (begun 1809), extending to the Tagus river, from behind which Wellington hindered the French march against Lisbon 1810 (Peninsular War); sulfur baths; old Moorish citadel.

Tor'reys Peak (tŏr'īz). Mountain 14,264 ft. in Clear Creek and Summit cos., cen. Colorado.

Tor'ridge (tŏr'ĭj). River ab. 40 m. long in Devonshire, SW England; flows SE and then curves to the NW and empties into Barnstaple Bay through an estuary at Bideford.

Tor'ri·don, Loch (lŏk tŏr'ĭ·d'n). Inlet on NW coast of Scotland, in Ross and Cromarty co.; extends inland ab. 12 m.

Tor'ring·ton (tŏr'ĭng·tŭn). **1** Industrial city, E cen. Litchfield co., NW Connecticut, on Naugatuck river 18 m. NNW of Waterbury; pop. 30,045; incorp. 1923; manufactures brass and copper products, hardware, textiles, engines and machines, tobacco products. The town (incorp. 1740) is coextensive with the city.
2 River, ⊗ of Goshen co., SE Wyoming, on North Platte river 7 m. W of Nebraska border; pop. 4188; trade center in section growing sugar beets, potatoes, alfalfa; petroleum and coal deposits nearby; beet-sugar refinery.

Tor'toise Islands (tŏr'tŭs; -tĭs). = GALÁPAGOS ISLANDS.

Tor·to'la (tŏr·tō'lä). Largest of the Virgin Is. in the West Indies, chief island of the British Virgin Is., in Leeward Islands group; 24 sq. m.; pop. ab. 4000; chief town Road Town.

Tor'to·li'ta Mountains (tŏr'tŏ·lē'tá). Small range in E Pinal co., S cen. Arizona.

Tor·to'na (tŏr·tō'nä); anc. **Der·to'na** (dûr·tō'ná). Manufacturing commune, Alessandria prov., Piedmont,

NW Italy, 13 m. E of Alessandria; pop. 20,361; 16th-cent. cathedral.

Tor·to·ri'ci (tôr·tô·rē'chĕ). Commune, Messina prov., NE Sicily, 42 m. WSW of Messina; pop. 11,398.

Tor·to'sa (tôr·tō'sá; Span. -sä). **1** anc. **Der·to'sa** (dûr·tō'sá). City, Tarragona prov., NE Spain, on Ebro river 40 m. SW of Tarragona; pop. 38,269; manufactures paper, leather, pottery, porcelain, faïence, glass, soap, hats; marble and alabaster quarries nearby; fisheries; ancient city walls; 12th-cent. cathedral; Roman ruins. Conquered by Rome 218 B.C.; made episcopal see under Goths; captured by Moors 713; captured 1148 by Ramón Berenguer IV; occupied by French 1648 and 1708.
2 (tôr·tō'sá) Town, Syria. See TARTUS.

Tor·to'sa, Cape (tôr·tō'sá; Span. -sä). Cape on E coast of Spain, E of Tortosa.

Tor'tue' (tôr'tü'), or **Tor·tu'ga** (tôr·tōo'gá), **Island.** Island 25 m. long in the West Indies, off N coast of Haiti; in 17th cent. a resort of pirates.

Tortuga, La. See LA TORTUGA.

Tor·tu'ga, Point (tôr·tōo'gá; Span. -gä). Cape extending into Pacific Ocean on NW coast of Ecuador.

To'ruń (tô'rōon·y'); Ger. **Thorn** (tôrn; Ger. tōrn). Industrial and commercial city, ✱ of Pomorze dept., N Poland, on Vistula river 110 m. NW of Warsaw; pop. (1938–39 est.) 81,215; railroad junction; fortress; 14th-cent. town hall with 13th-cent. tower; manufactures machinery, iron goods, beer, lumber, furniture, chemicals; trades in textiles, grain, cattle. Birthplace of the astronomer Copernicus.

History: Founded 1231 by Teutonic Knights; made city 1232; became member of Hanseatic League; to kingdom of Poland 1411; two treaties signed here (1411, 1466) by which the Poles gained territory; occupied by Charles XII of Sweden 1703; to Prussia 1793 (Second Partition of Poland); to Grand Duchy of Warsaw 1807 (Peace of Tilsit); to Prussia 1815 (Congress of Vienna); to Poland after World War I (Treaty of Versailles); held by Germans in World War II 1939–44; bypassed by Russians Jan. 1945 in invasion of Germany.

To'ry (tōr'ĭ). Small island in Atlantic Ocean off extreme NW coast of Ireland, and administratively part of co. Donegal; lighthouse; lobster fisheries. Ruins of churches, perhaps founded by St. Columba; a pirate stronghold of the legendary Fomorians.

Törz'bur'ger Pass (tûrts'bŏor'gĕr). Mountain pass, altitude 4065 ft., in the Transylvanian Alps, Romania, 25 m. SW of Braşov.

To·sa (tô·sä). Old province in S Shikoku I., Japan, now Kochi prefecture. Home of the Tosa clan, esp. influential at the time of the Restoration 1868.

Tosa Bay. Inlet of the Pacific Ocean on S coast of Shikoku I., Japan.

To·sa'ri (tô·sä'rĕ). Village on N slopes of Tengger Mts., E Java, Indonesia; alt. 5963 ft.; has fine climate and scenery, said to be best health resort in Java.

Toscana. See TUSCANY.

Tos'ca·nel'la (tŏs'kä·nĕl'á; Ital. tôs·kä·nĕl'lä); anc. and officially since 1912 **Tus·ca'ni·a** (tŭs·kä'nĭ·á; -kän'yá; Ital. tōos·kä'nyä). Commune, Viterbo prov., N Latium, cen. Italy, W of Viterbo; pop. (1931) 5408; Etruscan tombs; medieval walls; four Romanesque churches.

Toscano or **Tosco–Emiliano, Appennino.** See *Tuscan Apennines* at APENNINES.

Toscano, Arcipelago. See TUSCAN ARCHIPELAGO.

Töss (tûs). Former commune in Zurich canton, NE cen. Switzerland, on the **Töss River,** now a part of Winterthur.

To·sya' (tô·syä'). Town, Kastamonu vilayet, N Turkey in Asia, on a tributary of the Kızıl Irmak; pop. 10,081.

To·ta'na (tô·tä'nä). Manufacturing commune, Murcia prov., SE Spain, 25 m. SW of Murcia; pop. 15,264; produces linen, pottery.

Tót'kom·lós (tōt'kŏm·lōsh'). Commune, SE Hungary, on Mureş river 30 m. ENE of Szeged; pop. 10,992.

Tot′nes (tŏt′nĕs; -nĭs). Municipal borough, Devonshire, SW England, 20 m. SSW of Exeter; pop. 5534; brewing, flour milling; remains of ancient castle whose grounds are a public garden; very old, important in Saxon times.

To·to·mi Sea (tō·tō·mĕ). Inlet of W Pacific Ocean on S coast of Honshu, Japan, outside of Ise Bay.

To·to′ni·ca·pán (tō·tō′nē·kä·pän′). **1** Department, W cen. Guatemala; 410 sq. m.; pop. 92,292; ✳ Totonicapán. **2** Industrial city, its ✳, on high plateau; pop. 5623; center of an independence movement in 1838.

To′to·wa (tō′tō·wȧ). Residential borough, Passaic co., N New Jersey, 3 m. W of Paterson; pop. 10,897; encampment of Washington and his men during Revolution.

Tot′ten Coast (tŏt′′n). Section of coast of Wilkes Land, Antarctica, at ab. 120°E long.

Tot′ten·ham (tŏt′năm; tŏt′′n·ăm). Urban district, Middlesex, SE England, N suburb of London; pop. 157,772, (1951 pop.) 126,921; part of Greater London.

Tot′ten·ville (tŏt′′n·vĭl). Formerly an incorporated village, since 1898 part of borough of RICHMOND (*q.v.*), New York City, New York.

Tot′ting·ton (tŏt′ĭng·tŭn). Urban district, Lancashire, NW England, 10 m. NNW of Manchester; pop. 5824.

Tot·to·ri (tŏt·tō·rē). **1** Prefecture of Japan. See *Table* at JAPAN. **2** Seaport city, its ✳, 90 m. NW of Kyoto; pop. (1945) 51,848. Formerly the castle town of a daimio; became prosperous in recent times on the opening of the railroad. Manufactures silk and cotton goods.

Touamotou. French var. of *Tuamotu*: see TUAMOTU ARCHIPELAGO.

Toub′kal (tōōb′kăl). Mountain peak 13,661 ft. in Grand Atlas Mts., Morocco, S of Marrakesh; highest known peak in the Atlas range.

Toubouaï. French var. of *Tubuaï*: see TUBUAÏ ISLANDS.

Toug·gourt′ or **Tug·gurt′** (tōō·gōōrt′). **1** Territory of Algeria, S of Constantine dept. See *Table* at ALGERIA. **2** Town and oasis, ✳ of Touggourt territory, NE Algeria, 100 m. S of Biskra; pop. of town ab. 12,000 and of commune 61,198.

Toul (tōōl); *anc.* **Tul′lum** (tŭl′ŭm). City, Meurthe-et-Moselle dept., NE France, on Moselle river 13 m. WSW of Nancy; pop. 13,267; fortified place; 13th-cent. cathedral and church; 18th-cent. episcopal palace (now town hall).

History: Ancient capital of the Leuci; made episcopal see in 4th cent. (discontinued in Napoleonic times); important in Middle Ages; with Metz and Verdun (*Les Trois-Évêchés*, the three bishoprics) was captured by French 1552, and acquisition by France confirmed by Treaty of Westphalia 1648; fortified by Vauban; became important center for production of faïence in 18th cent.; capitulated to Germans after 5-weeks siege 1870; headquarters of Second American Army in World War I.

Tou·lon (tōō′lŏn). City, ⊗ of Stark co., NW cen. Illinois; pop. 1213.

Tou·lon′ (tōō·lŏn′; tōō′lŏn; *Fr.* tōō′lôɴ′); *anc.* **Te′lo Mar′ti·us** (tē′lō mär′shĭ·ŭs; -shŭs). Fortified seaport, Var dept., SE France, on Mediterranean 30 m. ESE of Marseilles; pop. 150,310; important chiefly as naval station and arsenal, ranking second in France; shipbuilding, marine foundry, etc.; episcopal see (since 5th cent.); 13th-cent. cathedral, 17th-cent. town hall, marine school, botanical gardens, etc.; winter resort; in addition to staple naval manufactures, produces machinery, iron goods, leather, clothing, footwear; trades in wine, fruit, oil.

History: Of pre-Roman origin; sacked by Saracens 889 A.D.; captured by Charles V 1524 and 1536; became important naval station under Louis XIV; French and Spanish fleets defeated English here 1744; Napoleonic victory over English and Spaniards 1793; important port of entry and naval station in World War I; large

part of French fleet interned here after armistice with Germany and Italy 1940, many scuttled by French when Germans occupied the whole of France Nov. 1942; captured by French Aug. 26, 1944.

Tou′louse′ (tōō′lōōz′); *anc.* **To·lo′sa** (tō·lō′sȧ). City, ✳ of Haute-Garonne dept., S France, on Garonne river 133 m. SE of Bordeaux; pop. 213,220; railroad center; 13th-cent. cathedral, 11th-cent. church of St-Sernin (largest Romanesque church in France) town hall, courthouse, museum, observatory, botanical garden, public library, professional and technical schools, academies of art, science, and literature, a national university (founded 1230), and a large Catholic institution of higher learning; manufactures include textiles, steam engines, leather, tobacco, cannon, brandy.

History: Sacked by Romans 106 B.C.; Visigoth capital 419–508 A.D.; taken by Franks under Clovis 508; foremost city in S Gaul for many centuries; taken by Saracens 718; capital of Aquitaine; center of countship 9th–14th cents.; tribunal of Inquisition established here; Huguenot massacres 1562 and 1572; captured by English under Wellington 1814. See LANGUEDOC.

Toun′goo (toung′gōō; toung′ōō). **1** District, Tenasserim division, Lower Burma; 6456 sq. m.; pop. 428,670; ✳ Toungoo. **2** Town, its ✳, on Sittang river 150 m. N of Rangoon; pop. 23,223; capital of an independent kingdom from 14th to 16th cents. Town and airdrome, defended by Chinese troops, lost to Japanese Mar. 30, 1942; retaken Apr. 26, 1945.

Tou·raine′ (tōō·rān′; *Fr.* tōō′rân′). Historical region of NW cen. France; bounded anciently on N by Le Maine, NE by Orléanais, SE by Berry, S by Marche, SW by Poitou, W by Saumurois, NW by Anjou; ✳ Tours; watered by Indre, Cher, and Loire rivers; sometimes called the "Garden of France"; province under the ancien régime.

Tou·rane′ (tōō·rän′) or **Da Nang** (dä′ näng′). Seaport city, cen. Annam, S Vietnam, on coastal railroad 50 m. SE of Hué; pop. 108,800.

Tour·coing′ (tōōr′kwăn′). Manufacturing city, Nord dept., N France, on Belgian frontier 8 m. NE of Lille; pop. 78,393; one of principal textile centers of France; soap works, sugar refineries. In World War I captured by Germans 1914 and seriously damaged.

Tour′la·ville (tōōr′lȧ·vēl′). Commune, Manche dept., NW France, 3 m. E of Cherbourg of which it is a suburb; pop. (1931) 7501; château; 14th-cent. church.

Tour·nai′ or **Tour·nay′** (tōōr·nā′; *Fr.* tōōr′-); *Flemish* **Door′nik** (dōr′nĭk). Commercial and manufacturing commune, Hainaut prov., SW Belgium, on the Schelde 45 m. SW of Brussels; pop. (1938 est.) 35,463; manufactures Brussels carpets, embroideries, cement; its cathedral of Notre-Dame, begun in 1030, has fine belfry. Captured by the Germans Aug. 1914 and held throughout World War I; severely damaged.

Tour′non′ (tōōr′nôɴ′). Town, Ardèche dept., SE France, on Rhone river 58 m. by rail S of Lyons; pop. 3740; remains of ancient fortifications.

Tour′nus′ (tōōr′nü′). Town, Saône-et-Loire dept., E cen. France, on the Saône ab. 15 m. N of Mâcon; pop. 3854; site of Benedictine abbey founded 7th or 8th cent.; remarkable abbey church. Birthplace of the painter Jean Baptiste Greuze.

Tours (tōōr; *Fr.* tōōr); *anc.* **Cae′sa·ro·du′num** (sē′zȧ·rō·dū′nŭm), *later* **Tu′ro·ni** (tū′rō·nī). Manufacturing and commercial city, ✳ of Indre-et-Loire dept., NW cen. France, 129 m. SW of Paris; pop. 83,753; 12th-cent. Gothic cathedral; archiepiscopal palace; two towers of old cathedral of St. Martin of Tours; fine bridges over Loire; manufactures include silk goods, serge, rugs, cloth, ribbons, leather, chemical goods, iron and steel goods, pottery; trades in brandy, wine, corn, dried fruits, wax, hemp, wool.

History: Important under Romans; Charles Martel defeated Saracens nearby 732 (sometimes called battle of

Poitiers) checking the Moslem invasion; became famous for manufacture of silk; Protestant stronghold; largely depopulated by revocation of Edict of Nantes 1685; seat of French government Sept.–Dec. 1870, during siege of Paris in Franco-Prussian War. Birthplace of Balzac.

Tou'si.dé (tōō'sē'dā'). Peak 10,709 ft. in Tibesti Mts. in N Chad, N cen. Africa.

Tou'tle (tōō't'l). River ab. 40 m. long, SW Washington; flows W in N Cowlitz co. into Cowlitz river.

Touva. = *Tannu Tuva:* see TUVA.

To.wa.da (tô-wä-dä). Lake in N Honshu, Japan, 25 m. in circumference, elevation 1476 ft.; resort, ab. 25 m. S of Aomori.

To.wan'da (tô-wŏn'då). Borough and summer resort, ⊗ of Bradford co., N Pennsylvania, on Susquehanna river 50 m. WNW of Scranton; pop. 4293; shipping point for nearby agricultural region; manufactures silk, hosiery, paper, X-ray screens.

Tow'ces.ter (tōs'tēr). Parish, S Northamptonshire, cen. England; pop. 2592; site of Roman camp on Watling Street; important in Saxon times.

Tow'er City (tou'ēr). Borough, Schuylkill co., E cen. Pennsylvania, 28 m. (50 m. by highway) NE of Harrisburg; pop. 1968; coal mining; textile mills, shirt factories.

Tower Falls. Waterfall 132 ft. in Yellowstone National Park, NW Wyoming.

Tower Hamlets. Former parliamentary borough in E London, England; the Tower of London stood at its SW end.

Tower Island. See GENOVESA island.

Tower Peak. Mountain 11,704 ft. in Sierra Nevada, in E Tuolumne co., cen. California.

Tow'ner (tou'nēr). **1** County in North Dakota. See *Table* at NORTH DAKOTA.

2 City, ⊗ of McHenry co., N cen. North Dakota; pop. 948; ships hay and stock; agriculture.

Towns (tounz). County in Georgia. See *Table* at GEORGIA.

Town'send (toun'zĕnd). **1** Town, Middlesex co., NE Massachusetts, 7 m. NE of Fitchburg; pop. 3650.

2 Town, ⊗ of Broadwater co., SW cen. Montana; pop. 1528.

Town'sends Inlet (toun'zĕndz). Narrow strait leading from Atlantic Ocean through barrier reefs in E Cape May co., S New Jersey.

Towns'ville (tounz'vĭl). City, E Queensland, Australia, on Halifax Bay 380 m. NW of Rockhampton; pop. 25,872; has active port, second largest in Queensland.

To.woe'ti or **To.wu'ti, Lake** (tô-wōō'tē). Lake in SE cen. Celebes I., Malay Archipelago.

Tow'son (tou's'n). Unincorporated locality, ⊗ of Baltimore co., N Maryland, N of Baltimore; pop. 19,090. Maryland State Teachers Coll. (founded 1865 in Baltimore, moved to Towson 1915) located here.

Tow'ton (tou't'n). Parish in West Riding, Yorkshire, N England; scene of battle Mar. 29, 1461 (the Wars of the Roses) in which Edward IV defeated the Lancastrians, a victory which confirmed his accession to the throne.

Tow'y (tou'ĭ). River ab. 50 m. long, SW Wales; flows SW to Carmarthen Bay.

To.ya.ma (tô-yä-mä). **1** Prefecture of Japan. See *Table* at JAPAN.

2 Seaport city, its ✳, on Honshu I. near S shore of Toyama Bay 110 m. N of Nagoya; pop. (1945) 100,775; manufactures patent medicines. From 16th cent. an important seat of daimios under Tokugawa Shogunate. In World War II bombed by American planes Aug. 2, 1945.

Toyama Bay. Inlet of the Sea of Japan on the W cen. coast of Honshu, Japan; enclosed on W by Noto Penin.

To'yen' Shan (dō'yĕn' shän'). Mountain range in W cen. Kwangsi prov., SE China, bet. the Hungshui and Siang rivers, highest ab. 5250 ft.

To.yo.ha.ra (tô-yô-hä-rä). Town, ✳ of Karafuto when under Japanese, in S part of Sakhalin I. on railroad 20 m.

N of Otomari; pop. (1939 est.) 37,922; on a plateau covered with forests; railroad extends N to Sakaehama and Shikuka.

To.yo.ha.shi (tô-yô-hä-shĕ). City, Aichi prefecture, S Honshu, Japan, 38 m. SE of Nagoya and near E shore of inlet of E Ise Bay; pop. (1945) 105,840.

To'zeur' (tô'zûr'). Town and large oasis, W Tunisia, on W shore of Chott Djerid.

Tpilisi. See TIFLIS.

Trab.zon' (träb-zŏn') or **Treb'i.zond** (trĕb'ĭ-zŏnd). **1** Vilayet, NE Turkey in Asia; 1787 sq. m.; pop. 360,679.

2 *anc.* **Trap'e.zus** (trăp'ē-zŭs). Seaport city, its ✳, on the SE coast of the Black Sea; pop. (1940) 33,040. For centuries a trade route terminus of importance; old route to Persia and Central Asia began here. Climate is good but harbor is merely a roadstead. Ancient Trapezus was a Greek colony of Sinope; held by Roman and Byzantine empires. Seat of Greek Empire of Trebizond (*q.v.*).

Trach'o.ni'tis (trăk'ô-nī'tĭs). District of N Palestine beyond (E of) the Jordan, S of Damascus, and E of Gaulanitis; formed a part of the Tetrarchy of Philip 4 B.C.–34 A.D.

Tra'cy (trā'sĭ). **1** Industrial city, San Joaquin co., cen. California, 18 m. SSW of Stockton; pop. 11,289; shipping point for San Joaquin valley.

2 City, Lyon co., SW Minnesota, 18 m. SSE of Marshall; pop. 2862.

Tracy City. Town, Grundy co., S cen. Tennessee, ab. 30 m. NW of Chattanooga; pop. 1577; coal mines.

Tra.fal'gar, Cape (trá-fǎl'gēr; trǎf''l-gär). Cape on SW coast of Spain, SE of Cádiz and WNW of the Strait of Gibraltar; scene of naval battle and Nelson's victory over French and Spanish fleets and scene of his death Oct. 21, 1805.

Traf'ford (trǎf'ērd). Borough, Allegheny and Westmoreland cos., SW Pennsylvania, 14 m. E of Pittsburgh; pop. 4330.

Tragurium. See TROGIR.

Trai.guén' (trī-gān'). **1** Island in Chonos Archipelago, in Pacific Ocean off SW coast of Chile.

2 Town, Malleco prov., S cen. Chile, ab. 45 m. S of Angol; pop. 8828.

Trail (trāl). Mining city, SE Brit. Columbia, Canada, on Columbia river 7 m. N of U.S. border; pop. 11,430; has large smelters; lead, silver, zinc, gold, cadmium, and bismuth all mined in the neighborhood.

Traill (trāl). County in North Dakota. See *Table* at NORTH DAKOTA.

Train'er (trān'ēr). Borough, Delaware co., SE Pennsylvania, on Delaware river 16 m. WSW of Philadelphia; pop. 2358; oil refineries.

Trajani Portus. See CIVITAVECCHIA.

Tra'kai (trä'kī). District of Lithuania. See *Table* at LITHUANIA.

Tra.lee' (trá-lē'). Urban district and seaport, ⊗ of co. Kerry, SW Eire, at head of **Tralee Bay** (inlet of Atlantic Ocean N of Dingle Bay); pop. 10,285; butter processing; site of Norman castle, seat of earls of Desmond. At nearby Ardfert are the ruins of 13th-cent. cathedral on site of earlier (6th-cent.) foundation of St. Brendan.

Trälleborg. See TRELLEBORG.

Tralles. See AYDIN.

Tra.nent' (trá-nĕnt'). Burgh, East Lothian, SE Scotland, ab. 9 m. E of Edinburgh near Prestonpans (*q.v.*); pop. (1951) 5639; coal mined here since 13th cent.

Trang (träng). **1** Province, SW Thailand; 1920 sq. m.; pop. 125,507.

2 Town, its ✳, on branch railroad 15 m. from the Strait of Malacca at Kantang and 85 m. ESE of Phuket.

Trang.an' (?träng-än'). Island ab. 50 m. long by 30 m. wide, S cen. part of Aru Is., Indonesia.

Tra'ni (trä'nē). Commercial seaport, Bari prov., Apulia, SE Italy, on Adriatic 26 m. WNW of Bari; pop. 31,175; seaside resort; cathedral of 11th to 13th cents.; 13th-cent. castle.

Tran′que·bar (trăng′kwĕ·bär; trăng′kĕ-). Town, E Madras state, S Indian Union, 50 m. NE of Tanjore; pop. 12,796. Formerly a seaport of importance; Danish settlement established here 1616; taken by British 1801, restored 1814, but bought with other Danish settlements in India in 1845.

Trans A·lai′ (trăns′ ä·lī′; *the prefix* trans[-] *is frequently* trănz *or* tränz *in England, but in the interest of space these pronunciations have been omitted from the entries that follow*). Mountain range in NW Pamirs, Central Asia, extending E and W bet. Kirgiz S.S.R. and the Gorno-Badakhshan Region, Tadzhik S.S.R., Soviet Central Asia; highest point Lenin Peak 23,386 ft. Cf. ALAI.

Transalpine Gaul. See GAUL.

Trans–Ap′pa·lach′i·a (trăns′ăp′a·lăch′ĭ·a; -lā′chĭ·a). Region W of the Appalachian Mts. in E cen. United States; used historically, esp. of period of late 18th and early 19th cents., to designate region drained by Ohio river.

Trans′bai·ka′li·a (trăns′bī·kä′lĭ·a) or **Trans′bai·kal′** (-bī·kàl′). Former Russian government in Asia E of Lake Baikal, now included in Buryat-Mongol A.S.S.R., Chita Region, and Khabarovsk Territory of Soviet Russia, Asia.

Trans′car·pa′thi·an Region (trăns′kär·pā′thĭ·ăn). English name for the Zakarpatskaya Region, the extreme W subdivision of the Ukraine, U.S.S.R.; formerly known as Carpathian Ruthenia.

Trans′cas′pi·an Region (trăns·kăs′pĭ·ăn) or **Trans-cas′pi·a** (-a). Former Russian government in Asia E of the Caspian Sea, roughly equivalent to the present Turkmen S.S.R. and a part of SW Kazakh S.S.R. of Soviet Central Asia.

Trans′cau·ca′sia (trăns′kô·kā′zha; -sha). **1** Region S of the Caucasus Mts. comprising, before 1917, various Russian governments, provinces, and districts. After that date a general name for the entire area embracing the three constituent Soviet Socialist Republics of Georgia, Azerbaidzhan, and Armenia which on Sept. 20, 1917 first formed a federation (see TRANSCAUCASIAN FEDERATION).
2 = TRANSCAUCASIAN FEDERATION.

Trans′cau·ca′sian Federation (-zhăn; -shăn) or, *frequently,* **Transcaucasia;** *officially* **Transcaucasian Soviet Federated Socialist Republic.** Formerly a federated union of what are now the three Soviet Socialist Republics of Transcaucasia, namely, Armenia, Azerbaidzhan, and Georgia; ✳ Tiflis. First formed Sept. 20, 1917 after the Russian Revolution; soon dissolved into separate republics of Georgia, Azerbaidzhan, and Armenia (*qq.v.*); scene of fighting in 1919–21 when Turkish Nationalists struggled with the Bolshevists for control of the region; re-formed Mar. 12, 1922 and entered the U.S.S.R. July 6, 1923; separated again into three autonomous republics Dec. 1936 when the U.S.S.R. adopted a new constitution.

Trans·co′na (trăns·kō′na). Industrial town, S Manitoba, Canada, 8 m. E of Winnipeg; pop. 6752; railroad shops.

Trans–Dnies′tri·a (trăns·nēs′trĭ·a). Region bet. the Dniester and Bug rivers in SW Ukraine, U.S.S.R., which, together with Bessarabia, was given 1941 to Romania by Germany during World War II; retaken by Russian armies 1944–45.

Transilvania. See TRANSYLVANIA region, Romania.

Trans·jor′dan (trăns·jôr′d'n); *or* **Jor′dan** (see below); *formerly* **Trans′jor·da′nia** (trăns′jôr·dān′ya; -dä′-nĭ·a); Arab. **Sharq el Ur′dunn** (shŭrk′ ăl ŏŏr′dŏŏn). Kingdom in NW Arabia, E of Palestine and Jordan river; 36,715 sq. m.; pop. 1,824,614; ✳ Amman; became in 1921 a British mandate, closely connected with administration of mandate of Palestine. Includes territories of ancient emirate of Kerak and of lands of Gilead, Moab, and Edom of earlier Bible times. Bounded on N by Syria and Jebel ed Druz, on NE by Iraq, on E and S by Saudi

Arabia, and on W by the Wadi el ‘Araba, Dead Sea, and Jordan river. Largely desert, mountainous in W. Traversed by railroad from N border to Ma‘an, whence a highway extends S to ‘Aqaba, only seaport of the country. Chief industries agriculture and cattle raising. Potash is obtained from the Dead Sea. Chief towns Amman, Ma‘an, Es Salt, Irbid, and El Kerak. See *Map* at PALESTINE.

History: Created 1921 out of former Turkish territory and proclaimed an independent state 1923 under Amir Abdullah ibn-Husein, but a mandate under British protection; first legislative council assembled 1929; mandate revoked 1946 and by treaty of Mar. 22, 1946 became an independent kingdom; engaged in war with Jewish republic of Israel 1948–49; at signing of armistice agreement with Israel Apr. 1949 held the cen. part of Palestine and adopted name of **Jordan,** *in full* **Hash′-em·ite Kingdom of Jordan** (hăsh′ĕm·ĭt).

Trans–Juba. See JUBALAND.

Trans·kei′ (trăns·kā′). **1** = TRANSKEIAN TERRITORIES. **2** One of the Transkeian Territories, E Cape Province, Republic of So. Africa, on coast N of Great Kei river; 2504 sq. m.; pop. 241,377; ✳ Butterworth. Comprises three districts, inhabited by Kaffir tribes: Fingoland, Galekaland, and the Idutywa Reserve.

Trans·kei′an Territories (trăns·kā′ăn). Division of Cape Province, Republic of So. Africa, in E part bet. Great Kei river and Natal; 16,351 sq. m.; pop. 961,000 (chiefly Kaffirs); ✳ Umtata; comprises four territories of Transkei, Tembuland, Griqualand East, and Pondoland; in early times known as Kaffraria. White pop. (1936) 17,624. Different regions annexed to Cape Colony at various dates bet. 1879 and 1894. Purely native affairs are dealt with by the Transkeian Territories General Council.

Trans′lei·tha′nia (trăns′lī·thăn′ya; -thā′nĭ·a). A region of Hungary; the part of former Austria-Hungary E of Leitha river.

Trans′ox·i·a′na (trăns′ŏk·sĭ·ā′na; -ăn′a). Region beyond (N of) the Oxus (modern Amu Darya) and NE of Khurasan, W Asia, including Bukhara and Samarkand. In ancient times known as Sogdiana (*q.v.*).

Trans′pa·dane Gaul (trăns′pa·dān; trăns·pā′dān). See GAUL.

Transpadane Republic. Provisionally organized republic in N Italy, created by Napoleon 1796–97 from lands N of Po around Milan, Bergamo, Brescia, and Cremona; incorporated into Cisalpine Republic 1797. See GAUL.

Trans·vaal′ (trăns·väl′); *formerly, as independent state,* **South African Republic** (*q.v.*). Province, NE Republic of South Africa; 110,450 sq. m.; pop. (1936) 3,341,470 (of which 2,520,714 are non-European); ✳ Pretoria. Bounded on N by Southern Rhodesia, on E by Mozambique and Swaziland, on S by Natal and Orange Free State, and on W by Cape Province and Bechuanaland Protectorate; lies bet. Limpopo river (on N) and Vaal river (on S). Chief tributaries of Limpopo are Olifants and its headstream, the Crocodile. Plateau land (high veld), averaging 5000 to 6400 ft. covers nearly one third of province in SE; drained by Komati, Pongola, and other rivers flowing E to Indian Ocean. In W plateau slopes to ab. 4000 ft. average. Has abundant mineral resources, esp. gold in Witwatersrand near Johannesburg (richest gold field in the world) and diamonds around Pretoria; also deposits of platinum, coal, iron, silver, etc. Agriculture second to mining in importance; stock raising is main industry; grain, fruit, cotton also raised. Chief towns Pretoria, Johannesburg with suburbs of Germiston and Boksburg, Klerksdorp, Middelburg, and Barberton.

History: About 1800 region was sparsely inhabited by Bantu Negroes, Bushmen, and Hottentots; later dominated by Zulus; few white persons crossed Vaal before 1836 when great trek of Boers began; first settlement at

Potchefstroom 1838. Independence acknowledged by British in Sand River Convention 1852. South African Republic formed 1856; civil war, financial difficulties, discovery of diamonds 1867 led to loss of Griqualand West 1871 and annexation by British 1877–81; rebellion of Boers 1880–81 and restoration of republic 1881; discovery of gold 1886 brought in many foreigners (uitlanders); Jameson's Raid 1895; joined Orange Free State in war with Great Britain 1899–1900; annexed as Transvaal as British crown colony 1900; granted self-government 1906; joined Union of South Africa 1910.

Trans-Volta Togoland. See TOGOLAND.

Tran'syl·va'nia (trăn'sĭl·văn'yȧ; -vā'nĭ·ȧ). **1** County in North Carolina. See *Table* at NORTH CAROLINA.

2 *Rom.* **Tran'sil·va'nia** (trän'sĕl·vä'nyä); *Hung.* **Er'dély** (ĕr'dā). Region, NW and cen. Romania, a province 1918–40; 24,020 sq. m.; a plateau (averaging 1000 to 1600 ft.) of triangular shape, shut in on N, E, and S by the Carpathian Mts. and Transylvanian Alps and drained chiefly by tributaries of the Tisza, esp. the Someş and Mureş. In Roman times included in the province of Dacia; later overrun by various Germanic and other tribes; conquered by Hungarians 1003; settled after the 9th cent. in many places by Szeklers, Vlachs, and Saxons; called Siebenbürgen by the Saxons; set up as a principality 1540; subject to the Ottoman Empire in the 17th cent.; scene of frequent racial and religious disturbances; became a grand principality in 1765 within the Austro-Hungarian Empire; scene of much fighting in Revolution of 1848; became integral part of Hungary 1867; united with Romania 1918 but its N part assigned to Hungary by the Axis powers Aug. 30, 1940 (area ab. 17,040 sq. m., pop. 2,500,000); restored to Romania after World War II.

Tran'syl·va'nian Alps (trăn'sĭl·văn'yăn; -vā'nĭ·ăn); *sometimes* **South Carpathians.** Mountain range ab. 230 m. long extending E and W in cen. Romania, along the boundary bet. N Walachia and S Transylvania; highest point Negoi 8346 ft. See SOUTH CARPATHIANS.

Tra'pa·ni (trä'pä·nĕ). **1** Province of Italy. See *Table* at ITALY.

2 *anc.* **Drep'a·num** (drĕp'ȧ·nŭm). Seaport, ✳ of Trapani prov., Sicily, on Mediterranean Sea at NW tip of the island 48 m. W by S of Palermo; pop. 63,540; 17th-cent. cathedral; fine churches of 14th, 15th, and 17th cents.; exports salt, Marsala wine, fish. Founded by Carthaginians; important naval station in First Punic War (264–241 B.C.); scene of Carthaginian victory over Roman fleet 249 B.C.; according to Vergil's *Aeneid*, death place of Anchises; conquered by Vandals 440 A.D., Saracens 1077, and later by Normans who made it part of kingdom of the Two Sicilies.

Trapezus. See TRABZON.

Trappe, La. Monastery. See SOLIGNY-LA-TRAPPE.

Trap'per Peak (trăp'ĕr). Mountain 10,175 ft. on SW border of Ravalli co., W Montana.

Tras'i·mene (trăs'ĭ·mēn) *or* **Pe·ru'gia** (pȧ·rōō'jä), **Lake;** *Ital.* **Tra·si·me'no** (trä'zĕ·mâ'nô); *anc.* **Tras'-i·me'nus** (trăs'ĭ·mē'nŭs). Lake in Umbria, cen. Italy, 10 m. W of Perugia; scene of Hannibal's victory over the Romans 217 B.C.; also of severe fighting June 28–July 3, 1944 in World War II bet. British and German armies.

Trás-os-Mon'tes e Al'to Dou'ro (trȧ'zōōzh·mōNnt'zĕ äl'tŏō thŏ'rŏō); *formerly* **Trás-os-Mon'tes** (-mŏNn'tĕsh). Province of Portugal. See *Table* at PORTUGAL.

Tras·par'ga (träs·pär'gä). Commune, Lugo prov., NW Spain, 16 m. NW of Lugo; pop. 11,909.

Tras·te've·re (träs·tā'vā·rå). The region across the Tiber (*Ital.* Tevere) from Rome, Italy.

Trat (trät) *or* **Bang Phra** (bäng p'hrä). **1** Province, S Thailand; 1077 sq. m.; pop. 39,029; ✳ Trat.

2 Town and port, its ✳, on NE coast of Gulf of Siam near Cambodia border; end of highway from Bangkok.

Traù, Trau. See TROGIR.

Trau'ger (trô'gẽr). Locality, Westmoreland co., SW Pennsylvania, ab. 6 m. SE of Greensburg.

Traun (troun). River 112 m. long, W cen. Austria; rises in a series of lakes in the Salzkammergut and flows N out of Styria through the Hallstätter and Traun lakes in Upper Austria prov. into Danube river 4 m. below Linz.

Traun, Lake; *Ger.* **Traun'see'** (troun'zā'). Lake ab. 7 m. long and 2 m. wide in S Upper Austria prov. of Austria, formed by Traun river.

Traun'stein (troun'shtīn). Commune, Upper Bavaria govt. dist., S Bavaria, Germany; pop. (1933) 9886; salt springs and baths.

Trautenau. See TRUTNOV.

Trav'an·core (trăv'ăn·kōr). Region, former state, one of the Madras States, S Indian Union; 7662 sq. m.; pop. 6,070,018; ✳ Trivandrum; extends 150 m. along Malabar Coast as far S as Cape Comorin. Has many hills and valleys and within its borders Western Ghats reach height of 8000 ft. Chief stream the Periyar; ports are Alleppey and Quilon. Chief crop rice; has world's largest supply of monazite sand, source of thorium. Its ruler, the maharaja, was direct descendant of Hindu Chera dynasty of early Christian Era; since establishment of first British factory 1684 was always firm ally of British; formal treaty concluded 1795. See COCHIN, KERALA.

Tra'ven·dal (trä'vĕn·däl). Village, S Schleswig-Holstein state, Germany, 15 m. W of Lübeck; treaty signed here Aug. 18, 1700 by which Charles XII of Sweden forced a peace on the Danes.

Trav'erse (trăv'ẽrs). County in Minnesota. See *Table* at MINNESOTA.

Traverse, Lake. Lake 30 m. long on boundary bet. Roberts co., NE South Dakota, and Traverse co., W Minnesota; outlet on N is the Bois de Sioux river, headstream of Red River of the North.

Traverse City. City, ⊗ of Grand Traverse co., NW Michigan, at S end of W arm of Grand Traverse Bay; pop. 18,432; trade and supply center of a boating, fishing, and hunting region; former lumbering center.

Trav'is (trăv'ĭs). County in Texas. See *Table* at TEXAS.

Travis, Lake. See UNITED STATES, *Dams and Reservoirs* (Mansfield Dam).

Trav'nik (trăv'nĕk). Town, Bosnia and Herzegovina, W cen. Yugoslavia, 45 m. NW of Sarajevo; pop. 6803; stock-breeding center. Has Roman remains, a Turkish citadel; from 1686 to 1850 was capital of Bosnia.

Treas'ure (trĕzh'ẽr). County in Montana. See *Table* at MONTANA.

Treasure Island. Man-made island (begun 1936) in San Francisco Bay, California; site of Golden Gate International Exposition 1939, now a naval base.

Treas'ur·y Islands (trĕzh'ẽr·ĭ). Group of small islands off S end of Bougainville I. and SSW of Shortland Is., NW Solomon Is., W Pacific Ocean; includes Mono I. and Stirling I.; occupied by Americans Oct. 26–30, 1943.

Treb'bia (trĕb'byȧ); *anc.* **Tre'bi·a** (trē'bĭ·ȧ). River 71 m. long in NW Italy; rises NE of Genoa, flows N into Po river 3 m. NW of Piacenza; scene of two battles: (1) 218 B.C. in which Hannibal defeated the Romans under Publius Scipio; (2) June 17–19, 1799 in which Suvorov defeated the French under Macdonald.

Tře'bíč (tēr·zhĕ'bĕch); *Ger.* **Tre'bitsch** (trā'bĭch). Town, SW Moravia prov., cen. Czechoslovakia, 36 m. W of Brno; pop. (1930) 13,295.

Treb'i·zond (trĕb'ĭ·zŏnd). **1** Greek empire, 1204–1461, founded by Alexius I (Comnenus) as an offshoot of Byzantine Empire; included at greatest extent Georgia, Crimea, and the entire S shore of Black Sea E of Sakarya river; ✳ Trebizond (mod. Trabzon); last Greek state to be captured by Ottoman Turks 1461.

2 See TRABZON.

Tre·blin'ka (trĕ·blĕng'kä). German concentration camp on Bug river, cen. Poland, ab. 50 m. NE of Warsaw; during World War II site of an extermination camp, esp. for the Jews of the Warsaw ghetto.

Tre·ca'te (trā·kä'tā). Commune, Novara prov., NE Piedmont, NW Italy, E of Novara; pop. (1931) 10,068.

Tre·de'gar (trĕ·dē'gẽr). Urban district, Monmouthshire, W England, on the Sirhowy 33 m. WNW of Bristol; pop. 20,375; iron and steel manufacturing; coal.

Tre'go (trē'gō). County in Kansas. See *Table* at KANSAS.

Tre·grosse' Islets (trĕ·grōs'). Group of coral islets and reefs in Coral Sea outside Great Barrier Reef, Queensland, Australia, 17°30'S.

Tre'ia (trā'yä). Commune, Macerata prov., Marches, cen. Italy, 7 m. W of Macerata; pop. (1931) 10,642; 15th-cent. cathedral.

Trein'ta y Tres (trĕ'ĕn·tä [trän'tä] ē träs'). 1 Department of Uruguay. See *Table* at URUGUAY.
2 Town, its ✳, E Uruguay, 140 m. NE of Montevideo; pop. ab. 21,500.

Tré'la·tête', Ai'guille' de (ā'gü·ē'y' dē trā'lä'tât'). Peak 12,832 ft. in the French Alps, SW of Mont Blanc.

Tré'la·zé' (trā'lä'zā'). Commune, Maine-et-Loire dept., W France; pop. (1931) 6304; E suburb of Angers; slate quarries.

Tre·lew' (trā·lā'ŏŏ). Commercial town, NE Chubut territory, S Argentina, W of Rawson; pop. (est.) 7000; in sheep-raising district. Founded by Welshmen 1881.

Trel'le·borg *or* **Träl'le·borg** (trĕl'ĕ·bôr'y'). Seaport, Malmöhus prov., SW Sweden, on the Baltic Sea; pop. 15,311; shipping center; sugar refineries; machinery, rubber, and cement works.

Tre'mi·ti Islands (trā'mē·tē). Italian group of 5 small islands in Adriatic Sea N of Mount Gargano; largest island **San Do'mi·no** (sän dô'mē·nō), ab. 5 m. in circumference.

Tremonia. See DORTMUND.

Tre'mont (trē'mŏnt). Borough, Schuylkill co., E cen. Pennsylvania, 11 m. WSW of Pottsville; pop. 1893; coal mining; manufactures shirts, clothing.

Trem'pea·leau (trĕm'pä·lō). 1 River ab. 50 m. long, W Wisconsin; rises in W Jackson co., flows SW into Mississippi river on line bet. Buffalo and Trempealeau cos.
2 County in Wisconsin. See *Table* at WISCONSIN.

Tren'čín (trĕn'chēn); *Hung.* **Tren'csén** (trĕn'chän); *Ger.* **Trent'schin** (trĕn't'chĭn). Town, W Slovakia prov., E cen. Czechoslovakia, on the Váh river ab. 70 m. NE of Bratislava; pop. (1930) 11,796.

Treng·ga'nu (trĕng·gä'nŏŏ). 1 One of the nine states of the Federation of Malaya, in E part of S Malay Penin.; 5050 sq. m.; pop. 179,789, (1941 est.) 211,041; ✳ Kuala Trengganu; formerly one of the Unfederated States under British protection. Bounded on N and E by the South China Sea, on S and SW by Pahang, and on W by Kelantan; has several small islands some distance off the coast. Rice is chief product but has to be imported also; exports rubber, tin, iron, copra. Has several local industries, esp. the weaving of silk sarongs.
History: For several centuries disputed by Malacca and Siam until downfall of former; became British dependency 1909; overrun by Japanese Dec. 1941.
2 River ab. 70 m. long in Trengganu state; flows NE into South China Sea at Kuala Trengganu.

Trent (trĕnt). 1 River 40 m. long, SE North Carolina; flows W to E across Jones and Craven cos. into Neuse river at New Bern.
2 River ab. 150 m. long, Victoria, Peterborough, and Northumberland cos., SE Ontario, Canada; has its source in the Kawartha chain of lakes, thence flows S (here called the Otonabee) past Peterborough to Rice Lake, from which it winds generally SE to Trenton on the Bay of Quinte. Its entire course either used or paralleled by the **Trent Canal** system (or **Trent Waterways**); in W part canal connects Kawartha Lakes with Lake Simcoe and thence by Severn river to Georgian Bay, total length 224 m. and 42 locks. Also it has branch S by way of Scugog river past Lindsay, ab. 35 m.
3 River 170 m. long in cen. England; rises in Stafford-

shire, flows NNE and unites with the Ouse ab. 15 m. W of Hull to form the Humber; navigable as far as Gainsborough.
4 *Ital.* **Tren'to** (trän'tō); *Ger.* **Tri·ent'** (trē·ĕnt'); *anc.* **Tri·den'tum** (trī·dĕn'tŭm). Commune, ✳ of Trento prov., Venezia Tridentina, NE Italy, on Adige river 106 m. ENE of Milan; pop. 56,017; manufactures pottery, silks, wine, confections; buildings include 16th-cent. town hall, 12th-cent. cathedral, and 16th-cent. church of Santa Maria Maggiore.
History: Thought to have been founded by Celts 4th cent. B.C.; fortified by Augustus; point of departure for expedition 15 B.C. of Drusus Senior; in Christian era, captured by Ostrogoths, Lombards, and Franks; became episcopal principality 11th cent. A.D.; passed to Austria 16th cent.; seat of famous Council of Trent 1545–63; center of Italian Irridentist agitation 19th cent.; ceded to Italy by Treaty of St-Germain 1919.

Tren·ti'no (trän·tē'nō). Region in NE Italy, roughly equivalent to Trento prov., Venezia Tridentina, NE Italy; formerly the Italian-speaking portion of S Tirol, annexed to Austria 1814. Scene of much fighting throughout World War I; by Treaty of St-Germain 1919 ceded to Italy as part of Venetia.

Tren'to (trän'tō). 1 Province of Italy. See *Table* at ITALY.
2 See TRENT.

Tren'ton (trĕn't'n; -tŭn). 1 City, ⊗ of Gilchrist co., NW Florida penin.; pop. 941.
2 Town, ⊗ of Dade co., NW corner of Georgia; pop. 1301.
3 City, Wayne co., SE Michigan, on Detroit river 15 m. SSW of Detroit; pop. 18,439; trading center in agricultural section; limestone deposits.
4 City, ⊗ of Grundy co., N Missouri, 22 m. N of Chillicothe; pop. 6262; trade center in grain, livestock-raising, and coal-mining section.
5 Village, ⊗ of Hitchcock co., S Nebraska; pop. 914.
6 Manufacturing city, ✳ of New Jersey and ⊗ of Mercer co., W cen. New Jersey, at head of navigation on Delaware river 28 m. NE of Philadelphia; pop. 114,167; manufactures wire rope and cables, pottery and porcelain, rubber goods, cigars, linoleum, parachutes, airplane equipment, woolens, foundry products. New Jersey State College (1855; coed.); Rider Coll. (1865; coed.). Battle monument (estab. 1893; marks spot where Washington opened fire on British 1776).
History: Settled by English Quakers c. 1679; became trade center and shipping point for grain, etc.; incorporated as borough and town under royal grant 1745; surrendered charter voluntarily 1750; remained part of Trenton township until beginning of constitutional period; scene of Provincial Congress meeting 1775; important center in Revolution; near Washington Crossing, where Washington crossed the Delaware 1776; scene of capture of Hessian garrison in surprise attack (battle of Trenton Dec. 26, 1776); proposed as capital of the U.S. 1783, but defeated by opposition of southern states; made state capital 1790; incorporated as city 1792; temporary headquarters of Federal government during epidemics in Philadelphia before removal of national offices to Washington; became industrially more active following construction of bridge across Delaware river 1806, development of a canal connecting the Delaware and Raritan rivers, building of railroad, etc.; became port for seagoing vessels 1932.
7 Town, ⊗ of Jones co., SE North Carolina; pop. 404.
8 City, ⊗ of Gibson co., NW Tennessee, 26 m. NNW of Jackson; pop. 4225; taken from Union forces by Gen. Forrest 1862; produces cotton, fruit, livestock; cotton gins, cotton and cottonseed-oil mills, lumber yards.
9 Town, Pictou co., N Nova Scotia, Canada, on Pictou Harbor 3 m. N of New Glasgow; pop. 3089.
10 Industrial town, Hastings co., SE Ontario, Canada, on Bay of Quinte 12 m. W of Belleville; pop. 10,085; exports timber; E terminus of Trent Canal system.

Trenton Falls. Cascades in West Canada Creek, cen. New York, 15 m. N of Utica; furnish water power for Utica; the creek cuts through limestone which was laid down in what geologists call the Trenton period, named after these formations.

Trentschin. See TRENČÍN.

Tre·pas′sey (trĕ-păs′ĭ). Seaport town, SE Newfoundland, on inlet of Atlantic 65 m. SSW of St. John's; pop. 552; base for transatlantic airplane flights.

Tréport, Le. See LE TRÉPORT.

Treptow am Rega. See TRZEBIATÓW.

Tres Ar·ro′yos (trās är-rō′yŏs). City, Buenos Aires prov., E Argentina, ab. 70 m. NE of Bahía Blanca and nearly 300 m. SW of Buenos Aires; pop. (est.) ab. 52,000; agricultural and cattle-raising center.

Tresck′ow (trĕs′kō). Locality, Carbon co., E Pennsylvania, ab. 2 m. SE of Hazleton; pop. 1145.

Tres Cru′ces (trās krōō′sās). Mountain 20,853 ft. in N Chile, NE of Copiapó, on Argentine boundary.

Tres For′cas, Cape (trās fôr′käs). Cape on NE coast of Morocco; Melilla is on it.

Tres Ma·rí′as (trās mä-rē′äs). Group of small islands in the Pacific Ocean, off the state of Nayarit, W Mexico, comprising María Madre, María Magdalena, María Cleofás, and San Juanito.

Tres Mon′tes Gulf (trās môn′tās). Inlet of Gulf of Peñas on S coast of Taitao Penin., SW Chile.

Tres Montes Peninsula. Peninsula extending from SW Taitao Penin., SW Chile.

Tres Mor′ros (trās môr′rōs) *or* **So·cor′ro** (sŏ-kôr′rō). Peak 11,155 ft. in NW cen. Colombia, in the Cordillera Occidental.

Tres Pun′tas, Cape (trās pōōn′täs). **1** Cape on NE coast of Santa Cruz territory, S Argentina, at S side of entrance to the Gulf of San Jorge.
2 Cape in E Guatemala, extending into the Gulf of Honduras and enclosing Honduras Bay.

Tres Tabernae. See SAVERNE.

Tres Za·po′tes (trās sä-pō′tās). Village just W of San Andrés Tuxtla in E Veracruz state, E Mexico; colossal sculptured head of stone and inscribed monuments, chiefly of a pre-Maya culture dating back nearly 300 years B.C.; discovered 1939.

Treut′len (troot′lĕn). County in Georgia. See *Table* at GEORGIA.

Tre Venezie. See VENETIA.

Treves *or* **Trèves.** See TRIER city.

Tre·vi′glio (trā-vēl′yō). Commune, Bergamo prov., Lombardy, N Italy, 12 m. SSW of Bergamo; pop. 19,164.

Tre·vi′ño (trā-vē′nyō). Exclave of Burgos in Álava prov., Spain.

Tre·vi′so (trā-vē′zō). **1** Province of Italy. See *Table* at ITALY.
2 *anc.* **Tar·vi′si·um** (tär-vĭzh′ĭ-ŭm). Commune, its ✻, Venezia Euganea, NE Italy, 17 m. N by W of Venice; pop. 53,886; surrounded by medieval ramparts; 11th-cent. cathedral, 13th-cent. palaces, 12th-cent. Loggia dei Cavalieri.
  History: Ancient Roman municipium; center of Lombard duchy; taken by Charlemagne 776 A.D. and made center of March of Treviso; independent from 1020; supported Lombard League against Emperor Frederick I 12th cent.; under the Ghibelline leader Ezzelino da Romano 1237–59; passed to Venice 1389, Austria 1797, kingdom of Naples 1805, Austria 1815, Italy 1866; bombed from air in World War I.

Trev′or·ton (trĕv′ĕr-t'n; -tŭn). Locality, Northumberland co., E cen. Pennsylvania, ab. 6 m. W of Shamokin; pop. 2597.

Tre·vose′ Head (trĕ-vōs′). Promontory on W coast of Cornwall, SW England; lighthouse.

Tré′voux′ (trā′vōō′). Commune, SW Ain dept., E France, on the Saône; pop. (1931) 3093; capital of Dombes 11th–16th cent.; noted for Jesuit press 1801–30 which published a newspaper and a dictionary.

Triangle, the. A name formerly given to the loosely administered territory, ab. 59,000 sq. m., of E Burma, formed by the Northern Shan and Southern Shan States and Karenni dist.; base of the triangle was roughly the 96th meridian.

Trib′une (trĭb′ūn). City, ⊗ of Greeley co., W Kansas; pop. 1036.

Tricca. See TRIKKALA city.

Trich′i·nop′o·ly (trĭch′ĭ-nŏp′ō-lĭ) *or* **Ti·ru′chi·rap′al·li** (tĭ-rōōch′ĭ-răp′ā·lĭ). City, cen. Madras state, S India, on right bank of the Cauvery river 200 m. SSW of Madras; pop. (1941) 159,566; important rail and trade center; silk mills, soap and cigar factories, jewelry industry. Has several notable Dravidian temples and ruins of an old fort which encloses the Rock of Trichinopoly (273 ft.). Scene of fighting bet. French and English during Carnatic wars 1749 to 1761; annexed by British 1801.

Tri·chur′ (trĭ-chōōr′). Town, N Kerala state, S Indian Union, 40 m. N of Cochin; pop. (1941) 57,524; site of one of India's oldest temples.

Tridentine Alps. = *Dolomites:* see *Table* at ALPS.

Tridentum. See TRENT commune, Italy.

Trient. See TRENT commune, Italy.

Trier (trēr; *Ger.* trēr). **1** Government district of former Rhine Province, Prussia, Germany; 2200 sq. m.
2 *Eng.* **Treves** (trēvz); *Fr.* **Trèves** (trâv); *anc.* **Augus′ta Trev′e·ro′rum** (ô-gŭs′tà trĕv′ĕ-rōr′ŭm). Manufacturing city, its ✻, on Moselle river near Luxembourg border 58 m. SW of Koblenz; pop. 58,140; contains most important Roman remains in N Europe, which include a large amphitheater built by Trajan, the Porta Nigra (a fortified gate), baths, imperial palace, piers of bridge across Moselle; 13th-cent. Gothic church; fine cathedral; manufactures iron goods, textiles, leather, machinery; lead and copper mines and gypsum quarries nearby; center of Moselle vineyards. One of most ancient towns in cen. Europe, ancient capital of the Treviri or Treveri; occasional Roman imperial residence; first episcopal see in N Europe; seat of powerful archbishops until beginning of 19th cent.; capital of former French department of the Sarre under Napoleon; passed to Prussia after fall of Napoleon; in World War II captured by American armies Mar. 1–2, 1945. Since 1945 in Rhineland-Palatinate state of West Germany.

Tri·e′ste (trē·ĕs′tà; *Angl.* trē·ĕst′). **1** Former province of Italy. See *Table* at ITALY.
2 *Ger.* **Tri·est′** (trē·ĕst′); *Serbo-Croatian* **Trst** (tûrst); *anc.* **Ter·ges′te** (tĕr·jĕs′tĕ). Commercial seaport at head of the Adriatic Sea on the **Gulf of Trieste**, bet. NE Italy and NW Yugoslavia on NW side of Istrian Penin.; pop. 248,379; has university and professional schools; zoological station; numerous museums and fine public library; cathedral of 11th or 14th cent.; remains of ancient Roman theater and aqueduct; tourist resort; manufactures include ships, oil, blast-furnace products, silk, jute, liquors, soap; formerly headquarters of Austrian Lloyd.
  History: Became Roman colony under Augustus; under episcopal rule from 10th cent.; became free at end of 13th cent.; under Austrian rule 1382 ff.; made free port 1719 by Emperor Charles VI (remaining so till 1891); under French rule 1809–14; reverted to Austria 1814; Austrian crownland 1867 ff.; ceded to Italy by Treaty of St-Germain 1919; became capital of Trieste prov., Venezia Giulia e Zara compartimento, Italy; in World War II taken by the Yugoslavs May 1945.
3 *in full* **Free Territory of Trieste.** Area on the W side of Istrian Penin., surrounding and including city of Trieste, established 1947 as a free territory under the United Nations; divided for administrative purposes into two zones: Zone A in N, including city, 86 sq. m., pop. (1951 est.) 292,000, under British and Americans; Zone B in S, 199 sq. m., pop. (1949 est.) 70,000, under Yugoslavs; Zone B virtually incorporated into Yugoslavia; Zone A turned over to Italy 1953.

Trigarta. See JULLUNDUR.

Trigg (trĭg). County in Kentucky. See *Table* at KENTUCKY.

Trig·gia′no (trēd·jä′nô). Commune, Bari prov., Apulia, SE Italy, near the Adriatic 5 m. ESE of Bari; pop. (1931) 12,557.

Tri′glav (trē′gläv); *Ger.* **Ter′glou** (tĕr′glōō). Highest peak 9394 ft. in the Julian Alps, NW Yugoslavia, near Italian border.

Tri′gnac′ (trē′nyȧk′). Commune, Loire-Atlantique dept., NW France, near Saint-Nazaire; pop. (1931) 5671; iron foundries.

Trik′ka·la (trĭk′ȧ·lȧ; *Gr.* trē′kä·lä). **1** Department of Greece. See *Table* at GREECE.

2 *anc.* **Tric′ca** (trĭk′ȧ). City, its ✱, W Thessaly, cen. Greece, N of Salambria river and ab. 35 m. W of Larissa; pop. 18,682. Temple of Asclepius anciently situated here.

Tril′by (trĭl′bĭ). Village, Lucas co., NW Ohio, ab. 7 m. NW of Toledo; pop. (est.) 3500.

Trim (trĭm). Urban district, ⊗ of co. Meath, E Eire, on the Boyne; pop. 1455; ruins of 12th-cent. castle which housed several Irish parliaments (to 15th cent.) and a mint.

Trim′ble (trĭm′b'l). County in Kentucky. See *Table* at KENTUCKY.

Trinacria. See SICILY.

Trin·che′ra Peak (trĭn·châr′ȧ). Mountain 13,540 ft. in Las Animas, Costilla, and Huerfano cos., S Colorado.

Trin·co·ma·lee′ or **Trin·ko·ma·li′** (trĭng′kô·mȧ·lē′). Seaport town, ✱ of Eastern Province in N part, E Ceylon, on Bay of Bengal 110 m. SE of Jaffna; pop. 10,160; built on a peninsula on N side of Bay of Trincomalee; has one of world's greatest natural harbors, but, since it is not on the regular sea lanes, has comparatively little trade; exports rice, coconuts, timber, tobacco, dried fish. One of first Tamil settlements in Ceylon, has ruins of "Temple of a Thousand Columns," a place of pilgrimage before destruction by Portuguese in 1622. Taken by Portuguese 1622, by Dutch 1639, by French 1673, recovered by Dutch 1674; retaken by French 1782; taken by British 1795. Former British fleet station; in World War II after loss of Singapore, chief British naval station in Far East; bombed by Japanese Apr. 1942. British control of base ceased 1958.

Tring (trĭng). Urban district, Hertfordshire, SE England, 30 m. NW of London; pop. 5018; small industries; natural-history museum, estab. by Lionel Walter, 2d Baron Rothschild.

Trin′i·dad (trĭn′ĭ·dăd). **1** Commercial city, ⊗ of Las Animas co., SE Colorado, on Purgatoire river 80 m. S of Pueblo; pop. 10,691; made ⊗ 1866; incorp. as town 1866; coal-mining and agricultural center; ships cattle, wool, coal; manufactures dairy products, lumber, brick and tile.

2 *Port.* **Trin·da′de** (trēɴn·dȧ′thĕ). Small rocky volcanic island, South Atlantic Ocean, 20°30′32″S, 29°50′W; belongs to Brazil.

3 Island of the West Indies in the Atlantic Ocean off NE coast of Venezuela; 1864 sq. m.; pop. 792,624; chief town Port of Spain, ✱ of Trinidad and Tobago (*q.v.*). See *Map* at LESSER ANTILLES. Nearly square in shape with two peninsulas extending from NW and SW corners enclosing the Gulf of Paria, the N peninsula and adjacent islands are separated by channel of Dragon's Mouths from Paria Penin. of Venezuela. Ranges of hills along N and S shores, several swamp areas on E and W, and Pitch Lake with large asphalt deposits at La Brea in SW. In addition to asphalt and petroleum chief exports are sugar, cocoa, lime oil, bitters, tonka beans, and rum. Discovered by Columbus July 31, 1498; Spanish settlement made ab. 1577 but destroyed by Sir Walter Raleigh 1595; occupied by British 1797 and ceded to Great Britain by Treaty of Amiens 1802; in World War II in 1942 four areas leased to U.S. for seaplane base and naval station; two largest were on N shore of Gulf of Paria and in N cen. part. See TRINIDAD AND TOBAGO.

Trin′i·dad (trĭn′ĭ·dăd; *Span.* trē′nē·thä[th]′). **1** Island in Bahía Blanca, a bay on SE coast of Buenos Aires prov., Argentina.

2 Town, ✱ of El Beni dept., N Bolivia, ab. 6 m. E of the Mamoré river; pop. (1943 est.) 8000; cattle market.

3 Peak 3206 ft. in S Las Villas prov., W cen. Cuba.

4 Municipality and town, Las Villas prov., W cen. Cuba; town near S coast 40 m. S of Santa Clara, pop. 15,453. Founded 1514.

5 Town, ✱ of Flores dept., SW Uruguay, 105 m. NNW of Montevideo; pop. ab. 15,700.

Trinidad, La. See LA TRINIDAD.

Trin′i·dad and To·ba′go (trĭn′ĭ·dăd, tô·bā′gō). Dominion of the British Commonwealth, formerly a territory of the West Indies Federation and until 1958 a colony of the British West Indies; comprises the islands of Trinidad and Tobago; 1980 sq. m.; pop. 827,957; ✱ Port of Spain. By order in council Oct. 1898 union of two islands authorized and colony brought into effect Jan. 1, 1899. For *Histories,* see TRINIDAD island and TOBAGO.

Trin′i·dad Gulf (trĭn′ĭ·dăd). Inlet of Pacific Ocean SW of S Wellington I., off SW coast of Chile.

Tri′nil (trē′nĭl. Village on Solo river, Surakarta, S cen. Java, at base of Mt. Lawu. Fossil skullcap found here 1891 and additional parts found 1936–37 of Java man or Trinil man (*Pithecanthropus erectus*).

Tri·ni·ta′po·li (trē·nē·tä′pô·lē). Commune, Foggia prov., Apulia, SE Italy, on S shore of Lake Salpi 29 m. ESE of Foggia; pop. 12,424.

Trinité, La. See LA TRINITÉ.

Trin′i·ty (trĭn′ĭ·tĭ). **1** River ab. 130 m. long, NW California; rises in NE Trinity co., flows SW and then NW into the Klamath river.

2 River 360 m. long, E Texas; formed by confluence of West Fork and Elm Fork just NW of Dallas; flows SE into Trinity Bay.

3 Name of counties in two states of the U.S. See *Tables* at CALIFORNIA and TEXAS.

4 City, Trinity co., E Texas, on Trinity river 45 m. SW of Lufkin; pop. 1787; railroad center.

5 Seaport, E Newfoundland, at mouth of Trinity Bay 65 m. NNW of St. John's; pop. 780; has fine harbor and is an active whaling and fishing port.

Trinity, Cape. Promontory 1700 ft. high, Quebec, Canada, on S shore of Saguenay river ab. 40 m. from its mouth and opp. Cape Eternity (*q.v.*).

Trinity Bay. **1** Northeast arm of Galveston Bay, Texas.

2 Inlet of Pacific Ocean forming the harbor of Cairns, Queensland, NE Australia.

3 Inlet ab. 75 m. long in SE Newfoundland; terminal of first Atlantic cable from Ireland 1866.

Trinity Peak. Mountain 9473 ft. in N Elmore co., SW cen. Idaho.

Trinity Peaks. Mountain 13,811 ft. in San Juan co., SW Colorado.

Trinity Range. Range in NW Nevada chiefly in W Pershing co.

Trinkomali. See TRINCOMALEE.

Tri′no (trē′nô). Commune, Vercelli prov., Piedmont, NW Italy, 12 m. SW of Vercelli; pop. 10,702.

Tri′on (trī′ŏn). Town, Chattooga co., NW Georgia, 22 m. NNW of Rome; pop. 2227.

Tri·phyl′i·a (trī·fĭl′ĭ·ȧ). Southern district of ancient Elis (*q.v.*) in W Peloponnesus, S Greece, **S** of the Alpheus river.

Tri′ple Di·vide′ Peak (trĭp′l dĭ·vīd′). **1** Mountain 11,613 ft. in Sierra Nevada in E Madera co., cen. California.

2 Peak 12,651 ft. in Sierra Nevada in N Tulare co., S cen. California, on border bet. Kings Canyon National Park and Sequoia National Park.

3 Mountain 8001 ft. in Glacier National Park, NW Mon-

tana. Water from the sides of this peak flows into three oceans, Pacific, Arctic, and Atlantic.

Trip′o·li (trĭp′ô·lĭ). **1** Region in N Africa; originally a Phoenician colony, **Trip′o·lis** (trĭp′ô·lĭs), literally "with three cities," named for its three chief cities Oea (Tripoli), Leptis Magna, and Sabrata, founded on the coast bet. Syrtis Major and Syrtis Minor; the E part of Carthaginian territory; under Romans called **Re′gi·o Syr′ti·ca** (rē′jǐ·ō sûr′tǐ·kȧ) until made a separate province, **Trip′o·li·ta′na** (trĭp′ô·lǐ·tā′nȧ; trĭ·pŏl′ǐ-), by Septimus Severus (193–211 A.D.); overrun by Vandals 5th cent.; recaptured 534 by Belisarius (see BYZANTINE EMPIRE); conquered by Islam in 7th cent.; ruled by successive Arab and Berber dynasties; the city of Tripoli captured by Ferdinand the Catholic 1510 and entrusted by Spanish to Knights of St. John (cf. MALTA) 1530–51; state became part of Ottoman Empire 1551 (Pashalik of Tripoli); achieved practical independence 1714; one of the Barbary States (see BARBARY), engaged in piracy; after war with United States 1801–05 (in which Decatur burned the *Philadelphia* in Tripoli harbor) and U.S. war with Algiers (q.v.) 1815, ceased to levy tribute on U.S. ships; became vilayet under direct Turkish administration 1835; long the object of Italian designs, finally ceded to Italy by Turkey as result of Tripolitan War (1911–12); under Italians the entire W part of colony of Libya (q.v.) 1912–19 became known as **Trip′o·li·ta′nia** (trĭp′-ô·lǐ·tān′yȧ; trĭ·pŏl′ǐ-; *Ital.* trĕ·pô·lĕ·tä′nyä); interior not conquered until after World War I; separated from Cyrenaica 1919, reunited 1929; in 1934 settled portion in N divided into four provinces for administrative purposes, one of which was Tripoli (see 2, below).
2 Former province of NW (Italian) Libya, N Africa; 73,803 sq. m.; pop. (1936) 351,774.
3 *Arab.* **Ta·ra′bu·lus el Gharb** (tȯ·rä′bŏō·lŏŏs ăl gȯrb′); *anc.* **Oe′a** (ē′ȧ). City, N Tripolitania, ✳ of Tripolitania and of Libya, N Africa; pop. (1958) 172,202; built on a promontory with sheltered harbor on E; remains of walls date from Roman times; Spanish citadel and Turkish mosques; modern part of city built by Italians. Site of Wheelus Field, U.S. Air Force base. Held by Axis powers 1941–42 but surrendered to British Jan. 24, 1943. See also 1, above.
4 *Arab.* **Ta·ra′bu·lus esh Sham** (tȯ·rä′bŏō·lŏŏs ăsh shăm′); *anc.* **Trip′o·lis** (trĭp′ô·lĭs). Commercial town and seaport, NW Lebanon republic, 43 m. NNE of Beirut; pop. (1935) 37,260; has active export trade in oranges, eggs, and cotton; connected by rail via Homs and Damascus with Turkey and Jordan; terminal of oil pipeline from Iraq; airport. Founded probably in 7th cent. B.C.; capital of **Tripolis**, a Phoenician federation of three cities (Greek *tripolis*, literally "with three cities"): Sidon, Tyre, and Aradus; held by Seleucids and Romans and taken by Moslems 638; after 5-year siege during Crusades taken 1109 and its great library destroyed; often fought for by princes of Alep and Acre; occupied by British 1918 and by British and Free French 1941.
5 Medieval county in Syria, N of the kingdom of Jerusalem; ✳ Tripoli.
Trip′o·lis (trĭp′ô·lĭs; *Mod. Gr.* trē′pô·lyĕs). **1** *also called* **Tri′po·li′tsa** *or* **Tri′po·li′tza** (trē′pô·lyē′tsä). City, ✳ of Arcadia dept., cen. Peloponnesus, S Greece; pop. 14,397; manufactures leather goods, tapestries. Regional capital under Turks; taken by Greek insurgents 1821; retaken and destroyed by Ibrahim Pasha 1825.
2 Ancient Phoenician colony in N Africa. See TRIPOLI, 1.
3 Ancient confederacy in Phoenicia comprising Sidon, Tyre, and Aradus; ✳ Tripolis. See TRIPOLI, 4.
Tripolitana. See TRIPOLI region.
Tripolitania. Province, W part of Libya, N Africa; ✳ Tripoli; ab. 136,250 sq. m.; pop. 746,064. See TRIPOLI.
Tripp (trĭp). County in South Dakota. See *Table* at SOUTH DAKOTA.

Tri′pu·ra (trē′pŏō·rä); *formerly known as* **Hill Tip′-pe·ra** (tĭp′ĕ·rä). Territory, NE Indian Union; 4049 sq. m.; pop. (1941) 513,010; ✳ Agartala; formerly one of the states in the Eastern States Agency. On N, W, and S borders on East Bengal, Pakistan. Area comprises parallel ranges of hills (highest 3200 ft.), covered with forests and jungle and the shelter of many wild animals; by tradition connected with very ancient kingdom; conquered by Moguls in 1733; since 1808 in direct relations with British government.
Tris′tan da Cu′nha (trĭs′tăn dȧ kōō′nȧ). Island in the South Atlantic Ocean; 45 sq. m.; highest point 7640 ft.; pop. (1944) 222; important meteorological and radio station; chief of the **Tristan da Cunha Islands,** a group of British volcanic islands in ab. lat. 37° to 39°S and long. 11°10′ to 12°15′W, which include also Gough, Inaccessible, and Nightingale Is.; total area 52 sq. m.; since Jan. 12, 1938 a dependency of St. Helena I.
Tris′te, Gol′fo (gôl′fô trĕs′tä). Bay on the N coast of Venezuela, bet. Carabobo and Falcón states, W of Caracas.
Tri·sul′ (trĭ·sōōl′). Peak 23,382 ft. in the Himalayas, United Provinces, N Indian Union.
Tri′umph, Mount (trī′ŭmf). Peak 7150 ft. in Skagit co., NW Washington.
Tri·van′drum (trĭ·văn′drŭm). Seaport city, ✳ of Kerala state and formerly ✳ of Travancore and Cochin state, SW India, on Arabian Sea 140 m. SW of Madura; pop. (1941) 128,365; built around old fort containing palaces and temple, visited by pilgrims; has maharaja's palace, observatory, zoological garden, and museum. Seat of maharaja's college, Sanskrit college.
Tr′na·va (tûr′nȧ·vȧ); *Hung.* **Nagy′szom·bat′** (nŏd′y′-sŏm·bŏt′); *Ger.* **Tyr′nau** (tür′nou). Town, SW Slovakia prov., E cen. Czechoslovakia, 23 m. NE of Bratislava; pop. (1930) 23,971; market town; manufactures esp. cloth; Gothic cathedral, dating from 14th cent.
Tr′no·va′ny (tûr′nô·vä′nǐ); *Ger.* **Turn** (tŏŏrn). Town, NW Bohemia prov., W Czechoslovakia, on the Ohře river 40 m. WNW of Prague; pop. (1930) 16,637.
Tr′no·vo (tûr′nô·vô) *or* **Tir′no·vo** (tûr′-). City, N cen. Bulgaria, 55 m. ESE of Pleven on the Yantra river; pop. (1926) 12,750; former capital of Bulgaria 1186 to 1394, replaced 1879 by Sofia. Remarkably situated in a deep gorge with two high promontories and a connecting ridge. Probably in early times a Roman fortress and an important city under the Bulgars; held by Turks from 1394 to 1877; independent kingdom of Bulgaria proclaimed here Oct. 5, 1908.
Tro *or* **Tro La** (trō lä). Mountain pass (*la*) 17,100 ft. in E part of the Tanglha Range, W Sikang, China, on highway bet. Lhasa and Chamdo.
Tro′as (trō′ăs). **1** *or* **the Tro′ad** (trō′ăd). Territory surrounding the ancient city of Troy in NW Mysia, Asia Minor, extending along Aegean coast from the Sigeum promontory (mod. Yeniṣehir) S to Cape Lectum (mod. Baba) and eastward to include the Ida Mts. and plain of Scamander river (mod. Menderes).
2 *later* **Al′ex·an′dri·a Troas** (ăl′ĕg·zăn′drǐ·ȧ; ăl′ĭg-; *Brit. also* -zän′-). Seaport of Mysia, in SW part of the ancient region of the Troas, and S of the site of Troy; visited by St. Paul on his second (*Acts* xvi. 8–11) and third journeys.
Tro′bri·and Islands (trō′brē·änd). Group of small coral islands in Solomon Sea N of E end of New Guinea I. and N of D'Entrecasteaux Is., largest Kiriwina I.; total area 170 sq. m.; pop. ab. 8500; chief town Losuia; attached to the Territory of Papua. According to some includes Woodlark I. group. Natives are Melanesian with noticeable Polynesian traits. Has fertile soil; grows esp. yams; produces pearl shell, pearls, and bêche-de-mer. Occupied by Allies June 30, 1943.
Troe′zen (trē′z'n; -zĕn). Town, SE ancient Argolis, E Peloponnesus, S Greece, near the coast of the Saronic Gulf; celebrated in mythology as the home of Theseus.

Tro′gen (trō′gĕn). Commune, Appenzell Outer Rhodes demicanton, NE Switzerland, ab. 5 m. SE of St. Gallen; pop. (1930) 1967.

Tro′gir (trō′gĕr); *Ital.* **Tra·ù′** (trä·ōō′); *Ger.* **Trau** (trou); *anc.* **Tra·gu′ri·um** (trȧ·gūr′ĭ·ŭm). Seaport, Dalmatia, W Yugoslavia, near Split; pop. 23,468; located on an island joined to mainland by a bridge; cathedral, dating in part from 13th cent., Dominican monastery, museum. Colonized by Greeks from Syracuse in 4th cent. B.C.; since medieval times has been held by many states (Venice, Hungary, Byzantium, Italy); since 1918 in Yugoslavia.

Troia. See TROY ancient ruined city.

Tro·i′na (trō·ē′nä). Commune, Enna prov., cen. Sicily, 24 m. NE of Enna on W slope of Mt. Etna; pop. 12,024; Capuchin convent. In World War II scene of severe fighting July 29–Aug. 5, 1943.

Trois–Évêchés, Les. See LES TROIS-ÉVÊCHÉS.

Trois Pis′toles′ (trwä′ pēs·tôl′). Town, Témiscouata co., S Quebec, Canada, on right bank of St. Lawrence river 25 m. NE of Rivière du Loup; pop. 3537; summer resort; agricultural center.

Trois-Ri′vières′ (trwä′rē′vyâr′). **1** See THREE RIVERS city, Canada.

2 Maritime village, S Basse-Terre, Guadeloupe; pop. ab. 9000.

Tro′itsk (trô′ĭtsk; troitsk). City, S Chelyabinsk Region, Soviet Russia, Asia, on a tributary of the upper Tobol river 75 m. S of Chelyabinsk; pop. 40,500; railroad junction point; supply and trading center for the S Ural mining district.

Troja. See TROY.

Tro La. See TRO.

Trold′tin′der (trôl′tĭn′ĕr). Mountain, Norway. See ROMSDAL.

Troll′hät′tan (trôl′hĕt′än). Town, Älvsborg prov., SW Sweden, on Göta river near Lake Vänern; pop. 20,091; falls in the river here which descends 108 ft. in ab. 1 m. provide water power for the hydroelectric works; rolling mills, chemical works, cellulose factories.

Trom·be′tas (trōNm·bā′tȧs). River ab. 350 m. long in NW Pará state, N Brazil; flows S from British Guiana border into Amazon river.

Tro′me·lin′ (trôm′lăN′). Small French island in the Indian Ocean 260 m. off NE Madagascar in 54°E long.

Tro′men (trō′mĕn). Volcanic peak 12,795 ft. in N Neuquén territory, W Argentina.

Troms (trŏms; trōōms). County in Norway. See *Table* at NORWAY.

Troms′ö′ (trŏm′sû′; trōōm′sû′; *Angl.* trŏm′sō′). Seaport, ⊗ of Troms co., N Norway, located on a small island bet. South Kvalöy and the mainland; pop. 10,336; chief city in N Norway; founded c. 1870 esp. as a center for herring fisheries; shipbuilding yards; exports fish, fish products, and furs.

Tro′na (trō′nȧ). Village, NW San Bernardino co., SE California, on Searles Lake; pop. 1138; produces potassium chloride, borax, and soda products.

Tronador, El. See EL TRONADOR.

Tron′chiennes′ (trôn′shyĕn′). Commune, East Flanders prov., NW cen. Belgium, just W of Gent; pop. 5799.

Trond′heim (trôn′hām), *formerly* **Trond′hjem** (trôn′yĕm); *also* **Ni′dar·os′** (nē′dä·rōs′; -rōōs′). Fortified seaport, ⊗ of Sör-Tröndelag co., cen. Norway, on S side of Trondheim Fjord; pop. 54,458; 3d largest city in Norway; commercial center in agricultural section; hydroelectric power plant; shipbuilding yards; exports fish, lumber, copper ore, wood pulp; museum; has technical university for engineering courses. Founded 996 by Olaf Tryggvesson; has finest cathedral in Norway where all kings are required to be crowned; capital to 1380; occupied by Germans Apr. 9, 1940 and used as German base in campaign in Norway Apr.–June 1940.

Trondheim Fjord. Inlet of Norwegian Sea on lower W cen. coast of Norway; extends inland 80 m.

Tro′noh (trō′nō). Town, cen. Perak state, Federation of Malaya, SSW of Ipoh; rich tin mines.

Tron′to (trŏn′tō; *Ital.* trôn′tō). River ab. 50 m. long, cen. Italy; flows N and E to the Adriatic.

Tro′o·dos *or* **Tro′ö·dos** (trō′ô·thôs). Mountain 6403 ft., highest point on island of Cyprus, in W cen. part.

Troon (trōōn). Burgh, Ayr co., SW Scotland; pop. 8544; watering place; shipbuilding, coal and iron exporting.

Trop′a·co Point (trŏp′ȧ·kō). Cape on N coast of St. Thomas I., Virgin Is. of the United States, West Indies, on W side of Magens Bay.

Troppau. See OPAVA.

Tros′sachs (trŏs′ăks; -ăks). Wooded valley in Perth co., cen. Scotland, bet. Loch Katrine and Loch Achray; immortalized by Scott's *Lady of the Lake* and *Rob Roy*.

Trotskoe. See GATCHINA.

Troup (trōōp). **1** County in Georgia. See *Table* at GEORGIA.

2 City, Cherokee and Smith cos., E Texas, 18 m. SSE of Tyler; pop. 1667.

Trous′dale (trouz′dāl). County in Tennessee. See *Table* at TENNESSEE.

Trout Lake (trout). Name of several lakes in Canada, esp.: (1) A source of English river, SW Ontario, 134 sq. m. (2) Source of Mattawa river, SE Ontario, separated from Lake Nipissing to the W by watershed.

Trou′ville′–sur–Mer (trōō′vēl′sür·mâr′). Seaport, Calvados dept., NW France, ab. 25 m. NE of Caen just NE of Deauville; pop. 5869; resort; imports timber, coal, cement.

Trow′bridge (trō′brĭj). Urban district, ⊗ of Wiltshire, S England; pop. 13,844; market town, known esp. for its manufacture of broadcloth and other woolen goods.

Troy (troi). **1** Commercial city, ⊗ of Pike co., SE Alabama, 48 m. SSE of Montgomery; pop. 10,234; settled 1824; distributing center for cotton, peanuts, livestock; manufactures cottonseed oil, peanut oil, fertilizers, veneer. Troy State Coll. (1887; coed.).

2 City, ⊗ of Doniphan co., NE Kansas; pop. 1051.

3 City, Oakland co., SE Michigan, SE of Pontiac; pop. 19,058.

4 City, ⊗ of Lincoln co., E Missouri; pop. 1779.

5 Commercial and industrial city, ⊗ of Rensselaer co., E New York, on E bank of Hudson river 8 m. NE of Albany; pop. 67,492; at head of tidewater navigation on Hudson river, opp. mouth of Mohawk river and outlet of N.Y. State Barge Canal system; manufacturing and distributing point; has extensive system of docks; manufactures collars and cuffs, shirts, women's clothing, machinery, engineering and surveying instruments, valves, bells, stoves and ranges. Rensselaer Polytechnic Institute (1824; coed.); Russell Sage Coll. for Women (1916); Emma Willard School for girls (estab. 1814 in Middlebury, Vermont; removed to Troy 1821).

History: Part of patroonship granted Van Rensselaer by Dutch West India Co.; passed to Vanderheyden family 1707; became ⊗ 1793; incorp. as village 1798; home of Samuel Wilson, known locally as "Uncle Sam," who acted as inspector for a government contractor supplying provisions to American soldiers during War of 1812 and is said to have been the original of *Uncle Sam* as applied to the United States; important iron and steel manufacturing center until after Civil War, produced armor and part of machinery for the *Monitor;* chartered as city 1816; annexed village of Lansingburgh (formerly called New City, now residential section) and other territory 1901.

5 Town, ⊗ of Montgomery co., S cen. North Carolina, 40 m. S of High Point; pop. 2346; rayon, rugs, lumber.

6 Industrial city, ⊗ of Miami co., W Ohio, 19 m. N of Dayton; pop. 13,685; settled 1807; airplanes, dishwashing machines, steel houses, furniture, air compressors.

7 *or* **Il′i·um** (ĭl′ĭ·ŭm); *anc.* **Tro′ia** (trō′yȧ) *or* **Tro′ja** (trō′jȧ) *or* **Il′i·on** (ĭl′ĭ·ŏn). Ancient ruined city in Troas, NW Asia Minor, S of the Dardanelles; an archaeological

site (mod. Hissarlik) on Menderes river, said to have nine cities built each on the ruins of its predecessor, Stone Age to Roman. In Greek legend besieged by the confederated Greek armies during a ten-year war (Trojan War), captured, and destroyed, c. 1200 B.C.; its story told in the *Iliad, Odyssey,* and *Aeneid,* by the cyclic poets, and in medieval romances.

Troyes (trwä); *anc.* **Au'gus·tob'o·na Tri·cas'si·um** (ô'gŭs·tŏb'ô·nȧ trĭ·kăs'ĭ·ŭm). City, ✻ of Aube dept., NE France, on Seine river 92 m. SE of Paris; pop. 57,961; manufactures textiles, hosiery, paper, gloves, soap; trades in grain, wine, brandy, sausage, wool, wood, iron, hemp; 13th-cent. Gothic cathedral, 17th-cent. town hall.
History: Existed in pre-Roman times; made capital of Champagne 1019; from 11th to 13th cent. a prosperous trading town; gave its name to system of measuring (*troy weights*) first used at fairs here; treaty bet. Charles VI and Henry V of England 1420; English expelled by Joan of Arc 1429.

Trst. See TRIESTE seaport.

Tru·an'do (trŏō·än'dô). River ab. 60 m. long, W Colombia, a W tributary of the Atrato flowing E.

Tru'chas Peak (trŏō'chȧs); *also known as* **North Truchas Peak.** Mountain peak in SE Rio Arriba co., N New Mexico, NE of Santa Fe; 13,110 ft.; the highest of three peaks forming **Truchas Peaks.**

Tru'cial O·man' (trŏō'shȧl ô·mȧn') *or* **Trucial States** *or* **Trucial Coast;** *formerly* **Pi'rate Coast** (pī'rĭt). Region W of Oman, SE Arabia, extending along the S coast of the Persian Gulf bet. Qatar Penin. and Cape Musandam, a distance of ab. 300 m.; pop. ab. 80,000; ✻ Dubai, important town Abu Dhabi. Comprises seven (originally five) Arab sheikdoms (now, Abu Dhabi, Dubai, Sharjah and Kalba, Ajman, Umm al Qaiwain, Ras al Khaimah, and Fujairah) that entered into treaty arrangement with Great Britain 1820 following war with East India Company; by series of agreements with British promised to suppress slave trade, piracy, relations with other foreign powers (esp. 1853, 1892); supervised by a British residency agent (see PERSIAN GULF RESIDENCY).

Truck'ee (trŭk'ē). River 120 m. long, W Nevada; rises in Placer co., E California, flows E and NE into Pyramid Lake, S Washoe co., NW Nevada.

Trues'dell Heights (trŏōz'd'l; -děl). Elevation 2809 ft. in Garrett co., NW corner of Maryland.

Tru·jil'lo (trŏō·hē'yô). **1** Province, S Dominican Republic. See *Table* at DOMINICAN REPUBLIC.
2 City, Dominican Republic. See CIUDAD TRUJILLO.
3 Seaport, ✻ of Colón dept., Honduras, 58 m. NE of Tegucigalpa; pop. (1940) 4514; founded c. 1525.
4 Coastal city, ✻ of La Libertad dept., NW Peru, 9 m. from its port Salaverry and ab. 315 m. NW of Lima; pop. (1940 est.) 38,961; commercial center; has cathedral, national college, and university; 4 m. to the W are the ruins of the pre-Incan city Chan-Chan.
5 (trŏō·hē'[l]yô) Commune, Cáceres prov., W Spain, 25 m. ENE of Cáceres; pop. 13,753; manufactures leather, chocolates, chinaware, pottery; stock raising, esp. for the bull ring; birthplace of Francisco Pizarro.
6 State of Venezuela. See *Table* at VENEZUELA.
7 Town, ✻ of Trujillo state, W cen. Venezuela, on W slope of the Cordillera Mérida ab. 60 m. E of Lake Maracaibo; pop. (1941 est.) 12,688.

Tru·jil'lo, Mon'te (mŏn'tå trŏō·hē'yô) *or* **Monte Tina** *or* **Lo'ma Ti'na** (lô'mä tē'nä); *now* **Pi'co Duar'te** (pē'kô dwär'tå). Mountain, Dominican Republic, in Cordillera Central; 10,417 ft.

Tru·jil'lo Al'to (trŏō·hē'yô äl'tô). Municipality (pop. 18,251) and town (pop. 1297), NE Puerto Rico.

Truk (trŏōk; trŏōk; trŭk), *or* **Ho'go·leu** (hô'gô·lŏō), **Islands.** Island group in cen. Caroline Is., W Pacific Ocean, ab. 925 m. E of Yap I., 1500 m. W of Tarawa in the Gilbert Is., and 800 m. N of Rabaul; 50 sq. m.; pop. (1938 est.) 17,133; chief town Truk on SE coast of

Dublon I. Group comprises ab. 11 major islands and many islets; chief islands Dublon, Moen, Tol, Udot, Fefan, and Uman; all within a lagoon ab. 38 m. in diameter, encircled by a reef which is pierced by 20 passes (only 4 navigable) allowing access to several fine harbors and anchorages within. Chief anchorage is enclosed by Dublon I., Fefan I., and Uman I. and was developed by Japanese into great naval base; airfield on Dublon. Larger islands have several peaks above 1000 ft. Strongly fortified by Japanese; in World War II raided and bombed by American naval and air forces 1944–45 but not invaded by Americans.

Tru'mann (trŏō'mȧn). City, Poinsett co., NE Arkansas, 15 m. S of Jonesboro; pop. 4511; lumber center.

Trum'bull (trŭm'bŭl). **1** County in Ohio. See *Table* at OHIO.
2 Town, SE Fairfield co., SW Connecticut, N of Bridgeport; pop. 20,379; incorp. 1797; manufactures cigars.

Trumbull, Mount. Peak 7700 ft. in N Mohave co., NW Arizona.

Trüm'mel·bach Falls (trüm'ĕl·bäк). Waterfall 950 ft. near Lauterbrunnen, S Bern canton, Switzerland.

Tru'ro (trŏōr'ô). **1** Town, Barnstable co., SE Massachusetts, ab. 10 m. from Provincetown; pop. 1002.
2 Town, ⊗ of Colchester co., cen. Nova Scotia, Canada, near head (E end) of Minas Basin; pop. 10,756; a railroad junction town. Nova Scotia Normal Coll. One of the largest Acadian settlements to be destroyed 1755, when its inhabitants were expelled by the English; resettled c. 1761 by New England colonists.
3 Municipal borough, ⊗ of Cornwall, SW England, at head of Falmouth Harbor 40 m. W of Plymouth; pop. 12,851; cathedral; former tin-mining center; pottery.

Trust Territory of the Pacific Islands. See Trust Territory of the PACIFIC ISLANDS.

Truth or Consequences. See HOT SPRINGS, N.Mex.

Trut'nov (trŏōt'nôf); *Ger.* **Trau'te·nau** (trou'tĕ·nou). Town, NE Bohemia prov., W Czechoslovakia, 83 m. NE of Prague at foot of the Riesen Gebirge; pop. (1930) 15,923; linen weaving; founded in 13th cent. by German colonists.

Tru·xil'lo (trŏō·hē'[l]yô). Var. of TRUJILLO.

Try'on (trī'ŭn). **1** Village, ⊗ of McPherson co., W cen. Nebraska; pop. (est.) 120.
2 Town and resort, Polk co., SW North Carolina, in Blue Ridge on South Carolina border 32 m. SE of Asheville; pop. 2223; center of hand-weaving, toymaking, and woodcarving industries.

Trze·bia'tów (chĕ·byä'tŏōf); *Ger.* **Trep'tow am Re'ga** (trāp'tô äm rā'gä). Town, N Szczecin dept., NW Poland, on river near Baltic WSW of Kołobrzeg; pop. (1946) 10,184; formerly in Germany.

Tsai'dam' (tsī'däm'). Sandy swamp region with salt lakes in a depression (alt. 9000 ft.) bet. Nan Shan and Astin Tagh ranges on the N and the E end of Kunlun Mts. on the S, cen. Tsinghai prov., W cen. China.

Tsal'a A·pop'ka (tsăl'ȧ ȧ·pŏp'kȧ). Lake ab. 15 m. long in E Citrus co., W Florida penin.; outlet through Withlacoochee river; has many islands.

Tsana, Lake. See Lake TANA.

Tsang'po' (tsäng'pô') *or* **Tsan'po'** (tsän'pô'). Name of the upper Brahmaputra river in S Tibet, Outer China.

Tsang'wu' (tsäng'wŏō'); *formerly* **Wu'chow'** (wŏō'jô'). City and treaty port, E Kwangsi prov., SE China, on N bank of Si river at confluence with the Kwei, 130 m. W of Canton (220 m. by river); pop. (1931 est.) 90,000; on border of W Kwangtung and distributing center for Kwangsi and Kweichow of goods from Canton; has export trade in tung oil, aniseed, and hides; situated in Si river gorge and area subject to disastrous floods when water rises 50 to 60 ft. Made treaty port 1897; important American air base in World War II, which, because of Japanese advance in S China, was destroyed by U.S. Air Force Sept. 22, 1944.

Tsa'ra·ta'na·na' Massif (tsä'rä·tä'nä·nä'). Mountain

group in N Madagascar; highest peak 9449 ft., the highest point in Madagascar.

Tsar·grad' (tsŭr·y'·grät'). Russian name of ÌSTANBUL.

Tsaribrod. See CARIBROD.

Tsa'ri·grad (tsä'rï·grät). Bulgarian name of ÌSTANBUL.

Tsaritsyn. See STALINGRAD.

Tsarskoe Selo. See PUSHKIN.

Tsa'vo (tsä'vō). River ab. 80 m. long in SE Kenya, E Africa, flowing from Mt. Kilimanjaro into the Sabaki river.

Tschaslau. See ČÁSLAV.

Tscheliads. See CZELADŹ.

Tse'la Dzong (tsä'lä dzong'). Fortress (dzong) on N bank of the Tsangpo, SE Tibet, 180 m. E of Lhasa.

Tser'na·go'ra (tsûr'nä·gō'rä). = Crna Gora: see MONTENEGRO.

Tse'sis (tsä'sïs); Latvian **Cē'sis** (tsä'sïs); Ger. **Wen'den** (vĕn'dĕn). Town, Vidzeme prov., N Latvia, in the Gauya river valley 45 m. NE of Riga; pop. (1935) 8748; paper mills; tourist center. Formerly seat of the Livonian Knights; alternated bet. Swedish and Polish rule from 1600 until it was taken over by Russia 1721; battlefield June 1919 where the Latvian army with Estonian aid defeated the Germans and drove them out of Latvia; held by Germans in World War II 1941–44.

Tshua'pa (chwä'pä) or **Chua'pa** (chwä'-). River ab. 420 m. long in S cen. Africa; flows W in N cen. Congo and empties into Busira river.

Tsi. Var. of Tze: see TZU.

Tsien Tang or **Tsientang.** See FUCHUN.

Tsil'ma (tsĭl'mä; Russ. tsyēl'y'·mä). River ab. 125 m. long, NW Komi Republic, Soviet Russia, Europe, a W tributary of the Pechora, flowing N and E to the Pechora at Ust Tsilma; navigable.

Tsim·lyansk' (tsĭm·lyänsk'). Town, E Rostov Region, SE Soviet Russia, Europe, on N bank of the Don ab. 120 m. ENE of Rostov; severe fighting during German advance on Stalingrad July 1942.

Tsi'nan' or **Chi'nan'** (jē'nän'). City, ✳ of Shantung prov., NE China, in NW part of province on old course of the Hwang Ho, ab. 225 m. S of Peiping; pop. (1936 est.) 472,300; in alluvial plain at foot of Tai Mt.; important railroad junction point; surrounded by double walls and has Confucian library, temples, and Shantung Christian Univ. Associated by tradition with early rulers, many centuries B.C.; made administrative center of newly organized province of Shantung under the Mings; opened to foreign commerce 1906; point of clashes 1928 bet. Japanese and Chinese Nationalists in civil war; in civil war that followed World War II captured by Communist forces Sept. 1948.

Tsinchow. See TIENSHUI.

Tsing'hai' or **Ching'hai'** (chĭng'hī'); also **Ko'ko Nor** (kō'kō nôr'; native kŭ'kŭ nōr'). Province, W cen. China, now a province of China Proper but formerly considered an outer dependency; 269,117 sq. m.; pop. (1936 est.) 1,196,054, (1940 est.) 1,512,823; ✳ Sining; bounded on the NW by Sinkiang, on N, NE, and E by Kansu prov., on S by Sikang, on SW by Tibet, and on W by Tibet and Sinkiang. Area much increased 1944 by relocation of the SW boundary; the new line begins at ab. 90°E long., 36°20'N lat., running S to ab. 90°30'E, 32°N, then E to join the new NW boundary of Sikang, thus taking a large section of NE Tibet; no new area figures available. Forms NE part of Tibetan plateau with the greater part above 10,000 ft.; at the NW and in the center is Tsaidam swamp at an elevation of ab. 9000 ft. On the N border, partly in Kansu prov., is the Nan Shan range; in the W cen. part is the E end of the Kunlun Mts., the E extension of which is the Amne Machin Shan reaching heights from 18,000 ft. to 25,000 ft. or possibly higher for Amne Machin, its highest peak; in this range the Hwang Ho has its source, winding in its upper course through E end of the province in tremendous gorges. Tsing Hai (or Koko Nor) is large lake in the NE part. Chief inhabi-

tants are Moslems and Tibetan nomad tribes (Buddhist). Only town of size is Sining.

Tsing Hai (chĭng' hī') or **Chinghai;** also **Koko Nor.** Lake (hai, nor), NE Tsinghai prov., China; 2300 sq. m.; lies at ab. 10,000 ft. bet. Nan Shan range on N and E end of Kunlun Mts. on S.

Tsing'kiang' (chĭng'jĭ·äng'). Town, cen. Kiangsi prov., SE China, on Kan river ab. 55 m. SSW of Nanchang; fighting 1943–44.

Tsing'tao' (chĭng'dou'); Ger. **Tsing'tau'** (tsĭng'tou'). City and treaty port on SE shore of Kiaochow Bay, S coast of Shantung Penin., NE China, equidistant (ab. 345 m.) from Peiping and Shanghai; pop. ab. 60,000; has rail connection with Tsinan and has large maritime trade; a favorite resort for foreigners because of its healthful climate and excellent beach. Until recent years merely a fishing village; acquired some importance 1891 by the establishment of a naval station and fort; part of Kiaochow territory seized by Germany 1897 in retaliation for the murder by Chinese of two German missionaries; leased by treaty 1898 to Germany for 99 years; established as open port 1899; built up on shore and hills as a fine modern city by Germany 1898–1914; besieged by combined Japanese and British (small force only) armies Aug. 23–Nov. 7, 1914; occupied by Japanese 1914–22; returned to China 1922; reoccupied by Japanese 1937–45. Headquarters for U.S. naval forces in W Pacific after end of World War II.

Tsing'yuan' (chĭng'yü·än'); formerly **Pao'ting'** (bou'dĭng'). City, cen. Hopei prov., NE China, on railroad ab. 90 m. SSW of Peiping; pop. ab. 100,000; surrounded by a wall built in Ming period. In civil war following World War II taken by Communists Nov. 22, 1948.

Tsi'ning' (jē'nĭng'). Manufacturing city, W Shantung prov., NE China, on the Grand Canal 80 m. SSW of Tsinan; pop. ab. 73,000.

Tsin'kiang' (jĭn'jĭ·äng'); formerly **Chuan'chow'** (chü·än'jō'). Seaport city, Fukien prov., SE China, 50 m. NE of Amoy (ab. 68 m. by water) on Tsinkiang Harbor; pop. ab. 75,000. Known as Chuanchow in time of T'ang dynasty (618–907); has been identified with Zayton (or Zaitun) described by Marco Polo as one of the great ports of the East in the time of Kublai Khan (1260–94); frequented by ships from the Malay Archipelago and India and was the point of departure of the Polos on their return to Europe. The modern city formerly had a prosperous local trade but it suffered great damage in the Taiping Rebellion.

Tsinling Shan. See CHIN LING SHAN.

Tsitsihar. See LUNGKIANG city.

Tskhinvali. See STALINIR.

Tsu (tsōō). Seaport city, ✳ of Mie prefecture, on W shore of Ise Bay in S Honshu, Japan, 37 m. SW of Nagoya; pop. (1945) 58,554. Bombed by American planes July–Aug. 1945.

Tsu·ga·ru Strait (tsōō·gä·rōō). Channel 15 to 25 m. wide bet. islands of Honshu and Hokkaido, Japan.

Tsu·gi·ta·ka (tsōō·gē·tä·kä); also **Mount Syl'vi·a** (sĭl'vĭ·à). Mountain peak 12,895 ft., N cen. Formosa.

Tsu'meb (tsōō'mĕb). Town, N South-West Africa, 225 m. NNE of Windhoek; chief copper-mining center in the protectorate; lead, silver, and vanadium also mined.

Tsung'ming' (chŏŏng'mĭng'). Island ab. 40 m. long at mouth of Yangtze river, SE Kiangsu prov., E China.

Tsun'yi' (dzŏŏn'ē'). Town, N cen. Kweichow prov., S China, on highway ab. 75 m. NNE of Kweiyang; pop. ab. 40,000; near **Tsunyi Pass.**

Tsu·ru·ga (tsōō·rōō·gä). Seaport, Fukui prefecture, W coast of Honshu, Japan, 60 m. NW of Nagoya; pop. ab. 18,000; has become base for steamship service with Vladivostok and Korean ports. Bombed by American planes July–Aug. 1945.

Tsu·ru·mi (tsōō·rōō·mē). Town, Kanagawa prefecture, SE Honshu, Japan, on W shore of Tokyo Bay 6 m. N of Yokohama; in recent years has come to be an important

industrial town in the Tokyo area because of its plants for the manufacture of chemicals, steel, automobiles, and synthetic oil.

Tsu·ru·o·ka (tsŏŏ·rŏŏ·ŏ·kä). City, Yamagata prefecture, N Honshu, Japan, near W coast S of Sakata; pop. (1945) 39,856; produces silk and cotton fabrics.

Tsu·shi·ma (tsŏŏ·shē·mä). Island in Korea Strait, constituting a former province of Japan; now part of Nagasaki prefecture; ab. 40 m. long; 271 sq. m.; pop. (1945) 52,046; separates Chosen Strait from Tsushima Strait.

Tsushima Strait. Channel ab. 63 m. wide bet. Tsushima I. and NW Kyushu, connecting the Sea of Japan with the East China Sea and forming the SE part of Korea Strait. Site of battle (called also "Battle of Sea of Japan") in the Russo-Japanese War in which the Russian fleet under Rozhdestvenski was destroyed or captured May 27–28, 1905 by Japanese fleet under Admiral Togo.

Tsu·ya·ma (tsŏŏ·yä·mä). Inland town, Okayama prefecture, in center of W extension of Honshu, Japan, 30 m. N of Okayama; pop. (1945) 48,607.

Tsu'yung' (tsŏŏ'yŏŏng'). Town, cen. Yunnan prov., S China, on Burma Road ab. 120 m. W of Kunming; alt. 6000 ft.

Tu'am (tū'ăm). Town, N co. Galway, W Eire; pop. 4181; seat of a Catholic archbishop and of a Church of Ireland bishop.

Tu'a·mo'tu (tŏŏ'ä·mō'tŏŏ), *or* **Pa'u·mo'tu** (pä'ŏŏ·mō'tŏŏ), *or* **Low** (lō), **Archipelago.** Extensive group of ab. 80 small islands, mostly low coral atolls, in S Pacific Ocean, included in French Polynesia, E of Society Is. and S of Marquesas; ab. lat. 14° to 23°S and long. 134° to 149°W; 330 sq. m.; pop. 4681; ✳ Apataki. Chief islands Makatéa, Fakarava, Rangiroa, Anaa, Hao, and Réao; includes also the Gambier and Duke of Gloucester Is. Part of group first discovered by Spanish navigator Pedro Fernandes de Queirós 1606; seized by France 1844 and annexed 1881; now form a part of Tahiti dependency.

Tua'pi Lagoon (twä'pĕ). Inlet of the Caribbean Sea on NE coast of Nicaragua.

Tu·ap·se' (tŏŏ·ŭp·syĕ'). Seaport town, S Krasnodar Territory, Soviet Russia, Europe, on Black Sea coast 62 m. S of Krasnodar; pop. 12,142; terminus of oil pipelines from Grozny through Armavir and Maikop; ships oil; has large cement works; health resort. Just beyond the limit reached by German drive toward the Caucasus 1942.

Tuban. See TOEBAN.

Tub'ber·gen (tŭb'ĕr·ᴋĕ[n]). Commune, Overijssel prov., E Netherlands, just NE of Almelo near German border; pop. 9530.

Tu·bi'gon (tŏŏ·bē'gôn). Municipality on W coast of Bohol I., Phil. Is., on Bohol Strait 22 m. NNE of Tagbilaran; pop. 21,766.

Tü'bing·en (tü'bǐng·ĕn). Manufacturing city, Baden-Württemberg state, West Germany, on Neckar river 17 m. S of Stuttgart; pop. 20,276; manufactures surgical instruments, machinery, paper, cement, knit goods; famed for its university (founded 1477) with which the names of Melanchthon, Reuchlin, Baur, and many others are connected; 15th-cent. town hall, ancient Cistercian abbey, old ducal castle. First mentioned 1078; first mentioned as city 1231; sold to Württemberg 1342; taken by Swabian League 1519; occupied by France 1647, 1688.

Tu'bize (tü'bēz'). Commune, Brabant prov., cen. Belgium, SSW of Brussels; pop. 8833; sandstone quarries.

Tu'bu·aï (tŏŏ'bŏŏ·ī'), *or* **Aus'tral** (ôs'trăl), **Islands.** Group of small volcanic islands in S French Polynesia, S Pacific Ocean, S of Society Is. and SW of Tuamotu Archipelago; form a chain ab. 850 m. long bet. lat. 21°50' to 27°41'S and long. 144°22' to 155°W; 115 sq. m.; pop. 3621. The inhabited islands of the group, from NW to SE, are Rimatara, Rurutu, Tubuaï, Raïvavaé, Rapa (*q.v.*). Islands are well-watered and fertile; natives are

Polynesians. Visited by Capt. Cook 1769 and 1777 and by Vancouver 1791; taken over by French bet. 1850 and 1889.

Tubuaï Ma'nu (mä'nŏŏ) *or* **Mai·a'o** (mī·ä'ŏ). Small island of the Society Is., S Pacific Ocean, 45 m. W of Mooréa; ab. 3 sq. m.; pop. (1936) ab. 100; most easterly of the Leeward Is.

Tu·bu'ran (tŏŏ·bŏŏ'rän). Municipality on NW coast of Cebu I., Phil. Is.; pop. 45,750; on Tañon Strait ab. 30 m. NNW of City of Cebu; has good port.

Tu·ca'cas (tŏŏ·kä'käs). Coastal town, E Falcón state, NW Venezuela; pop. ab. 2000; exports copper, cacao, coffee, hides.

Tuch'kov (tŏŏch'kŭf). Former Russian name of Izmail (*q.v.*).

Tuck'a·hoe (tŭk'á·hō). **1** River, SE New Jersey; flows from W Atlantic co. S and E into Great Egg Bay. **2** Village, Westchester co., SE New York, 18 m. NNE of New York; pop. 6423; residential suburb of Yonkers and New York City; marble quarries; lime, stucco.

Tuck'a·sei'gee (tŭk'á·sē'jĕ). River in SW North Carolina in which is located Glenville Dam, one of the dams of the Tennessee Valley Authority (*q.v.*).

Tuck'er (tŭk'ĕr). County in West Virginia. See *Table* at WEST VIRGINIA.

Tuck'er·man Ravine (tŭk'ĕr·măn). Gorge on S side of Mt. Washington, Presidential Range, White Mts., New Hampshire; popular ski slopes; trail from Pinkham Notch to the summit of Mt. Washington.

Tuck'er·nuck Island (tŭk'ĕr·nŭk). Island in Atlantic Ocean S of Cape Cod, Massachusetts, and a part of Nantucket co., Massachusetts.

Tuck'er·ton (tŭk'ĕr·t'n; -tŭn). Borough, Ocean co., E New Jersey, on Tuckerton river 18 m. NNE of Atlantic City; pop. 1536; founded c. 1699; port of entry in Colonial days; formerly produced flax and molasses, and cultivated silkworms; marine radio station.

Tu·co'pi·a (tŏŏ·kō'pǐ·á). Small island, E Santa Cruz Is., SW Pacific Ocean, ESE of Vanikoro.

Tuc·son' (tŏŏ·sŏn'; tŏŏ'sŏn). Commercial and residential city, ⊗ of Pima co., S Arizona, on Santa Cruz river 103 m. SE of Phoenix; pop. 212,892; winter and health resort; railroad junction and distributing center for irrigated agricultural and livestock region; tuberculosis sanitariums; Univ. of Arizona (1885); Davis-Monthan Air Force Base; Indian reservations nearby; San Xavier del Bac Indian mission (founded 1700) in vicinity. Became Spanish presidio 1776 under name of Presidio de San Augustín de Tuguison; acquired by United States through Gadsden Purchase 1853; occupied by Confederate troops 1862; territorial capital 1867–77; incorp. as city 1883.

Tu'cu·mán' (tŏŏ'kŏŏ·män'). **1** Province of Argentina. See *Table* at ARGENTINA. **2** City, its ✳, N Argentina, at foot of E ranges of the Andes on a tributary of the Dulce river; pop. (est.) 169,566; center of sugar industry. Founded 1565; in 1776 became part of viceroyalty of La Plata; independence of Argentina was first proclaimed here at the first congress of the republic which met here July 1816. See *History* at ARGENTINA.

Tu'cum·car'i (tŏŏ'kŭm·kâr'ĭ). City, ⊗ of Quay co., E New Mexico, 60 m. NNW of Clovis; pop. 8143; made ⊗ 1903; railroad division point; tourist center; ships cattle; produces wheat, corn; manufactures sisal, brooms.

Tu'cu·pi'ta (tŏŏ'kŏŏ·pē'tä). Town in the Orinoco delta, ✳ of Delta Amacuro territory, NE Venezuela.

Tu·de'la (tŏŏ·thä'lä); *anc.* **Tu·te'la** (tū·tē'lá). Commune, Navarra prov., N Spain, on Ebro river 52 m. S of Pamplona; pop. 13,134; stock raising, esp. for the bull ring; Romanesque collegiate church (1188). Conquered by Arabs 716; reconquered by Alfonso I of Aragon 1115; made episcopal see 1783; occupied by French 1808–13.

Tuder. See TODI.

Tug'a·loo (tŏŏg'á·lō) *or* **Tug'a·lo.** River, NE Georgia;

forms section of NE Georgia boundary with South Carolina and unites with the Seneca river in W Anderson co., NW South Carolina, to form the Savannah river. Upper course known as Chattooga river.

Tu·ge'la (tōō·gā'lá). River ab. 300 m. long in cen. Natal, E Union of South Africa; rises in Mont aux Sources, where it plunges through a gorge forming the **Tugela Falls** 2810 ft., and flows E to the Indian Ocean; not navigable; scene of battles of the Boer War Oct. 1899 to Feb. 1900, esp. at Colenso.

Tug Fork (tŭg). River, SW West Virginia; rises in McDowell co., flows NW and forms Kentucky-West Virginia boundary until it unites with Levisa Fork to form Big Sandy river (*q.v.*).

Tuggurt. See TOUGGOURT.

Tugh·lak'a·bad' (tōōg·lŭk'á·bäd'). Name of one of the cities built ab. 4 m. to the E of the site of Old Delhi; erected c. 1321 by Ghiyas-ud-din Tughlak, founder of the Tughlak dynasty. Only the ruins of its walls and fort remain. See DELHI.

Tu'gue·ga·ra'o (tōō'gá·gä·rä'ō). Municipality, ✳ of Cagayan prov., Luzon, Phil. Is., in S part of province on E side of Cagayan river, 270 m. by highway N of Manila and ab. 215 m. by air; pop. 27,643. In World War II taken by Japanese Dec. 25, 1941 and held until retaken by Filipino guerrillas June 1945.

Tuin'dorp Oost'zaan (toin'dôrp ōst'zàn). Town, suburb of Amsterdam, Netherlands; pop. 7725.

Tui'ra (twē'rä). River ab. 90 m. long, Panama prov., E cen. Panama; rises near Colombian border, flows N and NW to Gulf of San Miguel.

Tu·jun'ga (tú·hŭng'gá). Former suburban residential city, Los Angeles co., California; pop. (est.) 15,000; incorp. 1925; annexed to Los Angeles 1932, is in N part of city at foot of San Gabriel Mts.

Tukangbesi Islands. See TOEKANGBESI ISLANDS.

Tu'ko (tōō'kō). Village, N end of island of Manihiki, Manihiki Is., cen. Pacific Ocean.

Tuk'uh·nik'i·vatz, Mount (tŭk'ŭ·nĭk'ĭ·väts). Peak 12,004 ft. in N San Juan co., SE Utah.

Tu'kums (tōō'kōōms). Town, NW Zemgale prov., N Latvia, on railroad 40 m. W of Riga; pop. (1935) 8144.

Tu·ku'yu (tōō·kōō'yōō); *formerly* **Neu–Lang'en·burg** (noi·läng'ĕn·bŏŏrk). Town, SW Tanganyika, SE Africa, just NW of Lake Nyasa.

Tu'la (tōō'lá). **1** (*Span.* -lä) Town, SW Hidalgo state, cen. Mexico, 45 m. N of Mexico City; pop. ab. 2000. Excavations have revealed ruins of ancient capital of the Toltecs, dating back probably to 12th cent. A.D.
2 City, ✳ of Tula Region, Soviet Russia, Europe, on a tributary of the Oka river 110 m. S of Moscow; pop. 272,403; an industrial city long known for its metal manufactures, esp. rifles and samovars. Founded in 12th cent.; at first a frontier fortress against the Tatars, strengthened by stone fort or citadel 1514–21; here Tsar Boris Godunov established 1595 first Russian gun factory, a line further developed by Peter the Great 1712; in World War II fiercely defended against Germans' first invasion Oct. 1941.

Tu·la'gi (tōō·lä'gē). Small island in S cen. Solomon Is., W Pacific Ocean, off S coast of Florida I. and 22 m. N of Guadalcanal I.; chief town **Tulagi**, on SE coast, former ✳ of British Solomon Islands protectorate, has fine harbor. Seized by U.S. Marines Aug. 7–10, 1942.

Tu'la·in'yo Lake (tōō'lá·in'yō). Lake, elevation 12,865 ft., in Tulare and Inyo cos., California, 1½ m. NE of Mt. Whitney; highest lake in the United States having an area of more than one tenth of a sq. m.

Tu'lan' (dōō'län'). Town, E cen. Tsinghai prov., W cen. China, W of Tsing Hai (lake) and ab. 160 m. W of Sining; on trade route from Sining to towns of Sinkiang.

Tu'lan·cin'go (tōō'län·sēng'gō). Town, Hidalgo state, cen. Mexico, 65 m. NE of Mexico City; pop. 12,552.

Tu·lar'e (tōō·lâr'ĕ; tōō·lâr'). **1** Former lake Kings co., S cen. California; 220 sq. m.; reclaimed for farm land.

2 County in California. See *Table* at CALIFORNIA.
3 City, Tulare co., S cen. California, 42 m. SE of Fresno; pop. 13,824; founded 1872; shipping center for fruit, sugar beets, dairy products, cereals.

Tu'la Region (tōō'lá). Region, cen. Soviet Russia, Europe, part of western plateau; (before 1945) 12,661 sq. m.; pop. 2,049,950; ✳ Tula. Traversed by upper Don and tributaries and by the Oka; has rich soil in S part; produces rye, oats, wheat and other grains, hemp, sugar beets, vegetables; has important heavy industries. Chief cities Tula, Stalinogorsk. Became a part 1928 of Western Area, but reorganized 1936 as a separate region; again lost territory 1945 when Kaluga Region was formed from its W part; most of it came under German control in their first offensive 1941 but their advance stopped at Tula (city); recovered by Russians in winter campaign of 1941–42.

Tu'la·ro'sa (tōō'lá·rō'sá). Village, Otero co., S New Mexico, 65 m. NNE of Las Cruces; pop. 3200; lumber, cotton, cattle.

Tul·cán' (tōōl·kän'). Town, ✳ of Carchi prov., N Ecuador, near Colombian frontier and 90 m. NE of Quito; pop. (1944 est.) 12,828.

Tul'cea (tōōl'chä). Town, SE Romania, in Dobruja region in Danube delta; pop. 20,104.

Tu'lé'ar' *or* **Tul'le'ar'** (tü'lä'är'). Seaport, SW Madagascar; pop. (1936) 15,180.

Tu'le Lake (tōō'lē). Small lake in NE corner of Siskiyou co., N California; site of Japanese Relocation Camp in World War II.

Tu'le Mountain (tōō'lē). Peak 3833 ft. in S Brewster co., W Texas.

Tu'lia (tōōl'yá). City, ⊗ of Swisher co., NW Texas, in the panhandle 25 m. N of Plainview; pop. 4410; market for grain and dairy products; oil wells.

Tul·karm' *or* **Tul Karm** (tōōl·kärm'). **1** Subdistrict, Samaria dist., N cen. Palestine; 294 sq. m.; pop. 46,328, (1938 est.) 65,561.
2 Town, its ✳, 24 m. NE of Jaffa; pop. 5368; railroad junction point.

Tul'la·ho'ma (tŭl'á·hō'má). City and summer resort, Coffee and Franklin cos., S cen. Tennessee, 25 m. ENE of Fayetteville; pop. 12,242; in farming and lumbering area; manufactures gloves, baseballs, shoes, cheese, condensed milk.

Tul'la·more' (tŭl'á·mōr'). Urban district, ⊗ of co. Offaly, cen. Eire; pop. 5135; brewing, distilling.

Tulle (tül; *Angl.* tōōl); *Lat.* **Tu·te'la** (tū·tē'lá). Industrial city, ✳ of Corrèze dept., S cen. France, 47 m. SSE of Limoges; pop. 15,617; manufactures textiles, metal goods; government armament manufactory; 12th-cent. cathedral, 17th-cent. church; fine bridge. Founded in 7th cent.; taken by English 1346, 1369; devastated by Black Death; retaken by Charles V 1370; taken by Protestants 1585.

Tullear. See TULÉAR.

Tullum. See TOUL.

Tu·lo·ma' (tōō·lŭ·má'). River ab. 175 m. long, NW Murmansk Region, Soviet Russia, Europe; flows E to head of Kola Bay; its chief tributary is the Kola.

Tul'sa (tŭl'sá). **1** County in Oklahoma. See *Table* at OKLAHOMA.
2 City, its ⊗, NE Oklahoma, on Arkansas river ab. 15 m. NE of Sapulpa; pop. 261,685; financial, commercial, and transportation center of mid-continent agricultural and oil-producing country; chief industry petroleum refining; manufactures oil-well tools and equipment, glass, cotton textiles, chemicals, furniture, steel, airplanes, automobile bodies, brick and tile, oxygen; gas and oil wells; lead, zinc, coal mines. Univ. of Tulsa (1894; coed.; moved from Muskogee 1907). Formerly home of Creek Indians; settled c. 1880; incorp. 1898.

Tu·luá' (tōō·lwä'). Town, Valle dept., W Colombia, ab. 50 m. NNE of Cali; pop. 12,017.

Tu·lun' (tōō·lōōn'). Town, W Irkutsk Region, Soviet

Russia, Asia, on Trans-Siberian R.R. 225 m. NW of Irkutsk; pop. ab. 7000.

Tulungagung. See TOELOENGAGOENG.

Tu·ma·ca'co·ri National Monument (tōō'mȧ·kä'-kō·rė̇). See UNITED STATES, *National Monuments.*

Tu·ma'co (tōō·mä'kô). Seaport, W Nariño dept., SW Colombia; located on an island; southernmost Pacific port of Colombia; pop. 9671; exports ivory nuts, cacao, tobacco.

Tu'ma·tu·ma'ri Falls (tōō'mȧ·tōō·mä'rė̇). Waterfall in the Essequibo river in cen. British Guiana.

Tum'ba, Lake (tŭm'bȧ). Lake 23 m. long, 8–12 m. wide, in W Congo, SW of Coquilhatville and NW of Lake Leopold II; the Ubangi and Congo rivers meet just W of the lake.

Tum'bes (tōōm'bâs). **1** Department of Peru. See *Table* at PERU.

2 Town, its ✳, on Tumbes river ab. 645 m. NW of Lima, near Ecuador border; pop. (1940 est.) 6355. Pizarro landed here for his invasion of Peru 1527.

Tu'men' (tōō'mŭn'). River ab. 220 m. long, boundary bet. NE Korea and SE Manchuria; rises in Changpai Shan, NE Korea, flows generally N and NE but in its lower course turns sharply SE to the Sea of Japan; for ab. 11 m. from its mouth forms boundary of Korea with Maritime Territory, U.S.S.R. (see CHANGKUFENG); navigable for light craft for ab. 30 m.

Tum·kur' (tōōm·kōōr'). **1** District, E Mysore state, S Indian Union; 4082 sq. m.; pop. 861,405.

2 Town, its ✳, ab. 40 m. NW of Bangalore; pop. 18,196; health resort.

Tumluk. Var. of TAMLUK.

Tum'mo (tōōm'ō). Town and oasis, SW Libya, N Africa, SE of Gat, in the mountains on the border of Niger Republic, West Africa.

Tum'pat (tōōm'pät). Town, N Kelantan state, Federation of Malaya, on coast; port of Kota Bharu.

Tu·muc'–Hu·mac' Mountains (tōō·mōōk'ōō·mäk'). Range in NE Brazil, extending W to E along the boundary bet. Surinam and French Guiana on the N, and Brazil on the S; averages 2000 to 3000 ft.

Tum'wa'ter (tŭm'wô'tẽr, -wŏt'ẽr). Town, Thurston co., Washington, SW of Olympia; pop. 3885; first permanent settlement in state 1845.

Tun. See FIRDAUS.

Tu'na, Point (tōō'nȧ). Cape, SE Puerto Rico.

Tu·na'ri (tōō·nä'rė̇). Peak 17,060 ft. in W Cochabamba dept., cen. Bolivia.

Tunas. See VICTORIA DE LAS TUNAS.

Tun'bridge Wells (tŭn'brĭj). Municipal borough, Kent, SE England, 29 m. SSE of London; pop. 38,397; health resort, with chalybeate springs.

Tun'dzha *or* **Tun'ja** (tōōn'jä). River ab. 160 m. long in SE Bulgaria; rises in Balkan Mts. W of Kazanlik, flows E then S into the Maritsa river at Edirne in Turkey in Europe.

Tu'ne·mah Peak (tōō'nė̇·mä). Mountain 11,873 ft. in Sierra Nevada, E Fresno co., S cen. California.

Tunes. See TUNIS.

Tung (dōōng). River ab. 280 m. long, Kwangtung prov., SE China; rises in S Kiangsi and flows SW and W into upper Pearl river ab. 25 m. below Canton.

Tun'ga·bha'dra (tōōng'gäb·hŭd'rä). River ab. 400 m. long, S India; formed by confluence of Tunga and Bhadra rivers in W Mysore; flows NE along N border of Andhra Pradesh to the Kistna river.

Tungchow. 1 See NANTUNG.

2 See TALI.

3 See TUNGHSIEN.

Tungchwan. See HWEITSEH.

Tung'hai' (tōōng'hī'); *formerly* **Hai'chow'** (hī'jō'). Town, N Kiangsu prov., E China, near coast; E terminal of railroad running W to Kaifeng and Sian.

Tung'hsien' (tōōng'shǐ·ĕn'); *formerly* **Tung'chow'** (tōōng'jō'). City, NE Hopeh prov., NE China, 12 m. E

of Peiping on Pei river; pop. ab. 50,000; an old settlement known since the Earlier Han dynasty 202 B.C.

Tung'hwa' (tōōng'hwä') *or* **Tung'hua'**. **1** Former province (1932–45), SE Manchukuo; 12,216 sq. m.; pop. (1940 est.) 982,942.

2 City, SE Liaoning prov., S Manchuria, in mountainous region on Hun river, a tributary of the Yalu, 140 m. E of Mukden; pop. 42,539; ✳ of former Tunghwa prov., SW Manchukuo; important timber market.

Tung'kiang' (tōōng'jǐ·äng'). Town, NW Kirin prov., E Manchuria, on the Sungari at its junction with the Amur; pop. 96,652. In World War II taken by Russians Aug. 10, 1945.

Tung'kwan' (tōōng'gwän'). Town and fortress, E Shensi, NE cen. China, on S bank of Hwang Ho at its turning E where the Wei joins it; pop. ab. 80,000; controls the narrow valley bet. great walls of loess where the Hwang Ho is rapid and unnavigable; gateway to Shensi and Szechwan provs.

Tung'liao' (tōōng'lǐ·ou'). Town, W Liaoning prov., S Manchuria, on railroad 60 m. W of Liaoyuan; pop. 40,448.

Tung'shan' (tōōng'shän') *or* **Su'chow'** (sōō'jō'). Town, NW Kiangsu prov., E China, 185 m. NW of Nanking; point where Tientsin-Pukow R.R. crosses the Lunghai R.R. Object of heavy attack by Communist forces Nov. 1948 and taken by them Dec. 1948.

Tung'ting' Hu (dōōng'tǐng' hōō'). Shallow lake (*hu*), NE Hunan, SE cen. China; 1930 sq. m., but 3500 to 4000 sq. m. at high water in summer; receives the Siang, Yuan, Tzu, and Lin rivers; main outlet on NE at Yoyang to the Yangtze; also connects with the Yangtze on NW by the Sungtze river. Its dry bed in winter noted for its rice production.

Tun'gu·ra'gua (tōōng'gōō·rä'gwä) *or* **Tun'gu·ra'hua** (-rä'wä). **1** Volcano 16,684 ft. in the Andes Mts., in Ecuador.

2 Province of Ecuador. See *Table* at ECUADOR.

Tun·gu'ska (tŏōn·gōō'skȧ). Name of three rivers in cen. Siberia, Soviet Russia, Asia, tributaries of Yenisei river: (1) **Lower Tunguska;** *Russ.* **Nizh'nya·ya Tunguska** (nyēsh'nyȧ·yȧ), ab. 2000 m. long, rises in N cen. Irkutsk Region and flows N, crossing into Evenki National District at ab. 63°30'N, then flowing W to the Yenisei at Turukhansk; Tura, capital of Evenki, is on it. (2) **Stony Tunguska;** *Russ.* **Pod·ka'men·na·ya Tunguska** (pŭt·kä'myĭn·nȧ·yȧ), ab. 1000 m. long, rises in SE corner of Evenki National District and flows WNW into the Yenisei at ab. 61°30'N. (3) **Upper Tunguska;** *Russ.* **Verkh'nya·ya Tunguska** (vyẽrk'nyȧ·yȧ), the lower course of the Angara river (*q.v.*) in Krasnoyarsk Territory; enters the Yenisei just S of Yeniseisk.

Tun'hwang' (tōōn'hwäng'). Town, W end of Kansu prov., N cen. China, WSW of Ansi and at NW end of Nan Shan range; station on the Silk Route (*q.v.*) from China to Turkistan and India and in early times division point for "North Road" and "South Road."

Tu'ni·ca (tū'nǐ·kȧ). **1** County in Mississippi. See *Table* at MISSISSIPPI.

2 Town, its ⊗, NW Mississippi; pop. 1445.

Tu'nis (tū'nǐs). **1** Former Barbary state in N Africa; the region S and W of the ancient city of Carthage (*q.v.*); Roman province of Africa from 2d cent. B.C. to 5th cent. A.D. when it was overrun by Vandals; reconquered by Byzantine Empire 534; taken by Mohammedans 7th cent.; invaded by Louis IX of France on 7th Crusade 1270; attacked by Emperor Charles V as stronghold of Barbary Corsair, Barbarossa, 1535; conquered by Turks 1575; engaged in piracy (see BARBARY); in 1869, because of debts of its bey, accepted financial control by England, France, Italy; internal independence recognized by Turkey 1871; scene of rivalry bet. French and Italians 1879–81; forced by invasion to become French protectorate 1881. See TUNISIA.

2 *anc.* **Tu'nes** (tū'nēz). City, ✳ of Tunisia, in NE part;

pop. (1936) 219,578; near site of ancient Carthage; situated on hilly isthmus bet. two lagoons; E lagoon is **Lake of Tunis**, at E end of which is La Goulette, port of the city of Tunis; extensive trade passes through it. Has old town and European town, and many mosques. Existed as small place in Carthaginian times; not important until Moslem conquest.

Tunis, Gulf of. Inlet of Mediterranean Sea on NE coast of Tunisia; limited on E by Cape Bon Penin.; at its head is the seaport La Goulette, the Lake of Tunis, and the city of Tunis.

Tu·ni'si·a (tụ̄·nĭzh'ĭ·ȧ; -nĭzh'ȧ) or **Tu'nis** (tū'nĭs); *Fr.* **Tu'ni'sie'** (tü'nē'zē') Republic on the coast of N Africa; bounded on N and E by Mediterranean Sea, on S by Sahara Desert and Libya, on W by Algeria (province of Constantine); ab. 48,300 sq. m.; pop. (1936 est.) 2,608,313; ✶ Tunis. Plateau region in W and W cen. parts with highest points ab. 4500 ft.; coastal region low

TUNISIA
Statute Miles
0   50   100

in N and esp. along E; three indentations on E coast: Gulf of Tunis at N end, shut in on E by Cape Bon Penin.; Gulf of Hammamet, S of the peninsula; and Gulf of Gabès in S. Cape Blanc on N coast is northernmost point of Africa in 37°14′N; in S, on SE side of Gulf of Gabès, is large island of Djerba. Chief river the Medjerda in N flowing E to Gulf of Tunis; has no other sizable streams. In S is large Chott Djerid; along E coast are several marshy lakes, esp. Sidi-el-Hani, and in N are Lakes Bizerte and Achkel near Bizerte. Long S tract of country extends into the Sahara. Chief industry agricul-

ture; main products dates, citrus fruits, olives, grains, and the mineral phosphate. Chief cities Tunis, Sfax, Bizerte, Sousse, Kairouan, Gabès.

History: Became French protectorate 1881 (see TUNIS former Barbary state); French occupation the cause of long-standing Franco-Italian enmity and Italian accession to Triple Alliance 1882; government reorganized 1922; cession demanded by Italy, esp. in 1938. Goal of Allied campaign in North Africa 1942–43; invaded by American forces from the W Jan.–Feb. 1943 and by British from SE Mar. 1943; captured by May 12, 1943. Became an associated state of the French Union 1946; recognized by France as independent 1956.

Tun'ja. 1 (tо̄о̄n'jä) See TUNDZHA river, Bulgaria.
2 (tо̄о̄ng'hä) Town, ✶ of Boyacá dept., cen. Colombia; pop. 16,597; in the Cordillera Oriental of the Andes on the Trans-Andean highway 85 m. NE of Bogotá; one of the oldest cities in the new world.

Tunk, Mount (tŭngk). Peak 6065 ft. in Okanogan co., N Washington.

Tunk·han'nock (tŭngk·hăn'ŭk). Borough, ⊗ of Wyoming co., NE Pennsylvania, on Susquehanna river 18 m. WNW of Scranton; pop. 2297; settled 1775; in agricultural section; former hunting resort. A few miles to the NE, at Nicholson, is **Tunkhannock,** *or* **Nich'olson** (nĭk'ŭl·s'n; nĭk''l-), **Viaduct**, one of the largest concrete railroad bridges in the world, 240 ft. high and 2375 ft. long, crossing **Tunkhannock Creek**, tributary of the Susquehanna.

Tun'ni·bu'li (tо̄о̄n'ē·bо̄о̄'lē). Town and government station on E coast at S end of Santa Isabel I., E Solomon Is., W Pacific Ocean; has good harbor.

Tun'stall (tŭn'st'l). See the POTTERIES.

Tu'nu·yán' (tо̄о̄'nо̄о̄·yän'). River ab. 200 m. long in W Argentina; rises in Andes Mts. E of Santiago, Chile, flows E, chiefly in Mendoza prov.

Tu·ol'um·ne (tо̄о̄·ŏl'ů·mê). **1** River 155 m. long, cen. California; rises in Yosemite National Park and flows W into San Joaquin river in Stanislaus co. W of Modesto; contains Hetch Hetchy and Don Pedro Reservoirs. The **Grand Canyon of the Tuolumne** is a scenic feature of Yosemite National Park.
2 County in California. See *Table* at CALIFORNIA.

Tuolumne Peak. Mountain 10,875 ft. in Sierra Nevada, E Tuolumne co., cen. California.

Tu·par'ro (tо̄о̄·pär'rô). River ab. 200 m. long in NE Colombia; flows E into Orinoco river.

Tu·pe·lo (tū'pê·lō). City, ⊗ of Lee co., NE Mississippi, 57 m. NNW of Columbus; pop. 17,221; cotton and cottonseed-oil mills, clothing factories, dairies; scene of battle July 14, 1864 in Civil War in which Union forces under Gen. A. J. Smith defeated Confederate forces under Gen. Nathan Forrest.

Tupelo Battlefield Site. See UNITED STATES, *National Historical Parks.*

Tu·pi·za (tо̄о̄·pē'sä). Town, Potosí dept., SW Bolivia, 125 m. S of Potosí; alt. 9800 ft.; flour mills, and center of mining industries (silver, tin, bismuth, and lead); on railroad from La Paz to Argentina.

Tup'per Lake (tŭp'ēr). Village and resort, Franklin co., NE New York, 45 m. S of Malone; pop. 5200; alt. 1569 ft.; former lumbering center.

Tupper Lakes. Lakes in NE New York, **Great** *or* **Big Tupper Lake** in S Franklin co., and **Little Tupper Lake** in N Hamilton co. Great Tupper Lake is ab. 7 m. long; Little Tupper Lake, ab. 4 m. long; both are summer resorts.

Tu'pun·ga'to (tо̄о̄'pо̄о̄ng·gä'tô). Peak 22,300 ft. in Andes Mts. on the Chile-Argentina boundary ab. 40 m. ENE of Santiago, Chile.

Tuque, La. See LA TUQUE.

Tur, Jebel et. See Mount GERIZIM.

Tu'ra (tо̄о̄r'ä). Chief town in the Garo Hills, W Assam, NE Indian Union, at W end of Khasi Hills E of the Jamuna.

Tu·ra′ (tōō·rä′). **1** River ab. 400 m. long, a tributary of the Tobol, in Sverdlovsk and Tyumen Regions, Soviet Russia, Asia; rises in the Ural Mts. and flows E past Tyumen. Its valley much used by early Russian colonizers of Siberia for access to the region.
2 Town, ✳ of Evenki National District, Soviet Russia, Asia, on right bank of the Lower Tunguska river in cen. part of district.

Tu·ran′ (tōō·rän′). Ancient Persian name for the desert and steppe lands of Central Asia N of Iran, roughly equivalent to the regions around the Syr Darya (Jaxartes) and Amu Darya (Oxus) in modern Uzbek and Kazakh Republics of Soviet Russia in Asia; home of the Turanian peoples.

Tur·ba′co (tōōr·vä′kô). Town, Bolívar dept., N Colombia, just SE of Cartagena; pop. 8977.

Tur·bat′-i-Hai′da·ri′ (tōōr·bät′ė·hī′dá·rē′). Town, Khurasan prov., NE Iran; pop. ab. 4000; on trade route 75 m. S of Meshed; center of fertile agricultural region; chief trade is in grains.

Turck′heim′ (tür′kěm′); *Ger.* **Türk′heim** (türk′hīm). Village, Haut-Rhin dept., NE France, near Colmar; pop. (1931) 2532; scene of battle Jan. 5, 1675 in which Turenne defeated the Imperial forces (Thirty Years' War).

Tur′co·man (tûr′kô·măn; -măn). Var. of TURKOMEN.

Tur′da (tōōr′dä); *Hung.* **Tor′da** (tôr′dô). City, Transylvania region, NW cen. Romania, SSE of Cluj; pop. 20,057; salt mines.

Tur′fan′ (tōōr′fän′). **1** *formerly* **Luk′chun′** (lōōk′-chōōn′). Depression, NE part of Tarim basin, E Sinkiang, W China, said to be 426 ft. below sea level at lowest point; partly filled with salt lakes; soil fertile but cannot be irrigated.
2 Town, E cen. Sinkiang, W China, 30 m. N of Turfan depression and ab. 90 m. SE of Urumchi; pop. ab. 20,000; at foot of Tien Shan range on old caravan road from China via Qomul to Urumchi; in vicinity are many relics of early periods. As center of earlier kingdoms several times destroyed; ruled by the Uigurs in the 8th and 9th cents. but influences of Buddhism retained down to modern times.

Tur′gu–Jiu (tĭr′gōō·zhyōō′). = TÂRGU-JIU.

Tur′gut·lu′ (tōōr′[g]ōōt·lōō′); *formerly* **Ka′sa·ba′** (kä′-sä·bä′; *Angl.* kả·sä′bả). City, Manisa vilayet, Turkey in Asia, on Gediz river and on railroad 32 m. E of İzmir; pop. 21,672; noted for its production of the casaba melon.

Tü′ri (tü′rĭ); *Russ.* **Tyu′ri** (tū′ryĭ). Town, Järva prov., N cen. Estonia; pop. (1937) 3173; railroad junction point 7 m. S of Paide.

Tu·rí′, Point (tōō·rē′). Cape extending into Atlantic Ocean on N coast of Maranhão state, NE Brazil.

Tu′ria (tōō′ryä). = GUADALAVIAR.

Tu′rias·sú′ Bay (tōō′ryà·sōō′). Bay on NE coast of Brazil, in NW Maranhão state, at the mouth of the Turiassú river.

Tu′rin (tūr′ĭn; tụ·rĭn′); *Ital.* **To·ri′no** (tô·rē′nô); *anc.* **Tau·ra′sia** (tô·rä′zhả), *later* **Au·gus′ta Tau′ri·no′-rum** (ô·gŭs′tả tô′rĭ·nōr′ŭm). Commercial and manufacturing commune, ✳ of Torino prov., Piedmont, NW Italy, on Po river 78 m. NW of Genoa; pop. 629,115; military station; notable buildings include the 15th-cent. Renaissance cathedral, basilica of La Suporga (burial chapel of house of Savoy), the Castello Medioevale, Castello del Valentino, royal and other palaces (Madama, Carignano, dei Torri, etc.), academy of science, town hall, museums, Royal Albertine Library, exchange, arsenal, university (founded 1405), and national and municipal libraries; manufactures include autos, rubber, machinery, iron and steel goods, rolling stock, furniture, leather, and paper; exports silk and wine.

History: Capital of ancient Taurini; became Roman colony under Augustus; seat of Lombard duchy 590–636 A.D.; seat of government under Charlemagne and remained capital till 1032; passed to house of Savoy 1045;

free city for short time; scene of victory of Prince Eugene of Savoy over French 1706; capital of French department of Po 1800–14; reverted to house of Savoy 1815; capital of kingdom of Italy till 1865; important industrial center for Axis forces in World War II; taken by Americans Apr. 30, 1945.

Tu′ri·ya (tōō′ryĭ·yá); *Pol.* **Tur′ja** (tōōr′yä). River ab. 100 m. long in NW Ukraine, U.S.S.R.; formerly in Wołyń and Polesie depts., E Poland; flows N into the Pripyat river.

Tur′ka (tōōr′kả). Town, SW Ukraine, U.S.S.R., 67 m. SW of Lvov (formerly in Lwów dept., Poland); pop. 10,145; lumber; stone quarries.

Tur·ka′na (tōōr·kä′nả). Former extraprovincial district, NW Kenya colony, E Africa, W of Lake Rudolf; 26.547 sq. m.; pop. 79,918; ✳ Kapenguria; includes former Rudolf prov., transferred from Uganda protectorate.

Tur′ke·stan′ (tûr′kĕ·stăn′; -stän′). **1** Region, Central Asia. See TURKISTAN.
2 Town, S Kazakh S.S.R., Soviet Central Asia, on the Chkalov-Tashkent R.R. 140 m. NNW of Tashkent, ab. 20 m. E of the Syr Darya river; an ancient town with a fine mosque.

Túr′ke·ve′ (tōōr′kĕ·vĕ′). City, 50 m. SW of Debrecen, E Hungary; pop. 13,805.

Tur′key (tûr′kĭ). **1** *Turk.* **Tür′ki·ye′** (tür′kĭ·yĕ′). Republic, SE Europe and SW Asia, including Asia Minor: Turkey in Europe 9254 sq. m. with pop. 1,267,857; Turkey in Asia 285,162 sq. m. with pop. 14,890,161; total area 294,416 (exclusive of Hatay), pop. 16,158,018, (1940) 17,869,901; area including water 298,123 sq. m.; ✳ Ankara. Divided roughly (not politically) into Turkey in Europe (Eastern Thrace), Anatolia (W and cen. Turkey in Asia), Armenia (NE), and Kurdistan (SE). Turkey in Europe bounded on N by Bulgaria, on E by Black Sea and the Bosporus, on S by Sea of Marmara and Dardanelles, and on W by Aegean Sea and Greece (Meriç river); Turkey in Asia bounded on N by the Straits, Sea of Marmara, Black Sea, on NE by U.S.S.R., on E by Iran, on SE by Iraq, on S by Syria and the Mediterranean Sea, and on W by the Aegean Sea. A mountainous country with extensive plateau

covering cen. Asia Minor; highest ranges are in NE and E in Armenia (highest peak Ararat 16 873 ft.); along N coast are the Şmali Anadolu Dağları and on S coast the Taurus Range. Its rivers comprise the upper courses of Tigris and Euphrates (Frat) in the E, the Kızıl Irmak in the N, Sakarya in NW and Menderes in W with many other smaller but important streams; its lakes are numerous, esp. Lake Van in the E and several large ones in cen. and W cen. Anatolia. Its long coast line has few islands except in the Aegean and there most of them belong to Greece. Agriculture is chief industry and main products are cereals, tobacco, cotton, figs, raisins, olives,

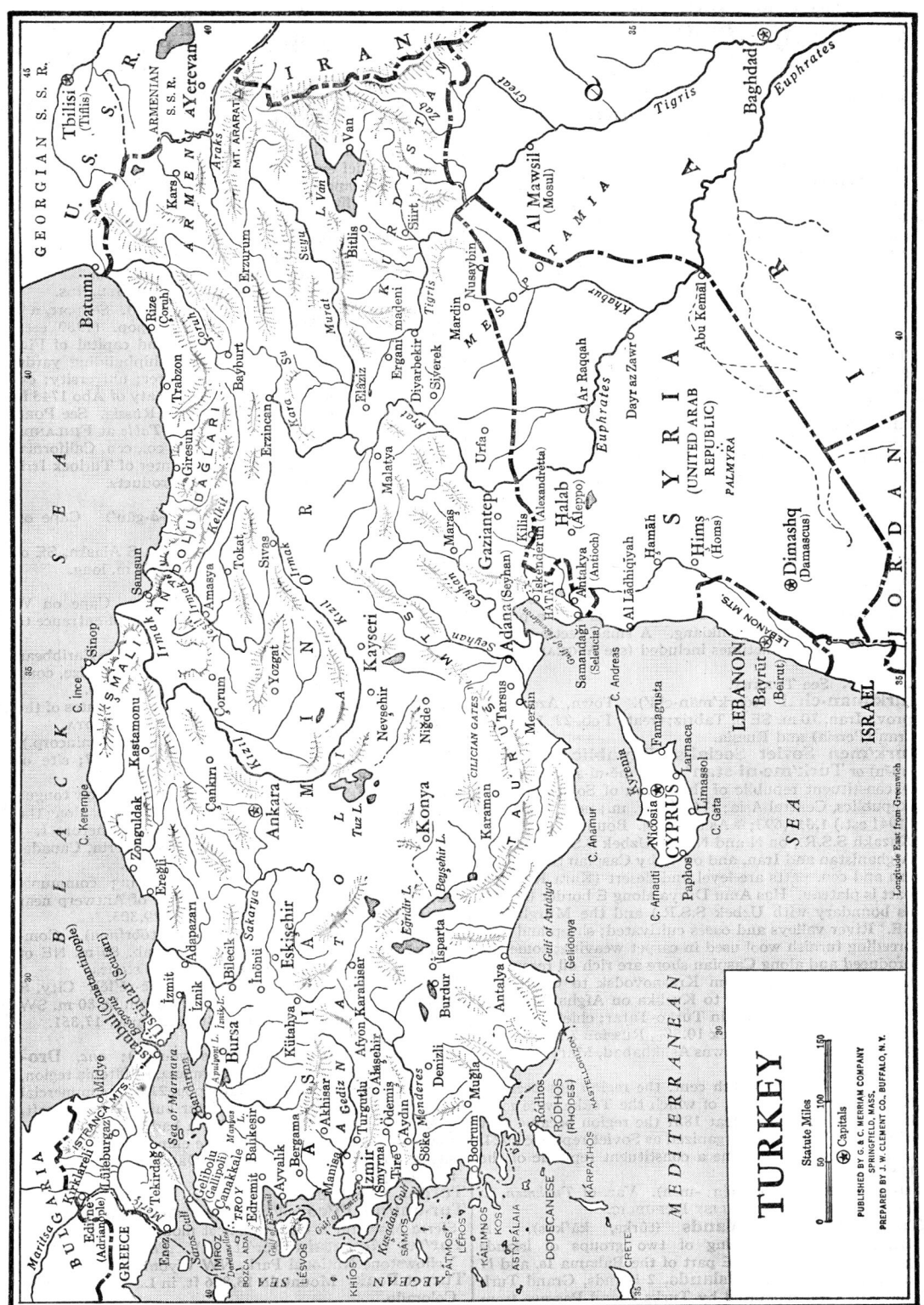

TURKEY

Statute Miles

⊛ Capitals

0   50   100   150

PUBLISHED BY G. & C. MERRIAM COMPANY
SPRINGFIELD, MASS.

PREPARED BY J. W. CLEMENT CO., BUFFALO, N.Y.

nuts, opium, and silk goods; animal husbandry is important; in minerals chief value is in coal and chrome. Administratively divided into 58 vilayets, five in Europe (two of them, İstanbul and Çanakkale, also having portions in Asia) and 53 in Asia. Chief cities İstanbul, İzmir, Ankara, Adana, and Bursa.

History: For earlier history, see OTTOMAN EMPIRE; beginning with Young Turk movement, which led revolt 1908, a nationalist group sought reform in Ottoman Empire; the nationalists, under Mustafa Kemal Pasha, later known as Kemal Atatürk, set up government at Ankara 1919; repudiated Sèvres treaty, defeated Greece (*q.v.*) 1920–22, adopted constitution 1921 (later amended), and formally proclaimed Turkish republic 1923; abolished caliphate 1924 and Islam as state religion 1928; joined Balkan Pact 1934 and nonagression pact with Iraq, Iran, and Afghanistan 1937; remilitarized the Straits (*q.v.*) 1936; incorporated Republic of Hatay (see ALEXANDRETTA) 1939; remained neutral throughout World War II (1939–45). See *Eastern Thrace* at THRACE.

2 River ab. 135 m. long, NE Iowa; rises in Howard co., flows SE into Mississippi river in SE Clayton co.

Türkheim. See TURCKHEIM.

Turkish Armenia. See Turkish ARMENIA.

Turkish Empire. = OTTOMAN EMPIRE.

Tur′ki·stan′ (tûr′kĭ·stăn′; -stän′) *or* **Tur′ke·stan′** (tûr′kĕ-). Region, Central Asia, now in U.S.S.R., China, and Afghanistan. Its W part (**Russian,** *or* **Western, Turkistan**), a former Russian government-general; total area ab. 57,700 sq. m. Conquered by Russia 1859–65. Chief cities Tashkent, Samarkand, and Bukhara. Between 1920 and 1925 divided by Soviet government into the Turkmen, Uzbek, Tadzhik, Kazakh, and Kirgiz Soviet Socialist Republics. (See these terms.) Its E part (**Chinese,** *or* **Eastern, Turkistan**) is now a part of Chinese province of Sinkiang. A small section of NE Afghanistan is sometimes included (see AFGHAN TURKISTAN).

Türkiye. See TURKEY.

Turk′man·chai′ (tōork′män·chī′). Town, Azerbaijan prov., Iran, 70 m. SE of Tabriz; treaty Feb. 22, 1828 bet. Iran (Persia) and Russia.

Turk′men Soviet Socialist Republic (tûrk′mĕn; -mĕn) *or* **Turk′me·ni·stan′** (tûrk′mĕ·nĭ·stăn′; -stän′). A constituent republic of the Union of Soviet Socialist Republics, Central Asia; 171,249 sq. m.; pop. 1,253,985, (1941 est.) 1,317,693; ✱ Ashkhabad. Bounded on NW by Kazakh S.S.R., on N and NE by Uzbek S.S.R., on S by Afghanistan and Iran, and on W by Caspian Sea. Western and cen. parts are level and desert (Kara Kum); E part is plateau. Has Amu Darya along E border (in part as boundary with Uzbek S.S.R.) and the Murghab in SE. River valleys and oases cultivated; sheep and goat breeding furnish wool used in carpet weaving; some silk produced and along Caspian shore are rich oil resources. Crossed by railroad from Krasnovodsk to Chardzhou with branch from Mary to Kushka on Afghan frontier. Predominant ethnic strain Turko-Tatar; chief nationalities Turkmen 72%, Uzbek 10.5%, Russian 7.5%; nearly ¾ in oases areas. Chief towns Ashkhabad, Mary, Krasnovodsk, Chardzhou.

History: Since the 10th cent. the region has been inhabited by Turki tribes, of which the Tekke were most important; by their defeat 1881 the region became part of Russian Turkistan; organized as Soviet republic 1924, and in May 1925 became a constituent republic of the U.S.S.R.

Tur′ko·men (tûr′kŏ·mĕn; -mĕn). Var. of *Turkmen,* in TURKMEN SOVIET SOCIALIST REPUBLIC.

Turks and Cai′cos Islands (tûrks, kā′kŭs). A British colony consisting of two groups of islands geographically in the SE part of the Bahama Is. and N of Hispaniola: **Turks Islands,** 2 islands, Grand Turk and Salt Cay, separated by Turks Island Passage from

Caicos Is. to the W; **Caicos Islands,** a group of small islands comprising **South Caicos, East Caicos, Grand Caicos, North Caicos, Prov′i·den′ci·a′les** (prŏv′ĭ·dĕn′shĭ·ä′lĕs), **West Caicos,** and numerous small cays ENE of Great Inagua I. Total area 166 sq. m.; pop. (1940 est.) 5300; ✱ Grand Turk. Turks Is. are separated by Mouchoir Passage from Mouchoir Bank to the SE, and Caicos Is. by Caicos Passage from Mayaguana I. to the NW. Chief industries collecting salt and sponges; chief exports sponges and sisal hemp. Has frequent hurricanes. Discovered c. 1512; visited by traders after 1678; first permanent settlement c. 1781; at first under Bahamas government but a dependency of Jamaica 1848–62. See *Map* at BAHAMA ISLANDS.

Turks Island Passage. Channel in the N cen. West Indies, SE of Caicos Is. and NW of Turks Is.

Turks Islands. See TURKS AND CAICOS ISLANDS.

Tur′ku (tōōr′kōō); *Swedish* **A′bo** (ō′bōō). Seaport, a ✱ of Turku-Pori dept., SW Finland; pop. (1939 est.) 73,700; 3d largest city in Finland, and capital of Finland until 1812; excellent harbor; shipbuilding yards, sawmills, textile mills; shipping center; university; cathedral; scene of the signing of the Treaty of Åbo 1743 in which Sweden ceded Viipuri dept. to Russia. See PORI.

Tur′ku-Po′ri (tōōr′kōō-pô′rĭ). See *Table* at FINLAND.

Tur′lock (tûr′lŏk). City, Stanislaus co., cen. California, 38 m. SE of Stockton; pop. 9116; center of Turlock Irrigation District; dairy and poultry products.

Turn. See TRNOVANY.

Turn′a·gain, Cape (tûrn′ȧ·gĕn′; -ȧ·gān′). Cape on SE coast of North I., New Zealand.

Turnagain Arm. Arm of Cook Inlet, S Alaska, SE of Anchorage and N of Kenai penin.; ab. 50 m. long.

Turnau. See TURNOV.

Turn′ber′ry Point (tûrn′bĕr′ĭ; -bĕr·ĭ). Cape on W coast of Ayrshire, SW Scotland, on E side of entrance to Firth of Clyde; lighthouse.

Tur′neffe Islands (tûr′nĕf). Island group in Caribbean Sea off coast of E cen. Brit. Honduras opp. Belize, comprising **Turneffe Island** and numerous islets.

Tur′ner (tûr′nẽr). Name of counties in two states of the U.S. See *Tables* at GEORGIA and SOUTH DAKOTA.

Tur′ners Falls (tûr′nẽrz fôlz′). Village (unincorp.), Franklin co., NW Massachusetts; pop. 4917; site of earliest dam on Connecticut river.

Tur′ner′s Peninsula (tûr′nẽrz). Long narrow tongue of land, actually an island, extending ab. 60 m. along the S shore of Sierra Leone, W Africa, SE of Sherbro I.

Tur′ner Valley (tûr′nẽr). Town, SW Alberta, Canada, 26 m. SSW of Calgary; pop. 719; oil field.

Turn′hout (tûrn′hout). Manufacturing commune, Antwerp prov., N Belgium, 26 m. NE of Antwerp near Netherlands border; pop. (1938 est.) 29,305.

Tur′nov (tōōr′nôf); *Ger.* **Tur′nau** (tōōr′nou). Commune, NW Bohemia, Czechoslovakia, ab. 80 m. NE of Prague; pop. (1930) 8594; semiprecious stones.

Tur′nu-Mă·gu·re′le (tōōr′nōō·mȧ·gōō·rĕ′lĕ). City, S Muntenia region, S Romania, on the Danube 80 m. SW of Bucharest opp. Nikopol in Bulgaria; pop. 17,351.

Turnu Roşu. See ROŞU.

Tur′nu-Se′ve·rin (tōōr′nōō-sĕ′vĕ·rēn′); *anc.* **Dro·be′ta** (drŏ·bē′tȧ). City, SW Romania, in Oltenia region, on Danube river near Iron Gate; pop. 21,073; commercial center; large government yards for building river craft. Ancient Roman town of Drobeta had commemorative tower (Turris Severi) built by the emperor Severus; also site of Trajan's bridge over the Danube, largest in Roman Empire.

Turoni. See TOURS.

Tur·qui′no, Pi′co (pē′kŏ tōōr·kē′nŏ). Peak 6560 ft. in Sierra Maestra, E Cuba; highest mountain in Cuba.

Tur′ret Mountain (tûr′ĕt; -ĭt). Peak 10,400 ft. in Yellowstone National Park, NW Wyoming.

Turret Peak. Mountain 13,826 ft. in La Plata co., SW Colorado.

Tur·rial′ba (tŏor·ryäl′vä). Volcano 10,900 ft. in Costa Rica, NE of Cartago.

Turris Libisonis. See PORTO TORRES.

Turt·kul′ (tŏort·kŏol′); *formerly* **Pe′tro·a′le·ksan′-drovsk** (pĕt′rô·ăl′ĕg·zăn′drôfsk; *Russ.* pyē′trŭ·ŭ·lyĭ-ksän′drŭfsk). Town on right bank of lower Amu Darya, W Uzbek S.S.R., Soviet Central Asia, just above Urgench; pop. ab. 1000; former capital of Kara-Kalpak Republic. Originally a Russian fort.

Tur′tle Creek (tûr′t′l). Borough, Allegheny co., SW Pennsylvania, 11 m. E of Pittsburgh; pop. 10,607; settled c. 1765; manufactures electrical equipment; coal mines.

Turtle Islands. 1 Group of small islands off W point of Sherbro I., Sierra Leone, W Africa.
2 See SCHILDPAD ISLANDS.
3 Group of islets in SW Sulu Sea off North Borneo coast ab. 25 m. N of Sandakan; annexed by Republic of the Philippines 1948.

Turtle Mountains. Small range in N North Dakota, in Bottineau and Rolette cos.

Tur′ton (tûr′t′n). Urban district, Lancashire, NW England, 13 m. NNW of Manchester; pop. 10,951; cotton goods; stone quarrying.

Tur′tu·ca′ia (tŏor′tŏo·kä′yä); *Bulg.* **Tu′tra·kan′** (tŏo′trä·kän′). Town, NE Bulgaria, in Dobruja region, on the Danube; pop. 11,103; in Romania 1913–40.

Tu′ru·gart′ Pass (tŏo′rŏo·gärt′). Mountain pass 12,155 ft. through W end of Tien Shan range, Central Asia, on highway from Kashgar in W Sinkiang, China, to towns of Kirgiz S.S.R.

Tu·ru·khansk′ (tŏo·rŏo·kánsk′). Town, W cen. Evenki National District, Soviet Russia, Asia, at junction of Lower Tunguska with the Yenisei.

Tu′run–Po′rin (tŏo′rŏon·pô′rĭn). = *Turku-Pori:* see *Table* at FINLAND.

Tus′ca·loo′sa (tŭs′ka·lŏo′sa). **1** County in Alabama. See *Table* at ALABAMA.
2 Commercial city, its ⊗, W cen. Alabama, on Black Warrior river 50 m. SW of Birmingham; pop. 63,370; manufactures paper, paper bags, dairy products, iron products, brick, lumber; coal fields in vicinity. Univ. of Alabama (founded 1831; located in E suburb called University; coed.); Stillman Coll. (coed.; 1876). Settled 1816; state capital 1826–46; captured by Federal troops 1865.

Tus′can Apennines (tŭs′kan). See APENNINES.

Tuscan Archipelago; *Ital.* **Ar′ci·pe′la·go To·sca′no** (är′chĕ·pä′lä·gô tôs·kä′nô). The group of small islands bet. Corsica and Italy; includes Elba, Pianosa, Montecristo, Giglio, and Giannutri.

Tuscania. See TOSCANELLA.

Tus′ca·ny (tŭs′ka·nĭ); *Ital.* **To·sca′na** (tôs·kä′nä). Compartimento of cen. Italy; for provincial divisions, area, and pop., see *Table* at ITALY; on Tyrrhenian and Ligurian Seas. bet. Latium and Liguria; generally mountainous; coastal area marshy and unhealthful; watered by Arno, Cecina, Serchio, and Ombrone rivers; extensive mineral wealth (iron, copper, marble, mercury, lignite, etc.); fertile valleys produce wheat, corn, olives, tobacco, wine; active industrial exploitation. Chief cities Florence, Leghorn, Apuania, Lucca, Pisa, Pistoia, and Arezzo. Early in medieval period a margraviate; later (11th cent.) a Lombard duchy; subdivided in 12th and 13th cents. into small republics, subsequently reunited under the Medici dukes of Florence (see FLORENCE); passed to house of Lorraine, and subsequently to Sardinia and the kingdom of Italy. Tuscan dialect now standard Italian. Region of severe fighting during latter part of World War II, esp. July–Sept. 1944.

Tus′ca·ra′was (tŭs′ka·rô′wăs). **1** River ab. 125 m. long, NE Ohio; rises in Summit co., flows S and joins Walhonding river in Coshocton co. to form Muskingum river.
2 County in Ohio. See *Table* at OHIO.

Tus′ca·ro′ra Deep (tŭs′ka·rōr′a). Ocean depth 32,644 ft. in W Pacific Ocean off SE coast of Honshu, Japan.

Tuscarora Mountains. 1 Range in N Nevada, chiefly in Eureka and Elko cos.
2 Ridge in S Pennsylvania extending along the boundary bet. Juniata, Huntingdon, and Fulton cos. on the NW, and Perry and Franklin cos. on the SE.

Tus·co′la (tŭs·kō′la). **1** County in Michigan. See *Table* at MICHIGAN.
2 City, ⊗ of Douglas co., E cen. Illinois, 36 m. E of Decatur; pop. 3875.

Tus′cu·lum (tŭs′kŭ·lŭm). Ancient town in Latium, Italy, ab. 12 m. SE of Rome and just N of Lake Albano and the Alban Hills; alt. ab. 2200 ft.; many interesting ruins. In very early times a rival of Rome, by which it was made subject after battle of Lake Regillus 496 B.C.; furnished many prominent citizens of Rome in time of the Republic; home of Cicero.

Tus·cum′bi·a (tŭs·kŭm′bĭ·a). **1** Manufacturing city, ⊗ of Colbert co., NW Alabama, on Tennessee river 10 m. from Wilson Dam; pop. 8994; founded 1817; fertilizers, jute, ginned cotton.
2 Town, ⊗ of Miller co., cen. Missouri; pop. 231.

Tus·ke′gee (tŭs·kē′gĕ). City, ⊗ of Macon co., E Alabama, 38 m. E of Montgomery; pop. 1750; incorp. as borough 1800, as city 1820; cotton gins, cottonseed-oil mills, brick kilns, lumber mills; Tuskegee Institute (1881; coed.) nearby.

Tus′sey Mountain (tŭs′ĭ). Peak 2225 ft. on boundary bet. Blair, Bedford, and Huntingdon cos., S Pennsylvania.

Tus·sum′ (tŏo·sŏom′). Village on W bank of Suez Canal, Egypt, near Ismailia; Turks defeated here 1915.

Tu′sta·no·wi′ce (tŏo′stä·no·vē′tsĕ). Former commune in Lwów dept., Poland, now part of Borislav, W Ukraine.

Tutela. 1 See TULLE city, France.
2 See TUDELA commune, Spain.

Tu′ti·co·rin′ (tŏo′tĭ·kô·rĭn′). Town, S Madras state, S Indian Union, on Gulf of Mannar 75 m. S of Madura; pop. (1941) 75,614; second port of Madras with good trade and steamer connection with Colombo; has large Roman Catholic mission. Very old town, in possession of Portuguese in 1540 and of Dutch in 1658; acquired by British 1825.

Tutrakan. See TURTUCAIA.

Tutt′ling·en (tŏot′lĭng·ĕn). Manufacturing city, Baden-Württemberg state, West Germany, on Danube river 45 m. E of Freiburg; pop. 16,281; shoes, woolen goods, precision tools.

Tu′tu·i′la (tŏo′tŏo·ē′lä). Chief island of American Samoa, in SW cen. Pacific Ocean; 25 m. long by 2 to 6 m. wide; 52 sq. m.; pop. 16,814; chief town Pago Pago, ✳ of American Samoa, at head of deep indentation on S coast, forming Pago Pago Harbor, one of the best in the South Pacific. Has mountain range running length of island; highest point Mt. Matafao 2141 ft.; is densely wooded with beautiful scenery. U.S. naval station on W coast of Pago Pago Harbor.

Tu′tu·pa′ca (tŏo′tŏo·pä′kä). Volcano 18,960 ft. in the Andes Mts., S Peru; ab. 55 m. E of Moquegua.

Tu′va (tŏo′va); *in full* **Tuva Autonomous Soviet Socialist Republic;** *formerly* **Tan′nu Tu′va** (tăn′ŏo tŏo′va; *native* täng′nŏo tŏo·vä′) *or* **U′rian·khai′** (ŏo′-ryäng·kī′). Autonomous republic, Soviet Russia, Asia, bet. Sayan and Tannu Ola Mts.; 64,000 sq. m.; pop. 213,000; ✳ Kyzyl (Kizil Khoto). Bounded on N by Khakass Autonomous Region, Krasnoyarsk Territory, and Irkutsk Region, on E by Buryat-Mongol A.S.S.R., on E and S by Outer Mongolia, and on W by the Oirot Autonomous Region. Mountainous and well-watered; crossed from E to W by the Bei Kem and Khua Kem, headstreams of the Yenisei. See *Map* at CHINA. Inhabitants are 50,000 Tuvinians, 12,000 Russians, and the rest Chinese and Mongols; mainly herdsmen and cattle farmers. Has some mineral resources, esp. asbestos and gold.

History: Until **1911** a part (Uriankhai) of **Outer**

Mongolia but had come gradually under Russian influence since c. 1870; nominally independent 1911–14; a Russian protectorate 1914–17 but again under Chinese influence until 1921; definitely proclaimed independent (as Tannu Tuva) 1921 and signed treaties of friendship with Russia and with Outer Mongolia 1926; incorporated in U.S.S.R. 1945; became an autonomous republic 1961.

Tu·waiq′, Ja′bal (jă′băl tōō·wīk′; -wāk′). Highland area ab. 400 m. long in cen. Saudi Arabia.

Tux·e′do Park (tŭk·sē′dō). Village and resort, Orange co., SE New York, bet. **Tuxedo Lake** and Palisades Interstate Park, on Ramapo river; pop. 723.

Tux′pan (tōōs′pän). **1** Town, S Jalisco state, W cen. Mexico, near Colima border; pop. 6763.
2 Town, Nayarit state, W Mexico, 35 m. NW of Tepic on San Pedro river; pop. 10,315.
3 or **Túx′pam** (tōōs′pän). Town, Veracruz state, E Mexico, on coast 145 m. NW of Veracruz; pop. 13,381.

Tuxpan Reef. Reef in Gulf of Mexico off the seaport town of Tuxpan in N Veracruz state, Mexico.

Tux·te·pec′ (tōōs′tä·pĕk′). Town, NE Oaxaca state, SE Mexico, 80 m. NNE of Oaxaca; pop. 5360; Plan of Tuxtepec issued Jan. 1876 as statement against policies of Pres. Lerdo de Tejada.

Tux′tla (tōōs′tlä). **1** Volcano 5095 ft. in Veracruz state, E Mexico, 75 m. SE of the city of Veracruz and just N of San Andrés Tuxtla; violent eruption 1793, and only mildly active since then.
2 in full **Tuxtla Gu·tiér′rez** (gōō·tyĕr′rás). Town, SE Mexico, ✳ of Chiapas state; pop. 15,883; altitude 1500 ft.; distributing center for sisal, tobacco, coffee, cattle.
3 Town, Veracruz state, E Mexico. See SAN ANDRÉS TUXTLA.

Tú′y (tōō′ē). Commune, Pontevedra prov., NW Spain, 30 m. S of Pontevedra; pop. 13,500; mineral baths; 9th-cent. cathedral; captured several times by Portuguese, notably in 1388, 1397.

Tu′zi·goot National Monument (tōō′zĭ·gōōt). See UNITED STATES, National Monuments.

Tuz′la or **Dol′nja Tuzla** (dȯl′nyä tōōz′lä). Town, Bosnia and Herzegovina, cen. Yugoslavia, 50 m. NNE of Sarajevo; pop. 16,711; trade center in coal and lumber; salt springs; salt mines.

Tuz Lake; *Turk.* **Tuz Gö·lü′** (tōōz gû·lü′); *anc.* **Pa′lus Tat·tae′us** (pā′lŭs tă·tē′ŭs). Salt lake (*gölü*) 45 m. long in W cen. Turkey in Asia; alt. 3100 ft.; at times dried up.

TVA. See TENNESSEE VALLEY AUTHORITY.

Tver. See KALININ.

Tver·tsa′ (tvyĕr·tsȧ′). River ab. 110 m. long in Kalinin Region, Soviet Russia, Europe; flows SE to the Volga at Kalinin. Joined by canal with the Msta.

Tvin. See DWIN.

Tweed (twēd). River 96 m. long in SE Scotland and NE England; rises in Peebles co., SE Scotland, flows E, forming a section of the boundary bet. Scotland and England, crosses the extreme NE border of England and empties into North Sea at Berwick.

Tweeddale. See PEEBLES.

Tweeds′muir Park (twēdz′mŭr). Canadian provincial park, Brit. Columbia; 5400 sq. m.; in Rocky Mts. W of Fraser river and SE of the Skeena; has many lakes, rivers, and mountains; largest lake is Eutsuk Lake, highest point 7562 ft.

Twelve Apostles. See APOSTLE ISLANDS.

Twelve Pins, or **Bens, of Bunnabeola.** See Twelve Pins of BUNNABEOLA.

Twenty–four Par′ga·nas (pŭr′gȧ·näz). District, Presidency division, West Bengal, NE Indian Union; 3696 sq. m.; pop. (1941) 3,536,386; ✳ Alipore (S suburb of Calcutta).

Twick′en·ham (twĭk′′n·ȧm; twĭk′năm). Municipal borough, Middlesex, SE England, on the Thames 11 m. SW of London; pop. 39,906, (1951 pop.) 105,645; part of Greater London, a residential suburb; home of Alexander Pope, Horace Walpole, Catherine of Aragon, Lord Tennyson. Noted Rugby football stadium; motion-picture center.

Twiggs (twĭgz). County in Georgia. See *Table* at GEORGIA.

Twil′lin·gate (twĭl′ĭng·gāt). Town, E Newfoundland, on island at entrance of Notre Dame Bay; pop. (1942 est.) 3300; has fine harbor facilities.

Twin Falls. 1 County in Idaho. See *Table* at IDAHO.
2 City, its ⊗, S Idaho, 110 m. W of Pocatello; pop. 20,126; 4th largest city in the state; trading center in irrigated area producing fruits, wheat, vegetables, potatoes, sugar beets; incorp. as city 1907. About 8 m. NE of the city in the Snake river are the **Twin Falls** at a place where the river divides into two channels to reunite after falling ab. 200 ft.; the S fall is now used for power.

Twin Lakes. Two lakes (Washinee and Washining) in extreme NW Connecticut; resort.

Twin Lakes Reservoir. Reservoir, S Lake co., W cen. Colorado; formed from two small lakes, stores water for irrigation; on its SW shore is the village of **Twin Lakes,** resort.

Twin Mounds. Heights 4309 ft. and 4349 ft. in Cheyenne co., W Nebraska.

Twin Mountain. Peak 8920 ft. in Blue Mts., NE Oregon.

Twin Mountains. 1 Two peaks, North Twin 4769 ft. and South Twin 4926 ft., in the Franconia Mts., N Grafton co., New Hampshire.
2 Peaks 6500 and 6700 ft. in S Jeff Davis co., W Texas.

Twin Peaks. Mountain 10,328 ft. on W cen. boundary of Lemhi co., E cen. Idaho.

Twin Rocks. Locality, Cambria co., SW cen. Pennsylvania, ab. 13 m. N of Johnstown.

Twins, the (twĭnz). Two mountain peaks in S Jasper National Park, SW Alberta, Canada; N peak 12,085 ft. and S peak 11,675 ft.

Twins′burg (twĭnz′bûrg). Village in Twinsburg township (pop. 5848), Summit co., NE Ohio, ab. 17 m. NNE of Akron; pop. 4098.

Twofold Bay. Inlet of Tasman Sea, SE New South Wales, Australia. Eden on N shore has excellent harbor.

Two Harbors. City, ⊗ of Lake co., NE Minnesota, on Lake Superior 26 m. NE of Duluth; pop. 4695; terminal shipping point for iron ore, pulpwood, lumber.

Two Medicine Lake. Small lake in S Glacier National Park, NW Montana.

Two Mountains; *Fr.* **Deux–Mon′tagnes′** (dû′môn′-tän′y′). County, Quebec, Canada. See *Table* at QUEBEC.

Two Mountains, Lake of; *Fr.* **Lac des Deux–Mon′-tagnes′** (lȧk′ dā dû′môn′tän′y′). Expansion of the Ottawa river at its junction with the St. Lawrence, W of Montreal I., Quebec prov., Canada; bordered on SE by Île Perrot and has two outlets to the NE, the Rivière des Mille Îles and Rivière des Prairies.

Two Rivers. City, Manitowoc co., E Wisconsin, on Lake Michigan 7 m. NE of Manitowoc; pop. 12,393; commercial fishing; manufactures aluminum.

Two Sicilies, the. See *the Two Sicilies* in *History* at SICILY.

Ty·a·na (tī′ȧ·nȧ). Ancient city, SW Cappadocia, Asia Minor, on N slope of Taurus Mts.; birthplace of Apollonius, Greek philosopher.

Tyan–Shan (tyȧn′shȧn′). **1** Russian form of TIEN SHAN mountain range.
2 Subdivision of Kirgiz Soviet Socialist Republic, in SE part, Soviet Central Asia, bordering on E on Tien Shan range and Sinkiang prov. of China; ✳ Naryn.

Ty′bee Island (tī′bē). Island 6 m. long in Chatham co., SE Georgia, at mouth of the Savannah river.

Ty′burn (tī′bẽrn). **1** A former small tributary of the Thames in London, England, now underground.
2 A former place of execution on the stream, near where is now the Marble Arch, Hyde Park.

Ty·bur′ni·a (tī-bûr′nĭ-a̍). A residential quarter of London, England, N and E of Hyde Park—so called from the Tyburn.

Ty′ee′, Mount (tī′ē′). Peak 6688 ft. in Chelan co., cen. Washington.

Ty′gart (tī′gẽrt). River ab. 160 m. long, N West Virginia; rises in Randolph co., flows N and unites with West Fork of Monongahela river near Fairmont to form the Monongahela river.

Tygart River Dam. Dam completed 1938 across Tygart river, S of Grafton, Taylor co., N West Virginia; height 232 ft.; impounds water for flood control.

Tyldes′ley (tĭl[d]z′lĭ). Urban district, Lancashire, NW England, 10 m. WNW of Manchester; pop. 18,096; cotton mills; collieries.

Ty′ler (tī′lẽr). 1 Name of counties in two states of the U.S. See *Tables* at TEXAS and WEST VIRGINIA.
2 Locality, Clearfield co., W cen. Pennsylvania, ab. 15 m. NE of Du Bois.
3 Commercial and industrial city, ⊗ of Smith co., NE Texas, 85 m. ESE of Dallas; pop. 51,230; ships quarried limestone, oil, agricultural products (esp. peaches, tomatoes), rose plants; commercial nurseries; oil refineries, cotton and peanut processing plants, lumber mills. Texas Coll. (1894; coed.). Settled c. 1840, incorp. 1846, became city 1875.

Ty′ler·town (tī′lẽr-toun). Town, ⊗ of Walthall co., S Mississippi; pop. 1532.

Tý′lis·sos (tē′lyẽ̍·sôs). Archaeological site near N coast of cen. Crete, SW of Candia; relics of Late Minoan period.

Tylos. See BAHREIN ISLANDS.

Tym·pá′kion (tĕm·pä′kyôn). Village on S coast of Crete, on the Bay of Messara S of Mt. Ida.

Tyn′dall (tĭn′d'l). City, ⊗ of Bon Homme co., SE South Dakota; pop. 1262.

Tyndall, Mount. 1 Peak 14,025 ft. in Sierra Nevada, in Tulare co., S cen. California.
2 Mountain 8280 ft. in Southern Alps, South I., New Zealand, on border bet. Westland and Canterbury provincial dists., NE of Aorangi (Mt. Cook).

Tyne (tīn). 1 River in N England, in Northumberland; formed by confluence of **North Tyne** and **South Tyne;** flows E into North Sea bet. the cities of Tynemouth and South Shields; 35 m. long; including North Tyne, 80 m. long.
2 River 28 m. long, SE Scotland; rises in Midlothian co. and flows NE through East Lothian to the North Sea near Dunbar.

Tyne′mouth (tīn′mouth; -mŭth; tĭn′mŭth). County borough, Northumberland, N England, on North Sea at mouth of the Tyne on its N bank 9 m. E of Newcastle; pop. 64,922, (1951 pop.) 66,544; seaport and shipping point; residential resort; shipbuilding yards; distributing center for coal-mining and metal-manufacturing section.

Tyngs′bor′ough *or* **Tyngs′bor′o** (tĭngz′bûr′ō). Residential town, Middlesex co., NE Massachusetts, on Merrimack river 6 m. WNW of Lowell; pop. 3302.

Tyn′set (tün′sĕt). Town, Hedmark co., E Norway, on the Glomma river; pop. 3780.

Ty′pee (tī′pĕ; *now, more correctly*, **Tai′pi** (tī′pĕ). Beautiful valley in E cen. part of Nuku Hiva I., largest of the Marquesas Is.; scene of Herman Melville's novel *Typee* (1846).

Tyras. 1 See BELGOROD-DNESTROVSKI.
2 See DNIESTER.

Tyre (tīr; *Fr.* **Tyr** (tēr) *or* **Sour** (so͞or); *Arab.* **Es Sur** (ăs so͞or′); *Heb.* **Zor** (tsōr; zōr); *anc.* **Ty′rus** (tī′rŭs). Town in S Lebanon, on the coast of the Mediterranean Sea; pop. ab. 5700; famous maritime city of antiquity; capital of Phoenicia from ab. 11th cent. to 774 B.C. In early times an island with two harbors; now a peninsula formed by the widening of the causeway or mole built by Alexander. Was for centuries a great commercial city, center of Phoenician civilization and mistress of the seas; famous for its silken garments and Tyrian purple. Probably founded in 15th cent. B.C., a colony of Sidon. In Biblical history well known from its king, Hiram (*1 Kings* v, *2 Sam.* v). Withstood attacks from Assyrians and Babylonians but forced to pay tribute; successfully resisted in 6th cent. B.C. a siege of 13 years by Nebuchadnezzar II but was besieged and captured by Alexander 332 B.C.; under control of Seleucids and Romans and in 7th cent. A.D. passed over to Moslems; captured by Crusaders 1124 and became chief city of kingdom of Jerusalem.

Tyree. See TIREE.

Ty′ri·fjord′ (tü′rĕ·fyŏr′; -fyo͞or′). Lake 16 m. long and 7 m. wide in SE Norway, 16 m. W of Oslo; on the N receives the Begna, which issues from it on the SW as the Drammenselv.

Tyrnau. See TRNAVA.

Tyr′na·vos (tẽr′nä·vôs); *Mod. Gr.* **Týr′na·vos.** Town, Larissa dept., E Thessaly, NE Greece, ab. 10 m. NW of Larissa; pop. 7158.

Tyrol. See TIROL.

Ty′rone (tī′rōn). Borough, Blair co., S cen. Pennsylvania, 15 m. NE of Altoona; pop. 7792; settled 1850; manufactures paper, textiles, lumber.

Ty·rone′ (tĭ·rōn′). County, W cen. Northern Ireland; 1218 sq. m.; pop. 132,049; ⊗ Omagh; agriculture, livestock raising, coal mining, whisky distilling.

Ty·ron′za Lake (tĭ·rŏn′za̍). Lake in cen. Mississippi co., NE Arkansas; outlet, **Tyronza River,** flowing S.

Tyr′o·poe′on (tĭr′ō̍·pē′ŏn). Valley within the walled city of Jerusalem, W of Zion, the City of David.

Tyros. See BAHREIN ISLANDS.

Tyr′rell (tĭr′ĕl). County in North Carolina. See *Table* at NORTH CAROLINA.

Tyrrha. See TIRE.

Tyr·rhe′ni·an Sea (tĭ·rē′nĭ·ăn); *Ital.* **Ma′re Tir·re′no** (mä′rĕ tĕr·râ′nō); *anc.* **Ma′re Tyr·rhe′num** (mā′rē tĭ·rē′nŭm). The part of the Mediterranean Sea W of Italy, N of Sicily, and E of Sardinia and Corsica.

Tyrus. See TYRE.

Tys Fjord (tüs). Inlet extending S from upper Vest Fjord on NW coast of Norway.

Ty′tär·saa′ri (tü′tär·sä′rĭ). Island in Gulf of Finland off coast of Estonia, NW of Narva.

Tyu·men′ (tu̍·mĕn′; *Russ.* -myän′y′). City, ✳ of Tyumen Region, Soviet Russia, Asia, in W part on Tura river 125 m. SW of Tobolsk and 190 m. E of Sverdlovsk; pop. 75,537; has rail connections with Sverdlovsk and Omsk but river navigation is difficult; has many and varied industries. Established as a fort 1585 and became the first settled Russian town beyond the Urals.

Tyumen Region. New region of Soviet Russia, Asia, created 1945; ✳ Tyumen.

Tyuri. See TÜRI.

Tza·rá′ra·cua (tsä·rä′rä·kwä). Waterfall 6 m. SE of the town of Uruapan del Progreso, Michoacán state, SW Mexico.

Tze′liu′tsing′ (dzŭ′lū′jĭng′). City, S Szechwan prov., S cen. China, bet. Min and To rivers 110 m. W of Chungking; pop. ab. 100,000.

Tzu *or* **Tze** (dzŭ). River ab. 375 m. long, cen. Hunan prov., SE cen. China; flows into Tungting Hu (lake) just W of mouth of the Siang.

U

U′a Hu′ka (ōō′ä hōō′kä). Small island of Marquesas Is., S Pacific Ocean, ab. 30 m. E of Nuku Hiva I.

Ualual. See WALWAL.

Uap. See YAP.

U′a Pu (ōō′ä pōō′) or Ua Pau (pou′). One of the Marquesas Is., French Polynesia, S Pacific Ocean, ab. 25 m. S of Nuku Hiva; has peak 4040 ft. high.

Uaso Nyiro. = WASO NYIRO.

Ua′tu·má′ (wä′tōō·má′). River 350 m. long, N Brazil; flows SE into the Amazon near E border of Amazonas state.

Uau·pés′ (wou·pās′). River ab. 700 m. long in NW South America; rises in S cen. Colombia where it is called the Vau·pés′ (bou·pās′), flows ESE across Brazilian border into Rio Negro; forms small section of Colombia-Brazil boundary.

Ua′xac·tún′ (wä′shäk·tōōn′). Ruins of an ancient town in N Guatemala, one of the oldest known centers of Maya civilization, founded probably in 1st cent. A.D.

U·bá′ (ōō·vá′). City, SE Minas Gerais state, E Brazil, 130 m. N of Rio de Janeiro; pop. (1940 est.) 11,101.

'U·baid′, al– (äl′ōō·bäd′; -bid′). = TELL EL-OBEID.

U·ban′gi (ü·bäng′[g]ē; ōō·bäng′[g]ē); Fr. Ou′ban′-gui′ (ōō′bän′gē′). River in cen. Africa; formed by confluence of Bomu and Uele rivers on N cen. border of Republic of Congo; 700 m. long, with longest headstream ab. 1400 m.; flows W and S, forming section of boundary bet. Republic of Congo, Congo Republic, and Central African Republic; empties into Congo river W of Lake Tumba; sometimes called Ma′ku·a (mä′kōō·ä) in its upper course and Mo·ban′gi (mō·bäng′[g]ē; -bäng′-[g]ē) in its lower course.

U·ban′gi–Sha′ri (ü·bäng′[g]ē·shä′rē; ōō·bäng′-); Fr. Ou′ban′gui′–Cha′ri′ (ōō′bän′gē′shä′rē′). Former territory in French Equatorial Africa, since 1958 the Central African Republic, Fr. République Centrafricaine, of the French Community, N of Ubangi and Bomu rivers and bet. Cameroun and the Republic of the Sudan; ab. 241,700 sq. m.; pop. (1959 est.) 1,117,000; ✳ Bangui. Plateau region, its N half above 7°N an open savanna country drained by tributaries of the Chari river, its S half thickly forested and marking N edge of Congo basin. Trade is in forest products, palm oil, and rubber. Only important town is Bangui. Became part of French Equatorial Africa 1910 when it included Chad colony and was called Ubangi-Shari-Chad (-chăd′), Fr. Oubangui-Chari-Tchad (-chäd′); lost Chad colony 1920; given territorial status 1946; became a republic Dec. 1, 1958.

U′bay (ōō′bī). Municipality, NE coast of Bohol I., Phil. Is.; pop. 21,213.

U′be (ōō′bĕ; Jap. ōō·bĕ). Seaport city, Yamaguchi prefecture, SW Honshu, Japan, at W end of Inland Sea 18 m. E of Shimonoseki; pop. (1945) 82,122; bombed by Allied planes July 1945.

U′be·da (ōō′vä·t̲hä). Commercial commune, Jaén prov., S Spain, 22 m. NE of Jaén; pop. 31,093; stock raising, esp. horses. Reconquered from Moors in 1212.

U′be·ra′ba (ōō′vĕ·rá′vä). City, W Minas Gerais state, E Brazil; pop. (1940 est.) 33,786; altitude 2278 ft.; equidistant (ab. 260 m.) W of Belo Horizonte and N of São Paulo; center of extensive cattle-raising district.

U′ber·lân′dia (ōō′vēr·länn′dyä). City, Minas Gerais state, E Brazil, on railroad 60 m. N of Uberaba; pop. (1940 est.) 21,837.

U·bi′na (ōō·vē′nä). Peak 16,830 ft. in Potosí dept., SW Bolivia.

U·bi′nas (ōō·vē′näs). Peak 17,390 ft. in Moquegua dept., S Peru.

U·bon (ōō·bŭn) or U·bol Ra·ja·dha·ni (ōō·bŭn [sic] rät·chä·t'hä·nē). 1 Province, SE Thailand; 8759 sq. m.; pop. 745,307.

2 Town, its ✳, E terminal of railroad from Ayudhya and ab. 40 m. W of French Indochina border; on left bank of Mun river just below its junction with the Si.

Ub′su Nur (ōōb′sōō nōōr′). Lake (nur) 1500 sq. m., NW Outer Mongolia, on S border of Tuva Autonomous Region, U.S.S.R.

U′ca·ya′li (ōō′kä·yä′lē). River ab. 1200 m. long in cen. and N Peru; chief headstream of Amazon river; formed by confluence of Apurímac and Urubamba rivers in cen. Peru, flows N to unite with Marañón river and form Amazon river; navigable for 600 m.

Uccle. See UKKEL.

U·chi·u·ra Bay (ōō·chē·ōō·rä). Inlet of W Pacific Ocean on E coast of S extension of Hokkaido I., Japan, lat. 42°20′N.

Uck′field (ŭk′fēld). Former urban district, East Sussex, S England; pop. (1931) 3557; near Piltdown (q.v.).

U·da′ (ōō·dà′); formerly Chu·na′ (chōō·nà′). River ab. 470 m. long, Irkutsk Region and Krasnoyarsk Territory, Soviet Russia, Asia; flows N and W to Upper Tunguska river, which empties into the Yenisei.

U·dai′pur (ōō·dī′pōōr; ōō′dī·pōōr′) or Oo·dey′pore (ōō·dī′pōr; ōō′dī·pōr′). 1 Former Indian state, Eastern States, SE India; 1045 sq. m.; pop. (1941) 118,331; ✳ Dharmjaygarh.

2 also Me·war′ (mà·wär′). Former Indian state, S Rajputana, NW India; 13,170 sq. m.; pop. (1941) 1,926,698. Region mostly level plain but part of Aravalli Range lies in SW. Its ruler, the maharana, was recognized as highest in rank of all Rajput princes. In relation to British government was organized as Mewar Residency. Offered strong resistance to Mogul emperors; in 18th cent. suffered from civil wars and attacks by Marathas; in June 1947 joined Union of Rajasthan.

3 City, ✳ of former Udaipur (Mewar) state, now in Rajasthan, 208 m. SSW of Jaipur; altitude 2469 ft.; pop. (1941) 59,648; picturesque city on shore of Lake Pichola, with numerous attractive palaces and temples.

Udayadhani. See UTHAI THANI.

Ud′de·val′la (ŭd′ĕ·väl′à). Town, Göteborg and Bohus prov., SW Sweden, near coast 45 m. N of Göteborg; pop. 18,408; textile mills, match factories.

Udd′jaur (ŭd′your). Lake 92 sq. m. in Västerbotten prov., N Sweden, connecting Hornavan and Storavan lakes, and drained by the Skellefte river.

U·dham′pur (ōōd·hŭm′pōōr). Town, Jammu div., Jammu and Kashmir state, N India, ab. 20 m. NE of Jammu; pop. 3633.

U′di·ne (ōō′dĕ·nä). 1 Former name of Friuli prov.: see Table at ITALY.

2 anc. U′ti·na (ū′t'n·à). Commune, ✳ of Friuli prov., Venezia Euganea, NE Italy, 61 m. NE of Venice; pop. 63,098; 13th-cent. cathedral, 15th-cent. town hall (restored after fire 1876); ancient city walls; seat of several learned societies; manufactures silk, iron, leather, paper, metalware. In World War I an Italian military base of operations against Austria 1915–18; occupied by Austrian troops Oct. 1917.

Ud′murt Republic (ōōd′mōōrt; Russ. ōōt·mōōrt′), officially Udmurt Autonomous Soviet Socialist Republic; formerly Vo·tyak′ (vŭ·tyák′). Autonomous republic, E Soviet Russia, Europe; 14,494 sq. m.; pop. 1,220,007, (1941 est.) 1,282,987; ✳ Izhevsk; a subdivision of the R.S.F.S.R. Bounded on W and N by Kirov Region, on E by Molotov Region, and on S by Tatar Republic; touches Bashkir Republic on SE. In W foothills of Ural Mts. in region bet. the Kama (q.v.) and Vyatka rivers. Has extensive forests and lumbering is one of its main industries; others are stock raising and agriculture (raising of rye, oats, flax, potatoes). Products of its peasant crafts are important in the trade. Crossed at the N and S by main E and W trunk railroads, with a

branch to Izhevsk and Votkinsk. Predominant ethnic strain is Finno-Ugrian; chief nationalities Udmurt 52%, Russian 43%. The Udmurts, also known as the Votyaks, represent eastern branch of the Finno-Ugrian peoples, speaking a Finnish dialect akin to Permian. Russian penetration began in 12th cent. and colonization three centuries later; after the Revolution created an autonomous area; suffered greatly in famine 1921–22; made autonomous republic 1936; in World War II its citizens by their skill in operating modern machinery contributed greatly to development of Ural Industrial Area.

U·don Tha·ni or **U·dorn·dha·ni** (ōō·dôn·t'hä·nē); also **Ban Mak Khaeng** (bän mäk k'hăng). **1** Province, NE Thailand; 4592 sq. m.; pop. 262,819.
2 Town, its ✱, 40 m. S of Vientiane, Laos, and terminus of railroad from Nakhon Ratchasima.

U′dot (ōō′dôt). Island in cen. part of Truk (q.v.).

Uea. See UVÉA.

Uebi Scebeli. See Webbe SHIBELI.

U·e·da (ōō·ĕ·dä) or **U·ye·da** (ōō·yĕ·dä). Town, Nagano prefecture, cen. Honshu, Japan; pop. (1945) 39,783; center of silkworm culture; has Government Sericultural School.

Ue′le (wĕ′lå); also **Wel′le** (wĕ′lå). River ab. 700 m. long in cen. Africa; flows W across N Congo to unite with Bomu river and form Ubangi river.

Ue·len′ (wĕ·lĕn′); also **Wel·len′**. Village, Far Eastern Region, Soviet Russia, Asia, at tip of Chukotski Penin., on Bering Strait near East Cape; Soviet airfield.

Uel′zen or **Ül′zen** (ül′tsĕn). City, Lower Saxony state, W Germany, in the former province of Hannover, Prussia, 21 m. SSE of Lüneburg; pop. 11,809; manufactures sugar, asbestos, roofing. Became city 1270.

Uer′ding·en (ür′dĭng·ĕn) or **Uerdingen am Rhein** (äm rīn′). Former city (pop. 11,779), Düsseldorf govt. dist., Rhine Province, Prussia, Germany; since 1929 part of city of Krefeld-Uerdingen am Rhein (q.v.).

U·fa′ (ōō·få′). **1** River ab. 430 m. long in Bashkir Republic, Soviet Russia, Europe; rises in W Chelyabinsk Region and flows NW and SW through the Southern Ural Mts. to join the Belaya river at Ufa; partly navigable.
2 City, ✱ of Bashkir Republic, in cen. part at junction of Belaya and Ufa rivers, 250 m. NE of Kuibyshev; pop. 245,863; in Ural Industrial Area; the industrial and cultural center of the republic with large percentage of the population Russian; has smelting and metallurgical plants developed here because of the rich mineral resources of the Southern Urals; also has other important mills and factories; rich oil fields nearby. Founded 1574; prominent point of conflict in civil war 1918–20.

U·gan′da (ū·găn′då; ōō·gän′dä). Country, E Africa, N of Lake Victoria; 93,981 sq. m., including 13,680 sq. m. of water (N half of Lake Victoria); pop. 6,845,000; ✱ Kampala; a dominion of the British Commonwealth; for administrative purposes, divided into four provinces, Buganda, Eastern, Northern, and Western; principal native kingdom is Buganda. Bounded on N by Republic of Sudan, on E by Kenya, on S by Lake Victoria and Tanganyika, on SW by Rwanda, and on W by Republic of Congo. On E are high mountains along Kenya boundary, highest Mt. Elgon 14,176 ft.; high Ruwenzori group on W, highest 16,791 ft.; plateau region (Ankole) in SW, dense forests in W part, and marshes on N shore of Lake Victoria and around Lake Kyoga in S cen. part. Traversed by the Nile which issues from Lake Victoria at Ripon Falls, flows through Lakes Kyoga and Albert on the W and then N in NW corner of Uganda into Republic of Sudan; Lakes Edward and George are in the SW. Cotton is chief product; coffee, oil seeds, ivory, tin ore, sugar, and rubber also exported. Chief towns Kampala, Jinja, and Entebbe.
History: Native kingdom crossed by explorers Grant and Speke 1862; soon after arrival of first group of missionaries 1877, religious factions developed which com-

bined with political rivalry to produce civil strife; in 1890 agent of British East Africa Co. arrived; formally proclaimed British protectorate 1894; granted self-rule Mar. 1962; became a dominion of the British Commonwealth Oct. 9, 1962.

U′ga·rit′ (ōō′gä·rēt′). Ancient city on site of modern Ras Shamra (q.v.), on E coast of the Mediterranean Sea N of Latakia, Syria, flourishing c. 1400 to 1360 B.C., and mentioned in Egyptian inscriptions, in the Tell el 'Amarna letters, and in Hittite records. Its remains have contributed much to our knowledge of Western Semitic religion and language. Destroyed by an earthquake c. 1350.

Ugernum. See BEAUCAIRE.

Ugliano. See ULJAN.

U·har′ie (û·här′ĭ) or **U·whar′rie** (û·hwär′ĭ). River, cen. North Carolina; rises in NW Randolph co., flows S into Montgomery co., and joins Yadkin river 10 m. W of Troy to form Pee Dee river (q.v.).

Uh′richs·ville (ūr′ĭks·vĭl). City, Tuscarawas co., E Ohio, 28 m. S of Canton; pop. 6201; forms single community with Dennison to the E (called "Twin Cities"); settled 1804; manufactures clay products (esp. sewer tile); fire-clay deposits, coal mines nearby.

U·i′ha (ōō·ē′hä). Island in E Haabai group, Tonga Is., SW cen. Pacific Ocean.

U·in′ka·ret Plateau (ōō·ĭng′kȧ·rĕt). Tableland 5400 to 6100 ft. in N Mohave co., NW Arizona S of Colorado river.

U·in′ta (û·ĭn′tȧ). **1** River, NE Utah; rises in Uinta Mts., flows SE into Duchesne river in W Uintah co; 50 m. long.
2 County in Wyoming. See *Table* at WYOMING.

U·in′tah (û·ĭn′tȧ). County in Utah. See *Table* at UTAH.

Uinta Mountains. Range chiefly in NE Utah, extending along the boundary bet. Summit and Daggett cos. on the N and Duchesne and Uintah cos. on the S; highest point Kings Peak 13,498 ft.

U′ist (ū′ĭst; ōō′ĭst). Two islands in Outer Hebrides off W coast of Scotland: see NORTH UIST and SOUTH UIST.

Ui·ten·hage (ū′t'n·häg; S. Afr. Du. oi′t'n·hä′kĕ). Town, S Cape Province, S Republic of South Africa, 20 m. NW of Port Elizabeth; pop. 20,584; wool-washing plants.

U·ja′e (ōō·jä′ȧ). Atoll in the Marshall Is., W Pacific Ocean, in the Ralik Chain W of Kwajalein.

Ujain. See UJJAIN.

Ujda. See OUDJDA.

Uj′fe′hér·tó′ (ōō′y′·fě′hār·tō′). Commune, NE Hungary, 19 m. N of Debrecen; pop. 14,694.

U·ji (ōō·jē). **1** *Jap.* **U·ji·ga·wa** (ōō·jē·gä·wä). River, W cen. Honshu, Japan, immediate outlet of Lake Biwa; joins the Hozu to form the Yodo.
2 See UJIYAMADA.

U·ji′ji (ōō·jē′jē) Town, Western Province, Tanganyika, on E shore of Lake Tanganyika; pop. ab. 5000; formerly an important trading town, harbor now very shallow; place where Stanley found Livingstone Oct. 28, 1871.

U·ji·na (ōō·jē·nä). Seaport, Hiroshima prefecture, SW Honshu, Japan, ab. 4 m. from Hiroshima; port for Hiroshima and a military transportation base; has steamer connections with ports on Inland Sea and with Formosa. Greatly damaged Aug. 6, 1945 when Hiroshima was hit with atomic bomb.

U′ji·tze (ōō′zhĕ·tsĕ). Var. of UŽICE.

U·ji·ya·ma·da (ōō·jē·yä·mä·dä). City, Mie prefecture, S Honshu, Japan, S of Ise Bay and 75 m. E of Osaka; pop. (1945) 60,787; consists of Uji and Yamada, formerly separate towns, now one municipality; the sacred city of Japan, containing the Great Shrines (Shinto) of Ise; visited by many pilgrims. Bombed by American planes July 29, 1945.

Uj′jain (ōō′jīn) or **U′jain**. City, W Madhya Pradesh, W cen. India, ab. 200 m. E of Ahmadabad; pop. 53,779. One of the oldest cities of India and ranked as one of its seven holy cities; ancient capital of Avanti kingdom (6th to 4th cents. B.C.) and of legendary Hindu

ruler, Vikramaditya; capital of Malwa c. 120 to c. 395 A.D., when it was a center of Sanskrit learning; also the seat of the Maratha dynasty of Sindhia in 18th cent. Possesses splendid examples of Mohammedan and Hindu architecture—temples, mosques, palaces, mausoleums, and a famed old observatory.

Új′pest (ōō′y′·pĕsht); *Ger.* **Neu′pest** (noi′pĕst). City, cen. Hungary, on Danube river N of Budapest; pop. (1939) 72,940; a N suburb of Budapest.

Újvidék. See Novi Sad.

U·kam′ba (ōō·käm′bà). Former province, SE Kenya colony, E Africa; 29,321 sq. m.; pop. 415,689; ✻ Machakos.

U·khrul′ (ōōk·hrōōl′). Town, NE Manipur state, NE India, ab. 38 m. NNE of Imphal near Burma border; in World War II used by Japanese as base in their invasion of India 1944; retaken by British July 1944.

U·ki′ah (û·kī′à). City, ⊗ of Mendocino co., W California, on Russian river 54 m. NNW of Santa Rosa; pop. 9900; founded 1856, made ⊗ 1859; sheep ranches; produces wine; fruit-packing center. Site of International Latitude Observatory, on 39°8′N lat., one of five such observatories in the world: see Gaithersburg, Maryland; San Pietro I., Sardinia (Carloforte); Kitab, Uzbek S.S.R., Mizusawa, Japan.

Uk′kel (ük′ĕl) *or* **Uc′cle** (ük′l′). Commune, Brabant prov., cen. Belgium, a suburb of Brussels; pop. (1938 est.) 52,818.

Uk′mer·ge′ (ōōk′mĕr·gā′); *Russ.* **Vil′ko·mir′** (vĭl′kō·mĭr′; *Russ.* vyĭl·kŭ·myēr′); *Ger.* **Wil′ko·mir** (vĭl′kō·mĭr). **1** District of Lithuania. See *Table* at Lithuania. **2** Town, its ✻, E Lithuania, on tributary of Neman river 43 m. NE of Kaunas; pop. (1938 est.) 12,292.

U·kraine′ (û·krān′; ū′krān; û·krīn′; ū′krīn); *Russ.* **U·krai′na** (ōō·krī′nà); *officially* **U·krai′ni·an Soviet Socialist Republic** (û·krā′nĭ·ăn; -krī′-). A constituent republic of the U.S.S.R. in SW part, on N shore of Black Sea in E cen. Europe; 171,770 sq. m.; pop. (1939) 30,960,221; with increased territory (6 regions from SE Poland, 2 from Romania, and 1 from Czechoslovakia), 213,473 sq. m., pop. 39,830,982, (1941 est.) 42,272,943; ✻ Kiev (✻ Kharkov 1921–34). Bounded on N by White Russia, on N and E by regions of the R.S.F.S.R., on S by Sea of Azov and the Black Sea, on SW by Moldavian S.S.R., and on W by Czechoslovakia and Poland. Original area divided into 16 administrative regions. Chiefly a wide extent of steppe land covered with fertile black earth (*chernozem*); its S border is a less fertile stretch of clayey soil and marshland along the Black Sea; in E and W are low hills. Traversed by three great rivers, Dnieper, Bug, and Donets, and is bordered on the SW by a fourth, the Dniester; in the S are two smaller streams, the Ingul and Ingulets (tributaries of the Bug and Dnieper); all others except the Donets (a tributary of the Don) flow into the Black Sea. In early times had large forests, now mostly disappeared. By far the greater part of the inhabitants are engaged in agriculture. Chief crops grains (rye, barley, wheat), fruits, vegetables; stock raising is also important. In the cities manufacturing industries of all kinds have been greatly developed in recent years, utilizing the coal of the Donbas, the iron of Krivoi Rog, manganese of Nikopol region, etc., and the power of the hydroelectric station of Dneprostroi (partially destroyed in 1941). Predominant ethnic strain Slav; chief nationalities Ukrainian (Little Russian) 80%, Russian 9%, Jew 5.4%. Has many large cities, the most important being Kiev, Kharkov, Odessa, Dnepropetrovsk, Stalino, Zaporozhe, Zhdanov, Voroshilovgrad; in new territory from Poland, Lvov, Stanislav, Rovno, Lutsk; and from Romania, Chernovtsy. See Little Russia.

History: Early history dates back to 6th and 7th cents.: settled by Ukrainians (Little Russians) and Ruthenians; Kiev (*q.v.*), its chief town, was leading principality of Russia until Tatar conquest in 13th cent.; taken by

Lithuania (*q.v.*); in 1667 by Treaty of Andrusovo Russia acquired region E of middle Dnieper and in 1680 the region of the Cossacks; the rest acquired in partition of 1793; Ukrainian People's Republic, established 1917, declared its independence from Russia 1918; part taken by Poland 1919–38; remainder reconquered by Russia, it became a soviet republic; entered U.S.S.R. 1923; a central theater of warfare in World War I and World War II; overrun by Axis armies in 1941; gradually rewon by Russians Sept. 1943 to spring of 1944.

U·ku (ōō·kōō). Island in Goto Archipelago (*q.v.*), Japan.

Ulala. See Oirot Tura.

Ulan Bator, Ulan Bator Khoto. See Urga.

U′lan–U·de′ (ōō′län ōō·dĕ′); *formerly* **Verkh′ne-u′dinsk** (vyĕrk′nyĕ·ōō′dyĭnsk). City, ✻ of Buryat Republic, Soviet Russia in Asia, on Selenga river ab. 70 m. SE of the S end of Lake Baikal; pop. 129,417; a modern industrial city on the Trans-Siberian R.R. with largest railroad locomotive and car factories and repair shops in Russian Far East; also has glassworks, meat-packing plant, sawmills, and a broadcasting station; connected by rail with Kyakhta to the S.

Ulasutai. Var. of Uliassutai.

U·la′wun (ōō·lä′wōōn) *or* **the Fa′ther** (fä′thēr). Active volcano 7546 ft., Whiteman Range, on the island of New Britain, near N coast at E end, W Pacific Ocean; highest point on the island.

Ul′cinj (ōōl′tsēn·y′); *Ital.* **Dul·ci′gno** (dōōl·chēn′yō); *anc.* **Ol·cin′i·um** (ŏl·sĭn′ĭ·ŭm). Seaport, Montenegro, S Yugoslavia, on Adriatic Sea near Albanian border; pop. 3748; market center and health resort; cathedral. Captured by Romans 167 B.C.; pirate stronghold during the Middle Ages; taken from the Venetians 1571 by the Turks and held by them until 1880 when they gave it up only under pressure from the Great Powers.

Uleåborg. See Oulu.

Uleelheue. See Oeleëheue.

Ulianovsk. See Ulyanovsk.

Uliarus. See Île d'Oléron.

Uliassutai. See Dzhibkhalantu.

U·lin′di (ōō·lĭn′dĕ). River ab. 100 m. long in S cen. Africa; rises in E cen. Congo, flows WNW into the Lualaba river.

U·li′thi (ōō·lē′thĕ). Islands (atoll group), W Caroline Is., W Pacific Ocean, 10°N lat. and 139°43′E long., 108 m. ENE of Yap, and 400 m. SW of Guam. Chief islands Falalop and Asor on the E and Mogmog on the N. Lagoon is 19 m. long by 5 to 10 m. wide and is exceptionally fine anchorage. Discovered 1791; in World War II taken by Americans Sept. 20–21, 1944 and developed into advance fleet base.

U′ljan (ōō′lyän); *Ital.* **U·glia′no** (ōōl·yä′nō). Island in Adriatic Sea off coast of Bosnia and Herzegovina, Yugoslavia, opp. Zadar; 20 sq. m.; pop. ab. 6000.

Ul′la·pool (ŭl′à·pōōl). Village, Ross and Cromarty co., N Scotland, on Loch Broom; fishing; good harbor.

Ul·lo′a (ōō·yō′ä). Var. of Ulúa.

Ulls′wa′ter (ŭlz′wô′tĕr; -wŏt′ĕr). Lake in the Lake District, NW England; on border bet. Cumberland and Westmorland; 7½ m. long; maximum depth 205 ft.

Ulm (ōōlm). Manufacturing and commercial city, Baden-Württemberg state, W Germany, on Danube river near mouth of Iller 45 m. SE of Stuttgart; pop. 57,427; 14th-cent. cathedral, one of largest Gothic churches in Europe; town hall of 14th and 15th cents.; manufactures include metal goods, leather, machinery, hats, textiles, motor vehicles, furniture, beer, butter, cheese. First mentioned 854; chartered 1027; imperial city 1155–1802; member of League of Schmalkalden; scene of battle Oct. 17, 1805 in which Napoleon defeated the Austrians; fortified 1871; in World War II occupied by French troops Apr. 24, 1945.

Ul′ster (ŭl′stĕr). **1** County in New York. See *Table* at New York.

2 Former province, N Ireland; 8331 sq. m., including

water 8567 sq. m.; pop. 1,560,000; now forms Northern Ireland (6 counties) and Ulster prov. of Eire (3 counties).

History: Ancient Irish kingdom; a center of Irish missionary enterprise from 6th cent. A.D.; home of O'Neills (earls of Tyrone) who rebelled against English rule 1598–1603; most of land forfeited to English crown by James I and planted with Protestant Scots, Welsh, and English; further colonized after Cromwellian settlement; its Protestant majority made it oppose union of Northern Ireland (*q.v.*) with Eire (see IRELAND).

3 Province, N Eire, comprising counties of Cavan, Donegal, and Monaghan; 3093 sq. m.; pop. 280,269.

U·lú′a (ठठ·lठठ′ä). River ab. 160 m. long in NW Honduras; flows NE into the Gulf of Honduras. See Lake YOJOA.

U′lu Dağ (ठठ′lठठ dä′); *anc.* **O·lym′pus** (ô·lĭm′pŭs). Mountain 8224 ft., Bursa vilayet, NW Turkey in Asia, SE of Bursa.

U·lugh Muz·tagh′ (ठठ′lठठ mठठz·tä′). Mountain peak 25,340 ft. high, highest in Kunlun Mts., on border bet. S Sinkiang, W China, and N Tibet, ab. 36°N, 87°30′E.

U·lun′di (ठठ·lठठn′dĕ). Village (*kraal*), Natal, E Republic of So. Africa, ab. 115 m. NNE of Durban; formerly capital of Zululand; nearby Lord Chelmsford defeated the Zulus July 4, 1879.

Ul′ver·ston (ŭl′vẽr·stŭn). Urban district, Lancashire, NW England, on Morecambe Bay 55 m. N of Liverpool; pop. 10,076; iron-manufacturing center.

Ul·ya′novsk (ठठl·yȧ′nŭfsk), *also* **Ul·ia′novsk**; *formerly* **Sim·birsk′** (sĭm·bĭrsk′; *Russ.* syĭm·byẽrsk′). City, * of Ulyanovsk Region, Soviet Russia, Europe, on right bank of the Volga 485 m. ESE of Moscow; pop. 102,106; built on hill along the river; has much traffic on river and on railroad E and W; bridge across Volga is one of longest in Soviet Union. A growing industrial city with mills, factories, breweries, etc.; also a cultural center; noted as birthplace of Nikolai Lenin (V. I. Ulyanov); its name changed from Simbirsk to Ulyanovsk in 1924 in his honor. Founded 1648.

Ulyanovsk Region. Region, E Soviet Russia, Europe, on both sides of the middle Volga; * Ulyanovsk. Formerly part of Kuibyshev Region.

U·lys′ses (ū·lĭs′ēz). City, ⊗ of Grant co., SW Kansas; pop. 3157.

Ülzen. See UELZEN.

U·man′ (ठठ·män′; *Russ.* ठठ·män′y′). City, S Kiev Region, cen. Ukraine, U.S.S.R., 125 m. S of Kiev; pop. 40,471; center of a farming district. Formerly a Polish town; long fought over by Cossacks and Poles; in World War II held by Germans 1941–44; retaken by Russians Mar. 15, 1944.

U′man (ठठ′män). Island in SE part of Truk Is. (*q.v.*).

U′ma·nak (ठठ′mȧ·năk). Settlement on S shore of **Umanak Fjord** (inlet N of Nûgssuaq Penin.), W Greenland, ab. 70°20′N; pop. 1400.

U′ma·nan′da (ठठ′mä·nŭn′dȧ). See GAUHATI.

U′mar·kot′ (ठठ′mär·kōt′). Town, Thar and Parkar dist., E Sind dist., Pakistan, in SW Thar Desert; pop. 3841; birthplace of Akbar.

U′ma·til′la (ū′mȧ·tĭl′ȧ). **1** River ab. 80 m. long, NE Oregon; rises in N Union co., flows W and N into Columbia river in NW Umatilla co.

2 County in Oregon. See *Table* at OREGON.

3 Town, Lake co., cen. Florida penin., 33 m. NW of Orlando; pop. 1717; citrus-growing center.

Um′ba (ŭm′bȧ). River ab. 60 m. long, Tanganyika and Kenya, E Africa, flowing E into the Indian Ocean in Kenya just N of Tanganyika boundary.

Um·ba′gog Lake (ŭm·bä′gŏg). Lake 10 m. long, part in Coos co., New Hampshire, and part in Oxford co., Maine; source of the Androscoggin river.

Um·bal′la (ŭm·bä′lä). = AMBALA.

Um·be·lu′zi (ŭm′bĕ·lठठ′zĕ) *or* **Um·be·lo′si** (-lō′zĕ). River ab. 120 m. long, SE Africa, in Swaziland and S Mozambique; flows E into Delagoa Bay.

Um·ber′ti·de (ठठm·bĕr′tĕ·dâ). Commune, Perugia prov., Umbria, cen. Italy, on Tiber river 14 m. NNW of Perugia; pop. 15,146.

Um′boi (ठठm′boi) *or* **Rooke** (rठठk). Island ab. 25 m. long by 15 m. wide bet. W end of New Britain I., Bismarck Archipelago, and Huon Penin., E New Guinea; separated from New Britain by Dampier Strait and from New Guinea by Vitiaz Strait; highest point 4500 ft. Taken by Allies Feb. 12, 1944 to cover operations on New Britain I.

Um·brel′la Point (ŭm·brĕl′ȧ). Cape on NW coast of the island of Jamaica, West Indies.

Um′bri·a (ŭm′brĭ·ȧ; *Ital.* ठठm′brĕ·ä). Compartimento of cen. Italy (for provincial divisions, area, and pop., see *Table* at ITALY); in Apennines; hemmed in by Tuscany, Latium, and the Marches; agriculture; produces electric power.

History: Inhabited by ancient Umbrians, known through the Eugubine tables found at Gubbio 1444 A.D.; conquered by Etruscans, in turn conquered (295 B.C.) by Romans; crossed by Flaminian Way; during Christian era became part of States of the Church (*q.v.*); seat of Umbrian school of painting during Middle Ages; home of St. Francis of Assisi and Jacopone da Todi. In World War II occupied by Allies June–July 1944.

Umbrian Apennines; *Ital.* **Appennino Umbro.** See APENNINES.

Umbro. See OMBRONE.

Umbro–Marchigiano, Appennino. = *Roman Apennines:* see APENNINES.

U′me (ठठ′mĕ). River ab. 290 m. long in Västerbotten prov., N Sweden; flows SE into upper Gulf of Bothnia.

U′me·å′ (ठठ′mĕ·ō′). Seaport, * of Västerbotten prov., N Sweden, on the Gulf of Bothnia at the mouth of Ume river; pop. 14,948; manufactures wood pulp, machinery, furniture; exports tar; burned by Russians 1720.

Um′fo·lo′zi (ŭm′fō·lō′zĕ). Town, Zululand, NE Natal, E Republic of So. Africa, ab. 100 m. NE of Durban; center of sugar-cane district.

Um·ge′ni (ठठm·gā′nĕ). River ab. 100 m. long, S Natal, E Republic of So. Africa; flows SE to Indian Ocean just N of Durban; noted for its waterfall 364 ft. high at Howick, NW of Pietermaritzburg.

U·ming′an (ठठ·mēng′än). Municipality, SE Pangasinan prov., Luzon, Phil. Is., 40 m. ESE of Lingayen; pop. 24,960.

Um′ma (ŭm′ȧ). Important city of ancient Sumer, flourishing in the 3d millennium B.C.; its site is in S Mesopotamia, WNW of Lagash.

Umm al Hanna. See HANNA.

Um′nak (ठठm′năk). Large island ab. 70 m. long and 12 m. wide in W part of Fox Is. group, Aleutian Is., SW Alaska, separated from Unalaska I. on the NE by **Umnak Pass;** highest point 7236 ft.

Ump′qua (ŭmp′kwô). River ab. 200 m. long, SW Oregon; formed by union of two branches (North Umpqua and South Umpqua) in W cen. Douglas co., flows N and W into Pacific Ocean. Navigable for 20 m.

Um·ta′li (ठठm·tä′lĕ). Town, Mashonaland, NE Southern Rhodesia, S Africa, on Mozambique border 130 m. ESE of Salisbury; pop. 5606; E gate of Southern Rhodesia; distribution and trade center for mining and agricultural section; silver, lead, copper, iron, and especially gold found in neighborhood; soil particularly adapted to tobacco.

Um·tam·vu′na (ठठm′tăm·vठठ′nȧ). River ab. 50 m. long, E Republic of So. Africa; flows into Indian Ocean and marks part of boundary bet. Cape Province and Natal.

Um·ta′ta (ठठm·tä′tȧ). **1** River 50 m. long, E Republic of South Africa; divides Tembuland from Pondoland.

2 Town, E Cape Province, S Republic of So. Africa, on Umtata river 114 m. NNE of East London; pop. 5530; * of Transkeian Territories and of Tembuland.

U′mur·bro′gol (ठठ′mठठr·brō′gôl). Mountain, Peleliu Is., Palau Is. See BLOODY NOSE RIDGE.

Um'zim·ku'lu (ŏŏm'zĭm·kŏŏ'lŏŏ). River ab. 125 m. long, S Natal, E Union of South Africa; flows SE into Indian Ocean at Port Shepstone.

Um'zim·vu'bu (ŏŏm'zĭm·vŏŏ'bŏŏ). River 140 m. long, Cape Province, S Union of South Africa; flows SE into Indian Ocean at Port St. Johns.

U'na (ŏŏ'nä). River 110 m. long, NW cen. Yugoslavia; flows NW past Bihać, then turns NE and flows into Sava river; forms NW boundary of Bosnia and Herzegovina federated republic, separating it from Croatia.

U'na, Mount (ŏŏ'nà). Peak 7540 ft. in N South I., New Zealand.

U'na·dil'la (ū'nà·dĭl'à). Village, Otsego co., cen. New York, on the Susquehanna river 36 m. ENE of Binghamton; pop. 1586; manufactures silos and farm equipment.

U·na'ka Mountains (ů·nä'kà). Range of the Appalachian Mts. in Unicoi and Carter cos., NE Tennessee, along the Tennessee-North Carolina boundary; includes **Mount Unaka** 5258 ft. in Unicoi co.

U'na·lak'leet (ŏŏ'nà·lăk'lēt). Village on Norton Sound, W Alaska, ab. 150 m. ESE of Nome; pop. (est.) 445.

Un'a·las'ka (ŭn'à·lăs'kà). 1 Large island of the Aleutian Is., SW Alaska, in Fox Is. group, next to Unimak in size; 75 m. long, greatest width ab. 25 m. On it is Makushin volcano 6680 ft. and at E end on Amaknak I. in Unalaska Bay is the U.S. naval base of Dutch Harbor (*q.v.*).
2 Town on Unalaska Bay, E end of island opp. Dutch Harbor; pop. 218; oldest settlement of Aleutian Is., established by Russians 1760–65.

Unalaska Bay. Inlet on N coast at E end of Unalaska I., E Aleutian Is., ab. 12 m. long and 9 m. wide at its mouth; Amaknak I. is in S cen. part. See DUTCH HARBOR.

U'nao (ŏŏ'nou). Town, Lucknow division, S cen. Uttar Pradesh, N Indian Union, 12 m. NE of Cawnpore; pop. 16,282.

Un'cas·ville (ŭng'kăs·vĭl). Village, SE Connecticut, in towns of Montville and Waterford; pop. 1381.

Unci. See ALMERÍA.

Un'com·pah'gre Peak (ŭn'kŭm·pä'grê). Mountain 14,306 ft. in Hinsdale co., SW Colorado, highest in the San Juan Mts.

Undavalle. See BEZWADA.

Un'der·berg (ŭn'dēr·bûrg). Town, S Natal, E Union of South Africa, ab. 55 m. W of Durban; terminus of railroad from Kelso (on the coast S of Durban).

Unĕtice. See AUNJETITZ.

Unfederated Malay States. Formerly, the Malay states of British Malaya on the Malay Penin. not federated: Johore, Kedah, Kelantan, Perlis, Trengganu; total area 22,276 sq. m.; pop. 1,526,604, (1940–41 est.) 1,912,497. See Federation of MALAYA, MALAY STATES, and names of individual states.

Ung (ŏŏng). Former county in Hungary, later in Carpathian Ruthenia, Czechoslovakia, and now in SW Ukraine, U.S.S.R.

Un'ga (ŏŏng'gà). 1 Island ab. 20 m. long in the Shumagin Is. group off S end of Alaska Penin.
2 Village on island; pop. (1950) 107.

Ungarn. See HUNGARY.

Un·ga'va (ŭn[g]·gä'và; -gä'và). Region, Canada, E of Hudson Bay and N of Eastmain river, separated from Labrador on the E by the height of land. Organized 1895 as a part of Northwest Territories; transferred 1912 as New Quebec to province of Quebec; divided 1927 with larger part remaining as New Quebec (*q.v.*) and E part assigned to Newfoundland as part of Labrador. Covered with hills, lakes, and rivers; largely unexplored and sparsely inhabited (chiefly nomadic Eskimos). Has considerable mineral wealth.

Ungava Bay. Large inlet of S Hudson Strait, NE Quebec prov., E Canada; receives several large rivers, as the Koksoak, Leaf, and Payne.

Ungava Peninsula. The N part of New Quebec dist. in the province of Quebec, Canada.

Ungvár. See UZHGOROD.

U·ni·ão' (ŏŏ·nyoun'). City, Alagoas state, E Brazil, 40 m. NW of Maceió; pop. 6191.

U'ni·coi (ū'nĭ·koi). County in Tennessee. See *Table* at TENNESSEE.

Unicoi Mountains. Range of the Appalachian Mts., chiefly in Monroe co., SE Tennessee, along the Tennessee-North Carolina boundary.

U'nieux' (ü'nyû'). Commune, Loire dept., SE cen. France; pop. (1931) 5914; steelworks.

Unie van Suid–Afrika. See UNION OF SOUTH AFRICA.

U'ni·je (ŏŏ'nĕ·yĕ); *Ital.* **U·ni'e** (ŏŏ·nē'å). Small island in the Veliki Kvarner W of the island of Lošinj, NW Yugoslavia; pop. (1931) ab. 1000; formerly Italian.

U'ni·mak (ū'nĭ·măk). Largest island of the Aleutian Is., in Fox Is. group SW of tip of Alaska Penin.; 65 m. long by 25 m. wide. On it is Shishaldin volcano 9978 ft.

Unimak Pass. Wide passage bet. Bering Sea and North Pacific Ocean SW of Unimak I.

Un'ion (ŭn'yŭn). 1 River ab. 50 m. long in Hancock co., SE Maine; flows S into Bluehill Bay.
2 Name of a parish in Louisiana and of counties in seventeen states of the U.S. See *Tables* at ARKANSAS, FLORIDA, GEORGIA, ILLINOIS, INDIANA, IOWA, KENTUCKY, LOUISIANA, MISSISSIPPI, NEW JERSEY, NEW MEXICO, NORTH CAROLINA, OHIO, OREGON, PENNSYLVANIA, SOUTH CAROLINA, SOUTH DAKOTA, TENNESSEE.
3 Town, Neshoba and Newton cos., E cen. Mississippi, 27 m. WNW of Meridian; pop. 1726.
4 City, ⊗ of Franklin co., E Missouri, 50 m. WSW of St. Louis; pop. 3937; in an agricultural section; shoes.
5 Township, Union co., NE New Jersey, 5 m. WNW of Elizabeth; pop. 51,499; manufactures brick, limestone, plate glass. Settled c. 1749 by people from Connecticut, hence its original name Connecticut Farms; figured in Revolutionary War (battle of Connecticut Farms 1780).
6 City, Union co., NE Oregon, 30 m. N of Baker; pop. 1490; agriculture; Eastern Oregon State Experiment Station.
7 City, ⊗ of Union co., NW South Carolina; pop. 10,191; settled 1791; cotton, hosiery, lumber.
8 Town, ⊗ of Monroe co., SE West Virginia; pop. 411.
9 Islands, cen. Pacific Ocean. See TOKELAU.

Union, La. Philippine province. See LA UNION.

Unión, La. See LA UNIÓN.

Un'ion, Mount (ŭn'yŭn). Peak 7971 ft. in cen. Yavapai co., cen. Arizona.

Union Beach. Borough and summer resort, Monmouth co., E cen. New Jersey, on Raritan Bay 7 m. SE of Perth Amboy; pop. 5862.

Union City. 1 City, Alameda co., W California, S of Oakland; pop. 6618.
2 Subdivision (est. pop. 6000) of town and borough of NAUGATUCK, Connecticut.
3 City, Randolph co., E Indiana, 30 m. E of Muncie on the Ohio border; pop. 4047; market center for agricultural section; manufactures furniture, carriages, trunks.
4 Industrial city, Hudson co., NE New Jersey, on Hudson river 3 m. N of and adjoining Jersey City; pop. 52,180; formed by merger of West Hoboken and Union Hill 1925; manufactures embroidery, soaps and perfumes, incandescent lights.
5 Village, Darke co., W Ohio, on state border adjoining Union City, Indiana; pop. 1657.
6 Borough, Erie co., NW corner of Pennsylvania, 20 m. SE of Erie; pop. 3819; in agricultural and oil region.
7 Town, ⊗ of Obion co., NW Tennessee, 34 m. NNE of Dyersburg; pop. 8837; commercial center in lake and agricultural district; outfitting station for fishermen and hunters; ships cotton, fish, farm and dairy products, livestock, lumber; varied manufactures.

Uniondale. Urban community (unincorporated), Nassau co., SE New York, on Long I.; pop. 20,041.

U·nión′ de Re′yes (ōō·nyôn′ dā rrĕ′yăs). Municipality and town, Matanzas prov., W cen. Cuba; town is junction point on railroad 17 m. S of Matanzas; pop. 6743.

Un′ion Island (ūn′yŭn). One of the Grenadines, West Indies; 4 sq. m.; pop. 1129; administratively a part of St. Vincent territory, West Indies Federation.

Union Islands. See TOKELAU.

Union Lake. Lake ab. 3½ m. long in cen. Cumberland co., SW New Jersey; a widening of the Maurice river.

Union of India. See INDIAN UNION.

Union of South Africa; *S. Afr. Du.* **U′nie van Suid-A′fri·ka** (ü′nĕ fän soit′ä′frĭ·kä). Country, formerly a British dominion, now a republic (**Republic of South Africa**) comprising the provinces of Cape of Good Hope (Cape Province), Natal, Transvaal, and Orange Free State; 472,550 sq. m.; white pop. (1936) 2,003,857, total pop 9,589,898 (including 6,596,000 Bantu) administrative ✳ Pretoria, legislative ✳ Cape Town judicial ✳ Bloemfontein. Bounded on the E, S, and W by the Indian and Atlantic Oceans (conventional boundary bet the oceans at 20°E) on the N by South-West Africa Bechuanaland Protectorate, and Southern Rhodesia, and on the NE by Mozambique Does not adm nister Basutoland and Swaziland although they are wholly within the Republic. A plateau region with Drakensberg Mts. in E along boundary bet. Orange Free State and Natal (highest Mont aux Sources 10 761 ft.); in Cape Province an inner plateau is bordered on S by an escarpment roughly parallel with the coast which contains many short ranges 6000 to 8000 ft. in height; S of this escarpment is the Great Karroo, 2000 to 3000 ft. high, separated by the Zwartberg Mts. from the Little Karroo, 1000 to 2000 ft. high, along the S coast (see KARROO). Has fertile agricultural areas along the coast and river courses; has much grassland (veld)—bush veld in Cape Province bet. the Great Karroo and the Orange river, and grass veld in the Transvaal and Natal; has

desert or semidesert land in much of the W and S part; bet. the Orange river and the Molopo (British Bechuanaland) is the S part of the Kalahari Desert. Chief river the Orange, which with its tributary the Vaal traverses whole cen. part, flowing W to the Atlantic Ocean; many short streams along S and SE coast. Chief occupations raising of sheep and cattle; produces maize, citrus fruits, sugar, hides and skins; mines gold, diamonds, coal, copper   Chief towns Cape Town, Pretoria Durban, Port Elizabeth, Johannesburg, Pietermaritzburg, Bloemfontein, and East London.

History: Cape settlement ceded by Dutch to British 1814 (see CAPE OF GOOD HOPE); in 1836 Dutch settlers (Boers) left Cape in great trek north and east of Orange river; Orange Free State and Transvaal (*qq.v.*) founded by Boers; Natal (*q.v.*) annexed to Cape Colony 1844, given separate government 1845; in 1877 British annexed South African Republic which had been guaranteed its independence by Sand River Convention 1852; Kaffraria, Griqualand West, British Bechuanaland, Zululand, and Tongaland were annexed to provinces later in Union 1865-98; after Boers were defeated in South African (Boer) War 1899-1902, former Boer states met with Cape and Natal in constitutional convention 1908; federal union went into effect 1910; received mandate to former German Southwest Africa 1919. Voted to become a republic Oct. 5, 1960; withdrew from Briti h Commonwealth May 31, 1961.

Union of So′vi·et Socialist Republics (sō′vĭ·ĕt; sō′vĭ·ĕt′; sŏ·vyĕt′; sŏv′ĭ·ĕt), *commonly shortened to* **Soviet Union** *or* **U.S.S.R.**; *often popularly,* **Russia.** A state of E Europe and N and W Asia, formerly an empire (see RUSSIA); 8,354.198 sq. m.; pop. (1939) 193,871,069; ✳ Moscow; comprises 16 constituent republics: the Russian Soviet Federated Socialist Republic (ab. 72% of the total area), and the Armenian, Azerbaidzhan, Estonian, Georgian, Karelo-Finnish Kazakh,

REPUBLIC OF SOUTH AFRICA

Statute Miles
0   100   200   300

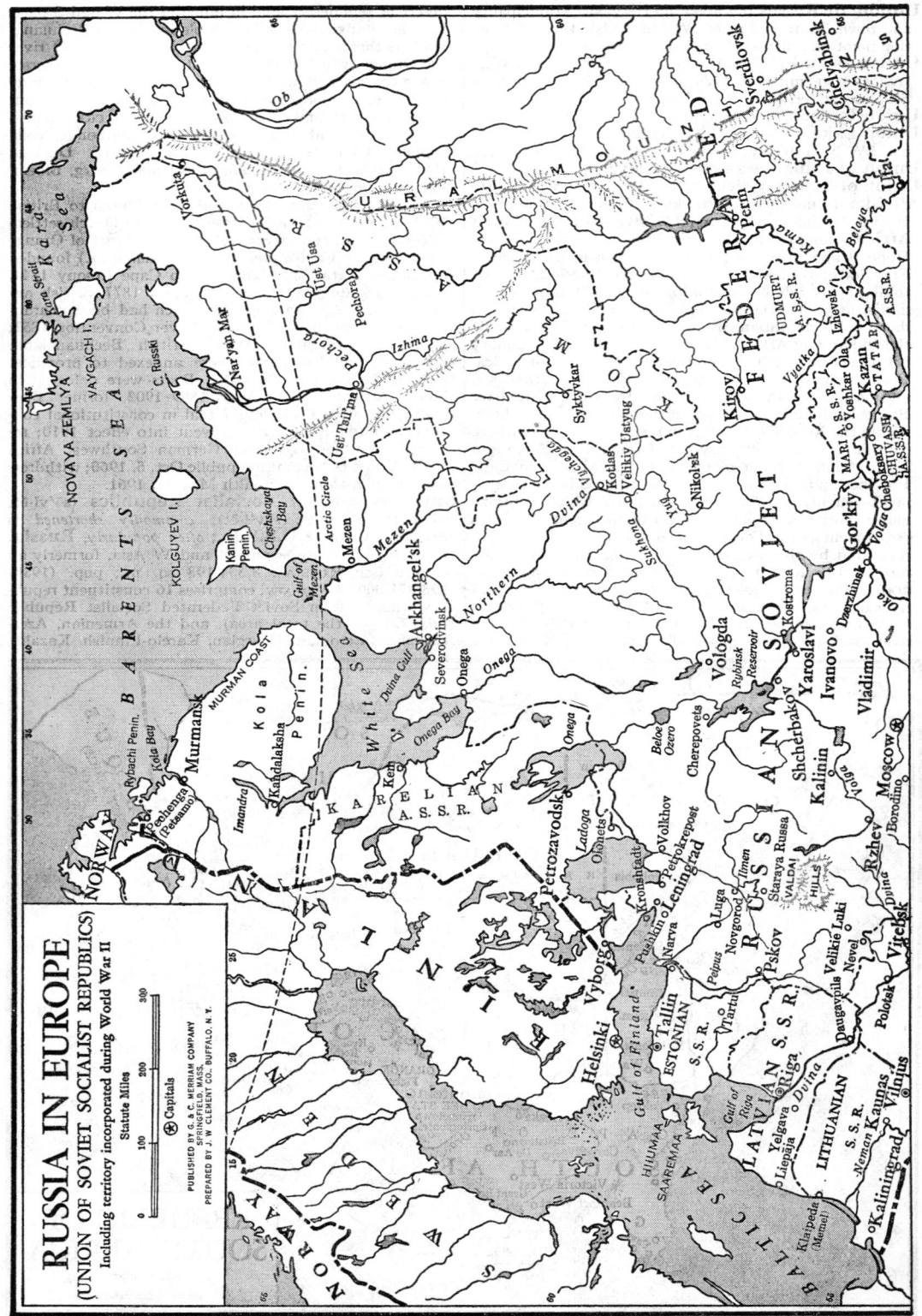

RUSSIA IN EUROPE
(UNION OF SOVIET SOCIALIST REPUBLICS)
Including territory incorporated during World War II

Statute Miles

⊕ Capitals

0   100   200   300

PUBLISHED BY G. & C. MERRIAM COMPANY
SPRINGFIELD, MASS.
PREPARED BY J. W. CLEMENT CO. BUFFALO, N. Y.

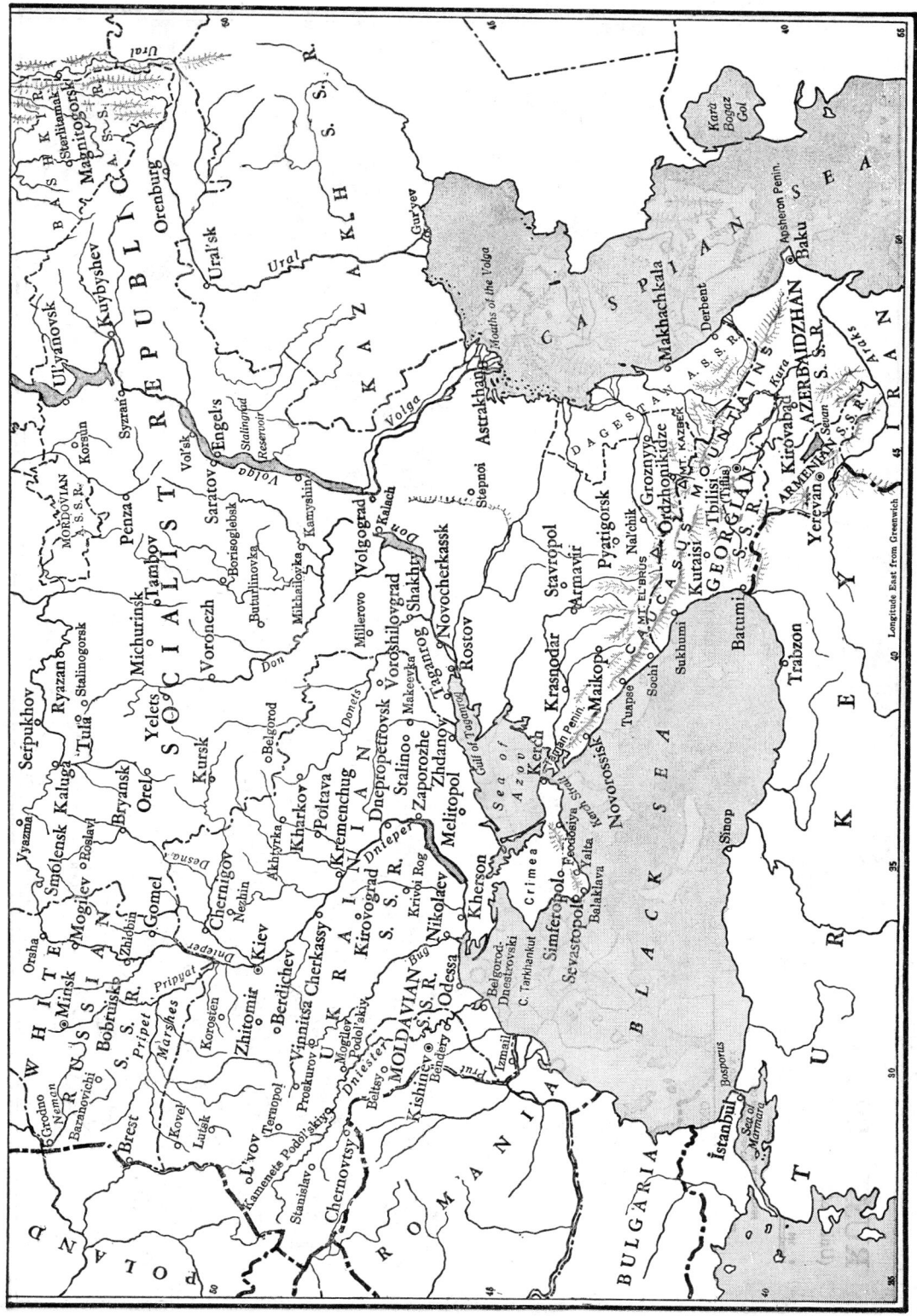

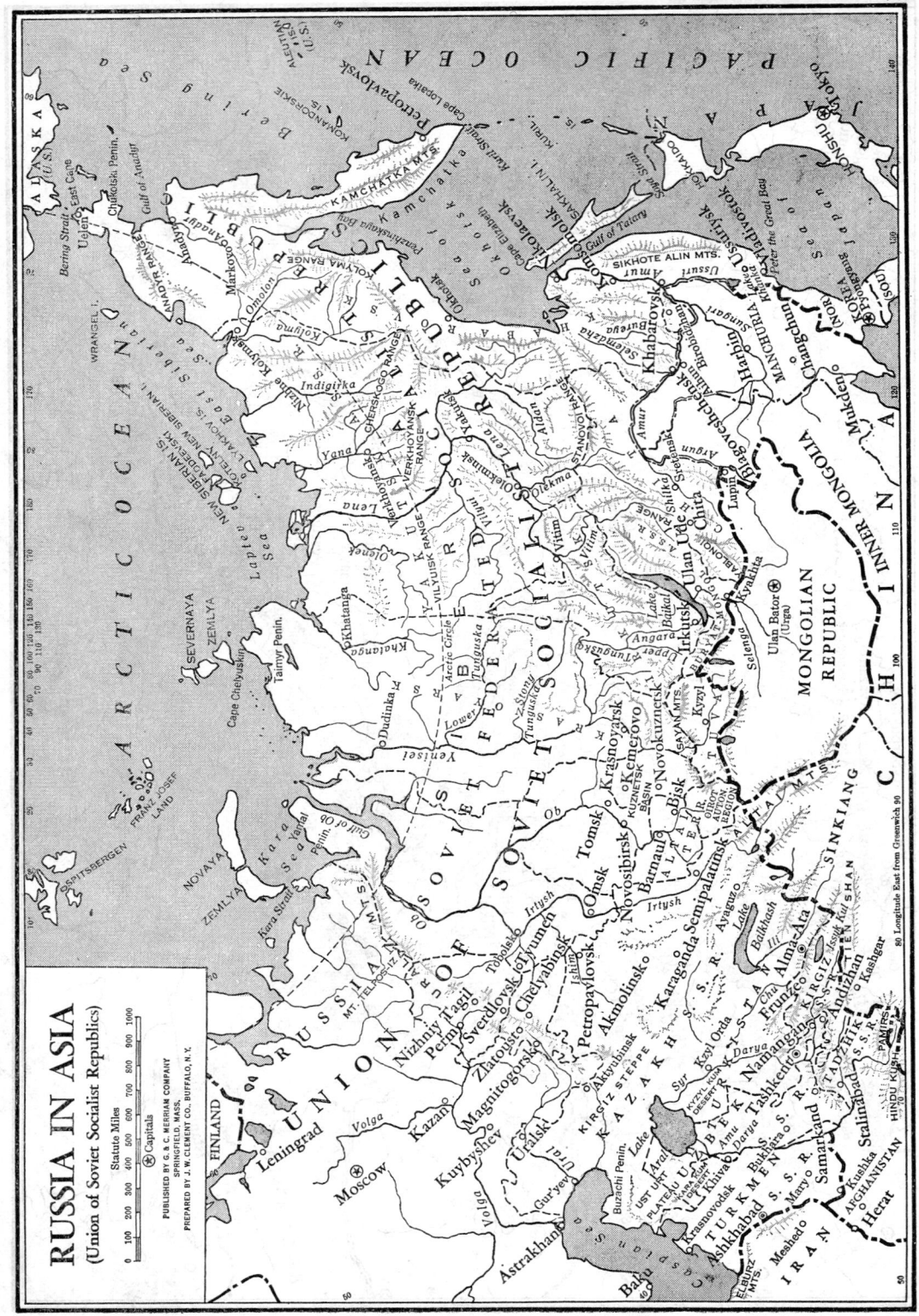

RUSSIA IN ASIA
(Union of Soviet Socialist Republics)

PUBLISHED BY G. & C. MERRIAM COMPANY
SPRINGFIELD, MASS.
PREPARED BY J. W. CLEMENT CO. BUFFALO, N.Y.

Statute Miles
0 100 200 300 400 500 600 700 800 900 1000

⊕ Capitals

Kirgiz, Latvian, Lithuanian, Moldavian, Tadzhik, Turkmen, Ukrainian, Uzbek, and White Russian Soviet Socialist Republics; the first Russian Soviet Federated Socialist Republic (R.S.F.S.R.) contains many subdivisions (territories, regions, autonomous republics, autonomous regions, and national districts); others contain several similar subdivisions each. In extent of territory the largest country on the globe stretching 5300 m. from East Cape on Bering Strait to Odessa on the Black Sea and 2900 m. from Cape Chelyuskin on the Siberian coast to the Pamirs on the borders of India; in area ab. 42% of the continent of Europe and 43% of Asia. Includes all types of physical features, from the fertile black-earth lands of Ukraine to the deserts of Central Asia, the tundra of the north and the high mountains of the Pamirs, Caucasus, Urals, and Kamchatka (see the various subdivisions for chief physical features of each region). Politically it borders in Asia on China, Outer Mongolia, Afghanistan, and Iran on the S, on Turkey on the SW, and in Europe on Romania, Poland, and Finland on the W. Contains some of the great rivers of the world: Volga, Ob, Yenisei, Lena, and many smaller but important streams, as the Dnieper, Don, Ural, Amur, etc. In the SW in Europe borders on the Black Sea and in the NW on the Baltic; its N coast line extends ab. 3000 m. on the Arctic Ocean and for more than 1000 m. along the Pacific. Most of the Caspian Sea lies within its borders; other large inland waters are Lake Aral and Lakes Baikal and Balkhash. In economic resources, esp. food crops and minerals, practically self-sufficient. Inhabitants chiefly Slavic in origin but are also represented by many Asiatic races; it is estimated that ab. 130 different languages are spoken within its borders. Chief cities Moscow, Leningrad, Kiev, Kharkov, Baku, Gorki, Odessa, and Tashkent. See *Map* at KURIL ISLANDS.

History: See RUSSIA for earlier history. By treaty of Brest Litovsk (signed with Germany Mar. 3, 1918) the government of soviets gave up Finland, Poland, Estonia, Latvia, Lithuania, Moldavia, Ukraine, Transcaucasia, but terms of this treaty abrogated by Treaty of Versailles June 28, 1919; period of unrest and civil war (1918–20) followed by severe famine 1921; state Communist methods modified 1921 by New Economic Policy (NEP); Union of Soviet Socialist Republics organized 1922 from soviet republics of Russia (see RUSSIAN SOVIET FEDERATED SOCIALIST REPUBLIC), Ukraine, White Russia, and Transcaucasia; with death of Lenin 1924 began struggle for power among leaders which ended with victory of Stalin 1926 and expulsion of Trotsky from the country 1929; by two Five-Year Plans (1928 and 1933) stimulated the industrial and agricultural development of the country; adopted new constitution 1936, providing for 11 soviet republics; purged country of "disloyal" persons 1936–39; launched third Five-Year Plan 1938. Signed nonaggression pact with Germany Aug. 1939; occupied E Poland 1939; took from Finland (*q.v.*) Karelian Isthmus and other territories 1939–40; in 1940 incorporated Bessarabia and N Bucovina and the Baltic countries; invaded June 22, 1941 by Germany, whose armies approached but did not take Moscow and Leningrad 1941–42; Kuibyshev temporary capital 1941–42; Ukraine and Crimea overrun and Stalingrad (farthest point reached) entered by Germans Sept. 16, 1942. First Russian counteroffensive regained some ground Nov. 1941–June 1942; second begun Jan. 1943 and continued through 1943 to 1945; expelled last Germans from Russian territory 1944 and Russian troops reached Berlin Apr. 1945; one of the four powers occupying Germany after the end of the war; invaded Manchuria Aug. 8, 1945; received Tuva Autonomous Region 1945 and S part of Sakhalin I. 1946 (see KARAFUTO); started on fourth Five-Year Plan 1946.

Union Pass. Mountain pass, W Wyoming, crossing the Wind River Range; used 1807 by John Colter, trapper and explorer, member of Lewis and Clark Expedition.

Union Point. Town, Greene co., NE cen. Georgia, 30 m. SE of Athens; pop. 1615; railroad junction point; hosiery mill; lumber.

Union Springs. City, ⊗ of Bullock co., SE Alabama; pop. 3704.

Un′ion·town (ūn′yŭn·toun). 1 Town, Perry co., W cen. Alabama, 29 m. W of Selma; pop. 1993; dairying. 2 City, ⊗ of Fayette co., SW Pennsylvania, SSE of Pittsburgh; pop. 17,942; bituminous coal mines. Founded 1769; to SE is site of Fort Necessity (*q.v.*) built 1754.

Un′ion·ville (ūn′yŭn·vĭl). 1 Urban community (unincorporated) pop. 2246; in the town of FARMINGTON, Connecticut; paper, nuts and bolts, cutlery, and tools. 2 City, ⊗ of Putnam co., N Missouri, 30 m. NW of Kirksville; pop. 1896.

United Arab Republic; *abbr.* **U.A.R.** Country, NE Africa and SW Asia, equivalent to Egypt; until 1961 a union of Egypt and Syria, formed Feb. 1, 1958; ✳ Cairo.

United Deccan State. Former state in W India formed Aug. 26, 1947 by the union of seven Deccan states: Aundh, Bhor, Kurundwad (Sr.), Miraj (Jr.), Phaltan, Ramdurg, and Sangli.

United Kingdom. Short form of *United Kingdom of Great Britain and Northern Ireland* or of earlier (1801–1922) *United Kingdom of Great Britain and Ireland:* see *History* at GREAT BRITAIN.

United Nations; *abbr.* **UN** *or* **U.N.** International territory, a small enclave in New York City, in E cen. Manhattan overlooking East River; site, since 1951, of permanent headquarters of the United Nations.

United Provinces. 1 *in full* **United Provinces of A′gra and Oudh** (ä′grȧ, ä′grä; oud), *since 1950 called* **Ut′tar Pra·desh** (ŏŏt′ĕr prȧ·dāsh′). State, N India, including former Agra and Oudh provs.; 106,247 sq. m.; pop. (1941) 55,020,617; ✳ Lucknow, former ✳ Allahabad; contains two former Indian states (Benares and Rampur, 1760 sq. m.). Bounded on N and NE by Tibet and Nepal, on E by Bihar state, on S and SW by Madhya Pradesh, and on W by Punjab state. N part lies in the Himalayas (high peaks Nanda Devi, Trisul, Kedarnath) and the remainder comprising most of its area, forms the plains of the Ganges and Jumna and their tributaries (Gogra, Gumti, Ramganga, Rapti, etc.), a region corresponding roughly to the Hindustan of the early Mohammedan period. Exceptionally fertile and populous; wheat, millet, rice, and other cereals are the chief crops, with some cotton, tobacco, and sugar. Population is chiefly Hindu and rural, but with following cities above 100,000: Cawnpore, Lucknow, Agra, Benares, Allahabad, Bareilly, Meerut, Moradabad. Area of present Uttar Pradesh, nearly all of the Gangetic basin, was the scene (with Delhi on the W and Patna on the E) of the greater part of Indian history. It was the country of the two great epics, the *Mahabharata* and *Ramayana*, of the rise of Buddhism, of Asoka's empire and the region ruled by the Guptas and Harsha, followed by the Moguls in the 16th cent. in which the city of Agra (*q.v.*) became a chief center. The British first came into the region (see OUDH) in the latter half of the 18th cent.; sovereignty of certain regions passed to them bet. 1798 and 1833, in which year province of Agra was formed out of Bengal; became 1835 the North-West Provinces, to which Oudh was annexed in 1856; placed under one administration 1877. United Provinces of Agra and Oudh formed 1902; placed under a governor 1921; since 1937 (by virtue of Government of India Act 1935), an autonomous government with a two-chamber legislature. 2 The seven provinces, Holland, Zeeland, Utrecht, Friesland, Groningen, Overijssel, and Gelderland, which formed a union under the Treaty of Utrecht in 1579, that led to the establishment of the Dutch republic, or the Netherlands (*q.v.*).

UNITED STATES—STATES, TERRITORIES, AND POSSESSIONS

STATES

Name	Area[1]	Rank in Area	Pop.[2]	Rank in Pop.	Date of Admission[3]	Rank of Admission	Capital	Nickname	Motto
Alabama	51,609	29th	3,266,740	19th	Dec. 14, 1819	22d	Montgomery	Cotton State	We Dare Defend Our Rights
Alaska[4]	586,400	1st	226,167	50th	Jan. 3, 1959	49th	Juneau		
Arizona	113,909	6th	1,302,161	35th	Feb. 14, 1912	48th	Phoenix	Grand Canyon State	Ditat Deus (God Enriches)
Arkansas	53,104	27th	1,786,272	32d	June 15, 1836	25th	Little Rock	Wonder State	Regnat Populus (The People Rule)
California	158,693	3d	15,717,204	2d	Sept. 9, 1850	31st	Sacramento	Golden State	Eureka (I Have Found It)
Colorado	104,247	8th	1,753,947	33d	Aug. 1, 1876	38th	Denver	Centennial State	Nil Sine Numine (Nothing Without the Divine Will)
Connecticut[3]	5,009	48th	2,535,234	25th	Jan. 9, 1788	5th	Hartford	Nutmeg State	Qui Transtulit Sustinet (He Who Transplanted Sustains)
Delaware[3]	2,057	49th	446,292	46th	Dec. 7, 1787	1st	Dover	Diamond State	Liberty and Independence
Florida	58,560	22d	4,951,560	10th	Mar. 3, 1845	27th	Tallahassee	Sunshine State	In God We Trust
Georgia[3]	58,876	21st	3,943,116	16th	Jan. 2, 1788	4th	Atlanta	Empire State of the South	Wisdom, Justice, Moderation
Hawaii[4]	6,424	47th	632,772	43d	Aug. 21, 1959	50th	Honolulu	Aloha State	Ua Mau Ke Ea O Ka Aina I Ka Pono (The Life of the Land is Perpetuated in Righteousness)
Idaho	83,557	13th	667,191	42d	July 3, 1890	43d	Boise	Gem State	Esto Perpetua (May She Endure Forever)
Illinois	56,400	24th	10,081,158	4th	Dec. 3, 1818	21st	Springfield	Prairie State	State Sovereignty—National Union
Indiana	36,291	38th	4,662,498	11th	Dec. 11, 1816	19th	Indianapolis	Hoosier State	The Crossroads of America
Iowa	56,290	25th	2,757,537	24th	Dec. 28, 1846	29th	Des Moines	Hawkeye State	Our Liberties We Prize and Our Rights We Will Maintain
Kansas	82,276	14th	2,178,611	28th	Jan. 29, 1861	34th	Topeka	Sunflower State	Ad Astra per Aspera (To the Stars by Hard Ways)
Kentucky	40,395	37th	3,038,156	22d	June 1, 1792	15th	Frankfort	Bluegrass State	United We Stand, Divided We Fall
Louisiana	48,523	31st	3,257,022	20th	Apr. 30, 1812	18th	Baton Rouge	Pelican State	Union, Justice, Confidence
Maine	33,215	39th	969,265	36th	Mar. 15, 1820	23d	Augusta	Pine Tree State	Dirigo (I Direct)
Maryland[3]	10,577	42d	3,100,689	21st	Apr. 28, 1788	7th	Annapolis	Old Line State	Fatti Maschii, Parole Femine (Deeds Masculine, Words Feminine)
Massachusetts[3]	8,257	45th	5,148,578	9th	Feb. 6, 1788	6th	Boston	Bay State	Ense Petit Placidam Sub Libertate Quietem (With the Sword She Seeks Calm Repose under Liberty)
Michigan	58,216	23d	7,823,194	7th	Jan. 26, 1837	26th	Lansing	Wolverine State	Si Quaeris Peninsulam Amoenam, Circumspice (If You Seek a Beautiful Peninsula, Look Around)
Minnesota	84,068	12th	3,413,864	18th	May 11, 1858	32d	St. Paul	Gopher State	L'étoile du Nord (Star of the North)
Mississippi	47,716	32d	2,178,141	29th	Dec. 10, 1817	20th	Jackson	Magnolia State	Virtute et Armis (By Valor and Arms)
Missouri	69,674	19th	4,319,813	13th	Aug. 10, 1821	24th	Jefferson City	Show Me State	Salus Populi Suprema Lex Esto (Let the Welfare of the People Be the Supreme Law)
Montana	147,138	4th	674,767	41st	Nov. 8, 1889	41st	Helena	Treasure State	Oro y Plata (Gold and Silver)
Nebraska	77,227	15th	1,411,330	34th	Mar. 1, 1867	37th	Lincoln	Cornhusker State	Equality Before the Law
Nevada	110,540	7th	285,278	49th	Oct. 31, 1864	36th	Carson City	Silver State	All for Our Country
New Hampshire[3]	9,304	44th	606,921	45th	June 21, 1788	9th	Concord	Granite State	Live Free or Die

UNITED STATES—STATES, TERRITORIES, AND POSSESSIONS (Cont.)

STATES (Cont.)

Name	Area[1]	Rank in Area	Pop.[2]	Rank in Pop.	Date of Admission[3]	Rank of Admission	Capital	Nickname	Motto
New Jersey[3]	7,836	46th	6,066,782	8th	Dec. 18, 1787	3d	Trenton	Garden State	Liberty and Prosperity
New Mexico	121,666	5th	951,023	37th	Jan. 6, 1912	47th	Santa Fe	Land of Enchantment	Crescit Eundo (It Grows as It Goes)
New York[3]	49,576	30th	16,782,304	1st	July 26, 1788	11th	Albany	Empire State	Excelsior (Ever Upward)
North Carolina[3]	52,712	28th	4,556,155	12th	Nov. 21, 1789	12th	Raleigh	Tarheel State	To Be Rather Than to Seem
North Dakota	70,665	17th	632,446	44th	Nov. 2, 1889	39th	Bismarck	Flickertail State	Liberty and Union
Ohio	41,222	35th	9,706,397	5th	Feb. 19, 1803	17th	Columbus	Buckeye State	None
Oklahoma	69,919	18th	2,328,284	27th	Nov. 16, 1907	46th	Oklahoma City	Sooner State	Labor Omnia Vincit (Labor Conquers All)
Oregon	96,981	10th	1,768,687	31st	Feb. 14, 1859	33d	Salem	Sunset State	Alis Volat Propriis (She Flies with Her Own Wings)
Pennsylvania[3]	45,333	33d	11,319,366	3d	Dec. 12, 1787	2d	Harrisburg	Keystone State	Virtue, Liberty, and Independence
Rhode Island[3]	1,214	50th	859,488	39th	May 29, 1790	13th	Providence	Little Rhody	Hope
South Carolina[3]	31,055	40th	2,382,594	26th	May 23, 1788	8th	Columbia	Palmetto State	Dum Spiro, Spero (While I Breathe, I Hope)
South Dakota	77,047	16th	680,514	40th	Nov. 2, 1889	40th	Pierre	Sunshine State	Under God the People Rule
Tennessee	42,244	34th	3,567,089	17th	June 1, 1796	16th	Nashville	Volunteer State	Agriculture, Commerce
Texas	267,339	2d	9,579,677	6th	Dec. 29, 1845	28th	Austin	Lone Star State	Friendship
Utah	84,916	11th	890,627	38th	Jan. 4, 1896	45th	Salt Lake City	Beehive State	Industry
Vermont	9,609	43d	389,881	47th	Mar. 4, 1791	14th	Montpelier	Green Mountain State	Freedom and Unity
Virginia[3]	40,815	36th	3,966,949	14th	June 25, 1788	10th	Richmond	Old Dominion	Sic Semper Tyrannis (Ever Thus to Tyrants)
Washington	68,192	20th	2,853,214	23d	Nov. 11, 1889	42d	Olympia	Evergreen State	Alki [Chinook Jargon] (By and By)
West Virginia	24,181	41st	1,860,421	30th	June 20, 1863	35th	Charleston	Mountain State	Montani Semper Liberi (Mountaineers [are] Always Free Men)
Wisconsin	56,154	26th	3,951,777	15th	May 29, 1848	30th	Madison	Badger State	Forward
Wyoming	97,914	9th	330,066	48th	July 10, 1890	44th	Cheyenne	Equality State	Cedant Arma Togae (Let Arms Yield to the Toga)
District of Columbia[5]	69	—	763,956	—	—	—	Washington		E Pluribus Unum (One Out of Many)
	3,615,211[6]		179,323,175						

TERRITORIES AND POSSESSIONS[7]

Name	Total Area	Pop.	Capital
American Samoa[8]	76	20,051	Pago Pago
Guam	212	67,044	Agana
Panama Canal Zone	553	42,122	Balboa Heights[9]
Puerto Rico[10]	3,435	2,349,544	San Juan
Virgin Islands of U.S.	133	32,099	Charlotte Amalie
Other (Trust Territory of the Pacific Islands, etc.)	8,520	76,553	
	12,929	2,587,413	
Totals for States, Territories, Possessions	3,628,140	181,910,588	

[1] Area in square miles: total land and inland water.
[2] Population from 1960 Census.
[3] Date of admission of the 13 original colonies is that of ratification of the Constitution. See *Map* on p. 1193 and *Color Plate* XII.
[4] The Alaska Statehood Act was signed by the President July 7, 1958; the Hawaii Statehood Act, Mar. 18, 1959.
[5] Coextensive with the city of Washington.
[6] Total land and inland water; does not include 74,364 sq. m. of Great Lakes and other primary bodies of water, of which total the state of Michigan has 38,575 sq. m.
[7] The Philippine Is., acquired in 1899, became the independent Republic of the Philippines July 4, 1946.
[8] Including Swains I.
[9] Administrative center.
[10] Adopted constitution 1952 establishing it as a commonwealth with autonomy in internal affairs.

UNITED STATES—DAMS AND RESERVOIRS

This *Table* includes the names of 40 important dams, with their location, year of first use, maximum height, purpose, and other facts when important. Some large dams, still uncompleted (1948) as Clearwater, John Martin, Santa Fe, Wolf Creek, are not included; nor are dams of the TENNESSEE VALLEY AUTHORITY, which are treated in a *Table* at that entry. Various other American dams, as well as the more important dams in foreign countries, are given individual vocabulary entries.

Name of Dam	Year of First Use	Max. Height (in Feet)	Location	Purpose for which Water Impounded	Name of Lake or Reservoir Created by Dam
American Falls	1927	94	Snake riv., N Power co., SE Idaho	irrigation	American Falls Res.
Anderson Ranch	[under cons. 1948]	456	South Fork of Boise riv., Elmore co., SW Idaho, above Arrowrock Res.	irrigation, power, and flood control	
Ariel	1931	313	Lewis riv., bet. Cowlitz and Clarke cos., SW Washington	power	Lake Merwin
Arrowrock	1915[1]	350[1]	Boise riv., bet. Boise and Elmore cos., SW Idaho	irrigation	Arrowrock Res.
Bagnell	1931	148	Osage riv., W Miller co., cen. Missouri	power[2]	Lake of the Ozarks[2]
Bonneville	1937	170	Columbia riv., bet. Skamania co., Washington, and Multnomah co., Oregon, ab. 40 m. above Portland	power and navigation[3]	
Boulder			See *Hoover Dam*, below		
Buffalo Bill, or Shoshone	1910	325	Shoshone riv., Park co., NW Wyoming, just W of Cody	irrigation and power	Buffalo Bill Res.
Coolidge	1928	250	Gila riv., bet. Pinal and Gila cos., Arizona	irrigation and power	San Carlos Res., or Coolidge Res.
Denison[4]	1944	165	Red riv., bet. Bryan co., Oklahoma, and Grayson co., Texas, ab. 5 m. NW of Denison, Texas	flood control and power	Lake Texoma
Diablo	1930	386	Skagit riv., E Whatcom co., NW Washington	power	Diablo Res.
Dreher Shoals			See *Saluda Dam*, below		
Elephant Butte[5]	1916	301	Rio Grande, Sierra co., New Mexico	irrigation and power	Elephant Butte Res., or Hall Lake
Exchequer	1926	326	Merced riv., W Mariposa co., cen. California, 60 m. SE of Stockton	irrigation and power	Exchequer Res.
Fort Peck[6]	1940	250	Missouri riv., bet. Valley and McCone cos., NE Montana, near Glasgow	flood control, power, and navigation	Fort Peck Res.
Friant	1944	320	San Joaquin riv., bet. Madera and Fresno cos., cen. California, 17 m. N of Fresno	irrigation and flood control	Millerton Lake
Grand Coulee[7]	1942	550	Columbia riv., at junction of Douglas, Okanogan, and Lincoln cos., NE cen. Washington	flood control, irrigation, power, and river regulation	Franklin D. Roosevelt Lake
Green Mountain	1943	309	Blue riv., tributary of Colorado riv., N Summit co., N cen. Colorado	irrigation and power	Green Mountain Res.
Hansen	1940	100	Tujunga Wash, tributary of Los Angeles riv., Los Angeles co., S California	flood control	
Hetch Hetchy			See *O'Shaughnessy Dam*, below		
Hoover, or Boulder[8]	1936	726	Colorado riv., bet. Clark co., Nevada, and Mohave co., Arizona	flood control, irrigation, power, and river regulation	Lake Mead (*q.v.*)
Horse Mesa	1927	300	Salt riv., Maricopa co., S cen. Ariz., ab. 20 m. W of Roosevelt Dam	irrigation and power	Apache Lake
Kensico	1916	307	Bronx riv., just N of White Plains, SE New York	water supply for New York City	Kensico Res.
Kingsley, or Keystone	1941	162	North Platte riv., Keith co., W Nebraska, 50 m. W of North Platte	irrigation, power, flood control	Lake McConaughy
Mansfield, or Marshal Ford	1942	270	Colorado riv., Travis co., cen. Texas, a few miles above Austin	flood control, irrigation, power, and river regulation	Lake Travis

UNITED STATES—DAMS AND RESERVOIRS (Cont.)

Name of Dam	Year of First Use	Max. Height (in Feet)	Location	Purpose for which Water Impounded	Name of Lake or Reservoir Created by Dam
Morris	1934	328	San Gabriel riv., Los Angeles co., S California, E of Pasadena	water supply for Pasadena	Morris Res.
Mud Mountain, or Stevens	[under cons. 1948]	425	White riv., bet. Pierce and King cos., W cen. Washington, near Enumclaw	flood control	
New Croton	1906	294	Croton riv., Westchester co., SE New York	water supply for New York City	New Croton Res.
O'Shaughnessy, or Hetch Hetchy	1923[9]	430[9]	Tuolumne riv., in Yosemite National Park, E California	power, and water supply for San Francisco	Hetch Hetchy Res.[9]
Owyhee	1932	417	Owyhee riv., Malheur co., SE Oregon	irrigation	Owyhee Res.
Pacoima, or Reagan	1928	372	Pacoima riv., tributary of Los Angeles riv., Los Angeles co., S California, NW of Los Angeles city	flood control	
Pardee	1929	358	Mokelumne riv., bet. Amador and Calaveras cos., E cen. California, ab. 30 m. NE of Stockton	water supply	Pardee Res.
Parker	1938	320	Colorado riv., bet. San Bernardino co., California, and Yuma co., Arizona, at mouth of Williams riv.	water supply and power	Havasu Lake[10]
Pathfinder	1913	214	North Platte riv., S Natrona co., E cen. Wyoming	irrigation	Pathfinder Res.
Quabbin	See *Winsor Dam*, below				
Reagan	See *Pacoima Dam*, above				
Roosevelt	1911	280	Salt riv., bet. Gila and Maricopa cos., Arizona, 55 m. ENE of Phoenix	irrigation, power, flood control	Roosevelt Lake[11]
Ross	[under cons. 1948]	545	Skagit riv., E Whatcom co., NW Washington	power	
Salt Springs	1931	328	North Fork of Mokelumne riv., bet. Calaveras and Amador cos., E cen. California	power	
Saluda, or Dreher Shoals	1930	208	Saluda riv., Lexington co., South Carolina, 11 m. W of Columbia	power	Lake Murray
San Gabriel No. 1	1938	381	San Gabriel riv., Los Angeles co., S California	flood control	
San Gabriel No. 2	1935	290	San Gabriel riv., Los Angeles co., S California	flood control	
Sardis	1940	117	Little Tallahatchie riv., Panola co., N Mississippi	flood control	Sardis Res.[12]
Shasta[13]	1945	602	Sacramento riv., Shasta co., N California	flood control, power, and irrigation	Shasta Res.
Shoshone	See *Buffalo Bill Dam*, above				
Stevens	See *Mud Mountain Dam*, above				
Winsor, or Quabbin	1939	280	Swift riv., W cen. Massachusetts, near Ware	water supply for Boston[14]	Quabbin Res.

[1] Dam raised in 1937 from 345 ft. to 350 ft.
[2] Has largest hydroelectric generating plant in Missouri. Lake of the Ozarks is 130 m. long, with shore line of ab. 1300 m.
[3] Has a single-lift lock and fishways to permit salmon to ascend the Columbia.
[4] Forms lake with shore line of more than 1200 m.
[5] Made after treaty with Mexico, because Mexico also uses waters of Rio Grande for irrigation.
[6] One of the largest earth-filled dams in the world, 128,000,000 cu. yds.; lake (reservoir) 189 m. long.
[7] Third highest dam in the United States; the reservoir extends 146 m. to Canadian border.
[8] Highest dam in the United States; called originally and from 1933–47 Boulder Dam; called Hoover Dam 1932–33 and officially so renamed 1947.
[9] Dam raised in 1938 from 345 ft. to 430 ft. Water flows through tunnel 18.3 m. long.
[10] About 50 m. long.
[11] Twenty-five miles long, in Gila co.; Tonto National Monument is S of it.
[12] In Panola and Lafayette cos.; ab. 32 m. long, 150 sq. m.
[13] Second largest concrete dam and highest overflow dam in the world.
[14] Water flows by gravity through 24½-mile tunnel to Wachusett Reservoir (*q.v.*).

UNITED STATES—NATIONAL MONUMENTS

Name	Estab-lished	Area (in acres)	Location	Features and Facts of Interest
Ackia Battleground	1938	49.15	Near Tupelo, NE Mississippi	Site of battle May 26, 1736 in which Chickasaw Indians defeated the French
Andrew Johnson	1942	17.08	Greeneville, Tennessee	Andrew Johnson's homestead
Appomattox Court House	1940	968.25	Appomattox, Virginia	Scene of surrender Apr. 9, 1865 of Confederate army under Gen. R. E. Lee
Arches	1929	33,769.94	E Utah	Wind-eroded natural arch formations
Aztec Ruins	1923	27.14	Near Aztec, NW N.M.	Prehistoric pueblo
Badlands	1939	122,972.46	SW South Dakota	Eroded formations; fossils
Bandelier	1916	27,048.89	N cen. New Mexico, 18 m. W of Santa Fe	Cliff-dweller ruins
Big Hole Battlefield	1910	200	SW Montana, 55 m. SW of Butte	Site of battle Aug. 9, 1877 bet. U.S. troops and Nez Percé Indians under Chief Joseph
Black Canyon of the Gunnison	1933	13,176.02	NE Montrose co., W Colorado	Deep gorge formed by Gunnison river; see BLACK CANYON
Cabrillo	1913	0.5	San Diego Bay, SW California	Land first sighted 1542 by Juan Rodríguez Cabrillo (d. 1543)
Canyon de Chelly	1931	83,840	NE Arizona	Cliff-dweller ruins
Capitol Reef	1937	33,068.74	S cen. Utah	Cliff dwellings, fossils, petrified trees, strange geologic formations
Capulin Mountain	1916	680.42	NE New Mexico	Site of ancient volcano, 8368 ft.
Casa Grande	1918	472.5	S Arizona	Prehistoric ruins, discovered 1694
Castillo de San Marcos	1924[1]	18.51	St. Augustine, Florida	Old Spanish fort, dating from 1672; see ST. AUGUSTINE
Cedar Breaks	1933	6,172.20	SW Utah; N of Zion National Park	Canyons and cliffs, vast natural highly-colored amphitheater
Chaco Canyon	1907	18,039.39	NW New Mexico, NE of Gallup	Cliff-dweller ruins
Channel Islands	1938	1,119.98	Parts of Anacapa Is. and Santa Barbara I., California	Fossils, examples of volcanic action, specimens of marine life
Chiricahua	1924	10,529.8	Cochise co., SE Arizona, NE of Tombstone	Curious natural rock formations
Colorado	1911	18,120.55	Mesa co., W Colorado	Monoliths and eroded formations
Craters of the Moon	1924	47,210.67	Butte and Blaine cos., S cen. Idaho	Lava flows in strange landscape effects
Custer Battlefield	1946	765.34	Big Horn co., S Montana, on Little Bighorn river	Site where Gen. Custer and his command were slain by Indians June 25, 1876; made national cemetery 1886
Death Valley	1933	1,850,565.2	Inyo co., E California	Ancient pictographs, curious geological formations; see DEATH VALLEY
Devils Postpile	1911	798.46	NE Madera co., cen. California	Peculiar hexagonal columns, like a pile of fence posts
Devils Tower	1906	1,193.91	On Belle Fourche river, NW of Black Hills, Wyoming	Rock tower 1200 ft. high, of volcanic origin
Dinosaur	1915	190,798.49	NE Utah	Fossil remains of prehistoric animals
El Morro	1906	240	Valencia co., W New Mexico	Ruins of ancient pueblos; castellated sandstone with inscriptions by early Spanish explorers
Fort Frederica	1945	74.53	W coast of Saint Simon I., Georgia	Site of fort built by Oglethorpe 1736 to protect against Spaniards from Florida
Fort Jefferson	1935	86.82	Florida, in Dry Tortugas, islands W of Key West	Marine exhibit, remains of fortifications built in 1846
Fort Laramie	1938	214.41	Goshen co., SE Wyoming	Site of outpost for traders and miners on the Oregon Trail in 1849 ff.
Fort McHenry	1925[2]	47.64	Baltimore, Maryland	Bombardment by British 1814, occasion of writing of *Star Spangled Banner*
Fort Matanzas	1924	227.76	NE Florida, S of St. Augustine	Relics of Spanish occupation; see MATANZAS RIVER
Fort Pulaski	1924	5,427.39	Island in mouth of Savannah river	Fort built 1829–47 to replace Revolutionary Fort Greene
Fort Sumter	1948	2.4	Charleston, South Carolina	Object of attack Apr. 12–13, 1861 which began Civil War
George Washington Birthplace	1930	393.68	NE Virginia	Part of family plantation and site of house where George Washington was born
Gila Cliff Dwellings	1907	160	SW New Mexico, 50 m. NE of Silver City	Cliff dwellings
Glacier Bay	1925	2,297,456.27	SE Alaska, at S end of St. Elias Range	Large tidewater glaciers

UNITED STATES—NATIONAL MONUMENTS (Cont.)

Name	Established	Area (in acres)	Location	Features and Facts of Interest
Grand Canyon	1932	196,051	NW Arizona	Inner gorge of Grand Canyon, with Colorado river 3000 ft. below rim of canyon
Gran Quivira	1909	450.94	S Torrance co., cen. New Mexico	Pueblo ruins and ruins of an early Spanish mission
Great Sand Dunes	1932	35,908.19	S cen. Colorado	Sand dunes of San Luis Park
Homestead	1939	162.73	SE Nebraska	Site of first homestead entered under the General Homestead Act of 1862
Hovenweep	1923	299.34	SE Utah and SW Colorado	Prehistoric towers, pueblos, cliff dwellings
Jackson Hole	1943	173,064.62	W Wyoming at S end of Grand Teton Nat. Park	Formerly important hunting grounds, now wildlife sanctuary
Jewel Cave	1908	1,274.56	Custer co., SW South Dakota	Cave of limestone formation
Joshua Tree	1936	655,961.33	S California	Desert flora
Katmai	1918	2,697,590	S Alaska, on N end of Alaska Penin.	Katmai volcano (7000 ft.) and Valley of Ten Thousand Smokes
Lava Beds	1925	46,027.56	N California	Lava and ice caves; battleground of Modoc Wars 1872–73
Lehman Caves	1922	640	E Nevada	Natural caves of limestone formation
Meriwether Lewis	1925	300	W cen. Tennessee	Grave of Capt. Meriwether Lewis
Montezuma Castle	1906	783.09	cen. Arizona	Prehistoric cliff dwellings
Mound City Group	1923	57	S Ohio, near Chillicothe	Prehistoric mounds
Muir Woods	1908	424.56	12 m. NW of San Francisco, California	Fine redwood grove
Natural Bridges	1908	2,649.7	SE Utah	Three large natural bridges, largest 221 ft. high with span of 261 ft.
Navajo	1909	360	N Arizona	Cliff-dweller ruins
Ocmulgee	1936	683.48	cen. Georgia	Indian mounds
Old Kasaan	1916	38	E shore of Prince of Wales I., SE Alaska	Abandoned Haida Indian village (Kasaan)
Oregon Caves	1909	480	Josephine co., SW Oregon	Caves of limestone formation
Organ Pipe Cactus	1937	328,161.73	S Arizona	Specimens of a species of cactus, the organ pipe cactus, and other plants
Perry's Victory and International Peace Memorial	1936	14.25	N Ohio	Commemorates Perry's victory over British Sept. 10, 1813 at Put in Bay, Lake Erie, and the years of peace thereafter
Petrified Forest	1906	85,303.63	E Arizona	Petrified coniferous trees
Pinnacles	1908	12,817.77	W cen. California, SE of Salinas	Spirelike rock formations
Pipe Spring	1923	40	NW Arizona	Old stone fort and a spring of pure water in a desert region
Pipestone	1937	115.6	SW Minnesota	Quarry from which Indians obtained material for ceremonial peace pipes
Rainbow Bridge	1910	160	SW San Juan co., SE Utah	Natural bridge 309 ft. above creek, 235 ft. above top of inner canyon, span 278 ft.
Saguaro	1933	53,669.24	E Pima co., S Arizona	Giant cacti, or saguaro
Scotts Bluff	1919	2,196.44	Scotts Bluff co., W Nebraska	Landmark on old Oregon Trail
Shoshone Cavern	1909	212.37	Park co., NW Wyoming	Large cave
Sitka	1910	57	Baranof I., SE Alaska	Sixteen totem poles; scene of a massacre of Russians by Tlingit Indians 1802
Statue of Liberty	1924	10.38	Liberty I., New York Harbor, N.Y.	Bartholdi's statue, Liberty Enlightening the World (unveiled 1886)
Sunset Crater	1930	3,040	Coconino co., N Arizona	Volcanic crater: lava flows, ice caves
Timpanogos Cave	1922	250	cen. Utah	Limestone cavern
Tonto	1907	1,120	80 m. E of Phoenix, Arizona	Cliff-dweller ruins
Tumacacori	1908	10	57 m. S of Tucson, Arizona	17th-cent. Spanish mission ruins
Tuzigoot	1939	42.67	On Verde river, cen. Arizona	Ruins of prehistoric pueblo
Walnut Canyon	1915	1,641.62	Near Flagstaff, Arizona	Cliff dwellings in canyon
Wheeler	1908	300	Mineral co., S Colorado	Valley in eroded volcanic rock
White Sands	1933	140,247.04	S cen. New Mexico	Dunes of gypsum sands
Whitman	1940	45.84	Near Walla Walla, SE Washington	Site of mission of Dr. Marcus Whitman and wife, massacred by Indians 1847
Wupatki	1924	34,853.03	Near Flagstaff, Arizona	Prehistoric Indian dwellings
Yucca House	1919	9.60	Montezuma co., SW Colorado	Prehistoric ruins

[1] Formerly called Fort Marion; name changed by act of Congress 1942.
[2] Date of creation as national park; changed to national monument 1939.

UNITED STATES—NATIONAL HISTORICAL PARKS, NATIONAL MILITARY PARKS, AND BATTLEFIELD SITES

Name	Estab-lished	Area (in acres)	Location	Features and Facts of Interest
Abraham Lincoln National Historical Park	1939	117	Hodgenville, Kentucky	Memorial building enclosing log cabin believed to be Lincoln's birthplace
Antietam Battlefield Site	1890	183	Sharpsburg, Maryland	Site of battle Sept. 17, 1862 where Federal army checked Lee's first invasion of the North in the Civil War; see SHARPSBURG
Brices Cross Roads Battlefield Site	1929	1	Bethany, Lee co., NE Mississippi	Battlefield 1864 of the Civil War
Chalmette National Historical Park	1939	33	E of New Orleans, Louisiana	Commemorates battle of New Orleans Jan. 8, 1815
Chickamauga and Chattanooga National Military Park	1890	8,149	NW Georgia and SE Tennessee	Includes battlefields of Chickamauga and Missionary Ridge in the Civil War
Colonial National Historical Park	1936	7,233	SE Virginia	Includes sites of Jamestown, Williamsburg, and Yorktown
Cowpens Battlefield Site	1929	1	Spartanburg co., NW South Carolina	Site of a battle Jan. 17, 1781 of American Revolution; see COWPENS
Fort Donelson National Military Park	1928	103	NW Tennessee	Includes site of a Civil War fort, captured by Gen. Grant 1862
Fort Necessity Battlefield Site	1931	2	Near Pittsburgh, Pennsylvania	Site of entrenchments thrown up by Major George Washington in the French and Indian War, finally surrendered by Washington July 3, 1754
Fredericksburg and Spotsylvania National Military Park	1927	2,421	Spotsylvania co., NE Virginia	Includes battlefields of Fredericksburg, Chancellorsville, Spotsylvania Court House and the Wilderness
Gettysburg National Military Park	1895	2,463	S Pennsylvania	Battlefield of Gettysburg
Guilford Courthouse National Military Park	1917	149	N cen. North Carolina	Site of battle Mar. 15, 1781 in which Americans defeated British and ended British control of the Carolinas
Kings Mountain National Military Park	1931	4,012	York co., N South Carolina	Includes site of battle Oct. 7, 1780 in which Americans defeated British in important battle of American Revolution
Moores Creek National Military Park	1926	30	Pender co., SE North Carolina	Site of battle Feb. 27, 1776 of the American Revolution; the "Lexington and Concord" of the South
Morristown National Historical Park	1933	958	Morristown, New Jersey	Main camp site of American armies during winters of 1776–77 and 1779–80
Petersburg National Military Park	1926	1,325	SE Virginia	Site of Civil War battles 1864–65; see PETERSBURG, Virginia
Saratoga National Historical Park	1948	1,865	Saratoga co., E New York	Scene of victory of Americans over British Oct. 1777; turning point of American Revolution
Shiloh National Military Park	1894	3,729	Hardin co., SW Tennessee	Site of battle of Shiloh Apr. 1862 in Civil War; see PITTSBURG LANDING
Stones River National Military Park	1927	324	cen. Tennessee, near Murfreesboro	Site of battle 1862–63 of Civil War; see MURFREESBORO
Tupelo Battlefield Site	1929	1	Lee co., NE Mississippi	Site of battle July 14, 1864 during Civil War; see TUPELO
Vicksburg National Military Park	1899	1,324	W Mississippi	Includes site of siege of Vicksburg 1862–63 in Civil War
White Plains Battlefield Site	1926		White Plains, Westchester co., SE New York	Area marked with memorials showing positions held by Washington's army at the battle of White Plains Oct. 28, 1776

UNITED STATES—NATIONAL PARKS

Name	Established	Area[1] (in sq. m.)	Location	Features and Facts of Interest
Acadia, formerly Lafayette (created 1919)	1929	44.2	Maine coast	Granite peaks on Mount Desert I. and promontory on mainland across Frenchman Bay
Big Bend	1944	1,080	W Texas, on Mexico border in big bend of Rio Grande	Mountain and desert scenery
Bryce Canyon	1928	56	Garfield and Kane cos., S Utah	Canyon with curiously eroded pinnacles of various brilliant colors
Carlsbad Caverns	1930	71	Eddy co., SE New Mexico	Huge natural caves; see CARLSBAD CAVERNS
Crater Lake	1902	250.4	Klamath co., S Oregon	Lake, maximum depth 2000 ft., in crater of extinct volcano in Cascade Range
Everglades	1947	423.4	S Florida penin.	See EVERGLADES
Glacier	1910	1,558.2	NW Montana; U.S. part of Waterton-Glacier International Peace Park (q.v.)	Mountain region with many lakes and small glaciers
Grand Canyon	1919	1,008.2	NW Arizona	Canyon of the Colorado river; see GRAND CANYON
Grand Teton	1929	148.2	Teton co., NW Wyoming	Most spectacular part of Teton Range including Grand Teton 13,766 ft.
Great Smoky Mountains	1930	720.3	Along S section of Tennessee-North Carolina boundary	Great Smoky Mts. (q.v.); dense forests, flowering shrubs and many varieties of flowers
Haleakala[2]	1961	27	Hawaii	Large extinct volcanic crater in E Maui I.
Hawaii	1916	244	Hawaii	Volcanic area including active volcanoes Kilauea and Mauna Loa on Hawaii I.
Hot Springs	1921	1.59	Garland co., W cen. Arkansas, in Ouachita Mts.	Forty-seven hot springs (147°F.)
Isle Royale	1940	209.1	Michigan, in NW Lake Superior	Isle Royale (q.v.) and more than 100 surrounding islands; forested wilderness, cascades, inland lakes; old Indian copper pits
Kings Canyon	1940	707.6	Fresno co., S cen. California, in the Sierra Nevada	Canyon of Middle and South Branches of Kings river; snow-covered mountains, giant sequoias in General Grant Grove Section and Redwood Mountain
Lassen Volcanic	1916	161.3	N California at S end of Cascade Range	Lassen Peak, recently active (1914–16) volcano; hot springs, mud geysers
Mammoth Cave	1936	79	Edmonson and Hart cos., SW cen. Kentucky	Series of huge caves; see MAMMOTH CAVE
Mesa Verde	1906	79.7	Montezuma co., SW Colorado	Prehistoric cliff dwellings
Mount McKinley	1917	3,030.2	S cen. Alaska	Mount McKinley 20,300 ft., highest peak in North America; wildlife, esp. caribou and white Alaska mountain sheep
Mount Rainier	1899	377.4	W cen. Washington	Mount Rainier with extensive glacier systems; wild flowers in parks at its base
Olympic	1938	1,323	NW Washington	Olympic Mts., virgin forests including temperate rain forests; glaciers
Platt	1906	1.42	Murray co., S Oklahoma	Springs: 18 sulfur, 6 fresh water, 4 iron, 3 bromide, and several smaller ones
Rocky Mountain	1915	395	N cen. Colorado	Heart of the Rockies; Longs Peak 14,255 ft. dominates region; interesting records of glacial period
Sequoia	1890	601.7	Tulare co., S cen. California, S of Kings Canyon National Park	Fine stands of sequoias; over 300 lakes; high mountains, Sierra Nevada, including Mount Whitney 14,495 ft.
Shenandoah	1935	302.3	N Virginia	Section of Blue Ridge; Hawksbill Mt. 4049 ft.; Skyline Drive part of Appalachian Trail (Maine to Georgia)
Wind Cave	1903	41.5	Custer co., SW South Dakota	Cavern with intermittent air current; boxwork formations
Yellowstone	1872	3,458.13	NW Wyoming (3199.48 sq. m.), S Montana (222.65 sq. m.), and E Idaho (36 sq. m.)	Geysers, hot springs; lakes and waterfalls; Grand Canyon of the Yellowstone, see YELLOWSTONE river, MAMMOTH HOT SPRINGS
Yosemite	1890	1,181.9	cen. California	Lofty cliffs; high waterfalls; groves of giant sequoias
Zion	1919	206.8	SW Utah	Zion Canyon cut by Virgin river; sandstone cliffs, remarkable for colors; includes (since 1956) former Zion National Monument

[1] Includes water area.
[2] Formerly included in Hawaii National Park.

United States of America; *commonly called for short* **United States**, *or, often,* **America.** Early in Revolutionary period known as *United Colonies;* this name changed in Declaration of Independence (July 4, 1776) to *United States of America*, also in Articles of Confederation (first draft 1777) and Constitution (1787). Federal republic of North America, comprising (since 1959) 50 states and District of Columbia; area 3,552,214 sq. m. (including inland water area, 3,615,222 sq. m.); including water area other than inland water (82% in Great Lakes region), 3,688,882 sq. m.; pop. 179,323,175; ✳ Washington; with outlying possessions (Puerto Rico, Guam, American Samoa, Virgin Islands, and Panama Canal Zone), land and inland water, 3,619,110 sq. m. Bounded on N by Canada and Great Lakes and (in Alaska) by Arctic Ocean, on W by the Pacific Ocean, on S by Mexico and Gulf of Mexico, and on E by the Atlantic Ocean. Easternmost point West Quoddy Head, Maine, 66°57′W long.; westernmost point (excluding Alaska and Hawaii) Cape Alava, Washington, 124°44′W; northernmost point (excluding Alaska) Northwest Angle, Minnesota, ab. 49°23′N lat.; southernmost point Cape Sable, Florida (mainland), ab. 25°7′N lat. *Chief rivers:* Mississippi system (including Missouri, Ohio, Platte, Red, Arkansas), Colorado, Columbia, Rio Grande, and many important industrial streams (300 to 900 m. long) on Atlantic seaboard and Gulf coast. *Lakes:* Great Lakes in N (U.S.-Canada boundary runs through Ontario, Erie, Huron, and Superior; Michigan is wholly within boundary); Great Salt Lake in Utah and Okeechobee in Florida. *Mountains:* Appalachian system (including White Mts. and Green Mts. in New England, Adirondacks and Catskills in New York, Blue Ridge and Great Smoky Mts. in SE), Ozark Plateau in Missouri, Arkansas, and Oklahoma, Rocky Mts. across (N to S) the W (including Bitterroot Range in N, Wasatch, Uinta, and Front Ranges in cen. part), and ranges along Pacific coast (Cascade Range, Sierra Nevada, and Coast Ranges); highest point Mt. McKinley, Alaska, 20,300 ft.; lowest point Death Valley, California, 280 ft. below sea level; highest point (excluding Alaska) Mt. Whitney, California, 14,495 ft.; highest point E of Mississippi river Mt. Mitchell, North Carolina, 6684 ft. *Largest cities:* New York, Chicago, Los Angeles, Philadelphia, Detroit, Baltimore, Houston, Cleveland, Washington, St. Louis. *Economic resources:* In world production: ab. 60% of petroleum, 35% of steel, nearly 30% of pig iron, 52% of corn, 17% of wheat, 29% of cotton, 36% of tobacco. For further data, see under separate states. *History:* Period of discovery: see NORTH AMERICA. Period of colonization: first permanent settlement, Spanish, at St. Augustine, Florida, 1565; English settlements in Virginia 1607 Massachusetts 1620, Maryland 1634, Pennsylvania 1681; English defeat of French in French and Indian War 1754–63 decided British political control over thirteen colonies along Atlantic seaboard. Period of political unrest caused by English colonial policy, and culminating in Revolutionary War 1775–83, and Declaration of Independence 1776. Period of political organization, first under the Articles of Confederation 1781–89 and finally under the Constitution, adopted 1787 and in effect 1789, and of increase of power as a nation; Louisiana Territory purchased from France 1803; War of 1812 with Great Britain; Florida purchased from Spain 1819; Monroe Doctrine announced 1823. Periods of westward expansion, notably into Middle West as result of acquisition of Louisiana Territory, and to Far West after discovery of gold in California 1848; Texas annexed 1845; northwest boundary fixed by treaty with Great Britain 1846; New Mexico and California ceded by Mexico 1848 by Treaty of Guadalupe Hidalgo ending Mexican War; southern Arizona acquired from Mexico by Gadsden Purchase 1853. Period of disunity, caused by development of slave cotton-growing plantation economy in South contrasted with

free industrial and diversified agricultural economy in North, and culminating in War between the States 1861–65. Period of reconstruction 1865–70. Period of rapid growth, urbanization, industrial development, and European immigration. Period of internationalism, caused by development of foreign trade and rapid communication and transportation, and marked by participation in foreign wars, Spanish-American War 1898, World War I 1914–18 (American participation Apr. 6, 1917–Nov. 11, 1918), World War II 1939–45 (American participation Dec. 8, 1941–Aug. 13, 1945). *Territorial acquisition:* Alaska (1867: by purchase from Russia); Midway Is. (1867: by occupation); Hawaiian Is. (July 1898: by annexation); Philippine Is., Puerto Rico, and Guam (Dec. 1898: by treaty with Spain ending Spanish-American War); Wake I. (1898–99: by occupation); American Samoa (1899: by treaty with Germany); Panama Canal Zone (1903: by purchase from Panama); Virgin Is. of the United States (1916: by purchase from Denmark). Philippine Islands granted independence July 4, 1946; Puerto Rico became an autonomous commonwealth 1952; Alaska and Hawaii admitted 1959.

United States of Brazil. See BRAZIL.

United States of Colombia. A former name of COLOMBIA.

United States of Indonesia. See *History* at NETHERLANDS INDIES.

United States of Mexico. = MEXICO.

United States of Venezuela. See VENEZUELA.

United States Range. Mountain range in N Ellesmere I., NE Franklin District, Northwest Territories, N Canada; highest point 9000 ft.

U·ni·ver′sal City (ū′nĭ·vûr′s'l). Suburb, NW of Los Angeles, California; motion-picture studios.

U·ni·ver′si·ty (ū′nĭ·vûr′sĭ·tĭ). **1** See TUSCALOOSA.
2 Suburb of GRAND FORKS, North Dakota.

University City. City, St. Louis co., E Missouri, 8 m. WNW of St. Louis; pop. 51,249; suburb of St. Louis.

University Heights. Residential city, Cuyahoga co., N Ohio, 8 m. E of Cleveland; pop. 16,641. John Carroll Univ. (1886; men).

University Park. 1 Town, Mahaska co., Iowa, adjacent to Oskaloosa; pop. 569.
2 City, Dallas co., NE Texas, entirely within city of Dallas; pop. 23,202.

University Peak. Mountain 13,588 ft. in Sierra Nevada, on NE boundary of Tulare co., S cen. California.

Un·kiar′–Ske′les·si′ (ŏong·kyär′skĕ′lĕ·sē′); *now* **Hunkyar′ I′ske·le·si′** (hŏong·kyär′ ĭ′skĕ·lĕ·sē′). Village on the Bosporus, 8 m. NNE of İstanbul, Turkey; treaty of mutual assistance signed here July 8, 1833 bet. Russia and Turkey (abrogated 1841).

Un′ley (ŭn′lĭ). City, in SE South Australia, a S suburb of Adelaide; pop. 41,004.

Un′na (ŏon′ä). Industrial city, in North Rhine-Westphalia state, W Germany, 10 m. E of Dortmund; pop. 18,594; coal mining; wire and machinery.

Unst (ŭnst). One of the Shetland Is., NE of N Scotland; 38 sq. m.; pop. 1326. Cf. MUCKLE FLUGGA.

Un′ter·fran′ken (ŏon′tĕr·fräng′kĕn). Bavarian government district. See *Lower Franconia* in *Table* at BAVARIA.

Un′ter·wal′den (ŏon′tĕr·väl′dĕn). Swiss canton; divided into demicantons: **Nid′wal′den** (nēt′väl′dĕn) and **Ob′wal′den** (ôp′väl′dĕn). See *History* and *Table* at SWITZERLAND.

U′nyam·we′zi (ōō′nyäm·wā′zĕ). Plateau region in Western Province, Tanganyika, East Africa, around Tabora.

Un·zen (ŏon·zĕn). Active volcano 4462 ft., Nagasaki prefecture, NW Kyushu, Japan, on peninsula at S end of Shimabara Bay and opp. Kumamoto.

Un′zha (ōōn′zhä). River ab. 365 m. long, cen. Soviet Russia, Europe; rises in Vologda Region, flows S through Kostroma and Ivanovo Regions to the Volga below Kineshma. Navigable for ab. 250 m.

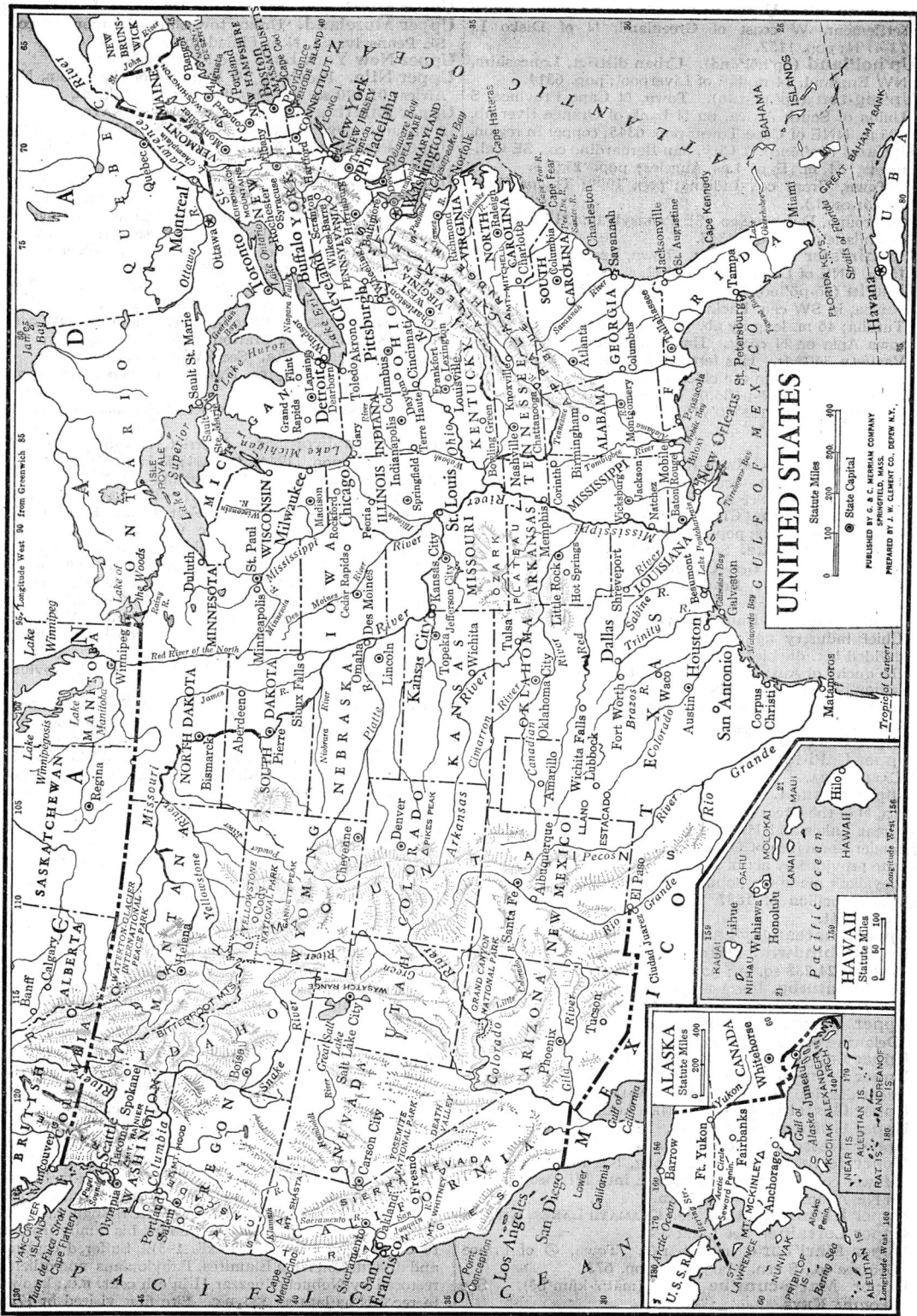

UNITED STATES

Statute Miles

PUBLISHED BY G. & C. MERRIAM COMPANY
SPRINGFIELD, MASS.
PREPARED BY J. W. CLEMENT CO., DEPEW N.Y.

⊙ State Capital

ALASKA
Statute Miles

HAWAII
Statute Miles

U·per′na·vik *or* U·per′ni·vik (ōō·pûr′nȧ·vĕk). Danish settlement, W coast of Greenland, N of Disko I., 72°47′N; pop. 1152.

Up′hol′land (ŭp′hŏl′ănd). Urban district, Lancashire, NW England, 14 m. NE of Liverpool; pop. 6314.

Up′ing·ton (ŭp′ĭng·tŭn). Town, N Cape Province, S Union of South Africa, on N bank of Orange river ab. 405 m. NNE of Cape Town; pop. 6345; copper in region.

Up′land (ŭp′lănd). 1 City, San Bernardino co., SE California, 34 m. E of Los Angeles; pop. 15,918.
2 Town, Grant co., Indiana; pop. 1999; Taylor Univ. (1846; coed.).
3 Borough, Delaware co., SE Pennsylvania, 15 m. WSW of Philadelphia; pop. 4343.

Up′min′ster (ŭp′mĭn′stēr). Town, Essex, SE England, 15 m. ENE of London; pop. 5732.

U·po′lu (ōō·pō′lōō). Island in the Territory of Western Samoa, in SW cen. Pacific Ocean, ab. 38 m. W by N of Tutuila; 46 m. long by ab. 16 m. wide; 430 sq. m.; chief town Apia on N coast. Has many mountains, highest Vaaifetu 3608 ft. Has fertile soil; chief product copra. Apia and Saluafata are chief harbors.

U·po′lu Point (ōō·pō′lōō). Cape on N tip of Hawaii I., Hawaii, 20°17′N, 155°50′W.

Upper A′di·ge (ä′dē·jâ). Italian name for S part of the Tirol (*q.v.*).

Upper Alsace. = HAUT-RHIN department, E France.

Upper Andalusia. See ANDALUSIA.

Upper Angara. See ANGARA.

Upper Arlington. City, Franklin co., cen. Ohio, 8 m. NNW of Columbus; pop. 28,486.

Upper Arrow Lake. See ARROW LAKE.

Upper Austria; *Ger.* O′ber·ö′ster·reich′ (ō′bēr·ŭ′-stēr·rīk′; -û′strīk). Province of Austria. See *Table* at AUSTRIA. Region bet. Lower Austria and Bavaria and mostly W of the Enns river; crossed by the Danube. Chief industry agriculture. In Hohenstaufen period divided bet. duchies of Styria and Bavaria; later part of the duchy of Austria, then of the archduchy and empire.

Upper Bann. See BANN.

Upper Bavaria. Bavarian government district. See *Table* at BAVARIA.

Upper Burma. See BURMA.

Upper Cal′i·for′nia (kăl′ĭ·fôrn′yȧ; -fôr′nĭ·ȧ). = ALTA CALIFORNIA.

Upper Canada. Old British province in North America, N of the Great Lakes and S of the watershed bet. the Great Lakes and Hudson Bay, equivalent to S part of modern province of Ontario, Canada. Erected as separate province by act of 1791; its settlement by American Loyalists made its population predominantly English; after rebellion of 1837, reunited with Lower Canada (*q.v.*) 1841.

Upper Chateaugay Lake. See CHATEAUGAY LAKES.

Upper Chindwin. District, Sagaing division, W Upper Burma; 24,238 sq. m.; pop. 204,982; ✽ Mawlaik.

Upper Danube. Former province of Austria (Ostmark). See *Upper Austria* in *Table* at AUSTRIA.

Upper Dar′by (där′bǐ). Urban district (township), Delaware co., SE Pennsylvania; pop. 93,158.

Upper Egypt. See EGYPT.

Upper Fran·co′ni·a (frăng·kō′nĭ·ȧ). Bavarian government district. See *Table* at BAVARIA.

Upper Gastein. See GASTEINER ACHE.

Upper Guinea. See GUINEA.

Upper Hesse. See *Oberhessen* in *Table* at HESSE.

Upper Iowa. River 135 m. long, NE Iowa; rises in S Mower co., S Minnesota, flows E into Mississippi river in NE Allamakee co., NE Iowa.

Upper Klamath Lake. See KLAMATH LAKES, Oregon.

Upper Lorraine. See LORRAINE.

Upper Marl′bor′o (märl′bûr′ō). Town, ⊗ of Prince Georges co., S cen. Maryland; pop. 673.

Upper Mat′e·cum′be Key (măt′ē·kŭm′bē). See FLORIDA KEYS.

Upper Montclair. See MONTCLAIR.

Upper Moreland. Urban township, Montgomery co., SE Pennsylvania, N of Philadelphia; pop. 21,032.

Upper New York Bay. See NEW YORK BAY.

Upper Nile. Province, SE Republic of the Sudan, NE Africa; 91,190 sq. m.; pop. 888,611; ✽ Malakal.

Upper Palatinate. 1 See Upper PALATINATE.
2 Bavarian government district. See *Table* at BAVARIA.

Upper Peninsula. North part of Michigan, bet. Lakes Superior and Michigan.

Upper Peru. Earlier name for region corresponding approximately to Bolivia; originally the audiencia of Charcas, a part (1559–1776) of the Spanish viceroyalty of Peru, capital Chuquisaca (modern Sucre); in 1776 became N part of new viceroyalty of La Plata; erected into the independent state of Bolivia 1825.

Upper Rhine; *Ger.* O′ber·rhein′ (ō′bēr·rīn′). The section of the Rhine river bet. Basel and Mainz.

Upper Sandusky. Village, ⊗ of Wyandot co., NW cen. Ohio, 18 m. NNW of Marion; pop. 4941.

Upper Saranac Lake. See SARANAC LAKES.

Upper Senegal–Niger. Name of French Sudan (*q.v.*) before 1920.

Upper Silesia. Former province of Prussia. See *Silesia* in *Table* at PRUSSIA.

Upper Sind Frontier. District, N Sind, Pakistan; 1969 sq. m.; pop. (1941) 304,034; ✽ Jacobabad.

Upper Tunguska. See TUNGUSKA.

Upper Vol′ta (vŏl′tȧ); *Fr.* Haute–Vol′ta′ (ōt′vôl′tä′). Former Territory in French West Africa, S of French Sudan; since 1958 a republic (sometimes called the Vol·ta′ic Republic [vŏl·tā′ĭk]); ab. 105,839 sq. m.; pop. (1959 est.) 4,000,000; ✽ Ouagadougou. Organized as separate colony 1919; its territory divided bet. Ivory Coast, Niger, and French Sudan 1933; re-established as separate political unit with territorial status 1947; became an autonomous republic of the French community 1958; gained full independence 1960.

Upp′sa′la *or* Up′sa′la (ŭp′säˈlȧ; *Swed.* -lȧ). 1 Province of Sweden. See *Table* at SWEDEN.
2 City, its ✽, E Sweden, 40 m. NNW of Stockholm; pop. 44,686; publishing houses, iron foundries, machine-manufacturing works; seat of the archbishop of Sweden, and of Uppsala Univ., founded by the archbishop 1477; cathedral, dating from 13th cent., contains the tombs of Gustavus Vasa, Linnaeus, and Swedenborg; an ancient capital of Sweden.

Up′shur (ŭp′shēr). Name of counties in two states of the U.S. See *Tables* at TEXAS and WEST VIRGINIA.

Up′son (ŭp′s′n). County in Georgia. See *Table* at GEORGIA.

Up′ton (ŭp′tŭn). 1 County in Texas. See *Table* at TEXAS.
2 Town, Worcester co., cen. Massachusetts, 12 m. ESE of Worcester; pop. 3127.
3 Locality on Long I., New York, in Suffolk co.; site of former Camp Upton (*q.v.*) and since 1947 of the Brookhaven National Laboratory for Nuclear Research.

Uqair. See OQAIR.

Uqsor, El. See LUXOR.

Ur (ûr); *Bib.* Ur of the Chal·dees′ (kăl·dēz′; kăl′dēz). City and district in ancient Sumer, S Babylonia, the modern Mu·qai′yir (mōō·kī′yǐr; -kā′-), ab. 12 m. SW of An Nasiriya, S Iraq, on a former channel of the Euphrates river and near the Baghdad-Basra railroad. One of the oldest cities of Mesopotamia; its First Dynasty ruled c. 3000–c. 2600 B.C.; probably settled 1000 years earlier; seat of worship of Sin, the moon-god. Declined, but again powerful under a new dynasty, the Third, c. 2300–2200 B.C., founded by Ur-Engur. Birthplace of Abraham c. 2000 B.C. who led his family from it to Canaan (*Gen.* xi. 27–31, xii. 1–5). Suffered capture and destruction from Elamites, Babylonians, and others; restored by Nebuchadnezzar II in 6th cent. B.C.; known in records as late as 324 B.C. Site first visited in 17th

cent.; excavations have uncovered remains of great archaeological value.

U'ra·bá', Gulf of (ōō'rä·vä'). Bay on the NW coast of Colombia, at the inner end of the Gulf of Darien (q.v.).

U·ra·ga (ōō·rä·gä). Seaport, Kanagawa prefecture, SE Honshu, Japan, 5 m. SE of Yokosuka on **Uraga Strait**; pop. (1945) 28,073. Port where first American emissaries under Commodore Biddle attempted 1846 to establish relations with the Japanese; their repulse led to Commodore Perry's expedition; 1 m. to the S is Kurihama, where Perry's four ships anchored July 8, 1853.

U'ral (ūr'ăl; *Russ.* ōō·räl'). Unnavigable river ab. 1400 m. long in Soviet Russia in Europe and Asia; rises at the S end of the Ural Mts. on the E border of Bashkir A.S.S.R., flows S, then W through Chkalov Region, crossing its SW border to flow S through W Kazakh S.S.R. to the Caspian Sea at Gurev. Magnitogorsk, Orsk, Chkalov, and Uralsk are on its banks.

Ural Area or **U·ralsk' Area** (ū·rälsk'; *Russ.* ōō·räl'-y'sk). Former subdivision of Soviet Russia in Asia; 696,380 sq. m.; * Sverdlovsk; included territory on both sides of the N and cen. Ural Mts.; after World War I its S part around Sverdlovsk developed into the Ural Industrial Area (q.v.).

Ural Industrial Area. A highly developed mining and manufacturing region on both sides of the cen. Ural Mts., Soviet Russia in Europe and Asia; comprises the Chelyabinsk, Sverdlovsk, and Molotov Regions, and parts of Bashkir and Udmurt A.S.S. Republics; approximately 200,000 sq. m.; pop. ab. 8,000,000. Has great deposits of coal, iron, copper, platinum, gold, oil, and nonferrous metals; second to Ukraine in total electric power developed for heavy industry. Has great railroad workshops; in World War II center for manufacture of machine tools, tractors, tanks, planes, etc. Chief cities Sverdlovsk, Chelyabinsk, Magnitogorsk, Nizhni Tagil, Molotov, Tyumen, Ufa, and Kurgan.

Ural Mountains. Mountain range, NW Asia, ab. 1640 m. long extending S from Kara Sea to the W Kirgiz Steppe region of Kazakh S.S.R., averaging 3000 to 4000 ft.; one of highest Telpos Iz 5558 ft. is in N (64°). Central part (**Middle U'rals** [ūr'ălz]) is ab. 80 m. broad and lower in altitude, actually a plateau region 1000 to 2000 ft.; densely forested and very rich in minerals; this region now developed into the Ural Industrial Area (q.v.). **Southern Urals** have three parallel ranges, with rich pasture grounds. Geographically constitutes the natural boundary bet. Europe and Asia, but under the Soviet Union Molotov Region, W of Middle Urals, is administered as part of Soviet Russia, Asia.

U·ralsk' (ū·rälsk'; *Russ.* ōō·räl'y'sk). Town, W Kazakh S.S.R., Soviet Central Asia, on Ural river at its lower bend near the Chkalov Region; * of West Kazakhstan; pop. 66,201; a trading center for cattle and grain.

Uralsk Area. See URAL AREA.

U·ra'ri·coe'ra (ōō·rä'rĕ·kwä'rä) or **U·ra'ri·cue'ra** (-kwä'rä). River ab. 360 m. long in N Brazil; rises in Serra Parima near S Venezuelan border, flows E to unite with Takutú river to form Rio Branco.

U·rar'tu (ōō·rär'tōō) or **Van** (vän). *Heb.* **Ar'a·rat** (ăr'à·răt). Ancient kingdom around Lake Van (ancient Thospitis), N of Assyria—the Assyrian name for the region. Kingdom lasted from c. 1270 to 750 B.C.; first inscriptions date from time of King Shalmaneser I (c. 1276–1257) oi Assyria; repeatedly attacked by Assyrian kings and weakened so that in 8th cent. B.C. it ceased to exist after invasions by Scythians and Medes. Its peoples were of Hurrian and Vannic stock. See ARMENIA ancient country.

U'ra Tyu·be' (ōō'rä tü·bĕ'). Town, NW Tadzhik S.S.R., Soviet Russia, Asia, 40 m. WSW of Leninabad.

U·ra'wa (ōō·rä'wä; *Jap.* ōō·rä·wä). Town, * of Saitama prefecture, SE cen. Honshu, Japan, 13 m. N of Tokyo; pop. (1945) 93,871; has an ancient Shinto shrine and groves of hinoki, cryptomeria, and cherry trees.

Ur·ban'a (ûr·băn'à). **1** City, ⊗ of Champaign co., E cen. Illinois, 47 m. ENE of Decatur; pop. 27,294; settled 1824, incorp. as town 1833, as city 1860; adjoins city of Champaign (combination often known as Urbana-Champaign); commercial center in agricultural section. Univ. of Illinois (1867; coed.).
2 City, ⊗ of Champaign co., W Ohio, 13 m. N of Springfield; pop. 10,461; manufactures strawboard, furniture, tools and dies, food products; farming, cattle raising.

Urbandale. Town, Polk co., S cen. Iowa, NW suburb of Des Moines; pop. 5821.

Ur·bi'no (ōōr·bē'nō); *anc.* **Ur·bi'num Hor·ten'se** (ûr·bī'nŭm hôr·tĕn'sĕ) or **Ur·vi'num Met'au·ren'se** (ûr·vī'nŭm mĕt'ô·rĕn'sĕ). Commune, Pesaro e Urbino prov., Marches, cen. Italy, 19 m. SW of Pesaro; pop. 22,248; manufactures silk, brick, oil, cheese, and dairy products; cathedral (rebuilt after earthquake of 1789), 15th-cent. ducal palace, 14th-cent. churches, university. Birthplace of Raphael. Capital of duchy of Urbino 1474–1626 after which it fell to Papal States.

Urbino, Pesaro e. See PESARO E URBINO.

Urbinum Hortense. See URBINO.

Urbs Vetus. See ORVIETO.

Ur'cos (ōōr'kôs). Town, Cuzco dept., Peru, SE of Cuzco on railroad in upper Urubamba valley.

Ur'da·ne'ta (ōōr'thä·nä'tä). Municipality, E cen. Pangasinan prov., Luzon, Phil. Is., 20 m. E of Lingayen; pop. 29,120.

Urdingen. = UERDINGEN.

Ure (ūr). River ab. 50 m. long in Yorkshire, N England; unites with the Swale river to form the Ouse.

Ur·fa' (ōōr·fä'). **1** Vilayet, SE Turkey in Asia, SE of the Euphrates river; 6597 sq. m.; pop. 229,614.
2 *anc.* **E·des'sa** (ĕ·dĕs'à). City, its *, 75 m. E of Gaziantep; pop. (1940) 34,829; a frontier trading town with remains of ancient walls and citadel.

History: Ancient Edessa had independent dynasty just before Christian Era, but its history is little known; an early center of Syriac-speaking Christianity until conquered by Arabs 639 A.D.; Bardesianism, a Gnostic sect, founded here in 2d cent. A.D.; conquered from Seljuk Turks by Baldwin I of Flanders who erected Christian county of Edessa 1098; reconquered by Moslems 1144; under Turkish rule from 1639; modern Urfa scene of massacres of Armenians 1895.

Ur'ga (ōōr'gä) or **U'lan Ba'tor** (ōō'län bä·tôr); *Chin.* **Ku'lun'** (kōō'lōōn'); *also* **Ulan Bator Kho'to** [ĸō'tō] (*khoto* = Mongol for "town"). Commercial and sacred town, * of Mongolian People's Republic (Outer Mongolia), in N cen. part; pop. ab. 100,000; junction point of main camel caravan and motor highways crossing Mongolia and terminus of railroad S (165 m.) from Kyakhta in U.S.S.R.; ab. 720 m. NW of Peiping. Divided into three sections: monastery, or residence of the Living Buddha (Hutukhtu of Urga); Mongol city; and Chinese quarter. Chief center of Mongol revolt 1912; successively under control of Mongols, Chinese, Russians.

Ur·gel', Seo de (sā'ô thä ōōr·hĕl'). Commune, Lérida prov., Catalonia, NE Spain, on the Segre river 10 m. SSW of Andorra; pop. 4116; episcopal see (Span. *seo*) founded 820; late Romanesque cathedral. Its bishop has joint suzerainty with France over Andorra (q.v.).

Ur·gench' (ōōr·gĕnch'). **1** or **No'vo Urgench** (nô'vŭ). *Eng.* **New Urgench.** Industrial town, Kara-Kalpak A.S.S.R., W Uzbek S.S.R., Soviet Central Asia, on left bank of the Amu Darya (ancient Oxus); pop. 5200.
2 Ancient town ab. 85 m. to the NW of Novo Urgench; has some architectural remains; once dominated the lower Oxus region.

U'ri (ōō'rĕ). Swiss canton. See *History* and *Table* at SWITZERLAND.

Uri, Bay, or **Lake, of.** SE extension of Lake of Lucerne, cen. Switzerland; receives river Reuss at its S end.

U'rian·ga'to (ōō'ryäng·gä'tō). Town, Guanajuato state, cen. Mexico, just N of Lake Cuitzeo; pop. 5201.

U'riang·hai' (ōō'ryäng·kī'). Var. of *Uriankhai:* see TUVA.

Uriankhai. See TUVA.

U·ri'bia (ōō-rē'vyä). Town, * of Guajira commissary, NE Colombia, 135 m. ENE of Santa Marta.

Uriburu, General J. F. See GENERAL J. F. URIBURU.

Uriconium. See WROXETER.

Ur'mi·a (ōōr'mĭ·à; *Pers.* ōōr'mē·yä'). See RIZAIYEH.

Urmia, Lake; *Pers.* Sha·hi' (shä·hē') *or* U'ru·mi·yeh' (ōō'rōō·mē·yĕ'); *anc.* Mat'i·a'nus (măt'ĭ·ā'nŭs). Shallow saline lake in NW Iran, E of Rizaiyeh and W of Tabriz; area varies bet. 1500 and 2300 sq. m. according to the season. Shahi I. is in N cen. part and a group of smaller islands in S cen. part; Sharifkhaneh on NE shore is only lake port; it is connected by branch railroad with Tabriz and is operation center for fleet of Iranian motor boats.

Urm'ston (ûrm'stŭn). Urban district, Lancashire, NW England, on the Mersey 5 m. WSW of Manchester; pop. 39,233.

Ur of the Chaldees. See UR.

Ur're Lau·quén' (ōōr'rĕ lou·kän'). Lake in the marshy area in S La Pampa territory, S cen. Argentina.

Urseren. See ANDERMATT.

Urso. See OSUNA.

U·rua'pan (ōō·rwä'pän), *in full* Uruapan del Pro·gre'so (dĕl prō·grä'sō). City, Michoacán state, SW Mexico, 50 m. SW of Morelia; pop. 20,583; lacquer work; in center of rich agricultural region and just E of new volcano, Parícutin. One of the chief towns of the Tarascan Indians; founded 1540.

U'ru·bam'ba (ōō'rōō·väm'bä). 1 River ab. 450 m. long in cen. Peru; rises in Andes Mts. and flows NNW bet. parallel ranges of the Andes to unite with Apurímac river at ab. 10°45'S and form Ucayali river; Cuzco on it. 2 Town, Cuzco dept., Peru, 20 m. N of Cuzco; mining town.

U'ru·gua·ia'na (ōō'rōō·gwà·yä'nà). City, W Rio Grande do Sul state, S Brazil, on Argentine border; pop. (1940 est.) 21,774; a center of the cattle industry.

U'ru·guay (ûr'ŭ-gwĭ; -gwä; ōōr'ŭ-; *Span.* ōō'rōō-gwī'). 1 River ab. 980 m. long in SE South America; flows W in Santa Catarina state, S Brazil, forming section of boundary bet. Santa Catarina and Rio Grande do Sul states; turns SW and forms boundary bet. S Brazil and Argentina, and bet. Uruguay and Argentina; empties into Río de la Plata.

2 *officially* Re·pú'bli·ca O'rien·tal' del U'ru·guay' (rrĕ·pōō'vlĕ·kä ō'ryän·täl' dĕl ōō'rōō·gwī'). Republic, SE cen. South America, E of the lower Uruguay river; bounded on N by Brazil, on E by the Atlantic Ocean, on S by the La Plata river, and on W by Argentina; 72,172 sq. m.; pop. (1941 est.) 2,185,626; * Montevideo; divided into the following 19 departments (for pronunciation of their names, see their individual entries):

NAME	LOCA-TION	AREA[1]	POP.[1]	CAPITAL
Artigas	NW	4,393	55,748	Artigas
Canelones	S	1,835	199,232	Canelones
Cerro Largo	E	5,764	96,488	Melo
Colonia	SW	2,194	129,322	Colonia
Durazno	cen.	5,527	94,291	Durazno
Flores	SW	1,745	35,835	Trinidad
Florida	S cen.	4,675	105,932	Florida
Lavalleja	S	4,820	115,181	Minas
Maldonado	S	1,587	66,539	Maldonado
Montevideo	S	256	536,533	Montevideo
Paysandú	W	5,117	83,490	Paysandú
Río Negro	N	3,271	47,147	Fray Bentos
Rivera	N	3,795	74,746	Rivera
Rocha	SE	4,281	82,156	Rocha
Salto	NW	4,866	99,754	Salto
San José	S	2,688	97,301	San José
Soriano	SW	3,561	92,167	Mercedes
Tacuarembó	N cen.	8,114	104,889	Tacuarembó
Treinta y Tres	E	3,683	68,371	Treinta y Tres

[1] Area in sq. m. Pop. is 1941 est.

Generally flat country (pampas region) with low range of Brazilian highlands in NE, less than 2000 ft. Trav-ersed from NE to SW by the Río Negro; has rich soil favorable to agriculture, but main industry is cattle raising; chief exports meat, wool, skins, and hides. Chief cities Montevideo, Paysandú, Salto, Mercedes, Rocha.

History: Río de la Plata discovered by Solís 1516; Colonia founded by Portuguese 1680 and Montevideo (*q.v.*) in 1726; region (called Banda Oriental by the Spaniards) long in dispute bet. Portuguese and Spanish, the latter finally securing control; in Spanish viceroyalty of La Plata 1776; with Buenos Aires, obtained independence from Spain 1811–14; incorporated in Brazil as Cisplatine Province 1821; revolted from Brazil 1825 and was recognized as independent state 1828; in war against Paraguay (*q.v.*) 1865–70; adopted present constitution 1934; did not take active part in either World War I or II, but broke off relations with Germany Oct. 7, 1917 and with the Axis powers in 1942.

Uruk. See ERECH.

U'ruk·tha'pel (ōō'rōōk·tä'pĕl). Second largest island of Palau Is. group, W Pacific Ocean, S of Babelthuap I.

U·rum'chi (ōō·rōōm'chē) *or* Ti'hwa' (dē'hwä'); *also* U·rum'tsi (ōō·rōōm'chē). City, * of Sinkiang prov., W China, in cen. part of province ab. 1000 m. NW of Lanchow in Kansu prov.; pop. (1953) 140,700; also chief town of Dzungaria; on N side of Tien Shan range at ab. 3000 ft. alt. Administrative center and important commercially in trade with Russia and India, on the N caravan and motor highway. A cosmopolitan town with representatives esp. of Chinese, Turki, Russians, and Mongolians.

Urumiyeh. See Lake URMIA.

U·run'di (ōō·rōōn'dē); *now* Bu·run'di (bōō·rōōn'dē). Country, cen. Africa, S of Rwanda; an independent kingdom, * Usumbura (now Bujumbura); 10,747 sq. m.; pop. 2,213,280; until 1962 part of Ruanda-Urundi trust territory. See RUANDA-URUNDI.

U·rup·pu (ōō·rōōp·pōō). One of the Kuril Is. (*q.v.*), NE of Etorofu.

U·ru·san (ōō·rōō·sän). Coastal town, South Keisho prov., SE Korea, 35 m. NE of Fusan; pop. 15,340.

Urville, Cape d'. See Cape D'URVILLE.

Urvinum Metaurense. See URBINO.

U·sa (ōō·sä). Town, Oita prefecture, NE Kyushu, Japan, near coast 45 m. NW of Oita; pop. 5115.

U·sa' (ōō·sä'). River 350 m. long, NE Komi Republic, Soviet Russia, Europe, an E tributary of the Pechora; rises at N end of Ural Mts. and flows SW to Pechora at Ust Usa; navigable.

U'sa·ga'ra (ōō'sá·gär'à). Hill region at E edge of the cen. plateau in Tanganyika, E Africa, traversed by the Ruaha River.

U·şak' (ōō·shäk') *or* U·shak'. Manufacturing town, Kütahya vilayet, W Turkey in Asia, on railroad 55 m. W of Afyon Karahisar; pop. 17,948; carpets.

U·sa'kos (ōō·sä'kŭs). Town, W cen. South-West Africa, 100 m. NW of Windhoek; pop. 3100.

U'sam·ba'ra (ōō'säm·bär'à). Highlands in NE Tanga prov., NE Tanganyika, E Africa.

Us'borne (ŭz'bērn). Peak 2245 ft. in East Falkland I. of the Falkland Is. (*q.v.*).

U'se·dom (ōō'zĕ·dôm); *Pol.* Uz'nam (ōōz'näm). Island 30 m. long off the coast of Pomerania, N Germany, bet. Stettiner Haff and the Bay of Pomerania (inlet of the Baltic Sea); 170 sq. m.; pop. ab. 47,000; since 1945 divided bet. Poland and Germany, with E third (Uznam) now in Szczecin dept., NW Poland; chief town is port of Świnoujście (formerly Swinemünde) in Polish section.

Useless Bay. See INÚTIL BAY.

U. S. Grant Peak (grànt). Mountain 13,692 ft. in San Juan and San Miguel cos., SW Colorado

Ush'ant (ŭsh'ănt); *Fr.* Île d'Oues'sant' (ēl' dwĕ'säN'); *anc.* Ux·an'tis (ŭk·săn'tĭs). Island 4½ m. long off tip of Brittany, NW France; 6 sq. m.; pop. ab. 2000; scene of naval battles 1778 and 1794 bet. French and English.

Ush'ba (ōōsh'bä). Peak in W cen. Caucasus Mts. in

ARGENTINA, CHILE, PARAGUAY, URUGUAY

Statute Miles

0   100   200   300

⊕ Capitals of Countries

PUBLISHED BY G. & C. MERRIAM COMPANY
SPRINGFIELD, MASS.
PREPARED BY J. W. CLEMENT CO., BUFFALO, N. Y.

Georgian Republic, U.S.S.R., SE of Mt. Elborus; a double peak 15,400 ft. high; glaciers.

U'shi·tse (ōō'zhĕ·tsĕ). = Užice.

Ush'nu·i·yeh' (ōōsh'nōō·wē·yĕ'). Town, NW Iran, W of S end of Lake Urmia.

Us·hua'ia (ōōs·wä'yä). Town, * of Tierra del Fuego territory, S Argentina, on S Tierra del Fuego I., on Beagle Channel; pop. ab. 1600; farthest S city in the world in 54°50'S.

Usk (ŭsk). River 60 m. long in S Wales and W England; rises in S cen. Wales, flows E and S into the Severn estuary just below Newport in Monmouthshire.

Üsküb. See Skoplje.

Üs'kü·dar' (üs'kü·där'); *formerly* **Scu'ta·ri** (skōō'-tä·rĭ; *Ital.* -tä·rē); *anc.* **Chry·sop'o·lis** (krĭ·sŏp'ŏ·lĭs). Town, İstanbul vilayet, Turkey in Asia, across the Bosporus from İstanbul; pop. (1935) 54,848; commercial and manufacturing suburb of İstanbul. Base of British Army in Crimean War and site of hospital under charge of Florence Nightingale. Ancient Chrysopolis was port of Chalcedon.

Üs·küp' (üs·küp'). = *Üsküb:* see Skoplje.

Us'pal·la'ta Pass (ōōs'pä·yä'tä; -pä·zhä'-) *or* **La Cum'bre** (lä kōōm'brä). Pass in the Andes Mts.; see Andes.

Us·su'ri (ōō·sōōr'ĭ; *Russ.* ōōs·sōō'ryĭ). River ab. 450 m. long, Soviet Russia, Asia, forming boundary bet. W Maritime Territory and E Manchuria, N of Vladivostok; rises in mountains at extreme S end of Maritime Territory and flows N to join the Amur near Khabarovsk; a W tributary of upper course is outlet for Lake Khanka. Chief Russian town on its bank is Iman.

Ussuri Bay. Northeast extension of Peter the Great Bay, Maritime Territory, Soviet Russia, Asia, just E of Vladivostok.

Ussuriysk. See Voroshilov.

Ust Bol'she·retsk' (ōōst' bôl'shĕ·rĕtsk'; *Russ.* ōōst'y' bŭl·shĭ·ryĕtsk'). Town, SW coast of Kamchatka Penin., Khabarovsk Territory, on Sea of Okhotsk, Soviet Russia, Asia, ab. 100 m. W of Petropavlovsk; airport.

Ust Dvinsk. See Daugavgrīva.

U'ster (ōōs'tẽr). Manufacturing commune, Zurich canton, Switzerland, 8 m. ESE of Zurich; pop. 10,588.

Ú'stí *or* **Ústí nad La'bem** (ōō'stye nàd là'bĕm); *Ger.* **Aus'sig** (ous'ĭk). City, N Bohemia prov., W Czechoslovakia, on Labe (Elbe) river; pop. (1930) 43,793; manufactures chemicals, textiles, glass; Dominican monastery, dating from 10th cent.

U'sti·ca (ōōs'tē·kä). Small island in Tyrrhenian Sea NW of Sicily; isolated, place of exile for prisoners.

Ust I·shim' (ōōst' ĭ·shĭm'; *Russ.* ōōst'y' ĭ·shĭm'). Town on Irtysh river where it is joined by the Ishim, 110 m. E of Tobolsk, E Tyumen Region, Soviet Russia, Asia.

Ust–Ka·me'no·gorsk (ōōst' kà·mĕn'ŏ·gôrsk; *Russ.* ōōst'y' kà·myĭ·nŭ·gôrsk'). Town, * of East Kazakhstan, E Kazakh S.S.R., Soviet Central Asia, on the Irtysh river 100 m. E of Semipalatinsk; on a branch of the Turkistan-Siberian R.R.

Ust Kut (ōōst' kōōt'; *Russ.* ōōst'y'). Town, N cen. Irkutsk Region, Soviet Russia, Asia, ab. 310 m. N of Irkutsk on the new Baikal-Amur-Magistral R.R.

Ust Nyuk'zha (ōōst' nük'zhà; *Russ.* ōōst'y'). Town, N Chita Region, Soviet Russia, Asia, on Olekma river where the new Baikal-Amur-Magistral R.R. crosses it.

Ust Or·da' (ōōst' ôr·dä'; *Russ.* ōōst'y' ŭr·dà'). Town, * of Ust-Ordin Buryat-Mongol National District, Soviet Russia, Asia, 40 m. N of Irkutsk, W of Lake Baikal.

Ust–Or·din' Buryat–Mongol National District (ōōst'ôr·dēn'; *Russ.* ōōst'y'·ŭr·dyēn'). National district, SE Irkutsk Region, Soviet Russia, Asia, W of Lake Baikal; 10,923 sq. m.; pop. (1941 est.) 110,000; * Ust Orda.

Ust Sysolsk. See Syktyvkar.

Ust Tsil'ma (ōōst' tsĭl'mà; *Russ.* ōōst'y' tsyĕl'y'·mà). Town, NW Komi Republic, Soviet Russia, Europe, on

right bank of the Pechora opp. the Tsilma tributary, 350 m. E of Arkhangelsk.

Ust Urt (ōōst' ōōrt'; *Russ.* ōōst'y' ōōrt'). Plateau ab. 92,000 sq. m. in SW Kazakh S.S.R., Soviet Central Asia, extending bet. the Caspian Sea and Lake Aral.

Ust U·sa' (ōōst' ōō·sá'; *Russ.* ōōst'y'). Town, N Komi Republic, Soviet Russia, Europe, at junction of the Usa river with the Pechora just S of the Arctic Circle.

Ustyug Veliki. = Veliki Ustyug.

U·su·ki (ōō·sōō·kĕ). Town, Oita prefecture, NE Kyushu, Japan, ab. 12 m. SE of Oita; pop. (1945) 23,876; has good harbor on Bungo Strait.

U'su·lu·tán' (ōō'sōō·lōō·tän'). **1** Department, SE El Salvador; 1291 sq. m.; pop. (1942 est.) 164,967. **2** Town, its *, near coast 55 m. ESE of San Salvador; pop. (1942 est.) 8622; produces tobacco, bananas, corn, beans.

U'su·ma·cin'ta (ōō'sōō·mä·sēn'tä). River ab. 330 m. long, N Guatemala and SE Mexico; rises in W Guatemala, flows NW forming section of Guatemala-Mexico (Chiapas state) boundary, empties into Grijalva river near its mouth in N Tabasco state, Mexico; navigable for a short distance; known as the **Chi·xoy'** (chē·hoi') river in its upper course.

U'sum·bu'ra (ōō'sŏŏm·bōōr'à); *now* **Bu'jum·bu'ra** (bōō'jŭm·bōōr'á). Town, * of Burundi and formerly of Ruanda-Urundi, on E side of N end of Lake Tanganyika.

Usuri. = Ussuri.

U·su'tu (ōō·sōō'tōō). River 135 m. long in S Africa; flows E in E Transvaal. Republic of So. Africa, and in Swaziland and unites with Pongola river in Mozambique to form the Maputo river.

U'tah (ū'tô; ū'tä). **1** Western state of U.S.A., 45th state admitted to Union (1896); bounded on N by Idaho and Wyoming, on E by Colorado, on S by Arizona, and on W by Nevada; 11th state in area, 84,916 sq. m. (land area 82,346 sq. m.); 38th state in population, 890,627; * Salt Lake City. See *Table of States* at United States. Divided into the following 29 counties (for pronunciation of their names, see their individual entries):

NAME	LOCATION	AREA	POP.[1]	CO. SEAT
Beaver	SW	2,587	4,331	Beaver
Box Elder[2]	NW corner	5,594	25,061	Brigham
Cache	N	1,175	35,788	Logan
Carbon	E cen.	1,474	21,135	Price
Daggett	NE	708	1,164	Manila
Davis[2]	N	268	64,760	Farmington
Duchesne	NE cen.	3,260	7,179	Duchesne
Emery	E cen.	4,442	5,546	Castle Dale
Garfield[2]	S	5,217	3,577	Panguitch
Grand	E	3,692	6,345	Moab
Iron[4]	SW	3,300	10,795	Parowan
Juab	W	3,412	4,597	Nephi
Kane[3,4]	S	4,105	2,667	Kanab
Millard[5]	W	6,648	7,866	Fillmore
Morgan	N	610	2,837	Morgan
Piute	S cen.	753	1,436	Junction
Rich	N	1,022	1,685	Randolph
Salt Lake[2]	N	764	383,035	Salt Lake City
San Juan[6]	SE corner	7,884	9,040	Monticello
Sanpete	cen.	1,597	11,053	Manti
Sevier	cen.	1,932	10,565	Richfield
Summit	NE	1,860	5,673	Coalville
Tooele[2]	NW	6,911	17,868	Tooele
Uintah	E	4,476	11,582	Vernal
Utah[7]	N cen.	1,998	106,991	Provo
Wasatch	N cen.	1,194	5,308	Heber
Washington[4]	SW corner	2,425	10,271	St. George
Wayne	S cen.	2,489	1,728	Loa
Weber[2]	N	549	110,744	Ogden

[1] Area = land area in sq. m. Pop. from 1960 Census.
[2] Upper part of Great Salt Lake in cen. and SE Box Elder co.; lower part in Weber, Davis, Salt Lake and Tooele cos.
[3] Bryce Canyon National Park in SW Garfield co. and NW Kane co.
[4] Zion National Park in NE and E Washington co., with small areas in abutting S part of Iron co. and W part of Kane co.
[5] Includes Sevier Lake and several smaller lakes.
[6] SE point of county the only point in U.S. common to four states (Utah, Colorado, New Mexico, Arizona).
[7] Utah Lake in W cen. part.

Nickname: Beehive State; also Mormon State. *State flower:* Sego lily. *Motto:* Industry. *Chief cities:* Salt Lake

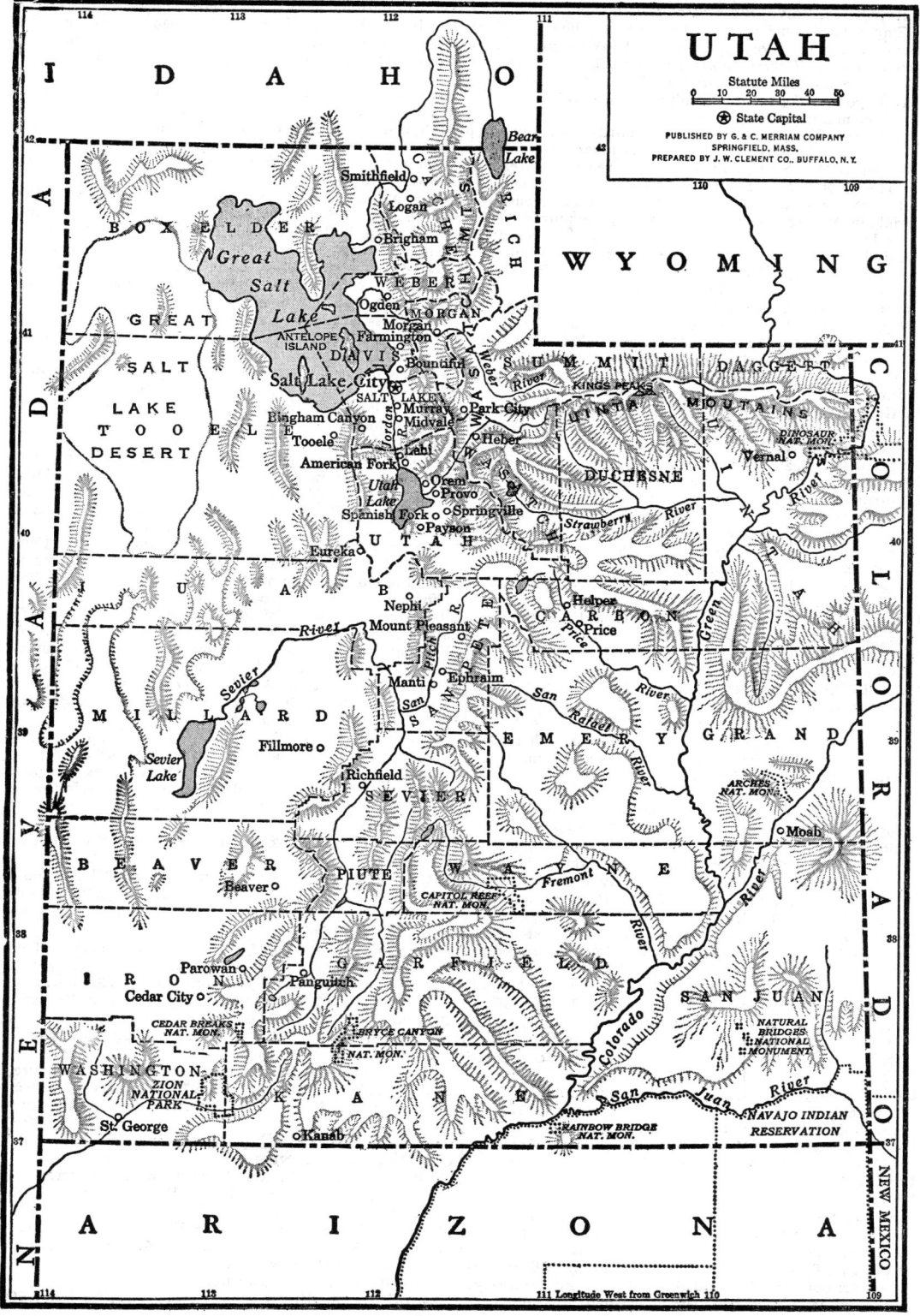

City, Ogden, Provo, *Rivers:* Colorado flowing SW across SE area; Green in E area flowing S to join the Colorado; Sevier in SW cen. area, flowing N and SW to empty into Sevier Lake. *Highest point:* Kings Peak 13,498 ft. in Duchesne co. *Chief industries:* Mining (lead, copper, silver, gold, zinc, sulfur, uranium), sheep raising, agriculture, manufacturing (metals).

History: First explored by Spaniards sent out by Coronado 1540; Great Salt Lake discovered by James Bridger 1824; acquired by United States from Mexico in Treaty of Guadalupe Hidalgo 1848; first permanent settlers were Mormons, led from Illinois and Missouri by Brigham Young 1847; Utah Territory organized 1850 (see DESERET); conflict bet. Mormon authorities and United States, known as Utah War (1857–58); admitted to Union Jan. 4, 1896.

2 County in Utah. See *Table* at UTAH.

Utah Beach. Name given by Allied commanders to the W part of the American sector of Normandy beaches, marked for invasion June 1944; extended from the estuary of the Douve N along E coast of Cotentin Penin. beyond Quinéville. Taken after slight resistance June 6, 1944.

Utah Lake. Lake ab. 30 m. long in Utah co., N cen. Utah; 150 sq. m.; has outlet, Jordan river, flowing N into SE Great Salt Lake.

Utaidhani. See UTHAI THANI.

U'ta·ka·mand' (ōō'tá·ka·mŭnd'). = OOTACAMUND.

U'te·na' (ōō'tĕ·nä'). **1** District of Lithuania. See *Table* at LITHUANIA.

2 Town, its ✳, E Lithuania, on railroad line near Polish border 78 m. NE of Kaunas; pop. (1938 est.) 6241.

Ute Pass (ūt). Mountain pass 7600 ft., Teller co., cen. Colorado, near Pikes Peak; used by Indians before 1800; road.

Ute Peak. 1 Mountain 12,298 ft., Grand and Summit cos., Colorado, S of Middle Park.

2 Mountain 10,151 ft., Taos co., N New Mexico, on Colorado boundary.

U·thai Tha·ni *or* **U·tai·dha·ni** (ōō·t'hī·t'hä·nē); *also* **U·da·ya·dha·ni** (ōō·t'hī·t'hä·nē—*sic*). **1** Province, W cen. Thailand; 2443 sq. m.; pop. 86,131.

2 Town, its ✳, on the Chao Phraya where the Tha Chin distributary leaves it; 25 m. S of Nakhon Sawan.

U'ti·ca (ū'tĭ·ká). **1** Manufacturing city and port of entry, a ⊗ of Oneida co., cen. New York, on Mohawk river 50 m. E of Syracuse; pop. 100,410; near geographic center of state, at gateway to the Adirondacks; in agricultural and dairying region; manufactures textiles, firearms, heating, ventilating, and refrigeration equipment, machinery, beds. Site included in Cosby Manor (granted 1734); Cosby tract bought 1772 by Palatine descendants and settled 1773; became trade and transportation center; incorporated as village 1798; developed industrially following opening of Erie canal 1825; chartered as city 1832.

2 Large ancient coastal city in N Africa, 15 m. NW of ancient Carthage (and modern Tunis) and 10 m. SE of modern Porto Farina. Captured by Agathocles 310 B.C.; place where Cato the Younger committed suicide 46 B.C. after the battle of Thapsus; taken in successive conquests of North Africa and destroyed by Arabs.

U·tiel' (ōō·tyĕl'). Manufacturing commune, Valencia prov., E Spain, 42 m. W by N of Valencia; pop. 12,411; French defeated here 1812.

U·ti'la Island (ōō·tē'lä). Island in Caribbean Sea N of N Honduras, near S entrance to Gulf of Honduras.

Utina. See UDINE commune.

U'trecht (ū'trĕkt; *Du.* ü'trĕĸt). **1** Province, cen. Netherlands; 535 sq. m.; pop. (1939) 479,743; ✳ Utrecht; smallest province of Netherlands, traversed by branches of the Rhine river.

2 City, its ✳, on the Oude Rijn river 20 m. SSE of Amsterdam; pop. (1939) 165,028; chiefly a residential city; cathedral of St. Martin, Archiepiscopal museum, uni-

versity, national mint. Very old city; see established c. 695 by St. Willibrord; one of the powerful commercial cities of the Middle Ages; came under control of Holy Roman emperors 1481–1527; scene of signing 1579 of Union of Utrecht (see NETHERLANDS) and of series of treaties 1713–14 ending War of Spanish Succession.

3 Village, NW Natal, E Union of South Africa; pop. 3448; center of a district settled by Boers after the great trek of 1836 and declared by them a republic (see also LYDENBURG and VRYHEID); originally in Transvaal, ceded to Natal 1903.

U·tre'ra (ōō·trā'rä). Commune, Sevilla prov., SW Spain, 19 m. SSE of Seville; pop. 30,440; stock raising, esp. for the bull ring; 14th-cent. Gothic church, 13th-cent. tower.

U·tsu·no·mi·ya (ōō·tsōō·nō·mē·yä). City, ✳ of Tochigi prefecture, cen. Honshu, Japan, 60 m. N of Tokyo; pop. (1945) 80,790; just S of Nikko and has fine view of Nikko Mts. Bombed by American planes July 1945.

U·tsu·ryo (ōō·tsōō·ryō). Island in SW Sea of Japan ab. 90 m. off E cen. coast of Korea.

Ut·ta·ra·dit *or* **U·ta·ra·dit** (ōōt·tä·rä·dĭt). **1** Province, NW cen. Thailand; 2979 sq. m.; pop. 147,838.

2 Town, its ✳, on right bank of Nan river 55 m. N of Phitsanulok.

Uttar Pradesh. See UNITED PROVINCES.

Ut·tox'e·ter (ŭ·tŏk'sĕ·tẽr; ŭ·tŏk'sĕ·tẽr; ŭk'sĕ·tẽr). Urban district, Staffordshire, W cen. England; pop. 7440.

U·tua'do (ōō·twä'thŏ). Municipality (pop. 40,449) and town (pop. 9870), W cen. Puerto Rico; town 13 m. S of Arecibo.

U'tu·pu'a (ōō'tōō·pōō'ä). Small island in Santa Cruz group 62 m. SE of Ndeni I., SW Pacific Ocean; a circular island ab. 8 m. in diameter, with a large inlet Basilisk Harbour, extending into its center.

Uu'si·kau'pun·ki (ōō'sĭ·kou'pŏong·kĭ); *Swedish* **Ny'-stad'** (nü'stä[d]'). Seaport town, Turku-Pori dept., SW Finland, on the Baltic Sea; pop. 4234; exports lumber and stone; scene of the signing of a treaty of peace (Treaty of Nystad) Aug. 30, 1721 bet. Russia and Sweden by which Russia restored Finland and Sweden ceded certain regions to Russia.

Uu'si·maa' (ōō'sĭ·mä'); *Swedish* **Ny'land'** (nü'län[d]'). Department of Finland. See *Table* at FINLAND.

U'va. 1 (ōō'vä) Province, SE Ceylon; 3277 sq. m.; pop. 303,243; ✳ Badulla; high plain and mountains in the W part.

2 (ōō'vä) See VUA river, Colombia.

U·val'de (ū·väl'dĕ). **1** County in Texas. See *Table* at TEXAS.

2 City, its ⊗, SW Texas, 65 m. ESE of Del Rio; pop. 10,293; in farming and livestock-raising section; ships cattle, wool, mohair, pecans, honey, asphalt; tourist resort. Settled 1853; incorp. 1921.

U·vé'a (ōō·vā'ä) *or* **U·e'a** (ōō·ā'ä). **1** Northernmost island of the chain of the Loyalty Is., E of New Caledonia and NW of Lifu; 23 sq. m.; pop. (1936) 1782; low, narrow island ab. 30 m. long, with large lagoon on W side.

2 Main island of Wallis Is., ab. 8 m. long by 3 m. wide, enclosed by oval coral reef; pop. ab. 4000; chief village Matautu.

U·wa·ji·ma (ōō·wä·jĕ·mä). Town, Ehime prefecture, NW Shikoku I., Japan; pop. (1945) 40,381; on E side of Bungo Strait. Bombed by American planes July–Aug. 1945.

Uweinat, Jebel. See Jebel OWEINAT.

Uxantis. See USHANT.

Ux'bridge (ŭks'brĭj). **1** Industrial town, Worcester co., cen. Massachusetts, 15 m. SSE of Worcester; pop. 7789; textiles.

2 Urban district, Middlesex, SE England, on the Colne 16 m. WNW of London; pop. 55,944; part of Greater London; engineering works.

Uxellodunum. See ISSOUDUN.

Ux·mal' (ōōz·mäl'). Ancient city in Yucatán state, SE

Mexico, S of Mérida; capital of the later Maya empire; Mayan ruins.

Uyeda. See UEDA.

U'yu (o͞o'yo͞o). River ab. 140 m. long in Upper Burma, the most important tributary of the Chindwin river; rises in mountains S of Hukawng valley, flows SW to the Chindwin at ab. 25°N; navigable for small boats.

U·yu'ni (o͞o·yo͞o'nē). Town, Potosí dept., SW Bolivia; on railroad 191 m. S of Oruro; railroad junction and importing and exporting center bet. Antofagasta, Chile, and S Bolivia.

Uyuni, Salar de. See SALAR DE UYUNI.

Uz'bek Soviet Socialist Republic (o͞oz'bĕk; ŭz'-) *or* **Uz'bek·i·stan'** (o͞oz'bĕk·i·stăn'; ŭz'-; -stän'). A constituent republic of the Union of Soviet Socialist Republics, Central Asia; 146,000 sq. m.; pop. 6,282,446, (1941 est.) 6,601,619; ✳ Tashkent. Bounded on N and W by Kazakh S.S.R., on E by Kirgiz and Tadzhik S.S. Republics, on S by Afghanistan and Turkmen S.S.R. In its NW part it includes the Kara-Kalpak A.S.S.R. (*q.v.*). For the most part plain and desert (Kyzyl Kum) regions but in SE bordering Tadzhik S.S.R. has plateau and high ranges. Includes S half of Lake Aral, the lower course and delta of the Amu Darya, and in S cen. part the Zeravshan river. In irrigated districts raises much cotton; other products are grain and rice and stock raising is important. Has rich mineral wealth, largely undeveloped. Between Tashkent and Moscow are direct rail and air services and on the Amu Darya are steamer lines. Predominant ethnic strain Turko-Tatar; chief nationalities Uzbek 76%, Russian ab. 6%. Chief cities Tashkent (largest city in Soviet Russia in Asia), Samarkand, Andizhan, Bukhara, Margelan, and Kokand.

History: Region once settled by Golden Horde, from one of whose chiefs, Uzbeg Khan (d. 1340), the Uzbeks, prevailing Moslem people of Turkish origin, received their name; from 8th to 19th cent. Moslem emirates flourished at Khiva, Bukhara, and Samarkand (*qq.v.*); see also KHWARIZM; in early 19th cent. visited by Russian geographers and scientists; Tashkent occupied by Russian forces 1865, Samarkand and Bukhara 1868, but Khiva not overcome until 1873; as emirates these remained vassal states of Russian Empire until 1917; after the Revolution, Soviet governments set up but conditions unstable until organization 1924 of Uzbek S.S.R.; made a constituent republic 1925.

U'zès' (ü'zĕs'). Manufacturing town, Gard dept., S France, ab. 15 m. N of Nîmes; pop. 3688; cathedral; ducal castle.

Uzh'go·rod (o͞ozh'gô·rŏd; *Russ.* -gŭ·rŭt); *Hung.* **Ung'vár** (o͞ong'vär); *Slovak* **Už'ho·rod** (o͞ozh'hô·rŏt). City, ✳ of Zakarpatskaya Region in SW Ukraine, U.S.S.R., on a headstream of the Tisza; pop. (1930) 26,670; lumber and cattle-trading center. Formerly a Hungarian city; from 1918 to 1939 chief town of Carpathian Ruthenia in Czechoslovakia; taken over by Soviet Russia 1946.

Uzhitse. Var. of UŽICE.

U'zhok; *Czech* **U'žok** (o͞o'zhôk). Mountain pass in E Carpathian Mts. just N of Uzhok village and 36 m. NE of Uzhgorod; leads from Zakarpatskaya Region, SW Ukraine, to the valley of the San river.

U'ži·ce (o͞o'zhĕ·tsĕ). Town, W Serbia, Yugoslavia, ab. 65 m. SE of Sarajevo; pop. 7481; seat of Saint Sava, first bishop (1219–34) of Serbia.

Uz'nam (o͞oz'näm). Polish name of Usedom I. (*q.v.*), at mouth of the Oder river; its E third, on which the Polish port of Świnioujście is located, is since 1945 a part of Szczecin dept., N W Poland.

V

Vaag'ö' (vôg'û'). Island of W part of the Faeroes (*q.v.*); 69 sq. m.; pop. (1925) 1923.

Va'ai·fe'tu, Mount (vä'ï·fä'tōō). Peak 3608 ft., highest on Upolu I., Samoa, SW cen. Pacific Ocean, 9 m. SE of the town of Apia.

Vaal (väl). River ab. 700 m. long in Union of South Africa; rises in SE Transvaal prov.; flows W, forming boundary bet. Transvaal and Orange Free State; empties into Orange river in N Cape Province.

Vaal Krantz or **Vaal'krantz'** (väl'kränts'; fäl'-). Village on the Tugela river, W Natal, Union of South Africa, just SW of Ladysmith; scene of defeat of British by Boers Feb. 5, 1900.

Vaals (väls). Commune, Limburg prov., Netherlands, at the place where boundaries of Netherlands, Belgium, and Germany meet, just W of Aachen; pop. 8080; castle; wool weaving.

Vaa'sa (vä'sà). **1** Department of Finland. See *Table* at FINLAND.
2 *formerly* **Ni'ko·lain·kau'pun·ki** (nï'kô·lïn·kou'-pōong·kï); *Swedish* **Va'sa'** (vä'sà'), *formerly* **Ni·ko·lai'stad** (nï·kōō·lï'stä[d]). Seaport city, its ✱, W Finland, on Gulf of Bothnia, built partly on an island; pop. (1939 est.) 31,100; textiles, glass; iron foundries.

Vác (väts); *Ger.* **Wait'zen** (vït'sĕn). City, N Hungary, on left bank of the Danube ab. 20 m. N of Budapest; pop. 20,434; cathedral and episcopal palace.

Vac'a·ville (väk'à·vïl). City, Solano co., cen. California, 33 m. WSW of Sacramento; pop. 10,898; founded 1850; fruitgrowing.

Vacca. See BÉJA.

Vache Island (vàsh). Island in Caribbean Sea off S coast of W Hispaniola.

Väddö' (vĕd'û'). Island off the SE coast of Sweden, opp. Ahvenanmaa in W entrance to the Gulf of Bothnia.

Vads'ö' (väd'sû'). Seaport, Finnmark co., N Norway, on N shore of Varanger Fjord; pop. 2031; ice-free harbor, used as whaling base; trades in reindeer meat and hides, dried fish, whale oil, guano.

Vad'ste'na (väd'stä'nà). Town, Östergötland prov., SE Sweden, on E shore of Lake Vättern 25 m. W of Linköping; pop. (1933) 2956; site of convent founded by Saint Bridget, founder c. 1344 of the Brigittine order for men and women.

Va·duz' (fä·dōōts'). Commune, ✱ of principality of Liechtenstein, on right bank of Upper Rhine ab. 27 m. S of Bregenz; pop. (1941) 2020. Greatly damaged in 1499 in war bet. the Swiss and the emperor, rebuilt 1523–26; came into possession of Liechtenstein family 1712.

Va·e'a, Mount (vä·ā'à). See VAILIMA.

Vaer'öy' (vâr'û'ü). Island of the Lofoten, in the Norwegian Sea off NW coast of Norway, S of Moskenes.

Va'ga. 1 (và'gà) River ab. 220 m. long, SW Arkhangelsk Region, Soviet Russia, Europe; flows N to the Northern Dvina river.
2 (vä'gà) Var. of *Vacca*: see BÉJA town, N Tunisia.

Va'gar·sha·pat' (vä'gär·shä·bäd'; -shä·pät'). Town, 12 m. W of Yerevan, Armenian S.S.R., Soviet Union; in valley of the Araks. An old town dating from 6th cent. B.C.; capital of old kingdom of Armenia 184 to 344 A.D. See ECHMIADZIN.

Váh (väk); *Hung.* **Vág** (väg); *Ger.* **Waag** (väk). River ab. 210 m. long in W Slovakia prov., Czechoslovakia; rises in the Tatra Mts., flows W and S into the Danube at Komárno.

Vahalis. See WAAL.

Vai'den (vä'd'n). Town, a ⊗ of Carroll co., cen. Mississippi; pop. 475.

Vai'gach (vï'gàch). Island 68 m. long, 1400 sq. m., NE Nenets National District, Soviet Russia, Europe, bet. the mainland and Novaya Zemlya, SE of Kara Strait; visited by Samoyed hunters and fishers.

Vai'gai (vï'gï). River ab. 180 m. long, SE India; rises in the Cardamom Hills, flows NE and ESE in SE Madras state into Palk Strait.

Vai·li'ma (vï·lē'mà). Estate of Robert Louis Stevenson (1889–94) on Upolu I., Territory of Western Samoa, ab. 4 m. S of Apia; his home now the administrator's residence. On top of Mt. Vaea nearby is his tomb with the famous epitaph ("Requiem") written by himself.

Vakh (vàk). River ab. 550 m. long, mostly in SE Khanty-Mansi National District, Soviet Russia, Asia; rises in W Krasnoyarsk Territory and flows W into Ob river.

Vaksh (väksh). River ab. 400 m. long, a N tributary of the Amu Darya, in SW Tadzhik S.S.R., Soviet Central Asia; flows W and SW.

Va·la·am' (và·lŭ·äm'); *Finnish* **Va'la·mo** (và'là·mô). Island group in N Lake Ladoga, in Karelo-Finnish S.S.R.; formerly belonged to Finland; site of Greek Orthodox monastery, founded in 10th cent.

Va'lais (và'lĕ'); *Ger.* **Wal'lis** (väl'ïs). Swiss canton; see *History* and *Table* at SWITZERLAND.

Val'cour Island (väl'kōōr). Island in Lake Champlain, 5 m. SE of Plattsburg, New York; battle 1776 (see PLATTSBURG, N.Y.).

Val'cov (väl'kŭf); *Romanian* **Vâl'cov** (vïl'kôv). Town, Izmail Region, SW Ukraine, U.S.S.R., on N side of the Kiliya mouth of the Danube; pop. (1930) 7405; fishing. Originally a Russian town 1877 to 1918; in Bessarabia, Romania 1918 to 1940.

Val·da'gno (väl·dän'yô). Commune, Vicenza prov., Venezia Euganea, NE Italy, in Alps 15 m. NW of Vicenza; pop. 20,836; manufactures linen; lignite mining.

Val·dai' Hills (vŭl·dï'). Hills and plateau in N Kalinin and S Novgorod Regions, W Soviet Russia, Europe; average height 600 to 1000 ft.; highest point 1053 ft., highest in the interior of Russia in Europe. Source of the Volga, Dvina, and Dnieper, and rivers flowing into Lake Ilmen; many lakes and marshes. In World War II overrun by Germans Oct. 1941 and controlled by them until winter of 1942–43.

Val d'Ajol, Le. See LE VAL D'AJOL.

Val'de·pe'ñas (bäl'dà·pā'nyäs). Commune, Ciudad Real prov., S cen. Spain, 33 m. SE of Ciudad Real; pop. 30,409; red wines, cooperage works.

Val'de·ra·duey' (bäl'dà·rä·thwĕ'ĕ; -thwä'). = ARA-DUEY.

Val'dese (väl'dēz). Manufacturing town, Burke co., W North Carolina, in foothills of Blue Ridge Mts. 12 m. S of Lenoir; pop. 2941; manufactures textiles, shoes, boxes; vineyards.

Val·dez' (väl·dēz'). Town and port at head of inlet on NE shore of Prince William Sound, S Alaska; pop. 555; starting point of Richardson Highway N to Fairbanks; military base in World War II.

Vál'dez Peninsula (bäl'dās). Peninsula extending into Atlantic Ocean from NE coast of Chubut territory, S Argentina, S of the Gulf of San Matías; encloses Gulf of San José on N.

Val di Gardena. See Val di GARDENA.

Val·di'via (bäl·dē'vyä; *Angl.* väl·dïv'ï·à). **1** River ab. 100 m. long in Valdivia prov., S cen. Chile; rises in Andes Mts., flows W into Pacific Ocean.
2 Province of Chile. See *Table* at CHILE.
3 City, ✱ of Valdivia prov., S cen. Chile, on the Valdivia river 16 m. from its mouth; pop. 34,496; in lake region.

Val'dob·bia'de·ne (väl'dôb·byä'dà·nà). Commune, Treviso prov., Venezia Euganea, NE Italy, 22 m. NW of Treviso; pop. 10,425; ferruginous springs.

Val d'Or (väl' dôr'). Town, Abitibi co., SW Quebec, Canada; pop. 8685; incorp. 1935.

Val·dos'ta (väl·dŏs'tà). City, ⊗ of Lowndes co., S Georgia, 57 m. WSW of Waycross; pop. 30,652; railroad

center; cotton mills, machine shops, peanut-processing plants, sawmills. Georgia State Womans Coll. (1906).

Vale (vāl). Town, ⊗ of Malheur co., SE Oregon, on Malheur river 62 m. SSE of Baker; pop. 1491; shipping point for large agricultural and range area; headquarters for the Vale Irrigation Project; hot springs.

Va·len'ça (vȧ·län'sȧ). **1** City, Baía state, E Brazil, on coast 50 m. SW of Salvador; pop. (1940 est.) 9754.

2 City, Rio de Janeiro state, SE Brazil, 40 m. NNW of Rio de Janeiro; pop. (1940 est.) 10,709.

Va'lence' (vȧ'läns'); *anc.* **Ven'ti·a** (věn'shĭ·ȧ; -shȧ), *later* **Va·len'ti·a** (vȧ·lěn'shĭ·ȧ; -shȧ). Manufacturing commune, ✳ of Drôme dept., SE France, on left bank of Rhone river 116 m. NNW of Marseilles; pop. 36,582; 11th-cent. Romanesque cathedral; manufactures textiles, hats, baskets, alimentary pastes, liqueurs; ancient Roman remains; university suppressed 1790.

Va·len'ci·a (vȧ·lěn'shĭ·ȧ; -shȧ). County in New Mexico. See *Table* at NEW MEXICO.

Va·len'ci·a (vȧ·lěn'shĭ·ȧ; -shȧ; *Span.* bä·län'thyä, -syä). **1** Region and ancient kingdom, E Spain; 8886 sq. m.; ✳ Valencia; bounded on N by Aragon and Catalonia, on E by the Mediterranean, on S by Murcia, and on W by Murcia, New Castile, and Aragon; comprises modern provinces of Alicante, Castellón de la Plana, and Valencia; watered by the Segura, Guadalaviar, Júcar, and Mijares rivers; generally mountainous, broken by coastal and inland plains; numerous salt lagoons on coast; wide variety of agricultural produce owing to wide variations in temperature and rainfall; sheep and goat raising; small deposits of lignite, iron, lead, zinc; well developed industrially, having numerous textile mills, iron and copper foundries, distilleries, sugar mills, potteries, fisheries, and fish-preserving establishments.

History: Conquered successively by Romans, Visigoths, and Moors; part of Caliphate of Córdoba until its dissolution in early 11th cent.; became independent Moorish kingdom; held by the Cid 1094–99, but after his death again lost to Moors; reconquered 1238 by James I of Aragon.

2 Province of Spain. See *Table* at SPAIN.

3 *anc.* **Va·len'ti·a** (vȧ·lěn'shĭ·ȧ; -shȧ). Commune, ✳ of Valencia prov., E Spain, on Mediterranean at mouth of Guadalaviar, 188 m. ESE of Madrid; pop. (1941 est.) 459,460; manufactures silk, paper, soap, hats, hardware, pottery, cigars, oil, brick, leather goods, plush, gloves, chocolates, felt, velvet, fans, hempen and linen goods; archiepiscopal palace, 13th-cent. cathedral, 15th-cent. exchange (Lonja de la Seda, *Span.*, silk exchange); university (founded 1441); seaside resort. Conquered by Romans, Visigoths, Moors; capital of kingdom of Valencia; occupied by French under Suchet 1812–13; temporary capital of Spain 1937 during Civil War.

Va·len'ci·a (vȧ·lěn'shĭ·ȧ; -shȧ; *Span.* bä·län'syä). **1** *or* **Ta'ca·ri'gua** (tä'kä·rē'gwä). Lake 216 sq. m. in N Venezuela, SW of Caracas and ab. 20 m. S of coast of Caribbean Sea.

2 Commercial city, ✳ of Carabobo state, N Venezuela, 80 m. W of Caracas and near W end of Lake Valencia; pop. (1941 est.) 54,037; third largest city in Venezuela and its most important manufacturing city; its port is Puerto Cabello ab. 30 m. to N; a social and political as well as trading center; cathedral. Founded 1555.

Va·len'ci·a *or* **Va·len'ti·a** (vȧ·lěn'shĭ·ȧ; -shȧ). **1** Island 7 m. long off SW coast of Ireland, S of entrance to Dingle Bay; administratively in co. Kerry; eastern terminus of the first transatlantic cable (to Newfoundland), laid by "Great Eastern" in 1866.

2 Town, SE Valencia I., the extreme W port of Europe.

Va·len'ci·a, Gulf of (vȧ·lěn'shĭ·ȧ; -shȧ; *Span.* bä·län'thyä, -syä). Widemouthed inlet of Mediterranean Sea on E coast of Spain bet. Cape Tortosa and Cape Nao.

Va·len'ci·a de Al·cán'ta·ra (vȧ·lěn'shĭ·ȧ dě äl·kän'tȧ·rȧ; *Span.* bä·län'thyä [-syä] thä äl·kän'tä·rä). Commune, Cáceres prov., W Spain, near Portuguese

border 47 m. W of Cáceres; pop. 15,415; cork; antimony and calcium phosphate mines.

Va'len'ciennes' (vȧ'län'syěn'; *Angl.* vȧ·lěn'sĭ·ěnz'). Industrial city, Nord dept., N France, on the Schelde 29 m. SE of Lille; pop. 42,564; in coal-producing region; manufactures iron, salt, potash, glass, soap, woolens, linen, gloves; once famous for manufacture of Valenciennes lace; 17th-cent. town hall, museum, arsenal and barracks, municipal library, hospital, lyceum.

History: Held by Charlemagne 711; part of Holy Roman Empire; became capital of Hainaut; conquered by Louis XIV 1677; ceded to France 1678; taken by Austrians 1793, retaken 1794; besieged 1814; in World War I captured and occupied by Germans 1914–18; almost completely demolished 1918.

Valentia. **1** See VALENCE commune, France.

2 See VALENCIA, Ireland.

3 See VALENCIA commune, Spain.

Val'en·tine (văl'ěn·tīn). City, ⊗ of Cherry co., N Nebraska, on Niobrara river 10 m. S of South Dakota border; pop. 2875; trade center in livestock-raising section.

Va·len'za (vä·lěn'tsä). Manufacturing commune, Alessandria prov., Piedmont, NW Italy, on Po river 9 m. N of Alessandria; pop. 11,743.

Va·len·zue'la (bä'län·swä'lä). Town, S Cordillera dept., cen. Paraguay; pop. ab. 7300.

Va·le'ra (bä·lā'rä). Town, Trujillo state, W cen. Venezuela, 25 m. from Trujillo; pop. (1941 est.) 10,553; trading center.

Va·le'ri·an Way (vȧ·lēr'ĭ·ăn); *Lat.* **Vi'a Va·le'ri·a** (vī'ȧ vȧ·lēr'ĭ·ȧ). Ancient Roman road from Tibur (Tivoli) along the N bank of the Anio (Aniene) E and NE through the Apennines to Aternum (Pescara) on the Adriatic, then N along the coast.

Va'lé'rien', Mont (môn vȧ'lā'ryăn'). Hill 532 ft., W of Paris, France, near Suresnes; site of a fort, built 1841–43, important defense in siege of Paris during Franco-Prussian War 1870–71.

Valetta. Var. of VALLETTA.

Val'ga (väl'gä). **1** Province of Estonia. See *Table* at ESTONIA.

2 Town, its ✳, S Estonia, on main Riga-Leningrad R.R. at Latvian boundary; pop. (1937) 10,309. See VALK.

Valgrund. See VALLGRUND.

Val'guar·ne'ra Ca'ro·pe'pe (väl'gwär·nâ'rä kä'rô·pā'pä). Commune, Enna prov., cen. Sicily, 9 m. SE of Enna; pop. 13,696.

Va·lien'tes, Cape (bä·lyän'tâs). Cape on NW coast of Panama, enclosing Chiriquí Lagoon.

Va·li'ra *or* **Gran Va·li'ra** (grän' bä·lē'rä). River in Andorra, among the Pyrenees, SW Europe; flows into the Segre river at Seo de Urgel in Spain.

Va'lje·vo (vä'lyě·vô). Town, NW Serbia, Yugoslavia, ab. 45 m. SW of Belgrade; pop. 11,055; trade in cattle; first open opposition to the Turks here 1804.

Valk (vȧlk). Former Russian town which became object of a boundary dispute bet. Estonia and Latvia 1919, after World War I; dispute settled by dividing the town, one section becoming Valga in S Estonia, and the other section, Valka in N Latvia.

Val'ka (väl'kä). **1** Administrative district, N Vidzeme prov., N Latvia; 1846 sq. m.

2 Town in Valka dist., on main Riga-Leningrad R.R. at Estonian boundary; pop. (1930) 3341. See VALK.

Val'la·do·lid' (văl'ȧ·dô·lĭd'; -lē[th]'; *Span.* bä'yä·thô-lē[th]', *Castilian* bä'lyä-). **1** Town, E Yucatán state, on Yucatán penin., SE Mexico; pop. 6402; railroad terminus E of the ruins of Chichén Itzá.

2 Municipality, W Negros Occidental, Negros, Phil. Is., on Guimaras Strait 16 m. SSW of Bacolod; pop. 14,636.

3 Province of Spain. See *Table* at SPAIN.

4 Commune, ✳ of Valladolid prov., NW cen. Spain, on Pisuerga river 98 m. NNW of Madrid; pop. (1941 est.) 116,084; manufactures leather, textiles, gold and silver wares, pottery, chemicals, paper, chocolates, bronze and

iron work, flour; 16th-cent. cathedral, 12th-cent. church of Santa María la Antigua, 17th-cent. royal palace, home where Columbus died; university (founded in 13th cent.); site of several autos-da-fé. Recovered from Moors 10th cent.; capital of Castile 1454–1598.

Val·lau·ris' (vȧ·lō'rēs'). Commune, Alpes-Maritimes dept., SE France, 13 m. SW of Nice; pop. 4337; winter resort; manufactures faïence, perfumes; site of Picasso's Museum of Peace.

Val'le (bä'yȧ). **1** or **Valle del Cau'ca** (ŧħĕl kou'kä). Department of Colombia. See *Table* at COLOMBIA.
2 Department, S Honduras; 815 sq. m.; pop. (1945 est.) 58,355; ✻ Nacaome.

Valle, El. See EL VALLE.

Val·le'cas (bä·[l]yä'käs). Commune, Madrid prov., cen. Spain, SE suburb of Madrid; pop. 60,614.

Val·le·ci'to Dam (vī·sē'tŭ). Dam completed 1941 across Pine (or Los Pinos) river, tributary of San Juan river, E La Plata co., SW Colorado; height 143 ft.; impounds water for irrigation, forming **Vallecito Reservoir**.

Val'le de San·tia'go (bä'yȧ ŧħä sän·tyä'gô). Town, Guanajuato state, cen. Mexico, 40 m. S of Guanajuato; pop. 12,278.

Valle di Pompei. See POMPEI.

Val'le·her·mo'so (bä'yȧ·ĕr·mō'sô). Municipality, NE Negros Oriental prov., Negros, Phil. Is., on Tañon Strait 34 m. SE of City of Bacolod; pop. 21,677.

Val·le'jo (vȧ·lā'ō). Commercial city, Solano co., cen. California, on San Pablo Bay 20 m. N of Oakland; pop. 60,877; port; trade and shipping center for agricultural region; flour milling, leather tanning, fish packing; opp. Mare Island Navy Yard. Settled c. 1850; state capital 1851–53; chartered 1866.

Val'le·nar' (bä'yȧ·när'). Town, Atacama prov., N cen. Chile, ab. 80 m. SSW of Copiapó; pop. 8472.

Val'les (bä'yäs). **1** River in E cen. Mexico, a tributary of the Pánuco river.
2 officially **Ciu·dad' de Val'les** (syōō·ŧħä' ŧħä vä'yäs). Town, San Luis Potosí state, cen. Mexico, on railroad from Tampico to San Luis Potosí; pop. 7240.

Val·let'ta (vȧ·lĕt'ȧ). Seaport city on the NE coast of the island of Malta; ✻ of Malta since 1570; pop. (1931) 22,779; pop. including the suburb Floriana, ab. 30,000; built on rocky promontory with harbors on either side; has governor's palace, library and museum, cathedral, and government buildings; relics of the long residence of the Knights of Malta (Hospitalers); port for much local and transit trade; important British naval base; in World War II frequently bombed 1941–43.

Val'ley (văl'ĭ). Name of counties in three states of the U.S. See *Tables* at IDAHO, MONTANA, NEBRASKA.

Valley City. City, ⊗ of Barnes co., E North Dakota, 60 m. W of Fargo; pop. 7809; first settled 1872; commercial center for grain, stock, and dairy-farming area; manufactures flour, processed dairy products. State Teachers Coll. (1889; coed.).

Valley Falls. Industrial village, Providence co., N Rhode Island, 2 m. N of Central Falls; pop. (est.) 4000; governmental center for Cumberland.

Val'ley·field (văl'ĭ·fēld), formerly **Sal'a·ber'ry de Valleyfield** (săl'ȧ·bĕr'ĭ dĕ). City, Beauharnois co., S Quebec, Canada, on S shore of Lake St. Francis 35 m. SW of Montreal; pop. 22,414; industrial center at head of Beauharnois canal; has cathedral, college, and schools. Founded c. 1840.

Valley Forge (fôrj; fōrj). Locality, Chester co., SE Pennsylvania, on Schuylkill river ab. 4 m. SE of Phoenixville; winter headquarters of Washington and his army 1777–78; state park.

Valley Junction. See WEST DES MOINES.

Valley of Ten Thousand Smokes. Volcanic region, SW Alaska, in Katmai National Monument W of Mt. Katmai; formed at the eruption of Katmai in June 1912 when the valley—17 m. long by 4 m. wide—was covered

by a flow of incandescent sand; later (1915), when discovered by an expedition of the National Geographic Society, its floor was found to have not 10,000, but actually millions of steam jets, large and small (largest 150 ft. in diameter) some of which had a temperature as high as 1200°F.

Valley Park. City, St. Louis co., E Missouri, 16 m. W of St. Louis; pop. 3452.

Valley Station. Urban area, Jefferson co., N cen. Kentucky, S of Louisville; pop. 10,553.

Valley Stream. Residential village, Nassau co., SE New York, on Long I. 16 m. ESE of New York; pop. 38,629; incorporated 1925; Curtis airport.

Valley View. Locality, Schuylkill co., E cen. Pennsylvania, ab. 17 m. W of Pottsville; pop. 1540.

Vall'grund or **Val'grund** (väl'gründ). Island in Gulf of Bothnia, Vaasa dept., Finland, opp. city of Vaasa.

Val'lo del'la Lu·ca'nia (väl'lô däl'lä lōō·kä'nyä). Commune, Salerno prov., Campania, S Italy, 43 m. SE of Salerno; pop. 10,722; cathedral.

Val'lom·bro'sa (väl'ŏm·brō'sä; -zȧ; *Ital.* väl'lôm·brō'sä). Literally "Shady valley"; resort in Firenze prov., Tuscany, cen. Italy, 16 m. ESE of Florence; celebrated abbey (founded in 11th cent.), now used as a forestry school.

Vallona. Var. of *Valona*: see VLONA.

Valls (väls). Commune, Tarragona prov., NE Spain, 11 m. N of Tarragona; pop. 10,866.

Val'me·ra (väl'mĕ·rä). **1** Administrative district, N cen. Vidzeme prov., N Latvia; 1785 sq. m.
2 *Ger.* **Wol'mar** (vôl'mär). Town in Valmera dist., 65 m. NE of Riga; pop. (1935) 8482.

Val'mon·to'ne (väl'mŏn·tō'nä). Town, Roma prov., W Latium, cen. Italy, at head of Liri valley NE of Velletri and 23 m. SE of Rome; pop. 7514; severe fighting May and June 1944, taken by Americans June 2.

Val'my (văl'mĭ; -mē; *Fr.* väl'mē'). Village, Marne dept., NE France; pop. 294; scene of victory of French revolutionary army under Dumouriez and Kellermann over combined Austrian-Prussian force under the duke of Brunswick Sept. 20, 1792.

Va'lognes' (vȧ·lôn'y'). Commercial town, Manche dept., NW France, SSE of Cherbourg; pop. 4051; church of 15th–17th cents.; a few Roman remains in vicinity.

Va'lois' (vȧ·lwä'; *Angl.* văl'wä). Medieval county and duchy in NE Île-de-France, N France, now included in modern departments of Aisne and Oise; ✻ Crépy-en-Valois. County (10th to 12th cent.) united to crown by King Philip Augustus 1214, but soon detached; granted 1285 by Philip III to his son Charles (Charles de Valois), whose son Philip VI became first ruler of the House of Valois 1328; its last representative, Henry III, was succeeded 1589 by the House of Bourbon.

Valona. See VLONA.

Valona, Bay of. See Bay of VLONA.

Val'pa·rai'so. 1 (văl'pȧ·rī'zō) City, Okaloosa co., NW Florida, on Choctawhatchee Bay; pop. 5975; Eglin Air Force Base, with air proving ground.
2 (văl'pȧ·rā'zō) Residential city, ⊗ of Porter co., NW Indiana, 12 m. S of Lake Michigan; pop. 15,227; manufactures magnets. Valparaiso U. (1859; coed.; Lutheran).

Val'pa·ra·i'so (bäl'pä·rä·ē'sô); *Eng.* **Val'pa·rai'so** (văl'pȧ·rā'zō; -rī'-). **1** Province of Chile. See *Table* at CHILE.
2 Seaport in cen. Chile, ✻ of Valparaíso prov., 75 m. WNW of Santiago on the **Bay of Valparaíso**; pop. 209,945; most important commercial town on W coast of South America; connected by rail with Buenos Aires; naval academy. Its suburban resort is Viña del Mar (q.v.). Founded 1536; not important in early history of Chile; has suffered much from earthquakes; modern growth began after quakes of 1906–07; bombarded by Spanish fleet Mar. 31, 1866; treaty signed here Apr. 4, 1884 giving Chile possession of coast region, won from Bolivia, which contained rich nitrate deposits.

Vals, *in full* **Vals–les–Bains** (våls′lä·băɴ′). Town, cen. Ardèche dept., SE France; pop. 2867; mineral springs.

Valsch, Kaap (kåp′ väls′); *Eng.* **False Cape.** Cape on SW tip of Frederik Hendrik I., off S coast of Neth. New Guinea.

Val Su·ga′na (väl′ sōō·gä′nä). = SUGANA valley.

Valua. See SADDLE island.

Val·ver′de (bäl·vĕr′thä). Chief town, Hierro I., Canary Is., Spain; pop. 5520.

Val Ver′de (väl vûr′dĕ). County in Texas. See *Table* at TEXAS.

Valyevo. = VALJEVO.

Vam′sa·dha′ra (vŭm′shåd·hä′rä). River 170 m. long, SW Orissa and NE Andhra Pradesh; rises in Eastern Ghats and flows S to Bay of Bengal.

Van (văn; *Angl.* văn). **1** *anc.* **Thos·pi′tis** (thŏs·pī′tĭs); *Turk.* **Van Gö·lü′** (vän gû·lü′). Large salt lake (*gölü*), E Turkey in Asia; ab. 1425 sq. m.; at altitude of 5260 ft.; has no apparent outlet.
2 Ancient kingdom, known as Urartu (*q.v.*) to the Assyrians. See ARMENIA ancient country.
3 Vilayet, E Turkey in Asia; 13,583 sq. m.; pop. 96,479; * Van. Includes E part of Lake Van.
4 Town, its *, on S shore of Lake Van; pop. 9402. An ancient town with citadel, formerly commercially important; dates back to Vannic kingdom of Urartu (see ARMENIA ancient country) of which it was made capital c. 832 B.C. when it was fortified; became subject successively to many peoples down to its absorption into Ottoman Empire 1543; seized by Russians Apr. 5, 1918 but later restored.

Van Al′styne (văn ăl′stīn). Town, Grayson co., NE Texas, 16 m. S of Sherman; pop. 1608.

Van Bu′ren (văn bûr′ĕn). **1** Name of counties in four states of the U.S. See *Tables* at ARKANSAS, IOWA, MICHIGAN, TENNESSEE.
2 City, ⊗ of Crawford co., NW Arkansas, on Arkansas river 6 m. NE of Fort Smith; pop. 6787; founded 1836; shipping point for agricultural area producing fruits (esp. strawberries), vegetables, and cotton; zinc smelting; deposits of coal, building stone, and natural gas in vicinity.
3 Town, Aroostook co., N Maine, on St. John river 34 m. N of Presque Isle; pop. 4679; port of entry; lumbering and potato growing.
4 Town, ⊗ of Carter co., SE Missouri; pop. 575.

Vance (văns). County in North Carolina. See *Table* at NORTH CAROLINA.

Vance′bor′o (văns′bûr′ô). Town (unincorporated), Washington co., Maine, on St. Croix river NE of Bangor; pop. (est.) 450; highway and railroad entrance to New Brunswick, Canada.

Vance′burg (văns′bûrg). City, ⊗ of Lewis co., NE Kentucky; pop. 1881.

Van·cou′ver (văn·kōō′vẽr). **1** City, ⊗ of Clark co., SW Washington, on Columbia river ab. 8 m. N of Portland, Oregon; pop. 32,464; shipping center; lumber and paper mills, canneries, packing plants, aluminum and wool manufactures, breweries, grain elevators; farming (esp. fruits); timber. Founded 1825 by Hudson's Bay Co. as trading post of Fort Vancouver; served as terminus of Oregon Trail; became U.S. territory 1846; recognized as military post 1848 (renamed Vancouver Barracks 1879); platted as Vancouver City 1848; became ⊗ 1854, town 1857, city 1889, port of entry 1912.
2 City, S British Columbia, Canada, on S side of Burrard Inlet at its mouth; pop. 344,833; third city in size in Canada and chief Canadian seaport for the Pacific; has fine natural harbor and is western terminus for transcontinental railroads; manufactures pulp and paper, machinery, textiles, sugar, and food products; has shipbuilding yards, grain elevators, cold-storage plants, and salmon canneries; center of immense lumber trade. Point Grey, a suburb, is site of Univ. of British Columbia (1912; coed.). Founded 1881.

Vancouver, Mount. Peak 15,700 ft. in St. Elias Range,

SW Yukon Territory, Canada, near Alaska boundary SE of Mt. Logan.

Vancouver Island. Island 285 m. long, 40 to 80 m. wide, off SW British Columbia, Canada; largest island off W coast of Canada; 13,024 sq. m.; pop. 210,876, with adjacent islands 215,003; chief city Victoria. On the S separated from Washington, U.S.A., by Juan de Fuca Strait and on E from Canadian mainland by Strait of Georgia, Johnstone Strait, and Queen Charlotte Sound. Has several fine harbors—Esquimalt in the S, Ladysmith and Nanaimo on the Strait of Georgia, Nootka Sound and Barkley Sound with Alberni Canal on the Pacific coast. Mountainous, averaging 2000 to 3000 ft.; highest Mt. Victoria 7484 ft. Contains Strathcona Park (provincial). Has extensive forests, coal and iron deposits, and profitable fisheries. Visited by early Spanish and English explorers and at Nootka Sound by Capt. Cook 1778; made a British crown colony 1849 and united with British Columbia 1866.

Van·da′lia (văn·dāl′yå). **1** City, ⊗ of Fayette co., S cen. Illinois, 30 m. N of Centralia; pop. 5537; capital of Illinois 1820–39. Illinois State Penal Farm.
2 City, Audrain co., NE cen. Missouri, 29 m. SSW of Hannibal; pop. 3055; near ceramic-clay deposits.
3 City, Montgomery co., SW Ohio, N of Dayton; pop. 6342.

Van′der·burgh (văn′dẽr·bûrg). County in Indiana. See *Table* at INDIANA.

Van′der·grift (văn′dẽr·grĭft). Industrial borough, Westmoreland co., SW Pennsylvania, on Kiskiminetas river 25 m. ENE of Pittsburgh; pop. 8742; platted as "workingman's paradise" 1896.

Van Die′men, Cape (văn dē′mĕn). Northwest point of Melville I., Northern Territory, Australia.

Van Diemen Gulf. Inlet of Arafura Sea, N Northern Territory, Australia, shut in by Melville I. and Cobourg Penin.; connected on the N by Dundas Strait with Arafura Sea and on the W by Clarence Strait with Timor Sea.

Van Die′men's Land (văn dē′mĕnz). Early name of Tasmania (*q.v.*).

Van Diemen Strait. See OSUMI ISLANDS.

Vä′nern (vâ′nẽrn) *or* **Ve′ner** (vâ′nẽr). Large lake in SW Sweden; 2141 sq. m.; W section is called **Dal′bo** (däl′bōō).

Vä′ners·borg′ (vâ′nẽrs·bôr′y′). Town, * of Älvsborg prov., SW Sweden, at S end of Lake Vänern; pop. 13,948.

Van Gölü. See VAN lake.

Vang′u·nu (väng′ōō·nōō). One of the New Georgia Is., off SE end of New Georgia, cen. Solomon Is., W Pacific Ocean. Mountainous, its highest point 3686 ft.; its N coast encloses Marovo lagoon (see NEW GEORGIA).

Van Horn (văn hôrn′). Village, ⊗ of Culberson co., W Texas; pop. 1953.

Van Horn Mountains. Range 5786 ft. in SW Culberson co., W Texas.

Va′ni·ko′ro (vä′nē·kō′rō) *or* **La Pé·rouse′ Island** (lä′ pē·rōōz′; *Fr.* lå pā′rōōz′). Island, S Santa Cruz Is., SW Pacific Ocean, 20 m. SE of Utupua I.; lat. 11°36′S and long. 166°53′E; scene of the wreck of La Pérouse's fleet 1788.

Va′ni·mo (vä′nĭ·mō; văn′ĭ-). Settlement on NW coast of North-East New Guinea, ab. 20 m. E of Neth. New Guinea boundary.

Va′ni·yam·ba′di (vä′nĭ·yȧm·bä′dĭ). Town, N Madras state, S Indian Union, on two islands in Palar river 118 m. WSW of Madras; pop. 22,940.

Van Lear (văn lẽr′). City, Johnson co., E Kentucky, 23 m. NNW of Pikeville; pop. 921.

Vannes (văn); *anc.* **Dar′i·or′i·gum** (dår′ĭ·ôr′ĭ·gŭm). Manufacturing and commercial seaport, * of Morbihan dept., NW France, 67 m. WNW of Nantes; pop. 24,068; railroad junction; cathedral; town hall, college; museum of Celtic and Roman antiquities; manufactures cotton

goods, rope, lace, leather, iron goods; shipyards; trades in agricultural products. Ancient capital of the Veneti, for whom it was named.

Vann'öy' (vän'ü'ü). Island in Arctic Ocean off NW coast of Norway; pop. 1016.

Van'port (văn'pōrt). Former community, NW Oregon, N part of Portland near confluence of Willamette and Columbia rivers, opp. Vancouver, Washington; built during World War II by Kaiser Shipbuilding Co. to house workers in nearby shipyards; wartime pop. ab. 40,000. Practically destroyed by Columbia river flood waters May 1948.

Van Rhyns'dorp (văn rānz'dôrp). Town, W Cape Province, Union of South Africa, ab. 145 m. NNE of Cape Town; pop. 1566; center of grazing district, on an auto highway.

Va·nu'a La'va (vȧ·nōō'ȧ lä'vȧ). Largest of the Banks Is., N New Hebrides, SW Pacific Ocean, ab. 15 m. long and 12 m. wide. Of volcanic origin, highest point 3120 ft.; has excellent harbor, Port Patteson, on SE coast.

Vanua Le'vu (lě'vōō). Island, second in size of the Fiji Is., in SW Pacific Ocean, 38 m. NE of Viti Levu; 2128 sq. m. Covered with mountains, highest Mt. Thurston 3134 ft. Its coast line irregular, esp. on E end where Natewa Bay makes deep indentation bet. mainland and Natewa Penin. (40 m. long). Chief river is the Dreketi. Has many small coastal villages most of them active in sugar industry; long reef and islets along its N shore.

Vanua Mba·la'vu ('m·bä·lä'vōō). One of the Fiji Is., SW Pacific Ocean, largest of the Exploring Is. group, 14 m. long and from ½ to 2½ m. wide; chief town Lomaloma.

Vanves (väNv). Commune, Seine dept., N France, SW suburb of Paris; pop. 20,157; bronze and aluminum foundries; manufactures metal goods, chemical products; stone quarries.

Van Wert (văn wûrt'). **1** County in Ohio. See *Table* at OHIO.
2 City, its ⊗, NW Ohio, 26 m. WNW of Lima; pop. 11,323; settled 1835; manufactures fiber drums, uniforms, oil seals for motors, cheese.

Van Zandt (văn zănt'). County in Texas. See *Table* at TEXAS.

Vaph'i·o (văf'ĭ·ō; *Gr.* vä·fyô'). Site of a beehive tomb, on Eurotas river 5 m. S of Sparta, Laconia dept., SE Peloponnesus, S Greece; tomb was excavated 1889 by Tsountas; among other important discoveries were two finely ornamented gold cups (the Vaphio cups), dating from c. 1500 B.C. (Late Minoan).

Vapincum. See GAP.

Var (vȧr). **1** *Ital.* **Va'ro** (vä'rô); *anc.* **Va'rus** (vâr'ŭs). River 70 m. long in extreme SE France; rises in the Alps, in Alpes-Maritimes dept., flows SE and S into Mediterranean Sea 4 m. SW of Nice.
2 Department of France. See *Table* at FRANCE.

Va·ra·de'ro (bä'rä·thā'rô). Seaside resort, barrio (pop. 861) on peninsula in N part of Cárdenas municipality, Matanzas prov., W cen. Cuba.

Varanasi. See BENARES.

Va·rang'er Fjord (vä·räng'ẽr). Inlet of the Arctic Ocean on the extreme NE coast of Norway, NW of Pechenga (Petsamo), U.S.S.R.; ab. 42 m. long.

Va·ra'no, Lake (vä·rä'nô). Lagoon of the Adriatic Sea on N side of Mount Gargano, SE Italy.

Va·raž'din (vä·räzh'dēn); *Hung.* **Va'rasd** (vŏ'rŏsht); *Ger.* **Wa'ras·din** (vä'räs·dēn). Town, N Croatia, N Yugoslavia, on Drava river ab. 38 m. NE of Zagreb; pop. 14,609; industrial and commercial center; radioactive springs nearby; occupied by Italians in World War II.

Va·raz'ze (vä·rät'tsȧ). Commune, Savona prov., Liguria, NW Italy, on Gulf of Genoa 7 m. NE of Savona; pop. 11,769; seaside resort.

Var'berg (vär'bȧr·y'). Town, Halland prov., SW Sweden, on the Kattegat ab. 45 m. S of Göteborg; pop. 11,270; port; museum; fishing.

Var'dar (vär'där; *Angl.* -dẽr); *anc.* **Ax'i·us** (ăk'sĭ·ŭs); *in Greece called* **Var·da'res** (vär·dä'rĕs). River ab. 200 m. long, SE Yugoslavia and N Greece; rises in mountains on Albanian border, flows S into the Gulf of Salonika. Chief tributary the Crna in Yugoslavia. In World War II its valley used by German forces in conquest of Yugoslavia Apr. 1941 and invasion of Greece.

Var'dar·ska (vär'där·skä). Former county, SE Yugoslavia; 15,007 sq. m.; pop. 1,656,348; ⊗ Skoplje; now mostly included in the federated republic of Macedonia, but N part in Serbia federated republic.

Var'de (vär'dĕ). River ab. 45 m. long in cen. Jutland, Denmark; flows SW into North Sea NW of Esbjerg.

Vard'ö' (vär'dü'). Port on island off NE tip of Norway N of entrance to Varanger Fjord; pop. 3587.

Va'rennes' (vȧ'rĕn'), *officially* **Va'rennes'–en–Ar'gonne'** (-äN-när'gôn'). Commune, Meuse dept., NE France; pop. 738; place where Louis XVI was arrested June 21, 1791 in his flight from Paris; during World War I held by Germans until captured by Americans Sept. 26, 1918.

Va·re'se (vä·rā'sā). **1** Province of Italy. See *Table* at ITALY.
2 Commune, ⁕ of Varese prov., Lombardy, N Italy, near Lake Varese 30 m. NW of Milan; pop. 44,832; summer resort; 12th-cent. baptistery, 16th-cent. basilica, 18th-cent. town hall; center of silk-spinning industry.

Var·gi'nha (vẽr·zhē'nyȧ). City, Minas Gerais state, E Brazil, 170 m. NW of Rio de Janeiro; pop. (1940 est.) 11,123.

Värm'land (värm'länd). Province of Sweden. See *Table* at SWEDEN.

Var'na (vär'nä; *Angl.* -nȧ); *anc.* **O·des'sus** (ō·dĕs'ŭs); *also,* 1949–57, *officially called* **Sta'lin** (stä'lĭn). Fortified seaport, Shumen dept., NE Bulgaria, on Black Sea; pop. (1934) 69,944; ships esp. grain, cattle, and dairy products; seaside resort; scene of battle Nov. 10, 1444 in which Murad II defeated Hungarian forces under János Hunyadi and in which Ladislas, King of Poland and Hungary, was killed; ceded to Bulgaria 1878.

Varns'dorf (värns'dôrf); *Ger.* **Warns'dorf** (värns'dôrf). City, N Bohemia, Czechoslovakia, 58 m. N of Prague near Saxony border; pop. (1930) 22,793; textilemanufacturing center.

Varo. See VAR.

Va·ro'sha (vȧ·rō'shȧ). See FAMAGUSTA.

Var·sha'va (vŭr·shä'vȧ). Russian form of *Warszawa:* see WARSAW.

Varus. See VAR.

Vary Karlovy. = KARLOVY VARY.

Vasa. See VAASA.

Vasconia. See GASCONY.

Vash'on Island (văsh'ŏn). Island 14 m. long in Puget Sound midway bet. Seattle and Tacoma, Washington; belongs to King co.

Va'sil·kov' (văs'ĭl·kôf'; *Russ.* vȧ·syĭl·kôf'). Town, Kiev Region, NW Ukraine, U.S.S.R., 19 m. S of Kiev; pop. 20,743. Dates back to 10th cent.; destroyed by Mongols 1239–42; restored, but later taken by Lithuanians and Poles; became Russian 1686.

Vas·lui' (väs·lōō'ē). City, Moldavia region, E Romania, 35 m. S of Iaşi; pop. 15,388.

Vas'quez Peak (văs'kĕz). Mountain 12,800 ft. high, Clear Creek and Grand cos., N Colorado.

Vas'sal·bor'ough (văs'ʾl·bûr'ō). Town, Kennebec co., SW Maine, on Kennebec river 6 m. S of Waterville; pop. 2446.

Vas'sar (văs'ẽr). City, Tuscola co., E Michigan, 19 m. ESE of Saginaw; pop. 2680.

Vas·sou'ras (vȧ·sō'rȧs). City, Rio de Janeiro state, SE Brazil, 45 m. NW of Rio de Janeiro; pop. 5025.

Väs'ter·ås' (vĕs'tẽr·ōs'). City, ⁕ of Västmanland prov., E Sweden, at mouth of Svart river on Lake Mälaren; pop. 44,306; manufactures electrical equipment and supplies; cathedral and castle dating from 12th cent.

Väs′ter·bot′ten (věs′tẽr·bôt′ĕn). Province of Sweden. See *Table* at SWEDEN.

Väster Dal. See DAL.

Väs′ter·norr′land (věs′tẽr·nôr′lånd). Province of Sweden. See *Table* at SWEDEN.

Väs′ter·vik′ (věs′tẽr·věk′). Seaport, Kalmar prov., SE Sweden, on the Baltic 73 m. N of Kalmar; pop. 13,263; manufactures machinery, matches; stone quarries.

Väst′man·land (věst′mån·lånd′). Province of Sweden. See *Table* at SWEDEN.

Va′sto (väs′tŏ); *anc.* **His·to′ni·um** (hĭs·tō′nĭ·ŭm). Commune, Chieti prov., Abruzzi e Molise, cen. Italy, on Adriatic 32 m. ESE of Chieti; pop. 18,401; 13th-cent. castle; 11th-cent. church; cathedral.

Vas′vár (vŏsh′vär); *Ger.* **Ei′sen·burg** (ī′zĕn·bŏŏrK). Commune, W Hungary, SE of Szombathely; pop. ab. 4000; treaty signed here Aug. 10, 1664 after battle of Saint Gotthard (see SZENTGOTTHÁRD) concluding by 20-year truce war bet. Emperor Leopold I and the Turks.

Vaté. See EFATE.

Va′ter·nish Point (wô′tẽr·nĭsh; wŏt′ẽr–). Cape on NW coast of the island of Skye in the Inner Hebrides, off NW coast of Scotland; bet. Loch Dunvegan and Loch Snizort.

Va′ter·say (vä′tẽr·sā). See BARRA.

Va·thy′ (vä·thē′). 1 *or* **Li·men′ Va·the′os** (lyě·měn′ vä·thä′ŏs). Seaport city, ✳ of Samos dept., Aegean Is., Greece, on NE coast of Samos I.; pop. 8636.
2 Chief town on Ithaca I., Ionian Is., Greece. See ITHACA island.

Vat′i·can City (văt′ĭ·kăn); *Ital.* **Cit·tà′ del Va′ti·ca′no** (chět·tä′ däl vä′tē·kä′nŏ). Independent papal state, within commune of Rome, Italy, on right bank of Tiber river, covering an area of 108.7 acres; pop. 1025; created Feb. 11, 1929 by the Lateran Pact as a settlement of the Roman question; extraterritoriality of the state extends to Castel Gandolfo and to 13 churches and palaces in Rome proper; under jurisdiction of the state are the Basilica of St. John Lateran (the cathedral church of Rome and highest ranking of all Roman Catholic churches), the Basilica of St. Peter (founded by Constantine on site of Circus of Caligula where St. Peter is said by tradition to have suffered martyrdom), the Vatican (collection of papal palaces, containing the Sistine Chapel, the Loggie, and the Stanze), papal gardens, Villa Pia, churches of Santa Maria Maggiore, San Paolo fuori le mura, San Lorenzo, and San Sebastiano, Pontifical Gregorian University (opened 1930), etc.; railroad station, radio station; independent postal and monetary systems; industries, esp. publishing. Holy See, or Apostolic See, designates Rome as the official seat of the Pope. For *History* of temporal domain of the Popes 755–1870, see STATES OF THE CHURCH.

Va′ti·ca′no, Cape (vä′tē·kä′nŏ). Cape on SW coast of Calabria, the "toe" of Italy, extending into Tyrrhenian Sea S of Gulf of Sant' Eufemia.

Va′ti·lau′ (vä′tē·lä′ŏŏ) *or* **Bue′na Vis′ta** (bwā′nä vēs′tä). Small island in SE Solomon Is., in W Pacific Ocean, off NW coast of Florida I. beyond Olevuga I.

Va′ti·u′ (vä′tē·ŏŏ′). Var. of ATIU.

Vat′na·jö′kull (vät′nä·yû′küt·l′), *or* **Klo′fa·jö′kull** (klŏ′vä–). Snow field in SE Iceland; 3300 sq. m.; average elevation 2000 to 3000 ft.

Va·to′a Island (vä·tō′ä). Small island, Fiji Is., SW Pacific Ocean, S end of Lau group in 20°S.

Vät′tern (vět′ẽrn) *or* **Vet′ter** (vět′ẽr). Lake in S Sweden, E of Lake Vänern; 733 sq. m.; connected with the Baltic by the Göta Canal. Jönköping is at its S end.

Vau′clin′ (vō′klăn′). Seaport commune, SE Martinique, French West Indies; pop. ab. 9000.

Vau′cluse (vŏ′klōōz; vō·klōōz′). Town, E New South Wales, SE Australia, NE suburb of Sydney on S side of entrance to Port Jackson; pop. 7205.

Vau′cluse′ (vō′klüz′). Department of France. See *Table* at FRANCE.

Vaud (vō); *Ger.* **Waadt** (vät). Swiss canton; includes part of Lake of Geneva and Lake of Neuchâtel; watered by Rhone river. Conquered by Romans 58 B.C ; taken by Franks; passed to Bern 1536 and forced to accept Reformation; former canton of Leman (1798–1803) in Helvetic Republic. See *Table* at SWITZERLAND.

Vau–de–Vire (vōd′vēr′). See VIRE town, France.

Vau′dreuil′ (vō′drû′y′; *Angl.* vô·droi′). 1 County, Quebec, Canada. See *Table* at QUEBEC.
2 Village, its ⊗, S Quebec, Canada, on Ottawa river near its mouth ab. 24 m. WSW of Montreal; pop. 714.

Vaughn (vôn). Village, Guadalupe co., E cen. New Mexico, 84 m. SSE of Santa Fe; pop. 1170.

Vaught, Mount (vôt). Peak 8840 ft. in Glacier National Park, NW Montana.

Vau·pés′ (bou·pās′). 1 Spanish spelling of Uaupés (*q.v.*). 2 Commissary of Colombia. See *Table* at COLOMBIA.

Vaux (vō). 1 Village, Aisne dept., N France, 4 m. W of Château-Thierry; captured by Americans in battle of July 1, 1918.
2 Village, Meuse dept., NE France, 3 m. NE of Verdun; Fort de Vaux in vicinity; very severe fighting Mar.–June, 1916; captured June 7 by Germans.

Vaux′hall′ (vŏks′hôl′). District, London, England, in Lambeth metropolitan borough on S bank of the Thames; site of Vauxhall Gardens 1661–1859, pleasure resort.

Va·va′u (vä·vä′ŏŏ). 1 Island group in N Tonga Is., SW cen. Pacific Ocean; includes island of Vavau and ab. 30 islets; ab. 60 sq. m.; pop. (1937) 8158. Mountainous, of volcanic origin.
2 Chief island of the Vavau group in N Tonga Is., SW cen. Pacific Ocean; 10 m. long; 56 sq. m. Chief town is Neiafu. Island noted for its caves.

Väx′jö′ (věk′shû′). Town, ✳ of Kronoberg prov., S Sweden, 60 m. WNW of Kalmar; pop. 16,900; manufactures matches; cathedral, traditionally founded in 11th cent. by an English missionary, St. Siegfrid.

Vech′te (fěK′tě); *Du.* **Vecht** (věKt). River ab. 125 m. long, W Germany and Netherlands; flows NW through German provinces of Westphalia and Hannover, and W through province of Overijssel, Netherlands, into IJsselmeer.

Vectis. See Isle of WIGHT.

Ve′dea (vě′dyä). River ab. 130 m. long in S Romania, E of the Olt; flows SE into the Danube near Giurgiu.

Ve·de·la′go (vä·dä·lä′gŏ). Commune, Treviso prov., Venezia Euganea, NE Italy, 14 m. W of Treviso; pop. (1931) 10,829.

Vee′ders·burg (vē′dẽrz·bûrg). Town, Fountain co., W Indiana, 22 m. SW of Lafayette; pop. 1762; brick kilns.

Veen·dam′ (vān·däm′). Commune, Groningen prov., NE Netherlands, 14 m. SE of Groningen; pop. 13,383.

Vee′nen·daal (vā′něn·dàl). Commune, Utrecht prov., cen. Netherlands, just N of the Neder Rijn SE of Utrecht; pop. 8393.

Ve′ga (vā′gȧ). Town, ⊗ of Oldham co., NW Texas; pop. 658.

Vega, La. See LA VEGA.

Ve′ga Al′ta (bā′gä äl′tä). Municipality (pop. 17,603) and town (pop. 3182), N Puerto Rico; town is 14 m. SW of San Juan.

Ve′ga Ba′ja (bā′gä vä′hä). Municipality (pop. 30,189) and town (pop. 3718), N Puerto Rico; town is 18 m. WSW of San Juan.

Vega Re·al′ (rrě·äl′). Valley in N Dominican Republic; formed by two streams flowing in opposite directions.

Ve′ge·sack (fā′gě·zäk). Town, W Germany, just NW of Bremen on the Weser; pop. (1933) 4547; port; shipbuilding; heavily bombed during World War II.

Veglia. See KRK.

Veg′re·ville (věg′rě·vĭl). Town, E Alberta, Canada, on a tributary of the North Saskatchewan river 57 m. E of Edmonton; pop. 2223.

Ve′ii (vē′[y]ī). Ancient city of Etruria, ab. 12 m. N of Rome, Italy; an Etruscan stronghold, one of the twelve

cities of the confederation; for 350 years almost continually at war with Rome; captured by Camillus 396 B.C. after a ten-year siege.

Ve·jer′ de la Fron·te′ra (bĕ·hĕr′ thä lä frôn·tā′rä). Commune, Cádiz prov., SW Spain, 26 m. SE of Cádiz; pop. 10,110; stock raising, esp. for the bull ring; textiles.

Vej′le (vī′lĕ). **1** County of Denmark. See *Table* at DENMARK.

2 Seaport, its ⊗, SE Jutland Penin., Denmark, at the head of **Vejle Fjord** (inlet 15 m. long); pop. (1945) 27,107; distributing center for dairy products; shipbuilding yards, textile mills, ironworks, breweries; St. Nicholas Church, dating from 13th cent.

Vej′pr·ty (vā′pēr·tĭ); *Ger.* **Wei′pert** (vī′pĕrt). Town, NW Bohemia, W Czechoslovakia, 68 m. NW of Prague; pop. (1930) 11,443.

Ve′la·de′ro (bā′lä·thā′rŏ) *or* **Ve′la·de′res** (-räs). Peak 20,735 ft. in NW La Rioja prov., NW Argentina, near border of Chile.

Vé·lan′ (vā′län′). Mountain 12,353 ft. in the Pennine Alps, on the Swiss-Italian border.

Ve′la·nai Island (vā′lä·nī). Island in N Palk Bay, off N tip of Ceylon.

Ve′las, Cape (bā′läs; vä′läs). Cape on NW coast of Costa Rica, extending into the Pacific Ocean.

Vel′bert (fĕl′bĕrt). Manufacturing city, cen. North Rhine-Westphalia state, West Germany, in the Ruhr valley 14 m. NE of Düsseldorf; pop. 25,721; manufactures locks, iron goods.

Ve′le·bit (vĕ′lĕ·bĕt). Mountain range in W Yugoslavia, extending from NW to SE along the Adriatic coast from ab. 44° to 45°N; greatest heights ab. 5700 ft.

Ve′les (vĕ′lĕs); *Turk.* **Kö′pri·li′** (kû′prü·lü′). Town, Macedonia, SE Yugoslavia, on the Vardar ab. 30 m. SE of Skoplje; pop. 13,440; commercial center, esp. for silks.

Ve·le′ta, Pi·ca′cho de (pĕ·kä′chŏ thä vä·lā′tä). Peak 11,378 ft. in the Sierra Nevada, Granada prov., S Spain, just WNW of Mulhacén.

Vé′lez–Má′la·ga (bā′läth·mä′lä·gä; bā′läz-). Commune, Málaga prov., S Spain, on Mediterranean 16 m. ENE of Málaga; pop. 28,894; in agricultural and fruit-growing region; sugar refining; ancient Moorish castle. Recaptured from Moors 1487 by Ferdinand the Catholic.

Ve′lho, *in full* **Pôr′to Velho** (pōr′tŏͦ vä′lyŏͦ). Town, ✷ of Guaporé territory, W Brazil, on the Madeira river; pop. 2284.

Ve′li·a (vē′lĭ·ȧ; vēl′yȧ) *or* **E′le·a** (ē′lĕ·ȧ). Ancient town of Lucania, S Italy, ruins in modern Campania compartimento near coast ab. halfway bet. Gulf of Salerno and Gulf of Policastro; remains of walls; founded c. 530 B.C. by Phocaeans; home of Parmenides and Zeno of the *Eleatic* school of philosophers, reputedly founded by Xenophanes.

Ve′li·ka Ki′kin·da (vĕ′lĕ·kä kē′kĕn·dä); *Hung.* **Nagy′ki′kin·da** (nŏd′y′·kĭ′kĭn·dŏ). City, Voivodina autonomous prov., NE Yugoslavia, near Romanian border; pop. 28,400; trade center in wheat-growing area.

Ve·li′ka·ya (vĕ·lē′kȧ·yȧ; *Russ.* vyĭ·lyē′kȧ·yȧ). River ab. 230 m. long in W Velikie Luki Region and W Pskov Region, Soviet Russia, Europe, flowing N into Lake Pskov.

Veliki Bečkerek. See PETROVGRAD.

Ve·li′kie Lu′ki (vĕ·lē′kĭ lōō′kĭ; *Russ.* vyĭ·lyē′kĭ·yĕ). Town, ✷ of Velikie Luki Region, Soviet Russia, Europe, on right bank of upper Lovat river 200 m. W of Kalinin; railroad junction point. Seized by Germans Aug. 21, 1941 and held by them through 1941–42; a key point in Russian counterattacks; surrounded by Russians Jan. 1943, and retaken in great March offensive.

Velikie Luki Region. Region, NW Soviet Russia, Europe; ✷ Velikie Luki.

Ve′li·ki Kvar′ner (vĕ′lĕ·kĕ kvär′nĕr); *Ital.* **Quar-ne′ro** (kwär·nâ′rŏ). Inlet or gulf of N Adriatic Sea on E side of Istria Penin., NW Yugoslavia; Cres I. is to the E and Rieka at its head.

Ve·li′ki U·styug′ (vĕ·lē′kĭ ōͦo·stŭk′; *Russ.* vyĭ·lyē′kĭ). Town, NE Vologda Region, Soviet Russia, Europe, on the left bank of the Northern Dvina river just below the junction of the Sukhona and the Yug; pop. 23,382; manufactures leather and textiles; sawmills; has old buildings of architectural interest. An old colony of Novgorod; formerly an important post road junction; in 17th cent. was noted for its wood carvings, silver engravings, embroideries.

Ve·li′no (vā·lē′nŏ). River 54 m. long in cen. Italy; flows out of the Apennines into Nera river; contains noted waterfall, **Cas·ca′te del′le Mar′mo·re** (käs-kä′tä dâl′lä mär′mŏ·rä), in three separate cascades.

Ve·lizh′ (vyĭ·lyēsh′). Town, NW Smolensk Region, W Soviet Russia, Europe, on upper Dvina river ab. 60 m. NNW of Smolensk; pop. 10,167.

Vel′ký Sev′luš (vĕl′y′·kē sĕv′lŏͦosh); *Hung.* **Nagy′-szől′lős** (nŏd′y′·sûl′lûsh). Town, Zakarpatskaya Region, W Ukraine, U.S.S.R., just W of Chust; pop. (1930) 11,049; before World War II in Czechoslovakia.

Vel′ký Žitný. See GREAT SCHÜTT.

Vel′la Gulf (vĕl′ȧ). Open water area in Solomon Is., W Pacific Ocean, SE of Vella Lavella I. and NW of Kolombangara I.; partly closed on the W by Ganongga I.; scene of American naval victory over Japanese Aug. 6, 1943, following battle in Kula Gulf.

Vel′la La·vel′la (vĕl′ȧ lȧ·vĕl′ȧ). Island in the New Georgia Is., cen. Solomon Is., W Pacific Ocean, NW of Kolombangara I. and separated from it by Vella Gulf; ab. 200 sq. m.; pop. 600; surrounded by coral reefs which prevent use of its many bays; copra. Highest point 3000 ft. Occupied Aug. 15, 1943 by American troops.

Vel·le′tri (vâl·lā′trĕ). Commune, Roma prov., W Latium, cen. Italy, 20 m. SE of Rome; pop. 31,029; cathedral (probably from 4th cent.); 16th-cent. town hall. In World War II strong German defense point in Rome area; taken by Americans after severe fighting June 2, 1944.

Vel·lore′ (vĕ·lōr′). City, Madras state, S Indian Union, on Palar river 80 m. WSW of Madras; pop. (1941) 71,502; has temple to Siva and a strong fortress that gained renown in Carnatic wars. Occupied by British in 1765; withstood two-year siege by Haidar Ali, 1780–82; after 1799 became residence of sons of Tipu Sahib who instigated Sepoy Mutiny here in 1806.

Vel′sen (vĕl′sĕ[n]). Commune, North Holland prov., W Netherlands, at the mouth of the North Sea Canal; pop. (1939) 48,730; serves as the outer port of Amsterdam.

Velsuna. See ORVIETO.

Velt′heim (fĕlt′hīm). Former commune in Zurich canton, NE cen. Switzerland, now part of Winterthur.

Vel′u·we (vĕl′ü·vĕ). Range of hills in Gelderland prov., E Netherlands N of Arnhem; highest point 351 ft.

Vel′va (vĕl′vȧ). City, McHenry co., N cen. North Dakota; pop. 1330; lignite coal mines; agriculture.

Ve·na′fro (vā·nä′frŏ); *anc.* **Ve·na′frum** (vē·nā′frŭm). Commune, Campobasso prov., Abruzzi e Molise, cen. Italy, 32 m. WSW of Campobasso; pop. 10,137.

Venaissin. See COMTAT VENAISSIN.

Ve·nan′go (vē·năng′gō). County in Pennsylvania. See *Table* at PENNSYLVANIA.

Ve·na·ri′a Re·a′le (vā·nä·rē′ä rā·ä′lä). Commune, Torino prov., Piedmont, NW Italy, 5 m. NNW of Turin; pop. 11,744.

Vence (väns). Commune, Alpes-Maritimes dept., SE France, W of Nice; medieval walls; Romanesque cathedral dating from 12th cent.; pop. 5635.

Ven·dée′ (vän′dā′). **1** River ab. 45 m. long, in Vendée dept., France, flowing to the Sèvre-Niortaise.

2 Department of France. See *Table* at FRANCE. Formed at the time of the Revolution out of the W part of the ancient region of Poitou (*q.v.*); became, with adjoining regions of Poitou, Anjou, and Brittany, the scene of the Wars of the Vendée, a series of peasant insurrections against the Revolutionary government 1793–96.

Ven'dôme' (vän'dōm'). Manufacturing town, Loir-et-Cher dept., N cen. France; pop. 7383; ancient countship, in 1515 made duchy whose dukes included César de Bourbon, natural son of Henry IV, and Louis Joseph, marshal of France during time of Louis XIV; 11th-cent. castle; abbey of the Trinity.

Vend'sys'sel–Thy (věn'süs'ĕl·tü'). Island N of Lim Fjord, forming the N end of the peninsula of Jutland, Denmark; 1792 sq. m.; pop. (1925) 233,838; chief town Hjörring. The E section (larger part of Hjörring co.) is called **Vendsyssel**; the W section (part of Thisted co.) **Thy'land** (tü'làn).

Ve·ne'dig (vå·nā'dĭk). German for VENICE.

Vener. See VÄNERN.

Veneta, Laguna. See Lagoon of VENICE.

Ven'e·tae, Al'pes (ăl'pēz věn'ē·tē). = *Dolomites:* see *Table* at ALPS.

Ve·ne'ti·a (vē·nē'shǐ·à; -shà). **1** Ancient Roman division of NE Italy including the territory bet. the Po river and the Alps and including the Istrian Penin.; named for its ancient inhabitants, the Veneti; principal towns included Aquileia, Pola, Tergeste, Tarvisium, Patavium, Atria, Vicentia, Tridentum, Verona, Mantua, Brixia, Cremona; prosperous under Roman rule; overrun by N barbarians in early Christian era.

2 *Ital.* **Ve·ne'zia** (vā·nā'tsyä). Modern region in Italy generally equivalent in extent to ancient region (see **1**, above); descends from Julian and Carnic Alps and Dolomites to fertile basins of Adige and Po rivers; produces cereals, rice, wine, silk, wool; rich in mineral wealth, including esp. coal, zinc, bauxite, mercury; industrial enterprises have centered chiefly at Trieste (*q.v.*), Venice, Monfalcone, Rovigno (now Rovinj). For history, see VENICE, ISTRIA peninsula, TRENTINO. Forms three modern compartimenti (for provincial divisions, area, and pop., see *Table* at ITALY), known collectively as the **Tre Ve·ne'zie** (trā' vå·nā'tsyä), i.e., the Three Venetias: (1) **Venezia Eu·ga'ne·a** (à·ōō·gä'nà·ä), *or simply*

Venezia; *formerly* **Ve'ne·to** (vâ'nā·tô); *anc.* **Ve·ne'ti·a Eu·ga'ne·a** (vē·nē'shǐ·à [-shà] ū·gā'nē·à); extends from Carnic Alps to Po river and from Dolomites to Adriatic. (2) **Venezia Tri·den·ti'na** (trē·dĕn·tē'nä); *anc.* **Venetia Tri'den·ti'na** (trī'dĕn·tī'nà); bet. Lombardy and Venezia Euganea, extending from Lake Garda to German border. (3) **Venezia Giu'lia e Za'ra** (jōō'lyä â dzä'rä); before 1947 comprised former Austrian province of Küstenland (including Istria), part of Carniola, Fiume, and Zara in Dalmatia; all of this, except for city of Gorizia and small area W of the Isonzo, ceded to Yugoslavia by treaty of Feb. 10, 1947; small region remaining, extending from Julian Alps to Adriatic, is known as **Venezia Giulia** (*Eng.* **Venetia Ju'lia** [jōō'lyà; jōō'lǐ·à]). See VENEZIA GIULIA.

3 See VENICE.

Venetian Republic. See *History* at VENICE.

Ve·ne'zia (vå·nā'tsyä). **1** Province of Italy. See *Table* at ITALY.

2 See VENETIA region, Italy.

3 See VENICE.

Venezia, Golfo di. See Gulf of VENICE.

Venezia Euganea, *or* **Venezia.** See under VENETIA, **2**.

Ve·ne'zia Giu'lia (vå·nā'tsyä jōō'lyä). The narrow strip of territory along the Isonzo left to Italy after the formation of the Free Territory of Trieste and cession of the greater part of Istria Penin. and the city of Zara (Zadar) to Yugoslavia by treaty of Feb. 1947; chief town Gorizia. See *Table* at ITALY.

Ven'e·zu·e'la (věn'ē·zē·wē'là, -zwē'-; -zē·wā'-, -zwä'-), *officially* **Republic of Venezuela,** *Span.* **Re·pú'bli·ca de Ve'ne·zue'la** (rrē·pōō'vlĕ·kä thä vā'nā·swā'lä), *until* 1953 **United States of Venezuela,** *Span.* **Es·ta'dos U·ni'dos de Ve'ne·zue'la** (ās·tä'thôs ōō·nē'thôz thä vā'nā·swā'lä). Republic, N South America; bounded on the N by the Caribbean Sea, on the E by British Guiana, on the S by Brazil, and on the W by Colombia; 352,141 sq. m.; pop. (1941 est.)

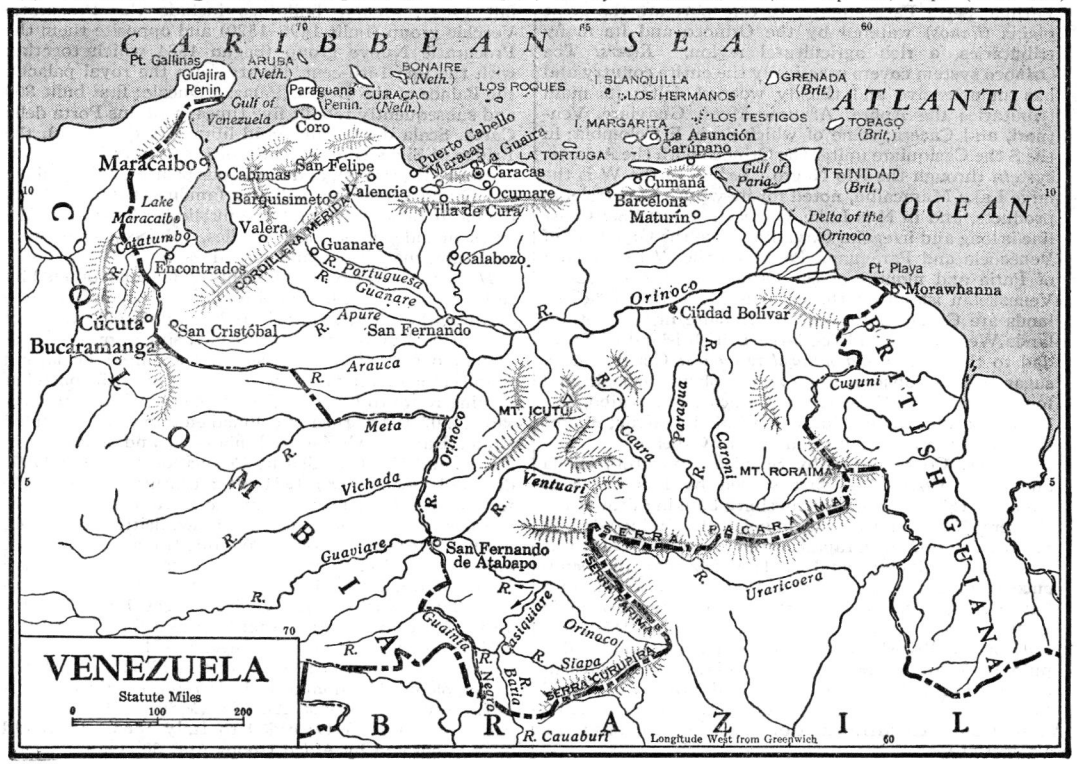

3,951,381; * Caracas; divided into the following 20 states, Federal District, and 2 territories (for pronunciation of their names, see their individual entries):

NAME	LOCA-TION	AREA[1]	POP.[1]	CAPITAL
Federal District	N	745	380,099	Caracas
		STATES		
Anzoátegui	N	16,718	156,946	Barcelona
Apure	W	29,537	84,569	San Fernando
Aragua	N	2,162	138,235	Maracay
Barinas	W cen.	13,591	62,959	Barinas
Bolívar	SE	91,892	112,523	Ciudad Bolívar
Carabobo	N	1,795	191,442	Valencia
Cojedes	NW cen.	5,714	49,769	San Carlos
Falcón	NW	9,575	232,644	Coro
Guárico	N cen.	25,637	135,089	San Juan de los Moros
Lara	NW	7,645	332,975	Barquisimeto
Mérida	W	4,363	192,994	Mérida
Miranda	N	3,069	227,604	Los Teques
Monagas	NE	11,158	122,901	Maturín
Nueva Esparta[2]	N coast	444	69,195	La Asunción
Portuguesa	W cen.	5,869	87,151	Guanare
Sucre	N	4,556	291,452	Cumaná
Táchira	W	4,286	245,722	San Cristóbal
Trujillo	W cen.	2,857	264,270	Trujillo
Yaracuy	NW	2,741	127,030	San Felipe
Zulia	NW	24,363	360,667	Maracaibo
		TERRITORIES		
Amazonas	S	67,857	47,128	Puerto Ayacucho
Delta Amacuro	NE	15,521	37,165	Tucupita
Federal Dependencies		120	852	

[1] Area in sq. m. Pop. is 1941 est.
[2] Comprises island group in the Caribbean Sea; chief island Margarita.

Mountains, etc.: In the W are the highest ranges, the Cordillera Mérida, a NE spur of the Andes E of Lake Maracaibo; highest point Pico Bolívar, over 16,000 ft.; along Caribbean coast extends the Cordillera de Venezuela, ranging from 5000 to 8530 ft. Lower ranges are in the S, esp. along the Brazilian border (Serra Parima, Serra Pacaraima). In cen. part are the great plains (*llanos*) watered by the Orinoco and its many tributaries, a rich agricultural region. *Rivers:* The Orinoco system covers practically the entire country and has an extensive and thickly wooded delta; its main tributaries the Apure, Arauca, Meta, Guaviare, Ventuari, and Cacera, some of which drain E Colombia; in the S the Casiquiare unites the Orinoco with the Amazon system through the Rio Negro. *Lakes:* In the W is the large Lake Maracaibo, noted for its wealth in petroleum products, and in N is Lake Valencia. *Coast line:* Coast line is long and irregular extending from the large Gulf of Venezuela and Paraguaná Penin. on the W to the Gulf of Paria and mouths of the Orinoco on the E. Chief Venezuelan island off the coast is Margarita; other islands are Curaçao, Aruba, and Bonaire in the Netherlands West Indies and the large British island of Trinidad to the NE. *Chief natural resources:* Coffee, cacao, sugar, cotton, tobacco, iron ore, petroleum, asphalt, and forest products. *Chief cities:* Caracas, Maracaibo, Valencia, Barquisimeto, Maracay, Ciudad Bolívar; important ports are La Guaira and Puerto Cabello.

History: Coast traced by Spanish navigators Ojeda and de la Cosa 1499; first settled by Las Casas at Cumaná 1520; granted to Augsburg banking firm of the Welsers 1528–46; Caracas founded 1567; included in viceroyalty of New Granada (see COLOMBIA) 1718; was made a captaincy-general 1731; Venezuelan independence from Spain, proclaimed 1811, not assured until battle of Carabobo 1821; part of Greater Colombia 1819–29; formally separated from Colombia 1830; lost territory to British Guiana (Venezuelan boundary dispute 1895–96), Brazil, and Colombia; adopted present constitution 1936; neutral in World War I; in World War II severed relations with Axis powers Dec. 31, 1941.

Venezuela, Cordillera de. See CORDILLERA DE VENEZUELA.

Venezuela, Gulf of. Inlet of Caribbean Sea in NW Venezuela, bet. Guajira Penin., Colombia, and Paraguana Penin., Venezuela; extends S as Lake Maracaibo (*q.v.*).

Veng′e·tind′er (věng′ě-tǐn′ẽr). Mountain 5960 ft., Norway. See ROMSDAL.

Ven′gi (věng′gē). Hindu kingdom of the Andhras, 1st–3d cents. A.D., E India, bet. lower Godavari and Krishna rivers; * Amaravati (*q.v.*).

Ven·gur′la (věn·gŏor′lȧ). Town, SW Maharashtra, W Indian Union, on Arabian Sea 220 m. S of Bombay and N of Goa; pop. 20,158; seaport with varied trade.

Ven′ice (věn′ĭs). 1 Former town, Los Angeles co., SW California; part of Los Angeles since 1925; amusement center.

2 City, Madison co., SW Illinois, on Mississippi river 5 m. N of East St. Louis; pop. 5380.

3 *Ital.* **Ve·ne′zia** (vȧ·nā′tsyȧ); *Lat.* **Ve·ne′ti·a** (vē·nē′shǐ·ȧ; -shȧ). Seaport, * of Venezia prov., Venezia Euganea, NE Italy, on 118 islands in Lagoon of Venice 162 m. E of Milan; pop. 264,027; archiepiscopal see; often called "Queen of the Adriatic"; majority of islands separated only by narrow canals (Ital. *rio;* pl. *rii*) crossed by some 378 bridges; main part of city traversed by S-shaped Grand Canal crossed by famous Rialto bridge (marble arch lined with double row of shops with broad footway between; built 1588–91) connecting Rialto I. (site of the exchange and center of commercial activity) and San Marco I.; intracity transportation facilities include gondolas, barcas, motorboats, and steamers; islands not forming part of main mass of city include Giudecca, San Giorgio Maggiore, Murano (group), Cimitero, Burano, Torcello, San Lazzaro, and San Servolo; sand banks and reefs (Ital. *lido;* pl. *lidi*) popular as bathing resorts, esp. the Lido di Malamocco; cathedral of St. Mark (begun in Romanesque style 830, with additions representing Byzantine, Gothic, Greek, and Oriental architecture; the separate Campanile rebuilt after its fall 1902); secular buildings include the Procuratie Vecchie group (built 1496–1520) and opposite them the Procuratie Nuove group (begun 1584 which together with the fine 16th-cent. library form the royal palace), the Palace of the Doges (Palazzo Ducale; first built 800 and subsequently rebuilt five times; contains Porta della Carta, Scala dei Giganti, and library of St. Mark), the Bridge of Sighs (Ponte dei Sospiri; connects Doges' palace and the prisons), and numerous palaces, chiefly along the Grand Canal; art galleries (among them the Accademia di Belle Arti), and fine public gardens; manufactures include glass, lace, textiles, tobacco, soap, wax, furniture, machinery, and torpedoes.

History: Grew from settlements on lagoons founded by refugees from barbarian invasion of mainland (see AQUILEIA) 5th cent. A.D.; elected first doge 697; vassal of Byzantine Empire until 10th cent.; spread onto coastal mainland east of Adige river, and acquired Istria and islands along Dalmatian coast; beginning with control of trading route to Levant, Venice emerged from 4th Crusade (1202–04) as ruler of colonial empire which included Crete, Euboea, Cyclades, Ionian Is., and footholds in Morea and Epirus; ruled by Council of Ten 1310–1797; defeated Genoa (*q.v.*) 1381 after century-long struggle for commercial supremacy in the Levant and E Mediterranean; in 15th cent., with acquisition of Friuli, Padua, Vicenza, Verona, Polesine, Brescia, Bergamo, and Crema, Venetian Republic became an extensive Italian state; gradually lost eastern possessions to Ottoman Turks with whom Venice fought intermittently 15th–18th cents.; driven from Cyprus 1571, Crete 1669, and Tenos, its last hold in Aegean, 1715; republic dissolved and territory ceded to Austria 1797; incorporated in Napoleon's kingdom of Italy 1805; restored to Austria 1815; revolted against Austria (Manin's Republic of Saint Mark) 1848–49; ceded to Italy 1866. In World War II entered by Allied troops Apr. 30, 1945.

Venice, Gulf of; *Ital.* **Gol'fo di Ve·ne'zia** (gôl'fô dĕ vä·nâ'tsyä). North section of the Adriatic Sea; sometimes, the entire Adriatic Sea.

Venice, Lagoon of; *Ital.* **La·gu'na Ve'ne·ta** (lä-gōō'nä vâ'nä·tä). Inlet of the Gulf of Venice, NE Italy, forming a shallow bay with more than 100 small islands on which the city of Venice is built; separated from the Gulf of Venice by a bar, the Lido; area 95 to 210 sq. m., according to season.

Vé'nis'sieux' (vä·nē'syû'). Industrial commune, Rhône dept., E cen. France, 3 m. SSE of Lyons; pop. (1931) 16,157; textiles.

Ven'lo *or* **Ven'loo** (vĕn'lō). Commune, Limburg prov., SE Netherlands, on Maas (Meuse) river on German border; pop. (1939) 27,872; fortified town; 16th-cent. stadhouse, 15th-cent. Gothic Church of Saint Martin.

Ven'na·char, Loch (lŏк vĕn'à·кär). Lake in Perth co., cen. Scotland; maximum depth 210 ft.

Ve·no'sa (vä·nō'sä); *anc.* **Ve·nu'si·a** (vê·nū'zhĭ·à). Commune, Potenza prov., Lucania, S Italy, 22 m. N of Potenza; pop. 11,045; 15th-cent. castle; 11th-cent. abbey (containing tomb of Robert Guiscard); 15th-cent. cathedral; Jewish catacombs nearby. Roman colony 291 B.C.; important as fulcrum of Roman attack on Pyrrhus and Hannibal. Birthplace of Horace.

Ven'ray *or* **Ven'raij** (vĕn'rī). Commune, Limburg prov., SE Netherlands, 21 m. S of Nijmegen; pop. 12,360.

Ven'ta (vĕn'tä); *Russ. formerly* **Vin·da'va** (vyĭn·dä'và); *Ger.* **Win'dau** (vĭn'dou). River ab. 200 m. long in Lithuania and Latvia; rises in W Lithuania and flows NNW into Baltic Sea at Ventspils.

Venta, La. See LA VENTA.

Venta Belgarum. See WINCHESTER.

Ventana, Sierra de la. See SIERRA DE LA VENTANA.

Ventia. See VALENCE.

Ven·ti·mi'glia (vän·tê·mēl'yä); *Fr.* **Vin'ti'mille'** (văN'tē'mēl'). Commune, Imperia prov., W Liguria, NW Italy, on Ligurian Sea 21 m. WSW of Imperia and just across the border from Menton, France; pop. 15,787; French-Italian border railroad station; bathing and winter resort; 11th-cent. cathedral. See GRIMALDI caves.

Vent'nor (vĕnt'nẽr). 1 City and shore resort, Atlantic co., SE New Jersey, on Atlantic Ocean 3 m. WSW of Atlantic City; pop. 8688.

2 Urban district, S Isle of Wight, S England, on English Channel 15 m. SSW of Portsmouth; pop. 7308; health resort. Burial place of Algernon Charles Swinburne is at nearby Bonchurch.

Ven·to·te'ne (vän·tô·tâ'nä). Italian island in the Tyrrhenian Sea W of Naples, Italy, SW of Pontine Is., and S of the Gulf of Gaeta.

Vents'pils (vĕnts'pĭls). 1 Administrative district, NW Kurzeme prov., W Latvia, U.S.S.R.; 1250 sq. m.

2 *Ger.* **Win'dau** (vĭn'dou). Seaport city in Ventspils dist., Latvia, U.S.S.R., on the Baltic Sea at the mouth of Venta river N of Lepaya and 100 m. WNW of Riga; pop. (1935) 15,671; exports lumber, flax, hemp, grain, and butter; seaside resort; has castle dating from 1290. Founded 1343; an important Russian port before World War I; in World War II held by Germans until end of war.

Ven·tua'ri (bân·twä'rê). River ab. 350 m. long in S Venezuela; flows W into Orinoco river near Colombian boundary.

Ven·tu'ra (vĕn·tōōr'à; -tûr'à). 1 County in California. See *Table* at CALIFORNIA.

2 *officially* **San Buen'a·ven·tu'ra** (săn bwĕn'à·vĕn-tōōr'à). Seaport city, its ⊗, SW California, on Santa Barbara Channel 23 m. SE of Santa Barbara; pop. 29,114; founded 1782; oil, lumber, machinery, oil-well supplies; old Spanish mission.

Venue, Ben. See BEN VENUE.

Venusberg. See HÖRSEL BERGE.

Venusia. See VENOSA.

Ve'ra·cruz' (vĕr'à·krōōz'; *Span.* bā'rä·krōōs'). 1 State, E Mexico. See *Table* at MEXICO.

2 Seaport, Veracruz state, E Mexico, on the Gulf of Mexico 264 m. from Mexico City; pop. 71,679; one of the chief ports of Mexico and terminal of several railroads. Settlement (original name, **Vil'la Ri'ca de Ve'ra Cruz** [bē'yä rē'kä thä vä'rä krōōs']) dates from 1519 at time of landing of Cortes; starting point of his march up to Mexico City; settlement soon removed but reestablished 1599; port for arrival and departure of the fleets of Spain in 16th and 17th cents.; pillaged by pirates, esp. 1653 and 1712; fort of San Juan de Ulúa built to strengthen it; captured by the French, 1838 and 1861; by Gen. Winfield Scott Mar. 29, 1847 on invasion of Mexico; scene of Mexican revolt against Madero 1912 and occupied by U.S. troops for 7 months, Apr. to Nov. 1914, in conflict with Pres. Huerta.

Ve·ra'gua (bä·rä'gwä). Region, W part of Isthmus of Panama, discovered and named by Christopher Columbus 1502; later included Nombre de Dios, Portobelo, and Panama City. In 1537 Luis Columbus, son of Christopher, granted title of duke of Veragua by Charles I.

Ve·ra'guas (bä·rä'gwäs). Province, SW cen. Panama; 4669 sq. m.; pop. 84,994; ✳ Santiago.

Ve·ra'val (vâ·rä'vàl). Town, SW Gujerat state, W India, in S Kathiawar penin., on Arabian Sea 210 m. NW of Bombay; pop. 21,114. Seaport of great age. Nearby is the old port of Somnath (*q.v.*).

Ver·ba'nia (vâr·bä'nyä). Commune, Novara prov., Piedmont, NW Italy, on W shore of Lake Maggiore (anc. Lacus Verbanus) 34 m. N of Novara; pop. 21,753; museum; 15th-cent. church; summer resort; formed 1939 by union of former communes of Intra and Pallanza.

Verbanus Lacus. See Lake MAGGIORE.

Ver·cel'li (vâr·chĕl'lē). 1 Province of Italy. See *Table* at ITALY.

2 *anc.* **Ver·cel'lae** (vûr·sĕl'ē). Commune, ✳ of Vercelli prov., Piedmont, NW Italy, on Sesia river 39 m. WSW of Milan; pop. 38,956; cathedral (remodeled 1572), 13th-cent. castle, early 13th-cent. basilica; trade center of rice-growing region. Cimbri annihilated by Marius 101 B.C. nearby; city-state in Middle Ages; under Visconti family of Milan 1335 ff. and dukes of Piedmont-Savoy 1427 ff.

Ver'chères' (vĕr'shâr'). 1 County, Quebec, Canada. See *Table* at QUEBEC.

2 Village, its ⊗, S Quebec, Canada, on S bank of St. Lawrence river 22 m. NE of Montreal; pop. 1201; site of a fort in 17th cent.

Ver'de. 1 (vûr'dĕ) River ab. 120 m. long, cen. Arizona; formed by confluence of forks in N cen. Yavapai co., flows SE into Salt river ab. 20 m. E of Phoenix.

2 (vâr'dĕ) River ab. 200 m. long in S Mato Grosso state, SW Brazil; flows SE into Paraná river.

Verde, Cape. See Cape VERT.

Ver'de Island (bĕr'thä). Island in center of Verde Island Passage S of Batangas, Luzon, Phil. Is.; 7 sq. m.; 5 m. long; pop. 2974; part of Batangas municipality; ab. 3 m. from mainland. Seized by American forces Feb. 26, 1945.

Verde Island Passage. Channel bet. SW Luzon and N Mindoro, Phil. Is., connecting waters S of Luzon with South China Sea; ab. 80 m. long and 9 to 22 m. wide; the W end of main interisland passage for ocean-going vessels from U.S. to Manila. See SAN BERNARDINO STRAIT.

Verde Islands, Cape. See CAPE VERDE ISLANDS.

Ver'den (fär'dĕn); *also* **Verden an der Al'ler** (än dĕr äl'ẽr). City, Lower Saxony state, W Germany, formerly in Hannover prov., on Aller river 57 m. SW of Hamburg; pop. 10,073; manufactures cigars, soap, furniture, tile, brandy. A bishopric founded c. 800; later became a duchy and was ceded 1648 to Sweden; passed to Hannover 1719.

Ver'di·gris (vûr'dĭ·grēs). River 280 m. long, SE Kansas

and NE Oklahoma; rises in SE Chase co., E cen. Kansas, flows S across Oklahoma border and into Arkansas river in N Muskogee co., E Oklahoma.

Ver'don' (vĕr'dôN'). River ab. 100 m. long in Basses-Alpes dept., SE France; flows into Durance river.

Ver·dun' (vĕr·dŭn'; vûr-; *Fr.* vĕr'dûN'). **1** Manufacturing city, Montreal I., S Quebec, Canada, on St. Lawrence river SE of Montreal city; pop. 77,391. **2** *or* **Ver'dun'-sur-Meuse** (vĕr'dûN'sür·mûz'); *anc.* **Ver'o·du'num** (vĕr'ô·dū'nŭm). Manufacturing city, Meuse dept., NE France, on Meuse river 29 m. NNE of Bar-le-Duc; pop. 19,460; one of chief citadels of France, its fortifications once having been among the most advanced in Europe; 12th-cent. cathedral; 18th-cent. episcopal palace; 17th-cent. town hall.

History: Treaty dividing Charlemagne's territory among his three grandsons signed here 843 A.D.; passed to Germany in 10th cent. and made free city; with Metz and Toul (*Les Trois-Évêchés*, the three bishoprics) taken by Henry II of France 1552, and acquisition by France acknowledged by Treaty of Westphalia 1648; taken by Prussians 1792 and 1871; scene of prolonged battle Feb. 21, 1916 through Dec. 1916, the longest and bitterest contest in World War I in which the Germans were held back by resistance of French under Pétain; two million troops engaged, nearly one million killed; French sustained by the famous battle phrase: "Ils ne passeront pas!" ("They shall not pass!") Later battle Aug. 20–24, 1917 a French success; entered by Americans under Pershing Sept. 1918; town practically destroyed. In World War II occupied by Germans June 1940; captured by Americans Aug. 3, 1944. For some of the battles of World War I around Verdun, see DOUAUMONT, FLEURY, LE MORT HOMME, VAUX, WOËVRE.

Ve·ree'ni·ging (fĕ·rē'nĭ·kĭng). Town, S Transvaal, NE Union of South Africa, on Vaal river 35 m. S of Johannesburg; pop. 18,856; industrial community in coal-mining district. Founded 1892; treaty ending Boer War signed here May 31, 1902.

Ver'en·drye National Monument (vĕr'ĕn·drī). Former national monument, South Dakota, abolished 1956; site now partly a state historical area, partly inundated by Garrison Reservoir.

Ver'ga, Cape (vûr'gà). Cape extending into Atlantic Ocean on W coast of Guinea, ab. lat. 10°S.

Ver·ga'ra (bĕr·gä'rä). Commune, Guipúzcoa prov., N Spain; pop. (1930) 9307; Convention of Vergara Aug. 31, 1839 concluded Carlist war.

Ver·gennes' (vĕr·jĕnz'). City, Addison co., W Vermont, on Otter Creek near Lake Champlain; pop. 1921; settled 1766; naval depot in War of 1812; fleet commanded by Macdonough at Plattsburg (1814) built here.

Verkh'ne An·ga·ra' (vyĕrK'nyĕ ŭn·gŭ·rà'). See ANGARA.

Verkhne Ko·lymsk' (kŭ·lĭmsk'). Village, NE Yakutsk Republic, Soviet Russia, Asia, on left bank of the Kolyma river; N terminus of highway from Magadan on the Sea of Okhotsk.

Verkhneudinsk. See ULAN-UDE.

Verkhnyaya Tunguska. See Upper TUNGUSKA.

Ver'kho·yansk' (vûr'kŏ·yänsk'; *Russ.* vyĭr·Kŭ·yänsk'). **1** Mountain range, N cen. Yakutsk Republic, Soviet Russia, Asia; extends for ab. 950 m. in a semicircle along right banks of the Lena and lower Aldan rivers; heights range from 1600 ft. to ab. 8000 ft. Source of the headstreams of the Indigirka, Yana, and Omoloi rivers and of many short (eastern) tributaries of the Lena and Aldan. **2** Town, N cen. Yakutsk Republic, on right bank of Yana river 400 m. NNE of Yakutsk, 67°32′N, 133°50′E; mining and fur-trading town; formerly a place of political exile. One of the poles of cold in the Northern Hemisphere; has January mean of −59°, absolute minimum of −90° (coldest climatic temperature ever recorded, Feb. 1892), and a range bet. Jan. and July means of 119°F. See OIMYAKON, FORT CONGER.

Ver'man'dois' (vĕr'män'dwä'). Ancient district of N France, in E Picardy; now included in the departments of Aisne, Somme, and Oise.

Ver·me'jo (bĕr·mĕ'hō). Var. of BERMEJO.

Ver·mil'ion (vĕr·mĭl'yŭn). **1** River 50 m. long, N cen. Illinois; formed by the junction of two forks in Livingston co., flows NW into Illinois river in La Salle co. **2** River in N Minnesota. See VERMILION LAKE. **3** River ab. 100 m. long, SE South Dakota; rises in Lake co., flows S into Missouri river on S boundary of Clay co. **4** Name of a parish in Louisiana and of a county in Illinois. See *Tables* at ILLINOIS and LOUISIANA. **5** Village, Erie and Lorain cos., N Ohio, on Lake Erie E of Sandusky; pop. 4785; fishing center; tourist resort.

Vermilion Bay. Inlet of Gulf of Mexico in SW Iberia parish and SE Vermilion parish, S Louisiana.

Vermilion Lake. Lake in N Saint Louis co., NE Minnesota; outlet, **Vermilion River** (ab. 50 m. long) flowing N into Crane Lake, at SE end of Rainy Lake.

Vermilion Peak. Mountain 13,870 ft. in San Juan and San Miguel cos., SW Colorado.

Vermilion Sea. Former name of Gulf of CALIFORNIA.

Ver·mil'lion (vĕr·mĭl'yŭn). **1** County in Indiana. See *Table* at INDIANA. **2** City, ⊗ of Clay co., SE South Dakota, on Missouri river where the Vermilion unites with it, 27 m. ESE of Yankton; pop. 6102; Univ. of South Dakota (1862; coed.). Founded 1859 W of Fort Vermillion, an American Fur Co. trading post (established 1835).

Ver·mont' (vĕr·mŏnt'). A northeastern state of U.S.A., 14th state admitted to Union (1791); bounded on N by Canadian province of Quebec, on E by New Hampshire (boundary line is W bank of Connecticut river), on S by Massachusetts, and on W by New York (boundary line goes through Lake Champlain); 43d state in area, 9609 sq. m. (land area 9278 sq. m.); 47th state in population, 389,881; ✳ Montpelier. See *Table of States* at UNITED STATES. Divided into the following 14 counties (for pronunciation of their names, see their individual entries):

NAME	LOCATION	AREA[1]	POP.[1]	CO. SEAT
Addison	W[2]	785	20,076	Middlebury
Bennington	SW corner	672	25,088	Bennington and Manchester
Caledonia	NE	614	22,786	St. Johnsbury
Chittenden	NW[2]	532	74,425	Burlington
Essex	NE corner	664	6,083	Guildhall
Franklin	NW; borders Quebec[2]	659	29,474	St. Albans
Grand Isle	NW corner[3]	77	2,927	North Hero
Lamoille	N	475	11,027	Hyde Park
Orange	E	690	16,014	Chelsea
Orleans	N; borders Quebec	715	20,143	Newport
Rutland	W[4]	929	46,719	Rutland
Washington	N cen.	708	42,860	Montpelier
Windham	SE corner	793	29,776	Newfane
Windsor	E	965	42,483	Woodstock

[1] Area = land area in sq. m. Pop. from 1960 Census.
[2] On W borders Lake Champlain.
[3] Major portion of county composed of islands in Lake Champlain (Grand Isle, North Hero, and Isle La Motte).
[4] On W borders lower end of Lake Champlain and New York state.

Nickname: Green Mountain State. *State flower:* Red clover. *Motto:* Freedom and Unity. *Chief cities:* Burlington, Rutland, Bennington. *Rivers:* Flowing into Lake Champlain on W boundary are the Lamoille and Winooski rivers, Otter Creek, and the Poultney river, which forms for a short distance the state boundary with New York; chief Vermont tributary of the Connecticut river is the White river in cen. part. *Highest point:* Mount Mansfield 4393 ft., in Lamoille co. in N Green Mts. *Chief industries:* Agriculture, dairying, quarrying (marble).

History: Explored 1609 by Samuel de Champlain, who discovered the lake now bearing his name; temporary settlement by French at Fort Ste. Anne on Isle La Motte 1666; Massachusetts established Fort Dummer on site of present Brattleboro 1724; Bennington set-

NEW HAMPSHIRE AND VERMONT

Statute Miles

10   20   30

✪ State Capital

PUBLISHED BY G. & C. MERRIAM COMPANY
SPRINGFIELD, MASS.
PREPARED BY J. W. CLEMENT CO., BUFFALO, N.Y.

tled 1761; Green Mountain boys organized 1764 and under Ethan Allen captured Ticonderoga from the British May 10, 1775, and under Seth Warner captured Crown Point May 12, 1775; claims to the region relinquished by Massachusetts 1781, by New Hampshire 1782, and New York 1790; admitted to the Union Mar. 4, 1791.

Ver'nal (vûr'n'l). City, ⊗ of Uintah co., E Utah, ab. 25 m. W of Colorado border; pop. 3655; manufactures leather goods; in section raising sheep and cattle.

Vernal Falls. Waterfall 317 ft. in Yosemite National Park, E cen. California.

Ver'neuil' (vĕr'nû'y'). Town, S Eure dept., N France, ab. 25 m. SW of Évreux; pop. 3551; 11th–17th cent. church; 12th-cent. keep built by Henry I of England; scene of battle 1424 in which John of Lancaster, Duke of Bedford, defeated the French and Scotch.

Vernoleninsk. See NIKOLAEV.

Ver'non (vûr'nŭn). **1** Name of a parish in Louisiana and of counties in two states of the U.S. See *Tables* at LOUISIANA, MISSOURI, WISCONSIN.
2 Town, ⊗ of Lamar co., NW Alabama; pop. 1492.
3 Town, W Tolland co., N Connecticut, NE of Manchester; pop. 16,961; incorp. 1808; shipping center for surrounding agricultural area producing esp. sweet potatoes; manufactures silk, cotton, and woolen goods; includes city of Rockville (*q.v.*).
4 Town, ⊗ of Jennings co., SE Indiana; pop. 461.
5 City, ⊗ of Wilbarger co., N Texas, 45 m. WNW of Wichita Falls; pop. 12,141; oil wells and refineries; cotton gins and compress; manufactures cottonseed oil, flour and feed, mattresses.
6 City, S Brit. Columbia, Canada, 5 m. E of N end of Okanagan Lake; pop. 7822; distributing center for rich farming and fruitgrowing district.

Ver'non' (vĕr'nôN'). Commune, Eure dept., N France, on Seine river 17 m. ENE of Évreux; pop. 11,330; tourist resort; mineral springs; manufactures military equipment. Taken by king of France 1198; held by English 1419–49.

Ver'non Valley (vûr'nŭn). Urban community (unincorporated), Suffolk co., SE New York, on Long I. ENE of Huntington; pop. 5998.

Vernyi. See ALMA ATA.

Ve'ro Beach (vē'rō). City, ⊗ of Indian River co., E Florida, on Indian river 70 m. NNW of West Palm Beach; pop. 8849; fishing and bathing resort; citrus fruits. In World War II site of naval air base.

Verőcze. See VIROVITICA.

Verodunum. See VERDUN.

Ve'roi·a or **Ver'roi·a** (vâ'ryä); *Mod. Gr.* **Ve'roi·a** (vâ'ryä); *anc.* **Be·roe'a, Be·re'a** (bĕ·rē'á); *Turk.* **Ka'ra·fe'ri·eh'** (kä'rä·fĕ'rĭ·yĕ'). Town, Thessalonike dept., W cen. Macedonia, Greece, 40 m. W of Salonika; pop. 14,589. According to *Acts* xvii. 10, Paul and Silas preached here.

Ve'ro·la·nuo'va (vâ'rô·lä·nwô'vä). Commune, Brescia prov., Lombardy, N Italy, 16 m. SSW of Brescia; pop. 11,078.

Ve'ro·li (vâ'rô·lē). Commune, Frosinone prov., Latium, cen. Italy, 4 m. NE of Frosinone; pop. 18,258; 11th-cent. church; cathedral.

Ve·ro'na (vĕ·rō'na). **1** Borough, Essex co., NE New Jersey, 7 m. SSW of Paterson; pop. 13,782.
2 Borough, Allegheny co., SW Pennsylvania, on Allegheny river 10 m. ENE of Pittsburgh; pop. 4032; manufactures foundry and machine-shop products, glass, powder and dynamite.

Ve·ro'na (vĕ·rō'na; *Ital.* vå·rō'nä). **1** Province of Italy. See *Table* at ITALY.
2 Commune, ✳ of Verona prov., Venezia Euganea, NE Italy, on Adige river 92 m. E of Milan; pop. 153,708; city walls flanked by bastions and towers; fine city gates; notable buildings include the ancient Roman amphitheater (of end of 1st cent. A.D.), ab. 50 churches, including

the 14th-cent. Gothic cathedral with 12th-cent. Romanesque façade; 15th-cent. Loggia del Consiglio, 12th-cent. town hall, 19th-cent. municipal palace, 14th-cent. Gothic tombs of the Scaligeri (or della Scala) family, and the 14th-cent. Castelvecchio (now a museum); manufactures include textiles.

History: Came under Roman rule 89 B.C.; after fall of Roman Empire, captured by Goths; here Odoacer was defeated by Theodoric 489; captured 774 A.D. by Charlemagne; became independent republic 1107; under della Scala family 1260–1387, the Visconti family of Milan 1387–1405, Venice 1405–1797; passed to Austria under whom it gained great strategic importance as a member of the Mantua-Verona-Peschiera-Legnago Quadrilateral; Congress of Verona held here 1822; became part of kingdom of Italy 1866.

Ve·ró'ni·ca (vĕ·rŏn'ĭ·ká; *Span.* bâ·rō'nĕ·kä). Peak 19,342 ft. in Andes in Peru, 30 m. NW of Cuzco.

Ver·sailles' (vĕr·sālz'). **1** Subdivision of town of SPRAGUE, Connecticut.
2 Town, ⊗ of Ripley co., SE Indiana; pop. 1158.
3 City, ⊗ of Woodford co., E cen. Kentucky, 13 m. W of Lexington; pop. 4060; in bluegrass section.
4 City, ⊗ of Morgan co., cen. Missouri; pop. 2047.
5 Village, Darke co., W Ohio, 35 m. NNW of Dayton; pop. 2159; agriculture, stock raising.
6 Borough, Allegheny co., SW Pennsylvania, on Youghiogheny river 13 m. SE of Pittsburgh; pop. 2297.
7 (vĕr·sī'; vĕr·sī'; vĕr·sālz'; *Fr.* vĕr'sä'y') City, ✳ of Seine-et-Oise dept., N France, 10 m. WSW of Paris; pop. 73,839; fine cathedral and 17th-cent. church; famous palace built by Louis XIV served as royal palace until 1793, converted into national historical museum by Louis Philippe; beautiful fountains, parks, and gardens; Grand Trianon and Petit Trianon villas; hippodrome, military hospital, public library; considered one of handsomest towns in Europe, having been lavishly embellished by kings of France, particularly Louis XIV.

History: Built by French kings on site of hunting lodge of Louis XIII; famed royal residence; seat of court of Louis XIV; place where States-General met 1783; negotiations for peace treaty bet. U.S. and Great Britain ending American Revolution concluded here 1782 and preliminary treaty signed (final treaty signed at Paris 1783); treaty bet. France and Great Britain recognizing sovereignty and independence of U.S. signed 1783; German headquarters during Franco-Prussian War Sept. 1870–Mar. 1871; place where Wilhelm I was declared Emperor of Germany and where treaty bet. France and Germany ending Franco-Prussian War was signed 1871; seat of French government 1871–79; at end of World War I scene of signing of treaty bet. Allies and Germany 1919; treaty (Grand Trianon) bet. Allies and Hungary signed here June 4, 1920.

Versecz. See VRŠAC.

Ver'shetz (vĕr'shĕts). = VRŠAC.

Vert (vûrt) or **Verde** (vûrd), **Cape.** Promontory, the westernmost point of Africa, 17°30'W, on the coast of Senegal, West Africa, bet. the Senegal and Gambia rivers; site of the port of Dakar. Its W tip known as Cape Almadies.

Verte, Aiguille. See AIGUILLE VERTE.

Ver'u·lam (vĕr'û·lăm; vĕr'ŏo-). Village, E Natal, E Union of South Africa, pop. 1878; founded 1850.

Verulamium. See SAINT ALBANS.

Ver'viers' (vĕr'vyā'). Manufacturing commune, Liège prov., E Belgium, on the Vesdre river 13 m. E of Liège; pop. (1938 est.) 42,931; textile mills (wool and cotton), also metal and glass works.

Ver'vins' (vĕr'văN'). Town, Aisne dept., N France; pop. 2791; treaty May 2, 1598 bet. Philip II of Spain and Henry IV of France, ending religious wars.

Ves'dre (vâ'dr'); *Ger.* **We'ser** (vā'zēr). River ab. 45 m. long in Liège prov., E Belgium; flows W out of Germany into the Ourthe river S of Liège.

Vésinet, Le. See LE VÉSINET.

Vesle (vâl). River 90 m. long in France, flowing from NE of Châlons-sur-Marne past Reims into the Aisne river.

Vesontio. See BESANÇON.

Ve·soul' (vĕ·zōōl'); *Lat.* **Ves'u·lum** (vĕs'ủ·lŭm) *or* **Ve·su'li·um** (vĕ·sū'lĭ·ŭm). Commune, * of Haute-Saône dept., E France, 58 m. ENE of Dijon; pop. 11,926; agricultural trade center; manufactures millstones. Pillaged by Germans 1369; depopulated by plague 1586; citadel razed by Spanish 1595; annexed to France 1678; made capital of Haute-Saône dept. 1790; occupied by Germans 1870.

Ves'per Peak (vĕs'pēr). Mountain 6190 ft. in Snohomish co., NW cen. Washington.

Ves Spišská Nová. = SPIŠSKÁ NOVÁ VES.

Vest–Ag'der (vĕst'äg'dēr). County of Norway. See *Table* at NORWAY.

Ves'tal Peak (vĕs't'l). Mountain 13,853 ft. in San Juan co., SW Colorado.

Ves'ter·å'len (vĕs'tēr·ô'lĕn). Island group in the Norwegian Sea off NW Norway, N of the Lofoten; includes islands of Hinnöy, Langöy, and Andöy; pop. 29,130.

Vest Fjord (vĕst). Inlet of Norwegian Sea extending NNE for 95 m. bet. the Lofoten and the Norwegian mainland.

Vest'fold' (vĕst'fôl'). County of Norway. See *Table* at NORWAY.

Vest'man'na·ey'jar (vĕst'män'ä·ā'yär) *or* **West'man Islands** (wĕst'măn). Small island group S of Iceland; on one of the islands is the town of **Vestmannaeyjar**, pop. (1942) 3513; fisheries.

Vest'våg·öy' (vĕst'vôg·ủ'ü). Island in the Lofoten, NE of Moskenes, in the Norwegian Sea off NW coast of Norway; 159 sq. m.; pop. 10,528.

Vesulium *or* **Vesulum.** See VESOUL.

Vesuna. See PÉRIGUEUX.

Ve·su'vi·us (vĕ·sū'vĭ·ŭs); *Ital.* **Ve·su'vio** (vå·zōō'vyō). Volcano 3877 ft. on E side of Bay of Naples; the cone is half encircled on N side by **Mon'te Som'ma** (môn'tä sôm'mä), part of the wall of a large crater in which the present cone has formed; numerous destructive eruptions, esp. Aug. 24, 79 A.D. when Pompeii and Herculaneum were destroyed, Dec. 16, 1631, and in 1906 when height was greatly reduced.

Vesz'prém (vĕs'prām). City, W Hungary, N of Lake Balaton; pop. 15,666; coal mines; manufactures iron products; cathedral.

Vet (fĕt). River 130 m. long, N Orange Free State, Union of South Africa; flows NW into Vaal river.

Veta Pass, La. See LA VETA PASS.

Vet·lu'ga (vĕt·lōō'gȧ; *Russ.* vyĕt-). River ab. 500 m. long, cen. Soviet Russia, Europe; rises in E Vologda Region, flows S through Kostroma and Gorki Regions to join the Volga in SW Mari A.S.S.R. Important channel for lumber floated down it; navigable to **Vetluga** (pop. 6606) town in N Gorki Region.

Vetter. See VÄTTERN.

Vet'tis·foss' (vĕt'ĭs·fôs'). Waterfall 850 ft. in the Mörkedola river, a small stream in the Sogne Fjord region of W Norway.

Vet·to're, Mon'te (môn'tä vät·tô'rä). Mountain 8128 ft. in Sibillini Mts., SW Marches, cen. Italy; highest peak in Roman Apennines.

Vet'u·lo'ni·a (vĕt'ủ·lō'nĭ·ȧ). Ancient city of Etruria, one of twelve in the Etruscan confederation, site ab. 10 m. NW of Grosseto in SW Tuscany, cen. Italy; tombs, acropolis walls, Roman houses.

Ve'vay (vē'vĭ). Town, ⊗ of Switzerland co., SE Indiana; pop. 1503.

Ve·vey' (vẽ·vā'); *Ger.* **Vi'vis** (vē'vĭs); *anc.* **Vi·bis'cum** (vĭ·bĭs'kŭm; vī-). Commune, Vaud canton, W Switzerland, on NE shore of Lake of Geneva 11 m. ESE of Lausanne; pop. (1941) 12,598; tourist resort; 12th-cent. church, castle, town hall; manufactures machinery, chocolates, condensed milk, tobacco; trades in wine.

Vex'in' (vĕk'săN'). Ancient district of France, N of the Seine and the Oise, bounded on NW by Normandy; * Gisors; divided in 911, part (including Gisors) going to Normandy, and part remaining French as a dependency of Île-de-France; Norman part ceded to Philip Augustus by Richard Coeur de Lion 1196.

Ve'zen·berg (vā'zĕn·bĕrK). = *Wesenberg:* see RAKVERE.

Vé'zère' (vā'zâr'). River ab. 120 m. long in SW cen. France; rises in Corrèze dept., flows SW into Dordogne river.

Via Appia. See APPIAN WAY.

Via Aurelia. See AURELIAN WAY.

Via Cassia. See CASSIAN WAY.

Via'cha (byä'chä). Town, La Paz dept., W Bolivia, 18 m. SW of La Paz; pop. 2000; railroad junction; cement plant.

Via·da'na (vyä·dä'nä). Commune, Mantova prov., Lombardy, N Italy, on Po river 22 m. SW of Mantua; pop. 18,165.

Viadua. See ODER.

Via Flaminia. See FLAMINIAN WAY.

Via Latina. See LATIN WAY.

Via'na do Cas·te'lo (vyȧ'nȧ thōō kȧsh·tâ'lōō). 1 District of Portugal. See *Table* at PORTUGAL.
2 Commercial seaport, its *, NW Portugal, near Atlantic Ocean 42 m. N by W of Oporto; pop. 11,819.

Via Ostiensis. See OSTIAN WAY.

Via·reg'gio (vyä·räd'jō). Seaport, Lucca prov., Tuscany, cen. Italy, on Ligurian Sea 12 m. W by N of Lucca; pop. 35,594; seaside resort; monument to Shelley, whose body was cast ashore here.

Via Salaria. See SALARIAN WAY.

Viatka. Var. of VYATKA.

Via Valeria. See VALERIAN WAY.

Vibiscum. See VEVEY.

Vibo, Gulf of. See Gulf of SANT' EUFEMIA.

Vi'borg (vē'bôrg; *Dan.* -bôr). 1 County of Denmark. See *Table* at DENMARK.
2 City, its ⊗, N cen. Jutland Penin., Denmark; pop. (1945) 20,084; manufactures machinery, textiles, and tobacco products; Gothic cathedral founded 1130.
3 (*Angl.* vē'bôrg; *Russ.* vî'bērk) City, formerly in Finland since 1940 in SW Karelia, U.S.S.R. See VYBORG.

Vi'bo Va·len'tia (vē'bô vä·lĕn'tyä); *formerly* **Mon'te·le·o'ne di Ca·la'bri·a** (môn'tä·lå·ō'nä dĕ kä·lä'brē·ä); *anc.* **Hip·po'ni·um** (hĭ·pō'nĭ·ŭm). Commune, Catanzaro prov., Calabria, S Italy, 30 m. SW of Catanzaro; pop. 16,151; earthquakes 1783 and 1905.

Vi·cál'va·ro (bē·käl'vä·rô). Commune, Madrid prov., cen. Spain, E suburb of Madrid; pop. 21,182.

Vic'chio (vĕk'kyô). Commune, Firenze prov., Tuscany, cen. Italy, 15 m. NNE of Florence; pop. (1931) 12,080.

Vi·cen'te, Point (vĭ·sĕn'tē). Point on SW coast of Los Angeles co., SW California, W of Long Beach.

Vi·cen'te Ló'pez (bē·sän'tā lō'pās). City, Buenos Aires prov., E Argentina; pop. (est.) 95,770.

Vi·cen'za (vē·chĕn'tsä). 1 Province of Italy. See *Table* at ITALY.
2 *anc.* **Vi·cen'ti·a** (vī·sĕn'shĭ·ȧ). Commune, its *, Venezia Euganea, NE Italy, 40 m. W of Venice; pop. 69,379; numerous medieval remains; 12th-cent. cathedral with 15th-cent. façade, 13th-cent. churches of Santa Corona and San Lorenzo, 16th-cent. Basilica Palladiana, Loggia del Capitanio, and Teatro Olimpico, and palaces of 14th, 15th, and 16th cents.; fine campanile in Piazza dei Signori; nearby is noted pilgrimage church, the 15th-cent. Basilica di Monte Berico; manufactures silk goods, leather, earthenware, hats.

History: Founded c. 1st cent. B.C. by Ligurians; capital of Lombard duchy in early Middle Ages; gained independence 1164 and joined Lombard League; destroyed by Emperor Frederick II 1236; ruled by della Scala family of Verona 1314 ff., Visconti of Milan 1387 ff., Venetian Republic 1404 ff., Emperor Maximilian I

1509–16, Austria 1797 ff.; became part of kingdom of Italy 1866. Held by Axis powers throughout World War II; occupied by Allies Apr. 28–29, 1945.

Vich (bĕk); *anc.* **Au′sa** (ô′sȧ), *later* **Vi′cus Au′so·nen′-sis** (vī′kŭs ô′sŏ·nĕn′sĭs). Commune, Barcelona prov., NE Spain, 38 m. N by E of Barcelona; pop. 15,516; manufactures textiles, hats, paper; 11th-cent. cathedral.

Vi·cha′da (vǐ·chä′dä; *Span.* bĕ·chä′t͟hä). **1** River 335 m. long in cen. and E Colombia; flows ENE into Orinoco river on Venezuelan border.
2 Commissary of Colombia. See *Table* at COLOMBIA.

Vichegda. *Var.* of VYCHEGDA.

Vi·chu′ga (vǐ·chōō′gȧ; *Russ.* vyǐ-). Town, Ivanovo Region, Soviet Russia, Europe, on railroad SW of Kineshma; pop. ab. 33,000.

Vi′chy (vĭsh′ĭ; vē′shǐ; *Fr.* vē′shē′). Commune, Allier dept., cen. France, on Allier river 200 m. SSE of Paris; pop. 25,074; famous spa and health resort; many thermal alkaline springs celebrated since Roman times; Vichy water and salts exported in large quantities. Taken by Charles VII 1440; as result of French armistice with Germany 1940, made capital, July 2, of unoccupied France; seat of French government until complete occupation of France by Germany Nov. 1942.

Vicks′burg (vĭks′bûrg). **1** Village, Kalamazoo co., SW Michigan, 7 m. S of Kalamazoo; pop. 2224.
2 City, ⊗ of Warren co., W Mississippi, on Mississippi river 40 m. W of Jackson; pop. 29,130; chief river port of the state; center of cotton-growing section; ships cotton, lumber, and cattle. During Civil War besieged 1862–63; final siege operations Apr.–June 1863, captured July 4 by Union forces under Gen. Grant. See CHICKASAW BAYOU.

Vicksburg National Military Park. See UNITED STATES, *National Historical Parks.*

Vi′co E·quen′se (vē′kŏ ā·kwĕn′sȧ). Commune, Napoli prov., Campania, S Italy, on Bay of Naples 15 m. SSE of Naples; pop. 12,625; seaside resort; mineral baths.

Vi·ço′sa (vē·sô′zä). City, SE Minas Gerais state, E Brazil, 85 m. SE of Belo Horizonte; pop. 6424.

Vic′tor (vĭk′tēr). City, Teller co., cen. Colorado, 18 m. SW of Colorado Springs; pop. 434; founded c. 1892 as gold-mining town.

Vic·to′ri·a (vĭk·tôr′ĭ·ȧ; *Span.* bēk·tō′ryä). **1** County in Texas. See *Table* at TEXAS.
2 City, ⊗ of Victoria co., S Texas, 20 m. WNW of Matagorda Bay; pop. 33,047; settled as Spanish colony 1824; cotton industries; oil and gas wells; sand, gravel, clay.
3 Industrial town, Lunenburg co., S Virginia, 51 m. WSW of Petersburg; pop. 1737.
4 City, Entre Ríos prov., E Argentina, ab. 40 m. NE of Rosario; pop. (est.) 21,850.
5 River 400 m. long, NW Northern Territory, Australia; flows N and NW to Queen Channel; navigable for ab. 100 m.
6 State, SE Australia; 87,884 sq. m.; pop. (1933) 1,820,261, (1963 est.) 3,055,731; ✳ Melbourne. Separated on N from New South Wales by Murray river which forms almost entire boundary from its source in Australian Alps to point at 34°S where it crosses into South Australia. W and NW (Mallee dist.) parts sandy desert and lowland; cen. and E parts are highlands forming S end of Great Dividing Range (here known as Australian Alps). Highest part is Darg Plateau with Mt. Bogong 6509 ft. SW coastal region known as Gippsland. In cen. part of S coast is spacious Port Phillip Bay, harbor of Melbourne; on coast SE of it is Wilson's Promontory, most southerly point of Australia. Separated on S from Tasmania by Bass Strait. *Chief exports:* Wool, wheat and flour, butter and other dairy products, meats, hides and skins; mineral products, gold and coal. *Chief cities:* Melbourne, Geelong, Ballarat, Bendigo, and Warrnambool.
History: Discovered by Capt. Cook 1770, a few days before his arrival at Botany Bay to the N; Port Phillip Bay discovered 1802; first settled at Melbourne 1835 by immigrants from Tasmania; set off 1851 from New South Wales as separate colony; received many new settlers as result of discovery of gold in Ballarat region 1851; local self-government introduced 1853 and responsible government established 1855; joined confederation to form Commonwealth 1901.
7 Town, port, and seat of government of Labuan settlement, on Labuan I., NW Borneo; pop. 2022; has excellent harbor.
8 County, New Brunswick, Canada. See *Table* at NEW BRUNSWICK.
9 County, Nova Scotia, Canada. See *Table* at NOVA SCOTIA.
10 County, Ontario, Canada. See *Table* at ONTARIO.
11 City, ✳ of British Columbia, Canada, on SE Vancouver I. and at E end of Juan de Fuca Strait; pop. 51,331; has large harbor; trades in lumber, canned salmon, coal, rice, grains and has varied manufactures. Seat of Victoria Coll., Dominion Astrophysical Observatory, and a provincial normal school. Founded 1843; selected as capital 1866 when Vancouver I. united with British Columbia.
12 Town, Malleco prov., S cen. Chile, 110 m. SE of Concepción; pop. 9039.
13 *or* **Hong Kong** (hŏng′kŏng′). Seaport city, NW Hong Kong I.; ✳ of Hong Kong colony, China; pop. 674,962; urban area (including suburbs, island villages, and population afloat) ab. 1,000,000; extends along NW shore of island; has extensive wharves; Univ. of Hong Kong (estab. 1912); headquarters for administration of Southern District of New Territories.
14 Chief town, Gozo I., in Malta group; pop. ab. 6000.
15 Seaport town, SW Cameroun, Africa, on Bight of Biafra; port of Buea and chief trading town of former British Cameroons trust territory.
16 Seaport and chief town on Mahé I., Seychelles Is., Indian Ocean; ✳ of Seychelles Is.; pop. (1931) ab. 5000.
17 *or* **Fort Victoria.** Town, Southern Rhodesia, S Africa, 188 m. S of Salisbury; pop. 364; gold fields; nearby are the Zimbabwe ruins.

Victoria. For cities in Brazil see VITÓRIA; in Sicily, VITTORIA; also see CIUDAD VICTORIA.

Victoria, La. See LA VICTORIA.

Victoria, Lake. 1 *or* **Victoria Ny·an′za** (nǐ·ăn′zȧ; nǐ-). Large lake of E cen. Africa, second largest freshwater body in the world; area 26,828 sq. m.; S half in Tanganyika and N half in Uganda, borders on Kenya in NE; alt. ab. 3720 ft., ab. 250 m. long (N to S) and 200 m. wide; greatest known depth ab. 270 ft.; has indented coast line with deep gulfs, numerous islands; many tributaries (largest, Kagera) draining nearby uplands of East Africa, but chief source of water supply is rainfall; only outlet is Nile (*q.v.*). Discovered 1858 by J. H. Speke in search for source of Nile; further explored 1862 by Speke and J. A. Grant and 1863 by Sir Samuel Baker; circumnavigated by H. M. Stanley 1875; ownership divided 1890 by England and Germany on E and W line 1°S; entirely British after 1920 when Tanganyika became British mandate. Steamer service bet. chief ports (Kisumu, Entebbe, Bukoba, Mwanza).
2 Small lake in high Pamirs, Tadzhik S.S.R., Soviet Central Asia, on N border of Wakhan dist.; alt. 13,400 ft.; source of the Murghab.

Victoria, Mount. 1 Peak 10,016 ft. in W cen. Upper Burma at N end of Arakan Yoma and NE of Akyab.
2 Peak 11,355 ft. on the boundary bet. Alberta and British Columbia, SW Canada, behind Lake Louise.
3 Mountain 7484 ft., N cen. Vancouver I., British Columbia, Canada; highest point on the island.
4 *or* **Mount Tom′a·ni′vi** (tŏm′ȧ·nē′vē). Peak 4341 ft. in N cen. Viti Levu I., Fiji Is., SW Pacific Ocean; highest point in the archipelago.
5 Peak 13,240 ft., highest in the Owen Stanley Range, Territory of Papua, New Guinea, NE of Port Moresby.

Victoria de Durango. See DURANGO.

Vic·to′ria de las Tu′nas (bĕk·tō′ryä thǎ läs tōō′näs), *sometimes called* **Tunas.** Municipality and town, Oriente prov., E Cuba; pop. (town) 12,300; town on central railroad 100 m. NW of Santiago de Cuba.

Vic·to′ri·a Falls (vĭk·tōr′ĭ·à). **1** Former name of IGUASSÚ FALLS, Brazil.

2 Falls in the Zambezi river, at a place where river is 5580 ft. wide, on the boundary bet. Northern Rhodesia and Southern Rhodesia, S Africa, near the town of Livingstone; surpassed only by Niagara in grandeur; broken by islands on precipice edge into four parts; height varies from 350 to 400 ft. and volume varies with the seasons; water of falls drops into narrow chasm, hitting opp. wall 80 to 240 ft. above chasm floor. Railroad bridge (650 ft. long) crosses Zambezi just below falls. Surrounding land is Rhodesian public park. Falls discovered by Livingstone Nov. 17, 1855 who named them after Queen Victoria.

Victoria Fjord. Large fiord 140 m. long on the N coast of Greenland, W of Peary Land.

Victoria Island. 1 Third largest island 74,400 sq. m. of Arctic Archipelago, SW Franklin District, Northwest Territories, Canada; separated from mainland (Mackenzie District) by Dolphin and Union Strait, Coronation Gulf, and Dease Strait.

2 Island in Chonos Archipelago, in Pacific Ocean off SW coast of Chile.

Victoria Land, *formerly* **South Victoria Land.** Section of Antarctica on W shore of Ross Sea and Ross Shelf Ice, lat. 70°–78°S and long. 164°E; largely included in Ross Dependency (*q.v.*). Has high mountain ranges and peaks. In NW part is area designated as South Magnetic Pole Area, visited 1909 by Prof. T. W. E. David and Douglas Mawson, members of the Shackleton Expedition, who tentatively placed the South Magnetic Pole at 72°25′S lat. and 155°16′E long., at alt. of 7000 ft. More recent determination has shifted its probable location W to a point in George V Coast at ab. 70°S and 148°E, but according to scientists it cannot be exactly fixed because of variations due to several causes.

Victoria Nile. See NILE.

Victoria Nyanza. See Lake VICTORIA, Africa.

Victoria Peak. 1 See COCKSCOMB MOUNTAINS, British Honduras.

2 Hill above Victoria city, NW Hong Kong I., Hong Kong colony, SE China, highest point on island, 1825 ft.; has exceptional view of Hong Kong harbor; residential section for Europeans. Last point surrendered to Japanese by British in fall of Hong Kong Dec. 25, 1941.

Victoria Point. Cape at extreme S of Burma, ab. 10°N, W of the mouth of Pakchan river.

Victoria Quadrant. Formerly the quarter section of Antarctica (*q.v.*) bet. 90°E and 180°E; now chiefly Wilkes Land and Victoria Land (W part of Ross Dependency).

Victoria River. See VICTORIA river, Australia.

Victoria Strait. Channel bet. SE Victoria I. and King William I., off N Canada mainland, S Franklin District, Northwest Territories.

Vic·to′ri·a·ville (vĭk·tōr′ĭ·à·vĭl). Manufacturing town, Arthabaska co., S Quebec, Canada, 36 m. SE of Three Rivers; pop. 13,124; railroad junction; furniture factories; agricultural center. Incorporated 1890.

Victoria West. Town, cen. Cape Province, S Union of South Africa, 230 m. NW of Port Elizabeth; pop. 2292; sheep, Angora goats, and ostriches raised in vicinity.

Vic′tor·ville (vĭk′tẽr·vĭl). Township, San Bernardino co., SE California, N of San Bernardino; pop. (est.) 5000; site of U.S. Air Force base.

Vicus Ausonensis. See VICH.

Vicus Elbii. See VITERBO.

Vicus Julii. 1 See AIRE commune, Landes dept., SW France.

2 See GERMERSHEIM commune, Bavaria, Germany.

Vid (vĭt). River ab. 130 m. long in NW cen. Bulgaria; flows from the Balkan Mts. N into Danube river 8 m. above Nikopol.

Vi·da′lia (vī·dāl′yà). City, Toombs co., SE cen. Georgia, 76 m. W of Savannah; pop. 7569.

Vi·dal′ia (vī·dăl′yà). Town, ⊗ of Concordia parish, E cen. Louisiana; pop. 4313.

Vi′din (vī′dĭn); *anc.* **Bo·no′ni·a** (bô·nō′nĭ·à; -nōn′yà). City, Vrattsa dept., NW Bulgaria, on Danube river near Yugoslav border; pop. (1934) 18,465; trade center, with important fisheries and factories. On site of Roman town Bononia; seat of small independent state in 14th cent.; under Turks 1396 to 1807.

Vid′ze·me (vĭd′zĕ·mĕ). Province, N Latvia, U.S.S.R., a part of former Livonia; 8988 sq. m.; pop. (1938 est.) 801,547; ✱ Riga; drained by Gauya river and in SW traversed by lower Dvina; livestock raising, paper manufacture (at Cēsis).

Vied′ma (byäth′mä). Town, ✱ of Río Negro territory, S cen. Argentina, on the Río Negro ab. 19 m. above its mouth; pop. (est.) 6000.

Viedma, Lake. Lake 53 m. long in W Santa Cruz territory, S Argentina, S of Lake San Martín and N of Lake Argentino.

Viejo, El. See EL VIEJO.

Vi·en′na (vī·ĕn′à). **1** City, ⊗ of Dooly co., SW cen. Georgia, 40 m. NE of Albany; pop. 2099; became ⊗ 1839; pecans; shipping point for peaches.

2 City, ⊗ of Johnson co., S Illinois; pop. 1094.

Vi·en′na (vĕ·ĕn′à). **1** Town, ⊗ of Maries co., S cen. Missouri; pop. 536.

2 Town, Fairfax co., NE Virginia, NW of Alexandria; pop. 11,440.

3 City, Wood co., W West Virginia, on Ohio river 5 m. N of Parkersburg; pop. 9381; glass products, thread.

4 *Ger.* **Wien** (vēn). District of Austria. See *Table* at AUSTRIA.

5 *Ger.* **Wien** (vēn); *anc.* **Vin·dob′o·na** (vĭn·dŏb′ô·nà; vĭn′dô·bō′nà) *or* **Vin·dob′na** (vĭn·dŏb′nà). Manufacturing and commercial city, NE Austria, on Danube river; pop. (1939) 1,920,390; previous to 1918 capital of Austrian empire; capital of Vienna dist. 1934–38 and of Austrian republic 1918–38; 1938–45 capital of Nazi state of Ostmark (*q.v.*); Roman Catholic archiepiscopal see; leading Austrian commercial port; famous center of learning (esp., in recent years, in medicine and psychology) and culture; seat of university founded c. 1365; among its many noteworthy buildings, parks, institutions, etc., are St. Stephen's cathedral, the Hofburg (former seat of the Hapsburgs), Imperial Library, Imperial Opera, archiepiscopal palace, 14th-cent. Minorite church the Maria am Gestade church, the Volksgarten, the Liechtenstein Palace and gallery, the Gothic Votivkirche (church), the Rathaus which includes two municipal historical museums, the Palace of Justice, the Burg theater, the botanical gardens, the Prater (imperial park since the 16th cent.; now the principal public park), the arsenal, the Schloss (Castle) Schönbrunn, the Winter Palace, and the famous Museum of Industrial Arts; manufactures include machinery, tools, scientific instruments, textiles, pottery, chemicals, furniture, arms, leather, musical instruments, porcelain, beer, art objects.

History: Founded by Celts; became important Roman military station; taken by Avars and later (6th cent.) by Franks; to Magyars 907; to Leopold I of Babenberg 976; became seat of dukes of Babenberg; important trade center during Crusades; conquered and fortified by Ottokar of Bohemia 1251; taken by Rudolf of Hapsburg 1278, remaining the seat of the Hapsburgs until 1918; besieged by Turks 1529, 1683; refortified 1704; under Maria Theresa (reigned 1740–80) became important cultural center, attracting such musicians as Haydn, Mozart, Beethoven, and John and Richard Strauss; became capital of Austrian empire under Francis I; occupied by Napoleon 1805–09; seat of Congress of Vienna 1814–15;

scene of revolution 1848; fortifications replaced 1857 by the famous Ringstrasse boulevard; on abdication of Emperor Charles 1918 became capital of Austrian republic. Administrative center of German Austria after Mar. 13, 1938. Bombed by Allies during latter part of World War II; captured by Russians after 7-day battle, Apr. 6–13, 1945.
6 See VIENNE, France.
Vienne (vyĕn). **1** Navigable river 217 m. long in SW cen. France; rises in Corrèze dept., flows NW through Limoges and Chinon into Loire river.
2 Department of France: **Haute–Vienne** (ōt'vyĕn') and **Vienne**. See *Table* at FRANCE.
3 *anc.* **Vi·en'na** (vĕ·ĕn'à). Manufacturing city, Isère dept., SE France, on the Rhone 47 m. NW of Grenoble; pop. 25,436; 11th-cent. Romanesque-Gothic cathedral; Roman remains include a Corinthian temple of Augustus and Livia, water conduits, theater, and obelisk; manufactures woolens, silks, leather, paper, gloves, iron goods.
History: Anciently chief town of the Allobroges and rival of Lyons; capital of Burgundy 413–534 and 879–933; formerly capital of Viennois; council held here 1311–12 in which Knights Templars were suppressed.
Vien'nois' (vyĕ'nwä'). Ancient county of SE France, in Dauphiné; now in Drôme and Isère depts.; ≈ Vienne.
Vien'tiane' (vyăn'tyän'). City, ≈ of Laos, Indochina, on the Mekong; pop. ab. 100,000.
Vie'ques (byä'kås). **1** *or* **Crab Island** (krăb). Fertile island off E coast of Puerto Rico, 21 m. long by 6 m. wide; administratively a part of Puerto Rico, forming a municipality, pop. 7210. East half leased by U.S. Navy.
2 Chief town on Vieques I., on N coast; pop. 2487; raises sugar.
Viern'heim (fērn'hīm). Agricultural commune, Hesse, Germany, NE suburb of Mannheim; pop. 10,868.
Vier'sen (fēr'zĕn). City, W Germany, 18 m. W of Düsseldorf; pop. 32,169; 12th-cent. late-Gothic church; manufactures textiles, machinery.
Vier'straat (vēr'strät). Village, West Flanders prov., Belgium, S of Ieper (Ypres); monument to American soldiers who fought in the region Aug. 18–Sept. 4, 1918.
Vier Waldstätter, Die. See the Four FOREST CANTONS.
Vierwaldstättersee. See Lake of LUCERNE.
Vier'zon' (vyĕr'zôn'). A group of towns, Cher dept., cen. France, on the Cher river 18 m. NW of Bourges; includes **Vierzon–Vil'lages'** (-vē'läzh'), pop. (1931) 7325, and **Vierzon–Ville** (-vēl'), pop. 10,070; railroad junction; manufactures machinery, glass, porcelain.
Vie'ste (vyĕs'tä). Commune, Foggia prov., Apulia, SE Italy, 43 m. NE of Foggia; pop. 10,309; castle.
Vi·et'nam' *or* **Vi·et-Nam** *or* **Vi·et Nam** (vĕ·ĕt'năm' -năm'; vēt'-; vē'ĕt-). Literally "Southern Land."
1 Annam, Indochina—its ancient name.
2 State set up in Tonkin and N Annam, Indochina, 1945–46; recognized by the French Mar. 6, 1946; torn by outbreak of war Dec. 1946 as group under Communist domination set up rival government recognized only by Russia and her satellites; extended territory to include all of Tonkin, Annam, and Cochin China and became an associated state of French Union 1950, ≈ Saigon; remained at war until armistice signed in Geneva July 1954 establishing the (Communist-dominated) Democratic People's Republic of Vietnam, ≈ Hanoi, N of the 17th parallel and the Republic of Vietnam, ≈ Saigon, S of the 17th parallel. See *Map* at BURMA.
Vieux–Con'dé' (vyû'kôn'dā'). Commune, Nord dept., N France, N of Valenciennes; pop. (1931) 9529; customs.
Vieux Fort (vyû' fôr'). **1** Town at S end of St. Lucia I., Windward Is., West Indies; first sugar works on the island established here 1765.
2 Point, S tip of Basse-Terre, Guadeloupe I., French West Indies.
Vi'ga (vē'gä). Municipality, N cen. Catanduanes subprov., Albay, Phil. Is., ab. 3 m. from coast; pop. 11,232.

Vi'gan (vē'gän). Municipality, ≈ of Ilocos Sur prov., Luzon, Phil. Is., just N of the mouth of the Abra; pop. 20,939; the most important town of N Luzon; its port is Pandan. Founded by Juan de Salcedo 1572; seized by Japanese Dec. 10, 1941.
Vi·ge'va·no (vĕ·jâ'vä·nō). Manufacturing commune, Pavia prov., Lombardy, N Italy, near Ticino river 18 m. NW of Pavia; pop. 38,039; 10th-cent. cathedral.
Vi·gi'a (vĕ·zhē'à). City, E Pará state, N Brazil, at the mouth of Pará river on E bank; pop. 6163.
Vigne'male', Pic de (pēk' dĕ vēn'y'·mȧl'). Peak 10,820 ft. in the Pyrenees Mts., in S France; highest peak in the French Pyrenees.
Vi'go. 1 (vē'gō; vī'gō) County in Indiana. See *Table* at INDIANA.
2 (vē'gō; *Span.* bē'gŏ) Seaport, Pontevedra prov., NW Spain, on the **Estuary of Vigo**, an inlet of Atlantic Ocean 17 m. S by W of Pontevedra; pop. (1941 est.) 125,262; manufactures lumber, leather, paper, petroleum, flour, chocolates, soap, brandy, sugar, machinery, tools; tunny and sardine fisheries. Under attack by Drake 1585, 1589; scene of French and Spanish naval defeat by English and Dutch 1702.
Vi·gon'za (vĕ·gŏn'tsä). Commune, Padova prov., Venezia Euganea, NE Italy, NE of Padua; pop. 10,100.
Vii'pu·ri (vē'pŏŏ·rĭ). **1** Department of Finland. See *Table* at FINLAND.
2 City, formerly in Finland, since 1940 in SW Karelia, U.S.S.R. See VYBORG.
Vi'ja·ya·na'gar (vĭj'à·yà·nŭg'ẽr) *or* **Bi'ja·na'gar** (bĭj'à·nŭg'ẽr). **1** Hindu kingdom in S India S of the Kistna, established 1336 by two brothers of the Kanarese race; for more than two centuries formed bulwark of Hindu peoples against Mohammedan raiders from the N; was an important center of Brahman culture and Dravidian art. Finally overthrown at Talikota 1565 by confederate (Bijapur, Ahmadnagar, and Golconda) of Deccan Moslem sultans.
2 City, its ≈, destroyed 1565; its ruins now at modern Hampi on S bank of the Tungabhadra, SW Andhra Pradesh, Indian Union, ab. 30 m. WNW of Bellary.
Vi·jo'së (vĕ·yō'sĕ); *also* **Vi·o'sa** (vĕ·ō'sà), **Vo·yu'tsa** (vȯ·yōō'tsä). River ab. 130 m. long, NW Greece and S Albania; rises in Pindus Mts., Greece, flows NW across Albania into Adriatic Sea 14 m. N of Vlona.
Vík (vēk). Hamlet on most southerly point of Iceland, ab. 63°25'; loran station.
Vik'na (vĭk'nä). Small island in the Norwegian Sea off W cen. coast of Norway; ab. lat. 64°46'N.
Vi'la (vē'là). **1** Seaport on Vila harbor, SW Efate I., New Hebrides Is., SW Pacific Ocean; ≈ of New Hebrides; pop. (1938 est.) 1200.
2 Village, SE coast of Kolombangara I., on Kula Gulf, cen. Solomon Is., W Pacific; in World War II a Japanese base, evacuated Oct. 1943.
Vi'la de Jo·ão' Be'lo (vē'là thĕ zhwouɴ' vä'lŏŏ). Seaport town at the mouth of the Limpopo river, S Mozambique, SE Africa; pop. (1935 est.) 4000.
Vilafro, Lake. See VILLAFRO.
Vi'laine' (vē'lĕn'). Navigable river ab. 140 m. long in NW France; rises in Mayenne dept., flows W to Rennes, and turns SW through Morbihan dept. into the Bay of Biscay.
Vi'la No'va de Por·ti·mão' (vē'là nŏ'vȧ thĕ pŏŏr·tĕ·mouɴ'). Commune, Faro dist. S Portugal, near Atlantic Ocean 24 m. WNW of Faro; pop. 14,712; fisheries; fish canneries, esp. for tuna, sardines.
Vila Re·al' (rĕ·äl'). **1** District of Portugal. See *Table* at PORTUGAL.
2 *sometimes spelled* **Vila Ri·al'** (rĕ·äl'). Commune, its ≈, N Portugal, 45 m. ENE of Oporto; pop. 6602; ≈ of Trás-os-Montes e Alto Douro prov.; episcopal see.
Vi'las (vī'lǎs). County in Wisconsin. See *Table* at WISCONSIN.
Vil'ca·no'ta Knot (bēl'kä·nō'tä). Mountain mass,

highest point ab. 18,000 ft., in the Andes Mts., in S Peru NW of Lake Titicaca; junction point of ranges entering Peru from Bolivia and Chile.

Vild′mo′se (vĭl′mō′sĕ). Swampy area in N Jutland Penin., Denmark, N of Lim Fjord.

Vi·lei′ka (vĭ·lā′kȧ; *Russ.* vyī-); *Pol.* **Wi·lej′ka** (vĕ-lā′kä). Town, Molodechno Region, NW White Russia, U.S.S.R., 50 m. NW of Minsk; pop. 5595.

Vilich. See BEUEL.

Viliya. See NERIS.

Vil′jan·di (vĭl′yȧn·dĭ). = VILYANDI.

Vil′ka·vish′kis (vĭl′kä·vĭsh′kĭs). 1 District of Lithuania. See *Table* at LITHUANIA.
2 Town, its *, SW Lithuania, 35 m. SW of Kaunas; pop. (1938 est.) 8699.

Vil·kits′ki Strait (vĭl·kĭts′kĭ; *Russ.* vyĭl·kēts′kĭ). Channel on N coast of Taimyr Penin., Taimyr National District, Soviet Russia, Asia; separates Bolshevik I. of the Severnaya Zemlya Is. from mainland and connects Laptev and Kara Seas.

Vilkomir. See UKMERGE.

Vil′la A·cu′ña (bē′yä ä-kōō′nyä). Town, NE Coahuila state, NE Mexico, on the Rio Grande opp. Del Rio, Texas; pop. 5607.

Villa A′le·ma′na (ä′lä·mä′nä). Town, Valparaíso prov., cen. Chile, just E of Valparaíso; pop. 5615.

Vil′la Bel′la (bē′yä vā′yä). Frontier town at confluence of the Beni and Mamoré rivers, El Beni dept., N Bolivia; customs post and trading center.

Villa Bens. See CABO YUBI.

Vil′la·car·ril′lo (bē′[l]yä·kär·rē′[l]yȯ). Commune, Jaén prov., S Spain, 41 m. NE of Jaén; pop. 18,234; produces oil, wine, vegetables, woolens.

Villa Cecilia. See CIUDAD MADERO.

Vil′lach (fĭl′äк); *Slovenian* **Be′ljak** (bĕ′lyäk). City, Carinthia prov., Austria, on Drau river 21 m. W of Klagenfurt; pop. (1939) 26,094; tourist resort; manufactures iron, leather, lumber, beer; radioactive thermal springs nearby.

Vil′la Cis·ne′ros (bē′lyä thĕz·nā′rȯs; bē′yä sĕz-). Seaport on Río de Oro Bay, SW cen. coast of Río de Oro, Spanish Sahara, NW Africa; * of Spanish Sahara; pop. ab. 1000; military post; airport.

Villa Concepción. See CONCEPCIÓN, Paraguay.

Vil′la Cons′ti·tu·ción′ (bē′yä [bē′zhä] kȯns′tĕ·tōō-syôn′); *also* **Constitución.** Port, Santa Fe prov., E cen. Argentina, on Paraná river 23 m. SE of Rosario.

Vil′la·cou′blay′ (vē′lä′kōō′blä′). Village 4 m. E of Versailles, Seine-et-Oise dept., N France; airport.

Vil′la de Cu′ra (bē′yä thä kōō′rä) *or* **Cura.** Town, Aragua state, N Venezuela, 50 m. SW of Caracas; pop. (1941 est.) 8208.

Vil′la Del·ga′do (bē′yä thĕl·gä′thȯ). Town, San Salvador dept., SW cen. El Salvador; pop. (1942 est.) 6579.

Villa del Pilar. See PILAR.

Vil′la Do·lo′res (bē′yä [bē′zhä] thȯ·lō′räs). Town, W Córdoba prov., N cen. Argentina, 75 m. SW of Córdoba; pop. (est.) 13,800; resort.

Vil′la·fran′ca de los Bar′ros (bē′[l]yä·fräng′kä thä lȯz vär′rȯs). Commune, Badajoz prov., SW Spain, 37 m. SE of Badajoz; pop. 15,360.

Vil′la·fran′ca di Ve·ro′na (vēl′lä·fräng′kä dē vä-rō′nä). Commune, Verona prov., Venezia Euganea, NE Italy, 10 m. SW of Verona; pop. 14,479; treaty bet. Austria and France signed here July 11, 1859.

Vil·la′fro, Lake (bē·yä′frȯ); *also* **Vi·la′fro** (bē·lä′frȯ). Lake in N Arequipa dept., S Peru; regarded as remotest source of Amazon river through the Apurímac.

Vil′la Fron·te′ra (bē′yä frȯn·tā′rä). Town, Coahuila state, NE Mexico; pop. 6035.

Vil′la·gar·cí′a de A·ro′sa (bē′lyä·gär·thē′ä [bē′yä·gär-sē′ä] thä ä·rō′sä). Seaport, Pontevedra prov., NW Spain, on Atlantic Ocean 13 m. NNW of Pontevedra; pop. 23,705; flour, chocolate, soap, brick, tile, nails.

Village, The. See THE VILLAGE.

Vil·la′gio Du′ca de′gli A·bruz′zi (vĕl·lä′jŏ dōō′kä däl′yĕ ä·brōōt′tsĕ). Town, S Somalia, E Africa; ab. 50 m. N of Mogadishu.

Vil′la Giu′sti (vĕl′lä jōōs′tē). Villa near Padua, Padova prov., Venezia Euganea, NE Italy, where armistice bet. Italy and Austria-Hungary was signed Nov. 4, 1918.

Vil′la Grove (vĭl′ȧ). City, Douglas co., E cen. Illinois, 20 m. S of Champaign; pop. 2308.

Vil′la·guay′ (bē′yä-gwī′; bē′zhä-). Town, Entre Ríos prov., E Argentina, 90 m. E of Paraná; pop. (est.) 14,108.

Vil′la Hayes (bē′yä ĭs′; hāz′). Town, * of Presidente Hayes dept., W cen. Paraguay, on right bank of the Paraguay river 9 m. N of Asunción; pop. ab. 4500; named for Rutherford B. Hayes, president of the U.S. who arbitrated Argentina-Paraguay boundary.

Vil′la·her·mo′sa (bē′yä-ĕr·mō′sä); *formerly* **San Juan Bau·tis′ta** (säng hwäm′ bou·tēs′tä). City, SE Mexico, * of Tabasco state, on the Grijalva river; pop. 25,114; distributing center for tobacco, coffee, sugar, cacao, bananas, and rubber, produced in vicinity.

Vil′la·jo·yo′sa (bē′[l]yä·hȯ·yō′sä). Seaport town and commune, Alicante prov., SE Spain, 20 m. NE of Alicante; pop. of commune (1930) 8715.

Vil·lal′ba. 1 (bē·yäl′vä) Municipality (pop. 16,239) and town (pop. 1892), S cen. Puerto Rico; town is in hilly region 9 m. NE of Ponce.
2 (bē·[l]yäl′vä) Commune, Lugo prov., NW Spain, 16 m. NNW of Lugo; pop. 17,935; textiles.

Vil′la Ma·rí′a (bē′yä [bē′zhä] mä·rē′ä). City, cen. Córdoba prov., N cen. Argentina, 343 m. NW of Buenos Aires; pop. (est.) 32,158.

Vil′la Mer·ce′des (bē′yä [bē′zhä] mĕr·sā′thȧs). = MERCEDES.

Vil′la Mon′tes (bē′yä môn′tȧs). Town on Pilcomayo river, Tarija dept., S Bolivia; Bolivian military headquarters for El Chaco.

Vil′la·no′va (vĭl′ȧ·nō′vȧ). Locality, Delaware co., SE Pennsylvania, ab. 6 m. W of Philadelphia; pop. (est.) 6000. Villanova Univ. (1842; coed.).

Vil′la·nue′va de Cór′do·ba (bē′[l]yä·nwä′vä thä kȯr′thȯ·vä). Commune, Córdoba prov., S Spain, 31 m. NNE of Córdoba; pop. 16,037; soap, flour, woolens.

Villanueva del Ar′zo·bis′po (thĕl är′thȯ·vēs′pȯ är′sȯ-). Commune, Jaén prov., S Spain, 47 m. NE of Jaén; pop. 14,739; produces wine, oil, flax; manufactures soap; stock raising.

Villanueva y Gel·trú′ (ē hĕl·trōō′). Commune, Barcelona prov., NE Spain, on Mediterranean 26 m. WSW of Barcelona; pop. 17,091; manufactures textiles, flour, preserves, alimentary pastes, iron pipe.

Vil′lány (vĭl′län·y′). Town, S Hungary, near Yugoslav border SSE of Pécs. pop. 2239; produces wine.

Vil′la O′bre·gón′ (bē′yä ō′vrä·gôn′). Town, Federal District, cen. Mexico; pop. 9121.

Villa O·li′va (ȯ·lē′vä). Town, Neembucú dept., SW corner of Paraguay, on the Paraguay river 55 m. S of Asunción; pop. ab. 3900.

Villa Orotava. See LA OROTAVA.

Vil′la Park (vĭl′ȧ). Village, Du Page co., NE Illinois, 25 m. W of Chicago; pop. 20,391.

Vil′lard′–Bon′not′ (vē′lär′bȯ′nō′). Commune, Isère dept., SE France, on the Isère; pop. (1931) 5654.

Vil′la·re·al′ (bē′yär·rĕ·äl′). Municipality, SW Samar, Phil. Is., on S shore of **Villareal Bay** (ab. 12 m. wide and long) 13 m. S of Catbalogan; pop. 13,807.

Vil′la Ric′a (vĭl′ȧ rĭk′ȧ). City, Carroll and Douglas cos., W Georgia, 30 m. W of Atlanta; pop. 3450; gold discovered here 1826; incorp. 1830; cottonseed-oil mill and cotton gin.

Villa Rica de Vera Cruz. See VERACRUZ.

Vil′la·ro′sa (vĕl′lä·rō′zä). Commune, Enna prov., cen. Sicily, just WNW of Enna; pop. (1931) 9772.

Vil′lar·re·al′ (bē′[l]yär·rĕ·äl′). Commune, Castellón de la Plana prov., E Spain, 7 m. SSW of Castellón de la Plana; pop. 20,025; manufactures liquors, paper.

Vil'lar·ri'ca. 1 (bē'yär·rē'kä; bē'zhär-). Volcanic peak 9314 ft. in S cen. Chile, near Argentina border and bet. provinces of Cautín and Valdivia.
2 (bē'yär·rē'kä) City, * of Guairá dept., S cen. Paraguay, 70 m. SE of Asunción; pop. ab. 31,000; founded 1570; has sugar refineries, distilleries, sawmills, flour mills, brick and tile works; seat of a national college.

Vil'lar·ro·ble'do (bē'[l]yär·rô·vlä'tฎô). Commune, Albacete prov., SE Spain, 42 m. WNW of Albacete; pop. 20,362; iron products, earthenware.

Villas, Las. See LAS VILLAS.

Vil'la San Gio·van'ni (vēl'lä sän' jô·vän'nê). Commune, Reggio di Calabria prov., Calabria, S Italy, on Strait of Messina 10 m. N of Reggio di Calabria; pop. 14,934.

Vil·la'sis (bê·yä'sês). Municipality, SE Pangasinan prov., Luzon, Phil. Is., near right bank of Agno river 25 m. ESE of Lingayen; pop. 18,452.

Vil'la·vi·cen'cio. 1 (bē'yä·vê·sän'syô; bē'zhä-) Town, NW Mendoza prov., W Argentina, 28 m. N of Mendoza; altitude 5900 ft.; curative waters; resort.
2 (bē'yä·vê·sän'syô) Town, cen. Colombia, on Meta river S of Bogotá; * of Meta intendancy; pop. 6074.

Vil'la·vi·cio'sa (bē'lyä·vê·thyô'sä; bē'yä·vê·syô'sä). Commune, Oviedo prov., NW Spain, on inlet of Bay of Biscay 21 m. ENE of Oviedo; pop. 22,029; agricultural produce; fisheries; jet mines; manufactures paper.

Ville'franche' (vēl'fränsh'). **1** Seaport, Alpes-Maritimes dept., SE France, on coast E of Nice; pop. 4071; resort.
2 *sometimes* **Villefranche-sur-Saône'** (-sür·sōn'). Commune, Rhône dept., E cen. France, on Saône river 16 m. NNW of Lyons; pop. 18,871; manufactures textiles, machinery; trades in wine.

Villefranche-de-Rou·er'gue' (-dĕ·rwĕrg'). Commune, Aveyron dept., S France, ab. 26 m. W of Rodez; pop. (1931) 7908; 13th–16th cent. church, 15th–16th cent. Carthusian monastery. Founded c. 1252.

Ville'juif' (vēl'zhü·ēf'). Commune, Seine dept., N France, S suburb of Paris; pop. 27,540; glassworks.

Ville Ma'rie' (vïl' mà'rē'). Village, ⊗ of Timiskaming co., SW Quebec, Canada, on E shore of Lake Timiskaming ab. 72 m. N of North Bay, Ontario; pop. 1316.

Ville–Marie de Montréal. See MONTREAL.

Ville'mom'ble (vēl'môɴ'bl'). Commune, Seine dept., N France, ENE suburb of Paris; pop. (1931) 17,199.

Vil·le'na (bê·[l]yä'nä). Commune, Alicante prov., SE Spain, 26 m. NW of Alicante; pop. 19,065; produces wine, oil, fruits; manufactures liquors, flour, soap.

Ville'nave'–d'Or'non' (vēl'nàv'dôr'nôɴ'). Commune, Gironde dept., SW France, just S of Bordeaux in the Graves dist.; pop. (1931) 6215; wine (Château Carbonnieux).

Ville'neuve'–le–Roi (vēl'nûv'lē·rwä') . Commune, Seine-et-Oise dept., N France, SSE suburb of Paris; pop. (1931) 13,747.

Villeneuve–Saint–Georges (-săn'zhôrzh'). Commune, Seine-et-Oise dept., N France, on the Seine 7 m. SSE of Paris; pop. 21,237; shipbuilding.

Villeneuve–sur–Lot (-sür·lôt'); *sometimes* **Villeneuve–d'A'gen'** (-dä'zhăɴ'); *early medieval* **Ga'jac'** (gà'zhàk') . Commune, Lot-et-Garonne dept., SW France, on Lot river 13 m. N of Agen; pop. 12,665; manufactures paper, cloth, copper goods, table linen.

Ville'nour' (vēl'nŏŏr'). Commune, SE India, suburb of Pondicherry; pop. (1941) 25,751.

Ville Platte (vēl' plăt'). Town, ⊗ of Evangeline parish, S cen. Louisiana, 35 m. NNW of Lafayette; pop. 7512.

Vil'lers'–Cot'te·rêts' (vē'lâr'kô'trē'). Town, Aisne dept., N France, 14 m. SW of Soissons; pop. 3512; birthplace of Alexandre Dumas père; forest in vicinity was a battlefield in World War I; captured by Germans Aug. 1914; severe fighting June–July 1918 when it was the scene July 18 of the opening action of the great Allied offensive.

Ville'rupt' (vēl'rüp'). Industrial commune, Meurthe-et-Moselle dept., NE France, on Alzette river on Luxembourg border 36 m. N of Metz; pop. (1931) 11,005; coal mines; steel mills; iron foundries.

Vil·le'ta (vě·yä'tä). Town, Central dept., S Paraguay, S of Asunción; pop. ab. 12,600.

Ville'ur'banne' (vēl'ür'bàn'). Industrial commune, Rhône dept., E cen. France, E suburb of Lyons; pop. 81,322; chemicals, bronze goods, distillery products.

Vil'liers·dorp (vïl'yĕrz·dôrp). Town, SW Cape Province, S Union of South Africa, 50 m. E of Cape Town; pop. 1271.

Vil'ling·en (fïl'ïng·ĕn). Manufacturing city, Baden-Württemberg, W Germany, 30 m. ENE of Freiburg; pop. 13,982; airport; manufactures clocks, radios, meters, furniture, cutlery, electrical goods.

Vil·lis'ca (vĭ·lïs'kà). City, Montgomery co., SW Iowa, 53 m. SE of Council Bluffs; pop. 1690.

Villuercas, Las. See LAS VILLUERCAS.

Vil'lu·pu'ram (vïl'ú·pŏŏr'ám). Town, NE Madras state, SE Indian Union, 92 m. SSW of Madras; pop. 20,127.

Vilna, Vilnius, Vilno. See VILNYUS.
Vil'ny·us *or* **Vil'ni·us** (vĭl'nĭ·ús; *Lithuanian* -ŏŏs); *Pol.* **Wil'no** (vïl'nô; *Pol.* vēl'nô); *Russ.* **Vil'na** (vĭl'nà; *Russ.* vyēl'y'·nà) *or* **Vil'no** (vïl'nô; *Russ.* vyēl'y'·nú); *Ger.* **Wil'na** (vïl'nä). Commercial and administrative city, * of Lithuania and of former Wilno dept., Poland, in SE Lithuania 57 m. ESE of Kaunas; pop. (1938–39 est.) 208,770; Lithuanian and Polish commercial and cultural center; seat of Roman Catholic and Orthodox archbishoprics and of head of Polish Mohammedan Church; university (founded 1578; closed 1832; reopened 1919); important railroad junction; manufactures lumber, leather, foodstuffs, chemicals, matches, paper. Founded in 10th cent.; in 1323 became capital of principality, later kingdom, of Lithuania; made capital of Russian administrative district 1795; captured by Germans 1915; occupied by Russians 1919 and by Poles 1919 and 1920. After 1920 its status was in dispute; its occupation by Polish forces in that year was in direct opposition to the League of Nations, but in 1923 Poland was confirmed in her possession. Occupied by Russians 1939 and by Germans June 1941; retaken by Russian armies July 13, 1944 and restored to Lithuania and made capital in place of Kaunas.

Vilp'pu·la (vïlp'pŏŏ·là). Town, SW Finland, in Häme dept., on railroad 45 m. NNE of Tampere; pop. 4699.

Vil'vorde' (vēl'vôrd'). Manufacturing commune, Brabant prov., cen. Belgium, on Senne river just N of Brussels; pop. (1938 est.) 26,110.

Vil'yan·di (vïl'yàn·dĭ). **1** Province of Estonia. See *Table* at ESTONIA.
2 *Ger.* **Fel·lin'** (fĕ·lēn'). Town, its *, S cen. Estonia, 42 m. E of Pärnu; pop. (1937) 12,629.

Vi·lyui' (vyĭ·lū'ĭ). River ab. 1500 m. long in W Yakutsk Republic, Soviet Russia, Asia; rises in E Evenki National District, flows E into Lena river; as chief tributary on the W, it enters the Lena ab. 200 m. below Yakutsk; navigable for 900 m.

Vi·lyu'isk (vyĭ·lū'ĭsk). Town, W cen. Yakutsk Republic, Soviet Russia, Asia, on S bank of Vilyui river, 285 m. NW of Yakutsk on connecting highway; pop. 630.

Vilyuisk Range. Mountain range, W Yakutsk Republic, Soviet Russia, Asia, W of Lena river and serving as watershed bet. Olenek and tributaries and the Vilyui tributaries; highest point ab. 3500 ft.

Vi·mei'ro (vê·mā'ê·rŏŏ). Village, Lisboa dist., W Portugal, near Atlantic Ocean 32 m. N by W of Lisbon; pop. 781; famous victory Aug. 21, 1808 (Peninsular War) of Wellington over French under Junot.

Vi·mer·ca'te (vê·mär·kä'tā). Commune, Milano prov., Lombardy, N Italy, 14 m. NE of Milan; pop. 11,776.

Vim'i·nal (vïm'ĭ·n'l). One of the seven hills of Rome. See SEVEN HILLS.

Vi'mou'tiers' (vē'mōō'tyä'). Town, Orne dept., NW France, NE of Argentan; pop. 2071; center for Camembert cheese, first made in village 3 m. SW (see CAMEMBERT).

Vi'my Ridge (vĭm'ĭ; vē'mĭ; *Fr.* vē'mē'). Ridge near Vimy commune, Pas-de-Calais dept., N France, 10 m. N of Arras; captured by Canadians Apr. 9–10, 1917.

Vi'ña del Mar (bē'nyä thĕl mär'). City and seaside resort, a residential suburb 6 m. E of Valparaíso, Chile; pop. 65,916; has casinos, racecourse, etc.

Vi'nai'gre, Mont (môn' vē'nâ'gr'). Mountain, Var dept., S France; highest point 2020 ft. in the Estérel.

Vi·ña'les (bě·nyä'läs). Municipality, Pinar del Río prov., W Cuba, 15 m. N of Pinar del Río; pop. 15,460.

Vi'nal·ha'ven (vī'n'l·hā'vĕn). **1** Island at mouth of Penobscot Bay off S cen. Maine coast, part of Knox co. **2** Town on S end of Vinalhaven I.; pop. 1273; summer resort and fishing center; granite quarries nearby.

Vin·cennes'. **1** (vĭn·sĕnz'; *esp. attributively*, vĭn'sĕnz) City, ⊗ of Knox co., SW Indiana on Wabash river 55 m. S of Terre Haute; pop. 18,046; in agricultural and coalmining area; manufactures steel products, glass, farm implements, buttons, flour. Oldest town in Indiana; on site of a French mission; fortified c. 1732 by François Marie Bissot, Sieur de Vincennes; town received present name c. 1736; remained French to 1763, when it was ceded to Great Britain; seized by George Rogers Clark 1779; capital of Indiana Territory 1800–13 (see NORTHWEST TERRITORY). Has memorial to George Rogers Clark, established by Congress and dedicated Feb. 25, 1929. **2** (vĭn·sĕnz'; vĭn'sĕnz; *Fr.* văn'sĕn') Manufacturing commune, Seine dept., N France, 5 m. E of Paris; pop. 48,967; ancient castle, once residence of French kings, later a state prison, and now an arsenal; beautiful park (**Bois de Vin'cennes'** [bwäd' văn'sĕn']); military school, hospital; hardware, chemicals, pharmaceuticals.

Vin'ces (bēn'sâs). City, Los Ríos prov., W cen. Ecuador, just N of Guayaquil; pop. (1944 est.) 21,860.

Vin'dau (vĭn'dou). = *Windau:* see VENTSPILS seaport.

Vindava. See VENTA.

Vin'del (vĭn'dĕl). River ab. 225 m. long in Västerbotten prov., N Sweden; flows SE into Ume river.

Vin·de·li·ci·a (vĭn'dě·lĭsh'ĭ·à; -lĭsh'à). Ancient Roman province in cen. Europe S of the Danube river, including modern S Baden, Württemberg, and Bavaria, Germany; later called **Rae'ti·a Se·cun'da** (rē'shĭ·à [-shà] sě·kŭn'dà).

Vin'dhya Mountains (vĭnd'hyà). Mountain range extending ENE across India from Gujerat to the Ganges valley near Benares, dividing the Ganges basin from the Deccan; greatest elevation bet. 4500 and 5000 ft. N of and parallel with the Narbada river.

Vin'dhya Pra·desh' (vĭnd'hyà prà·dāsh'). Former state of the Indian Union, in NE cen. India between Uttar Pradesh and Madhya Pradesh; merged 1956 in reorganized Madhya Pradesh.

Vindobona or **Vindobna.** See VIENNA.

Vin'e·gar Hill (vĭn'ě·gẽr). Hill 398 ft., co. Wexford, SE Eire, E of Enniscorthy on the Slaney river; scene of defeat of Irish rebels by General Lake June 21, 1798.

Vine'land (vīn'lănd). **1** City, Cumberland co., SW New Jersey, 11 m. ENE of Bridgeton; pop. 37,685; settled 1861; business center for S New Jersey; manufactures glassware, clothing, chemicals. Vineland Training School (1888). **2** See VINLAND.

Vineta. See JULIN.

Vine'yard Haven (vĭn'yērd). Town, N Martha's Vineyard, SE Massachusetts, on W shore of **Vineyard Haven Harbor**, inlet of Nantucket Sound; summer resort. See TISBURY.

Vineyard Sound. Body of water lying SE of Elizabeth Is. and NW of Martha's Vineyard, SE Massachusetts; connects with Nantucket Sound on the NE and the Atlantic Ocean on the SW.

Vinh (vĭn'y'). Town near coast, N Annam, N Vietnam, 190 m. NW by N of Hue; pop. 20,000; important market for products of Laos, coming by highway from Luangprabang.

Vinh'long' (vĭn'y'·lông'). Town, cen. Cochin China, S Vietnam, on right bank of the Mekong in the delta 65 m. SW of Saigon; produces much rice.

Vi·ni'ta (vĭ·nē'tà). City, ⊗ of Craig co., NE Oklahoma; pop. 6027; oil wells; machine shops; meat packing.

Vin'kov·ci (vēng'kŏv·tsē). Town, E Croatia federated republic, N Yugoslavia, ab. 85 m. NW of Belgrade; pop. 13,266.

Vin'land (vĭn'lănd); *also* **Wine'land** (wīn'-) *or* **Vine'land** (vīn'-). A portion of the coast of North America visited and so called by Norse voyagers, c. 1000 A.D., according to whose accounts it was well wooded and produced agreeable fruits, esp. grapes; has been variously located from Labrador to New Jersey.

Vin'ni·tsa (vĭn'ĭt·sà; *Russ.* vyēn'nyĭ·tsà). **1** Region, W cen. Ukraine, U.S.S.R., N of Dniester river. **2** City, its ✳, on left bank of the upper Bug and on main railroad line 130 m. SW of Kiev; pop. 92,868; has large factories for making sugar and phosphates. In World War II held by Germans 1941–Mar. 30, 1944.

Vi'no·hra'dy Krá'lov·ské (vĭ'nô·hrà'dĭ krä'lôf·skâ); *Ger.* **Kö'nig·li·che Wein'ber'ge** (kû'nĭk·lĭ·Kě vīn'bĕr'gě). Former city in Bohemia, Czechoslovakia, now part of Prague.

Vintimille. See VENTIMIGLIA.

Vin'ton (vĭn't'n; -tŭn). **1** County in Ohio. See *Table* at OHIO. **2** City, ⊗ of Benton co., E cen. Iowa, 19 m. NW of Cedar Rapids; pop. 4781; corn canneries. **3** Town, Calcasieu parish, SW Louisiana, 23 m. W of Lake Charles; pop. 2987; oil fields. **4** Town, Roanoke co., W cen. Virginia, 4 m. NE of Roanoke; pop. 3432.

Vin'ton·dale (vĭn't'n·dāl; vĭn'tŭn-). Borough, Cambria co., SW cen. Pennsylvania, 11 m. N of Johnstown; pop. 938.

Vion'ville' (vyôn'vēl'). Village, NE France, near Metz and near Mars-la-Tour (*q.v.*).

Viosa. See VIJOSË.

Vi·pi·te'no (vě·pē·tâ'nô); *Ger.* **Ster'zing** (shtĕr'tsĭng). Town, Bolzano prov., N Venezia Tridentina, NE Italy, just S of the Brenner Pass; pop. (1931) 2180. At end of World War II in Europe American armies from N and S Italy met here May 4, 1945 and surrender of Germans in Italy May 5 ended fighting.

Vipuri. Var. of *Viipuri:* see VYBORG.

Vi·rac' (vē·räk'). Municipality, ✳ of Catanduanes subprov., Albay, Phil. Is., pop. 19,279; port on S coast 45 m. from Legaspi.

Vir'den (vûr'd'n). **1** City, Macoupin co., SW cen. Illinois, 23 m. SSW of Springfield; pop. 3309; coal mining. **2** Market town, SW Manitoba, Canada, 47 m. W of Brandon; pop. 1746; has grain elevators.

Vire (vēr). **1** River ab. 75 m. long, Normandy, NW France; flows N past Vire and St-Lô to the Bay of the Seine near Isigny; its estuary in the invasion of June 1944 was the dividing point bet. the two American landing beaches, Omaha Beach and Utah Beach. **2** Town, Calvados dept., NW France, on Vire river 32 m. SW of Caen; pop. 5466; manufactures cloth, trades in horses and cattle; Tour de l'Horloge; important Norman stronghold in Middle Ages. Nearby is the valley (*Vau-de-Vire*) where Olivier Basselin lived in 15th cent. and supposedly composed the lively drinking songs by which the name of the valley became the source of the word *vaudeville.* In World War II occupied by Allies in Normandy invasion ab. July 29, 1944.

Vír'ge·nes (bēr'hā·nâs); *Angl.* **Vir'gins** (vûr'jĭnz; -j'nz); *also* **Cape of the Eleven Thousand Virgins.** Headland on the N side of the E entrance to the Strait of Magellan, S Argentina; adjoins Point Dungeness.

Vir·gi′lio (vĕr·jē′lyô); *formerly* **Pie′to·la** (pyȧ′tô·lä). Commune, Lombardy, Italy ab. 3 m. S of Mantua; pop. (1931) 4514; on site of ancient **An′des** (ăn′dēz), birthplace of Vergil.

Vir′gin (vûr′jĭn; -j′n). **1** River 200 m. long, SW Utah and SE Nevada; rises in W Kane co., S Utah, flows SW across NW corner of Arizona and across border of Nevada, then S into Lake Mead. In Utah portion is Zion Canyon, now included in Zion National Park (see UNITED STATES, *National Parks*). **2** Peak 1370 ft. in Virgin Gorda I., Virgin Is., West Indies.

Virgin Gor′da (gôr′dȧ). One of the Virgin Is., West Indies; ab. 9 m. long; belongs to Great Britain.

Vir·gin′ia (vĕr·jĭn′yȧ; -jĭn′ĭ·ȧ). **1** Eastern state of U.S.A., an original state of the Union, the 10th to ratify the Federal Constitution (June 25, 1788); bounded on N by West Virginia and Maryland, on E by Maryland, Chesapeake Bay, and Atlantic Ocean, on S by North Carolina and Tennessee, on W by Kentucky and West Virginia; 36th state in area, 40,815 sq. m. (land area 39,838 sq. m.); 14th state in population, 3,966,949; ✳ Richmond. See *Table of States* at UNITED STATES. Divided into the following 98 counties (for pronunciation of their names, see their individual entries) and 32 independent cities:

NAME	LOCATION	AREA[1]	POP.[1]	CO. SEAT
Accomac	N part of E penin.; coastal	470	30,635	Accomac
Albemarle	cen.	739	30,969	Charlottesville
Alleghany	W	446	12,128	Covington
Amelia	SE cen.	366	7,815	Amelia Courthouse
Amherst	cen.	467	22,953	Amherst
Appomattox	cen.	343	9,148	Appomattox
Arlington	N	24	163,401	Fort Myer Heights
Augusta	N cen.	986	37,363	Staunton
Bath	W	540	5,335	Warm Springs
Bedford	SW cen.	770	31,028	Bedford
Bland	W	369	5,982	Bland
Botetourt	W cen.	548	16,715	Fincastle
Brunswick	S	579	17,779	Lawrenceville
Buchanan	SW	508	36,724	Grundy
Buckingham	cen.	576	10,877	Buckingham
Campbell	S cen.	524	32,958	Rustburg
Caroline	E	544	12,725	Bowling Green
Carroll	S	494	23,178	Hillsville
Charles City	E	184	5,492	Charles City
Charlotte	S	467	13,368	Charlotte Courthouse
Chesterfield	SE cen.	460	71,197	Chesterfield
Clarke	N	174	7,942	Berryville
Craig	W	336	3,356	New Castle
Culpeper	N	389	15,088	Culpeper
Cumberland	cen.	288	6,360	Cumberland
Dickenson	SW	335	20,211	Clintwood
Dinwiddie	SE	507	22,183	Dinwiddie
Essex	E	250	6,690	Tappahannock
Fairfax	NE	405	275,002	Fairfax
Fauquier	N	660	24,066	Warrenton
Floyd	SW	383	10,462	Floyd
Fluvanna	cen.	282	7,227	Palmyra
Franklin	SW cen.	718	25,925	Rocky Mount
Frederick	N	433	21,941	Winchester
Giles	W	356	17,219	Pearisburg
Gloucester	E	225	11,919	Gloucester
Goochland	E cen.	289	9,206	Goochland
Grayson	SW	450	17,390	Independence
Greene	N cen.	153	4,715	Stanardsville
Greensville	S	301	16,155	Emporia
Halifax	S	800	33,637	Halifax
Hanover	E cen.	466	27,550	Hanover
Henrico	E cen.	232	117,339	Richmond
Henry	S	384	40,335	Martinsville
Highland	W	416	3,221	Monterey
Isle of Wight	SE	319	17,164	Isle of Wight
James City	E	148	11,539	Williamsburg
King and Queen	E	318	5,889	King and Queen Courthouse
King George	E	178	7,243	King George
King William	E	278	7,563	King William
Lancaster	E	142	9,174	Lancaster
Lee	SW tip	434	25,824	Jonesville
Loudoun	N	517	24,549	Leesburg
Louisa	cen.	514	12,959	Louisa
Lunenburg	S	443	12,523	Lunenburg
Madison	N	327	8,187	Madison
Mathews	E	87	7,121	Mathews

NAME	LOCATION	AREA[1]	POP.[1]	CO. SEAT
Mecklenburg	S	626	31,428	Boydton
Middlesex	E	132	6,319	Saluda
Montgomery	W	395	32,923	Christiansburg
Nansemond	SE	402	31,366	Suffolk
Nelson	cen.	468	12,752	Lovingston
New Kent	E	212	4,504	New Kent
Norfolk	SE	337	51,612	Portsmouth
Northampton	S part of E penin.	226	16,966	Eastville
Northumberland	E	200	10,185	Heathsville
Nottoway	S cen.	308	15,141	Nottoway
Orange	N cen.	354	12,900	Orange
Page	N	316	15,572	Luray
Patrick	S	469	15,282	Stuart
Pittsylvania	S	1,012	58,296	Chatham
Powhatan	E cen.	268	6,747	Powhatan
Prince Edward	S cen.	357	14,121	Farmville
Prince George	SE	281	20,270	Prince George
Princess Anne	SE corner	253	77,127	Princess Anne
Prince William	NE	345	50,164	Manassas
Pulaski	SW	327	27,258	Pulaski
Rappahannock	N	267	5,368	Washington
Richmond	E	192	6,375	Warsaw
Roanoke	W cen.	277	61,693	Salem
Rockbridge	W cen.	604	24,039	Lexington
Rockingham	N	868	40,485	Harrisonburg
Russell	SW	483	26,290	Lebanon
Scott	SW	539	25,813	Gate City
Shenandoah	N	507	21,825	Woodstock
Smyth	SW	435	31,066	Marion
Southampton	SE	607	27,195	Courtland
Spotsylvania	NE	409	13,819	Spotsylvania
Stafford	NE	271	16,876	Stafford
Surry	SE	280	6,220	Surry
Sussex	SE	496	12,411	Sussex
Tazewell	SW	522	44,791	Tazewell
Warren	N	219	14,655	Front Royal
Washington	SW	579	38,076	Abingdon
Westmoreland	E	236	11,042	Montross
Wise	SW	411	43,562	Wise
Wythe	SW	460	21,975	Wytheville
York	SE	123	21,583	Yorktown

[1] Area = land area in sq. m. Pop. from 1960 Census.

INDEPENDENT CITIES

NAME[1]	COUNTY	AREA[2]	POP.[2]
Alexandria	Arlington	15	91,023
Bristol	Washington	4	17,144
Buena Vista	Rockbridge	3	6,300
Charlottesville	Albemarle	6	29,427
Clifton Forge	Alleghany	2	5,268
Colonial Heights	Chesterfield	8	9,587
Covington	Alleghany	4	11,062
Danville	Pittsylvania	14	46,577
Falls Church	Fairfax	2	10,192
Fredericksburg	Spotsylvania	6	13,639
Galax		3	5,254
Hampton[3]		57	89,258
Harrisonburg	Rockingham	3	11,916
Hopewell	Prince George	7	17,895
Lynchburg	Campbell	23	54,790
Martinsville	Henry	10	18,798
Newport News[4]		75	113,662
Norfolk	Norfolk	50	304,869
Norton	Wise	3	5,013
Petersburg	Dinwiddie	8	36,750
Portsmouth	Norfolk	18	114,773
Radford	Montgomery	5	9,371
Richmond	Henrico	37	219,958
Roanoke	Roanoke	26	97,110
South Boston	Halifax	2	5,974
South Norfolk	Norfolk	7	22,035
Staunton	Augusta	9	22,232
Suffolk	Nansemond	2	12,609
Virginia Beach	Princess Anne	2	8,091
Waynesboro	Augusta	7	15,694
Williamsburg	James City and York	3	6,832
Winchester	Frederick	3	15,110

[1] These 32 cities have the status of counties. They are located geographically in the counties named, which do not include their area and population figures.
[2] Area = land area in sq. m. Pop. from 1960 Census.
[3] Area includes former Elizabeth City co., which was consolidated with Hampton city 1952.
[4] Area includes former Warwick co., which was incorporated as Warwick city 1952 and consolidated with Newport News city 1958.

Nickname: Old Dominion, also Mother of Presidents, Mother of States. *State flower:* American dogwood. *Motto:* Sic Semper Tyrannis (Ever Thus to Tyrants). *Chief cities:* Norfolk, Richmond, Portsmouth, Newport News, Roanoke. *Rivers:* Potomac, forming N cen., NE, an upper E boundary; Shenandoah, flowing NE to the

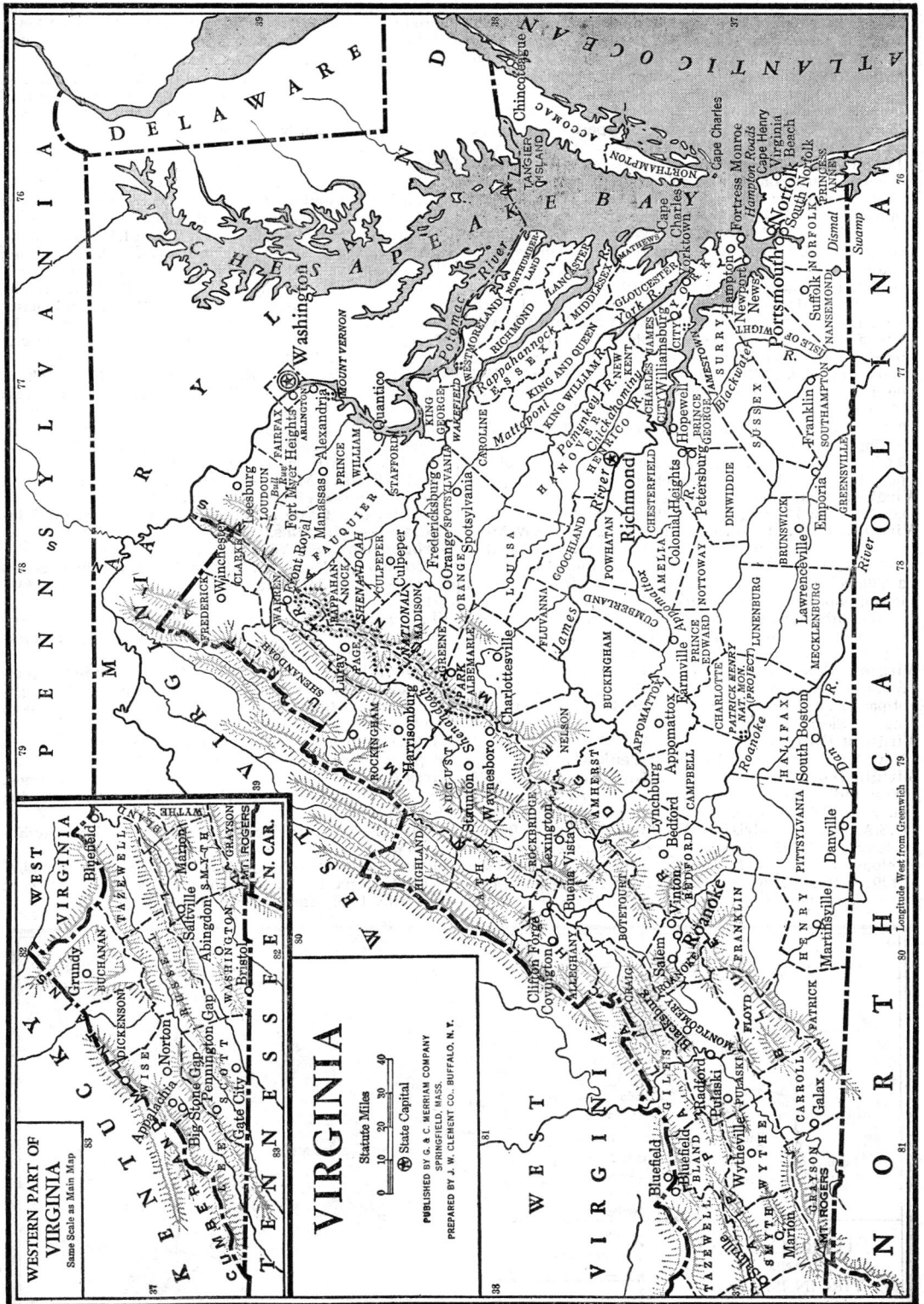

VIRGINIA

Statute Miles

⊕ State Capital

PUBLISHED BY G. & C. MERRIAM COMPANY
SPRINGFIELD, MASS.
PREPARED BY J. W. CLEMENT CO. BUFFALO, N.Y.

WESTERN PART OF
VIRGINIA
Same Scale as Main Map

Potomac in West Virginia; James, flowing from W cen. area E into Atlantic Ocean; Roanoke flowing from W area SE across North Carolina border. *Highest point:* Mount Rogers 5929 ft. in Grayson and Smyth cos. *Chief industries:* Agriculture (corn, tobacco), lumbering.

History: Attempts made by Sir Walter Raleigh to found settlements 1584–87; 1st royal charter to London (Virginia) Company 1606, and 1st permanent settlement, made by colonists sent out by this Company, at Jamestown 1607; first popular assembly in America convened 1619; one of first colonies to express resistance to the Stamp Act and other British taxes 1765; active in movement for independence; scene of surrender of Lord Cornwallis at Yorktown 1781; NW part of western lands ceded to U.S. 1784, S part admitted to the Union as the state of Kentucky 1792; ratified the Federal Constitution June 25, 1788; passed ordinance of secession Apr. 17, 1861; western counties remained loyal to the Union, separated from Virginia 1861 and admitted to the Union as the state of West Virginia 1863; scene of many battles of the Civil War, notably Bull Run (first and second), Fair Oaks, Chancellorsville, Fredericksburg, Wilderness, Cold Harbor, and many engagements in Shenandoah Valley; readmitted to Union Jan. 26, 1870.

2 City, ⊗ of Cass co., W cen. Illinois, 30 m. NW of Springfield; pop. 1669.

3 City, St. Louis co., NE Minnesota, 20 m. E of Hibbing; pop. 14,034; in iron-mining section in Mesabi Range.

Virginia Beach. Independent city, SE Virginia, on Atlantic Ocean 18 m. E of Norfolk; pop. 8091; fisheries.

Virginia City. 1 Town, ⊗ of Madison co., SW Montana; pop. 194; founded 1863, after discovery of gold in Alder Gulch nearby; territorial capital 1865–75.

2 Village, ⊗ of Storey co., W Nevada, 16 m. SSE of Reno; pop. (est.) 500; settled 1859 at time of discovery on this site of the Comstock Lode, a gold and silver lode with many bonanzas, which until c. 1886 yielded half the silver output of the U.S.; now a ghost town.

Virginia Pass. Mountain pass 10,500 ft., Tuolumne co., cen. California, at N end of Yosemite National Park; one of passes most used by emigrants and explorers in crossing the Sierra Nevada Mts.

Virginia Range. Small range W of Pyramid Lake, W Nevada; highest point **Virginia Peak** 8340 ft.

Vir′gin Islands (vûr′jǐn; -j′n). Group of islands in NE West Indies, westernmost of the Lesser Antilles, ab. 60 m. E of Puerto Rico, divided bet. Great Britain and U.S.A.: (1) The **British Virgin Islands,** a British colony, until 1958 a presidency of the Leeward Islands Colony, Brit. West Indies; 58 sq. m.; pop. (1943 est.) 7129; ✳ Road Town (on Tortola I.); chief islands Tortola, Virgin Gorda, Anegada, Jost Van Dyke, Peter, and

Norman; includes also ab. 24 other small islands. Chief products fruit and tobacco. (2) *Officially,* the **Virgin Islands of the United States,** *before 1917* **Danish West Indies,** consisting of the islands St. Thomas, St. Croix, and St. John, and ab. 50 islets; 133 sq. m.; pop. 32,099; ✳ Charlotte Amalie. Virgin Islands National Park, opened 1956, is situated on St. John I. Chief products sugar, cattle, bay oil, bay rum.

History: Discovered and named by Columbus 1493; St. Croix occupied by Dutch, English, Spanish; St. Thomas occupied by Denmark 1666 and 1672, St. John in 1684 and St. Croix in 1733; British group, part of Leeward Islands colony until formation of West Indies Federation, of which the British Virgin Islands are not a member, acquired by England 1666. Danish group, known as Danish West Indies, subject of treaties of sale bet. U.S. and Denmark in 1867 and 1902, but finally acquired by U.S. by purchase 1916–17 and name changed to Virgin Islands; until 1931 administered by Navy Department; given Organic Act 1936 and universal suffrage 1938.

Virgin Mountains. Range in extreme NW Mohave co., NW Arizona, extending along E bank of Virgin river into SE Nevada.

Virgin Passage. Channel ab. 9 m. wide bet. W St. Thomas I. of the Virgin Is. of the United States and Culebra I., off E end of Puerto Rico.

Virgin Peak. Mountain 7250 ft. in E Clark co., SE Nevada, in the **Virgin Range.**

Virgins, *also* **Cape of the Eleven Thousand Virgins.** See VÍRGENES.

Viroconium. See WROXETER.

Vi·ro·flay (vǐr′ô·flā; *Fr.* vē′rô′flā′). Commune, Seine-et-Oise dept., N France, near Versailles; pop. (1931) 9182.

Vi·ro′qua (vǐ·rō′kwà). City, ⊗ of Vernon co., SW Wisconsin, 25 m. SE of La Crosse; pop. 3926; in dairy-farming and tobacco-raising section.

Vi·ro·vi′ti·ca (vě·rô·vē′tē·tsä); *Hung.* **Ve′rö·cze′** (vě′-rû·tsě′). Town, Croatia federated republic, N Yugoslavia, near Hungarian border 65 m. E of Zagreb; pop. 10,653.

Vir′rat (vǐr′ràt). Town, SW cen. Finland, in Vaasa dept., at N end of Nasijärvi; pop. 11,269.

Virts (vǐrts). Lake in S cen. Estonia; 95 sq. m., largest entirely within the country; its outlet is the Ema, flowing E to Lake Peipus.

Vi′ru (vǐ′rōō). Province of Estonia. See *Table* at ESTONIA.

Vi′ru Harbour (vē′rōō). Harbor on W side of S end of New Georgia I., cen. Solomon Is., W Pacific Ocean; taken by U.S. Marines June 30, 1943.

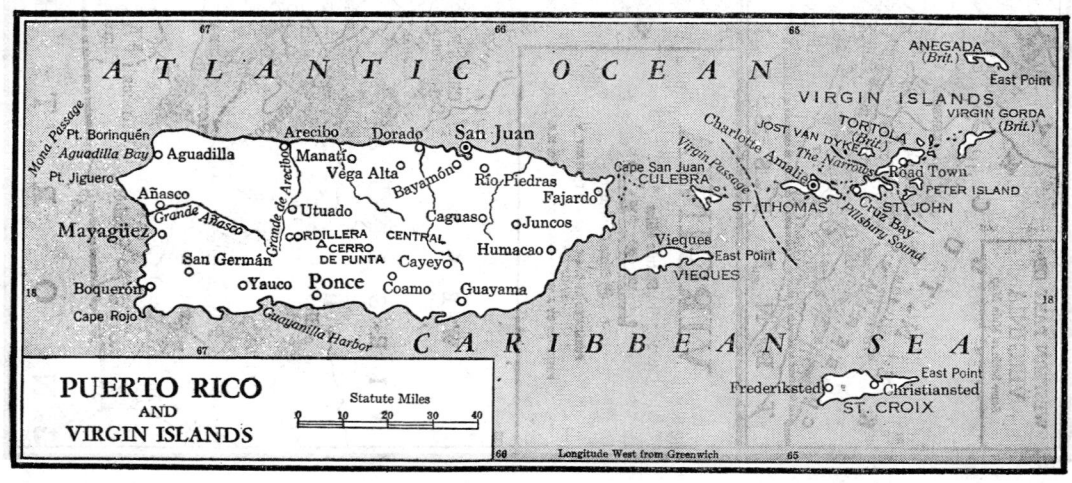

PUERTO RICO
AND
VIRGIN ISLANDS

Vi·run'ga (vĭ·rŏŏng'gȧ), *or* **Mfum'bi·ro** ('m·fōōm'-bē·rō), **Mountains.** Range of volcanic mountains in E Congo and SW Uganda, E Africa, N of Lake Kivu; highest peak Karisimbi 14,786 ft.

Vi'ry'-Cha'til'lon' (vē'rē'shä'tē'yôN'). Commune, Seine-et-Oise dept., N France, S of Paris; pop. 8442.

Vis (vēs); *Ital.* **Lis'sa** (lĭs'ȧ; *Ital.* lēs'sä); *anc.* **Is'sa** (ĭs'ȧ). **1** Yugoslav island in the Adriatic Sea SSW of Split; 33 sq. m.; pop. ab. 10,000; has fertile central plain; highest point 1942 ft. in SW; viticulture. Ruled by Venice from 996, held by French during Napoleonic Wars until British victory over Franco-Venetian squadron Mar. 13, 1811 in nearby waters; ceded to Austria 1815; nearby waters again scene of naval battle July 20, 1866 in which Austrians under Admiral Tegetthoff defeated Italians under Persano; island became Yugoslav after World War I; occupied by Italy in World War II. **2** Chief town on the island; palace of Venetian counts; ruins of ancient city of Issa.

Visakhapatnam. See VIZAGAPATAM.

Vi·sa'le (vĭ·sä'lĕ). Village at Cape Esperance, NW point of Guadalcanal I., SE Solomon Is., W Pacific Ocean; Japanese beachhead 1942.

Vi·sa'lia (vĭ·sāl'yȧ). City, ⊗ of Tulare co., S cen. California, 38 m. SE of Fresno; pop. 15,791; founded 1852, made ⊗ 1853, incorp. 1874; fruit canning.

Vi·sa'yan Islands (vė·sä'yăn) *or* **Bi·sa'yas** (bė·sä'yȧz; *Span.* bė·sä'yäs). Large group of islands in cen. Philippines, inhabited chiefly by the Visayan peoples; chief islands Panay, Samar, Leyte, Cebu, Negros, Bohol, Masbate, and the Romblon group; adjacent are many smaller islands; ab. 23,535 sq. m.; pop. 5,871,954. Bounded on the N by Luzon, on the E by the Pacific Ocean, on the S by Mindanao, and on the W by Mindoro and the Sulu Sea.

Visayan Sea. Open body of interisland water in cen. Phil. Is., bordered on N by Masbate, on E by Leyte and Cebu, on S by Negros, and on W by Panay. Connects with Sibuyan Sea by Jintotolo Channel, with Mindanao Sea by Tañon Strait, and with Sulu Sea by Guimaras Strait.

Vi·sa'yas (vė·sä'yȧz; *Span.* bė·sä'yäs). = VISAYAN ISLANDS.

Vis'by (vĭz'bĭ; *Swed.* vēs'bü); *Ger.* **Wis'by** (wĭz'bĭ; *Ger.* vĭs'bė). Seaport on Gotland I. in the Baltic Sea; ⁂ of Gotland prov., Sweden; pop. 13,626; seaside resort; sugar refineries; commercial center of northern Europe from 10th to 14th cent.; member of Hanseatic League.

Vis'count Mel'ville Sound (vĭ'kount mĕl'vĭl); *formerly* **Melville Sound.** Body of water in Franklin District, Northwest Territories, N Canada, bet. Melville I. on the N and N Victoria I.

Vi·sé' (vē'zā'). Commune, Liège prov., Belgium, NE of Liège; pop. 4651; burned Aug. 1914; rebuilt.

Vi·seu (vė·zā'ōō). **1** District of Portugal. See *Table* at PORTUGAL.
2 Commune, its ⁂, N cen. Portugal, 41 m. NE of Coimbra; pop. 9471; ⁂ of Beira Alta prov.; 12th-cent. cathedral; Roman, Visigothic, and Moorish ruins.

Visla. See VISTULA.

Vi'so, Mount (vē'zō); *also* **Mon·vi'so** (mŏm·vē'zō). Peak 12,605 ft. in Torino prov., Piedmont, Italy, 40 m. SW of Turin near the French border; highest in Cottian Alps.

Vis'ta (vĭs'tȧ). Urban community (unincorporated), San Diego co., SW California, N of San Diego; pop. 14,795.

Vis'ta Her·mo'sa de Ne·gre'te (bēs'tä ĕr·mō'sä thä nȧ·grä'tȧ). Town, Michoacán state, SW Mexico; pop. 5548.

Vi·stri'tsa (vė·strē'tsȧ); *anc.* **Hal'i·ac'mon** (hăl'ĭ·ăk'-mŏn). River ab. 140 m. long in W Macedonia, N Greece; rises near Florina and flows SE and NE into head of Gulf of Salonika.

Vis'tu·la (vĭs'tū·lȧ); *Pol.* **Wis'la** (vēs'lä); *Russ.* **Vis'la** (vyēs'lä); *Ger.* **Weich'sel** (vīk'sĕl). River of N and cen.

Poland, 652 m. long; rises on N slope of the Carpathian Mts. in SW Poland; flows in a great curve NE, N, and NW through Warsaw and Toruń; then N into the Baltic Sea at Danzig. Navigable for most of its course. Its chief tributaries on left are Bzura and Pilica; on right the Bug, San, Wisłoka, and Dunajec.

Visurgis. See WESER.

Vi'tebsk (vē'tĕpsk; *Russ.* vyĕ'tyĕpsk). City, ⁂ of Vitebsk Region, NE White Russia, U.S.S.R., on both banks of the Dvina 140 m. NE of Minsk; pop. 167,424; on the Riga-Moscow railroad; center of an old province largely agricultural; has many industries, especially those connected with lumber, flax, linseed, and the manufacture of machinery, boots and shoes; many churches. An old town dating back to the 11th cent. when it belonged to the Polotsk principality; chief town of an independent principality for nearly 200 years; came under Lithuania 1320 and under Poland in 16th cent.; suffered much in wars bet. Poland and Russia; finally annexed by Russia 1772. In World War I occupied by Germans 1918 and in World War II again in their first drive in the summer of 1941; retaken by Russians June 24–26, 1944.

Vitebsk Region. Region, NE White Russia, U.S.S.R.; ⁂ Vitebsk.

Vi·ter'bo (vė·tĕr'bō). **1** Province of Italy. See *Table* at ITALY.
2 *anc.* **Vi'cus El'bi·i** (vī'kŭs ĕl'bĭ·ī). Commune, ⁂ of Viterbo prov., Latium, cen. Italy, 42 m. NNW of Rome; pop. 36,123; 12th-cent. Gothic cathedral; 13th-cent. episcopal palace; 13th-cent. town hall; 15th-cent. Farnese palace; churches of 9th, 11th, and 12th cents.; medieval walls and gates; sulfur baths nearby; manufactures paper, leather, textiles; trades in sulfur and iron. Principal town in Countess Matilda's alods bequeathed to pope at end of 11th cent., forming part of the Patrimony of St. Peter.

Vi'ti·az Strait (vē'tĭ·ăz). Channel ab. 35 m. wide and 150 m. long off NE coast of North-East New Guinea, separates New Guinea from Long I. and Umboi I. and connects Bismarck Sea with Solomon Sea.

Vi'ti Islands (vē'tē). = FIJI ISLANDS.

Viti Le'vu (lĕ'vōō). Largest of the Fiji Is., in SW Pacific Ocean; 90 m. from E to W and 50 m. from N to S; 4053 sq. m.; chief town Suva, ⁂ of the colony. Most of it mountainous; highest point Mt. Victoria 4341 ft. Has several sizable streams; largest is the Rewa in the E. Most of its villages on the coast on a highway that completely encircles the island. Grows coffee, sugar, cinchona, coconuts, and tropical fruits and vegetables; exports copra and sugar.

Vi·tim' (vĭ·tēm'; *Russ.* vyĭ·tyēm'). **1** River ab. 1100 m. long, S Siberia, Soviet Russia, Asia; rises in cen. Buryat-Mongol Republic, flows NE and N forming in part the E boundary of the republic, then across NE Irkutsk Region to join the Lena on SW border of Yakutsk Republic.
2 Town, SW Yakutsk Republic, on left bank of the Lena opp. the mouth of the Vitim river.

Vi·ti'mo-O·lek'minsk (vĭ·tē'mŏ·ô·lĕk'mĭnsk; *Russ.* vyĭ·tyē'mŭ·ŭ·lyäk'myĭnsk, -ŭ·lyĭk·myēnsk'). Former national district, Soviet Russia, Asia, in N part of Chita Region; 81,000 sq. m.; pop. ab. 9000; ⁂ Ust-Miya; liquidated 1937.

Vít'ko·vi'ce (vēt'kô·vĭ'tsĕ); *Ger.* **Wit'ko·witz** (vĭt'kô·vĭts). Former commune, now part of Moravská Ostrava, Moravia, Czechoslovakia.

Vi·tor' (bė·tôr'). Town, Arequipa dept., S Peru, 30 m. E of Arequipa; important junction point on Pan American Highway.

Vi·to'ri·a (vĭ·tōr'ĭ·ȧ; *Span.* bė·tō'ryä). City, ⁂ of Álava prov., N Spain, 50 m. W of Pamplona; pop. (1941 est.) 51,162; manufactures wine, liquors, candles, chocolates, soap, pottery, leather and leather goods, chemicals, textiles, furniture; trades in iron, grain, and manufactured products; 12th-cent. fortress-cathedral; 13th-cent.

Franciscan monastery; scene of battle June 21, 1813 in which Wellington defeated the French, driving them from Spain (Peninsular War).

Vi·tó'ri·a (vĭ·tōr'ĭ·à; *Port.* vĕ·tô'ryà). 1 Seaport, E Brazil, * of Espírito Santo state, on Espírito Santo I.; pop. (1940 est.) 42,873; ships iron ore of the Doce river region. **2** City, E Pernambuco state, E Brazil, on railroad just W of Recife; pop. (1940 est.) 12,563.

Vi'tré' (vē'trā'). Manufacturing and commercial town, Ille-et-Vilaine dept., NW France, 22 m. E of Rennes; pop. 6584; formerly a Huguenot stronghold.

Vi'try'–le–Fran'çois' (vē'trē'lē·frän'swä'). Town, Marne dept., NE France, on the Marne 20 m. SE of Châlons-sur-Marne; pop. 8727; built 1545 by Francis I; scene of fighting during battle of the Marne 1914; ab. 2½ m. to the NE is the village of **Vitry–en–Per'thois'** (-än·pĕr'twä'), *formerly* **Vitry–le–Brû'lé'** (-lē·brü'-lä'), which suffered the burning of its church 1142 by Louis VII and destruction at hands of Charles V 1544.

Vitry–sur–Seine (-sür·sân'). Commune, Seine dept., N France, SSE suburb of Paris; pop. 46,945; manufactures chemicals; machinery.

Vit'tel' (vē'tĕl'). Town, Vosges dept., NE France, ab. 30 m. W of Épinal; pop. (1931) 3106; mineral waters; fashionable resort.

Vit·to'ri·a (vĭ·tōr'ĭ·à; *Ital.* vēt·tô'ryä). Commune, Ragusa prov., SE Sicily, 11 m. W of Ragusa; pop. 37,575; cathedral; wine market.

Vittoriosa. See COSPICUA.

Vit·to'rio Ve'ne·to (vēt·tô'ryŏ vā'nä·tŏ). Commune, Treviso prov., Venezia Euganea, NE Italy, 23 m. N of Treviso; pop. 23,475; cathedral; mineral baths; summer resort; scene of last decisive battle bet. Austrian and Italian forces Oct. 24–Nov. 3, 1918, culminating in Italian victory and armistice of Villa Giusti Nov. 4, 1918.

Vi'tu Islands (vē'tōō). Group of small islands in S Bismarck Sea off the N coast of W end of New Britain I., Bismarck Archipelago, W Pacific; largest is Garove I.

Vitz'nau (fĭts'nou). Village near Rigi Mt. in Lucerne canton, cen. Switzerland, on Lake of Lucerne; pop. (1930) 1038; resort.

Vi'va'rais' (vē'và'rĕ'). Ancient district of SE France, now mostly in department of Ardèche; * Viviers.

Vi·va'rio Cays (bĕ·vä'ryŏ). Group of small islands in Caribbean Sea E of NE coast of Honduras.

Vi·ve'ro (bĕ·vä'rŏ). Commune, Lugo prov., NW Spain, on Bay of Biscay 42 m. N of Lugo; pop. 13,930; agricultural produce; commercial fishing; fish-salting works.

Vive–Saint–Éloi. = SINT-ELOOIS-VIJVE.

Viv'i·an (vĭv'ĭ·ăn; vĭv'yăn). Town, Caddo parish, NW corner of Louisiana, 28 m. NNW of Shreveport; pop. 2624.

Vi'viers' (vē'vyā'). Town, Ardèche dept., SE France, on the Rhone SSE of Privas; pop. (1931) 1787; cathedral with six Gobelin tapestries; capital of ancient Vivarais.

Vivis. See VEVEY.

Vi·za'ga·pa'tam (vĭ·zä'gà·pŭt'ăm) *or* **Vi·sa'kha·pat'nam** (vĭ·sä'kà·pŭt'năm). City, NE Andhra Pradesh, E India, on Bay of Bengal 380 m. NE of Madras; pop. 108,042; increasingly important seaport with exports of manganese ore, groundnuts, and sugar; has good textile industry. European quarter and bathing resort of **Wal'tair** (wôl'târ) at N end of bay. Site of English factory in 1683; captured by French in 1757 and regained 1758.

Viz·ca'ya (bĕth·kä'yä), *also* **Bis·ca'ya** (bĕs·kä'yä); *Eng.* **Bis'cay** (bĭs'kā; -kĭ). Province of Spain. See *Table* at SPAIN.

Vizcaya, Gulf of. = Bay of BISCAY.

Vi·zeu' (vē·zā'ŏŏ). = VISEU.

Viz'i·a·nag'ram (vĭz'ĭ·à·năg'răm). Town, NE Andhra Pradesh, E India, 410 m. NNE of Madras and just NNE of Vizagapatam; pop. 67,104; has old fort and small military cantonment.

Vi'zille' (vē'zēl'). Town, Isère dept., SE France, S of

Grenoble; pop. 3912; Roman military post; château where the estates of Dauphiné met July 21, 1788 in the tennis court (a year before the Oath of the Tennis Court taken by the National Assembly) and made a protest which foreshadowed the Revolution.

Viz·zi'ni (vēt·tsē'nē). Commune, Catania prov., E Sicily, 30 m. SW of Catania; pop. 14,706.

Vlaanderen. Flemish form of FLANDERS.

Vlaar'ding·en (vlär'dĭng·ĕ[n]). Commune, South Holland prov., SW Netherlands, on the Nieuwe Maas (Meuse) river 6 m. W of Rotterdam; pop. (1939) 31,038; center of herring and cod fisheries.

Vladikavkaz. See DZAUDZHIKAU.

Vlad'i·mir (vlăd'ĭ·mĭr; *Russ.* vlŭ·dyē'myĭr). 1 Principality, cen. Russia, 12th to 15th cent.; * Vladimir; founded by Andrei Bogolyubski from Kiev c. 1150; later, with Suzdal and Rostov, a part of joint principality under princes of Vladimir. Its last ruler, Ivan I (Kalita) removed court to Moscow; absorbed by Moscow in 15th cent.

2 City, * of Vladimir Region, Soviet Russia, Europe, on N bank of Klyazma river 110 m. E of Moscow; pop. 66,761; on the railroad from Moscow to Gorki, has several industries, esp. cotton factories; has part of its ancient walls and two very old cathedrals (built in 12th cent.; restored in 19th). One of the oldest towns of Russia, founded in the 12th cent. (c. 1150); plundered by Mongols 1237 and by Tatars 1410; capital of Vladimir principality until reign (1328–41) of Prince Ivan I, who transferred court to Moscow, but remained coronation city until 1431; became dependent on Moscow.

Vla·di'mi·rov'ka (vlŭ·dyē'myĭ·rôf'kà). Town, SE Stalingrad Region, Soviet Russia, Europe, on E bank of the Volga ab. 85 m. SE of Stalingrad.

Vladimir Region. Region, cen. Soviet Russia, Europe; * Vladimir.

Vlad'i·mir Vo·lynsk' (vlăd'ĭ·mĭr vŏ·lĭnsk'; *Russ.* vlŭ·dyē'myĭr vŭ·lĭnsk'); *Pol.* **Wło·dzi'mierz** (vlô·jē'myĕsh). City, Volyn Region, NW Ukraine, U.S.S.R., 45 m. WNW of Lutsk; formerly in Wołyń dept., Poland; pop. 24,581; on Kovel-Lvov railroad; formerly important as the ancient capital of Volhynia, a principality known in the 12th and 13th cents. as Vladimir in Volhynia. Its name was Latinized as Lodomeria (*q.v.*).

Vla·di·vos·tok' (vlăd'ĭ·vŏs·tŏk'; -vŏs'tŏk; *Russ.* vlà-dyĭ·vŭ·stôk'). Seaport city, * of Maritime Territory (Primorski Krai), Soviet Russia, Asia, at the S tip of a peninsula extending into Peter the Great Bay; pop. 206,432; its harbor, the Golden Horn, is an inlet of Amur Bay; most important and most southerly port in E part of Russian Asia; its harbor kept open in winter by icebreakers; has dockage, storage capacity, shipyards, cranes, etc., capable of handling large maritime trade; shipping point for soybeans, soybean oil, timber, fish. Site selected 1860 for settlement under Treaty of Aigun; made Russian Pacific naval base 1872; connected by Chinese Eastern Railway (then under Russian lease) with Lake Baikal and Europe 1897; became free commercial port 1904; suffered from civilian revolt 1905–06, but with growth of trade prosperity returned; became terminal of Trans-Siberian R.R., completed 1917; since World War I has been developed into great naval and aviation base.

Vlagt'wed'de (vläkt'vĕd'ĕ). Commune, Groningen prov., NE Netherlands, 25 m. SE of Groningen near German border; pop. 13,798.

Vlie'land (vlē'länt). Island of Netherlands in the West Frisian Is., N of Texel I.; 10 m. long; administratively a part of North Holland prov.

Vlie Stroom (vlē' strōm). Strait bet. Vlieland I. and Terschelling I. in the West Frisian Is., connecting the North Sea with Wadden Zee.

Vlis'sing·en (vlĭs'ĭng·ĕ[n]); *Eng.* **Flush'ing** (flŭsh'-ing). Commune and seaport, Zeeland prov., SW Netherlands; chief town on Walcheren I., on its S shore and

on Schelde estuary; pop. (1939) 23,002; commercial and naval port and seaside resort; steamer line to Harwich, England. Birthplace of Admiral de Ruyter. Objective of Allied Walcheren expedition, Oct.–Nov. 1944, to clear Schelde estuary for access to Antwerp.

Vlodava. See WŁODAWA.

Vlo'na (vlō'nä) *or* **Va·lo'na** (vä·lō'nä; *Ital.* vä·lō'nä). **1** Prefecture, SW Albania; 525 sq. m.; pop. 53,461. **2** *also* **Av·lo'na** (äv·lō'nä); *Albanian also* **Vlo'rë** (vlō'rĕ); *anc.* **Au'lon** (ô'lŏn). Seaport town, Vlona prefecture, SW Albania, on Bay of Vlona; pop. 9100; excellent harbor, best on Albanian coast; protected by island of Saseno on N; market and shipping center for grain, olives, salt, bitumen; fisheries. Important in wars bet. Normans and Byzantines in 11th and 12th cents.; under Turkish rule 1464–1912; place where Albanian independence was proclaimed 1912; held by Italians 1914 to 1920; suffered during war 1940–41 bet. Greeks and Italians and during bombing by British Dec. 18, 1940.

Vlona, *or* **Valona, Bay of.** Inlet of SE Adriatic Sea on SW coast of Albania; harbor for the city of Vlona.

Vlorë. See VLONA.

Vlotslavsk. See WŁOCŁAWEK.

Vl'ta·va (vŭl'tà·và); *Ger.* **Mol'dau** (môl'dou). River 270 m. long in Bohemia, Czechoslovakia; flows SE, then N through České Budějovice and Prague into the Labe (Elbe) river 20 m. N of Prague; navigable as far as České Budějovice.

Vluck Point (vlŭk). Cape on NW coast of St. Thomas I., Virgin Is. of the U.S., West Indies, on E side of entrance to Santa Maria Bay.

Vly, Mount (vlī; flī). Peak 3476 ft. in the Catskill Mts., Greene co., SE New York.

Vodena. See EDESSA.

Vo'gel·kop' (vō'gĕl·kôp'); *formerly* **Be·rau'** (bĕ·rou'). Peninsula, NW extension of West New Guinea, SW Pacific Ocean, N of McCluer Gulf; shaped like a bird's head, hence the Dutch name *Vogelkop*, literally "bird head." Arfak Mts. extend along N coast; highest point Kwoka 9842 ft. Sorong and Manokwari are chief towns. In World War II secured by Allies July 30, 1944, by landing at Sansapor.

Vo'gels·berg (fō'gĕls·bĕrĸ). Mountain range in W Germany, in Oberhessen, Hesse, Germany; highest point 2539 ft.

Vogesus. See VOSGES.

Vo·ghe'ra (vō·gā'rä). Commune, Pavia prov., Lombardy, N Italy, 15 m. SSW of Pavia; pop. 30,180; 14th-cent. castle; churches of San Lorenzo (rebuilt 1605) and Sant'Ilario (remodeled 12th cent.).

Vogt'land (fōkt'länt). Old district of Germany, later included in SW Saxony and SE Thuringia.

Voh'win'kel (fō'ving'kĕl). Former city (pop. 16,093), Düsseldorf govt. dist., Rhine Province, Prussia, Germany; since 1929 part of Wuppertal (*q.v.*).; metal goods, textiles.

Voi (voi). Town, SE Kenya colony, E Africa, 90 m. NW of Mombasa; railroad junction on the Mombasa-Nairobi line.

Voiotia. Modern Greek form of BOEOTIA.

Voi'ron' (vwà'rôN'). Industrial commune, Isère dept., SE France, 15 m. NNW of Grenoble; pop. 12,444; manufactures textiles, paper, liqueurs, chemical products, lumber.

Voi'vo·di'na (voi'vō·dē'nä). Former region in S Hungary, N of Danube river; later included in Dunavska co., NE Yugoslavia, and the Banat, Romania. Since 1945 the area in NE Yugoslavia, N of Serbia, has been established as an autonomous province, in some administrative matters attached to Serbia; chief town Novi Sad.

Volaterrae. See VOLTERRA.

Vol·cán' (bôl·kän'). Peak 18,077 ft. in E Coquimbo prov., cen. Chile, near Argentina border.

Vol·ca'no Bay (vŏl·kä'nō). = UCHIURA BAY.

Volcano Island. 1 See TINAKULA ISLAND.

2 Island in Lake Taal, Batangas, Phil. Is. See TAAL.

Volcano Islands; *Jap.* **Ka·zan Ret·to** (kä·zän rĕt·tō), *also* **I·wo Retto** (ē·wō). Group of three small islands in W Pacific Ocean S of Bonin Is., 25°N, 143°E; comprise Iwo Jima (*q.v.*) or Naka Iwo, Kita Iwo, and Minami Iwo; formerly Japanese, now administered by U.S.

Vol·chansk' (vŭl·chánsk'). Town, NE Ukraine, U.S.S.R., NE of Kharkov; pop. 20,810.

Vo'len·dam' (vō'lĕn·däm'). Town, North Holland prov., NW Netherlands, NE of Amsterdam on the IJsselmeer opp. Marken I.; tourist resort; pop. 6900.

Vol'ga (vŏl'gà; *Russ.* vôl'-); *anc.* **Rha** (rä). River of Soviet Russia in Europe, 2325 m. long; rises W of Lake Seliger in the Valdai Hills in N Kalinin Region, flows with greatly winding course E and SE to Kazan in Tatar A.S.S.R., then S in great bend at Kuibyshev, SW to Stalingrad and SE to the Caspian Sea near Astrakhan. Longest river in Europe and most important in U.S.S.R. Its basin estimated at 560,000 sq. m. and because its entire course is through steppe and lowland the fall from source to mouth is less than 650 ft. Navigable for almost its entire course but in some sections too shallow for large vessels; subject to great floods. Has extensive delta ab. 75 m. wide. Fed by many tributaries; on left bank: Tvertsa, Mologa, Kostroma, Unzha, Vetluga, Kama, and Samara; on right bank: Oka, Sura. Chief cities on its banks are Kalinin, Rybinsk, Yaroslavl, Kostroma, Gorki, Kazan, Kuibyshev, Saratov, Volgograd, and Astrakhan. Fishing is important on its lower course; connects by canals in several places with Baltic rivers (see MARIINSK CANAL SYSTEM) and in lower course near Volgograd with the Don. "Great Volga" government projects are concerned with construction of dams for power, irrigation, and flood control (see RYBINSK RESERVOIR), deeper channels for better transportation, and additional canal systems. See STALINGRAD.

Volga German Republic. See GERMAN VOLGA REPUBLIC.

Volgograd. See STALINGRAD.

Volgograd Region. See STALINGRAD REGION.

Vol·hyn'i·a (vŏl·hĭn'ĭ·à; vō·lĭn'-); *Russ.* **Vo·lyn'** (vŭ·lĭn'y'); *Pol.* **Wo'łyń** (vō'lĭn·y'). Region of E cen. Europe around the headstreams of the Pripyat and Bug rivers; well forested, with marshlands and many lakes; originally a Russian medieval principality, SW of Polotsk and W of Pinsk and Kiev. In 14th cent. a smaller area in Lithuania; in 1569 to Poland; in 1796 became a government of Russia. Divided 1921 by Treaty of Riga bet. Poland (Wołyń) and Soviet Russia (Volyn). Population is largely Ukrainian. Polish section taken by Russia in partition of 1939 and retained as Volyn Region of NW Ukraine after 1945.

Vol'khov (vôl'ĸŭf). Navigable river 140 m. long, Leningrad Region, Soviet Russia, Europe; outlet of Lake Ilmen; flows N to Lake Ladoga; bisects Novgorod and, at **Volkhov** near Lake Ladoga, forms rapids (fall nearly 30 ft.) that develop power at Lenin Hydroelectric Station, opened 1926. Area held by Germans in early part of World War II.

Völk'ling·en (fŭlk'ling·ĕn). Commune, Saarland, on the Saar, just W of Saarbrücken; pop. (1927) 20,059; ironworks.

Vol·ko'vysk (vŭl·kô'vĭsk); *Pol.* **Woł·ko'wysk** (vôl·kô'vĭsk). Town, W White Russia, U.S.S.R., 55 m. E of Belostok; formerly in Białystok dept., Poland; pop. (1938–39 est.) 17,000; lumber agricultural machinery.

Volks'rust (vŏlks'rŭst). Town, S Transvaal, NE Republic of So. Africa, 134 m. SE of Johannesburg on Natal border in Drakensberg Mts.; pop. 4792; center of extensive pastoral region.

Vo'log·da (vô'lŭg·dà). City, ✱ of Vologda Region, N cen. Soviet Russia, Europe, in S part of region on the **Vologda River** (tributary of upper Sukhona river) and SE of Lake Kubenskoe; pop. 95,194; on main railroad line from Leningrad to Kirov, ab. 330 m. E of Leningrad;

has several technical schools, research laboratories, museums, etc.; location of railroad repair yards; has developed many new factories in recent years. Has been a trading town since very early times; became a colony of Novgorod 1147; plundered by Tatars 1273; annexed to Moscow 1447 (early Russian cathedral, built 1537–42); declined in 18th cent. but coming of railroads has again made it prosperous; during World War II transshipment point for lend-lease goods shipped from Arkhangelsk.

Vologda Region. Region, N cen. Soviet Russia, Europe; 57,514 sq. m.; pop. 1,662,258; ✻ Vologda. Level area with marshes, many lakes and streams, and extensive forests. Beloe and Kubenskoe are largest lakes and chief rivers are the Sukhona and Sheksna; includes part of Mariinsk Canal System. Has long winters and poor soil; chief crops winter rye and oats. Chief towns Vologda, Cherepovets, and Veliki Ustyug. In medieval times a part of the Novgorod principality; in 15th cent. most of it came under Moscow principality; part of Leningrad Area 1918 until made separate region 1936.

Vo·lo·ko'lamsk (vŭ·lŭ·kô'lämsk). Town, Moscow Region, cen. Russia in Europe, ab. 65 m. WNW of Moscow and E of Rzhev; reached by Germans Nov. 22, 1941 but retaken in winter campaign of 1942–43.

Vo'los (vō'lŏs); *Gr.* **Vó'los** or **Bo'los** (vô'lôs). Seaport city, Larissa dept., E Thessaly, NE Greece, on Gulf of Volos; pop. 41,706. Many ancient ruins found in vicinity; sites of ancient Iolcus and Demetrias nearby.

Volos, Gulf of; *anc.* **Si'nus Pag'a·sae'us** (sī'nŭs păg'à·sē'ŭs). Inlet of the Aegean Sea on E coast of Greece, in Larissa dept., E Thessaly; shut in on E by peninsula of Magnesia.

Vol'scian Mountains (vŏl'shăn). See LEPINI MOUNTAINS.

Volsinii. 1 Commune, Latium, cen. Italy. See BOLSENA. **2** Commune, Umbria, cen. Italy. See ORVIETO.

Volsk (vŏlsk; *Russ.* vôl'y'sk). Town, cen. Saratov Region, Soviet Russia, Europe, on W bank of the Volga 70 m. NE of Saratov; pop. 55,053; important river port; has large cement works and other industries, esp. those of the peasant type in textiles and leather.

Vol'ta (vŏl'tà). River in W Africa; formed by confluence of Black Volta and White Volta in N cen. Ghana; flows S bet. Ashanti prov. and Trans-Volta Togoland and empties into Bight of Benin; ab. 250 m. long, or, with the Black Volta, ab. 790 m. long.

Volta, Black; *Fr.* **Vol'ta' Noire** (vŏl'tà' nwàr'). Chief headstream of Volta river in the Gold Coast region, W Africa; rises in N Ivory Coast, flows S, forming section of NW boundary of Ghana, turns E and unites with White Volta river to form the Volta; ab. 540 m. long.

Volta, Red; *Fr.* **Vol'ta' Rouge** (vŏl'tà' rōozh'). Tributary of the White Volta in N Ghana and Upper Volta.

Volta, Upper. See UPPER VOLTA.

Volta, White; *Fr.* **Vol'ta' Blanche** (vŏl'tà' bläNsh'). River ab. 450 m. long rising in Upper Volta, West Africa; flows SW and S to unite with Black Volta river in cen. Ghana and form the Volta river.

Voltaic Republic. See UPPER VOLTA.

Vol'ta Re·don'da (vŏl'tà rĕ·thōNn'dà). Town, Rio de Janeiro state, E Brazil, on the Paraíba river near city of Rio de Janeiro; Brazil's first steel-manufacturing town, started 1942 on site of abandoned coffee plantation; produced first steel June 23, 1946.

Vol·ter'ra (vŏl·tĕr'rä); *anc.* **Vol'a·ter'rae** (vŏl'à·tĕr'ē). Commune, Pisa prov., Tuscany, cen. Italy, 29 m. SE of Pisa; pop. 20,638; notable buildings include the citadel, several palaces (13th to 17th cent.), cathedral (remodeled 13th cent.), churches of 13th and 14th cents., and an old abbey; Etruscan antiquities; produces alabaster products; home of ancient Roman poet Persius. In World War II scene of hard fighting in Allied advance northward July 1944.

Vol'tri (vŏl'trĕ). Former seaport commune, now part of Genoa, Genova prov., Liguria, NW Italy; pop. 16,000.

Vol·tur'no (vŏl·tōōr'nŏ). River 110 m. long in S cen. Italy; flows S and SE out of the Apennines, then turns W through Capua into the Gulf of Gaeta, 20 m. SE of Gaeta. German line of defense in World War II; after severe fighting crossed by Allies Oct. 12–14, 1943.

Vo·lu'bi·lis (vŏ·lū'bĭ·lĭs). Ancient Roman town, W Mauretania; now ruins in N Morocco E of Rabat and ab. 19 m. N of Meknes; ruins extensive, esp. of walls; most notable Roman remains in Morocco.

Vo·lu'sia (vŏ·lōō'shà). County in Florida. See *Table* at FLORIDA.

Volyn. See VOLHYNIA.

Volynia. Var. of VOLHYNIA.

Vo·lyn' Region (vŭ·lĭn'y'). Region, NW Ukraine, U.S.S.R.; ✻ Lutsk; formerly part of Volhynia (*Russ. Volyn, Pol.* Wo'łyń [vô'lĭn·y']) and a province of Poland.

Voor'burg (vōr'bûrK). Commune, South Holland prov., SW Netherlands; pop. (1939) 28,349; E suburb of The Hague.

Voor'ne (vōr'nĕ). Island, South Holland prov., SW Netherlands, bet. the estuary of the Nieuwe Maas and the Haringvliet; chief town Brielle (*q.v.*).

Voorst (vōrst). Commune, Gelderland prov., E Netherlands, just NW of Zutphen; pop. 13 812.

Vop'na Fjord (vôp'nä). Inlet of Norwegian Sea, NE Iceland, SE of Thistil Fjord.

Vor'arl'berg (fōr'ärl'bĕrK). A province of Austria, in extreme W part; area 1005 sq. m.; ✻ Bregenz; bounded by Bavaria on N, Switzerland and Liechtenstein on W, Switzerland on S, and Tirol on E; a mountainous region, including source of the Lech and several upper tributaries of the Rhine, and noted for its Alpine scenery and glaciers. See *Table* at AUSTRIA.

Vor'der Rhein (fôr'dĕr rīn'). River in SE Switzerland; flows E to unite with the Hinter Rhein and form the Rhine river.

Vor'ding·borg' (vôr'dĭng·bôrK'). Town, Præstö co., SE Sjælland, Denmark, on coast opp. Falster I.; pop. (1945) 9681.

Voreiai Sporades. = *Northern Sporades:* see SPORADES.

Vö'ring·foss' (vû'rĭng·fôs'). Waterfall 535 ft. in the Bjoreia river, a small stream in SW Norway E of Hardanger Fjord.

Vor·ku'ta (vôr·kōō'tà). Town, E Nenets National District, Soviet Russia, Europe, at N end of Ural Mts.; terminus of railroad from Kotlas and Ust Usa; coal mines.

Vorlich, Ben. See BEN VORLICH.

Vorm'si (vôrm'sĭ), *Ger.* **Worms** (vôrms). Small island in Baltic Sea off W coast of Estonia, bet. Hiiumaa and the mainland; 36 sq. m.; a part of Lääne prov.

Vo·ro'na (vŏ·rô'nà; *Russ.* vŭ·rô'nà). River ab. 200 m. long Penza and Tambov Regions, Soviet Russia, Europe; flows S to the Khoper near Borisoglebsk in E Voronezh Region.

Vo·ro'nezh (vŭ·rô'nĕsh; *Russ.* -nyĕsh). **1** Navigable river 290 m. long, cen. Soviet Russia, Europe; rises in S Ryazan Region, flows S to the Don just S of Voronezh. **2** City, ✻ of Voronezh Region, Soviet Russia, Europe in W part of the region on right bank of Voronezh river near its junction with the Don, 165 m. NE of Kharkov; pop. 326,836; on the main railroad line S from Moscow to Rostov; important industrial city with factories (esp. for making machines), mills, cold-storage plants, railroad shops, etc.; a collecting center for agricultural products; has a university and institute. In early times a Khazar town but not occupied by Russians until 1586 when a fort was built; starting point 1696 for Peter the Great's successful flotilla expedition down the Don against Azov; has been several times destroyed by fire; in World War II captured by German armies July 7, 1942; retaken Jan. 25, 1943.

Voronezh Region. Region, S cen. Soviet Russia, Europe, traversed NW to SE by the Don; 26,866 sq. m.;

pop. 3,551,009; * Voronezh. Chiefly in the valley of the Don bet. the two plateau areas of cen. Russia, but W part is hilly. Has rich soil (black earth) but agriculture until recently has been carried on under many handicaps; principal crops are grains (rye, oats, wheat, millet), hemp, and sunflower seeds. Inhabitants are mainly Great Russians, with some Tatars. Chief towns Voronezh, Buturlinovka. In early times on the S border of Moscow principality; came entirely under Russian tsars in 16th cent.; was a part of Central Black Earth Area 1928 and made a separate region 1936; part W of the Don taken by Germans in 1942 campaign but regained early in 1943.

Vo'ro·shi'lov (vŏr'ŏ·shē'lŏf; *Russ.* vŭ·rŭ·shī'lŭf; *before 1935 called* **Ni·kolsk'–Us·su·rii'ski** (nyĭ·kôl'y'sk-ōōs·sŏō·rē'skĭ), *since 1957* **Us·su·riysk'** (ōōs·sŏō·rēsk'). City, SW Maritime Territory, Soviet Russia, Asia, 50 m. N of Vladivostok; pop. 70,628; junction point of railroad (formerly Russian) across Manchuria with Trans-Siberian R.R.; has railroad-building shops, agricultural machinery factory, sugar factory, oil refinery; important agricultural center.

Vo'ro·shi'lov·grad (vŏr'ŏ·shē'lŭf·grăd; *Russ.* vŭ·rŭ-shī'lŭf·gràt'); *before 1935 and since 1957 called* **Lugansk'** (lŏŏ·gånsk'). City, E Ukraine, U.S.S.R., on a tributary of the Donets 100 m. N of Rostov; pop. 213,007; center of coal-mining region in Donbas; has many engineering works, factories, foundries, mills. Founded c. 1795 when coal mines were opened; has grown rapidly since 1923; in World War II captured by Germans in 1941 and Aug. 3, 1942, and held until Feb. 14, 1943.

Vo'ro·shi'lovsk (vŏr'ŏ·shē'lŏfsk; *Russ.* vŭ·rŭ·shī'lŭfsk).
1 See STAVROPOL.
2 *before 1935 and since 1957 called* **Al·chevsk'** (ŭl-chĕfsk'). City, SW Voroshilovgrad Region, Ukraine, U.S.S.R., ab. 30 m. W of Voroshilovgrad; pop. 54,794; industrial city of the Donbas.

Vorpommern. = *Hither Pomerania:* see POMERANIA.

Vor'skla (vôr'sklà). River ab. 270 m. long, cen. Ukraine, U.S.S.R.; rises in S Kursk Region and flows S past Poltava to the Dnieper above Dnepropetrovsk.

Vorst (vôrst); *Fr.* **Fo'rest'** (fô'rĕ'). Commune, Brabant prov., cen. Belgium, a suburb of Brussels; pop. 39,594.

Võ'ru (vŭ'rŏō). **1** Province of Estonia. See *Table at* ESTONIA.
2 *Ger.* **Wer'ro** (vĕr'ō). Town, its *, SE Estonia, 35 m. E of Valga; pop. (1937) 6144; on railroad bet. Valga and Pskov.

Vosges (vōzh; vôzh). **1** *anc.* **Vos'e·gus** (vŏs'ē·gŭs) *or* **Vog'e·sus** (vŏj'ē·sŭs). Mountain range in NE France, extending bet. Haut-Rhin and Vosges depts.; separated on S from Jura Mts. by Belfort Gap; highest point Ballon de Guebwiller 4667 ft.; has many rounded summits, called (Fr.) *ballons* or (Ger.) *Belchen*.
2 Department of France. See *Table at* FRANCE.

Voss (vôs). Town, Hordaland co., SW Norway, ab. 44 m. ENE of Bergen; pop. 8321.

Vos·tok' (vŭs·tŏk'). Small British uninhabited island of the Line Is. in cen. Pacific Ocean, in 10°6'S lat., 152°23'W long., and ab. 100 m. W by S of Caroline I. Discovered 1820.

Votiak. = *Votyak:* see UDMURT REPUBLIC.

Vot'kinsk (vŏt'kĭnsk; *Russ.* vôt'kĭnsk). Town, E Udmurt Republic, Soviet Russia, Europe, on right bank of Kama river; pop. 19,479; terminus of branch railroad 35 m. E of Izhevsk; famous for its ironworks, established 1759; has produced much agricultural machinery, engines, and other metal goods for the region. Birthplace of Tchaikovsky.

Votyak. See UDMURT REPUBLIC.

Voûxa, Akrotērion. See Cape BUSA.

Vou'ziers' (vŏō'zyä'). Commune, Ardennes dept., NE France, on Aisne river; pop. 2507; fighting Oct. 1918.

Voyutsa. See VIJOSË.

Voyvodina. Var. of VOIVODINA.

Voz'ne·sensk' (vŏz'nĕ·sĕnsk'; *Russ.* vŭz·nyĭ·syĕnsk'). Town, E Odessa Region, S Ukraine, U.S.S.R., at head of navigation of the Bug river 80 m. NNE of Odessa; pop. 20,813; on the Odessa-Cherkassy railroad.

Vraca. See VRATTSA city.

Vrakhori. See AGRINION.

Vrangelya, Ostrov. See WRANGEL ISLAND.

Vra'nja, Vra'nya (vrä'nyä). = VRANJE.

Vra'nje (vrä'nyĕ). Town, Kosovo-Metohija autonomous prov., SE Yugoslavia, near Morava river; pop. 9817; manufactures shoes, textiles, iron products.

Vra'tsa, Vra'tza (vrä'tsä). = VRATTSA.

Vrat'tsa (vrä'tsä). **1** Department, NW Bulgaria; 4298 sq. m.; pop. (1934) 739,366.
2 *or* **Vra'ca** (vrä'tsä). City, its *, 35 m. NNE of Sofia; pop. (1934) 16,177.

Vr'bas (vûr'bäs). River 107 m. long in W Yugoslavia, flowing N into Sava river.

Vr'bas·ka (vûr'bäs·kä). Former county (1929–45), NW cen. Yugoslavia; 7888 sq. m.; pop. 1,008,190; ⊗ Banja Luka; now forms NW part of Bosnia and Herzegovina federated republic.

Vre'de (frē'dĕ; vrēd). Town, NE Orange Free State, E cen. Union of South Africa, 105 m. SE of Johannesburg; pop. 4301; center of region excellent for breeding cattle, sheep, and horses.

Vreed–en–Hoop (vrēd'ĕn·hōōp'). Town, N British Guiana, in Demerara co., ¾ m. by ferry across the Demerara river from Georgetown; pop. (1931) 1531.

Vries Island (vrēs). = O SHIMA, 2.

Vriesland. Var. of FRIESLAND.

Vrie'zen·veen (vrē'zĕn·vān). Commune, Overijssel prov., Netherlands, just N of Almelo; pop. 8576.

Vr'šac (vûr'shäts); *Hung.* **Ver'secz** (vĕr'shĕts); *Ger.* **Wer'schetz** (vĕr'shĕts). City, Voivodina autonomous prov., NE Yugoslavia, near Romanian frontier; pop. 29,411; trade center in grape-growing region; produces red wines and brandy, and grains. Serbs defeated here by Hungarians during Revolution of 1848–49.

Vr'šo·vi'ce (vûr'shô·vi'tsĕ); *Ger.* **Wr'scho·witz** (vûr'-shô·vĭts). Former commune, now part of Prague, Bohemia, Czechoslovakia; pop. ab. 40,000.

Vry'burg (frī'bûrg; frä'-). Town, N Cape Province, S Union of South Africa, on a tributary of Vaal river 125 m. N of Kimberley; pop. 5026; capital of the part of Bechuanaland (British Bechuanaland) included in Union of South Africa; center of pastoral and grazing region. Occupied by Boers during Boer War. See STELLALAND.

Vry'heid (frī'hāt; frä'-). Town, NW Natal, E Union of South Africa, 140 m. N of Durban; pop. 6440; large deposits of iron ore and coal in neighborhood; operates coke plants. Chief town of a district ceded to Boers by a Zulu chief 1884 and declared by them a republic (New Republic); in 1888 incorporated in Transvaal and after Boer War 1899–1902 transferred to Natal.

Vu'a (bŏō'ä) *or* **U'va** (ŏō'vä). River in E Colombia; flows from **Lake Vua** E into Guaviare river.

Vuel'ta A·ba'jo (bwĕl'tä ä·vä'hô). Literally "Lower turn," popular name for the section of Cuba W of the meridian of Havana, mostly Pinar del Río prov.; famous for its production of tobacco.

Vught (vûkt). Commune, North Brabant prov., S Netherlands; pop. 10,135; S suburb of 's Hertogenbosch.

Vu'ko·var (vŏō'kŏ·vär). Town, E Croatia federated republic, N Yugoslavia, on the Danube ab. 83 m. NW of Belgrade; pop. 10,862.

Vul'can, Mount (vŭl'kăn). Volcano, Blanche Bay, SSW of Rabaul and Matupi volcano, E New Britain I., Bismarck Archipelago; formed May 29–30, 1937, at time of eruption of Matupi, by crater being built up on **Vulcan Island** in the bay (island formed by eruption of Mt. Mother 1878).

Vulcan Crest. Peak 13,722 ft. in Mineral and Saguache cos., S Colorado.

Vul·ca′no (vōōl·kä′nô); *anc.* **Hi′er·a** (hī′ĕr·à). Southernmost of the Lipari Is.; erupted 1890.

Vul·can′ Pass (vōōl·kän′; *Angl.* vŭl′kăn). Mountain pass 5000 ft. in W Transylvanian Alps, Romania.

Vul′ture Peak (vŭl′tụr). Mountain 9611 ft. in Glacier National Park, NW Montana.

Vuok′si (vwôk′sĭ) *or* **Vuok′sen** (vwôk′s'n). River in SE Finland and SW Karelia; flows out of Lake Saimaa E into Lake Ladoga.

Vyat′ka *or* **Viat′ka** (vyàt′kà). **1** River ab. 800 m. long, E Soviet Russia, Europe; rises in N Udmurt A.S.S.R. and flows W, S, and SE into Kama river in N Tatar A.S.S.R. **2** Region and city. See KIROV.

Vyaz′ma (vyàz′mà). Town, E Smolensk Region, Soviet Russia, Europe, 125 m. WSW of Moscow on a tributary of the Desna; pop. 17,217; on the Moscow-Smolensk highway and railroad, and a junction railroad point for Rzhev, Kaluga, and Bryansk; has some important industries. In 11th cent. carried on trade with Narva; held alternately by Lithuania, Russia, and Poland, 15th to 17th cent.; became permanently Russian 1634. In World War II occupied by Germans Oct. 1941 and was a strong point in their front line until Russian winter campaign of 1942–43; retaken Mar. 12, 1943.

Vy′borg (vē′bôrg; *Russ.* vī′bĕrk); *Swedish* **Vi′borg** (vē′bôrg; *Swed.* vē′bôr·y'); *Finnish* **Vii′pu·ri** (vē′-pŏŏ·rĭ). Seaport city, NW Leningrad Region, Soviet Russia, Europe, on Vyborg Bay 70 m. NW of Leningrad; pop. 74,247; commercial city on main railroad from Leningrad to Helsinki; has large export trade esp. in lumber, cement, farm products, and ironware; at mouth of canal connecting with interior lakes. Originated as a Swedish castle, built 1293; for centuries was an important cultural and trading town; incorporated 1403; belonged to the republic of Finland after 1917; ceded to Russia, Mar. 12, 1940, as result of Russo-Finnish War 1939–40; retaken by Axis forces (Germans and Finns) Aug. 30, 1941 but again became Russian in collapse of Finnish state June 1944.

Vyborg Bay; *formerly* **Viipuri Bay.** Inlet of NE Gulf of Finland on SW coast of Karelia, U.S.S.R.; at its head is the city of Vyborg.

Vy′cheg·da *or* **Vi′cheg·da** (vĭ′chĕg·dà). River ab. 700 m. long, chiefly in Komi A.S.S.R., Soviet Russia, Europe; flows W to the Northern Dvina river near Kotlas.

Vyernyi. Var. of *Vernyi:* see ALMA ATA.

Vyr′nwy (vûr′nŏŏ·ĭ). River 35 m. long in N cen. and E Wales; flows E into the Severn; **Lake Vyrnwy,** a reservoir ab. 5 m. long in N Montgomeryshire, was created 1880–90 by damming up the river, and is the largest lake in Wales. Cf. BALA LAKE.

Vysh′ni Vo·lo′chek (vĭsh′nyĭ vŭ·lô′chĕk). Town, N Kalinin Region, Soviet Russia, Europe, near source of Tvertsa river 70 m. NW of Kalinin; pop. 63,642; on the Moscow-Leningrad R.R. and on the canal system bet. the Baltic and the Volga inaugurated by Peter the Great, now largely superseded; has sawmills, textile plants, and some manufacturing industries.

Vy′so·ké Mý′to (vĭ′sô·kâ mē′tô); *Ger.* **Ho′hen·mauth** (hō′ĕn·mout). Town, E Bohemia, W Czechoslovakia, on the upper Labe river 75 m. E of Prague; pop. (1930) 10,818.

Vysoké Tatry. See TATRA MOUNTAINS.

Vy′te·ġra (vĭ′tyĭ·grà). Town, NW Vologda Region, Soviet Russia, Europe, near SE shore of Lake Onega on the **Vytegra River,** a short stream flowing into Lake Onega and forming part of the Mariinsk Canal System; pop. ab. 5000.

W

Wa (wä). **1** Town, NW Northern Region, Ghana, West Africa, 120 m. NW of Tamale near Ivory Coast border; pop. 5223.
2 See WA STATES.
Waadt. See VAUD.
Waag. See VÁH.
Waal (väl); *anc.* **Va′ha·lis** (vä′[h]à·lĭs). River in Netherlands, being the S branch of the Lower Rhine; unites with estuaries of the Maas (Meuse) river at Gorinchem. Its course to the North Sea continues as the Merwede and its two branches, the Nieuwe Maas and the Oude Maas.
Waal′wijk (väl′vīk). Commune, North Brabant prov., S Netherlands, N of Tilburg; pop. 9919.
Waas, Mount (wäs). Peak 12,586 ft. in S Grand co., E Utah.
Waasten. See WARNETON.
Wa′bash (wô′băsh). **1** River 475 m. long in Indiana and Illinois; rises in Darke co., W Ohio, flows W and SW across Indiana to form S section of Indiana-Illinois boundary, and empties into Ohio river at SW extremity of Indiana.
2 Name of counties in two states of the U.S. See *Tables* at ILLINOIS and INDIANA.
3 City, ⊗ of Wabash co., N Indiana, 20 m. NNW of Marion; pop. 12,621; trading center in agricultural area; manufactures tractors, trucks, office supplies.
Wa′ba·sha (wô′bá·shô). **1** County in Minnesota. See *Table* at MINNESOTA.
2 City, its ⊗, SE Minnesota, on Mississippi river 30 m. NW of Winona; pop. 2500; wheat collection and shipping center.
Wa·baun′see (wǒ·bôn′sē). County in Kansas. See *Table* at KANSAS.
Wac′ca·maw (wŏk′à·mô). River ab. 130 m. long, S North Carolina and NE South Carolina; flows through **Waccamaw Lake**, in Columbus co., North Carolina, SW across South Carolina border into Pee Dee river near its mouth.
Wac′ca·sas′sa Bay (wŏ′kà·săs′à). Inlet of Gulf of Mexico on SW coast of Levy co., NW Florida penin.
Wa·cho′vi·a (wŏ·chō′vĭ·à). Region, W cen. North Carolina, E of Yadkin river; settled and named by Moravians from Bethlehem, Pennsylvania, in 1752–53; Bethabara the first settlement (now a small village), and Salem, now part of Winston-Salem.
Wa·chu′sett Mountain (wŏ·chōō′sět; -sĭt). Isolated peak 2006 ft. in Worcester co., cen. Massachusetts.
Wachusett Reservoir. Reservoir 18½ m. long in E cen. Worcester co., cen. Massachusetts, formed by **Wachusett Dam.** A rock tunnel 24½ m. long connected with Quabbin Reservoir (see UNITED STATES, *Dams and Reservoirs*) furnishes constant water supply for Boston.
Wa′co (wā′kō). City, ⊗ of McLennan co., cen. Texas, on Brazos river 82 m. S of Fort Worth; pop. 97,808; founded 1849; incorp. 1850; commercial and shipping center in agricultural region (cotton, grain); cotton market; manufactures cotton products, textiles and clothing, furniture, saddles. Baylor Univ. (1845; coed.); Paul Quinn Coll. (1881; coed.).
Wad, El. See EL OUED.
Wa·dai′ (wä·dī′); *Fr.* **Oua′daï′** (wȧ′dī′). Former independent sultanate in E Chad, NE cen. Africa; ab. 80,000 sq. m.; pop. (est.) ab. 1,000,000; ✳ Abéché; a fertile plateau region with some hilly sections; inhabited by warlike Negroid tribes. Sultanate (kingdom) dates back to middle of 17th cent.; came under French influence 1899 and made a protectorate 1903.
Wadan. See OUADANE.
Wad′den Zee (väd′ĕ[n] zā). Outer section of the former Zuider Zee, bet. the outer islands and the dike enclosing IJsselmeer.

Wad′ding·ton (wŏd′ĭng·tŭn). Parish, Lincolnshire, E England, just S of Lincoln; pop. 1140; airfield.
Wad′ding·ton, Mount (wŏd′ĭng·tŭn). Peak 13,260 ft. in SW Brit. Columbia, Canada, near head of Knight Inlet; a peak of the Coast Mts. and highest point in Brit. Columbia.
Wad Dra. See Wad DRA.
Wa′de·lai (wä′dĕ·lī). Town, NW Uganda protectorate, on Nile river N of Lake Albert, where the river narrows suddenly to ab. 500 ft. width.
Wa·de′na (wŏ·dē′nà). **1** County in Minnesota. See *Table* at MINNESOTA.
2 Village, its ⊗, cen. Minnesota, 43 m. WNW of Brainerd; pop. 4381; railroad and agricultural trade center.
Wä′dens·wil (vâ′dĕns·vēl). Commune, Zurich canton, NE cen. Switzerland, on S shore of Lake of Zurich 12 m. SSE of Zurich; pop. (1930) 9501; manufactures silk, woolen goods; produces wine, fruit.
Wades′bor′o (wādz′bûr′ō). Town, ⊗ of Anson co., S North Carolina, 46 m. ESE of Charlotte; pop. 3744; manufactures lumber, cotton, cottonseed products, textiles, flour.
Wadh·wan′ (wȧd·hwän′). **1** Former Indian state, NE Kathiawar, Western India States, W Indian Union; 242 sq. m.; pop. (1941) 50,915; joined new confederation of states July 7, 1947.
2 Town, state ✳, railroad junction 65 m. WSW of Ahmadabad; pop. 18,269.
Wa′di (wȧ′dĭ; *Angl.* wŏd′ĭ). In the Near East and Northern Africa an Arabic term used in place names, meaning "valley, river, dry river bed," as Wadi el 'Araba, Wadi Mojib. For names beginning with this term, see the second element, as 'ARABA, MOJIB, etc.
Wadi el Kebir. See GUADALQUIVIR.
Wa′di Hal′fa (wä′dĭ hăl′fà; -fä) or **Halfa.** Commercial town, Northern prov., N Republic of Sudan, on the Nile river; ✳ of former Halfa prov.; pop. (1938 est.) 10,597; at the S boundary of Egypt just below the 2d Cataract; S terminus of steamboat service on the Nile and N terminus of railroad (232 m.) to Abu Hamed to the SE on the big bend of the Nile.
Wadi Musa. See PETRA.
Wad Me′da·ni (wäd mě′dä·nĭ). City, ✳ of Blue Nile prov., E Sudan, SSE of Khartoum; pop. 47,677.
Wads′worth (wŏdz′wûrth; -wērth). Industrial city, Medina co., N Ohio, 11 m. WSW of Akron; pop. 10,635; settled 1814; manufactures matches, valves, lubricators, locomotive appliances.
Wae′re·ghem (vȧ′rĕ·кĕm). Commune, West Flanders prov., NW Belgium, 43 m. W of Brussels; pop. 10,167; site of Flanders Field Cemetery, the only American military cemetery in Belgium for soldiers of World War I.
Waes (vàs) or **Pays de Waes** (pā′ēd′ vàs′). Ancient district comprising part of the modern provinces of East Flanders in Belgium and Zeeland in the Netherlands.
Wagadugu. See OUAGADOUGOU.
Wa′ge·ning′en (vȧ′кĕ·nĭng′ĕ[n]). Commune, Gelderland prov., E Netherlands, on N bank of Neder Rijn 11 m. W of Arnhem; pop. 13,167.
Wa′ger Bay (wā′jẽr). Inlet ab. 160 m. long and 38 m. wide at greatest width, NE Keewatin District, Northwest Territories, Canada, opening into Roes Welcome.
Wag′ga Wag′ga (wŏg′à wŏg′à). Town, S New South Wales, SE Australia, on Murrumbidgee river 100 m. W of Canberra; pop. 11,631; center of wheat, fruit, and grazing district (see RIVERINA).
Wa·gi′na (wä·gĭn′à). Small island W of Manning Strait and off SE end of Choiseul I., E Solomon Is., W Pacific Ocean.
Wag′ner (wăg′nẽr). City, Charles Mix co., S South Dakota, 47 m. SSW of Mitchell; pop. 1586.

Wag′on·er (wăg′ŭn·ēr). **1** County in Oklahoma. See *Table* at OKLAHOMA.
2 City, its ⊗, NE Oklahoma, 14 m. N of Muskogee; pop. 4469; estab. 1886; cottonseed oil, brick and clay products, cotton gins; gas and oil wells; coal mines.

Wa′gram (vä′gräm). Village, Lower Austria, in the Marchfeld 11 m. NE of Vienna; battle July 5 and 6, 1809 in which Napoleon defeated the Austrians under Archduke Charles Louis.

Wa·ha Lake (wô′hô). Lake, Nez Percé co., W Idaho, 18 m. SE of Lewiston; source of the Waha Lake trout (*Salmo bouvieri*).

Wa·hi·a·wa′ (wä′hĕ·ȧ·wä′). **1** District, Honolulu co., cen. Oahu I., Hawaii; pop. 34,595; pineapple plantations.
2 City in district on cen. plateau; pop. 15,512; U.S. Army post of Schofield Barracks adjoins it.

Wahiawa Bay. Bay on S coast of Kauai I., Hawaii, bet. Lawai Bay and Hanapepe Bay.

Wa·hi′e Point (wä·hē′ä). Cape on NE coast of Lanai I., Hawaii.

Wah·ki′a·kum (wô·kĭ′ȧ·kŭm). County in Washington. See *Table* at WASHINGTON.

Wahl′statt (väl′shtät). Village just SE of Legnica (Liegnitz), Wrocław dept., SW Poland, before 1945 in Silesia prov., Prussia, Germany; scene of battle Apr. 9, 1241 in which Batu Khan defeated Henry, Duke of Silesia.

Wa′hoo (wä′hōō). City, ⊗ of Saunders co., E Nebraska, 17 m. SSW of Fremont; pop. 3610.

Wah′pe·ton (wô′pĕ·tŭn). City, ⊗ of Richland co., SE corner of North Dakota, on Red river 44 m. S of Fargo; pop. 5876; manufactures processed dairy and poultry products; pottery; printing and binding establishments.

Wahsatch. Var. of WASATCH.

Wah Wah Mountains (wä′ wä′). Range in W Utah, in S Millard and N Beaver cos.

Wai′a·la′e Bay (wī′ä·lä′ä). = MAUNALUA BAY.

Wai·a′le·a′le (wī·ä·lä·ä′lä). Mountain 5080 ft., cen. Kauai I., Hawaii.

Wai·a·lu′a (wī′ä·lōō′ä). **1** District, Honolulu co., N Oahu I., Hawaii; pop. 8221.
2 *or* **Waialua Mill.** Town in district near N coast of Oahu; pop. 2689.

Waialua Bay. Bay on N coast of Oahu I., Hawaii, bet. Kaiaka Bay and Waimea Bay.

Wai·a·na′e (wī′ä·nä′ä). **1** District, Honolulu co., W Oahu I., Hawaii; pop. 16,452.
2 Village in district on W coast of Oahu; pop. (with Makaha) 6844.

Waianae Range. Mountain range extending along SW side of Oahu I., Hawaii; highest peak Kaala 4030 ft.

Wai·a′u (wī·ä′ōō). River ab. 60 m. long in S South I., New Zealand; flows S from Te Anau Lake and Manapouri Lake into Tewaewae Bay on Foveaux Strait.

Waichow. See WAIYEUNG.

Wai·ge′o (wī·gä′ô). Island 80 m. long and 28 m. wide, NE Moluccas, Indonesia, off NW end of Neth. New Guinea; highest point 3281 ft.; pop. ab. 2400; nearly divided in two parts by long inlet; covered with dense forests.

Wai′he′ki (wī′hä′kĕ). Island in Hauraki Gulf, N coast of North I., New Zealand.

Wai·hi′ (wī·hē′). Borough, Auckland provincial dist., N North I., New Zealand, 75 m. ESE of Auckland; pop. 3150.

Wai′ka′to (wī′kä′tō). River 220 m. long in NW North I., New Zealand; flows N and W into Pacific Ocean S of Manukau Harbor.

Wai·ki·ki′ Beach (wī′kĭ·kē′). Pleasure resort on SE Oahu I., Hawaii, SE section of Honolulu, near Diamond Head; bathing and boating.

Wai′lang′i La′la (wī′läng′ē lä′lä). Small island, NE Fiji Is., SW Pacific Ocean; lighthouse for ships passing through Nanuku Passage.

Wai·lu′a Bay (wī·lōō′ä). Bay on E coast of Maui I., Hawaii.

Wai·lu′ku (wī·lōō′kōō). **1** District, Maui co., Hawaii, W cen. Maui I.; pop. 6969; sugar plantations.
2 Village in district on N coast of Maui I.; chief town and ⊗ of Maui co.; an educational center since early days; schools established 1835–37.

Wailuku Valley. See IAO VALLEY.

Wai·ma′ka·ri′ri (wī·mä′kä·rē′rē). River ab. 90 m. long in NE cen. South I., New Zealand; flows SE into Pegasus Bay ab. 12 m. N of Port Lyttelton.

Wai′ma′te (wī′mä′tä). Borough, Canterbury provincial dist., E South I., New Zealand, 80 m. NNE of Dunedin; pop. 2315; in grazing and farming district.

Wai·me′a (wī·mä′ä). **1** District, W Kauai I., Kauai co., Hawaii; pop. (with Kekaha) 3969; also includes Nuhau I. (to SW).
2 Village, South Kohala dist., Hawaii co., Hawaii, in N part of island; pop. (1950) 560; its post office is Kamuela; a place of importance in the early wars of the kingdom.
3 Village, Waimea dist., SW coast of Kauai I., Hawaii; pop. 1312; canyon nearby 3000 ft. deep.

Waimea Bay. 1 Harbor of Waimea village, SW coast of Kauai I., Hawaii; first anchorage of Capt. Cook Jan. 1778; visited by Vancouver 1792.
2 Bay on N coast of Oahu I., Hawaii.

Wain·gan′ga (wǐn·gŭng′gä) *or* **Wain River** (wǐn). River (*ganga*) ab. 360 m. long in Madhya Pradesh and Maharashtra, cen. India; rises in Seoni dist., flows S to unite with Wardha and form the Pranhita river.

Wain·ga′poe *or* **Wain·ga′pu** (wǐn·gä′pōō). Seaport and chief town of Sumba I., Lesser Sunda Is., Indonesia, on N coast; pop. 2127; has good harbor.

Wai′ni (wī′nē). River ab. 140 m. long in NW British Guiana; flows NE, then curves to NW and empties into Atlantic Ocean near border of Venezuela.

Wain′wright Buffalo Park (wān′rīt). = *Buffalo National Park* now included in *Wood Buffalo National Park:* see CANADA, *National Parks.*

Wai·pa′ (wī·pä′). River ab. 60 m. long, S tributary of Waikato river in SW Auckland provincial dist., North I., New Zealand.

Wai·pa′hu (wī·pä′hōō). City, Ewa dist., Honolulu co., S Oahu I., Hawaii, on NW shore of Pearl Harbor just W of Pearl City; pop. (est.) 9000; suffered damage in Japanese attack on Pearl Harbor Dec. 7, 1941.

Wai′pa′pa Point (wī′pä′pä). Cape on NE coast of South I., New Zealand, at mouth of Clarence river.

Wai′rau (wī′rou). River ab. 100 m. long in N South I., New Zealand; flows ENE into Cloudy Bay.

Wai·ro′a (wī·rō′ä). **1** River ab. 60 m. long in E cen. North I., New Zealand; flows S into N Hawke Bay.
2 River ab. 70 m. long in N extension of North I., New Zealand; flows S into Kaipara Harbor on W coast.
3 Seaport borough, Hawke′s Bay provincial dist., E North I., New Zealand, on Hawke Bay at mouth of Wairoa river; pop. 2490.

Wai′ta′ki (wī′tä′kē). River 135 m. long in SE cen. South I., New Zealand; flows ESE into Pacific Ocean N of Oamaru.

Wai′tang′i (wī′täng′ē). Village, Auckland provincial dist., N North I., New Zealand, on Bay of Islands 115 m. NNW of Auckland. In 1840 treaty signed here bet. Maori chiefs and British Empire.

Wai·ta·ra (wī′tȧ·rȧ). Coast borough on North Taranaki Bight, Taranaki provincial dist., W North I., New Zealand, NE of New Plymouth; pop. 1810.

Wai·te·ma′ta Harbor (wī′tä·mä′tä). Inlet at SW corner of Hauraki Gulf, on N coast of North I., New Zealand; harbor for Auckland.

Wai·to′mo Caves (wī·tō′mō). Underground caverns near Te Kuiti, W North I., New Zealand; their Glowworm Grotto is illuminated by myriads of glowworms.

Waitzen. See VÁC.

Wai′yeung′ (wī′yüng′); *formerly* **Wai′chow′** (wī′jō′). City, Kwangtung prov., SE China, on Tung river 70 m. E of Canton; pop. ab. 40,000.

Wa·ka·ma·tsu (wä·kä·mä·tsoō). **1** Former city, Fukuoka prefecture, N Kyushu I., Japan, opp. Tobata and 3 m. N of Yawata; pop. (1945) 68,199; an important seaport. See KITA-KYUSHU.

2 City, Fukushima prefecture, N cen. Honshu, Japan, 35 m. SW of Fukushima; pop. (1945) 56,230; produces lacquer wares, pottery, and fabrics. In early times an important daimio city; almost entirely destroyed in fighting at time of Restoration 1868.

Wakasa Bay. Inlet of the Sea of Japan on the W coast of Honshu I., Japan, in Fukui prefecture.

Wa'ka·ti'pu Lake (wä'kä·tē'pōō; wä'kä·tĭp). Lake in SW South I., New Zealand; 54 m. long; 112 sq. m.

Wa·ka·ya·ma (wä·kä·yä·mä). **1** Prefecture of Japan. See *Table* at JAPAN.

2 Seaport city, its ✳, SW Honshu, 35 m. SSW of Osaka on Kii Channel; pop. (1945) 147,523; produces cotton cloth and lacquer ware. Was seat of one of the Tokugawa branches; has large castle built in 16th cent. by Hideyoshi. Earthquake and tidal wave Dec. 21, 1946.

Wak'de (wäk'dĕ). Group of small islands off NE coast of Neth. New Guinea halfway bet. Tanahmerah Bay and the mouth of the Mamberamo river; site of Japanese airdrome seized by Allied Nations forces May 21, 1944.

Wake (wāk). County in North Carolina. See *Table* at NORTH CAROLINA.

Wa'Kee'ney (wô'kē'nĭ). City, ⊗ of Trego co., W cen. Kansas, 78 m. NW of Great Bend; pop. 2808.

Wake'field (wāk'fēld). **1** Town, Middlesex co., NE Massachusetts, 10 m. N of Boston; pop. 24,295; site of first rattan factory in the world.

2 City, Gogebic co., NW Michigan penin., 12 m. E of Ironwood; pop. 3231; iron mining.

3 Village and summer resort, Washington co., S Rhode Island, ab. 3 m. SSE of Kingston; pop. 5569 (with Peacedale); administrative center of South Kingstown; manufactures woolen and cotton goods.

4 *or* **Bridg'es Creek** (brĭj'ĕz; -ĭz). Estate on S bank of Potomac river and near mouth of Popes Creek, Westmoreland co., Virginia; birthplace of George Washington. Estate acquired by Augustine Washington 1718; became property 1923 of Wakefield National Memorial Association which later conveyed its acres to the United States as the George Washington Birthplace National Monument (see UNITED STATES, *National Monuments*).

5 City and county borough, ⊗ of West Riding, Yorkshire, N England, on the Calder 10 m. S of Leeds; pop. (1951) 60,380; woolens, chemicals, and machinery; coal mining. Scene of battle (Wars of the Roses) at which Richard, Duke of York, was captured and beheaded by Lancastrians; possibly scene, ab. 15th cent., of presentation of the Towneley Mysteries or Wakefield Plays, one of the four collections of English miracle plays (see CHESTER, COVENTRY, YORK).

Wake Forest (wāk). Town, Wake co., E cen. North Carolina, 16 m. NNE of Raleigh; pop. 2664. Wake Forest Coll. established here 1833, moved 1956 to Winston-Salem.

Wake Island. Small sandy island in N Pacific Ocean, 480 m. N of N Marshall Is., 1180 m. W of Midway and 1500 m. ENE of Guam; lat. 19°18′N and long. 166°35′E; actually three islets around a lagoon: Wake, the largest, on the E, Peale on the N, and Wilkes on the SW; total area 3 sq. m.; highest point 21 ft. Long uninhabited but had many sea birds, rats, and crabs. Acquired by United States July 4, 1898, by expeditionary force on the way to Manila; became an important civil aviation station 1935 and naval and air station 1939–41. Captured by Japan Dec. 23, 1941, after heroic resistance of 15 days by small contingent of U.S. Marines. Frequently raided 1942–44.

Wake'ly, Mount (wāk'lĭ). Peak 3617 ft. in the Adirondack Mts., Hamilton co., NE cen. New York.

Wa'ke·naam' (wä'kĕ·näm'). Island at mouth of Essequibo river, off NE coast of British Guiana.

Wa·khan' (wä·kän'). **1** High narrow valley in NE Afghanistan in the Pamirs, forming a district extending E to long. 75°E bet. Tadzhik S.S.R. of Soviet Central Asia and NW India (Kashmir and Chitral).

2 River flowing W through the valley, an upper tributary of the Ab-i-Pandj forming in part its NW boundary.

Wak·ka·nai (wäk·kä·nĭ). Seaport town, Hokkaido prefecture, N extremity of Hokkaido, Japan, on S side of Soya Strait; pop. (1945) 26,962.

Wa·kul'la (wŏ·kŭl'à). **1** County in Florida. See *Table* at FLORIDA.

2 Village, N Wakulla co., NW Florida, S of Tallahassee; nearby is **Wakulla Springs**, a pool (ab. 4 acres) out of which flows the **Wakulla River.**

Wa·la'chi·a *or* **Wal·la'chi·a** (wŏ·lā'kĭ·à). Former principality bet. Danube river and Transylvanian Alps, S Romania; 29,561 sq. m.; includes Muntenia and Oltenia. Plain region along the Danube with plateau and mountains in N part; traversed by many tributaries of the Danube flowing S. Chief towns Bucharest, Ploeşti, Brăila, Craiova.

History: Inhabited by a people which combines Slavic stock with strain probably derived from Roman colonists of Dacia (*q.v.*); established as principality by Radul Negru (d. 1310), a vassal of Hungary; Târgovişte its capital 1383–1698; made tributary to Turks in 15th cent.; under Prince Michael the Bold (1593–1601) annexed Moldavia and Transylvania (*qq.v.*); from 1716 ruled by Phanariots from Constantinople instead of by dependent native princes; Little Walachia held by Austria 1713–39; occupied by Russia 1769; for history after 1774, see DANUBIAN PRINCIPALITIES.

Wa·law'bum (wà·lô'bŭm). Village, N Burma, on Stilwell Road S of Hukawng valley; captured by Allies Mar. 4, 1944.

Wał'brzych (väl'bzhĭk); *Ger.* **Wal'den·burg** (väl'dĕn-bŏŏrk), *also* **Waldenburg in Schle'si·en** (ĭn shlā'zĕ·ĕn). Industrial city, S Wrocław dept., SW Poland, on the Bobr in foothills of Riesen Gebirge 42 m. SW of Wrocław; pop. (1946) 66,372; formerly in Germany; coal mining; manufactures porcelain, iron goods, ceramic ware. Assigned to Poland by Potsdam Conference 1945.

Wal'che·ren (väl'ĸĕ·rĕ[n]). Island of Netherlands, in Zeeland prov., in the North Sea off the SW coast; 11 m. in diameter; area 82 sq. m.; pop. ab. 66,000; chief towns Vlissingen and Middelburg. Scene of earl of Chatham's disastrous expedition 1809 during Napoleonic Wars in attempt to capture Antwerp; in World War II strongly defended by German force but after Allied bombing of dikes occupied by British Nov. 1–3, 1944; drained again by Dec. 1945.

Wałcz (välch); *Ger.* **Deutsch–Kro'ne** (doich'krō'nĕ). Town, SE Szczecin dept., NW Poland, NW of Piła; pop. (1946) 13,359; formerly in Grenzmark Posen-Westpreussen.

Wald (vält). **1** Former city (pop. 27,560), Düsseldorf govt. dist., Rhine Province, Prussia, Germany; since 1929 part of Solingen (*q.v.*); iron goods.

2 Industrial commune, E Zurich canton, Switzerland, 18 m. ESE of Zurich; pop. (1930) 6936.

Wal'deck (väl'dĕk). **1** Former state of Germany, bet. Westphalia and Hesse-Nassau; part of Hesse-Nassau prov., Prussia, 1929–45; now in N Hesse; 407 sq. m.; pop. ab. 56,000; ✳ Arolsen. In Middle Ages a county; in 1712 raised to a principality; became part of Prussia 1867 and 1918–29 a republic, forming a constituent state of the Weimar Republic.

2 Town, N Hesse, Germany, on the Eder river S of Arolsen; pop. ab. 1000.

Wal'den (wôl'dĕn). **1** Town, ⊗ of Jackson co., N Colorado; pop. 809.

2 Village, Orange co., SE New York, 10 m. WNW of Newburgh; pop. 4851; settled before 1768; farming; manufactures cutlery, women's underwear, hats, engines.

Waldenburg, Waldenburg in Schlesien. See WAŁBRZYCH.

Wal′den Pond (wôl′dĕn). Pond in Middlesex co., NE Massachusetts, near Concord; on its shore Henry Thoreau lived 1845–47; results of his study and thought and observations of nature published 1854 as series of essays in *Walden, or Life in the Woods*.

Walden Ridge. Ridge extending from NE to SW in E cen. Tennessee.

Wald′heim (vält′hīm). City, Leipzig dist., East Germany, 32 m. W of Dresden; pop. 12,394; manufactures perfumes, toilet soap, cigars, wooden goods; serpentine quarrying.

Wal′do (wôl′dō; wŏl′-). County in Maine. See *Table* at MAINE.

Wal′do·bor′o (wôl′dō·bûr′ō; wŏl′-). Town, Lincoln co., S Maine, 26 m. ESE of Augusta; pop. 2882; tourist and fishing resort.

Wal′dron (wôl′drŭn). City, ⊗ of Scott co., W Arkansas; pop. 1619; farm trade center.

Waldstätter, Die Vier. See the Four FOREST CANTONS.

Wald′wick (wôld′wĭk). Residential borough, Bergen co., NE New Jersey, 7 m. N of Paterson; pop. 10,495.

Walensee. See Lake WALLEN.

Wales (wālz). 1 Principality forming wide peninsula on W of island of Great Britain; part of the United Kingdom of Great Britain and Northern Ireland; area 7469 sq. m.; pop. (1951) 2,172,339; ✻ Cardiff; bounded on N by Irish Sea, on E by England, on S by Bristol Channel, on W by St. George's Channel; St. David's Head, Pembrokeshire, its westernmost point, 5°20′W; divided into the following 12 counties (for pronunciation of their names, see their individual entries):

NAME[1]	LOCA-TION	AREA[2]	POP.[2]	CO. SEAT
Anglesey	NW	276	50,637	Llangefni
Brecknockshire	SE	733	56,484	Brecknock
Caernarvonshire	NW	569	124,074	Caernarvon
Cardiganshire	W	692	53,267	Aberystwyth
Carmarthenshire	S	919	171,742	Carmarthen
Denbighshire	N	669	170,699	Ruthin
Flintshire	NE	256	145,108	Mold
Glamorganshire	SE	813	1,201,989	Cardiff
Merionethshire	W	660	41,456	Dolgelley
Montgomeryshire	E	797	45,989	Welshpool
Pembrokeshire	SW	614	90,896	Haverfordwest
Radnorshire	E	471	19,998	Llandrindod Wells

[1] For county names ending in *-shire*, the *-shire* is often omitted in informal use when there is no ambiguity. In legal use, *county of Caernarvon, Denbigh, Flint*, etc., not *Caernarvonshire, Denbighshire*, etc., is preferred. The redundant *county of Caernarvonshire*, etc. is regarded as incorrect. Monmouthshire (*q.v.*) is sometimes regarded as a part of Wales.

[2] Area in sq. m. Pop. is 1951 Census.

Almost entirely an upland region, known generally as the Cambrian Mts.; highest mountains Snowdon massif in NW 3560 ft., highest point in England and Wales; Berwyn Mts. in NE and Brecon Beacons in SE. Its chief streams are the Dee in N, upper course of Severn in E, and Conway in N; numerous small lakes. Coast line irregular, indented by wide bays, esp. Cardigan Bay on W, enclosed on N by Lleyn Penin. and bounded on S by the large peninsula formed by counties of Pembroke, Cardigan, and Carmarthen. Only large island is Anglesey off NW coast, separated from mainland by narrow Menai Strait. Stock raising, coal mining, and textile industries are important. Chief cities Cardiff, Swansea, Rhondda, and Merthyr Tydfil.

History: Inhabited in prehistoric times by the insular branch of the Celts, the Cymric, or Brythonic, people, whose land covered much larger area than present Wales, extending into W and SW England; conquered by Romans in their occupation of Britain (see GREAT BRITAIN); remained Celtic during Anglo-Saxon invasions; in 12th cent. Normans established marches on Welsh border and in S Wales; N Wales conquered by Edward I 1277–84 and Wales made an English principality by

Statute of Wales 1284; since 1301 the heir to the English throne has been Prince of Wales; incorporated with England by series of statutes drawn up in reign of Henry VIII.

2 Village on Cape Prince of Wales, W Alaska; westernmost point, 168°W, of mainland of North America; pop. (1950) 141.

Walfischbai. See WALVIS BAY town.

Walfish Bay. See WALVIS BAY.

Wal′green Coast (wôl′grēn). Region on coast of Antarctica forming part of Marie Byrd Land, W of Thurston Penin. (*q.v.*) and bordering on Amundsen Sea; W boundary undetermined.

Wal·hal′la (wŏl·hăl′à). 1 City, Pembina co., NE corner of North Dakota, 80 m. NNW of Grand Forks; pop. 1432; site of early mission for Indians (1848) and fur trading post; mountain resort; clay pits; agriculture.

2 Town, ⊗ of Oconee co., NW South Carolina, near Blue Ridge Mts. 31 m. WNW of Anderson; pop. 3431; summer resort; manufactures cotton goods, bedspreads.

Wal·hon′ding (wŏl·hŏn′dĭng). River, Coshocton co., cen. Ohio, formed by junction of forks 16 m. NW of Coshocton; flows SE and joins Tuscarawas river to form Muskingum river.

Walk. See VALK.

Walk′er (wôk′ẽr). 1 River ab. 50 m. long, W cen. Nevada; formed in Lyon co. by branches which rise in California, flows N and then SE through Walker River Indian Reservation into Walker Lake.

2 Name of counties in three states of the U.S. See *Tables* at ALABAMA, GEORGIA, TEXAS.

3 Village, ⊗ of Cass co., N cen. Minnesota; pop. 1180.

Walker Lake. Lake ab. 28 m. long in NW Mineral co., SW Nevada; no outlet.

Walker Pass. Mountain pass 5248 ft., Kern co., S California, in S end of the Sierra Nevada; named for the American trapper and guide, Joseph Walker, who explored this region 1834 ff.

Walk′er·ton (wôk′ẽr·tŭn; -t′n). Industrial town, ⊗ of Bruce co., SE Ontario, Canada, on Saugeen River 33 m. S of Owen Sound; pop. 3264; flour and planing mills, foundries, tanneries, rope and furniture factories.

Walk′er·ville (wôk′ẽr·vĭl). 1 City, Silver Bow co., SW Montana, N suburb of Butte; pop. 1453; copper mines.

2 Former town, Essex co., SE Ontario, Canada; annexed to Windsor 1935.

Wall (wôl). Borough, Allegheny co., SW Pennsylvania, 12 m. E of Pittsburgh; pop. 1493.

Wall′a·bout′ Bay (wŏl′à·bout′). Inlet of the East river on N shore of W end of Long I., New York, and opp. SE corner of Manhattan I.

Wal′lace (wŏl′ĭs). 1 County in Kansas. See *Table* at KANSAS.

2 City, ⊗ of Shoshone co., NE Idaho, 45 m. ESE of Coeur d'Alene; pop. 2412; incorp. as town 1888, as city 1893; in heart of silver and lead-mining district.

Wal′lace·burg (wŏl′ĭs·bûrg). Industrial town, Kent co., SE Ontario, Canada, 17 m. NW of Chatham; pop. 7688; glass, brass and iron products, dies, sugar, flour.

Wallachia. See WALACHIA.

Wal′la·roo (wŏl′à·rōō). Seaport town, SE South Australia, on E shore of Spencer Gulf 90 m. NW of Adelaide; pop. 2741; mining center; has copper smelters.

Wal′la·sey (wŏl′à·sĭ). County borough, Cheshire, NW England, on Irish Sea 9 m. W of Liverpool; pop. 97,626, (1951) 101,331; has extensive docks.

Wal′la Wal′la (wŏl′à wŏl′à). 1 County in Washington. See *Table* at WASHINGTON.

2 City, its ⊗, SE Washington, ab. 118 m. SW of Spokane near Walla Walla river; pop. 24,536; trading and distributing point in agricultural and lumbering country; manufactures processed foods, cans, agricultural implements, flour. Whitman Coll. (1859; coed.); Walla Walla Coll. (1892; coed.) in College Place, a suburb. Settled around U.S. Army fort (first estab. 1856) at

time of Indian wars of 1855–58; became outfitting point for Idaho gold rush 1860; incorp. as city 1862.

Wal′len, Lake (väl′ĕn); *Ger.* **Wa′len·see′** *or* **Wal′len-see′** (väl′ĕn·zā′). Lake 9 sq. m. in NE Switzerland, in Saint Gallen canton; receives the Linth river from the S; linked by canal (Linth Canal) with the Lake of Zurich to the W.

Wal′len·pau′pack, Lake (wŏl′ĕn·pô′păk). Lake 9 sq. m. on boundary bet. Wayne and Pike cos., NE Pennsylvania; formed by dam in **Wallenpaupack Creek.**

Wal′ler (wŏl′ēr). County in Texas. See *Table* at TEXAS.

Wall′face′ Mountain (wôl′fās′). Peak 3860 ft. in the Adirondack Mts., Essex co., NE New York.

Wal′ling·ford (wŏl′ĭng·fērd). **1** Town, NE New Haven co., S Connecticut, S of Meriden; pop. 29,920; agriculture, manufacturing. Includes industrial borough of Wallingford on Quinnipiac river 12 m. NE of New Haven; manufactures sterling and plated silverware, steel, nickel, and brassware, hardware, tools, wire; Choate School (boys' preparatory school).
2 Municipal borough, Berkshire, S England; pop. 3514; treaty 1153 (negotiated here but signed at Westminster) bet. King Stephen and Prince Henry, by which Stephen kept throne for his lifetime only, and Henry succeeded him.

Wal′ling·ton (wŏl′ĭng·tǔn). Borough, Bergen co., NE corner of New Jersey, on Passaic river 6 m. SSE of Paterson; pop. 9261; manufactures curtains, paints.

Wallis. See VALAIS canton, Switzerland.

Wal′lis and Fu·tu′na Islands (wŏl′ĭs, fōō·tōō′nà). French territory in SW Pacific Ocean, until 1959 a dependency of New Caledonia territory; ab. 100 sq. m.; pop. ab. 10,000; comprises the two groups of Wallis Is. and Futuna Is.

Wal′lis Islands (wŏl′ĭs). Island group in SW Pacific Ocean, a part of Wallis and Futuna Islands territory; 40 sq. m.; pop. ab. 10,000; comprises the main island of Uvéa and eight islets, all enclosed in one coral reef. Discovered by Samuel Wallis, English navigator, 1767; occupied by French 1842; joined with Futuna Is. 1887 and attached to New Caledonia colony until 1959.

Wal′lo (wŏl′ō; *native* wûl·lō). Region, N cen. Ethiopia; very mountainous, some peaks above 12,000 ft. Chief towns Dessie and Magdala.

Wal·lo′ni·a (wŏ·lō′nĭ·à; -lōn′yà); *Fr.* **Wal·lo′nie′** (wȧ′lô′nē′). Name sometimes applied to the French-speaking part of Belgium, comprising provs. of Hainaut, Liège, Luxembourg, Namur, and S part of Brabant.

Wal′lops Island (wŏl′ŭps). Island, Accomac co., E Virginia, in Atlantic Ocean NE of Assawaman Inlet; rocket-launching base.

Wal·low′a (wŏ·lou′à). **1** River ab. 50 m. long, NE Oregon; rises in Wallowa Lake, S Wallowa co., flows NW into Grande Ronde river on Wallowa co. boundary.
2 County in Oregon. See *Table* at OREGON.

Wallowa Lake. Lake, S Wallowa co., NE corner of Oregon.

Wallowa Mountains. Range in NE Oregon, in S Wallowa, N Baker, and E Union cos.

Walls′end′ (wôlz′ĕnd′). **1** Town, E New South Wales, SE Australia, W suburb of Newcastle; pop. 6934; collieries.
2 Municipal borough, Northumberland, N England, on the Tyne 4 m. ENE of Newcastle; pop. 48,645; in coal-mining section (*Wallsend coal* takes its name from this place); shipbuilding yards. At eastern end of Hadrian's Wall, hence the name.

Wal′mer (wôl′mēr). **1** Former urban district, Kent, SE England, on Strait of Dover 6 m. NNE of Dover; now in Deal municipal borough; watering place.
2 Residential town, SE Cape Province, S Union of South Africa, suburb of Port Elizabeth; pop. 11,130.

Wal′ney (wôl′nĭ). Island off NW coast of England, N of entrance to Morecambe Bay; bridge connects with Barrow in Furness, Lancashire.

Wal′nut (wôl′nǔt; -nǔt). River ab. 90 m. long, SE Kansas; rises in N Butler co., flows S into Arkansas river at Arkansas City, S Cowley co., S Kansas.

Walnut Canyon National Monument. See UNITED STATES, *National Monuments.*

Walnut Creek. City, Contra Costa co., W California, 10 m. S of Suisun Bay; pop. 9903; shipping center for soft-shell walnuts.

Walnut Heights. Urban area, Contra Costa co., W California, NE of Oakland; pop. 5080.

Walnut Ridge. City, a ⊗ of Lawrence co., NE Arkansas; pop. 3547.

Wal′pole (wôl′pōl; wŏl′-). **1** Industrial town, Norfolk co., E Massachusetts, 18 m. SW of Boston; pop. 14,068; manufactures roofing materials and hospital supplies; state prison (from 1956).
2 Town, Cheshire co., SW New Hampshire, on Connecticut river 13 m. NW of Keene; pop. 2825; settled 1749.

Walpole Island. Island ab. 154 m. SE of Nouméa, New Caledonia, SW Pacific Ocean; ab. 310 acres; owned by France; guano deposits.

Wal′sall (wôl′sôl; -s′l). County borough, Staffordshire, W cen. England, 10 m. NNW of Birmingham; pop. 103,059, (1951 pop.) 114,514; coal mining, iron mining, iron foundries, limestone quarries.

Wal′sen·burg (wôl′s′n·bûrg). City, ⊗ of Huerfano co., S Colorado, 45 m. S of Pueblo; pop. 5071; trade center for region producing beans, wheat, hay, corn; coal.

Walsh (wôlsh). County in North Dakota. See *Table* at NORTH DAKOTA.

Wal′sing·ham, Cape (wôl′sĭng·ǎm; -hǎm). Cape on E Baffin I., E Franklin District, Northwest Territories, Canada, extending into Davis Strait, ab. 66°N.

Wal′sum (väl′zōōm). Industrial commune, in North Rhine-Westphalia state of West Germany, NNW suburb of Duisburg, on the Rhine river; pop. 20,063; manufactures paper, steel, tile.

Waltair. See VIZAGAPATAM.

Wal′ter·bor′o (wôl′tēr·bûr′ō). Town and winter resort, ⊗ of Colleton co., S South Carolina, 45 m. W of Charleston; pop. 5417; settled in early 18th cent.; cotton.

Wal′ters (wôl′tērz). City, ⊗ of Cotton co., SW Oklahoma, 17 m. S of Lawton; pop. 2825; agriculture.

Wal′thall (wôl′thôl). **1** County in Mississippi. See *Table* at MISSISSIPPI.
2 Village, ⊗ of Webster co., N cen. Mississippi; pop. 153.

Wal′tham (*pronounced* wôl′thǎm, -thǎm *in U.S.*, wôl′thǎm, -tǎm *in England*). Industrial city, Middlesex co., NE Massachusetts, 9 m. W of Boston; pop. 55,413; best known for the manufacture of Waltham watches; also manufactures electronic equipment, precision instruments, tools, dresses; had first paper mill in America 1788 and first power loom for manufacture of cotton cloth 1814. Incorporated 1738. Middlesex Univ. (1849–1947; charter given up); Brandeis Univ. (1947; coed.).

Waltham Cross. Parish, Hertfordshire, SE England; Eleanor Cross, marking one of stopping places of funeral cortege of Eleanor, queen of Edward I.

Waltham Holy Cross *or* **Waltham Abbey.** Urban district, Essex, SE England, NE suburb of London, 1 m. E of Waltham Cross; pop. 8197; part of Greater London. Has remains (nave and Lady chapel) of oldest Norman building in England, the abbey church in which the Saxon king Harold, slain at Hastings, was buried.

Wal′tham·stow (wôl′thǎm·stō; wôl′tǎm-). Municipal borough Essex, SE England, NE industrial suburb of London; pop. 132,972, (1951 pop.) 121,069; part of Greater London; birthplace of William Morris.

Wal′ton (wôl′t′n). **1** Name of counties in two states of the U.S. See *Tables* at FLORIDA and GEORGIA.
2 Village, Delaware co., S New York, on Delaware river 42 m. E of Binghamton; pop. 3855.

Walton le Dale (lĕ dāl′). Urban district, Lancashire, NW England, on the Ribble 26 m. NW of Manchester; pop. 14,711; cotton mills, iron foundries.

Walton Mountain. Peak 8931 ft. in Glacier National Park, NW Montana.

Walton on Thames (tĕmz′) *or* **Walton upon Thames.** Former urban district, Surrey, S England, 17 m. WSW of London; pop. (1931) 17,953; site of palace of Oatlands Park (destroyed in Civil War) of Henry VIII, often used by Queen Elizabeth.

Wal′trop (väl′trôp). Commune, in North Rhine-Westphalia state, West Germany, NNW suburb of Dortmund; pop. 11,044; coal mining; manufactures tile.

Wal′vis Bay (wôl′vĭs). **1** *also* **Wal′fish Bay** (wôl′fĭsh). Inlet of Atlantic Ocean on W cen. coast of South-West Africa, lat. 22°56′S.

2 *Ger.* **Wal′fisch·bai′** (väl′fĭsh·bī′). Town, W South-West Africa, on Atlantic Ocean 170 m. W of Windhoek and 710 m. N of Cape Town by sea; town, harbor, and immediate vicinity (374 sq. m., pop. 30,410) an exclave of Cape Province; only good harbor in the protectorate; trades esp. in frozen meats with Great Britain; connected by rail with Windhoek; whaling and fishing industries.

Wal′wal (wôl′wôl; *native* wûl·wûl); *also* **Ual′ual.** Town, Ogaden, SE Ethiopia, ab. 7°N near Somalia border; scene of clash bet. Italian and Ethiopian forces Dec. 5, 1934. See ETHIOPIA.

Wal′worth (wôl′wûrth; -wērth). Name of counties in two states of the U.S. See *Tables* at SOUTH DAKOTA and WISCONSIN.

Wa·me′go (wŏ·mē′gō). City, Pottawatomie co., NE Kansas, on Kansas river E of Manhattan; pop. 2363.

Wamps′ville (wŏmps′vĭl). Village, ⊗ of Madison co., cen. New York, 25 m. E of Syracuse; pop. 564.

Wa′na (wä′nȧ). Village and frontier post, South Waziristan, North-West Frontier Province, Pakistan, 85 m. WNW of Dera Ismail Khan, beyond Gomal Pass and near Afghanistan border; inhabited by a Wazir tribe. Occupied 1894 by British expedition; later (1922) abandoned but reoccupied 1929.

Wa′na·ka, Lake (wä′nȧ·kȧ). Lake 75 sq. m. in SW cen. South I., New Zealand.

Wan′a·mie (wŏn′ȧ·mĭ). Locality, Luzerne co., E Pennsylvania, ab. 9 m. SW of Wilkes-Barre; pop. (1950) 1092.

Wan′a·pi·tei′ Lake (wŏn′ȧ·pĭ·tā′). Lake in S cen. Sudbury dist., SE Ontario prov., Canada; drains S through the **Wanapitei River** (ab. 60 m. long) into Georgian Bay.

Wan′a·que (wŏn′ȧ·kū). Borough, Passaic co., N New Jersey, 10 m. NW of Paterson; pop. 7126.

Wanaque Reservoir. Reservoir in N Passaic co., N New Jersey.

Wa′na Wa′na (wä′nȧ wä′nȧ). Small island off NW coast of New Georgia I., cen. Solomon Is., W Pacific Ocean, S of Arundel I.

Wan′chuan′ (wän′chü·än′); *formerly* **Kal′gan′** (käl′-gän′) *and* **Chang′kia′kow′** (jäng′jĭ·ä′kō′). City and treaty mart, ✻ of Chahar prov., E Inner Mongolia, N China, just inside the Great Wall ab. 100 m. NW of Peiping; pop. ab. 70,000, (1945 est.) 130,000; station on Peiping-Suiyuan R.R. at alt. 2800 ft. on edge of rich loess plain; starting point of camel caravan and motor routes to Urga and through Suiyuan to Sinkiang. Under Ming and Manchu dynasties was a city of military and commercial importance; formerly in Chihli prov., China; through it large amount of China tea trade with Russia has passed; more recently has exported cattle, skins, etc. Railroad opened in 1911; extended to Kweisui 1921. Has been called the "Gate to Mongolia." Guards Nankow Pass to the SE. Occupied by Japanese 1937–1945; taken over by Communist forces Dec. 1948.

Wan·da′men Bay (?wän·dä′mĕn). Inlet, W Geelvink Bay, on NW coast of Neth. New Guinea, nearly opp. McCluer Gulf.

Wan′di·wash *or* **Wan′de·wash** (wŭn′dĭ·wäsh). Town, Madras state, S Indian Union, 60 m. SW of Madras; scene of several conflicts bet. French and British 1752 to 1759, and especially of victory Jan. 22, 1760 of British under Col. (later Sir) Eyre Coote over the French under Lally.

Wan′dle (wŏn′d′l). River 9 m. long, Surrey co., S England; flows NW into the Thames at Wandsworth.

Wands′bek (vänts′bĕk; -bāk). Former city, Schleswig-Holstein prov., Prussia, Germany; since 1937 a part of Hamburg.

Wandsworth. Metropolitan borough of London. See *Table* at LONDON.

Wang (wäng). River ab. 150 m. long, N tributary of the Ping river, NW Thailand; flows S from hills S of Chiang Rai to the Ping above Rahaeng.

Wang′a·nu′i (wông′ȧ·nōō′ē). **1** River ab. 150 m. long in SW cen. North I., New Zealand; rises in Tongariro National Park, flows W and S into N part of Cook Strait. Notable for its scenery; flows through region which was original home of Maoris.

2 Seaport city, Wellington provincial dist., W North I., New Zealand, at mouth of Wanganui river 95 m. N of Wellington; pop. (1941 est.) 26,000; center of pastoral region; has export trade in wool, meat, and dairy produce. Founded 1842; Maoris and British engaged in conflicts in this locality in 1847, 1864, and 1868.

Wan′ga·rat′ta (wăng′gȧ·răt′ȧ; wŏng′-). Town, N Victoria, SE Australia, 130 m. NE of Melbourne; pop. 4794.

Wang′er·oo′ge (väng′ēr·ō′gĕ). Island 6 m. long, most easterly of the East Frisian Is., in North Sea off NW coast of Germany; NNW of Jade Bay.

Wang′i·wang′i (wäng′ē·wäng′ē). Island in Banda Sea, 25 m. off E coast of Butung I., and in NW part of the Tukangbesi Is.; lighthouse.

Wang Mai Khon. See SAWANKHALOK.

Wang′yeh′miao′ (wäng′yĕ′mĭ·ou′). Town, N Liaoning prov., S Manchuria; ✻ of former South Hsingan prov., W Manchukuo; on a tributary of the Nonni river 200 m. NW of Changchun; pop. 9544.

Wan′hsien′ (wän′shǐ·ĕn′). City, E Szechwan prov., S cen. China, on left bank of Yangtze river 130 m. below Chungking in mountainous district at upper end of Yangtze Gorges; pop. (1931 est.) 210,837; carries on large junk trade; opened to foreign trade 1917; has temple dedicated to Li Po, famous Chinese poet who resided here.

Wan·ka′ner (wäng·kä′nēr). Former Indian state, N Kathiawar, Western India, Indian Union, S of Morvi.

Wan′kie (wŏng′kĭ). Town, W Southern Rhodesia, near Victoria Falls; pop. (white) 586; in coal district.

Wanks. See SEGOVIA.

Wan′ne-Eick′el (vän′ĕ·ī′kĕl). Industrial city, North Rhine-Westphalia state, W Germany, N suburb of Bochum in Ruhr valley; pop. 91,024.

Wan–shou–shan (wän′shō′shän′). Literally "Mountain of 10,000 Ancients"; park, N Hopeh prov., NE China, 8 m. NW of Peiping. Nearby was the celebrated Summer Palace, resort of imperial family, built by Emperor Yung Chêng in early 18th cent.; original palaces destroyed 1860 by British under orders from Lord Elgin; rebuilt by Empress Dowager Tzu Hsi.

Wan′stead and Wood′ford (wŏn′stĭd, wŏŏd′fērd). Municipal borough, Essex, SE England, 7 m. NE of London; pop. 61,620; part of Greater London.

Wan′tage (wŏn′tĭj). Town and urban district, cen. Berkshire, England, in the Vale of the White Horse (*q.v.*); pop. 5089; birthplace of Alfred the Great.

Wan′tagh′ (wŏn′tô′). Urban community (unincorporated), Nassau co., SE New York, on Long I., SE of Hempstead; pop. 34,172.

Wan′ting′ (wän′tĭng′). Frontier customs town on E bank of Shweli river, W Yunnan, S China, N of Namhkam on Burma Road; alt. 3200 ft.; held nearly three years by Japanese during World War II but retaken by Chinese and American forces Jan. 17–18, 1945.

Waoe·ka′ra *or* **Wau·ka′ra** (wou·kä′rȧ). Mountain 10,259 ft. in NW part of cen. Celebes I., Indonesia, near W coast.

Wa′pa·ko·net′a (wô′pô·kô·nĕt′à). City, ⊗ of Auglaize co., W Ohio, 13 m. S of Lima; pop. 6756; manufactures furniture, toys, churns, planing-mill products.

Wap′el·lo (wŏp′ĕ·lō). **1** County in Iowa. See *Table* at IOWA.
2 City, ⊗ of Louisa co., SE Iowa, 19 m. SSW of Muscatine; pop. 1745; in agricultural section; manufactures buttons, tiles; prehistoric Indian mounds nearby.

Wap′ping (wŏp′ĭng). Parish in the Tower ward, Stepney metropolitan borough, London, England.

Wap′pin·gers Falls (wŏp′ĭn·jẽrz). Village, Dutchess co., SE New York, near Hudson river 8 m. S of Poughkeepsie; pop. 4447; water power supplied by 75-ft. cascade in **Wappinger Creek**; printworks, gristmill, creameries; manufactures overalls, sheeting, machinery.

Wap′si·pin′i·con (wŏp′sĭ·pĭn′ĭ·kŭn). River 255 m. long, E Iowa; rises in S Mower co., S Minnesota, flows SE into Mississippi river forming most of boundary bet. Clinton and Scott cos., E Iowa.

Wa·quoit′ Bay (wŏ·kwoit′). Inlet of Nantucket Sound on S coast of W Barnstable co. in SE Massachusetts.

Wa′ra·maug, Lake (wŏr′rà·môg). Lake in W cen. Litchfield co., NW Connecticut; resort.

Wa′ran·gal (wŭ′răng·găl). City, N Andhra Pradesh, S cen. India, 86 m. ENE of Hyderabad; pop. 62,119; 12th-cent. capital of Telugu kingdom.

Warasdin. See VARAŽDIN.

War′a·tah (wŏr′à·tä). **1** City, E New South Wales, SE Australia, suburb of Newcastle; pop. 20,313; coal and copper mines.
2 Town, NW Tasmania, Australia, 90 m. W of Launceston; alt. 2000 ft.; pop. 1009; mining center, esp. for tin at nearby Mt. Fischoff, the "mountain of solid tin."

War′burg (wôr′bŭrg; *Ger.* vär′boͦoͦrĸ). Town, in North Rhine-Westphalia, western Germany; scene of battle July 31, 1760 in which Duke Ferdinand of Brunswick defeated the French (Seven Years' War).

War′bur·ton, the (wôr′bẽr·t′n; -bûr′t′n). River 275 m. long, NE South Australia; flows SW into Lake Eyre.

Ward (wôrd). Name of counties in two states of the U.S. See *Tables* at NORTH DAKOTA and TEXAS.

Wardastalla. See GUASTALLA.

War′dha (wŭrd′hä). **1** River ab. 290 m. long, E Maharashtra, cen. India; rises in NW, flows SE to unite on the S border with Wainganga river and form the Pranhita river; receives the Penganga from the W.
2 Town, E Maharashtra, Indian Union, 45 m. SW of Nagpur; pop. 19,571; occasional residence and retreat of Gandhi during his last years.

Ward Hunt, Cape (wôrd hŭnt). Cape on N coast of SE Papua, near North-East New Guinea boundary, New Guinea I., on Solomon Sea, 8°S lat.

Ward Hunt Strait. Passage ab. 20 m. wide and 75 m. long bet. D'Entrecasteaux Is. and mainland of SE Papua, New Guinea, connecting Collingwood Bay and Solomon Sea on the NW with Goschen Strait on SE.

Ward′s Island (wôrdz). Island of 255 acres in East river, New York, part of Manhattan borough, just S of Randall's I. Crossed by Triborough Bridge.

Ware (wâr). **1** River ab. 40 m. long, cen. Massachusetts; rises in Worcester co., flows SW into Swift river near N border of Hampden co.
2 County in Georgia. See *Table* at GEORGIA.
3 Town, Hampshire co., W Massachusetts, 21 m. ENE of Springfield; pop. 7517; manufactures paper, textiles, leather and metal goods.
4 Urban district, Hertfordshire, SE England, on the Lea 23 m. N of London; pop. 8253; market town in agricultural section. The "great bed of Ware," mentioned in Shakespeare's *Twelfth Night*, formerly at the Saracen's Head inn here, was removed to Rye House (*q.v.*).

Ware′ham (wâr′ăm; *Mass. also* wâr′hăm). **1** Town, Plymouth co., SE Massachusetts, 13 m. ENE of New Bedford; pop. 9461; cranberries; oyster fisheries.
2 Municipal borough, SE Dorsetshire, S England, on

NW edge of the Isle of Purbeck; pop. (1951) 2750; very old town, has remains of ancient earthworks.

Ware′house′ Point (wâr′hous′). Subdivision (pop. 1936) of town of EAST WINDSOR, Connecticut.

Wa′ren (vä′rĕn). City, Mecklenburg, East Germany, 60 m. E of Schwerin; pop. 10,363; summer resort; dairy products, lumber.

Ware Shoals (wâr). Village, Greenwood co., W South Carolina, on Saluda river ab. 17 m. N of Greenwood; pop. 2671; produces cotton.

Wargla. See OUARGLA.

Warka. See ERECH.

Wark′worth (wôrk′wûrth; -wẽrth). Town, Northumberland, N England, ab. 1½ m. from the North Sea coast; pop. ab. 1000; Norman castle; hermitage and remains of Benedictine priory nearby.

Warm′bad (*Ger.* värm′bät; *Angl.* wôrm′băd). Town, S South-West Africa, near Orange river 350 m. N of Cape Town; pop. (of the district) 5818.

War′min·ster (wôr′mĭn′stẽr). **1** Urban township, Bucks co., SE Pennsylvania; pop. 15,994.
2 Urban district, Wiltshire, S England; pop. 8236; market town in agricultural region; several prehistoric barrows nearby.

Warm Springs. **1** City, S Meriwether co., W Georgia; pop. 538; health resort; site of Warm Springs Foundation, estab. 1927 by Franklin D. Roosevelt for treatment of infantile-paralysis patients, and of Franklin D. Roosevelt Museum.
2 Village, ⊗ of Bath co., W Virginia 23, m. NNE of Covington; pop. (est.) 300; warm sulfur springs.

Warm Springs Reservoir. Irrigation reservoir in middle fork of Malheur river, bet. Harney and Malheur cos., E Oregon; formed by **Warm Springs Dam**.

War′ne·mün′de (vär′nĕ·mün′dĕ). Seaport town at mouth of Warnow river. Mecklenburg, East Germany; pop. 6500; outer port of Rostock.

War′ner (wôr′nẽr). Town, Muskogee co., E Oklahoma, ab. 18 m. S of Muskogee; pop. 881.

Warner Mountains. Range in E Modoc co., NE California, and S Lake co., S Oregon; called **Warner Range** in Oregon.

Warner Rob′ins (rŏb′ĭnz). City, Houston co., cen. Georgia, S of Macon; pop. 18,633.

War′ne·ton′ (vàr′nĕ·tôn′); *Flem.* **Waa′sten** (väs′tĕ[n]). Commune, West Flanders prov., NW Belgium, on Lys river SSE of Ieper; pop. 3269.

Warn′ham (wôr′năm). Village just N of Horsham, Sussex, S England; birthplace of Percy Bysshe Shelley.

War′now (vär′nō). Stream ab. 80 m. long, Mecklenburg, East Germany; flows N to Gulf of Mecklenburg; navigable for seagoing vessels to Rostock.

Warnsdorf. See VARNSDORF.

Warq′la (wärk′là). = *Wargla:* see OUARGLA.

Warr Acres (wôr). City, Oklahoma co., cen. Oklahoma, W suburb of Oklahoma City; pop. 7135.

War′re·go (wŏr′ĕ·gō). River ab. 400 m. long in Australia, flowing SSW from S cen. Queensland to the Darling in N New South Wales.

War′ren (wŏr′ĕn; -ĭn). **1** Name of counties of fourteen states of the U.S. See *Tables* at GEORGIA, ILLINOIS, INDIANA, IOWA, KENTUCKY, MISSISSIPPI, MISSOURI, NEW JERSEY, NEW YORK, NORTH CAROLINA, OHIO, PENNSYLVANIA, TENNESSEE, VIRGINIA.
2 City, ⊗ of Bradley co., S Arkansas, 46 m. E of Camden; pop. 6752; lumber mills; manufactures unassembled furniture, skis, handles; cotton market.
3 Town, Worcester co., cen. Massachusetts, 20 m. W of Worcester; pop. 3383; paper, textiles, metal goods.
4 City, Macomb co., SE Michigan, NNE of Detroit; pop. 89,246.
5 City, ⊗ of Marshall co., NW Minnesota, 27 m. WNW of Thief River Falls; pop. 2007.
6 City, ⊗ of Trumbull co., NE Ohio, 13 m. NW of Youngstown; pop. 59,648; settled 1798; incorp. as village

1834, as city 1869; manufactures steel and steel products, motors, fire equipment.

7 Borough, ⊗ of Warren co., NW Pennsylvania, 30 m. WSW of Bradford; pop. 14,505; oil refineries; manufactures iron and steel products, furniture, tanks, tools.

8 Town and summer resort, Bristol co., E Rhode Island, on Narragansett Bay 10 m. SE of Providence; pop. 8750; manufactures cotton goods, automotive equipment; oyster and shellfish industries. Settled 1632; originally part of Swansea, Massachusetts; annexed by Rhode Island and incorporated as town 1747; seat of Rhode Island Coll. (now Brown Univ.) 1764–70; pillaged and burned by British in Revolutionary War 1778.

War'rens·burg (wôr'ĕnz·bûrg; wŏr'ĭnz-). City, ⊗ of Johnson co., W Missouri, 30 m. W of Sedalia; pop. 9689; limestone quarries nearby. Central Missouri State Coll. (1871; coed.).

War'ren·ton (wôr'ĕn·tŭn; wŏr'ĭn-). **1** City, ⊗ of Warren co., E cen. Georgia; pop. 1770.

2 City, ⊗ of Warren co., E Missouri; pop. 1869.

3 Town, ⊗ of Warren co., N North Carolina; pop. 1124.

4 Town, ⊗ of Fauquier co., N Virginia, in foothills of Blue Ridge 35 m. NNW of Fredericksburg; pop. 3522.

5 Town, E British Bechuanaland, N Union of South Africa, on the Vaal river; pop. ab. 1600.

War'ri (wôr'ē). **1** Province of Nigeria. See *Table* at NIGERIA.

2 Town, its ✳, S Western Region, Nigeria, 190 m. ESE of Lagos in Niger delta; pop. ab. 11,000.

War'rick (wôr'ĭk). County in Indiana. See *Table* at INDIANA.

War'ring·ton (wôr'ĭng·tŭn). **1** Urban area, Escambia co., NW Florida, W of Pensacola; pop. 16,752.

2 County borough, Lancashire, NW England, on the Mersey 14 m. E of Liverpool; pop. 79,317, (1951 pop.) 80,681; cotton, iron, and leather goods, chemicals.

Warr'nam·bool (wôr'năm·bōōl). Seaport town, SW Victoria, SE Australia, 140 m. WSW of Melbourne; pop. 8909; trade center for dairying and farming section.

War'saw (wôr'sô). **1** City, Hancock co., W Illinois, on Mississippi river 30 m. N of Quincy; pop. 1938.

2 City, ⊗ of Kosciusko co., N Indiana, 36 m. SE of South Bend; pop. 7234; resort center in lake region.

3 City, ⊗ of Gallatin co., N Kentucky; pop. 981.

4 City, ⊗ of Benton co., W cen. Missouri; pop. 1054.

5 Village, ⊗ of Wyoming co., W New York, 39 m. SW of Rochester; pop. 3653; dairying, farming.

6 Town, ⊗ of Richmond co., E Virginia; pop. 549.

War'saw (wôr'sô); *Pol.* **War·sza'wa** (vär·shä'vä). **1** A grand duchy in E Europe, being a partial restoration of Poland 1807–15; ✳ Warsaw.

2 Department of Poland. See WARSZAWA.

3 *Ger.* **War'schau** (vär'shou). Commercial and manufacturing city, ✳ of Warszawa dept. and ✳ of Poland, on both banks of Vistula river 325 m. E of Berlin (Germany); pop. (1938–39 est.) 1,300,000; largest city of Poland and chief railroad and commercial center; seat of all Polish Protestant sects and of Roman Catholic and Orthodox archbishoprics; university (suppressed 1830; reopened 1864); noteworthy buildings included Roman Catholic and Orthodox cathedrals, ancient royal castle (Zamek), government buildings, town hall, mint, arsenal, exchange, customhouse, and barracks; manufactures metals, textiles, chemicals, tobacco, furniture, beer.

History: Succeeded Kraków as residence of sovereign and actual capital of Polish kingdom 1595 although not formally capital until 1609; occupied by Charles X Gustavus of Sweden 1656; successfully defended for a time by Polish army against Russians 1794; successful Russian assault 1794 led to Russian massacre of Polish defenders and civilians and to partial destruction of the city by fire; made capital of grand duchy of Warsaw by Napoleon 1807; taken by Russia 1813 and in 1815 became capital of kingdom under Russian crown; seat of

Polish War 1831; occupied by Germans 1915; after World War I capital of Polish republic; in World War II occupied by Germans after severe bombing Sept. 27, 1939 when city was nearly destroyed; retaken by Russians Sept. 1944 to Jan. 17, 1945.

Warschau. See WARSAW city, Poland.

War'sop (wôr'sŭp). Urban district, Nottinghamshire, N cen. England, on the Meden 18 m. N of Nottingham; pop. 10,888.

War·sza'wa (vär·shä'vä); *Eng.* **War'saw** (wôr'sô). **1** Polish department, in E cen. part; 12,239 sq. m.; pop. 2,530,675; ✳ Warsaw.

2 See WARSAW.

War'ta (vär'tä); *Ger.* **War'the** (vär'tĕ). River 445 m. long in Poland; rises 35 m. NW of Kraków, flows NW and W into the Oder at Kostrzyn; navigable for 250 m. Its lower course formerly in Germany, now in part assigned to Poland by Potsdam Conference 1945. Its chief tributaries are the Prosna and Notec.

Wart'burg. 1 (wôrt'bûrg) Village, ⊗ of Morgan co., NE cen. Tennessee; pop. (est.) 800.

2 (värt'bōōrк; *Angl.* wôrt'bûrg) Castle of the landgraves of Thuringia, in the Thuringian Forest on a steep hill near Eisenach, Germany; here Martin Luther translated the New Testament 1521–22; traditional site of medieval contests of minnesingers.

War'wick (*outside England:* wôr'ĭk, wôr'wĭk; *in England:* wôr'ĭk). **1** Former county in Virginia, incorporated 1952 as independent city of Warwick and consolidated 1958 with city of Newport News.

2 Village, Orange co., SE New York, 40 m. NNW of New York; pop. 3218; in farming country.

3 City and summer resort, Kent co., cen. Rhode Island, on Narragansett Bay 10 m. S of Providence; pop. 68,504; comprises many scattered villages; textile center; also manufactures stapling machines, brass castings, and pipe fittings; ships shellfish. Settled 1643; admitted to "Incorporation of Providence Plantations" 1647.

4 Former city, Virginia: see **1**, above.

5 Town, SE Queensland, Australia, 80 m. WSW of Brisbane; pop. 6664; viticulture, agriculture, and grazing.

6 Village, Arthabaska co., S Quebec, Canada, 37 m. N of Sherbrooke; pop. 2094; founded 1841.

7 County in England. See WARWICKSHIRE.

8 Municipal borough, ⊗ of Warwickshire, cen. England, on the Avon 20 m. SSE of Birmingham; pop. 15,350; Norman castle, with notable collection of pictures.

War'wick·shire (wôr'ĭk·shĭr; -shēr) *or* **War'wick** (wôr'ĭk). County, cen. England; area 976 sq. m.; pop. (1951) 1,860,874; ⊗ Warwick; other towns Birmingham, Coventry, Leamington, Nuneaton, Kenilworth, Rugby, Stratford on Avon; rivers Avon, Cole, Blythe; farming, grazing, coal and iron mining, limestone quarrying, manufacturing (esp. iron and steel products).

Wa'satch (wô'săch). County in Utah. See *Table* at UTAH.

Wasatch Mountain. Peak 13,551 ft. in San Miguel co., SW Colorado.

Wasatch Range. Range averaging 10,000 ft. extending from Bannock co., SE Idaho, S along the E boundary of the Great Basin to Sanpete co., cen. Utah; highest peak Mount Timpanogos 12,008 ft.

Was'co (wôs'kō). **1** County in Oregon. See *Table* at OREGON.

2 City, Kern co., S California, NW of Bakersfield; pop. 6841.

Wa·se'ca (wô·sē'kà). **1** County in Minnesota. See *Table* at MINNESOTA.

2 City, its ⊗, S Minnesota, 23 m. ESE of Mankato; pop. 5898; shipping point for wheat; canneries.

Wash, the (wŏsh). Shallow bay 22 m. long and 15 m. wide, an inlet of the North Sea, on the E coast of Norfolk and Lincolnshire, E England; includes the estuaries of several rivers, including the Witham, Welland, Nene, and Ouse.

Wash'a·baugh (wŏsh'á·bô). County in South Dakota. See *Table* at SOUTH DAKOTA.

Wash'a·kie (wŏsh'á·kê). County in Wyoming. See *Table* at WYOMING.

Wash'burn (wŏsh'bẽrn; -bûrn). **1** County in Wisconsin. See *Table* at WISCONSIN.

2 Town, Aroostook co., N Maine, 10 m. NW of Presque Isle; pop. 2083.

3 City, ⊗ of McLean co., W cen. North Dakota, on Missouri river 35 m. N of Bismarck; pop. 993; trading post in pioneer days, and one of earliest Missouri river boat landings; site of a Sioux-Arikara battle (1869) nearby; lignite coal mines.

4 City, ⊗ of Bayfield co., NW Wisconsin, on Lake Superior 7 m. N of Ashland; pop. 1896; shipping and trade center for lumbering and fruitgrowing section.

Washburn, Mount. Peak 10,317 ft. in N part of Yellowstone National Park, NW Wyoming, W of the Grand Canyon of the Yellowstone.

Wash'ing·ton (wŏsh'ing·tŭn). **1** A northwestern state of U.S.A., 42d state admitted to Union (1889); bounded on N by Canadian province of British Columbia, on E by Idaho, on S by Oregon, and on W by the Pacific Ocean, Juan de Fuca Strait, and Strait of Georgia; 20th state in area, 68,192 sq. m. (land area 66,786 sq. m.); 23d state in population, 2,853,214; ✳ Olympia. See *Table of States* at UNITED STATES. Divided into the following 39 counties (for pronunciation of their names, see their individual entries):

NAME	LOCATION	AREA[1]	POP.[1]	CO. SEAT
Adams	E	1,895	9,929	Ritzville
Asotin	SE corner	627	12,909	Asotin
Benton	S	1,738	62,070	Prosser
Chelan	cen.	2,931	40,744	Wenatchee
Clallam[2]	NW; coastal	1,753	30,022	Port Angeles
Clark	SW	633	93,809	Vancouver
Columbia	SE	860	4,569	Dayton
Cowlitz	SW	1,146	57,801	Kelso
Douglas	cen.	1,841	14,890	Waterville
Ferry	NE	2,197	3,889	Republic
Franklin	SE	1,262	23,342	Pasco
Garfield	SE	714	2,976	Pomeroy
Grant[3]	cen.	2,691	46,477	Ephrata
Grays Harbor	W; coasta.	1,905	54,465	Montesano
Island[4]	NW	206	19,638	Coupeville
Jefferson[2]	W; coastal	1,812	9,639	Port Townsend
King	W cen.	2,134	935,014	Seattle
Kitsap	W[5]	402	84,176	Port Orchard
Kittitas	cen	2,315	20,467	Ellensburg
Klickitat	S	1,912	13,455	Goldendale
Lewis[6]	SW	2,447	41,858	Chehalis
Lincoln	E	2,300	10,919	Davenport
Mason[2]	W	967	16,251	Shelton
Okanogan	N	5,294	25,520	Okanogan
Pacific	SW corner; coastal	925	14,674	South Bend
Pend Oreille	NE corner	1,406	6,914	Newport
Pierce[6]	W cen.	1,676	321,590	Tacoma
San Juan[7]	NW	172	2,872	Friday Harbor
Skagit[8]	NW	1,735	51,350	Mount Vernon
Skamania	S	1,676	5,207	Stevenson
Snohomish	NW cen.	2,100	172,199	Everett
Spokane	E	1,763	278,333	Spokane
Stevens	NE	2,486	17,884	Colville
Thurston	W	717	55,049	Olympia
Wahkiakum	SW	269	3,426	Cathlamet
Walla Walla	SE	1,288	42,195	Walla Walla
Whatcom	NW	2,151	70,317	Bellingham
Whitman	SE	2,167	31,263	Colfax
Yakima	S	4,273	145,112	Yakima

[1] Area = land area in sq. m. Pop. from 1960 Census.
[2] Olympic National Park occupies adjoining areas in S Clallam co., cen. Jefferson co., and NW corner of Mason co.
[3] Grand Coulee Dam at NE corner.
[4] Composed of islands lying N of Puget Sound and E of Admiralty Inlet.
[5] Between Hood Canal (on its W) and Puget Sound.
[6] Mount Rainier National Park occupies SE corner of Pierce co. and adjoining smaller area in NE Lewis co.
[7] Composed of islands lying NE of Juan de Fuca Strait and S of Strait of Georgia.
[8] Includes islands separated from San Juan co. by Rosario Strait.

Nickname: Evergreen State, also Chinook State. *State flower:* Rhododendron. *Motto:* Alki (By and By). *Chief cities:* Seattle, Spokane, Tacoma, Yakima, Everett.

Rivers: Columbia, flowing from NE area to cen. area, then S to the border and W to form boundary bet. Washington and Oregon; its tributaries, Pend Oreille in NE area, Snake in SE area, and Yakima in S cen. area. *Highest point:* Mount Rainier 14,410 ft. in Pierce co. *Chief industries:* Agriculture (esp. fruitgrowing), lumbering, quarrying (granite, sandstone, marble), fishing and canning (esp. salmon), machinery, paper.

History: Region visited by Spanish, Russian, British, and French explorers 1543–1792 (short-lived settlement 1791 at Neah Bay, *q.v.*) and by Lewis and Clark, who sailed down Columbia river 1805; part of Oregon Country; occupied jointly by Great Britain and United States 1818–46; first permanent settlement at Tumwater 1845; by treaty with Great Britain 1846 N boundary set at 49th parallel; settlement at Seattle 1851, at Tacoma 1852; region organized as Washington Territory 1853, admitted to Union as state Nov. 11, 1889.

2 Name of a parish of Louisiana and of counties in thirty states. See *Tables* at ALABAMA, ARKANSAS, COLORADO, FLORIDA, GEORGIA, IDAHO, ILLINOIS, INDIANA, IOWA, KANSAS, KENTUCKY, LOUISIANA, MAINE, MARYLAND, MINNESOTA, MISSISSIPPI, MISSOURI, NEBRASKA, NEW YORK, NORTH CAROLINA, OHIO, OKLAHOMA, OREGON, PENNSYLVANIA, RHODE ISLAND, TENNESSEE, TEXAS, UTAH, VERMONT, VIRGINIA, WISCONSIN.

3 City, Hempstead co. SW Arkansas, 33 m. NE of Texarkana; pop. 321; cotton gins; shipping point for cotton, tobacco, etc. Settled 1824; field headquarters for American forces in Mexican War 1846; state capital 1863–65; ⊗ to 1939. Cf. HOPE.

4 Residential town, S cen. Litchfield co., NW Connecticut, NE of New Milford; pop. 2603; watered by Shepaug river; incorp. 1779; in farming region.

5 Capital city of the U.S.A., coextensive with the District of Columbia (area 69 sq. m., including 8 sq. m. of water), bet. Maryland and Virginia on the E bank of the Potomac river at the head of navigation and at its confluence with the Anacostia river ab. 40 m. SW of Baltimore, Maryland; pop. 763,956; 9th largest city in the United States. Considered one of most beautiful cities in the world and a world political, cultural, and educational center. Served by numerous railroads, excellent highways, two airfields (Washington National Airport and Bolling Field), and steamboat lines. Parks include the Mall (oldest park in city), Potomac Park, Rock Creek Park, National Zoological Park, Anacostia Park (containing the National Arboretum), Palisades Park, and ab. 700 other public open spaces, including esp. Du Pont Circle, Mount Vernon Square, Fort Slocum Park, and Washington Circle; among the outstanding government buildings and monuments are the Capitol (located on Capitol Hill, 88 ft. above the Potomac; cornerstone first laid Sept. 18, 1793; restored 1819; extensions built 1851), White House (the oldest government building in Washington; cornerstone laid 1792), Library of Congress (completed 1897; largest library in world) and the Annex Building of Georgia (1940), Senate Office Building, Treasury Building, State Department Building (begun 1871), Lincoln Memorial, Washington Monument (555 ft. 5⅛ in. high; cornerstone laid 1848, opened to public 1888), Jefferson Memorial, National Archives (1935), Supreme Court (1935), Federal Reserve Board (1937), Department of Justice (1934), Post Office Department, Department of Interior (1937), Department of Agriculture, Department of Commerce (1932), Bureau of Engraving and Printing, Government Printing Office (largest printing establishment in world), and the Pentagon Building (War Department; begun 1940; in Virginia 3 m. from White House); among the outstanding nongovernment buildings are the Pan-American Union Building, Union R.R. Station, Constitution Hall, and Washington Cathedral (Episcopal Cathedral of Saint Peter and Saint Paul); institutions include St. Elizabeth's Hospital, Freedmen's Hospital,

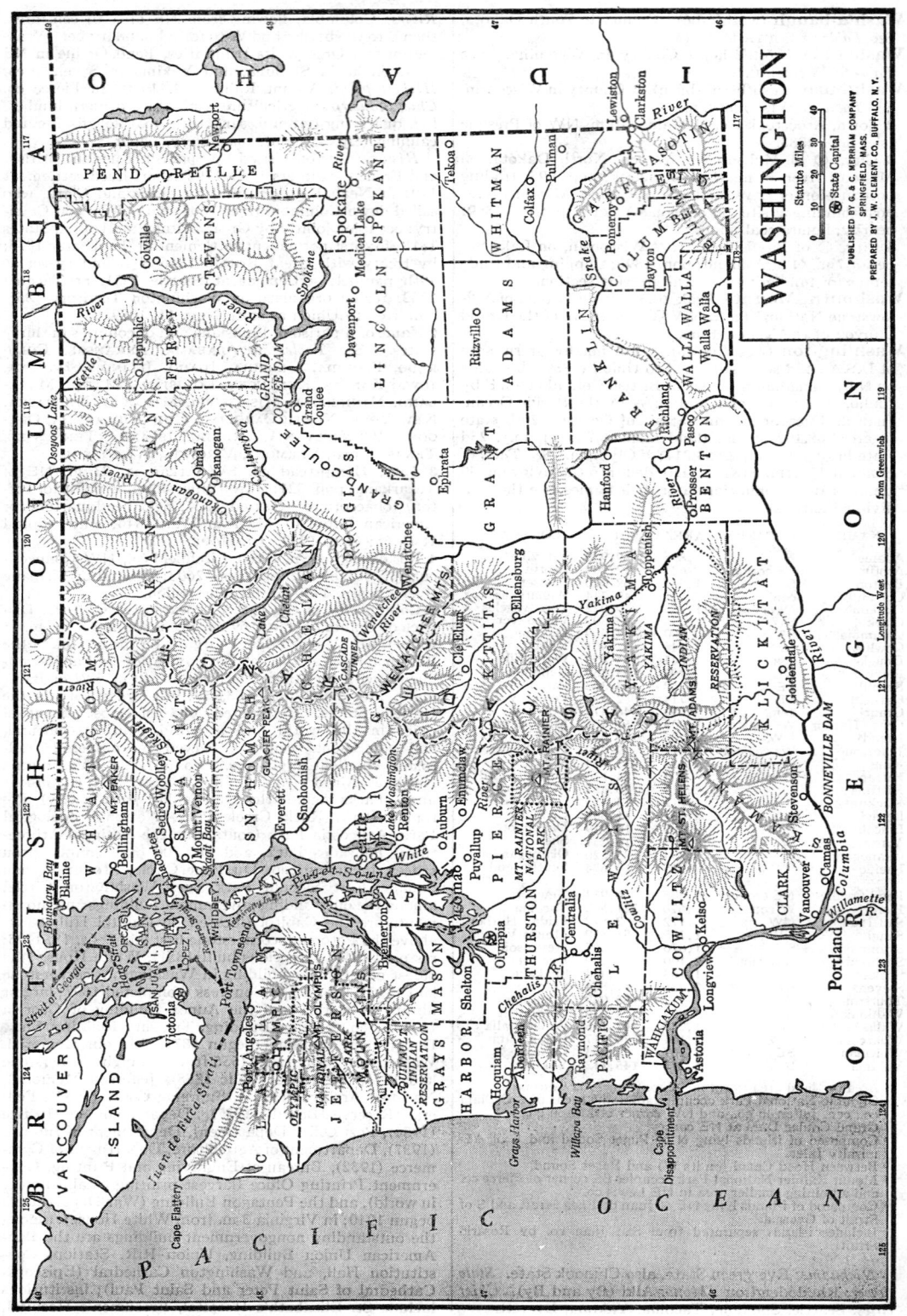

WASHINGTON

Statute Miles

🅝 State Capital

PUBLISHED BY G. & C. MERRIAM COMPANY
SPRINGFIELD, MASS.
PREPARED BY J. W. CLEMENT CO., BUFFALO, N.Y.

Walter Reed Hospital, U.S. Soldiers' Home, Home for the Aged and Infirm, National Training School for Boys, and many others; one of principal retail centers in U.S.; limited manufactures include printed matter, dairy and other foods, paper, steel products, naval equipment; among its many educational institutions are the Catholic Univ. of America (1887; coed.), Georgetown Univ. (1789; men), George Washington Univ. (1821; coed.), Howard Univ. (1867; coed.), American Univ. (1891; coed.), National Univ. (1869; coed.), Southeastern Univ. (1917; coed.), Trinity Coll. (1897; women), Gallaudet Coll. (1857; coed.; for deaf, dumb, and blind), U.S. Department of Agriculture Graduate School (1921; coed.); other cultural agencies include the Smithsonian Institution, Washington Public Library, Folger Shakespeare Library, departmental government libraries, National Museum, Corcoran Gallery, old National Gallery of Art, Freer Gallery, Phillips Memorial Gallery, and new National Gallery of Art (opened 1941).

History: Site chosen by President Washington in 1790 and planned by French engineer Major L'Enfant; occupied by Federal government 1800; incorp. as city 1802; occupied by British troops and burned 1814; lost charter as city 1871 and, with annexation of Georgetown 1878, became coterminous with District of Columbia (*q.v.*).

6 City, ⊗ of Wilkes co., NE Georgia, 40 m. ESE of Athens; pop. 4440; platted 1780; many fine old homes.

7 City, Tazewell co., cen. Illinois, 10 m. E of Peoria; pop. 5919.

8 Industrial and commercial city, ⊗ of Daviess co., SW Indiana, 18 m. E of Vincennes; pop. 10,846.

9 City, ⊗ of Washington co., SE Iowa, 25 m. SSW of Iowa City; pop. 6037; trading center in agricultural section; manufactures buttons, calendars; canneries.

10 City, ⊗ of Washington co., N Kansas, 52 m. NNW of Manhattan; pop. 1506.

11 City, Franklin co., E Missouri, on Missouri river 50 m. E of St. Louis; pop. 7961.

12 Borough, Warren co., NW New Jersey, 12 m. ENE of Phillipsburg; pop. 5723; once piano-manufacturing center; in farming country; manufactures hosiery and underwear, porcelain and brass articles. Laboratories of Consumers Research.

13 City, ⊗ of Beaufort co., E North Carolina, on Pamlico river at head of navigation 30 m. N of New Bern; pop. 9939; market center for cotton, tobacco, and garden produce; fish, oysters; manufactures lumber, fertilizers, flour, and feed.

14 Industrial city, ⊗ of Washington co., SW Pennsylvania, 25 m. SW of Pittsburgh; pop. 23,545; oil, clay, limestone, sand, bituminous coal deposits; gas wells; manufactures glass and glassware, steel, tin plate, chemicals. Washington and Jefferson Coll. (1780; men).

15 Village, Kent co., cen. Rhode Island; governmental seat of Coventry; settled c. 1750; manufactures lace, cotton, woolen goods.

16 Town, ⊗ of Rappahannock co., N Virginia; pop. 255.

17 Urban district, Durham, N England, 6¼ m. SSE of Newcastle; pop. 17,795.

Washington, Lake. Lake ab. 20 m. long, 4 m. wide, with maximum depth of 225 ft. in King co., W cen. Washington; forms E boundary of city of Seattle; completion 1916 of ship canal 8 m. long, 100 ft. wide and 30 ft. deep bet. the lake and Puget Sound gave Seattle a waterfront 140 m. long and a fresh-water, nontidal harbor; Lake Washington floating bridge, completed 1940, is largest concrete pontoon bridge in the world (floating portion 6561 ft. long); shipyards; U.S. naval air station.

Washington, Mount. **1** Peak 2624 ft., SW corner of Massachusetts, in Berkshire co.

2 Peak 6288 ft. in the Presidential Range of the White Mts., in S Coos co., N New Hampshire; highest point in NE United States; cog railway.

Washington Court House. City, ⊗ of Fayette co., SW Ohio, 27 m. WNW of Chillicothe; pop. 12,388; live-

stock center; manufactures shoes, gloves, canned goods, cheese, store furniture.

Washington Crossing. **1** Recreational areas (state parks) in Pennsylvania (440 acres) and New Jersey (292 acres) on both sides of the Delaware river ab. 8 m. NNW of Trenton, New Jersey; established to commemorate the crossing of the river by Washington and his army Dec. 25–26, 1776, prior to the battle of Trenton.

2 Hamlet and post office, Bucks co., SE Pennsylvania, within the state park.

Washington Island. **1** Island in NW Lake Michigan, S of entrance to Green Bay, in Door co., NE Wisconsin.

2 One of the Line Is. (*q.v.*) in the cen. Pacific Ocean in 4°40′N lat. and 140 m. SE of Palmyra I.; 6 sq. m.; pop. (1942) 99; included 1916 in the British colony of Gilbert and Ellice Is.; administered by the district commissioner of Fanning I. Cf. AMERICA ISLANDS.

Washington Land. Section of NW Greenland along E shore of Kennedy Channel.

Washington Mills. Village, Oneida co., cen. New York, ab. 5 m. SW of Utica; pop. ab. 500.

Washington Park. Village, St. Clair co., SW Illinois, near St. Louis; pop. 6601.

Washington's Birthplace. See WAKEFIELD estate, Virginia.

Washington Sound. Body of water bet. Juan de Fuca Strait and the Strait of Georgia, off SE Vancouver I. and NW Washington; has many islands, most of them forming San Juan co., Washington.

Washington Terrace. City, Weber co., N Utah; pop. 6641.

Wash′i·ta (wŏsh′ĭ·tô). **1** River 500 m. long, W and S cen. Oklahoma; rises in Hemphill co., NW Texas, flows E across Oklahoma boundary, then SE to S cen. Oklahoma, and S into Red river.

2 County in Oklahoma. See *Table* at OKLAHOMA.

3 Var. of OUACHITA.

Wash′oe (wŏsh′ō). County in Nevada. See *Table* at NEVADA.

Wash′te·naw (wŏsh′tĕ·nô). County in Michigan. See *Table* at MICHIGAN.

Wasmes (väm). Commune, Hainaut prov., SW Belgium, 6 m. SW of Mons; pop. 15,401.

Wa′so Nyi′ro (wä′sō nyē′rō) or **Gua′so Nyiro** (wä′sō). River in cen. Kenya, E Africa; flows NE 350 m. into Lorian Swamp in E Kenya; issues from the swamp as the **Lach De′ra** (läk dĕ′rä) and in certain seasons empties into the Juba river in S Somalia.

Was′que·hal′ (väs′kál′). Industrial commune, Nord dept., N France, 4 m. E of Lille; pop. (1931) 11,707.

Was′se·naar (väs′ĕ·när). Commune, South Holland prov., SW Netherlands, just SSW of Leiden; pop. 13,027.

Was′ser·kup′pe (väs′ĕr·kŏŏp′ĕ). Mountain 3116 ft. in SE Hesse, Germany; highest peak in the Rhön mountain region.

Was′suk Range (wŏs′ŭk). Range in W Mineral co., SW Nevada.

Wa States (wä). Native states on E frontier of Burma, E of the Salween; now considered a part of the Federated Shan States; 3332 sq. m. Inhabited by the Wa, perhaps an aboriginal people of the region; they may be connected with the Negritos. Some of the tribes have been somewhat civilized.

Wast Water (wŏst). Lake 3 m. long in the Lake District, NW England, in Cumberland 14 m. SW of Keswick; maximum depth 258 ft.

Wa·tau′ga (wŏ·tô′gá; wŏt·ô′gá). **1** River ab. 60 m. long, NE Tennessee; rises in NW North Carolina, flows NW into south fork of Holston river SE of Kingsport, S Sullivan co., Tennessee. It contains **Watauga Dam,** one of the dams in the Tennessee Valley Authority (*q.v.*). In its valley were established 1769–75 the **Watauga Settlements** of early settlers crossing the mountains by Boone's Gap from North Carolina and

Virginia; they were the nucleus and starting point of further settlements in Tennessee and other states.
2 County in North Carolina. See *Table* at NORTH CAROLINA.

Watch Hill (wŏch). Village and summer resort in Westerly town, Washington co., S Rhode Island, on Block Island Sound ab. 3 m. SE of Stonington, Connecticut.

Watch Hill Point. Promontory ab. 1 m. E of Napatree Point, SW extremity of Washington co., S Rhode Island.

Watenstedt–Salzgitter. See SALZGITTER.

Wa'ter·bur'y (wŏ'tẽr·bĕr'ĭ; -bẽr·ĭ; wŏt'ẽr-). **1** Industrial city, a ⊗ of New Haven co., S Connecticut, at confluence of Naugatuck and Mad rivers 18 m. NNW of New Haven; pop. 107,130; incorp. as borough 1825, as city 1853; center of U.S. brass industry; produces buttons, buckles, pins, clocks, watches, sheet metal, wire, rivets, tubing, lamps, kettles, boilers, percussion caps, photographic materials, coins for South American countries, machine-shop products, paper boxes, cutlery, silverware, chemical products, foundry products, batteries. The town (settled 1677, incorp. 1686) and the city were consolidated and made coextensive 1931.
2 Village in Waterbury town (pop. 4303), Washington co., N cen. Vermont, on Winooski river 10 m. WNW of Montpelier; pop. 2984; dairy and maple products, woodworking; granite quarries, talc mines.

Wa'ter·ee' (wŏ'tẽr·ē'; wŏt'ẽr·ē'). River, cen. South Carolina; enters state from North Carolina as Catawba river (*q.v.*) but known as Wateree river in South Carolina and joins the Congaree to form Santee river; length of Wateree-Catawba river 395 m.

Wateree Pond. Long narrow lake in N cen. South Carolina, formed by a dam in the Wateree river; extends along boundary bet. Kershaw and Fairfield cos.

Wa'ter·ford (wŏ'tẽr·fẽrd; wŏt'ẽr-). **1** Town, S New London co., SE Connecticut, on Thames river and Long Island Sound adjoining New London on E; pop. 15,391; incorp. 1801; agriculture, manufacturing, quarrying.
2 Village, Saratoga co., E New York, on Hudson river 10 m. N of Albany; pop. 2915; part of industrial section including Cohoes and Troy. See CHAMPLAIN CANAL.
3 County, S Eire, in Munster prov.; 710 sq. m.; pop. 77,614; ⊗ Waterford; rivers Suir, Blackwater; livestock grazing, dairy farming, quarrying (limestone, marble), fishing, textile manufacture.
4 Seaport city, ⊗ of co. Waterford, S Eire, on Suir river; pop. 27,968; large livestock and agricultural exports; brewing, ironfounding. A historic seaport at which many English sovereigns landed; James II left from here for France after his defeat at the Boyne; successfully resisted siege by Cromwell 1649 but fell to Ireton 1650.

Waterford Harbour. Inlet of St. George's Channel on SE coast of Ireland, in co. Waterford; the city of Waterford is at the head of the inlet.

Waterford Works. Village, Camden co., SW New Jersey, 21 m. SE of Camden; pop. (est.) 700.

Wa'ter·graafs'meer' (vä'tẽr·kräfs'mār'). Former commune, now a SE suburb of Amsterdam, Netherlands.

Wa'ter·loo' (wŏ'tẽr·lōō'; wŏt'ẽr-; -'--). **1** City, ⊗ of Monroe co., SW Illinois, 22 m. S of East St. Louis; pop. 3739.
2 City, ⊗ of Black Hawk co., NE cen. Iowa, on Cedar river 52 m. NW of Cedar Rapids; pop. 71,755; trading center in agricultural and livestock-raising section; manufactures creamery separators, tractors, farm implements. Founded 1846 and laid out in 1854.
3 Village, a ⊗ of Seneca co., W cen. New York, 15 m. W of Auburn; pop. 5098; in farming country; manufactures automobile bodies, lumber, flour, dairy products.
4 Town, on railroad in N cen. part of Sierra Leone Penin., Sierra Leone, W Africa, 14 m. SE of Freetown; pop. 2312.
5 Town, E New South Wales, SE Australia, S suburb of Sydney; pop. 11,657.

6 (*Flem.* vä'tẽr·lô') Commune, Brabant prov., cen. Belgium, ab. 12 m. S of Brussels; pop. 5735; battle called Waterloo nearby (at La Belle Alliance, 3 m. to SE) June 18, 1815 in which the British under Wellington and the Prussians under Blücher decisively defeated Napoleon and ended his power.
7 County, Ontario, Canada. See *Table* at ONTARIO.
8 Town, Waterloo co., SE Ontario, Canada, NW suburb of Kitchener; pop. 11,991; iron foundries; manufactures textiles, agricultural implements; insurance companies.
9 Town, ⊗ of Shefford co., S Quebec, Canada, 30 m. W of Sherbrooke; pop. 4054; trades in lumber and farm produce. Founded by Loyalists 1796.

Waterloo with Sea'forth (sē'fôrth). Former urban district, Lancashire, NW England, at mouth of the Mersey 4 m. N of Liverpool; watering place.

Wa'ter'mael'–Boits'fort' (vä'tẽr'mäl'bwä'fôr'). Commune, Brabant prov., cen. Belgium, a suburb of Brussels; pop. 16,138.

Wa'ter Rock Knob (wô'tẽr; wŏt'ẽr). Peak 6399 ft. in Haywood co., W North Carolina.

Waters of Merom. See Waters of MEROM.

Wa'ter·ton–Glacier International Peace Park (wŏ'tẽr·t'n; -tŭn; wŏt'ẽr-). International park, estab. 1932, comprising Waterton Lakes National Park in S Alberta and Glacier National Park in NW Montana. See CANADA, *National Parks*; UNITED STATES, *National Parks*.

Waterton Lakes National Park. See CANADA, *National Parks*.

Wa'ter·town (wŏ'tẽr·toun; wŏt'ẽr-). **1** Industrial town, SE Litchfield co., NW Connecticut, on W bank of Naugatuck river NW of Waterbury; pop. 14,837; incorp. 1780; manufactures silk, rayon, hardware, plastics, wire products, pins, tacks. Taft School (preparatory school for boys).
2 Town, Middlesex co., NE Massachusetts, 7 m. W of Boston; pop. 39,092; founded 1630; U.S. Arsenal located here 1816; manufactures textiles and rubber goods; home of Charles Pratt (1830–91), founder of Pratt Institute in Brooklyn, New York.
3 Manufacturing city, ⊗ of Jefferson co., N New York, 10 m. E of Lake Ontario; pop. 33,306; bisected by Black river, with falls of 120 ft. within city; settled 1800; trading and industrial center; manufactures paper and papermaking machinery, railroad air brakes, metal products, optical goods, flour, plumbers' supplies.
4 City, ⊗ of Codington co., NE South Dakota, 70 m. ENE of Huron; pop. 14,077; platted 1878, incorp. 1885. Railroad, shipping, and trading center for agricultural and stock-raising area; food processing, packing plants for meat and poultry, creameries, flour mills, machine and bottling works; farm implements, cement products; sand and gravel deposits nearby.
5 City, Dodge and Jefferson cos., SE Wisconsin, 32 m. E of Madison; pop. 13,943; railroad, shipping, and industrial center in agricultural and dairy-farming section; home of Carl Schurz 1855–61; reputed site of first kindergarten in America, estab. by Mrs. Carl Schurz 1856; Northwestern Coll. (1865; coed.).

Water Valley. City, a ⊗ of Yalobusha co., N Mississippi, 53 m. E of Clarksdale; pop. 3206; in agricultural section; shipping point for watermelons.

Wa'ter·ville (wŏ'tẽr·vĭl; wŏt'ẽr-). **1** Subdivision of town and city of WATERBURY, Connecticut.
2 City, Kennebec co., SW Maine, on Kennebec river 18 m. N of Augusta; pop. 18,695; railroad terminal, and commercial and industrial center; textile mills, iron foundry. Colby Coll. (1813; coed.; Baptist).
3 City, Le Sueur co., S Minnesota, 20 m. E of Mankato; pop. 1623; summer resort.
4 Village, Oneida co., cen. New York, 13 m. SW of Utica; pop. 1901; formerly a hop-raising center, now industrial. Birthplace of George Eastman.
5 Town, ⊗ of Douglas co., cen. Washington; pop. 1013.

Wa′ter·vliet (wô′tēr·vlēt; wŏt′ēr-). Industrial city, Albany co., E New York, on Hudson river opp. Troy near terminus of N.Y. State Barge Canal, 6 m. N of Albany; pop. 13,917; manufactures textiles, wooden, leather, and metal articles, machine-shop products, boats. Seat of U.S. Arsenal, established 1813, producing arms for War of 1812 and all subsequent wars; specializes in heavy ordnance.

Wat′ford (wŏt′fērd). Municipal borough, Hertfordshire, SE England, on the Colne 17 m. NW of London; pop. 56,805, (1951 pop.) 73,072; commercial center; a small part (pop. 2636) lies within Greater London.

Watford City. Village, ⊗ of McKenzie co., W North Dakota, 28 m. SE of Williston; pop. 1865; railroad terminus; lignite coal mines; grain, stock, dairy farms.

Wath upon Dearne (wŏth [wăth], dûrn). Urban district, West Riding, Yorkshire, N England, 8 m. SE of Barnsley; pop. 13,927.

Wat′kins Glen (wŏt′kĭnz). Village, ⊗ of Schuyler co., SW cen. New York, at S end of Seneca Lake 18 m. N of Elmira; pop. 2813; shopping, industrial, and tourist center; mineral springs, saltworks nearby; also **Watkins Glen**, a gorge 2 m. long, 100–300 ft. deep, the stream falling 1200 ft. in many cascades.

Wat′kins·ville (wŏt′kĭnz·vĭl; *Sou. also* -v′l). Town, ⊗ of Oconee co., NE cen. Georgia; pop. 758.

Wat′lings Island *or* **Wat′lings** (wŏt′lĭngz); *sometimes*, *unofficially*, **Wat′ling′s** (-lĭngz), *or* **Wat′ling** (-lĭng), **Island.** See SAN SALVADOR island, Bahama Is.

Wat′ling Street (wŏt′lĭng). Roman road in Britain extending from London to Wroxeter (near Shrewsbury) in a general northwesterly direction; by some it is held to be the road that began at Richborough, or Dover, ran through Canterbury to London, and continued from Wroxeter to Chester. Southwest of Leicester it was intersected by Fosse Way. In 9th cent. divided Mercia (*q.v.*). Cf. ERMINE STREET.

Watling Town. See WELLINGTON.

Wa·ton′ga (wȧ·tŏng′gȧ). City, ⊗ of Blaine co., W cen. Oklahoma, 50 m. SW of Enid; pop. 3252; in agricultural country; cotton gins, grain elevators.

Wat′on·wan′ (wŏt′′n·wŏn′). County in Minnesota. See *Table* at MINNESOTA.

Wa′trous (wô′trŭs; wŏt′rŭs). Village, S Mora co., NE New Mexico; ruins of Fort Union (*q.v.*) nearby.

Wat·se′ka (wŏt·sē′kȧ). City, ⊗ of Iroquois co., E Illinois, 27 m. SSE of Kankakee; pop. 5219.

Wat′son, Mount (wŏt′s′n). Peak 11,473 ft. in S Summit co., NE Utah.

Watson Lake. Village on left bank of Liard river, S Yukon, Canada, on Brit. Columbia border near Lower Post; station on the Alaska Highway.

Wat′son·town (wŏt′s′n·toun). Borough, Northumberland co., E cen. Pennsylvania, 16 m. SSE of Williamsport; pop. 2431.

Wat′son·ville (wŏt′s′n·vĭl). City, Santa Cruz co., W California, near Monterey Bay 30 m. S of San Jose; pop. 13,293; founded 1852; shipping center for apples, strawberries, lettuce, apricots; canneries, evaporating plants.

Wat′ten·scheid (vät′ĕn·shīt). Industrial city, in North Rhine-Westphalia, West Germany, in Ruhr valley, E suburb of Essen; pop. 60,823; coal mining; manufactures brushes, pianos, wooden shoes, iron goods.

Wat′ti·gnies′, *in full* **Wattignies–la–Vic′toire′** (vȧ·tē′nyē′lȧ·vēk′twȧr′). Village in Nord dept., N France; pop. (1931) 191; battle Oct. 16, 1793 in which the French under Jourdan defeated the Austrians.

Wat′tre·los′ (vȧ′trē·lō′). Industrial commune, Nord dept., N France, 9 m. NE of Lille; pop. 31,084; suburb of Roubaix; coal mines; textile manufactures; petroleum refinery.

Watts Bar Dam (wŏts). See *Table* at TENNESSEE VALLEY AUTHORITY.

Watts Island. Island in lower Chesapeake Bay, W cen. coast of Accomac co., Virginia.

Watt′wil (vät′vēl). Commune, St. Gallen canton, Switzerland; pop. (1930) 6330; Capuchin convent; castle ruins.

Wau (wou). **1** Town Equatoria prov., S Sudan, ✳ of Bahr el Ghazal prov., on the Jur river ab. 300 m. NW of Mongalla.

2 Settlement and active mining town, SE North-East New Guinea, 32 m. SW of Salamaua; situated high (alt. 3500 ft.) in Bulolo Valley, in the mountains of the Morobe dist. where the gold fields are, it has an airstrip and is connected with Lae to the NNE by airline (46 m.) and road (93 m.). Settlement begun c. 1925; in World War II seized by Japanese but retaken by Australians and Americans bet. Feb. and Sept. 1943.

Wau′bay Lake (wô′bā). Lake in Day co., NE South Dakota.

Wau·be′sa, Lake (wô·bē′sȧ). See FOUR LAKES.

Wau·chu′la (wô·choo′lȧ). City, ⊗ of Hardee co., cen. Florida penin., 37 m. S of Lakeland; pop. 3411; fruit and frogs′ legs.

Waugh Mountain (wô). Peak 8882 ft. in SE Idaho co., N cen. Idaho.

Waukara. See WAOEKARA.

Wau·ke′gan (wô·kē′găn). Residential city, ⊗ of Lake co., NE corner of Illinois, on Lake Michigan 40 m. N of Chicago; pop. 55,719; settled 1835, incorp. as town 1849, as city 1859; manufactures wire and wire products, iron castings; summer resort; just S of the town is the Great Lakes Naval Training Station.

Wau′ke·sha (wô′kĕ·shô). **1** County in Wisconsin. See *Table* at WISCONSIN.

2 City, its ⊗, SE Wisconsin, 15 m. W of Milwaukee; pop. 30,004; commercial and industrial center in agricultural and livestock-raising section; medicinal springs and limestone quarries nearby. Carroll Coll. (1840; coed.; Presbyterian).

Wau·kon′ (wô·kŏn′). City, ⊗ of Allamakee co., NE corner of Iowa, 17 m. E of Decorah; pop. 3639; in agricultural and dairy section; iron deposits nearby.

Waum′bek Mountain (wôm′bĕk). Peak 4005 ft. in S Coos co., N New Hampshire.

Wau·pac′a (wô·păk′ȧ). **1** County in Wisconsin. See *Table* at WISCONSIN.

2 City, its ⊗, E cen. Wisconsin, 32 m. WNW of Appleton; pop. 3984; market center in potato-growing section; vacation and fishing resorts nearby.

Wau·pés′ (wou·pās′). = UAUPÉS.

Wau·pun′ (wô·pŏn′—*sic*). City, Dodge and Fond du Lac cos., SE cen. Wisconsin, 17 m. SW of Fond du Lac; pop. 7935; trade center in agricultural and dairy-farming section.

Wau·ri′ka (wô·rē′kȧ). City, ⊗ of Jefferson co., S Oklahoma, 38 m. SSE of Lawton; pop. 1933; agriculture; oil and gas wells.

Wau′sau (wô′sô). City, ⊗ of Marathon co., cen. Wisconsin, on Wisconsin river 84 m. WNW of Green Bay (city); pop. 31,943; trade and industrial center in agricultural section; manufactures motors, dairy products, flour, shoes, wood products.

Wau′se·on (wô′sē·ŏn; wŏ′sē·ŏn′). Village, ⊗ of Fulton co., NW Ohio, 32 m. W of Toledo; pop. 4311; settled 1835; manufactures canned foods, cement blocks.

Wau·shar′a (wô·shär′ȧ). County in Wisconsin. See *Table* at WISCONSIN.

Wau·to′ma (wô·tō′mȧ). City, ⊗ of Waushara co., cen. Wisconsin; pop. 1466.

Wau′wa·to′sa (wô′wȧ·tō′sȧ). City, Milwaukee co., SE Wisconsin, 5 m. W of Milwaukee; pop. 56,923; suburb of Milwaukee.

Waveney. See the BROADS.

Wa′ver·ley (wā′vēr·lĭ). Municipality, E New South Wales, SE Australia, E suburb of Sydney, on Pacific Ocean; pop. 55,911.

Wa′ver·ly (wā′vēr·lĭ). **1** City, ⊗ of Bremer co., NE Iowa, 15 m. NNW of Waterloo; pop. 6357; in agricul-

tural section; produces butter, canned corn, condensed milk. Wartburg Coll. (1868; coed.; Lutheran).

2 Village, Tioga co., S New York, on Pennsylvania border 15 m. ESE of Elmira; pop. 5950; shipping point for farming and stock-raising country.

3 Village, ⊗ of Pike co., S Ohio, 15 m. S of Chillicothe; pop. 3830; farm and market center.

4 Town, ⊗ of Humphreys co., W Tennessee; pop. 2891.

Wa'vre (và'vr'). Manufacturing commune, Brabant prov., cen. Belgium, 14 m. SE of Brussels; pop. 8258. Battle here June 18, 1815, a phase of Waterloo, in which French general, Grouchy, drove back part of Blücher's force but failed to aid Napoleon.

Wavre–Sainte–Catherine. See SINT-KATELIJNE-WAVER.

Wa'wa (wä'wä). Village, Rizal prov., Luzon, Phil. Is., NE of Manila; **Wawa Dam,** E of Montalban, in the Manila water system held by Japanese as defense point during fighting in 1945; taken by Americans May 28, 1945.

Wa'wa·see' Lake (wô'wà·sē'). Lake in NE Kosciusko co., N Indiana; largest lake in Indiana.

Wax'a·hach'ie (wôk'sà·hăch'ê). City, ⊗ of Ellis co., NE cen. Texas, 30 m. S of Dallas; pop. 12,749; cotton market; cottonseed-oil and textile mills, cotton compress. Site of Trinity Univ. 1902–42, moved to San Antonio (q.v.).

Wax'haw (wăks'hô). Village, Lancaster co., N South Carolina; birthplace of Andrew Jackson, 7th president of the U.S.

Way'ah Bald (wī'à). Peak 5336 ft. in N Macon co., SW North Carolina.

Way'cross (wā'krŏs). City, ⊗ of Ware co., SE Georgia, 50 m. W of Brunswick; pop. 20,944; railroad and commercial center; honey, naval stores, tobacco, furs.

Way'land (wā'lănd). **1** City, Floyd co., E Kentucky, 17 m. W of Pikeville; pop. 1340; in coal-mining section.

2 Town, Middlesex co., NE Massachusetts, 15 m. W of Boston; pop. 10,444.

3 Village, Steuben co., S New York, 16 m. NNE of Hornell; pop. 2003; produces potatoes, peas, beans, corn; dairy farms, canneries.

Wayne (wān). **1** Name of counties in sixteen states of the U.S. See *Tables* at GEORGIA, ILLINOIS, INDIANA, IOWA, KENTUCKY, MICHIGAN, MISSISSIPPI, MISSOURI, NEBRASKA, NEW YORK, NORTH CAROLINA, OHIO, PENNSYLVANIA, TENNESSEE, UTAH, WEST VIRGINIA.

2 Village, Wayne co., SE Michigan, 19 m. W of Detroit; pop. 16,034.

3 City, ⊗ of Wayne co., NE Nebraska, 26 m. ENE of Norfolk; pop. 4217. Nebraska State Teachers Coll. (1891; coed.).

4 Urban township, Passaic co., N New Jersey, 6 m. W of Paterson; pop. 29,353.

5 Residential locality, Delaware co., SE Pennsylvania, ab. 6 m. SSW of Norristown; pop. (est.) 6000.

6 Town, ⊗ of Wayne co., SW West Virginia; pop. 1274.

Waynes'bor'o (wānz'bûr'ô). **1** City, ⊗ of Burke co., E Georgia, 28 m. S of Augusta; pop. 5359; cotton center.

2 Town, ⊗ of Wayne co., SE Mississippi; pop. 3892.

3 Borough and resort, Franklin co., S Pennsylvania, 14 m. S of Chambersburg; pop. 10,427; storage and shipping point for fruit (esp. peaches and apples); manufactures textiles, shoes, iron fences, steel, machinery.

4 City, ⊗ of Wayne co., S Tennessee; pop. 1343.

5 Independent city, Augusta co., N Virginia, in Shenandoah Valley at foot of Blue Ridge Mts. 12 m. ESE of Staunton; pop. 15,694; manufactures rayon, silk, woven fabrics, furniture, flour and feed, dairy products, food, stoves; agriculture (apples, livestock, wheat). Site first settled c. mid-18th cent.; scene of battle Mar. 2, 1865 in which Confederate forces under Gen. Early were badly defeated.

Waynes'burg (wānz'bûrg). Borough, ⊗ of Greene co., SW corner of Pennsylvania, 26 m. W of Uniontown; pop.

5188; agricultural center; gas wells, stone quarries. Waynesburg Coll. (1850; coed.).

Waynes'ville (wānz'vĭl; *Sou. also* -v'l). **1** City, ⊗ of Pulaski co., S cen. Missouri; pop.2377 .

2 Town, ⊗ of Haywood co., W North Carolina, 26 m. WSW of Asheville; pop. 6159; vacation and health resort.

Way·no'ka (wā·nō'kà). Town, Woods co., NW Oklahoma, 32 m. ENE of Woodward; pop. 1794; railroad division point; farming.

Wazan. = *Wazzan:* see OUEZZANE.

Wa'ziers' (và'zyā'). Commune, Nord dept., N France; pop. (1931) 9959; ENE suburb of Douai.

Wa·zir'a·bad' (wà·zēr'à·bäd'). **1** See BALKH ancient city.

2 Town, Gujranwala dist., N West Punjab, Pakistan, on Chenab river 60 m. N of Lahore; pop. 20,707; important railroad junction, with Alexandra bridge over the Chenab; has boatbuilding business.

Wa·zir'i·stan' (wà·zēr'ĭ·stän'). Mountain tract, SW North-West Frontier Province, Pakistan; 5218 sq. m.; pop. 201,783; divided into **North Waziristan** (*formerly* **To'chi** [tō'chĭ]), pop. 93,570, and **South Waziristan** (*formerly* **Wa'na** [wä'nà]), pop. 108,213; lies NE of Baluchistan and along border of Afghanistan; inhabited by Wazirs, a Pathan tribe of low civilization, divided into the Darwesh Khel and Mahsuds; their chief town is Kaniguram. Since 1860 there have been several uprisings in Waziristan (see WANA); most serious, called Third Afghan War, was in 1919–22 when Mahsuds rose in revolt. Kaniguram and Wana subdued; last Mahsud tribes submitted Feb. 1922.

Wazzan. See OUEZZANE.

We or **Weh** (wā). Small island ab. 14 m. off extreme NW tip of Sumatra, Indonesia, directly N of Kutaradja; 65 sq. m.; has irregular coast line with large bay on N coast, on which is Sabang, an important free port with fine harbor.

Weak'ley (wēk'lĭ). County in Tennessee. See *Table* at TENNESSEE.

Weald, the (wēld). Wooded district in Kent, Surrey, and Sussex cos., SE England, lying bet. the North Downs and South Downs; formerly heavily forested; in 17th cent. covered ab. 325 sq. m.

Weald'stone (wēld'stōn). Former urban district, Middlesex, SE England, 12 m. WNW of London; pop. (1931) 27,019; now in Harrow.

Wear (wēr). River 67 m. long in Durham, N England; flows E and NE into North Sea at Sunderland.

Wearmouth. See SUNDERLAND, England.

Weath'er·ford (wĕth'ēr·fērd). **1** City, Custer co., W Oklahoma, 11 m. E of Clinton; pop. 4499; agriculture. Southwestern Institute of Technology (1901; coed.).

2 City, ⊗ of Parker co., N cen. Texas, 25 m. W of Fort Worth; pop. 9759; ships watermelons and melon seeds; limestone and clay deposits nearby.

Weath'er·ly (wĕth'ēr·lĭ). Borough, Carbon co., E Pennsylvania, 21 m. S of Wilkes-Barre; pop. 2591.

Wea'ver (wē'vēr). River ab. 45 m. long in Cheshire, NW England; rises near border of Shropshire, flows NE, and then NW into the Mersey; navigable as far as Winsford.

Wea'ver·ville (wē'vēr·vĭl). Village, ⊗ of Trinity co., NW California; pop. 1736.

Webb (wĕb). County in Texas. See *Table* at TEXAS.

Webb City. City, Jasper co., SW Missouri, 6 m. N of Joplin; pop. 6740; zinc and lead deposits nearby.

Web'be (wĕb'ā; *native* wûb·bā) or **Web** (wĕb). River ab. 280 m. long, SE Ethiopia; flows S to join the Ganale Dorya and Dawa rivers to form the Juba.

Webbe Mana. See Webbe MANA.

Webbe Shibeli. See Webbe SHIBELI.

We'ber (wē'bēr). **1** River ab. 100 m. long, N Utah; rises in S Summit co., flows NW into Great Salt Lake.

2 County in Utah. See *Table* at UTAH.

We'bi Shi·be'li (wā'bĭ shĭ·bā'lĭ). = Webbe SHIBELI.

Web′ster (wĕb′stẽr). **1** Name of a parish in Louisiana and of counties in seven states of the U.S. See *Tables* at GEORGIA, IOWA, KENTUCKY, LOUISIANA, MISSISSIPPI, MISSOURI, NEBRASKA, WEST VIRGINIA.
2 Town, Worcester co., cen. Massachusetts, 15 m. S of Worcester; pop. 13,680; has textile mills and shoe factories.
3 Village, Monroe co., W New York, 10 m. ENE of Rochester; pop. 3060; farming.
4 City, ⊗ of Day co., NE South Dakota, 37 m. NNW of Watertown; pop. 2409.
Webster, Lake. See Lake CHAUBUNAGUNGAMAUGG.
Webster, Mount. Peak 3876 ft. in S Coos co., N New Hampshire.
Webster City. Industrial city, ⊗ of Hamilton co., N cen. Iowa, 20 m. E of Fort Dodge; pop. 8520.
Webster Groves. City, St. Louis co., E Missouri, 8 m. W of St. Louis; pop. 28,990. Eden Theological Seminary (1850; Evangelical and Reformed Church); Webster Coll. (1915; women; Roman Catholic).
Webster Springs. Town, ⊗ of Webster co., E cen. West Virginia, 43 m. SW of Elkins; pop. (1950) 1313; incorporated 1892 as **Ad′di·son** (ăd′ĭ·s′n), but better known as Webster Springs, its post-office name.
Wed, El. Var. of EL OUED.
Wed′dell Island (wĕd′′l). One of the Falkland Is. (*q.v.*), W of West Falkland.
Weddell Quadrant. Formerly, the quarter section of Antarctica (*q.v.*) bet. Greenwich meridian and 90°W; now chiefly W Queen Maud Land, Weddell Sea and Coats Land, and Palmer Archipelago and Palmer Penin. (Falkland Islands Dependencies).
Weddell Sea. Arm of S Atlantic Ocean in Antarctica SE of Palmer Penin.; discovered 1823 by Capt. James Weddell. Its W shore is along 60th meridian, W long.; its E shore is Coats Land (*q.v.*); Filchner Shelf Ice is at its S end. See FALKLAND ISLANDS DEPENDENCIES.
Wed′more (wĕd′mōr). Village, N cen. Somerset, SW England; in 878 scene of signing of peace bet. King Alfred and Guthrum, Danish king of East Anglia, by which Danes were restricted to territory (the Danelaw) in NE England, N of Watling Street.
Wednes′bur·y (wĕnz′bẽr·ĭ; wĕj′-; -brĭ). Municipal borough, Staffordshire, W cen. England, on the Tame 8 m. NW of Birmingham; pop. 34,758; in coal-mining section; iron and steel works.
Wednes′field (wĕns′fēld; wĕj′-). Urban district, Staffordshire, W cen. England; pop. 17,422.
We·dow′ee (wĕ·dou′ĕ). Town, ⊗ of Randolph co., E Alabama; pop. 917.
Wee·haw′ken (wē·hô′kĕn; *attributively, also* wē′hô′-). Township, Hudson co., NE New Jersey, on Hudson river opp. New York City (connected by Lincoln Tunnel), 5 m. N of Jersey City; pop. 13,504; coal depot and railroad center; manufactures; scene of Hamilton-Burr duel July 11, 1804.
Weeks′bur·y (wēks′bẽr′ĭ; -bẽr·ĭ). Town, Floyd co., E Kentucky, 13 m. SW of Pikeville; pop. (1950) 1340; in Cumberland Mts.
Wee′nen (vē′nĕn). Town, cen. Natal, E Union of South Africa, 85 m. NW of Durban; pop. 2759; founded 1838, second oldest settlement in Natal; scene of massacre of Boer Voortrekkers by Zulus under Dingaan 1838—hence its name, literally "place of weeping."
Weert (vārt). Commune, Limburg prov., SE Netherlands, near Belgian border 16 m. SE of Eindhoven; pop. 14,144.
Weesp (vāsp). Commune, North Holland prov., W Netherlands, 7 m. SE of Amsterdam; pop. 7227.
Weets′lade (wēts′lād). Former urban district, Northumberland, N England; now in Seaton Valley.
Wę′go·rze′wo (vĕnng′gô·zhĕ′vô); *Ger.* **Ang′er·burg** (äng′ẽr·bŏŏrk). Town, NE Olsztyn dept., N Poland, 60 m. NE of Olsztyn; pop. (1946) 2200; terminus on Angerapp river at N end of Lake Mamry for motorboat

line serving Masurian Lakes; near Russian border, formerly in East Prussia, Germany; manufactures small machinery and clay products. Founded 1571 in connection with religious structure built 1328; battle 1914; assigned to Poland by Potsdam Conference 1945.
Weh. See WE.
Weh′lau (vā′lou). Town, formerly in East Prussia, Germany, on S bank of the Pregel at the mouth of the Alle, 30 m. E of Königsberg (Kaliningrad); pop. (1933) 7534; in part of Prussia assigned to the U.S.S.R. 1945. Has late-Gothic church of 16th cent. and several other earlier structures. Treaty signed here Sept. 19, 1657 bet. Brandenburg and Poland by which Poland renounced sovereignty over duchy of Prussia and Brandenburg restored territory seized from Poland.
Wei (wā). **1** River 400 m. long, rises in mountains of SE Kansu prov., N cen. China, flows E across Shensi to join the Hwang Ho at Tungkwan, the point where it turns E; on its S bank in Shensi is Sian. Its fertile valley shut in on the S by the Chin Ling Shan; a cultural center in early Chinese history.
2 = WEIHSIEN town, China.
Wei′chow′ (wā′jō′). Island in NE Gulf of Tonkin, Kwangtung prov., SE China, S of Pakhoi.
Weichsel. See VISTULA.
Wei′da (vī′dä). City, Thuringia, E Germany, WNW of Zwickau; pop. 10,040; 12th-cent. Gothic church, 12th-cent. castle; manufactures leather, shoes, jute, textiles.
Wei′den (vī′dĕn). Manufacturing city, Lower Bavaria and Upper Palatinate govt., Bavaria, W Germany, on Naab river 31 m. SE of Bayreuth; pop. 19,536; 16th-cent. town hall, 17th-cent. church; manufactures porcelain, lumber, glass; trades in cattle.
Wei′de·nau (vī′dĕ·nou), *also* **Weidenau an der Sieg** (än dẽr zēk′). Commune, in North Rhine-Westphalia state, West Germany, formerly in Westphalia prov., Prussia, on Sieg river 48 m. E of Cologne; pop. 10,913; ore mining; manufactures iron, steel, copper.
Wei′hai′wei′ (wā′hī·wā′). Seaport and treaty port, NE Shantung prov., NE China, at E end of peninsula on N coast 40 m. E of Chefoo; pop. ab. 7000; on S shore of Strait of Pohai nearly opp. Dairen. Chinese fleet destroyed here and town seized by Japanese 1895 in war with China; occupied by Japanese 1895–98. Leased with adjacent waters and territory (285 sq. m., pop. 154,416) to Great Britain 1898; used as a naval base; returned to China Oct. 1, 1930. Has considerable trade and exceptionally fine climate; its harbor is protected by Liukung I. (2 m. long), lying across its mouth.
Wei′hsien′ (wā′shĭ·ĕn′). Commercial walled town, E cen. Shantung prov., NE China, on railroad 85 m. NW of Tsingtao; pop. ab. 80,000.
Wei′mar (vī′mär). City, Thuringia, E Germany, 13 m. E of Erfurt; pop. 45,957; once the leading cultural center of Germany as the residence of Herder, Wieland, Goethe, and Schiller, among others, and often called on this account the "German Athens"; buildings include grand ducal palace, Goethe's and Schiller's residences, Stadtkirche, modern Gothic town hall, museum, library, etc.; relatively unimportant trade and manufactures. After World War I German national assembly met here and ratified Treaty of Versailles, formed German republic (often called the "Weimar Republic"), and formulated republican constitution (often called the "Weimar Constitution") 1919. Weimar Republic and Constitution superseded (although not formally abrogated) by Act of 1933 granting Hitler and National Socialist Party absolute power. In World War II taken by American forces Apr. 12, 1945.
Wein′heim (vīn′hīm). City, Baden-Württemberg, W Germany, 10 m. NE of Mannheim; pop. 15,793; health resort; 13th-cent. Gothic chapel, 16th-cent. Gothic town hall; manufactures leather, machinery, brushes, chairs, rubber goods, soap.

Weins'berg (vīns'bĕrʀ). Commune, Baden-Württemberg, W Germany, on a tributary of the Neckar just E of Heilbronn; pop. 3658; scene of defeat 1140 of Welf VI by Conrad III of Germany; free imperial city, in league of Swabian cities 1331–1440.

Wei Pei Dam (wā' pā'). Dam on King river NW of Sian, SW Shensi prov., N cen. China; part of International Famine Relief project, opened June 1932.

Weipert. See VEJPRTY.

Weir'ton (wĕr't'n). City, Brooke and Hancock cos., N West Virginia, on Ohio river ab. 26 m. NNE of Wheeling; pop. 28,201; steel manufactures. Incorp. 1947.

Weirton Heights. Former town, N West Virginia, in Hancock co.; incorp. in Weirton city 1947.

Wei'ser (wē'sĕr). City, ⊗ of Washington co., W Idaho, on Snake river 62 m. NW of Boise; pop. 4208; grain, fruit, dairy products.

Weissbad. See APPENZELL.

Weisse Elster. See ELSTER.

Weis'sen·burg (vī'sĕn·bŏŏrʀ). **1** Town, NE France. See WISSEMBOURG.

2 *formerly* **Weissenburg–am–Sand** (-äm·zänt'). Fortified town, Middle Franconia, Bavaria, Germany, ab. 30 m. SW of Nürnberg; pop. (1939) 8894; dates from 8th cent.; has old walls, Gothic town hall.

Weis'sen·fels (vī'sĕn·fĕls). Manufacturing commune, E Germany, in what was formerly Saxony prov., Prussia; pop. 36,756; an old town, of considerable importance in 17th and 18th cents.

Weissenstein. See PAIDE.

Weisser Berg. See WHITE MOUNTAIN.

Weiss'horn' (vīs'hôrn'). Peak 14,804 ft. in Valais canton, SW cen. Switzerland, in Pennine Alps.

Weisskirchen. See BELA CRKVA.

Weiss'ku'gel (vīs'kōō'gĕl); *Ital.* **Pa'la Bian'ca** (pä'lä byäng'kä). Peak 12,291 ft. in the Ötztaler Alps, on the border bet. Austrian Tirol and the Italian compartimento of Venezia Tridentina.

Weiss'mies (vīs'mēs). Mountain 13,226 ft. in SW cen. Switzerland, in E part of the Pennine Alps.

Weiss–stein. See BIAŁY KAMIEŃ.

Weiss'was'ser (vīs'väs'ĕr). Commune, E Germany, in what was Silesia province of Prussia, 25 m. NNE of Bautzen; pop. 12,388; manufactures glass, porcelain, lumber, tile; lignite mining.

Weit'mar (vīt'mär). Former commune in Westphalia, now part of Bochum, North Rhine-Westphalia state, West Germany.

Wejh (wăj'h'). Port on the Red Sea, N Hejaz, W Arabia, 260 m. NW of Medina.

Wej'he·ro'wo (vā'hĕ·rô'vô). Commune, Pomorze dept., Poland, 23 m. NW of Danzig; pop. (1938–39 est.) 14,556; on railroad from Gdynia to Stettin (Szczecin).

Welch (wĕlch). City, ⊗ of McDowell co., S West Virginia, 24 m. WNW of Bluefield; pop. 5313; coal mines; lumber.

Wel'come Bay (wĕl'kŭm); *Du.* **Wel'komst Baai** (vĕl'kômst bä'ī). Inlet of Sunda Strait on W end of Java, Indonesia.

Weld (wĕld). County in Colorado. See *Table* at COLORADO.

Wel'don (wĕl'dŭn). Town, Halifax co., NE North Carolina, on Roanoke river at head of navigation 34 m. NNE of Rocky Mount; pop. 2165; in peanut-growing region.

We·leet'ka (wĕ·lēt'kà). City, Okfuskee co., E cen. Oklahoma, 23 m. SSW of Okmulgee; pop. 1231; agriculture (watermelons, etc.).

Wel'fare' Island (wĕl'fâr'). Island in East river, New York, 1½ m. long by ⅛ m. wide, part of Manhattan borough; municipal hospital, and formerly a penal institution; known as **Black'wells Island** (blăk'wĕlz; -wĕlz) until 1921.

Wel'land (wĕl'ănd). **1** County, Ontario, Canada. See *Table* at ONTARIO.

2 Industrial city, its ⊗, SE Ontario, Canada, on Welland Ship Canal 14 m. S of St. Catharines; pop. 15,382; cordage mills, iron and brass foundries, cotton mills, boilerworks; manufactures agricultural and electrical equipment, fertilizer, rubber goods. Founded 1830 and incorp. as a city 1917.

3 River 70 m. long, E cen. England; rises in Northamptonshire and flows NE into the Wash.

Welland Ship Canal; *formerly* **Welland Canal.** Canadian government-owned ship waterway connecting Lake Erie with Lake Ontario in Welland and Lincoln cos., SE Ontario, 27.6 m. long and having 8 locks and minimum depth of 25 ft.; extends from Port Colborne on Lake Erie to Port Weller on Lake Ontario, with a rise of 326 ft. bet. the two. Old canal had 25 locks, was first built 1824–33, reconstructed 1872–87, and entirely rebuilt as a ship canal 1914–32.

Welle. See UELE.

Wellen. See UELEN.

Welles'ley (wĕlz'lĭ). Residential town, Norfolk co., E Massachusetts, 12 m. WSW of Boston; pop. 26,071; Wellesley Coll. (1870; women).

Wellesley, Province. See PROVINCE WELLESLEY.

Wellesley Islands. Group of islands off N coast of Queensland, Australia, at head of Gulf of Carpentaria.

Well'fleet (wĕl'flēt). Town, Barnstable co., SE Massachusetts, on Cape Cod Bay ab. 15 m. from Provincetown; pop. 1404; inlet of the bay here called **Wellfleet Harbor.**

Wel'ling·bor·ough (wĕl'ing·bŭ·rŭ; -brŭ). Urban district, Northamptonshire, cen. England, on the Nene 60 m. NNW of London; pop. 28,220; industrial and commercial center.

Wel'ling·ho'fen (vĕl'ing·hō'fĕn). Former commune (pop. 11,134), Arnsberg govt. dist., Westphalia prov., Prussia, Germany; since 1929 part of Dortmund (*q.v.*).

Wel'ling·ton (wĕl'ing·tŭn). **1** City, ⊗ of Sumner co., S Kansas, 30 m. S of Wichita; pop. 8809; in agricultural section; therapeutic mineral springs nearby.

2 Village, Lorain co., N Ohio, 35 m. SW of Cleveland; pop. 3599; settled 1818; abolitionist center prior to Civil War; manufactures gray-iron castings, warehouse trucks, automobile parts.

3 City, ⊗ of Collingsworth co., NW Texas, in the panhandle 87 m. ESE of Amarillo; pop. 3137; cotton, livestock, grain, poultry.

4 County, Ontario, Canada. See *Table* at ONTARIO.

5 Island 110 m. long and 40 m. wide in S Pacific Ocean W of SW Chile, N of Madre de Dios Archipelago.

6 *orig.* **Wat'ling Town** (wŏt'lĭng). Urban district, Shropshire, W England, 30 m. WNW of Birmingham; pop. 11,412.

7 Urban district, Somersetshire, SW England, 44 m. SW of Bristol; pop. 7298; manufactures textiles.

8 Town and cantonment, SW Madras, S Indian Union, 9 m. SE of Ootacamund; pop. 7289.

9 Provincial district of New Zealand. See *Table* at NEW ZEALAND.

10 City, ✳ of Wellington provincial dist. and of New Zealand, S North I., on Port Nicholson, an inlet of Cook Strait; pop. with suburbs (1941 est.) 160,500. Founded 1840; capital transferred here from Auckland 1865. Has deep, capacious harbor; center of interisland and coastal shipping and conducts large transoceanic trade. Has Houses of Parliament and other public buildings. Seat of Wellington Coll., St. Patricks Coll., and Victoria Univ. (part of New Zealand Univ.).

11 Town, SW Cape Province, S Union of South Africa, 38 m. NE of Cape Town; pop. 6842; founded 1840; fruit orchards, stock raising. Seat of Huguenot Univ., a branch of the Univ. of South Africa.

Wellington, Mount. Mountain 4166 ft., S Tasmania, Australia, 4 m. WSW of Hobart; large part of its slope now a national park.

Wells (wĕlz). **1** Name of counties in two states of the U.S. See *Tables* at INDIANA and NORTH DAKOTA.

2 Town, York co., SW Maine, 12 m. SSW of Biddeford; pop. 3528; in agricultural section; beach resort nearby.

3 Village, Faribault co., S Minnesota, 18 m. WNW of Albert Lea; pop. 2897.

4 City, Elko co., NE corner of Nevada, ab. 48 m. NE of Elko; pop. 1071.

5 Municipal borough, Somersetshire, SW England, at foot of Mendip Hills 17 m. S of Bristol; pop. 7298; an old town, important in ancient Wessex; its origin and development have been chiefly ecclesiastical; its cathedral (begun 1186) one of the smaller but also one of the most beautiful of English cathedrals.

Wells, Lake. Lake, cen. Western Australia, in region of salt lakes bordering Gibson Desert.

Wells'bor'o (wĕlz'bûr'ŏ). Borough and resort, ⊗ of Tioga co., N Pennsylvania, 38 m. NNW of Williamsport; pop. 4369; coal mines, gas wells, timber; glass.

Wells'burg (wĕlz'bûrg). Industrial city, ⊗ of Brooke co., N West Virginia, in N panhandle on Ohio river 15 m. NNE of Wheeling; pop. 5514; manufactures glassware, paper and paper bags, flour, cement; coal mines.

Wells Gray Park. Canadian provincial park, S Brit. Columbia, just N of Kamloops; 1820 sq. m.; big-game area.

Wells River. Industrial village, Orange co., E Vermont, at junction of Wells and Connecticut rivers ab. 19 m. S of St. Johnsbury; pop. 472; gateway bet. White Mts. and Green Mts.

Wells'ton (wĕl'stŭn) **1 City**, St. Louis co., E Missouri, NW suburb of St. Louis; pop. 7979.

2 Manufacturing city, Jackson co., S Ohio, 26 m. ESE of Chillicothe; pop. 5728; manufactures metal containers, furniture, wood products; former coal-mining and smelting center.

Wells'ville (wĕlz'vĭl). **1 Village**, Allegany co., SW New York, 20 m. SW of Hornell; pop. 5967; settled 1795; oil-refining center in agricultural and dairying region.

2 City, Columbiana co., E Ohio, on Ohio river 16 m. N of Steubenville; pop. 7117; founded 1797; manufactures pottery and clay products, foundry and machine-shop products; clay deposits; in farming, dairy, fruitgrowing, and coal-mining region.

Well'ton (wĕl't'n; -tŭn). Village, Yuma co., SW corner of Arizona; farming.

Wels (vĕls); *anc.* **O'vi·la'va** (ō'vĭ·lä'vả). Manufacturing and commercial city, Upper Austria prov., Austria, on Traun river 26 m. SW of Linz; pop. (1939) 26,656; manufactures machinery, leather, paper, rope; produces natural gas.

Welsh (wĕlsh). Town, Jefferson Davis parish, SW Louisiana, 25 m. E of Lake Charles; pop. 3332; in rice-producing section; petroleum deposits nearby.

Welsh'pool' (wĕlsh'pōōl'). Municipal borough, ⊗ of Montgomeryshire, E Wales; pop. 6034; site of a 12th-cent. castle, residence of the earls of Powis (or Powys).

Wel'te·vre'den (vĕl'tĕ·vrā'dĕ[n]). Part of Djakarta, Java, Indonesia, residential section where formerly the Dutch and other foreigners lived; on both sides of the Tjiliwong river S of old city. See BATAVIA.

Wel'wyn Garden City (wĕl'ĭn). Urban district, Hertfordshire, SE England, on tributary of the Lea 24 m. N of London; pop. 18,296; established as the second English garden city in 1920, Letchworth, the first, dating from 1903.

Wem'bley (wĕm'blĭ). Municipal borough, Middlesex, SE England, W suburb of London; pop. 131,369; part of Greater London; scene of the British Empire Exhibition 1924–25.

Wemyss (wēmz). Civil parish, Fife co., E Scotland, on N shore of Firth of Forth; pop. 28,465; Wemyss castle where Mary, Queen of Scots, met Darnley 1565; caves (*Scot.* weems) along the coast of the district.

We·natch'ee (wĕ·năch'ē). **1 River** ab. 60 m. long, cen. Washington; flows SE in Chelan co. into Columbia river at Wenatchee.

2 City, ⊗ of Chelan co., cen. Washington, at confluence of Columbia and Wenatchee rivers 30 m. S of Lake Chelan; pop. 16,726; fruitgrowing, esp. apples; asbestos processing, lumber; resort region (Wenatchee National Forest and Chelan National Forest nearby)

Wenatchee Lake. Lake in cen. Chelan co., cen. Washington.

Wenatchee Mountains. Range in cen. Washington, extending along boundary bet. Chelan and Kittitas cos.

Wenchow. See YUNGKIA.

Wenden. See TSESIS.

Wen'do'ver (wĕn'dō'vẽr). Town, Tooele co., W Utah, on W edge of Great Salt Lake Desert, on Nevada boundary; pop. 609; railroad town; military base established during World War II; U.S. Air Force base.

We'ner, Wen'ner (vå'nẽr). = VÄNERN.

Wen'lock (wĕn'lŏk). Municipal borough, Shropshire, W England, on the Severn 30 m. W of Birmingham; pop. 15,093; coal mines, limestone quarries, ironworks. It includes the market town of **Much Wenlock** (mŭch), noted for its ruined Early English priory church.

Wensuh. See AQSU.

Went'worth (wĕnt'wûrth; -wẽrth). **1 Village**, ⊗ of Rockingham co., N North Carolina.

2 County, Ontario, Canada. See *Table* at ONTARIO.

Wentworth Lake. Lake 4 m. long in S Carroll co. E New Hampshire.

We'pe·ner (vē'pĕ·nẽr). Town, S Orange Free State, E cen. Union of South Africa, near Caledon river 63 m. SE of Bloemfontein; pop. 2844; founded 1871; located near W border of Basutoland and has considerable trade with it; vicinity devoted to agriculture and stock raising.

Wer'dau (vär'dou). Manufacturing city, East Germany, in Karl-Marx-Stadt dist. on Pleisse river 5 m. WNW of Zwickau; pop. 21,047; 18th-cent. church; textiles, machinery.

Wer'den (vär'dĕn), *also* **Werden an der Ruhr** (än dẽr rōōr'). Former city (pop. 13,232), Düsseldorf govt. dist., Rhine Province, Prussia, Germany; since 1929 part of Essen (*q.v.*).

Wer·dohl' (vĕr·dōl'). Industrial commune, in North Rhine-Westphalia state, West Germany, 41 m. E of Düsseldorf; pop. 12,253; manufactures iron, steel, wire, metal goods.

Wer'mels·kir'chen (vĕr'mĕls-kĭr'ĸĕn). Industrial city, in North Rhine-Westphalia state, West Germany, 19 m. ESE of Düsseldorf; pop. 15,638; 11th-cent. church; shoes, iron, silk.

Wer'ne (vĕr'nĕ). **1 Former commune** (pop. 18,883), Arnsberg govt. dist., Westphalia prov., Prussia, Germany; since 1929 part of Bochum (*q.v.*).

2 also Werne an der Lip'pe (än dẽr lĭp'ĕ). Coal-mining city, in North Rhine-Westphalia state, West Germany, on Lippe river 22 m. S Münster; pop. 11,627.

Wer'ner Peak (wûr'nẽr). Mountain 7000 ft. in W Flathead co., NW Montana.

Wer'ners·ville (wûr'nẽrz·vĭl). Borough, Berks co., SE Pennsylvania, 10 m. W of Reading; pop. 1462; summer and health resort.

Wer'ni·ge·ro'de (vĕr'nĕ·gĕ·rō'dĕ). City, E Germany, in Magdeburg dist., formerly in Saxony province of Prussia, 30 m. SSE of Brunswick; pop. 19,636; tourist and health resort. Founded in middle of 9th cent.; became city 1229; member of Hanse 1267 ff.

Wer'ra (vĕr'ä). River ab. 280 m. long in cen. Germany; flows S to unite with Fulda river at Münden and form the Weser river.

Werro. See VÕRU.

Werschetz. See VRŠAC.

Wert'heim (vārt'hīm). Town, N Baden-Württemberg, Germany, at the confluence of the Tauber and the Main; pop. (1933) 3676; Wertheim Bible published 1735.

Wer'vicq (vĕr'vēk'). Commune, West Flanders prov., W Belgium, 8 m. SE of Ieper; pop. 11,288; tobacco factories.

We'sel (vā'zĕl). Manufacturing city in North Rhine-Westphalia state, W Germany, on the Rhine at mouth of Lippe river 49 m. WSW of Münster; pop. 24,136; harbor; railroad junction; old structures include a castle, 15th-cent. Gothic church, 14th-cent. Gothic town hall; manufactures machinery, porcelain, cement, lumber, tile, soap, wire, flour, oil; salmon fisheries. First mentioned c. 750 A.D.; became city 1241; joined Hanseatic League 1350; under French rule 1808–14; to Prussia 1814; in World War II taken Mar. 23, 1945 when Allied troops crossed the Rhine.

Wesenberg. See RAKVERE.

We'ser (vā'zēr); *anc.* **Vi·sur'gis** (vĭ·sûr'jĭs). **1** Navigable river ab. 280 m. long in W Germany; formed by confluence of Fulda and Werra rivers at Münden in SE Lower Saxony, flows NW into the North Sea through a large estuary; its chief tributary is the Aller from the E, joining it near Verden.
2 River in E Belgium. See VESDRE.

We'ser·mün'de (vā'zēr·mün'dĕ); *now* **Brem'er·ha'ven** (brĕm'ēr·hä'vĕn; *Ger.* brā'mēr·hä'fĕn). Seaport city, Bremen state, W Germany, formerly in Hannover prov., Prussia, on E side of Weser estuary 58 m. W of Hamburg; pop. 72,065; formed 1924 from former cities of Geestemünde and Lehe, later included Bremerhaven and name of entire city changed 1947 to Bremerhaven; excellent harbors, docks, dry docks, shipyards; harbor fortifications; important fish market; foundries, fisheries, engineering works, lumber mills, ropeworks. Bremerhaven founded 1827 by free state of Bremen; Geestemünde founded 1857. As important naval base in World War II, often bombed.

Wes'la·co (wĕs'lá·kō). City, Hidalgo co., S Texas, 17 m. E of McAllen; pop. 15,649; in farming section.

Wes'ley·ville (wĕs'lĭ·vĭl). Borough, Erie co., NW corner of Pennsylvania, on Lake Erie 5 m. E of Erie; pop. 3534; manufactures flour, electrical parts.

Wes'se·ling (vĕs'ĕ·lĭng). Town, North Rhine-Westphalia, W Germany, on left bank of Rhine just S of Cologne; pop. (1933) 4229; synthetic oil plant.

Wes'sel Islands (wĕs'l). Island group NW of Gulf of Carpentaria, off coast of N Northern Territory, Australia.

Wes'sex (wĕs'ĕks; -ĭks). Ancient Anglo-Saxon kingdom in S Britain; ✳ Winchester; also, the corresponding section of modern England, used esp. with reference to the novels of Thomas Hardy; approximately the modern counties of Berkshire, Dorsetshire, Hampshire, Somersetshire, and Wiltshire.
   History: Kingdom founded, traditionally, by Saxon invaders of Britain; conquered Kent and Sussex (*qq.v.*) and, in 9th cent. A.D., leader of the Anglo-Saxon Heptarchy (*q.v.*); under Alfred the Great 871–899, successfully kept Danes from conquest of England south of Danelaw; by c. 954 Wessex had reconquered the Danelaw and become ruler of all England; important Anglo-Saxon earldom.

Wes'sing·ton Springs (wĕs'ĭng·tŭn). City, ⊗ of Jerauld co., SE cen. South Dakota; pop. 1488; mineral springs.

West (wĕst). **1** River ab. 50 m. long in Windham co., SE corner of Vermont; formed by confluence of forks in NW part of the county, flows SE into Connecticut river above Brattleboro.
2 City, McLennan co., cen. Texas, 19 m. N of Waco; pop. 2352.

West Al'lis (ăl'ĭs). City, Milwaukee co., SE Wisconsin, 6 m. WSW of Milwaukee; pop. 68,157; residential and industrial suburb of Milwaukee; manufactures trucks, tractors, farm machinery, steel castings.

West Antarctica. See ANTARCTICA.

West Australian Current. Warm ocean current flowing N off W coast of Australia.

West Ba'den (bā'd'n). Town, Orange co., Indiana; pop. 879; mineral springs; resort. West Baden Coll. (men; part of Loyola Univ., Chicago).

West Baton Rouge. Parish in Louisiana. See *Table* at LOUISIANA.

West Belmar. Village, E Monmouth co., E New Jersey; pop. 2511.

West Bend. City, ⊗ of Washington co., SE Wisconsin, 29 m. NNW of Milwaukee; pop. 9969; manufactures aluminum products, automobile parts, farm machinery, leather products, evaporated milk.

West Bengal. State, NE Indian Union, established Aug. 15, 1947; comprises all of Burdwan division of Bengal, India; Calcutta, 24 Parganas, and Murshidabad dists. of Presidency division; Darjeeling dist. of Rajshahi division; parts of Nadia and Jessore dists. of Presidency division; and parts of Dinajpur, Jalpaiguri, and Malda dists. of Rajshahi division; total est. area 29,664 sq. m.; total est. pop. (1931) ab. 17,290,000; chief city Calcutta.

West Beskids. See BESKIDS.

West Bloc'ton (blŏk'tŭn). Town, Bibb co., cen. Alabama, 30 m. SSW of Birmingham; pop. 1156; settled 1890, incorp. 1901; cotton, corn, potatoes; coal mines; lumber mills.

West'bor'ough *or* **West'bor'o** (wĕst'bûr'ō). Town, Worcester co., cen. Massachusetts, 9 m. E of Worcester; pop. 9599.

West Boyls'ton (boil'stŭn). Residential town, Worcester co., cen. Massachusetts, 7 m. N of Worcester; pop. 5526.

West Branch. **1** Town, Cedar co., E Iowa, just E of Iowa City; pop. 1053; birthplace of Herbert C. Hoover, 31st president of the U.S.
2 City, ⊗ of Ogemaw co., NE Michigan, 50 m. N of Bay City; pop. 2025; in agricultural section; oil field nearby.

West Branch of Susquehanna River. See SUSQUEHANNA river.

West Bridgewater. **1** Town, Plymouth co., SE Massachusetts, 4 m. S of Brockton; pop. 5061; in agricultural section.
2 See BRIDGEWATER borough, Pennsylvania.

West Bridg'ford (brĭj'fērd). Urban district, Nottinghamshire, N cen. England, SE suburb of Nottingham; pop. 24,838.

West Brom'wich (brŭm'ĭj; -ĭch; brŏm'-; -wĭch). County borough, Staffordshire, W cen. England, 5 m. NW of Birmingham; pop. 81,303, (1951 pop.) 87,985; iron and coal mines; has iron foundries and hardware factories.

West'brook (wĕst'brŏŏk). **1** Agricultural town, Middlesex co., S Connecticut, on Long Island Sound 4 m. W of mouth of Connecticut river; pop. 2399; incorp. 1840; fishing.
2 Industrial city, Cumberland co., SW Maine, 7 m. W of Portland; pop. 13,820; textile and paper mills.

West Brookfield. Town, Worcester co., cen. Massachusetts, 18 m. W of Worcester; pop. 2053.

West Brownsville. Borough, Washington co., SW Pennsylvania, on Monongahela river 13 m. NW of Uniontown; pop. 1907; coal mining.

West Burlington. Town, Des Moines co., SE Iowa, W of Burlington; pop. 2560.

West'bur'y (wĕst'bĕr'ĭ; -bēr·ĭ; -brĭ). **1** Residential village, Nassau co., SE New York, on Long I. 23 m. E of New York; pop. 14,757; Meadowbrook polo fields.
2 Town, N Tasmania, Australia, 17 m. WSW of Launceston; pop. 836; center of dairying and farming section.

Westbury Down. See SALISBURY PLAIN.

West'by (wĕst'bĭ). City, Vernon co., SW Wisconsin, N of Viroqua; pop. 1544.

West Caldwell. Borough, Essex co., NE New Jersey, 9 m. SW of Paterson; pop. 8314.

West Canada Creek. Stream ab. 55 m. long, cen. New York; flows S into Mohawk river at Herkimer; contains Trenton Falls (*q.v.*).

West Cape. Cape on W coast of Guadalcanal I., SE Solomon Is., W Pacific Ocean.

West Carroll. Parish in Louisiana. See *Table* at LOUISIANA.

West Carrollton. Village, Montgomery co., SW Ohio, on Miami river 8 m. S of Dayton; pop. 4749.

West Carthage. Village, Jefferson co., N New York, 15 m. E of Watertown; pop. 2167.

West Charlevoix. See CHARLEVOIX.

West'ches'ter (wĕst'chĕs'tẽr). **1** County in New York. See *Table* at NEW YORK.
2 Village, Cook co., NE Illinois, W suburb of Chicago; pop. 18,092.

West' Ches'ter. Borough, ⊗ of Chester county, SE Pennsylvania, 26 m. W of Philadelphia; pop. 15,705; became ⊗ 1784. West Chester State Coll. (1812; coed.).

West Chicago. City, Du Page co., NE Illinois, 30 m. W of Chicago; pop. 6854.

West Cho·sen Bay (chō·sĕn). Inlet of the Yellow Sea on the NW coast of Korea, bet. North Heian prov. and South Heian prov.; an inlet of Korea Bay.

West'cliffe (wĕst'klĭf). Town, ⊗ of Custer co., S cen. Colorado; pop. 306.

West Coast. Residency, W North Borneo; 4715 sq. m.; pop 109,566; * Jesselton.

West Columbia. 1 City, Lexington co., cen. South Carolina, on Congaree river W of Columbia; pop. 6410. Known until 1938 as **Brook'land** (brōok'lănd).
2 City, Brazoria co., SE Texas, 19 m. ENE of Bay City; pop. 2947; estab. 1826; temporary capital of Republic of Texas in 1836.

West Concord. Urban area, Cabarrus co., SW North Carolina, NE of Charlotte; pop. 5510.

West Conshohocken. Borough, Montgomery co., SE Pennsylvania, 12 m. NW of Philadelphia; pop. 2254.

West Covina. City, Los Angeles co., SW California, W of Los Angeles; pop. 50,645.

West Des Moines. City, Polk co., S cen. Iowa, 7 m. W of Des Moines; pop. 11,949; name changed from Valley Junction in 1938.

West Dundee. Village, Kane co., Illinois, ab. 35 m. NW of Chicago; pop. 2530.

West Elmira. Urban community (unincorporated), Chemung co., S New York; pop. 5763.

West End. 1 Town on W tip of Grand Bahama I., Bahama Is., West Indies; pop. 407; 64 m. directly E of Palm Beach, Florida.
2 The western portion of London, England, including the regions of Westminster, Belgravia, and Brompton on the S, Hyde Park and Mayfair in the center, and Bayswater and Marylebone on the N.

West Englewood. Village, Bergen co., NE corner of New Jersey, in Teaneck township.

We'ster·land (vĕs'tẽr·länt). Town, northwestern Germany, on the island of Sylt. (1933) 3992; resort.

Wes'ter·ly (wĕs'tẽr·lĭ). Town, Washington co., S Rhode Island, on Pawcatuck river and Connecticut state boundary 27 m. WSW of Newport; pop. 14,267; comprises several villages including Westerly village; settlement by whites 1648; involved in the boundary dispute bet. Rhode Island and Connecticut until 1728; early shipbuilding center. Granite quarries; textile mills.

Western Area. Former subdivision of W Soviet Russia, Europe; 62,904 sq. m.; * Smolensk.

Western Australia. State, Australia, W of 129°E long.; 1490 m. long, 850 m. broad; 975,920 sq. m.; pop. (1933) 438,852 (excluding ab. 21,800 full-blooded aboriginals), (1963 est.) 772,511; * Perth. Extensive interior area covered by three deserts, Great Sandy, Gibson, and Great Victoria; in W part is plateau and semidesert with numerous salt lakes. Coast along Timor Sea and Indian Ocean generally rugged with promontories, islands, and coral reefs with only a few good harbors; notable inlets are Joseph Bonaparte Gulf, King Sound, Exmouth Gulf, and Shark Bay. *Rivers:* Swan (with estuary forming excellent natural harbor of Fremantle), Murchison, Fortescue, and Fitzroy. *Mountains:* Highest point Mt.

Bruce in NW, 4024 ft.; Darling Range along SW coast. Its great extent from N to S affords several distinct climatic regions. Fine pastoral country in the Kimberleys in the N; rich gold mines in the SW around Kalgoorlie. *Chief towns:* Perth, Fremantle, Bunbury, and Geraldton on the coast, Kalgoorlie and Boulder in mining region.

History: West coast first visited 1616 by Dirck Hartog; explored by Dampier 1688, 1699; Vancouver, English navigator, took formal possession 1791 of region about King George Sound; New South Wales formed small settlement there in 1826 but permanent colonization began in 1829 when Capt. Fremantle founded Swan River Settlement; made penal settlement 1850–88; became part of colonial government 1886; granted responsible government 1890; last state to ratify the federation 1900.

Western Carolines. The Palau Is.

Western Desert. 1 Desert of W cen. Egypt, approximately 25° to 30°N lat., 26° to 30°E long.; includes Siwa, Baharîya, and Farafra oases; actually a part of the greater Libyan Desert.
2 Province, W Egypt. See *Table* at EGYPT.

Western Dvina. See DVINA.

Western Empire *or* **Western Roman Empire.** The western part of the Roman Empire, first set apart 286 A.D. by Emperor Diocletian with the establishment of joint emperors of the East and West; later in 395 after the death of Theodosius I (the Great) on the actual division of the Empire (see BYZANTINE EMPIRE) the western part comprising Italy, Spain, Gaul, Britain, Illyricum, and Africa; it ceased to exist 476 on the death of Romulus Augustulus. By some considered to have been revived by Charlemagne 800 (see HOLY ROMAN EMPIRE).

Western Erg. = *Grand Erg Occidental:* see El ERG.

Western Euphrates. See KARA SU.

Western Ghats. See GHATS.

Western India States. Formerly an agency (formed 1924), W India, comprising a group of states in Kathiawar and Gujarat, formerly under Bombay presidency; 37,894 sq. m.; pop. (1941) 4,904,156; * Rajkot, in Kathiawar; comprised 17 salute states, 34 nonsalute states, and 84 talukas; some areas (Sabar Kantha) in N Gujarat were included in the former Banas Kantha and Mahi Kantha agencies. Among the more important salute states were Cutch, Idar, Junagarh, Navanagar, Bhaunagar, Porbandar. Since 1947 in Indian Union.

Western Islands. See HEBRIDES.

Western Kathiawar. Former agency, forming a part of Western India States agency; 2552 sq. m.; pop. (1941) 435,858; chief town Jetpur.

Western Locris. See LOCRIS.

Western Manych. See MANYCH.

Western Morava. Branch of Morava river, Yugoslavia. See MORAVA.

West'ern·port (wĕs'tẽrn·pōrt). Town, Allegany co., NW Maryland, on Potomac river 20 m. SW of Cumberland; pop. 3559; head of navigation on north branch of the Potomac river.

Western Province. 1 Province, SW Ceylon, on Indian Ocean; 1432 sq. m.; pop. 1,445,034; * Colombo. Other important towns are Mount Lavinia, Kalutara, Negombo, Panadura, and Moratuwa.
2 Province, W Tanganyika, E Africa; 102,900 sq. m.; pop. 846,778; * Tabora; includes former Tabora prov. and Kigoma prov.
3 Province, W Uganda, E Africa; * Fort Portal; includes native kingdoms of Toro, Ankole, and Bunyoro.

Western Provinces; *now* **Western Region.** Southwestern division of Nigeria protectorate. See *Table* at NIGERIA.

Western Punjab. = WEST PUNJAB.

Western Rajputana States. Western part of former Rajputana Agency, NW India, comprising Danta, Jaisalmer, Jodhpur, Palanpur, and Sirohi states.

Western Reserve. Tract of ab. 3,500,000 acres in NE corner of Ohio on S shore of Lake Erie forming the part of the western lands of Connecticut not included in area surrendered to Congress in 1786; extended southward to ab. 41°N and westward as far as Willard and Port Clinton; sold in part to immigrants from Connecticut 1786–1800; ceded 1800 to Ohio to form Trumbull co., later divided into many counties. Western Reserve Univ. in Cleveland is named from it. See NORTHWEST TERRITORY.

Western Samoa. Group of islands of Samoa (*q.v.*) in SW cen. Pacific Ocean W of long. 171°W; 1133 sq. m.; pop. 113,567; a Brit. dominion; ✳ Apia; chief islands Savaii and Upolu. See AMERICAN SAMOA.

History: Apia granted to Germany by treaty with native ruler 1879; after period of joint administration of Samoan Is. (see SAMOA) by England, U.S., and Germany (1889–99), Savaii and Upolu recognized as German 1899–1900; occupied by New Zealand expeditionary force during World War I 1914–20; surrendered by Germany as part of terms of Versailles Treaty 1919; became mandate of New Zealand 1920 and United Nations trust territory (administered by New Zealand) 1947–61; became an independent member of British Commonwealth Jan. 1, 1962.

Western Sierra Madre. = SIERRA MADRE OCCIDENTAL.

Western Springs. Village, Cook co., NE Illinois, 15 m. W of Chicago; pop. 10,838.

Western Thrace. See THRACE.

Western Turkistan. See TURKISTAN.

Western U·krai′ni·a (û·krā′nĭ·à; -krĭ′-). Republic in E Galicia 1918–19; soon taken over by Poland; now in W Ukrainian S.S.R.

Westerplatte. See NEUFAHRWASSER.

Wes′ter·ville (wĕs′tēr·vĭl). Village, Franklin co., cen. Ohio, 12 m. N of Columbus; pop. 7011. Otterbein Coll. (1847; coed.).

We′ster·wald′ (vās′tēr·vält′). Mountainous region in W Germany, stretching NE from near Koblenz for ab. 70 m. bet. the rivers Rhine, Sieg, and Lahn; highest peak 2156 ft.

West Fairview. Borough, Cumberland co., S Pennsylvania, on Susquehanna river 4 m. NW of Harrisburg; pop. 1718.

West′fa′len (vĕst′fä′lĕn). Province of former Prussia. See *Westphalia* in *Table* at PRUSSIA.

West Falkland. See FALKLAND ISLANDS.

West Fargo. See FARGO, North Dakota.

West Fe·li′ci·an′a (fĕ·lĭsh′ĭ·ăn′à). Parish in Louisiana. See *Table* at LOUISIANA.

West′field (wĕst′fēld). **1** Unnavigable river ab. 50 m. long, W Massachusetts; rises in NE Berkshire co., NW Massachusetts, flows SE into Connecticut river opp. Springfield.
2 City, Hampden co., SW Massachusetts, on Westfield river 8 m. W of Springfield; pop. 26,302; formerly known as whip-manufacturing center; now manufactures bicycles, boilers, machinery, envelopes and paper products. State sanatorium; Massachusetts State Coll. (1839; coed.). Trading post, part of Springfield 1640–69; chartered as city 1921.
3 Residential town, Union co., NE New Jersey, 7 m. W of Elizabeth; pop. 31,447; figured in Revolutionary War.
4 Village, Chautauqua co., SW corner of New York, on Lake Erie 23 m. WNW of Jamestown; pop. 3878; founded 1802; in Chautauqua grape belt; manufactures unfermented grape juice, tomato juice, canned fruits.

West Flanders. Province, NW Belgium; 1248 sq. m.; pop. (1941 est.) 971,472; ✳ Brugge (Bruges); agriculture, livestock raising; manufactures linen and lace.

West Florida. See *History* at FLORIDA.

West′ford (wĕst′fērd). Town, Middlesex co., NE Massachusetts, 8 m. SW of Lowell; pop. 6261; in fruit-growing section.

West Frank′fort (frăngk′fērt). City, Franklin co., S Illinois, 33 m. S of Mount Vernon; pop. 9027; coal-mining center.

West Frisian Islands. See FRISIAN ISLANDS.

West Gaspé. See GASPÉ.

West Glacier; *formerly* **Bel′ton** (bĕl′t'n). Village, Flathead co., NW Montana; pop. ab. 150; W entrance to Glacier National Park.

West Greenville. Former town, Greenville co., NW South Carolina; in 1948 annexed to Greenville.

West Ham (hăm). County borough, Essex, SE England, suburb of London; pop. 294,278, (1951 pop.) 170,987; industrial section, a part of Greater London.

West Hartford. Suburban residential town, cen. Hartford co., N Connecticut, W of Hartford; pop. 62,382; settled 1679, incorp. 1854; shipping center for surrounding district devoted to tobacco culture, dairying, and truck farming; manufactures steel balls, burial vaults, tools and dies, sheet-metal products, nipples. Birthplace of Noah Webster. St. Joseph Coll. (1925; women).

West Hartlepool. County borough, Durham, N England, on North Sea 28 m. SSE of Newcastle; pop. 68,135, (1951) 72,597.

West Haven. Suburban residential town, SW New Haven co., S Connecticut, separated from New Haven by West river; pop. 43,002; incorp. as borough 1873, became part of town of Orange 1911, incorp. as independent town 1921; manufactures pianos, pipe organs, safes, beer, glazed paper, elastic fabrics. Raided by British 1779.

West Haverstraw. Village, Rockland co., SE New York, W of Hudson river 34 m. N of New York; pop. 5020; site of Treason House, where Benedict Arnold and Major John André plotted betrayal of West Point to the British.

West Hazleton. Borough, Luzerne co., E Pennsylvania, 20 m. SSW of Wilkes-Barre; pop. 6278; residential suburb of Hazleton.

West Helena. City, Phillips co., E Arkansas, near Mississippi river 85 m. ENE of Pine Bluff; pop. 8385; founded 1909; industrial extension of Helena (*q.v.*); manufactures boxes, crates, wooden automobile parts.

West Hempstead. Urban area, Nassau co., SE New York, on Long I., pop. (with Lakeview) 24,783.

West Hickory. Former town, Catawba co., North Carolina, annexed to HICKORY 1931.

West Hoboken. See UNION CITY, New Jersey.

West Hollywood. Urban area, Los Angeles co., SW California, NE of Beverly Hills; pop. 28,870.

West Homestead. Borough, Allegheny co., SW Pennsylvania, on Monongahela river adjacent to Homestead and 5 m. ESE of Pittsburgh; pop. 4155.

West′hough′ton (wĕst′hô′t'n; -hou′-). Urban district, Lancashire, NW England, 13 m. WNW of Manchester; pop. 15,002.

West Hsingan. Former province (1932–45), W Manchukuo; 31,038 sq. m.; pop. (1940 est.) 763,804; ✳ Tapanshang.

West Hungary. Name applied to Burgenland (*q.v.*) when it was part of Hungary.

West In′dies (ĭn′dĭz; -dēz). **1** Islands lying bet. SE North America and N South America, enclosing the Caribbean Sea; grouped in 3 divisions: **Greater Antil′les** (ăn·tĭl′ēz; -ēz; *Fr.* äN′tē′y′) including Cuba, Hispaniola (Haiti and Dominican republics), Jamaica, and Puerto Rico; **Lesser Antilles** *or* **Car′ib·bees** (kăr′ĭ·bēz) including Virgin Is., Windward Is., Leeward Is., and the islands in the S Caribbean Sea N of Venezuela (generally considered to include Trinidad and Tobago); **Bahama Islands** (*q.v.*). See *Maps* at CUBA, HISPANIOLA, JAMAICA, PUERTO RICO, LESSER ANTILLES, BAHAMA ISLANDS.

History: San Salvador (Watlings I.) in the Bahamas was first land in New World reached by Columbus Oct. 12, 1492; Cuba, Hispaniola, Dominica, Puerto Rico,

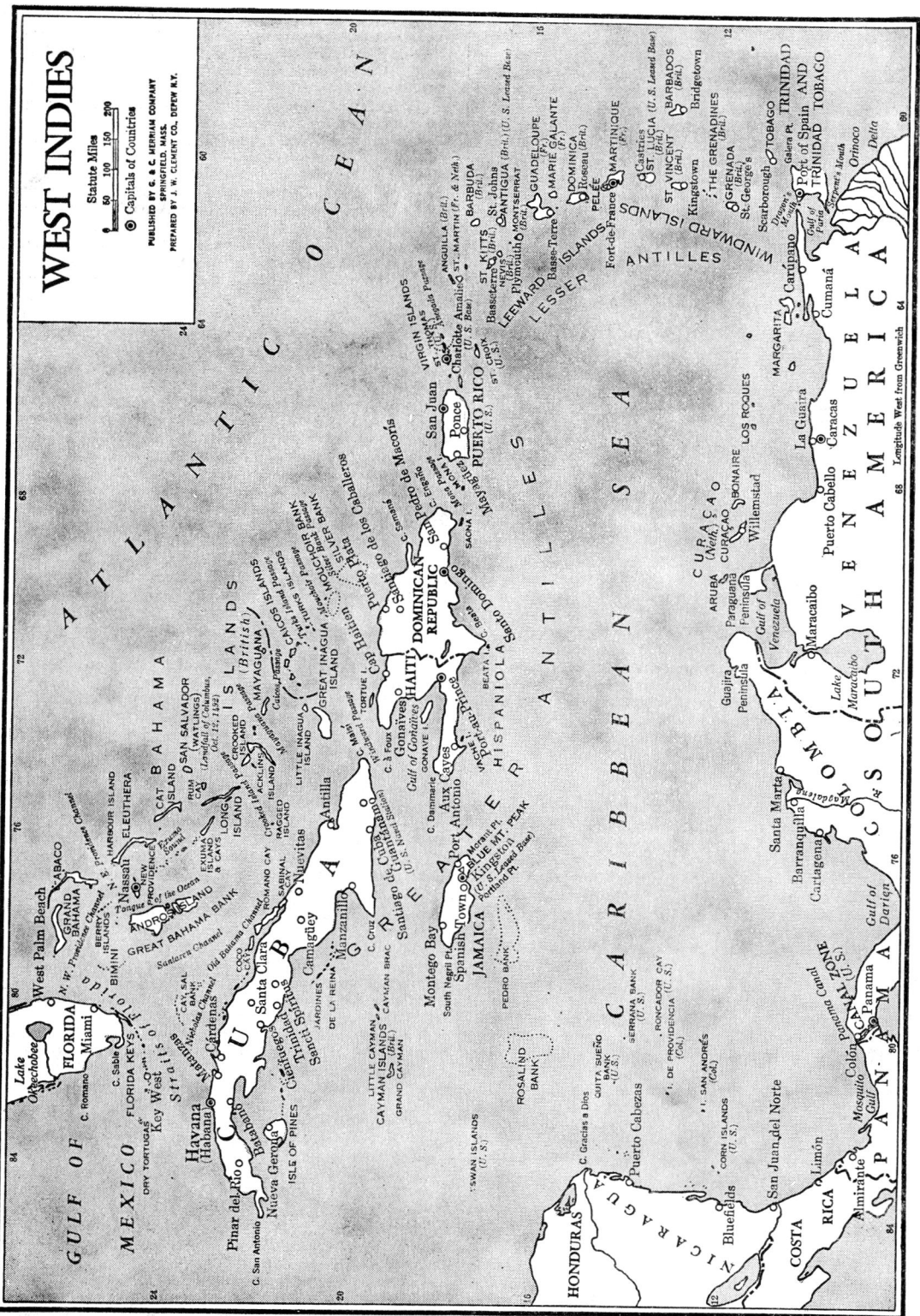

WEST INDIES

Statute Miles

50 100 150 200

◎ Capitals of Countries

PUBLISHED BY G. & C. MERRIAM COMPANY
SPRINGFIELD, MASS.
PREPARED BY J. W. CLEMENT CO., DEPEW N.Y.

Virgin Is., Jamaica, and Trinidad were among the islands discovered by Columbus during his voyages 1492–1504; Santo Domingo, founded 1496, was seat of Spanish rule in West Indies and base for expansion to American mainland; the English settled Barbados 1626, Dutch captured Curaçao 1634, and French occupied Guadeloupe and Martinique 1635; Jamaica was taken from Spanish by English 1655; St. Thomas in Virgin Is. came into Danish hands 1666; became a central theater of bitter Anglo-French colonial rivalry; by 1814 British had acquired the islands of Dominica, Grenada, Saint Lucia, and Tobago from France and Trinidad from Spain; Santo Domingo and Haiti became independent republics in 19th cent. (see DOMINICAN REPUBLIC and HAITI); Cuba and Puerto Rico (qq.v.), last of the Spanish colonies in America, became dependencies of U.S. 1898 (Cuba became a republic 1902); Virgin Is. purchased from Denmark by U.S. 1916–17. See INDIES.

2 or **West Indies Federation,** also **Federation of the West Indies.** Former country, including all of the British West Indies except the Bahama Is. and the British Virgin Is. colonies; a member of the British Commonwealth, established April 1958, dissolved 1962; its ✳ was Port of Spain.

West I′ri·an (ē′rē·än). The western section of New Guinea, since 1963 belonging to Indonesia. See NETHERLANDS NEW GUINEA.

West Ja′va (jä′vȧ; jȧv′ȧ). Province of Indonesia and of the former Netherlands Indies, comprising the W section of the island of Java; ✳ Djakarta (Batavia).

West Jersey. Western and southern New Jersey constituting a Quaker colony under William Penn from 1676 to 1702 when it was united with East Jersey to form the royal province of New Jersey (q.v.); ✳ (from 1681) Burlington.

West′ka·pel′le (vĕst′kȧ·pĕl′ĕ). Town, Zeeland prov., SW Netherlands, at W tip of Walcheren I. NW of Vlissingen; pop. 2194; lighthouse in church tower. Occupied by British commando units Nov. 1, 1944; with Vlissingen came under Allied control by Nov. 3, insuring free entry of the Schelde estuary.

West Kazakhstan Region. Large subdivision, W Kazakh S.S.R., Soviet Central Asia; ✳ Uralsk.

West Kill, Mount (kĭl). Peak 3777 ft. in the Catskill Mts., Greene co., SE New York.

West Kingston. Village in South Kingstown town, ⊗ of Washington co., S Rhode Island; pop. (est.) 900.

West Lafayette. City, Tippecanoe co., W cen. Indiana, suburb of Lafayette across Wabash river; pop. 12,680.

West′lake′ (wĕst′lāk′); formerly **Do′ver** (dō′vĕr). City, Cuyahoga co., N Ohio, W suburb of Cleveland; pop. 12,906.

West Lake St. John. See LAKE ST. JOHN.

West′land (wĕst′lănd). Provincial district of New Zealand. See Table at NEW ZEALAND.

West Lawn (lôn). Borough, Berks co., SE Pennsylvania, 5 m. W of Reading; pop. 2059.

West Lebanon. Town, Grafton co., W New Hampshire, ab. 19 m. N of Claremont; pop. (est.) 2000.

West Lei′sen·ring (lī′s′n·rĭng). Locality, Fayette co., SW Pennsylvania, near Connellsville; pop. (est.) 496.

West Liberty. 1 Town, Muscatine co., E Iowa, 17 m. NW of Muscatine; pop. 2042; center of a livestock-raising section; melons, vegetables, condensed milk.

2 City, ⊗ of Morgan co., E Kentucky; pop. 1165.

3 Village, West Virginia, ab. 9 m. NE of Wheeling; pop. (est.) 1400. West Liberty State Coll. (1837; coed.).

West Linn (lĭn). City, Clackamas co., NW Oregon, on Willamette river 10 m. S of Portland; pop. 3933.

West Long Branch. Borough, Monmouth co., E cen. New Jersey, 4 m. N of Asbury Park; pop. 5337.

West Lothian; formerly **Lin·lith′gow** (lĭn·lĭth′gō) or **Lin·lith′gow·shire** (-gō·shīr; -shēr). County, SE Scotland; area 120 sq. m.; pop. (1951) 88,576; ⊗ Linlithgow; rivers Almond, Avon; agriculture, dairy farming.

Westman Islands. See VESTMANNAEYJAR.

West′meath′ (wĕst′mēth′; Ir. -mēth′). County, N cen. Eire, in Leinster prov.; 681 sq. m.; pop. 54,706; ⊗ Mullingar; rivers Shannon, Brosna; agriculture.

West Memphis. City, Crittenden co., E Arkansas, 8 m. W of Memphis, Tennessee; pop. 19,374; formerly Bragg's Spur; incorp. under present name 1927.

West Miami. Town, Dade co., SE Florida, N of Coral Gables; pop. 5296.

West Mifflin. Borough, Allegheny co., SW Pennsylvania, SE suburb of Pittsburgh; pop. 27,289.

West Milwaukee. Village, Milwaukee co., SE Wisconsin; pop. 5043; suburb of Milwaukee.

West′min′ster (wĕs[t]′mĭn′stẽr). **1** City, Orange co., SW California, SE of Long Beach; pop. 25,750.

2 City, Adams co., NE cen. Colorado, NW of Denver; pop. 13,850.

3 City, ⊗ of Carroll co., N Maryland, 30 m. NW of Baltimore; pop. 6123; seat of Western Maryland Coll. (1867; coed.; Methodist).

4 Town, Worcester co., cen. Massachusetts, 7 m. WSW of Fitchburg; pop. 4022.

5 Town, Oconee co., NW South Carolina, 29 m. WNW of Anderson; pop. 2413; suburb of Milwaukee.

6 anc. **West′mon′as·te′ri·um** (wĕst′mŏn′ăs·tẽr′ĭ·ŭm). City and metropolitan borough, cen. part of London, England, on N bank of the Thames; 3.91 sq. m.; pop. 98,895; bounded on N by Paddington, St. Marylebone, and Holborn metropolitan boroughs, on E by the City, on S by the Thames, and on W by Chelsea and Kensington. Includes the Houses of Parliament, Westminster Abbey, Buckingham Palace, St. James's Park and Palace, Whitehall, New Scotland Yard, Hyde Park, Strand and Charing Cross, Knightsbridge, and the districts of Belgravia and Mayfair; in common use the term Westminster is generally restricted to the area including the Houses of Parliament, Whitehall and government buildings, the Abbey, and the Westminster, or Roman Catholic, Cathedral.

West Monroe. City, Ouachita parish, N Louisiana; pop. 15,215; paper, cottonseed oil, carbon black.

West′mont (wĕst′mŏnt). **1** Village, Du Page co., NE Illinois, 20 m. W of Chicago; pop. 5997.

2 Borough, Cambria co., SW cen. Pennsylvania, near Altoona; pop. 6573.

West·more′land (Pa., Kan., wĕs[t]·mōr′lănd; Va., wĕs[t]′mẽr·lănd). **1** Name of counties in two states of the U.S. See Tables at PENNSYLVANIA and VIRGINIA.

2 City, ⊗ of Pottawatomie co., NE Kansas; pop. 460.

West′mor·land (wĕs[t]′mẽr·lănd). **1** County, New Brunswick, Canada. See Table at NEW BRUNSWICK.

2 County, NW England; area 789 sq. m.; pop. (1951) 67,383; ⊗ Kendal; other towns Appleby, Windermere; lakes include Windermere, Hawes Water, Rydal Water; rivers include Eden and Kent; woolen goods, grazing, quarrying (granite, slate).

West′mount (wĕst′mount). Residential city, Montreal I., S Quebec, Canada, entirely enclosed by Montreal city in its W part; pop. 25,222; part of Greater Montreal.

West New Brigh′ton (brī′t′n). See RICHMOND borough, New York City.

West Newbury. Town, Essex co., NE corner of Massachusetts, 19 m. NE of Lowell; pop. 1844.

West New Guinea. 1 Formerly, a subdivision of Ternate division, Moluccas residency, Neth. Indies, comprising greater part of Vogelkop Penin. and W coastal region of Neth. New Guinea SE of McCluer Gulf as far as and including Kaukenau; 35,717 sq. m.; pop. 44,473.

2 See WEST IRIAN.

West Newton. 1 See NEWTON, Massachusetts.

2 Borough, Westmoreland co., SW Pennsylvania, on Youghiogheny river 20 m. SE of Pittsburgh; pop. 3982; bituminous coal mines.

West New York. Manufacturing town, Hudson co., NE New Jersey, on Hudson river 4 m. N of Jersey City; pop.

35,547; docks and grain elevators; manufactures textiles, rubber goods.

West Nor′ri·ton (nŏr′ĭ·tŭn; -t′n). Urban township, Montgomery co., SE Pennsylvania, W of Philadelphia; pop. 8342.

Wes′ton (wĕs′tŭn). **1** County in Wyoming. See *Table* at WYOMING.

2 Residential town, Middlesex co., NE Massachusetts, 12 m. W of Boston; pop. 8261. Regis Coll. (1927; women).

3 City, ⊗ of Lewis co., N cen. West Virginia, on West Fork of Monongahela river 18 m. SSW of Clarksburg; pop. 8754; glassware; coal mines; oil, gas wells.

4 Town, W British North Borneo, port at head of Brunei Bay and railroad terminus SW of Beaufort; occupied by Allied troops June 19–21, 1945.

5 Town, York co., SE Ontario, Canada, 10 m. WNW of Toronto; pop. 8677.

Weston Peak. Mountain 13,500 ft. in Park co., cen. Colorado.

Weston su′per Mare (sū′pẽr mâr′). Municipal borough, Somersetshire, SW England, on Bristol Channel at mouth of the Severn 20 m. WSW of Bristol; pop. 40,165; watering place.

West Orange. Town, Essex co., NE New Jersey, 5 m. NW of Newark; pop. 39,895; with the other "Oranges" and Maplewood, forms residential suburban community; separated from Orange 1862; incorp. 1890; "Glenmont," home of Thomas A. Edison after 1887 (made a national monument 1961), in Llewellyn Park nearby. Manufactures storage batteries, cement, electrical controls, calculating machines.

West′o′ver (wĕs′tō′vẽr). City, Monongalia co. N West Virginia, on Monongahela river 3 m. SW of Morgantown; pop. 4749.

West Pakistan. The part of Pakistan in the west of the peninsula of India; since 1955 a province, formed by merger of West Punjab, Sind, Baluchistan, and North-West Frontier Province; ✳ Lahore.

West Palm Beach. City, ⊗ of Palm Beach co., SE Florida, on Lake Worth 65 m. N of Miami and 40 m. E of Lake Okeechobee; pop. 56 208; popular winter resort; fishing; market center.

West Paterson. Borough, Passaic co., N New Jersey, SW suburb of Paterson; pop. 7602.

West Peak (wĕst) *or* **Mount Se′a·tu′ro** (sā′ä·tōō′rō). Peak 2760 ft. in SW Vanua Levu I., Fiji Is., SW Pacific Ocean.

West·pha′lia (wĕst·fāl′yȧ; -fä′lĭ·ȧ). Province of Prussia. See *Table* at PRUSSIA. Region a level plain, crossed by the Ems, Lippe, and Ruhr rivers, with hills in S and SE parts (highest point 2756 ft.). Mineral wealth is very great, esp. coal and iron in the Ruhrgebiet (see RUHR), and industries, esp. the heavy industries, have had extensive development. Chief cities, in addition to those of the Ruhr valley, are Münster, Bielefeld, Hamm, Bocholt, and Paderborn. Now part of North Rhine-Westphalia state of West Germany.

History: Duchy created in 12th cent.; for several centuries administered for the archbishop of Cologne. Peace of Westphalia terminating Thirty Years' War and in large measure determining political status of modern Europe, signed at Münster Oct. 24, 1648. In 1803 divided bet. Prussia and Hesse-Darmstadt; created a kingdom 1807 by Napoleon for his brother, Jérôme Bonaparte, with boundaries extended eastward and with capital at Kassel; reorganized by Congress of Vienna 1815; became province of Prussia 1816. Its cities suffered many and severe bombings in World War II; came under control of Allies Apr.–May 1945.

West Pittston. Residential borough, Luzerne co., E Pennsylvania, on Susquehanna river 8 m. NNE of Wilkes-Barre; pop. 6998; manufactures silk, machine-shop products; coal mines nearby.

West Plains. City, ⊗ of Howell co., S Missouri, 90 m. ESE of Springfield; pop. 5836; trade and shipping center

for agricultural, dairy-farming, and livestock-raising section.

West Point. 1 City, Troup co., W Georgia, 14 m. SW of La Grange; pop. 4610; incorp. as Franklin 1831, but changed name to West Point 1832; cotton market; iron-works and textile mills; sacked during the Civil War; scene of the battle of West Point Apr. 16, 1865.

2 City, ⊗ of Clay co., E Mississippi, 16 m. NW of Columbus; pop. 8550; trade center in agricultural section; cotton gins, cottonseed-oil mills, lumber mills.

3 City, ⊗ of Cuming co., NE Nebraska, 30 m. NNW of Fremont; pop. 2921; trade center in corn-growing and livestock-raising section.

4 United States military post, Orange co., SE New York, on W bank of Hudson river just SE of Storm King and Crow's Nest Mts.; about 50 miles by railroad N of New York; 3500-acre reservation on W bank of Hudson river and (since 1908) Constitution I. in river; occupied as military post and fortified by Americans 1778, and has served as military post since Revolution; iron chain stretched across Hudson bet. West Point and Constitution I. to block British ships as Revolutionary defense measure; center of Benedict Arnold's plot in 1780; seat of U.S. Military Academy (founded by act of Congress 1802).

5 Town, King William co., E Virginia, on York river at junction of Pamunkey and Mattaponi rivers 38 m. E of Richmond; pop. 1678; made port of entry 1691, free borough 1705; manufactures paper processed cotton, fertilizer; oyster packing.

6 West tip of Anticosti I., at the mouth of the St. Lawrence river, E Canada.

West′port (wĕst′pōrt). **1** Residential town, S Fairfield co., SW Connecticut, on Long Island Sound at mouth of Saugatuck river; pop. 20,955; settled 1645, incorp. 1835; resort, has artists' colony, summer theater; manufactures woolen goods, twine, soap, disinfectants, embalming fluid, boats.

2 Town, Bristol co., SE Massachusetts, 8 m. W of New Bedford; pop. 6641; textiles.

3 Former town, W Missouri, on Missouri river, now residential district of Kansas City (*q.v.*); scene of battle (see also INDEPENDENCE, Missouri) Oct. 21–23, 1864 in which Federal forces defeated Confederates under Price.

4 Urban district and seaport, SW co. Mayo, on shore of Clew Bay, NW Eire; pop. 3409; resort, angling center.

5 Seaport, Nelson provincial dist., NW South I., New Zealand, at mouth of Buller river 90 m. WSW of Nelson; pop. 3910; center of extensive coal region; principal coal-shipping point of New Zealand.

West Preanger. See PREANGER.

West′preus′sen (vĕst′proi′sĕn). **1** See WEST PRUSSIA.

2 Former government district, SW East Prussia prov., Prussia, Germany; 1141 sq. m.; ✳ Marienwerder.

West Prussia; *Ger.* **West′preus′sen** (vĕst′proi′sĕn). **1** Region in Pomerania along the Baltic, of varying boundaries and ownership, 13th–18th cents.; after 1772 part of Prussia (see 2, below).

2 Former province of Prussia on Baltic coast, NE Germany; in 1919 divided into Pomorze prov., Poland, Free City of Danzig, West Prussia govt. dist. in East Prussia prov. of Germany, and part of Grenzmark Posen-Westpreussen. Entire region assigned to Poland by Potsdam Conference 1945.

3 = WESTPREUSSEN govt. dist., Prussia, Germany.

West, *or* **Western, Punjab.** Former province, Pakistan; the W part of the province of Punjab of British India, comprising Rawalpindi and Multan divisions, the Sialkot, Gujranwala, and Sheikhupura dists. of Lahore division, and parts of Lahore and Gurdaspur dists. of Lahore division; ab. 61,469 sq. m.; chief city Lahore; merged 1955 in province of West Pakistan.

West Quoddy Head. Cape, NE Maine, S of Eastport at S entrance to Passamaquoddy Bay; lighthouse; eastern-most point of the U.S., 66°57′W long., 44°49′N lat.

Wes·tra′lia (wĕs·trāl′yȧ; -trä′lĭ·ȧ). = WESTERN AUSTRALIA.

Wes′tray (wĕs′trā). One of the Orkney Is., off N coast of Scotland; ab. 10 m. long; pop. 1091; 15th-cent. castle.

Westray Firth. Channel bet. islands of Westray on the N and Rousay on the S in the N Orkney Is., off N coast of Scotland.

West Reading. Industrial borough, Berks co., SE Pennsylvania, across Schuylkill river 2 m. W of Reading; pop. 4938; manufactures paper, textiles.

West Riding. See YORKSHIRE.

West River. 1 See WEST river, Vermont.
2 See SI river, SE China.

West Roxbury. Former town, E Massachusetts, became part of Boston 1874; site of Brook Farm where a communistic experiment was tried 1841–47 by a group of famous Americans, including George Ripley (the leader), Hawthorne, George W. Curtis, Charles A. Dana, and Margaret Fuller; figures in Hawthorne's *Blithedale Romance* (1852).

West Rutland. Town, Rutland co., W Vermont; pop. 2302; center of marble industry.

West Saint Paul. City, Dakota co., SE Minnesota, 5 m. S of St. Paul; pop. 13,101.

West Schelde Estuary *or* **Hon′te** (hôn′tĕ). Inlet of the North Sea on SW coast of Netherlands, at the mouth of the Schelde river, extending S of Walcheren I. and South Beveland I.

West Seneca. Urban community (unincorp.), Erie co., NW New York, SE suburb of Buffalo; pop. 23,138.

West Siberia, *or* **Western Siberian, Region.** Formerly one of the three subdivisions of Russia in Asia, consisting of the W part of Siberia (see SIBERIA, 2); its chief town and capital was Novosibirsk.

West Side. The W part of Manhattan borough, New York City, New York, traversed at lower end by West Street, merging into West Side Highway and, above 72d Street, into the Henry Hudson Parkway; includes several miles of docks along E Hudson river water front, esp. of transatlantic liners.

West Smithfield. See SMITHFIELD, London, England.

West Spanish Peak. Mountain 13,623 ft. in Huerfano and Las Animas cos., S Colorado.

West Spitsbergen. Chief island of Spitsbergen (*q.v.*); 14,600 sq. m.; highest point Mt. Newton 5445 ft.

West Springfield. Town, Hampden co., SW Massachusetts, on Connecticut river across from Springfield; pop. 24,924; paper mills, petroleum storage and distributing plant; also manufactures oil burners, air-conditioning equipment, magnetos. Eastern States Exposition grounds.

West′stel′ling·werf′ (vĕst′stĕl′ĭng·vĕrf′). Commune, Friesland prov., N Netherlands; pop. 18,291.

West Suffield. Subdivision of town of SUFFIELD, Connecticut.

West Suffolk. See SUFFOLK.

West Sussex. See SUSSEX.

West Terre Haute. City, Vigo co., W Indiana, suburb of Terre Haute; pop. 3006.

West Union. 1 City, ⊗ of Fayette co., NE Iowa, 25 m. S of Decorah; pop. 2551; in agricultural, dairy, and corn-canning section.
2 Village, ⊗ of Adams co., S Ohio; pop. 1762.
3 Town, ⊗ of Doddridge co., N West Virginia; pop. 1186.

West University Place. City, Harris co., SE Texas, entirely within city of Houston; pop. 14,628.

West View. Borough, Allegheny co., SW Pennsylvania, 6 m. N of Pittsburgh; pop. 8079; residential suburb.

West′ville (wĕst′vĭl). 1 Village, Vermilion co., E Illinois, 6 m. S of Danville; pop. 3497.
2 Borough, Gloucester co., SW New Jersey, 5 m. S of Camden; pop. 4951.
3 Town, Pictou co., N Nova Scotia, Canada, ab. 5 m. W of New Glasgow; pop. 4301; coal-mining, lumbering, and brickmaking industries.

West Virginia. An east central state of U.S.A., 35th state admitted to Union (1863); bounded on N by Ohio, Pennsylvania, and Maryland, on E and S by Virginia, and on W by Kentucky and Ohio; 41st state in area, 24,181 sq. m. (land area 24,080 sq. m.); 30th state in population, 1,860,421; ✱ Charleston. See *Table of States* at UNITED STATES. Divided into the following 55 counties (for pronunciation of their names, see their individual entries):

NAME	LOCATION	AREA[1]	POP.[1]	CO. SEAT
Barbour	N	336	15,474	Philippi
Berkeley	NE	316	33,791	Martinsburg
Boone	SW	501	28,764	Madison
Braxton	cen.	517	15,152	Sutton
Brooke	N; in pan-handle	89	28,940	Wellsburg
Cabell	W	279	108,202	Huntington
Calhoun	cen.	281	7,948	Grantsville
Clay	cen.	342	11,942	Clay
Doddridge	N	319	6,970	West Union
Fayette	S cen	659	61,731	Fayetteville
Gilmer	cen.	339	8,050	Glenville
Grant	NE	477	8,304	Petersburg
Greenbrier	SE	1,026	34,446	Lewisburg
Hampshire	NE	639	11,705	Romney
Hancock	N tip of pan-handle	82	39,615	New Cumberland
Hardy	NE	585	9,308	Moorefield
Harrison	N	418	77,856	Clarksburg
Jackson	W	463	18,541	Ripley
Jefferson	NE	211	18,665	Charles Town
Kanawha	W cen.	908	252,925	Charleston
Lewis	N cen.	392	19,711	Weston
Lincoln	W	438	20,267	Hamlin
Logan	SW	456	61,570	Logan
McDowell	S	533	71,359	Welch
Marion	N	309	63,717	Fairmont
Marshall	N; in pan-handle	306	38,041	Moundsville
Mason	W	432	24,459	Point Pleasant
Mercer	S	417	68,206	Princeton
Mineral	NE	330	22,354	Keyser
Mingo	SW	423	39,742	Williamson
Monongalia	N	365	55,617	Morgantown
Monroe	SE	473	11,584	Union
Morgan	NE	233	8,376	Berkeley Springs
Nicholas	cen.	649	25,414	Summersville
Ohio	N; in pan-handle	107	68,437	Wheeling
Pendleton	E	695	8,093	Franklin
Pleasants	N W	130	7,124	St. Marys
Pocahontas	E cen.	943	10,136	Marlinton
Preston	N	645	27,233	Kingwood
Putnam	W	349	23,561	Winfield
Raleigh	S	604	77,826	Beckley
Randolph	NE cen.	1,036	26,349	Elkins
Ritchie	NW	452	10,877	Harrisville
Roane	W cen.	486	15,720	Spencer
Summers	S	359	15,640	Hinton
Taylor	N	170	15,010	Grafton
Tucker	NE	421	7,750	Parsons
Tyler	NW	256	10,026	Middlebourne
Upshur	NE cen	352	18,292	Buckhannon
Wayne	SW	513	38,977	Wayne
Webster	E cen.	551	13,719	Webster Springs
Wetzel	N	362	19,347	New Martinsville
Wirt	W	234	4,391	Elizabeth
Wood	W	368	78,331	Parkersburg
Wyoming	S	504	34,836	Pineville

[1] Area = land area in sq. m. Pop. from 1960 Census.

Nickname: Mountain State. *State flower:* Rhododendron. *Motto:* Montani Semper Liberi (Mountaineers [are] Always Free Men). *Chief cities:* Huntington, Charleston, Wheeling, Clarksburg, Parkersburg. *Rivers:* Ohio, forming large section of upper W boundary, and its tributaries Big Sandy, Guyandot, Great Kanawha, Little Kanawha, Monongahela; Potomac, forming section of N boundary. *Highest point:* Spruce Knob 4860 ft. in Pendleton co. *Chief industries:* Mining (coal), petroleum production; manufacturing of iron and steel, chemicals, and glass.

History: A part of Virginia until the Civil War; voted against ordinance of secession May 23, 1861; loyal government organized at Wheeling June 11–25, 1861; admitted to Union June 20, 1863.

West′wall′ (wĕst′wôl′; *Ger.* vĕst′väl′); *often called also, especially by the Germans,* **Sieg′fried Line** (sēg′frēd; *Ger.* zēк′frēt). In World War II the strong defense

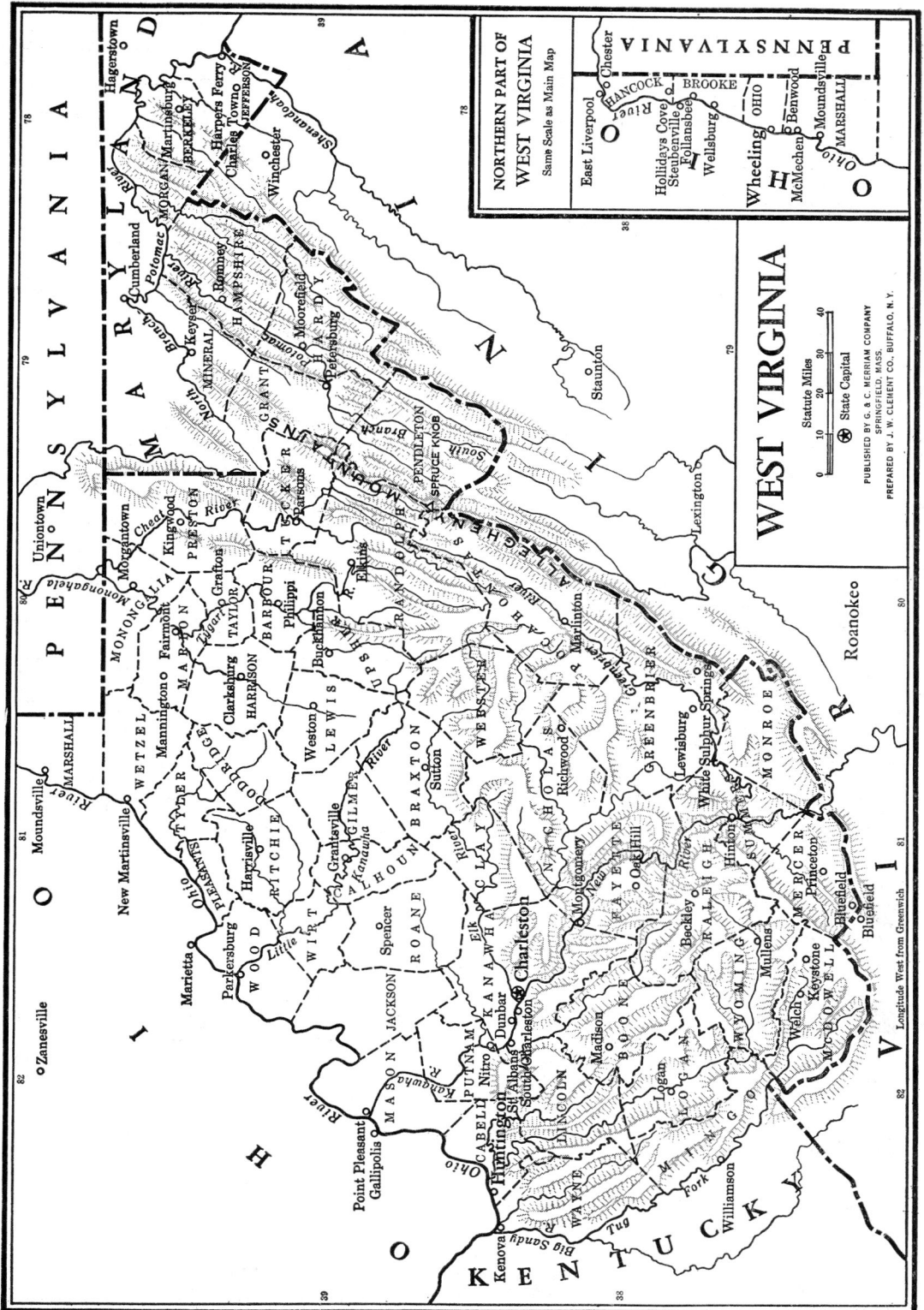

NORTHERN PART OF
WEST VIRGINIA
Same Scale as Main Map

WEST VIRGINIA

Statute Miles

PUBLISHED BY G. & C. MERRIAM COMPANY
SPRINGFIELD, MASS.
PREPARED BY J. W. CLEMENT CO., BUFFALO, N.Y.

⊛ State Capital

line in W Germany, prepared in great depth and extending from Swiss border on the S to Cleve on the N, generally parallel with the Rhine and in the S opposite to the French Maginot Line. Penetrated by Allied forces 1944–45.

West Warwick. Town, Kent co., cen. Rhode Island, 11 m. WSW of Providence; pop. 21,414; governmental center River Point village; separated from Warwick and incorp. 1913; textile industries (lace, etc.).

West·we′go (wĕst·wē′gō). Town, Jefferson parish, SE Louisiana, 8 m. WSW of New Orleans; pop. 9815.

West Winter Haven. Urban community (unincorporated), Polk co., cen. Florida, W of Lakeland; pop. 5050.

West′wood (wĕst′wŏŏd). **1** Town, Norfolk co., E Massachusetts, 12 m. SW of Boston; pop. 10,354.
2 Residential borough, Bergen co., NE corner of New Jersey, 9 m. NE of Paterson; pop. 9046.

Westwood Lakes. Urban community (unincorporated), Dade co., SE Florida; pop. 22,517.

West Wyoming. Borough, Luzerne co., E Pennsylvania, 5 m. N of Wilkes-Barre; pop. 3166.

West York. Borough, York co., S Pennsylvania, 2 m. W of York; pop. 5526; machinery, pottery, hosiery, furniture manufactures.

We′tar (wĕ′tär). Island, Indonesia, 30 m. N of E Portuguese Timor and WNW of the Leti group; ab. 80 m. long by 23 m. wide; ab. 1200 sq. m.; pop. 2571; chief settlement Ilwaki on SE coast. Mountainous and undeveloped, with scant population for the area.

Wetar Strait. Channel ab. 30 m. wide bet. NE Portuguese Timor and Wetar I., Malay Archipelago.

We·tas′ki·win (wĕ·tăs′kĭ·wĭn). City, S cen. Alberta, Canada, 40 m. S of Edmonton; pop. 3824; in wheat belt.

Weth′ers·field (wĕth′ĕrz-fēld). Suburban town, S cen. Hartford co., N Connecticut, on Connecticut river S of Hartford; pop. 20,561; settled 1635 by colonists from Massachusetts Bay Colony; named 1637; manufactures agricultural implements; seed cultivation, packing, and shipping; Wethersfield state prison.

We′ti (wā′tē). Township on Pemba I., N of Zanzibar, off NE coast of Tanganyika, E Africa.

Wet′ter (wĕt′ĕr). Var. of WETAR Island, Indonesia.

Wet′ter (vĕt′ĕr). = *Vetter:* see VÄTTERN lake, Sweden.

Wet′te·ren (vĕt′ĕ·rĕ[n]). Manufacturing commune, East Flanders prov., NW cen. Belgium, on Schelde river just ESE of Gent; pop. 17,925.

Wet′ter·horn (vĕt′ĕr·hôrn). Peak 12,149 ft. in the Bernese Alps, SW cen. Switzerland, N of the Finsteraarhorn.

Wet′ter·horn Peak (wĕt′ĕr·hôrn). Mountain 14,020 ft. in Hinsdale and Ouray cos., SW Colorado.

Wet′ter·stein Mountains (vĕt′ĕr-shtīn); *Ger.* **Wet′ter·stein·ge·bir′ge** (-gĕ-bĭr′gĕ). Mountains in S Bavaria, Germany; include Zugspitze 9719 ft., highest peak in Germany.

Wet′ting·en (vĕt′ĭng·ĕn). Commune, Aargau canton, Switzerland, ab. 10 m. NW of Zurich; pop. (1930) 8505; Cistercian abbey, now a school.

We·tum′ka (wĕ·tŭm′kà). City, Hughes co., E cen. Oklahoma, 32 m. SSW of Okmulgee; pop. 1789; cotton, peanuts, watermelons; manufactures cottonseed oil, caskets; gas and oil wells.

We·tump′ka (wĕ·tŭm[p]′kà). City, ⊗ of Elmore co., E cen. Alabama, on Coosa river 12 m. NE of Montgomery; pop. 3672; agricultural distributing center.

Wet′zel (wĕt′s'l). County in West Virginia. See *Table* at WEST VIRGINIA.

Wet′zi·kon (vĕt′sĕ·kôn). Commune, Zurich canton, Switzerland, ab. 12 m. ESE of Zurich; pop. (1930) 6904; railroad junction point near Lake of Pfäffikon (see PFÄFFIKON).

Wetz′lar (vĕts′lär). City, Hesse state, W Germany, on Lahn river 30 m. N of Frankfurt am Main; pop. 16,482; manufactures optical goods, ironware; old Romanesque cathedral (founded in 12th cent.). Became free city in 12th cent.

We′vel·gem (vā′vĕl·ĸĕm). Commune, West Flanders prov., NW Belgium, just W of Kortrijk; pop. 10,769.

We′wa·hitch′ka (wē′wô-hĭch′kä). Town, ⊗ of Gulf co., NW Florida; pop. 1436.

We′wak (wā′wäk; *Angl.* wē′wăk). Coastal town, NW North-East New Guinea, New Guinea I., ab. 75 m. W of the mouth of the Sepik river; has good harbor. Japanese base in early part of World War II; severely bombed by American planes Aug. 17, 1943; bypassed in Allied advance along N New Guinea coast.

We·wo′ka (wĕ·wō′kà). City, ⊗ of Seminole co., cen. Oklahoma, 28 m. ESE of Shawnee; pop. 5954; oil and gas wells; agriculture (esp. corn, cotton); manufactures gasoline, carbon black, brick, oil-well supplies.

Wex′ford (wĕks′fĕrd). **1** County in Michigan. See *Table* at MICHIGAN.
2 County, SE Eire, in Leinster prov.; 908 sq. m.; pop. 94,245; ⊗ Wexford; chief river Slaney; agriculture, livestock raising, dairy farming, fishing.
3 Municipal borough and seaport, ⊗ of co. Wexford, SE Eire; pop. 12,247; shipbuilding, distilling, rope and twine, farm implements; salmon and sea fisheries. An early settlement of Danish marauders and later of Anglo-Normans, it was sacked 1649 by Cromwell with great destruction and slaughter.

Wexford Harbour. Inlet of St. George's Channel on SE coast of Ireland, in co. Wexford; the city of Wexford is at the head of the inlet.

Wey (wā). River 35 m. long flowing NE in Hampshire and Surrey, S England, and emptying into the Thames 2 m. SE of Chertsey.

Wey′bridge (wā′brĭj). Town, Surrey, S England, near the confluence of the Wey and Thames; pop. (1931) 7364. Brooklands motor-racing track is nearby.

Wey′burn (wā′bĕrn). Market city, SE Saskatchewan, Canada, on Souris river 65 m. SE of Regina; pop. 7148; has grain elevators and flour mills.

Wey′mouth (wā′mŭth). Town, Norfolk co., E Massachusetts, 11 m. SSE of Boston; pop. 48,177; shoe factories, granite quarries.

Weymouth and Mel′combe Re′gis (mĕl′kŭm rē′jĭs). Contiguous towns forming municipal borough, Dorsetshire, S England, on Weymouth Bay of English Channel 53 m. WSW of Southampton; pop. 37,097; seaport and watering place.

Weymouth Fore River. See FORE RIVER.

Wezzan. = *Wazzan:* see OUEZZANE.

Wha′ka·ta′ne (hwä′kä·tä′nà). **1** River ab. 70 m. long in N cen. North I., New Zealand; flows N into Bay of Plenty.
2 Borough, Auckland provincial dist., N North I., New Zealand, on Bay of Plenty; pop. 1460.

Whale Islands (hwāl). See HVALER.

Whales, Bay of (hwälz). Inlet of Ross Sea in Ross Shelf Ice, Ross Dependency, Antarctica, 78°30′S, 163°50′W; used since 1911 as a base for Antarctic exploring expeditions (see LITTLE AMERICA).

Whal′sey *or* **Whal′say** (hwôl′sĭ). One of the Shetland Is., NE of N Scotland; noted sea-fishing center.

Wham′po·a′ (hwäm′pō′à′). Seaport town, Kwangtung, SE China, on island on S side of upper Pearl river in Si delta 12 m. below Canton; outport of Canton where in early trade British and American clippers anchored. Whampoa Military Academy established 1924.

Whang′a·rei′ (hwäng′à·rā′). Borough, Auckland provincial dist., N North I., New Zealand, on Whangarei Harbor 85 m. N of Auckland; pop. (1941 est.) 7600.

Whangarei Harbor *or* **Bay.** Inlet of Pacific Ocean on E coast of N extension of North I., New Zealand.

Whangpoo. See HWANG PU.

Wharfe (hwôrf). River in N cen. England, in W Yorkshire; flows ESE into the Ouse.

Whar′ton (hwôr′t'n). **1** County in Texas. See *Table* at TEXAS.
2 Borough, Morris co., N New Jersey, 10 m. NNW of

Morristown; pop. 5006; in old iron-mining region; manufactures.

3 City, ⊗ of Wharton co., SE Texas, on Colorado river 28 m. N of Bay City; pop. 5734; sulfur deposits.

Wharton Deep. See JAVA TROUGH.

Wharton Peninsula. Peninsula extending from SW cen. Wellington I., off SW coast of Chile.

What'com (hwŏt'kŭm). County in Washington. See *Table* at WASHINGTON.

Wheat'land (hwēt'lănd). **1** County in Montana. See *Table* at MONTANA.

2 Town, ⊗ of Platte co., SE Wyoming, 43 m. W of Torrington; pop. 2350; sugar beets, livestock.

Wheatland Reservoir. Reservoir in Laramie river, cen. Albany co., SE Wyoming.

Whea'ton (hwē't'n). **1** City, ⊗ of Du Page co., NE Illinois, 25 m. W of Chicago; pop. 24,312; in agricultural and livestock-raising section. Wheaton Coll. (1843; coed.).

2 Urban community (unincorporated), Montgomery co., cen. Maryland, SW of Baltimore; pop. 54,635.

3 Village, ⊗ of Traverse co., W Minnesota, 39 m. SSW of Fergus Falls; pop. 2102; duck and pheasant shooting.

Wheat Ridge (hwēt). Urban area, Jefferson co., cen. Colorado, WNW of Denver; pop. 21,619.

Whee'ler (hwē'lẽr). Counties in four states of the U.S. See *Table* at GEORGIA, NEBRASKA, OREGON, TEXAS.

2 Town, ⊗ of Wheeler co., NW Texas; pop. 1174.

Wheeler Dam. Dam across Tennessee river, NW Alabama, at head of Lake Wilson, forming **Wheeler Lake** 74 m. long. See *Table* at TENNESSEE VALLEY AUTHORITY.

Wheeler National Monument. See UNITED STATES, *National Monuments.*

Wheeler Peak. **1** Mountain 13,063 ft., second highest in the state, in Snake Range, SE White Pine co., E Nevada.

2 Mountain 13,160 ft. in Taos co., N New Mexico; highest point in the state.

Whee'ling (hwē'lĭng). **1** Village, Cook co., NE Illinois, SW of Highland Park; pop. 7169.

2 Commercial and manufacturing city and port of entry, ⊗ of Ohio co., N West Virginia, on Ohio river in N panhandle; pop. 53,400; part of residential section on Wheeling I., connected by bridges with mainland and with Ohio; manufactures iron and steel products, tin plate, nails, stogies, tobacco, glassware, china and porcelain, canned foods, packed meats, textiles, lumber products, patent medicine, paper boxes; coal fields; gas wells. Settled 1769; Fort Fincastle (renamed Fort Henry 1776) built as defense against Indians 1774, attacked by Indians and British 1777, 1781, 1782; incorp. 1793, incorp. 1795, became ⊗ 1797; chartered as city 1836, and developed as important trading post on Cumberland Road; became capital of "restored government of Virginia" 1861, state capital 1863–70, 1875–85.

Wheel'wright (hwēl'rīt). City, Floyd co., E Kentucky, 15 m. SW of Pikeville; pop. 1518.

Whern'side (hwûrn'sīd). Mountain 2414 ft. in Yorkshire, N England; a peak in the Pennine Chain.

Whet'stone' (hwĕt'stōn'). Village, Middlesex, SE England, 10 m. N of London; fine suburban residences.

Whetstone Buttes. Isolated peaks in NW Adams co., SW North Dakota.

Whick'ham (hwĭk'ăm). Urban district, Durham, N England, 6 m. SW of Newcastle; pop. 23,116.

Whid'bey, or Whid'by, Island (hwĭd'bĭ). Island 40 m. long in upper Puget Sound, E of Admiralty Inlet, Washington, a part of Island co.; chief town Coupeville.

Whid'dy Island (hwĭd'ĭ). Island in Bantry Bay on SW coast of Ireland; ruins of old castle.

Whirlwind Peak. Mountain 11,000 ft. in W Park co., NW Wyoming.

Whit'a·ker (hwĭt'à·kẽr). Borough, Allegheny co., SW Pennsylvania, 7 m. E of Pittsburgh; pop. 2130.

Whit'by (hwĭt'bĭ). **1** Town, ⊗ of Ontario co., SE Ontario, Canada, a port of entry on Lake Ontario 5 m. W of Oshawa; pop. 7267; iron foundries, tanneries; manufactures mill machinery, agricultural implements, musical instruments.

2 Urban district, North Riding, Yorkshire, N England, on the seacoast at mouth of the Esk river; pop. 11,668; site of an abbey founded by St. Hilda (657); meeting place of the Synod of Whitby 664, at which the Irish system of computing the date of Easter was abandoned in favor of the Roman system; destroyed by the Danes 867, and founded again for the Benedictines in 1078; Anglo-Saxon poet Caedmon (fl. 670) was a monk of Whitby. See NORTHUMBRIA.

Whit'church (hwĭt'chûrch). Urban district, Shropshire, W England, 32 m. SSE of Liverpool; pop. 6856; formerly noted for turret clocks.

White (hwīt). **1** River 690 m. long in Arkansas; navigable for 260 m.; rises in Boston Mts., Madison co., NW Arkansas, bends N into Missouri, then SE across Arkansas to empty into the Mississippi on E boundary of Desha co., SE Arkansas.

2 River ab. 160 m. long, NW Colorado and E Utah; rises in NE Garfield co., Colorado, flows W across Utah border into Green river in cen. Uintah co., E Utah.

3 River 50 m. long, SW Indiana; formed by confluence of West Fork 300 m. long rising in Randolph co., E Indiana, and East Fork 250 m. long rising in Henry co., E cen. Indiana; flows W into Wabash river in NW corner of Gibson co., SW Indiana. See BLUE river.

4 River ab. 325 m. long, SW and S cen. South Dakota; rises in NW Nebraska, flows NE across South Dakota border, then E into Missouri river on SE boundary of Lyman co.

5 River ab. 75 m. long, NW Texas; formed by confluence of Callahan Draw and Running Water Draw in N Hale co., flows SE into Salt Fork in Kent co.

6 River ab. 50 m. long, E cen. Vermont; rises in E Addison co., flows S, then E and SE into Connecticut river at White River Junction.

7 River ab. 60 m. long, W cen. Washington; rises in Mt. Rainier National Park, flows NW and unites with Green river in SW King co. to form Duwamish river.

8 Name of counties in five states of the U.S. See *Tables* at ARKANSAS, GEORGIA, ILLINOIS, INDIANA, TENNESSEE.

9 River 185 m. long, SW Yukon Territory, Canada; rises in Wrangell Mts. in Alaska, flows E, then N in Yukon to the Yukon river above Dawson. Its upper course crossed by Alaska Highway.

10 River in Iceland. See HVÍTÁ.

White Bay. Inlet of Atlantic Ocean ab. 60 m. long on N coast of Newfoundland.

White Bear Lake. **1** Lake on border of Ramsey and Washington cos., E Minnesota; resort.

2 City, Ramsey co., E Minnesota, 11 m. NNE of St. Paul; pop. 12,849; summer resort.

White Carpathian Mountains, *also* **White Carpathians.** Mountain range, cen. Czechoslovakia, a SW spur of the Carpathian Mts. running NE and SW and forming boundary bet. Moravia and Slovakia; highest point 3514 ft.

White Castle. Town, Iberville parish, S Louisiana, on Mississippi river 20 m. S of Baton Rouge; pop. 2253.

White'chap'el (hwĭt'chăp'ĕl). Three wards of Stepney metropolitan borough, London, England, E of the City of London and N of the Thames; pop. 21,213; Whitechapel Art Gallery, London Hospital.

White Cloud. City, ⊗ of Newaygo co., W Michigan; pop. 1001.

White'cross' Mountain (hwīt'krȯs'). Peak 13,550 ft. in Hinsdale co., SW Colorado.

White Dome. Peak 13,614 ft. in San Juan co., SW Colorado.

White Earth. River ab. 60 m. long, NW North Dakota; rises in NE Williams co., flows S into Missouri river on SW boundary of Mountrail co.

White'face' (hwīt'fās'). River ab. 60 m. long, NE Minnesota; rises in E cen. St. Louis co., flows SW into St. Louis river, SW St. Louis co.

Whiteface Mountain. Peak 4872 ft. in the Adirondack Mts., Essex co., NE New York.

White'field (hwīt'fēld). **1** Town, Coos co., N New Hampshire, 21 m. WSW of Berlin; pop. 1581; summer resort and winter sports center. **2** Urban district, Lancashire, NW England, 5 m. N of Manchester; pop. 12,912.

White'fish' (hwīt'fĭsh'). City, Flathead co., NW Montana, 15 m. N of Kalispell; pop. 2965; in lumbering section.

Whitefish Bay. 1 Inlet of Lake Superior on N coast of Chippewa co., E Michigan penin. **2** Village, Milwaukee co., SE Wisconsin, on Lake Michigan 5 m. N of Milwaukee; pop. 18,390; residential.

Whitefish Lake. Lake, N Crow Wing co., cen. Minnesota.

Whitefish Mountain. Peak 8000 ft. in Glacier National Park, NW Montana.

Whitefish Point. Point on extreme N coast of Chippewa co., E Michigan penin., at W entrance to Whitefish Bay.

Whitefish Range. A range of the Rocky Mts. in NW Montana, extending along N section of boundary bet. Lincoln and Flathead cos.

White'fri'ars (hwīt'frī'ẽrz). Section of London, England, in cen. part of the City, deriving its name from a Carmelite monastery (c. 1241–1538) in Fleet Street, whose precincts were a sanctuary till 1697; became a refuge for lawless characters who gave the district the name Alsatia; now includes Whitefriars Street and has many journalistic offices.

White'hall (hwīt'hôl). **1** Industrial village, Washington co., E New York, on Vermont border at S end of Lake Champlain and N terminus of Champlain Canal, 10 m. E of Lake George; pop. 4016; settled by British 1759. **2** City, Franklin co., cen. Ohio, E suburb of Columbus; pop. 20,818. **3** Borough, Allegheny co., SW Pennsylvania, S suburb of Pittsburgh; pop. 16,075. **4** City, ⊗ of Trempealeau co., W Wisconsin; pop. 1446. **5** Wide thoroughfare in Westminster metropolitan borough, London, England, running N and S bet. Trafalgar Square and the Houses of Parliament; lined with the chief government offices of the British Empire and hence frequently used figuratively for the British Government or its policies. Originally site of Whitehall Palace (from 1529 to 1698 when it was destroyed by fire), the chief residence of the Court of London.

White Hall (hwīt' hôl'). City, Greene co., W Illinois, 48 m. WSW of Springfield; pop. 3012.

White'ha'ven (hwīt'hā'vĕn). **1** Urban area, Shelby co., Tennessee, S suburb of Memphis; pop. 13,894. **2** Municipal borough, Cumberland, NW England, on Irish Sea SW of Carlisle; pop. 24,624; shipbuilding.

White Haven. Borough, Luzerne co., E Pennsylvania, on Lehigh river 14 m. S of Wilkes-Barre; pop. 1778.

White'horse' *or* **White Horse** (hwīt'hôrs'). Town, S Yukon, Canada, on left bank of Lewes river ab. 52 m. N of British Columbia border; pop. 2594; terminus of railroad from Skagway, Alaska, and one of most important stations on Alaska Highway; active trading town in Klondike gold-rush days; head of navigation on Lewes river; became ✳ of the Yukon 1953.

White Horse, Vale of the. Valley, Berkshire, S England; named from the *White Horse*, a figure of a horse 374 ft. long, formed by cutting away the turf on the side of a chalk hill; many ancient earthworks in the valley which contains the town of Wantage (*q.v.*).

Whitehorse Rapids. Rapids on the Lewes river at the town of Whitehorse, Yukon Territory, Canada.

White'house' Mountain (hwīt'hous'). Peak 13,493 ft. in Ouray co., SW Colorado.

White Island. 1 Small island in the Bay of Plenty off NE cen. coast of North I., New Zealand. **2** *or* **Gil'lis Island** (gĭl'ĭs). Island of the Spitsbergen archipelago (Svalbard), bet. NE Spitsbergen and Franz Josef Land.

White Lake. Lake in SW Vermilion parish, S Louisiana; connected by intracoastal canal with Vermilion Bay.

White'man Range (hwīt'măn). Mountain range traversing the length of New Britain I., W Pacific Ocean; highest peak Ulawun (the Father) 7546 ft.

White'marsh' (hwīt'märsh'). Village, Montgomery co., SE Pennsylvania, on Wissahickon Creek 14 m. N of Philadelphia; pop. (est.) 500; in Revolutionary War Washington's encampment 1777 during battle of Germantown and before retirement to Valley Forge.

White Mountain. 1 Peak 14,242 ft. in Sierra Nevada, on line bet. Alpine and Mono cos., E cen. California. **2** See SIERRA BLANCA PEAK, New Mexico. **3** *or* **White Hill;** *Ger.* **Weis'ser Berg** (vī'sẽr bĕrҡ); *Czech* **Bi'lá Ho'ra** (bĭ'lä hô'rȧ). Hill 1244 ft. in Bohemia, Czechoslovakia, W of Prague; scene of battle Nov. 8, 1620 in which the Catholic forces (commanded by the count of Tilly) of Maximilian I, Duke of Bavaria, defeated the Bohemian Protestants under Frederick V (commander in the field, Christian of Anhalt); Bohemia lost its independence.

White Mountains. 1 Mountains, E California and SW Nevada, on boundary bet. Esmeralda co., Nevada, and Mono co., California; contain Boundary Peak 13,145 ft., highest peak in Nevada. **2** Mountains of the Appalachian range, in N New Hampshire; highest point Mt. Washington 6288 ft. in Presidential Range (*q.v.*).

Whit'en Head (hwīt''n). Cape on N coast of Scotland, in Sutherland co., 15 m. E of Cape Wrath.

White Nile. 1 See NILE. **2** Former province, E cen. Sudan, NE Africa, bet. lat. 12°N and 15°30′N; 16,700 sq. m.; pop. ab. 540,000; ✱ Ed Dueim; now part of Blue Nile prov.

White Oak. 1 Locality, Montgomery co., cen. Maryland, 12 m. NE of Washington, D.C.; 938 acres here set aside 1944 for new naval ordnance laboratory; central unit dedicated Jan. 1949. **2** Borough, Allegheny co., SW Pennsylvania, SSE suburb of Pittsburgh; pop. 9047.

White Pass. Pass in mountains N of Skagway, SE Alaska; highest point 2885 ft.; superseded Chilkoot Pass ab. 1900 as easier route to Klondike gold fields; now traversed by White Pass and Yukon R.R. **White Pass** post is Canadian border station ab. 14 m. N of Skagway.

White Peak. Mountain 13,600 ft. in Saguache co., S Colorado.

White Pine. County in Nevada. See *Table* at NEVADA.

White Pine Mountains. Range in SW White Pine co., E Nevada; at S end is **White Pine Peak** 11,493 ft.

White Plains. City, ⊗ of Westchester co., SE New York, 25 m. NNE of New York; pop. 50,485; residential suburb of New York City; settled 1683; active in iron mining until end of 18th cent.; meeting place of Provincial congress 1776, which ratified Declaration of Independence; scene of Washington's retreat from Manhattan and of British attack under Howe and battle at Chatterton Hill Oct. 28, 1776 (commemorative area set aside as **White Plains Battlefield Site:** see UNITED STATES, *National Historical Parks*); incorp. as village 1866, as city 1916. Good Counsel Coll. (1923; women).

White River. 1 Name of several rivers of the U.S. and one of Canada: see WHITE, above. **2** Town, ⊗ of Mellette co., S South Dakota; pop. 583. **3** See HVÍTÁ.

White River Junction. Village, Windsor co., E Vermont, at junction of Connecticut and White rivers ab. 9 m. NNE of Woodstock; pop. 2546; railroad center.

White Rock Mountain. Peak 13,532 ft. in Gunnison co., W cen. Colorado.

White Russia; *Russ.* **Bye·lo·rus′si·a** *or* **Be·lo·rus′-si·a** (byĭ·lŭ·rōōs′syĭ·y*à*). **1** Former region of eastern Europe, indefinitely bounded, inhabited by the White Russians; after World War I comprised the territory divided bet. S Latvia, E Poland, and W Soviet Union (the White Russian republic). The S part includes the Pripet Marshes.
2 *or* **White Russian Soviet Socialist Republic;** *officially* **Bye′lo·rus′sian Soviet Socialist Republic** (byě′lŏ·rŭsh′*ăn*). A constituent republic of the Union of Soviet Socialist Republics, in W part; 49,022 sq. m.; pop. 5,567,976; ✱ Minsk. Bounded on N by Velikie Luki Region, on E by Smolensk and Bryansk Regions, all three in the R.S.F.S.R., on the SE and S by Ukraine, on W by Poland, and on NW by Lithuanian and Latvian Soviet Republics; divided administratively into 12 regions. To this area was added after World War II most of NE Poland (all of departments of Nowogródek and Wilno, and parts of Białystok and Polesie), ab. 39,022 sq. m. and a pop. (estimated on basis of Polish 1931 census) of 4 586,287; total area 88,044 sq. m. and (est.) pop. 10,154,287. The N part is crossed by the Dvina, past low hills in the NW; through the E cen. part flows from N to S the upper course of the Dnieper, which has as tributaries the Berezina, Sozh, and Pripyat; along the Pripyat in the S extend the Pripet Marshes. In the W (former Poland) is upper course of Neman river and its tributaries and on the SW the Bug forms part of the boundary. Had great forested areas, now much reduced by unscientific cutting and by destruction in wars. Chief occupations are agriculture and stock raising. The predominant ethnic strain is Slav; chief nationalities before 1945: White Russian (Byelorussian) 80.6%, Jewish 8%, Russian 7%. Chief towns Minsk, Vitebsk, Gomel, Mogilev, Bobruisk; and in former Polish territory Grodno, Brest, and Pinsk.

History: In medieval times region was subject to Lithuanians and Poles; small section came under Ivan the Great 1503 but reconquered by Poles and continued as part of Poland until 1656; for the next century a prize of war; E part to Russia in First Partition of Poland 1772 and remainder by Second 1793; continual wars left country devastated and made worse by Napoleon's Campaign 1812 (see BEREZINA); again overrun in World War I and occupied by Poles 1919; in 1921 W part assigned to Poland; in 1922 became part of U.S.S.R.; in 1924 and 1926 E boundary adjusted by Russia to include Vitebsk and Gomel; in World War II overrun by German armies in summer of 1941; recovered by Russians 1944; after World War II increased by parts of NE Poland nearly equal to original republic in area and population.

White Sands National Monument. See UNITED STATES, *National Monuments.*

White Sands Proving Ground. Area ab. 125 m. long of white (gypsum) sand dunes, Dona Ana co., S New Mexico, SE of San Andres Mts. and SW of the White Sands National Monument; U.S. testing ground for rockets and guided missiles; Holloman Air Force Base adjacent.

Whites′bor′o (hwīts′bûr′ō). **1** Village, Oneida co., cen. New York, on Mohawk river 5 m. WNW of Utica; pop. 4784; settled 1784; manufactures knit goods, furniture.
2 Town, Grayson co., NE Texas, 18 m. W of Sherman; pop. 2485; cotton gins; cottonseed, feed, flour mills.

Whites′burg (hwīts′bûrg). Town, ⊗ of Letcher co., SE Kentucky, 30 m. SW of Pikeville; pop. 1774; in the Cumberland region; coal mining.

White Sea; *Russ.* **Be′lo·e Mo′re** (byě′lŭ·yě mô′ryě). Large inlet, or gulf, of the Barents Sea on N coast of Soviet Russia in Europe, enclosed on the N by Kola Penin.; 36,000 sq. m.; chief port Arkhangelsk, on Dvina Gulf; on S borders on Arkhangelsk Region and on W on Karelian Republic. Receives the Northern Dvina and Onega rivers.

White Settlement. Town, Tarrant co., N Texas, W suburb of Fort Worth; pop. 11,513.

White′shell′ Forest Reserve (hwīt′shĕl′). Canadian provincial park, SE Manitoba, S of Winnipeg river; 1088 sq. m.; area of primitive forest with more than 200 lakes and rivers. Characterized by volcanic rock cliffs.

White′side′ (hwīt′sīd′). County in Illinois. See *Table* at ILLINOIS.

White′stone′ (hwīt′stōn′). Community on North Shore, N Queens co., New York, at W end of Long I. N of Flushing; terminus of bridge across East river to the Bronx. Settled by Dutch farmers c. 1645.

White Sulphur Springs. 1 City, ⊗ of Meagher co., cen. Montana; pop. 1519.
2 Residential city, Greenbrier co., SE West Virginia, near Virginia border 36 m. ENE of Hinton; pop. 2676; resort; mineral springs; served as summer White House for Presidents Van Buren, Tyler, Fillmore; Japanese diplomats interned here 1942.

White′tail′ Butte (hwīt′tāl′). Isolated peak 3000 ft. in Kootenai co., N Idaho.

White Top Mountain. Peak 5520 ft. in Smyth co., SW Virginia.

White′ville (hwīt′vĭl; *Sou.* also -v'l). Town, ⊗ of Columbus co., S North Carolina, 44 m. W of Wilmington; pop. 4683; tobacco warehouses; lumber and veneer mills.

White Volta. See White VOLTA.

White′wa′ter (hwīt′wô′tẽr; -wŏt′ẽr). **1** River 100 m. long, E Indiana; rises in E cen. Indiana, flows S, then E across Ohio border to empty into the Miami river just above its junction with the Ohio river, SE Ohio.
2 City, Walworth co., S Wisconsin, 18 m. NE of Janesville; pop. 6380; Wisconsin State Coll. (1868; coed.).

Whitewater Bald′y (bôl′dĭ). Mountain 10,892 ft. in S Catron co., W New Mexico.

Whitewater Bay. Inlet of Gulf of Mexico, Monroe co., SW Florida, bet. the mainland and Cape Sable.

Whitewater Lake. Lake ab. 10 m. long in SW Manitoba, Canada, 42 m. SSW of Brandon.

White′wood′ Peak (hwīt′wŏŏd′). Mountain 5140 ft. in Lawrence co., W South Dakota.

White′wright (hwīt′rīt). Town Grayson co., NE Texas, 15 m. SE of Sherman; pop. 1315.

Whit′field (hwĭt′fēld). County in Georgia. See *Table* at GEORGIA.

Whit′horn′ (hwĭt′hôrn′). Burgh, Wigtown, SW Scotland, in S part near Burrow Head; pop. ab. 1068; an old town, with first stone church in Scotland built 397 by St. Ninian; 12th-cent. priory.

Whit′ing (hwīt′ĭng). City, Lake co., NW corner of Indiana, on Lake Michigan 17 m. SE of Chicago; pop. 8137; oil refinery, chemical works.

Whit′ing·ham, Lake (hwĭt′ĭng·hăm). Reservoir in Deerfield river, SW Windham co., S Vermont, formed by 200-ft. earthen **Har′ri·man Dam** (hăr′ĭ·măn), completed 1924.

Whit′ins·ville (hwīt′ĭnz·vĭl). Urban community (unincorporated), Worcester co., cen. Massachusetts, SE of Worcester; pop. 5102.

Whit′ley (hwĭt′lĭ). Name of counties in two states of the U.S. See *Tables* at INDIANA and KENTUCKY.

Whitley Bay; *formerly* **Whitley and Monks′ea′ton** (mŭngks′ē′t'n). Urban district, Northumberland, N England, on North Sea 9 m. ENE of Newcastle; pop. 32,257; summer resort.

Whitley City. Town, ⊗ of McCreary co., SE Kentucky; pop. 1034.

Whit′man (hwĭt′măn). **1** County in Washington. See *Table* at WASHINGTON.
2 Town, Plymouth co., SE Massachusetts, 4 m. E of Brockton; pop. 10,485; shoe manufacturing.

Whitman National Monument. See UNITED STATES, *National Monuments.*

Whit′mire (hwĭt′mīr). Town, Newberry co., NW cen. South Carolina, 35 m. SE of Spartanburg; pop. 2663.

Whit′ney (hwĭt′nĭ). Urban community (unincorporated), Ada co., SW Idaho, WSW of Boise; pop. 13,603.

Whitney, Mount. Peak 14,495 ft. in Sierra Nevada, on boundary bet. Tulare and Inyo cos., SE cen. California, in Sequoia National Park; highest point in the state, and in continental U.S. outside of Alaska. See DEATH VALLEY.

Whit′sta·ble (hwĭt′stȧ·b′l). Urban district, Kent, SE England, on North Sea 50 m. E of London; pop. 17,467; oyster fisheries.

Whit′sun′day Island (hwĭt′sŭn′dĭ; hwĭt′s'n·dā′). Island, N of Cumberland Is. off E coast of Queensland, Australia, SE of Townsville, 20°8′S.

Whit′ti·er (hwĭt′ĭ·ēr). 1 Suburban residential city, Los Angeles co., SW California, 12 m. ESE of Los Angeles; pop. 33,663; founded 1887, incorp. as city 1898; in region producing esp. avocados, citrus fruits, walnuts; Whittier Coll. (1891; coed.), Chapman Coll. (1861; coed.).
2 Seaport village on W shore of Prince William Sound, S Alaska; connected by rail with Fairbanks; pop. (est.) 1000.

Whit′tle·sey or **Whit′tle·sea** (hwĭt′'l·sĭ). Urban district, Isle of Ely, E England, 43 m. E of Leicester; pop. 8609; bricks and tiles.

Whit′well (hwĭt′wĕl; -wĕl). City, Marion co., S Tennessee, ab. 18 m. NW of Chattanooga; pop. 1857.

Whit′wood (hwĭt′wŏŏd). Former urban district, West Riding, Yorkshire, N England; now in Castleford.

Whit′worth (hwĭt′wûrth; -wẽrth). Urban district, Lancashire, NW England, N of Manchester; pop. 7442.

Whydah. See OUIDAH.

Wiak. See BIAK.

Wi′ar·ton (wĭ′ẽr·t'n; -tŭn). Town, Bruce co., SE Ontario, Canada, at head of an inlet of Georgian Bay 15 m. NW of Owen Sound; pop. 1955.

Wi′baux (wē′bō). 1 County in Montana. See *Table* at MONTANA.
2 Town, its ⊗, E Montana; pop. 766.

Wich′i·ta (wĭch′ĭ·tô). 1 River 230 m. long, N Texas; flows ENE into Red river; contains Wichita Falls Dam.
2 Name of counties in two states of the U.S. See *Tables* at KANSAS and TEXAS.
3 City, ⊗ of Sedgwick co., S cen. Kansas, on Arkansas river 177 m. SW of Kansas City; pop. 254,698; trade and industrial center in agricultural and oil-producing section; stockyards, grain elevators, flour mills, oil refineries, packing houses; manufactures airplanes, farm machinery, machine tools. Municipal Univ. of Wichita (1892; coed.); Friends Univ. (1898; coed.; Quaker).

Wichita Falls. City, ⊗ of Wichita co., N Texas, 105 m. NNW of Fort Worth; pop. 101,724; a center of oil industry; oil fields in vicinity; oil refineries; manufactures oil-field equipment, dairy and machine-shop products.

Wichita Falls Dam. Dam completed 1924 across Wichita river, Baylor co., N Texas; height 100 ft.; impounds water for irrigation, forming **Lake Kemp** (kĕmp).

Wichita Mountains. Range ab. 1000 ft. in SW Oklahoma, chiefly in Comanche and Kiowa cos.

Wick (wĭk). Burgh, ⊗ of Caithness co., N Scotland, at mouth of the Wick river; pop. 7161; herring fisheries.

Wick′en·burg (wĭk′ĕn·bûrg). Town, Maricopa co., SW cen. Arizona; pop. 2445; trading center.

Wick′ford (wĭk′fẽrd). Village, Washington co., S Rhode Island, on Narragansett Bay ab. 8 m. NE of Kingston; pop. 2934; administrative center of North Kingstown.

Wick′ham (wĭk′ăm). Town, E New South Wales, SE Australia, suburb of Newcastle; pop. 12,001.

Wick′liffe (wĭk′lĭf). 1 City, ⊗ of Ballard co., W Kentucky; pop. 917.
2 City, Lake co., NE Ohio, on Lake Erie 13 m. NE of Cleveland; pop. 15,760.

Wick′low (wĭk′lō). 1 County, E Eire, in Leinster prov.; 782 sq. m.; pop. 58,569; ⊗ Wicklow; stock raising, agriculture, granite quarrying.
2 Urban district and seaport, its ⊗, E Eire; pop. 3183; anciently settled by the Danes; ruins of Franciscan abbey and 12th-cent. castle.

Wicklow Head. Cape on E coast of Ireland, E of Wicklow; lighthouse.

Wicklow Mountains. Range extending along E coast of co. Wicklow, E Ireland; highest peak **Lug′na·quil′la** (lŭg′nȧ·kŭl′yȧ) 3039 ft.

Wi·com′i·co (wī·kŏm′ĭ·kō). County in Maryland. See *Table* at MARYLAND.

Wic′o·nis′co (wĭk′ō·nĭs′kō). Locality in Wiconisco township (pop. 1801), Dauphin co., SE cen. Pennsylvania, ab. 23 m. NW of Lebanon; pop. 1402.

Wida. See OUIDAH.

Wid′nes (wĭd′nĕs; -nĭs). Municipal borough, Lancashire, NW England, on the Mersey 10 m. E of Liverpool; pop. 48,795; manufactures paint, soap, chemicals, metal goods.

Wid′ows′ Tears (wĭd′ōz tẽrz′). Waterfall 1170 ft. in Yosemite National Park, E cen. California.

Wie·licz′ka (vyĕ·lēch′kä). Commune, Kraków dept., Poland, 8 m. SE of Kraków; pop. (1938–39 est.) 11,631; celebrated rock salt mines, said to be most ancient in the world.

Wie′luń (vyĕ′lōon·y′). Commune, Łódź dept., Poland, 61 m. SW of Łódź; pop. (1938–39 est.) 15,536; limestone quarries nearby; manufactures sugar products, beer, lumber.

Wien (vēn). See VIENNA.

Wie′ner Neu′stadt (vē′nēr noi′shtät). Manufacturing city, Lower Austria prov., Austria, 24 m. SSW of Vienna; pop. (1939) 39,394; railroad junction; manufactures locomotives, tools, leather, paper, beer. Founded 1192. In World War II taken by Russians Apr. 3, 1945.

Wie′ner·wald′ (vē′nēr·vält′). A spur of the Eastern Alps in Lower Austria, W and NW of Vienna and S of the Danube, covered with forests; in N part is the Kahlenberg.

Wieprz (vyĕpsh). River ab. 150 m. long in cen. Poland; rises in S Lublin dept., flows NW and W into the Vistula river.

Wier′den (vēr′dĕ[n]). Commune, Overijssel prov., E Netherlands, just W of Almelo; pop. 10,831.

Wie′ring·en (vē′rĭng·ĕ[n]). Commune, North Holland prov., W Netherlands, at W end of dike enclosing IJsselmeer; pop. 5465; formerly an island in Zuider Zee, now constitutes N section of Wieringermeer.

Wie′ring·er·meer′ (vē′rĭng·ēr·mār′). Polder 80 sq. m. in NW part of former Zuider Zee, Netherlands; flooded by Germans Apr. 18, 1945, reclaimed again by May 1946.

Wies′ba′den (vēs′bä′dĕn; *local pron.* vīs′-). 1 Government district of former Hesse-Nassau prov., Prussia, Germany; 2169 sq. m.
2 City, its ✳ and ✳ of Hesse, on the Rhine 20 m. W of Frankfurt am Main; pop. (1957) 249,900; warm alkaline springs; tourist resort; royal and ducal palaces, town hall, courthouse, museum, art gallery, library, royal theater, Kurhaus; remains of 3d-cent. Roman wall; trades in wine; manufactures chocolate, surgical instruments. Saline springs known from Roman times; made city before 1242; capital of former duchy of Nassau 1815–66; seat of Rhineland Commission 1918–29 under French and English occupation; in World War II entered by American forces ab. Mar. 23, 1945.

Wies′dorf (vēs′dôrf). Former city (pop. 30,178), Düsseldorf govt. dist., Rhine Province, Prussia, Germany; since 1930 part of Leverkusen (*q.v.*).

Wig′an (wĭg′ăn). County borough, Lancashire, NW England, on the Douglas 18 m. W of Manchester; pop. 85,357, (1951 pop.) 84,546; manufactures cotton goods and machinery; former pottery and bell-founding center.

Wig′gins (wĭg′ĭnz). Town, ⊗ of Stone co., SE Mississippi; pop. 1591.

Wight, Isle of (wīt); *anc.* **Vec′tis** (vĕk′tĭs). Adminis-

trative county constituted by the Isle of Wight; part of former county of Hampshire (*q.v.*); 147 sq. m.,; pop. (1951) 95,594; ⊗ Newport; includes many watering places and holiday resorts, as Ryde, Ventnor, Cowes; other towns Shanklin, Sandown, Carisbrooke.

Wigs'ton Mag'na (wĭg'stŭn măg'nȧ). Urban district, Leicestershire, cen. England, 4 m. S of Leicester; pop. 15,452.

Wig'town (wĭg'tŭn; -toun). 1 *or* **Wig'town·shire** (-shĭr; -shēr). County, SW Scotland; 487 sq. m.,; pop. (1951) 31,625; ⊗ Wigtown; hilly region; rivers Cree, Bladenoch; agriculture, livestock raising.
2 Burgh, its ⊗, SW Scotland, on Wigtown Bay; pop. 1376.

Wigtown Bay. Inlet of Irish Sea on S coast of Scotland; extends 15 m. inland in Wigtown co.

Wij'de Bay (vī'dĕ). Fiord 70 m. long on the N coast of the island of West Spitsbergen, Spitsbergen archipelago.

Wijk aan Zee en Duin (vīk' än zā' ĕn doin'). Commune, North Holland prov., W Netherlands; pop. 6304; seaside resort NNW of Haarlem.

Wijm·brit'se·ra·deel' (vĭm·brĭt'sĕ·rȧ·dāl'). Commune, Friesland prov., N Netherlands; pop. 11,659.

Wijn'koops, *or* **Wyn'coops,** Bay (vīn'kōps). Inlet of the Indian Ocean on the S side of the W end of Java, Indonesia.

Wiju. See GISHU.

Wil (vēl). Commune, NW Saint Gallen canton, NE Switzerland; pop. (1930) 7514; cotton spinning.

Wil'bar'ger (wĭl'bär'gẽr). County in Texas. See *Table* at TEXAS.

Wil'ber (wĭl'bẽr). City, ⊗ of Saline co., SE Nebraska; pop. 1358.

Wil'ber·force (wĭl'bẽr·fôrs). Village, Greene co., SW Ohio, ab. 3 m. NE of Xenia; pop. (est.) 1800. Wilberforce University (1856; coed.); Central State College (1887; coed.).

Wilberforce, Cape. Point on N coast of Australia. Northern Territory, just NW of Cape Arnhem, ab. 12°S.

Wil'bra·ham (wĭl'brȧ·hăm). Town, Hampden co., SW Massachusetts, 8 m. E of Springfield; pop. 7387; Wilbraham Academy, founded 1817.

Wil'bur, Mount (wĭl'bẽr). Peak 9293 ft. in Glacier National Park, NW Montana.

Wilbur Dam. See *Table* at TENNESSEE VALLEY AUTHORITY.

Wil'bur·ton (wĭl'bẽr·t'n; -tŭn). City, ⊗ of Latimer co., E Oklahoma, 28 m. E of McAlester; pop. 1772; coal mining.

Wil'cox (wĭl'kŏks). Name of counties in two states of the U.S. See *Tables* at ALABAMA and GEORGIA.

Wil'czek Land (vĭl'chĕk). See FRANZ JOSEF LAND.

Wild'bad (vĭlt'bät). Commune, Baden-Württemberg state, West Germany; pop. (1939) 5307; mineral springs; resort.

Wild'cat' Mountain (wīld'kăt'). 1 Peak 1757 ft. in Iron co., SE Missouri; connected with Taum Sauk by a saddle.
2 Peak 5082 ft. in Banner co., W Montana.

Wil'der·ness (wĭl'dẽr·nĕs; -nĭs). 1 Region, Orange and Spotsylvania cos., N Virginia, S of Rapidan river; battles 1863 (Chancellorsville) and May 5–7, 1864 bet. Federals under Grant and Confederates under Lee, one of the bloodiest battles of the Civil War.
2 Any of several extensive tracts of desert land mentioned in the Bible; as the **Wilderness of Judah,** a tract of E Judaea along W shore of the Dead Sea; sometimes, **the Wilderness,** the Wilderness of Paran. See (Wilderness of) PARAN, SHUR, SIN, ZIN.

Wilderness Road. Road from E Virginia, through Cumberland Gap and cen. Kentucky to the Ohio river; trail blazed and cleared as far as Boonesborough by Daniel Boone 1775, later enlarged and used by many early pioneers to the West.

Wil'der·vank (vĭl'dẽr·vängk). Commune, Groningen

prov., NE Netherlands, 15 m. SE of Groningen; pop. 10,179.

Wild'spit'ze (vĭlt'shpĭt'sĕ). Highest peak 12,382 ft. in Ötztaler Alps, in S Tirol-Vorarlberg prov., Austria.

Wil'dung·en *or* **Bad Wildungen** (bät vĭl'dŏong·ĕn). Commune, W Germany, in Hesse state; pop. ab. 5000; formerly in Waldeck; mineral springs.

Wild'wood (wĭld'wŏod). City and seaside resort, Cape May co., S New Jersey, on Atlantic Ocean 33 m. SW of Atlantic City; pop. 4690; port of call for Atlantic fishing fleet.

Wilejka. See VILEIKA.

Wil'hel·mi'na (wĭl'hĕl·mē'nȧ; wĭl'ĕ·mē'nȧ); *Du.* **Wil'-hel·mi'na Top** (vĭl'hĕl·mē'nȧ tôp). Peak 15,584 ft. in cen. Neth. New Guinea, in the Orange Range; highest in the range and second highest in Neth. New Guinea.

Wilhelmina Mountains. Mountain range in cen. Surinam; highest 4200 ft.

Wil'helms·burg (vĭl'hĕlms·bŏorK). Former commune (pop. 32,504) and island in the Elbe, Lüneburg govt. dist., Hannover prov., Prussia, Germany; became part of Harburg-Wilhelmsburg (*q.v.*) 1927.

Wil'helms·ha'ven (vĭl'hĕlms·hä'fĕn). Seaport city, Lower Saxony state, W Germany, formerly in Hannover prov., Prussia, on W shore of Jade Bay 19 m. W of Wesermünde; pop. 25,403; founded 1854–69 as German North Sea naval station; important navy yard until 1945. Bombed repeatedly by Allies during World War II; occupied on termination of the war May 8, 1945.

Wil'helm II Coast, *formerly* **Kai'ser Wil'helm II Land** (kī'zẽr vĭl'hĕlm thē sĕk'ŭnd). Section of coast of Antarctica ab. lat. 66°30'S and long. 86° to Cape Filchner at 91°52'E separating it from Queen Mary Coast. Formerly claimed by Germany; now lies within region claimed by Great Britain.

Wi'lis (vē'lĭs). Mountain group 7872 ft. including also Mt. Liman, E cen. Java, Indonesia.

Wilja. See NERIS.

Wil'jan·di (vĭl'yȧn·dĭ). Var. of VILJANDI.

Wilkes (wĭlks). Name of counties in two states of the U.S. See *Tables* at GEORGIA and NORTH CAROLINA.

Wilkes–Bar're (wĭlks'băr'ĕ; -bär'ĕ). Commercial and industrial city, ⊗ of Luzerne co., E Pennsylvania, on Susquehanna river 18 m. SW of Scranton; pop. 63,551; settled 1769, and Fort Durkee erected; settlement burned by British and Indians 1778, 1784; became ⊗ 1786; center of anthracite coal-mining region; redistribution point for farm produce, etc.; manufactures textiles, silk, and lace, mining and railroad supplies, machinery, locomotives, iron products, tobacco and lumber products. Wilkes Coll. (1933; coed.).

Wilkes'bor'o (wĭlks'bûr'ō). Town, ⊗ of Wilkes co., NW cen. North Carolina; pop. 1568.

Wilkes Land (wĭlks). Coast region of Antarctica, not fully delimited but extending approximately through lat. 66° to 70°S and long. 102° to 142°20'E along the Indian Ocean from Queen Mary Coast to George V Coast. Includes French Claim of Adélie Coast (*q.v.*). Discovered 1839 by Charles Wilkes, American naval officer, who coasted along this part of Antarctic barrier from ab. 150°E to 108°E. As result of explorations of T. W. E. David and Douglas Mawson, British explorers, region (coastal area and interior extending to South Pole) claimed 1908 by Great Britain. Except for Adélie Coast, part of the Australian claim as established 1933 and 1936, with concurrence of Great Britain.

Wil'kin (wĭl'kĭn). County in Minnesota See *Table* at MINNESOTA.

Wil'kins (wĭl'kĭnz). 1 Township, Allegheny co., SW Pennsylvania, E suburb of Pittsburgh; pop. 8272.
2 Locality, Beaufort co., S South Carolina, on an island ab. 6 m. N of Beaufort; pop. (1950) 500.

Wil'kins·burg (wĭl'kĭnz·bûrg). Residential borough, Allegheny co., SW Pennsylvania, 7 m. E of Pittsburgh;

pop. 30,066; settled 1780; manufactures machinery, railroad supplies, chromium plating, mine safety appliances.

Wil'kin·son (wĭl'kĭn·s'n). Name of counties in two states of the U.S. See *Tables* at GEORGIA and MISSISSIPPI.

Wilkomir. See UKMERGE.

Will (wĭl). County in Illinois. See *Table* at ILLINOIS.

Wil'la·cy (wĭl'å·sĭ). County in Texas. See *Table* at TEXAS.

Wil·lam'ette (wĭ·lăm'ĕt; -ĭt). River 190 m. long, NW Oregon; formed by junction of forks in cen. Lane co., flows N into Columbia river near Portland.

Wil'la·pa Bay (wĭl'å·på). Inlet of Pacific Ocean on W coast of Pacific co., SW Washington.

Wil'lard (wĭl'ẽrd). Village, Huron co., N Ohio, 26 m. S of Sandusky; pop. 5457; manufactures steel burial vaults, rubber and lumber-mill products.

Wil'lau'mez' Peninsula (vĕ'yō'mĕz'). Long point of land extending from cen. part of N coast of New Britain I. into Bismarck Sea, Bismarck Archipelago, W Pacific Ocean; Cape Hollman is at N extremity, Kimbe Bay to the E, and Talasea on its E shore.

Wil'le·broeck (vĭl'ĕ·brōōk). Manufacturing commune, Antwerp prov., N Belgium, halfway bet. Antwerp and Brussels; pop. 13,895.

Wil'lem·stad (vĭl'ĕm·stät). City at S end of Curaçao I., Neth. West Indies; ✱ of Curaçao colony; pop. (1942) 33,062. Built in Dutch style, has fine harbor; shipping point for oil refinery, one of the largest and most modern in the world, treating oil from the Lake Maracaibo district of Venezuela.

Wil'len·dorf (vĭl'ĕn·dôrf). Village, Austria, on the Danube near Krems; site of paleolithic station where the Venus of Willendorf (a limestone statuette ab. 4½ inches tall representing a female, assigned to the Aurignacian period) was discovered.

Wil'len·hall (vĭl'ĕn·hôl). Urban district, Staffordshire, W cen. England, 10 m. NW of Birmingham; pop. 30,695.

Willes'den (wĭlz'dĕn). Municipal borough, Middlesex, SE England, 7 m. W of London; pop. 184,434, (1951) 179,647; part of Greater London; railroad center.

Wil'ley, Mount (wĭl'ĭ). Peak 4261 ft. on W side of Crawford Notch, White Mts., New Hampshire, in NE Grafton co.

Wil'liam, Mount (wĭl'yăm). See the GRAMPIANS, Australia.

Wil'liams (wĭl'yămz). 1 River ab. 50 m. long, W cen. Arizona; formed by confluence of Big Sandy and Santa Maria rivers on SE boundary of Mohave co., flows W into Colorado river.

2 Name of county in two states of the U.S. See *Tables* at NORTH DAKOTA and OHIO.

3 Town, Coconino co., N Arizona, 28 m. W of Flagstaff; pop. 3559; settled 1878; lumber; tourist trade and railroad junction point for visitors to Grand Canyon; livestock distributing point.

Williams Bay. Village, Walworth co., S Wisconsin, 24 m. ESE of Janesville; pop. 1347; site of Yerkes Observatory (founded 1892; belongs to Univ. of Chicago).

Wil'liams·burg (wĭl'yămz·bûrg). 1 County in South Carolina. See *Table* at SOUTH CAROLINA.

2 City, ✱ of Whitley co., SE Kentucky, 28 m. WNW of Middlesborough; pop. 3478; in agricultural and coal-mining section.

3 Town, Hampshire co., W Massachusetts, 15 m. SSW of Greenfield; pop. 2186.

4 District of BROOKLYN (*q.v.*), New York.

5 Borough, Blair co., S cen. Pennsylvania, 12 m. ESE of Altoona; pop. 1792.

6 City and tourist resort in SE Virginia, in James City and York cos., ✱ of James City co., but politically independent; on peninsula bet. James and York rivers 27 m. NNW of Newport News; 1 sq. m.; pop. 6832; settled 1633; designated new capital of Virginia 1699; incorp. as city 1722 (first incorporated municipality in Virginia);

became political, educational, and social center of Virginia; declined following removal of capital to Richmond 1780; headquarters of British, then of Continental and French forces before and after siege of Yorktown 1781; battle May 5, 1862. Has been restored to its colonial appearance, 572 modern buildings having been destroyed and many old ones restored (eventually 250 will have been restored); restoration begun 1927; became part of Colonial National Historical Park 1936. College of William and Mary (1693; coed.).

Wil'liam·son (wĭl'yăm·s'n). 1 River ab. 70 m. long, Klamath co., S Oregon; flows NW then S to N end of Upper Klamath Lake; receives the Sprague near its mouth.

2 Name of counties in three states of the U.S. See *Tables* at ILLINOIS, TENNESSEE, TEXAS.

3 Village in Williamson town (pop.5294), Wayne co., W New York, ab. 22 m. NE of Rochester; pop. 1690; farming.

4 City, ✱ of Mingo co., SW West Virginia, 52 m. S of Huntington; pop. 6746; coal mining and shipping point; manufactures armatures, machinery.

Williamson, Mount. Peak 14,384 ft. in Sierra Nevada, in W Inyo co., SE cen. California.

Williamson Head. Headland on Oates Coast, Antarctica, W of Ross Sea at ab. 69°S, 158°10′E.

Wil'liams·port (wĭl'yămz·pōrt). 1 Town, ✱ of Warren co., W Indiana; pop. 1353.

2 Town, Washington co., N Maryland, on Potomac river 7 m. WSW of Hagerstown; pop. 1853; tannery, silk mill, limestone quarries.

3 Manufacturing city, ✱ of Lycoming co., N cen. Pennsylvania, on West Branch of Susquehanna river 70 m. N of Harrisburg; pop. 41,967; settled in 1770's on site of Indian village; became ✱ 1795; formerly important lumbering center; manufactures airplane motors, steel rails, cables, sole leather, wood products (esp. furniture), textiles. Lycoming Coll. (1812; coed.).

Wil'liams·ton (wĭl'yăm·stŭn). 1 City, Ingham co., S Michigan, 13 m. E of Lansing; pop. 2214; clay and soft-coal deposits nearby.

2 Town, ✱ of Martin co., E North Carolina, on Roanoke river 42 m. E of Rocky Mount; pop. 6924; tobacco market; manufactures peanut products, fertilizer, lumber.

3 Town, Anderson co., NW South Carolina, 13 m. NE of Anderson; pop. 3721; former health resort (mineral spring).

Wil'liams·town (wĭl'yămz·toun). 1 City, ✱ of Grant co., N Kentucky; pop. 1611.

2 Town, Berkshire co., N Massachusetts, 19 m. N of Pittsfield; pop. 7322. Williams Coll. (1793; men).

3 Town, Gloucester co., SW New Jersey, ab. 14 m. SE of Woodbury; pop. 2722; former glassmaking center; fruit and vegetable canneries.

4 Borough, Dauphin co., SE cen. Pennsylvania, 26 m. NE of Harrisburg; pop. 2097; manufactures hosiery; anthracite coal mines.

5 City, Wood co., W West Virginia, on Ohio river across from Marietta, Ohio; pop. 2632; manufactures art glass, ceramics.

6 City, E Victoria, SE Australia; SW suburb of Melbourne at mouth of Yarra Yarra river on Port Phillip Bay; pop. 22,206; seaport with floating docks, shipbuilding yards, and a navy depot.

Wil'liams·ville (wĭl'yămz·vĭl). Residential village, Erie co., W New York, 10 m. NE of Buffalo; pop. 6316.

Willimansett. See CHICOPEE.

Wil'li·man'tic (wĭl'ĭ·măn'tĭk). 1 River ab. 30 m. long, NE Connecticut; rises in S Massachusetts, flows S across cen. Tolland co. and unites with the Natchaug river at Willimantic to form the Shetucket river.

2 Manufacturing city (pop. 13,881) in town of WINDHAM, Connecticut, at junction of Natchaug and Willimantic rivers; a ✱ of Windham co.; incorp. as borough 1833, as city 1893; known esp. for the manufacture of

spooled thread; manufactures also cotton, velvet, silk, and rayon goods, clothing, foundry products, silk machinery, machine-shop products. Willimantic State Coll. (1889; coed.).

Wil'ling·ton (wĭl'ĭng·tŭn). **1** Town, NW cen. Tolland co., N Connecticut, on E bank of Willimantic river opp. Tolland; pop. 2005; incorp. 1727; manufactures pearl buttons, lumber, thread.
2 Former urban district, Durham, N England, 18½ m. S of Newcastle; pop. (1931) 8964.

Wil'lis Islands (wĭl'ĭs). Group of coral islets and reefs in Coral Sea outside Great Barrier Reef, Queensland, Australia, 16°15'S.

Wil'lis·ton (wĭl'ĭs·tŭn). City, ⊗ of Williams co., NW North Dakota, on Missouri river 20 m. E of Montana border; pop. 11,866; stockyards; turkey market; large co-operative enterprises, including creamery, grain elevator, poultry plant; lignite coal mines.

Williston Park. Residential village, Nassau co., SE New York, on Long I. 18 m. E of New York; pop. 8255.

Wil'lits (wĭl'ĭts). City, Mendocino co., W California, 73 m. NNW of Santa Rosa; pop. 3410; stock raising; poultry; hay.

Will'mar (wĭl'mär). City, ⊗ of Kandiyohi co., SW cen. Minnesota, 52 m. SW of St. Cloud; pop. 10,417; shipping point for grain and livestock; railroad division point.

Wil'lough·by (wĭl'ŏ·bĭ). **1** City, Lake co., NE Ohio, on Lake Erie 18 m. NE of Cleveland; pop. 15,058.
2 City, E New South Wales, SE Australia, N suburb of Sydney; pop. 42,521.

Willoughby Lake. Lake ab. 6 m. long and 2 m. wide in E Orleans co., N Vermont; summer resort.

Wil'low Glen (wĭl'ō). Former city, Santa Clara co., California; annexed to San Jose 1936.

Willow Grove. Locality, Montgomery co., SE Pennsylvania, 13 m. N of Philadelphia; pop. (est.) 6000; Willow Grove Park, amusement center; naval air station.

Wil'lo·wick (wĭl'ō·wĭk). City, Lake co., NE Ohio, E suburb of Cleveland; pop. 18,749.

Wil'low·more (wĭl'ō·mōr). Town, S Cape Province, S Union of South Africa, 130 m. WNW of Port Elizabeth; pop. 2073; in E part of the Great Karroo; mohair, wool, and ostrich feathers produced in this region. Twice unsuccessfully attacked by Boers in 1901.

Wil'low Mountain (wĭl'ō). Peak 3830 ft. in SW Brewster co., W Texas.

Willow Run. Site near Ypsilanti, Washtena co., Michigan, W of Detroit; pop. (est.) 4100; huge bomber plant built by government in World War II to be run by Henry Ford; after the war plant sold by government; now manufactures automobiles.

Wil'lows (wĭl'ōz). City, ⊗ of Glenn co., N California, 42 m. NE of Clear Lake; pop. 4139; in irrigated region producing rice, wheat, barley, sugar beets, citrus fruits.

Willow Springs. City, Howell co., S Missouri, 18 m. N of West Plains; pop. 1913; market for dairy products.

Wills'bor'o (wĭlz'bûr'ō). Village in Willsboro town (pop. 1716), Essex co., NE New York, ab. 25 m. S of Plattsburg; settled 1765; scene of Burgoyne's encampment 1777; tourist center.

Wills Point. City, Van Zandt co., NE Texas, 40 m. E of Dallas; pop. 2281; marketing and shipping center; oil, lignite, salt, clay deposits nearby.

Willyama. See BROKEN HILL.

Wil'mer·ding (wĭl'mĕr·dĭng). Borough, Allegheny co., SW Pennsylvania, 11 m. E of Pittsburgh; pop. 4349; manufactures air brakes.

Wil'mers·dorf (vĭl'mĕrs·dôrf). City, SW suburb of Berlin, part of Greater Berlin, Germany.

Wil·mette' (wĭl·mĕt'). Residential village, Cook co., NE Illinois, 15 m. N of Chicago; pop. 28,268.

Wil'ming·ton (wĭl'mĭng·tŭn). **1** Former city, Los Angeles co., SW California, NE of San Pedro; annexed to Los Angeles 1909; harbor protected by an island.
2 Commercial and industrial city, ⊗ of New Castle co.,

N Delaware, at junction of Delaware and Christina rivers and Brandywine creek; largest city in the state; pop. 95,827; port of entry; municipal marine terminal; airports; shipyards, tanneries; manufactures rubber goods, vulcanized fiber, iron and steel, textiles, kid and morocco leather, machinery, building materials, railroad cars, chemicals, powder, etc.; seat of DuPont industries. Fort Christina (q.v.) settled by Swedes 1638; capital of New Sweden (q.v.) until 1643 and again 1654; captured by Dutch 1655 and by English 1664; named Willington 1731; chartered as borough and renamed Wilmington 1739; battle of Brandywine fought just N of city 1777; captured by British; incorp. as city 1832. Landmarks include old Swedish church (1698), George Washington's headquarters, town hall (1798), and several old churches and meeting houses (1740, 1776).
3 City, Will co., NE Illinois, 15 m. S of Joliet; pop. 4210.
4 Town, Middlesex co., NE Massachusetts, 9 m. SE of Lowell; pop. 12,475.
5 City, ⊗ of New Hanover co., SE North Carolina, on Cape Fear river 30 m. N of its mouth; pop. 44,013; port of entry and commercial and railroad center; export trade in cotton, tobacco, peanuts, lumber, fertilizer, naval stores; shipyards and shipbuilding; petroleum products terminal; chemical industries; manufactures lumber, creosoting, fertilizer, textiles. Settled 1730; incorp. as town 1739; scene of armed resistance to Stamp Act 1765; occupied by Cornwallis 1781; chief port of entry for Confederate blockade runners during Civil War; surrendered following bombardment and capture of Fort Fisher by Federals 1865; chartered as city 1866.
6 City, ⊗ of Clinton co., SW Ohio, 29 m. SE of Dayton; pop. 8915; founded 1810; manufactures steel drill bits, bridges. Wilmington Coll. (1863; coed.; since 1917 merged with Lebanon National Normal Univ.); Clinton County Air Force Base.

Wil'more (wĭl'mōr). City, Jessamine co., E cen. Kentucky, 17 m. SW of Lexington; pop. 2773. Asbury Coll. (1890; coed.; Methodist).

Wilms'low (wĭlmz'lō; wĭmz'lō). Urban district, Cheshire, NW England, on the Bollin 12 m. S of Manchester; pop. 19,531.

Wilna. See VILNYUS.

Wil'no (vĭl'nō; *Pol.* vēl'nô). **1** Former Polish department, in NE part; 11,196 sq. m.; pop. 1,275,269; an area for several centuries of racial conflict bet. Lithuanians, Poles, and White Russians; in 1922 in region ceded by plebiscite to Poland; part ceded to Lithuania by Russia 1939.
2 City. See VILNYUS.

Wil'ryck (vĭl'rĭk). Commune, Antwerp prov., N Belgium; pop. (1938 est.) 25,752; S suburb of Antwerp.

Wil'son (wĭl's'n). **1** Name of counties in four states of the U.S. See *Tables* at KANSAS, NORTH CAROLINA, TENNESSEE, TEXAS.
2 Subdivision (est. pop. 2500) of town of WINDSOR, Connecticut.
3 City, ⊗ of Wilson co., E North Carolina, 18 m. SSW of Rocky Mount; pop. 28,753; tobacco market; in cotton and tobacco region; manufactures cotton yarns, cottonseed meal and oil, fertilizer, lumber, veneer, wagons. Atlantic Christian Coll. (1902; coed.).
4 City, Carter co., S Oklahoma, 20 m. W of Ardmore; pop. 1647; cottonseed-oil, flour, feed mills; cotton gin; oil and gas wells.
5 Borough, Northampton co., E Pennsylvania, 14 m. ENE of Allentown; pop. 8465; manufactures foundry products, knit goods, paper cups.

Wilson, Mount. 1 Peak 5704 ft. in San Gabriel Mts., Los Angeles co., SW California, just NE of Pasadena; Mount Wilson Observatory operated by the Carnegie Institution and possessing a 100-inch telescope.
2 Peak 14,250 ft. in San Juan Mts., Dolores co., SW Colorado.

Wilson Dam. Dam across Tennessee river, NW Alabama, forming **Lake Wilson** 15½ m. long submerging

Muscle Shoals. See TENNESSEE river; *Table* at TENNESSEE VALLEY AUTHORITY.

Wilson Peak. 1 Peak 14,026 ft. in San Miguel co., SW Colorado.

2 Mountain 13,095 ft. in E Summit co., NE Utah.

Wil′son′s Creek (wĭl′s′nz). Small stream near Springfield, Greene co., SW Missouri; battle Aug. 10, 1861 in which Confederates under Price defeated Federals under Lyon.

Wilson′s Promontory. Cape, S Victoria, most southerly point of Australia, 39°5′S.

Wil′ton (wĭl′t′n; -tŭn). **1** Residential and agricultural town, W Fairfield co., SW Connecticut, on New York border N of Norwalk; pop. 8026; settled 1701, incorp. 1802.

2 Town, Franklin co., W Maine, 29 m. NW of Augusta; pop. 3274.

3 Town, Hillsboro co., S New Hampshire, 15 m. WNW of Nashua; pop. 2025; summer resort; woolen and lumber mills.

4 Municipal borough, Wiltshire, S England; pop. 2857; Wilton rugs first manufactured here; former seat of kings of Wessex; battle 871 bet. Alfred the Great and the Danes.

Wilton Manor. Village, Broward co., SE Florida, NW of Fort Lauderdale; pop. 8257.

Wilt′shire (wĭlt′shĭr; -shēr) *or* **Wilts** (wĭlts). County, S England; area 1345 sq. m.; pop. (1951) 387,379; ⊗ Trowbridge; other towns Salisbury, Swindon, Wilton, Malmesbury, Devizes, Chippenham; rivers Avon, Kennet; agriculture, dairy farming, manufacturing (carpets, locomotives and rolling stock). Inhabitants are known as *moonrakers* from a story of rustics seeing the moon's reflection in water and attempting to rake it out.

Wim′ble·don (wĭm′b′l-dŭn). Municipal borough, Surrey, S England; SW suburb of London and part of Greater London; pop. 59,524, (1951 pop.) 58,158; known for its sports facilities, esp. for cricket and lawn tennis ("All-England") championships); ranges of National Rifle Association transferred from here to Bisley 1890.

Wim′borne (wĭm′bôrn). Town and urban district, Dorsetshire, S England, ab. 7 m. NNW of Bournemouth; pop. (1951) 4488; important in Anglo-Saxon times; college (founded 1043) and church (Wimborne Minster).

Wim′mer·a (wĭm′ēr·à). **1** River 228 m. long, W Victoria, SE Australia; flows N into Lake Hindmarsh.

2 District, W Victoria, SE Australia, S of Murray river.

Win′a·mac (wĭn′à·măk). Town, ⊗ of Pulaski co., NW Indiana, 23 m. W of Logansport; pop. 2375.

Win′burg (wĭn′bûrg). Town, cen. Orange Free State, E cen. Union of South Africa, 65 m. NE of Bloemfontein; pop. 3722. Founded 1836.

Win′chell, Mount (wĭn′chĕl). Peak 13,749 ft. high in the Sierra Nevada, California, on boundary bet. Fresno and Inyo cos.

Win′chel·sea (wĭn′chĕl·sĭ). Village, East Sussex, S England, near coast just SW of Rye and ab. 9 m. NE of Hastings; famous seaport 13th–15th cents., one of the Cinque Ports (*q.v.*); remains of Church of St. Thomas à Becket include chancel and aisles in beautiful Decorated style.

Win′chen·don (wĭn′chĕn·dŭn). Town, Worcester co., cen. Massachusetts, 14 m. WNW of Fitchburg; pop. 6237; manufactures toys.

Win′ches′ter (wĭn′chĕs′tēr; -chĭs·tēr). **1** Manufacturing town, NE Litchfield co., NW Connecticut, N of Torrington; pop. 10,496; incorp. 1771; in lake and forest region of Litchfield hills; watered by Mad and Still rivers; includes city of Winsted (*q.v.*).

2 City, ⊗ of Scott co., W Illinois, 45 m. WSW of Springfield; pop. 1657.

3 City, ⊗ of Randolph co., E Indiana, 20 m. E of Muncie; pop. 5742; glass manufactories.

4 City, ⊗ of Clark co., E cen. Kentucky, 20 m. E of Lexington; pop. 10,187; in bluegrass section; agricultural

trading center; tobacco and livestock market; petroleum and natural-gas deposits nearby. Kentucky Wesleyan Coll. (1866; coed.; Methodist).

5 Residential town, Middlesex co., NE Massachusetts, 8 m. NW of Boston; pop. 19,376.

6 Town, Cheshire co., SW corner of New Hampshire, on Ashuelot river 12 m. SSW of Keene; pop. 2411; settled 1732; state fish hatchery nearby.

7 Town, ⊗ of Franklin co., S Tennessee, 25 m. E of Fayetteville; pop. 4760; dairy products, canned goods, flour, patent medicines; mining, lumbering.

8 City, ⊗ of Frederick co. (but politically independent), N Virginia, in Shenandoah Valley 70 m. WNW of Alexandria; 4 sq. m.; pop. 15,110; manufactures cider, vinegar, and other apple products, woolens, knit goods, brick; apple-growing center. Site of National and Confederate cemeteries. Founded 1744; headquarters of George Washington (who started career here as surveyor 1748) after Braddock's defeat in 1755; Fort Loudoun built by Washington in French and Indian War 1756–57; incorp. as town 1779, as city 1874; strategic point in Civil War; battles May 25, 1862 and Sept. 19, 1864 (the latter sometimes known as battle of Opequon Creek).

9 *anc.* **Ven′ta Bel·ga′rum** (vĕn′tà bĕl·gâr′ŭm). Municipal borough, ⊗ of Hampshire, S England, on the Itchin 21 m. NNW of Portsmouth; pop. 25,710; cathedral. Ancient capital of Wessex and seat of government of Alfred the Great, Canute (who is buried here), and, with London, of William the Conqueror; known formerly as a seat of learning. Winchester Coll. was founded by William of Wykeham in 1387.

Wind (wĭnd). River ab. 120 m. long, W cen. Wyoming; rises in NW Fremont co., flows SE along E slopes of Wind River Range and unites with Popo Agie river in cen. Fremont co. to form Big Horn river.

Windau. 1 River. See VENTA.

2 City. See VENTSPILS.

Wind′ber (wĭn[d]′bēr). Borough, Somerset co., S Pennsylvania, 8 m. SE of Johnstown; pop. 6994; soft-coal mines; brick and lumber yards.

Wind Cave National Park (wĭnd). See UNITED STATES, *National Parks*.

Win′der (wĭn′dēr). City, ⊗ of Barrow co., N Georgia, 20 m. W of Athens; pop. 5555; incorp. 1893; scene of a skirmish Aug. 3, 1864 during the Civil War; textile mills.

Win′der·mere (wĭn′dēr·mēr). **1** Lake 10½ m. long in the Lake District, NW England, on border bet. Westmorland and Lancashire; maximum depth 219 ft.; largest lake in England.

2 Urban district, Westmorland, NW England, on Lake Windermere 33 m. S of Carlisle; pop. 6306.

Wind′ham (wĭn′dăm). **1** Name of counties in two states of the U.S. See *Tables* at CONNECTICUT and VERMONT.

2 Town, SW Windham co., NE Connecticut; pop. 16,973; watered by Willimantic, Natchaug, and Shetucket rivers; incorp. 1692; agriculture, manufacturing; includes industrial city of Willimantic (*q.v.*).

3 Town, Cumberland co., SW Maine, 15 m. NW of Portland; pop. 4498.

Wind′hoek (vĭnt′hook). Town, * of South-West Africa, in cen. part, 400 m. N of mouth of Orange river; pop. (1936) 10,585; in good pasturage region at elevation of 5428 ft.; lead, silver, copper, and salt found in vicinity; important educational center.

Win′dle·sham (wĭn′d′l-shăm; *formerly* wĭn′săm). Former urban district, Surrey, S England; pop. (1931) 5257.

Win′dom (wĭn′dŭm). City, ⊗ of Cottonwood co., SW Minnesota, 30 m. NE of Worthington; pop. 3691.

Windom Peak. Mountain 14,091 ft. in La Plata co., SW Colorado.

Wind River. See WIND.

Wind River Range (wĭnd). Range of the Rocky Mts. in W cen. Wyoming, extending along the boundary bet. Sublette and Fremont cos.; highest point Gannett Peak 13,785 ft.

Wind′sor (wĭn′zẽr). **1** County in Vermont. See *Table* at VERMONT.
2 Town, Weld co., N Colorado; pop. 1509.
3 Town, N cen. Hartford co., N Connecticut, on Connecticut river N of Hartford; pop. 19,467; in region growing tobacco, tomatoes, and squash; sorts and packs tobacco, cans tomatoes; has machine shops and brickyards; manufactures airplanes. Settled 1635 by colonists from Massachusetts Bay Colony; named in 1637.
4 City, Henry co., W Missouri; pop. 2714.
5 Town, ⊗ of Bertie co., NE North Carolina, 15 m. W of Albemarle Sound; pop. 1813; former port of entry; grows cotton, tobacco, peanuts; manufactures lumber, barrels.
6 Village in Windsor town (pop. 4468), Windsor co., E Vermont, on Connecticut river 13 m. N of Springfield; pop. 3256; settled 1764.
7 Former town, Queensland, Australia, now part of Brisbane.
8 Town, ⊗ of Hants co., cen. Nova Scotia, Canada, on inlet of Minas Basin 37 m. NW of Halifax; pop. 3439; locale of large gypsum quarries and noted for tremendous tides, sometimes reaching 50 feet. Once contained King's Coll., oldest (1789) English college in Canada, now part of Dalhousie Univ. in Halifax. Settled as Pisiquid by the French in 1710; into English hands in 1750 just before expulsion of Acadians 1755; renamed Windsor 1764. Home of public fair, chartered 1815, probably oldest in America; birthplace and home of Thomas C. Haliburton.
9 Industrial city, ⊗ of Essex co., SE Ontario, Canada, on Detroit river opp. Detroit, Michigan; pop. 120,049; important railroad terminus; has large flour mills; chief automobile-manufacturing city of Canada; outlet for fertile farming district; connected with Detroit by tunnel (1 m. long, built 1928–30) and Ambassador Bridge. Has one of Canada's chief airports. Founded 1834 on land that was earlier a mission station and trading post; in 1935 annexed three adjacent urban areas—the city of East Windsor and the towns of Sandwich and Walkerville.
10 Town, Richmond co., S Quebec, Canada, on St. Francis river 12 m. N of Sherbrooke; pop. 4714; has large pulp and paper mill; settled c. 1800.
11 *officially* **New Windsor**. Municipal borough, Berkshire, S England, on the Thames 20 m. W of London; pop. 23,181; seat of Windsor Castle, principal residence of England's sovereigns since the time of William the Conqueror; St. George's Chapel, burial place of many English kings; to the S is a park ab. 1500 acres.
12 Town, cen. Newfoundland, near Grand Falls; pop. (1951) 3674.
Windsor Heights. Town, Polk co., S cen. Iowa, W of Des Moines; pop. 5906.
Windsor Locks. Industrial town, NE Hartford co., N Connecticut, on Connecticut river S of Suffield; pop. 11,411; settled c. 1663, incorp. 1854; named from locks in canal (completed 1828) to take traffic around Connecticut river rapids and to provide water power. In farming and tobacco-growing region; manufactures silk, cotton yarns, knit goods, paper, machinery, lathe chucks; tobacco sorting and packing. Bradley Field, airport.
Wind′ward Islands (wĭnd′wẽrd). **1** The islands forming the southern chain of the Lesser Antilles, West Indies, extending from Martinique S to 12°N; they do not include Barbados, Trinidad, and Tobago. See LEEWARD ISLANDS.
2 Division of the West Indies Federation comprising the territories of St. Lucia, St. Vincent, and Grenada in the Windward Is. group (see **1**, above), and Dominica in the Leeward Is.; total area 821 sq. m.; pop. ab. 260,000; administrative ✳ St. George's, on the island of Grenada.
3 *Fr.* **Îles du Vent** (ēl′ dü väɴ′). Eastern group in the Society Is., French Polynesia, S Pacific Ocean; chief islands Tahiti and Moorea.
Windward Passage. Channel bet. the E end of Cuba and the NW tip of Hispaniola.

Wind′y Butte (wĭn′dĭ). Isolated peak 3563 ft. in Fall River co., SW corner of South Dakota.
Wind′y·gate Hill (wĭn′dĭ·gĭt; -gāt). Peak 2034 ft. in the Cheviot Hills along the border bet. England and Scotland.
Wineland. See VINLAND.
Win′field (wĭn′fēld). **1** City, ⊗ of Cowley co., S Kansas, 13 m. N of Arkansas City; pop. 11,117; railroad and trade center in agricultural, livestock-raising, and oil-producing area. Southwestern Coll. (1885; coed.; Methodist).
2 Town, ⊗ of Putnam co., W West Virginia; pop. 318.
Wing′ham (wĭng′ăm). Industrial town, Huron co., SE Ontario, Canada, 24 m. ENE of Goderich; pop. 2642; a grain-shipping center; has varied manufactures.
Win′isk (wĭn′ĭsk). River ab. 400 m. long in N cen. Ontario prov., Canada; flows N and NW into Hudson Bay.
Wink (wĭngk). City, Winkler co., W Texas, 33 m. NNE of Pecos; pop. 1863; oil wells; stock raising.
Wink′ler (wĭngk′lẽr). County in Texas. See *Table* at TEXAS.
Winn (wĭn). Parish in Louisiana. See *Table* at LOUISIANA.
Win·ne′ba (?wĭ·nā′bȧ). Coast town, S Ghana, W Africa, ab. 35 m. WSW of Accra; pop. 10,926.
Win′ne·ba′go (wĭn′ĕ·bā′gō). **1** Name of counties in three states of the U.S. See *Tables* at ILLINOIS, IOWA, WISCONSIN.
2 Village, Faribault co., S Minnesota, 17 m. ENE of Fairmont; pop. 2088.
Winnebago, Lake. Lake in E Wisconsin, bounded by Winnebago, Calumet, and Fond du Lac cos.; ab. 30 m. long and 10 m. wide at its greatest extent; the Fox river enters from the W and flows out from the N. The cities of Menasha, Oshkosh, Fond du Lac, and Neenah are on its shores.
Win′ne·muc′ca (wĭn′ĕ·mŭk′ȧ). City, ⊗ of Humboldt co., NW Nevada, on Humboldt river 77 m. NE of Humboldt Lake; pop. 3453; in mining and cattle-raising area; smelters; ships cattle and sheep.
Winnemucca Lake. Lake ab. 20 m. long in NW Nevada, ab. 6 m. E of Pyramid Lake; often dry.
Win′ner (wĭn′ẽr). City, ⊗ of Tripp co., S South Dakota, 33 m. SW of confluence of White and Missouri rivers; pop. 3705; agriculture; livestock raising.
Win′ne·sheik (wĭn′ĕ·shēk). County in Iowa. See *Table* at IOWA.
Win·net′ka (wĭ·nĕt′kȧ). Residential village, Cook co., NE Illinois, 19 m. N of Chicago; pop. 13,368; famous school system.
Win′nett (wĭn′ĕt; -ĭt). Town, ⊗ of Petroleum co., cen. Montana; pop. 360.
Winn′field (wĭn′fēld). City, ⊗ of Winn parish, N cen. Louisiana, 45 m. N of Alexandria; pop. 7022; limestone quarries, salt pits, lumber.
Win′ni·bi·go′shish Lake (wĭn′ĭ·bĭ·gō′shĭsh). Lake on boundary of Itasca and Cass cos., N cen. Minnesota; ab. 14 m. long.
Win′ni·peg (wĭn′ĭ·pĕg). **1** River 140 m. long, SW Ontario and SE Manitoba, Canada; outlet of Lake of the Woods flowing NW to SE part of Lake Winnipeg. Near Ontario border receives tributary, English river, outlet of a number of large lakes in SW Ontario.
2 City, ✳ of Manitoba, Canada, at confluence of Assiniboine and Red rivers and 45 m. S of Lake Winnipeg; pop. 235,710; largest grain market in British Empire; extensive train yards; important cattle market; flour and grist milling, slaughtering, meat packing; dairy produce; foundry and machine-shop products, lumber products; printing and publishing. Has large airport. Seat of Univ. of Manitoba (1877; coed.); United Coll. (1938; coed.; formed by union of Manitoba and Wesley Colleges), part of Univ. of Manitoba. Music festival held here every spring. Founded 1860 on the site of Fort Rouge, erected in 1738; followed 1806 by Fort Gibraltar and 1821 by Fort Garry.

WISCONSIN

Statute Miles

0 10 20 30 40 50

⊛ State Capital

PUBLISHED BY G. & C. MERRIAM COMPANY
SPRINGFIELD, MASS.
PREPARED BY J. W. CLEMENT CO., BUFFALO, N.Y.

Winnipeg, Lake. Lake 9460 sq. m., 275 m. long, S cen. Manitoba, Canada; receives the Red and Winnipeg rivers in the S and the Saskatchewan in the N; outlet is the Nelson. Remnant of Lake Agassiz, ancient Pleistocene lake. Much boating and fishing in the summer. Discovered by the La Vérendryes in 1733.

Win′ni·peg·o′sis, Lake (wĭn′ĭ·pĕg·ō′sĭs). Lake 2086 sq. m., ab. 122 m. long, W Manitoba, Canada, W of Lake Winnipeg; connects with Lake Manitoba.

Win′ni·pe·sau′kee (wĭn′ĭ·pĕ·sô′kĕ); formerly **Win′ne·pe·sau′kee** (wĭn′ĕ-). Short river, cen. New Hampshire; flows SW out of Lake Winnipesaukee to unite with the Pemigewasset river at Franklin and form the Merrimack river.

Winnipesaukee, Lake; formerly **Winnepesaukee.** Lake in cen. New Hampshire, in Carroll and Belknap cos.; largest lake in New Hampshire, 71 sq. m., 25 m. long; summer resort.

Win′nis·quam Lake (wĭn′ĭs·kwŏm). Lake in Belknap co., cen. New Hampshire, W of Lake Winnipesaukee.

Winns′bor′o (wĭnz′bŭr′ō). **1** Town, ⊗ of Franklin parish, NE Louisiana, 33 m. SE of Monroe; pop. 4437; trade center; cotton gins, sawmills.

2 City, ⊗ of Fairfield co., N cen. South Carolina, 27 m. N of Columbia; pop. 3479; settled c. 1755; in cotton-growing section; manufactures cord for automobile tires, textiles; granite works.

3 City, Franklin and Wood cos., NE Texas, 40 m. N of Tyler; pop. 2675; manufactures pottery, lumber.

Wi·no′na (wĭ·nō′nà). **1** County in Minnesota. See *Table* at MINNESOTA.

2 City, ⊗ of Winona co., SE Minnesota, on Mississippi river 40 m. E of Rochester; pop. 24,895; former lumbering and wheat-shipping center; trading center for agricultural section; limestone quarries, brickworks, meatpacking plants. Winona State Coll. (1858; coed.); Coll. of St. Teresa (1907; women; Roman Catholic); St. Mary's Coll. (1912; men; Roman Catholic).

3 City, ⊗ of Montgomery co., N cen. Mississippi, 25 m. E of Greenwood; pop. 4282; in cotton and livestock-raising section; shipping point for cotton; cotton gins, cottonseed-oil mills.

Wi·noos′ki (wĭ·nōōs′kĭ). **1** or **On′ion** (ŭn′yŭn). River ab. 100 m. long, N cen. Vermont; rises in NE Vermont, flows S to Montpelier, turns NW into Lake Champlain in W Chittenden co.

2 Industrial city, Chittenden co., NW Vermont, on Winooski river 3 m. NE of Burlington; pop. 7420; settled 1787; manufactures textiles, screens, furniture, doors and sash. St. Michael's Coll. (1904; men; Roman Catholic).

Win′scho′ten (vĭn′sĸō′tĕ[n]). Commune, Groningen prov., NE Netherlands, 19 m. ESE of Groningen, near German border; pop. 13,342.

Winschoten Canal. Canal 18 m. long in NE Netherlands, in Groningen prov., joining the city of Groningen with the Dollart.

Wins′ford (wĭnz′fĕrd). Urban district, Cheshire, NW England, on the Weaver river 23 m. SE of Liverpool; pop. 12,745.

Wins′low (wĭnz′lō). **1** City, Navajo co., NE Arizona, near Little Colorado river 58 m. E of Flagstaff; pop. 8862; stock raising; settled 1882.

2 Town, Kennebec co., SW Maine, SE suburb of Waterville; pop. 5891.

Win′sor Dam (wĭn′zẽr). See UNITED STATES, *Dams and Reservoirs.*

Win′sted (wĭn′stĕd; -stĭd). Manufacturing city (pop. 8136) in town of WINCHESTER, Connecticut; settled 1758, incorp. as borough 1858, as city 1917; resort and commercial center; manufactures hosiery, cutlery, clocks, spool silk, knit goods, wire, chairs.

Win′ston (wĭn′stŭn). Name of counties in two states of the U.S. See *Tables* at ALABAMA and MISSISSIPPI.

Winston–Sa′lem (-sā′lĕm). Industrial city, ⊗ of Forsyth co., N cen. North Carolina, in piedmont section 68 m. NNE of Charlotte; pop. 111,135; Salem (founded by Moravian church colony 1766; incorp. 1856–57) and Winston (estab. 1849; incorp. 1859) consolidated as Winston-Salem 1913. Leaf-tobacco market; manufactures tobacco products (esp. cigarettes), textiles and knit goods, woolen blankets, furniture, air-conditioning machinery, wagons. Salem Coll. (1888; women); Winston-Salem State Coll. (1892; coed.); Wake Forest Coll. (1833; coed.).

Win′ter·berg (wĭn′tẽr·bûrg). Mountains, SE Cape Province, Republic of South Africa; highest 7778 ft.

Winter Garden. City, Orange co., cen. Florida penin., 12 m. W of Orlando; pop. 5513; citrus-fruit packing.

Winter Haven. City, Polk co., cen. Florida penin., 15 m. E of Lakeland; pop. 16,277; citrus-fruit packing.

Winter Park. Resort city, Orange co., cen. Florida penin., 5 m. NE of Orlando; pop. 17,162; founded as Lakeview 1858, name changed to Osceola 1870, and Winter Park 1881. Rollins Coll. (1885; coed.).

Win′ter·port (wĭn′tẽr·pōrt). Town, Waldo co., S Maine, on Penobscot river 12 m. S of Bangor; pop. 2088.

Win′ters (wĭn′tẽrz). City, Runnels co., W cen. Texas, 37 m. S of Abilene; pop. 3266.

Win′ter·set (wĭn′tẽr·sĕt). City, ⊗ of Madison co., S cen. Iowa, 30 m. SW of Des Moines; pop. 3639; in agricultural and livestock-raising section.

Win′ters·wijk′ (vĭn′tẽrs·vĭk′). Commune, Gelderland prov., E Netherlands, ab. 33 m. E of Arnhem near German border; pop. 17,939.

Win′ter·thur′ (vĭn′tẽr·tōōr′). Industrial commune, Zurich canton, NE cen. Switzerland, 12 m. NE of Zurich; pop. (1941) 58,883; important railroad junction; 16th-cent. late-Gothic church; old town hall; manufactures machinery, silk and cotton goods. Passed to Hapsburg family 1264; made imperial city 1415; reverted to Hapsburgs 1442; to Zurich 1467.

Win′throp (wĭn′thrŭp). **1** Town, Kennebec co., SW Maine, 10 m. W of Augusta; pop. 3537; oilcloth and woolen mills.

2 Town, Suffolk co., E Massachusetts, 4 m. ENE of Boston; pop. 20,303; summer resort and yachting center.

Win′ton (wĭn′t'n; -tŭn). **1** Town, ⊗ of Hertford co., NE North Carolina, 43 m. W of Elizabeth City; pop. 835.

2 Borough, Lackawanna co., NE Pennsylvania, 9 m. NE of Scranton; pop. 5456; coal mining, silk manufactures.

Win′yah Bay (wĭn′yô). Inlet of Atlantic Ocean on SE coast of Georgetown co., E South Carolina, receiving the Black river on the NW and the Pee Dee river on the N.

Wi′pers (wī′pẽrz). Common British Army spelling and pronunciation of *Ypres* (see IEPER).

Wirt (wûrt). County in West Virginia. See *Table* at WEST VIRGINIA.

Wi′ru (vĭ′rōō). = VIRU.

Wis′bech (wĭz′bēch). Municipal borough, Isle of Ely, E England, on the Nene 83 m. N of London; pop. 17,430; agricultural center; seaport.

Wisby. See VISBY.

Wis·cas′set (wĭs·kăs′ĕt; -ĭt). Seaport town, ⊗ of Lincoln co., S Maine; pop. 1800; picturesque town with good harbor; artist resort. Settled 1734.

Wisch (vĭs). Commune, Gelderland prov., E Netherlands, E of Arnhem near German border; pop. 10,679.

Wis·con′sin (wĭs·kŏn′s'n; -sĭn). **1** River 430 m. long, cen. and SW Wisconsin; rises in Lac Vieux Desert in N Vilas co., flows S through cen. Wisconsin, turns W and enters Mississippi river on boundary line bet. Crawford and Grant cos.; navigation, difficult because of shifting sandbars, is possible for small craft for ab. 200 m. See FOX river.

2 A northern state of U.S.A., 30th state admitted to Union (1848); bounded on N by Lakes Superior and Michigan, on E by Lake Michigan, on S by Illinois, and on W by Iowa and Minnesota; 26th state in area, 56,154 sq. m. (land area 54,705 sq. m.); in addition to this Wisconsin has 10,062 sq. m. of water of Lake Michigan; 15th state

in population, 3,951,777; ✳ Madison. See *Table of States* at UNITED STATES. Divided (until 1961—see Footnote 4, below) into the following 71 counties (for their pronunciations, see individual entries):

NAME	LOCATION	AREA[1]	POP.[1]	CO. SEAT
Adams	cen.	677	7,566	Friendship
Ashland	N	1,037[1]	17,375	Ashland
Barron	NW	866	34,270	Barron
Bayfield	NW	1,474[2]	11,910	Washburn
Brown	E	525	125,082	Green Bay
Buffalo	W	712	14,202	Alma
Burnett	NW	840	9,214	Grantsburg
Calumet	E[3]	315	22,268	Chilton
Chippewa	W	1,025	45,096	Chippewa Falls
Clark	Wcen.	1,222	31,527	Neillsville
Columbia	S cen.	778	36,708	Portage
Crawford	SW	586	16,351	Prairie du Chien
Dane	S	1,197	222,095	Madison
Dodge	SE cen.	892	63,170	Juneau
Door	NE	491	20,685	Sturgeon Bay
Douglas	NW corner	1,310	45,008	Superior
Dunn	W	858	26,156	Menomonie
Eau Claire	W	649	58,300	Eau Claire
Florence	NE	489	3,437	Florence
Fond du Lac	E[3]	724	75,085	Fond du Lac
Forest	NE	1,010	7,542	Crandon
Grant	SW corner	1,168	44,419	Lancaster
Green	S	586	25,851	Monroe
Green Lake	cen.	355	15,418	Green Lake
Iowa	SW	761	19,631	Dodgeville
Iron	N	746	7,830	Hurley
Jackson	W cen.	1,000	15,151	Black River Falls
Jefferson	SE	564	50,094	Jefferson
Juneau	cen.	795	17,490	Mauston
Kenosha	SE corner	273	100,615	Kenosha
Kewaunee	E	331	18,282	Kewaunee
La Crosse	W	469	72,465	La Crosse
Lafayette	S	643	18,142	Darlington
Langlade[4]	NE	858	19,916	Antigo
Lincoln	N	900	22,338	Merrill
Manitowoc	E	589	75,215	Manitowoc
Marathon	cen.	1,584	88,874	Wausau
Marinette	NE	1,388	34,660	Marinette
Marquette	cen.	457	8,516	Montello
Milwaukee	SE	239	1,036,041	Milwaukee
Monroe	W cen.	915	31,241	Sparta
Oconto[4]	NE	1,106	25,110	Oconto
Oneida	N	1,114	22,112	Rhinelander
Outagamie	E	634	101,794	Appleton
Ozaukee	E	235	38,441	Port Washington
Pepin	W	237	7,332	Durand
Pierce	W	591	22,503	Ellsworth
Polk	NW	934	24,968	Balsam Lake
Portage	cen.	810	36,964	Stevens Point
Price	N	1,268	14,370	Phillips
Racine	SE	337	141,781	Racine
Richland	SW	584	17,684	Richland Center
Rock	S	721	113,913	Janesville
Rusk	NW	910	14,794	Ladysmith
Saint Croix	W	736	29,164	Hudson
Sauk	S cen.	840	36,179	Baraboo
Sawyer	NW	1,273	9,475	Hayward
Shawano[4]	E cen.	1,176	34,351	Shawano
Sheboygan	E	506	86,484	Sheboygan
Taylor	W	979	17,843	Medford
Trempealeau	W	739	23,377	Whitehall
Vernon	SW	805	25,663	Viroqua
Vilas	N	867	9,332	Eagle River
Walworth	S	560	52,368	Elkhorn
Washburn	NW	816	10,301	Shell Lake
Washington	SE	428	46,119	West Bend
Waukesha	SE	556	158,249	Waukesha
Waupaca	E cen.	751	35,340	Waupaca
Waushara	cen.	628	13,497	Wautoma
Winnebago	E[3]	454	107,928	Oshkosh
Wood	cen.	812	59,105	Wisconsin Rapids

[1] Area = land area in sq. m. Pop. from 1960 Census.
[2] Most of Apostle Is. in Ashland co., rest in Bayfield co.
[3] Upper (larger) part of Lake Winnebago in Winnebago and Calumet cos., lower part in Fond du Lac co.
[4] The Menominee Indian reservation, formerly in parts of Langlade, Oconto, and Shawano counties, was constituted the county of Menominee May 1, 1961.

Nickname: Badger State. *State flower:* Violet. *Motto:* Forward. *Chief cities:* Milwaukee, Madison, Racine, West Allis, Kenosha. *Rivers:* Mississippi, forming lower W boundary; St. Croix (forming section of upper W boundary), Wisconsin (see 1, above), Black, and Chippewa rivers flowing into the Mississippi; Menominee, forming NE boundary. *Lakes:* Winnebago in E; Mendota in S. *Highest point:* Rib Mt. 1940 ft., in Marathon co. in cen. area. *Chief industries:* Agriculture (oats,

corn, barley, wheat), stock raising, lumbering, mining (esp. zinc), dairying.

History: Area visited by Jean Nicolet 1634; first permanent settlement 1717; French settlement at Green Bay 1745; French claim ceded to Great Britain 1763; recognized by Great Britain as part of United States 1783; claims relinquished by Virginia 1784, Massachusetts 1785, Connecticut 1786; part of Northwest Territory 1787 and of Indiana Territory 1800; Wisconsin Territory organized 1836; admitted to Union May 29, 1848.

Wisconsin Dells. City, Columbia co., S cen. Wisconsin, on Wisconsin river; pop. 2105; tourist resort.

Wisconsin Rapids. City, ⊗ of Wood co., cen. Wisconsin, on Wisconsin Rapids 40 m. S of Wausau; pop. 15,042; railroad center; manufactures paper, dairy products, refrigeration equipment.

Wise (wīz). **1** Name of counties in two states of the U.S. See *Tables* at TEXAS and VIRGINIA.
2 Town, ⊗ of Wise co., SW Virginia; pop. 2614.

Wish'ek (wĭsh'ĭk). City, McIntosh co., S North Dakota, 63 m. SW of Jamestown; pop. 1290; wheat, flax.

Wish'kah (wĭsh'kȧ) *or* **Wy·noo'che** (wĭ·nōō'chê). River 40 m. long, W Washington; flows S in Grays Harbor co. into Chehalis river near its mouth.

Wisła. See VISTULA.

Wis·ło'ka (vēs·lô'kä). River ab. 125 m. long, Rzeszów dept., SE Poland; flows N from Carpathian Mts. to the Vistula.

Wis'mar. **1** (wĭz'mär) Town, N British Guiana, in Demerara co., on Demerara river ab. 50 m. S of Georgetown.
2 (vĭs'mär) Seaport and manufacturing city, Mecklenburg, Germany, on **Wismar Bay** (arm of Bay of Mecklenburg) 19 m. N of Schwerin; pop. 26,016; manufactures vehicles and airplanes, machinery, sugar; fisheries; important shipping center; trades in coal, potatoes, wood, sugar beets, sugar, paper, cattle. First mentioned as city 1229; free Hanse city 13th cent.; to Sweden 1649, Denmark 1675; to Mecklenburg-Schwerin 1828. In World War II taken by British forces May 4, 1945.

Wis'sa·hick'on Creek(wĭs'ȧ·hĭk'ŭn). Short stream, SE Pennsylvania; flows SE through Whitemarsh to Schuylkill river in Philadelphia; furnished power for mills before the Revolution, esp. first paper mill in America 1690.

Wis'sem'bourg' *or* **Weis'sen·burg** (vē'sĕn'bōōr') (vī'sĕn·bŏŏrk). Town, Bas-Rhin dept., NE France, ab. 40 m. NE of Strasbourg; pop. 5738; 13th-cent. church of the Benedictine abbey founded 7th cent. by Dagobert II; place where Otfrid completed his Old High German poetical version of the life of Jesus c. 868; scene of two battles: (1) Oct. 1793 in which Count Wurmser was defeated by the French; (2) Aug. 4, 1870 in which Prussians defeated the French under MacMahon.

Wis·so'ta, Lake (wĭ·sō'tȧ). Lake in S Chippewa co., W Wisconsin.

Wis'ter, Mount (wĭs'tēr). Peak 11,480 ft. in cen. Grand Teton National Park, NW Wyoming.

Wit'bank (wĭt'băngk). Town, S cen. Transvaal, NE Union of South Africa, 60 m. E of Pretoria; pop. 8263; center of large coal-mining industry; carbide factory.

With'am (wĭth'ăm). River 80 m. long in E England; rises in Rutlandshire, flows N into Lincolnshire, passing Grantham and Lincoln, turns SE and continues past Boston into the Wash.

With'la·coo'chee (wĭth'lȧ·kōō'chê). **1** River ab. 120 m. long, W Florida penin.; forms boundary bet. Levy and Citrus cos. and empties into Gulf of Mexico; outlet for Lake Tsala Apopka in Citrus co.
2 River ab. 110 m. long, N Florida; rises in S Georgia, flows S across state border forming Madison-Hamilton co. boundary and empties into Suwannee river.

Witkowitz. See VÍTKOVICE.

Wit'ney (wĭt'nĭ). Urban district, Oxfordshire, cen. England, ab. 60 m. WNW of London; pop. (1951) 6553; very old blanket-making industry.

Wit'tels'heim' (vĕ'tĕl'zĕm'; *Ger.* vĭt'ĕls·hīm). Commune, Haut-Rhin dept., NE France, pop. (1931) 7105; potash mines.

Wit'ten (vĭt'ĕn). Industrial city, in North Rhine-Westphalia state, West Germany, on Ruhr river 9 m. SW of Dortmund; pop. 45,295; iron goods, glass, refractories.

Wit'ten·berg (wĭt''n·bûrg; *Ger.* vĭt'ĕn·bĕrK). Manufacturing city, East Germany, in former Saxony prov. of Prussia, on the right bank of the Elbe river 19 m. E of Dessau; pop. 23,457; railroad junction; manufactures include machinery, textiles, paper, hosiery, spirits, leather, soap powder, pottery, electrical apparatus, cement; famous as home of the Reformation (1517) and as the residence of Luther, Melanchthon, and Bugenhagen; numerous historical structures connected with the Reformation, including the 15th-cent. Schlosskirche (castle church) to the door of which Luther nailed his 95 theses, the Stadtkirche (city church) in which Luther preached, the remains of the 16th-cent. Augustinian monastery in which Luther lived, and the home of Melanchthon; university (joined to Halle 1817) in which Luther taught. First mentioned 1180; became city 1293; residence of dukes and electors of Saxe-Wittenberg to 1422; to Prussia 1815. In World War II taken by Russian forces Apr. 27, 1945.

Wit'ten·berg, Mount (wĭt''n·bûrg). Peak 3802 ft. in the Catskill Mts., Ulster co., SE New York.

Wit'ten·ber'ge (vĭt'ĕn·bĕr'gĕ). Industrial city, East Germany, in Brandenburg, on Elbe river 80 m. SE of Hamburg and 78 m. NW of Berlin; pop. 25,652; river port. Taken by Russians and held as key point in last days of World War II May 1945.

Wit'ten'heim' (vĕ'tĕ'nĕm'; *Ger.* vĭt'ĕn·hīm). Commune, Haut-Rhin dept., NE France, near Mulhouse; pop. (1931) 7053; potash mines.

Witt'stock (wĭt'stŏk; *Ger.* vĭt'shtôk). Town, N Brandenburg, East Germany, 58 m. NW of Berlin; pop. (1933) 8313; scene of battle Oct. 4, 1636 in which Swedes under Banér defeated imperial and Saxon forces.

Wi'tu (wē'tōō). **1** Protected sultanate in E Coast Province, Kenya Protectorate, E Africa; ab. 1200 sq. m. Proclaimed German protectorate 1885, but given up to British in agreement of 1890.
2 Town, its ✱, near the mouth of the Tana river.

Wit·wa'ters·rand (wĭt·wô'tĕrz·rănd; -wŏt'ĕrz-), *colloquially* **the Rand** (rănd). A ridge of auriferous rock ab. 62 m. long and 23 m. wide, S Transvaal, NE Union of South Africa. Johannesburg located nearly at its center. Watershed for streams on N to Olifants river and on S to Vaal. Richest gold fields in world; gold first discovered 1886; deepest mine shaft 7630 ft.

Wling'i (vlĭng'ē). Town, East Java prov., Indonesia, ab. 20 m. W of Malang; pop. 10,383.

Wło·cła'wek (vlô·tslä'vĕk); *Russ.* **Vlo·tslavsk'** (vlŭ-tslȧfsk'). Commune, Pomorze dept., N cen. Poland, on Vistula river 87 m. WNW of Warsaw; pop. (1938–39 est.) 66,739; Roman Catholic episcopal see; 14th-cent. cathedral; manufactures paper, machinery, stoneware, brick and tile, organs, beer. Founded at end of 11th cent.; Russians defeated here 1914; held by Germans 1941–45.

Wło·da'wa (vlô·dä'vä); *Russ.* **Vlo·da'va** (vlŭ·dȧ'vȧ). Commune, Lublin prov., E Poland, on W bank of the Bug 36 m. S of Brest; pop. 8519; battle Aug. 15, 1915.

Włodzimierz. See VLADIMIR VOLYNSK.

Wo'burn. **1** (wō'bĕrn; wōō'-) City, Middlesex co., NE Massachusetts, 10 m. NNW of Boston; pop. 31,214; leather and leather goods, machinery, chemicals.
2 (wōō'bĕrn) Parish, Bedfordshire, SE cen. England; pop. 1062; estate of duke of Bedford.

Woer'den (vōōr'dĕ[n]). Commune, South Holland prov., SW Netherlands, just W of Utrecht; pop. 7649.

Woë'vre (vwä'vr'). Plateau E of Verdun, NE France, extending N and S parallel with the Meuse for 15 to 20 m.; many battles in World War I, 1914–18, esp. artillery duels.

Woh'len (vō'lĕn). Commune, Aargau canton, Switzerland; pop. (1930) 5862; center of straw-hat industry.

Wo'kam (wō'käm). Island ab. 30 m. by 35 m., N cen. Aru Is., Indonesia, N of Kobroor I.

Wo'king (wō'kĭng). Urban district, Surrey, S England, on the Wey 22 m. WSW of London; pop. 47,612; vacation resort.

Wo'king·ham (wō'kĭng·ăm). Municipal borough, Berkshire, S England, 32 m. WSW of London; pop. 8716.

Wol'cott (wōōl'cŭt). Town, N New Haven co., S Connecticut, NE of Waterbury; pop. 8889; incorp. 1796.

Wolds, the (wōldz). Highland plain district in NE England, esp. in E Yorkshire and NE Lincolnshire, on both sides of the Humber.

Wo'le·ai' (wō'lä·ī'). Island (atoll), W Caroline Is., W Pacific, 7°23'N lat. and 144°E long., 560 m. W of Truk. Attacked by American task force Mar. 31, 1944 and Japanese ships destroyed.

Wolf (wōōlf). **1** River 100 m. long, Mississippi and Tennessee; flows WNW from Benton co., Mississippi, to Mississippi river just above Memphis, Tennessee.
2 River ab. 200 m. long, E Wisconsin; rises in N Langlade co., flows S into Lake Poygan, and then E into Fox river near Oshkosh.

Wolfe (wōōlf). **1** County in Kentucky. See *Table* at KENTUCKY.
2 County, Quebec, Canada. See *Table* at QUEBEC.

Wolfe'bor'o (wōōlf'bûr'ō). Town, Carroll co., E New Hampshire, on Lake Winnipesaukee 13 m. ENE of Laconia; pop. 2689; resort.

Wolfe Island. Island 18 m. long at NE end of Lake Ontario, in Ontario prov., Canada; divides head of St. Lawrence river, S of Kingston, but channel most used is on S or U.S. side.

Wol'fen·büt·tel (vôl'fĕn·büt'ĕl). Manufacturing city, Lower Saxony, W Germany, on Oker river S of Brunswick; pop. 18,479; late 16th-cent. town hall, 17th-cent. castle, 17th-cent. armory; manufactures preserved foodstuffs, machinery. Residence of dukes of Brunswick to 1753. Taken in Apr. 1945 by Allied forces.

Wolf Jaws. Mountain 4225 ft. in the Adirondack Mts., Essex co., NE New York.

Wolf'pin' Ridge (wōōlf'pĭn'). Ridge 4251 ft. in Towns co., N Georgia.

Wolf Point. City, ⊗ of Roosevelt co., NE Montana, on Missouri river 48 m. E of Glasgow; pop. 3585.

Wolf River. See WOLF.

Wolf Rock. Elevation 2796 ft. in Allegany co., NW corner of Maryland.

Wolfs'berg (wōōlfs'bûrg; *Ger.* vôlfs'bĕrK). Manufacturing commune, Carinthia prov., S Austria; pop. 6165; summer resort.

Wolfs'burg (wōōlfs'bûrg; *Ger.* vôlfs'bŏŏrK). City, Lower Saxony state, West Germany, 15 m. NE of Brunswick; pop. (1961) ab. 62,000; founded 1938; manufactures automobiles.

Wolf'ville (wōōlf'vĭl). Town, Kings co., W Nova Scotia, Canada, on Minas Basin 15 m. NW of Windsor; pop. 2313. Center of land of Evangeline near the original settlement of Grand Pré (*q.v.*); founded by the English in 1760. Seat of Acadia Univ. (founded 1838).

Wo'lin (vō'lĕn); *Ger.* **Wol·lin'** (vô·lēn'). **1** Island off the NW coast of Szczecin dept., NW Poland, bet. Stettiner Haff and the Baltic Sea, E of Usedom (Uznam); 95 sq. m.; pop. ab. 17,000; formerly in Pomerania, Germany. By Potsdam Conference 1945 assigned to Poland.
2 Commune on SE point of Wolin I.; pop. (1946) 800. See JULIN.

Wołkowysk. See VOLKOVYSK.

Wol'las·ton, Mount (wōōl'ăs·tŭn; *in U.S., sometimes* wôl'-). See QUINCY, Massachusetts.

Wollaston Islands. Chilean island group in S Tierra del Fuego Archipelago (*q.v.*); largest islands are Wollaston, Hermite, Grévy; includes also, at S extremity, Horn I. on which is Cape Horn.

Wollaston Lake. Lake 906 sq. m. in NE Saskatchewan, Canada; connected through its outlet with Reindeer Lake and Churchill river.

Wollaston Peninsula. Peninsula on SW part of Victoria I., Franklin District, Northwest Territories, N Canada; bet. Prince Albert Sound and Dolphin and Union Strait.

Wollin. See WOLIN.

Wol′lon·gong (wŏŏl′ŭn·gŏng). Seaport, E New South Wales, SE Australia, on Pacific Ocean 40 m. S of Sydney; pop. 11,402; center of Illawarra dairy and farm district.

Wolmar. See VALMERA.

Wo·ło′min (vô·lô′mēn). Commune, Warszawa dept., Poland, 15 m. ENE of Warsaw; pop. 13,114.

Wol′stan′ton United (wŏŏl′stăn′t′n; wŏŏl′stŭn). Former urban district, Staffordshire, W cen. England; pop. (1931) 30,525; now in Newcastle under Lyme.

Wo′lu′we′–Saint–Lam′bert′ (vô′lü′vă′săN′läN′bâr′); *Flemish* **Sint–Lam′brechts–Wo′lu·we** (sĭnt·läm′-brĕkts·vō′lü·vĕ). Commune, Brabant prov., cen. Belgium, a suburb of Brussels; pop. 18,244.

Wo′lu′we′–Saint–Pierre (vô′lü′vă′săN′pyâr′). Commune, Brabant prov., cen. Belgium; pop. 13,512.

Wol′ver·hamp′ton (wŏŏl′vĕr·hăm[p]′tŭn). County borough, Staffordshire, W cen. England, 12 m. NW of Birmingham; pop. 133,212, (1951 pop.) 162,669; in coal-mining and iron-mining section; manufacturing.

Wol′ver·ton (wŏŏl′vĕr·t′n; -tŭn). Urban district, Buckinghamshire, SE cen. England, on the Ouse 48 m. NW of London; pop. 13,421; railroad rolling stock.

Wo′łyń (vô′lĭn·y′). **1** See VOLHYNIA.
2 Former Polish department, in SE part; 13,780 sq. m.; pop. 2,084,791; ✳ Łuck.
3 See VOLYN REGION.

Wom′an Bay (wŏŏm′ăn). Inlet of Gulf of Alaska, E coast of Kodiak I., S Alaska, ab. 8 m. SW of Kodiak.

Womb′well (wŏŏm′b′l; wŏŏm′wĕl; wŏŏm′′l). Urban district, West Riding, Yorkshire, N England; pop. 18,837.

Wo′no·so′bo (wō′nô·sō′bô), Town, Central Java prov., Indonesia, 45 m. WNW of Magelang; pop. 10,701.

Wonsan. See GENZAN.

Won′se·ra·deel′ (vôn′sĕ·rà·dāl′). Commune, Friesland prov., N Netherlands, on NE coast of IJsselmeer S of Harlingen; pop. 13,409.

Won·thag′gi (wŏn·thăg′ĭ). Town on coast of S Victoria, SE Australia, 65 m. SE of Melbourne; pop. 5593.

Wood (wŏŏd). Name of counties in four states of the U.S. See *Tables* at OHIO, TEXAS, WEST VIRGINIA, WISCONSIN.

Wood, Mount. Peak 15,880 ft. in St. Elias Range, SW Yukon Territory, Canada, N of Mt. Logan.

Wood′bine′ (wŏŏd′bīn′). **1** City, ⊗ of Camden co., SE corner of Georgia; pop. 845.
2 Borough, Cape May co., S New Jersey, 22 m. WSW of Atlantic City; pop. 2823; clothing, hats, rubber goods.
3 Urban community (unincorporated), Davidson co., N cen. Tennessee, SSW suburb of Nashville; pop. (with Radnor and Glen Cliff) 14,485.

Wood′bridge (wŏŏd′brĭj). **1** Suburban residential town, SW New Haven co., S Connecticut, NW of New Haven; pop. 5182; incorp. 1784; agriculture.
2 City, before 1964 an urban township, Middlesex co., cen. New Jersey, 4 m. N of Perth Amboy; pop. 78,846; settled 1665; fashionable watering place until 1880's; clay deposits; terra cotta, tile, brick.
3 Urban district, East Suffolk, SE England, just ENE of Ipswich at head of wide inlet; pop. 5310; residence of Edward FitzGerald and Bernard Barton.

Wood Buffalo Park. See CANADA, *National Parks.*

Wood′burn (wŏŏd′bērn). City, Marion co., NW Oregon; pop. 3120; lumber; bulb culture; canneries.

Wood′bur′y (wŏŏd′bĕr′ĭ; -bēr·ĭ). **1** County in Iowa. See *Table* at IOWA.
2 Agricultural and manufacturing town, S Litchfield co., NW Connecticut; pop. 3910; settled 1672.

3 Residential city, ⊗ of Gloucester co., SW New Jersey, 8 m. S of Camden; pop. 12,453; settled c. 1665; in agricultural region; truck, dairy, and poultry farms.
4 Town, ⊗ of Cannon co., cen. Tennessee; pop. 1562.

Wood′ford (wŏŏd′fērd). **1** Counties in two states of the U.S. See *Tables* at ILLINOIS and KENTUCKY.
2 Former urban district, Essex, SE England; now part of Wanstead and Woodford municipal borough.

Wood Green. Urban district, Middlesex, SE England, N suburb of London on New river; pop. 54,181, (1951) 52,224; part of Greater London; residential section.

Wood′land (wŏŏd′lănd). City, ⊗ of Yolo co., N cen. California, 15 m. WNW of Sacramento; pop. 13,524; founded 1855, made ⊗ 1862; agricultural trade center; beet-sugar refining, rice and feed milling.

Wood′lands (wŏŏd′lăndz). Village, N Singapore I., on Johore Strait opp. Johore Bahru; terminus of railroad across the island from Singapore.

Wood′lark′ (wŏŏd′lärk′) *or* **Mu′ru·a** (mŏŏr′ŏŏ·ä). Island in Solomon Sea, ab. 38 m. long by 12 m. wide, ab. 400 sq. m., NE of SE end of New Guinea I.; lat. 9°S and long. 153°E; attached to the Territory of Papua; its chief village, Kulamadau, is a port of entry. Together with small island groups surrounding it, known as **Woodlark Islands** group and sometimes considered a part of the Trobriand Is. Low and hilly with good harbor and profitable gold fields. Used by Japanese as an air base 1942–43 but seized by Allied forces June 30, 1943.

Wood′lawn (wŏŏd′lôn). Urban community (unincorporated), Baltimore co., N Maryland, W of Baltimore; pop. (with Rockdale and Milford Mills) 19,254.

Wood′–Lynne′ (wŏŏd′lĭn). Borough, Camden co., S New Jersey, 2 m. SSE of Camden; pop. 3128.

Wood′mere (wŏŏd′mēr). Urban community (unincorporated), Nassau co., SE New York, on Long I. SW of Hempstead; pop. 14,011.

Wood′mont (wŏŏd′mŏnt). Urban community (unincorporated), Davidson co., N cen. Tennessee; pop. (with Green Hills and Glendale) 23,161.

Wood Mountain. Peak 13,640 ft. in Hinsdale and San Juan cos., SW Colorado.

Wood′–Ridge′ (wŏŏd′rĭj′). Residential borough, Bergen co., NE New Jersey, 7 m. SSE of Paterson; pop. 7964.

Wood′ River. City, Madison co., SW Illinois, 15 m. N of East St. Louis; pop. 11,694; oil refinery.

Wood′roffe, Mount (wŏŏd′rŭf). Mountain 4970 ft. in Musgrave Range, South Australia, near boundary bet. SW Northern Territory and NW South Australia.

Wood′ruff (wŏŏd′rŭf). **1** County in Arkansas. See *Table* at ARKANSAS.
2 Town, Spartanburg co., NW South Carolina, 17 m. SSW of Spartanburg; pop. 3679.

Woodruff Place. Town, Marion co., cen. Indiana, suburb of Indianapolis; pop. 1501.

Woods (wŏŏdz). County in Oklahoma. See *Table* at OKLAHOMA.

Woods, Lake of the. See LAKE OF THE WOODS.

Woods′field (wŏŏdz′fēld). Village, ⊗ of Monroe co., SE Ohio, 30 m. NE of Marietta; pop. 2956.

Woods Hole. See FALMOUTH, Massachusetts.

Wood′side′ National Historic Park (wŏŏd′sīd′). See CANADA, *National Historic Parks.*

Wood′son (wŏŏd′s′n). County in Kansas. See *Table* at KANSAS.

Woodson Terrace. City, St. Louis co., E Missouri, NW of St. Louis; pop. 6048.

Wood′stock (wŏŏd′stŏk). **1** Town, NE Windham co., NE Connecticut, NW of Putnam; pop. 3177.
2 City, ⊗ of McHenry co., N Illinois, 33 m. W of Waukegan; pop. 8897; county market center; manufactures typewriters and metal products.
3 Village in Woodstock town (pop. 3836), Ulster co., SE New York, ab. 12 m. NW of Kingston; artists' colony.
4 Village in Woodstock town (pop. 2786), ⊗ of Windsor co. E Vermont, 23 m. E of Rutland; pop. 1415.

5 Town, ⊗ of Shenandoah co., N Virginia, 30 m. SW of Winchester; pop. 2083; creameries, apple-grading plants.
6 Market town, ⊗ of Carleton co., W New Brunswick, Canada, on St. John river 48 m. WNW of Fredericton; pop. 3996; center of prosperous agricultural section; seat of a provincial agricultural school.
7 City, ⊗ of Oxford co., SE Ontario, Canada, on Thames river 26 m. ENE of London; pop. 15,544; railroad center; manufactures furniture and agricultural implements.
8 Municipal borough, Oxfordshire, cen. England, 8 m. NW of Oxford; pop. 1713; medieval royal residence.
9 *formerly* **Pa′pen·dorp** (pä′pĕn·dôrp). Town, SW Cape Province, S Union of South Africa, E suburb of Cape Town; pop. ab. 20,000 (white).

Woods′town (wo͝odz′toun). Borough, Salem co., SW New Jersey, 16 m. NNW of Bridgeton; pop. 2942; Quaker center since early 1700's.

Woods′ville (wo͝odz′vĭl). Town, ⊗ of Grafton co., W New Hampshire, on Connecticut river 17 m. SW of Littleton; pop. 1596; a section of Haverhill (*q.v.*).

Wood′ville (wo͝od′vĭl; *Sou.* also -v'l). **1** Town, ⊗ of Wilkinson co., SW corner of Mississippi; pop. 1856.
2 Town, ⊗ of Tyler co., E Texas; pop. 1920; lumber.
3 Borough, Hawke's Bay provincial dist., E North I., New Zealand; pop. 1031.

Wood′ward (wo͝od′[w]ẽrd). **1** County in Oklahoma. See *Table* at OKLAHOMA.
2 City, its ⊗, NW Oklahoma, 35 m. E of Oklahoma panhandle; pop. 7747; farming, ranching, dairying; manufactures butter, brooms; clay pits; U.S. Great Plains Field and Experiment Station.

Wood′y Mountain (wo͝od′ĭ). Peak 8064 ft. in S cen. Coconino co., near Flagstaff, Arizona.

Wool·lah′ra (wo͝o·lär′à). City, E New South Wales, SE Australia, E suburb of Sydney on S shore of Port Jackson; pop. 34,737.

Woolwich. Metropolitan borough of London. See *Table* at LONDON.

Woo′mer·a (wo͝o′mẽr·à). Township, SE cen. South Australia, 100 m. NNW of Port Augusta; pop. 4600; rocket range and satellite-tracking base, estab. 1945.

Woon·sock′et (wo͝on′sŏk′ĕt; -ĭt; wo͝on′sŏk′-). **1** Industrial city, Providence co., N Rhode Island, 13 m. NNW of Providence; pop. 47,080; settled 1666; separated from Cumberland in 1867 and from North Smithfield in 1871; incorp. as city 1888; manufactures textiles (esp. woolens), rubber rollers, washers, textile machinery.
2 City, ⊗ of Sanborn co., South Dakota; pop. 1035.

Woos′ter (wo͝os′tẽr). City, ⊗ of Wayne co., NE cen. Ohio, 27 m. W of Canton; pop. 17,046; settled 1807; manufactures brushes, aluminum goods, oil and gas well tools. Coll. of Wooster (1866; coed.).

Woosung. See SHANGHAI.

Worces′ter (wo͝os′tẽr). **1** Counties in two states of the U.S. See *Tables* at MARYLAND and MASSACHUSETTS.
2 City, a ⊗ of Worcester co., cen. Massachusetts, 37 m. W of Boston; pop. 186,587; first settled c. 1668; industrial center, manufacturing wire and wire products, textile machinery, tools, carpets, envelopes. Clark Univ. (1887; coed.); Worcester Polytechnic Institute (1865; men); Coll. of the Holy Cross (1843; men; Roman Catholic); Assumption Coll. (1904; men; Roman Catholic); Massachusetts State Coll. (1871; coed.).
3 Village in Worcester town (pop. 1946), Otsego co., cen. New York, ab. 18 m. NE of Oneonta.
4 County in England. See WORCESTERSHIRE.
5 County borough, ⊗ of Worcestershire, W cen. England, on the Severn 25 m. SSW of Birmingham; pop. 50,546, (1951 pop.) 59,700; manufactures porcelain, gloves, Worcestershire sauce, metal goods, and machinery; cathedral. Battle Sept. 3, 1651 in which Charles II and his Scottish army were routed by Cromwell and Parliamentarian army.
6 Town, SW Cape Province, S Union of South Africa, on Breede river 60 m. ENE of Cape Town; pop. 12,515; in Little Karroo region; viticulture; fruit farming and horse breeding.

Worces′ter·shire (wo͝os′tẽr·shĭr; -shẽr) *or* **Worcester.** County, W cen. England; area 699 sq. m.; pop. (1951) 522,974; ⊗ Worcester; other towns Dudley, Oldbury, Stourbridge, Stourport, Kidderminster, Malvern; rivers Severn, Avon, Stour, Teme; agriculture, grazing, iron working, porcelain, carpets.

Wor′dens Pond (wûr′d'nz). Small lake in S cen. Washington co., S Rhode Island.

Wor′king·ton (wûr′kĭng·tŭn). Municipal borough, Cumberland, NW England, on Irish Sea at mouth of the Derwent 32 m. SW of Carlisle; pop. 28,882; steel and iron manufactures; paper mills; coal mines nearby.

Work′sop (wûrk′sŭp; -sŏp). Urban district, Nottinghamshire, N cen. England, on the Ryton 17 m. ESE of Sheffield; pop. 31,038; in coal-mining section.

Wor′land (wûr′lănd). Town, ⊗ of Washakie co., N cen. Wyoming, on Big Horn river 78 m. SW of Sheridan; pop. 5806; sugar refinery.

World's View. Height 23 m. SW of Bulawayo, in the Matopo Hills, S Southern Rhodesia, S Africa; burial place of Cecil Rhodes.

Wormatia. See WORMS city, Germany.

Wor′mer·veer′ (vôr′mẽr·vär′). Commune, North Holland prov., W Netherlands, just N of Amsterdam; pop. 8802.

Worms. 1 (vôrms) See VORMSI island in Baltic Sea.
2 (vôrms; *Angl.* wûrmz; *anc.* **Bor′be·tom′a·gus** (bôr′bĕ·tŏm′à·gŭs), *later* **Au·gus′ta Van′gi·o′num** (ô·gŭs′tà văn′jĭ·ō′nŭm) *and* **Wor·ma′ti·a** (wôr·mā′-shĭ·à; -shà). City, Hesse, W Germany, on the Rhine 10 m. NNW of Mannheim; pop. 47,015; in region now noted for its wines; 11th-cent. Romanesque cathedral; fine monument to Luther 1868; river port with active trade; leather, machinery, textiles, soap, slate, asphalt.
History: Destroyed by Attila and rebuilt by Clovis I 486; episcopal see to 1806; synod declared Gregory VII no longer pope 1076; Concordat of Worms concluded here 1122; free imperial city from early 13th-cent.; member of Rhenish Confederation in 1255; seat of numerous imperial diets, including esp. the famous Diet of Worms 1521 convoked by Charles V at which Luther made his defense; destroyed by French 1689, 1792; to France by Peace of Lunéville 1801, to Germany 1814, to Hesse-Darmstadt 1815; occupied by French 1918–30; taken by Allied forces Mar. 20, 1945 in World War II; much devastated but cathedral still stands.

Worm's Head (wûrmz). Cape on SW Gower Penin. off S coast of Wales.

Wor′ring·en (vôr′ĭng·ĕn). Former commune, NE part of Cologne (*q.v.*), Germany.

Wors′bor·ough (wûrz′bŭ·rŭ; -brŭ). Urban district, West Riding, Yorkshire, N England; pop. 14,155.

Wors′ley (wûrs′lĭ). Urban district, Lancashire, NW England, 6 m. WNW of Manchester; pop. 27,363;

Wor′stead (wo͝os′tĕd; -tĭd). Parish and village, Norfolk, E England; 14th-cent. church; settled 12th cent. by Flemish weavers who manufactured wool fabric.

Worth (wûrth). **1** Name of counties in three states of the U.S. See *Tables* at GEORGIA, IOWA, MISSOURI.
2 Village, Cook co., NE Illinois, SW of Chicago; pop. 8196.

Wörth (vûrt). Commune, Bas-Rhin dept., NE France; pop. 1095; scene of battle Aug. 6, 1870 in which French under Marshal MacMahon were defeated by Crown Prince Frederick of Prussia. By the French called the battle of **Frösch′wil′ler** (frĕsh′vē′lär′).

Worth, Lake (wûrth). **1** Lagoon 18 m. long, SE Florida, in Palm Beach co. bet. mainland and coastal island.
2 Lake, N Texas, in Tarrant co. 9 m. NW of Fort Worth; formed by dam in West Fork of Trinity river.

Wör′ther See (vûr′tẽr zä). Lake (*see*) ab. 11 m. long, largest in Carinthia, S Austria, in valley of the Drau (Drava) just W of Klagenfurt; watering place.

Wor'thing (wûr'thĭng). Municipal borough, West Sussex, S England, on English Channel 47 m. S of London; pop. 69,375; seaside resort.

Wor'thing·ton (wûr'thĭng·tŭn). **1** Town, Greene co., SW Indiana, 24 m. WSW of Bloomington; pop. 1635. **2** City, ⊗ of Nobles co., SW Minnesota, 55 m. W of Fairmont; pop. 9015; railroad and trade center. **3** City, Franklin co., cen. Ohio, 9 m. N of Columbus; pop. 9239.

Worthington Peak. Mountain 8400 ft. in NW Lincoln co., E Nevada.

Wö'ru (vû'rōō). Var. of VŌRU.

Wot'ho (wŏt'hō). Island (atoll) in N cen. part of Ralik Chain, W Marshall Is., W Pacific, ab. 10°N lat. Occupied by U.S. forces Mar. 1944.

Wot'je (wŏt'jĕ). Island (atoll) in cen. part of Ratak Chain, E Marshall Is., W Pacific, ab. 9°N lat.; has 65 islets. Bombed by American forces 1943–44 but bypassed in attack on Japan.

Wo·wo'ni (wō·wo'nĕ). Island in W Banda Sea off SE coast of Celebes I., Indonesia, N of Butung I.

Wran'gel Island (răng'gĕl); *Russ.* **O'strov Vran'-ge·lya** (ŏ'strŭf vrȧn'gĭ·lyȧ). Island ab. 2000 sq. m. in the Arctic Ocean, ab. 100 m. off N coast of Chukot National District, Soviet Russia, Asia; crossed by the 180th meridian; site of a meteorological station. Known to Siberian natives; sought for by Baron Wrangel 1823 but not found; discovered 1867 by Long, an American whaler, and named for Wrangel by him.

Wran'gell (răng'gĕl). **1** Island, SE Alaska, NE of Prince of Wales Island. **2** Town on N tip of Wrangell I. and just S of mouth of Stikine river; pop. 1315; one of the oldest communities in SE Alaska; has large lumber, fishing, and canning industries; extensive hunting in region makes it important fur market. Numerous totem poles.

Wrangell, Mount. Mountain 14,000 ft. in cen. part of Wrangell Mts., S Alaska.

Wrangell Mountains. Range, S Alaska, near Yukon border; highest Mt. Bona 16,420 ft., Mt. Sanford 16,208 ft., and Mt. Blackburn 16,140 ft.

Wrath, Cape (rȧth). Extreme NW point of Scotland, 58°35'N; lighthouse.

Wray (rā). Town, ⊗ of Yuma co., NE Colorado, 65 m. SE of Sterling; pop. 2082.

Wreak (rēk). River 18 m. long, Leicestershire, cen. England; flows SW to the Soar.

Wreck Island (rĕk). Island in Atlantic Ocean, E coast of Northampton co., Virginia.

Wreck Point. Cape extending into Atlantic Ocean on extreme NW coast of Cape Province, Union of South Africa, S of Alexander Bay.

Wreck Reef. Coral reef in South Pacific 300 m. off E coast of Queensland, Australia, 22°15'S, 155°30'E.

Wre'kin, the (rē'kĭn). A sugar-loaf hill 1335 ft. high, an extinct volcano, in Shropshire, W England.

Wren'tham (rĕn'thăm). Town, Norfolk co., E Massachusetts, 15 m. W of Brockton; pop. 6685; settled 1669; burned during King Philip's War 1675.

Wrex'ham (rĕk'săm). Manufacturing and commercial municipal borough, Denbighshire, N Wales; pop. 30,962; in coal-mining section; burial place of Elihu Yale.

Wright (rīt). **1** Name of counties in three states of the U.S. See *Tables* at IOWA, MINNESOTA, MISSOURI. **2** Municipality, W Samar, Phil. Is., at head of an inlet of Villareal Bay ab. 9 m. E of Catbalogan; pop. 17,716.

Wrights'town (rīts'toun). Borough, Burlington co., S cen. New Jersey, ab. 10 m. NNE of Mount Holly; pop. 4846; on edge of Fort Dix Military Reservation and army training camp.

Wrights'ville (rīts'vĭl; *Sou. also* -v'l). **1** City, ⊗ of Johnson co., cen. Georgia, 53 m. E of Macon; pop. 2056. **2** Industrial borough, York co., S Pennsylvania, on Susquehanna river 12 m. ENE of York; pop. 2345; settled 1736; manufactures dresses, hosiery, iron castings.

Wrig'ley Gulf (rĭg'lĭ). Inlet of South Pacific Ocean E of Hobbs Coast in Marie Byrd Land, Antarctica, ab. 74°S, 129°W; separated from Amundsen Sea by Mt. Siple.

Wro'claw (vrô'tslȧf). **1** New department of SW Poland; bounded on N by Poznań dept., on E by Śląsk dept., on S by Czechoslovakia, and on W by Germany; formed after 1945 from former German Lower Silesia and part of Brandenburg and at first called **Śląsk Dol'ny** (shlônsk dôl'nĭ). **2** *Ger.* **Bres'lau** (brĕs'lou; *in English, also* brĕz'-). Commercial city, its ✻, on Oder (Odra) river 183 m. ESE of Berlin; pop. (1950) 341,419; formerly in Lower Silesia, Germany, and its capital and capital of former Breslau govt. dist.; promenades (on site of ancient fortifications), 12th-cent. cathedral, Gothic town hall, royal residence; university (founded 1702) includes botanic gardens, observatory, library, art gallery, museum; manufactures machinery, iron goods, railroad cars, bells, musical instruments, oil, liquors; trades chiefly in wool, corn, coal, metals, glass. Made episcopal see before 11th cent.; independent duchy 1163–1335; ceded to Austria 1527; conquered by Frederick II of Prussia 1741; occupied by French 1807 and 1813; important industrial center in World War II; besieged by Russians Feb. to May 1945, captured May 7; assigned to Poland by Potsdam Conference 1945.

Wrough'ton (rô't'n). Former village in Wiltshire, S England, now part of Swindon; transatlantic radio receiving station.

Wrox'e·ter (rŏk'sĕ·tẽr). Village on the Severn river, Shropshire, W England, just below Shrewsbury, on the site of an ancient Roman town **U'ri·co'ni·um** (ū'rĭ·kō'nĭ·ŭm) or **Vir'o·co'ni·um** (vĭr'ô-) of which the public baths, town hall, and market have been excavated.

Wrschowitz. See VRŠOVICE.

Wu (wōō). **1** River ab. 500 m. long, cen. China; rises in W Kweichow, flows NE, N, and NW through Szechwan into Yangtze river ab. 50 m. below Chungking; navigable for much of its course. **2** See LI. **3** River ab. 150 m. long in Chekiang prov., E China; rises on SW border of province and flows E to East China Sea at Yungkia.

Wu'chang' (wōō'chäng'). City, Hupeh prov., E cen. China, part of city of Wuhan (q.v.), in SE Hupeh on S bank of the Yangtze, 425 m. by air W of Shanghai, 585 m. by river; pop. ab. 500,000; oldest of the Han Cities, dating from several centuries B.C. as an important town. Capital of kingdom of Chu 300 B.C. and of Wu in 3d cent. A.D.; under Yüan dynasty (1206–1368) capital of Hukwang prov. and, later, on establishment of Hupeh prov. continued as its capital; starting point of Revolution against Imperialist China Oct. 1911.

Wuchow. See TSANGWU.

Wu'han' (wōō'hän'). City, actually a group of three cities called the **Han Cities** (hän)—Hankow, Hanyang, and Wuchang—at the junction of the Han with the Yangtze, SE Hupeh prov., E cen. China; pop. (1931 est.) 777,993, (1953) 1,427,300; capital of Hupeh prov.

Wu'hing' (wōō'hĭng'); *formerly* **Hu'chow'** (hōō'jō'). City, N Chekiang prov., E China, near SE shore of Tai Hu 40 m. N of Hangchow; pop. ab. 100,000.

Wu'hsien' (wōō'shĭ·ĕn'); *formerly* **Soo'chow'** (sōō'jō'). City and treaty port, S Kiangsu prov., E China, on the Grand Canal near the E shore of Tai Hu, ab. 55 m. W of Shanghai; pop. (1931 est.) 260,000, (1953) 474,000; has abundant waterways and is sometimes called the "Venice of China"; surrounded by rectangular walls (built 1662) ab. 15 m. in length, with six gates; famous for its bridges, palaces, temples, etc., for its many pagodas, esp. the Great Pagoda, one of the finest and largest in China (built c. 1131 A.D.), and for its silk industries. One of the oldest and most famous of Chinese cities; founded c. 525 B.C.; capital of Wu, ancient feudal kingdom, 513–473 B.C.; received its present name under Sui dynasty

6th cent. A.D.; partly destroyed by Mings 14th cent.; restored under Emperor K'ang-hsi 1662; destroyed 1853 in Taiping Rebellion but again rebuilt; opened as treaty port 1896; seized by Japanese Nov. 1937.

Wu'hu' (woo'hoo'). City and treaty port, E Anhwei, E China, on right bank of the Yangtze 50 m. SSW of Nanking and 260 m. by river above Shanghai; pop. (1931 est.) 135,385; connected by canals with neighboring towns; important trade center for rice tea, cotton, wheat, and lumber. Opened to foreign trade 1877.

Wu'kang' (woo'käng'). City, SW Hunan prov., E cen. China, near source of Tzu river ab. 110 m. W of Hengyang; scene of fighting May 1945.

Wu'lar Lake (woo'lĕr). Lake in course of the Jhelum, W Kashmir, N India, 25 m. NW of Srinagar; ab. 10 m. long by 12 m. wide; largest natural fresh-water body in India. Noted for its beauty, with background of lofty mountains E and N.

Wülf'rath (vülf'rät). Industrial city, in North Rhine-Westphalia state of Germany, NE suburb of Düsseldorf; pop. 11,264; textiles, leather, iron goods.

Wul'sten Peak (wool'stĕn). Mountain 13,659 ft. in Custer co., S cen. Colorado.

Wun'tho' (woon'thō'). Town, Katha dist., Upper Burma, on railroad WSW of Katha and ab. 135 m. N of Mandalay; fighting in vicinity 1943–44.

Wu·pat'ki National Monument (woo·păt'kĭ). See UNITED STATES, *National Monuments*.

Wup'per (voop'ĕr). River ab. 65 m. long on S edge of the Ruhrgebiet, W Germany; with many windings flows generally W and SW past Wuppertal to the Rhine just N of Cologne.

Wup'per·tal (voop'ĕr·täl). Industrial city in North Rhine-Westphalia state of Germany, on Wupper river in Ruhr valley 16 m. ENE of Düsseldorf; pop. (1939) 398,099; formed 1929 from several former cities, including Barmen, Elberfeld, and Ronsdorf; manufactures textiles, chemicals, leather, furniture, carpets, rubber goods, paper, machinery, glass, firearms, metal goods; mineral spring and bathing establishment in Barmen; Elberfeld well known through Elberfeld System of poor relief.

Würm (vürm); *Ger.* **Würm'see'** (vürm'zā') *or* **Wür'mer See** (vür'mĕr zā'); *also* **Starn'ber'ger See** (shtärn'bĕr'gĕr). Lake in Bavaria, S Germany, 15 m. SSW of Munich; 12 m. long and 3 m. wide at its greatest extent; altitude 1915 ft.

Wür'se·len (vür'zĕ·lĕn). Industrial city in North Rhine-Westphalia state of Germany, N suburb of Aachen; pop. 14,591; manufactures needles, cigars; coal mining.

Würt'tem·berg (vür'tĕm·bĕrк; *Angl.* wûr'tĕm·bûrg). Former German state, S Germany; 7530 sq. m.; pop. (1933) 2,696,324, (1939) 2,907,166; * Stuttgart; other important cities of region include Esslingen, Ulm, Tübingen, Reutlingen, Friedrichshafen; watered by Danube and Neckar rivers among others; diversified topography; agricultural; manufactures textiles and metal goods. Divided into the following four circles (Kreise), which were abolished 1934:

NAME	LOCATION IN WÜRT-TEMBERG	AREA IN SQ. M.	POPULA-TION (1933 CENSUS)	CAPITAL
Donau[1]	E	2,417	609,313	Ulm
Jagst	NE	2,021	430,202	Ellwangen
Neckar	NW	1,249	1,036,298	Stuttgart
Schwarzwald[2]	W	1,843	620,511	Reutlingen

[1] Sometimes Anglicized as Danube.
[2] Sometimes Anglicized as Black Forest.

History: Originally inhabited by Celts; later occupied successively by Suevi, Romans, Alamanni; became part of duchy of Swabia; ruled by counts 11th–15th cents.; became duchy 1495; suffered in wars of 17th and 18th cents.; became electorate 1803, kingdom 1813; constitutional monarchy 1819–1918; republic 1918–34; lost sovereignty to Reich 1934; in World War II overrun by

Allies Apr.–May 1945. See BADEN-WÜRTTEMBERG.

Würz'burg (vürts'boorк; *Angl.* wûrts'bûrg). Manufacturing city, * of Lower Franconia govt. dist., Bavaria, Germany, on Main river 60 m. ESE of Frankfurt am Main; pop. (1939) 108,617; 11th-cent. Romanesque cathedral, 14th-cent. Gothic chapel, 15th-cent. bridge, 18th-cent. palace; manufactures wine, beer, machinery, lacquer, paper, furniture; university (founded 1582). Episcopal see founded here 741 (secularized 1801; reestablished 1817); made grand duchy 1805 under Ferdinand III, former grand duke of Tuscany; passed to Bavaria 1815; Roentgen discovered X-rays at university here; in World War II occupied by Allied troops Apr. 1945.

Wur'zen (voor'tsĕn). City, Leipzig dist., East Germany, on Mulde river 16 m. E of Leipzig; pop. 18,286; 12th-cent. cathedral (remodeled 1932), 15th-cent. episcopal palace; manufactures carpets, farm machinery, furniture, cardboard. First mentioned as German town 961 A.D.

Wu'sih' (woo'shē'). City, S Kiangsu prov., E China, on Grand Canal 70 m. WNW of Shanghai; pop. ab. 200,000; a progressive walled city that has grown rapidly in recent years; has large rice and silk trade; intersected by many canals.

Wu·ster·hau'sen (voo'stĕr·hou'zĕn). Town, Brandenburg, eastern Germany, on a tributary of the Havel river 50 m. NW of Berlin; pop. 2671; treaty signed here 1726 bet. Austria and Prussia.

Wu Tai Shan (woo' tī' shän'). Mountain ab. 10,000 ft., NE Shansi, NE China, ab. 100 m. N of Yangku; one of the four mountains of China sacred to Buddhism; visited the whole year round by many pilgrims. Its top and slopes covered with temples, monasteries, lamaseries—some said to date back to 1st cent. A.D.

Wu'tsin' (woo'jĭn'); *formerly* **Chang'chow'** (chäng'-jō'). City, S Kiangsu prov., E China, ab. 60 m. SE of Nanking on the Grand Canal; known in ancient times, received its name of Changchow under Sui dynasty; has extensive trade by junk, esp. with Wuhsien.

Wu'wei' (woo'wā'); *formerly* **Liang'chow'** (lĭ-äng'jō'). City, cen. Kansu prov., N cen. China, 150 m. NNW of Lanchow; pop. 200,000; on highway to Sinkiang and Europe S of Great Wall; has been greatly damaged by earthquakes.

Wy'a·lu'sing (wī'à·loo'sĭng). Town, NW Grant co., SW Wisconsin, on the Mississippi river; pop. 485; nearby is Elephant Mound (q.v.).

Wy'an·dot (wī'ăn·dŏt). County in Ohio. See *Table* at OHIO.

Wy'an·dotte (wī'ăn·dŏt). **1** County in Kansas. See *Table* at KANSAS.
2 City, Wayne co., SE Michigan, on Detroit river 11 m. SW of Detroit; pop. 43,519; salt and limestone deposits; manufactures soda ash, caustic soda, baking soda, calcium chloride, magnesium, bromine, drugs, dyes, disinfectants; first Bessemer steel in America manufactured here 1864.

Wyck'off (wĭk'ŏf). Town, Bergen co., NE corner of New Jersey, 7 m. N of Paterson; pop. (est.) 8800.

Wye (wī). **1** River 130 m. long in E Wales and W England; rises in Montgomeryshire, cen. Wales, flows SE across English border W of Hereford, and continues S into the Severn estuary 2 m. S of Chepstow; the ruins of Tintern Abbey are on its banks a few miles N of Chepstow.
2 Small stream, tributary of the Thames, Buckinghamshire, SE cen. England.
3 River 20 m. long, Derbyshire, N cen. England; flows E to the Derwent.

Wy'lie (wī'lĭ). City, Collin co., NE Texas, SE of McKinney; pop. 1804; agricultural center.

Wy'man Dam (wī'măn). Dam completed 1931 across Upper Kennebec river, cen. Maine, NW of Bingham; height 155 ft.; impounds water for water power, forming **Wyman Lake.**

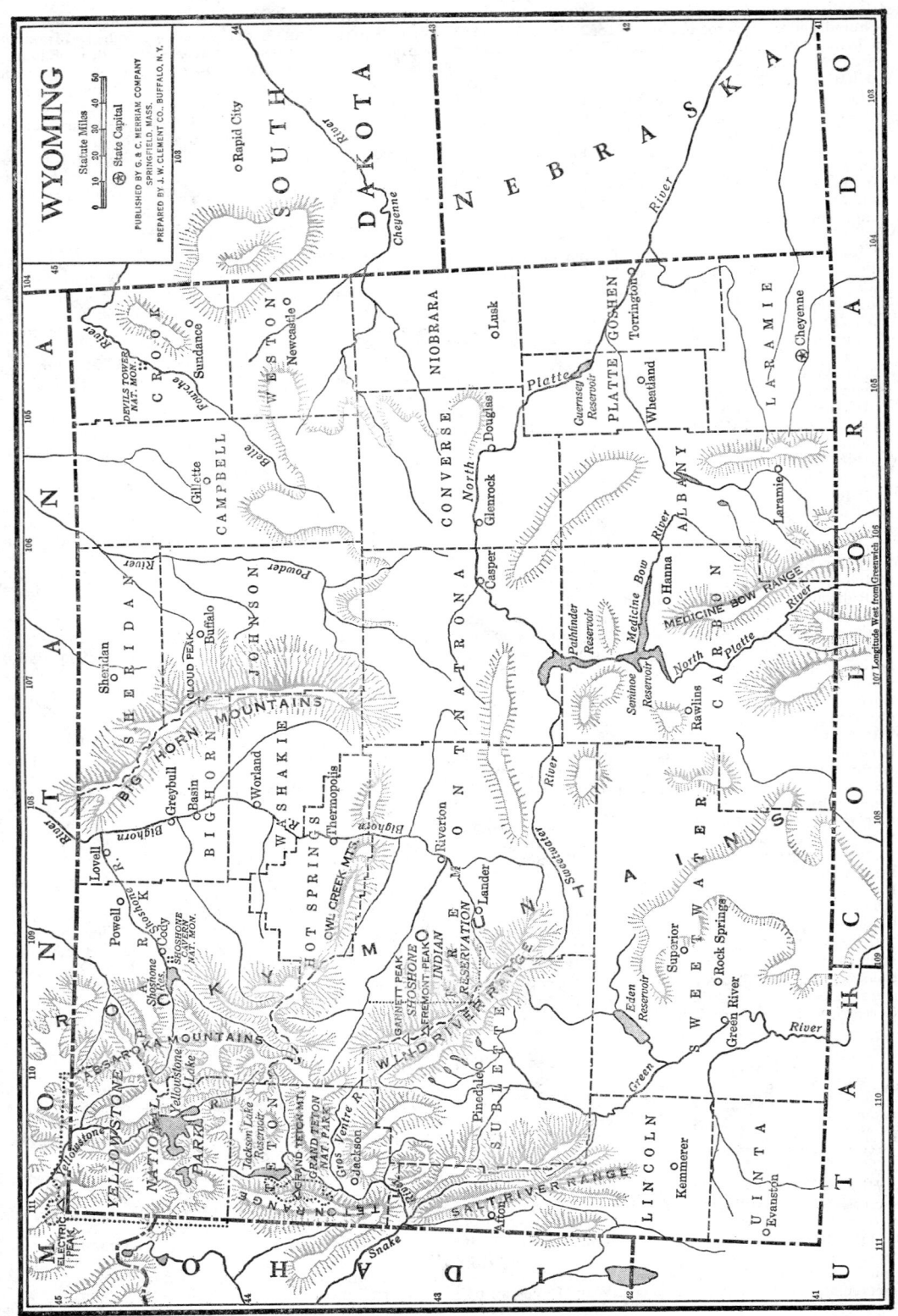

WYOMING

Statute Miles

0 10 20 30 40 50

⊕ State Capital

PUBLISHED BY G. & C. MERRIAM COMPANY
SPRINGFIELD, MASS.
PREPARED BY J. W. CLEMENT CO. BUFFALO, N.Y.

Wy′more (wī′mōr). City, Gage co., SE Nebraska, 12 m. S of Beatrice; pop. 1975; trade center; flour mill.

Wyn′berg (wĭn′bûrg). Town, SW Cape Province, S Republic of So. Africa, a suburb of Cape Town, incorp. with it in 1927; pop. 112,764.

Wyncoops Bay. See WIJNKOOPS BAY.

Wyn′cote (wĭn′kōt). Locality, Montgomery co., SE Pennsylvania, near Jenkintown; pop. (est.) 6000.

Wynd′ham (wĭn′dăm). Town, NE Western Australia, near mouth of the Ord river; pop. 576; has a port; meat-packing industry.

Wynne (wĭn). City, ⊗ of Cross co., E Arkansas, 46 m. W of Memphis, Tennessee; pop. 4922; shipping point for fruits, esp. peaches.

Wyn′ne·wood (wĭn′ĕ·wŏŏd). City, Garvin co., S cen. Oklahoma, on Washita river 33 m. N of Ardmore; pop. 2509; produces cotton, alfalfa, pecans; shipping point for livestock and poultry; cottonseed-oil mill, oil refinery.

Wynooche. See WISHKAH.

Wyn′yard (wĭn′yĕrd); *formerly* **Ta′ble Cape** (tā′b'l). Town on NW coast of Tasmania, Australia, 12 m. W of Burnie; pop. 1387; agricultural center and tourist resort.

Wy·o′ming (wī-ō′mĭng; *attributively, also* wī′ō′-). **1** A western state of U.S.A., 44th state admitted to Union (1890); bounded on N by Montana, on E by South Dakota and Nebraska, on S by Colorado and Utah, and on W by Utah and Idaho; 9th state in area, 97,914 sq. m. (land area 97,506 sq. m.); 48th state in population, 330,066; ✳ Cheyenne. See *Table of States* at UNITED STATES. Divided into the following 23 counties and Yellowstone National Park (for pronunciation of their names, see their individual entries):

NAME	LOCATION	AREA[1]	POP.[1]	CO. SEAT
Albany	SE	4,400	21,290	Laramie
Big Horn	N	3,176	11,898	Basin
Campbell	NE	4,755	5,861	Gillette
Carbon	S	7,965	14,937	Rawlins
Converse	E	4,167	6,366	Douglas
Crook	NE corner	2,897	4,691	Sundance
Fremont	cen.	9,244	26,168	Lander
Goshen	SE	2,230	11,941	Torrington
Hot Springs	NW cen.	2,022	6,365	Thermopolis
Johnson	N	4,175	5,475	Buffalo
Laramie	SE corner	2,703	60,149	Cheyenne
Lincoln	SW	4,101	9,018	Kemmerer
Natrona	cen.	5,342	49,623	Casper
Niobrara	E	2,613	3,750	Lusk
Park	NW	5,217	16,874	Cody
Platte	SE	2,114	7,195	Wheatland
Sheridan	N	2,531	18,989	Sheridan
Sublette	W	4,876	3,778	Pinedale
Sweetwater	SW	10,492	17,920	Green River
Teton[2]	NW	2,815	3,062	Jackson
Uinta	SW corner	2,070	7,484	Evanston
Washakie	N cen.	2,262	8,883	Worland
Weston	NE	2,408	7,929	Newcastle
Yellowstone National Park	NW corner	2,931	420	

[1] Area = land area in sq. m. Pop. from 1960 Census.
[2] Contains Grand Teton National Park in W and NW part.
[3] Main part of Yellowstone National Park is within Wyoming state boundaries (2930.8 sq. m.), with adjacent strips in Montana (268.9 sq. m.) and Idaho (57.6 sq. m.). Total area with inland waters 3419 sq. m.

Nickname: Equality State. *State flower:* Indian paintbrush. *Motto:* Cedant Arma Togae (Let Arms Yield to the Toga). *Chief cities:* Cheyenne, Casper. *Rivers:* Green, with its tributaries, draining SW corner of state and flowing S across border into Utah; Bighorn, flowing from cen. area N into Montana; Yellowstone, rising in NW area and flowing N into Montana; Powder, flowing from cen. area E of the Bighorn, N into Montana; North Platte, flowing from S area N and then SW across border into Nebraska, receiving waters of the Laramie near the border; Snake, rising in NW corner of state and flowing S then NW across border into Idaho. *Highest point:* Gannett Peak 13,785 ft. in Fremont co. *Chief industries:* Cattle and sheep raising, lumbering, mining (uranium), petroleum production.

History: Originally a part of Louisiana region claimed by France; greater part acquired from France by United States under Louisiana Purchase 1803; part of area under joint British-American occupation 1818–46; Great Britain relinquished claim 1846 and Texas transferred its claim to United States 1850; Wyoming Territory organized 1868; adopted woman suffrage, first instance in United States, 1868; admitted to Union July 10, 1890; Mrs. Nellie Tayloe Ross governor 1925–27, first woman governor of an American state.

2 Name of counties in three states of the U.S. See *Tables* at NEW YORK, PENNSYLVANIA, WEST VIRGINIA.

3 City, Kent co., W Michigan, SW of Grand Rapids; pop. 45,829.

4 City, Hamilton co., SW corner of Ohio, 8 m. N of Cincinnati; pop. 7736.

5 Borough, Luzerne co., E Pennsylvania, in Wyoming Valley on Susquehanna river 6 m. NNE of Wilkes-Barre; pop. 4511; anthracite coal mining; silk, metal industries. See WYOMING VALLEY.

Wyoming Mountain. Ridge ab. 18 m. long in Luzerne co., E Pennsylvania, extending along SE bank of Susquehanna river and bordering Wyoming Valley.

Wyoming Peak. Mountain 11,418 ft. in N Lincoln co., W Wyoming, at S end of Wyoming Range.

Wyoming Range. Range in W Wyoming, extending along boundary bet. Sublette and N Lincoln cos.

Wyoming Valley. Valley ab. 20 m. long and 3 m. wide in Luzerne co., E Pennsylvania, along Susquehanna river; noted for beautiful scenery; old Forty Fort, near borough of Wyoming, was scene of an Indian and British attack on the settlers, the "Wyoming Massacre," July 3, 1778. Valley was settled from Connecticut and from 1753 to 1800 was subject of controversy bet. Connecticut and Pennsylvania.

Wy′o·mis′sing (wī′ō·mĭs′ĭng). Borough, Berks co., SE Pennsylvania, 3 m. W of Reading; pop. 5044; manufactures textile machinery, hosiery, brick.

Wysz′ków (vĭsh′kŏŏf). Commune, Warszawa dept., Poland, on Bug river 33 m. NE of Warsaw; pop. 10,768.

Wythe (wĭth). County in Virginia. See *Table* at VIRGINIA.

Wythe′ville (wĭth′vĭl; *Sou. also* -v′l). Town, ⊗ of Wythe co., SW Virginia, 19 m. WSW of Pulaski; pop. 5634; in agricultural and livestock-raising section; manufactures flour, lumber, textiles.

Wyt′schae′te (vĭt′sкȧ′tĕ). Village in West Flanders prov., NW Belgium, S of Ieper (Ypres); scene of battles during 1914, 1917, and 1918, esp. as phase of the battle of Messines Ridge June 7, 1917.

Wyvis, Ben. See BEN WYVIS.

X

Xalapa. See JALAPA.

Xal'to·cán' (häl'tô·kän'). Lake in the Valley of Mexico, cen. Mexico, NNE of Mexico City and N of Lake Texcoco.

Xan'ten (ksän'těn; *Angl.* zăn't'n). Town, W North Rhine-Westphalia state, West Germany, on left bank of the Rhine 7 m. W of Wesel; pop. (1933) 5057; has fine cathedral; treaty signed here 1614 settling inheritance dispute of the elector of Brandenburg. In latter part of World War II scene of severe fighting Mar. 1945; taken by Allies Mar. 9.

Xan'the (zăn'thĕ); *Mod. Gr.* **Xan'thē** (ksän'thē); *Turk.* **Es'ki·je'** (ĕs'kĕ·jĕ'). City, Rhodope dept., Western Thrace, NE Greece, 30 m. W of Komotinē and near E bank of Nestos river; pop. 33,712.

Xan'thus (zăn'thŭs). **1** *mod.* **Ko·ca'** (kô·jä'). River ab. 75 m. long, ancient Lycia, SW Asia Minor, flowing SW and S to the Mediterranean.
2 *mod.* **Gü·nük'** (gü·nük'). Ancient city of Lycia, Asia Minor, near mouth of Xanthus river; its ruins, including the theater, a stele, temples, and the bases of tombs which are now in the British Museum, are in SE Muğla vilayet, SW Turkey in Asia; twice besieged and destroyed: (1) in 546 B.C. by the Persians under General Harpagus; (2) in 42 B.C. by Romans under Marcus Junius Brutus.

Xátiva. See JÁTIVA.

Xau'en (hou'än). Town, N Morocco, NW Africa, S of Tetuán; pop. (1936) 6065.

Xa'vi·er (ză'vĭ·ẽr). A southern suburb of Leavenworth, Leavenworth co., NE Kansas; Saint Mary College (1923; women).

Xe'nia (zēn'yá; zē'nĭ·á). City, ⊗ of Greene co., SW Ohio, 15 m. ESE of Dayton; pop. 20,445; settled 1803; manufactures rope and twine, furniture, and shoes;

trade center for the surrounding farm region; ab. 3 m. to the NE is Wilberforce village, site of Wilberforce University (1856).

Xeres. See JEREZ.

Xi'nan·te'catl (shē'nän·tä'kät·'l). = Nevado de TOLUCA.

Xin·gu' (shĕNng·gōō'). River ab. 1300 m. long in cen. and N Brazil; rises in several headstreams in N part of the Plateau of Mato Grosso and flows N through NE Mato Grosso state and cen. Pará state into the Amazon river near its mouth; in its cen. part goes through a series of rapids 400 m. long. Explored by Karl von den Steinen 1884–87.

Xi·pho'ni·a (zĭ·fō'nĭ·á; -fōn'yá; zī-). See AUGUSTA, Sicily.

Xo'chi·mil'co (sō'chĕ·mēl'kô). **1** Lake in Valley of Mexico, cen. Mexico, 7 m. SE of Mexico City; only a few inches deep.
2 Town, Federal District, cen. Mexico, 10 m. S of Mexico City on W shore of Lake Xochimilco; pop. 14,385; site of chinampas or "Floating Gardens," actually gardens on made land that is interlaced by canals. The original chinampas of the Aztecs were formed by piling mud onto rafts which were composed of interlacing twigs and floated in the water until the roots of the plants that were grown on them finally anchored the rafts to the bottom of the lake, the number of these artificial islands being multiplied until they formed a meadow interlaced by waterways.

Xo'ïs (zō'ĭs). Ancient city, Lower Egypt, in the middle of the Nile delta ab. 20 m. NW of Busiris; capital of Egypt under the XIVth (Xoite) dynasty c. 17th cent. B.C.

Xulla Islands. Former name of the SULA ISLANDS, Indonesia.

Y

Ya'an' (yä'än'); *formerly* **Ya'chow'** (yä'jō'). Town, E Sikang, S China, on Szechwan border and on tributary of Min river 70 m. SW of Chengtu; center for tea trade; residence of some of Sikang government officials; highway junction point.

Ya·blo·noi' (yĭ·blŭ·noi'), *or* **Ya·blo·no·voi'** (yĭ·blŭ-nŭ·voi'), **Mountains.** Range along border bet. W Chita Region, Soviet Russia, Asia, and E Buryat-Mongol Republic; highest peak Sokhondo 8228 ft., at its S end near Outer Mongolian border; forms watershed for rivers flowing to Arctic and Pacific Oceans.

Ya'bu·co'a (yä'vōō·kō'ä). Municipality (pop. 29,782) and town (3734), SE Puerto Rico; town is 16 m. ENE of Guayama.

Yacarana. See JAVARÍ.

Yachow. See YAAN.

Ya·cui'ba (yä·kwē'vä). Town on Argentine frontier, Tarija dept., S Bolivia; port of entry and trading center for Chaco region.

Ya·cu'ma (yä·kōō'mä). River nearly 200 m. long in NW Bolivia; flows NE into Mamoré river.

Yad'kin (yăd'kĭn). **1** River 202 m. long, cen. North Carolina; rises in Watauga co., flows E, then S, and joins Uharie river to form Pee Dee river (*q.v.*). See also YADKIN DAM and HIGH ROCK LAKE.

2 County in North Carolina. See *Table* at NORTH CAROLINA.

Yadkin, *or* **Yadkin Narrows, Dam.** Dam completed across narrows of Yadkin river bet. Stanly and Montgomery cos., S cen. North Carolina; height 217 ft.; impounds water, **Ba'din Lake** (bä'dĭn; -d'n), for power.

Yad'kin·ville (yăd'kĭn·vĭl; *Sou.* also -v'l). Town, ⊗ of Yadkin co., NW cen. North Carolina; pop. 1644.

Ya·e·ju Hill (yä·ĕ·jōō). Elevation ab. 1840 ft., highest point in S Okinawa, Ryukyu Is., S Japan; captured by Americans June 14, 1945.

Ya·e·ya·ma Islands (yä·ĕ·yä·mä). Group of islands in S Ryukyu Is., part of Sakishima Is.; 246 sq. m.; pop. (1940) 34,395; chief islands Iriomote and Ishigaki.

Yafa. See JAFFA.

Ya·gua'chi (yä·gwä'chě). Town, Guayas prov., W Ecuador, just ENE of Guayaquil; pop. (1944 est.) 8699.

Ya'gua·jay (yä'gwä·hī'). Municipality and town, Las Villas prov., W cen. Cuba; town 45 m. E of Santa Clara, pop. 8796.

Ya'gua·rón' (yä'gwä·rôn'). **1** River. See JAGUARÃO.

2 Town, E Central dept., S Paraguay, 20 m. SE of Asunción; pop. ab. 13,000; noted for its old Jesuit church San Roque.

Yahata. See YAWATA.

Yai'la Range (yī'lȧ). Mountain range along SE coast of Crimea Penin.; highest peak ab. 5000 ft.

Yai'nax (yī'năks). Mountain 7277 ft. in SE Klamath co., S Oregon.

Yak'i·ma (yăk'ĭ·mȯ). **1** River ab. 200 m. long, S cen. Washington; flows SE through Kittitas and Yakima cos. into Columbia river in Benton co.

2 County in Washington. See *Table* at WASHINGTON.

3 City, ⊗ of Yakima co., S Washington, on Yakima river 5 m. N of Yakima Indian Reservation; pop. 43,284; commercial center of agricultural region (esp. apples); manufactures lumber, flour, cider, clay products.

Ya·kob·shtat' (yĭ·kŭp·shtät'). = YEKABPILS.

Ya·ku (yä·kōō); *Jap.* **Yaku Shi·ma** (shě·mä). One of the Osumi Is. (*q.v.*) off S tip of Kyushu, S Japan; with adjacent small island, 208 sq. m.; pop. (1945) 18,015.

Yak'u·tat (yăk'ū·tăt; yŭk'ū-). Village at Ocean Cape on S shore of Yakutat Bay, SE Alaska; pop. 230; airport.

Yakutat Bay. Inlet of Gulf of Alaska, SE Alaska, 60°N, 140°W, S of St. Elias Range.

Ya·kutsk' (yĕ·kōōtsk'). Town, ✱ of Yakutsk A.S.S.R., Soviet Russia, Asia, on Lena river in 62°N, 129°50′E;

pop. 10,513; chief town of Lena valley; trade center for furs, hides, cattle, ivory; has large airport.

Yakutsk Autonomous Soviet Socialist Republic; *also* **Ya·kut'** A.S.S.R. (yĕ·kōōt') *and* **Ya·ku'ti·a** (yȧ·kōō'shĭ·ȧ). An autonomous republic of the R.S.F.S.R. in E cen. Siberia, Asia; 1,169,927 sq. m.; pop. 400,544, (1941 est.) 420,892; ✱ Yakutsk. In area the largest unit of the U.S.S.R.; bounded on the N by the Arctic Ocean (Laptev and East Siberian Seas), on the E by Khabarovsk Territory, on S by Chita and Irkutsk Regions, and on W by Krasnoyarsk Territory (Evenki and Taimyr National Districts). Includes nearly all of the great basin of the Lena (*q.v.*), as well as the valleys of the Olenek, Yana, Indigirka, and Kolyma; largely plain, with tundra in the N and mountain ranges (Verkhoyansk and Cherskogo) in the E; highest peaks 8000 to 10,200 ft. Includes New Siberian and Lyakhov Is. in the Arctic. Climate is severe, the towns of Verkhoyansk and Oimyakon being two of the coldest places on the globe. Has great timber resources and probably rich deposits of various minerals, but these, except for gold, not yet exploited; mammoth ivory is also a valuable product. Predominant ethnic strain Turko-Tatar; chief nationalities Yakut 81.6%, Russian ab. 10%. Trapping, hunting, and stock raising are chief occupations of Yakuts. Has no railroads, but several excellent highways have been built recently. Chief towns Yakutsk, Verkhoyansk, Vilyuisk, Olekminsk, Aldan. The least explored of all Soviet republics; fort at Yakutsk founded 1632 and gold mines near Olekminsk worked as early as 1850; organized as an autonomous republic 1922.

Ya·la (yä·lä). **1** Province, SW Thailand; 1893 sq. m.; pop. 76,086.

2 Town, its ✱, 22 m. S of Pattani.

Yale, Mount (yāl). Peak 14,172 ft. in Sawatch Range, Chaffee co., cen. Colorado.

Yales'ville (yālz'vĭl). Subdivision (1950 pop. 1122) of town of WALLINGFORD, Connecticut.

Ya·lias' (yä·lyäs'); *anc.* **I·da'lia** (ī·dāl'yȧ; -dā'lĭ·ȧ). River 45 m. long on the island of Cyprus, flowing E into Famagusta Bay.

Yai'o·bush'a (yăl'ō·bōōsh'ȧ). **1** River ab. 80 m. long, N cen. Mississippi; rises in Chickasaw co., flows W and SW to unite with Tallahatchie river in Leflore co. and form the Yazoo river.

2 County in Mississippi. See *Table* at MISSISSIPPI.

Yal'pukh (yăl'pōōK); *Romanian* **Ial'pug** (yäl'pōōg). Lake 89 sq. m. in Izmail Region, SW Ukraine, U.S.S.R.; outlet is into Danube river near the delta.

Yal'ta (yôl'tȧ; yäl'tȧ; *Russ.* yȧl'tȧ). Town, S coast of Crimea, Soviet Russia, Europe, 30 m. E of Sevastopol; pop. 28,800; has long been a resort; site of winter palace of former tsars. Held by Germans 1941–44; retaken by Russians Apr. 1944; scene of "Big Three Conference" (President Roosevelt, Prime Minister Churchill, and Premier Stalin) Feb. 3–11, 1945.

Ya'lu' (yä'lōō'). **1** *or* **Am'nok** (äm'nŏk); *Jap.* **O·ryok·ko** (ō·ryŏk·kō). River ab. 300 m. long bet. SE Manchuria and Korea; rises in Chang Pai Shan on N border of Korea, flows N, W, and SW to Korea Bay. Near its mouth is Antung, important city of Manchuria; crossed here by railroad bridge 3000 ft. long. Has many tributaries, esp. in Manchuria; navigable for most of its course for smaller vessels. Naval battle off its mouth (Haiyang I.) 1894 in which Japanese defeated the Chinese; land battle May 1, 1904, first in Russo-Japanese War, in which Russians were defeated.

2 *Jap.* **Cha'lan'tun'** (jä'län'tōōn'). Town, W cen. Heilungkiang prov., N Manchuria (Japanese ✱ of former East Hsingan prov., NW Manchukuo) on Yali river (tributary of Nonni) 75 m. NW of Lungkiang.

Yal'u·it (yăl'ōō·ĭt). = JALUIT.

Ya′lung′ (yä′lōōng′). River ab. 725 m. long, E Sikang prov., S China; rises in Amne Machin Shan in Tsinghai prov. and flows S into the Yangtze on the Yunnan border W of Hweili; unnavigable.

Ya·lu′to·rovsk (yĕ·lōō′tŭ·rŭfsk). Town, SW Tyumen Region, Soviet Russia, Asia, on left bank of the Tobal river 50 m. SE of Tyumen.

Yal·vaç′ (yäl·väch′). Town, N Isparta vilayet SW Turkey in Asia, 48 m. NE of Isparta; pop. 8349. Ruins of ancient city of Pisidian Antioch lie nearby; founded c. 290 B.C. by Seleucus Nicator and made free city by the Romans 189 B.C.; established as a colony by Augustus and became important Roman administrative center in S Galatia; visited by Saint Paul on first missionary journey c. 46 A.D.; source of many inscriptions.

Yama. See KINGISEPP.

Ya′ma′chiche′ (yȧ′mȧ′shĭsh′). Village, ⊗ of Saint Maurice co., S Quebec, Canada, on N shore of Lake St. Peter; pop. 875; transatlantic receiving station.

Ya·ma·da (yä·mä·dä). City, Mie prefecture, S Honshu, Japan, now a part of Ujiyamada (q.v.).

Ya·ma·ga·ta (yä·mä·gä·tä). 1 Prefecture of Japan. See *Table* at JAPAN.

2 City, its ✳, on Mogami river 30 m. W of Sendai; pop. (1945) 89,531; a center of the silk industry; also produces copper and iron wares. Residence of daimios from early 17th cent. to 1868.

Ya·ma·gu·chi (yä·mä·gōō·chē). 1 Prefecture of Japan. See *Table* at JAPAN.

2 City, its ✳, 35 m. NE of Shimonoseki; pop. (1945) 89,042; has several fine temples. From 14th to 16th cents. under the Ouchi family one of the leading cities of feudal Japan; visited c. 1550 by the Jesuit missionary Francis Xavier; important during Restoration period 1862–68.

Ya·mal′ (yĕ·mál′). Peninsula ab. 380 m. long and 150 m. wide in NW Siberia, bet. Kara Sea and Gulf of Ob, N Yamalo-Nenets National District, Soviet Russia, Asia.

Ya·ma′lo–Ne·nets′ (yĕ·mä′lŭ·nyĭ·nyĕts′). National district, N part of former Omsk Region, Soviet Russia, Asia; 179,876 sq. m.; pop. (1941 est.) 12,753; ✳ Salekhard; includes Yamal Penin., region on E coast of Gulf of Ob, and the tundra along the lower Ob river and to the E of it. Organized 1930.

Ya′man (yȧ′măn). = YEMEN.

Ya·ma·na·ka (yä·mä·nä·kä). Lake, S Honshu, Japan, highest of lakes on slopes of Fuji; alt. 3270 ft.

Ya·ma·na·shi (yä·mä·nä·shē). Prefecture of Japan. See *Table* at JAPAN.

Ya·mas′ka (yȧ·mäs′kȧ). 1 River ab. 75 m. long, S Quebec, Canada; flows N to Lake St. Peter.

2 County, Quebec, Canada. See *Table* at QUEBEC.

Ya·ma·to (yä·mä·tō). Old province in W cen. Honshu, Japan, now Nara prefecture; in legendary Japan, the region of the original settlement of the imperial clan; here Jimmu Tenno first ruled 660 B.C.; in early centuries Japanese were called "people of Yamato."

Yam′bol (yäm′bŏl); *Turk.* **Yan′bo·li′** (yän′bŏ·lĭ′). City, Burgas dept., E Bulgaria, on Tundzha river; pop. (1934) 24,920; trade center in wool and wine. First mentioned in 11th cent., then in Byzantine Empire.

Yamburg. See KINGISEPP.

Yamchow. See YAMHSIEN.

Yamdena. See JAMDENA.

Yam′drok′ Tso (yäm′drŏk′ tsô′) or **Pal′ti** (päl′tē). Lake (Tibetan *tso*), SE Tibet, Outer China, ab. 45 m. S of Lhasa; alt. 13,800 ft.

Ya·me′thin (yȧ·mā′thĭn). 1 District, Mandalay division, Upper Burma; 4196 sq. m.; pop. 390,820.

2 Town, its ✳, on Rangoon-Mandalay railroad 105 m. S of Mandalay; pop. 9291.

Yam′hill (yăm′hĭl). County in Oregon. See *Table* at OREGON.

Yam′hsien′ (yäm′shĭ·ĕn′); *formerly* **Yam′chow′** (yäm′jō′). Town, W Kwangtung prov., SE China, at head of Gulf of Tonkin ab. 50 m. NW of Pakhoi.

Y′A′mi (yä′mē). Islet 1 sq. m., N Batan Is., N Philippine Is.; the northernmost point of the Philippine Is.

Yam′pa (yăm′pȧ). River 200 m. long, NW Colorado; rises in S Routt co., flows N then W into the Green river near Utah boundary.

Yam′pol (yäm′pŭl·y′). Town, Ukraine, U.S.S.R., on the Dniester ab. 85 m. SE of Khobin; recent improvements at rapids in the river here have made navigation possible to Khobin.

Yam′say Peak (yăm′zī). Mountain 8248 ft. in E Klamath co., S Oregon.

Yamundá. = JAMUNDÁ.

Ya′na (yá′nȧ). River ab. 750 m. long in N cen. Yakutsk Republic, Soviet Russia, Asia; rises in Verkhoyansk Mts. and flows N into Laptev Sea.

Ya′na′on′ (yȧ′ná′ŏn′; *Angl.* yä·noun′) or **Ya·nam′** (yä·näm′). Town and seaport, E India, on the N mouth of Godavari delta 290 m. NNE of Madras, formerly a free city of French India; 6 sq. m.; pop. (1941) 5711; founded 1750; captured by British and returned to French in 1817; all that remained to France from conquests of Bussy and Dupleix; to India 1954.

Yanboli. See VAMBOL.

Yanbu′. See YENBO′.

Yan′cey (yăn′sĭ). County in North Carolina. See *Table* at NORTH CAROLINA.

Yan′cey·ville (yăn′sĭ·vĭl; *Sou.* also -v′l). Village, ⊗ of Caswell co., N North Carolina; pop. 1113.

Yan′da·bu′ (yän′dȧ·bōō′). Town in Sagaing dist. on the Irrawaddy river 40 m. W of Mandalay, Upper Burma; treaty signed here Feb. 24, 1826, by which the king of Ava abandoned his claim to Assam and ceded to the British the provinces of Arakan and Tenasserim.

Yangchow. See KIANGTU.

Yang′ku′ (yäng′chü′); *formerly* **Tai′yuan′** (tī′yü·än′). City, ✳ of Shansi prov., NE China, in center of province on the Fen 265 m. SW of Peiping; pop. ab. 230,000; in fertile region at alt. 2600 ft. near rich coal deposits; railroad terminus. Has fine historical museum, Shansi Univ. Known since 450 A.D.; a strategic center in time of Mongols, scene of massacre of missionaries in Boxer uprising; besieged by Communist forces 1948–49.

Yang′pi′ (yäng′pē′). 1 River 170 m. long, W Yunnan, S China, flowing S to the Mekong; crossed by Burma Road at 5000 ft. altitude; outlet of the lake Erh Hai.

2 Town on E bank of Yangpi river where it is crossed by Burma Road ab. 20 m. WSW of Tali.

Yang′so′ (yäng′sō′). Town, NE Kwangsi prov., SE China, just S of Kweilin; American air base in World War II; captured by Japanese Sept. 1944; retaken by Chinese July 27, 1945.

Yang′tze′ (yäng′[t]sē′; *Chin.* yäng′dzŭ′) or **Yang′tze′ Kiang** (yäng′[t]sē′ kĭ·äng′; *Chin.* yäng′dzŭ′ ji·äng′). Literally "Yang kingdom river," the principal river (*kiang*) in China, ab. 3200 m. long; rises in E Kunlun Mts. in SW Tsinghai, flows SE through deep gorges in Sikang, then E across the plateau of Yunnan and finally ENE across the entire width of China Proper to the East China Sea near Shanghai (see *Map* at SHANGHAI). Known as the Kinsha (q.v.) in its upper course. Navigable for vessels of large draft 585 m. to Hankow; above Ichang navigation difficult and dangerous because of rapids in the Yangtze Gorges (q.v.); on some sections above the gorges navigable for smaller vessels. Its chief tributaries on the N are the Yalung, Min, Kialing, and Han; on the S the Wu and the outlets of (lakes) Tungting Hu and Poyang Hu. In its upper course 8000 to 10,000 ft. above sea level, at Paan 8540 ft., at Chungking 630 ft., at Ichang (below the gorges) 130 ft. and for the last 200 m. of its course practically at sea level.

Yangtze Gorges. Series of remarkable gorges in the Yangtze river, in Hupeh and Szechwan provs., cen. China, bet. the cities of Chungking (at 630 ft. above sea level) and Ichang (at 130 ft.), caused by the river forcing its passage through the Ta Pa Shan. Most famous of the

gorges are bet. Ichang and Fengkieh (120 m.); noted for beauty and grandeur of scenery.

Yang′tze′poo′ (yăng′[t]sē′pŏ′; *Chin.* yăng′dzŭ′-). The northern district of the city of Shanghai, China, from 1932 to 1945 held by the Japanese.

Yanina, Yannina. = IOANNINA.

Ya′nis·yar′vi (yả′nĭs·yăr′vĭ); *Finnish* **Jä′nis·jär′vi** (yä′nĭs·jär′vĭ). Lake, SW Karelia, U.S.S.R., near Finnish border; formerly in Finland.

Yank′ton (yăngk′tŭn). 1 County in South Dakota. See *Table* at SOUTH DAKOTA.

2 City, its ⊗, SE South Dakota, on Missouri river 60 m. SW of Sioux Falls; pop. 9279; railroad center; manufactures flour, fireworks, cement, dairy products; Yankton Coll. (1881; coed.). Settled 1858; capital of Dakota Territory 1861–83; scene of Indian uprising 1862.

Yannitsa. See GENITSA.

Yan′tic (yăn′tĭk). River ab. 20 m. long, SE Connecticut; formed by confluence of forks in W cen. New London co., flows E to join the Shetucket river at Norwich and form the Thames river.

Yan′tra (yän′trä). River ab. 110 m. long in NE cen. Bulgaria; flows N into Danube river E of Nikopol.

Ya′oun·dé′ (yả′ōōn′dā′) *or* **Yaun′de** (youn′dä). Town, ✳ of Republic of Cameroun, 125 m. E of coast of the Gulf of Guinea, W Africa; pop. (1955) 38,000.

Yap (yăp; yäp) *or* **Uap** (wäp). Island group, W Caroline Is., in W Pacific Ocean ab. 225 m. NE of Palau Is.; lat. ab. 9°30′N and long. 138°E; 80 sq. m.; pop. (1938 est.) 6939; comprises four islands close together, of which Yap is largest. One of most beautiful and productive of the Carolines; covered with hills and notable for its numerous remains of an early people, esp. ancient stone platforms and large pieces of circular stone money (hence, often called "Island of Stone Money"). Site of transpacific cable station. Seized by Germany 1885 (see CAROLINE ISLANDS); after World War I became subject of dispute 1920–21 bet. Japan and U.S.; settled at Washington Conference by inclusion in Japanese mandate but with cable and radio rights secured to U.S.; raided and bombed by American naval and air forces 1944–45; bypassed in advance on Japan.

Yap′hank (yăp′hăngk). Village, Suffolk co., SE New York, on Long I. ab. 7 m. NE of Patchogue. Camp Upton was located nearby (see UPTON).

Yapurá. ═ JAPURÁ.

Ya·qui′ (yä·kē′). River ab. 420 m. long in the state of Sonora, NW Mexico; rises near U.S. border, flows S and SW into the Gulf of California.

Ya′ra·cuy′ (yä′rä·kwē′). State of Venezuela. See *Table* at VENEZUELA.

Yard′ville (yärd′vĭl). Village, Mercer co., W cen. New Jersey, ab. 5 m. SW of Trenton; pop. (est.) 3000; manufactures rubber goods and floor coverings.

Yare. See the BROADS.

Ya·ri (yä·rē̇) *or* **Ya·ri·ga·ta·ke** (-gä·tä·kě). Peak 10,467 ft., cen. Honshu, Japan, on W border of Nagano prefecture.

Ya′ri·ta′gua (yä′rė̇·tä′gwä). Town, Yaracuy state, NW Venezuela, SW of San Felipe; pop. (1941 est.) 5495.

Yar′kand′ (yär·kănd′). 1 River 500 m. long, W Sinkiang prov., W China; rises on N slopes of Karakoram Range in Kashmir, N India; flows N and W forming part of Kashmir-Sinkiang border, then N around W end of Kunlun Shan, then N and NE to join the Khotan at ab. 41°N, 81°E and form the Tarim river.

2 *Turki* **Yar·kend′** (yär·kĕnd′); *Chin.* **So′che′** (swä′-chŭ′). Town and oasis, SW Sinkiang, W China, on Yarkand river at edge of Takla Makan Desert 100 m. SE of Kashgar; pop. ab. 70,000; altitude 3900 ft., at foot of N slope of Kunlun Mts.; on S caravan and motor road across Sinkiang; has for centuries been a trade center; irrigation highly developed; grows wheat, barley, beans, and oil plants. Visited by Marco Polo.

Yar′mouth (yär′mŭth). 1 Seaport town, Cumberland

co., SW Maine, on Casco Bay 10 m. N of Portland; pop. 3517; fishing and crab-meat packing; formerly a shipping and shipbuilding center.

2 Town, Barnstable co., SE Massachusetts, 4 m. E of Barnstable; pop. 5504; summer resort.

3 County, Nova Scotia, Canada. See *Table* at NOVA SCOTIA.

4 Resort town, ⊗ of Yarmouth co., SW Nova Scotia, Canada, on Atlantic Ocean; pop. 8106; makes sailing ships, exports fish, lumber. Founded 1759 by settlers from New England; in early days ranked high in tonnage of wooden sailing vessels.

5 *or* **Great Yarmouth.** County borough, Norfolk, E England, on North Sea at mouth of the Yare 110 m. NE of London; pop. 56,771, (1951 pop.) 51,105; port and watering place; largest herring fishing port in the world. Settled as a fishing village before the Conquest; Church of St. Nicholas, founded 1101, destroyed by bombs 1942.

Yar·muk′ (yär·mōōk′). River ab. 50 m. long in NW Jordan, flowing W into the Jordan just S of the Sea of Galilee and in its course forming a section of the boundary bet. Syria and Jordan; in Biblical times separated Gilead on S from Bashan and Gaulanitis on N.

Yaroslav. Russian form of JAROSŁAW.

Ya′ro·slavl′ (yär′ō̇·släv′′l; *Russ.* yĭ·rŭ·släv′′l·y̆′). Industrial city, ✳ of Yaroslavl Region, Soviet Russia, Europe, on the Volga ab. 160 m. NE of Moscow; pop. 298,065; on main railroad N from Moscow; manufactures tobacco, leather, lacquer, and esp. textiles; has cathedral, monasteries, university, and technical schools. Founded c. 1026, an important town in the early Rostov-Suzdal principality.

Yaroslavl Region. Region, N cen. Soviet Russia, Europe, part of level plain traversed by upper Volga; 23,507 sq. m.; pop. 2,271,307; ✳ Yaroslavl. In NW is large Rybinsk Reservoir (*q.v.*); in S part is the small but historically famous Lake Pereslavl. About one third covered with forests and large area is marshland. Agriculture is restricted but well developed; dairying is important. Chief towns Yaroslavl and Shcherbakov (Rybinsk). In early times part of Rostov-Suzdal principality; in 15th cent. came under Moscow principality; after Revolution was a part of Ivanov Industrial Area; reorganized as separate region 1936.

Yar′ra; *formerly* **Yar′ra Yar′ra** (yăr′á yăr′á). River 150 m. long, Victoria, SE Australia; flows W to Port Phillip Bay at Melbourne.

Yar′row (yăr′ō) *or* **Yarrow Water.** Small river in SE Scotland, in Selkirk co.; flows into the Ettrick and on into the Tweed; celebrated by Wordsworth in his verse.

Yar′tse·vo (yär′tsyĭ·vŭ). 1 Town, W Krasnoyarsk Territory, Soviet Russia, Asia, on left bank of the Yenisei, ab. 140 m. NNW of Yeniseisk.

2 Town, W cen. Smolensk Region, Soviet Russia, Europe, on Moscow-Smolensk R.R. ab. 35 m. ENE of Smolensk; cotton mill. Held by Germans 1941–43.

Ya′ru·mal′ (yä′rōō·mäl′). Town, Antioquia dept., NW Colombia, 50 m. N of Medellín; pop. 8693.

Yarva. See JÄRVA.

Yar′vi·co′ya (yär′vė̇·kō′yä). Peak 17,390 ft. in E Tarapacá prov., N Chile.

Ya·sa′wa Islands (yä·sä′wá). Chain of islands and rocky islets extending NNE and SSW for 45 m. NW of Viti Levu I., W Fiji Is., SW Pacific Ocean; in early times inhabited by a savage people.

Ya·sel′da (yả·sĕl′dả; *Russ.* yĭ·syĕl′-); *Pol.* **Ja·siol′da** (yä·shŏl′dä). River ab. 120 m. long, SW White Russia, U.S.S.R., formerly in Polesie dept., E Poland; flows SE into the Pripyat river.

Ya′se·nya (yả·syĭ·nyả); *Czech* **Ja′si·ňa** (yä′sĭ·nyả); *Hung.* **Kő·rös·me′zö** (kû′rŭsh·mě′zŭ). Town, E Carpatho-Ukraine, U.S.S.R., in Carpathian Mts. at W end of Jablonica Pass; pop. (1930) 10,615.

Yas′na·ya Po·lya′na (yȧs′nȧ·yȧ pŭ·lyä′nȧ). Village ab. 13 m. S of Tula, cen. Tula Region, Soviet Russia,

Europe; birthplace and residence of Count Lev Tolstoi. Tolstoi Museum, national shrine, destroyed by Germans in World War II, restored 1946.

Yass (yås). Town, SE New South Wales, SE Australia, on tributary of Murrumbidgee river 32 m. N of Canberra; pop. 2866; located in **Yass–Can'ber·ra** (yås'-kăn'bĕr·à) district, a part of which (Canberra) was set aside 1911 as the Federal Capital Territory (now Australian Capital Territory). See CANBERRA.

Yassy. Var. of *Jassy:* see IAŞI.

Ya·sun', Cape (yä·sŏon'); *Turk.* **Ya·sun' Bur·nu'** (yä·sŏon' bŏor·nŏo'). Cape on Black Sea on N coast of Turkey in Asia, bet. Samsun and Giresun.

Ya·te'ras (yä·tä'räs). Municipality, Oriente prov., E Cuba, just N of Guantánamo; pop. 25,112.

Yates (yäts). County in New York. See *Table* at NEW YORK.

Yates'bor'o (yäts'bûr'ŏ). Locality, Armstrong co., W Pennsylvania, ab. 17 m. NW of Indiana; pop. (1950) 1264.

Yates Center (yäts). City, ⊗ of Woodson co., SE Kansas, NW of Chanute; pop. 2080; near limestone and sandstone quarries, oil and natural-gas deposits.

Yath'ky·ed' Lake (yăth'kĭ·ĕd'). Lake 858 sq. m. in S cen. Keewatin District, Northwest Territories, Canada; in course of Kazan river.

Yathrib. See MEDINA.

Ya·tsu·shi·ro (yä·tsŏo·shĕ·rŏ). Town, Kumamoto prefecture, W cen. Kyushu, Japan, on NE coast of Yatsushiro Bay 25 m. S of Kumamoto; pop. (1945) 41,281.

Yatsushiro Bay. Inlet of East China Sea on W coast of Kyushu I., Japan, ab. 50 m. long by 5 to 15 m. wide; shut in on W by Amakusa Is.

Ya'tung' (yä'tŏong'). Town in Chumbi valley, S Tibet, Outer China, on Sikkim frontier 50 m. NE of Darjeeling; pop. ab. 2000; treaty mart.

Yauapery. = JAUAPERÍ.

Yau'co (you'kô). Municipality (pop. 34,780) and town (pop. 8996), SW Puerto Rico; town is in sugar-growing section 15 m. W of Ponce, near the coast.

Yaunde. See YAOUNDÉ.

Yaun'lat'ga·le; *Latvian* **Jaun'lat'ga·le** (youn'lät'-gä·lĕ). Administrative district, NE Latgale prov., E Latvia; 1657 sq. m.

Yaun'yel'ga·va (youn'yĕl'gà·và); *Latvian* **Jaun'jel'-ga·va** (youn'yĕl'gä·vä); *Ger.* **Frie'drich·stadt** (frē'-drĭk·shtät). Town, E Zemgale prov., S Latvia, on Dvina river 40 m. ESE of Riga; pop. (1930) 2299.

Yav'a·pai (yăv'à·pī). County in Arizona. See *Table* at ARIZONA.

Yavarí. = JAVARÍ.

Ya·vo'rov (yĕ·vô'rŭf); *Pol.* **Ja·wo'rów** (yä·vô'rŏof). Town, SW Ukraine, U.S.S.R., 35 m. WNW of Lvov (formerly in Lwów dept., Poland); pop. 10,690; agricultural trade center; sulfur baths nearby.

Ya·wa·ta (yä·wä·tä) *or* **Ya·ha·ta** (yä·hä·tä). Seaport city, Fukuoka prefecture, N Kyushu, Japan, ab. 13 m. SW of Moji; pop. (1938 est.) 237,900, (1945) 151,378; has great government ironworks (founded 1897), largest in Japan; hence sometimes called the "Pittsburgh of Japan." With Fukuoka forms an important industrial center; shipbuilding; electrical equipment, automobiles, ordnance, light-metals products. Bombed by Americans June 15–16, 1944 and often later. See KITA-KYUSHU.

Ya·wa·ta·ha·ma (yä·wä·tä·hä·mä). Seaport town, Ehime prefecture, NW Shikoku I., Japan, on Bungo Strait; pop. (1945) 33,682; trades esp. with Kyushu.

Yawng'hwe' (young'hwä'). 1 State of the Southern Shan States, Burma; 1389 sq. m.; pop. ab. 127,000. 2 Town, its *, 110 m. SE of Mandalay; pop. 4705.

Yaz'oo (yăz'ŏo). 1 Navigable river 188 m. long, W cen. Mississippi; formed by confluence of Tallahatchie and Yalobusha rivers in Leflore co., flows SW into Mississippi river above Vicksburg; in W part of the 35,000,000 acres sold for $500,000 (the Yazoo Fraud) by Act of the State of Georgia Jan. 7, 1795 to four land companies whose shareholders were discovered to include members of the Georgia legislature. 2 County in Mississippi. See *Table* at MISSISSIPPI.

Yazoo City. City, ⊗ of Yazoo co., W cen. Mississippi, 42 m. N of Jackson; pop. 11,236; cotton trade center.

Ybbs (ĭps). River ab. 70 m. long in W Lower Austria; flows N into Danube river 25 m. W of Sankt Pölten.

Y'by·ty·mí' (ē'vĕ·tĕ·mē'). Town, Paraguarí dept., S Paraguay; pop. ab. 7700.

Yea'don (yā'd'n). Borough, Delaware co., SE Pennsylvania, 5 m. W of Philadelphia; pop. 11,610.

Yead'on (yăd''n). Former urban district, West Riding, Yorkshire, N England; pop. (1931) 7672.

Yea'ger·town (yā'gĕr·toun). Locality, Mifflin co., cen. Pennsylvania, ab. 3 m. N of Lewistown; pop. 1349.

Ye·ba'la (yä·vä'lä; jà-) *or* **Ge·ba'la** (hâ-). Mountainous region in N Morocco, NW Africa, S of Tangier.

Ye'cla (yā'klä). Commune, Murcia prov., SE Spain, 43 m. N by E of Murcia; pop. 22,371; produces oil, esparto, and, esp., wines; manufactures soap, leather.

Yed'do (*Angl.* yĕd'ō). Var. of *Yedo:* see TOKYO.

Yedo. See TOKYO.

Ye·gor'evsk *or* **E·gor'evsk** (yĕ·gôr'yĕfsk). City, Moscow Region, W cen. Soviet Russia, Europe, on branch railroad 60 m. SE of Moscow; pop. 56,340; a manufacturing city with cotton and dye factories.

Ye'gros (yā'grŏs). Town, Caazapá dept., S Paraguay; pop. ab. 9400.

Ye'guas, Point (yà'gwäs). Cape, SE Puerto Rico.

Yehcheng. See QARGHALIQ.

Ye'hsien' (yĕ'shĭ·ĕn'); *formerly* **Lai'chow'** (lī'jō'). City, N Shantung prov., NE China, near S coast of Gulf of Po Hai 80 m. NNW of Tsingtao; pop. ab. 100,000.

Yeisk *or* **Eisk** (yā'ĕsk). Seaport town, NW Krasnodar Territory, Soviet Russia, Europe, on Gulf of Taganrog; pop. 49,280; terminus of branch railroad 80 m. WSW of Rostov; important fisheries; resort.

Ye'ji (yā'jĕ). Town, SE Northern Region, Ghana, West Africa, on the Volta and on Kumasi-Tamale highway ab. 130 m. NE of Kumasi.

Ye'kab·pils (yĕ'kàp·pyĭls); *Latvian* **Jē'kab·pils** (yā'-käb·pĭls); *Ger.* **Ja'kob·stadt** (yä'kôp·shtät). Town, Latvia, on S bank of Dvina river 70 m. ESE of Riga; pop. (1935) 5826; manufactures woolens and wood products. Founded 1650; capitulated to Germans 1917 in World War I after long siege; held by Germans in World War II 1941–44.

Yekaterinburg. Var. of EKATERINBURG.

Yekaterinenshtadt. Var. of EKATERINENSTADT.

Yekaterinodar. Var. of EKATERINODAR.

Yekaterinoslav. Var. of *Ekaterinoslav:* see DNEPROPETROVSK.

Ye·la'bu·ga *or* **E·la'bu·ga** (yĕ·lä'bŏo·gà). Town, N Tatar Republic, Soviet Russia, Europe, on Kama river 100 m. E of Kazan; pop. 8223; active grain trade; notable for discovery 1858 on the Kama 3 m. above the town of ancient burial place in a large mound, where were found skeletons, urns, weapons, bronze decorations, and other artifacts of Stone, Bronze, and Iron Ages.

Ye·lets' *or* **E·lets'** (yĭ·lyĕts'). City, E Orel Region, Soviet Russia, Europe, on the Sosna river ab. 100 m. E of Orel; pop. 50,888; an important railroad junction bet. Tula and Voronezh, has active trade in grain and cattle. Mentioned in 12th cent. when it was an outlying fort of Ryazan principality; destroyed by Mongols 1239 and 1305 and plundered by Tatars 15th cent. when for a time it was entirely abandoned; its modern prosperity dates from 17th cent.; in World War II twice taken by Germans 1941 and 1942.

Yel'ga·va (yĕl'gà·và); *Latvian* **Jel'ga·va** (yĕl'gä·vä); *Ger.* **Mi'tau** (mē'tou). City, * of Zemgale prov., S Latvia, on Lielupe river 20 m. SSW of Riga; pop. (1935) 34,099; manufactures linen, ink, soap; breweries, sugar refineries. Founded 1266 by Teutonic Knights; became

capital of duchy of Kurland 1561; fell under Russian rule 1795; headquarters Oct. 1919 of Bolshevik troops, who were expelled from the city by a combined Latvian and Lithuanian army; in World War II held by German forces 1941–44.

Yelizavetgrad, Yelizavetpol. Vars. of ELISAVET-GRAD, ELISAVETPOL.

Yelizavety, Cape. See Cape ELIZABETH.

Yell (yěl). **1** County in Arkansas. See *Table* at ARKAN-SAS.
2 One of the Shetland Is., NE of N Scotland; 55 sq. m.; pop. 1883.

Yel'low (yěl'ō). **1** River ab. 90 m. long, flowing SW across border from S Alabama into NW Florida; empties into NE Pensacola Bay.
2 River ab. 75 m. long, cen. Wisconsin; rises in E Clark co., flows S into Wisconsin river in E cen. Juneau co.
3 River ab. 70 m. long, NW cen. Wisconsin; rises in cen. Taylor co., flows SW into Lake Wissota near Chippewa Falls.
4 River in China—so called because of the great quantities of yellowish-brown loess it carries in flood. See HWANG HO.

Yel'low·head' Pass (yěl'ō-hěd'). Mountain pass 3723 ft. in Canadian Rocky Mts. on border bet. Jasper National Park, Alberta, and Mount Robson Provincial Park, Brit. Columbia; railroad.

Yel'low·knife (yěl'ō-nīf'). Town, since 1967 ✳ of Northwest Territories, Canada, in S Mackenzie District, on NW shore of Great Slave Lake at mouth of Yellowknife river; pop. 3500; gold mining; airfield.

Yellowknife Preserve. Extensive area, cen. Mackenzie District, Northwest Territories, Canada, bet. Great Bear and Great Slave Lakes, set aside as reservation for Yellowknife Indians.

Yellow Medicine. County in Minnesota. See *Table* at MINNESOTA.

Yellow Mountain. Peak 8900 ft. in Glacier National Park, NW Montana.

Yellow River. 1 Name of several rivers in the U.S.: see YELLOW, above.
2 Name of river in China. See YELLOW and HWANG HO.

Yellow Sea; *Chin.* Hwang Hai (hwäng' hī'). Large inlet of Pacific Ocean bet. NE China and Korea; N inlets are Po Hai and Korea Bay; connects with East China Sea on the S; Shantung Penin. extends into it from W.

Yellow Springs. Residential village, Greene co., SW Ohio, 8 m. S of Springfield; pop. 4167; Antioch Coll. (1852; coed.; co-operative educational plan).

Yel'low·stone' (yěl'ō·stōn'). **1** River, NW Wyoming and S and E Montana; 671 m. long, navigable for 300 m. during high water; rises in Park co., Wyoming, flows N through Yellowstone Lake and Yellowstone National Park, continues N across Montana border, then flows E and NE into Missouri river on boundary bet. Montana and North Dakota; the Grand Canyon of the Yellowstone is the valley, 2000 ft. wide and 1200 ft. deep, of this river in Yellowstone National Park; in the park also includes **Yellowstone Falls,** upper fall 109 ft., lower fall 308 ft.
2 County in Montana. See *Table* at MONTANA.

Yellowstone Lake. Lake in Yellowstone National Park, NW Wyoming; ab. 20 m. long; area 139 sq. m.; elevation 7731 ft.; largest body of water in North America at so great an altitude. Yellowstone river flows through the lake from S to N.

Yellowstone National Park. See UNITED STATES, *National Parks.*

Yel'low·tail' Dam (yěl'ō·tāl'). Dam in Bighorn river, S Montana, forming **Yellowtail Reservoir** (71 m. long) in Montana and Wyoming.

Yell'ville (yěl'vĭl; *Sou,* also -v'l). City, ⊗ of Marion co., N Arkansas; pop. 636; lead and zinc mines nearby.

Yel'mo (yěl'mō). Highest peak 5927 ft. in Segura Mts., SE Spain.

Yem'en (yěm'ěn; *Arab.* yă'măn). Country, SW part of peninsula of Arabia, SW Asia; 75,000 sq. m.; pop. ab. 4,000,000; ✳ San'a. Triangular in shape, bounded by Asir (Saudi Arabia) on the N, by the desert (Rub'al Khali) on the NE, by Aden Protectorate on the E and SE, and by the Red Sea on the W. Quite mountainous, esp. in the S part where peaks exceed 10,000 ft.; has numerous fertile valleys and oases. Known to ancients as Arabia Felix (*q.v.*) although by some early geographers the term was applied to a larger area. Inhabitants engaged generally in agriculture and trade. Chief towns San'a, its port Hodeida, Ta'izz, Mocha, and Maidi.

History: Seat of ancient Minaean kingdom; conquered by Egypt c. 1600 B.C.; invaded by Ethiopians and Romans; converted to Islam 628 A.D., ruled under caliphate; under Turkish control 16th cent.; practically independent until establishment of Egyptian control along coast by Mehemet Ali 1819; autonomy guaranteed by Porte 1913 following serious revolts; successful maintenance of independence by its imam following World War I; independence guaranteed by Great Britain 1934 following its conquest by ibn-Saud; imam assassinated and republic proclaimed Sept. 1962.

Yemen, South. See SOUTH YEMEN.

Yen (yěn). **1** Feudal state of early China under the Chou dynasty (1122–255 B.C.), in the extreme NE. Also so called under the Later Han and Wei dynasties.
2 Early name of Peking (see PEIPING), chief town in the state.

Ye·na·ki'ye·vo (yĭ·nŭ·kē'yĭ·vŭ); *formerly* **Or'dzho·ni·kid'ze** (ôr'jŏn·ĭ·kĭd'zě; *Russ.* ŭr·jŭ·nyĭ·kēd'zě). City, E Stalino Region, E Ukraine, U.S.S.R.; pop. 88,246; manufacturing suburb of Stalino.

Yen'an' (yěn'än'); *officially* **Fu'shih'** (foo'shĭr'). Town, N Shensi prov., NE cen. China, on S bank of a tributary of the Hwang Ho; pop. ab. 50,000. After 1938 became headquarters of Eighth Route (Communist) Army which in the war against the Japanese controlled ab. 1,500,000 people in parts of Shensi, Kansu, and Ningsia provs.; also capital of Communists in Chinese civil war which followed World War II; captured by Nationalist forces Mar. 19, 1947; reoccupied by Communists Apr. 1948 and remained their capital until their capture of Peiping Jan. 1949.

Ye'nan·gyat' (yā'nän·jät'). Town, cen. Burma, on the Irrawaddy 50 m. N of Yenangyaung; oil field.

Ye'nan·gyaung' (yā'nän·joung'). Town on the Irrawaddy river in Magwe dist., Upper Burma, 130 m. SW of Mandalay; pop. 11,098; has extensive oil fields, the most important in Burma and among the largest in the Far East; destroyed when abandoned by the British Apr. 17, 1942; retaken Apr. 16, 1945.

Yen'bo' (yěn'bō) or **Yan'bu'** (yăn'boō). Port on the Red Sea, Hejaz, W Arabia, 185 m. NNW of Jidda; seaport of Medina.

Yen'cheng' (yěn'chŭng'). City, N cen. Kiangsu prov., E China, near coast 125 m. NE of Nanking.

Yen'di (yěn'dĭ). Town, NE Ghana, West Africa, E of Tamale; chief town of N Togoland.

Yeni Foça. See FOÇA.

Ye'ni·şe·hir' (yě'nĭ·shě·hĭr') or **Ye'ni·shehr'** (yě'nĭ-shě'h'r). **1** Town, Bursa vilayet, NW Turkey in Asia, 30 m. E of Bursa; pop. 6893.
2 Village and promontory (*anc.* **Si·ge'um** [sī·jē'ŭm]), Çanakkale vilayet, NW Turkey in Asia, on coast S of the entrance to the Dardanelles; near the site of ancient Troy; the village where Homer places the anchorage of the Greek fleet and their camp during the Trojan War.

Ye'ni·sei' or **Ye'ni·sey'** or **E'ni·sei'** (yěn'ĭ·sā'; *Russ.* yĭ·nyĭ·syā'ĭ). River ab. 2300 m. long, W Siberia, Soviet Russia, Asia; formed by confluence of the Bei Kem and the Khua Kem, with many tributaries rising in the mountains of E Tuva; flows W, then N through the Sayan Mts. past Minusinsk and Krasnoyarsk through Krasnoyarsk Territory into Yenisei Bay at 71°45'N.

Receives the three great Tunguska streams (Upper, Stony, and Lower) from the plateau region to the E; its basin estimated at more than 1,000,000 sq. m. At the delta frozen over generally from Oct. to June, at Minusinsk from Nov. to May. First visited by Cossacks c. 1618; delta first entered by Nordenskjöld 1875.

Yenisei, or **Enisei, Bay.** Inlet of Arctic Ocean (Kara Sea) on coast of NW Siberia W of Taimyr Penin. in Krasnoyarsk Territory, ab. 73°N lat. and 80°E long.

Ye′ni·seisk′ or **E′ni·seisk′** (yĕn′ĭ-sāsk′; Russ. yĭ-nyĭ-syä′ĭsk). Town, W Krasnoyarsk Territory, Soviet Russia, Asia, on left bank of the Yenisei just below the point where it receives the Upper Tunguska, ab. 150 m. N of Krasnoyarsk; pop. 5957; has steamer connection with Krasnoyarsk; center for fur trade and gold mining. Founded 1618.

Yen′ki′ (yĕn′jē′). **1** Town, China. See QARA SHAHR.

2 or **Yen′chi′** (yĕn′jē′). Town, SE Kirin prov., E Manchuria (* of former Chientao prov., SE Manchukuo), ab. 135 m. W of Vladivostok; pop. 24,824.

Yen Mên (yĕn′ mŭn′). See GREAT WALL.

Yenping. See NANPING.

Yentai. See CHEFOO.

Ye·ot′mal (yȧ-ōt′mäl). Town, E Maharashtra state, E cen. India, 85 m. SW of Nagpur; pop. 20,967; trade center with cotton industry.

Yeo′vil (yō′vĭl). Municipal borough, Somersetshire, SW England, on the Yeo 36 m. S of Bristol; pop. 23,337; manufactures gloves, agricultural machinery, bricks.

Yer′ba Bue′na Island (yĕr′bȧ bwā′nȧ; yûr′bȧ); formerly **Goat Island** (gōt). Island in San Francisco Bay, California; bridges from the island to San Francisco and to Oakland joined by a 540-ft. tunnel (76-ft. by 50-ft. cross section) through the island form the San Francisco–Oakland Bay or Transbay bridge (longest bridge in the world, a double-deck structure; bridge proper, including island crossing 4.5 m.; overall length with approaches, ab. 8 m.; 2 center spans of western section of bridge, each 2310 ft. in length, 216 ft. above water; in eastern section, main cantilever span 1400 ft.).

Ye·re·van′ (yĕ·rĕ·vän′) or **E·re·van′** (ĕ·rĕ·vän′); also **E·ri·van′** (Russ. ĕ·ryĭ·vän′y′). City, * of Armenian S.S.R., Soviet Union, in W part on Zanga river 110 m. S of Tiflis; pop. 200,031; on a spur track of the Tiflis–Leninakan-Tabriz R.R. at altitude of 3170 ft.; in recent years has developed many industries, esp. since establishment 1926 of a hydroelectric station on the Zanga; manufactures machinery, furniture, brick, leather products, silk, glycerine, wine and brandy. Has Armenian State Univ. (founded 1921), a Tropical Institute, the Blue Mosque, a Greek church, several Persian palaces, and the ruins of a 16th-cent. Turkish fortress. Founded c. 661 A.D.; scene of much conflict, fought for many times by Persia and Turkey; taken by Russians 1827 and ceded by Persia 1828; became capital of Armenian Republic 1921.

Yer′ing·ton (yĕr′ĭng·tŭn). City, ⊗ of Lyon co., W Nevada, 30 m. ESE of Carson City; pop. 1764.

Yer′wa (yĕr′wȧ). See MAIDUGURI.

Ye·şil′ Ir·mak′ (yĕ·shēl′ ĭr·mäk′); anc. **I′ris** (ī′rĭs). River ab. 200 m. long, chiefly in Tokat and Amasya vilayets, N Turkey in Asia; rises in Akdağ range W of Sivas, flows generally N into Black Sea, with wide delta just E of Samsun. Receives the Kelkit from the E.

Yeşilköy. See SAN STEFANO.

Ye·so (yĕ·zō). Var. of Yezo: see HOKKAIDO.

Yes′te (yās′tā). Commune, Albacete prov., SE Spain, 48 m. SE of Albacete; pop. 9997.

Ye·to·ro·fu (yĕ·tô·rô·fōō). = ETOROFU.

Ye′u′ or **Ye–u** (yä′ōō′). Town, Shwebo dist., Upper Burma, on Mu river 70 m. NW of Mandalay; pop. 3739.

Yeu, Île d′ (ēl′ dyü′). Island 6 m. long and 2 m. wide in Bay of Biscay off coast of Vendée dept., W France; pop. ab. 4000; Pétain imprisoned here Nov. 1945.

Yev·pa·to′ri·ya (Russ. yĭf·pŭ·tô′ryĭ·[y]ȧ) or **Ev′pa-**

to′ri·a (ĕf′pȧ·tōr′ĭ·ȧ); also **Eu′pa·to′ri·a** (ū′pȧ·tōr′ĭ·ȧ). Town and seaport, W coast of Crimea, Soviet Russia, Europe, ab. 45 m. NW of Simferopol; pop. ab. 30,000; taken from Turks by Russians 1783; landing place for Allied armies in Crimean War Sept. 1854; in World War II site of unsuccessful landing of Russian forces Jan. 7–13, 1942 to relieve Sevastopol.

Yezd (yĕzd). **1** Province, cen. Iran; 11,079 sq. m.

2 Industrial city, its *, 170 m. SE of Isfahan; pop. ab. 60,000; on main highway from Tehran and Qum to Kerman; its central position makes it a junction point for several trade routes.

Yezhovo–Cherkessk. See CHERKESSK.

Yezo. See HOKKAIDO.

Y·hú′ or **I·hú′** (ē·ōō′). Town, Caaguazú dept., E cen. Paraguay, ab. 105 m. ENE of Asunción; pop. ab. 5200.

Yi (yē). River ab. 120 m. long in cen. Uruguay; flows W into Río Negro.

Yiews′ley and West Dray′ton (yōōz′lĭ, drā′t′n). Urban district, Middlesex, SE England, 17 m. W of London; pop. 20,488; part of Greater London.

Ying′kow′ (yĭng′kō′) or **New′chwang′** (nū′chwäng′; Chin. nĭ-ū′jōō·äng′). City and treaty port, SW Liaoning prov., S Manchuria, on left bank of Liao ab. 13 m. from its mouth, 120 m. N of Dairen; pop. (1940 est.) 180,871; manufactures cotton cloth. Formerly only the port of inland Newchwang but in 1864 actually became the trading port opened by treaty because of its superior location; only open port of Manchuria until 1907, was main export town for soybeans, bean cake, bean oil, cotton, and coal; in 20th cent. has lost trade in competition with Dairen and Antung.

Yis′ra·el′ (yĭs′rä-āl′). Anglicized form of the Hebrew name of ISRAEL (Heb. Yisrä′ēl).

Y·mui′den (ī·moi′dĕ[n]). = IJMUIDEN.

Yngaví. See INGAVI.

Yoa′kum (yō′kŭm). **1** County in Texas. See Table at TEXAS.

2 City, S Texas, in De Witt and Lavaca cos. 36 m. N of Victoria; pop. 5761; manufactures leather goods; farming (esp. tomatoes, poultry).

Yo′be (yō′bȧ). Stream ab. 100 m. long in NE Nigeria; formed by confluence of Hadejia and another headstream in Bornu prov., flows E to NW Lake Chad.

Yochow. See YOYANG.

Yo·do (yô·dô). **1** Lake, Kyoto prefecture, just S of Kyoto, W cen. Honshu, Japan, near junction of Uji and Hozu rivers which form the Yodo river.

2 Jap. **Yo·do·ga·wa** (yô·dô·gä·wä). River W cen. Honshu, Japan; formed by the Uji and Hozu in S Kyoto prefecture S of Kyoto, flows S into Osaka Bay at Osaka through two mouths, the Ajikawa and the Kizugawa. See UJI.

Yog Point (yōg). Point, 14.6°N, N Catanduanes I., E Phil. Is.

Yo′ho (yō′hō). River and scenic valley in Yoho National Park, SE Brit. Columbia; contains Takkakaw waterfall; joins Kicking Horse river to flow into the Columbia.

Yoho National Park. See CANADA, National Parks.

Yo·jo′a, Lake (yō·hō′ä). Lake 25 m. long and 6 m. wide in W cen. Honduras; affords water communication via the Blanco river and the Ulúa river with the seaport town of Puerto Cortés.

Yok·kai·chi (yŏk·kĭ·chĕ). City, Mie prefecture, S Honshu, Japan, on NW shore of Ise Bay 25 m. SW of Nagoya; pop. (1945) 94,696; special trading port; large import and export business; chief exports cotton fabrics and banko ware. Bombed by Americans 1945.

Yo′ko·ha′ma (yō′kô·hä′mȧ; Jap. yô·kô·hä·mä). Commercial seaport city, * of Kanagawa prefecture, SE Honshu, Japan, on W shore of Tokyo Bay 18 m. S of Tokyo; pop. (1940) 968,091, (1945) 624,994; chief port of Japan and leading silk port in the world; ranks first in shipbuilding and is important in manufacture of auto-

mobiles and heavy electrical equipment. Only a fishing village in feudal period of Japan; visited by Commodore Perry 1854; opened to foreign trade 1859; harbor completed 1896; expanded 1901 to include Kanagawa (q.v.); almost completely destroyed 1923 by earthquake and fire; rebuilt on more modern plan. Severely bombed by American planes May 28, 1945 and often in June–July 1945.

Yo′ko·su′ka (yō′kô·sōō′kà; *Jap.* yô·kôs·kä). Seaport city and naval base, Kanagawa prefecture, SE Honshu, Japan, on Tokyo Bay 12 m. S of Yokohama; pop. (1945) 202,038; harbor is shut in by two promontories; has Admiralty Office, shipyard, naval school, etc. Contains tomb of Will Adams, English navigator and pilot, who lived here 1600–20. A fishing village before 1865 when it was selected as naval port; bombed July 18, 1945 by Americans with heavy damage to Japanese fleet.

Yo′la (yō′là). Town, * of Adamawa prov., E Northern Region, Nigeria, on the upper Benue river near Cameroun border; pop. ab. 5000; ab. 480 m. by river above Lokoja and reached by steamers of light draft in flood season; a former Fulah capital.

Yo′lo (yō′lō). County in California. See *Table* at CALIFORNIA.

Yom (yŭm; *Angl.* yŏm). River ab. 300 m. long, NW Thailand; flows S from mountains on N border to join the Nan just above its confluence with the Ping.

Yo·me Ji·ma (yô·mĕ jê·mä). One of the Bonin Is., Japan.

Yo·na·ba·ru (yô·nä·bä·rōō). Locality on E coast of Okinawa I., Ryukyu Is., Japan, at S end across from Naha on S shore of Buckner Bay; pop. ab. 5000; airfield; severe fighting May 1945; airfield captured May 14.

Yo·na·go (yô·nä·gô). Town, Tottori prefecture, W Honshu, Japan; pop. (1945) 47,929; a rail and shipping center N of Okayama, with good harbor on Sea of Japan.

Yo·ne·za·wa (yô·nĕ·zä·wä). City, Yamagata prefecture, N Honshu, Japan, 55 m. E of Niigata; pop. (1945) 53,768; its chief industry for 150 years has been the weaving of silken fabrics.

Yon′kers (yŏng′kẽrz). City, Westchester co., SE New York, on Hudson river adjoining Greater New York on the N; center of city is ab. 15 m. N of S end of Manhattan I.; pop. 190,634; residential suburb of New York City; produces elevators, hats, refined sugar, carpets, patent medicines, wire and cable. St. Joseph's Seminary and Coll. (1831; men). Part of purchase made by Dutch West India Co. from Indians c. 1639; included in grant of land made 1646 to "Jonker" or "Jonkheer" Van der Donck; became part of Philipse Manor after 1672; was disputed territory in Revolutionary War; incorp. as village 1855, chartered as city 1872.

Yonne (yôn). **1** River 120 m. long in cen. France; flows N out of Nièvre dept. into Seine river at Montereaufaut-Yonne.
2 Department of France. See *Table* at FRANCE.

Yon·tan (yŏn·tän). Village and airfield on W coast of Okinawa I., Ryukyu Is., Japan, ab. 13 m. N of Naha; airfield seized by U.S. troops early in Apr. 1945.

York (yôrk). **1** Estuary ab. 40 m. long, E Virginia; formed by confluence of Pamunkey and Mattaponi rivers at West Point, flows SE into Chesapeake Bay.
2 Name of counties in five states of the U.S. See *Tables* at MAINE, NEBRASKA, PENNSYLVANIA, SOUTH CAROLINA, VIRGINIA.
3 Town, Sumter co., W Alabama, 5 m. E of Mississippi border and 18 m. W of Tombigbee river; pop. 2932.
4 Town, York co., SW Maine, on Atlantic Ocean 25 m. SSW of Biddeford; pop. 4663. Includes **York Beach** and **York Harbor,** summer resorts. Settled 1624; object of Indian raid 1692 in which town was burned and inhabitants killed or made captive; ⊗ 1760–1832.
5 City, ⊗ of York co., SE Nebraska, 41 m. E of Grand Island; pop. 6173; trade center in agricultural section. York Coll. (1890; coed.; United Brethren in Christ).

6 Industrial city, ⊗ of York co., S Pennsylvania, 23 m. S of Harrisburg; pop. 54,504; rifle-making center before Revolution; manufactures safes and locks, cigars, ice machinery, air-conditioning equipment, pianos, farm machinery, turbines, metal products, textiles. Settled by Germans 1735; became ⊗ 1749; capital of American Colonies during British occupation of Philadelphia 1777–78; occupied by Confederates under Gen. Jubal Early 1863; chartered as city 1887.
7 Town, ⊗ of York co., N South Carolina, 13 m. WNW of Rock Hill; pop. 4758; settled c. 1757; manufactures cotton goods, lumber products, meal.
8 County, New Brunswick, Canada. See *Table* at NEW BRUNSWICK.
9 County, Ontario, Canada. See *Table* at ONTARIO.
10 County in England. See YORKSHIRE.
11 *anc.* **Eb′o·ra′cum** (ĕb′ô·rā′kŭm) *or* **Eb′u·ra′cum** (ĕb′ú·). City and county borough, Yorkshire, N England, at confluence of Foss and Ouse rivers 20 m. ENE of Leeds; pop. 84,813, (1951 pop.) 105,336; manufactures iron and steel goods, glass, chemicals, and leather products; cathedral (York Minster) noted for stained glass. A (Celtic) British, Roman, Angle, Danish, and Norman settlement; Constantine the Great proclaimed Roman emperor here 306; several English parliaments 1175 ff.; site of Council of the North 1537, which dealt with problems caused by the insurrectionary Pilgrimage of Grace; during 15th–16th cents. scene of presentation of plays of the York Cycle, one of the four collections of English mystery plays (see CHESTER, COVENTRY, WAKEFIELD).

York, Cape. 1 Northern point of Cape York Penin., Queensland, Australia, on E side of Gulf of Carpentaria, 10°45′S; extends into Torres Strait.
2 Point, SW Hayes Penin., NW Greenland, on N shore of Baffin Bay, 76°N, 68°W. Station here used by Peary and Bartlett on Polar expeditions. Noted for its large iron meteorites, one of which (weighing 100 tons) was brought by Peary to American Natural History Museum in New York. Monument erected here 1932 to Peary.

Yorke (yôrk), *or* **Yorke's** (yôrks), **Peninsula.** Peninsula ab. 100 m. long, SE South Australia, bet. Spencer Gulf on W and Gulf of St. Vincent on E.

York Factory. Trading post on Hudson Bay, NE Manitoba prov., Canada, at the mouth of Hayes river; with Port Nelson, pop. 506.

York′shire (yôrk′shĭr; -shẽr) *or* **York.** County, N England; area 6089 sq. m.; pop. (1951) 4,621,698; includes three administrative counties, North Riding (⊗ Northallerton), East Riding (⊗ Beverly), West Riding (⊗ Wakefield), and the City of York, which is a county of itself, outside the ridings; see *Table* at ENGLAND. Towns include Hull, Bradford, Leeds, Sheffield, Wakefield, Middlesbrough, Rotherham; rivers include Ouse, Swale, Wharfe, Aire, Derwent; agriculture, livestock raising, fisheries, coal and iron mining, iron and steel manufacturing, manufacturing of wool and cotton textiles, leather goods.

York′ton (yôrk′tŭn). City, SE Saskatchewan, Canada, 110 m. ENE of Regina; pop. 7074; railroad junction.

York′town (yôrk′toun). **1** Town, De Witt co., S Texas, 30 m. WNW of Victoria; pop. 2527; in farming section.
2 Town, ⊗ of York co., SE Virginia, on York river 20 m. N of Newport News; pop. 311; in Colonial National Historical Park; scene in 1781 of siege of British forces under Cornwallis by Washington and Rochambeau in Revolution and of surrender of Cornwallis; besieged by Union forces under McClellan in Civil War and evacuated 1862; U.S. naval base established 1917.

York′ville (yôrk′vĭl). **1** City, ⊗ of Kendall co., NE Illinois; pop 1568.
2 Village, Oneida co., cen. New York, on Mohawk river 3 m. WNW of Utica; pop. 3749; residential suburb.
3 Village, Belmont and Jefferson cos., E Ohio, on Ohio river 15 m. S of Steubenville; pop. 1801; steel manufactures.

Yo'ro (yō'rô). **1** Department, N Honduras; 4030 sq. m.; pop. (1945 est.) 78,359.

2 Town, its ✳; pop. (1935) 1419.

Yor'tan Te·pe' (yôr'tän tĕ·pĕ'). Locality, W Turkey in Asia; archaeological site, ruins of ancient city of W Lydia, ESE of Pergamum.

Yor'u·ba·land' (yôr'ŭ·bà·lănd'). Country of the Yorubas, a former kingdom, now included in Western Region and part of SW Northern Region, Nigeria; ab. 35,000 sq. m.; pop. 3,166,000.

Yo·sem'i·te Falls (yŏ·sĕm'ĭ·tĕ). Two falls, upper 1430 ft., lower 320 ft., total drop including a series of cascades 2525 ft., in Yosemite National Park, E cen. California.

Yosemite National Park. See UNITED STATES, *National Parks.*

Yosemite Valley. Famous valley 6 m. long of the upper Merced river, cen. California, in S Yosemite National Park; valley floor ab. 4000 ft. above sea level, walls 3000–4000 ft. high; many waterfalls.

Yo·shi·no (yŏ·shē·nŏ). River 146 m. long in NE Shikoku I., Japan; flows E into Kii Channel at Tokushima.

Yoshkar Ola. See IOSHKAR OLA.

Youghal (yôl). Urban district and commercial seaport, E co. Cork, SW Eire, on **Youghal Bay,** estuary of Blackwater river; pop. 5131; resort. A Norse settlement in 9th cent.; site of first Franciscan monastery in Ireland (1224); Sir Walter Raleigh was mayor 1588–89 and is said to have planted the first potato here.

Yough'io·ghe'ny (yŏk'io·gā'nĭ; *attributively, usu.* yŏk'ŏ·gā'nĭ). River ab. 150 m. long, NW Maryland and SW Pennsylvania; flows N through NW Maryland into Pennsylvania, and NW into Monongahela river at McKeesport. Navigable for 9 m.

Young (yŭng). County in Texas. See *Table* at TEXAS.

Young Island. One of the Balleny Is., Antarctica, ab. 19 m. long by 5 m. wide; rises to a plateau ab. 4000 ft.

Youngs'town (yŭngz'toun). City, Mahoning and Trumbull cos., NE Ohio on Mahoning river 43 m. E of Akron; ⊗ of Mahoning co.; pop. 166,689; iron and steel center; limestone deposits, once also had iron, coal; makes finished steel products, brick and cement, electric lamps, coke and coke by-products, chemicals, rubber goods. Youngstown Univ. (1908). Settled 1797; incorp. as town 1848, as city 1867; became ⊗ 1876.

Youngs'ville (yŭngz'vĭl). Borough, Warren co., NW Pennsylvania, 36 m. NNE of Oil City; pop. 2211; settled 1795; makes colored shale brick, furniture, mirrors.

Young'wood (yŭng'wŏŏd). Industrial borough, Westmoreland co., SW Pennsylvania, 27 m. ESE of Pittsburgh; pop. 2813; manufactures scientific instruments.

Yo'yang' (yō'yäng'); *formerly* **Yo'chow'** (yō'jō'). Treaty port, NE Hunan prov., SE cen. China, on NE shore of Tungting Hu (lake) at its outlet and ab. 6 m. S of the Yangtze; pop. (1931 est.) 4800; on Hankow-Canton R.R. Built 1371 and surrounded by a wall; made a treaty port in 1898.

Yoz·gat' (yôz·gät'). **1** Vilayet, cen. Turkey in Asia; 5385 sq. m.; pop. 261,821.

2 Town, its ✳, 100 m. E of Ankara; pop. 13,615.

Y'pa·ca'ra·í' (ē'pä·kä'rä·ē') *or* **Y'pa·ca·ray'** (ē'pä·kä·rī'). **1** Lake in S cen. Paraguay, near Asunción; pleasure resort.

2 Town, Central dept., S Paraguay, ab. 160 m. ESE of Asunción; pop. ab. 8200.

Y'pa·né' (ē'pä·nä'). Town, Central dept., S Paraguay, ab. 80 m. SE of Asunción; pop. ab. 5000.

Y'pi·ran'ga (ē'pĕ·răNNg'gà); *modern spelling* **I'pi·ran'ga.** Plain near São Paulo, in São Paulo state, SE Brazil; site where independence of Brazil from Portugal was declared Sept. 7, 1822 by Prince Pedro.

Y·po'a, Lake (ē·pō'ä). Lake ab. 100 sq. m. in S Paraguay; navigable for small boats.

Ypres. See IEPER.

Yp'si·lan'ti (ĭp'sĭ·lăn'tĭ). Industrial city, Washtenaw co., SE Michigan, 8 m. SE of Ann Arbor; pop. 20,957;

trading center for agricultural section. Eastern Michigan Univ. (1849; coed.).

Yp'si·lon Mountain (ĭp'sĭ·lŏn). Peak 13,507 ft. in Larimer co., N Colorado.

Y·re'ka *or* **Yreka City** (wī·rē'kà). Town, ⊗ of Siskiyou co., N California, 100 m. NE of Eureka; pop. 4759; founded as mining town 1851; in agricultural and lumbering region; fruit; stock raising.

Ys'a·bel (ĭz'à·bĕl; *Span.* ē'sä·vĕl'). Var. of *Isabel:* see SANTA ISABEL.

Ys'a·bel Channel (ĭz'à·bĕl). Passage bet. New Hanover I. and the Saint Matthias Group, N Bismarck Archipelago, connecting Pacific Ocean with Bismarck Sea.

Y'sel (ī'sĕl). = IJSSEL.

Y'ser' (ē'zâr'). River 55 m. long in Nord dept., N France, and in Belgium, flowing into North Sea; battles 1914–18.

Yssel. See IJSSEL.

Y'stad (ü'städ). Commercial seaport, Malmöhus prov., SW Sweden, on the Baltic Sea; pop. 12,109; iron foundries, steelworks, dairies.

Ystrad Fflur. See STRATA FLORIDA.

Ystradyfodwg. See RHONDDA.

Yst'wyth (ĭst'wĭth; *Welsh* ûst'-). Small river in cen. Wales; flows W into cen. Cardigan Bay at Aberystwyth.

Y'than (ī'thăn). River 35 m. long in NE Scotland; flows SE in Aberdeen co. and empties into North Sea ab. 12 m. N of Aberdeen.

Yu. See SIANG, 2.

Yuan (yü·än'). **1** Name of the Coi (river of N Indochina) in Yunnan, S China.

2 *or* **Yuen** (yü·än'). River ab. 500 m. long, SE cen. China; rises in cen. Kweichow near Kweiyang, flows NE in Hunan prov. to Tungting Hu (lake); navigable for most of its course.

Yuanchow. See CHIHKIANG.

Yu'ba (yōō'bà). **1** River in N cen. California; its branches from Sierra and Nevada cos. join in Yuba co., then flow SW into Sacramento river N of Sacramento. See BULLARD'S BAR DAM and LAKE SPAULDING DAM.

2 County in California. See *Table* at CALIFORNIA.

Yuba City. City, ⊗ of Sutter co., N cen. California, on Feather river 42 m. N of Sacramento; pop. 11,507; opp. Marysville with which it forms one commercial community; founded 1849, made ⊗ 1856; peach canning.

Yu'bi (yōō'bĭ; *Span.* yōō'vĕ) *or* **Ju'by** (jōō'bĭ; *Span.* hōō'vĕ), **Cape.** Cape on SW coast of Morocco, NW Africa, E of Canary Is.; on boundary bet. Morocco and the Saquiet el Hamra zone of Spanish Sahara. See CABO YUBI.

Yu'ca·ma'ni (yōō'kä·mä'nĕ). Peak 17,860 ft. in the Andes Mts. in Moquegua dept., S Peru.

Yu'ca·tán' (yōō'kä·tän'; -tän'). **1** Peninsula comprising the states of Campeche and Yucatán and the territory of Quintana Roo in SE Mexico, and British Honduras and the N section of Guatemala in Central America; separates Gulf of Mexico from Caribbean Sea; its NE point, Cape Catoche, extends into Yucatán Channel; Bay of Campeche to the W and Cozumel I. off NE coast. Rich in historical associations; seat of Maya civilization (1st empire 100 B.C. to 630 A.D.; transitional period 630 to 930; 2d empire 960–1200) and of Toltecs 1200 to 1450. Many magnificent ruins of cities, temples, pyramids, esp. Chichén Itzá, Uaxactún, Uxmal (*qq.v.*).

2 State, N Yucatán penin., SE Mexico. See *Table* at MEXICO.

Yucatán Channel. Channel bet. W end of Cuba and Yucatán penin., Mexico, connecting the Caribbean Sea with the Gulf of Mexico.

Yuc'ca House National Monument (yŭk'à). See UNITED STATES, *National Monuments.*

Yug (yōōk). River 330 m. long, E Vologda Region, Soviet Russia, Europe; flows N to unite with the Sukhona and form the Northern Dvina just above Veliki Ustyug.

Yu·go·sla′vi·a (yōō′gṓ·slä′vĭ·à; -släv′ĭ·à); *Serb.* **Ju′go-sla′vi·ja** (yōō′gṓ·slä′vĕ·yä); *formerly* **Kingdom of the Serbs, Cro′ats, and Slo′venes** (sûrbz′, krō′ăts, slō′vĕnz′); *also* **Ju′go·sla′vi·a** (yōō′gṓ·slä′vĭ·à; -släv′ĭ·à). Federal republic, SE Europe, officially a "federal people's republic"; 96,201 sq. m.; pop. (1931) 13,934,038, (1947 est.) 15,324,500; ✳ Belgrade. Bounded on N by Austria and Hungary, on E by Romania and Bulgaria, on S by Greece and Albania, and on W by Adriatic Sea and Italy. Comprises the six federative units (republics) of Serbia, Croatia, Bosnia and Herzegovina, Slovenia, Macedonia, and Montenegro and two autonomous provinces, Voivodina and Kosovo-Metohija, temporarily attached to Serbia. *Mountains:* Country has almost no coastal plain, the coastal region being a white limestone plateau (karst) including the Dinaric Alps and the Velebit range; in NW are the Karawanken Alps on Austrian border and the Julian Alps (highest point Triglav 9394 ft.) on Italian border; in S is a part of the North Albanian Alps; in cen. part is plateau (Slav *planina,* "mountain pasture") region 2000 to 8200 ft.; highest inland peak Durmitor 8294 ft. in S. *Chief rivers:* In E is a section of the Danube which in Yugoslavia receives the Tisza and the Drava rivers from the N, the Sava (its chief tributaries the Una, Vrbas, Drina) from the W, and the Morava (its chief tributary the Ibar) from the S; in SE flowing through Greece into Gulf of Salonika is the Vardar. *Lakes:* Parts of Scutari, Ohrid, and Prespa on SW border. *Chief occupations:* Agricul-ture (grains, fruits, olives, and tobacco) and mining (coal, iron, copper, chrome). *Chief cities:* Belgrade, Zagreb, Subotica, Ljubljana, Sarajevo, and Skoplje.

History: At collapse of Dual Monarchy proclaimed Kingdom of Serbs, Croats, and Slovenes, 1918 (see AUSTRIA-HUNGARY, SERBIA, CROATIA, BOSNIA AND HERZEGOVINA, MONTENEGRO, DALMATIA, and SLOVENIA for earlier history of component parts); engaged in dispute with Italy over Fiume (*q.v.*) 1919–24; signed treaties with Czechoslovakia 1920, with Romania 1921, the beginning of Little Entente; ruled by absolute monarchy from 1929, at which time name was changed officially to Yugoslavia and the country was divided into 9 counties not based on racial lines, to 1931; tried to end struggle bet. federalist minorities (Croats, Slovenes) and the predominantly Serbian government by providing for greater autonomy of Croatia and Slovenia in federalized constitution 1939; overthrew the government which had signed Axis pact Mar. 1941; invaded by German forces Apr. 6, 1941 and during rest of war was occupied by German, Italian, Hungarian, and Bulgarian troops; elected Nov. 11, 1945 a new government under Marshal Josip Broz (Tito) who had previously (Nov. 1943) formed a provisional government repudiating the monarchy; adopted new constitution and proclaimed Nov. 29, 1945 the Federal People's Republic of Yugoslavia.

Yu′ki (yōō′kẻ). Seaport, North Kankyo prov., extreme NE Korea, N of Rashin close to Soviet Russia border; pop. 22,473; occupied by Russians Aug. 12, 1945.

YUGOSLAVIA

Statute Miles
0   50   100

✳ Capitals

Yu′kon (yōō′kŏn). **1** City, Canadian co., cen. Oklahoma, 13 m. W of Oklahoma City; pop. 3076; milling center.
2 Locality, Westmoreland co., SW Pennsylvania, ab. 9 m. SW of Greensburg; pop. 1062.
3 River formed by union of Lewes and Pelly rivers in SW Yukon Territory, Canada, ab. 2300 m. long from the headwaters of the Lewes; flows NW across Yukon border into Alaska, then SW from its junction with the Porcupine across cen. Alaska to Bering Sea S of Norton Sound. Receives Stewart and Klondike tributaries from the E in Yukon Territory, the Porcupine (q.v.) from the NE, the Koyukuk from the N, and the Tanana from the S, in Alaska; has delta 80 to 90 m. wide with only one mouth navigable. Third longest river highway in North America; its entire course of 1260 m. in Alaska is navigable, also as far as Dawson and to Whitehorse for smaller vessels. Frozen over Oct. to June. Its lower course is broad and muddy flowing through a marshy plain. At its bend in NE Alaska it widens into the **Yukon Flats** (10 to 20 m. wide for ab. 200 m.).
4 Territory, NW Canada; land area 205,346 sq. m.; pop. 9096; ✱ Whitehorse. Bounded on N by Arctic Ocean, E by Mackenzie District, Northwest Territories, on S by British Columbia, and on W by Alaska. A plateau region with several mountain ranges. St. Elias, across SW corner (containing Mt. Logan, highest mountain in Canada, 19,850 ft.); N end of Rocky Mts. in S, including Stikine Mts.; the Mackenzie Mts. along Mackenzie District border; and the Ogilvie Range in cen. part. Chief river the upper Yukon, with its tributaries and headstreams, the Porcupine, Klondike, White, Lewes, and Pelly; in the N is the Peel, a tributary of the Mackenzie and in the S the upper Liard. No large lakes (largest Kluane 184 sq. m.), but many small ones. Whitehorse is head of navigation of the Yukon (Lewes) and also terminus of only railroad, running S through White Pass to Skagway in Alaska. Many river valleys have extensive forests and mineral resources are very great, esp. gold (see KLONDIKE). Chief towns Whitehorse, Dawson, Carcross, Selkirk. Formed from Northwest Territories in 1898, soon after the Klondike gold rush.
Yu′lin′ (yü′lĭn′). Town, N Shensi prov., NE cen. China, 265 m. N of Sian, just inside the Great Wall.
Yu′ma (yōō′mȧ). **1** Name of counties in two states of the U.S. See *Tables* at ARIZONA and COLORADO.
2 City, ⊗ of Yuma co., SW corner of Arizona, on Colorado river 20 m. N of Mexican border; pop. 23,974; incorp. 1871; commercial center for agricultural region.
3 Town, Yuma co., NE Colorado, 43 m. SE of Sterling; pop. 1919; in region producing oats, rye, wheat.
Yun·gay′ (yōōng-gī′). City, Ancash dept., NW Peru, W of Mt. Huascarán; scene of a battle in which Chilean troops under Manuel Bulnes overthrew the Peruvian-Bolivian confederation Jan. 20, 1839.
Yungchang. See PAOSHAN.
Yung′ki′ (yōōng′jē′); *Jap. official name* **Ki′rin′** (kē′rĭn′; *Pekingese* jē′lĭn′). City and treaty port, ✱ of Kirin prov., E Manchuria, in SW part of province (also ✱ of former Kirin prov., SE cen. Manchukuo), on left bank of Sungari river ab. 60 m. E of Changchun; pop. (1940 est.) 173,624; has long been an important trade center; trades esp. in lumber and tobacco. Seat of a Chinese military government 1750–1911; opened to foreign trade 1905; almost entirely destroyed by fire 1911; captured by Communist forces Mar. 1948.
Yung′kia′ (yōōng′jĭ·ä′); *formerly* **Wen′chow′** (wŭn′-jō′). City and treaty port, SE Chekiang prov., E China, at the mouth of the Wu river, 160 m. S of Hangchow and 150 m. NNE of Minhow; pop. (1931 est.) 631,276. Founded in 4th cent. A.D.; has many old buildings; opened to foreign trade 1876 by Chefoo Convention; in World War II occupied by Japanese; taken by Chinese June 1949.
Yung′nien′ (yōōng′nĭ·ĕn′). Town, S Hopeh prov., NE China, ab. 125 m. W of Tsinan.

Yung′ning′ (yōōng′nĭng′) *or* **Nan′ning′** (nän′nĭng′). Town and treaty port, ✱ of Kwangsi prov., SE China, on left bank of Siang river ab. 30 m. below its junction with the Li and 360 m. above Tsangwu; pop. (1931 est.) 68,110; walled town; exports chiefly aniseed, beans, ground nuts, tin, antimony. Opened to foreign trade 1907; in World War II taken by Japanese Nov. 1944; recaptured by Chinese May 1945.
Yung′ting′ (yōōng′dĭng′) *or* **Hun** (hōōn). River ab. 300 m. long; rises in N Shansi prov., NE China, flows generally E and SE to the Peh at Tientsin.
Yun′kang′ (yün′gäng′). See TATUNG.
Yun·nan′ (yōō·nän′; *Chin.* yün′nän′). **1** *formerly also* **Yün′nan′** (yün′nän′). Province, S China; 123,539 sq. m.; pop. (1936 est.) 11,994,549; ✱ Kunming. Bounded on N by Sikang and Szechwan, on E by Kweichow and Kwangsi, on S by French Indochina and Burma, and on W by Burma. Third largest province of China Proper; very mountainous esp. in N and W; its cen. part a plateau averaging 6500 ft. and sloping to SE. Has many small lakes; crossed by 3 great river systems—the Yangtze (here known as the Kinsha), the Mekong and Salween—and the source of two others—the Si (Hungshui) and the Yuan (Coi); the N courses of the first three flow through great gorges. Chief occupation agriculture, with rice, maize, wheat, tea, sugar, and cotton as the main crops; has great mineral resources, as yet only little developed, such as coal, iron, tin, copper, lead, precious stones. A large part of its population consists of Miaos, Lolos, Shans, and other non-Chinese elements. Chief cities Kunming, Tali, Mengtsz, Szemao, Likiang. Long independent, because of its isolation, during the historical development of China; overrun by Kublai Khan in 13th cent., completely conquered 1382, and became part of empire in 17th cent.; scene of great Panthay (Mohammedan) revolt 1855–73; trade routes through it sought by British but difficult terrain delayed them until Burma Road (q.v.) was opened 1939; part of road and S section of province seized by Japanese 1942.
2 See KUNMING.
Yün′nan′fu′ (yün′nän′fōō′). A former name of KUNMING.
Yunque, El. See EL YUNQUE.
Yura Strait. See KITAN STRAIT.
Yu·ré′cua·ro (yōō·rā′kwä·rô). Town, Michoacán state, SW Mexico, 60 m. NNW of Uruapan; pop. 8956.
Yurev. See TARTU.
Yu·ri·ma′guas (yōō′rĕ·mä′gwäs). Town, Loreto prov., NE Peru, on Huallaga river; pop. (1940 est.) 5918.
Yu·ri′ria (yōō·rē′ryä). Town, Guanajuato state, cen. Mexico, W of Salvatierra; pop. 5698.
Yus′ca·rán′ (yōōs′kä·rän′). Town, ✱ of El Paraíso dept., Honduras, 35 m. SE of Tegucigalpa; pop. 1214; cereals, fruits, coffee, silver.
Yu′sef, Bahr (bä′h′r yōō′sĕf). Dry bed of the Nile, Egypt, on its W side, used as an artificial irrigation channel; extends ab. 270 m. from near Asyût to El Faiyûm region.
Yutien. See KERIYA.
Yu′ty (yōō′tĕ). Town, S Caazapá dept., S Paraguay; pop. ab. 18,200.
Yuzovka. See STALINO.
Y′ver′don′ (ē′vĕr′dôn′) *or* **Y′ver′dun′** (-dûn′); *Ger.* **I′fer·ten** (ē′fĕr·tĕn); *anc.* **Eb′u·ro·du′num** (ĕb′ū̇·rô-dū′nŭm). Commune, Vaud canton, W Switzerland, 18 m. N of Lausanne; pop. (1930) 9715; 12th-cent. castle, 18th-cent. church; sulfur baths nearby; tourist resort; manufactures locomotives and railroad cars, cigars.
Y′ve·tot′ (ēv′tô′). Town, Seine-Maritime dept., N France, 20 m. NW of Rouen; pop. 7214; a small monarchy 15th–16th cents., the title of king being applied to its lords who became subject of one of Béranger's most famous songs, *Le Roi d'Yvetot* (1813).
Y′za·bal′, Lake (ē′sä·väl′). = Lake IZABAL.

Z

Zaan·dam′ (zän·däm′). Commune, North Holland prov., W Netherlands, on Zaan river; pop. (1939) 38,023; lumber center, with many windmills; place where Peter the Great of Russia lived while he studied shipbuilding 1697.

Zab, Great (zăb); *Arab.* **Zab al Ka·bir′** (zăb′ ăl kä·bēr′). River ab. 260 m. long in SE Turkey in Asia and N Iraq; rises in mountains of Kurdistan and flows S and SW into the Tigris river below Mosul.

Zab, Little; *Arab.* **Zab al As′fal** (zăb′ ăl ăs′făl). River ab. 230 m. long in NW Iran and N Iraq; flows SW into the Tigris river ab. 50 m. below the Great Zab.

Za′bai·kal′ (zä′bī·käl′). = TRANSBAIKALIA.

Zabern. See SAVERNE.

Ząb′ko·wi′ce (zônmp′kô·vē′tsĕ), *in full* **Ząbkowice Śląs′kie** (shlôns′kyĕ); *Ger.* **Fran′ken·stein** *or* **Fran·kenstein in Schle′si·en** (frängk′ĕn·shtīn ĭn shlä′zĕ·ĕn). City, S Wrocław dept., SW Poland, 39 m. SSW of Wrocław; pop. (1946) 10,857; formerly in Prussia, Germany; late-Gothic church; manufactures hats, horsehair. Founded 13th cent.; sold to Prussia 1791; assigned to Poland by Potsdam Conference 1945.

Zab Mountains (zăb). Range of the Atlas Mts. along the NW boundary of Touggourt territory, N Algeria; highest ab. 4300 ft.

Za·bo′rze (zä·bô′zhĕ). Former commune (pop. 29,208), Oppeln govt. dist., Silesia prov., Prussia, Germany; in 1927 became part of Hindenburg, Germany, which in 1945 again became Polish under the name Zabrze.

Zab′rze (zäb′zhĕ); *Ger.* **Hin′den·burg** (hĭn′dĕn·bûrg; *Ger.* -bŏŏrk), *also* **Hin′den·burg in O′ber·schle′si·en** (-bŏŏrk ĭn ō′bēr·shlä′zĕ·ĕn). Industrial city, E cen. Śląsk dept., SW Poland, WNW of Katowice; pop. (1946) 126,079; formerly in Silesia, Germany; coal mining; iron foundries, rolling mills, steelworks, glassworks, breweries, production of small tools, machinery. Founded c. 1300; an obscure village until end of 19th cent. when it grew rapidly; became German 1915, when it was renamed Hindenburg; increased 1927 by consolidation of several towns; in World War II taken by Russians Jan. 1945; assigned to Poland by Potsdam Conference 1945; its earlier Polish name, Zabrze, again taken as its official name.

Za·ca′pa (sä·kä′pä). 1 Department, SE Guatemala; 1039 sq. m.; pop. 145,797.
2 Town, its *; pop. 14,443; sulfur springs; in tobacco-growing area.

Za′ca·te′cas (sä′kä·tā′käs). 1 State, cen. Mexico. See *Table* at MEXICO.
2 City, its *, 65 m. NNW of Aguascalientes; pop. 21,846; altitude 8075 ft.; cathedral; large mines and smelters.

Za′ca·te′co·lu′ca (sä′kä·tä′kô·lōō′kä). City, S El Salvador, * of La Paz dept.; pop. (1942 est.) 10,822; commercial and industrial center.

Za′co·al′co (sä′kô·äl′kô), *in full* **Zacoalco de Tor′res** (tħä tôr′rĕs). Town, Jalisco state, W cen. Mexico, 35 m. SSW of Guadalajara; pop. 6227.

Zacynthus. See ZANTE.

Za′dar (zä′där); *Ital.* **Za′ra** (dzä′rä; *Angl.* zär′à); *anc.* **I·ad′er·a** (ĭ·ăd′ĕr·à). Port on the Adriatic, in Croatia federated republic, W Yugoslavia, on Dalmatian coast 70 m. NW of Split; formerly an exclave of Italy constituting a province; pop. 20,055; seaside resort; fortified till 1873; ancient Roman triumphal arch; 13th-cent. Lombardesque cathedral, 8th to 13th-cent. churches; manufactures glass, rosolio, and, esp., maraschino. Became Roman colony under Augustus; captured by Venice 1202 A.D.; taken by Hungary; purchased by Venice 1409; taken by Austria 1797; held by Napoleon 1805–13, Austria 1813 ff.; ceded to Italy by Treaty of Rapallo 1920; made free port 1923; returned to Yugoslavia by treaty of Feb. 10, 1947.

Zafarin Islands. See CHAFARINAS ISLANDS.

Ża′gań (zhä′gän·y′); *Ger.* **Sa′gan** (zä′gän). City, NW Wrocław dept., SW Poland, on Bobr river 47 m. NW of Legnica; pop. (1946) 8000; formerly in Silesia prov., Prussia, Germany; railroad junction; manufactures textiles, paper, shoes. First mentioned 1202; site of prison camp in World War II.

Ża·ga′rė (zhä·gä′rä). Town, N Shaulyai dist., N Lithuania, 28 m. N of Shaulyai; pop. (1938 est.) 5445.

Zag′a·zig (zăg′à·zĭg); *Arab* **Za·qa·zîq′** (zŭ·kä·zēk′). Commercial city, * of Sharqiya prov., Lower Egypt; pop. (1937) 59,793; ruins of ancient Bubastis (q.v.) are at Tell Basta nearby.

Zagh·ouan′ (zäg·wän′). Town, N Tunisia, N Africa, ab. 25 m. W of Hammamet; railroad terminus and road junction; battles 1943.

Za·gorsk′ (zŭ·gôrsk′); *before 1930* **Ser′gi·ev** (syär′gĭ-[y]ĕf). Town, Moscow Region, Soviet Russia, Europe; pop. 27,813; on railroad 45 m. NE of Moscow; has some commercial activity but is famous as site of early Troitsko-Sergievskaya monastery, architecturally important and long venerated as a place of pilgrimage. Original wooden church, built by monk Sergius, was destroyed by Tatars 1391; two cathedrals built in monastery 1422 and 1585; also had famous bell tower and acquired great wealth.

Za′greb (zä′grĕb); *Hung.* **Zá′gráb** (zä′gräb); *Ger.* **A′gram** (ä′gräm); *anc.* **Za·gra′bi·a** (zà·grä′bĭ·à). City, * of Croatia federated republic, NW Yugoslavia, near Sava river; pop. 185,581; 2d largest city in Yugoslavia; commercial and industrial center; manufactures wood products, chemicals, textiles, processed foods, machinery; 15th-cent. cathedral; university.

Zag′ros Mountains (zăg′rŏs). Mountain system in many parallel ranges, S and SW Iran, extending along and across the Iran-Iraq border; many peaks above 9000 ft., highest Zardeh Kuh 14,921 ft.

Zagy′va (zŏd′y′·vŏ). River ab. 100 m. long in E cen. Hungary; flows S into Tisza river at Szolnok.

Za′hi·dan′ (zä′hĕ·dän′); *formerly* **Duz·dab′** (dōōz-däb′). Town, E Iran, near the border of Baluchistan; terminus of railroad from Baluchistan and on motor highway from Meshed S to Gulf of Oman.

Zah′le (zä′h′·lĕ); *Fr.* **Zah′lé′** (zà′lā′). Town, cen. Lebanon republic, on railroad 23 m. E of Beirut; pop. (1935) 20,985; at foot of E slope of Lebanon Mts. in El Bika valley.

Zairam Nor. See SAIRAM NOR.

Za·i′re (*Port.* zà·ē′rĕ; *Fr.* zà′ēr′). Early name of the Congo river.

Zai′san (zī′sän). Lake 270 sq. m. in NE Kazakh S.S.R., Soviet Central Asia, in the Alatau Mts.; traversed by Irtysh river.

Zai·tun′ (zä·tōōn′). Var. of ZAYTON.

Zakarpatskaya. See CARPATHIAN RUTHENIA.

Za′kho (zä′ĸō). Frontier town, N Iraq, on an E tributary of the Tigris 60 m. NW of Mosul.

Za′ko·pa′ne (zä′kô·pä′nĕ). Commune, Kraków dept., S Poland, in Tatra Mts. 52 m. S of Kraków; pop. (1938–39 est.) 23,000; chief summer resort and winter sports center in Poland; alt. ab. 3300 ft. Founded in 16th cent.

Zakynthos. See ZANTE.

Zalaca. See ZALLAKA.

Za′la·e′ger·szeg (zŏ′lŏ·ĕ′gĕr·sĕg′). City, W Hungary, W of Lake Balaton; pop. 13,271.

Za′la·me′a la Re·al′ (thä′lä·mā′ä [sä′-] lä rrĕ·äl′). Commune, Huelva prov., SW Spain, 36 m. NNE of Huelva; pop. (1930) 11,418; iron pyrites and copper sulfide mines.

Ză·lă′u (zà·lŭ′ŏŏ); *Hung.* **Zi′lah** (zĭ′lŏ). Commune, Transylvania, Romania, ab. 55 m. ENE of Oradea; pop. 8154; trade in wines.

Za·leshch′ki (zŭ·lyāshch′kĭ); *Pol.* **Za′lesz·czy′ki** (zä′-lĕsh·chĭ′kĕ). Town, Ternopol Region, W Ukraine, U.S.S.R.; formerly in Tarnopol dept., Poland; pop. ab. 4000; battles 1915–16.

Zal·la′ka *or* **Za·la′ca** (zȧ·lä′kȧ); *Arab.* **al–Zal·lā′qah** (äl′zȧl·lä′kŏ·h'); *Span.* **Sa·cra′lias** (sä·krä′lyäs). Ancient town, SW Spain, N of Badajoz; scene of battle Oct. 23, 1086 in which Yusuf ibn-Tashfin defeated Alfonso VI of León and Castile.

Za′ma (zā′mȧ). Ancient town in N Africa, SW of Carthage; scene of decisive defeat of the Carthaginians under Hannibal by the Romans under Scipio Africanus 202 B.C.

Zam·ba′les (säm·bä′läs). Province, W Luzon, Phil. Is.; 1408 sq. m.; pop. 106,945; ✳ Iba. Traversed N to S by the Zambales Mts., consisting of more or less isolated volcanic cones; highest High Peak 6683 ft. in N cen. part and Pinatubo 5842 ft. on Pampanga border. Coast irregular with fine sheltered anchorage of Subic Bay in S. Lumbering and stock raising important industries; has large deposits of chromite and uranium ore discovered in recent years. Inhabitants Sambals, Ilokanos, Negritos, and some Tagalogs. Chief towns Iba, Subic, and Santa Cruz.

History: Coast explored by Juan de Salcedo 1572 and region organized as a province immediately; of slow growth at first but progressed rapidly in 19th cent.; civil government established by Americans Aug. 1901; American force landed near San Narciso Jan. 1945.

Zambales Mountains. Mountain range in W Luzon, Phil. Is., running from Lingayen Gulf in N to entrance to Manila Bay in S, in Zambales and Bataan provs.; many peaks from 2500 to 5000 ft.; highest point High Peak 6683 ft. in N cen. Zambales; Mt. Mariveles 4700 ft. is highest in Bataan.

Zam·be′zi *or* **Zam·be′si** (zăm·bē′zĭ); *Port.* **Zam·be′ze** (zănm·bā′zĕ). River ab. 1650 m. long in S cen. and SE Africa; rises in NW Northern Rhodesia, flows S across E Angola and W Northern Rhodesia to the border of Bechuanaland Protectorate; turns E and forms boundary bet. Northern Rhodesia and Southern Rhodesia; crosses cen. Mozambique and empties into Mozambique Channel at Chinde; navigable in three long stretches, separated by rapids and by the Victoria Falls (*q.v.*). Has many headstreams in the marshlands of SE Angola and W Northern Rhodesia; its chief tributaries on the N are the Kafue and Luangwa in Northern Rhodesia and the Shire, outlet of Lake Nyasa; on the S the Chobe bet. Caprivi Concession and Bechuanaland Protectorate and the Sanyati in Southern Rhodesia. First visited by Livingstone 1851–53 and later 1858–60 by Dr. John Kirk; little additional information gained about it before end of 19th cent.

Zam·be′zi·a *or* **Zam·be′si·a** (zăm·bē′zhĭ·ȧ; -zhȧ).
1 Name formerly applied to the British territories in the Zambezi basin (Rhodesia and Nyasaland).
2 Province, E cen. Mozambique, N of Zambezi river; chief town Quelimane.

Zambia. See NORTHERN RHODESIA.

Zam′bo·an′ga (säm′bŏ·äng′gä). **1** Province, W Mindanao, Phil. Is.; 6517 sq. m.; pop. 355,984; ✳ City of Zamboanga; comprises Mindanao W of Misamis Occidental and Lanao provs., the long SW peninsula, and Basilan I.; touches Mindanao Sea on NE, Moro Gulf on S, and Sulu Sea on W and NW. Very mountainous, with range through cen. part; highest is Mt. Dapiak in NE 8620 ft. Coast line has many bays, largest being Sindangan and Sibuguey. Forest resources are large; chief products hemp (abacá), copra, and rice. Inhabitants are Christians on N coast and around Zamboanga, Moros on other coasts, and the pagan tribe of Subanun in the interior. Chief towns Zamboanga, Pagadian, Katipunan, Sindangan, and Dipolog.

History: Visited by Legaspi 1565 and by missionaries 1631 and after; its Spanish population had frequent en-counters with Moros in 17th and 18th cents.; made a military government 1837 and became part of Moro prov. 1903; civil government established 1914.

2 *officially* City of Zamboanga. Chartered city, its ✳, at S tip of W peninsula on Basilan Strait, including Basilan I.; 1124 sq. m.; pop. 131,455; port of call 600 m. S of Manila; has good roadstead but not a safe anchorage in SW monsoon. Founded 1635 as a fort for protection of Christian settlers; during American possession was rebuilt into a fine town and the chief market of S Philippines. The City of Zamboanga was created c. 1940; in World War II a Japanese defense headquarters, taken by Americans Mar. 10, 1945.

Zámky Nové. = NOVÉ ZÁMKY.

Za·mo′ra (zȧ·mōr′ȧ; *Span.* sä·mō′rä, *in Spain also* thä-). **1** River 190 m. long in S and SE Ecuador; flows E and N to join Paute river and form Santiago river, a tributary of the Marañón.
2 Town, Michoacán state, SW Mexico, 80 m. SE of Guadalajara; pop. 15,447; in center of rich agricultural region. Founded 1540.
3 Province of Spain. See *Table* at SPAIN.
4 City, ✳ of Zamora prov., NW Spain, on Duero river 129 m. NW of Madrid; pop. 32,383; manufactures brandies, pottery, leather, textiles; 12th-cent. Gothic cathedral. Notable defense against Moorish invasion 939 A.D.
5 Former name of *Barinas* state, Venezuela: see *Table* at VENEZUELA.

Za′mość (zä′môshch); *Russ.* **Za·most′e** (zŭ·môst′yĕ). Fortified commune, Lublin dept., Poland, 48 m. SE of Lublin; pop. (1938–39 est.) 28,000; has a university (founded 1773); noted for fine Renaissance architecture; manufactures furniture, concrete goods. Seat of the Zamojski family.

Za·mu′ro, Point (sä·mōō′rŏ). Cape extending into Caribbean Sea on NW coast of Venezuela, S of island of Curaçao.

Zancle. See MESSINA seaport.

Zand′voort (zänt′vōrt). Commune, North Holland prov., Netherlands, on the North Sea coast W of Haarlem; pop. 8280; watering place.

Zanes′ville (zānz′vĭl). Manufacturing city, ⊗ of Muskingum co., SE cen. Ohio, on Muskingum river 50 m. E of Columbus; pop. 39,077; produces clay products (esp. floor and wall tile), pottery, glass, porcelain, brick, iron and steel, shoes, machinery; clay, oil, coal, gas, limestone-sand deposits nearby. Platted 1797; incorp. 1800; became ⊗ 1804, capital of Ohio 1810–12, city 1850.

Zan·ga′ (zän·gä′). River ab. 65 m. long, the outlet of Lake Sevan in the Armenian S.S.R., Soviet Union, flowing from its N end to the Araks S of Yerevan. Has powerful hydroelectric station established 1926.

Zan′gue·bar (zăng′gĕ·bär) *or* **Zenj** (zĕnj) *or* **Zinj** (zĭnj) *or* *later* **Zan′zi·bar** (zăn′zĭ·bär). Arab and Persian land or empire on the E coast of Africa (✳ Kilwa), destroyed by the Portuguese, and restored (subject to Masqat) in the 16th cent.; mainland territories leased or purchased by Italy, Germany, and Great Britain in the 19th cent. See ZANZIBAR.

Zan′te (zăn′tĕ; *Ital.* dzän′tä); *Gr.* **Za·kyn′thos** (zȧ·kĭn′thŏs; *Mod. Gr.* zä′kyĕn·thôs); *anc.* **Za·cyn′thus** (zȧ·sĭn′thŭs). **1** One of the Ionian Is. in Ionian Sea off NW coast of Peloponnesus, Greece, 8 m. S of Cephalonia; 25 m. long by 12 m. wide; area 156 sq. m.; pop. (1938 est.) 44,750; constitutes Zante dept. (see *Table* at GREECE). Has wide fertile plain in cen. part with low hills on W; produces currants for export. Subject to frequent earthquakes. In tradition belonged to Ulysses, king of Ithaca; historically, in classical period, came under possession of various states—Athens, Macedon, Rome—usually as a military base; in 11th cent. held by Norman kings of Sicily; then by Epirus, and from 1482 to 1797 belonged to Venice whose influence on its people and culture has been greatest.

2 Town, ✳ of Zante dept., Ionian Is., Greece, on E coast of Zante I.; pop. 11,609; traditionally said to have been founded by Zacynthus, son of the Arcadian chief Dardanus.

Zan′zi·bar (zăn′zĭ·bär). **1** Former sultanate in E Africa, comprising Zanzibar and Kenya protectorates; formerly included also Mafia I., the coast of Tanganyika, and the coast of Somalia S of lat. 3°N.
2 Former British protectorate comprising Zanzibar I., Pemba I., and adjacent small islands; 1020 sq. m.; pop. 235,428; ✳ Zanzibar; became independent Dec. 10, 1963 and a republic Jan. 12, 1964; united with Tanganyika Apr. 1964 in republic of Tanzania. See TANGANYIKA.
3 Chief island of the republic, in the Indian Ocean off NE coast of Tanganyika, E Africa; area 640 sq. m.; pop. 137,741; world's chief source of cloves; also produces copra, coconut oil, mangrove bark.
History: Formerly under Arab rulers, became dominated by Portuguese c. 1505; conquered by ruler of Oman (*q.v.*) in 18th cent.; came under Masqat when in 1832 the town of Zanzibar became capital of the sayid of Masqat whose successor received European recognition of his independence from Oman; granted part of mainland holdings to German East Africa Co. (see TANGANYIKA TERRITORY) 1895 and to British (see KENYA) 1887; became British protectorate 1890.
4 Commercial seaport on W coast of the island of Zanzibar, ✳ of Zanzibar republic; pop. 45,276; was capital of Masqat 1832–56 and later in 19th cent. the starting point for explorers and missionaries to Africa.

Zapadnaya Dvina. See DVINA river, Europe.

Za·pa′la (sä·pä′lä). Town, cen. Neuquén territory, W Argentina, 50 m. W of Plaza Huincul oil field; railroad terminus.

Za·pa′ta (zȧ·pä′tȧ; *Span.* sä·pä′tä). **1** County in Texas. See *Table* at TEXAS.
2 Village, its ⊗, S Texas; pop. 2031.
3 Swamp, SW Las Villas prov., Cuba; 600 sq. m.

Zapata Peninsula. Peninsula extending from SW coast of Las Villas prov., W cen. Cuba; encloses Broa Bay from the S.

Za′po·ro′zhe (zä′pŭ·rô′zhĕ; *Russ.* zȧ·pŭ·rôzh′yĕ). **1** Region, SE Ukraine, U.S.S.R.
2 *formerly* **A·le·ksan′drovsk** (ŭ·lyĭ·ksȧn′drŭfsk). City, its ✳, on the left bank of the Dnieper 45 m. S of Dnepropetrovsk; pop. 289,188; on the main railroad from Moscow to Sevastopol, at the bend of the Dnieper below the Dneprostroi (*q.v.*), near the Donbas; has developed into an important industrial center, with a great metallurgical plant and chemical works. In 16th cent. and later the surrounding country was the home of the Zaporogian Cossacks whose chief camp was on Khortitsa I. opposite in the Dnieper.

Za·po′til·tic′ (sä·pō′tĕl·tēk′). Town, Jalisco state, W cen. Mexico, S of Lake Chapala; pop. 5522.

Zaqaziq. See ZAGAZIG.

Za′ra (dzä′rä; *Angl.* zär′ȧ). **1** Former province of Italy.
2 City. See ZADAR.

Za′ra·go′za (thä′rä·gō′thä; sä′rä·gō′sä). **1** Province of Spain. See *Table* at SPAIN.
2 City. See SARAGOSSA.

Zaraka. See STYMPHALIS.

Za·ra·sai′ (zä·rä·sī′). **1** District of Lithuania. See *Table* at LITHUANIA.
2 *formerly* **No′vo·a·le·ksan′drovsk** (nô′vŭ·ŭ·lyĭ·ksȧn′-drŭfsk). Town, its ✳, NE Lithuania, near Polish and Latvian borders ab. 20 m. S of Daugavpils; pop. 3785.

Zárate. See GENERAL J. F. URIBURU.

Zar′deh Kuh (zär′dĕ kōō′; *Iranian* zär′dȧ kōō′h′). Peak 14,921 ft. in W Iran, W of Isfahan; highest point in the Zagros Mts.

Zar′e·phath (zăr′ĕ·făth). Ancient town of Phoenicia, subject to Sidon, on the coast ab. 8 m. S of it; residence of Elijah (*1 Kings* xvii. 8–24). Near the modern village of **Sar′a·fand** (săr′ȧ·fănd; *Arab.* sȯ′rȯ·fănd′).

Za′ri·a (zär′ĭ·ȧ). **1** Province of Nigeria; region of open rolling country, generally fertile and healthy; site of former Hausa state, at one time subject to Sokoto. See *Table* at NIGERIA.
2 Town, its ✳, on railroad ab. 87 m. SW of Kano; pop. (with township) 28,121.

Za·ru′ma (sä·rōō′mä). Town, El Oro prov., SW Ecuador, in the Andes SSW of Cuenca; pop. (1944 est.) 13,657; gold mining.

Ża′ry (zhä′rĭ); *Ger.* **So′rau** (zō′rou), *in full* **Sorau in der Nie′der·lau′sitz** (ĭn dĕr nē′dĕr·lou′zĭts). Manufacturing city, NW Wrocław dept., SW Poland, bet. Bobr and Nysa rivers 56 m. SSE of Frankfurt; pop. (1946) 15,200; formerly in Brandenburg, Germany; early 14th-cent. castle; manufactures textiles, porcelain. Assigned to Poland by Potsdam Conference 1945.

Zas′tron (zăs′trŭn). Town, S Orange Free State, E cen. Republic of So. Africa, bet. Caledon and Orange rivers 95 m. SSE of Bloemfontein; pop. 3477; agriculture.

Ża′tec (zhä′tĕts); *Ger.* **Saaz** (zäts). Town, NW Bohemia prov., W Czechoslovakia, on Ohře river; pop. (1930) 18,061; in hop-growing area; military airfield.

Za·va′la (zȧ·vä′lä). County in Texas. See *Table* at TEXAS.

Za·wier′cie (zä·vyĕr′chĕ). Industrial commune, NE Śląsk dept., SW Poland, 60 m. SW of Kielce; pop. (1938–39 est.) 32,872; coal and iron mining; manufactures glass, textiles.

Zay·ton′ (zä·tōn′). Seaport of China, described by Marco Polo. See TSINKIANG.

Zba′razh (zbä′räsh); *Pol.* **Zba′raż** (zbä′räsh). Town, W Ukraine, just NE of Ternopol (formerly in Tarnopol dept., SE Poland); pop. 7673; famous in Polish wars in 17th cent.

Zbruch (zbrōōch); *Pol.* **Zbrucz** (zbrōōch). River ab. 100 m. long, formerly on border bet. Ukraine and Poland; flows S into the Dniester; now bet. Ternopol and Kamenets-Podolski Regions of W Ukraine.

Zdol·bu′nov (zdŭl·bōō′nŭf); *Pol.* **Zdoł·bu′nów** (zdôl-bōō′nōōf). Town, W Ukraine, U.S.S.R., 44 m. ESE of Lutsk (formerly in Wołyń dept., Poland); pop. 10,228; railroad junction point just S of Rovno.

Zduń′ska Wo′la (zdōōn′y′·skä vô′lä). Commune, W Łódź dept., cen. Poland, 28 m. WSW of Łódź; pop. 22,904; manufactures textiles, leather.

Zea. See KEOS.

Zealand. See SJÆLLAND.

Zeb′u·lon (zĕb′ū·lŭn). City, ⊗ of Pike co., W Georgia; pop. 563.

Zee′brug′ge (zā′brüg′ĕ). Seaport, West Flanders prov., NW Belgium, port of the city of Brugge (Bruges) with which it is connected by canal; occupied by the Germans 1914 and used as a submarine base; raided by British naval contingents 1918, who succeeded in destroying the mole and blocking the harbor by sinking vessels at its mouth.

Zee′han (zē′ăn). Mining town, W Tasmania, Australia, 18 m. N of upper end of Macquarie Harbour; pop. 1010.

Zee′land. 1 (zē′lănd) City, Ottawa co., W Michigan, 21 m. WSW of Grand Rapids; pop. 3702; poultry center.
2 (zē′lănd; *Du.* zä′länt) Province, SW Netherlands, composed of several islands (esp. Walcheren, North and South Beveland, Schouwen, and Tholen) on the North Sea coast, and a part of the mainland S of the Schelde estuary; 1040 sq. m.; pop. (1939) 254,854; ✳ Middelburg, on Walcheren I.; largely below sea level, protected by dikes. Other towns Vlissingen, Neuzen, Zieriksee. United with Holland and Hainaut in 14th cent.

Zee′rust (zā′rŭst). Town, W Transvaal, NE Republic of So. Africa, 135 m. W of Pretoria; pop. 4046; center of fertile Marico valley producing citrus fruits, wheat, oats, and cotton; district is rich in various minerals.

Że′gań (zhĕ′gän·y′). Var. of ŻAGAŃ.

Zeig′ler (zīg′lēr). City, Franklin co., S Illinois, 32 m. SSW of Mount Vernon; pop. 2133.

Zei′la or **Zei′lah** (zā′là). Seaport town, NW Somalia, E Africa, SE of Djibouti in French Somaliland; pop. ab. 5000.

Zeist (zīst). Commune, Utrecht prov., cen. Netherlands, 6 m. E of Utrecht; pop. (1939) 33,642.

Zeitz (tsīts). Manufacturing city, E Germany, in what was formerly Saxony prov., Prussia, on Weisse Elster river 21 m. SSW of Leipzig; pop. 34,590; machinery, pianos, perambulators, chocolate. sugar, textiles.

Zela. See ZILE.

Ze·la′ya (sȧ·lä′yä). **1** Town, Buenos Aires prov., E Argentina, ab. 30 m. NW of Buenos Aires.
2 Department, E Nicaragua; 27,819 sq. m.; pop. (1943 est.) 72,300; * Bluefields. See MOSQUITO COAST.

Ze′le (zā′lĕ). Commune, East Flanders prov., NW cen. Belgium, E of Gent; pop. 15,168.

Ze′lee′, Cape (zā′lā′) Cape, S end of Maramasike I., SE Solomon Is., W Pacific Ocean.

Ze′li·e·no′ple (zē′li·ė·nō′p'l; zēl′yē-). Borough, Butler co., W Pennsylvania, 18 m. SE of New Castle; pop. 3284; clay, lumber; manufactures metal products.

Zei′la–Meh′lis (tsĕl′ä·mā′lis). City, Thuringia, E Germany, 28 m. SW of Erfurt; pop. 14,423; manufactures office machinery, weapons, bicycle parts, tools.

Zel′le (tsĕl′ĕ). Var. of CELLE.

Zem′ga·le (zĕm′gä·lĕ) or **Zem·gal′ia** (zĕm·gäl′yȧ). Province, S Latvia; 5259 sq. m.; pop. (1938 est.) 306,635; * Yelgava; traversed by Lielupe river and bordered on NE by the Dvina.

Zem′po·al′te·pec′ (säm′pō·äl′tȧ·pĕk′) or **Zem′po·al·te′petl** (-äl·tā′pĕt·'l). Mountain 11,138 ft. in SE Mexico, in Oaxaca state 55 m. E of the city of Oaxaca; stands at the convergence of the Sierra Madre Occidental and the Sierra Madre Oriental.

Ze′mun (zĕ′mōōn); Ger. **Sem·lin′** (zĕm·lēn′). City, S Voivodina autonomous prov., NE Yugoslavia, on Danube river WNW of Belgrade; pop. 28,083; commercial center and shipping point.

Zengg. See SENJ.

Zenj. See ZANGUEBAR.

Zen·jan′ (zĕn·jän′) or **Zin·jan′** (zĭn-). City, NW Iran, SW of the Caspian Sea and at W end of Elburz Mts.; * of Khamseh prov.; pop. ab. 24,100; on the main Tehran-Tabriz trade route ab. 90 m. WNW of Kazvin.

Zenra Hoku, Zenra Nan. See NORTH ZENRA, SOUTH ZENRA.

Zen·shu (zĕn·shōō) or **Chon·ju** (jûn·jōō). Town, * of North Zenra prov., SW Korea, 80 m. W of Taikyu; pop. 40,593; railroad and highway center in region producing great quantities of rice.

Zenta. See SENTA.

Zen·tsu·ji (zĕn·tsōō·jĕ). Town, Kagawa prefecture, NE Shikoku I., Japan, SW of Takamatsu; pop. (1945) 17,146. Birthplace of the founder (Kobo Daishi) of the Buddhist sect Shingon-shu; has large temple. Camp for American war prisoners in World War II.

Ze′rav·shan′ (zȧ′rȧf·shän′). River ab. 400 m. long in Soviet Central Asia; rises at W end of Alai Mts., flows W through NW Tadzhik S.S.R. and the oasis region of Samarkand in SE Uzbek S.S.R. to the desert near Bukhara.

Zerbst (tsĕrpst). City, Anhalt, East Germany, NW of Dessau; pop. 19,470; 13th-cent. church, 17th-cent. castle; manufactures machinery, tools, leather goods, celluloid goods, thermometers, beer; important trade in vegetables and cattle.

Ze′ri·a (zĕr′ĭ·à; Gr. zē′ryà). Var. of Ziria: see CYLLENE.

Zer·matt′ (tsĕr·mät′). Village in Valais canton, SW cen. Switzerland; pop. (1930) 962; elevation 5315 ft., in the Pennine Alps; surrounded by meadows (Matten) forming a beautiful valley from which can be seen the Matterhorn to the SW.

Zerqa, Wadi. See JABBOK.

Zet′land (zĕt′lănd) or **Shet′land** (shĕt′-). Scottish county comprising the Shetland Is. (q.v.); 550 sq. m.;

pop. (1940 est.) 19,700; ⊗ Lerwick; agriculture, herring fisheries, livestock raising (Shetland ponies), knitted goods, tweeds.

Zet′ska (zĕt′skä). Former county, S Yugoslavia; 11,866 sq. m.; pop. 910,350; ⊗ Cetinje.

Zeu′len·ro′da (tsoi′lĕn·rō′dä). Industrial city, Thuringia, East Germany, WSW of Zwickau; pop. 11,047; 15th-cent. town hall; textiles, hosiery, rubber, woven goods, machinery.

Ze′ven (tsā′fĕn; Angl. zā′vĕn). Town, Lower Saxony state, West Germany, 24 m. NE of Bremen; scene Sept. 8, 1757 during the Seven Years' War of duke of Cumberland's capitulation to the French (the Convention of Kloster-Zeven) by which Hannover was abandoned.

Ze′ve·naar′ (zā′vĕ·när′). Town, Gelderland prov., Netherlands, SE of Arnhem near the German border on the Rhine; pop. 6429; customs station.

Ze′ya (zyä′yȧ). River 768 m. long in SE Soviet Russia, Asia; rises in Stanovoi Mts. in E Chita Region and flows S and SE into the Amur river in Khabarovsk Territory; joined by the Selemdzha in its lower course.

Ze′ze·re (zä′zĕ·rĕ). River ab. 110 m. long, cen. Portugal; rises near Spanish border and flows SW to the Tagus below Abrantes; water-power development.

Zgierz (zgyĕsh); Russ. **Zgerzh** (zgĕrsh). Commune, Łódź dept., Poland, 4 m. N of Łódź; pop. (1938–39 est.) 28,114; textiles, esp. linen.

Zgorzelec. See GÖRLITZ.

Zhda′nov (zhdä′nŭf); formerly **Ma′ri·u′pol** (mȧr′ĭ·ōō′pŏl; Russ. mȧ·ryĭ·ōō′pŭl·y′). City, S Stalino Region, E Ukraine, U.S.S.R., on N shore of Sea of Azov 60 m. W of Taganrog; pop. 222,427; at mouth of the Kalmius with a good harbor and export trade in grain, coal, iron, and oilcake; graphite mine nearby; connected by rail with Stalino. Probable site of ancient Greek colony, but modern town founded 1779; in World War II held by Germans Oct. 7, 1941–Aug. 30, 1943.

Zhi·to′mir (zhĭ·tô′myĭr); also **Ji·to′mir** (zhĭ-). **1** Region, W Ukraine, U.S.S.R.; formerly on the border of SE Poland.
2 Industrial city, its *, on the Teterev river 85 m. W of Kiev; pop. 95,090; manufactures machinery and has breweries and lumber mills. An old town on the early trade route from Scandinavia to Constantinople and on the direct route W from Kiev; plundered by Tatars in medieval times; belonged to Lithuania after 1320, then to Poland, and was sacked by the Cossacks in 1648; incorporated in Russia 1778; occupied by Axis forces Aug. 2, 1941 in World War II; retaken by Russians after much severe fighting Dec. 31, 1943.

Zhlo′bin (zhlô′byĭn). Town, SE White Russia, U.S.S.R., on right bank of the Dnieper ab. 75 m. S of Mogilev; pop. 11,010; a railroad junction point for lines to Mogilev, Bobruisk, Gomel and S to Zhitomir in Ukraine; bitterly contested point in Russian campaign of 1944; retaken by Russians in June.

Zhme·rin′ka (zhmyĭ·ryēn′kȧ; Angl. zhmĕ·rĭng′kȧ). Town, W Vinnitsa Region, W cen. Ukraine, U.S.S.R., 20 m. SW of Vinnitsa; pop. 22,240; railroad junction point, a key communication center in World War II campaigns of 1944; taken by Russians Mar. 30, 1944.

Zhob (zhōb). District, NE Baluchistan; 10,478 sq. m.; pop. (1941) 61,499; * Fort Sandeman. Occupies extensive valley of the **Zhob River** (a tributary of the Gumal) which is direct route bet. North-West Frontier Province and Quetta, in Pakistan. First opened up in 1884 by Zhob Valley Expedition; formed into a political agency 1890; scene of several frontier disturbances (1884, 1890, 1919).

Ži′de·ni′ce (zhĭ′dĕ·nyĭ′tsĕ); Ger. **Schi′mitz** (shē′mĭts). Commune, suburb of Brno, Moravia, Czechoslovakia; pop. (1921) 14,170.

Zidon. See SIDON.

Zie′bach′ (zē′bäk′; -bä′; -bô′). County in South Dakota. See Table at SOUTH DAKOTA.

Ziel, Mount (zēl). Mountain 4955 ft., highest point in Macdonnell Ranges, Northern Territory, Australia, on Tropic of Capricorn ab. 132°30′E.

Zie·lo′na Gó′ra (zhĕ·lŏ′nä gōō′rä); *Ger.* **Grün′berg** (grün′bĕrκ), *also* **Grünberg in Schle′si·en** (ĭn shlā′zĕ·ĕn). Industrial city, SW Poznań dept., W cen. Poland, S of the Odra (Oder) 58 m. NNW of Legnica; pop. 24,898; formerly in Silesia, Germany; manufactures brandy, wine, textiles, machinery, artistic stonework, vehicles; lignite mining; metal foundries. Assigned to Poland by Potsdam Conference 1945.

Zie′rik·zee′ (zē′rĭk·sā′). Commune, Zeeland prov., SW Netherlands, on S shore of Schouwen I.; pop. 6771.

Zi·ga·na′ Si·ra′ Da·ǧla·ri′ (zĭ·gä·nä′ sĭ·rä′ dä·lä·rĭ′). = ŞMALİ ANADOLU DAĞLARI.

Zi′guin′chor′ (zē′gän′shôr′). Port on Casamance river 45 m. from its mouth, ✳ of Casamance territory, SW Senegal, West Africa.

Zilah. See ZĂLĂU.

Zi·le′ (zĭ·lĕ′); *anc.* **Ze′la** (zē′lä). Town, Tokat vilayet, N cen. Turkey in Asia, on railroad and on tributary of Yeşil Irmak; pop. 15,167. In a battle here 47 B.C. Pharnaces II, king of Pontus, was defeated by Caesar who announced his victory to the senate at Rome by his famous laconic message: *Veni, Vidi, Vici.*

Ži′li·na (zhĭ′lĭ·nȧ); *Hung.* **Zsol′na** (zhŏl′nŏ); *Ger.* **Sil·lein′** (zĭ·līn′). Town, NW Slovakia prov., E cen. Czechoslovakia, on S slope of West Beskids; pop. (1930) 17,473.

Zil′le·be′ke (zĭl′ĕ·bā′kĕ). Commune, West Flanders prov., NW Belgium, near Ieper (Ypres); pop. 1642; held by the British in World War I.

Zil′ler·ta′ler Alps (tsĭl′ĕr·tä′lĕr). Subsidiary range of the E Alps along boundary bet. NE Italy and the Tirol, Austria, at W end of the Hohe Tauern; highest peak Hochfeiler 11,555 ft.

Zil′ling Tso (zĭl′ĭng tsō′) *or* **Sel′ling Tso** (sĕl′ĭng). Lake, E cen. Tibet, Outer China, at alt. 15,120 ft.

Zim·ba′bwe (zĭm·bä′bwā). Site of ruins 17 m. SE of Victoria, Mashonaland, NE Southern Rhodesia, S Africa; from Bantu words meaning "houses" and "stones." Distinguished as **Great Zimbabwe** from a smaller and more recent group of ruins 8 m. distant (**Little Zimbabwe**). Ruins comprise a probable citadel or acropolis, a temple, and huge walls of granite monoliths fitted without mortar. Discovered by Adam Benders in 1868. Origin a subject of controversy but probably Bantu and not earlier than 14th or 15th cent.; may have been a stone kraal serving as distributing center in early gold traffic.

Zim′ni·cea (zēm′nĕ·chä). Town, S Romania, on the Danube ab. 27 m. SW of Bucharest; pop. 10,933.

Zi′mony (zĭ′mŏn·y′). = ZEMUN.

Zin, Wilderness *or* **Desert of** (zĭn). Desert region SW of the Dead Sea, S Palestine; in Biblical times the region bet. W Edom and SE Judaea, traversed by the Israelites on their journey to Canaan (*Num.* xx. 1).

Zi·nal′ Rot′horn′ (tsē·näl′ rōt′hôrn′). Peak 13,855 ft. in SW cen. Switzerland, in the Pennine Alps near Zermatt.

Zin′der (zĭn′dĕr). Commercial town and military headquarters, S Niger Republic, West Africa, ab. 65 m. N of the Nigeria border; pop. ab. 16,000; since latter part of 19th cent. an administrative and trading town and center for exploration.

Zinj. See ZANGUEBAR.

Zinjan. See ZENJAN.

Zinovievsk. See KIROVOGRAD.

Zi′on (zĭ′ŭn). **1** City, Lake co., NE corner of Illinois, on Lake Michigan 5 m. N of Waukegan; pop. 11,941; founded as Zion City by John Alexander Dowie, head of the Christian Catholic Church, 1901; incorp. 1902; developed and industrialized by Dowie's successor, Wilbur Glenn Voliva, 1907–39; manufactures candy, lace, cement; trading center for dairy products and vegetables.

2 *or* **Si′on** (sī′ŭn; zī′-). Height in NE part of the city of Jerusalem, Palestine; originally the Jebusite stronghold captured by David (*2 Sam.* v). On it was built the Temple, residence of David, and other buildings so that it became the center of Jewish national life and came to be used as synonym for Jerusalem and the symbol of Zionism.

Zion National Monument. Former national monument, SW Utah; 33,920 acres; established 1937, incorporated 1956 in Zion National Park.

Zion National Park. See UNITED STATES, *National Parks.*

Zi·pan′gu (zĭ·păng′gōō). Marco Polo's name for Japan. See NIPPON.

Zi′pa·qui·rá′ (sē′pä·kĕ·rä′). Town, Cundinamarca dept., cen. Colombia N of Bogotá; pop. 6955; center of salt-mining, cattle-raising district; site of underground Salt Cathedral, carved in a salt mountain.

Zipfer Neudorf. See SPIŠSKÁ NOVÁ VES.

Zips. See SZEPES.

Zi·ra′ni·an (zĭ·rä′nĭ·ăn), **Zir′i·an** (zĭr′ĭ·ăn). ⇒ ZYRIAN (Autonomous Area).

Ziria. See CYLLENE.

Zi′sters·dorf (tsĭs′tĕrs·dôrf; *Angl.* zĭs′tĕrz-). Town, Lower Austria prov., NE Austria, ab. 27 m. NE of Vienna; pop. 2280; extensive oil fields developed since 1933; in 1946–48 in Russian zone.

Zi·tá′cua·ro (sĕ·tä′kwä·rō). Town, E Michoacán state, SW Mexico, 80 m. W of Mexico City; pop. 11,434.

Zit′tau (tsĭt′ou). Manufacturing city, Dresden dist., East Germany, on left bank of Neisse river 46 m. ESE of Dresden; pop. 38,353; promenades on site of old fortifications; manufactures textiles, metal goods, chemicals, organs, pianos, beer, soap, cordage, blankets. Became city 1255; important medieval textile-manufacturing center.

Zituni. See LAMIA.

Žiž′kov (zhĭsh′kŏf). Former city, now part of Prague, Bohemia, Czechoslovakia; pop. ab. 91,000.

Zla·to·ust′ (zlȧ·tŭ·ōōst′). City in S part of Ural Mts., W Chelyabinsk Region, Soviet Russia, Asia, 75 m. W of Chelyabinsk; pop. 99,272; on railroad bet. Chelyabinsk and Ufa; since middle of 18th cent. has been a center of the ironworking industry; manufactures machinery. Has a meteorological observatory.

Zlín (zlēn); *Ger.* **Zlin** (zlēn). Town, SE Moravia prov., cen. Czechoslovakia; pop. (1930) 21,584; manufactures shoes; renamed **Gott′wald·ov** (gŏt′vȧl·dôf) in 1948.

Zlo′chev (zlŏ′chĕf); *Pol.* **Zło′czów** (zlŏ′chōōf). Town, W Ukraine, U.S.S.R., on railroad 35 m. NW of Ternopol (formerly in Tarnopol dept., Poland); pop. 13,265; fortified castle (now a prison); manufactures metal goods, candy, leather. Battle fought here June–July 1917.

Zło′ta Li′pa (zlŏ′tä lē′pä). Small stream 65 m. long in SW Ukraine, U.S.S.R., flowing S into Dniester river; battle line 1914. Formerly in SE Poland.

Zmei′no·gorsk′ (zmā′nŭ·gôrsk′). Town, S Altai Territory, SW Soviet Russia, Asia, 165 m. SW of Barnaul at NW end of Altai Mts.; rich mining region (gold, silver, lead, zinc).

Zna′men·ka (znä′myĕn·kȧ). Town, cen. Kirovograd Region, S cen. Ukraine, U.S.S.R., 20 m. NNE of Kirovograd; pop. 9070; railroad communications center.

Znoj′mo (znoi′mô); *Ger.* **Zna′im** (tsnä′ĭm; tsnīm). City, S Moravia prov., cen. Czechoslovakia; pop. (1930) 25,832; manufacturing and commercial center in agricultural region; armistice signed here July 12, 1809 after Napoleon's victory in the battle of Wagram.

Zoan. See TANIS.

Zoar (zōr). Village, Tuscarawas co., E Ohio, N of Dover; pop. 191; site of Separatist community founded 1817 by group of German Protestant peasants, disbanded 1898.

Zo·a′ra (zō·ä′rȧ). Var. of ZUARA.

Zo′fing·en (tsō′fĭng·ĕn). Commune, Aargau canton, Switzerland; pop. 5563; textiles.

Żół'kiew (zhool'kyĕf). Town, W Ukraine, U.S.S.R., 13 m. NNW of Lvov (formerly in Lwów dept., Poland); pop. (1938–39 est.) 11,000; Renaissance church. Founded 1603; battle 1915.

Zol'lern (tsôl'ẽrn). Mountain 2805 ft., West Germany, near Hechingen, in former Hohenzollern prov., Prussia; site of castle Hohenzollern.

Zólyom. See ZVOLEN.

Zom'ba (zŏm'bȧ). Town, ✳ of Nyasaland protectorate, SE Africa, in Shire Highlands (elevation averages 3000 ft.) ab. 70 m. S of Lake Nyasa; pop. ab. 3000.

Zombor. See SOMBOR.

Zone of the Straits. Demilitarized zone around the Bosporus, the Dardanelles, and the Sea of Marmara, administered 1920–22 by the League of Nations; mostly returned to Turkey 1923. See the STRAITS, 2.

Zon·gul·dak' (zông'gool·däk'). **1** Vilayet, NW Turkey in Asia; 2937 sq. m.; pop. 322,108; coal mines. **2** Seaport city, its ✳, on the Black Sea 140 m. E of the Bosporus; pop. (1940) 37,420.

Zon'ne·be'ke (zôn'ĕ·bā'kĕ). Small commune, West Flanders prov., NW Belgium; pop. 3484; battlefield 1915 and 1917 in World War I.

Zoppot. See SOPOT.

Zor. 1 (tsôr; zōr) Town, Lebanon. See TYRE. **2** (zōr) Former region of Turkey in Asia, extending on both sides of Euphrates river; ✳ Deir-ez-Zor; now divided bet. Turkey and Syria.

Zorn'dorf (tsôrn'dôrf). Village, formerly in Brandenburg, Prussia; now in W Poland near Kostrzyń; scene of battle Aug. 25, 1758 during the Seven Years' War in which the Prussians under Frederick the Great defeated the Russians under Count William of Fermor.

Zout'pans'berg' (sō'ŏŏt·pans'bĕrκ'). Literally "Salt pan hill," a mountain range (highest peak ab. 6700 ft.) in N Transvaal, NE Union of South Africa, a continuation of the Drakensberg.

Zsolna. See ZILINA.

Zsom'bo·lya (zhŏm'bŏ·lyŏ). = JIMBOLIA.

Zua'ra (zwä'rȧ). Seaport town, NW Tripolitania, Libya, N Africa, 66 m. W of Tripoli; pop. ab. 11,000.

Zuetina, Ez. See Ez ZUETINA.

Zuf'fen·hau'sen (tsŏŏf'ĕn·hou'zĕn). Former city (pop. 15,455), Neckar circle, Württemberg, Germany; since 1931 part of Stuttgart (q.v.).

Zug (tsŏŏκ). **1** Swiss canton. See *Table* at SWITZERLAND. **2** Commune, its ✳, N cen. Switzerland, on Lake of Zug 15 m. S of Zurich; pop. 12,372; tourist resort; manufactures liqueurs; trades in cattle.

Zug, Lake of; Ger. **Zu'ger·see'** or **Zu'ger See** (tsŏŏ'gẽr·zā'). Lake in N cen. Switzerland, in Zug and Schwyz cantons, N of Lake of Lucerne; area 15 sq. m.; elevation 1368 ft.; depth 650 ft.

Zug'spit'ze (tsŏŏκ'shpĭt'sĕ). Peak 9719 ft. in Wetterstein Mts. of the Bavarian Alps, S Bavaria, S Germany, on border of the Tirol 54 m. SSW of Munich; highest mountain in the former German Reich.

Zugur. See ZUQAR.

Zuh·reh' (zŏŏ·rȧ'); *formerly* **Tab** (täb). River ab. 150 m. long in SW Iran; flows W and SW into the head of the Persian Gulf along the boundary bet. Khuzistan and Fars provs.

Zuid Afrikaansche Republiek. See SOUTH AFRICAN REPUBLIC.

Zuid–Bali. See SOUTH BALI.

Zui'der Zee (zī'dẽr zā'; zī'dẽr zē'; zoi'-); *anc.* **Fle'vo La'cus** (flē'vō lā'kŭs). Formerly a landlocked inlet of the North Sea on N coast of Netherlands; extended inland ab. 80 m.; originally a lake, but was joined to the North Sea by inundations; now again separated from the North Sea by a dike (completed 1932), and is called IJsselmeer (q.v.); partly drained, two polders already having been formed, the NE polder (completed 1942) and the Wieringermeer (q.v.), of the four which are planned. See WADDEN ZEE.

Zuidholland. See SOUTH HOLLAND.

Zuid–Nieuw–Guinee. See SOUTH NEW GUINEA.

Zui'len (zoi'lĕ[n]). Commune, Utrecht prov., cen. Netherlands; pop. 10,580; NW suburb of Utrecht.

Zú'jar (thōō'här; sōō'-). River 100 m. long in Badajoz prov., SW Spain, flowing into Guadiana river.

Zu'la (zōō'lȧ). Seaport town, Eritrea, Africa, on Gulf of Zula; ancient ruins nearby; became Italian protectorate 1888, part of Eritrea 1890.

Zula, Gulf of; *or* **Annes'ley Bay** (ănz'lĭ). Inlet of the Red Sea on the coast of Eritrea, NE Africa.

Zul'fi·kar' (zōōl'fē·kär'). Mountain pass and village on the Hari Rud river at NW corner of Afghanistan, on Turkmen S.S.R. border.

Zu'lia (sōō'lyä). State of Venezuela. See *Table* at VENEZUELA.

Zül'pich (tsül'pĭk); *anc.* **Tol·bi'a·cum** (tŏl·bī'ȧ·kŭm). Commune, in North Rhine-Westphalia, W Germany, SW of Cologne; pop. 3543; at Tolbiacum Clovis I, king of the Franks, defeated the Alamanni 496.

Zu·lue'ta (sōō·lwā'tä). Municipality and town, Las Villas prov., W cen. Cuba; pop. (town) 5905.

Zu'lu·land' (zōō'lōō·lănd'). Territory, NE Natal, E Union of South Africa; 10,427 sq. m.; pop. 362,438; chief town Eshowe; includes Ingwavuma dist. and Tongaland; borders on E on Indian Ocean. Consists of native reserves of Zulus, a Bantu nation that first came into prominence in early part of 19th cent. Chiefs Chaka and Dingaan noted for their cruelty and for the fighting efficiency of their *impis* (regiments); under both Dingaan and Cetewayo fought with Boers and British; Cetewayo defeated in battle 1879 and finally overcome 1883; land of Zulus taken under British control 1887 and annexed to Natal 1897; known as "Province of Zululand" 1898–1910.

Zu·mar'ra·ga (sōō·mär'rä·gä). Municipality on W coast of Buad I. off W Samar, Phil. Is., 9 m. S of Catbalogan; pop. 21,225; includes barrios on Daram I.

Zum'bo (zŏŏm'bō; zŭm'-). Westernmost town of Mozambique, SE Africa, 600 m. up the Zambezi river.

Zum·pan'go (sŏŏm·päng'gō). **1** Lake in the Valley of Mexico, cen. Mexico, ab. 30 m. N of the city of Mexico. **2** *in full* **Zumpango de O·cam'po** (thä ō·käm'pō). Town, México state, cen. Mexico; pop. 5583.

Zungaria. See DZUNGARIA.

Zu'ni (zōō'nyĕ; sōō'-). **1** River ab. 90 m. long rising in W New Mexico and flowing W into the Little Colorado river in Arizona. **2** *or* **Zu'ñi** (zōō'nyĕ; sōō'-). Indian pueblo and village, McKinley co., NW New Mexico, in Zuni Indian Reservation, on Zuni river ab. 32 m. S of Gallup; pop. 3585; inhabited by descendants of people of Cibola, reported in 1539 by the Spaniards; agriculture, weaving, pottery.

Zuni Mountains. Range in W New Mexico, in McKinley and Valencia cos.

Zu'po, Piz (pēts' pō). Mountain 13,120 ft., second highest of the Bernina Mts. of the Rhaetian Alps, on the Swiss-Italian border; its peak is hidden (*zupô*).

Zu'qar (zōō'kär) *or* **Zu'gur** (zōō'gẽr). Island at S end of Red Sea, bet. Yemen and Eritrea, ab. 14°N; belongs to Eritrea.

Zu'rich (zōōr'ĭk); *Ger.* **Zü'rich** (tsü'rĭκ). **1** Swiss canton. See *Tables* at SWITZERLAND. **2** Industrial city and popular resort, its ✳, NE cen. Switzerland, at foot of Alps on Limmat river at NW end of Lake of Zurich 60 m. NE of Bern; pop. (1941) 336,395; largest city in Switzerland; among its buildings are an 11th-13th-cent. Byzantine cathedral, 12th-cent. Fraumünster, town hall, and museums; university (founded 1832), and the Swiss Polytechnic School (founded 1860); botanical and zoological gardens; extensive silk and cotton manufactories; also manufactures calico, machinery, candles, soap, tobacco, paper, leather.

History: Occupied by lake dwellers before Roman occupation 58 B.C.; became free imperial city 1219; joined

Swiss Confederation 1351; Swiss defeated Austrians here 1443; center of Swiss Reformation; residence of Zwingli; scene of French victory over Russians 1799; place where treaty ending Franco-Italian war was concluded 1859.

Zurich, Lake of; *Ger.* **Zü'rich·see'** (tsü'rĭк·zā') *or* **Zü'ri·cher See** (tsü'rĭ· кēr zā'). Lake in N cen. Switzerland, for the most part in Zurich canton; 25 m. long; area 34 sq. m.

Zu'shi (zōō'shĭ; *Jap.* zōō·shĕ). Town, Kanagawa prefecture, SE Honshu, Japan, ab. 30 m. SW of Tokyo near Kamakura; pop. (1945) 24,119; bathing resort.

Zus'mars·hau'sen (tsōōs'märs·hou'zĕn). Village in Swabia, Bavaria, ab. 14 m. W of Augsburg; pop. (1933) 1117; battle May 17, 1648 in which Count Wrangel and Turenne defeated the Imperialists and Bavarians.

Zut'phen (zŭt'fĕ[n]; *Angl.* zŭt'fĕn). Manufacturing commune, Gelderland prov., E Netherlands, on IJssel river; pop. (1939) 21,525; formerly a fortified town; Church of St. Walpurgis, 12th-cent. Gothic structure; battlefield on which Sir Philip Sidney was mortally wounded Sept. 1586.

Zuyder Zee. = ZUIDER ZEE.

Zvo'len (zvô'lĕn); *Hung.* **Zó'lyom** (zō'lyôm); *Ger.* **Alt'sohl** (ält'zōl). Town, cen. Slovakia prov., E cen. Czechoslovakia, on the Hron river 100 m. NE of Bratislava; pop. (1930) 11,217.

Zwai, Lake (zwī). Lake in cen. Ethiopia, S of Addis Ababa.

Zwart'berg (swôrt'bûrg); *S. Afr. Du.* **Zwaar'te·berg** (svär'tĕ·bĕʀк). Mountains separating Great Karroo from Little Karroo, S Cape Province, S Union of South Africa; contains the Cango Caves; traversed by a pass at alt. 5000 ft.

Zwei'brück'en (tsvī'brük'ĕn); *Fr.* **Deux'ponts'** (dû'pôɴ'); *Lat.* **Bi·pon'ti·um** (bī·pŏn'shĭ·ŭm). Manufacturing city, Rhineland-Palatinate state, West Germany, 53 m. WSW of Mannheim; pop. 15,783; 18th-cent. town hall and baroque castle; manufactures machinery, tex-

tiles, shoes, cigars, tile. Known to scholars for its early editions of Greek and Latin classics. War factories bombed in World War II; taken by the Allies Mar' 20, 1945.

Zwel'len·dam (swĕl'ĕn·dăm). = SWELLENDAM.

Zwick'au (tsvĭk'ou). **1** Circle of Saxony. See *Table* at SAXONY.

2 Manufacturing and mining city, East Germany, on the Mulde river 42 m. S of Leipzig; pop. 80,358; 14th and 15th-cent. churches, 16th-cent. town hall, old castle; coal mines; manufactures textiles, chemicals, machinery, leather, porcelain, dyes. Birthplace of composer Robert Schumann. Founded in 11th cent.; became city 1220; free imperial city 1290–1323; prominent in rise of Anabaptists 1524; occupied by Allies Apr. 1945.

Zwijn'drecht (zvīn'drĕкt). **1** See ZWYNDRECHT, Belgium.

2 Commune, South Holland prov., Netherlands; pop. 12,139; suburb of Dordrecht.

Zwil'ling·e (tsvĭl'ĭng·ĕ). Two peaks in Pennine Alps. See CASTOR.

Zwittau. See SVITAVY.

Zwol'le. 1 (zwŏl'ĕ) Town, Sabine parish, W Louisiana, 61 m. S of Shreveport; pop. 1326.

2 (zvôl'ĕ) Commune, ✻ of Overijssel prov., E Netherlands, on IJssel river; pop. (1939) 42,525; shipbuilding yards, iron foundries; railroad junction; Church of St. Michael, dating from 15th cent.; provincial museum; Church of our Lady, 15th-cent. Gothic building; Stadhuis. Thomas a Kempis lived for 64 years in a monastery on Agnietenberg, 3 m. from Zwolle.

Zwyn'drecht *or* **Zwijn'drecht** (zvīn'drĕкt). Commune, Antwerp prov., Belgium; pop. 6194; W suburb of Antwerp.

Ży·rar'dów (zhĭ·rär'dōōf). Commune, Warszawa dept., cen. Poland, 25 m. WSW of Warsaw; pop. (1938–39 est.) 28,870; important textile center, esp. linen.

Zyrian Autonomous Area. See KOMI REPUBLIC.

OTHER FINE DICTIONARIES
PREPARED BY
The Merriam-Webster Editorial Staff

WEBSTER'S THIRD NEW INTERNATIONAL DICTIONARY
UNABRIDGED

From the first word to the last—in contents, size, shape, and design—this is a completely new unabridged dictionary. It presents the English language in a new modern way to give you the most useful, understandable, and enjoyable fund of word information ever available and covering every area of human thought. A masterpiece of modern defining, every definition is given in a single phrase of precise meaning. Thousands of quotations from well-known writers demonstrate word usage to make meanings clearly understandable. 450,000 entries, including 100,000 new words or meanings never before covered in the unabridged Merriam-Webster. 3,000 terms newly illustrated with twenty true-to-life plates in glorious color. Simplified pronunciation key, clear and informative etymologies, 1,000 synonym articles. This is one of the most remarkable literary achievements of all time. 2,728 pages.

WEBSTER'S SEVENTH NEW COLLEGIATE DICTIONARY

This new desk dictionary is the latest in the famous Merriam-Webster Collegiate series, the outstanding favorite in schools, homes, and offices. 130,000 entries include 20,000 new words and new meanings for more complete coverage than any other desk dictionary. Precise, clear definitions with 10,000 usage examples assure full understanding and accurate use of words. 1244 pages.

WEBSTER'S NEW PRACTICAL SCHOOL DICTIONARY

This dictionary has been specifically written for teen-age needs in junior high school and higher grades. 45,000 entries and 800 new illustrations. A special 50-page introduction teaches each student how to use the dictionary. An everyday aid to better understanding and improved grades.

WEBSTER'S ELEMENTARY DICTIONARY

The only dictionary specifically written for boys and girls in the fourth, fifth, sixth, and seventh grades. 18,000 vocabulary entries selected for elementary-school needs. 1,600 pictures to increase understanding and interest. Large, clear, easily readable type with simplified pronunciation. Sturdily bound.

CAUTION: The Merriam series of Webster's Dictionaries can be identified by a circular trademark on the cover and also by the trademark *a Merriam-Webster* on the title page. Only in this series are to be found the most authoritative dictionaries, based on the experience of more than a century of dictionary making. These trademarks insure accuracy, reliability, and up-to-dateness. To be sure you're right, insist on a Merriam-Webster.

G. & C. MERRIAM COMPANY, Publishers, Springfield, Mass.

Merriam-Webster Pronunciation Key

Symbol	Example	Name
ā	āle	long a
ā̍	chā̍otic	half-long a
â	câre	circumflex a
ă	ădd	short a
ă	*ă*ccount	italic short a
ä	ärm	two-dot a
ȧ	ȧsk	one-dot a
ȧ	sof*ȧ*	italic one-dot a
b	but	
ch	chair	
d	day	
d͜ū	verd͜ūre	ligatured d-u
ē	ēve	long e
ę̄	hę̄re	hooked long e
ē̍	ē̍vent	half-long e
ĕ	ĕnd	short e
ĕ	sil*ĕ*nt	italic short e
ẽ	makẽr	tilde e
f	fill	
g	go	
h	hat	
ī	īce	long i
ĭ	ĭll	short i
ĭ	char*ĭ*ty	italic short i
j	joke	
k	keep	
ᴋ	=ch in German **ich**	small-capital k
l	late	
m	man	
n	nod	

Symbol	Example	Name
ɴ	boɴ (French **bon**)	small-capital n
ng	sing	
ō	ōld	long o
ō̍	ō̍bey	half-long o
ô	ôrb	circumflex o
ŏ	ŏdd	short o
ŏ̂	sŏ̂ft	short-circumflex o
ŏ	c*ŏ*nnect	italic short o
oi	oil	
o͞o	fo͞od	long double o
o͝o	fo͝ot	short double o
ou	out	
p	pen	
r	rat	
s	sit	
sh	she	
t	to	
th	thin	plain t-h: voiceless
~~th~~	~~th~~en	barred t-h: voiced
t͜ū	nat͜ūre	ligatured t-u
ū	cūbe	long u
ū̍	ū̍nite	half-long u
û	ûrn	circumflex u
ŭ	ŭp	short u
ŭ	circ*ŭ*s	italic short u
ü	German **grün**	umlaut u
v	van	
w	win	
y	yet	
z	zone	
zh	=z in azure	

For a fuller description of these sounds, see GUIDE TO PRONUNCIATION.

c is used only in the combination **ch**; **q**, **x** are not used in the respelling for pronunciation.

Foreign sounds for which no special symbols are provided are represented by the nearest English equivalents.

For the apostrophe as in *Eton* (ē′t'n), *Ypres* (ē′pr'), see §§ 66, 66.1, 63.3 in the GUIDE TO PRONUNCIATION.

The principal accent is indicated by a heavy mark (′), and the secondary accent by a lighter mark (ʹ), at the end of the syllable. Foreign words of more than one syllable bearing no accent marks at the ends of syllables have approximately equal accent on all syllables. Syllabic division is indicated by a centered period, or an accent mark, or a hyphen used to join the members of words written or printed with a hyphen.

Equal-Area

Lambert's Azimuthal Equal-Area represents square mileage correctly, showing areas of continental size to best advantage.

MAP

Mollweide

An equal-area projection in ellipse form; scales along equator and parallels constant and equal; outer areas progressively distorted.

Mercator

Starts with central cylindrical projection; both meridians and parallels are straight lines and at true distance apart at equator.

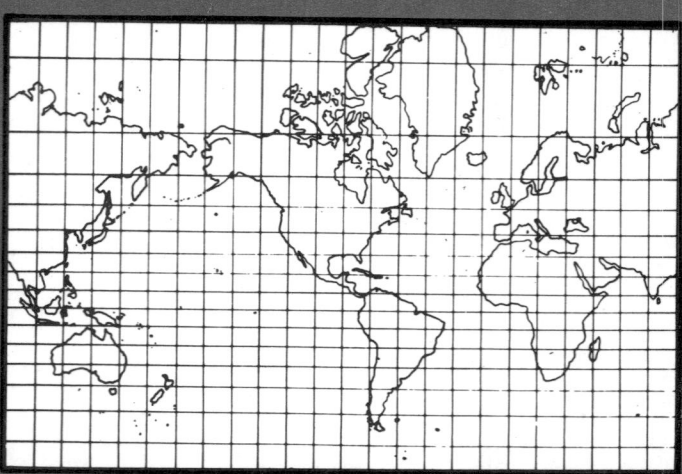